CASSELL'S SPANISH-ENGLISH
ENGLISH-SPANISH DICTIONARY

CASSELL'S

SPANISH DICTIONARY

SPANISH-ENGLISH   ENGLISH-SPANISH

EDITED BY

EDGAR ALLISON PEERS
Late Gilmour Professor of Spanish
University of Liverpool

JOSÉ V. BARRAGÁN
Senior Lecturer in Spanish
Queen Mary College, University of London

FRANCESCO A. VINYALS, L.F. y L.

JORGE ARTURO MORA
Latin-American Supervisor at the B.B.C.

FUNK & WAGNALLS

NEW YORK

CASSELL'S SPANISH DICTIONARY
First Published in the United States
in 1960 by Funk & Wagnalls, *A Division of* Reader's Digest Books, Inc.

© *Cassell & Co. Ltd.*, 1959
New Material © *Cassell & Co. Ltd.*, 1963, 1964, 1966, 1967, 1968

11—269

Library of Congress Catalog Card Number: 60-7806
Printed in the United States of America

CONTENTS

[v]

PREFACE

THE compilation of an entirely new, fully comprehensive dictionary is always a formidable task. In addition to scholarship and an intimate understanding of the living language it demands the unstinting devotion of a team of skilled collaborators for a period of many years. CASSELL'S SPANISH DICTIONARY is the fruit of such an endeavour.

In the course of its preparation the Dictionary has undergone a number of vicissitudes that could not have been foreseen when Edgar Allison Peers, at that time Lecturer at the Institute of Hispanic Studies, first commenced to plan the work some years before the outbreak of World War II. In order to ensure complete copyright protection in America (under Copyright Law as it then existed) it was decided that the text should be set up in the United States, where composition began in the mid-thirties. When war came, all further work on the Dictionary was suspended and the existing material shipped back to Great Britain—surviving the perils of submarine attack only to fall victim two years later to a massive fire-bomb raid on London in 1941, when a large part of the manuscript was irretrievably lost in the total destruction of 'La Belle Sauvage,' Cassell's headquarters since 1851.

When, after the war, the work of compilation was resumed, much of it had to be begun again almost from scratch. By this time E. A. Peers' increasing academic commitments as visiting lecturer and professor in Madrid, Oxford, and New York, and professor in Liverpool, had made it necessary for him to withdraw from active participation, although, until his untimely death in 1952, his valuable advice remained at the disposal of those who carried on the task—Mr. J. V. Barragán, Mrs. Rose Barragán and, later, Mr. F. A. Vinyals who gave much time and thought to bringing the whole text completely up to date. The publishers were especially fortunate in being able to enlist the aid, also, of Mr. J. A. Mora, whose wide knowledge of South and Central American usage has been responsible for the inclusion in the Spanish-English section of terms and idioms peculiar to Spanish America—one of the Dictionary's most important features. Finally, the whole work was revised and enlarged by Mr. R. O. Jones and Mr. J. W. Sage.

A dictionary of this size must of necessity be highly selective. We believe, however, that the present work will be found adequate for the reading of both the Classics and standard modern literature in English and Spanish (many archaisms have been included with this purpose in mind); for the comprehension of current colloquialisms in both languages; and for a wide range of modern technical usage. Its strength in Spanish-American terms has already been referred to. In short, our aim has been to provide a dictionary which, though compendious, could be of service to student, business man and general reader alike.

ADVICE TO THE USER

GROUPING OF WORDS. Alphabetical order has been generally adopted, but where it was thought clearer or more convenient compounds were grouped under key-words. Key-words which are spelt alike, but which differ in origin and meaning, are given separate entries where that seems necessary to avoid gross confusion.

PUNCTUATION. In principle, synonyms or near-synonyms are separated by commas, and wider differences of meaning indicated by semicolons. In practice a clear distinction is impossible to observe and some apparent inconsistency is inevitable. Where clear demarcation in meaning or usage can be established, the semicolon is used; otherwise a comma is preferred.

GENDER. In the English-Spanish section the gender of Spanish nouns is given only when it does not obey a simple rule which is given separately (see p. xiv).

ADVERBS. English adverbial forms ending in '-ly' have generally been omitted except when there is some special feature in their Spanish equivalents.

USE OF BRACKETS. Brackets are used in various ways:

(1) They enclose words or parts of words which may be omitted or included without changing the sense.

(2) When a word or phrase enclosed in brackets in one language is followed by a word or phrase in brackets in the other language, the contents of the one bracket are to be understood as translating the contents of the other.

(3) In order to indicate the range of usage of a word with the help of the appropriate abbreviation in italics or in some other way. Thus, (aer.) limits the word to an aeronautical, and (igl.) to an ecclesiastical context. In an attempt to give some guidance in distinguishing between other uses, a hint has often been given by a word in brackets in roman type where no appropriate abbreviation existed. For example, under **distinction** one of the equivalents is given as '(examen) sobresaliente', to indicate the term used in examinations.

(4) In order to indicate the stratum of language to which a word belongs. Here there are not always clear dividing lines, but the following are some of the distinctions borne in mind:

(i) (obs.) or (ant.): the Dictionary includes a large number of archaic and obsolete terms. Many archaic terms survive in, for example, legal use, but we have set our bounds wider than this. A Spanish student of English will wish to possess a dictionary that will cover adequately the vocabulary of Shakespeare, Milton and Scott.

(ii) (poet.): here most of the foregoing applies with equal force. The indication should be taken as a warning that the form is no longer part of the living language.

(iii) (coll.) and (fam.) indicate language which would not be used in dignified prose or even in conversation with respected strangers. It would be normal in polite conversation with one's equals.

(iv) (vulg.) indicates language which is considered embarrassing in polite conversation. It is not synonymous with obscenity. So far as possible renderings have been chosen from the same layer of language, though this is often difficult, but sometimes it was considered necessary to avoid ambiguity by giving a more conventional equivalent as well.

(v) (Am.) and more specific references to particular Latin-American countries indicates usage peculiar to those areas. This Dictionary carries an unusually high proportion of Spanish-American vocabulary and this is, we believe, one of the most important features of the work.

PRONUNCIATION. In the English-Spanish section the International Phonetic Alphabet is used to indicate pronunciation. The stress mark precedes the syllable which carries the stress. Since Spanish already is an approximation to a phonetic transcription, pronunciation has not been indicated in the Spanish-English section, though some simple rules for the English user are given. In both sections the 'standard' pronunciation has been used in each case (that is, Castilian and Southern English).

AMERICAN ENGLISH. Where English and American usage differ, dictionaries tend to be unjust to one or the other. This Dictionary attempts to do justice to both. Differences of spelling (pyjama and pajama), of meaning (the two senses of truck) and of terminology (elevator and lift) are catered for and clearly distinguished.

ABREVIATURAS ESPAÑOLAS

a.	adjectivo		**filos.**	filosofía
abrev.	abreviatura		**fís.**	física
adv.	adverbio		**fisiol.**	fisiología
aer.	aeronáutica		**for.**	forense
agr.	agricultura		**fort.**	fortificación
alb.	albañilería		**foto.**	fotografía
álg.	álgebra		**fr.**	francés
Am.	América		**frenol.**	frenología
anat.	anatomía		**fund.**	fundición
ant.	anticuado		**gen.**	generalmente
anglo-ind.	anglo-indio		**geog.**	geografía
apl.	aplícase		**geol.**	geología
arit.	aritmética		**geom.**	geometría
arq.	arquitectura		**ger.**	gerundio
art.	artículo		**gram.**	gramática
arti.	artillería		**herr.**	herraduría
astr.	astronomía		**hidr.**	hidráulica
astrol.	astrología		**hist.**	historia
aut.	automovilismo		**hist. nat.**	historia natural
aux.	auxiliar		**ict.**	ictiología
azú.	industria azucarera		**igl.**	iglesia
b.a.	bellas artes		**impers.**	impersonal
bact.	bacteriología		**impr.**	imprenta
bib.	bíblico		**ind.**	industria
biol.	biología		**indef.**	indefinido
blas.	blasón		**indic.**	indicativo
bot.	botánica		**ing.**	ingeniería
cant.	cantería		**Ingl.**	Inglaterra
carp.	carpintería		**interj.**	interjección
carr.	carruajería		**irr.**	irregular
caz.	caza		**joy.**	joyería
célt.	céltico		**lat.**	latín
cerá.	cerámica		**lóg.**	lógica
cir.	cirugía		**ll.**	llámase
coc.	cocina		**magn.**	magnetismo
com.	comercio		**mar.**	marina
comp.	comparativo		**mat.**	matemáticas
conj.	conjunción		**mec.**	mecánica
constr.	construcción		**med.**	medicina
contr.	contracción		**metal.**	metalurgia
cost.	costura		**meteorol.**	meteorología
danz.	danza		**Méx.**	México
defec.	defectivo		**mil.**	milicia
dep.	deporte		**min.**	minería
der.	derecho		**mit.**	mitología
despec.	despectivo		**mús.**	música
dial.	dialecto		**numis.**	numismática
dib.	dibujo		**obst.**	obstetricia
dim.	diminutivo		**ópt.**	óptica
dip.	diplomacia		**orn.**	ornitología
elec.	electricidad		**p.a.**	participio activo
enc.	encuadernación		**pal.**	paleontología
e.p.	economía política		**pat.**	patología
equit.	equitación		**pers.**	personal
esc.	escultura		**pint.**	pintura
Esco.	Escocia		**piro.**	pirotecnia
esgr.	esgrima		**pl.**	plural
esp.	especialmente		**poét.**	poético
E.U.	Estados Unidos		**pol.**	política
fam.	familiar		**pos.**	posesivo
farm.	farmacia		**p.p.**	participio pasado
f.c.	ferrocarriles		**prep.**	preposición
fig.	figurado		**pret.**	pretérito

[x]

P. Rico	Puerto Rico	tec.	tecnología
pron.	pronombre	tej.	tejidos
prov.	proverbio	tele.	telefonía
psic.	psicología	ten.	tenería
quím.	química	teo.	teología
rad.	radio	tint.	tintorería
radtlf.	radiotelefonía	tip.	tipografía
radtlg.	radiotelegrafía	tlg.	telegrafía
relig.	religión	top.	topografía
ret.	retórica	ú.	úsase
s.	substantivo	u. ref.	usado reflexivamente
S.A.	Sud América	v.	véa(n)se
sast.	sastrería	v.i.	verbo intransitivo
sing.	singular	v.r.	verbo reflexivo
somb.	sombrerería	v.t.	verbo transitivo
subj.	subjuntivo	vulg.	vulgarismo
super.	superlativo	zap.	zapatería
t.	también	zool.	zoología
teat.	teatro	[. . .]	véase

ENGLISH ABBREVIATIONS

a.	adjective	Dom.	Dominican Republic
abbr.	abbreviation	dynam.	dynamics
abl.	ablative	Ec.	Ecuador
acc.	accusative	eccles.	ecclesiastical
adv.	adverb	econ.	economics
aer.	aeronautics	e.g.	for instance
agric.	agriculture	elec.	electricity
alch.	alchemy	ellip.	elliptical
alg.	algebra	embryol.	embryology
Am.	South America	Eng.	English
anat.	anatomy	engin.	engineering
anc.	ancient	entom.	entomology
Ant.	Antilles	equit.	equitation
anth.	anthropology	ES.	El Salvador
Arab.	Arabic	ethn.	ethnology
arch.	architecture	etym.	etymology
archæol.	archæology	f.	feminine
Arg.	Argentine	fam.	familiar
arith.	arithmetic	fenc.	fencing
art.	artistic	fig.	figuratively
artill.	artillery	for.	foreign
astrol.	astrology	fort.	fortification
astron.	astronomy	freq.	frequentative
augm.	augmentative	fut.	future
aux. v.	auxiliary verb	G.	German
Bibl.	Biblical, Bible	Gael.	Gaelic
bibliog.	bibliography	gen.	genitive
biol.	biology	geneal.	genealogy
Bol.	Bolivia	geog.	geography
bot.	botany	geol.	geology
build.	building	geom.	geometry
c.	circa, about	ger.	gerund
Carib.	Caribbean	Goth.	Gothic
carp.	carpentry	Gr.	Greek
Cat.	Catalonia	gram.	grammar
Celt.	Celtic	Guat.	Guatemala
Cent. Am.	Central America	Heb.	Hebrew
ceram.	ceramics	her.	heraldry
Ch.	Church	hist.	history
chem.	chemistry	Hond.	Honduras
Chi.	Chile	hort.	horticulture
civ. eng.	civil engineering	hunt.	hunting
class.	classical	hydrost.	hydrostatics
C.O.D.	Concise Oxford Dictionary	hyg.	hygiene
Col.	Colombia	ichth.	ichthyology
coll.	colloquial	i.e.	that is
com.	commerce	imper.	imperative
conch.	conchology	imperf.	imperfect
conj.	conjunction	indic.	indicative
contempt.	contemptuously	indef. art.	indefinite article
contr.	contraction	inf.	infinitive
cook.	cooking	int.	interjection
CR.	Costa Rica	interrog.	interrogative
craniol.	craniology	intr.	intransitive
cryst.	crystallography	iron.	ironical
Cub.	Cuba	irreg.	irregular
dat.	dative	jewel.	jewellery
def.	definitive	joc.	jocular
defect.	defective verb	L.	Latin
deriv.	derivation	Lit.	literature
dial.	dialect	lit.	literally
dim.	diminutive	log.	logic
diplom.	diplomatics	m.	masculine

mach.	machinery	poss.	possessive
mas.	masonry	p.p.	past participle
math.	mathematics	pref.	prefix
mech.	mechanics	prep.	preposition
med.	medicine	pres.	present
med.	mediæval	pres. p.	present participle
metal.	metallurgy	PR.	Puerto Rico
metaph.	metaphysics	print.	printing
meteor.	meteorology	pron.	pronoun
Mex.	Mexico	pros.	prosody
mil.	military	Prov.	Provençal
min.	mineralogy	prov.	provincial
mint.	minting	psych.	psychology
motor.	motoring	pugil.	pugilism
mus.	music	r., reflex.	reflexive
myth.	mythology	railw.	railway
n.	noun	R.C.	Roman Catholic
N. Am.	North America	relig.	religion
nat. hist.	natural history	rel. pron.	relative pronoun
naut.	nautical	remonstr.	remonstrative
neg.	negative	rhet.	rhetoric
neol.	neologism	Rom.	Roman
neut.	neuter	s.	south
newsp.	newspaper	sci.	science
Nic.	Nicaragua	sculp.	sculpture
nom.	nominative	sing.	singular
N.T.	New Testament	sl.	slang
numis.	numismatics	Span.	Spanish
obj.	objective	Stock Exch.	Stock Exchange
obs.	obsolete	subj.	subjunctive
onomat.	onomatopœic	suf.	suffix
O. Prov.	Old Provençal	superl.	superlative
opt.	optics	surg.	surgery
orig.	origin	surv.	surveying
orn.	ornithology	syl.	syllable
O. Sp.	Old Spanish	tail.	tailoring
p.	past	teleg.	telegraphy
palæont.	palæontology	theat.	theatre
Par.	Paraguay	theol.	theology
parl.	parliamentary	therap.	therapeutics
part.	participle	therm.	thermionics
pass.	passive	tr., t.	transitive
path.	pathology	trig.	trigonometry
pej.	pejorative	typ.	typography
Per.	Peru	univ.	university
perf.	perfect	Ur.	Uruguay
pers.	person; personal	U.S.A.	United States of America
petrol.	petrology	usu.	usually
pharm.	pharmacology	v.	verb
phil.	philosophy	Ven.	Venezuela
Philip.	Philippines	verb. a.	verbal adjective
philol.	philology	vet.	veterinary
phon.	phonetics	v.i.	intransitive verb
photo.	photography	v.r., v. refl.	reflexive verb
phrenol.	phrenology	v.t.	transitive verb
phys.	physics	vulg.	vulgar
physiol.	physiology	W. Indies	West Indies
pl.	plural	wire.	wireless, radio
p.n.	proper noun	zool.	zoology
poet.	poetry, poetical	[. . .]	see, see also
polit.	politics		

Nouns ending in -a, -ción, -gión, -sión, -tión, -xión, -umbre, -dad, -tad, -tud, -ez, are feminine. Nouns with other terminations are masculine. (Exceptions to these rules are noted in the body of the dictionary.)

In a few cases, even where these rules apply, the gender has been indicated when doubt might arise: e.g. tiralíneas, *m.*

KEY TO PRONUNCIATION

The English equivalents of the sounds of the Spanish language, given below, are only approximations, but they will aid the user in acquiring a reasonably satisfactory pronunciation of Spanish. Those who wish to make a more thorough study are referred to *Manual de pronunciación española* by Navarro Tomás (Hafner Publ. Co., New York, 1957).

VOWELS

In Spanish it is very important to pronounce the vowels clearly and distinctly. They always have the same sound, whether stressed or unstressed. There are two tendencies, common in English, that should be carefully avoided in Spanish pronunciation: (1) the dropping or slurring of an unstressed vowel (p'lite *vs.* polite), and (2) the glide sound commonly found in such English words as *there* (frequently pronounced they-er) or *more* (frequently pronounced mow-er).

The Spanish vowels are: **a, e, i, o, u,** and occasionally **y.**

a   is pronounced like the *a* in English *bah, father.*
   Spanish examples: **la** (the) ; **da** (give)

e   has two sounds: (1) in an open syllable (i.e. a syllable not closed by a consonant) it is pronounced like the first *a* in *fatality.*
   Spanish examples: **me-sa** (table) ; **pa-dre** (father)
   (2) in a syllable closed by a consonant, it is pronounced like the *e* in *let, met,* or *set.*
   Spanish examples: **em-bar-go** (embargo) ; **pa-pel** (paper)

i   pronounced like the *i* in *machine.*
   Spanish examples: **vi-no** (wine) ; **des-ti-no** (destiny)

o   has two sounds: (1) in an open syllable (i.e. a syllable not closed by a consonant) it is pronounced like the *o* in *halo.*
   Spanish examples: **pe-so** (weight) ; **so-lo** (alone)
   (2) in a syllable closed by a consonant, it is pronounced like *o* in *storm.*
   Spanish examples: **me-nor** (less) ; **tor-men-ta** (storm)

u   pronounced like the *oo* in *boot.*
   Spanish examples: **lu-na** (moon) ; **mu-cho** (much)

y   is a vowel only when it stands alone, or when it ends a word. In these cases it has the same sound as the Spanish **i** (*See* **i** above).
   Spanish examples: **y** (and) ; **hay** (there is, there are) ; **soy** (I am)

CONSONANTS

b , v These letters are identical in sound, but vary in pronunciation according to their position: (1) after a pause or after the consonants **m** or **n**, they are pronounced exactly like English *b.*
   Spanish examples: **ban-di-do** (bandit) ; **em-bar-go** (embargo) ; **en va-no** (in vain)
   (2) in all other positions, both **b** and **v** have approximately the same sound as the English *v* in *give* (i.e. they are pronounced between the lips without a complete contact of the lips).
   Spanish examples: **ha-blar** (to speak) ; **pa-vo** (turkey)

c   has three sounds: (1) before **a, o,** and **u,** and at the end of a syllable or a word, it has the sound of English *k*.

     Spanish examples: **ca-sa** (house); **co-sa** (thing); **cu-na** (cradle); **ac-to** (act); **cinc** (zinc)

     (2) in standard Castilian pronunciation, **c** before **e** and **i** is pronounced like *th* in English *thin*.

     Spanish examples: **ce-na** (supper); **cin-ta** (ribbon, tape)

     (3) in parts of southern Spain and in Latin America, **c** before **e** and **i** is pronounced like English *s* in *say*.

ch   is treated (and alphabetized) as a single consonant. It is pronounced like the *ch* in *church*.

     Spanish examples: **chin-che** (bedbug); **mu-cha-cha** (girl)

d   has two distinct sounds: (1) after a pause, and after **n** and **l**, the pronunciation is similar to the *d* in *dog*.

     Spanish examples: **¿Dón-de?** (Where?); **fal-da** (skirt)

     (2) between vowels and at the end of a word, the pronunciation is similar to the *th* in *though*.

     Spanish examples: **la-do** (side); **mi-tad** (half)

f   similar to the English *f,* except that the Spanish **f** is formed by the two lips, rather than by lip and teeth.

     Spanish examples: **fi-no** (fine); **fa-vor** (favor)

g   has two sounds: (1) before **a, o,** and **u,** and before a consonant, it is pronounced like the *g* in *go*.

     Spanish examples: **ga-to** (cat); **go-ta** (drop); **gus-to** (taste); **mag-ní-fi-co** (magnificent)

     (2) before **e** and **i**, **g** has no equivalent sound in English. The closest approximation is that of the *ch* in the Scottish *loch* (Loch Lomond) or the German *Bach* (Johann Sebastian Bach).

     Spanish examples: **gen-te** (people); **gi-gan-te** (giant)

     NOTE: In the combinations **gue** and **gui,** the **u** is not pronounced and the **g** has the sound of the *g* in English *go*. (Examples: **gue-rra** [war]; **gui-ta-rra** [guitar].) However, if the **u** carries a dieresis (**ü**), it is pronounced like the English *w*. (Examples: **a-güe-ro** [omen]; **güi-ro** [gourd].)

h   is never sounded in Spanish.

     Spanish example: **ho-ra** (hour) is pronounced as if it were spelled "ora."

j   has the same sound as **g** before **e** and **i** (*See* **g** above)

     Spanish examples: **je-fe** (chief); **hi-jo** (son)

k   has the same sound as in English.

     Spanish example: **ki-lo-gra-ma** (kilogram)

l   pronounced approximately as the *l* in *limp*.

     Spanish examples: **lu-na** (moon); **ma-lo** (bad)

ll   is treated (and alphabetized) as a single consonant. The sound in Castilian is very much like the English *lli* in *billiard*. In parts of southern Spain and in Latin America **ll** is pronounced like the English *y* in *yet*.

     Spanish examples: **vi-lla** (town); **lla-ve** (key)

m   has the same sound as in English.

     Spanish example: **mu-cho** (much)

n   has three sounds in Spanish: (1) approximately like the *n* in *normal.*

     Spanish examples: **nú-me-ro** (number); **can-to** (chant)

[xv]

(2) before **b** or **v**, it is pronounced like the English *m*.
    Spanish examples: **en bo-ga** (in style); **in-vi-tar** (to invite)
(3) before hard **c** and **g**, it is similar to the *ng* in *wringer*.
    Spanish examples: **fran-co** (frank); **len-gua** (tongue)

ñ   is pronounced like the *ny* in *canyon*.
    Spanish example: **ma-ña-na** (tomorrow)

p   is similar to English *p,* but without the explosive sound.
    Spanish examples: **pa-tio** (courtyard); **ma-pa** (map)
NOTE: the **p** is silent in two Spanish words—**sép-ti-mo** (seventh) and **sep-tiem-bre** (September).

q   occurs only in the combinations **que-** and **qui-** and is pronounced like English *k* (the **u** is silent).
    Spanish examples: **que-so** (cheese); **quin-to** (fifth)

r   after a pause, and when preceded by **l, n,** or **s,** this letter is strongly trilled.
    Spanish examples: **al-re-de-do-res** (environs); **hon-ra** (honor); **is-ra-e-li** (Israeli)
In all other positions, it is pronounced with one tap of the tongue against the sockets of the upper front teeth.
    Spanish examples: **pe-ro** (but); **can-tar** (to sing)

rr   is treated (and alphabetized) as a single consonant. It is strongly trilled, in much the same manner as the Scottish *r* is trilled.
    Spanish examples: **pe-rro** (dog); **ca-rro** (cart)

s   has two sounds: (1) in general it is pronounced like the *s* in *case*.
    Spanish examples: **so-lo** (alone); **ca-sa** (house)
(2) before **b, d, g, l, m,** and **n,** it is pronounced like the *z* in *haze*.
    Spanish examples: **es-bo-zar** (to sketch); **des-de** (since)
        tras-go (goblin); **is-la** (island)
        fan-tas-ma (phantom); **fres-no** (ash tree)

t   similar to the English *t,* but without the explosive sound.
    Spanish examples: **tan-go** (a dance); **pa-to** (duck)

v   *See* under letter **b** above.

w   This letter does not belong to the Spanish alphabet and is found only in foreign words. *See* the letter *W* in the Spanish-English section of this dictionary.

x   The usual sound of Spanish **x** is somewhere between the *x* in *axe* and the sound of the *x* in *exaggerate*.
    Spanish examples: **e-xa-mi-nar** (examine); **bo-xe-ar** (to box)
However, in the prefix **ex** followed by a consonant, the **x** is generally pronounced like the *s* in *case*.
    Spanish example: **ex-pli-car** (to explain)
NOTE: In the word **México** and its derivatives, the **x** is prononuced like the Spanish **j**.

y   For the pronunciation of the letter **y** as a vowel, *see* the letter **y** above under the heading of *Vowels*.
As a consonant, **y** before a vowel is pronounced like the *y* in *yet*.
    Spanish examples: **yo** (I); **yu-go** (yoke)

z   In Castilian, **z** is pronounced like the *th* in *thin*. But in parts of southern Spain and in Latin America, the **z** is pronounced like the *s* in *case*.
    Spanish examples: **ca-zar** (to hunt); **zo-na** (zone)

CASSELL'S
SPANISH-ENGLISH DICTIONARY

CASSELL'S
SPANISH-ENGLISH DICTIONARY

A

A, a, *n.f.* first letter of the alphabet; pronounced invariably as the open English *a* in *far.* *No sabe ni la a,* he is a perfect ignoramus; *a por a y be por be,* point by point, minutely.

a, *prep.* to, at, on, by, in, up to, according to, as, as if, for, against, with, toward, up on, until, of, after, etc. It governs the dative and accusative cases: *lo doy a mi padre,* I give it to my father. Before proper nouns, personified nouns and occasionally before other nouns, in the accusative case, *a* is a symbol of that case and is not translated: *veo a mi madre,* I see my mother; *conozco a Juan,* I know John. It indicates direction, purpose, limit, approval, interval, action, location, rate or quantity, request, time, distance, command, manner, instrument or means, e.g.: *voy a París,* I am going to Paris; *ella me enseñó a cantar,* she taught me (how) to sing; *voy a verle,* I am going to see him; *de tres a cuatro,* from three to four; *de mes a mes,* from month to month; *de casa a casa,* from house to house; *a mi gusto,* to my taste; *a mi pesar,* to my regret; *con el agua a la cintura,* with water up to the waist; *a la orilla del río,* on the bank of the river; *a mi lado,* at my side; *el azúcar se vende a tres pesos el quintal,* sugar is sold at three dollars per hundredweight; *hacer el seguro a tres por ciento,* to effect the insurance at three per cent; *a instancias de mi hermano,* at my brother's request; *a mediodía,* at midday; *a la española,* in or after the Spanish fashion; *morir a hierro,* to die by the sword; *oler a vino,* to smell of wine; *a su disposición,* at your disposal; *a voluntad,* at will; *a manos llenas,* liberally, by handfuls; *a mano,* by hand; *a máquina,* by machine; *a fuerza bruta,* by brute force; *a pedazos,* by pieces; *paso a paso,* step by step; *poco a poco,* little by little; *a caballo,* on horseback; *a pie,* on foot; *a bordo,* on board, aboard; *a mi fe,* upon my honour. It forms many idiomatic and adverbial phrases: *a mi llegada,* on my arrival; *a oscuras,* in the dark; *a lo que parece,* as it seems; *a sabiendas,* on purpose, deliberately; *a trueque,* in exchange; *a deshora,* unseasonably; *a la verdad,* truly; *a lo menos,* at least; *a ojos vistos,* plainly, publicly; *a veces,* sometimes; *a pesar de,* in spite of. When followed by an infinitive, it represents: if, if . . . not, but for: e.g.: *a ser yo,* if I were; *a mal dar,* if it should turn out badly; *a no haber sido,* if it had not been; *a no ser zahorí,* but for his being a wizard; *a no venir José,* but for Joseph's coming; *a no ser por Vd,* but for you. It coalesces with the article *el,* forming *al; al hombre,* to the man; *traducir al inglés,* translate into English. This masculine article is also used before the infinitive of verbs used as nouns: *al entrar,* on entering. It is used before the infinitive of verbs of action governed by other verbs: *vamos a pasear, a comer, a beber,* let us go for a walk, (let us) eat, (let us) drink.

a-, *pref.* denotes privation or negation as, *acromático,* achromatic; *ateísmo,* atheism; *amoral,* amoral.

A., contraction for *Alteza,* Highness; (*com.*) on a bill of exchange signifies 'accepted'; (*naut.*) on the anchor of a ship, 'insured'; 'approved' (on examination papers).

AA., contraction for *autores,* authors.

aarónico, aaronita, *a.* Aaronic, pertaining to Aaron or his descendants.

aba, *n.f.* an obsolete unit of lineal measure, about 6 feet.

¡ aba !, *interj.* look out! beware!

abab, *n.m.* Turkish volunteer sailor employed in the galleys.

ababa, *n.f.* red poppy [AMAPOLA].

ababán, *n.m.* (*Arg.*) fruit tree (*Caesalpinia*).

ababillarse, *n.m.* (*Chi.*) animal sickness.

ababol, *n.m.* red poppy [AMAPOLA]; (*fig.*) simpleton, stultified, silly.

abacá, *n.m.* plant of the banana family; fibre of the plant called Manila hemp; material made of this fibre.

abacería, *n.f.* retail grocery.

abacero, -ra, *n.m.f.* retail grocer.

abacial, *a.* abbatial.

ábaco, *n.m.* (*arch.*) abacus, plate on a capital; calculating frame; washing-trough in mining.

abacorar, *v.t.* (*Ven.*) to pursue close, to attack, to subject.

abad, *n.m.* abbot; *abad bendito, mitrado,* crosiered and mitred abbot; *abad avariento, por un bodigo pierde ciento,* avarice recoils on the miser; *si bien canta el abad, no le va en zaga el monacillo,* if the abbot sings well the acolyte is not far behind him; *el abad de lo que canta yanta,* it's by his singing that the abbot gets his dinner.

abada, *n.f.* rhinoceros.

abadanar, *v.t.* to dress or finish like sheepskin.

abadejo, *n.m.* codfish; pollack [BACALAO]; Spanish fly or blistering beetle; (*orn.*) kinglet, golden-crested wren.

abadengo, -ga, *a.* abbatial.

abadernar, *v.t.* (*naut.*) to fasten with short ropes called *badernas.*

abadesa, *n.f.* abbess.

abadí, *a.* applied to the descendants of Mohammed ben Ismail ben Abad, founder of the kingdom of Seville (11th cent.).

abadía, *n.f.* abbey.

abadiato, *n.m.* dignity of an abbot, abbotship.

abajadero, *n.m.* downhill, slope.

abajador, *n.m.* (*min.*) stable-man; helper; abater.

abajamiento, *n.m.* depression; humiliation; discount, reduction.

abajar, *v.t., v.i.* [BAJAR].

abajeño, - ña, *a.* (*Mex., P. Rico*) lowlander.

abajera, *n.f.* (*Arg.*) horse blanket.

abajino, -na, *a.* (*Chi.*) inhabitant of the northern territories.

abajo, *adv.* under, underneath, below; down; *venirse abajo,* to fall; (*interj.*) *¡abajo!* down with! *cuesta abajo,* downhill; *dar abajo,* to descend.

abalanzar, *v.t.* (*pret.* **abalancé**; *pres. subj.* **abalance**) to balance, compare; to throw, impel. — *v.r.* to throw oneself, dart, rush impetuously; to venture; *abalanzarse a los peligros,* to rush into danger.

abalaustrado, -da, *a.* balustered. — *p.p.* [ABALAUSTRAR].

abaldonar, *v.t.* to debase, revile.

abaleador, -ra, *n.m.f.* grain cleaner or separator.

abaleaduras, *n.f.pl.* siftings, chaff.

abalear, *v.t.* to clean or separate grain from chaff.

abaleo, *n.m.* (*agric.*) cleaning or separating of grain.

abalizamiento, *n.m.* (*naut.*) buoying.

abalizar, *v.t.* (*pret.* **abalicé**; *pres. subj.* **abalice**) (*naut.*) to lay down buoys. — *v.r.* (*naut.*) to take bearings.

abalorio, *n.m.* glass bead; bead-work; (*fig.*) showy article of little value; *no valer un abalorio,* of little value.

abalsamado, -da, *a.* like, or impregnated with balsam. — *p.p.* [ABALSAMAR].

abalsamar, *v.t.* to give the consistence or quality of balsam to a liquid.

aballestar, *v.t.* (*naut.*) to haul a cable.

abámeas, *n.f.pl.* (*bot.*) Abama.

abanar, *v.t.* to ventilate with fans.

abanderado, *n.m.* standard-bearer; colour-sergeant. — *p.p.* [ABANDERAR].

abanderamiento, *n.m.* registration (ship); conscription.

abanderar, *v.t., v.r.* to register (a ship), give a certificate of registration; to conscript.

abanderizador, -ra, *n.m.f., a.* ringleader.

abanderizamente, *adv.* in bands, in revolt.

abanderizante, *a.* [ABANDERIZADOR].

abanderizar, *v.t.* (*pret.* **abandericé**; *pres. subj.* **abandericé**) to organize in bands; to stir up revolution. — *v.r.* to band together.

abandonadamente, *adv.* carelessly, negligently.

abandonado, -da, *a.* abandoned, forsaken; helpless; forlorn; lost; profligate; slovenly.— *p.p.* [ABANDONAR].

abandonamiento, *n.m.* forlornness; slovenliness; profligacy, debauchery.

abandonar, *v.t.* to forsake, leave, give up. — *v.r.* to give oneself up to; to despond; *abandonarse a* (or *en manos de*) *la suerte,* to give oneself up to chance, to trust to luck.

abandono, *n.m.* [ABANDONAMIENTO].

abanicamiento, *n.m.* [ABANIQUEO].

abanicar, *v.t.* (*pret.* **abaniqué**; *pres. subj.* **abanique**) to fan. — *v.r.* to fan oneself.

abanicazo, *n.m.* stroke with a fan.

abanico, *n.m.* fan; (*coll.*) sword; (*naut.*) derrick; crane; spritsail; (*fort.*) defensive parapet of wood; (*arch.*) fan-light; (*arch.*) winding stairs; semicircular window; (*min.*) ventilator; *en abanico,* fan-shaped; *tirar del abanico,* to draw the sword; *abanico de culpas,* talebearer, informer; *parecer un abanico de tonta,* to be very restless.

abanillo, *n.m.;* **abanino,** *n.m.* pleated collar; modesty vest; ruffle, frill.

abaniqueo, *n.m.* fanning; swinging motion; (*fig.*) exaggerated gesturing in speaking.

abaniquería, *n.f.* fan shop or factory.

abaniquero, *n.m.* fan-maker; fan-dealer.

abano, *n.m.* fan; hanging-fan, punkah, ventilator.

abanto, *n.m.* (*orn.*) African vulture. — *a.* (*fam.*) timid (bull); undecided.

abañar, *v.t.* to grade (seeds, etc.).

abaratable, *a.* that can be cheapened.

abaratablemente, *adv.* cheaply.

abaratador, -ra, *a.* that cheapens.

abaratadura, *n.f.;* **abaratamiento,** *n.m.* cheapness.

abaratar, *v.t.* to cheapen; to abate. — *v.i., v.r.* to fall in price.

abarbar, *v.i.* to raise bees; (*agric.*) to take root.

abarbetación, *n.f.* hold, grasp; (*naut.*) fastening by gaskets.

abarbetador, -ra, *a.* that holds fast.

abarbetar, *v.t.* to grasp firmly; (*naut.*) to fasten with gaskets; (*mil.*) to fortify.

abarca, *n.f.* sandal of rubber or leather, worn by peasants.

abarcado, -da, *a.* sandalled; embraced; contained. — *p.p.* [ABARCAR].

abarcador, -ra, *a.* clasping; monopolistic.

abarcadura, *n.f.;* **abarcamiento,** *n.m.* embracing, comprising.

abarcar, *v.t.* (*pret.* **abarqué**; *pres. subj.* **abarque**) to clasp, embrace, contain; to comprise; to monopolize; (*fig.*) to undertake too many things at once; *quien mucho abarca, poco aprieta,* grasp all, lose all. (*Ec.*) to brood, hatch; (*Mex.*) to monopolize.

abarcía, *n.f.* (*prov.*) inordinate hunger.

abarcón, *n.m.* iron ring, hoop; pole-ring in carriages; large iron clamp.

abarloar, *v.t., v.r.* (*naut.*) to dock; to bring alongside a ship; to moor at a wharf.

abarquería, *n.f.* *abarca* or sandal shop or factory.

abarquero, -ra, *n.m.f.* maker or seller of coarse sandals or *abarcas.*

abarquillado, -da, *a.* rolled up; curled up. — *p.p.* [ABARQUILLAR].

abarquillador, -ra, *a.* that curls or rolls up.

abarquillamiento, *n.m.* curling up into a roll; warping.

abarquillar, *v.t., v.r.* to curl up; shape into a roll; to warp.

abarracado, -da, *a.* (*mil.*) disposed in the form of barracks. — *p.p.* [ABARRACAR].

abarracador, -ra, *a.* that barracks.

abarracadura, *n.f.;* **abarracamiento,** *n.m.* (*mil.*) hutting.

abarracar, *v.i., v.r.* (*mil.*) to encamp in huts or barracks.

abarrado, -da, *a.* said of corded or striped material.

abarraganamiento, *n.m.* concubinage.

abarraganarse, *v.r.* to live in concubinage.

abarrajar, *v.t.* to throw, hurl, fling with force and violence; (*Per.*) to become a ruffian.

abarrancadero, *n.m.;* **abarrancadura,** *n.f.* heavy road; precipice; [ATASCADERO, ATOLLADERO]; (*fig.*) difficult business, embarrassment.

abarrancado, -da, *a.* embarrassed, stranded.— *p.p.* [ABARRANCAR].

abarrancamiento, *n.m.* embarrassment; fall into a pit; (*naut.*) stranding.

abarrancar, *v.t.* (*pret.* **abarranqué**; *pres. subj.* **abarranque**) to ditch; to form a ravine.— *v.r.* to fall into a pit; to get into difficulties, become embarrassed. — *v.i.* (*naut.*) to run aground.

abarrar, *v.t.* [GOLPEAR].

abarraz, *n.m.* (*bot.*) louse-wort.

abarredera, *n.f.* broom, carpet-sweeper; anything that sweeps and cleans.

abarrotar, *v.t.* to tie, bind; to bar, strengthen with bars; (*naut.*) to stow a cargo; to over-stock.

abarrote, *n.m.* a small package for filling up; stop-gap; *tienda de abarrotes*, (*Am.*) retail grocery.

abarrotero, *n.m.* (*Am.*) grocer.

abarse, *v.r.* (defective, used only in the infinitive and the second person (sing. & pl.) of the imperative: *ábate, abáos*) to go; to move aside; to get away.

abasí, *a.* (*hist.*) Abbasid.

abastamiento, *n.m.* provisioning; supplying with stores, provisions, etc.

abastar, *v.t.* to provision, supply.

abastecedor, -ra, *n.m.f.,* *a.* caterer, provider, purveyor.

abastecer, *v.t., v.r.* (*pres. ind.* **abastezco**; *pres. subj.* **abastezca**) to supply, provision, purvey.

abastecimiento, *n.m.* provisioning, provisions, supplies.

abastero, *n.m.* (*Cub., Chi.*) purveyor of live-stock, fruit, vegetables.

abastionado, -da, *a.* similar to or protected by bastions. — *p.p.* [ABASTIONAR].

abastionar, *v.t.* (*mil.*) to fortify with bastions.

abasto, *n.m.* supply of provisions; (*fig.*) anything abundant; (*com.*) supply; *plaza de abastos*, public market; *dar*, or *no dar, abasto a una cosa*, to be equal, or not, to all exigencies (used usually in the negative); *no darse abasto*, to have too much to do.

abatanar, *v.t.* to beat or full (cloth).

abate, *n.m.* abbé, French or Italian priest.

abatí, *n.m.* (*Arg., Par.*) maize; liquor of maize.

abatida, *n.f.* (*mil.*) abattis.

abatidamente, *adv.* dejectedly.

abatidero, *n.m.* drain trench.

abatido, -da, *a.* dejected; spiritless; discouraged; crestfallen; faint; dismayed; abject; mean; (*coll.*) knocked down (in value or price); (*com.*) depreciated or fallen in price or demand. — *p.p.* [ABATIR].

abatidura, *n.f.* sudden descent of a bird of prey on its quarry.

abatimiento, *n.m.* depression, low spirits; (*naut.*) *abatimiento del rumbo*, leeway of a ship; (*aer.*) drift.

abatir, *v.t.* to throw down, bring down, knock down, undo; to flatten; to humble, debase; to overwhelm; to discourage, dishearten; to lay down, demolish; (*mech.*) to lower, depress; to dismount, take apart. — *v.i.* to descend, stoop. — *v.r.* to be disheartened, dismayed, depressed; to swoop; (*naut.*) to have leeway; (*aer.*) to drift; *abatirse al suelo*, to come down to the ground; *abatirse con dificultad*, to be not easily disheartened; *abatirse de ánimo*, to become discouraged;

abatirse en, or *por los contratiempos*, to become depressed by, through difficulties.

abayado, -da, *a.* (*bot.*) similar to a berry.

abazón, *n.m.* cheek-pouch.

abdicación, *n.f.* abdication; renunciation.

abdicar, *v.t.* (*pret.* **abdiqué**; *pres. subj.* **abdique**) to abdicate.

abdomen, *n.m.* abdomen.

abdominal, *a.* abdominal.

abducción, *n.f.* (*anat.*) abduction; (*log.; math.; law*) abduction.

abducir, *v.t.* (*log., math.*) to abduce.

abductor, *n.m.,* *a.* (*anat.*) abducent muscle; abductors.

abecé, *n.m.* A.B.C., the alphabet; rudiments; *no saber el abecé*, to be a dunce.

abecedario, *n.m.* alphabet; spelling-book, primer.

abedul, *n.m.* birch-tree.

abeja, *n.f.* bee; *abeja machiega, maesa, maestra, reina, madre*, queen bee; breeding bee; *abeja neutra, obrera*, working bee.

abejar, *n.m.* bee-hive; apiary; [COLMENA, COLMENAR]. — *a.*; *uva abejar*, grape much liked by bees.

abejarrón, *n.m.* bumble-bee.

abejaruco, *n.m.* (*ornith.*) bee-eater.

abejeo, *n.m.* buzz, hum (of crowd).

abejera, *n.f.* bee-hive; (*bot.*) bee-wort, balm-mint.

abejero, *n.m.* bee-keeper.

abejeruco, *n.m.* (*orn.*) bee-eater.

abejilla, -jita, -juela, *n.f.* little bee.

abejón, *n.m.* drone; hornet; rustic game; *jugar al abejón con*, to depreciate, despise.

abejorro, *n.m.* bumble-bee; (*fig.*) heavy, tedious person.

abejuno, -na, *a.* relating to the bee.

abelmosco, *n.m.* (*bot.*) abelmosk (*Hibiscus abelmoschus*); musk-okra, moschatel, *Adoxa moschatellina*.

abellacado, -da, *a.* mean-spirited, degraded. — *p.p.* [ABELLACAR].

abellacar, *v.t.* to vilify, debase. — *v.r.* to lower or degrade oneself.

abellotado, -da, *a.* in the form of an acorn. — *p.p.* [ABELLOTAR].

abellotar, *v.r.* to shape like an acorn. — *v.r.* to take the shape of an acorn.

abemoladamente, *adv.* softly.

abemolar, *v.t.* to soften (the voice); (*mus.*) to flat.

abéndula, *n.f.* blade of water-wheel.

aberenjenado, -da, *a.* egg-plant coloured; lilac. — *p.p.* [ABERENJENAR].

aberenjenar, *v.t., v.r.* to give or become egg-plant colour.

aberración, *n.f.* aberration; deviation; mania.

aberrar, *v.i.* to be mistaken or misled; to deviate.

aberrugado, -da, *a.* [AVERRUGADO].

abertal, *a.* soil easily cleft or cracking with drought. — *n.m.* crack; small opening.

abertura, *n.f.* aperture, opening; cleft, crevice; fissure, gap; outset; (*fig.*) openness of mind, sincerity.

abesana, *n.f.* [BESANA].

abestiado, -da, *a.* beast-like.

abestiarse, *v.r.* to become brutalized, stupid, besotted.

abetal, *n.m.* place covered with silver firs.

abete, *n.m.* (*bot.*) silver fir-tree; hook for holding cloth while cutting it.

abético, -ca, *a.* relating to *abeto.*

abetina, *n.f.* (*chem.*) abietin.

abetinote, *n.m.* rosin of the silver fir.

abeto, *n.m.* (*bot.*) silver-tree; yew-leaved fir; spruce; hemlock.

abetuna, *n.f.* fir-tree sprout.

abetunado, -da, *a.* resembling bitumen. — *p.p.* [ABETUNAR].

abetunar, *v.t.* to cover with pitch [EMBETUNAR].

abey, *n.m.* (*bot.*) a hardwood tree of the West Indies; *abey macho* (*bot.*) jacaranda.

abiar, *n.m.* camomile [ALBIHAR].

abiertamente, *adv.* openly, frankly, candidly.

abierto, -ta, *a.* open, clear; sincere, candid, frank, outspoken; (*bot.*) full-blown; *campo abierto,* open country; *carta abierta,* open letter; (*com.*) *cuenta abierta,* open account; (*com.*) *letra abierta,* open credit; *libro abierto,* at sight; *pueblo abierto,* unfortified town; *puerto abierto,* free port; *a pecho abierto,* openly, candidly. — *p.p. irreg.* [ABRIR].

abietina, *n.f.* [ABETINA].

abietíneas, *n.f.pl.* (*bot.*) plants forming the genus Abies.

abietino, *n.m.* [ABETINOTE].

abigarradamente, *adv.* in a variegated manner.

abigarrado, -da, *a.* variegated, motley, mottled, speckled. — *p.p.* [ABIGARRAR].

abigarrar, *v.t.* to paint with diverse ill-matched colours; to fleck, variegate.

abigeato, *n.m.* (*law*) theft of cattle.

abigeo, *n.m.* (*law*) cattle-thief.

abigotado, -da, *a.* wearing a heavy moustache [BIGOTUDO].

abimástico, -ca, *a.* abysmal.

abintestato, *n.m.* legal adjudication of an intestate estate.

abiótico, -ca, *a.* not life-producing or life-supporting.

abipón, -na, *a.* (*Am.*) Indian of a tribe on the river Paraná.

abirritar, *v.t.* (*med.*) lessen irritation.

abisagrar, *v.t.* to nail, fix hinges to doors, windows, etc.

abiselación, *n.f.* bevelling.

abiselado, -da, *a.* bevelled. — *p.p.* [ABISELAR].

abiseladura, *n.f.* bevelment.

abiselar, *v.t.* to bevel.

abisinio, -nia, *n.m.f., a.* Abyssinian.

abismado, -da, *a.* dejected, depressed; absorbed in thought.

abismal, *a.* abysmal. — *n.m.* clasp-nail, shingle-nail.

abismar, *v.t., v.r.* to depress, humble, destroy. — *v.r.* (*fig.*) to think *or* feel deeply.

abismo, *n.m.* abyss, gulf; immense depth; hell; (*fig.*) anything profound and unfathomable, as of ignorance *or* degradation.

abita, *n.f.* (*naut.*) bitt.

abitadura, *n.f.* (*naut.*) a turn of the cable round the bitts.

abitaque, *n.m.* (*arch.*) rafter; joist.

abitar, *v.t., v.r.* (*naut.*) to bitt.

abitas, *n.m.pl.* (*naut.*) bitts; *abitas del molinete,* carrick-bitts.

abitón, *n.m.* (*naut.*) topsail-sheet bitt.

abizcochado, -da, *a.* in the form of a biscuit. — *p.p.* [ABIZCOCHAR].

abjuración, *n.f.* abjuration, recantation.

abjurar, *v.t.* to abjure, forswear.

ablación, *n.f.* (*surg.*) ablation.

ablactación, *n.f.* weaning.

ablactar, *v.t.* to wean.

ablandabrevas, *n.m.f.* (*coll.*) good-for-nothing.

ablandador, -ra, *n.m.f.* mollifier.

ablandahigos, *n.m.f.* [ABLANDABREVAS].

ablandamiento, *n.m.* softening, pacification.

ablandante, *a.* soothing, mollifying.

ablandar, *v.t., v.i.* to soften, mollify, mellow, mitigate, assuage; to loosen; to melt, relent; to soothe; *ablandar las piedras,* to melt a heart of stone; to inspire great pity.

ablandativo, -va, *a.* mollifying.

ablandecer, *v.t.* [ABLANDAR].

ablanedo, *n.m.* (*prov.*) hazel-nut *or* filbert plantation [AVELLANEDO].

ablano, *n.m.* hazel-tree; filbert-tree [AVELLANO].

ablativo, *n.m.* (*gram.*) ablative case.

ablator, *n.m.* (*vet.*) ablator, instrument for removing the tails of sheep.

ablegado, *n.m.* ablegate, papal envoy charged with the delivery of the red biretta (*zucchetto*) to newly created cardinals. — *p.p.* [ABLEGAR].

ablepsia, *n.f.* (*med.*) ablepsia, lack of sight; (*fig.*) loss of mental powers.

ablución, *n.f.* ablution, washing, cleansing.

abnegación, *n.f.* abnegation, self-denial.

abnegar, *v.t., v.r.* (*pres. indic.* **abniego;** *pres. subj.* **abniegue**) to renounce; to deny oneself.

abobado, -da, *a.* stupid, silly; stupefied. — *p.p.* [ABOBAR].

abobamiento, *n.m.* stupidity; stupefaction.

abobar, *v.t.* to stupefy. — *v.r.* to grow stupid; to stand aghast.

abocadear, *v.t.* to bite.

abocado, *a.* mild, agreeable (applied to wine). — *p.p.* [ABOCAR].

abocamiento, *n.m.* meeting, interview; parley.

abocar, *v.t.* (*pret.* **aboqué;** *pres. subj.* **aboque**) to take *or* catch with the mouth; to open the mouth of (bag); to decant; to cause to approach, bring near; *abocar la artillería,* to bring the guns to bear; *abocar un estrecho,* (*naut.*) to enter the mouth of a channel or strait. — *v.r.* to meet by agreement, have an interview.

abocardado, -da, *a.* wide-mouthed. — *p.p.* [ABOCARDAR].

abocardar, *v.t.* to widen or expand the mouth (of tube, hole, etc.); to ream; to countersink.

abocardo, *n.m.* (*min.*) large drill.

abocetado, -da, *a.* unfinished, rough (of pictures).

abocetar, *v.t.* to make a rough sketch; to scribble.

abocinado, -da, *a.* bent; (*arch.*) depressed; shaped like a trumpet. — *p.p.* [ABOCINAR].

abocinadura, *n.f.* (*arch.*) arch.

abocinamiento, *n.m.* (*arch.*) arch.

abocinar, *v.i.* to fall upon the face. — *v.t.* to shape like a trumpet.

abochornado, -da, *a.* out of countenance, flushed, put to shame; (*bot.*) scorched. — *p.p.* [ABOCHORNAR].

abochornar, *v.t.* to overheat; (*fig.*) to become embarrassed; to shame, provoke. — *v.r.* (*fig.*) to blush; (*agric.*) to wilt, dry up from excessive heat. *abochornarse de algo,* to be ashamed of something; *abochornarse por alguno*, to feel ashamed for someone.

abofeteable, *a.* capable or deserving of slapping.

abofeteador, -ra, *n.m.f., a.* buffeter; one who insults.

abofeteamiento, *n.m.* slapping.

abofetear, *v.t.* to slap; to insult.

abogacía, *n.f.* profession of a lawyer or advocate; law (as a subject or profession).

abogada, *n.f.* mediatrix; counsellor's wife; lady barrister.

abogadear, *v.i.* to play the advocate (used contemptuously).

abogaderas, *f.pl.* (*Am.*) captious or insidious arguments.

abogadesco, -ca, *a.* appertaining to the *abogado* (only used contemptuously).

abogadillo, *n.m.* pettifogger.

abogado, *n.m.* lawyer, advocate, barrister; counsellor; mediator; *abogado de secano*, quack lawyer, charlatan; *abogado sin pleitos*, briefless lawyer; *abogado del diablo*, Devil's advocate. — *p.p.* [ABOGAR].

abogador, *n.m.* [MUÑIDOR].

abogar, *v.i.* (*pret.* **abogué;** *pres. subj.* **abogue**) to advocate, plead; (*fig.*) to intercede, mediate; *abogar por alguno*, to plead for someone.

abohetado, -da, *a.* inflated, swollen [ABUHADO].

abolengo, *n.m.* ancestry, lineage; (*law*) inheritance.

abolible, *a.* abolishable.

abolición, *n.f.* abolition, abrogation, extinction.

abolicionismo, *n.m.* abolitionism.

abolicionista, *n.m., a.* abolitionist.

abolir, *v.t. and defective* (the only moods and persons used are those which end in **i**), to abolish, annul, revoke, repeal.

abolitivo, -va, *a.* that abolishes.

abolorio, *n.m.* [ABOLENGO].

abolsado, -da, *a.* purse-shaped, pursed up, puckered.

abollado,-da, *a.* curled, fluted, plaited. — *p.p.* [ABOLLAR]. — *n.m., a.* [ALECHUGADO].

abolladura, *n.f.* unevenness, inequality; dent, bruise; embossment.

abollar, *v.t.* to emboss, bruise, dent; to annoy; to stun, confound; (*fig.*) to fatigue. — *v.r.* to get bruised, dented.

abollón, *n.m.* (*bot.*) bud, first shoot (vine).

abollonadura, *n.f.* embossment.

abollonamiento, *n.m.* (*bot.*) budding.

abollonar, *v.t.* to emboss. — *v.i.* to bind.

abomaso, *n.m.* (*vet.*) abomasus [CUAJAR].

abombado, -da, *a.* convex, arched; (*fig.*) deafened, stunned, giddy. — *p.p.* [ABOMBAR].

abombar, *v.t.* to give a convex form to; (*fig. & fam.*) to deafen, confuse; (*Am.*) tainted, approaching putrefaction.

abominable, *a.* abominable, detestable, odious, heinous.

abominablemente, *adv.* abominably.

abominación, *n.f.* abomination; detestation; execration.

abominar, *v.t.* to abominate; to detest, abhor.

abonable, *a.* which can be subscribed to; that can be improved; credited.

abonadamente, *adv.* with security or guarantee.

abonado, -da, *n.m.f.* subscriber; holder of a season-ticket; (*N. Amer.*) commuter. — *a.* rich; creditable, substantial; fit for. — *p.p.* [ABONAR].

abonador, -ra, *n.m.f., a.* (*com.*) person who goes bail or surety. — *n.m.* barrel-maker's auger.

abonamiento, *n.m.* bail, security [ABONO].

abonanzar, *v.i.* (*v. impers.: pres. subj.* **abonance**) (*naut.*) to grow calm; to clear up.

abonar, *v.t.* to bail, guarantee, insure, endorse, answer for; to give credit; (*com.*) to credit with, to put to the credit (of a person or commercial firm); to indemnify, compensate, pay; to improve; to manure. — *v.r.* to subscribe to; to buy a season or commutation ticket for. — *v.i.* to grow calm, clear up.

abonaré, *n.m.* promissory note; bill [PAGARÉ].

abono, *n.m.* security, guarantee; subscription; allowance, discount; receipt, voucher; manure, fertilizer.

abonuco, *n.m.* (*Cub.*) [BABUNUCO].

aboquillar, *v.t.* to add a mouthpiece; (*arch.*) to enlarge an opening on one side and narrow it on the other; (*arch.*) to bevel, chamfer.

abordable, *a.* (*naut.*) accessible.

abordador, *a.* (*naut.*) boarder; intruder.

abordaje, *n.m.* (*naut.*) the act of boarding a ship.

abordar, *v.t.* (*naut.*) to board a ship; to run foul of a ship; (*fig.*) to approach (a person); to undertake (business). — *v.i.* to put into a port; *abordar* (*una nave*) *a, con otra*, to run foul (one ship) of another.

abordo, *n.m.* the act of boarding a ship [ABORDAJE].

aborigen, *a.* aboriginal.

aborígenes, *n.m.pl.* aborigines.

aborlonado, -da, *a.* (*Chi., Col.*) ribbed, striped (cloth).

aborrachado, -da, *a.* high-coloured red; inflamed, flushed, purplish.

aborrajarse, *v.r.* the drying of the stalk before the ears are properly formed (corn, barley, etc.).

aborrascado, -da, *a.* hazardous, dangerous, exposed to storms. — *p.p.* [ABORRASCARSE].

aborrascarse, *v.r.* to become stormy.

aborrecedor, -ra, *n.m.f.* hater, detester. — *a.* detestable, odious.

aborrecer, *v.t.* (*pres. ind.* **aborrezco;** *pres. subj.* **aborrezca**) to hate, abhor; to desert (of birds); to weary, bore. — *v.r.* to hate each other; to become bored, weary; *aborrecer de muerte*, to hate like poison, to death.

aborrecible, *a.* hateful, detestable; forbidding.

aborreciblemente, *adv.* **aborrecidamente,** *adv.* hatefully, odiously.

aborrecido, -da, *a.* weary, bored [ABURRIDO]. — *p.p.* [ABORRECER].

aborrecimiento, *n.m.* hate, detestation, dislike; grudge; abhorrence, tediousness; boredom.

aborregado, -da, *a.* fleecy (sky). — *p.p.* [ABORREGARSE].

aborregarse, *v.r.* to become fleecy (sky).

abortamiento, *n.m.* abortion.

abortar, *v.i.* (*med.*) to miscarry; to abort (a disease); (*fig.*) to fail; (*bot.*) not to ripen.

abortivamente, *adv.* abortively; untimely, inopportunely.

abortivo, -va, *a.* abortive; producing abortion. — *n.m.* abortive remedy.

aborto, *n.m.* miscarriage, abortion; monster; (*fig.*) failure.

abortón, *n.m.* the miscarriage of an animal; unborn lamb's skin.

aborujar, *v.t.* to make lumps. — *v.r.* to become lumpy; to muffle up.

abotagarse, *v.r.* to become swollen, inflated; (*fig.*) to become silly.

abotinado, -da, *a.* shaped like a half-gaiter.

abotonador, *n.m.* button-hook.

abotonar, *v.t.* to button. — *v.i.* to bud; germinate. — *v.r.* to button up (one's coat).

abovedado, -da, *a.* (*arch.*) arched, vaulted. — *p.p.* [ABOVEDAR].

abovedar, *v.t.* (*arch.*) to arch, vault, make vault-shaped.

aboyado, -da, *a.* rented with oxen for ploughing (of a farm).

aboyar, *v.t.* (*naut.*) to lay down buoys. *v.i.* to float.

abozalar, *v.t.* to muzzle.

abra, *n.f.* bay, haven; cove, creek; valley, dale; gorge, fissure; (*Col.*) half section of a door or window.

abracar, *v.t.* (*CR., Cub., Ec., Per.*) to gird, surround, embrace.

abracijo, *n.m.* (*coll.*) embrace, hug.

abrahonar, *v.t.* (*coll.*) to hold one fast by the garment.

abrandecosta, *n.m.* (*Cub.*) a hard-wood tree (*Bunchosia nitida*).

abrasadamente, *adv.* ardently.

abrasado, -da, *a.* red-hot, burning; (*fig.*) flushed, angry. — *p.p.* [ABRASAR].

abrasador, -ra, *a.* burning, exceedingly hot.

abrasamiento, *n.m.* burning; inflammation; excess of passion.

abrasante, *a.* burning.

abrasar, *v.t.* to burn; to set on fire; to dry up; to provoke; (*fig.*) to squander. — *v.r.* to glow; to be agitated by any violent passion; *abrasarse vivo*, to be hot with passion; (*agric.*) to wither; (*fig.*) to make ashamed; *abrasarse las pajarillas*, to feel great heat; *muchas hijas en casa, todo se abrasa*, many daughters are expensive; *abrasarse de amor*, to become passionately in love; *abrasarse en deseos*, to become full of desires.

abrasilado, -da, *a.* of the colour of brazil-wood.

abrasión, *n.f.* (*geol., med.*) abrasion.

abraxas, *n.m.* abraxas; abraxas stone.

abrazadera, *n.f.* clasp, clamp, cleat, band; (*print.*) brace, bracket. — *a.* [SIERRA ABRAZADERA].

abrazado, -da, *a.* (*sl.*) imprisoned. — *p.p.* [ABRAZAR].

abrazador, -ra, *n.m.f.* embracer; hook; thief-catcher; kind of bolster used in the Philippines. — *a.* embracing.

abrazamiento, *n.m.* embracing.

abrazante, *a.* embracing.

abrazar, *v.t.* (*pret.* **abracé**; *pres. subj.* **abrace**) to embrace, hug, clasp; to clamp, cleat; to contain, comprise; to surround; to accept, follow; to take charge of; *abrazar la vida religiosa*, to adopt a religious vocation. — *v.r.* to embrace; to be attached to each other.

abrazo, *n.m.* embrace, clasp, hug.

ábrego, *n.m.* south wind.

abrelatas, *n.m.* tin-opener.

abrenuncio, *Lat. interj.* far be it from me; fie!

abrepuño, *n.m.* (*bot.*) lesser burdock; milk thistle.

abretonar, *v.t.* (*naut.*) to lash the guns to the ship's side.

abrevadero, *n.m.* watering-place for cattle; drinking trough.

abrevado, -da, *a.* watered; steeped (leather); moistened; (*med.*) damp. — *p.p.* [ABREVAR].

abrevador, *n.m.* one who waters cattle; drinking trough.

abrevar, *v.t.* to water cattle; to irrigate; to moisten skins with water.

abreviación, *n.f.* abbreviation, shortening; abridgment; reduction; hastening, acceleration.

abreviadamente, *adv.* briefly, in short.

abreviador, -ra, *n.m.f.,* *a.* one who shortens, abridges. — *n.m.* (*eccl.*) a pontifical officer who issues briefs and bulls.

abreviaduría, *n.f.* office of the pontifical issuer of briefs.

abreviamiento, *n.m.* abbreviation.

abreviar, *v.t.* to abridge, shorten, cut short, reduce; to hasten, accelerate.

abreviativo, -va, *a.* abbreviatory, abridging.

abreviatura, *n.f.* abbreviation; contraction; shorthand; *en abreviatura*, in abbreviation; (*coll.*) hastily.

abreviaturía, *n.f.* office of the pontifical issuer of briefs.

abribonarse, *v.r.* to become lazy; to loaf; to become a rascal.

abridero, -ra, *a.* easily opened; free-stone, free-shell (of peaches); aperitive. — *n.m.* (*bot.*) sort of free-stone peach.

abridor, -ra, *a.* open, opening. — *n.m.* nectarine, free-stone peach-tree; ear-drop or wire to keep ears pierced; opener; grafting-knife; *abridor de láminas*, engraver; *abridor en hueco*, die or punch-sinker; *abridor de guantes*, glove-stretcher; *abridor de latas*, tin-opener.

abrigadero, *n.m.* (*naut.*) sheltered place, shelter.

abrigado, -da, *a.* warm (of clothes), sheltered, covered. — *n.m.* shelter. — *p.p.* [ABRIGAR].

abrigador, -ra, *a.* (*Mex., Per.*) that which covers or protects well; *gabán muy abrigador*, very warm overcoat; (*Mex.*) concealer of a crime.

abrigaño, *n.m.* shelter for cattle; (*agric.*) matting for protecting plants; brick and tile kilns.

abrigar, *v.t.* (*pret.* **abrigué**; *pres. subj.* **abrigue**) to shelter, protect, cover, lodge; (*fig.*) to patronize, nourish; to cherish, warm. — *v.r.* to take shelter; to put on a wrap; *abrigarse bajo techado*, to shelter oneself under a roof; *abrigarse con ropa*, to protect oneself with clothes; *abrigarse del aguacero*, to shelter from the heavy rain; *abrigarse en el portal*, to take shelter in the doorway.

abrigo, *n.m.* shelter, protection, cover; aid, support; overcoat, wrap; (*naut.*) harbour, haven; *al abrigo de*, sheltered from; under protection of; shielded by.

abril, *n.m.* April. *n.m.pl.* (*fig.*) years; youth; *los dieciseis abriles*, sweet sixteen; *estar hecho*, or *parecer un abril*, to be gay, smart, handsome; *abril, aguas mil*, April showers; *estar hecho un abril*, to be dressed up smartly.

abrileño, -ña, *a.* April (used adjectively), relating to, or like, April.

abrillantado, -da, *a.* brilliant, shining, sparkling. — *n.m.* operation of imparting brilliance. — *p.p.* [ABRILLANTAR].

abrillantador, *n.m.* diamond cutter (workman or instrument).

abrillantar, *v.t.* to cut diamonds; to make sparkle; polish, brighten; to impart brilliance.

abrimiento, *n.m.* opening.

abrir, *v.t.* (*p.p.* **abierto**) to open, unlock, unfasten, uncover, unseal; to begin, inaugurate; to remove obstacles, force a path; to engrave; to expand, separate, distend; to cut open, cleave, rend, dig. — *v.i.* to open, unfold, unclose; to extend; to display. — *v.r.* to open, expand, crack, gape, yawn; to confide, unbosom oneself, communicate; *abrir la corona*, to shave the tonsure; *abrir el día*, to dawn; *abrir el ojo*, to be on the alert; *abrir paso*, to clear the way; *abrir la mano*, to accept bribes, be generous; *abrir la mano al caballo*, to give rein to a horse; *abrir registro*, (*naut.*) to begin to take in cargo; *abrir(se) una vía de agua*, (*naut.*) to spring a leak; *abrir las zanjas*, to lay the foundations of a building; *abrir la procesión*, to head the procession; *abrir brecha en un muro*, to make a breach in a fortress; *abrir brecha*, to make advances to someone; to tempt; *abrir camino*, to clear the way; (*fig.*) to advance, facilitate, give the means of success; *abrir trincheras*, to open trenches; to begin a siege; *en un abrir y cerrar de ojos*, in the twinkling of an eye; *abrirse las cataratas del cielo*, to rain heavily; to pour; *abre el tiempo*, the weather clears up; *la madera se abre*, the wood cracks; *abrir puerta a la puerta*, to afford an opportunity; *abre el ojo que asan carne*, improve the opportunity; *abrir los oídos*, to open one's ears; *abrir los ojos a uno*, to undeceive someone; to open one's eyes; *abrir tanto ojo*, to stare with joy; *abrir a chasco*, to mock, to jest; *abrir las ganas*, to awaken the appetite; *abrir su pecho a alguno*, *abrirse con alguno*, to confide in someone; *abrir (una lámina) a buril*, to engrave; *abrir de arriba abajo*, to open from top to bottom; *abrir en canal*, to dig a trench; *abrirse a, con los amigos*, to confide in one's friends.

abrochador, *n.m.* button-hook.

abrochadura, *n.f.*; **abrochamiento,** *n.m.* buttoning, fastening or lacing on.

abrochar, *v.t.* to button on, clasp, buckle, fasten with hooks and eyes; (*Chi., Ec.*) to chastise, punish, reprehend; (*Chi.*) to scuffle, come to blows.

abrogación, *n.f.* (*law*) abrogation, repeal.

abrogar, *v.t.* (*pret.* **abrogué;** *pres. subj.* **abrogue**) (*law*) to abrogate, annul, repeal.

abrogatorio, -ria, *a.* abrogative.

abrojal, *n.m.* thistly ground.

abrojillo, *n.m.* small thistle.

abrojín, *n.m.* (*ichth.*) purple sea-snail.

abrojo, *n.m.* thistle; thorn; prickle; (*mil.*) caltrop; (*bot.*) crowfoot. — *pl.* (*naut.*) hidden rocks in the sea; (*fig.*) difficulties.

abromado, -da, *a.* (*naut.*) hazy, foggy; worm-eaten. — *p.p.* [ABROMARSE].

abromarse, *v.r.* (*naut.*) to become worm-eaten.

abroncar, *v.t., v.r.* (*fam.*) to annoy, vex, irritate.

abroquelado, -da, *a.* (*bot.*) in the form of a shield. — *p.p.* [ABROQUELAR].

abroquelar, *v.t.* (*naut.*) to box-haul. — *v.r.* to shield or defend oneself; *abroquelarse con* or *de su inocencia*, to defend oneself by one's innocence.

abrótano, *n.m.* (*bot.*) southern-wood.

abrotoñar, *v.i.* (*bot.*) to bud, germinate, sprout; to burst (water).

abrumado, -da, *a.* weary; overwhelmed, overcome; *abrumado bajo*, bending under. — *p.p.* [ABRUMAR].

abrumador, -ra, *a.* vexatious; oppressive; wearying.

abrumar, *v.t.* to crush, overwhelm, oppress; to weary, annoy. — *v.r.* to become foggy; to worry.

abrupto, -ta, *a.* craggy, rugged, abrupt.

abrutado, -da, *a.* brutish, bestial. — *p.p.* [ABRUTAR].

abruzo, -za, *n.m.f., a.* Abruzzian.

absceso, *n.m.* (*med.*) abscess.

abscisa, *n.f.* (*geom.*) abscissa.

abscisión, *n.f.* (*med.*) incision.

absentismo, *n.m.* absenteeism.

ábside, *n.m.f.* (*arch.*) apse.

absintina, *n.f.* (*chem.*) absinthin.

absintio, *n.m.* (*bot.*) wormwood [AJENJO].

absintismo, *n.m.* (*med.*) absinthism.

absolución, *n.f.* absolution, pardon, acquittal; *absolución de la demanda*, (*law*) finding for the defendant; *absolución libre*, acquittal, verdict of not guilty.

absoluta, *n.f.* dogma; universal proposition; ipse dixit, dictum; total liberation from military service; (*fig.*) *tener su absoluta*, to have a pension.

absolutamente, *adv.* absolutely.

absolutismo, *n.m.* autocracy; despotism.

absolutista, *n.m.f., a.* absolutist.

absoluto, -ta, *a.* absolute, unconditional; imperious, despotic. — *adv. en absoluto*, absolutely (not).

absolutorio, -ria, *a.* (*law*) absolving, absolutory.

absolvederas, *n.f.pl.* (*fam.*) facility with which some priests give absolution; *buenas absolvederas*, facility for pardoning.

absolvente, *a.* absolving.

absolver, *v.t.* (*pres. ind.* **absuelvo;** *pres. subj.* **absuelva;** *p.p.* **absuelto**) to absolve; to acquit; *absolver del cargo*, to absolve from the charge; *absolver las preguntas*, to answer questions; *absolver de la instancia*, to pardon a criminal.

absorbencia, *n.f.* absorbability; absorption.

absorbente, *n.m., a.* absorbefacient, absorbent; absorber; engrossing.

absorber, *v.t.* (*p.p.* **absorbido, absorto**) to absorb, imbibe; to engross.

absorbible, *a.* (*physiol.*) absorbable.

absorbimiento, *n.m.* [ABSORCIÓN].

absorción, *n.f.* absorption.

absortar, *v.t.* to cause rapture; to strike with amazement.

absorto, -ta, *a.* absorbed in thought; amazed. — *p.p. irreg.* [ABSORBER].

abstemio, -mia, *a.* abstemious.

abstención, *n.f.* abstention; self-denial; forbearance.

abstencionista, *n.m.f., a.* abstentionist (politics).

abstenerse, *v.r.* (*pres. ind.* **abstengo;** *pret.* **abstuve;** *pres. subj.* **abstenga**) to abstain, forbear; *abstenerse de lo vedado*, to abstain from what is prohibited.

abstergente, *n.m.,* *a.* (*med.*) cleansing; detergent; abstergent.

absterger, *v.t.* (*med.*) to absterge; to cleanse, sterilize.

abstersión, *n.f.* (*med.*) abstersion, cleansing, purification.

abstersivo, -va, *a.* (*med.*) cleansing; detergent.

abstinencia, *n.f.* abstinence; forbearance; fasting; *día de abstinencia*, fast-day.

abstinente, *a.* abstemious, abstinent.

abstinentemente, *adv.* abstinently.

abstracción, *n.f.* abstraction; preoccupation.

abstractivamente, *adv.* abstractedly.

abstractivo, -va, *a.* abstractive.

abstracto, -ta, *a.* abstract; imaginary; *en abstracto*, in the abstract. — *p.p.* *obs.* [ABSTRAER].

abstraer, *v.t.* (*pres. indic.* **abstraigo;** *pret.* **abstraje;** *pres. subj.* **abstraiga;** *p.p.* **abstraído**) to abstract (idea, etc.). — *v.i. abstraer de*, to do without, leave aside. — *v.r.* to concentrate one's mind; to be or become absorbed.

abstraído, -da, *a.* retired, secluded; absent-minded. — *p.p. irreg.* [ABSTRAER].

abstraigo; abstraiga, *pres. indic.; pres. subj.* [ABSTRAER].

abstraje, *pret.* [ABSTRAER].

abstruso, -sa, *a.* difficult, abstruse.

abstuve, *pret.* [ABSTENERSE].

absuelto, -ta, *a.* acquitted, absolved. — *p.p. irreg.* [ABSOLVER].

absuelvo; absuelva, *pres. indic.; pres. subj.* [ABSOLVER].

absurdamente, *adv.* absurdly.

absurdidad, *n.f.* absurdity.

absurdo, -da, *a.* absurd, nonsensical. — *n.m.* absurdity, nonsense; *reducción al absurdo*, reductio ad absurdum.

abubilla, *n.f.* (*orn.*) hoopoe.

abubo, *n.m.* (*prov.*) (*bot.*) fruit of *cermeño;* (*fig.*) simpleton, ninny.

abuchear, *v.t.* (*coll.*) to scoff.

abucheo, *n.m.* (*coll.*) outcry.

abuela, *n.f.* grandmother; old woman, crone; *no necesita* (or *no tiene* or *se le ha muerto la*) *abuela*, he doesn't need a trumpeter (*i.e.* he is continually praising himself); *cuénteselo a su abuela*, (ironically) tell that to your grandmother.

abuelo, *n.m.* grandfather; (mainly as plural) ancestor; old man.

abuhardillado, -da, *a.* like a garret or skylight.

abuinche, *n.m.* (*Col.*) machete used to fell and strip the bark of cinchona trees.

abuje, *n.m.* (*Cub., PR.*) a tick attacking human beings.

abultadamente, *adv.* in bulk.

abultado, -da, *a.* big, bulky, massive; (*fig.*) exaggerated; *abultado de facciones*, coarse, big-featured; *abultado de carnes*, squat, thick-set. — *p.p.* [ABULTAR].

abultar, *v.t.* to enlarge, augment; (*fig.*) to exaggerate. — *v.i.* to be large or bulky.

abundamiento, *n.m.* abundance, plenty. — *adv. a mayor abundamiento*, moreover, furthermore, in confirmation.

abundancia, *n.f.* abundance, plenty; opulence;

fertility, fruitfulness; *cuerno de la abundancia*, horn of plenty; *de la abundancia del corazón habla la boca*, one speaks of what is nearest one's heart.

abundancial, *a.* abundant; (*gram.*) *adjetivo abundancial*, augmentative adjective.

abundante, *a.* abundant, plenteous, copious.

abundantemente, *adv.* abundantly.

abundar, *v.i.* to abound, have plenty; *lo que abunda, no daña*, you can't have too much of a good thing; *abundar de* or *en riqueza*, to abound in riches; *abundar en su sentido*, to adhere to one's opinion.

abundosamente, *adv.* abundantly, plentifully.

abundoso, -sa, *a.* abundant, plentiful.

abuñolado, -da, *a.* [ABUÑUELADO]. — *p.p.* [ABUÑOLAR].

abuñolar, abuñuelar, *v.t.* to turn eggs in frying; to shape like a fritter.

abuñuelado, -da, *a.* turned, fritter-shaped (of fried eggs).

¡abur!, *interj.* adieu, farewell, good-bye [¡AGUR!].

aburar, *v.t.* to burn, scorch.

aburelado, -da, *a.* of dark red wool; like fustian; [BURIELADO]. — *p.p.* [ABURELAR].

aburelar, *v.t.* to give a reddish colour.

aburilar, *v.t.* to engrave.

aburrado, -da, *a.* brutish; (*Mex.*) applied to a brood-mare kept for breeding mules. — *p.p.* [ABURRARSE].

aburrarse, *v.r.* to become brutish.

aburrición, *n.f.* (*coll.*) annoyance; weariness.

aburrido, -da, *a.* weary, bored. — *p.p.* [ABURRIR].

aburridor, -ra, *n.m.f.* bore. — *a.* tiresome, boring.

aburrimiento, *n.m.* annoyance, weariness; tediousness, boredom.

aburrir, *v.t.* to annoy, vex, tire, bore, weary, perplex; (*fam.*) to venture, hazard; to spend. — *v.r.* to grow tired, weary of, be bored; *aburrirse con* (or *de* or *por*) *todo*, to become bored with everything; *aburrirse en casa*, to be bored at home.

aburujado, -da, *a.* pressed together; perplexed. — *p.p.* [ABURUJAR].

aburujar, *v.t.* to make into lumps. — *v.r.* to clot.

abusador, -ra, *n.m.f.* abuser. — *a.* abusive.

abusante, *a.* abusing.

abusar, *v.t.* to abuse, misapply, profit unduly by; to impose upon; *abusar de la amistad*, to abuse friendship.

abuse, *n.m.* (*Cub., PR.*), see **abuje.**

abusión, *n.f.* abuse; superstition.

abusionero, -ra, *a.* superstitious. — *n.m.* fortune-teller, soothsayer.

abusivamente, *adv.* abusively.

abusivo, -va, *a.* abusive.

abuso, *n.m.* abuse, misuse; *eso es un abuso de confianza*, that is taking an unfair advantage.

abyección, *n.f.* abjectness; servility.

abyecto, -ta, *a.* abject, dejected; servile.

acá, *adv.* here, this way, hither, this side; *¿de cuándo acá?* since when? *ven acá*, come along, come here; *acá no se estila*, that is not the custom here; *acá y allá* (or *acá y acullá*), here and there; *desde entonces acá*, since that time; *acá en la tierra, acá abajo*, here below; *por acá*, here, hereabouts, this way; *para acá*, hither, here; (*coll.*) *acá estamos todos*, here we are; *sin más acá, ni más allá*, without more ado.

acabable, *a.* that can be finished, practicable; achievable.

acabadamente, *adv.* completely, perfectly.

acabado, -da, *a.* perfect, complete, consummate, well-finished, faultless; (*fam.*) old; shabby, ill-dressed; dejected; worn-out, dilapidated, ruined. — *n.m.* (*art*) the last touch; to touch up, finish. — *p.p.* [ACABAR].

acabador, -ra, *n.m.f.* finisher, completer. — *a.* finishing.

acabalar, *v.t.* to complete, finish.

acaballadero, *n.m.* the time when and place where horses cover mares.

acaballado, -da, *a.* like a horse; *cara acaballada,* horse-faced; *narices acaballadas,* horse-like nostrils. — *p.p.* [ACABALLAR].

acaballar, *v.t.* to cover, serve (mares).

acaballerado, -da, *a.* gentlemanlike, ladylike; noble. — *p.p.* [ACABALLERAR].

acaballerar, *v.t.* to render genteel; to make a person behave as a gentleman. — *v.r.* to conduct oneself as a gentleman.

acaballonar, *v.t.* (*agric.*) to ridge land.

acabamiento, *n.m.* end, completion, death; consummation.

acabar, *v.t.,* *v.i.* to finish, end, conclude, complete, make, achieve; to harass, exhaust; to destroy; to die; to fail; to consume; to extinguish; ¡*acabara ya!* or ¡*acabáramos!* (*coll.*) at last, at long last! *acabar con,* to obtain; to finish, destroy, extirpate; *acabar con el negocio,* to make an end of an affair; *acabar con su hacienda,* to finish with his property; *acabar de* (foll. by *inf.*), to have just (foll. by *p.p.*); *acaba de salir, venir,* he has just gone out, arrived; *está acabado de salir . . . ,* it is fresh from . . . ; *la espada acaba en punta,* the sword ends in a point; *acabar en bien,* to terminate successfully; *acabar por negarse,* to end by refusing. — *v.r.* to die, end, be finished; to fail; to grow feeble or less; to diminish; to become exhausted; to be, or run out of; *se me acaba el agua,* the water is running out, I am short of water; *se me ha acabado la paciencia,* my patience is exhausted; *es cosa de nunca acabarse,* it is an endless affair; *la vela se está acabando,* the candle is flickering; *acabados son cuentos,* there is an end to it (conversation or dispute); ¡*se acabó!* it's all up, all over; (*Ec.*) to defame *or* discredit a person.

acabellado, -da, *a.* light chestnut colour.

acabestrado, -da, *a.* similar to a halter.

acabestrar, *v.t.* to accustom to the halter.

acabestrillar, *v.i.* to go fowling with a stalking-horse or ox.

acabijo, *n.m.* (*coll.*) end, termination, conclusion.

acabildar, *v.t.* to unite persons by persuasion to do something.

acabo, *n.m.* [ACABAMIENTO].

acabóse, *n.m.* (*fam.*) end (usually tragic or disastrous); *ser una cosa el acabóse,* that is the limit.

acabronado, -da, *a.* resembling a buck; bold, unembarrassed.

acacia, *n.f.* (*bot.*) acacia.

acacharse, *v.r.* (*coll.*) [AGACHARSE]; (*Chi.*) to rig the market.

acachetar, *v.t.* to strike the bull with the poniard.

academia, *n.f.* academy; school; university; literary society; (*art*) nude study from nature.

académicamente, *adv.* in an academic sense.

académico, -ca, *a.* academical. — *n.m.* academician.

acadenillar, *v.t.* to form like a small chain.

acaecedero, -ra, *a.* eventual, contingent.

acaecer, *v.i. def.* (*subj.* **acaezca**) to happen, come to pass; *acaecer en tal tiempo,* to happen at a certain time; *acaecer* (*algo*) *a alguno,* to happen (something) to someone.

acaecimiento, *n.m.* event, incident.

acaezca, *pres. subj.* [ACAECER].

acahé, *n.m.* (*Par.*) magpie.

acahual, *n.m.* (*bot.*) (*Mex.*) sunflower.

acahualillo, *n.m.* (*Mex.*) herbaceous plant.

acal, *n.m.* (*Mex.*) canoe; any vessel.

acalabazado, -da, *a.* similar to a pumpkin or gourd. — *p.p.* [ACALABAZARSE].

acalabazarse, *v.r.* to become like a pumpkin or gourd; (*fig.*) to become brutish.

acalabrotar, *v.t.* (*naut.*) to make a cable by intertwining three ropes each containing three strands.

acalaca, *n.f.* (*Am.*) ant.

acaldar, *v.t.* (*Per.*) to intimidate, overwhelm, oppress.

acalefo, -fa, *n.m.f., a.* (*zool.*) acalephan. — *n.m.pl.* Acalephæ, a class of marine animals containing sea-nettles, jelly-fish, etc.

acalenturado, -da, *a.* feverish. — *p.p.* [ACALENTURARSE].

acalenturarse, *v.r.* to become feverish.

acalia, *n.f.* (*bot.*) marsh-mallow.

acaloradamente, *adv.* warmly; excitedly.

acalorado, -da, *a.* excited, heated, fiery, angry, irritated. — *p.p.* [ACALORAR].

acaloramiento, *n.m.* ardour, heat, excitement.

acalorar, *v.t.* to warm; to inflame, overheat, urge on; to encourage, forward, promote. — *v.r.* to grow warm, excited; *acalorarse por, en, con la disputa,* to become heated by, in, because of the debate.

acaloro, *n.m.* overheating, suffocation.

acalote, *n.m.* (*Mex.*) (*orn.*) wading bird (*Tantalus mexicanus*).

acallantar, *v.t.* [ACALLAR].

acallar, *v.t.* to quiet, hush; to mitigate, assuage.

acamar, *v.t.* to blow down; to lay plants flat (by a storm). — *v.r.* to be blown down.

acamastronarse, *v.i.* (*Per.*) to become sly, crafty, cunning.

acambrayado, -da, *a.* cambric-like.

acamellado, -da, *a.* camel-like.

acamellonar, *v.i.* (*Mex., Cent. Am.*) to make ridges with plough or spade.

acampado, -da, *a.* encamped. — *p.p.* [ACAMPAR].

acampamento, *n.m.* (*mil.*) encampment, camp.

acampanado, -da, *a.* bell-shaped. — *p.p.* [ACAMPANAR].

acampanar, *v.t., v.r.* to shape like a bell.

acampar, *v.t., v.r., v.i.* to encamp.

acampo, *n.m.* waste land, common pasture [DEHESA].

ácana, *n.f.* a hard reddish wood of Cuba.

acanalado, -da, *a.* passing through a channel; channelled, striate, fluted, corrugated. —*p.p.* [ACANALAR].

acanalador, *n.m.* (*mech.*) grooving-plane.

acanalados, *n.m.pl.* ridge of a horse's back.
acanaladura, *n.f.* (*arch.*) groove, stria, striation.
acanalar, *v.t.* to make a channel; to flute, groove, corrugate.
acanallarse, *v.r.* to become a ruffian; to keep low company.
acandilado, -da, *a.* made with sharp points; in the form of a lamp; shaped like a three-cornered hat; dazzled. — *p.p.* [ACANDILAR].
acandilar, *v.t.* to shape like a lamp.
acanelado, -da, *a.* cinnamon-coloured or flavoured.
acanillado, -da, *a.* making furrows; ribbed, striped (of cloth).
acantáceas, *n.f.pl.* (*bot.*) Acanthaceæ.
acantáceo, -cea, (*bot.*) acanthaceous.
acantalear, *v. impers.* to hail large hailstones.
acantarar, *v.t.* to measure by *cántaras*.
acantilado, -da, *a.* bold, steep, sheer; *costa acantilada*, inaccessible coast.—*n.m.* cliff. — *p.p.* [ACANTILAR].
acantilar, *v.t.*, *v.r.* (*naut.*) to founder in a rocky cove.
acanto, *n.m.* (*bot.*) prickly thistle; (*arch.*) acanthus.
acántolis, *n.m.* (*Cub.*) reptile covered with sharp-pointed tubercles.
acantonamiento, *n.m.* cantonment; military depot.
acantonar, *v.t.* to quarter troops. — *v.r.* to be provided with quarters.
acañaverear, *v.t.* to wound with sharp-pointed canes.
acañoneamiento, *n.m.* cannonade.
acañonear, *v.t.* to cannonade.
acañutado, -da, *a.* [ACANUTILLADO].
acaparador, -ra, *a.* monopolizing. — *n.m.f.* monopolizer.
acaparamiento, *n.m.* monopoly.
acaparar, *v.t.* to monopolize; to corner, control a market.
acaparrarse, *v.r.* to come to terms, to close a bargain.
acaparrosado, -da, *a.* copperas-hued.
acapillar, *v.t.* to grasp, seize.
acápite, *n.m.* (*Am.*) separate paragraph.
acapizarse, *v.r.* (*coll.*, *prov.*) to grapple; clinch.
acaponado, -da, *a.* capon-like; effeminate; *rostro acaponado*, hairless face; *voz acaponada*, shrill voice.
acaracolado, -da, *a.* spiral-shaped; winding.
acaraira, *n.f.* (*Cub.*) bird of prey.
acarambanado, -da, *a.* forming icicles.
acaramelado, -da, *a.* caramel-like; (*fam.*) over-polite, mealy-mouthed, spoony, mawkish. — *p.p.* [ACARAMELAR].
acaramelar, *v.t.* to make caramel or like caramel. — *v.r.* (*fig.*) to show oneself over-polite, hypocritical.
acarar, *v.t.* to confront, face, brave.
acardenalado, -da, *a.* covered with weals, livid. — *p.p.* [ACARDENALAR].
acardenalar, *v.t.* to beat black and blue. — *v.r.* to be covered with weals.
acareamiento, *n.m.* confronting, facing.
acarear, *v.t.* to confront, face, brave.
acariciador, -ra, *a.* fondling, caressing. — *n.m.f.* fondler.
acariciar, *v.t.* to fondle, caress, embrace, hug; to cherish, love devotedly; to touch lightly.
acarminado, -da, *a.* carmine-coloured.

acarnerado, -da, *a.* said of horses having the head shaped like sheep.
ácaro, *n.m.* (*zool.*) acarus; *ácaro de queso*, cheese-mite.
acarralar, *v.t.*, *v.r.* to miss a thread in weaving.
acarrarse, *v.r.* to go under the shade (applied to sheep).
acarrazar, *v.t.*, *v.r.* (*coll.*, *prov.*) to grab, hold hard in a scuffle.
acarreadizo, -za, *a.* portable.
acarreador, -ra, *n.m.f.*, *a.* carrier, porter.
acarreamiento, *n.m.* carrying, cartage. — *n.pl.* supplies.
acarrear, *v.t.* to carry, cart, convey, transport, forward; to cause, occasion; *acarrear a lomo*, to carry on the back; *acarrear en ruedas*, to carry on wheels; *acarrear por agua*, to carry by water. — *v.r.* to bring upon oneself.
acarreo, *n.m.* carrying, cartage. — *pl.* supplies; *cosas de acarreo*, freight; *tierras de acarreo*, alluvium.
acarreto (**hilo de**), *n.m.* packthread [BRAMANTE].
acarroñar, *v.i.* (*Col.*) to cower, quail; to flag.
acartonado, -da, *a.* pasteboard-like; dried-up by age (persons). — *p.p.* [ACARTONAR].
acartonamiento, *n.m.* hardening like cardboard (said specially of organic bodies).
acartonar, *v.t.* to give or have the appearance or consistency of cardboard. — *v.r.* (*fam.*) to become dried up by age.
acasamatado, -da, *a.* (*mil.*) having or resembling a casemate.
acasanate, *n.m.* (*Mex.*) black bird which destroys the maize lands.
acaseramiento, *n.m.* (*Per.*) to patronize a shop.
acaserarse, *v.r.* (*Chi.*, *Per.*) to become a regular customer; to become fond of.
acaso, *n.m.* chance; accident. — *adv.* by chance, by accident; maybe, mayhap, perhaps; ¿*acaso*? how? how now? *por si acaso*, in case (anything should happen).
acastañado, -da, *a.* reddish-brown.
acastillaje, *n.m.* (*naut.*) upper works of a ship [OBRAS MUERTAS].
acastillar, *v.t.* to put the upper works on a ship.
acastorado, -da, *a.* similar to beaver fur.
acatable, *a.* venerable.
acatadamente, *adv.* respectfully.
acataléctico, acatalecto, *a.* (*poet.*) acatalectic.
acatalepsia, *n.f.* (*med.*) acatalepsy.
acataléptico, -ca, *a.* acataleptic.
acatamiento, *n.m.* esteem, respect; veneration, reverence, obeisance; acknowledgment; presence, view.
acatante, *n.m.f.*, *a.* one who respects; respectful.
acatar, *v.t.* to respect, revere, do homage to; *acatar abajo*, to belittle.
acatarrado, *p.p.* [ACATARRARSE].
acatarrarse, *v.r.* to catch cold; (*Mex.*) to importune, pester.
acatéchili, *n.m.* (*orn.*) (*Mex.*) kind of green finch (*Fringila mexicana*).
acates, *n.m.* Achates, true friend.
acatitado, *a.* similar to *catite*, sugar-loaf; *sombrero acatitado*, sugar-loaf hat.
acato, *n.m.* [ACATAMIENTO]; *darse uno acato*, to realize, understand.

acaudalado, -da, *a.* wealthy, opulent. — *p.p.* [ACAUDALAR].

acaudalador, -ra, *n.m.f.,* *a.* hoarder.

acaudalar, *v.t.* to hoard up riches; (*fig.*) to acquire wealth, reputation.

acaudillador, -ra, *a.* commanding, leading. — *n.m.* commander of troops; leader.

acaudillamiento, *n.m.* command of troops; leadership of a group.

acaudillar, *v.t.* to command troops; lead (party, band).

acaule, *a.* (*bot.*) wanting a stem; short-stemmed.

accedente, *a.* acceding.

acceder, *v.t.* to accede, agree, consent; *acceder al dictamen de alguno,* to accept someone's advice; *acceder a la petición,* to accede to the request.

accesibilidad, *n.f.* accessibility.

accesible, *a.* accessible, approachable; attainable; *accesible a todos,* accessible to all.

accesión, *n.f.* accession; accessory; (*med.*) access of a fever; paroxysm.

accésit, *n.m.* (*Lat.*) second prize or award.

acceso, *n.m.* access; carnal intercourse; accession to property; (*med.*) access; *es persona de fácil acceso,* he is very approachable.

accesoria, *n.f.* outbuilding.

accesoriamente, *adv.* accessorily.

accesorio, -ria, *a.* accessory, additional; *obras accesorias,* the outworks of a fortress.

accidentado, -da, *a.* agitated, perturbed; given to fits; full of incidents, eventful; broken, irregular. — *p.p.* [ACCIDENTARSE].

accidental, *a.* accidental, casual, fortuitous, contingent.

accidentalmente, *adv.* accidentally.

accidentario, -ria, *a.* accidental.

accidentarse, *v.r.* to be seized with a fit or sudden illness.

accidente, *n.m.* accident, chance; sudden fit or illness; casualty; (*gram.*) accidence; *accidente del trabajo,* occupational accident; *de* or *por accidente,* by chance.

acción, *n.f.* action; feat; act; gesticulation; gesture; lawsuit; battle, action; (*com.*) stock, capital in a company; action in drama, plot; (*art*) posture; *acción de gracias,* thanksgiving; *acción de guerra,* battle; *acción de presencia,* (*chem.*) catalysis; *coger* or *ganar a uno la acción,* to forestall someone in his plans; *acción industrial,* share in a company; *acción liberada,* free share.

accionado, -da, *p.p.* [ACCIONAR]. — *n.m.* (*theat.*) action.

accionar, *v.t.* to gesticulate; (*mech.*) to operate, move.

accionista, *n.m.* (*com.*) shareholder, stockholder.

accípitre, *n.m.* (*orn.*) accipiter; bird of prey.

accipitrino, -na, *a.* accipitral; rapacious, predatory; keen-sighted.

acebadamiento, *n.m.* (*vet.*) surfeit [ENCEBADAMIENTO].

acebal, *n.m.* plantation of holly-trees.

acebedo, -da, *n.m.f.* plantation of holly-trees.

acebo, *n.m.* (*bot.*) holly-tree.

acebolladura, *n.f.* damage to a tree from splitting of the woody layers.

acebrado, -da, *a.* [CEBRADO].

acebuchal, *n.m.* plantation of wild olives. — *a.* belonging to wild olives.

acebuche, *n.m.* (*bot.*) wild olive-tree.

acebucheno, -na, *a.* belonging to the wild olive.

acebuchina, *n.f.* fruit of the wild olive.

acecinado, -da, *a.* smoked, dried (meat); (*fig.*) dried-up, old, withered (people). — *p.p.* [ACECINAR].

acecinar, *v.t.* to salt and dry meat. — *v.r.* to grow old and withered.

acechadera, *n.f.* place from which one can observe, pry or spy.

acechador, -ra, *n.m.f.* one who lies in ambush; look-out, observer; prier, intruder. — *a.* prying, intruding; spying; ambushing.

acechanza, *n.f.* [ACECHO].

acechar, *v.t.* to waylay, lie in ambush, lurk; to pry; to follow closely up; to spy, watch.

aceche, *n.m.* copperas.

acecho, *n.m.* waylaying, lying in ambush; *al* or *en acecho,* in wait, in ambush.

acechón, -na, *n.m.f.,* *a.* [ACECHADOR]; *hacer la acechona,* to scrutinize, be inquisitive.

acedable, *a.* liable to become sour, acid.

acedamente, *adv.* sourly, bitterly.

acedar, *v.t.* to sour, embitter; to displease, vex. — *v.r.* to become acid, sour, vexed, displeased; (*bot.*) to turn yellow (the leaves).

acedera, *n.f.* (*bot.*) sorrel; *sal de acedera,* (*chem.*) oxalate of potash.

acederaque, *n.m.* (*bot.*) bead-tree.

acederilla, *n.f.* (*bot.*) wood-sorrel.

acederón, *n.m.* (*bot.*) variety of sorrel.

acedía, *n.f.* acidity, sourness, roughness; heartburn; (*fig.*) asperity of address; (*ichth.*) flounder or plaice.

acedo, -da, *a.* acid, sour; (*fig.*) harsh, unpleasant.

acefalía, *n.f.;* **acefalismo,** *n.m.* headlessness.

acéfalo, -la, *a.* (*zool.*) acephalous, headless.

aceguero, *n.m.* woodman.

aceitada, *n.f.* oil spilled; cake kneaded with oil.

aceitar, *v.t.* to oil; to rub with oil.

aceitazo, *n.m.* thick oil.

aceite, *n.m.* oil; essential or volatile oils; *aceite de abeto,* resin; *aceite de comer,* olive, or sweet oil; *aceite de trementina,* oil of turpentine; *aceite de pescado,* train-oil; *aceite de linaza,* linseed-oil; *aceite de carbón, aceite mineral,* coal-oil, petroleum; *aceite de vitriolo,* oil of vitriol (sulphuric acid); *aceite de anís,* sweet aniseed brandy; *aceite de ballena,* whale oil; *aceite de cada,* juniper oil; *aceite de hígado de bacalao,* cod-liver oil; *aceite de palo,* balsam of copaiba; *aceite virgen,* virgin olive-oil; *aceite de arder,* lamp, or fuel oil; *aceite volátil,* or *esencial,* or *de olor,* essential oil; *aceite graso, litargiriado, secante,* boiled linseed-oil, or linseed-oil mixed with litharge; *aceite de cáñamón,* hemp-oil; *aceite de patas de vaca,* neat's-foot oil; *cundir como mancha de aceite,* to spread like an oil-stain; *quien el aceite mesura, las manos se unta,* he who measures out oil has greasy fingers; *caro como aceite de Aparicio,* excessively dear; *echar aceite al fuego,* (*fig.*) to add fuel to the flames.

aceitera, *n.f.* woman who sells oil; oil-jar, oil-cruet, oil-horn, oil-can; (*mech.*) oil-cup; *pl. aceiteras,* cruets for oil and vinegar (VINAGRERAS).

aceitería, *n.f.* oil-shop.

aceitero, -ra, *n.m.f.* oil-seller; oiler; vessel for

holding oil. — *a.* appertaining to oil. — *n.m.* (*W. Indies*) satin-wood.

aceitillo, *n.m.* very light oil; (*Cub., PR., Mex.*) a tree.

aceitón, *n.m.* lubricating olive-oil; (*agric.*) fungus attacking olive-trees, orange-trees and lemon-trees.

aceitoso, -sa, *a.* oily, greasy.

aceituna, *n.f.* olive; *aceituna corval,* olive larger than usual; *aceituna de la reina,* or *gordal,* queen olive; *aceituna zorzaleña,* or *picudilla,* crescent olive; *aceituna manzanilla,* manzanilla olive; *llegar a las aceitunas,* to arrive at the end of a banquet, spectacle or entertainment; *aceitunas zapateras,* olives over ripe and off-colour; *aceituna, una, y si es buena, una docena,* or *aceituna una es oro, dos plata, y la tercera mata,* or *aceituna una, dos mejor, y tres peor,* a reference to the need for moderation in eating olives.

aceitunada, *n.f.* the season for gathering olives.

aceitunado, -da, *a.* olive-coloured.

aceitunero, -ra, *n.m.f.,* a person who gathers, carries, or sells olives. — *n.m.* olive depot.

aceituní, *n.m.* arabesque work.

aceitunil, *a.* olive-coloured.

aceitunillo, *n.m.* (*bot.*) satin-wood.

aceituno, *n.m.* (*bot.*) olive-tree; *aceituno silvestre,* satin-wood; (*Hond.*) Talcochote tree.

acelajado, -da, *a.* with clouds of various colours. — *p.p.* [ACELAJARSE].

aceleración, *n.f.* acceleration; hastening, haste.

aceleradamente, *adv.* speedily, swiftly, hastily.

acelerado, -da, *a.* accelerated. — *p.p.* [ACELERAR].

acelerador, *n.m.* accelerator; (*aut.*) accelerator, foot throttle; (*med.*) accelerator.

aceleramiento, *n.m.* acceleration; hastening.

acelerante, *a.* accelerating.

acelerar, *v.t.* to accelerate, hasten, hurry, forward, expedite. — *v.r.* to make haste; to move quickly.

aceleratriz, *a.* (*mech.*) accelerative; *fuerza aceleratriz,* *n.f.* (*mech.*) accelerated motion.

acelerómetro, *n.m.* (*aer.*) accelerometer.

acelga, *n.f.* (*bot.*) salt-wort; *cara de acelga,* pale-faced person.

acémila, *n.f.* mule; beast of burden; (*fam.*) enduring person.

acemilar, *a.* belonging to mules and muleteers.

acemilería, *n.f.* stable where mules are kept.

acemilero, -ra, *a.* belonging to mules. — *n.m.* a muleteer.

acemita, *n.f.* bread made of fine bran.

acemite, *n.m.* fine bran, porridge.

acendrado, -da, *a.* purified; refined; stainless. — *p.p.* [ACENDRAR].

acendramiento, *n.m.* refinement (metals).

acendrar, *v.t.* to purify or refine metals; (*fig.*) to free from stain; *acendrarse* (*el amor*) *con* or *en las contrariedades,* (love) to become purified by adversities.

acensuado, -da, *p.p.* [ACENSUAR]. — *a.pl.* (*law*) taxed (property).

acensuar, *v.t.* to lease at a rent; to tax (property).

acento, *n.m.* accent; tone, modulation; inflection of the voice; *acento ortográfico,* graphic accent; *acento prosódico* or *tónico,* tonic accent, emphasis.

acentuación, *n.f.* accentuation.

acentuado, -da, *a.* (*fig.*) exaggerated, prominent. — *p.p.* [ACENTUAR].

acentuar, *v.t.* to accentuate.

aceña, *n.f.* water-mill; *andando gana la aceña, que no estándose queda,* one who lives by his work must work hard to be successful; *más vale aceña parada que molinero amigo,* a good opportunity is better than a friend.

aceñero, *n.m.* water-mill keeper.

acepar, *v.i.* to take root.

acepción, *n.f.* acceptation; (*gram.*) meaning; *acepción de personas,* favouritism.

acepillador, -ra, *n.m.f.,* *a.* planer. — *n.f.* planing-machine.

acepilladura, *n.f.* planing; wood-shavings.

acepillar, *v.t.* to plane; to brush clothes; (*fam.*) to polish manners.

aceptable, *a.* acceptable; admissible.

aceptablemente, *adv.* acceptably.

aceptación, *n.f.* acceptation; approbation; (*com.*) acceptance of a draft; *aceptación de personas,* favouritism.

aceptado, -da, *a.* accepted. — *p.p.* [ACEPTAR].

aceptador, -ra, *n.m.f.,* *a.* acceptor; *aceptador de personas,* one who favours persons.

aceptante, *n.m.* acceptant. — *a.* accepting.

aceptar, *v.t.* to accept; (*com.*) *aceptar una letra,* to accept or honour a bill.

acepto, -ta, *a.* acceptable, agreeable; *acepto a la nobleza y plebe,* agreeable to the nobility and people.

aceptor, *n.m.* used only in *aceptor de personas,* one who favours persons.

acequia, *n.f.* canal, trench, drain, channel, flume; (*Per.*) rivulet.

acequiado, -da, *a.* intersected by canals. — *p.p.* [ACEQUIAR].

acequiador, *n.m.* canal-maker.

acequiar, *v.t.* to construct canals or drains.

acequiero, *n.m.* canal-keeper.

acera, *n.f.* pavement, sidewalk; row of houses on either side of a street; *tomar la acera,* to walk near the wall of the street; (*arch.*) surface (wall); stone slab of wall.

aceración, *n.f.* acierage.

acerado, -da, *a.* made of steel; (*fig.*) strong; sharp (of voice). — *p.p.* [ACERAR].

acerar, *v.t.* to point or edge with steel; to impregnate liquors with steel; to strengthen; (*fig.*) to fortify, give courage to; to put stone slabs or flagstones; to strengthen (wall) with stone slabs. — *v.r.* to take courage.

acerbamente, *adv.* harshly, cruelly, rudely.

acerbidad, *n.f.* acerbity, asperity; rigour, cruelty.

acerbo, -ba, *a.* tart, rough to the taste; (*fig.*) severe, cruel.

acerca de, *adv.* about, concerning, relating to; *acerca de,* with regard to; *acerca de lo dicho,* concerning, relating to what has been said.

acercamiento, *n.m.* approximation, approaching.

acercar, *v.t.* (*pret.* **acerqué;** *pres. subj.* **acerque**) to place near, approach. — *v.r.* (with *a*) to approach, accost; to come near to.

ácere, *n.m.* (*bot.*) maple-tree.

acerico, acerillo, *n.m.* pin-cushion; small pillow.

aceríneas, *n.f.pl.* (*bot.*) Aceraceæ.
acerino, -na, *a.* (*poet.*) of steel, steel-like.
acernadar, *v.t.* (*vet.*) to apply ash poultices (to horses).
acero, *n. n.* steel; (*fig.*) sword; edged or pointed small arms; *acero de herramientas,* tool-steel; *acero moldeado, colado, fundido,* cast steel; *espada de buenos aceros,* sword of well-tempered steel; *pl.* (*fig.*) courage, spirit; appetite; *buenos, valientes aceros,* good appetite.
acerola, *n.f.* haw, the fruit of the hawthorn.
acerolo, *n.m.* (*bot.*) hawthorn.
acérrimamente, *adv.* strenuously; vigorously.
acérrimo, -ma, *a. superl.* of *acre;* very strong (taste, odour); very vigorous, very harsh; (*fig.*) very staunch or stalwart.
acerrojar, *v.t.* to bolt, lock; [AHERROJAR].
acertable, *a.* ascertainable.
acertadamente, *adv.* opportunely, fitly; correctly, properly.
acertado, -da, *a.* right, correct; fit, proper. — *p.p.* [ACERTAR].
acertador, -ra, *n.m.f.,* *a.* one who hits the nail on the head; good guesser.
acertajo, *n.m.* (*fam.*) [ACERTIJO].
acertamiento, *n.m.* [ACIERTO].
acertar, *v.t.* (*pres. ind.* **acierto;** *pres. subj.* **acierte**) to hit the mark; to be right; to hit by chance. — *v.i.* to succeed; to conjecture right; *acertar a,* to happen unexpectedly; to thrive; *no acertar a decir alguna cosa,* not to find the right word; *aciértalo tú, que yo lo diré,* guess and I'll tell you; *acertar a, con la casa,* to find, come upon the house; *acertar en el pronóstico,* to prophesy correctly.
acertijo, *n.m.* riddle, conundrum; *ponerse acertijos,* to propose riddles.
aceruelo, *n.m.* small packsaddle.
acervo, *n.m.* heap; (*law*) undivided estate.
acescencia, *n.f.* acescence, turning sour; inclination to acidity.
acescente, *a.* (*chem.*) acescent; turning sour, acid.
acetábulo, *n.m.* cruet; Roman measure; (*anat.*) acetabulum.
acetal, *n.m.* (*chem.*) acetal.
acetanilida, *n.f.* (*chem.*) acetanilide.
acetato, *n.m.* acetate.
aceteria, *n.f.* pickled vegetables.
acético, -ca, *a.* acetic; vinegary.
acetificación, *n.f.* acidification.
acetificar, *v.t.* to convert into vinegar.
acetileno, *n.m.* gas acetileno, acetylene gas.
acetílico, -ca, *a.* (*chem.*) acetylic.
acetilo, *n.m.* (*chem.*) acetyl.
acetímetro, *n.m.* acetimeter.
acetín, *n.m.* (*bot.*) satin-wood.
acetona, *n.f.* acetone.
acetosa, *n.f.* (*bot.*) sorrel.
acetosidad, *n.f.* acidity.
acetosilla, *n.f,* wood-sorrel [ACEDERILLA].
acetoso, -sa, *a.* acetous.
acetre, *n.m.* small bucket; holy-water basin.
acetrinarse, *v.r.* to become jaundiced, melancholy.
acezar, *v.i.* (*pret.* **acecé;** *pres. subj.* **acece**) to pant, be winded.
acezo, *n.m.* pant; short-windedness.
acezoso, -sa, *a.* panting, short-winded.
aciago, -ga, *a.* unfortunate, melancholy, sad.
acial, aciar, *n.m.* (*vet.*) barnacle, twitch;

(*Cent. Am.*) whip; *más vale acial que fuerza de oficial,* persuasion is better than force.
aciano, *n.m.* (*bot.*) corn-flower.
acíbar, *n.m.* aloes; aloe-tree; (*fig.*) harshness; bitterness; displeasure.
acibaradamente, *adv.* bitterly, harshly.
acibarado, -da, *a.* embittered. — *p.p.* [ACIBARAR].
acibarador, -ra, *a.* aloetic.
acibaramiento, *n.m.* embitterment.
acibarar, *v.t* to put aloes into anything; (*fig.*) to make bitter; to embitter, cause displeasure.
aciberar, *v.t.* to grind very fine.
acicalada, -da, *a.* flashing; affected (in dress). — *p.p.* [ACICALAR]. — *n.m.* act of polishing any weapon; polishing.
acicalador, -ra, *a.* embellishing, polishing, burnishing, furbishing. — *n.m.* burnishing tool.
acicaladura, *n.f.;* **acicalamiento,** *n.m.* burnishing; polish, glossiness.
acicalar, *v.t.* to polish, burnish; dress, adorn, embellish. — *v.r.* (*fig.*) to make an elaborate toilet.
acicate, *n.m.* long-pointed Moorish spur; (*fig.*) inducement; goad.
acicatear, *v.t.* (*Ven.*) to spur.
acíclo, -cla, *a.* (*elec.*) acyclic.
acicular, *a.* needle-shaped; (*bot.*) acicular.
aciche, *n.m.* paving-hammer; brick-hammer; tiling-trowel.
acidamente, *adv.* acidly.
acidaque, *n.m.* Mohammedan marriage settlement.
acidez, *n.f.* acidity, sourness.
acidia, *n.f.* laziness, sloth; weakness.
acidificación, *n.f.* (*chem.*) acidification.
acidificado, -da, *a.* acidified. — *p.p.* [ACIDIFICAR].
acidificante, *a.* acidifying.
acidificar, *v.t.* to acidify.
acidimetría, *n.f.* acidimetry.
acidímetro, *n.m.* acidimeter.
acidioso, -sa, *a.* lazy; weak; lax.
ácido, -da, *a.* acid, sour; harsh; tart. — *n.m.* (*chem.*) acid.
acidulado, -da, *a.* acidulated; sour. — *p.p.* [ACIDULAR].
acidular, *v.t.* to acidulate; make sour.
acídulo, -la, *a.* (*chem.*) acidulous; sour; tart.
acierto, *n.m.* hitting the mark, good hit; ability; tact; knack; dexterity.
acierto; acierte, *pres. indic.; pres. subj.* [ACERTAR].
acigarrado, -da, *adj.* (*Chi.*) rough, hoarse (of voice).
aciguatado, -da, *a.* jaundiced. — *p.p.* [ACIGUATARSE].
aciguatarse, *v.r.* to be seized with jaundice.
acijado, -da, *a.* copper-coloured or copperas-coloured.
acije, *n.m.* copperas; ferrous sulphate.
acijoso, -sa, *a.* brownish.
acimboga, *n.f.* a variety of citron tree.
ácimo, -ma, *a.* [ÁZIMO].
acimut, *n.m.* (*astron.*) azimuth.
acimutal, *a.* (*astron.*) azimuthal.
acina, *n.f.* [HACINA].
acinar, *v.t.* [HACINAR].
acincelar, *v.t.* to engrave, carve, chisel.
acinesia, *n.f.* (*med.*) akinesia.

ácino, *n.m.* (*bot.*, *anat.*) acinus.
ación, *n.f.* stirrup-leather.
acionera, *f.* (*Arg.*, *Chi.*) part of a saddle.
acionero, *n.m.* maker of stirrup-leathers.
acipado, -da, *a.* well-milled (said of cloth).
acirate, *n.m.* landmark; limit; elevated ground.
acitara, *n.f.* partition-wall; rail of a bridge; cover of chair or saddle; zither.
acitrón, *n.m.* candied citron.
acivilarse, *v.t.* (*Chi.*) to marry before a registrar.
aclamable, *a.* laudable.
aclamación, *n.f.* acclamation; *por aclamación,* unanimously.
aclamado, -da, *a.* acclaimed, applauded. — *p.p.* [ACLAMAR].
aclamador, -ra, *n.m.f.* applauder. — *a.* applausive.
aclamar, *v.t.* to shout, acclaim, applaud; (*obs.*) (*hunt.*) call back (dogs).
aclamatoriamente, *adv.* applausively.
aclamatorio, -ria, *a.* applausive.
aclarable, *a.* explainable.
aclaración, *n.f.* illustration, explanation.
aclarador, -ra, *n.m.f.* explainer. — *a.* explanatory, illustrative. — *n.m.* a kind of comb in looms.
aclarar, *v.t.* to make clear; to illustrate; to explain; to widen; to clarify, thin; to rinse. — *v.i.*, *v.r.* to clear up (weather), recover brightness; (*naut.*) to disentangle, untie; (*min.*) to rinse ore; *aclarar la voz,* to clear the throat; *aclarar los colores,* to soften the colours.
aclaratoriamente, *adv.* explanatorily.
aclaratorio, -ria, *a.* that makes clear; explanatory.
aclarecer, *v.t.* to lighten, illuminate; to enlighten, elucidate, explain.
acle, *n.m.* (*Philip.*) tree of the Leguminosæ family.
aclimatación, *n.f.* acclimatizing, acclimatization.
aclimatar, *v.t.*, *v.r.* to acclimatize.
aclocado, -da, *a.* stretched. — *p.p.* [ACLOCAR].
aclocadura, *n.f.*; aclocamiento, *n.m.* stretching, lying down.
aclocar, *v.i.* (*pres. indic.* aclueco; *pret.* acloqué; *pres. subj.* aclueque) to brood, hatch eggs. — *v.r.* (*fig.*) to stretch oneself, lie down; to become broody.
acmé, *n.m.* top, highest point, culmination.
acné, *n.m.* (*med.*) acne.
acobardamiento, *n.m.* terror, fear, cowardice.
acobardar, *v.t.* to daunt, intimidate, terrify. — *v.r.* to become frightened; to lose courage.
acobijar, *v.t.* (*agric.*) to mulch.
acobijo, *n.m.* (*agric.*) mulch.
acobrado, -da, *a.* copper-hued.
acoceador, -ra, *a.* kicking (horses).
acoceamiento, *n.m.* kicking.
acocear, *v.t.* to kick; (*fig.*) oppress, ill-treat, debase.
acocil, -ile, -ili, *n.m.* (*Mex.*) kind of freshwater shrimp.
acocotar, *v.t.* to kill by a blow on the neck; [ACOGOTAR].
acocote, *n.m.* (*Mex.*) long gourd used to extract the juice of maguey.
acocharse, *v.r.* to stoop, squat down.
acochinadamente, *adv.* filthily.

acochinado, -da, *a.* dirty, filthy, neglected. — *p.p.* [ACOCHINAR].
acochinar, *v.t.* (*coll.*) to murder, assassinate; to obstruct a law-suit; to hush up; (*fig.*, *fam.*) to humble; to corner (a pawn in chess).
acodado, -da, *a.* elbowed; cranked (axle); (*naut.*) toggled. — *p.p.* [ACODAR].
acodadura, *n.f.* bending, leaning on the elbow; nudging, jostling; (*agric.*) layering.
acodalamiento, *n.m.* (*arch.*) propping; staying.
acodalar, *v.t.* (*arch.*) to prop; shore; stay.
acodamiento, *n.m.* [ACODADURA].
acodar, *v.t.* to elbow, bend; to lean the elbow upon; (*agric.*) to layer, plant cuttings; (*arch.*) to prop, stay; (*carp.*) to square (timber). — *v.r.* to lean or rest on one's elbow.
acoderamiento, *n.m.* (*naut.*) bringing the broadside to bear.
acoderar, *v.t.*, *v.r.* (*naut.*) to put a spring on a cable; to bring the broadside to bear.
acodiciar, *v.t.* to covet, long for; to urge on. — *v.r.* to become covetous; to be provoked.
acodillado, -da, *a.* elbowed; bent into an angle. — *p.p.* [ACODILLAR].
acodillar, *v.t.* to bend into an elbow or angle; to make tricks (in shadow, at cards). — *v.i.* to touch the ground with knee (animals); (*fig.*) *acodillar con la carga,* to sink under a burden.
acodo, *n.m.* (*agric.*) shoot, scion.
acogedizo, -za, *a.* gathered or collected promiscuously.
acogedor, -ra, *n.m.f.* harbourer, protector; host. — *a.* sheltering, protecting.
acoger, *v.t.* (*pres. indic.* acojo; *pres. subj.* acoja) to welcome, receive; (*fig.*) to accept (opinions); to protect, shelter; to admit cattle to pasture land. — *v.r.* to take shelter in; (*fig.*) to resort to (pretext); to apply or appeal to; *acoger en casa,* to receive in the house; *acogerse bajo,* or *a sagrado,* to shelter oneself in a place of safety.
acogeta, *n.f.* shelter, cover, place of safety; evasion.
acogible, *a.* receivable, acceptable.
acogida, *n.f.* reception; place of meeting; asylum; confluence; *dar acogida a una letra,* (*com.*) to honour a bill or draft; *buena* or *mala acogida,* welcome, good or bad reception.
acogido, -da, *n.m.f.* collection of breeding mares given to the owner of the principal steed, to keep them at a certain price; temporary admission of flocks into pasture. — *a.* received; welcome. — *p.p.* [ACOGER].
acogolladamente, *adv.* securely.
acogollado, -da, *a.* (*agric.*) grown to a head, budded. — *p.p.* [ACOGOLLAR].
acogolladura, *n.f.* earthing up of plants.
acogollar, *v.t.* to cover up plants for protection. — *v.i.* to bud forth. — *v.r.* to grow to a round head.
acogombradura, *n.f.* (*agric.*) digging up the ground about plants.
acogombrar, *v.t.* to dig up the ground about plants; to bank; to cover plants with earth.
acogotado, -da, *a.* killed by a blow on the neck. — *p.p.* [ACOGOTAR].
acogotador, -ra, *n.m.f.*, *a.* (*prov.*) slaughterer, feller (of oxen, etc.); (*fam.*) bore.
acogotar, *v.t.* to kill by a blow on the neck.
acohombrar, *v.t.* (*agric.*) [APORCAR].

acojinamiento, *n.m.* (*mech.*) cushioning of the piston.

acojinar, *v.t.* to quilt; to cushion.

acolada, *n.f.* accolade.

acolar, *v.t.* (*her.*) to quarter or unite two coats of arms together.

acolchado, -da, *a.* quilted. — *p.p.* [ACOLCHAR].

acolchador, -ra, *n.m.f.* quilter.

acolchamiento, *n.m.* quilting.

acolchar, *v.t.* to quilt; (*naut.*) to intertwine.

acolchonar, *v.t.* (*Am.*) to quilt, to cushion.

acólita, *n.f.* (*Chi.*) female acolyte in a convent.

acolitado, *n.m.* acolyte.

acolitar, *v.i.* (*Am.*) to serve as an acolyte.

acólito, *n.m.* acolyte; assistant.

acolladores, *n.m.pl.* lanyards.

acolladura, *n.f.* covering of earth round the base of a trunk.

acollar, *v.t.* (*pres. indic.* **acuello**; *pres. subj.* **acuelle**) (*agric.*) to hill up earth round the base of a trunk; (*naut.*) to caulk a ship; to haul by the lanyards.

acollarado, -da, *a. pájaros acollarados*, birds having about their necks a ring of feathers of a different colour. — *p.p.* [ACOLLAR].

acollarar, *v.t.* to yoke or harness horses, oxen, etc.; to leash hounds; (*Arg., Chi.*) horses in double harness.

acollonar, *v.t.* (*coll.*) to intimidate. — *v.r.* to become frightened [ACOBARDAR].

acombado, -da, *a.* warped. — *p.p.* [ACOMBAR].

acombar, *v.t.* to bend, crook, warp. — *v.r.* to become warped.

acomedido, *adj.* (*Am.*) obsequious, obliging, compliant.

acomedirse, *v.i.* (*Am.*) to offer oneself, to volunteer.

acometedor, -ra, *n.m.f.* aggressor, attacker. — *a.* aggressive, enterprising.

acometer, *v.t.* to attack, assault; (*fig.*) to go for; to undertake; to overtake; *acometer con dinero*, to attempt to bribe; *acometer por la espalda*, to assault in the back; *ser acometido de un síncope*, to be overcome by a fainting fit; *ser acometido por un flanco*, to be attacked from the side, flank; *le acometió el sueño*, sleep overtook him; *acometerse mutuamente*, to jostle one another.

acometible, *a.* attackable.

acometida, *n.f.*; **acometimiento**, *n.m.* attack, assault; fit of illness; outlet in a sewer.

acometiente, *a.* attacking.

acometividad, *n.f.* combativeness.

acomodable, *a.* easily arranged.

acomodación, *n.f.* accommodation.

acomodadamente, *adv.* commodiously, conveniently, suitably.

acomodadizo, -za, *a.* accommodating.

acomodado, -da, *a.* convenient, fit; rich, well-to-do; fond of comfort; moderate, reasonable. — *p.p.* [ACOMODAR].

acomodador, -ra, *n.m.f.* one who accommodates; usher or boxkeeper in a theatre. — *a.* conciliating.

acomodamiento, *n.m.* accommodation.

acomodar, *v.t.* to accommodate, put up, arrange; to bestow conveniently; to rectify; to reconcile, compound, compromise; to supply with; to take in, lodge. — *v.i.* to fit, suit. — *v.r.* to condescend, comply, put up with; *acomodarse al tiempo*, to be content with things as they are; *acomodarse a*, or

con otro dictamen, to conform to another judgment; *acomodarse de criado*, to become suited with a servant; *acomodarse en una casa*, to make oneself at home.

acomodaticio, -cia, *a.* compliant, accommodating; (*Bibl.*) metaphorical.

acomodativo, -va, *a.* accommodative.

acomodo, *n.m.* employment, place, situation; lodgings; (*Chi.*) finery, ornament.

acompañado, -da, *a.* accompanied; (*coll.*) frequented (thoroughfare). — *n.m.* (*law*) assistant judge, lawyer, etc. — *p.p.* [ACOMPAÑAR].

acompañador, -ra, *n.m.f.* chaperon, companion; attendant; (*mus.*) accompanist. — *a.* accompanying.

acompañamiento, *n.m.* attendance, retinue; (*mus.*) accompaniment; supernumeraries at a theatre; (*her.*) ornament round an escutcheon.

acompañante, *n.m.f., a.* companion, chaperon, etc.; [ACOMPAÑADOR].

acompañar, *v.t.* to accompany, attend, conduct, follow; to lead along; to join, unite; to enclose; (*mus.*) to accompany; *acompaño a Vd.*, (*in letters*) I send you herewith; *acompañar a paseo*, to accompany for a walk; *acompañar con, de pruebas*, to accompany with proofs. — *v.r.* to hold a consultation; (*mus.*) to accompany oneself; *acompañarse con el piano*, to accompany oneself at the piano.

acompasadamente, *adv.* rhythmically.

acompasado, -da, *a.* measured by the compass; rhythmic; (*coll.*) quiet and slow in tone; of fixed, regular habits. — *p.p.* [ACOMPASAR].

acompasar, *v.t.* to measure with dividers and rule; (*mus.*) to divide a score into equal parts.

acomplexionado, -da, *a.* of good (or bad) complexion *or* constitution.

acomunarse, *v.r.* to band together; to league for a common purpose, combine.

aconchabarse, *v.r.* to unite for some evil purpose; to plot, conspire.

aconchar, *v.t.* to push to a place of safety; (*naut.*) to run aground.

acondicionado, -da, *a.* of good (or bad) disposition (persons) *or* condition (goods). — *p.p.* [ACONDICIONAR].

acondicionamiento, *n.m.* drying (silk) after manufacture.

acondicionar, *v.t.* to dispose, affect, constitute; to prepare, arrange, fix. — *v.r.* to acquire a certain quality or condition; to qualify.

acongojadamente, *adv.* sorrowfully, with grief.

acongojado, -da, *a.* anguished, grieved. — *p.p.* [ACONGOJAR].

acongojador, -ra, *n.m.f.* vexer, oppressor. — *a.* vexing, afflicting.

acongojar, *v.t.* to vex, sadden, oppress, afflict. — *v.r.* to become vexed, grieved.

aconitina, *n.f.* (*chem.*) aconitine.

acónito, *n.m.* aconite, wolf's-bane.

aconsejable, *a.* advisable.

aconsejadamente, *adv.* with advice from another.

aconsejado, -da, *p.p.* [ACONSEJAR]. — *a. bien aconsejado*, prudent, well-advised; *mal aconsejado*, ill-advised, imprudent.

aconsejador, -ra, *n.m.f.* adviser, counsellor. — *a.* advising, counselling.

aconsejamiento, *n.m.* counselling.

aconsejante, *a.* advising.

aconsejar, *v.t.* to advise, counsel. — *v.r.* (*de*, of, *con*, with), to take counsel of, consult; *aconsejarse mejor*, to think better of it; *aconsejarse con la almohada*, to consult one's pillow, sleep on a thing; *aconsejarse con*, or *de sabios*, to take advice from the wise.

aconsonantar, *v.t.* to make a word rhyme with another; to use rhymes in prose. — *v.i.* to rhyme.

aconstelado, -da, *a.* (*astron.*) constellated.

acontecedero, -ra, *a.* possible, probable, eventual.

acontecer, *v. impers.* (used only in the inf. and third person sing. and pl.) (*pres. subj.* **acontezca**) to happen, come about, fare; *hacer y acontecer*, a common phrase signifying the promises of any good or benefit; also a threat; *lo acontecido*, that which has or had occurred; *acontecer a todos*, to happen to everybody; *acontecer con todos lo mismo*, to happen the same with everybody.

acontecimiento, *n.m.* event, incident, occurrence.

acontezca, *pres. subj.* [ACONTECER].

acopado, -da, *a.* shaped like a cup or vase. — *p.p.* [ACOPAR].

acopar, *v.i.* (*bot.*) to grow in the form of a cup. — *v.t.* (*naut.*) to trim; to hollow.

acopetado, -da, *a.* tufted. — *p.p.* [ACOPETAR].

acopetadura, *n.f.*; **acopetamiento,** *n.m.* tuft-making.

acopetar, *v.t.* to make tufts.

acopiador, -ra, *n.m.f.*, *a.* (*com.*) one who collects or stores up, who corners the market in goods.

acopiamiento, *n.m.* the gathering and buying up of goods.

acopiar, *v.t.* to gather, store up; to forestall; to corner goods.

acopio, *n.m.* gathering, storing; *acopio usurario*, illicit or unfair buying up of goods.

acoplado, -da, *a.* fitted, adjusted; coupled; scarfed; *acoplado directamente*, (*mech.*) direct-coupling. — *p.p.* [ACOPLAR].

acopladura, *n.f.* coupling, junction; scarfing.

acoplar, *v.t.* to couple, join, adjust, fit; to yoke, hitch; to pair, mate (animals); to settle differences, to frame timber. — *v.r.* to make up matters, be agreed; (*coll.*) to become intimate.

acoplo, *n.m.* [ACOPLADURA].

acoquinado, -da, *a.* terrified.

acoquinamiento, *n.m.* intimidation.

acoquinar, *v.t.* (*fam.*) to terrify, intimidate. — *v.r.* to be terrified.

acorador, -ra, *n.m.f.* oppressor. — *a.* oppressing.

acoralado, -da, *a.* coralline.

acorar, *v.t.* to afflict, sadden. — *v.r.* to be grieved. — *v.i.* (*bot.*) to fade.

acorazado, -da, *a.* ironclad; shell (applied to transformers). — *n.m.* armoured ship; ironclad. — *p.p.* [ACORAZAR].

acorazamiento, *n.m.* supplying armour to ships.

acorazar, *v.t.* (*pret.* **acoracé;** *pres. subj.* **acorace**) to armour ships.

acorazonado, -da, *a.* heart-shaped. — *p.p.* [ACORAZONAR].

acorchado, -da, *a.* corked (bottles); spongy

(fruits); (*fig.*) torpid (limbs). — *p.p.* [ACORCHAR].

acorchamiento, *n.m.* shrivelling; sponginess; (*fig.*) torpidity.

acorchar, *v.t.* to line with cork. — *v.r.* to shrivel; become stale (fruits); (*fig.*) to become torpid.

acordable, *a.* tunable.

acordada, *n.f.* (*law*) order, decision, resolution.

acordadamente, *adv.* by common consent; with mature deliberation; harmoniously.

acordado, -da, *a.* agreed; done with mature deliberation. — *p.p.* [ACORDAR].

acordar, *v.t.* (*pres. indic.* **acuerdo;** *pres. subj.* **acuerde**) to resolve by common consent, agree; to remind; to tune musical instruments; to dispose figures in a picture; to make flush, level, smooth. — *v.i.* to agree, become uniform. — *v.r.* (with *de*) to remember, recollect; to come to an agreement; *no me acuerdo de eso*, I do not remember it; *acordarse con uno*, to come to an agreement with someone; *acordarse remotamente de*, to have a confused recollection of; *acordar (la voz) con un instrumento*, to tune (the voice) to an instrument; *acordarse de lo pasado*, to remember the past; *acordarse con los contrarios*, to agree with opposites; *si mal no me acuerdo*, if my memory does not fail me.

acorde, *a.* agreed; in tune; in agreement; conformable, according; coinciding in opinion; to the point, in harmony. — *n.m.* (*mus.*) chord; harmony of sound or colours.

acordelado, -da, *a.* ranged into line; corded; surveyed. — *p.p.* [ACORDELAR].

acordeladura, *n.f.*; **acordelamiento,** *n.m.* measuring by cord or rule.

acordelar, *v.t.* to measure with a cord; to survey, align; to cord.

acordemente, *adv.* by common consent, harmoniously.

acordeón, *n.m.* accordion.

acordonado, -da, *a.* surrounded; made in the form of a cord; (*Mex.*) lean (of animals). — *p.p.* [ACORDONAR].

acordonamiento, *n.m.* act of lacing; milling; cording.

acordonar, *v.t.* to make in the form of a cord or rope; to lace (shoes, etc.); to mill a coin; to cord, twine; to surround.

acores, *n.m.pl.* (*med.*) achore, eruption on the face and head (in infants).

acornar, acornear, *v.t.* to butt with the horns.

acorneador, -ra, *n.m.f.*, *a.* a butting animal.

ácoro, *n.m.* (*bot.*) sweet-smelling flag, sweet cane, sweet grass.

acorralamiento, *n.m.* corralling.

acorralar, *v.t.* to shut up cattle or sheep in pens; to corral; (*fig.*) to surround; to intimidate; to silence.

acorrer, *v.t.* to help, succour. — *v.i.* to run to, hasten. — *v.r.* to take shelter.

acorrucarse, *v.r.* to fold oneself up (from cold, etc.); [ACURRUCARSE].

acortable, *a.* reducible, shrinkable.

acortamiento, *n.m.* shortening; (*astron.*) difference between the real distance of a planet to the sun or to the earth and the projection of that distance on the plane of the ecliptic.

acortar, *v.t.* to shorten, lessen, reduce; to

obstruct; *acortar la vela*, (*naut.*) to shorten sail; *acortar de palabras*, to say very little. — *v.r.* to shrivel, contract, shrink, to be bashful; to fall back, retire.

acorullar,*v.t.*(*naut.*)to bridle or hold up the oars.

acorvar, *v.t.* to double, bend.

acosado, -da, *a.* pursued, persecuted, importunated; *acosado de hambre*, pinched with hunger. — *p.p.* [ACOSAR].

acosador, -ra, *n.m.f.* pursuer, persecutor. — *a.* persecutory, pursuing.

acosamiento, *n.m.* pursuit, persecution, molestation.

acosar, *v.t.* to pursue closely; to vex, molest, harass; *ser acosado de los perros*, to be harassed by the dogs.

acosijar, *v.t.* (*Mex.*) to pursue relentlessly; to vex, harass.

acosmismo, *n.m.* (*phil.*) acosmism.

acostado, -da, *a.* stretched, laid down, retired; in bed. — *p.p.* [ACOSTAR].

acostamiento, *n.m.* stretching, laying down; stipend, emolument.

acostar, *v.t.* (*pres. indic.* **acuesto**; *pres. subj.* **acueste**) to lay down; to put to bed. — *v.i.* to approach; (*naut.*) to bring a ship alongside the shore; to lie along; to have a list. — *v.r.* to lie down, go to bed; *acostarse con las gallinas*, (*coll.*) to go to bed very early; *más vale acostarse sin cena que amanecer con deudas*, it is better to go to bed supperless than wake up in debt.

acostumbradamente, *adv.* customarily.

acostumbrado, -da, *a.* accustomed; customary, usual. — *p.p.* [ACOSTUMBRAR].

acostumbrar, *v.t.* to accustom, use. — *v.i.* to be accustomed, used, habituated; *no acostumbro fumar tanto*, I am not used to smoking so much. — *v.r.* to get used to, become accustomed to; *acostumbrarse a los trabajos*, to accustom oneself to work.

acotación, *n.f.* bounds, limit; annotation, marginal note; (*theat.*) directions; (*surv.*) elevation marked on a map.

acotamiento, *n.m.* limitation.

acotada, *n.f.* (*bot.*) nursery.

acotar, *v.t.* to limit, set bounds; to fix, mark; (*surv.*) to put altitude figures on map; to quote, annotate, make marginal notes; to accept for a certain price; to witness, vouch for; to prune trees; (*fam.*) to select. — *v.r.* to seek refuge outside the boundary line.

acotiledóneo, -nea, *a.* (*bot.*) acotyledonous, not provided with seed leaves. — *n.f.pl.* (*bot.*) Acotyledons.

acotillo, *n.m.* sledge-hammer.

acoyundar, *v.t.* to yoke oxen to a load.

acoyuntar, *v.t.* to form a partnership between two one-horse farmers.

acracia, *n.f.* (*polit.*) doctrine of the ácratas.

ácrata, *a.* (*polit.*) one opposed to all authority.

acre, *a.* sour; pungent; tart; hot; mordant; keen; acrimonious; *acre de condición*, acrid by nature. — *n.m.* acre (= 40 áreas).

acrebite, *n.m.f.* sulphur.

acrecencia, *n.f.* (*law*) increase, augmentation, growth.

acrecentadamente, *adv.* increasingly.

acrecentado, -da, *a.* promoted, augmented, increased. — *p.p.* [ACRECENTAR].

acrecentador, -ra, *n.m.f.* one that increases. — *a.* increasing.

acrecentamiento, *n.m.* increase, growth.

acrecentante, *n.m.f.* one that increases. — *a.* increasing.

acrecentar, *v.t.*, *v.r.* (*pres. indic.* **acreciento**; *pres. subj.* **acreciente**), **acrecer,** *v.t.*, *v.r.* (*pres. indic.* **acrezco**; *pres. subj.* **acrezca**) to increase; to promote, advance.

acreditadamente, *adv.* creditably.

acreditado, -da, *a.* distinguished, famous; accredited. — *p.p.* [ACREDITAR].

acreditar, *v.t.* to assure, affirm; to verify, prove; to give credit to; (*com.*) to credit, recommend; to answer for, guarantee; to accredit, authorize. — *v.r.* to gain a reputation; *acreditarse de loco*, to act like a madman; *acreditarse con*, or *para con alguno*, to gain someone's confidence; *acreditarse de necio*, to be considered a fool; *acreditado en*, or *para su oficio*, considered suitable for his position.

acreditativo, -va, *a.* creditable.

acreedor, -ra, *a.* deserving, meritorious; *acreedor a la gratitud de la patria*, worthy of the country's gratitude. — *n.m.* creditor. — *n.f.* creditrix, creditress.

acremente, *adv.* sourly, bitterly; with acrimony.

acrezco; acrezca, *pres. indic.; pres. subj.* [ACRECER].

acribador, -ra, *n.m.f.* sifter. — *a.* sifting.

acribadura, *n.f.* sifting. — *pl.* siftings.

acribar, *v.t.* to sift; to riddle with holes, pierce like a sieve; (*fig.*) to cover with wounds.

acribillado, -da, *a.* pierced like a sieve; covered with wounds; molested, tormented. — *p.p.* [ACRIBILLAR].

acribillador, -ra, *n.m.f.* one who pierces; tormentor, molester. — *a.* sieve-like; tormenting, molesting.

acribillar, *v.t.*, *v.r.* to pierce like a sieve; to riddle (with shot); (*coll.*) to molest, torment; to ply anyone with (questions); *le acribillan los acreedores*, his creditors torment him.

acrídidos, *n.m.pl.* (*ent.*) Acridids, locusts.

acridófago, -ga, *n.m.f.*, *a.* living on locusts.

acriminable, *a.* incriminatory.

acriminación, *n.f.* accusation, crimination.

acriminador, -ra, *n.m.f.* accuser, informer. — *a.* accusing; informing.

acriminar, *v.t.* to accuse, impeach; (*law*) to aggravate a fault or crime.

acrimonia, *n.f.* acrimony, sharpness, sourness; asperity of expression; sharpness of temper; vehemence in talking.

acrimonial, *a.* acrimonious.

acrimoniosamente, *adv.* acrimoniously.

acrimonioso, -sa, *a.* acrimonious.

acriollarse, *v.t.* (*Am.*) to adopt national customs.

acrisolación, *n.f.* purification.

acrisoladamente, *adv.* in a pure way, honestly.

acrisolado, -da, *a.* pure, honest. — *p.p.* [ACRISOLAR].

acrisolador, -ra, *n.m.f.* refiner, assayer (metals). — *a.* clean, refining.

acrisolar, *v.t.*, *v.r.* to refine, purify, or assay metals; (*fig.*) to cleanse; (*fig.*) to clear up, prove by means of witnesses.

acristianar, *v.t.* (*coll.*) to baptize, christen.

acritud, *n.f.* acrimony; sharpness; asperity.

acróbata, *n.m.f.* acrobat, rope-dancer.

acrobático, -ca, *a.* acrobatic.
acromático, -ca, *a.* achromatic.
acromatismo, *n.m.* achromatism.
acromatizar, *v.t.* to achromatize.
acromial, *a.* (*anat.*) acromial.
acrómico, -ca, *a.* achromic.
acromio, acromión, *n.m.* (*anat.*) acromion.
acrónicamente, *adv.* (*astron.*) acronychally.
acrónico, -ca, *a.* (*astron.*) acronychal.
acróstico, -ca, *a.* acrostic.
acrotera, *n.f.* (*arch.*) acroterium.
acta, *n.f.* act or record of proceedings; certificate of election. — *pl.* the acts, minutes or records of communities, chapters, councils; papers, file, etc.; *libro de actas*, minute-book; *acta notarial*, notarial certificate; *levantar acta*, to draw up and execute a certificate or affidavit; *actas de los santos*, lives of the saints.
actínico, -ca, *a.* actinic.
actinio, *n.m.* actinium, metallic element.
actinométrico, -ca, *a.* (*opt.*) actinometric.
actinómetro, *n.m.* (*opt.*) actinometer.
actinota, *n.f.* actinium.
actitud, *n.f.* attitude, position, posture.
activamente, *adv.* actively.
activar, *v.t.* to push, make brisk, hasten, hurry, expedite, rush.
actividad, *n.f.* activity, quickness, liveliness, nimbleness, hurry; *poner en actividad*, to put in operation, ply.
activo, -va, *a.* active, quick, diligent; *voz activa*, suffrage. — *n.m.* (*com.*) assets, outstanding claims.
acto, *n.m.* act, action; event; ceremony; public function; opening of a term in universities; Roman lineal measure of about 120 feet or 36 metres; act of a play; thesis defended in universities; *acto continuo*, immediately afterwards; *en el acto*, at once, instantly; *actos públicos*, public or official occasions; *Actos de los Apóstoles*, Acts of the Apostles.
actor, *n.m.* performer, player; (*law*) claimant, plaintiff; proctor, attorney.
actora, *n.f.* (*law*) plaintiff; *parte actora*, prosecution.
actriz, *n.f.* actress.
actuación, *n.f.* actuation; moving; action. — *pl.* (*law*) proceedings.
actuado, -da, *a.* actuated; skilled, experienced. — *p.p.* [ACTUAR].
actual, *a.* present, belonging to the present time, actual (in the sense of 'present').
actualidad, *n.f.* the actual or present state of things, actuality; *en la actualidad*, at present, at the present time.
actualmente, *adv.* at present.
actuante, *n.m.f.* defender of a thesis (in universities, etc.).
actuar, *v.t.* to put a thing in action. — *v.i.* to digest; to perform or discharge a duty; to consider, weigh maturely; to perform judicial acts; to support a thesis (in universities, etc.); *actuar en los negocios*, to act in business. — *v.r.* to move oneself.
actuario, *n.m.* clerk of a court of justice, actuary.
acuadrillar, *v.t.* to form parties; to collect or head a band of armed men.
acuafortista, *n.m.* etcher.
acuantiar, *v.t.* to determine a quantity.
acuarela, *n.f.* painting in water-colours.
acuarelista, *n.m.f.* painter in water-colours.

acuario, *n.m.* aquarium; (*astron.*) Aquarius, a sign of the zodiac.
acuartelado, -da, *a.* (*her.*) divided into quarters; billeted. — *p.p.* [ACUARTELAR].
acuartelamiento, *n.m.* quartering troops; quarters.
acuartelar, *v.t.* to quarter, billet troops; to confine troops to barracks; *acuartelar las velas*, (*naut.*) to flatten the sails.
acuartillar, *v.i.* to bend in the quarters under a heavy load (beasts of burden).
acuate, *n.m.* (*Mex.* **acoatl**) water snake.
acuático, -ca; acuátil, *a.* aquatic.
acuatinta, *n.f.* aquatint.
acuatizaje, *n.m.* (*aer.*) alighting on the water; place for alighting on the water.
acuatizar, *v.i.* (*aer.*) to alight on the water.
acuatubular, *a.* pertaining to a water-tube (boiler).
acubado, -da, *a* resembling a bucket or pail. — *p.p.* [ACUBAR].
acubar, *v.t.* to shape like a pail or bucket. — *v.r.* (*fam.*) to become intoxicated.
acubilar, *v.t.* to shelter (cattle).
acucia, *n.f.* zeal, diligence, haste; eagerness, longing; covetousness.
acuciadamente, *adv.* [ACUCIOSAMENTE].
acuciador, -ra, *n.m.f.* coveter. — *a.* stimulating.
acuciamiento, *n.m.* stimulation, urgency, haste.
acuciar, *v.t.* to stimulate, hasten; to covet.
acuciosamente, *adv.* zealously, actively; diligently; eagerly; covetously.
acuciosidad, *n.f.* (*Ven.*) [ACTIVIDAD].
acucioso, -sa, *a.* zealous, hasty, eager.
acuclillado, -da, *a.* cowering, squatting. — *p.p.* [ACUCLILLARSE].
acuclillarse, *v.r.* to crouch, squat.
acucharado, -da, *a.* spoon-like.
acucharar, *v.t.* to shape like a spoon.
acuchillado, -da, *a.* cut, slashed, stabbed; (*fig.*) experienced, skilful after long practice; slashed (of garments). — *p.p.* [ACUCHILLAR].
acuchillador, -ra, *n.m.f.* bully; gladiator. — *a.* quarrelsome.
acuchillar, *v.t.* to cut, stab, hack, slash (clothes). — *v.r.* to fight with knives or swords.
acuchuchar, *v.t.* (*Chi.*) [APLASTAR].
acudimiento, *n.m.* aid, assistance.
acudir, *v.i.* to assist, attend; to go; to come; to succour, support; to be present; (*agric.*) to respond; to produce; to run in, come in or up to, rush; to go *or* come to the rescue; to resort or repair to; *acudir al, con el remedio*, to have recourse to, arrive with the remedy.
acueducto, *n.m.* aqueduct.
acuello; acuelle, *pres. indic.; pres. subj.* [ACOLLAR].
ácueo, -a, *a.* watery, aqueous.
acuerdado, -da, *a.* constructed by line or rule.
acuerdo, *n.m.* resolution, determination; opinion, advice; reflection, prudence; remembrance, recollection; harmony of colours; body of the members of a tribunal assembled in the form of a court; concurrence, agreement, accord; *de acuerdo*, by agreement, unanimously; agreed; of the same opinion; in accordance, complying; *ponerse* or *estar de acuerdo*, to agree unani-

mously, to come to an understanding; *estar en*, or *fuera de su acuerdo*, to be, or not to be in one's proper senses; *volver sobre su acuerdo*, to change one's mind; *volver en su acuerdo*, to regain one's senses; *acuerdos*, book of resolutions.

acuerdo; acuerde, *pres. indic.; pres. subj.* [ACORDAR].

acuesto; acueste, *pres. indic.; pres. subj.* [ACOSTAR].

acuidadarse, *v.r.* to take care, be vigilant.

acuitadamente, *adv.* grievously.

acuitado, -da, *a.* afflicted, grieved. — *p.p.* [ACUITAR].

acuitador, -ra, *n.m.f., a.* one who afflicts.

acuitar, *v.t.* to afflict, oppress. — *v.r.* to grieve.

acular, *v.t.* (*coll.*) to make an animal curl up; to force one into a corner; to compel one to retreat; to make an animal back up. — *v.r.* to set one's back against something; (*naut.*) to be down at the stern; to retreat.

aculebrinado, -da, *a.* made in the form of a culverin.

aculeiforme, *a.* in the form of a goad or sting.

acúleo, -lea, *a.* (*zool.*) aculeate, armed with a sting.

acullá, *adv.* there; yonder, on the other side; opposite; *aquí y acullá*, here and there.

acumen, *n.m.* acumen, discernment.

acuminado, -da, *a.* (*bot.*) acuminate, ending in a point.

acumíneo, -a, *a.* ending in a point.

acumuchar, *v.t.* (*Chi.*) [AGLOMERAR].

acumulable, *a.* that can be accumulated.

acumulación, *n.f.* accumulation, gathering, storing up.

acumuladamente, *adv.* in quantity.

acumulado, -da, *a.* accumulated, hoarded up. — *p.p.* [ACUMULAR].

acumulador, -ra, *n.m.f.* accumulator; (*elec.*) electric storage battery. — *a.* accumulating, amassing.

acumulante, *a.* amassing, accumulating.

acumular, *v.t.* to accumulate, heap together, treasure up, hoard, lay up; to impute a fault; (*law*) to try or dispose of jointly.

acumulativamente, *adv.* jointly, accumulatively; (*law*) by way of prevention or precaution.

acumulativo, -va, *a.* joint, cumulative.

acunar, *v.t.* to rock a child in the cradle.

acuñación, *n.f.* coinage, milling, minting; wedging.

acuñador, -ra, *a.* coining, minting; wedging. — *n.m.f.* minter, coiner; wedge; (*print.*) shooting-stick.

acuñar, *v.t.* to coin, mint; to wedge, fasten with wedges; to key, lock; (*print.*) to quoin; *acuñar dinero*, to mint money.

acuosidad, *n.f.* wateriness.

acuoso, -sa, *a.* watery, aqueous.

acupuntura, *n.f.* (*surg.*) acupuncture.

acure, *n.m.* (*Col., Ven.*) guinea pig.

acurito, *n.m.* (*Col., Ven.*) [ACURE].

acurrado, *a.* (*Cub.*) [CURRUTACO].

acurrarse, *v.r.* (*Cub.*) to imitate Andalusian pronunciation.

acurrucado, -da, *a.* curled up (like a cat or dog). — *p.p.* [ACURRUCARSE].

acurrucarse, *v.r.* to huddle, muffle, oneself up (from cold, fear, etc.).

acusable, *a.* accusable, indictable.

acusación, *n.f.* accusation, impeachment, charge.

acusado, -da, *n.m.f., a.* defendant, accused. — *p.p.* [ACUSAR].

acusador, -ra, *n.m.f.* accuser, prosecutor; informer. — *a.* accusing, prosecuting.

acusante, *a.* accusing, prosecuting.

acusar, *v.t.* to accuse, blame, criminate, charge, prosecute, indict; at cards, to announce in due time that one holds certain cards that count so many points; *acusar recibo*, to acknowledge the receipt; (*obs.*) *acusar a pena*, to file a complaint; *acusar* or *acusarse de un delito ante el juez*, to accuse someone, or oneself of a crime to the judge; *acusar las cuarenta*, to call out the forty honour points (at cards); (*coll.*) to give a piece of one's mind; *acusar la conciencia*, to have remorse; *acusar la rebeldía*, (*law*) to summon a defaulter. — *v.r.* to acknowledge sins to a confessor.

acusativo, *n.m.* the accusative case.

acusatorio, -ria, *a.* accusatory.

acuse, *n.m.* accusation; each of the cards duly announced (in certain games of cards); *acuse de recibo*, acknowledgment of receipt.

acusetas, *n.m.* (*Am.*) [ACUSÓN].

acusón, -na, *n.m.f., a.* talebearer, tell-tale.

acústica, *n.f.* acoustics.

acústico, -ca, *a.* acoustic; *tubo acústico*, speaking-tube; *trompetilla acústica*, ear-trumpet, auriphone.

acustión, *n.m.* electric sound-amplifier.

acutángulo, *a.* (*geom.*) acute-angled.

acutí, *n.m.* (*Arg.*) [ACURE].

acuznador, *n.m.* polisher, burnisher.

achacable, *a.* imputable.

achacani, *n.m.* (*Bol.*) species of potatoes used to cure quicksilver miners.

achacar, *v.t.* to impute, blame; to frame an excuse.

achacosamente, *adv.* sickly; in an unhealthy manner; maliciously, dissemblingly.

achacoso, -sa, *a.* sickly, unhealthy.

achachay, *n.m.* (*Col.*) children's game.

achaflanadura, *n.f.* bevelling, chamfering.

achaflanar, *v.t.* to make chamfers; to chamfer, bevel.

achagual, *n.m.* (*Am.*) South American fish.

achahuistlarse, *v.r.* (*Mex.*) to contract a disease from a plant.

achajuanarse, *v.r.* (*Col.*) to suffer from working in hot weather (animals).

achamparse, *v.r.* (*Chi.*) to keep someone else's property.

achancharse, *v.r.* (*Per.*) to become lazy.

achantarse, *v.r.* (*coll.*) to hide during danger; to submit, agree.

achaparrado, -da, *a.* stunted (tree); *hombre achaparrado*, short and thick-set man.

achaparrarse, *v.r.* to grow stunted.

achaque, *n.m.* theme, matter; (*coll.*) excuse, pretext; habitual failing, vice or indisposition; (*coll.*) monthly courses; pregnancy; *saber poco de achaques de amores*, to know little of love matters.

achaquiento, -ta, *a.* sickly, unhealthy.

achares, *n.m.pl.* jealousy; suspicions.

acharolado, -da, *a.* resembling patent leather; treated with japan varnish. — *p.p.* [ACHAROLAR].

acharolador, -ra, *n.m.f.* japan varnisher.

— *a.* that varnishes, makes to resemble patent leather.

acharoladura, *n.f.* japan varnishing.

acharolar, *v.t.* to varnish, make to resemble patent leather.

achatadamente, *adv.* flatly.

achatado, -da, *a.* flat; *nariz achatada,* flat nose. — *p.p.* [ACHATAR].

achatamiento, *n.m.* flattening.

achatar, *v.t.* to flatten. — *v.r.* to become flat.

achicado, -da, *a.* diminished; childish. — *p.p.* [ACHICAR].

achicador, -ra, *n.m.f.* reducer, diminisher; (*naut.*) scoop for bailing boats; (*min.*) baler, scooper. — *a.* reducing, baling; belittling.

achicadura, *n.f.*; **achicamiento,** *n.m.* reduction, diminution; (*naut.*) baling.

achicar, *v.t.* to reduce, diminish, lessen; (*coll.*) to humble, belittle; to bale a boat or drain a mine; *achicar un cabo,* to shorten a rope; *achicar el agua del navío,* to free the ship of water; *tuvo que achicar sus pretensiones,* he had to reduce his demands; (*Chi.*) [ENCHIQUERAR]; (*Col.*) to kill. — *v.r.* to humble oneself, feel small; *Fulano se achica demasiado,* So-and-so belittles himself too much.

achicopalarse, *v.r.* (*Mex.*) to dishearten, to discourage.

achicoria, *n.f.* (*bot.*) chicory.

achicorial, *n.m.* ground where chicory is grown.

achicharradero, -ra, *n.m.* place where the heat is oppressive; *el teatro es un achicharradero,* the theatre is like an inferno.

achicharrador, -ra, *n.m.f.,* *a.* that burns, overheats.

achicharrar, *v.t.* to fry, cook, roast, toast anything too much; (*fig.*) to overheat; to annoy. — *v.r.* to become overdone, overheated (cooking).

achichinque, *n.m.* (*min.*) scooper, baler; (*Mex.*) lackey, servile follower.

achiguarse, *v.r.* (*Arg., Chi.*) to warp, bulge, sag.

achilenado, *a.* (*Per.*) pro-Chilean.

achimero, *n.m.* (*Guat., ES.*) pedlar, hawker.

achinado, -da, *a.* (*Am.*) like a Chinaman; (*Arg.*) dark-red.

achinar, *v.t.* (*coll.*) to murder; to corner (a checker).

achinelado, -da, *a.* slipper-shaped.

achinelar, *v.t.* to give shoes the form of a slipper.

achiote, achote, *n.m.* (*bot.*) (*Mex.*) arnotto-tree; (*com.*) anatta.

achique, *n.m.* scooping, baling, draining.

achispado, -da, *a.* tipsy. — *p.p.* [ACHISPAR].

achispar, *v.t.* (*coll.*) to make a person tipsy. — *v.r.* to get tipsy.

achocadura, *n.f.* knock against an object.

achocar, *v.t.* to throw one against the wall, wound, strike (with stick, stone, etc.); to knock asunder; (*coll.*) to hoard money.

achocolatado, -da, *a.* chocolate-coloured.

achocharse, *v.r.* (*coll.*) to become senile.

acholado, -da, *a.* (*Am.*) half Indian; half-breed.

acholar, *v.t.* (*Chi., Per.*) to disconcert, rattle, make blush; to shame; to cow.

achorizado, -da, *a.* similar to *chorizo* in shape and taste.

achubascarse, *v.r.* (*naut.*) to get squally and showery.

achuchador, -ra, *n.m.f.* bully. — *a.* bullying.

achuchadura, *n.f.*; **achuchamiento,** *n.m.* blow, thrust, jostling.

achuchar, *v.t.* (*coll.*) to crush with a blow; (*coll.*) to thrust, push roughly, jostle.

achuchón, *n.m.* (*coll.*) push, squeeze.

achucutarse, achucuyarse, *v.r.* (*Cent. Am.*) to become down-hearted; to lose courage; to wither.

achulado, -da, *a.* (*coll.*) playful; rough; pimp, man kept by prostitutes. — *p.p.* [ACHULARSE].

achulaparse, *v.r.* [ACHULARSE].

achularse, *v.r.* to become waggish, frolicsome; to become a knave.

achunchar, *v.t.* (*Chi.*) to foil, frustrate.

achupalla, *n.f.* (*Am.*) a plant of the Bromeliaceæ family.

achura, *n.f.* (*Arg.*) gut of cattle.

adafina, *n.f.* stew used by the Jews in Spain.

adagio, *n.m.* proverb; saying; adage; (*mus.*) adagio, slow time.

adalid, *n.m.* chief, commander, champion, leader.

adamado, -da, *a.* ladylike (applied to vulgar women); effeminate; delicate, elegant, graceful. — *p.p.* [ADAMARSE].

adamadura, *n.f.* infatuation.

adamantino, -na, *a.* (*poet.*) adamantine.

adamarse, *v.r.* to become effeminate; to degenerate.

adamascado, -da, *a.* damask-like. — *p.p.* [ADAMASCAR].

adamascador, -ra, *n.m.f.,* *a.* that manufactures damask.

adamascar, *v.t.* to damask.

adámico, -ca, *a.* said of sand accumulated by the tide.

adamismo, *n.m.* doctrine of the Adamites.

adamita, *n.m.* Adamite.

Adán, *n.m.* Adam; (*coll.*) slovenly man.

adanismo, *n.m.* doctrine and sect of the Adamites.

adaptabilidad, *n.f.* adaptability.

adaptable, *a.* adaptable; suitable.

adaptación, *n.f.* adaptation; fitting; accommodation.

adaptadamente, *adv.* adapted in a fit manner; fitly, justly.

adaptado, -da, *a.* suited, adapted. — *p.p.* [ADAPTAR].

adaptador, -ra, *n.m.f.* adapter. — *a.* adapting.

adaptante, *n.m.f.* adapter. — *a.* adapting.

adaptar, *v.t.* to adapt, fit, apply; to make suitable; to fashion. — *v.r.* to adapt oneself to; get used to; to cohere; *adaptar (algo)* or *adaptarse al uso,* to adapt (something), or become adapted to.

adaraja, *n.f.* (*arch.*) toothing.

adarce, *n.m.* dry sea-froth. — *pl.* carbonate of lime deposited by certain mineral waters.

adarga, *n.f.* oval or heart-shaped leather shield.

adargar, *v.t.* to shield, protect, defend.

adarguero, *n.m.* maker of shields.

adarguilla, *n.f.* small shield.

adarme, *n.m.* half a drachm, sixteenth part of an ounce; 179 centigrams; *por adarmes,* very sparingly.

adarvar, *v.t.* to paralyse, bewilder, stun. — *v.r.* to faint, become unconscious.

adarve, *n.m.* (*mil., arch.*) way behind the parapet; (*fig.*) protection, defence.

adatar, *v.t.* to open an account; to credit; to annotate, comment.

adaza, *n.f.* (*bot.*) common panic-grass.

adazal, *n.m.* esparto thread.

adecenamiento, *n.m.* forming by tens.

adecenar, *v.t.* to form or count by tens.

adecentar, *v.t.* to render decent. — *v.r.* to become decent.

adecuación, *n.f.* fitness; adequateness.

adecuadamente, *adv.* fitly, properly, to the purpose.

adecuadamiento, *n.m.* fitness.

adecuado, -da, *a.* adequate, fit, competent. — *p.p.* [ADECUAR].

adecuar, *v.t.* to fit, accommodate; to render suitable; *adecuar(se)*, or *ser adecuado al asunto*, to fit, become adequate, or be adequate to the matter.

adefagía, *n.f.* (*zool.*) voracity.

adéfago, -ga, *a.* (*zool.*) voracious; adephagous.

adefesio, *n.m.* (*coll.*) extravagance, folly; anything not to the purpose; ridiculous attire; extravagant, ridiculous person.

adefesios, (*coll.*) nonsensically; absurdly.

adefina, *n.f.* [ADAFINA].

adehala, *n.f.* gratuity, perquisite, tip.

adehesado, *n.m.* place converted into pasture. —*p.p.* [ADEHESAR].

adehesamiento, *n.m.* converting land into pasture; pasturage.

adehesar, *v.t.* to convert land into pasture.

adelantadamente, *adv.* beforehand; in anticipation.

adelantado, -da, *a.* anticipated, advanced, proficient, precocious, bold, forward; early (fruit, etc.); fast (clock or watch). — *n.m.* an appellation formerly given to the governor of a province; *por adelantado*, in advance. — *p.p.* [ADELANTAR].

adelantador, -ra, *n.m.f.* one that advances, extends, amplifies.— *a.* advancing, extending.

adelantamiento, *n.m.* progress, improvement, increase; growth, furtherance; cultivation; anticipation; betterment, promotion; the dignity of the governor formerly called *adelantado*, and the district of his jurisdiction.

adelantar, *v.t.* to advance, accelerate, promote, forward; to anticipate; to pay beforehand. — *v.i.* to advance, keep on; to grow; to improve. — *v.r.* to take the lead, outrun, come forward; to excel, outdo; to go forward in advance, to go ahead; *adelantar como el cangrejo*, to move backwards; *adelantar(se) a otros*, to overtake, or surpass others; *adelantar en algo*, to improve in, at something.

adelante, *adv.* ahead; forward, onward; higher up; farther off; **¡ adelante!** *interj.* ' Come in '; go on; forward!; *en adelante*, *de hoy en adelante*, *de aquí en adelante*, henceforth, in future, for the future; *más adelante*, later on; *quien adelante no mira, atrás se queda*, look before you leap.

adelanto, *n.m.* advance, progress; (*com.*) advance payment.

adelfa, *n.f.* (*bot.*) oleander; rose-bay.

adelfal, adelfar, *n.m.* (*bot.*) plantation of rose-bay trees.

adélfico, -ca, *a.* (*poet.*) bitter, cruel.

adelfilla, *n.f.* (*bot.*) the flowering osier, mezereon.

adelgazado, -da, *a.* made slender or thin; attenuated. — *p.p.* [ADELGAZAR].

adelgazador, -ra, *a.* one that makes thin or slender.

adelgazamiento, *n.m.* making slender; slenderness, thinness.

adelgazar, *v.t.* (*pret.* **adelgacé;** *pres. subj.* **adelgace**) to attenuate, to make thin, slender; to lessen; refine; to taper; to discuss with subtlety. — *v.i.*, *v.r.* to become slender or thin; to taper off.

adema, *n.f.*; **ademe,** *n.m.* (*min.*) shore; strut; prop.

ademador, *n.m.* mine carpenter who places props.

ademán, *n.m.* gesture; look, manner; attitude; (*pl.*) breeding, manners; *en ademán de*, about to, prepared to; *hacer ademanes de*, to assume the airs of; *con un ademán me impuso silencio*, he silenced me with a gesture; *no pude reprimir un ademán de impaciencia*, I could not refrain from a gesture of impatience.

ademar, *v.t.* (*min.*) to shore, prop.

además, *adv.* moreover, likewise, further; furthermore; short of this; besides; *además de*, besides; *además de lo referido*, in addition to, besides the matter referred to.

adenografía, *n.f.* (*med.*) a treatise on the glands.

adenoideo, -dea, *a.* adenoid; *tumor adenoideo*, *vegetación adenoidea*, adenoids.

adenología, *n.f.* (*med.*) part of anatomy dealing with the glands.

adenoso, -sa, *a.* glandular.

adentelladura, *n.f.* biting; (*arch.*) toothing.

adentellar, *v.t.* to bite, catch with the teeth; (*fig.*) to mutter; *adentellar una pared*, to leave toothing-stones or bricks to continue a wall. — *v.r.* to become angry.

adentro, *adv.* within, inwardly, internally, inside; *de botones adentro*, in my heart; *ser muy de adentro*, to be intimate in a house; *¡adentro!* come in! *tierra adentro*, in the interior of the country; *nunca me entró de dientes adentro*, I never could endure him. — *pl.* the innermost thoughts; *pensé para mis adentros*, I thought to myself, within myself.

adepto, *n.m.* adept; initiated; expert.

aderezadamente, *adv.* with seasonings, adornments, embellishments.

aderezador, -ra, *n.m.f.*, *a.* that adorns, dresses, embellishes. — *n.m.* (*carp.*) jointing-plane.

aderezadura, *n.f.* [ADEREZO].

aderezamiento, *n.m.* adorning, embellishing, dressing.

aderezar, *v.t.* (*pret.* **aderecé;** *pres. subj.* **aderece**) to adorn, embellish, dress; to prepare; to season; *aderezar la comida*, to cook the dinner; to dress (salad); to clean, repair; to mix (drinks); to blend (wines or tea); to gum (silks); to size (stuffs). — *v.r.* to adorn, embellish, dress oneself.

aderezo, *n.m.* dressing and adorning; finery; gum, starch, etc., used for stiffening; set of jewellery; trappings of a horse; furniture; hilt, hook, and other appendages of a sword; *aderezo de mesa*, oil, vinegar, salt, etc., for the table; *aderezo de comida*, condiment.

aderra, *n.f.* rush rope.

adestrado, -da, *a.* broken in; (*her.*) on the dexter side of the escutcheon. — *p.p.* [ADESTRAR].

adestrador, -ra, *n.m.f.* teacher; censor; critic. — *a.* instructive, censorious, critical.

adestramiento, *n.m.* teaching; criticizing; censorship.

adestrar, *v.t.* (*pres. indic.* **adiestro;** *pres. subj.* **adiestre**) to guide, lead; to teach; to train; to make dexterous. — *v.r.* to train oneself, practise; [ADIESTRAR].

adeudado, -da, *a.* indebted. — *p.p.* [ADEUDAR].

adeudamiento, *n.m.* indebtedness.

adeudar, *v.t.* to owe; to be dutiable; (*com.*) to charge, debit. — *v.r.* to incur debt. — *v.i.* to become related by marriage.

adeudo, *n.m.* indebtedness; custom-house duty; (*com.*) debit, charge.

adherencia, *n.f.* alliance; adherence; (*fig.*) relationship; bond, friendship.

adherente, *a.* adhesive, attached, adherent. — *n.m.* follower, adherent. — *n.m.pl.* equipment, accessories.

adherido, -da, *a.* glued to. — *p.p.* [ADHERIR].

adherir, *v.i.* (*pres. indic.* **adhiero;** *pres. subj.* **adhiera**) to adhere, stick to. — *v.r.* to hold, stick fast; *adherir(se) a un dictamen,* to adhere to an opinion.

adhesión, *n.f.* adhesion; cohesion, following, attachment.

adhesividad, *n.f.* adhesiveness.

adhesivo, -va, *a.* adhesive.

adhiero; adhiera, *pres. indic.; pres. subj.* [ADHERIR].

adiafa, *n.f.* tip given to seamen at the end of a voyage.

adiamantado, -da, *a.* adamantine. — *p.p.* [ADIAMANTAR].

adiamantar, *v.t.* to adorn with diamonds.

adición, *n.f.* addition, extension; remark or note put to accounts; advance of salary; *adición de la herencia,* acceptance of an inheritance.

adicionable, *a.* addible, that can be added.

adicionador, -ra, *n.m.f.* one who makes an addition. — *a.* that adds.

adicional, *a.* supplementary, additional.

adicionalmente, *adv.* additionally.

adicionar, *v.t.* to make additions, add to; to extend, prolong.

adicto, -ta, *n.m.f.* supporter, follower. — *a.* addicted, attached.

adiestrable, *a.* trainable.

adiestrador, -ra, *n.m.f.* [ADESTRADOR].

adiestramiento, *n.m.* [ADESTRAMIENTO].

adiestrar, *v.t., v.r.* [ADESTRAR]; *adiestrarse a esgrimir, en la lucha,* practise fencing, boxing or wrestling.

adiestro; adiestre, *pres. indic.; pres. subj.* [ADESTRAR; ADIESTRAR].

adietar, *v.t.* to put on a diet. — *v.r.* to diet oneself.

adinamia, *n.f.* (*med.*) debility, adynamia, prostration.

adinámico, -ca, *a.* (*med.*) lacking force.

adinerado, -da, *a.* rich, wealthy. — *p.p.* [ADINERAR].

adinerar, *v.t.* (*prov.*) to convert into currency. — *v.r.* (*coll.*) to become rich.

adintelado, -da, *a.* (*arch.*) falling from an arch gradually into a straight line.

adiós, *interj.* good-bye, adieu.

adipal, *a.* greasy.

adipocira, *n.f.* adipocere.

adiposidad, *n.f.* fatness, adiposity.

adiposo, -sa, *a.* fat, adipose; *tejido adiposo,* adipose tissue.

adir, *v.t.* (*law*) to accept or receive an inheritance.

aditamento, *n.m.* addition.

aditivo, -va, *a.* additive.

adiva, *n.f.;* **adive,** *n.m.* jackal.

adivas, *f.pl.* (*vet.*) fives.

adivinable, *a.* that can be divined.

adivinación, *n.f.* divination.

adivinador, -ra, *n.m.f.* diviner, soothsayer. — *a.* divining.

adivinaja, *n.f.* (*coll.*) puzzle, riddle, conundrum.

adivinamiento, *n.m.* divination.

adivinanza, *n.f.* (*coll.*) prophecy; prediction; enigma, riddle; guess; divination.

adivinar, *v.t.* to predict, foretell future events; to conjecture, divine, guess; to solve a riddle.

adivinatorio, -ria, *a.* divinatory.

adivino, -na, *n.m.f.* soothsayer; foreboder, fortune-teller; wizard; guesser.

adjetivación, *n.f.* adjectival use; (*gram.*) agreement.

adjetivadamente, *adv.* adjectively.

adjetival, *a.* adjectival.

adjetivar, *v.t.* to make agree; (*gram.*) to give adjectival value. — *v.r.* to be used adjectivally.

adjetivo, -va, *a.* adjective; *adjetivo calificativo,* qualifying adjective; *adjetivo comparativo,* comparative adjective; *adjetivo determinativo,* limiting adjective; *adjetivo gentilicio,* proper adjective. — *n.m.* adjective.

adjudicación, *n.f.* adjudication; auction-sale; 'knocking-down' at auction.

adjudicador, -ra, *n.m.f.* adjudger; adjudicator. — *a.* adjudging, adjudicating.

adjudicar, *v.t.* to adjudge, adjudicate; to sell at auction. — *v.r.* to appropriate.

adjudicatario, -ria, *n.m.f.* grantee.

adjudicativo, -va, *a.* adjudicative; adjudicating.

adjunción, *n.f.* (*law*) adjunction; (*gram.*) zeugma.

adjunta, *n.f.* (*com.*) letter enclosed in another.

adjuntamente, *adv.* jointly; in the same place.

adjunto, -ta, *a.* joined, annexed, enclosed; associate, adjunct. — *n.m.* addition; adjective. — *n.m.f.* enclosure; partner.

adjutor, -ra, *a.* helping, adjuvant. — *n.m.f.* helper; assistant.

ad lítem, *Lat.* (*law*) legal representative of a minor person.

adminicular, *v.t.* (*law*) to increase the power of a thing by collateral aids; to support, corroborate.

adminículo, *n.m.* aid, prop, support. — *pl.* articles carried for emergency use.

administrable, *a.* administrable.

administración, *n.f.* administration, management; office of an administrator; *en administración,* in trust; *administración militar,* commissariat; *administración económica,* treasury department; *administración activa,* executive office; *administración contenciosa,* administración de justicia, legal, judicial administration; *administración pública,* executive office; *por administración,* by the government; officially; by the management, company, etc.

administrador, -ra, *a.* administrating. — *n.m.f.* administrator, manager; steward, director, trustee; *administrador de aduanas,* collector of the customs; *administrador de correos,* postmaster; *administrador que administra y enfermo que se enjuaga, algo traga,* money is apt to stick to the fingers of trustees.

administradorcillo, *n.m. dim.* of *administrador (contempt.).*

administrar, *v.t.* to administer, govern, manage; to serve an office; to apply a remedy; to give, bestow.

administrativamente, *adv.* administratively.

administrativo, -va, *a.* administrative, managerial.

administratorio, -ria, *a. (law)* belonging to an administration or administrator.

admirable, *a.* admirable, excellent; wonderful, marvellous.

admirablemente, *adv.* admirably.

admiración, *n.f.* admiration; wonder; *(gram.)* exclamation mark (¡ !); prodigy; *es una admiración,* it is a thing worthy of admiration.

admirado, -da, *a.* astonished; admired *(de, by).* — *p.p.* [ADMIRAR].

admirador, -ra, *n.m.f.* admirer. — *a.* admiring.

admirando, -da, *a.* worthy of admiration.

admirar, *v.t.* to admire, marvel, contemplate. — *v.r.* to wonder, be astonished; to be surprised at, regard with admiration; *admirarse de un suceso,* to wonder at an occurrence.

admirativamente, *adv.* in a wondering manner; admiringly.

admirativo, -va, *a.* admiring, wondering; admirable; admired; filled with admiration.

admisible, *a.* admissible.

admisión, *n.f.* admission, acceptance.

admitido, -da, *a.* admitted, accepted. — *p.p.* [ADMITIR].

admitir, *v.t.* to receive, admit; to concede; to accept; to permit; to find; to allow, suffer, brook; *el asunto no admite dilación,* the affair admits of no delay; *admitir en cuenta,* to take into consideration.

admonición, *n.f.* warning, counsel, advice.

admonitor, *n.m.* monitor (in some religious communities).

adnado, -da, *n.m.f. (obs.)* [ALNADO].

adnata, *n.f. (anat.)* conjunctiva.

adnato, -ta, *a. (bot., physiol.)* adnate.

adobado, *n.m.* pickled pork. — *a.* pickled; dressed; curried; preserved. — *p.p.* [ADOBAR].

adobador, -ra, *n.m.f.* dresser, preparer. — *a.* pickling, preserving.

adobamiento, *n.m.* dressing; preserving; cooking; tanning.

adobar, *v.t.* to dress, prepare, pickle pork or other meats; to cook; to tan hides.

adobasillas, *n.m.* chair-mender.

adobe, *n.m.* unburnt brick dried in the sun; fetters, irons, shackles.

adobera, *n.f.* mould for making bricks; *(Mex.)* cheese in brick shape; *(Chi.)* mould for making cheese.

adobería, *n.f.* brickyard; tannery.

adobío, *n.m.* front wall of a blast-furnace.

adobo, *n.m.* repairing, mending; pickle, sauce; dressing for seasoning; ingredients

for dressing leather or cloth; pomade, cosmetic.

adocenadamente, *adv.* in a common, ordinary, vulgar manner.

adocenado, -da, *a.* common, ordinary, vulgar; counted by the dozen, numerous. — *p.p.* [ADOCENAR].

adocenamiento, *n.m.* counting, selling by dozens; vulgarity; depreciation.

adocenar, *v.t.* to count or sell by dozens; to despise, depreciate, underrate. — *v.r.* to lower oneself; to become despicable.

adoctrinar, *v.t.* to instruct.

adolecente; adoleciente, *a.* suffering, patient.

adolecer, *v.i. (pres. indic.* **adolezco;** *pres. subj.* **adolezca)** to be seized with illness; to suffer, be subject to; to grow; *adolecer de alguna enfermedad,* to suffer from some illness. — *v.r.* to condole.

adolescencia, *n.f.* youth, adolescence.

adolescente, *a.* young, adolescent. — *n.m.f.* adolescent.

adolezco; adolezca, *pres. indic.; pres. subj.* [ADOLECER].

adolorado, -da; adolorido, -da, *a.* afflicted; heart-sick.

adomiciliar, *v.i.* to domicile. — *v.r.* to take up one's abode.

adonde, *conj.* where; *¿adónde?* *adv.* whither? to what place? *¿adónde bueno?* whither away?

adondequiera, *adv.* wherever, to whatever place you please; anywhere.

adónico; adonio, *n.m.* a Latin verse consisting of a dactyl and a spondee.

adónide, *n.m.* greenhouse.

Adonis, *n.m.* Adonis; *(fig.)* handsome youth; *(bot., ent., ichth.)* adonis.

adonizar, *v.r.* to adorn oneself.

adopción, *n.f.* adoption.

adopcionismo, *n.m.* adoptionism, an ancient Spanish sect.

adopcionista, *n.m.* Adoptionist.

adoptable, *a.* adoptable.

adoptado, -da, *a.* adopted. — *p.p.* [ADOPTAR]. — *n.m.f.* adopted person.

adoptador, -ra, *n.m.f.* adopter. — *a.* adopting.

adoptante, *n.m.f.* adopter. — *a.* adopting.

adoptar, *v.t.* to adopt, father; to embrace an opinion; to adopt a resolution; *adoptar por hijo,* to adopt as a son.

adoptivamente, *adv.* adoptively.

adoptivo, -va, *a.* adoptive; adopted.

adoquier; adoquiera, *adv.* anywhere, where you please.

adoquin, *n.m.* paving-stone; *(coll.)* dull, sluggish person.

adoquinado, -da, *a.* paved. — *p.p.* [ADOQUINAR]. — *n.m.* pavement; paving.

adoquinar, *v.t.* to pave.

ador, *n.m.* time for watering land, where water is officially distributed.

adorable, *a.* adorable, worshipful.

adorablemente, *adv.* adorably.

adoración, *n.f.* adoration, worship.

adorado, -da, *a.* adored, well-beloved. — *p.p.* [ADORAR].

adorador, -ra, *n.m.f.* adorer; worshipper. — *a.* adoring.

adorante, *n.m.f.* adorer; worshipper. — *a.* adoring.

adoratorio, *n.m. (Am.)* Indian temple, teocalli.

adorar, *v.t.* to adore, worship, idolize; (*fig.*) to love excessively; *adorar a Dios*, to adore God; *adorar en una persona*, to respect a person.

adoratriz, *n.f.* nun of a religious order that befriends reformed women.

adormecedor, -ra, *a.* soporiferous, soporific.

adormecer, *v.t.* (*pres. indic.* **adormezco;** *pres. subj.* **adormezca**) to cause drowsiness or sleep; (*fig.*) to lull asleep; (*fig.*) to calm, lull. — *v.r.* to fall asleep; to grow benumbed or torpid; (*fig.*) to grow or persist in vice.

adormecido, -da, *a.* mopish; sleepy, drowsy. — *p.p.* [ADORMECER].

adormeciente, *a.* soporific.

adormecimiento, *n.m.* drowsiness, slumber, sleepiness, numbness, mopishness.

adormezco; adormezca, *pres. indic.; pres. subj.* [ADORMECER].

adormidera, *n.f.* (*bot.*) poppy; poppy-head.

adormilarse, *v.r.* to doze, drowse.

adormir, *v.t., v.r.* [ADORMECER].

adormitarse, *v.r.* to doze, drowse.

adornable, *a.* that can be adorned.

adornado, -da, *a.* ornamented, adorned. — *p.p.* [ADORNAR].

adornador, -ra, *n.m.f.* adorner, decorator. — *a.* adorning, decorating.

adornamiento, *n.m.* embellishment, adornment.

adornante, *n.m.f.* adorner, decorator. — *a.* decorating, adorning.

adornar, *v.t.* to adorn, beautify, embellish, grace, decorate, ornament; to furnish, garnish; to be distinguished by certain gifts, talents, etc.; *adornar con*, or *de tapices*, to adorn with tapestries. — *v.r.* to adorn oneself; to become distinguished by certain gifts, talents, etc.

adornista, *n.m.* painter, decorator.

adorno, *n.m.* adorning, accomplishment; ornament, finery; decoration, habiliment; garniture; *adorno de una casa*, furniture; (*bot.*) balsam.

adosado, -da, *a.* (*her.*) placed back to back. — *p.p.* [ADOSAR].

adosar, *v.t.* (*her.*) to place back to back; to support, unite.

adquiero; adquiera, *pres. indic.; pres. subj.* [ADQUIRIR].

adquirente; adquiriente, *n.m.f.* acquirer. — *a.* acquiring.

adquirido, -da, *a.* acquired. — *p.p.* [ADQUIRIR]; *bienes mal adquiridos nunca han enriquecido*, illgotten gains never prosper.

adquiridor, -ra, *n.m.f.* acquirer; *a buen adquiridor, buen expendedor*, after a gatherer comes a scatterer. — *a.* acquiring.

adquirimiento, *n.m.* acquisition.

adquirir, *v.t.* (*pres. indic.* **adquiero;** *pres. subj.* **adquiera**) to acquire, obtain, get.

adquisición, *n.f.* acquisition, attainment.

adquisidor, -ra, *n.m.f.* acquirer. — *a.* acquiring.

adquisitivo, -va, *a.* (*law*) acquisitive.

adquisito, *p.p. irreg.* (*obs.*) [ADQUIRIR].

adquisitorio, -ria, *a.* referring to *adquisición*.

adquisividad, *n.f.* acquisitiveness.

adra, *n.f.* turn, time, successive order; portion of the inhabitants of a town.

adragante, *a.* tragacanth.

adraganto, *n.m.* tragacanth.

adrales, *n.m.pl.* hurdles, side-boards (of carts).

adrazo, *n.m.* alembic for distilling sea-water.

adrede; adredemente, *adv.* purposely, knowingly.

adrenalina, *n.f.* (*chem.*) adrenaline.

adrián, *n.m.* bunion; (*orn.*) magpie's nest.

adriático, -ca, *n.m.f., a.* Adriatic.

adrizado, -da, *a.* (*naut.*) righted. — *p.p.* [ADRIZAR]. — *n.m.* (*naut.*) set of halyards.

adrizar, *v.t.* (*naut.*) to right. — *v.r.* (*naut.*) to right itself.

adrolla, *n.f.* fraud, trick.

adrollado, -da, *a.* vain, deceptive, muddled.

adrollero, *n.m.* one who buys or sells dishonestly.

adscribir, *v.t.* to appoint a person to a place or employment. — *v.r.* to inscribe oneself.

adscripción, *n.f.* nomination, appointment; adscription.

adscripto, -ta; adscrito, -ta, *a.* adscript. — *p.p. irreg.* [ADSCRIBIR].

aduana, *n.f.* custom-house; *en la aduana*, in bond; *arancel de aduanas*, tariff; *corredor de aduana*, custom-house broker; *derecho de aduana*, duty; *pasar por todas las aduanas*, to undergo a close examination.

aduanar, *v.t.* to enter goods at the custom-house; to pay customs duty; to put in bond.

aduanero, -ra, *a.* belonging to the custom-house. — *n.m.* custom-house officer; revenue officer.

aduar, *n.m.* horde, migratory crew; village of Arabs; ambulatory Arab camp; horde of gipsies; (*Am.*) Indian settlement.

adúcar, *n.m.* silk from outer part of cocoon and the cloth made from it.

aducción, *n.f.* adduction.

aducir, *v.t.* (*pres. indic.* **aduzco;** *pres. subj.* **aduzca;** *pret.* **aduje**) to adduce, cite; to add, join; to guide; to bring.

aductor, *n.m.* (*anat.*) adductor (muscle). — *a.* adducent.

aduendado, -da, *a.* fairy-like, ghost-like.

adueñarse, *v.r.* to take possession of, seize.

adufa, *n.f.* (*prov.*) half-door; sluice; lock (canals).

adufe, *n.m.* timbrel or tambourine; (*coll.*) silly talker.

adufero, -ra, *n.m.f.* tambourine-player.

adujadas; adujas, *n.f.pl.* (*naut.*) coil or a coiled cable.

adujar, *v.t.* (*naut.*) to coil (cable, chain). — *v.r.* to twist, curl oneself up in a small space.

aduje, *pret.* [ADUCIR].

adula, *n.f.* common pasture-ground.

adulación, *n.f.* flattery, fawning, coaxing; adulation.

adulador, -ra, *n.m.f.* flatterer, fawner, coaxer. — *a.* flattering, fawning, coaxing.

adular, *v.t.* to flatter, soothe, coax, court, compliment; to fawn, creep, crouch, grovel.

adularia, *n.f.* (*min.*) variety of feldspar.

adulatorio, -ria, *a.* flattering, honey-mouthed; parasitical.

adulear, *v.i.* (*prov.*) to bawl, cry out.

adulero, *n.m.* driver of horses or mules.

adulón, -na, *n.m.f.* gross flatterer; toady. — *a.* cringing, toadying.

adúltera, *n.f.* adulteress [ADÚLTERO].

adulterable, *a.* liable to adulteration.

adulteración, *n.f.* adulteration, sophistication.
adulterado, -da, *a.* adulterated, sophisticated. — *p.p.* [ADULTERAR].
adulterador, -ra, *n.m.f.* adulterator, adulterant; falsifier. — *a.* adulterating, adulterant.
adulterante, *n.m.f.* adulterant. — *a.* adulterating.
adulterar, *v.t.* to adulterate, corrupt, falsify. — *v.i.* to commit adultery. — *v.r.* to become corrupted, adulterated.
adulterinamente, *adv.* in an adulterous manner, adulterously.
adulterino, -na, *a.* adulterine, begotten in adultery; (*fig.*) adulterated, falsified, forged.
adulterio, *n.m.* adultery.
adúltero, -ra, *n.m.f.* adulterer, adulteress. — *a.* adulterous; (*fig.*) base, corrupted.
adulto, -ta, *n.m.f., a.* adult, grown-up.
adulzamiento, *n.m.* action and effect of moulding metals.
adulzar, *v.t.* to sweeten; soften; to render (metals) more ductile.
adumbración, *n.f.* adumbration, shade in a picture.
adunar, *v.t.* to unite, join; to unify. — *v.r.* to become associated.
adunco, -ca, *a.* curved; warped.
adunia, *adv.* abundantly.
adustamente, *adv.* austerely, severely.
adustez, *n.f.* disdain, aversion, asperity.
adusto, -ta, *a.* adust; scorched, parched; (*fig.*) gloomy, austere, intractable, sullen (of persons).
aduzco; aduzca, *pres. indic.; pres. subj.* [ADUCIR].
advenedizo, -za, *n.m.f., a.* foreign, strange; newcomer, stranger, immigrant; parvenu.
advenidero, -ra, *a.* future, coming.
advenimiento, *n.m.* arrival; advent; *esperar uno el santo advenimiento,* to wait for something that is long in coming.
advenir, *v.i.* to come, arrive; to occur.
adventicio, -cia, *a.* accidental, adventitious; (*law*) coming otherwise than by direct succession.
adventismo, *n.m.* (*relig.*) doctrine of the Adventists.
adventista, *n.m.f., a.* (*relig.*) Adventist.
adverar, *v.t.* to certify, authenticate.
adverbial, *a.* adverbial.
adverbialmente, *adv.* adverbially.
adverbio, *n.m.* adverb.
adversamente, *adv.* adversely, unfortunately; contrariwise.
adversario, -ria, *n.m.f.* opponent; antagonist, foe. — *n.m.pl.* tabulated notes for reference purposes.
adversativo, -va, *a.* (*gram.*) adversative.
adversidad, *n.f.* calamity, adversity, misfortune, affliction.
adverso, -sa, *a.* adverse, calamitous, afflictive; opposite, averse; favourless; facing; in front of.
advertencia, *n.f.* warning, advice; foreword; remark, notice.
advertidamente, *adv.* advisedly, deliberately.
advertido, -da, *a.* noticed; skilful, clever; expert; intelligent; acting with deliberation; sagacious. — *p.p.* [ADVERTIR].
advertimiento, *n.m.* warning, advice; remark; notice.

advertir, *v.t.* (*pres. indic.* **advierto**; *pres. subj.* **advierta**; *pret.* (él) **advirtió**) to take notice of, observe; to instruct, advise, give notice or warning; to acquaint; to mark, note; to inform; to perceive; to state; to consider; *es de advertir,* it is proper to state, or, it must be remembered; *he de advertir,* I must observe. — *v.r.* to notice, think of.
adviento, *n.m.* Advent, season before Christmas.
advierto; advierta; (él) advirtió, *pres. indic.; pres. subj.; pret.* [ADVERTIR].
advocación, *n.f.* title given to a church, chapel, or altar dedicated to the Blessed Virgin or a saint.
adyacencia, *n.f.* adjacency.
adyacente, *a.* adjacent, contiguous.
adyuntivo, -va, *a.* conjunctive; joining.
aechadero, *n.m.* (*prov.*) [AHECHADERO].
aechador, -ra, *n.m.f.* [AHECHADOR].
aechaduras, *n.f.pl.* [AHECHADURAS].
aechar, *v.t.* (*prov.*) [AHECHAR].
aecho, *n.m.* [AHECHO].
aeración, *n.f.* aeration, charging with gas or air; (*med.*) action of atmospheric air in treatment of disease; ventilation.
aéreo, -rea, *a.* aerial; (*fig.*) airy, fantastic.
aerífero, -ra, *a.* aeriferous, air-conducting.
aerificación, *n.f.* gasification.
aerificar, *v.t.* to gasify. — *v.r.* to be converted into gas.
aeriforme, *a.* (*chem.*) aeriform, gaseous.
aerio, -ria, *a.* aerial.
aerobio, *n. & a.* aerobian.
aerobús, *n.m.* aerobus.
aerodinámica, *n.f.* aerodynamics.
aerodinámico, -ca, *a.* relating or appertaining to aerodynamics.
aeródromo, *n.m.* aerodrome; airport.
aerofagia, *n.m.* (*med.*) spasmodic deglutition of air in some neuroses.
aeréfano, -na, *a.* diaphanous, transparent.
aerofobia, *n.f.* aversion to air; aerophobia.
aeréfobo, -ba, *a.* suffering from aerophobia.
aeréfono, -na, *a.* amplifying (voice). — *n.m.* aerophone.
aeréforo, -ra, *a.* air-conducting.
aerégamo, -ma, *a.* (*bot.*) flowering.
aerografía, *n.f.* aerography.
aerograma, *n.m.* wireless message, aerogram.
aerolito, *n.m.* aerolite, meteoric stone.
aerología, *n.f.* aerology.
aeromancía, *n.f.* aeromancy.
aeromántico, -ca, *n.m.f.* professor or student of aeromancy. — *a.* appertaining or relating to aeromancy.
aerometría, *n.f.* aerometry.
aerómetro, *n.m.* aerometer.
aeromotor, *n.m.* aeromotor.
aeronato, -ta, *a.* born in a plane during a flight.
aeronauta, *n.m.f.* aeronaut.
aeronáutica, *n.f.* aeronautics.
aeronáutico, -ca, *a.* aeronautic.
aeronave, *n.f.* airship, dirigible.
aeroplano, *n.m.* aeroplane, airplane.
aeropostal, *n. & a.* air mail.
aeropuerto, *n.m.* airport.
aeréscafo, *n.f.* sailing boat.
aeroscopia, *n.f.* aeroscopy.

[25]

aerostación, *n.f.* aerostation; air navigation.
aeróstata, *n.m.f.* aerostat, balloonist.
aerostática, *n.f.* aerostatics.
aerostático, -ca, *a.* aerostatic.
aeróstato, *n.m.* aerostat, air balloon.
aerostero, *n.m.* (*mil.*) air soldier.
aerotecnia, *n.f.* application of air in industry.
aerotermo, -ma, *a.* (*phys.*) applied to hot-air furnaces.
afabilidad, *n.f.* affability, graciousness, courtesy; civility of address.
afabilísimo, -ma, *a. superl.* of *afable,* extremely affable, very kind.
afable, *a.* affable, kind, agreeable, courteous; *afable con,* or *para,* or *para con todos,* affable to, with everyone; *afable en el trato,* affable in his manners.
afablemente, *adv.* affably, good-naturedly; familiarly.
afabulación, *n.f.* morality or explanation of fable.
afabular, *v.t.* to explain a fable; to relate a story in the form of a fable.
áfaca, *n.f.* (*bot.*) yellow vetch.
afamable, *a.* that deserves or may acquire fame.
afamado, -da, *a.* celebrated, noted, famous. — *p.p.* [AFAMAR].
afamar, *v.t.* to make famous, give fame to. — *v.r.* to become renowned.
afán, *n.m.* anxiety, solicitude, trouble; eagerness. — *pl.* **afanes,** labours, toils.
afanadamente, *adv.* anxiously, eagerly; laboriously.
afanador, -ra, *n.m.f.* one eager for riches; painstaker, painstaking, laboriousness; hustler. — *a.* painstaking, hustling, hurrying; laborious, toilsome.
afanaduría, *n.f.* (*Mex.*) casualty ward.
afanar, *v.t.* to urge, press, hurry. — *v.i.* to toil, labour; be too solicitous; *afanar, afanar y nunca medrar,* much toil and little profit. — *v.r.* to toil, etc., too much; *afanarse por nada,* to fidget; *afanarse en la labor,* to work eagerly; *afanarse por ganar,* to work anxiously for gain.
afaneso, *n.f.* arsenite of copper.
afaníptero, -ra, *a.* wingless; (*zool.*) aphanipterous. — *n.m.pl.* Aphaniptera, Siphonaptera.
afanita, *n.f.* (*geol.*) [ANFIBOLITA].
afanosamente, *adv.* anxiously.
afanoso, -sa, *a.* anxious, solicitous; laborious, painstaking; anxious.
afantasmado, -da, *a.* (*fam.*) vain, presumptuous; phantasmal.
afarallonado, -da, *a.* steep, with steep cliffs.
afarolarse, *v.r.* (*coll. Am.*) to become excited; to make a fuss; to lose one's temper.
afasia, *n.f.* (*med.*) aphasia.
afeable, *a.* that can, or deserves to, be made ugly; censurable.
afeador, -ra, *n.m.f.* one that deforms or makes ugly. — *a.* deforming, distorting, that makes homely.
afeamiento, *n.m.* defacing; ugliness; calumny.
afear, *v.t.* to deform, disfigure, deface, misshape; to make look ugly; to be a blemish to; (*fig.*) to decry, condemn; to calumniate. — *v.r.* to become impaired, faulty.
afeblecerse, *v.r.* (*pres. ind.* **me afeblezco;** *pres. subj.* **me afeblezca**) to grow feeble or delicate.

afección, *n.f.* affection, inclination, fondness; (*med.*) affection.
afectable, *a.* affectible; impressionable.
afectación, *n.f.* affectation, artificial appearance, daintiness; presumption, pride.
afectadamente, *adv.* affectedly.
afectado, -da, *a.* affected, formal, conceited, foppish. — *p.p.* [AFECTAR].
afectador, -ra, *n.m.f.* one who behaves affectedly. — *a.* affecting.
afectar, *v.t.* to make a show of something, to feign; to affect, assume a manner; to affect, influence; (*law*) to charge, impose, encumber. — *v.r.* to be moved, feel emotion.
afectibilidad, *n.f.* affectibility.
afectísimo, -ma, *a.* (*superl.* of *afecto*), very affectionate, most loving.
afectividad, *n.f.* affectibility; affectionateness.
afectivo, -va, *a.* affective, proceeding from affection.
afecto, -ta, *a.* affectionate, fond, inclined; well-affected; (*law*) subject to some charge or encumbrance; *ser afecto a una persona,* to feel friendly towards someone; *ser afecto de un achaque,* to be affected by an illness. — *n.m.* affection, love, fondness, fancy, concern; passion, sensation; pain, disease; (*paint.*) lively interpretation.
afectuosamente, *adv.* fondly, affectionately.
afectuosidad, *n.f.* fondness; affection.
afectuoso, -sa, *a.* loving, fond; kind, gracious.
afeitado, -da, *a.* shaved; painted, made-up. — *p.p.* [AFEITAR].
afeitar, *v.t.* to shave; to beautify; to clip plants, trees, etc.; to trim the tail and mane of a horse. — *v.r.* to shave oneself; to use cosmetics.
afeite, *n.m.* paint, rouge, cosmetic; make-up.
afelio, *n.m.* (*astron.*) aphelion.
afelpado, -da, *a.* like plush or velvet; (*fig.*) shaggy; (*naut.*) *palletes afelpados,* cased mats. — *n.m.* grass mat. — *p.p.* [AFELPAR].
afelpar, *v.t.* to make like plush or velvet; (*naut.*) to pad.
afeminación, *n.f.* effeminacy, emasculation.
afeminadamente, *adv.* effeminately; in a womanly way.
afeminado, -da, *a.* effeminate. — *p.p.* [AFEMINAR].
afeminamiento, *n.m.* effeminacy, emasculation.
afeminar, *v.t.* to effeminate, unman; to enervate. — *v.r.* to become weak, feeble, lose courage.
aferente, *a.* (*med.*) afferent.
aféresis, *n.f.* (*gram.*) aphæresis.
aferradamente, *adv.* tenaciously, obstinately.
aferrado, -da, *a.* headstrong. — *p.p.* [AFERRAR].
aferrador, -ra, *n.m.f.* one that grapples or grasps. — *a.* grappling, grasping.
aferramiento, *n.m.* grasping, grappling, seizing, binding; headstrongness, obstinacy; *aferramiento de las velas,* the furling of the sails.
aferrar, *v.t., v.i.* to grasp, grapple, seize, bind; (*naut.*) to furl; to moor, anchor. — *v.r.* (*naut.*) to fasten to each other; *aferrarse a,* or *con,* or *en su opinión,* to become determined in one's opinion; to interlock; (*fig.*) to persist obstinately in an opinion.
aferravelas, *n.f.pl.* (*obs.*) (*naut.*) rope bands, gaskets; furling-lines.

aferruzado, -da, *a.* angry, irate.
afestonado, -a, *a.* festooned. — *p.p.* [AFESTONAR].
afestonar, *v.t.* to festoon.
afgano, -na, *n.m.f.*, *a.* Afghan.
afianzado, -da, *a.* guaranteed; secured; bailed. — *p.p.* [AFIANZAR].
afianzador, -ra, *n.m.f.* guarantor. — *a.* guaranteeing.
afianzamiento, *n.m.* security, guarantee, bail; prop, support; fastening, securing.
afianzar, *v.t.* (*pret.* **afiancé**; *pres. subj.* **afiance**) to become bail or security for; to guarantee; to prop, secure, buttress, make fast, clinch; *afianzar con sus bienes*, to guarantee with his property; *afianzar de calumnia*, to affirm by calumny. — *v.r.* to prop, support oneself; *afianzarse en*, or *sobre los estribos*, to make oneself secure in the stirrups.
afición, *n.f.* love, affection, fondness (*a*, for); eagerness, efficiency; taste, inclination; *afición ciega razón*, love is blind.
aficionadamente, *adv.* fondly, with liking; as an amateur.
aficionado, -da, *a.* fond (*a*, of). — *n.m.f.* amateur. — *p.p.* [AFICIONAR].
aficionador, -ra, *a.* that inspires, causes affection; attractive.
aficionar, *v.t.* to cause, inspire affection or fondness. — *v.r.* ; *aficionarse a*, to fancy, grow fond of; *aficionarse a*, or *de alguna cosa*, to fancy something.
aficioncilla, *n.f.* sneaking kindness, cool regard, slight affection; secret love.
afidávit, *n.m.* affidavit.
afijo, -ja, *n.m.f.* (*gram.*) affix. — *a.* affixed.
afiladera, *n.f.* whetstone.
afilado, -da, *a.* sharp, keen; slender, thin, tapering. — *p.p.* [AFILAR].
afilador, -ra, *a.* sharpening. — *n.m.* sharpener; leather razor-strop.
afiladura, *n.f.* sharpening, whetting.
afilamiento, *n.m.* slenderness of the face, nose, or fingers; sharpening, whetting.
afilar, *v.t.* to whet, grind; to render keen, sharpen; to taper; *afilar el ingenio*, to make a great effort for a special purpose; *afilar las uñas*, to sharpen one's wit; to make an intelligent effort; *afilar en la piedra*, to sharpen on a stone; *afilar con la navaja*, to sharpen with the knife. — *v.r.* to grow thin; to taper.
afiliación, *n.f.* affiliation.
afiliado, -da, *a.* adopted; affiliated. — *p.p.* [AFILIAR].
afiliar, *v.t.* to adopt; to affiliate. — *v.r.* to join a body or society.
afiligranado, -da, *a.* filigree, filigreed; ornamented; slender, thin, delicate, neat. — *p.p.* [AFILIGRANAR].
afiligranar, *v.t.* to make filigree work; to polish, embellish, ornament.
áfilo, -la, *a.* (*bot.*) leafless.
afilón, *n.m.* whetstone; steel, knife-sharpener, razor-strop.
afilosofado, -da, *a.* eccentric; applied to the person who sets up as a philosopher or savant.
afín, *a.* close; contiguous, adjacent. — *n.m.f.* relation by affinity.
afinación, *n.f.* completion; last touch; refining (metals); tuning (of musical instruments).

afinadamente, *adv.* completely, perfectly, finally; delicately; politely; in tune.
afinado, -da, *a.* well-finished, perfect; refined, minute; well tuned. — *p.p.* [AFINAR].
afinador, -ra, *n.m.f.* finisher; piano-tuner; tuning-key. — *a.* finishing, tuning.
afinadura, *n.f.* completion; refining.
afinamiento, *n.m.* completion; refining; refinement; fineness of manners.
afinar, *v.t.* to complete; to polish; to trim (binding); to tune (instruments, voice); to refine (metals); (*Chi.*) to finish, to conclude. — *v.r.* to become polished, refined, civilized, astute, keen, sagacious.
afincado, -da, *p.p.* [AFINCAR] bought (real estate).
afincar, *v.i.*, *v.r.* to buy up real estate.
afine, *a.* related, analogous; adjoining.
afinidad, *n.f.* analogy, resemblance; relationship; (*chem.*) affinity.
afino, *n.m.* refinement of metals.
afión, *n.m.* opium.
afir, *n.m.* (*vet.*) horse medicine made up of juniper-berries.
afirmación, *n.f.* affirming, assertion, affirmation.
afirmadamente, *adv.* firmly.
afirmado, -da, *p.p.* [AFIRMAR] affirmed. — *n.m.* road-bed.
afirmador, -ra, *n.m.f.* affirmer. — *a.* affirming.
afirmante, *n.m.f.* affirmer. — *a.* affirming.
afirmar, *v.t.* to affirm, assert, contend; to make fast, secure, clinch. — *v.r.* to maintain firmly; to hold fast; to steady oneself, make oneself firm; *afirmarse en lo dicho*, to confirm the statement.
afirmativa, *n.f.* affirming, assertion.
afirmativamente, *adv.* affirmatively.
afirmativo, -va, *a.* affirmative.
afistular, *v.t.* to render fistulous. — *v.r.* to become fistulous.
aflato, *n.m.* breath, wind; (*fig.*) inspiration.
aflautada, *a.* screechy, shrill (voice).
aflechado, -da, *a.* (*bot.*) arrow-shaped (said of leaves).
aflicción, *n.f.* affliction, sorrow, grief, anguish.
aflictivo, -va, *a.* afflicting, distressing, grievous; (*law*) *pena aflictiva*, corporal punishment.
aflicto, -ta, *p.p. irreg.* [AFLIGIR] grieved (used only in poetry).
afligidamente, *adv.* grievously, sadly, sorrowfully.
afligido, -da, *a.* grieved, sad. — *p.p.* [AFLIGIR].
afligimiento, *n.m.* affliction, sorrow, grief, anguish.
afligir, *v.t.* (*pres. indic.* **aflijo**; *pres. subj.* **aflija**) to afflict, cause pain to. — *v.r.* to grieve, languish, repine; to become despondent; *afligirse por pequeños males*, to worry over trifles; *afligirse de todo*, to worry over everything; *afligirse con sus propios sentimientos*, to be worried by one's own feelings.
aflojador, -ra, *a.* slackening. — *n.m.* weaver's instrument.
aflojadura, *n.f.* ; **aflojamiento,** *n.m.* relaxation, loosening, slackening.
aflojar, *v.t.* to loosen, slacken, relax, let loose; to debilitate; *aflojar el ánimo*, to take things easy awhile, take a rest; *aflojar la cuerda*, to give pause to fatiguing work; *aflojó en el*

estudio, he slackened in his studies; *aflojar la bolsa*, to open one's purse; (*naut.*) *aflojar los obenques*, to ease the shrouds; *aflojar las riendas*, to relax watchfulness or authority. — *v.i.* to grow weak, abate; *aflojó la calentura*, the fever abated. — *v.r.* to grow cool in fervour or zeal; to lose courage; to relent.

aflorado, -da, *a.* flowered or figured goods; made of the finest flour; choice, exquisite; best, most perfect; (*min.*) outcropped. — *p.p.* [AFLORAR].

afloramiento, *n.m.* (*min.*) outcrop; sifting (flour, grain).

aflorar, *v.i.* (*min.*) to crop out. — *v.t.* to sift; to purify, refine.

afluencia, *n.f.* plenty, abundance; (*fig.*) fluency, volubility; crowd.

afluente, *a.* copious, abundant, affluent; loquacious; *afluente en palabras*, fluent in speech. — *n.m.* affluent, tributary of a river.

afluir, *v.i.* (*pres. indic.* **afluyo**; *pres. subj.* **afluya**) to congregate, assemble; to discharge into another stream, lake or sea.

aflujo, *n.m.* (*med.*) afflux, affluxion.

afofado, -da, *a.* spongy, soft. — *p.p.* [AFOFAR].

afofar, *v.t.* to make spongy. — *v.r.* to become soft, spongy.

afogarar, *v.t.* to scorch. — *v.r.* to become scorched; to become irritated or distressed.

afolador, -ra, *a.* caulking.— *n.m.* caulking-iron.

afolar, *v.t.* to caulk.

afoliado, -da, *a.* (*bot.*) leafless.

afollado, -da, *a.* blown up by bellows. — *n.m.* bellows. — *n.m.pl.* wide trousers. — *p.p.* [AFOLLAR].

afollador, -ra, *a.* that blows by bellows. — *n.m.f.* bellows-blower. — *n.m.* (*Mex.*). [FOLLADOR].

afolladura, *n.f.*; **afollamiento,** *n.m.* action and effect of blowing by bellows.

afollar, *v.t.* to blow with bellows; (*fig.*) to pleat; (*build.*) to work badly. — *v.r.* (*build.*) to become blistered, puff up, hollow (walls).

afondado, -da, *p.p.* [AFONDAR] submerged, sunk, foundered.

afondar, *v.t.* to put under water. — *v.i.*, *v.r.* (*naut.*) to sink, founder.

afonía, *n.f.* (*med.*) aphonia; loss of voice through disease of the throat.

afónico, -ca; áfono, -na, *a.* aphonic; silent.

aforado, -da, *a.* privileged, favoured; appraised, measured. — *n.m.f.* privileged person. — *p.p.* [AFORAR].

aforador, *n.m.* gauger, appraiser.

aforamiento, *n.m.* gauging, appraisement; duty on foreign goods.

aforar, *v.t.* to gauge, measure (vessels or quantities); to appraise; to give privileges.

aforisma, *n.f.* (*vet.*) tumour (in animals).

aforismo, *n.m.* aphorism, brief sentence, maxim.

aforístico, -ca, *a.* aphoristical.

aforo, *n.m.* gauging; appraisement.

aforrador, -ra, *n.m.f.* one who lines clothes.

aforrar, *v.t.* to line (clothes, vessels, tubes, etc.); to cover books; *aforrar una casa*, to ceil a room or house; (*naut.*) to sheathe; *aforrar un cabo*, to serve a cable; *aforrar con*, or *de*, or *en piel*, to line with fur. — *v.r.* to put on heavy underclothing; (*coll.*) to gorge.

aforro, *n.m.* lining; (*naut.*) rounding, sheathing; (*naut.*) waist of a ship.

afortunadamente, *adv.* luckily, fortunately.

afortunado, -da, *a.* fortunate, happy, lucky. — *p.p.* [AFORTUNAR].

afortunar, *v.t.* to make happy.

afosarse, *v.r.* (*mil.*) to entrench oneself.

afoscarse, *v.r.* (*naut.*) to become hazy.

afrailado, -da, *a.* monk-like; (*agric.*) pruned; (*print.*) applied to a print having a friar patch. — *p.p.* [AFRAILAR].

afrailamiento, *n.m.* (*agric.*) pruning.

afrailar, *v.t.* (*agric.*) to prune, trim trees.

afrancesado, -da, *a.* frenchified, French-like. — *n.m.f.* a Spanish sympathizer with the French, especially during the Napoleonic invasion (1808–1813). — *p.p.* [AFRANCESAR].

afrancesamiento, *n.m.* frenchification.

afrancesar, *v.t.* to gallicize, frenchify; to give a French termination or turn to words. — *v.r.* to imitate the French; to be naturalized in France.

afranelado, -da, *a.* flannelly.

afrecharse, *v.r.* (*Chi.*) to get sick through overeating (animals).

afrecho, *n.m.* bran.

afrenillar, *v.i.* (*naut.*) to bridle the oars.

afrenta, *n.f.* affront, dishonour, outrage, insult, abuse, infamy, disgrace, stigma.

afrentador, -ra, *a.* outraging, insulting. — *n.m.f.* abuser, insulter.

afrentar, *v.t.* to affront, insult; *afrentar con denuestos*, to injure by insults. — *v.r.* to be affronted; be shamed; to blush; *afrentarse de su estado*, to be ashamed of one's position.

afrentosamente, *adv.* ignominiously.

afrentoso, -sa, *a.* ignominious; insulting; outrageous.

afretado, -da, *a.* (*naut.*) clean, scrubbed. — *p.p.* [AFRETAR].

afretar, *v.t.* (*naut.*) to scrub and clean the bottom of a vessel; to rub, scour.

africanista, *n.m.f.* one interested in Africa. — *a.* appertaining to African studies.

africano, -na, *n.m.f.*, *a.* African.

áfrico, *n.m.* the south-west wind [ABREGO].

afrisonado, -da, *a.* resembling a Frisian horse.

afrodisia, *n.f.* aphrodisia.

afrodisíaco, -ca, *a.* aphrodisiac, aphrodisian. — *n.m.* aphrodisiac.

afrodita, *n. & a.* (*zool.*) aphroditidæ.

afroditario, *n.m.* aphrodisiac.

afrontado, -da, *a.* confronted; (*her.*) face to face; endangered. — *p.p.* [AFRONTAR].

afrontamiento, *n.m.* confrontation.

afrontar, *v.t.* to confront; to defy; to reproach. — *v.i.* to face.

afrontilar, *v.t.* (*Mex.*) to tie cattle by the horns.

afta, *n.f.* (*med.*) aphthæ, thrush.

aftoso, -sa, *a.* aphthous.

afuera, *adv.* outside, outward, in public; (*obs.*) besides, moreover. — *n.f.pl.* **afueras,** suburbs, outskirts, environs; (*fort.*) open ground around a fortress; ¡*afuera!* clear the way, stand out of the way!

afufa, *n.f.* (*coll.*) flight; *estar uno sobre las afufas*, to be arranging to escape; *tomar las afufas*, (*coll.*) to run away.

afufar, *v.i.*, *v.r.* to run away, escape.

afusión, *n.f.* (*med.*) affusion, shower-bath.

afusionar, *v.t.* (*med.*) to administer an affusion.

afuste, *n.m.* gun-carriage; *afuste de mortero*, mortar-bed; emplacement.

agá, *n.m.* Turkish officer.

agabachado, -da, *a.* Frenchified. — *p.p.* [AGABACHAR].

agabachar, *v.t.* to Frenchify. — *v.r.* to become frenchified.

agabanado, -da, *a.* resembling an overcoat.

agacé, *a.* (*Par.*) Indian aboriginal.

agachadiza, *n.f.* (*orn.*) snipe; *hacer la agachadiza,* (*coll.*) to crouch down, conceal oneself.

agachado, -da, *a.* stooping, bent, crouched. — *p.p.* [AGACHAR].

agachaparse, *v.r.* (*prov.*) (*coll.*) [AGAZAPARSE].

agachar, *v.t.* to lower, bow down, bend. — *v.r.* (*coll.*) to stoop, squat, crouch, cower; to go into seclusion for a while; *agachar las orejas,* (*coll.*) to be humble; to be dejected, dispirited, crestfallen.

agachona, *n.f.* (*Mex.*) wading bird.

agafar, *v.t.* (*coll.*) (*prov.*) to seize, grasp.

agafita, *n.f.* oriental turquoise.

agalbanado, -da, *a.* indolent, lazy, shiftless.

agalerar, *v.t.* (*naut.*) to tip an awning.

agalgado, -da, *a.* similar to a greyhound.

agalibar, *v.t.* (*naut.*) to squadron.

agáloco, *n.m.* aloe plant.

agalla, *n.f.* (*bot.*) gall-nut; *agalla de ciprés,* cypress gall; (*pl.*) tonsils; fish-gills; (*vet.*) windgalls of a horse; screw-thread of boring rod; the side of the head of birds corresponding to the temple; (*Cub.*) (*bot.*) wild shrub (used in dyeing); (*Ec.*) hook of a hanging lamp; *quedarse de la agalla,* or *colgado de la agalla,* to be deceived in one's hopes. — *pl.* (*coll.*) courage, cheek, gall; *tener muchas,* or *buenas agallas,* to be very audacious, unscrupulous.

agallado, -da, *a.* (*Cub.*) steeped in an infusion of agalla.

agalladura, *n.f.* cicatricule, tread (of egg).

agallato, *n.m.* gallate.

agállico, -ca, *a.* gallic, derived from nut-galls.

agallón, *n.m.* large gall-nut; (*arch.*) echinus. — *pl.* strings of large silver beads hollowed like gall-nuts; wooden beads put to rosaries.

agallonado, -da, *a.* (*arch.*) ornamented with echinus.

agalludo, -da, *a.* (*Am.*) cunning, astute, foxy.

agalluela, *n.f.* small gall-nut.

agamitar, *v.t.* to imitate the voice of a fawn.

ágamo, -ma, *a.* (*biol.*) agamic, asexual.

agamuzado, -da, *a.* chamois-coloured, buff, like chamois-leather. — *p.p.* [AGAMUZAR].

agamuzar, *v.t.* to dress skins like chamois-leather.

agangrenarse, *v.r.* to gangrene.

ágape, *n.m.* agape.

agarabar, *v.t.* (*coll.*) to wait for, expect.

agarbado, -da, *a.* comely, neat; bent, crouched. — *p.p.* [AGARBARSE].

agarbanzado, -da, *a.* chick-pea coloured, buff; (*prov.*) (*agric.*) sprouted, budded. — *p.p.* [AGARBANZAR].

agarbanzar, *v.t.* (*prov.*) (*agric.*) to bud, sprout.

agarbarse, *v.r.* to bend, stoop down, crouch.

agarbillar, *v.t.* (*agric.*) to bind or tie in sheaves.

agardamarse, *v.r.* (*prov.*) to become worm-eaten (wood).

agarduñar, *v.t.* to steal.

agareno, -na, *a.* Mohammedan.

agárico, *n.m.* (*bot.*) agaric, fungus.

agarrada, *n.f.* (*coll.*) altercation, wrangle.

agarradero, *n.m.* hold, haft, handle; (*naut.*) anchorage; (*coll.*) protection, patronage.

agarrado, -da, *a.* (*coll.*) miserable, stingy, close-fisted; held, gripped. — *p.p.* [AGARRAR].

agarrador, -ra, *a.* grasping, seizing. — *n.m.f.* grasper, seizer; sad-iron holder; catchpole; (*coll.*) bailiff.

agarrafar, *v.t.* (*coll.*) to grasp; grapple hard in a struggle. — *v.r.* to come to close grips.

agarrama, *n.f.* [GARRAMA].

agarrante, *a.* grasping.

agarrar, *v.t.* to grasp, seize, lay hold of; (*coll.*) to obtain; to come upon; *por fin agarró el destino que pretendía,* he obtained at last the situation he desired; *se le agarró la calentura,* the fever had a firm hold on him. — *v.r.* to clinch, grapple, hold on; *agarrarse de un pelo,* to support an opinion; to furnish an excuse; to split hairs; *agarrarse a* (or *de*) *buenas aldabas,* to avail oneself of an influential protector; *agarrarse de un clavo ardiendo,* to seize a red-hot nail, to take any means, however dangerous, to accomplish one's object; *agarrarse a,* or *de un hierro,* to hold on tightly to an iron.

agarre, *n.m.* [AGARRADERO].

agarro, *n.m.* grasp, seizure.

agarrochador, *n.m.* pricker, goader.

agarrochar, *v.t.* to prick with a spike or spear; to goad; (*naut.*) to brace (the yards).

agarrón, *n.m.* (*Am.*) grasp, clutch, hold [AGARRADA].

agarrotado, -da, *a.* garrotted; (*coll.*) stiff, rigid. — *p.p.* [AGARROTAR].

agarrotar, *v.t.* to compress bales with ropes and cords; to garrotte; to compress, bind tightly.

agasajador, -ra, *n.m.f.,* *a.* attentive, kind, obliging person.

agasajar, *v.t.* to receive and treat kindly; to fondle; to regale, entertain.

agasajo, *n.m.* graceful and affectionate reception; attention shown; friendly present; consideration, kindness, regard; afternoon refreshment or collation.

ágata, *n.f.* agate.

agatoideo, -dea, *a.* that leads to good; that seems good.

agavanza, *n.f.;* **agavanzo,** *n.m.* hip-tree, dog-rose.

agave, *n.m.* (*bot.*) agave, century-plant; fibre of the agave.

agavillado, -da, *a.* (*agric.*) sheaved; (*coll.*) ruffian-like. — *p.p.* [AGAVILLAR].

agavillar, *v.t.* (*agric.*) to bind or tie in sheaves. — *v.r.* (*coll.*) to associate with a gang of sharpers; (*fig.*) to give cause for thought.

agazapada, *n.f.* refuge of game.

agazapar, *v.t.* (*coll.*) to nab a person. — *v.r.* (*coll.*) to hide oneself; to crouch.

agencia, *n.f.* agency; ministration; commission; agent's bureau, office; diligence, activity.

agenciador, -ra, *n.m.f.* agent, promoter, negotiator. — *a.* negotiating, promoting.

agenciar, *v.t.,* *v.i.* to solicit, promote, negotiate.

agencioso, -sa, *a.* diligent, active; officious.

agenda, *n.f.* note-book; memorandum.

agenesia, *n.f.* (*med.*) impotence; sterility.

agente, *n.m.* agent, actor, minister; solicitor, attorney; *agente de cambio y bolsa,* stockbroker, bill-broker; *agente de negocios,* promoter; *agente fiscal,* assistant attorney;

agente de policía, police officer, detective. — *a.* acting.

agerasia, *n.f.* old age free from indispositions.

agérato, *n.m.* (*bot.*) sweet milfoil or maudlin.

agermanado, -da, *a.* belonging to a sect called *germanía* (1519–22). — *p.p.* [AGERMANARSE].

agermanarse, *v.r.* to become a partisan of a *germanía.*

agestado, -da, *a.* [(**bien** *or* **mal**), (well *or* ill)] featured. — *p.p.* [AGESTARSE].

agestarse, *v.r.* to make a definite grimace.

agestión, *n.f.* accumulation, agglomeration.

agibílibus, *n.m.* (*coll.*) application and industry to obtain the conveniences of life; hustling; hustler.

agible, *a.* feasible, practicable.

agigantado, -da, *a.* gigantic; (*coll.*) exaggerated, extraordinary; out of the common; *a pasos agigantados,* by leaps and bounds. — *p.p.* [AGIGANTAR].

agigantar, *v.t.* (*fig.*) to exaggerate. — *v.r.* to become exaggerated, extraordinary.

ágil, *a.* nimble, active, agile, fast, light; keen; *ágil de pies,* agile on his feet.

agilidad, *n.f.* agility, nimbleness, activity, lightness, liveliness, sprightliness; keenness.

agilitar, *v.t.* to render nimble; make active. — *v.r.* to become nimble, active.

ágilmente, *adv.* nimbly, actively; keenly.

agio, *n.m.;* **agiotaje,** *n.m.* (*com.*) agio, agiotage; exchange of paper money for coin, or coin for bills; premium; stock-jobbing.

agiotador, agiotista, *n.m.* money-changer, bill-broker, stock-jobber.

agitable, *a.* agitable; that can be shaken.

agitación, *n.f.* agitation, flurry, flutter, fluctuation, fidget, fretting; excitement.

agitado, -da, *a.* agitated, stormy. — *p.p.* [AGITAR].

agitador, -ra, *n.m.f.* fretter, agitator.

agitanado, -da, *a.* gipsy-like. — *p.p.* [AGITANARSE].

agitanarse, *v.r.* to become gipsy-like.

agitar, *v.t.* to agitate, ruffle, fret, irritate; to move, stir, discuss. — *v.r.* to flutter, palpitate; to move about; to become agitated, disturbed, excited.

aglomeración, *n.f.* agglomeration, heaping up.

aglomerado, -da, *a.* agglomerate. — *n.m.* briquette, brick made with coal-dust and tar, used for fuel. — *p.p.* [AGLOMERAR].

aglomerador, -ra, *a.* agglomerative. — *n.m.* machine for making briquettes.

aglomerante, *a.* agglomerative.

aglomerar, *v.t.* to heap up or upon, agglomerate. — *v.r.* to gather in a mass; to become agglomerated.

aglutinación, *n.f.* agglutination.

aglutinado, -da, *a.* agglutinate. — *p.p.* [AGLUTINAR].

aglutinante, *a.* agglutinating, cementing. — *n.m.* cementing material; (*med.*) sticking-plaster.

aglutinar, *v.t.* to glue together, to agglutinate.

aglutinativo, -va, *a.* agglutinative.

agnación, *n.f.* (*law*) agnation.

agnado, -da, *a.,* *n.m.f.* agnate.

agnaticio, -cia, *a.* agnatic.

agnición, *n.f.* (*poet.*) recognition of a person in a poem or drama.

agnocasto, *n.m.* chaste-tree, Agnus Castus.

agnomento, *n.m.* agnomen, nickname.

agnominación, *n.f.* (*rhet.*) paronomasia.

agnosia, *n.f.* ignorance.

agnosticismo, *n.m.* agnosticism.

agnóstico, -ca, *a.* *n.m.f.* agnostic.

agnusdéi, *n.m.* Agnus Dei, a small thin wax cake, with the figure of a lamb, blessed by the Pope; a part of the service of the Mass; a coin of the time of John I of Castile, of copper and silver alloy.

agobiado, -da, *a.* bent, oppressed. — *p.p.* [AGOBIAR].

agobiar, *v.t.* to bend the body down; (*fig.*) to oppress, overwhelm, grind; *le agobian los quehaceres, los años, las penas,* he is overwhelmed by his duties, age, worries. — *v.r.* to bow, couch; *agobiarse con,* or *de,* or *por los años,* to become oppressed by age.

agobio, *n.m.* bending down; oppression, grinding; dejection, load.

agogía, *n.f.* drain; water outlet in mines.

agolar, *v.t.* (*naut.*) to furl (sails).

agolpamiento, *n.m.* crowding, rush.

agolpar, *v.t.* to heap, pile up. — *v.r.* to crowd, rush.

agonal, *a.* agonistic (said of games in honour of Janus).

agonía, *n.f.* agony, death-agony, pangs of death; violent pain of body or mind; (*fig.*) vehement desire.

agónico, -ca, *a.* agonizing, painful, in agony.

agonioso, -sa, *a.* (*coll.*) anxious, eager; persistent; importunate; *niño agonioso,* insistent, importunate child.

agonística, *n.f.* athletics; science of combat.

agonístico, -ca, *a.* agonistic.

agonizadamente, *adv.* agonizingly.

agonizante, *a.,* *n.m.f.* dying, dying person; a monk who assists a dying person; in some universities, one who assists students in their examinations.

agonizar, *v.t.* to assist dying persons; (*coll.*) to annoy, importune. — *v.i.* to be dying; *estar agonizando,* to be in the agony of death.

agono, -na, *a.* agonic, without angles.

agora, *adv.* (*Am.*) [AHORA].

agorador, -ra, *n.m.f.,* *a.* [AGORERO].

agorafobia, *n.f.* (*path.*) agoraphobia, dread of open spaces.

agorar, *v.t.* (*pres. ind.* **agüero;** *pres. subj.* **agüere**) to divine, foretell, prognosticate.

agorería, *n.f.* divination.

agorero, -ra, *n.m.* fortune-teller, soothsayer, diviner. — *a.* divinatory, augural; superstitious.

agorgojarse, *v.r.* (*agric.*) to be destroyed by grubs (seeds, etc.).

agostadero, *n.m.* summer pasture.

agostado, -da, *a.* parched, consumed, extinguished; gathered; ploughed. — *p.p.* [AGOSTAR].

agostador, -ra, *n.m.f.,* *a.* that dries up, parches; (*coll.*) spendthrift.

agostamiento, *n.m.* parching up.

agostar, *v.t.* to parch; to consume, extinguish; to plough in August. — *v.i.* to pasture cattle on stubbles in summer. — *v.r.* to become parched, scorched.

agostero, *n.m.* harvest-man; religious mendicant who begs corn in August.

agostizo, -za, *a.* (person) born in August; said of a colt foaled in that month; weak.

agosto, *n.m.* August; harvest-time; harvest; (*coll.*) pauper; *hacer su agosto,* to make hay while the sun shines; to feather one's nest; to strike while the iron is hot; to improve the opportunity.

agotable, *a.* exhaustible.

agotación, *n.f.;* **agotadura,** *n.f.;* **agotamiento,** *n.m.* exhaustion, debility.

agotado, -da, *a.* exhausted; out of print (of books). — *p.p.* [AGOTAR].

agotador, -ra, *n.m.f.* exhauster. — *a.* exhausting, exhaustible.

agotante, *a.* exhausting.

agotar, *v.t.* to drain off liquids; to run through a fortune; to exhaust. — *v.r.* to become exhausted; to be out of print.

agoticado, -da, *a.* Gothic.

agovía, *n.f.* [ALBORGA].

agracejina, *n.f.* (*bot.*) barberry fruit.

agracejo, *n.m.* unripened grape; unripe fallen olive; (*bot.*) barberry; (*Cub.*) tree of the terebinth family.

agraceño, -a, *a.* resembling verjuice; acrid, sour, acid.

agracero, -ra, *a.* applied to vines when their fruit never ripens. — *n.f.* verjuice cruet.

agraciadamente, *adv.* graciously, gracefully.

agraciado, -da, *a.* graceful, gracious, favoured, genteel. — *p.p.* [AGRACIAR].

agraciador, -ra, *n.m.f.,* *a.* pleasing, pleasant, gracious person or thing.

agraciar, *v.t.* to adorn, embellish; to favour; to grace; to give employment; *agraciar con una cruz,* to reward with a cross. — *v.i.* to please, like, be pleasing.

agracillo, *n.m.* (*bot.*) barberry.

agradabilidad, *n.f.* agreeableness.

agradabilísimo, -ma, *a. superl.* most agreeable.

agradable, *a.* agreeable, pleasing, pleasant, enjoyable; *agradable al,* or *para el gusto,* agreeable to the taste; *agradable con,* or *para,* or *para con todos,* agreeable to everybody; *agradable de gusto,* agreeable in taste.

agradablemente, *adv.* agreeably, pleasantly.

agradar, *v.i.* to please, gratify, humour. — *v.r.* to be pleased; *me agrada,* (*impers.*) I like; (*lit.*) (it) pleases me.

agradecer, *v.t.* (*pres. indic.* **agradezco;** *pres. subj.* **agradezca**) to acknowledge (a favour); to thank; to show gratitude; to reward, recompense.

agradecidamente, *adv.* gratefully.

agradecido, -da, *a.* thankful, grateful; acknowledged; *pan agradecido,* (*coll.*) grateful person; *al agradecido, más de lo pedido,* to the grateful one more than he asks for; *agradecido a los beneficios, por los favores,* grateful for kindnesses, for favours. — *p.p.* [AGRADECER].

agradecimiento, *n.m.* gratefulness; thankfulness, acknowledgment.

agradezco; agradezca, *pres. indic.; pres. subj.* [AGRADECER].

agrado, *n.m.* affability, agreeableness; grace; gratefulness; pleasure; taste; will, inclination; liking; *esto no es de mi agrado,* that does not please me, I do not like that.

agrafia, *n.f.* (*path.*) agraphia.

agraja, *n.f.* (*carp.*) [ADARAJA].

agramadera, *n.f.* brake for dressing flax or hemp; scutcher.

agramado, -da, *p.p.* [AGRAMAR] broken, scutched. — *n.m.* braking, scutching.

agramador, -ra, *n.m.f.* flax or hemp dresser. — *n.m.* brake, scutch.

agramar, *v.t.* to brake, scutch flax or hemp.

agramilador, -ra, *a.* (*build.*) pointing. — *n.m.* (*build.*) pointer.

agramilar, *v.t.* to point and colour (a brick wall); (*arch.*) to imitate a brick wall by painting; to make even, adjust (the bricks).

agramiza, *n.f.* the stalk of hemp; refuse of dressed hemp; hemp; tow.

agrandable, *a.* increasable, expansible, extensible.

agrandamiento, *n.m.* enlargement, expansion, aggrandizement.

agrandar, *v.t.* to enlarge, increase, aggrandize. — *v.r.* to increase, grow larger.

agranujado, -da, *a.* filled with grain; rough-grained, grain-shaped; (*coll.*) roguish, urchin-like.

agranujarse, *v.r.* to become grain-shaped; to be covered in pimples; (*coll.*) to become a ragamuffin, rogue.

agrario, -ria, *a.* agrarian; rustic.

agrarismo, *n.m.* agrarianism.

agravación, *n.f.* aggravation.

agravador, -ra, *n.m.f.* aggravator, oppressor. — *a.* oppressing, aggravating.

agravamiento, *n.m.* aggravation; getting worse.

agravante, *a.* aggravating.

agravantemente, *adv.* aggravatingly; with unnecessary increase or pressure.

agravar, *v.t.* to oppress with taxes, etc.; to aggrieve; to exaggerate; to add to a load; to complicate. — *v.r.* to become worse, graver; *la enfermedad se agrava,* (*coll.*) the illness is getting worse; *el pesquisidor agravaba el delito,* the prosecutor exaggerated the crime.

agravatorio, -ria, *a.* (*law*) confirmatory, compulsory, aggravating.

agraviadamente, *adv.* offensively, insultingly.

agraviado, -da, *p.p.* [AGRAVIAR] injured, offended; (*com.*) amended.

agraviador, -ra, *n.m.f.* injurer, wronger, offender; (*coll.*) incorrigible delinquent. — *a.* offending, wrongful, injurious.

agraviamiento, *n.m.* wrong, offence, injury.

agraviante, *a.* wronging, offending, aggravating.

agraviar, *v.t.* to wrong, offend, injure, harm, grieve; (*law*) to amend (accounts). — *v.r.* to be aggrieved, take offence, be piqued; *agraviarse de alguno,* to become offended by someone; *agraviarse por una chanza,* to become offended by a joke.

agravio, *n.m.* offence, insult, injury, affront, damage, harm; grievance; *deshacer agravios,* to right wrongs; *escrito de agravios,* (*law*) appeal.

agravión, *n.m.* (*Chi.*) touchy.

agravioso, -sa, *a.* offensive, insulting, aggravating.

agraz, *n.m.* verjuice; unripe grape; (*coll.*) displeasure, disgust; (*bot.*) barberry; *en agraz,* unseasonably; *echar a uno el agraz en el ojo,* to say something unpleasant.

agrazada, *n.f.* verjuice-water with sugar.

agrazar, *v.t.* (*coll.*) to disgust, vex. — *v.i.* to taste sour.

agrazón, *n.m.* wild grape, grape which does not ripen; gooseberry-bush; (*coll.*) displeasure, resentment, disgust.

agrecillo, *n.m.* unripe grape or olive; barberry [AGRACILLO].

agredido, -da, *n.m.f.,* *a.* assaulted, injured person.

agredir, *v.t.* to assume the aggressive, assault, attack.

agredón, *n.m.* (*prov.*) wool for quilting.

agregable, *a.* that can be collected together.

agregación, *n.f.* aggregation, collection, aggregate.

agregado, -da, *p.p.* [AGREGAR]. — *n.m.* aggregate; congregation; assistant; supernumerary; attaché; (*Arg., Col., Ven.*) tenant-farmer; (*eng.*) aggregate (of concrete).

agregamiento, *n.m.* [AGREGACIÓN].

agregar, *v.t.* to aggregate, collect and unite, heap together; to collate; to nominate; to muster; to annex. — *v.r.* to become united, added.

agregatorio, -ria, *a.* aggregative.

agremán, *n.m.* passementerie, trimming.

agremiar, *v.t., v.r.* to form a guild or union.

agresión, *n.f.* aggression, attack, assault.

agresivamente, *adv.* aggressively.

agresividad, *n.f.* aggressiveness.

agresivo, -va, *a.* aggressive, hostile.

agresor, -ra, *n.m.f.* aggressor, assaulter; (*law*) one who tramples on another's rights. — *a.* aggressive, assaulting.

agresorio, -ria, *a.* aggressive.

agreste, *a.* rustic, country-like, wild; (*coll.*) clownish, uncultured, rude, uncouth.

agrete, *a.* sourish, tartish. — *n.m.* sourness with a mixture of sweet.

agria, *n.f.* (*med.*) herpes, tetter; (*min.*) very sloping gallery.

agriado, -da, *a.* soured, turned acid; (*coll.*) irritated. — *p.p.* [AGRIAR].

agriamente, *adv.* (*coll.*) sourly, harshly, bitterly, severely.

agriar, *v.t.* to make sour; (*coll.*) to irritate, exasperate. — *v.r.* to turn sour or acid; (*coll.*) to become irritated, exasperated.

agriaz, *n.m.* (*bot.*) bead-tree.

agrícola, *a.* agricultural. — *n.m.f.* agriculturist.

agricultor, *n.m.* husbandman, farmer, agriculturist.

agricultora, *n.f.* woman farmer.

agricultura, *n.f.* agriculture.

agridulce, *a.* bitter-sweet.

agridulzura, *n.f.* bitter-sweetness.

agrietado, -da, *a.* cracked, defective. — *p.p.* [AGRIETAR].

agrietamiento, *n.m.* cracking.

agrietar, *v.t., v.r.* to crack, split.

agrifolio, *n.m.* (*bot.*) holly-tree.

agrilla, *n.f.* (*bot.*) sorrel.

agrillado, -da, *a.* (*agric.*) sprouted; (*ent.*) similar to the cricket. — *p.p.* [AGRILLARSE].

agrillarse, *v.r.* (*agric.*) to shoot, sprout [GRILLARSE].

agrillo, -lla, *a.* sourish, tartish.

agrimensor, *n.m.* land-surveyor.

agrimensorio, -ria, *a.* appertaining to surveying.

agrimensura, *n.f.* land surveying; survey.

agrimonia, *n.f.* (*bot.*) agrimony, liverwort.

agringarse, *v.r.* (*Am.*) to imitate North-American manners.

agrio, -ria, *a.* sour, acrid; (*coll.*) rough (road); sharp, rude, unpleasant; *una respuesta agria,* a tart reply; brittle, unmalleable (metals); bad taste (colouring or drawing); crude; *agrio al gusto,* acid to the taste; *agrio de gusto,* acid in taste. — *n.m.* acidity (fruits); sourness; citric acid. — *n.m.pl.* (*bot., com.*) citrus fruits; *mascar las agrias,* to hide one's distaste or bad humour.

agrión, *n.m.* (*vet.*) callosity in a horse's knee; (*bot.*) bead-tree.

agripalma, *n.f.* (*bot.*) motherwort.

agripeno, *n.m.* (*Cub.*) migratory bird (*Paserinus americanus; Icterus agripennis*).

agrisado, -da, *a.* greyish. — *p.p.* [AGRISAR].

agrisar, *v.t.* to colour grey. — *v.r.* to become greyish.

agrisetado, -da, *a.* like flowered silk; grey-coloured. — *p.p.* [AGRISETAR].

agro, -ra, *a.* acid, sour; (*coll.*) tart, sharp, irritating. — *n.m.* citron; *jalea del agro,* citron preserve.

agrología, *n.f.* ecology.

agronomía, *n.f.* agronomy, agronomics.

agronómico, -ca, *a.* agronomic, agronomical.

agrónomo, -ma, *n.m.f.* agronomist, writer on agriculture. — *a.* agronomic.

agropecuario, -ria, *a.* appertaining to land and cattle; *riqueza agropecuaria,* land and cattle wealth.

agropila, *n.m.* German bezoar; panacea.

agrostema, *n.f.* corn-cockle; rose-campion.

agrósteo, -ea, *a.* gramineous. — *n.f.pl.* (*bot.*) Agrostis.

agróstide, *n.f.* (*bot.*) bent-grass.

agrostografía, *n.f.* agrostography, the division of botany dealing with grasses.

agrucho, -cha, *a.* disagreeably acid.

agrumación, *n.f.* clotting, curdling.

agrumar, *v.t.* to curdle, clot. — *v.r.* to curdle, become clotted.

agrupable, *a.* that can be grouped.

agrupación, *n.f.* cluster, crowd, group; gathering, groupage.

agrupado, -da, *a.* (*art*) arranged in a group; grouped. — *p.p.* [AGRUPAR].

agrupamiento, *n.m.* [AGRUPACIÓN].

agrupar, *v.t.* to group, cluster. — *v.r.* to gather in groups, crowd together.

agrura, *n.f.* acidity; acerbity; orchard of citrus trees.

agua, *n.f.* water, liquid, fluid, rain; the sea; (*chem.*) liquor distilled from herbs, flowers, or fruit; lustre of diamonds; (*naut.*) leak; (*arch.*) slope of a roof; *¡agua!* man overboard; *agua bendita,* holy water; *agua de Colonia,* eau-de-Cologne; *agua de cepas,* (*coll.*) wine; *agua dulce,* fresh water; *agua fuerte,* aqua fortis, nitric acid; *grabado al agua fuerte,* etching; *de agua y lana,* of little or no value or importance; *agua de olor,* scented water; *agua oxigenada,* peroxide of hydrogen; *agua del pantoque,* bilge-water; *agua rica,* scented water (in Peru); *agua llovediza, agua lluvia,* rain-water; *agua del timón,* wake of a ship; *¡agua va!* a notice to passers-by that water will be thrown; (*coll.*) said when someone forgets himself in conversation; *agua viva,* running water; *agua abajo,* downstream; *agua arriba,* upstream; with great difficulty. — *pl.* mineral waters in general; gloss (feathers, stone, wood, etc.); clouds in silk and other stuffs; urine; tide; *aguas chifles*, *aguas muertas*, neap-tides; *aguas vivas*, spring-tides; *entre dos aguas*, between wind and water; in doubt, perplexed; *nadie diga, de esta agua yo no beberé*, let no one say, I will not drink of this water; *cada uno quiere llevar el agua a su molino, y dejar en seco el del vecino*, everyone has his own axe to grind; *coger agua en cesto* (or *en harnero*), to labour in vain; *correr el agua por donde solía*, to return to one's old customs; *del agua mansa me libre Dios*, or, *guárdate del agua mansa*, still waters run deep; *sin tomar agua bendita*, without breaking any laws, legitimately; *sin decir agua va*, without premeditation, precipitately; *echar agua en el mar*, to carry coals to Newcastle; *del agua vertida, alguna cogida*, half a loaf is better than no bread, or, better to recover something than nothing; *ahogarse uno en poca agua*, to be troubled without cause; *agua de coco*, coco-nut milk; *agua muerta*, still water, without current; *agua de nafa*, orange-flower water; *agua cruda*, hard water; *agua de manantial*, spring water; *agua de nieve*, ice water; *agua de pozo*, well water; *agua fresca*, cold water; *agua gorda*, hard water; *agua nieve*, sleet; *agua sal*, salty water; *agua salobre*, salt water unfit for drinking; *agua termal*, hot-spring water; *agua viento*, wind and rain storm; *agua gaseosa*, aerated water; *agua de pie*, spring water; *aguas jurisdiccionales*, territorial waters; *aguas madres*, (*chem.*) mother-liquor; *aguas mayores*, stools (evacuation); (*naut.*) greatest equinoctial tides; *aguas menores*, urine; (*naut.*) daily tides; *aguantar aguas*, (*naut.*) to backwater with the oars; *como agua*, (*coll.*) abundantly; *como el agua de mayo*, (*coll.*) welcome, appreciated; *agua vertida, no toda cogida*, the damage is done; *algo tendrá el agua cuando la bendicen*, there must be something wrong when they praise that person so much; *arrollar agua*, (*naut.*) to go at great speed; *bailarle el agua delante*, (*coll.*) to be very officious, gushing to anyone; *bañarse en agua rosada*, (*coll.*) to rejoice at someone's good or bad fortune; *echar agua*, to baptize; *echar a uno un jarro de agua fría*, to discourage someone; *echarse al agua*, to face boldly, risk; *deshacerse una cosa como la sal en el agua*, to vanish; *echar toda el agua al molino*, to do one's utmost to reach one's aim; *hacérsele una agua la boca*, to make one's mouth water; *hacerse una agua*, *estar hecho una agua*, to be in a state of perspiration; *estar con el agua a*, or *hasta, la boca, el cuello*, or *la garganta*, to be in great danger; *no alcanzar para agua*, to earn very little; *no hallar agua en el mar*, to be blind to what is obvious; *parecer que uno no enturbia el agua*, to look very innocent; *hay más que agua*, he is very rich; *lo que por agua viene, por agua va*, easy come, easy go.

aguacatal, *n.m.* plantation of avocado pear-trees.

aguacate, *n.m.* the avocado pear-tree and its fruit; alligator-pear; (*min.*) pear-shaped emerald.

aguacatillo, *n.m.* variety of the avocado pear-tree.

aguacero, *n.m.* heavy shower.

aguacibera, *n.f.* water used for irrigating ground sowed when dry.

aguacha, *n.f.* (*coll.*) muddy, marshy water.

aguachar, *n.m.* pool, puddle.

aguachar; aguacharnar, *v.t.* to flood; (*Chi.*) to tame (horses). — *v.r.* to become flooded; (*Arg.*) to get fat in idleness (horses).

aguachento, -ta, *a.* (*Art.*) moist, sodden.

aguachirle, *n.f.* inferior wine; (*coll.*) any inferior liquor; trifle, frivolity.

aguada, *n.f.* (*build.*) first coat of paint; watering-station; (*min.*) flood in a mine; (*naut.*) fresh water on board a ship; (*art*) water-colour sketch or outline; *hacer aguada*, (*naut.*) to take fresh water; *a la aguada*, water-colour (picture).

aguadera, *n.f.* wing-feather; *pl.* frames for water jars carried by horses.

aguadero, *a.* waterproof; *capa aguadera*, waterproof cape. — *n.m.* drinking-trough; drinking-pool (wild animals); (*lumbering*) log pond.

aguadija, *n.f.* water, humour in pimples or sores.

aguado, -da, *a.* watered; watery, diluted; abstemious, teetotaller; ruined, spoilt; *fiesta aguada*, spoilt feast; (*vet.*) catarrhal (horses). — *p.p.* [AGUAR].

aguador, -ra, *n.m.f.* water-carrier; sprocket of a water-wheel; (*mil.*) *aguador del real*, sutler.

aguaducho, *n.m.* heavy shower; stall for selling water; (*prov.*) place where earthen vessels with drinking water are kept.

aguadura, *n.f.* (*vet.*) catarrh (in horses); abscess in the hoofs of horses.

aguafiestas, *n.m.f.* kill-joy, spoil-sport, (*coll.*) wet blanket.

aguafuerte, *n.f.* etching; etched plate.

aguagoma, *n.f.* gum-water.

aguaitador, -ra, *n.m.f.* (*obs.*) spy, detective. — *a.* detecting, spying.

aguaitamiento, *n.m.* action of spying, watching, detecting.

aguaitar, *v.t.* (*prov., Am.*) to lie in ambush; to spy, watch, detect.

aguajaque, *n.m.* fennel gum.

aguajas, *n.f.pl.* (*vet.*) ulcers above the hoofs.

aguaje, *n.m.* sea current or stream; (*naut.*) watering station; tidal wave; whirlpool, eddy at rudder; wake of a ship; *hacer aguaje*, violent rush of a stream.

aguají, *n.m.* (*ichth.*) an acanthopterygian fish of the Caribbean Sea.

aguajoso, -sa, *a.* aqueous, watery, humid.

agualdar, *v.t.* to colour like dyer's weed [GUALDA].

agualí, *n.f.* (*slang*) office, fees of assessor.

agualó, *n.m.* (*slang*) assessor, adviser.

aguallevado, *n.m.* method of canal dredging.

agualluvia, *n.f.* rain-water.

aguamala, *n.f.;* **aguamar**, *n.m.* (*ich·h.*) medusa, jelly-fish.

aguamanil, *n.m.* water-jug, wash-basin; wash-stand.

aguamanos, *n.m.* water for washing the hands; wash-basin, wash-stand.

aguamarina, *n.f.* pale green precious stone; beryl.

aguamelado, -da, *a.* washed over with water and honey. — *p.p.* [AGUAMELAR].

aguamelar, *v.t.* to mix with water and honey; to sweeten water.

aguamiel, *n.f.* hydromel, honey and water, mead; (*Am. Mer.*) sugar cane and water; (*Mex.*) unfermented juice of maguey.

aguamiento, *n.m.* watering (wine, etc.); (*fig.*) spoiling (pleasure).

aguamotor, *n.m.* water motor.

aguana, *n.f.* (*Am.*) wood used for canoes.

aguanafa, *n.f.* (*prov.*) orange-flower water.

aguanieve, *n.f.* (*orn.*) magpie; sleet, snow.

aguanosidad, *n.f.* serous humours; wateriness.

aguanoso, -sa, *a.* extremely moist; watery.

aguantable, *a.* tolerable, bearable.

aguantadero, -ra, *a.* bearable, endurable.

aguantar, *v.t.* to sustain, suffer, bear, endure, abide, put up with; to maintain; (*naut.*) to carry a stiff sail; move or turn in bull-fighting; *aguantar la mecha,* or *el pujo,* to be patient, resign oneself. — *v.r.* to forbear.

aguante, *n.m.* fortitude, firmness; endurance under toil or fatigue; resistance; patience; tolerance; *navío de aguante,* ship that carries a stiff sail.

aguañón, *n.m.* constructor of hydraulic machines.

aguapié, *n.m.* small wine; inferior liquor.

aguar, *v.t.* to dilute with water; to mar pleasure; *aguar la fiesta,* to spoil a pleasure; to arrive inopportunely. — *v.r.* to become inundated; (*vet.*) to become ill from drinking water when perspiring (horses).

aguará, *n.m.* (*Arg.*) a large fox.

aguardado, -da, *p.p.* [AGUARDAR] expected, awaited.

aguardador, -ra, *n.m.f.* expecter. — *a.* expecting.

aguardar, *v.t., v.r.* to wait for, await, expect; to grant, extend time, e.g. to a debtor; *aguardar a otro día,* to wait another day; *aguardar en casa,* to wait at home. — *v.i.* to wait, take time, hold on.

aguardentado, -da, *a.* addicted to drinking *aguardiente;* containing *aguardiente.*

aguardentera, *n.f.* spirit-flask.

aguardentería, *n.f.* spirits-shop.

aguardentero, -ra, *n.m.f.* maker or retailer of spirits.

aguardentoso, -sa, *a.* mixed with, or similar to spirits; harsh, raucous (said of the voice).

aguardiente, *n.m.* spirituous liquor; brandy; *aguardiente de caña,* rum; *aguardiente de cabeza,* the first spirits drawn from the still; *aguardiente anisado,* anisette.

aguardillado, -da, *a.* garret-like.

aguardo, *n.m.* covert.

aguarrás, *n.m.* oil of turpentine.

aguasol, *n.m.* (*bot.*) blight.

aguatinta, *n.f.* etching.

aguatocha, *n.f.* pump; fire-engine.

aguaturma, *n.f.* (*bot.*) Jerusalem artichoke.

aguavientos, *n.m.* (*bot.*) yellow sage-tree.

aguavilla, *n.f.* (*bot.*) red-berried arbutus.

aguay, *n.m.* (*Arg.*) a tree of the apocynaceæ family.

aguaza, *n.f.* aqueous humour; sap extracted from trees.

aguazal, *n.m.* marsh, fen.

aguazar, *v.t.* to form puddles. — *v.r.* to become marshy.

aguazo, *n.m.*; *pintura de aguazo,* painting in gouache.

aguazoso, -sa, *a.* aqueous.

aguazul, *n.m.* (*bot.*) salt-wort.

aguazur, *n.m.* (*bot.*) kind of salt-wort.

agudamente, *adv.* sharply, keenly, lively; ingeniously; finely; clearly.

agudeza, *n.f.* sharpness (instruments); acute-ness, subtlety, fineness; witty saying, repartee; lightness, velocity; smartness; (*obs.*) acidity (of fruits and plants).

agudo, -da, *a.* sharp-pointed, keen-edged (arms or instruments); clever, keen, acute, witty; brisk, ready, active; smart, sharp; (*mus.*) high-pitched; (*med.*) acute, of rapid development; *palabra aguda,* word accented on the last syllable; *agudo como punta de colchón,* as sharp as the corner of a mattress (said of a stupid person); *agudo de ingenio,* or *en sus ocurrencias,* quick-witted; *ángulo agudo,* (*geom.*) acute angle.

aguedita, *n.f.* (*Am.*) a tree of the terebinth group.

agüela, *n.f.* (*slang*) cloak, mantle.

agüera, *n.f.* trench for irrigation.

agüero, *n.m.* augury, prognostication, omen.

agüero; agüere, *pres. indic.; pres. subj.* [AGORAR].

aguerrido, -da, *a.* inured to war; veteran; *aguerrido en los combates,* accustomed to fighting. — *p.p.* [AGUERRIR].

aguerrir, *v.t.* (*defective*), to accustom to war. — *v.r.* (*defective*) to become inured to war, hardships.

aguijada, *n.f.* spur, goad.

aguijadamente, *adv.* goadingly, spurringly.

aguijador, -ra, *n.m.f.* goader, spurrer; insti-gator, stimulator. — *a.* goading, spurring, stimulating.

aguijadura, *n.f.* spurring; stimulation.

aguijar, *v.t.* to prick, spur, goad; to incite, stimulate. — *v.i.* to march fast.

aguijatorio, -ria, *a.* (*law*) mandatory.

aguijón, *n.m.* sting of a bee, wasp, etc.; prick, spur, goad; thorn (plants); stimulus; *dar coces contra el aguijón,* to kick against the pricks (or goad).

aguijonamiento, *n.m.* pricking, stinging.

aguijonazo, *n.m.* thrust with a goad.

aguijoncillo, *n.m.* petty exciter, disturber.

aguijoneador, -ra, *n.m.f.* one who pricks or goads. — *a.* pricking, stinging.

aguijoneadura, *n.f.* goading, spurring.

aguijoneamiento, *n.m.* goading, spurring.

aguijonear, *v.t.* to prick, thrust; incite.

águila, *n.f.* eagle; *ve más que un águila,* he is more sharp-sighted than an eagle; Roman standard; a gold coin with an eagle of the reign of Charles V.; ten-dollar gold piece of the United States; Mexican twenty-dollar gold piece; *media águila,* (*Mex.*) ten-dollar gold piece; *águila barbuda,* lammergeyer; *águila blanca,* Andine vulture; *águila cabdal, caudal, real,* royal or golden eagle; *águila de mar,* frigate-bird; (*ichth.*) fish similar to the ray; (*astron.*) Aquila; good cigar; *ser un águila,* to be a lynx; to be extremely efficient at anything; *un águila del foro,* a genius of the legal profession; (*slang*) astute thief.

aguilando, *n.m.* [AGUINALDO].

aguileña, *n.f.* (*bot.*) columbine.

aguileño, -ña, *a.* aquiline; hooked, hawk-nosed; (*slang*) thief [AGUILUCHO].

aguilera, *n.f.* rock where eagles nest.

aguilillo, -lla, *n.m.f.* little eagle, eaglet; kestrel; sparrow-hawk.

aguilón, *n.m.* boom of a crane, used for lifting heavy weights; square clay tube; (*arch.*) gable wall; large eagle [ÁGUILA].

aguilucho, *n.m.* young eagle, eaglet; (*slang*) thief who shares the booty taking no part in the robbery.

aguinaldo, *n.m.* New Year's gift; Christmas-box; (*Cub.*) reed.

agüista, *n.m.f.* frequenter of spas.

aguja, *n.f.* needle, knitting-needle, hatpin, bodkin; spire of an obelisk, steeple; (*ichth.*) needle-fish, horn-fish; needle-shell; hand of a watch, style of a dial; switch-rail; spindle; pin (in typography and in artillery); a brad; (*agric.*) graft; under-pinning beam (bridge); meat-stuffed pastry roll; goad-stick [PICADOR]; customs officer's spike; *aguja colchonera,* quilting, tufting needle; *aguja de arria, de enjalmar, salmera, saquera,* saddler's or packing-needle; *aguja de fogón,* gun-pin; *aguja de gancho,* crochet-hook; *aguja de marcar,* theodolite; *aguja de mechar, aguja mechera,* larding-needle, skewer; *aguja de tejer,* knitting-needle; *aguja de toque,* needle of assaying instrument; *aguja de verdugado,* largest needle used by tailors; *aguja loca,* compass which does not point to N; (*naut.*) *aguja de bitácora, aguja magnética, aguja de marear,* mariner's compass; *aguja de cámara,* hanging compass; *aguja capotera,* darning-needle; *aguja de relinga,* boltrope-needle; *aguja de hacer media,* knitting-needle; *aguja de pastor, aguja de Venus,* (*bot.*) shepherd's needle; *buscar una aguja en un pajar,* to look for a needle in a bundle of hay; *conocer la aguja de marear,* to know how to manage a person; *meter aguja y sacar reja,* to give a sprat to catch a herring; to do a favour in order to receive a greater one; *alabar uno sus agujas,* to blow one's own trumpet. — *pl.* ribs of the fore quarter of an animal: distemper of horses, affecting the legs, neck and throat; *vino de agujas,* wine of a sharp, acrid taste.

agujadera, *n.f.* needlewoman, knitter.

agujal, *n.m.* hole left by beams, props.

agujazo, *n.m.* prick with a needle.

agujerar, *v.t.* [AGUJEREAR].

agujerazo, *n.m.* wide hole [AGUJERO].

agujereable, *a.* pierceable.

agujereado, -da, *a.* full of holes. — *p.p.* [AGUJEREAR].

agujereador, -ra, *n.m.f.* pricker, borer, piercer. — *a.* pricking, boring, piercing.

agujereamiento, *n.m.* pricking, boring, piercing.

agujerear, *v.t.* to pierce, bore, prick. — *v.r.* to become full of holes.

agujero, *n.m.* hole; den; needle-maker, needle-seller; opening in the coast; dug-out; *quien acecha por agujero, ve su duelo,* listeners hear no good of themselves.

agujeta, *n.f.* lace, string, or latchet, tipped with tags. — *pl.* tip formerly given to post-boys; pains from fatigue; *alabar sus agujetas,* to praise one's own merchandise.

agujetear, *v.t.* to sew or join together pieces of leather with strips or thongs.

agujetería, *n.f.* shop where *agujetas* are made or sold.

agujetero, -ra, *n.m.f.* maker or seller of *agujetas;* (*Am.*) needle-case.

agujón, *n.m.* large needle; hatpin.

agujuela, *n.f.* brad.

aguosidad, *n.f.* lymph.

aguoso, -sa, *a.* aqueous.

¡agur! *interj.* (*coll.*) adieu, farewell, good-bye.

agusanado, -da, *a.* wormy, worm-eaten. — *p.p.* [AGUSANAR].

agusanamiento, *n.m.* worminess.

agusanarse, *v.r.* to become worm-eaten.

agustina, *n.f.* (*bot.*) variety of anemone.

agustiniano, -na, *a.* Augustinian.

agustino, -na, *n.m.f., a.* Augustinian, Austin (monk, nun).

agutí, *n.m.* agouti, a rodent of tropical America.

aguzable, *a.* that can be sharpened.

aguzadero, -ra, *n.m.f.* sharpener. — *n.f.* whetstone. — *n.m.* haunt of wild boars. — *a.* sharpening.

aguzado, -da, *a.* sharp, pointed, keen. — *p.p.* [AGUZAR].

aguzador, -ra, *a.* sharpening. — *n.m.f.* sharpener.

aguzadura, *n.f.* sharpening, whetting; steel used to forge new cutting edge or point on plough.

aguzamiento, *n.m.* sharpening, whetting.

aguzanieve, *n.f.* (*orn.*) wagtail.

aguzar, *v.t.* (*pret.* **agucé;** *pres. subj.* **aguce**) to whet, sharpen; to stimulate, excite; *aguzar el ingenio,* to sharpen the wit; *aguzar las orejas,* to prick up the ears, listen intently; *aguzar los dientes,* to whet the appetite; *aguzar la vista,* to sharpen the sight.

aguzonazo, *n.m.* thrust with a sword.

¡ah! *interj.* ah! alas!

ahebrado, -da, *a.* fibrous, thread-like.

ahechadero, *n.m.* place for winnowing.

ahechador, -ra, *n.m.f.* sifter, winnower. — *a.* sifting, winnowing.

ahechaduras, *n.f.pl.* winnowings.

ahechar, *v.t.* to sift, winnow.

ahecho, *n.m.* winnowing.

aheleado, -da, *a.* bitter, embittered. — *p.p.* [AHELEAR].

aheleador, -ra, *n.m.f.* embitterer. — *a.* embittering.

aheleamiento, *n.m.* embitterment.

ahelear, *v.t.* to gall, embitter. — *v.i.* to taste bitter.

ahelgado, -da, *a.* jag-toothed.

aherrojable, *a.* easily shackled, chained.

aherrojamiento, *n.m.* putting in irons; shackling, enchainment.

aherrojar, *v.t.* to put in irons; to chain, shackle; (*fig.*) to subdue, oppress.

aherrumbrarse, *v.r.* to have the taste and colour of iron (as water); to become ferruginous; to rust.

aherrumbroso, -sa, *a.* rusty, rusted.

ahervorarse, *v.r.* to become heated (cereals).

ahí, *adv.* there, in that place; yonder; in, within, in it; *de por ahí,* anything common; one who makes himself cheap; *por ahí,* about, all over, everywhere, that way (in the street).

ahidalgado, -da, *a.* gentlemanly.

ahigadado, -da, *a.* brave, courageous; liver-coloured.

ahijada, *n.f.* god-daughter; (*agric.*) paddle-staff.

ahijadero, *n.m.* sheep nursery, breeding place for sheep.

ahijado, *n.m.* godchild; protégé. — *p.p.* [AHIJAR].

ahijador, *n.m.* shepherd in charge of a sheep nursery.

ahijar, *v.t.* to adopt; to put every lamb with its dam; (*fig.*) to impute. — *v.i.* to bring forth young (applied only to cattle); (*agric.*) to bud, shoot.

ahijonear, *v.t.* to prick, goad, urge on.

¡ahijuna! *interj.* (*Arg., Chi.*) expressing admiration, surprise or insult.

ahilado, -da, *p.p.* [AHILAR]. — *a.* faint, weak, mouldy, thin, withered; gentle (breeze).

ahilar, *v.t.* to form single file. — *v.r.* to become faint, weak; to turn sour; to grow thin; to go in single file; to grow weak (plants); *ahilarse el vino,* to turn ropy (applied to wine).

ahilo, *n.m.* faintness, weakness; mould.

ahincadamente, *adv.* eagerly, earnestly, ardently.

ahincado, -da, *a.* efficient, vehement. — *p.p.* [AHINCAR].

ahincar, *v.t.* (*pres. ind.* ahinco; *pres. subj.* ahinque) to urge, press, drive. — *v.r.* to make haste.

ahinco, *n.m.* earnestness, eagerness, insistence.

ahitado, -da, *a.* satiated. — *p.p.* [AHITAR].

ahitar, *v.t.* (*p.p.* ahito) to surfeit, cloy, satiate. — *v.i.* to be satiated. — *v.r.* to become surfeited; *ahitarse de manjares,* to become gorged with food.

ahitera, *n.f.* (*coll.*) violent or continued indigestion.

ahito, -ta, *a.* gorged, satiated, full; disgusted, bored; attacked with indigestion. — *p.p.* [AHITAR]. — *n.m.* indigestion, surfeit, repletion.

¡aho!, *interj.* (*naut.*) ahoy!

ahobachonado, -da, *a.* (*coll.*) dull, slovenly, lazy; cowardly. — *p.p.* [AHOBACHONARSE].

ahobachonarse, *v.r.* to become lazy, slovenly.

ahocicar, *v.i.* (*naut.*) to pitch or plunge.

ahocinarse, *v.r.* to run in deep and narrow ravines (stream).

ahogadamente, *adv.* (*fig.*) oppressively, in an anguished manner.

ahogadero, *n.m.* hangman's rope; stifling, overcrowded place; throat-band; halter.

ahogadizo, -za, *a.* easily drowned; harsh, unpalatable (fruits); heavier than water, nonfloating (wood); *carne ahogadiza,* flesh of drowned or suffocated animals.

ahogado, -da, *a.* suffocated; drowned; close; unventilated; *dar mate ahogado,* to pin up the king at chess; to insist upon things being done without delay; *estar ahogado or verse ahogado,* to be overwhelmed with business or trouble. — *p.p.* [AHOGAR].

ahogador, -ra, *n.m.f.* hangman; suffocator; throat-band.

ahogamiento, *n.m.* drowning, suffocation; pain; distress.

ahogar, *v.t.* (*pret.* ahogué; *pres. subj.* ahogue) to choke, throttle, stifle; smother; to drown, oppress; to quench, extinguish; to water plants to excess; *ahogar las odios,* to forget enmities. — *v.r.* to become suffocated; to drown oneself; (*naut.*) to founder; *ahogarse de risa,* to choke with, die of (laughter); *ahogarse de*

calor, to become suffocated by the heat; *ahogarse en poca agua,* to come to grief over trifling difficulties; *ahogarse el grano,* the grain is smothered by the weeds; *ahogarse de gente,* to become overcrowded.

ahogaviejas, *n.f.* (*bot.*) dill.

ahogo, *n.m.* oppression; anguish; tightness (chest), suffocation; pain; severe affliction; embarrassment; penury; *pasar un ahogo,* to be in financial difficulties.

ahoguido, *n.m.* [AHOGUÍO].

ahoguijo, *n.m.* (*vet.*) quinsy, swelled throat.

ahoguío, *n.m.* oppression in the chest.

ahojar, *v.t.* (*prov.*) (*agric.*) to browse.

ahombrado, -da, *a.* (*coll.*) manly, mannish.

ahondable, *a.* penetrable.

ahondado, -da, *a.* deep. — *p.p.* [AHONDAR].

ahondar, *v.t.* to dig, deepen, sink; to go deep into. — *v.i.* to penetrate into a thing; to go deep; to advance in knowledge; to investigate. — *v.r.* to become deeper.

ahonde, *n.m.* excavation; (*Am.*) shaft which must be sunk within three months to acquire title to a mine.

ahora, *adv.* now, at present, just now; *por ahora,* for the present; *hasta ahora,* hitherto, so far, until now; *ahora bien,* now then; well then (argumentative); well; granted; nevertheless; *desde ahora,* henceforth, from this day; *ahora mismo,* at once, this moment; this very instant; *de ahora,* of the present day; *ahora ahora,* just now; *ahora entro yo,* now it's *my* turn; *ahora sí que digo yo,* now *I* tell you (que, that). — *conj.* whether, or; *ahora estudies, ahora medites, no perderás el tiempo,* whether you study or meditate, you will not waste time.

ahorcadizo, -za, *a.* (*obs.*) deserving of hanging.

ahorcado, -da, *n.m.f.* hanged man, hanged woman; *no se ha de mentar la soga en casa del ahorcado,* avoid painful topics of conversation; *no llora, or no suda el ahorcado, y llora,* or *suda el teatino,* he worries more over the matter than the interested person. — *p.p.* [AHORCAR].

ahorcadora, *n.f.* (*Guat., Hond.*) a large wasp whose sting is believed to be fatal.

ahorcadura, *n.f.* act of hanging.

ahorcajado, -da, *a.* seated astride. — *p.p.* [AHORCAJARSE].

ahorcajadura, *n.f.* sitting astride.

ahorcajarse, *v.r.* to sit astride.

ahorcalobo, *n.m.* (*bot.*) herb Paris.

ahorcamiento, *n.m.* hanging.

ahorcaperro, *n.m.* (*naut.*) running knot.

ahorcar, *v.t.* (*pret.* ahorqué; *pres. subj.* ahorque) to hang (to kill by hanging); *ahorcar los hábitos,* to abandon the clerical profession; *que me ahorquen si lo hago,* I'll be hanged if I do it. — *v.r.* to hang oneself; to be extremely worried; *ahorcarse en una rama,* to sit astride a branch; *ahorcarse de un árbol,* to hang oneself from a tree; *ahorcarse por los pies,* to hang by the feet.

ahorita, *adv.* (*coll.*) just now; this minute; *ahorita mismo,* this very moment; right away, at once.

ahormar, *v.t.* to fit, shape, adjust; to break in (shoes, etc.); to block (hats); (*fig.*) to bring to reason. — *v.r.* to adjust oneself to; to become adapted to.

ahornado, -da, *a.* dried-up (bread). — *p.p.* [AHORNAR].

ahornagamiento, *n.m.* (*agric.*) drying up; dryness.

ahornagarse, *v.r.* (*agric.*) to get, become parched or burned.

ahornar, *v.t.* to put in an oven. — *v.r.* to be scorched in an oven without being baked through.

ahorquillado, -da, *a.* forked. — *p.p.* [AHORQUILLAR].

ahorquillar, *v.t.* to stay, prop up with forks. — *v.r.* to become forked.

ahorrable, *a.* savable.

ahorradamente, *adv.* freely.

ahorrado, -da, *a.* unencumbered, free, exempt; saving, economizing. — *p.p.* [AHORRAR].

ahorrador, -ra, *n.m.f.* economizer, saver; emancipator. — *a.* emancipating; economizing.

ahorramiento, *n.m.* saving, emancipation, enfranchisement.

ahorrar, *v.t.* to enfranchise, emancipate; to economize, save, spare; (*fig.*) to shun, avoid labour, danger, or difficulties; *ahórrese Vd. palabras*, spare yourself the trouble of talking; *¡ahorra palabras!* obey, without further excuse! *no ahorrarse con nadie*, not to care a hang for anyone; *ahorrar de razones*, to save excuses; *no ahorrárselas con nadie*, not to mince one's words; to be afraid of nobody.

ahorrativa, *n.f.* (*coll.*) parsimony, saving.

ahorratividad, *n.f.* predisposition to economy; (*coll.*) avarice.

ahorrativo, -va, *a.* frugal, thrifty, saving, sparing; *andar* (or *ir*) *a la ahorrativa*, to go frugally to work.

ahorro, *n.m.* parsimony, frugality, husbandry; saving, economy, sparingness; (*pl.*) savings; *banco* (or *caja*) *de ahorros*, savings-bank.

ahoyador, *n.m.* (*prov.*) one who makes holes for planting; (*fig.*) grave-digger.

ahoyadura, *n.f.* digging, making holes in the ground.

ahoyamiento, *n.m.* hole digging.

ahoyar, *v.t.* to dig holes.

ahuate, *n.m.* (*Mex., Hond.*) prickly hair (sugar cane, maize).

ahuchador, -ra, *n.m.f.* hoarder, miser. — *a.* hoarding, miserly.

ahuchamiento, *n.m.* hoarding, miserliness.

ahuchar, *v.t.* to hoard up.

ahuecable, *a.* that can be excavated, made hollow.

ahuecadera, *n.f.* pick.

ahuecado, -da, *a.* hollow, excavated; affectedly deep (voice). — *p.p.* [AHUECAR].

ahuecamiento, *n.m.* hollowing, excavation.

ahuecar, *v.t.* (*pret.* **ahuequé**; *pres. subj.* **ahueque**) to excavate, make hollow, scoop out; to loosen close-pressed or matted things; to affect gravity of the voice. — *v.i.* (*coll.*) to leave a meeting, gathering, etc. — *v.r.* to become loosened; (*coll.*) to grow haughty, proud, elated.

ahuehué, ahuehuete, *n.m.* (*bot.*) a Mexican conifer.

ahuesado, -da, *a.* bone-coloured; bone hard.

ahuevar, *v.t.* to clarify wine with the white of eggs.

ahuizote, *n.m.* (*Mex.*) amphibian as yet unclassified.

ahulado, -da, *a.* (*Am.*) waterproof cloth.

ahumado, -da, *a.* smoky, smoked, cured. — *n.f.* smoke signal from coast, watch-towers, or high places. — *n.m.* smoking, curing. — *p.p.* [AHUMAR].

ahumador, -ra, *n.m.f.* smoker, curer. — *a.* smoking, curing.

ahumadura, *n.f.;* **ahumamiento,** *n.m.* smoking, curing.

ahumar, *v.t.* to smoke; to cure in smoke; to fill with smoke. — *v.i.* to fume, smoke, emit smoke. — *v.r.* to become smoky, smoked; to look smoky; (*coll.*) to become intoxicated.

ahur, *interj.* (*coll.*) adieu, farewell, good-bye.

ahurrugado, -da, *a.* (*agric.*) badly tilled or cultivated.

ahusado, -da, *a.* spindle-shaped, slender, tapering. — *p.p.* [AHUSAR].

ahusar, *v.t.* to make slender as a spindle; to taper. — *v.r.* to taper; to become slender.

ahuyentador, -ra, *n.m.f.* scarecrow. — *a.* scaring, frightening.

ahuyentar, *v.t.* to drive away; to frighten away, put to flight; to overcome a passion; to banish care. — *v.r.* to flee, run away.

aijada, *n.f.* goad.

ailanto, *n.m.* (*bot.*) ailanthus tree.

aimará, *a.* (*Am.*) pertaining to an Indian race on lake Titicaca (Peru-Boliv.).

aína, aínas, *adv.* (*obs.*) quickly; almost; easily, well-nigh; *no tan aínas*, not so easily.

ainado, -da, *a.* weary, tired.

aínda, *adv.* moreover, besides.

aindamáis, *adv.* (*coll.*) moreover, besides.

aindiado, *a.* (*Am.*) a person with Indian features.

airadamente, *adv.* angrily, hastily.

airado, -da, *a.* angry, wrathful, furious, vexed; (*fig.*) depraved, perverse. — *p.p.* [AIRAR].

airamiento, *n.m.* wrath, anger.

airar, *v.t.* to anger, irritate. — *v.r.* to grow angry; *airarse con, contra alguno*, to become irritated by, against somebody; *airarse de, por lo que se oye*, to become irritated by, through that which one hears.

airampo, *n.m.* (*bot.*) (*Per.*) a tinctorial cactus.

aire, *n.m.* air; atmosphere, wind; briskness (of a horse); air, carriage, demeanour, gait, aspect, countenance, look; vanity; beauty; hability; vigour, enterprise; (*coll.*) attack of paralysis; (*slang*) hair (head); musical composition; trifle, frivolity; *aire colado*, a cold draught; *aires naturales*, native air; *beber los aires* (or *los vientos*), to desire anxiously; *azotar el aire*, to act to no purpose, to labour in vain; *creerse del aire*, to be credulous; *darle a uno el aire de alguna cosa*, to give a person wind of an affair; *hablar al aire*, to talk idly; *tomar el aire*, to take a walk; *¿qué aires le traen a Vd. por acá?* what good wind brings you here? *al aire libre*, in the open air, out of doors; *en aire*, in a good humour; *en el aire*, quickly, in a moment, instantly; in the air, in suspense; *de buen* (*mal*) *aire*, in a pleasing (or peevish) manner, or humour; *estar en el aire*, to be pending; *empañar el aire*, to obscure the sky (of clouds, etc.); *fundar en el aire*, (*fig.*) to build on insufficient foundations; *aire de taco*, graceful, elegant movement; *se da un aire a*, it has a look like, it rather resembles; *aire de suficiencia*, (*fig.*) air of conceit; *aire popular*,

popular song; *castillos en el aire*, castles in the air; *guarnición al aire*, (*jew.*) open setting; *palabras al aire*, idle talk; *cortarlas uno en el aire*, *matarlas uno en el aire*, (*coll.*) to answer quick-wittedly; *dar aire*, (*coll.*) to spend (money) quickly; *dar con*, or *de buen aire*, to give a blow violently; *disparar al aire*, to fire off (arms) in the air; *echar al aire*, to uncover some part of the body; *guardarle*, or *llevarle el aire a uno*, to accommodate oneself to someone's mood; *hacer aire a uno*, or *hacerse aire*, to fan someone, or oneself; (*coll.*) to do someone a bad turn; *herir el aire con voces*, *quejas*, to lament loudly; *mudar* (*de*) *aires*, to visit health resorts; (*coll.*) to be exiled, to escape; *mudarse uno a cualquier aire*, (*fig.*) to be a turncoat; *mudarse el aire*, (*fig.*) to turn (luck, fortune); *ofenderse uno del aire*, (*fig.*) to be very touchy; *por el aire*, or *los aires*, very lightly, very quickly (with verbs *ir*, *venir*, *llevar*, etc.); *ser una cosa aire*, or *un poco de aire*, to be of little value; *sustentarse uno del aire*, (*coll.*) to eat very little; to live on vain hopes; to be taken in by flattery; *todo es aire lo que echa la trompeta*, it is all boasting; *tomar aires*, to visit health resorts. — *n.m.* (*Cub.*) an insectivorous mammalian about 1 foot long.

airear, *v.t.* to give air, ventilate; to aerate, charge with gas. — *v.r.* to take the air; to cool oneself.

airecico; airecillo; airecito, *n.m.* (*dim.*) a gentle breeze; *airecillo protector*, something of a patronizing air.

airón, *n.m.* violent gale; ornament of plumes; crest; purple-crested heron, egret; deep Moorish well.

airosamente, *adv.* gracefully, lightly.

airosidad, *n.f.* graceful deportment.

airoso, -sa, *a.* airy, windy; graceful, genteel; lively; successful; *salir airoso*, to come forth triumphant.

aislable, *a.* separable; that can be isolated, insulated.

aisladamente, *adv.* isolatedly; separately; singly.

aislado, -da, *a.* isolated; (*elec.*, *phys.*) insulated, separate. — *p.p.* [AISLAR].

aislador, -ra, *n.m.f.* isolator; (*elec.*, *phys.*) insulator. — *a.* isolating, insulating.

aislamiento, *n.m.* isolation; (*elec.*, *phys.*) insulation; loneliness; retirement.

aislar, *v.t.* to surround with water; to insulate, isolate. — *v.r.* to isolate, seclude oneself; to become isolated.

aislatorio, -ria, *a.* relating to *aislamiento*.

¡ajá!, ¡ajajá!, *interj.* aha!, ha! ha! that's right!

ajabeba, *n.f.* Moorish flute.

ajable, *a.* that can be withered, faded.

ajacintado, -da, *a.* hyacinth-like.

ajada, *n.f.* garlic sauce.

ajadamente, *adv.* sadly, languidly.

ajadizo, -za, *a.* easily faded, withered, crumpled.

ajado, -da, *a.* garlicky; withered, crumpled, languid. — *p.p.* [AJAR].

ajador, -ra, *n.m.f.* crumpler, disfigurer, one that withers. — *a.* crumpling, withering, disfiguring.

ajamiento, *n.m.* disfiguration; deformity; crumpling, rumpling.

ajamonarse, *v.r.* (*coll.*) to grow stout (of women).

ajaquecarse, *v.r.* to have a headache.

ajar, *v.t.* to spoil, mar; to tarnish, fade; to crumple, rumple; *ajar la vanidad a alguno*, to humble a person. — *v.r.* to become spoiled, crumpled. — *n.m.* garlic field.

ajaraca, *n.f.* (*arch.*) bow, knot or ornament (Arabic and Mudejar).

ajarafe, *n.m.* table-land, terrace.

aje, *n.m.* (*usu. pl.*) chronic complaint; (*Cub.*) a plant of the dioscorea or yam family; (*Hond.*) a kind of cochineal.

ajea, *n.f.* brushwood for fuel.

ajear, *v.i.* to cry like a pursued partridge.

ajebe, *n.m.* rock alum.

ajedrea, *n.f.* (*bot.*) winter savory.

ajedrecista, *n.m.f.* chess-player.

ajedrez, *n.m.* chess; (*naut.*) netting, grating.

ajedrezado, -da, *a.* chequered. — *p.p.* [AJE-DREZAR].

ajedrezamiento, *n.m.* chequer-work.

ajedrezar, *v.t.* to chequer-work.

ajenabe; ajenabo, *n.m.* (*bot.*) wild mustard.

ajengibre, *n.m.* (*bot.*) ginger.

ajenjo, *n.m.* (*bot.*) wormwood; absinthe; (*fig.*) bitterness, displeasure.

ajeno, -na, *a.* another's; foreign, strange; abhorrent, contrary to, remote; ignorant; improper; *ajeno a*, foreign to, free from; *ajeno de*, devoid of, lacking, ignorant of; indifferent to; *estar uno ajeno de una cosa*, to be ignorant of an affair; *estar uno ajeno de sí*, to lack pride; *ajeno de cuidados*, careless; *ajeno de verdad*, void of truth; *al que de ajeno se viste*, *en la calle le desnudan*, he who assumes credit falsely, is apt to be shorn of it unexpectedly.

ajenuz, *n.m.* (*bot.*) field fennel-flower.

ajeo, *n.m.* cry (partridge); *perro de ajeo*, setter-dog.

ajero, -ra, *n.m.f.* vendor of garlic. — *n.m.* proprietor of garlic field.

ajesuitado, -da, *a.* Jesuitical; Jesuit-like. — *p.p.* [AJESUITAR].

ajete, *n.m.* young garlic; leek, garlic sauce.

ajetrearse, *v.r.* to become physically wearied; to fidget.

ajetreo, *n.m.* fatigue, agitation.

ají, *n.m.* (*bot.*) chilli; capsicum; chilli sauce.

ajiaceite, *n.m.* mixture of garlic and oil.

ajiaco, *n.m.* (*Am.*) a dish made of vegetables, meat and chilli.

ajicarar, *v.t.* to shape like a cup.

ajicero, -ra, *n.m.f.* (*Chi.*) seller of chilli; *n.m.* (*Chi.*) vase for keeping chilli. — *a.* (*Chi.*) pertaining to chilli.

ajicola, *n.f.* (*art*) glue made of kidskin boiled with garlic.

ajicomino, *n.m.* sauce made of garlic and cumin seed.

ajigotar, *v.t.* (*coll.*) to smash into bits.

ajilimoje; ajilimójili, *n.m.* sauce of pepper and garlic; (*coll.*) extras.

ajillo, *n.m.* young garlic.

ajimez, *n.m.* arched window, with pillar in centre; twin-window.

ajipuerro, *n.m.* (*bot.*) wild-leek.

ajironar, *v.t.* to patch; to tear, rent, slit.

ajizal, *n.m.* chilli field.

ajo, *n.m.* (*bot.*) garlic; garlic sauce for meat; (*coll.*) paint (for ladies); (*coll.*) oath, swear word; crooked affair; *diente de ajo,* clove of garlic; *andar en el ajo,* to be shady (business); *muchos ajos en un mortero, mal los maja un majadero,* Jack of all trades, master of none; *ajo de Valdestillas,* costly extras; *villano harto de ajos, (coll.)* ill-bred, uncouth person; *tieso como un ajo,* very proud; *revolver el ajo, (coll.)* to stir up trouble; *hacer morder el ajo,* to mortify; *(coll.) se fué echando ajos y cebollas,* he went off with oaths and imprecations; *ajo crudo y vino puro pasan el puerto seguro,* good food is necessary for physical exertion; *¡bueno anda el ajo! (iron.)* things are in a nice state! — *interj. ¡ajo! ¡ajó!* used to children beginning to speak.

ajobar, *v.t.* to carry on the back.

ajobilla, *n.f.* common sea-shell.

ajobo, *n.m.* burden, heavy load; **action of** carrying; *(fig.)* fatiguing work.

ajofaina, *n.f.* basin, washing-bowl.

ajolín, *n.m.* a bug (Hemiptera).

ajolio, *n.m. (prov.)* sauce made of oil and garlic.

ajolote, *n.m. (Mex.)* axolotl, an edible batrachian.

ajomate, *n.m. (bot.)* a kind of seaweed.

ajonje, *n.m.;* **ajonjo,** *n.m.* bird-lime.

ajonjera, *n.f.;* **ajonjero,** *n.m. (bot.)* the low carline thistle.

ajonjolí; aljonjolí, *n.m. (bot.)* sesame.

ajoqueso, *n.m.* dish made of garlic and cheese.

ajorar, *v.t.* to carry away by force (people, cattle).

ajorca, *n.f.* Moorish bracelet or anklet.

ajordar, *v.i. (prov.)* to bawl.

ajornalar, *v.t.* to hire by the day. — *v.r.* to hire oneself out by the day.

ajote, *n.m. (bot.)* water-germander.

ajuagas, *n.f.pl. (vet.)* malanders, ulcers over the hoofs, spavin.

ajuanetado, -da, *a.;* **ajuaneteado, -da,** *a.* bunion-like; bony protuberance; *rostro ajuanetado,* face with prominent cheekbones.

ajuar, *n.m.* bridal apparel; trousseau; bridal or household furniture.

ajudiado, -da, *a.* Jewish, Jew-like. — *p.p.* [AJUDIARSE].

ajuiciable, *a.* susceptible to judiciousness.

ajuiciado, -da, *a.* judicious, prudent. *p.p.* [AJUICIAR].

ajuiciamiento, *n.m.* judiciousness, sagacity.

ajuiciar, *v.t.* to reform. — *v.i.* to become prudent, acquire judgment.

ajustabilidad, *n.f.* adjustability.

ajustadamente, *adv.* justly, rightly, exactly.

ajustado, -da, *a.* exact, right; *(obs.)* close, mean, miserly; adapted; well fitted; tight. — *p.p.* [AJUSTAR].

ajustador, -ra, *a.* fitting, adjusting. — *n.m.* strait-waistcoat, -jacket; *(print.)* justifier; *(mech.)* adapter, fitter, adjuster, adjusting tool, coupler.

ajustamiento, *n.m.* agreement; fitting; settling of accounts, receipts.

ajustar, *v.t.* to adjust, fit, regulate; to compose; to guide; to measure; *(print.)* to justify (type); to bargain, make an agreement; to reconcile, heal; to settle accounts; to press close, oppress; to fashion, accommodate; to adapt; to engage, hire; to trim, size, true. — *v.r.* to settle matters; to

combine, conform; to approach; to engage, hire oneself; *ajustarse a la razón,* to conform to reason; *ajustarse con el amo,* to come to an agreement with an employer.

ajuste, *n.m.* proportionate measure of the parts of an object; adjustment; fit, agreement; contract; accommodation; *(print.)* making galleys into pages; settlement, engagement; *más vale mal ajuste que buen pleito,* better a poor settlement than a good lawsuit. — *pl.* couplings.

ajusticiado, -da, *n.m.f.* executed convict. — *p.p.* [AJUSTICIAR].

ajusticiar, *v.t.* to execute, put to death.

al, *art.* (formed of *a* and *el*) to the, at the (before masc. noun); used with *inf.* of verbs with equivalence of English *on + pres. part.;* it also indicates immediate moment of action or co-existence; *al salir del sol,* at sunrise; *al anochecer,* at nightfall; *al acabar la vida,* at the moment of dying.

ala, *n.f. (naut., bot., aer., arch.)* wing, row, file; *(mil.)* flank; brim (hat); *(anat.)* auricle (of ear, heart); *(aer.)* blade of a screw propeller; fin of a fish; *(bot.)* sneeze-weed; *(arch.)* eaves; *(fig.)* presumption; leaf of a door, of a table; *pl. (naut.)* upper studding-sails; *ala de gavia, (naut.)* main-top studding-sails; *(fort.)* curtain; *ala de mosca, (slang)* cheating at cards; *ala de proa, (naut.)* head of the ship; *ala de sobremesana, (naut.)* mizzen-top studding-sails; *ala de velacho, (naut.)* fore studding-sails; *arrastrar el ala,* to court, make love to. — *pl. (fig.)* boldness, protection; *(poet.)* speed, rapidity; *caérsele a uno las alas del corazón,* to be dismayed, to be lacking in constancy; *cortar las alas,* to clip someone's wings; to deprive of ways and means of prospering; to discourage; to deprive of liberty; to take someone down a peg; *ahuecar el ala, (coll.)* to take wing, disappear; *tomar alas,* to take liberties; *volar con propias alas,* to be independent; *dar alas,* to protect, encourage; *estar bajo el ala de,* to be under someone's wing.

Alá, *n.m.* Allah.

¡ala!, *interj. (naut.),* pull!, haul!

alabado, -da, *a.* praised. — *p.p.* [ALABAR]. — *n.m.* hymn in praise of the Sacrament; *al alabado, (Chi.)* at daybreak.

alabador, -ra, *n.m.f.* applauder, praiser. — *a.* praiseworthy, laudable.

alabamiento, *n.m.* praise.

alabancia, *n.f.* praise, laudation.

alabancioso, -sa, *a. (coll.)* boastful, ostentatious.

alabandina, *n.f.* manganese sulphide; kind of garnet, almandine (alabandicus).

alabanza, *n.f.* praise, commendation, glory; *la alabanza propia envilece,* self-praise debaseth; *cantar las alabanzas de uno,* to sing someone's praises.

alabar, *v.t.* to praise, extol, glorify, commend. — *v.r.* to praise oneself; to boast; to show oneself pleased at; *mucho me alabo de su triunfo,* I am very pleased at his success; *alabar de discreto,* to praise as discreet; *alabar (algo) en otro,* to praise (something) in another; *alabarse de valiente,* to boast of one's valour; *¡alabo la llaneza! (iron.)* I admire your taste! *cada ollero alaba su puchero,* each crow thinks its own young the whitest; *no se irá alabando*, he laughs best who laughs last; *quien no se alaba, de ruin se muere*, diffidence does not pay. — *v.i.* (*Mex.*) to sing the hymn '*Alabado*'.

alabarda, *n.f.* halberd.

alabardado, -da, *a.* halberd-shaped.

alabardazo, *n.m.* blow with a halberd.

alabardero, *n.m.* halberdier; (*theat.*) hired applauder, claqueur.

alabastrado, -da, *a.* alabaster-like. — *p.p.* [ALABASTRAR].

alabastrina, *n.f.* thin sheet of alabaster.

alabastrino, -na, *a.* alabastrine, made of alabaster.

alabastro, *n.m.* alabaster.

álabe, *n.m.* drooping branch of an olive or other tree; blade (water-wheel); (*mech.*) cam; mat (carts).

alabeado, -da, *a.* warped. — *p.p.* [ALABEAR].

alabear, *v.t.* to warp. — *v.r.* to become warped.

alabega, *n.f.* (*bot.*) sweet-basil.

alabeo, *n.m.* warping.

alabiado, -da, *a.* lipped or ragged (of coins).

alacayuela, *n.f.* (*bot.*) a plant of the Cistaceæ family.

alacena, *n.f.* cupboard, closet; (*naut.*) locker.

alaciar, *v.t.* make lax or languid. — *v.i.* to be lax, faded. — *v.r.* to become withered.

alacrán, *n.m.* scorpion; ring in bit of bridle; chain or link in sleeve-button; swivel; *quien del alacrán está picado, la sombra le espanta*, a burnt child dreads the fire.

alacranado, -da, *a.* bitten by a scorpion; infected by some vice or disease.

alacrancillo, *n.m.* (*Am.*) plant of the Boraginaceæ family.

alacranera, *n.f.* (*bot.*) scorpion-grass.

alacranino, -na, *a.* relating to scorpions.

alacridad, *n.f.* alacrity, eagerness, joyfulness.

alacha; **alache**, *n.f.* anchovy.

alachero, -ra, *n.m.f.* seller of anchovies.

alada, *n.f.* fluttering of the wings.

aladares, *n.m.pl.* forelocks over the temples.

aladierna, *n.f.* (*bot.*) mock-privet.

alado, -da, *a.* winged; (*fig.*) light, quick.

aladrada, *n.f.* (*prov.*) furrow.

aladrar, *v.t.* (*prov.*) to plough the ground. — *v.r.* to become tainted (meat).

aladrería, *n.f.* (*prov.*) agricultural implements.

aladrero, *n.m.* (*carp.*) prop-maker (mines); (*prov.*) plough-maker.

aladro, *n.m.* (*prov.*) plough, ploughed land.

aladroque, *n.m.* (*prov.*) unsalted anchovy.

alafia, *n.f.* (*coll.*) *pedir alafia*, to beg pardon.

álaga, *n.f.* species of yellow wheat.

alagadizo, -za, *a.* easily flooded.

alagar, *v.t.* to make ponds or lakes in. — *v.r.* to become flooded.

alagartado, -da, *a.* variegated, motley; lizard-like.

alagunado, -da, *a.* lagoon-like.

alajor, *n.m.* ground rent.

alajú, *n.m.* paste made of almonds, walnuts, honey, etc.; gingerbread.

alalá, *n.m.* popular song in the north of Spain.

alalagmo, *n.m.* [LELILÍ] war-whoop of the Moors.

alalía, *n.f.* (*med.*) aphonia.

alalimón, *n.m.* a children's game.

alalino, -na, *a.* dumb.

alama, *n.f.* (*bot.*) a fodder plant.

alamar, *n.m.* frog and braid trimming; gimp.

alambicadamente, *adv.* subtly, with subtlety.

alambicado, -da, *a.* distilled; (*fig.*) euphuistic, exaggerated (of style); given sparingly. — *p.p.* [ALAMBICAR].

alambicamiento, *n.m.* distillation; subtlety; euphuism, exaggeration (of style).

alambicar, *v.r.* to distil; to investigate, scrutinize, examine closely; *alambicar los sesos*, to cudgel one's wits.

alambique, *n.m.* still; *por alambique*, sparingly.

alambor, *n.m.* (*arch.*) face of a hewn stone; (*fort.*) inside slope.

alambrada, *n.f.* (*mil.*) wire entanglements.

alambrado, -da, *a.* wiry, wired. — *p.p.* [ALAMBRAR]. — *n.m.* wire netting, wire fence, screen; wire cover; electric wiring.

alambrador, -ra, *a.* wiring. — *n.m.* wirer.

alambrar, *v.t.* to surround with wire (fencing); to fasten with wire; *v.i.* (*prov.*) to clear up (sky).

alambre, *n.m.* wire; copper wire; cattle bells; (*fig.*) very thin (person, animal); *alambre conejo*, rabbit-wire (for snares, etc.); *alambre de latón*, brass wire.

alambrera, *n.f.* wire netting; wire fire-screen; wire (food) cover.

alambrería, *n.f.* wire shop; agglomeration of wire.

alameda, *n.f.* poplar grove; public walk; avenue.

alamín, *n.m.* clerk appointed to inspect weights and measures; surveyor of buildings; irrigation inspector.

alamina, *n.f.* fine paid by potters for transgressing the law.

alaminazgo, *n.m.* office of the *alamín*.

alamirré, *n.m.* (*obs.*) sign in musical notation.

álamo, *n.m.* (*bot.*) poplar; *álamo blanco*, white poplar; *álamo temblón*, aspen.

alampar, *v.t.; ***alamparse***, *v.r.* to long for, crave after (esp. food and drink).

alamud, *n.m.* square bolt for a door.

alanceador, -ra, *n.m.f.* lancer. — *a.* lancing.

alanceadura, *n.f.;* **alanceamiento**, *n.m.* lancing, spearing.

alancear, *v.t.* to dart; to spear.

alandrearse, *v.r.* to become dry, stiff, and blanched (silk-worms).

alandro, *n.m.* (*fig.*) trifle.

alanés, *n.m.* (*Mex.*) a large deer.

alangarí, *n.m.* (*slang*) pardon, excuse; pain, cramp.

alano, -na, *a.* belonging to the Vandals. — *n.m.f.* large mastiff; (*coll.*) sticky person.

alanzado, -da, *a.* lance-like, spear-like; lanced, speared. — *p.p.* [ALANZAR].

alanzar, *v.t.* to throw lances, spear.

alaqueca, *n.f.;* **alaqueque**, *n.m.* bloodstone.

alar, *n.m.* overhanging roof; (*pl.*) horse-hair snare (birds); (*slang*) breeches.

alar, *v.t.* (*naut.*) to haul [HALAR].

alárabe; **alarbe**, *n.m.f.*, *a.* Arabian. — *n.m.* (*fig.*) unmannerly person; *portarse como un alarbe*, to behave badly.

alarconiano, -na, *a.* proper and characteristic of Juan Ruiz de Alarcón (dramatic poet).

alarde, *n.m.* review of soldiers, parade, muster; ostentation, boasting, vanity; *hacer alarde*, to boast or brag; to make a show.

alardear, *v.i.* to brag, boast.

alardeo, *n.m.* boastfulness.

alardoso, -sa, *a.* ostentatious, boastful.

alargada, *n.f.* (*naut.*) cessation of wind.

alargadera, *n.f.* (*chem.*) nozzle; lengthening tube; (*naut.*) lengthening bar (compasses).

alargadero, -ra, *a.* that can be lengthened.

alargado, -da, *a.* extended, long; (*fig.*) remote. — *p.p.* [ALARGAR].

alargador, -ra, *a.* stretching, lengthening.

alargamiento, *n.m.* lengthening; (*eng.*) elongation.

alargar, *v.t.* (*pret.* **alargué;** *pres. subj.* **alargue**) to lengthen, extend; to protract, prolong, increase; to reach or hand something to somebody; (*naut.*) to pay out cable; to make people advance; (*fig.*) to augment; *alargar el salario, el sueldo, la ración,* to increase the salary, wage, ration; *alargar el paso,* to take long strides, to hurry; *alargar la mecha,* to protract a negotiation; *alargar la bolsa,* to prepare for some great expenditure; *alargar los dientes,* to show one's teeth. — *v.r.* to become prolonged; to expatiate; to move away; to become longer, last longer; (*naut.*) to change in direction (wind); *alargarse en una carta, en un discurso,* to write at length, to give a long lecture; *alargarse a,* or *hacia la ciudad,* to move away to the town; *se alargan los días,* the days get longer.

alarguez, *n.m.* (*bot.*) dog-rose.

alaria, *n.f.* potter's finishing iron.

alarida, *n.f.* hue and cry.

alarido, *n.m.* outcry, shout; howl, scream; *dar alaridos,* to shout, scream.

alarifazgo, *n.m.* office of *alarife,* or builder (*Arab.*).

alarife, *n.m.* architect, builder.

alarije, *n.f.* large kind of grape [ARIJE].

alarma, *n.m.* (*mil.*) alarm, warning; (*fig.*) anxiety; *dar la alarma,* to raise the alarm; *vivir en perpetua alarma,* to live in a state of perpetual anxiety.

alarmador, -ra, *a.* alarming. — *n.m.f.* alarmist.

alarmante, *a.* alarming.

alarmar, *v.t.* to alarm; to sound the warning to arms. — *v.r.* to become alarmed.

alarmativo, -va, *a.* alarming.

alármega, *n.f.* (*bot.*) wild rue.

alarmista, *n.m.,* *a.* alarming, alarmist, panic-monger.

alastrar, *v.t.* to throw back the ears; (*naut.*) to ballast. — *v.r.* to squat close, lie flat (of game).

alaterno, *n.m.* (*bot.*) mock-privet.

alatinadamente, *adv.* according to the Latin language; in a Latinized form or manner.

alatrón, *n.m.* froth of saltpetre; purified saltpetre.

alaureado, -da, *a.* laurel-like.

alavanco, *n.m.* kind of wild duck.

alavense; alavés, -sa, *n.m.f.,* *a.* of or from Alava, Alavese.

alazán, -na; alazano, -na, *a.* sorrel-coloured, chestnut-coloured. — *n.m.f.* horse so coloured; *alazán tostado, antes muerto que cansado,* sorrel horse sooner dead than tired. — *n.f.* oil-press.

alazo, *n.m.* stroke with the wings.

alazor, *n.m.* (*bot.*) bastard saffron.

alba, *n.f.* dawn of day; (*slang*) sheet; alb, white vestment worn by priests and others; *al alba,* at daybreak; *al quebrar, romper, reír,* or *rayar del alba,* at the first flush of day.

albaca, *n.f.* (*bot.*) sweet-basil [ALBAHACA].

albacara, *n.f.* (*fort.*) round tower, enclosing bailey.

albacea, *n.m.* testamentary executor. *n.f.* testamentary executrix.

albaceazgo, *n.m.* executorship.

albacora, *n.f.* (*ichth.*) tunny; (*bot.*) early large fig.

albada, *n.f.* morning serenade; (*prov., bot.*) soapwort; (*Mex.*) attack at dawn.

albahaca, *n.f.* (*bot.*) sweet-basil.

albahaquero, *n.m.* flowerpot.

albaida, *n.f.* (*bot.*) shrubby gypsophila.

albaire, *n.m.* (*slang*) hen's egg.

albalá, *n.m.f.* royal letters patent; a public instrument.

albanado, -da, *a.* (*slang*) sleepy, asleep.

albando, -da, *a.* incandescent, white-hot (metals).

albanega, *n.f.* hair-net; net for catching partridges or rabbits.

albaneguero, -ra, *n.m.f.* (*slang*) player at dice.

albanés, -nesa, *a.* Albanian; (*slang*) dice-player. — *n.m.pl.* dice.

albañal, *n.m.* common sewer; garbage heap, dump; waste; drain; *salir uno por el albañal,* to come out badly in an affair.

albañil, *n.m.* mason, bricklayer.

albañilear, *v.t.* to build, construct.

albañilería, *n.f.* masonry.

albaquía, *n.f.* remnant, residue, balance.

albar, *a.* white.

albara; albarás, *n.f.* (*med.*) white leprosy.

albaracino, -na, *a.* leprous.

albarada, *n.f.* dry-stone wall; temporary whiteness.

albarán, *n.m.* placard announcing apartments to let; note of hand or other private instrument.

albarazado, -da, *a.* affected with white leprosy; marbled; variegated; pale, whitish; *uva albarazada,* marble-coloured grape; (*Mex.*) cross-bred of Chinese and Indian.

albarazo, *n.m.* white leprosy.

albarca, *n.f.* [ABARCA].

albarcoque, *n.m.* apricot.

albarcoquero, *n.m.* apricot-tree.

albarda, *n.f.* packsaddle; lardon; *albarda sobre albarda,* unnecessary repetition; *como ahora llueven albardas,* (*iron.*) that's very likely! *coser,* or *labrar albardas, todo es dar puntadas,* saying applied to a malapropism; *echar un albarda a uno,* to take advantage of someone's patience; *venirse,* or *volverse la albarda a la barriga,* to turn out contrary to expectations.

albardado, -da, *a.* having different-coloured skin at the loins (cattle); (*prov.*) meat in butter. — *p.p.* [ALBARDAR].

albardar, *v.t.* to put on a packsaddle; to lard (fowls).

albardela, *n.f.* small saddle.

albardería, *n.f.* packsaddle shop or trade.

albardero, -ra, *n.m.f.* packsaddle maker or seller.

albardilla, *n.f.* batter; small packsaddle; coping-stone; border of a garden bed; wool-tuft; sadiron holder; lardon.

albardillar, *v.t.* to hoodwink a hawk; to lard (fowls).

albardín, *n.m.* (*bot.*) mat-weed.

albardón, *n.m.* large packsaddle, panel.

albardoncillo, *n.m.* small packsaddle.

albardonería, *n.f.* packsaddle trade or shop.
albardonero, *n.m.* packsaddle maker.
albarejo; albarigo, *n.m.* kinds of wheat.
albareque, *n.m.* fishing-net.
albaricoque, *n.m.* apricot.
albaricoquero, *n.m.* apricot-tree.
albarillo, *n.m.* tune on the guitar; (*bot.*) white apricot.
albarino, *n.m.* (*obs.*) white cosmetic.
albarizo, -za, *a.* whiting (earth). — *n.m.* dishcloth. — *n.f.* salt-water lagoon.
albarrada, *n.f.* dry wall; earth fence; trench, ditch for defence; enclosure; earthenware jar.
albarrana, *n.f.* (*bot.*) *cebolla albarrana,* squill; blue-flowered onion; *torre albarrana,* watch-tower.
albarranilla, *n.f.* blue-flowered species of onion.
albarraz, *n.m.* (*bot.*) louse-wort; (*med.*) white leprosy.
albarrazado, -da, *a.* marbled; dyed. — *p.p.* [ALBARRAZAR].
albarrazar, *v.t.* to dye (beard, hair).
albarsa, *n.f.* fisherman's basket.
albatoza, *n.f.* small covered boat.
albatros, *n.m.* (*orn.*) albatross.
albayaldado, -da, *a.* cerused. — *p.p.* [ALBAYALDAR].
albayaldar, *v.t.* to cover with, give the colour of white lead.
albayalde, *n.m.* white-lead, ceruse.
albazano, -na, *a.* of dark chestnut colour (horse).
albear, *v.i.* to whiten, show white. — *n.m.* clay-pit, marl-pit, loam-pit.
albedrío, *n.m.* free-will; (*law*) precedent; *libre albedrío,* liberty, free-will; will; impulsiveness, wilfulness; *al albedrío de uno,* according to one's pleasure or desire, as one likes; *hazlo a tu albedrío,* do as you please; *rendir el albedrío,* to give way through love.
albéitar, *n.m.* farrier; veterinary surgeon.
albeitería, *n.f.* farriery; veterinary surgery.
albellón, *n.m.* common sewer.
albenda, *n.f.* hangings of white linen.
albendera, *n.f.* woman who makes *albendas;* (*fig.*) woman who gads about.
albengala, *n.f.* kind of gauze worn in turbans.
albéntola, *n.f.* fine fishing-net.
alberca, *n.f.* pond, pool; reservoir, tank; sink; vat; *en alberca,* roofless.
albercón, *n.m.* large pool or pond.
albercoque, *n.m.* apricot.
albérchiga, *n.f.;* albérchigo, *n.m.* kind of peach.
alberchiguero, *n.m.* peach-tree.
albergador, -ra, *n.m.f.* shelterer. — *a.* sheltering.
albergar, *v.t.* (*pret.* albergué; *pres. subj.* albergue) to lodge, shelter, harbour; to keep (lodgers). — *v.i., v.r.* to lodge, take a lodging.
albergue, *n.m.* lodging, shelter; den; orphan asylum.
alberguería, *n.f.* poor-house; asylum; place of shelter.
albericoque, *n.m.* apricot.
albero, -ra, *a.* white. — *n.m.* whitish earth; dishcloth.
alberquero, *n.m.* caretaker of pools [ALBERCAS].
alberquilla, *n.f.* little pool.

albicante, *a.* whitening, bleaching.
albicaudo, -da, *a.* (*zool.*) white-tailed.
albicaulo, -la, *a.* (*bot.*) white-stemmed.
albiceps, *a.* (*zool.*) white-headed, white-faced.
albicerato, -ta, *a.* colour of white wax. — *n.m.* variety of fig.
albicie, *n.f.* whiteness.
albicolo, -la, *a.* (*zool.*) white-necked.
albiflor, -ora, *a.* (*bot.*) white-flowered.
albigense, *n.m.f., a.* Albigensian. — *n.pl.* Albigenses.
albihar, *n.m.* (*bot.*) ox-eye.
albilabro, -ra, *a.* white-lipped.
albilla, *n.f.;* albillo, *n.m.* early white grape.
albillo, *n.m.* wine of white grape.
albimano, -na, *a.* white-handed.
albín, *n.m.* bloodstone; carmine pigment.
albina, *n.f.* salt-water marsh; salt; nitre.
albinismo, *n.m.* albinism.
albino, -na, *a., n.m.* albino; (*Mex.*) octoroon. — *n.f.* albiness.
Albión, *n.f.* Albion; (*poet.*) England.
albita, *n.f.* (*min.*) white feldspar, albite.
albitana, *n.f.* fence to enclose plants; (*naut.*) apron; *albitana del codaste,* (*naut.*) inner post.
albo, -ba, *a.* (*poet.*) snow white.
alboaire, *n.m.* glazed tile-work.
albogalla, *n.f.* a kind of gall-nut.
albogue, *n.m.* pastoral flute; cymbal.
alboguear, *v.i.* to play the *albogue.*
alboguero, -ra, *n.m.f.* maker, seller, or player of *albogues.*
alboheza, *n.f.* (*bot.*) marsh-mallow.
albohol, *n.m.* (*bot.*) red poppy; bindweed.
albollón, *n.m.* drain, sewer.
albóndiga, *n.f.* ball of forcemeat with eggs and spice; *picar a alguien para albóndigas; hacer a alguien albondiguillas,* to make mincemeat of (threat used in a comic sense).
albondiguilla, *n.f.* small ball of forcemeat.
albor, *n.m.* (*poet.*) brightness; whiteness; dawn; *albor* or *albores de la vida,* youth, childhood.
alborada, *n.f.* dawn of day; (*mil.*) action fought at dawn; réveillé; morning serenade.
albórbola, *n.f.* shouting and yelling (for joy).
alborear, *v.i.* to dawn.
alborga, *n.f.* mat-weed sandal.
albornía, *n.f.* large glazed jug.
alborno, *n.m.* (*bot.*) alburnum.
albornoz, *n.m.* coarse woollen stuff; Moorish cloak; burnoose.
alboronía, *n.f.* dish of egg-plant, tomatoes, pumpkins and pimento.
alboroque, *n.m.* treat at the conclusion of a bargain; good-will.
alborotadamente, *adv.* noisily, confusedly.
alborotadizo, -za; alborotado, -da, *a.* restless, restive, excited, turbulent, agitated. — *p.p.* [ALBOROTAR].
alborotador, -ra, *a.* riotous; agitating. — *n.m.f.* agitator, rioter.
alborotapueblos, *n.m.* mover of sedition; (*coll.*) good fellow.
alborotar, *v.t.* to disturb, excite, agitate; *alborotar la calle,* to disturb the neighbourhood. — *v.i., v.r.* to get excited; to riot; to make a fuss; (*naut.*) to become rough (sea); *ni te alborotes, ni te enfotes,* do not believe or disbelieve blindly.

alboroto, *n.m.* disturbance, riot, tumult; outcry, hubbub.

alborozadamente, *adv* jubilantly, mirthfully.

alborozador, -ra, *n.m.f.* promoter of mirth or gaiety. — *a.* mirthful, gay.

alborozar, *v.t.* (*pret.* **alborocé;** *pres. subj.* **alboroce**) to promote mirth or gaiety; to exhilarate; to gladden. — *v.r.* to become happy.

alborozo, *n.m.* merriment, gaiety, exhilaration.

albotín, *n.m.* (*bot.*) terebinth.

albrán, *n.m.* young duck.

albricias, *n.f.pl.* reward for good news; (*Ec., ES.*) a present; (*Mex.*) holes in casting moulds; ¡ **albricias!** *interj.* an expression of joy; *ganar las albricias,* to be the first to congratulate a person; *albricias, padre; que el obispo es chantre,* said to persons who ask for *albricias* not deserved by them.

albuco, *n.m.* (*bot.*) asphodel.

albudeca, *n.f.* inferior watermelon.

albufera, *n.f.* large salt lagoon.

albugíneo, -nea, *a.* (*zool.*) entirely white.

albugo, *n.m.* (*med.*) leucoma.

albuhera, *n.f.* lake or reservoir.

álbum, *n.m.* album.

albumen, *n.m.* (*bot.*) albumen.

albúmina, *n.f.* (*chem.*) albumin.

albuminado, -da, *a.* albuminous. — *p.p.* [ALBUMINAR].

albuminar, *v.t.* (*phot.*) to albumenize.

albuminoídeo, -dea, *a.* albuminoid.

albuminoso, -sa, *a.* albuminous.

albur, *n.m.* (*ichth.*) dace; risk, chance; first draw at monte; *correr un albur,* to venture, chance, risk. — *pl.* game of cards.

albura, *n.f.* perfect whiteness; white of egg; (*bot.*) alburnum.

alburero, *n.m.* player of *albures*.

alburno, *n.m.* (*bot.*) alburnum; (*ichth.*) ablet.

alca, *n.f.* (*orn.*) razorbill.

alcabala, *n.f.* excise; *alcabala del viento,* duty paid by a visiting merchant; *el caudal de fulano está en alcabala de viento,* So-and-so lives on what he earns.

alcabalatorio, *n.m.* tax-register.

alcabalero, *n.m.* tax-gatherer, revenue officer.

alcabor, *n.m.* (*prov.*) flue of a chimney.

alcacel; alcacer, *n.m.* green barley; barley field; *ya está duro el alcacer para zampoñas,* he is too old; it is too late; *retozarle a uno el alcacer,* to romp, skip about.

alcací; alcacil, *n.m.* (*bot.*) wild artichoke.

alcachofa, *n.f.* (*bot.*) artichoke.

alcachofado, -da, *a.* like an artichoke. — *n.m.* dish of artichokes.

alcachofal, *n.m.* artichoke-bed.

alcachofar, *v.t.* (*fig.*) to extend, enlarge, overflow.

alcachofera, *n.f.* artichoke-plant; seller of artichokes.

alcachofero, -ra, *a.* (*bot.*) producing or selling artichokes. — *n.m.* seller of artichokes.

alcahaz, *n.m.* large bird-cage, aviary.

alcahazada, *n.f.* number of birds in a cage.

alcahazar, *v.t.* to cage birds.

alcahuete, -ta, *n.m.f.* procurer, bawd; blind, cover; (*coll.*) concealer; gossip; (*theat.*) entr'acte curtain.

alcahuetear, *v.t.* to pander, bawd; to procure women; (*coll.*) to conceal; to gossip. — *v.i.* to act as *alcahuete.*

alcahuetería, *n.f.* bawdry; concealment; (*coll.*) dodge.

alcaicería, *n.f.* raw silk exchange.

alcaico, *a.* alcaic verse in Latin poetry.

alcaide, *n.m.* governor of a castle, gaoler, warden.

alcaidesa, *n.f.* wife of a governor or gaoler.

alcaidía, *n.f.* office, dwelling, territory of a governor or gaoler.

alcairía, *n.f.* (*ES.*) [ALQUERÍA].

alcaldada, *n.f.* indiscreet action of a mayor (*alcalde*); abuse of authority.

alcalde, *n.m.* mayor; justice of the peace; leader; game of cards; *alcalde de barrio,* justice of the peace of a ward; selectman; *alcalde del mes de enero,* (*fig.*) new broom; *quien padre tiene alcalde, seguro va a juicio,* he whose father is mayor goes to court with a light heart. *¿Soy alcalde o no soy alcalde, o esta vara la tengo de balde?* (Comic demand made of a person for recognition).

alcaldear, *v.i.* (*coll.*) to play the *alcalde.*

alcaldesa, *n.f.* wife of an *alcalde.*

alcaldía, *n.f.* office or jurisdiction of an *alcalde.*

alcalescencia, *n.f.* (*chem.*) alkalization; alkalescence.

alcalescente, *a.* (*chem.*) alkalescent.

alcalescer, *v.t.* (*chem.*) to alkalify.

álcali, *n.m.* (*chem.*) alkali.

alcalífero, -ra, *a.* alkaline.

alcalificable, *a.* (*chem.*) alkalifiable.

alcalígeno, -na, *a.* alkaligenous, producing alkali.

alcalímetro, *n.m.* alkalimeter.

alcalinidad, *n.f.* alkalinity.

alcalino, -na; alcalizado, -da, *a.* (*chem.*) alkaline.

alcalización, *n.f.* (*chem.*) alkalization.

alcalizar, *v.t.* (*pret.* **alcalicé;** *pres. subj.* **alcalice**) (*chem.*) to alkalize.

alcaloide, *n.m.* alkaloid.

alcaloídeo, -dea, *a.* alkaloid.

alcaller, *n.m.* potter.

alcallería, *n.f.* pottery.

alcam, *n.m.* (*bot.*) bitter apple.

alcamonías, *n.f.pl.* spices; (*coll.*) [ALCAHUETE-RÍAS]. — *n.m.* (*coll.*) [ALCAHUETE].

alcana, *n.f.* (*bot.*) privet.

alcance, *n.m.* pursuit; arm's length, reach; (*com.*) deficit; scope, extent; range (firearms); compass; capacity, ability; supplement; extra collection (post); (*mil.*) soldier's net pay after official deductions; (*print.*) copy; stop-press; result; (*vet.*) tumour in the pastern; *ir a los alcances de una cosa,* to be on the point of gaining, or attaining something; *seguir el alcance,* (*mil.*) to pursue the enemy; *andarle,* or *irle a,* or *en los alcances a uno,* to spy on, watch someone; *dar alcance a uno,* to overtake someone.

alcancía, *n.f.* money-box; earthenware ball filled with ashes or flowers for missiles; *pl.* (*mil.*) combustible balls; (*slang*) brothel-keeper.

alcanciazo, *n.m.* blow with an *alcancía.*

alcándara, *n.f.* perch of a falcon; clothes-horse.

alcandía, *n.f.* (*bot.*) Turkey millet.

alcandial, *n.m.* millet field.

alcandora, *n.f.* beacon, bonfire; white tunic.

alcanfor, *n.m.* camphor.

alcanforada, *n.f.* camphor-scented shrub.
alcanforado, -da, *a.* camphorated. — *p.p.* [ALCANFORAR].
alcanforar, *v.t.* to camphorate; *v.r.* (*Hond.*, *Ven.*) to vaporize, vanish, disappear.
alcanforero, *n.m.* camphor-tree.
alcántara, *n.f.* wooden receptacle for velvet in the loom.
alcantarilla, *n.f.* small bridge; culvert, drain, underground sewer.
alcantarillado, *n.m.* sewerage. — *p.p.* [ALCANTARILLAR].
alcantarillar, *v.t.* to make sewers.
alcantarillero, *n.m.* sewer-man.
alcanzadizo, -za, *a.* within reach; obtainable; easily attained.
alcanzado, -da, *a.* necessitous, impecunious, in debt, indebted; *alcanzado de recursos,* short of money. — *p.p.* [ALCANZAR].
alcanzador, -ra, *n.m.f.* pursuer. — *a.* pursuing.
alcanzadura, *n.f.* (*vet.*) tumour in the pastern.
alcanzar, *v.t.* (*pret.* **alcancé;** *pres. subj.* **alcance**) to follow; overtake, come up to, reach; *alcanzar con,* to get, acquire, attain, obtain; to be contemporary; to comprehend; (*com.*) to find debtor of. — *v.i.* to share; *alcanzar a,* to attain, reach; *alcanzar para,* to suffice; *alcanzar de uno,* to prevail upon anyone; *alcanzar en días,* to survive; *alcanzar a ver,* to make out, descry; *alcancé a mi bisabuelo,* I knew my great-grandfather. — *v.r.* (*vet.*) to suffer from *alcanzaduras; alcanzársele poco a alguno,* or *no alcanzársele más,* to be of a weak understanding.
alcaparra, *n.f.;* **alcaparro,** *n.m.* (*bot.*) caper-bush, caper.
alcaparrado, -da, *a.* dressed with capers. — *n.f.* portion of capers.
alcaparral, *n.m.* caper-field.
alcaparrero, -ra, *n.m.f.* seller of capers. — *n.f.* container for capers.
alcaparrón, *n.m.* large caper.
alcaparrosa, *n.f.* (*min.*) copperas.
alcaraván, *n.m.* (*orn.*) bittern.
alcaravanero, *n.m.* hawk trained to pursue the bittern.
alcaravea, *n.f.* (*bot.*) caraway-seed.
alcarceña, *n.f.* (*bot.*) bitter-vetch.
alcarceñal, *n.m.* tare-field.
alcarcil, *n.m.* (*bot.*) wild artichoke.
alcarracero, -ra, *n.m.f.* potter; shelf for earthenware.
alcarraza, *n.f.* unglazed porous clay jar.
alcarrecería, *n.f.* earthenware factory or shop.
alcarria, *n.f.* high plain.
alcartaz, *n.m.* paper cone, cornucopia.
alcatifa, *n.f.* fine carpet or rug; (*mas.*) layer of earth.
alcatife, *n.m.* (*slang*) silk.
alcatifero, *n.m.* (*slang*) silk thief.
alcatraz, *n.m.* pelican; cornucopia; (*bot.*) arum.
alcaucil, *n.m.* wild artichoke.
alcaudón, *n.m.* (*orn.*) butcher-bird.
alcayata, *n.f.* spike; hook.
alcazaba, *n.f.* (*fort.*) keep, donjon.
alcázar, *n.m.* castle; fortress; (*naut.*) quarter-deck.
alcazuz, *n.m.* liquorice.
alce, *n.m.* (*zool.*) moose, elk; (at cards) part of the pack after being shuffled; (*print.*)

gathering for binding; (*Cub.*) gathering of the sugar cane after cutting.
alcedo, *n.m.* maple grove.
alcino, *n.m.* (*bot.*) wild basil.
alción, *n.m.* (*orn.*) Chinese swallow; (*ichth.*) halcyon, kingfisher; (*astron.*) principal star of the Pleiades.
alcista, *n.m.f.* bull (in finance).
alcoba, *n.f.* alcove, bedroom; case for tongue of a balance; fishing smack; place for public weighing.
alcobilla; alcobita, *n.f.* small alcove; *alcobilla de lumbre,* (*prov.*) fireplace.
alcocarra, *n.f.* gesture, grimace.
alcohol, *n.m.* alcohol; spirit of wine; antimony; galena; cosmetic used for eyebrows; *alcohol amílico,* amyl alcohol; *alcohol metílico,* methyl alcohol; *alcohol de arder,* methylated spirit.
alcoholado, -da, *a.* of a darker colour round the eyes (cattle); alcoholized. — *n.m.* (*med.*) alcoholized compound. — *p.p.* ([ALCOHOLAR].
alcoholador, -ra, *n.m.f.* rectifier of spirits.
alcoholar, *v.t.* to distil alcohol from; to dye or paint with antimony; (*naut.*) to tar after caulking; to pulverize.
alcoholato, *n.m.* alcoholate.
alcoholera, *n.f.* vessel for alcohol or antimony.
alcohólico, -ca, *a.* alcoholic.
alcoholímetro, *n.m.;* **alcoholómetro,** *n.m.* alcoholometer.
alcoholismo, *n.m.* alcoholism.
alcoholización, *n.f.* (*chem.*) alcoholization.
alcoholizado, -da, *a.* alcoholized. — *n.m.f.* sufferer from alcoholism. — *p.p.* [ALCOHOLIZAR].
alcoholizar, *v.t.* (*pret.* **alcoholicé;** *pres. subj.* **alcoholice**) to alcoholize.
alcolla, *n.f.* large glass bulb or decanter.
alcor, *n.m.* hill.
Alcorán, *n.m.* the Koran, Alkoran.
alcoranista, *n.m.* Koran expounder or scholar.
alcorcí, *n.m.* an Arab jewel or valuable trinket.
alcornocal, *n.m.* plantation of cork-trees.
alcornoque, *n.m.* (*bot.*) cork-tree; (*fig.*) blockhead, stupid fellow.
alcornoqueño, -ña, *a.* belonging to the cork-tree.
alcorque, *n.m.* cork-wood clogs or soles; hollow for water around trees.
alcorza, *n.f.* sugar icing; (*fig.*) refined, finical person.
alcorzado, -da, *a.* iced (cake); *n.m.* group in icing.
alcorzar, *v.t.* to ice (cake); *v.r.* to polish, adorn.
alcotán, *n.m.* (*orn.*) lanner.
alcotana, *n.f.* (*build.*) pickaxe, gurlet, mattock.
alcotancillo, *n.m.* (*orn.*) young lanner.
alcrebite, *n.m.* sulphur.
alcribís, *n.m.* tuyère, tewel.
alcubilla, *n.f.* reservoir, basin, mill-pond.
alcucero, -ra, *n.m.f.* maker or seller of tin oil-bottles, cruets. — *a.* (*coll.*) greedy.
alcucilla, *n.f.* small oil-can.
alcuña; alcurnia, *n.f.* ancestry, lineage.
alcuza, *n.f.* oil-bottle or cruet; oil-can, oiler; *razonar como una alcuza,* to use absurd arguments.
alcuzada, *n.f.* cruetful of oil.
alcuzazo, *n.m.* blow with an oil-cruet or oil-can.

alcuzón, *n.m.* large oil-can.

alcuzcuz, *n.m.* balls of flour, honey and water.

aldaba, *n.f.* knocker, clapper; door-handle, door-latch; cross-bar securing door or window; *agarrarse de,* or *tener buenas aldabas,* to rely on powerful protection.

aldabada, *n.f.* rap with knocker; (*fig.*) sudden fear; twinges of conscience.

aldabazo; aldabonazo, *n.m.* loud knocking.

aldabear, *v.i.* to rap or knock at the door.

aldabeo, *n.m.* continuous knocking.

aldabía, *n.f.* horizontal cross-beam.

aldabilla, *n.f.* small knocker, latch.

aldabón, *n.m.* large knocker; trunk-handle or haft.

aldea, *n.f.* small village, hamlet.

aldeana, *n.f.* villager, countrywoman, country-girl.

aldeanamente, *adv.* in village style, in country fashion; rudely, roughly.

aldeaniego, -ga, *a.* belonging to a village; rustic.

aldeano, *n.m.* villager, countryman. — *a.* rustic, boorish, uncultured.

aldehída, *n.f.* aldehyde.

aldehuela; aldeílla; aldeíta, *n.f.* small village; *más mal hay en la aldehuela del que se suena,* there's more mischief done in the village than is spoken about.

aldeorrio; aldeorro, *n.m.* (*contempt.*) insignificant little village.

alderredor, *adv.* [ALREDEDOR] around.

aldino, *a.* Aldine (editions).

aldiza, *n.f.* (*bot.*) cornflower.

aldrán, *n.m.* one who sells wine in country districts.

aleación, *n.f.* art of alloying metals; alloy; mixture.

aleador, *n.m.* alloyer.

alear, *v.t.* to alloy. — *v.i.* to flutter; to move the wings (or arms) quickly; (*fig.*) to recover from sickness or fatigue.

aleatorio, -ria, *a.* uncertain, hazardous; relating to games of chance; (*law*) aleatory.

alebrado, -da, *a.* hare-like; timid, fearful. — *p.p.* [ALEBRARSE].

alebrarse; alebrastarse; alebrestarse, *v.r.* to squat; (*fig.*) to cower; become frightened.

alebronarse, *v.r.* to become dispirited; to cower; to squat.

aleccionable, *a.* teachable.

aleccionamiento, *n.m.* lesson, coaching, instruction.

aleccionar, *v.t.* to teach, instruct, coach.

alece, *n.m.* (*ichth.*) anchovy; ragout of fish-liver.

alecrín, *n.m.* (*Am.*) verbenaceous tree; (*Cub.*) fish of the selachian group.

alectoria, *n.f.* stone in an old cock's liver.

alectórico, -ca, *a.* relative to cocks; cock-like.

alechigar, *v.t.* (*obs.*) to soften; to sweeten. — *v.r.* to turn milky.

alechugado, -da, *a.* curled like a lettuce; fluted; plaited. — *p.p.* [ALECHUGAR].

alechugar, *v.t.* to curl like lettuce leaf; to plait; to flute.

alechuguinado, -da, *a.* dandy-like, dude-like.

aleda, *n.f.*; *cera aleda,* propolis or bee-glue.

aledaño, *n.m.* common boundary, border, limit. — *a.* bordering, confining.

alefanginas, *n.f.pl.* purgative pills made of spices.

alefris; alefriz, *n.m.* (*naut.*) mortise, rabbet (on the keel, stem and sternpost).

alefrizar, *v.t.* (*pret.* **alefricé;** *pres. subj.* **alefrice**) (*naut.*) to mortise, rabbet.

alegación, *n.f.* allegation, argument.

alegamar, *v.t.* to fertilize with mud or silt.

alegar, *v.t.* (*pret.* **alegué;** *pres. subj.* **alegue**) to allege, affirm, quote, adduce, maintain.

alegato, *n.m.* (*law*) allegation, presentation, summing-up.

alegoría, *n.f.* allegory.

alegóricamente, *adv.* allegorically.

alegórico, -ca, *a.* allegorical.

alegorista, *n.m.f.* allegorist.

alegorizar, *v.t.* (*pret.* **alegoricé;** *pres. subj.* **alegorice**) to turn into allegory, allegorize.

alegra, *n.f.* (*naut.*) reamer, auger.

alegrador, -ra, *a.* causing mirth. — *n.m.* paper spill to light cigars.

alegrar, *v.a.* to make merry, gladden, exhilarate, comfort; to stir up (fire); to enliven; to beautify; (*naut., mech.*) to bore, round, ream, widen. — *v.r.* to rejoice, exult, be glad; to get tipsy.

alegre, *a.* merry, joyful, contented, light-hearted, gleeful; tipsy; comic, ludicrous, facetious; gay, showy; fine, clear, brilliant, pleasant, pleasing; indelicate (story); fortunate, lucky; risky, reckless, optimistic; *un cielo alegre,* a clear (or brilliant) sky; *alegre de cascos,* hare-brained.

alegremente, *adv.* merrily, gladly, gaily; laughingly, good-humouredly; facetiously.

alegrete, -ta, *a.* frolicsome, gay, waggish.

alegría, *n.f.* mirth, merriment, gaiety, glee, rejoicing, ecstasy, joy, pleasure; (*slang*) tavern; (*bot.*) sesame, oily grain; (*naut.*) opening of a loop-hole or gun-port; *alegría secreta, candela muerta,* joy must be shared to be felt. — *pl.* rejoicings, public festivals.

alegrillo, -a, *a.* sprightly, gay.

alegro, *n.m.* (*mus.*) allegro.

alegrón, *n.m.* (*coll.*) sudden, unlooked-for joy; blaze.

alejamiento, *n.m.* elongation; retiring, withdrawal; distance; strangeness.

Alejandría, *n.f.* Alexandria; Alessandria.

alejandrino, -na, *a.* of or from Alexandria; relating to Alexander the Great; (*poet.*) *verso alejandrino,* Alexandrine verse.

Alejandro, *n.m.* Alexander.

alejar, *v.t.* to remove to a distance; to separate; to estrange; to withdraw. — *v.r. alejarse de su tierra,* to move away, recede from one's country.

alejijas, *n.f.pl.* barley porridge.

alejur, *n.m.* paste of nuts and honey.

alelamiento, *n.m.* stupidity, foolishness.

alelar, *v.t.* to make stupid; to bewilder. — *v.r.* to become stupid.

alelí, *n.m.* [ALHELÍ].

aleluya, *n.f.* hallelujah; joy, merriment; Eastertime; (*bot.*) wood-sorrel. — *pl.* small prints thrown among the people on Easter-Eve; (*coll.*) poor verses, doggerel; very thin person or animal.

alema, *n.f.* allotted quantity of water for purposes of irrigation.

alemán, -na, *n.m.f., a.* German. — *n.m.* German language.

alemana; alemanda, *n.f.* ancient Spanish dance of German or Flemish origin.

Alemania, *n.f.* Germany.

alemánico, -ca, *a.* Germanic.

alemanisco, -ca, *a.* applied to cloth made in Germany; huckaback; damask (table-linen).

alenguamiento, *n.m.* agreement relative to pasture.

alenguar, *v.t.* to agree about pasture lands or pasturage.

alentada, *n.f.* long breath.

alentadamente, *adv.* bravely, gallantly.

alentado, -da, *a.* spirited, courageous, valiant. — *p.p.* [ALENTAR].

alentador, -ra, *n.m.f.* one who inspires courage. — *a.* encouraging, cheering.

alentar, *v.i.* (*pres. indic.* **aliento;** *pres. subj.* **aliente**) to breathe. — *v.t.* to encourage, inspire, cheer; to comfort; *alentar con la esperanza,* to inspire with hope. — *v.r.* to become inspired, encouraged.

aleonado, -da, *a.* lion-like; tawny.

alepín, *n.m.* a kind of very fine bombazine.

alerce, *n.m.* (*bot.*) larch-tree.

alero, *n.m.* projecting part of a roof; eaves, gable-end, corona; water-table; hood-moulding; splash-board of a carriage. — *pl.* snares for partridges.

alerón, *n.m.* (*aer.*) aileron.

alerta, *n.f.* (*mil.*) watchword.

alerta; alertamente, *adv.* vigilantly, carefully; *estar alerta,* to be on the alert.

alertar, *v.t.* to make watchful; to put on guard. — *v.i.* to be on one's guard.

alerto, -ta, *a.* vigilant, alert, guarded.

alerzal, *n.m.* larch grove.

alesna, *n.f.* awl.

alesnado, -da, *a.* awl-shaped, pointed.

aleta, *n.f.* small wing, fish's fin; (*arch.*) aletta; (*mech.*) leaf of a hinge, teeth of a pinion, blade of a screw-propeller. — *pl.* (*naut.*) fashion pieces.

aletada, *n.f.* motion of the wings.

aletado, -da, *a.* winged, finned.

aletargado, -da, *a.* lethargic. — *p.p.* [ALETARGAR].

aletargamiento, *n.m.* lethargy.

aletargar, *v.t.* to lethargize. — *v.r.* to fall into lethargy; to become lethargic.

aletazo, *n.m.* blow with the wing or fin.

aletear, *v.i.* to flutter, flap wings or fins; (*fig.*) to move the arms like wings; to recover strength after illness.

aleteo, *n.m.* flapping of wings; (*fig.*) palpitation.

aleto, *n.m.* kind of falcon.

aletón, *n.m.* large wing.

aletría, *n.f.* (*prov.*) a kind of paste; vermicelli.

aleudar, *v.t.* to leaven. — *v.r.* to become fermented.

aleve, *a.* treacherous, perfidious, guileful. — *n.m.* traitor. — *n.f.* traitress.

alevilla, *n.f.* white moth resembling the silkworm's moth.

alevinador, -ra, *n.m.f.,* *a.* one who stocks ponds with fry.

alevinamiento, *n.m.* breeding young fish; stocking (water) with young fish.

alevinar, *v.t.* to stock with fry.

alevino, *n.m.* (*ichth.*) fry, young fish.

alevosa, *n.f.* (*vet.*) ranula, tumour under the tongue.

alevosamente, *adv.* guilefully, treacherously.

alevosía, *n.f.* perfidy, breach of faith; *con alevosía,* treacherously.

alevoso, -sa, *a.* treacherous. — *n.m.* traitor. *n.f.* traitress.

alexifármaco, -ca, *a.* (*med.*) alexipharmic, antidotal. — *n.m.* antidote.

aleya, *n.f.* verse of Koran.

alezna, *n.f.* (*prov.*) black mustard seed.

alezo, *n.m.* (*med.*) draw-sheet; large bandage (maternity).

alfa, *n.f.* first letter of Greek alphabet, alpha; beginning, commencement.

alfábega, *n.f.* (*bot.*) sweet-basil.

alfabéticamente, *adv.* alphabetically.

alfabético, -ca, *a.* alphabetical.

alfabetista, *n.m.f.,* *a.* one who studies the alphabet; reader.

alfabeto, *n.m.* alphabet.

alfaguara, *n.f.* copious stream.

alfahar, *n.m.* [ALFAR].

alfaharería, *n.f.* [ALFARERÍA].

alfaharero, *n.m.* [ALFARERO].

alfajía, *n.f.* (*carp.*) wood frame for windows and doors; lintel.

alfajor, *n.m.* cake made with nuts and honey.

alfalfa, *n.f.;* **alfalfe,** *n.m.* (*bot.*) lucerne, alfalfa.

alfalfal; alfalfar, *n.m.* lucerne-field.

alfana, *n.f.* strong and spirited horse.

alfandoque, *n.m.* (*Am.*) paste made with molasses, cheese and ginger.

alfaneque, *n.m.* (*orn.*) white eagle; tent, booth.

alfanjado, -da, *a.* shaped like a cutlass.

alfanjazo, *n.m.* wound with a cutlass.

alfanje, *n.m.* cutlass, hanger, scimitar; (*ichth.*) sword-fish.

alfanjete, *n.m.* small cutlass.

alfanjón, *n.m.* large, powerful cutlass.

alfanjonazo, *n.m.* cut with a large cutlass.

alfaque, *n.m.* shoal, sand-bar.

alfaquí, *n.m.* Mohammedan doctor of laws.

alfar, *n.m.* potter; clay. — *v.i.* to rear (horse).

alfaraz, *n.m.* Moorish horse for light cavalry.

alfarda, *n.f.* (*prov.*) duty paid for the irrigation of lands; (*arch.*) thin beam.

alfardero, *n.m.* (*prov.*) collector of duty for irrigation.

alfardilla, *n.f.* gold or silver braid; (*prov.*) small tax for cleaning culverts.

alfardón, *n.m.* duty paid for irrigation; (*mech.*) washer.

alfareme, *n.m.* Arab head-dress.

alfarería, *n.f.* the art of the potter; pottery shop or factory.

alfarero, -ra, *n.m.,* *a.* potter.

alfargo, *n.m.* master beam of an oil-mill.

alfarje, *n.m.* lower stone of an oil-mill; ceiling ornamented with carved work; wainscot.

alfarjía, *n.f.* (*carp.*) wood frame for windows and doors.

alfarma, *n.f.* (*bot.*) wild rue.

alfayate, *n.m.* (*obs.*) tailor.

alféizar, *n.m.* (*arch.*) embrasure; splay of a door or window.

alfeñicado, -da, *a.* weakly, delicate; (*coll.*) affected, prudish, finical. — *p.p.* [ALFEÑICARSE].

alfeñicarse, *v.r.* to become thin; (*coll.*) to 'mince' or affect a peculiar delicacy.

alfeñique, *n.m.* sugar paste; (*coll.*) delicate person; affectation; make-up.

alferazgo, *n.m.;* **alferecía,** *n.f.* ensigncy, dignity of an ensign.

alferecía, *n.f.* epilepsy (in infants); [ALFERAZGO].

alférez, *n.m.* ensign, second lieutenant· *alférez de navío,* lieutenant.

alficoz, *n.m.* cucumber.·

alfil, *n.m.* bishop (in game of chess).

alfiler, *n.m.* pin, scarf-pin, brooch; *alfiler de París,* wire nail; (*pl.*) pin-money, tip; *alfileres de gancho* (or *de pelo*), hairpins; *con todos sus alfileres* or *con veinticinco alfileres,* dressed up, pranked up; *no estar con sus alfileres,* to be of ill humour; *pegado, prendido,* or *preso con alfileres,* very unstable.

alfilerazo, *n.m.* pinprick; large pin.

alfilerera, *n.f.* (*bot.*) seed of the geranium and other plants of the same natural order.

alfilerero, -ra, *n.m.f.* maker or seller of pins.

alfiletero, *n.m.* pin-case, needle-case, pin-cushion.

alfiltete, *n.m.* paste made of coarse wheat flour or semolina.

alfolí, *n.m.* granary; salt warehouse.

alfoliero; alfolinero, *n.m.* keeper of a granary or salt depot.

alfombra, *n.f.* carpet; (*poet.*) cover, ornament; *una alfombra de rosas,* a carpet of roses, etc.; (*med.*) measles.

alfombrado, -da, *a.* carpeted. — *n.m.* aggregate of carpets; *alfombrado de una escalera,* the whole staircase carpet. — *p.p.* [ALFOMBRAR].

alfombrar, *v.t.* to carpet, spread with carpets.

alfombrero, -ra, *n.m.f.* carpet-maker or seller.

alfombrilla, *n.f.* small carpet, rug; (*med.*) measles.

alfombrista, *n.m.* carpet dealer, sewer and layer.

alfóncigo; alfónsigo, *n.m.* pistachio; pistachio-tree.

alfonsearse, *v.r.* (*obs.*) (*coll.*) to mock, banter.

alfonsí; alfonsino, -na, *a.* relating to the kings of Spain named Alfonso.

alfonsina, *n.f.* solemn rite performed in the University of Alcalá.

alforfón, *n.m.* (*bot.*) buckwheat.

alforja, *n.f.* saddle-bag, knapsack; provision; *qué alforjas,* used to express discontent.

alforjero, *a.* relating to *alforja.* — *n.m.f.* maker or seller of saddle-bags; one who carries the bags with provisions. — *n.m.* lay brother who begs alms; sportsman's dog.

alforjilla; alforjita; alforjuela, *n.f.* small saddle-bag, small knapsack.

alforza, *n.f.* horizontal plait, tuck, pleat, hem; (*coll.*) clipping; large seam, scar; secret place (heart).

alforzar, *v.t.* to tuck, pleat.

alfoz, *n.m.* borough, district, or dependence.

alga, *n.f.* (*bot.*) alga, seaweed.

algaba, *n.f.* wood, forest.

algaceo, -cea, *a.* (*bot.*) like seaweed.

algadonera, *n.f.* (*bot.*) cudweed.

algaida, *n.f.* ridge of shifting sand; sand-dune; jungle, brush.

algaido, -da, *a.* (*prov.*) thatched.

algalaba, *n.f.* (*bot.*) white bryony, wild hops.

algalia, *n.f.* civet, civet-cat; (*med.*) catheter.

algaliado, -da, *a.* civet-like; perfumed with civet. — *p.p.* [ALGALIAR].

algaliar, *v.t.* to perfume with civet.

algaliero, -ra, *n.m.f., a.* one who likes perfumes, especially civet.

algara, *n.f.* thin film covering an egg, onion, etc.; foraging party of cavalry.

algarabía, *n.f.* Arabic; (*coll.*) gabble, jargon; scribble; din, clamour, confused noise; (*bot.*) centaury.

algarada, *n.f.* loud cry; sudden onslaught; surprise attack; ancient battering-ram.

algarero, -ra, *a.* prating, chattering, talkative.

algarrada, *n.f.* driving bulls into the pen; bull-baiting· battering-ram.

algarroba, *n.f.* (*bot.*) smooth-podded tare; carob bean.

algarrobal, *n.m.* carob-tree plantation.

algarrobera, *n.f.;* **algarrobo,** *n.m.* (*bot.*) carob-tree.

algazara, *n.f.* hurrah; cry of applause; shout of a crowd.

algazul, *n.m.* seaweed which produces barilla.

álgebra, *n.f.* algebra; (*med.*) art of setting joints.

algebraico, -ca; algébrico, -ca, *a.* algebraic.

algebrista, *n.m.* algebraist; bone-setter.

algente, *a.* (*poet.*) algid, cold.

algidez, *n.f.* (*med.*) icy coldness.

álgido, -da, *a.* (*med.*) algid, icy.

algo, *pron.* something. — *a.* some. — *adv.* somewhat, a little, rather; *más vale algo que nada,* or *algo es algo,* a little is better than nothing; *mientras se gana algo, no se pierde nada,* so long as something is gained, nothing is lost; *algo ajeno no hace heredero,* ill-gotten property does no good to those who inherit it; *algo qué,* rather, somewhat important; not a little.

algodón, *n.m.* cotton; (*bot.*) cotton-plant; *algodón en rama,* raw cotton. — *pl.* silk or cotton fibres; ear plugs; *estar criado entre algodones,* to be brought up in cotton-wool; *llevar, meter,* or *tener entre algodones,* to treat with consideration.

algodonado, -da, *a.* filled with cotton. — *p.p.* [ALGODONAR].

algodonal, *n.m.* cotton-plantation; cotton-plant.

algodonar, *v.t.* to cover or fill with cotton.

algodoncillo, *n.m.* a plant of the Asclepiadaceæ family.

algodonería, *n.f.* cotton-factory; cotton-trade.

algodonero, -ra, *a.* cottony, appertaining to cotton. — *n.m.f.* cotton dealer. — *n.m.* cotton; cotton-plant; cottonwood poplar.

algodonoso, -sa, *a.* cottony, woolly, covered with thick down; insipid, tasteless (of certain fruits).

algorfa, *n.f.* garret for storing grain, etc.

algorín, *n.m.* place in oil-mills for receiving olives.

algoritmia, *n.f.;* **algoritmo,** *n.m.* algorithm; arithmetic.

algoso, -sa, *a.* weedy, full of seaweed.

alguacil, *n.m.* constable, peace-officer; short-legged spider.

alguacilazgo, *n.m.* alguacil's office.

alguarín, *n.m.* (*prov.*) store-room; bucket in which flour falls from the mill-stones.

alguaza, *n.f.* (*prov.*) hinge.

alguien, *pron.* somebody, someone.

algún; alguno, -na, *a.* some, any (*algún* before *n.m.*). — *pron.* someone; something, anyone; *algún tiempo,* sometime; *algún tanto,* somewhat, rather, a little; *alguna vez,* sometimes, now and then; *alguno que otro,* some, a few.

alhadida, *n.f.* (*obs.*) copper sulphate.

alhaja, *n.f.* showy furniture; gaudy ornament; something of great value; jewel, gem; (*coll.*) excellent (person, animal); necessary utensil; *es una buena alhaja,* he's a good-for-nothing; (ironically) he's a fine fellow; *quien trabaja tiene alhaja,* he that labours spins gold.

alhajar, *v.t.* to adorn; to fit up; to furnish.

alhajuela, *n.f.* little jewel; toy.

alhamel, *n.m.* (*prov.*) beast of burden; labourer; muleteer.

alhana, *n.f.* alhanna, Tripoli earth.

alhandal, *n.m.* (*pharm.*) coloquintida, colocynth, bitter apple.

alharaca, *n.f.* clamour, complaint, angry vociferation.

alharaquiento, -ta, *a.* noisy, clamorous, complaining.

alhárgama; alharma, *n.f.* (*bot.*) wild rue.

alhelí, *n.m.* (*bot.*) stock, wallflower.

alheña, *n.f.* privet; flower of privet; powdered Egyptian privet (henna); blasting of corn.

alheñar, *v.t.* to dye with privet (henna). — *v.r.* to become mildewed (of corn).

alhoja, *n.f.* small bird resembling a lark.

alholva, *n.f.* (*bot.*) fenugreek.

alholvar, *n.m.* (*bot.*) fenugreek field.

alhóndiga, *n.f.* public granary; wheat exchange.

alhondiguero, *n.m.* keeper of a public granary.

alhorma, *n.f.* Moorish camp or royal tent.

alhorre, *n.m.* (*med.*) meconium; skin eruption in the newly born.

alhoz, *n.m.* limit or lot of land; borough, district.

alhucema, *n.f.* (*bot.*) lavender.

alhuceña, *n.f.* a plant of the Cruciferæ family.

alhumajo, *n.m.* pine-needles.

ali, *n.m.* a sequence of two or three playing cards.

aliabierto, -ta, *a.* open-winged, with wings expanded.

aliacán, *n.m.* jaundice.

aliacanado, -da, *a.* jaundiced.

aliáceo, -cea, *a.* aliaceous, like garlic.

aliado, -da, *n.m.f.* ally. — *a.* allied, confederate. — *p.p.* [ALIARSE].

aliadófilo, -la, *a.* applied to the Spaniards who in the 1914–18 war sided with the Allies.

aliaga, *n.f.* (*bot.*) furze, gorse.

aliagar, *n.m.* place covered with furze.

alianza, *n.f.* alliance, confederacy, league, coalition; agreement, convention; alliance contracted by marriage; (*Bibl.*) covenant.

aliara, *n.f.* horn goblet.

aliaria, *n.f.* (*bot.*) garlic hedge-mustard.

aliarse, *v.r.* to become allied; to be in a league, in coalition; to form an alliance.

alible, *a.* nutritive, nourishing.

álica, *n.f.* pottage of spelt and pulse.

alicaído, -da, *a.* with drooping wings; (*coll.*) weak, extenuated, exhausted; discouraged, depressed; fallen from high estate; *sombrero alicaído,* an uncocked hat.

alicántara, *n.f.;* **alicante,** *n.m.* venomous snake, like a viper. — *n.m.* variety of nougat; wine.

alicantina, *n.f.* (*coll.*) artifice, stratagem, cunning.

alicantino, -na, *n.m.f., a.* native of Alicante.

alicaria, *n.f.* receptacle for spelt.

alicario, -ria, *a.* relating to spelt. — *n.m.* spelt-miller.

alicatado, *n.m.* work inlaid with arabesque tiles; tiled. — *p.p.* [ALICATAR].

alicatar, *v.t.* (*build.*) to tile.

alicates, *n.m.pl.* fine-pointed pliers, pincers, nippers.

aliciente, *n.m.* inducement, excitement, attraction.

alicortar, *v.t.* to clip wings.

alicuanta, *a.* aliquant; *parte alicuanta,* aliquant number.

alícuota, *a.* aliquot, proportional; *parte alícuota,* aliquot number or part.

alidada, *n.f.* alidade, index of a quadrant; geometrical ruler.

alídeo, -dea, *a.* (*bot.*) similar to garlic.

alídico, -ca, *a.* mixed with garlic.

alidona, *n.f.* stone in the intestines of a swallow.

alienable, *a.* alienable, capable of alienation.

alienación, *n.f.* (*law, med.*) alienation.

alienado, -da, *a.* insane; alienated. — *p.p.* [ALIENAR].

alienar, *v.t.* to alienate; to transfer (of property).

alienista, *n.m.* (*med.*) alienist.

aliento, *n.m.* breath, inspiration; spirit; enterprise, vigour; courage; scent; *de un aliento,* in one breath, without stopping, continuously; *cobrar aliento,* to take courage again; *dar aliento,* to encourage; *sin aliento,* breathless, out of breath.

aliento; aliente, *pres. indic.; pres. subj.* [ALENTAR].

alier, *n.m.* (*naut.*) rower; marine on watch.

alifa, *n.f.* (*prov.*) second-year sugar-cane.

alifafe, *n.m.* callous tumour on horse's hock; (*coll.*) chronic complaint.

alifar, *v.t.* (*prov.*) to polish, burnish.

alifara, *n.f.* (*prov.*) gratuity, tip; collation, lunch.

alífero, -ra, *a.* aliferous, winged.

aliforme, *a.* aliform, wing-shaped.

aligación, *n.f.;* **aligamiento,** *n.m.* alligation, mixture, union; tying or binding together.

aligar, *v.t.* (*pret.* **aligué;** *pres. subj.* **aligue**) to tie; to unite. — *v.r.* to become united, allied.

aliger, *n.m.* cross guard of a sword.

aligeramiento, *n.m.* alleviation, lightening.

aligerar, *v.t.* to lighten; to alleviate; to ease; to hasten; to shorten. — *v.r.* to become lighter.

alígero, -ra, *a.* (*poet.*) winged, fast, fleet.

alijado, -da, *a.* (*naut.*) buoyant; eased, lightened, shortened. — *p.p.* (ALIJAR).

alijador, -ra, *n.m.f.* smuggler; (*naut.*) lighterman; *lanchón alijador,* (*naut.*) lighter; one who separates the seed from cotton.

alijar, *n.m.* uncultivated ground; (*pl.*) common pasture land.

alijar, *v.t.* (*naut.*) to lighten; to separate cotton from the seed; to smuggle; (*carp.*) to sand-paper.

alijarar, *v.t.* to divide (waste lands) for cultivation.

alijarero, *n.m.* sharer of waste lands to cultivate.

alijares, *n.m.pl.* royal pleasure resort of Granada.

alijariego, -ga, *a.* relating to waste lands.

[48]

alijo, n.m. (naut.) lightening of a ship; alleviation; smuggled goods; embarcación de alijo, (naut.) lighter.

alilla, n.f. small wing; fin of a fish.

alim, n.m. (Philip.) (bot.) small medicinal tree of the Euphorbiaceæ family.

alimaña, n.f. animal which destroys game.

alimañero, n.m. gamekeeper who destroys alimañas.

alimentación, n.f. feeding; board, meals; nutrition.

alimentador, -ra, a. nourishing, feeding. — n.m. feed-tank (engine).

alimental, a. alimental, nutritive.

alimentante, n.m.f. (law) maintainer.

alimentar, v.t. to feed, nourish, nurse; to supply a person with the necessaries of life; to fatten; to nurture, fondle, sustain; to cultivate, tend, encourage; to foment; to cherish (hope, illusion, etc.). — v.r. to feed oneself; alimentarse con (de) carne, to feed oneself on meat.

alimentario, -ria, n.m.f.; **alimentista,** n.m.f. one who enjoys a maintenance, pensioner.

alimenticio, -cia, a. nutritious; pastas alimenticias, Italian pastes like macaroni, etc.

alimento, n.m. nourishment, nutriment, food; incentive, encouragement; alimento combustible, or respiratorio, carbohydrate food; alimento plástico, or reparador, nitrogenous, protein food. — pl. (law) allowance, pension, alimony.

alimentoso, -sa, a. alimentary, nutritious.

alimo, n.m. (bot.) orach, mountain spinach.

alimoche, n.m. (orn.) African bird of prey.

alimonarse, v.r. to turn yellowish from disease (said of leaves).

alindado, -da, a. affectedly elegant or nice. — p.p. [ALINDAR].

alindamiento, n.m. act of putting limits (property).

alindar, v.t. to mark limits; to embellish, adorn. — v.i. to be contiguous; alindar con, to border on. — v.r. to adorn, embellish oneself.

alineación, n.f. alinement.

alinear, v.t. to aline, align. — v.r. (mil.) to fall into line.

aliñado, -da, a. dressed, embellished, seasoned. — p.p. [ALIÑAR].

aliñador, -ra, n.m.f. one who embellishes; one who prepares, seasons or dresses victuals; (Chi.) bonesetter.

aliñar, v.t. to arrange, adorn; to dress, cook or season victuals.

aliño, n.m. dress, ornament, decoration; cleanliness; dressing or seasoning for victuals; preparation.

aliñoso, -sa, a. dressed, decked out, decorated; careful, attentive.

alioli, n.m. sauce of garlic and oil.

alionín, n.m. (orn.) blue-feathered duck.

alipata, n.m. (Philip.) poisonous tree.

alípede, a. (poet.) with winged feet, swift, nimble.

alípedo, -da, a. (zool.) cheiropterous, alipedous.

aliquebrado, -da, a. broken-winged; dejected. — p.p. [ALIQUEBRAR].

aliquebrar, v.t. to break a wing. — v.r. to become weak; to break one's wing.

alirrojo, -ja, a. with red wings.

alisador, -ra, n.m.f. polisher, planisher, smoothing-iron; silk-stick; tool to shape wax candles. — a. polishing, smoothing.

alisadura, n.f. planing, smoothing, polishing; (pl.) shavings, cuttings.

alisar, v.t. to plane, make smooth (hair), polish, burnish; to mangle. — v.r. to become smooth, polished.

alisar, n.m.; **aliseda,** n.f. plantation of aldertrees.

alisios, n.m.pl. east winds, trade winds.

alisma, n.f. (bot.) water-plantain.

aliso, n.m. (bot.) alder-tree.

alistado, -da, a. enlisted; striped. — p.p. [ALISTAR].

alistador, n.m. one who enrols or enlists; one who keeps accounts.

alistamiento, n.m. enrolment, conscription, levy.

alistar, v.t., v.r. to enlist, enrol, recruit; to get ready; alistarse por socio, to enrol as a member; alistarse en un cuerpo, to enlist in a corps; alistarse para la partida, to get ready for the game.

aliteración, n.f. alliteration.

alitierno, n.m. (bot.) mock privet.

aliviadero, n.m. overflow canal or sewer. — n.m.

aliviador, -ra, n.m.f. helper, assistant. — n.m. spindle to raise or lower a running millstone; (slang) receiver of stolen goods. — a. helping, assisting, labour-saving.

aliviar, v.t. to lighten, help, loose; to relieve, mitigate, assuage, soothe; to exonerate; to hasten; to move swiftly; aliviar del or en el trabajo, to exonerate from, lighten the work. — v.r. to become lighter, relieved.

alivio, n.m. alleviation, ease; mitigation of pain; relief, improvement; comfort, calm; (law-slang) plea; attorney.

alizace, n.m. trench or excavation for the foundations of a building.

alizar, n.m. dado or wainscoting of tiles.

aljaba, n.f. quiver.

aljafana, n.f. wash-bowl, basin for washing.

aljafifar, v.t. to mop, clean, wash.

aljama, n.f. assembly of Moors or Jews; mosque; synagogue.

aljamía, n.f. Moorish document written in Spanish with Arabic letters; Moorish name for the Spanish language.

aljamiar, v.t. (coll.) to speak brokenly; to jabber.

aljarafe, n.m. roof, terrace.

aljarfa, n.f.; **aljarfe,** n.m.; **aljerife,** n.m. tarred fishing-net with small meshes.

aljévena, n.f. (prov.) wash-bowl.

aljez, n.m. crude gypsum, plaster of Paris.

aljezar, n.m. pit of gypsum.

aljezón, n.m. gypsum, plaster of Paris.

aljibe, n.m. cistern, reservoir of water; (naut.) tank boat for supplying vessels with water, petrol or oil; (naut.) water-tank.

aljibero, n.m. one who takes care of cisterns; cistern-keeper.

aljimierado, -da, a. shaved, trimmed.

aljofaina, n.f. wash-bowl; basin for washing; basin, earthen jug.

aljófar, n.m. misshapen pearl; (poet.) drops of water, dewdrops.

aljofarado, -da, a. (poet.) full of little drops or pearls. — p.p. [ALJOFARAR].

aljofarar, v.a. to adorn with pearls; to imitate pearls.

aljofifa, *n.f.* mop for floors.

aljofifar, *v.t.* to rub with a cloth; to mop, wash, clean, scour.

aljonje, *n.m.* bird-lime [AJONJE].

aljonjera, *n.f.; ;* **aljonjero,** *n.m.; ;* **aljonjolí,** *n.m.* [AJONJERA; AJONJERO; AJONJOLÍ].

aljor, *n.m.* crude gypsum.

aljorra, (*Cub.*) *n.f.* a very small insect, harmful to agriculture.

aljuba, *n.f.* Moorish garment.

alma, *n.f.* soul, mind, spirit; being, human being; strength, vigour; substance; staff, frame; web (of beam, nail, etc.); (*mech.*) attic ridge, scaffolding pole; (*arm.*) bore, core (of a rope, of a cable); (*naut.*) body of a mast; ghost, phantom, apparition; soundpost (violin, etc.); mould for casting statues; *estar con el alma entre los dientes,* to be dead with fear; *el alma me da,* my heart tells me; *dar, despedir, entregar, exhalar, rendir, salírsele el alma,* to expire; *alma mía,* or *mi alma,* my love, my dear, dear heart; *alma de caballo, alma de Judas* or *alma de Caín,* bad, unscrupulous person; *alma de cántaro,* fool; *alma de Dios,* bountiful or goodhearted, simple, inoffensive person; *romperse el alma,* to break one's neck in a fall; *tocar en el alma,* to touch one to the quick; *alma nacida* (or *viviente*) used in negative as English 'not a soul'; *arrancársele* (or *partírsele*) *a uno el alma,* to feel very much for a person; *como alma que lleva el diablo,* with great agitation of mind; *con el alma y la vida,* with great pleasure, very willingly; *estar como el alma de Garibay,* to take no side in a matter; *estar con el alma en un hilo,* to be worried by the fear of some grave danger; *tener el alma bien puesta,* to have courage and resolution; *paseársele el alma por el cuerpo,* to be very indolent; *caérsele el alma a los pies,* to be bitterly disappointed; *alma en pena,* soul in purgatory; lonely person; *en el alma,* keenly, deeply; *alma del negocio,* the crux of the business; *dar el alma al diablo,* to sacrifice everything to one's desires; *dolerle el alma de una cosa,* to be tired of something; *echar el alma atrás,* or *a las espaldas,* to be unscrupulous; *hablar al alma,* to speak frankly, with fervour; *irse el alma por,* or *tras alguna cosa,* to desire something ardently; *llevar en el alma,* to love deeply; *llevar tras sí el alma,* to move, attract greatly; *manchar el alma,* to commit a sin; *no tener alma,* to be soulless, unfeeling; *partir el alma,* to cause pain, sorrow; *perder el alma,* to be damned; *pesarle en el alma,* to repent; *sacar el alma a otro,* to kill or injure someone; to threaten to kill or injure; to make someone spend his all; *sentir en el alma,* to feel and deplore deeply; *tener uno el alma parada,* to waste one's possibilities; *volverse el alma al cuerpo,* to deliver from danger or fear; *alma perdida,* (*Per.*) the rock-thrush, solitaire bird.

almacén, *n.m.* store, shop, warehouse; depot; magazine, naval arsenal, dockyard; (*naut.*) *almacén de agua,* water-cask; (*naut.*) *almacén de una bomba de agua,* chamber of a pump; *gastar* (*mucho*) *almacén,* to wear much trash; to talk much about trivialities.

almacenado, -da, *a.* warehoused, bonded, stored. — *p.p.* [ALMACENAR].

almacenador, *n.m.* warehouseman.

almacenaje, *n.m.* warehouse rent.

almacenamiento, *n.m.* warehousing, storing.

almacenar, *v.t.* to store, deposit, keep, put in warehouse; to hoard.

almacenero, -ra, *n.m.f.* warehouse-keeper.

almacenista, *n.m.* warehouse owner; salesman; shopkeeper; wholesale merchant, large retail store; (*Cub.*) wholesale grocer.

almáciga, *n.f.* (*bot.*) mastic; nursery of trees.

almacigado, -da, *a.* perfumed with mastic. — *p.p.* [ALMACIGAR].

almacigar, *v.t.* to perfume with mastic.

almácigo, *n.m.* mastic-tree; plant nursery.

almaciguero, -ra, *a.* relating to a tree nursery.

almádana; ; almádena; ; almádina, *n.f.* large stone hammer.

almadaneta; ; almadeneta, *n.f.* *dim.* [ALMÁDANA].

almadén, *n.m.* mine.

almadía, *n.f.* canoe used in India, raft.

almadiar, *v.i., v.r.* to become or get sea-sick.

almadiero, *n.m.* raft-pilot.

almadraba, *n.f.* tunny-fishery; net used in the tunny-fishery season for fishing tunny.

almadrabero, *n.m.* tunny-fisher.

almadraque, *n.m.* (*obs.*) quilted cushion, mattress.

almadreña, *n.f.* wooden shoe, sabot; clog.

almaganeta, *n.f.* large stone hammer.

almagesto, *n.m.* Almagest.

almagra, *n.f.; ;* **almagre,** *n.m.* red earth, red ochre, Indian red; mark, sign.

almagral, *n.m.* place abounding in red ochre.

almagrar, *v.t.* to colour with red ochre; to defame; to mark; (*vulg.*) to draw blood in a quarrel.

almagre, [ALMAGRA].

almaizal; ; almaizar, *n.m.* gauze veil worn by Moors; sash worn by priests.

almajaneque, *n.m.* (*mil.*) battering-ram.

almajara, *n.f.* ground well manured, forcing-bed.

almajo, *n.m.* seaweed yielding barilla.

almaleque, *n.f.* long robe worn by Moors.

almanac; ; almanaque, *n.m.* almanac, calendar; *hacer almanaques,* to muse, to be pensive; to make hasty predictions.

almanaquero, -ra, *n.m.f.* maker or vendor of almanacs.

almancebe, *n.m.* fishing-net used in Andalusia.

almandina; ; almandino, *n.f.* red garnet; almandine.

almanguena, *n.f.* red ochre, Indian red.

almanta, *n.f.* space between rows of vines and olive-trees; ridge between two furrows; tree nursery; *poner a almanta,* (*agric.*) to plant vines closely and in disorder.

almarada, *n.f.* triangular poniard; needle for making rope sandals; tool used for removing sulphur from steel furnaces.

almarbatar, *v.t.* to join two pieces of wood.

almarcha, *n.f.* town on marshy ground.

almarga, *n.f.* marl-pit.

almario, *n.m.* wardrobe, clothes-press.

almarjal, *n.m.* plantation of glasswort; marshy ground.

almarjo, *n.m.* (*bot.*) glasswort.

almaro, *n.m.* (*bot.*) germander.

almarrá, *n.m.* cotton-gin.

almarraja; almarraza, *n.f.* sprinkling glass bottle.

almártaga; almártega; almártiga, *n.f.* (*chem.*) litharge; sort of halter; massicot; (*Col.*) *n.f.* incapable; good-for-nothing.

almartigón, *n.m.* rough halter.

almástiga, *n.f.* mastic.

almastigado, -da, *a.* containing mastic.

almatrero, *n.m.* one fishing with shad-nets.

almatriche, *n.m.* irrigation canal.

almazara, *n.f.* (*prov.*) oil-mill.

almazarero, *n.m.* oil-miller.

almazarrón, *n.m.* red ochre; Indian red.

almea, *n.f.* Oriental poetess and dancer; bark of the storax-tree; (*bot.*) star-headed water-plantain.

almear, *n.m.* stack of hay, corn or straw.

almecina, *n.f.* (*prov.*) fruit of the lotus-tree.

almeja, *n.f.* mussel, clam, shell-fish.

almejar, *n.m.* mussel-bed, mussel-pool.

almejía, *n.f.* small cloak used by poor Moors.

almena, *n.f.* turret; merlon of a battlement.

almenado; almenaje, *n.m.* series of merlons; battlement.

almenado, -da, *a.* embattled, crowned with merlons. — *p.p.* [ALMENAR].

almenar, *v.t.* to crown with merlons. — *n.m.* cresset.

almenara, *n.f.* beacon; (*prov.*) outlet channel for surplus irrigation water.

almendra, *n.f.* almond; kernel; almond-shaped diamond; cut-glass drop; fine cocoon; *almendras garapiñadas,* sugared almonds; *almendras confitadas,* pralines; *almendras de cacao,* cocoa-beans, chocolate nuts; *almendra mollar,* soft-shelled almond; *dama de la media almendra,* finical, prudish lady.

almendrada, *n.f.* almond milk; *dar una almendrada,* pay a compliment.

almendrado, -da, *a.* almond-like. — *n.m.* macaroon.

almendral, *n.m.* almond-tree; plantation of almond-trees.

almendrera, *n.f.;* **almendrero,** *n.m.* almond-tree; almond salver.

almendrica; almendrilla; almendrita, *n.f.* small almond.

almendrilla, *n.f.* almond-shaped file (locksmith's); gravel for road repair; (*pl.*) almond-shaped diamond ear-rings.

almendro, *n.m.* almond-tree.

almendrón, *n.m.* a Jamaica tree and its fruit.

almendruco, *n.m.* green almond.

almenilla, *n.f.* battlemented ornament, fringe, etc. [ALMENA].

almete, *n.m.* helmet; soldier wearing a helmet.

almez; almezo, *n.m.* (*bot.*) lotus-tree; Indian nettle-tree.

almeza, *n.f.* (*bot.*) fruit of the lotus-tree.

almiar, *n.m.* haystack.

almíbar, *n.m.* syrup.

almibarado, -da, *a.* (*coll.*) soft, endearing (applied to words); effeminate. — *p.p.* [ALMIBARAR].

almibarar, *v.t.* to preserve (fruit) in sugar; to conciliate with soft words.

almíbares, *n.m.pl.* preserved fruit.

almicantarat, *n.f.* (*astron.*) circle parallel to the horizon.

almidón, *n.m.* starch; amylum.

almidonado, -da, *a.* starched; (*coll.*) dressed with affected precision or elegance; spruce; stiff. — *n.m.* starching. — *p.p.* [ALMIDONAR].

almidonar, *v.t.* to starch; *sin almidonar,* unstarched.

almidonería, *n.f.* starch factory or shop.

almidonero, -ra, *n.m.f.* starcher; maker or seller of starch.

almifor, *n.m.* (*slang*) horse.

almifora, *n.f.* (*slang*) she-mule.

almiforero, *n.m.* horse-thief.

almijara, *n.f.* oil-depot, oil-tank (in the Almadén mines).

almijarero, *n.m.* keeper of the *almijara.*

almila, *n.f.* potter's oven.

almilla, *n.f.* close-fitting jacket; short military jacket worn beneath armour; (*carp.*) tenon; breast of pork.

almimbar, *n.m.* pulpit of a mosque.

alminar, *n.m.* minaret, turret of a mosque.

almiranta, *n.f.* (*naut.*) vice-admiral's ship; flagship; admiral's wife.

almirantazgo, *n.m.* (*naut.*) board of admiralty; admiralty court; admiral's dues; admiralship.

almirante, *n.m.* admiral, commander of a fleet; women's headgear; (*prov.*) swimming-master; a kind of shell; *contraalmirante,* rear-admiral.

almirez, *n.m.* brass mortar; wood-engraver's tool of tempered steel.

almirón, *n.m.* (*prov., bot.*) wild chicory.

almizclar, *v.t.* to perfume with musk.

almizcle, *n.m.* musk.

almizcleña, *n.f.* (*bot.*) musk, grape-hyacinth.

almizcleño, -ña, *a.* musky.

almizclera, *n.f.* musk-rat.

almizclero, -ra, *a.* musky. — *n.m.* musk-deer.

almo, -ma, *a.* (*poet.*) creating, vivifying; holy, venerable, sacred; beneficent.

almocadén, *n.m.* captain of infantry (*obs.*); n.c.o. commanding a cavalry platoon; (*Morocco*) justice of peace; sergeant of Moorish levies.

almocafrar, *v.t.* to dibble.

almocafre, *n.m.* gardener's hoe, dibble.

almocárabes; almocarbes, *n.m.pl.* (*arch.*) bow-knot or loop-shaped ornaments.

almocatracía, *n.f.* duty on broadcloths and woollen goods.

almoceda, *n.f.* (*prov.*) impost on water for irrigation; right of irrigation on certain days.

almocela, *n.f.* ancient hood.

almocrate, *n.m.* sal-ammoniac.

almocrí, *n.m.* reader of the Koran in a mosque.

almodí; almudí; almudín, *n.m.* public granary; (*prov.*) measure containing six *cahices* or bushels.

almodón, *n.m.* baking-flour.

almodrote, *n.m.* sauce for egg-plant; (*coll.*) hotch-potch.

almófar, *n.m.* mail head-cover under the helmet.

almofía, *n.f.* wash-bowl, basin.

almoflate, *n.m.* saddler's round knife.

almofrej, *n.m.* travelling canvas or leather bag for mattress; (*Am.*) [ALMOFREZ].

almogama, *n.f.* (*naut.*) stern-post of a ship.

almogárabe; almogávar, *n.m.* expert forager; highly trained soldier in raiding

[51]

enemy's territory (an ancient commando force).

almogavarear, *v.i.* (*mil.*) to make a raid.

almogávares, *n.m.pl.* light Catalan troops who harassed the ancient Moors.

almogavaría; almagavería, *n.f.* body of raiding troops.

almohada, *n.f.* pillow, bolster, cushion; pillow-case; (*arch.*) projecting wall stone; (*naut.*) piece of timber on which the bowsprit rests; *aconsejarse,* or *consultar con la almohada,* to sleep upon it (an idea); *dar almohada,* court function at which the queen used to bestow the grandeeship on a lady; *tomar la almohada,* phrase used of a lady who takes possession of a grandeeship; *hacer la cuenta con la almohada,* to take time for mature consideration.

almohades, *n.m.,* *a.* Almohades.

almohadilla, *n.f.* small bolster or pillow; working case; (*Chi.*) sewing cushion; pads of a harness; (*arch.*) stone projecting from a wall; (*vet.*) callous excrescence on the backs of mules and horses; *cantar a la almohadilla,* to sing to oneself.

almohadillado, -da, *a.* (*arch.*) cushioned. — *n.m.* (*arch.*) relief. — *p.p.* [ALMOHADILLAR].

almohadillar, *v.t.* (*arch.*) to work in relief; to make like ashlar stone.

almohadón, *n.m.* large cushion, large pillow.

almohatre; almojatre, *n.m.* sal-ammoniac.

almohaza, *n.f.* curry-comb; *anda el almohaza, y toca en la matadura,* to hurt someone's feelings in conversation unknowingly.

almohazado, -da, *a.* curried, groomed. — *p.p.* [ALMOHAZAR].

almohazador, *n.m.* groom.

almohazar, *v.t.* to curry, groom with a curry-comb.

almojábana, *n.f.* cake made of cheese and flour; paste of butter, eggs and sugar; cruller.

almojarifadgo; almojarifalgo; almojarifazgo, *n.m.* ancient duty on imports and exports; jurisdiction of the *almojarife.*

almojarife, *n.m.* tax-gatherer for the king; custom-house officer.

almojatre, *n.m.* [ALMOHATRE].

almojaya, *n.f.* putlog, piece of wood inserted in a wall.

almona, *n.f.* public stores; shad-fishery; (*prov.*) soap-manufactory.

almóndiga; almondiguilla, *n.f.* ball of forcemeat.

almoneda, *n.f.* public auction.

almonedear, *v.t.* to sell by auction.

almoradux, *n.m.* (*bot.*) sweet marjoram.

almorávides, *n.m.f.,* *a.* (*pl.*) ancient Moorish tribe; Almoravides.

almorejo, *n.m.* (*bot.*) kind of grass.

almorí; almurí, *n.m.* sweetmeat or cake.

almoronia, *n.f.* [ALBORONÍA].

almorranas, *n.f.pl.* (*med.*) piles.

almorraniento, -ta, *n.m.f.,* *a.* sufferer, suffering from piles.

almorrefa, *n.f.* triangular tile; mosaic floor.

almorta, *n.f.* (*bot.*) blue vetch.

almorzada, *n.f.* double-handful; as much as is contained in the hollow of both hands placed together.

almorzado, -da, *a.* one who has breakfasted or lunched. — *p.p.* [ALMORZAR].

almorzador, *n.m.* breakfast-case.

almorzar, *v.i.* (*pret.* **almorcé;** *pres. indic.* **almuerzo;** *pres. subj.* **almuerce**) to breakfast or lunch (a mid-day meal). — *v.t.* to eat (something) at lunch; *almorzar chuletas,* to eat chops at lunch.

almotacén, *n.m.* inspector of weights and measures; inspector's office; (*Morocco*) overseer of markets.

almotacenazgo, *n.m.* inspector's office and duty.

almotacenía, *n.f.* fee paid to the market-clerk or inspector; inspectorship.

almozárabe, *n.m.f.,* *a.* Christian subject to the Moors in Spain.

almud, *n.m.* measure of grain (about 4·625 litres); *almud de tierra,* a measure of about half an acre.

almudada, *n.f.* ground which takes one *almud* of seed.

almudejo, *n.m.* each of the weights kept by the *almudero.*

almudero, *n.m.* keeper of weights and measures for grain.

almudí; almudín, *n.m.* Castilian measure containing about 4000 litres.

almuecín; almuédano, *n.m.* muezzin.

almuerce, *pres. subj.* [ALMORZAR].

almuérdago, *n.m.* bird-lime.

almuertas, *n.f.pl.* (*prov.*) duty on cereals sold.

almuerza, *n.f.* double-handful.

almuerzo, *v.t.,* *v.i.,* *pres. indic.* [ALMORZAR]. — *n.m.* late breakfast, luncheon; breakfast, luncheon service.

almunia, *n.f.* orchard, vegetable garden.

almutazaf, *n.m.* (*prov.*) inspector of weights and measures.

alnado, -da, *n.m.f.* stepchild.

alo, (*Mex.*) *n.m.* a kind of crested parrot.

aloaria, *n.f.* (*arch.*) vault.

alobadado, -da, *a.* bitten by a wolf; (*vet.*) suffering from anthrax.

alobunado, -da, *a.* wolf-coloured (hair).

alocadamente, *adv.* rashly, inconsiderately.

alocado, -da, *a.* half-witted, foolish; wild.

alocución, *n.f.* allocution, address, harangue; speech.

alodial, *a.* (*law*) allodial, free, exempt.

alodio, *n.m.* freehold possession.

áloe, *n.m.* (*bot.*) aloes-tree, aloes; *palo áloe,* aloes-wood.

aloético, -ca, *a.* aloetic.

aloína, *n.f.* aloin, active principle of aloes.

aloja, *n.f.* metheglin, mead.

alojado, -da, *p.p.* [ALOJAR] (*mil.*) billeted, lodged. — *n.m.* billeted soldier.

alojamiento, *n.m.* lodging, quartering, billeting soldiers; (*naut.*) steerage. — *pl.* (*mil.*) camp, quarters.

alojar, *v.i.,* *v.t.* to lodge, let lodgings; to live, dwell, reside; to quarter, billet troops. — *v.r.* to lodge, put up, take lodgings; (*mil.*) to station; to become sweet, suave (like *aloja*).

alojería, *n.f.* a place where mead is made or sold.

alojero, -ra, *n.m.f.* one who mixes or sells mead; box near the pit in theatres.

alomado, -da, *a.* (*vet.*) having a curved back; (*agric.*) furrowed; equally distributed (load); strong, vigorous (horse). — *p.p.* [ALOMAR].

alomar, *v.t.* to distribute equally the load on a horse; (*agric.*) to furrow. — *v.r.* to grow strong and vigorous (of horses).

alón, *n.m.* plucked wing of any bird.

alondra, *n.f.* (*orn.*) lark.

alongadero, -ra, *a.* dilatory.

alongamiento, *n.m.* delay; distance; separation.

alongar, *v.t.* to enlarge, extend, stretch, lengthen, prolong; to separate. — *v.r.* to become lengthened; to move away.

alonso, *a. trigo alonso*, bearded wheat.

alópata, *n.m.* allopath, allopathist.

alopatía, *n.f.* allopathy.

alopático, -ca, *a.* allopathic.

alopecia, *n.f.* (*med.*) alopecia, baldness.

alopiado, -da, *a.* opiate, composed of opium.

aloque, *a.* of clear white wine, or of red and white wine. — *n.m.* mixture of red and white wine.

aloquín, *n.m.* stone enclosure in a wax bleachery.

alosa, *n.f.* (*ichth.*) shad.

alosna, *n.f.* (*bot.*). wormwood.

alotar, *v.t.* (*naut.*) to reef, stow, lash; *alotar las anclas*, to stow the anchors.

alotropía, *n.f.* (*chem.*) allotropy.

alotrópico, -ca, *a.* (*chem.*) allotropic.

alpaca, *n.f.* alpaca; wool of this animal; fabric made from it; nickel silver.

alpamato, *n.m.* (*Arg.*) (*bot.*) shrub of the Myrtaceæ family used as tea.

alpañata, *n.f.* piece of chamois-skin used for polishing.

alpargata, *n.f.*; **alpargate,** *n.m.* hempen sandal.

alpargatado, -da, *a.* wearing *alpargatas*. — *p.p.* [ALPARGATAR].

alpargatar, *v.i.* to make *alpargatas*.

alpargatazo, *n.m.* blow with an *alpargata*.

alpargatería, *n.f.* manufactory or shop of *alpargatas*.

alpargatero, -ra, *n.m.f.* manufacturer of *alpargatas*.

alpargatilla, *n.f.* small *alpargata*; (*coll.*) crafty, designing person.

alpechín, *n.m.* juice which oozes from a heap of olives.

alpechinera, *n.f.* well or large jar to hold *alpechín*.

alpende, *n.m.* shed for mining tools.

alpes, *n.m.pl.* Alps.

alpestre, *a.* Alpine; (*fig.*) mountainous, wild.

alpicoz, *n.m.* (*prov.*) kind of cucumber.

alpinismo, *n.m.* Alpinism, mountain-climbing.

alpinista, *n.m.f.* Alpinist, mountain-climber.

alpino, -na, *a.* Alpine.

alpiste, *n.m.* canary-seed; *dejar a uno alpiste*, to disappoint; to leave someone out (of a party, project, etc.); *quedarse alpiste*, to be disappointed.

alpistela; alpistera, *n.f.* cake made of flour, eggs, sesame and honey.

alpistero, *n.m.* sieve for canary-seed.

alquequenje, *n.m.* Barbados winter-cherry, used as diuretic.

alquería, *n.f.* grange, farm-house.

alquermes, *n.m.* kermes, cordial; (*pharm.*) medicinal syrup.

alquerque, *n.m.* place in oil-mills where the bruised olives are heaped.

alquez, *n.m.* wine measure containing twelve *cántaras* (*q.v.*).

alquibla, *n.f.* point of the horizon, or mosque, towards which the Mohammedan looks when at prayer.

alquicel; alquicer, *n.m.* Moorish cloak; cover for benches, tables, etc.

alquifol, *n.m.* (*min.*) zaffre, zaffer.

alquil, *n.m.* remuneration, salary.

alquila, *n.f.* " for hire " indicator on vehicles.

alquiladizo, -za, *a.* that which may be let or hired.

alquilador, -ra, *n.m.f.* one who lets coaches or horses on hire.

alquilamiento, *n.m.* act of hiring or letting.

alquilar, *v.t.* to let, hire, rent; to fee. — *v.r.* to serve for wages; to hire oneself.

alquilate, *n.m.* duty paid in Murcia on sales.

alquiler, *n.m.* wages, hire, fee; the act of letting or hiring; *de alquiler*, for hire, to let, rentable; *alquiler de una casa*, house-rent, rental.

alquilón, -na, *a.* which can be let or hired. — *n.m.* vehicle for hire. — *n.f.* woman hired occasionally for odd work.

alquimia, *n.f.* alchemy.

alquímico, -ca, *a.* alchemistic, alchemical, alchemistical.

alquimila, *n.f.* (*bot.*) lady's mantle.

alquimista, *n.m.* alchemist.

alquinal, *n.m.* veil or head-dress for women.

alquitara, *n.f.* still; *por alquitara*, sparingly.

alquitarar, *v.t.* to distil.

alquitira, *n.f.* tragacanth.

alquitrán, *n.m.* pine-tar, liquid pitch; (*naut.*) mixture of pitch, grease, resin and oil; *alquitrán mineral*, coal-tar.

alquitranado, -da, *a.* tarred. — *n.m.* (*naut.*) tarpaulin, tarred cloth; *cabos alquitranados*, (*naut.*) black or tarred cordage. — *p.p.* [ALQUITRANAR].

alquitranar, *v.t.* to tar.

alrededor, *adv.* around; *alrededor de*, about, around. — *n.m.pl.* environs, outskirts.

alrota, *n.f.* coarse kind of tow.

alsaciano, -na, *n.m.f., a.* Alsatian.

alsine, *n.f.* (*bot.*) scorpion-grass.

alta, *n.f.* kind of court dance; dancing exercise; fencing bout; (*mil.*) record of entry into service; discharge from a hospital; (*slang*) window, tower, belfry; *darse de alta*, to enter a profession; *dar de alta*, (*mil.*) to register the return of men to their respective units; *dar de alta*, or *el alta*, (*mil.*) to declare cured and fit for service; *ser alta*, (*mil.*) to return to a regiment after illness.

altabaque, *n.m.* needle-work basket; work-basket.

altabaquillo, *n.m.* (*bot.*) small bindweed or convolvulus.

altamente, *adv.* highly, strongly, extremely, perfectly, entirely; (*fig.*) in a distinguished manner.

altamisa, *n.f.* (*bot.*) mugwort.

altana, *n.f.* (*slang*) temple.

altanado, -da, *a.* (*slang*) married.

altanería, *n.f.* hawking; haughtiness, pride, loftiness, contemptuousness.

altanero, -ra, *a.* soaring, towering (of birds of prey); haughty, arrogant, insolent, proud.

altanos, *a.* (*naut.*) wind blowing alternately from the sea and the land.

altar, *n.m.* stone for sacrifices; altar; communion table; the Church; (*astron.*) southern constellation (*Ara*); *altar mayor*, main altar, high altar; *conducir,* or *llevar al altar a una mujer,* to marry; get married.

altarejo, *n.m.* little altar.

altarero, -ra, *n.m.f.* altar-maker or dresser; one who decks or adorns altars.

altarreina, *n.f.* (*bot.*) milfoil.

altavoz, *n.m.* loud-speaker (of a wireless set).

altea, *n.f.* (*bot.*) marsh-mallow.

altear, *v.t., v.r.* (*naut.*) to rise above the land; to present inequalities (ground).

alterabilidad, *n.f.* changeableness, mutability.

alterable, *a.* changeable, alterable.

alteración, *n.f.* alteration, mutation; change for the worse; unevenness of the pulse; strong emotion; disturbance, commotion, tumult.

alterado, -da, *a.* agitated, disturbed; altered; *caldo alterado,* medicated broth. — *p.p.* [ALTERAR].

alterador, -ra, *n.m.f.* alterer disturber. — *a.* altering, disturbing.

alterante, *a.* altering; (*med.*) alterative.

alterar, *v.t.* to alter, change, transform; to change for the worse; to disturb, stir up; to fling; *alterar la moneda,* to debase the coinage. — *v.r.* to become altered, agitated, disturbed, angry.

alterativo, -va, *a.* alterative.

altercación, *n.f.;* **altercado,** *n.m.* controversy, altercation, contest, strife, wrangle, quarrel.

altercador, -ra, *n.m.f.* wrangler, arguer. — *a.* wrangling, arguing.

altercar, *v.i.* to contend, quarrel, bicker, dispute or argue obstinately, expostulate, wrangle.

alternación, *n.f.* alternation.

alternadamente, *adv.* alternatively, by turns.

alternador, *n.m.* (*elec.*) alternator.

alternar, *v.t.* to alternate, perform by turns, change for something else. — *v.i.* to happen by turns; (*elec.*) to change from positive to negative and back again in turns; *alternar con gente,* to have friendly relations with people; *alternar en el servicio,* to serve alternatively; *alternar entre uno y otro,* to take it in turns.

alternativa, *n.f.* alternative, option, choice; service by turn; (bullfight) ceremony of becoming a full matador.

alternativamente, *adv.* alternatively, by turns.

alternativo, -va, *a.* alternate; *cultivo alternativo,* rotation of crops.

alterno, -na, *a.* alternate.

alteza, *n.f.* Highness (title); height, elevation, sublimity.

altibajo, *n.m.* kind of embossed velvet; downright blow in fencing; (*pl.*) the sinuosities of uneven ground; (*fig.*) vicissitudes, ups and downs.

altilocuencia, *n.f.* grandiloquence.

altilocuente; altílocuo, -cua, *a.* pompous, high-sounding, grandiloquent.

altillo, *n.m.* hillock.

altimetría, *n.f.* (*geom.*) altimetry.

altimétrico, -ca, *a.* (*geom.*) altimetric.

altímetro, -tra, *a.* altimetric. — *n.m.* (*aer.*) altimeter.

altiplanicie, *n.f.* high plateau, tableland.

Altísimo, *n.m.* the Most High; *El Altísimo,* God.

altisonante; altísono, -na, *a.* altisonant, high-sounding.

altitonante, *a.* (*poet.*) thundering.

altitud, *n.f.* altitude, height.

altivamente, *adv.* highly, loftily, in a haughty or lordly way.

altivarse; altivecerse, *v.r.* to put on airs.

altivez; altiveza, *n.f.* haughtiness, insolence, arrogance, pride.

altivo, -va, *a.* haughty, proud, lofty, lordlike; high, high-minded; overbearing.

alto, -ta, *a.* high, lofty elevated, tall; eminent; difficult, arduous; superior; grave, enormous (offence); deep; late; loud, strong (voice); *alta mar,* (*naut.*) high seas; *pasar por alto,* to overlook, *altas horas,* late at night. — *n.m.* height; high ground; story, floor (house); *casa de tres altos,* three-storied house; place or time of rest; (*mus.*) notes put over the bass; (*mil.*) halt! command to stop. — *interj.* stop! *¡alto de aquí!* go away! *¡alto ahí!* stop there! halt there!; *hacer alto,* to halt, stop. — *pl.* (*Chi., Mex., Per.*) stories (as opposed to ground). — *adv.* loudly; highly; *de lo alto,* from above, from heaven; *altos y bajos,* ups and downs; *de alto a abajo,* from top to bottom, from head to foot; *en alto,* up high, above; *lo alto,* the highest point; the sky; *por alto,* by stealth; *por todo lo alto,* very well; *alto horno,* blast-furnace; *alto relieve,* high-relief; *de alto bordo,* large, sea-going (vessel).

altoparlante, *n.m.* wireless loud-speaker.

altor, *n.m.* height.

altozano, *n.m.* height; hill; (*Am.*) atrium; paved terrace or platform in front of a church.

altramuz, *n.m.* (*bot.*) lupine. — *pl. altramuces,* voting black balls.

altruísmo, *n.m.* altruism.

altruísta, *n.m.f.* altruist. — *a.* altruistic.

altura, *n.f.* height, loftiness; elevation, sublimity; summits of mountains; altitude; (*naut.*) latitude; exaltation of spirits; (*geom.*) altitude (of a plane figure); height (of a solid); *las alturas,* the heavens, Heaven; *altura meridiana,* meridian altitude.

alúa, *n.f.* (*Arg.*) glow-worm.

alubia, *n.f.* (*bot.*) French bean.

aluciar, *v.t.* to give a lustre, polish, burnish, brighten. — *v.r.* to become polished, bright.

alucinación, *n.f.;* **alucinamiento,** *n.m.* hallucination.

alucinadamente, *adv.* erroneously, by hallucination.

alucinador, -ora, *n.m.f.* hallucinator.

alucinar, *v.t.* to deceive, delude, fascinate. — *v.i., v.r.* to deceive oneself; *alucinarse con promesas,* to delude oneself with promises; *alucinarse en el negocio,* to become fascinated by business.

alucón, *n.m.* (*orn.*) barn-owl.

alud, *n.m.* avalanche.

aluda, *n.f.* (*ent.*) winged ant or emmet.

aludel, *n.m.* (*chem.*) sublimating pots; aludel.

aludir, *v.i.* to allude, refer.

aludo, -da, *a.* winged, large-winged.

alumbrado, -da, *a.* aluminous; alum-treated; lighted; illuminated; enlightened; (*coll.*) tipsy. — *n.m.* lighting. — *n.m.pl.* the Illuminati. — *p.p.* [ALUMBRAR].

alumbrador, -ora, *n.m.f.* link-boy, lighter. — *a.* illuminating.

alumbramiento, *n.m.* illumination; childbirth.

alumbrante, *a.* illuminating. — *n.m.* (*theat.*) lighting operator.

alumbrar, *v.t.* to light, lighten; to enlighten, shed light, illuminate, instruct; to dip cloth into alum water (in dyeing); (*agric.*) to dig about the roots of vines. — *v.i.* to give light; to give birth to a child. — *v.r.* (*coll.*) to become intoxicated.

alumbre, *n.m.* alum; *alumbre catino,* alkali from glasswort; *alumbre de rasuras,* salt of tartar; *alumbre sacarino,* alum-whey.

alumbrera, *n.f.* (*min.*) alum mine.

alumbrería, *n.f.* alum factory.

alumbrico, -ca; alumbrífero, -ra, *a.* aluminous.

alumbroso, *a.* containing alum.

alúmina, *n.f.* (*chem.*) alumina.

aluminato, *n.m.* (*chem.*) aluminate.

alumínico, -ca, *a.* containing alumina; aluminous.

aluminífero, -ra, *a.* aluminiferous.

aluminio, *n.m.* (*chem.*) aluminium.

aluminita, *n.f.* aluminite.

aluminoso, -sa, *a.* aluminous.

alumno, -na, *n.m.f.* foster-child; disciple, pupil, scholar, student; *alumno de las musas,* (*fig.*) poet.

alunado, -da, *a.* lunatic; spasmodic, jerky from constipation (of horses); long-tusked (boar); tainted (of meat).

alunamiento, *n.m.* (*naut.*) hollow, curve of sail.

alunarse, *v.r.* to become tainted (meat); (*Col.*) (*vet.*) to fester (a sore or gall of a horse).

alunita, *n.f.* (*min.*) alunite, alumstone.

alusión, *n.f.* reference, allusion, hint.

alusivo, -va, *a.* allusive, hinting.

alustrar, *v.t.* to give lustre to.

alutación, *n.f.* (*min.*) stratum of grains of gold.

alutrado, -da, *a.* otter-coloured.

aluvial, *a.* (*geol.*) alluvial.

aluvión, *n.m.* alluvion; alluvium.

alveario, *n.m.* (*anat.*) canal; alveary.

álveo, *n.m.* bed of a river.

alveolar, *a.* (*zool.*) alveolar.

alvéolo, *n.m.* alveolus, alveole, small cavity.

alverja; alverjana, *n.f.* (*bot.*) common vetch.

alvino, -na, *a.* (*med.*) alvine.

alza, *n.f.* piece of leather put round a last to make the shoe wider; (*artill.*) hind-sight; (*com.*) rise; *jugar al alza,* (*com.*) to speculate on a rise; (*print.*) overlay, frisket sheet; instrument used in rope-walks; *alza y baja,* rise and fall of stocks.

alzacuello, *n.m.* clergyman's collar; neck-stock or tie.

alzada, *n.f.* height, stature (of horses); appeal; *juez de alzadas,* judge in appeal cases.

alzadamente, *adv.* wholesale, in heaps, for a lump sum.

alzado, -da, *a.* fixed (sum); raised. — *n.m.* fraudulent bankrupt; (*arch.*) front elevation; (*print.*) co-ordinating the sheets of a work; (*prov.*) robbery, fraud. — *p.p.* [ALZAR].

alzador, -ra, *a.* lifting, raising. — *n.m.* (*print.*) gatherer; gathering-room.

alzadura, *n.f.*; **alzamiento,** *n.m.* elevation, raising, lifting; outbidding (auction); revolt; fraudulent bankruptcy.

alzafuelles, *n.m.f.* flatterer.

alzapaño, *n.m.* curtain-holder or loop.

alzapié, *n.m.* snare.

alzaprima, *n.f.* lever, wedge; (*naut.*) heaver; (*mech.*) fulcrum.

alzaprimar, *v.t.* to raise with a lever; (*fig.*) to incite, spur on.

alzapuertas, *n.m.* figurant; dumb player; supernumerary.

alzar, *v.t.* (*pret.* **alcé**; *pres. subj.* **alce**) to raise (price, load, siege, voice, etc.); to heave, lift up; to construct; to erect; to carry off; to displace; to hide; to lock up; to cut (cards); (*print.*) to collate printed sheets; to elevate the host in celebrating mass; (*naut.*) to heave; to recall from exile; to repeal a decree of excommunication; *alzar de precio,* to raise the price; *alzar de codo* (or *el codo*), to drink much; *alzar la cresta,* to be elated with pride; *alzar el dedo,* to raise the fore-finger in affirmation; *alzar la casa, los reales,* to leave a house, break up house or camp; *alzar velas,* (*naut.*) to set the sails; to move; *alzar cabeza,* to recover from a calamity or disease; *alzar figura,* to cut a dash, assume an air of importance; *alzar los naipes,* to cut the cards; *alzar un entredicho,* to raise an injunction; *alzar la mesa,* to clear away the table (after meals); *alzar la tienda,* to close the shop; *alzar el grito,* to cry out; to claim; *alzar la mano,* to threaten; *alzar mano,* to abandon; *alzar por jefe, rey,* to proclaim as chief, king. — *v.r.* to rise in revolt; (*law*) to appeal; to rise from one's knees; *alzarse los manteles,* to clear the table (after meals); *alzarse a las nubes,* to rise up to the clouds; *alzarse con el reino,* to usurp the kingdom; *alzarse en rebelión,* to rise in revolt; *alzarse con el banco,* to make a fraudulent bank-ruptcy; *alzarse con el dinero,* to abscond with, embezzle, run away with, steal (money); *alzarse con el santo y con la limosna,* to make off with everything.

alzatirantes, *n.m.pl.* harness-straps to suspend the traces.

allá, *adv.* there, yonder, in that place; thither; formerly, of old; *allá él,* (*allá Vd*) that's his (or your) look out; *allá en las Indias,* yonder in the Indies; *allá en mis mocedades,* formerly, in my young days; *¡allá va con Dios!* (*naut.*) about ship!; *¡allá va Sancho con su rocín!* there go the inseparables; *allá veremos,* we shall see, that remains to be seen; *tan allá,* far, beyond; *más allá,* farther; *muy allá,* much beyond, far beyond; *por allá,* there, thereabouts; *allá se las haya,* let him shift for himself; *¡allá va eso!,* look out!; *él allá, ella allá,* I don't care.

allanador, -ra, *n.m.f.* leveller. — *n.m.* gold-beater's paper. — *a.* levelling.

allanamiento, *n.m.* levelling; smoothing; consent; affability; (*law*) submission to a judicial decision; *allanamiento de morada,* (*law*) breaking and entering into.

allanar, *v.t.* to level, make even; to flatten; to remove difficulties; to pacify, quiet, subdue. — *v.r.* to acquiesce, conform; to fall to ruin; to abide by; *allanar el camino,* to pave the way for obtaining something; *allanar la casa,* to break into a house; *allanar hasta el suelo,* to raze to the ground; *allanarse a lo justo,* to acquiesce in what is right.

allariz, *n.m.* kind of linen manufactured at Allariz in Galicia.

allegadizo, -za, *a.* collected without choice.

allegado, -da, *n.m.f.* relation, intimate friend, ally; adept. — *a.* near, conjunct. — *p.p.* [ALLEGAR].

allegador, -ra, *a.* gathering, collecting. — *n.m.f.* gatherer, collector. — *n.m.* board for gathering threshed wheat; poker.

allegamiento, *n.m.* collection, union; collecting, uniting; reaping, gathering; close friendship, relationship.

allegar, *v.t.* (*pret.* **allegué;** *pres. subj.* **allegue**) to collect, reap, unite; to gather threshed corn or wheat; to solicit, procure. — *v.i.* to arrive. — *v.r.* to come near, approach; to be acquainted; to adhere, agree.

allende, *adv.* on the other side, beyond; besides; *allende el mar,* overseas.

allí, *adv.* there, yonder, in that place; then; *aquí y allí,* here and there; *de allí,* thence; *por allí,* there, through there, by there; *allí está,* there is; *allí mismo,* in that very place; *allí suena el timbre,* there goes the bell.

alloza, *n.f.* green wild almond.

allozar, *n.m.* ground planted with wild almond-trees.

allozo, *n.m.* (*bot.*) wild almond-tree.

alludel, *n.m.* [ALUDEL].

ama, *n.f.* mistress of the house; landlady; woman owner; *ama de llaves, ama de gobierno,* housekeeper; *ama de cría, de leche,* wet-nurse; *ama seca,* children's nurse.

amabilidad, *n.f.* kindliness, amiability, charm.

amabilísimo, -ma, *a. superl.* extremely kind, affable, courteous.

amable, *a.* amiable, kindly, kind, affable.

amablemente, *adv.* amiably, courteously, kindly.

amacayo, *n.m.* (*Am.*) (*bot.*) flower-de-luce.

amaceno, -na, *a.* Damascene. — *n.m.* (*bot.*) damson, damson plum.

amacigado, -da, *a.* of yellowish or mastic colour.

amación, *n.f.* (mystic) love; deep love.

amacollarse, *v.r.* (*agric.*) to throw out shoots.

amacrático, -ca, *a.* amacratic.

amachetear, *v.t.* to strike and cut with a machete.

amachinarse, *v.r.* (*Cent. Am., Col., Mex.*) to live in concubinage.

amadamado, -da, *a.* effeminate. — *p.p.* [AMA-DAMARSE].

amadamarse, *v.r.* to become effeminate.

amado, -da, *n.m.f.* beloved, sweetheart. — *p.p.* [AMAR].

amador, -ra, *n.m.f.* lover, sweetheart, suitor. — *a.* loving.

amadrigar, *v.t.* (*pret.* **amadrigué;** *pres. subj.* **amadrigue**) to receive well, especially one not deserving. — *v.r.* to burrow; to live in retirement.

amadrinar, *v.t.* to couple, yoke together; (*naut.*) to join one thing to another; to act as godmother or bridesmaid; to favour, uphold. — *v.r.* to help mutually; (*Am.*) to become tame (horses).

amadroñado, -da, *a.* resembling arbutus-berries (*madroños*).

amaestradamente, *adv.* magisterially.

amaestrado, -da, *a.* taught, tutored, schooled, practised, versed, expert; *caballo amaestrado,* horse completely broken in. — *p.p.* [AMAES-TRAR].

amaestradura, *n.f.* artifice, deception, trickery, deceit.

amaestramiento, *n.m.* instruction, training, coaching.

amaestrar, *v.t.* to instruct; to break in, tame; to master, dominate; to lead; to train, coach; *amaestrar un caballo,* to break in a horse. — *v.r.* to train, teach oneself.

amagar, *v.t.* to threaten. — *v.i.* to show a threatening attitude; to have some symptoms of a disease; to manifest a desire; to design, feign; to hint; to be impending. — *v.r.* (*coll.*) to hide.

amago, *n.m.* threat, threatening; symptom of disease.

amago, *n.m.* bitter stuff found in some bee-cells; nausea, loathing.

amainar, *v.t.* (*naut.*) to lower the sails; to relax. — *v.i.* to subside, lessen, moderate. — *v.r.* to yield; to give way to.

amaine, *n.m.* the act of lowering the sails.

amaitinar, *v.t.* to observe attentively; to watch closely; to spy.

amajadar, *v.t.* to enclose sheep in a field in order to fertilize it. — *v.i.* to be in the fold (sheep, goats, etc.).

amalecita; amalequita, *n.m.f., a.* Amalekite.

amalgama, *n.f.* (*chem.*) amalgam.

amalgamación, *n.f.* amalgamation.

amalgamador, -ra, *n.m.f.* amalgamator. — *a.* amalgamating.

amalgamar, *v.t.* to amalgamate. — *v.r.* to become amalgamated.

amallarse, *v.r.* (*Chi.*) to leave a gambling party when winning money.

amamantamiento, *n.m.* suckling, nursing.

amamantar, *v.t.* to nurse; to suckle, give suck.

Amán, *n.m.* (Muscat and) Oman.

amán, *n.m.* (*Morocco*) peace, amnesty.

amancebamiento, *n.m.* concubinage.

amancebarse, *v.r.* to live in concubinage.

amancillar, *v.t.* to stain; to pollute; to offend; to injure; to tarnish someone's reputation; to defame.

amandina, *n.f.* (*chem.*) amandine.

amanear, *v.t.* to hobble (horse).

amanecer, *v.i.* (*pres. indic.* **amanezco;** *pres. subj.* **amanezca**) to dawn; to arrive at break of day; to begin to appear; *cuando Dios amanece, para todos aparece,* the sun shines on the just and the unjust; *por mucho madrugar, no amanece más temprano,* it dawns none the sooner because we rise early. — *n.m.* dawn; *al amanecer,* at daybreak.

amanecida, *n.f.* daybreak.

amaneciente, *a.* that which begins to appear, dawning; *arreboles al oriente, agua amaneciente,* red sky in the evening, rain in the morning.

amaneradamente, *adv.* affectedly.

amanerado, -da, *a.* full of mannerisms. — *p.p.* [AMANERARSE].

amanerarse, *v.r.* to adopt a mannerism; to become affected.

amanezco; amanezca, *pres. ind.; pres. subj.* [AMANECER].

amanita, *n.f.* (*bot.*) agaric.

amanojamiento; amanojeo, *n.m.* handful.

amanojar, *v.t.* to gather by handfuls.

amansador, -ra, *n.m.f.* tamer, subduer; appeaser; (*Chi., Ec., Mex.*) horse breaker. — *a.* taming, subduing, appeasing.

amansamiento, *n.m.* taming.

amansar, *v.t.* to tame, subdue, pacify; to domesticate. — *v.r.* to become tamed *or* domesticated.

amantar, *v.t.* (*coll.*) to cover with any loose garment; to cloak.

amante, *n.m.f.* lover, sweetheart. — *a.* loving. — *n.m.pl.* (*naut.*) moorings; hawser.

amantillar, *v.t.* (*naut.*) to top lifts; to hoist one end of the yard-arm higher than the other.

amantillo, *n.m.* (*naut.*) lift.

amanuense, *n.m.* amanuensis, clerk.

amanzamiento, *n.m.* (*Arg.*) dividing a plot of land into squares.

amanzanar, *v.t.* (*Arg.*) to divide an area into squares so that each side faces a street.

amañar, *v.t.* to do a thing cleverly. — *v.r.* to be handy, to accustom oneself to do things with skill; *amañarse a escribir*, to get used to writing; *amañarse con cualquiera*, to get on well with anybody.

amaño, *n.m.* cleverness, cunning way of doing a thing. — *pl.* tools, instruments; intrigue, machinations.

amapola, *n.f.* (*bot.*) poppy, papaver.

amar, *v.t.* to love, like, fancy; to have a tendency to; *quien feo ama, hermoso le parece*, love is blind; *amar de corazón*, to love wholeheartedly; *amar con locura*, to love madly.

amaracino, *a.* (*pharm.*) containing marjoram. — *n.m.* ointment made of marjoram.

amáraco, *n.m.* (*bot.*) marjoram.

amaraje, *n.m.* (*aer.*) seaplane alighting or landing on the water.

amarantáceo, -cea, *a.* (*bot.*) amaranthine. — *n.f.pl.* (*bot.*) Amaranthaceæ.

amarantina, *n.f.* (*bot.*) amaranthine.

amaranto, *n.m.* (*bot.*) amaranth.

amarar, *v.t.* (*aer.*) to alight on the water.

amargado, -da, *a.* embittered. — *p.p.* [AMARGAR].

amargaleja, *n.f.* (*bot.*) bitter or wild plum.

amargamente, *adv.* bitterly.

amargar, *v.t.* (*pret.* **amargué**; *pres. subj.* **amargue**) to make bitter; to cause bitterness; to give pain, exasperate, offend; *cada día gallina, amarga la cocina*, constant repetition wearies; *la verdad amarga*, truth is bitter. — *v.i.* to be bitter. — *v.r.* to become bitter.

amargo, -ga, *a.* bitter; with an acrid taste; painful, dolorous. — *n.m.* bitterness, bitter taste; sweetmeat of bitter almonds; (*pl.*) bitters; *amargo al gusto*, bitter to the taste; *amargo de sabor*, bitter in taste.

amargón, *n.m.* (*bot.*) dandelion.

amargor, *n.m.* bitterness; vexation; sorrow; *quitarse el amargor de la boca*, to satisfy a whim or desire.

amargosamente, *adv.* bitterly.

amargoso, -sa, *a.* bitter.

amarguera, *n.f.* (*bot.*) wild horse-radish.

amarguillo, -lla, *a.* rather bitter. — *n.m.* bitter-almond sweetmeat.

amargura, *n.f.* bitterness, acerbity; sorrow.

amaricado, -da, *a.* (*coll.*) effeminate, womanish.

amarilídeo, -dea, *a.* (*bot.*) amaryllidaceous; *n.f.pl.* (*bot.*) amaryllidaceæ.

amarilis, *n.f.* (*bot.*) amaryllis.

amarilla, *n.f.* gold coin, especially the *onza;* liver disease of sheep.

amarillazo, -za, *a.* of a pale yellow colour.

amarillear, *v.i.* to incline to yellow; to be yellowish. — *v.t.* to make yellow.

amarillecer, *v.i.* to turn, become yellow.

amarillejo, -ja; amarillento, -ta, *a.* yellowish, inclining to yellow, yellowy.

amarillez, *n.f.* yellowness (of the body); paleness, pallor.

amarillo, -lla, *a.* yellow, gold colour. — *n.m.* yellow; jaundice; yellow fever; disease of silkworms; (*Arg.*) large tree with fine wood, of Leguminosæ family and order of the Mimosa.

amarilloso, -sa, *a.* yellowish.

amarinado, -da, *a.* accustomed to the sea; salted (fish). — *p.p.* [AMARINAR].

amarinar, *v.t.* to salt (fish); (*naut.*) to man (a ship).

amariposado, -da, *a.* (*bot.*) papilionaceous; butterfly-like.

amaro, *n.m.* (*bot.*) common clary.

amarra, *n.f.* (*naut.*) cable, hawser; martingale; (*naut.*) a word of command, corresponding to the English belay, lash or fasten; (*fig.*) protection shelter; *cortar las amarras*, to cut the cable; to be independent; to go off on one's own account.

amarraco, *n.m.* score of five points (card game).

amarradero, *n.m.* tying, hitching post; (*fig.*) tie, obligation, restriction; (*naut.*) mooring berth.

amarrado, -da, *a.* fastened; moored. — *p.p.* [AMARRAR].

amarradura, *n.f.* tying, fastening; (*naut.*) moorage.

amarraje, *n.m.* (*naut.*) moorage tax.

amarrar, *v.t.* to tie, fasten, lash; to cheat (at cards); *amarrar a un tronco*, to tie on a post.

amarrazones, *n.m.pl.* (*naut.*) ground-tackle.

amarre, *n.m.* (*naut.*) tying, fastening, mooring; cheating (at cards).

amarrido, -da, *a.* dejected, gloomy, melancholy.

amarro, *n.m.* [AMARRA].

amartelado, -da, *a.* madly in love. — *p.p.* [AMARTELAR].

amartelamiento, *n.m.* (*coll.*) excessive gallantry.

amartelar, *v.t.* to enamour; to court a woman; to love devotedly. — *v.r.* to fall in love.

amartillar, *v.t.* to hammer; to cock (a gun or pistol).

amarulencia, *n.f.* resentment, bitterness.

amasadera, *n.f.* kneading-trough.

amasadero, *n.m.* kneading-place.

amasador, -ra, *n.m.f.* kneader; mason's labourer who mixes the mortar. — *a.* kneading.

amasadura, *n.f.* kneading.

amasamiento, *n.m.* act of uniting or joining; kneading; (*med.*) massage.

amasar, *v.t.* to knead, mould; to arrange matters for some purpose (usually bad); (*med.*) to massage.

amasijo, *n.m.* dough; the act of kneading; a quantity of mortar; medley; task; plotting agreement; kneading-place.

amatar, (*Ec.*) *v.t.* to cause a sore on a horse.

amate, (*Mex.*) *n.m.* a fig-tree whose juice is used as a resolvent.

amatista, *n.f.* (*min.*) amethyst.

amatividad, *n.f.* (*phrenol.*) amativeness.
amatorio, -ria, *a.* amatory, loving.
amaurosis, *n.f.* (*med.*) amaurosis.
amaurótico, -ca, *a.* (*med.*) amaurotic.
amauta, *n.m.* (*Am.*) sage among the ancient Incas.
amayorazgado, -da, *a.* entailed. — *p.p.* [AMAYORAZGAR].
amayorazgar, *v.t.* to entail.
amazacotado, -da, *a.* heavy, roughly made, thick; incoherent, dull, clumsy (writings).
amazona, *n.f.* Amazon; mannish woman; lady rider; riding-habit; (*Brazil*) a large parrot.
amazónico, -ca; amazonio, -nia, *a.* Amazonian.
amazorcado, -da, *a.* terminating in different colours (flowers).
amba, *n.f.* (*bot.*) fruit of the mangrove.
ambages, *n.m.pl.* maze; circumlocution; roundabout expression.
ambagioso, -sa, *a.* ambiguous.
ámbar, *n.m.* amber; *ámbar gris,* ambergris; *ámbar negro,* jet; *es un ámbar,* it is excellent; it is very sweet (wine, liquor).
ambarar, *v.t.* to perfume with amber.
ambarilla, *n.f.* (*bot.*) amber-seed.
ambarina, *n.f.* (*chem.*) ambrine.
ambarino, -na, *a.* relating to amber; amberlike.
ambición, *n.f.* aspiration, ambition; envy, greed.
ambicionar, *v.t.* to aspire to; to covet.
ambiciosamente, *adv.* ambitiously, highly.
ambicioso, -sa, *a.* ambitious, aspiring; highminded; covetous; greedy; (*bot.*) climbing. — *n.m.f.* glutton; (*bot.*) climber.
ambidextro, -tra, *a.* ambidextrous.
ambiente, *a.* ambient; surrounding. — *n.m.* atmosphere, environment, surroundings.
ambigú, *n.m.* collation (evening); refreshment bar, buffet, refreshment place or room.
ambiguamente, *adv.* ambiguously, doubtfully, uncertainly.
ambigüedad, *n.f.* ambiguity, doubt, uncertainty.
ambiguo, -gua, *a.* ambiguous, doubtful.
ámbito, *n.m.* circuit, circumference, compass, limited space; scope, limit.
amblador, -ra, *n.m.f.* ambler. — *a.* ambling (animals).
amblar, *v.i.* to amble, pace.
ambleo, *n.m.* short and thick wax-candle; candlestick for same.
ambligonio, -nia, *a.* obtuse-angled.
ambliopía, *n.f.* (*med.*) amblyopia, weakness of sight.
ambo, *n.m.* combination of two numbers in lotto.
ambón, *n.m.* ambon; (*eccles.*) either of two pulpits on each side of the altar in some churches.
ambos, -bas, *a.pl.* both; *ambos a dos, ambas a dos,* both, both together.
ambrosía, *n.f.* ambrosia; (*fig.*) any delicious viand or liquor; *ambrosía campestre,* (*bot.*) buckthorn.
ambrosiano, -na, *a.* Ambrosian.
ambuesta, *n.f.* contents held in the hollow of two hands.
ambulación, *n.f.* ambulation.
ambulancia, *n.f.* (*mil.*) ambulance; field-hospital; *ambulancia de correos,* mail coach.

ambulanciero, -ra, *n.m.f.* ambulance attendant; nurse.
ambulante, *a.* ambulatory, roving, of no fixed abode. — *n.m. ambulante de correos,* mailcoach official.
ambular, *v.i.* to go from place to place; to have no fixed abode.
ambulativo, -va, *adv.* of a roving turn, ambulatory, shifting.
ambulatorio, -ria, *a.* ambulatory.
amebeo, -bea, *n.m.f., a.* dialogue in verse.
amechar, *v.t.* to put wicks in lamps, candles; to lard (meat).
amedrentador, -ra, *n.m.f.* threatener, discourager. — *a.* threatening, terrifying, frightening.
amedrentar, *v.t.* to frighten, discourage, deter, intimidate. — *v.r.* to become terrified or frightened.
ámel, *n.m.* chief of an Arabian district.
amelar, *v.i.* to make honey (bees).
amelcochar, *v.t.* (*Am.*) to pulp molasses into syrup.
amelga, *n.f.* ridge between two furrows.
amelgado, *n.m.* (*prov.*) hillock, boundary; unevenly grown wheat. — *p.p.* [AMELGAR].
amelgar, *v.t.* to open furrows; to mark boundaries with mounds.
amelía, *n.f.* district governed by an ámel.
amelo, *n.m.* (*bot.*) golden starwort.
amelonado, -da, *a.* melon-shaped; (*coll.*) stupid.
amén, *n.m.* amen, so be it; *amén de,* besides, in addition to; *ser sacristán de amén, decir a todo amén,* to be always of the same opinion as others; *en un decir amén,* in an instant. — *adv.* with the exception of; besides.
amenaza, *n.f.* threat, menace.
amenazador, -ra, *n.m.f.* one who threatens. — *a.* threatening.
amenazante, *a.* minacious, menacing, impending.
amenazar, *v.t.* (*pret.* **amenacé;** *pres. subj.* **amenace**) to threaten, menace, be impending; *amenazar de muerte,* to threaten with death; *amenazar con multa,* to menace with a fine.
amencia, *n.f.* (*obs.*) dementia.
amenguamiento, *n.m.* diminution, shortage.
amenguar, *v.t.* to defame, dishonour; to diminish, grow short or less.
amenidad, *n.f.* amenity, agreeableness; pleasantness of language.
amenizar, *v.t.* (*pret.* **amenicé;** *pres. subj.* **amenice**) to make pleasant or agreeable; to adorn (a speech).
ameno, -na, *a.* pleasant, delicious, delightful; elegant.
amenorrea, *n.f.* (*med.*) amenorrhœa, suppression of the menses.
amentáceo, -cea, *a.* (*bot.*) amentaceous.
amentar, *v.t.* to lace (shoes, etc.).
amento, *n.m.* shoe-lace; leather string; (*bot.*) ament.
amerar, *v.t.* to soak, mix liquids with water. — *v.r.* to percolate, soak.
amerengado, -da, *a.* like meringue, containing meringue; (*coll.*) affected, prudish.
americana, *n.f.* coat, jacket.
americanismo, *n.m.* (*gram.*) Americanism (applied to S. American words and phrases); admiration, sympathy for anything American.

americanista, *n.m.f.* one who studies American matters.

americanizar, *v.t.* to Americanize. — *v.r.* to become American.

americano, -na, *n.m.f., a.* American (particularly applied to Hispanic America).

amerindo, -da, *a.* American Indian.

amestizado, -da, *a.* mestizo-like.

ametalado, -da, *a.* brass-coloured; sonorous as metal.

ametista, *n.f.; ametisto,* *n.m.* (*min.*) amethyst.

ametralladora, *n.f.* mitrailleuse, machine-gun.

ametrallar, *v.t.* to fire shrapnel; to machine-gun.

amia, *n.f.* shark.

amianto, *n.m.* (*min.*) amianthus, asbestos.

amiba, *n.f.* amœba.

amiboideo, -dea, *a.* amœboid, amœbic.

amicísimo, -ma, *a. superl.* most friendly.

amida, *n.f.* (*chem.*) amide.

amidina, *n.f.* (*chem.*) amidin.

amidol, *n.m.* (*phot.*) amidol.

amiento, *n.m.* leather strap to secure helmet; shoelace; leather string.

amiga, *n.f.* (*prov.*) school for girls; mistress at such a school; female friend; mistress, concubine.

amigable, *a.* friendly; fit, suitable.

amigablemente, *adv.* amicably, in a friendly way.

amigar, *v.t.* to make (others) friends; to make acquainted. — *v.r.* to become friends; to live in concubinage.

amigdaláceo, -cea, *a.* (*bot.*) amygdalaceous. — *n.f.pl.* Amygdalaceæ.

amígdalas, *n.f.pl.* (*med.*) amygdalæ; tonsils.

amigdalina, *n.f.* (*chem.*) amygdalin.

amigdalitis, *n.f.* amygdalitis, tonsillitis.

amigo, -ga, *n.m.f.* friend, comrade; lover. — *n.m.* man living in concubinage. — *a.* friendly, fond; *muy amigo mío,* a great friend of mine; *un amigo del asa,* an intimate, a familiar friend; *es amigo de dar consejos,* he is fond of giving advice; *no hay mejor amigo que un duro en la faltriquera,* money is the best friend after all; *no hay amigo para amigo,* friendship is a poor stand-by; *al amigo y al caballo, no apretallo,* don't overwork a friend; *amigo reconciliado, enemigo doblado,* don't trust a reconciled friend; *a muertos y a idos, no hay (más) amigos,* out of sight, out of mind; *cuanto más amigos, más claros,* let there be no secrets between friends; *entre amigos y soldados, cumplimientos son excusados,* friends never stand on ceremony; *más vale un amigo que pariente ni primo,* a friend is often better than a relative; *cara de pocos amigos,* stern-faced, austere; *al amigo con su vicio,* a friend, in spite of his faults; *al amigo que no es cierto, con un ojo cerrado y el otro abierto,* be cautious with an uncertain friend; *aquel es tu amigo, que te quita de ruidos,* a friend in need is a friend indeed; *amigo de taza de vino,* friend through motives of interest, sponger.

amigote, *n.m.* (*coll.*) great friend.

amiláceo, -cea, *a.* amylaceous, starchy.

amilanado, -da, *a.* terrified, cowed. — *p.p.* [AMILANAR].

amilanamiento, *n.m.* terror, fright; abject fear; cowardice.

amilanar, *v.t.* to frighten, terrify; to stupefy; to cow. — *v.r.* to become terrified, cowed.

amillaramiento, *n.m.* assessment of a tax.

amillarar, *v.t.* to assess a tax on.

amillonado, -da, *a.* liable to pay a tax called *millones;* wealthy, opulent. — *n.m.f.* millionaire, very rich person.

amimar, *v.t.* to wheedle, flatter, fondle.

amín, *n.m.* (*Morocco*) tax collector.

aminorar, *v.t.* to diminish, lessen.

amir, *n.m.* ameer, amir.

amiri, *a.* applied to the descendants of Ibn Abī'Āmir Mohammed (called Almanzor in Spain).

amistad, *n.f.* friendship, amity; concubinage; commerce; gallantry; *amistad de yerno, sol en invierno,* friendships between fathers-in-law and sons-in-law are short-lived; *hacer las amistades,* to become reconciled, make up; *romper las amistades,* to fall out.

amistar, *v.t.* to reconcile enemies, to make (others) friends. — *v.r.* to become reconciled; to become acquainted, or friends.

amistosamente, *adv.* in a friendly way, amicably.

amistoso, -sa, *a.* friendly, amicable, cordial.

amito, *n.m.* (*eccles.*) amice.

amnesia, *n.f.* (*med.*) amnesia, loss of memory.

amnios, *n.m.* (*zool.*) amnion, fœtal envelope.

amniótico, -ca, *a.* amniotic.

amnistía, *n.f.* amnesty.

amnistiar, *v.t.* to give amnesty, grant pardon.

amo, *n.m.* master; master of a house; employer; head of a family; proprietor; overseer; foster-father; lord; (*coll.*) boss; (*Chi., Mex.*) *nuestro amo,* the consecrated host; *amo de casa,* householder; *el ojo del amo engorda el ganado,* the best work is done in the master's presence; *asentar con amo,* to contract for service.

amoblar, *v.t.* to furnish.

amoceto, *n.m.* larva of river lamprey.

amodita, *n.f.* kind of horned serpent.

amodorrado, -da, *a.* heavy with sleep; drowsy. — *p.p.* [AMODORRARSE].

amodorramiento, *n.m.* drowsiness, sleepiness.

amodorrarse, *v.r.* to be drowsy, grow heavy with sleep.

amodorrido, -da, *a.* heavy with sleep; drowsy.

amogotado, -da, *a.* (*naut.*) like a hillock; pap-like.

amohecerse, *v.r.* (*pres. indic.* **amohezco**; *pres. subj.* **amohezca**) to grow rusty or mouldy.

amohinar, *v.t.* to irritate, worry; fret. — *v.r.* to become annoyed, fretful, peevish.

amojamado, -da, *a.* (*fig.*) dried-up, thin; like dried, smoked tunny-fish.

amojamar, *v.t.* to dry and smoke (tunny-fish). — *v.r.* to become dried up.

amojonador, *n.m.* one who sets landmarks.

amojonamiento, *n.m.* setting of landmarks.

amojonar, *v.t.* to set landmarks to.

amoladera, *n.f.* whetstone, grindstone.

amolador, *n.m.* whetter, grinder; sharpener; (*coll.*) bore, tiresome person. — *a.* grinding, sharpening, whetting.

amoladura, *n.f.* whetting *or* grinding. — *pl.* grit.

amolar, *v.t.* (*pres. indic.* **amuelo**; *pres. subj.*

amuele) to whet, grind; (*coll.*) to bore, weary.

amoldador, -ra, *n.m.f.* moulder. — *a.* moulding.

amoldar, *v.t.* to figure, cast in a mould; to polish (needles); (*obs.*) to brand (cattle); to adjust. — *v.r.* to adapt, adjust oneself.

amole, *n.m.* (*Mex.*) name of several plants whose bulbs and rhizomes are used as soap.

amollador, -ra, *n.m.f.* one who lets pass a winning card.

amollar, *v.t.* to play an inferior card to a winning one; (*naut.*) to ease off. — *v.i.* to cede; to weaken, desist.

amolletado, -da, *a.* shaped like a French loaf.

amomo, *n.m.* (*bot.*) grain of paradise.

amondongado, -da, *a.* (*coll.*) sallow, coarse; fat.

amonedación, *n.f.* coinage; coining.

amonedado, -da, *a.* coined; (*coll.*) rich. — *p.p.* [AMONEDAR].

amonedar, *v.t.* to coin.

amonestación, *n.f.* advice, admonition, warning; marriage banns; *correr las amonestaciones,* to publish banns of marriage.

amonestador, -ra, *n.m.f.* monitor; admonisher. — *a.* admonishing, warning.

amonestar, *v.t.* to advise, counsel, forewarn, admonish; to publish banns of marriage. — *v.r.* to be advised or admonished.

amoniacal, *a.* ammoniacal, ammoniated.

amoníaco, *n.m.* ammoniac, ammonia; gum resin.

amónico, -ca, *a.* ammoniac, ammoniacal; ammoniated.

amonio, *n.m.* (*chem.*) ammonium.

amonita, *n.f.* (*zool.*) ammonite.

amontarse, *v.r.* to take to the mountains.

amontillado, *n.m.* variety of sherry.

amontonadamente, *adv.* in heaps.

amontonador, -ra, *n.m.f.* heaper, gatherer, accumulator.

amontonamiento, *n.m.* act of heaping, accumulating, gathering; conglomeration.

amontonar, *v.t.* to heap, pile or throw things together, without order or choice; to accumulate, gather, hoard, lay up, congest, agglomerate; to group a crowd of figures in a painting; *amontonar dinero,* (*fig.*) to coin money. — *v.r.* (*coll.*) to fly into a passion; (*coll.*) to live in concubinage.

amor, *n.m.* love, tenderness, affection; fancy; object of one's love; word of endearment; (*bot.*) great bur parsley, burdock; *amor de hortelano,* (*bot.*) goosegrass; *amor al uso,* (*bot.*) kind of abelmosk; *amor patrio,* love of country; *amor con amor se paga,* diamond cut diamond; the payment should fit the debt; *al amor del fuego,* or *de la lumbre,* by the fireside, or firelight; *amor loco, yo por vos y vos por otro,* love is sometimes perverse; *a su amor,* comfortably, easily; *dar como por amor de Dios,* to give with a bad grace; *en amor y compaña,* in friendship, harmoniously; *por amor de,* on account of, because of; *amor al arte,* love of art; *amor a Dios,* love of God; *al amor de agua,* with the current; *amor mío,* my love; *por amor de Dios,* for God's sake; *amor propio,* self-esteem, amour propre, love of oneself, conceit; *amor de niños, agua en cestillo,* youthful love soon passes; *amor de padre, que todo lo*

demás es aire, a father's love alone can be depended on; *donde hay dolor, hay dolor,* a friend will bear a friend's infirmities. — *pl.* **amores,** gallantry; amours; love affairs; *con* (or *de*) *mil amores,* with the greatest pleasure.

amoral, *a.* amoral, non-moral.

amoralidad, *n.f.* amorality.

amoralismo, *n.m.* (*phil.*) amoralism.

amoratado, -da, *a.* livid, ghastly. — *p.p.* [AMORATAR].

amoratar, *v.t.* to make livid or violet-coloured. — *v.r.* to become livid or purple-coloured.

amorcillo, *n.m.* figurine of Cupid.

amordazar, *v.t.* (*pret.* **amordacé**; *pres. subj.* **amordace**) to gag, muzzle; (*naut.*) to fasten with bitts; to deprive of the liberty of speaking or writing.

amorecer, *v.t.* to mate the ram with the ewe.

amores; amores mil, *n.m.* (*bot.*) red valerian.

amorfia, *n.f.* amorphism; organic deformity.

amorfo, -fa, *a.* amorphous.

amorgado, -da, *a.* stupefied from eating the lees of pressed olives (*alpechín, morga,* or *murga*) (applied to fish), greased with *alpechín;* egg-plant-coloured. — *p.p.* [AMORGAR].

amorgar, *v.t.* to stupefy fish with *morga* or *murga.* — *v.r.* to become stupefied through eating *morga, murga* or *alpechín.*

amoricones, *n.m.pl.* (*coll.*) looks, gestures and actions expressive of love.

amorío, *n.m.* love-affair, love-making, amour.

amoriscado, -da, *a.* Moor-like.

amormado, -da, *a.* applied to horses having the glanders.

amormío, *n.m.* (*bot.*) sea-daffodil.

amorosamente, *adv.* lovingly.

amorosidad, *n.f.* amorousness, love, affection.

amoroso, -sa, *a.* kind, affectionate, loving; pleasing; gentle, mild, serene; *amoroso con, para, para con los suyos,* kind, affectionate to his family.

amorrar, *v.i.* (*coll.*) to hold down the head; to muse; to be sullen; (*naut.*) to pitch. — *v.r.* to sulk.

amorreo, -a, *a.* concerning or pertaining to the biblical Amorites.

amorronar, *v.t.* (*naut.*) to hoist a flag to signal for help.

amortajador, -ra, *n.m.f.* one who puts a shroud on a corpse.

amortajar, *v.t.* to shroud (a corpse).

amortecer, *v.t.* (*pres. indic.* **amortezco**; *pres. subj.* **amortezca**) to deaden. — *v.r.* to faint, be in a faint or swoon.

amortecimiento, *n.m.* swoon, fainting.

amortiguación, *n.f.;* **amortiguamiento,** *n.m.* mortification; softening, lessening, mitigation.

amortiguador, -ra, *n.m.f.* softener, reducer. — *n.m.* (*mech.*) shock-absorber. — *a.* reducing, softening, mitigating.

amortiguar, *v.t.* to mortify, deaden; to temper, moderate, calm, mitigate, soften (colours); to absorb (shocks).

amortizable, *a.* redeemable (of annuities, etc.), inalienable, payable.

amortización, *n.f.* liquidation, paying off (a debt), amortization; (*com.*) redemption, the paying off of mortgages and debentures; *caja* (or *fondo de*) *amortización,* sinking fund.

amortizar, *v.t.* (*pret.* **amorticé**; *pres. subj.* **amortice**) to amortize; to liquidate (a debt); to recoup, recover (money sunk in business); to render an estate inalienable by transferring it to a community; to suppress (offices, etc.); to refund.

amoscar, *v.t.* (*pret.* **amosqué**; *pres. subj.* **amosque**) to flap (flies). — *v.r.* to shake off flies; (*coll.*) to become irritated.

amosquilado, -da, *a.* (*prov.*) tormented with flies (cattle).

amostachado, -da, *a.* bearded; moustached.

amostazar, *v.t.* (*pret.* **amostacé**; *pres. subj.* **amostace**) (*coll.*) to exasperate, provoke. — *v.r.* to fly into a violent passion; to become vexed, irritated.

amotinadamente, *adv.* mutinously, riotously, tumultuously.

amotinado, -da, *n.m.f.* [AMOTINADOR]. — *a.* mutinous, rebellious, seditious. — *p.p.* [AMOTINAR].

amotinador, -ra, *n.m.f.* mutineer, rioter, rebel. — *a.* [AMOTINADO].

amotinamiento, *n.m.* mutiny, rebellion, insurrection.

amotinar, *v.t.* to excite to rebellion; to cause sedition; (*fig.*) to disorder (the mind). — *v.r.* to mutiny, riot.

amover, *v.t.* to remove; to dismiss.

amovibilidad, *n.f.* revocableness; removability.

amovible, *a.* removable; revocable.

ampac, *n.m.* (*bot.*) champac.

ampara, *n.f.* (*prov., law*) seizure of movable property, sequestration.

amparador, -ra, *n.m.f.* protector, defender. — *a.* protecting, defending.

amparar, *v.t.* to shelter; to protect, help, support, assist; (*prov.*) to seize goods and chattels; to sequestrate; (*Chi.*) to fulfil the requirements for registering and working a mine; *amparar de la persecución*, to protect from persecution; *amparar en la posesión*, (*law*) to maintain in possession. — *v.r.* to enjoy favour or protection; to defend oneself; to seek shelter; *ampararse con*, or *de algo*, to seize something.

amparo, *n.m.* favour, aid, protection; guardianship; refuge; (*law*) sequestration; (*prov.*) fragment, chip; (*slang*) prisoner's advocate; asylum, shelter.

ampelídeo, -dea, *a.* (*bot.*) ampelideous. — *n.f.pl.* ampelopsis.

ampelita, *n.f.* soft slate used for carpenters' pencils.

ampelografía, *n.f.* viticulture.

ampelográfico, -ca, *a.* viticultural.

ampelógrafo, -fa, *n.m.f.* viticulturist.

amper, amperio, *n.m.* (*elec.*) ampere; *amperio hora*, ampere hour; *amperio vuelta*, ampere turn.

amperaje, *n.m.* amperage.

amperímetro, *n.m.* amperemeter.

amplexicaulo, -la, *a.* (*bot.*) amplexicaul.

amplexo, -xa, *a.* (*bot.*) amplexifoliate.

ampliación, *n.f.* enlargement, extension, expansion.

ampliador, -ra, *n.m.f.* amplifier, enlarger. — *a.* amplifying.

ampliamente, *adv.* largely, copiously, fully, amply.

ampliar, *v.t.* to amplify, enlarge, distend, extend.

ampliativo, -va, *a.* amplifying, enlarging.

amplificación, *n.f.* enlargement; (*rhet.*) amplification.

amplificador, -ra, *n.m.f.* (*phot.*) amplifier, enlarger; (*wire.*) amplifier. — *a.* amplifying, enlarging.

amplificar, *v.t.* to amplify, enlarge, extend, exaggerate; to dilate, expatiate.

amplificativo, -va, *a.* amplifying, enlarging.

amplio, -lia, *a.* ample, extensive; large, roomy; absolute.

amplitud, *n.f.* extent, greatness, largeness; (*astron.*) amplitude.

ampo, *n.m.* whiteness; *blanco como los ampos de la nieve*, white as snow.

ampolla, *n.f.* blister on the skin; vial, cruet; small bubble of water; lamp bulb.

ampollar, *v.t.* to blister; to make hollow, excavate. — *v.r.* to become blistered, hollow, bulb-like; to bubble up. — *a.* resembling a bladder, bubble or blister.

ampolleta, *n.f.* small vial or cruet; hourglass; bulb; (*naut.*) sand-glass; time taken by the hour-glass; *no soltar*, or *tomar uno la ampolleta*, (*coll.*) to speak excessively and prevent anyone else from taking part in the conversation.

ampón, -na, *a.* frothy, redundant; bulky, large, puffed up.

amprar, *v.i.* (*prov.*) to borrow.

ampulosidad, *n.f.* pomposity, verbosity.

ampuloso, -sa, *a.* grand, pompous, sonorous, resounding, emphatic.

amputación, *n.f.* amputation.

amputar, *v.t.* to amputate.

amuchachado, -da, *a.* boyish, childish.

amueblar, *v.t.* to furnish; *amueblar con lujo*, to furnish luxuriously; *amueblar de nuevo*, to furnish anew.

amueblo; amueble, *pres. ind.; pres. subj.* [AMOBLAR].

amuelo; amuele, *pres. ind.; pres. subj.* [AMOLAR].

amugamiento, *n.m.* act of setting landmarks.

amugronador, -ra, *n.m.f., a.* one who trains vine-shoots.

amugronar, *v.t.* to lay the shoot of a vine.

amujerado, -da, *a.* effeminate.

amujeramiento, *n.m.* effeminacy.

amular, *v.i.* to be sterile (mares).

amulatado, -da, *a.* mulatto-like.

amuleto, *n.m.* amulet.

amunicionar, *v.t.* to supply with ammunition.

amuñecado, -da, *a.* puppet-like.

amura, *n.f.* (*naut.*) beam of a ship at one-eighth of its length from the bow; exterior sides of ship corresponding to this section; tack of a sail.

amurada, *n.f.* (*naut.*) interior side of a ship.

amurallado, -da, *a.* surrounded with walls, walled.

amurallar, *v.t.* to surround with walls, to wall.

amurar, *v.t.* (*naut.*) to haul the tack aboard.

amurcar, *v.t.* to gore with the horns.

amurco, *n.m.* blow or stroke with the horns.

amurillar, *v.t.* (*agric.*) to earth up.

amurriarse, *v.r.* (*prov.*) to become melancholic *or* sullen; (*Hond.*) to become affected with murrain.

amusco, -ca, *a.* brown.

amusgar, *v.t.* to throw back the ears (horses and mules); to contract the eyes to see better.

amuso, *n.m.* (*hist.*) marble slab with the signs of the compass; mariner's compass.

ana, *n.f.* ell; abbreviation used by medical men to signify equal parts.

anabaptismo, *n.m.* Anabaptism.

anabaptista, *n.m.f.,* *a.* Anabaptist.

anacarado, -da, *a.* like mother-of-pearl.

anacardino, -na, *a.* mixed with anacardium. — *n.f.* confection made of anacardium or cashew-nut.

anacardo, *n.m.* cashew-tree, cashew-nut.

anacatártico, -ca, *a.* (*med.*) emetic.

anaclástica, *n.f.* (*opt.*) anaclastics.

anaco, (*Per., Bol.*) *n.m.* dress of Indian women; (*Ec.*) women's hairdressing.

anaconda, *n.f.* (*Am.*) anaconda, a large boa.

anacoreta, *n.m.f.* anchorite, hermit.

anacorético, -ca, *a.* anchoretical.

anacreóntico, -ca, *a.* Anacreontic.

anacrónico, -ca, *a.* anachronic.

anacronismo, *n.m.* anachronism.

ánade, *n.m.f.* duck.

anadear, *v.i.* to waddle.

anadeja, *n.f.* duckling.

anadino, -na, *n.m.f.* duckling, young duck.

anadón, *n.m.* young duck; non-floating wood.

anadoncillo, *n.m.* grown duckling.

anaerobio, *a.* (*biol.*) anaerobic.

anafalla; anafaya, *n.f.* kind of thick corded silk.

anafe; anafre, *n.m.* portable furnace or stove.

anafilaxis, *n.f.* (*med.*) anaphylaxis.

anáfora, *n.f.* (*rhet.*) anaphora.

anafrodisia, *n.f.* (*med.*) anaphrodisia.

anafrodisíaco, -ca, *a.* (*med.*) anaphrodisiac.

anafrodita, *n.m.f.,* *a.* abstaining from sexual pleasures.

anáglifo, *n.m.* (*arch.*) vase, vessel, or other work adorned with sculpture in bas-relief.

anagnórisis, *n.f.* (*poet.*) anagnorisis, recognition.

anagoge; anagogía, *n.f.* anagoge, anagogy.

anagógicamente, *adv.* anagogically.

anagógico, -ca, *a.* anagogical.

anagrama, *n.m.* anagram.

anagramáticamente, *adv.* anagrammatically.

anagramático, -ca, *a.* anagrammatical.

anagramatizador, -ra, *n.m.f.* anagrammatist.

anagramatizar, *v.t.* to anagrammatize.

anaiboa, *n.m.* (*Cuba*) poisonous juice extracted from the cassava root.

anal, *a.* anal, relating to the anus.

analectas, *n.m.pl.* analects, literary gleanings.

analéptico,-ca, *a.* (*med.*) analeptic; comforting, restorative.

anales, *n.m.pl.* annals.

analfabetismo, *n.m.* ignorance, illiteracy.

analfabeto, -ta, *n.m.f.,* *a.* illiterate; ignorant person.

analgesia, *n.f.* (*med.*) analgesia, insensibility to pain.

analgésico, -ca, *a.* (*med.*) anodyne.

analgesina, *n.f.* (*chem.*) antipyrine.

análisis, *n.m.f.* analysis; (*gram.*) parsing; (*math.*) analysis.

analista, *n.m.* annalist; analyst.

analíticamente, *adv.* analytically.

analítico, -ca, *a.* analytical. — *n.f.* analytics.

analizable, *a.* analysable.

analizador, -ra, *n.m.f.* analyst; analyser. — *a.* analysing.

analizar, *v.t.* (*pret.* **analicé;** *pres. subj.* **analice**) to analyse; (*gram.*) to parse.

análogamente, *ad*·. analogically.

analogía, *n.f.* analogy, resemblance.

analógicamente, *adv.* analogically.

analógico, -ca; análogo, -ga, *a.* analogous; analogic, analogical.

analogismo, *n.m.* (*med.*) empiricism.

anamorfosis, *n.f.* (*phys.*) anamorphosis.

ananá; ananás, *n.f.* (*bot.*) pine-apple.

anapelo, *n.m.* (*bot.*) wolf's-bane.

anapesto, *n.m.* anapæst.

anaquel, *n.m.* shelf.

anaquelería, *n.f.* shelving, case of shelves.

anaranjado, -da, *a.* orange-coloured. — *n.m.* orange (colour).

anarquía, *n.f.* anarchy.

anárquico, -ca, *a.* anarchical.

anarquismo, *n.m.* anarchism.

anarquista, *n.m.f.* anarchist. — *a.* anarchical.

anasarca, *n.f.* (*med.*) general dropsy.

anascote, *n.m.* twilled woollen stuff like serge.

anastasia, *n.f.* (*bot.*) mugwort.

anastomosis, *n.f.* (*anat.*) anastomosis.

anástrofe, *n.f.* (*rhet.*) anastrophe, inversion of words.

anata, *n.f.* annates, yearly income; *media anata,* the annates of the half-year.

anatema, *n.f.; anatematismo,* *n.m.* anathema, curse, imprecation; excommunication.

anatematizar, *v.t.* (*pret.* **anatematicé;** *pres. subj.* **anatematice**) to anathematize, excommunicate; to curse.

anatife, *n.m.* (*ichth.*) goose-barnacle, a variety of shell-fish.

anatista, *n.m.* officer for the half-year's annates.

anatomía, *n.f.* anatomy; dissection.

anatómicamente, *adv.* anatomically.

anatómico, -ca, *n.m.f.* anatomist. — *a.* anatomical.

anatomista, *n.m.f.* professor of anatomy.

anatomizar, *v.t.* (*pret.* **anatomicé;** *pres. subj.* **anatomice**) to anatomize, dissect; (*art*) to indicate the bones and muscles in statues and figures.

anavajado, -da, *a.* knife-scarred.

anca, *n.f.* croup of a horse; haunch; (*coll.*) buttock; *a ancas, a las ancas,* behind; *llevar, traer uno a las ancas a otro,* (*coll.*) to keep, maintain somebody; *no sufrir ancas,* (*coll.*) to be rather intolerant of jokes.

ancado, *n.m.* (*vet.*) distemper; contraction of the hind-leg muscles.

ancianidad, *n.f.* old age; antiquity.

anciano, -na, *n.m.f.,* *a.* elderly (man, woman); person advanced in years; one of the elders of the Sanhedrin.

ancla, *n.f.* anchor; (*slang*) hand; *ancla de la esperanza,* (*naut.*) sheet-anchor; *ancla de servidumbre,* bower anchor; *zafar el ancla para dar fondo,* to clear the anchor for coming to; *uñas del ancla,* anchor arms; *pico del ancla,* bill of the anchor; *echar anclas,* to anchor; *levar anclas,* to weigh anchor; *estar sobre el ancla,* or *las anclas,* to be anchored, be at anchor.

ancladero, *n.m.* anchorage, anchoring-place.

anclaje, *n.m.* casting anchor; anchoring-ground; *derecho de anclaje,* anchorage dues.

anclar, *v.i.* to anchor, cast anchor.

anclote, *n.m.* stream-anchor, grapnel, kedge.

anclotillo, *n.m.* kedge-anchor.

ancón, *n.m.;* **anconada,** *n.f.* small cove, inlet, bay; (*Mex.*) corner, angle, nook.

áncora, *n.f.* anchor.

ancoraje, *n.m.* anchorage.

ancorar, *v.i.* to anchor, cast anchor.

ancorca, *n.f.* yellow ochre.

ancorel, *n.m.* large stone serving as anchor to net-float.

ancorería, *n.f.* anchor-forge.

ancorero, *n.m.* anchor-smith.

ancusa, *n.f.* (*bot.*) alkanet.

ancuviña, *n.f.* (*Chi.*) grave of the Chilean Indians.

anchamente, *adv.* widely, broadly, largely.

ancharia, *n.f.* width of cloth (among merchants and traders).

ancheta, *n.f.* small quantity of goods ventured in commerce; profit in a bargain.

anchicorto, -ta, *a.* wider than it is long.

ancho, -cha, *a.* broad, wide, large. — *n.m.* width, breadth. — *n.f.* (*slang*) large city; *a sus anchas,* at one's ease, at one's will; *tener la conciencia ancha,* to have an elastic conscience; *ancho de vía,* gauge of a railway line; *tantas en ancho como en largo,* quite freely, satisfactorily; *a todos anchos,* unrestrictedly; *estar,* or *ponerse muy ancho,* or *tan ancho,* to boast, swell with pride; *¡ancha Castilla!* just as you please, frankly; *ancho de boca,* wide-mouthed.

anchoa, *n.f.;* **anchova,** *n.f.* anchovy.

anchor, *n.m.;* **anchura,** *n.f.* largeness, extensiveness, breadth, width, latitude, laxity.

anchuroso, -sa, *a.* large, extensive, broad, spacious, wide.

anda, *n.f.* (*Chi., Guat., Per.*) stretcher; litter; bier.

andábata, *n.m.* gladiator who fought hoodwinked.

andaboba, *n.f.* card-game.

andada, *n.f.* thin hard-baked cake; track, trail, pathway; (*pl.*) traces of game; *volver a las andadas,* to return to bad habits; to backslide.

andaderas, *n.f.pl.* go-cart.

andadero, -ra, *a.* easy for walking (place, ground); running. — *n.m.f.* runner.

andado, -da, *a.* beaten, trodden (path); worse for use; elapsed; threadbare; customary. — *n.m.f.* (*coll.*) stepchild. — *p.p.* [ANDAR].

andador, -ra, *a.* swift, good at walking or running. — *n.m.f.* good walker. — *n.m.* inferior minister of justice; messenger of a court; (*naut.*) fine sailor; alley or small walk in a garden; (*pl.*) leading strings; *no necesito* (or *puedo andar sin*) *andadores,* I need no help with my own business.

andadura, *n.f.* gait, pacing; amble.

andaluz, -za, *n.m.f. a.* Andalusian.

andaluzada, *n.f.* boasting, exaggeration; (*coll.*) yarn; fishy story.

andamiada, *n.f.;* **andamiaje,** *n.m.* scaffolding.

andamio, *n.m.* scaffold, platform; (*coll.*) footgear; (*naut.*) gang-board.

andana, *n.f.* row, line; tier; *llamarse andana,* (*coll.*) not to fulfil a promise.

andanada, *n.f.* (*naut.*) broadside; grandstand (bull-ring); (*coll.*) reproof, reprimand, tirade.

andancio, *n.m.* (*prov., Cub.*) light epidemic illness.

andaniño, *n.m.* kind of go-cart in which children learn to walk.

andante, *n.m.* (*mus.*) andante. — *a.* walking, errant.

andantesco, -ca, *a.* belonging to knighthood or knight-errantry.

andanza, *n.f.* occurrence, event; *buena* (or *mala*) *andanza,* good (or bad) fortune.

andar, *v.i.* (*pret.* **anduve;** *impf. subj.* **anduviese; anduviera;** *fut. subj.* **anduviere**) to go, come; to walk, move (person, machine, watch, etc.) move along; to act, behave; to transact; to elapse; run, function (of machines); to be; to get along; to be going on; *los negocios andan bien,* business is good; *andar alegre,* to be merry; *andar arrastrando,* to eke out a wretched existence; *andar de barrio,* to wear a plain dress; *andar de boca en boca, en coplas,* to be well-known, to be the talk of the town; *andar en buena vela,* (*naut.*) to be under full sail; *andar de capa caída,* to be crestfallen; *andar a caza,* to go hunting; *andar a caza de una cosa,* to go in pursuit of something; *andar por una cosa,* to strive for something; *andar con la cara descubierta,* to act openly; *andar en carnes* (or *en cueros*) to go stark-naked; *andar por los cerros de Úbeda,* to be at sixes and sevens; *andar en coche,* to ride; *andar en cuentos,* to come to loggerheads; *andar en cuerpo,* to go out without a cloak or overcoat; *andar de ceca en meca,* to go wandering or roaming about; *andar en dares y tomares* (or *en dimes y diretes*) to deal in 'ifs and ands'; *andar a derechas,* to act honestly; *andar las estaciones,* to mind one's own business; *andar a gatas,* to walk timidly, to crawl, to creep along; *a más andar, a todo andar,* at full speed; *andar a la gineta,* to go at a trot; *¡anda listo!* be quick! *andar en malos pasos,* to be up to mischief, to lead a bad life; *andar al estricote,* or *a mía sobre tuya,* or *al morro,* or *al pelo,* to come to blows, to quarrel; *¡anda a pasear! ¡ anda a paseo!* get out! be off with you! *andar al pescuezo,* to fly at each other's throats; *andar con pies de mar,* (*naut.*) to have found one's sea-legs; *andar con pies de plomo,* to go very cautiously; *andar de pie quebrado,* to be poverty-stricken; *andar prudente,* to act prudently; *andar a puñetazos,* to fight with fists; *andar a puñaladas,* to fight with knives; *andar sin recelo,* to have no fear; *andando el tiempo,* in course of time; *andar a tientas,* to grope, feel one's way in the dark; *andar todo,* (*naut.*) to put up the helm; *andar tras,* to follow, run after; *andar a la tuna,* to play truant; *andar al uso,* to conform to the times; *andar la villa,* to scour the town; *andar de zoco en colodro* or *de Herodes a Pilatos,* to escape Scylla and fall into Charybdis; *dime con quién andas, decirte he quién eres,* a man is known by the company he keeps; *anda que andarás, que nunca llegarás,* (*coll.*) do what you like, you will never achieve anything; *andarse en cumplimientos,* to stand upon ceremony; *andarse por las márgenes,* or *las ramas,* to beat about the bush; *¡anda!* stand out of the way! get up! let it go! gracious! *¡andar!* all right; go ahead; *el tiempo anda,* time flies; *andar por las nubes el mar,* the sea runs mountains

[63]

high; *andar estaciones*, to pray at the 14 shrines in a Roman-Catholic church; *tornar a andar las estaciones*, to backslide; *andar en palmas*, to be universally applauded; *anden y ténganse*, play fast and loose; *andar de rama en rama*, to dwell upon unimportant details; *andar en retruécanos*, to make puns; *andar de una camada*, like seeks like; *andar como el cangrejo*, to go backward or very slowly, like a crab; *andar con dilatorias*, to waste another's time with false promises; *andar el mundo al revés*, to reverse the order of nature; *andar por hacer, decir una cosa*, to be about to do, say a thing; *andar con las manos en la cinta*, not to have anything to do; *andar de acá para allá* or *para acullá*, *andar a la flor del berro, a la gandaya, de bardanza* or *trastejando*, to wander, gad, roam about; to be unsettled; *andar a la briba*, or *a la sopa*, or *buscando*, to beg; *andar a tres menos cuartillo*, to be very short of anything; *andar tentando*, to grope where one cannot see; to make efforts or trials; *andar a sombra de tejado*, (naut.) to be under the hatches; to hide; to abscond; *andar a monte*, to flee; to skulk; *andar aperreado*, to be harassed or fatigued; *andar de nones*, to be idle; *andar a grillos, andarse a picos pardos*, to waste time in idle pursuits; *andar manga por hombro*, to be very careless and untidy in domestic affairs; *andar por su cabal*, to live selfishly; *¡ande yo caliente, y ríase la gente!* if I am comfortable, what care I for ridicule! *andar con un palmo de lengua*, to be overheated; *anda mal*, he is a bad walker; it is going badly; *andar sin sombra, andar balando por algo*, to crave, long anxiously for something; *quien mal anda, mal acaba*, he who lives ill, dies ill; *quien con lobos anda, a aullar se enseña*, he who lives with wolves will learn to howl; evil communications corrupt good manners; *andar* or *estar en la danza*, to be implicated in an affair; *andarse tocando tabletas*, to be disappointed; *andar como ardilla*, to be as active as a squirrel; *andar en balanza*, to be in danger of losing property or place; *andar con mosca*, to fly into a passion; *andar de*, or *en puntas*, or *en quintillas*, or *a capazos*, to quarrel; *andar a la que salta*, to go to the dogs; *andar en opiniones*, to throw a doubt upon a person's credit; *andar a malas*, to go away in enmity; *andar en gerigonzas*, to quibble; to evade; *andar a coz y bocado*, to play roughly; *¡anda noramala! ¡anda a freír espárragos!* be off! go away! *andar con un ten con ten*, to act cautiously and justly; *andar de ganancia*, to pursue a thing successfully; *andar de prisa*, to be in haste; to be very busy; *andar con reserva*, to proceed cautiously; *entre bobos anda el juego*, this affair is in the hands of experts; *andar listo*, to be active or diligent; *andar en pretensiones*, to seek office importunately; *mal me andarán las manos*, if nothing prevents, I will do it; *andar por el pleito*, to have charge of a lawsuit; *andar un negocio*, to undertake the charge of a case or business; *andar a caza con hurón muerto*, to undertake a business without adequate means; *andar con el tiempo*, to conform to the times; *andar con cuidado*, to be careful; *andar holgado*, to be well provided for; *andar a caza de gangas*, to hunt for bargains; to try for a sinecure; *andar a las bonicas*, to take things easily; *andar cazando*, to hunt; to seek; *andar en los cuernos del toro*, to be in imminent danger; *andársele a uno la cabeza*, to become dizzy; *andarse en flores*, to decline entering into a debate; *andar en mangas de camisa*, to be in one's shirt-sleeves; *cuando la zorra anda a caza de grillos, mal para ella, y peor para sus hijos*, the fox and her young must be badly off when she goes hunting for crickets; *andar a viva quien vence*, rats always leave a sinking ship; *andar tropezando y cayendo*, to commit mistakes or be in danger; *todo se andará*, that's all right; it shall be done; *andar en una cosa, en algo*, to interfere, intervene in an affair; *andar con miedo*, to fear; *andar a la pierna*, to walk on the side (horse); *andar a las vueltas* or *a las alcances*, to watch, spy on someone; *andar buscando tres pies al gato*, to provoke someone; *andar de mala con alguno*, to bear a grudge; *andar tierras*, to travel; *andar las siete partidas*, to travel all over the world; *andar a caballo*, to ride on horseback; *andar en bicicleta*, to ride a bicycle; *andar en coche, en automóvil*, to ride in a carriage, in a motor-car; *anda mal de dinero*, he is badly off; *anda por ahí*, he is somewhere around.

andar, *n.m.* gait (horse); pace; walking; *a largo andar*, in the long run; *a mayor andar*, at best, at most; *a peor andar*, at worst; *el poco andar del barco*, (naut.) the slow way of the ship; *estar a un andar*, to be on the same level, on the same story or floor.

andaraje, *n.m.* wheel of a well; frame of a garden-roller.

andariego, -ga, *a.* restless, of a restless or roving disposition; begging. — *n.m.f.* fast walker or runner; beggar.

andarín, -na, *n.m.f.* (coll.) good walker, fast walker; professional runner. — *a.* running, walking. — *n.m.pl.* young partridges. — *n.f.* (orn.) swallow.

andarivel, *n.m.* (naut.) girt-line; ferry cable, safety-ropes on board ship.

andarraya, *n.f.* kind of game of draughts played with stones.

andarrío, *n.m.* wagtail.

andas, *n.f.pl.* kind of bier or litter with shafts; stretcher.

andén, *n.m.* sidewalk; pier; platform of a railway station; path for a horse round the draw-well or in a mill; sidewalk by a road, wharf or bridge.

andero, *n.m.* stretcher-bearer.

andilú, *n.m.* shoemaker's burnishing stick.

andino, -na, *a.* Andean.

ándito, *n.m.* gallery, corridor round a building; sidewalk of a street.

andolina; andorina, *n.f.* (orn.) swallow.

andón, *a.* (Col., Cub., Ven.) roving, one who walks a great deal (of horses).

andorga, *n.f.* paunch; *llenar la andorga*, to eat a great deal, to gorge.

andorina, *n.f.* (orn.) swallow [ANDOLINA].

andorra, *n.f.* street-walker.

andorrear, *v.i.* to gad about.

andorrero, -ra, *n.m.f.* gadabout; loiterer, vagabond. — *n.f.* street-walker. — *a.* loitering, rambling.

andosco, -ca, *n.m.f., a.* two years old (sheep).
andrajero, -ra, *n.m.f.* rag-picker.
andrajo, *n.m.* rag of worn clothes; despicable person.
andrajosamente, *adv.* raggedly.
andrajoso, -sa, *a.* ragged.
andriana, *n.f.* gown formerly worn by women.
andrina, *n.f. (bot.)* sloe.
andrino, *n.m. (bot.)* sloe-tree, blackthorn.
androfobia, *n.f.* fear, aversion to men.
andrógino, -na, *n.m.f. (bot., zool.)* androgyny. — *a.* androgynous.
androide, *n.m.* automaton, shaped like a man.
Andrómeda, *n.f. (astron.)* Andromeda.
andrómina, *n.f. (coll.)* trick, fraud, artifice.
androsemo, *n.m. (bot.)* St. John's wort.
andularios, *n.m.pl. (coll.)* long and wide gown.
andullo, *n.m.* bale of tobacco; plug tobacco; *(naut.)* canvas shield on harpings and blocks.
andurriales, *n.m.pl.* by-roads, retired places.
anduve; anduviese, *pret.; imperf. subj.* [ANDAR].
anea, *n.f. (bot.)* cat's-tail, rush; *silla de anea,* basket chair.
aneaje, *n.m.* alnage, ell measure.
anear, *v.t.* to measure by ells; *(prov.)* to rock a cradle.
aneblar, *v.t. (pres. indic.* **anieblo;** *pres. subj.* **anieble)** to cloud; to darken. — *v.r.* to become cloudy.
anécdota, *n.f.* anecdote, tale, relation, story.
anecdótico, -ca, *a.* anecdotal.
anecdotista, *n.m.f.* anecdotist.
aneciarse, *v.r.* to become imbecile.
anegable, *a.* submersible.
anegación, *n.f.* overflowing, inundation.
anegadizo, -za, *a.* frequently inundated.
anegado, -da, *a.* inundated, submerged; *(naut,.)* low-lying; waterlogged. — *p.p.* [ANEGAR].
anegar, *v.t.* to inundate, submerge; to flush; to drown. — *v.r.* to become flooded, submerged, wet, soaked; to sink, drown; *anegar en sangre,* to drown in blood; *navío anegado,* waterlogged ship.
anegociado, -da, *a.* greatly occupied.
anejín; anejir, *n.m.* popular proverb put to music.
anejo, -ja, *a.* annexed, joined. — *n.m.* benefice or church dependent upon another.
aneldo, *n.m. (bot.)* common dill.
aneléctrico, -ca, *a. (phys.)* anelectrical, non-electric.
anélido, -da, *n.m.f. (zool.)* annelid; *(pl.)* Annelida.
anemia, *n.f. (med.)* anæmia.
anémico, -ca, *a.* affected with anæmia, anæmic.
anemografía, *n.f.* anemography.
anemográfico, -ca, *a.* anemographic.
anemometría, *n.f.* anemometry.
anemómetro, *n.m.* anemometer.
anémona; anémone, *n.f. (bot.)* anemone; windflower; *anémone de mar,* sea-anemone.
anemoscopio, *n.m.* anemoscope.
anepigráfico, -ca, *a.* without title or inscription.
anequín (a, or **de),** *adv.* so much a head (applied to the shearing of sheep).
aneroide, *n.m., a. (phys.)* aneroid (barometer).

anestesia, *n.f. (med.)* anæsthesia.
anestesiar, *v.t.* to anæsthetize.
anestésico, -ca, *n.m., a.* anæsthetic.
aneurisma, *n.m.f. (med.)* aneurism.
anexar, *v.t.* to annex, join, unite, add to.
anexidades, *n.f.pl.* annexes, belongings, appurtenances.
anexión, *n.f.* union, annexation.
anexionismo, *n.m.* annexationism.
anexionista, *n.m.f., a.* annexationist.
anexo, -xa, *a.* joined, annexed.
anfibio, -bia, *a.* amphibious. — *n.m.f.* amphibian.
anfibiografía, *n.f. (zool.)* amphibiography.
anfibiográfico, -ca, *a. (zool.)* amphibiographic.
anfíbol, *n.m. (min.)* amphibole.
anfibólico, -ca, *a.* amphibolous, doubtful.
anfibolita, *n.f. (geol.)* amphibolite.
anfibología, *n.f. (rhet.)* amphibology.
anfibológicamente, *adv.* amphibologically.
anfibológico, -ca, *a. (rhet.)* amphibological, doubtful.
anfíbraco, *n.m. (poet.)* amphibrach.
anfímacro, *n.m. (poet.)* amphimacer.
anfión, *n.m.* a name given to opium in the East Indies.
anfioxo, *n.m. (zool.)* amphioxus.
anfípodo, -da, *a.* amphipod. — *n.m.pl.* Amphipoda.
anfipróstilo, *n.m. (arch.)* amphiprostyle.
anfisbena; anfisbena, *n.f.* amphisbæna.
anfiscios, *n.m.pl. (geog.)* amphiscii.
anfiteatro, *n.m.* amphitheatre.
anfitrión, *n.m.* host.
Anfitrite, *n.f. (myth., astron.)* Amphitrite.
ánfora, *n.f.* amphora. — *pl.* cruets.
anfractuosidad, *n.f. (anat.)* anfractuosity; crookedness.
anfractuoso, -sa, *a.* anfractuous; sinuous, unequal.
angaria, *n.f.* ancient form of servitude; forced delay in the sailing of a ship due to its use in the public service.
angarillado, -da, *a.* provided with panniers. — *p.p.* [ANGARILLAR].
angarillar, *v.t.* to put panniers on horses, etc.
angarillas, *n.f.pl.* hand-barrow; panniers; cruet-stand.
angarillón, *n.m.* large basket; large hand-barrow; *(coll.)* large clumsy body.
angaripola, *n.f.* kind of striped calico. — *n.f.pl.* gaudy, ostentatious ornaments on clothes.
ángaro, *n.m.* fire beacon.
angazo, *n.m.* instrument for catching shell-fish.
ángel, *n.m.* angel, spiritual being; term of affection; *(ichth.)* angel-fish; *(artill.)* cross-bar shot; *ángel custodio, ángel de la guarda,* guardian angel; *ángel malo,* evil angel, devil; *ángel patudo,* wolf in sheep's clothing; *tener ángel,* to have the gift of pleasing.
angélica, *n.f. (bot.)* garden angelica; *(pharm.)* purgative mixture; *angélica palustre,* wild angelica; *angélica carlina,* carline thistle.
angelical; angélico, -ca, *a.* angelic, angelical.
angelicalmente, *adv.* angelically.
angelico; angelito, *n.m.* little angel; baby; *estar con los angelitos, (coll.)* to be asleep or distrait.
angelón, *n.m.* great angel; *angelón de retablo,* fat child.

angelote, *n.m.* large figure of an angel; large or fat good-natured child; simple person; (*ichth.*) angel-fish.

ángelus, *n.m.* Angelus.

angina, *n.f.* (*med.*) angina, quinsy; sore throat; pharyngitis; *angina de pecho,* angina pectoris.

anginoso, -sa, *a.* (*med.*) anginal, anginose.

angiografía, *n.f.* angiography.

angiospermo, -ma, *a.* (*bot.*) angiosperm. — *n.f.pl.* Angiospermæ.

angla, *n.f.* cape (of land).

anglesita, *n.f.* (*min.*) anglesite.

anglicanismo, *n.m.* Anglicanism.

anglicano, -na, *n.m.f.,* *a.* Anglican; *la iglesia anglicana,* the Anglican church.

anglicismo, *n.m.* Anglicism.

anglo, -gla, *a.* Anglian. — *n.m.f.* Angle; English.

angloamericano, -na, *n.m.f.,* *a.* Anglo-American.

anglófilo, -la, *n.m.f.,* *a.* Anglophile.

anglófobo, -ba, *n.m.f.,* *a.* Anglophobe.

anglomanía, *n.f.* Anglomania; enthusiasm for England or English things.

anglómano, -na, *n.m.f.,* *a.* Anglomaniac.

anglosajón, -na, *n.m.f.,* *a.* Anglo-Saxon.

angolán, *n.m.* (*bot.*) alangium, East India tree.

angorra, *n.f.* canvas or leather apron.

angostamente, *adv.* narrowly.

angostar, *v.t.,* *v.i.* to narrow, contract.

angosto, -ta, *a.* narrow, close, insufficient.

angostura, *n.f.* narrowness; narrows; narrow pass; strait; distress.

angra, *n.f.* small bay, cove.

angrelado, -da, *a.* (*her.*) engrailed.

anguarina, *n.f.* loose coat hanging down to the knees.

anguiforme, *a.* anguiform, serpent-like.

anguila, *n.f.* (*ichth.*) eel; (*pl.*) (*naut.*) launching-ways; *anguila de cabo,* port-rope to flog sailors (on galleys); *escurrirse como una anguila,* to be as slippery as an eel.

anguilazo, *n.m.* stroke with a port-rope.

anguilero, -ra, *n.m.f.* basket for eels. — *n.f.* eel-buck, eel-pot; tank for live eels.

anguiliforme, *a.* (*ichth.*) eel-like.

anguililla, *n.f.* small irrigating canal.

anguina, *n.f.* (*vet.*) vein of the groins.

angula, *n.f.* elver.

angulado, -da, *a.* formed by one or more angles.

angular, *a.* angular; *piedra angular,* corner-stone.

angularmente, *adv.* angularly.

angulema, *n.f.* kind of coarse linen, manufactured at Angoulême; (*coll.*) fulsome flatteries.

ángulo, *n.m.* angle, corner, nook; *ángulo acimutal,* (*astron.*) azimuth; *ángulo de ataque,* (*aer.*) angle of attack; *ángulo de balance,* (*aer.*) angle of bank or roll; *ángulo de contingencia,* (*railw.*) interior intersection angle (of two tangents); *ángulo de resistencia nula,* (*aer.*) angle of zero lift; *ángulo entrante,* re-entrant angle; convex angle; *ángulo externo, interno,* (*geom.*) exterior, interior angle; *ángulo horario,* (*astron.*) hour angle; *ángulo recto,* right angle; *ángulo tangencial,* (*railw.*) deflection angle (from a tangent to a curve); *ángulos alternos externos, internos,* alternate exterior, interior angles; *ángulos correspondientes,* corresponding, or interior-exterior

angles; *ángulos opuestos por el vértice,* vertical angles.

anguloso, -sa, *a.* angular, sharp, sharp-cornered.

angurria, *n.f.* (*coll.*) strangury.

angustia, *n.f.* anguish, affliction, pang, heaviness of mind; (*slang*) prison; (*pl.*) (*slang*) galleys.

angustiadamente, *adv.* painfully, with affliction.

angustiado, -da, *a.* painful, worried; grieved, sorrowful, miserable; narrow-minded. — *n.m.* (*slang*) prisoner; galley-slave. — *p.p.* [ANGUSTIAR].

angustiar, *v.t.* to cause anguish, afflict, worry, distress. — *v.r.* to torment oneself.

angustiosamente, *adv.* with anguish.

angustioso, -sa, *a.* causing or suffering anguish or worry; full of anguish.

anhelación, *n.f.* (*med.*) anhelation; panting; longing.

anhelar, *v.i.,* *v.t.* to breathe with difficulty; to desire anxiously, long for, covet; to gape, gasp; *anhelar honores,* to desire honours; *anhelar a más,* to aspire higher; *anhelar por mayor fortuna,* to long for better fortune.

anhélito, *n.m.* difficult respiration.

anhelo, *n.m.* anxiousness, eagerness, vehement desire.

anheloso, -sa, *a.* difficult (of breathing), panting, breathless; anxious, very desirous.

anhídrico, -ca; anhidro, -dra, *a.* anhydrous.

anhídrido, *n.m.* (*chem.*) anhydride; *anhídrido carbónico,* carbon dioxide, carbonic acid gas; *anhídrido sulfúrico,* sulphur trioxide.

anhidrita, *n.f.* anhydrite.

anhidro, -dra, *a.* (*chem.*) anhydrous.

anhidrosis, *n.f.* (*med.*) anhydrosis.

aní, (*Am.*) *n.m.* a pretty creeping bird common in Mexico and Brazil.

aniaga, *n.f.* (*prov.*) annual wage.

anidar, *v.i.* to nestle; (*fig.*) to dwell, reside. — *v.t.* to cherish, shelter.

anidiar, *v.t.* (*prov.*) to whitewash; to spring-clean (house). — *v.r.* to comb oneself.

anidio, *n.m.* (*prov.*) whitewashing; spring-cleaning.

anieblar, *v.t.* to cloud, darken, obscure; to mystify. — *v.r.* to become cloudy, dark; (*prov.*) to become foolish.

anieblo; anieble, *pres. ind.; pres. subj.* [ANEBLAR].

aniego, *n.m.* abnegation.

anilina, *n.f.* (*chem.*) aniline.

anilla, *n.f.* curtain ring, hoop.

anillado, -da, *a.* (*zool.*) ringed, annulated. — *n.m. pl.* Annelida. — *p.p.* [ANILLAR].

anillar, *v.t.* to form rings or circles; to fasten with rings.

anillejo; anillete, *n.m.* small ring.

anillo, *n.m.* ring, circuit; finger ring; ring of a turbine; circular band; (*arch.*) astragal; (*naut.*) hank or grommet; (*slang*) fetters, irons; *venir como anillo al dedo,* to fit like a glove; to happen (or be said or be done) in the nick of time; *cuando te dieren el anillo, pon el dedillo,* when you get an opportunity, seize it; *de anillo,* honorary (of posts, dignities, etc.); *anillo del Pescador,* Fisher's Seal; *anillo en dedo, honra sin provecho,* much cuff, and little shirt.

ánima, *n.f.* soul; (*artill.*) bore of a gun. —

n.f.pl. ringing of bells at sunset; *descargar el ánima de otro*, to carry out someone's last wishes; *en mi ánima*, on my conscience.

animable, *a.* which can be animated.

animación, *n.f.* animation, bustle, liveliness.

animado, -da, *a.* manful; lively, animated. — *p.p.* [ANIMAR].

animador, -ra, *n.m.f.* animator, enlivener. — *a.* animating, enlivening.

animadversión, *n.f.* animadversion, remark.

animal, *n.m.,* *a.* animal; brute; dunce, blockhead; *animal de bellota*, hog; (*fig.*) a rough, rude person; *el peor mal de los males, es tratar con animales* (said of rude, unmannerly people).

animalada, *n.f.* (*coll.*) asinine word or action.

animalazo; animalote, *n.m.* big animal; (*coll.*) extremely rude, ignorant person.

animálculo, *n.m.* animalcule.

animalejo; animalico; animalillo, *n.m.* small animal; animalcule.

animalidad, *n.f.* animality.

animalismo, *n.m.* animalism.

animalización, *n.f.* (*med.*) animalization.

animalizar, *v.t.* to animalize; to make into animal substance.

animalucho, *n.m.* ugly, hideous animal.

animar, *v.t.* to animate, enliven, revive; to inspire, incite, excite; to encourage, comfort; to give power or vigour to; *animar al certamen*, to encourage for the contest. — *v.r.* to grow lively, to feel encouraged, energetic, cheer up, be merry.

anime, *n.f.* (*bot.*) locust-tree; its resin.

animero, *n.m.* one who asks charity for souls in purgatory.

anímico, -ca, *a.* psychic.

animismo, *n.m.* animism.

ánimo, *n.m.* soul; spirit; courage, valour, fortitude, bravery, hardiness; thought, mind, attention, intention, meaning; *¡ánimo! ¡buen ánimo!* cheer up! come on! *ánimo y adelante*, forward and never fear; *¡ánimo a las gachas, que son de arrope!* joking encouragement to do an easy and agreeable task; *caer(se) de ánimo*, to lose courage; *dilatar el ánimo*, to become hopeful, resigned, consoled; *estrecharse de ánimo*, to become cowardly; *hacer*, or *tener ánimo*, to have the intention of doing something.

animosamente, *adv.* courageously, bravely.

animosidad, *n.f.* valour, daring, courage, boldness; active enmity, animosity.

animoso, -sa, *a.* brave, courageous; *animoso para emprender*, bold to undertake.

aniñadamente, *adv.* childishly.

aniñado, -da, *a.* childish. — *p.p.* [ANIÑARSE].

aniñarse, *v.r.* to grow childish.

aniquilable, *a.* annihilable, destructible.

aniquilación, *n.f.* annihilation, extinction.

aniquilador, -ra, *n.m.f.* destroyer. — *a.* destroying.

aniquilamiento, *n.m.* annihilation, destruction.

aniquilar, *v.t.* to annihilate, destroy, overthrow, reduce to nothing, crush, ruin. — *v.r.* (*fig.*) to decline, decay, waste away; to become emaciated; to humble oneself.

anís, *n.m.* (*bot.*) anise; aniseed; anisette; (*pl.*) sugar-coated aniseeds; small sweets; *llegar a los anises*, to arrive late at a function.

anisado, -da, *a.* mixed with aniseed; anise-

like. — *n.m.* action of adding anise; *aguardiente anisado*, aniseed brandy. — *p.p.* [ANISAR].

anisar, *v.t.* to tincture with anise. — *n.m.* ground planted with anise.

anisete, *n.m.* anisette.

anisodonte, *a.* (*zool.*) of unequal or unsymmetrical teeth or tusks.

anito, *n.m.* (*Philip.*) familiar god of the Indians.

anivelar, *v.t.* to make even or equal.

aniversario, -ria, *a.* annual, yearly. — *n.m.* anniversary, holiday; yearly requiem.

anjeo, *n.m.* coarse sort of linen.

ano, *n.m.* (*anat.*) anus.

anoa, *n.f.* anoa, kind of buffalo.

anoche, *adv.* last night.

anochecedor, -ra, *n.m.f.,* *a.* person who retires late at night; (*coll.*) night-bird.

anochecer, *v.i.* (*pres. indic.* anochezco; *pres. subj.* anochezca) to grow dark (at the approach of nightfall); to be, or reach somewhere at nightfall. — *v.r.* to become dark at nightfall; (*poet.*) to become deprived of light. — *n.m.* dusk, nightfall; *anochecer y no amanecer*, to run away suddenly and secretly; *anochecerle (a uno) en alguna parte*, to be somewhere at nightfall; *al anochecer*, at nightfall.

anochecida, *n.f.* nightfall.

anodinar, *v.t.* to administer anodyne medicines to.

anodinia, *n.f.* (*med.*) anodynia, absence of pain.

anodino, -na, *n.m.,* *a.* (*med.*) anodyne; (*coll.*) insipid, graceless.

ánodo, *n.m.* (*phys.*) anode, positive pole of a generator.

anofeles, *n.f.* anopheles, mosquito.

anomalía, *n.f.* anomaly; (*astron.*) anomaly.

anomalístico, -ca, *a.* anomalistic.

anómalo, -la, *a.* anomalous.

anón, *n.m.* (*bot.*) custard-apple-tree.

anona, *n.f.* (*bot.*) anona, custard-apple; store of provisions.

anonáceo, -cea, *a.* (*bot.*) anonaceous. — *n.f.pl.* Anonaceæ.

anonadación, *n.f.;* **anonadamiento,** *n.m.* annihilation, self-contempt.

anonadar, *v.t.* to annihilate, destroy, exterminate; to diminish. — *v.r.* to humble oneself greatly.

anónimamente, *adv.* anonymously.

anónimo, -ma, *a.* anonymous, nameless. — *n.m.* anonym; anonymity.

anoria, *n.f.* draw-well; chain-pump, noria.

anormal, *a.* abnormal.

anormalidad, *n.f.* abnormality.

anormalmente, *adv.* abnormally.

anortita, *n.f.* (*min.*) anorthite.

anorza, *n.f.* (*bot.*) white bryony.

anotación, *n.f.* annotation note.

anotador, -ra, *n.m.f.* commentator, annotator. — *a.* annotating.

anotar, *v.t.* to write notes or comment upon; to annotate.

anquera, *n.f.* (*Mex.*) hind covering (for horses).

anqueta, *n.f.* [ANCA]; *estar de media anqueta*, to be incommodiously seated.

anquialmendrado, -da, *a.* having an almond-shaped croup.

anquiboyuno, -na, *a.* (*vet.*) having a croup like an ox.

anquilosis, *n.f.* (*anat.*, *vet.*) anchylosis, stiff joint.

anquirredondo, -da, *a.* (*vet.*) having a rounded croup.

anquiseco, -ca, *a.* lean-crouped.

ansa, *n.f.* Hanse, Hanseatic League.

ánsar, *n.m.* goose; *ánsar macho*, gander; *el ánsar de Cantimpalos, que salió al lobo al camino*, said of those who needlessly encounter danger.

ansarería, *n.f.* place where geese are reared.

ansarero, -ra, *n.m.f.* gooseherd.

ansarino, -na, *a.* goosy; relating to geese. — *n.m.* gosling.

ansarón, *n.m.* great goose.

anseático, -ca, *a.* Hanseatic.

ansí, *adv.* (*obs.*) so, thus.

ansia, *n.f.* anxiety; anguish, ardent desire; longing, hankering, greediness.

ansiadamente, *adv.* anxiously.

ansiar, *v.t.* to desire anxiously; to long, hanker after; *ansío saber*, I long to know.

ansiedad, *n.f.* anxiety.

ansiosamente, *adv.* anxiously, earnestly.

ansioso, -sa, *a.* anxious; eager, greedy; *ansioso de triunfo*, anxious for triumph; *ansioso por la comida*, eager for the meal.

anta, *n.f.* (*zool.*) elk; obelisk; needle; (*arch.*) antæ, pillars of a building.

antagallas, *n.f.pl.* (*naut.*) spritsail reef-bands.

antagónico, -ca, *a.* antagonistic.

antagonismo, *n.m.* antagonism.

antagonista, *n.m.f.* antagonist, adversary, competitor, opposer, foeman.

antana, *n.f. llamarse uno antana*, to go back on one's promise.

antañazo, *adv.* (*coll.*) a long time since.

antaño, *adv.* last year, formerly; long ago; yore; *en los nidos de antaño no hay pájaros hogaño*, take time by the forelock.

antártico, -ca, *a.* antarctic.

ante, *n.m.* (*zool.*) elk; African antelope; dressed buck or buffalo skin; buckskin; suède; (*paint.*) buff-colour; first dinner course; (*Per.*) refreshing beverage; (*Mex.*) dessert made of egg, coconut, almond, etc.; (*Guat.*) syrup. — *prep.* in presence of; in comparison with; in respect of; before; *ante mí*, before me, in my presence; *ante todo*, above all.

anteado, -da, *a.* buff-coloured.

antealtar, *n.m.* the space in front of the steps of the altar, chancel.

anteanoche, *adv.* the night before last.

anteanteayer, *adv.* three days ago.

anteantenoche, *adv.* three nights ago.

anteantier, *adv.* (*coll.*) three days ago.

antear, *v.t.* to cover with, or make like chamois leather.

anteayer, *adv.* the day before yesterday.

antebrazo, *n.m.* fore-arm; (*vet.*) shoulder or fore-thigh.

antecama, *n.f.* bedside carpet, rug.

antecámara, *n.f.* antechamber; lobby, hall.

antecapilla, *n.f.* ante-chapel, room before a chapel.

antecedencia, *n.f.* antecedence; lineage, origin.

antecedente, *n.m.*, *a.* antecedent.

antecedentemente, *adv.* antecedently, previously, beforehand.

anteceder, *v.t.* to precede, go before, or in front of.

antecesor, -ra, *n.m.f.* predecessor. — *n.m.* forefather. — *n.m.pl.* ancestors. — *a.* antecedent.

anteco, -ca, *a.* (*geog.*) relating to the Antœci. — *n.m.pl.* Antœci.

antecoger, *v.t.* (*pres. indic.* **antecojo**; *pres. subj.* **antecoja**) to grasp and carry, or lead in front of one; (*prov.*) to gather in fruit before the due time.

antecolumna, *n.f.* (*arch.*) column of a portico.

antecoro, *n.m.* entrance leading to the choir.

Antecristo, *n.m.* Antichrist.

antecuerpo, *n.m.* (*arch.*) projection, balcony.

antedata, *n.f.* antedate.

antedatar, *v.t.* to antedate.

antedecir, *v.t.* (conjugated like DECIR) to predict, foretell.

antedía, *adv.* before the fixed day.

antedicho, -cha, *a.* aforesaid. — *p.p. irr.* [ANTEDECIR].

antediluviano, -na, *a.* antediluvian.

antefirma, *n.f.* address before the signature; description of signatory before the signature.

antefoso, *n.m.* (*fort.*) second ditch.

antehistórico, -ca, *a.* prehistoric.

anteiglesia, *n.f.* (*prov.*) parochial church and municipal district of some places in Vizcaya; church-porch.

anteislámico, -a, *a.* relating to the Arab people before Muhammad.

antejo, *n.m.* (*Cub.*) a wild tree with valuable wood.

antelación, *n.f.* preference; precedence in order of time.

antemano, (de), *adv.* beforehand.

antemeridiano, -na, *a.* in the forenoon.

antemural, *n.m.;* **antemuro**, *n.m.;* **antemuralla**, *n.f.* fort, rock, or mountain serving as defence to a fortress; safeguard.

antena, *n.f.* (*naut.*) lateen yard; (*ent.*) horn or antenna; (*wire.*) aerial. — *pl.* antennæ.

antenacido, -da, *a.* premature (baby).

antenatal, *a.* pre-natal.

antenífero, -ra, *a.* (*ent.*) antenniferous.

anteniforme, *a.* (*ent.*) antenniform.

antenoche, *adv.* the night before last; dusk, twilight.

antenombre, *n.m.* title prefixed to a proper name, as *don*, *san*, etc.

anténula, *n.f.* antennule.

antenupcial, *a.* before marriage, antenuptial.

anteojera, *n.f.* spectacle-case; *pl.* blinkers.

anteojero, -ra, *n.m.f.* spectacle maker or seller.

anteojo, *n.m.* spy-glass; eye-glass; *anteojo de larga vista*, telescope; *mirar*, or *ver con anteojo de aumento*, or *de larga vista*, to anticipate greatly; to exaggerate; *anteojo de puño* or *de teatro*, opera-glass; (*pl.*) spectacles, eye-glasses; *anteojos de camino* or *de enfermos*, goggles; (*bot.*) honesty.

antepagar, *v.t.* to pay in advance.

antepalco, *n.m.* (*theat.*) private room attached to a box.

antepasado, -da, *a.* passed, elapsed. — *n.m.pl.* ancestors, predecessors, forefathers.

antepasto, *n.m.* appetizer.

antepechado, -da, *a.* having railings.

antepecho, *n.m.* breastwork, parapet, battlement; balcony, bridge-rail, sill, railing;

footstep of a coach; breast harness; breast-beam of a loom; (*min.*) breast.

antependio, *n.m.* antependium.

antepenúltimo, -ma, *n.m.f.,* *a.* antepenultimate, antepenult.

anteponer, *v.t.* (conjugated like PONER) to prefer, place before. — *v.r.* to push oneself forward.

anteportada, *n.f.* fly-leaf bearing the title only of a book, half-title.

anteproyecto, *n.m.* preliminary plans for architectural or engineering work.

antepuerta, *n.f.* portière, curtain placed before a door; (*fort.*) anteport.

antepuerto, *n.m.* (*naut.*) outer port, anteport.

antepuesto, -ta, *p.p. irr.* [ANTEPONER] placed before, preferred.

antequino, *n.m.* (*arch.*) quarter-round moulding.

antera, *n.f.* (*bot.*) anther.

anterior, *a.* anterior, former, previous; *anterior a tal fecha,* previous to such-and-such a date.

anterioridad, *n.f.* priority, preference; *con anterioridad,* previously.

anteriormente, *adv.* previously, antecedently.

antero, *n.m.* worker in buckskin.

antes, (with *de* or *que*) *adv.* before. — *conj.* on the contrary; (with *de que* or *que*) before. — *adv.* beforehand; first; rather, better; heretofore; *haga Vd. esto antes,* do this first; *antes bien,* on the contrary; rather; *antes con antes, cuanto antes,* as quickly as you can, as soon as possible; *antes hoy que mañana,* better to-day than to-morrow; *de antes,* (*coll.*) of old.

antesacristía, *n.f.* room leading to the sacristy.

antesala, *n.f.* anteroom, antechamber; *hacer antesala,* to dance attendance in an antechamber; to wait a long time for someone in his house.

antestatura, *n.f.* (*fort.*) small entrenchment of palisades and sandbags.

antetemplo, *n.m.* portico of a church.

antever, *v.t.* (conjugated like VER) to foresee.

antevíspera, *n.f.* the day before yesterday.

antevisto, -ta, *p.p. irr.* [ANTEVER] foreseen.

anti, *prep.* anti, against; before.

antia, *n.f.* (*ichth.*) lampuga, mutton-fish.

antiácido, *a.* antacid.

antiafrodisíaco, -ca, *a.* antaphrodisiac.

antiálcali, *n.m.* antalkali.

antiapoléctico, -ca, *a.* (*med.*) antiapoplectic.

antiapóstol, *n.m.f.* anti-apostle.

antiar, *n.m.* (*bot., chem.*) antiar resin; antiar (poison).

antiarina, *n.f.* (*chem.*) antiarin.

antiaris, *n.m.* (*bot.*) upas-tree.

antiartístico, -ca, *a.* inartistic.

antiartrítico, -ca, *n.m., a.* (*med.*) antarthritic.

antiasmático, -ca, *n.m., a.* (*med.*) antasthmatic.

antibaquio, *n.m.* (*poet.*) antibacchic.

antibilioso, -sa, *a.* antibilious.

anticardenal, *n.m.* schismatic cardinal.

anticatarral, *n.m., a.* (*med.*) anticatarrhal.

anticausótico, -ca, *a.* febrifugal. — *n.m.* febrifuge.

anticiclón, *n.m.* anticyclone.

anticipación, *n.f.* anticipation, foretaste; *con anticipación,* in advance.

anticipada, *n.f.* unexpected thrust or blow (in fencing).

anticipadamente, *adv.* prematurely, beforehand.

anticipado, -da, *a.* premature; (*agric.*) early; (*com.*) advanced, in advance (payment). — *p.p.* [ANTICIPAR].

anticipador, -ra, *n.m.f.* anticipator. — *a.* anticipating.

anticipamiento, *n.m.* anticipation.

anticipante, *a.* anticipating; (*med.*) anticipant. — *n.m.f.* one who anticipates or forestalls.

anticipar, *v.t.* to anticipate, forestall; to take up beforehand; to advance.

anticipo, *n.m.* anticipation; advance, anticipated payment; money lent.

anticívico, -ca, *a.* anticivic.

anticlerical, *a.* anticlerical. — *n.m.f.* irreligious person.

anticlímax, *n.m.f.* (*rhet.*) anticlimax.

anticlinal, *a.* (*geol.*) anticlinal. — *n.m.* anticline.

anticohesor, *n.m.* (*wire.*) anti-coherer.

anticombustible, *n.m., a.,* non-inflammable (material).

anticonstitucional, *a.* unconstitutional, anticonstitutional.

anticonstitucionalmente, *adv.* unconstitutionally.

anticosmético, -ca, *a.* anticosmetic.

anticresis, *n.f.* (*law*) agreement to yield the fruits of a farm till a debt is paid.

anticresista, *n.m.f.* the creditor in *anticresis.*

anticrético, -ca, *a.* (*law*) relating to *anticresis.*

anticristiano, -na, *a.* antichristian.

Anticristo, *n.m.* Antichrist.

anticrítica, *n.f.* counter-criticism.

anticrítico, *n.m.* opponent to a critic.

anticuado, -da, *a.* antiquated, out of date, out of use. — *p.p.* [ANTICUAR].

anticuar, *v.t.* to antiquate, outdate. — *v.r.* to become antiquated, old-fashioned.

anticuario, -ria, *n.m.f.* antiquarian.

antidisentérico, -ca, *a.* antidysenteric.

antidoral, *a.* (*law*) remuneratory, remunerative.

antidotario, *n.m.* pharmacopœia; place in a pharmacy for antidotes; dispensary.

antídoto, *n.m.* antidote, counter-poison.

antiemético, -ca, *a.* (*med.*) antemetic.

antiepiléptico, -ca, *a.* (*med.*) antepileptic.

antier, *adv.* (*coll.*) [ANTEAYER].

antiesclavista, *n.m.f., a.* anti-slavery.

antiescorbútico, -ca, *a.* antiscorbutic.

antiescrofuloso, -sa, *a.* antiscrofulous.

antiespasmódico, -ca, *n.m., a.* antispasmodic.

antiestético, -ca, *a.* unæsthetic; ungainly.

antifaz, *n.m.* veil covering the face; mask.

antifebril, *a.* (*med.*) antifebrile, febrifugal.

antifernales, *a.pl.* said of possessions given by the husband to the wife as security for her dowry.

antiflogístico, -ca, *n.m., a.* (*med.*) antiphlogistic.

antífona, *n.f.* antiphon, anthem.

antifonal, *n.f.;* **antifonario,** *n.m., a.* antiphonal, antiphonary.

antifonero, *n.m.* precentor.

antífrasis, *n.f.* (*rhet.*) antiphrasis.

antifricción, *n.f.* (*mech.*) anti-friction.

antigramatical, *a.* ungrammatical.

antigualla, *n.f.* monument of antiquity; antique, antiquity; ancient custom or object.

antiguamente, *adv.* anciently, formerly, heretofore.

antiguar, *v.i., v.r.* to obtain seniority (as member of a tribunal, college, etc.). — *v.t.* to antiquate. — *v.r.* to become out of date, antiquated.

antigüedad, *n.f.* antiquity, oldness; ancient times; the ancients; antique; seniority.

antiguo, -gua, *a.* antique, ancient, old; having been long in a position or employment; *a la antigua,* or *a lo antiguo,* after the manner or custom of the ancients; *de antiguo,* of old; from times of yore; *en lo antiguo,* in remote times; *Antiguo Testamento,* Old Testament. — *n.m.* aged member of a community; senior of a college; (*pl.*) the ancients.

antihelio, *n.m.* anthelion.

antihelmíntico, -ca, *n.m., a.* anthelmintic.

antiherpético, -ca, *a.* (*med.*) antiherpetic.

antihigiénico, -ca, *a.* unhealthy, unhygienic.

antihistérico, -ca, *a.* (*med.*) antihysteric.

antihumano, -na, *a.* inhuman.

antilogía, *n.f.* contradiction.

antilógico, -ca, *a.* illogical.

antílope, *n.m.* (*zool.*) antelope.

antillano, -na, *n.m.f., a.* native of or relating to the Antilles; West-Indian.

Antillas, *n.f.pl.* West Indies, Antilles.

antimilitarista, *n.m.f., a.* anti-militarist.

antiministerial, *a.* anti-ministerial.

antimonárquico, -ca, *a.* antimonarchical.

antimonial, *a.* antimonial.

antimoniato, *n.m.* antimoniate.

antimónico, -ca, *a.* antimonic.

antimonio, *n.m.* antimony.

antinacional, *a.* anti-national.

antinatural, *a.* unnatural.

antinefrítico, -ca, *a.* (*med.*) antinephritic.

antinomia, *n.f.* (*law*) conflict between laws or parts of a law; antinomy.

antinómico, -ca, *a.* implying antinomy; contradictory.

antioqueno, -na, *n.m.f., a.* Antiochian.

Antioquía, *n.f.* Antioch.

antipalúdico, -ca, *n.m., a.* (*med.*) anti-malarial.

antipapa, *n.m.* anti-pope.

antipapado, *n.m.* dignity of anti-pope.

antipapal, *a.* anti-papal.

antipapista, *n.m.f., a.* anti-papal.

antipara, *n.f.* screen; legging covering the front part of leg and foot.

antiparalítico, -ca, *a.* (*med.*) antiparalytic.

antiparras, *n.f.pl.* (*coll.*) spectacles.

antipatía, *n.f.* antipathy, aversion, dislike.

antipático, -ca, *a.* repugnant, antipathetic, displeasing.

antipatizar, *v.i.* to find uncongenial, dislike.

antipatriótico, -ca, *a.* unpatriotic.

antiperistáltico, -ca, *a.* (*med.*) antiperistaltic.

antiperistasis, *n.f.* antiperistasis.

antiperistático, -ca, *a.* belonging to antiperistasis.

antipestilencial, *a.* (*med.*) antipestilential.

antipirético, -ca, *n.m., a.* (*med.*) antipyretic.

antipirina, *n.f.* (*chem.*) antipyrine.

antipoca, *n.f.* (*law, prov.*) agreement to lease; obligation for a tenant to pay a certain rent.

antipocar, *v.t.* (*law, prov.*) to execute a lease; to acknowledge by deed the obligation to pay a certain rent; to resume the performance of a duty.

antípoda, *a.* (*geog.*) antipodal. — *n.f.pl.* antipodes; (*coll.*) persons of opposite dispositions or manners.

antipolítico, -ca, *a.* impolitic.

antipolo, *n.m.* antipole.

antipútrido, -da, *a.* (*med.*) antiseptic.

antiquísimo, -ma, *a. superl.* very ancient.

antiquismo, *n.m.* archaism.

antirrábico, -ca, *a.* (*med.*) useful in the treatment of rabies.

antirreligioso, -sa, *n.m.f., a.* anti-religious; irreligious person.

antirreumático, -ca, *n.m., a.* (*med.*) antirheumatic.

antirrevolucionario, -ria, *n.m.f., a.* anti-revolutionary.

antirrino, *n.m.* (*bot.*) antirrhinum, snapdragon.

antisabático, -ca, *n.m.f., a.* anti-Sabbatarian.

antiscio, -cia, *n.m.f., a.* (*geog.*) [ANTECO].

antisemita, *n.m.f.* anti-Semite.

antisemitismo, *n.m.* anti-Semitism.

antisepsia, *n.f.* (*med.*) antisepsy.

antiséptico, -ca, *a.* antiseptic.

antisifilítico, -ca, *n.m., a.* (*med.*) antisyphilitic.

antisocial, *a.* antisocial; opposed to society and order.

antisocialista, *n.m.f., a.* anti-socialist.

antistrofa, *n.f.* antistrophe.

antiteísmo, *n.m.* antitheism.

antitérmico, -ca, *a.* (*phys.*) non-conducting (heat).

antítesis, *n.f.* (*rhet.*) antithesis; (*phil.*) opposition in two assertions.

antitético, -ca, *a.* antithetic, antithetical.

antitípico, -ca, *a.* antitypal, antitypical.

antitipo, *n.m.* antitype.

antitóxico, -ca, *a.* (*med.*) antitoxic, preventing poison.

antitoxina, *n.f.* antitoxin.

antitrinitario, -ria, *n.m.f., a.* anti-Trinitarian.

antituberculoso, -sa, *n.m.f., a.* (*med.*) anti-tuberculous.

antivarioloso, -sa, *a.* (*med.*) efficacious against smallpox.

antivenenoso, -sa, *n.m.f.* antidote. — *a.* antidotal.

antivenéreo, -a, *a.* (*med.*) anti-venereal.

antiverminoso, -sa, *a.* vermifugal.

antizímico, -ca, *a.* (*chem.*) non-fermenting.

antófago, -ga, *a.* anthophagous.

antojadizamente, *adv.* capriciously, whimsically; in a fickle manner.

antojadizo, -za, *a.* capricious, whimsical, fickle.

antojado, -da, *a.* anxious, longing; (*slang*) in fetters (prisoner). — *p.p.* [ANTOJARSE].

antojarse, *v.r.* to long for, fancy, desire greatly; to surmise, imagine; *antojársele a uno una cosa,* to desire or fancy something suddenly; *no hace más que lo que se le antoja,* he only does what he pleases; *se me antoja que va a llover,* I think it is going to rain; *se me antoja que no va a pagar,* I have a feeling that he will not pay.

antojera, *n.f.* spectacle-case; blinker (for horses).

antojero, *n.m.* spectacle maker.

antojo, *n.m.* whim, caprice, fancy; longing, hankering after, vehement desire; surmise; eye-glass; (*pl.*) moles, beauty-spots; birthmark; (*slang*) fetters.

antojuelo, *n.m.* slight desire.
antología, *n.f.* anthology.
antónimo, -ma, *n.m., a.* (*gram.*) antonym.
antonomasia, *n.f.* (*rhet.*) antonomasia.
antonomástico, -ca, *a.* antonomastic.
antor, -ra, *n.m.f.* (*law, prov.*) vendor of stolen goods.
antorcha, *n.f.* torch, taper, flambeau; cresset.
antorchero, *n.m.* cresset.
antoría, *n.f.* (*law, prov.*) right against the seller of stolen goods.
antracita, *n.f.* anthracite coal.
antracítico, -ca, *a.* anthracitic.
ántrax, *n.m.* (*med.*) anthrax.
antro, *n.m.* (*poet.*) cavern, den, grotto.
antropofagía, *n.f.* anthropophagy.
antropófago, -ga, *n.m.f.* cannibal. — *a.* cannibalistic.
antropografía, *n.f.* anthropography.
antropoide, *a.* anthropoid.
antropología, *n.f.* anthropology.
antropológico, -ca, *a.* anthropological.
antropólogo, *n.m.* anthropologist.
antropómetra, *n.m.* anthropometrist.
antropometría, *n.f.* anthropometry.
antropomorfismo, *n.m.* anthropomorphism.
antropomorfita, *n.m.f.* anthropomorphist.
antropomorfo, -fa, *a.* anthropomorphous.
antroposofía, *n.f.* anthroposophy.
antruejar, *v.t.* (*prov.*) to wet with water; to play carnival tricks.
antruejo, *n.m.* the three days of Carnival before Ash Wednesday.
antucá, *n.m.* parasol, umbrella.
antuerpiense, *n.m.f.* native, inhabitant of Antwerp. — *a.* appertaining to Antwerp.
antuviada, *n.f.* (*coll.*) blow or stroke.
antuviar, *v.t.* to forestall, anticipate; (*coll.*) to be first in striking or attacking.
antuvión, *n.m.* (*coll.*) sudden, unexpected blow or attack; *de antuvión*, unexpectedly.
antuzano, *n.m.* (*prov.*) small terrace in front of house.
anual, *a.* annual, yearly.
anualidad, *n.f.* annual recurrence; annuity, yearly pension or rent.
anualmente, *adv.* annually, yearly.
anuario, *n.m.* year-book, trade directory, yearly report.
anúbada, *n.f.* call to war.
anubarrado, -da, *a.* clouded, cloudy; (*paint.*) with cloud effects.
anublado, -da, *a.* overcast, clouded, dim, misty; (*slang*) blind. — *p.p.* [ANUBLAR].
anublar, *v.t.* to cloud, darken, overcast, obscure. — *v.r.* to become cloudy; (*agric.*) to become blasted, withered, mildewed; (*fig.*) to fall through.
anublo, *n.m.* mildew.
anudadura, *n.f.*; **anudamiento,** *n.m.* knotting, tying, joining; withering, pining.
anudar, *v.t.* to knot; to join, unite; to continue something interrupted. — *v.r.* to become knotted, joined; to wither, fade, pine away; *anudarse la voz*, to become speechless.
anuencia, *n.f.* compliance, consent.
anuente, *a.* complying, consenting.
anuir, *v.i.* to assent, agree, consent.
anulable, *a.* that can be annulled; revocable.
anulación, *n.f.* nullification, abrogation.
anulador, -ora, *n.m.f.* repealer. — *a.* repealing.
anular, *v.t.* to annul, make void, frustrate; to cancel, rescind, take away (authority). — *v.r.* to humble oneself, submit.
anular, *a.* ring-shaped, annular; *dedo anular,* the fourth finger, ring-finger.
anulativo, -va, *a.* having the power of making void.
anuloso, -sa, *a.* annular.
anunciación, *n.f.* announcement; Annunciation; Day of the Annunciation or Lady Day (March 25).
anunciador, -ra, *n.m.f.* announcer; advertiser. — *n.m.* (*elec.*) annunciator. — *a.* announcing; advertising.
anunciante, *n.m.f., a.* [ANUNCIADOR].
anunciar, *v.t.* to announce, proclaim; to notify (arrival); to advertise; to foretell. — *v.r.* to make oneself known.
anuncio, *n.m.* announcement; advertisement, notice; omen; prediction; (*com.*) advice.
anuo, -ua, *a.* annual, yearly.
anúteba, *n.f.* call to war; ancient tax for defence.
anverso, *n.m.* obverse.
anvir, *n.m.* (*West Ind.*) beverage from fermented tobacco leaves.
anzolero, -ra, *n.m.f.* maker of or dealer in fish-hooks.
anzuelo, *n.m.* fish-hook; (*coll.*) allurement, incitement; fritters; *caer*, or *picar en el anzuelo*, to be tricked, defrauded; *echar el anzuelo*, to angle; *tragar el anzuelo*, to swallow the bait; *roer el anzuelo*, to escape a danger.
aña, *n.f.* hyena.
añacal, *n.m.* carrier of wheat to mills; baker's board for carrying bread.
añacalero, *n.m.* (*prov.*) carrier of building materials.
añada, *n.f.* good or bad season; moiety of arable land.
añadido, -da, *p.p.* [AÑADIR] added. — *n.m.* hair-switch; (*print.*) addition.
añadidura, *n.f.*; **añadimiento,** *n.m.* addition, excess, increase; make-weight; *por añadidura,* further, what is more.
añadir, *v.t.* to add, join; to increase, augment; *añadir a lo expuesto*, to add to what has already been said; to exaggerate.
añafea, *n.f.*; *papel de añafea*, brown paper.
añafil, *n.m.* Moorish musical trumpet.
añafilero, *n.m.* player on the *añafil*.
añagaza, *n.f.* lure, decoy (birds); allurement, enticement.
añal, *a.* annual; *cordero añal*, yearling lamb. — *n.m.* anniversary; offering for some person deceased made one year after funeral.
añalejo, *n.m.* ecclesiastical almanac.
añás, *n.f.* (*Per.*) kind of South American fox.
añascar, *v.t.* (*pret.* **añasqué**; *pres. subj.* **añasque**) to collect small trinkets by degrees; to entangle, muddle. — *v.r.* to become twisted, entangled.
añasco, *n.m.* entanglement, muddle.
añejar, *v.t.* to make old. — *v.r.* to change, grow old; to become stale.
añejo, -ja, *a.* old (wine, bacon); (*coll.*) stale (news); musty.
añicos, *n.m.pl.* bits or small pieces of anything; smithereens; *hacer añicos*, to break into fragments; *hacerse añicos*, to take great pains.
añil, *n.m.* (*bot.*) indigo plant; indigo dye-stuff.

añilar, *v.t.* to blue laundry clothes; to dye with indigo.

añilería, *n.f.* indigo plantation.

añinero, -ra, *n.m.f.* dealer in lambskins.

añinos, *n.m.pl.* the unshorn coats of yearling lambs; lambs' wool.

año, *n.m.* year; crop; valentine drawn by lot on New Year's Eve. — *pl.* birthday; old age; *entre año,* during the year; *¡mal año!* an imprecatory exclamation; *por (al, cada) año,* yearly; *tener — años,* to be — years old; *año bisiesto,* or *intercalar,* leap-year; *año económico,* fiscal year; *año de gracia,* or *de nuestra salud,* year of grace; *año climatérico,* climacteric year; *año escolar,* school year; *año secular,* the last year in each century; *año y vez,* (*agric.*) cultivated or bearing fruit in alternate years; *por los años de* 1878, about the year 1878; *año de la nanita,* (*comic*) donkeys' years ago; *estar de buen año,* to be healthy and fleshy; *día de año nuevo,* New Year's Day; *celebrar,* or *dar los años,* to keep a birthday; *entrado en años,* elderly; *no en los años están todos los engaños,* youth can deceive as well as age; *no digáis mal del año hasta que sea pasado,* it's a long lane that has no turning; *más vale año tardío que vacío,* better late than never; *ganar* (or *perder*) *año,* to pass (or fail) in one's examinations (of students); *lo que no fué en mi año, no fué en mi daño,* it's no use crying over spilt milk; *no hay quince años feos,* youth is better than beauty (said of girls); *jugar los años,* to play without stakes.

añojal, *n.m.* fallow land.

añojo, -ja, *n.m.f.* yearling calf.

añoranza, *n.f.* homesickness, nostalgia; regret.

añorar, *v.t.* to regret, mourn for. — *v.r.* to feel homesick.

añoso, -sa, *a.* old, stricken in years.

añublado, -da, *a.* (*slang*) blind. — *p.p.* [AÑUBLAR].

añublar, *v.t.* [ANUBLAR].

añublo, *n.m.* mildew.

añudador, -ra, *n.m.f.* one who knots or ties. — *a.* knotty, tying.

añudadura, *n.f.;* añudamiento, *n.m.* [ANUDADURA].

añudar, *v.t.* to make fast, knot, unite, tie close; *añudar los labios,* to impose silence. — *v.r.* to become knotted, tied.

añusgar, *v.i.* to choke; to be displeased, vexed.

aojado, -da, *a.* bewitched, affected by the evil eye. — *p.p.* [AOJAR].

aojador, -ra, *n.m.f., a.* one with the evil eye.

aojadura, *n.f.;* aojamiento, *n.m.* witchcraft, fascination, evil eye.

aojar, *v.t.* to charm, bewitch; to spoil; to send wrong.

aojo, *n.m.* fascination, charm, evil eye.

aojusgar, *v.i.* to choke while eating.

aónides, *n.f.pl.* the Muses.

aoristo, *n.m.* (*gram.*) aorist, past tense.

aorta, *n.f.* (*anat.*) aorta.

aorteurismo, *n.m.* aneurism of the aorta.

aórtico, -ca, *a.* aortic.

aovado, -da, *a.* ovate, oviform, egg-shaped. — *p.p.* [AOVAR].

aovar, *v.i.* to lay eggs.

aovillar, *v.t.* to wind into balls or clues. — *v.r.* to crumple oneself up like a clue or ball of thread.

apabellonado, -da, *a.* tent-like.

apabilar, *v.t.* to trim the wick of a candle. — *v.r.* to lose courage.

apabullar, *v.t.* (*coll.*) to flatten, crush; to silence.

apabullo, *n.m.* (*coll.*) flattening, crushing; silencing.

apacentadero, *n.m.* pasture-land.

apacentador, -ra, *n.m.f.* one who tends cattle. — *n.m.* herdsman, pasturer.

apacentamiento, *n.m.* the act of tending grazing cattle; pasturage.

apacentar, *v.t.* (*pres. indic.* apaciento; *pres. subj.* apaciente) to tend grazing cattle; to graze; (*fig.*) to teach, instruct spiritually; (*fig.*) to inflame the passions. — *v.r.* to graze; to become excited; *apacentarse con, de memorias,* to feed on memories.

apacibilidad, *n.f.* affability, mildness, meekness; *con apacibilidad,* peacefully.

apacibilísimo, -ma, *a. superl. irr.* [APACIBLE] extremely meek.

apacible, *a.* peaceable, peaceful, pleasant, affable, meek, gentle; still, quiet, placid, calm; *tiempo apacible,* (*naut.*) moderate weather.

apaciblemente, *adv.* pleasantly, quietly, gently.

apaciento; apaciente, *pres. indic.; pres. subj.* [APACENTAR].

apaciguador, -ra, *n.m.f.* pacifier. — *a.* pacifying.

apaciguamiento, *n.m.* pacification.

apaciguar, *v.t.* to appease, pacify, calm, still. — *v.i.* (*naut.*) to abate. — *v.r.* to become calm; to calm down.

apacorral, *n.m.* (*Hond.*) gigantic tree with bitter medicinal bark.

apache, *n.m., a.* Apache; thug.

apacheta, (*Per.*) *n.f.* cairn on hilltops worshipped by the Peruvians.

apachurrar, *v.t.* (*Am.*) to crush, to flatten.

apadrinador, -ra, *n.m.f.* patron, patroness, defender, protector, protectress; second in a duel; person who accompanies another while riding. — *a.* protecting, defending.

apadrinamiento, *n.m.* patronage.

apadrinar, *v.t.* to act as second in a duel; to act as godfather; to accompany another while riding; to protect, favour, patronize, support.

apagable, *a.* extinguishable, quenchable, effaceable.

apagadizo, -za, *a.* of difficult combustion.

apagado, -da, *a.* humble-minded, submissive, pusillanimous; dull, faded (of colours); extinguished, quenched. — *p.p.* [APAGAR].

apagador, -ra, *n.m.f.* one who quenches or extinguishes; damper, extinguisher; damper (in pianos). — *a.* extinguishing.

apagaincendios, *n.m.* fire-engine, fire-extinguisher.

apagamiento, *n.m.* extinguishment, quenching.

apagapenoles, *n.m.pl.* (*naut.*) leech-ropes, leech-lines.

apagar, *v.t.* (*pret.* apagué; *pres. subj.* apague) to quench, put out, extinguish; to efface, destroy; (*art*) to soften colours; (*mech.*) to deaden; (*artill.*) to silence the enemy's guns; *apagar la sed,* to quench thirst; *apagar la cal,* to slake lime; *apagar la voz*, to mute a musical instrument; *¡apaga y vámonos!* (*coll.*) leave off! — *v.r.* to become extinguished; to die out, go out; *apagarse* (*la lumbre, la luz, el fuego*), to go out (of light, fire, etc.).

apagavelas, *n.m.* candle-extinguisher.

apainelado, -da, *a.* (*arch.*) elliptical.

apaisado, -da, *a.* (painting or frame) broader than its height; oblong.

apalabrar, *v.t.* to agree to something by word of mouth; to bespeak, engage beforehand; to appoint a meeting for consultation. — *v.r.* to come to an agreement.

apalancar, *v.t.* (*pret.* **apalanqué;** *pres. subj.* **apalanque**) to move with a lever.

apaleador, -ra, *n.m.f.* cudgeller. — *a.* cudgelling.

apaleamiento, *n.m.* beating, drubbing.

apalear, *v.t.* to cane, whip, drub, cudgel, maul, beat (clothes, carpets, etc.); to beat down (fruit) with a pole; to winnow grain.

apaleo, *n.m.* winnowing grain; period of winnowing.

apalmada, *a.* (*her.*) *mano apalmada*, outstretched palm of the hand.

apanalado, -da, *a.* honey-combed.

apancora, *n.f.* (*ichth.*) sea-hedgehog.

apandar, *v.t.* (*coll.*) to pilfer, steal, rob. — *v.r.* (*prov.*) to keep immobile.

apandillar, *v.t., v.r.* to form a league, party or faction; (*slang*) to cheat at cards.

apandorgarse, *v.r.* (*coll.*) to grow stout (of women).

apanojado, -da, *a.* (*bot.*) paniculate.

apantanar, *v.t.* to flood, inundate. — *v.r.* to become flooded, inundated.

apantuflado, -da, *a.* shaped like a slipper.

apañado, -da, *a.* resembling woollen cloth; (*fig.*) dexterous, skilful; seized; pilfered; (*fig.*) (*coll.*) adequate, suitable. — *p.p.* [APAÑAR].

apañador, -ra, *n.m.f.* one who grasps or seizes; pilferer. — *n.m.* orator. — *a.* seizing, grasping.

apañadura, *n.f.; ***apañamiento,** *n.m.* act of seizing or grasping, snatching. — *n.f.pl.* trimming on counterpanes.

apañar, *v.t.* to grasp or seize; to pilfer; to carry away; to dress, adorn, clothe; (*coll.*) to fit close, protect, wrap; (*prov.*) to mend, patch; *estar apañado*, to be well suited or fitted to its use. — *v.r.* (*coll.*) to become skilful, handy.

apaño, *n.m.* act of seizing or grasping; knack; (*coll.*) patch, mend, repair; (*coll.*) mistress, concubine.

apañuscador, -ra, *n.m.f.* (*coll.*) crumpler. — *a.* crumpling.

apañuscar, *v.t.* (*pret.* **apañusqué;** *pres. subj.* **apañusque**) (*coll.*) to rumple, crush, crumple; to pilfer.

apapagayado, -da, *a.* parrot-like, aquiline (nose).

aparador, -ra, *n.m.f.* closer of shoes. — *n.m.* sideboard, cupboard, dresser; credence-table; workshop of an artisan; show-window; *estar de aparador una mujer*, to be dressed up to receive visitors (said of a woman).

aparadura, *n.f.* (*naut.*) garbel, garboard-plank.

aparar, *v.t.* to stretch out the hands or skirts for catching anything; (*agric.*) to dress,

weed plants; to close the uppers of shoes; to prepare, arrange; to dress with an adze, dub; *aparar un navio*, (*naut.*) to dub a ship; *aparar en, con la mano*, to catch in, with the hand. — *v.r.* to prepare, adorn, arrange oneself.

aparasolado, -da, *a.* umbrella-like; (*bot.*) umbelliferous.

aparatado, -da, *a.* prepared, disposed; adorned; overcast (sky). — *p.p.* [APARATARSE].

aparatarse, *v.r.* (*Col.*) to become overcast; to threaten snow or hail (sky); to adorn oneself ostentatiously.

aparatero, -ra, *a.* (*prov. & Chi.*) boasting, exaggerating.

aparato, *n.m.* apparatus, preparation, system; pomp, show, ceremony, ostentation; signs, symptoms; machine, appliance; (*surg.*) external application. — *pl.* (*coll.*) exaggerations; (*theat.*) elaborate scenic display; associated organs.

aparatoso, -sa, *a.* pompous, showy; (*coll.*) exaggerating.

aparcar, *v.t.* to park (artillery, cars, etc.).

aparcería, *n.f.* partnership.

aparcero, -ra, *n.m.f.* partner, associate, co-proprietor.

apareamiento, *n.m.* matching, mating; pairing.

aparear, *v.t.* to match, mate, couple. — *v.r.* to become paired, matched, mated; to form a pair.

aparecer, *v.i., v.r.* (*pres. indic.* **aparezco;** *pres. subj.* **aparezca**) to appear, turn up unexpectedly, show up; *aparecerse a alguno*, to see a ghost; *aparecerse en casa*, to arrive home unexpectedly; *aparecerse entre sueños*, to see someone in dreams.

aparecido, -da, *a.* appeared. — *n.m.* ghost. — *p.p.* [APARECER].

aparecimiento, *n.m.* apparition, appearance.

aparejadamente, *adv.* aptly.

aparejado, -da, *a.* apt, fit, ready. — *p.p.* [APAREJAR].

aparejador, -ra, *n.m.f.* one who prepares or gets ready; overseer of a building; (*naut.*) rigger.

aparejar, *v.t.* to get ready; to prepare; to saddle or harness; (*naut.*) to rig; to furnish; to size work before painting or gilding; (*paint.*) to prime; to prepare for building. — *v.r.* to get ready; to equip oneself; *aparejarse al*, or *para el trabajo*, to get ready for work.

aparejo, *n.m.* preparation, disposition; harness, gear; (*paint.*) priming; sizing canvas or board; (*mech.*) tackle, set of pulleys; (*build.*) bond; (*naut.*) tackle and rigging on a ship; furniture; *aparejo real*, main-tackle. — *pl.* apparatus, tools, instruments or materials necessary for a trade.

aparejuelo, *n.m.* small apparatus [APAREJO]; (*naut.*) small tackle.

aparentar, *v.t.* to pretend; to feign, affect.

aparente, *a.* apparent but not real; seeming; feigned, false; convenient, fit, suited; evident, conspicuous.

aparentemente, *adv.* apparently, outwardly; seemingly.

aparezco; aparezca, *pres. indic.; pres. subj.* [APARECER].

aparición, *n.f.* apparition, appearance, vision; (*eccl.*) feast of the Apparition of Christ to the Apostles after Easter.

apariencia, *n.f.* appearance, aspect, outside; face, likeness, looks; resemblance; vestige; pageant, outward show; probability, conjecture; (*pl.*) (*theat.*) scenic effects.

aparrado, -da, *a.* (*bot.*) shrubby, vine-like, crooked; with branches growing horizontally; (*fig.*) short, thick-set. — *p.p.* [APARRAR].

aparrar, *v.t.* (*hort.*) to train branches horizontally.

aparroquiado, -da, *n.m.f.* customer; parishioner. — *a.* introduced as a client; established in a parish. — *p.p.* [APARROQUIAR].

aparroquiar, *v.t.* to bring customers to a shop.

apartación, *n.f.* distribution, division.

apartadamente, *adv.* privately, apart; separately.

apartadero, *n.m.* side-track, parting-place; street-refuge; (*railw.*) siding, railway-switch; sorting-room (for wool); (*agric.*) free pasture place (beside a road); place for bulls (before bullfight).

apartadijo, *n.m.* small part, share, portion; room partitioned off another; *hacer apartadijos,* to divide a whole into shares.

apartadizo, -za, *a.* unsociable. — *n.m.f.* recluse. — *n.m.* small room partitioned off another.

apartado, -da, *a.* separated; distant, remote, retired; distinct, different. — *n.m.* room apart or shut off; smelting-house; mail separated for early or special delivery; post office private letter-box; separation of cattle; shutting up of bulls (before bullfight); board of cattle-ranchers; (*min.*) smelting; assaying; (*Mex.*) department in the Mint for separating and purifying gold. — *p.p.* [APARTAR].

apartador, -ra, *n.m.f.* one who divides or separates; sorter in paper-mills; wool-sorter; separator of cattle; smelter (of metals); *apartador de ganado,* (*slang*) cattle-thief. — *a.* sorting, separating.

apartamiento, *n.m.* separation; retirement; secluded place or room; apartment, flat, habitation; (*law*) renouncement; *apartamiento de ganado,* (*slang*) cattle-stealing.

apartar, *v.t.* to part, separate, divide; to dissuade; to remove, dislodge; to sort (letters, wool); *apartar el grano de la paja,* to winnow the grain from the chaff, to distinguish essentials from non-essentials; *apartar de sí,* to push away; (*Mex.*) to separate gold from silver ingots. — *v.r.* to withdraw, hold off; to become divorced; (*law*) to desist from a claim, action or plea; *apartarse a un lado,* to move aside; to make way for; *apartarse de la ocasión,* to miss the opportunity.

aparte, *n.m.* (*prov.*) space between two words; paragraph; (*theat.*) aside. — *adv.* separately, apart; aside (on the stage); *dejar aparte,* to lay aside; *dejando aparte chanzas,* joking apart.

apartidar, *v.t.* to side with. — *v.r.* to become biased, prejudiced.

aparvar, *v.t.* to heap grain for threshing; to heap, throw together.

apasionadamente, *adv.* passionately; in a prejudiced or bigoted way.

apasionado, -da, *a.* passionate; affected with pain; devoted, passionately fond of. — *n.m.* admirer; (*slang*) governor of a prison; partisan. — *p.p.* [APASIONAR].

apasionamiento, *n.m.* the inspiring or suffering of a passion.

apasionar, *v.t.* to inspire a passion; to torment, afflict. — *v.r.* (with *de* or *por*) to become passionately fond of, to dote on.

apaste, *n.m.* (*Guat., Hond., Mex.*) earthenware tub with handles.

apasturar, *v.t.* (*obs.*) to pasture, forage.

apatán, *n.m.* (*Philip.*) a dry measure of capacity containing 2 minims.

apatanado, -da, *a.* rustic, boorish.

apatía, *n.f.* apathy, impassibility.

apático, -ca, *a.* apathetic, indifferent.

apatuscar, *v.t.* to work carelessly.

apatusco, *n.m.* (*coll.*) ornament, adornment.

apea, *n.f.* rope fetter, hobble (for horses).

apeadero, *n.m.* landing, alighting-place; horse-block; small railway station, halt; house temporarily rented.

apeador, -ra, *n.m.f.* one who dismounts, alights. — *n.m.* land-surveyor. — *n.m.pl.* (*arch.*) props, supports. — *a.* alighting, dismounting.

apeamiento, *n.m.* survey of land.

apear, *v.t.* to help alight, step down, dismount; to measure lands, tenements, buildings; to set landmarks; to fell (a tree); to block or scotch a wheel; to take something down from its place; (*artill.*) to dismount a gun; to dissuade; to ford (a river); to remove, surmount difficulties; to shackle (a horse); (*arch.*) to prop a building; *apear una caballería,* to hobble a horse; *nadie le apea de su error.* — *v.r.* to alight; *apearse por la cola* (or *por las orejas*), to be thrown from one's horse; (*coll.*) to give some absurd answer; *apearse para merendar,* to alight for lunch; *apearse de la mula,* to dismount from the mule.

apechugar, *v.i.* (*pret.* **apechugué;** *pres. subj.* **apechugue**) to push with the breast; (*coll.*) to face, undertake with spirit; (*coll.*) to give in unwillingly; *apechugar con todo,* to accept with repugnance.

apedazar, *v.t.* (*pret.* **apedacé;** *pres. subj.* **apedace**) to tear into pieces; to patch, mend, repair.

apedernalado, -da, *a.* flinty, hard, insensible.

apedreadero, *n.m.* place where boys stone one another.

apedreado, -da, *a.* stoned, pelted; spattered, spotted, variegated; pitted with smallpox. — *p.p.* [APEDREAR].

apedreador, -ra, *n.m.f.* thrower of stones.

apedreamiento, *n.m.* lapidation, stoning; hailing.

apedrear, *v.t.* to stone; to lapidate. — *v. impers.* to hail. — *v.r.* to become injured by hail.

apedreo, *n.m.* [APEDREAMIENTO].

apegadamente, *adv.* devotedly.

apegarse, *v.r.* (with *a*) to attach oneself to.

apego, *n.m.* attachment, fondness; inclination.

apegualar, *v.i.* (*Arg., Chi.*) to use a girth for fastening and securing horses, etc.

apelable, *a.* appealable.

apelación, *n.f.* (*law*) appeal; (*med., coll.*) consultation; *dar por desierta la apelación,* (*law*) expiration of period for appeal; *desamparar la apelación,* (*law*) to abandon the appeal; *interponer apelación,* (*law*) to appeal; *no haber (tener) apelación,* to be hopeless, without remedy.

apelado, -da, *a.* (*law*) successful in appeal; of the same coat or colour (of horses). — *p.p.* [APELAR].

apelambrar, *v.t.* to soak skins in limewater.

apelante, *n.m.f.* appellant. — *a.* appellate.

apelar, *v.i.* (*law*) to appeal, have recourse to; to refer, have relation to; to be of the same colour; to match (said of a pair of horses); *apelar a otro medio,* to have recourse to other measures; *apelar de la sentencia,* to appeal against the sentence; *apelar para ante el tribunal superior,* to appeal to the higher court; *apelar una cosa a otra,* to tally, correspond, match; *apelar el enfermo,* to recover from serious illness; *estas yeguas apelan bien,* these mares go or match well together. — *v.r.* to have recourse to; to seek remedy for.

apelativo, -va, *n.m.f.,* *a.* (*gram.*) appellative; *nombre apelativo,* appellative name.

apeldar, *v.i.* (*coll.*) *apeldarlas,* to flee, take to flight, run away. — *v.r.* (*prov.*) to come together.

apelde, *n.m.* (*coll.*) flight, escape; bell rung before daybreak in Franciscan convents.

apelmazado, -da, *a.* compressed, compact. — *p.p.* [APELMAZAR].

apelmazadura, *n.f.;* **apelmazamiento,** *n.m.* compactness.

apelmazar, *v.t.* (*pret.* **apelmacé;** *pres. subj.* **apelmace**) to compress and so render less spongy.

apelotonar, *v.t., v.r.* to form into balls.

apellar, *v.t.* to dress leather.

apellidado, -da, *a.* named, by name; called; called up. — *p.p.* [APELLIDAR].

apellidador, -ra, *n.m.f.* namer. — *a.* naming. — *n.m.* [APELLIDERO].

apellidamiento, *n.m.* naming.

apellidar, *v.t.* to call one by his name; to proclaim; to call to arms; to name; (*law*) to appeal. — *v.r.* to be called; to call oneself.

apellidero, *n.m.* (*mil.*) called-up man.

apellido, *n.m.* surname; special name given to things; nickname, epithet; call to arms; force called to arms; mobilization order; cry.

apenar, *v.t.* to cause pain, grief or sorrow. — *v.r.* to grieve.

apenas, *adv.* scarcely, hardly; with difficulty; no sooner than; as soon as.

apencar, *v.i.* (*pret.* **apenqué;** *pres. subj.* **apenque**) (*coll.*) to accept with repugnance; [APECHUGAR].

apéndice, *n.m.* appendix, supplement; *apéndice cecal, vermiforme,* or *vermicular,* (*anat.*) vermiform appendix.

apendicitis, *n.f.* (*med.*) appendicitis.

apendicular, *a.* appendicular.

apenino, -na, *a.* Apennine.

apeo, *n.m.* survey, mensuration of lands and buildings; (*arch.*) propping; prop, stay.

apeonar, *v.i.* to walk or run swiftly (of birds, especially partridges).

apepsia, *n.f.* (*med.*) apepsy, indigestion.

aperador, *n.m.* farmer; wheelwright; foreman in a mine.

aperar, *v.i.* to carry on the trade of a wheelwright.

apercibimiento, *n.m.* preparation; foresight; arrangement; advice, warning; (*law*) threat, summons.

apercibir, *v.t.* to provide, get ready; to warn, advise; (*law*) to summon; *hombre apercibido,*

nunca combatido, preparation is half the battle, forewarned is forearmed. — *v.r.* to prepare oneself; to get oneself ready; *apercibirse a,* or *para la batalla,* to prepare oneself for the battle; *apercibirse contra el enemigo,* to get ready against the enemy; *apercibirse para el viaje,* to get ready for the journey; *apercibirse de ropa,* to equip oneself with clothes.

aperción, *n.f.* opening.

apercollar, *v.t.* (*coll.*) to collar, seize by the neck; to steal, snatch.

aperdigar, *v.t.* (*pret.* **aperdigué;** *pres. subj.* **aperdigue**) to broil (partridges, meat) slightly.

apergaminado, -da, *a.* parchment-like; (*fig.*) dried-up (person). — *p.p.* [APERGAMINARSE].

apergaminarse, *v.r.* (*coll.*) to become dried up.

aperiódico, *n.m. a.* (*phys.*) aperiodic.

aperitivo, -va, *a.* aperitive; appetizing. — *n.m.* aperient; appetizer.

aperlado, -da, *a.* of pearly colour.

apernador, *n.m.* dog which seizes the game by the legs.

apernar, *v.t.* (*pres. indic.* **apierno;** *pres. subj.* **apierne**) to seize by the legs.

apero, *n.m.* sheep-fold; set of implements; outfit of tools; (*Am.*) riding accoutrements.

aperreado, -da, *a.* thrown to the dogs; (*coll.*) annoyed; fatigued, harassed. — *p.p.* [APERREAR].

aperreador, -ra, *n.m.f.* (*coll.*) intruder; importunate person, nuisance. — *a.* harassing.

aperrear, *v.t.* to throw to the dogs; (*fig.*) to annoy, bother. — *v.r.* to toil, overwork oneself.

aperreo, *n.m.* (*coll.*) fatigue, annoyance.

apersogar, *v.t.* (*Mex.*) to tether a horse by the neck.

apersonado, -da, *p.p.* [APERSONARSE] present; visible, manifest; appeared; *bien,* or *mal apersonado,* of good, or bad appearance or presence.

apersonarse, *v.r.* (*law*) to appear in person; to appear as an interested party; to meet on business.

apertura, *n.f.* solemn opening of assemblies, corporations, etc.; reading of a will.

apesadumbrado, -da, *a.* sad, grief-stricken; mournful. — *p.p.* [APESADUMBRAR].

apesadumbrar, *v.t.* to vex, sadden, cause affliction. — *v.r.* to grieve; to become sad.

apesaradamente, *adv.* mournfully.

apesarar, *v.t.* to vex, cause grief. — *v.r.* to become sad.

apesgamiento, *n.m.* sinking beneath a load.

apesgar, *v.t.* (*pret.* **apesgué;** *pres. subj.* **apesgue**) to overburden. — *v.r.* to become oppressed, aggrieved.

apestado, -da, *a.* infected, plague-stricken; tainted; foul-smelling, stinking; pestered, annoyed; full, sated; overstocked. — *p.p.* [APESTAR].

apestar, *v.t.* to infect with the plague; (*fig.*) to corrupt, turn putrid; to pester, vex, annoy. — *v.i.* to be foul-smelling, stinking; to be overstocked; *la plaza está apestada de verduras,* there is a glut of greens in the market; *aquí apesta,* there is a foul smell here. — *v.r.* to become infected.

apestoso, -sa, *a.* pestilent, foul-smelling, sickening, nauseating.

apétala, *a.* (*bot.*) apetalous.

apetecedor, -ra, *n.m.f.* one who longs for something. — *a.* covetous.

apetecer, *v.t.* (*pres. indic.* **apetezco**; *pres. subj.* **apetezca**) to long for; to crave or hanker after.

apetecible, *a.* desirable.

apetencia, *n.f.* appetite, hunger, desire, eagerness.

apetezco; apetezca, *pres. indic.; pres. subj.* [APETECER].

apetite, *n.m.* sauce, appetizer; inducement.

apetitivo, -va, *a.* appetitive, appetizing.

apetito, *n.m.* appetite, hunger, desire; *apetito concupiscible,* concupiscence; *abrir,* or *despertar el apetito,* to whet the appetite.

apetitoso, -sa, *a.* savoury, palatable; appetizing; epicurean; capricious.

apezonado, -da, *a.* nipple-shaped.

apezuñar, *v.i.* to sink the edge of the hoof into the ground.

apiadadamente, *adv.* compassionately, with pity.

apiadador, -ra, *a.* (said of one) who pities.

apiadar, *v.t.* to cause pity; to pity. — *v.r.* to pity; *apiadarse de,* to take, have pity on, have mercy on.

apiaradero, *n.m.* shepherd's reckoning of his flock.

apiario, -a, *a.* bee-like.

apicarado, -da, *a.* roguish, knavish, impudent. — *p.p.* [APICARARSE].

apicararse, *v.r.* to become roguish.

ápice, *n.m.* apex, summit, top, pinnacle, utmost height; ascent; trifle, jot, iota; (*gram.*) graphic accent; most intricate part of a question; *estar en los ápices de una cosa,* to have thorough knowledge of a thing; *no falta un ápice,* there is not an iota missing.

ápices, *n.m.pl.* (*bot.*) anthers.

apícola, *a.* appertaining to bee-keeping.

apículo, *n.m.* (*bot.*) small, keen point.

apicultor, -ra, *n.m.f.* bee-keeper, apiarist.

apicultura, *n.f.* bee-keeping, apiculture.

apierno; apierna, *pres. indic.; pres. subj.* [APERNAR].

apilado, -da, *p.p.* [APILAR] piled up. — *a.f.* dried, peeled (chestnut).

apilador, -ra, *n.m.f.* piler. — *a.* piling.

apilar, *v.t.* to pile up, heap up.

apimpollarse, *v.r.* to put forth bud, germinate.

apiñado, -da, *a.* shaped like a pine-cone; crowded, close together. — *p.p.* [APIÑAR].

apiñadura, *n.f.;* **apiñamiento,** *n.m.* pressing together, crowd, jam.

apiñar, *v.t.* to press together, join, unite. — *v.r.* to clog, crowd; to throng.

apio, *n.m.* (*bot.*) celery; *apio caballar,* or *equino,* (*bot.*) smallage, wild chicory; *apio de ranas,* (*bot.*) buttercup, crowfoot.

apiolar, *v.t.* to gyve a hawk; to tie by the legs; (*met.*) to seize, apprehend; (*coll.*) to kill, murder.

apiparse, *v.r.* (*coll.*) to gorge.

apirético, -ca, *a.* (*med.*) apyretic.

apirexia, *n.f.* (*med.*) apyrexia.

apisonar, *v.t.* to ram.

apitonado, -da, *a.* touchy, peevish; having tenderlings, buds. — *p.p.* [APITONAR].

apitonamiento, *n.m.* (*zool.*) putting forth tenderlings; (*agric.*) sprouting, budding; passion, anger.

apitonar, *v.i.* to put forth tenderlings; (*agric.*) to bud, germinate. — *v.t.* to break with bill or horn; to shell; to peck like chickens in the egg-shell. — *v.r.* to abuse each other.

apívoro, -ra, *a.* bee-eating.

apizarrado, -da, *a.* slate-coloured.

aplacable, *a.* placable; complacent.

aplacación, *n.f.* (*obs.*); **aplacamiento,** *n.m.* appeasement; stay of execution.

aplacador, -ra, *n.m.f.* one who placates or appeases. — *a.* appeasing.

aplacar, *v.t.* (*pret.* **aplaqué**; *pres. subj.* **aplaque**) to appease, pacify, mitigate, calm down. — *v.r.* to become tranquil.

aplacer, *v.i.* (conjugated like PLACER) to please, content. — *v.r.* to please oneself.

aplacerado, -da, *a.* (*naut.*) level and shallow; (*Am.*) open, cleared of trees.

aplacible, *a.* pleasant.

aplaciente, *a.* pleasing.

aplacimiento, *n.m.* pleasure.

aplanadera, *n.f.* roller for levelling; beetle, rammer.

aplanador, -ra, *a.* levelling. — *n.m.* leveller; (*mech.*) battledore, brusher, riveter; cylinder roller; (*typ.*) planer, planishing mallet.

aplanamiento, *n.m.* levelling.

aplanar, *v.t.* to level, make level or even, flatten; (*coll.*) to terrify or astonish, to dismay. — *v.r.* to tumble down (building); to weaken.

aplanchado, -da, *p.p.* [APLANCHAR] ironed. — *n.m.* ironing, linen ironed or for ironing.

aplanchador, -ra, *n.m.f.* ironer.

aplanchar, *v.t.* to iron linen.

aplanético, -ca, *a.* (*opt.*) aplanatic.

aplantillar, *v.t.* to adjust or fit (stones, etc.) according to pattern.

aplastado, -da, *a.* caked; crushed, dispirited. — *p.p.* [APLASTAR].

aplastador, -ra, *n.m.f.* one who crushes or flattens. — *a.* crushing, flattening.

aplastar, *v.t.* to cake, flatten, crush, smash; (*coll.*) to disconcert, floor an opponent. — *v.r.* to become flat; to collapse.

aplaudidor, -ra, *n.m.f.* one who applauds. — *a.* applauding.

aplaudir, *v.t.* to applaud, extol.

aplauso, *n.m.* applause; praise, approbation.

aplayar, *v.i.* to overflow the banks.

aplazamiento, *n.m.* convocation, citation; summons; deferring, postponement.

aplazar, *v.t.* (*pret.* **aplacé**; *pres. subj.* **aplace**) to convene, invest, concert, summon; to defer, adjourn, postpone.

aplebeyar, *v.t.* to render vile; to debase. — *v.r.* to degrade, lower oneself, to become mean.

aplegar, *v.t.* (*pret.* **aplegué**; *pres. subj.* **aplegue**) (*prov.*) to join, unite; to put beside, bring near.

aplicable, *a.* applicable.

aplicación, *n.f.* application, assiduity, laboriousness, close study; (*sew.*) appliqué.

aplicado, -da, *a.* studious, industrious, laborious, intent; applied. — *p.p.* [APLICAR].

aplicar, *v.t.* (*pret.* **apliqué**; *pres. subj.* **aplique**) to apply; to destine, intend; to clap; to attribute or impute; (*law*) to adjudge. — *v.r.* to apply oneself; *aplicarse a los estudios,* to study assiduously; *aplicar el oído,* to listen attentively; *aplicar las espuelas,* to spur a horse.

aplomado, -da, a. lead-coloured, leaden, containing lead; (fig.) heavy, dull, lazy; prudent, discreet; (build.) plumb, perpendicular. — p.p. [APLOMAR].

aplomar, v.t. to overload, crush; (build.) to plumb; (arch.) to put vertically. — v.i. (build.) to plumb; to be perpendicular. — v.r. to get out of plumb; to tumble, fall to the ground.

aplomo, n.m. tact, prudence, serenity, self-possession; (mus.) exactness in time; (art) due proportion; plumb, plumb-bob, plummet.

apnea, n.f. (med.) apnœa; want of respiration.

apocado, -da, a. pusillanimous, mean-spirited, cowardly; of mean, low extraction. — p.p. [APOCAR].

apocador, -ra, n.m.f. reducer, diminisher. — a. lessening, diminishing.

Apocalipsis, n.m. Apocalypse, Book of Revelation.

apocalíptico, -ca, a. apocalyptical.

apocamiento, n.m. bashfulness, diffidence; pusillanimity, depression.

apocar, v.t. (pret. apoqué; pres. subj. apoque) to lessen; to humiliate; to cramp, contract. — v.r. to humble, belittle oneself.

apócema; apócima, n.f. (med.) apozem.

apocopar, v.t. (gram.) to make use of apocope, take away last letter or syllable of a word.

apócope, n.f. (gram.) apocope.

apócrifamente, adv. apocryphally.

apócrifo, -fa, a. apocryphal.

Apócrifos, n.pl. (Bibl.) Apocrypha.

apodador, -ra, n.m.f. one who gives nick-names; wag. — a. scoffing, ridiculing.

apodar, v.t. to give nick-names; to scoff at, ridicule.

apodencado, -da, a. pointer-like, hound-like.

apoderado, -da, a. empowered, authorized. — n.m. proxy, attorney; constituir apoderado, (law) to appoint a proxy. — p.p. [APODERAR].

apoderar, v.t. to empower, grant power of attorney. — v.r. to possess oneself of, take possession of.

apodíctico, -ca, a. convincing; demonstrative; indisputable.

apodo, n.m. nick-name.

ápodo, -da, a. (zool.) apodal, without feet.

apofige, n.f. (arch.) apophyge.

apófisis, n.f. (med.) apophysis, prominent part of bones.

apogeo, n.m. (astron.) apogee; (fig.) highest degree (of fame, power, grandeur, etc.).

apógrafo, n.m. transcript, copy of manuscript.

apolillado, -da, a. moth-eaten, mothy, worm-eaten. — p.p. [APOLILLAR].

apolilladura, n.f. moth-hole.

apolillar, v.t. to gnaw, eat, or infest clothes, etc. (moths). — v.r. to become moth-eaten.

apolinar; apolíneo, -ea, a. (poet.) of or belonging to Apollo.

apologético, -ca, a. apologetic, excusatory.

apología, n.f. apology, defence, eulogy.

apológico, -ca, a. relating to an apologue.

apologista, n.m.f. apologist.

apólogo, -ga, a. [APOLÓGICO]. — n.m. apologue, fable, moral story.

apoltronarse, v.r. to grow lazy, cowardly.

apomazar, v.t. (pret. apomacé; pres. subj. apomace) to glaze, burnish with pumice-stone.

aponeurosis, n.f. (med.) aponeurosis, fascia.

apopar, v.t., v.i. (naut.) to present the stern of vessel to wind, tide, or current.

apoplejía, n.f. (med.) apoplexy.

apoplético, -ca, a. apoplectic.

aporcadura, n.f. (agric.) hilling, earthing-up, banking-up.

aporcar, v.t. (pres. indic. apuerco; pret. aporqué; pres. subj. apuerque) (agric.) to hill, earth up.

aporcelanado, -da, a. resembling porcelain.

aporisma, n.m. (surg.) ecchymosis.

aporismarse, v.r. to become an ecchymosis.

aporracear, v.t. (prov.) to pommel.

aporrar, v.i. (coll.) to be mute, tongue-tied. — v.r. (coll.) to become importunate.

aporreado, -da, a. cudgelled; dragged along. — n.m. (Cub.) a spiced-meat dish. — p.p. [APORREAR].

aporreamiento, n.m. beating, pommelling.

aporreante, n.m.f. (coll.) cudgeller. — a. cudgelling.

aporrear, v.t. to beat, cudgel, knock, maul. — v.r. to beat, cudgel each other; aporrearle a uno los oídos, to box someone's ears; (fig.) to study with intense application; aporrearse en la jaula, to drudge, toil needlessly.

aporreo, n.m. the act of cudgelling, pommelling or beating; drudgery, toil.

aporrillarse, v.r. to swell in the joints.

aportación, n.f. contribution; share.

aportaderas, n.f.pl. chests for stores carried on horses or mules; boxes for provisions; wooden tubs for carrying grapes.

aportadero, n.m. place where a ship or person may stop; landing-stage.

aportar, v.i. to make a port, arrive; to reach an unexpected place; aportar a Barcelona, to call or arrive at Barcelona. — v.r. to cause, occasion; (law) to contribute a share to a society, company, or in marriage.

aportillar, v.t. to breach a wall or rampart; to break down, break open. — v.r. to tumble down, fall into ruins.

aposentador, -ra, n.m.f. lodging-house keeper, inn-keeper; usher in a theatre.

aposentamiento, n.m. lodgement.

aposentar, v.t. to lodge, give lodging to. — v.r. to take lodgings.

aposento, n.m. room, apartment; temporary habitation; inn; (obs.) box in theatre.

aposesionar, v.t. to give possession. — v.r. to take possession.

aposición, n.f. (gram.) apposition.

apositivo, -va, a. (gram.) appositional.

apósito, n.m. (med.) external application.

aposta; apostadamente, adv. designedly, on purpose.

apostadero, n.m. naval station; dock-yard.

apostador, -ra, n.m.f. one who bets, better.

apostal, n.m. (prov.) good fishing-place in a river.

apostáleos, n.m.pl. (naut.) thick planks for gun platforms.

apostar, v.t. (pres. indic. apuesto; pres. subj. apueste) to bet, lay a wager; to place relays, post soldiers; apostar carreras, to run races. — v.i. (fig.) to emulate, rival, compete; apostarlas, apostárselas a or con alguno, to challenge someone; to contend, compete with someone; (coll.) to threaten someone. — v.r. to place, station oneself; to compete with one another.

apostasía, *n.f.* apostasy.

apostasis, *n.f.* (*med.*) abscess.

apóstata, *n.m.f.* apostate; forsaker, abjurer.

apostatar, *v.i.* to apostatize, abjure, forsake, fall away; *apostatar de la fe,* to abjure one's religion.

apostema, *n.f.* (*med.*) abscess, tumour.

apostemación, *n.f.* (*obs.*) formation of an abscess.

apostemar, *v.t.* (*med.*) to form, cause an abscess. — *v.r.* to get an abscess; to become an abscess; *no apostemársele a uno alguna cosa,* to be unable to keep a secret.

apostemero, *n.m.* (*med.*) bistoury, scalpel.

apostemoso, -sa, *a.* apostematous.

apostilla, *n.f.* marginal note, annotation, rider, apóstil.

apostillamiento, *n.m.* breaking out in pimples.

apostillar, *v.t.* to make marginal notes. — *v.r.* to break out in pimples.

apóstol, *n.m.* apostle. — *pl.* (*naut.*) hawsepieces.

apostolado, *n.m.* apostleship; the twelve apostles.

apostólicamente, *adv.* apostolically; (*coll.*) simply; on foot.

apostólico, -ca, *a.* apostolic.

apostrofar, *v.t.* to apostrophize.

apóstrofe, *n.m.f.* (*rhet.*) apostrophe; (*fig.*) taunt, insult.

apóstrofo, *n.m.* (*gram.*) apostrophe.

apostura, *n.f.* gentleness, gentility, neatness, agreeable behaviour, pleasant disposition.

aposturaje, *n.m.* (*naut.*) top-timber, futtock.

apote, *adv.* (*coll.*) abundantly.

apotegma, *n.m.* apophthegm, maxim.

apoteosis, *n.f.* apotheosis, deification; exaltation.

apoyadero, *n.m.* prop, support.

apoyador, -ra, *a.* supporting. — *n.m.* support, prop.

apoyadura, *n.f.* flow of milk from the breasts.

apoyar, *v.t.* (with *en*) to rest on; (*fig.*) to protect, patronize, favour; to countenance, abet; to confirm, prove, corroborate; to hold up; (*equit.*) to bear upon the bit; to droop, or incline the head. — *v.i.* (with *en* or *sobre*) to rest on. — *v.r.* (with *en*) (*fig.*) to depend on; to lean upon; *apoyar una proposición,* to second a motion; *apoyar con citas,* to corroborate with proofs.

apoyatura, *n.f.* (*mus.*) appoggiatura.

apoyo, *n.m.* prop, stay, support; fulcrum; (*fig.*) help, protection, patronage; maintenance; *el apoyo de la vejez,* the staff of old age; [APOYADURA].

apozarse, *v.r.* (*Col., Chi.*) to form a pool; to accumulate; (*fig.*) to be stopped or checked.

apreciabilidad, *n.f.* appreciability.

apreciable, *a.* appreciable, valuable, respectable, worthy of esteem; having a price; saleable.

apreciación, *n.f.* estimation, valuation, appraisement, appreciation.

apreciadamente, *adv.* valuably, respectably; appreciatively.

apreciador, -ra, *n.m.f.* estimator, appraiser; appreciator. — *a.* appreciating.

apreciar, *v.t.* to appreciate; to appraise, esteem, estimate, price, value; (*fig.*) to graduate; *apreciar en mucho,* to appreciate greatly; *apreciar por sus prendas,* to appreciate because of his qualities; *apreciar un libro en or por su valor,* to appreciate a book at its value.

apreciativo, -va, *a.* appreciative; relative to the value set on something.

aprecio, *n.m.* appreciation, approbation, regard, esteem; appraisement, valuation.

aprehender, *v.t.* to apprehend, seize; (*phil.*) to fancy, conceive, imagine.

aprehensión, *n.f.* seizure, capture; apprehension, fear; misapprehension; acuteness.

aprehensivo, -va, *a.* apprehensive, timid, fearful; quick to understand.

aprehensor, -ra, *n.m.f.* one who apprehends. — *a.* apprehending.

aprehensorio, -ria, *a.* apprehending, seizing.

apremiador, -ra, *n.m.f.* one who presses, urges. — *a.* compelling.

apremiante, *a.* urgent, pressing.

apremiar, *v.t.* to press, urge; to compel, oblige.

apremio, *n.m.* pressure, constraint; constriction; (*law*) judicial compulsion.

aprendedor, -ra, *n.m.f.* learner. — *a.* one who learns or is capable of or apt at learning.

aprender, *v.t.* to learn, acquire knowledge; *aprender a escribir,* to learn to write; *aprender de memoria,* to learn by heart; *aprender con Fulano,* to learn, study with So-and-so; *aprender de Fulano,* to learn from So-and-so; *aprender por aprender,* to learn for the sake of learning; *lo que se aprende en la cuna, siempre dura,* what is learnt in childhood is never forgotten.

aprendiz, -za, *n.m.f.* apprentice; *aprendiz de todo, oficial de nada,* Jack of all trades, master of none.

aprendizaje, *n.m.* apprenticeship.

aprensador, -ra, *n.m.f.* presser, calenderer, mangler. — *a.* pressing, calendering, mangling.

aprensar, *v.t.* to dress, press, calender; (*fig.*) to vex, crush, oppress.

aprensión, *n.f.* apprehension; scruple, fear; mistrust, suspicion; (*fig.*) delicacy, bashfulness.

aprensivo, -va, *a.* apprehensive, fearing illness or disease; bashful. — *n.f.* imagination.

apresador, -ra, *n.m.f.* privateer, cruiser; captor, captress. — *a.* seizing, capturing.

apresamiento, *n.m.* clutch, hold; capture.

apresar, *v.t.* to seize, grasp (with claws, fangs); to imprison; (*naut.*) to capture an enemy's ship.

aprestar, *v.t.* to prepare, make ready, arrange; to gum, size (materials). — *v.r.* to get ready, prepare oneself.

apresto, *n.m.* preparation, accoutrement; dressing (materials).

apresuración, *n.f.* acceleration, haste.

apresuradamente, *adv.* hastily.

apresurado, -da, *a.* brief, hasty, acting quickly. — *p.p.* [APRESURAR].

apresuramiento, *n.m.* eagerness, hastiness; forwardness; acceleration.

apresurar, *v.t.* to accelerate, hasten, hurry, forward. — *v.r.* to make haste; *apresurarse a venir,* to come quickly; *apresurarse en la réplica,* to give a quick answer; *apresurarse por llegar a tiempo,* to hurry in order to be in time.

apretadamente, *adv.* tightly, closely, fast.
apretadera, *n.f.* strap or rope to tie anything with. — *pl.* (*coll.*) pressing requests, entreaties.
apretadero, *n.m.* truss for ruptures.
apretadizo, -za, *a.* which can be easily bound or compressed.
apretado, -da, *a.* tight, difficult, arduous, dangerous; mean, close-fisted; pressing, urgent; afflicted; necessitous. — *n.m.* minute handwriting; (*slang*) jacket; *estar muy apretado*, to be in great danger (invalids). — *p.p.* [APRETAR].
apretador, -ra, *a.* pressing, tightening. — *n.m.f.* one who presses. — *n.m.* presser, rammer; quoin-wedge; waistcoat; soft stays for children; broad bandage for infants; hairnet.
apretadura, *n.f.* compression, constriction.
apretamiento, *n.m.* crowd, jam, crush; closeness; conflict.
apretar, *v.t.* (*pres. indic.* **aprieto;** *pres. subj.* **apriete**) to compress, tighten, press down; to constrict, contract; to crowd, constrain; to clutch; (*fig.*) to distress, harass, vex; (*fig.*) to act with more vigour and efficiency; to urge, spur (a horse); (*art*) to enhance the colour contrast. — *v.i.* to pinch (shoes); *apretar la mano*, to shake hands; (*fig.*) to correct with severity; *apretar a alguien con fuertes razones*, to press anyone with urgent reasons; *apretar los talones*, to take to one's heels; *apretar los puños*, to exercise care and energy in the execution of anything; *apretar a correr*, to start off running; *apretar a uno las clavijas*, to put someone in a difficult situation; *apretar con uno*, to come to grips with someone; *apretar con las manos*, to squeeze with the hands; *apretar entre los brazos*, to press in one's arms; *apretar hasta que salte la cuerda*, to exhaust someone's patience; *apretar a uno la nuez*, to strangle someone; *apretar frenos*, to apply the brakes; *apretar los dientes*, to gnash, grind one's teeth; *apretar el paso*, to hasten; *mucho aprieta este testigo*, this witness is significant; *¡aprieta!* good gracious!
apretón, *n.m.* pressure; struggle, conflict; rapid and brief race, or run; gripes; (*paint.*) dash of dark colour; *apretón de manos*, handshake.
apretujar, *v.t.* (*coll.*) to squeeze, press repeatedly.
apretujón, *n.m.* tight pressure.
apretura, *n.f.* narrow, confined place, crowd, crush; narrowness; distress, anguish; straits.
apriesa, *adv.* in haste, in a hurry, hastily.
aprieto, *n.m.* crowd, crush; stringency; risk, danger, difficulty.
aprieto; apriete, *pres. indic.; pres. subj.* [APRETAR].
apriorismo, *n.m.* method of reasoning a priori.
aprisa, *adv.* swiftly, promptly, fast.
apriscar, *v.t.* to gather the sheep in the fold.
aprisco, *n.m.* sheep-fold.
aprisionar, *v.t.* to confine, imprison; to put in chains; (*fig.*) to bind.
aproar, *v.t.* (*naut.*) to turn the prow.
aprobable, *a.* approvable.
aprobación, *n.f.* approbation, concurrence; consent, approval, applause; probation, trial.
aprobado, -da, *a.* admitted, accepted; approved; passed (examination); *aprobado por*

mayoría, accepted by the majority. — *n.m.* pass mark (examination). — *p.p.* [APROBAR].
aprobador, -ra, *n.m.f.* approver. — *a.* approving.
aprobante, *n.m.f.* approver, examiner; censor (of books). — *a.* approving, examining.
aprobar, *v.t.* (*pres. indic.* **apruebo;** *pres. subj.* **apruebe**) to approve; to like; to praise; to pass (an examination); *aprobar en alguna facultad al estudiante*, to pass the student in a certain subject.
aprobativo, -va, *a.* approbatory.
aprobatorio, -ria, *a.* approbatory, approving.
aproches, *n.m.pl.* (*mil.*) approaches.
aprontar, *v.t.* to prepare or deliver with despatch, hastily.
apropiación, *n.f.* appropriation, assumption.
apropiadamente, *adv.* fitly, properly, conveniently.
apropiado, -da, *a.* appropriate, fit; appropriated. — *p.p.* [APROPIAR].
apropiador, -ra, *n.m.f.* appropriator. — *a.* appropriating.
apropiar, *v.t.* to appropriate, assume; to accommodate, fit, apply. — *v.r.* to possess oneself of, to appropriate to oneself; *apropiar a su idea*, to adapt to one's idea; *apropiar para sí*, to appropriate to oneself.
apropincuación, *n.f.* approach.
apropincuarse, *v.r.* (*coll.*) to approach, draw near.
aprovechable, *a.* profitable, serviceable; available.
aprovechadamente, *adv.* profitably.
aprovechado, -da, *a.* improved, made use of; economical, saving; studious, diligent; advanced, proficient. — *p.p.* [APROVECHAR].
aprovechador, -ra, *a.* that makes good use of.
aprovechamiento, *n.m.* profit, advantage; utilization, exploitation, development; progress, proficiency; *aprovechamiento de aguas*, water-supply; *aprovechamiento forestal*, forest products.
aprovechar, *v.t.* to profit by, make good use of. — *v.i.* to be useful or profitable; to avail; to progress; *aprovechar en el estudio*, to progress in one's studies. — *v.r.* to avail oneself; *aprovecharse de la ocasión*, to profit by the opportunity.
aprovisionador, -ra, *n.m.f.* provider, purveyor; caterer, victualler.
aprovisionar, *v.t.* to victual, stock, supply with necessaries.
aproximación, *n.f.* approximation; nearness; bringing near.
aproximadamente, *adv.* nearly, about, approximately.
aproximado, -da, *a.* approximate; next; proximate; *aproximado hasta*, (*arith.*) approximate to. — *p.p.* [APROXIMAR].
aproximar, *v.t., v.r.* to approximate; to bring, move near; to approach; *aproximarse al altar*, to approach the altar.
aproximativo, -va, *a.* approaching; approximate.
apruebo; apruebe, *pres. indic.; pres. subj.* [APROBAR].
ápside, *n.m.* (*astron.*) apsis, apogee (of the moon); (*arch.*) apse, apsis.
aptamente, *adv.* fitly, aptly.
áptero, -ra, *a.* (*ent.*) apterous, wingless.
aptitud, *n.f.* aptitude, fitness, ability, capacity.

apto, -ta, *a.* able, fit, apt, competent, capable, meet; *apto para todo,* fit for all, competent for anything.

apuerco; apuerque, *pres. indic.; pres. subj.* [APORCAR].

apuesta, *n.f.* betting, bet, wager; *de apuesta,* in competition.

apuesto, -ta, *a.* elegant, genteel, well-dressed, spruce.

apuesto; apueste, *pres. indic.; pres. subj.* [APOSTAR].

apulgarar, *v.t.* to force with the thumb. — *v.r.* to be spotted by moisture (of linen).

apunarse, *v.r.* (*Am.*) contract mountain-sickness.

apunchar, *v.t.* twinning or parting (comb making).

apuntación, *n.f.* annotation, note, memorandum, memorial; musical notation.

apuntado, -da, *a.* indicated, noted; pointed at both ends. — *p.p.* [APUNTAR].

apuntador,-ra, *n.m.f.* observer, one who notes or marks. — *n.m.* (*naut.*) gunner; (*theat.*) prompter; (*slang*) constable. — *a.* observing, noting.

apuntalamiento, *n.m.* propping, scaffolding, supporting.

apuntalar, *v.t.* to prop, support; (*naut.*) to shore a vessel.

apuntamiento, *n.m.* abstract, summary; annotation; judicial report.

apuntar, *v.t.* to aim, level at; to point out, indicate, mark; to note; to hint; to sketch; to stitch, tack lightly; to mend; to wager (in games); (*print.*) to fasten the sheets in the register points; to sharpen; (*theat.*) to prompt; *apuntar a un blanco,* to aim at a target; *apunta el día,* the day peeps; *apuntar y no dar,* to promise and not perform. — *v.r.* to begin to turn (wine, etc.); (*coll.*) to be half-seas over; (*Mex.*) to sprout in the open air (seeds, etc.).

apunte, *n.m.* annotation, memorandum; mark (examination); rough sketch; stake (in games); (*theat.*) prompt-book, prompting; (*coll.*) rascal, crafty person; aim.

apuñadar, *v.t.* (*prov.*) to strike with the fist.

apuñalado, -da, *a.* shaped like a dagger; stabbed with a dagger. — *p.p.* [APUÑALAR].

apuñalar, *v.t.* to thrust, stab with a dagger.

apuñar, *v.t.* to seize with the fist. — *v.i.* to tighten, clench the fist.

apuñear, *v.t.* (*coll.*) to strike with the fist.

apuracabos, *n.m.* candlestick; save-all.

apuración, *n.f.* investigation; trouble, misfortune.

apuradamente, *adv.* (*coll.*) in the nick of time, punctually, exactly; surely, precisely.

apurado, -da, *a.* poor, destitute, needy; exhausted, over-spent; difficult; dangerous; conscientious, scrupulous; *apurado de medios,* short of funds. — *p.p.* [APURAR].

apurador, -ra, *n.m.f.* refiner, purifier; candlestick. — *a.* refining, purifying; consuming.

apuramiento, *n.m.* research, enquiry, verification; purification; exhaustion; hurry.

apurar, *v.t.* to purify; to clear up, verify, investigate minutely; to consume, exhaust, drain; to tease; to hurry, push; to annoy; *apurar la paciencia de uno,* to exhaust one's patience; *apurar todos los recursos,* to exhaust every expedient. — *v.r.* to grieve, worry, fret; to exert oneself; *apurarse en los contratiempos,*

to worry over disappointments; *apurarse por poco,* to worry over trifles.

apurativo, -va, *a.* (*med.*) detersive.

apuro, *n.m.* stringency, strait, want; anguish, affliction, grievance.

aquebrazarse, *v.r.* (*prov.*) to become chapped, cracked (hands, feet).

aquejar, *v.t.* to complain, lament, grieve; to fatigue, afflict.

aquejoso, -sa, *a.* afflicted, grieved.

aquel, *m.*; **aquella,** *f.*; **aquellos,** *m.pl.*; **aquellas,** *f.pl.* dem. pron. & *a.* that (one), those (ones) yonder, farthest away. — *aquello,* neut. dem. pron. that; that matter; the common belief, notion; *no creo en aquello que se dice,* I do not believe what is said. — **aquél, aquélla,** *n.m.f.;* **aquéllos, aquéllas,** *n.m.f.pl.* the former, the first mentioned. — *n.m.* indescribable quality; charm, air, grace; *Juana tiene mucho aquel,* Jane has charm; *ya apareció aquello,* (*coll.*) I guessed that would happen.

aquelarre, *n.m.* witches' Sabbath; (*fig.*) noise, confusion.

aquende, *adv.* on this side, hither, here.

aqueo, -ea, *n.m.f., a.* Achæan.

aquerenciarse, *v.r.* to become fond of a place or person (animals).

aquese, *m.*; **aquesa,** *f.*; **aqueso,** neut. pron. dem. (*poet.*) that. — *pl.* **aquesos,** *m.*; **aquesas,** *f.*, those.

aqueste, *m.*; **aquesta,** *f.*; **aquesto,** neut. pron. dem. (*poet.*) this, that. — *pl.* **aquestos,** *m.*; **aquestas,** *f.* these.

áqueta, *n.f.* (*ent.*) cicada, harvest fly.

aquí, *adv.* here, hither; now; then; *he aquí,* behold, look here; *de aquí para allí,* to and fro, up and down; *de aquí,* from here, from this place, hence; *por aquí,* this way, through here; here, hereabouts; *de aquí en adelante,* from now onward, henceforth; *hasta aquí,* hitherto; *aquí hay gato encerrado,* there's some mystery here; *aquí mando yo,* I am master here; *aquí me nacieron los dientes,* I was born and bred here; *aquí fué Troya,* (in a comic sense) and here was the disaster! *aquí para entre los dos,* between us.

aquiesciencia, *n.f.* (*law*) acquiescence, consent.

aquietar, *v.t.* to quiet, lull, pacify, hush, allay; to set at rest. — *v.r.* to grow calm; to quiet down; *aquietarse con la explicación,* to become pacified by the explanation.

aquifolio, *n.m.* (*bot.*) holly-tree.

aquilatación, *n.f.*; **aquilatamiento,** *n.m.* assay; assaying; examination.

aquilatar, *v.t.* to assay (gold, silver, gems; graduation of pearls); to examine closely.

aquilea, *n.f.* (*bot.*) milfoil, yarrow.

aquileño, *n.m.* (*slang*) promising thief.

aquilino, -na, *a.* (*poet.*) aquiline.

aquilón, *n.m.* north wind; north pole.

aquilonal; aquilonar, *a.* northerly, northern; wintry.

aquillado, -da, *a.* keel-shaped; (*naut.*) said of a ship with very long keel.

Aquisgrán, *n.m.* Aachen, Aix-la-Chapelle.

aquistar, *v.t.* to acquire; to conquer.

aquivo, -va, *a.* Achæan.

ara, *n.f.* altar, communion-table; *acogerse a las aras,* to take refuge or shelter; *amigo hasta las aras,* a good and faithful friend. — (*astron.*) Ara, a constellation; *n.m.* (*orn.*) a blue and yellow macaw.

árabe, *n.m.f.* Arab. — *n.m.* Arabic. — *a.* Arabian.

arabesco, -ca, *a.* Arabian. — *n.m.* arabesque.

arábico, -ca; arábigo, -ga, *a.* Arabian. — *n.m.* Arabic; *estar una cosa en arábigo,* to be gibberish, *goma arábiga,* gum arabic.

arabio, -bia, *n.m.f.* Arab. — *a.* Arabian, Arabic.

arabismo, *n.m.* Arabic expression.

arabista, *n.m.f.* Arabic scholar.

arabizar, *v.i.* to imitate Arabian customs, language, etc.

arable, *a.* (*agric.*) arable.

arácnido, -da, *a.* (*zool.*) arachnidan, arachnidean. — *n.m.* arachnid; (*pl.*) Arachnida.

aracnoides, *n.f.* (*anat.*) arachnoid membrane.

aracnología, *n.f.* (*nat. hist.*) arachnology.

arada, *n.f.* (*agric.*) ploughing; ploughed ground; husbandry; land ploughed in a day.

arado, *n.m.* plough; ploughing.

arador, -ra, *a.* that ploughs; ploughing. — *n.m.* ploughman; (*ent.*) harvest-mite; handworm, ring-worm.

aradro, *n.m.* (*prov.*) plough.

aradura, *n.f.* act or practice of ploughing; (*prov.*) land ploughed in a day.

aragonés, -esa, *n.m.f., a.* Aragonese.

aragonito, *n.m.* (*min.*) aragonite.

araguato, *n.m.* (*Am.*) American monkey.

araguirá, *n.m.* (*Arg.*) small bird.

aralia, *n.f.* shrub of the Araliaceæ family.

arambel, *n.m.* (*fig.*) rag, tatter.

arambeloso, -sa, *a.* covered in rags; ragged.

arameo, -a, *a.* Aramæan.

aramio, *n.m.* piece of ploughed ground left fallow. ·

arán, *n.m.* (*prov., bot.*) sloe-tree and fruit.

arana, *n.f.* imposition, trick; (*Cub.*) kind of grass.

arancel, *n.m.* tariff of duties, fees, etc.; book of rates; *arancel de aduanas,* customs duties, tariff.

arancelar, *v.t.* (*coll.*) to list, put in order.

arancelario, -ria, *a.* referring to the tariff of customs duties.

arandanedo, *n.m.* cranberry patch.

arándano, *n.m.* cranberry.

arandela, *n.f.* socket-pan of a candlestick; (*mech.*) washer, axle-guard; rivet-plate, collar-plate; (*obs.*) guard round the staff of a lance; nave-box of gun-carriage; (*naut.*) half-ports; glass candelabrum.

arandillo, *n.m.* grey bird with white breast and red feet; (*prov.*) hip-pad, bustle.

aranero, -ra, *n.m.f.* trickster, cheat. — *a.* deceitful, tricky.

arangorri, *n.m.* (*ichth.*) fish of the Acanthopterygii order, very common in the Gulf of Biscay.

araniego, -ga, *a.* taken in a net (*arañuelo*) (said of young hawks).

aranoso, -sa, *n.m.f., a.* [ARANERO].

aranzada, *n.f.* measure of land (447 deciares; in Córdoba 367 deciares; in Sevilla 475 deciares).

araña, *n.f.* (*ent.*) spider; (*ichth.*) sting-bull; common weaver, sea-spider; water-skater; spider-crab; chandelier, girandole, sconce; (*bot.*) crowfoot; bird net or trap; (*coll.*) thrifty, economical person; (*fig.*) prostitute; (*prov.*) scuffle, scramble; (*Chi.*) a light two-wheeled carriage.

arañada, *n.f.* collection of spiders; scratch.

arañador, -ra, *n.m.f.* scratcher, scraper. — *a.* scratching, scraping.

arañamiento, *n.m.* scratch; the act of scratching.

arañar, *v.t.* to scratch, claw, scrabble; (*coll.*) to scrape (stringed instruments); (*coll.*) to scrape together, scrape up (of money, etc.). — *v.r.* to scratch oneself.

arañazo, *n.m.* slight scratch; (*coll.*) prick.

arañero, -ra, *a.* (*prov.*) wild, untameable (bird). — *n.m.* spider-catcher.

araño, *n.m.* scratch, nipping, slight wound.

arañón, *n.m.* (*prov.*) sloe-tree and fruit.

arañuela, *n.f.* small spider; (*bot.*) crowfoot.

arañuelo, *n.m.* small spider; variety of grub which spins a web; sheep-, cattle-tick; net.

arapenne, *n.m.* (*obs.*) ancient measure of 120 square feet.

aráquida, *n.f.* (*bot.*) peanut.

arar, *v.t.* to plough; labour; to scan carefully; (*fig.*) to scratch. — *v.r.* (*fig.*) to become wrinkled, furrowed; *arar con el ancla,* (*naut.*) to drag the anchor.

arar, *n.m.* African coniferous tree.

aratada, *n.f.* (*prov.*) bad turn.

arate cavate, (*phrase*) foolishness; heaviness.

araticú, *n.m.* (*Am.*) (*bot.*) kind of cherimoya.

aratoso, -sa, *a.* (*prov.*) heavy, annoying.

araucano, -na, *a.* araucanian, araucarian.

araucaria, *n.f.* (*bot.*) araucaria, tall pine.

arauja, *n.f.* (*Brazil*) creeping plant (Asclepiadaceæ).

aravico, *n.m.* ancient Peruvian bard.

arazá, *n.m.* (*Arg., Par., Ur.*) fruit tree (Myrtaceæ).

arbalestrilla, *n.f.* an old surveying instrument.

arbellón, *n.m.* (*prov.*) gutter, draining channel.

arbitrable, *a.* arbitral.

arbitración, *n.f.* (*law*) arbitration.

arbitrador, -ra, *a.* arbitrating. — *n.m.* arbitrator, umpire, referee, judge. — *n.f.* arbitress.

arbitraje, *n.m.* arbitration; (*com.*) arbitrage.

arbitral, *a.* arbitral.

arbitramento; arbitramiento, *n.m.* arbitration; (*law*) arbitrament.

arbitrante, *a.* arbitrating.

arbitrar, *v.t.* to arbitrate, adjudge; to act unhampered. — *v.r.* to contrive ways and means.

arbitrariamente, *adv.* arbitrarily.

arbitrariedad, *n.f.* arbitrariness.

arbitrario, -ria; arbitrativo, -va, *a.* arbitrary; depending on arbitration; (*law*) arbitral.

arbitratorio, -ria, *a.* arbitral.

arbitrio, *n.m.* free will; means, expedient; arbitration; arbitrariness; (*fig.*) caprice, inconstancy; (*law*) discretionary judgment. — *pl.* rates and taxes; *propios y arbitrios,* ways and means.

arbitrista, *n.m.f.* schemer, projector, contriver.

arbitro, -ra, *n.m.f.* one who is master of his or her actions. — *n.f.* arbitress. — *n.m.* arbitrator, arbiter, referee, umpire.

árbol, *n.m.* (*bot.*) tree; (*naut.*) mast; (*mech.*) arbor, upright shaft, axle, drill, spindle; body of shirt; (*slang*) body; crown post of winding stairs; *árbol de costados,* or *genealógico,* genealogical tree; *árbol de amor,* (*bot.*) Judas-tree; *árbol de la vida*, tree of life; (*bot.*) thuya; *árbol de ruedas*, spindle of clock wheels; *árbol de pie*, seed-grown tree; *árbol de Paraíso*, flowering ash-tree; *árbol del pan*, breadfruit tree; *árbol de transmisión*, or *de asiento*, main horizontal shaft; transmission belt shaft; *árbol motor*, driving shaft or axle; *árbol de fuego*, or *de pólvora*, props for fireworks; *quien a buen árbol se arrima, buena sombra le cobija*, who leans against a good tree, enjoys good shade; *del árbol caído todos hacen leña*, everyone can kick a man who is down; *no halla ni un árbol de donde ahorcarse*, he has not a single resource left.

arbolado, -da, *a.* wooded; (*naut.*) masted. — *n.m.* woodland; (*slang*) tall man. — *p.p.* [ARBOLAR].

arboladura, *n.f.* (*naut.*) masts and spars; hoisting.

arbolar, *v.t.* to hoist, set upright; (*naut.*) to mast a ship, ensign, flag. — *v.r.* to rear (horse).

arbolario, -ria, *n.m.f.* (*coll.*) madcap, spendthrift. — *a.* thoughtless.

arboleda, *n.f.* grove, plantation of trees, wooded ground.

arboledo, *n.m.* woodland.

arbolejo, *n.m.* small tree.

arbolete, *n.m.* branch of a tree for fastening lime twigs on; (*fig.*) trap.

arbolillo, *n.m.* small tree; (*min.*) side of a blast-furnace.

arbolista, *n.m.f.* arboriculturist; dealer in trees.

arbolito, *n.m.* small tree.

arbollón, *n.m.* outlet, conduit; gutter; *salir por el arbollón*, to have the worst of an affair.

arbóreo, -rea, *a.* arboreal, arboraceous.

arborescencia, *n.f.* arborescence.

arborescente, *a.* arborescent.

arboricultura, *n.f.* arboriculture.

arboriforme, *a.* tree-like in shape.

arborista, *n.m.f.* [ARBOLISTA].

arborización, *n.f.* (*min., med.*) arborization.

arborizado, -da, *a.* having the appearance of foliage; arborescent, dendritic.

arborizar, *v.t.* to make tree-like. — *v.i.* to cultivate trees.

arbotante, *n.m.* vault supporting arch; flying buttress.

arbusto, *n.m.* shrub.

arca, *n.f.* chest, coffer, safe; tempering oven for blown glass; *arca del diluvio*, or *de Noé*, Noah's ark; lumber chest; (*ichth.*) mollusc; *arca cerrada*, reserved person; *arca de agua*, reservoir, cistern; *arca de la alianza*, or *del testamento*, Ark of the Covenant; *arca del cuerpo*, (*anat.*) human trunk; *arca del pan*, (*coll.*) abdomen; *arca llena y arca vacía*, vicissitudes; *en arca abierta, el justo peca*, opportunity makes the thief; *en arca de avariento, el diablo yace dentro*, the devil lurks in the miser's coffer; *hacer arcas*, to open the coffers or treasury-chest; *en el arca se vende el buen paño*, good wine needs no bush. — *pl.* cavities of the body under the ribs; treasury.

arcabucear, *v.t.* to shoot, execute with an harquebus.

arcabucería, *n.f.* (*mil.*) troop of harquebusiers; salvo of harquebuses; factory and shop.

arcabucero, *n.m.* harquebus maker, gunsmith; harquebusier.

arcabucete, *n.m.* small harquebus.

arcabuco, *n.m.* densely wooded mountain.

arcabuz, *n.m.* harquebus.

arcabuzazo, *n.m.* harquebus shot or wound.

arcacil, *n.m.* (*bot.*) species of wild artichoke.

arcada, *n.f.* retch, retching; (*arch.*) arcade, row of arches.

árcade, *n.m.f.; a.* **arcadio, -dia,** *a.* Arcadian.

arcador, *n.m.* wool-beater.

arcaduz, *n.m.* conduit, pipe; bucket; (*met.*) channel for obtaining something; *llevar una cosa por sus arcaduces*, to conduct an affair through its proper channels.

arcaico, -ca, *a.* archaic, ancient, antiquated.

arcaísmo, *n.m.* archaism.

arcaísta, *n.m.f.* archaist.

arcaizar, *v.t., v.i.* to archaize.

arcanamente, *adv.* mysteriously, secretly.

arcángel, *n.m.* archangel.

arcangélical; arcangélico, -ca, *a.* archangelic.

arcano, -na, *a.* secret, recondite, reserved. — *n.m.* arcanum.

arcar, *v.t.* to arch; to beat wool.

arcaz, *n.m.* large chest.

arcazón, *n.m.* (*prov.*) osier; willow-plot.

arce, *n.m.* (*bot.*) maple-tree.

arcedianato, *n.m.* archdeaconship, archdeaconry.

arcediano, *n.m.* archdeacon.

arcedo, *n.m.* maple grove.

arcén, *n.m.* border, brim, edge; curbstone (well).

arcifinio, -nia, *a.* having natural boundaries (territory).

arcilla, *n.f.* argil, clay.

arcillar, *v.t.* to cover with clay; to improve the soil with clay.

arcilloso, -sa, *a.* clayey, argillaceous.

arciprestazgo, *n.m.* office of archpriest.

arcipreste, *n.m.* archpriest.

arco, *n.m.* (*geom.*) arc; (*arch.*) arch, bridge; bow; fiddle-bow; hoop; *arco de iglesia*, (*fam.*) something difficult of execution; *arco iris*, rainbow; *arco siempre armado, o flojo o quebrado*, things cannot remain in a state of violence indefinitely; *arco de San Martín*, or *arco iris*, rainbow.

arcón, *n.m.* large chest, bin.

arcosa, *n.f.* (*min.*) variety of sandstone.

archicofradía, *n.f.* confraternity enjoying more privileges than others.

archidiácono, *n.m.* archdeacon.

archiducado, *n.m.* archdukedom, archduchy.

archiducal, *a.* archducal.

archiduque, *n.m.* archduke.

archiduquesa, *n.f.* archduchess.

archilaúd, *n.m.* musical instrument resembling a large lute.

archimillonario, -ria, *n.m.f., a.* multimillionaire.

archipámpano, *n.m.* (*coll.*) imaginary dignity or authority; *archipámpano de las Indias*, (*coll.*) a pretentious person of no great merit.

archipiélago, *n.m.* archipelago; (*fig.*) something difficult to count due to its abundance.

archivar, *v.t.* to file; to deposit in an archive; (*coll.*) to keep very secret.

archivero; archivista, *n.m.* archivist, keeper of the records.

archivo, *n.m.* archive, archives; file, files; (*coll.*) secret place.

archivolta, *n.f.* (*arch.*) archivolt.
arda, *n.f.* squirrel.
ardalear, *v.i.* to yield thin bunches of grapes.
ardea, *n.f.* bittern.
ardentía, *n.f.* heat; phosphorescence (of sea); heartburn.
ardentísimamente, *adv.* very ardently, with much ardour.
ardentísimo, **-ma**, *a. superl.* [ARDIENTE], extremely ardent.
ardeola, *n.f.* (*orn.*) squacco heron.
arder, *v.i.* to burn, blaze, glow; (*poet.*) to glitter, glisten, shine; to rot (manure); to be inflamed. — *v.t.* to burn, kindle. — *v.r.* (*agric.*) to become ruined, destroyed through heat and moisture; to become agitated or consumed by some passion; *ardiendo de*, or *en cólera*, fuming with rage; *arderse en pleitos*, to be entangled in lawsuits; *la mar arde*, the sea sparkles; *arder verde por seco*, the innocent suffers for the guilty; *arder en deseo de hacer una cosa*, to burn with desire to do anything.
ardero, **-ra**, *a.* squirrel-hunter (dog).
ardeviejas, *n.f.* (*bot.*, *coll.*) gorse, furze.
ardid, *n.m.* stratagem, artifice, cunning trick; *usar de ardides*, to act in an underhand way. — *a.* astute, cunning.
ardido, **-da**, *a.* brave, courageous; daring, bold, fearless. — *p.p.* [ARDER].
ardiente, *a.* ardent, burning, hot, fervent; (*fig.*) fiery, feverish; passionate; (*poet.*) glowing red, like fire.
ardientemente, *adv.* ardently, fervidly; fearlessly.
ardilla, *n.f.* squirrel; *andar como ardilla*, to fly about from place to place; *listo como una ardilla*, extremely intelligent or efficient.
ardimiento, *n.m.* conflagration; intrepidity, valour, courage.
ardínculo, *n.m.* (*vet.*) abscess (of horses).
ardiondo, **-da**, *a.* valiant, courageous.
ardite, *n.m.* ancient coin of small worth; *no importar*, or *no valer un ardite*, not to be worth a red cent.
ardor, *n.m.* ardour, great heat, hotness, fieriness; vivacity; efficiency; valour, vigour; fervency, eagerness; (*med.*) fever; *en el ardor de la batalla, de la disputa*, in the heat of the battle, of the dispute.
ardoroso, **-sa**, *a.* fiery; ardent, vigorous.
arduamente, *adv.* arduously.
arduo, **-dua**, *a.* arduous, difficult; (*poet.*) steep, lofty.
área, *n.f.* plot of land; area; are, square decametre; (*agric.*) threshing-floor; (*geom.*) area within a perimeter.
areca, *n.f.* palm-tree of the Philippines.
arefacción, *n.f.* act of drying; dryness; arefaction.
areito, *n.m.* popular song and dance of the Caribbean.
arel, *n.m.* large sieve.
arelar, *v.t.* to sift corn with the *arel*.
arena, *n.f.* sand, grit; arena, circus; (*pl.*) (*med.*) gravel; *arena movediza*, quicksand; *sembrar en arena*, to labour in vain; *comer arena antes que hacer vileza*, to be flayed alive rather than do a base deed; *edificar sobre arena* or *escribir en la arena*, to build upon foundations of sand.
arenáceo, **-cea**, *a.* arenaceous, gravelly, sandy.

arenal, *n.m.* sandy ground, sandy beach, quicksand bed.
arenalejo, *n.m.* small sandy place.
arenar, *v.t.* to sand; to rub or cover with sand.
arencado, **-da**, *a.* herring-like; (*fig.*) dried-up, skinny. — *p.p.* [ARENCAR].
arencar, *v.t.* (*pret.* **arenqué**; *pres. subj.* **arenque**) to salt and dry sardines, etc.
arencón, *n.m.* (*ichth.*) variety of herring.
arenería, *n.f.* sand-pit.
arenero, **-ra**, *n.m.f.* dealer in sand. — *n.m.* sand-box.
arenga, *n.f.* harangue, speech, address.
arengador, **-ra**, *n.m.f.* speech-maker, haranguer. — *a.* haranguing.
arengar, *v.i.*, *v.t.* (*pret.* **arengué**; *pres. subj.* **arengue**) to harangue, deliver a speech.
arenilla, *n.f.* moulding sand; powder to dry writing; (*med.*) calculus. — *pl.* granulated saltpetre.
arenisca, *n.f.* (*min.*) rock of quartz and silex; sandstone.
arenisco, **-ca**; **arenoso**, **-sa**, *a.* sandy, gravelly, arenose.
arenque, *n.m.* (*ichth.*) herring; *arenque ahumado*, red herring.
arenquera, *n.f.* herring fishing-net.
arenquería, *n.f.* herring shop.
arenquero, **-ra**, *n.m.f.* herring dealer. — *n.f.* (*slang*) coarse, low woman.
aréola, *n.f.* (*anat.*, *biol.*, *med.*) areola; circle round the nipple.
areómetro, *n.m.* aræometer; hydrometer.
areopagita, *n.m.* areopagite.
areópago, *n.m.* Areopagus; important tribunal.
areóstilo, *n.m.* (*arch.*) aræostyle.
areotectónica, *n.f.* areotectonics.
arepa, *n.f.* (*Am.*) corn griddle cake.
arestil; **arestín**, *n.m.* (*bot.*) perennial umbelliferous plant with dark blue flowers; (*vet.*) skin eruption, rash.
arestinado, **-da**, *a.* (*vet.*) afflicted with thrush.
arete, *n.m.* small hoop; ear-drop, ear-ring.
aretino, **-na**, *n.m.f.*, *a.* native of Arezzo.
arfada, *n.f.* (*naut.*) pitching (a ship).
arfar, *v.i.* (*naut.*) to pitch.
argadijo; **argadillo**, *n.m.* reel, bobbin, winder; (*prov.*) large wicker basket; (*coll.*) blustering, noisy, interfering person.
argado, *n.m.* trick, artifice; absurdity, nonsense.
argal, *n.m.* argol, crude tartar.
argalia, *n.f.* catheter.
argallera, *n.f.* (*carp.*) saw for cutting grooves.
argamandel, *n.m.* rag, tatter.
argamandijo, *n.m.* collection of small tools or implements.
argamasa, *n.f.* mortar, cement for building.
argamasado, **-da**, *a.* cemented; containing mortar. — *n.m.* quantity of mortar. — *p.p.* [ARGAMASAR].
argamasar, *v.t.* to make mortar; to cement.
argamasón, *n.m.* large dry piece of mortar.
argamula, *n.f.* (*bot.*, *prov.*) bugloss.
árgana, *n.f.*; **árgano**, *n.m.* (*mech.*) crane. — *n.f.pl.* wicker baskets on a horse.
arganel, *n.m.* ring in an astrolabe.
arganeo, *n.m.* (*naut.*) anchor-ring.
argavieso, *n.m.* whirlwind.
argayar, *v. impers.* to fall down (said of landslide).
argayo, *n.m.* landslide; *argayo de nieve*, (*prov.*) avalanche; monk's woollen cloak.

argel, *a*. said of a horse whose right hind foot is white.

Argel, *n.m.* Algiers.

Argelia, *n.f.* Algeria.

argelino, -na, *n.m.f.*, *a*. native of Algeria.

argema; argemón, *n.m.* (*med.*) argema.

argemone, *n.f.* (*bot.*) prickly or horned poppy.

argén, *n.m.* (*her.*) white or silver colour, argent.

argentada, *n.f.* ladies' cosmetic.

argentado, -da, *a*. silvered, silvery; slashed (shoes). — *p.p.* [ARGENTAR].

argentador, -ra, *a*. silvery. — *n.m.* silversmith.

argentar, *v.t.* to plate, adorn with silver; to polish like silver.

argentario, *n.m.* silversmith; governor of the mint.

argénteo, -tea, *a*. silvery, silver-plated; silver-white.

argentería, *n.f.* embroidery in gold or silver.

argentero, *n.m.* silversmith.

argentífero, -ra, *a*. silver-bearing.

argentina, *n.f.* (*bot.*) satin cinquefoil.

argentinismo, *n.m.* (*Am.*) expression peculiar to Argentina.

argentino, -na, *a*. silvery, argentine; belonging to the Argentine Republic. — *n.m.* Argentine gold coin, worth five gold pesos.

argento, *n.m.* (*poet.*) silver; *argento vivo*, quick-silver; *argento vivo sublimado*, (*chem.*) corrosive sublimate.

argentoso, -sa, *a*. mixed with silver.

argila; argilla, *n.f.* argil, clay.

argiloso, -sa, *a*. argillaceous.

argiritas, *n.m.pl.* white pyrites.

argo, *n.m.* (*chem.*) argon.

argolla, *n.f.* large ring, collar, hoop, staple; ring in bowling game; pillory.

argolleta, *n.f.* small staple or ring.

argollón, *n.m.* very large ring or staple.

árgoma, *n.f.* (*bot.*) furze, gorse.

argomal, *n.m.* furze plantation.

argomón, *n.m.* large, prickly furze.

argonauta, *n.m.* Argonaut; (*zool.*) paper-nautilus; cuttlefish.

Argos, *n.m.* (*myth.*) Argus; (*fig.*) a very obser-vant person.

argucia, *n.f.* subtlety, sophistry.

argüe, *n.m.* (*naut.*) windlass, capstan.

arguellarse, *v.r.* (*prov.*) to become emaciated.

arguello, *n.m.* (*prov.*) lack of health, faintness, indisposition.

árguenas; árgueñas, *n.f.pl.* handbarrows, panniers; saddlebags; (*Chi.*) wicker baskets on a horse.

argüidor, -ra, *n.m.f.* arguer. — *a*. argumen-tative.

argüir, *v.i.* (*pres. indic.* **arguyo**; *pres. subj.* **arguya**) to argue, dispute, oppose. — *v.t.* to infer, imply; to reveal, prove; to accuse, charge; *argüir de falso*, to imply falsely; *argüir (ignorancia, malicia, etc.) en una persona*, to imply (ignorance, malice, etc.) in a person; *argüirle a uno su conciencia*, to be pricked by one's conscience.

argumentación, *n.f.* argumentation, argu-mentativeness.

argumentador, -ra, *n.m.f.* arguer, reasoner, disputer. — *a*. argumentative; reasoning.

argumentante, *n.m.f.* arguer. — *a*. arguing.

argumentar, *v.i.* to argue, dispute.

argumentista, *n.m.f.* arguer, reasoner.

argumento, *n.m.* argument; plot of a story or play; summary, synopsis; sign, token, indica-tion; *argumento cornuto*, dilemma; *apretar el argumento*, (*log.*) to reinforce an argument in order to make its solution more difficult; *desatar el argumento*, to settle a question.

arguyente, *n.m.f.* arguer. — *a*. arguing, op-posing.

aria, *n.f.* song for a single voice; tune, air.

ariano, -na, *a*. Aryan.

aribar, *v.t.* (*obs.*) to reel yarn into skeins.

aribo, *n.m.* (*obs.*) reel for making skeins.

aricar, *v.t.* (*agric.*) to plough across sown ground.

aridecer, *v.t.*, *v.i.*, *v.r.* (*pres. indic.* **aridezco**; *pres. subj.* **aridezca**) to render, be, or be-come arid.

aridez, *n.f.* drought; barrenness, aridity, aridness.

árido, -da, *a*. arid, dry, barren; (*fig.*) mono-tonous, uninteresting. — *n.m.pl.* dry goods (vegetables, grain, etc.) which can be meas-ured with dry measure.

arienzo, *n.m.* old Castilian coin.

arieta, *n.f.* arietta, short song for one voice.

arietar, *v.t.* to ram.

ariete, *n.m.* battering-ram; (*naut.*) ram; *ariete hidráulico*, hydraulic ram.

arietino, -na, *a*. resembling a ram's head.

arigue, *n.m.* Philippine timber.

arije, *a*. applied to a kind of grape.

arijo, -ja, *a*. (*agric.*) light, easily tilled.

arillo, *n.m.* ear-ring; neck-stock frame.

arimez, *n.m.* prominence or extension of a building.

ario, -ria, *n.m.f.*, *a*. Aryan.

arisaro, *n.m.* (*bot.*) wake-robin.

arisblanco, -ca, *a*. white-bearded (of wheat).

arisco, -ca, *a*. churlish, shy, cross, stubborn, surly; fierce, wild; harsh, rough, unpolished.

arisnegro, -ra; arisprieto, -ta, *a*. black-bearded (of wheat).

arista, *n.f.* (*bot.*) arista; beard or awn of grains; hemp-stalk; edge; (*slang*) stone; (*geom.*) intersection. — *pl.* (*mil.*) salient angles.

aristado, -da, *a*. awned, bearded, aristate.

aristarco, *n.m.* Aristarch, severe but capable critic.

aristino, *n.m.* (*vet.*) thrush; wheals.

aristocracia, *n.f.* aristocracy.

aristócrata, *n.m.f.* aristocrat.

aristocráticamente, *adv.* aristocratically.

aristocrático, -ca, *a*. aristocratic.

aristoloquia, *n.f.* (*bot.*) birthwort.

aristón, *n.m.* (*arch.*) edge, corner; (*arch.*) groin, groin-rib; (*mus.*) kind of barrel-organ.

aristoso, -sa, *a*. having many beards or awns.

aristotélico, -ca, *a*. Aristotelian.

aristotelismo, *n.m.* Aristotelianism.

aritmancia; aritmomancia, *n.f.* arithmancy, arithmomancy.

aritmética, *n.f.* arithmetic.

aritméticamente, *adv.* arithmetically.

aritmético, -ca, *a*. arithmetical. — *n.m.f.* arithmetician, accountant.

aritmómetro, *n.m.* calculating machine.

arjorán, *n.m.* ciclamor, an ornamental tree.

arlar, *v.t.* to hang fruit in bunches for preser-vation.

arlequín, *n.m.* harlequin, buffoon; Neapolitan ice-cream.

arlequinado, -da, *a*. parti-coloured (clothes). — *n.f.* harlequin's trick or joke.

[84]

arlo, *n.m.* (*bot.*) barberry; fruit hung in bunches to be preserved.

arlota, *n.f.* tow of flax or hemp.

arma, *n.f.* weapon, arms; (*mil.*) division of military forces; *arma de infantería*, infantry; *arma de caballería*, cavalry, etc. — *pl.* troops, armies; armorial ensigns; coat of arms; (*fig.*) means, power, reason; *arma negra*, fencing foil; *armas vedadas*, illicit means; *¡arma, arma! ¡a las armas! ¡al arma!* to arms! *alzarse en armas*, to rise up in arms; *armas y dinero, buenas manos quieren*, arms and money should be in wise hands; *dejar las armas*, to retire from military life; *hacer armas*, to fight; to threaten with weapon in hand; to fight hand to hand; *hecho de armas*, fight; *suspensión de armas*, armistice; *probar las armas*; (*fencing, fig.*) to put to the test; *medir las armas*, to fight; to dispute verbally; *poner en arma*, to alarm; *poner en armas*, to arm; *ponerse en arma*, (*coll.*) to get ready, prepare oneself; *dar arma*, (*mil.*) to call out the guard; *arma falsa*, false attack, feint; *arma arrojadiza*, missile weapon; *arma de fuego*, fire-arms, gun; *arma blanca*, side-arms, steel arms; *hombre de armas*, military man; *maestro de armas*, fencing-master; *pasar por las armas*, (*mil.*) to shoot, execute; *rendir las armas*, to surrender; *publicar armas*, to challenge to public combat; *sobre las armas*, under arms, alert and prepared; *armas de agua*, (*Mex.*) waterproof skins for riding.

armada, *n.f.* navy; fleet, squadron; (*slang*) cheating trick (cards); (*hunt.*) party of beaters.

armadera, *n.f.* keel, main timber of a ship.

armadía, *n.f.* raft, float.

armadijo, *n.m.* trap, snare for game.

armadilla, *n.f.* (*slang*) money given to another to play for one.

armadillo, *n.m.* (*zool.*) armadillo.

armado, -da, *a.* weaponed, armed; (*her*) gold or silver placed on other metal; (*mech.*) mounted, set. — *n.m.* man in armour (in religious processions). — *p.p.* [ARMAR].

armador, *n.m.* outfitter, shipowner; privateer, cruiser; one who fits out whale-ships; (*mech.*) framer, adjuster, fitter; jacket.

armadura, *n.f.* armour; (*mil.*, *elec.*) armature; (*elec.*) yoke of a magnet; framework, shell of a building; (*mech.*) fitting, setting; truss; (*anat.*) skeleton; *armadura del tejado*, frame of a roof; trestle, mounting; *armadura de la cama*, bedstead.

armajal, *n.m.* glasswort field.

armajara, *n.f.* (*agric.*) land prepared for tree nursery.

armajo, *n.m.* (*bot.*) glasswort.

armamento, *n.m.* armament, warlike preparations; accoutrements; (*naut.*) equipment.

armar, *v.t.* to arm; to man; (*carp.*) to bind, mount, truss, put together; (*mech.*) to set, frame, mount, piece, adjust, make true, rig up; to plate (with gold or silver); (*coll.*) to lend money to; (*naut.*) to equip, fit out, put a ship in commission; *armarla*, to cheat at cards; to cause an altercation; *armar una bronca*, to make a row; *armar en corso*, to privateer; *armar caballero*, to knight; *armar un escándalo*, to kick up a shindy; *armar en guerra*, to arm a merchantman; *armar los remos*, (*naut.*) to man the oars; *armar ruido*, to raise a disturbance; *armar la gorda*, to cause an altercation; *se arma una tempestad*, a storm is brewing; *armar un baile, una fiesta*, to prepare a ball, a feast; *¡buena se va a armar!* there's trouble brewing! — *v.i.* to suit, fit, go together. — *v.r.* to prepare oneself, arm oneself; *armarse de paciencia*, to prepare oneself with patience.

armario, *n.m.* clothes-press, cabinet, wardrobe, bookcase, closet, cupboard; *armario de luna*, wardrobe with mirror.

armatoste, *n.m.* hulk; unwieldy machine; heavy or ill-made piece of furniture; trap, snare; (*coll.*) corpulent, worthless person.

armayada, *n.f.* fishing net for lobsters.

armazón, *n.f.* framework, skeleton, frame; adjustment, mounting; hulk of a ship. — *n.m.* (*anat.*) skeleton.

armelina, *n.f.* ermine skin.

armella, *n.f.* screw-eye.

armelluela, *n.f.* small screw-eye.

arménico, -ca, *a.* Armenian. — *n.m.* Armenian bole; Armenian stone.

armenio, -nia, *n.m.f.*, *a.* Armenian.

armería, *n.f.* armoury, arsenal; gunsmith's trade or shop; heraldry.

armero, *n.m.* armourer, gunsmith; keeper of arms; (*mil.*) rack or stand for fire-arms.

armífero, -ra; **armígero, -ra**, *a.* warlike; (*poet.*) armed, armour-bearing. — *n.m.* squire, shield-bearer.

armila, *n.f.* (*arch.*) part of base of a column.

armilar, *a. esfera armilar*, armillary sphere.

armilla, *n.f.* (*arch.*) astragal; surbase of column.

armillado, -da, *a.* armillary; surrounded by rings.

armiñado, -da, *a.* trimmed or lined with ermine fur; ermine-white.

armiño, *n.m.* (*zool.*) ermine.

armipotente, *a.* (*poet.*) mighty in war.

armisonante, *a.* (*poet.*) bearer of resounding arms.

armisticio, *n.m.* armistice.

armón, *n.m.* (*mil.*) limber, forecarriage of a piece of artillery.

armonía, *n.f.* harmony; concord; (*mus.*) harmonization; (*fig.*) peace, friendship.

armónicamente, *adv.* harmoniously.

armónico, -ca, *a.* harmonical, harmonious; proportionate, musical, rhythmical. — *n.f.* harmonica.

armonio, *n.m.* harmonium, small reed-organ.

armoniosamente, *adv.* harmoniously.

armonioso, -sa, *a.* harmonious, sonorous, pleasing to the ear, consonous.

armonista, *n.m.f.* harmonist.

armonización, *n.f.* harmonization.

armonizar, *v.t.* (*pret.* **armonicé**; *pres. subj.* **armonice**) to harmonize; *armonizar con*, to be in keeping with. — *v.r.* to conform, adapt oneself.

armosín, *n.m.* thin silk, taffeta.

armuelle, *n.m.* (*bot.*) orach, mountain spinach.

arna, *n.f.* (*prov.*) beehive.

arnacho, *n.m.* (*bot.*) rest-harrow.

arnaute, *n.m.f.*, *a.* Albanian.

arnera, *n.f.* difficult to work, hard (land).

arnés, *n.m.* harness; coat of mail, armour. — *pl.* harness, trappings; (*coll.*) necessary implements or tools; *blasonar del arnés*, to boast of imaginary exploits.

árnica, *n.f.* (*bot.*) arnica; wolf's-bane.

arnillo, *n.m.* West Indian fish of the Acanthopterygii order.

aro, *n.m.* hoop of wood or metal; staple; serviette-ring; children's game; *entrar por el aro,* to submit unwillingly; (*bot.*) wild arum, lords-and-ladies; *¡aro!* (*Chi.*) interj. word with which a singer, dancer or talker is stopped, and presented with a drink.

aroca, *n.f.* kind of linen made in Arouca (Portugal).

aroma, *n.f.* flower of the aromatic myrrh-tree. — *n.m.* any aromatic gum, balsam, wood or herb; perfume, fragrance.

aromaticidad, *n.f.* aromatic quality, perfume.

aromático, -ca, *a.* aromatic, fragrant.

aromatización, *n.f.* aromatization.

aromatizador, -ra, *a.* perfuming. — *n.m.* aromatizer; atomizer.

aromatizante, *a.* fragrant, aromatizing.

aromatizar, *v.t.* (*pret.* **aromaticé;** *pres. subj.* **aromatice**) to aromatize, perfume.

aromo, *n.m.* (*bot.*) aromatic myrrh-tree.

aromoso, -sa, *a.* aromatic, fragrant.

arón, *n.m.* (*bot.*) arum.

aroza, *n.m.* foreman in iron-works or forges.

arpa, *n.f.* (*mus.*) harp, lyre; *tronar como arpa vieja,* (*coll.*) to finish disastrously and suddenly.

arpado, -da, *a.* serrated, toothed; (*poet.*) sweetly singing (bird). — *p.p.* [ARPAR].

arpador, *n.m.* (*obs.*) harper.

arpadura, *n.f.* scratch.

arpar, *v.t.* to rend, scratch, claw, tear to pieces.

arpegio, *n.m.* (*mus.*) arpeggio.

arpella, *n.f.* (*orn.*) harpy-eagle.

arpeo, *n.m.* (*naut.*) grappling-iron.

arpía, *n.f.* (*myth., coll.*) harpy, fiend; ugly shrew; (*slang*) constable; greedy person.

arpillera, *n.f.* sackcloth, burlap.

arpista, *n.m.f.* (*mus.*) harper, harpist; (*Chi.*) common thief.

arpón, *n.m.* harpoon, harping iron; clamp.

arponado, -da, *a.* harpooned; harpoon-like. — *p.p.* [ARPONAR].

arponar; arponear, *v.t.* to throw the harpoon. — *v.i.* to manipulate the harpoon dexterously.

arponero, *n.m.* harpooner; harpoon-maker.

arqueada, *n.f.* stroke with the fiddle-bow; retching; *dar arqueadas,* (*coll.*) to show symptoms of nausea.

arqueador, *n.m.* ship-gauger; wool-beater; one who forms arches.

arqueaje; arqueamiento, *n.m.* gauging of a ship.

arquear, *v.t.* to arch; to beat wool; (*naut.*) to gauge ships; *arquear las cejas,* to arch the brows. — *v.i.* to feel nausea.

arqueo, *n.m.* the act of arching; (*naut.*) tonnage or burden of a ship; (*com.*) verification of money and papers in a safe.

arqueología, *n.f.* archæology.

arqueológico, -ca, *a.* archæologic, archæological.

arqueólogo, *n.m.* archæologist.

arquería, *n.f.* series of arches; (*Mex.*) aqueduct.

arquero, *n.m.* treasurer, cashier; archer, bow-maker; hooper.

arqueta, *n.f.* small chest.

arquetipo, *n.m.* archetype.

arquetón, *n.m.* large chest.

arquibanco, *n.m.* bench with drawers.

arquidiócesis, *n.f.* archdiocese.

arquiepiscopal, *a.* archiepiscopal.

arquilla; arquita, *n.f.* little chest; coach-box.

arquillo, *n.m.* small bore (locksmiths').

arquimesa, *n.f.* writing-desk, escritoire.

arquisinagogo, *n.m.* principal in the synagogue.

arquitecto, *n.m.* architect.

arquitectónico, -ca, *a.* architectural; architectonic.

arquitectura, *n.f.* architecture.

arquitrabe, *n.m.* architrave.

arquivolta, *n.f.* archivolt.

arrabal, *n.m.* suburb. — *pl.* environs, outskirts.

arrabalero, -ra, *n.m.f.,* *a.* suburban; (*coll.*) ill-bred (person).

arrabillado, -da, *a.* (*agric.*) blighted (wheat).

arrabio, *n.m.* cast-iron fused for making steel.

arracada, *n.f.* ear-ring with pendant.

arracimado, -da, *a.* clustered, in racimes. — *p.p.* [ARRACIMARSE].

arracimarse, *v.t.* to cluster; to form racimes.

arraclán, *n.m.* alder-tree; (*prov.*) scorpion.

arráez, *n.m.* captain or master of Arab ship.

arraigadamente, *adv.* fixedly, rootedly, securely.

arraigadas, *n.f.pl.* (*naut.*) futtock-shrouds.

arraigado, -da, *a.* owning real estate; fixed, rooted, secure, inveterate; *del hombre arraigado no te verás vengado,* you cannot be revenged on a man who is well established. — *n.m.* (*naut.*) mooring. — *p.p.* [ARRAIGAR].

arraigar, *v.i.* to root; (*law*) to pledge land as guarantee. — *v.r.* to settle down; to become rooted.

arraigo, *n.m.* settling in a place; landed property; *hombre (persona) de arraigo,* landlord, property-owner; *tener arraigo,* to own property; *fianza de arraigo,* guarantee by mortgage.

arraigue, *n.m.* settling down, taking root.

arralar, *v.i.* to become thin or sparse; (*agric.*) to yield thin bunches of grapes.

arramblar, *v.t.* to leave covered with sand and gravel (after floods); (*fig.*) to sweep away. — *v.r.* to become covered in sand through floods.

arranca, *n.f.* plucking (fruit).

arrancaclavos, *n.m.* nail-puller.

arrancada, *n.f.* (*coll.*) sudden departure; violent sally; (*naut.*) sudden increase in speed.

arrancadera, *n.f.* leading bell for cattle.

arrancadero, *n.m.* starting-point; (*prov.*) thickest part of a gun-barrel.

arrancado, -da, *a.* poor, penniless; uprooted, extirpated. — *p.p.* [ARRANCAR].

arrancador, -ra, *n.m.f.* extirpator, destroyer. — *a.* extirpating, destroying.

arrancadura, *n.f.;* **arrancamiento,** *n.m.* extirpation, pulling out, destroying.

arrancapinos, *n.m.* (*coll.*) dwarf, small person.

arrancar, *v.t.* (*pret.* **arranqué;** *pres. subj.* **arranque**) to extirpate, root out, force out, wrest, pull out, tear out, draw out; to carry off; to force up (sighs, voices); to expectorate. — *v.i.* to start off; (*coll.*) to leave; to originate in; (*arch.*) to begin arch; (*naut.*) to set sail; *arrancar la espada*, to unsheathe the sword; *arrancar de raíz*, to root or pull up; *arrancar la rosa al, del suelo*, to pull up the rose from the ground; *arrancar de cuajo*, to eradicate; *arrancar a uno alguna cosa*, to obtain something by importunity; *arrancársele el corazón a alguno*, to feel great sympathy for someone; *arrancársele a uno el alma*, to die broken-hearted.

arrancasiega, *n.f.* (*agric.*) poor grain half mowed and half pulled up; (*prov.*) quarrel, dispute.

arranciarse, *v.r.* to grow rancid.

arranchar, *v.t.* (*naut.*) to coast; (*naut.*) to brace. — *v.r.* to mess together.

arranque, *n.m.* extirpation, wrench; impetuousness, fit (of passion, love, etc.); sudden start, sudden impulse; (*arch.*) springer of an arch; (*mech.*) start; (*motor.*) starter; starting gear.

arranquera, *n.f.* (*Cub., Mex.*) financial straits.

arrapar, *v.t.* (*vulg.*) to snatch away, carry off.

arrapiezo; **arrapo**, *n.m.* tatter, rag; urchin, ragamuffin.

arras, *n.f.pl.* security, earnest of a contract; the 13 coins given by the bridegroom to the bride at a wedding; dowry; earnest-money, pledge, handsel.

arrasado, *a.* satiny; levelled, razed, filled. — *p.p.* [ARRASAR].

arrasadura, *n.f.* levelling with a strickle.

arrasamiento, *n.m.* levelling, demolition.

arrasar, *v.t.* to level; to raze, demolish, destroy; to level with a strickle; to obliterate; to well up (tears); to fill to the brim. — *v.i.*, *v.r.* to clear up, grow fine (of the weather); *arrasarse (los ojos) de, en lágrimas*, to become filled with tears (the eyes).

arrastrada, *n.f.* prostitute.

arrastradamente, *adv.* defectively, imperfectly; painfully, wretchedly.

arrastraderas, *n.f.pl.* (*naut.*) lower studding-sails.

arrastradero, *n.m.* road by which logs are dragged; spot whence dead bulls are taken off; (*naut.*) careening place.

arrastrado, -da, *a.* dragged along; (*coll.*) rascally, knavish; (*coll.*) destitute. — *p.p.* [ARRASTRAR].

arrastramiento, *n.m.* creeping, dragging along.

arrastrante, *a.* dragging, crawling. — *n.m.* applicant for a scholarship or a degree in colleges.

arrastrapiés, *n.m.* shuffling *or* dragging feet.

arrastrar, *v.t.* to drag along; to convince; to drag down, degrade; to haul; to attract; to prompt, move, urge. — *v.i.* to creep, crawl; to hang down to the ground; (*naut.*) to be urged along (by wind or current); to follow suit (at cards); *arrastrar en su caída*, to drag down in its fall; *arrastrar por tierra*, to drag on the ground; *arrastrar bayetas*, to apply for a scholarship; *arrastrar coche*, to own a carriage; *arrastrar los pies*, to shuffle, to move with a dragging gait; *hacer una cosa arrastrando*, to do a thing on compulsion, badly. — *v.r.* to humiliate oneself vilely.

arrastre, *n.m.* dragging, haulage, drayage; leading a trump; slope in a mining shaft; claiming a degree; (*Mex.*) mining mill.

arrate, *n.m.* pound of sixteen ounces.

arratonado, -da, *a.* gnawed by mice.

arrayán, *n.m.* (*bot.*) myrtle.

arrayanal, *n.m.* plantation of myrtles.

¡arre! *interj.* gee! get up! gee up! *¡arre allá!* get out of the way!

arreada, *n.f.* herding the grazing flock; (*mil.*) recruiting; (*Arg., Mex.*) robbery, theft of cattle, horses or any livestock.

arreado, -da, *p.p.* [ARREAR] driven.

arreador, *n.m.* (*Arg., Col., Per.*) driving whip; beater of olive-trees; (*prov.*) foreman, overseer.

arreala, *n.f.* pasturage toll.

arrear, *v.t.* to drive, urge horses, mules, etc.; to urge, hurry, press on; (*Arg., Mex.*) to steal, rob cattle, livestock; to put on ornaments, trappings; *el que venga detrás que arree*, there's nothing left for the last comer; the devil take the hindmost; *¡arrea!* hurry up!

arrebañaderas, *n.f.pl.* grappling-irons for dragging a well.

arrebañador, -ra, *n.m.f.* gleaner, gatherer. — *a.* gleaning, gathering.

arrebañadura, *n.f.* gleaning, picking up. — *pl.* scraps, remains (food).

arrebañar, *v.t.* to glean, gather; to scrape up; to snatch.

arrebatadamente, *adv.* precipitately, headlong, violently.

arrebatadizo, -za, *a.* prone to violence.

arrebatado, -da, *a.* sudden, rapid, violent; rash, precipitate, impetuous; inflamed (face). — *p.p.* [ARREBATAR].

arrebatador, -ra, *n.m.f.* violent snatcher. — *a.* snatching; (*fig.*) captivating, arresting.

arrebatamiento, *n.m.* carrying off by violence; (*fig.*) rage, fury; ecstasy, rapture.

arrebatar, *v.t.* to carry off, snatch; to attract (the attention, etc.); to captivate, charm; to move, stir; (*agric.*) to parch; *arrebatar de*, or *de entre las manos*, to snatch from the hands. — *v.r.* to develop, grow; to become burnt, overcooked; (*agric.*) to become parched; *arrebatarse de ira*, to be led away by passion.

arrebatiña, *n.f.* scrimmage (to pick up something).

arrebato, *n.m.* surprise; sudden attack, paroxysm; fit, fury, rage; rapture; (*law*) a mitigating circumstance.

arrebatoso, -sa, *a.* prompt, sudden.

arrebol, *n.m.* red sky or cloud; rouge.

arrebola, *n.f.* group of red clouds.

arrebolar, *v.t.* to paint red. — *v.r.* to rouge.

arrebolera, *n.f.* rouge-box, rouge-seller; (*bot.*) four o'clock, marvel of Peru.

arrebollarse, *v.r.* (*prov.*) to precipitate oneself, fall headlong.

arrebozar, *v.t.* (*pret.* **arrebocé**; *pres. subj.* **arreboce**) (*cook.*) to dip in, cover with butter, sugar, etc.; to wrap up. — *v.r.* to muffle or wrap oneself up; to swarm; *arrebócese con ello*, you keep it, have it.

arrebozo, *n.m.* muffling oneself up; muffler; pretext.

arrebujadamente, *adv.* confusedly, in a disorderly fashion.

arrebujar, *v.t.* to jumble together; to huddle. — *v.r.* to wrap or huddle oneself up.

arreciar, *v.i.* to increase in strength or intensity; *arrecia la borrasca*, the storm increases. — *v.r.* to grow stronger.

arrecido, -da, *n.m.f., a.* benumbed; frozen to death. — *p.p.* [ARRECIRSE].

arrecife, *n.m.* road paved with stone; *(naut.)* reef.

arrecirse, *v.r.* to become numb; *arrecirse de frío,* to grow stiff with cold.

arrechucho, *n.m.* fit of anger; impulse; *(coll.)* sudden and passing indisposition.

arredilar, *v.t.* to fold sheep; to pen cattle.

arredomado, -da, *a.* artful, cunning; joined, united. — *p.p.* [ARREDOMAR].

arredomar, *v.t.* *(slang)* to join. — *v.r.* *(slang)* to be scandalized, shocked.

arredondar; arredondear, *v.t.* to round. — *v.r.* to become round.

arredramiento, *n.m.* moving back, removing to a greater distance; backing out; dismay, fear.

arredrar, *v.t.* to remove, cause to move back, separate; to terrify. — *v.r.* to be, or become terrified; to fear; to remove oneself.

arregazado, -da, *a.* tucked up; *(fig.)* with the point turned up; *nariz arregazada,* snub nose. — *p.p.* [ARREGAZAR].

arregazar, *v.t.* *(pret.* **arregacé;** *pres. subj.* **arregace)** to tuck up the skirts; to truss.

arregladamente, *adv.* regularly, in an orderly way.

arreglado, -da, *a.* regular, moderate; regulated, arranged; *arreglado a las leyes,* in accordance with the laws; *arreglado en la conducta,* of good, regular behaviour; *a un precio arreglado,* at a reasonable price. — *p.p.* [ARREGLAR].

arreglador, *n.m.* *(com.)* surveyor, valuer (of averages).

arreglar, *v.t.* to guide, regulate; to frame; *(min.)* to level; *(com.)* to arrange, settle, adjust; to bring into a rule; *arreglar el velamen,* *(naut.)* to trim the sails; *arreglar a uno,* to dictate to someone; *arreglar uno sus cosas,* to get one's things ready, put them in order. — *v.r.* to conform oneself; to settle; to come to an agreement; *arreglarse por las buenas,* to settle matters amicably; *arreglárselas,* to manage as best one can; *arreglarse, a, con lo que uno tiene,* to cut one's coat according to one's cloth; *arreglarse a la razón,* to conform to reason; *arreglarse con el acreedor,* to settle with the creditor.

arreglo, *n.m.* rule, order; disposition, adjustment; *(com.)* settlement, compromise, arrangement; *(coll.)* concubinage; *con arreglo a,* according to, conformably with.

arregostarse, *v.r.* (with *a*) to become fond of; to relish.

arrejacar, *v.t.* *(pret.* **arrejaqué;** *pres. subj.* **arrejaque)** to plough across for clearing weeds.

arrejaco, *n.m.* *(orn.)* swift, martin.

arrejada, *n.f.* *(agric.)* paddle of a plough.

arrejaque, *n.m.* fishing-fork with three prongs; fish-spear; *(orn.)* swift, martin.

arrejerar, *v.t.* *(naut.)* to make a ship fast by casting two anchors fore and one aft.

arrela; arrelde, *n.m.* weight of four pounds.

arrellanarse, *v.r.* to sit at ease; to be satisfied with one's employment; to make oneself comfortable.

arremangado, -da, *a.* tucked up; lifted upward; *arremangado de nariz,* with a turned-up nose. — *p.p.* [ARREMANGAR].

arremangar, *v.t.* *(pret.* **arremangué;** *pres. subj.* **arremangue)** to tuck up the sleeves or petticoats. — *v.r.* to be, or become determined.

arremango, *n.m.* tucking up the clothes.

arrematar, *v.t.* *(coll.)* to complete, finish.

arremedar, *v.t.* to copy, mimic.

arremetedero, *n.m.* *(mil.)* point of attack; weak point.

arremetedor, -ra, *n.m.f.* assailant, aggressor. — *a.* assaulting, aggressive.

arremeter, *v.t.* to assail, attack, seize violently or briskly. — *v.i.* to launch forth; *(coll.)* to shock.

arremetida, *n.f.* assault, attack, invasion, start of horses.

arremolinado, -da, *a.* whirled, eddied; *(coll.)* crowded. — *p.p.* [ARREMOLINAR].

arremolinar, *v.t., v.r.* to whirl, eddy; to form a crowd, throng together.

arrempujar, *v.t.* to push, jostle.

arremueco; arremuesco, *n.m.* *(Col.)* caress, fondling.

arrendable, *a.* rentable, farmable, tenantable.

arrendación, *n.f.* renting, letting; lease; rental.

arrendadero, *n.m.* ring to tie horses to.

arrendado, -da, *a.* obedient to the reins; rented, leased. — *p.p.* [ARRENDAR].

arrendador, -ra, *n.m.f.* landlord, lessor; hirer, tenant, lessee, holder; farmer; *(slang)* receiver of stolen goods, fence; horsetrainer; [ARRENDADERO].

arrendadorcillo, *n.m.* petty tenant.

arrendajo, *n.m.* *(orn.)* mocking bird; *(coll.)* mimic, buffoon; *ser uno el arrendajo de otro,* to be someone's double.

arrendamiento, *n.m.* renting, letting, hiring, lease, rental.

arrendante, *n.m.f.* lessor.

arrendar, *v.t.* *(pres. indic.* **arriendo;** *pres. subj.* **arriende)** to rent, let, lease, hire; to bridle, tie a horse; to train a horse; to imitate; *arrendar a diente,* to let on condition of allowing commonage; *no le arriendo la ganancia,* I don't envy him; I should not like to be in his shoes.

arrendatario, -ria, *n.m.f.* lessee, tenant. — *a.* renting, hiring.

arrentado, -da, *a.* *(obs.)* receiving large rental.

arreo, *n.m.* dress, ornament, decoration. — *pl.* harness, trappings, appurtenances, accessories.

arreo, *adv.* successively, uninterruptedly.

arrepápalo, *n.m.* fritter, pancake.

arrepentido, -da, *n.m.f.* penitent. — *n.f.* reformed penitent woman. — *a.* regretted; repentant; *de los arrepentidos nacen los afligidos,* repentance is bitter (used as a warning against sin). — *p.p.* [ARREPENTIRSE].

arrepentimiento, *n.m.* repentance, contrition, compunction; lock of hair; *(paint.)* correction; *(law)* mitigating circumstance.

arrepentirse, *v.r.* *(pres. indic.* **me arrepiento;** *pres. subj.* **me arrepienta;** *pret.* *(él)* **se arrepintió;** *imperf. subj.* **me arrepintiese, -tiera;** *fut. subj.* **me arrepintiere)** (with *de*) to repent, rue, regret.

arrepistar, *v.t.* to grind rags into pulp (in paper making).

arrepisto, *n.m.* grinding or pounding rags.

arrepollado, -da, *a.* cabbage-like.

arrepsia, *n.f.* irresolution.

arrepticio, -cia, *a.* possessed by the devil.

arrequesonarse, *v.r.* to curdle, become curdled or coagulated (milk).

arrequife, *n.m.* singeing-iron (in cotton gins).

arrequives, *n.m.pl.* dress trimmings; (*coll.*) ornaments, adornments; (*coll.*) circumstances; requisites.

arrestado, -da, *a.* intrepid, bold, audacious; (*mil.*) arrested. — *p.p.* [ARRESTAR].

arrestar, *v.t.* to arrest, confine, imprison. — *v.r.* (with *a*) to venture, undertake boldly.

arresto, *n.m.* imprisonment, detention; (*mil.*) prison, arrest; spirit, enterprise.

arretín, *n.m.* moreen, woollen cloth.

arretranca, *n.f.* (*Col., Ec., Mex.*) brake (horses).

arrevesado, -da, *a.* frisky, difficult.

arrezafe, *n.m.* (*bot.*) spear-plume thistle; place full of brambles or thistles.

arrezagar, *v.t.* to raise; to turn up, tuck up.

arria, *n.f.* drove of beasts. — *interj.* (*naut.*) lower away.

arriada, *n.f.* flood, freshet, wash-out; (*naut.*) taking in (of sails).

arrial; arriaz, *n.m.* hilt-bar of a sword.

arrianismo, *n.m.* Arianism.

arriano, -na, *n.m.f., a.* Arian.

arriar, *v.t.* (*naut.*) to lower; to strike; to inundate; *arriar la bandera,* to strike the colours; *arriar un cabo,* (*naut.*) to pay out a cable; *arriar las velas,* (*naut.*) to take in sail. — *v.r.* to become flooded.

arriata, *n.f.; arriate,** *n.m.* border, edge in gardens; trellis; causeway, path.

arriaz, *n.m.* hilt-bar of a sword.

arriba, *adv.* above, over, up, high; on high, overhead; upstairs; (*naut.*) aloft; *¡arriba!* hurry up! *de arriba,* (*fig.*) from above, from God; *de cinco pesetas para arriba,* from 5 pesetas upwards; *no costará arriba de un dólar,* it will not cost more than one dollar; *arriba dicho,* above-mentioned; *ir agua arriba,* (*naut.*) to work up the river; *de arriba abajo,* from head to foot; from top to bottom; from beginning to end.

arribada, *n.f.* arrival (of a vessel in port); *de arribada,* putting into a port by stress.

arribaje, *n.m.* (*naut.*) arrival.

arribar, *v.i.* to arrive; (*naut.*) to put into a harbour; to fall off to leeward; to reach; (*coll.*) to recover from an illness or financial calamity; (*coll.*) to accomplish one's desire.

arribazón, *n.f.* great influx of fish to coasts and ports at certain seasons.

arribeño, -ña (*Mex., Arg., Per.*) *n.m.f., a.* a person from the highlands.

arribo, *n.m.* arrival.

arricés, *n.m.* buckle of stirrup-strap.

arricete, *n.m.* shoal, sand-bank.

arridar, *v.t.* (*naut.*) to haul taut.

arriendo, *n.m.* letting, renting, hiring.

arriendo; arriende, *pres. indic.; pres. subj.* [ARRENDAR].

arriería, *n.f.* occupation of muleteer, driving of mules.

arriero, *n.m.* (*dim.* **arrierico; arrierillo; arrierito**) muleteer.

arriesgadamente, *adv.* dangerously, hazardously, riskily.

arriesgado, -da, *a.* risked; perilous, dangerous, hazardous, risky, daring. — *p.p.* [ARRIESGAR].

arriesgar, *v.t.* (*pret.* **arriesgué;** *pres. subj.*

arriesgue) to risk, hazard. — *v.r.* (with *a* or *en*) to expose oneself to danger; to dare.

arrimadero, *n.m.* scaffold, stool, stand, support.

arrimadillo, *n.m.* mat; wainscot; dado.

arrimadizo, -za, *a.* made to be placed against or joined to a thing; (*fig.*) parasitic, sponging.

arrimador, *n.m.* log placed in a fireplace to support those in front of it.

arrimadura, *n.f.* act of approaching.

arrimar, *v.t.* to approach, draw near; to place near; to add; to give (blow); to displace, dismiss; (*naut.*) to stow the cargo; to lay aside, put by, reject; *arrimar una cosa,* to put something out of the way; *arrimar el hombro,* to lend a hand, assist; to work actively; *arrimar las espuelas al caballo,* to spur a horse. — *v.r.* (with *a*) to lean against or upon; to join others; to seek the protection of; to come to the knowledge of a thing; *arrimarse al parecer de otro,* to espouse another's opinion; *arrimarse a una persona,* to place oneself under another's protection; *arrímate a los buenos, y serás uno de ellos,* consort with good people, and you will become one of them.

arrime, *n.m.* mark for balls to arrive at (in bowls).

arrimo, *n.m.* placing against, beside, near; staff, stick, crutch; abandonment, giving up; protection; help, support; (*arch.*) idle wall, wall bearing no load; (*Cub.*) wall, fence or hedge separating ownership.

arrimón, *n.m.* idler, loafer; *hacer el arrimón* (*coll.*) to stagger along a wall; *estar de arrimón,* to stand and keep watch.

arrinconado, -da, *a.* distant, out of the way; put away, neglected, forgotten. — *p.p.* [ARRINCONAR].

arrinconamiento, *n.m.* retreat, retirement.

arrinconar, *v.t.* to put in a corner; to corner, drive into a position of difficulty; to neglect; to dismiss; to lay aside; to reject; to withdraw one's favour or protection. — *v.r.* to retire from the world; *arrinconarse en casa,* to live in retirement.

arriñonado, -da, *a.* kidney-shaped.

arriostrar, *v.t.* (*naut.*) to brace a frame.

arrisado, -da, *a.* agreeable, pleasing; affable, benign, peaceable. — *p.p.* [ARRISAR].

arrisar, *v.t.* to make pleasant, agreeable. — *v.r.* to become pleasant, agreeable.

arriscadamente, *adv.* boldly, audaciously.

arriscado, -da, *a.* risked; craggy; forward, bold, audacious, intrepid, rash, impudent; brisk; *caballo arriscado,* high-mettled horse. — *p.p.* [ARRISCAR].

arriscador, -ra, *n.m.f.* (*prov.*) gleaner of olives.

arriscamiento, *n.m.* intrepidity, daring.

arriscar, *v.t.* (*pret.* **arrisqué;** *pres. subj.* **arrisque**) to risk. — *v.r.* to dare; to be proud, arrogant; to plunge over a cliff (flocks); to ascend (cliff). — *v.t.* (*Per., ES.*) to dress smartly.

arrisco, *n.m.* risk.

arritranca, *n.f.* broad crupper of packsaddle.

arrizafa, *n.f.* garden, park.

arrizar, *v.t.* (*pret.* **arricé;** *pres. subj.* **arrice**) (*naut.*) to reef; to stow; to lash, tie; *arrizar el ancla,* to stow the anchor.

arroaz, *n.m.* (*ichth.*) dolphin.

arroba, *n.f.* variable liquid measure according to province and liquids; weight of about twenty-five pounds (11·5 kgs.); *echar por arrobas,* to exaggerate.

arrobadizo, -za, *a.* (*coll.*) feigning ecstasy and rapture.

arrobado, -da, *a.* ecstatic, rapturous. — *p.p.* [ARROBAR].

arrobador, -ra, *a.* charming, enchanting.

arrobamiento, *n.m.* enchantment; ecstasy, rapture; bliss, trance.

arrobar, *v.t.* to charm, enchant. — *v.r.* to be in rapture; to be out of one's senses.

arrobero, -ra, *a.* weighing an *arroba.* — *n.m.f.* baker for a community.

arrobeta, *n.f.* (*prov.*) measure of liquid (olive oil) about ⅔ of one *arroba.*

arrobinador, -ra, *a.* consuming, corrupting.

arrobinar, *v.t.* to consume, corrupt. — *v.r.* to rust; to become corrupted.

arrobiñar, *v.t.* (*slang*) to pick up.

arrobo, *n.m.* rapture, ecstasy; trance.

arrocabe, *n.m.* (*arch.*) wooden frieze; frieze-like ornament.

arrocado, -da, *a.* distaff-like; cut or slashed (of clothes).

arrocero, -ra, *n.m.f.* grower of rice, dealer in rice. — *a.* of rice; *molino arrocero,* rice mill.

arrocinado, -da, *a.* stupid, stubborn; hacklike, worn-out (horse). — *p.p.* [ARROCINAR].

arrocinar, *v.t.* to reduce one to a state of coarseness or vulgarity. — *v.r.* to become dull, stupid; (*fig., coll.*) to become blindly enamoured.

arrodajarse, *v.r.* (*CR.*) to sit on the ground with crossed legs.

arrodear, *v.t., v.i.* to surround, encircle.

arrodelarse, *v.r.* to arm oneself with a buckler or round shield.

arrodeo, *n.m.* [RODEO].

arrodillada, *n.f.* (*Chi.*) genuflexion.

arrodilladura, *n.f.;* **arrodillamiento,** *n.m.* action of kneeling.

arrodillar, *v.t.* to make kneel down. — *v.i.* to bend the knee. — *v.r.* to kneel down.

arrodrigar; arrodrigonar, *v.t.* to prop vines.

arrogación, *n.f.* arrogation; (*law*) child adoption.

arrogador, -ra, *n.m.f.* adopter; one who makes a proud claim. — *a.* arrogant.

arrogancia, *n.f.* arrogance, haughtiness, loftiness, valour, courage; stately carriage.

arrogante, *a.* arrogant, overbearing; spirited, high-minded; (*law*) adopting; haughty, proud.

arrogantemente, *adv.* arrogantly, haughtily.

arrogar, *v.t.* (*pret.* **arrogué;** *pres. subj.* **arrogue**) to arrogate; (*law*) to adopt a child. — *v.r.* to appropriate to oneself; to claim unjustly, usurp.

arrojadamente, *adv.* audaciously, impetuously, rashly.

arrojadizo, -za, *a.* easily cast, thrown, or darted; *arma arrojadiza,* dart, arrow.

arrojado, -da, *a.* thrown, flung; rash, inconsiderate; *arrojado de carácter,* bold, intrepid, fearless, resolute. — *n.m.pl.* (*slang*) trousers. — *p.p.* [ARROJAR].

arrojador, -ra, *a.* a throwing, flinging.

arrojar, *v.t.* to dart, fling, hurl, jerk, launch, dash; (*agric.*) to shoot, sprout; to emit (fragrance, light); to shed (blood); (*prov.*) to make red-hot; to turn away, dismiss, drive out; (*naut.*) to drive or cast on rocks; (*com.*) to show balance; *arrojar de sí,* to dismiss angrily; *arrojar el guante,* to challenge. — *v.r.* to launch, throw oneself forward impetuously; to venture or launch out upon an enterprise; *arrojarse de, por la ventana,* to throw oneself out of the window.

arroje, *n.m.* man who drops as counterweight to raise the curtain in a theatre.

arrojo, *n.m.* boldness, intrepidity, fearlessness.

arrollable, *a.* that can be rolled.

arrollado, -da, *a.* rolled. — *n.m.* (*Chi.*) a dish of pork meat. — *p.p.* [ARROLLAR].

arrollador, -ra, *a.* rolling, winding; violent, sweeping. — *n.m.* roller.

arrollamiento, *n.m.* (*elec.*) winding, rolling.

arrollar, *v.t.* to roll up, wind; to roll or sweep away; (*fig.*) to trample down; to insult; to roll round, wrap, twist; (*fig.*) to confound an opponent; (*fig.*) to subjugate; to dominate; *arrollar a un niño,* to dandle, rock (a child).

arromadizar, *v.t.* to cause, give a cold. — *v.r.* to catch cold.

arromanzar, *v.t.* to translate into the vernacular.

arromar, *v.t.* to blunt, dull. — *v.r.* to become blunt, dull.

arronzar, *v.t.* (*pret.* **arroncé;** *pres. subj.* **arronce**) (*naut.*) to raise with levers. — *v.i.* (*naut.*) to incline too much to leeward.

arropado, -da, *a.* mixed with *arrope* (must). — *p.p.* [ARROPAR].

arropamiento, *n.m.* act of clothing or dressing; mixing with boiled must.

arropar, *v.t.* to dress, cover, wrap, clothe; *arropar el vino,* to mix wine with boiled must; *arropar las viñas,* to cover the roots of the vines. — *v.r.* to wrap, clothe oneself; *arrópese con ello,* you can keep it (used contemptuously).

arrope, *n.m.* must boiled to a syrup; (*prov.*) conserve made of boiled honey; (*chem.*) concentrated syrup.

arropea, *n.f.* iron, fetter, shackle.

arropera, *n.f.* vessel for holding boiled must.

arropia, *n.f.* (*prov.*) toffee, taffy.

arropiero, -ra, *n.m.f.* (*prov.*) maker or seller of *arropia.*

arrostrar, *v.i.* to set about dauntlessly. — *v.t.* to defy, face; to encounter; *arrostrar los peligros* (*la muerte*), to brave dangers (death). — *v.r.* to fight face to face.

arroyada, *n.f.;* **arroyadero,** *n.m.* valley through which a rivulet runs; channel of a rivulet; gully; flood; freshet.

arroyar, *v.t.* to inundate. — *v.r.* to form, or run in gullies; (*agric.*) to become smutted (of grain).

arroyo, *n.m.* rivulet, small river, stream, brook; watercourse of a street, gutter; (*fig.*) street; *plantar,* or *poner en el arroyo,* to put out in the street; *arroyos de sangre,* streams of blood.

arroyuela, *n.f.* (*bot.*) salicaceous shrub; [SALICARIA].

arroyuelo, *n.m.* rill, small brook, rivulet.

arroz, *n.m.* rice; *más pesado que el arroz,* more tiresome than rice.

arrozal, *n.m.* rice-field.

arrozar, *v.t.* (*pret.* **arrocé;** *pres. subj.* **arroce**) to ice a liquid.

arruar, *v.i.* to grunt (said of hunted wild boar).

arrufadura, *n.f.* (*naut.*) sheer of a ship.

arrufaldado, -da, *a.* proud; with raised brim (of a hat). — *p.p.* [ARRUFALDARSE].

arrufaldarse, *v.r.* (*prov.*) to become proud, haughty.

arrufamiento, *n.m.* ire, irritation.

arrufar, *v.t.* (*naut.*) to incurvate; to form the sheer of a ship. — *v.r.* (*obs.*) to snarl.

arrufianado, -da, *a.* ruffianly, roguish, knavish, scoundrelly, impudent.

arrufo, *n.m.* (*naut.*) [ARRUFADURA].

arruga, *n.f.* wrinkle; corrugation; fold, crease.

arrugación, *n.f.*; **arrugamiento,** *n.m.* corrugation, wrinkling.

arrugar, *v.t.* (*pret.* **arrugué;** *pres. subj.* **arrugue**) to wrinkle, crumple, cockle; to rumple, plait, gather, fold, crease; *arrugar el entrecejo, la frente,* to knit the brow, frown; *no se le arruga el ombligo,* he never retreats before a peril. — *v.r.* to become wrinkled; (*slang*) to flee, escape.

arrugia, *n.f.* (*min.*) gold-mine.

arrugón, *n.m.* decoration of carved work.

arruinador, -ra, *n.m.f.* ruiner, demolisher. — *a.* ruinous, destructive.

arruinamiento, *n.m.* ruin, destruction, ravage, overthrow.

arruinar, *v.t.* to throw down, demolish; to ruin; to destroy. — *v.r.* to become ruined, demolished, destroyed.

arrullador, -ra, *n.m.f.* one who lulls babies to rest; flatterer, cajoler. — *a.* lulling, soothing.

arrullar, *v.t.* to bill; to lull babies; (*fig.*) to bill and coo; to court.

arrullo, *n.m.* cooing and billing of doves; lullaby.

arruma, *n.f.* (*naut.*) cargo space in the hold.

arrumaco, *n.m.* caress; (*coll.*) eccentric dress or ornament.

arrumaje, *n.m.* (*naut.*) stowage.

arrumar, *v.t.* (*naut.*) to stow. — *v.r.* (*naut.*) to become overcast (horizon).

arrumazón, *n.m.* (*naut.*) stowage; overcast horizon.

arrumbación, *n.f.* ranging wine-casks in cellars.

arrumbadas, *n.f.pl.* (*naut.*) bulwarks at bow of rowing-galley.

arrumbador, -ra, *n.m.f.* heaper, piler. — *n.m.* (*naut.*) steersman; workman in Jerez wine-cellars. — *a.* heaping, piling.

arrumbamiento, *n.m.* (*naut.*) direction, relative bearing.

arrumbar, *v.t.* to put anything away in a lumber-room; to refute in conversation; to debate; to range wine-casks; to remove one from a trust; (*naut.*) to determine the direction. — *v.i.* (*naut.*) to steer the proper course. — *v.r.* (*naut.*) to take bearings.

arrunflarse, *v.r.* to have a flush of cards of the same suit.

arrurruz, *n.m.* arrowroot.

arsáfragra, *n.f.* (*bot.*) water-parsnip.

arsenal, *n.m.* arsenal; dockyard, shipyard, navy-yard.

arseniato, *n.m.* (*chem.*) arsenate.

arsenical, *a.* arsenical.

arsénico, *n.m.* arsenic.

arsenioso, -sa, *a.* arsenious.

arsenito, *n.m.* arsenite.

arsolla, *n.f.* (*bot.*) lesser burdock, milk-thistle.

arsonvalización, *n.f.* (*med.*) high-frequency treatment.

arta, *n.f.* (*bot.*) plantain, ribwort.

artalejo; artalete, *n.m.* sort of tart or pie.

artanica; artanita, *n.f.* cyclamen, sowbread.

arte, *n.m.f.* art; skill, craft, cunning; intrigue, machination, plot, artifice; trade, profession; machine; fishing-net; *usar de arte,* to be astute, artful, cunning; *no tener arte ni parte en alguna cosa,* to have neither art nor part in a thing; to have nothing to do with the business; *buen arte,* gracefulness of manners or gait; *mal arte,* awkwardness of manners or gait. — *f.pl.* arts; *curso de artes,* course of logic, physics, and metaphysics; *de mal arte,* badly; *por arte del diablo,* by unnatural means; *quien tiene arte, va por toda parte,* no craftsman need starve; *artes liberales,* liberal arts; *las bellas artes,* the fine arts.

artefacto, *n.m.* manufacture, anything artificially made; handiwork; appliance, device.

artejo, *n.m.* finger-joint, knuckle.

artemisa; artemisia, *n.f.* (*bot.*) artemisia, mugwort.

artera, *n.f.* (*prov.*) iron instrument for marking bread before it is baked.

arteramente, *adv.* artfully, astutely, fraudulently.

arteria, *n.f.* (*anat.*) artery; (*fig.*) main road; (*railw.*) trunk line; (*elec.*) feeder.

artería, *n.f.* artifice, stratagem, cunning; sagacity.

arterial, *a.* arterial.

arteriografía, *n.f.* arteriography.

arteriola, *n.f.* small artery.

arteriología, *n.f.* (*anat.*) arteriology.

arteriosclerosis, *n.f.* (*med.*) arteriosclerosis.

arterioso, -sa, *a.* arterial; abounding in arteries.

arteriotomía, *n.f.* (*anat.*) arteriotomy.

artero, -ra, *a.* dexterous, cunning, artful.

artesa, *n.f.* trough in which dough is worked; canoe; *artesa de panaderos,* kneading-trough.

artesano, *n.m.* artisan, artist, manufacturer, mechanic.

artesiano, -na, *a.* Artesian.

artesilla, *n.f.* a small trough; game or exercise on horseback; trough for a *noria* or draw-well.

artesón, *n.m.* wash-tub; (*arch.*) carved panel on ceilings and vaults; carved and panelled ceiling.

artesonado, -da, *a.* (*arch.*) panelled. — *n.m.* carved, panelled ceiling.

artesonar, *v.t.* to make troughs; (*arch.*) to panel ceilings or vaults.

artesuela, *n.f.* small kneading-trough.

artete, *n.m.* drag-net.

artético, -ca, *a.* afflicted with arthritis; arthritic.

ártico, -ca, *a.* arctic, northern; *polo ártico,* the arctic (or north) pole.

articulación, *n.f.* articulation; joint; clear pronunciation; (*bot.*) geniculation.

articuladamente, *adv.* distinctly, articulately.

articulado, -da, *a.* articulate. — *n.m.* (*law*) entirety of articles forming law, treaty, etc.; series of clauses in legal papers. — *n.m.pl.* (*zool.*) Articulata. — *p.p.* [ARTICULAR].

articulador, -ra, *a.* articulating, pronouncing.

articular, *v.t.* to articulate, pronounce distinctly; to unite, join; (*law*) to propound the articles of evidence, or interrogatories. — *a.* articular.

articulista, *n.m.f.* writer of articles, journalist.

artículo, *n.m.* joint, knuckle, article; section; clause; (*law*) incidental question; plea; question or query of an interrogatory; (*gram.*) article, part of speech; cause, condition; (*anat.*) joint of movable bones; *artículo de comercio,* commodity, merchandise; *artículo de fondo,* newspaper leader, editorial; *artículo de la muerte,* the last moment prior to death; *hacer el artículo,* to promulgate some cause in which one is interested.

artifara; artife, *n.m.* (*slang*) bread.

artifero, *n.m.* (*slang*) baker.

artifice, *n.m.f.* artificer, artist; inventor, contriver; (*fig.*) author.

artificial, *a.* artificial, made by artifice or art; *fuegos artificiales,* fireworks.

artificialmente, *adv.* artificially.

artificiero, *n.m.* (*artill.*) artificer.

artificio, *n.m.* workmanship, craft; trick, cunning, artifice; guilefulness, finesse; (*mech.*) contrivance, device, appliance.

artificiosamente, *adv.* artificially; artfully, craftily.

artificioso, -sa, *a.* skilful, ingenious; artful, crafty.

artiga, *n.f.* breaking up new land; land newly broken up.

artigar, *v.t.* to break, burn, and level land before cultivation.

artilugio, *n.m.* worthless mechanical contrivance.

artillado, -da, *p.p.* [ARTILLAR]. — *n.m.* artillery.

artillar, *v.t.* to furnish with artillery. — *v.r.* (*slang*) to arm, prepare oneself.

artillería, *n.f.* gunnery; artillery, ordnance; *parque de artillería,* park of artillery; *artillería de sitio,* siege guns; *artillería gruesa,* heavy artillery; *artillería de avancarga,* muzzle-loading artillery; *artillería de retrocarga,* breech-loading artillery; *artillería de montaña,* light mountain artillery; *artillería de campaña,* field artillery.

artillero, *n.m.* gunner; artillery-man.

artimaña, *n.f.* trap, snare, gin; stratagem, artifice.

artimón, *n.m.* (*naut.*) mizen-sail.

artina, *n.f.* fruit of the box-tree.

artista, *n.m.f.* artist; craftsman. — *a.* said of one following a *curso de artes.*

artísticamente, *adv.* artistically.

artístico, -ca, *a.* artistic.

artizar, *v.t.* to perform ingeniously.

arto; artos, *n.m.* (*bot.*) box-tree.

artocárpeo, -pea, *a.* (*bot.*) artocarpous.

artolas, *n.f.pl.* back-to-back seats for two persons on the same horse.

artrítico, -ca, *a.* arthritic.

artritis, *n.m.* (*med.*) arthritis.

artritismo, *n.m.* (*med.*) arthritism.

artrodia, *n.f.* (*anat.*) arthrodia.

artrografía, *n.f.* description of the joints.

artrón, *n.m.* (*anat.*) arthrosis, articulation.

artrópodo, -da, *a.* (*zool.*) arthropodal, arthropodous. — *n.m.f.* (*zool.*) arthropod. — *n.m.pl.* (*zool.*) Arthropoda.

artuña, *n.f.* ewe whose lamb has perished.

Arturo, *n.m.* (*astron.*) Arcturus; Arthur.

arugas, *n.f.* (*bot.*) feverfew.

árula, *n.f.* (*archæol.*) small altar.

arundense, *n.m.f., a.* native of Arunda (modern Ronda).

arundíneo, -nea, *a.* (*bot.*) arundinaceous, arundineous, reedy.

aruñar, *v.t.* (*coll.*) to scratch.

aruñazo, *n.m.* (*coll.*) slight scratch, prick.

aruño, *n.m.* (*coll.*) scratch, nipping.

arúspice, *n.m.* haruspex; augurer, soothsayer.

aruspicina, *n.f.* haruspicy.

arveja, *n.f.* (*bot.*) honey mesquit; carob-tree; *arveja silvestre,* vetch, tare; (*Chi.*) green pea.

arvejal; arvejar, *n.m.* field sown with *arveja.*

arvejana; arvejera, *n.f.* (*bot.*) honey mesquit; carob-tree.

arvejo, *n.m.* (*bot.*) pea.

arvejón, *n.m.* (*bot., prov.*) chickling-vetch, blue vetch.

arvejona, *n.f.; *arvejote,** *n.m.* (*prov.*) a kind of vetch or tare.

arvela, *n.f.* (*orn.*) martin-fisher.

arvense, *a.* growing in sown fields.

arza, *n.f.* (*naut.*) hoisting-tackle; (*naut.*) sling, strap for blocks.

arzobispado, *n.m.* archbishopric.

arzobispal, *a.* archiepiscopal.

arzobispo, *n.m.* archbishop.

arzolla, *n.f.* (*bot.*) lesser burdock, milk-thistle.

arzón, *n.m.* fore or hind bow of a saddle; saddle-tree.

asa, *n.f.* handle, ear of a vase; juice of certain plants; (*fig.*) occasion, pretext; (*prov.*) holly-tree; (*coll.*) ear; *asa dulce,* gum benzoin, gum benjamin; *asa fétida,* asafœtida, a gum resin; *amigo del asa,* or *ser del asa,* to be a bosom friend; to be on intimate terms; *en asas,* akimbo.

así, *adv. así que así* , so-so, middling.

asacar, *v.t.* to withdraw; to invent; to pretend; to impute.

asación, *n.f.* (*pharm.*) decoction.

asadero, *-ra, a.* fit for roasting.

asado, -da, *a.* roasted, dressed. — *n.m.* roast. — *p.p.* [ASAR].

asador, *n.m.* spit; jack; *asador de bomba,* (*naut.*) pump-hook; *parece que come asadores,* he looks as stiff as if he had swallowed a poker.

asadura, *n.f.* entrails of an animal, chitterlings; liver, lights; *echar las asaduras,* to work very hard; *asadura de puerco,* haslet, pig's fry; cattle-toll.

asaeteador, -ra, *a.* (*fig.*) harassing, annoying. — *n.m.* archer, bowman. — *n.f.* archeress.

asaetear, *v.t.* to attack, wound, kill with arrows; (*fig.*) to annoy, harass repeatedly.

asaetinado, -da, *a.* resembling satin.

asainetado, -da, *a.* (*theat.*) farcical.

asalariado, -da, *p.p.* [ASALARIAR] salaried. — *n.m.* wage-earner, employee.

asalariar, *v.t.* to give a fixed salary or pay.

asalmonado, -da, *a.* salmon-like.

asaltador, -ra, *n.m.f.* assailant, assaulter. — *n.m.* highwayman. — *a.* assaulting, assailing.

asaltar, *v.t.* to assault, storm; to surprise, fall upon; (*fig.*) to occur suddenly.

asalto, *n.m.* assault; *asalto de armas,* fencing bout; *dar asalto,* to assault; *por asalto,* by storm.

asamblea, *n.f.* assembly, meeting, congress; (*mil.*) assembly (bugle-call).

asambleísta, *n.m.f.* member of an assembly.

asar, *v.t.* to roast; *asar a la lumbre,* to roast at the open fire; *asar en la parrilla,* to grill. — *v.r.* to be excessively hot; *asarse de calor, asarse vivo,* to feel the heat intensely; *aun no asamos y ya pringamos,* said of someone who wishes to be perfect in something without due practice or instruction.

asarabácara; asáraca, *n.f.* (*bot.*) wild ginger or nard.

asarcia, *n.f.* emaciation.

asarero, *n.m.* (*bot.*) blackthorn, sloe-tree.

asargado, -da, *a.* serge-like.

asarina, *n.f.* (*bot.*) bastard asarum.

ásaro, *n.m.* (*bot.*) asarum.

asativo, -va, *a.* (*pharm.*) dressed or boiled in its own juice.

asaz, *adv.* (*poet.*) enough, abundantly.

asbestino, -na, *a.* belonging to asbestos.

asbesto, *n.m.* asbestos.

ascalonia, *n.f.* (*bot.*) seed onion; shallot.

áscar, *n.m.* army (in Morocco).

áscari, *n.m.* Moroccan infantryman.

ascárides, *n.f.pl.* ascarides, small threadlike worms infesting the intestines.

ascendencia, *n.f.* ancestry, origin.

ascendente, *a.* ascendant; ascending.

ascender, *v.i.* (*pres. indic.* **asciendo;** *pres. subj.* **ascienda**) to ascend, mount, climb; (*fig.*) to be promoted; *ascender a,* (*com.*) to amount to. — *v.t.* to grant promotion to; *ascender a otro empleo,* to be promoted to another post; *ascender en la carrera,* to rise in one's career; *ascender por los aires,* to rise in the air.

ascendiente, *n.m.f.* ancestor, forefather. — *n.m.* ascendency, influence, power. — *a.* ascendant, ascending.

ascensión, *n.f.* ascension; exaltation; feast of the Ascension of Our Lord; exaltation to the papal throne; rising point of the equator; *ascensión recta,* (*astron.*) right ascension.

ascensional, *a.* (*astron.*) ascensional.

ascensionista, *n.m.f.* balloonist; climber. — *a.* climbing, ascending.

ascenso, *n.m.* rise, promotion.

ascensor, *n.m.* lift; *ascensor de municiones,* ammunition hoist.

asceta, *n.m.* ascetic.

ascético, -ca, *a.* ascetic. — *n.f.* ascetics.

ascetismo, *n.m.* asceticism.

ascidia, *n.f.* (*bot.*) pitcher-like leaf; (*zool.*) Ascidium, ascidian. — *a.* ascidian.

ascidio, -dia, *a.* (*bot.*) pitcher-like.

asciendo; ascienda, *pres. ind.; pres. subj.* [ASCENDER].

asciro, *n.m.* (*bot.*) St. Peter's wort, St. Andrew's cross.

ascítico, -ca, *a.* (*med.*) dropsical.

ascitis, *n.f.* (*med.*) ascites, dropsy.

asclepiadea, *n.f.* (*bot.*) swallow-wort.

asclepiadeo, *n.m.* Asclepiad, a Greek and Latin verse.

asco, *n.m.* nausea, loathsomeness; (*coll.*) fear; *es un asco,* it is a mean, despicable thing; it is worthless; *hacer ascos,* to turn up one's nose; *estar hecho un asco,* to be very dirty.

ascosidad, *n.f.* loathsomeness.

ascoso, -sa, *a.* loathsome, repulsive.

ascua, *n.f.* red-hot coal; *ascua de oro,* anything that glitters. — *pl.* (as *interj.*) how it hurts! *estar en ascuas,* to be very uneasy; to be on thorns; *cada cual arrima el ascua a su sardina,*

everyone looks after himself first; *sacar el ascua con la mano del gato,* to make a cat's paw of someone.

aseadamente, *adv.* cleanly, elegantly, neatly.

aseado, -da, *a.* clean, elegant, neatly finished. — *p.p.* [ASEAR].

asear, *v.t.* to set off, adorn, embellish; to polish, clean. — *v.r.* to make oneself clean and tidy.

asechador, -ra, *n.m.f.* ensnarer, waylayer, deceiver. — *a.* ensnaring, deceiving.

asechamiento, *n.m.;* **asechanza,** *n.f.* waylaying; artifice, trick, stratagem.

asechar, *v.t.* to waylay, be on the watch for, lie in ambush for.

asedado, -da, *a.* silky. — *p.p.* [ASEDAR].

asedar, *v.t.* to work flax and hemp so as to make them feel like silk.

asediador, -ra, *n.m.f.* besieger. — *a.* besieging.

asediar, *v.t.* to besiege, blockade; (*fig.*) to importune.

asedio, *n.m.* siege, blockade.

aseglararse, *v.r.* to secularize oneself; to make oneself worldly.

asegundar, *v.t.* to repeat with little or no intermission of time.

asegurable, *a.* insurable.

aseguración, *n.f.* insurance contract.

asegurado, -da, *a.* secured, fixed; assured; guaranteed; decided. — *n.m.f.* insured (person). — *p.p.* [ASEGURAR].

asegurador, -ra, *n.m.f.* insurer, assurer, underwriter. — *a.* insuring, assuring.

aseguramiento, *n.m.* the act of securing; (*law*) security, safety; insurance, assurance.

asegurar, *v.t.* to secure, fasten, fix; to affirm, assure; to preserve; to imprison; (*com.*) to guarantee; to insure. — *v.r.* to feel secure; to make sure; to become insured; *asegurar contra el granizo,* to protect against hail; *asegurar de incendios,* to preserve against fires; *asegurarse de la verdad,* to make sure of the truth.

aseidad, *n.f.* self-existence (attribute of the Deity).

aselarse, *v.r.* (*prov.*) to roost.

asemejar, *v.t.* to make similar. — *v.i.* to favour. — *v.r.* to resemble.

asendereado, -da, *a.* beaten, frequented (applied to roads); worn-out by anxiety; persecuted. — *p.p.* [ASENDEREAR].

asenderear, *v.t.* to persecute, pursue; to open a path.

asengladura, *n.f.* (*naut.*) day's run.

asenso, *n.m.* assent, consent, acquiescence, credence, credit; *no dar asenso,* not to credit (or believe); *no dar su asenso,* not to agree to.

asentada, *n.f.* session, sitting; *de una asentada,* all at once, at one heat, without leaving, without rising at one sitting.

asentaderas, *n.f.pl.* (*coll.*) buttocks, seat.

asentadillas, (a), *adv.* sitting on horseback on side-saddle, woman-fashion.

asentado, -da, *a.* seated; planted, situated; clear, serene, calm; stable, permanent. — *p.p.* [ASENTAR].

asentador, *n.m.* bricklayer; plate-layer; setter-up; razor-strop; blacksmith's turning chisel.

asentamiento, *n.m.* (*law*) possession of goods given by a judge to the plaintiff on non-appearance of the defendant; establishment, settlement; prudence, sanity.

asentar, *v.t.* (*pres. indic.* **asiento**; *pres. subj.* **asiente**) to seat; to stop at; to suppose, affirm, assure; to adjust, contract; to note, register, assess; to place in employment; to fix; to deal (blows); to plane, smooth; to enter (accounts); to found, establish; to hone; to estimate; (*law*) to put a plaintiff in possession of goods claimed on non-appearance of the defendant; *asentar casa*, to set up house for oneself; *asentar plaza*, to enlist in the army. — *v.i.* to fit (as clothes); to sit down; to settle, establish a residence. — *v.r.* to subside, clarify (as of liquors); to perch or settle after flying; (*arch.*) to sink, settle; to remain undigested.

asentimiento, *n.m.* assent, consent.
asentir, *v.i.* (*pres. indic.* **asiento**; *pres. subj.* **asienta**) to agree; to acquiesce; to concede.
asentista, *n.m.* contractor.
aseñorado, -da, *a.* gentlemanly, ladylike.
aseo, *n.m.* cleanliness, neatness.
asépalo, -la, *a.* (*bot.*) without sepals.
asepsia, *n.f.* (*med.*) asepsia.
aséptico, -ca, *a.* (*med.*) aseptic.
asequi, *n.m.* (*prov.*) cattle duty.
asequible, *a.* attainable, obtainable.
aserción, *n.f.* assertion, affirmation.
aserenar, *v.t.* to calm, pacify; to settle. — *v.r.* to become serene; to clear up.
aserradero, *n.m.* saw-pit, sawmill, saw-horse.
aserradizo, -za, *a.* that can be sawn or sawn easily.
aserrado, -da, *a.* serrate, serrated, dented; saw-like. — *p.p.* [ASERRAR].
aserrador, -ra, *n.m.f.* sawyer.
aserradura, *n.f.* sawing; cut in sawing. — *pl.* sawdust.
aserrar, *v.t.* (*pres. indic.* **asierro**; *pres. subj.* **asierre**) to saw, cut with the saw; to scrape.
aserrín, *n.m.* sawdust.
aserruchar, *v.t.* (*Col., Chi., Hond., Per.*) to saw, cut with the handsaw.
asertivamente, *adv.* assertively, affirmatively.
asertivo, -va, *a.* assertive.
aserto, *n.m.* assertion, affirmation.
asertorio, -ria, *a.* affirmatory.
asesar, *v.i.* to become prudent; to acquire discretion.
asesinar, *v.t.* to assassinate; to afflict greatly; (*fig.*) to betray.
asesinato, *n.m.* assassination, murder; treachery.
asesino, *n.m.f.* assassin, murderer, murderess; impostor, cheat.
asesor, -ra, *n.m.f.* counsellor, adviser, conciliator; assessor. — *a.* advising; assessing.
asesorar, *v.t.* to advise, counsel. — *v.r.* to take advice; *asesorarse con*, or *de letrados*, to consult a lawyer; to take the assistance of counsel.
asesoría, *n.f.* office or place of an assessor; payment and fees of an assessor.
asestadero, *n.m.* (*prov.*) resting-place for cattle.
asestador, *n.m.* gunner.
asestadura, *n.f.* aim, pointing fire-arms, taking aim.
asestar, *v.t.* to aim, point, level; to deal (blow); to fire a cannon, gun or pistol; (*fig.*) to try to injure; (*prov.*) to take a nap.
aseveración, *n.f.* asseveration, affirmation.
aseveradamente, *adv.* affirmatively.

aseverar, *v.t.* to asseverate, affirm.
aseverativo, -va, *a.* affirming, asseverating.
asfaltado, -da, *a.* asphalted. — *n.m.* asphalt pavement. — *p.p.* [ASFALTAR].
asfaltar, *v.t.* to cover with asphalt.
asfáltico, -ca, *a.* asphaltic, bituminous.
asfalto, *n.m.* asphalt; kind of bitumen.
asfíctico, -ca; **asfíxico, -ca**, *a.* asphyxial.
asfixia, *n.f.* (*med.*) asphyxia.
asfixiado, -da, *a.* asphyxiated. — *p.p.* [ASFIXIAR].
asfixiador, -ra, *a.* asphyxiating.
asfixiante, *a.* asphyxiating.
asfixiar, *v.t.* (*med.*) to asphyxiate, suffocate. — *v.r.* to asphyxiate oneself.
asfódelo, *n.m.* (*bot.*) asphodel.
asgo; **asga**, *pres. indic.*, *pres. subj.* [ASIR].
así, *adv.* so, thus, in this way, like this; also, therefore, so that, equally; (followed by a verb in the subjunctive mood) would that; *así como*, in the same proportion or manner; as soon as; after; *así bien*, as well, equally; *así que*, as soon as; so that, therefore; *así así*, so-so; middling; *así que llegó*, as soon as he arrived; *así que asá*, or *asado*, anyway; be it as it will; *así me estoy*, it's all the same to me; *así pues*, therefore; thus then; so, in this way; *así como*, or *que así*, anyway; *así sea*, so be it; *así estaba escrito*, it had to be so; it could not be otherwise; *así se me figuraba*, I thought as much; *así y todo*, in spite of it; notwithstanding.
asiático, -ca, *n.m.f.*, *a.* Asiatic. — *a.* (*fig.*) luxurious.
asidera, (*Arg.*) *n.f.* a strap with rings for fastening the lasso.
asidero, *n.m.* handle, holder; (*fig.*) occasion, pretext.
asido, -da, *p.p.* [ASIR] caught, grasped, held.
asiduamente, *adv.* frequently, assiduously; punctually.
asiduidad, *n.f.* assiduity.
asiduo, -dua, *a.* assiduous, laborious.
asiento, *n.m.* chair, stool, bench, seat; seat in tribunal or court of justice; bottom of a vessel; sediment; treaty; spot, site; settling; (*fig.*) solidity; stability, permanence, order; contract; (*fig.*) prudence, discretion, judgment; registry, list, roll; indigestion; bit (bridle); *hombre de asiento*, prudent man; *asiento de los esmaltes*, the edging of enamels; *asiento de puente levadizo*, the bed of a drawbridge; *asiento de plaza*, enlistment; *asiento del estómago*, indigestion; *estar de asiento*, to be established in a sure place; *tomar asiento*, to take a seat; *asiento de colmenas*, open apiary; *asiento de molino*, or *de tahona*, millstone; *asiento de negros*, asiento or contract for supplying slaves; *no calentar el asiento*, to stay a short time; *quedarse de asiento*, to remain in a place; *hacer*, or *tomar asiento*, to establish oneself. — *pl.* posteriors, seat; bindings; collar and cuff bands; variety of pearls flat on one side.
asiento; **asienta**, *pres. indic.*; *pres. subj.* [ASENTIR].
asiento; **asiente**, *pres. indic.*; *pres. subj.* [ASENTAR].
asierro; **asierre**, *pres. indic.*; *pres. subj.* [ASERRAR].
asignable, *a.* assignable.

asignación, *n.f.* assignation; grant, subsidy; salary; distribution, partition; destination.

asignado, *p.p.* [ASIGNAR] assigned. — *n.m.* assignat.

asignar, *v.t.* to assign, mark out; to ascribe, attribute.

asignatura, *n.f.* subject of study. — *pl.* curriculum, course of study.

asilar, *v.t.* to shelter; to place in an asylum.

asilo, *n.m.* asylum, sanctuary, place of shelter and refuge; harbourage; protection; (*entom.*) asilus, hornet-fly; *asilo de huérfanos*, orphan asylum; *asilo de locos*, asylum for the insane; *dar asilo*, to protect, shelter.

asilla, *n.f.* small handle; slight pretext; collarbone.

asimetría, *n.f.* asymmetry.

asimétrico, -ca, *a.* asymmetrical.

asimiento, *n.m.* grasp; (*fig.*) attachment, affection.

asimilable, *a.* assimilable.

asimilación, *n.f.* assimilation.

asimilar, *v.t.* to make similar; to compare; to grant (rights or honours); (*bot.*, *zool.*) to assimilate. — *v.i.* to resemble, be like. — *v.r.* to become assimilated; to resemble.

asimilativo, -va, *a.* assimilating, assimilative.

asimismo, *adv.* even so, exactly so, identically, precisely, likewise.

asimplado, -da, *a.* like a simpleton.

asincrónico, -ca, *a.* asynchronous.

asincronismo, *n.m.* asynchronism.

asindeton, *n.m.* (*rhet.*) suppression of conjunctions; asyndeton.

asinino, -na, *a.* asinine, ass-like.

asíntota, *n.f.* (*geom.*) asymptote.

asir, *v.t.* (*pres. indic.* **asgo;** *pres. subj.* **asga**) to grasp or seize with the hand; to hold; to come upon; to grip. — *v.i.* (*agric.*) to strike or take root; *asir de los cabellos*, to take time by the forelock. — *v.r.* to take hold of; to take advantage of; to dispute, contend with each other; *asirse de otras aldabas*, to avail oneself of different means; *asirse a las ramas*, to make frivolous excuses.

asiriano, -na; asirio, -ria, *n.m.f.*, *a.* Assyrian.

asiriología, *n.f.* Assyriology.

asiriológico, -ca, *a.* Assyriological.

asiriólogo, *n.m.* Assyriologist.

asistencia, *n.f.* actual presence; reward gained by personal attendance; attendance; assistance, favour, help, aid, comfort; board, meals; (*Mex.*) intimate drawing-room. — *pl.* allowance; alimony.

asistenta, *n.f.* handmaid; servant-maid.

asistente, *n.m.* assistant, helper, helpmate; assistant bishop at consecration of bishops; (*mil.*) orderly; (*obs.*) chief officer of justice in certain cities of Spain. — *a.* assisting, helping.

asistido, -da, *p.p.* [ASISTIR] assisted.

asistir, *v.i.* to be present; to live in a house or frequent it much; to follow suit (cards). — *v.t.* to accompany; to attend; to assist, help, serve; *asistir a los enfermos*, to minister to, to take care of the sick; *asistir de oyente*, to attend as a listener; *asistir en tal caso*, to help in such a case; *asistir a un moribundo*, to close the eyes of one who is dying; *asistir a uno la razón*, to be right.

asistolia, *n.f.* (*med.*) syndrome (connected with cardiac systole).

asma, *n.f.* (*med.*) asthma.

asmático, -ca, *a.* asthmatic.

asna, *n.f.* she-ass. — *pl.* (*carp.*) rafters of a house.

asnacho, asnallo, *n.m.* (*bot.*) rest-harrow, cammock.

asnada, *n.f.* (*coll.*) asininity, foolish action.

asnado, *n.m.* prop, side-wall timber in mines.

asnal, *a.* asinine; (*coll.*) stupid, obstinate; brutal.

asnalmente, *adv.* (*coll.*) mounted on an ass; foolishly, stupidly.

asnería, *n.f.* (*coll.*) stud of asses; (*coll.*) foolish action.

asnico, *n.m.* little ass; (*prov.*) fire-irons.

asnilla, *n.f.* stanchion or prop supporting a ruinous building.

asnillo, *n.f.* little ass; (*entom.*) field-cricket.

asnino, -na, *a.* asinine, like an ass.

asno, *n.m.* ass; (*fig.*) dull, stupid fellow; *cada asno, con su tamaño*, birds of a feather flock together; everyone must associate with his equals; *caer de su asno*, to admit an error; to open the eyes to reason; *asno de muchos, lobos le comen*, everybody's business is nobody's business; *un asno cargado de oro, sube ligero por una montaña*, an ass laden with gold goes lightly up a mountain; *el asno sufre la carga, mas no la sobrecarga*, the last straw breaks the camel's back; *la culpa del asno no se ha de echar a la albarda*, the ass's fault must not be ascribed to the packsaddle; *al asno muerto, la cebada al rabo*, an opportunity past is lost; to lock the stable door after the horse is stolen; *asno con oro, alcánzalo todo*, money surmounts all difficulties; *bien sabe el asno en cuya cara*, or *casa rebuzna*, too great familiarity engenders disrespect; *burláos con el asno, daros ha en la barba con el rabo*, it is unwise to joke with ignorant persons; *no ver tres sobre un asno*, to see very little.

asobarcar, *v.t.* (*pret.* **asobarqué;** *pres. subj.* **asobarque**) (*coll.*) to carry a weighty thing under the arm; to raise to the armpits (clothes).

asobiar, *v.t.* (*prov.*) to whistle.

asobinarse, *v.r.* to fall face downwards (horses).

asobío, *n.m.* (*prov.*) whistle.

asocairarse, *v.r.* (*naut.*) to shelter behind a cape or point; (*fig.*) to fail in one's promise.

asocarronado, -da, *a.* crafty, sly, cunning.

asociación, *n.f.* association; fellowship, co-partnership.

asociado, -da, *n.m.f.* associate, comrade; (*com.*) partner. — *a.* associate, associated. — *p.p.* [ASOCIAR].

asociar, *v.t.* to associate, conjoin. — *v.r.* to form a partnership; to consociate; *asociarse a*, to become a partner; *asociarse con*, to associate with; *estar asociado con otro*, (*com.*) to be in partnership with someone.

asolación; asoladura, *n.f.* desolation, devastation.

asolador, -ra, *a.* destroying, desolating.

asolamiento, *n.m.* depopulation, destruction, devastation, desolation.

asolanar, *v.t.* to parch, dry up. — *v.r.* to become destroyed by the easterly wind.

asolapar, *v.t.* to make lapels (tailoring); to overlap (tiles).

asolar, *v.t.* (*pres. indic.* **asuelo;** *pres. subj.*

asuele) to level with the ground, destroy, lay waste, pillage, devastate; to burn, parch. — *v.r.* to settle, clarify (of liquids); (*agric.*) to become parched, dried up.

asoldadar; asoldar, *v.t.* (*pres. ind.* **asueldo**; *pres. subj.* **asuelde**) to hire, employ. — *v.r.* to engage oneself as employee.

asolear, *v.t.* to sun, expose to the sun. — *v.r.* to sun oneself; to become sunburnt; (*vet.*) to become affected by the sun (horses).

asoleo, *n.m.* (*vet.*) suffocation.

asomada, *n.f.* appearance, apparition; point from which something is first seen.

asomar, *v.i.* to begin to appear, become visible; (*naut.*) to loom. — *v.t.* to show. — *v.r.* (*coll.*) to be flustered with wine; to peep; *asomarse a, por la ventana,* to look out of the window.

asombradizo, -za, *a.* fearful, timid.

asombrador, -ra, *n.m.f.* terrifier; shader. — *a.* wondrous; shading.

asombramiento, *n.m.* amazement, astonishment.

asombrar, *v.t.* to shade, darken; to frighten, terrify; to astonish, cause admiration. — *v.r.* to take fright; to be astounded; *asombrarse del éxito,* to be amazed at the success.

asombro, *n.m.* dread, fear, terror, consternation; amazement, astonishment.

asombrosamente, *adv.* amazingly, wonderfully.

asombroso, -sa, *a.* wonderful, astonishing, marvellous, admirable.

asomo, *n.m.* mark, token, sign; supposition, presumption; *ni por asomo,* by no means.

asonada, *n.f.* tumultuous crowd of people, mutiny, riot.

asonancia, *n.f.* assonance, consonance; harmony.

asonantado, -da, *a.* assonant.

asonantar, *v.t.* (*poet.*) to mix assonant with consonant verses. — *v.i.* to be assonant.

asonante, *n.m.f., a.* assonant.

asonar, *v.i.* (*pres. indic.* **asueno**; *pres. subj.* **asuene**) to be assonant; to accord.

asordar, *v.t.* to deafen; to stun.

asosegar, *v.t.* to appease. — *v.r.* to grow calm.

asotanado, -da, *a.* cellar-like; vaulted. — *p.p.* [ASOTANAR].

asotanar, *v.t.* to vault; to make cellars.

aspa, *n.f.* cross; beams placed in form of a cross; reel, winder; sails of a windmill; *aspa de San Andrés,* St. Andrew's cross.

aspadera, *n.f.* (*mech.*) reel.

aspado, -da, *a.* with the arms extended like a cross; (*coll.*) with the arms confined. — *p.p.* [ASPAR].

aspador, -ra, *n.m.f.* reeler. — *n.m.* reel. — *a.* winding, reeling.

aspálato, *n.m.* (*bot.*) rosewood.

aspalto, *n.m.* (*paint.*) dark-coloured paint.

aspar, *v.t.* to reel; (*coll.*) to vex, mortify; to crucify. — *v.r.* to show great grief or pain; to work eagerly, anxiously; *asparse a gritos,* to give loud or piercing cries; *que me aspen si eso es cierto,* I'll be hanged if it's true; *así lo aspen no hará eso,* he wouldn't do it if they were to flay him alive.

aspaventar, *v.i., v.r.* to be, or become extremely horrified; to exaggerate one's emotions.

aspaventero, -ra; aspaventoso, -sa, *n.m.f., a.* one showing exaggerated or affected emotion.

aspaviento, *n.m.* excessive or affected demonstration of fear, admiration, or emotion.

aspearse, *v.r.* to become sore through much walking (feet, hoofs).

aspecto, *n.m.* sight, appearance, look, aspect, countenance; (*arch.*) outlook; (*astron.*) aspect, relative positions of stars and planets; *a primer aspecto,* at first sight.

ásperamente, *adv.* rudely, gruffly, harshly.

ásperarteria, *n.f.* windpipe, trachea.

asperear, *v.i.* to be rough and acrid to the taste.

asperete; asperillo, *n.m.* sour taste of unripe fruit.

aspereza, *n.f.* asperity, acerbity, acrimony; roughness, ruggedness (of ground); austerity, sourness.

aspergear; aspergiar, *v.t.* to sprinkle.

asperges, *n.m.* (*eccles.*) asperges; aspergillum, sprinkler; *quedarse asperges,* to be disappointed in one's expectations.

asperidad, *n.f.* asperity; roughness; harshness; rough place.

asperiego, -ga, *a.* applied to a sour apple.

asperilla, *n.f.* (*bot.*) sweet-smelling plant with bluish flowers.

asperillo, *n.m.* [ASPERETE]. — *a.* tartish, sourish.

asperjar, *v.t.* to sprinkle; to spray.

áspero, -ra, *a.* rough, rugged, cragged, knotty; rough and uneven to the touch; (*fig.*) harsh to the ear; (*fig.*) sour, sharp, acid; (*fig.*) gruff, hard, severe; *áspero al,* or *para el gusto,* acid to the taste; *áspero con los inferiores,* severe with dependents; *áspero en las palabras,* harsh, gruff in speech.

asperón, *n.m.* grindstone; flagstone.

aspérrimo, -ma, *a. sup.* [ÁSPERO].

aspersión, *n.f.* aspersion, sprinkling, spraying.

aspersorio, *n.m.* water-sprinkler; (*eccles.*) aspersorium.

áspid; áspide, *n.m.* (*zool.*) aspic, asp; *lengua de áspid,* venomous tongue; small ancient gun.

aspidistra, *n.f.* (*bot.*) aspidistra.

aspilla, *n.f.* (*prov.*) dip-stick.

aspillera, *n.f.* (*mil.*) loophole, battlement, embrasure, crenel.

aspillerar, *v.t.* to construct battlements.

aspiración, *n.f.* aspiration; inspiration; (*mus.*) short pause.

aspiradamente, *adv.* with aspiration.

aspirado, -da, *a.* (*gram.*) aspirate; aspirated. — *p.p.* [ASPIRAR].

aspirante, *n.m.f.* aspirant. — *n.m.* successful candidate for public office. — *a.* aspiring; aspirating.

aspirar, *v.t.* to inspire the air, draw breath; to inspire (gas, etc.); (*gram.*) to aspirate; (*fig.*) to aspire, covet, long for; *aspirar a mayor fortuna,* to aspire to greater fortune; *aspirar a la mano de una mujer,* to desire to marry a woman.

aspirina, *n.f.* (*chem.*) aspirin.

aspro, *n.m.* asper, a Turkish coin.

asquear, *v.t., v.i.* to consider with disgust; to feel nausea.

asquerosamente, *adv.* nastily, nauseously, foully.

asquerosidad, *n.f.* nastiness, filthiness, foulness.

asqueroso, -sa, *a.* nasty, filthy, nauseous, loathsome, disgusting; *asqueroso a la vista,* objectionable to the sight; *asqueroso de ver,* loathsome to see; *asqueroso en su aspecto,* of filthy aspect.

asta, *n.f.* lance; pikestaff; part of the deer's head which bears the antlers; horn; handle of a pencil or brush; (*carp.*) tenon; shaft, spindle; (*naut.*) anchor-shank; pole, flagstaff; *asta de tope,* flagstaff; *arriar bandera a media asta,* to hoist a flag half-mast high. — *pl.* horns of animals; *darse de las astas,* to carp at each other; *dejar en las astas del toro,* to desert someone in difficulties.

astaco, *n.m.* river lobster; crawfish, crayfish.

astado; astero, *n.m.* Roman pikeman.

astático, -ca, *a.* astatic.

asteísmo, *n.m.* (*rhet.*) delicate irony.

astenia, *n.f.* (*med.*) asthenia, debility.

asténico, -ca, *a.* (*med.*) asthenic.

asteria, *n.f.* (*min.*) star-stone, cat's-eye; (*zool.*) asteria, starfish.

asterisco, *n.m.* asterisk.

asterismo, *n.m.* (*astron., min.*) asterism.

asteroide, *n.m., a.* asteroid.

astigmático, -ca, *a.* astigmatic.

astigmatismo, *n.m.* (*med.*) astigmatism.

astil, *n.m.* handle of an axe, hatchet, etc.; shaft of an arrow; beam of a balance; steelyard; quill.

astilla, *n.f.* chip, splinter; (*slang*) cheating trick (cards); *de tal palo, tal astilla,* a chip of the old block; like father, like son; *sacar astilla,* to benefit out of something.

astillar, *v.t.* to chip, break into splinters.

astillazo, *n.m.* crack, noise made by a splinter when torn from the block; blow from flying chip or splinter; damage, injury.

astillejos; astilejos, *n.m.pl.* (*astron.*) Castor and Pollux.

astillero, *n.m.* rack for lances, spears, pikes, etc.; shipwright's yard, dockyard; (*Mex.*) clearing in the forest; *en astillero,* in an honourable post.

astillón, *n.m.* large splinter or chip of stone.

astilloso, -sa, *a.* chippy, easily splintered.

astracán, *n.m.* astrakhan (cloth or fur).

astrágalo, *n.m.* (*arch.*) astragal; (*bot.*) milk-vetch; (*artill.*) mouldings on a cannon; (*anat.*) astragalus; round moulding.

astral, *a.* astral. — *n.m.* (*prov.*) small hatchet or axe.

astreñir, *v.t.* (*pres. indic.* **astriño;** *pres. subj.* **astriña**) to astringe, contract, compress.

astricción, *n.f.* astriction; (*med.*) costiveness.

astrictivo, -va, *a.* astrictive, astringent, styptic.

astricto, -ta, *a.* contracted, compressed; bound, obliged, constrained. — *p.p. irreg.* [ASTRINGIR].

astrífero, -ra, *a.* (*poet.*) starry.

astringencia, *n.f.* astringency, astriction; (*med.*) costiveness.

astringente, *n.m.f., a.* (*med.*) astringent.

astringir, *v.t.* (*pres. indic.* **astrinjo;** *pres. subj.* **astrinja**) (*med.*) to astringe, contract, compress; (*fig.*) to oblige, bind, constrain.

astriño; astriña, *pres. indic.; pres. subj.* [ASTREÑIR].

astro, *n.m.* heavenly body; (*fig.*) star, illustrious person.

astrografía, *n.f.* astrography.

astroite, *n.m.* (*min.*) astroite.

astrolabio, *n.m.* astrolabe.

astrólatra, *n.m.f.* astrolater.

astrolatría, *n.f.* astrolatry.

astrología, *n.f.* astrology.

astrológico, -ca, *a.* astrological, astrologic.

astrólogo, -ga, *n.m.f.* astrologer. — *a.* astrologic.

astronomía, *n.f.* astronomy.

astronómicamente, *adv.* astronomically.

astronómico, -ca, *a.* astronomical.

astrónomo, *n.m.* astronomer.

astrosamente, *adv.* slovenly, coarsely, sluttishly.

astroso, -sa, *a.* wretched, miserable; (*fig.*) base, vile.

astucia, *n.f.* cunning, craft, finesse, astuteness.

astucioso, -sa, *a.* astute, shrewd.

astur, -ra, *n.m.f., a.* native of N.W. Spain; (*poet.*) Asturian; (*orn.*) goshawk.

asturiano, -na, *n.m.f., a.* Asturian; native of Asturias.

asturión, *n.m.* pony, small horse; (*ichth.*) sturgeon.

astutamente, *adv.* cunningly, craftily, astutely.

astuto, -ta, *a.* astute, cunning, sly.

asuardado, -da, *a.* stained, spotted (cloth).

asubiar, *v.i.* (*prov.*) to guard against the rain.

asuejón, *n.m.* great ass; very stupid person.

asueldo; asuelde, *pres. indic.; pres. subj.* [ASOLDAR].

asuelo; asuele, *pres. indic.; pres. subj.* [ASOLAR].

asueno; asuene, *pres. indic.; pres. subj.* [ASONAR].

asueto, *n.m.* short school holiday, vacation.

asumir, *v.t.* to assume, take upon oneself; (*law*) [AVOCAR].

asunción, *n.f.* assumption; postulate; ascent, elevation to a higher dignity; ascent of the Blessed Virgin Mary to Heaven; feast of the Assumption.

asunto, *n.m.* matter; (*art*) subject; affair, business. — *pl.* effects, business, stock; *desflorar un asunto,* to treat an affair superficially; *en asunto de,* in the matter of.

asuramiento, *n.m.* burning (of food whilst cooking).

asurar, *v.t.* to burn (food whilst cooking); (*agric.*) to parch, scorch; (*fig.*) to worry, annoy. — *v.r.* to be burnt in the pot or pan; to be parched with drought; (*fig.*) to be roasting or very hot; to be disquieted.

asurcano, -na, *a.* adjacent, neighbouring.

asurcar, *v.t.* (*pret.* **asurqué;** *pres. subj.* **asurque**) to furrow; to plough.

asuso, *adv.* upwards.

asustadizo, -za, *a.* easily frightened, excessively timid.

asustar, *v.t.* to frighten, terrify, scare. — *v.r.* (with *de, con, por*) to be frightened by.

atabaca, *n.f.* (*bot., prov.*) groundsel.

atabacado, -da, *a.* tobacco-coloured.

atabal, *n.m.* kettle-drum; timbrel; kettle-drummer.

atabalear, *v.i.* to imitate the noise of a kettle-drum; to clatter; to paw, stamp (horses).

atabalejo; atabalete, *n.m.* small kettle-drum.

atabalero, *n.m.* kettle-drummer.

atabanado, -da, *a.* (*vet.*) spotted white.

atabardillado, -da, *a.* applied to spotted fever, or to diseases of a similar nature.

atabe, *n.m.* small vent or spiracle left in water-pipes.

atabernado, -da, *a.* retailed in taverns (wine).

atabillar, *v.t.* to fold cloth with selvedges out.

atabladera, *n.f.* roller to level sown land.

atablar, *v.t.* to level sown land.

atacable, *a.* attackable.

atacadera, *n.f.* blast rammer.

atacado, -da, *a.* (*fig.*, *coll.*) irresolute, undecided; miserable, mean; attacked; (*slang*) stabbed to death. — *p.p.* [ATACAR].

atacador, -ra, *n.m.f.* aggressor. — *n.m.* ramrod or rammer for a gun; (*slang*) dagger. — *a.* attacking, aggressive.

atacadura, *n.f.*; **atacamiento,** *n.m.* fitting, tightening (of clothes).

atacamita, *n.f.* (*min.*) atacamite, native oxychloride of copper.

atacar, *v.t.* (*pret.* **ataqué**; *pres. subj.* **ataque**) to fit clothes tight to the body; to button; to ram or force the charge into fire-arms; to attack, assault, assail, provoke; to corner.

atacir, *n.m.* (*astrol.*) division of the celestial arch into twelve parts.

ataderas, *n.f.pl.* (*coll.*) garters.

atadero, *n.m.* cord, rope; place where a thing is tied; tying; halter-ring; (*fig.*) subjection, slavery; *no tener atadero*, to have neither head nor tail.

atadijo, *n.m.* (*coll.*) ill-shaped little bundle.

atado, -da, *a.* tied; bound; pusillanimous, good-for-nothing. — *n.m.* bundle, parcel, something tied together; *atado de cebollas*, string of onions. — *p.p.* [ATAR].

atador, -ra, *n.m.f.* (*agric.*) binder. — *a.* tying, binding.

atadura, *n.f.* fastening; cord; tying together; (*fig.*) union, connexion; knot, loop; lace.

atafagar, *v.t.* to stupefy, stun; (*fig.*) to tease, importunate to distraction.

atafetanado, -da, *a.* resembling taffeta.

atagallar, *v.t.* (*naut.*) to crowd sail.

ataguía, *n.f.* coffer-dam.

ataharre, *n.m.* broad crupper of a packsaddle.

atahona, *n.f.* bakery; mill.

atahonero, *n.m.* baker; miller.

atahorma, *n.f.* osprey.

atahulla, *n.f.* plot of arable land.

ataifor, *n.m.* deep dish; Moorish round table.

atairar, *v.t.* to cut mouldings in panels; to mould panels and frames.

ataire, *n.m.* moulding in the panels and frames of doors and windows.

atajadero, *n.m.* barrage; sluice-gate.

atajadizo, *n.m.* partition of boards dividing land; smaller portion of such divided ground.

atajador, -ra, *a.* intercipient. — *n.m.f.* interceptor; (*mil.*) scout; (*Chi.*) lad who tends the horses; *atajador de ganado*, sheepstealer.

atajamiento, *n.m.* interception.

atajante, *a.* intercepting.

atajar, *v.i.* to go the shortest way. — *v.t.* to overtake; to divide or separate by partitions, to cut (MSS., play, etc.); to interrupt; to intercept, stop, obstruct. — *v.r.* to be confounded with shame or fear.

atajea; atajía, *n.f.* [ATARJEA].

atajo, *n.m.* short-cut (road or path); division; cut (in MS., play, etc.); ward or guard made

by a weapon in fencing; obstruction; interception, stopping; *echar por el atajo*, to take the easiest way out of a difficulty; *dar atajo*, to cut short; *no hay atajo sin trabajo*, there is no convenience without some inconvenience; *salir al atajo*, to interrupt another's speech; *tomar por el atajo*, not to do things frankly or sincerely.

atajuelo, *n.m.* small short-cut.

atalajar, *v.t.* (*artill.*) to harness and hitch horses to a carriage.

atalaje, *n.m.* (*coll.*) tools, implements; (*artill.*) breast-harness; draft.

atalantar, *v.t.* to agree; to please; to bewilder, daze. — *v.r.* to become dazed, bewildered, stunned.

atalaya, *n.f.* watch-tower; high view-point. — *n.m.* guard placed in a watch-tower; lookout; (*slang*) thief.

atalayador, -ra, *n.m.f.* guard or sentry stationed in a watch-tower; (*fig.*, *coll.*) observer; (*fig.*, *coll.*) investigator, prier. — *a.* investigating, prying.

atalayar, *v.t.* to observe country and coast from a watch-tower; to watch, guard; (*fig.*) to pry, spy.

atalayero, *n.m.* advance scout.

atalayuela, *n.f.* small watch-tower.

ataluzar, *v.t.* to slope; to embank.

atalvina, *n.f.* porridge of almond-meal.

atamiento, *n.m.* (*coll.*) pusillanimity, poor-spiritedness, want of courage; meekness.

atanasia, *n.f.* (*bot.*) costmary, alecost; (*print.*) type between pica and English.

atanor, *n.m.* tile-drain; tile (for drains).

atanquia, *n.f.* depilatory; refuse of silk.

atañer, *v.i.* to belong, concern, appertain.

atapar, *v.t.* to cover, cover up; to hide.

ataque, *n.m.* attack, onset; (*mil.*) offensive works; (*fig.*) fit of palsy, apoplexy, etc.; verbal dispute, wrangle; *ataque cerebral*, cerebral hæmorrhage.

ataquiza, *n.f.* (*agric.*) layering (vine).

ataquizar, *v.t.* to layer or lay a vine.

atar, *v.t.* to tie, bind, fasten, knit, lace; to stop, deprive of motion; *loco de atar*, a fool or madman who should be put into the straitwaistcoat; *atar cabos*, to mass one's evidence; to draw one's own conclusions; *atar la lengua*, or *las manos*, to prevent from speaking or acting; *atar corto a uno*, (*coll.*) to repress someone; *ni atar, ni desatar*, (*coll.*) to speak at random; *quien bien ata, bien desata*, fast bind, safe find; *atar por la cola*, to put the cart before the horse; *atar a un árbol*, to tie to a tree; *atar con cuerdas*, to tie with cords; *atar de pies y manos*, to tie hand and foot; *atar por la cintura*, to tie from the waist. — *v.r.* to become embarrassed, perplexed; *atarse en las dificultades*, to be at a loss to know how to free oneself from perplexities; *atarse a una sola opinión*, to limit, confine oneself to a determined opinion; *atarse las manos*, to bind oneself by a promise.

ataracea, *n.f.* marquetry, chequers, chequer-work.

ataracear, *v.t.* to chequer, inlay, variegate.

atarantado, -da, *a.* bitten by a tarantula; (*coll.*) restless, wild; amazed, astonished. — *p.p.* [ATARANTAR].

atarantamiento, *n.m.* stunning, bewilderment.

atarantar, v.t. (coll.) to stun, bewilder. — v.r. to become stunned, bewildered.

ataraxia, n.f. ataraxia, ataraxy.

atarazana, n.f. arsenal, public dockyard; shed in rope-walks; (prov.) cellar; (slang) fence, receiver of stolen goods.

atarazar, v.t. to bite, wound, tear with the teeth.

atardecer, v.i. to grow late; to draw towards evening.

atareado, -da, a. exceedingly busy or occupied; engrossed. — p.p. [ATAREAR].

atarear, v.t. to task, impose a task, exercise. — v.r. to overdo oneself; to be exceedingly busy; atarearse a escribir, to become engrossed in writing; atarearse con, en los negocios, to become much taken up by business.

atarjea, n.f. small vault over the pipes of an aqueduct, to preserve them from harm; small sewer or house drain.

atarquinar, v.t. to bemire. — v.r. to become covered with mire.

atarraga, n.f. (bot.) elecampane.

atarragar, v.t. to fit a shoe to a horse's foot.

atarrajar, v.t. to cut the thread of a screw.

atarraya, n.f. casting-net.

atarugado, -da, a. wedged, plugged; (coll.) silenced. — p.p. [ATARUGAR].

atarugamiento, n.m. act and effect of wedging.

atarugar, v.t. (pret. atarugué; pres. subj. atarugue) to fasten or straighten with wedges; to plug, bung; (coll.) to silence, confound someone; to cram, stuff. — v.r. (coll.) to become confused; to overeat; to choke.

atasajado, -da, a. (coll.) stretched on a horse; jerked (beef). — p.p. [ATASAJAR].

atasajar, v.t. to jerk beef.

atascadero; atascamiento, n.m. deep, miry place where traffic sticks fast; (fig.) obstruction, impediment.

atascar, v.t. (pret. atasqué; pres. subj. atasque) (naut.) to stop a leak; (fig.) to obstruct. — v.r. atascarse en el barro, to stick in a miry place; to stop short in a discourse; to lose the thread of a speech; atascarse de comida, to gorge.

atasco, n.m. obstacle, barrier, obstruction.

ataúd, n.m. coffin, hearse; ancient grain measure.

ataudado, -da, a. made in the shape of a coffin.

ataujia, n.f. damascening.

ataurique, n.m. ornamented plaster-work.

ataviar, v.t. to deck out, trim, adorn, embellish, accoutre. — v.r. to adorn, embellish oneself.

atávico, -ca, a. atavistic.

atavío, n.m. dress; ornament; finery; gear, accoutrement.

atavismo, n.m. atavism.

ataxia, n.f. (med.) ataxy.

atáxico, -ca, a. (med.) ataxic.

atediar, v.t. to bore, tire. — v.r. to become vexed; to become tired, bored.

ateísmo, n.m. atheism.

ateísta, n.m.f. atheist, infidel. — a. atheist, atheistic.

ateje, n.m. (Cub.) (bot.) hardwood tree of the Boraginaceæ family.

atejo, n.m. (Col.) parcel, bundle.

atelaje, n.m. (artill.) team; harness.

atemorizar, v.t. (pret. atemoricé; pres. subj.

atemorice) to terrify, strike with terror. — v.r. atemorizarse de, por algo, to become terrified at, of, by something.

atemperación, n.f. act and effect of tempering.

atemperante, a. soothing, cooling, modifying, tempering.

atemperar, v.t. to temper; to soften, mollify, assuage, calm, cool; to modify, accommodate. — v.r. to habituate oneself.

atenacear; atenazar, v.t. to tear off flesh with pincers.

atenazado, -da, a. like pincers; tortured. — p.p. [ATENAZAR].

atención, n.f. heed, attention; attentiveness; civility, kindness; contract of sale (in wool trade); (pl.) business, affairs; en atención a sus méritos, in consideration of his merits; en atención, considering, bearing in mind; in consideration, seeing. — (int., mil.) attention!; attitude of readiness.

atendedor, -ra, n.m.f. (print.) one who checks from original MSS.

atendencia, n.f. attention.

atender, v.t., v.i. (p.p. atendido, atento; pres. indic. atiendo; pres. subj. atienda) to attend, be attentive, mind; to heed, hearken; to expect, wait; to show civility, attention, courtesy; (print.) to check from original MSS; atender a la conversación, to pay attention to the conversation.

atendible, a. worthy of consideration or attention.

atenebrarse, v.r. (poet.) to become obscured.

ateneísta, n.m.f. member of an athenæum.

ateneo, n.m. athenæum.

atenerse, v.r. (pres. indic., me atengo; pret. me atuve; pres. subj. me atenga) (with a) to depend, rely on; atenerse a lo seguro, to keep on the safe side; atenerse a la letra, to keep to the letter of the text; atenerse a alguna cosa, to abide by something.

ateniense, n.m.f., a. Athenian.

atentación, n.f. (law) illegal procedure.

atentadamente, adv. cautiously, prudently; illegally, contrary to law.

atentado, -da, a. prudent, moderate; noiseless, tactful. — p.p. [ATENTAR]. — n.m. (law) abuse of authority; outrage; excess, transgression; attempted crime.

atentamente, adv. attentively; civilly, politely.

atentar, v.t. (pres. indic. atiento; pres. subj. atiente) to attempt to commit a crime; atentar contra la vida de, to attempt the life of; atentar contra la propriedad, to attack property. — v.r. to act with great circumspection; to refrain, moderate oneself.

atentatorio, -ria, a. (law) illegal, unlawful; prejudicial.

atento, -ta, a. attentive; polite, civil, courteous; atento con los mayores, polite to grown-ups. — p.p. irr. [ATENTAR]. — adv. seeing that, in consideration of; atento a la explicación, in view of the explanation.

atenuación, n.f. attenuation, extenuation, diminution; intentional understatement.

atenuante, a. attenuant; diluent; extenuating (circumstances).

atenuar, v.t. to attenuate, extenuate, diminish; to thin.

ateo, -ea, a. atheistic. — n.m.f. atheist.

atepocate, n.m. (Mex.) frog spawn, tadpole.

atercianado, -da, *n.m.f.*, *a.* afflicted with a tertian fever.

aterciopelado, -da, *a.* velvet-like.

aterimiento, *n.m.* act of growing stiff or benumbed with cold.

aterino, *n.m.* atherine, sand smelt.

aterirse, *v.r.* (*pres. indic.* **me atiero;** *pres. subj.* **me atiera**) to grow stiff with cold.

atermancia, *n.f.* (*phys.*) athermancy.

atérmano, -na, *a.* (*phys.*) athermanous.

aterrador, -ra, *a.* horrible, dreadful, frightful.

aterrajar, *v.t.* to work with the draw-plate; to thread a screw; to tap with the die.

aterraje, *n.m.* (*naut.*) landfall; (*aer.*) landing.

aterramiento, *n.m.* ruin, destruction; terror.

aterrar, *v.t.* (*pres. indic.* **atierro;** *pres. subj.* **atierre**) to destroy; to pull down, strike down; to cover with earth; (*min.*) to dump (rubbish); (*reg. conj.*) to terrify. — *v.i.* (*naut.*) to make the land; (*aer.*) to land.

aterrerar, *v.t.* (*min.*) to dump (rubbish).

aterrizaje, *n.m.* (*aer.*) landing.

aterrizar, *v.t.* (*aer.*) to land.

aterronar, *v.t.* to clod; to make lumpy. — *v.r.* to coagulate; to grow lumpy.

aterrorizar, *v.t.* to frighten, terrify. — *v.r.* to become frightened, terrified.

atesador, *n.m.* (*mech.*) stretcher, tightener; brace pin.

atesar, *v.t.* (*pres. indic.* **atieso;** *pres. subj.* **atiese**) (*naut.*) to haul taut; to brace, tighten.

atesorador, -ra, *n.m.f.* hoarder.

atesorar, *v.t.* to treasure up, hoard up; (*fig.*) to possess many amiable qualities.

atestación, *n.f.* attestation, deposition, testimony, affidavit.

atestado, -da, *a.* attested, witnessed; stubborn. — *n.m.* authentic proof; (*pl.*) testimonials. — *p.p.* [ATESTAR].

atestadura, *n.f.* cramming, stuffing; extra must poured into pipes and butts as an allowance for wastage during fermentation.

atestamiento, *n.m.* cramming, stuffing, filling.

atestar, *v.t.* (*pres. indic.* **atiesto;** *pres. subj.* **atieste**) to cram, stuff; to overstock; to crowd; to put one thing inside another; to refill pipes or butts of wine with must; (*law*) to attest, witness; to affirm.

atestiguación, *n.f.;* **atestiguamiento,** *n.m.* deposition, testimony, affidavit.

atestiguar, *v.t.* to depose, witness, give evidence, testify; *atestiguar con otro,* to give evidence with another; *atestiguar de oídas,* to testify by hearsay.

atetado, -da, *a.* mammillated, mammiform; suckled. — *p.p.* [ATETAR].

atetar, *v.t.* to suckle, give suck; (*prov.*) to suck.

atetillar, *v.t.* (*agric.*) to dig a trench round the roots of trees.

atezado, -da, *a.* black, blackened. — *p.p.* [ATEZAR].

atezamiento, *n.m.* the act or effect of blackening.

atezar, *v.t.* (*pret.* **atecé;** *pres. subj.* **atece**) to blacken. — *v.r.* to grow black.

atibar, *v.t.* (*min.*) to fill up (excavations).

atiborrar, *v.t.* to stuff with locks of wool, tow, etc.; (*coll.*) to cram with victuals. — *v.r.* to gormandize.

aticismo, *n.m.* Atticism; concise and elegant expression.

aticista, *n.m.f.*, *a.* Attic, elegant (writer).

ático, -ca, *a.* Attic, elegant. — *n.m.* Attic dialect; (*arch.*) ornamental masonry set above the cornice; (*arch.*) upper part of a building, attic.

atiendo; atienda, *pres. indic.; pres. subj.* [ATENDER].

atiento; atiente, *pres. indic.; pres. subj.* [ATENTAR].

atiero; atiera, *pres. indic.; pres subj.* [ATERIR].

atierre, *n.m.* (*min.*) caving in; landslide, collapse.

atierro; atierre, *pres. indic.; pres. subj.* [ATERRAR].

atiesar, *v.t.* to harden, stiffen. — *v.r.* to become hard or stiff.

atieso; atiese, *pres. indic.; pres. subj.* [ATESAR].

atiesto; atiesta, *pres. indic.; pres. subj.* [ATESTAR].

atifle, *n.m.* potter's trivet.

atigrado, -da, *a.* marked like a tiger's skin.

atijara, *n.f.* merchandise, freight; recompense.

atijarero, *n.m.* carrier.

atildado, -da, *a.* dressed, adorned; punctuated. — *p.p.* [ATILDAR].

atildadura, *n.f.;* **atildamiento,** *n.m.* punctuation; censure; tidiness, nicety.

atildar, *v.t.* to punctuate, place a dash or stroke (*tilde*) over a letter; (*fig.*) to censure (speeches or actions); (*fig.*) to dress, adorn. — *v.r.* to dress, adorn oneself.

atinadamente, *adv.* cautiously, prudently; pertinently, appositely; considerately.

atinado, -da, *a.* opportune; prudent. — *p.p.* [ATINAR].

atinar, *v.i.* to touch the mark; (*fig.*) to hit upon, guess; to find out; *atinar al blanco,* to hit the mark; *atinar con la solución,* to hit upon the solution.

atíncar, *n.m.* (*chem.*) tincal, borax.

atinconar, *v.t.* (*min.*) to prop up.

atinente, *a.* touching, belonging, appertaining.

atingencia, *n.f.* relation; contiguity.

atiplar, *v.t.* to raise the pitch of a musical instrument. — *v.r.* (*mus.*) to become sharp or acute.

atirantar, *v.t.* (*arch.*) to truss, stay, fix collar-beams in a building.

atiriciarse, *v.r.* to contract jaundice.

atisbadero, *n.m.* peep-hole.

atisbador, -ra, *n.m.f.* prier, searcher, observer, curious person. — *a.* prying, observing.

atisbadura, *n.f.* prying, observation.

atisbar, *v.t.* to scrutinize, pry, spy, examine closely.

atisbo, *n.m.* prying, observing cautiously; conjecture, surmise.

atisuado, -da, *a.* like gold or silver tissue.

atizadero, *n.m.* fire-poker; (*min.*) furnace door.

atizador, -ra, *a.* poking, fire-trimming. — *n.m.* workman in oil-mills who passes the olives under the millstones; fire-poker.

atizar, *v.t.* (*pret.* **aticé;** *pres. subj.* **atice**) to stir the fire with a poker; to snuff, trim; (*fig.*) to stir up or rouse the passions; to incite; (*fig.*) to slap, give a blow; *¡atiza!* good gracious!

atizonar, *v.t.* (*build.*) to bond with headers; to embed a beam in a wall. — *v.r.* (*agric.*) to be smutted (of grain).

atlante, *n.m.* (*arch.*) telamon. — *pl.* (*arch.*) atlantes.

atlántico, -ca, *a.* Atlantic. — *n.m.* the Atlantic Ocean.

atlas, *n.m.* atlas, book of maps; (*anat.*) first cervical vertebra.

atleta, *n.m.* athlete, gymnast, wrestler.

atlético, -ca, *a.* athletic, robust.

atletismo, *n.m.* athletics.

atmósfera, *n.f.* atmosphere, air; (*fig.*) sphere of influence; (*mech.*) measure of force.

atmosférico, -ca, *a.* atmospherical.

atoaje, *n.m.* (*naut.*) towage, tow, towing.

atoar, *v.t.* (*naut.*) to tow; (*naut.*) to pull ahead.

atoba, *n.f.* (*prov.*) adobe, brick.

atocinado, -da, *a.* (*coll.*) corpulent, fat, fleshy. — *p.p.* [ATOCINAR].

atocinar, *v.t.* to cut up a pig; to make bacon; to salt bacon; (*coll.*) to assassinate. — *v.r.* (*coll.*) to become exasperated; (*coll.*) to fall madly in love.

atocha, *n.f.* (*bot.*) esparto.

atochal; atochar, *n.m.* esparto field.

atochar, *v.t.* to fill with esparto.

atochón, *n.m.* panicle of esparto; esparto cane or rush.

atol, atole, *n.m.* (*Cub., Guat., Ven.*) corn-flour gruel; (*Mex.*) (*fig.*) deceit, trick.

atoleadas, *n.f.pl.* (*Hond.*) festivities celebrated between July and December.

atolillo, *n.m.* (*CR., Hond.*) gruel made of flour, sugar and eggs.

atolondradamente, *adv.* giddily, thoughtlessly.

atolondrado, -da, *a.* hare-brained, giddy, thoughtless, careless, unreflective; confused. — *p.p.* [ATOLONDRAR].

atolondramiento, *n.m.* stupefaction, confusion, amazement; giddiness.

atolondrar, *v.t.* to stun, stupefy, perplex, confound, amaze. — *v.r.* to become stupefied, giddy, confused; to grow stupid.

atolladero, *n.m.* deep miry place; (*fig.*) obstacle, impediment.

atollar, *v.i., v.r.* to fall into the mire; *atollarse en el lodo,* to be or become involved in great difficulties.

atomicidad, *n.f.* atomicity.

atómico, -ca, *a.* atomic.

atomismo, *n.m.* atomism.

atomista, *n.m.f.* atomist.

atomístico, -ca, *a.* atomical.

atomizar, *v.t.* to atomize.

átomo, *n.m.* atom; iota, jot; mote; corpuscle; *no exceder en un átomo,* to stick closely to instructions; *reparar en un átomo,* to remark the minutest detail.

atona, *n.f.* ewe that rears another's lamb.

atondar, *v.t.* to urge on a horse with the legs.

atonía, *n.f.* (*med.*) atony.

atónico, -ca, *a.* (*gram., med.*) atonic.

atónito, -ta, *a.* astonished, amazed; *atónito con la desgracia,* amazed at the misfortune.

átono, -na, *a.* (*gram.*) atonic, unaccented.

atontadamente, *adv.* foolishly, stupidly, indiscreetly.

atontado, -da, *a.* foolish, stupid; confused. — *p.p.* [ATONTAR].

atontamiento, *n.m.* stupefaction.

atontar, *v.t.* to stun, stupefy, confuse, confound. — *v.r.* to become stupid, dull, confused.

atopile, *n.m.* (*Mex.*) foreman in charge of irrigation waters.

atora, *n.f.* (*Bibl.*) Mosaic Law.

atoramiento, *n.m.* choking, obstruction.

atorar, *v.t.* to obstruct; to choke, jam; to cut firewood. — *v.r.* to stick in the mire; to choke, suffocate.

atorgar, *v.t.* [OTORGAR].

atormentadamente, *adv.* anxiously, tormentingly.

atormentador, -ra, *n.m.f.* tormentor, tormentress. — *a.* tormenting.

atormentar, *v.t.* to torment; to cause pain, affliction, vexation; to rack, torture, harass; to shell a fortress, etc. — *v.r.* to become agitated.

atornillar, *v.t.* to screw; to fix with screws.

atorozonarse, *v.r.* (*vet.*) to suffer from colic or gripes.

atorra, *n.f.* (*prov.*) linen petticoat.

atorrante, *n.m.* (*Arg.*) vagabond, loafer; vagrant; beggar.

atortolar, *v.t.* (*coll.*) to confound, intimidate. — *v.r.* to become intimidated.

atortorar, *v.t.* (*naut.*) to frap; (*naut.*) to strengthen by means of a tourniquet.

atortujar, *v.t.* to squeeze, flatten.

atosigador, -ra, *a.* poisonous; (*fig.*) worrying, oppressive. — *n.m.* poisoner; (*fig.*) worrier, oppressor.

atosigamiento, *n.m.* poisoning.

atosigar, *v.t.* (*pret.* **atosigué;** *pres. subj.* **atosigue**) to poison; (*fig.*) to harass, oppress. — *v.r.* to become worried, harassed.

atoxicar, *v.t.* to poison.

atóxico, -ca, *a.* non-poisonous.

atrabajar, *v.t.* to keep someone very busy; to make work hard.

atrabancar, *v.t.* (*pret.* **atrabanqué;** *pres. subj.* **atrabanque**) to huddle; to perform in a hurry; (*prov.*) to overfill.

atrabanco, *n.m.* the act of huddling, or acting hurriedly.

atrabiliario, -ria; atrabilioso, -sa, *a.* atrabiliary, melancholy; splenetic, bitter-tempered; (*med.*) bilious; *cápsula atrabiliaria,* (*med.*) atrabiliary capsule.

atrabilis, *n.f.* (*med.*) atrabiliousness, black bile; (*coll.*) melancholy, bad temper.

atracable, *a.* (*naut.*) approachable.

atracada, *n.f.* (*naut.*) berthing, docking; (*Cub., Mex.*) overeating, gluttony.

atracadero, *n.m.* (*naut.*) landfall; landing-place.

atracado, -da, *p.p.* [ATRACAR] satiated; approached; (*naut.*) berthed, docked.

atracador, *n.m.* (*slang*) highwayman.

atracar, *v.t.* (*pret.* **atraqué;** *pres. subj.* **atraque**) (*coll.*) to cram with food and drink; (*naut.*) to overtake, approach; to rob on the highway. — *v.i.* (*naut.*) to berth, come alongside a quay or pier. — *v.r.* to gorge; to pamper oneself; *atracarse de dulces,* to stuff oneself with sweets.

atracción, *n.f.* attraction.

atraco, *n.m.* highway robbery.

atracón, *n.m.* overeating, gluttony.

atractivo, -va, *a.* attractive, engaging, enchanting. — *n.m.* charm, gracefulness, inducement.

atractriz, *a.f.* (*phys.*) attracting; *fuerza atractriz,* attractive power.

atraer, *v.t.* (*pres. indic.* **atraigo;** *pret.* **atraje;** *pres. subj.* **atraiga**) to attract, lead, lure; to charm, captivate; to conciliate; *atraer a su bando*, to attract to his party; *atraer con promesas*, to lure with promises.

atrafagado, -da, *a.* much occupied, laborious; fatigued; fidgety. — *p.p.* [ATRAFAGAR].

atrafagar, *v.i.* to toil; to be exhausted with fatigue.

atragantarse, *v.r.* to choke, stick in the throat; to stop short, lose the thread in conversation; *atragantarse con una espina*, to choke on a fish-bone.

atraíble, *a.* attractable.

atraicionar, *v.t.* to betray.

atraidorado, -da, *a.* treacherous, faithless, perfidious.

atraigo; atraiga; atraje, *pres. indic.; pres. subj.; pret.* [ATRAER].

atraillar, *v.t.* to leash; to follow game guided by a dog in leash; (*fig.*) to dominate, hold fast.

atramento, *n.m.* black colour.

atrampar, *v.t.* to trap, snare, entrap. — *v.r.* to become trapped, snared; to become choked, blocked up (drain); to become bolted (door); (*coll.*) to become involved in difficulties.

atramuz, *n.m.* (*bot.*) lupine.

atrancar, *v.t.* (*pret.* **atranqué**; *pres. subj.* **atranque**) to bar a door; to block up. — *v.i.* (*coll.*) to take long steps; to read hurriedly. — *v.r.* to become blocked up.

atranco; atranque, *n.m.* [ATOLLADERO].

atrapamoscas, *n.f.* (*bot.*) Venus's fly-trap.

atrapar, *v.t.* (*coll.*) to overtake; to grab, catch; to gain; to trap, ensnare, deceive.

atrás, *adv.* backwards, towards the back, behind; past; previously; ¡*atrás!* back! go back! go behind! *hacia atrás,* (*coll.*) on the contrary; *hacerse atrás*, to fall back; *quedarse atrás*, to remain behind.

atrasado, -da, *a.* short of means, poor; backward; behindhand, behind the times; late; slow (clock); in arrears; ignorant; *atrasado de noticias*, ignorant of common things; *atrasado en el estudio*, backward in study; *atrasado de medios*, short of means, needy. — *p.p.* [ATRASAR].

atrasar, *v.t.* to protract, postpone, retard, delay, detain. — *v.i.* to be slow (as a watch); *atrasar las pagas*, to suspend or delay payments; *atrasar el reloj*, to retard the motion of a watch. — *v.r.* to remain behind; to be in debt; to be late; to lose time (watch).

atraso, *n.m.* backwardness; delay; slowness (watch). — *pl.* arrears.

atravesado, -da, *a.* squint-eyed; oblique; crossed; pierced; perverse, cross-grained, troublesome; mongrel; (*prov.*) mulatto or half-breed; *atravesado de dolor*, grief-stricken; *atravesado por una bala*, pierced by a bullet; *atravesado en una caballería*, stretched across a horse. — *p.p.* [ATRAVESAR].

atravesador, -ra, *a.* traversing, crossing.

atravesaño, *n.m.* cross-timber, transverse beam, cross-piece.

atravesar, *v.t.* (*pres. indic.* **atravieso**; *pres. subj.* **atraviese**) to stretch across a horse; to pierce; to run through with a sword; to cross, cross over, pass over, go through; to wager, bet; (*coll.*) to bewitch; to lay a trump (at cards); (*naut.*) to lie to; *atravesar la ciudad*, to pass through the city; *atravesar un madero*

en la calle, to lay a beam athwart the street; *atravesar con alguno una palabra*, to speak with a person; *atravesar el corazón*, (*fig.*) to move to compassion; *atravesar los géneros*, to buy wholesale and sell retail; *no atravesar los umbrales*, not to darken one's door; not to put foot in a house; *atravesar el pecho de un balazo*, to shoot in the breast. — *v.r.* to be obstructed by something thrown in the way; to interfere; to have a dispute; to interrupt; to mingle; (*naut.*) to cross the course of another vessel; to bet, stake, wager; *atravesarse en medio del camino*, to spring up suddenly (obstacle); *atravesarse en el juego*, to bet; *se atravesaron veinte duros*, they staked twenty dollars; *atravesarse a uno un nudo en la garganta*, to choke with emotion.

atrayente, *a.* attractive.

atreguado, -da, *a.* foolish; lunatic; under truce. — *p.p.* [ATREGUAR].

atreguar, *v.t.* to give a truce. — *v.r.* to agree to a truce.

atrenzo, *n.m.* (*Am.*) conflict, difficulty.

atresia, *n.f.* (*med.*) atresia.

atresnalar, *v.t.* (*agric.*) to shock or stook.

atreverse, *v.r.* to be too forward; to dare to; to venture, adventure; to run a risk; *atreverse a cosas grandes*, to venture on big things; *atreverse con todos*, to be bold, forward with everyone.

atrevidamente, *adv.* audaciously, daringly, boldly.

atrevido, -da, *a.* bold, audacious, daring, fearless; forward, insolent. — *p.p.* [ATREVERSE].

atrevimiento, *n.m.* boldness, audacity, daring; effrontery, impudence.

atribución, *n.f.* conferring; prerogative; attribute.

atribuible, *a.* attributable.

atribuir, *v.t.* (*pres. indic.* **atribuyo**; *pret.* **él atribuyó**; *pres. subj.* **atribuya**) to attribute, ascribe, impute; to count; *atribuir a otro*, to attribute to another. — *v.r.* to assume, arrogate to oneself.

atribulación, *n.f.* tribulation, affliction.

atribuladamente, *adv.* distressfully, afflictedly.

atribular, *v.t.* to vex, afflict, annoy, worry, torment. — *v.r.* to be or become vexed; to suffer tribulation; *atribularse con, en, por los trabajos*, to feel overwhelmed through troubles.

atributivo, -va, *a.* attributive.

atributo, *n.m.* attribute; (*log.*) predicate.

atribuyo; atribuya, *pres. indic.; pres. subj.* [ATRIBUIR].

atriceses, *n.m.pl.* stirrup-strap rings.

atrición, *n.f.* attrition; (*vet., obs.*) contraction of the principal nerve; contrition, grief for sin.

atril, *n.m.* desk, lectern, music-stand; easel.

atrilera, *n.f.* ornamental cover for a lectern.

atrincheramiento, *n.m.* entrenchment.

atrincherar, *v.t.* to entrench, fortify with a trench. — *v.r.* to entrench oneself.

atrio, *n.m.* atrium; porch, portico, courtyard.

atrípedo, -da, *a.* (*zool.*) having black feet.

atrirrostro, -tra, *a.* (*orn.*) black-beaked.

atrito, -ta, *a.* contrite.

atrocidad, *n.f.* atrocity, atrociousness, heinousness, wickedness, cruelty; (*coll.*) a very stupid or foolish action; (*coll.*) excess; *es una atrocidad lo que come*, he eats to excess.

atrochar, *v.i.* to go through by-paths.

atrofia, *n.f.* (*med.*) atrophy.

atrofiarse, *v.r.* (*med.*) to fall into a state of atrophy; to waste away.

atrófico, -ca, *a.* atrophic.

atrojar, *v.t.* (*agric.*) to garner. — *v.r.* (*Mex., coll.*) to be stumped.

atrompetado, -da, *a.* trumpet-like.

atronadamente, *adv.* precipitately; recklessly, hastily.

atronado, -da, *a.* unreflecting, inconsiderate, precipitate. — *n.m.f.* blunderer. — *p.p.* [ATRONAR].

atronador, -ra, *a.* thundering.

atronadura, *n.f.* crack or split in wood; (*vet.*) tumour in the pastern.

atronamiento, *n.m.* thundering; stupefaction caused by a blow; (*vet.*) ulcer in the feet or legs of horses.

atronar, *v.t.* (*pres. indic.* atrueno; *pres. subj.* atruene) to make a great noise; to stun, stupefy, deafen; to thunder; to stop the ears of horses; to kill a bull. — *v.r.* to be thunderstruck (silk-worms, chicks, etc.).

atronerar, *v.t.* to make loopholes.

atropado, -da, *a.* (*agric.*) grouped, clumped. — *p.p.* [ATROPAR].

atropar, *v.t.* to group together, assemble in groups. — *v.r.* to form or fall into a group.

atropelladamente, *adv.* tumultuously, confusedly, helter-skelter, pell-mell.

atropellado, -da, *a.* hasty. — *p.p.* [ATROPELLAR].

atropellador, -ra, *n.m.f.* trampler, transgressor, violator. — *a.* trampling, violating.

atropellamiento, *n.m.* trampling under foot; confusedness.

atropellar, *v.t.* to trample, tread under foot; to push through; to knock down; (*fig.*) to violate; to insult with abusive language; *atropellar las leyes,* to act in defiance of the law. — *v.r.* to hurry overmuch; to be very hasty; *atropellarse en las acciones,* to act hastily; *atropellarse con, por todo,* to push everything aside.

atropello, *n.m.* upset; trampling; insult, abuse, outrage.

atropina, *n.f.* (*chem.*) atropine.

atroz, *a.* atrocious, cruel, heinous, inhuman, barbarous; (*coll.*) enormous; vast, immense.

atrozar, *v.t.* (*naut.*) to truss a yard to the mast.

atrozmente, *adv.* atrociously, heinously; excessively, enormously.

atruchado, -da, *a.* trout-coloured (cast-iron graining).

atruendo; atuendo, *n.m.* pomp, ostentation.

atrueno; atruene, *pres. indic.; pres. subj.* [ATRONAR].

atruhanado, -da, *a.* scurrilous, rascally.

atufadamente, *adv.* peevishly, morosely, angrily.

atufamiento; atufo, *n.m.* vexation, angry feeling, annoyance.

atufar, *v.t.* to vex, plague, irritate. — *v.r.* to inhale or become suffocated by deleterious vapours; to fret, turn sour (liquors); to be angry; *atufarse por todo,* to become angry on the slightest provocation; *atufarse de, con poca cosa,* to become easily annoyed.

atufo, *n.m.* vexation, irritation, annoyance.

atumultuar, *v.t.* to incite to a tumult.—*v.r.* to rise in arms.

atún, *n.m.* tunny, tunny-fish; *pedazo de atún,* stupid person.

atunara, *n.f.* tunny-fishing-ground.

atunera, *n.f.* tunny-fish-hook.

atunero, *n.m.* tunny-fisherman or salesman.

aturar, *v.i.* to act judiciously. — *v.t.* (*coll.*) to close tightly.

aturdido, -da, *a.* hare-brained, mad-brained; giddy. — *p.p.* [ATURDIR].

aturdidor, -ra, *a.* that makes giddy; stupefying.

aturdimiento, *n.m.* physical disorder; moral perturbation; dullness; bewilderment, confusion, amazement; (*med.*) giddiness.

aturdir, *v.t.* to perturb, bewilder, confuse; (*fig.*) to amaze; to stupefy, stun. — *v.r.* to go out of one's wits; to become dazed, perturbed, stupefied, bewildered, stunned, amazed.

aturrullar, *v.t.* (*coll.*) to confuse, disconcert, confound, perplex, bewilder. — *v.r.* to become confused; to lose one's presence of mind.

atusador, -ra, *n.m.f.* hairdresser; one who trims plants. — *a.* trimming, clipping.

atusar, *v.t.* to cut, trim, comb and smooth the hair even; to trim plants. — *v.r.* (*fig.*) to dress oneself with affectation.

atutía, *n.f.* (*chem.*) tutty; oxide of zinc ointment.

atuve, atuvo, *pret.* (*yo me atuve, él se atuvo*). [ATENERSE].

auca, *n.f.* goose.

auca, *n.m., a.* Indian of an Araucanian tribe.

audacia, *n.f.* audacity, boldness.

audaz, *a.* bold, audacious, brave, valiant, daring.

audazmente, *adv.* boldly, audaciously, fearlessly.

audible, *a.* audible.

audición, *n.f.* audition, hearing.

audiencia, *n.f.* audience, hearing, reception; audience-chamber; a court of oyer and terminer; law officers appointed to institute some judicial inquiry; (*obs.*) *audiencia de los grados,* Seville court of appeal; *dar audiencia,* to hold a levee; to give audience; *hacer audiencia,* (*law*) to sit and determine lawsuits.

audífono, *n.m.* audiphone.

audiofrecuencia, *n.f.* audiofrequency.

audiómetro, *n.m.* audiometer.

auditivo, -va, *a.* auditive, auditory. — *n.m.* telephone ear-piece.

auditor, *n.m.* judge; auditor; telephone earpiece; *auditor de la nunciatura,* Papal legal adviser in Spain; *auditor de guerra, de marina,* military, naval legal adviser.

auditoría, *n.f.* auditorship; office of *auditor.*

auditorio, -ria, *a.* auditory. — *n.m.* auditorium, audience.

auge, *n.m.* apogee; acme, culmination.

augita, *n.f.* (*min.*) augite.

augur, *n.m.* augur.

auguración, *n.f.* augury.

augural, *a.* augural.

augurar, *v.t.* to augur, foretell, prophesy.

augurio, *n.m.* augury.

augustal, *a.* Augustan.

augusto, -ta, *a.* august, venerable, magnificent, majestic.

aula, *n.f.* lecture hall; class room; (*poet.*) palace.

aulaga, *n.f.* (*bot.*) furze, whin, gorse.

aulagar, *n.m.* gorse-field.
áulico, -ca, *a.* aulic, courtly. — *n.m.* courtier.
aulladero, *n.m.* place where wolves meet and howl.
aullador, -ra, *a.* howling.
aullante, *a.* howling.
aullar, *v.i.* to howl, yell, cry.
aullido; aúllo, *n.m.* howl, cry of horror.
aumentable, *a.* augmentable.
aumentación, *n.f.* increase; (*rhet.*) climax.
aumentador, -ra, *a.* augmenting.
aumentante, *a.* augmenting, increasing.
aumentar, *v.t.* to augment, increase, enlarge, multiply, magnify. — *v.r.* to gather; to grow larger.
aumentativo, -va, *a.* (*gram.*) augmentative.
aumento, *n.m.* augmentation, increase, enlargement, access, accession, growth; the magnifying power of a telescope or lens. — *pl.* promotion, advancement.
aun; aún, *adv.* yet, as yet, nevertheless, notwithstanding, still, even, further. — *conj. aun cuando,* although.
aunar, *v.t.* to unite, join, assemble; to incorporate, mix. — *v.r.* to become united, confederated; *aunarse con otro,* to combine with another.
auniga, *n.f.* web-footed bird of the Philippines.
aunque, *conj.* though, notwithstanding, howsoever; *aunque más,* however much.
¡aúpa! *interj.* (*coll.*) up, up! (to children).
aupar, *v.t.* (*coll.*) to help a child get up.
aura, *n.f.* (*orn.*) bird of the vulture kind; (*poet.*) gentle breeze; (*fig.*) favour, applause; (*med.*) epileptic, aura; *aura popular,* popularity.
auranciáceo, -cea, *a.* (*bot.*) orange-like.
áureo, -rea, *a.* (*bot.*) golden, gold; (*poet.*) aureate; *áureo número,* golden number, the lunar cycle. — *n.m.* ancient gold coin; weight of four scruples.
auréola; aureola, *n.f.* aureola.
aureolar, *v.t.* to adorn as with an aureole.
aurero, *n.m.* (*Cub.*) place where vultures gather.
auricalco, *n.m.* copper, bronze or brass.
aurícula, *n.f.* (*anat.*) auricle; (*bot.*) lobe on leaf (as on bear's ear).
auricular, *a.* auricular. — *n.m.* telephone earpiece.
aurífero, -ra, *a.* auriferous.
auriga, *n.m.* (*poet.*) coachman; (*astron.*) Auriga, Wagoner.
aurígero, -ra, *a.* auriferous.
aurista, *n.m.f.* (*med.*) aurist, ear specialist.
aurívoro, -ra, *a.* (*poet.*) greedy for gold.
aurora, *n.f.* dawn, daybreak, peep of day, morning; roseate colour; east; (*fig.*) first appearance of something; beverage of almond milk and cinnamon; (*naut.*) morning-watch gun; *aurora boreal,* aurora borealis, northern lights; *despuntar* or *romper la aurora,* dawning; *llorar la aurora,* fall of dew at sunrise.
aurragado, -da, *a.* badly tilled and cultivated.
auscultación, *n.f.* (*med.*) auscultation.
auscultar, *v.t.* (*med.*) to auscultate.
ausencia, *n.f.* absence; period of absence; *hacer buenas, malas ausencias,* to speak well, ill of the absent.
ausentado, -da, *a.* absent, absented. — *p.p.* [AUSENTARSE].

ausentarse, *v.r.* to absent oneself.
ausente, *a.* absent, distant.
ausentismo, *n.m.* absenteeism.
auspicio, *n.m.* auspice; presage, prediction; protection, favour, patronage. — *pl.* auspices
austeramente, *adv.* austerely, frowningly, roughly.
austeridad, *n.f.* austerity, severity, rigour.
austero, -ra, *a.* austere; severe, harsh, rigid; astringent, acrid; mortified, retired and penitent.
austral; austrino, -na, *a.* austral, southern.
australiano, -na, *n.m.f.,* *a.* Australian.
austríaco, -ca, *n.m.f.,* *a.* Austrian.
austrino, -na, *a.* belonging to the house of Austria.
austro, *n.m.* south wind; south.
austrohúngaro, -ra, *n.m.f.,* *a.* Austro-Hungarian.
auténtica, *n.f.* original, authentic text; certificate, attestation.
autenticación, *n.f.* authentication.
auténticamente, *adv.* authentically.
autenticar, *v.t.* (*pret.* **autentiqué**; *pres. subj.* **autentique**) to authenticate, attest.
autenticidad, *n.f.* authenticity.
auténtico, -ca, *a.* authentic, genuine; (*law*) attested.
autillo, *n.m.* particular Inquisition act or decree; (*orn.*) barn-owl, screech-owl.
auto, *n.m.* act; judicial decree or sentence; writ, warrant, edict, ordinance; (*coll.*) motor-car, automobile; (*pl.*) pleadings and proceedings in a lawsuit; *auto de fe, auto-da-fé,* sentence given by the Inquisition; *auto interlocutorio,* interlocutory sentence; *auto sacramental,* allegorical or religious play; *estar en* (*los*) *autos,* (*fam.*) to know a thing profoundly; to be well up in something; *poner en autos,* to inform.
autobiografía, *n.f.* autobiography.
autobiográfico, -ca, *a.* autobiographical.
autobombo, *n.m.* blowing one's own trumpet.
autobús, *n.m.* motor omnibus.
autocamión, *n.m.* motor-lorry.
autoclave, *a.* self-regulating (cooking vessel). — *n.m.* steam-pressure saucepan; steam-pressure sterilizing apparatus.
autocopiar, *v.t.* (*com.*) to duplicate, multiply.
autocopista, *n.m.* (*com.*) autocopyist; duplicator; duplicating machine.
autocracia, *n.f.* autocracy.
autócrata, *n.m.f.* autocrat.
autocrático, -ca, *a.* autocratical.
autocrítica, *n.f.* critical review of one's own work.
autóctono, -na, *a.* autochthonic, aboriginal. — *n.m.f.* autochthon.
autodidacto, -ta, *n.m.f.* self-taught person.
autodidaxia, *n.f.* facility for self-teaching.
autógamo, -ma, *a.* (*bot.*) autogamous.
autogénesis, *n.f.* (*physiol.*) autogeny, autogony.
autógeno, -na, *a.* welding by means of oxygen and acetylene.
autogiro, *n.m.* (*aer.*) helicopter.
autografía, *n.f.* autography; facsimile reproduction; duplicating office.
autografiar, *v.t.* to autograph; to duplicate.
autográfico, -ca, *a.* autographical, facsimile.
autógrafo, -fa, *a.* autograph, autographic. — *n.m.* autograph.
autoinducción, *n.f.* (*elec.*) self-induction.

autointoxicación, *n.f.* (*path.*) autointoxication, autotoxæmia.

automación, *n.f.* automation.

autómata, *n.m.* automaton; (*coll.*) weak person.

automáticamente, *adv.* automatically.

automático, -ca, *a.* automatic.

automatismo, *n.m.* automatism.

automedonte, *n.m.* (*myth.*) Automedon; (*fig., coll.*) coachman.

automotor, -ra; automotriz, *n.m.f.,* *a.* self-acting, self-moving, self-propelling (thing).

automóvil, *n.m.* motor-car, automobile. — *a.* self-moving.

automovilismo, *n.m.* automobilism.

automovilista, *n.m.f.* motorist.

autonomía, *n.f.* autonomy, home rule; (*fig.*) independence, self-determination.

autonómicamente, *adv.* autonomously.

autonómico, -ca, *a.* autonomous.

autonomista, *a., n.m.f.* autonomist.

autónomo, -ma, *a.* autonomous, free.

autopista, *n.f.* autobahn.

autoplastia, *n.f.* (*surg.*) autoplasty.

autopsia, *n.f.* (*med.*) autopsy, post-mortem.

autópsido, -da, *a.* (*min.*) glittering, having a metallic lustre.

autor, -ra, *n.m.f.* author, authoress; maker, composer; writer; manager of a theatre; (*law*) plaintiff, claimant; perpetrator, abettor, inciter (of crime).

autorcillo, *n.m.* scribbler.

autoría, *n.f.* direction of a theatrical company.

autoridad, *n.f.* authority, credit; ostentation, display of grandeur; quotation.

autoritariamente, *adv.* authoritatively; imperiously.

autoritario, -ria, *a.* despotic; authoritative; assuming or upholding authority.

autoritativo, -va, *a.* authoritative.

autorizable, *a.* authorizable.

autorización, *n.f.* authorization.

autorizadamente, *adv.* authoritatively.

autorizado, -da, *a.* respectable, commendable; authorized. — *p.p.* [AUTORIZAR].

autorizador, -ra, *n.m.f.* one who authorizes. — *a.* authorizing.

autorizamiento, *n.m.* authorization.

autorizar, *v.t.* (*pret.* **autoricé;** *pres. subj.* **autorice**) to authorize; to attest, legalize, confirm; to qualify, exalt, extol; *autorizar con su firma,* to confirm with his signature; *autorizar para algún acto,* to grant authority for, authorize a certain act.

autorretrato, *n.m.* self-portrait.

autorzuelo, *n.m.* scribbler.

autosugestión, *n.f.* (*med.*) auto-suggestion.

autotipia, *n.f.* (*photo.*) autotype.

autumnal, *a.* autumnal.

auxiliador, -ra, *n.m.f.* auxiliary, assistant, saver, helper. — *a.* auxiliary, helping.

auxiliante, *a.* aiding, assisting.

auxiliar, *v.t.* to aid, help, assist; to attend a dying person. — *a.* (*gram.*) auxiliary; helping, assistant. — *n.m.* assistant, auxiliary.

auxiliatorio, -ria, *a.* (*law*) auxiliary.

auxilio, *n.m.* aid, help, assistance.

avacado, -da, *a.* cow-like in body (horse).

avadarse, *v.r.* to become fordable.

avahar, *v.t.* to warm with breath or vapour. — *v.i., v.r.* to fume; to give off vapour.

aval, *n.m.* guarantee, surety; (*com.*) endorsement; (*polit.*) guarantee of conduct.

avalancha, *n.f.* avalanche.

avalar, *v.t.* (*com.*) to guarantee by endorsement.

avalentado, -da; avalentonado, -da, *a.* bragging, boasting, arrogant.

avalo, *n.m.* slight movement; earthquake.

avalorar, *v.t.* to estimate, price, value; (*fig.*) to inspire, animate, encourage.

avaluación, *n.f.* valuation, rate, appraisement.

avaluar, *v.t.* to value, appraise, estimate.

avalúo, *n.m.* valuation, appraisement.

avallar, *v.t.* to barricade, fence in.

avambrazo, *n.m.* armlet, piece of ancient armour that served to cover the arm.

avampiés, *n.m.* spatterdash.

avancarga (de), *n.f.* muzzle loader.

avance, *n.m.* (*mil.*) advance, attack, assault; (*com.*) account, statement, balance-sheet; payment in advance; (*Gallicism*) temerity, boldness.

avanecerse, *v.r.* to become stale (fruit).

avantrén, *n.m.* (*mil.*) limbers of a gun-carriage.

avanzada, *n.f.* (*mil.*) van, outpost, reconnoitring troop.

avanzado, -da, *a.* advanced, mature; progressive; *avanzado de edad,* stricken in years. — *p.p.* [AVANZAR].

avanzar, *v.i.* (*pret.* **avancé;** *pres. subj.* **avance**) (*mil.*) to advance, attack, engage, come on, go forward; to have a balance in one's favour. — *v.t., v.r.* to advance, push forward.

avanzo, *n.m.* (*com.*) estimate, tender; balance-sheet.

avaramente, *adv.* avariciously, miserably.

avaricia, *n.f.* avarice, cupidity.

avariciosamente, *adv.* avariciously.

avaricioso, -sa; avariento, -ta, *a.* avaricious, covetous, niggardly, miserly, miserable. — *n.m.f.* miser, niggard.

avaro, -ra, *a.* avaricious, miserly; *avaro de gloria,* eager for glory. — *n.m.f.* miser.

avasallador, -ra, *a.* enslaving. — *n.m.f.* enslaver.

avasallamiento, *n.m.* enslavement, servitude.

avasallar, *v.t.* to subdue, subject, enslave, reduce to vassalage. — *v.r.* to become subject; to become a vassal.

ave, *n.f.* bird, fowl; *ave brava* or *silvestre,* wild bird; *ave de cuchar* or *cuchara,* spoonbill; *ave del Paraíso,* bird of paradise; *ave pasajera* or *de paso,* migratory bird; *ave fría,* lapwing; (*coll.*) poor-spirited person; *ave ratera,* low-flying bird; *ave de rapiña, ave rapaz* or *rapiega,* bird of prey; *ave tonta* or *zonza,* sparrow-like bird, easily caught and tamed; (*fam.*) simpleton; *al ave de paso, cañazo,* have nothing to do with strangers; *ser un ave,* (*fam.*) to be very quick, or nimble.

avecica; avecilla; avecita, *n.f.* small bird; *las avecitas del campo tienen a Dios por su proveedor y despensero,* even the birds of the field have God for their purveyor and caterer.

avecinar, *v.t., v.i.* to approach; to come near. — *v.r.* to domicile oneself.

avecindamiento, *n.m.* domiciliation, domicile.

avecindar, *v.t.* to enrol in the number of citizens. — *v.r.* to domicile oneself.

avechucho, *n.m.* (*orn.*) sparrow-hawk; ugly bird; (*coll.*) ragamuffin.

avejentado, -da, *a.* appearing older than one really is. — *p.p.* [AVEJENTAR].

avejentar, *v.t., v.r.* to make or appear older than one is; to look old; to age.

avejigar, *v.t.* to produce blisters. — *v.i., v.r.* to blister.

avellana, *n.f.* filbert, hazel-nut.

avellanado, -da, *a.* countersunk; (*fig.*) dried up; nut-brown; *coco avellanado,* dry coconut. — *p.p.* [AVELLANAR].

avellanador, *n.m.* tool used by blacksmiths and carpenters; fraise, countersink-bit, rose-bit.

avellanal; avellanar, *n.m.* plantation of hazels or nut-trees.

avellanar, *v.t.* to countersink. — *v.r.* to shrivel; to grow as dry as a nut.

avellanero, -ra, *n.m.f.* dealer in nuts and filberts. — *n.f.* hazel-tree, filbert-tree.

avellanica, *n.f.* small filbert.

avellano, *n.m.* common hazel-nut tree.

avemaría, *n.f.* Ave Maria; Hail Mary; rosary bead; *al avemaría,* at nightfall; *en un avemaría,* in an instant.

¡Ave María! *interj.* good gracious!

avena, *n.f.* (*bot.*) oats; (*poet.*) pastoral flute or pipe.

avenáceo, -cea, *a.* oat-like.

avenado, -da, *a.* fickle, inconstant; drained. — *p.p.* [AVENAR].

avenal, *n.m.* oatfield.

avenamiento, *n.m.* draining, drainage.

avenar, *v.t.* to drain or draw off water.

avenate, *n.m.* water-gruel, oatmeal-gruel; (*prov.*) fit of madness.

avenenar, *v.t.* to poison.

avenencia, *n.f.* agreement, stipulation, bargain, contract, arrangement; conformity; *más vale mala avenencia que buena sentencia,* a bad agreement is better than a good lawsuit.

avengo; avenga, *pres. indic.; pres. subj.* [AVENIR].

avenible, *a.* adjustable.

aveníceo, -cea, *a.* oaten.

avenida, *n.f.* flood, inundation; (*fig.*) concurrence of several things; (*prov.*) agreement, concord; avenue; country road or lane; (*mil.*) approaches, way of access.

avenido, -da, *a.* agreed; *bien (mal) avenidos,* living on good (bad) terms. — *p.p.* [AVENIR].

avenidor, -ra, *n.m.f.* mediator, pacificator. — *a.* mediating, pacifying.

avenimiento, *n.m.* convention, accord, arrangement.

avenir, *v.t.* (*pres. indic.* **avengo;** *pret.* **avine;** *pres. subj.* **avenga**) to reconcile. — *v.r.* to settle differences in a friendly way; to join, unite; to accord, agree; to compromise; *avenirse a todo,* to conform to everything; *avenirse con cualquiera,* to agree with anyone.

aventador, -ra, *n.m.f.* (*agric.*) fanner, winnower. — *n.m.* (*agric.*) pitchfork; esparto scoop or fan; (*min.*) pump-valve. — *a.* fanning, winnowing.

aventadura, *n.f.* (*vet.*) wind-gall.

aventajadamente, *adv.* advantageously.

aventajado, -da, *a.* advantageous, profitable; notable, excellent. — *n.m.* (*mil.*) (*obs.*) soldier having additional pay. — *p.p.* [AVENTAJAR].

aventajar, *v.t.* to improve; to meliorate; to prefer; to surpass; *aventajar a todos en los deportes,* to surpass everyone in games or sports. — *v.r.* to exceed, excel, advance, rise.

aventamiento, *n.m.* fanning, moving the air; winnowing.

aventar, *v.t.* (*pres. indic.* **aviento;** *pres. subj.* **aviente**) to fan, winnow; (*coll.*) to expel, drive away; (*Cub.*) to expose sugar to sun and air (cane-mills). — *v.r.* to become inflated; (*coll.*) to escape, run away; (*prov.*) to become tainted; (*naut.*) to burst.

aventura, *n.f.* adventure, enterprise; event, incident; contingency, hazard, risk.

aventuradamente, *adv.* adventurously.

aventurar, *v.t.* to venture, hazard, risk, endanger, expose. — *v.r.* to venture oneself; *quien no se aventura no pasa el mar,* faint heart never won fair lady.

aventureramente, *adv.* by chance, riskily, hazardously.

aventurero, -ra, *a.* adventurous. — *n.m.* adventurer, knight-errant, volunteer; itinerant merchant; free-lance; soldier of fortune. — *n.f.* adventuress.

averdugado, -da, *a.* blotchy, pimply.

avergonzar, *v.t.* (*pres. indic.* **avergüenzo;** *pret.* **avergoncé;** *pres. subj.* **avergüence**) to shame, abash, cover with confusion, make ashamed. — *v.r.* to feel shame, blush for, be ashamed; *avergonzarse a pedir,* to humble oneself to ask; *avergonzarse de pedir,* to be ashamed of asking; *avergonzarse por sus acciones,* to blush for his actions.

avería, *n.f.* damage sustained by merchandise during transport; breakdown; (*naut.*) average; collection of birds, poultry-yard, aviary; *avería gruesa,* general average.

averiado, -da, *a.* damaged, harmed. — *p.p.* [AVERIARSE].

averiarse, *v.r.* to become damaged.

averiguable, *a.* investigable, ascertainable, verifiable.

averiguación, *n.f.* investigation, inquiry, inquest.

averiguadamente, *adv.* certainly, surely, incontestably.

averiguador, -ra, *n.m.f.* searcher, inquirer, investigating, inquiring.

averiguar, *v.t.* to inquire, investigate, ascertain, find out; to pry into; *averiguarse con alguno,* to agree with anyone; *no hay quien se averigüe con Juan,* no one can get on with John.

averío, *n.m.* flock of birds; (*prov.*) beast of burden.

averno, -na, *a.* avernian; infernal. — *n.m.* (*poet.*) hell; (*myth.*) Avernus.

averroismo, *n.m.* Averroism.

averroísta, *n.m.f.* Averroist.

averrugado, -da, *a.* having many pimples or warts.

aversión, *n.f.* aversion, antipathy, opposition, dislike, repugnance; malevolence; apprehension.

avertín, *n.m.* (*med.*) melancholia; (*vet.*) colic (in cattle).

avestruz, *n.m.* ostrich; (*coll.*) ignoramus.

avetado, -da, *a.* veined, streaked.

avetarda, *n.f.* (*zool.*) bustard.

avetoro, *n.m.* (*orn.*) variety of heron.

avezar, *v.t.* (*pret.* **avecé;** *pres. subj.* **avece**) to accustom, get used to, habituate. — *v.r.* to accustom oneself; *avezarse a la vagancia*, to get used to vagrancy.

aviación, *n.f.* aviation.

aviado, -da, *a.* equipped, prepared; financed; (*min.*) enlarged. — *p.p.* [AVIAR].

aviador, -ra, *a.* equipping, providing. — *n.m.* aviator; provider; caulking-auger; (*Chi.*) one who supplies money to work mines; (*Am.*) one who lends money or implements to farmers. — *n.f.* aviatrix.

aviar, *v.t.* to prepare, arrange; to provide articles for a journey; to finance; to accoutre; to hasten the execution of a thing; (*min.*) to enlarge (blast-hole); (*naut.*) to caulk; *estar aviado*, (*fam.*) to be surrounded by difficulties. — *v.r.* to get ready, prepare oneself; *aviarse de ropa*, to rig oneself out; *aviarse para salir*, to dress oneself to go out.

aviciar, *v.t.* (*agric.*) to encourage luxuriant growth; (*prov.*) to manure.

avicultor, -ra, *n.m.f.* aviarist.

avicultura, *n.f.* aviculture.

avichucho, *n.m.* (*slang*) ragamuffin.

ávidamente, *adv.* greedily, covetously.

avidez, *n.f.* covetousness, avidity.

ávido, -da, *a.* greedy, covetous, eager, anxious.

aviejarse, *v.r.* to grow old.

avienta, *n.f.* (*agric.*) winnowing.

aviento, *n.m.* pitchfork.

aviento; **aviente**, *pres. indic.*; *pres. subj.* [AVENTAR].

aviesamente, *adv.* sinistrously, perversely.

avieso, -sa, *a.* irregular, crooked, out of rule; (*fig.*) perverse, mischievous.

avigorar, *v.t.* to invigorate, animate, revive.

avilantarse, *v.r.* to become insolent.

avilantez; **avilanteza**, *n.f.* forwardness, boldness, insolence.

avillanado, -da, *a.* rustic, boorish, mean. — *p.p.* [AVILLANAR].

avillanar, *v.t.* to debase. — *v.r.* to grow mean, abject; to degenerate.

avinado, -da, *a.* wine-coloured; bibulous; wine-soaked (cask).

avinagradamente, *adv.* sourly, harshly.

avinagrado, -da, *a.* vinegary, sour; (*coll.*) harsh-tempered; crabbed, peevish, morose. — *p.p.* [AVINAGRAR].

avinagrar, *v.t.* to sour, make acid. — *v.r.* to become sour.

avine, *pret.* [AVENIR].

avío, *n.m.* preparation, provision; (*prov.*) rations; (*Am.*) money advanced. — *pl.* (*coll.*) equipment, tackle; *avíos de pescar*, fishing-tackle; ¡*al avío*! hurry up! get ready!

avión, *n.m.* (*orn.*) martin, martlet, swift; (*aer.*) aeroplane.

avioneta, *n.f.*) light airplane.

avisadamente, *adv.* prudently, sagaciously, discreetly.

avisado, -da, *a.* prudent, cautious, judicious; expert; sagacious, clear-sighted; *mal avisado*, indiscreet, ill-advised. — *n.m.* (*slang*) judge. — *p.p.* [AVISAR].

avisador, -ra, *n.m.f.* adviser, admonisher; announcer, informer; messenger. — *a.* advising, informing.

avisar, *v.t.* to inform, give notice, announce, acquaint; to advise, admonish; (*slang*) to notice, observe; *avisar con tiempo*, to warn, advise in time.

aviso, *n.m.* information, intelligence, notice; announcement; advertisement; advice, warning; prudence, care, attention; counsel; (*naut.*) advice-boat, despatch-boat; (*slang*) pimp, pander; *andar* or *estar sobre aviso*, to be on one's guard.

avispa, *n.f.* wasp.

avispado, -da, *a.* (*coll.*) lively, brisk, clever, vigorous; stimulated; roused; (*slang*) suspicious, circumspect. — *p.p.* [AVISPAR].

avispar, *v.t.* to whip, spur, lash; (*coll.*) to stimulate, excite, rouse; (*Chi.* and *slang*) to scare, frighten; to spy, investigate. — *v.r.* to fret, become peevish, worry; (*slang*) to become astonished; to rouse oneself, become lively.

avispedar, *v.t.* (*slang*) to look with suspicion, carefully.

avispero, *n.m.* wasps' nest; swarm of wasps; (*med.*) carbuncle; (*coll.*) muddled, troublesome affair; *no quiero meterme en tal avispero*, I prefer not to get involved in this troublesome affair.

avispón, *n.m.* hornet; (*slang*) thief who spies out likely places to rob.

avistar, *v.t.* to descry at a distance. — *v.r.* to have an interview.

avitelado, -da, *a.* parchment-like.

avituallamiento, *n.m.* victualling.

avituallar, *v.t.* (*mil.*) to victual, supply with provisions.

avivadamente, *adv.* in a lively manner, briskly.

avivado, -da, *p.p.* [AVIVAR] enlivened, animated; revived, heightened. — *n.m.* heightening (textile colours); first operation in mirror silvering; pumice rubbing before gilding (bronze statues); jewellery's final polish; (*art*) final touch.

avivador, -ra, *n.m.f.* enlivener, hastener. — *n.m.* (*carp.*) fluting-plane; rabbet-plane; (*arch.*) ornamental line; (*arch.*) quirk; (*prov.*) perforated paper for raising silkworms. — *a.* enlivening, reviving.

avivamiento, *n.m.* enlivening, quickness.

avivar, *v.t.* to quicken, enliven, encourage, hasten, animate; to heat, inflame; to revive, vivify; to heighten colours; (*carp.*) to rabbet; *avivar el ojo*, to be watchful; *avivar el paso*, to hasten one's steps. — *v.i.*, *v.r.* to hatch, be hatched (silkworm eggs); to revive, cheer up, grow gay.

avizor, -ra, *a.* watchful. — *n.m.* spy; (*pl.*) (*slang*) eyes; *estar ojo avizor*, to keep a sharp look-out, be on the alert.

avizorador, -ra, *a.* watching, spying. — *n.m.f.* watcher, spy.

avizorar, *v.t.* to watch attentively, spy.

avocación, *n.f.*; **avocamiento**, *n.m.* (*law*) evocation; (*law*) removing a lawsuit to a higher court.

avocar, *v.t.* (*pret.* **avoqué**; *pres. subj.* **avoque**) (*law*) to evoke.

avoceta, *n.f.* (*orn.*) avocet, a wading bird.

avolcanado, -da, *a.* volcanic.

avucasta, *n.f.* (*orn.*) [AVUTARDA].

avugo, *n.m.* (*bot.*) fruit of *avuguero*, very small early pear.

avuguero, *n.m.* (*bot.*) kind of pear-tree.

avulsión, *n.f.* (*surg.*) extirpation.

avutarda, *n.f.* (*orn.*) bustard, wild turkey.

avutardado, -da, *a.* bustard-like.

¡**ax**! *interj.* exclamation of pain.

axil, *a.* axial; (*zool.*) axillary.

axila, *n.f.* (*bot.*) axilla; (*med.*) armpit.

axilar, *a.* (*bot., zool.*) axillar, axillary.

axinita, *n.f.* (*min.*) axinite.

axioma, *n.m.* axiom, maxim.

axiomáticamente, *adv.* axiomatically.

axiomático, -ca, *a.* axiomatic, axiomatical.

axiómetro, *n.m.* (*naut.*) axiometer.

axis, *n.m.* (*anat.*) axis, second vertebra.

axo, *n.m.* (*Per.*) woollen garment worn by Indian women.

axoideo, -dea, *a.* (*anat.*) axoid, axoidean.

¡ay! *interj.* alas! followed by *de* denotes fear, pain, commiseration, threat; *¡ay de mí!* alas, poor me! *¡ay de los vencidos!* woe to the vanquished! *¡ay del que me ofenda!* let my offender beware! — *n.m.* sigh, moan; *tiernos ayes*, tender sighs; *estar en un ay*, to be in pain.

aya, *n.f.* governess, instructress.

ayacuá, *n.m.* (*Arg.*) small devil in Indian folklore.

ayahuasa, *n.f.* (*Ec.*) narcotic plant used by Indians.

ayate, *n.m.* (*Mex.*) cloth made of maguey fibre.

ayear, *v.i.* to wail, bemoan.

ayeaye, *n.m.* small lemur from Madagascar.

ayecahue, *n.m.* (*Chi.*) nonsense, absurdity.

ayer, *adv.* yesterday; (*fig.*) formerly; lately, not long ago; *de ayer acá, de ayer a hoy*, from yesterday to this moment; not long ago. — *n.m.* time just elapsed; *de ayer a hoy*, from yesterday to today, in the immediate past.

ayermado, -da, *a.* deserted, desolate. — *p.p.* [AYERMAR].

ayermar, *v.t.* to make waste, desert; to demolish, raze.

¡aymé! *interj.* (*poet.*) woe is me!

ayo, -ya, *n.m.f.* tutor, teacher.

ayocote, *n.m.* (*Mex.*) kidney bean.

ayocuantoto, *n.m.* (*Mex.*) a mountain bird.

ayote, *n.m.* (*Am.*) pumpkin.

ayotera, *n.f.* (*Am.*) pumpkin, gourd plant.

ayúa, *n.f.* (*Am.*) tree of the Rutaceæ family.

ayuda, *n.f.* help, aid, assistance, comfort; water-carrier (shepherds); support, succour, friendship; injection; syringe, enema, clyster; (*naut.*) preventer-rope; *ayuda de cámara*, valet; *ayuda de costa*, financial help; gratification; *ayuda de parroquia*, chapel of ease; *ayuda de vecino*, (*coll.*) outside, foreign help.

ayudador, -ra, *a.* helping, assisting. — *n.m.f.* assistant, helper; chief shepherd.

ayudanta, *n.f.* woman assistant.

ayudante, *n.m.* (*mil.*) adjutant; (*mil.*) aide-de-camp; assistant. — *a.* helping, assisting.

ayudantía, *n.f.* adjutancy; office of adjutant.

ayudar, *v.t.* to aid, help, favour, assist, succour, protect. — *v.r.* to adopt measures to attain success; to avail oneself of help; *ayudar a misa*, to serve at Mass; *a quien madruga, Dios le ayuda*, the early bird catches the worm; *ayúdate, y ayudarte he*, God helps those who help themselves; *ayudar en un apuro*, to come to the rescue, to help in need.

ayuga, *n.f.* (*bot.*) ground-pine; (*bot.*) summer cypress goose-foot.

ayunador, -ra; ayunante, *n.m.f., a.* one who fasts; who observes fast-days.

ayunar, *v.i.* to fast; *ayunar después de harto*, (*coll.*) to fast after a good meal; *harto ayuna quien mal come*, a bad meal is no better than fasting; *ayunarle a uno*, (*coll.*) to fear, respect someone.

ayuno, -na, *a.* fasting, abstemious; (*fig.*) ignorant. — *n.m.* fast, abstinence; *estoy ayuno*, I have not yet broken my fast; *quedarse en ayuno* (or *en ayunas*), (*coll.*) to be ignorant of an affair, to miss the point.

ayunque, *n.m.* anvil.

ayuntador, -ra, *n.m.f.* one who unites. — *a.* uniting, joining.

ayuntamiento, *n.m.* union, joint; corporation or body of magistrates in cities or towns; municipal government; *casa de ayuntamiento*, town-hall, guild-hall; carnal copulation.

ayuso, *adv.* below.

ayustar, *v.t.* (*naut.*) to splice.

ayuste, *n.m.* (*naut.*) splice, splicing; scarf, scarfing.

azabachado, -da, *a.* black as jet.

azabache, *n.m.* (*min.*) jet; (*orn.*) titmouse. *pl.* trinkets of jet.

azabara, *n.f.* (*bot.*) common aloe.

azacán, -na, *a.* toiling, labouring. — *n.m.* water-carrier; labourer; *andar*, or *estar hecho, un azacán*, (*coll.*) to toil, labour, be extremely busy.

azacaya, *n.f.* (*prov.*) conduit of water, water-pipe.

azache, *a.* silk of an inferior quality.

azada, *n.f.* (*agric.*) spade, hoe.

azadada, *n.f.; azadazo*, *n.m.* blow with a spade or hoe; pickaxe.

azadilla, *n.f.* gardener's hoe.

azadón, *n.m.* mattock, hoe; *azadón de peto* or *de pico*, pickaxe.

azadonada, *n.f.* blow with pickaxe or hoe; *a la primera azadonada*, (*coll.*) lucky first stroke; at first sight; at once.

azadonar, *v.t.* to dig with a spade, hoe or pickaxe.

azadonazo, *n.m.* stroke with a mattock.

azadonero, *n.m.* digger.

azafata, *n.f.* lady of the queen's wardrobe.

azafate, *n.m.* low, flat-bottomed basket or tray.

azafatero, *n.m.* tray maker or seller.

azafrán, *n.m.* (*bot.*) saffron; stigma of this plant; (*paint.*) saffron colour; *azafrán bastardo, romí* or *romín*, safflower or bastard saffron; *azafrán de Marte*, (*chem.*) iron rust; *azafrán del timón*, after-piece of the rudder.

azafranado, -da, *a.* saffron-coloured; saffrony. — *p.p.* [AZAFRANAR].

azafranal, *n.m.* plantation of saffron.

azafranamiento, *n.m.* saffron-dyeing.

azafranar, *v.t.* to tinge, mix, dye with saffron.

azafranero, -ra, *n.m.f.* dealer in saffron.

azafranina, *n.f.* (*chem.*) safranin.

azagadero; azagador, *n.m.* path or pass for cattle.

azagaya, *n.f.* javelin, spear, half-pike.

azagayada, *n.f.* cast of a javelin.

azagor, *n.m.* verdigris.

azahar, *n.m.* orange, lemon or citron flower; *agua de azahar*, orange-flower water.

azainadamente, *adv.* perfidiously.

azainado, -da, *a.* (*prov.*) perfidious, treacherous. — *p.p.* [AZAINAR].

azainador, -ra, a. (prov.) treacherous. —
n.m. (prov.) traitor. — n.f. traitress.
azainamiento, n.m. (prov.) perfidy, treachery.
azainar, v.t. (prov.) to make treacherous. —
v.r. (prov.) to turn traitor.
azalá, n.m. Mohammedan prayer.
azalea, n.f. (bot.) azalea.
azamboa, n.f. fruit of a kind of citron-tree.
azamboero; azamboo, n.m. (bot.) kind of
citron-tree.
azanahoriate; azanoriate, n.m. preserved
carrot; (coll.) flattery.
azanca, n.f. (min.) subterranean spring.
azandar, n.m. (bot., prov.) sandalwood.
azanoria, n.f. carrot; [ZANAHORIA].
azaque, n.m. tax paid by Moslems.
azar, n.m. unforeseen disaster, accident, disappointment; (ball game) impediment,
obstruction; hazard, chance; unfortunate
card or throw at dice; cushion sides of a
billiard-pocket; echar azar, to be unlucky, to
turn out badly.
azarado, -da, a. crooked; spoiled; alarmed. —
p.p. [AZARAR].
azarandar, v.t. (agric.) to winnow, sift.
azarar, v.t. (coll.) to perturb, trouble. — v.i.
to turn out badly; to become anxious,
alarmed. — v.r. to get rattled, bewildered.
azarbe, n.m. irrigation trench or drain.
azarbeta, n.f. small irrigation trench.
azarcón, n.m. red oxide of lead; (paint.)
vermilion; bright orange colour; (prov.)
earthen pot.
azarja, n.f. instrument for winding raw silk.
azarolla, n.f. (bot.) haw; (prov.) fruit of the
true service-tree.
azarollo, n.m. (bot., prov.) true service-tree.
azarosamente, adv. unfortunately, hazardously.
azaroso, -sa, a. unlucky, unfortunate.
azaúcho, n.m. (bot.) wild fig.
azaya, n.f. (bot., prov.) spike, French lavender.
azcón, n.m.; azcona, n.f. dart, javelin.
azemar, v.t. to fit; to smooth.
azenoria, n.f. (bot.) carrot.
azi, n.m. curd of milk and vinegar used for
cheese-making.
azímico, -ca, a. opposed to fermentation.
azimitas, n.m.pl. Azymites.
ázimo, -ma, a. azymous, unleavened.
azimut, n.m. (astron.) azimuth.
azimutal, a. azimuthal.
aznacho; aznallo, n.m. (bot.) Scotch fir;
species of rest-harrow.
azoado, -da, a. nitrogenous. — p.p. [AZOAR].
azoar, v.t. (chem.) to azotize.
azoato, n.m. (chem.) nitrate.
azocar, v.t. (naut.) to tighten; (Cub.) to over-
tighten.
ázoe, n.m. (chem.) nitrogen.
azofaifa; azufaifa, n.f. (bot.) jujube berry.
azofaifo; azufaifo, n.m. (bot.) jujube-tree.
azófar, n.m. latten, brass.
azofra, n.f. personal assistance; (prov.) ridge-
band of harness.
azofrar, v.i. (prov.) to assist personally.
azogadamente, adv. (coll.) quickly, restlessly.
azogado, -da, a. (coll.) restless, trembling;
quick-silvered, tinned; slaked. — p.p.
[AZOGAR].
azogamiento, n.m. tinning; slaking lime;
agitation, trepidation; quicksilvering.

azogar, v.t. (pret. azogué; pres. subj. azogue)
to quicksilver; to slake lime. — v.r. to become salivated; to be affected by mercury
vapours; (coll.) to become agitated, perturbed.
azogue, n.m. (min.) quicksilver; market-
place; ship carrying quicksilver (to Spanish
America); ser un azogue, tener azogue en las
venas, to be restless or vivacious.
azoguejo, n.m. small market-place.
azoguería, n.f. (min.) amalgamating works.
azoguero, n.m. (min.) amalgamator.
azoico, -ca, a. (geol.) azoic; (chem.) nitric.
azolar, v.t. (pres. indic. azuelo; pres. subj.
azuele) (carp.) to adze.
azolvar, v.t. to obstruct water-conduits. —
v.r. to become obstructed, choked.
azolve, n.m. (Mex.) sludge obstructing a water-
conduit.
azor, n.m. (orn.) goshawk; (slang) thief.
azoradamente, adv. uneasily, anxiously.
azorado, -da, a. uneasy; distrustful. — p.p.
[AZORAR].
azoramiento, n.m. trepidation, tremor, uneasiness, confusion.
azorar, v.t. to terrify, confound, frighten; to
prompt, agitate, incite. — v.r. to become
anxious, agitated, excited; to tremble convulsively.
azorero, n.m. (slang) accomplice of a thief; receiver of stolen goods.
azorrado, -da, a. fox-like; drowsy, sleepy;
(naut.) water-logged. — p.p. [AZORRARSE].
azorramiento, n.m. heaviness of the head,
drowsiness.
azorrarse, v.t. to become drowsy from heaviness; (naut.) to pitch through being waterlogged.
azotable, a. deserving a whipping.
azotacalles, n.m.f. (coll.) street-lounger, idler.
azotada, n.f. severe whipping or spanking.
azotado, -da, a. whipped; variegated (flowers).
— n.m. publicly whipped criminal; (obs.)
flagellant, one who lashes himself for mortification. — p.p. [AZOTAR].
azotador, -ra, n.m.f. whipper. — a. whipping.
azotaina; azotina, n.f. (coll.) drubbing,
flogging.
azotalengua, n.f. (bot., prov.) goose-grass.
azotamiento, n.m. whipping.
azotaperros, n.m. church beadle appointed to
enforce silence and throw out dogs.
azotar, v.t. to whip, lash, horsewhip, flagellate; to afflict, punish; azotar las calles, to
lounge about the streets; azotar el aire, to
act to no purpose; el mar azota los peñascos,
the sea lashes the rocks.
azotazo, n.m. severe lash or spank.
azote, n.m. whip, lash; spank; (fig.) calamity,
affliction; (fig.) scourge (person). — pl. (obs.)
public whipping; besar el azote, to kiss the
rod, resign oneself to punishment; si buenos
azotes me daban, bien caballero me iba, if
they whipped me well, I went at least
mounted like a gentleman (of rogues who,
mounted on an ass, were whipped through
the streets); no salir de azotes y galeras,
never to prosper; azotes y galeras, plain,
unvaried food.
azotea, n.f. flat roof of a house; platform.
azótico, -ca, a. (chem.) azotic.
azozobrar, v.t. to fill with anguish; to worry
unduly.

azre, *n.m.* (*bot.*) maple-tree.

azteca, *n.m.f.*, *a.* Aztec. — *n.m.* Aztec language.

azúcar, *n.m.f.* sugar; *azúcar blanco* (*-ca*), *de flor, de florete, refino* (*-na*), first quality refined sugar; *azúcar cande, candi, piedra,* candy; *azúcar de leche,* (*chem.*) milk-sugar; *azúcar de lustre,* caster sugar; *azúcar de pilón,* loaf-sugar; *azúcar de plomo,* (*chem.*) sugar of lead; *azúcar de redoma,* crystallized sugar in syrup-jars; *azúcar de Saturno,* (*chem.*) sal Saturni; *azúcar mascabado* (*-da*), *quebrado* (*-da*), *muscovado* (*-da*), unclarified sugar; *azúcar moreno* (*-na*), *negro* (*-gra*), *terciado* (*-da*), brown sugar; *azúcar en terrón,* lump-sugar; *azúcar en polvo,* granulated, caster sugar ; *azúcar y canela,* sorrel-grey (horse); *azúcar rosado* (*-da*), rose-coloured *azucarillo.*

azucarado, -da, *a.* sugared; sugary, sweet; (*coll.*) affable, pleasing. — *n.m.* cosmetic. — *p.p.* [AZUCARAR].

azucarar, *v.t.* to sugar, sweeten; to ice or coat with sugar; (*fig.*) to conciliate with soft words; (*Mex.*) crystallization of conserves.

azucarero, -ra, *a.* relating to sugar. — *n.m.* foreman in sugar factory; (*orn.*) tropical bird. — *n.m.f.* sugar-basin.

azucarí, *a.* (*prov.*) sugary, sweet (fruits).

azucarillo, *n.m.* sweetmeat made of syrup, white of egg and lemon juice; (*theat.*) cut in orchestral piece; (*mil., slang*) shoe.

azucena, *n.f.* (*bot.*) white lily.

azucenal, *n.m.* white lily nursery.

azuche, *n.m.* (*engin.*) pile ferrule.

azud, *n.f.*; **azuda,** *n.f.* dam with a sluice or floodgate; Persian wheel for irrigation.

azuela, *n.f.* adze; *azuela de construcción,* shipwright's adze; *azuela curva,* hollow adze.

azuelo; azuele, *pres. ind.; pres. subj.* [AZOLAR].

azufaifa, azufeifa, *n.f.* jujube berry.

azufaifo, azufeifo, *n.m.* jujube-tree.

azufrado, -da, *a.* sulphureous; sulphuretted; sulphury. — *p.p.* [AZUFRAR].

azufrador, *n.m.* sulphurator, machine for drying and bleaching linen; instrument for sulphuring vines.

azufral, *n.m.*; **azufrera,** *n.f.* sulphur mine.

azuframiento, *n.m.* sulphuration; sulphurization.

azufrar, *v.t.* to sulphurate; to sulphurize.

azufre, *n.m.* sulphur.

azufrín, *n.m.* sulphurous wick or candle.

azufrón, *n.m.* (*min.*) powder pyrites.

azufroso, -sa, *a.* sulphureous.

azul, *a.* blue. — *n.m.* blue; *azul celeste,* sky blue; *azul oscuro,* dark blue; *azul de Prusia,* Prussian blue; *azul turquí,* indigo.

azulado, -da, *a.* blue, bluish. — *p.p.* [AZULAR].

azulador, -ra, *n.m.f.*, *a.* one who (that which) dyes blue.

azulamiento, *n.m.* act of dyeing blue.

azulaque, *n.m.* (*hydrost.*) packing stuff; (*naut.*) stuff for caulking bottom of ship.

azular, *v.t.* to dye or colour blue.

azulear, *v.i.* to have a bluish shade; to show blue.

azulejado, -da, *a.* tiled. — *p.p.* [AZULEJAR].

azulejar, *v.t.* to tile.

azulejería, *n.f.* tile-works; tiling.

azulejero, *n.m.* tiler.

azulejo, *n.m.* glazed tile; (*bot.*) cornflower; (*orn.*) bee-eater.

azulete, *n.m.* slight tinge of blue given to linen to make it look white.

azulino, -na, *a.* bluish.

azuloso, -sa, *a.* blue, bluish.

azumar, *v.t.* to dye the hair.

azumbar, *n.m.* (*bot.*) star-headed water-plantain; spikenard; storax-tree gum.

azumbrado, -da, *a.* measured by *azumbres*; (*coll.*) inebriate.

azumbre, *n.f.* liquid measure of four pints.

azuquero, *n.m.* (*prov.*) sugar-basin.

azur, *n.m.*, *a.* (*her.*) azure.

azurita, *n.f.* (*min.*) azurite.

azut, *n.m.* (*prov.*) [AZUD].

azutero, *n.m.* (*prov.*) sluice-master.

azuzador, -ra, *n.m.f.* instigator. — *a.* inciting, instigating.

azuzar, *v.t.* (*pret.* **azucé;** *pres. subj.* **azuce**) to hallo; to set dogs on to; (*fig.*) to incite.

azuzón, -na, *n.m.f.* instigator.

B

B, b, *n.f.* the second letter of the Spanish alphabet; pronounced as a plosive (similarly to English *b*) after a pause and after a nasal consonant; pronounced as a bi-labial fricative (a sound with no exact correspondence in English; rather softer than the English *b*, it is produced by joining the lips without pressure) in all other positions; *saber algo b por b*, or *b por c,* or *c por b,* to know something in all its details.

baba, *n.f.* drivel, spittle; *se le cae la baba,* he raves about it; he is rather silly.

babibuí, *n.m.* (*Am.*) mocking bird.

babada, *n.f.* muscles about the knee of quadrupeds; thigh-bone.

babadero; babador, *n.m.* bib, chin-cloth.

babaza, *n.f.* slime; slug.

babazorro, *n.m.* (*coll., prov.*) clown, ill-bred man. — *a.* (*prov.*) uncouth, rustic.

babear, *v.i.* to dribble, slaver; (*coll.*) to court, woo with excessive gallantry.

babel, *n.m.f.* Babel; (*coll.*) babel; confusion, disorder.

babeo, *n.m.* drivelling, slavering.

babera, *n.f.* beaver of a helmet; bib.

babero, *n.m.* bib, chin-cloth.

baberol, *n.m.* beaver of a helmet.

Babia, *n.f.* ; *estar en Babia,* (*coll.*) to be absent in mind, distrait.

babieca, *n.m.f.*, *a.* ignorant, stupid (person); idiot.

Babilonia, *n.f.* (*coll.*) babel, crowd, uproar, confusion.

babilónico, -ca, *a.* Babylonian; gigantic, magnificent; (*coll.*) noisy.

babilonio, -nia, *n.m.f.*, *a.* Babylonian.

babilla, *n.f.* [BABADA]; thin skin about the flanks of cattle.

babirusa, *n.m.* (*zool.*) babiroussa.

bable, *n.m.* Asturian dialect.

babón, -na, *a.* [BABOSO].

babor, *n.m.* (*naut.*) port, larboard; *a babor todo,* hard a-port; *de babor a estribor,* athwart ship.

babosa, *n.f.* slug; (*prov.*) young onion; (*slang*) silk; (*agric.*) vine which produces malmsey wine.

babosear, *v.t.* to dribble, slaver. — *v.r.* (*coll.*) to woo, court with exaggerated gallantry.

baboseo, *n.m.* (*coll.*) infatuation.

babosilla, *n.f.* small slug.

babosillo, -lla; babosuelo, -uela, *a.* drivelling, slavering; (*coll.*) spoony.

baboso, -sa, *n.m.f.* driveller, slaverer. — *a.* drivelling, slavering; (*coll.*) impudent (child); (*coll.*) spoony, over-affectionate.

babucha, *n.f.* Turkish heelless slipper.

babuino, *n.m.* (*zool.*) baboon; (*med.*) pustule on lips; (*fig.*) grotesque figure; dwarf; idiot; coward.

baca, *n.f.* top of a stage-coach; leather cover for a stage-coach; awning for a wagon; (*mech.*) press belting; chain-link; (*min.*) pearl-like metal; (*bot.*) berry; (*orn.*) African falcon or eagle.

bacalada, *n.f.* whole dried codfish.

bacalao; bacallao, *n.m.* codfish; (*coll.*) skinny person; *te conozco bacalao, aunque vengas 'disfrazao'* (*disfrazado*), (*coll.*) you can't take *me* in (frequently shortened to *te conozco*); *cortar el bacalao,* to be master, take the upper hand.

bacalar, *n.m.* (*prov.*) early fig.

bacallar, *n.m.* rustic.

bacanal, *a.* bacchanal. — *n.f.* (*fig.*) orgy. — *n.f.pl.* bacchanals, bacchanalia.

bacante, *n.f.* bacchante; (*coll.*) low drunken woman.

bácara; bácaris, *n.f.* (*bot.*) common clary.

bacará; bacarrat, *n.m.* baccarat.

bacelar, *n.m.* arbour with grape-vines.

bacera, *n.f.* (*vet.*) swelling of the belly.

baceta, *n.f.* (*obs.*) basset; stock (card-playing).

bacía, *n.f.* metal basin; shaving-dish; barber's basin; wash-pot.

bacífero, -ra, *a.* (*bot.*) bacciferous.

baciforme, *a.* (*bot.*) bacciform.

báciga, *n.f.* a game played with three cards.

bacilar, *a.* (*biol.*) bacillary; (*min.*) of coarse fibre.

baciliforme, *a.* bacilliform.

bacilo, *n.m.* bacillus, bacterium.

bacillar, *n.m.* new vineyard; [BACELAR].

bacín, *n.m.* chamber-utensil; alms-dish; (*coll.*) despicable man.

bacina, *n.f.* (*prov.*) poor-box.

bacinada, *n.f.* filth, slops; (*coll.*) despicable action.

bacinejo, *n.m.* small chamber-utensil.

bacinero, -ra, *n.m.f.* collector of oblations in church.

bacineta, *n.f.* small bowl; offertory box; *bacineta de arma de fuego,* pan of a gun-lock.

bacinete, *n.m.* basnet, bacinet, basinet; (*anat.*) pelvis.

bacinica; bacinilla, *n.f.* small chamber-utensil; small alms-dish.

bacívoro, -ra, *a.* (*zool.*) baccivorous.

baconiano, -na, *a.* Baconian.

bacteria, *n.f.* bacterium.

bacteriología, *n.f.* bacteriology.

bacteriológico, -ca, *a.* bacteriological.

bacteriólogo, -ga, *n.m.f.* bacteriologist.

bactris, *n.m.* (*bot.*) South American palm.

báculo, *n.m.* walking-stick, staff; (*fig.*) support, relief, comfort, aid; *báculo pastoral,* bishop's crozier; *José es el báculo de mi vejez,* Joseph is the comfort of my old age.

bache, *n.m.* deep hole in street or road; sweating place (for sheep before shearing).

bachear, *v.t.* to repair ruts in roads.

bacheo, *n.m.* road repair.

bachiller; bachillero, -ra, *n.m.f.* bachelor (i.e. one who has passed the first university examination, corresponding to the matriculation of an English university); babbler, prater; *es un(a) bachiller (a),* he (she) is an officious fraud; *bachiller en artes, burro en todas partes,* a bachelor in arts but an ass in everything else (a student's saying). — *a.* garrulous, loquacious.

bachilleramiento, *n.m.* conferring or obtaining the degree of bachelor.

bachillerar, *v.t.* to confer the degree of bachelor. — *v.r.* to graduate as bachelor.

bachillerato, *n.m.* baccalaureate.

bachillerear, *v.i.* (*coll.*) to prattle, babble.

bachillerejo, -ja, *n.m.f.* talkative little person.

bachillería, *n.f.* (*coll.*) prattle, babble.

bada, *n.f.* rhinoceros.

badajada, *n.f.* stroke of the clapper (of bell); (*coll.*) idle talk.

badajear, *v.i.* (*coll.*) to chatter.

badajo, *n.m.* clapper of a bell; (*coll.*) idle talker.

badajuelo, *n.m.* small clapper (of bell).

badal, *n.m.* (*obs.*) muzzle; (*vet.*) barnacle, twitch; (*prov.*) shoulder and ribs of butcher's meat.

badallar, *v.i.* (*prov.*) to yawn.

badán, *n.m.* (*anat.*) trunk of a body.

badana, *n.f.* dressed sheep-skin, basil; *zurrar a uno la badana,* to give someone a flogging or dressing-down; to insult.

badano, *n.m.* (*carp.*) chisel.

badaza, *n.f.* cord for lacing bonnets to sails.

badea, *n.f.* (*bot.*) bad melon or water-melon; insipid yellowish cucumber; (*coll.*) dull, insipid fellow; (*coll.*) insubstantial thing.

badelico, *n.m.* (*slang*) fire-shovel.

badén, *n.m.* channel made by rain-water; catch-drain.

badeón, *n.m.* (*bot.*) melon.

baderna, *n.f.* (*naut.*) cable.

badernón, *n.f.* (*naut.*) large cable.

badián, *n.m.*; **badiana,** *n.f.* (*bot.*) Indian anise; aniseed.

badil, *n.m.*; **badila,** *n.f.* fire-shovel; *dar con la badila en los nudillos,* to scold, reprehend, rebuff.

badilazo, *n.m.* blow with a fire-shovel.

badina, *n.f.* (*prov.*) puddle.

badomía, *n.f.* nonsense, absurdity.

badulacada, (*Chi., Per.*) *n.f.* knavish action.

badulaque, *n.m.* (*obs.*) cosmetic; (*obs.*) ragout of stewed livers; (*coll.*) unreliable fellow.

bafea, *n.f.* waste, rubbish, filth.

bafear, *v.i.* (*prov.*) to emit fumes or vapour.

bafetas, *n.f.pl.* (*com.*) white cotton cloth, indiana.

baga, *n.f.* (*prov.*) rope to tie burdens on the backs of beasts; little head of flax; (*Cub.*) (*bot.*) tree of the Annonaceæ family.

bagacera, *n.f.* (*Cub.*) place in sugar-mills where the bagasse is dried in the sun.

bagaje, *n.m.* (*mil.*) baggage; beast of burden; *bagaje mayor,* horse, mule; *bagaje menor,* donkey; (*Gallicism*) luggage.

bagajero, *n.m.* driver of military baggage.

bagar, *v.i.* to yield the seed (flax).

bagarino, *n.m.* free sailor in a galley as opposed to a galley-slave.

bagasa, *n.f.* prostitute, harlot.

bagatela, *n.f.* bagatelle, trifle; (*Chi.*) bagatelle billiard table and game.

bagazo, *n.m.* bagasse; oil-cake; husk (flax); remains of sugar-canes, grapes, olives, etc., after pressing.

bago, *n.m.* (*prov.*) payment.

bagre, *n.m.* (*Am.*) fresh-water fish.

bagual, *n.m.*, *a.* (*Arg.*) wild (horses and cattle); (*Chi.*) big, lusty or stupid(man).

bagualada, *n.f.* (*Arg.*) drove of *bagual* animals.

baguarí, *n.m.* (*Arg.*) species of stork.

¡ bah ! *interj.* bah!

baharí, *n.m.* (*orn.*) sparrow-hawk.

bahía, *n.f.* bay, harbour.

bahorrina, *n.f.* (*coll.*) slops; collection of filthy things; (*coll.*) rabble.

bahuno, -na, *a.* base, vile.

baila, *n.f.* (*ichth.*) sea-trout.

bailable, *a.* danceable. — *n.m.* ballet.

bailadero, *n.m.* public dancing-place.

bailador,-ra, *n.m.f.* dancer. — *n.m.* (*slang*) thief.

bailar, *v.i.* to dance, spin; to be roused (emotions). — *v.t.* to dance; (*slang*) to steal; *bailar el agua adelante*, to dance attendance; *bailar al son que se toca* or *que tocan*, to do as others do; *bailar a compás*, to dance in time; *bailar el corazón de alegría*, to experience great joy.

bailarín, -ina, *n.m.f.* professional dancer. — *n.m.* (*zool.*) small water coleopter. — *a.* dancing.

baile, *n.m.* dance, dancing, ballet, ball; (*prov.* & *Andorra*) bailiff; (*slang*) thief; *baile de candil, de botón* or *de cascabel gordo*, rustic dance; *baile de disfraces, máscaras*, or *trajes*, fancy-dress ball, masquerade; *baile de cuenta* or *de figuras*, figure or square dance; *baile de San Vito*, (*med.*) chorea, St. Vitus's dance; *baile serio*, formal dance; *puede el baile continuar*, a bitter phrase condemnatory of politics, customs, etc. (*cf.* Eng.: 'the same old game').

bailete, *n.m.* short ballet.

bailía, *n.f.*; **bailiazgo**, *n.m.* bailiwick.

bailiaje, *n.m.* commandery of the Order of Malta.

bailío, *n.m.* knight commander of the Order of Malta.

bailotear, *v.i.* (*coll.*) to dance frequently and ungracefully.

bailoteo, *n.m.* ungraceful dancing, jigging.

baivel, *n.m.* square bevel used by stonemasons.

bajá, *n.m.* pasha, bashaw.

baja, *n.f.* fall of price; [ALEMANDA]; (*mil.*) casualty; casualty list; vacancy; *dar baja*, to fall in value; *dar de baja*, (*mil.*) to report as casualty; to remove from membership of a society; *darse de baja*, (*fig.*) to retire from business or profession; to resign voluntarily membership of a society; *jugar a la baja*, (*com.*) to bear, speculate on a fall; *ser baja*, (*mil.*) to cease belonging to a corps; *estar en baja*, to be on the decline or wane; to droop; to fail, diminish.

bajada, *n.f.* descent, slope; inclination of an arch; *bajada de agua*, rain-water pipe.

bajadizo, -za, *a.* descending, sloping easily.

bajado, -da, *a.* lowered, fallen, reduced, diminished; *bajado del cielo*, heaven-sent; excellent; unexpected. — *p.p.* [BAJAR].

bajalato, *n.m.* office or territory of a pasha.

bajamanero, *n.m.* (*slang*) pickpocket.

bajamano, *n.m.* (*slang*) shop-thief; shoplifter. — *adv.* (*slang*) under the arm.

bajamar, *n.f.* low water, low tide.

bajamente, *adv.* basely, meanly, abjectly.

bajar, *v.i.* to descend, go or come down, fall, alight; to go down in price, lower, lessen, diminish; *bajar a la arena*, to take up the cudgels; *bajar de ley el oro*, to alloy gold; *bajar al jardín*, to go down to the garden; *bajar a la mina*, to go down the mine; *bajar de la torre*, to come down from the tower; *bajar hacia el valle*, to go down towards the valley; *bajar por la escalera*, to go downstairs; *bajar de punto*, to decline, decay; *bajar la tierra*, to lay out the land. — *v.t.* to lower, let down; to bring or take down; to reduce; to humble; *bajar el punto*, to temper; *bajar los humos*, to become more humane; *bajar los ojos*, to cast one's eyes down; to be ashamed; *bajar la cabeza*, to bow one's head; to humble oneself; to obey without objection; *bajar la voz*, to speak softly; *bajar las orejas*, to humble oneself; to yield. — *v.r.* to crouch, grovel; to stoop; to dismount, get down; to humble oneself.

bajareque, *n.m.* (*Cub.*) ruinous hut, hovel or cabin; (*Guat.*, *Hond.*) lath-and-mud for walls.

bajel, *n.m.* (*naut.*) ship, boat, vessel.

bajelero, *n.m.* owner, master of a vessel.

bajero, -ra, *a.* (*prov.*) lower, under; *sábana bajera*, under-sheet.

bajete, *n.m.* short person; (*mus.*) baritone, counterpoint exercise.

bajeza, *n.f.* meanness; vile action; (*fig.*) lowliness, lowness; fawning; *bajeza de ánimo*, weakness of mind; *bajeza de nacimiento*, meanness of birth.

bajial, *n.m.* (*Per.*) marsh.

bajillo, *n.m.* (*prov.*) stand-cask for wine.

bajío, *n.m.* shoal, sand-bank, flat; (*Am.*) lowland; *dar en un bajío*, (*fig.*) to meet with a grave obstacle.

bajista, *n.m.* (*com.*) bear (of stocks).

bajito, -ta, *a.* very low. — *adv.* softly, quietly (voice).

bajo, -ja, *a.* short, low, shallow; inferior; downcast; dull, faint; (*fig.*) humble, despicable, abject; (*fig.*) common, vulgar, coarse; *bajo de cuerpo*, low in stature; *bajo en su estilo*, vulgar in his style; *cuarto bajo*, ground-floor room; *bajo de ley*, debased, alloyed; *Los Países Bajos*, the Netherlands; *con los ojos bajos*, with downcast eyes; *azul bajo*, dull blue; *sentimientos bajos*, sordid, vulgar sentiments; *hablar bajo*, or *en voz baja*, to speak in a low voice. — *n.m.* deep place; shoal, sand-bank; (*mus.*) bass (voice, instrument, player, score); (*pl.*) lower portion of feminine undergarments; hoofs; ground floor; *bajo de arena*, sand-bank; *bajo relieve*, bas-relief.

bajo, *adv.* below. — *prep.* under, beneath; *por lo bajo*, secretly, dissimulatingly; *bajo mano*, underhand, secretly; *bajo condición*, conditionally; *bajo pena de muerte*, on pain of death; *bajo palabra de caballero*, on the word of a gentleman; *bajo techado*, sheltered, protected; *bajo tutela*, under the care of a guardian.

bajoca, *n.f.* (*prov.*, *bot.*) French bean; (*prov.*) dead silkworm.
bajocar, *n.m.* (*prov.*) plot of French beans.
bajón, *n.m.* (*mus.*) bassoon; bassoon-player; (*coll.*) great reverse, decline (in health, fortune, etc.).
bajonazo, *n.m.* blow with a bassoon; discordant sound of same; (*bullfight*) low thrust with the sword.
bajoncillo, *n.m.* fagottino, descant bassoon.
bajonista, *n.m.* bassoon-player.
bajuelo, -la, *a.* lowish, shortish.
bajuno, -na, *a.* vile, low, contemptible.
bajura, *n.f.* shortness; lowland.
bal, *n.m.* (*slang*) hair.
bala, *n.f.* ball, bullet, shot; sweetmeat; bale; wax ball filled with water or perfume used in carnival; printers' inking-ball; paper packet of ten reams; *bala de cadena*, or *encadenada*, chain-shot; *bala enramada*, bar-shot; *bala fría*, spent bullet; *bala perdida*, stray bullet; *bala roja*, red-hot incendiary ball; *balas de metralla*, grape-shot; *bala rasa*, cannon-ball; *como una bala*, with immense velocity.
balada; balata, *n.f.* ballad, song; (*slang*) arrangement, agreement.
baladí, *a.* weak, frail, worthless.
balador, -ra, *a.* bleating.
baladrar, *v.i.* to cry out, shout, storm, cry.
baladre, *n.m.* (*bot.*) rose-bay.
baladrero, -ra, *a.* shouting, crying, noisy.
baladro, *n.m.* shout, outcry, clamour, howl.
baladrón, -na, *a.* a boaster, bragger, bully.
baladronada, *n.f.* boast, brag, bravado; rodomontade.
baladronar; baladronear, *v.i.* to boast, brag, bully.
balagar, *n.m.* (*prov.*) haystack, hayrick.
bálago, *n.m.* grain-stalk, straw; rick; soap-bubble; *sacudir, menear* or *zurrar el bálago*, to give a sound drubbing.
balagre, *n.m.* (*Hond.*) (*bot.*) kind of rush.
balaguero, *n.m.* rick of straw.
balaj; balaje, *n.m.* balas, spinel ruby.
balance, *n.m.* oscillation, swinging; (*fencing*) poise, poising, equilibrium; (*naut.*) rolling, rocking; dance step or setting; (*fig.*) vacillation, fluctuation; (*com.*) balance, balancing, balance-sheet; (*Cub.*) rocking-chair; (*Col.*) affair, business; (*naut., aer.*) rolling.
balanceable, *a.* balanceable.
balanceador, -ra, *a.* (*naut.*) rolling, rocking.
balancear, *v.i., v.r.* (*naut., aer.*) to roll, rock; (*fig.*) to waver; to be perplexed; to swing. — *v.t.* to balance; to poise; *balancear en la duda*, to waver, hesitate.
balanceo, *n.m.* balancing, oscillation, rocking.
balancero, *n.m.* weigh-master in the mint.
balancín, *n.m.* splinter-bar, futchel, whipple-tree, swingle-tree, whiffle-tree; (*mech.*) cross-beam, balance-beam; minting-mill; (*zool.*) balancer; rope-walker's balancing pole. — *pl.* (*naut.*) yard-lifts.
balandra, *n.f.* (*naut.*) sloop.
balandrán, *n.m.* cassock; *sacudir a uno el balandrán*, to reprimand, scold.
balandro, *n.m.* (*naut.*) small sloop; (*Cub.*) fishing smack.
balanitis, *n.f.* (*med.*) inflammation of the penis.
bálano; balano, *n.m.* (*anat.*) penis; (*ichth.*) barnacle.

balante, *a.* bleating.
balanza, *n.f.* scales; balance; (*slang*) gallows; (*fig.*) comparative estimate, judgment; (*astron.*) Libra, the Balance; *balanza de comercio*, balance of trade; *en balanza, en balanzas*, doubtful, in danger; *poner en balanza*, (*fig.*) to hesitate, waver.
balanzario, *n.m.* balancer, weigh-master in the mint.
balanzón, *n.m.* cleaning-pan used by jewellers, platers, etc.
balar, *v.i.* to bleat; *balar por*, (*coll.*) to crave.
balastaje, *n.m.* ballasting (road).
balastar, *v.t.* to ballast a track.
balaste; balasto, *n.m.* (*railw.*) ballast, layer of gravel.
balastera, *n.f.* (*railw.*) quarry of stone or gravel used for ballasting.
balata, *n.f.* dancing-song.
balate, *n.m.* terrace margin; sloping terrace; border of a trench; (*zool.*) sea-slug.
balausta, *n.f.* (*bot.*) fruit of a variety of pomegranate.
balausta; balaustra, *n.f.* (*bot.*) variety of pomegranate.
balaustrada; (obs.) balaustrería, *n.f.* balustrade.
balaustrado, -da, *a.* balustered. — *p.p.* [BALAUSTRAR].
balaustral; balaustrado, *a.* balustered.
balaustrar, *v.t.* to put balusters.
balaustre; balaústre, *n.m.* baluster.
balay, *n.m.* (*Am.*) wicker basket; (*Cub.*) wooden-plate for winnowing rice.
balazo, *n.m.* shot; gunshot wound.
balboa, *n.m.* (*Panama*) gold coin.
balbuceamiento, *n.m.; **balbucencia**, *n.f.; **balbuceo**, *n.m.* stammer, lisp, stutter.
balbucear; balbucir, *v.i.* to stutter, stammer; to mumble; to lisp.
balbuciente, *a.* stammering, stuttering.
balbusardo, *n.m.* (*orn.*) osprey, sea-eagle.
balcánico, -ca, *a.* Balkan.
balcarrotas, *n.f.pl.* (*Mex.*) plaited hair style adopted by the Indians.
balcón, *n.m.* balcony, open gallery, mirador.
balconaje, *n.m.; **balconería**, *n.f.* range of balconies.
balconazo, *n.m.* large balcony.
balconcillo, *n.m.* small balcony.
balda, *n.f.* shelf; trifle; (*prov.*) large knocker or handle.
baldado, -da, *a.* paralysed; crippled. — *p.p.* [BALDAR].
baldadura, *n.f.; **baldamiento**, *n.m.* physical disability; impediment.
baldanza, (de), *adv.* idly, lazily.
baldaquín; baldaquino, *n.m.* canopy, dais.
baldar, *v.t.* to cripple; to trump; (*obs.*) to obstruct, hinder, interrupt; (*fig.*) to annoy greatly; (*prov.*) to impair, take away a part of. — *v.r.* to become crippled, maimed; *baldarse con la humedad*, to become crippled through the damp; *baldarse de un lado*, to become maimed on one side.
balde, *n.m.* bucket (especially leather or canvas); (*de*) *balde*, *adv.* gratis, free of charge; *en balde*, in vain, of no use, to no purpose; *estar de balde*, to be too many, too much; to be lazy, unoccupied.
baldear, *v.i.* (*naut.*) to wash the deck; to bale (water); to clean with buckets of water.

[113]

baldeo, *n.m.* washing by throwing buckets of water; (*slang*) sword.

baldés, *n.m.* soft dressed skin for gloves, etc.

baldiamente, *adv.* vainly.

baldío, -día, *a.* untilled, uncultivated; useless, vain; unappropriated; common, public (land); idle, lazy; vagabond.

baldo, -da, *a.* having to renounce (at cards). — *n.m.* renounce (at cards).

baldón, *n.m.* affront, reproach, insult.

baldonado, -da, *p.p.* [BALDONAR] insulted.

baldonador, -ra, *n.m.f.* insulter. — *a.* insulting.

baldonar; baldonear, *v.t.* to affront, insult, stigmatize.

baldosa, *n.f.* ancient string instrument; fine square tile; flat paving-stone, flag.

baldosado, -da, *p.p.* [BALDOSAR] tiled, paved. — *n.m.* tiled floor, pavement.

baldosar, *v.t.* to tile, flag.

baldosín, *n.m.* small square tile.

baldosón, *n.m.* large tile or flagstone.

baldragas, *n.m.* weak, soft man.

balduque, *n.m.* narrow red tape.

balear, *v.t.* (*prov.*) [ABALEAR]; (*Am.*) to kill or wound by bullets.

balear; baleárico, -ca; baleario, -ria, *n.m.f., a.* Balearic.

balénidos, *n.m.pl.* (*ichth.*) family, of the Cetacea order, which includes the whales.

baleo, *n.m.* rug, mat; (*prov.*) esparto scoop or fan.

balería, *n.f.; balerío,* *n.m.* (*artill.*) pile of balls or shot.

balero, *n.m.* bullet-mould; (*Mex.*) toy called cup and ball.

baleta, *n.f.* small bale of goods.

balhurria, *n.f.* (*slang*) rabble.

balido, *n.m.* bleat, bleating.

balimbín, *n.m.* (*bot.*) (*Philip.*) tree of the Geraniaceæ family.

balín, *n.m.* small-bore bullet.

balista, *n.f.* ballista.

balístico, -ca, *a.* ballistic.

balita, *n.f.* land measure used in Philippine Islands equivalent to 27 are, 95 centiare.

balitadera, *n.f.* call, reed instrument for calling fawns.

balitar, *v.i.* to bleat frequently.

baliza, *n.f.* (*naut.*) buoy.

balizamiento, *n.m.* [ABALIZAMIENTO].

balneario, -ria, *a.* pertaining to baths. — *n.m.* watering-place, spa.

balompié, *n.m.* (*obs.*) football.

balón, *n.m.* large ball, game of ball; balloon; large bale; (*motor.*) balloon tyre; *balón de papel,* bale of paper (24 reams).

baloncesto, *n.m.* basket-ball.

balota, *n.f.* ballot; small voting ball.

balotada, *n.f.* leap of a horse.

balotar, *v.i.* to ballot.

balsa, *n.f.* pool, pond; (*naut.*) raft, float; (*prov.*) half a butt of wine; in oil-mills, pond where the oil residue is sent; (*slang*) impediment, obstacle; *una balsa de aceite,* (*coll.*) quiet gathering of people; *balsa de sangre,* (*prov.*) pond from which water is drawn with much difficulty.

balsadera, *n.f.; balsadero,* *n.m.* ferry.

balsamera, *n.f.* flask for balsam.

balsamerita, *n.f.* small flask for balsam.

balsámico, -ca, *a.* balsamic, balmy.

balsamina, *n.f.* balsam-apple; balsamine.

balsamita, *n.f.* (*bot.*) hedge-mustard; *balsamita mayor* watercress.

bálsamo, *n.m.* balsam, balm; (*med.*) purest part of the blood; *bálsamo de Judea* or *de Meca,* true balsam, balm of Gilead; *bálsamo del Canadá,* Canada balsam; *bálsamo del Perú,* Peru balsam; *ser un bálsamo,* (*fig.*) to be very fragrant, generous, perfect (old wine).

balsar, *n.m.* marshy and brambly ground.

balsear, *v.t.* to ferry or cross a river on rafts, or floats.

balsero, *n.m.* ferryman.

balsete, *n.m.* (*prov.*) small puddle, pool.

balso, *n.m.* (*naut.*) rope with loops for raising men or goods on board ship; sling; (*Am.*) a tree of light wood used for making rafts.

balsopeto, *n.m.* (*coll.*) large pouch carried near the breast; (*coll.*) bosom.

bálteo, *n.m.* officer's belt.

báltico, -ca, *a.* Baltic. — *n.m.* the Baltic Sea.

baltra, *n.f.* (*prov.*) belly, paunch.

baluarte, *n.m.* bastion, bulwark; (*fig.*) defence, support; *baluarte de la fe,* bulwark of the faith.

balumba, *n.f.* bulk, heap.

balumbo, (*obs.*) balume; *n.m.* bulky thing.

ballena, *n.f.* (*zool.*) whale; train-oil; whalebone; (*astron.*) Whale, Cetus, a southern constellation.

ballenato, *n.m.* whale-calf.

ballener, *n.m.* medieval vessel.

ballenero, -ra, *a.* appertaining to whaling. — *n.m.* whale-boat; whaler.

ballesta, *n.f.* cross-bow, ballista; snare for birds; carriage-spring; (*pl.*) (*slang*) saddlebags; *a tiro de ballesta,* at a great distance.

ballestada, *n.f.* shot from a cross-bow.

ballestazo, *n.m.* blow from the arrow of a cross-bow.

ballesteador, *n.m.* cross-bowman, arbalister.

ballestear, *v.t.* to shoot with a cross-bow.

ballestera, *n.f.* loopholes for cross-bows.

ballestería, *n.f.* big-game hunting; archery; armoury for cross-bows; number of cross-bows or bowmen.

ballestero, *n.m.* archer, arbalister, cross-bowman; cross-bow maker; king's armourer; *ballestero de maza,* mace-bearer; *ballestero de corte,* king's porter.

ballestilla, *n.f.* small whiffle-tree; (*vet.*) fleam; cross-staff; (*naut.*) forestaff; (*slang*) cheating trick (at cards).

ballestón, *n.m.* large cross-bow, arbalest; (*slang*) cheating trick (at cards).

ballestrinque, *n.m.* (*naut.*) clovehitch.

ballico, *n.m.* (*bot.*) rye-grass.

ballueca, *n.f.* (*bot.*) wild oats.

bamba, *n.f.* fluke (billiards); (*prov.*) swing on cords; (*prov.*) sponge roll.

bambalear; bambanear; bambolear; bambonear, *v.i., v.r.* to reel, stagger, totter.

bambalina, *n.f.* fly in theatrical scenery.

bambarria, *n.f.* fluke (billiards); (*coll.*) fool, idiot.

bambarrión, *n.m.* (*coll.*) great fluke.

bambochada, *n.f.* painting representing a banquet or drunken feast, with grotesque figures.

bamboche, *n.m.* (*coll.*) short person with a full red face.

bamboleación, *n.f.* staggering, tottering.

bamboleo; bamboleón; bamboneo, *n.m.* reeling, staggering, tottering, swaying.

bambolla, *n.f.* (*coll.*) ostentation; humbug, sham; *vendiendo bambolla,* displaying much ostentation.

bambollero, -ra, *a.* ostentatious. — *n.m.f.* humbug (person).

bambú; bambuc, *n.m.* (*bot.*) bamboo.

bambuco, *n.m.* (*Col.*) a folk-dance.

bambusáceo, -cea, *a.* bamboo-like. — *n.f.pl.* bamboos.

bamía, *n.f.* (*bot.*) malvaceous plant used as emollient.

banaba, *n.f.* (*bot.*) tree of the Philippines.

banana, *n.f.;* **bananero; banano,** *n.m.* banana, banana plantain-tree.

banas, *n.f.pl.* (*Mex.*) matrimonial banns.

banasta, *n.f.* large wicker basket.

banastero, -ra, *n.m.f.* basket-maker, basket-dealer. — *n.m.* (*slang*) prison governor.

banasto, *n.m.* large round basket; (*slang*) prison.

banca, *n.f.* form, bench; washing-box; market-stand; (*com.*) banking; card game; money staked by dealer or banker (at cards); Philippine canoe; *hacer saltar la banca,* to break the bank; *banca de hielo,* ice-field.

bancable, *a.* (*com.*) bankable.

bancada, *n.f.* bench for shearing cloth; quantity of cloth prepared for shearing; (*arch.*) piece of masonry; (*naut.*) rower's bench; (*min.*) step.

bancal, *n.m.* oblong plot used as orchard or garden; terrace; bench-cover.

bancalero, *n.m.* weaver of bench-covers.

bancario, -ria, *a.* banking, financial.

bancarrota, *n.f.* bankruptcy, failure; *hacer bancarrota,* to go bankrupt.

bancaza, *n.m.* (*naut.*) bench.

bancazo, *n.m.* blow given with a bench.

banco, *n.m.* form, bench, seat, settee; pew; (*mech.*) bed, table, frame, horse; planing-bench; bench for rowers; (*arch.*) pediment; (*naut.*) course; school, shoal of fishes; (*naut.*) large sand-bank, shoal; (*com.*) bank; (*geol.*) stratum; (*slang*) prison; (*pl.*) cheeks of the bit of a bridle; *banco de liquidación,* clearing-house; *banco de ahorros,* savings bank; *banco de hielo,* ice-field; *banco de río,* sand-bank in a river.

banda, *n.f.* sash, scarf, ribbon; band, gang, party, crew; military band, brass band; covey; bank, border, edge; side of a ship; cushion (of billiard-table); (*eccles.*) humeral veil; (*prov.*) felloe (wheel); (*print.*) platen-rail; *arriar en banda,* (*naut.*) to loose the ropes; *cerrarse a la banda,* to be firm and resolute; *caer* or *estar en banda,* (*naut.*) to be hanging loosely; *dar a la banda,* (*naut.*) to heel; *de banda, a banda,* from party to party, from side to side.

bandada, *n.f.* covey; flock of birds.

bandarria, *n.f.* (*naut.*) iron maul.

bandazo, *n.m.* (*naut.*) breaking of a wave on the side of a ship; heave of a ship.

bandeado, -da, *a.* striped.

bandear, *v.t.* to conduct. — *v.i.* (*obs.*) to band. — *v.r.* to shift for oneself; (*prov.*) to swing oneself.

bandeja, *n.f.* tray.

bandera, *n.f.* banner, standard, flag, ensign, colours of an infantry regiment; (*mil.*) a subdivision of an infantry battalion in certain corps; *bandera blanca, bandera de paz,* flag of truce; (*fig.*) reconciliation; *bandera de popa,* (*naut.*) ensign; *bandera de proa,* (*naut.*) jack; *bandera de inteligencia,* (*naut.*) signalling flag; *bandera de recluta,* recruiting party; *afianzar, afirmar, asegurar la bandera,* (*naut.*) fire a salute; *arriar la bandera,* (*naut.*) to strike the colours, surrender; *a banderas desplegadas,* (*fig.*) openly, freely; *con banderas desplegadas,* with flying colours; *alzar, levantar bandera,* to call to arms; to put oneself at the head of a party; *batir banderas,* (*mil.*) to salute; *dar a uno la bandera,* (*fig.*) to acknowledge someone's superiority or advantage; *llevarse la bandera,* (*fig.*) to carry the day; *militar* or *seguir debajo de la bandera de otro,* (*fig.*) to side with someone; *rendir la bandera,* (*naut.*) to strike the flag as sign of courtesy; (*mil.*) to strike the flag in honour of the Sacred Sacrament.

bandereta; banderita, *n.f.* bannerette, small flag.

banderetas, *n.f.pl.* (*mil.*) camp colours.

bandería, *n.f.* band, faction.

banderica; banderilla; banderilleta, *n.f.* bannerette, small flag.

banderilla, *n.f.* small dart with a bannerol for baiting bulls; *clavar, plantar, poner a uno una banderilla,* to taunt, ridicule, revile, vex.

banderillear, *v.t.* to put *banderillas* on bulls.

banderillero, *n.m.* one who thrusts *banderillas* into the bull.

banderín, *n.m.* camp colours; small flag; railway signal; soldier who carries a flag in his gun, file-leader; recruiting post.

banderizar, *v.t., v.r.* to divide into bands or parties.

banderizo, -za, *a.* factious; (*fig.*) turbulent, seditious.

banderola, *n.f.* banderol, camp colours; signalling flag; streamer, pennon.

bandidaje, *n.m.* banditti; brigandage.

bandido, *n.m.* bandit, highwayman, outlaw.

bandín, *n.m.* (*naut.*) seat in a row-galley.

bando, *n.m.* proclamation, edict; faction, party; shoal of fishes; *echar bando,* to publish a law.

bandola, *n.f.* bandore, mandolin; (*naut.*) jury-mast.

bandolera, *n.f.* bandolier; bandit's wife; woman bandit.

bandolerismo, *n.m.* banditti; brigandage.

bandolero, *n.m.* highwayman, robber.

bandolín, *n.m.* small bandore or mandolin.

bandolina, *n.f.* bandoline, hair fixative.

bandolón, *n.m.* (*mus.*) large *bandola.*

bandujo, *n.m.* large sausage; (*prov., coll.*) bowel, intestine.

bandullo, *n.m.* (*vulg.*) belly, bowels, intestines.

bandurria, *n.f.* bandurria, bandore.

bandurrista, *n.m.* (*mus.*) player of *bandurria.*

bánova, *n.f.* (*prov.*) bed-quilt, bed-cover.

banquera, *n.f.* (*prov.*) bee-house; site or frame for beehives.

banquero, *n.m.* banker; exchanger; dealer, banker (cards); (*slang*) prison governor.

banqueta, *n.f.* tripod, three-legged stool, foot-stool; (*mil.*) banquette; sidewalk, pavement; small chest; *banqueta de cureña,* (*artill.*) gun-carriage bed; *banqueta de calafate,* (*naut.*) caulking-stool.

banquete, *n.m.* small bench; banquet; great feast.

banquetear, *v.i., v.t., v.r.* to banquet, feast.

banquillo, *n.m.* little stool; *banquillo de los acusados,* (*law*) dock, enclosure for prisoners; (*law*) seat in the dock.

banquito, *n.m.* stool, foot-stool.

banzo, *n.m.* cheek of embroidering-frame; jamb; sloping bank of canal.

baña, *n.f.* (*prov.*) [BAÑADERO].

bañadera, *n.f.* (*naut.*) skeet.

bañadero, *n.m.* puddle; bathing-place of wild animals.

bañado, *p.p.* [BAÑAR] bathed, washed; irrigated, watered; coated. — *n.m.* chamberpot; (*Am.*) marsh land.

bañador, -ra, *n.m.f.* bather. — *n.m.* dipping-tub (of candle-makers); bathing costume. — *a.* bathing.

bañar, *v.t.* to bathe, wash, lave; to water, irrigate; to dip; (*fig.*) to fill to the brim, flood; to moisten, wet copiously; to leave extra border on shoe sole; to glaze, coat, ice with sugar; (*art*) to cover a painting with a coat of transparent colours; *el río baña las murallas de la ciudad,* the river washes the walls of the city; *bañar el sol (algún espacio),* to flood (a place) with sunlight; *bañar la luz (algún espacio),* to light up, illuminate (some place); *bañar un papel con, en, de lágrimas,* to write a tearful letter *or* story. — *v.r.* to bathe; to take a bath; to go into the water; *bañarse en agua rosada,* to look through rose-coloured spectacles.

bañera, *n.f.* bath-tub; woman bathing-attendant.

bañero, -ra, *n.m.f.* bath-owner; bath-keeper. — *n.m.* male bathing-attendant; bathing costume.

bañil, *n.m.* (*prov.*) pool in which cattle bathe.

bañista, *n.m.f.* bather in or drinker of mineral or medicinal waters.

baño, *n.m.* bath; bath-water; bath-tub; bath-room; bathing; coat of sugar, wax, paint, silver, etc.; (*chem.*) bath; (*obs.*) Moorish prison; (*coll., prov.*) water-closet; *baño de asiento,* hip-bath; *baño de ducha* or *regadera,* shower-bath; *baño turco,* Turkish bath; *baño de María,* bain-marie; *dar un baño a alguno,* beat a professional rival (used of bull-ring and also generally). — *pl.* bathing-place; spa; watering-place.

bañon, *n.m.; palo de bañon,* (*bot.*) mock privet.

bañuelo, *n.m.* little bath.

bao, *n.m.* (*naut.*) beam, cross-timber.

baobab, *n.m.* (*bot.*) baobab.

baptisterio, *n.m.* baptistery.

baque, *n.m.* blow in falling; thud.

baqueano, -na, *a.* experienced, expert. — *n.m.* guide.

baquear, *v.i.* (*naut.*) to sail with the current.

baqueta, *n.f.* ramrod; switch used for breaking in young horses; *tratar a la baqueta,* to treat harshly. — *pl.* drumsticks; *carrera de baquetas,* (*mil.*) running the gauntlet; *mandar a (la) baqueta,* to command imperiously.

baquetazo, *n.m.* blow with a *baqueta.*

baqueteado, -da, *a.* experienced, inured, habituated. — *p.p.* [BAQUETEAR].

baquetear, *v.t.* to inflict the punishment of the gauntlet; to vex.

baqueteo, *n.m.* (*mil.*) gauntlet; (*fig.*) annoyance, vexation.

baquetilla, *n.f.* small rod or switch.

baquetón, *n.m.* (*mil.*) worm for drawing wad.

baquía, *n.f.* practical acquaintance with the roads, forests, etc. of a country; (*Am.*) skill in handwork, handy.

baquiano, -na, *a.* skilful, experienced. — *n.m.f.* one acquainted with particular tracks or roads. — *n.m.* mountain and road guide.

báquico, -ca, *a.* bacchanal, bacchic.

baquio, *n.m.* (*poet.*) metrical foot.

báquira, *n.f.* (*Am.*) species of wild-hog.

bar, *n.m.* bar, place of refreshment.

baraca, *n.f.* (*Morocco*) divine gift ascribed to sherifs and hermits.

barago, *n.m.* wicker tray for drying chestnuts.

barahá, *n.f.* Jewish term for prayer.

barahunda, *n.f.* great uproar and confusion.

baraja, *n.f.* complete pack of cards; game of cards, deck; (*pl.*) quarrel; *echarse en la baraja, entrarse* or *meterse en baraja, irse a la baraja,* to hold a losing hand (at cards); (*fig.*) to give up, renounce; *jugar con dos barajas,* (*coll.*) to act with duplicity; *peinar la baraja,* to shuffle the cards.

barajado, -da, *a.* shuffled; (*coll.*) confused, topsy-turvy. — *p.p.* [BARAJAR].

barajador, -ra, *n.m.f.* chicaner, caviller.

barajadura, *n.f.* shuffling of cards; dispute.

barajar, *v.t.* to shuffle (cards); (*fig.*) to entangle; to jumble together; (*horsemanship*) to draw the reins; *barajar la costa,* (*naut.*) to sail close to the shore; *barajar un negocio,* to jumble an affair; *barajar una proposición,* to reject a proposal; *paciencia y barajar,* work on and be patient. — *v.i.* to quarrel, contend; *barajar con el vecino,* to quarrel with a neighbour.

baraje, *n.m.* [BARAJADURA].

barajón, *n.m.* snow-shoe.

baranda, *n.f.* railing, banister; cushion of billiard-table; *echar de baranda,* to exaggerate, boast.

barandado; barandaje, *n.m.* balustrade.

barandal, *n.m.* upper- and under-piece of a balustrade; railing.

barandilla, *n.f.* balustrade, small railing.

barangay, *n.m.* (*Philip.*) tribal government.

barangayán, *n.m.* (*Philip.*) large clinker-built canoe.

baraño, *n.m.* (*prov.*) new-mown hay.

barata, *n.f.* barter; (*Mex.*) reduction sale; bargain; sham sale; move in backgammon; *a la barata,* confusedly.

baratador, -ra, *n.m.f.* barterer, trader. — *a.* trading.

baratamente, *adv.* (*fig.*) at little cost or effort.

baratar, *v.t.* to barter, traffic.

baratear, *v.t.* to cheapen, undersell.

baratería, *n.f.* (*law*) fraud, deception; *baratería de capitán* or *patrón,* (*law*) barratry.

baratero, *n.m.* one who exacts money from winning gamblers.

baratía, *n.f.* (*Col.*) cheapness.

baratijas, *n.f.pl.* trifles, toys, trinkets.

baratillero, -ra, *n.m.f.* pedlar; seller of second-hand goods or articles; keeper of second-hand shop.

baratillo, *n.m.* second-hand shop; bargain counter; heap of trifling articles for sale.

baratista, *n.m.f.* barterer, trafficker.

barato, -ta, *a.* cheap, low-priced; easy. — *n.m.* bargain or reduction sale; money given by winning gamblers; *cobrar el barato,* to dominate over; *dar de barato,* to admit for the sake of argument; *echar* or *meter a barato,* to confuse, interrupt (a speaker); *lo barato es caro,* cheap things are dear in the long run. — *adv.* cheaply; *de barato,* gratuitously, without interest.

báratro, *n.m.* (*poet.*) hell; (*Bibl.*) Sheol; abysm.

baratura, *n.f.* cheapness, little value.

baraúnda, *n.f.* noise, hurly-burly, confusion.

baraustado, -da, *a.* aimed, pointed; (*slang*) stabbed to death. — *p.p.* [BARAUSTAR].

baraustador, *n.m.* (*slang*) dagger.

baraustar, *v.t.* to aim, point; to ward off, deflect (blow).

barba, *n.f.* chin; beard; shave, shaving; goat's whiskers; first swarm of bees; top of a bee-hive; wattle. — *n.m.* player who takes old men's parts; *barba cerrada,* thick strong beard; *barbas de chivo* or *de macho,* (*coll.*) pointed beard; man having such a beard; *barbas de zamarro,* heavy curly beard; *a barba regada,* very abundantly; *andar con la barba por el suelo,* to be very old, decrepit; *andar, estar con, traer la barba sobre el hombro,* to be on the alert, cautious; *llevar de la barba,* to rule, domineer; to lead by the nose; *tirarse, pelarse (de) las barbas,* to fly into a rage; *temblarle a uno la barba,* to be afraid; *tener una mujer buenas barbas,* to be a good-looking woman; *tentarse la barba,* to stroke one's beard; *mentir por la barba,* to tell a barefaced lie; *barba cabruna,* (*bot.*) yellow goat's beard; *barba de Aarón,* (*bot.*) green dragon arum; *barba a barba,* face to face; *por barba,* per head, apiece; *hacer la barba,* shave; (*coll.*) to annoy, irritate; to flatter; *a poca barba, poca vergüenza,* youth is rash and daring. — *pl.* (*astron.*) beard (comet); slender roots; fibres; rough edges of paper; vanes of a quill; (*vet.*) ranula; *a la barba, en sus barbas,* in his beard, to his face; *barbas de ballena,* whalebone; *barbas de gallo,* wattle; *barba honrada,* honourable man; *subirse a las barbas,* to show disrespect, to fly in one's face; *tener pocas barbas,* to be young or without experience; *echarlo a las barbas,* to reproach a man with something.

barbacana, *n.f.* (*mil.*) barbican; churchyard wall; loophole.

barbacoa; barbacuá, *n.f.* (*Am.*) barbecue.

barbada, *n.f.* lower jaw of a horse; bridle-curb; (*ichth.*) dab, small flatfish.

barbadamente, *adv.* strongly, vigorously.

barbado, -da, *a.* bearded, barbed, barbated. — *n.m.* full-grown man; vine or tree transplanted; (*bot.*) shoot, sucker; (*slang, zool.*) buck; *plantar de barbado,* to plant a sucker with roots. — *p.p.* [BARBAR].

barbaja, *n.f.* (*bot.*) cut-leaved viper's-grass. — *pl.* (*agric.*) first roots of plants.

barbaján, *n.m., a.* (*Cub., Mex.*) coarse, clumsy, brutish.

barbajuelas, *n.f.pl.* small roots.

barbar, *v.i.* to grow a beard; to rear bees; (*agric.*) to strike root.

bárbaramente, *adv.* barbarously, savagely, coarsely, rudely.

barbáricamente, *adv.* like barbarians.

barbárico, -ca, *a.* barbarous, barbarian.

barbaridad, *n.f.* barbarity, barbarism, cruelty; (*fig.*) temerity, rashness; rudeness; wild expression or action; lack of breeding; (*coll.*) nonsense; blunder; (*coll.*) great quantity; *comer una barbaridad,* to eat enormously; *¡qué barbaridad!* (*coll.*) what a scandal! how absurd!

barbarie, *n.f.* (*fig.*) barbarousness, incivility; rusticity; cruelty.

barbarismo, *n.m.* barbarism, barbarousness; (*poet.*) crowd of barbarians.

barbarizar, *v.t.* (*pret.* **barbaricé;** *pres. subj.* **barbarice**) to barbarize. — *v.i.* (*fig.*) to make wild statements.

bárbaro, -ra, *a.* barbaric, barbarous, barbarian; (*coll.*) fierce, cruel; (*fig.*) rash, reckless; rude, unpolished; (*coll.*) very big. — *n.m.f.* barbarian.

barbarote, -ta, *a.* (*coll.*) very fierce, cruel; very reckless; extremely rude, ill-bred.

barbato, -ta, *a.* having the tail before the nucleus (of comets).

barbaza, *n.f.* long beard.

barbear, *v.t.* to reach with the chin; (*Mex.*) to shave; (*Mex.*) to throw down a steer. — *v.i.* to be almost as high (one thing) as (another); *barbear con la pared,* to be nearly as high as the wall; *barbeando,* (*naut.*) lying alongside. — *v.r.* (*fig.*) to be very stiff with someone.

barbechada, *n.f.* (*agric.*) ploughing.

barbechar, *v.t.* (*agric.*) to fallow; to prepare ground for sowing.

barbechera, *n.f.* series of ploughings; act of ploughing; fallowing season.

barbecho, *n.m.* fallow; first ploughing of the ground; ploughed land ready for sowing; *firmar como en un barbecho,* (*coll.*) to sign without due examination or reflection.

barbera, *n.f.* barber's wife.

barbería, *n.f.* barber's shop or trade.

barberil, *a.* pertaining to a barber, barber-like.

barberillo, *n.m.* little barber.

barbero, *n.m.* barber; (*prov.*) net for barbel; (*Mex.*) flatterer, fawner; (*ichth.*) fish of the Caribbean Sea; *ni barbero mudo, ni cantor sesudo,* the barber is as talkative as the actor is improvident.

barbeta, *n.f.* (*naut.*) gasket; (*artill.*) barbette; *a barbeta,* (*artill., fort.*) en barbette.

barbi, *a.* (*slang*) generous, very good.

barbián, -na, *a.* (*coll.*) bold, forward; free, easy.

barbiblanco, -ca, *a.* grey or white-bearded.

barbicacho, *n.m.* ribbon tied under the chin.

barbicano, -na, *a.* grey-bearded.

barbicastaño, *a.* with chestnut-coloured beard.

barbiespeso, -sa, *a.* having a thick beard.

barbihecho, -cha, *a.* freshly shaven.

barbijo, *n.m.* (*Arg. & prov.*) chin-strap; scar on face.

barbilampiño, -ña, *a.* smooth-chinned; with a thin beard.

barbilindo, -da, *a.* well-shaved and trimmed; effeminate and pretty; foppish, dandyish.

barbilucio, -cia, *a.* smooth-faced, pretty, genteel.

barbiluengo, *a.* long-bearded.

barbilla, *n.f.* point of the chin; (*ichth.*) barbel, fleshy filament; (*carp.*) rabbet; (*vet.*) ranula, tumour under the tongue; (*Col.*) man with thin beard.

barbillera, *n.f.* roll of tow (in wine casks); bandage put under the chin of a dead person.

barbimoreno, *a.* brown-bearded.

barbinegro, -gra, *a.* black-bearded.

barbiponiente, *a.* (*coll.*) having the beard beginning to grow; apprenticed.

barbipungente, *a.* just growing a beard; with thin beard.

barbiquejo, *n.m.* bonnet-string; guard ribbon for a hat; curb chain (for horses); (*Per.*) handkerchief placed under the chin as a bandage; (*naut.*) bobstay.

barbirrapado, *a.* having a cropped beard.

barbirrojo, *a.* red-bearded.

barbirrubio, -bia, *a.* blond-bearded.

barbirrucio, -cia, *a.* grey-bearded, colour of pepper-and-salt.

barbitaheño, -ña, *a.* having a red beard.

barbiteñido, -da, *a.* having a dyed beard.

barbo, *n.m.* (*ichth.*) barbel, river fish; *barbo de mar,* surmullet.

barbón, *n.m.* full-bearded man; Carthusian lay-brother; (*zool.*) buck.

barboquejo; barbuquejo, *n.m.* chin-strap, hatguard.

barbotar, *v.t., v.i.* to mumble, mutter.

barbote, *n.m.* beaver of a helmet.

barbudo, -da, *a.* having a long beard; *a la mujer barbuda, desde lejos se saluda,* a warning against masculine women. — *n.m.* vine transplanted with the roots; (*slang, zool.*) buck.

barbulla, *n.f.* babble, noisy talk.

barbullar, *v.i.* to talk loud and fast.

barbullón, -na, *n.m.f.* (*coll.*) loud, fast talker. — *a.* talking noisily.

barbusano, *n.m.* (*bot.*) lofty tree of the Canaries belonging to the Lauraceæ family.

barca, *n.f.* (*naut.*) boat, barge, bark; *barca chata,* or *de pasaje,* ferry-boat.

barcada, *n.f.* passage in a boat; boat-load.

barcaje, *n.m.* ferryage; freightage, freight.

barcal, *n.m.* (*prov.*) wooden trough, pan or tray.

barcarola, *n.f.* barcarole.

barcaza, *n.f.* barge, lighter; privilege of loading and unloading.

barcelonés, -sa, *a., n.m.f.* of or from Barcelona.

barceno, -na, *a.* dappled.

barceo, *n.m.* dry bass or sedge for mats, ropes, etc.

barcia, *n.f.* chaff, siftings.

barcina, *n.f.* (*Mex. & prov.*) esparto net-bag; (*Mex. & prov.*) large truss of straw.

barcinador, *n.m.* (*prov. & agric.*) one who loads sheaves.

barcinar, *v.i.* (*prov.*) to load with sheaves.

barcino, -na, *a.* dappled.

barco, *n.m.* boat, barge, vessel, ship; shallow gorge; *barco que mandan muchos pilotos va a pique,* too many cooks spoil the broth; *por viejo que sea el barco, pasa una vez el vado,* however old a thing may be, it will still serve for some purpose.

barcolongo; barcoluengo, *n.m.* (*hist.*) swift-sailing ship; oblong boat with a large bow.

barcón; barcote, *n.m.* large vessel carried in tow by the galleys.

barchilón, *n.m.* (*Am.*) male nurse in hospitals.

barchilla, *n.f.* (*prov.*) measure for grain.

barda, *n.f.* (*obs.*) bard, horse-armour; thatch; reed; (*prov.*) hawthorn hedge or fence; (*prov.*) young oak-tree; (*naut.*) large threatening cloud; *aún hay sol en las bardas,* there's hope yet.

bardado, -da, *a.* (*obs.*) barded, caparisoned; thatched. — *p.p.* [BARDAR].

bárdago, *n.m.* (*naut.*) pendant.

bardaguera, *n.f.* (*bot.*) willow.

bardaja; bardaje, *n.m.* sodomite.

bardal, *n.m.* thatched wall or fence; mud wall covered at the top with straw or brushwood, *saltando bardales,* overcoming all difficulties.

bardana, *n.f.* (*bot.*) burdock.

bardanza, *n.f.; andar de bardanza,* to go here and there.

bardar, *v.t.* to thatch fences.

bardiota, *a., n.m.* Byzantine soldier.

bardiza, *n.f.* (*prov.*) cane fence.

bardo, *n.m.* bard, poet.

bardoma, *n.f.* (*prov.*) filth, mud.

bardomera, *n.f.* (*prov.*) brush or weeds carried off by a stream.

barí; baril, *a.* (*prov.*) excellent.

baría, *n.f.* (*Cub.*) tree of the Boraginaceæ family.

bario, *n.m.* (*min.*) barium.

barisfera, *n.f.* (*geol.*) the centre of mass of the earth.

barita, *n.f.* (*min.*) baryta, barytes.

baritel, *n.m.* (*min.*) hoisting machine.

barítico, -ca, *a.* baric, relating to barium.

baritina, *n.f.* barium sulphate, heavy spar.

barítono, *n.m.* (*mus.*) baritone.

barjuleta, *n.f.* knapsack, haversack, tool-bag.

barloa, *n.f.* cable for mooring a ship to another.

barloar, *v.t., v.i., v.r.* to bring alongside a ship or wharf.

barloventear, *v.i.* (*naut.*) to ply to windward; (*coll.*) to beat about, tack about, rove about.

barlovento, *n.m.* (*naut.*) windward; *costa de barlovento,* weather shore; *costado de barlovento,* weather side; *ganar el barlovento,* (*coll.*) to get to windward of.

barnacla, *n.m.* (*orn.*) barnacle, sea-goose.

barniz, *n.m.* varnish, japan, lacquer, gloss, glaze; cosmetic for the face; printer's ink; superficial or partial knowledge.

barnizado, -da, *p.p.* [BARNIZAR] glazed, lacquered, varnished. — *n.m.* (*art*) varnishing-day.

barnizador, -ra, *n.m.f.* varnisher. — *a.* varnishing.

barnizar, *v.t.* (*pret.* **barnicé;** *pres. subj.* **barnice**) to varnish, gloss, lacquer, glaze.

barógrafo, *n.m.* barograph.

barología, *n.f.* barology.

barometría, *n.f.* barometry.

barométrico, -ca, *a.* barometric, barometrical.

barómetro, *n.m.* barometer.

barón, *n.m.* baron.

baronesa, *n.f.* baroness.

baronía, *n.f.* barony, baronage.

baroscopio, *n.m.* baroscope.

baroto, *n.m.* (*Philip.*) small boat.

barquear, *v.t.* to cross (river or lake) by boat.— *v.i.* to go about in a boat.

barqueo, *n.m.* boating.

barquero, *n.m.f.* person guiding a boat.—*n.m.* bargeman, waterman, ferryman, boatman, rower; (*entom.*) water-bug.

barqueta, *n.f.; barquete,** *n.m.* small boat.

barquía, *n.f.* (*naut.*) fishing-boat; fishing-net.

barquichuelo, *n.m.* small bark or boat.

barquilla, *n.f.* conical mould for wafers; little

boat, wherry; airship-car; balloon-basket; (*naut.*) log; *barquilla de la corredera*, log.

barquillero, -ra, *n.m.f.* maker or seller of rolled wafers. — *n.m.* wafer-mould.

barquillo, *n.m.* cock-boat; thin rolled wafer.

barquín, *n.m.;* **barquinera,** *n.f.* large bellows for furnaces.

barquinazo, *n.m.* violent swaying or upset of vehicle.

barquinero, *n.m.* bellows-maker.

barquino, *n.m.* wine-skin.

barra, *n.f.* (*mech.*) bar, beam, rod; strip; crowbar, lever; (*naut.*) sand-bar; ingot; Spanish game played with iron bars; barrier (of court-room); gross-spun thread in defective cloth; (*her., mus., naut.*) bar; chase bar; shaft of a carriage, thill; (*naut.*) spar. — *pl.* saddle-trees; (*Am.*) mining shares; (*her., vulg.*) stripes, bars; clamps of embroidery-frame; *barra fija,* (*gymn.*) fixed bar; *barras paralelas,* (*gymn.*) parallel bars; *a barras derechas,* without deceit; *de barra a barra,* from side to side and from one end to the other; *estirar la barra,* (*coll.*) to do one's utmost to attain something; *llevar a la barra,* (*fig.*) to impeach; *sin mirar, pararse, reparar o tropezar en barras,* regardless of obstacles; *tirar a la barra,* to play the game of *barra; tirar la barra,* (*coll.*) to get the highest price possible; to do all in one's power to attain anything; *sin daño de barras,* without injury or danger; *estar en barras,* to be on the point of settling an affair.

Barrabás, *n.m.* (*coll.*) bad, ungovernable, contrary person.

barrabasada, *n.f.* (*coll.*) serious mischief; hasty action.

barraca, *n.f.* barrack, cabin, hut; (*prov.*) cottage, rustic dwelling; (*Am.*) storage, warehouse.

barraco, *n.m.* ancient naval gun.

barracón, *n.m.* large hut or cabin.

barrado, -da, *a.* corded; ribbed; striped; (*her.*) barred. — *p.p.* [BARRAR].

barragán, *n.m.* barracan, camlet; waterproof woollen stuff; overcoat of such material.

barragana, *n.f.* concubine; (*obs.*) morganatic wife.

barraganería, *n.f.* concubinage.

barraganete, *n.m.* (*naut.*) top-timber, futtock.

barral, *n.m.* (*prov.*) demijohn containing twenty-five pints.

barranca, *n.f.;* **barrancal,** *n.m.* deep cleft, or hollow; gorge, ravine; *a trancas y a barrancas,* with many difficulties and obstacles.

barranco, *n.m.* precipice; cleft, gorge, ravine; (*fig.*) great difficulty; *no hay barranco sin atranco,* there is no undertaking without risk; *salir del barranco,* to get out of the difficulty.

barrancoso, -sa, *a.* broken, uneven, full of breaks and holes.

barranquera, *n.f.* obstruction, embarrassment; [BARRANCA].

barraquero, *n.m.* (*prov.*) hut-constructor; (*Am.*) owner of a store or warehouse.

barraquillo, *n.m.* (*obs.*) short light field-piece.

barrar, *v.t.* to stain, smear with mud; (*prov.*) to plaster roughly; to daub, smear; to bar, barricade.

barrate, *n.m.* little joist or rafter.

barrear, *v.t.* to bar, barricade; (*prov.*) to can-

cel, cross off. — *v.i.* to graze a knight's armour with a lance. — *v.r.* (*obs.*) to entrench oneself; (*prov.*) to wallow (pigs and boars).

barreda, *n.f.* barricade, barrier, fence.

barredera, *n.f.* road-sweeping machine. — *pl.* (*naut.*) studding sail.

barredero, -ra, *a.* that drags along; sweeping; *red barredera,* drag-net, sweep-net. — *n.m.* baker's long-handled oven mop or swab.

barredor, -ra, *n.m.f.* sweeper. — *a.* sweeping.

barreduela, *n.f.* (*prov.*) small enclosed square or place.

barredura, *n.f.* sweeping. — *pl.* sweepings, remains, residue, refuse, chaff.

barrelotodo, *n.m.* one who collects and makes use of everything.

barrena, *n.f.* gimlet, borer, drill; *barrena grande,* auger, borer; *barrena pequeña* or *de mano,* gimlet; *barrena de gusano,* (*obs.*) wimble, rock-drill; *barrena de disminución,* taper auger; *barrena de guía,* centre-bit; *entrar en barrena,* (*aer.*) to spin.

barrenado, -da, *a.* bored, drilled. — *p.p.* [BARRENAR].

barrenador, *n.m.* blaster, driller; (*naut.*) auger, borer.

barrenamiento, *n.m.* boring, drilling.

barrenar, *v.t.* to bore, auger, drill; (*fig.*) to foil, frustrate, defeat someone's intentions; (*fig.*) to violate laws, rights; *barrenar un navío,* (*naut.*) to scuttle a ship; *barrenar una roca* or *mina,* to blast a rock or mine.

barrendero, -ra, *n.m.f.* sweeper, cleaner. — *n.m.* dustman.

barrenero, *n.m.* maker or seller of augers or drills; blaster, driller.

barrenillo, *n.m.* (*ent.*) borer; (*bot.*) disease in trees caused by borer.

barreno, *n.m.* large borer or auger; bored hole, blast-hole; (*fig.*) vanity; *dar barreno,* (*naut.*) to sink a ship.

barreña, *n.f.;* **barreño,** *n.m.* earthen pan, tub.

barrer, *v.t.* to sweep; (*fig.*) to carry off everything; (*mil.*) to enfilade; (*naut.*) to rake; *barrer hacia dentro,* to behave from interested motives.

barrera, *n.f.* barricade, barrier, parapet, fence; clay-pit; mound of earth; cupboard for crockery; bar; (*fig.*) obstacle, difficulty; tollgate, turnpike; (bullfight-ring) front seat. *barrera de golpe,* automatically self-closing gate; *ver los toros desde la barrera,* not to interfere; *salir a barrera,* to expose oneself to censure.

barrero, *n.m.* potter; clay-pit; (*prov.*) eminence, ridge of hills; bog, quagmire; (*Am.*) salty soil.

barreta, *n.f.* small bar; shoe-lining; (*prov.*) bar of toffee.

barretear, *v.t.* to fasten with bars; to line a shoe.

barretero, *n.m.* (*min.*) one who works with a pick, wedge or crow.

barretina, *n.f.* Phrygian cap; Catalonian cap.

barriada, *n.f.* city ward, district, precinct, suburb.

barrial, *a.* clayey. — *n.m.* (*obs.*) muddy spot.

barrica, *n.f.* cask; *barrica bordelesa,* cask containing about 50 gallons.

barricada, *n.f.* barricade.

barrido, -da, *a.* swept. — *n.m.* sweeping; sweepings, remains. — *p.p.* [BARRER].

barriga, *n.f.* abdomen, belly, bowels; (*fig.*) belly of a flask; bulge (in a wall); *estar, hallarse con,* or *tener la barriga a la boca,* to be big with child; *de los cuarenta para arriba, no te mojes la barriga,* sea baths should not be taken by persons over forty; *sacar la barriga de mal año,* to have a good feed.

barrigón, -na; barrigudo, -da, *a.* (*coll.*) big-bellied, pot-bellied.

barriguera, *n.f.* belly-band.

barril, *n.m.* barrel, jug; (*naut.*) water cask; *barril bizcochero,* biscuit-cask.

barrila, *n.f.* (*prov.*) short, round jug.

barrilamen, *n.m.;* **barrilería,** *n.f.* stock of casks or barrels; barrel factory or shop.

barrilejo, *n.m.* rundlet, small barrel.

barrilero, *n.m.* cooper, barrel-maker or vendor.

barrilete, *n.m.* (*carp.*) holdfast, dog, clamp; (*zool.*) crab covered with prickles; keg; (*prov.*) kite (toy); (*mus.*) part of a clarinet near mouthpiece; (*naut.*) mouse.

barrilla, *n.f.* (*bot.*) saltwort, glasswort.— *pl.* saltwort ashes.

barrillar, *n.m.* barilla plantation; barilla pits.

barrillero, -ra, *a.* (*bot.*) salsolaceous.

barrillo, *n.m.* pimple.

barrio, *n.m.* city district, ward, quarter or suburb; *el otro barrio,* (*coll.*) eternity; *andar* or *estar de barrio* (or *vestido de barrio*), to wear plain, simple dress.

barriscar, *v.t.* (*prov.*) to sell in bulk; (*prov.*) to sweep brusquely.

barrisco, (a), *adv.* jointly, without exception; (*fig.*) pell-mell.

barrita, *n.f.* small bar.

barrizal, *n.m.* clay-pit, muddy place.

barro, *n.m.* clay, mud, mire; earthenware drinking vessel; *dar* or *tener barro a mano,* to give or have the money to do a thing; *barro cocido,* terra-cotta; *barro y cal encubren mucho mal,* rouge and paint hide many defects; *dejar en el barro,* (*slang*) to leave in the gutter. — *pl.* pimples on the face; (*vet.*) fleshy tumours (on mules and cattle).

barroco, -ca, *a.* baroque.

barrocho, *n.m.* barouche.

barrón, *n.m.* graminaceous plant growing in sand-dunes [BARRA].

barroquismo, *n.m.* extravagance, bad taste.

barroso, -sa, *a.* muddy, full of mire; pimpled; reddish, terra-cotta colour.

barrote, *n.m.* short and thick iron bar; iron band; table-clamp; (*carp.*) brace.

barrotín, *n.m.* (*naut.*) wooden lattice-lath.

barrueco, *n.m.* pearl of irregular form; (*geol.*) nodule.

barrumbada, *n.f.* (*coll.*) extravagant expense; boastful saying.

barruntador, -ra, *a.* conjecturing; foreseeing.

barruntamiento, *n.m.* conjecturing, guessing.

barruntar, *v.t.* to foresee, conjecture, guess; (*slang*) to smell.

barrunte, *n.m.* indication, presentiment, sign.

barrunto, *n.m.* conjecture.

bartola, *n.f.* (*coll.*) paunch; *echarse, tenderse,* or *tumbarse a la bartola,* to lie back lazily.

bartolillo, *n.m.* small three-cornered meat or cream pie.

bartolina, *n.f.* (*Mex.*) small, narrow and dark dungeon.

bartulear, *v.i.* (*Chi.*) to cavil.

bartuleo, *n.m.* (*Chi.*) action and effect of *bartulear.*

bártulos, *n.m.pl.* household goods; tools; business; *preparar los bártulos,* to arrange ways and means; *liar los bártulos,* to get ready for a journey.

baruca, *n.f.* (*coll.*) artifice, cunning, deceit.

barulé, *n.m.* upper part of the stockings rolled over the knee.

barullero, -ra, *n.m.f.* busybody.

barullo, *n.m.* (*coll.*) confusion, disorder, tumult.

barzal, *n.m.* bramble-patch.

barzón, *n.m.* idle walk; (*agric.*) ring of a yoke; (*CR.*) leather strap for yoking oxen; *dar, hacer barzones,* to loiter, idle about.

barzonear, *v.i.* to loiter about.

barzoque; berzoque, *n.m.* (*coll.*) Satan; evil spirit.

basa, *n.f.* (*arch.*) pedestal, base; (*fig.*) basis, foundation; (*prov.*) pool, pond.

basácula, *n.f.* locker of the thumb-plate in a stocking-frame.

basada, *n.f.* (*naut.*) cradle, stocks.

basal, *a.* basal, basic.

basáltico, -ca, *a.* basaltic, of basalt.

basalto, *n.m.* (*min.*) basalt.

basamento, *n.m.* (*arch.*) base and pedestal, basement.

basanita, *n.f.* (*min.*) basanite; touchstone; (*zool.*) variety of crustacean.

basar, *v.t.* to fix, establish upon a base; (*fig.*) to found, rest upon; to set up a theory; (*surv.*) to start from a fixed base-line. — *v.r.* (with *en*) to base one's opinion (on).

basáride, *n.f.* (*zool.*) bassariscus, a species of racoon.

basca, *n.f.* squeamishness; nausea; (*vet.*) distemper; (*coll.*) fit of anger.

bascosidad, *n.f.* nastiness, filth.

báscula, *n.f.* platform-scale; weighing-machine; (*fort.*) bascule-bridge.

bascuñana, *n.f.* (*bot.*) variety of Barbary wheat.

base, *n.f.* base, basis; ground, foot, footing; ground-work; (*surv.*) base-line; *base aérea,* military airport.

basicidad, *n.f.* (*chem.*) basicity.

básico, -ca, *a.* basic.

báside; basideo, *n.m.* (*bot.*) basidium.

basilea, *n.f.* (*slang*) gallows, gibbet.

basílica, *n.f.* royal palace; public hall; privileged church; *vena basílica,* (*anat.*) basilic vein.

basilicón, *n.m.* (*med.*) basilicon, ointment.

basilio, -lia, *n.m.f., a.* Basilian (monk or nun).

basilisco, *n.m.* basilisk, cockatrice; ancient cannon; (*Ec.*) reptile not unlike a small iguana; *estar hecho un basilisco,* (*coll.*) to be very cross.

basquear, *v.i.* to be squeamish or nauseated.

basquilla, *n.f.* disease in sheep.

basquiña, *n.f.* outer skirt.

basta, *n.f.* basting, tacking; mattress tufting.

bastaje, *n.m.* porter, carrier.

bastante, *a.* sufficient, enough; competent. — *adv.* rather; not too little not too much; sufficiently.

bastantear, *v.i.* (*law*) to acknowledge the validity of a power of attorney.

bastantemente, *adv.* sufficiently.

bastanteo, *n.m.* acknowledgment of a power of attorney.

bastantero, *n.m.* (*law*) officer who examined powers of attorney.

bastar, *v.i.* to suffice, be enough; to abound; *¡basta!* or *¡basta con esto!* stop! that's enough! *¡basta ya!* leave off! that will do! *¡basta de bulla!* that's enough noise! *¡basta para chanza!* that will do for a joke! *basta a*, or *para enriquecerse*, that is sufficient to get rich. — *v.t.* (*Ven.*) to baste.

bastarda, *n.f.* locksmith's fine file; (*obs.*) piece of ordnance; (*naut.*) lateen mainsail.

bastardeamiento, *n.m.* degeneracy, degeneration; depravation; bastardy.

bastardear, *v.i.* to degenerate, bastardize, debase; *bastardear de su naturaleza*, to degenerate in its nature; *bastardear en sus acciones*, to be debased in his ways.

bastardelo, *n.m.* notary's draft book; blotter.

bastardía, *n.f.* bastardy; meanness; corruption, depravity.

bastardillo, **-lla**, *n.m.f.*, *a.* (*print.*) italic (type). — *n.f.* (*mus.*) kind of flute.

bastardo, **-da**, *a.* bastard, illegitimate; spurious, (*print.*) bastard (type). — *n.m.* bastard; (*zool.*) boa (snake); kind of saddle; (*naut.*) parrel rope.

baste, *n.m.* (*sew.*) basting, tacking; kind of cushion placed under saddles for comfort of horses.

bastear, *v.t.* to baste; to stitch loosely, sew slightly.

basterna, *n.m.* Bastarnæ (people). — *n.f.* cart; horse-drawn Roman litter.

bastero, *n.m.* maker or retailer of packsaddles.

basteza, *n.f.* coarseness; rudeness.

bastidor, *n.m.* easel, frame; embroidery-frame; stretcher for canvas; window-sash; wing of stage scenery; (*naut.*) frame of a screw propeller; holder for photographic plates; stage scenery; (*motor.*) frame of a chassis; *entre bastidores*, behind the scenes; intimately.

bastilla, *n.f.* hem; the Bastille.

bastillado, **-da**, *a.* hemmed; (*her.*) with merlons pointing downwards. — *p.p.* [BASTILLAR].

bastillar, *v.t.* to hem.

bastimentar, *v.t.* to victual, supply with provisions.

bastimento, *n.m.* supply of provisions; (*naut.*) vessel, boat; building, structure; mattress tufting.

bastión, *n.m.* bulwark.

bastionado, **-da**, *a.* fortified; provided with bulwarks.

basto, **-ta**, *a.* coarse, homespun, unpolished; clumsy, clownish, gross, rude. — *n.m.* packsaddle for beasts of burden; pad; ace of clubs in several games of cards. — *pl.* clubs (in cards); *bastos son triunfos*, clubs are trumps; the hardest hitter has won; (*Am.*) the two pads forming the packsaddle.

bastón, *n.m.* cane, stick, truncheon, baton; roller of a silk-frame; (*bot.*, *prov.*) young reed or shoot; (*arch.*) fluted moulding; (*her.*) vertical bars; *dar bastón*, to stir wine when ropy; *empuñar el bastón*, to take the command; *bastón de Jacob*, Jacob's staff; *meter el bastón*, to intervene, make peace.

bastonada, *n.f.*; **bastonazo**, *n.m.* blow with a stick, bastinado.

bastoncillo, *n.m.* small cane or stick (used in velvet-loom); narrow lace trimming.

bastonear, *v.t.* to cane, beat with a stick; to stir must with a stick. — *v.i.* (*prov.*) to eat young shoots (cattle).

bastonera, *n.f.* umbrella-stand.

bastonería, *n.f.* walking-stick shop.

bastonero, *n.m.* marshal or manager of a ball, steward of a feast, master of ceremonies; cane-maker or seller; assistant jail-keeper; cotillion leader.

basura, *n.f.* sweepings, filth swept away; dung, manure, ordure, refuse.

basurero, *n.m.* dustman; dust-bin; dump, refuse heap; dung-yard, dunghill.

bata, *n.f.* morning-gown, dressing-gown, wrapper; (*obs.*) frock with train; *n.m.*, *a.* (*Philip.*) child; young Indian servant.

batacazo, *n.m.* noisy violent fall; (*fig.*) calamity, failure.

batahola, *n.f.* (*coll.*) hurly-burly, bustle, clamour, hubbub, clatter.

batalla, *n.f.* battle, fight, combat; fencing bout; joust, tournament; saddle seat; distance between the axles of four-wheeled carriage; (*artill.*) battle-piece; struggle or agitation of the mind; *campo de batalla*, battlefield; *batalla campal*, decisive battle; *dar la batalla*, to face difficulties; *en batalla*, (*mil.*) with extended front; *presentar la batalla*, to offer battle; *batalla de flores*, carnival, pageantry.

batallador, **-ra**, *n.m.f.* battler, combatant, fighter, warrior; fencer with foils. — *a.* battling, combating, fighting, pugnacious; fencing.

batallante, *a.* battling, fighting.

batallar, *v.i.* to battle, fight; to fence with foils; (*fig.*) to contend, strive, struggle, argue, dispute; (*fig.*) to vacillate, fluctuate; *batallar con los enemigos*, to contend with enemies.

batallón, *n.m.* battalion.

batallona, *n.f.* (*coll.*) cause of dispute.

batán, *n.m.* fulling-mill. — *pl.* boyish game.

batanar, *v.t.* to full cloth.

batanear, *v.t.* (*coll.*) to bang, beat, handle roughly.

batanero, *n.m.* fuller; cloth-worker.

batanga, *n.f.* (*Philip.*) bamboo outrigger in boats.

bataola, *n.f.* [BATAHOLA].

batata, *n.f.* (*bot.*) sweet-potato; *batata en polvo*, preserve of *batata*.

batatar, *n.m.* sweet-potato-field.

batatero, **-ra**, *n.m.f.* *batata* vendor.

batatín, *n.m.* (*prov.*) small sweet-potato.

bátavo, **-va**, *n.m.f.*, *a.* Batavian.

batayola, *n.f.* (*naut.*) rail.

batea, *n.f.* painted wooden tray or trough; (*naut.*) punt, boat; open wagon with low sides; (*Per.*) washing trough.

batehuela, *n.f.* small wooden bowl or tray.

batel, *n.m.* (*naut.*) small vessel. — *pl.* (*slang*) gang of roughs or thieves.

batelada, *n.f.* boat-load.

batelejo, *n.m.* small boat.

batelero, **-ra**, *n.m.f.* one who guides a *batel*. — *n.m.* boatman.

bateo, *n.m.* (*coll.*) baptism.

batería, *n.f.* (*mil.*, *elec.*) battery; (*naut.*) range of guns, broadside; breach; (*theat.*) footlights; (*fig.*) deep mental depression; assault, blow; (*mus.*) aggregate of percussion instruments in an orchestra; repeated importunities; *batería a barbeta*, barbette battery; *batería de campo*, field battery; *batería de cocina*, metal kitchen utensils; *batería cruzante*, cross-battery; *batería eléctrica*, electric battery; *batería enterrada*, sunk battery; *hacer batería*, to assault, strike; *preparar las baterías*, to get ready one's fighting forces; to prepare for a tussle; *batería a rebote*, ricochet battery.

batero, -ra, *n.m.f.* ladies' tailor; dressmaker.

batey, *n.m.* (*Cub.*) sugar plant (factory, workers' dwellings, warehouse, etc.).

batiboleo, *n.m.* (*Mex.*) noisy stir; bustle.

batiborrillo; batiburrillo, *n.m.* [BATURRILLO].

baticola, *n.f.* crupper.

baticulo, *n.m.* (*naut.*) cordage, rigging; lateen mizen-sail.

batida, *n.f.* (*sport.*) battue, hunting-party; reconnaissance.

batidera, *n.f.* (*build.*) beater; instrument for cutting honeycombs.

batidero, *n.m.* continuous beating or striking; beating-place; collision; uneven ground. — *pl.* (*naut.*) wash-boards; sail-tablings; *guardar los batideros*, to drive carefully over bad roads; (*fig.*) to prevent and avoid all difficulties.

batido, -da, *a.* beaten, changeable, shot, chatoyant (silk); well-trodden (roads). — *n.m.* wafer or biscuit batter; beaten eggs; beating. — *p.p.* [BATIR].

batidor, -ra, *a.* beating. — *n.m.* (*mech.*) beater; scout, pioneer; (*prov.*, *hunt.*) beater; lifeguard who rides before a royal coach; outrider; haircomb; *batidor de cáñamo*, hemp-dresser; *batidor de oro*, gold-beater.

batiente, *n.m.*, *a.* beating. — *n.m.* jamb; leaf of door; place where the sea beats against shore or dyke; damper (of a piano); (*naut.*) vertical frame of gun-port; *tambor batiente*, (*mil.*) with drums beating.

batihoja, *n.m.* gold-beater; sheet-metal-worker.

batimento, *n.m.* (*paint.*) shade.

batimetría, *n.f.* bathymetry.

batimiento, *n.m.* beating.

batín, *n.m.* smoking-jacket.

batintín, *n.m.* Chinese gong.

bationdeo, *n.m.* fluttering of a banner or curtain.

batiportar, *v.t.* (*naut.*) to house a gun so that it rests against upper part of port-hole.

batiporte, *n.m.* (*naut.*) upper or lower frame of gun-port.

batir, *v.t.* to beat, dash, strike; to clash, clout, clap; to raze, pull down, demolish; to flap; to mix, pound, stir; to fluff (hair); to move in a violent manner; to adjust reams of paper; to roll a drum; to strike or fall on (said of the sun and wind); (*mus.*) to beat time; (*prov.*) to throw out, down; to drop; to vanquish; *batir el agua por la ventana*, to throw water out of the window; *batir el campo*, to reconnoitre the enemy's camp; *batir banderas*, (*naut.*) to salute with the colours; to strike colours; *batir la catarata*, (*med.*) to couch; *batir el cobre*, to pursue an enterprise energetically; *batir hoja*, to foliate; *batir moneda*, to coin money; *batir las olas*, to ply the seas; *batir tiendas*, to break up the camp. — *v.r.* to fight, engage in a duel; to swoop (bird of prey); *batirse a puñetazos*, to beat one another.

batista, *n.f.* batiste, fine cambric.

bato, *n.m.* simpleton, ninny, rustic.

batochar, *v.t.* to mix the hairs and fibres in hat-making.

batojar, *v.t.* to beat down the fruit of a tree.

batología, *n.f.* tautology, needless repetition.

batológico, -ca, *a.* tautological.

batometría, *n.f.* bathymetry.

batómetro, *n.m.* batometre, bathymetre.

batracio, -cia, *a.*, *n.m.f.* (*zool.*) batrachian. — *n.m.pl.* Batrachia.

batraco, *n.m.* tumour on the tongue.

batuda, *n.f.* spring-board jumps.

Batuecas, *pr.n.*; *estar en las Batuecas*, (*coll.*) to be absent-minded.

batueco, *n.m.* (*prov.*) addled egg.

batuque, *n.m.* rowdy dance; confusion, disorder.

batuquear, *v.t.* (*Col.*, *Cub.*, *Guat.*, *Ven.*) to flap, to move in a violent manner.

baturrada, *n.f.* rustic, uncouth act or expression.

baturrillo, *n.m.* hotchpotch, mash, salmagundi; (*coll.*) medley, potpourri.

baturro, -rra, *n.m.f.* peasant from Aragon; (*fig.*) simpleton, rustic. — *a.* appertaining to the *baturro*; uncouth.

batuta, *n.f.* (*mus.*) conductor's baton; *llevar la batuta*, to lead, preside, manage.

baúl, *n.m.* coffer, chest, trunk; (*coll.*) belly; *henchir* or *llenar el baúl*, (*coll.*) to fill the paunch; *baúl mundo*, Saratoga trunk.

baulero, *n.m.* trunk maker or seller.

bauprés, *n.m.* (*naut.*) bowsprit.

bausán, -na, *n.m.f.* effigy; mannikin; (*coll.*) fool, idiot.

bautismal, *a.* baptismal.

bautismo, *n.m.* baptism, christening; *fe de bautismo*, certificate of baptism; *romper a uno el bautismo*, (*fam.*) to give one a blow on the head.

bautista, *n.m.* one who baptizes; Baptist; *San Juan Bautista* or *El Bautista*, St. John the Baptist.

bautisterio, *n.m.* baptistry.

bautizante, *a.* baptizing, christening.

bautizar, *v.t.* (*pret.* **bauticé**; *pres. subj.* **bautice**) to baptize, christen; to name, call; (*coll.*) to nick-name; to throw water in fun; *bautizar el vino*, to mix water with wine.

bautizo, *n.m.* baptism, christening party.

bauyúa, *n.f.* (*Cub.*) tree of the Lauraceæ family.

bauza, *n.f.* rough chunk or piece of wood.

bauzado, *n.m.* (*prov.*) roof of a hut.

bávaro, -ra, *n.m.f.*, *a.* Bavarian.

bayá, *n.m.f.*, *a.* Indian living west of the Paraguay river near Bahia.

baya, *n.f.* (*bot.*) berry, small fruit; variety of hyacinth; (*zool.*, *prov.*) lobster.

bayadera, *n.f.* bayadère, Oriental dancer.

bayal, *a.* long-stemmed, fine-fibred (flax). — *n.m.* lever used in raising millstones.

bayeta, *n.f.* baize, a sort of flannel; *arrastrar bayetas*, to apply for a scholarship, (*coll.*) to study at a university, (*coll.*) to have great pretensions.

bayetón, *n.m.* blanket-cloth, heavy coating, cloth for coats; (*Am.*) long baize poncho.

bayetuno, -na, *a.* appertaining to baize.

bayo, -ya, *a.* bay, yellowish-white (horse). — *n.m.f.* bay (horse). — *n.m.* silkworm moth (used as bait by anglers); *pescar de bayo*, to fly-fish; *uno piensa el bayo y otro el que le ensilla*, each one judges according to his position.

bayoco, *n.m.* Italian copper coin; *(prov.)* unripe or withered fig.

bayón, *n.m.* (*Philip.*) sack made of matting for bailing.

bayona, *pr.n.; arda Bayona*, (*coll.*) never mind the expense. — *n.f.* bow oar; scull used for steering.

bayoneta, *n.f.* bayonet; *a la bayoneta*, with fixed bayonets; *armar, calar la bayoneta*, to fix bayonets; *bayoneta calada*, fixed bayonet.

bayonetazo, *n.m.* bayonet thrust or wound.

bayoque, *n.m.* Italian copper coin.

bayosa, *n.f.* (*slang*) sword.

bayú, *n.m.* (*Cub.*) house of ill repute.

bayuca, *n.f.* (*coll.*) tavern.

baza, *n.f.* trick (at cards); *asentar uno bien su baza*, to establish firmly one's credit, interests or opinion; *asentar la baza*, to gather up a won trick (cards); *hacer baza*, (*coll.*) to prosper; *no dejar meter baza*, to monopolize the conversation; *sentada esta (la) baza*, accepting this (the) principle.

bazagón, -na, *a.* chattering, gossiping.

bazar, *n.m.* bazaar, market-place; department store.

bazo, -za, *a.* brownish-yellow; *pan bazo*, brown bread. — *n.m.* (*anat.*) spleen, milt.

bazofia, *n.f.* offal, waste meat, refuse, hog-wash, food remnants; dirt, filth.

bazucar; bazuquear, *v.t.* (*pret.* **bazuqué**; *pres. subj.* **bazuque**) to stir liquids by shaking; to agitate, shake.

bazuqueo, *n.m.* shaking, stirring of liquids; (*fig.*) jumble.

be, *n.m.* baa (the cry of sheep); bleating. — *n.f.* name of B, the second letter of the alphabet; *be por be*, in detail.

beata, *n.f.* [BEATO].

beatería, *n.f.* act of affected piety; bigotry.

beaterio, *n.m.* house inhabited by pious women.

beático, -ca, *a.* hypocritical.

beatificación, *n.f.* beatification.

beatíficamente, *adv.* (*theol.*) beatifically.

beatificar, *v.t.* to beatify; to render venerable; to render happy.

beatífico, -ca, *a.* (*theol.*) beatific, beatifical.

beatilla, *n.f.* sort of fine linen.

beatísimo, -ma, *a. superl.* most holy, most blessed; *beatísimo padre*, most holy father (the Pope).

beatitud, *n.f.* beatitude, blessedness, holiness; *su beatitud*, his Beatitude (a title of Greek bishops).

beato, -ta, *a.* happy, blessed; beatified; devout. — *n.m.f.* one wearing a religious habit for piety; one engaged in works of charity; one living in pious retirement; devotee; (*coll.*) bigot, hypocrite, fanatic.

beatón, -na, *n.m.f.* hypocrite, bigot. — *a.* bigoted, hypocritical.

beatuco, -ca, *a.* bigoted, hypocritical.

bebedero, -ra, *a.* potable, drinkable. — *n.m.* drinking-trough (for birds); place where birds resort to drink; spout. — *n.m.pl.* strips for facing revers and sleeves.

bebedizo, -za, *a.* drinkable, potable. — *n.m.*

medicinal potion; love potion; philtre; poisonous draught.

bébedo, -da, *a.* (*prov.*) drunk, intoxicated.

bebedor, -ra, *n.m.f.* tippler, toper. — *a.* tippling.

beber, *n.m.* drinking; beverage, drink. — *v.t.* to drink, swallow. — *v.i.* to pledge, toast; (*coll.*) to drink to excess; (*fig.*) to absorb, imbibe; to learn quickly. — *v.r.* (*prov.*) to execute work rapidly; *beber agua*, (*naut.*) to ship a sea; *beber a bocados* or *de bruces*, to drink face downwards from a fountain or stream; *beber con* or *en blanco*, to have a white under-lip (horse); *beber en buenas fuentes*, (*coll.*) to get information from good sources; *beber de, en una fuente*, to drink from a spring; *beber fresco*, to be tranquil, unconcerned; *beber el cáliz*, to drink the cup of bitterness; *beberse las lágrimas*, to keep back one's tears; *beber a, por la salud de alguno*, to drink to another's health; *beber de codos*, to drink luxuriously, at one's ease or leisure; *beber como una cuba*, to drink like a fish; *beber una doctrina*, to imbibe a doctrine; *beber palabra y semblante*, to listen intently; *beber los pensamientos a alguno*, to anticipate someone's thoughts; *beber a tragantadas*, to drink huge draughts; *beber los vientos*, to desire with great eagerness; *beber el freno*, to take the bit between the teeth (of horse); *beber los sesos*, to bewitch; *estar delgado que se puede beber*, to exaggerate the fineness of a thing; *sin comerlo ni beberlo*, to suffer innocently; *querer beber la sangre a otro*, to hate another mortally; *al pie del coco se bebe el agua*, opportunities should not be lost.

beberrón, -na, *a.* tippling. — *n.m.f.* tippler.

bebible, *a.* drinkable, pleasant to drink.

bebida, *n.f.* drink, beverage, potion; (*prov.*) time allowed to workmen for drinks.

bebido, -da, *a.* drunk, swallowed; intoxicated. — *p.p.* [BEBER].

bebienda, *n.f.* beverage.

bebiente, *a.* drinking.

bebistrajo, *n.m.* (*coll.*) irregular and extravagant mixture of drinks; unpleasant or nauseating drink.

beborrotear, *v.i.* (*coll.*) to sip often.

beca, *n.f.* part of a collegian's dress worn over the gown; fellowship, scholarship, pension; tippet worn by ecclesiastics; alumnus, fellow, collegian.

becabunga, *n.f.* (*bot.*) brooklime.

becada, *n.f.* (*orn.*) woodcock.

becafigo, *n.m.* (*orn.*) fig-pecker.

becardón, *n.m.* (*prov., orn.*) snipe.

becario, *n.m.* holder of a scholarship.

becerra, *n.f.* heifer; (*bot.*) snapdragon; (*prov.*) lump of dough in cakes and bread.

becerrada, *n.f.* bullfight with young bulls.

becerrero, *n.m.* cowherd.

becerril, *a.* concerning cows or bulls; bovine; calf (as adjective).

becerrilla, *n.f.* very young heifer.

becerrillo, *n.m.* tanned and dressed calfskin.

becerro, *n.m.* young bull; calfskin tanned and dressed; church register; register of privileges and nobility; *becerro marino*, (*zool.*) sea-calf, seal; *el culto del becerro de oro*, the worship of the golden calf; excessive respect paid to wealth. — *n.f.* heifer; (*bot.*) snapdragon.

becoquín, *n.m.* cap with ear-flaps; coif.
becoquino, *n.m.* (*bot.*) honeywort.
becuadrado, *n.m.* (*mus.*) natural; first property in plain-song, or Gregorian mode.
becuadro, *n.m.* (*mus.*) sign (♮) denoting a natural tone.
becuna, *n.f.* (*ichth.*) becuna.
bedano, *n.m.* (*prov.*) large chisel.
bedel, *n.m.* beadle, porter, warden.
bedelía, *n.f.* beadleship, wardenship.
bedelio, *n.m.* bdellium, an aromatic gum.
bederre, *n.m.* (*slang*) hangman, executioner.
beduíno, -na, *n.m.f., a.* Bedouin. — *n.m.* (*fig.*) brutal, lawless man.
beduro, *n.m.* (*mus.*) natural.
befa, *n.f.* derision, scoffing, jeering, taunt.
befabemí, *n.m.* (*mus.*) Hypophrygian mode, as in plainchant.
befadura, *n.f.* scoffing, taunt; moving of lips (horse).
befar, *v.t.* to mock, scoff, ridicule, laugh at, jeer at, taunt. — *v.i.* to move the lips, and endeavour to catch the chain of the bit (said of horses).
befedad, *n.f.* the deformity of bandy-legs.
befo, -fa, *a.* blubber-lipped; knock-kneed. — *n.m.* lip of an animal; (*zool.*) kind of monkey.
begardo, -da, *n.m.f.* Beghard.
begonia, *n.f.* (*bot.*) begonia.
begoniáceo, -cea, *a.* relating to the begonia.
beguino, -na, *n.m.f.* [BEGARDO]; Beghard, Beguine.
behetría, *n.f.* town whose inhabitants were free and could elect any lord; (*fig.*) confusion, disorder.
bejín, *n.m.* (*bot.*) puff-ball; person easily irritated; whining, peevish child.
bejucal, *n.m.* place where *bejucos* grow.
bejuco, *n.m.* (*bot.*) bindweed; thin reed; rattan.
bejuqueda, *n.f.* [BEJUCAL].
bejuquillo, *n.m.* small gold chain made in China; (*bot.*) root of ipecacuanha.
belcho, *n.m.* (*bot.*) horse-tail tree.
beldad, *n.f.* beauty; beautiful woman, belle.
beldar, *v.t.* (*agric.*) to winnow.
belemnita, *n.f.* (*geol.*) belemnite.
belemnítico, -ca, *a.* (*geol.*) belemnitic.
Belén, *n.m.* Bethlehem; crib, group of figures representing the Nativity (shown at Christmas); (*coll.*) Bedlam, confusion, disorder, noise; (*coll.*) gossip, mischief; business in jeopardy; *estar* or *estar bailando en Belén,* (*coll.*) to be absent-minded; *meterse en Belenes,* to get into difficulties; *¡Qué Belén!* What a din!
beleño, *n.m.* (*bot.*) henbane; poison.
belérico, *n.m.* (*bot.*) myrobalan.
belez, *n.f.;* **belezo,** *n.m.* receptacle, vessel; household goods; (*prov.*) jar for oil or wine; (*slang*) household article.
belfo, -fa, *a.* blubber-lipped. — *n.m.* lip (animals).
belga; bélgico, -ca, *n.m.f., a.* Belgian, Belgic.
bélicamente; belicosamente, *adv.* in a bellicose manner.
bélico, -ca, *a.* warlike, martial, military.
belicosidad, *n.f.* bellicosity, inclination to war.
belicoso, -sa, *a.* warlike, martial, military; (*fig.*) quarrelsome, aggressive.
beligerancia, *n.f.* belligerence, belligerency.
beligerante, *n.m.f., a.* belligerent.

belígero, -ra, *a.* (*poet.*) warlike, belligerent.
belísono, -na, *a.* with martial, warlike sound.
belitre, *a.* (*coll.*) low, mean, vile, vulgar. — *n.m.* (*coll.*) rascal, rogue.
belitrería, *n.f.* knavishness, rascality.
belitrero, *n.m.* (*slang*) rogue who swindles thieves.
belorta, *n.f.* (*agric.*) clasp-ring of plough.
Beltrán, *pr.n.; quien bien quiere a Beltrán, bien quiere a su can,* love me, love my dog.
bellacada, *n.f.* nest of rogues; knavish act or deed.
bellacamente, *adv.* knavishly, rascally.
bellaco, -ca, *a.* artful, sly; cunning, mean, vile, deceitful. — *n.m.* rogue, villain, swindler, knave.
bellacón, -na; bellaconazo, -za, *a.* very artful, extremely cunning. — *n.m.f.* aug. great knave, arrant rogue.
bellacuelo, -la, *a.* rather sly, cunning. — *n.m.* artful, cunning little fellow.
belladona, *n.f.* (*bot.*) belladonna, deadly nightshade.
bellamente, *adv.* prettily, gracefully, beautifully.
bellaquear, *v.i.* to cheat, swindle; play roguish, knavish tricks.
bellaquería, *n.f.* knavery, roguery; cunning, cheating; vile act or word.
bellerife, *n.m.* (*slang*) judge's servant.
belleza, *n.f.* beauty, fairness, handsomeness; flourish; ornament, decoration; *decir bellezas,* to say something with charm and wit.
bellico, *n.m.* (*bot.*) variety of oat.
bello, -lla, *à.* beautiful, handsome, fair, fine, perfect; *el bello sexo,* the fair sex; *Bellas Artes,* fine arts; *bella pedrería,* fine jewels.
bellorio, -ria, *à.* greyish, mouse-coloured (horse).
bellota, *n.f.* acorn; acorn-shaped balsam or perfume box; carnation bud; acorn-shaped fringeless tassel.
bellote, *n.m.* large, round-headed nail.
bellotear, *v.i.* to feed on acorns.
bellotera, *n.f.* woman who gathers or sells acorns; season for gathering acorns and pig fattening; acorn crop; holm-oak grove.
bellotero, *n.m.* man who gathers or sells acorns; oak tree.
belloto, *n.m.* (*Chi.*) a tree of the Lauraceæ family.
bemol, *a.* (*mus.*) flat. — *n.m.* (*mus.*) flat; the sign ♭; softness, smoothness; *tener* (*tres*) *bemoles,* (*coll.*) to be very difficult.
bemolado, -da, *a.* (*mus.*) flatted, lowered a semitone. — *p.p.* [BEMOLAR].
ben, *n.m.* (*bot.*) behen, plant of the Leguminosæ family producing oil used by watch-makers.
bencina, *n.f.* (*chem.*) benzine; (*Spain*) petrol (motor).
bendecidor, -ra, *a.* blessing, blesser.
bendecir, *v.t.* (*p.p.*(**bendito**)**bendecido;** *pres. indic.* **bendigo;** *pret.* **bendije;** *imperative* **bendice;** *pres. subj.* **bendiga**) praise, exalt; to render happy and prosperous (by Providence); to devote to the service of the church; to bless; to consecrate; *bendecir la bandera,* to consecrate the colours; *bendice Dios a las criaturas,* God blesses his creatures; *¡Dios te bendiga!* God bless thee! *¡bendito sea Dios!* praise be to God!

bendición, *n.f.* benediction, blessing; *echar la bendición,* to invoke God's blessing on someone accompanied by the sign of the cross; *(coll.)* to have nothing more to do with a person or thing; *es una bendición, es bendición, (coll.)* it does one's heart good to see what a plenty there is; *hijo y fruto de bendición,* child born in wedlock; *hacerse con la bendición, (coll.)* to be done successfully; *miente que es una bendición, (iron.)* it's a blessing to hear how he lies. — *pl. bendiciones nupciales,* marriage ceremony.

bendigo; bendije; bendiga, *pres. indic.; pret.; pres. subj.* [BENDECIR].

bendito, -ta, *a.* sainted, blessed; fortunate, happy; *(euphemistic)* cursed; *(coll.)* simple, silly. — *n.m.f.* simpleton. — *n.m.* prayer; *ser un bendito,* to be a ninny, a simpleton. — *p.p. irreg.* [BENDECIR].

benedícite, *n.m.* travel permission sought by ecclesiastics; grace before meat; Song of the Three Holy Children.

benedicta, *n.f. (med.)* benedict, electuary.

benedictino, -na, *a.* Benedictine. — *n.m.* Benedictine (monk or liqueur).

benedictus, *n.m. (mus.)* benedictus.

benefactor, -ra, *n.m.f.* benefactor, benefactress.

beneficencia, *n.f.* beneficence, kindness, charity; *función de beneficencia,* charity performance; *el hombre nació para la beneficencia,* man was born to do good.

beneficentísimo, -ma *a.* extremely beneficent, charitable, kind.

beneficiable, *a.* deserving of charity, kindness.

beneficiación, *n.f.* benefaction.

beneficiado, -da, *a.* benefited. — *n.m.f.* *(theat.)* person or charity for whom a benefit is held. — *n.m.* curate, beneficiary.

beneficiador, -ra, *n.m.f.* benefactor; improver. — *a.* beneficent, doing good.

beneficial, *a. (eccl.)* relating to benefices.

beneficiar, *v.t.* to benefit, do good to; to improve; *(agric.)* to cultivate; to work (mines); *(min.)* to subject to metallurgical process; to purchase a place or employ; to administer excise revenue; *(com.)* to sell at a discount; *(eccl.)* to confer a benefice; *beneficiar de, (Gallicism)* to benefit, profit by.

beneficiario, *n.m.* beneficiary.

beneficio, *n.m.* benefit, favour, kindness, benefaction; utility, profit; *(agric.)* cultivation; *(min.)* development of a mine; *(min.)* metallurgical process; buying of place or employ; *(com.)* selling at a discount; *(theat.)* benefit (performance, proceeds); *(law)* benefit, right by law or charter; *(eccl.)* benefice, ecclesiastical living; *beneficio bruto,* gross profit; *beneficio neto,* net profit; *beneficio de bandera,* reduction in customs dues; *a beneficio de inventario, (fig.)* with prudence, reserve; *no tener* or *estar sin oficio ni beneficio,* to have neither profession nor property; *desconocer el beneficio,* to be ungrateful.

beneficioso, -sa, *a.* beneficial, advantageous, profitable.

benéfico, -ca, *a.* beneficial; beneficent, kind, charitable; *benéfico para la salud,* beneficial to health; *benéfico con sus contrarios,* charitable to his enemies.

benemérito, -ta, *a.* meritorious, worthy;

benemérito de la patria, well-deserving of the country. — *n.f. La Benemérita,* the Civil Guard *(Guardia Civil).*

beneplácito, *n.m.* goodwill, approbation, consent.

benévolamente, *adv.* benevolently.

benevolencia, *n.f.* benevolence, goodwill, kindness.

benevolente, *a.* benevolent, gentle, kind.

benévolo, -la, *a.* benevolent, kind, gentle.

bengala, *n.f. (bot.)* cane; *(mil.)* baton, sceptre; Bengal stripes; *luz de bengala,* Bengal light.

bengalí, *n.m.f., a.* Bengali, Bengalee. — *n.m.* Bengali language; *(orn.)* Bengal finch.

benignamente, *adv.* kindly, graciously, mercifully, benevolently, favourably.

benignidad, *n.f.* benignity, kindness, graciousness, mercifulness; mildness (of climate, weather, etc.).

benigno, -na, *a.* benign, merciful, kind, gracious, pious; *(fig.)* mild, temperate, inoffensive.

benito, -ta, *n.m.f., a.* Benedictine friar or nun.

Benjamín, *n.m.* Benjamin, youngest son, darling.

benjamita, *n.m.f., a.* descending from Benjamin tribe.

benjuí, *n.m.* benzoin.

benzoato, *n.m. (chem.)* benzoate.

benzoico, *a. (chem.)* benzoic.

benzol, *n.m. (chem.)* benzol.

benzolina, *n.f. (chem.)* benzoline.

beocio, -cia, *a.* Bœotian; *(fig.)* stupid, dull. — *n.m.f.* dunce.

beodez, *n.f.* drunkenness.

beodo, -da, *a.* drunk, drunken. — *n.m.f.* drunkard, inebriate.

beorí, *n.m. (zool.)* American tapir.

beque, *n.m. (naut.)* head of a ship; crew's water-closet; *(fig.)* chamber-pot.

béquico, -ca, *a.* efficacious against coughs.

berberecho; berbericho; berbiricho, *n.m. (ichth.)* cockle, shell-fish.

berberí; berberisco, -ca, *n.m.f., a.* native of Barbary, Berber.

Berbería, *n.f.* Barbary.

berberis, *n.m. (bot.)* barberry, berberry.

bérbero; berberos, *n.m.* barberry (tree and fruit); confection made of barberry fruit.

berbí, *n.m.* kind of woollen cloth.

berbiquí, *n.m. (carp.)* brace and bit.

berceo, *n.m. (bot.)* bass, sedge.

bercería, *n.f.* vegetable market.

bercero, -ra, *n.m.f.* greengrocer.

berciano, -na, *n.m.f.* native of Bierzo.

bereber, *n.m.f., a.* native of Barbary, Berber.

berenjena, *n.f. (bot.)* egg-plant.

berenjenal, *n.m.* egg-plant plantation; *(fig.)* difficulties, troubles; *meterse en un berenjenal,* to involve oneself in difficulties.

berenjenín, *n.m. (bot.)* variety of egg-plant.

bergamota, *n.f. (bot.)* bergamot (fruit, essence or snuff); kind of pear.

bergamote; bergamoto, *n.m. (bot.)* bergamot-tree.

bergante, *n.m.* brazen-faced villain, ruffian, rascal.

bergantín, *n.m. (naut.)* brig, brigantine; *ser* or *estar bergantín,* to hold only two suits (cards).

bergantinejo, *n.m. (naut.)* small brig.

bergantón; bergantonazo, *n.m.* great villain.

beriberi, *n.m.* (*med.*) beriberi.

berilo, *n.m.* (*min.*) beryl.

berlanga, *n.f.* card game.

berlina, *n.f.* landau, berlin, closed carriage; front compartment of a stage-coach or railway carriage; *estar, poner, quedar en berlina*, to be, put, remain in a difficult or ridiculous position.

berlinés, -esa, *n.m.f.* native of Berlin. — *a.* concerning Berlin.

berlinga, *n.f.* pole of green wood used for stirring molten metal; (*prov.*) clothes-line post; (*prov.*) tall, gawky person; (*naut.*) round timber.

berlingar, *v.t.* to stir molten metal with a *berlinga*.

berma, *n.f.* (*fort.*) berm, ground at the foot of a rampart.

bermejal, *n.m.* (*Cub.*) the red lands of Cuba.

bermejear; bermejecer, *v.i.* to be of a reddish colour.

bermejizo, -za, *a.* reddish. — *n.m.* (*zool.*) large Australian herbivorous bat.

bermejo, -ja, *a.* of a bright reddish colour.

bermejón, -ona, *a.* reddish.

bermejuelo, -la, *a.* a little reddish. — *n.f.* (*ichth.*) rochet; (*prov., bot.*) heather.

bermejura, *n.f.* reddishness, ruddy colour.

bermellón, *n.m.* vermilion.

Bernabé, *n.m.* Barnabas.

bernardina, *n.f.* (*coll.*) lie; fanfaronade, false boast.

bernardo, -da, *a.* Bernardine (monk or nun). — *n.m.* (*zool.*) variety of hermit-crab.

bernegal, *n.m.* bowl, drinking-cup, cup with scalloped edges; (*Ven.*) earthen jar to collect filtered water.

bernés, -esa, *n.m.f., a.* Bernese.

bernia, *n.f.* rug; cloak made of rug.

berniz, *n.m.* (*prov.*) [BARNIZ].

berquera, *n.f.* confectioner's wire sieve or tray.

berra, berraza, *n.f.* watercress plant.

berraña, *n.f.* species of common inedible watercress.

berrazal; berrizal, *n.m.* cress-bed.

berrear, *v.i.* to bleat like a calf; to low; (*fig.*) to bellow. — *v.r.* (*slang*) to confess, disclose.

berrenchín, *n.m.* odour emitted by furious wild boar; (*coll.*) cry of wayward children.

berrendearse, *v.r.* (*prov.*) to grow yellow (of wheat).

berrendo, -da, *a.* stained or tinged with two colours; (of wheat) having the husk tinged with dark blue spots; (*prov.*) brown (silkworm); (*Mex.*) species of deer.

berreón, -na, *a.* (*prov.*) bawling, screeching; whining.

berrera, *n.f.* (*bot.*) watercress.

berrido, *n.m.* bellow (of calf); bawl, screech.

berrín, *n.m.* child or other person in a violent passion.

berrinche, *n.m.* (*coll.*) anger, passion, sulkiness of children.

berro, *n.m.* (*bot.*) watercress.

berrocal, *n.m.* craggy or rocky place.

berroqueña, *a.* granitic. — *n.f.* granite; *piedra berroqueña*, dark grey granite.

berrueco, *n.m.* (*med.*) tumour in the pupil of the eye; rock.

berso; berzo, *n.m.* (*prov.*) cradle.

berta, *n.f.* lace collar or pelerine.

berza, *n.f.* (*bot.*) cabbage; *berza de pastor*, (*bot.*) white goosefoot; *berza de perro* or *perruna*, (*bot.*) milkweed; *estar en berza*, to be in the blade (of corn); *mezclar berzas con capachos*, (*coll.*) to say something irrelevant; *picar la berza*, (*coll.*) to make little progress in a new study.

berzal, *n.m.* cabbage field.

berzo, *n.m.* (*prov.*) heather.

besable, *a.* kissable.

besador, -ra, *a.* kissing.

besalamano, *n.m.* unsigned note bearing the abbreviation B. L. M. and written in the third person.

besamanos, *n.m.* levee, court-day; salute performed by kissing someone's hand; *dar besamanos*, to reward.

besana, *n.f.* first furrow opened with a plough; series of parallel furrows; agrarian measure of 2187 square metres (Catalonia); (*prov.*) tillable land.

besante, bezante, *n.m.* (*numis., her.*) bezant.

besapiés, *n.m.* kissing of the foot (formula of etiquette addressed to ladies).

besar, *v.t.* to kiss; (*coll.*) to touch closely (inanimate objects); *besar el azote*, to kiss the rod; *besar en la frente*, to kiss on the brow; *besar el suelo*, to fall face downwards; *llegar y besar*, no sooner said than done; *besar la mano* (or *los pies*) expressions of respect and courtesy, often used in letters in abbreviated forms (Q.B.S.M., Q.B.S.P., etc.). — *v.r.* (*coll.*) to knock accidentally against each other's face or head.

besico; besito, *n.m.* a little kiss; *besico de monja* (*bot.*) Indian heart-seed.

beso, *n.m.* kiss; (*fig.*) collision of persons or things; *beso de Judas*, treacherous kiss; false caress; *beso de paz*, kiss of peace; *comerse a besos*, (*coll.*) to kiss repeatedly and vehemently.

besotear, *v.t.* to kiss excessively.

besoteo, *n.m.* excessive kissing.

besque, *n.m.* (*prov.*) bird-lime.

bestezuela, *n.f.* small beast.

bestia, *n.f.* beast; (*fig.*) dunce, idiot, ill-bred fellow; *bestia de silla*, saddle-mule; *bestia de carga*, beast of burden; *gran bestia*, elk; tapir; *a la bestia cargada el sobornal la mata*, it's the last straw that breaks the camel's back; *quedarse por bestia*, to remain behind for lack of mount; *quien quiere bestia sin tacha, a pie se anda*, it's wise to take things as they come; *reniego de bestia que en invierno tiene siesta*, I have no time for lazy people.

bestiaje; bestiame, *n.m.* assembly of beasts of burden.

bestial, *a.* bestial, brutal, irrational; (*coll.*) enormous. — *n.m.* animal, quadruped.

bestialidad, *n.f.* bestiality, filthiness.

bestializarse, *v.r.* to bestialize oneself.

bestialmente, *adv.* bestially, brutally.

bestiario, *n.m.* bestiary.

bestión, *n.m.* (*arch.*) great beast.

bestionazo, *n.m.* big idiot.

béstola, *n.f.* paddle for cleaning the coulter of the plough.

besucador, -ra, *n.m.f.* kisser, spooner. — *a.* kissing.

besucar, *v.t.* (*pret.* besuqué, *pres. subj.* besuque) to give many kisses; (*coll.*) to spoon.

besucón, -na, *n.m.f.* kisser. — *n.m.* (*vulgar*)

hearty, resounding kiss. — *a.* kissing, spooning.

besugada, *n.f.* luncheon or supper of sea-bream.

besugo, *n.m.* (*ichth.*) sea-bream; red gilt-head; *ojo de besugo*, (*coll.*) squint-eye; *ya te veo, besugo, que tienes el ojo claro*, (*coll.*) I see through you.

besuguero, -ra, *n.m.f.* vendor of sea-bream. — *n.m.* sea-bream transporter; (*prov.*) fishing-tackle for sea-bream. — *n.f.* fish-kettle.

besuguete, *n.m.* (*ichth.*) red sea-bream.

besuquear, *v.t.* to kiss heartily and repeatedly.

besuqueo, *n.m.* hearty and repeated kissing.

beta, *n.f.* piece of thread or tape; (*naut.*) esparto cord; (*naut.*) piece of cordage used as tackle; *beta de la madera*, grain of the wood.

betarraga; betarrata, *n.f.* (*bot.*) beetroot.

betel, *n.m.* (*bot.*) betel, betel-pepper.

betería, *n.f.* (*naut.*) all the cordage aboard a ship.

bético, -ca, *n.m.f.*, *a.* Andalusian.

betlemita, *n.m.f.* native of Bethlehem.

betlemítico, -ca, *a.* appertaining to Bethlehem.

betón, *n.m.* concrete, hydraulic cement; bee-glue; (*med.*) colostrum.

betónica, *n.f.* (*bot.*) betony.

betuláceo, -cea, *a.* (*bot.*) birchen. — *n.f.* belonging to the genus birch.

betuminoso, -sa, *a.* bituminous.

betún, *n.m.* bitumen, pitch; (*hydr.*) packing for pipe-joints; cement; shoe-blacking; coarse wax; *betún judaico*, asphalt.

betunería, *n.f.* bitumen; shoe-polish factory or shop.

betunero, *n.m.* maker or seller of *betún*.

beuna, *n.f.* (*prov.*) a gold-coloured wine, made of a red grape of the same name.

bezaar; bezar; bezoar, *n.m.* (*med.*) bezoar.

bezante, *n.m.* [BESANTE].

bezo, *n.m.* thick lip; lip; (*med.*) proud flesh in a wound.

bezoar, *n.m.* (*zool.*) bezoar.

bezoárdico, -ca; bezoárico, -ca, *a.* relating to bezoar. — *n.m.* antidote; *bezoar mineral*, peroxide of antimony.

bezote, *n.m.* (*Am.*) ring worn by Indians in lower lip.

bezudo, -da, *a.* blubber-lipped.

biajaiba, *n.f.* fish of the Caribbean Sea.

biangulado, -da; biangular, *a.* biangular.

biazas, *n.f.pl.* saddlebags.

bíbaro, *n.m.* (*zool.*) beaver.

bibero, *n.m.* kind of linen cloth.

biberón, *n.m.* infant's feeding-bottle.

bibijagua, *n.f.* a very harmful ant of Cuba.

Biblia, *n.f.* Bible.

bíblico, -ca, *a.* biblical.

bibliófilo, *n.m.* book-lover, bookworm, biblio-phile.

bibliografía, *n.f.* bibliography.

bibliográfico, -ca, *a.* bibliographical.

bibliógrafo, *n.m.* bibliographer.

bibliología, *n.f.* bibliology.

bibliomanía, *n.f.* bibliomania.

bibliomancia; bibliomancía, *n.f.* biblio-mancy.

bibliómano; bibliomaníaco, -ca, *n.m.f.* bibliomaniac.

biblioteca, *n.f.* library.

bibliotecario, -ria, *n.m.f.* librarian.

bica, *n.f.* (*prov.*) unleavened maize-tart, maize-cake.

bical, *n.m.* (*ichth.*) male salmon.

bicapsular, *a.* (*bot.*) bicapsular.

bicarbonato, *n.m.* (*chem.*) bicarbonate.

bíceps, *n.m.* biceps muscle. — *a.* biceps.

bicerra, *n.f.* (*zool.*) kind of wild goat.

bicicleta, *n.f.* bicycle.

biciclista, *n.m.f.* bicyclist.

biciclo, *n.m.* large bicycle.

bicipital, *a.* (*anat.*) bicipital.

bicípite, *a.* bicephalous.

bicloruro, *n.m.* (*chem.*) bichloride.

bicoca, *n.f.* shanty; sentry-box; small fort; (*coll.*) thing of small value.

bicolor, *a.* two-coloured.

bicóncavo, -va, *a.* concavo-concave.

biconvexo, -xa, *a.* convexo-convex.

bicoquete; bicoquín, *n.m.* cap with ear-flaps.

bicorne, *a.* (*poet.*) two-horned.

bicornio, -nia, *a.* two-horned. — *n.m.* hat with two points.

bicorpóreo, -rea, *a.* bicorporal, bicorporate.

bicos, *n.m.pl.* gold trimmings on skullcaps.

bicromato, *n.m.* (*chem.*) bichromate.

bicromía, *n.f.* two-colour print.

bicuadrado, -da, *a.* (*math.*) biquadratic; *ecuación bicuadrada*, biquadratic equation.

bicuento, *n.m.* billion.

bicuspidado, -da; bicúspide, *a.* bicuspid.

bicha, *n.f.* (*coll.*) used instead of 'snake' by superstitious people; (*arch.*) fantastic cary-atid; (*Col.*) small grubs or insects.

bichar; bichear, *v.t.*, *v.i.* to pry, spy on.

bicharraco, *n.m.* (*coll.*) repugnant beast; (*coll.*) ugly, repulsive person.

bichero, *n.m.* (*naut.*) boat-hook.

bichillo, *n.m.* (*prov.*) sirloin.

bichito, *n.m.* diminutive insect.

bicho, *n.m.* general name for small insects; vermin; creature; fighting bull; (*fig.*) ridiculous person; *mal bicho*, mischievous creature or urchin; *bicho viviente*, (*coll.*) living soul.

bidé, *n.m.* bidet, toilet requisite.

bidente, *n.m.* (*poet.*) two-pronged fork; ancient weapon in the form of crescent; sheep. — *a.* (*poet.*) bidentate.

biela, *n.f.* (*mech.*) connecting-rod; axle-tree.

bielda, *n.f.* pitchfork with six or seven prongs; rake.

bieldar, *v.t.* to winnow corn by means of a *bieldo*.

bieldero, -ra, *n.m.f.* maker or vendor of *bieldos*.

bieldo; bielgo, *n.m.* winnowing fork with four prongs; rake.

bien, *n.m.* good; well-being, welfare; utility, benefit; object of esteem or love; supreme goodness. — *pl.* property, fortune, riches, land; *el bien de la patria*, the public welfare; *mi bien*, my darling or dearest; *hombre de bien*, honest man; *bienes dotales*, dower; *bienes de fortuna*, worldly treasures; *bienes libres*, unencumbered estate; *bienes mos-trencos*, ownerless property reverting to the state; *bienes muebles*, goods and chattels; *bienes inmuebles, raíces, sedientes, sitos* or *sitios*, real estate; *bienes semovientes*, cattle; *el bien y el mal a la cara sale*, good or bad conduct leave their marks on the countenance; *bien con bien se paga*, one good turn deserves another;

bien vengas mal, si vienes sólo, misfortunes never come singly; *cuando viene el bien, mételo en tu casa,* take the gifts of fortune when they come to thee; *el bien no es conocido, hasta que es perdido,* one never knows one's good fortune until it is lost; *quien bien tiene y mal escoge, del mal que le viene no se enoje,* he who has good and seeks for evil let him not complain if it comes to him; *lo bien ganado se pierde, y lo malo ello y su dueño,* well-gotten gain can itself be lost, but ill-gotten gain causes its owner to be lost into the bargain; *del bien al mal no hay un canto de real,* the good and the bad are often not far apart; *el bien suena y el mal vuela,* ill news flies apace; *hacer bien nunca se pierde,* good deeds are never lost; *contar, decir mil bienes de uno,* to speak well of someone; *no hay bien ni mal que cien años dure,* do not despair, it cannot last for ever. — *adv.* well, right; happily, prosperously; willingly, heartily, readily, very; fully; perfectly; much; *Juan se conduce siempre bien,* John always behaves well; *Pablo lo hace todo bien,* Paul does everything well; *el plan salió bien,* the plan turned out well; *el enfermo va bien,* the invalid is progressing; *yo bien aceptaría tu invitación, pero no puedo,* I would willingly accept your invitation, but I cannot; *bien se puede hacer esta tarea en una hora,* this task can be done easily in an hour; *bien se conoce que tienes dinero,* it is easy to see you have money; *bien tendrá sesenta años,* he is fully sixty years old; *entérate bien,* inform yourself thoroughly; *bien tarde,* rather late; *bien desdichadamente,* very unfortunately; *bien rico,* very rich; *bien malo está,* he is very ill; *bien malo es ese chico,* this child is very naughty, wicked; *bien criado,* well brought up; *bien andaríamos cinco leguas,* we would walk quite five miles; *bien habrán transcurrido veinte años,* it is quite twenty years ago; *¿iremos al baile esta noche? bien,* shall we go to the ball to-night? very well; *iremos bien por tranvía bien por tren,* we shall go either by tram or train; *bien (así) como,* as soon as; in the same manner as, like; *(de) bien a bien,* readily, willingly; *de bien en mejor,* better and better; *haz bien y guárdate,* do good but expect ingratitude; *haz bien y no cates or mires,* do good disinterestedly; *no bien había llegado,* hardly had he arrived; *por bien de paz,* amicably; *y bien,* well! *bien avenidos,* on good terms; *ha vivido bien,* he has lived uprightly; *he comido bien,* I have dined heartily; *bebió bien,* he drank a great deal; *vamos bien,* we are getting on nicely; *estar bien,* to be in good health; *caminar bien,* to walk much, at a great rate; *tener a or por bien,* to be kind enough, deign; *bien que,* although; *ahora bien,* now this being so; well now; *más bien,* rather; *si bien,* although, though.

bienal, *a.* biennial.

bienamado, -da, *a.* cherished, well-beloved.

bienandante, *a.* happy, successful, prosperous.

bienandanza, *n.f.* felicity, prosperity, success.

bienaventuradamente, *adv.* fortunately, happily.

bienaventurado, -da, *a.* blessed, happy; fortunate, successful; *(iron.)* simple, silly, harmless; *bienaventurados los mansos,*

blessed are the meek (used ironically of hen-pecked husbands).

bienaventuranza, *n.f.* beatitude; prosperity, felicity, happiness. — *pl.* the eight beatitudes.

bienestar, *n.m.* well-being, comfort, commodiousness; felicity, happiness; peace of mind, tranquillity, calm.

bienfortunado, -da, *a.* fortunate, successful.

biengranada, *n.f.* curl-leaved goose-foot.

bienhablado, -da, *a.* speaking clearly; civilly spoken.

bienhadado, -da, *a.* lucky, fortunate, happy.

bienhecho, -cha, *a.* having a good figure; well-made (body).

bienhechor, -ra, *n.m.f.* benefactor, benefactress. — *a.* charitable, kind.

bienintencionadamente, *adv.* with good intentions, well-meaning.

bienintencionado, -da, *a.* well-intentioned, well-meaning.

bienio, *n.m.* biennium, term or period of two years.

bienllegado, -da, *a., n.f.* welcome.

bienmandado, -da, *a.* obedient, submissive.

bienmesabe, *n.m.* meringue.

bienoliente, *a.* fragrant.

bienparecer, *n.m.* compromise to save one's face.

bienquerencia, *n.f.* goodwill, esteem.

bienquerer, *v.t.* (*conj. like* QUERER) to wish another well; to appreciate, like, esteem. — *n.m.* esteem, goodwill.

bienqueriente, *n.m.f.* well-wisher.

bienquistar, *v.t., v.r.* to conciliate, reconcile.

bienquisto, -ta, *a.* generally esteemed and respected. — *p.p. irr.* [BIENQUERER].

bienteveo, *n.m.* hut built on piles for watching vineyards.

bienvenida, *n.f.* safe arrival; welcome.

bienvivir, *v.i.* to live well, uprightly or in comfort.

bienza, *n.f.* (*prov.*) pellicle (of egg, onion); membrane.

bierva, *n.f.* (*prov.*) milch-cow.

bierzo, *n.m.* kind of linen made in Bierzo.

bies, *n.m.* bias (of materials); *al bies,* on the bias or cross.

bifásico, -ca, *a.* (*elec.*) two-phase.

bifero, -ra, *a.* (*bot.*) fructifying twice a year.

bífido, -da, *a.* (*bot.*) bifid.

bifilar, *a.* (*elec.*) two-wired.

biflor; bifloral; bifloro, -ra, *a.* (*bot.*) bi-florate, bi-florous.

bifoliado, -da, *a.* (*bot.*) bifoliate.

biforme, *a.* (*poet.*) biformed, biform.

bifronte, *a.* (*poet.*) double-fronted, double-faced.

biftec, *n.m.* beefsteak.

biftequera, *n.f.* (*Chi.*) beefsteak broiler.

bifurcación, *n.f.* bifurcation; railway branch; road junction.

bifurcado, -da, *a.* bifurcated, forked, branched. — *p.p.* [BIFURCARSE].

bifurcarse, *v.r.* to bifurcate, fork.

biga, *n.f.* (*poet.*) team of two horses pulling a biga.

bigamia, *n.f.* bigamy; (*law*) second marriage.

bígamo, -ma, *n.m.f.* bigamist; twice-married person; person married to widow or widower. — *a.* bigamous.

bigarada, *n.f.* (*bot.*) variety of sour orange.

bigarda, *n.f.* (*prov.*) tip-cat (a game).

bigardear, *v.i.* (*coll.*) to live aimlessly, lazily.
bigardía, *n.f.* jest, fiction, dissimulation.
bigardo, -da, *a.* lazy; licentious. — *n.m.* (*fig.*) rascal, scoundrel; licentious friar.
bigardón, -na, *n.m., a.* [BIGARDO].
bigardonear, *v.i.* (*prov., coll.*) to tramp about begging.
bigardonería, *n.f.* (*coll.*) state or life of a tramp.
bígaro; bigarro, *n.m.* (*ichth.*) large sea-snail.
bigarra, *n.f.* (*mech.*) horse-power pole in horse-mill.
bigarrado, -da, *a.* mottled, variegated.
bigeno, -na, *a.* producing twice yearly.
bignonia, *n.f.* (*bot.*) bignonia.
bigorella, *n.f.* heavy stone for sinking fykes.
bigorneta, *n.f.* small anvil.
bigornia, *n.f.* anvil of two beaks or bicks; (*slang*) *los de la bigornia*, gang of bullies.
bigornio, *n.m.* (*slang*) boaster; bully, rough.
bigorrilla, *n.f.* (*naut.*) round seam (in material).
bigotazo, *n.m.* large moustache.
bigote, *n.m.* whisker, mustachio, moustache; (*print.*) ornamental horizontal line; (*min.*) hole in trough or vat through which the scoria falls. — *n.m.pl.* moustaches; (*min.*) flames coming out of the vat-hole; infiltrations of metals in the cracks of foundries; *no tener malos bigotes*, to be good-looking (woman); *hombre de bigote*, man of spirit and vigour; *tener bigotes*, to have resolution and courage.
bigotera, *n.f.* leather cover for moustaches; ribbon bow formerly worn by women on the breast; folding seat put in the front of a carriage; small compass; fur edging of slippers; toe-cap; (*min.*) hole in vats for the discharge of scoria; (*prov.*) swindle, trick.— *n.f.pl.* marks left on the upper lip after drinking; *pegar una bigotera*, to play a trick; *tener buenas bigoteras*, to have a pleasing face.
bigotudo, -da, *a.* having large moustache.
bija, *n.f.* (*bot.*) heart-leaved arnotto, bixa; (*com.*) anatta; (*Am.*) concoction of seeds of this plant and vermilion used by Indians to daub their body.
bijago, *n.m.* (*ichth.*) voracious fish of the Cantabrian sea.
bijón, *n.m.* kind of gum.
bilabiado, -da, *a.* (*bot.*) bilabiate.
bilabial, *a.* (*gram.*) labial.
bilao, *n.m.* (*Philip.*) tray made of reed.
bilateral, *a.* bilateral.
bilateralmente, *adv.* bilaterally.
bilbaíno, -na, *n.m.f., a.* of Bilbao.
biliar; biliario, -ria, *a.* (*med.*) biliary.
bilimbin, *n.m.* small tree of the Philippines belonging to the Oxalidaceæ family.
bilingüe, *a.* bilingual, bilinguous.
bilioso, -sa, *a.* (*med.*) bilious.
bilis, *n.f.* bile, gall; (*fig.*) irritability, anger, wrath, fury; *cortar la bilis*, to take antibilious medicine; *exaltársele* or *revolvérsele a uno la bilis*, to get in a rage, be enraged.
bilítero, -ra, *a.* biliteral, of two letters.
bilma, *n.f.* (*Cub., Chi., Mex.*) poultice.
bilmar, *v.t.* (*Cub., Chi., Mex.*) to place poultices.
bilobado, -da, *a.* (*anat.*) bilobate.
bilocación, *n.f.* (*theol.*) bilocation.
bilocarse, *v.r.* (*pret.* **biloqué;** *pres. subj.* **biloque**) to be in two places simultaneously.

bilogía, *n.f.* book in two parts.
biltrotear, *v.i.* (*coll.*) to ramble about the streets; to gad about.
biltrotero, -ra, *n.m.f.* gossip; gadabout.
billa, *n.f.* hazard, in the game of billiards; pocketing a ball after it has struck another.
billalda; billarda, *n.f.* tip-cat (children's game).
billar, *n.m.* game of billiards; billiard-table; billiard-hall; *billar romano*, pin-table.
billarda; billalda, *n.f.* (*Hond.*) trap to catch lizards.
billarde, *n.m.* (*coop.*) instrument for curving staves.
billarista, *n.m.f., a.* billiard player.
billete, *n.m.* note, letter; ticket; lottery ticket; brief letter; love letter; (*arch., her.*) billet; *billete de abonado*, season or commutation ticket; *billete de ida y vuelta*, return ticket; *billete kilométrico*, mileage ticket; *billete de banco*, bank-note; *billete del Tesoro*, Treasury note.
billón, *n.m.* billion (Eng., a million millions; U.S.A. and France, a thousand millions).
billonésimo, -ma, *n.m., a.* one part of a billion.
bimaculado, -da, *a.* two-coloured.
bimano, -na, *a.* bimanal, bimanous. — *n.m.f.* bimane.
bimba, *n.f.* (*coll.*) top-hat.
bimbalete, *n.m.* (*Mex.*) prop; buttress, pillar.
bimbral, *n.m.* plantation of osiers.
bimbre, *n.m.* (*bot.*) osier, willow.
bimembre, *a.* having two members.
bimensual, *a.* twice-monthly.
bimestral, *a.* bimensal, bimestrial.
bimestre, *a.* [BIMESTRAL]. — *n.m.* period of two months' duration; two months' rent, pension, salary, etc.
bimetálico, -ca, *a.* bimetallic.
bimetalismo, *m.* bimetallism.
bimetalista, *n.m.f.* bimetallist. — *a.* bimetallic.
bimotor, -ra, *a.* (*aer.*) two-motor.
bina, *n.f.;* **binazón,** *n.m.* digging or ploughing a second time.
binación, *n.f.* (*eccl.*) celebration of Mass twice on a feast day.
binadera, *n.f.* (*agric.*) hoe.
binado, -da, *a.* (*bot.*) geminative.
binador, *n.m.* digger; hoe, weeding-fork.
binar, *v.t.* to plough or dig ground for the second time; to hoe and weed vines for the second time. — *v.i.* (*eccl.*) to celebrate two Masses on a feast day.
binario, -ria, *a.* binary.
binocular; biocular, *a.* (*med.*) binocular.
binóculo; bióculo, *n.m.* binocle, dioptric telescope; field-glasses; opera glasses; (*surg.*) eye-bandage.
binomio, *n.m.* (*alg.*) binomial; *binomio de Newton*, binomial theorem.
binubo, -ba, *n.m.f., a.* twice-married (person).
binza, *n.f.* pellicle (of egg, onion); any thin membrane; (*prov.*) tomato or capsicum seed.
bioblasto, *n.m.* bioblast.
bioculado, -da, *a.* two-eyed.
biodinámica, *n.f.* biodynamics.
biogénesis; biogenia, *n.f.* biogenesis.
biogenético, -ca; biogénico, -ca, *a.* biogenetic.
biografía, *n.f.* biography.

biografiado, -da, *n.m.f.* subject of a biography.
biografiar, *v.t.* to write a biography.
biográfico, -ca, *a.* biographical.
biógrafo, -fa, *n.m.f.* biographer.
biología, *n.f.* biology.
biológicamente, *adv.* biologically.
biológico, -ca, *a.* biological.
biólogo, *n.m.* biologist.
biomagnetismo, *n.m.* biomagnetism.
biombo, *n.m.* folding screen.
biometría, *n.f.* biometry.
biomía, *n.f.* (*entom.*) cattle-fly.
bionomía, *n.f.* bionomics.
bioplasma, *n.m.* bioplasm.
bioquímica, *n.f.* biochemistry.
bioscopia, *n.f.* observation of life's phenomena.
bioscopio, *n.m.* (*physiol.*) kind of hygrometer to help to distinguish real from apparent death.
biósfera, *n.f.* bioplasm, protoplasm.
biotecnia, *n.f.* art of utilizing animals and plants.
biótico, -ca, *a.* biotic.
biotita, *n.f.* (*min.*) biotite.
bióxido, *n.m.* (*chem.*) dioxide.
bipartición, *n.f.* bipartition.
bipartido, -da, *a.* (*poet.*) bipartite.
bipedal, *a.* bipedal.
bípede, *a.* biped.
bípedo, -da, *n.m.f.* biped. — *a.* [BÍPEDE].
bipétalo, -la, *a.* (*bot.*) bipetalous.
biplano, -na, *n.m.*, *a.* (*aer.*) biplane.
bipolar, *a.* bipolar.
bipontino, -na, *n.m.f.*, *a.* native of or relating to Zweibrücken in the Palatinate.
biribís, *n.m.* game like roulette.
biricú, *n.m.* sword-belt.
birimbao, *n.m.* (*mus.*) jew's-harp *or* jew's-trump.
birla, *n.f.* (*prov.*) ninepin, skittle.
birlador, *n.m.f.*, *a.* one who bowls a second time from where the ball stopped the first time. — *n.m.* (*slang*) swindler.
birlar, *v.t.* to bowl a second time from the place where the ball stopped the first time; (*coll.*) to kill, knock down at a blow; to snatch away; to dispossess; (*slang*) to defraud, swindle.
birlesca, *n.f.* (*slang*) assembly of thieves and ruffians.
birlesco, *n.m.* (*slang*) thief, ruffian.
birli, *n.m.* (*print.*) blank space at bottom of printed page; printer's earnings.
birlibirloque, *n.m.*; *por arte de birlibirloque,* (*coll.*) by occult and extraordinary means.
birlo; birloche, *n.m.* (*slang*) thief.
birlocha, *n.f.* paper-kite.
birlocho, *n.m.* barouche.
birlón, *n.m.* (*prov.*) jack pin, large middle skittle in the game of ninepins.
birlonga, *n.f.* manner of playing ombre; *a la birlonga,* confusedly, carelessly.
Birmania, *n.f.* Burma.
birmano, -na, *n.m.f.*, *a.* native of or appertaining to Burma.
birrectángulo, -la, *a.* (*geom.*) having two right angles; *triángulo esférico birrectángulo,* spherical triangle with two right angles.
birreme, *a.*, *n.m.* bireme; having two banks of oars.
birreta, *n.f.* biretta, cardinal's cap.

birrete, *n.m.* biretta; official head-gear of university professors, judges, and lawyers; béret.
birretina, *n.f.* small biretta or cap; grenadier or hussar's cap.
bis, *adv.* twice, repeated *or* second; ¡bis! ¡bis! encore!
bisabuelo, *n.m.*; **bisabuela,** *n.f.* great-grandfather (or -mother).
bisagra, *n.f.* hinge; shoemaker's boxwood polisher; *bisagras y pernos,* hooks and hinges.
bisagüelo, -la, *n.m.f.* (*obs.*) grandfather, grandmother.
bisalto, *n.m.* (*prov.*) pea.
bisanual; bisanuo, -nua, *a.* (*bot.*) biennial.
bisar, *v.t.* to repeat (music).
bisasado, -da, *a.* twice-roasted.
bisbís, *n.m.* game resembling roulette.
bisbisar; bisbisear, *v.i.*, *v.t.* (*coll.*) to mumble, mutter.
bisbiseo, *n.m.* muttering, mumbling.
bisecar, *v.t.* to bisect.
bisección, *n.f.* bisection.
bisector, -triz, *a.* (*geom.*) bisecting. — *n.f.* bisector (of an angle).
bisecular, *a.* two centuries old.
bisel, *n.m.* bevelled edge of a looking-glass; bevel; chamfer.
biselado, -da, *a.* bevelled. — *n.m.* bevelling. — *p.p.* [BISELAR].
biselamiento, *n.m.* bevelling.
biselar, *v.t.* to bevel.
bisemanal, *a.* occurring twice weekly.
bisexual, *a.* (*bot.*) bisexual.
bisiesto, -na, *a.* bissextile (year); *año bisiesto,* leap-year; *mudar uno de bisiesto,* (*coll.*) to change one's conduct or language.
bisilábico, -ca; bisílabo, -ba, *a.* disyllabic, consisting of two syllables.
bismuto, *n.m.* (*min.*) bismuth.
bisnieto, -ta, *n.m.f.* great-grandson, great-granddaughter.
bisojo, -ja, *a.* squinting, squint-eyed. — *n.m.f.* squinter.
bisonte, *n.m.* (*zool.*) bison.
bisoñada; bisoñería, *n.f.* (*coll.*) novice's rash or inconsiderate speech or action; practical joke played on new boy at school.
bisoñé, *n.m.* small wig, toupee.
bisoño, -ña, *a.* (*mil.*) raw, undisciplined; inexperienced. — *n.m.f.* novice.
bispón, *n.m.* roll of oilcloth or tarpaulin used by sword-cutlers.
bistec, *n.m.* beefsteak.
bístola, *n.f.* (*prov.*) paddle of a plough.
bistorta, *n.f.* (*bot.*) bistort, snake-weed.
bistraer, *v.t.* (*pres. indic.* bistraigo; *pres. subj.* bistraiga; *pret.* bistraje) (*prov.*) to advance or receive in advance (money); (*coll.*) to pilfer; to draw out, entice.
bistre; bistro, *n.m.* (*art*) bistre.
bistrecha, *n.f.* (*law*) payment made in advance.
bisturí, *n.m.* (*surg.*) bistoury, scalpel.
bisulco, -ca, *a.* (*zool.*) bisulcate, cloven-footed, cloven-hoofed.
bisulfato, *n.m.* bisulphate.
bisulfito, *n.m.* bisulphite.
bisulfuro, *n.m.* disulphide.
bisunto, -ta, *a.* dirty, greasy.
bisutería, *n.f.* jewellery.
bisutero, *n.m.* jeweller (imitation).

bita, *n.f.* (*naut.*) bitt; *contrabitas,* standards of the bitts.

bitácora, *n.f.* (*naut.*) binnacle.

bitadura, *n.f.* (*naut.*) cable coiled on deck in preparation for letting go the anchor.

bitango, *a.; pájaro bitango,* kite (toy).

bitar, *v.t.* (*naut.*) to bitt.

bitola, *n.f.* callipers.

bitones, *n.m.pl.* (*naut.*) pins of the capstan.

bitongo, -ga, *a.;* (*prov.*) *niño bitongo,* overgrown child.

bitoque, *n.m.* bung, stopple; *ojos de bitoque,* cross-eyes.

bitor, *n.m.* (*orn.*) rail, king of quails.

bitumen, *n.m.* bitumen.

bituminización, *n.f.* bituminization.

bituminizar, *v.t.* to bituminize.

bituminoso, -sa, *a.* bituminous.

bivalvo, -va; bivalvulado, -da; bivalvular, *a.* bivalve, bivalvular.

bixineas, *n.f.pl.* (*bot.*) bixaceæ.

biza, *n.f.* (*ichth.*) bonito, fish of the tunny tribe.

Bizancio, *n.m.* Byzantium.

bizantinismo, *n.m.* corruption by luxury (society); excessive ornamentation (art); predilection for irrelevant discussions.

bizantino, -na, *a.* Byzantian; insignificant, irrelevant (discussion). — *n.m.f.* Byzantine.

bizarramente, *adv.* courageously, gallantly, with spirit.

bizarrear, *v.i.* to act in a spirited and gallant manner.

bizarría, *n.f.* gallantry, valour, fortitude, mettle; liberality, splendour.

bizarro, -ra, *a.* gallant, brave, high-spirited; generous, high-minded, liberal.

bizazas, *n.f.pl.* saddlebags.

bizcacha, *n.f.* (*Am.*) a rodent.

bizcar; bizquear, *v.i.* (*pret.* **bizqué;** *pres. subj.* **bizque**) to squint. — *v.t.* to wink.

bizco, -ca, *a.* cross-eyed, squinting, squint-eyed. — *n.m.f.* squinter; *dejar a uno bizco,* to make one blind with surprise.

bizcochada, *n.f.* biscuit and milk soup; long split French roll.

bizcochar, *v.t.* to bake bread a second time.

bizcochería, *n.f.* art of biscuit-making; (*Am.*) cake shop.

bizcochero, -ra, *n.m.f.* biscuit maker or seller. — *n.m.* biscuit-cask.

bizcochito; bizcochuelo, *n.m.* small biscuit or sponge cake.

bizcocho, *n.m.* biscuit; hard-tack; bisque; plaster; whiting; sponge cake; *con esto y un bizcocho, hasta mañana a las ocho,* an ironical comment on a worthless gift or concession; *embarcarse con poco bizcocho,* to plunge into an affair inconsiderately.

bizcorneado, -da, *a.* (*print.*) folded crookedly (page); (*Cub.*) cross-eyed, squinting.

bizcorneto, -a, *a.* (*Col.*) cross-eyed, squinting.

bizcotela, *n.f.* sweet biscuit, biscuit with sugar icing.

bizma, *n.f.* cataplasm, poultice.

bizmar, *v.t.* to poultice, apply a cataplasm.

bizna, *n.f.* zest, woody membrane separating walnut-kernel.

biznaga, *n.f.* (*bot.*) umbelliferous plant; a cactus of Mexico.

biznieto, -ta, *n.m.f.* [BISNIETO,-TA].

bizquear, *v.i.* to squint.

blanca, *n.f.* old copper coin of the value of half

a *maravedí*; mite; brass farthing; (*prov., orn.*) magpie; (*mus.*) minim; *blanca morfea,* [ALBARAZO]; (*vet.*) white scurf, tetter, ringworm; *no tener blanca* or *estar sin blanca,* not to have a copper to bless oneself with.

blancal, *a.* white-footed (partridge).

blancamente, *adv.* whitely.

blancarte, *n.m.* (*min.*) residue, rubbish.

blancazo, -za, *a.* very white, whitish.

blanco, -ca, *a.* white; blank, hoar, hoary, light-coloured; fair, light (complexion); (*coll.*) cowardly, white-livered.—*n.m.f.* white person; coward. — *n.m.* white colour; white spot or hairs (on animals); (*theat.*) interval; (*fig.*) aim, goal; (*slang*) fool; (*print.*) recto form; (*chem.*) bleach, white dye; blank; blank space; blank, mark or target to shoot at; *blanco de huevo,* eggshell cosmetic; *blanco de la uña,* half-moon of the nail; *dar en el blanco,* to hit the mark; *blanco de ballena,* spermaceti; *blanco de España,* Spanish white, whiting; *blanco de plata* or *plomo,* white lead; *blanco del ojo,* (*anat.*) cornea; *blanca de tez,* white-faced, of fair complexion; *tela* or *ropa blanca,* linen; *arma blanca,* side-arms; *de punta en blanco,* cap-à-pie, in full regalia; *tirar al blanco,* to shoot at the target; *ejercicios de tiro al blanco,* target practice; *en blanco,* blank; *muebles en blanco,* unpainted furniture; *no distinguir lo blanco de lo negro,* to be very ignorant; *quedarse en blanco,* not to grasp the meaning, to be frustrated, disappointed; *en el blanco de la uña,* in the very least; *pasar en blanco,* to omit, make no mention of; *armas blancas,* (*her.*) argent.

blancor, *n.m.;* **blancura,** *n.f.* whiteness; *blancura del ojo,* (*vet.*) white film on the eye.

blancote, -ta, *a.* very white; (*coll.*) cowardly. — *n.m.f.* coward.

blancuzco, -ca, *a.* whitish, dirty white.

blanda, *n.f.* (*slang*) bed.

blandamente, *adv.* softly, smoothly, mildly, sweetly.

blandeador, -ra, *a.* softening.

blandeamiento, *n.m.* softening.

blandear, *v.t.* to soften, render mild, persuade, make one modify or change his opinion; to brandish, flourish. — *v.i., v.r.* to yield; to be or become softened, mollified; *blandear con otro,* to fall in with another's opinion.

blandengue, *n.m.f., a.* bland, suave (person); (*prov.*) coward. — *n.m.* (*Arg.*) pikeman, lancer.

blandicia, *n.f.* adulation, flattery; gentleness.

blandiente, *a.* brandishing, quivering.

blandir, *v.t.* to brandish; to hurtle, whirl round, swing, wave, flourish, sway. — *v.r.* to quiver, to move tremulously.

blando, -da, *a.* soft, lithe, pliant, flabby; bland, gentle; temperate, mild, pleasing, moderate; (*fig.*) effeminate, delicate; tractable, good-natured, kindly; (*coll.*) cowardly; (*mus.*) flatted; *blando de boca,* tender-mouthed (horse); *blando de carona,* (*fig.*) easily infatuated man; *blando de ojo,* tender-eyed; *ojos blandos,* (*coll.*) watery eyes; *hombre blando,* gentle or mild man; *llevar blanda la mano,* to have a gentle hand. — *adv.* gently, suavely.

blandón, *n.m.* large wax torch with one wick; large church-candlestick.

blanducho, -cha; blandujo, -ja, *a.* (*coll.*) flabby, loose, soft.

blandura, *n.f.* softness; litheness; daintiness, delicacy; affability; weakness (character); gentleness; (*med.*) lenitive or emollient application; white cosmetic; mild temperature; blandishment; soft, endearing language.

blandurilla, *n.f.* kind of fine soft hair-pomade.

blanqueación, *n.f.* blanching (metals); bleaching; whitewashing.

blanqueado, -da, *a.* blanched, bleached; whitewashed. — *p.p.* [BLANQUEAR].

blanqueador, -ra; blanqueante, *n.m.f.* blancher, bleacher, whitener, whitewasher. — *a.* bleaching; whitening; whitewashing.

blanqueadura; blanqueamiento, *n.f.* whitening, bleaching.

blanquear, *v.t.* to blanch, bleach, whiten, whitewash; to give coarse wax to bees in winter; to clean, burnish (metal); *blanquear cera,* to bleach wax. — *v.i.* to show whiteness, be whitish.

blanquecedor, *n.m.* officer in the mint who burnishes coins.

blanquecer, *v.t.* (*pres. indic.* **blanquezco**; *pres. subj.* **blanquezca**) to blanch, burnish (gold, silver, etc.), to bleach.

blanquecimiento, *n.m.* blanching, burnishing (metals).

blanquecino, -na, *a.* whitish, hoary.

blanqueo, *n.m.* whitewash, whitening, bleaching.

blanquería, *n.f.* bleaching-place, bleach-field.

blanquero, *n.m.* (*prov.*) tanner.

blanqueta, *n.f.* coarse blanket.

blanquete, *n.m.* cosmetic for whitening the skin; whitewash.

blanquezco; blanquezca, *pres. indic.; pres. subj.* [BLANQUECER].

blanquición, *n.f.* blanching of metals.

blanquillo, -lla, *a.* very white (flour, bread); *n.m.* (*Chi., Per.*) white peach; (*Am.*) small fish; *soldado blanquillo,* foot-soldier dressed in white.

blanquimento; blanquimiento, *n.m.* bleaching liquid.

blanquinoso, -sa, *a.* whitish.

blanquizal; blanquizar, *n.m.* clay-pit.

blanquizco, -ca; blanquizo, -za, *a.* whitish.

blao, *n.m., a.* (*her.*) azure.

Blas, *n.m.* Blaise; *díjolo Blas, punto redondo,* (*iron.*) you're always right.

blasfemable, *a.* blameworthy, vituperable.

blasfemador, -ra, *n.m.f.* blasphemer, swearer. — *a.* blaspheming, swearing.

blasfemamente, *adv.* blasphemously, impiously.

blasfemante, *n.m.f., a.* [BLASFEMADOR].

blasfemar, *v.i.* to blaspheme; to curse; *blasfemar de la virtud,* to rail at virtue.

blasfematorio, -ria, *a.* blasphemous, impious.

blasfemia, *n.f.* blasphemy, blaspheming; gross insult; *decir blasfemias,* to blaspheme.

blasfemo, -ma, *a.* blasphemous; cursing. — *n.m.f.* blasphemer, curser, swearer.

blasido, *n.m.* yellowing of linen through use.

blasón, *n.m.* heraldry, blazon, blazonry; arms, coat of arms, armorial bearings; honour, glory; *hacer blasón,* to boast.

blasonador, -ra, *a.* boasting, bragging.

blasonante, *a.* vainglorious, boasting.

blasonar, *v.t.* to blazon. — *v.i.* (*fig.*) to boast, brag; *blasonar de valiente,* to brag of one's courage.

blasonería, *n.f.* boasting, bravado.

blasónico, -ca, *a.* relating to heraldry.

blasonista, *n.m.* heraldry expert.

blastema, *n.m.* (*biol.*) blastema.

blastodermo, *n.m.* (*biol.*) blastoderm.

blata, *n.f.* (*entom.*) cockroach.

blaterón, -na, *a.* chattering, gossipy (person).

blavo, -va, *a.* yellowish-grey and reddish colour.

ble, *n.m.* handball game.

bledo, *n.m.* (*bot.*) wild amaranth; *no se me da un bledo, no vale* or *no importa un bledo,* it is not worth a rush.

bledomora, *n.f.* (*bot., prov.*) spinach.

blefaritis, *n.f.* (*med.*) blepharitis, inflammation of the eyelids.

blefaroplastia, *n.f.* (*surg.*) blepharoplasty.

blefaróstato, *n.m.* (*surg.*) blepharostat.

blenda, *a.* (*min.*) blende.

blenia, *n.m.; blénidos,** *n.m.pl.* (*ichth.*) hake, blenny.

blenorragia, *n.f.* (*med.*) blennorrhœa.

blenorrágico, -ca, *a.* belonging to blennorrhagia.

blenorrea, *n.f.* (*med.*) chronic blennorrhœa, gleet.

bletonismo, *n.m.* water-divining power.

blinda, *n.f.* (*fort.*) blindage.

blindado, -da, *a.* (*fort.*) protected with blindage; (*naut.*) iron-plated, armoured. — *p.p.* [BLINDAR].

blindaje, *n.m.* (*mil.*) blindage; *planchas de blindaje,* (*naut.*) armour-plate.

blindar, *v.t.* (*mil., naut.*) to protect with blindage.

blocao, *n.m.* (*mil.*) block-house.

blonda, *n.f.* silk lace, blonde lace.

blondina, *n.f.* narrow silk lace, narrow blonde lace.

blondo, -da, *a.* flaxen, flaxy, light, blond.

bloque, *n.m.* block of stone.

bloqueador, -ra, *a.* blockading. — *n.m.f.* blockader.

bloquear, *v.t.* (*naut.*) to blockade; to lay siege; (*print.*) to replace temporarily missing letters by others turned upside down to facilitate recognition when changing.

bloqueo, *n.m.* blockade; *bloqueo en el papel,* paper blockade.

blusa, *n.f.* blouse.

boa, *n.f.* (*zool.*) boa, large serpent; fur or feather stole, tippet.

boalaje, *n.m.* pasture ground; (*prov.*) tax paid by cattle-owner.

boato, *n.m.* ostentation, pompous show; shout of acclamation.

bobada, *n.f.* silly speech *or* deed.

bobalías, *n.m.f.* (*coll.*) stupid person, dolt, blockhead.

bobalicón, -na; bobazo, -za, *n.m.f., a.* [BOBO].

bobamente; bobáticamente, *adv.* foolishly, stupidly; (*coll.*) without trouble or care.

bobarrón, -na, *n.m.f., a.* very silly or foolish person.

bobatel, *n.m.* (*coll.*) dolt, fool, simpleton.

bobático, -ca, *a.* silly, stupid, foolish.

bobear, *v.i.* to act or talk in a foolish manner; to dally, fribble.

bobería, *n.f.* foolery, folly, foolishness, idle conceit.

bobiculto, -ta, *a.* ignorant yet affecting culture.

bóbilis, *adv.; de bóbilis bóbilis,* (*coll.*) without labour, study or merit; (*coll.*) for nothing, gratis.

bobillo, *n.m.* big-bellied jug; modesty-piece, vest, neckerchief.

bobina, *n.f.* reel or bobbin (for winding silk, cables, etc.); (*elec.*) coil.

bobitonto, -ta, *a.* (*coll.*) extremely foolish, stupid.

bobo, -ba, *n.m.f.,* *a.* dunce, dolt, fool; one easily cheated; (*coll.*) ample, plentiful.—*n.m.* kind of ruff worn by women; stage buffoon; (*Cub.*) old maid (card game); (*Guat., Mex.*) fresh-water fish; (*slang*) stolen goods recovered by owner; *pájaro bobo* (*orn.*) penguin; *bobo de Coria,* great fool, fools in general; *manga boba,* bell or wide sleeve; *a bobas,* foolishly; *entre bobos anda el juego,* said ironically of an affair between very astute persons; *el bobo, si es callado, por sesudo es reputado,* a fool who talks little passes for a wise man; *a los bobos se les aparece la madre de Dios,* fools find fortune they know not how; *bobos van al mercado, cada cual con su asno,* fools are the most obstinate of all men; *al bobo, múdale el juego,* with a conceited man change the subject and show up his ignorance.

bobote, -ta, *n.m.f.,* *a.* great idiot or simpleton.

boca, *n.f.* mouth; entrance, opening, hole; nozzle; muzzle; pincers (of crustaceans); taste, flavour (of wine); organ of speech; dependant (person, animal); distance between compass points; (*naut.*) hatchway; hole of fish-trap; approaches (to a tunnel, etc.); cutting part of edged tools. — *pl.* outfall (river); *a boca,* or *boca a boca,* verbally, by word of mouth; *boca de bajada,* water-pipe outlet; *boca de chimenea,* chimney hole; *boca de espuerta* or *rasgada,* very large mouth; *boca de gachas,* mumbling, sputtering speaker; *boca de infierno,* volcanic crater; *boca de lobo,* (*naut.*) hole in deck for mast; (*fig.*) pitch-black darkness; *boca regañada,* mouth with disfiguring pucker; *boca de riego,* hydrant; *boca de risa,* smiling face; *boca de taco,* tip of billiard-cue; *boca de verdades,* frank person; (*iron.*) liar; *a boca de cañón,* at close range; *a boca de costal,* without measure; *a boca llena,* frankly, openly; *boca de escorpión,* (*fig.*) evil-speaking person, calumniator; *boca del estómago,* pit of the stomach; *boca de fuego,* fire-arm; *hablar por boca de ganso,* to say what another has suggested; *boca de una arma de fuego,* muzzle of a fire-arm; *andar de boca en boca,* to be the talk of the place; *andar en boca de alguno,* to be the object of someone's talk; *a una boca una sopa,* fair distribution; *blando de boca,* sensitive to the bit, tender-mouthed (horse); imprudent talker; *buscar a uno la boca,* to provoke someone to speak; *calentársele a uno la boca,* to speak at great length; to speak incoherently through excitement; *callar, cerrar* or *coserse uno la boca,* to be silent; *cerrar la boca a uno,* to silence someone; *decir lo que se viene a la boca,* to speak heedlessly; *despegar, desplegar uno la boca,* to speak; *duro de boca,* insensitive to the bit, hard-mouthed (horse);

echar boca, to sharpen (tools); to replace (billiard-cue tips); *estar con la boca a la pared,* to be in extreme want and have no one to appeal to; *ganar a uno la boca,* to induce someone to change his opinion; *guardar la boca,* to eat in moderation; to keep a still tongue in a wise head; *hacer boca,* to take an appetizer; *hacer la boca a una caballería,* to train a horse to the use of the bit; *halagar con la boca y morder con la cola,* to be false; *heder* or *oler la boca a uno,* to sponge on someone; *boca de oro,* mellifluous tongue; great orator; *decir una cosa con la boca chica* or *chiquita,* to offer a thing merely for form's sake; *estar* or *quedarse con la boca abierta,* to gape at; *irse de boca,* to become slave of a vice; to speak much without reflection; *irse la boca donde está el corazón,* to advocate one's own wishes; *la boca hace juego,* to be as good as one's word; *la boca y la bolsa abierta, para hacer casa cierta,* kind words and open-handedness ensure success; *llorar a boca cerrada, y no dar cuenta a quien no se le da nada,* do not tell your sorrows to those who will neither sympathize nor help you; *mentir con toda la boca,* to lie shamelessly; *no abrir* or *no descoser la boca,* to keep silence when one should speak; *no caérsele a uno de la boca una cosa,* to repeat a thing continually; *poner* (*la*) *boca en uno,* to speak ill of someone; *poner la boca al viento,* to be without food; *quien tiene boca, no diga a otro sopla,* one should look after one's interests in person; *quitar a uno de la boca alguna cosa,* to take the words out of someone's mouth; *quitárselo de la boca,* to deprive oneself for the sake of another; *repulgar uno la boca,* to purse up one's lips; *tener buena* (or *mala*) *boca,* to speak well (or ill) of others; *no decir esta boca es mía,* (*fam.*) not to speak a word; *respirar por boca de otro,* to be completely subjected to another; *saber algo de* (*la*) *boca de otro,* to know of something by hearsay; *tapar bocas,* to stop people slandering someone; *tapar la boca a uno,* to buy someone's silence; *traer en bocas a uno,* to speak frequently of someone; to gossip, grumble about someone; *traer siempre en la boca una cosa,* to repeat something frequently; *venírsele a la boca alguna cosa,* to repeat (food); to be on the tip of one's tongue; *en boca cerrada no entran moscas,* silence is best; *torcer la boca,* to curl the lip, pout; *no tomar a una persona en* (*la*) *boca,* not to make mention of a person; *de la mano a la boca desparece la sopa,* there's many a slip twixt cup and lip; *en la boca del discreto lo público es secreto,* prudence and reserve are best in all things; *pegar la boca a la pared,* to hide one's misery or want; *írsele la boca a uno,* to speak inconsiderately or inadvisedly; *a boca de invierno,* about the beginning of winter; *a boca de jarro,* drinking without measure; point-blank; *a boca de noche,* at nightfall; *boca arriba,* reversed, upside down, on one's back; *boca abajo,* face downwards; *¡boca abajo todo el mundo!* silence! no more argument! *boca con boca,* face to face; *a pedir de boca* or *a qué quieres boca,* according to one's desire; very well; *de manos a boca,* unexpectedly; *estar uno a qué quieres boca,* to be satisfied about everything; *de boca,* viva voce, verbally; (*iron.*) words (of boasting); *de boca en boca*, from mouth to mouth; *tu boca será medida*, what you ask shall be done; *quien tiene boca se equivoca*, the wisest of us goes astray at times; *por la boca muere el pez*, the rogue hangs himself (i.e. gives himself away).

bocabarra, *n.f.pl.* (*naut.*) bar-hole in the capstan or windlass.

bocacalle, *n.f.* entry, end or opening of a street; street intersection.

bocacaz, *n.m.* opening left in the weir or dam of a river.

bocací; bocacín, *n.m.* fine glazed buckram.

bocacha, *n.f.* large mouth; blunderbuss with trumpet-like mouth.

bocadear, *v.t.* to divide into bits or mouthfuls.

bocadillo, *n.m.* morsel, bit; thin kind of linen; narrow ribbon or tape; early luncheon given to labourers; sandwich; (*Ven., Col.*) guava jelly wrapped in banana leaves; (*Hond., Mex.*) coconut preserve; (*Cub.*) sweet potato jelly.

bocado, *n.m.* mouthful, morsel of food; gobbet; modicum, small portion; bite; bit of a bridle; poison given in food. — *pl.* dried fruit preserve; *a bocados*, piecemeal; *bocado sin hueso*, profitable employment without labour; sinecure; *buen bocado*, (*fig.*) good thing; *caro bocado*, (*fig.*) expensive and unsatisfactory item; *a buen bocado, buen grito*, you have done wrong, now take the punishment; *comer en un bocado*, to gulp; *contarle a uno los bocados*, to give someone very little to eat; *dar un bocado*, to give alms in the form of food; *con el bocado en la boca*, immediately after dinner or supper; *más valen dos bocados de vaca que siete de patata*, little and good is better than much and bad; *no tener para un bocado*, to be in extreme distress.

bocal, *n.m.* wide-mouthed wine pitcher; mouthpiece; (*prov.*) dam.

bocallave, *n.f.* keyhole.

bocamanga, *n.f.* part of sleeve near wristband.

bocamina, *n.f.* entrance to a mine; shaft.

bocanada, *n.f.* mouthful of liquid; puff of smoke; *bocanada de gente*, crowd, rush of people; *bocanada de viento*, sudden blast of wind; *echar bocanadas*, to boast of one's valour; *echar bocanadas de sangre*, to brag of one's grand relations; *hablar a bocanadas*, to speak senselessly.

bocarón, *n.m.* wind-chest of an organ, wind-trunk.

bocarte, *n.m.* ore-crusher, stamp-mill; (*prov.*) sardine-breeding.

bocartear, *v.t.* to crush ore.

bocateja, *n.f.* front tile on each line of roof-tiling.

bocatijera, *n.f.* socket for pole of a four-wheeled coach.

bocaza, *n.f.* large mouth. — *n.m.* indiscreet speaker.

bocazo, *n.m.* (*min.*) fizzled-out explosion.

bocear; bocezar, *v.i.* (*vet.*) to move the lips from one side to another (horses, etc.).

bocel, *n.m.* (*arch.*) fluted moulding; fluting-plane.

bocelar, *v.t.* to make fluted mouldings.

bocelete, *n.m.* small moulding-plane [BOCEL].

bocelón, *n.m.* large moulding-plane [BOCEL].

bocera, *n.f.* crumbs sticking to the lip after eating.

boceto, *n.m.* sketch, delineation, drawing, cartoon.

bocezar, *v.i.* [BOCEAR].

bocín, *n.m.* round piece of bass mat put about the hubs of wheels as a cap of defence; feed-pipe to overshot wheel.

bocina, *n.f.* sort of large trumpet; megaphone; bugle; motor-horn; fog-horn, huntsman's horn; speaking-trumpet; gramophone-horn; receiver (telephone); (*astron.*) Little Bear; shell used as trumpet; (*mech.*) bushing.

bocinal, *a.* appertaining to *bocín*.

bocinar, *v.i.* to sound the trumpet, bugle-horn or huntsman's horn.

bocinero, *n.m.* trumpeter, horn-blower.

bocio, *n.m.* (*med.*) tumour in the neck.

bocón, -na, *n.m.f., a.* wide-mouthed (person); (*coll.*) braggart; species of sardine of the West Indies.

bocoy, *n.m.* hogshead, large barrel or cask.

bocudo, -da, *a.* wide-mouthed.

bocha, *n.f.* bowl, wooden ball for bowls; (*prov.*) fold or bag in misfit clothes. — *pl.* game of bowls.

bochado, *n.m.* (*slang*) executed prisoner.

bochar, *v.t.* to throw a ball so that it dislodges another ball.

bochazo, *n.m.* blow of one bowl against another.

boche, *n.m.* hole in cherry-pit, chuck-farthing games; (*slang*) executioner.

bochero, *n.m.* (*slang*) executioner's servant.

bochinche, *n.m.* (*coll.*) row, tumult, noisy crowd.

bochinchero, -ra, *a.* agitating. — *n.m.* agitator.

bochista, *n.m.f.* good bowler.

bochorno, *n.m.* hot, sultry weather, suffocating heat; blush, flushing; shame, humiliation, embarrassment; rush of blood to the head.

bochornoso, -sa, *a.* embarrassing; shameful; reproachful; sultry; insufferable.

boda, *n.f.* marriage, nuptials, wedding; wedding party; *bodas de diamante, de oro, de plata*, diamond, golden, silver wedding; *boda de hongos*, (*coll.*) poor wedding; *bodas largas, barajas nuevas*, weddings too long delayed rarely take place; *de tales bodas, tales costras* or *tortas*, evil-doers come to a bad end; *lo que no viene a la boda, no viene a toda hora*, if the promises of parents-in-law are not fulfilled before the wedding, there is little likelihood of realization afterwards; *ni boda pobre ni mortuario rico*, it is usual to exaggerate one's wealth at weddings and depreciate it at funerals; *no hay boda sin doña toda*, some women are seen at every festivity; *no ir uno a bodas*, not to go amusing oneself, but to work; *boda de negros*, boisterous feast; *perrito de todas bodas*, parasite who runs from wedding to wedding; *quien bien baila, de boda en boda se anda*, the clever person is welcomed everywhere; *en la boda, quien menos come es la novia*, the host is he who least enjoys the feast; *irse con la boda*, (in gambling) to sweep the stakes; *a boda ni bautizado no vayas sin ser llamado*, don't meddle in other people's concerns.

bode, *n.m.* he-goat, buck.

bodega, *n.f.* wine-vault, cellar; store-room, warehouse, magazine; abundant vintage; retail grocery; (*prov.*) basement dwelling; (*naut.*) hold of a ship; *la bodega huele al vino que tiene,* everyone gives himself away by his words and actions.

bodegaje, *n.m.* (*Am.*) warehousing.

bodegón, *n.m.* mean eating-house, chop-house or cook-shop; tippling-house; (*paint.*) still-life; *¿en qué bodegón hemos comido juntos?* out of which platter did we eat together? a rebuke to anyone unduly familiar.

bodegoncillo, *n.m.* [BODEGÓN]; *bodegoncillo de puntapié,* travelling refreshment-stall.

bodegonear, *v.i.* to run from one tippling-house to another.

bodegoneo, *n.m.* tippling.

bodegonero, -ra, *n.m.f.* keeper of a low eating-house or tavern.

bodeguero, -ra, *n.m.f.* butler, one who has the care of a cellar; (*Am.*) retail grocer.

bodigo, *n.m.* manchet brought as church offering.

bodijo, *n.m.* (*coll.*) unequal match; misalliance; marriage with little ceremony.

bodocal, *a.* applied to a kind of black grape.

bodocazo, *n.m.* blow of a pellet shot from a cross-bow.

bodollo, *n.m.* (*prov.*) pruning-hook *or* knife.

bodón, *n.m.* pool that dries up in summer.

bodoque, *n.m.* clay pellet; lump of pressed wool, etc.; dunce, idiot; *estar haciendo bodoques,* (*coll.*) to be reduced to dust; (*Mex.,* *fig.*) bump, lump, any morbid swelling.

bodoquera, *n.f.* mould in which pellets are formed; cradle of cross-bow; pea-shooter, blowgun, blow-pipe.

bodorrio, *n.m.* (*coll.*) unequal match, misalliance.

bodrio, *n.m.* soup; broken meat and garden stuff given to the poor; hodge-podge; badly cooked meal; mixture of hog's blood and onions for sausages.

bóer, *n.m.f.,* *a.* Boer.

boezuelo, *n.m.* stalking-ox used in partridge shooting.

bofada, *n.f.* stew; large quantity of lungs and lights.

bofe, *n.m.;* **bofena,** *n.f.* lungs, lights; *echar el bofe* (or *los bofes*) to labour very hardly; to gape for.

bofeña, *n.f.* (*prov.*) sausage of pork lights and lungs.

bófeta, *n.f.* thin stiff cotton material.

bofetada, *n.f.* slap, buffet, box; *dar una bofetada,* to treat with the utmost contempt.

bofetón, *n.m.* hard slap; (*theat.*) revolving-door trick.

bofo, -fa, *a.* soft, spongy.

boga, *n.f.* (*ichth.*) kind of edible fish, mendole; (*naut.*) act of rowing; vogue, fashion; (*prov.*) small two-edged knife; *estar en boga,* to be fashionable, commonly used; *boga arrancada,* quick, strong rowing; *boga larga,* slow rhythmic rowing. — *n.m.f.* (*naut.*) rower.

bogada, *n.f.* distance covered with one rowing-stroke; (*prov.*) bucking of clothes with lye.

bogador, -ra, *n.m.f.* rower.

bogadura, *n.f.* rowing.

bogante, *a.* rowing.

bogar, *v.i.* (*pret.* **bogué;** *pres. subj.* **bogue**) to row; (*Chi.*) to skim molten mineral.

bogavante, *n.m.* (*naut.*) strokesman of a row-galley; (*zool.*) large lobster.

bogotano, -na, *n.m.f.,* *a.* of or from Bogotá (Col.).

boguear, *v.i.* to fish *boga.*

boguera, *n.f.* net for catching *boga.*

bohardilla, *n.f.* garret; skylight.

bohemiano, -na, *n.m.f.,* *a.* Bohemian.

bohémico, -ca, *a.* appertaining to Bohemia.

bohemio, -mia, *n.m.f.,* *a.* Bohemian; bohemian; gipsy. — *n.m.* short cloak, formerly worn by the royal archers. — *n.f.* bohemianism.

bohemo, -ma, *n.m.f.,* *a.* (*geog.*) Bohemian.

bohena; boheña, *n.f.* (*prov.*) sausage of pork lights and lungs.

bohío, *n.m.* (*Am.*) Indian hut.

bohordar, *v.i.* to throw *bohordos* in tournaments.

bohordo, *n.m.* (*bot.*) blade of flag; (*bot.*) scape; short spear or dart used in tournaments; stalk of a cabbage run to seed.

boicot, *n.m.* boycott.

boicotear, *v.t.* to boycott.

boicoteo, *n.m.* boycotting.

boil, *n.m.* ox-stall.

boina, *n.f.* béret, flat round cap without peak, worn in Navarre and Biscay.

boira, *n.f.* (*prov.*) fog.

boj, *n.m.* (*bot.*) box, box-tree, box-wood; shoemaker's box-wood tool; (*naut.*) [BOJEO].

boja, *n.f.* (*bot.*) southern-wood.

bojar; bojear, *v.t.* (*naut.*) to sail round an island or cape; to scrape off the stains on leather. — *v.i.* to measure around; to contain.

boje, *n.m.* (*prov.*) dolt, simpleton; (*prov.*) box-tree.

bojedal, *n.m.* plantation of box-trees.

bojeo; bojo, *n.m.* (*naut.*) the act of sailing round an island and measuring it; perimeter of an island or cape.

bojiganga, *n.f.* company of strolling players.

bojote, *n.m.* (*Col., Hond., Ven.*) bundle, parcel.

bojotero, *n.m.* (*Col.*) worker in a sugar mill.

bol, *n.m.* Armenian bole, red earth; punch-bowl; fishing-smack; casting a net.

bola, *n.f.* ball, globe, pellet, circlet; bolus; marble; blacking for shoes; billiard-ball; game of bowls; grand slam (at cards); (*coll.*) lie, falsehood, humbug, hoax; (*naut.*) truck; signalling-ball; (*slang*) fair, market; (*Ven.*) tamale; (*Cub., Chi.*) game resembling croquet; *a bola vista,* frankly, openly; *bola de nieve,* (*bot.*) viburnum; *escurrir la bola,* to flee; *hacer bolas,* to play truant; *dale bola,* what, again! *bola de jabón,* wash-ball; *dejar que ruede la bola,* to let well alone.

bolada, *n.f.* throw or cast of a ball or bowl; stroke (in billiards); (*artill.*) chase.

bolado, *n.m.* (*prov.*) [AZUCARILLO].

bolaga, *n.f.* (*prov., bot.*) flax-leaved daphne.

bolandistas, *n.m.pl.* Bollandists.

bolantín, *n.m.* fine sort of packthread.

bolaño, *n.m.* stone missile.

bolar, *a.; tierra bolar,* bole earth, bole armeniac.

bolazo, *n.m.* violent blow with a bowl; *de bolazo,* hurriedly, carelessly.

bolchaca, *n.f.;* **bolchaco,** *n.m.* (*prov.*) purse; pocket.

bolchevique, *n.m.f.*, *a.* Bolshevik, Bolshevist.
bolcheviquismo, *n.m.* Bolshevism.
boldina, *n.f.* (*chem.*) alkaloid from jalap.
boldo, *n.m.* (*bot.*) jalap from Chile.
bolea, *n.f.* (*artill.*) whipple-tree of a carriage.
boleador, *n.m.* (*vulg.*) wrestler; (*slang*) thief at fairs and markets.
boleadoras, *n.f.pl.* (*Arg.*) lariat with balls at one end to catch animals by the legs.
bolear, *v.i.* to play at billiards for amusement only; to throw wooden or iron balls for a wager; (*prov.*) to boast, lie; (*Arg.*) to throw the *boleadoras* at an animal; (*Arg.*, *fig.*) to confuse, entangle; to cheat, deceive; (*slang*) to fall down. — *v.t.* to dart, launch.
bolecha, *n.f.* cup and ball (toy).
boleo, *n.m.* bowling; bowling-green, place where balls are thrown.
bolero, *n.m.f.* dancer; (*coll.*) liar. — *n.m.* popular Spanish dance and song; short feminine jacket; kind of black-beetle. — *n.f.* bowling-green; (*Guat.*, *Hond.*) scoop or racket fastened to the hand for playing ball. — *a.* truant.
boleta, *n.f.* admission-ticket; ticket or slip directing soldiers where they are billeted; ticket or warrant for receiving money; small package of tobacco.
boletar, *v.t.* to roll up tobacco in small bits of paper.
boletería, *n.f.* (*Am.*) (*theat.*) box-office, booking office.
boletero, *n.m.* (*mil.*) billeting officer.
boletín, *n.m.* bulletin; voting-paper; pay-warrant, pay-bill; admission-ticket; lodging-billet; (*com.*) price-list.
boleto, *n.m.* (*bot.*) mushroom; (*Am.*) ticket.
bolichada, *n.f.* game of *boliche*; throw of bag-net; fish caught in a drag-net; (*fig.*) lucky stroke; *de una bolichada*, at one throw, all at once.
boliche, *n.m.* jack, small ball in bowls; skittles (game, ground); furnace for lead-smelting or charcoal-burning; inferior tobacco (from Puerto Rico); small drag-net and all the small fish caught at once in it; cup and ball (toy); (*vulg.*) gaming-house.—*pl.* (*naut.*) foretop bowlines and top-gallant bowlines; *juego de boliche*, pigeon-holes, an old game.
bolichero, -ra, *n.m.f.* one who keeps a pigeon-hole or troll-madam table; (*prov.*) fisherman who uses a drag-net; seller of small fish caught in drag-nets.
bolichillo, *n.m.* small drag-net.
bolicho, *n.m.* (*prov.*) shrimp-net.
bólido, *n.m.* bolide; fiery meteor, shooting star.
bolillo, *n.m.* lace-bobbin; iron pin in the game of pool billiards; (*vet.*) bone to which hoof is joined; mould for starching lace cuffs; starched lace cuff. — *pl.* bars of sweet paste.
bolín, *n.m.* jack, small bowl (game); *de bolín, de bolán*, (*coll.*) at random, inconsiderately.
bolina, *n.f.* (*naut.*) bowline; sounding-line; (*naut.*) (*obs.*) a punishment; (*coll.*) noise of a scuffle; turmoil; *ir* or *navegar de bolina*, (*naut.*) to sail close to the wind; *echar de bolina*, to make idle boasts.
bolineador, -ra; bolinero, -ra, *a.* (*naut.*) good at bowline sailing.
bolinear, *v.i.* (*naut.*) to haul up the bowline; to sail close to the wind.

bolinga, *n.f.* (*naut.*) main-topsail.
bolingrín, *n.m.* turf, lawn.
bolisa, *n.f.* (*prov.*) embers, hot cinders.
bolívar, *n.m.* (*Ven.*) silver coin, the monetary unit of Venezuela.
bolivariano, -na, *a.* relating to Simón Bolívar.
boliviano, -na, *a.* from or of Bolivia. — *n.m.* monetary unit of Bolivia.
bolo, *n.m.* skittle; grand slam (in the game of 'tresillo'); misère (in the game of 'cargadas'); large piece of timber; (*med.*) bolus; (*prov.*) round or lace cushion; axis of a winding staircase; (*coll.*) dolt, idiot; actor engaged for one performance; (*Philip.*) large knife, like a machete, used by the Indians. — *pl.* game of nine-pins; *diablos son bolos*, contingencies cannot be depended upon; *echar a rodar los bolos*, (*coll.*) to start trouble; *mudarse, trocarse los bolos*, to take a turn for the better or worse; *quedarse* or *volver bolo*, to come back empty-handed from the hunt; *tener bien puestos los bolos*, to make good plans for success.
bolómetro, *n.m.* (*phys.*) bolometer.
bolón, *n.m.* (*artill.*) square bolt or mortar-bed pintle; (*Chi.*) large stone for foundations.
bolonio, -nia, *n.m.f.*, *a.* student of the Spanish College at Bologna; (*coll.*) ignorant, rattle-brained (person).
boloñés, -esa, *a.* Bolognese, of Bologna.
bolsa, *n.f.* purse; money, wealth; stock-exchange; bag, fold, pouch (in clothes); game-bag; foot-muff; (*min.*) pocket, vein containing the purest gold or any other mineral; (*med.*) sac, morbid swelling full of matter; old-fashioned hair-bag for men; (*anat.*) scrotum; *alargar la bolsa*, to save money against a rainy day; *bolsa de hierro*, avaricious person; *bolsa de pastor*, (*bot.*) shepherd's purse; *bolsa rota*, spendthrift; *bolsa de corporales*, (*eccl.*) corporals holder; *bolsa turca*, folding drinking-cup; *bajar, subir la bolsa*, (*com.*) to fall, rise on the stock-exchange; *jugar a la bolsa*, (*com.*) to speculate on the stock-exchange; *llevar* or *tener bien herrada la bolsa*, to have a well-lined purse; *bolsa sin dinero, llámola cuero*, as useless as an empty purse; *tener una cosa como en la bolsa*, to have a thing securely (or, in one's gift); *castigar en la bolsa*, to fine, to impose pecuniary punishment.
bolsada, *n.f.* (*min.*) pocket.
bolsear, *v.i.* (*prov.*) to purse up, pucker, pouch (clothes, materials, etc.). — *v.t.* (*Guat.*, *Hond.*, *Mex.*) to pick the pocket of someone.
bolsera, *n.f.* hair-bag or net (for ladies).
bolsería, *n.f.* place where purses or bags are made or sold; trade of bag-making; collection of bags or purses.
bolsero, -ra, *n.m.f.* maker or seller of purses.
bolsico, *n.m.* (*obs.*) money, wealth; (*Chi.*) pocket.
bolsicón, *n.m.* (*Ec.*) baize skirt worn by poor Indian women.
bolsicona, *n.f.* (*Ec.*) woman who wears *bolsicón*.
bolsilla, *n.f.* (*slang*) false pocket used by card-sharpers.
bolsillo, *n.m.* purse, pocket; money; *consultar con el bolsillo*, to see whether one can afford a certain thing; *de bolsillo*, pocket-size; *no echarse nada en el bolsillo*, to make no benefit out of a thing; *rascarse el bolsillo*, to spend

(usually unwillingly); *tener uno en el bolsillo a otro*, to be absolutely sure of someone.

bolsín, *n.m.* gathering of brokers out of exchange hours; little stock-exchange.

bolsista, *n.m.* stock-broker, speculator.

bolso, *n.m.* purse of money, money-bag; (*naut.*) bulge in sail.

bolsón, *n.m.* large purse; (*build.*) large iron ring to hold braces of arches; board lining of the oil-reservoir (in oil-mills).

bolla, *n.f.* duty on woollens and silks formerly levied in Catalonia; tax on the manufacture of playing-cards; (*prov.*) milk-roll; (*Am.*) great richness of gold or silver ore.

bolladura, *n.f.* unevenness, dent, bruise.

bollar, *v.t.* to put a leaden seal on cloths to indicate their manufactory; to emboss, raise figures.

bollería, *n.f.* bakery, pastry-shop.

bollero, -ra, *n.m.f.* baker, pastry-cook, seller of sweet cakes.

bollico; bollito, *n.m.* (*prov.*) small loaf or roll [BOLLO].

bollo, *n.m.* small loaf or roll, penny cake or loaf; small biscuit; puff in dress; tuft in upholstery; boss; bruise made in metal; bruise, bump; (*Per.*) silver ingot; (*Col.*) tamale; (*Hond.*) a blow; *bollo maimón*, round cake; cake filled with sweetmeats; *bollo de relieve*, boss (of embossed or raised work); *ese bollo no se ha cocido en su horno*, not written or said by its reputed author; *no cocérsele a uno el bollo* or *el pan*, to be uneasy or anxious; *perdonar el bollo por el coscorrón*, the game is not worth the candle.

bollón, *n.m.* boss; brass-headed nail; (*agric., prov.*) button or bud; vine-bud; button ear-ring, pendant.

bollonado, -da, *a.* bossed, bossy, studded with bosses.

bolluelo, *n.m.* [BOLLO].

bomba, *n.f.* pump, pumping-engine, fire-engine; bomb, shell, bomb-shell; lamp-globe; electric bulb; piece of wind-instrument; earthen jar for skimming oil from water; impromptu verses; (*Col., Hond.*) bubble; (*Guat., Hond., Per.*) drunkenness, orgy; (*Cub., Mex.*) scoop or racket fastened to the hand for playing ball; (*mus.*) sliding tube; *bomba alimenticia* or *de alimentación*, feed-pump; *bomba de achique*, bilge-pump; *caer como una bomba*, to fall like a bomb-shell; *estar echando bombas*, to be very heated, at boiling point; *estar a tres bombas*, (*prov.*) to be very irritated; *bomba aspirante*, suction-pump; *bomba atómica*, atom(ic) bomb; *bomba centrifuga* or *rotatoria*, centrifugal-pump; *bomba impelente*, force-pump; *bomba de fuego* or *de vaho*, steam-engine; *bomba marina*, water-spout; *bomba neumática*, pneumatic pump; *bomba de vacío*, vacuum pump; *bomba de guimbalete* (*naut.*) common pump; *bomba de carena*, bilge-pump; *cargar la bomba*, to fetch the pump; *dar a la bomba*, to pump ship; *estar a prueba de bomba*, to be bomb-proof; *¡bomba!* listen! (calling attention to a toast).

bombáceo, -cea, *a.*, (*bot.*) bombacaceous. — *n.f.pl.* bombacaceae.

bombacino, *n.m.* bombasine, bombazine.

bombachas, *n.f.pl.* (*Arg.*) balloon trousers fastened at the bottom.

bombacho, *n.m., a.* short, wide (breeches); *pantalón bombacho*, balloon trousers.

bombar, *v.t.* to pump.

bombarda, *n.f.* (*mil., mus.*) bombard; (*naut.*) bomb-ketch, bomb-vessel; bombardone, bass reed-stop of a pipe-organ.

bombardear; bombear, *v.t.* (*artill.*) to bombard; to bomb.

bombardeo, *n.m.* bombardment.

bombardero, -ra, *a.* bombarding. — *n.m.* bombardier; (*entom.*) bombardier-beetle.

bombardino; bombardón, *n.m.* (*mus.*) bombardone.

bombasí, *n.m.* bombazine, dimity.

bombástico, -ca, *a.* bombastic, high-sounding.

bombax, *n.m.* (*bot.*) bombax.

bombazo, *n.m.* blow, damage, report of a bursting bomb.

bombé, *n.m.* light two-wheeled carriage open in front.

bombear, *v.t.* to bomb, bombard; to pump; to praise excessively; to write up.

bombeo, *n.m.* bulge, convexity.

bombero, *n.m.* fireman; pumper; howitzer.

bómbice, *n.m.* (*entom.*) bombyx.

bombicidos, *n.m.pl.* (*entom.*) bombycidae.

bombicino, -na, *a.* (*bot.*) silk-like. — *n.m.pl.* (*entom.*) variety of lepidoptera.

bombilla, *n.f.* (*Am.*) tube for drinking maté; (*elec.*) bulb, electric-light globe; (*naut.*) hand lantern.

bombillo, *n.m.* water-closet trap; sample or thief tube; (*naut.*) small hand-pump, fire-extinguisher.

bombista, *n.m.* manufacturer of glass bulbs or pumps.

bombo, -ba, *a.* astounded, stunned; (*Am.*) lukewarm. — *n.m.* bass-drum; player on bass-drum; (*naut.*) barge, lighter; leather container for numbered balls (in billiards, lottery, etc.); revolving lottery box; (*fig.*) excessive praise, puff; *dar bombo*, to over-praise, write up, puff; *de bombo y platillos*, said of literary works without merit.

bombomido, -da, *a.* (*entom.*) buzzing.

bombón, *n.m.* bonbon, sweet stuff, candy; (*Philip.*) vessel made of cane.

bombona, *n.f.* carboy.

bombonaje, *n.m.* (*bot.*) screw-pine.

bombonera, *n.f.* box for bonbons.

Bona, *n.f.* Bonn.

bonachón, -na, *n.m.f., a.* good-natured, kind (person); (*coll.*) credulous, simple-minded (person).

bonaerense, *n.m.f., a.* of Buenos Aires.

bonancible, *a.* moderate, calm, fair, serene (weather, sea).

bonanciblemente, *adv.* calmly, mildly.

bonanza, *n.f.* fair weather; (*fig.*) prosperity, success; (*min.*) bonanza; *ir en bonanza*, to sail with fair wind and weather; (*fig.*) to be prosperous.

bonanzoso, -sa, *a.* prosperous; kind; favourable, serene, tranquil.

bonapartismo, *n.m.* Bonapartism.

bonapartista, *n.m.f., a.* Bonapartist.

bonazo, -za, *a.* [BUENO] (*fam.*) good-natured, kind-hearted; credulous.

bondad, *n.f.* goodness, excellence; kindness, kindliness, goodwill, clemency; frankness, suavity, graciousness, courteousness.

bondadosamente, *adv.* kindly, graciously.

bondadoso, -sa; bondoso, -sa, *a.* kind, generous, beautiful.

boneta, *n.f.* (*naut.*) bonnet.

bonetada, *n.f.* (*fam.*) salutation by taking off the hat.

bonetazo, *n.m.* blow given with a bonnet.

bonete, *n.m.* bonnet, college cap; (*fig.*) secular clergyman; bonnet of a fortress; preserve jar; (*anat.*) reticulum of ruminants; *hasta* or *a tente bonete,* eagerly, persistently; *bravo bonete,* (*iron.*) idiot, stupid person; *gran bonete,* big-wig, person of importance; (*iron.*) idiot; *bonete y almete hacen casas de copete,* letters and arms bring glory to a family; *tirarse los bonetes,* to quarrel bitterly.

bonetería, *n.f.* bonnet factory or shop.

bonetero, -ra, *n.m.f.* one who makes or sells bonnets; (*bot.*) common spindle-tree, dog-wood.

bonetillo, *n.m.* small cap or bonnet; ornament for the hair.

bonetón, *n.m.* (*Chi.*) game of forfeits.

bonga, *n.f.* (*Philip.*) species of palm tree.

bongo, *n.m.* (*Cent. Am.*) Indian canoe; (*Cub.*) boat, barge.

boniatillo, *n.m.* (*Cub.*) sweet made of sweet-potato and sugar.

boniato; buniato; moniato, *n.m.* (*bot.*) sweet-potato.

bonicamente, *adv.* prettily, neatly, slyly, cleverly, dexterously, politely.

bonico, -ca, *a.* [BUENO]; pretty, neat, sly; *a bonico,* (*prov.*) in a low voice; in silence.

bonificación, *n.f.* amelioration, improvement; (*com.*) allowance, discount, bonus.

bonificar, *v.t.* (*pret.* **bonifiqué;** *pres. subj.* **bonifique**) (*com.*) to receive on account; to credit; to ameliorate, improve.

bonijo, *n.m.* (*prov.*) ground olive stone.

bonina, *n.f.* (*bot.*) ox-eye camomile.

bonísimo, -ma, *a. superl.* [BUENO] very good.

bonítalo, *n.m.* (*ichth.*) [BONITO].

bonitamente, *adv.* prettily, neatly; gradually, slowly.

bonitera, *n.f.* bonito fishing and season for same.

bonitillo, -lla, *a.* rather pretty [BONITO].

bonito, -ta, *a.* pretty good, passable; pretty, graceful, gallant, elegant; neat, nice, dainty [BUENO].

bonito, *n.m.* (*ichth.*) bonito, striped tunny; (*slang*) short capeless cloak.

bonitolera, *n.f.* (*prov.*) imitation fish-bait used in tunny fishing.

bonizal, *n.m.* (*bot.*) panic-field.

bonizo, *n.m.* (*bot.*) variety of panic growing wild in Asturias.

bono, *n.m.* relief ticket (charity), voucher; (*com.*) bond, certificate.

bonote, *n.m.* coconut fibre; (*naut.*) coir.

bonzo, *n.m.* bonze, a priest of Buddha.

boñiga, *n.f.* cow-dung.

boñigar, *n.m.* kind of round white fig.

boñigo, *n.m.* piece of cow-dung.

bootes, *n.m.* (*astron.*) Bootes, a northern constellation.

boque, *n.m.* (*prov., zool.*) buck.

boqué; boquí, *n.m.* (*slang*) hunger.

boqueada, *n.f.* gasp, gasping (used only when referring to imminent death of person or animal); *dar la última boqueada,* to be at the last gasp, at the point of death; *dar* or *estar dando las boqueadas,* (*coll.*) to be terminating.

boquear, *v.i.* to gape, gasp; to breathe one's last, expire; (*coll.*) to be ending, terminating. — *v.t.* to pronounce, utter.

boquera, *n.f.* sluice in irrigation canal; door of hayloft; (*prov.*) opening in enclosures for cattle; (*prov.*) cesspool; (*med.*) excoriation of the angles of the lips; (*vet.*) ulcer in the mouth.

boquerón, *n.m.* wide opening, large hole [BOQUERA]; (*ichth.*) anchovy.

boquete, *n.m.* gap, narrow entrance.

boquiabierto, -ta, *a.* open-mouthed; (*fig.*) gaping, astonished.

boquiancho, -cha, *a.* wide-mouthed.

boquiangosto, -ta, *a.* narrow-mouthed.

boquiblando, -da, *a.* tender-mouthed (horse); (*fig.*) indiscreet (speaker).

boquiconejuno, -na, *a.* rabbit-mouthed; hare-lipped (horse).

boquiduro, -ra, *a.* hard-mouthed (horse).

boquifresco, -ca, *a.* fresh-mouthed (horse); (*coll.*) frank, outspoken.

boquifruncido, -da, *a.* having the corners of the mouth low or narrow (horse); pucker-mouthed.

boquihendido, -da, *a.* large-mouthed (horse).

boquihundido, -da, *a.* having the corners of the mouth placed very high (horse).

boquilla, *n.f.* lower opening of breeches; opening in irrigation canal; chisel-cut, mortise; cigar- or cigarette-holder; mouthpiece of a wind-instrument; bomb-hole; burner of lamp; mouth of a scabbard; lighting tip of cigar; cigarette tip (of cardboard, cork, etc.); (*build.*) verge, course; (*mech.*) nozzle; *de boquilla,* in jest; *boquilla de bolsillo,* purse-clasp .

boquimuelle, *a.* tender-mouthed (horse); (*fig.*) easily imposed upon.

boquín, *n.m.* coarse kind of baize; executioner, hangman.

boquina, *n.f.* (*prov.*) buckskin.

boquinatural, *a.* well-mouthed (horse).

boquinegro, -gra, *a.* black-mouthed (of animals). — *n.m.f.* kind of snail.

boquipando, -da, *n.m.f.*, *a.* prudent, discreet, slow (speaker); (*iron.*) gossip, chatterbox.

boquirrasgado, -da, *a.* deep-mouthed.

boquirroto, -ta, *a.* deep-mouthed; (*coll.*) loquacious, garrulous.

boquirrubio, -bia, *a.* simple, artless. — *n.m.* conceited youth.

boquiseco, -ca, *a.* dry-mouthed (horse); (*fig.*) showy, unsubstantial.

boquisumido, -da, *a.* [BOQUIHUNDIDO] with a sunken mouth.

boquita, *n.f.* small mouth.

boquitorcido, -da; boquituerto, -ta, *a.* wry-mouthed, having a crooked mouth.

boquiverde, *n.m.f.*, *a.* plain-spoken about improper subjects.

boracita, *n.f.* (*min.*) boracite.

borásico, -ca, *a.* (*chem.*) boracic.

boratado, -da, *a.* mixed with boric acid.

boratera, *n.f.* (*Chi.*) borate mine.

boratero, -ra, *a.* (*Chi.*) belonging to borate. — *n.m.* (*Chi.*) worker in a borate mine.

borato, *n.m.* (*chem.*) borate.

bórax, *n.m.* (*chem.*) borax, sodium biborate.

borbollar; borbollear; borbollonear, *v.i.* to bubble out, gush out (water).

borbolleamiento, *n.m.* bubbling.

borbollón; borbotón, *n.m.* bubbling, gushing up of water; flash; *a borbollones* or *borbotones,* impetuously, bubbling over; *hablar a borbotones,* to speak hastily and incorrectly.

borbónico, -ca, *a.* relating to the Bourbons.

borbonismo, *n.m.* Bourbonism.

borbonista, *n.m.f., a.* Bourbonist.

borbor, *n.m.* action of bubbling.

borborigmo, *n.m.* (*med.*) rumbling in the bowels.

borboritar, *v.i.* to flow or rush out with violence; to outburst.

borborito, *n.m.* (*prov.*) [BORBOTÓN].

borbotar, *v.i.* to gush out, boil over (water).

borbotón, *n.m.* [BORBOLLÓN].

borceguí, *n.m.* buskin, half-boot; laced shoe.

borceguinería, *n.f.* shop where laced shoes are made or sold.

borceguinero, -ra, *n.m.f.* maker or retailer of laced shoes.

borcelana, *n.f.* (*prov.*) wash-bowl.

borcellar, *n.m.* brim of a vessel.

borda, *n.f.* hut, cottage; (*naut.*) main-sail (of a galley); gunwale.

bordada, *n.f.* (*naut.*) board, tack; (*coll.*) promenade, stroll; *dar una bordada,* (*naut.*) to tack; (*coll.*) to promenade.

bordadillo, *n.m.* (*obs.*) double-flowered taffeta.

bordado, -da, *a.* embroidered; *bordado a cadeneta,* chain-stitch embroidery; *bordado a canutillo,* embroidered with gold or silver twist; *bordado al* or *de pasado,* embroidered both sides alike; *bordado de imaginería,* embroidered picture; *bordado de recamado,* raised embroidery; *bordado de sobrepuesto,* appliqué. — *n.m.* embroidery. — *p.p.* [BORDAR].

bordador, -ra, *n.m.f.* embroiderer.

bordadura, *n.f.* embroidery; embroidering; (*her.*) bordure.

bordaje, *n.m.* (*naut.*) side-planks of a ship.

bordar, *v.t.* to embroider; (*fig.*) to perform a thing prettily and artistically; *bordar al tambor,* to tambour; *bordar de realce,* to do raised embroidery; *bordar con* or *de oro,* to embroider with gold; *bordar en cañamazo,* to embroider on canvas.

borde, *n.m.* border, outer edge, margin, fringe, ledge, verge; hem of a garment; brim of a vessel; (*naut.*) board; *a borde,* on the brink, on the eve. — *a.* wild, savage, uncultivated; bastard (child).

bordear, *v.i.* to walk on the edge or border; (*naut.*) to ply to windward.

bordelés, -sa, *n.m.f., a.* of or from Bordeaux.

bordeo, *n.m.* (*naut.*) boarding, tacking.

bordo, *n.m.* (*naut.*) side of a ship; tack; border, outer edge; *a bordo,* on board ship; *al bordo, bordo con bordo,* alongside the ship; *de alto bordo,* large sea-going (vessel); (*fig.*) important person or business; *dar bordos,* (*naut.*) to tack; *rendir el bordo en,* (*naut.*) to arrive at.

bordón, *n.m.* Jacob's staff, pilgrim's staff; guide and support of another; refrain or burden of a song; bass-string; snares (of side drum); (*surg.*) gut for certain operations; (*print.*) omission in setting-up; vicious repetition of words; *bordón y calabaza, vida holgada,* said of vagabonds.

bordonado, -da, *a.* (*her.*) pommée, pommetty.

bordoncillo, *n.m.* catchword, refrain.

bordoneado, -da, *a.* beaten, pommelled. — *p.p.* [BORDONEAR].

bordonear, *v.i.* to try the ground with a staff or stick; to beat, cudgel, club; (*fig.*) to rove or wander about.

bordonería, *n.f.* wandering idly about, on pretence of devotion.

bordonero, -ra, *n.m.f.* vagrant, vagabond, tramp.

bordura, *n.f.* (*her.*) bordure.

boreal, *a.* boreal, northern.

bóreas, *n.m.* Boreas, the north wind.

Borgoña, *n.f.* Burgundy.

borgoña, *n.m.* Burgundy wine.

borgoñón, -na, *n.m.f., a.* of or from Burgundy; *a la borgoñona,* in the Burgundy fashion.

borgoñota, *n.f.* sort of ancient helmet; *a la borgoñota,* in the Burgundy fashion.

borguil, *n.m.* (*prov.*) haystack.

bórico, -ca, *a* (*chem.*) boric, boracic.

borinqueño, -ña, *n.m.f.* a native of Puerto Rico.

borla, *n.f.* tassel, tuft, lock; doctor's bonnet or doctorship in universities. — *pl.* (*bot.*) amaranth; *borla para polvos de tocador,* toilet powder-puff; *tomar la borla,* to graduate as a doctor or master.

borlica; borlita, *n.f.* small tassel.

borlilla, *n.f.* (*bot.*) anther.

borlón, *n.m.* large tassel [BORLA]; napped, tufted stuff, made of thread and cotton yarn. — *pl.* (*bot.*) amaranth.

borne, *n.m.* end of a lance; (*bot.*) kind of oak; (*elec.*) binding post, binding screw; terminal; (*slang*) gallows, gibbet. — *a.* brittle, splintery (wood).

borneadero, *n.m.* (*naut.*) berth of a ship at anchor; swinging berth.

borneadizo, -za, *a.* pliant, flexible, easily warped or bent.

bornear, *v.t.* to bend, turn, twist; (*arch.*) to model and cut pillars all round; (*arch.*) to hoist, move and set down building blocks, etc.; (*arch.*) to mark out; to make sure something is level or straight. — *v.i.* (*prov.*) to edge, sidle, pirouette; (*naut.*) to swing around the anchor. — *v.r.* to warp, turn.

borneo, *n.m.* turning or winding a thing; swinging motion in dancing; warping; (*naut.*) swinging around the anchor.

bornero, -ra, *a.* blackish (mill-stone); ground (by such a stone).

borní, *n.m* (*orn.*) kind of falcon.

bornido, *n.m.* (*slang*) hanged man.

bornizo, *a.* said of cork obtained from the first stripping. — *n.m.* (*prov., agric.*) stem, sucker.

boro, *n.m.* (*chem.*) boron, borax.

borococo, *n.m.* (*prov.*) dish of fried tomatoes and eggs.

borona, *n.f.* (*bot.*) millet, maize; Indian corn; (*prov.*) bread made from this grain; (*Am.*) crumb or bit of bread.

boronía, *n.f.* [ALBORONÍA].

borra, *n.f.* yearling ewe; coarsest part of wool; goat's hair; nap (of cloth); floss, fluff; cotton; tax or duty on sheep; lees, sediment, waste; silk waste; (*coll.*) idle talk, trash; borax; *borra de lana,* flock wool; *borra de seda,* silk waste; *¿acaso es borra?* perhaps you think it is rubbish? *meter borra,* to introduce trash in writings, etc.

borrable, *a.* effaceable, erasable, eradicable.

borracha, *n.f.* (*coll.*) borachio, a leather wine-bag.

borrachada, *n.f.* [BORRACHERA].

borrachear, *v.i.* to be often drunk.

borrachera; borrachería, *n.f.* drunkenness, hard-drinking; carousal, revelry, drunken feast; (*coll.*) madness, great folly.

borrachero, *n.m.* (*Am.*) shrub of the Solanaceæ family whose fruit, ingested, cause delirium.

borrachez, *n.f.* intoxication; (*fig.*) perturbation of the judgment or reason; *borrachez de agua nunca se acaba,* vices grow with opportunities.

borrachico, *n.m.* (*prov., bot.*) madroño fruit.

borrachín, *n.m.* habitual drunkard [BORRACHO].

borracho, -cha, *a.* drunk, intoxicated; (*coll.*) inflamed by passion; applied to fruits and flowers of a violet colour, and to biscuits, cakes, etc., soaked in wine; *sopa borracha,* wine-cake; *borracho de cerveza,* drunk on beer.

borrachón; borrachonazo, *n.m.* great drunkard, tippler [BORRACHO].

borrachuelo. -la, *n.m.f.,* *a.* little tippler [BORRACHO]. — *n.f.* (*bot.*) bearded darnel, ray-grass.

borrado, -da, *a.* (*Per.*) pock-marked. — *p.p.* [BORRAR].

borrador, *n.m.* rough copy or draft; blotter; waste-book; *sacar de borrador a uno,* (*coll.*) to clothe someone decently.

borradura, *n.f.* erasure, scratching out, effacement.

borragíneo, -a, *a.* (*bot.*) applied to plants of the Boraginaceæ family.

borraj, *n.m.* borax; tincal.

borraja, *n.f.* (*bot.*) borage.

borrajear, *v.i.* to scribble, scrawl.

borrajo, *n.m.* embers, hot ashes, cinders; dead pine leaves.

borrar, *v.t.* to cross out, strike out; to scratch out, blot, efface, erase, rub out; (*fig.*) to expunge, obliterate; *borrar de la matrícula,* to strike out from the list; *la ausencia borra los recuerdos,* out of sight, out of mind. — *v.r.* to disappear; *borrarse de la memoria,* to forget.

borrasca, *n.f.* storm, tempest, squall; (*fig.*) hazard, danger, obstruction; (*coll.*) orgy; (*Mex.*) exhaustion of a mine.

borrascoso, -sa, *a.* stormy, gusty; (*fig.*) boisterous, tempestuous; (*coll.*) disorderly (life).

borrasquero, -ra, *a.* (*coll.*) revelling.

borregada, *n.f.* large flock of sheep or lambs.

borrego, -ga, *n.m.f.* lamb not yet two years old; (*coll.*) simpleton; (*Cub., Mex.*) hoax, practical joke. — *n.m.pl.* (*coll.*) fleecy clouds; *no haber tales borregos,* not to be any such thing.

borregoso, -sa, *a.* curly.

borreguero, -ra, *a.* suitable for lambs (pasture land); fleecy (sky). — *n.m.f.* shepherd, shepherdess who tends lambs.

borreguil, *a.* appertaining to *borrego.*

borreguillo, *n.m.* isolated cloudlet.

borreguito, *n.m.* little lamb [BORREGO].

borrén, *n.m.* panel of saddle.

borrica, *n.f.* she-ass; (*coll.*) ignorant woman; *a la borrica arrodillada, doblarle la carga,* said of those who overwork others.

borricada, *n.f.* drove of asses; cavalcade on asses; (*coll.*) silly or foolish word or action.

borricalmente, *adv.* (*coll.*) in an asinine manner.

borrico, *n.m.* ass; (*coll.*) fool; (*carp.*) trestle; *caer de su borrico,* to acknowledge one's error; *poner sobre un borrico,* to threaten with a public whipping; *puesto en el borrico,* determined to accomplish something at all costs; *ser un borrico,* to be patient and hard-working.

borricón; borricote, *n.m.* (*coll.*) plodder; laborious man.

borrilla, *n.f.* lamb's first coat; downy matter enveloping fruits.

borrina, *n.f.* (*prov.*) dense fog.

borriqueño, -na, *a.* asinine.

borriquería, *n.f.* [BORRICADA].

borriquero, *n.m.* ass-driver or keeper.

borriquete, *n.m.* (*carp.*) trestle; (*naut.*) fore-topsail.

borriquillo, -lla; borriquito, -ta, *n.m.f.* little ass [BORRICO].

borro, *n.m.* lamb not two years old; duty on sheep.

borrón, *n.m.* blot of ink, blur; rough draft, first sketch; (*fig.*) blemish; stigma; (*prov.*) pile of weeds burnt for manure. — *pl.* (*print.*) excess of paste on overlay.

borronazo, *n.m.* great blot or blur [BORRÓN].

borroncillo, *n.m.* small blot or stain [BORRÓN].

borronear, *v.t.* to sketch; to waste paper by scribbling on it.

borronista, *n.m.f.* careless writer, scribbler; one who makes blots when writing.

borroso, -sa, *a.* full of dregs, thick, turbid, muddy; blurred; badly written and full of blots and corrections; *letra borrosa,* illegible writing.

borrufalla, *n.f.* (*prov., coll.*) empty sounds or words, bombast.

borrumbada, *n.f.* extravagant expense; boastful saying.

bortal; borto, *n.m.* (*prov., bot.*) madroño.

boruca, *n.f.* (*fam.*) noise, hubbub, uproar.

boruga, *n.f.* (*Cub.*) curd mixed with sugar.

borujo; burujo, *n.m.* small lump; mass of ground and pressed olive stones; oilcake.

borujón; burujón, *n.m.* bump on the head caused by a blow; protuberance; lump; (*fam.*) untidy heap; disorderly crowd [BORUJO, BURUJO].

boruquiento, -ta, *a.* (*Mex.*) boisterous, noisy, lively.

borusca, *n.f.* withered leaf.

boscaje, *n.m.* cluster of trees, boscage, grove; (*paint.*) landscape.

Bósforo, *n.m.* Bosphorus; channel by which two seas communicate.

bosníaco, -ca; bosnio, -nia, *n.m.f., a.* Bosnian.

bosque, *n.m.* bosk, wood, forest, grove; (*slang*) moustache; *bosque maderable,* timber-yielding grove.

bosquecillo, *n.m.* small wood, coppice, grove [BOSQUE].

bosquejar, *v.t.* to make a rough sketch; to plan, draw, design, project; to explain an idea in rather an obscure way; to make a rough model of a figure or bas-relief.

bosquejo, *n.m.* (*paint.*) sketch; any unfinished

work, writing or composition; *en bosquejo*, in an unfinished state, in the rough.

bosquete, *n.m.* bosket, artificial grove [BOSQUE].

bosta, *n.f.* dung, manure.

bostear, *v.i.* (*Arg., Chi.*) to excrete (animals).

bostezador, -ra, *a.* gaping, yawning. — *n.m.f.* gaper, yawner.

bostezante, *a.* gaping, yawning.

bostezar, *v.i.* (*pret.* **bostecé;** *pres. subj.* **bostece**) to yawn, gape, oscitate; *bostezar de aburrimiento*, to yawn with boredom.

bostezo, *n.m.* yawn, yawning.

bota, *n.f.* small leather wine-bag; butt or pipe for wine or other liquids; liquid measure equal to about 113 gallons; boot; (*naut.*) water-cask; *bota de montar*, riding-boot; *bota fuerte*, strong riding-boot; *estar de botas* or *con las botas puestas*, to be ready for a journey; to be ready for any emergency; *ponerse las botas*, to become very rich or extraordinarily successful; *sentar las botas*, to stack the wine-butts (in Jerez).

botabala, *n.f.* kind of ramrod.

botacuchar, *v.i.* to meddle, interfere.

botada, *n.f.* quantity of staves; (*naut.*) launch, launching.

botado, -da, *a.* launched; thrown; (*fig.*) bold, shameless. — *p.p.* [BOTAR].

botador, -ra, *n.m.f.* thrower, pitcher. — *n.m.* punch, instrument for driving out nails; dentist's crow-bill; (*naut.*) starting-pole, boat-hook; (*print.*) quoin-adjusting tool. — *a.* throwing, pitching.

botadura, *n.f.* (*naut.*) launch, launching.

botafuego, *n.m.* (*artill.*) linstock, match-staff; (*coll.*) irritable, quick-tempered person.

botagueña, *n.f.* sausage made of pigs' haslets.

botalón, *n.m.* (*naut.*) jib boom.

botamen, *n.m.* (*naut.*) collection of water-casks; all the pots and jars in a chemist's shop.

botana, *n.f.* patch or plug to stop up a hole in a leather wine-bag or cask; (*coll.*) plaster on a wound; (*coll.*) scar.

botanero, *n.m.* instrument for applying patches to casks and leather wine-bags.

botánica, *n.f.* botany.

botánico, -ca, *a.* botanic, botanical. — *n.m.f.* botanist.

botanista, *n.m.f.* botanist.

botanizar, *v.i.* to botanize.

botanomancia, *n.f.* superstitious divination by herbs.

botante de caza, *n.m.* (*naut.*) cradle used for launching ships.

botar, *v.t.* to cast, pitch, throw, launch, fling; (*Am.*) to dismiss, to throw away; (*naut.*) to shift the helm. — *v.i.* to bound, rebound; to jump. — *v.r.* (*equit.*) to buck-jump; *botar al agua*, (*naut.*) to launch.

botaratada, *n.f.* rash, thoughtless action, frivolity.

botarate, *n.m., a.* (*coll.*) madcap, thoughtless, blustering (person).

botarel, *n.m.* (*arch.*) buttress, abutment, spur, counterfort.

botarete, *a.* (*arch.*) vault-supporting (arch).

botarga, *n.f.* (*obs.*) loose breeches, galligaskins; motley dress; harlequin, buffoon; kind of large sausage; (*prov.*) tumbler (toy) used at bull-fights.

botasilla, *n.f.* bugle signal for the cavalry to saddle.

botavante, *n.m.* (*naut.*) boarding-pike.

botavara, *n.f.* (*naut.*) boom or pole, gaff, sprit; boat-hook; *botavara de cangreja*, gaff-sail boom.

bote, *n.m.* thrust with a pike, lance, or spear; rebound of a ball; frolicsome bound of a horse; jump; gallipot; toilet-box; pot or jar; chuck-farthing hole; (*naut.*) row-boat; *bote de carnero*, buck-jump; *bote de metralla*, barrel of grape-shot; *bote salvavidas*, life-boat; *bote de tabaco*, snuff-canister; *bote de lastre*, ballast-lighter; *estar de bote en bote*, to be full of people; *de bote y voleo*, instantly, without delay.

botecario, *n.m.* war tribute.

botecico; botecillo; botecito, *n.m.* small canister; skiff [BOTE].

botella, *n.f.* bottle, flask; liquor contained in a bottle; measure equal to 1⅓ pints; *botella de Leiden*, (*phys.*) Leyden jar.

botellazo, *n.m.* blow with a bottle.

botellería, *n.f.* bottle factory.

botellero, *n.m.* bottle manufacturer or dealer; wire basket for bottles; bin, bottle-rack in wine-cellars.

botellón, *n.m.* large bottle, demijohn [BOTELLA].

botequín, *n.m.* (*naut.*) cock-boat, small boat.

botería, *n.f.* (*naut.*) collection of casks of wine; shop for the sale of leather wine-bags and casks.

botero, *n.m.* maker or vendor of leather bags and bottles for wine, oil, etc.; boatman, wherry-man.

botete, *n.m.* kind of mosquito.

boteza, *n.f.* (*obs.*) rudeness, boorishness.

botica, *n.f.* apothecary's shop; medicine in general; shop; (*slang*) drapery shop; *haber de todo como en botica*, to sell everything under the sun; *recetar de buena botica*, to spend extravagantly, depending on generous parents or friends.

boticaria, *n.f.* woman chemist; apothecary's wife.

boticario, *n.m.* apothecary; (*slang*) draper; *venir como pedrada en ojo de boticario*, to come in the nick of time.

botifuera, *n.f.* (*prov.*) discount, bonus to purchaser; (*prov.*) wine-measurer's perquisite; (*prov.*) tip, gratuity.

botiga, *n.f.* (*prov.*) shop.

botiguero, *n.m.* (*prov.*) shopkeeper.

botiguilla, *n.f.* small shop [BOTIGA].

botija, *n.f.* earthen jug; *estar hecho una botija*, said of a peevish child; also of a stout person.

botijero, -ra, *n.m.f.* maker or seller of *botijas* or *botijos*.

botijo, *n.m.* round earthen jar with spout and handle; *tren botijo*, (*fam.*) excursion train.

botijón, *n.m.* large earthen jar [BOTIJO].

botijuela, *n.f.* small jar; tip; discount, bonus [BOTIJA].

botilla, *n.f.* small wine-bag; (*obs.*) woman's half-boot.

botiller; botillero, *n.m.* maker or seller of icecream and light refreshments.

botillería, *n.f.* soda-fountain and light refreshments saloon; war tribute; pantry, larder.

botillo, *n.m.* small leather wine-bag.

botín, *n.m.* buskin, half-boot; spatterdash, gaiter, legging; booty, spoils of war.

botina, *n.f.* modern boot.

botinería, *n.f.* shoe shop or factory.

botinero, -ra, *a.* black-footed (cattle). — *n.m.* shoemaker; soldier who guards or sells booty.

botinico; botinillo; botinito, *n.m.* little gaiter or spatterdash [BOTÍN].

botiquín, *n.m.* medicine-chest.

botito, *n.m.* man's spring-side or buttoned boot.

botivoleo, *n.m.* recovering a ball at the rebound.

boto, -ta, *a.* blunt; (*fig.*) torpid; *boto de ingenio,* dull of understanding. — *n.m.* small skin for wine, oil, etc.; (*prov.*) large gut filled with lard.

botón, *n.m.* (*bot.*) sprout, bud; button; tip of a foil (in fencing); knob of doors, windows, furniture; annulet of balusters, and of keys; (*prov.*) piece of wood which fastens a fowling-net; crank-pin; dowel; handle; *botón de cerradura,* button of a lock; *botón eléctrico,* electric button; *botón de fuego,* cautery in the form of a button; *botón de oro,* (*bot.*) creeping double-flowered crowfoot; *de botón gordo,* rustic, coarse, ill-bred, clumsy; *contarle los botones a otro,* (in fencing) to give another as many thrusts as one pleases; *de botones adentro,* inwardly.

botonadura, *n.f.* set of buttons.

botonar, *v.i.* to germinate, bud.

botonazo, *n.m.* thrust given with a fencing-foil.

botoncito, *n.m.* small button [BOTÓN].

botonería, *n.f.* button-maker's shop.

botonero, -ra, *n.m.f.* button-maker; button-seller. — *n.f.* (*carp.*) socket for stanchion, dowel.

botones, *n.m.* page-boy, groom; buttons.

botor, *n.m.* tumour.

bototo, *n.m.* (*Am.*) gourd or calabash for water.

botulina, *n.f.* (*med.*) botuline.

botulismo, *n.m.* botulism.

botuto, *n.m.* (*Am.*) stem of papaw fruit; war trumpet of the Orinoco Indians.

bou, *n.m.* joint casting of a net by two boats.

bourel, *n.m.* cork buoy with flag signal.

bovage; bovático, *n.m.* ancient duty on horned cattle, levied in Catalonia.

bovátilmente; bovinamente, *adv.* in a bovine manner.

bóveda, *n.f.* (*arch.*) arch, vault; cave, cavern; vault for the dead in churches; *bóveda celeste,* the firmament; *bóveda cranial,* cranial cavity; *bóveda palatina,* (*anat.*) palate; *bóveda de jardín,* bower.

bovedilla, *n.f.* (*arch.*) small vault, cove; (*naut.*) counter; *subirse a las bovedillas,* to become nettled.

bóvido, *n.m.* (*zool.*) an animal of the bovini group. — *pl.* Bovidæ.

bovino, -na, *a.,* bovine.

box, *n.m.* shoemaker's box-wood tool.

boxeador, *n.m.* boxer, pugilist.

boxear, *v.i.* to box.

boxeo, *n.m.* boxing.

bóxer, *n.m.* a member of a secret society in China, Boxer; boxer (*dog*). (*pl.* **bóxers**)

boya, *n.f.* (*naut.*) beacon; buoy; net-float; *boya salvavidas,* life-buoy; *estar de buena boya,* to be fortunate, prosperous.

boyada, *n.f.* drove of oxen.

boyal, *a.* relating to cattle (pasture ground).

boyante, *a.* buoyant, floating; (*naut.*) drawing light, sailing well; (*fig.*) prosperous, successful; *boyante en la fortuna,* fortunate.

boyar, *v.i.* (*naut.*) to float, be afloat, refloat.

boyarin, *n.m.* small buoy or net-float [BOYA].

boyazo, *n.m.* large ox [BUEY].

boyera; boyeriza, *n.f.* ox-stall, cow-house.

boyero, *n.m.* ox-herd, ox-driver, cowherd.

boyezuelo, *n.m.* young or small ox [BUEY].

boyo, *n.m.* variety of serpent.

boyuda, *n.f.* (*slang*) pack of cards.

boyuno, -na, *a.* bovine.

boza, *n.f.* (*naut.*) rope with one end fast in a ring-bolt; (*naut.*) stopper.

bozal, *n.m.f., a.* (applied to) newly imported slave; (*coll.*) novice, inexperienced, green-horn; stupid, foolish; wild, not broken in, untamed (horse). — *n.m.* muzzle; bells on a harness; (*Am.*) temporary headstall.

bozalejo, *n.m.* small muzzle [BOZAL].

bozo, *n.m.* down, preceding the beard; exterior of mouth; headstall.

braba, *n.f.* large net.

brabante, *n.m.* Brabant or Flemish linen.

brabanzón, -na, *n.m.f., a.* native of Brabant.

brabera, *n.f.* (*arch.*) vent or air-hole of cave, etc.

brabio, *n.m.* prize, reward.

bracarense, *n.m.f., a.* of or from Braga (Portugal).

braceada, *n.f.* violent extension of the arms.

braceado, *n.m.* action of stirring molten metal; brewing, mashing.

braceador, -ra, *a.* (*riding*) drawing up the front legs too much. — *n.m.* coiner, minter.

braceaje, *n.m.* coinage; beating the metal for coining in the mint; (*naut.*) depth of water, sounding, soundings.

bracear, *v.i.* to move or swing the arms; to swim hand over hand; (*fig.*) to strive, struggle; to do the crawl (swimming); (*prov., equit.*) to draw up the fore-feet; to stir molten metal. — *v.t.* (*naut.*) to brace.

braceo, *n.m.* repeated swinging of the arms.

braceral, *n.m.* brace (armour).

bracero, -ra, *a.* thrown by hand (weapon, dart, etc.). — *n.m.* one who offers his arm to a lady for support; day-labourer; strong-armed man; *ir de bracero,* to walk arm in arm. — *n.f.* tenon-saw.

bracete, *n.m.* small arm [BRAZO]; *de bracete,* arm in arm.

bracillo, *n.m.* branch of the bridle-bit.

bracio, *n.m.* (*slang*) arm; *bracio godo,* (*slang*) right arm; *bracio ledro,* (*slang*) left arm.

bracitendido, -da, *a.* indolent, lazy.

bracito, *n.m.* little arm [BRAZO].

bracmán, *n.m.* Brahmin, Hindu priest.

braco, -ca, *a.* (*coll.*) pug-nosed; *perro braco,* pointer dog.

bráctea, *n.f.* (*bot.*) bract.

bracteal, *a.* (*bot.*) bracteal.

bractéola, *n.f.* (*bot.*) bracteole.

bradipepsia, *n.f.* (*med.*) bradypepsia, slow digestion.

brafonera, *n.f.* brace (armour).

braga, *n.f.* hoisting-rope; nursery diaper or square; (*pl.*) panties; breeches, knicker-bockers; *calzarse las bragas,* to wear the breeches; *al que no está hecho a bragas, las costuras le hacen llagas,* it is distasteful to have to do that to which one is not accustomed.

bragada, *n.f.* (*vet.*) flat or inside part of the thigh.

bragado, -da, *a.* (*vet.*) having the *bragadura* of a different colour from the rest of the body; (*fig.*) ill-disposed, of depraved sentiments; (*coll.*) energetic, firm.

bragadura, *n.f.* (*anat.*) crotch, part of the body where it begins to fork; fork of a pair of breeches; [BRAGADA].

bragar, *v.t.* (*artill.*) to suspend in the prolonge.

bragazas, *n.m.,* *a.* easily ruled, hen-pecked (man).

braguerista, *n.m.* surgical-truss maker or vendor.

braguero, *n.m.* (*med.*) surgical truss, brace, bandage for a rupture; (*artill., naut.*) breeching; (*Per.*) martingale.

bragueta, *n.f.* fly of breeches, cod-piece.

braguetero, -ra, *a.* (*fam.*) lecherous, lascivious. — *n.m.* lecher.

braguillas, *n.m.* (*fig.*) newly breeched child; (*fig.*) ugly, undersized child.

brahmán; brahmín, *n.m.* Brahmin, Hindu priest.

brahmánico, -ca; brahmínico, -ca, *a.* Brahminic(al).

brahmanismo, *n.m.* Brahminism.

brahón, *n.m.; **brahonera,** *n.f.* fold surrounding the upper part of the sleeve.

brama, *n.f.* rut, mating season of deer and other wild animals.

bramadera, *n.f.* rattle (toy); call or horn used by shepherds and keepers of plantations; (*Col., Cub.*) vent, chimney (of furnaces).

bramadero, *n.m.* rutting-place of deer and other wild animals; (*Am.*) post in corral for tying animals.

bramador, -ra, *a.* roaring, bawling. — *n.m.f.* roarer, bawler. — *n.m.* (*slang*) town-crier.

bramante, *a.* roaring. — *n.m.* pack-thread, hemp-cord, twine; Brabant linen.

bramar, *v.i.* to roar, groan, bellow; to storm, bluster; (*slang*) to fret, rage, cry.

bramido, *n.m.* bellow; (*fig.*) bawl; (*fig.*) tempestuous roaring of the elements.

bramil, *n.m.* (*barbarism for*) [GRAMIL]; (*carp.*) marking-gauge.

bramo, *n.m.* (*slang*) bawl, cry; alarm.

bramón, *n.m.* (*slang*) sneak.

bramona, *n.f.; soltar la bramona,* (*vulg.*) to use foul language (amongst gamblers).

bran de Inglaterra, *n.m.* an old Spanish dance.

branca, *n.f.* point of a horn; *branca ursina,* (*bot.*) brank ursine, bear's breech.

brancada, *n.f.* drag-net, sweep-net.

branchas, *n.f.* gills of fish.

brandales, *n.m.pl.* (*naut.*) ladder-ropes.

brandar, *v.i.* (*naut.*) to rock.

brandís, *n.m.* (*obs.*) great-coat.

branque, *n.m.* (*naut.*) stem.

branquia, *n.f.* gill of fish.

branquiado, -da, *a.* branchiate.

branquial, *a.* branchial.

branquífero, *a.* branchiferous.

branza, *n.f.* fastening ring of galley-slave's chain.

braña, *n.f.* (*prov.*) summer pasture; (*prov.*) brushwood.

braquiado, -da, *a.* (*bot.*) brachiate.

braquial, *a.* brachial.

braquicéfalo, -la, *a.* brachycephalic.

braquigrafía, *n.f.* shorthand.

braquígrafo, *n.m.* shorthand-writer.

braquiópodo, -da; braquípodo, -da, *a.* brachiopodous. — *n.m.f.* brachiopod.

braquiotomía, *n.f.* (*surg.*) arm amputation.

brasa, *n.f.* live coal, red-hot coal or wood; (*slang*) thief; *estar hecho unas brasas,* to be flushed, red-faced; *estar en brasas,* to be on pins and needles; *salir de llamas y caer en brasas,* to fall from the frying pan into the fire; *pasar como sobre brasas,* to mention, touch upon superficially; *sacar la brasa con mano ajena* or *de gato,* to use someone as a cat's paw.

brasca, *n.f.* (*chem., min.*) coating of coal-powder and clay in furnaces.

brascar, *v.t.* (*chem.*) to cover the interior of crucibles with *brasca.*

braserillo, *n.m.* small fire-pan; small cigar-lighter [BRASERO].

braserito, *n.m.* small pan to hold coals.

brasero, *n.m.* brazier, pan to hold coals; fire-pan; funeral-pile, pyre, stake; (*slang*) theft; (*Mex.*) hearth, fireplace.

Brasil, *n.m.* Brazil.

brasil, *n.m.* (*obs.*) rouge, used by ladies; *palo brasil,* Brazil wood.

brasilado, -da, *a.* of a red or Brazil-wood colour; ruddy.

brasileño, -ña, *a.* Brazilian.

brasilete, *n.m.* inferior Brazil wood, Jamaica wood.

brasilina, *n.f.* (*chem.*) brazilin.

brasmología, *n.f.* science which treats of the tides.

bravamente, *adv.* bravely, gallantly; cruelly, barbarously; finely, extremely well; plentifully, copiously.

bravata, *n.f.* bravado, boast, brag; threat.

bravatero, *n.m.* (*slang*) bully, hector.

braveador, -ra, *a.* bullying, hectoring. — *n.m.f.* bully, hector.

bravear, *v.i.* to bully, hector, menace.

bravera, *n.f.* vent or chimney of ovens.

braveza, *n.f.* bravery, vigour, valour; ferocity; fury of the elements.

bravío, -vía, *a.* ferocious, savage, wild, untamed (animals); uncultivated (plants); (*fig.*) coarse, unpolished. — *n.m.* fierceness or savageness of wild beasts.

bravo, -va, *a.* brave, valiant, strenuous, manful, hardy, fearless; (*fam.*) bullying, hectoring; savage, wild, fierce; (*coll.*) severe, intractable; rude, unpolished, uncivilized; (*coll.*) luxurious, sumptuous, expensive; excellent, fine. — *n.m.* (*slang*) judge; *¡bravo!* bravo! *mar bravo,* swollen sea.

bravonel, *n.m.* bravo, hector, braggart.

bravosidad, *n.f.* elegance; arrogance, bravado.

bravote, *n.m.* (*slang*) bravo, bully.

bravucón, -na, *a.* (*fam.*) boastful, braggart. — *n.m.f.* boaster, braggart.

bravura, *n.f.* ferocity, fierceness; courage, manliness; bravado, boast, brag.

braza, *n.f.* (*naut.*) fathom, measure of about 5½ ft.; (*Philip.*) land measure of 36 square feet; (*naut.*) brace.

brazada, *n.f.* uplifting of the arms; armful.

brazado, *n.m.* armful, truss (of hay).

brazaje, *n.m.* [BRACEAJE]; (*naut.*) depth of water.

brazal, *n.m.* brace (armour), clasp of shield; brassard; bracelet; channel or ditch from a river or canal, to irrigate land; mourning band on the arm; wooden instrument for playing balloons; (*naut.*) rail.

brazalete, *n.m.* armlet, bracelet; brace (armour).

brazalote, *n.m.* (*naut.*) brace pendant.

brazo, *n.m.* arm (of the body, the sea, of a balance-beam, a lever, a chair); upper part of arm; branch (of a chandelier, a tree); fore-leg, fore-foot of quadrupeds; (*fig.*) valour, strength, power; (*pl.*) protectors, defenders; hands, labourers; *brazo de araña,* or *de candelero,* branch of girandole, lustre or chandelier; *brazo de caballo,* fore-foot of horse; *brazo de cruz,* cross-bar; *brazo de Dios,* the omnipotence of God; *brazo de mar,* arm of the sea; *brazos del reino,* states of the realm; *brazo real, secular* or *seglar,* the temporal authority; *abiertos los brazos* or *con los brazos abiertos,* with open arms; *a brazo partido,* hand to hand, without weapons; (*fig.*) by main force, with the utmost effort; *andar* (*venir*) *a los brazos con uno,* to come to blows with someone; *brazo a brazo,* arm to arm, with equal weapons; *con los brazos cruzados,* with folded arms; idly; *cruzarse de brazos,* to remain idle; *dar el brazo a uno,* to offer one's arm to someone; (*fig.*) to help someone; *dar los brazos a uno,* (*coll.*) to embrace someone; *dar su brazo a torcer,* to give oneself up; to desist; *dar un brazo por una cosa,* to offer something precious for anything coveted; *echarse, entregarse* or *ponerse en brazos de uno,* to place oneself in someone's hands; *entregar al brazo secular una cosa,* to place a matter in the hands of someone who will deal promptly with it; *ir, venir* or *estar hecho un brazo de mar,* to be gorgeously attired; *no dar su brazo a torcer,* not to give in; to maintain one's opinion; *ponerse* or *tomarse a brazos,* to struggle, fight; *quedar a uno el brazo sabroso,* to be proud of something done and with desire to repeat it; *ser el brazo derecho de uno,* to be someone's right-hand man; *soltar uno los brazos,* to let one's arms drop; *tener brazo,* to be very robust and strong; *venirse* or *volverse con los brazos cruzados,* to return empty-handed; *vivir por su brazo,* to live by one's labours.

brazolas, *n.f.pl.* (*naut.*) coamings of the hatchways.

brazuelo, *n.m.* small arm [BRAZO]; shoulder or fore-thigh of beasts; branch of bridle-bit.

brea, *n.f.* resin, pitch, tar, artificial bitumen; coarse canvas; sackcloth.

brear, *v.t.* to pitch, tar; (*coll.*) to vex, molest, maltreat, plague, thwart; to play a joke (upon someone); *brear a golpes,* to beat, strike.

brebaje, *n.m.* beverage, potion (generally disagreeable); (*naut.*) grog.

brebajo, *n.m.* [BREBAJE]; (*prov., vet.*) drench.

breca, *n.f.* (*ichth.*) bleak.

brecol, *n.m.*; **brecolera,** *n.f.* (*bot.*) broccoli.

brecha, *n.f.* beach, opening; (*fig.*) impression made upon the mind; (*slang*) dice; one who completes the number of players (at cards); *abrir brecha,* (*mil.*) to make a breach; (*fig.*) to persuade someone, make an impression on his mind; *batir en brecha,* (*fort.*) to batter a breach; (*fig.*) to persecute; *estar siempre en la brecha,* to be always on the defensive;

montar la brecha, to attack by the breach.

brechador, *n.m.* (*slang*) one who comes into a game to complete the number of players.

brechar, *v.i.* (*slang*) to play with loaded dice.

brechero, *n.m.* (*slang*) player with loaded dice.

brecho, *n.m.* (*ichth.*) kind of mutton-fish.

brega, *n.f.* strife, contest, affray; (*fig.*) practical joke, jest, trick; *dar brega,* to play a trick; *andar a la brega,* to work arduously.

bregar, *v.i.* (*pret.* **bregué,** *pres. subj.* **bregue**) to contend, struggle; to struggle with difficulties. — *v.t.* to work dough with a rolling-pin; *bregar con alguno,* to struggle with someone.

bregón, *n.m.* baker's rolling-pin.

brema, *n.m.* (*prov., ichth.*) sheepshead.

bren, *n.m.* bran.

brenca, *n.f.* sluice-post; (*bot.*) maidenhair.

brenga, *n.f.* (*prov.*) bundle of fibres and filaments twisted round a trunk.

breña, *n.f.;* **breñal; breñar,** *n.m.* craggy, broken, and brambled ground.

breñoso, -sa, *a.* craggy and brambled.

breque, *n.m.* (*ichth.*) bleak; *ojo de breque,* bleary eye.

bresca, *n.f.* honeycomb.

brescar, *v.t.* (*pret.* **bresqué,** *pres. subj.* **bresque**) to extract honeycombs from a beehive.

breslinga, *n.f.* (*bot.*) variety of strawberry.

bretador, *n.m.* call or whistle to call birds.

Bretaña, *n.f.* Brittany; *Gran Bretaña,* Great Britain.

bretaña, *n.f.* fine linen made in Brittany; (*bot.*) hyacinth.

brete, *n.m.* shackle, fetter; (*fig.*) perplexity, difficulty; (*Arg.*) place in the corral where beasts are branded; (*Philip.*) leaves of betel; *estar* or *poner en un brete,* to be hard put to.

bretesado, -da, *a.* scalloped, serrated (sash, band, etc.).

bretón, -na, *n.m.f., a.* Breton. — *n.m.* Breton language; (*bot.*) borecole, kale.

breva, *n.f.* early fruit of a fig-tree; early large acorn; choice cigar; (*coll.*) any valuable thing obtained easily, bargain; *es más blando que una breva,* he is very soft-hearted.

breval, *n.m.* (*bot.*) early fig-tree.

breve, *a.* brief, short, concise, laconic, compact, compendious, close. — *n.m.* apostolic brief. — *n.f.* breve, longest note in music; *en breve,* shortly, in a little time.

brevedad, *n.f.* brevity, briefness, shortness; conciseness, compendiousness.

brevemente, *adv.* briefly, concisely, shortly.

brevera, *n.f.* (*prov.*) [BREVAL].

brevete, *n.m.* memorandum [BREVE].

brevetín, *n.m.* [EVANGELIOS].

breviario, *n.m.* breviary; abridgment, epitome; (*print.*) brevier, small size of type; (*slang*) quick worker.

brevipenne, *a.* (*zool.*) brevipennate.

brevípodo, -da, *a.* (*zool.*) breviped.

brevirrostro, -tra, *a.* (*orn.*) brevirostrate.

brezal, *n.m.* heath, heather; heathery place.

brezo, *n.m.* (*bot.*) heath, heather.

briaga, *n.f.* thick bass-weed rope; hoisting rope.

brial, *n.m.* rich silken skirt or petticoat.

briba, *n.f.* truantship, idleness; *andar* or *echarse a la briba,* to live in an idle and negligent way; *hombre de la briba,* good-for-nothing fellow.

bribar, *v.i.* to lead a vagabond life.

bribia, *n.f.* (*slang*) beggar's tale of woe; *echar la bribia*, to go a-begging.

bribión, *n.m.* (*slang*) master in the art of begging.

bribón, -na, *n.m.f.*, *a.* vagrant; impostor; knave, scoundrel, rascal.

bribonada, *n.f.* knavery, petty villainy, mischievous trick or practice.

bribonazo, -za, *a.* [BRIBÓN]. — *n.m.f.* great cheat, big rascal, impudent impostor.

bribonear, *v.i.* to loaf, loiter about; to cheat, pilfer.

bribonería, *n.f.* vagrancy, vagabondage; roguery, cheating.

bribonesco, -ca, *a.* knavish, rascally.

bribonzuelo, -la, *n.m.f.*, *a.* young impostor or rascal [BRIBÓN].

bricbarca, *n.f.* three-masted ship, square-rigged on mainmast and foremast, barque.

bricho, *n.m.* spangle, tinsel.

brida, *n.f.* bridle; bridle-rein; horsemanship; (*pl., surg.*) fibrous membranes in wounds; *a la brida*, riding with low saddle and long stirrup; *a toda brida*, at full speed.

bridecú, *n.m.* sword-belt.

bridón, *n.m.* horseman riding *a la brida;* horse accoutred *a la brida;* small bridle; snaffle-bit; (*poet.*) fine horse.

briega, *n.f.* (*prov.*) [BREGA].

brigada, *n.f.* (*mil.*) brigade; a certain number of soldiers; beasts of burden for an army; group of workers; *sargento brigada*, or *sargento mayor de brigada*, sergeant-major.

brigadero, *n.m.* civilian who tends beasts of burden in the army.

brigadier, *n.m.* (*mil.*) brigadier or general commanding a brigade; (*naut.*) officer commanding a division of a fleet.

brigadiera, *n.f.* (*fam.*) brigadier's wife.

brigantina, *n.f.* brigandine (armour for a brigand).

brigantino, -na, *a.* of or from La Coruña. — *n.f.* brigantine.

brigola, *n.f.* (*mil.*) battering-ram.

Briján, *pr.n.; saber más que Briján*, to be very wise and cautious.

brillador, -ra, *a.* brilliant, sparkling, radiant, glittering.

brillante *a.* brilliant, bright, shining, sparkling, radiant, fulgent; glossy, resplendent, golden, lustrous, light, lucid, glittering; gaudy, gay, gorgeous, grand. — *n.m.* brilliant, diamond.

brillantemente, *adv.* brilliantly, brightly, resplendently, splendidly.

brillantez, *n.f.* brilliance, brilliancy; (*fig.*) success, splendour.

brillantina, *n.f.* brilliantine, cosmetic; percaline; mineral powder for polishing metal.

brillar, *v.i.* to shine, sparkle, glisten, glitter, gleam, flare, glare; (*fig.*) to outshine in talents or merits.

brillo, *n.m.* brilliancy, brilliance, brightness, luminousness, lustre, splendour, glitter, resplendence; (*fig.*) distinction, glory.

brin, *n.m.* (*prov.*) fragment or pistil of saffron; fine canvas, sail-cloth.

brincador, -ra, *a.* leaping, jumping.

brincar, *v.i.* (*pret.* **brinqué**, *pres. subj.* **brinque**) to leap, jump, frisk, skip, gambol, hop; (*coll.*) to omit a subject purposely and pass to another; (*coll.*) to fly into a passion,

become resentful. — *v.t.* to bounce (a child); to step over others in promotion.

brincia, *n.f.* [BRIZNA].

brinco, *n.m.* leap, jump, frisk, hop, jerk, skip, gambol, bounce, bound; small jewel for head-dress.

brincho, *n.m.* flush in the game of cards called *quínolas*.

brindador, -ra, *a.* inviting; toasting. — *n.m.f.* inviter; toaster.

brindar, *v.i.* to drink someone's health, toast. — *v.i., v.t.* to offer cheerfully, invite; (*fig.*) to entice, allure. — *v.r.* to offer one's services; *brindar a la salud de alguno*, to drink someone's health; *brindar con regalos*, to entice with presents; *se brindó a pagar*, he offered to pay.

brindis, *n.m.* health, drinking the health of another; toast.

brinete, *n.m.* sail-cloth.

bringulata, *n.f.* (*naut.*) pump handle or brake.

brinquillo; brinquiño, *n.m.* hop, jump; gewgaw, small trinket (*brinco*); sweetmeat from Portugal; *estar* or *ir hecho un brinquiño*, to be very spruce.

brinzal, *n.m.* (*bot.*) blade, slip, sprig, shoot.

briñolas, *n.f.pl.* prunes.

briñolero, *n.m.* (*bot.*) kind of olive-tree.

briñón, *n.m.* (*bot.*) nectarine.

brío, *n.m.* strength, force, vigour, manliness, spirit, resolution, courage, mettle; *bajar los bríos*, to humble.

briol, *n.m.* (*naut.*) brail.

briolín, *n.m.* (*naut.*) bunt-line.

briología, *n.f.* bryology.

brión, *n.m.* (*naut.*) fore-foot.

brionia, *n.f.* (*bot.*) briony.

brios, *interj. ¡voto* or *juro a brios!*, by the Almighty! (a jocular oath).

briosamente, *adv.* spiritedly, courageously, vigorously, in a lively way.

brioso, -sa, *a.* vigorous, spirited, high-minded, courageous, lively.

briqueta, *n.f.* briquette, briquet.

brisa, *n.f.* breeze, light wind; bagasse of pressed grapes.

brisada; brisura, *n.f.* (*her.*) label.

brisca, *n.f.* card game.

briscado, -da, *a.* mixed with silk, gold, or silver twist embroidered with *briscado*. —*p.p.* [BRISCAR].

briscar, *v.t.* to embroider or weave with gold or silver twist.

brisera, *n.f.* glass screen for a candle.

británico, -ca, *a.* British, Britannic. — *n.f.* (*bot.*) great water dock.

britano, -na, *n.m.f.*, *a.* Briton; English; British, Britannic.

briza, *n.f.* fog, haze; (*bot.*) graminaceous plant.

brizar, *v.t.* to rock the cradle.

brizna, *n.f.* (*bot.*) filament, string (of beans, etc.); fragment, splinter, chip; morsel, minute piece.

briznoso, -sa, *a.* full of fragments or scraps.

brizo, *n.m.* rocking cradle.

broa, *n.f.* (*naut.*) shallow dangerous creek or cove; kind of biscuit or cracker.

broca, *n.f.* (weaving) reel for twist, silk or thread; conical drill for boring in iron; shoemaker's tack.

brocadillo, *n.m.* brocade of inferior quality.

brocado, -da, *a.* brocaded with gold or

silver. — *n.m.* gold, silver or silk brocade; gilt or silvered embossed leather.

brocadura, *n.f.* bear's bite.

brocal, *n.m.* curb-stone of a well; metal ring of the scabbard of a sword; *brocal de bota*, mouthpiece of a leathern wine-bottle; steel ornament on shield; (*min.*) mouth of a shaft. (*mil.*) bush, reinforcement of cannon's mouth.

brocamantón, *n.m.* brooch set with gems.

brocatel, *n.m.* brocade, damask of hemp and silk; *mármol brocatel*, Spanish marble with white veins; *brocatel de seda*, silk brocade.

brocato, *n.m.* (*prov.*) [BROCADO].

brocino, *n.m.* bump on the head.

brocúl, *n.m.* (*prov.*) broccoli; cauliflower.

brócula, *n.f.* drill for piercing metals.

bróculi, *n.m.* (*bot.*) broccoli.

brocha, *n.f.* painter's brush; cogged dice; *de brocha gorda*, poorly done or written (said of painter or painting of doors, windows, etc.).

brochado, -da, *a.* brocaded. — *n.f.* stroke of the brush as made in painting.

brochadura, *n.f.* set of hooks and eyes.

brochal, *n.m.* (*arch.*) joist.

brochar, *v.i.* to daub, paint badly.

brochazo, *n.m.* (*paint.*) [BROCHADA].

broche, *n.m.* clasp; hook and eye; locket; hasp; brooch.

brocheta, *n.f.* skewer.

brochón, *n.m.* large brush, whitewash brush [BROCHA].

brochuela, *n.f.* small brush [BROCHA].

brodio, *n.m.* [BODRIO] soup given to the poor in convents; hodge-podge; mixture of hog's blood and onions for sausages.

brodista, *n.m.f.* poor person or student who comes for a portion of *bodrio* or hotch-potch.

brollador, -ra, *a.* gushing out, boiling over; spitting. — *n.m.* fountain, jet.

brollar, *v.i.* to gush out, boil over. — *v.t.* to spit.

broma, *n.f.* gaiety, jollity, merriment; clatter, confused noise; noisy gathering; joke, jest; ship-worm; oatmeal gruel; (*build.*) riprap, mixture of gravel and mortar for filling up; *dar broma*, to tease; *meter broma*, to use many words to express very little; *broma pesada*, offensive or practical joke.

bromado, -da, *a.* worm-eaten. — *p.p.* [BROMAR].

bromar, *v.t.* to gnaw, like the ship-worm.

bromato, *n.m.* (*chem.*) bromate.

bromatografía, *n.f.* description of alimentary substances.

bromatología, *n.f.* treatise on foods.

bromatometría, *n.f.* calculation of food quantity necessary to maintain the human body in good condition.

bromazo, *n.m.* stupid joke [BROMA].

bromear, *v.i.*, *v.r.* to joke, make fun, jest.

bromelia, *n.f.* (*bot.*) pineapple.

bromhidrato, *n.m.* (*chem.*) hydrobromate, hydrobromide.

bromhídrico, -ca, *a.* (*chem.*) hydrobromic.

bromhidrosis; bromidrosis, *n.f.* (*med.*) fetid sweating.

brómico, -ca, *a.* (*chem.*) bromic.

bromífero, -ra, *a.* containing bromine.

bromismo, *n.m.* (*med.*) bromism.

bromista, *n.m.f.*, *a.* merry person, practical joker.

bromo, *n.m.* (*chem.*) bromine; (*bot.*) brome grass.

bromurado, -da, *a.* (*chem.*, *med.*) bromic, bromine.

bromuro, *n.m.* (*chem.*) bromide.

bronca, *n.f.* (*coll.*) pleasantry, practical joke; wrangle, quarrel; (*prov.*) anger, annoyance.

broncamente, *adv.* peevishly, snappishly, morosely, crustily.

bronce, *n.m.* bronze, brass; (*art*) bronze; (*poet.*) trumpet, bell, cannon; anything strong and hard; (*numis.*) copper coin; *edad de bronce*, Bronze Age; *gente del bronce*, (*coll.*) gay, determined people; *bronce de aluminio*, aluminium bronze; *escribir en bronce una cosa*, to remember something constantly; *ser de bronce* or *un bronce*, to be hard-hearted; to be robust and indefatigable.

bronceado, -da, *a.* bronze, bronzy; bronzed; tanned, sunburnt. — *n.m.* bronzing. — *p.p.* [BRONCEAR].

bronceadura, *n.f.* bronzing.

broncear, *v.t.* to bronze.

broncería, *n.f.* collection of brass or bronze articles.

broncia, *n.f.* (*min.*) pyrites.

broncina, *n.f.* bronze-powder.

broncíneo, -ea, *a.* bronze, bronzy.

broncista, *n.m.* worker in bronze.

bronco, -ca, *a.* rough, coarse, unpolished; brittle (metals); (*fig.*) rude, hard, abrupt (character); harsh, hoarse (voice, instrument); *bronco de genio*, crusty, morose, crabbed.

broncocele, *n.m.* (*surg.*) bronchocele.

bronconeumonía, *n.f.* (*med.*) broncho-pneumonia.

broncotomía, *n.f.* (*surg.*) bronchotomy.

broncha, *n.f.* short poniard; jewel; white-washing brush.

bronquedad, *n.f.* harshness, roughness, rudeness; brittleness.

bronquial, *a.* (*anat.*) bronchial.

bronquina, *n.f.* (*fam.*) dispute, contention, quarrel.

bronquio, *n.m.* (*anat.*) bronchus, bronchial tube.

bronquitis, *n.f.* (*med.*) bronchitis.

broquel, *n.m.* shield, buckler; (*fig.*) support, protection; (*naut.*) position of sails when taken aback.

broquelarse, *v.r.* [ABROQUELARSE] to shield oneself.

broquelazo, *n.m.* stroke with shield or buckler.

broquelero, *n.m.* maker or wearer of shields or bucklers; (*fig.*) wrangler, disputer.

broquelete, *n.m.* small buckler [BROQUEL].

broquelillo, *n.m.* small ear-ring.

broquer, *n.m.* small door of fyke.

broqueta, *n.f.* skewer.

bróquil, *n.m.* (*prov.*) [BRÉCOL].

brosquil, *n.m.* (*prov.*) sheep-fold, sheep-cote.

brota, *n.f.* bud, shoot.

brotación; brotadura, *n.f.* budding.

brotador, -ra, *a.* budding.

brótano, *n.m.* (*bot.*) southern-wood; bud, shoot.

brotar, *v.i.* to bud, germinate, put forth shoots or germs; to come out, gush, flow or rush out; (*fig.*) to issue, break out, appear. — *v.t.* to grow, bring forth; (*fig.*) to throw out, produce, originate; *brotar de, en un peñascal*, to grow in a rocky place.

brote; broto, *n.m.* germ, budding, sprouting; bud; (*prov.*) fragment, crumb, bit.

brotón, *n.m.* (*obs.*) large clasp; bud, shoot, tender twig, thicket, brushwood; (*fig.*) useless stuff.

broza, *n.f.* dead leaves, branches, etc.; chaff, rubbish (spoken or written); (*print.*) brush; *gente de toda broza,* people without trade or employment; *meter broza,* to introduce irrelevant matter; *servir de toda broza,* to be a Jack of all trades.

brozador, *n.m.* (*print.*) [BRUZADOR].

brozar, *v.t.* (*print.*) to brush the types.

broznamente, *adv.* roughly, harshly; (*obs.*) rudely, uncouthly.

brozno, -na, *a.* [BRONCO]; (*fig.*) rough, coarse, uncouth.

brozoso, -sa, *a.* bushy, covered with bushes.

brucero, *n.m.* brush and broom maker and seller.

bruces (a *or* **de),** *adv.* face downwards, on one's stomach; *caer (dar) de bruces,* to fall headlong.

brucita, *n.f.* (*min.*) hydrate of magnesia, brucite.

bruco, *n.m.* plant-louse.

brugo, *n.m.* moth larva which destroys oak-leaves; plant-louse.

bruja, *a.* very fine (sand). — *n.f.* (*orn.*) owl; witch, sorceress; (*coll.*) hag, ugly old woman; *creer en brujas,* to be very credulous, simple-minded; *parece que le han chupado brujas,* she looks as pale and lean as if she had been sucked by witches.

brujear, *v.i.* to practise witchcraft.

brujería, *n.f.* witchcraft, sorcery.

brujesco, -ca, *a.* appertaining to witchcraft, magic.

brujido, *n.m.* diamond dust.

brujidor, *n.m.* glazier's nippers.

brujir, *v.t.* to trim glass with a *brujidor.*

brujo, *n.m.* sorcerer, conjurer, wizard. — *a.* (*Chi.*) false, fraudulent; (*Cub., Mex., PR.*) impoverished, without means.

brújula, *n.f.* magnetic needle; (*naut.*) compass; sight, small hole to point a gun; peep-hole; (*fig.*) perception, intention; *perder la brújula,* to lose control of an affair.

brujularmente, *adv.* inquisitively, with curiosity.

brujulear, *v.t.* at cards, to examine one's hand by the top of cards; (*coll.*) to discover by conjectures.

brujuleo, *n.m.* examining one's hand by the top of cards; scrutiny, close examination; guess, conjecture.

brulote, *n.m.* (*naut.*) fire-ship.

bruma, *n.f.* mist rising from the sea; fog, brume, haziness, haze.

brumador, -ra, *a.* crushing, oppressing, wearisome.

brumal, *a.* brumous, foggy; hazy; brumal.

brumamiento, *n.m.* oppression, weariness, lassitude.

brumar, *v.t.* to oppress, weary, annoy.

brumazón, *n.m.* thick fog or mist at sea [BRUMA].

brumo, *n.m.* refined wax (used for polishing tapers, etc.).

brumoso, -sa, *a.* foggy, hazy, misty.

brunella, *n.f.* (*bot.*) self-heal.

bruno, -na, *a.* dark brown, darkish. - *n.m.* black plum or damson; plum or damson tree.

bruñidera, *n.f.* board for polishing wax.

bruñido, -da, *a.* burnished, polished, glossy. — *n.m.* polish, burnish. — *p.p.* [BRUÑIR].

bruñidor, -ra, *a.* burnishing, polishing. — *n.m.f.* burnisher, polisher. — *n.m.* burnisher (tool).

bruñidura, *n.f.* burnishing, polishing.

bruñimiento, *n.m.* polishing, burnishing; polish.

bruñir, *v.t.* to burnish, polish; (*coll.*) to put on rouge; to fard; *bruñir los diamantes,* to cut diamonds.

bruño, *n.m.* (*bot.*) damson (fruit and tree).

brusca, *n.f.* (*Ven.*) plant of the Leguminosæ family; (*Cub.*) brushwood; bursh fire.

bruscamente, *adv.* abruptly, peevishly.

bruscate, *n.m.* hash of lambs' and goats' chitterlings.

brusco, -ca, *a.* rough, brusque, rude, peevish. — *n.m.* (*bot.*) knee-holly, butcher's broom; trifling remains at harvesting. — *n.f.* (*naut.*) bevel, sweep or rounding of masts.

brusela, *n.f.* lesser periwinkle. — *pl.* jeweller's tongs or tweezers.

Bruselas, *n.f.* Brussels.

bruselense, *n.m.f., a.* of or from Brussels.

brusquedad, *n.f.* brusqueness; rudeness.

brusquería, *n.f.* (*fam.*) brusqueness.

brutal, *a.* brutal, brutish; savage, ferocious, bestial. — *n.m.* brute.

brutalidad, *n.f.* brutality, savageness, brutishness.

brutalizarse, *v.r.* to become brutal.

brutalmente; brutamente, *adv.* brutally, brutishly, ferociously.

brutaña, *n.f.* (*comic*) roughness, uncouthness.

brutesco, -ca, *a.* grotesque.

bruteza, *n.f.* roughness, want of polish; brutality.

bruto, -ta, *a.* coarse, beastly, brutish, gross, unpolished, rough. — *n.m.* brute, beast; *en bruto,* in a rough state; *madera en bruto,* (*naut.*) rough timber; *diamante en bruto,* rough diamond; *peso bruto,* gross weight; *beneficio bruto,* gross profit; *noble bruto,* (*poet.*) horse; *pedazo de bruto,* ignorant, rude man.

bruza, *n.f.* horse-brush; stove-brush; scrubbing-brush; printer's brush.

bruzador, *n.m.* (*print.*) inclined table for cleaning type.

bruzar, *v.t.* to brush with a *bruza.*

bu, *n.m.* (*coll.*) bogy, bugbear; *hacer el bu,* to frighten, terrify; *mira que viene el bu,* here comes the hobgoblin; (*coll.*) scarecrow.

búa; buba, *n.f.* (*med.*) pustule, small tumour; (*pl.*) buboes; *el que tiene búa, ése la estruja,* everyone knows where his own shoe pinches.

buaro; buarillo, *n.m.* [BUHARRO].

búbalo, -la, *n.m.f.* African antelope.

bubático, -ca, *a.* bubonic, having buboes or glandular tumours.

bubón, *n.m.* morbid tumour.

bubónico, -ca, *a.* bubonic; *peste bubónica,* bubonic plague.

buboso, -sa, *a.* afflicted with pustules.

bucal, *a.* relating to the mouth.

bucanero, *n.m.* buccaneer.

bucara, *n.f.* (*bot.*) variety of grape.

bucarán, *n.m.* (*prov.*) buckram.

bucardo, *n.m.* (*prov.*) buck of wild goat.

bucare, *n.m.* (*Ven.*) shade tree.

bucarito, *n.m.* small earthen vessel of odoriferous earth.

búcaro, *n.m.* vessel made of an odoriferous earth of the same name; (*Col.*) [BUCARE].

buccelación; bucelación, *n.f.* action of stopping hæmorrhage; (*med.*) ligature of open vein or artery.

buccino, *n.m.* buccinum, whelk.

buceamiento, *n.m.* diving.

bucear, *v.i.* (*naut.*) to dive.

bucéfalo, *n.m.* (*coll.*) stupid, dull man.

bucentauro, *n.m.* (*myth.*) centaur with bull's body; Bucentaur.

buceo, *n.m.* diving; searching.

bucero, -ra, *a.* black-nosed (applied to a dog).

buces (de), *adv.* [DE BRUCES].

bucinador, *n.m.* (*anat.*) buccinator.

bucle, *n.m.* ringlet, curl, lock of hair; (*fig.*) loop.

buco, *n.m.* opening, aperture, gap; (*zool.*) buck (of goat).

bucólico, -ca, *a.* bucolic, relating to pastoral poetry. — *n.m.* bucolic poet. — *n.f.* bucolic, pastoral poetry; food.

bucosidad, *n.f.* (*naut.*) tonnage.

bucranio, *n.m.* (*arch.*) bucranium.

buchada, *n.f.* mouthful.

buche, *n.m.* (*orn.*) craw, crop; maw, stomach (of quadrupeds); mouthful of a fluid; young sucking ass, foal; bag, wrinkle or pucker in clothes; (*coll.*) bosom, breast; (*coll.*) human stomach; tunny-fish net; *sacar el buche a alguno,* to extract someone's secrets.

buchete, *n.m.* puffed out, inflated cheek.

buchillo, *n.m.* (*prov.*) large knife or dagger.

buchón, -na, *a.* baggy, pouched, wrinkled; *paloma buchona,* pouter pigeon.

budare, *n.m.* (*Ven.*) large baking pan.

búdico, -ca, *a.* Buddhic, Buddhistic.

budín, *n.m.* pudding.

budinera, *n.f.* pudding-basin.

budión, *n.m.* (*ichth.*) peacock-fish.

budismo, *n.m.* Buddhism.

budista, *n.m.f.* Buddhist.

buega, *n.f.* (*prov.*) landmark, boundary, term.

buen, *a.* apocope of BUENO, good, used before a singular masculine noun and before an infinitive verb used as a substantive; *buen dinero,* a safe debt; *el buen señor,* the good gentleman; *el buen decir,* the correct way of speaking; *buen Juan,* Simple Simon; *El Buen Pastor,* The Good Shepherd; *el buen ladrón,* the good thief (New Testament); *¡buen apunte es!* (*iron.*) a nice fellow he is! *buen principio, la mitad es hecho,* well begun is half done.

buenaboya, *n.m.* volunteer seaman aboard a galley.

buenamente, *adv.* freely, spontaneously; conveniently, easily, commodiously.

buenandanza, *n.f.* prosperity, felicity, success.

buenaventura, *n.f.* fortune, good luck; prediction of fortune-tellers.

bueno, -na, *a.* good, kind; upright, virtuous; simple, plain; fair; serviceable, useful; fit, proper; sociable; agreeable, gracious, pleasant, loving; great, strong; violent; healthy, sound; savoury, palatable, delicious; (*iron.* with verb *ser*) strange, extraordinary, wonderful; sufficient. — *adv.* very well, all right; enough, no more. — *n.m.* superior mark to "pass" in examinations; *buena calentura,* a strong fever; *buenos días,* good day, good morning; *buenas palabras,* conciliatory language, a soft answer; *buenas tardes,* good afternoon, good evening; *buenas noches,* good evening, good night; *¿adónde bueno?* where are you going? *¿de dónde bueno?* where are you coming from? *¡bueno anda el ajo!* (*iron.*) a pretty state of things! *de buenas a primeras,* suddenly, unexpectedly; at first sight, from the beginning; *de bueno a bueno* or *de buenas a buenas,* freely, willingly, gratefully; *a* or *por buenas,* willingly; *¡buena es ésa (ésta)!* or *¡eso (esto) es bueno!* (*iron.*) expression of surprise and disapproval; *¡buenas y gordas!* no, really I can't believe that! *bueno está,* that's all right; enough, no more; *bueno está lo bueno,* leave well alone; *estar de buenas,* to be in a good mood; *estoy bueno,* I am well; *lo bueno es que quiera enseñar a su maestro,* the extraordinary thing is that he now presumes to teach his master; *bueno fuera que ahora negase lo que ha dicho tantas veces,* would it not be strange were he to deny what he has said so often; *buenas son mangas después de Pascua,* better late than never; *allégate, arrímate,* or *júntate a los buenos, y serás uno de ellos,* go with the good and you will grow like them; *nunca lo bueno fué mucho,* good people are scarce.

buenparecer, *n.m.* good looks or appearance.

bueña, *n.f.* (*prov.*) sausage.

buera, *n.f.* (*prov.*) pustule or pimple (in the mouth).

buey, *n.m.* ox, bullock; *pl.* (*slang*) cards; *buey marino,* sea-calf; *buey de cabestrillo* or *caza,* stalking-ox; *a paso de buey,* at a snail's pace; *buey de agua,* a measure for water; body of water coming from a conduit or spring; *buey viejo, surco derecho,* an old ox makes a straight furrow; experienced, competent person; *¿a dó irá el buey que no are?* every mode of life has its difficulties; *el buey harto no es comedor,* surfeit brings boredom; *habló el buey y dijo mu,* to put one's foot in it; *el buey suelto bien se lame,* liberty is the most appreciated gift.

bueyazo, *n.m.* big ox.

bueyecillo; bueyezuelo, *n.m.* little ox [BUEY].

bueyerizo, *n.m.* ox-driver, cowherd.

bueyuno, -na, *a.* bovine, oxlike.

bufa, *n.f.* flatulence; joke, buffoonery.

bufado, -da, *a.* puffed up; blown (applied to glass drops blown extremely thin). — *p.p.* [BUFAR].

bufador, -ra, *a.* puffing, blowing. — *n.m.* volcanic eruption.

bufalino, -na, *a.* belonging to buffalo.

búfalo, -la, *n.m.f.* buffalo. — *n.m.* buff-stick, buff-wheel.

bufanda, *n.f.* muffler, comforter, scarf.

bufante, *a.* puffing, blowing.

bufar, *v.i.* to puff and blow with anger (animals); to snort; *bufar de ira,* (*coll.*) to swell with indignation.

bufarda, *n.f.* garret window; (*prov.*) lower opening of a charcoal-burner's furnace.

bufete, *n.m.* bureau; desk or writing-table; (*fig.*) lawyer's office and clientele; *abrir bufete,* to start practice as a lawyer.

bufetillo, *n.m.* small desk or writing-table; small chest [BUFETE].

buffet, *n.m.* sideboard; (*railw.*) buffet, refreshment-bar.

bufi, *n.m.* kind of watered camlet.

bufia, *n.f.* (*slang*) bag, butt of wine.

bufido, *n.m.* bellow, roar, snort; (*coll.*) huff, fit of sudden anger; (*slang*) shout.

bufo, -fa, *a.* comic, farcical; *ópera bufa,* comic opera. — *n.m.f.* comic singer, harlequin, buffoon.

bufón, -na, *a.* funny, comical. — *n.m.* pedlar, hawker. — *n.m.f.* buffoon, harlequin, merry-andrew, mimic, humourist, fool, clown, jester.

bufonada; bufonería, *n.f.* buffoonery, waggery, jest, mimicry, raillery.

bufonearse, *v.r.* to jest, turn into ridicule, be jocose.

bufonería, [BUFONADA].

bufonesco, -ca, *a.* comic, farcical.

bufonizar, *v.i.* to jest.

bugada, *n.f.* buck, lye, clothes-bleach.

bugalla, *n.f.* (*bot.*) gall-nut, gall-apple.

buganvilla, *n.f.* (*bot.*) bougainvillæa.

bugir, *v.i.* (*naut.*) to caulk.

bugle, *n.f.* (*mus.*) bugle.

buglosa, *n.f.* (*bot.*) alkanet, bugloss.

búgula, *n.f.* (*bot.*) bugle.

buhar, *v.t.* (*slang*) to discover, denounce.

buharda; buhardilla, *n.f.* dormer-window; garret; skylight.

buhardo; buharro, *n.m.* eagle-owl.

buhedera, *n.f.* embrasure, loop-hole.

buhedo, *n.m.* marly earth; pondlet.

buhero, *n.m.* owl-keeper.

buho, *n.m.* owl; (*coll.*) unsocial person; (*slang*) sneak, spy.

buhonería, *n.f.* pedlar's box, pedlary.

buhonero, *n.m.* pedlar, hawker; *cada buhonero alaba sus agujas,* to blow one's own trumpet.

buido, -da, *a.* burnished, polished; pointed, sharp; striated, grooved. — *p.p.* [BUIR].

buir, *v.t.* to polish, burnish; to sharpen.

buitre, *n.m.* vulture.

buitrero, -ra, *a.* vulturine, vulturish, vulturous. — *n.f.* place to catch vultures. — *n.m.* vulture-fowler.

buitrón, *n.m.* osier basket to catch fish; partridge net; snare for game; (*Am.*) furnace where silver is smelted.

bujarasol, *n.m.* (*prov., bot.*) fig with reddish pulp.

bujarrón, *n.m., a.* (*vulg.*) Sodomite.

buje, *n.m.* axle-box, bush-box, iron ring; pillow of a shaft.

bujeda, *n.f.; bujedal; bujedo, n.m.* plantation of box-trees.

bujería, *n.f.* gewgaw, bauble, toy, knick-knack.

bujeta, *n.f.* wooden box; perfume box; case for a perfume-bottle.

bujía, *n.f.* wax candle, stearine candle; candle-stick; candle, candle-power, the unit for measuring light; (*med.*) bougie, catheter; (*motor.*) sparking-plug (also BUJIA DEL ENCENDIDO).

bujier, *n.m.* chief or head of the *bujiería.*

bujiería, *n.f.* office at court where wax candles were kept.

bula, *n.f.* bulla; bull, seal; papal bull; (*fig.*) favour, privilege; *bula de carne,* dispensation by the Pope to eat meat on fast days; *echar las bulas a uno,* to impose a burden or troublesome duty on someone; to reprimand severely; *haber bulas para difuntos,* there is a remedy for everything; *no poder con la bula,* to be worn out, extremely weak; *tener bula para todo,* to act as one pleases.

bulado, -da, *a.* (*obs.*) branded; officially recognized. — *p.p.* [BULAR].

bular, *v.t.* (*obs.*) to brand (prisoners, slaves).

bulario, *n.m.* collection of papal bulls.

bulbar, *a.* (*med.*) bulbaceous, bulbous, bulbose.

bulbífero, -ra, *a.* (*bot.*) bulbiferous.

bulbiforme, *a.* bulbiform.

bulbillo, *n.m.* (*bot.*) bulbil.

bulbo, *n.m.* (*bot., anat.*) bulb.

bulboso, -sa, *a.* bulbous.

bulero, *n.m.* one who distributes bulls of crusades.

buleto, *n.m.* brief granted by the Pope or his legate; apostolic letter.

bulevar, *n.m.* boulevard.

búlgaro, -ra, *n.m.f., a.* Bulgarian. — *n.m.* Bulgarian language.

bulí, *n.m.* (*Philip.*) a palm-tree [BURÍ].

bulimia, *n.f.* (*med.*) bulimia, voracious appetite.

bulista, *a.* in charge of the register of Papal bulls.

bultito, *n.m.* little lump, small bundle.

bulto, *n.m.* bulk, anything which appears bulky; any object not clearly seen; protuberance; tumour, swelling; massiness; (*art*) bust; pillow-case; bundle, package, parcel; *figura* or *imagen de bulto,* figure (image) in sculpture; *bulto redondo,* round sculpture; *a bulto,* indistinctly, confusedly, at guess-work; *buscar a uno el bulto,* to persecute, harass someone; *coger* or *pescar el bulto,* to lay hold of, seize; *escurrir, guardar* or *huir el bulto,* to avoid, sneak out of doing something; *comprar las cosas a bulto,* to buy things wholesale, by the lump; *menear, tentar* or *tocar a uno el bulto,* to give someone a sound drubbing; *poner de bulto,* to make conspicuous, prominent; *ser de bulto,* to be clear, evident.

bululú, *n.m.* strolling protean comedian; (*Ven.*) tumult, riot, commotion.

bulla, *n.f.* noise, bustle, fuss, clatter, shout; noisy stir, crowd, mob; (*prov.*) [BOLLA]; *meter bulla,* to make a noise; *meter a bulla,* to confuse, obstruct.

bullaje, *n.m.* noisy crowd.

bullanga, *n.f.* tumult, riot.

bullanguero, -ra, *a.* riotous. — *n.m.f.* rioter, turbulent person.

bullar, *v.t.* (*prov.*) to mark goods with lead seal to show origin; (*hunt.*) to kill the boar while the dogs hold him down.

bullarengue, *n.m.* (*fam.*) bustle (dress); (*Cub.*) feigned, artificial thing.

bullebulle, *n.m.f.* (*fam.*) busybody, bustler, hustler.

bullente, *a.* bubbling, boiling.

bullicio, *n.m.; bulliciosidad, n.f.* bustle, noise, tumult, uproar; sedition; heat.

bulliciosamente, *adv.* noisily, tumultuously.

bullicioso, -sa, *a.* lively, restless, merry, playful, noisy, clamorous, busy; seditious, turbulent; boisterous (the sea). — *n.m.f.* rioter, sedition-monger.

bullidor, -ra, *a.* lively, restless.
bullir, *v.i.* to boil, bubble up; (*fig.*) to swarm
(insects); (*fig.*) to move about, fidget; (*fig.*)
to occur frequently. — *v.t.* to move, stir.
— *v.r.* to stir, give signs of life; *Don Quijote
no bullía pie ni mano,* Don Quixote did not
stir hand or foot; *le bullen los pies a la chica,*
the girl is itching to dance; *bullirle a uno una
cosa,* to desire something vehemently.
bullón, *n.m.* dye bubbling up in a boiler;
metallic ornament for large books; (*sew.*)
puff.
buneto, *n.m.* hedge sparrow.
bunga, *n.f.* (*Cub.*) a small orchestra; deceit, lie.
bungo, *n.m.* (*Nic.*) flat-boat.
buniatal, *n.m.* plantation of *buniatos.*
buniato, *n.m.* [BONIATO].
bunio, *n.m.* (*bot.*) turnip grown for seed.
buñolería, *n.f.* fritter or waffle shop.
buñolero, -ra, *n.m.f.* maker or seller of
waffles or fritters.
buñuelo, *n.m.* fritter, pancake, bun, waffle;
(*coll.*) anything poorly done or spoiled;
failure; *esto no es hacer buñuelos,* it is not a
light matter, it cannot be done in a hurry.
buque, *n.m.* (*naut.*) bulk, capacity, burden of
a ship; hull of a ship; vessel, ship, steamer;
buque a la carga, ship in port awaiting cargo;
buque escuela, training-ship; *buque insignia,*
flag-ship; *buque de guerra,* man-of-war;
buque de hélice, screw-steamer; *buque de
torres,* turreted man-of-war; *buque de
transporte,* transport ship; *buque de vapor,*
steamer; *buque de vela,* sailing ship; *buque en
lastre,* ship in ballast; *buque en rosca,* newly-
built ship, a hull without equipment;
buque mercante, merchant vessel; *buque
mixto,* vessel equipped to sail under canvas
or steam; *buque submarino,* submarine.
buqué, *n.m.* bouquet (of wine).
buquetino, *n.m.* (*zool.*) bouquetin, the ibex.
buratado, -da, *a.* crapy.
buratina, *n.f.* silk or wool cloth; Persian silk.
burato, *n.m.* crape, crape cloth; transparent
veil.
burba, *n.f.* African coin of small value.
burbuja, *n.f.* bubble, bleb.
burbujear, *v.i.* to bubble.
burbujeo, *n.m.* bubbling.
burbujita, *n.f.* small bubble [BURBUJA].
burchaca, *n.f.* pilgrim's leather bag.
burche, *n.m.* tower (fort).
burcho, *n.m.* (*naut.*) large sloop or barge.
burda, *n.f.* (*naut.*) back-stay.
burdégano, *n.m.* hinny.
burdel, *n.m.* brothel; (*coll.*) disreputable place
or house. — *a.* libidinous.
burdinalla, *n.f.* (*obs.*) sprit-topsail-stay.
burdo, -da, *a.* coarse, common, ordinary;
paño burdo, coarse cloth.
burel, *n.m.* (*her.*) bar, the ninth part of a
shield; (*naut.*) fid, marline-spike; (*naut.*)
wooden mould of scupper-plug.
burelado, *a.* (*her.*) with five bars of gold and
five of silver.
burelete, *n.m.* (*her.*) cord tying plumes and
lambrequins.
burengue, *n.m.* (*prov.*) mulatto slave.
bureo, *n.m.* court of justice; entertainment,
amusement, diversion, spree.
bureta, *n.f.* (*chem.*) burette, dropping-tube.
burga, *n.f.* spa, hot spring.

burgado, *n.m.* edible snail.
burgalés, -sa, *n.m.f.,* *a.* native of Burgos; ancient coin made at Burgos.
burgo, *n.m.* borough.
burgomaestre, *n.m.* burgomaster.
burgués, -sa, *n.m.f.,* *a.* burgess; appertaining
to a borough. — *n.m.f.* middle-class citizen.
burguesía, *n.f.* burgess-ship; bourgeoisie.
burguesismo, *n.m.* bourgeois qualities.
burí, *n.m.* (*Philip.*) buri, talipot palm.
buriel, *a.* reddish, dark red. — *n.m.* kersey,
dark red coarse cloth.
buril, *n.m.* burin, engraver's tool, graver; *buril
de punta,* sharp-pointed burin; *buril chaple
redondo,* gouge-pointed burin; *buril chaple
en forma de escoplo,* chisel-pointed burin.
burilada, *n.f.* line or stroke of a burin; silver
taken by an assayer for testing.
buriladura, *n.f.* engraving with a burin.
burilar, *v.t.* to engrave with a burin or
graver; *burilar en cobre,* to engrave on
copper.
burjaca, *n.f.* pilgrim's leather bag.
burla, *n.f.* scoff, flout, mockery, fling, sneer;
trick, jest, practical joke, hoax; gibe, jeer;
cheat, deceit; (*pl.*) falsities uttered in a
jocular style; *burla pesada,* biting jest, bad
trick; *burla burlando,* in an easy way, without
effort; *burlas aparte,* joking aside; *de burlas,*
in jest; *a la burla dejarla cuando más agrada,*
it is wise not to carry a joke too far; *burla
burlando vase el lobo al asno,* it is very easy
to do what we like; *decir una cosa entre
burlas y veras,* to say something unpleasant
jestingly; *mezclar burlas con veras,* to introduce serious and frivolous matters in an
article or conversation; to say home-
truths jestingly; *ni en burlas ni en veras, con
tu amo no partas peras,* it is wise to refrain
from familiarity with one's superiors; *hablar
de burlas,* to speak with one's tongue in one's
cheek; *hacer burla de,* to mock, make fun of;
hombre de burlas, scoffer; *no aguantar burlas,*
to have no sense of humour; to stand no
nonsense; *no es hombre de burlas,* he is a
serious man; *quien hace la burla, guárdese de
la escarapulla,* those who play tricks must
put up with the consequences; *no son burlas
las que duelen,* jests that wound are no jests
at all; *no hay peor burla que la verdadera,*
there is no more cutting gibe than an apposite
one.
burladero, -ra, *a.* joking, scoffing. — *n.m.*
refuge or covert in a bullring; island, street-
refuge; (*railw.*) vaulted niche in tunnels.
burlador, -ra, *a.* joking, mocking. — *n.m.f.*
wag, jester, scoffer, mocker, practical joker.
— *n.m.* libertine, seducer; conjurers' cup;
concealed squirt.
burlar, *v.t.* to ridicule, mock, hoax, laugh,
scoff, gibe; to abuse; to deceive, disappoint,
frustrate, evade. — *v.r.* to jest, laugh at,
make fun of, gibe, chaff, banter. *burlar a
alguno,* to deceive someone; *burlarse de uno,*
to make fun of someone; *burlar la ley,* to
evade the law; *burlarse de lo que dirán,* not to
care what people say.
burlería, *n.f.* fun, drollery; pun; artifice; yarn,
romantic story; deceit, illusion; derision, reproach; chaff, banter, ridicule.
burlescamente, *adv.* burlesquely, comically,
ludicrously.

burlesco, -ca, *a.* burlesque, jocular, ludicrous, comical, funny.

burleta, *n.f.* (*fam.*) little trick, fun, joke [BURLA].

burlete, *n.m.* weather-strip.

burlón, -na, *a.* bantering, mocking. — *n.m.f.* banterer, jester, mocker, scoffer. — *n.m.* mocking-bird.

burlonamente, *adv.* mockingly, scoffingly.

burlote, *n.m.* small bank (gambling).

buro, *n.m.* (*prov.*) chalk, marl.

buró, *n.m.* bureau, writing-desk.

burocracia, *n.f.* bureaucracy; officialism.

burócrata, *n.m.f.* bureaucrat.

burocrático, -ca, *a.* bureaucratic.

burra, *n.f.* she-ass; (*fig.*) dirty, ignorant and quite unteachable woman; (*coll.*) laboriously inclined and patient woman; *panza de burra,* parchment inscribed with university degree; *caer de su burra,* to acknowledge one's error; *descargar la burra,* to shift the work on to someone else; *estarle a uno una cosa como a la burra las arracadas,* to be unsuitable, inappropriate; *írsele a uno la burra,* to give free vent to (one's tongue); *la burra que tiene pollino, no va derecha al molino,* one possessed by a passion cannot act straightforwardly.

burrada, *n.f.* drove of asses; (*coll.*) asininity, stupid action or saying; (*fig.*) play contrary to the rule in the game of *burro.*

burrajear, *v.t.* [BORRAJEAR].

burrajo, *n.m.* dry stable-dung for fuel.

burral, *a.* (*fam.*) brutal.

burreño, *n.m.* hinny.

burrero, *n.m.* ass-keeper or -driver who sells asses' milk.

burriciego, -ga, *a.* said of a bull with defective vision; (*fam.*) short-sighted person; (*coll.*) slow-witted.

burrillo, *n.m.* (*coll.*) ecclesiastical almanac.

burrito, *n.m.* little ass [BURRO].

burro, *n.m.* ass; (*fig.*) stupid, ignorant being; sawyer's jack or horse; wheel of a reel; card game; (*fig.*) loser at this card game; (*naut.*) windlass; *burro de carga,* laborious and patient man; *caer de su burro,* [CAER DE SU BURRA]; *puesto en el burro,* to be resolved to see something through to the end; *burro cargado de letras,* one who has studied a great deal but lacks intelligence and talent.

burrumbada, *n.f.* (*fam.*) boastful saying.

bursario, -ria, *a.* baggy, purse-like.

bursátil, *a.* fiscal; (*com.*) relating to the bourse or exchange.

burujo, *n.m.* lump of pressed wool or other matter; parcel, package; bagasse from olives, grapes, etc.

burujón, *n.m.* [BORUJÓN].

burujoncillo, *n.m.* [BORUJÓN].

busaca, *n.f.* (*Col., Ven.*) a bag.

busardas, *n.f.pl.* (*naut.*) breast-hooks, compass-timbers.

busardo, *n.m.* buzzard.

busca, *n.f.* search, research; pursuit; hunting-dog; hunting-party.

buscada, *n.f.* search, research.

buscadero, -ra, *a.* findable.

buscador, -ra, *a.* searching, investigating. — *n.m.f.* searcher, investigator. — *n.m.* finder (optical appliance).

buscaniguas, *n.m.* (*Col., Guat.*) squib, cracker.

buscapié, *n.m.* hint dropped in a conversation or otherwise and leading to some other subject.

buscapiés, *n.m.* squib-cracker; serpent fire-cracker.

buscapleitos, *n.m.f.* (*Am.*) a touting lawyer.

buscar, *v.t.* (*pret.* **busqué**; *pres. subj.* **busque**) to seek, search; to look for, look after, look out, hunt after; (*slang*) to pinch, pilfer; *buscar a tientas,* to grope for (something) in the dark; *buscar la madre gallega,* to earn one's own living; *buscar tres* or *cinco pies al gato,* to seek or pick a quarrel; *buscársela, buscar la vida,* to find ways and means of earning a living; *buscar el flanco al enemigo,* to threaten the enemy's flank; *buscar a uno, buscar la lengua,* to irritate, provoke someone; *buscar pan de trastrigo,* to look for the impossible; *buscar por donde salir,* to look for a way out; *buscar por todos lados,* to hunt everywhere; *buscar rodeos,* to seek devious means; *cada uno busca a los suyos,* like seeks like; *andar buscando,* to beg; *ir a buscar,* to go for, look for; *quien busca halla,* he that seeks shall find.

buscarruidos, *n.m.f.* (*coll.*) mischief-maker, quarrelsome person; (*naut.*) scout ship.

buscavida; buscavidas, *n.m.f.* (*coll.*) busybody; gossip-monger; hustler; thrifty person.

busco, *n.m.* threshold of a sluice-gate; track of an animal.

buscón, -na, *a.* searching. — *n.m.f.* searcher; cheat, pilferer, filcher, petty robber. — *n.f.* harlot, prostitute.

busilis, *n.m.* (*coll.*) riddle, question, knotty point, root of a difficulty; *dar en el busilis,* to hit the mark.

busingote, *n.m.* certain kind of hat.

búsqueda, *n.f.* search.

busquillo, *n.m.* (*bot.*) myosotis; (*zool.*) variety of tiny dog; (*Chi., Per.*) diligent, active.

busquizal, *n.m.* (*prov.*) very brambly place.

busto, *n.m.* (*art*) bust.

bustrófedon, *n.m.* a method of writing from left to right and right to left alternately.

butaca, *n.f.* arm-chair, easy-chair; (*theat.*) orchestra-chair or stall.

butano, *n.m.* (*chem.*) butane.

buten, *adv.* ser de buten, (*slang*) to be A 1 or first-rate.

butifarra, *n.f.* pork sausage made in Catalonia, Valencia, and Balearic Is.; (*coll.*) baggy loose socks or stockings; (*Per.*) ham sandwich.

butifarrería, *n.f.* art of making, and shop for selling *butifarras.*

butifarrero, -ra, *a.* maker and seller of *butifarras.*

butilo, *n.m.* (*chem.*) butyl.

butiondo, -da, *a.* lustful, lewd, obscene.

butiráceo, -cea, *a.* butyraceous.

butirato, *n.m.* (*chem.*) butyrate.

butírico, -ca, *a.* butyric.

butirina, *n.f.* (*chem.*) butyrine.

butiro, *n.m.* butter.

butiroso, -sa, *a.* buttery.

butomeo, -mea, *a.* (*bot.*) butomaceous.

butomo, *n.m.* (*bot.*) butomus.

butrino; butrón, *n.m.* osier basket to catch fish.

buya, *n.m.* (*zool.*) beaver.

buyador, *n.m.* (*prov.*) brazier, worker in brass.

buyes, *n.m.pl.* (*slang*) cards.

buyo, *n.m.* (*Philip.*) leaf of the betel-vine.

buz, *n.m.* kiss of respect and reverent regard; lip; *hacer el buz,* to do homage and pay respect.

buzamiento, *n.m.* (*geol.*) dip, inclination of a stratum.

búzano, *n.m.* diver; kind of culverin.

buzar, *v.i.* (*geol.*) to dip downward.

buzardas, *n.f.pl.* (*naut.*) breast-hooks, forehooks.

buzcorona, *n.f.* blow on the head given in fun while the hand is being kissed.

buzo, *n.m.* diver; ancient kind of ship; (*slang*) alert thief.

buzón, *n.m.* conduit, canal; letter-box, pillarbox; bung, lid or cover; hook to remove the lids of melting pots; sluice of a mill.

buzonera, *n.f.* (*prov.*) drain or gutter in a court-yard.

C

C, c, *n.f.* third letter of the Spanish alphabet.

ca, *conj.* (*obs.*) because, for.

¡ca! *interj.* oh no! come now! no, indeed!

cabal, *a.* just, exact; (*fig.*) perfect, complete, full, accomplished; faultless, consummate. — *adv.* justly, exactly; *por sus cabales,* exactly, perfectly; *according* to rule and order; at its just price.

cábala, *n.f.* cabbala, secret science of the Hebrew rabbis; (*fig.*) superstitious divination; (*coll.*) cabal, intrigue, plot, combination, confederacy.

cabalar, *v.t.* to complete.

cabalgada, *n.f.* foray; cavalcade; booty.

cabalgador, -ra, *n.m.f.* rider, horseman, horsewoman; (*obs.*) horse-block.

cabalgadura, *n.f.* mount, animal for riding; sumpter, beast of burden.

cabalgante, *a.* on horseback.

cabalgar, *v.i.* (*pret.* **cabalgué,** *pres. subj.* **cabalgue**) to get or mount on horseback; to ride; to horse; to parade on horseback; to go in a cavalcade. — *v.t.* to horse, cover a mare; to take horse; *cabalgar la artillería,* to mount cannon on their carriages; *cabalgar a mujeriegas,* to ride side-saddle; *cabalgar a mula,* to ride a mule.

cabalgata, *n.f.* cavalcade.

cabalhuste, *n.m.* saddle with high semicircular pommel and cantle.

cabalino, -na, *a.* (*poet., myth.*) applied to Pegasus, Mount Helicon, and the Hippocrene spring.

cabalismo, *n.m.* cabbalism.

cabalista, *n.m.* cabbalist.

cabalísticamente, *adv.* cabbalistically.

cabalístico, -ca, *a.* cabbalistic.

cabalito, *adv.* (*fam.*) [CABALMENTE].

cabalmente, *adv.* exactly, completely, precisely, perfectly, fully.

caballa, *n.f.* (*ichth.*) horse-mackerel.

caballada, *n.f.* a number of horses; (*Am.*) asinine word or action.

caballaje, *n.m.* serving of mares and she-asses; money paid for that service.

caballar, *a.* equine.

caballear, *v.i.* (*fam.*) to ride on horseback often.

caballejo, *n.m.* little horse, nag; rack, instrument of torture.

caballerato, *n.m.* ecclesiastical title and benefice granted by the Pope to a married layman; privilege of gentleman or esquire in Catalonia.

caballerear, *v.i.* to set up for a gentleman.

caballerescamente, *adv.* in a gentlemanly or a knightly way.

caballeresco, -ca, *a.* knightly, chivalrous; belonging to or having the appearance of a gentleman; romantic (of books on knight-errantry).

caballerete, *n.m.* young knight or gentleman [CABALLERO]; (*coll.*) spruce presumptuous young gentleman.

caballería, *n.f.* riding beast; cavalry, horsetroops; art of riding, horsemanship; chivalry; order of knights, military order, knighthood, martialism; cavalcade; share of spoils given to a knight; (*prov.*) pension given by grandees to knights fighting for them; agrarian measure of 60 *fanegas* or 96 acres; (*Cub.*) of 33 acres; (*PR.*) of 190 acres; *caballería mayor,* saddle-horse, mule; *caballería menor,* ass, jackass; *libros de caballería,* books of knight-errantry; *caballería andante,* knight-errantry; *caballería de carga,* sumpter cattle; *andarse en caballerías,* to make fulsome and exaggerated compliments.

caballerito, *n.m.* young gentleman.

caballeriza, *n.f.* stable; stud of horses, mules; staff of grooms, ostlers, etc.

caballerizo, *n.m.* head groom of a stable; *caballerizo de campo* or *del rey,* equerry to the king; *caballerizo mayor del rey,* master of the horse to the king.

caballero, -ra, *a.* riding (on animal's back); (*fig.*) (followed by *en* and words expressing acts of will or intelligence, as *propósito, opinión,* etc.) obstinate, determined. — *n.m.* knight, nobleman, cavalier; rider, horseman; gentleman; mister, sir; (*orn.*) gambet, the redshank; Spanish dance; (*fort.*) cavalier; surplus mound of earth in a clearing; *espuela de caballero,* (*bot.*) larkspur; *caballero andante,* knight-errant; (*fig.*) poor idle nobleman; *caballero aventurero,* knighterrant; *caballero cubierto,* grandee who keeps his head covered in the king's presence; (*coll.*) man who does not remove his hat when etiquette requires it; *caballero de industria,* swindler; *caballero del hábito,* knight of certain military orders; *caballero de mohatra,* swindler, sharper; *caballero en plaza,* mounted toreador; *caballero novel,* novice knight; *caballero en su porte,* gentleman in his demeanour; *iba caballero sobre un asno,* he was riding on an ass; *a caballero,* above, in a superior degree; *armar a uno caballero,* to knight; *de caballero a caballero,* as between gentlemen; *poderoso caballero es don dinero,* money is power.

caballerosamente, *adv.* generously, nobly, in a gentlemanly manner, in a knightly way.

caballerosidad, *n.f.* gentlemanhood, gentlemanship; gentlemanliness, nobleness, honourable behaviour, generosity.

caballeroso, -sa, *a.* noble; gentlemanly, urbane, polished; generous,

caballerote, *n.m.* (*coll.*) graceless, unpolished man.

caballeta, *n.f.* (*entom.*) grasshopper.

caballete, *n.m.* little horse [CABALLO]; (*arch.*) ridge of a gable-roof; carpenter's horse; stand for saddles; bench, trestle; horse, instrument of torture; chimney cap or cowl; ridge between furrows; bridge (of the nose); brake, for dressing hemp and flax; painter's easel; potter's trivet; (*orn.*) breast-bone; (*print.*) gallows of a printing-press; (*Mex.*) knight (chess); *caballete de aserrar,* sawyer's trestle, saw-horse.

caballico, *n.m.* little horse, pony; (*prov.*) mould for convex tiles.

caballino, -na, *a.* equine. — *n.m.* (*bot.*) variety of aloes used by veterinarians.

caballista, *n.m.* horseman, good rider, connoisseur of horses; (*prov.*) mounted highwayman; (*prov.*) horse-trainer.

caballito, *n.m.* small horse [CABALLO]; (*naut.*) trestle; (*pl.*) game of chance; roundabout, merry-go-round (circus); (*Per.*) kind of Indian coracle; *caballito del diablo,* dragonfly; *caballito de Bamba,* worthless person or thing.

caballo, *n.m.* horse; figure on horseback equivalent to the queen (Spanish cards); knight (chess); (*carp.*) trestle; cross-thread in reel or skein; (*med.*) bubo; (*prov.*) strong vine-shoot; (*mil., min.*) horse; *pl.* (*mil.*) horse, cavalry; *caballo aguililla,* (*Am.*) very swift horse; *caballo de alquiler,* hack, hackney, hired horse; *caballo alazán (tostado),* (dark) sorrel horse; *caballo de batalla,* battle-horse, charger; (*fig.*) forte, speciality; main point (of discussion); *caballo bayo (dorado),* (bright) bay horse; *caballo blanco,* (*coll.*) pigeon, gull; *caballo de buena boca,* person easily satisfied, especially as regards food; *caballo de carga,* pack-horse; *caballo castrado* or *capado,* gelding; *caballo de caza,* hunter; *caballo corredor* or *de carrera,* race-horse; *caballo del diablo,* dragonfly; *caballo desbocado,* run-away horse; *caballo de escuela,* horse well broken-in at the manège; *caballo frisón,* draught-horse; *caballo de Fris(i)a,* (*mil.*) cheval-de-frise; *caballo de guerra,* battle-horse, charger; *caballo ligero,* light-armed horse; *caballos ligeros,* light horse; *caballo de mano,* horse on the right-hand side of coach-pole; led horse; *caballo medroso* or *espantadizo,* skittish horse; *caballo matado,* galled horse; *caballo marino, de agua, de mar,* river-horse; (*ichth.*) hippopotamus; (*ichth.*) hippocampus, sea-horse; *caballo de montar* or *de silla,* saddle-horse; *caballo moro,* piebald horse; *caballo overo,* red and white spotted horse; *caballo padre,* stallion; *caballo pardo,* brown or dark grey horse; *caballo picazo,* pied horse; *caballo de palo,* (*coll.*) any vessel fit for sea; rack for criminals; *caballo de posta,* post-horse; *caballo rabón,* docked horse; *caballo de regalo* or *de albda,* state horse; *caballo retinto,* shining black horse; *caballo rubicán,* speckled white horse; *caballo rucio rodado,* dapple-grey horse; *caballo de silla,* horse on left-hand side of coach-pole; *caballo de tiro,* draught-horse; *caballo tordo rodado,* dapple bay horse; *caballo de vapor,* horse-power; *caballo de vara,* shaft-horse; *caballo que vuela, no quiere espuela,* don't flog a willing horse; *a caballo,* on horse-back; *a caballo presentado (regalado) no hay*

que mirarle el diente, one should not look a gift horse in the mouth; *a mata caballo,* at break-neck speed; *caer (ponerse) bien* or *mal a (en un) caballo,* to sit a horse well or badly; *de caballo de regalo a rocín de molinero,* from wealth to poverty; *ir en el caballo de San Francisco,* to go on foot; *huir a uña de caballo,* to have a hairbreadth escape; *montar (subir) a caballo,* to get on horseback; *poner a uno a caballo,* to initiate someone in horsemanship; *sacar bien limpio el caballo,* to come well out of a difficulty.

caballón, *n.m.* border, bank of earth; ridge between two furrows.

caballona, *n.f.* queen (chess).

caballote, *n.m.* horse, torture rack.

caballuelo, *n.m.* little horse [CABALLO].

caballuno, -na, *a.* equine, horse-like.

cabana, *n.f.* (*naut.*) customs-officer's office; strong boat.

cabaña, *n.f.* shepherd's hut, cottage, cot, cabin; hole, hovel, poor or mean dwelling; large flock of ewes or breeding sheep; drove of mules for carrying grain; baulk-line (in billiards); (*paint.*) landscape with cottage and domestic animals.

cabañal, *a.* used by sheep or cattle (road). — *n.m.* village of huts; (*prov.*) cattle-shelter.

cabañería, *n.f.* rations for a week allowed to shepherds.

cabañero, -ra, *a.* belonging to or of a drove or flock. — *n.m.* drover, shepherd. — *n.f.* (*prov.*) cattle road, drove; *perro cabañero,* sheep-dog.

cabañil, *a.* belonging to a shepherd's hut. — *n.m.* muleteer.

cabañuela, *n.f.* small hut or cottage [CABAÑA]; weather prognostication made in August for the following year. — *pl. fiesta de las Cabañuelas,* Jewish feast of the tabernacles.

cabás, *n.m.* small pannier, shopping-bag.

cabe, *n.m.* stroke by which two balls are hit in the game of *argolla; cabe de pala,* lucky chance; *dar un cabe al bolsillo,* to hurt one in his business, fortune, etc.

cabe, *prep.* (*poet.*) near, hard by, nigh.

cabeceado, -da, *a.* nodding; rocking. — *n.m.* thickening of line in a letter. — *p.p.* [CABECEAR].

cabeceador, -ra, *a.* nodding; (*naut.*) pitching.

cabeceamiento; cabeceo, *n.m.* nodding, nod of the head; (*naut.*) pitching.

cabecear, *v.i.* to nod (in sleep, in assent); to shake the head in disapprobation; to raise or lower the head (said of horses); to lurch (of carriages); to incline to one side, to hang over (of a load); (*naut.*) to pitch. — *v.t.* in writing to make letters with thick loops; in bookbinding, to put the head-band to a book; to bind clothes or rugs; to foot (stockings); (*agric.*) to plough headland; to head wine (by adding old wine to give it strength).

cabeceo, *n.m.* [CABECEAMIENTO].

cabecequia, *n.m.* inspector of sluices and drains.

cabecera, *n.f.* head (of bed, table); beginning or principal part of something; upper end; head-waters; head-board (bed); seat of honour; capital of province, region or district; bridge-head; head-line; head-band (book); head-piece or vignette; pillow, bolster; chief, leader; fixed bank (gambling); (*arch.*) sanctuary; (*min.*) foreman of drillers; (*prov.*) head of family; *pl.* (*print.*) quoins, wedges; *asistir* (*estar*) *a la cabecera del enfermo*, to nurse, attend an invalid continually; *nunca dejó la cabecera de su padre*, he never left his father's bedside.

cabecería, *n.f.* obstinacy, stubbornness; (*fig.*) primacy, primateship.

cabecero, *n.m.* (*carp.*) hood-mould, hood-moulding.

cabeciancho, -cha, *a.* broad- or flat-headed (nails or studs).

cabecil, *n.m.* padded ring for carrying objects on the head.

cabecilla, *n.f.* small head [CABEZA]. — *n.m.f.* wrong-headed person. — *n.m.* leader of rebels; ringleader.

cabellar, *v.i., v.r.* to grow hair; to put on false hair.

cabellejo, *n.m.* little hair [CABELLO].

cabellera, *n.f.* long hair; false hair, switch (of hair); tail of a comet.

cabello, *n.m.* hair of the head. — *pl.* large sinews in mutton; fibres of maize; *cabellos de ángel*, sweetmeat made with *cidra cayote;* preserve of fruit cut into small threads; *cabello liso* or *llano*, smooth, straight hair; *cabello merino*, thick, curly hair; *cabello rizado*, curly hair; *asirse de un cabello*, to adopt the slightest pretext, to catch at a straw; *traer alguna cosa por los cabellos*, to say something inappropriate or illogical; *tomar la ocasión por los cabellos*, to seize time by the forelock; *cada cabello hace su sombra en el suelo*, there is nothing insignificant; *cortar, hender* or *partir un cabello en el aire*, to be very quick-witted; *en cabello*, with hair hanging loose; *en cabellos*, bare-headed; *estar uno colgado de los cabellos*, to be on tenter-hooks; *estar* (*una cosa*) *pendiente de un cabello*, (something) to be in imminent danger; *llevar a uno de un cabello*, to influence someone easily; *llevar* (*tirar*) *de* or *por los cabellos*, to carry off violently or against one's will; *no faltar un cabello*, to a hair; *no montar un cabello*, not to be worth a rush; *podérsele ahogar con un cabello*, to be in great distress; *ponérsele los cabellos de punta* or *tan altos*, to make one's hair stand on end; *tocar a uno en un cabello* or *en la punta de un cabello*, to offend someone's susceptibilities easily; *tropezar en un cabello*, to be discouraged easily.

cabelludo, -da, *a.* hairy; (*bot.*) fibrous; *cuero cabelludo*, scalp.

cabelluelo, *n.m.* thin, short hair [CABELLO].

caber, *v.i.* (*pres. indic.* **quepo, cabe, cabemos;** *pret.* **cupe;** *pres. subj.* **quepa, quepamos**) to be able or capable of being contained; to have room or entry; to fit; to be possible or natural; to be entitled to something; to fall to one's share; to befall (good or bad luck). — *v.t.* to contain; to comprise, include; to admit; *no caber de gozo*, to be overjoyed; *no caber de pies*, to have no room to stand; *no cabe en sí*, he is very conceited; *todo cabe*, everything is possible; *todo cabe en él*, he is capable of any evil; *no cabe duda*, there is no doubt; *no caber en uno alguna cosa*, to be incapable of something; *no cabe más*, there is no

more room; there is no more to be desired; *no más de lo que cabe en la mano*, not more than will go in the hollow of the hand; *honra y provecho no caben en un saco*, honour and riches are seldom found united; *a mí me cupo en suerte venir a Europa*, it was my lot to come to Europe; *no caber en toda la casa*, to quarrel with the whole household; *no caber en el pellejo*, to be extremely fat; *me ha cabido buena suerte*, good luck has befallen me.

cabero, *n.m.* (*prov.*) maker of handles for tools. — *a.* (*Mex.*) last, final.

cabestraje, *n.m.* halter; fee paid to a drover.

cabestrante, *n.m.* (*naut.*) capstan.

cabestrar, *v.t.* to halter. — *v.i.* to fowl with a stalking-ox.

cabestrear, *v.i.* to follow docilely when led by a halter, (said of beasts).

cabestrería, *n.f.* shop where halters and collars are made and sold.

cabestrero, -ra, *a.* that can be led by a halter. — *n.m.* halter and collar maker or seller; fishing-net. — *n.f.* fishing-net cord.

cabestrillo, *n.m.* sling; gold or silver chain; (*carp.*) kind of hoop; (*naut.*) small cord; *buey de cabestrillo*, stalking-ox.

cabestro, *n.m.* halter; bell-ox; gold or silver chain; *llevar* (*traer*) *del cabestro*, to lead by the nose.

cabeza, *n.f.* head; cranium; chief, leader, principal person; individual person; understanding, judgment, mind, intelligence, intellect; talent; beginning; extremity; origin, source; top (of book, page, bell, mountain); principal town or capital of a province, region or district; (*anat.*) rounded part of certain bones; (*naut.*) head; head of nail, pin. — *pl.* (*naut.*) bow and stern; an equestrian game; *cabeza de ajo(s)*, head of garlic; *cabeza de casa* or *de linaje*, first-born, head of the family; *cabeza de chorlito*, hare-brained, foolish person; *cabeza de gigante*, (*prov., bot.*) sunflower bud; *cabeza de hierro*, obstinate, determined man; one able to withstand prolonged mental work; *cabeza de ganado mayor*, head of neat cattle; *cabeza mayor*, head of family; head of neat cattle; *cabeza menor*, head of sheep, goat, etc.; *cabeza de la Iglesia*, the Pope; *cabeza del Dragón*, (*astron.*) ascendant node; *cabeza de olla*, scum, skimmings; *cabeza de partido*, capital of province, region or district; *cabeza de perro*, (*bot.*) common celandine; *cabeza de proceso*, writ to commence a process; *cabeza de puente*, (*mil.*) bridge-head; *cabeza de tarro*, big-headed person; simpleton; *cabeza de testamento*, introductory part of a will; *cabeza de turco*, scapegoat; *cabeza moruna*, light-coloured horse with black head; *cabeza redonda*, blockhead; round-head (English Parliamentarian, 17th cent.); *cabeza torcida*, hypocrite; *cabeza vana*, head weakened by overwork or illness; *mala cabeza*, hare-brained irresponsible person; *abrir la cabeza*, to wound in the head; *a la cabeza*, in front, at the head; *alzar* (*levantar*) *la cabeza*, to retrieve one's health or fortune; *andársele* (*írsele*) *a uno la cabeza*, to feel giddy; to be threatened with loss of position; *a un volver de cabeza*, in a trice; *bajar* (*doblar*) *la cabeza*, to bow to the inevitable; *calentarle a uno la cabeza*, to annoy, irritate someone;

to buoy up with vain hopes and flatteries; *calentarse la cabeza*, to study hard, swot; *cargársele la cabeza*, to feel heavy, drowsy; *dar con la cabeza en las paredes*, to run into an affair at one's disadvantage; *dar uno de cabeza*, to lose one's position or fortune; *dar en la cabeza a uno*, to defeat, frustrate someone; *de cabeza*, headlong, head first; *aprender* or *hablar de cabeza*, to learn by or speak from memory, by heart; *de mi (su) cabeza*, out of my (his) own head, original; *descomponérsele a uno la cabeza*, to lose one's reason; *dolerle a uno la cabeza*, to have a headache; to be on the point of losing one's position; *echar (hundir) de cabeza*, (*agric.*) to plant cuttings; *encajársele (metérsele, ponérsele) a uno en la cabeza alguna cosa*, to get a notion; to be bent upon a thing; *encasquetarle en la cabeza*, to clap on the head; *en volviendo la cabeza*, in a trice; *escarmentar en cabeza ajena*, to learn from another's mistakes; *flaco de cabeza*, weak-minded; *hacer cabeza*, to be the leader; *henchir (llenar) la cabeza de viento*, to flatter; *ir cabeza abajo*, to become ruined gradually; *la cabeza blanca y el seso por venir*, old yet foolish; *levantar (sacar) uno de su cabeza alguna cosa*, to fancy, imagine something; *llevar en la cabeza*, to be frustrated, disappointed; *más vale ser cabeza de ratón que cola de león*, it is better to be a triton among minnows; *meter la cabeza en alguna parte*, to get a look in; *meter la cabeza en un puchero*, to continue obstinately in one's error; *meter en la cabeza*, to persuade, convince; to teach; *meterse de cabeza*, to go into an affair wholeheartedly; *no haber (tener) donde volver la cabeza*, not to know which way to turn; *no levantar cabeza*, to be very busy reading or writing; to make no progress or remain in poor health or fortune; *otorgar de cabeza*, to nod assent; *pagar a tanto por cabeza*, to pay so much a head; *pasarle por la cabeza*, to get a whim; *pasársele la cabeza*, to catch cold; *perder (volvérsele a uno) la cabeza*, to lose one's senses; to be at a loss how to act; *por su cabeza*, according to his own bent; *quebrantar la cabeza*, to humble, humiliate; to annoy, bore; *quebrarle a uno la cabeza*, to annoy, bore someone; *quebrarse (romperse) la cabeza*, to cudgel one's wits; *quitar de la cabeza*, to dissuade, get out of one's head; *romper a uno la cabeza*, to break someone's head; to annoy, bore; *sacar la cabeza*, to show, come to a head; to assume an air of importance; *sentar la cabeza*, to settle down, become sensible; *subirse a la cabeza*, to go to one's head (wine, fame, etc.); *tener mala cabeza*, to act foolishly; *tocado de la cabeza*, mentally unbalanced; *torcer la cabeza*, to fall ill; to die; *tornar (volver) la cabeza a alguna cosa*, to pay attention to something.

cabezada, *n.f.* head-shake; blow or butt given with or received on the head; nod; halter, nose-band; (*naut.*) pitching; headstall; cord for stitching headband of a book; instep, upper of a boot; highest part of piece of ground; *dar cabezadas*, to nod in sleep, fall asleep; *darse de cabezadas (por las paredes)*, to cudgel one's wits fruitlessly; *cabezada potrera*, halter for colts.

cabezal, *n.m.* small pillow; (*surg.*) compress; long, round bolster; forepart of a carriage;

post of a door; narrow mattress used by labourers.

cabezalejo, *n.m.* little pillow or bolster; small compress [CABEZAL].

cabezalero, -ra, *n.m.* executor, executrix of a will.

cabezazo, *n.m.* blow given with the head.

cabezo, *n.m.* summit of a mountain; hillock; (*naut.*) reef; shirt collar.

cabezón, -na, *n.m.f., a.* big-headed (person); (*coll.*) obstinate (person). — *n.m.* large head [CABEZA]; tax list or register; shirt collar; opening of a garment for the head; *cabezón de cuadra*, halter, nose-band; *cabezón de serreta*, serrated nose-ring; *llevar (traer) de cabezones*, to carry away by force; to lead by the nose.

cabezonada, *n.f.* (*fam.*) obstinacy.

cabezorro, *n.m.* (*fam.*) large or disproportionate head.

cabezota, *n.f.* large head [CABEZA]. — *n.m.f., a.* (*coll.*) big-headed, club-headed (person); obstinate (person).

cabezudo, -da, *a.* large-headed; (*coll.*) headstrong, obstinate, stubborn; (*coll.*) heady (liquors); (*agric.*) headed (runner, stem). — *n.m.* (*ichth.*) mullet; large-headed dwarfs in procession.

cabezuela, *n.f.* small head [CABEZA]; coarse flour; wine sediment; rosebud from which rose water is distilled; (*bot.*) eryngo, ragwort-leaved centaury. — *n.m.f.* dolt, blockhead, simpleton, hare-brained fellow.

cabezuelo, *n.m.* little head or top [CABEZO].

cabido, -da, *a.* contained; befallen; appropriate. — *n.m.* landmark; knight of the Order of Malta. — *n.f.* content, space, room, capacity; (*fig.*) influence; *tener (gran) cabida con alguna persona* or *en alguna parte*, to have (great) influence with someone or somewhere. — *p.p.* [CABER].

cabila, *n.f.* tribe of Berbers in Morocco.

cabildada, *n.f.* (*fam.*) hasty, ill-advised proceeding of a corporation or chapter.

cabildante, *n.m.* (*Am.*) councillor.

cabildear, *v.i.* to lobby; to influence or win votes in a corporation or chapter.

cabildeo, *n.m.* lobbying, intrigue.

cabildero, *n.m.* lobbyist, intriguer.

cabildo, *n.m.* chapter of a cathedral or collegiate church; meeting of a chapter; place where such a meeting is held; municipal council.

cabileño, -ña, *a.* belonging to a *cabila*. — *n.m.* individual of a *cabila*.

cabilla, *n.f.* dowel; (*naut.*) treenail; belaying-pin.

cabillador, *n.m.* maker of belaying-pins.

cabillería, *n.m.* number of *cabillas*.

cabillero, *n.m.* (*naut.*) rack for holding belaying-pins.

cabillo, *n.m.* (*bot.*) flower-stalk, leaf-stalk; fruit-stem.

cabimiento, *n.m.* capacity, content, space; right of claiming a commandery in the Order of Malta.

cabio, *n.m.* lintel; flooring joist; breastsummer of a chimney; top and bottom pieces of a window- or door-frame; kind of rafter.

cabizbajarse, *v.r.* to lower one's head.

cabizbajo, -ja, *a.* crestfallen; thoughtful; pensive; melancholy.

cabizcaído, -da, *a.* [CABIZBAJO].

cabizmordido, -da, *a.* with depressed nape.

cable, *n.m.* thick rope; (*naut.*) cable (111¼ fathoms); *cable de alambre,* wire rope; *cable de cadena,* chain cable; *cable eléctrico,* electric cable; *cable submarino,* submarine cable.

cablegrafiar, *v.t.* to cable (message).

cablegráfico, -ca, *a.* cablegraphic, cablegrammic.

cablegrama, *n.m.* cablegram.

cablero, -ra, *a.* cable-laying (ship).

cabo, *n.m.* extreme, extremity, tip; stub, stump; bit; cape, headland, promontory, foreland; place, situation; handle, holder, haft; cord, rope, thread; lowest card in the game called *revesino;* chief, head, commander; end, finish, termination; (*mil.*) corporal; (*prov.*) paragraph, article; parcel or package at the custom-house smaller than a bale; (*naut.*) cord. — *pl.* tail and mane of horses; loose pieces of apparel, such as shoes, stockings, hats, etc.; divisions of a discourse; *cabo blanco,* untarred cord; *cabo de ala* or *fila,* (*mil.*) guide, fugleman; *cabo de armería,* (*prov.*) manorial residence; *cabo de barra,* last payment or balance of account; *cabo de columna,* (*naut.*) guide; *cabo suelto,* unforeseen or pending circumstance; *al (hasta el) cabo del mundo,* to the ends of the earth; *al cabo de un año tiene el mozo las mañas de su amo,* like master like man; *al cabo de cien años todos seremos calvos,* it will be all the same a hundred years hence; *estar (muy) al cabo,* to be at death's door; *llevar a (al) cabo,* to complete, conclude; tó perfect; to carry through to the end; *no tener cabo ni cuerda,* to have neither head nor tail; to be very perplexing; *por (el) cabo,* extremely; *volver a coger el cabo,* to resume the thread of a discourse; *cabo de año,* anniversary; *cabo de escuadra,* (*mil.*) corporal; *cabo de maestranza,* foreman of a workmen's brigade; *cabo de presa,* (*naut.*) prize-master; *al cabo, al cabo de la jornada, al cabo y a la postre,* at last; *al fin y al cabo,* finally, in the end; *estar* or *ponerse al cabo de,* to be or make oneself conversant with, or well informed about; *atar (juntar, recoger, unir) cabos,* to collect and study the circumstances of a case; *cabos negros,* black hair, eyes and eyebrows of a woman; *dar cabo a una cosa,* to finish or perfect a thing; *dar cabo de una cosa,* to destroy a thing; *de cabo a cabo* or *a rabo,* from head to tail, from top to bottom, from end to end; *por ningún cabo,* by no means.

Cabo, *n.m.* the Cape; *Cabo de Buena Esperanza,* Cape of Good Hope; *Cabo de Hornos,* Cape Horn.

cabotaje, *n.m.* (*naut.*) coasting-trade, pilotage; *gran cabotaje,* (*naut.*) coastal trade between Spain and Northwest Africa, and the Mediterranean.

cabra, *n.f.* goat; (*mil.*) engine formerly used for throwing stones; (*astron.*) Capella, star in the Auriga; (*Col., Cub.*) loaded dice; (*Chi.*) light two-wheeled carriage; *barba de cabra,* (*bot.*) goat's-beard; *pata de cabra,* shoemaker's burnishing tool; *pie de cabra,* two-pronged lever; *cabra coja no tiene siesta,* the person with little talent needs to work harder; *cargar (echar) las cabras a uno,* to make one person pay all the losses; to throw the blame

on another; *echar (las) cabras,* to play among the losers who will pay the reckoning; *la cabra siempre tira al monte,* what is bred in the bone will out in the flesh; *meterle a uno las cabras en el corral,* to intimidate someone; *cabra montés,* wild goat; *piel de cabra,* goatskin; (*pl.*) red marks on legs caused by fire.

cabrahigal; cabrahigar, *n.m.* grove or plantation of wild fig-trees.

cabrahigar, *v.t.* to caprificate.

cabrahigo, *n.m.* the male wild fig-tree; its fruit.

cabreo, *n.m.* (*prov.*) church register.

cabrería, *n.f.* goat's shelter; goat's milk dairy.

cabrerizo, -za, *a.* caprine, goatish, hircine. — *n.m.f.* goatherd. — *n.f.* hut for goatherds.

cabrero, -ra, *n.m.f.* goatherd, wife of goatherd.

cabrestante, *n.m.* (*naut.*) capstan.

cabrevación, *n.f.* (*prov.*) survey of royal property.

cabrevar, *v.t.* (*prov.*) to survey royal property.

cabreve, *n.m.* (*prov.*) survey of royal property.

cabria, *n.f.* crane; wheel and axle; winch, windlass; hoist; axle-tree; (*naut.*) sheers.

cabrieta, *n.f.* (*mach.*) jack.

cabrihigación; cabrahigadura, *n.f.* caprification.

cabrilla, *n.f.* (*ichth.*) a fish; (*carp.*) trestle, bench. — *pl.* (*astr.*) Pleiades; marks on the legs, produced by continual proximity to the fire; (*naut.*) whitecaps on the water; ducks and drakes (game).

cabrillear, *v.i.* (*naut.*) to form whitecaps.

cabrilleo, *n.m.* waves forming whitecaps.

cabrio, *n.m.* (*carp.*) bridging-joist; rafter, beam.

cabrío, *a.* caprine, goatish, hircine. — *n.m.* herd of goats; *macho cabrío,* buck.

cabriola, *n.f.* caper; nimble leap; gambol; hop, skip, jump.

cabriolar; cabriolear, *v.i.* to caper, cut capers; to jump, curvet, frisk.

cabriolé, *n.m.* a kind of cloak, without sleeves; cabriolet, two-wheeled hooded carriage.

cabriolista, *n.m.* caperer, dancer.

cabrión, *n.m.* (*naut.*) piece of wood at the back of a gun-carriage.

cabrionar, *v.t.* (*naut.*) to put *cabriones* to gun-carriages.

cabrita, *n.f.* ancient engine to cast stones.

cabritero, -ra, *n.m.f.* dealer in kid-skins.

cabritilla, *n.f.* dressed lamb or kid-skin.

cabritillo, *n.m.* corset.

cabrito, *n.m.* kid, kidling.

cabrituno, -na, *a.* appertaining to the kid.

cabro; cabrón, *n.m.* buck, he-goat; (*coll.*) cuckold; (*Chi.*) pimp, pander.

cabronada, *n.f.* (*vulg.*) infamous action which a man permits against his own honour; (*coll.*) great annoyance or nuisance.

cabronzuelo, *n.m.* little he-goat [CABRÓN].

cabruno, -na, *a.* caprine, goatish, goat-like, hircine.

cabruñar, *v.t.* (*prov.*) to sharpen a scythe by hammering the edge.

cabruño, *n.m.* (*prov.*) sharpening a scythe.

cabú, *n.m.* (*prov.*) barren ground.

cabujón, *n.m.* (*jewel.*) cabochon.

caburé, *n.m.* (*Par., Arg.*) small bird of prey.

cabuya, *n.f.* (*bot.*) common American agave; sisal-grass, sisal-hemp; (*prov. and Am.*)

cord or rope made of aloes; *dar cabuya,* *(fig.)* *(Am.)* to tie, fasten; *ponerse en la cabuya, (Am.)* to begin to understand, to see daylight.

cabuyera, *n.f.* cords supporting a hammock.

cabuyeria, *n.f. (naut.)* small cordage.

caca, *n.f. (fam.)* excrements of a child; word used by children who wish to go to stool; *(coll.)* fault, vice, defect; dishonesty; scandal.

cacahual, *n.m.* plantation of cacao-trees.

cacahuate; cacahuete; cacahuey, *n.m. (bot.)* peanut, American earth-nut.

cacahuetero, -ra, *n.m.f. (Mex.)* pea-nut seller.

cacalote, *n.m. (Mex.)* raven; *(Am.) (metal.)* rosette copper.

cacao, *n.m. (bot.)* cacao-tree; cacao-nut, chocolate-nut; *manteca de cacao,* cacao-butter; *no valer un cacao,* to be of very little value; *pedir cacao (Col., Guat., Mex., Ven.)* to beg pardon, quarter.

cacaotal, *n.m.* cacao plantation.

cacaraña, *n.f.* pit caused by small-pox.

cacarañado, -da, *a.* pock-marked, pitted.

cacareador, -ra, *a.* cackling (hen); crowing (cock); *(coll.)* boastful. — *n.m.f.* cackler; cock that crows; hen that cackles; *(coll.)* boaster, braggart.

cacarear, *v.i.* to crow, cackle. — *v.t.* to brag, boast; *cacarear y no poner huevo,* to promise and not perform.

cacareo, *n.m.* crowing, cackling; *(coll.)* boasting, bragging.

cacarizo, -za, *a. (Mex.)* pock-marked.

cacarro, *n.m. (prov.)* oak-gall.

cacatúa, *n.f. (orn.)* cockatoo.

cacaxtle, *n.m. (Mex.)* crate to carry goods.

cacaxtlero, *n.m. (Mex.)* Indian porter with a *cacaxtle.*

cacear, *v.t.* to stir with a dipper or ladle.

caceo, *n.m.* stirring with a ladle.

cacera, *n.f.* irrigating canal; channel, conduit.

cacería, *n.f.* hunting-party; quantity of dead game; *(paint.)* landscape representing field-sports.

cacerina, *n.f.* cartridge-box or pouch.

cacerola, *n.f.* stew-pan, saucepan.

caceta, *n.f.* small colander used by apothe-caries.

cacica, *n.f.* wife of a *cacique.*

cacical, *a.* appertaining to a *cacique.*

cacicazgo, *n.m.* dignity of a chief or *cacique* or his territory; *(coll.)* wire-pulling.

cacillo, *n.m.* small saucepan, dipper or ladle.

cacimba, *n.f.* hole dug on the sea-shore for drinking-water; bucket; fishing-net; *(coll.)* top-hat.

cacique, *n.m.* cacique, Indian chief; *(coll.)* political leader, wire-puller or boss.

caciquería, *n.f.* reunion of *caciques* or in-fluential persons.

caciquismo, *n.m. (coll.)* political leadership; wire-pulling.

caciquista, *a.* appertaining to *or* partisan of a *cacique* or *caciquismo.*

cacle, *n.m. (Mex.)* leather sandal.

caco, *n.m.* thief, pickpocket; *(coll.)* coward, poltroon.

cacodilato, *n.m. (chem.)* cacodylate.

cacodílico, -ca, *a. (chem.)* cacodylic.

cacodilo, *n.m. (chem.)* cacodyl.

cacofonía, *n.f.* cacophony.

cacofónico, -ca, *a.* cacophonous.

cacogástrico, -ca, *a. (med.)* cacogastric.

cacografía, *n.f.* cacography.

cacomite, *n.m. (Mex.)* a flower plant.

cacomiztle, *n.m. (Mex.) (zool.)* cacomistle.

cacomorfia, *n.f. (med.)* cacomorphia.

cacoquimia, *n.f. (med.)* cachæmia.

cacoquímico, -ca, *a. (med.)* cacochymic.

cacoquimio, -mia, *n.m.f.* one suffering from melancholy.

cácteo, -tea, *a. (bot.)* cactaceous, cactal, cactoid. — *n.f.pl.* cacti.

cacto, *n.m. (bot.)* cactus.

cacumen, *n.m.* top, height; *(coll.)* head, understanding, acumen.

cacha, *n.f.* each of the two leaves of a razor or knife handle; buttock of hare or rabbit; cheek; *(prov.)* buttock, seat; *hasta las cachas,* up to the hilt.

cachaco, *(Col., Ec., Ven.) n.m.* dandy.

cachada, *n.f.* stroke of one top against another when boys play at tops; *(Col., Hond.)* thrust with the horns (from animals).

cachado, -da, *a.* broken; sliced. — *n.m. (carp.)* wood sawn in the middle. — *p.p.* [CACHAR].

cachalote, *n.m.* sperm whale.

cachamarín, *n.m. (naut.)* coasting lugger.

cachano, *n.m. (fam.)* the devil; *llamar a cachano,* to ask, call in vain.

cachapa, *n.f. (Ven.)* corn bread with sugar.

cachapucha, *n.f. (coll.)* hotchpotch.

cachar, *v.t.* to break in pieces; to divide a plank in two lengthwise by a saw or axe.

cacharpari, *n.m. (Per.)* farewell supper and dance.

cacharrazo, *n.m. (fam.)* large draught of liquor.

cacharrería, *n.f.* crockery-store; collection of earthen pots.

cacharrero, -ra, *n.m.f.* maker or seller of crockery.

cacharro, *n.m.* coarse earthen pot; piece of an earthen pot.

cachava, *n.f.* children's sport resembling hockey or golf; stick for driving the ball; shepherd's crook.

cachavazo, *n.m.* stroke of the *cachava.*

cachavona, *n.f. (prov.)* kind of cudgel or club.

cachaza, *n.f.* slowness, tardiness, inactivity; forbearance; *(Am.)* rum; first froth on cane-juice when boiled to make sugar.

cachazudo, -da, *n.m.f., a.* slow, calm, phleg-matic, cool, tranquil (person). — *n.m. (Cub.)* worm which attacks the tobacco-plant.

cache, *(Arg.) a.* coarse, unpolished (person).

cachear, *v.t.* to search a person for hidden weapons.

cachemarín, *n.m.* coasting lugger.

cachemir, *n.m.; cachemira, n.f.* cashmere.

cacheo, *n.m.* search for arms and weapons on suspects.

cachera, *n.f.* coarse shaggy cloth or baize.

cacheta, *n.f.* tooth or ward in a lock or latch.

cachete, *n.m.* blow, slap on the face; fat cheek; poniard for cattle killing.

cachetear, *v.t.* to slap, smack on the face.

cachetero, *n.m.* short poniard; bull-fighter who delivers the *coup de grâce; (coll.)* last of many persons to damage someone or some-thing.

cachetina, *n.f.* hand-to-hand fight.

cachetudo, -da, *a.* plump-cheeked, fleshy.

cachicamo, *n.m.* (*Am.*) armadillo.

cachicán, *n.m.* overseer of a farm; (*coll.*) smart, cunning; clever man.

cachicuerno, -na, *a.* having a horn handle or haft.

cachidiablo, *n.m.* (*fam.*) hobgoblin, one disguised in a devil's mask.

cachifo, -fa, *n.m.f.* (*Col., Ven.*), (*coll.*) boy, girl.

cachifollar, *v.t.* (*coll.*) to vex, disappoint; to humble; to banter; to trick.

cachigordete, -ta; cachigordito, -ta, *a.* (*fam.*) squat and plump [CACHIGORDO].

cachigordo, -da, *a.* (*fam.*) short and plump.

cachillada, *n.f.* litter of young animals.

cachimán, *n.m.* (*fam.*) hiding-place.

cachimba, *n.f.* **cachimbo,** *n.m.* (*Arg.*) hole dug on the seashore for drinking water; (*Am.*) tobacco pipe; (*Per.*) (*contempt.*) national guard; *chupar cachimba,* (*Ven.*) to smoke a pipe; to suck one's thumb (of children).

cachipolla, *n.f.* (*entom.*) day-fly; May-fly.

cachiporra, *n.f.;* **cachiporro,** *n.m.* (*prov.*) stick with a big knob; club, cudgel.

cachiporrazo, *n.m.* blow with a club.

cachirulo, *n.m.* earthen, glass or tin pot for liquors; head ornament formerly worn by women; (*vulg.*) paramour; (*prov.*) small cup; small three-masted vessel; (*Mex.*) lining of chamois for riding trousers.

cachivache, *n.m.* (*fig.*) lying, worthless fellow. — *pl.* pots and pans; broken crockery.

cachizo, -za, *a.* that can be hewn; *madero cachizo,* log.

cacho, *n.m.* slice, piece; card game; (*ichth.*) surmullet; *cacho de pan,* slice of bread; (*Am.*) horn; (*Chi., Guat.*) drinking horn.

cacho, -cha, *a.* bent, crooked.

cacholas, *n.f.pl.* (*naut.*) cheeks of the masts; (*naut.*) bee-blocks of bowsprit.

cachón, *n.m.* breaker (wave); small waterfall.

cachondearse, *v.r.* (*vulg.*) to joke slyly.

cachondeo, *n.m.* sly joke.

cachondez, *n.f.* sexual appetite, lust.

cachondo, -da, *a.* ruled by sexual appetite; in heat (bitch).

cachopo, *n.m.* (*prov.*) dry trunk, stump of a tree.

cachorra, *n.f.* (*prov.*) soft hat.

cachorreña, *n.f.* (*prov., fam.*) tardiness, slowness. — *pl.* (*prov.*) a kind of soup made of garlic, oil, chillies, vinegar and salt.

cachorrillo, *n.m.* pocket pistol.

cachorro, -ra, *n.m.f.* puppy; cub, whelp; pocket pistol.

cachú, *n.m.* catechu, cutch.

cachúa, *n.f.* (*Per., Ec., Bol.*) Indian dance.

cachucha, *n.f.* row-boat; man's cloth or fur cap; Andalusian dance and song in triple measure.

cachuchear, *v.t.* (*prov., fam.*) to coax; to indulge.

cachuchero, *n.m.* maker or seller of caps, or of pin-and-needle-cases; (*slang*) gold thief.

cachucho, *n.m.* oil-measure, containing 2·8 fl. oz.; pin- or needle-case; row-boat; (*prov.*) earthen pot; (*slang*) gold; gold currency; (*ichth.*) a fish of West Indies sea.

cachuela, *n.f.* fricassee of rabbits' livers and lights; gizzard.

cachuelo, *n.m.* (*ichth.*) small river fish resembling an anchovy.

cachulera, *n.f.* (*prov.*) cavern, hiding-place.

cachumba, *n.f.* (*Philip.*) plant of the Compositæ family used as a substitute for saffron.

cachumbo, *n.m.* (*Am.*) hard shell of coconut or other fruit.

cachunde, *n.f.* cachou, aromatic chewing paste of amber, musk and catechu; catechu.

cachupanda, *n.f.* jolly meal, picnic; (*prov.*) hotchpotch, mess.

cachupin, -na, *n.m.f.* Spaniard who settles in Central America or U.S.A.

cada, *n.m.* (*bot.*) juniper-tree. — *a.* every, each; *cada uno, cada cual, cada quisque,* everyone, each one; *cada loco con su tema,* everyone has his hobby; *cada vez,* every time; *cada vez más,* more and more; *cada que, cada vez que,* every time that; whenever; *cada (y) cuando que,* whenever, as soon as; *cada tres días,* every three days.

cadahalso, *n.m.* shed, cabin, hut, shanty; scaffold [CADALSO].

cadalecho, *n.m.* (*prov.*) bed made of the branches of trees.

cadalso, *n.m.* platform, stage, stand; scaffold or gallows for capital punishment.

cadañal, *a.* annual, yearly.

cadañego, -ga, *a.* annual, yearly; (*bot.*) bearing abundant fruit yearly.

cadañero, -ra, *a.* lasting a year; annual, yearly. — *n.f., a.* giving birth every year.

cadarzo, *n.m.* coarse, entangled silk which cannot be spun; cover of the cocoon; (*prov.*) narrow silk ribbon.

cádava, *n.f.* (*prov.*) burnt stump of furze.

cadaval, *n.m.* (*prov.*) ground strewn with *cádavas.*

cadáver, *n.m.* corpse, dead body.

cadavérico, -ca, *a.* cadaveric; (*fig.*) cadaverous.

cadejo, *n.m.* entangled hair; small skein; threads put together to make tassels.

cadena, *n.f.* chain, links joined together; surveying measure (32′ 9″); (*fig.*) bond, tie; fetters; (*fig.*) series of events; imprisonment for life; number of criminals chained together to be led to the galleys; (*arch.*) buttress; frame; wooden hearth-fender; figure in dancing; *balas de cadena,* chainshot; *cadena de montañas,* range of hills; *cadena de puerto,* boom of a harbour; *cadena de rocas,* ledge or ridge of rocks; *cadena sin fin,* endless, circular chain; *estar en cadena,* to be in prison; (*fig.*) to be oppressed; *renunciar la cadena,* in ancient Castile, to renounce all one's effects and wear an iron collar until settlement of one's debts in order to get out of prison.

cadencia, *n.f.* cadence, measure, rhythm; fall of the voice; flow of verses or periods; harmony of motion and music (in dancing); (*mus.*) cadenza.

cadenciado, -da; cadencioso, -sa, *a.* rhythmical, harmonious.

cadeneta, *n.f.* lace or needle-work wrought in the form of a chain; chain-stitch; headband of a book.

cadenilla, *n.f.* small ornamental chain; *cadenilla y media cadenilla,* graduated pearls.

cadenita, *n.f.* small chain [CADENA].

cadente, *a.* decaying, declining; going to ruin; well-modulated, rhythmical.

cadera, *n.f.* hip, hip-joint. — *pl.* [CADERILLAS]; *silla de caderas,* easy chair; *derribar las caderas a un caballo,* to overthrow a horse.

caderillas, *n.f.pl.* bustle; dress-hoops.

caderudo, -da, *a.* large-hipped.

cadetada, *n.f.* (*fam.*) injudicious, thoughtless action; schoolboy prank.

cadete, *n.m.* (*mil.*) cadet, youth in any military school; *hacer el cadete,* to play the fool.

cadi, *n.m.* (*Ec.*) ivory-nut palm.

cadí, *n.m.* cadi, Moorish magistrate.

cadillar, *n.m.* place where bur-parsley grows.

cadillo, *n.m.* (*bot.*) great bur-parsley; prickly burweed; common burdock; wart (on skin); (*prov.*) puppy. — *pl.* first warp threads.

cadmía, *n.f.* sublimated oxide of zinc, tutty.

cadmio, *n.m.* (*min.*) cadmium; calamine; *amarillo de cadmio,* cadmium yellow.

cado, *n.m.* (*prov.*) ferret-hole.

cadoce; cadoz, *n.m.* (*ichth.,* *prov.*) gudgeon.

cadozo, *n.m.* whirlpool.

caducamente, *adv.* weakly, feebly, dotingly.

caducante, *a.* doting.

caducar; caduquear, *v.i.* to dote; to be worn out by service; to fall into disuse; to become extinct or superannuated; (*com.,* *law*) to lapse.

caduceador, *n.m.* king at arms, who proclaimed peace and carried the caduceus.

caduceo, *n.m.* caduceus.

caducidad, *n.f.* (*law*) caducity; decrepitude.

caducífloro, -ra, *a.* (*bot.*) caducous.

caduco, -ca, *a.* worn out, senile, enfeebled by age; decrepit; perishable, frail; broken; *mal caduco,* epilepsy. — *membrana caduca, n.f.* (*anat.*) decidua.

caduquez, *n.f.* dotage, senility.

caedizo, -za, *a.* ready to fall; (*bot.*) deciduous.

caedura, *n.f.* loose threads dropping from the loom.

caer, *v.i.* (*pres. indic.* **caigo**; *pret.* él **cayó**; *pres. subj.* **caiga**) to fall, drop, tumble down; to light on; to hang down, droop; to fall off; to fit, suit, become; to fall due; to fall into an error or danger; to be situated; to decrease, decline; to deviate from one's path; to fall due; to befall, happen, come to pass; to fall to one's lot; to die; to come to an end; (*mil.*) to surrender, yield, fall; to come upon; to grasp, realize, understand; to fade (colours); to be included, numbered amongst. — *v.r.* to languish, become low-spirited; to fall; *caer a (hacia) esta parte,* to be situated on (towards) this side; *las ventanas caen al río,* the windows overlook the river; *caer bien (una cosa),* to fit, suit, become (a thing); *caer bien o mal (una persona),* to be well or unfavourably received (a person); *caer bien a caballo,* to sit a horse well; *caer de pies,* to fall on one's feet; *caer de su estado,* to fall senseless; to lose one's position; *caer a plomo* or *de plano,* to fall down flat, stretched; *caer una cosa por defuera,* to make little impression; *caer que hacer,* to get unexpected work; to come in for troubles and worries; *caer(se) redondo,* to drop down unconscious; *caer en culpa,* to commit a fault; *con las orejas caídas,* disappointed; *caerle a uno en suerte,* to fall to one's lot; *el castillo cayó,* the fortress surrendered; *el sol se deja caer,* the heat lessens; *la Pascua cae en Abril,* Easter falls in April; *caer en el*

mes del obispo, to fill a vacancy; *caer en color,* to fade; *caer en mal caso,* to fall into bad repute; *caer en las mientes,* to guess, imagine something; *caer debajo del número,* to be included, numbered amongst; *caer* or *morir como chinches,* to die off in great numbers; *en el mejor paño cae una mancha,* there is nothing free from imperfections; *pájaro viejo no cae en el lazo,* old birds are not caught with chaff; *le ha caído la lotería,* he has won a lottery prize; (*iron.*) said of an unlucky stroke; *el que no cae no se levanta,* one learns by one's errors; *estar una cosa al caer,* to be ripe, ready to fall; *caer con otro,* to match; *caer de lo alto,* to fall from above; *caer en tierra,* to fall to the ground; *caer por Pascua,* to fall at Easter; *caer sobre el enemigo,* to fall upon the enemy; *cayendo y levantando,* ups and downs (especially in illness); *la conversación cae,* the conversation languishes; *caer (una costumbre, una raza),* to die out, become extinct (a custom, a race); *dejar caer la voz,* to drop one's voice; *todo cae en el dedo malo,* everything falls on the tender spot; *del árbol caído todos hacen leña,* it is easy to kick a man when he is down; *ya caigo en ello* or *en la cuenta,* I see, I understand; *caer de bruces, de cabeza, de espaldas,* to fall face downward, headlong, backward; *caer en cama, enfermo* or *malo,* to fall ill; *caer en una cosa,* to remember or realize something; *caer en la cuenta,* to bethink oneself; to grasp, realize, see the point; *caer en el chiste,* to guess rightly; *el día cae,* day draws to a close; *caer en falta,* to fail to perform one's pledges; *caer en flor,* to be cut off in one's youth, to die prematurely; *caer de golpe,* to fall suddenly; *caer de la gracia de alguno,* or *en desgracia,* to lose someone's favour; *caer en gracia,* or *en gusto,* to please, be agreeable, find favour; *al caer de la hoja* or *de la pámpana,* at the end of autumn; *el que hoy cae puede levantarse mañana,* he who falls to-day may rise again to-morrow; *caer el plazo,* to arrive (of an allotted time); *caer en la trampa,* to fall into the trap. Among the idiomatic reflexive uses of *caer* are: *caerse de suyo,* to fall spontaneously; to be obvious, self-evident; *caerse (una cosa) de su peso,* to be evident; *caerse muerto de risa, de susto,* to drop with laughing, with fear; *caerse muerto de sueño,* to be dead-tired; *caérsele a uno la cara de vergüenza,* to blush deeply with shame; *caerse de la memoria,* to forget; *caerse de maduro* or *de viejo,* to be senile, decrepit; *caerse los pájaros,* to be insufferably hot; *caerse de inanición,* to break down through weakness; *caerse a pedazos,* to fall to pieces; to walk with a shambling gait; *caerse de ánimo,* to be dejected; *caérsele el moco a uno,* to be a booby; *caérsele a uno las alas del corazón,* to be discouraged; *caerse la sopa en miel,* to succeed beyond all expectations; *caérsele a uno la casa a cuestas,* to suffer a great calamity; to have the house fall about one's ears; *se le caen los dientes y el pelo,* he is losing his teeth and hair.

cafar, *v.i.* (*slang*) to escape.

café, *n.m.* coffee; coffee-tree; coffee-berry; coffee-house, café.

cafeíco, -ca, (*chem.*) caffeic.

cafeína, *n.f.* caffeine.

cafería, *n.f.* village.

cafetal, *n.m.* coffee plantation.

cafetalista, *n.m.f.* (*Cub.*) owner of coffee plantation.

cafetero, -ra, *a.* appertaining to coffee. — *n.m.f.* one who gathers coffee-berries; coffee-maker or seller; owner of coffee-house or café. — *n.f.* coffee-pot; kettle.

cafetín, *n.m.* small café.

cafeto, *n.m.* (*bot.*) coffee-tree.

cafetucho, *n.m.* small, untidy café.

cáfila, *n.m.* (*fam.*) series, string of people, things or animals; caravan.

cafiroleta, *n.f.* (*Cub.*) sweetmeat made of sweet-potatoes, grated coconut and sugar.

cafre, *n.m.f.*, *a.* Kafir; (*fig.*) savage, inhuman (person); clownish, rude, uncivil (person).

caftán, *n.m.* caftan.

cagaaceite, *n.m.* thrush-like bird.

cagachín, *n.m.* small reddish mosquito; tiny bird.

cagada, *n.f.* excrement; (*com.*) blunder, mistake.

cagadero, *n.m.* public water-closet, latrine.

cagado, -da, *a.* excreted; (*coll.*) soiled, spoiled; (*coll.*) cowardly, mean-spirited. — *p.p.* [CAGAR].

cagafierro, *n.m.* scoria, dross of iron.

cagajón, *n.m.* dung of horses, mules and asses.

cagalaolla, *n.m.* masquerader who dances in processions; harlequin.

cagalar, *n.m.* (*anat.*) cæcum.

cagalera, *n.f.* diarrhœa.

cagaluta, *n.f.* [CAGARRUTA].

cagancia, *n.f.* diarrhœa.

caganidos, *n.m.* (*prov.*) one who frequently changes his residence.

cagaoficios, *n.m.f.* (*fam.*) rolling stone.

cagar, *v.i.*, *v.t.*, *v.r.* (*pret.* **cagué;** *pres. subj.* **cague**) to go to stool; (*coll.*) to soil, stain, defile; to make a botch of something.

cagarrache, *n.m.* one who washes the olive-pits in an oil-mill; (*orn.*) thrush-like bird.

cagarria, *n.f.* morel, an edible mushroom.

cagarropa, *n.m.* a small reddish mosquito.

cagarruta, *n.f.* dung of sheep, goats, hares and mice.

cagatinta, *n.m.* contemptuous nickname given to clerks.

cagatorio, *n.m.* public water-closet, latrine.

cagón, -na, *n.m.f.*, *a.* person troubled with diarrhœa; (*coll.*) cowardly, timorous person.

caguama, *n.f.* turtle of the Caribbean Sea.

cagueta, *n.m.f.* (*fam.*) worthless, cowardly person.

cahinza, *n.f.* (*bot.*) medicinal plant.

cahiz, *n.m.* a nominal measure of twelve *fanegas*, or 18½ bushels.

cahizada, *n.f.* land sufficient to contain one *cahiz* of seed.

caico, *n.m.* (*Cub.*) large reef or shoal.

caíd, *n.m.* (*hist.*) judge or governor of Algiers, kadi.

caída, *n.f.* fall, falling; tumble, downfall; falling off, drop, lapse; diminution; droop; hanging drapery; (*slang*) affront; (*slang*) prostitute's earnings; declination, declension, declivity, descent; landslip; (*geol.*) dip; (*Philip.*) interior gallery overlooking the courtyard; *caída de una vela,* (*naut.*) depth or drop of a sail; *ir* or *andar de* (*capa*) *caída,*

to decline in fortune and credit; *a la caída de la tarde,* at the close of the evening; *a la caída del sol,* at sunset. — *pl.* coarse wool cut off the skirts of a fleece; witty remarks; repartee.

caído, -da, *a.* fallen, dropped; (*fig.*) languid, downfallen. — *n.m.* sloping line to show proper slant when learning to write. — *pl.* arrears (of rents, taxes). — *p.p.* [CAER].

caigo; caiga, *pres. indic.; pres. subj.* [CAER].

caigua, *n.f.* (*Per.*) cucurbitaceous plant.

caiguá, *n.m.f.*, *a.* (*Am.*) Indian inhabiting the mountains of Uruguay, Paraná and Paraguay.

caimacán, *n.m.* vizier.

caimán, *n.m.* cayman, alligator, American crocodile; (*fig.*) cunning man.

caimiento, *n.m.* fall, drop; droop; (*fig.*) dejection, languidness, lowness of spirits.

caimito, *n.m.* (*Am.*) star apple.

caique, *n.m.* (*naut.*) caïque, skiff, small boat, ketch.

cairel, *n.m.* false hair or wig worn by women to embellish their head-dress; fringe trimming; furbelow, flounce; silk threads for fastening the hair of wigs to the net foundation.

cairelado, -da, *a.* fringed. — *p.p.* [CAIRELAR].

cairelar, *v.t.* to fringe.

cairelota, *n.f.* (*slang*) striped, multicoloured shirt.

caja, *n.f.* box, case; coffin; chest; body (of carriage); safe, cash-box; sheath; gun-stock; socket; cavity, hole; (*mil.*) drum, drum case or frame; frame; (*com.*) cash, funds; cashier's office; central or distributing post office; printer's case; portable writing equipment; well (of staircase); wooden case of an organ, piano, etc.; (*bot.*) seed-case; (*naut.*) block, pulley; *caja alta, caja baja,* (*typ.*) upper case, lower case; *caja de ahorros,* savings-bank; *caja de amortización,* Department of Public Debts; Sinking Fund Department; *caja de balas,* shot-locker; *caja de brasero,* wooden stand for a brazier; *caja de caudales,* (*com.*) safe; *caja de coche,* body of a coach; *caja de consulta,* (*law*) brief; *caja del cuerpo,* thorax; *caja de escopeta,* stock of a musket; *caja de engranajes,* gear-box; *caja de las muelas,* (*fam.*) the gums; the whole mouth; *caja de música,* musical-box; *caja de reclutamiento,* (*mil.*) recruiting-office; *caja registradora,* (*com.*) cash register; *caja del tambor,* (*anat.*) drum, middle ear cavity; *cajas en ternos,* nest of boxes; *libro de caja,* cash-book; *despedir, echar* (*a uno*) *con cajas destempladas,* to turn (someone) harshly away; *en caja,* in hand (cash); *entrar* (*estar*) *en caja,* to be in good health or order; *no estar en caja,* to feel out of sorts.

cajear, *v.t.* (*carp.*) to make sockets in wood.

cajel, *a.; naranja cajel,* blood-orange.

cajera, *n.f.* woman cashier; (*naut.*) sheave-hole.

cajería, *n.f.* shop for boxes, cases, etc.

cajero, *n.m.* box-maker; cashier, cash-keeper, treasurer; reservoir in irrigation canals.

cajeta, *n.f.* little box; (*prov.*) poor-box; (*naut.*) plaited cord; (*Cub.*) tobacco pouch; (*Mex., CR.*) box of jelly.

cajete, *n.m.* (*Mex., Guat.*) flat earthen bowl.

cajetilla, *n.f.* packet of cigarettes.

cajetín, *n.m.* very small box; (*typ.*) fount-case, letter-case; stamp (mark and instrument).

cají, *n.m.* (*Cub.*) a fish.

cajiga, *n.f.* (*bot.*) muricated oak.

cajigal, *n.m.* plantation of muricated oaks.

cajilla, *n.f.* (*bot.*) capsule.

cajista, *n.m.f.* (*print.*) compositor.

cajita, *n.f.* small box [CAJA].

cajo, *n.m.* bookbinder's groove.

cajón, *n.m.* large box, case, chest [CAJA]; drawer, till, money-drawer, locker; space between shelves of a book-case; (*arch.*) space between buttress and wall; mould for casting; wooden stand or shed for selling provisions; (*Mex.*) dry-goods store; (*Chi.*) ravine; *cajón de dique* or *grada*, (*naut.*) dam, caisson; dock-gate; *ser de cajón*, to be a matter of course, usual; *cosas de cajón*, commonplace things; *cajón de sastre*, confused mass, odds and ends; muddle-headed person.

cajonada, *n.f.* (*naut.*) locker.

cajoncito, *n.m.* small box; little drawer.

cajonera, *n.f.* chest of drawers in a vestry; box in which flowers or shrubs are grown.

cajonería, *n.f.* set of drawers in a piece of furniture; tall-boy or chiffonier.

cajonero, *n.m.* (*min.*) operative in charge of water-extracting implements.

cajonga, *n.f.* (*Hond.*) omelet of maize.

cajuela, *n.f.* small box [CAJA].

cal, *n.f.* lime; *ahogar la cal*, to slake lime; *cal viva*, quick or unslaked lime; *cal hidráulica*, hydraulic lime; *cal muerta*, slaked lime; *pared de cal y canto*, wall of rough stone and mortar; *ser de cal y canto*, to be very strongly built.

cala, *n.f.* cove, creek, small bay; fishing-ground; small piece cut out of a melon to try its flavour; action of testing melon's flavour; hole made in a wall to try its thickness; (*med.*) probe; (*med.*) suppository; (*naut.*) hold of a ship; (*bot.*) calla-lily; (*slang*) hole; *hacer cala y cata*, to test for quantity or quality.

calaba, *n.m.* (*bot.*) [CALAMBUCO].

calabacear, *v.t.* (*col.*) [DAR CALABAZAS].

calabacera, *n.f.* (*bot.*) pumpkin, gourd-plant; woman vendor of this fruit.

calabacero, *n.m.* retailer of pumpkins; (*slang*) picklock, burglar.

calabacica, *n.f. dim.* [CALABAZA] small pumpkin; [CALABACINO].

calabacil, *a.*, *pera calabacil*, calabash pear.

calabacilla, *n.f.* bitter gherkin; core of gourd-shaped tassel; pear-shaped ear-ring.

calabacín, *n.m.* small, young, tender vegetable marrow; (*coll.*) dolt, silly person.

calabacinate, *n.m.* fried *calabacines*.

calabacino, *n.m.* dry gourd, calabash, bottle.

calabacita, *n.f.* small calabash; young vegetable marrow [CALABAZA].

calabaza, *n.f.* (*bot.*) pumpkin, squash, gourd; (*fig.*) stupid, ignorant person; (*slang*) picklock, skeleton-key; (*naut.*) lumbering old boat; *calabaza vinatera*, bottle-gourd, calabash; *dar calabazas*, to pluck, not to pass (in examination); to reject (a lover), give the mitten; *llevar calabazas*, to be dismissed, sent away; *salir calabazas*, to fail to come up to expectations; to be ploughed in an examination; *calabaza bonetera* or *pastelera*, large

bonnet-like gourd; *calabaza confitera* or *totanera*, pumpkin; *echar en calabaza*, to waste time through someone failing to keep his word; *nadar sin calabazas*, *no necesitar de calabazas para nadar*, to stand on one's own legs.

calabazada, *n.f.* knock with the head against something; *darse de calabazadas*, to labour in vain to ascertain something.

calabazano, -na, *a.* unsuccessful (in examination).

calabazar, *n.m.* pumpkin orchard.

calabazate, *n.m.* candied pumpkin; piece of pumpkin steeped in honey or syrup.

calabazazo, *n.m.* blow with a pumpkin; (*fam.*) blow received on the head.

calabazo, *n.m.* gourd, calabash; pumpkin; (*naut.*) heavy ship in bad condition; (*Cub.*) musical instrument used by negroes.

calabazón, *n.m.* large gourd or pumpkin [CALABAZA].

calabazona, *n.f.* (*prov.*) large winter pumpkin.

calabazuela, *n.f.* plant grown in the Sierra de Sevilla and used against viper bites.

calabobos, *n.m.* (*fam.*) drizzle, mizzle, gentle rain.

calabocero, *n.m.* jailer, warden.

calabozaje, *n.m.* fee paid by prisoners to the jailer.

calabozo, *n.m.* dungeon, cell, jail; pruning-hook, pruning-knife; (*Cub.*) small sickle.

calabrés, -sa, *n.m.f.*, *a.* Calabrian.

calabriada, *n.f.* mixture of different things; mixture of red and white wine; balderdash.

calabriar, *v.t.* to confuse, embroil, mix.

calabrotar, *v.t.* (*naut.*) [ACALABROTAR].

calabrote, *n.m.* (*naut.*) laid rope.

calacuerda, *n.f.* beat of drums summoning to attack the enemy resolutely.

calada, *n.f.* soaking, wetting through; rapid flight of birds of prey; *dar una calada*, to reprimand severely.

caladera, *n.f.* (*prov.*) net for fishing mullet.

caladero, *n.m.* suitable place for casting fishing-nets.

caladio, *n.m.* (*bot.*) caladium.

caladizo, -za, *a.* (*fig.*) intelligent, perspicacious, sharp.

calado, -da, *a.* soaked, steeped; perforated, pierced. — *n.m.* open-work in metal, stone, wood, or linen; fretwork; (*naut.*) draught of a vessel; (*slang*) recovered theft. — *pl.* lace cape or deep collar. — *pp.* [CALAR].

calador, *n.m.* perforator, borer; one who makes open-work; (*naut.*) caulking iron; (*surg.*) bougie, probe.

caladora, *n.f.* (*Ven.*) large piragua.

caladre, *n.f.* (*orn.*) lark.

caladura, *n.f.* cutting and tasting of fruits.

calafate; calafateador, *n.m.* (*naut.*) caulker; shipwright.

calafateado, -da, *a.* (*naut.*) caulked. — *n.m.* caulking; staff of caulkers. — *p.p.* [CALAFATEAR].

calafateadura, *n.f.* caulking.

calafatear; calafetear, *v.t.* (*naut.*) to caulk.

calafateo, *n.m.* caulking.

calafatería, *n.f.* caulking.

calafatín, *n.m.* caulker's boy or mate.

calafraga, *n.f.* (*bot.*) saxifrage.

calagozo, *n.m.* bill-hook or hedging-hook.

calagraña, *n.f.* table grape, not fit for wine.

calaguala, *n.f.* (*Per.*) medicinal fern.

calaguasca, *n.f.* (*Col.*) anisette.

calahorra, *n.f.* public office where bread was distributed in times of scarcity.

calaíta, *n.f.* (*min.*) turquoise.

calaje, *n.m.* (*prov.*) chest, trunk, coffer.

calajería, *n.f.* (*prov.*) [CAJONERÍA].

calalú, *n.m.* (*Cub.*) potage of vegetables.

calaluz, *n.m.* (*Philip.*) (*naut.*) small vessel.

calamaco, *n.m.* calamanco, a woollen stuff.

calamar, *n.m.* calamary, squid, sea-sleeve.

calambac, *n.m.* (*bot.*) aloes-wood, kalamba, eaglewood.

calambre, *n.m.* spasm; cramp.

calambuco, *n.m.* (*bot.*) an American resinous tree; *a.* (*Cub.*) hypocritical.

calamento, *n.m.* soaking of fishing-nets; [CALAMINTA].

calamidad, *n.f.* misfortune, calamity; misery, grievousness; *ser* (*uno*) *una calamidad,* to be a nuisance (a person).

calamillera; caramilleras, *n.f.* pot-hook of a crane.

calamina; piedra calaminar, *n.f.* calamine.

calaminta, *n.f.* (*bot.*) calamint.

calamita, *n.f.* loadstone; magnetic needle; [CALAMITE].

calamitación, *n.f.* (*phys.*) magnetization.

calamite, *n.m.* little green tree-frog.

calamiteas, *n.f.* (*bot.*) calamite.

calamitosamente, *adv.* calamitously; unfortunately, disastrously.

calamitoso, -sa, *a.* calamitous; unfortunate, wretched.

cálamo, *n.m.* calamus; (*poet.*) pen; ancient flute; *cálamo aromático,* (*bot.*) sweet-flag.

calamocano, -na, *a.* fuddled, tipsy, unsteady; doting.

calamoco, *n.m.* icicle.

calamocha, *n.f.* dull yellow ochre.

calamochazo, *n.m.* (*fam.*) [CALAMORRAZO].

calamón, *n.m.* (*orn.*) purple water-hen, gallinule; round-headed nail; stay which supports the beam of an oil-mill.

calamonarse, *v.r.* (*prov.*) to rot, ferment, become heated (grass, vegetables).

calamorra, *a.* woolly-faced (sheep). — *n.f.* (*coll.*) head.

calamorrada, *n.f.* blow with or on the head; nod (in sleep).

calamorrar, *v.t.* to butt.

calamorrazo, *n.m.* (*fam.*) blow on the head.

calamorro, *n.m.* (*Chi.*) coarse and rough shoe.

calandraca, *n.f.* (*naut.*) mess of hard-tack.

calandrajo, *n.m.* (*fam.*) rag hanging from a garment; old rag; (*coll.*) ragamuffin; (*prov.*) invention, supposition.

calandria, *n.f.* (*orn.*) lark; calender; (*slang*) town-crier; winch, windlass. — *n.m.f.* malingerer in hospital in order to obtain food and shelter.

cálanis, *n.m.* (*bot.*) sweet-flag.

calaña, *n.f.* pattern; sample; model, form; (*fig.*) character, quality; cheap cane-ribbed fan.

calañés, -sa, *n.m.f.*, *a.* native of Calañas; *sombrero calañés,* Andalusian hat.

calapatillo, *n.m.* weevil, or its grub.

calapé, *n.m.* (*Am.*) turtle roasted in its shell.

calar, *v.t.* to penetrate, soak through, permeate, drench; to go through, pierce, perforate; (*coll.*) to discover, see through, com-prehend a design or motive; to plug; to make open-work in metal, wood, linen or paper; (*mech.*) to wedge; (*slang*) to pick pockets; (*naut.*) to raise or lower by means of a pole; (*naut.*) to soak, submerge (fishing-tackle); (*Col.*) to crush, vex, humble; (*Mex.*) to take out a sample (from a bale). — *v.i.* (*naut.*) to draw. — *v.r.* to introduce, enter, insinuate oneself; to become wet through, soaked; to swoop, dart down on prey; (*slang*) to burgle, rob; *calar la bayoneta,* (*mil.*) to fix the bayonet; *calar el can de una escopeta,* to cock a gun; *calar las cubas,* to gauge a barrel or cask; *calar el melón* or *la sandía,* to tap (or plug) a water melon to try its flavour; *calar el palo,* (*naut.*) to step the mast; *calar los pensamientos a alguno,* to guess someone's thoughts; *calar el puente,* to let down the drawbridge; *calarse el sombrero,* to press down one's hat; *calar tantos pies,* (*naut.*) to draw so many feet; *calar el timón,* (*naut.*) to hang the rudder; *calarse hasta los huesos,* to become wet through.

calar, *a.* calcareous. — *n.m.* lime-quarry.

calasancio, -cia, *a.* [ESCOLAPIO].

calato, -ta, *a.* (*Per.*) naked.

Calatrava, *n.pr.* Calatrava, a military order of knighthood.

calatravo, -va, *n.m.f.*, *a.* appertaining to, member of the Order of Calatrava.

calavera, *n.f.* skull. — *n.m.* madcap, hotbrained fellow.

calaverada, *n.f.* ridiculous, foolish, or ill-timed action; tomfoolery.

calaverear, *v.i.* to act foolishly, without judgment or prudence.

calaverilla; calaverita, *n.f.* little skull [CALAVERA].

calavernario, *n.m.* charnel-house, ossuary.

calaverón, *n.m.* dissipated, loose-living man; madcap, dare-devil [CALAVERA].

calboche, *n.m.* (*prov.*) perforated earthenware pan for roasting chestnuts.

calbote, *n.m.* (*prov.*) bread made of acorns or chestnuts; roasted chestnut.

calca, *n.f.* (*slang*) road, highway. — *pl.* footsteps, footprints.

calcable, *a.* fordable, navigable.

calcado, *n.m.* action of tracing (drawing). — *p.p.* [CALCAR].

calcador, -ra, *n.m.f.* copier, tracer, draughtsman. — *n.m.* style (instrument).

calcamar, *n.m.* Brazilian sea-bird.

calcáneo, *n.m.* (*anat.*) calcaneum.

calcañal; calcañar, *n.m.* heel, heel-bone.

calcañuelo, *n.m.* disease of bees.

calcar, *v.t.* (*pret.* **calqué;** *pres. subj.* **calque**) to trace (drawing); to trample upon; (*fig.*) to copy, imitate.

calcáreo, -rea, *a.* calcareous.

calcatrife, *n.m.* (*slang*) drudge; common labourer.

calce, *n.m.* tyre of a wheel; iron or steel shoe added to the coulter of a plough, when it is worn; wedge; wheel shoe, brake; (*Mex.,* *Guat.*) bottom, foot, end of a writing.

calcedonia, *n.f.* chalcedony.

calceolaria, *n.f.* (*bot.*) calceolaria, slipperwort.

calcés, *n.m.* (*naut.*) mast-head.

calceta, *n.f.* hose, stocking; (*fig.*) fetter worn by criminals; (*prov.*) kind of sausage; *hacer calceta,* to knit.

calcetería, *n.f.* hosier's shop; hosier's trade; hosiery.
calcetero, -ra, *n.m.f.* one who makes, mends or sells stockings; hosier. — *n.m.* (*slang*) one who puts the fetters on.
calcetín, *n.m.* half-hose, sock [CALCETA].
calceto, *a.* (*Col., CR.*) chicken with feathers covering its legs.
calcetón, *n.m.* large stocking worn under boots [CALCETA].
calcicloro, *n.m.* chloride of lime.
cálcico, -ca, *a.* (*chem.*) calcic.
calciferrita; calcioferrita; calcoferrita, *n.f.* (*min.*) calcio-ferrite.
calcificación, *n.f.* (*med.*) calcification.
calcificar, *v.t.* to calcify.
calcil, *n.m.* light tawny colour.
calcilla, *n.f.* (*prov.*) footless stocking; gaiter. — *pl.* short, narrow breeches; (*fam.*) timid man; short man; *poner calcilla,* to praise unduly.
calcímetro, *n.m.* instrument to determine the lime-content in soils.
calcina, *n.f.* mortar.
calcinable, *a.* able to undergo calcination.
calcinación, *n.f.;* **calcinamiento,** *n.m.* (*chem.*) calcination.
calcinador, -ra, *a.* calcining. — *n.m.f.* calciner.
calcinar, *v.t.* to calcine.
calcinatorio, -ria, *a.* calcinatory.
calcinero, *n.m.* lime-burner.
calcio, *n.m.* calcium.
calcita, *n.f.* (*min.*) calcite.
calco, *n.m.* tracing (drawing); (*slang*) shoe.
calcografía, *n.f.* chalcography; place where engravings are made.
calcografiar, *v.t.* to engrave on copper.
calcógrafo, *n.m.* chalcographer, engraver; engraving machine.
calcomanía, *n.f.* transfer (drawing); pastime using transfers.
calcopirita, *n.f.* (*min.*) chalcopyrite.
calcorrear, *v.i.* (*slang*) to run.
calcorreo, *n.m.* (*slang*) running.
calcorro, *n.m.* (*slang*) shoe.
calculable, *a.* calculable.
calculación, *n.f.* calculation, computation, estimate.
calculadamente, *adv.* in a calculating manner.
calculador, -ra, *a.* calculating. — *n.m.f.* calculator; calculating machine; accountant.
calcular, *v.t.* to calculate, reckon, count, compute, estimate.
calculativo, -va, *a.* calculative.
calculatorio, -ria, *a.* calculating.
calculiforme, *a.* pebble-shaped.
calculista, *a.* scheming. — *n.m.* schemer.
cálculo, *n.m.* calculation, computation; estimate; count, account; conjecture; (*math.*) calculus; (*med.*) calculus, gravel, stone. — *pl.* (*med.*) lithiasis.
calculoso, -sa, *n.m.f., a.* (*med.*) calculous (sufferer).
calcha, *n.f.* (*Chi.*) fetlock of a horse; (*Chi., Arg.*) workman's clothing and bedding.
calchacura, *n.f.* (*Chi.*) lichen used in medicine.
calchona, *n.f.* (*Chi.*) fantastic and malevolent being who frightens lone travellers; (*Chi.*) old, ugly woman.
calda, *n.f.* act of warming or heating; stoking (furnaces, etc.). — *pl.* thermal springs; *dar*

(*una*) *calda a uno,* to encourage, stimulate someone; *dar una calda,* to reheat (in the forge).
caldaico, -ca, *n.m.f., a.* Chaldean, Chaldee; Chaldaic. — *n.m.* Chaldean language.
caldaria, *n.f. ley caldaria,* ordeal of water.
caldario, *n.m.* caldarium.
caldeado, -da, *a.* heated, warmed; hot, warm. — *p.p.* [CALDEAR].
caldeamiento, *n.m.* heating; heat.
caldear, *v.t.* to warm, heat; to weld iron. — *v.r.* to become heated, welded.
caldeo, -dea, *a.* Chaldaic.
caldera, *n.f.* cauldron, boiler; sugar-kettle; shell of kettle-drum; kettleful; (*min.*) sump of well; (*Arg.*) coffee-pot, kettle; (*Chi.*) tea-pot; *caldera de jabonería,* soap factory; *calderas de Pero Botero,* (*coll.*) hell; *caldera de vapor,* steam-boiler; *caldera tubular,* tubular boiler.
calderada, *n.f.* cauldronful.
calderería, *n.f.* boiler-maker's or brazier's shop or trade.
calderero, *n.m.* brazier, coppersmith, boiler-maker, tinker.
caldereta, *n.f.* small cauldron, kettle, pot [CALDERA]; kettleful; stoup, holy-water basin; stew of fish; lamb stew; (*Mex.*) chocolate-pot; (*Am.*) thunderstorm.
calderil, (*prov.*) *n.m.* notched pole for supporting cooking pots.
calderilla, *n.f.* holy-water basin; copper coin; (*bot.*) grossulaceous plant.
caldero, *n.m.* bucket-like semi-spherical cauldron; copper; cauldronful; *con un caldero viejo se compra otro nuevo,* applied to a young person who marries an old one in the hope of inheriting the latter's property; *quién dice a quién: el caldero a la sartén,* the pot called the kettle black.
calderón, *n.m.* large copper cauldron or kettle [CALDERA]; (*prov.*) tip-cat; (*arith.*) mark of a thousand (.Ð); (*gram., print.*) orthographic sign denoting paragraph (¶); (*mus.*) sign indicating pause (⌒); (*mus.*) pause and flourish executed during same.
calderoniano, -na, *a.* proper and characteristic of Pedro Calderón de la Barca.
calderuela, *n.f.* small kettle [CALDERA]; dark lantern used to drive partridges into the net.
caldibache; caldivache, *n.m.* [CALDUCHO].
caldillo, *n.m.* gravy; (*Mex.*) sauce with ragout or fricassee.
caldito, *n.m.* light broth.
caldo, *n.m.* broth; beef-tea, bouillon; sauce, gravy; (*Mex.*) juice of sugar cane; (*Mex.*) marigold; salad dressing; juice; *caldo alterado,* alterative or medicated broth; *caldo de carne,* consommé, beef-tea; *caldo de cultivo,* culture (of microbe); *caldo esforzado,* strengthening broth; *amargar el caldo,* to cause someone grief; *hacer a uno el caldo gordo,* to enable someone to gratify his wishes (usually unwittingly); *revolver caldos, revolver uno el caldo,* to revive disputes. — *pl.* (*com.*) wine, oil and all juices extracted from fruits.
caldoso, -sa, *a.* having plenty of broth; thin.
calducho, *n.m.* ill-seasoned thin broth, hogwash.
calduda, *n.f.* (*Chi.*) moist pie made with eggs, sultanas, olives, etc.

cale, *n.m.* light blow or tap.

calé, *n.m.* (*Col., Ec.*) small coin.

calecer, *v.i.* to become heated.

calecico, *n.m.* small chalice [CÁLIZ].

caledonio, -nia, *n.m.f. a.* Caledonian.

calefacción, *n.f.* heating; system of heating, calefaction; *calefacción central,* central heating.

calefactorio, *n.m.* calefactory, place in convents for warming.

calembé, *n.m.* (*Cub.*) bathing trunks.

calenda, *n.f.* part of the martyrology which treats of the acts of the saints of the day. — *pl.* kalends; *las calendas griegas,* the Greek Kalends, never.

calendario, *n.m.* almanac, calendar; *hacer calendarios,* to muse; to forecast hastily.

calendarista, *n.m.f.* calendarer.

caléndula, *n f.* marigold.

calentador, *a.* heating, warming. — *n.m.* heater, warmer, warming-pan; (*coll.*) large, clumsy watch.

calentamiento, *n.m.* calefaction, warming, heating; a disease of horses.

calentano, -na, *a.* (*Am.*) lowlander.

calentar, *v.t.* (*pres. indic.* **caliento;** *pres. subj.* **caliente**) to warm, heat; to roll and heat a ball in one's hand before it is played; (*fig.*) to urge, press forward; (*fig.*) to despatch speedily; (*coll.*) to beat, cudgel. — *v.r.* to be in heat, rut; to grow hot; to become angry; *calentar a uno las orejas,* to scold a person; *calentar el asiento, la silla,* to bore by a long visit; *no calentar la silla,* not to stay long anywhere; *calentarse a la lumbre,* to warm oneself by the fire; *calentarse con el ejercicio,* to grow hot through exercise; *calentarse en la disputa,* to dispute warmly; *calentarse la cabeza, los sesos,* to rack one's brains.

calentito, -ta, *a.* (*coll.*) recent, fresh, piping-hot.

calentón, *n.m.* (*fam.*) action of warming oneself quickly; *darse un calentón,* to take a bit of a warming.

calentura, *n.f.* fever; *calentura de pollo por comer gallina,* malingering.

calenturiento, -ta, *n.m.f., a.* feverish (person); (*Chi.*) consumptive.

calenturilla, *n.f.* slight fever [CALENTURA].

calenturón, *n.m.* violent fever [CALENTURA].

calenturoso, -sa, *a.* feverish.

caleño, -ña, *a.* producing lime. — *n.f.* (*prov.*) limestone.

calepino, *n.m.* (*coll.*) Latin dictionary.

calería, *n.f.* place where lime is burnt, or sold.

calero, -ra, *a.* calcareous. — *n.m.* lime-burner, lime-maker, lime-seller. — *n.f.* lime-kiln; lime-quarry; fishing smack, in Biscay.

calés, *n.m.; calesa,* *n.f.* two-wheeled calash, chaise; (*prov.*) maggot.

calesera, *n.f.* Andalusian bolero-jacket, kind of vest.

calesero, *n.m.* driver of a calash.

calesín, *n.m.* light chaise.

calesinero, *n.m.* owner or driver of a *calesín.*

caleta, *n.f.* (*naut.*) cove, creek, small bay or inlet [CALA]; (*Am.*) ship plying small cabotage; (*Ven.*) guild of carriers; (*slang*) thief who steals through a hole.

caletero, *n.m.* (*Ven.*) carrier (workman); (*slang*) thief's accomplice.

caletre, *n.m.* (*fam.*) understanding, judgment, discernment, acumen; (*fig.*) head.

cali, *n.m.* (*chem.*) alkali.

calibeo, -bea, *a.* (*med.* chalybeate.

cálibes, *n.m.pl.* Chalybes.

calibo, *n.m.* (*prov.*) embers, hot ashes.

calibración, *n.f.* calibration.

calibrador, *n.m.* calibre-gauge; callipers.

calibrar, *v.t.* to calibrate a ball or firearm; to gauge, size, graduate.

calibre, *n.m.* calibre; *compás de calibres,* callipers; *ser de buen* or *mal calibre,* to be large or small in size; to be of good or bad quality.

calicanto, *n.m.* (*bot.*) allspice; stone masonry.

calicata, *n.f.* (*min.*) trial pit; sounding of a ground.

caliciflora, *a.* (*bot.*) calyciflorate.

caliciforme, *a.* (*bot.*) calyciform.

calicillo, *n.m.* (*bot.*) calycle.

calicinal; caliciniano, -na, *a.* (*bot.*) calycine.

calicó, *n.m.* calico.

calicud; calicut, *n.f.* silk stuff from India.

caliculado, -da, *a.* (*bot.*) calycled.

calicular, *a.* (*bot.*) calyculate.

calículo, *n.m.* calycle.

caliche, *n.m.* pebble burnt in a brick; crust of lime flaking from a wall; (*prov.*) crack (in vessel); (*prov.*) game of quoits; (*Chi.*) saltpetre; (*Per.*) mound of earth left in extracting saltpetre.

calidad, *n.f.* quality, condition, character, kind, nature; nobility, rank; requisite; (*fig.*) importance, seriousness; (*med.*) fever, heat; stipulation. — *pl.* conditions, rules (in card games); personal qualifications, gifts, parts; *a calidad de que,* on condition that; *en calidad de,* as, in the capacity of.

calidez, *n.f.* (*med.*) heat, fever.

cálido, -da, *a.* warm, hot; piquant; heating (seasonings); (*art*) warm (colouring); crafty, artful.

calidoscópico, -ca, *a.* kaleidoscopic.

calidoscopio, *n.m.* kaleidoscope.

calientacamas, *n.m.* warming-pan, bed-warmer.

calientapiés, *n.m.* foot-warmer.

calientaplatos, *n.m.* plate-warmer.

caliente, *a.* warm, hot, scalding; fiery, feverish, vehement; (*art*) warm (colouring); *caliente de cascos,* hot-headed; *hierro caliente,* red-hot iron; *en caliente,* piping-hot, instantly; *estar caliente,* to be in heat, rut; *ande yo caliente, y ríase la gente,* people may laugh, but I am all right.

caliento; caliente, *pres. indic.; pres. subj.* [CALENTAR].

califa, *n.m.* caliph.

califato, *n.m.* caliphate.

calífero, -ra, *a.* calciferous.

calificable, *a.* qualifiable.

calificación, *n.f.* qualification, judgment, censure, proof, habilitation; mark (in examination).

calificadamente, *adv.* qualifiedly, qualifyingly.

calificado, -da, *a.* qualified, authorized, competent. — *p.p.* [CALIFICAR].

calificador, *n.m.* qualifier; censor; *calificador del Santo Oficio,* ecclesiastical censor of books.

calificar, *v.t.* (*pret.* **califiqué;** *pres. subj.* **califique**) to qualify, discriminate, determine the quality of a person or thing; to authorize, empower; (*fig.*) to certify, attest; (*fig.*) to illustrate, ennoble. — *v.r.* to prove one's noble birth and descent according to law; *calificar alguno de docto,* to consider someone as being learned.

calificativo, -va, *a.* (*gram.*) qualifying.

californiano, -na; californio, -nia, *n.m.f.*, *a.* Californian.

califórnico, -ca, *a.* relating to California.

cáliga, *n.f.* sandal worn by Roman soldiers. — *pl.* bishop's gaiters.

calígine, *n.f.* mist, obscurity, darkness.

caliginoso, -sa, *a.* dark, dim.

caligrafía; calografía, *n.f.* calligraphy, penmanship.

caligrafiar, *v.t.* to calligraph.

caligráfico, -ca, *a.* calligraphic.

calígrafo, *n.m.* calligrapher.

calilla, *n.f.* suppository; (*Chi., Guat., Hond.*) vexatious or bothersome person; (*Am.*) annoyance, bother; (*Chi.*) hardship, grievance.

calima, *n.f.* (*naut.*) buoy of strung cork-floats; [CALINA].

calimaco, *n.m.* calamanco.

calimba, *n.f.* (*Cub.*) branding-iron.

calimbar, *v.t.* (*Cub.*) to brand animals, etc.

calimbo, *n.m.* (*min.*) kernel of eagle-stone.

calimoso, -sa, *a.* [CALINOSO].

calimote, *n.m.* centre cork-float of seine.

calina, *n.f.* thick vapour, light haze or mist.

calinda, *n.f.* (*Cub.*) popular creole dance.

calino, -na, *a.* containing lime.

calinoso, -sa, *a.* vapoury, misty, hazy.

calípedes, *n.m.* (*zool.*) sloth.

caliptriforme, *a.* (*bot.*) calyptriform.

caliptro, *n.m.* (*bot.*) calyptra.

calisaya, *n.f.* esteemed variety of cinchona.

calistenias, *n.f.pl.* callisthenics.

cáliz, *n.m.* chalice; cup used for Holy Communion; (*bot.*) calyx; (*poet.*) cup, vase; *apurar el cáliz de la amargura,* to drain the bitter cup of grief and affliction.

calizo, -za, *a.* calcareous, limy, calc-spar. — *n.f.* calcite.

calma, *n.f.* (*naut.*) calm; calmness, tranquillity, composure, quiet, stillness; slowness, tardiness; cessation (of pain); suspension (of business); *calma chicha,* (*naut.*) dead calm; (*coll.*) laziness, indolence; *en calma,* (*naut.*) motionless (sea).

calmadamente, *adv.* quietly, calmly.

calmado, -da, *a.* quiet, calm; soothed, pacified, calmed; (*prov.*) tired, perspiring. — *p.p.* [CALMAR].

calmante, *a.* calmative, mitigating, mitigant. — *n.m.* (*med.*) narcotic, anodyne, sedative.

calmar, *v.t.* to calm, quiet, compose, pacify, still, lull, hush, soothe; to alleviate, allay, mitigate, moderate, soften. — *v.i.* to be calm, becalmed. — *v.r.* to become pacified, soothed; to abate, calm down; to compose oneself.

calmazo, *n.m.* great calm; indolence; (*naut.*) dead calm [CALMA].

calmear, *v.i.* to become calm; to calm little by little.

calmil, *n.m.* (*Mex.*) a tilled and sown field adjoining a farmhouse.

calmita, *n.f.* calmness, gentleness [CALMA].

calmo, -ma, *a.* uncultivated, untilled; treeless,

barren; fallow; *tierras calmas,* flat, bleak country.

calmoso, -sa, *a.* calm, tranquil, quiet, soothing; (*coll.*) slow, tardy.

calmuco, *n.m.f.*, *a.* Kalmuck.

calo, *n.m.* (*Ec.*) thick cane containing water.

caló, *n.m.* cant, slang of gipsies and ruffians.

calobiótica, *n.f.* art of living well; natural tendency of man to live an orderly, harmonious life.

calocéfalo, -la, *a.* having a beautiful head.

calofilo, -la, *a.* (*bot.*) having beautiful leaves.

calofriado, -da, *a.* chilly, shivery, shivering with cold. — *p.p.* [CALOFRIARSE].

calofriarse; calosfriarse, *v.r.* to shiver with cold; to feel chilly.

calofrío; calosfrío, *n.m.* chill, shiver.

calología, *n.f.* æsthetics.

calomel, *n.m.*; **calomelanos,** *n.m.pl.* (*med.*) calomel.

calón, *n.m.* pole for keeping fishing-nets extended; fathom (pole); (*min.*) sand-covered iron vein, in Vizcaya.

caloña, *n.f.* fine or damages for slander.

calóptero, -ra, *a.* handsome-winged.

calor, *n.m.* (*phys.*) heat, hotness, glow; warmth, ardour, fieriness, fervour; fever; excitement, feeling; animation, fire, vivacity; brunt of a battle; favour, kind reception; *calor canicular,* sweltering heat; *calor del hígado,* flush, high colour; *ahogarse (freírse) uno de calor,* to be overcome by the heat; *asarse uno de calor,* to be roasting, feel very hot; *coger (entrar en) calor,* to get warm; *dar calor,* to encourage; *hace calor,* it is hot weather; *dejarse caer el calor,* to be very hot (weather); *gastar uno el calor natural en una cosa,* to pay more attention to a thing than it is worth; to pay the greatest attention to a matter; *meter en calor,* to espouse warmly; *tomar calor (una cosa),* to progress (of an affair); *tomar con calor una cosa,* to carry out a thing earnestly, with great zeal; *de todo calor,* ardently, intensely; *hablar con calor,* to speak fervently; *eso no le da ni frío ni calor,* he is very indifferent to the matter.

calorescencia, *n.f.* calorescence.

caloría, *n.f.* calorie.

caloriamperímetro, *n.m.* (*elec.*) ammeter.

caloricidad, *n.f.* caloricity.

calórico, *n.m.* caloric; heat; *calórico radiante,* radiant heat.

calorífero, -ra, *a.* giving heat. — *n.m.* stove, heater, furnace; foot-warmer; *calorífero de aire,* hot-air radiator; *calorífero de vapor,* steam-radiator.

calorificación, *n.f.* caloricity.

calorífico, -ca, *a.* calorific.

calorífugo, -ga, *a.* non-conducting; incombustible.

calorimetría, *n.f.* (*phys.*) calorimetry.

calorimétrico, -ca, *a.* (*phys.*) calorimetric.

calorímetro, *n.m.* (*phys.*) calorimeter.

calorimotor, *n.m.* (*phys.*) calorimotor.

calorina, *n.f.* (*prov.*) [CALINA].

calorosamente; calurosamente, *adv.* warmly, excitedly, passionately, hotly, ardently.

caloroso, -sa; caluroso, -sa, *a.* warm, hot, heating; (*fig.*) excited, passionate, enthusiastic.

caloso, -sa, *a.* porous (paper).

calostro, *n.m.* colostrum.
calota, *n.f.* medicated ringworm cap.
calote, *n.m.* (*prov.*) fraud, hoax.
calotipia, *n.f.* calotype.
caloyo, *n.m.* unborn or new-born lamb or kid; (*mil., prov.*) raw recruit, newly enlisted.
calpamulo, -la, *a.* (*Mex.*) half-breed.
calpixque, *n.m.* (*Mex.*) collector of taxes from Indians.
calpul, *n.m.* (*Guat.*) meeting, unlawful assembly; (*Hond.*) the site of ancient aboriginal villages.
calquín, *n.m.* (*Arg.*) an eagle of the Andes.
calseco, -ca, *a.* cured with lime.
calta, *n.f.* (*bot.*) caltha, marsh marigold.
calucha, *n.f.* (*Bol.*) inner rind of coconut, almond, etc.
caluma, *n.f.* (*Per.*) a gorge of the Andes mountains; (*Per.*) Indian village, hamlet, etc.
calumbarse, *v.r.* (*prov.*) to plunge, dive.
calumbo, *n.m.* (*prov.*) plunge, dive, diving.
calumnia, *n.f.* calumny, slander.
calumniador, -ra, *a.* calumniating, slanderous. — *n.m.f.* slanderer, calumniator.
calumniar, *v.t.* to calumniate, slander.
calumniosamente, *adv.* calumniously, slanderously.
calumnioso, -sa, *a.* calumnious, slanderous.
calungo, *n.m.* (*Col.*) kind of dog with curly hair.
caluro, *n.m.* (*Am.*) a climbing bird.
calurosamente, *adv.;* **caluroso, -sa,** *a.* [CALOROSAMENTE] [CALOROSO].
caluyo, *n.m.* (*Bol.*) Indian dog-dance.
calva, *n.f.* bald crown of the head; treeless, bare spot in a grove; threadbare, napless spot (on cloth, skin, etc.); game played among country people; *calva de almete,* crest of a helmet.
calvar, *v.t.* to hit the top of the post or horn in the game of *calva;* to cheat, deceive.
calvario, *n.m.* Calvary; (*coll.*) great tribulation; (*coll.*) debt; tally; score.
calvatorio, -ria, *a.* appertaining to baldness.
calvatrueno, *n.m.* (*fam.*) baldness of the whole head; (*coll.*) wild person.
calvaza, *n.f.* large bald head.
calverizo, -za, *a.* having many bare or barren spots (ground).
calvero; calvijar; calvitar, *n.m.* bare spot in a grove; clay-pit.
calvete, *n.m., a.* little bald head [CALVO].
calvez; calvicie, *n.f.* baldness.
calvijar, *n.m.* [CALVERO].
calvilla, *n.f.* little baldness.
calvinismo, *n.m.* Calvinism.
calvinista, *n.m.f., a.* Calvinist.
calvitar, [CALVERO].
calvo, -va, *a.* bald, hairless, bald-headed, bald-pated; barren, treeless; napless, threadbare; *tierra calva,* barren soil. — *n.m.f.* bald-head, bald-pate.
calza, *n.f.* long, loose breeches or trousers; (*fam.*) hose, stockings; garter or ribbon tied on certain animals; wedge, scotch (of a wheel, etc.). — *pl.* (*slang*) fetters; *calzas acuchilladas,* slashed trousers; *calza de arena,* sand-bag; *meter en una calza,* to screw up (a person); *medias calzas,* stockings reaching to the knees; *tomar las calzas de Villadiego,* to make a hurried escape or flight; *echarle una calza a*

uno, to take note of a person to be avoided; *poner a uno* (or *verse*) *en calzas prietas,* to put someone (*or* to be) in difficulties.
calzacalzón, *n.m.* galligaskins.
calzada, *n.f.* causeway, paved highroad, main road, avenue; *calzada romana,* Roman road.
calzadera, *n.f.* hempen cord; lace for *abarcas;* shoe, drag (wheel).
calzadito, *n.m.* small shoe [CALZADO].
calzado, -da, *a.* shod (monk or nun); with feathers on the legs and feet (birds); with extremities of a different colour to the rest of the body (animals); wedged, scotched; *frente calzada,* narrow brow. — *n.m.* footwear in general, including stockings and garters; (*slang*) person in fetters. — *p.p.* [CALZAR].
calzador, *n.m.* shoe-horn; (*Arg.*) pen-holder; *entrar una cosa con calzador,* to require an effort.
calzadura, *n.f.* act of putting on the shoes; tip for this service; felloe of a cart-wheel.
calzar, *v.t., v.r.* (*pret.* **calcé;** *pres. subj.* **calce**) to put on gloves; to put on shoes, spurs, etc.; to scotch a wheel; to strengthen with wood or iron; to carry a ball of a definite size (of fire-arms); to wedge, chock, key; (*print.*) to overlay, raise, underlay; *calzar el ancla,* (*naut.*) to shoe the anchor; *calzarse los guantes,* to put on gloves; *calzar las herramientas,* to put a steel edge to iron tools; *calzárselas al revés,* to do precisely the contrary; *calzarse las bragas,* to wear the breeches; *calzar las mesas,* to make tables stand fast; *calzar tantos puntos,* to take a certain size in footwear; *calzar pocos* or *muchos puntos,* to have little or great ability; *calzar ancha,* not to be very nice or scrupulous; *calza como vistes y viste como calzas,* it is wise to observe harmony and proportion in everything; *calzarse a alguno,* to govern or manage someone; *calzarse uno alguna cosa,* to obtain something; *el que primero llega, ese la calza,* first come, first served; *el mismo que viste y calza,* that is the man in question.
calzo, *n.m.* (*print.*) frisket-sheet, overlay; (*mech.*) wedge, quoin; shoe of a felloe; (*naut.*) skid, chock, bed, shoe; (*rail.*) block, brake-shoe.
calzón, *n.m.* long trouser [CALZA]; safety rope used by masons and painters; ombre, card game; (*Mex.*) disease of the sugar cane from lack of water. — *pl.* breeches, trousers; *en calzones,* (*naut.*) sails arranged as goose-wings; *calzon(es) blanco(s),* pants, trunks (underwear); *calzon(es) bombacho(s),* breeches slit on one side; *calzon(es) corto(s),* knickerbockers; *calzarse* or *ponerse una mujer los calzones,* to wear the breeches; *tener buen puesto los calzones* or *tener muchos calzones,* to be very manly.
calzonarias, *n.f.pl.* (*Col.*) braces (Gt. Brit.); suspenders (U.S.A.).
calzonazos, *n.m.* (*coll.*) weak, soft fellow.
calzoncillos, *n.m.pl.* pants, trunks, drawers, under-garments.
calzoneras, *n.f.pl.* (*Mex.*) trousers buttoned all the way down both sides.
calzorras, *n.m.* (*coll.*) [CALZONAZOS].
calla, *n.f.* (*Am.*) (*agric.*) dibble.
callada, *n.f.* meal consisting principally of tripe; silence (in certain phrases); (*naut.*) lull; *a las calladas,* or *de callada,* privately,

on the quiet; *dar la callada por respuesta*, to answer by silence.

calladamente, *adv.* silently, tacitly, privately, secretly.

calladito, *n.m.* (*Chi.*) popular dance without song.

callado, -da, *a.* silent, noiseless, reserved; discreet, prudent. — *p.p.* [CALLAR].

callana, *n.f.* (*Am.*) flat earthen bowl for toasting maize or corn; metallic scoria; crucible for assaying metals; (*Chi.*) big pocket-watch; (*Per.*) flowerpot.

callandicamente; callandito; callandito, *adv.* (*fam.*) in a low voice, quietly, softly, without noise, silently; secretly, slyly.

callandriz, *n.m.* sly, secretive person.

callao, *n.m.* river pebble; flat ground covered with boulders (in Canary Islands).

callapo, *n.m.* (*Chi.*, *min.*) prop, stay, step of a ladder or stairs in mines; (*Per.*) stretcher (in mines).

callar, *v.i.*, *v.r.* to be silent, keep silence, be quiet; to stop talking, playing, etc.; to dissemble; (*poet.*) to abate, become moderate, calm, muted. — *v.t.*, *v.r.* to conceal, hush up, not to mention a thing; *al buen callar llaman Sancho* or *santo*, silence is golden; *¡calla!* or *¡calle!* you don't say! you can't mean that! *calla callando*, or *mátalas callando*, slyly, on the quiet; *calla y cuez*, get on with the work; *calle el que dió y hable el que tomó*, let the giver be silent and the receiver loud with gratitude; *el callar y el hablar no caben en un lugar*, loquacity and discretion do not go hand in hand; *más vale callar que mal hablar*, it is better to be silent than say the wrong thing; *¡cortapicos y callares para los preguntones!* be quiet! (said especially to inquisitive children); *quien calla, piedras apaña*, he who listens carefully may make use of what he has heard; *callar la verdad a otro*, to conceal the truth from a person; *callar de (por) miedo*, to keep silent through fear; *quien calla otorga*, silence gives consent; *callar el pico* or *la boca*, to hold one's tongue; *cállate y callemos, que sendas nos tenemos*, those who live in glass houses should not throw stones.

calle, *n.f.* street, paved way, lane, alley; garden walk; (*slang*) liberty; (*print.*) vertical or oblique space spoiling a printed page; *calle arriba* or *abajo*, up or down the street; *calle de árboles*, garden walk or alley; *calle hita*, from house to house, from street to street; *calle mayor*, main street, high street; *calle sin salida*, alley without egress, blind alley; *calle traviesa*, cross-street; *abrir* or *hacer calle*, to clear a passage; to make way; *alborotar la calle*, to disturb the neighbourhood; *azotar calles*, to lounge about the streets; *coger uno la calle (puerta)* to escape, run away; *coger las calles*, to obstruct the streets; *dejar a uno en la calle*, to leave one penniless, destitute; *doblar uno la calle*, to turn the corner; *echar a uno a la calle*, to dismiss someone; *echar a* or *en la calle alguna cosa*, to make something publicly known; *echar (tirar) uno por la calle de en medio*, to attain one's aim notwithstanding all obstacles; *echarse a (ponerse en) la calle*, to go out into the street; to mutiny, rebel; *ir uno desempedrando las calles*, to go at a

great speed; *llevar(se) a uno de calle*, to carry all before one; to overmaster; to confound, silence; *llevarse (hacer huir) una calle de hombres*, to scatter a crowd; *pasear* or *rondar la calle (a una mujer)*, to court (a woman) from the street; *plantar* or *poner a uno en la calle*, to throw out, dismiss someone; *por la calle de 'después' se va a la casa de 'nunca,'* by the street of 'By and by' one arrives at the house of 'Never'; *quedar en la calle*, to be in the greatest distress.

callear, *v.t.* to clear the walks in a vineyard.

callecalle, *n.m.f.* (*Chi.*) a medicinal plant of the Iridaceæ family.

calleja, *n.f.* small street, alley [CALLE]; [CALLEJUELA]; (*slang*) escape; *sépase* or *ya se verá* or *ya verán quién es Calleja*, they will soon know with whom they have to deal.

callejear, *v.i.* to walk or loiter about the streets; to gad; to ramble.

callejeo, *n.m.* idling, loitering, strolling.

callejero, -ra, *a.* fond of gadding about. — *n.m.f.* gadabout, gadder, loiterer. — *n.m.* street directory and guide; publisher's list of subscribers.

callejo, *n.m.* (*prov.*) pit or trap for game.

callejón, *n.m.* narrow long lane between two walls; narrow mountain pass [CALLEJA]; *callejón sin salida*, blind alley, deadlock.

callejoncillo, *n.m.* narrow passage; small lane.

callejuca, *n.f.* very narrow lane.

callejuela, *n.f.* alley, lane, narrow passage [CALLEJA]; (*coll.*) subterfuge, shift, evasion; *todo se sabe, hasta lo de la callejuela*, truth will out, though hid in a well.

callialto, -ta, *a.*, *n.m.f.* horse-shoe having swelling welts or borders.

callicida, *n.f.* substance acting as corn extirpator.

callista, *n.m.f.* chiropodist.

callizo, *n.m.* (*prov.*) [CALLEJÓN]; (*prov.*) [CALLEJUELA].

callo, *n.m.* corn, callosity, callousness on the feet, hands, etc.; (*surg.*) callus; extremity of a horse-shoe. — *pl.* tripe; *callo de herradura*, either end of a horse-shoe; *criar, hacer* or *tener callos*, to become inured to work, ill-treatment or vices.

callón, -na, *a.* silent, reserved. — *n.m.* whetstone, rubber (for awl).

callosidad, *n.f.* callosity, callousness. — *pl.* wens.

calloso, -sa, *a.* callous, corny, corneous, horny.

cama, *n.f.* bed, couch; bedstead; bed hangings and furniture; place (in hospitals, schools); floor of a cart; lair or couch of wild animals; litter (brood); litter, straw, bedding for animals and plants; part of a melon touching the ground; (*mech.*) cam; cog; catch; tooth; bed plate; base; (*geol.*) layer, stratum; slice of meat put upon another, in cooking; felloe of a wheel; sheath of a plough; cheek of a bridle. — *pl.* V-shaped pieces in a cloak; (*geol.*) layer, stratum; *cama de galgos* or *de podencos*, untidy, uncomfortable bed; *media cama*, bed with only one mattress, sheet, blanket, and pillow; also used to explain that two persons share a bed; *a mala cama, colchón de vino*, when expecting to have a bad night, drink plenty of wine; *caer uno en (la) cama*, to fall ill; *échate en tu* *cama y piensa en lo de tu casa*, go to bed and think matters over; *estar en, guardar, hacer cama*, to be confined to bed; *hacer la cama*, to make the bed; *hacerle la cama a uno*, to injure a person secretly; *la cama y la cárcel son prueba de amigos*, adversity tests one's friends; *la mala cama hace la noche larga*, our own troubles loom larger than they really are; *no hay tal cama como lo de la enjalma*, there is no hard bed to the truly weary person; *quien mala cama hace, en ella se yace*, as you make your bed so you must lie; *saltar uno de la cama*, to jump out of bed.

camacero, *n.m.* tree of the Solanaceæ family.
camachil, *n.m.* (*Philip.*) a lofty tree.
camachuelo, *n.m.* linnet.
camada, *n.f.* litter, brood of young animals; layer; (*min.*) floor of struts; (*coll.*) band of thieves; *una camada de huevos en una caja*, a layer of eggs in a box.
camafeo, *n.m.* cameo.
camagón, *n.m.* (*Philip.*) tree with very fine wood.
camagua, *a.* (*CR., ES., Hond., Mex.*) said of maize beginning to ripen. — *n.f.* (*Cub.*) tree with white, hard wood.
camaguira, *n.f.* (*Cub.*) wild tree of hard rich yellow wood.
camahuas, *n.m.pl.* wild tribe which used to inhabit the banks of the river Ucayali, in Peru.
camahueto, *n.m.* (*Chi.*) fabulous animal of enormous strength.
camal, *n.m.* hempen halter; pole for suspending dead pig; chain for slaves; (*prov.*) thick branch; (*Per.*) principal slaughterhouse.
camáldula, *n.f.* religious order of Benedictines.
camaldulense, *n.m.f.*, *a.* of or belonging to the order of Camáldula.
camaleón, *n.m.* (*zool.*) chameleon; (*coll.*) changeable, self-interested person; (*Bol.*) iguana; (*Cub.*) green tree-climbing lizard; (*CR.*) small bird of prey; *camaleón mineral*, permanganate of potash; *como el camaleón, que se muda de colores do se pon*, censuring servility and fickleness.
camaleonesco, -ca, *a.* chameleonic.
Camaleopardo, *n.m.* (*astron.*) Camelopardalis.
camalero, *n.m.* (*Per.*) slaughterman; butcher.
camalote, *n.m.* (*Am.*) river plant forming a floating island.
camama, *n.f.* (*coll.*) sham, humbug.
camambú, *n.m.* (*Am.*) wild plant with white flower and very sweet small fruit.
camamila, *n.f.* (*bot.*) common camomile.
camanance, *n.m.* (*CR.*) dimple (in face).
camanchaca, *n.f.* (*Chi., Per.*) thick fog in the Tarapacá desert.
camándula, *n.f.* [CAMÁLDULA]; chaplet or rosary of one or three decades; (*coll.*) hypocrisy, astuteness; *tener muchas camándulas*, to be very tricky.
camandular; camandulear, *v.i.* to feign religious devotion, be a hypocrite.
camandulense, *n.m.f.*, *a.* belonging to the religious order of Camaldula or reformed Benedictines.
camandulería, *n.f.* hypocrisy, insincerity, dissimulation; prudery.
camandulero, -ra, *a.* tricky, dissembling,

hypocritical. — *n.m.f.* hypocrite, trickster, rogue.
camanonca, *n.f.* stuff formerly used for linings.
camao, *n.m.* (*Cub.*) small wild pigeon.
cámara, *n.f.* hall; parlour; chamber, board, council; each of the two legislative houses; granary, barn; (*naut.*) cabin; chamber (of fire-arm, mine); evacuation, stool; (*aer.*) cockpit; (*phot.*) camera. — *pl.* diarrhœa, laxity; *cámara apostólica*, pontifical exchequer; *cámara lúcida* or *clara*, camera lucida; *cámara de aire*, inner tube of tyres; *cámara del rey*, royal exchequer; *cámara doblada*, suite of rooms; *cámara mortuoria*, funeral chamber; *cámara obscura*, camera obscura; *cámara de comercio*, chamber of commerce; *cámara de seda*, breeding-room for silkworms; *ayuda de cámara*, valet; *moza de cámara*, chambermaid; *de cámara*, attached to the court; *irse uno de cámaras*, to suffer from involuntary evacuation; *padecer cámaras*, to suffer from diarrhœa.
camarada, *n.m.* comrade, partner, companion, fellow, chum.
camaraje, *n.m.* rent for a granary.
camaranchón, *n.m.* garret, attic.
camarera, *n.f.* head waiting-maid, housekeeper in great houses; chambermaid; waitress; keeper of the queen's wardrobe.
camarería, *n.f.* place or employment of a chambermaid; ancient perquisite of the lord chamberlain.
camarero, *n.m.* chamberlain; steward; keeper of stores; valet, waiter.
camareta, *n.f.* small bed-chamber [CÁMARA]; (*naut.*) small cabin; deck-cabin; midshipman's cabin; (*Arg., Chi., Per.*) maroon, a detonating firework.
camareto, *n.m.* (*Cub.*) kind of sweet potato.
camarico, *n.m.* (*Am.*) offering of the Indians to their priests and afterwards to the Spaniards; (*Chi.*) favourite place; (*Chi.*) love affair.
camariento, -ta, *a.* having diarrhœa.
camarilla, *n.f.* coterie of the king's private advisers; small band of influential persons.
camarín, *n.m.* small room [CÁMARA]; place behind an altar where images are dressed and ornaments destined for that purpose are kept; (*theat.*) dressing-room; closet; private office.
camarista, *n.m.* member of the supreme council. — *n.f.* maid of honour to the queen and the *infantas* of Spain.
camarlengato, *n.m.* dignity of a *camarlengo*.
camarlengo, *n.m.* lord of the bed-chamber of the kings of Aragon; chamberlain to the Pope.
cámaro; camarón, *n.m.* common prawn, shrimp; (*CR.*) tip, gratuity; *camarón y cangrejo, corren parejo*, used to compare persons or things very much alike; *camarón que se duerme se lo lleva la corriente*, the shrimp that sleeps is carried away by the stream.
camaronero, -ra, *n.m.f.* prawn or shrimp seller; shrimper. — *n.f.* shrimp-net. — *n.m.* (*Per.*) (*orn.*) kingfisher.
camarote, *n.m.* (*naut.*) state-room, berth, cabin.
camarotero, *n.m.* (*Am.*) cabin steward.

camarroya, *n.f.* (*bot.*) wild chicory.

camasquince, *n.m.f.* meddlesome person.

camastra, *n.f.* (*Chi.*) cunning, trickery.

camastrear, *v.t.* (*Chi.*) to dissemble.

camastro, *n.m.* poor, wretched bed.

camastrón, -na, *n.m.f.,* *a.* (*coll.*) sly, cunning, artful (person).

camastronería, *n.f.* cunning, artifice.

camatón, *n.m.* (*prov.*) small bundle of fire-wood.

camauro, *n.m.* Pope's red cap.

camba, *n.f.* cheek of a bridle; (*prov.*) felloe. — *pl.* gores, V-shaped pieces in garments.

cambado, -da, *a.* (*Arg.*) bowlegged.

cambalache, *n.m.* (*coll.*) barter; (*Arg.*) second-hand shop.

cambalachear, *v.t.* to barter.

cambalachero, -ra, *a.* bartering. — *n.m.f.* barterer.

cambalada, *n.f.* (*prov.*) stagger, drunken person.

cambaleo, *n.m.* strolling troupe of players.

cambar, *v.t.* (*Arg., Ven.*) to bend; to curve.

cámbaro, *n.m.* crab, crustacean.

cambera, *n.f.* net for crab and shrimp fishing.

cambeto, -ta, *a.* (*Ven.*) bowlegged.

cambiable, *a.* fit to be bartered; exchange-able.

cambiada, *n.f.* (*equit.*) change of gait; (*naut.*) change (of course, etc.).

cambiadizo, -za, *a.* inconstant, changing.

cambiador, -ra, *a.* changing. — *n.m.* bar-terer, money-changer; (*slang*) brothel pro-prietor; (*Chi., Mex.*) (*rail.*) switchman.

cambiamiento, *n.m.* change, alteration, mutation.

cambiante, *a.* bartering, exchanging. — *n.m.* banker, money-changer. — *n.m.pl.* irides-cence; shot, chatoyant fabrics.

cambiar, *v.t., v.i.* to barter, exchange; to change, shift, alter, remove; to commute, transfer, replace; to negotiate bills and exchange them for money; (*naut.*) to change the course. — *v.i., v.r.* to veer (wind). — *v.i., v.t., v.r.* (*equit.*) to change a horse's gait; *cambiar la comida* or *la peseta*, to be seasick; *cambiar de propósito*, to change one's plans; *cambiar el seso,* to lose one's senses; *cambiar las velas,* (*naut.*) to shift the sails; *cambiar de manos,* (*equit.*) to change hands; *cambiar (alguna cosa) con, por otra,* to exchange one thing for another; *cambiar plata en calderilla,* to change silver into small copper coins; *se cambió su alegría en tristeza,* his *or* her joy turned to sadness.

cambiavía, *n.m.* (*Cub., Mex.*) (*rail.*) switch; switchman.

cambiazo, *n.m.* great change [CAMBIO]; *dar el cambiazo,* to make a fraudulent exchange.

cambija, *n.f.* reservoir, basin of water.

cambín, *n.m.* round rush fishing-basket or net.

cambio, *n.m.* change, alteration; small change; (*com.*) premium paid or received for negotiating bills, changing money, etc.; (*com.*) quotation price of stocks and shares; (*com.*) rate of exchange (of money); (*rail.*) switch, point; (*law*) barter, exchange; *letra de cambio,* bill of exchange; *libre cambio,* free trade; *cambio minuto,* rate of money exchange; *a las primeras de cambio,* (*com.*) at first sight; *en cambio,* instead of, on the other hand, in exchange.

cambista, *n.m.* banker, money-broker; *libre cambista,* free-trader.

cambray, *n.m.* cambric, fine linen.

cambrayado, -da, *a.* resembling cambric.

cambrayón, *n.m.* coarse cambric.

cambriano, -na; cámbrico, -ca, *a.* (*geol.*) Cambrian. — *n.m.f., a.* Cambrian, Welsh.

Cambrige, Cambrigia, *n.f.* Cambridge.

cambrillón, *n.m.* inner sole of shoe.

cambrón, *n.m.* (*bot.*) buckthorn; hawthorn. — *pl.* brambles.

cambronal, *n.m.* thicket of briars, brambles, etc.

cambronera, *n.f.* (*bot.*) box-thorn.

cambrún, *n.m.* (*Col.*) home-made wool cloth.

cambucho, *n.m.* (*Chi.*) paper cone; cornu-copia; waste-basket; hut, hovel; straw envelope for bottles; small kite (toy).

cambuí, *n.m.* American myrtle-tree.

cambuj, *n.m.* child's cap; veil; mask.

cambujo, -ja, *a.* reddish-black (donkey); (*Mex.*) mestizo; half-breed.

cambullón, *n.m.* (*Per.*) imposition, swindle; (*Col., Mex.*) second-hand shop; barter.

cambur, *n.m.* a species of banana; *cambur amarillo* or *criollo,* yellow or Johnson banana; *cambur higo* or *titiaro,* very small variety of banana; *cambur manzano,* small banana with apple flavour; *cambur morado,* red banana.

camedafne, *n.f.* (*bot.*) dwarf-bay; daphne.

camedrio; camedris, *n.m.* (*bot.*) wall-ger-mander, germander speedwell.

camedrita, *n.f.* germander wine.

camelador, -ra, *a.* gallant; flirty.

camelar, *v.t.* (*fam.*) to flirt, pay attention, court, woo; (*fam.*) to seduce, deceive; (*Mex.*) to see; to look; to look into, at, upon or towards; to spy on.

camelete, *n.f.* kind of large cannon.

camelia, *n.f.* (*bot.*) camellia; (*Cub.*) poppy.

camélidos, *n.m.pl.* mammalians belonging to the camel and dromedary group.

camelo, *n.m.* (*fam.*) flirtation, gallantry, courtship; disappointment, deceit; joke, jest; mockery.

camelote, *n.m.* (*bot.*) a tropical weed; camlet; *camelote de aguas,* lustrous, shining camlet; *camelote de pelo,* cameline, fine camlet.

camelotero, -ra, *n.m.f.* maker or vendor of camlets.

camelotina, *n.f.* cameline, fine camlet.

camelotón, *n.m.* coarse camlet.

camella, *n.f.* she-camel; ridge in ploughed land; wooden trough or milk-pail; bow (of animal's yoke).

camellar, *a.,* camel-like, camelish.

camellejo, *n.m.* small camel [CAMELLO].

camellería, *n.f.* employment of a camel-driver.

camellero, *n.m.* keeper or driver of camels.

camello, *n.m.* (*zool.*) camel; ancient cannon; (*naut.*) camel, engine for setting ships afloat in shoal water; *camello pardal,* giraffe.

camellón, *n.m.* ridge turned up by the plough or spade; drinking-trough for cattle; camlet.

camena, *n.f.* (*poet.*) Muse.

camera, *n.f.* (*Col.*) kind of wild rabbit.

camero, -ra, *a.* belonging to a double bed. — *n.m.f.* upholsterer; one who lets beds on hire.

Camerón, *n.m.* Cameroons.

camia, *n.f.* (*Philip.*) a fruit tree.

camibar, *n.m.* (*CR., Nic.*) copaiba tree; balsam of copaiba.

cámica, *n.f.* (*Chi.*) slope of the roof.

camilucho, -cha, *a.* (*Am.*) said of an Indian farm labourer.

camilla, *n.f.* small bed, pallet, cot; litter, stretcher; clothes-horse.

camillero, *n.m.* stretcher-bearer; (*mil.*) ambulance man.

caminada, *n.f.* [JORNADA].

caminador, -ra, *n.m.f.* good walker.

caminante, *n.m.f.* traveller, walker. — *n.m.* running footman; (*Chi.*) small bird like a lark.

caminar, *v.i.* to travel, march, walk, go; move along, act. — *v.t.* to walk; *caminar con pies de plomo,* to act with prudence; *caminar derecho,* to act uprightly; *caminar a, para Madrid,* to go, travel to Madrid; *caminar de concierto,* to act by, in agreement; *los ríos, los planetas caminan,* the rivers, the planets move along; *hoy he caminado* 25 *kilómetros de una tirada,* I have walked 25 kilometres today at one stretch; *caminar sobre un supuesto falso,* to act upon erroneous data.

caminata, *n.f.* (*fam.*) long walk for exercise; promenade; excursion, outing, trip, jaunt.

caminero, -ra, *a.* relating to the road; *peón caminero,* road-man.

camini, *n.m.* (*Arg.*) the best quality maté.

camino, *n.m.* road, highroad, beaten track, way, path, pass; route, passage, trip, journey (of a water-carrier, etc.); manner or method of doing a thing; *camino asenderado, trivial,* or *trillado,* beaten track, frequented road; *camino carretero* or *carretil,* roadway, drive, vehicle road; routine; commonplace; *camino carril,* road for one carriage; *camino cubierto,* (*mil.*) covert-way; *camino de cabaña,* road for nomadic cattle; *camino de herradura,* path, bridle-road; *camino de hierro,* railway; *camino derecho,* (*fig.*) straight ahead (to one's goal); *camino de ruedas,* roadway; *camino de Santiago,* Milky Way; *camino de sirga,* towing-path; *camino real,* highroad, highway; (*fig.*) royal road; *camino vecinal,* municipal road; *abrir camino,* to clear, lead the way; pave the way for; *abrise uno camino,* to make one's way, get on; *al mal camino darle priesa,* unpleasant matters should be dealt with quickly; *andar uno al camino,* to become a highwayman or smuggler; *camino de Roma, ni mula coja ni bolsa floja,* count the cost before beginning anything difficult; *cegar los caminos,* to obstruct the roads; *coger uno el camino,* to go out; *de camino,* on the way, by the way; in travelling costume; *de un camino dos mandados,* to kill two birds with one stone; *echar (ir) cada cual por su camino,* to take one's own way; to disagree; *en luengos caminos se conocen los amigos,* one learns to know one's friends on long journeys; *entrar, meter a uno por camino,* or *traer a uno a buen camino,* to bring someone to reason, put in the right way; *ir, ser (una cosa) fuera de camino,* to be incorrect (a thing); *ir uno fuera de camino,* to act mistakenly; to act without method, order or reason; *ir uno su camino,* to continue on one's way; to pursue one's aim; *llevar camino (una cosa),* to be founded on fact or reason (a thing); *no llevar camino (una cosa),* to be without foundation or reason (a thing); *partir el camino,* to meet half-way; *ponerse*

uno en camino, tomar el camino en las manos, to set off on a journey; *procurar el camino,* to clear the way; *quedarse a medio camino,* to stop half-way; *romper un camino,* to open up a new road; *salir al camino,* to go to meet (someone); (*fig.*) to rob on the highway.

camión, *n.m.* dray, truck; lorry.

camionaje, *n.m.* truck transport; truckage.

camioneta, *n.f.* light motor-van.

camisa, *n.f.* shirt, shift, chemise; coat of whitewash; slough of a serpent; thin skin of almonds or other fruit; (*mil.*) chemise; jacket, case, casing; internal lining of a furnace; incandescent gas-mantle; paper wrapper of documents; (*print.*) linen case for roller; (*Chi.*) paper-lining; *camisa alquitranada, embreada* or *de fuego,* (*naut.*) fire-chemise; *camisa de fuerza,* strait-jacket; *camisa de una vela,* (*naut.*) body of a sail; *dejar a uno sin camisa,* or *no dejar a uno ni aun camisa,* to ruin, rob someone completely; *jugar (empeñar, vender) hasta la camisa,* to play (pawn, sell) the very shirt off one's back; *más cerca está la camisa de la carne que el jubón,* blood is thicker than water; *meterse en camisa de once varas,* to meddle with other people's business; *no llegarle a uno la camisa al cuerpo,* to be frightened, anxious; *primero es la camisa que la saya,* do everything in due order; *tomar la mujer en camisa,* to marry a woman without money; *no tener camisa,* to be destitute; *en mangas de camisa,* in shirt sleeves.

camisería, *n.f.* shirt-factory; shirt-shop, haberdashery.

camisero, -ra, *n.m.f.* shirt-maker, haberdasher.

camiseta, *n.f.* vest, undershirt; short shirt with wide sleeves.

camisilla, *n.f.* small shirt [CAMISA]; torn, ragged shirt.

camisola, *n.f.* ruffled (or day) shirt; (*Chi.*) doublet, jacket; blouse.

camisolín, *n.m.* shirt-front; tucker; camisole; dicky; chemisette, modesty vest.

camisón, *n.m.* long and wide shirt [CAMISA]; night-shirt; (*West Indies, CR.*) woman's chemise; (*Col., Chi., Ven.*) dress, costume of any material other than black silk; *tu camisón no sepa tu intención,* don't let your left hand know what your right is doing; discretion is wise in all matters.

camisote, *n.m.* ancient hauberk.

camistrajo, *n.m.* (*fam.*) pallet, poor bed.

camita, *n.m.f.,* *a.* Hamite.

camítico, -ca, *a.* Hamitic.

camoatí, *n.m.* (*River Plate*) kind of wasp and its nest.

camocán, *n.m.* variety of brocade.

camodar, *v.t.* (*slang*) to disarrange, muddle.

camomila, *n.f.* (*bot.*) camomile.

camón, *n.m.* large bed [CAMA]; portable throne; conservatory, glass-enclosed balcony; curved piece of a water-wheel frame; (*arch.*) lath frame. — *pl.* oak tyres of cart-wheels; *camón de vidrios,* glass partition.

camoncillo, *n.m.* stool in a drawing-room.

camorra, *n.f.* (*fam.*) quarrel, wrangle, dispute.

camorrear, *v.i.* (*fam.*) to annoy, pester, harass.

camorrista, *n.m.f.,* *a.* noisy, quarrelsome (person).

camote, *n.m.* (*Am.*) sweet potato; (*Am.*) infatuation; (*Am.*) lover, mistress; (*Am.*) lie, fib; (*Mex.*) knave, scoundrel; (*ES.*) wale, welt; (*Ec., Mex.*) silly, stupid.

camotear, *v.i.* (*Mex.*) to roam, loiter.

camotero, -ra, *n.m.f., a.* (*Mex.*) seller of sweet potatoes.

camotillo, *n.m.* (*Per.*) sweet potato jam; (*Mex.*) violet coloured wood with black streaks; (*ES., Guat., Hond.*) curcuma; (*CR.*) sago.

campa, *a. tierra campa,* plain; treeless (ground).

campal, *a.* belonging to the field, camp, open country; *batalla campal,* pitched battle.

campamento, *n.m.* camping, camp, encampment.

campana, *n.f.* bell; (*fig.*) anything bell-shaped; bottom of a well shaped like a bell; (*fig.*) parish church, parish; children's game; curfew; (*slang*) top skirt; *campana de chimenea,* bell-shaped hood or mantel of a chimney; *campana de buzo,* diving-bell; *campana de rebato,* alarm-bell; *campana de cristal,* bell-glass; *a campana herida* or *tañida,* at the sound of the bell; *campana cascada, nunca sana,* it is no use crying over spilt milk; *cual es la campana, tal la badajada,* the actions reflect the doer; *doblar las campanas,* to knell, toll the bell; *echar las campanas a vuelo,* to announce, proclaim joyfully; *no haber oído uno campanas,* to be ignorant of the most ordinary things; *oír campanas y no saber dónde,* to have heard a fact incorrectly, or give a wrong version of it; *picar la campana,* (*naut.*) to sound the bell.

campanada, *n.f.* stroke, ring, sound of a bell; (*fig.*) scandal, sensational report; *dar una campanada,* to make a noise, cause scandal.

campanario, *n.m.* belfry; *de campanario,* mean, despicable (action).

campanear, *v.i.* to ring frequently, reverberate (bells); to chime.

campanela, *n.f.* fancy step in dancing; (*mus.*) natural stroke (guitar).

campaneo, *n.m.* bell-ringing, chime; (*coll.*) affected gait, strut.

campanero, *n.m.* bell-founder; bell-ringer; (*Ven.*) (*orn.*) bellbird.

campaneta, *n.f.* small bell [CAMPANA].

campanil, *n.m.* belfry. — *a. metal campanil,* bell-metal.

campanilla, *n.f.* small bell, door-bell, hand-bell; (*naut.*) cabin-bell; (*bot.*) bell-flower; small bubble; (*anat.*) epiglottis, uvula; little tassel, bell-shaped dress fringe; (*print.*) loose, ill-adjusted type; (*Cub.*) wild creeping plant (bejuco); *persona de (muchas) campanillas,* distinguished person, one with many titles and honours.

campanillazo, *n.m.* violent ringing of a bell; signal given with a bell.

campanillear, *v.i.* to ring often, reverberate (small bell).

campanilleo, *n.m.* continuous ringing of small bell.

campanillero, *n.m.* bellman, public crier.

campano, *n.m.* cattle-bell; (*bot.*) American tree the wood of which is used in ship-building.

campanología, *n.f.* campanology.

campanológico, -ca, *a.* campanological.

campanólogo, -ga, *n.m.f.* (*mus.*) campanologist.

campante, *a.* excelling, surpassing; (*fam.*) cheerful, buoyant, contented.

campanudo, -da, *a.* bell-shaped; puffed up (clothes); (*fig.*) resonant, ringing; pompous, lofty, high-sounding; (*bot.*) campanulate, campanular. — *n.m.* (*slang*) shield, body protector.

campánula, *n.f.* (*bot.*) bell-flower, campanula.

campanuláceo, -cea, *a.* (*bot.*) campanulaceous. — *n.f.pl.* Campanulaceæ.

campaña, *n.f.* level country; (*Am.*) country; (*mil.*) campaign; (*mil.*) each year of active service; *campaña naval,* (*naut.*) cruise; *batir* or *correr la campaña,* to reconnoitre; *estar* or *hallarse en campaña,* (*mil.*) to serve on a campaign; *salir a (la) campaña,* (*mil.*) to go to war, take the field.

campañista, *n.m.* (*Chi.*) highland shepherd.

campañol, *n.m.* (*zool.*) field-mouse.

campar, *v.i.* to excel, surpass in ability, talent or position; (*mil.*) to encamp, be encamped; *campar con su estrella,* to be fortunate; *campar por su respeto,* to act independently.

campeador, *a.* surpassingly valiant. — *n.m.* combatant, warrior.

campear, *v.i.* to be in the field; to pasture; to frisk about; to grow, crop out; to excel, be eminent; (*mil.*) to campaign; reconnoitre; *ya campear los trigos,* the corn is sprouting already; *campear de sol a sombra,* to work in the fields from morning to night.

campecico; campecillo; campecito, *n.m.* small field [CAMPO].

campechana, *n.f.* (*Cub., Mex.*) refreshing drink; (*Ven.*) hammock; (*Ven.*) harlot.

campechanamente, *adv.* heartily, generously.

campechanía, *n.f.* (*prov.*) cheerfulness, generosity.

campechano, -na, *a.* frank, hearty, cheerful, generous; native of or belonging to Campeche (*Mex.*). — *n.f.* (*naut.*) grating, lattice-work on exterior of certain boats.

campeche, *n.m.* Campeche wood, log-wood.

campeón; campión, *n.m.* champion, combatant, defender, hero.

campeonato, *n.m.* championship.

campero, -ra, *a.* exposed to the weather in the open field; unsheltered, unhoused, sleeping out (cattle); (*Mex.*) having a gait like gentle trotting horses. — *n.m.* friar who superintends a farm; field-guard.

campesino, -na, *a.* rural, rustic, country. — *n.m.f.* countryman, countrywoman.

campilán, *n.m.* (*Philip.*) straight, long sabre broadening at the point.

campillo, *n.m.* small field [CAMPO]; common, public land.

campiña, *n.f.* flat tract of arable land, field; country; landscape.

campirano, -na, *a.* (*CR.*) churlish, unmannerly; (*Mex.*) countryman; (*Mex.*) expert in farming; (*Mex.*) tamer; horse-breaker.

campista, *n.m.* (*Am.*) owner or partner of a mine; (*Hond.*) foreman inspecting cattle on the savanna.

campo, *n.m.* open country, field; arable land; country as opposed to town and mountain; crops, trees, plantations; district; (*fig.*) scope, range, space; (*mil.*) field, ground, camp; body of troops; (*her.*) field; ground of patterned materials, papers, etc.; (*paint.*) background, groundwork; *campo de Agramante*, babel, place of great confusion and disagreement; *campo de batalla*, battlefield; *campo de honor*, duelling-ground; field of honour; *campo magnético*, magnetic field; *campo raso*, flat, treeless, houseless country; plain; *campo regadío*, permanently irrigated land; *campo santo*, burial-ground, cemetery; *campo visual*, field of vision; *campos Elíseos* or *Elisios*, Elysian fields; *hombre de campo*, lover of country-life; *hombre del campo*, countryman; *a campo raso*, in the open field, out of doors; *a campo traviesa* or *travieso*, cross-country; *batir, descubrir* or *reconocer el campo*, to reconnoitre, investigate; *campo a campo*, (*mil.*) force to force; *dejar uno el campo abierto* (*expedito, libre*), to give up a claim, to withdraw from a competition; *dar campo a*, to give free range to; *el campo fértil, no descansando, tórnase estéril*, rest is essential in order to work better; *entrar en campo con uno*, to fight a duel with someone; *hacer campo*, to clear the way, make room; to fight hand to hand; *hacerse uno al campo*, to go into the country as a fugitive from danger or in order to rob; *juntar campo*, to raise an army; *levantar el campo*, to raise camp; to give up an undertaking; *partir el campo*, to mark out a duelling ground; *quedar el campo por uno*; *quedar uno señor del campo*, to hold the field; *quedar en el campo*, to be killed in battle or duel; *salir a* (*al*) *campo*, to go out to fight a duel.

camuatí, *n.f.* (*Arg.*) hut, rough cabin on the gorges of the Paraná.

camucha, *n.f.* (*fam.*) pallet, small rude bed.

camuesa, *n.f.* (*bot.*) pippin, apple.

camueso, *n.m.* (*bot.*) pippin-tree; (*coll.*) dunce, fool.

camuliano, -na, *a.* (*Hond.*) any fruit beginning to ripen.

camuñas, *n.f.pl.* all seeds except barley, wheat and rye.

camuza, *n.f.* (*zool.*) chamois.

camuzón, *n.m.* (*zool.*) large chamois [CAMUZA].

can, *n.m.* dog; (*arch.*) bracket, shoulder, corbel; modillion; (*astron., poet.*) dog-star; trigger of gun; ancient piece of ordnance; khan, Turkish title; *can de busca*, terrier; *Can Mayor*, Canis Major; *Can Menor*, Canis Minor; *can que mata al lobo*, mastiff; *calar el can*, to cock the trigger of a gun; *canes que ladran, ni muerden, ni toman caza*, applied to a boastful and lazy man, useless to himself and others; *can que mucho lame, saca sangre*, too much affection is harmful; *el can de buena raza, siempre ha mientes del pan e la casa*, good breeding and gratitude go hand in hand; *el pequeño can levanta la liebre, y el grande la prende*, those who take the initiative do not always reap the benefit; *¿quieres que te siga el can? Dale pan*, interest is a strong motive; *quien bien quiere a Beltrán, bien quiere a su can*, love me, love my dog.

cana, *n.f.* grey hair; Catalonian measure of about 63 in.; (*Cub.*) variety of the wild palm-tree; *a canas honradas, no hay puertas cerradas*, grey hairs command respect; *canas y*

armas vencen batallas, experience and strength are necessary for success; *echar uno una cana al aire*, to make merry; *no llegar a peinar canas*, not to make old bones; *peinar uno canas*, to be old; *quitar mil canas a uno*, to give great pleasure or satisfaction to someone; *tener canas*, to be grey-haired or old.

canabíneo, -nea, *a.* pertaining to the hemp family. — *n.f.pl.* the hemp family.

canaca, *n.m.* (*Chi.*) (*contempt.*) any individual of the yellow race; (*Chi.*) owner of a brothel.

canacuate, *n.m.* (*Mex.*) large aquatic serpent.

canadiense, *n.m.f., a.* Canadian.

canadillo, *n.m.* horse-tail tree.

canadio, *n.m.* metal of the platinum group.

canal, *n.m.* channel, canal, gutter, artificial waterway; deepest part of estuary; inlet, strait; (*anat.*) duct; pharynx. — *n.m.f.* natural waterway under the earth; long, narrow dell; gas- or water-pipe, conduit; gutter, duct, pantile; drinking-trough; (*arch.*) stria, groove; crease, slot in metal or wood-work; animal carcase cleaned and gutted; weaver's comb; hemp once hackled; front edge of a book; *canal maestra*, principal gutter of roof; *abrir en canal*, to cut from top to bottom; *canal de la Mancha*, English channel.

canalado, -da, *a.* fluted, corrugated. — *n.m.* (*prov.*) aqueduct cavity.

canaladura, *n.f.* (*arch.*) vertical groove.

canaleja, *n.f.* small canal; small drinking-trough [CANAL]; mill-hopper spout.

canalera, *n.f.* (*prov.*) roof-gutter; (*prov.*) rain falling from this gutter.

canaleta, *n.f.* (*Chi.*) mill-hopper spout.

canalete, *n.m.* single- or double-bladed paddle for canoeing; small oar; (*naut.*) winding-frame for spun yarn.

canalí, *n.m.* (*Cub.*) paddle for canoeing made of palm.

canalita, *n.f.* small channel or gutter.

canalizable, *a.* that can be canalized.

canalización, *n.f.* canalization; (*elec.*) wiring.

canalizar, *v.t.* to construct channels or canals; to canalize.

canalizo, *n.m.* narrow channel between two islands or sand-banks.

canalón, *n.m.* big gutter or spout; gargoyle; priest's hat.

canalla, *n.f.* mob, rabble. — *n.m.* (*coll.*) scoundrel.

canallada, *n.f.* knavery, blackguardism.

canallesco, -ca, *a.* low, rascally.

canalluza, *n.f.* big scoundrel [CANALLA].

canameño, *n.m.* (*Am.*) a hammock used esp. for travelling.

canana, *n.f.* cartridge-belt.

cananeo, -nea, *a.* Canaanitish. — *n.m.f.* Canaanite.

cananga, *n.f.* fragrant plant used in perfumery.

canapé, *n.m.* sofa, couch; settee; lounge.

canaria, *n.f.* female canary-bird.

Canarias, *n.f.pl.* Canary Islands.

canariense; canario, -ria, *n.m.f., a.* of or belonging to the Canary Islands.

canariera, *n.f.* large cage for canaries.

canario, *n.m.* canary-bird; dance originally performed in the Canary Islands; (*naut.*) barge used in the Canary Islands; (*Chi.*) generous tipper; (*Chi.*) water-filled toy-whistle which imitates the song of a canary;

(*CR.*) plant with yellow flowers growing in marshy land; *¡canario! interj.* zounds!

canasta, *n.f.* basket, hamper, crater; (*prov.*) olive measure of half a *fanega;* card game.

canastada, *n.f.* basketful, crateful.

canastero, -ra, *n.m.f.* basket-maker or seller; (*Chi.*) fruit and vegetables pedlar; (*Chi.*) assistant baker; (*Chi.*) kind of blackbird which builds a nest in basket form.

canastilla, *n.f.* small basket; gift to ladies of the court; layette.

canastillero, -ra, *n.m.f.* maker or seller of *canastillos.*

canastillo, *n.m.* small wicker tray; small basket.

canasto; canastro, *n.m.* basket with narrow opening; *¡canastos! interj.* an expression of surprise or annoyance.

canastrón, *n.m.* large basket [CANASTRO].

cancagua, *n.f.* (*Chi.*) fine sand used for brick-making and building.

cáncamo, *n.m.* a rare gum, resembling myrrh; (*naut.*) ring-bolt; *cáncamo de argolla,* ring-bolt; *cáncamo de gancho,* hook-bolt; *cáncamo de ojo,* eye-bolt; *cáncamo de mar,* surge, swell.

cancamurria, *n.f.* (*coll.*) sadness, melancholy.

cancamusa, *n.f.* (*coll.*) trick to deceive.

cancán, *n.m.* cancan (dance); (*CR.*) parrot which never learns to speak.

cáncana, *n.f.* cricket; punishment-stool for boys at school; kind of spider.

cancanear, *v.i.* (*fam.*) to rove, wander about; (*Col., Mex.*) to stammer.

cáncano, *n.m.* (*fam.*) louse.

cancel, *n.m.* wooden screen in churches, halls, etc.; glass case in chapel for the king.

cancela, *n.f.* front-door grating or screen in Spanish houses.

cancelación; canceladura, *n.f.* cancellation, obliteration, expunging; closing up.

cancelado, -da, *a.* (*bot.*) cancellate, cancellated, cancellous.

cancelar, *v.t.* to cancel, annul (a writing); (*fig.*) to efface from the memory.

cancelaría; cancelería, *n.f.* papal chancery.

cancelariato, *n.m.* chancellorship.

cancelario, *n.m.* chancellor of a university.

cáncer, *n.m.* (*med.*) cancer, virulent ulcer; (*astron.*) Cancer, one of the signs of the zodiac.

cancerado, -da, *a.* cancered, cancerous; (*med.*) cancroid; (*fig.*) corrupt. — *p.p.* [CANCERAR].

cancerar, *v.t.* (*fig.*) to consume, destroy; (*fig.*) to mortify, punish, reprove. — *v.r.* to be afflicted with a cancer; to turn cancerous, become a cancer (of ulcers).

Cancerbero, *n.m.* (*myth.*) Cerberus; (*fig.*) severe and incorruptible guard.

canceriforme, *a.* cancriform.

canceroso, -sa, *a.* cancerous.

cancilla, *n.f.* lattice or wicker door or gate.

canciller, *n.m.* chancellor.

cancillerato, *n.m.* chancellorship.

cancilleresco, -ca, *a.* belonging to chancellery.

cancillería, *n.f.* chancellery.

cancín, *n.m.* sheep between one and two years.

canción, *n.f.* song, lay, ballad, lyric poem; *mudar de canción,* to change the conversation; *volver a la misma canción,* to tell the old story.

cancioncica; cancionilla; cancionita, *n.f.* canzonet, little song.

cancionero, *n.m.* song-book.

cancioneta, *n.f.* little song, canzonet [CANCIÓN].

cancionista, *n.m.f.* author or composer of songs; songster, songstress, ballad-singer.

canco, *n.m.* (*Chi.*) kind of stewpot made of clay; (*Chi.*) flower-pot; (*Bol.*) buttock, rump. — *pl.* (*Chi.*) wide hips in a woman.

cancón, *n.m.* (*fam.*) [BU].

cancrinita, *n.f.* (*min.*) variety of nepheline with carbonate of lime.

cancro, *n.m.* canker; disease of bark in trees.

cancrófago, -ga, *a.* crab-eating.

cancroide, *n.m.* (*med.*) cancroid.

cancroideo, -dea, *a.* cancroid, cancriform.

cancha, *n.f.* cockpit; *pelota* or sports ground; (*Am.*) roasted corn or broad beans ; (*Am.*) wide, clear ground; (*Am.*) hippodrome; (*Col.*) charge levied by the owner of a gambling-house; *¡Cancha!, interj.* (*Arg.*) give way! out of the way!

canchal, *n.m.* rocky or bouldery ground, stony place.

canchalagua; canchelagua, *n.f.* (*Per.*) a medicinal plant.

cancho, *n.m.* big boulder or rock.

candadico; candadillo; candadito, *n.m.* small padlock.

candado, *n.m.* padlock; (*prov.*) tendril of vine; (*Col.*) goatee, imperial. — *pl.* cavities round the frog of horses' feet; *echar un candado a los labios,* to keep a secret.

candaliza, *n.f.* (*naut.*) brail.

candamo, *n.m.* ancient rustic dance.

candar, *v.t.* to lock, shut.

cándara, *n.f.* (*prov.*) sifting-screen, sieve.

cande; candi, *a.* candied; *azúcar cande,* sugar-candy.

candeal, *a.* white and of first quality (flour); *pan candeal,* bread made of white wheat; *trigo candeal,* white wheat, summer wheat.

candela, *n.f.* candle, taper; candlestick; flower or blossom of chestnut-tree; inclination of the balance-needle to the thing weighed; (*coll.*) light, fire; *acabarse la candela,* to sell by inch of candle; to be dying (person); *arrimar candela,* to give a drubbing; *arrimarse a la candela,* to draw near the fire; *como unas candelas,* bright, gay; *en candela,* (*naut.*) in a vertical position (masts); *estar con la candela en la mano,* to be dying.

candelabro, *n.m.* candelabrum, candelabra.

candelada, *n.f.* bonfire, blaze.

candelaria, *n.f.* Candlemas; (*bot.*) mullein.

candelecho, *n.m.* hut built on piles for watching a vineyard.

candeleja, *n.f.* (*Chi., Per.*) socket pan of a candlestick.

candelejón, *a.* (*Col., Chi., Per.*) candid; silly.

candelerazo, *n.m.* blow given with a candlestick.

candelero, *n.m.* candlestick; student's lamp; fishing-torch; candle-maker or seller; (*naut.*) stanchion; *candelero ciego,* (*naut.*) stanchion without top ring; *candelero de ojo,* (*naut.*) eye-stanchion; *estar en candelero,* to be high in office, to hold an exalted station.

candeleta, *n.f.* [CANDALIZA].

candelica; candelilla; candelita, *n.f.* small candle.

candelilla, *n.f.* (*surg.*) bougie, catheter; (*bot.*) blossom of holm-oak and cork-trees; (*bot.*) catkin, ament; children's game; (*Cub.*) hem; (*CR., Chi., Hond.*) glow-worm, firefly; (*Arg., Chi.*) jack-o'-lantern; will-o'-the-wisp, ignis fatuus; *le hacen candelillas los ojos,* (*coll.*) his eyes sparkle with the fumes of wine; *muchas candelillas hacen un cirio pascual,* many rivulets make a river.

candelizo, *n.m.* icicle, shoot of ice.

candelón, *n.m.* (*Dom.Rep.*) tree with a very hard wood.

candencia, *n.f.* candescence, incandescence, white heat.

candente, *a.* candescent, incandescent, red-hot; *cuestión candente,* burning question.

candi, *a. azúcar candi,* sugar-candy.

candial, *a.* [CANDEAL].

candidación, *n.f.* crystallization (of sugar).

cándidamente, *adv.* candidly.

candidato, *n.m.* candidate.

candidatura, *n.f.* candidacy; candidature, candidateship; list of candidates.

candidez, *n.f.* whiteness; candour, sincerity, candidness, ingenuousness, simplicity.

cándido, -da, *a.* white, snowy; candid, guileless, simple.

candiel, *n.m.* sweetmeat made of white wine, eggs, sugar, etc.

candil, *n.m.* kitchen or stable oil-lamp; Greek lamp; (*coll.*) point of cocked hat; (*coll.*) long irregular fold in petticoats; top of a stag's horn; (*Mex.*) chandelier; (*Cub.*) a phosphorescent pink fish. — *pl.* (*bot.*) wake-robin; *baile de candil,* rustic ball; *escoger una cosa a moco de candil,* to examine something very closely; *ni buscado con un candil,* said of a clever and efficient person; *puede arder en un candil,* said of a strong wine or a smart person or saying; *¿qué aprovecha candil sin mecha?* what is the use of a pump without a handle?

candilada, *n.f.* (*coll.*) oil spilt from a lamp.

candilazo, *n.m.* blow given with a kitchen lamp.

candileja, *n.f.* oil receptacle for a lamp; (*bot.*) lucerne; (*pl.*) footlights of a theatre.

candilejo, *n.m.* small kitchen-lamp [CANDIL]; (*bot.*) lucerne.

candilera, *n.f.* (*bot.*) labiate plant with yellow flowers.

candilero, *n.m.* (*prov.*) drilled slat for hanging lamps.

candiletear, *v.i.* (*prov.*) to idle, roam about.

candiletero, -ra, *n.m.f.* (*prov.*) idler, gossip.

candilillos, *n.m.pl.* (*bot.*) wake-robin.

candilón, *n.m.* large open lamp [CANDIL].

candiota, *n.m.f., a.* Candiot, Cretan. — *n.f.* barrel or keg for carrying wine; large earthen jar for wine.

candiotera, *n.f.* wine-cellar; collection of casks.

candiotero, *n.m.* cooper; maker or seller of *candiotas.*

candita, *n.f.* (*min.*) black variety of aluminate of magnesia.

candombe, *n.m.* (*Am. Mer.*) low, coarse Negro dance.

candongo, -ga, *n.m.f., a.* (*coll.*) cunning, fawning person; shirker. — *n.f.* (*coll.*) artful

flattery or caress intended to deceive; (*coll.*) merry, playful trick; practical joke; (*fam.*) draught-mule; (*Hond.*) (*med.*) binder; (*naut.*) storm-sail. — *pl.* (*Col.*) earrings.

candonguear, *v.t.* (*coll.*) to sneer, jeer, tease; to play practical jokes. — *v.i.* to shirk work.

candonguero, -ra, *a.* jocose, ludicrous. — *n.m.f.* (*coll.*) practical joker; deceiver by flattery.

candor, *n.m.* supreme whiteness; (*fig.*) ingenuousness, candour, purity of mind, sincerity, frankness.

candorosamente, *adv.* candidly.

candoroso, -sa, *a.* candid, frank, ingenuous.

candujo, *n.m.* (*slang*) padlock.

cané, *n.m.* game of chance at cards (played only in low-class gambling houses).

caneca, *n.f.* glazed stone bottle for gin and cordials; (*Arg.*) vessel or bucket of wood; (*Cub.*) stone hot-water bottle; (*Cub.*) measure of capacity about 4 gallons; (*Ec.*) unglazed porous jar; (*Ven.*) glazed clay bottle for gin or beer.

canecillo, *n.m.* (*arch.*) corbel, truss, modillion, cantilever; console.

caneco, -ca, *a.* (*Bol.*) intoxicated, drunk.

canéfora, *n.f.* canephorus.

canela, *n.f.* (*bot.*) canella, cinnamon; (*coll.*) anything exquisite, superbly fine.

canelado, -da, *a.* cinnamon-coloured.

canelar, *n.m.* cinnamon-tree plantation.

canelero, *n.m.* cinnamon-tree.

canelo, -la, *a.* cinnamon-coloured (horses, dogs). — *n.m.* (*bot.*) cinnamon-tree.

canelón, *n.m.* gargoyle; gutter; icicle; tubular fringe; bullion (on epaulets); cinnamon candy. — *pl.* ends of a cat-o'-nine-tails, thicker and more twisted than the rest.

canequí, *n.m.* Indian fine muslin.

canequita, *n.f.* (*Cub.*) measure of capacity of about 3½ pints.

canero, *n.m.* (*prov.*) coarse bran.

canesú, *n.m.* corset-cover; yoke of a shirt or blouse.

caney, *n.m.* (*Cub.*) bend of a river; (*Cub., Ven.*) log cabin.

canfeno, *n.m.* (*chem.*) carbohydrate made by treating artificial camphor with lime.

canfín, *n.m.* (*CR.*) petroleum.

canforado, -da, *a.* camphorated.

canforato, *n.m.* (*chem.*) camphorate.

canforero, *n.m.* (*bot.*) camphor-tree.

canfórico, -ca, *a.* (*chem.*) camphoric.

canforífero, -ra, *a.* (*bot.*) producing camphor.

canga, *n.f.* (*prov.*) coupling, yoking of any animals except oxen; cangue, cang; (*Am. Mer.*) iron ore mixed with clay.

cangagua, *n.f.* (*Ec.*) earth for adobe making.

cangalla, *n.f.* (*prov.*) rag, tatter; (*slang*) cart; (*Col.*) emaciated person or animal; (*Arg., Per.*) coward, poltroon; (*Arg., Chi.*) refuse of minerals; (*Bol.*) harness with pack-saddle.

cangallar, *v.t.* (*Chi.,Per.*) to steal ore or metals; (*Chi.*) to buy stolen ore; (*Per.*) to sell doubtful goods.

cangallero, *n.m.* (*slang*) carter, wagoner.

cangallo, *n.m.* (*prov.*) nickname given to a lanky person; (*prov.*) heel-bone; (*prov.*) damaged object; (*slang*) car, cart.

cangilón, *n.m.* earthen jar or pitcher; tankard

for wine; bucket of water-wheel; fluting, goffer of a frilled collar.

cangre, *n.m.* (*Cub.*) stem of yucca.

cangreja, *n.f., a.; vela cangreja,* boom-sail, gaff-sail.

cangrejal, *n.m.* (*River Plate*) place frequented by crabs or crayfish.

cangrejero, -ra, *n.m.f.* one who sells crabs or crayfish. — *n.m.* heron-like bird. — *n.f.* (*Chi.*) nest of crabs.

cangrejo, *n.m.* fresh-water lobster, crayfish; (*naut.*) boom, gaff; (*fam.*) red tram-car; (*astron.*) crab, cancer; *cangrejo de mar,* crab; *andar como el cangrejo,* to go backwards.

cangrejuelo, *n.m.* small crayfish [CANGREJO].

cangrena, *n.f.* gangrene.

cangrenarse, *v.r.* to be afflicted with gangrene or mortification.

cangrenoso, -sa, *a.* gangrenous, mortified.

cangro, *n.m.* (*Col., Guat., Mex.*) (*med.*) cancer.

canguelo, *n.m.* (*slang*) fear; *tener canguelo,* to show the white feather.

cangüeso, *n.m.* acanthopterygian fish.

canguil, *n.m.* (*Ec.*) maize of small grain, but of very good quality.

canguro, *n.m.* kangaroo.

cania, *n.f.* small nettle.

caníbal, *n.m., a.* cannibal, man-eater; (*fig.*) bloodthirsty, cruel man.

canibalismo, *n.m.* cannibalism; (*fig.*) barbarity.

canica, *n.f.* (*Cub.*) white wild cinnamon.

canicie, *n.f.* whiteness of the hair.

canícula, *n.f.* dog-star; dog-days.

canicular, *a.* canicular, belonging to the dog-star. — *n.m.pl.* dog-days.

caniculario, *n.m.* beadle who drags dogs out of church.

caniculoso, -sa, *a.* [CANICULAR].

cánidos, *n.m.pl.* (*zool.*) canidæ.

canijo, -ja, *n.m.f., a.* (*coll.*) weak, sickly, infirm (person).

canil, *n.m.* coarse bread, dog's bread; (*prov.*) canine tooth.

canilla, *n.f.* long bone of either extremity; any of the principal bones of the wing of a fowl; stopcock, faucet, spigot; reel, bobbin, spool; unevenness of the woof in thickness or colour; (*fam.*) slender legs; (*Per.*) game of dice; (*Arg.*) tap, cock; (*Col.*) calf of the leg; (*Mex.*) (*fig.*) strength, fortitude, courage; *irse de canilla* or *como una canilla,* to suffer from diarrhœa; to let the tongue run on forever.

canillado, -da, *a.* ribbed or striped cloth.

canillera, *n.f.* (*Col.*) awe, dread, a state of anxiety.

canillero, -ra, *n.m.f.* maker of weaver's quills. — *n.m.* faucet, spigot-hole in casks. — *n.f.* greave, jamb (armour).

canime, *n.m.* (*Col.*) tree producing medicinal oil.

canina, *n.f.* excrement of dogs.

caninamente, *adv.* ragingly, snarlingly.

caninero, *n.m.* one who gathers *canina* for the use of tan-yards.

caninez, *n.f.* canine, inordinate appetite.

canino, -na, *a.* canine; *hambre canina,* canine appetite, inordinate hunger; *dientes caninos,* eye-teeth, canine teeth.

caniquí, *n.m.* Indian fine muslin.

canísimo, -ma, *a., superl.* [CANO] very grey or white (hair).

canje, *n.m.* (*mil., dipl., com.*) exchange.

canjeable, *a.* exchangeable.

canjear, *v.t.* to exchange prisoners of war, treaties, credentials or newspapers.

canjura, *n.f.* (*Hond.*) a highly poisonous alkaloid.

canjuro, *n.m.* (*CR.*) tree giving a fruit used to feed the wild peacock.

cano, -na, *a.* hoary, hoar, frosty, grey-haired; (*fig.*) old, ancient; (*poet.*) white; *no todos los canos son viejos ni sabios,* age does not necessarily imply wisdom or knowledge.

canoa, *n.f.* canoe, Indian boat; *sombrero de canoa,* shovel-hat.

canoero, -ra, *n.m.f.* canoeist.

canoi, *n.m.* (*Am.*) fishing basket used by Indians.

canoita, *n.m.* small canoe.

canon, *n.m.* canon, rule, precept; catalogue, list; books which compose the Holy Scriptures; part of the Mass; (*mus.*) canon; (*print.*) canon; (*art*) standard measurements of human figure; governmental or municipal loan; (*law*) land tax; (*min.*) royalty. — *pl.* canons, canon law.

canonesa, *n.f.* canoness.

canónica, *n.f.* conventual life.

canonical, *a.* canonical, relating to canon, prebendary; (*coll.*) comfortable, easy (life).

canónicamente, *adv.* canonically.

canonicato, *n.m.* canonry; (*coll.*) sinecure.

canonicidad, *n.f.* canonicity.

canónico, -ca, *a.* canonical, canonic.

canóniga, *n.f.* (*coll.*) siesta; nap before a meal.

canónigo, *n.m.* canon, prebendary; *vida de canónigo,* comfortable life.

canonista, *n.m.* canonist.

canonizable, *a.* worthy of canonization.

canonización, *n.f.* canonization.

canonizar, *v.t.* to canonize; (*fig.*) to applaud, praise.

canonjía, *n.f.* canonry; (*coll.*) sinecure.

canope, *n.m.* (*archæol.*) canopic vase.

canoro, -ra, *a.* canorous, musical, melodious.

canoso, -sa, *a.* hoary, hoar-headed, grey-haired.

canotié, *n.m.* straw-hat.

canquén, *n.m.* (*Chi.*) wild goose.

cansable, *a.* easily tired.

cansadamente, *adv.* importunately, in a troublesome way; wearily.

cansado, -da, *a.* weary, wearied, exhausted, tired, spent, worn out; tedious, tiresome, troublesome; *una bala cansada,* a spent ball; *una lámina cansada,* a worn-out copper-plate; *una vista cansada,* an impaired eye-sight. — *p.p.* [CANSAR].

cansancio, *n.m.* weariness, fatigue, lassitude.

cansar, *v.t.* to weary, tire, fatigue, overcome; (*fig.*) to tease, harass, bore, molest; (*agric.*) to exhaust land. — *v.r.* to tire oneself, become fatigued, grow weary.

cansera, *n.f.* (*coll.*) fatigue, weariness, importunity.

cansí, *n.m.* (*Cub.*) hut or cabin of an Indian chief.

cansino, -na, *a.* worn by work (said of animals); (*fig.*) annoying, importunate.

canso, -sa, *a.* (*prov.*) [CANSADO].

cantable, *a.* singable; (*mus.*) that is sung slowly. — *n.m.* lyrics, musical part of a zarzuela; (*mus.*) cantabile; majestic, simple melody.

cantábrico, -ca; cántabro, -bra, *n.m.f., a.* Cantabrian, of Cantabria.

cantada, *n.f.* (*mus.*) cantata.

cantador, -ra, *n.m.f.* singer of popular songs; ballad-singer.

cantal, *n.m.* block of stone; stony ground.

cantalear, *v.i.* to coo, warble (doves).

cantaleta, *n.f.* charivari; tin-pan serenade; (*fig.*) pun, jest, joke, humbug; *dar cantaleta,* (*coll.*) to deride, laugh at, turn to ridicule.

cantaletear, *v.t.* (*Am.*) to nag, harp on; to be continually repeating a thing; (*Mex.*) to deride, laugh at; to sermonize.

cantalinoso, -sa, *a.* stony, pebbly.

cantante, *a.* singing. — *n.m.f.* professional singer.

cantar, *n.m.* song set to music, canticle; *Cantar de los Cantares,* Song of Solomon, Canticles; *cantar de gesta,* old legendary romance; *eso es otro cantar,* that's another pair of shoes.

cantar, *v.i., v.t.* to sing; (*poet.*) to compose, recite. — *v.i.* to chirp, chirr; (*fig.*) to announce the trump at cards; (*coll.*) to creak, make a harsh grinding noise; (*coll.*) to divulge a secret; (*naut.*) to inform; (*naut.*) to sound the whistle; (*naut.*) to sing shanties; (*mus.*) to play solo with accompaniment; *cantar a libro abierto,* to sing off-hand, at sight; *cantar de plano,* to make a full confession; *cantar siempre en el mismo tono,* to harp on; *cantarlas claras,* to speak out; *cantar la misa,* to say mass; *el gallo canta,* the cock crows; *al fin se canta la gloria,* don't hallo till you're out of the wood; *una ánima sola, ni canta, ni llora,* union accomplishes much; *los dineros del sacristán, cantando se vienen, y cantando se van,* easy come, easy go; *quien mal canta, bien le suena,* we are all blind to our own defects; *quien canta, sus males espanta,* he who sings frightens away his woes; *en menos que canta un gallo,* in a twinkling.

cántara, *n.f.* large, narrow-mouthed pitcher; cantar, wine-measure (about 32 pints).

cantarada, *n.f.* as much as will fill a *cántara.*

cantarcico; cantarcillo; cantarcito, *n.m.* little song [CANTAR].

cantarela, *n.f.* treble (of violin or guitar).

cantarera, *n.f.* shelf for jars, pitchers, etc.

cantarería, *n.f.* shop where pitchers and jars are sold.

cantarero, -ra, *n.m.f.* potter; dealer in earthen jars, pitchers, etc.

cantárida, *n.f.* cantharis, Spanish-fly; cantharides, blistering-plaster; blister raised by this plaster.

cantaridina, *n.f.* (*chem.*) cantharidine.

cantarillo, *n.m.* small pitcher [CÁNTARO].

cantarín, -ina, *a.* (*coll.*) singing constantly. — *n.m.f.* songster, songstress; professional singer.

cántaro, *n.m.* large, narrow-mouthed pitcher; liquid which it contains; wine-measure; measure for liquids, varying from $2\frac{1}{2}$ to 4 gals.; vessel into which votes are put; (*Mex.*) bassoon; *a cántaros,* in abundance, forcefully; *entrar en cántaro,* to draw lots; *estar en cántaro,* to be proposed for an office; *llover a cántaros,* to pour, rain in bucketfuls; *tantas veces va el cántaro a la fuente, que al fin se quiebra,* the pitcher which goes oft to the well gets broken at last.

cantata, *n.f.* (*mus.*) cantata.

cantatriz, *n.f.* professional singer (woman).

cantazo, *n.m.* throw of a stone; blow from a stone.

cante, *n.m.* (*prov.*) song; singing; *cante hondo* or *flamenco,* popular Andalusian gipsy song.

canteado, -da, *a.* on edge (position of brick, stone). — *p.p.* [CANTEAR].

cantear, *v.t.* to work the edge of stone; to put bricks on edge.

canteles, *n.m.pl.* (*naut.*) ends of old ropes put under casks to keep them steady.

cantera, *n.f.* quarry; (*fig.*) talents, genius.

cantería, *n.f.* art of hewing stone; building made of hewn stone; portion of hewn stone.

canterios, *n.m.pl.* transverse roof-beams.

canterito, *n.m.* small piece of bread.

cantero, *n.m.* stone-cutter; extremity of a hard substance which can easily be separated from the rest; *cantero de heredad,* (*prov.*) piece of ground; *cantero de pan,* crust of bread.

canticio, *n.m.* (*coll.*) frequent and annoying singing.

cántico, *n.m.* canticle.

cantidad, *n.f.* quantity; amount; measure; number; (*gram.*) duration of a syllable; sum of money; large portion; *cantidad alzada,* total sum necessary for any object; *cantidad concurrente,* amount necessary to complete a certain sum; *cantidad continua,* (*math.*) continued quantity; *cantidad discreta,* distinct or separate quantity; *hacer buena una cantidad,* to pay a sum of money due.

cantiga, *n.f.* poetical composition for a song.

cantil, *n.m.* steep rock; place where the shore is precipitous; (*Am. Mer.*) verge of a precipice; (*Guat.*) large snake.

cantilena; cantinela, *n.f.* a kind of ballad; (*coll.*) wearisome repetition of a subject.

cantillo, *n.m.* small pebble used in a children's game; corner, angle.

cantimpla, *a.* (*River Plate*) said of a quiet, silly, simple, giggling person.

cantimplora, *n.f.* siphon; water-cooler; (*Guat.*) goiter; (*Col.*) powder flask.

cantina, *n.f.* wine-cellar; canteen, public-house, saloon; canteen, double case for provisions, etc. (on a journey).

cantinela, *n.f.* [CANTILENA].

cantinera, *n.f.* vivandière.

cantinero, *n.m.* butler; sutler, canteen-keeper.

cantiña, *n.f.* (*coll.*) popular song.

cantizal, *n.m.* stony ground, place full of stones.

canto, *n.m.* singing; short poem of the heroic type; canto, division of a long poem; chant, song, canticle; end, extremity, point; border, corner, edge; crust (of a loaf); thickness of anything; back (of a knife); front edge (of a book); dimension less than square; stone, pebble; game of throwing the stone (duck on a rock); quarry-stone, block; *canto Gregoriano (llano),* Gregorian chant, plainsong; *a canto,* very near; *al canto,* by one's side; *al canto del gallo,* (*coll.*) at daybreak; *al canto de los gallos,* at midnight; *de canto,* on edge; *canto de las aves,* singing of birds; *con un canto a los pechos,* with alacrity, pleasure; *canto pelado* or *rodado,* boulder;

en canto llano, clearly, simply; usually, ordinarily; *echar cantos*, to throw stones; *por el canto se conoce el pájaro*, a man is known by his actions; *ser canto llano*, to be current, ordinary, usual; to be easy, plain.

cantollanista, *n.m.f.* expert in plain-song.

cantomanía, *n.f.* singing mania.

cantón, *n.m.* corner; canton, region, district; cantonment; (*her.*) canton; *cantón redondo*, (*carp.*) coarse file; (*Hond.*) isolated plateau; (*Mex.*) cloth imitation of cashmere.

cantonada, *n.f.* (*prov.*) corner; *dar cantonada*, to dodge, shake off, or evade (a person).

cantonal, *a.* cantonal. — *n.m.f.*, *a.* [CANTONALISTA].

cantonalismo, *n.m.* cantonal spirit; policy of decentralization into cantons.

cantonalista, *n.m.f.*, *a.* upholder of *cantonalismo*.

cantonar, *v.t.* to canton, quarter troops. — *v.r.* to take up a position, quarters, abode.

cantonear, *v.i.* to walk, roam from corner to corner. — *v.r.* to walk with an affected air, or gait.

cantoneo, *n.m.* (*fam.*) affected air or gait.

cantonero, -ra, *a.* loafing, idling. — *n.m.* loafer; bookbinder's gilding instrument. — *n.f.* plate nailed to the corners of a chest, etc.; corner-plate, clip; angle-iron, corner-bracket; street-walker.

cantor, -ra, *a.* singing, that sings. — *n.m.f.* singer; song-bird. — *n.m.* (*slang*) one who confessed under torture. — *n.f.pl.* order of song-birds.

cantoral, *n.m.* chorus-book.

Cantorbery, *n.m.* Canterbury.

cantorcillo, *n.m.* petty, worthless singer.

cantorral, *n.m.* [CANTIZAL].

cantoso, -sa, *a.* stony, pebbly (ground).

cantú, *n.m.* (*Per.*) garden plant of the Polemoniaceæ family.

cantúa, *n.f.* (*Cub.*) sweetmeat made of sweet potato, coconut, sesame and sugar.

cantuariense, *a.* of or belonging to Canterbury.

cantueso, *n.m.* (*bot.*) French lavender, spike.

canturía, *n.f.* singing exercise, vocal music, musical composition; monotonous singing; method of singing musical compositions.

canturrear; canturriar, *v.i.* (*fam.*) to hum, sing in a low voice.

canturria, *n.f.* (*Per.* and *prov.*) monotonous singing.

cantuta, *n.f.* (*Per.*) carnation plant (also called *flor de los Incas*).

cánula, *n.f.* small cane; (*med.*) clyster pipe, injection-tube.

canular, *a.* like a *cánula*.

canutero; canutillo; canuto, [CAÑUTERO, CAÑUTILLO, CAÑUTO].

caña, *n.f.* (*bot.*) cane, reed, bamboo; walking-stick, cane; stem, stalk; bone of arm or leg; (*min.*) gallery; (*arch.*) shaft of a column or pillar; (*anat.*) marrow; (*naut.*) helm, tiller; long, narrow tumbler for *manzanilla* wine; Andalusian song; flaw in a sword's blade; glass-blower's pipe; groove (for the barrel of a firearm); (*carp.*) shank; reed of wind-instruments; *¡ la caña a babor !* (*naut.*) port the helm! *caña de un cañón*, chase of a gun; *caña común*, cultivated reed; *caña dulce, de azúcar* or *melar*, sugar-cane; *caña de la bota*

or *media*, leg of a boot or stocking; *caña de pescar*, fishing-rod; *caña del ancla*, (*naut.*) anchor shank; *caña del timón*, (*naut.*) tiller; *caña del pulmón*, (*anat.*) windpipe; *caña del trigo*, stem of corn; *caña de vaca*, shin-bone of beef and its marrow; *cañas, correr cañas*, jousts, to joust with reed spears; *jugar a las cañas*, to wound with sharp-pointed canes; *las cañas se vuelven lanzas*, what began in jest may end in earnest; *ser brava, buena* or *linda caña de pescar*, to be very astute, cunning.

cañacoro, *n.m.* (*bot.*) Indian shot, Indian reed.

cañada, *n.f.* glen or dale between mountains; dell, glade; cattle-path; shin-bone marrow; (*prov.*) measure of wine.

cañadilla, *n.f.* edible mollusc, variety of the purple murex.

cañado, *n.m.* Galician liquid measure equivalent to about 8 gallons.

cañaduz, *n.m.* (*Col.* and *prov.*) sugar-cane.

cañafístola; cañafístula, *n.f.* (*bot.*) cassia-tree and its fruit.

cañaheja; cañaherla; cañajelga, *n.f.* (*bot.*) common fennel-plant; *cañaheja hedionda*, (*bot.*) madder, Thapsia.

cañahua, *n.f.* (*Per.*) Indian millet from which *chicha* is made.

cañahuate, *n.m.* (*Col.*) species of lignum vitæ.

cañal, *n.m.* cane or reed plantation; weir for fishing, made of canes or reeds; small sluice or channel, for catching fish.

cañaliega, *n.f.* cane or reed weir for fishing.

cáñama, *n.f.* assessment of taxes.

cañamacero, ra, *n.m.f.* canvas-maker or seller.

cañamal; cañamar, *n.m.* hemp-field.

cañamazo, *n.m.* coarse canvas, canvas for embroidery; embroidered canvas; burlap; (*Cub.*) wild plant used as fodder.

cañamelar, *n.m.* sugar-cane plantation.

cañameño, -ña, *a.* hempen, made of hemp.

cañamiel, *n.f.* sugar-cane.

cañamiza, *n.f.* bagasse of hemp.

cáñamo, *n.m.* hemp; cloth made of hemp; (*CR., Chi., Hond.*) hempcord; *cáñamo de Manila*, manila hemp; *cáñamo en rama*, undressed hemp.

cañamón, *n.m.* hempseed.

cañamoncillo, *n.m.* very fine sand.

cañamonero, -ra, *n.m.f.* vendor of hempseed.

cañar, *n.m.* cane or reed plantation; weir for catching fish.

cañareja, *n.f.* common fennel plant.

cañariego, -ga, *a.* accompanying a drove; *pellejos cañariegos*, skins of sheep that die on the road.

cañarroya, *n.f.* pellitory, wall-pellitory.

cañavera, *n.f.* common reed-grass.

cañaveral, *n.m.* plantation of canes or reeds.

cañaverear, *v.t.* to wound with sharp-pointed canes.

cañaverería, *n.f.* place where reeds are sold.

cañaverero, -ra, *n.m.f.* retailer of canes or reeds.

cañazo, *n.m.* blow with a cane; *dar cañazo*, to confound, sadden, make pensive.

cañedo, *n.m.* plantation of canes or reeds.

cañería, *n.f.* aqueduct, water- or gas-pipe; water- or gas-main.

cañero, *n.m.* conduit-maker, director of water- or gas-works; (*Mex.*) peon in a sugar mill;

(*Cub.*) seller of sugar-cane; (*Hond.*) owner of a sugar plantation; (*Mex.*) sugar-cane warehouse; (*prov.*) angler.

cañeta, *n.f.* reed-grass.

cañete, *n.m.* small tube [CAÑO]; *ajo cañete,* red-bulbed garlic.

cañí, *n.m.* (*slang*) gipsy.

cañihueco; cañivano, *a.* applied to a variety of wheat which gives good flour.

cañilavado, -da, *a.* thin, lank-limbed (horse).

cañilla; cañita, *n.f.* small cane or reed.

cañillera, *n.f.* jambe.

cañista, *n.m.f.* maker of *cañizos.*

cañiza, *a.* having the vein on one side (wood). — *n.f.* coarse linen; (*prov.*) sheepfold-fence, hurdle.

cañizal; cañizar, *n.m.* plantation of canes or reeds.

cañizo, *n.m.* hurdle; frame for rearing silkworms; frame of car-tilt; lath frame of plaster ceiling, etc.; (*prov.*) wicker door or gate; (*naut.*) flake.

caño, *n.m.* tube, pipe; common sewer, gutter; conduit, spout, spring, jet of water; cellar or other place for cooling water; organ-pipe; (*min.*) gallery; (*prov.*) warren, burrow; (*naut.*) channel at entrance to seaports.

cañocal, *a.* (*naut.*) easily split (wood).

cañón, *n.m.* cannon; gun; cylindrical tube or pipe; fold, quill (of garment); quill (feather stem and pen); down (feathers, hair); (*Col.*) tree-trunk; (*Mex.*) canyon, gorge; (*Per.*) road, highway; (*min.*) gallery; (*mech.*) socket; bit of a bridle; well (of a staircase); (*slang*) tramp, homeless rogue; *cañón de chimenea,* chimney flue; *cañón de fusil, de escopeta, de pistola,* barrel of a musket, fowling-piece, pistol; *cañón de órgano,* organ-pipe; *cañón obús,* howitzer; *cañón rayado,* rifle (gun).

cañonazo, *n.m.* cannon-shot; report and damage caused by a cannon-shot.

cañoncico; cañoncillo; cañoncito, *n.m.* small cannon; small tube or pipe [CAÑÓN].

cañonear, *v.t.* to cannonade. — *v.r.* to cannonade each other.

cañoneo, *n.m.* cannonade.

cañonería, *n.f.* collection of cannon; collection of organ-pipes.

cañonero, -ra, *a.* (*naut.*) carrying cannons. — *n.f.* embrasure for cannon; (*mil.*) large tent; (*naut.*) gun-port; (*Mex.*) holster; *lancha cañonera,* gun-boat.

cañota, *n.f.* panicled sorghum.

cañucela, *n.f.* slender cane or reed.

cañuela, *n.f.* [CAÑA] small reed; fescue-grass.

cañutazo, *n.m.* (*coll.*) hint, suggestion, whisper, tale, gossip.

cañutería, *n.f.* collection of organ-pipes; gold or silver embroidery.

cañutero, *n.m.* pin- or needle-case.

cañutillo, *n.m.* gold or silver twist; bugle for fringes, tassels, flounces, etc.; lobster's placenta; *de cañutillo,* (*agric.*) a method of grafting; *cañutillo de suplicaciones,* rolled wafer [BARQUILLO].

cañuto, *n.m.* part of a cane from knot to knot; small pipe, small tube; (*Mex.*) ice-cream cylinder; (*prov.*) informer, tale-bearer; *cañuto de jeringa,* clyster-pipe.

cao, *n.m.* (*Cub.*) black bird of the Corvus species.

caoba; caobana, *n.f.;* **caobo,** *n.m.* (*bot.*) mahogany-tree, mahogany-wood.

caolín, *n.m.* kaolin, china clay.

caos, *n.m.* chaos; (*fig.*) confusion, disorder.

caótico, -ca, *a.* chaotic, in disorder and confusion.

capa, *n.f.* cape, cloak, mantle; cover; layer, ledge, seam, vein, stratum; hider, harbourer; coat, coating, protective covering; (*slang*) night; colour of animal's coat; (*fig.*) cloak, pretence, mask, covering; coping; property, fortune; third mould in casting bells; (*build.*) bed, course; (*com.*) primage; cigar's outer leaf; *capa aguadera* or *gascona,* waterproof cape or cloak; (*naut.*) tarred canvas covering for mast; *capa del cielo,* canopy of heaven; *capa de fogonaduras,* (*naut.*) mast-coat; *capa consistorial* or *magna,* cope worn by officiating bishops; *capa de rey,* (*bot.*) three-coloured amaranth; *capa de coro* or *pluvial,* pluvial or choir-cope; *capa rota,* secret emissary; *capa torera,* toreador's cape; short, graceful cape; *capa del timón,* (*naut.*) rudder-coat; *de capa y gorra,* unceremoniously, informally; *comedia de capa y espada,* swashbuckler comedy; *gente de capa negra,* middle-class townspeople; *gente de capa parda,* rustics, country-people; *hombre de buena capa,* man of genteel bearing; *andar* or *ir de capa caída,* to be down in the mouth, crestfallen, seedy; *debajo de mala capa suele haber buen bebedor,* under a bad cloak there's often a good drinker, i.e. put no trust in appearances; *defender a capa y espada,* to defend with all one's might; *defender uno su capa,* to fight for one's rights or property; *dejar* or *soltar la capa al toro,* to lose something in order to save oneself from greater loss; *echar la capa a otro,* to shield someone; *echar la capa al toro,* (*fig.*) to risk all in one supreme effort; to expose oneself to great danger; *el que tiene capa, escapa,* the man with resources can get out of any difficulty; *esperar, estar, estarse* or *ponerse a la capa,* (*naut.*) to lie to; to watch for an opportunity; *hacer de su capa un sayo,* to do as one pleases with one's property; *hacer a uno la capa,* to hide, conceal someone; *no tener uno más que la capa en el hombro,* to be very poor; *pasear uno la capa,* to promenade, stroll, walk about; *quitar a uno la capa,* to rob; to overcharge; *sacar uno la* or *su capa,* to justify oneself; *sobre mí la capa cuando llueve,* never me be the cloak when it rains; *tirar a uno de la capa,* to warn someone against danger; *una buena capa todo lo tapa,* a good appearance is often deceitful.

capá, *n.m.* tree of the West Indies used in shipbuilding.

capacete, *n.m.* helmet, casque; (*Cub.*) apron, covering for the legs in an open carriage.

capacidad, *n.f.* capacity, extent; (*fig.*) opportunity, means; (*fig.*) genius, ability, talent, capability; (*law*) legal qualification.

capacitar, *v.t.* to capacitate, equip, qualify; (*Chi.*) to commission, empower, delegate. — *v.r.* to qualify oneself, make oneself competent.

capacha, *n.f.* frail, hamper.

capachazo, *n.m.* blow given with a basket.

capachero, *n.m.* one who carries things in baskets.

capacho, *n.m.* hamper, frail, large basket; hempen pressing-bag in oil-mills; (*orn.*)

common owl, barn owl; *capacho de albañil*, bricklayer's hod.

capada, *n.f.* (*coll.*) anything carried in a cloak.

capador, *n.m.* gelder; whistle used by gelders.

capadura, *n.f.* castration; castration scar; inferior quality tobacco leaf used for cigar-filling or as cut tobacco.

capar, *v.t.* to geld, castrate; (*coll.*) to curtail, diminish one's authority; income, etc.

capararoch, *n.m.* (*Am.*) a nocturnal bird of prey.

caparazón, *n.m.* caparison; saddle-cover, carriage-cover, piano-cover; hempen nose-bag; carcass of a fowl; shell of insects and crustaceans.

caparra, *n.f.* sheep-louse; money given to confirm a bargain, deposit; (*prov.*) caper-tree.

caparrilla, *n.f.* small tick which molests bees.

caparro, *n.m.* (*Per., Ven.*) small white monkey.

caparrós, *n.m.* (*prov.*); **caparrosa,** *n.f.* copperas; *caparrosa azul*, copper sulphate; *caparrosa blanca*, sulphate of zinc; *caparrosa verde*, iron sulphate.

capasurí, *n.m.* (*CR.*) deer.

capataz, *n.m.* overseer, foreman, steward, superintendent, warden; (*coll.*) leader, conductor; *capataz de cultivo*, practical agronomist or forester.

capaz, *a.* capacious, ample, roomy, spacious, wide, large; (*fig.*) capable, clever, ingenious, learned, fit, apt, competent, suitable; *capaz de diez litros*, able to contain ten litres; *capaz para el cargo*, fit, suitable for the post.

capaza, *n.f.* (*prov.*) hempen pressing-bag in oil-mills.

capazmente, *adv.* amply, capaciously.

capazo, *n.m.* large frail, hempen basket; esparto mat; blow given with a cloak; *acabarse* or *salir a capazos*, to end in a quarrel.

capazón, *n.m.* very large frail [CAPAZO].

capciosamente, *adv.* captiously, artfully, cunningly, insidiously.

capciosidad, *n.f.* captiousness, falsity, bad faith, dissimulation.

capcioso, -sa, *a.* captious, artful, cunning, insidious.

capea, *n.f.* cloak stealing; amateur bullfight with calf in which the animal is not killed.

capeado, -da, *a.* robbed of a cloak; deceived. — *p.p.* [CAPEAR].

capeador, *n.m.* bull-fighter who challenges and tricks the bull with his cloak; cloak-stealer.

capear, *v.t.* to strip or rob of a cloak; to challenge and trick a bull with a cloak; (*coll.*) to deceive; (*naut.*) to lay to.

capeja, *n.f.* small shabby cloak or cape.

capelán; caplán, *n.m.* (*ichth.*) capelin.

capelanero; caplanero, *n.m.* capelin fisher and vendor.

capelete, *n.m.* member of the Capulet family of Verona.

capelina, *n.f.* head bandage.

capelo, *n.m.* dues formerly received by bishops from their clergy; cardinal's hat; cardinalate; (*Am.*) glass bell.

capellada, *n.f.* toe-piece of a shoe; repair to the vamp of shoe.

capellán, *n.m.* chaplain, clergyman; *capellán de altar*, priest who assists at the Mass;

capellán castrense, army chaplain; *capellán de honor*, king's private chaplain; *capellán mayor de los ejércitos*, vicar-general of the army; *capellán de navío*, naval chaplain.

capellanía, *n.f.* chaplaincy.

capellar, *n.m.* Moorish cloak.

capellina, *n.f.* head-piece of a helmet or casque; hood worn by country-people; trooper armed with a helmet; (*surg.*) [CAPELINA].

capeo, *n.m.* challenging and teasing a bull with a cloak. — *pl.* amateur bullfight with calf.

capeón, *n.m.* young bull challenged with a cloak.

capero, *n.m.* priest wearing cope in church; cloak-rack.

caperol, *n.m.* (*naut.*) top of stem.

caperucear, *v.t.* to remove the headgear as salute.

caperuceta; caperucilla, *n.f.* small hood [CAPERUZA].

caperuza, *n.f.* hood or cap ending in a point; ulster cap; *dar en caperuza a uno*, (*coll.*) to frustrate someone's views and designs; *caperuza de chimenea*, chimney-cowl.

caperuzón, *n.m.* large hood [CAPERUZA].

capeta, *n.f.* short collarless cape or cloak [CAPA].

capetonada, *n.f.* violent vomiting affecting Europeans when in torrid zone.

capi, *n.m.* (*Chi.*) pod, capsule; (*Am.*) maize.

capia, *n.f.* (*Arg.*) sweetmeat made of maize and sugar; (*Col.*) tender maize.

capialzado, -da, *n.m.f.*, *a.* (*arch.*) arched cap-piece; rear-arch, rear-vault. — *p.p.* [CAPIALZAR].

capialzar, *v.t.* (*arch.*) to raise the front of a rear-arch.

capialzo, *n.m.* (*arch.*) slope of intrados.

capiati, *n.m.* (*Arg.*) medicinal plant.

capibara, *n.f.* (*zool.*) capybara.

capicatí, *n.m.* (*Par.*) herb of the Cyperaceæ family used in brewing a drink particular to Paraguay.

capicúa, *n.m.* palindrome.

capichola, *n.f.* ribbed silk stuff.

capicholado, -da, *a.* of or resembling *capichola*.

capidengue, *n.m.* small cloak worn by ladies.

capigorrista; capigorrón, *n.m.*, *a.* (*coll.*) vagabond; sloven, sly fellow; student who never takes a high degree; one who has taken minor orders.

capilar, *a.* capillary.

capilaridad, *n.f.* capillarity; (*phys.*) capillary attraction.

capilla, *n.f.* hood; cowl of monk or friar; chapel, small church; portable chapel for military corps; priests and others taking part in chapel services; band of musicians in a church; chapter or assembly of collegians; (*bot.*) pod, seed-vessel; (*print.*) proof-sheet; *capilla ardiente*, lighted room where a dead body lies in state; *caja de capilla*, (*naut.*) chest for chapel ornaments; *estar en capilla*, to be awaiting execution (of criminals); (*coll.*) to be anxiously awaiting the end of some matter; *no quiero, no quiero, mas echádmelo en la capilla*, I won't have it myself, but throw it into my hood.

capillada, *n.f.* hoodful of anything; blow given with a hood.

capilleja, *n.f.* [CAPILLA] small chapel; small hood.

capillejo, *n.m.* [CAPILLO] small christening-cap; skein of sewing-silk.

capiller; capillero, *n.m.* clerk or sexton of a chapel; churchwarden.

capilleta; capillita, *n.f.* [CAPILLA] small chapel; niche; shrine.

capillo, *n.m.* child's cap; baptismal cap; christening fee; hood (of hawk); cloth which covered a church-offering; rosebud; toe-piece lining; cap of a distaff; silk cocoon; net for catching rabbits; colander for wax; (*anat.*) prepuce; first wrapper of cigar-fillings; (*naut.*) tin or wooden binnacle-cover; (*naut.*) canvas covering of shroud ends; *capillo de hierro,* helmet, casque; *ponte el capillo ruin, que viene abril,* be prepared for emergencies.

capilludo, -da, *a.* resembling a monk's hood or cowl.

capín, *n.m.* (*Am.*) fodder plant.

capingo, *n.m.* (*Chi.*) short and narrow cape.

capipardo, *n.m.* artisan, working-man.

capirotada, *n.f.* batter made of herbs, eggs, etc.; (*Mex.*) pauper's grave.

capirotazo, *n.m.* fillip, blow.

capirote, *a.* said of cattle having head of a different colour from that of the body. — *n.m.* hood; sharp-pointed cap worn in processions; doctor graduate's hooded gown; half-gown worn by collegians; hood (of hawk, carriage); fillip, blow; *tonto de capirote,* blockhead, ignorant fool; *capirote de colmena,* cover of a beehive.

capirotero, *a.* accustomed to carry a hood (hawk).

capirucho, *n.m.* (*coll.*) [CAPIROTE].

capisayo, *n.m.* cloak, mantle, mantelet; vestment worn by bishops; (*Col.*) undervest.

capiscol, *n.m.* precentor; (*slang*) cock, rooster.

capiscolía, *n.f.* precentorship.

capita, *n.f.* small cloak [CAPA].

capitá, *n.m.* (*Am.*) small black bird.

capitación, *n.f.* capitation; poll-tax, head-money.

capital, *a.* capital, principal, relating to the head; leading, great; excellent, unsurpassed; essential. — *n.m.* capital, wealth; patrimony; money put out at interest; husband's fortune at marriage; (*com.*) capital stock. — *n.f.* (*fort.*) imaginary line bisecting a salient angle in a fortification; capital, metropolis, chief city of a country or province; *capital desembolsado,* (*com.*) paid-up capital; *capital líquido,* net balance of assets; *capital social,* nominal capital, authorized capital; *enemigo capital,* mortal enemy; *error capital,* capital error; *letra capital,* capital letter; *pecado capital,* deadly sin; *pena capital,* capital punishment.

capitalidad, *n.f.* condition of a city being a capital.

capitalismo, *n.m.* capitalism.

capitalista, *n.m.f.* owner of cash or bonds; (*com.*) capitalist.

capitalizable, *a.* that can be capitalized.

capitalización, *n.f.* capitalization.

capitalizador, -ra, *n.m.f.,* *a.* that capitalizes.

capitalizar, *v.t.* (*pret.* **capitalicé;** *pres. subj.* **capitalice**) to capitalize, realize; to add interest or dividends to the capital held.

capitalmente, *adv.* capitally, mortally.

capitán, *n.m.* captain; leader; chief or leader of a band of robbers; commander of a ship; *capitán de bandera,* (*naut.*) captain of the admiral's ship; *capitán de fragata,* navy officer ranking as lieutenant-colonel; *capitán general de ejército,* field-marshal; *capitán general de provincia,* commander-in-chief of a military district; *capitán de alto bordo* or *de navío,* navy officer ranking as colonel; commander of a man-of-war; *capitán del puerto,* (*naut.*) port-captain, harbour-master; *capitán vencido, ni loado ni bien recibido,* the fallen man, although innocent, finds little sympathy.

capitana, *n.f.* admiral's ship, flagship; (*fam.*) captain's wife; (*fam.*) woman leader of a troop.

capitanear, *v.t.* to have the command of an armed corps; (*fig.*) to head, lead.

capitanía, *n.f.* captainship, captaincy; (*mil.*) company commanded by a captain; tax paid to the port-captain by ships anchored in the harbour; *capitanía de puerto,* harbour-master's office; *capitanía general,* rank of a captain-general; residence and office of a captain-general.

capitel, *n.m.* (*arch.*) capital; spire.

capitelado, -da, *a.* (*arch.*) adorned with capitals; (*bot.*) capitate, capitated.

capitolino, -na, *a.* Capitolian, Capitoline.

capitolio, *n.m.* capitol; any lofty or majestic public building; acropolis.

capitón, *n.m.* mullet.

capítula, *n.f.* part of the prayers read during the divine office.

capitulación, *n.f.* capitulation, stipulation, agreement; surrender. — *pl.* marriage articles or contract; document embodying these articles.

capitulado, -da, *a.* abridged, condensed; capitulated. — *n.m.* capitulation, contract. — *p.p.* [CAPITULAR].

capitulador, -ra, *n.m.f.,* *a.* that capitulates.

capitulante, *a.* capitulating.

capitular, *a.* (*eccl.*) capitular. — *n.m.* (*eccl.*) capitular. — *n.f.pl.* capitulary.

capitular, *v.i.* to conclude an agreement; to draw up the articles of a contract; to compound; to dispose, resolve; to sing prayers at the divine office; (*mil.*) to capitulate. — *v.t.* (*law*) to impeach.

capitulario, *n.m.* book of prayers for the divine office.

capituliforme, *a.* (*bot.*) capitate.

capítulo, *n.m.* (*eccl.*) chapter; meeting of the prelates of religious orders; chapter-house; meeting of a secular community or other body; accusation, charge; (*eccl.*) public and severe reproof, reprimand; chapter (of a book); (*fig.*) determination, resolution; *capítulo de culpas,* impeachment; *capítulos matrimoniales,* marriage articles; *dar un capítulo,* to reprimand severely; *ganar* or *perder capítulo,* to gain or lose one's expectations; *llamar* or *traer a uno a capítulo,* to ask for an explanation of someone's conduct.

capizana, *n.f.* part of the armour of a horse protecting the upper side of the neck.

capnomancia; capnomancía, *n.f.* capnomancy.

capoc, *n.m.;* **capoca,** *n.f.* kapok.

capolado, -da, *a.* hashed, cut in pieces. — *n.m.* (*prov.*) hash, mince. — *p.p.* [CAPOLAR].

capolar, *v.t.* to cut into pieces; (*prov.*) to hash, mince or chop up meat; (*prov.*) to decapitate, behead.

capón, *a.* castrated, gelded. — *n.m.* eunuch; gelding; capon; (*coll.*) blow on the head with knuckle of middle finger; faggot, bundle of brushwood; (*naut.*) anchor-stopper at the cathead; *capón de ceniza,* blow on the forehead with rag filled with ashes; *capón de galera* [GAZPACHO]; *capón de leche,* capon fattened in a coop.

capona, *n.f.* epaulette without fringe; shoulder-knot; sleeveless surplice; *llave capona,* key worn by a lord of the bed-chamber.

caponado, -da, *a.* tied together, like runners of vines. — *p.p.* [CAPONAR].

caponar, *v.t.* to tie up the runners of vines; (*naut.*) to fasten the anchor to the cathead.

caponera, *n.f.* leading mare; coop, enclosure to fatten poultry; (*coll.*) jail; (*fort.*) caponiere; (*coll.*) place where one lives well at other people's expense; *estar metido en caponera,* to be locked up in gaol.

capoquero, *n.m.* kapok-tree.

caporal, *n.m.* chief, ringleader; (*Am.*) headman in a ranch, chief cowherd; (*slang*) cock, rooster; (*mil.*) corporal.

capota, *n.f.* head of the teasel or fuller's thistle; woman's light bonnet; adjustable hood of some vehicles; collarless cape.

capotazo, *n.m.* (*tauro.*) flourish of the *capote.*

capote, *n.m.* sort of raglan or cloak with sleeves to keep off rain; short, bright-coloured cloak, used by bull-fighters; (*fig.*) brow-beating; (*mil.*) greatcoat; (*coll.*) thick mist or cloud; *capote de montar,* soldier's riding greatcoat; *capote de monte,* kind of poncho; *a* or *para mi capote,* in my opinion; *dar capote,* grand slam (at cards); *dar capote a uno,* to silence someone in argument; to leave a guest without dinner for coming late; *dije para mi capote,* I said to myself; *llevar uno capote,* to be without a trick at cards; (*Chi., Mex.*) deceived, ridiculed; *de capote,* (*Mex.*) secretly, hiddenly.

capotear, *v.t.* to trick a bull with a *capote;* (*fig.*) to wheedle, bamboozle, mock; to get out of a promise and difficulties.

capoteo, *n.m.* [CAPOTAZO].

capotera, *n.f.* (*Am.*) hat or clothes rack; (*Ven.*) travelling-bag made of canvas.

capotero, *n.m.* maker of *capotes.*

capotillo, *n.m.* cape, mantlet; *capotillo de dos faldas,* short, loose jacket, open at the sides.

capotín, *n.m.* small cloak or *capote.*

capotudo, -da, *a.* frowning.

caprario, -ria, *a.* capric, caprine.

caprico, -ca, *a.* (*chem.*) capric.

capricornio, *n.m.* (*astron.*) Capricorn.

capricho, *n.m.* caprice, fancy, whim, humour, conceit, mood; longing; (*mus., art*) caprice, fantasy.

caprichosamente, *adv.* fancifully, capriciously, moodily, whimsically, humorously.

caprichoso, -sa, *a.* capricious, fanciful, whimsical; (*art*) fantastic.

caprichudo, -da, *a.* capricious, stubborn, obstinate.

caprificación, *n.f.* caprification.

caprino, -na, *a.* (*poet.*) caprine, goatish.

caprípede; caprípedo, -da, *a.* (*poet.*) goat-footed.

caproico, -ca, *a.* (*chem.*) caproic.

capsicina, *n.f.* (*chem.*) capsicine.

cápsico, *n.m.* (*bot.*) capsicum.

capsueldo, *n.m.* (*prov.*) discount for payment in advance.

cápsula, *n.f.* metal cap on bottles; capsule; cartridge shell.

capsulación, *n.f.* (*pharm.*) making into capsules.

capsular, *a.* capsular. — *v.t.* to put a top on a bottle.

captación, *n.f.* captation.

captador, -ra, *a.* captivating, fascinating. — *n.m.f.* inveigler, one who captivates.

captar, *v.t.* to captivate, attract, win; to collect mineral waters at the springs. — *v.r.* to attract, win.

captatorio, -ria, *a.* (*law*) underhand, undue.

captura, *n.f.* (*law*) capture, seizure.

capturar, *v.t.* (*law*) to apprehend, arrest.

capuana, *n.f.* (*coll.*) spanking.

capuceta, *n.f.; capucete,* *n.m.* (*prov.*) act of ducking (a person).

capucha, *n.f.* hood of woman's cloak; friar's cowl or hood; (*print.*) circumflex (^) accent.

capuchino, -na, *n.m.f., a.* Capuchin monk, nun. — *n.f.* (*bot.*) nasturtium; portable lamp with extinguisher; a confection of yolk of egg. — *pl.* (*print.*) two or more frames joined together at the top.

capucho, *n.m.* capuche, cowl, hood.

capuchón, *n.m.* lady's evening cloak with hood; short domino [CAPUCHO].

capuleto, *n.m.* [CAPELETE].

capulí, *n.m.* (*Am.*) kind of cherry; (*Cub.*) a tree of the Tiliaceæ family; (*Per.*) fruit of a Solanaceæ plant resembling grape and of bitter-sweet taste.

capúlidos, *n.m.pl.* (*zool.*) family of the limpets (mollusca).

capulina, *n.f.* (*Am.*) fruit of the capulí; (*Cub.*) tiliaceous tree (capulí); (*Mex.*) poisonous black spider; (*Mex.*) prostitute, harlot.

capultamal, *n.m.* (*Mex.*) tamale of capulí.

capullito, *n.m.* small pod of a silkworm; small bud [CAPULLO].

capullo, *n.m.* cocoon; rosebud; bunch of boiled flax knotted at the end; acorn-cup; chestnut bur; coarse stuff of floss-silk; (*anat.*) prepuce; *seda de capullos,* or *de todo capullo,* floss-silk; *capullo ocal,* cocoon made by two or more silkworms together.

capuz, *n.m.* act of ducking a person; old-fashioned gala cloak with a hood; long mourning gown.

capuzar, *v.t.* to duck, throw into water; *capuzar un bajel,* to sink a ship by the head.

caquéctico, -ca, *a.* cachectic. — *n.m.f.* (*med.*) person suffering from cachexia.

caquexia, *n.f.* (*med.*) cachexia; (*bot.*) chlorosis, etiolation.

caqui, *n.m.* Japanese fruit-tree; khaki (material and colour).

caquino, *n.m.* (*Mex.*) guffaw, loud laughter.

car, *n.m.* (*naut.*) lower and thicker end of a lateen-yard.

cara, *n.f.* face, visage, countenance, mien; front, surface, façade, facing; base of a sugar-loaf; obverse; aspect, expression, look; manner, presence; (*geom.*) face, plane surface of a polyhedron. — *adv.* forward, towards; *cara adelante*, forward; *cara al sol*, facing the sun; *cara apedreada*, *empedrada* or *de rallo*, pock-marked face; *cara con dos haces*, double-face; *cara de gualda*, very pale person; *cara de juez* or *de justo juez*, stern face; *cara de perro*, surly face; *cara de pocos amigos* or *de vinagre*, churlish, frowning face; *cara y cruz*, game of pitch-and-toss; *cara de acelga*, pale, sallow face; *cara a cara*, face to face; *cara de cartón*, wrinkled face; *cara de hereje*, ugly fellow; *cara de aleluya*, *de Pascua* or *de risa*, smiling, cheerful face; *cara de vaqueta* or *de bronce*, serious, hostile face; brazen face; *cara de viernes* or *Viernes Santo*, sad, lean face; *buena cara*, cheerful face (or manner); *mala cara*, frowning, cross demeanour; *de cara*, opposite, facing; *a primera cara*, at first sight; *a cara descubierta*, publicly, openly; *andar a cara descubierta*, to act frankly; *caérsele a uno la cara de vergüenza*, to blush with shame; *cara de beato y uñas de gato*, hypocrite; *cruzar la cara a uno*, to smack someone's face; *dar la cara*, to face the consequences of one's actions; *dar, sacar uno la cara por otro*, to defend someone; to be responsible for someone; *dar a uno con las puertas en la cara*, to shut the door in someone's face; *dar, echar en cara*, to reproach, upbraid; *dar el sol de cara*, to have the sun in one's face; *decírselo en su cara*, to tell one to his face; *en la cara se le conoce* or *la cara se lo dice*, his face betrays him; *escupir en la cara a uno*, to mock, ridicule someone to his face; *estar mirando* or *mirar a la cara a uno*, to make the greatest efforts to please someone; *guardar la cara*, to hide; to evade; *hacer cara*, to face, fulfil, meet; to oppose, resist; *hacer a dos caras*, to act deceitfully; *hombre de dos caras*, double-dealer; deceitful man; *lavar la cara a uno*, to flatter someone; *lavar la cara a una cosa*, to clean, polish something; *mírame esta cara* or *la cara*, look at me well, I don't think you know me! *no conocer la cara al miedo, a la necesidad*, to be a stranger to or ignorant of fear, necessity; *no haber visto la cara al enemigo*, (*mil.*) not to have seen any fighting; *no mirar la cara a uno*, to be angry with someone; *no saber uno donde tiene la cara*, to be ignorant of one's profession; *no tener uno a quien volver la cara*, not to have anywhere to turn for help; *no tener cara para*, not to have courage for; *no volver la cara atrás*, not to flinch; *poner buena* or *mala cara*, to welcome or disapprove of; *por su bella* or *linda cara*, (*iron.*) for his good looks; *sacar uno la cara*, to show one's face; *salir a la cara*, to show in one's face; to be ashamed; *saltar a la cara*, to fly in the face of; to be self-evident; *si me quiere, con esta cara; si no, vaya*, take me as you find me; *su cara defiende su casa*, his face is ugly enough to frighten anyone; *tener una cara de corcho*, to be brazen-faced; *tener cara para hacer una cosa*, to have the face (courage) to do something; *terciar a la cara a uno*, to scar someone's face; *verse las caras*, to have a crow to pluck with anyone; *volver a la cara una cosa*, to return a thing with contempt; *volver a la cara las palabras, las injurias*, to retort, return abusive language;

volver la cara al enemigo, to rally and face the enemy again.

cáraba, *n.f.* vessel used in the Levant.

carabalí, *a.* untameable as a Negro from Carabalí (Africa).

carabao, *n.m.* (*Philip.*) caraboo, buffalo.

cárabe, *n.m.* amber.

carabela, *n.f.* (*naut.*) carvel, caravel; (*prov.*) large basket or tray for provisions.

carabelón, *n.m.* (*naut.*) small caravel.

carábico, -ca, *a.* (*entom.*) similar or relating to the beetle.

carabina, *n.f.* fowling-piece; carbine, carabine; (*coll., Madrid*) chaperon; *carabina rayada*, rifle carbine; *ser (una cosa) la carabina de Ambrosio*, thing of no use.

carabinazo, *n.m.* report, firing of a carbine; effect, damage of a carbine-shot.

carabinero, *n.m.* carabineer; inland revenue, excise, customs guard.

carablanca, *n.m.* (*Col., CR.*) monkey of the genus Cebus; (*Col.*, also *mico maicero*).

cárabo, *n.m.* small Moorish vessel; (*entom.*) beetle; (*orn.*) large horned owl; kind of setter dog.

carabú, *n.m.* handsome Indian tree.

caraca, *n.f.* (*Cub.*) cake made of maize.

caracal, *n.m.* (*Am.*) kind of lynx.

caracará, *a.* (*Par.*) applied to an Indian tribe living on the banks of the river Paraná; (*Arg.*) bird of prey belonging to the Falconidæ family.

caracas, *n.m.* (*Ven.*) cacao from the coast of Caracas; (*coll.*) (*Mex.*) chocolate. — *n.m.pl.* tribe of the Guaraní.

caracatcy, *n.m.* (*Cub.*) crepuscular bird which feeds on mosquitoes, etc.

caracoa, *n.f.* (*Philip.*) small rowing-barge.

caracol, *n.m.* (*zool.*) snail; any spiral shell; (*mech.*) snail-wheel; (*arch., equit.*) caracole; (*anat.*) cochlea; twisted coil of hair worn on the temples; (*Mex.*) nightdress worn by women; (*Mex.*) embroidered blouse; *¡caracoles!* (*interj., coll.*) ha! bah! *hacer caracoles*, to reel, stagger; *no se le da, no importa, no vale un caracol* or *dos caracoles*, it does not matter in the least.

caracola, *n.f.* (*prov.*) small snail with whitish shell; conch-shell used as a horn.

caracolada, *n.f.* dish of snails.

caracolear, *v.i.* (*equit.*) to caracole.

caracolejo, *n.m.* small snail.

caracoleo, *n.m.* the act of caracoling; caracole.

caracolero, -ra, *n.m.f.* snail-gatherer, snail-seller.

caracolilla, *n.f.* small snail-shell [CARACOLA].

caracolillo, *n.m.* snail-flowered kidney-bean; veined mahogany; *café caracolillo*, pea-bean coffee. — *pl.* shell-like fringes, trimmings on clothes.

caracolito, *n.m.* small snail [CARACOL].

carácter, *n.m.* (*pl.* **caracteres**) character, reputation, standing, capacity, personal qualities, manners, temperament, humour, disposition, nature; firmness, energy, moral or spiritual nobility; handwriting, written sign, letter; mark, brand (on animals); character, type; style of speaking or writing; *de medio carácter*, of insufficiently defined characteristics (music, literature); *en su carácter de*, in his capacity as; *una mujer de buen* or *mal carácter*, a good- or bad-tempered woman; *caracteres de imprenta*, printing types.

caracterismo, *n.m.* characteristics.

característica, *n.f.* actress who plays the part of old ladies; feature, fundamental property; (*math.*) characteristic, logarithmic number preceding the period that divides the decimal fraction.

característicamente, *adv.* characteristically.

característico, -ca, *a.* characteristic, typical, distinctive. — *n.m.* actor playing old people's parts.

caracterizable, *a.* that may be characterized.

caracterizado, -da, *a.* charactered, characterized; distinguished, authorized, responsible; apt, competent. — *p.p.* [CARACTE-RIZAR].

caracterizar, *v.t.* (*pret.* **caractericé**; *pres. subj.* **caracterice**) to characterize, distinguish by peculiar qualities; to confer a distinguished employment, dignity or office; to act a part properly; to mark, point out.

caracú, *n.m.* (*Arg.*) race of cattle bred specially for meat.

caracha, *n.f.;* **carache**, *n.m.* (*Chi., Per.*) itch, scab; (*Per.*) mange of llamas.

carado, -da, *a.* found only in the compounds *biencarado, -da*, pleasant, cheerful; *malcarado, -da*, frowning, churlish, harsh.

caraguatá, *n.f.* (*Par.*) sisal.

caraguay, *n.m.* (*Bol.*) a large lizard.

caraira, *n.f.* (*Cub.*) diurnal bird of prey, kind of sparrow-hawk.

caraja, *n.f.* (*Mex.*) sail used by Veracruz fishermen.

caramanchel, *n.m.* (*naut.*) shed over the hatchways; (*Arg.*) eating house, lunch room; (*Chi.*) canteen; (*Col.*) den, low place; (*Ec.*) hawker's or pedlar's basket.

caramanchelero, *n.m.* (*Am. Mer.*) hawker, pedlar.

caramanchón, *n.m.* garret.

caramayola, *n.f.* (*Chi.*) (*mil.*) water-bottle.

¡caramba! *interj.* (*coll.*) ha! dear me! good gracious! — *n.f.* ancient headgear for women.

carambanado, -da, *a.* frozen, forming icicles.

carámbano, *n.m.* icicle, shoot of ice.

carambillo, *n.m.* (*bot.*) salt-wort.

carambola, *n.f.* carambole, cannon (in billiards); method of playing the card game called *revesino;* (*coll.*) double result from one act; (*coll.*) trick to deceive; (*bot.*) fruit of the *carambolo* tree; *por carambola*, (*coll.*) indirectly. — *interj.* [CARAMBA].

carambolaje, *n.m.* cannon (in billiards).

caramboleado, -da, *a.* cannoned. — *p.p.* [CARAMBOLEAR].

carambolear, *v.t.* to cannon (at billiards).

carambolero, *n.m.* player at *carambola*.

carambolista, *n.m.f.* good at making cannons (billiards).

carambolo, *n.m.* carambola-tree.

caramel, *n.m.* kind of pilchard or sardine.

caramelización, *n.f.* conversion of sugar to caramel.

caramelizar, *v.t., v.r.* to convert into caramel.

caramelo, *n.m.* caramel (sweetmeat); burnt sugar.

caramente, *adv.* dearly, expensively; exceedingly, highly; (*law*) rigorously.

caramera, *n.f.* (*Ven.*) badly fitting dental plate.

caramiello, *n.m.* kind of hat worn by women in Leon and Asturias.

caramillar, *n.m.* salt-wort plantation.

caramilleras, *n.f.pl.* (*prov.*) pot-hooks.

caramillo, *n.m.* flageolet, small flute; (*bot.*) salt-wort; deceit, trick; gossip, tale-telling; confused heap of things; *armar* or *levantar un caramillo*, to make mischief.

caramilloso, -sa, *a.* (*fam.*) peevish, touchy.

caramuzal, *n.m.* vessel used by the Turks.

carancho, *n.m.* (*Arg., Bol.*) bird of prey belonging to the Falconidæ family; (*Per.*) owl.

carandaí, *n.m.* (*Arg.*) tall palm-tree.

caranegra, *n.m.f.* (*Arg.*) a race of sheep with black faces; (*Col., CR., Ven.*) black-faced monkey of the Ateles group.

caranga, *n.f.;* **carángano**, *n.m.* louse.

carantamaula, *n.f.* (*coll.*) hideous mask; (*coll.*) ugly, hard-featured person.

carantoña, *n.f.* (*coll.*) old and ugly woman, who dresses up as though she were young. — *pl.* caresses, soft words, acts of endearment.

carantoñero, -ra, *n.m.f.* (*fam.*) flatterer, wheedler, cajoler.

caraña, *n.f.* (*CR.*) tree and resinous gum.

caráota, *n.f.* (*Ven.*) french bean.

carapacho, *n.m.* carapace; shell (of crustaceans); (*Cub.*) shell-fish cooked in the shell; (*Per.*) tribe of Indians of the Huánaco.

carapato, *n.m.* castor oil.

¡carape! *interj.* [CARAMBA].

carapucho, *n.m.* (*Per.*) gramineous plant whose intoxicating seeds produce delirium tremens.

carapulca, *n.f.* (*Per.*) dish made of meat, dry potato and chilli.

caraqueño, -na, *a.* of or belonging to Caracas.

carasol, *n.m.* sunny place, sun-gallery.

carate, *n.m.* (*Am. Cent.*) disease attacking the negroes.

carátula, *n.f.* mask, hideous face; (*fig.*) the histrionic art; bee-net.

caratulero, *n.m.* maker or seller of masks.

carava, *n.f.* holiday meeting of country people.

caravana, *n.f.* caravan; company of pilgrims or traders.

caravanera, *n.f.* caravanserai.

caravanero, *n.m.* caravaneer.

caravanista, *n.m.f.* caravanist.

caravanseray; caravanserrallo, *n.m.* caravanserai.

caray, *n.m.* tortoise-shell. — *interj.* ha! dear me!

carayá, *n.m.* (*Arg., Col.*) howling monkey.

caraza, *n.f.* large broad face [CARA].

cárbaso, *n.m.* kind of fine linen; ancient tunic made of this linen; (*poet.*) sail of a ship.

carbinol, *n.m.* methylic alcohol.

carbol, *n.m.* phenol, carbolic acid.

carbólico, -ca, *a.* carbolic.

carbón, *n.m.* coal, fuel, charcoal; cinder; crayon, carbon-pencil; carbon (arc lamp); coal-brand, wheat-smut; *carbón animal*, bone-black; *carbón de arranque*, root, charcoal; *carbón de canutillo*, charcoal of thin branches; *carbón mineral* or *de piedra*, coal, pit-coal; *carbón vegetal*, charcoal.

carbonada, *n.f.* coal charge put into a furnace; broiled chop or steak; grillade; kind of pancake.

carbonado, -da, *a.* carbonaceous; carbonized. — *n.m.* black diamond. — *p.p.* [CARBONAR].

carbonalla, *n.f.* mixture of coal, sand and clay (used for floor of reverberatory-furnaces).

carbonar, *v.t.* to carbonize. — *v.r.* to become carbonized.

carbonatado, -da, *a.* carbonated. — *p.p.* [CARBONATAR].

carbonatar, *v.t.* to carbonate. — *v.r.* to become carbonated.

carbonato, *n.m.* carbonate.

carboncillo, *n.m.* black crayon; carbon-pencil; (*bot.*) mushroom; variety of black sand.

carbonear, *v.t.* to char, make into charcoal.

carboneo, *n.m.* carbonization; charcoal-making, charring.

carbonera, *n.f.* wood prepared for burning into charcoal; coal house, coal cellar; woman who sells charcoal; (*Col.*) coal mine; (*Chi.*) tender of a locomotive; (*Hond.*) a garden plant; (*naut.*) common name of the main staysail.

carbonería, *n.f.* coal-yard, coal-shed, coal-shop.

carbonero, -ra, *a.* relating to coal or charcoal. — *n.m.* (*orn.*) colemouse, coal-titmouse; charcoal-maker or -seller; collier, coal-man, coal-miner; coal-merchant; (*Cub.*) tree with very hard wood.

carbónico, -ca, *a.* carbonic.

carbónidos, *n.m.pl.* carbon and its compounds.

carbonífero, -ra, *a.* carboniferous, coal-bearing.

carbonilla, *n.f.* coal-dust; cinder.

carbonización, *n.f.* carbonization.

carbonizado, -da *a.* carbonized, charred. — *p.p.* [CARBONIZAR].

carbonizar, *v.t.* (*pret.* **carbonicé;** *pres. subj.* **carbonice**) to carbonize, char. — *v.r.* to become carbonized, charred.

carbono, *n.m.* carbon.

carbonoso, -sa, *a.* carbonaceous, coaly.

carborundo, *n.m.* (*chem.*) carborundum.

carbuncal, *a.* carbuncular.

carbunclo; carbunco, *n.m.* carbuncle, a precious stone; carbuncle, anthrax.

carbuncoso, -sa, *a.* carbuncular.

carbúnculo, *n.m.* carbuncle, a precious stone.

carburación, *n.f.* carburization.

carburador, *n.m.* carburettor.

carburante, *a.* containing carbon-hydrate. — *n.m.* carburet.

carburar, *v.t.* to carburet, carburize.

carburo, *n.m.* (*chem.*) carbide; carburet.

carca, *n.m.*, *a.* contemptuous name applied to a Carlist.

carcaj; carcax, *n.m.; carcaza,* *n.f.* quiver; case in which the cross may be borne in a procession; Moorish anklet; (*Am.*) leather case for a rifle at the saddle bow.

carcajada, *n.f.* cachinnation, guffaw.

carcamal, *n.m.*, *a.* (*coll.*) decrepit old person.

carcamán, *n.m.* heavy, big unseaworthy vessel; (*Cub.*) foreigner of low status; (*Per.*) presumptuous, conceited, but unworthy person; (*Arg.*) Italian and especially Genoese.

cárcamo, *n.m.* hollow in which a water-wheel turns.

carcañal; calcañar, *n.m.* heel-bone, calcaneum.

cárcava; carcavina, *n.f.* gully made by tor-

rents of water; hedge; ditch; grave; mound; (*mil.*) enclosure.

cárcavo, *n.m.* [CÁRCAMO]; (*obs.*) pit or cavity of the abdomen.

carcavón, *n.m.* large, deep ditch [CÁRCAVA].

carcavuezo, *n.m.* deep pit.

carcax, *n.m.; carcaza,* *n.f.* [CARCAJ].

cárcel, *n.f.* prison, gaol; coulisse (of a sluice-gate); (*carp.*) clamp, cramp, clasp; (*print.*) cheek of a printing-press.

carcelaje; carceraje, *n.m.* gaoler's fees, prison fees.

carcelario, -ria, *a.* relating to a prison.

carcelería, *n.f.* imprisonment; bail offered for a prisoner; *guardar carcelería,* to be forced to keep within certain bounds (a prisoner).

carcelero, -ra, *a.* [CARCELARIO]; *fiador carcelero,* one who is bail or surety for a prisoner; *fianza carcelera,* bail, surety. — *n.m.* gaoler, keeper, warder. — *n.f.* gaoleress, wardress; popular Andalusian song dealing with prisoner's tribulations.

carcinoma, *n.f.* carcinoma.

carcinomatoso, -sa, *a.* carcinomatous.

carcinosis, *n.f.* carcinosis.

cárcola, *n.f.* treadle of a loom.

carcoma, *n.f.* death-watch beetle, wood-borer, wood-fretter; dust made by wood-borer; (*fig.*) grief, concern worry; spendthrift, prodigal; (*slang*) road, highway, footpath.

carcomer, *v.t.* to gnaw, corrode (of the wood-borer); to consume by degrees; to impair gradually. — *v.r.* to become worm-eaten.

carcomido, -da, *a.* worm-eaten; consumed; decayed, declined, impaired. — *p.p.* [CARCOMER].

carda, *n.f.* carding; card (instrument); (*bot.*) card-thistle, teasel; (*coll.*) severe reproof, censure; (*naut.*) small vessel like a galley; *gente de* (*la*) *carda,* bullies, ruffians; *dar una carda,* to reprimand severely; *todos somos de la carda,* we all belong to the same class (used contemptuously).

cardada, *n.f.* portion of wool carded at one operation.

cardadería; cardería, *n.f.* carding factory; card factory.

cardado, -da, *a.* carded, teased; combed. — *p.p.* [CARDAR].

cardador, -ra, *n.m.f.* carder, comber. — *n.m.* (*entom.*) myriapod.

cardadura, *n.f.* carding, combing (of wool).

cardamina, *n.f.* cardamine, lady's smock, cuckoo-flower.

cardamomo, *n.m.* cardamom.

cardar, *v.t.* to card or comb wool; to teasel; *cardarle a uno la lana,* to reprimand someone bitterly and severely; to win a large amount from someone at gambling.

cardelina, *n.f.* goldfinch.

cardenal, *n.m.* (*eccl.*) cardinal; (*orn.*) Virginia nightingale; cardinal-bird; weal raised by flogging; lividity.

cardenalato, *n.m.* cardinalate, cardinalship.

cardenalicio, -cia, *a.* belonging to a cardinal.

cardencha, *n.f.* (*bot.*) teasel; comb, card (instrument).

cardenchal, *n.m.* place where the teasels grow.

cardenchoso, -sa, *a.* like the teasel.

cardenillo, *n.m.* verdigris; paris green.

cárdeno, -na, *a.* livid; piebald (bull); opaline (water); *lirio cárdeno,* (*bot.*) purple iris.

cardería, *n.f.* [CARDADERÍA].

cardero, *n.m.* card-maker.

cardíaca, *n.f.* common motherwort.

cardiáceo, -cea, *a.* cardiac, heart-shaped.

cardíaco, -ca, *a.* cardiac, cardiacal; suffering from heart-disease. — *n.m.f.* person suffering from heart-disease.

cardialgia, *n.f.* cardialgy, heart-burn.

cardiálgico, -ca, *a.* cardialgic.

cardias, *n.m.* the upper or cardiac orifice of the stomach.

cardico; cardillo; cardito, *n.m.* small thistle.

cardillar, *n.m.* place where *cardillos* abound.

cardillo, *n.m.* golden thistle.

cardinal, *a.* cardinal (point); principal, fundamental.

cardiografía, *n.f.* cardiography.

cardiógrafo, *n.m.* cardiograph.

cardiología, *n.f.* cardiology.

cardítico, -ca, *a.* cardiac.

cardizal, *n.m.* land covered with thistles and weeds.

cardo, *n.m.* thistle; (*Par.*) sisal; *cardo alcachofero,* garden artichoke; *cardo ajonjero* or *aljonjero,* carline thistle; *cardo bendito* or *santo,* blessed thistle, centaury; *cardo corredor, estelado* or *setero,* creeping thistle, erigeron; *cardo huso,* bastard saffron; *cardo lechero* or *mariano,* milk-thistle; *cardo silvestre* or *borriqueño,* spear-plume thistle; *más áspero que un cardo,* harsher than a thistle (said of a disagreeable person).

cardón, *n.m.* (*bot.*) teasel; carding, teaseling.

Cardona, *n.pr.; más listo que Cardona,* said of a very clever fellow. — *n.f.* (*Cub.*) species of cactus growing on the coast.

cardonal, *n.m.* (*Arg., Chi., Ven.*) place abounding in thistles.

cardoncillo, *n.m.* milk-thistle.

carducha, *n.f.* large iron comb or card (for wool).

cardume; cardumen, *n.m.* shoal of fishes.

carduzador, -ra, *n.m.f.* carder; (*slang*) fence, receiver of stolen goods.

carduzal, *n.m.* [CARDIZAL].

carduzar, *v.t.* (*pret.* **carducé;** *pres. subj.* **carduce**) to card or comb wool.

carear, *v.t.* (*law*) to confront criminals; (*fig.*) to compare; to tend a flock of sheep or a drove of cattle; to clean the base of a sugarloaf. — *v.r.* to assemble, meet; to come face to face.

carecer, *v.i.* (*pres. indic.* **carezco;** *pres. subj.* **carezca**) to want, be wanting, need, lack; *carecer de medios,* to lack means; *la necesidad carece de ley,* necessity knows no law.

careciente, *a.* lacking.

carecimiento, *n.m.* [CARENCIA].

carena, *n.f.* (*naut.*) careenage, careening; (*coll.*) banter; *dar carena,* (*coll.*) to banter, reprove in jest; to blame.

carenadura, *n.f.* careenage.

carenar, *v.t.* (*naut.*) to careen; to repair a ship's hull; *carenar de firme,* to overhaul a ship completely.

carencia, *n.f.* need, want, lack, deprivation.

carenero, *n.m.* (*naut.*) careenage, careening-place.

careo, *n.m.* (*law*) confrontation of criminals or witnesses; act of meeting or bringing face to face; comparison; (*prov.*) corn-plot for hog-feeding; (*prov.*) fodder; (*prov.*) gossip, chat.

carero, -ra, *a.* (*coll.*) selling dearly, expensively.

carestía, *n.f.* scarcity, want, famine; high price, dearness.

careta, *n.f.* mask; (*fencing*) face-guard; beekeeper's wire face-covering; *quitarle a uno la careta,* to unmask, expose.

careto, -ta, *a.* having the forehead marked with a white spot or stripe (of horses).

carey, *n.m.* tortoise-shell turtle; tortoise-shell.

carezco, carezca, *pres. indic., pres. subj.* [CARECER].

carga, *n.f.* load, burden; freight, cargo, lading; charge (of fire-arms, mines, furnaces, etc.); nozzle of a flask to measure powder for charges; a corn measure of about 6 bushels; (*fig.*) duty, impost, imposition, toll, tax; (*fig.*) mental burden, heaviness; weight, load, pressure; hindrance, encumbrance; (*mil.*) charge, attack; (*vet.*) poultice; *a cargas,* abundantly, in great plenty; *bestia de carga,* beast of burden; *carga abierta,* bayonet or sword charge in open formation; *carga a fondo* or *de petral,* cavalry charge against cavalry; *carga cerrada,* bayonet or sword charge in close formation; (*mil.*) volley; (*coll.*) severe reprimand; *a carga cerrada,* in bulk; without reflection or consideration; all at once; *carga concejil* or *vecinal,* municipal office or obligatory service; *carga de caballería,* cavalry charge; *carga fija,* (*eng.*) dead load; *carga de fractura* or *de rotura,* breaking load; *carga hidrostática,* (*hydr.*) head; *carga mayor,* burden suitable for horse or mule; *carga menor,* load suitable for an ass; *cargo móvil,* (*eng.*) live load; *carga personal,* obligatory personal service; *carga real,* king's tax, land tax; *acodillar uno con la carga,* to sink down under a burden; to be unable to fulfil one's duties; *echar uno la carga a otro,* to transfer the hardest part to another; *echar uno la carga de sí,* to avoid a duty or responsibility; *echar uno las cargas a otro,* to throw the blame upon another; *echarse uno con la carga,* to give up in despair; *llevar una la carga,* to assume responsibilities; *sentarse la carga,* to chafe (the load on a beast of burden); (*coll.*) to become annoying (a duty or undertaking); *ser de ciento en carga (una cosa),* to be ordinary, of little value; *ser en carga,* to annoy, irritate; *soltar uno la carga,* to throw off a duty or responsibility; *terciar la carga,* to divide the load; *volver a la carga,* to insist on a thing; to harp on a subject.

cargable, *a.* that can be loaded.

cargadal, *n.m.* (*prov.*) silt in rivers and drains.

cargadamente, *adv.* heavily.

cargadas, *n.f.pl.* card game.

cargadera, *n.f.* (*naut.*) down-haul, brail; (*Col.*) suspenders.

cargadero, *n.m.* loading or unloading place; (*arch.*) lintel.

cargadilla, *n.f.* (*coll.*) increase of a debt through accumulation of interest.

cargadizo, -za, *a.* that can be loaded.

cargado, -da, *a.* loaded, full; fraught; sultry (weather); pregnant (sheep); strong (tea, coffee, etc.); *cargado de espaldas,* round-shouldered, stooping; *cargado de vino,* tipsy, drunk. — *n.m.* Spanish step in dancing.— *p.p.* [CARGAR].

cargador, *n.m.* merchant; shipper, freighter; (*Guat., Mex., Per.*) carrier, loader, porter; (*arch.*) post put in a door or window; pitchfork for straw; rammer, ramrod.

cargamento, *n.m.* (*naut.*) cargo.

cargante, *a.* annoying, burdensome.

cargar, *v.t.* (*pret.* **cargué**; *pres. subj.* **cargue**) to burden, load, freight; to charge, load (fire-arms, furnace, battery, etc.); to lay in a large stock; to overload, overweight; to impose (tax, duty, obligation); to impute, charge, arraign, impeach; to take a card with a higher one; to raise the stake (card games); (*fig.*) to vex, molest, annoy, worry, tease; (*com.*) to debit, book, charge to account; (*naut.*) to furl or unfurl; (*mil.*) to charge, attack; (*vet.*) to poultice. — *v.i.* to lean, incline towards; to undertake a charge or trust; to carry a load; to maintain, support; to rest or lean on; (*bot.*) to bear much fruit; to crowd together (people); (*gram.*) to stress one letter or syllable more than the rest; (with *con*) to take away; (with *sobre*) to throw the blame on; (with *sobre*) to urge, pester, importunate. — *v.r.* to lean (the body) towards; to incline towards; (*com.*) to agree with the sum debited to one's account; to become cloudy, denser or heavier (weather); to become peevish, vexed, tired; (with *de*) to become full, overburdened; *cargar de leña a alguno*, to thrash someone with a stick; *cargar la mano*, to pursue something eagerly; to overcharge; to be very strict; *cargar arriba una vela*, (*naut.*) to clew up a sail; *el viento se ha cargado al norte*, the wind has veered to the north; *cargársele a uno la cabeza*, to feel drowsy; *cargar delantero*, to be intoxicated; *cargar demasiado* or *mucho*, to overeat, drink too much; *cargar a flete*, to ship goods on freight; *cargar a, en hombros*, to carry on the shoulders; *cargar con todo*, to take away everything; *cargarse de razón*, to proceed deliberately, carefully; *cargar la conciencia*, to burden one's conscience with sin; *cargar el juicio en*, to reflect attentively on; *cargar los dados*, to cog dice; *cargar uno la mano en una cosa*, to use an ingredient in excess (in cookery, medicine).

cargareme, *n.m.* receipt, voucher.

cargazón, *n.f.* cargo; heaviness in any part of the body; cloudiness; (*Arg.*) work done in a clumsy way; (*Chi.*) abundance of fruit on trees, plants, etc.; *cargazón de cabeza*, heaviness of the head; *cargazón de tiempo*, cloudy, thick weather.

cargo, *n.m.* act of loading; load, weight, burden; number of baskets filled with crushed olives and piled one on the other and put in the oil-press; load of stones of one-third cubic metre; load of pressed grapes for repressing; (*com.*) total receipts; charge, accusation; (*law*) count; employment, office, dignity, honour; (*Chi.*) (*law*) certificate issued by the court and appended to legal documents indicating date and hour of receipt; care, charge, keeping; duty or obligation; ministry; command; management; fault or deficiency of duty; *cargo concejil*, compulsory municipal office; *cargo de conciencia*, remorse, sense of guilt; *cargo*

y data, (*com.*) creditor and debtor; *hacer cargo a uno de una cosa*, to charge one with a fault; to hold one responsible; *hacerse cargo de una cosa*, to take into consideration; to make oneself acquainted with something; to take something upon oneself; *ser uno en cargo a otro*, to be indebted to someone.

cargoso, -sa, *a.* heavy, grave, annoying, vexatious.

carguero, -ra, *a.* burden-bearing, freight-carrying; (*Arg.*) beast of burden.

carguío, *n.m.* cargo, freight; load.

cari, *a.* (*Arg., Chi.*) light brown colour; *n.m.* (*Am.*) blackberry; (*Arg.*) kind of poncho; (*Chi.*) Indian pepper.

caria, *n.f.* (*arch.*) shaft of column.

cariacedo, -da, *a.* disagreeable, ill-tempered.

cariaco, *n.m.* (*Cub.*) popular dance; (*Ec.*) beverage made from sugar-cane.

cariacontecido, -da, *a.* sad, mournful (face).

cariacos, *n.m.pl.* (*ethn.*) Caribs.

cariacuchillado, -da, *a.* scarred (face).

cariado, -da, *a.* carious, rotten. — *p.p.* [CARIARSE].

cariadura, *n.f.* (*med.*) caries.

cariaguileño, -ña, *a.* long-faced with aquiline or hooked nose.

carialegre, *a.* smiling, cheerful.

carialzado, -da, *a.* with uplifted face.

cariampollado, -da; cariampollar, *a.* round-faced, plump-cheeked.

cariancho, -cha, *a.* broad-faced, chubby, chub-faced.

cariarse, *v.r.* (*med.*) to become carious.

cariátide, *n.f.* (*arch.*) caryatid.

caríbal, *n.m.* cannibal, man-eater.

caribe, *n.m.f.*, *a.* Carib, Indian of the Antilles. — *n.m.* language of the Caribs; (*fig.*) cruel and inhuman man.

caribello, *a.* having white spots on the forehead (bull).

caribito, *n.m.* river fish of the bream species.

cariblanco, *n.m.* (*CR.*) small wild boar.

caribobo, -ba, *a.* stupid-looking.

caribú, *n.m.* caribou, cariboo.

carica, *n.f.* (*prov.*) sort of spotted kidney bean.

caricato, *n.m.* opera buffoon.

caricatura, *n.f.* caricature.

caricatural, *a.* caricatural.

caricaturar; caricaturizar, *v.t.* to caricature.

caricaturesco, -ca, *a.* caricatural.

caricaturista, *n.m.f.* caricaturist.

caricia, *n.f.* caress, petting; endearing expression; (*slang*) expensive thing.

cariciosamente, *adv.* caressingly, endearingly.

caricioso, -sa, *a.* fondling, endearing, caressing.

caricompuesto, -ta, *a.* with composed, circumspect face.

caricorto, -ta, *a.* small-featured.

caricoso, -sa, *a.* fig-shaped.

caricuerdo, -da, *a.* with a grave, reserved expression.

carichato, -ta, *a.* flat-faced.

caridad, *n.f.* charity, charitableness, kindness, benevolence, love; alms, refreshment given to travellers; *la caridad bien ordenada empieza por uno mismo*, charity begins at home.

caridelantero, -ra, *a.* (*coll.*) brazen-faced, impudent.

caridoliente, *a.* pained-looking.

cariedón, *n.m.* nut-weevil.

carientismo, *n.m.* (*rhet.*) dissimulated irony.

caries, *n.f.* (*med.*) caries; (*agric.*) smut, wheat-rust; *caries seca,* (*bot.*) caries.

cariexento, -ta, *a.* (*fam.*) shameless, brazen-faced.

carifruncido, -da, *a.* (*coll.*) cross-looking, frowning, wrinkled (face).

carigordo, -da, *a.* (*coll.*) full-faced; puffy.

cariharto, -ta, *a.* round-faced.

carihermoso, -sa, *a.* beautiful, handsome.

carijusto, -ta, *a.* hypocritical.

carilamido, -da, *a.* much kissed, petted.

carilampiño, *a.* (*Chi., Per.*) smooth-faced, beardless.

carilargo, -ga, *a.* long-faced.

carilavado, -da, *a.* [CARILUCIO].

carilucio, -cia, *a.* (*coll.*) shiny-faced.

carilla, *n.f.* bee-keeper's mask; page (of book); silver coin (Aragonese) worth eighteen *dinerillos.*

carilleno, -na, *a.* (*coll.*) plump-faced.

carillo, -lla, *a.* rather dear, expensive; loved, cherished. — *n.m.f.* beloved, betrothed, lover.

carillón, *n.m.* (*mus.*) carillon.

carimba, *n.f.* (*Per.*) branding mark on slaves; (*Cub.*) branding-iron (animals).

carimbo, *n.m.* (*Bol.*) branding-iron.

carinegro, -gra, *a.* dark, swarthy-complexioned.

carininfo, -fa, *a.* with girlish face, effeminate.

cariñana, *n.f.* ancient head-dress resembling a nun's wimple.

cariñar, *v.i.* (*prov.*) to be homesick.

cariñena, *n.f.* sweet red wine from Aragon.

cariño, *n.m.* love, affection, tenderness, fondness, kindness, solicitude; (*pl.*) tender or endearing expressions.

cariñosamente, *adv.* fondly, kindly, affectionately.

cariñoso, -sa, *a.* affectionate, loving, endearing, benevolent, good, kind.

caripálido, -da, *a.* pale-faced.

caripando, -da, *a.* foolish-looking.

cariparejo, -ja, *a.* (*coll.*) of an impassive countenance.

carirraído, -da, *a.* (*coll.*) brazen-faced, impudent.

carirrechoncho, -cha, *a.* (*fam.*) [CARIGORDO].

carirredondo, -da, *a.* round-faced.

carirromo, -ma, *a.* small-featured.

cariseto, *n.m.* coarse woollen cloth.

carisma, *n.m.* divine gift, grace or favour.

carita, *n.f.* small face.

caritán, *n.m.* (*Philip.*) gatherer of tuba.

caritativamente, *adv.* charitably.

caritativo, -va, *a.* benevolent, charitable, hospitable.

carite, *n.m.* (*Cub.*) species of sawfish.

caritieso, -sa, *a.* severe, austere.

cariucho, *n.m.* (*Ec.*) Indian national dish.

cariz, *n.m.* aspect of the atmosphere or of the horizon; (*coll.*) aspect (of an affair or reunion).

carla, *n.f.* coloured cloth.

carlán, *n.m.* person with certain rights and jurisdiction of a district in Aragon.

carlanca, *n.f.* mastiff's collar with spikes; (*slang*) shirt-collar; (*Col., CR.*) shackle, fetter; (*Ec.*) appliance placed on animals'

heads to prevent them entering cultivated fields; (*Chi., Hond.*) burdensome, onerous person. — *pl.* roguery, trickery; *tener muchas carlancas,* to be very cunning and crafty.

carlanco, -ca; carlancón, -na, *n.m.f., a.* cunning and crafty (person).

carlanga, *n.f.* (*Mex.*) rag, tatter.

carlanía, *n.f.* dignity and district of a *carlán.*

carlear, *v.i.* to pant.

carleta, *n.f.* file for smoothing (iron); (*min.*) Anjou slate.

carlín, *n.m.* an ancient silver coin.

carlina, *n.f.* carline thistle.

carlinga, *n.f.* (*naut.*) step of a mast.

carlismo, *n.m.* Carlism.

carlista, *n.m.f., a.* Carlist.

carlita, *n.f.* reading-glasses.

Carlos, *n.m.* Charles.

carlota, *n.f.* Charlotte pudding.

carlovingio, -gia, *n.m.f., a.* Carolingian.

carmañola, *n.f.* kind of jacket with narrow collar; carmagnole (song).

carme, *n.m.* (*prov.*) country-house and garden.

carmel, *n.m.* variety of plantain.

carmelina, *n.f.* second quality vicunia wool.

carmelita, *n.m.f., a.* Carmelite. — *n.f.* nasturtium flower. — *a.* (*Cub., Chi.*) hazel, brown.

carmelitano, -na, *a.* belonging to the order of the Carmelites.

carmen, *n.m.* (*prov.*) country-house and garden; villa; Carmelite order; verse, poem.

carmenador, *n.m.* teaser, comber (workman or machine); carding-engine or machine.

carmenadura, *n.f.* teasing (wool, silk, etc.).

carmenar, *v.t.* to tease, card, unravel wool or silk; to comb, disentangle hair; (*coll.*) to pull the hair; (*coll.*) to rob, cheat of valuables.

carmes, *n.m.* (*entom.*) kermes.

carmesí, *a.* carmine, scarlet, bright red. — *n.m.* cochineal powder; crimson, scarlet, bright red; red silk material.

carmín, *n.m.* carmine, colouring matter of cochineal; carmine (colour); (*bot.*) wild red rose; *carmín bajo,* pale rose-colour.

carminativo, -va, *n.m.f., a.* (*med.*) carminative.

carminoso, -sa, *a.* reddish.

carnación, *n.f.* carmine; (*her., paint.*) carnation.

carnada, *n.f.* bait; (*coll.*) artifice, trap.

carnadura, *n.f.* muscularity, robustness; (*surg.*) incarnation.

carnaje, *n.m.* salt beef; carnage.

carnal, *a.* carnal, sensual lustful, fleshly; (*fig.*) earthly, worldly; united by relationship; *primo carnal,* cousin-german. — *n.m.* time of the year when fasting or abstinence is not prescribed.

carnalidad, *n.f.* carnality, lustfulness.

carnalmente, *adv.* carnally, sensually, lust fully.

carnaval, *n.m.* carnival, feast held before Lent.

carnavalada, *n.f.* amusement or joke proper to carnival.

carnavalesco, -ca, *a.* belonging to or resembling carnival.

carnaza, *n.f.* fleshy side of a hide or skin; bait; (*coll.*) corpulence; (*Col., CR., Hond., Mex.*) *echar a uno de carnaza,* (*coll.*) to hold the baby.

carne, *n.f.* flesh, flesh-meat (food); pulp (of fruit); flesh, one of the evil temptations;

fleshly part of man as distinguished from the spiritual; kith and kin; concave part of knuckle-bone in the game of knuckle bones; *carne ahogadiza*, meat of a drowned animal; *carne asada en horno*, oven-roasted meat; *carne asada en parrillas*, broiled meat; *carne cediza*, tainted meat; *carne de cañon*, cannon-fodder; people treated inconsiderately; *carne fiambre*, cold meat; *carne de gallina*, (met.) goose-flesh; (bot.) tree disease; *carne magra* or *mollar*, lean meat; *carne de membrillo*, sweet of preserved quince pulp; *carne de pelo*, flesh of small quadrupeds, as rabbits; *carne de pluma*, flesh of fowls; *carne de sábado*, head, pluck, feet of slaughtered animals; giblets of fowls; *carne momia*, mummy; (coll.) choice, lean, boneless meat; *carne nueva*, first meat sold after Lent; *carne salvajina*, flesh of wild deer, boar, etc.; *carne sin hueso*, (fig.) sinecure; *carne trifa*, meat cut by a Hebrew butcher; *carne viva*, quick flesh in a wound; *carne viciosa*, proud flesh; *carnes blancas*, white meats; *a carne de lobo, diente de perro*, when one is hungry one cannot afford to be fussy; *carne de pluma quita del rostro la arruga*, sumptuous fare makes one fat; *carne que crece, no puede estar si no mece*, play and action are natural to the growing child; *carne y sangre*, flesh and blood, near relationship; *cobrar, echar* or *tomar carnes*, to recover one's weight; to pick up; *criar carnes*, to continue putting on flesh; *en (vivas) carnes*, naked; *en carne viva*, raw, with flesh exposed; *hacer carne*, to kill, slaughter (by carnivores); (coll.) to wound, ill-treat; *hacerse carne*, to gloat over pain; to flay oneself; *la carne en el techo, y la hambre en el pecho*, said against misers who deprive themselves of necessities; *ni es carne ni pescado*, (fig.) he is neither fish, flesh nor fowl; he is an insipid fellow; *no está la carne en el garabato por falta de gato*, referring to women who remain unmarried although courted by many suitors; *poner uno toda la carne en el asador*, to risk all at one venture; *quien come la carne, que roa el hueso*, one must take the good with the bad; *ser uña y carne*, (fig.) to be hand in glove, intimate, familiar; *ser uno de carne y hueso*, to be human; *envuelto en carnes*, fleshy, plump, buxom; *temblarle las carnes a uno*, to be afraid; *tener uno carne de perro*, to be very strong; *yo soy la carne y usted el cuchillo*, I am your slave.

carnear, *v.t.* (*Am.*) to slaughter beasts; (*Chi.*) to swindle, cheat; (*Mex.*) to kill, stab in a fight or brawl.

carnecería, *n.f.* [CARNICERÍA].

carnecilla, *n.f.* caruncle, small fleshy excrescence.

carnerada, *n.f.* flock of sheep.

carneraje, *n.m.* tax or duty on sheep.

carnerario, *n.m.* (*prov.*) charnel-house.

carnereamiento, *n.m.* poundage, penalty for the trespass of sheep.

carnerear, *v.t.* to fine the proprietor of cattle for damage done.

carnerero, *n.m.* shepherd.

carneril, *n.m.* sheep-walk, sheep-run.

carnero, *n.m.* ram, mutton; (*prov.*) sheepskin dressed and tanned; family vault, charnel-house, burying place; (*Arg., Bol., Per.*) llama; (*Arg., Chi.*) (coll.) weak-minded

person; *carnero manso para guía*, bell-wether; *carnero marino*, seal; *carnero de simiente*, ram kept for breeding; *carnero verde*, kind of mutton stew; *cada carnero cuelga de su piezgo*, a place for everything and everything in its place; *no hay tales carneros*, (coll.) there is no such thing.

carneruno; -na, *a.* belonging to sheep; sheep-like, sheepish.

carnestolendas, *n.f.pl.* three carnival days before Ash Wednesday.

carnet, *n.m.* memorandum book; season-ticket, commutation-ticket.

carnicería, *n.f.* meat-market, butcher's shop; (*fig.*) carnage, havoc, slaughter; (*Ec.*) slaughterhouse.

carnicero, -ra, *a.* carnivorous (of animals); (*fig.*) blood-thirsty, sanguinary; applied to pasture-grounds for cattle about to be slaughtered; (coll.) great meat-eater (of a person). — *n.m.f.* butcher, person who sells meat. — *n.m.pl.* (*zool.*) carnivora.

carnicol, *n.m.* hoof of cloven-footed animal. — *pl.* knuckle-bones (game).

carnificación, *n.f.* (*med.*) carnification.

carnificarse, *v.r.* (*med.*) to carnify.

carniforme, *a.* flesh-like, fleshy.

carniseco, -ca, *a.* lean, scraggy.

carnívoro, -ra, *a.* carnivorous (animal). — *n.m.* carnivore. — *n.m.pl.* carnivora.

carniza, *n.f.* (coll.) refuse of meat; cats' meat, dogs' meat; decayed flesh.

carnosidad, *n.f.* proud flesh; excrescence; corpulence; fatness, fleshiness.

carnoso, -sa; carnudo, -da, *a.* carnose, fleshy, fleshed; full of marrow; pulpy (fruit).

carnuz, *n.m.* (*prov.*) tainted meat.

carnuza, *n.f.* abundance of meat producing nausea or loathing.

caro, -ra, *a.* dear, costly, high-priced; dear, affectionate, beloved; *cara mitad*, better half. — *adv.* dear, dearly, at a high price, expensively; — *n.m.* (*Cub.*) dish made of crab roes and cassava.

caroba, *n.f.* carob.

caroca, *n.f.* decoration in public festivities; farcical piece; (coll.) caress; cajolery, cajolement.

carocha; carrocha, *n.f.* eggs of bees and other insects.

carochar; carrochar, *v.i.* to lay eggs (said of bees and other insects).

carola, *n.f.* carol, song and dance.

carolingio, -gia, *n.m.f.*, *a.* Carolingian.

carolino, -na, *n.m.f.*, *a.* Caroline, of or from Caroline Islands (Pacific).

cárolus, *n.m.* Flemish coin used in the time of Charles V.

caromomia, *n.f.* the dry flesh of a mummy.

carona, *n.f.* padding of the saddle which touches the animal's back; inside of saddle; part of the animal's back which bears the saddle; (*slang*) shirt; *a carona*, bare-backed; *esquilar* or *hacer la carona*, to shear the back of a mount; *blando de carona*, to have the back tender where the saddle goes; (coll.) said of a person who is lazy, feeble, or addicted to falling in love; *corto* or *largo de carona*, short- or long-backed (mount).

caroñoso, -sa, *a.* old and galled (of animals).

caroquero, -ra, *a.* caressing; honey-worded. — *n.m.f.* wheedler, flatterer.

carosiero, *n.m.* species of palm-tree from Brazil.

carosis, *n.f.* profound stupor accompanied by complete insensibility.

carótico, -ca, *a.* (*med.*) relating to *carosis*. — *n.m.* medicament curing this ailment.

carótido, -da, *a.* carotid. — *n.f.* the carotid artery.

caroto, *n.m.* (*Ec.*) tree with very heavy wood.

carozo, *n.m.* (*prov.*) core of apple, pear, etc.; cob of maize.

carpa, *n.f.* carp, fresh-water fish; part torn off from a bunch of grapes; (*Am.*) canvas tent.

carpanel, *n.m.* (*arch.*) elliptic arch.

carpanta, *n.f.* (*coll.*) keen appetite, hunger; (*prov.*) indolence, laziness; (*Mex.*) crowd of noisy people; gang of libertines.

carpe, *n.m.* hornbeam.

carpedal, *n.m.* plantation of hornbeam-trees.

carpelar, *a.* carpellary.

carpelo, *n.m.* carpel.

carpeta, *n.f.* table-cover; file, letter-file, portfolio; writing-case; docket (of stock-exchange quotations); small curtain or screen before the door of a tavern; (*prov.*) envelope.

carpetazo, *n.m.* blow or stroke with a *carpeta*; *dar carpetazo*, to lay by, lay aside, shelve, pigeon-hole.

carpiano, -na, *a.* (*zool.*) carpal.

carpidor, *n.m.* (*Am.*) hoe.

carpincho, *n.m.* (*Am.*) capybara.

carpintear, *v.i.* to carpenter; (*fam.*) to do carpenter's work as a hobby.

carpintería, *n.f.* carpentry; carpenter's shop.

carpintero, *n.m.* carpenter, joiner; *carpintero de blanco*, joiner; *carpintero de armar* or *de obras de afuera*, carpenter who timbers or roofs houses; *carpintero de prieto* or *de carretas*, cartwright, wheelwright; *carpintero real*, ivory-billed woodpecker; *carpintero de ribera* or *de navío*, ship-carpenter, shipwright; *maestro carpintero de remos*, master oar-maker; *pájaro carpintero*, (*orn.*) carpenter-bird, woodpecker; *segundo carpintero*, carpenter's mate.

carpir, *v.t.*, *v.r.* to wrangle, quarrel; to scrape, scratch, tear; to stun; (*Am.*) to clear the ground with a hoe.

carpo, *n.m.* carpus, wrist.

carpobálsamo, *n.m.* (*bot.*) carpobalsamum, fruit of balsam-fir.

carpófago -ga, *a.* carpophagous.

carpología, *n.f.* carpology.

carqueroles, *n.m.pl.* parts of velvet-loom.

carquesa, *n.f.* glass-furnace.

carquexia, *n.f.* species of medicinal broom.

carraca, *n.f.* carrack, large and slow-sailing merchant ship; rattle, ratchet; the navy-yard in Cadiz.

carraco, -ca, *n.m.*, *a.* old, withered, decrepit (person).

carrada, *n.f.* cart-load, cartful.

carragaheen, *n.m.* carrageen.

carral, *n.m.* barrel, butt, vat; (*prov.*) decrepit old man.

carraleja, *n.f.* black beetle with yellow stripes similar to the cantharis.

carralero, *n.m.* cooper.

carramplón, *n.m.* (*Col.*) rustic musical instrument used by Negroes.

carranca; carrancha, *n.* [CARLANCA].

carranque, *n.m.* (*Per.*) a bird resembling a crane.

carranza, *n.f.* each iron point of the *carlanca*.

carrao, *n.m.* (*Ven.*) bird resembling a crane; (*Col., Cub.*) heavy, coarse shoes.

carraón, *n.m.* short-stemmed wheat.

carrasca, *n.f.* holly-oak, holm-oak.

carrascal; carrascalejo, *n.m.* plantation of *carrascas*.

carrasco, *n.m.* holm-oak, Corsican pine.

carrascón, *n.m.* [CARRASCA] large *carrasca*.

carrascoso, -sa, *a.* abounding in *carrascas*.

carraspada, *n.f.* negus (beverage).

carraspante, *a.* acrid, harsh.

carraspear, *v.i.* to feel hoarse, suffer from hoarseness.

carraspeño, -ña, *a.* gruff, hoarse.

carraspeo, *n.m.* hoarseness.

carraspera, *n.f.* (*coll.*) hoarseness; sore throat, frog-in-the-throat.

carraspique, *n.m.* candytuft.

carrasposo, -sa, *a.* suffering from chronic hoarseness or sore throat; (*Ven., Col.*) rough to the touch.

carrasqueño, -ña, *a.* belonging to the holm-oak or *carrasca*; (*prov.*) harsh, sharp.

carrejo, *n.m.* corridor, passage.

carrera, *n.f.* run, race; race-track; high-road; (*astron.*) course; row of objects; range of iron teeth in combing-cards; line, parting of the hair; (*arch.*) beam, girder; broken stitch, ladder (in stocking); career, profession; method of life; course of life; conduct, mode of action; course of a pageant or procession; route of a line of steamers; coach or stage line; Spanish step in dancing; long, spacious avenue (in Madrid). — *pl.* races, horse-racing; *carrera de baquetas*, (*mil.*) gauntlet (punishment); (*fig.*) series of troubles; *de carrera*, swiftly, rashly, without consideration; *carrera del émbolo*, stroke of the piston; *carrera de Indias*, trade between Spain and South America; *carrera de válvula*, travel of a valve; *carrera del sol*, the sun's course; *a carrera abierta, tendida*, or *a la carrera*, at full speed; *dar carrera a uno*, to pay for someone's education; *entrar uno por carrera*, to see reason; *estar en carrera*, to begin to earn one's livelihood; *hacer carrera*, to take up a career or profession; *hacer la carrera*, to walk the streets; *no poder hacer carrera con* or *de alguno*, to be unable to bring one to reason; *partir de carrera*, (*fig.*) to act rashly and without consideration; *poner a uno en carrera*, to provide someone with a job.

carrerilla, *n.f.* rapid movement in a Spanish dance; (*mus.*) run, flourish, roulade of an octave.

carrerista, *n.m.f.* turfite; punter, better; racing cyclist. — *n.m.* outrider of the royal carriage.

carrero, *n.m.* carman, carrier, carter, ox-cart driver, vanman.

carreta, *n.f.* long, narrow cart.

carretada, *n.f.* cartful, cart-load; (*coll.*) abundance, profusion; (*Mex.*) measure used in buying or selling lime, equivalent to 3,042 lb.; *a carretadas*, (*coll.*) profusely, copiously, abundantly.

carretaje, *n.m.* cartage, trade with carts.

carretal, *n.m.* rough, ragged ashlar.

carrete, *n.m.* spool, bobbin, reel; fishing-reel;

(*elec.*, *wire*.) bobbin, wireless induction coil; *dar carrete*, to reel off (in fishing); *dar carrete a uno*, to keep someone dangling.

carreteador, *n.m.* carter, van-driver.

carretear, *v.t.* to cart, convey in a cart; to drive a cart. — *v.r.* to draw unevenly (of oxen and mules). — *v.i.* (*Cub.*) loud chatter made by parrots or parakeets especially when young.

carretel, *n.m.* (*prov.*) fishing-reel, line-reel; (*naut.*) log-reel.

carretela, *n.f.* calash; (*Chi.*) omnibus, stage-coach.

carreteo, *n.m.* cart transport.

carretera, *n.f.* high-road, main road.

carretería, *n.f.* number of carts; trade of a carman; cartwright's yard; wheelwright's shop.

carreteril, *a.* appertaining to *carreteros*.

carretero, *a.* *camino carretero*, vehicle-road, drive. — *n.m.* cartwright; carter, driver; (*slang*) card-sharper; [CARRERO]; *jurar como un carretero*, to swear like a trooper.

carretil, *a.* belonging to a cart; *camino carretil*, cart-road.

carretilla, *n.f.* small cart; push-cart, wheel-barrow, hand-cart; railway truck; child's go-cart (to learn walking); squib, cracker; instrument for adorning bread and cakes; (*Arg.*, *Ur.*) heavy goods vehicle drawn by three mules; (*Chi.*) long narrow cart, wagon; (*Arg.*, *Chi.*) jaw, jawbone; *de carretilla*, mechanically, by heart, without reflection or attention; *carretilla de equipaje*, baggage-truck; *saber de carretilla*, (*coll.*) to know by heart.

carretillada, *n.f.* wheelbarrow-load.

carretillero, *n.m.* one who guides or pushes a *carretilla*.

carretón, *n.m.* cart, go-cart; truck; dray; child's chair; knife-grinder's cart; *carretón de lámpara*, pulley used for raising and lowering lamps (in churches).

carretonada, *n.f.* truck-load, wagon-load.

carretoncillo, *n.m.* small go-cart [CARRETÓN]; sled, sledge, sleigh.

carretonero, *n.m.* drayman, truck-man.

carricoche, *n.m.* wagonette; (*coll.*) old-fashioned cart or coach; (*prov.*) muck-cart, dung-cart.

carricuba, *n.f.* water-cart.

carriego, *n.m.* osier fishing-trap; rough basket for bleaching flax-yarn.

carriel, *n.m.* (*Col.*, *Ec.*, *Ven.*) muleteer's girdle; (*CR.*) travelling valise; (*CR.*) reticule.

carril, *n.m.* rut, cart-rut; narrow road, cart-way; furrow; (*railw.*) rail.

carrilada; carrilera, *n.f.* rut, cart-rut; (*Cub.*) railway siding; (*Col.*) grate, grillage.

carrilano, *n.m.* (*Chi.*) railway worker; (*Chi.*) thief, bandit.

carrillada, *n.f.* oily or medullar substance of a hog's cheek.

carrillar, *n.m.* tackle used to hoist light goods from the hold of a ship. — *v.t.* (*naut.*) to hoist with a tackle.

carrillera, *n.f.* jaw; chin-strap, chin-stay.

carrillo, *n.m.* cheek; hoisting tackle, pulley; *carrillos de monja boba*, *de trompetero*, full, plump cheeks; *comer* or *masticar a dos carrillos*, to eat voraciously; to have two

strings to one's bow; to run with the hare and hunt with the hounds.

carrilludo, **-da**, *a.* plump or round-cheeked.

carriola, *n.f.* truckle-bed, trundle-bed; carriole, small chariot, curricle.

carriquí, *n.m.* (*Col.*) a singing-bird.

carrizada, *n.f.* line of barrels towed on the water.

carrizal, *n.m.* land full of reed-grass.

carrizo, *n.m.* (*bot.*) common reed-grass.

carro, *n.m.* cart, car; carriage; cart-load, carriageful; running gear of a carriage without the body; (*astron.*) the Great Bear, the Dipper; (*slang*) gambling; (*print.*) bed, carriage of press; carriage of a typewriter; (*CR.*) an edible fruit; *carro de oro*, fine shot camlet; *carro de basura*, dust-cart; *carro de mudanzas*, removal van; *carro de riego*, water-cart; *carro de volteo*, tip-car, tilt-car; *carro fuerte*, lorry, truck; *Carro Mayor*, (*astron.*) Great Bear; *Carro Menor*, (*astron.*) Little Bear; *carro triunfal*, triumphal car; *carro urbano* or *tranvía*, tramcar; *cogerle a uno el carro*, to be unlucky; *no se puede hacer el carro sin pisar el barro*, the good things of life are not attained without trouble; *pare Vd. el carro*, keep cool, don't upset yourself; *tirar del carro*, to bear alone the responsibilities that should be shared by others; *untar el carro*, (*fig.*) to bribe, wheedle.

carrocería, *n.f.* shop where carriages are made, repaired or sold; body (of motor-car).

carrocero, *n.m.* carriage-, coach-builder.

carrocilla, *n.f.* small coach.

carrocín, *n.m.* gig.

carrocha, *n.f.* seminal substance of insects; eggs of same.

carromatero, *n.m.* carter, carman.

carromato, *n.m.* long, narrow two-wheeled cart with tilt.

carrón, *n.m.* hodful of bricks.

carronada, *n.f.* short gun of large calibre.

carroña, *n.f.* carrion, putrid flesh.

carroñar, *v.t.* to infect sheep with the scab.

carroño, **-ña**, *a.* putrefied, putrid, rotten.

carroñoso, **-sa**, *a.* foul-smelling.

carroza, *n.f.* large or state coach; (*naut.*) awning.

carrozal, *a.* appertaining to coach-building.

carruaje, *n.m.* carriage or vehicle in general.

carruajero, *n.m.* carrier, wagoner, carter, driver.

carruata, *n.f.* a kind of agave from Guiana.

carruco, *n.m.* small cart used in the mountains; hodful of tiles.

carrucha, *n.f.* pulley.

carrucho, *n.m.* small or ill-conditioned carriage.

carrujado, **-da**, *a.* corrugated, wrinkled. — *n.m.* (*sew.*) fluting, gathering, shirring.

carrujo, *n.m.* tree-top.

carta, *n.f.* letter, epistle, note; playing card; map, chart; royal ordinance; charter, written constitution; *carta abierta*, open letter; (*com.*) letter of credit for unlimited amount; *carta blanca*, carte blanche; full powers; *carta credencial*, ambassador's credentials; *carta cuenta*, bill or statement; *carta de ahorría*, *de ahorro* or *de horro*, letters of enfranchisement; *carta de amparo*, *de encomienda* or *de seguro*, safe-conduct; *carta de contramarca*, letter of marque and reprisal; *carta de crédito*, letter of credit; *carta de creencia*, reference, testimonial; credentials; *carta de dote*, document detailing a wife's dowry; *carta de espera* or *moratoria*, (*law*) moratorium; *carta de examen*, diploma; *carta de fletamento*, (*com*.) charter-party; *carta de gracia* or *forera*, royal grant of privileges; (*law*) reversion contract; *carta de guía*, passport; *carta de hermandad*, (*eccl*.) introduction; *carta de hidalguía* or *ejecutoria* (*de hidalguía*), letters patent of nobility; *carta de libre*, (*law*) guardian's discharge; *carta de marca*, letters of marque; *carta de marear*, sea chart; *carta de naturaleza*, letters of naturalization; *carta de pago*, acquittance, receipt, discharge (of a debt, etc.); *carta de presentación* or *de recommendación*, letter of introduction; *carta desaforada*, cancellation of a privilege; *carta de sanidad*, bill of health; *carta de seguridad*, safeguard, protection; *carta de Urías*, trap, snare, treacherous letter; *carta de vecindad*, burghership certificate; *carta de venta*, bill of sale; *carta de vuelta*, dead letter; *carta en lista*, letter "to be called for," letter in *poste restante*; *carta familiar*, familiar, intimate letter; *carta forera*, judicial writ; (*law*) claim valid for one year only; *carta orden*, mandatory letter; *carta pastoral*, pastoral; *carta pécora*, document written on parchment; *carta plomada*, document with lead seals; *carta puebla*, document relating to settlers' territory; *carta receptoria*, warrant, voucher; *carta requisitoria*, letters requisitorial; *carta viva*, messenger who delivers a message verbally; *cartas* or *letras expectativas*, royal or papal announcement of forthcoming appointment; *a carta cabal*, irreproachably; completely; *a cartas, cartas; y a palabras, palabras*, one's behaviour to people should be governed by their attitude; *apartar las cartas*, to sort out letters for people having post-office boxes; *carta canta*, it may be proved by written documents; *echar las cartas*, to tell fortunes by cards; *enseñar* or *entregar uno las cartas*, to show one's hand, one's object or purpose; *hablen cartas y callen barbas*, statistics speak more truly than men; *irse de una buena carta*, to abandon an asset willingly; *jugar a cartas vistas*, to bet on a certainty; to put all one's cards on the table; to act frankly; *ni firmes carta que no leas, ni bebas agua que no veas*, safety first, though it may entail an effort; *no ver carta*, to have a bad hand (at cards); *perder uno con buenas cartas*, to fail notwithstanding merit and protection; *por carta de más o de menos*, to say or do either too much or too little; *por carta de más o de menos se pierden los juegos*, a miss is as good as a mile; extremes should be avoided; *tomar cartas* (*en algún negocio*), to take part, interfere (in an affair); *traer* or *venir con malas cartas*, to attempt something beyond one's means.

cartabón, *n.m.* drawing triangle; shoemaker's slide-rule; topographic octagonal prism; *echar el cartabón*, to adopt measures to attain one's end.

cartafolio, *n.m.* whole sheet of paper.

cartagenero, -ra, *n.m.f.*, *a.* of or from Cartagena.

cartaginense; cartaginés, -sa; cartaginiense, *n.m.f.*, *a.* Carthaginian, of Carthage.

cártama, *n.f.*; **cártamo**, *n.m.* bastard saffron.

cartapacio, *n.m.* memorandum-book; blotter, writing-case; student's exercise-book; batch or pile of papers; book-satchel.

cartapel, *n.m.* memorandum of useless matter.

cartazo, *n.m.* [CARTA] long letter; (*coll*.) letter or paper containing a severe reproof.

carteado, -da, *a.* applied to a card game after the tricks are taken up. — *n.m.* card game. — *p.p.* [CARTEAR].

cartear, *v.i.* to play out low cards to see how the game stands. — *v.r.* to correspond by letter.

cartel, *n.m.* placard, poster, hand-bill; mural reading-chart (for teaching children); cartel, written challenge; agreement; sardine fishing-net; lampoon, satire; *tener uno cartel*, to have a good reputation.

cartela, *n.f.* slip of paper or other form of memorandum; (*arch*.) modillion, console, bracket; iron stay supporting a balcony.

cartelera, *n.f.* bill-board, board for edicts.

cartelero, *n.m.* bill-poster, bill-sticker.

cartelón, *n.m.* long edict; show-bill [CARTEL].

carteo, *n.m.* correspondence, intercourse by letters.

cartera, *n.f.* portfolio; pocket-book, wallet, note-book; writing-case; letter-case; letter-book; pocket-flap; (*fig*.) portfolio (office of cabinet minister); (*com*.) assets.

cartería, *n.f.* employment of letter-carrier; distributing-room in a post office.

carterista, *n.m.* pickpocket.

cartero, *n.m.* postman.

cartesianismo, *n.m.* Cartesianism.

cartesiano, -na, *n.m.f.*, *a.* Cartesian.

carteta, *n.f.* card game.

cartica; cartita, *n.f.* [CARTA] small letter, note.

cartílago, *n.m.* cartilage, gristle.

cartilla, *n.f.* short letter, note; clergyman's certificate of ordination; children's primer, first book; horn-book; *no saber la cartilla*, to be extremely ignorant; *cantarle* or *leerle a uno la cartilla*, (*met*.) to read one a lecture; *no estar en la cartilla*, to be uncommon, out of the ordinary.

cartismo, *n.m.* Chartism.

cartista, *n.m.f.*, *a.* Chartist.

cartivana, *n.f.* linen or paper strip for binding single sheets.

cartografía, *n.f.* cartography, art of map-drawing.

cartográfico, -ca, *a.* cartographic.

cartógrafo, *n.m.* cartographer.

cartolas, *n.f.pl.* [ARTOLAS].

cartología, *n.f.* cartology.

cartomancia, *n.f.* cartomancy, fortune-telling by cards.

cartomántico, -ca, *a.* relating to cartomancy. — *n.m.f.* fortune-teller by cards.

cartómetro, *n.m.* curvimeter.

cartón, *n.m.* pasteboard, cardboard, cartonnage, millboard; cartoon, painting or drawing on stout paper; a kind of iron ornament imitating the leaves of plants; *cartón piedra*, (*art*) staff; papier-mâché.

cartonaje, *n.m.* making of cardboard articles.

cartonería, *n.f.* cardboard or millboard factory or shop.

cartonero, -ra, *a.* relating to cardboard. — *n.m.f.* maker or vendor of pasteboard, cardboard articles, bandboxes, etc. — *n.f.pl.* paper-making wasps.

cartuchera, *n.f.* cartridge-box or pouch; cartridge-belt.

cartuchería, *n.f.* cartridge-factory; quantity of cartridges and munitions.

cartucho, *n.m.* cartridge; roll of coins; fancy paper cornet; *quemar uno el último cartucho,* to use up one's last resource.

cartuja, *n.f.* Carthusian order or monastery.

cartujano, -na, *a.* Carthusian.

cartujo, *a.* Carthusian. — *n.m.* Carthusian monk; (*coll.*) taciturn man; hermit, recluse.

cartulario, *n.m.* cartulary, archives, registry; archivist.

cartulina, *n.f.* Bristol-board.

cartusana, *n.f.* galloon with curly fringe.

caruata, *n.f.* (*Ven.*) a kind of agave.

carúncula, *n.f.* caruncle; wattle; *carúncula lagrimal,* lachrymal glands.

carunculado, -da, *a.* carunculate, carunculated.

caruncular, *a.* caruncular.

caruto, *n.m.* genipap.

carvajal; carvallar; carvalledo, *n.m.* oak plantation.

carvajo; carvallo, *n.m.* (*prov.*) oak.

carvi, *n.m.* caraway-seed.

cas, *n.f.* (*vulg.*) apocope for house; (*CR.*) tree similar to the guava but with bitter fruit.

casa, *n.f.* house, dwelling, building, edifice; home, private house; household, family living in one house; state, property, revenue; establishment; business house, emporium; line or branch of a family; checkers, squares of a chessboard; *casa abierta,* residence and office or studio combined; shop; *casa a la malicia,* one-storied house to avoid paying rates; *casa celeste,* (*astron.*) house; *casa(s) consistorial(es),* town hall; *casa cuartel,* (*mil.*) barracks and residential quarters; *casa cuna,* orphan asylum; *casa de aposento,* house obliged to receive members of the king's household; *casa de banca,* bank, banking establishment; *casa de baños,* public baths; *casa de beneficencia,* asylum, poorhouse; *casa de camas, de mancebía* or *de trato, casa pública,* brothel; *casa de campo* or *de placer y recreo,* country-house; *casa de comidas,* dining-rooms, cheap restaurant; *casa de comercio,* commercial house, business firm; *casa de conversación,* seventeenth-century club or casino; *casa de corrección,* reformatory; *casa de devoción,* sanctuary; *casa de Dios, de oración* or *del Señor,* church; *casa de dormir,* inn, hostel; *casa de empeños* or *de préstamos,* pawnshop; *casa de expósitos,* foundling home; *casa de ganado,* (*prov.*) barn with stable beneath; *casa de huéspedes, de pupilos* or *de posada(s),* boarding-house; *casa de juego,* gambling-house; *casa de labor* or *de labranza,* farm; *casa de locos* or *de orates,* lunatic asylum, madhouse; (*fig.*) noisy, riotous house; *casa de maternidad,* maternity hospital; *casa de moneda,* mint; *casa de postas,* post-house; *casa de socorro,* emergency hospital; *casa de tía,* (*fam.*) prison; *casa de tócame Roque* or *de trueno,* very full and badly run house; *casa de vacas,* dairy; *casa de vecindad,* tenement; *casa fuerte,* castle; rich and powerful family; *casa llana,* unfortified country-seat; *casa mortuoria,* house of de-

ceased person; *casa paterna,* parents' home; *casa profesa,* convent, monastery; *casa real,* royal palace and family; *casa robada,* poorly furnished house; *casa santa,* Holy Sepulchre in Jerusalem; *casa solar* or *solariega,* ancient mansion house of a family; *a casa de tu hermano no irás cada serano. A casa de tu tía, mas no cada día,* do not abuse anyone's kindness however much they love you; *a mal decir no hay casa fuerte,* wealth and power cannot escape ill-luck; *apartar casa,* to take up separate residence; *arderse la casa,* to upset a household by quarrels; *armar una casa,* to put up the framework of a house; *alzar, arrancar* or *levantar la casa,* to move, change one's residence; to break up a home; to cease housekeeping; *asentar casa,* to start a fresh home; *cada uno en su casa y Dios en la de todos,* families should live separately in order to avoid quarrels; *caérsele a uno la casa a cuestas,* to have the house fall about one's ears; *casa con dos puertas mala es de guardar,* a house with many doors is difficult to guard; *casa hita* or *casa por casa,* from house to house; *casa reñida, casa regida,* severity is essential to a well-ordered house; *cuando fueres a casa ajena, llama de fuera,* knock before you enter; *cuando vieres tu casa quemar, llégate a escalentar,* it's no use crying over spilt milk; *de buena casa, buena brasa,* even the remnants from a rich house have some value; *de fuera vendrá quien de casa nos echará,* rebuke addressed to person presuming to give orders in another's house; *deshacerse una casa,* to lose one's position, come down in the world (of a family); *de su casa,* original; *echar uno la casa por la ventana,* to be a spendthrift; *en cada casa cuecen habas, y en la nuestra, a calderadas,* everyone has his troubles, but ours always seem the worst; *en casa de Gonzalo, más puede la gallina que el gallo,* applied to a household where the woman wears the breeches; *en casa del abad, comer y llevar,* in the abbot's house there is enough and to spare; *en casa del alboguero (gaitero) todos son albogueros (danzantes),* like father, like son; *en casa del herrero badil de madero (or cuchillo de palo or mangorrero),* the shoemaker's children go barefooted; *en casa del moro no hables algarabía,* avoid wounding anyone's feelings in your conversation; *en casa del oficial asoma el hambre, mas no osa entrar,* the skilled hard-working man need never fear hunger; *en casa de mujer rica, ella manda y ella grita,* the rich wife holds the reins; *en casa llena presto se guisa la cena,* with resources one can get over any difficulty; *en la casa donde no hay harina, todo es mohina,* when poverty comes in at the door, love flies out of the window; *entrar (el zapato, etc.) como por su casa,* to be easy, comfortable (shoe, etc.); *en tu casa no tienes sardina y en la ajena pides gallina,* rebuke to people who expect too much, and to those who are lenient at home and exigent with strangers; *estar de casa,* to be homely, to feel at home; *franquear a uno la casa,* to give a person the freedom of the house; *guardar la casa,* to stay at home compulsorily; *la casa quemada, acudir con el agua,* to lock the stable door after the steed is stolen; *llovérsele a uno la casa,* to begin to decline in prosperity; *mi casa y mi hogar cien doblas val*, there's no place like home; *mientras en mi casa estoy, rey me soy*, contentment makes one feel a king, every man's house is his castle; *no caber en toda la casa*, to be in a bad humour (said of the head of the family); *no hay casa que no tenga chiticalla*, or *do no haya su calla, calla*, every family has its skeleton in the cupboard; *no parar uno en casa*, to be a bird of passage, nev r at home; *no tener uno casa ni hogar*, to be destitute, homeless; *oler la casa a hombre*, implying that someone wishes to rule his own house, usually without success; *poner casa*, to found a household; *poner la casa a uno*, to furnish a house for someone; *quémese la casa y no salga humo*, do not wash your dirty linen in public; *ser uno muy de casa*, to be treated as one of the family, to be on intimate terms; *tener casa y tinelo*, (*prov.*) to keep open house; *tener la casa como una colmena*, to have the house well-stocked; *toma casa con hogar, y mujer que sepa hilar*, when marrying do not overlook the domestic qualities of your bride; *triste está la casa donde la gallina canta y el gallo calla*, pity the house where the woman wears the breeches; *unos por otros y la casa por barrer*, too many generals and no soldiers; *su casa* or *casa de Vd.*, a polite way of giving one's address and intimating that it is at the addressee's disposal.

casabe; **cazabe,** *n.m.* manioc cake.

casaca, *n.f.* coat, dress-coat; (*coll.*) marriage, wedding; *querer* (*no querer*) *casaca*, to wish to be married (or the reverse); *volver uno* (*la*) *casaca*, to become a turncoat.

casación, *n.f.* cassation, abrogation, repeal.

casacón, *n.m.* cassock; greatcoat [CASACA].

casadero, -ra, *a.* marriageable, fit for marriage.

casadilla, *n.f.* (*prov., fam.*) young married woman.

casado, -da, *n.m.f.,* *a.* married (person). — *n.m.* (*print.*) imposition; *casado y arrepentido*, tardy regrets are futile; *el casado casa quiere*, every newly wed couple should live independently. — *p.p.* [CASAR].

casaisaco, *n.m.* (*Cub.*) parasite plant of the palm-trees.

casal, *n.m.* manor, country-house; (*River Plate*) couple (male and female).

casalicio, *n.m.* house, edifice.

casamata, *n.f.* casemate.

casamentero, -ra, *a.* match-making. — *n.m.f.* match-maker, marriage-maker.

casamiento, *n.m.* marriage, wedding; matrimony; *no perderás por ese casamiento*, your reputation will not suffer by that affair.

casampulga, *n.f.* (*ES., Hond.*) poisonous spider.

casamuro, *n.m.* (*fort.*) single wall without a terreplein.

casapuerta, *n.f.* porch, entrance of a house.

casaquilla, *n.f.;* **casaquín,** *n.m.* kind of short jacket.

casar, *v.i., v.r.* to marry, get married, wed. — *v.t.* to marry, mate; couple, unite in marriage, join in wedlock; (*fig.*) to join, unite; to suit, match (things or colours); (*law*) to annul, abrogate, appeal; (*paint.*) to blend; (*typ.*) to impose; *casar una cosa con otra*, to match a thing with another; *casarse con un inglés*, to marry an Englishman; *casarse por poderes*, to

marry by proxy; *antes que te cases, mira lo que haces*, look well before you leap; *casarás y amansarás*, the responsibilities of marriage will soon teach you wisdom; *casar, casar, que bien que mal*, marriage is mankind's natural state; *casar y compadrar, cada cual con su igual*, keep within your station in life; *el que se casa por todo pasa*, marriage brings many responsibilities in its train; *quien mal casa, tarde enviuda*, unpleasant things seem everlasting; *casarse en segundas nupcias*, to remarry.

casar, *n.m.* hamlet, small village.

casarón, *n.m.* big house [CASA]; large ramshackle house.

casatienda, *n.f.* tradesman's shop and house (in one building).

casca, *n.f.* skin of pressed grapes; oak-bark; (*prov.*) bad liquor; ring-shaped fruit-cake; (*prov.*) [CASCARA].

cascabel, *n.m.* small bell, hawk-bell, sleighbell; cascabel (of a cannon); *culebra, serpiente de cascabel*, rattlesnake; *de cascabel gordo*, jingle; inartistic, vulgar (of writing or painting); *echar el cascabel*, to drop a hint in conversation to see how it is taken; *echar or soltar el cascabel a otro*, to shift the burden on someone else; *poner el cascabel al gato*, to bell the cat, undertake a risky thing; *ser un cascabel*, to be a rattle-brained fellow; *tener un cascabel*, to be worried, anxious.

cascabela, *n.f.* (*CR.*) rattlesnake.

cascabelada, *n.f.* rattle, jingling with small bells; (*coll.*) inconsiderate speech or action.

cascabelear, *v.t.* (*coll.*) to feed with vain hopes; to bamboozle. — *v.i.* to act without foresight and prudence.

cascabelero, -ra, *n.m.f., a.* light-witted, rattle-brained (person). — *n.m.* baby's rattle (toy).

cascabelillo, *n.m.* small black plum.

cascabillo, *n.m.* tiny bell [CASCABEL]; hawk-bell; (*bot.*) glume; cup of an acorn.

cascabullo, *n.m.* (*prov.*) acorn-cup.

cascaciruelas, *n.m.f.* (*coll.*) mean, despicable person; *hacer lo que Cascaciruelas*, to be a busybody, fuss needlessly.

cascada, *n.f.* cascade, waterfall.

cascado, -da, *a.* (*coll.*) broken, burst; decayed, infirm; dull, unresonant (voice). — *p.p.* [CASCAR].

cascadura, *n.f.* act of bursting or breaking asunder.

cascajal; **cascajar,** *n.m.* place full of gravel and pebbles; place in which the husks of grapes are thrown.

cascajera, *n.f.* gravelly, pebbly place.

cascajero, *n.m.* (*Col.*) [CASCAJAL].

cascajo, *n.m.* gravel; nuts in general; (*coll.*) old, useless crockery or furniture; (*coll.*) small copper money; *estar hecho un cascajo*, to be very old and infirm.

cascajoso, -sa, *a.* gravelly, full of stones.

cascamajar, *v.t.* to break a thing slightly.

cascamiento, *n.m.* breaking, bruising.

cascante, *a.* breaking, bursting.

cascanueces, *n.m.* nut-cracker.

cascapiedras, *n.m.* railway-sweeper.

cascapiñones, *n.m.* pine-nut cracker (instrument and operative).

cascar, *v.t.* (*pret.* **casqué**; *pres. subj.* **casque**) to crack, burst, break into pieces; to crunch;

(*coll.*) to strike, beat. — *v.i.* (*coll.*) to talk much. — *v.r.* to break, be broken open; to weaken in health; *cascar a uno las liendres*, to give someone a drubbing.

cáscara, *n.f.* rind, shell, peel, husk; (*prov.*) silk-cocoon; (*prov.*) dried red pepper; (*bot.*) bark. — *pl.* (*slang*) stockings reaching to the knee; *cáscara sagrada*, (*med.*) bark of the Californian buckthorn; *ser de la cáscara amarga*, to be full of mischief; to hold advanced views.

cascarada, *n.f.* (*slang*) quarrel, strife.

¡cáscaras! *interj.* really! great heavens!

cascarela, *n.f.* lansquenet, card game.

cascarero, -ra, *a.* that collects *cáscaras*. — *n.m.* place where *cáscaras* are stored.

cascarilla; cascarita, *n.f.* Peruvian bark, Jesuit's bark, quinine; cosmetic made of powdered eggshell; thin metal covering.

cascarillero, *n.m.* gatherer of Peruvian bark.

cascarillina, *n.f.* bitter principle of quinine.

cascarillo, *n.m.* (*Am. Mer.*) shrub from which the cinchona bark is obtained.

cascarón, *n.m.* thick rind, shell [CÁSCARA]; eggshell (especially when broken); (*arch.*) calotte, vault, arch; trick in *cascarela;* (*Mex.*) eggshell filled with confetti; (*Ur.*) tree of the cork order; *cascarón de nuez*, (*naut.*) cockleshell, boat too small for its purpose; *aún no ha salido del cascarón y ya tiene espolón*, rebuke to inexperienced youths who assume the airs of men of the world.

cascarrabias, *n.m.f.* (*coll.*) irritable person.

cascarria, *n.f.* [CAZCARRIA].

cascarrojas, *n.m.pl.* insects or worms in ships.

cascarrón, -na, *a.* (*coll.*) rough, harsh, rude. — *n.m.* (*naut.*) stiff wind.

cascarudo, -da, *a.* having a thick rind or shell.

cascaruleta, *n.f. cuchareta* wheat; (*coll.*) noise made by the teeth when one is chucked under the chin.

casco, *n.m.* skull, cranium; potsherd, fragment of an earthen vessel; (*prov.*) quarter of orange, lemon, etc.; coat of onion; crown of hat; casque, helmet, headpiece; cask, pipe, vat; saddle-tree; horse's hoof; hull of a ship. — *pl.* heads of sheep or bullocks without the tongues or brains; (*fam.*) head; talents; (*med.*) ringworm cap; *casco atronado*, (*vet.*) injured hoof; *casco de casa*, framework of house; *casco de mantilla*, foundation material of mantilla; *casco de un navío*, (*naut.*) hull of a ship; *casco y quilla*, bottomry; *casco* or *tapa de un barril*, head of a cask; *casco de población*, a city excluding its suburbs; *alegre* or *barrenado de cascos, de cascos lucios, ligero de cascos*, feather-brained person; *cortar a casco*, to prune cleanly; *lavar* or *untar el casco* or *los cascos a uno*, to adulate, flatter someone; *levantarle a uno de cascos*, to fill someone's head with idle and lofty ideas; *meter a uno en los cascos alguna cosa*, to convince someone; *metérsele a uno en los cascos alguna cosa*, to be stubborn; *parecerse los cascos a la olla*, like father, like son; *quitarle* or *raerle a uno del casco alguna cosa*, to deter, dissuade someone; *romper a uno los cascos*, to break someone's head; (*coll.*) to bore, vex, annoy; *romperse uno los cascos por una cosa*, to rack one's brains in doing something;

tener uno cascos de calabaza, or *a la jineta*, or *malos cascos*, to be irresponsible.

cascol, *n.m.* (*Ec.*) resin of a Guiana tree.

cascote, *n.m.* rubbish, rubble, ruins of a building.

cascotería, *n.f.* rubble-work.

cascudo, -da, *a.* large-hoofed.

casea, *n.f.* casein.

caseación, *n.f.* coagulation of milk for cheese-making.

caseasa, *n.f.* ferment which converts casein into peptone.

caseato, *n.m.* salt formed by combining lactic acid with a base.

caseico, -ca, *a.* caseic; caseous; lactic.

caseificación, *n.f.* transformation into casein.

caseificar, *v.t.* to transform into casein; to separate or precipitate the casein from the milk.

caseína, *n.f.* casein.

cáseo, -sea, *a.* caseous. — *n.m.* [CUAJADA].

caseoso, -sa, *a.* caseous; cheesy.

casera, *n.f.* (*prov.*) housekeeper, woman servant.

caseramente, *adv.* in a homely way, simply, informally, frankly.

casería, *n.f.* manor with out-buildings for farm-hands; housewifery.

caserillo, *n.m.* kind of homespun linen.

caserío, *n.m.* series of houses; village, settlement.

caserna, *n.f.* barrack.

casero, -ra, *a.* domestic, homely, home-bred; home-made. — *n.m.f.* landlord, landlady; house-agent; caretaker; tenant, lessee; familiar; *baile casero*, family dance; *lienzo casero*, home-spun linen; *mujer casera*, good housewife; *pan casero*, home-made bread; *remedio casero*, domestic remedy; *estar muy casera (una mujer)*, to be dressed in a plain and homely manner (a woman).

caserón, *n.m.* large, ill-proportioned house [CASA].

caseta, *n.f.* small house, hut, cottage [CASA]; *caseta de baño*, bathing-cabin.

casetón, *n.m.* (*arch.*) rosette.

casi, *adv.* almost, nearly, more or less, just, somewhat; *casi que* or *casi casi*, very nearly; *casi de balde*, (*coll.*) almost free; *casi nada*, (*coll.*) of little importance; *interj.* (*iron.*) a mere trifle! *casi regalado*, given away.

casia, *n.f.* bastard cinnamon; cassia, leguminous plant.

casica; casilla; casita, *n.f.* small house; cabin [CASA].

casicontrato, *n.m.* quasi-contract.

casilla, *n.f.* keeper's lodge; railway guard's hut; kiosk; booth; ticket office; (*Cub.*) trap, snare to catch birds; (*Ec.*) water-closet. — *pl.* pigeon-holes; ruled columns in accounts; squares of a chess-board; points of a backgammon-table; *sacarle a uno de sus casillas*, (*coll.*) to make a person change his habits; to vex a person beyond endurance; *salir de sus casillas*, to forget oneself.

casiller, *n.m.* palace servant who emptied slops, etc.

casillero, *n.m.* desk or cabinet with pigeon-holes; storekeeper in naval dockyards.

casillo, *n.m.* (*iron.*) trifling matter, slight case.

casimba, *n.f.* (*Cub., Per.*) water reservoir.

casimir; casimiro, *n.m.;* **casimira,** *n.f.* cashmere, cassimere, kerseymere.
casinete, *n.m.* (*Arg., Chi., Hond.*) low quality cashmere; (*Ec., Ven.*) cheap woollen cloth.
casinita, *n.f.* feldspar of barytes.
casino, *n.m.* casino, dancing-hall, club-house; social or political club.
casiopea, *n.f.* Cassiopeia, northern constellation.
casis, *n.m.* black currant.
casiterita, *n.f.* cassiterite, oxide of tin.
caso, *n.m.* case, event, occasion, occurrence; contingency, opportunity; casualty, accident; (*gram., law, med.*) case; *caso apretado,* intricate case; *caso de conciencia,* matter of conscience; *caso de honra,* matter of honour; *caso de menos valer,* discreditable action; *caso favorable,* favourable eventuality; *caso fortuito,* unforeseen occurrence; force majeure; *caso omiso,* case of omission; *caso raro,* rare occurrence; *caso reservado,* (*eccl.*) case to be decided by superior authority; *a caso hecho* or *de caso pensado,* deliberately, on purpose; successfully; *caer en mal caso,* to fall into disrepute; *caso que, en caso de que,* in case that, supposing that; *dado caso* or *demos caso,* supposing; *en tal caso,* in such an eventuality (or case); *en todo caso,* at all events, in any case; *estar uno en el caso,* to be well acquainted with the subject; *esto no hace al caso* or *no viene al caso* or *no es del caso,* this is not to the point; *hablar al caso,* to speak to the point; *hacer caso de,* to respect or esteem (persons); to take notice of (things); *no hacer caso,* not to mind; *esto no hace caso* or *no viene al caso,* this is not to the point; *hacer caso omiso,* to omit, pass over purposely; *pongo por caso,* let us assume, for example; *por el mismo caso,* for a similar reason; *prestar el caso,* (*law*) to be responsible for unforeseen contingencies; *ser caso negado,* to be practically an impossibility; *vamos al caso,* let us come to the point.
casoar, *n.m.* cassowary.
casolero, -ra, *a.* (*prov.*) home-loving, home-keeping.
casón, *n.m.* large house [CASA].
casorio, *n.m.* (*coll.*) hasty or unwise marriage; informal wedding.
caspa, *n.f.* dandruff, scurf; crust, scab (on scars).
caspera, *n.f.* scurf-comb.
caspia, *n.f.* (*prov.*) core of an apple.
caspicias, *n.f.pl.* (*fam.*) remains, trifles.
caspio, -pia, *n.m.f.,* *a.* Caspian.
caspiroleta, *n.f.* (*Am.*) egg-nog.
¡cáspita! *interj.* wonderful!; by Jove!; gracious me!
casposo, -sa, *a.* full of dandruff.
casquería, *n.f.* tripe-shop.
casquero, *n.m.* tripe-seller.
casquetazo, *n.m.* blow given with the head.
casquete, *n.m.* helmet, casque; skull-cap, cap; wig, periwig; (*mech.*) cap; (*conch.*) helmet-shell; cataplasm to remove scurf.
casquiacopado, -da, *a.* cup-hoofed (of horses).
casquiblando, -da, *a.* soft-hoofed.
casquiderramado, -da, *a.* wide-hoofed.
casquijo, *n.m.* gravel; ballast-material.
casquilucio, -cia, *a.* gay, frolicsome.
casquilla, *n.f.* cell of the queen-bee.

casquillo, *n.m.* metal; tip, cap; ferrule, socket; iron arrow-head; cartridge-cap; spent cartridge; (*Am.*) horseshoe; (*Hond.*) sweat-band (in hats).
casquimuleño, -ña, *a.* narrow-hoofed like mules (applied to horses).
casquivano, -na, *a.* feather-brained; foolishly conceited.
casta, *n.f.* caste, clan, particular breed, lineage; race, generation; kindred, offspring; (*fig.*) kind or quality of a thing; *cruzar las castas,* to cross breeds; *hacer casta,* to get a particular breed of some animal.
Castálidas, *n.f.pl.* the Muses.
castalio, -lia, *a.* castalian.
castamente, *adv.* chastely.
castaña, *n.f.* chestnut; chestnut-shaped jar, demijohn; chignon; (*Mex.*) small barrel; *castaña pilonga* or *apilada,* dried chestnut; *castaña regoldana,* wild or horse-chestnut; *dar a uno la castaña,* to play a trick on someone; *dar a uno para castaña,* to threaten someone; *sacar las castañas del fuego,* to play cat's paw; to expose oneself to danger for another's advantage.
castañal; castañar, *n.m.* chestnut-grove or plantation.
castañazo, *n.m.* blow from a chestnut.
castañeda, *n.f.;* **castañedo,** *n.m.* chestnut-grove.
castañero, -ra, *n.m.f.* dealer in chestnuts. — *n.m.* palmiped dove. — *n.f.* (*prov.*) district rich in chestnut-trees.
castañeta, *n.f.* snapping of the fingers; castanet.
castañetada, *n.f.;* **castañetazo,** *n.m.* blow with a castanet; sound made by a chestnut bursting in the fire; cracking of the joints.
castañete, *a.* [CASTAÑA] brownish.
castañeteado, -da, *p.p.* [CASTAÑETEAR] crackled, rattled. — *n.m.* sound of castanets.
castañetear, *v.t.* to rattle the castanets; *v.i.* to clatter the teeth; to crackle; to clack the knees; to cry (applied to partridges).
castañeteo, *n.m.* clacking.
castaño, -ña, *a.* chestnut, chestnut-coloured; reddish-brown. — *n.m.* common chestnut-tree; chestnut-wood; *castaño de Indias,* horse-chestnut-tree; *pasar de castaño obscuro,* (*coll.*) to be beyond reason or endurance; *castaño regoldano,* wild chestnut-tree.
castañola, *n.f.* large sea-fish found in the Mediterranean.
castañuela, *n.f.* castanet; round tuberous-rooted cyperus; *estar como unas castañuelas,* (*coll.*) to be very gay.
castañuelo, -la, *a.* [CASTAÑO] of a light chestnut colour (applied to horses).
castellán, *n.m.* castellan (only used in Aragon).
castellana, *n.f.* chatelaine, mistress of a castle; stanza in old Spanish poetry.
castellanamente, *adv.* in the Castilian manner.
castellanía, *n.f.* castellany.
castellanismo, *n.m.* expression peculiar to Castile.
castellanizar, *v.t.* to Castilianize; to turn a foreign word into a Spanish one.
castellano, -na, *n.m.f., a.* Castilian. — *a.* said of a mule got by a jackass and a mare. — *n.m.* the Castilian or Spanish language; castellan, or warden of a castle; an ancient Spanish

coin, the fiftieth part of a gold mark; *a la castellana*, in the Castilian or Spanish fashion; *en castellano*, clearly, in intelligible language.

castellar, *n.m.* St. John's wort, tutsan.

casticidad, *n.f.* correctness, purity (of language, customs, etc.).

casticismo, *n.m.* purism.

casticista, *n.m.f.* purist.

castidad, *n.f.* chastity, purity, continence, honour.

castigación, *n.f.* castigation, punishment; revision and correction of a written work.

castigadera, *n.f.* strap or rope for tying the clapper of a wether's bell.

castigador, -ra, *a.* castigating, chastising. — *n.m.f.* punisher, chastiser, castigator.

castigar, *v.t.* (*pret.* **castigué**; *pres. subj.* **castigue**) to chastise, castigate, punish; to scourge, grieve, pain, afflict; (*fig.*) to revise or correct the proof-sheets of writings; to break in, train (horses, bulls); (*naut.*) to exercise undue pressure or tension; *castigar en la bolsa*, to punish with a fine; *castigar el bolsillo*, to pay reluctantly; *castigar el cuerpo*, to overwork; to deprive of food, sleep; *castigar el estómago*, to fast, practise abstinence; to starve; *castigar la vista*, to strain one's sight by overwork or by working in a poor light; *ser castigado por desobediente*, to be punished for disobedience.

castigo, *n.m.* chastisement, punishment, correction; (*fig.*) alteration or correction made in a work; (*coll.*) tiresome person or child; *castigo de Dios*, the judgment of God; *castigo ejemplar*, exemplary punishment; *ser de castigo (una cosa)*, to be hard, unpleasant (something).

castila, *a.* (*Philip.*) nickname applied to Spaniards; *n.m.* Spanish language.

Castilla, *n.f.* Castile; *ancha Castilla*, (*coll.*) as you will, without hindrance; (*Chi.*) cloth for coats.

castillado, -da, *a.* (*her.*) castellated.

castillaje, *n.m.* castle-toll.

castillejo, *n.m.* small castle [CASTILLO]; scaffolding; go-cart.

castillería, *n.f.* toll for transit through castle property.

castillete, *n.m.* small castle [CASTILLO].

castillo, *n.m.* castle, fortress, fort; cell of queen-bee; mounting of a velvet-loom; (*mil.*) wooden tower on the back of an elephant; total capacity of cart; *castillo de fuego*, fireworks; *castillo de naipes*, house of cards, flimsy structure, castle in the air; *castillo de proa*, (*naut.*) forecastle; *castillo roquero*, castle built on a rock; *castillo apercibido, no es decebido*, forewarned is forearmed; *hacer castillos en el aire*, (*fig.*) to build castles in the air.

castilluelo, *n.m.* small castle [CASTILLO].

castina, *n.f.* (*chem., metal.*) flux.

castizamente, *adv.* correctly, in puristic manner.

castizar, *v.t.* (*fig.*) to purify, refine.

castizo, -za, *a.* of noble descent; of a good breed; pure-blooded; pure (language); very prolific; *caballo castizo*, blood-horse; *estilo castizo*, pure style. — *n.m.f.* (*Mex.*) quadroon.

casto, -ta, *a.* pure, chaste, clean, continent; honest; modest.

castor, *n.m.* beaver; beaver-skin, -cloth, and -felt; (*Mex.*) fine red baize.

Cástor, *n.m.* (*astron.*) Castor, a star in the constellation Gemini; *Castor y Pólux*, St. Elmo's fire.

castora, *n.f.* (*prov., fam.*) top-hat.

castorcillo, *n.m.* a kind of rough, hairy serge.

castoreño, -ña, *a.* made of beaver; *sombrero castoreño*, beaver hat.

castóreo, *n.m.* (*pharm.*) castoreum.

castórico, -ca, *a.* said of an acid extracted from *castorina*.

castorina, *n.f.* oil extracted from castoreum; beaverteen.

castra, *n.f.* pruning (trees or plants); pruning season.

castración, *n.f.* castration, gelding, spaying.

castradera, *n.f.* iron instrument with which honey is taken from a hive.

castrado, -da, *a.* castrated; pruned. — *n.m.* eunuch. — *p.p.* [CASTRAR].

castrador, *n.m.* gelder, castrator.

castradura, *n.f.* castration; scar which remains after castration.

castrametación, *n.f.* castrametation, encamping.

castrapuercas, *n.f.;* **castrapuercos,** *n.m.* gelder's whistle.

castrar, *v.t.* to geld, castrate, spay; to dry up sores, wounds; to prune (trees or plants); to cut the honeycombs from beehives. — *v.r.* to dry up (wounds).

castrazón, *n.f.* cutting of honeycombs out of hives; season when this is done.

castrense, *a.* belonging to the military profession.

castro, *n.m.* act of taking honeycombs from hives; game played by boys; (*prov.*) headland; (*prov.*) hill-top with castle in ruins.

castrón, *n.m.* castrated goat; (*Cub.*) hog.

casual, *a.* casual, accidental, contingent, occasional, fortuitous.

casualidad, *n.f.* chance, hazard, contingency, accident, coincidence; *por casualidad*, by chance.

casualismo, *n.m.* casualism.

casualista, *n.m.f.* casualist.

casualmente, *adv.* casually, accidentally, contingently.

casuáridos, *n.m.* family of the cassowaries.

casuario, *n.m.* cassowary.

casuca; casucha, *n.f.;* **casucho,** *n.m.* (*coll.*) crib, miserable hut or cottage.

casuísta, *a.* casuistic, casuistical. — *n.m.f.* casuist.

casuística, *n.f.* casuistry.

casuístico, -ca, *a.* casuistical.

casulla, *n.f.* chasuble; (*Hond.*) grain of rice with its husk.

casullero, *n.m.* maker of chasubles and other vestments.

cata, *n.f.* trying by tasting; trial, sample; plummet for measuring heights; (*Col., Mex.*) trial excavation of a mine; (*Col.*) hidden thing; *dar cata*, to examine, observe; *dar a cata*, to put on trial.

cata, *imper.* [CATAR] mark, beware, lo and behold!

catabre, catabro, *n.m.* (*Col.*) shell of calabash.

catacaldos, *n.m.f.* taster of wine, liquors, soup, etc.; (*fig.*) inconstant, fickle person.

catacáustico, -ca, *n.f., a.* catacoustic(s).

cataclismo, *n.m.* cataclysm, deluge, inundation; catastrophe, upheaval, appalling disaster; great social or political turmoil.

cataclismología, *n.f.* history of floods and terrestrial catastrophes.

cataclismológico, -ca, *a.* cataclysmal, cataclysmic.

cataclismólogo, *n.m.* cataclysmist.

catacresis, *n.f.* (*rhet.*) catachresis.

catacumbas, *n.f.pl.* catacombs.

catador, *n.m.* taster, sampler.

catadura, *n.f.* tasting; (*coll.*) gesture, face, countenance; *mala catadura,* repulsive face.

catafalco, *n.m.* temporary cenotaph, catafalque.

catafractarios, *n.m.pl.* mounted knights in armour.

catafractos, *n.m.pl.* cataphracted fish.

catalán, -na, *n.m.f.,* *a.* Catalan, of or belonging to Catalonia. — *n.m.* the language of Catalonia; *método catalán,* Catalan forge.

catalanismo, *n.m.* political party desiring autonomy for Catalonia; doctrine of this party; expression peculiar to Catalonia.

catalanista, *n.m.f.* partisan of *catalanismo.*

cataléctico, -ca; catalecto, -ta, *n.m.f.,* *a.* (*poet.*) catalectic (verse); *catalectos,* anthology.

catalejo, *n.m.* telescope.

catalepsia, *n.f.* catalepsy, trance.

cataléptico, -ca, *n.m.f.,* *a.* (*med.*) cataleptic.

catalicón, *n.m.* catholicon, panacea.

catalicores, *n.m.* pipette.

Catalina, *n.f.* Catherine; *rueda catalina,* principal wheel of a watch.

catalineta, *n.f.* West Indian fish.

catálisis, *n.f.* catalysis.

catalíticamente, *adv.* in a catalytic manner; from the point of view of catalysis.

catalítico, -ca, *a.* catalytic.

catalizador, *n.m.* catalytic.

catalogable, *a.* that can be catalogued.

catalogación, *n.f.* cataloguing.

catalogador, -ra; catalógrafo, -fa, *n.m.f.* cataloguer.

catalogar, *v.t.* to catalogue, list.

catálogo, *n.m.* catalogue, list, inventory, file, roll, schedule, table.

catalufa, *n.f.* kind of floor-carpet; (*Cub.*) [CATALINETA].

Cataluña, *n.f.* Catalonia.

catán, *n.m.; ***catana,** *n.f.* Indian cutlass.

catanga, *n.f.* (*Arg.*) black beetle; (*Chi.*) green scarab; (*Col.*) fish trap; (*Bol.*) one-horse cart.

catante, *a.* one who tastes or looks.

cataplasma, *n.f.* cataplasm, poultice. — *n.m.f.* (*coll.*) very tiresome person; anything badly done.

catapléctico, -ca, *a.* relating to cataplexy.

cataplexia, *n.f.* cataplexy.

¡cataplum! *interj.* bang!

catapulta, *n.f.* catapult, military engine.

catar, *v.t.* to taste, try by taste, sample; to view, examine, investigate, enquire, inspect; to judge, form an opinion; to bear in mind; to respect, esteem; to cut the combs out of beehives.

cataraña, *n.f.* sheldrake.

catarata, *n.f.* cataract, waterfall, cascade; (*med.*) cataract; *abrirse las cataratas del cielo,* to rain heavily, to pour; *batir la catarata,*

(*surg.*) to couch a cataract; *tener cataratas,* (*coll.*) not to understand clearly.

catarinita, *n.f.* (*Mex.*) variety of parakeet.

cátaros, *n.m.pl.* catharists.

catarral, *a.* catarrhal.

catarribera, *n.m.* falconer; manservant sent to follow the hawk on horseback and take its prey from it; (*iron.*) lawyer in search of briefs.

catarriento, -ta, *a.* catarrhous.

catarro, *n.m.* catarrh, cold; *catarro epidémico,* influenza.

catarroso, -sa, *n.m.f.,* *a.* catarrhal; (person) subject to colds; having a cold.

catarsis, *n.f.* catharsis.

catártico, -ca, *a.* cathartic, purging.

catartina, *n.f.* cathartin.

catasalsas, *n.m.f.* (*coll.*) [CATACALDOS].

catastral, *a.* relating to the *catastro* or census.

catastro, *n.m.* royal tax formerly imposed on real estate; census or list of real property of a county or state.

catástrofe, *n.f.* catastrophe; final point of a tragedy.

catata, *n.f.* (*Cub.*) variety of maté.

catatán, *n.m.* (*Chi.*) (*coll.*) punishment, penalty.

cataté, *a.* (*Cub.*) applied to a fatuous, stupid person of no importance.

cataviento, *n.m.* (*naut.*) dog-vane; weathercock.

catavino, *n.m.* small jug or cup for tasting wine; small hole in wine-vessel for tasting the wine.

catavinos, *n.m.* wine-taster, professional wine-sampler; (*coll.*) tippler who goes round from one tavern to another.

cate, *n.m.* (*prov.*) blow, slap; (*Philip.*) weight of half a pound.

cateador, *n.m.* (*Am.*) prospector; geologist's hammer.

catear, *v.t.* to procure, solicit; (*coll.*) to fail, suspend in an examination; (*Arg., Chi., Per.*) to prospect.

catecismo, *n.m.* catechism.

catecú, *n.m.* catechu.

catecumenado, *n.m.* state of preparation as catechumen.

catecuménico, -ca, *a.* catechumenical.

catecúmeno, -na, *n.m.f.* catechumen.

cátedra, *n.f.* cathedra, chair or seat of a professor; professorship, professorate; branch of study taught by a professor; lecture-room in a university; (*eccl.*) see; *cátedra del Espíritu Santo,* pulpit; *cátedra de San Pedro,* the Holy See; *pasear uno la cátedra,* to lecture to an empty class-room; *poder uno poner cátedra,* to master an art or science; *poner cátedra,* to speak pedantically.

catedral, *n.f.,* *a.* cathedral; *hacer de una ermita una catedral,* to make a mountain out of a molehill.

catedralidad, *n.f.* dignity of a cathedral church.

catedrático, -ca, *n.m.f.* professor in a university or college. — *n.m.* contribution paid to bishops and prelates. — *n.f.* professor's wife.

catedrilla, *n.f.* university chair occupied temporarily by an undergraduate.

categorema, *n.f.* (*log.*) the quality by which an object is classified in a certain category.

categoría, *n.f.* (*phil.*) predicament or category;

condition, class, character of a person; *hombre de categoría*, man of rank.

categóricamente, *adv.* categorically.

categórico, -ca, *a.* categorical, categoric.

catenaria, *n.f.*, *a.* catenary.

catenular, *a.* catenarian.

catequesis, *n.f.* catechizing.

catequismo, *n.m.* catechism; teaching by question and answer; instruction in religious doctrine.

catequista, *n.m.f.* catechist.

catequístico, -ca, *a.* catechetic, catechetical, catechistical.

catequización, *n.f.* catechizing, catechism.

catequizador, -ra, *n.m.f.* one who persuades.

catequizante, *a.* catechizing. — *n.m.f.* catechiser, catechist.

catequizar, *v.t.* (*pret.* **catequicé**; *pres. subj.* **catequice**) to catechize, instruct in religious doctrine; (*fig.*) to induce, persuade.

caterético, -ca, *a.* (*med.*) erosive.

caterva, *n.f.* multitude, throng, crowd, swarm.

catete, *n.m.* (*Chi.*) vulgar name for the devil.

catéter, *n.m.* (*surg.*) catheter.

cateterismo, *n.m.* sounding with a catheter or probe.

cateterizar, *v.t.* to sound with a catheter.

cateto, *n.m.* each of the two sides containing the right-angle in a rectangular triangle; (*fig.*) villager, countryman.

catey, *n.m.* (*Cub.*) small cockatoo; in some West Indies Isles, kind of palm-tree.

catilinaria, *a.* catilinarian. — *n.f.* speech or writing containing severe censure.

catimbao, *n.m.* (*Chi., Per.*) figures of pasteboard appearing in Corpus Christi procession; (*Chi.*) (*fig.*) ridiculously dressed person; (*Chi.*) clown; (*Per.*) squat, dumpy person.

catín, *n.m.* copper-refining crucible.

catinga, *n.f.* (*Am.*) bad smell (esp. that of sweat); (*Chi.*) (*contempt.*) nickname given by sailors to soldiers.

catión, *n.f.* (*elec.*) cation.

catire, *n.m.f.*, *a.* (*Am.*) blond, light-haired (offspring of mulatto and white).

catite, *n.m.* loaf of the finest refined sugar; slight slap; *dar catite a uno*, to beat someone.

cato, *n.m.* Japan earth, or catechu.

catoche, *n.m.* (*Mex.*) bad humour.

catódico, -ca, *a.* cathodic.

cátodo, *n.m.* cathode.

católicamente, *adv.* catholically, catholicly.

catolicidad, *n.f.* catholicity; Catholicism.

catolicísimo, -ma, *a. superl.* extremely Catholic.

catolicismo, *n.m.* Catholicism.

católico, -ca, *a.* Catholic; catholic, universal; true, infallible; *no estar muy católico*, (*coll.*) to feel out of sorts, in bad form. — *n.m.f.* Catholic.

catolicón, *n.m.* (*pharm.*) electuary.

catón, *n.m.* primer, reading-book for children; (*fig.*) severe censor.

catonizar, *v.t.* to censure severely.

catopter, *n.m.* (*opt.*) speculum.

catóptrica, *n.f.* catoptrics.

catóptrico, -ca, *a.* catoptric.

catoptromancia, *n.f.* catoptromancy.

catorce, *n.m.*, *a.* fourteen; fourteenth.

catorcena, *n.f.* conjunction of fourteen units.

catorceno, -na, *a.* fourteenth; aged fourteen.

catorzavo, -va, *n.m.*, *a.* one-fourteenth (part).

catre, *n.m.* cot, small bedstead; *catre de mar*, hammock, cot; *catre de tijera*, camp-bed, field-bed.

catrecillo, *n.m.* canvas camp-stool.

catricofre, *n.m.* folding-bed, bed-lounge, press-bed which shuts up.

catrintre, *n.m.* (*Chi.*) cheese made with skim-milk; (*Chi.*) beggar.

caturra, *n.f.* (*Chi.*) small parrot or parakeet.

catzo, *n.m.* (*Ec.*) kind of bumblebee.

cauba, *n.f.* (*Arg.*) small tree whose wood is used in cabinet-making.

cauca, *n.m.* (*Col., Ec.*) herb cultivated as fodder.

caucalis, *n.m.* (*bot.*) bur-parsley, bur-weed.

caucáseo, -sea; caucasiano, -na, *a.* Caucasian (region).

caucásico, -ca, *a.* Caucasian (race).

cauce, *n.m.* river-bed; ditch, trench.

caución, *n.f.* caution, precaution, warning, prevention, care; security or pledge given for the performance of an agreement; *caución de indemnidad*, (*law*) bail-bond; surety, guarantee, gage; *caución juratoria*, parole.

caucionar, *v.t.* to take precautions against loss or harm; to bail.

caucha, *n.f.* (*Chi.*) variety of thistle used as an antidote against the sting of poisonous spiders.

cauchal, *n.m.* rubber plantation or patch.

cauchera, *n.f.* rubber-yielding plant.

cauchero, *n.m.* collector of india-rubber.

cauchil, *n.m.* (*prov.*) small well or reservoir of water.

caucho, *n.m.* caoutchouc, India-rubber, gum-elastic.

cauchotina, *n.f.* rubber solution used in tanneries.

cauda, *n.f.* train of a bishop's robe.

caudal, *a.* having much water; (*zool.*) caudal. — *n.m.* property, fortune, means, wealth, fund; capital, principal sum, stock; volume (of water); (*fig.*) appreciation, esteem; (*fig.*) plenty, abundance; *águila caudal*, red-tailed eagle; *hacer caudal de una persona* or *cosa*, to hold a person or thing in high estimation; *echar caudal en alguna cosa*, to spend much money on something; *redondear uno su caudal*, to clear one's fortune of liabilities; *tras poco caudal, mala ventura*, troubles never come singly.

caudalejo, *n.m.* moderate fortune [CAUDAL].

caudalosamente, *adv.* copiously, abundantly, opulently.

caudaloso, -sa, *a.* having much water; copious, abundant; rich, wealthy.

caudatario, *n.m.* (*eccl.*) train-bearer; (*coll.*) adulator.

caudato, -ta, *a.* having a tail (said of a comet); having a refrain (sonnet).

caudatrémula, *n.f.* wagtail.

caudillaje, *n.m.* command; chief's power; (*Arg., Chi.*) tyranny.

caudillo, *n.m.* chief, leader, director, principal man; (*mil.*) commander; (*fig.*) hero.

caudimano, *a.* (*zool.*) having a prehensile tail.

caudón, *n.m.* bird of prey.

caula, *n.f.* (*Chi., Hond.*) trick, deceit, cunning.

caulescente, *a.* (*bot.*) caulescent.

caulícolo; cauliculo, *n.m.* (*arch.*) caulis, ornament of the capital of columns.

caulífero, -ra, *a.* (*bot.*) cauliferous.
caulifloro, -ra, *a.* (*bot.*) with flowers growing on the top of the stem.
cauliforme, *a.* (*bot.*) cauliform.
caulinario, -ria, *a.* (*bot.*) cauline.
caulote, *n.m.* (*Hond.*) malvaceous tree.
cauque, *n.m.* (*Chi.*) variety of large mackerel; (*Chi.*) (*fig.*) quick, clever person; (*Chi.*) (*iron.*) dull, stupid person.
cauro, *n.m.* north-west wind.
causa, *n.f.* origin, fundamentals; cause, motive, causality; consideration, occasion; movement, party, side, cause; (*law*) case, trial, lawsuit; criminal cause or information; (*Chi.*) light meal; (*Per.*) creole dish; *a causa de,* owing to, on account of, considering; *causa eficiente,* efficient cause; *causa final,* final cause; *causa primera,* first cause; *causa pública,* common weal; *acriminar la causa,* (*law*) to aggravate an action; *conocer de una causa,* (*law*) to judge an action; *dar la causa por conclusa,* (*law*) to wind up an action; *hacer causa,* (*law*) to bring an action; *hacer uno la causa de otro,* to take up someone's case; *quita la causa, quitarás el pecado,* remove the cause and you will remove the sin.
causador, -ra, *a.* causing, causative. — *n.m.f.* occasioner.
causahabiente, *n.m.* person holding a right from others.
causal, *a.* (*gram.*) causative, causal. — *n.f.* ground on which something is done.
causalidad, *n.f.* cause, origin; causality, causation.
causante, *a.* causative, causing, occasioning; (*coll.*) guilty, responsible. — *n.m.* causer, occasioner; (*law*) person from whom a right is derived.
causar, *v.t.* to cause, produce, generate, engender, create, make, bring about, occasion, originate; (*prov.*) to sue, enter an action.
causativo, -va, *a.* causative.
causear, *v.i.* (*Chi.*) to partake of a meal.
causeo, *n.m.* (*Chi.*) light lunch between meals.
causídico, -ca, *a.* (*law*) causidical, forensic. — *n.m.* advocate, counsellor.
causón, *n.m.* burning fever of short duration.
causticación, *n.f.* conversion into causticity; cauterization.
cáusticamente, *adv.* caustically.
causticar, *v.t.* to make caustic.
causticidad, *n.f.* causticity; pungent satire.
cáustico, -ca, *a.* caustic, burning; (*fig.*) aggressive, biting. — *n.m.* (*med.*) caustic. — *n.f.* (*math.*) caustic curve.
causticóforo, -ra, *a.* cauterizing (instrument). — *n.m.* cauter, cautery (instrument).
cautamente, *adv.* cautiously.
cautela, *n.f.* caution, care, foresight, prudence, prevention, precaution, reserve, heed, guard; artfulness, craft, cunning; *absolver a cautela,* (*eccl.*) to give the benefit of the doubt.
cautelar, *v.t.* to foresee, prevent, warn. — *v.r.* to take the necessary precautions; to proceed prudently.
cautelosamente, *adv.* cautiously, warily, guardedly.
cauteloso, -sa, *a.* cautious, wary, heedful, prudent.
cauterio, *n.m.* cauterization; cautery; (*fig.*) corrective; *cauterio actual,* actual cautery,

burning with hot iron; *cauterio potencial,* potential cautery, produced by chemicals.
cauterización, *n.f.* cauterization, cauterizing.
cauterizador, -ra, *a.* cauterizing. — *n.m.f.* one who or that which cauterizes.
cauterizante, *a.* cauterizing.
cauterizar, *v.t.* (*pret.* **cauxtericé,** *pres. subj.* **cauterice**) to cauterize; (*fig.*) to correct or reproach with severity; (*fig.*) to blame, to brand, stigmatize.
cautín, *n.m.* soldering-iron.
cautivador, -ra, *a.* captivating.
cautivante, *a.* captivating, interesting.
cautivar, *v.t.* to make prisoners of war; to imprison; (*fig.*) to captivate, charm, subdue. — *v.i.* to be imprisoned, fall a prisoner; *cautivar a alguno con promesas,* to win someone with promises.
cautiverio, *n.m.;* **cautividad,** *n.f.* captivity, confinement.
cautivo, -va, *n.m.f.,* *a.* captive; (*poet.*) captivated, (one) charmed by beauty.
cauto, -ta, *a.* cautious, wary, prudent, heedful.
cava, *n.f.* digging and earthing of vines; wine-cellar in the royal palace.
cavacote, *n.m.* mound made with the hoe, small hillock of earth.
cavadiza, *a.* dug out of a pit (as sand).
cavado, -da, *a.* hollow, hollowed, dug out. — *p.p.* [CAVAR].
cavador, *n.m.* digger.
cavadura, *n.f.* digging.
cavalillo, *n.m.* ditch, trench between two properties.
caván, *n.m.* (*Philip.*) dry measure of capacity (about 2 bushels).
cavar, *v.t.* to dig, excavate. — *v.i.* to penetrate far; (*fig.*) to think profoundly or intensely.
cavatina, *n.f.* cavatina.
cavazón, *n.f.* digging.
caverna, *n.f.* cave, cavern; (*med.*) ulcer or wound cavity; (*slang*) house.
cavernidad; cavernosidad, *n.f.* cave, cavern.
cavernilla, *n.f.* small cavern [CAVERNA].
cavernoso, -sa, *a.* cavernous, caverned.
caveto, *n.m.* (*arch.*) concave moulding forming quadrant of a circle.
caví, *n.m.* dried root of the Peruvian plant *oca.*
cavia, *n.f.* circular excavation made at the foot of a tree to collect water.
cavial; caviar, *n.m.* caviare, sturgeon's roe.
cavicornios, *n.m.pl.* family of hollow-horned ruminants.
cavidad, *n.f.* cavity, excavation.
cavilación, *n.f.* cavilling; captious objection.
cavilar, *v.t.* to cavil, find fault; to think deeply.
cavilosamente, *adv.* cavillously.
cavilosidad, *n.f.* cavilling, captiousness.
caviloso, -sa, *a.* captious, cavillous, subtle.
cay, *n.m.* (*Arg.*) capuchin monkey.
cayada, *n.f.;* **cayado,** *n.m.* shepherd's crook; bishop's crozier; walking-stick.
cayán, *n.m.* (*Philip.*) boat awning.
cayana, *n.f.* (*Arg., Col.*) large baking pan.
cayanco, *n.m.* (*Hond.*) poultice of hot herbs.
cayapear, *v.i.* (*Ven.*) to combine for assault and battery.
cayente, *a.* falling.
cayeputi, *n.m.* cajuput-tree; cajuput oil.
cayo, *n.m.* rock, shoal, islet, cay, key.
cayuco, *n.m.* (*Am.*) a fishing boat.

caz, *n.m.* canal, ditch, trench; conduit, mill-race.

caza, *n.f.* chase, hunting, fowling; (*naut.*) chase, pursuit; game (wild animals or birds); *caza mayor,* big-game hunting; *caza menor,* shooting, fowling; chasing hares and small game; (*obs.*) fine linen cloth; *partida de caza,* hunting-party; *trompa de caza,* hunting-horn; *alborotar* or *levantar la caza,* to start the game; to be the first to propose anything; *andar* or *ir a caza de una cosa,* (*fig.*) to go in pursuit of a thing; *andar a caza de gangas* or *de perdices,* to hunt for sinecures and profits; *dar caza,* to pursue; (*fig.*) to go after; in pursuit of (employment, secret, etc.); (*naut.*) to give chase to a vessel; *el que sigue la caza, ese la mata,* he who works for an aim attains it; *espantar la caza,* to spoil a transaction by acting inopportunely; *esperar la caza,* to be cautious, wait for an opportunity; *ponerse en la caza,* (*naut.*) to manœuvre an escape; *seguir uno la caza,* to follow the scent or trail; *uno levanta la caza y otro la mata,* one beats the bush, and another catches the bird.

cazabe, *n.m.* cassava; flour from the cassava-plant; bread made from this flour.

cazable, *a.* that can be hunted, runnable.

cazaclavos, *n.m.* nail-puller.

cazada, *n.f.* capacity of a *cazo,* ladleful.

cazadero, *n.m.* chase, hunting-grounds.

cazador, -ra, *a.* hunting, chasing; (*coll.*) prevailing upon. — *n.m.* hunter, huntsman, sportsman, chaser; *pl.* light infantry. — *n.f.* huntress; hunting-jacket; sack coat; (*CR.*) small insectivorous singing bird; *cazador de alforja,* one who sports with dogs, snares and other devices; *cazadores a caballo,* light cavalry.

cazar, *v.t.* (*pret.* **cacé**; *pres. subj,* **cace**) to chase, hunt, fowl; (*coll.*) to attain a difficult object by dexterity; (*coll.*) to charm and captivate by caresses and deceitful tricks; (*coll.*) to catch, surprise; *cazar una vela,* (*naut.*) to tally a sail, haul the sheet aft; *cazarlas al vuelo,* to divine another's intentions; *cazar con perdigones de plata,* said of those who buy game instead of killing it; *cazar muy largo,* to be far-sighted; *cazar moscas,* to waste time; *cazar en vedado,* to poach; to take an unfair advantage.

cazatorpedero, *n.m.* (*naut.*) destroyer.

cazcalear, *v.i.* (*coll.*) to fidget, fuss.

cazcarria, *n.f.* splashings of mud on the clothes.

cazcarriento, -ta, *a.* (*coll.*) splashed, bemired.

cazcorvo, -va, *a.* bow-legged (horse); (*Col., Ven.*) bowlegged.

cazo, *n.m.* dipper, ladle; glue-pot; melting-pan; size-kettle; founder's scoop.

cazolada, *n.f.* stew-panful.

cazoleja, *n.f.* small saucepan [CAZUELA]; pan of a musket-lock.

cazolero; cazoletero, *n.m., a.* (*coll.*) cotquean, man who does women's work in the kitchen.

cazoleta, *n.f.* small saucepan [CAZUELA]; pan of a musket-lock; boss or defence of a shield; hand-guard of a sword; kind of perfume; censer; pipe-bowl.

cazolilla; cazolita, *n.f.* small saucepan [CAZUELA].

cazolón, *n.m.* large earthen pot or stew-pan [CAZUELA].

cazón, *n.m.* dog-fish, small shark; brown sugar.

cazonal, *n.m.* fishing-tackle for the shark fishery; (*coll.*) difficulty, muddle.

cazonete, *n.m.* (*naut.*) toggle.

cazudo, -da, *a.* having a thick back (said of knives).

cazuela, *n.f.* earthen stewing-pan, crock; meat and vegetables cooked in such a pan; (*theat.*) gallery; (*theat.*) place reserved for women; (*print.*) wide composing stick holding several lines.

cazumbrar, *v.t.* to join staves with hempen cords.

cazumbre, *n.m.* hempen cord to join staves.

cazumbrón, *n.m.* cooper.

cazurro,-rra, *n.m.f., a.* (*coll.*) taciturn, sulky, sullen (person).

cazuz, *n.m.* ivy.

ce, *n.f.* the third letter of the Spanish alphabet; *¡ce!* hark! here! come here! *ce por be,* or *ce por ce,* minutely, in detail; *por ce o por be,* somehow or other.

cea, *n.f.* thigh-bone.

ceanoto, *n.m.* New Jersey tea, redroot.

cearina, *n.f.* white ointment of wax, liquid paraffin, etc.

ceática, *n.f.* sciatica.

ceático, -ca, *a.* sciatical.

ceba, *n.f.* fattening of domestic animals; (*fig.*) stoking (of furnaces).

cebada, *n.f.* barley; *cebada perlada,* pearl-barley; *dar cebada,* to attend to the horses.

cebadal, *n.m.* barley-field.

cebadar, *v.t.* to feed animals.

cebadazo, -za, *a.* belonging to barley; *paja cebadaza,* barley-straw.

cebadera, *n.f.* nose-bag; barley-bin; (*naut.*) sprit-sail; (*min.*) furnace-charger.

cebadería, *n.f.* barley-market.

cebadero, *n.m.* place where fowls or game are fed; breeder and feeder of hawks; ostler; mule carrying the feed; bell-mule; (*min.*) mouth for feeding a furnace; dealer in barley; (*art*) domestic birds feeding.

cebadilla, *n.f.* wild barley; (*bot.*) sneeze-wort; powdered hellebore-root used as snuff.

cebado, -da, *a.* fattened, fed; (*Am.*) said of a wild beast which has tasted human flesh; (*her.*) ravening. — *p.p.* [CEBAR].

cebador, *n.m.* priming-horn, powder-horn.

cebadura, *n.f.* feeding, fattening of domestic animals.

cebar, *v.t.* to fatten animals; to cram, stuff; to prime a fire-arm; to feed a fire, furnace or lamp; to bait a fish-hook; to start a hand-machine or apparatus; to light a rocket or other kind of fireworks; to remagnetize a needle; to cherish a passion or desire. — *v.t., v.i.* to penetrate; to take hold of; to stick fast to. — *v.r.* to be bent upon a thing; to prey upon; to give rein to one's passions; *cebar con maíz,* to fatten, feed with maize; *cebarse en su víctima,* to gloat over one's victim.

cebellina, *n.f.* sable; sable-fur.

cebetera, *n.f.* bag for priming materials.

cebiche, *n.m.* (*Per.*) dish made of fish and chilli.

cebil, *n.m.* (*River Plate*) the sumac tree.

cebo, *n.m.* fodder, food given to animals;

fattening of animals; bait; priming of guns; (*min.*) charge (of furnaces); incentive; kind of monkey; *cebo de pescar*, fishing-bait, bob; *cebo fulminante*, percussion-cap.

cebolla, *n.f.* onion; onion-bulb; bulbous root; round oil-receptacle of a lamp; rose-nozzle or -strainer; *cebolla albarrana*, (*bot.*) squill; *cebolla escalonia*, (*bot.*) shallot.

cebollada, *n.f.* onion ragout.

cebollana, *n.f.* chive.

cebollar, *n.m.* patch of onions.

cebollero, -ra, *n.m.f.* onion-seller.

cebolleta, *n.f.* tender onion.

cebollino, *n.m.* young onion fit for transplanting; onion seed; [CEBOLLANA]; *escardar cebollinos*, to do nothing useful; *enviar alguien a escardar cebollinos*, to tell someone to go to the devil.

cebollón, *n.m.* large onion [CEBOLLA].

cebolludo, -da, *a.* bulbous, having a bulb; (*coll.*) ill-shaped (person).

cebón, -na, *n.m.f., a.* fattened (animal).

ceboncillo, *n.m.* fatling.

cebra, *n.f.* zebra.

cebrado, -da, *a.* striped like the zebra.

cebratana, *n.f.* [CERBATANA].

cebruno, -na, *a.* having the colour of deer.

cebú, *n.m.* zebu; (*Arg.*) variety of howling-monkey.

ceburro, *a.* [CANDEAL].

ceca, *n.f.* mint for coining money; (*Sp. Mor.*) money; *de Ceca en Meca*, or *de la Ceca a la Meca*, to and fro, hither and thither.

cecal, *a.* appertaining to the blind gut; *apéndice cecal*, vermiform appendage.

ceceamiento, *n.m.* [CECEO].

cecear, *v.i.* to lisp, pronounce *s* as *c*. — *v.t.* to call anyone by using the word *ce-ce* (= I say).

ceceo, *n.m.* lisping, lisp; using the word *ce-ce*.

ceceoso, -sa, *n.m.f., a.* lisper, lisping.

cecesmil, *n.m.* (*Hond.*) plantation of early maize.

cecial, *n.m.* dried and cured hake, haddock, etc.

cecina, *n.f.* dried beef, corned beef, hung beef.

cecinado, -da, *a.* cured, dried. — *p.p.* [CECINAR].

cecinar, *v.t.* to salt and dry meat.

cecografía, *n.f.* braille, writing for the blind.

cecográfico, -ca, *a.* appertaining to *cecografía*.

cecógrafo, *n.m.* one practising this writing; braille writer.

ceda, *n.f.* z, zed, last letter of the alphabet; horse-hair.

cedacear, *v.i.* to fail, decrease (of the sight).

cedacería, *n.f.* shop where sieves are made or sold.

cedacero, *n.m.* maker or seller of sieves.

cedacillo; cedacito, *n.m.* small sieve [CEDAZO].

cedacillo, *n.m.* variety of quaking-grass.

cedazo, *n.m.* hair-sieve or strainer; bolt, bolter; kind of large fishing-net.

cedazuelo, *n.m.* small hair-sieve or strainer [CEDAZO].

cedente, *a.* ceding, granting. — *n.m.* conveyer, assigner, transferrer.

ceder, *v.t.* to grant, yield, give up, make over, convey, deliver up, transfer, cede, resign, assign. — *v.i.* to yield, yield to, submit, comply, give out, give over, give way, go back, come in; (*mech.*) to sag, slacken; to abate, grow less; to happen, turn out (well or ill); *ceder al torrente*, to be carried away by public opinion; *ceder a la razón*, to yield to reason; *ceder de su derecho*, to yield in spite of his rights; *ceder en favor de uno*, to give way in another's favour.

cedilla, *n.f.* cedilla.

cedizo, -za, *a.* putrid, rotten; *carne cediza*, tainted meat.

cedoaria, *n.f.* zedoary.

cedras, *n.f.pl.* saddle-bags of skin.

cedreleón, *n.m.* oil of cedar.

cedreno, *n.m.* base of the cedar oil.

cedria; cedrilla, *n.f.* resin from the cedar.

cédride, *n.f.* fruit of the cedar-tree.

cedrino, -na, *a.* cedarn, of cedar, cedar.

cedrito, *n.m.* beverage of sweet wine and cedar-resin.

cedro, *n.m.* cedar; *cedro de España*, savin, Spanish juniper; *cedro de las Antillas*, Spanish cedar; *cedro de la India*, deodar; *cedro del Líbano*, cedar of Lebanon.

cedróleo, *n.m.* essential oil of cedar.

cédula, *n.f.* scrip; slip of paper for writing or bearing written or printed matter; bill, decree; order; schedule, warrant; share; Government security, stock; *cédula de abono*, order to remit a tax; *cédula ante diem*, secretary's summons to members of a society; *cédula de cambio*, bill of exchange; *cédula personal* or *de vecindad*, official identity document declaring the name, occupation, address, etc., of the bearer; *cédula real*, royal letters patent; *echar cédulas*, to draw or cast lots.

cedulaje, *n.m.* fees or dues paid for a *cédula real*.

cedulario, *n.m.* collection of *cédulas reales*.

cedulilla; cedulita, *n.f.* small slip of paper.

cedulón, *n.m.* large bill; proclamation, public notice; long edict [CÉDULA]; (*fig.*) lampoon.

cefalalgia, *n.f.* headache.

cefalea, *n.f.* violent headache, migraine.

cefáleo, -lea, *a.* cephalous.

cefálico, -ca, *a.* cephalic.

céfalo, *n.m.* mullet.

cefaloídeo, -dea, *a.* cephaloid.

Cefeo, *n.m.* Cepheus, a constellation.

céfiro, *n.m.* zephyr, mild breeze; zephyr (material).

cefo, *n.m.* large African monkey.

cegador, -ra, *a.* that which causes blindness or dazzle.

cegajo, *n.m.* he-goat two years old.

cegajoso, -sa, *a.* blear-eyed, watery-eyed.

cegar, *v.i.* (*pres. indic.* **ciego;** *pret.* **cegué;** *pres. subj.* **ciegue**) to grow blind. — *v.t.* to blind, make blind; to obfuscate; to darken the light of reason; to close up (a door, window, channel, passage, road, well, etc.); *cegar una vía de agua*, (*naut.*) to stop a leak; *cegarse de cólera*, to be blinded by anger.

cegarra, *a.* (*coll.*) myopic, short-sighted.

cegarrita, *n.m.f., a.* (*coll.*) short-sighted (person); *a ojos cegarritas*, with the eyes half-shut to see at a distance.

cegato, -ta; cegatón, -na, *n.m.f., a.* [CEGARRA].

cegatoso, -sa, *a.* blear-eyed.

ceguecillo, -lla; ceguezuelo, -la, *n.m.f., a.* little blind child [CIEGO].

ceguedad, *n.f.* blindness; ignorance, intellectual darkness; hallucination, obfuscation.

ceguera, *n.f.* [CEGUEDAD]; a form of ophthalmia.

ceiba, *n.f.* silk-cotton tree; sea-moss, alga.

Ceilán, *n.m.* Ceylon.

ceja, *n.f.* eyebrow; edging of clothes, books, etc.; summit of a mountain; ridge of clouds round a hill, cloud-cap; bridge of stringed instruments; rim; (*arch.*) weather-moulding; (*carp.*) rabbet; (*Cub.*) narrow path in a forest; *arquear las cejas,* to raise one's eyebrows in surprise or wonder; *dar a uno entre ceja y ceja,* to tell someone painful truths to his face; *llevar* or *tener uno* or *metérsele, ponérsele a uno entre ceja y ceja alguna cosa,* to bear something in mind, to concentrate on something; *tener a uno entre ceja y ceja* or *entre cejas,* to take a dislike to someone; *fruncir las cejas,* to frown, knit one's brows; *hasta las cejas,* to the utmost, to the extreme; *quemarse las cejas,* (*fig.*) to study with intense application.

cejadero, *n.m.* hold-back strap of a harness; harness trace.

cejar, *v.i.* to go backward; to hold back; (*fig.*) to cede, relax, slacken.

cejijunto, -ta, *a.* having eyebrows that meet; (*fig.*) frowning.

cejilla, *n.f.* (*mus.*) bridge.

cejinegro, -ra, *a.* having black eyebrows.

cejo, *n.m.* fog which rises from rivers; esparto cord tied round a bundle of esparto-grass.

cejudo, -da, *a.* having long and heavy eyebrows.

cejuela, *n.f.* small eyebrow [CEJA].

celada, *n.f.* sallet, helm, helmet without visor; snare, ambush; artful dodge or trick; horse-soldier with helmet; part of the key of the cross-bow; *caer en la celada,* to fall into the trap; *celada borgoñota,* helmet without a visor; *en celada,* secretly.

celador, -ra, *a.* vigilant, watchful. — *n.m.f.* watcher, caretaker; curator; warden; monitor.

celaduría, *n.f.* office, position of *celador.*

celaje, *n.m.* skylight; skyscape; (*fig.*) presage; prognostic. — *pl.* cloud effects, coloured clouds; (*naut.*) scud, light clouds passing rapidly over the sky.

celajería, *n.f.* (*naut.*) scud (clouds).

celandés, -sa, *n.m.f., a.* of or belonging to Zealand (Netherlands).

celar, *v.t.* to fulfil the duties of an office with care; to watch, spy on (through fear, jealousy); to supervise, control; to cover, conceal; to carve, engrave.

celda, *n.f.* cell (in prison, convent, bee-hive).

celdilla, *n.f.* cell; cellule; niche.

celebérrimo, -ma, *a. superl.* most celebrated.

celebrable, *a.* worthy of celebration.

celebración, *n.f.* celebration, solemn performance; praise, acclamation, applause.

celebradamente, *adv.* with celebration.

celebrador, -ra, *a.* praising, applauding, celebrating.

celebrante, *a.* celebrating. — *n.m.* celebrant.

celebrar, *v.t.* to celebrate; to applaud, commend, praise, to rejoice at; to hold a conference, meeting; to venerate, respect, revere. — *v.t., v.i.* to say or sing mass.

célebre, *a.* celebrated, renowned, famous, noted; (*coll.*) gay, witty, facetious.

célebremente, *adv.* with celebrity; famously; merrily, facetiously.

celebridad, *n.f.* celebrity, renown, fame; pageant, public celebration or show.

celebro, *n.m.* skull, brain; prudence; fancy, imagination.

celemín, *n.m.* measure, equivalent to half a peck; quantity contained in such a measure.

celeminada, *n.f.* quantity of grain contained in a *celemín.*

celeminero, *n.m.* ostler.

celeque, *a.* (*ES., Hond.*) applied to tender fruits.

célere, *a.* quick, rapid. — *n.m.* one of the select three hundred knights of ancient Roman nobility. — *n.f.pl.* (*myth.*) the Hours.

celeridad, *n.f.* celerity, velocity.

celeste, *a.* celestial, heavenly; *azul celeste,* sky-blue, azure.

celestial, *a.* celestial, heavenly; excellent, perfect; delightful, agreeable; (*iron.*) silly, stupid; *música celestial,* (*coll.*) nonsense, moonshine.

celestialidad, *n.f.* glory; beatitude.

celestialmente, *adv.* celestially; divinely; perfectly; in a heavenly manner.

celestino, -na, *n.m.f., a.* Celestine, Celestinian (monk or nun). — *n.f.* (*min.*) celestine, celestite; (*coll.*) procuress.

celfo, *n.m.* (*zool.*) [CEFO].

celia, *n.f.* beverage made from wheat; a kind of beer.

celíaco, -ca, *a.* cœliac. — *n.f.* cœliac artery; chylific diarrhœa.

celibato, *n.m.* celibacy; (*coll.*) bachelor, single man.

célibe, *n.m.f.* bachelor, spinster, unmarried person, celibate.

célico, -ca, *a.* (*poet.*) celestial, heavenly.

celidonia, *n.f.* common celandine.

celinda, *n.f.* syringa.

celindrate, *n.m.* ragout made with coriander-seed.

celo, *n.m.* zeal, ardour; devotion; envy, rivalry; heat, rut. — *pl.* jealousy; suspicions; *dar celos,* to excite suspicions; *pedir celos,* to be jealous.

celosamente, *adv.* with zeal, zealously; jealously.

celosía, *n.f.* lattice of a window; venetian blind; jalousie.

celoso, -sa, *a.* zealous; jealous; suspicious; (*naut.*) light and swift-sailing; crank.

celotipia, *n.f.* jealousy.

celsitud, *n.f.* elevation, grandeur; highness, a title, now expressed by *alteza.*

celta, *n.m.f., a.* Celt, Celtic. — *n.m.* Celtic (language).

celtibérico, -ca; celtiberio, -ria; celtíbero, -ra, *n.m.f., a.* Celtiberian.

celticismo, *n.m.* Celticism.

céltico, -ca, *a.* Celtic.

celtismo, *n.m.* Celticism; love for the study of Celtic races.

celtista, *n.m.f.* Celtologist.

celtohispánico, -ca; celtohispano, -na, *a.* Celto-Spanish.

celtómano, -na, *n.m.f., a.* Celtomaniac.

célula, *n.f.* small cell or cavity; (*bot., zool.*) cell, cellule.

celulado, -da, *a.* cellulate, cellulated.

celular; celulario, -ria, *a.* cellular; system of isolation in prisons.

celuliforme, *a.* cellulated.

celulilla, *n.f.* very small cell; small cellule or cavity.

celuloide, *n.m.* celluloid.

celulosa, *n.f.* cellulose.

celulosidad, *n.f.* cellulosity.

celuloso, -sa, *a.* cellulose, cellulous.

celladura, *n.f.* repairing of broken cask-hoops.

cellar, *a.* forged (of iron).

cellenco, -ca, *a.* (*coll.*) decrepit.

cellisca, *n.f.* fine rain, snow or sleet; squall.

cellisquear, *v.i.* to sleet; to come down violently (of fine snow or rain); to blow a squall of snow.

cello, *n.m.* hoop used in cooperage.

cementación, *n.f.* cementation.

cementar, *v.t.* to cement; (*min.*) to precipitate.

cementatorio, -ria, *a.* relating to cementation.

cementerial, *a.* relating to a cemetery.

cementerio, *n.m.* cemetery, churchyard, graveyard.

cemento, *n.m.* cement; binding substance in rocks; bony covering of teeth; *cemento de Portland,* Portland cement; *cemento armado* or *hormigón armado,* reinforced concrete.

cementoso, -sa, *a.* like cement.

cena, *n.f.* supper, evening meal; *Jueves de la cena,* (*obs.*) Maundy Thursday.

cenaaoscuras, *n.m.f.* (*coll.*) recluse; miser.

cenáculo, *n.m.* cenacle, guest-chamber (where the Last Supper was taken).

cenacho, *n.m.* basket or hamper for fruit, vegetables, etc.

cenadero, *n.m.* summer-house; supper-room.

cenado, -da, *a.* that has supped.

cenador, -ra, *a.* supping. — *n.m.f.* one fond of suppers. — *n.m.* summer-house; arbour, bower; open gallery round a court-yard in a Spanish house.

cenaduría, *n.f.* (*Mex.*) eating-house where food is only served at night.

cenagal, *n.m.* slough, quagmire; (*coll.*) difficult or unpleasant affair.

cenagoso, -sa, *a.* muddy, miry, marshy.

cenal, *n.m.* topgallant sail of a felucca.

cenancle, *n.m.* (*Mex.*) cob, the spike of maize.

cenar, *v.i.* to sup, have supper. — *v.t.* to eat (something) at supper.

cenata, *n.f.* (*Col., Cub.*) convivial supper amongst friends.

cencapa, *n.f.* (*Per.*) llama's halter.

cenceño, -ña, *a.* lean, thin, slight, slender; *pan cenceño,* unleavened bread.

cencerra, *n.f.* [CENCERRO].

cencerrada, *n.f.* charivari; tin-pan serenade at the door of a widower on the night of his re-marriage.

cencerrear, *v.i.* to jingle continually (of cowbells, etc.); (*coll.*) to make a din or rattle (doors, windows, etc.); to play on an untuned guitar.

cencerreo, *n.m.* jingling, rattling noise.

cencerro, *n.m.* bell worn by cattle; *a cencerros tapados,* privately, by stealth; *cencerro zumbón,* bell worn by leading beast of a drove.

cencerrón, *n.m.* small bunch of grapes remaining ungathered.

cencido, -da, *a.* untilled, uncultivated.

cencuate, *n.m.* (*Mex.*) poisonous snake.

cendal, *n.m.* gauze, light thin stuff made of silk or thread; scarf used by the priest for the consecration at Mass; barbs of a feather; Moorish vessel with xebec rigging, and usually armed. — *pl.* cotton for an inkstand.

cendea, *n.f.* (*prov.*) in Navarre, municipal borough composed of several villages.

cendra; cendrada, *n.f.* bone-dust paste used for cupels; *ser (vivo como) una cendra,* (*fig.*) to be as lively as a cricket.

cenefa, *n.f.* border; band, hem, stripe on a piece of cloth, etc.; centre part of a chasuble; hangings, flounce, valance, trimming; (*naut.*) top rim, paddle-box rim; (*naut.*) awning.

ceni, *n.m.* fine brass or bronze.

cenia, *n.f.* irrigation water-wheel; plot watered in this way.

cenicero, *n.m.* ash-bin, ash-pit, ash-pan; ash-tray.

Cenicienta, La. Cinderella; person or thing unjustly ignored or despised (*n.f.* c-).

ceniciento, -ta, *a.* ash-coloured, ashen, cinerous.

cenicilla, *n.f.* (*bot.*) Oidium.

cenismo, *n.m.* mixture of dialects.

cenit, *n.m.* zenith.

ceniza, *n.f.* ash, ashes, cinders; (*paint.*) size on canvas; (*bot.*) Oidium. — *pl.* ashes, remains of the dead; *día* or *miércoles de ceniza,* Ash Wednesday; *cenizas azules,* lapis lazuli, blue paint; *cenizas de estaño,* putty; *cenizas graveladas,* weed-ashes; *cenizas de vegetales,* potash; *convertir en* or *reducir a cenizas* or *hacer ceniza(s),* to smash into smithereens, to lay in ashes; *descubrir la ceniza,* to stir up old quarrels; *huir de la ceniza y caer en las brasas,* to fall from the frying-pan into the fire; *poner a uno la ceniza en la frente,* to outdo someone; *tomar uno la ceniza,* to receive the ashes on Ash Wednesday.

cenizal, *n.m.* [CENICERO].

cenizo, -za, *a.* ash-coloured. — *n.m.* goose-foot.

cenizoso, -sa, *a.* ashen; ashy; covered with ashes.

cenobio, *n.m.* monastery.

cenobita, *n.m.f.* cœnobite monk, nun.

cenobítico, -ca, *a.* cœnobitical.

cenobitismo, *n.m.* cœnobitism.

cenojil, *n.m.* garter.

cenopegias, *n.f.pl.* Jewish feast of Tabernacles.

cenotafio, *n.m.* cenotaph, monument to the dead.

cenote, *n.m.* (*Mex.*) water reservoir in caves.

censal, *a.* (*prov.*) [CENSUAL]. — *n.m.* (*prov.*) annual ground-rent.

censalista, *n.m.f.* (*prov.*) [CENSUALISTA].

censatario, *n.m.* vassal; one who pays an annuity out of his estate; lessee; farmer.

censo, *n.m.* agreement for settling an annuity; annual ground-rent, rental, lease; income; census; poll-tax; (*fig.*) burden, charge; *censo de agua,* water-tax; *censo de por vida,* life annuity; *censo redimible,* redeemable annuity.

censontli; censontle, *n.m.* (*Mex.*) mockingbird.

censor, *n.m.* censor; censorious critic, censorious person.

censoría, *n.f.* censorship; censor's office.

censorino, -na; censorio, -ria, *a.* censorial; censorious.

censual, *a.* belonging to a lease, annuity or rent; rental.

censualista, *n.m.f.* lessor, annuitant; copyholder.

censura, *n.f.* censorship; office of a censor, act of exercising this office by examining books, etc., before publication; critical literary review; censure, blame, reproach, reprimand; spiritual punishment.

censurable, *a.* censurable.

censurador, -ra, *a.* censorious. — *n.m.* censor; fault-finder.

censurante, *a.* censorious, censoring.

censurar, *v.t.* to censor, criticize, review, judge; to blame, censure; to reprove, correct; to reprehend; to accuse.

censuratorio, -ria, *a.* censorial.

censurista, *a.* critical, carping. — *n.m.f.* critic, fault-finder.

centaura, *n.f.* (*bot.*) centaury; *centaura mayor,* great centaury; *centaura menor,* lesser centaury.

centaureo, -rea, *a.* gentianic. — *n.f.* [CENTAURA]; gentian. — *n.f.pl.* Gentiana.

centauro, *n.m.* (*myth.*) centaur; (*astron.*) Centaur.

centavo, -va, *a.* centesimal. — *n.m.* centesimal, hundredth part.

centella, *n.f.* lightning; flash of fire; spark of passion or discord; (*slang*) sword; (*Chi.*) crowfoot, buttercup.

centellador, -ra, *a.* brilliant, flashing.

centellante, *a.* sparkling, flashing.

centellar; centellear, *v.i.* to sparkle, flash, twinkle.

centelleo, *n.m.* sparkle, scintillation.

centellica; centellita, *n.f.* small spark or flash [CENTELLA].

centellón, *n.m.* large spark or flash [CENTELLA].

centén, *n.m.* a Spanish gold coin worth twenty-five *pesetas* (i.e. one hundred *reales*).

centena, *n.f.* hundred; century.

centenada, *n.f.* hundred; *a centenadas,* by hundreds.

centenal, *n.m.* centenary; rye-field.

centenar, *n.m.* hundred, centenary; rye-field; *a centenares,* by hundreds.

centenario, -ria, *a.* centenary, centennial, secular. — *n.m.* centenary, centennial. — *n.m.f.,* *a.* centenarian.

centenaza, *a.* belonging to rye; *paja centenaza,* rye-straw.

centenero, -ra, *a.* good for rye (soil).

centeno, *n.m.* rye.

centeno, -na, *a.* hundred.

centenoso, -sa, *a.* mixed with rye.

centesimal *a.* centesimal, hundredth.

centésimo, -ma, *n.m.f.,* *a.* centesimal, hundredth.

centiárea, *n.f.* centiare, square metre, hundredth part of an are.

centígrado, -da, *a.* centigrade.

centigramo, *n.m.* centigram.

centilitro, *n.m.* centilitre.

centiloquio, *n.m.* work divided into a hundred parts or chapters.

centillero, *n.m.* (*Chi.*) seven-light candelabra used in churches.

centimano, -na, *a.* (*poet.*) hundred-handed.

centímetro, *n.m.* centimetre.

céntimo, -ma, *a.* hundredth. — *n.m.* copper coin, centime; one-hundredth part of any monetary unit.

centinela, *n.m.f.* sentry, sentinel; person on watch; *centinela avanzada,* advance guard; *centinela a caballo,* mounted sentinel; *centinela perdida,* forlorn hope; *centinela de vista,* prisoner's guard; *hacer* or *estar de centinela,* (*mil.*) to stand sentry, to be on guard.

centinodia, *n.f.* knot-grass, persicaria.

centípedo, -da, *a.* centipedal. — *n.m.pl.,* (*entom.*) genus of centipedes.

centiplicado, -da, *a.* centuple, centuplicate, hundredfold.

centola; centolla, *n.f.* marine spider-crab.

centón, *n.m.* crazy-quilt; (*fig.*) cento, a literary composition; (*mil.*) coarse covering for war machines.

centonar, *v.t.* to pile, heap up untidily; (*fig.*) to compile centos.

centrado, -da, *a.* centred; (*her.*) having something on centre of globe or sphere.

central, *a.* central, centric. — *n.f.* central, head office; generating plant.

centralidad, *n.f.* centrality.

centralismo, *n.m.* centralism.

centralista, *n.m.f.,* *a.* centralist.

centralización, *n.f.* centralization.

centralizador, -ra, *n.m.f.,* *a.* centralizing, that centralizes; relating to centralization.

centralizar, *v.t.* (*pret.* **centralicé;** *pres. subj.* **centralice**) to centralize.

centralmente, *adv.* centrally.

centrar, *v.t.* to centre.

céntrico, -ca, *a.* central, focal; *punto céntrico,* axis, pivot; aim; centre of attraction.

centrifugación, *n.f.* action of separating by a centrifuge.

centrifugador, *n.m.* centrifuge.

centrifugar, *v.t.* to separate by means of a centrifuge.

centrífugo, -ga, *a.* centrifugal; *bomba centrífuga,* centrifugal pump; *fuerza centrífuga,* centrifugal force.

centrina, *n.f.* variety of crab.

centripetencia, *n.f.* tendency to approach the centre.

centrípeto, -ta, *a.* centripetal.

centrisco, *n.m.* trumpet-fish.

centro, *n.m.* centre, midst, middle; (*geom.*) centre, axis; headquarters, main office; core, innermost part; nucleus; political party of moderate views; circle in which one moves; club, reunion place; (*fig.*) principal aim; (*fig.*) principal street or district; (*Ec.*) short flannel dress worn by Indian women; (*Cub.*) transparent skirt used by mestizo women; (*Cub.*) suit comprising trousers, shirt and waistcoat; (*Hond., Mex.*) waistcoat; *centro de gravedad,* (*phys.*) centre of gravity; *centro de la batalla,* (*mil.*) centre, main body of troops; *centro de mesa,* centre-piece for a table; *centros nerviosos,* nerve centres; *estar en su centro,* (*fig.*) to be in one's element, content with one's lot.

Centroamericano, -na, *n.m.f.,* *a.* of or from Central America; native of Costa Rica, Nicaragua, Honduras, El Salvador, Guatemala.

centrobárico, -ca, *a.* centrobaric.

centroide, *n.m.* (*math.*) centrode.

centunviral, *a.* centunviral.

centunvirato, *n.m.* centumvirate.
centunviro, *n.m.* centumvir.
centuplicación, *n.f.* centuplication.
centuplicadamente, *adv.* in centuplicate, a hundredfold; considerably increased.
centuplicado, -da, *a.* centuplicated, multiplied a hundredfold. — *p.p.* (CENTUPLICAR).
centuplicador, -ra, *n.m.f.*, *a.* centuplicating, multiplying a hundredfold.
centuplicar, *v.t.*, *v.r.* to centuplicate.
céntuplo, -pla, *n.m.f.*, *a.* centuple, centuplicate.
centuria, *n.f.* century; one hundred soldiers (in Roman times).
centurión, *n.m.* centurion.
centurionazgo, *n.m.* office of a centurion.
cenzalino, -na, *a.* relating to a *cénzalo* or mosquito.
cénzalo, *n.m.* mosquito.
ceñido, -da, *a.* contracted, reduced, confined; moderate in expense or pleasure; narrow-waisted (insects). — *p.p.* [CEÑIR].
ceñidor, *n.m.* belt, sash, girdle.
ceñidura, *n.f.* act of girding; contraction, reduction, restriction.
ceñiglo, *n.m.* white goose-foot.
ceñir, *v.t.* (*pres. indic.* **ciño;** *pres. subj.* **ciña**) to gird, girdle, circle, surround; to environ, hem in; (*fig.*) to reduce, contract, abbreviate; *ceñir espada,* to gird or wear a sword; *ceñir la plaza,* to invest or besiege a place; *ceñir el viento,* (*naut.*) to haul the wind; *ceñir con* or *de flores,* to girdle with flowers. — *v.r.* to confine or limit oneself (to certain words); to reduce one's expenses, words, etc.; *ceñirse a lo justo,* to limit oneself to the strict necessities; *ceñirse a las circunstancias,* to adapt oneself to circumstances.
ceño, *n.m.* frown, browbeating; supercilious expression; hoop, ring, band; (*vet.*) circle round the top of a horse's hoof; (*poet.*) gloomy aspect of the sea or sky.
ceñoso, -sa, *a.* (*vet.*) hoof surrounded with rings; [CEÑUDO].
ceñudo, -da, *a.* frowning, supercilious; grim, gruff; browbeating.
ceo, *n.m.* dory.
cepa, *n.f.* vine-stock; underground butt-end of tree-stem; stump, stub; (*fig.*) origin, stock of a family; root of horns or tails of animals; (*arch.*) pier of an arch; *de buena cepa,* of good family, origin or stock.
cepeda; cepera, *n.f.* land overgrown with heath used in charcoal-making.
cepejón, *n.m.* butt-end of a branch torn from the trunk.
cepellón, *n.m.* earth left round the roots of a plant for transplanting.
cepilladura, *n.f.* planing. — *pl.* shavings.
cepillamiento, *n.m.* the act of planing.
cepillar, *v.t.* to brush; to plane; to polish.
cepillo, *n.m.* poor-box, charity-box; (*carp.*) plane; brush; *cepillo de dientes,* tooth-brush.
cepo, *n.m.* bough or branch of a tree; stock of an anvil; (*naut.*) bilboes; stocks (for punishment); shoemaker's horse; trap, snare (for wolves, etc); reel for winding silk; poor-box; stocks of gun-carriage; (*zool.*) [CEFO]; (*mech.*) block, socket, clasp, clamp, joining-press; *cepo del ancla,* anchor-stock. — *pl.* notched cleats; *cepos quedos,* (*interj.*, *coll.*) hands off! stop! no more of that!

cepón, *n.m.* large stub of tree or vine-stock [CEPA].
ceporro, *n.m.* old vine pulled up for fuel; (*fig.*) rough man.
cequí, *n.m.* sequin, Venetian gold coin.
cequia, *n.f.* [ACEQUIA].
cera, *n.f.* wax; wax tapers, wax candles; *cera aleda,* bee-glue, propolis; *cera de dorar,* gold size; *cera de los oídos,* ear-wax, cerumen; *cera toral,* unbleached wax; *cera vieja,* ends of wax candles; *cera virgen,* virgin wax; *hacer de uno cera y pabilo,* to turn a man which way you please; *no hay más cera que la que arde,* there is nothing more than what you see; *no quedar a uno cera en el oído,* to have spent the last of one's fortune; *ser una cera* or *como una cera,* or *hecho de cera,* to be pliable as wax, of a pliant or gentle disposition; *melar las ceras,* to fill the combs with honey.
ceracates, *n.f.* yellow agate.
ceráceo, -cea, *a.* cereous, waxy.
ceración, *n.f.* preparation of metal for fusion.
cerafolio, *n.m.* common chervil.
cerámica, *n.f.* ceramic art; ceramics.
cerámico, -ca, *a.* ceramic.
ceramista, *n.m.f.* ceramist.
ceramita, *n.f.* precious stone; brick stronger than granite.
cerapez, *n.f.* cobbler's wax.
cerasina, *n.f.* cerasin.
cerasiote, *n.m.* purge containing cherry-juice.
cerasta; cerastas, *n.f.;* **ceraste; cerastes,** *n.m.* cerastes, horned serpent.
ceratias, *n.m.* double-tailed comet.
cerato, *n.m.* oil and wax ointment.
ceratoideo, -dea, *a.* ceratoid.
ceratótomo, *n.m.* ceratotome.
ceraunia, *n.f.* thunderbolt (stone).
ceraunómetro, *n.m.* apparatus for measuring intensity of lightning.
ceraunoscopión, *n.m.* ceraunoscope.
cerbatana, *n.f.* pop-gun; pea-shooter; blow-pipe; acoustic trumpet for the deaf; ancient culverin; *hablar por cerbatana,* to speak through an intermediary.
cerbero, *n.m.* Cerberus; shrub with poisonous sap.
cerca, *n.f.* enclosure, hedge, fence. — *n.m.pl.* (*paint.*) objects in the foreground. — *adv.* near, nigh, close by; (requires *de* when preceding noun or pronoun); *cerca de tu tío,* near or close to your uncle; *son cerca de las ocho,* it is close on or nearly eight o'clock; *embajador cerca de Su Majestad Británica,* ambassador to Her Britannic Majesty; *aquí cerca* or *cerca de aquí,* just by, near here; *cerca de,* approximately, about, nearly; *de cerca,* close by, closely, near; *en cerca,* round about; *cerca le anduvo,* he had (that was) a close shave; *tener buen* or *mal cerca,* to admit or not to admit of close examination; *tocar de cerca,* to affect nearly, be nearly allied to, be greatly interested in, strike home.
cercado, -da, *a.* enclosed, fenced, walled in; *cercado de desdichas y trabajos,* involved in troubles and misfortunes. — *n.m.* enclosed garden, field, etc.; fence, enclosure; (*Per.*) territorial division. — *p.p.* [CERCAR].
cercador, -ra, *a.* enclosing. — *n.m.f.* hedger, encloser. — *n.m.* blunt chisel used in repoussé-work.
cercadura, *n.f.* enclosure, fence, wall.

cercamiento, *n.m.* act of enclosing.
cercanamente, *adv.* nigh, nearly.
cercanía, *n.f.* proximity. — *pl.* vicinity, neighbourhood; environment, surroundings.
cercano, -na, *a.* near, near to, close by, adjoining, neighbouring, approximate; *cercano a su fin,* nearing its end.
cercar, *v.t.* (*pret.* **cerqué;** *pres. subj.* **cerque**) to enclose, environ, fence, hem in, circle, encircle, gird, compass; to surround, crowd about; to pale; (*mil.*) to besiege, invest a town, fortress, etc.; to bring or put near.
cercen; cercén (a), *adv.* close to the root and all around; completely.
cercenadamente, *adv.* in a clipping manner, with retrenchment.
cercenadera, *n.f.* clipping-knife used by waxchandlers.
cercenador, -ra, *a.* clipping. — *n.m.f.* clipper.
cercenadura, *n.f.* clipping, retrenchment. — *pl.* cuttings.
cercenar, *v.t.* to pare, clip, lop off the ends or extremities; to abridge, curtail, cut away, lessen, reduce (expenses, etc.).
cercera, *n.f.* (*prov.*) strong northerly wind.
cerceta, *n.f.* widgeon. — *pl.* first growth of a deer's antlers.
cercillo, *n.m.* ear-ring; *cercillo de vid,* tendril of a vine.
cerciorar, *v.t.* to assure, affirm. — *v.r.* to ascertain, make sure.
cerco, *n.m.* hoop; ring; fence; rim, border, edge; halo; (*mil.*) blockade; circular motion; circle, small gathering; frame (of a door, picture or window); *en cerco,* round about; *alzar* or *levantar el cerco,* to raise a blockade; *poner cerco a,* to block up; to lay siege to, blockade.
cercopiteco, *n.m.* kind of long-tailed monkey.
cercote, *n.m.* fishing-net.
cercha, *n.f.* wooden rule for measuring convex or concave objects; skeleton pattern or frame for building vaults or arches; each segment of a rim; rim of a rudder.
cerchar, *v.t.* to plant vine-cuttings.
cerchearse, *v.r.* (*prov.*) to bend, curve under a load (beam, girder, etc.).
cerchón, *n.m.* (*arch.*) [CIMBRA; CIMBRIA].
cerda, *n.f.* hair of horse's tail or mane; bristle; new-mown but unthrashed cereals; bundle of unhackled flax; (*zool.*) sow. — *pl.* snares for partridges; *cerda de puerco,* hog's bristle; *ganado de cerda,* swine.
cerdada, *n.f.* herd of swine.
cerdamen, *n.m.* handful of bristles prepared for brush-making.
cerdear, *v.i.* to be weak in the fore-quarter (said of animals); to emit a harsh sound (musical instrument); (*coll.*) to decline a request by evasions.
Cerdeña, *n.f.* Sardinia.
cerdillo; cerdito, *n.m.* small hog or pig.
cerdo, *n.m.* hog, pig; *cerdo de muerte,* a pig fit to be killed; *cerdo de vida,* a pig not ready or not fit for killing; *cerdo marino,* porpoise.
cerdoso, -sa, *a.* bristly.
cerdudo, -da, *a.* [CERDOSO]; (*fig.*) bristly; hairy-chested.
cereal, *a.* cerealian, appertaining to the goddess Ceres. — *n.m.f.,* *a.* cereal.
cerealina, *n.f.* cerealin.

cerebelitis, *n.f.* inflammation of the cerebellum.
cerebelo, *n.m.* cerebellum.
cerebral, *a.* cerebral.
cerebralidad, *n.f.* cerebralism; intellectual vigour.
cerébrico, -ca, *a.* cerebric (acid).
cerebrina, *n.f.* cerebrin; anti-neuralgic drug.
cerebrino, -na, *a.* cerebral.
cerebritis, *n.f.* encephalitis.
cerebro, *n.m.* skull, brain, cerebrum; (*fig.*) head, talent.
cerebroespinal, *a.* cerebro-spinal.
cerebroideo, -dea, *a.* encephaloid.
cerebropatía, *n.f.* encephalopathy.
cereceda, *n.f.* cherry-orchard; (*slang*) galley-slaves' chain.
cerecilla, *n.f.* pod of red pepper.
cerecita, *n.f.* small cherry [CEREZA].
cereiforme, *a.* cherry-shaped.
cereleón, *n.m.* (*pharm.*) [CERATO].
ceremonia, *n.f.* ceremony, rite, solemnity, pomp, display, formality, form of civility; empty form, affected compliment; *de ceremonia,* formal, with ceremony (or pomp); *por ceremonia,* out of compliment; *guardar ceremonia,* to be formal, to stick to traditional ceremonies and customs; *lo hace de pura ceremonia,* he does it out of mere compliment (or form).
ceremonial, *a.* ceremonial, ceremonious. — *n.m.* book of ceremonies for public occasions.
ceremonialmente, *adv.* ceremonially, ceremoniously.
ceremoniáticamente, *adv.* ceremoniously.
ceremoniático, -ca, *a.* ceremonious.
ceremoniero, -ra, *a.* ceremonious.
ceremoniosamente, *adv.* ceremoniously.
ceremonioso, -sa, *a.* ceremonious, polite, formal.
cereño, -ña, *a.* wax-coloured (dog).
céreo, -rea, *a.* cereous.
cereolita, *n.f.* soft waxy-looking lava.
cerería, *n.f.* wax-chandler's shop; place in the royal palace where wax candles are kept.
cerero, *n.m.* wax-chandler; *cerero mayor,* royal chandler.
ceresina, *n.f.* mixture of zocerite and vegetable wax; *goma ceresina,* cerasin.
cerevisina, *n.f.* brewer's yeast.
cereza, *n.f.* cherry; cerise, cherry, ruddy colour; degree of incandescence of metals; *cereza garrafal,* large white-heart cherry; *cereza mollar,* cherry; *cereza póntica,* small black cherry; *cerezas y hadas malas, toman pocas, y llevan hartas* or *sartas,* troubles never come singly.
cerezal, *n.m.* plantation of cherry-trees.
cerezo, *n.m.* cherry-tree, cherry wood; *cerezo silvestre,* dog-cherry-tree.
ceribón, *n.m.* (*obs.*) surrender by an insolvent debtor of his estate to his creditors; *hacer ceribones,* (*obs.*) to make affectedly submissive compliments.
cérico, -ca, *a.* relating to an acid resulting from oxidization of cerium.
cerífero, -ra, *a.* producing, yielding wax.
cerífica, *a.* cerographical; *pintura cerífica,* encaustic or wax painting.
cerificación, *n.f.* purifying of wax.
cerificador, *n.m.* wax-purifying apparatus.
cerificar, *v.t.* to purify wax.

ceriflor, *n.m.* honey-wort, honey-flower.

cerilla, *n.f.* wax taper in rolls; wax match; (*chem.*) cerumen; kind of cold-cream or cosmetic.

cerillera, *n.f.;* **cerillero,** *n.m.* match-box.

cerillo, *n.m.* (*prov.*) wax match; (*Cub.*) tree, the wood of which is used for cabinet-making and walking-sticks.

cerina, *n.f.* wax extracted from the cork tree; substance obtained from white wax.

cerio, *n.m.* cerium; silicious oxide of cerium.

cerita, *n.f.* (*min.*) cerite.

cermeña, *n.f.* variety of pear.

cermeño, *n.m.* the *cermeña* tree; (*fig.*) coarse, rough man.

cernada, *n.f.* leached ashes; mixture of ashes and size laid on canvas to prepare it for painting; (*vet.*) plaster made of ashes, etc.

cernadero; cernaguero, *n.m.* coarse linen strainer for the leach-tub; material of linen or linen and silk for collars.

cernedero, *n.m.* apron worn in sifting flour; bolting-place.

cernedor, -ra, *n.m.f.* bolting-machine, bolter, sifter.

cerneja, *n.f.* fetlock (hair) of a horse.

cernejudo, -da, *a.* having shaggy fetlocks.

cerner, *v.t.* (*pres. indic.* **cierno**; *pres. subj.* **cierna**) to sift, bolt; (*fig.*) to scrutinize, examine minutely; (*fig.*) to refine, purify. — *v.i.* to bud and blossom; (*fig.*) to drizzle. — *v.r.* to move from side to side, waggle, waddle; to hover, soar (said of birds); to be impending, threatening; *cerner, cerner y sacar poca harina,* to make great efforts to obtain trifles.

cernícalo, *n.m.* kestrel, windhover; (*fig.*) ignorant, rough man; (*slang*) woman's cloak; *coger* or *pillar un cernícalo,* to be fuddled, to be half-seas over.

cernidillo, *n.m.* thick mist or small rain; (*fig.*) short and waddling gait.

cernido, -da, *a.* sifted. — *n.m.* sifting; sifted flour. — *p.p.* [CERNER].

cernidura, *n.f.* sifting.

cernir, *v.t.* [CERNER].

cero, *n.m.* cipher, zero, naught; *ser un cero,* or *un cero a la izquierda,* to be a mere cipher.

ceroferario, *n.m.* (*eccl.*) acolyte carrying the candelabrum.

cerografía, *n.f.* cerography.

cerográfico, -ca, *a.* cerographical.

cerógrafo, *n.m.* cerographist; (*archæol.*) Roman wax seal.

ceroideo, -dea, *a.* cereous; (*min.*) scaly.

ceroleína, *n.f.* constituent of bees-wax.

cerollo, -lla, *a.* said of grain reaped when green and soft.

ceroma, *n.f.* ointment used by Roman athletes.

ceromancia, *n.f.* ceromancy.

ceromático, -ca, *a.* containing oil and wax.

ceromiel, *n.m.* ointment of wax and honey.

cerón, *n.m.* dregs of pressed wax.

ceróneo, *n.m.* kind of embrocation.

ceronero, *n.m.,* *a.* buyer of *cerón.*

ceroplasta, *n.m.* modeller in wax.

ceroplástica, *n.f.* ceroplastics.

cerote, *n.m.* shoemaker's wax; (*coll.*) panic, fear.

cerotear, *v.t.* to wax thread (cobblers).

cerotero, *n.m.* piece of felt used to wax twine in making rockets.

ceroto, *n.m.* [CERATO] ointment of oil and wax.

cerquillo, *n.m.* small circle, hoop; seam or welt of a shoe; ring of hair or tonsure.

cerquita, *n.f.* small enclosure or fence. — *adv.* at a small distance; near in time or place; *aquí cerquita,* just by.

cerrada, *n.f.* part of the hide or skin covering the backbone of an animal.

cerradero, -ra, *a.* said of a place locked and of the thing which locks it. — *n.m.f.* lock; locker. — *n.m.* staple or hole which receives the bolt of a lock; purse-strings; *echar la cerradera,* to turn a deaf ear, to refuse flatly.

cerradizo, -za, *a.* that may be locked or fastened.

cerrado, -da, *a.* close, reserved, dissembling, secretive; secreted, concealed; incomprehensible, occult; inflexible, obstinate; speaking with typical local accent; overcast, cloudy. — *n.m.* enclosure, fence. — *hacer la cerrada,* to commit a gross fault or palpable error; *cerrado de cascos,* or *de mollera,* dull, stupid; *a puño cerrado,* with might and main; *cerrado americano,* downright American; *cerrado como pie de muleto,* as stubborn as a mule; *barba cerrada* or *cerrado de barba,* heavy, thick beard (also applied to a secretive or silent person); *a ojos cerrados,* without examination; *a puerta cerrada,* behind closed doors, privately, secretly; *a puerta cerrada el diablo se huye,* (*prov.*) avoid occasions of stumbling and you will not fall. — *p.p.* [CERRAR].

cerrador, -ra, *a.* locking, shutting. — *n.m.* locker, contrivance that locks, shutter; porter, door-keeper; tie, fastening.

cerradura, *n.f.* closure, act of locking or shutting up; lock; (*obs.*) ground surrounded by an enclosure; *cerradura embutida,* mortise lock; *cerradura de golpe* or *de muelle,* spring-lock; *cerradura de loba,* lock with wards shaped like a wolf's teeth; *cerradura de molinillo,* lock with revolving tube for key-shaft; *no hay cerradura donde es oro la ganzúa,* there's no lock proof against a golden key.

cerradurilla; cerradurita, *n.f.* small lock [CERRADURA].

cerraja, *n.f.* lock of a door; (*bot.*) common sow-thistle; *todo es agua de cerrajas,* it's nothing but empty words; it's perfectly useless.

cerrajear, *v.i.* to carry on the trade of a locksmith.

cerrajería, *n.f.* locksmith's trade, shop, or forge.

cerrajero, *n.m.* locksmith.

cerrajón, *n.m.* steep, craggy cliff.

cerramiento, *n.m.* closure, occlusion, act of shutting or locking up; lock; fence and enclosure; finishing of the roof of a building; partition wall of a house; *cerramiento de razones,* (*law*) conclusion of an argument, inference.

cerrar, *v.t.* (*pres. indic.* **cierro**; *pres. subj.* **cierre**) to close, shut, occlude, lock, fasten; to stop up, obstruct; to enclose, include, contain, fence in; to finish, terminate, put an end to; to engage the enemy. — *v.i.* to close; to become equal (horse's teeth). — *v.r.* to remain of fixed opinion, stand firm; to be shut or locked up; to heal up, become cicatrized; to grow cloudy and overcast; (*mil.*) to close in, unite; to close up (flowers); *cerrarse todas las puertas a uno*, to be completely destitute, to find all avenues closed; *cerrarse en falso*, to heal up partially; *cerrarse en callar*, to maintain an obstinate silence; *cerrarse las velaciones*, (*eccl.*) to forbid the issue of marriage licences during certain seasons; *cerrar la boca, el pico* or *los labios*, to be silent; *cerrar la carta*, to seal up a letter; *cerrar la cuenta*, to close an account; *cerrar la mollera*, to begin to get sense; *cerrar el ojo*, to die; *cerrar los ojos*, to close the eyes; to risk, venture; to die; *cerrar la oreja*, not to listen to what another is saying; *cerrar una procesión*, to bring up the rear of a procession; *cerrar la puerta*, to shut out, give a flat denial; *al cerrar del día*, at nightfall; *a cierra ojos*, blindly, inconsiderately; *cerrar el abono, el concurso, la lista*, to close the list, the competition; *cerrar el bufete*, to give up practice (lawyer); *cerrar el paso* or *el portillo*, to block the way; *cerrar el contrato*, to settle an agreement; *cerrar en falso*, to close insecurely, without locking; *cerrar la cola*, to close (of birds' tails); *cerrar la mano*, to close the hand; (*coll.*) to be tight-fisted; *cerrar la noche*, to get dark; *cerrar las filas*, to close the ranks; *cerrar las piernas*, to bring the legs together; *cerrar las Cortes, la universidad*, to end the session (of Spanish Parliament), to break up (school, university); *cerrar los estudios*, to finish one's studies; *cerrar con* or *contra el enemigo*, to close with, attack the enemy; *cuando una puerta se cierra, ciento se abren*, never lose hope of something turning up; *¡cierra España!* war-whoop of the ancient Spaniards.

cerrazón, *n.f.* dark and cloudy weather preceding tempests; (*Col.*) spur or ridge of a mountain range.

cerrejón, *n.m.* hillock.

cerrería, *n.f.* freedom, laxity, licence.

cerrero, -ra, *a.* untamed, running wild; lofty, haughty; (*Am.*) rude, rough; (*Ven.*) bitter; *caballo cerrero*, unbroken horse.

cerreta, *n.f.* (*naut.*) bulwarks.

cerril, *a.* mountainous, uneven, rough; wild, unbroken, untamed (of animals); (*coll.*) rude, unmannerly, unpolished; *puente cerril*, very narrow bridge.

cerrilmente, *adv.* roughly, wildly, rudely, curtly.

cerrilla, *n.f.* die for milling coins.

cerrillar, *v.t.* to mill coins.

cerrillo, *n.m.* (*bot.*) grama. — *pl.* dies for milling coined metal.

cerrión, *n.m.* icicle.

cerro, *n.m.* neck of an animal; backbone, ridge formed by the backbone; hill, high land; cleaned flax or hemp; (*fig.*) heap, pile; *en cerro*, bareback; unadorned; *cerro enriscado*, steep and inaccessible mountain; *pasar* or *traer la mano por el cerro*, to flatter, cajole; *como por los cerros de Úbeda*, irrelevant, foreign to the purpose; at random; *echar por esos cerros*, to go astray, off the road; to wander about.

cerrojazo, *n.m.* the loud noise of a bolt suddenly shot home.

cerrojillo; cerrojito, *n.m.* wagtail, warbler; small bolt.

cerrojo, *n.m.* bolt, latch; *tentar cerrojos*, to try all ways and means to succeed.

cerrón, *n.m.* kind of coarse fabric made in Galicia; (*slang*) [CERROJO].

cerruma; ceruma, *n.f.* pastern.

cerrumado, -da, *a.* having weak or defective pasterns (said of horses).

certamen, *n.m.* (*obs.*) duel, battle; literary controversy, disputation; competition.

certeneja, *n.f.* (*Mex.*) small and deep reservoir; (*Chi.*) pit dug in a river bed.

certeramente, *adv.* skilfully.

certería, *n.f.* dexterity (in shooting).

certero, -ra, *a.*, aiming well; well-aimed, certain, sure, knowing. — *n.m.* sharp-shooter; excellent shot.

certeza, *n.f.* certainty, certitude, assurance.

certidumbre, *n.f.* certainty; (*obs.*) security, obligation to fulfil an engagement.

certificable, *a.* certifiable; registrable.

certificación, *n.f.* certificate; certification; attestation of the truth of a fact or event; registration.

certificado, -da, *a.* certified; certificated; registered. — *n.m.* certificate. — *p.p.* [CERTIFICAR].

certificador, -ra, *a.* certifying, registering. — *n.m.f.* certifier.

certificar, *v.t.* (*pret.* **certifiqué**; *pres. subj.* **certifique**) to assure, affirm, certify; to register a letter or postal packet; (*law*) to prove by a public instrument. — *v.i.* [CERCIORAR].

certificativo, -va; certificatorio, -ria, *a.* certifying.

certinidad; certitud, *n.f.* certitude, certainty.

certísimo, -ma, *a. superl.* [CIERTO] most certain.

ceruleína; cerulina, *n.f.* (*chem.*) cerulein, cerulin.

cerúleo, -lea, *a.* cerulean, sky-blue.

cerumen, *n.m.* cerumen.

ceruminoso, -sa, *a.* ceruminous.

cerusa, *n.f.* ceruse, carbonate of lead.

cerusita, *n.f.* cerusite.

cerval; cervario, -ria, *a.* of or like a deer; *miedo cerval*, great timidity.

cervantesco, -ca; cervántico, -ca; cervantino, -na, *a.* like, in the style of, relating or peculiar to, Cervantes.

cervantismo, *n.m.* influence of or expression peculiar to Cervantes.

cervantista, *a.* admirer or student of Cervantes.

cervantófilo, -la, *n.m.f., a.* Cervantist; collector of Cervantes's works.

cervatica, *n.f.* species of locust.

cervatillo, *n.m.* musk-deer.

cervato, *n.m.* fawn.

cerveceo, *n.m.* fermentation of beer.

cervecería, *n.f.* brewhouse, brewery; alehouse; beer-saloon.

cervecero, -ra, *a.* appertaining to beer. — *n.m.f.* brewer, beer-seller. — *n.m.* set of beer-jugs and -glasses.

cerveza, *n.f.* beer, ale, malt liquor.

cervicabra, *n.f.* gazelle.

cervical; cérvico, -ca; cervicular, *a.* cervical.

cérvidos, *n.m.pl.* cervidæ, deer.

cervigudo, -da, *a.* high-necked, thick-necked; (*fig.*) obstinate, stubborn.

cerviguillo, *n.m.* thick nape of the neck.

cervillera, *n.f.* helmet, casque.

cervino, -na, *a.* cervine, resembling a deer.

cerviolas, *n.f.pl.* (*naut.*) cat-heads.

cerviz, *n.f.* cervix, nape of the neck; *doblar* or *bajar la cerviz,* to humble oneself; *levantar la cerviz,* to be elated, or proud; *ser de dura cerviz,* to be incorrigible, unruly.

cervuno, -na, *a.* cervine, resembling, belonging to a deer; of the colour of a deer.

cesación, *n.f.;* **cesamiento,** *n.m.* cessation, ceasing, pause; *cesación a divinis,* canonical suspension of divine service in a desecrated church.

cesante, *n.m.* a public officer dismissed but left with part of his salary. — *a.* ceasing; unemployed (state official).

cesantía, *n.f.* unemployment, state of retired official; pension of such an official.

César, *n.m.* Caesar, emperor; *o César o nada,* neck or nothing.

cesar, *v.i.* to cease, give over, forbear; to leave, leave off, desist; *cesar de correr,* to leave off running; *cesar en su empleo,* to leave his employment.

cesáreo, -rea, *a.* Caesarian, Caesarean, imperial; *operación cesárea,* the Caesarian operation.

cesariano, -na; cesarino, -na, *a.* Caesarian, Caesarean.

cesarismo, *n.m.* Caesarism, despotism.

cese, *n.m.* mark denoting that pay is to cease; stopping of pay.

cesible, *a.* (*law*) that may be ceded; transferable.

cesión, *n.f.* cession or transfer; assignment, conveyance; resignation; concession; *cesión de bienes,* surrender of property.

cesionario, -ria; cesonario, -ria, *n.m.f.* (*law*) cessionary.

cesionista, *n.m.f.* transferrer, assignor, grantor.

césped; céspede, *n.m.* sod, grass plot, turf, sward, clod, lawn; bark growing over cut made by pruning; *césped inglés,* rye-grass.

cespedera, *n.f.* field where grass sods are cut.

cespitar, *v.i.* to hesitate, vacillate.

cespitoso, -sa, *a.* cespitose.

cesta, *n.f.* basket, pannier, hamper; scoop or racket in the game of *pelota; llevar la cesta,* to contribute unwillingly to others' pleasure.

cestada, *n.f.* basketful.

cestería, *n.f.* basket-shop or factory; basket-making.

cestero, -ra, *n.m.f.* basket-maker, basket-seller.

cestica; cestilla, cestita, *n.f.* small basket, hand-basket.

cestico; cestillo, cestito, *n.m.* little basket.

cesto, *n.m.* hand-basket; hutch; cestus used by Roman pugilists; *coger agua en cesto,* to labour in vain; *estar hecho un cesto,* to be overcome (by sleep, by drink, etc.); *estar metido en el cesto,* to be spoiled (children); *quien hace un cesto hará ciento,* he that steals a pin will steal a pound; *ser un cesto,* (*coll.*) to be ignorant and rude.

cestodos, *n.m.pl.* Cestoidea.

cestoide; cestoideo, -dea, *a.* cestoid.

cestón, *n.m.* large pannier or basket; (*mil.*) gabion.

cestonada, *n.f.* (*mil.*) gabionade.

cesura, *n.f.* caesura.

ceta, *n.f.* [ZETA].

cetáceo, -cea, *a.* cetaceous. — *n.m.f.* cetacean. — *n.m.pl.* cetacea.

cetaria, *n.f.* hatchery.

cetarina, *n.f.* extract of Iceland lichen.

cetario, *n.m.* breeding place of whales.

cetina, *n.f.* spermaceti.

cetís, *n.m.* old Galician and Portuguese coin.

cetra, *n.f.* leather shield formerly used by the Spaniards.

cetrarina, *n.f.* bitter element found in certain lichens.

cetre, *n.m.* (*obs.*) holy-water basin; (*prov.*) assistant acolyte.

cetrería, *n.f.* falconry, hawking, fowling with falcons.

cetrero, *n.m.* verger; falconer; sportsman.

cetrífero, *n.m.* (*poet.*) one who bears a sceptre.

cetrino, -na, *a.* citrine; citrinous, lemon-coloured; (*fig.*) jaundiced, melancholy.

cetro, *n.m.* sceptre; (*fig.*) reign of a prince; rod or verge borne by canons on solemn occasions; wand or staff borne by the deputies of confraternities; perch or roost for birds; *cetro de locura,* jester's bauble with cap and bells; *empuñar el cetro,* to begin to reign.

ceugma, *n.f.* (*rhet.*) zeugma.

ceutí, *n.m.f.,* *a.* of or from Ceuta. — *n.m.* coin of Ceuta.

cía, *n.f.* hip-bone, huckle-bone.

ciaboga, *n.f.* act of putting a rowing-vessel about; *hacer ciaboga,* to turn the back, to flee.

ciaescurre, *n.m.* (*naut.*) putting about.

cianato, *n.m.* cyanate.

cianea, *n.f.* (*min.*) [LAZULITA].

cianhidrato, *n.m.* hydrocyanate.

cianhídrico, -ca, *a.* hydrocyanic.

ciánico, -ca, *a.* cyanic.

ciánido, *n.m.* cyanide.

cianina, *n.f.* cyanine.

cianita, *n.f.* cyanite.

cianoférrico, -ca, *a.* ferrocyanic.

cianoferro, *n.m.* ferrocyanide.

cianógeno, *n.m.* cyanogen.

cianómetro, *n.m.* cyanometer.

cianopatía, *n.f.;* **cianosis,** *n.m.* cyanosis.

cianosado, -da, *a.* suffering from cyanosis.

cianótico, -ca, *a.* relating to cyanosis. — *n.m.f.,* *a.* [CIANOSADO].

cianotipia, *n.f.* cyanotype.

cianuro, *n.m.* cyanide.

ciar, *v.i.* to back water with the oars and go astern; to retrograde; (*fig.*) to slacken in the pursuit of an affair.

ciática, *n.f.* sciatica, lumbago, hip-gout; (*Per.*) poisonous tree-fern.

ciático, -ca, *a.* sciatic.

ciatófero, -ra, *a.* cyathiform.

cibal, *a.* appertaining to food.

Cibeles, *n.f.* (*myth.*) Cybele; (*astron.*) earth.

cibera, *a.* suitable as fodder. — *n.f.* quantity of wheat put at once in the hopper; seeds or grains fit for animal food; coarse remains of crushed grain or fruit; (*prov.*) hopper in a corn-mill.

cibica, *n.f.* clout, hurter (of axle-tree); (*naut.*) staple, clamp.

cibicón, *n.m.* large kind of clout [CIBICA].

cíbolo, -la, *n.m.f.* bison, American buffalo.

ciborio, *n.m.* ciborium.

cibui, *n.m.* (*Per.*) cedar.

cicada, *n.f.* cicada.

cicadario, -ria, *a.* like the cicada.

cicatear, *v.i.* (*coll.*) to be sordidly parsimonious.

cicatería, *n.f.* niggardliness, parsimony.

cicaterillo, -lla, *n.m.f.,* *a.* sordid or avaricious little person.

cicatero, -ra, *a.* niggardly, sordid, parsimonious. — *n.m.f.* miser. — *n.m.* (*slang*) pickpocket.

cicateruelo, -la, *n.m.f.* avaricious little person; little skinflint or miser, curmudgeon [CICATERO].

cicatricera, *n.f.* volunteer military nurse.

cicatriz, *n.f.* cicatrice, cicatrix, scar, gash, mark of a wound; (*fig.*) impression remaining on the mind.

cicatrizado, -da, *a.* scarred; (*fig.*) healed, calmed, forgotten. — *p.p.* [CICATRIZAR].

cicatrizante, *a.* cicatrizing.

cicatrizar, *v.t.* (*pret.* **cicatricé;** *pres. subj.* **cicatrice**) to cicatrize, heal a wound. — *v.r.* to cicatrize, heal up, skin over.

cicatrizativo, -va, *a.* cicatrizing.

cícera; cicércula; cicercha, *n.f.* small kind of chick-pea.

cícero, *n.m.* (*print.*) pica; measure unit equivalent to 12 points.

Cicerón, *n.m.* (*fig.*) eloquent man.

cicerone, *n.m.* cicerone.

ciceroniano, -na, *n.m.f.,* *a.* Ciceronian (of style, etc.).

ción, *n.m.* (*prov.*) tertian, an intermittent fever.

ciclada, *n.f.* kind of undress formerly worn by ladies.

ciclamen; ciclamino, *n.m.* cyclamen.

ciclamor, *n.m.* tree with beautiful crimson flowers.

ciclán, *n.m.* having only one testicle; immature (ram or goat); (*fig.*) single, one having no companion.

ciclar, *v.t.* to polish, burnish, clean precious stones.

ciclatón, *n.m.* woman's tunic.

cíclico, -ca, *a.* cyclic, cyclical.

ciclismo, *n.m.* cycling.

ciclista, *n.m.f.* cyclist.

ciclo, *n.m.* cycle, round of time.

ciclógrafo, *n.m.* cyclograph.

cicloidal; cicloideo, -dea, *a.* cycloidal.

cicloide, *n.f.* cycloid.

ciclometría, *n.f.* cyclometry.

ciclométrico, -ca, *a.* relating to cyclometry.

ciclómetro, *n.m.* cyclometer.

ciclón, *n.m.* hurricane, cyclone.

ciclonal, *a.* cyclonic.

ciclope; ciclope, *n.m.* (*myth., zool.*) cyclops.

ciclópeo, -pea; ciclópico, -ca, *a.* cyclopean; gigantic.

ciclorama, *n.m.* cyclorama.

ciclosis, *n.f.* cyclosis.

ciclostilo, *n.m.* cyclostyle.

cicuración, *n.f.* taming of wild animals.

cicurar, *v.t.* to tame wild animals.

cicuta, *n.f.* hemlock; spotted cowbane.

cicutado, -da, *a.* impregnated with cicuta juice.

cicutina, *n.f.* poison obtained from hemlock.

cid, *n.m.* chief.

cidra, *n.f.* citron.

cidrada, *n.f.* preserve made of citrons.

cidral, *n.m.* plantation of citron-trees.

cidrayote; chilacayote, *n.m.* American gourd.

cidro, *n.m.* citron-tree.

cidronela, *n.f.* common balm.

ciegamente, *adv.* blindly.

ciegayernos, *n.m.* (*coll.*) showy but worthless thing; humbug.

ciego, -ga, *a.* blind; (*fig.*) swayed by violent passion; choked, shut up (of a passage, etc.). — *n.m.* (*anat.*) cæcum; large black-pudding; *a ciegas,* blindly, in the dark, carelessly, thoughtlessly; *ciego con los celos,* blinded by jealousy; *ciego de ira,* blind with rage; *obediencia ciega,* blind obedience; *muy ciego es el que no ve por tela de cedazo,* he is very blind who can't see through a sieve.

ciego, ciegue, *pres. indic., pres subj.* [CEGAR].

cieguecico, -ca; cieguillo, -lla; cieguito, -ta; cieguezuelo, -la, *n.m.f.,* *a.* little blind person.

cielito, *n.m.* (*Arg.*) tune and dance.

cielo, *n.m.* sky, firmament, heaven; God, the supreme power; glory, paradise, felicity; atmosphere, climate; roof, ceiling, cover; canopy (of bed); *bajado* or *venido del cielo,* heaven-sent; *un cielo benigno,* a mild climate; *cielo borreguero,* fleecy sky; *cielo de la boca,* roof of the mouth; *cielo de la cama,* tester, bed-canopy; *cielo de coche,* roof of a coach; *¡cielo de mi vida!* my darling! *¡cielo santo! ¡cielos!* good heavens! *cielo viejo,* (*naut.*) glimpse of blue sky seen in bad weather; *cielo raso,* flat roof, ceiling; *dormir a cielo raso,* to sleep in the open air; *cielo del toldo de un bote,* roof of a boat's awning; *a cielo abierto,* in the open air; *a cielo descubierto,* in the open; *al que al cielo escupe, en la cara le cae,* excessive arrogance recoils upon itself; *escupir al cielo,* to do an ill deed (which returns upon the doer); *cerrarse* or *entoldarse el cielo,* to become cloudy, overcast; *comprar, conquistar* or *ganar el cielo,* to be assured of heaven by good works; *desencapotarse* or *despejarse el cielo,* to clear up (of the weather); *desgajarse el cielo,* to rain in torrents; *estar hecho un cielo,* to be splendid, brilliant; *mudar (de) cielo,* to change the air; *llovido del cielo,* godsend; *aunque se suba al cielo,* even if one goes to the utmost extremes to save oneself; *coger* or *tomar el cielo con las manos,* to be transported with joy, grief or passion; *herir los cielos con voces, lamentos, etc.,* to rend the heavens with cries, lamentations, etc.; *mover cielo y tierra,* to move heaven and earth, make great exertions; *nublársele el cielo,* to be grieved, very sad; *poner en el cielo* or *los cielos,* to laud to the skies; *ver el cielo abierto,* to discover an unforeseen opportunity; *ver el cielo por embudo,* to be unsophisticated, unused to the world; *venirse el cielo abajo,* to pour, deluge; *irse al cielo vestido y calzado,* to gain heaven without passing through purgatory (said of an unusually good person); *volar al cielo,* to go to heaven (the soul).

ciempiés, *n.m.* centipede; (*coll.*) poor piece of literary work.

cien, *a.* one hundred (used before nouns for CIENTO).

ciénaga, *n.f.* marsh, bog, miry place.

ciencia, *n.f.* science; knowledge, certainty; *a* or *de ciencia cierta,* knowingly, with certainty; *a ciencia y paciencia,* by, with someone's knowledge and permission; *ciencias exactas,* exact sciences (mathematics, etc.); *gaya ciencia,* the art of poetry.

cienmilésimo, -ma, *a.* hundred-thousandth.

cienmilímetro, *n.m.* hundredth part of a millimetre.

cienmilmillonésimo, -ma, *a.* hundred-thousand-millionth.

cieno, *n.m.* mud, mire, marshy ground, slime, slough, bog.

ciente, *a.* learned, skilful.

científicamente, *adv.* scientifically.

científico, -ca, *a.* scientific.

ciento, *n.m., a.* one hundred; hundredth; a hundred. — *pl.* tax assessed at so much per cent.; piquet (card game).

cientopiés, *n.m.* centipede.

cierna, *n.f.* anther of blossom of vines, corn, and some other plants.

cierne, *n.m.* blossoming, flowering; *en cierne,* in bloom (of vine, corn, etc.); *estar en cierne,* to be in its infancy, far from perfect.

cierno; cierna, *pres. indic.; pres. subj.* [CERNER].

cierrapuertas, *n.m.* automatic door-closing apparatus.

cierre, *n.m.* closing, closure; fastening, locking, shutting; snap; clasp; plug of a valve; *cierre metálico,* flexible metal roller-shutter (for shops, etc.); *cierre hidráulico,* hydraulic or water seal.

cierro, *n.m.* closure; (*prov.*) *cierro de cristales,* glass-covered balcony or veranda.

cierro; cierre, *pres. indic.; pres. subj.* [CERRAR].

cierta, *n.f.* (*slang*) death.

ciertamente, *adv.* certainly, surely.

cierto, -ta, *a.* certain, sure, positive; evident, doubtless; constant; true; (*slang*) cheating, sharping. — *adv.* certainly, surely; *al* or *de cierto,* certainly; *cierto tal que,* so that, in such a way that; *cierto profesor,* a certain teacher (example of indeterminate use, preceding the noun); *cierto de su poder,* sure of his power; *dejar lo cierto por lo dudoso,* to leave the substance for the shadow; *no, por cierto,* no, certainly not; *sí, por cierto,* certainly, surely; *cierta y verdadera,* absolutely true; *ciertos son los toros,* the story is true; it is a fact; *por cierto,* certainly, surely, in truth; *me dan por cierto que,* I have been credibly informed that.

cierva, *n.f.* hind, female stag.

ciervo, *n.m.* deer, stag, hart; *ciervo volante,* stag-beetle.

cierzas, *n.f.pl.* shoots, suckers of vine.

cierzo, *n.m.* cold northerly wind; *tener ventana al cierzo,* to be haughty, lofty, elated in spirit.

cifac; cifaque, *n.m.* peritoneum.

cifosis, *n.f.* (*med.*) abnormal outward curvature of spine.

cifra, *n.f.* cipher, code, cryptography, secret or occult manner of writing; cipher, on seals, coaches, etc.; contraction, abbreviation; numerical character; monogram, device, emblem; arithmetical mark; music written with numbers; (*slang*) astuteness; *en cifra,* briefly, shortly; mysteriously, obscurely.

cifradamente, *adv.* briefly.

cifrado, -da, *a.* ciphered. — *p.p.* [CIFRAR].

cifrador, -ra, *n.m.f., a.* (one) writing in cipher.

cifrar, *v.t.* to cipher, write in cipher; (*fig.*) to abridge, summarize; to enclose; *cifrar en,* to place, make a thing depend exclusively, principally on another; *cifrar su dicha en dinero,* to set his whole heart on money.

cigala, *n.f.* variety of crayfish.

cigarra, *n.f.* grasshopper, cicada, harvest-fly; (*slang*) bag, purse.

cigarral, *n.m.* (in Toledo) country-house with orchard.

cigarralero, -ra, *n.m.f.* caretaker or inhabitant of a *cigarral.*

cigarrera, *n.f.* cigar-seller or maker; cigar-case, cigar-cabinet.

cigarrería, *n.f.* (*Am.*) tobacconist's shop.

cigarrero, *n.m.* cigar-maker or dealer.

cigarrillo, *n.m.* cigarette.

cigarrista, *n.m.* excessive smoker.

cigarro, *n.m.* cigar; *cigarro de papel,* cigarette; *cigarro puro,* cigar.

cigarrón, *n.m.* large grasshopper; (*slang*) large purse [CIGARRA].

cigofileo, lea-, *a.* (*bot.*) zygophyllaceous. — *n.f.pl.* zygophyllum.

cigoma, *n.m.* (*anat.*) zygoma.

cigomático, -ca, *a.* zygomatic.

cigoñal, *n.m.* swape-well; (*fort.*) beam for raising draw-bridge.

cigoñino, *n.m.* young stork.

cigoñuela, *n.f.* small bird resembling the stork.

cigua, *n.f.* a tree from West-Indies.

ciguapa, *n.f.* (*Cub.*) an owl-like bird.

ciguapate, *n.f.* (*Hond.*) a medicinal umbelliferous plant.

ciguaraya, *n.f.* (*Cub.*) a medicinal and industrial liliaceous plant.

ciguatera, *n.f.* (*Mex.*) jaundice, contracted by eating diseased fish.

cigüeña, *n.f.* (*orn.*) stork, crane; crank of a bell; (*mech.*) crane; winch.

cigüeñal, *n.m.* (*motor-car*) crank-shaft.

cigüeñear, *v.i.* to make a noise with the beak (stork).

cigüeño, *n.m.* (*obs.*) male stork; (*prov.*) tall and silly-looking person.

cigüeñuela, *n.f.* (*mech.*) small crank [CIGÜEÑA]; *cigüeñuela de la caña del timón,* (*naut.*) goose-neck of the tiller.

cigüete, *n.f.* variety of white grape.

cija, *n.f.* granary; building for sheltering sheep; (*prov.*) dungeon.

cilampa, *n.f.* (*CR., ES.*) drizzle.

cilanco, *n.m.* pool left by a river.

cilantro, *n.m.* (*bot.*) coriander.

ciliado, -da; cilífero, -ra, *a.* ciliate.

ciliar, *a.* ciliary, belonging to the eye-lids.

cilicio, *n.m.* hair-cloth; cilice, hair-shirt for the body, also girdle of bristles or netted wire with points worn as a penance; (*mil.*) coarse cover for armaments.

cilindrado, -da, *p.p.* [CILINDRAR]; *a.* rolled, calendered. — *n.m.* calendering, rolling.

cilindrar, *v.t.* to roll, calender.

cilíndricamente, *adv.* cylindrically.

cilíndrico, -ca, *a.* cylindrical; cilindriform.

cilindro, *n.m.* cylinder, roller; (*print.*) cylinder-press; (*mech.*) chamber; *cilindro compresor,* steam-roller for roads; *cilindro de escarchar,* silversmith's roll; *cilindro estriado,* fluted cylinder.

cilindroide, *n.m.* cylindroid.

cilindroideo, -dea, *a.* cylindrical.

cilla, *n.f.* granary for tithes and other grain.

cillazgo, *n.m.* store-house fees paid by persons concerned on tithes kept in a granary.

cillerero, *n.m.* cellarist or butler, in some religious houses.

cilleriza, *n.f.* nun who directs the domestic affairs of a convent.

cillero, *n.m.* keeper of a granary or store-house for tithes; granary; cellar, store-house.

cima, *n.f.* summit, top; height, crest, peak, apex, head, cap; (*fig.*) acme; end, extremity; finish, completion; (*bot.*) cyme; *a la por cima,* finally, ultimately; *dar cima a,* to conclude happily; *por cima,* at the uppermost part, at the very top; superficially; *mirar una cosa por cima,* to look at a thing superficially.

cimacio, *n.m.* (*arch.*) cyma, cymatium, ogee.

cimar, *v.t.* to clip the tops of hedges, plants, etc.

cimarrón, -na, *a.* (*Am.*) wild, unruly. — *n.m.f.* runaway slave, maroon; (*Arg.*) black maté. — *n.m., a.* (*naut.*) lazy (sailor).

cimbalaria, *n.f.* ivy-wort.

cimbalero; cimbalista, *n.m.* cymbalist.

cimbalillo; cimbanillo, *n.m.* small church-bell.

címbalo, *n.m.* cymbal.

címbara, *n.f.* short, broad scythe.

cimbel, *n.m.* decoy-pigeon; cord with which such pigeons are made fast.

cimboga, *n.f.* [ACIMBOGA].

cimborio; cimborrio, *n.m.* base of cupola; dome.

cimbornales, *n.m.pl.* (*naut.*) scupper-holes.

cimbra, *n.f.* (*arch.*) wooden frame for constructing an arch; cradling; (*naut.*) curvature; *cimbra de una tabla,* (*naut.*) bending of a board; *plena cimbra,* semicircular frame.

cimbrable, *a.* that can be brandished.

cimbrado, -da, *p.p.* [CIMBRAR] brandished, flourished; bent. — *n.m.* quick, bending movement in a Spanish dance; (*arch.*) fixing of the *cimbra.*

cimbrar; cimbrear, *v.t.* to brandish a rod; (*arch.*) to fix the *cimbra;* to place cradlings in; *cimbrar a alguno,* to give someone a drubbing. — *v.r.* to bend; to vibrate; sway.

cimbre, *n.m.* underground gallery or passage.

cimbreño, -ña, *a.* pliant, flexible, swaying, vibrating.

cimbreo, *n.m.* act of bending, swaying; bending or moulding of a plank.

cimbronazo, *n.m.* stroke given with a foil or the flat of a sword; (*Col., CR.*) violent nervous jerk.

cimbroso, -sa, *a.* flexible, pliable.

cimentación, *n.f.* foundation.

cimentado, -da, *a.* founded; (*min.*) refined. — *n.m.* refinement of gold; *p.p.* [CIMENTAR].

cimentador, -ra, *a.* founding; (*min.*) refining. — *n.m.f.* founder; (*min.*) refiner.

cimentar, *v.t.* (*pres. indic.* **cimiento;** *pres. subj.* **cimiente**) to found, ground, lay the foundation of a building; to refine gold; (*fig.*) to establish fundamental principles.

cimenterio, *n.m.* cemetery, churchyard.

cimento, *n.m.* cement.

cimera, *n.f.* crest of a helmet or of coat of arms.

cimero, -ra, *a.* placed at the top of some elevated spot; apical. — *n.m.* [CIMERA].

cimiento, *n.m.* foundation of a building; (*fig.*) basis, origin, base, root, groundwork; *cimiento real,* composition for purifying gold.

cimiento; cimiente, *pres. indic.; pres. subj.* [CIMENTAR].

cimillo, *n.m.* flexible twig to which decoy-bird is attached.

cimitarra, *n.f.* scimitar, falchion.

cimofana, *n.f.* cymofane, cat's-eye.

cimorra, *n.f.* (*vet.*) glanders.

cimótico, -ca, *a.* (*med.*) zymotic.

cinabrino, -na, *a.* resembling cinnabar.

cinabrio, *n.m.* cinnabar; vermilion.

cinámico, -ca, *a.* (*chem.*) cinnamonic.

cinamida, *n.f.* (*chem.*) cinnamate.

cinamomo, *n.m.* (*bot.*) bead-tree; cinnamon; (*Philip.*) privet.

cinc, *n.m.* zinc.

cinca, *n.f.* infraction of the rules of the game of ninepins; *hacer cinca en el juego de bolos,* to lose five points at ninepins.

cincel, *n.m.* chisel, engraver, burin, drove.

cincelado, -da, *p.p.* [CINCELAR] chiselled, engraved. — *n.m.* chiselling, engraving.

cincelador, *n.m.* engraver, sculptor, stone-cutter.

cinceladura, *n.f.* chasing, carving; fretwork, embossment, relief.

cincelar, *v.t.* to chisel, engrave, emboss, carve, sculpture, chase, cut.

cincelería, *n.f.* shop or factory where chiselling or engraving is done.

cincelito, *n.m.* small chisel [CINCEL].

cíncico, -ca, *a.* zinciferous, zincoid, zinky.

cinco, *n.m., a.* five, fifth; five-spotted (card); (*Ven.*) five-string guitar; (*CR., Chi.*) silver coin (5 centavos); *decir a uno cuántas son cinco,* to show a person what's what; to reprimand with a threat; *no sabe cuántas son cinco,* he can't say bo to a goose; *saber cuántas son cinco,* to be no fool; *las cinco,* five o'clock.

cincoañal, *a.* five years old (of animals).

cincoenrama, *n.f.* common cinquefoil.

cincograbado, *n.m.* zincograph.

cincografía, *n.f.* zincography.

cincomesino, -na, *a.* five months old.

cincona, *n.f.* (*bot.*) cinchona; quinine.

cinconáceo, -cea, *a.* cinchonaceous.

cinconina, *n.f.* (*chem.*) cinchonine.

cincuenta, *n.m., a.* fifty, fiftieth.

cincuentañal, *a.* fifty years old.

cincuentavo, -va, *n.m., a.* fiftieth.

cincuentén, *n.m., a.* plank 50 palms long, 3 wide, and 2 thick.

cincuenteno, -na, *a.* fiftieth.

cincuentón, -na, *n.m.f., a.* quinquagenarian.

cincuesma, *n.f.* Pentecost.

cincha, *n.f.* girth, cinch; *a revienta cinchas,* at breakneck speed; *ir* or *venir rompiendo cinchas,* to drive at full speed.

cinchadura, *n.f.* act of girthing.

cinchar, *v.t.* to girth, cinch up; to fasten with iron hoops.

cinchera, *n.f.* girth-place (on a mule, horse, etc.); (*vet.*) disorder affecting the girth-place.

cincho, *n.m.* belly-band; belt; girdle, sash; tyre; iron hoop; (*arch.*) projecting rib of arch; (*Mex.*) cinch; plaited esparto band of vessel for moulding cheese; (*vet.*) disorder in horse's hoofs.

cinchón, *n.m.* (*River Plate*) strip of rawhide used as a cinch; (*Ec.*) hoop of iron; (*Col.*) overload (horse).

cinchuela, *n.f.* small girth; narrow ribbon [CINCHA].

cine; cinema, *n.m.* (*coll.*) cinema, kinema.

cinefacción, *n.f.* cineration, reduction to ashes.

cinefacto, -ta, *a.* reduced to ashes.

cineficar, *v.t.* to reduce to ashes. — *v.r.* to become pulverized.

cinegética, *n.f.* art of hunting with dogs.

cinemadrama, *n.m.* kinematic melodrama.

cinemática, *n.f.* kinematics.

cinematicamente, *adv.* kinematically.

cinematografía, *n.f.* cinematography.

cinematográfico, -ca, *a.* cinematographic.

cinematógrafo, *n.m.* cinematograph.

cinematurgo, *n.m.* author of dramas for the cinematograph.

cinemógrafo, *n.m.* (*railw.*) apparatus measuring the velocity of trains, also arrival at and departure from stations.

cinemómetro, *n.m.* apparatus for measuring the velocity of movement.

cineración, *n.f.* cineration.

cinerario, -ria, *a.* cinerary; *urna cineraria*, cinerary urn. — *n.f.* (*bot.*) cineraria.

cinéreo, -rea, *a.* cinerious.

cinericio, -cia, *a.* ashy.

cineriforme, *a.* ash-like.

cingalés, -sa, *n.m.f.*, *a.* Cingalese.

cíngaro, -ra, *n.m.f.*, *a.* gipsy.

cinglado, -da, *p.p.* [CINGLAR]; *a.* beaten, hammered, forged. — *n.m.* blooming (of metals).

cinglador, *n.m.* large hammer for blooming metals.

cingladora, *n.f.* bloomery.

cinglar, *v.t.*, *v.i.* (*naut.*) to move a boat with only one oar aft; to bloom (metals).

cingleta, *n.f.* (*naut.*) rope with cork to buoy up a net.

cíngulo, *n.m.* girdle of priest's alb; ancient military badge.

cinicamente, *adv.* cynically.

cínico, -ca, *a.* cynical, satirical, impudent, barefaced; slovenly, unclean. — *n.m.* cynic.

cínife, *n.m.* mosquito.

cinismo, *n.m.* cynicism, shamelessness, barefacedness, impudence, ribaldry; slovenliness.

cinocéfalo, *n.m.* (*zool.*) cynocephalus, dog-faced baboon.

cinoglosa, *n.f.* (*bot.*) hound's tongue.

cinosura, *n.f.* (*astron.*) Cynosure; pole-star, lesser Bear.

cinquén, *n.m.* ancient Spanish coin.

cinqueño; cinquillo, *n.m.* game of ombre, played by five persons.

cinquero, *n.m.* zinc-worker.

cinta, *n.f.* ribbon, thread, tape; band, strip; (*obs.*) girdle; strong hempen net used in tunny-fishing; lowest part of pastern of a horse; first course of floor-tiles; kerb-stone; (*arch.*, *her.*) fillet; (*arch.*) scroll; surveyor's steel tape-measure; cinematograph film; *andar* or *estar con las manos en la cinta*, to be idle; *espada en cinta*, with one's sword on; *cintas galimas*, (*naut.*) bow-wales; *cinta de hilo* or *algodón*, thread or cotton tape; *cinta de hiladillo*, ferret ribbon; *cintas de navío*, (*naut.*) wales. — *adv. en cinta*, under subjection; liable to restraint.

cintadero, *n.m.* part of a cross-bow to which the string is fastened.

cintagorda, *n.f.* coarse hempen net for the tunny fishery.

cintajos; cintarajos, *n.m.pl.* knot or bunch of tumbled ribbons; tawdry ornaments in female dress.

cintar, *v.t.* (*arch.*) to adorn with fillets or scrolls.

cintarazo, *n.m.* stroke or blow with the flat of the sword.

cintarear, *v.t.* (*coll.*) to slap with a sword.

cinteado, -da, *a.* adorned with ribbons.

cintería, *n.f.* collection of ribbons; ribbon-shop or -trade.

cintero, -ra, *n.m.f.* seller or weaver of ribbons. — *n.m.* belt, girdle; (*prov.*) bandage, truss; halter, cable, rope.

cintilla, *n.f.* small ribbon; narrow tape [CINTA].

cintillo, *n.m.* hat-band; ring set with precious stones.

cinto, -ta, *p.p. irreg.* [CEÑIR] encircled, girdled, girt. — *n.m.* belt; waist; (*obs.*) *cinto de onzas* or *de oro*, inner belt for carrying money.

cintón, *n.m.* (*naut.*) strake.

cintra, *n.f.* (*arch.*) curve of an arch or vault.

cintrado, -da, *a.* (*arch.*) curved.

cintrel, *n.m.* (*arch.*) rule or line placed in the centre of a dome for arching.

cintura, *n.f.* girdle, belt; waist; throat of a chimney; (*naut.*) rope knot; *meter en cintura*, (*fig.*) to keep someone in subjection.

cinturica; cinturilla; cinturita, *n.f.* small girdle or belt [CINTA].

cinturón, *n.m.* large waist; large sword-belt; broad girdle or belt [CINTURA]; (*fig.*) series of things that surround another.

cinzolín, *n.m.* reddish-mauve colour.

ciño; ciña; ciñó, *pres. indic.*; *pres subj.*; 3rd *pers. sing. pret.* [CEÑIR].

cipariso, *n.m.* (*poet.*) cypress.

cipayo, *n.m.* Sepoy.

cipión, *n.m.* walking-stick.

cipo, *n.m.* (*arch.*) cippus, short stone pillar; milestone; sign-post.

cipolino, -na, *n.m.*, *a.* cipolin, cipollino.

cipote, *a.* (*Col.*) dull, stupid; (*Guat.*) chubby, obese; (*ES.*, *Hond.*) (*coll.*) urchin, little rogue.

ciprés, *n.m.* cypress.

cipresal, *n.m.* grove or plantation of cypress.

cipresino, -na, *a.* resembling or belonging to cypress.

ciprino, -na; ciprio, -ria; cipriota, *n.m.f.*, *a.* Cyprian, Cypriot.

ciprino, *n.m.* (*ichth.*) cyprine.

cipripedio, *n.m.* (*bot.*) cypripedium.

ciquiribaile, *n.m.* (*slang*) thief.

ciquiricata, *n.f.* (*coll.*) caress; flattery.

ciquitroque, *n.m.* fried tomatoes, pimentoes, etc.

circaeto, *n.m.* moor-buzzard.

circe, *n.f.* Circe; artful, deceitful woman.

circinado, -da, *a.* (*bot.*) circinate.

circo, *n.m.* circus; amphitheatre and occupants of same.

circón, *n.m.* zircon.

circona, *n.f.* zirconate.

circonio, *n.m.* zirconium.

circuición, *n.f.*; **circuimiento**, *n.m.* act of surrounding or encircling.

circuir, *v.t.* (*pres. indic.* **circuyo**; *pres. subj.* **circuya**) to surround, compass, encircle.

circuito, *n.m.* circuit, circle, extent; circumference, compass; *corto circuito,* short circuit.

circulación, *n.f.* circulation of currency or traffic; movement.

circulador, -ra, *a.* circulating, circulative. — *n.m.f.* circulator.

circulante, *a.* circulatory, circulating, circulative, circling.

circular, *a.* circular, circulatory, circling, circulating. — *n.f.* circular (letter). — *v.i.* to circulate, move, travel round, go from hand to hand, point to point. — *v.t.* to circularize; to circulate, diffuse, spread.

circularmente, *adv.* circularly.

circulatorio, -ria, *a.* circulatory.

círculo, *n.m.* circle, ring; orb; circlet; compass; circumference, district, social circle, club, casino; *círculo máximo* (*geom.*) great circle; *círculo menor* (*geom.*), lesser or small circle; *círculo vicioso,* (*rhet.*) vicious circle.

circumcirca, *adv.* (*coll.*) about, thereabout, almost.

circumpolar, *a.* circumpolar, near the pole.

circuncenital, *a.* (*astron.*) surrounding the zenith.

circuncidante, *a.* circumcising.

circuncidar, *v.t.* (*p.p.* **circunciso**) to circumcise; to diminish, clip, curtail, modify.

circuncisión, *n.f.* circumcision; festival of the Circumcision (New Year's Day).

circunciso, -sa, *a.* circumcised; (*fig.*) Jewish, Moorish. — *p.p. irreg.* [CIRCUNCIDAR].

circundante, *a.* surrounding, encircling.

circundar, *v.t.* to surround, encircle, compass.

circunferencia, *n.f.* circumference.

circunferencial, *a.* circumferential, circular, surrounding.

circunferencialmente, *adv.* in circumference.

circunferente, *a.* circumscribing.

circunflejo, -ja, *a.* (*anat., gram.*) circumflex; *acento circunflejo,* circumflex (ˆ) accent.

circunfuso, -sa, *a.* circumfluent.

circunlocución, *n.f.;* **circunloquio,** *n.m.* circumlocution, periphrasis, roundabout expression.

circunnavegable, *a.* circumnavigable.

circunnavegación, *n.f.* circumnavigation.

circunnavegante, *n.m.* circumnavigator.

circunnavegar, *v.t.* to circumnavigate; to sail round the world (a ship).

circunscribir, *v.t.* (*p.p.* **circunscripto, circunscrito**) to circumscribe, enclose, encircle; **circunscribirse,** *v.r.* to limit, restrict oneself to.

circunscripción, *n.f.* circumscription.

circunsolar, *a.* circumsolar.

circunspección, *n.f.* circumspection, prudence, watchfulness, general attention, decorousness.

circunspectamente, *adv.* circumspectly.

circunspecto, -ta, *a.* circumspect, prudent, cautious, judicious, grave.

circunstancia, *n.f.* circumstance; incident, event, detail; condition, state of affairs, particulars; *circunstancia agravante,* aggravating circumstance; *circunstancia atenuante,* extenuating circumstance; *circunstancia eximente,* circumstance which absolves of criminal responsibilities; *en las circunstancias presentes,* in the circumstances; *refirió el caso con todas sus circunstancias,* he gave a full, true and particular account of the matter.

circunstanciadamente, *adv.* circumstantially, minutely, in detail.

circunstanciado, -da, *a.* circumstantial, minute, according to circumstances. — *p.p.* [CIRCUNSTANCIAR].

circunstancial, *a.* circumstantial.

circunstante, *a.* surrounding; present, actually attending. — *n.m.pl.* bystanders, persons present; audience.

circunvalación, *n.f.* the act of surrounding; circumvallation; (*fort.*) line of trenches.

circunvalar, *v.t.* to surround, encircle; (*fort.*) to surround with trenches.

circunvecino, -na, *a.* neighbouring, contiguous, adjacent.

circunvención, *n.f.* circumvention.

circunvenir, *v.r.* to circumvent; to overreach.

circunvolar, *v.t.* to fly round.

circunvolución, *n.f.* circumvolution; *circunvolución cerebral,* cerebral convolution.

circunyacente, *a.* surrounding.

cirial, *n.m.* processional candlestick.

cirigallo, -lla, *n.m.f.* idler, wastrel.

cirigaña, *n.f.* (*prov.*) flattery; (*prov.*) practical joke; trifle.

cirineo, *n.m.* (*coll.*) mate, assistant.

cirio, *n.m.* long, thick wax taper; church candle; *cirio pascual,* paschal candle.

cirolar, *n.m.* plum-tree plantation.

cirolero, *n.m.* plum-tree.

ciroso, -sa, *a.* cereous.

cirro, *n.m.* (*surg.*) scirrhus; (*bot., meteor., zool.*) cirrus.

ciruela, *n.f.* plum; prune; *ciruela pasa,* dried plum, prune; *ciruela amacena* or *damascena,* damson plum; *ciruela claudia,* greengage; *ciruela de yema,* yellow plum.

ciruelar, *n.m.* plum plantation.

ciruelica; ciruelilla; ciruelita, *n.f.* small plum [CIRUELA].

ciruelillo, *n.m.* (*Arg., Chi.*) a tree with fine wood.

ciruelo, *n.m.* plum-tree; (*coll.*) fool, idiot.

cirugía, *n.f.* surgery.

cirujano, *n.m.* surgeon; *cirujano romancista,* surgeon who knows no Latin; *no hay mejor cirujano que el bien acuchillado,* there is no schoolmaster like experience.

cisalpino, -na, *a.* cisalpine.

cisca, *n.f.* reed-grass.

ciscar, *v.t.* (*pret.* **cisqué**; *pres. subj.* **cisque**) (*coll.*) to besmear, dirty. — *v.r.* to ease nature; *ciscarse de miedo,* to dirty oneself from fright.

cisco, *n.m.* coal-dust, broken coal, culm, slack; (*coll.*) noisy wrangle, hubbub, hue and cry; *hacer cisco,* to smash into smithereens.

ciscón, *n.m.* small coke and ashes.

cisión, *n.f.* incision.

cisípedo, *a.* having the foot divided into toes.

cisma, *n.m.f.* schism; disturbance in a community.

cismáticamente, *adv.* schismatically.

cismático, -ca, *n.m.f.,* *a.* schismatic.

cismontano, -na, *a.* situated on this side of the mountains.

cisne, *n.m.* (*orn.*) swan; (*astron.*) Cygnus; (*fig.*) great poet or musician; (*slang*) prostitute.

cisneo, -nea, *a.* swan-like.
cisoria, *a.; arte cisoria,* art of carving (meat).
cisquera, *n.f.* receptacle for coal-dust or slack.
cisquero, *n.m.* seller of coal-dust or slack; pounce-bag.
cista, *n.f.* (*archæol.*) cist.
ciste, *n.m.* (*surg.*) cyst.
cistel; cister, *n.m.* Cistercian order.
cisterciense, *n.m.f., a.* Cistercian.
cisterna, *n.f.* cistern, reservoir, water-tank, enclosed fountain.
cisticerco, *n.m.* cystic worm.
cístico, -ca, *a.* (*surg.*) cystic.
cistina, *n.f.* (*chem.*) cystine.
cisura, *n.f.* incisure, incision.
cita, *n.f.* assignation, appointment, rendezvous, interview; citation, quotation.
citable, *a.* citable, quotable.
citación, *n.f.* making an appointment; citation, quotation; (*law*) summons, judicial notice.
citado, -da, *a.* cited, quoted, summoned. — *p.p.* [CITAR]; *estar citado,* to have an appointment, engagement.
citador, -ra, *a.* citing; quoting; summoning. — *n.m.f.* citer; quoter; summoner.
citano, -na, *n.m.f.* (*coll.*) [ZUTANO].
citar, *v.t.* to make an appointment with; to convoke, convene; to quote, cite; (*law*) to summon; (*law*) to give judicial notice; to provoke (the bull); *citar a junta,* to call a meeting.
cítara, *n.f.* zither, cithern.
citara, *n.f.* partition-wall; (*mil.*) troops covering the flanks.
citarica; citarilla; citarita, *n.f.* small cithern or zither [CÍTARA].
citarilla, *n.f.* thin partition-wall [CITARA].
citarista, *n.m.f.* zither-player.
citarón, *n.m.* socle with wooden framework [CITARA].
citatorio, -ria, *a.* (*law*) summoning. — *n.f.* (*law*) summons.
citereo, -rea, *a.* (*poet.*) cytherean.
citerior, *a.* hither, nearer, towards this part; *España citerior,* (*hist.*) the north-eastern part of Spain.
cítiso, *n.m.* shrub-trefoil, cytisus.
¡cito!, *n.m.* word used to call dogs.
cítola, *n.f.* clack, clapper (in corn-mills).
citote, *n.m.* (*coll.*) summons, judicial citation.
citra, *adv.* on this side.
citramontano, -na, *a.* cismontane.
citrato, *n.m.* (*chem.*) citrate.
cítrico, -ca, *a.* (*chem.*) citric.
citrino, -na, *a.* citrine, citrinous, lemon-coloured. — *n.f.* (*min.*) citrine; (*chem.*) essential oil of lemon.
citrón, *n.m.* lemon; (*PR.*) lime.
ciudad, *n.f.* town, city; corporation, civic body.
ciudadanía, *n.f.;* **ciudadanismo,** *n.m.* citizenhood, citizenship.
ciudadano, -na, *a.* relating to a city; civil, citizen, town-bred; relating to any man as member of a community; citizen-like. — *n.m.* livery man of a city; citizen, freeman; inhabitant of a city; *¡ciudadano!* (*fam.*) comrade, friend.
ciudadela, *n.f.* citadel, stronghold.
civeta, *n.f.* civet-cat.
civeto, *n.m.* civet perfume.

cívico, -ca, *a.* civic.
civil, *a.* civil, relating to the community; civil, polite, courteous, gentlemanly; (*obs.*) of low rank or extraction; (*law*) civil. — *n.m.* (*coll.*) rural policeman in Spain.
civilidad, *n.f.* civility, politeness, urbanity, good manners, sociability; (*obs.*) misery, meanness, vileness.
civilismo, *n.m.* civicism.
civilista, *n.m.* attorney skilled in civil law; (*Am.*) opponent of militarism.
civilizable, *a.* civilizable.
civilización, *n.f.* civilization.
civilizado, -da, *a.* civilized; refined. — *p.p.* [CIVILIZAR]
civilizador, -ra, *a.* civilizing. — *n.m.f.* civilizer.
civilizar, *v.t.* (*pret.* **civilicé;** *pres. subj.* **civilice**) to civilize. — *v.r.* to become civilized.
civilmente, *adv.* civilly, courteously, politely; according to the common law; (*obs.*) poorly, miserably, meanly.
civismo, *n.m.* civicism, patriotism.
cizalla, *n.f.* shears for metal; metal clippings, fragments or filings.
cizallar, *v.t.* to shear metal.
cizaña, *n.f.* (*bot.*) darnel; (*fig.*) corrupting vice; discord, disagreement; pollution.
cizañador, -ra, *n.m.f., a.* one who sows discord, or enmity.
cizañar, *v.t.* to sow discord, provoke enmity.
cizañero, -ra, *n.m.f., a.* [CIZAÑADOR].
clac, *n.m.* opera-hat; cocked hat.
claco, *n.m.* (*Mex.*) ancient copper coin (about one farthing).
clacopacle, *n.m.* (*Mex.*) birth wort.
clacota, *n.f.* (*Mex.*) small tumour or boil.
clachique, *n.m.* (*Mex.*) unfermented pulque.
clamador, -ra, *a.* clamorous, insistent. — *n.m.f.* shouter, whiner.
clamar, *v.t.* to call; to whine, cry in a mournful tone; (*fig.*) to want, require, demand. — *v.i.* to clamour; *la tierra clama por agua,* the ground wants water; *clamar a Dios,* to implore God; *tal crimen clama castigo,* such a crime demands punishment.
clamor, *n.m.* clamour, outcry, scream, shriek; whine, plaint, cry; knell, sound of passing-bell.
clamoreada, *n.f.* whine; shriek, outcry, scream, clamour.
clamorear, *v.t.* to clamour; to implore insistently. — *v.i.* to toll the passing-bell; *clamorear a muerto las campanas,* to ring a knell.
clamoreo, *n.m.* repeated or prolonged clamour; importunate appeal; *el clamoreo de las campanas,* knell.
clamorosamente, *adv.* clamorously.
clamoroso, -sa, *a.* clamorous, loud, noisy.
clamosidad, *n.f.* clamorousness.
clandestinamente, *adv.* clandestinely, secretly.
clandestinidad, *n.f.* clandestineness, secrecy.
clandestino, -na, *a.* clandestine, secret.
clanga, *n.f.* [PLANGA].
clangor, *n.m.* (*poet.*) clarion, sound of a trumpet.
claque, *n.f.* claque.
clara, *n.f.* white of egg; thin part of badly woven cloth; (*coll.*) short interval of fine

weather on a wet day; bald spot; *a la(s) clara(s)*, clearly, evidently; *clara o turbia*, anyhow; *claras y oscuras* or *claras y turbias*, without exception, all together; *decir cuatro claras*, to tell one's mind bluntly and plainly.

claraboya, *n.f.* skylight; transom.

claramente, *adv.* clearly, openly, fairly, conspicuously, obviously, manifestly; (*coll.*) certainly.

clarea, *n.f.* beverage made of white wine, cinnamon, sugar and egg.

clarear, *v.i.* to dawn, grow light; to clear up, become fine (weather). — *v.t.* to light, give light to. — *v.r.* to become transparent or translucent; (*coll.*) to give oneself away; *clearearse de hambre*, to be very hungry.

clarecer, *v.i.* (*pres. subj.* **clarezca**) to dawn, grow light.

clarens, *n.m.* a four-seater carriage with hood.

clarete, *n.m.* claret (wine).

claridad, *n.f.* clarity, brightness, splendour, light; clearness, distinctness, freedom from obscurity and confusion; celebrity, fame; glory of the blessed. — *pl.* plain language, plain truths; *claridad de la vista* or *de los ojos*, clearness of sight; *con claridad*, distinctly, frankly; *entre más amistad más claridad*, the greater the friendship the more need for frankness; *salir a puerto de claridad*, to get well over an arduous undertaking; *le dije dos claridades*, I told him my mind very plainly.

clarificable, *a.* that can be clarified.

clarificación, *n.f.* clarification, refining.

clarificador, **-ra**, *a.* clarifying. — *n.m.f.* clarifier; (*Cub.*) clarifying pan (sugar).

clarificar, *v.t.* (*pret.* **clarifiqué**; *pres. subj.* **clarifique**) to brighten, illuminate; to clarify, purify, refine.

clarificativo, **-va**, *a.* clarifying, purifying.

clarífico, **-ca**, *a.* resplendent.

clarilla, *n.f.* (*prov.*) lye of ashes or any alkaline salt.

clarimente, *n.m.* beautifying lotion used by women; (*paint.*) cleanser and colour-reviver.

clarimentos, *n.m.pl.* (*paint.*) lights.

clarín, *n.m.* bugle, clarion, trumpet; organ-stop; bugler, trumpeter; fine cambric; (*Chi.*) sweet pea; (*orn.*) an American songbird.

clarinado, **-da**, *a.* (*her.*) applied to animals with bells in their harness. — *n.f.* sharp, uncalled-for remark.

clarinero, *n.m.* trumpeter, bugler.

clarinete, *n.m.* clarinet; clarinet-player.

clarión, *n.m.* white crayon, chalk.

clarioncillo, *n.m.* pastel, coloured crayon.

clarisa, *n.f.* nun of the order of St. Clare.

clarísimo, **-ma**, *a. superl.* [CLARO] very illustrious, very noble.

clarividencia, *n.f.* clear-sightedness, perspicacity, penetration; transparence of atmosphere.

clarividente, *n.m.f.*, *a.* clear-sighted, discerning (person).

claro, **-ra**, *a.* clear, bright, fine, transparent, pellucid, crystalline, limpid; thin, rare, sparse; serene, cloudless, fair; light (of colours); perspicuous, intelligible; obvious, explicit, evident, manifest, indisputable; open, frank, ingenuous; (*fig.*) celebrated, illustrious; (*fig.*) sagacious, quick of thought;

es una verdad clara, it is an undeniable truth.

claro, *n.m.* skylight; break (in a discourse); a space (in writing); void, gap, interval, lacuna; (*paint.*) light; (*naut.*) clear space in the sky. — *pl.* (*arch.*) loopholes; windows. — *adv.* clearly, openly; ¡*claro!* or ¡*claro está!* of course, naturally, evidently; *claro y oscuro*, (*paint.*) chiaroscuro; *claros y turbios*, uncertainty, vacillation; *de claro en claro*, evidently, manifestly; from beginning to end; *pasar la noche de claro en claro*, to spend the night without any sleep; *por lo claro*, clearly, manifestly, conspicuously; *poner en claro*, to place a matter in its true light; to expound, interpret, explain; *sacar en claro*, to deduce, arrive at a conclusion; *vamos claros*, let us be clear; let us speak frankly.

claror, *n.m.* resplendence, clearness.

claroscuro, *n.m.* chiaroscuro, light and shade; monochrome; combination of light and heavy strokes in penmanship.

clarucho, **-cha**, *a.* (*contempt.*) too thin, too watery.

clascal, *n.m.* (*Mex.*) omelet made of maize.

clase, *n.f.* class, rank, order, kind; category, species, family; division, form (in schools); lecture, lesson; classroom; (*com.*) sort, description, quality, rate, line; *clases de navío*, (*naut.*) rates of ships; *clases de tropa*, non-commissioned officers; *clase media*, middle-class; *clases pasivas*, pensioners, retired people.

clásicamente, *adv.* classically.

clasicidad, *n.f.* classicality.

clasicismo, *n.m.* classicism.

clásico, **-ca**, *a.* classic, classical; principal, remarkable, of the first order or rank. — *n.m.* classic; *autores clásicos*, classics; *error clásico*, gross error.

clasificación, *n.f.* classification.

clasificador, **-ra**, *a.* classifying, classificatory. — *n.m.f.* classifier. — *n.m.* filing-cabinet.

clasificar, *v.t.* (*pret.* **clasifiqué**; *pres. subj.* **clasifique**) to classify, arrange, class.

claudicación, *n.f.* limp, halting, lameness.

claudicante, *a.* halting, limping, lame.

claudicar, *v.i.* (*pret.* **claudiqué**; *pres. subj.* **claudique**) to halt, limp; (*fig.*) to bungle, proceed in a disorderly way.

claustral, *a.* claustral.

claustrero, **-ra**, *a.* applied to monks and nuns.

claustrillo, *n.m.* small hall in certain universities.

claustro, *n.m.* cloister, piazza, or gallery round a court; university council; (*fig.*) monastic state; room, chamber; *claustro de licencias*, faculty of medicine or theology; *claustro de profesores*, academic staff; *claustro materno*, womb.

claustrofobia, *n.f.* claustrophobia.

cláusula, *n.f.* (*gram., rhet.*) period, clause of a discourse, sentence; (*law*) clause, condition, particular stipulation, proviso.

clausulado, **-da**, *a.* (*rhet.*) written in short sentences; closed. — *n.m.* group of clauses. —*p.p.* [CLAUSULAR].

clausular, *v.t.* to close a period; to terminate a speech.

clausura, *n.f.* cloister, sanctum, inner recess of a convent; claustration, confinement, retirement; closure; cloture; *guardar* or *vivir en clausura*, to lead a retired or monastic life.

clausurar, *v.t.* to close, terminate, shut.

clava, *n.f.* cudgel, club; (*naut.*) scupper.

clavadizo, -za, *a.* adorned with nails.

clavado, -da, *a.* nailed, armed or furnished with nails; exact, precise; firm, sure; (*coll.*) adequate, fit; (*fig.*) cheated, exploited. — *p.p.* [CLAVAR]; *el reloj está clavado a las cinco,* it is just five by the clock; *tener los ojos clavados en el suelo,* to refuse to look up; *venir clavada una cosa a otra,* to fit exactly.

clavador, -ra, *n.m.f., a.* that nails on.

clavadura, *n.f.* pricking (in horse-shoeing).

clavar, *v.t.* to nail, fasten with nails; to fasten in, force in; to stick, prick; to cheat, deceive; (*artill.*) to spike, nail up (guns); to set in gold or silver; (*mil.*) to ground arms; (*coll.*) to fix, place; (*vet.*) to drive a nail to the quick; (*coll.*) to cheat, deceive. — *v.r.* to prick oneself; to be deceived; *clavar a* or *en la pared,* to shame, bewilder, confuse; *clavar un clavo con la cabeza,* to be very stubborn; *clavarle el diente,* to try, taste, begin something; *clavar las uñas,* to hang on grimly; *se clavó un alfiler,* he pricked himself with a pin; *clavarle a uno en el alma* or *en el corazón,* to affect someone deeply; *clavar los ojos* or *la vista,* to stare; *me lo claven en la frente,* I don't believe it.

clavario, -ria, *n.m.f.* keeper of the keys.

clavazón, *n.m.* set of nails.

clave, *n.m.* clavichord. — *n.f.* (*arch.*) keystone; key; code; (*mus.*) clef; *echar la clave,* to close a speech.

clavel, *n.m.* pink, carnation.

clavelito, *n.f.* plant which bears the pink; small pink.

clavellina, *n.f.* pink, carnation; (*artill.*) vent stopple.

claveque, *n.m.* rock crystal cut like a diamond.

clavera, *n.f.* mould for nail-heads; hole through which a nail is fastened; (*prov.*) boundary landmark.

clavería, *n.f.* office and dignity of key-bearer in certain military orders; (*Mex.*) treasury of a cathedral.

clavero, -ra, *n.m.f.* keeper of the keys; treasurer, cashier. — *n.m.* aromatic clove-tree; key-bearer of some military orders.

clavete, *n.m.* tack, small nail [CLAVO]; (*mus.*) plectrum.

clavetear, *v.t.* to nail, garnish with brass nails; to point or tag a lace; (*fig.*) to settle definitely (business, etc.).

clavicordio, *n.m.* clavichord.

clavicornio, -nia, *n.m.f., a.* (*entom.*) clavicorn.

clavícula, *n.f.* clavicle, collar-bone.

clavicular, *a.* clavicular.

clavija, *n.f.* pin, peg, tack, treenail, pintle, knag; peg of a stringed instrument; *clavija maestra,* fore axle-tree pintle; *apretar a uno las clavijas,* to drive home an argument; put on the screws.

clavijera, *n.f.* (*prov.*) opening in mud walls to let in the water.

clavijero, *n.m.* bridge of a clavichord; hat and coat rack.

clavillo; clavito, *n.m.* small nail, brad, tack; *clavillo de hebilla,* rivet (of a buckle); (*bot.*) clove.

clavímano, -na, *a.* having short fat hand.

claviórgano, *n.m.* instrument with strings like a clavichord and pipes like an organ.

clavo, *n.m.* nail, iron spike; corn (on the foot); spot in the eye; (*surg.*) tent, lint; (*bot.*) clove; (*naut.*) rudder; injury; (*vet.*) tumour between hair and hoof; (*surg.*) dead skin of furuncle; headache; *clavo pasado,* (*vet.*) tumour passing from one side to the other; *clavo de rosca,* screw nail; *clavo de gota de sebo,* nail with semispherical head; *clavo tachuela,* tack, small nail; *arrimar el clavo,* (*vet.*) to prick in shoeing; *clavo de herradura,* hobnail; *clavo plateado,* nail dipped in lead and solder; *clavo romano,* curtain knob, picture nail; *clavo trabadero,* bolt with key on opposite side; *no dejar clavo ni estaca en pared,* to leave nothing at all in a house; *de clavo pasado,* evident, well-known; easy; *dar en el clavo,* (*fig.*) to hit the mark; *dar una en el clavo y ciento en la herradura,* to be right by pure chance; *echar un clavo en la rueda de la fortuna,* to fix one's fortune; *clavar un clavo con la cabeza,* to be very obstinate and dictatorial; *hacer clavo,* to set (of mortar); *no importa un clavo,* it does not matter a pin; *por un clavo se pierde una herradura,* for want of a nail the shoe was lost; *remachar el clavo,* to add error to error; to overstate an argument; *sacar un clavo con otro clavo* or *un clavo saca otro,* (*fig.*) to cure one excess by another; *tener buen* or *mal clavo,* to have large or small pistils (saffron-flower).

clazol, *n.m.* (*Mex.*) bagasse of sugar cane.

clemátide, *n.f.* (*bot.*) traveller's joy, clematis, virgin's bower.

clemencia, *n.f.* clemency, mercy, forbearance.

clemente, *a.* merciful.

clementemente, *adv.* mercifully.

clepsidra, *n.f.* water-clock; hour-glass.

cleptomanía, *n.f.* kleptomania.

cleptomaníaco, -ca; cleptómano, -na, *n.m.f., a.* kleptomaniac.

clerecía, *n.f.* clergy; body of clerics.

clerical, *a.* clerical.

clericalismo, *n.m.* clericalism.

clericalmente, *adv.* clerically.

clericato, *n.m.* clericality, state and dignity of a clergyman.

clericatura, *n.f.* state of a clergyman, clergy.

clerigalla, *n.f.* (*contempt.*) bad clergy.

clérigo, *n.m.* clergyman, cleric, clerk; *clérigo de corona,* tonsured cleric; *clérigo de misa,* priest; *clérigo de misa y olla,* unlearned priest.

cleriguicia, *n.f.* (*contempt.*) body of clerics.

cleriguillo, *n.m.* petty clergyman [CLÉRIGO].

clerizón, *n.m.* (*prov.*) chorister.

clerizonte, *n.m.* layman wearing a clerical dress; ill-dressed or ill-mannered priest.

clero, *n.m.* clergy; *clero regular,* regular (i.e. monastic) clergy; *clero secular,* secular clergy (i.e. non-monastic).

clerofobia, *n.f.* hatred of clergy, anti-clericalism.

clerófobo, -ba, *a.* anti-clerical.

cliente, *n.m.f.* client; person under the protection and tutorage of another.

clientela, *n.f.* clientele, following; clientship, condition of a client; protection, patronage.

clima, *n.m.* climate; clime.

climatérico, -ca, *a.* climacteric; critical; *estar climatérico,* (*coll.*) to be ill-humoured.

climático, -ca, a. climatic; (fig.) changeable, fickle.
climatología, n.f. climatology.
climatológico, -ca, a. climatological.
clímax, n.m. (rhet.) climax.
clin, n.f. mane; (coll.) tenerse a las clines, (fig.) to make every effort not to decline in rank or fortune.
clínico, -ca, a. clinic, clinical. — n.m.f. (eccles.) clinic. — n.f. (med.) clinic (instruction); clinic ward of hospitals; clinique.
clinométrico, -ca, a. clinometrical.
clinómetro, n.m. (naut.) clinometer.
clinopodio, n.m. (bot.) wild basil, calamint.
clíper, n.m. (naut.) clipper.
clisado, -da, a. (print.) stereotyped. — n.m. stereotyping; stereotypography. — p.p. [CLISAR].
clisador, n.m. (print.) stereotyper.
clisar, v.t. (print.) to stereotype.
clisé, n.m. (print.) stereotype, cliché.
clistel; clister, n.m. (med.) clyster.
clistelera, n.f. woman who administers clysters.
clisterizar, v.t. to administer clysters.
clitómetro, n.m. (surveying) clinometer.
clivoso, -sa, a. (poet.) gradually descending, declivous, sloping.
clo, n.m. cluck (of a hen).
cloaca, n.f. cloaca; sewer, conduit for dirty water; (zool.) large intestine of fowls, etc.
clocar, v.i. to cluck.
cloque, n.m. boat-hook; gaff (used for tunny-fishing).
cloquear, v.i. to cluck, cackle, chuck, make a noise like a hen; to gaff (tunny fish).
cloqueo, n.m. chuck, cluck, cackle, the cry of a hen.
cloquera, n.f. broodiness (in fowls).
cloquero, n.m. one who handles the gaff in the tunny-fishery.
cloral, n.m. (chem.) chloral.
clorato, n.m. (chem.) chlorate.
clorhidrato, n.m. (chem.) chloral-hydrate.
clorhídrico, -ca, a. (chem.) hydrochloric.
clórico, -ca, a. chloric; ácido clórico, chloric acid.
clorita, n.f. (min.) chlorite.
clorítico, -ca, a. (min.) chloritic.
cloro, n.m. (chem.) chlorine.
clorofila, n.f. chlorophyll.
clorofílico, ca, a. appertaining to chlorophyll.
clorofilo, -la, a. (bot.) having green or yellow leaves.
clorofórmico, -ca, a. relating to chloroform.
cloroformización, n.f. chloroforming.
cloroformizador, -ra, n.m.f. anæsthetist.
cloroformizar, v.t. to chloroform.
cloroformo, n.m. chloroform.
clorosis, n.f. (med.) chlorosis, green-sickness.
cloroso, -sa, a. (chem.) chlorous.
clorótico, -ca, a. chlorotic. — n.f., a. suffering from chlorosis.
clorurado, -da, a. containing chloride.
clorurar, v.t. to chloridize.
cloruro, n.m. chloride; cloruro de cal, chloride of lime; cloruro de sodio or cloruro sódico, sodium chloride, common salt.
club, n.m. club, association of persons.
clubista, n.m. club-man, member of a club.
clueco, -ca, a broody; (coll.) decrepit, worn out with age. — n.f. broody hen.

coa, n.f. (Am.) stick used by Indians to till the land; (Mex.) kind of hoe; (Chi.) thieves and convicts' slang.
coacción, n.f. coaction, compulsion.
coacervación, n.f. coacervation.
coacervar, v.t. to heap together.
coacreedor, -ra, n.m.f. joint creditor.
coactivo, -va, a. coercive, compulsive.
coacusado, -da, a. (law) accused jointly. — n.m.f. (law) co-respondent; fellow-prisoner.
coacusar, v.t. (law) to accuse jointly with another.
coadjutor, n.m. coadjutor, assistant, associate.
coadjutora, n.f. coadjutrix.
coadjutoría, n.f. coadjutorship, office of a coadjutor; right of survivorship of a co-adjutor.
coadministrador, n.m. co-trustee (of a diocese).
coadquirente; coadquiriente, a. acquiring jointly.
coadquiridor, -ra; coadquisidor, -ra, n.m.f. joint-purchaser.
coadquirir, v.t. to acquire jointly.
coadquisición, n.f. joint-purchase.
coadunación, n.f.; coadunamiento, n.m. coadunation.
coadunar, v.t. to join things closely together.
coadyutor, n.m. coadjutor.
coadyutorio, -ria, a. co-operative.
coadyuvador, -ra, n.m.f. fellow-helper, assistant.
coadyuvante, a. helping, assisting.
coadyuvar, v.t. to help, assist.
coagente, n.m. coagent, associate.
coagulable, a. easily coagulating.
coagulación, n.f. coagulation.
coagulador, -ra, coagulante, a. coagulating.
coagular, v.t., v.r. to coagulate, curdle.
coágulo, n.m. coagulation of blood; clot; coagulum.
coaguloso, -sa, a. coagulating, coagulated.
coairón, n.m. (prov.) piece of timber.
coaita, n.f. (Am. Cent.) species of monkey.
coalescencia, n.f. coalescence.
coalición, n.f. coalition, confederacy.
coalicionar, v.t., v.r. to form a coalition.
coalicionista, n.m.f. coalitionist.
coaltar, n.m. coal-tar.
coalla, n.f. woodcock.
coapóstol, n.m. fellow-apostle.
coarrendador, n.m. joint-lessor.
coarrendamiento, n.m. joint-tenancy.
coarrendar, v.t. to rent jointly.
coarrendatario, n.m. joint-tenant.
coartación, n.f. limitation, restriction; (eccles.) obligation to be ordained within a given time.
coartado, -da, a. slave who has paid his master a sum to obtain freedom; limited, restricted. — n.f. alibi; probar la coartada, to prove an alibi. — p.p. [COARTAR].
coartador, -ra, a. restraining. — n.m.f. restrainer.
coartar, v.t. to limit, restrict.
coartatorio, -ria, a. limiting, restrictive.
coasignatorio, -ria, n.m.f. joint-assignee.
coasociación, n.f. co-partnership.
coasociado, -da, n.m.f. co-partner. — p.p. [COASOCIARSE].
coasociarse, v.r. to go into partnership.
coate, -ta, a. (Mex.) twin.

coautor, -ra, *n.m.f.* co-author, joint-author.

coba, *n.f.* (*coll.*) funny story; *dar la coba,* to indulge in small talk; (*Morocco*) Sultan's tent; (*Morocco*) dome, cupola; shrine or tomb of a dervish.

cobáltico, -ca, *a.* (*chem.*) cobaltic.

cobaltina, *n.f.* cobaltite.

cobalto, *n.m.* cobalt.

cobaltocre, *n.m.* cobalt-bloom.

cobanillo, *n.m.* small basket used during vintage.

cobarcho, *n.m.* part of tunny-fishing net.

cobarde, *a.* cowardly, timid, fearful; (*fig.*) weak, poor (sight). — *n.m.f.* coward.

cobardear, *v.i.* to be cowardly, timid, fearful.

cobardemente, *adv.* in a cowardly way.

cobardía, *n.f.* cowardliness, dastardly abjectness.

cobayo, *n.m.* (*Arg., Col.*) guinea-pig.

cobea, *n.f.* (*Cent. Am.*) climbing plant of the bellflower family.

cobertera, *n.f.* pot-lid, cover; bawd, procuress; (*prov.*) white water-lily. — *pl.* the two middle feathers of a hawk's tail.

cobertizo, *n.m.* pent-roof, penthouse; shed.

cobertor, *n.m.* coverlet, quilt, counterpane, bed-spread.

cobertura, *n.f.* cover, covering, wrapping; act of grandee of Spain in covering himself in the presence of the king.

cobija, *n.f.* ridge-tile; (*prov.*) short mantilla; cover; fine feather; (*Mex.*) shawl; *pl.* (*Col., Mex.*) bed-clothes.

cobijador, -ra, *a.* covering, protective.

cobijadura, *n.f.* act of covering.

cobijamiento; cobijo, *n.m.* act of covering; lodging.

cobijar, *v.t.* to cover, protect, overspread; to shelter, lodge. — *v.r.* to take shelter, lodging; protect oneself.

cobijón, *n.m.* (*Col.*) leather or hide covering for a pack-horse.

cobil, *n.m.* corner, angle.

cobla, copla, *n.f.* metrical composition in Provençal and Catalan poetry; (*mus.*) Sardana band.

cobo, *n.m.* (*Cub.*) gigantic snail; (*CR.*) blanket.

cobra, *n.f.* a number of mares for treading out the corn; rope for yoking oxen; (*zool.*) cobra; (*hunt.*) act of retrieving.

cobrable; cobradero, -ra, *a.* collectable, recoverable.

cobrado, -da, *a.* recovered, received; acquired; retrieved; complete, undaunted. — *p.p.* [COBRAR].

cobrador, -ra, *n.m.f.* receiver or collector of rents or other money; tram conductor; *perro cobrador,* retriever dog.

cobramiento, *n.m.* utility, profit, emolument; recovery, restoration.

cobranza, *n.f.* recovery or collection of money; (*hunt.*) retrieving game.

cobrar, *v.t.* to recover, collect, receive what is due; (*hunt.*) to retrieve game; to gain affection, esteem, fame, etc.; to charge (fee, price); to pull, draw in (cords, etc.); to acquire. — *v.r.* to recover, return to oneself; *cobrar afición al estudio,* to acquire a love of study; *cobrar ánimo* or *corazón,* to take courage; *cobrar cariño a Juan,* to take a liking to John; *cobrar carnes,* to become fat; *cobrar de los deudores,* to recover from the debtors;

cobrar en papel, to collect money in notes; *cobrar fuerzas,* to gather strength; *cobrar un cheque,* to cash a cheque; *cobra buena fama y échate a dormir,* once you get a good name, you need worry no more.

cobratorio, -ria, *a.* belonging to the collection of money; collectable.

cobre, *n.m.* copper; kitchen brass utensils; *cobre de cecial,* pair of dried hake; *cobre quemado,* sulphate of copper; *cobre verde,* malachite; *batir el cobre,* (*coll.*) to pursue with vigour; *batirse el cobre,* to work hard at profitable business; to dispute hotly; *cobre gana cobre, que no huesos del hombre,* money goes to money. — *pl.* brass instruments of an orchestra.

cobreño, -ña, *a.* made of copper.

cobrizo, -za, *a.* coppery, cupreous; (*min.*) cupric.

cobro, *n.m.* [COBRANZA]; receptacle, place of safety; *poner cobro,* to make efforts to recover; to be careful, take care; *poner en cobro,* to put in a safe place; *ponerse en cobro,* to find a sure refuge.

coca, *n.f.* (*bot.*) coca; (*prov.*) [TARASCA]; (*naut.*) small vessel; women's side-hair; (*coll.*) head; (*coll.*) rap on the head; (*prov.*) cake; (*naut.*) knot in cable; *coca de Levante,* Indian berry.

cocacho, *n.m.* (*Arg., Ec., Per.*) rap on the head.

cocada, *n.f.* (*Bol., Col.*) nougat, almond paste.

cocador, -ra, *a.* wheedling, coaxing, flattering. — *n.m.f.* coaxer, flatterer, wheedler.

cocaína, *n.f.* cocaine.

cocal, *n.m.* (*Per.*) grove of Indian berries; (*Ven.*) coconut plantation.

cocán, *n.m.* (*Per.*) breast of a fowl.

cocar, *v.t.* to make grimaces or wry faces; (*coll.*) to coax, flatter.

cocarar, *v.t.* to supply with coca-leaves.

cocaví, *n.m.* (*Am. Mer.*) coca and provisions for a journey.

coccicultura, *n.f.* cochineal-insect cultivation.

coccíneo, -nea, *a.* purple, purplish.

cocción, *n.f.* boiling, cooking.

coce, *n.f.* (*obs.*) kick.

coceador, -ra, *a.* kicking (animal). — *n.m.f.* kicker.

coceadura, *n.f.;* **coceamiento,** *n.m.* kicking.

cocear, *v.i.* to kick; *cocear contra el aguijón,* to kick against the pricks; (*coll.*) to repugn, resist.

cocedero, -ra, *a.* easily boiled or cooked. — *n.m.* kitchen; place where wine is boiled.

cocedizo, -za, *a.* easily boiled or cooked.

cocedor, *n.m.* one whose business is to boil must; baking-oven.

cocedura, *n.f.* boiling; cooking.

cocer, *v.t.* (*pres. indic.* **cuezo;** *pres. subj.* **cueza**) to boil, cook, dress victuals; to bake (bread, bricks, tiles or earthenware); to digest; (*surg.*) to maturate. — *v.i.* to boil, ferment, cook, seethe; to ret. — *v.r.* to suffer intense and continued pain; *duro de cocer y peor de comer,* things unpleasant do not become less so with use; *vieja fué y no se coció,* expression reproaching a vain excuse for leaving something undone; *cocer a la* or *con lumbre,* to cook on the fire.

coces, *n.f.pl.* [COZ] kicks.

cocido, -da, *n.m.* Spanish dish of boiled meat and vegetables. — *a.* boiled, baked, cooked. — *p.p.* [COCER]; *estar cocido en,* to be skilled at, experienced in.

cociembre, *n.f.* (*prov.*) fermentation of wine.

cociente, *n.m.* quotient.

cocimiento, *n.m.* boiling, cooking, decoction; bath or mordant for dyeing.

cocina, *n.f.* cookery; kitchen; broth; pottage of greens; *cocina económica,* cooking-range.

cocinar, *v.t.* to cook or dress victuals. — *v.i.* (*coll.*) to meddle in others' affairs.

cocinera, *n.f.* cook.

cocinero, *n.m.* cook, chef; *haber sido cocinero antes que fraile,* to have practical knowledge.

cocinilla; cocinita, *n.f.* small kitchen [COCINA]; camping-stove for paraffin, methylated spirit, etc.; chafing-dish; fireplace. — *n.m.* interfering, meddlesome man.

cocle, *n.m.* (*naut.*) [CLOQUE].

cóclea, *n.f.* Archimedean screw.

coclear, *a.* (*bot.*) cochlean, cochlear. — *n.m.* half a drachm.

coclearia, *n.f.* cochlearia, common scurvygrass.

coclero, -ra, *n.m.f.* harpooner.

coclillo, *n.m.* insect that destroys vines.

coco, *n.m.* (*bot.*) coco-palm; coco-nut; (*entom.*) coccus; (*prov.*) muslin, percale; bogy, bugbear; berry used for rosary beads; (*coll.*) gesture, grimace; (*Cub.*) a wading bird, kind of ibis; *agua de coco,* coconut milk; *hacer cocos,* (*fig.*) to flatter, wheedle; to flirt; *paracer* or *ser un coco,* (*coll.*) to be very ugly; *coco avellanado,* dry coco-nut.

cocó, *n.m.* (*Cub.*) whitish earth used in masonry and for concrete making.

cocobacilo, *n.m.* bubonic plague bacillus.

cocobacteria, *n.f.* primitive form of bacteria.

cocobálsamo, *n.m.* fruit of the balm of Gilead.

cocobolo; cocolobo, *n.m.* hardwood-tree.

cocodrilo, *n.m.* (*zool.*) crocodile; (*railw.*) alarm-signal; *lágrimas de cocodrilo,* crocodile tears; unreal, affected pity.

cocol, *n.m.* (*Mex.*) bread roll.

cocolero, *n.m.* (*Mex.*) baker of *cocoles.*

cocolía, *n.f.* (*Mex.*) spite, ill-will, dislike.

cocoliche, *n.m.* (*Arg.*) jargon used by foreigners, especially Italian immigrants; (*contempt.*) an Italian immigrant.

cocoliste, *n.m.* (*Mex.*) epidemic fever.

cocolita, *n.f.* (*min.*) coccolith.

cócora, *n.m.f.,* *a.* impertinent person, bore.

cocoso, -sa, *a.* worm-eaten, gnawed by grubs.

cocotal, *n.m.* coco-palm plantation.

cocote, *n.m.* occiput.

cocotero, *n.m.* coco-palm.

cocui, *n.m.* (*Ven.*) agave.

cocuiza, *n.f.* (*Mex., Ven.*) strong rope made of *cocui* fibre.

cocula, *n.f.* (*bot.*) cocculus.

cocuma, *n.f.* (*Per.*) roasted ear of corn.

cocuyo; cucuyo, *n.m.* cocujo, firefly, glowworm in the West Indies.

cocha, *n.f.* (*min.*) small reservoir of water; (*Per.*) large, clear space; (*Chi., Ec.*) lagoon, pool.

cochama, *n.m.* (*Col.*) large fish of the Magdalen river.

cochambre, *n.m.* (*coll.*) greasy, dirty, stinking thing.

cochambrería, *n.f.* (*coll.*) heap of filthy things.

cochambrero, -ra; cochambroso, -sa, *a.* dirty, nasty, stinking.

cocharro, *n.m.* wooden or stone dish, cup, platter.

cochastro, *n.m.* little sucking-boar.

cochayuyo, *n.m.* (*Am. Mer.*) an edible subaquatic plant.

coche, *n.m.* coach, carriage; *coche de alquiler, de plaza, de punto,* or *simón,* hack or hackney coach; *coche de colleras,* coach drawn by mules; *coche cama,* (*railw.*) sleeping-car; *coche comedor,* (*railw.*) dining-car; *coche de camino,* travelling coach; *coche parado,* (*fig.*) balcony or window giving on busy thoroughfare; *ir en el coche de San Francisco,* to go on foot, walk; *coche fúnebre,* hearse.

cochear, *v.i.* to drive a coach.

cochera, *n.f.* carriage house; (*railw.*) depot, roundhouse, garage; coach-house; coachman's wife.

cocheril, *a.* (*coll.*) relating to coachmen.

cochero, -ra, *a.* easily cooked. — *n.m.* coachman; (*astron.*) Auriga; *puerta cochera,* carriage-entrance.

cocherón, *n.m.* large coach-house; enginehouse.

cochevira, *n.f.* lard.

cochevís, *n.f.* [COGUJADA].

cochifrito, *n.m.* fricassee of kid or lamb.

cochigato, *n.m.* (*Mex.*) a wading bird.

cochina, *n.f.* sow.

cochinada, *n.f.* (*coll.*) mean, dirty action.

cochinamente, *adv.* (*fam.*) foully, hoggishly, filthily; (*coll.*) meanly, basely, nastily.

cochinata, *n.f.* (*naut.*) rider.

cochinear, *v.i.* (*fam.*) to behave basely, do nasty things.

cochinería, *n.f.* (*coll.*) dirtiness, filthiness, nastiness; meanness, niggardliness.

cochinero, -ra, *a.* of fruits poor in quality, given to hogs; (*coll.*) short, quick (gait).

cochinilla, *n.f.* small crustacean used in medicine; wood louse; cochineal-insect; cochineal.

cochinillo, *n.m.* sucking-pig.

cochino, -na, *a.* (*coll.*) dirty, filthy, nasty, mean, vile. — *n.m.f.* pig.

cochiquera, *n.f.* hog-sty, pig-sty; (*coll.*) small, filthy room.

cochistrón, -na, *n.m.f.* (*coll.*) very dirty, nasty person.

cochite hervite, *n.m.* (*coll.*) helter-skelter; feather-brained person.

cochitril, *n.m.* pig-sty; (*coll.*) filthy hovel.

cocho, -cha, *p.p. irreg.* [COCER] cooked. — *n.m.f.* (*prov.*) pig; (*prov.*) nasty person.

cochura, *n.f.* boiling; dough for a batch of bread; (*min.*) calcination.

cochurero, *n.m.* furnace-man, stoker.

cochurra, *n.f.* (*Cub.*) sweetmeat of guava with seeds.

coda, *n.f.* (*prov.*) tail; (*mus.*) coda; (*mus.*) repetition; (*carp.*) wedge.

codadura, *n.f.* (*agric.*) layer (of vine).

codal, *n.m.,* *a.* bent, cranked, elbowed; measuring a cubit. — *n.m.* one cubit in length; elbow-piece of armour; cubitlong wax candle; vine shoot; (*arch.*) buttress, counterfort; (*carp.*) frame of hand-saw; (*carp.*) square; (*min.*) prop, shore.

codaste, *n.m.* (*naut.*) stern-post.

codazo, *n.m.* blow with the elbow, hunch.

codeador, *n.m.* (*naut.*) timber-measurer.

codear, *v.i.* to elbow, jostle; *v.t.* (*naut.*) to measure timber into cubits. — *v.r.* to treat one another as equals; *codearse con,* to mix with (people).

codeína, *n.f.* (*chem.*) codeine.

codelincuencia, *n.f.* complicity, joint delinquency.

codelincuente, *n.m.f.,* *a.* accomplice, partner in crime.

codemandante, *n.m.f.,* *a.* co-plaintiff, joint-plaintiff.

codemandar, *v.t.* (*law*) to prosecute jointly.

codera, *n.f.* itch, scabbiness of elbow; piece put in the elbow of a jacket to strengthen it; (*naut.*) stern-fast.

codesera, *n.f.* plantation of *codesos.*

codeso, *n.m.* (*bot.*) hairy cytisus, bean-trefoil.

codetenido, -da, *n.m.f.* fellow-prisoner.

codetentar, *v.t.* to detain jointly (another's property).

codeudor, -ra, *n.m.f.* joint-debtor.

códex, *n.m.* pharmacopœia.

códice, *n.m.* manuscript volume, codex.

codicia, *n.f.* covetousness, cupidity; greediness, ardent desire; *la codicia rompe el saco,* covet all, lose all.

codiciable, *a.* covetable.

codiciador, -ra, *n.m.f.,* *a.* covetous (person).

codiciante, *a.* coveting.

codiciar, *v.t.* to covet, desire eagerly.

codicilar, *a.* codicillary, pertaining to a codicil.

codicilo, *n.m.* codicil.

codiciosamente, *adv.* covetously, greedily.

codicioso, -sa, *a.* greedy, covetous, avaricious; (*coll.*) diligent, laborious, thrifty; *codicioso de honores,* desiring honours.

codificación, *n.f.* codification.

codificador, -ra, *a.* codifying. — *n.m.f.* codifier.

codificar, *v.t.* (*pret.* **codifiqué;** *pres. subj.* **codifique**) to codify, digest (laws).

código, *n.m.* code of laws; *código de señales,* (*naut.*) signal code.

codillera, *n.f.* tumour on the knee of horses.

codillo, *n.m.* bend, elbow, angle; codille (a term at ombre); shoulder (of quadrupeds); stirrup of a saddle; part of the branch of a tree joining the trunk; *jugársela uno de codillo a otro,* (*fig.*) to trick or outwit a person; *tirar a uno al codillo,* to ruin, injure someone greatly.

codirector, -ra, *n.m.f.* joint-director, joint-directress.

codo, *n.m.* elbow; cubit; (*mech.*) angle, elbow, knee; shoulder (of quadrupeds); *apretar* or *hincar el codo,* to do all one can for a dying man; *beber de codos,* to drink at one's ease; *dar de codo,* to elbow; (*coll.*) to treat with contempt; *comerse los codos de hambre,* to be starving; *del codo a la mano,* expression denoting shortness of stature; *hablar por los codos,* to chatter, talk idly; *empinar, levantar* or *alzar el codo* or *de codo,* to crook or lift the elbow, tipple; *estar metido* or *meterse hasta los codos,* to be up to one's eyes in a thing.

codón, *n.m.* leather cover for a horse's tail.

codonante, *a.* giving jointly. — *n.m.f.* joint-donor.

codoñate, *n.m.* quince sweet.

codorniz, *n.f.* quail.

coeducación, *n.f.* coeducation.

coeducar, *v.t.* to coeducate.

coeficiencia, *n.f.* coefficiency.

coeficiente, *a.* co-operating. — *n.m.* (*alg.*) coefficient; *coeficiente de seguridad,* safety factor; *coeficiente de trabajo,* working stress.

coelector, -ra, *n.m.f.* joint-elector.

coemperador, *n.m.* associate emperor.

coendú, *n.m.* (*Am.*) porcupine.

coepíscopo, *n.m.* fellow bishop.

coercer, *v.t.* (*pres. indic.* **coerzo;** *pres. subj.* **coerza**) to coerce, check, restrain.

coercibilidad, *n.f.* (*phys.*) compressibility.

coercible, *a.* coercible, subject to check; (*phys.*) compressible.

coerción, *n.f.* (*law*) coercion, restraint, check.

coercitivo, -va, *a.* coercive, restraining.

coesencial, -a, *a.* coessential.

coetaneamente, *adv.* simultaneously.

coetáneo, -nea, *a.* coetaneous; *coetáneo de Cervantes,* contemporary with Cervantes.

coeternamente, *adv.* coeternally.

coeternidad, *n.f.* coeternity.

coeterno, -na, *a.* coeternal.

coevo, -va, *a.* coeval, contemporary.

coexistencia, *n.f.* coexistence.

coexistente, *a.* coexistent.

coexistir, *v.i.* to coexist; *coexistir con Calderón,* to live at the same time as Calderón.

coextenderse, *v.r.* to become coextensive.

coextenso, -sa, *a.* coextensive. — *p.p. irreg.* [COEXTENDERSE].

cofa, *n.f.* (*naut.*) topmast; look-out aloft for gun director, control top and range-finder.

cofia, *n.f.* head-dress, head-gear; coif; hair-net.

cofiador, -ra, *n.m.f.* (*law*) joint-guarantor.

cofiezuela, *n.f.* small hair-net or coif [COFIA].

cofín, *n.m.* small basket; fruit-box.

cofosis, *n.f.* complete deafness.

cofrade, *n.m.f.* confrère; member of a confraternity, sisterhood or brotherhood; *confrade de pala,* (*slang*) burglar's accomplice.

cofradía, *n.m.* confraternity, brotherhood; association of persons with a common purpose; trades union; (*slang*) reunion, gathering of thieves.

cofre, *n.m.* trunk for clothes, coffer; (*print.*) coffin.

cofrecillo, *n.m.* small trunk [COFRE].

cofrero, *n.m.* trunk-maker or seller.

cofto, -ta, *a.* [COPTO].

cofundador, -ra, *a.* co-founding.

cogedera, *n.f.* rod for gathering esparto-grass; box for catching swarming bees; pole for gathering fruit.

cogedero, -ra, *a.* ready to be collected, gathered. — *n.m.* handle.

cogedizo, -za, *a.* which can easily be collected or gathered.

cogedor, -ra, *a.* collecting, gathering. — *n.m.f.* collector, gatherer. — *n.m.* dustpan; coal or ash shovel; tax-gatherer.

cogedura, *n.f.* act of gathering or collecting.

coger, *v.t.* (*pres. indic.* **cojo;** *pres. subj.* **coja**) to catch, grasp, seize; to get, lay hold of; to come upon; to fetch, gather, collect; to imbibe, soak; to gather the produce of the ground; to have room; to hold; to occupy, take up; to find, procure; to surprise, discover; to attack unexpectedly; to gore, pierce with a horn (bullfighting); to follow, overtake, come up to; to intercept, obstruct. — *v.i.* to go in or into, fit, have room; *aquí te cojo, aquí te mato*, now I have my chance; *coger a mano*, to gather by hand; *coger con el hurto*, to surprise with the stolen goods; *coger de buen humor* or *de buenas*, to find in a good humour; *coger de malas*, to find in a bad temper; *coger de, por la mano*, to take by the hand; *coge bien*, it holds comfortably; *cógelas, que están maduras*, do it now, the time is propitious; *cógeme ésa*, what do you think of that? *coger en casa*, to catch, find at home; *coger a puñados*, to gather in handfuls, in great abundance; *esta noticia me cogió de nuevo*, this news surprised me; *coger a uno la palabra*, to take someone at his word, hold him to his promise; *coger buena idea a una persona*, to feel affection for a person; *coger casa*, to take a house or office; *coger el rábano por las hojas*, to misunderstand, usually to one's advantage; *coger infraganti*, to catch in the act; *coger la breva*, to secure a plum; *coger la ocasión por los cabellos*, to grasp the opportunity; *cogerle entre la espada y la pared* or *entre paredes*, to put someone between the devil and the deep sea; *cogerle las palabras*, to see through someone's story; *cogerle miedo*, to be terrified of someone; *cogerle un carro*, to be run over, knocked down by a vehicle; *cogerlo por carambola*, or *chiripa*, to get something by chance; *coger los trastos*, to collect one's belongings, get ready; *coger las aguas*, (*arch.*) to provide with gutters; *cogerlas al aire* or *al vuelo*, to be quick in the uptake; *coger las de Villadiego*, to escape, flee; *cogerle a solas*, to get someone alone; *cogerle coraje, inquina* or *tirria*, to feel animosity against someone; *cogerle de un brazo y ponerle de patitas en la calle*, to throw someone out of the house; *coger toda la calle*, to behave as if the street belonged to one; *coger una calle y seguirla*, to turn up a street and go straight on; *coger y* (followed by verb), to be determined, resolved (on the act expressed by second verb); *cogió y se acostó*, he went to bed without further ado; *coger a uno el paso*, to catch up to, overtake someone in order to speak to him; *coger al vuelo*, to sprint; *esta cámara coge mil fanegas de trigo*, this granary holds a thousand bushels of wheat; *me cogió descuidado*, he took me unawares; *coger la delantera*, to get the start (of a person); *coger la calle*, to bolt, abscond, run away; *coger las calles*, to obstruct the streets; *coger a deseo*, to obtain one's wishes; *coger cogorza, la gorda, la juma, una merluza, una mona, una turca*, to be tipsy, intoxicated; *coger laureles*, to win triumphs; *coger la puerta*, to go away; *coger las palabras*, to listen attentively; *¡cogite!* I have caught you, I have you there (phrase used in arguments).

cogetrapos, *n.m.* rag-dealer.

cogida, *n.f.* (*coll.*) fruit harvest; gathering or harvesting of fruits; act of the bull in catching the bull-fighter; catch (in fishing).

cogido, -da, *p.p.* [COGER] caught, held. — *n.m.* fold, gather, pleat (in clothes, curtains, etc.).

cogimiento, *n.m.* gathering, collecting, catching.

cogitabilidad, *n.f.* cogitativeness.

cogitable, *a.* cogitable.

cogitabundo, -da, *a.* pensive, musing, thoughtful.

cogitación, *n.f.* reflection, cogitation, meditation.

cogitar, *v.t.* to reflect, meditate, muse.

cogitativo, -va, *a.* cogitative, given to meditation.

cognación, *n.f.* cognation, kindred, relationship.

cognado, -da, *n.m.f.* cognate, blood relation.

cognaticio, -cia, *a.* cognate.

cognático, -ca, *a.* (*law*) cognate.

cognición, *n.f.* cognition.

cognomento, *n.m.* cognomen, surname.

cognominado, -da, *a.* named, surnamed, nicknamed.

cognominar, *v.t.* to call by the surname.

cognoscible, *a.* cognoscible.

cognoscitivo, -va, *a.* cognitive, having the power of knowing.

cogollero, *n.m.* (*Cub.*) worm which attacks the tobacco plant.

cogollico; **cogollito**, *n.m.* small heart or flower of garden plants.

cogollo, *n.m.* heart of cabbage, lettuce, etc.; shoot of a plant; tree-top, summit (of pine).

cogombrillo, *n.m.* [COHOMBRILLO].

cogón, *n.m.* (*Philip.*) bamboo used for thatching.

cogotazo, *n.m.* slap on the back of the neck.

cogote, *n.m.* occiput, back part of the neck; crest at the back of the helmet; *ser tieso de cogote*, (*fig.*) to be stiff-necked, headstrong, obstinate.

cogotera, *n.f.* linen nape-protector; sunbonnet for beasts of burden; hair combed down on the neck.

cogotudo, -da, *a.* thick-necked; (*coll.*) haughty, conceited.

cogucho, *n.m.* coarse, inferior sort of sugar.

cogujada, *n.f.* crested lark.

cogujón, *n.m.* corner of a mattress or bolster.

cogujonero, -ra, *a.* pointed (like the corners of mattresses and bolsters).

cogulla, *n.f.* cowl, hood or habit of a monk.

cogullada, *n.f.* pig's dewlap.

cohabitación, *n.f.* cohabitation.

cohabitador, -ra, *n.m.f., a.* (person) cohabiting, living with another.

cohabitar, *v.i.* to cohabit, live together.

cohecha, *n.f.* last tillage before sowing the crop.

cohechador, -ra, *a.* bribing. — *n.m.f.* briber, suborner; (*obs.*) bribed judge.

cohechar, *v.t.* to bribe, suborn, hire, fee; (*obs.*) to force, oblige; (*agric.*) to plough the ground for the last time before it is sown.

cohechazón, *n.m.* [COHECHA].

cohecho, *n.m.* bribery; (*agric.*) season for ploughing; *ni hagas cohecho, ni pierdas derecho*, take no bribe, but give up no right.

cohén, *n.m.f.* soothsayer; procurer, pimp.

coheredar, *v.t.* to inherit jointly.

coheredera, *n.f.* coheiress, joint-heiress.

coheredero, *n.m.* co-heir, joint-heir.

coherencia, *n.f.* coherence, connexion; (*phys.*) cohesion.

coherente, *a.* coherent, cohesive, consistent.

cohesión, *n.f.* cohesion.

cohesivo, -va, *a.* cohesive.

cohesor, *n.m.* (*wire.*) coherer.

cohete, *n.m.* rocket, sky-rocket; *cohete corredor,* rocket which runs along the ground; *cohetes para señales,* signal rockets; *salió como un cohete,* he went out like a flash.

cohetera, *n.f.* wife of a *cohetero.*

cohetería, *n.f.* artificial firework factory or shop.

cohetero, *n.m.* rocket-maker, firework-maker or -dealer.

cohibente, *a.* (*phys.*) applied to a bad conductor of electricity.

cohibición, *n.f.* prohibition, restraint.

cohibidor, -ra, *a.* prohibiting, restraining. — *n.m.f.* prohibitor.

cohibir, *v.t.* to prohibit; to restrain.

cohobación, *n.f.* (*chem.*) repeated distillation.

cohobar, *v.t.* to distil repeatedly.

cohobo, *n.m.* deer-skin; (*Ec., Per.*) deer.

cohollo, *n.m.* [COGOLLO].

cohombral, *n.m.* cucumber-bed.

cohombrar, *v.t.* (*agric.*) (*prov.*) to earth up (plants).

cohombrillo, *n.m.* gherkin [COHOMBRO].

cohombro, *n.m.* cucumber; kind of fritter; *cohombro de mar,* sea-cucumber.

cohonder, *v.t.* to corrupt; to vilify.

cohondimiento, *n.m.* corruption, reproach, infamy.

cohonestar, *v.t.* to give an honest or decent appearance to an action.

cohorte, *n.m.* cohort; (*fig.*) crowd, legion.

coigual, *a.* coequal.

coigualdad, *n.f.* coequality.

coila, *n.f.* (*Chi.*) fraud, lie.

coima, *n.f.* perquisite received by the keeper of a gaming-table; mistress, concubine.

coime; coimero, *n.m.* keeper of a gaming-table; scorer (at billiards).

coincidencia, *n.f.* coincidence, concurrence.

coincidente, *a.* coincident, coincidental; concurrent.

coincidir, *v.i.* to coincide, to concur.

coinquilino, -na, *n.m.f.* joint-tenant.

coinquinación, *n.f.* staining, stain.

coinquinado, -da, *a.* (*fig.*) sullied, dirty, impure. — *p.p.* [COINQUINAR].

coinquinar, *v.t.* to stain, sully. — *v.r.* to become stained, tarnished (good name, fame).

cointeresado, -da, *a.* jointly interested with another. — *n.m.f.* sharer, partner (in affairs).

coipo, *n.m.* (*Arg., Chi.*) coypu, mammal similar to the beaver.

coirón, *n.m.* (*Bol., Chi., Per.*) kind of thatching grass.

coironal, *n.m.* coiron field.

coito, *n.m.* coition, carnal copulation.

coja, *n.f.* (*coll.*) lewd woman.

cojal, *n.m.* knee-cap worn by carders.

cojear, *v.i.* to limp, halt, hobble; (*coll.*) to deviate from virtue; *cojear y no de los pies,* (*coll.*) to suffer from some vice or defect; *cojear del mismo pie,* to have the same defect or passion; *cojear del pie derecho,* to limp with the right foot; *el que no cojea, renquea,* nobody is perfect; *saber de qué pie cojea,* to know someone's weakness.

cojera, *n.f.* lameness, halt, limp; *en cojera de perro y en lágrimas de mujer, no hay que*

creer, do not be impressed by exaggerated lamentations.

cojijo, *n.m.* slight complaint or injury; grub, insect.

cojijoso, -sa, *a.* peevish, irritable.

cojín, *n.m.* cushion; saddle-pad; (*naut.*) pillow.

cojinete, *n.m.* cushionet, small pillow [COJÍN]; pad; (*railw.*) chair; (*mech.*) journal-bearing, shaft-bearing, pillow-block; (*print.*) roller-clamp; *cojinete de bolas,* ball-bearing.

cojitranco, -ca, *n.m.f., a.* (*contempt.*) applied as a nickname to evil-minded lame persons.

cojo, -ja, *a.* crippled; halt, lame; ill-balanced, unsteady, lop-sided (chair, table). — *n.m.f.* cripple; *cojo de nacimiento,* lame from birth; *no ser cojo ni manco,* to be clever, skilful.

cojobo, *n.m.* (*Cub.*) a hard-wood tree.

cojubo, *a.* entire, not gelt or castrated (animal).

cojuelo, -la, *n.m.f., a.* small cripple [COJO].

cok, *n.m.* coke; *cok metalúrgico,* furnace coke.

col, *n.f.* cabbage; *entre col y col, lechuga,* variation is necessary in all things.

cola, *n.f.* tail (of animal, bird); train (of dress); end of a piece of cloth; tail-end, hind part of anything; tail (of comet); extremity; appendage; queue (of people); (*carp.*) glue; (*arch.*) inside joint; (*fort.*) gorge; gum; (*mus.*) in singing, sustained note on final syllable; (*bot.*) cola, kola; lowest place in school or class; *cola de boca,* adhesive in the form of a pastille; *cola de caballo,* (*bot.*) horse-tail; *cola de golondrina,* (*fort.*) hornwork; *cola de milano* or *de pato,* (*carp.*) dovetail; swallow-tail, fan-tail; *a cola de milano,* (*arch.*) dovetail moulding; *cola de pescado,* isinglass; *cola de retal* or *de retazos,* painters' size; *cola fuerte,* adhesive gum; *a la cola,* at the end, right at the back; *apearse por la cola,* to say something absurd; *ser arrimado a la cola,* to be ignorant or rude; *hacer bajar la cola a alguno,* (*coll.*) to humble one's pride; *estar* or *faltar la cola por desollar,* there's the tail to be skinned yet (i.e. there's the worst to come); *hacer cola,* to line up in a queue; *tener* or *traer cola,* (*coll.*) to have serious consequences; *llevar la cola* or *ser cola,* to speak last, bring up the rear; *menea la cola el can, no por ti, sino por el pan,* proverb attributing something to 'cupboard love.'

colaboración, *n.f.* collaboration.

colaborador, -ra, *n.m.f.* collaborator.

colaborar, *v.i.* to work jointly, collaborate.

colación, *n.f.* collation; critical comparison; conferring of degrees; conference on spiritual matters; lunch, luncheon; sweetmeats given to servants on Christmas Eve; precinct or district of a parish; *sacar a colación,* to start talking about; *traer a colación,* to support with proofs or reasonings, to introduce irrelevant matter.

colacionar, *v.t.* to collate; to compare.

colactáneo, -nea, *n.m.f.* foster-brother, foster-sister.

colachón, *n.m.* guitar with a long handle.

colada, *n.f.* drenching, soaking; soaking of clothes or linen in lye; lye; linen soaked in lye; common, open ground; road for cattle; tap of a furnace; col (of mountain); (*coll.*) good sword; *todo saldrá en la colada,* 'twill all come out in the wash! truth will out; (*coll.*) you'll get paid out some day.

coladera, *n.f.* strainer, colander, wax-chandler's sieve; (*Mex.*) sewer, drain.

coladero, *n.m.* colander, drainer, strainer; filtering bag; narrow passage; (*min.*) hole for dumping ore.

coladizo, -za, *a.* penetrating, filtering through easily; (*coll.*) subtle, artful.

colado, -da, *a.* cold (air or draught); cast (iron); strained, filtered; bleached. — *p.p.* [COLAR].

colador, *n.m.* colander, (*eccles.*) collator; (*print.*) leach-tub.

coladora, *n.f.* laundress, washerwoman; washing machine.

coladura, *n.f.* straining, filtration; (*coll.*) fib, lie.

colágeno, -na, *a.* gummy, gummiferous.

colaina, *n.f.* [ACEBOLLADURA].

colaire, *n.m.* (*prov.*) draughty place.

colambre, *n.f.* [CORAMBRE].

colana, *n.f.* beverage, draught.

colanilla, *n.f.* small sliding bolt (for doors, windows).

colaña, *n.f.* railing or low partition on stairs or in granaries; (*prov.*) joist about 14 feet long, 6 inches wide, and 4 inches thick.

colapez; colapiscis, *n.f.* isinglass.

colapso, *n.m.* (*med.*) collapse, prostration.

colar, *v.t.* (*pres. indic.* **cuelo**; *pres. subj.* **cuele**) to strain, filter; to bleach linen in lye after washing; (*eccles.*) to collate. — *v.i.* to pass through a narrow passage; (*coll.*) to drink wine; to spread false news; to pass counterfeit money. — *v.r.* (*coll.*) to steal into a place *or* creep in by stealth; (*coll.*) to be displeased with a jest; to utter stupidities; to tell lies; *no colar* (*una cosa*), to be incredible; *colarse por el ojo de una aguja*, to be very clever, subtle; *colarse de rondón* or *de sopetón*, to enter suddenly and unexpectedly.

colateral, *a.* collateral.

colateralmente, *adv.* collaterally.

colativo, -va, *a.* straining, filtering; (*eccles.*) relating to collation.

colcótar, *n.m.* colcothar, jewellers' rouge.

colcha, *n.f.* coverlet, quilt, counterpane.

colchado, -da, *a.* quilted. — *p.p.* [COLCHAR].

colchadura, *n.f.* quilting.

colchar, *v.t.* to quilt; *colchar cabos*, (*naut.*) to lay or twist ropes.

colchero, -ra, *n.m.f.* quilt-maker.

cólchico, *n.m.* (*bot.*) [CÓLQUICO].

colchón, *n.m.* mattress; *colchón de pluma*, feather-bed; *colchón de muelles*, box-spring mattress; *colchón de tela metálica*, woven wire mattress; *colchón de viento*, air-cushion, air-bed.

colchoncillo, *n.m.* small mattress [COLCHÓN].

colchonería, *n.f.* mattress-shop.

colchonero, -ra, *n.m.f.* mattress-maker *or* vendor.

colchoneta, *n.f.* long thin cushion for sofa, etc.; (*naut.*) long thin mattress used for hammocks.

coleada, *n.f.* wag of the tail; (*Ven.*) act of felling a steer by twisting the tail.

coleador, *n.m.* (*Ven.*) man who throws a bull by twisting his tail.

coleadura, *n.f.* wagging of the tail; wriggling.

colear, *v.i.* to wag the tail; to wriggle or move ridiculously. — *v.t.* to fell a bull by twisting his tail (in bull-fights); *todavía colea*, it's not over yet.

colección, *n.f.* collection, aggregation, accumulation, set, suit, array, gathering.

coleccionador, -ra, *n.m.f.* collector.

coleccionar, *v.t.* to collect.

coleccionista, *n.m.f.* collector.

colecta, *n.f.* distribution of a tax; collection of voluntary offerings; (*eccles.*) collect.

colectación, *n.f.* levy; collecting of rates, taxes or dues.

colectar, *v.t.* to collect taxes, etc.

colecticio, -cia, *a.* raw, undisciplined (of troops); collectaneous (book).

colectivamente, *adv.* collectively.

colectividad, *n.f.* collectivity, mass of people

colectivismo, *n.m.* collectivism.

colectivista, *n.m.f.*, *a.* collectivist.

colectivo, -va, *a.* collective; gathered together; *nombre colectivo*, collective noun.

colector, *n.m.* collector, gatherer; tax- or rent-collector; (*eccles.*) collector of the retributions for masses; water-conduit; (*elec.*) commutator.

colecturía, *n.f.* collectorship; tax office.

colédoco, *n.m.* common bile duct.

colega, *n.m.* colleague, compeer, co-worker.

colegatario, -ria, *n.m.f.* co-legatee, co-heir.

colegiación, *n.f.* formation of collegiate group.

colegiadamente, *adv.* in the form of a college.

colegiado, -da, *a.* collegiate; united in a college. — *p.p.* [COLEGIARSE].

colegial, *a.* collegiate. — *n.m.* collegian, member of a college; (*coll.*) inexperienced, timid youth.

colegiala, *n.f.* woman-member of a college.

colegialico; colegialillo; colegialito, *n.m.* little collegian.

colegialmente, *adv.* in a collegial way.

colegiarse, *v.r.* to unite in a college those of the same profession or class.

colegiata, *n.f.* collegiate church.

colegiatura, *n.f.* fellowship in or scholarship at college.

colegio, *n.m.* college, school, seminary of education; body of students, dignitaries, electors, etc.; society of men in the same profession.

colegir, *v.t.* (*pres. indic.* **colijo**; *pret.* **él coligió**; *pres. subj.* **colija**) to collect, gather; *colegir por, de los antecedentes*, to infer, deduce from the antecedents.

colegislador, -ra, *a.* co-legislative (assembly, chamber).

coleo, *n.m.* [COLEADURA].

coleóptero, -ra, *a.* (*zool.*) coleopterous.

colera, *n.f.* ornament for a horse's tail.

cólera, *n.f.* choler, bile; (*fig.*) anger, fury, rage, passion. — *n.m.* (*med.*) cholera morbus; gummed cotton cloth; *cortar la cólera* or *la bilis*, to alleviate the attack of cholera; (*coll.*) to have a snack between meals; *cortar la cólera a uno*, to appease someone's wrath; *tomarse de la cólera*, to be carried away by passion; *montar en cólera*, to get into a passion; *cuando la cólera sale de madre, no tiene la lengua padre*, when a person is enraged he cannot measure his words; *descargar la cólera en uno*, to vent one's rage on someone.

coléricamente, *adv.* fumingly, passionately, angrily, wrathfully.

colérico, -ca, *a.* choleric, passionate, hasty, hotheaded, irascible, wrathful.

colero, *n.m.* (*Am.*) (*min.*) supervisor-assistant.

coleta, *n.f.* queue or tail of hair; (*coll.*) short addition to a discourse or writing; *cortarse la coleta,* to leave the profession of bull-fighter; to give up a career or custom; *tener* or *traer coleta,* to have serious consequences.

coletazo, *n.m.* blow with tail.

coletero, *n.m.* maker of doublets.

coletilla, *n.f.* small hair queue; postscript.

coletillo, *n.m.* small sleeveless doublet worn by Castilian women.

coleto, *n.m.* buff doublet or jacket; (*coll.*) body of a man; (*coll.*) interior of a person; *dije para mi coleto,* I said to myself; *echarse al coleto,* to read through; to eat or drink.

coletón, *n.m.* (*Ven.*) burlap; sackcloth.

colgable, *a.* suspensible.

colgadero, -ra, *a.* fit to be hung up. — *n.m.* hook to hang things upon.

colgadizo, -za, *a.* useful only when pendent, suspended. — *n.m.* pent-house, pent-roof.

colgado, -da, *a.* suspended; (*coll.*) disappointed, left. — *p.p.* [COLGAR]; *dejar a alguno colgado,* to frustrate someone's desires or expectations; *quedarse uno colgado,* to be disappointed, frustrated; *estar colgado de la ventana,* to be dangling from the window; *colgado de un cabello,* hanging by a hair.

colgadura, *n.f.* tapestry, hanging, drapery; bunting; *colgadura de cama,* bed-hangings; *colgaduras de papel pintado,* paper hangings.

colgajo, *n.m.* tatter or rag hanging from clothes; *colgajo de uvas,* bunch of grapes hung up to be preserved; (*surg.*) portion of healthy skin left to cover the wound.

colgamiento, *n.m.* hanging-up, suspension.

colgandero, -ra, *a.* hanging, pendent.

colgante, *a.* hanging, clinging, pendent. — *n.m.* (*arch.*) festoon; ear-ring, pendant; (*mech.*) hanger; *puente colgante,* suspension-bridge.

colgar, *v.t.* (*pres. indic.* **cuelgo;** *pret.* **colgué;** *pres. subj.* **cuelgue**) to hang, hoist, suspend; to adorn with tapestry or hangings; (*coll.*) to hang, kill by hanging; (*fig.*) to give an anniversary present; (*fig.*) to impute. — *v.i.* to hang, be suspended, dangle; (*fig.*) to be in a state of dependence; *colgar los hábitos,* to doff the cassock; *colgar a uno,* to compliment someone; *colgar de un clavo,* to hang from a nail; *colgar en la percha,* to hang on the clothes-rack.

colibacilo, *n.m.* inoffensive intestinal parasite.

coliblanco, -ca, *a.* white-tailed.

colibrí, *n.m.* colibri, humming-bird.

cólica, *n.f.* colic.

colicano, -na, *a.* having grey hair in the tail.

colicitante, *n.m.f.,* *a.* joint-bidder.

cólico, -ca, *a.* (*med.*) belonging to the colon. — *n.m.* colic, gripes. — *n.f.* slight colic, stomach-ache.

colicoli, *n.m.* (*Chi.*) kind of gadfly.

colicuable, *a.* easily dissolved.

colicuación, *n.f.* act of melting or dissolving; (*med.*) wasting away through excessive liquid discharge.

colicuante, *a.* dissolving.

colicuar, *v.t.* to melt, dissolve. — *v.r.* to become liquid.

colicuativo, -va, *a.* (*med.*) causing *colicuación.*

colicuecer, *v.t.* (*pres. indic.* **colicuezco;** *pres. subj.* **colicuezca**) to fuse, melt.

coliche, *n.m.* (*fam.*) informal party.

colidir, *v.t.* to collide, to dash or knock together.

colífero, -ra, *a.* cauliferous.

coliflor, *n.f.* cauliflower.

coligación, *n.f.* colligation, binding together; connexion of one thing with another; union, alliance.

coligado, -da, *a.* allied, colleagued. — *n.m.f.* leaguer, covenanter, one associated for some purpose with others. — *p.p.* [COLIGARSE].

coligadura, *n.f.; ***coligamiento,** *n.m.* colligation.

coligarse, *v.r.* (*pret.* **coligué;** *pres. subj.* **coligue**) to confederate, colligate; *coligarse con otro,* to ally oneself with another.

coligrueso, -sa, *a.* thick-tailed.

colijo; colija, *pres. indic.; pres. subj.* [COLEGIR].

colilla, *n.f.* train of a gown; stub of a cigar or cigarette.

colillero, -ra, *n.m.f.* one who gathers cigar-ends.

colín, *a.* short-tailed (horse). — *n.m.* (*Mex.*) bird, kind of quail.

colina, *n.f.* hill, hillock, hummock; [COLINO]; (*chem.*) cholestrin, cholesterine.

colinabo, *n.m.* variety of cabbage.

colindante, *a.* adjacent, contiguous.

colindar, *v.i.* to be adjacent, contiguous.

colineta, *n.f.* (*prov.*) table centrepiece of sweets, fruits, etc.

colino, *n.m.* cabbage-seed; small cabbage not transplanted.

colipava, *a.* broad-tailed (pigeon).

coliquidador, *n.m.* joint-liquidator.

colirio, *n.m.* (*med.*) collyrium, eye-wash.

colirrábano, *n.m.* kohlrabi.

colisa, *n.f.* swivel-gun; pivot for this.

coliseo, *n.m.* theatre, opera-house, play-house, coliseum, colosseum.

colisión, *n.f.* collision, crush, clash; bruise, chafe, soreness caused by friction; (*fig.*) opposition, clash of ideas.

colitigante, *n.m.f.* joint-litigant.

colitis, *n.f.* (*med.*) colitis.

coliza, *n.f.* (*naut.*) [COLISA].

colmadamente, *adv.* abundantly, plentifully.

colmado, -da, *a.* abundant, filled, heaped. — *n.m.* restaurant specializing in sea food. — *p.p.* [COLMAR].

colmar, *v.t.* to heap up; to fill to the brim; to stock, store (granary); (*fig.*) to give abundantly; *colmar de mercedes,* to confer great favours.

colmena, *n.f.* beehive; *tener la casa como una colmena,* to have one's house well stocked with provisions.

colmenar, *n.m.* apiary.

colmenero, -ra, *n.m.f.* bee-keeper; *oso colmenero,* bear who eats the honey from bee-hives.

colmenilla, *n.f.* morel, edible mushroom.

colmillada, *n.f.* injury made by a fang or tusk.

colmillar, *a.* belonging to the canine teeth.

colmillazo, *n.m.* [COLMILLO] large canine tooth; [COLMILLADA].

colmillo, *n.m.* eye-tooth, canine tooth; fang; long tusk; *mostrar los colmillos,* to show spirit and resolution; *tener colmillos retorcidos*, to be astute, sharp, not easily imposed upon; *escupir por el colmillo*, (*coll.*) to brag, boast.

colmilludo, -da, *a.* having prominent canine teeth, large fangs or tusks; (*fig.*) sagacious, quick-sighted, not easily imposed upon.

colmo, -ma, *a.* heaped up full to the top, overflowing. — *n.m.* heaping up above a full measure; (*fig.*) complement, finishing, completion, crown; summit, top; (*prov.*) thatched roof; overmeasure; full height; *a colmo, adv.* abundantly, plentifully; *es el colmo de la mezquindad*, it's the height of meanness; *llegar al colmo de sus deseos*, to attain the summit of one's desires; *no llegará a colmo*, it will not come to perfection.

colobo, *n.m.* (*Am.*) a catarrhine monkey.

colocación, *n.f.* employment, place, post, office; composition, distribution or arrangement of the parts of a whole; position, situation, location.

colocar, *v.t.* (*pret.* **coloqué,** *pres. subj.* **coloque**) to collocate, arrange, put into due place or order; to put in any place, rank, condition or office; to provide one with a place or employment. — *v.i.* to place, station oneself; to take one's place or seat; to obtain a post or situation; *colocar con, en* or *por orden*, to place in order; *colocar entre dos puertas*, to place between two doors.

colocolo, *n.m.* (*Chi.*) wild cat.

colocutor, -ra, *n.m.f.* collocutor.

colodión, *n.m.* collodion.

colodra, *n.f.* milk-pail, kit; wooden can with which wine is measured; tumbler; (*prov.*) wooden case for mower's whetstone; *ser una colodra*, (*coll.*) to be a toper or tippler.

colodrazgo, *n.m.* tax or duty on wine sold in small quantities.

colodrillo, *n.m.* occiput, back part of the head.

colodro, *n.m.* wooden shoe; (*prov.*) wine measure.

colofón, *n.m.* (*print.*) colophon.

colofonia, *n.f.* colophony, a kind of resin.

colofónico, -ca, *a.* colophonic.

colofonita, *n.f.* light-green or red garnet.

colofonona, *n.f.* (*chem.*) colophonate.

colografía, *n.f.* photographic impression.

cológrafo, *n.m.* collograph.

coloidal, *a.* colloidal.

coloide, *n.m.*, *a.* colloid.

coloídico, -ca; coloideo, -dea, *a.* colloid.

colombiano, -na, *n.m.f.*, *a.* Colombian.

colombino, -na, *a.* of or belonging to Columbus.

colombofilia, *n.f.* fancy for pigeon-breeding.

colombófilo, -la, *n.m.f.*, *a.* pigeon-fancier.

colombroño, *n.m.* namesake.

colon, *n.m.* colon; part of a period.

colón, *n.m.* (*CR., ES.*) silver coin.

colonato, *n.m.* system of colonization.

colonche, *n.m.* (*Mex.*) strong drink from cactus sap and sugar.

colonés, -sa, *n.m.f.*, *a.* of or from Cologne.

Colonia, *n.f.* Cologne.

colonia, *n.f.* colony; plantation; colonized country; silk ribbon two fingers wide; *media colonia*, narrow silk ribbon; *agua de colonia*, eau-de-Cologne.

colonial, *a.* colonial; (*com.*) oversea.

colónico, -ca, *a.* biliary.

colonizable, *a.* colonizable.

colonización, *n.f.* colonization.

colonizador, -ra, *a.* colonizing. — *n.m.f.* colonizer.

colonizar, *v.t.* (*pret.* **colonicé;** *pres. subj.* **colonice**) to colonize.

colono, *n.m.* colonist, planter; labourer, small-holder who lives on his plot of ground.

coloño, *n.m.* (*prov.*) load of wood which a person carries on his head or back.

coloquíntida, *n.f.* coloquintida, colocynth, bitter apple.

coloquintina, *n.f.* (*chem.*) colocynthin.

coloquio, *n.m.* colloquy, conversation, talk.

color, *n.m.* colour, hue; dye, paint; rouge; colouring; complexion, flush, blush; (*fig.*) colour, pretext, pretence, false show; (*fig.*) general character, tone, quality; *color cargado* or *lleno*, deep colour; *color de cera*, yellow colour; *color muerto* or *quebrado*, pale or faded colour; *color vivo*, bright colour; *de color*, coloured; *colores nacionales*, flag, colours; *dar color* or *colores*, to paint; to picture; *meter en color*, (*paint.*) to combine the colours; *mudar de color(es)*, (*fig.*) to change colour; *no distinguir uno de colores*, to be a poor judge of persons or things; *pintar con negros colores*, to consider things dismally; *ponerse uno de mil colores*, to change colour through repressed anger or shyness; *robar el color*, to take away colour, cause to lose colour; *sacarle a uno los colores (a la cara* or *al rostro)*, to make someone blush; *salirle a uno los colores (a la cara* or *al rostro)*, to flush up, blush; *so color*, under pretext, on pretence; *tomar color*, to begin to ripen; *tomar el color*, to take the dye well; *un color se le iba, y otro se le venía*, his colour came and went (i.e. in his perturbation); *ver de color de rosa*, to see in the best light.

coloración, *n.f.* colouring, coloration; blush; pretence, pretext.

coloradamente, *adv.* speciously, under pretext.

colorado, -da, *a.* coloured; ruddy, florid; (*fig.*) indelicate (of tales, etc.); (*fig.*) specious. — *p.p.* [COLORAR]; *poner a uno colorado*, to put someone to shame; *ponerse colorado*, to blush.

colorador, -ra, *a.* colouring, tinting. — *n.m.f.* colourist.

colorante, *a.* colorific. — *n.m.* dye.

colorar, *v.t.* to dye, colour, stain, paint, tint, tinge, lay colour on thickly; to make plausible. — *v.i.* to blush, colour up.

colorativo, -va, *a.* colorific, tingeing.

colorear, *v.t.* to colour, palliate, excuse, make plausible. — *v.i.* to redden, grow red.

colorete, *n.m.* rouge.

colorido, -da, *n.m.* (*art*) colouring, colour; (*fig.*) pretext, pretence. — *p.p.* [COLORIR].

coloridor, -ra, *n.m.f.* (*art*) colourist.

colorímetro, *n.m.* colorimeter.

colorín, *n.m.* (*orn.*) linnet; *pl.* glaring, showy colours.

colorir, *v.t.* to colour, mark with some hue or dye; (*fig.*) to make plausible. — *v.i.* to become coloured.

colorista, *n.m.f.* (*art*) colourist.

colosal, *a.* colossal, gigantic, huge; immense; extraordinary.

coloso, *n.m.* Colossus, giant; (*fig.*) exceptionally gifted person or remarkable thing.

colostro, *n.m.* colostrum.
colotipia, *n.f.* (*print.*) collotype.}
colpa, *n.f.* (*min.*) colcothar used as a flux.
cólquico, *n.m.* colchicum, meadow saffron.
colúbridos; colubrinos, *n.m.pl.* coluber.
coludir, *v.i.* (*law*) to conspire, act in collusion.
columbial, *a.* (*orn.*) columbine.
columbino, -na, *a.* columbine; dove-like, innocent, candid.
columbio, *n.m.* (*min.*) columbium, niobium.
columbrador, -ra, *n.m.f., a.* one who sees afar off, discerns, conjectures.
columbrar, *v.t.* to spy, perceive, discern at a distance, see afar off; (*fig.*) to form a conjecture from indications.
columbrete, *n.m.* (*naut.*) low islet suitable for anchoring.
columelar, *a.* canine (tooth).
columna, *n.f.* column; pillar, support; (*fig.*) supporter, protector, pile; body of troops; (*naut.*) line of warships; (*print.*) column; (*arith.*) row; (*phys.*) column of air or water; *columna miliaria,* milestone; *columna entorchada* or *salomónica,* twisted column; *columna vertebral,* spine.
columnación, *n.f.* (*arch.*) columnication.
columnario, -ria, *a.* relating to money struck in Spanish America.
columnata, *n.f.* colonnade.
columnilla, *n.f.* (*bot.*) columella.
columnita, *n.f.* short, slender column.
columpiar, *v.t.* to swing to and fro, rock. — *v.r.* to swing, rock oneself; (*coll.*) to waddle, walk unevenly.
columpio, *n.m.* swing.
coluna, *n.f.* [COLUMNA].
colurión, *n.m.* lesser butcher-bird, flusher.
colusión, *n.f.* collusion, deceitful agreement.
colusor, *n.m.* partner in collusion.
colusoriamente, *adv.* collusively, fraudulently.
colusorio, -ria, *a.* collusive.
colutorio, *n.m.* gargle.
coluvie, *n.f.* gang of ruffians; (*fig.*) sink of iniquity.
colza, *n.f.* (*bot.*) colza, rape.
colla, *n.f.* gorget, a piece of ancient armour; (*naut.*) last oakum placed in a seam; channel of an auger; (*Philip.*) storm from S.W. preceding the monsoons; (*Bol.*) Indian from the Andean plains; (*Arg.*) Indian mestizo.
collación, *n.f.* light repast.
collada, *n.f.* (*naut.*) long duration of wind.
colladía, *n.f.* series of hillocks.
collado, *n.m.* hill, fell, small eminence.
collar, *n.m.* necklace; chain; collar; (*mech.*) collet.
collarada, *n.f.* shirt-collar; wild pigeon.
collarcito, *n.m.* small necklace, string of beads.
collarejo, *n.m.* small collar or necklace [COLLAR].
collarín, *n.m.* small collar, necklet [COLLAR]; priest's collar or stock; coat-collar; ring of bomb-fuse.
collarino, *n.m.* half-circle at the top of a column.
collazo, *n.m.* ploughman, labourer, farmer.
colleja, *n.f.* lamb's lettuce, corn-salad; *pl.* thin nerves in sheep's neck.
collera, *n.f.* collar, horse-collar, breast-harness for draught cattle; gang of convicts

chained together; *collera de yeguas,* number of breeding mares used to thresh corn.
collerón, *n.m.* large harness collar [COLLERA]; light fancy collar for carriage horse.
colleta, *n.f.* (*prov.*) small cabbage.
collón, -na, *a.* cowardly. — *n.m.f.* (*coll.*) coward, poltroon.
collonada; collonería, *n.f.* cowardliness, cowardice.
coma, *n.f.* comma; (*mus.*) fifth part of a tone. — *n.m.* (*med.*) coma, stupor; tilting seat in choir-stalls; *punto y coma,* semicolon; *sin faltar una coma; sin faltar punto ni coma,* without omitting the least portion (in a narrative).
comadrazgo, *n.m.* spiritual relationship between a child's mother and godmother.
comadre, *n.f.* midwife; name given reciprocally by the mother and godmother of a child; (*coll.*) procuress; (*coll.*) intimate friend; gossip; *mal me quieren mis comadres porque digo las verdades,* expression denoting the unpopularity of tellers of truths; *riñen las comadres, y se dicen las verdades,* when gossips fall out they tell bitter truths.
comadrear, *v.i.* to gossip, tattle.
comadreja, *n.f.* weasel.
comadrería, *n.f.* gossip, tittle-tattle.
comadrero, -ra, *a.* lazy and gossiping. — *n.m.f.* lazy gossiper.
comadrón, *n.m.* man-midwife, accoucheur.
comadrona, *n.f.* midwife.
comal, *n.m.* (*Mex.*) flat earthenware pan for cooking maize cake.
comalia; comalición, *n.f.* epizootic disease among sheep.
comandado, -da, *a.* (*mil.*) officered. — *p.p.* [COMANDAR].
comandamiento, *n.m.* [MANDAMIENTO].
comandancia, *n.f.* command; office of a commander; province or district of a commander; headquarters; *comandancia general de Marina,* High Court of Admiralty; *comandancia militar,* military command.
comandanta, *n.f.* commandant's wife; (*naut.*) flagship.
comandante, *n.m.* commander, chief, commandant, leader; *comandante general,* commander-in-chief; *comandante mayor,* paymaster, generally a lieutenant-colonel.
comandar, *v.t.* to command, govern.
comandita, *n.f.* (*com.*) silent partnership; *compañía* or *sociedad en comandita,* limited or joint-stock company.
comanditar, *v.i.* (*com.*) to promote, act as promoter.
comanditariamente, *adv.* as a limited or joint-stock company.
comanditario, *n.m.* (*law*) joint-mandatary.
comanditario, -ria, *a.* (*com.*) relating to the *comandita.* — *n.m.f.* (*com.*) sleeping-partner; shareholder.
comando, *n.m.* (*mil.*) command.
comarca, *n.f.* territory; district; border, boundary, limit.
comarcano, -na, *a.* neighbouring, near, bordering upon.
comarcar, *v.t.* (*pret.* **comarqué;** *pres. subj.* **comarque**) to plant trees in lines. — *v.i.* to border upon, be on the borders.
comatoso, -sa, *a.* comatose.
comba, *n.f.* curve, bend, convexity, warp,

bulge; play of skipping-rope; skipping or jumping rope; *hacer combas*, waddle or swing the body.

combadura, *n.f.* curvature, convexity, warping, bending, bulging, belly.

combar, *v.t.* to bend, curve. — *v.r.* to warp, sag, jut, become crooked.

combate, *n.m.* combat, battle, conflict, fight, fray, engagement; (*fig.*) agitation of the mind.

combatible, *a.* combatable, conquerable.

combatidor, *n.m.* combatant, champion.

combatiente, *a.* combating, fighting. — *n.m.* combatant, fighter, soldier.

combatir, *v.i.* to combat, fight. — *v.t.* to attack; to beat, dash, strike (as waves, wind); (*fig.*) to contradict, oppose; (*fig.*) to agitate, ruffle the mind. — *v.r.* to fight one another; *combatir con, contra el enemigo*, to fight (against) the enemy; *combatir a la retreta*, (*naut.*) to keep up a running fight.

combatividad, *n.f.* combativeness.

combeneficiado, *n.m.* joint-curate or prebendary.

combés, *n.m.* (*naut.*) waist of a ship; open space.

combinable, *a.* combinable.

combinación, *n.f.* combination; concurrence; (*chem.*) compound; group of words beginning with the same syllable (in dictionary).

combinado, -da, *a.* combined, united; (*mil.*) allied. — *p.p.* [COMBINAR].

combinador, -ra, *a.* combining. — *n.m.f.* one that combines. — *n.m.* part of telegraph-receiving machine which translates the signal emitted; regulating apparatus of electric cars and trains which puts the circuits of the motor in combination.

combinar, *v.t.* to combine, join, unite, connect; (*chem.*) to compound. — *v.r.* (*chem.*) coalesce, unite; *combinar una cosa con otra*, to combine one thing with another.

combinatorio, -ria, *a.* combinative, combining, uniting, compounding.

combleza, *n.f.* mistress kept by a married man.

comblezo, *n.m.* one who lives in concubinage with a married woman.

combo, -ba, *a.* bent, warped, crooked. — *n.m.* stand or frame for casks; (*Chi.*) fisticuff; (*Arg.*) stone-breaking hammer.

comboso, -sa, *a.* curved, warped.

comburente, *a.* (*phys.*) inducing combustion.

combustibilidad, *n.f.* (*phys.*) combustibility.

combustible, *a.* combustible. — *n.m.* fuel.

combustión, *n.f.* combustion, burning; *combustión espontánea*, spontaneous combustion.

combusto, -ta, *a.* burnt, consumed.

comedero, -ra, *a.* eatable, edible. — *n.m.* dining-room, feeding-place, eating-trough; *limpiarle a uno el comedero*, to deprive someone of his livelihood.

comedia, *n.f.* comedy, play, farce; drama; theatre, play-house; laughable incident; *es una comedia*, it's a regular farce; *comedia de capa y espada*, cloak and sword play; *comedia de costumbres*, society play; *comedia de enredo*, play with complicated plot; *hacer la comedia*, to pretend; *comedia togada*, ancient Roman play (produced in Spanish).

comedianta, *n.f.* actress, comedienne; (*coll.*) hypocrite.

comediante, *n.m.* player, actor, comedian; (*coll.*) hypocrite.

comediar, *v.t.* to divide into equal shares; to average.

comedidamente, *adv.* gently, courteously, civilly; moderately.

comedido, -da, *a.* civil, gentle, polite, courteous, obsequious, obliging; moderate, prudent, discreet. — *p.p.* [COMEDIRSE].

comedimiento, *n.m.* civility, politeness, kindness, obsequiousness, urbanity; discretion, moderation.

comedio, *n.m.* middle of a kingdom or place; intermediate time between epochs.

comediógrafo, *n.m.* playwright.

comedión, *n.m.* (*contempt.*) long, tedious comedy [COMEDIA].

comedirse, *v.r.* to govern oneself; be moderate, obliging; *comedirse en la conducta*, to regulate one's conduct. (conj. like HERIR).

comedón, *n.m.* blackhead, pimple.

comedor, -ra, *a.* eating much. — *n.m.* dining-room, restaurant.

comején, *n.m.* wood-fretter moth; (*Am., Philip.*) white ant.

comejenera, *n.f.* breeding-place for *comején*; (*Ven.*) thieves-kitchen.

comelón, -na, *a.* [COMILÓN].

comendador, *n.m.* commander (of an order of knighthood); prefect (of religious houses).

comendadora, *n.f.* superior of certain convents.

comendatario, *n.m.* (*eccles.*) commendator.

comendaticio, -cia, *a.* (*eccles.*) commendatory (letter).

comendatorio, -ria, *a.* recommendatory (letters of introduction and recommendations).

comendero, *n.m.* commendator, beneficiary of the crown.

comensal, *a.* member of a household, table-companion.

comensalía, *n.f.* commensality, fellowship of house and table.

comentador, -ra, *n.m.f.* expositor, commentator, annotator, glosser, expounder; malicious gossip or critic.

comentar, *v.t.* to comment, explain, expound, gloss; (*fam.*) to gossip or criticize maliciously.

comentario, *n.m.* commentary. — *pl.* brief historical narrative; (*fam.*) malicious criticism.

comentarista, *n.m.f.* commentator, author of a commentary.

comento, *n.m.* comment, exposition, explanation.

comenzante, *a.* beginning. — *n.m.f.* beginner.

comenzar, *v.i., v.t.* (*pres. indic.* **comienzo**; *pret.* **comencé**; *pres. subj.* **comience**) to commence, begin; *comenzar a hablar*, to begin to speak; *comenzar por reñir*, to start by quarrelling.

comer, *v.i.* (*pres. indic.* **como**; *pret.* **comí**; *pres. subj.* **coma**) to eat, feed; to dine. — *v.t.* to eat; (*fig.*) to consume, corrode; to itch; (*fam.*) to enjoy an income; (*fig.*) to spend, squander, waste; to take (a piece in a game of draughts); to cause a colour to fade (by light). — *v.r.* to skip, omit, leave out; to eat up. — *n.m.* food, sustenance; *comer a destajo*, to eat much quickly and anxiously; *comer a dos manos*, to eat voraciously, to eat like a horse; *comer a escote*,

to pay one's share of a feast; *comer por cuatro*, to eat enough for four; *comerse de invidia*, to be consumed by envy; *comer de viernes* or *de vigilia*, to fast, abstain from meat; *comerse las palabras*, to enunciate indistinctly; *comerse unos a otros*, to be at daggers drawn; *comerse el capital*, to squander, dissipate one's fortune; *comerse una dama*, *un peon*, to take a queen, a pawn (in chess); *comer de gorra* or *de mogollón*, to sponge on others; *comerse a uno con los ojos*, to look daggers or stare fixedly or eagerly at a person; *comerse la risa*, to restrain one's laughter; *comer pan con corteza*, to be independent; *comer como un sabañón*, to eat to excess; *comer y callar*, best be silent about favours; *comer con gana*, to eat with an appetite; *el comer y el rascar, todo es empezar*, you won't dislike it so much once you start; *ganar de comer*, to earn one's living; *comerse vivo*, to be desperate, very impatient; *comerle a uno vivo*, to itch; (*fig.*) to hate, thirst for revenge; *lo que no has de comer, déjalo cocer*, let alone what doesn't concern you; *comer el pan a traición*, to receive a salary without working; *come que te come*, to keep on eating; *come que da gusto*, it's a pleasure to see how he enjoys his food; *come poco y cena más poco*, eat little at dinner and less at supper; *con su pan se lo coma*, let him get on with it; *no comer el pan de balde*, not to eat the bread of idleness; *quien come y condensa, dos veces pone la mesa*, a penny saved is a penny gained; *ser de buen comer*, to have a good appetite; *sin comerlo ni beberlo*, innocently; *tener que comer*, to have enough to get along with.
comerciable, *a.* merchantable, marketable; (*fig.*) sociable, affable, easy to get on with.
comercial, *a.* commercial, trading, mercantile.
comercialmente, *adv.* commercially.
comerciante, *a.* trading. — *n.m.f.* trader, merchant, trafficker.
comerciar, *v.i.* to trade, traffic; to have intercourse or communication; *comerciar con su crédito*, to trade on his credit; *comerciar con todo*, to deal in everything; *comerciar en granos*, to deal in grain; *comerciar por mayor*, to trade wholesale; *comerciar por menor*, to trade retail.
comercio, *n.m.* trade, commerce, traffic; mart, shop, business, commercial establishment; intercourse, communication; unlawful sexual connexion; business quarter of a town; body or company of merchants; a card game; *comercio de cabotage*, coasting trade; *comercio exterior*, foreign trade; *comercio interior*, home trade.
comestible, *a.* eatable, edible, comestible. — *n.pl.* provisions, food.
cometa, *n.m.* comet. — *n.f.* kite (a plaything); game of cards.
cometario, -ria, *a.* (*astron.*) cometic, cometary.
cometedor, -ra, *a.* offending, perpetrating. — *n.m.f.* offender, criminal, perpetrator.
cometer, *v.t.* to commit, charge, entrust; to undertake; to attempt; to commit a criminal act or an error; (*com.*) to order; (*gram.*) to use tropes and rhetorical figures.
cometido, *n.m.* commission, charge, trust; duty, task.

cometografía, *n.f.* cometography.
cometología, *n.f.* (*astron.*) cometology.
comezón, *n.f.* itch, itching; (*fig.*) desire, longing.
comible, *a.* eatable.
comicalla, *a.* reserved, taciturn. — *n.m.f.* sulky, taciturn person.
cómicamente, *adv.* comically.
comicidad, *n.f.* comicality.
comicios, *n.m.pl.* assembly; electoral meeting.
cómico, -ca, *a.* comic, ludicrous, funny, comical; relating to the stage, dramatic. — *n.m.f.* actor, actress, player, comedian; (*obs.*) writer of comedies; *cómico de la legua*, strolling player.
comida, *n.f.* food, nourishment, victuals; meal; dinner; eating; *cambiar la comida*, to vomit; *comida hecha, compañía deshecha*, expression denoting the getting rid of one's friends as soon as one has received their favours; *reposar la comida*, to rest after meals.
comidilla, *n.f.* (*coll.*) fancy, fad, favourite amusement; gossip, topic of conversation.
comido, -da, *a.* fed, sated, having eaten; satiated, full to satiety. — *p.p.* [COMER]; *comido por servido*, small return for work; *comido y bebido*, maintained, supported.
comido; comida, *pres. indic.; pres. subj.* [COMEDIR].
comienzo, *n.m.* origin, beginning, start, initiation, commencement, inauguration.
comienzo; comience, *pres. indic.; pres. subj.* [COMENZAR].
comihuelga, *a.* working little but eating heartily; lazy, good-for-nothing.
comilitón, *n.m.* fellow-soldier.
comilitona; comilona, *n.f.* (*coll.*) splendid and plentiful repast.
comilón, -na, *a.* gluttonous, greedy. — *n.m.f.* great eater, glutton.
comilla, *n.f.* small comma [COMA]. — *pl.* quotation marks.
cominear, *v.i.* (*coll.*) to meddle in women's affairs.
cominero, -ra, *a.* meddlesome, interfering. — *n.m.f.* busybody, meddler.
cominillo, *n.m.* darnel grass.
comino, *n.m.* cumin plant and seed; *no se me da* or *no montar* or *no valer un comino*, (*coll.*) I don't care a rush for it; it is not worth a rush.
comiquear, *v.i.* (*fam.*) to be a comedian (of amateur theatricals).
comiquería, *n.f.* group of poor comedians.
comisar, *v.t.* to confiscate, sequestrate, attach.
comisara, *n.f.* wife of *comisario*.
comisaria, *n.f.; comisariato, n.m.* commissaryship, commissariat.
comisario, *n.m.* commissary, delegate, deputy, manager; *comisario de cuartel* or *de barrio*, justice of the peace (of a ward); *comisario de entradas*, person who notes the patients who enter and leave (in hospitals); *comisario de guerra*, head of the commissariat; *comisario general*, commissary-general of the army; *comisario ordenador*, assistant quarter-master.
comiscar, *v.t.* to peck, eat in small quantities.
comisión, *n.f.* commission, trust; precept; mandate, charge; ministration, ministry; committee; perpetration; *comisión mercantil*,

(*com.*) order; commission, allowance, percentage.

comisionado, -da, *a.* commissional; commissioned, deputed, empowered. — *n.m.f.* commissioner; (*com.*) agent, proxy; *comisionado de apremios,* bailiff, sheriff's officer. — *p.p.* [COMISIONAR].

comisionar, *v.t.* to commission, depute, empower, appoint.

comisionista, *n.m.f.* (*com.*) commission-merchant, commission-agent.

comiso, *n.m.* (*law*) confiscation of prohibited goods; confiscated goods; (*com.*) seizure, attachment; (*law*) foreclosure of an emphyteusis.

comisorio, -ria, *a.* (*law*) binding, obligatory for a fixed period on pain of forfeiture (clauses).

comisquear, *v.t.* [COMISCAR].

comistión; conmistión, *n.f.* commixture, mixture.

comistrajo, *n.m.* (*coll.*) hodge-podge, mess of victuals, food.

comisura, *n.f.* (*anat.*) commissure, suture.

comisural, *a.* (*anat.*) commissural.

comital, *a.* relating to the dignity of a count or count-ship.

comité, *n.m.* committee.

comitente, *a.* commissioning. — *n.m.f.* client.

comitiva, *n.f.* suite, retinue, following, followers.

cómitre, *n.m.* boatswain on board a galley; sea-captain.

comiza, *n.f.* kind of surmullet or barbel.

como, *adv., conj.* how, in what manner, to what degree; why; as; if; because; that; in such a manner; like, in the same manner as; so that; such as; inasmuch as; about, approximately; *¡cómo!* what! why! can it be?; *¿cómo?* what is it? what did you say?; *¿cómo así?* how? how so?; *¿cómo se encuentra Vd.?* how do you feel?; *¿cómo no?* why not?; *¿cómo fué eso?* how was that? how did that happen? *como hay viñas,* as sure as fate; *como una leche,* as tender as chicken; *como quiera que,* notwithstanding, although, yet; *como quiera que sea,* however, at any rate; *como se viene, se va,* lightly come, lightly go; *como sigue,* as follows; *¿cómo sucede que . . . ?* how does it happen that . . . ?; *como aciertes lo que traigo,* if you guess what I've brought; *¿cómo a estas horas?* fancy coming now!; *está como a cinco kilómetros,* it's about five kilometres away; *el cómo y el cuándo,* the why and the wherefore. (*interr.* or *exclam.,* **cómo.**)

cómoda, *n.f.* chest of drawers; bureau.

comodable, *a.* (*law*) which can be lent or borrowed.

cómodamente, *adv.* conveniently; commodiously, comfortably.

comodante, *n.m.f.* (*law*) lender of a *comodato.*

comodatario, *n.m.* (*law*) borrower; 'in commodatum.'

comodato, *n.m.* (*law*) loan on condition that actual things lent are returned.

comodidad, *n.f.* comfort, convenience, accommodation; ease, leisure, freedom from want; opportunity; profit, advantage, interest. — *pl.* creature comforts.

comodín, *n.m.* joker, playing card of different values; (*coll.*) something of general utility; habitual and unjustified excuse, pretext.

comodista, *n.m.f.* selfish, self-interested person.

cómodo, -da, *a.* convenient, comfortable, commodious. — *n.m.* utility, profit, convenience.

comodón, -na, *a.* (*fam.*) comfort-loving.

comodoro, *n.m.* commodore.

comoforo, -ra, *a.* comose, hairy, filamentose.

comorar, *v.i.* to dwell, live together.

comótico, -ca, *a.* beautifying, embellishing.

compacidad, *n.f.* [COMPACTIBILIDAD].

compactar, *v.t.* (*Col., Chi.*) to consolidate.

compactibilidad, *n.f.* compactness.

compacto, -ta, *a.* compact, close, dense.

compadecer, *v.t.* (*pres. indic.* **compadezco;** *pres. subj.* **compadezca**) to pity; to be compassionate with. — *v.r.* to pity, condole, sympathize with; to concur, concord, conform, tally, accord; *compadecerse* (*una cosa*) *con otra,* to match, tally (one thing) with another; *compadecerse del desgraciado,* to sympathize with the unfortunate man.

compadraje, *n.m.* clique, ring; collusion.

compadrar, *v.i.* to become a godfather or godmother; to become a friend or sponsor.

compadrazgo, *n.m.* spiritual relationship between a child's parents and the godfather [COMPADRAJE].

compadre, *n.m.* name given reciprocally by the father and godfather of a child; godfather; protector, benefactor; friend, gossip.

compadrería, *n.f.* friendly intercourse between friends, godfathers or companions.

compaginación, *n.f.* compagination, arrangement, union.

compaginador, *n.m.* joiner, uniter, coupler; collator.

compaginar, *v.t.* (*fig.*) to join, compact, unite, couple, compaginate, arrange in order; (*print.*) to gather; to collate. — *v.r.* to assemble, congregate.

companage; compango, *n.m.* snack, anything eaten with bread, such as cheese, onion, etc.

compañerismo, *n.m.* good fellowship, comradeship.

compañero, -ra, *n.m.f.* companion, comrade, chum, friend, fellow, consort, equal, compeer; coadjutor, colleague, fellow-member, associate partner; (*fig.*) counterpart, match; *compañero de bromas,* boon-companion; *compañero de cuarto,* room-mate; *compañero de, en intrigas,* fellow-conspirator, accomplice.

compañía, *n.f.* companionship; (*com., mil., theat.*) company, society, co-partnership; assembly, meeting; fellowship, partnership; (*theat.*) troop; *compañía de la legua,* strolling company of players; *Compañía de Jesús,* Society of Jesus; *compañía del ahorcado, ir con él y dejarle colgado,* (*coll.*) person who leaves one in the lurch; *compañía de dos, compañía de Dios,* two is company, three is none; *compañía de seguros,* (*com.*) insurance company; *hacer compañía a alguno,* to accompany someone, be at his side; *ir en compañía,* to go together (with others); *trabajar en compañía,* to work together or in partnership.

compañón, *n.m.* testicle.

compar, *a.* (*mus.*) correlative; companion, comrade.

comparabilidad, *n.f.* comparability.
comparable, *a.* comparable.
comparablemente, *adv.* comparatively.
comparación, *n.f.* comparison, collation, simile; *toda comparación es odiosa,* all comparisons are odious; *correr la comparación,* to bear comparison.
comparado, -da, *a.* compared; comparative (grammar). — *p.p.* [COMPARAR].
comparador, *n.m.* (*phys.*) comparator.
comparanza, *n.f.* comparison.
comparar, *v.t.* to compare, estimate, collate; to confront; *comparar una cosa con otra,* to compare one thing with another.
comparativamente, *adv.* comparatively.
comparativo, -va, *a.* comparative.
comparecencia, *n.f.* (*law*) entering an appearance in court.
comparecer, *v.i.* (*pres. indic.* **comparezco**; *pres. subj.* **comparezca**) (*law*) to enter an appearance in court.
compareciente, *n.m.f.* (*law*) person appearing in court on a summons.
comparendo, *n.m.* (*law*) summons, citation.
comparición, *n.f.* (*law*) appearance; (*law*) summons.
compariente, *a.* akin, kin, kindred.
comparsa, *n.f.* (*theat.*) chorus; retinue, masquerade in carnival. — *n.m.f.* (*theat.*) supernumerary; figurant.
comparte, *n.m.* (*law*) joint-party in a civil, or accomplice in a criminal case.
compartimiento, *n.m.* division into parts; compartment, department, enclosure; (*aer.*) curtain of an airship; *compartimiento estanco,* (*naut.*) water-tight compartment.
compartir, *v.t.* to divide into equal parts; to share; *compartir las penas con otro,* to share another's troubles; *compartir la fruta en dos canastas,* to divide (the fruit) into two baskets; *compartir entre varios,* to divide amongst many.
compás, *n.m.* compass; size; pair of compasses; callipers; range of the voice in music; (*mus.*) measure, time, space between two bars upon the musical stave; (*mus.*) motion of a conductor's baton; (*naut.*) mariner's compass; territory assigned to a monastery; rule of life; pattern, standard; springs of coach-roof; *a compás,* in right (musical) time; *llevar el compás,* to beat time; to conduct a choir or orchestra; *ir con el compás en la mano,* to proceed with due order and circumspection; *compás de mar,* mariner's compass; *salir de compás,* to act in a way forgetful of one's duty; *compás de cinco por ocho,* (*mus.*) five-eight time; *compás de dos por cuatro,* (*mus.*) two-four time; *compás de espera,* (*mus.*) pause for the duration of a bar; (*fig.*) short break or interruption.
compasadamente, *adv.* by rule and measure.
compasado, -da, *a.* measured, judicious, sensible. — *p.p.* [COMPASAR].
compasamiento, *n.m.* measuring with compasses.
compasar, *v.t.* to measure with a rule and compass; (*fig.*) to regulate; (*mus.*) to divide a musical composition into bars; *compasar una carta de marear,* (*naut.*) to prick the chart.
compasible, *a.* compassionate, lamentable, deserving pity.

compasillo, *n.m.* quick musical time, quadruple measure.
compasión, *n.f.* compassion, pity, sympathy, mercifulness, commiseration.
compasivamente, *adv.* compassionately.
compasivo, -va, *a.* compassionate, merciful, humane, tender-hearted.
compaternidad, *n.f.* spiritual relationship between a child's parents and its godfather.
compatibilidad, *n.f.* compatibility, consistency.
compatible, *a.* compatible, suitable, fit; *compatible con la justicia,* consistent with justice.
compatricio, -cia; compatriota, *n.m.f.* countryman, countrywoman, compatriot, fellow-citizen.
compatrón, -na, *n.m.f.* fellow-patron or patroness.
compatronato, *n.m.* rights and duties of joint-patronage.
compatrono, -na, *n.m.f.* fellow-patron or patroness.
compelación, *n.f.* (*law*) interrogatory; (*rhet.*) apostrophe.
compelativo, -va, *a.* interrogative, interrogatory.
compeler, *v.t.* (*p.p.* **compulso**) to compel, constrain, oblige, force, extort; *compeler (a otro) al pago,* to compel payment (from another).
compendiador, -ra, *a.* compending. — *n.m.f.* epitomist, abridger.
compendiar, *v.t.* to epitomize, shorten, reduce, cut short, abridge, extract, contract.
compendiariamente, *adv.* compendiously, summarily.
compendio, *n.m.* compendium, abridgment, summary, epitome, abstract; *en compendio,* briefly.
compendiosamente, *adv.* compendiously, briefly, concisely.
compendioso, -sa, *a.* brief, abridged, compendious, laconic, compact.
compendista, *n.m.* author of a compendium.
compendizar, *v.t.* [COMPENDIAR].
compenetración, *n.f.* intermixture, mingling together.
compenetrarse, *v.recipr.* to intermix, pervade.
compensable, *a.* that can be compensated.
compensación, *n.f.* compensation; equivalent, recompense.
compensador, -ra, *a.* compensating. — *n.m.* compensator, balance or pendulum.
compensar, *v.t., v.r.* to compensate, counterbalance, countervail; to make amends, make up for, indemnify; *compensar una cosa con otra,* to counterbalance one thing with another; *compensarse a sí mismo,* to compensate oneself for loss incurred.
compensativo, -va; compensatorio, -ria, *a.* compensatory.
competencia, *n.f.* competition, rivalry; duty, obligation; competence, cognizance, fitness, aptitude; *a competencia,* competitively, contentiously, contestingly.
competente, *a.* competent, sufficient, able, adequate, compatible, capable, consistent.
competentemente, *adv.* competently.
competer, *v.i.* to belong, appertain, concern, be one's due.
competición, *n.f.* competition, rivalry.

competidor, -ra, *a.* competing, contesting. — *n.m.f.* competitor, rival, opponent, contender.
competir, *v.i.* (*pres. indic.* compito; *pres. subj.* compita) to vie, contest, contend; to rival, cope, strive, compete, race; to be on a level or par; *competir con alguno,* to compete with someone.
compilación, *n.f.* compilation.
compilador, -ra, *a.* compiling. — *n.m.f.* compiler, collector.
compilar, *v.t.* to compile.
compinche, *n.m.f.* (*coll.*) bosom friend, comrade, confidant, chum, crony.
compito; compita, *pres. indic.; pres. subj.* [COMPETIR].
complacedero, -ra, *a.* [COMPLACIENTE].
complacedor, -ra, *n.m.f., a.* complaisant, obliging (person).
complacencia, *n.f.* pleasure, gratification; complacency, satisfaction; complaisance, compliance; condescension.
complacer, *v.t.* (*pres. indic.* complazco; *pres. subj.* complazca) to please, humour, accommodate, content; to make oneself agreeable. — *v.r.* with con, de, en, to be pleased with, take delight in; *complacer a un amigo,* to please a friend.
complacido, -da, *a.* pleasant, willing; pleased. — *p.p.* [COMPLACER].
complaciente, *a.* complaisant, pleasing, accommodating.
complacientemente, *adv.* complaisantly, complacently.
complacimiento, *n.m.* [COMPLACENCIA].
complazco; complazca, *pres. indic., pres. subj.* [COMPLACER].
complectivo, -va; complectorio, -ria, *a.* (*bot.*) complected, joined together.
complejidad, *n.f.* complexity.
complejo, -ja, *a.* complex, complicated. — *n.m.* complex.
complementar, *v.t.* to complement, complete.
complementario, -ria, *a.* complementary, completing, perfecting.
complemento, *n.m.* complement; (*gram.*) predicate; perfection; accomplishment; completion.
completamente, *adv.* completely, entirely, perfectly, finally.
completar, *v.t.* to complete, perfect, finish, crown, accomplish, consummate.
completas, *n.f.pl.* (*eccles.*) compline.
completivamente, *adv.* completely.
completivo, -va, *a.* completive, absolute.
completo, -ta, *a.* complete, perfect, finished, absolute, full, concluded.
complexidad, *n.f.* complexity.
complexión, *n.f.* (*physiol.*) constitution, habit, nature, temperament.
complexionado, -da, *a.* constituted; *bien* (or *mal*) *complexionado,* of a good (or bad) constitution. — *p.p.* [COMPLEXIONAR].
complexional, *a.* constitutional, temperamental.
complexionar, *v.t.* to reform the constitution, disposition, nature.
complexo, -xa, *a.* complex, complicated, arduous, difficult. — *n.m.* complex; (*anat.*) complexus.
complicable, *a.* complicable.
complicación, *n.f.* complication, complex, complexity.

complicadamente, *adv.* complicatedly.
complicado, -da, *a.* complicated.
complicador, -ra, *n.m.f., a.* complicating (person or thing).
complicamiento, *n.m.* [COMPLICACIÓN].
complicar, *v.t.* (*pret.* compliqué; *pres. subj.* complique) to complicate; to jumble together. — *v.r.* to become complicated, entangled.
cómplice, *n.m.f.* accomplice, associate, abettor, accessory; *cómplice con otros,* accomplice with others; *cómplice de otro,* abettor of another; *cómplice en el delito,* accessory to the crime.
complicidad, *n.f.* complicity.
complot, *n.m.* (*coll.*) plot, conspiracy; intrigue.
componedor, -ra, *n.m.f.* constructor; repairer; contriver; composer, author. — *n.m.* (*print.*) composing-stick; *amigable componedor,* (*law*) arbitrator; *muchos componedores, descomponen la novia,* too many cooks spoil the broth.
componenda, *n.f.* arbitration; compromise; fees paid for bulls and licences in Rome.
componente, *n.m., a.* component.
componer, *v.t.* (*p.p.* compuesto; *pres. indic.* compongo; *pret.* compuse; *pres. subj.* componga) to compose, construct, put together; to arrange, compound; to garnish, prepare, mix (food, drinks); to sum up; to devise, invent; to repair, mend, put in order; to adorn, trim, decorate; to adjust, settle differences; to compromise; to moderate, correct, compose; to write, compose, produce; (*coll.*) to strengthen, restore, fortify; (*print.*) to compose. — *v.i.* to write verses; (*mus.*) to compose. — *v.r.* to form a composite; to deck oneself out; to settle differences amicably; *esa copa de coñac me ha compuesto,* that glass of brandy has done me good; *allá se las componga,* let him get on with it; *componer el semblante,* to put on a calm appearance; *componérselas,* to shift for oneself.
componible, *a.* mendable, compoundable.
comporta, *n.f.* (*prov.*) large basket for grape harvesting; (*Per.*) mould used in the solidification of refined sulphur.
comportable, *a.* supportable, tolerable.
comportación, *n.f.* joint-carrying; deportment, behaviour.
comportamiento, *n.m.* behaviour, deportment, conduct.
comportar, *v.t.* to carry jointly; (*fig.*) to tolerate, suffer. — *v.r.* to comport or behave oneself.
comporte, *n.m.* behaviour, conduct; deportment.
comportería, *n.f.* trade and shop of a *comportero.*
comportero, *n.m.* maker or vendor of *comportas.*
composición, *n.f.* composition; composing; making up, repair, mending, adjustment; agreement, compact; composure, modesty, discretion; *hacer composición de lugar,* to weigh the pros and cons.
compositivo, -va, *a.* (*gram.*) compositive, synthetic.
compositor, -ra, *a.* composing. — *n.m.f.* (*mus.*) composer. — *n.m.* (*print.*) compositor.
compostura, *n.f.* composition, accommodation, agreement, adjustment; repairing,

mending; neatness, cleanliness; adulterating mixture; composure, circumspection, modesty, sedateness.

compota, *n.f.* compote, stewed fruit, preserves.

compotera, *n.f.* dish for stewed fruit.

compra, *n.f.* purchase; marketing, buying; collection of necessaries bought for daily use; *hacer compras,* to shop, go shopping.

comprable; compradero, -ra; compradizo, -za, *a.* purchasable.

comprachilla, *n.f.* (*Guat.*) bird like the blackbird.

compradillo, *n.m.* card game (ombre).

comprado, -da, *p.p.* [COMPRAR] bought, purchased. — *n.m.* card game.

comprador, -ra; comprante, *n.m.f.,* *a.* buyer, purchaser, caterer; buying, purchasing.

comprar, *v.t.* to buy, purchase, shop, market, acquire; to bribe; *comprar al contado, al fiado, a plazos,* to buy for cash, on credit, by instalments; *comprar de comer,* to buy food; *comprar del comerciante,* to buy from the dealer; *comprar las cosas sueltas* or *a bulto,* to buy things singly or in bulk (wholesale); *comprar por kilos,* to buy in kilos; *lo compré en veinte dólares,* I bought it for twenty dollars; *comprar de primera mano,* to buy at first hand; *el que compra y miente, en su bolsa lo siente,* he who buys and lies feels it in his purse.

compraventa, *n.f.*; *contrato de compraventa,* contract of bargain and sale.

comprehensivo, -va, *a.* comprehensive.

comprendedor, -ra, *a.* comprehending, understanding, comprehensive.

comprender, *v.t.* (*p.p.* **comprendido** and **compreso**) to comprehend, embrace, encircle, comprise, include, contain; to comprehend, understand, conceive, know.

comprensibilidad, *n.f.* comprehensibility; comprehensiveness.

comprensible, *a.* comprehensible, conceivable; comprehensive; *comprensible al entendimiento,* intelligible; *comprensible para todos,* understandable to all.

comprensiblemente, *adv.* comprehensibly, comprehensively.

comprensión, *n.f.* comprehension, conceiving, conception; comprehensiveness.

comprensividad, *n.f.* comprehensiveness.

comprensivo, -va, *a.* comprehensive, capable of understanding; comprisable, comprising, containing.

comprenso, -sa, *p.p. irreg.* [COMPRENDER] understood; comprised.

comprensor, -ra, *n.m.f.,* *a.* one that understands, attains, embraces; (*theol.*) the blessed.

compresa, *n.f.* (*surg.*) compress.

compresbítero, *n.m.* fellow-priest.

compresibilidad, *n.f.* compressibility.

compresible, *a.* compressible.

compresión, *n.f.* compression, pressing together; (*gram.*) synæresis.

compresivamente, *adv.* compressibly, contractedly.

compresivo, -va, *a.* compressive, compressing, condensing.

compreso, -sa, *p.p. irreg.* [COMPRIMIR] compressed.

compresor, -ra, *a.* compressing. — *n.m.* compressor; *compresor de aire,* air-compressor.

comprimario, -ria, *n.m.f.* singer of secondary parts.

comprimente, *a.* compressing, oppressing, constraining.

comprimible, *a.* compressible.

comprimido, -da, *a.* compressed, condensed; repressed, restrained. — *p.p.* [COMPRIMIR].

comprimidor, -ra, *a.* compressive.

comprimir, *v.t.* (*p.p.* **comprimido** and **compreso**) to compress, condense; to constrain, repress, restrain, keep in awe. — *v.r.* to control oneself, refrain.

comprobación, *n.f.* check, checking, comparison; attestation, verification.

comprobadamente, *adv.* provably.

comprobador, -ra, *a.* checking, proving, verifying. — *n.m.f.* attestor, prover.

comprobante, *a.* proving, attesting, substantiating. — *n.m.* check, proof; voucher, schedule, document.

comprobar, *v.t.* (*pres. indic.* **compruebo;** *pres. subj.* **compruebe**) to verify, prove, give evidence, compare.

comprofesor, -ra, *n.m.f.* colleague.

comprometedor, -ra, *a.* compromising, jeopardizing. — *n.m.f.* compromiser, jeopardizer.

comprometer, *v.t.* to compromise, arbitrate; to expose, jeopardize, endanger; to engage, bind. — *v.r.* to compromise oneself; to make a compromise; to commit oneself, become liable; *comprometer a otro,* to jeopardize another; *comprometer en jueces árbitros,* to submit to arbitration; *comprometerse a pagar,* to pledge oneself to pay; *comprometerse con alguno,* to become engaged or betrothed to someone; *comprometerse en una empresa,* to assume responsibility in an undertaking.

comprometido, -da, *a.* compromised, pledged; embarrassing. — *p.p.* [COMPROMETER(SE)].

comprometimiento, *n.m.* compromise; compact, agreement, adjustment; predicament, embarrassment, jeopardy.

compromisario, *n.m.* arbitrator, umpire, referee; elector of political delegate.

compromiso, *n.m.* compromise; obligation, agreement, bond; difficulty, jeopardy, embarrassment, predicament; engagement, betrothal; *estar* or *poner en compromiso,* to place or be in doubt (of something which formerly was clear).

compromisorio, -ria, *a.* (*law*) pronounced by arbiters (decisions, etc.); stipulating arbitration (clauses, etc.).

comprovincial, *a.* suffragan (bishop).

comprovinciano, -na, *n.m.f.,* *a.* from the same province.

compruebo; compruebe, *pres. indic.*; *pres. subj.* [COMPROBAR].

compuerta, *n.f.* hatch, half-door; lock, sluice, flood-gate; door-curtain of coach; *compuerta de marea,* tide-gate.

compuertecilla, *n.f.* small lock-gate, valve [COMPUERTA].

compuestamente, *adv.* composedly, regularly, decently; in an orderly manner.

compuesto, -ta, *a.* composed; compound, complex; made up, repaired. — *n.m.* compound, commixture, composition. — *p.p. irreg.* [COMPONER].

compulsa, n.f. (law) authentic copy duly compared with original; collation, comparison.

compulsador, -ra, n.m.f. one who collates or compares.

compulsar, v.t. (law) to make an authentic copy or transcript; to compare, collate.

compulsión, n.f. compulsion, forcing, impulsion, restraint.

compulsivamente, adv. compulsively, compulsorily.

compulsivo, -va, a. compulsive.

compulso, -sa, p.p. irreg. [COMPELER] compelled.

compulsor, -ra, a. compulsory. — n.m.f. compelling, forceful person.

compulsorio, -ria, a. (law) relating to a judicial decree to obtain a compulsa. — n.m.f. (law) order for a compulsa.

compunción, n.f. compunction, contrition, repentance.

compungido, -da, a. compunctious; sad, mournful. — p.p. [COMPUNGIR].

compungir, v.t. (pres. indic. **compunjo**; pres. subj. **compunja**) to move to compunction. — v.r. to feel compunction, contrition, remorse.

compungivo, -va, a. pricking, stinging.

compurgación, n.f. (law) compurgation, vindication.

compurgador, n.m. (law) compurgator.

compurgar, v.t. (law) to prove one's innocence by compurgation.

computación, n.f. computation, calculation.

computadamente, adv. by computation.

computador, -ra, a. computing, calculating. — n.m.f. enumerator; accountant.

computar, v.t. to compute, calculate.

computista, n.m.f. enumerator, computer; accountant.

cómputo, n.m. computation, estimate, calculation, account.

comulación, n.f. accumulation.

comulgante, a. (eccles.) of an age to communicate. — n.m.f. (eccles.) communicant.

comulgar, v.t. (pret. **comulgué**; pres. subj. **comulgue**) to communicate, administer communion. — v.i. to communicate, receive the Sacrament; comulgar con ruedas de molino, (coll.) to be very credulous, swallow anything.

comulgatorio, n.m. communion altar.

común, a. common; usual, general, customary, ordinary, familiar; much used, current, habitual, frequent; low, vulgar, mean. — n.m. community, public; water-closet, lavatory; en común, in common, conjointly, collectively; por lo común, in general, generally; quien sirve al común, sirve a ningún, services rendered to public bodies receive few thanks; común de dos, (gram.) common gender; el común de las gentes, the majority, the general public; común a todo, common to all.

comuna, n.f. (prov.) principal canal of irrigation; main water-pipe.

comunal, a. common, commonable, communal. — n.m. commonalty.

comunalista, n.m.f. (eccles.) belonging to the community.

comunalmente, adv. in common.

comunero, -ra, a. popular, common, pleasing to the people; appertaining to the com-

munities of Castile. — n.m. commoner; joint-holder of a tenure of lands. — pl. villages with commonage.

comunes, n.m.pl. Commons, the Lower House of the British parliament.

comunial, a. communal, of the community.

comunicabilidad, n.f. communicability, communicableness.

comunicable, a. communicable, sociable, affable.

comunicación, n.f. communication; intercourse; conversation; connexion of one thing with another; official despatch or statement. — pl. posts, telegraphs, telephones, etc.

comunicado, -da, p.p. [COMUNICAR] communicated. — n.m. notice, article of a personal nature sent to a newspaper, comuniqué.

comunicador, -ra, a. communicating. — n.m.f. communicator.

comunicante, a. communicating. — n.m.f. communicant.

comunicar, v.t. (pret. **comuniqué**; pres. subj. **comunique**) to communicate, impart, extend; to reveal, make known; to consult, confer; to advise, announce, inform. — v.r. to communicate; to open into; to be connected; comunicarse entre sí, to interchange sentiments or ideas; comunicar con el exterior, to communicate with the outside world; comunicarse (dos lagos) entre sí, to be joined together (two lakes); comunicarse por señas, to communicate by signs.

comunicativamente, adv. communicatively.

comunicativo, -va, a. communicative, not reserved, liberal, open-hearted, approachable, accessible.

comunicatorio, -ria, a.; letras comunicatorias, testimonial letters.

comunidad, n.f. commonness; commonage, commonalty; community, corporation, guild, society; pl. popular risings in Castile (16th cent.); de comunidad, in common, conjointly, collectively.

comunión, n.f. communion, fellowship; congregation; political party; common possession; familiar intercourse; communion, act of receiving the Blessed Sacrament; the eucharist.

comunísimo, -ma, a. superl. [COMUN] extremely common, very general.

comunismo, n.m. communism.

comunista, a. communistic. — n.m.f. communist.

comúnmente, adv. commonly, usually, generally, customarily; frequently, often.

comuña, n.f. maslin, mixed corn and rye; (prov.) partnership. — pl. [CAMUÑAS].

comunitario, -ria, a. communistic, relating to communism.

con, prep. with; (preceding an infinitive) by (followed by English gerund); (followed by infinitive) although; in; toward; con pagar se eximió del servicio, by paying he was exempted from military service; con ser tan difícil lo hizo, notwithstanding its being so difficult he did it; con que Vd. me hubiera escrito, if you had only written to me; con que, así es, so that's that; afable con los niños, kind towards children; llevarse bien con otro, to be on good terms with another person.

conacho, *n.m.* (*Per.*) mortar for pounding gold-ore.

conato, *n.m.* endeavour, effort, exertion; propensity, tendency; (*law*) crime unsuccessfully attempted.

concadenamiento, *n.m.* concatenation.

concadenar, *v.t.* to concatenate, link together.

concambio, *n.m.* exchange.

concanónigo, *n.m.* fellow-canon.

concatedralidad, *n.f.* union of two cathedral churches.

concatenación, *n.f.* concatenation.

concausa, *n.f.* joint cause.

cóncava; concavidad, *n.f.* concavity, hollowness, hollow.

concavar, *v.t.* to dig jointly.

cóncavo, -va, *a.* concave, hollow. — *n.m.* concavity, hollow place.

cóncavoconvexo, *a.* concavo-convex.

concebible, *a.* conceivable.

concebir, *v.i.,* *v.t.* (*pres. indic.* **concibo**; *pres. subj.* **conciba**) to conceive, become pregnant; to imagine, conceive, have an idea of; to understand, comprehend. — *v.t.* to begin to feel (passion, sentiment).

concedente, *a.* conceding.

conceder, *v.t.* to give, bestow, grant, concede, allow; admit, permit.

concedible, *a.* allowable, admissible, permissible.

concejal, concejala, *n.m.f.* councillor.

concejalía, *n.f.* councillorship.

concejil, *a.* common; public; relating to the municipal council.

concejo, *n.m.* civic body of a small town or village; municipal council; council-board, session; foundling; *casa del concejo,* town-hall; *pon lo tuyo en el concejo, y unos dirán que es blanco, y otros dirán que es negro,* ask the opinion of a council, and you will receive conflicting advice.

concelebramiento, *n.m.* (*eccles.*) action and effect of concelebrating.

concelebrar, *v.t.* (*eccles.*) to concelebrate.

conceller, *n.m.* councillor (in Catalonia).

concento, *n.m.* concert, concord of voices, harmony.

concentrabilidad, *n.f.* quality of being concentrated.

concentrable, *a.* that which can be concentrated.

concentración, *n.f.* concentration.

concentrado, -da, *a.* concentrate, concentrated. — *p.p.* [CONCENTRAR].

concentrador, -ra, *a.* concentrating. — *n.m.f.* concentrator.

concentrar, *v.t.* to concentrate, concentre. — *v.r.* to concentrate one's mind; *concentrar (el poder) en una mano,* to concentrate power in one person.

concentratividad, *n.f.* concentrativeness.

concentricamente, *adv.* concentrically.

concentricidad, *n.f.* concentricity.

concéntrico, -ca, *a.* (*geom.*) concentric.

concentuoso, -sa, *a.* harmonious.

concepción, *n.f.* conception, act of conceiving; idea, comprehension, fancy; festival of the Immaculate Conception; picture representing the Blessed Virgin.

concepcional, *a.* (*phil.*) conceptional.

concepcionario, -ria, *n.m.f.* defender of the dogma of the Immaculate Conception.

conceptáculo, *n.m.* (*bot.*) conceptacle.

conceptear, *v.i.* to give smart repartees.

conceptibilidad, *n.f.* imaginativeness.

conceptible, *a.* conceivable, imaginable.

conceptismo, *n.m.* affected, exaggerated, witty style; conceit.

conceptista, *n.m.* wit, man of genius; humourist, punster; one who affects or overdoes witticisms.

conceptividad, *n.f.* conceivableness, conceivability.

conceptivo, -va, *a.* conceptive.

concepto, *n.m.* concept, thought, idea; pithy sentence, flash of wit, epigram, pun; sentiment; opinion, judgment; esteem, estimation; *formar un concepto,* to form an opinion.

conceptor, -ra, *a.* conceiving, imagining. — *n.m.f.* conceptionist, imaginer.

conceptuar, *v.t.* to conceive, judge, form an opinion; *ser conceptuado de inteligente,* to be considered intelligent.

conceptuosamente, *adv.* ingeniously, wittily; pithily expressed.

conceptuosidad, *n.f.* witticism, pithiness; ingenuity, ingeniousness.

conceptuoso, -sa, *a.* ingenious, witty.

concernencia, *n.f.* concernment, relation.

concerniente, *a.* concerning, touching, relating to; *en lo concerniente a,* as for, with regard to; *lo concerniente al negocio,* what concerns the business.

concernir, *v. impers.* (*pres. indic.* **ello concierne**; *pres. subj.* **ello concierna**) to regard, concern; to appertain, belong to.

concertadamente, *adv.* by agreement; in an orderly or regular manner, concertedly, methodically.

concertado, -da, *p.p.* [CONCERTAR] concerted.

concertador, -ra, *a.* adjusting, regulating. — *n.m.f.* regulator, expediter, adjuster; mediator, mediatrix; *maestro concertador,* choirmaster.

concertamiento, *n.m.* [CONCERTACIÓN].

concertante, *a.* concerting, arranging, planning; (*mus.*) concerted, arranged for two or more voices.

concertar, *v.t.* (*pres. indic.* **concierto**; *pres. subj.* **concierte**) to regulate, adjust, set to rights, settle, contrive, accord, harmonize; to bargain, covenant, conclude (an agreement); (*com.*) to close (a deal); to compose or adjust differences; to tune musical instruments; to compare, estimate relative qualities; (*hunt.*) to beat, to start or rouse the game. — *v.i.* to agree, accord, suit. — *v.r.* to be arranged; to go hand in hand; to contrive, design, covenant, concert; *concertar (uno) con otro,* to agree with another; *concertar en género y número,* to agree in gender and number; *concertar las paces entre dos contrarios,* to adjust differences between two parties.

concertina, *n.f.* (*mus.*) concertina.

concertino, *n.m.* orchestra leader.

concertista, *n.m.f.* (*mus.*) conductor; performer.

concesible, *a.* admissible, grantable.

concesión, *n.f.* concession; grant; acknowledgment.

concesionario, *n.m.* (*law*) grantee, concessionary.

concesivo, -va, *a.* that may be granted.

concia, *n.f.* preserved forest, prohibited part of a forest.

conciencia, *n.f.* conscience; conscientiousness; consciousness; scrupulosity; *a conciencia,* conscientiously; *ajustarse con su conciencia,* to follow one's own conscience; *ancho de conciencia,* not scrupulous; *cargar uno la conciencia,* to have a heavy conscience; load one's conscience; *descargar uno la conciencia,* to fulfil an obligation; to confess to the priest; *en conciencia,* in good earnest, in truth; *estrecho de conciencia,* scrupulously conscientious; *manchar uno la conciencia,* to have on one's conscience.

concienzudamente, *adv.* conscientiously, scrupulously.

concienzudo, -da, *a.* conscientious, scrupulous, thorough, assiduous.

concierto, *n.m.* concert; bargain, contract, agreement, accommodation; good order, arrangement; (*hunt.*) battue; *de concierto,* in concert; by agreement; *más vale mal concierto que buen pleito,* better a poor agreement than a good lawsuit.

concierto; concierte, *pres. indic.; pres. subj.* [CONCERTAR].

conciliabilidad, *n.f.* conciliatoriness, reconciliability.

conciliable, *a.* reconcilable, capable of conciliation.

conciliábulo, *n.m.* (*coll.*) illegal reunion; secret meeting.

conciliación, *n.f.* conciliation, reconcilement; affinity; favour, good will.

conciliador, -ra, *a.* conciliating. — *n.m.f.* conciliator.

conciliar, *a.* conciliar. — *n.m.* council-man, member of a council. — *v.t.* to reconcile; to conciliate, to reconcile two friends; *conciliarse el respeto de todos,* to win everyone's respect; *conciliar las amistades,* to make friends; *conciliar el sueño,* to induce sleep.

conciliativo, -va, *a.* conciliative. — *n.m.* conciliator.

conciliatorio, -ria, *a.* conciliatory; *palabras conciliatorias,* conciliatory words.

concilio, *n.m.* council, congress, meeting; collection of decrees of a council; *hacer* or *tener concilio,* (*coll.*) to hold unlawful meetings.

concino, -na, *a.* concinnous, harmonious (used of language).

concisamente, *adv.* concisely, laconically, shortly, briefly.

concisión, *n.f.* conciseness, brevity, terseness.

conciso, -sa, *a.* concise, short, brief, laconic.

concitación, *n.f.* commotion, disturbance; instigation, stirring up.

concitador, -ra, *a.* inciting, provoking. — *n.m.f.* instigator, inciter to ill.

concitamiento, *n.m.* [CONCITACIÓN].

concitar, *v.t.* to excite, stir up commotions.

concitativo, -va, *a.* inciting, stirring up commotions.

conciudadanía, *n.f.* affinity, relationship between fellow-citizens; quality of fellow-citizens.

conciudadano, -na, *n.m.f.* fellow-citizen, fellow-countryman.

conclave; cónclave, *n.m.* conclave, close or secret meeting.

conclavista, *n.m.* domestic attending on cardinals in a conclave.

concluidor, -ra, *a.* concluding, conclusive.

concluir, *v.t.* (*pres. indic.* **concluyo;** *pres. subj.* **concluya;** *p.p.* **concluido, concluso**) to conclude, terminate, end, finish, close, complete, expire, make up; to convince with reason, make evident, silence in argument; to infer, deduce; to close judicial proceedings; (*fenc.*) to disarm. — *v.r.* to finish, come to an end; *concluir con algo,* to finish with something; *concluir a uno de ignorante,* to consider someone an ignoramus; *concluir en vocal,* to end in a vowel.

conclusión, *n.f.* conclusion; end; settlement; decision, resolution; inference; (*law*) winding-up; (*pl.*) theses (in schools); *en conclusión,* finally, in conclusion; *sentarse en la conclusión,* to stick obstinately to an erroneous opinion.

conclusivo, -va, *a.* conclusive, final, concluding.

concluso, -sa, *a.* concluded, closed, terminated. — *p.p. irreg.* [CONCLUIR]; *dar por concluso,* (*law*) to wind up.

concluyente, *a.* concluding, conclusive, convincing.

concluyentemente, *adv.* conclusively, evidently.

concluyo; concluya, *pres. indic.; pres. subj.* [CONCLUIR].

concofrade, *n.m.* confrère, fellow of the same brotherhood.

concoidal, *a.* (*geom.*) conchoidal.

concoide, *a.* (*geom.*) conchoid. — *n.f.* (*math.*) conchoid.

concoideo, -dea, *a.* conchoidal, shell-like.

concolega, *n.m.* fellow-collegian.

concología, *n.f.* conchology.

concomerse, *v.r.* (*coll.*) to shrug the shoulders.

concomezón; concomimiento; concomio, *n.m.* (*coll.*) shrug, shrugging of the shoulders.

concomitancia, *n.f.* concomitance.

concomitante, *a.* concomitant, concurrent.

concomitar, *v.t.* to accompany.

concón, *n.m.* (*Chi.*) barn-owl; (*Chi.*) wind from land.

concordable, *a.* concordant, conformable, consistent, agreeable, accommodating.

concordación, *n.f.* co-ordination, combination, conformation.

concordador, -ra, *a.* conciliating, pacifying. — *n.m.f.* conciliator, moderator, peacemaker.

concordancia, *n.f.* concord, agreement, harmony. — *pl.* concordance, index.

concordante, *a.* concordant, agreeing.

concordar, *v.t., v.i.* (*pres. indic.* **concuerdo;** *pres. subj.* **concuerde**) to accord, agree, conform, regulate, make agree; to compromise, comply, be congenial; *la copia concuerda con el original,* the copy conforms to the original; *el adjetivo concuerda en género y número con el substantivo,* the adjective agrees with the noun in gender and number.

concordata, *n.f.; concordato,** *n.m.* concordat.

concordativo, -va; concorde, *a.* concordant, agreeing, tallying.

concordatorio, -ria, *a.* relating to a concordat.

concordemente, *adv.* concordantly.

concordia, *n.f.* concord, conformity, harmony, unity; (*law*) agreement, settlement;

linked finger-rings; *de concordia*, jointly, by common consent.

concorpóreo, -rea, *a.* (*theol.*) concorporate, of the same body.

concreado, -da, *a.* created simultaneously.

concreción, *n.f.* concretion.

concrecionado, -da, *a.* (*min.*) concreted; (*min.*) concrete. — *p.p.* [CONCRECIONAR].

concrecionar, *v.t.*, *v.r.* to concrete, form concretions.

concrecionario, -ria, *a.* (*min.*) concretionary.

concrescencia, *n.f.* (*bot.*) concrescence.

concrescible, *a.* capable of concreting.

concretación, *n.f.*; **concretamiento,** *n.m.* concreteness, concretion.

concretador, -ra, *a.* concreting.

concretamente, *adv.* concretely.

concretar, *v.t.* to combine, unite, concrete; to reduce to the simplest form. — *v.r.* to confine oneself to one subject.

concreto, -ra, *a.* concrete. — *n.m.* concretion; *en concreto*, in conclusion.

concubina, *n.f.* concubine, mistress.

concubinariamente, *adv.* in concubinage.

concubinario, *n.m.* concubinary, one who keeps a mistress.

concubinato; concubinismo, *n.m.* concubinage.

concúbito, *n.m.* coition.

concuerda, *adv.*; *por concuerda*, in accordance with, conforming to the original manuscript (copy).

concuerdo; concuerde, *pres. indic.*; *pres. subj.* [CONCORDAR].

conculcación, *n.f.* trampling; infringement.

conculcador, -ra, *a.* infringing, trampling. — *n.m.f.* infringer, trampler.

conculcar, *v.t.* (*pret.* **conculqué**; *pres. subj.* **conculque**) to trample under foot; to infringe.

concuna, *n.f.* (*Col.*) wild pigeon.

concuñado, -da, *n.m.f.* brother-in-law, sister-in-law (confined to persons married to two brothers or sisters).

concupiscencia, *n.f.* concupiscence, lust, cupidity, greed.

concupiscente, *a.* concupiscent.

concupiscible, *a.* that awakens desire.

concurrencia, *n.f.* concourse, convention, assembly, attendance; concurrence, coincidence; assistance, support, help, influence; competition.

concurrente, *a.* concurrent, coincident, competing. — *n.m.f.* competitor; contributor; person present at a function.

concurrido, -da, *a.* crowded; well-attended, frequented. — *p.p.* [CONCURRIR].

concurrir, *v.i.* to concur, agree; to coincide; to contribute, help; to attend, be present; to compete; *concurrir a algún fin*, to contribute to a cause; *concurrir en un lugar*, to frequent a place; *concurrir con otros*, to compete with others; *concurrir en un dictamen*, to concur in an opinion; *Antonio concurrió con mil pesetas*, Anthony subscribed 1,000 pesetas.

concursar, *v.t.* (*law*) to bankrupt, declare insolvent.

concurso, *n.m.* concourse, conflux, confluence, flux; crowd, congregation; assembly, aid, assistance; competition; competitive examination; call for tenders; *concurso de acreedores*, (*law*) meeting of creditors.

concusión, *n.f.* concussion, shaking, shock; (*law*) exaction, extortion, blackmailing.

concusionario, -ria, *a.* concussive; extortionate. — *n.m.* extortioner; extorter.

concha, *n.f.* shell, case, carapace; tortoise-shell; oyster; (*arch.*) volute; shell-guard of dagger or cutlass; shell-shaped covering of spike of Indian corn; prompter's box; nether millstone; ancient copper coin; little bay, cove, creek; any shell-shaped object; very good cigar; shell-shaped butter or jam-dish; (*coll.*) pet contraction of Concepción (girl's name); *concha auditiva*, (*anat.*) concha; *concha de perla* or *madreperla*, mother-of-pearl; *meterse en su concha*, to become a recluse; *tener muchas conchas* or *tener más conchas que un galápago*, to be very reserved and astute.

conchabanza, *n.f.* manner of making oneself comfortable; (*coll.*) plotting, conspiracy.

conchabar, *v.t.* to unite, join; to mix inferior and superior wool. — *v.r.* (*fam.*) to plot, conspire; to make oneself snug.

conchabo, *n.m.* (*Am. Mer.*) a domestic servant's contract.

concháceo, -cea, *a.* having a bivalve shell. — *n.m.f.* lamellibranch molluscs.

conchado, -da, *a.* crustaceous, shelly, scaly.

conchal, *a.* high-class (silk).

conchífero, -a, *a.* conchiferous, shell-bearing.

conchil, *n.m.* (*zool.*) murex.

Conchita, *n.f.* dear little Concha (girl's name) [CONCHA].

concho, -cha, *a.* (*Ec.*) of the same colour as the lees of beer and chicha; (*Am.*) *n.m.* bees, dregs.

conchoidal, *a.* (*zool.*) conchoid.

conchoso, -sa, *a.* (*zool.*) scaly, shelly.

conchudo, -da, *a.* scaly, shelly; (*coll.*) cunning, crafty, close, reserved.

conchuela, *n.f.* small shell [CONCHA]; sea-bed covered with broken shells.

condado, *n.m.* earldom, dignity of an earl; county.

condal, *a.* of an earl or count; relating to an earldom.

conde, *n.m.* earl, count; head or chief of gipsies; (*prov.*) overseer.

condecente, *a.* convenient, fit, proper.

condecoración, *n.f.* decoration, embellishment; badge, medal; insignia of knighthood, etc.

condecorar, *v.t.* to decorate, honour, reward, confer a decoration upon.

condena, *n.f.* sentence of a condemned criminal, term of imprisonment; penalty.

condenable, *a.* condemnable, blamable, culpable, damnable.

condenación, *n.f.* condemnation; eternal damnation; punishment, fine, sentence; *es una condenación*, (*coll.*) it is unbearable, intolerable.

condenado, -da, *a.* condemned, damned; devilish, perverse. — *n.m.f.* reprobate. — *p.p.* [CONDENAR].

condenador, -ra, *a.* condemning, damning. — *n.m.f.* condemner, blamer, censurer.

condenar, *v.t.* to condemn, pronounce judgment; to damn, censure, blame, disapprove; to refute a doctrine or opinion; to stop, shut or nail up (a door, window, passage, etc.). — *v.r.* to condemn oneself, acknowledge one's fault; to incur eternal punishment; *condenar con* or *en costas*, to sentence to pay costs; *condenar a trabajos forzados*, to sentence to penal servitude or hard labour.

condenatorio, -ria, *a.* (*law*) condemnatory; damnatory.

condensabilidad, *n.f.* condensability.

condensable, *a.* condensable.

condensación, *n.f.* condensation, compression.

condensador, -ra, *a.* condensing. — *n.m.* condenser, air-compressor; *condensador de fuerzas,* accumulator; *condensador eléctrico,* storage-battery; *condensador de chorro,* jet condenser; *condensador de mezcla,* mixing condenser; *condensador de superficie,* surface condenser.

condensamiento, *n.m.* [CONDENSACIÓN].

condensante, *a.* condensing.

condensar, *v.t.* to thicken, condense; (*fig.*) compress. — *v.r.* to condense, become condensed, compact.

condensativo, -va, *a.* condensing.

condenso, -sa, *p.p. irreg.* [CONDENSAR].

condesa, *n.f.* countess.

condescendencia, *n.f.* condescendence, condescension, compliance, complacency.

condescender, *v.i.* (*pres. indic.* **condesciendo;** *pres. subj.* **condescienda**) to condescend, be complacent, submit, comply, yield; *condescender a los ruegos,* to yield to the supplications; *condescender con la instancia,* to comply with the request; *condescender en reiterarse,* to condescend to repeat oneself.

condescendiente, *a.* complacent, compliant, acquiescent, condescending.

condesciendo; condescienda, *pres. indic.; pres. subj.* [CONDESCENDER].

condesil, *a.* (*iron.*) [CONDAL].

condesito, -ita, *n.m.f.* little or young earl or countess.

condestable, *n.m.* high constable, commander-in-chief of the army; master gunner.

condestablesa, *n.f.* high constable's wife.

condestablía, *n.f.* constableship, dignity of high constable.

condición, *n.f.* condition, quality, state; footing; disposition, temper; rank, high social position; primitive constitution (of a village); circumstance; conditional clause, stipulation, specification; *condición callada* or *tácita,* understood or tacit condition; *condición deshonesta* or *torpe* or *imposible de derecho,* illegal, immoral condition; *a condición de que* or *bajo la condición de que,* on condition that; *de condición,* so that, in such a manner; *hombre de condición,* nobleman; *persona de humilde condición,* person of humble birth; *precios y condiciones,*(to adhere to) terms; *estar en condiciones de,* to be in a position to; *quebrarle a uno la condición,* to break someone's pride; *poner en condición,* to hasard, expose to danger; *tener condición,* to be of a sharp disposition.

condicionado, -da, *a.* conditioned; conditional; agreed on. — *p.p.* [CONDICIONAR].

condicional, *a.* conditional; *libertad condicional,* (*law*) conditional discharge.

condicionalmente, *adv.* conditionally, hypothetically.

condicionar, *v.i.* to agree, accord, condition.

condicioncilla; condicioncita, *n.f.* hasty temper; small clause or stipulation.

condignamente, *adv.* condignly, deservedly.

condignidad, *n.f.* desert, merit, suitability.

condigno, -na, *a.* condign, suitable, deserved, merited.

condileo, -lea; condiloideo, -dea, *a.* (*anat.*) condylar, condyloid.

cóndilo, *n.m.* (*anat.*) condyle.

condimentador, -ra, *n.m.f.* seasoner, one adding condiments.

condimentar, *v.t.* to dress or season victuals.

condimenticio, -cia, *a.* condimental, suitable as seasoning.

condimento, *n.m.* condiment, seasoning, sauce.

condiscípulo, -la, *n.m.f.* fellow-scholar, fellow-student, schoolfellow.

condolecerse, *v.r.* (*pres. indic.* **me condolezco;** *pres. subj.* **me condolezca**) [CONDOLERSE].

condolencia, *n.f.* condolence.

condolerse, *v.r.* (*pres. indic.* **me conduelo;** *pres. subj.* **me conduela**) to condole, be sorry for, sympathize with regret; *condolerse de los desvalidos,* to sympathize with the destitute.

condominio, *n.m.* condominium, joint-ownership.

condómino, *n.m.f.* condominus, joint-owner.

condonación, *n.f.* condonation, pardoning.

condonante, *a.* condoning, forgiving, remitting.

condonar, *v.t.* to pardon, forgive, condone.

condonatario, *n.m.* joint-donatory.

condonatorio, -ria, *a.* (*law*) condoning, remitting (sentence).

cóndor, *n.m.* (*orn.*) condor; (*Chi., Ec.*) gold coin.

condotiero, *n.m.* condottiere.

cóndrico, -ca, *a.* relating to cartilage.

condrila, *n.f.* common gum-succory.

condrín, *n.m.* (*Philip.*) weight for precious metals (0·3768 grammes).

conducción, *n.f.* conveyance, carriage, transmission, transportation, cartage; conduct, leading, guiding, or bringing anything; contract at a stipulated rate; conduction (of liquids); driving (of vehicles).

conducencia, *n.f.* [CONDUCCIÓN].

conducente, *a.* conducive, conductive, conductible.

conducir, *v.t., v.i.* (*pres. indic.* **conduzco;** *pret.* **conduje;** *pres. subj.* **conduzca**) to conduct, guide, direct; to transport, convey; to manage, control (a business); to drive (a vehicle); to contract at a fixed rate or salary. — *v.r.* to behave, conduct oneself; *conducir al bien de otro,* to conduce to someone's benefit; *conducir en carreta,* to transport in a cart; *conducir por mar,* to convey by sea.

conducta, *n.f.* [CONDUCCIÓN]; transport of currency or bullion; the currency or bullion transported; command, direction, management; conduct, behaviour, deportment; contract with a doctor to attend the sick of a given district; the doctor's remuneration for this work; new recruits conducted to the regiments; stipulation, agreement.

conductero, *n.m.* one in charge of a convoy.

conductibilidad, *n.f.* conductibility.

conductible, *a.* conveyable, conductible.

conductividad, *n.f.* conveying power, conductivity.

conductivo, -va, *a.* conductive, conveying or transporting.

conducto, *n.m.* conduit, sewer, drain, duct, sink; channel (business); spout; mediator; water-main; steam-pipe; (*fig.*) salvo conducto, safe-conduct.

conductor, -ra, *a.* conducting, directing, guiding. — *n.m.* conductor, leader, guide; driver (of vehicle); usher; (*phys.*) conductor, conveyer. — *n.f.* conductress, directress.

conduelo; conduela, *pres. indic.; pres. subj.* [CONDOLER].

condueño, *n.m.f.* joint-owner.

conduerma, *n.f.* (*Ven.*) drowsiness, heaviness.

condumio, *n.m.* (*coll.*) food eaten with bread; *haber* or *hacer mucho condumio*, there is plenty of food.

conduplicación, *n.f.* reduplication.

conduplicado, -da; conduplicativo, -va, *a.* conduplicate.

condutal, *n.m.* spout (of roof-gutter).

conectador, *n.m.* connecter (contact-plug).

conectar, *v.t.* (*mech.*) to connect, couple, gear.

coneja, *n.f.* female of rabbit; *ser (una) una coneja*, to breed like a rabbit, have many children.

conejal; conejar, *n.m.* rabbit-warren.

conejear, *v.i.* to burrow, crouch, hide; to cower; (*fig.*) to evade a promise or responsibility.

conejero, -ra, *a.* rabbit-hunting (dog). — *n.m.f.* breeder and vendor of rabbits. — *n.f.* rabbit-warren; rabbitry; (*coll.*) burrow, den; (*coll.*) cellar, low haunt.

conejillo; conejito, *n.m.* young rabbit [CONEJO]; *conejillo de Indias,* guinea-pig.

conejo, -ja, *n.m.f.* rabbit; *alambre conejo,* rabbit-wire, copper-wire; *conejo albar,* white rabbit; *el conejo ido, el consejo venido,* to lock the stable-door after the horse has been stolen.

conejuelo, *n.m.* young rabbit [CONEJO].

conejuna, *n.f.* rabbit down or fur.

conejuno, -na, *a.* relating, similar to the rabbit.

coneo, -nea, *a.* conic.

conexidades, *n.f.pl.* rights annexed to another principal one.

conexión, *n.f.* connexion, conjunction, union, conjuncture, cohesion, coherence, closeness. — *pl.* acquaintanceship, friendship, connexions.

conexionarse, *v.r.* to form acquaintanceship, get in touch; to make (social, commercial) connexions.

conexivo, -va, *a.* connective.

conexo, -xa, *a.* connected; (*law*) united, linked.

confabulación, *n.f.* confabulation, conversation; conspiracy, leaguing, collusion, plot.

confabulador, -ra, *n.m.f.* schemer, plotter, story teller.

confabular, *v.i.* to confer, consult together. — *v.r.* to league, plot; *confabularse con los adversarios,* to enter into a conspiracy with the adversaries.

confalón, *n.m.* gonfalon, ensign, standard.

confalonier; confaloniero, *n.m.* gonfalonier, standard-bearer.

confarreación, *n.f.* confarreation.

confección, *n.f.* confaction, fabrication, manufacture, handiwork; (*pharm.*) compound remedy, electuary.

confeccionador, -ra, *a.* confectioning, manufacturing. — *n.m.f.* manufacturer (of wearing apparel or handiwork).

confeccionar, *v.t.* to make, put together, prepare, confection; to compound medicines, make up prescriptions.

confederación, *n.f.* confederation, coalition, league, union, confederacy, federation.

confederado, -da, *a.* confederate, confederated, confederal, allied. — *n.m.f.* ally, confederate; federalist. — *p.p.* [CONFEDERAR].

confederar, *v.t., v.r.* to confederate, join in a league; *confederarse con alguno,* to combine with someone.

confederativo, -va, *a.* confederative.

conferencia, *n.f.* conference, meeting, interview, conversation; daily lecture (in universities); public lecture; congress.

conferenciante, *a.* conferring, consulting. — *n.m.f.* lecturer; member of a conference.

conferenciar, *v.i.* to debate, confer, deliberate, hold a conference, take counsel;   to give a lecture.

conferimiento, *n.m.* conferment.

conferir, *v.t.* (*pres. indic.* **confiero;** *pres. subj.* **confiera**) to confer, compare; to deliberate, commune; to give, bestow, award. — *v.i.* [CONFERENCIAR]; *conferir (un asunto) con* or *entre amigos,* to discuss (a matter) with or among friends.

confesa, *n.f.* widow who became a nun.

confesable, *a.* avowable.

confesado, -da, *a.* avowed, confessed. — *n.m.f.* (*coll.*) confessant, penitent. — *p.p.* [CONFESAR].

confesante, *a.* confessing; (*law*) declaratory. *n.m.* (*obs.*) penitent, confessant.

confesar, *v.t.* (*pres. indic.* **confieso;** *pres. subj.* **confiese;** *p.p.* **confesado** and **confeso**) to confess, acknowledge, grant, avow, own; (*law*) to declare; to manifest or assert one's opinion; to hear or receive confessions, shrive. — *v.r.* to confess, make one's confession, be shriven; *confesar de plano,* to confess plainly or openly; *confesar (el delito) al juez,* to plead guilty to the judge; *confesarse con alguno,* to confess to someone; *confesarse de sus culpas,* to acknowledge one's faults.

confesión, *n.f.* confession, acknowledgment, avowal; (*law*) plea of guilty or not guilty; *oír de confesión,* to hear or receive a confession.

confesional, *a.* sectarian.

confesionario, *n.m.* confessional; treatise with rules for confession.

confesionista, *n.m.f.* confessionist, Lutheran.

confeso, -sa, *a.* (*law*) confessed; converted (Jew). — *n.m.* lay brother. — *p.p.* [CONFESAR].

confesor, *n.m.* confessor; father confessor; *confesor de manga ancha,* confessor who grants absolution easily.

confesorio, -ria, *a.* (*law*) appertaining to avowry.

confeti, *n.m.* confetti.

confiable, *a.* trusty.

confiadamente, *adv.* confidently, safely.

confiado, -da, *a.* confided, entrusted; confident, secure; forward, presumptuous, arrogant; trusting, unsuspicious. — *p.p.* [CONFIAR].

confiador, *n.m.* (*law*) joint surety.

confianza, *n.f.* confidence, trust, reliance, firm belief, faith, hope; presumptuousness, forwardness; boldness, courage; familiarity, intimacy; (*com.*) secret arrangement; *de confianza,* informally, without ceremony; *en confianza,* privately, secretly, confidentially, in confidence; *pida con confianza,* ask without hesitation.

confiar, *v.i.* to hope. — *v.t.* to confide, trust, entrust; to confide in; to give hope; *confiar de* or *en alguno,* to rely on someone.

confidencia, *n.f.* confidence, secret, trust.

confidencial, *a.* confidential.

confidentialmente, *adv.* confidentially.

confidente, *a.* faithful, sure, trusty. — *n.m.f.* confidant, confidante; secret agent, spy. — *n.m.* sofa for two, tête-à-tête.

confidentemente, *adv.* confidentially; faithfully; fiducially.

confiero; confiera, *pres. indic.; pres. subj.* [CONFERIR].

confieso; confiese, *pres. indic.; pres. subj.* [CONFESAR].

configuración, *n.f.* configuration.

configurar, *v.t.* to configure, dispose into form.

confín, *a.* [CONFINANTE]. — *n.m.* limit, boundary, confine, border.

confinación, *n.f.;* **confinamiento,** *n.m.* confining, confinement; banishing, exiling.

confinado, -da, *a.* exiled, banished; confined; limited. — *p.p.* [CONFINAR].

confinante, *a.* bordering upon, conterminous.

confinar, *v.t.* to banish, exile; to confine. — *v.i.* to border upon, abut; *confinar alguno a* or *en una isla,* to banish someone to an island; *confinar con,* to lie adjacent to, be bounded by.

confingir, *v.t.* (*pres. indic.* **confinjo;** *pres. subj.* **confinja**) (*pharm.*) to mix into one mass.

confirmación, *n.f.* confirmation, corroboration, attestation.

confirmadamente, *adv.* confirmedly, firmly, surely, assuredly.

confirmado, -da, *a.* confirmed, valid, corroborated, ratified. — *n.m.f.* confirmee. — *p.p.* [CONFIRMAR].

confirmador, -ra, *a.* confirming. — *n.m.f.* confirmer, attester.

confirmando, -da, *n.m.f.* confirmee.

confirmante, *a.* confirming. — *n.m.f.* confirmer.

confirmar, *v.t.* to confirm, corroborate, verify, ratify; to fortify, strengthen, support; *confirmarse en su dictamen,* to be confirmed, strengthened in one's opinion.

confirmativamente, *adv.* confirmingly.

confirmativo, -va; confirmatorio, -ria, *a.* confirmatory.

confiscable, *a.* confiscable, confiscatable.

confiscación, *n.f.* confiscation, forfeiture.

confiscado, -da, *a.* confiscate, confiscated. — *p.p.* [CONFISCAR].

confiscar, *v.t.* (*pret.* **confisqué;** *pres. subj.* **confisque**) to confiscate.

confitable, *a.* that can be candied.

confitado, -da, *a.* candied, preserved; (*fig.*) soft, effeminate; (*fig.*) satisfied, persuaded, won over. — *p.p.* [CONFITAR].

confitar, *v.t.* to candy with melted sugar; to sweeten; to make into sweetmeats.

confite, *n.m.* comfit, sugar-plum. — *pl.* dainties.

confectionery; *morder en un confite,* to be hand and glove, intimate, familiar.

confitente, *a.* confessed; penitent.

confitera, *n.f.* vessel or box for sweetmeats.

confitería, *n.f.* confectioner's shop, sweet-shop, confectionery.

confitero, -ra, *n.m.f.* confectioner. — *n.m.* tray for sweetmeats.

confítico; confitillo; confitito, *n.m.* ornamented coverlet.

confitura, *n.f.* confectionery, comfit, confection, sweetmeat, candied fruit, preserve.

confiturería, *n.f.* art of making confectionery.

confiturero, -ra, *n.m.f.* confectioner.

conflagración, *n.f.* conflagration; (*fig.*) sudden disturbance or uproar.

conflagrar, *v.t.* to inflame; set on fire, burn.

conflátil, *a.* fusible.

conflicto, *n.m.* conflict, struggle, strife, combat; (*fig.*) agony, pang.

confluencia, *n.f.* confluence, conflux.

confluente, *a.* confluent. — *n.m.* confluence (of rivers).

confluir, *v.i.* (*pres. indic.* **él confluye;** *pret.* **él confluyó;** *pres. subj.* **confluya**) to join, meet (of rivers, currents, etc.); (*fig.*) to assemble in one place.

conformación, *n.f.* conformation.

conformador, *n.m.* shaper, conformator (of hats).

conformar, *v.i., v.t., v.r.* to conform, adjust, fit. — *v.i., v.r.* to comply with, agree. — *v.r.* to yield, submit; to resign oneself; *conformar su opinión a* or *con la ajena,* to adjust one's opinion to another's; *conformarse al tiempo,* to accommodate oneself to the weather; *conformarse con la situación,* to resign oneself to the situation.

conforme, *a.* conformable, agreeable; correspondent, suitable, congruent, consistent, consonant, similar; compliant, resigned. — *adv.* (with *a* or *con*) in due proportion to, according to, consistent with.

conformemente, *adv.* conformably.

conformidad, *n.f.* conformity, congruence, likeness, resemblance, similitude, agreement; union, concord, concordance; symmetry; affinity, congeniality; close attachment; submission, resignation; patience; *de conformidad,* *adv.* conformably, by common consent; *en conformidad,* *adv.* agreeably, accordingly.

conformismo, *n.m.* (*eccles.*) conformity [CONFORMIDAD].

conformista, *n.m.f.* conformist.

confortable, *a.* comfortable.

confortación, *n.f.* comfort, consolation, encouragement.

confortador, -ra, *a.* comforting. — *n.m.f.* comforter, consoler, strengthener.

confortamiento, *n.m.* comfort, consolation.

confortante, *n.m.f., a.* [CONFORTADOR]. — *n.m.* mitten.

confortar, *v.t., v.r.* to comfort, strengthen, enliven, console, invigorate, cheer, solace.

confortativo, -va, *a.* comforting, encouraging, strengthening, cheering. — *n.m.* cordial; solace.

conforte, *n.m.* comfort, solace.

confracción, *n.f.* breaking.

confraguación, *n.f.* alloying, fusing (of metals).

confraguar, *v.t.* [FRAGUAR].

confraternidad, *n.f.* confraternity, brotherhood.
confraternizar, *v.t.* [FRATERNIZAR].
confricación, *n.f.* friction.
confricar, *v.t.* to rub, produce friction.
confrontación, *n.f.* confrontation; comparison, comparing one thing with another; sympathy, natural conformity.
confrontante, *a.* confronting.
confrontar, *v.t.* to confront, collate, compare. — *v.i.* to border upon. — *v.i.*, *v.r.* to be opposite, stand facing one another; (*fig.*) to agree in sentiments and opinion; *confrontar un texto con otro,* to compare one text with another.
confucianismo, *n.m.* Confucianism.
confuciano, -na; confucionista, *n.m.f.*, *a.* Confucian.
confulgencia, *n.f.* refulgence.
confundible, *a.* that can be confused, indistinguishable.
confundimiento, *n.m.* confusedness, confusion; perplexity.
confundir, *v.t.* (*p.p.* **confundido** and **confuso**) to confound, jumble; to perplex, confuse, darken, throw into confusion or disorder; to confute; to abase, humiliate; to disconcert. — *v.r.* to be bewildered, perplexed, confounded, rattled, mixed up; (*fig.*) ashamed, humbled; *confundirse de lo que se ve,* to be bewildered by what one sees; *confundirse (una cosa) con otra,* (one thing) to be mistaken for another; *confundirse en sus opiniones,* to become confused in one's opinions.
confusamente, *adv.* confusedly, helter-skelter.
confusión, *n.f.* confusion, tumult, medley, misrule, disorder; (*fig.*) perplexity, perturbation, entanglement, confusedness, obscuration; (*fig.*) ignominy, humiliation, shame, debasement of mind; (*slang*) jail, prison.
confuso, -sa, *a.* confused, mixed, perplexed, confounded, jumbled together; obscure, doubtful; timorous, fearful, perplexed; *en confuso,* confusedly. — *p.p. irreg.* [CONFUNDIR].
confutación, *n.f.* confutation, disproof, refutation.
confutador, -ra, *a.* confuting, refutatory. — *n.m.f.* refuter.
confutar, *v.t.* to confute, disprove.
confutatorio, -ria, *a.* [CONFUTADOR].
conga, *n.f.* (*Cub.*) hutia, a large rodent.
congelable, *a.* congealable.
congelación, *n.f.* congelation, freezing, congealing.
congelador, *n.m.* refrigerator; freezer.
congelamiento, *n.m.* congelation, congealing.
congelante, *a.* congealing.
congelar, *v.t.*, *v.r.* to congeal, coagulate, freeze.
congelativo, -va, *a.* having the power of congealing.
congénere, *a.* congeneric; congenerous, congenetic.
congenial, *a.* congenial; analogous.
congenialidad, *n.f.* congeniality.
congeniar, *v.i.* (with *con*) to be congenial, to sympathize with.
congénito, -ta, *a.* congenital, connate.
congerie, *n.f.* congeries, heap, mass.

congestibilidad, *n.f.* predisposition to congestion.
congestible; congestionable, *a.* liable to congestion.
congestión, *n.f.* congestion.
congestionado, -da, *a.* (*med.*) congested. — *p.p.* [CONGESTIONAR(SE)].
congestional, *a.* (*med.*) congestive.
congestionar, *v.t.*, *v.r.* (*med.*) to congest.
congestivo, -va, *a.* (*med.*) congestive.
conglobación, *n.f.* conglobation; (*fig.*) mixture and union of immaterial things; (*rhet.*) accumulation of proofs.
conglobar, *v.t.*, *v.r.* to conglobate, heap together.
conglomeración, *n.f.* conglomeration, accumulation, heterogeneous mixture.
conglomerado, -da, *a.* conglomerate, conglomerated. — *n.m.* conglomerate. — *p.p.* [CONGLOMERAR].
conglomerar, *v.t.* to conglomerate.
conglutinación, *n.f.* conglutination.
conglutinante, *n.m.*, *a.* conglutinant.
conglutinar, *v.t.* to conglutinate, cement, adhere. — *v.r.* to become glutinous.
conglutinativo, -va, *n.m.*, *a.* conglutinative.
conglutinoso, -sa, *a.* viscous, glutinous.
congo, -ga, *n.m.f.*, *a.* [CONGOLEÑO].
congo, *n.m.* (*Mex., Cub.*) the thigh bone of a pig; (*Cub.*) popular dance and music; (*Hond.*) an acanthopterygian fish; (*CR., ES.*) howler monkey.
congoja, *n.f.* anguish, dismay, anxiety of mind.
congojar, *v.t.* to oppress, afflict.
congojosamente, *adv.* anxiously, painfully.
congojoso, -sa, *a.* afflictive, painful, afflicted.
congoleño, -na; congolés, -sa, *n.m.f.*, *a.* relating to, of or from the Congo; Congolese.
congolona, *n.f.* (*CR.*) wild chicken.
congorocho, *n.m.* (*Ven.*) kind of centipede.
congosto, *n.m.* mountain-pass, canyon.
congraciador, -ra, *n.m.f.* flatterer, fawner, congratulator, wheedler.
congraciamento, *n.m.* flattery, false praise, obsequiousness.
congraciarse, *v.r.* to ingratiate oneself; *congraciarse con otro,* to get into someone's good graces.
congratulación, *n.f.* congratulation, felicitation.
congratulador, -ra, *a.* congratulating. — *n.m.f.* congratulator.
congratular, *v.t.* to congratulate, compliment, greet. — *v.r.* to congratulate oneself, rejoice; *congratularse con los suyos,* to rejoice with one's family; *congratularse de* or *por una cosa,* to delight in something.
congratulatorio, -ria, *a.* congratulatory.
congregación, *n.f.* congregation; fraternity, brotherhood; meeting, assembly; *congregación de los fieles,* Catholic or universal church.
congregacionalismo, *n.m.* Congregationalism.
congregacionalista, *n.m.f.*, *a.* Congregationalist.
congregante, -ta, *n.m.f.* congregant; member of a congregation.
congregar, *v.t.*, *v.r.* (*pret.* **congregué;** *pres. subj.* **congregue**) to assemble, meet, congregate, gather.
congresista, *n.m.f.* member of a congress.

congreso, *n.m.* congress; assembly, convention; sexual intercourse.

congrio, *n.m.* conger-eel.

congrua, *n.f.* income requisite for a priest.

congruamente, *adv.* congruously, conveniently, becomingly.

congruencia, *n.f.* convenience, congruence, fitness.

congruente, *a.* congruent, corresponding.

congruentemente, *adv.* suitably, congruously.

congruísmo, *n.m.* (*theol.*) congruism.

congruísta, *n.m.f.* (*theol.*) congruist.

congruo, -ua, *a.* congruous, apt, fit, suitable.

conicidad, *n.f.* (*geom.*) conicalness.

conicina; conina, *n.f.* (*chem.*) conine.

cónico, -ca, *a.* conical, conic.

conífero, -ra, *a.* coniferous. — *n.f.* conifer.

coniforme, *a.* coniform, conical.

conio, *n.m.* (*bot.*) conium.

conirrostro, -tra, *a.* (*orn.*) having a conical beak.

conivalvo, -va, *a.* (*zool.*) having a conical shell.

coniza, *n.f.* great flea-bane.

conjetura, *n.f.* conjecture, surmise, guess.

conjeturable, *a.* conjecturable.

conjeturador, -ra, *a.* conjecturing, guessing.

conjetural, *a.* conjectural.

conjeturalmente, *adv.* conjecturally, guessingly.

conjeturar, *v.t.* to conjecture, guess; *conjeturar* (*algo*) *de* or *por ciertos indicios,* to surmise (something) by certain signs.

conjuez, *n.m.* brother judge, assistant judge, co-judge.

conjugable, *a.* that may be conjugated.

conjugación, *n.f.* conjugation.

conjugado, -da, *a.* conjugated, inflected; (*math.*) conjugate. — *p.p.* [CONJUGAR].

conjugador, -ra, *a.* conjugating. — *n.m.f.* conjugate.

conjugar, *v.t.* (*gram.*) to conjugate.

conjunción, *n.f.* union, league, association, consolidation; (*astron., gram.*) conjunction.

conjuntamente, *adv.* conjunctly, conjointly.

conjuntivitis, *n.f.* conjunctivitis.

conjuntivo, -va, *a.* (*gram.*) conjunctive, copulative, connective.

conjunto, -ta, *a.* conjunct, united, contiguous; connected, allied by kindred or friendship; mixed, incorporated. — *n.m.* mass; whole; general effect.

conjura, conjuración, *n.f.* conspiracy, plot, machination.

conjurado, -da, *n.m.f., a.* conspirator, conspiratress.

conjurador, *n.m.* conjuror; exorcist; conspirator.

conjuramentar, *v.t.* to conjure, bind by an oath. — *v.r.* to be sworn in, take an oath.

conjurante, *a.* conjuring; conspiring. — *n.m.f.* conjuror; conspirator, conspiratress.

conjurar, *v.i.* to conjure, bind by oath; to conspire, plot. — *v.t.* to conjure, summon in a sacred name; to entreat, implore; (*fig.*) to avert, warn off. — *v.r.* to bind oneself by oath; to conspire together.

conjuro, *n.m.* conjuration; exorcism; incantation; entreaty.

conllevador, -ra, *a.* assisting, helping. — *n.m.f.* helper, assistant.

conllevar, *v.t.* to aid, assist, support; to bear with, endure.

conmemorable, *a.* commemorable.

conmemoración, *n.f.* remembrance, anniversary, commemoration, public celebration.

conmemorador, -ra; conmemorante, *a.* commemorating. — *n.m.f.* commemorator.

conmemorar, *v.t.* to commemorate.

conmemorativo, -va, *a.* commemorative.

conmemoratorio, -ria, *a.* commemorative.

conmensal, *n.m.* commensal, mate, messmate, fellow-boarder.

conmensalía, *n.f.* commensality.

conmensurabilidad, *n.f.* commensurability.

conmensurable, *a.* commensurable.

conmensuración, *n.f.* commensuration.

conmensurar, *v.t.* to measure equally, in proportion.

conmensurativo, -va, *a.* serving to measure equally.

conmigo, *ablative, pers. pron. m. & f.* with me, with myself.

conmilitón, *n.m.* comrade; fellow-soldier.

conminación, *n.f.* commination, threat.

conminador, -ra, *n.m.f.* threatener.

conminar, *v.t.* to comminate, threaten; (*law*) to denounce.

conminativo, -va, *a.* threatening.

conminatorio, -ria, *a.* comminatory. — *n.f.* threatening order.

conmiseración, *n.f.* commiseration, pity, compassion, sympathy.

conmistión; conmistura; conmixtion, *n.f.* commixion, commixture.

conmisto, -ta; conmixto, -ta, *a.* mixed, mingled.

conmoción, *n.f.* commotion, stir; concussion; excitement, flurry, fretting; disturbance, convulsion.

conmonitorio, *n.m.* written narration of an event; (*law*) reminder to subordinate judge.

conmovedor, -ra, *a.* disturbing, fretting, affecting, harrowing, moving.

conmover, *v.t.* (*pres. indic.* **conmuevo;** *pres. subj.* **conmueva**) to disturb, agitate; to affect, move to pity. — *v.r.* to be affected, moved, disturbed, agitated, stirred.

conmutabilidad, *n.f.* commutability.

conmutable, *a.* commutable.

conmutación, *n.f.* commutation, exchange.

conmutador, -ra, *a.* commutating. — *n.m.* (*elec.*) commutator.

conmutar, *v.t.* to commute, exchange, barter; *conmutar una cosa con* or *por otra,* to exchange one thing for another; *conmutar una pena en otra,* to commute one penalty for another.

conmutativo, -va, *a.* commutative.

conmutatriz, *n.f.* apparatus for converting alternating current to direct current or vice-versa.

connato, -ta, *a.* (*bot.*) connate.

connatural, *a.* connatural, inborn.

connaturalidad, *n.f.* inherency.

connaturalización, *n.f.* naturalization.

connaturalizarse, *v.r.* to accustom oneself, become inured or acclimatized.

connaturalmente, *adv.* connaturally.

connivencia, *n.f.* connivance; plotting.

connotación, *n.f.* connotation; distant relationship.

connotado, *n.m.* relationship, kindred. — *p.p.* [CONNOTAR] connoted.
connotante, *a.* connoting.
connotar, *v.t.* to connote; (*gram.*) to imply.
connotativo, -va, *a.* (*gram.*) connotative.
connovicio, -cia, *n.m.f.* (*eccles.*) fellow-novice.
connubial, *a.* connubial, matrimonial.
connubio, *n.m.* (*poet.*) matrimony, marriage, wedlock.
connumerar, *v.t.* to enumerate, include in a number.
cono, *n.m.* (*bot.*, *geom.*) cone.
conocedor, -ra, *a.* skilled, expert. — *n.m.f.* connoisseur, judge, critic. — *n.m.* (*prov.*) chief, herdsman.
conocencia, *n.f.* (*law*) confession.
conocer, *v.t.* (*pres. indic.* conozco; *pres. subj.* conozca) to know, be acquainted with; to perceive, comprehend, experience, observe, conjecture; (*fig.*) to know carnally. — *v.r.* to know each other; to appreciate one's own good or bad qualities; *antes que conozcas, ni alabes ni cohondas*, never praise or censure anyone before knowing him; *conocer a otro*, to know someone; *conocer de vista*, to know by sight; *conocer de or en tal asunto*, to be experienced in a certain matter; *conocer por su fama*, to know by repute; *conocer el terreno que pisa*, to mind one's P's and Q's; *conocerle el juego* or *la trampa*, to see through another's designs; *conocer de una causa* or *un pleito*, said of the judge who tries a lawsuit; *dar a conocer*, to introduce, make known; *darse a conocer*, to make oneself known; *quien no te conozca que te compre*, once bit, twice shy, or you won't catch me again.
conocible, *a.* cognoscible, cognizable, knowable.
conocidamente, *adv.* evidently, clearly.
conocido, -da, *a.* known; eminent, well-known. — *n.m.f.* acquaintance. — *p.p.* [CONOCER].
conocimiento, *n.m.* knowledge, skill, comprehension, understanding, mastership, cleverness, cognition, notice, experience; consciousness, sense; slight friendship, acquaintance; (*com.*) note of hand; (*law*) cognizance; *conocimiento de embarque*, (*com.*) bill of lading; receipt, acknowledgment; (*pl.*) science, knowledge, learning; *venir en conocimiento*, to recollect a thing distinctly.
conopeo, *n.m.* canopy.
conopial, *a.* (*arch.*) relating to a canopy; *arco conopial*, ogee arch.
conozco; conozca, *pres. indic.; pres. subj.* [CONOCER].
conque, *conj.* so there; now then; well then. — *n.m.* (*coll.*) condition, circumstance.
conquiforme, *a.* conchiform.
conquilifero, -ra, *a.* [CONCHIFERO].
conquiliología, *n.f.* conchology.
conquiliológico, -ca, *a.* conchological.
conquiliólogo, -ga, *n.m.f.* conchologist.
conquista, *n.f.* conquest, subjection, acquisition by victory, thing gained; winning another's affections.
conquistable, *a.* conquerable; attainable, accessible.
conquistador, -ra, *a.* conquering. — *n.m.f.* conqueror, victress; conquistador.
conquistar, *v.t.* to conquer, overcome, subdue; to acquire, win another's affections.

conrear, *v.t.* to grease wool; (*agric.*) to hoe the soil; to treat or apply a particular process to (land, cloth, etc.).
conregnante, *a.* co-regent.
conreinar, *v.i.* to reign with another.
conreo, *n.m.* application of particular process (to land, etc.).
consabido, -da, *a.* already known, alluded to, beforementioned, aforesaid.
consabidor, -ra, *n.m.f.* one possessing knowledge jointly with others.
consagrable, *a.* consecratable.
consagración, *n.f.* consecration.
consagrado, -da, *a.* consecrate, consecrated, sacred; (*fig.*) devoted. — *p.p.* [CONSAGRAR].
consagrante, *a.* consecrating, consecrative. — *n.m.* consecrator.
consagrar, *v.t.* to consecrate, hallow, make sacred; to deify; to devote; (*fig.*) to dedicate; to erect (a monument). — *v.r.* (with *a*) to devote oneself to.
consanguíneo, -nea, *a.* consanguineous, cognate, kindred. — *n.m.f.* kin, blood relation; half-brother (sister) by the same father.
consanguinidad, *n.f.* consanguinity.
consciente, *a.* conscious, of sound mind.
conscientemente, *adv.* consciously.
conscripción, *n.f.* (*mil.*) conscription.
consectario, *a.* consecutive, consequent; belonging to the same sect. — *n.m.f.* co-religionist. — *n.m.* consectary, corollary.
consecución, *n.f.* attainment, acquisition.
consecuencia, *n.f.* consequence, conclusion, issue; inference; *en consecuencia*, consequently, therefore; *guardar consecuencia*, to be consistent; *por consecuencia*, therefore; *ser de consecuencia*, to be important; *tener* or *traer consecuencias*, to entail consequences; *traer a consecuencia*, to consider, weigh up; *traer en consecuencia*, to adduce.
consecuencial, *a.* consequential, resulting indirectly.
consecuente, *a.* consequent, coherent, consistent, following. — *n.m.* consequence, (*math.*) consequent.
consecuentemente, *adv.* consequently, in consequence, necessarily, inevitably.
consecutivamente, *adv.* consecutively.
consecutivo, -va, *a.* consecutive.
conseguimiento, *n.m.* attainment, obtainment.
conseguir, *v.t.* (*pres. indic.* consigo; *pres. subj.* consiga) to attain, get, gain, obtain.
conseja, *n.f.* fable, story, fairy-tale; illegal assembly; *el lobo está en la conseja*, a wolf in sheep's clothing.
consejera, *n.f.* counsellor's wife; woman adviser.
consejero, *n.m.* counsellor, adviser, member of a council; (*fig.*) warning; *consejero de la corona*, minister of the crown.
consejo, *n.m.* counsel, advice, monition; council, court; council-house; advisory board, consulting body; *consejo de familia*, (*law*) family council; *consejo de guerra*, court-martial; council of war; *consejo de ministros*, cabinet council; *entrar en consejo*, consult or confer as to what should be done; *presidente del consejo de ministros*, Prime Minister; *tomar consejo de*, to take counsel of, consult; *quien no oye consejo, no llega a viejo*, prudent men listen to others' counsel.

consenso, *n.m.* consensus, general assent.

consentido, -da, *a.* spoiled (child); willing (cuckold); allowed, permitted. — *p.p.* [CONSENTIR].

consentidor, -ra, *a.* consenting, conniving. — *n.m.f.* complier, conniver.

consentimiento, *n.m.* consent, connivance, compliance, acquiescence, concurrence; pampering, coddling; *por consentimiento,* (*med.*) by consensus.

consentir, *v.t.* (*pres. indic.* **consiento;** *pres. subj.* **consienta**) to consent, agree, allow, comply, acquiesce, permit, tolerate, accede, condescend; to believe for certain, rely, depend; to accept, admit, suffer, concur; to coddle, spoil, over-indulge, pamper. — *v.i.* (*mech.*) to relax, weaken, become loose, give way, flag. — *v.r.* to crack, spring, begin to break; *consentir con los caprichos,* to give way to whims; *consentir en algo,* to consent, agree to something.

conserje, *n.m.* keeper, warden; concierge, caretaker, janitor.

conserjería, *n.f.* janitorship, wardenship; warden's dwelling, janitor's office.

conserva, *n.f.* conserve, preserve jam, marmalade; pickles; fleet of merchantmen under convoy; *conservas alimenticias,* canned goods; *conserva trojezada,* jam, marmalade; *navegar en conserva,* to sail under convoy.

conservable, *a.* conservable, preservable.

conservación, *n.f.* conservation, preservation.

conservador, *a.* conserving, preserving. — *n.m.f.* conserver, preserver, (*polit.*) conservative. — *n.m.* conservator; *juez conservador,* (*eccles.*) person appointed to defend the rights of a community.

conservaduría, *n.f.* guardianship; dignity in the Order of Malta.

conservante, *a.* conserving, preserving.

conservar, *v.t.* to conserve, preserve, maintain; to guard, keep, hold, take care of, observe; to candy, can or pickle goods. — *v.r.* to last, keep; *conservarse con salud,* to keep in good health; *conservarse en su opinión,* to maintain one's opinion.

conservativo, -va, *a.* conserving, preservative.

conservatoría, *n.f.* place or office of a *juez conservador;* also privilege or exemption issued by him.

conservatorio, -ria, *a.* conserving, preservative.—*n.m.* conservatoire, place of instruction in the fine arts.

conservería, *n.f.* art of preserve-making or canning; cannery, place where canned goods are made or sold.

conservero, -ra, *a.* preparer of conserves.

considerable, *a.* considerable; important; large.

considerablemente, *adv.* considerably.

consideración, *n.f.* consideration, regard, notice, sake, account; reflection, contemplation, meditation, circumspection; importance, claim to notice, worthiness of regard; urbanity, respect; *en consideración,* considering, in consideration; *ser de consideración,* to be of great moment; *tomar en consideración,* to consider worthy of attention.

consideradamente, *adv.* considerately; calmly, with consideration.

considerado, -da, *a.* considered, examined; prudent, thoughtful; considerate, circumspect; esteemed, respected, distinguished. — *p.p.* [CONSIDERAR].

considerador, -ra, *a.* considering. — *n.m.f.* one who considers.

considerando, *n.m.* (*law*)whereas; each of the principal arguments in the preamble of the text of a law, edict, etc.; reason, reasoning.

considerante, *a.* considering.

considerar, *v.t.* to consider, think over, cogitate, meditate; to judge, estimate; to treat with consideration or respect; *considerar un asunto bajo* or *en todos sus aspectos,* to consider a matter in all its aspects; *considerar por todos lados,* to consider all round.

consiento; consienta, *pres. indic.; pres. subj.* [CONSENTIR].

consiervo, *n.m.* fellow-slave.

consigna, *n.f.* (*mil.*) watchword, countersign.

consignación, *n.f.* consignation, apportionment, consignment, cargo.

consignador, *n.m.* (*com.*) consignor.

consignar, *v.t.* to assign, set apart; to deposit; to countersign, ratify; (*com.*) to consign (goods); (*law*) to deposit in trust.

consignatario, *n.m.* (*law*) trustee, mortgagee; (*com.*) consignee.

consigo, *pers. pron.* with oneself, with himself, herself, themselves, yourself, yourselves; *consigo mismo, propio* or *solo,* by oneself.

consigo; consiga, *pres. indic.; pres. subj.* [CONSEGUIR].

consiguiente, *a.* consequent, consequential, consecutive. — *n.m.* (*log.*) consequent; consequence, result; *de* (or *por el*) *consiguiente,* consequently, pursuantly; *ir* or *proceder consiguiente,* to act in accordance with prearranged principles.

consiguientemente, *adv.* consequently.

consiliario, -ria, *n.m.f.* adviser; counsellor to heads of associations.

consintiente, *a.* consenting, agreeing.

consistencia, *n.f.* consistence, consistency; firmness, solidity; duration, stability; coherence, cohesion; conformity.

consistente, *a.* firm, solid.

consistir, *v.i.* (with *en*) to consist, be founded or constituted in; to be the effect of; to be comprised or contained in.

consistorial, *a.* consistorial; *casa consistorial,* senate house, court-house, town-hall, guildhall.

consistorialmente, *adv.* in or by consistory.

consistorio, *n.m.* (*eccles.*) consistory; municipal council; *consistorio divino,* tribunal of God.

consocio, -cia, *n.m.f.* consociate, partner, companion, fellow, associate.

consol, *n.m.* (*Per.*) [CONSOLA].

consola, *n.f.* console-table, pier-table.

consolable, *a.* consolable, relievable.

consolablemente, *adv.* consolatorily, cheeringly.

consolación, *n.f.* consolation, comfort; forfeit (at cards).

consolador, -ra, *a.* consolatory, comforting. — *n.m.f.* consoler, comforter.

consolante, *a.* comforting, consoling, soothing.

consolar, *v.t.* (*pres. indic.* **consuelo;** *pres. subj.* **consuele**) to console, comfort, reanimate, cheer, soothe. — *v.r.* to become resigned, comforted; to console, solace oneself; *con-*

solar a alguien en su dolor, to console someone in his sorrow; *consolarse en Dios*, to find
consolation in God; *consolarse con su suerte*,
to be resigned to one's fate.
consolativo, -va; consolatorio, -ria, *a.*
consolatory, comforting.
consólida, *n.f.* comfrey; *consólida real*, larkspur.
consolidable, *a.* that can be consolidated.
consolidación, *n.f.* consolidation.
consolidado, -da, *a.* consolidated. — *n.m.*
consolidated fund. — *p.p.* [CONSOLIDAR].
consolidar, *v.t.* to consolidate, compact; to
harden, strengthen; to fund (debts). — *v.r.*
to consolidate, grow firm, hard or solid;
(*law*) to unite.
consolidativo, -va, *a.* consolidating, con-
solidatory.
consonancia, *n.f.* consonance, harmony;
assonance; rhyme; conformity, consistency,
congruency, consent.
consonante, *a.* consonant, concordant, consistent, conformable; rhyming. — *n.m.* rime,
rhyme; (*mus.*) consonous or corresponding
sound. — *n.f.* (*gram.*) consonant.
consonantemente, *adv.* consonantly, agreeably.
consonar, *v.i.* (*pres. indic.* **consueno**; *pres.
subj.* **consuene**) to harmonize; to rhyme; to
agree, conform, fit with one another.
cónsone, *a.* concordant; consonous. — *n.m.*
chord.
cónsono, -na, *a.* consonous; consonant, harmonious.
consorcio, *n.m.* companionship, partnership;
marital union.
consorte, *n.m.f.* consort; husband, wife; mate;
companion. — *pl.* (*law*) accomplices, con-
federates; associates, joint-parties to a lawsuit.
conspicuo, -cua, *a.* conspicuous, obvious;
eminent, famous, distinguished, notorious.
conspiración, *n.f.* conspiracy, plot.
conspirador, -ra, *n.m.f.* conspirator, plotter,
traitor.
conspirar, *v.i.* to conspire, plot, agree together, co-operate; (*fig.*) to concur.
constancia, *n.f.* constancy, immutability,
perseverance, steadiness.
constante, *a.* constant, firm, unalterable,
persevering, loyal; manifest, apparent, clear;
consisting in, composed of; *constante en la
amistad*, steadfast in friendship. — *n.f.*, *a.*
(*math.*) constant.
constantemente, *adv.* constantly; firmly,
evidently, undoubtedly; unalterably.
constantinopolitano, -na, *n.m.f.*, *a.* native of
or pertaining to Constantinople.
constar, *v. impers.* to be clear, evident, certain;
to be composed of; to consist in; (*poet.*) to
be in metre; to be recorded, registered,
entered; *constar por escrito*, to be in writing,
written down; *el libro consta de tres partes*,
the book consists of three parts; *constar en las
actas*, to be recorded in the minutes; *me
consta que Juan lo hizo*, I know for certain
that John did it.
constelación, *n.f.* constellation; climate,
temperature; *correr una constelación*, an
epidemic prevails.
consternación, *n.f.* consternation, amazement,
horror, panic, dismay.

consternar, *v.t.* to consternate, terrify, confound. — *v.r.* to be dismayed.
constipación, *n.f.* cold, chill; *constipación de
vientre*, constipation, costiveness.
constipado, -da, *p.p.* [CONSTIPAR] chilled,
suffering from cold. — *n.m.* cold, chill,
catarrh.
constipar, *v.t.* to cause a cold, give one a cold;
to obstruct perspiration. — *v.r.* to catch cold.
constipativo, -va, *a.* constrictive.
constitución, *n.f.* constitution; composition;
temper, temperament; peculiar structure;
statutes, by-laws.
constitucional, *a.* constitutional. — *n.m.* constitutionalist.
constitucionalidad, *n.f.* constitutionality.
constitucionalismo, *n.m.* constitutionalism.
constitucionalmente, *adv.* constitutionally.
constituidor, -ra, *a.* constituting, establishing.
— *n.m.f.* constitutor.
constituir, *v.t.* (*pres. indic.* **constituyo**; *pres.
subj.* **constituya**) to constitute, form, compose; (with *en apuro* or *obligación*) to impose,
enjoin, compel; to establish, arrange; to give
a definite quality or condition. — *v.r.* (with
en or *por*) to constitute oneself as; to bind
oneself to; to be responsible for.
constitutivo, -va, *a.* constitutive. — *n.m.*
constitutor.
constituyente, *a.* constituting, constituent. —
n.f.pl. Cortes constituyentes, constitutional
assembly.
constreñidamente, *adv.* compulsively, compulsorily.
constreñimiento, *n.m.* constraint, compulsion.
constreñir, *v.t.* (*pres. indic.* **constriño**; *pres.
subj.* **constriña**) to constrain, compel, force;
(*med.*) to bind, make costive.
constricción, *n.f.* constriction, contraction.
constrictivo, -va, *a.* (*med.*) binding, astringent; constrictive, constringent.
constrictor, -ra, *a.* constrictive. — *n.m.* (*med.*)
constrictor.
constringente, *a.* constringent.
constriño; constriña, *pres. indic.*; *pres. subj.*
[CONSTREÑIR].
construcción, *n.f.* construction, building,
fabrication; edifice, structure; shipbuilding,
naval architecture; interpretation; (*gram.*)
syntax.
constructor, -ra, *a.* constructing, constructive. — *n.m.f.* builder, constructor, framer,
fabricator, maker; *constructor de buques*,
ship-builder.
construir, *v.t.* (*pres. indic.* **construyo**; *pres.
subj.* **construya**) to form, build, frame,
fabricate, construct; to translate literally
Latin or Greek to Castilian, construe.
construpador, *n.m.* debaucher, defiler, corrupter.
construpar, *v.t.* to ravish, defile.
consubstanciación, *n.f.* consubstantiation.
consubstancial, *a.* consubstantial.
consubstancialidad, *n.f.* consubstantiality.
consuegrar, *v.i.* to become reciprocal fathers-
or mothers-in-law.
consuegro, -gra, *n.m.f.* term of address used
reciprocally by the parents of a married
couple.
consuelda, *n.f.* comfrey.
consuelo, *n.m.* consolation, relief, comfort;

joy, merriment; *sin consuelo*, out of proportion, to excess.

consuelo; consuele, *pres. indic.; pres. subj.*
[CONSOLAR].

consueno; consuene, *pres. indic.; pres. subj.*
[CONSONAR].

consueta, *n.m.* (*theat.*) prompter. — *n.f.*
(*eccles., prov.*) almanac. — *pl.* short prayers.

consuetudinal; consuetudinario, -ria, *a.*
consuetudinary, customary, generally practised; (*eccles.*) habitually sinning.

cónsul, *n.m.* consul; *cónsul general*, consul-
general.

consulado, *n.m.* consulate, consulship.

consular, *a.* consular.

consulta, *n.f.* consultation, conference; question proposed; report in writing; (*med.*)
consulting hours.

consultable, *a.* consultable.

consultación, *n.f.* consultation, conference,
meeting.

consultante, *n.m., a.* consultant.

consultar, *v.t.* to consult; to deliberate; to
take counsel of; to advise; *consultar con la
almohada*, (*coll.*) to sleep on a matter, give it
mature consideration; *consultar con el
bolsillo*, to cut one's coat according to one's
cloth.

consultivamente, *adv.* in consultation, deliberately.

consultivo, -va, *a.* consultative, advisory.

consultor, -ra, *a.* advising, consulting. —
n.m.f. consultant, consulter, consultee; consultor; adviser, counsel, counsellor.

consultorio, *n.m.* information bureau; clinic,
consulting-room, dispensary, surgery.

consumación, *n.f.* consummation, perfection,
finishing, end, completion, accomplishment;
destruction, suppression; *la consumación de
los siglos*, the end of the world.

consumadamente, *adv.* perfectly, consum-
mately, completely.

consumado, -da, *a.* consummated, finished;
consummate, complete, perfect, accomplished, exquisite. — *n.m.* jelly-broth, consommé. — *p.p.* [CONSUMAR].

consumador, -ra, *a.* consummating, con-
summative. — *n.m.f.* consummator.

consumar, *v.t.* to consummate, perfect, finish,
complete.

consumativo, -va, *a.* consummate, consum-
mative.

consumero, *n.m.* (*contempt.*) excise-officer,
exciseman.

consumición, *n.f.* [CONSUMO].

consumido, -da, *a.* consumed; (*coll.*) lean,
meagre, exhausted, spent; (*coll.*) easily
afflicted. — *p.p.* [CONSUMIR].

consumidor, -ra, *a.* destroying. — *n.m.f.*
consumer; destroyer.

consumimiento, *n.m.* consumption, utilization.

consumir, *v.t.* (*p.p.* **consumido** or **consunto**)
to consume; to destroy, extinguish; to eat,
use up; (*coll.*) to afflict, grieve. — *v.i., v.t.*
(*eccles.*) to communicate. — *v.r.* to be consumed, burned, destroyed; to waste away;
to wear out; to fret, pine, be grieved; *consumir el caudal*, to run through one's fortune;
consumirse a fuego lento, to burn away slowly;
consumirse con la fiebre, to waste away
through fever; *consumirse de fastidio*, (*coll.*)

to be bored beyond measure; *consumirse en
meditaciones*, to be lost in meditation.

consumo, *n.m.* consumption of provisions
and merchandise. — *pl.* municipal excise-
duty.

consunción, *n.f.* consumption, decline, waste;
phthisis, tuberculosis.

consuno, *adv.; de consuno*, jointly, unanimously.

consuntivo, -va, *a.* consuming, consumptive.

consunto, -ta, *p.p. irreg.* [CONSUMIR].

consustancial, *a.* consubstantial.

consustancialidad, *n.f.* consubstantiality.

contabilidad, *n.f.* book-keeping, art of keeping accounts, accounting; calculability.

contable, *n.m.* accountant.

contacto, *n.m.* contact, touch, union, impact.

contadero, -ra, *a.* countable, numerable. —
n.m. narrow passage where sheep are
counted; *entrar* or *salir por el contadero*, to
go in or out through a very narrow passage.

contado, -da, *a.* counted; scarce, rare, infrequent, uncommon; distinguished, noted. —
p.p. [CONTAR]; *al contado*, with ready money,
for cash; *de contado*, instantly, immediately,
in hand; *por de contado*, certainly, of course;
contadas veces, rarely.

contador, -ra, *a.* counting. — *n.m.f.* book-
keeper, accountant, auditor, cashier. — *n.m.*
official receiver; counter, desk; compto-
meter; meter (for gas, etc.); automatic
counter; cash register.

contaduría, *n.f.* accountantship, accountancy;
counting-house; auditorship; cashier's office;
(*theat.*) box-office.

contagiar, *v.t.* to infect, spread by contagion,
communicate disease; to corrupt, pervert.
— *v.r.* to become infected, perverted; *contagiarse con el, del* or *por el roce*, to become
infected by contact.

contagio, *n.m.;* **contagión,** *n.f.* contagion,
infection; contagious disease; contagium;
corruption, perversion.

contagiosamente, *adv.* in a contagious
manner.

contagiosidad, *n.f.* contagiousness.

contagioso, -sa, *a.* contagious, malign; (*fig.*)
infectious, perverting.

contal, *n.m.* string of beads for counting.

contaminable, *a.* contaminable.

contaminación, *n.f.* contamination, pollution; defilement, blot, stain.

contaminado, -da, *a.* contaminated, polluted, defiled. — *p.p.* [CONTAMINAR].

contaminador, -ra, *a.* contaminating, con-
taminative.

contaminar, *v.t.* to contaminate, pollute,
infect, stain, corrupt; to profane, vitiate,
violate; to destroy the integrity of an
original text. — *v.r.* (with *con* or *de*) to be
corrupted, become infected by.

contante, *a.; dinero contante y sonante*, ready
money, cash; ready coin.

contar, *v.t.* (*pres. indic.* **cuento;** *pres. subj.*
cuente) to count, reckon, number, compute,
enumerate; to relate, tell, narrate; to book,
charge to an account; to class, rate, range;
to consider, look (upon); (with *con*) to depend, rely, reckon (on). — *v.i.* to calculate;
contar por hecha una cosa, to consider a thing
as though it had been done; *cuéntaselo a su
abuela* or *a su tía!* tell that to your grand-

mother or to the marines!; *no ser bien contada una cosa*, to have bad results; *contarle las pisadas a uno*, to watch someone zealously; *contar cuentos*, to relate, tell stories; *contar por verdadero*, to relate as true.

contemperante, *a.* temperate, tempering, moderating.

contemperar, *v.t.* to temper, moderate.

contemplación, *n.f.* contemplation, meditation; compliance, complaisance.

contemplado, -da, *a.* spoiled, pampered; studied, contemplated. — *p.p.* [CONTEMPLAR].

contemplador, -ra, *a.* contemplating, contemplative. — *n.m.f.* contemplator.

contemplar, *v.t., v.i.* to contemplate, study; to meditate, muse; to assent, flatter, condescend; to be lenient, coddle, pamper; *contemplar en Dios*, to meditate on God.

contemplativamente, *adv.* attentively, thoughtfully, contemplatively.

contemplativo, -va, *a.* contemplative, studious, meditative; lenient, condescending.

contemporaneamente, *adv.* contemporaneously, at the same time.

contemporaneidad, *n.f.* contemporaneousness, contemporaneity.

contemporáneo, -nea, *a.* contemporaneous, coeval, contemporary. — *n.m.f.* contemporary.

contemporización, *n.f.;* **contemporizamiento**, *n.m.* temporization, compliance.

contemporizador, -ra, *a.* complying, temporizing. — *n.m.f.* complier, temporizer.

contemporizar, *v.i.* (*pret.* **contemporicé**; *pres. subj.* **contemporice**) to temporize, comply.

contención, *n.f.* check, curb; (*law*) contention, emulation, contest; dispute, strife, struggle.

contenciosamente, *adv.* contentiously, contestingly.

contencioso, -sa, *a.* contentious, quarrelsome, litigious, contradictive, disputatious.

contendedor, *n.m.* contender, antagonist.

contender, *v.i.* (*pres. indic.* **contiendo**; *pres. subj.* **contienda**) to contend, fight, strive, combat; to contest, conflict, debate, litigate; to discuss, argue, expostulate; *contender en caballerosidad*, to compete in gentlemanliness; *contender por las armas*, to contest, fight with weapons; *contender sobre alguna cosa*, to contend over something.

contendiente, *n.m.f., a.* a disputant, litigant.

contendor, *n.m.* contender, antagonist.

contenedor, -ra, *a.* containing, holding. — *n.m.f.* holder, container, receptacle.

contenencia, *n.f.* suspension in the flight of birds; a movement in the Spanish dance; *contenencia a la demanda*, (*obs. law*) demurer.

contener, *v.t.* (*pres. indic.* **contengo**; *pret.* **contuve**; *pres. subj.* **contenga**) to comprise, contain, hold, embrace, enclose, comprehend; (*fig.*) to refrain, curb, restrain, coerce, repress; to detain, check, stop. — *v.r.* to keep one's temper, hold oneself in check; *como en ello se contiene*, exactly as said; *contenerse en sus deseos*, to curb, repress one's desires.

contenido, -da, *a.* contained; moderate, prudent, temperate, modest. — *n.m.* contents, context, tenor, enclosure. — *p.p.* [CONTENER].

conteniente, *a.* containing, comprising.

contenta, *n.f.* satisfactory gift, present; (*mil., naut.*) certificate of good conduct; (*com.*) endorsement.

contentadizo, -za, *a.* acquiescent; *bien contentadizo*, easily contented; *mal contentadizo*, hard to please.

contentamiento, *n.m.* contentment, joy, satisfaction.

contentar, *v.t.* to content, please, gratify, satisfy; (*com.*) to endorse; *ser de buen* or *mal contentar*, to be easily or not easily pleased. — *v.r.* to be contented, satisfied, pleased; *contentarse con el olor*, to be satisfied with little; *contentarse con su suerte*, to be contented with one's lot; *contentarse del parecer*, to be satisfied with the opinion; *contentarse a medias*, to be only half-satisfied.

contentible, *a.* contemptible.

contentivo, -va, *a.* containing, comprising; (*surg.*) covering, binding (bandages).

contento, -ta, *a.* glad, pleased, satisfied, contented, full of joy, mirthful. — *n.m.* contentment, joy, mirth, pleasure, satisfaction; (*law*) discharge, release (of debt); *a contento*, to one's satisfaction; *no caber de contento*, to be overjoyed.

contera, *n.f.* chape (of a scabbard); button of the cascabel of a gun; ferrule (of an umbrella or walking-stick); refrain (of song); end, completion; *echar la contera*, to finish, end, terminate; *por contera*, ultimately, finally; *temblarle a uno la contera*, to feel terrified.

contérmino, -na, *a.* conterminous, contiguous, bordering upon.

conterráneo, -nea, *a.* compatriotic. — *n.m.f.* countryman, countrywoman.

contertuliano, -na; contertulio, -lia, *n.m.f.* one belonging to the same social set or circle.

contestable, *a.* contestable, disputable, controvertible.

contestación, *n.f.* answer, reply; contestation, debate, strife, altercation, disputation, contention; *contestación a la demanda*, (*law*) demurrer; *sin contestación*, incontestably, indisputably.

contestar, *v.t.* to answer, reply; to confirm; to prove, attest; to plead to an action. — *v.i.* to accord, agree; *contestar una carta*, to reply to a letter; *contestar a la pregunta*, to answer the question; *contestar con mucho aire*, to reply impertinently; *contestar en el mismo tono*, to answer in the same tone.

conteste, *a.* (*law*) confirming the evidence of another witness.

contexto, *n.m.* contexture; context of a discourse.

contextuar, *v.t.* to prove textually.

contextura, *n.f.* contexture; context; frame and structure of the human body.

conticinio, *n.m.* dead of night.

contienda, *n.f.* contest, dispute, debate, conflict, contention, strife, fray, struggle, fight, jarring, clashing.

contiendo; contienda, *pres. indic.; pres. subj.* [CONTENDER].

contignación, *n.f.* floor-boards; lath-work (of ceiling).

contigo, *pron.* with thee; *contigo pan y cebolla*, anything will do as long as I am with you.

contiguamente, *adv.* contiguously.

contigüidad, *n.f.* contiguity, proximity.

contiguo, -gua, *a.* contiguous, close, adjacent; *contiguo al jardín,* next to the garden.

continencia, *n.f.* continence, abstinence, moderation; graceful bow in a dance; capacity, action of containing.

continental, *a.* continental.

continente, *a.* containing; continent, chaste, abstinent, moderate, abstemious. — *n.m.* container; continent, mainland; countenance, air, gait, mien.

continentemente, *adv.* moderately, abstemiously, chastely, continently.

contingencia, *n.f.* contingent, contingency, possibility, risk.

contingente, *a.* contingent, fortuitous, accidental. — *n.m.* contingent, quota, share; contingency.

contingentemente, *adv.* casually, contingently, accidentally.

contingible, *a.* that may happen, possible.

continuación, *n.f.* continuation, continuity, uninterrupted connexion, continuance, stay; protraction, lengthening.

continuadamente, *adv.* continually, uninterruptedly, continuously.

continuador, -ra, *a.* continuing. — *n.m.f.* continuer, continuator.

continuamente, *adv.* continually, incessantly.

continuar, *v.t.* to continue, pursue, protract. — *v.i.* to endure, last, remain. — *v.r.* to go on, continue, extend; *continuar en su puesto,* to remain at his post; *continuar con salud,* to keep in good health; *continuar por buen camino,* to keep on the right road.

continuativo, -va, *a.* implying continuation.

continuidad, *n.f.* continuity, cohesion.

continuo, -nua, *a.* continuate, continuous, continual; continuant, constant, lasting; persevering. — *n.m.* whole, composition of united parts; yeoman of the guard; *a la continua, de continuo,* continually, continuously.

contonearse, *v.r.* to strut, waddle.

contoneo, *n.m.* waddle, waddling.

contorcerse, *v.r.* (*pres. indic.* **me contuerzo;** *pres. subj.* **me contuerza**) to contort, twist, writhe one's body.

contorción, *n.f.* contortion; twisting, writhing.

contornado, -da, *a.* contoured; (*her.*) distorted, turned towards the sinister side of the shield. — *p.p.* [CONTORNAR].

contornar, contornear, *v.t.* to contour, outline; to go or wind round (a place).

contorneado, -da, *a.* (*bot.*) convoluted; contoured, outlined. — *p.p.* [CONTORNEARSE].

contorneo, *n.m.* turning, winding; contouring, outlining.

contorno, *n.m.* environs, vicinity, contour, outline; *en contorno,* round about.

contorsión, *n.f.* contortion, twist; grimace, wry motion, queer gesture.

contorsionista, *n.m.f.* acrobat, contortionist.

contra, *prep.* contra, against, contrary to, opposite to, counter, in opposition to, athwart. — *n.m.* opposite, opposite sense; (*mus.*) organ-pedal. — *pl.* organ-pipes forming lowest bass. — *n.f.* (*coll.*) difficulty, obstacle; counter (in fencing); *en contra de,* against, in opposition to; *hacer* or *llevar la contra,* to go counter, run counter; *el pro y el contra,* the pros and cons.

contraabertura, *n.f.* (*surg.*) counter-opening.

contraabrir, *v.t.* (*surg.*) to make a counter-opening.

contraábside, *n.m.* western apsis.

contraaletas, *n.f.pl.* (*naut.*) counter-fashion pieces.

contraalmirante, *n.m.* rear-admiral.

contraalmohadón, *n.m.* (*arch.*) voussoir on coussinet.

contraamantillos, *n.m.pl.* (*naut.*) preventer-lifts, counter-braces.

contraamura, *n.f.* (*naut.*) preventer-tack.

contraaproches, *n.m.pl.* (*fort.*) counter-approaches.

contraarmiños, *n.m.pl.* (*her.*) black field with white spots.

contraataguía, *n.f.* second or reinforcing coffer-dam.

contraataque, *n.m.* counter-attack. — *pl.* counter-approaches.

contraaviso, *n.m.* counter-advice.

contrabajo, *n.m.* double-bass; bass (voice and singer).

contrabalancear, *v.t.* to counterbalance, counterpoise; (*fig.*) to compensate.

contrabalanceo, *n.m.* counterbalancing.

contrabalanza, *n.f.* counterbalance, counterpoise.

contrabanda, *n.f.* (*her.*) band sinister.

contrabandear, *v.i.* to engage in contraband.

contrabandista, *a.* smuggling. — *n.m.f.* smuggler, contrabandist.

contrabando, *n.m.* contraband trade, smuggling; prohibited commodity; *contrabando de guerra,* contraband of war; *ir* or *venir de contrabando,* to go or come by stealth.

contrabarrado, -da, *a.* (*her.*) counter-barred shield.

contrabarrera, *n.f.* second row of seats in the inner barrier in a bull-ring.

contrabasa, *n.f.* pedestal.

contrabatería, *n.f.* (*mil.*) counter-battery.

contrabatir, *v.t.* to fire upon the enemy's batteries.

contrabolina, *n.f.* (*naut.*) preventer-bowline.

contrabracear, *v.t.* (*naut.*) to counter-brace.

contrabranque, *n.m.* (*naut.*) stemson.

contrabraza, *n.f.* (*naut.*) preventer-brace.

contrabrazola, *n.f.* (*naut.*) coaming (of a scuttle).

contracaja, *n.f.* (*print.*) right-hand upper.

contracalcar, *v.t.* to trace the reversed impression of a drawing.

contracambiada, *n.f.* changing of the forefoot by a horse.

contracambio, *n.m.* (*com.*) re-exchange; *en contracambio,* in exchange.

contracanal, *n.m.* counter-channel; branch trench or canal.

contracandela, *n.f.* (*Cub.*) back-fire made to prevent the spread of a forest fire.

contracarrera, *n.f.* reinforcement to joist or girder.

contracarril, *n.m.* check-rail, guard-rail, safety-rail.

contracarta, *n.f.* [CONTRAESCRITURA].

contracción, *n.f.* contraction, shrivelling, shrinking, constriction, corrugation; abbreviation, abridgement; (*gram.*) synæresis.

contracebadera, *n.f.* sprit-topsail.

contracédula, *n.f.* counter-decree.

contracifra, *n.f.* cipher-key.

contraclave, *n.f.* (*arch.*) voussoir next to key-stone.

contracodaste, *n.m.* (*naut.*) inner stern-post.

contracorriente, *n.f.* (*meteor.*) reverse current.

contracosta, *n.f.* coast opposite another.

contracostado, *n.m.* (*naut.*) sheathing.

contracruz, *n.f.* (*naut.*) spilling-line.

contractable, *a.* contractible.

contráctil, *a.* contractile, contractible.

contractilidad, *n.f.* contractility, contractibility.

contractivo, -va, *a.* contractive.

contracto, -ta, *p.p. irreg.* [CONTRAER].

contractual, *a.* contractual.

contractura, *n.f.* (*med.*) persistent contraction of muscles; (*arch.*) upward diminution of column's diameter.

contracuartel, *n.m.* (*her.*) quarter.

contracuartelado, -da, *a.* (*her.*) having the quarters opposed in colour or metal.

contracuerdas, *n.f.pl.* (*naut.*) outward deck-planks.

contracurva, *n.f.* (*railw.*) reversed curved rail.

contradancista, *n.m.f.* dancer of country-dance.

contradanza, *n.f.* quadrille, cotillon, cotillion.

contradecir, *v.t.* (*p.p.* **contradicho;** *pres. indic.* **contradigo;** *pret.* **contradije;** *fut.* **contradiré;** *pres. subj.* **contradiga**) to contradict, gainsay. — *v.r.* to contradict oneself, be inconsistent.

contradenuncia, *n.f.* (*law*) counter-claim.

contradicción, *n.f.* contradiction, gainsaying, opposition; controversy, clashing, resistance; inconsistency, incongruity; *espíritu de contradicción,* contradictory temper, contradictiousness.

contradictor, -ra, *a.* contradictive. — *n.m.f.* contradictor.

contradictoria, *n.f.* (*log.*) contradictory.

contradictoriamente, *adv.* contradictorily.

contradictorio, -ria, *a.* contradictory.

contradicho, -cha, *p.p. irreg.* [CONTRADECIR] contradicted.

contradigo; contradiga; contradije, *pres. indic.; pres. subj.; pret.* [CONTRADECIR].

contradique, *n.m.* embankment or dike for strengthening another.

contradriza, *n.f.* (*naut.*) second halliard.

contradurmente; contradurmiente, *n.m.* (*naut.*) clamp.

contraedicto, *n.m.* counter-edict.

contraeje, *n.m.* countershaft.

contraemboscada, *n.f.* counter-ambuscade.

contraembozo, *n.m.* strap of cape.

contraemergente, *a.* (*her.*) counter-salient.

contraendosar, *v.t.* to repass a bill of exchange to the first endorser.

contraendoso, *n.m.* repassing of a bill of exchange to the first endorser.

contraer, *v.t., v.i.* (*p.p.* **contraído** or **contracto, -ta,** *p.p. indic.* **contraigo;** *pret.* **contraje;** *pres. subj.* **contraiga**) to contract, join, tighten, unite; to get, incur, acquire; to abbreviate. — *v.r.* to contract or shrink up (of nerves, etc.); to crumple; to be reduced to an idea or phrase (a discourse); *contraer amistad con alguno,* to make friends with someone; *contraer deudas,* to run into debt; *contraer enfermedad,* to contract a disease; *contraer matrimonio,* to marry.

contraescarpa, *n.f.* counterscarp.

contraescota, *n.f.* (*naut.*) preventer-sheet.

contraescotín, *n.m.* (*naut.*) preventer topsail-sheet.

contraescritura, *n.f.* (*law*) deed revoking a former one.

contraestay, *n.m.* (*naut.*) preventer-stay.

contrafacción, *n.f.* (*Gallicism*) imitation, counterfeit.

contrafactor, *n.m.* counterfeiter.

contrafajado, -da, *a.* (*her.*) having the fillets opposed in colour or metal.

contrafallar, *v.t.* to trump at cards after another.

contrafallo, *n.m.* the act of trumping after another.

contrafianza, *n.f.* indemnity-bond.

contrafigura, *n.f.* (*theat.*) double.

contrafilo, *n.m.* sharp back edge of sword near point.

contraflorado, -da, *a.* (*her.*) having flowers opposed in metal or colour.

contrafoque, *n.m.* fore-top staysail.

contraforjar, *v.t.* to beat iron on the flat and side alternately.

contrafoso, *n.m.* (*theat.*) second cellar under stage; (*fort.*) outer ditch.

contrafuero, *n.m.* infringement of a charter or privilege.

contrafuerte, *n.m.* strap of leather on saddle for securing the cinch; stiffener (in a shoe); (*arch.*) counterfort, abutment, buttress; spur (of mountain); (*fort.*) fort opposite another.

contrafuerzas, *n.f.pl.* opposing forces.

contrafuga, (*mus.*) counterfugue.

contragolpe, *n.m.* (*med.*) effect produced by a blow on a place distinct from the one suffering a contusion.

contraguardia, *n.f.* (*fort.*) counter-guard.

contraguía, *n.f.* near or left-hand mule (of a team).

contrahacedor, -ra, *a.* counterfeiting, imitating. — *n.m.f.* imitator, counterfeiter.

contrahacer, *v.t.* (*p.p.* **contrahecho;** *pres. indic.* **contrahago;** *pret.* **contrahice;** *pres. subj.* **contrahaga**) to counterfeit, mimic, falsify, forge; to imitate, copy; to pirate an author's works. — *v.r.* to feign, dissemble.

contrahaz, *n.f.* wrong side of a piece of cloth.

contrahecho, -cha, *a.* hump-backed, deformed; forged, counterfeit, fictitious. — *p.p.* [CONTRAHACER].

contrahechura, *n.f.* copy, imitation.

contrahierba, *n.f.* a South American medicinal plant used as an antidote.

contrahilera, *n.f.* (*arch.*) second ridge-piece for reinforcing another.

contrahilo, *a.* cross-grain; *a contrahilo,* on the cross (of material).

contrahojas, *n.f.pl.* (*naut.*) dead lights of the cabin.

contrahoradar, *v.t.* to bore on the opposite side.

contrahuella, *n.f.* (*arch.*) rise (of step or stair).

contraído, -da, *p.p.* [CONTRAER].

contraigo; contraje; contraiga, *pres. indic.; pret.; pres. subj.* [CONTRAER].

contraindicación, *n.f.* (*med.*) contraindication.

contraindicante, *n.m.* (*med.*) contraindicant.

contraindicar, *v.t.* (*pret.* **contraindiqué,** *pres. subj.* **contraindique**) (*med.*) to contraindicate.

contralecho, *adv.; a contralecho,* (*arch.*) set in surbed manner.

contralibrar, *v.t.* to draw a bill to cover oneself.

contraliga, *n.f.* counter-league.

contralínea, *n.f.* fosse with parapet for defence.

contralizo, *n.m.* (*weav.*) back leash.

contralmirante, *n.m.* rear-admiral.

contralor, *n.m.* (*mil.*) controller, inspector.

contraloría, *n.f.* controllership; controller's office.

contralto, *n.m.f.* contralto, counter-tenor.

contraluz, *n.f.* cross-light.

contramaestra, *n.f.* mainsail.

contramaestre, *n.m.* boatswain; overseer, foreman.

contramalla; contramalladura, *n.f.* double-meshed net for catching fish.

contramallar, *v.t.* to make double-meshed nets.

contramandar, *v.t.* to countermand.

contramangas, *n.f.pl.* oversleeves.

contramaniobra, *n.f.* counter-manœuvre or movement.

contramano, (a), *adv.* against the natural flow.

contramarca, *n.f.* countermark; duty on goods.

contramarcar, *v.t.* (*pret.* **contramarqué;** *pres. subj.* **contramarque**) to countermark.

contramarco, *n.m.* interior frame (of french window, etc.).

contramarcha, *n.f.* countermarch, retrocession; (*mil., naut.*) evolution.

contramarchar, *v.i.* to countermarch.

contramarea, *n.f.* counter-tide.

contramesana, *n.f.* mizen-mast.

contramina, *n.f.* countermine; (*min.*) driftway, heading.

contraminar, *v.t.* (*mil.*) to countermine; (*fig.*) to counterwork.

contramolde, *n.m.* second mould wrapping another to replace same, if necessary.

contramotivo, *n.m.* melody contrary to another; phrase in double counterpoint.

contramuelle, *n.m.* counter-mole; duplicate spring.

contramuñones, *n.m.pl.* (*artill.*) metallic reinforcements of the trunnions.

contramuralla, *n.f.; contramuro,* *n.m.* (*fort.*) countermure.

contranatural, *a.* unnatural, against or contrary to nature.

contraorden, *n.f.* countermand.

contrapalanquín, *n.m.* (*naut.*) preventer clew-garnet.

contrapalmejar, *n.m.* (*naut.*) kelson.

contrapar, *n.m.* (*arch.*) rafter.

contraparte, *n.f.* opposite side; flat side of embossed work; (*mus.*) counterpoint.

contrapartida, *n.f.* (*com.*) cross-entry, correction in double-entry book-keeping.

contrapás, *n.m.* step or figure in the quadrille.

contrapasar, *v.i.* to join an opposite party.

contrapaso, *n.m.* back step in walking or dancing; second or lower part of melody.

contrapeado, -da, *a.* two-ply (wood); made into two-ply. — *p.p.* [CONTRAPEAR].

contrapear, *v.t.* to make into two-ply (wood).

contrapechar, *v.t.* to strike breast against breast (horses in jousts).

contrapelo, *adv.; a contrapelo,* against the grain, against one's natural inclination.

contrapesar, *v.t.* to counterpoise, counterbalance; countervail, offset.

contrapeso, *n.m.* counterpoise, counterbalance, equipollence; makeweight; rope / dancer's pole; plummet.

contrapeste, *n.m.* remedy against pestilence.

contrapié, *n.m.* (*hunt.*) failure of scent, losing of trail; (*fig.*) trap, snare.

contrapilastra, *n.f.* reinforcement on either side of a pilaster; wooden draught-excluder on doors and windows.

contraplancha, *n.f.* second plate (in engraving).

contrapolicía, *n.f.* secret police watching ordinary police.

contrapóliza, *n.f.* (*com.*) policy which annuls another.

contraponedor, -ra, *a.* comparing, contrasting; opposing. — *n.m.f.* comparer; opposer.

contraponer, *v.t.* (*p.p.* **contrapuesto;** *pres. indic.* **contrapongo;** *pret.* **contrapuse;** *pres. subj.* **contraponga**) to compare, contrast, to oppose. — *v.r.* to set oneself against; *contraponer una cosa a* or *con otra,* to compare one thing with another.

contraposición, *n.f.* contraposition, counterview, contrast.

contrapozo, *n.m.* fougade in countermine.

contrapresión, *n.f.* back-pressure.

contraprincipio, *n.m.* assertion contrary to a principle.

contraproducente, contraproducéntem, *a.* self defeating, producing the opposite of the desired effect.

contrapromesa, *n.f.* cancellation of promise; opposition of promise to promise.

contraproposición, *n.f.* counter-proposition.

contrapropósito, *n.m.* change of purpose; cross-purpose.

contraprotesta, *n.f.* protest opposed to another.

contraprotesto, *n.m.* (*com.*) objection to meeting a bill because it has already been paid.

contraproyectar, *v.t.* to counterplan; to prepare a counterplan.

contraproyecto, *n.m.* counter-project; change of plan.

contraprueba, *n.f.* counter-proof; (*print.*) second proof.

contrapuerta, *n.f.* front or main door (of house); screen-door, double door; (*fort.*) second gate.

contrapuesto, -ta, *a.* compared, contrasted, opposed. — *p.p. irreg.* [CONTRAPONER].

contrapugnar, *v.t.* to fight, combat.

contrapuntante, *n.m.* singer in counterpoint.

contrapuntarse, *v.r.* to revile, spite each other.

contrapuntear, *v.t.* to sing in counterpoint; to taunt, revile. — *v.r.* [CONTRAPUNTARSE]; *contrapuntearse con alguno,* to wrangle, dispute with someone; *contrapuntearse de palabras,* to abuse, insult each other.

contrapuntista, *n.m.* contrapuntist.

contrapunto, *n.m.* counterpoint, harmony.

contrapunzar, *v.t.* to punch, use a punch-tool.

contrapunzón, *n.m.* punch for driving in a nail; punch for stamping-die; gunsmith's countermark on guns.

contraquerella, *n.f.* (*law*) cross-action.

contraquilla, *n.f.* (*naut.*) false keel.

contrariamente, *adv.* contrarily, contrariwise, contrary.

contrariar, *v.t.* to contradict, oppose, counteract, run counter, thwart; to disappoint, upset, vex.

contrariedad, *n.f.* contrariety, contrariness, contradiction, opposition; disappointment, obstacle, impediment, inconvenience.

contrario, -ria, *a.* hurtful, mischievous, contrary, repugnant, contradictory; opposite, adverse; dissimilar, loath, abhorrent, cross. — *n.m.f.* opponent, antagonist, competitor, rival, contrary. — *n.m.* impediment, contradiction, obstacle. — *n.f.* opposition, repugnance; *contrario a* or *de muchos,* contrary, opposite to many; *contrario en ideas,* dissimilar in ideas; *tiempo contrario,* foul weather; *al contrario; por el* or *lo contrario,* on the contrary; *en contrario,* against, in opposition; *llevar la contraria,* to contradict, go counter.

contrarraya, *n.f.* cross-hatching line (in engraving).

contrarrayar, *v.t.* to cross-hatch.

contrarreforma, *n.f.* counter-reformation.

contrarregistro, *n.m.* control or second checking of excise or customs register.

contrarreguera, *n.f.* lateral ditch or drain (in irrigated ground).

contrarreparo, *n.m.* (*fort.*) countermure, counterscarp.

contrarréplica, *n.f.* rejoinder, counter-reply, retort.

contrarrestar, *v.t.* to resist, oppose; check, counteract, countercheck; to strike back a ball.

contrarresto, *n.m.* check, contradiction, opposition; player who is to return the ball at the service.

contrarretablo, *n.m.* back of altar-piece.

contrarrevolución, *n.f.* counter-revolution.

contrarrevolucionario, -ria, *n.m.f., a.* counter-revolutionary.

contrarroda, *n.f.* (*naut.*) stemson.

contrarronda, *n.f.* (*mil.*) second round (night patrol).

contrarrotura, *n.f.* (*vet.*) plaster, poultice.

contrasalida, *n.f.* (*mil.*) counter-sally.

contrasalva, *n.f.* (*mil.*) counter-salute.

contrasazón, *n.f.* unseasonableness, inopportunity.

contraseguro, *n.m.* re-insurance contract.

contrasellar, *v.t.* to counter-seal.

contrasello, *n.m.* small seal placed next to a large one; the impression made by this seal.

contrasentido, *n.m.* contrary sense; misinterpretation; false deduction.

contraseña, *n.f.* countersign; countermark; (*mil.*) watch-word; *contraseña de salida,* (*theat.*) re-admission ticket.

contrasignar, *v.t.* [CONTRASELLAR].

contrasignatorio, *n.m.* one who countersigns.

contrasol, *n.m.* (*hort.*) bell-glass, sunshade.

contrastable, *a.* contrastable.

contrastador, -ra, *a.* contrasting.

contrastante, *a.* contrasting; resisting.

contrastar, *v.t.* to oppose, resist; to assay metals; to test weights and measures. — *v.i.* to contrast, be different.

contraste, *n.m.* contrast, opposition, counterview; dissimilitude, strife; assayer of weights and measures or metals; assayer's office; sudden change of the wind; public weighing of raw silk.

contrata, *n.f.* contract, deed; *contrata de arriendo,* lease; *contrata de fletamento,* charter-party.

contratablacho, *n.m.* lock, floodgate, sluice close to another.

contratación, *n.f.* trade, commerce, traffic, transaction, undertaking, enterprise.

contratajamar, *n.m.* buttress of bridge-piles.

contratante, *a.* contracting. — *n.m.* contractor, party to a contract.

contratapa, *n.f.* reinforcement of cover or lid.

contratar, *v.t.* to trade, traffic, deal; to contract, stipulate, bargain, covenant.

contratecho, *n.m.* roof-reinforcement.

contratela, *n.f.* (*hunt.*) second enclosure of canvas to trap game.

contratiempo, *n.m.* disappointment, mishap, misfortune, contretemps, calamity; *a contratiempo,* syncopated time. — *pl.* (*equit.*) unruly movements.

contratista, *n.m.f.* contractor, lessee, grantee.

contrato, *n.m.* contract, convention, pact, agreement, stipulation, covenant; deed, indenture; *hacer un contrato,* to enter into a bargain, strike a bargain; *contrato a la gruesa* or *a riesgo marítimo,* respondentia; *contrato de arrendamiento,* lease; *contrato de compra y venta,* contract of bargain and sale; *contrato de retrovendendo,* contract of sale and return; *contrato leonino,* (*fig.*) one-sided pact.

contratorpedero, *n.m.* torpedo-boat destroyer.

contratreta, *n.f.* counterplot.

contratrinchera, *n.f.* (*fort.*) counter-approaches.

contravalación, *n.f.* (*fort.*) contravallation.

contravalar, *v.t.* to form a line of contravallation.

contravalor, *n.m.* equivalent (value).

contravapor, *n.m.* *dar contravapor,* to reverse steam in locomotives.

contravención, *n.f.* contravention, transgression, violation.

contraveneno, *n.m.* counter-poison, antidote.

contravenir, *v.i.* (*pres. indic.* **contravengo;** *pret.* **contravine;** *pres. subj.* **contravenga**) (with *a*) to contravene, transgress, violate; to oppose, obstruct.

contraventana, *n.f.* window-shutter.

contraventor, -ra, *a.* contravening, infringing. — *n.m.f.* transgressor.

contravertiente, *n.m.* unevenness opposing the free flow of waters.

contravidriera, *n.f.* double window.

contravirar, *v.t.* (*naut.*) to turn in an opposite direction.

contravisita, *n.f.* second visit (as check on previous visit).

contravoluta, *n.f.* (*arch.*) inner volute.

contray, *n.m.* kind of fine cloth.

contrayente, *n.m.f., a.* betrothed; (person) contracting marriage.

contrecho, -cha, *a.* crippled, maimed.

contribución, *n.f.* contribution, tax, impost; *contribución de sangre,* military service.

contribuidor, -ra, *a.* contributing. — *n.m.f.* contributor.

contribuir, *v.t.* (*pres. indic.* **contribuyo;** *pres.*

subj. **contribuya**) to contribute; to pay tax; (*fig.*) to give, furnish; to concur, promote.

contribulado, -da, *a.* grieved, afflicted.

contributario, -ria, *n.m.f.* contributor, tax-payer.

contributivo, -va, *a.* contributive.

contribuyente, *a.* contributing, contributory. — *n.m.f.* tax-payer.

contrición, *n.f.* contrition, penitence, compunction.

contrín, *n.m.* weight used in the Philippines (about 6 grains).

contrincante, *n.m.* competitor, rival, opponent.

contristar, *v.t.* to afflict, sadden. — *v.r.* to become sad, grieved.

contrito, -ta, *a.* contrite, compunctious, penitent.

controversia, *n.f.* controversy, debate.

controversista, *n.m.* controversialist, disputant.

controvertible, *a.* controvertible, disputable, litigious.

controvertir, *v.i.*, *v.t.* (*pres. indic.* **controvierto**; *pres. subj.* **controvierta**) to controvert, dispute in writing, discuss, argue against.

contubernio, *n.m.* cohabitation, concubinage; (*fig.*) infamous alliance.

contuerzo(me), contuerza(me), *pres. indic.*, *pres. subj.* [CONTORCERSE].

contumacia, *n.f.* obstinacy, perverseness, stubbornness; (*law*) contumacy, non-appearance, contempt of court, default.

contumaz, *a.* obstinate, stubborn, contumacious, perverse, disobedient; (*med.*) germ-carrying (substances).

contumazmente, *adv.* contumaciously, obstinately, perversely.

contumelia, *n.f.* contumely, insolence, abuse.

contumeliosamente, *adv.* contumeliously, abusively.

contumelioso, -sa, *a.* contumelious, abusive.

contundente, *a.* blunt, bruising, producing a contusion; (*fig.*)impressing the mind deeply; clinching, forcible (argument).

contundir, *v.t.* (*p.p.* **contuso**) to contuse, bruise. — *v. recip.* to bruise, pound mutually.

conturbación, *n.f.* perturbation, uneasiness of mind.

conturbado, -da, *a.* turbulent, troublesome. — *p.p.* [CONTURBAR].

conturbador, -ra, *a.* disturbing, perturbing. — *n.m.f.* perturber, disturber.

conturbar, *v.t.* to perturb, disquiet, disturb. — *v.r.* to become uneasy, agitated, anxious.

conturbativo, -va, *a.* troubling, disturbing, disquieting.

contusión, *n.f.* contusion, bruise.

contuso, -sa, *a.* bruised. — *p.p. irreg.* [CONTUNDIR].

contutor, *n.m.* assistant tutor, fellow-tutor.

contuve, *pret.* [CONTENIR].

conuco, *n.m.* (*Col., Cub., Ven.*) small plot of land.

convalaria, *n.f.* convallaria, lily of the valley.

convalecencia, *n.f.* convalescence; convalescent hospital.

convalecer, *v.i.* (*pres. indic.* **convalezco**; *pres. subj.* **convalezca**) to convalesce, be convalescent; (*fig.*) to regain lost prosperity

or success; *convalecer de una enfermedad*, to recover from sickness.

convaleciente, *n.m.f.*, *a.* convalescent.

convalidación, *n.f.* (*law*) confirmation, corroboration.

convalidar, *v.t.* (*law*) to ratify, confirm.

convecino, -na, *a.* neighbouring. — *n.m.f.* neighbour.

convelerse, *v.r.* (*med.*) to shrink, contract, twitch.

convencedor, -ra, *a.* convincing. — *n.m.f.* convincer.

convencer, *v.t.* (*p.p.* **convencido** or **convicto**; *pres. indic.* **convenzo**; *pres. subj.* **convenza**) to convince. — *v.r.* to become convinced, assured; *convencerse con las razones*, to be satisfied with the explanations; *convencerse de la razón* (*de una cosa*), to become convinced of the reason (of something).

convencido, -da, *a.* convinced, persuaded. — [CONVENCER].

convencimiento, *n.m.* conviction, belief; act of convincing; state of being convinced; *en el convencimiento de que*, in the belief or believing that.

convención, *n.f.* convention, contract, agreement, pact; convenience, conformity; meeting, convening, congress, assembly.

convencional, *a.* conventional, conventionary. — *n.m.* conventionalist.

convencionalismo, *n.m.* conventionalism, conventionality.

convencionalmente, *adv.* conventionally.

convengo; convenga, *pres. indic.*; *pres. subj.* [CONVENIR].

convenible, *a.* docile, tractable; moderate, reasonable (price).

convenido, -da, *a.* settled by consent. — *interj.* agreed, done. — *p.p.* [CONVENIR].

conveniencia, *n.f.* conformity, congruity; utility, profit, advantage; convention, adjustment, agreement; service, employ, servant's place in a house; convenience, comfort. — *pl.* (*obs.*) emoluments, perquisites; income, property; *he hallado conveniencia*, I have got a place.

conveniente, *a.* useful, good, advantageous, profitable, convenient; conformable, agreeable, suitable, accordant, expedient, fit; opportune, timely, commodious; decent, discreet.

convenientemente, *adv.* conveniently, fitly, expediently, suitably.

convenio, *n.m.* convention, agreement, pact.

convenir, *v.i.* (*pres. indic.* **convengo**; *pret.* **convine**; *pres. subj.* **convenga**) to agree, coincide; to cohere, fit, harmonize, belong to, correspond; to convene, assemble. — *v. impers.* to suit, be to the purpose, be fitting, meet. — *v.r.* to compound; to agree, suit, close, make a deal; *conviene a saber*, that is, to wit; *convenir con*, to agree with; *convenir en*, to agree to, on or about; *convenir* (*una cosa*) *al niño*, to be suitable for the child (something).

conventícula, *n.f.*; **conventículo,** *n.m.* conventicle.

convento, *n.m.* convent, monastery, nunnery, religious community.

conventual, *a.* conventual, monastic. — *n.m.* conventual, monk; member of landed Franciscan order.

conventualidad, *n.f.* conventual life; assignment of monk to certain convent.

conventualmente, *adv.* in community, monastically.

convenzo; convenza, *pres. indic.; pres. subj.* [CONVENCER].

convergencia, *n.f.* convergence.

convergente, *a.* converging, convergent.

converger; convergir, *v.i.* to converge; (*fig.*) to agree in opinions.

conversable, *a.* conversable, sociable.

conversación, *n.f.* conversation, talk, chat, converse, conference, society, communication, colloquy; commerce, intercourse, company; illicit intercourse; *conversación tirada,* long-drawn-out conversation; *dejar caer una cosa en la conversación,* to let a remark drop offhandedly; *dirigir la conversación a uno,* to address someone in particular; *la mucha conversación es causa de menosprecio,* familiarity breeds contempt; *hacer que caiga la conversación sobre una cosa,* to direct the conversation to a definite matter; *sacar la conversación,* to touch on a certain point in conversation; *trabar conversación,* to start a conversation.

conversador, -ra, *n.m.f.* good, witty talker.

conversar, *v.i.* to converse, talk together, discourse familiarly; to have social intercourse; to live together with others; (*mil.*) to change front, wheel; *conversar con,* to talk to or with; *conversar en, sobre,* to talk on, about.

conversión, *n.f.* conversion, change, transformation, reform; (*rhet.*) apostrophe; (*mil.*) wheel, wheeling; (*com.*) conversion (of treasury bonds, etc.).

conversivo, -va, *a.* having the power of converting or changing.

converso, -sa, *a.* changed, converted. — *n.m.f.* convert. — *n.m.* lay brother. — *p.p. irreg.* [CONVERTIR].

convertible, *a.* convertible, movable.

convertibilidad, *n.f.* convertibility.

convertido, -da, *a.* converted, changed. — *p.p.* [CONVERTIR].

convertidor, -ra, *a.* converting. — *n.m.* (*metal., elect.*) converter.

convertir, *v.t.* (*p.p.* **convertido** or **converso;** *pres. indic.* **convierto;** *pres. subj.* **convierta**) to convert, reform, change, transform. — *v.r.* to become converted, undergo a change; *el agua se convirtió en hielo,* the water turned into ice; *se ha convertido al catolicismo,* he has become converted to Catholicism.

convexidad, *n.f.* convexity.

convexo, -xa, *a.* convex.

convexocóncavo, -va, *a.* convexo-concave.

convicción, *n.f.* conviction, convincement.

conviccional, *a.* convincing.

convicto, -ta, *a.* (*law*) convicted, guilty. — *p.p. irreg.* [CONVENCER].

convictor, *n.m.* (*prov.*) boarder, pensioner in a college.

convictorio, *n.m.* student's quarters (in Jesuit colleges).

convidado, -da, *n.m.f.* guest, person invited to a party. — *n.f.* (*coll.*) invitation to drink, treat. — *p.p.* [CONVIDAR].

convidador, -ra, *a.* inviting. — *n.m.f.* inviter.

convidante, *a.* inviting, requesting.

convidar, *v.t.* to invite, bid, stand treat; to offer; (*fig.*) to allure, incite, persuade, induce.

— *v.r.* to offer one's services spontaneously; *convidar a comer,* to invite to dinner; *convidar con un billete,* to offer, present a ticket; *convidar para el baile,* to suggest coming to the ball; *el frío convida a andar,* the cold tempts one to walk.

convierto; convierta, *pres. indic.; pres. subj.* [CONVERTIR].

convincente, *a.* convincing, convincible.

convincentemente, *adv.* convincingly, convincedly.

convite, *n.m.* invitation; feast, treat.

convival, *a.* convivial.

convivencia, *n.f.* living together with others.

conviviente, *n.m.f., a.* (one) living together with others.

convivir, *v.i.* to live together with others.

convocación, *n.f.* convocation.

convocador, -ra, *a.* convening, convoking. — *n.m.f.* convener, convoker.

convocar, *v.t.* (*pret.* **convoqué;** *pres. subj.* **convoque**) to convene, convoke, summon, call together, congregate; to acclaim; *convocar a junta,* to summon a meeting.

convocatoria, *n.f.* letter of convocation.

convocatorio, -ria, *a.* convocational, convoking.

convolución, *n.f.* convolution.

convóluto, -ta, *a.* (*bot., zool.*) convolute, convoluted.

convoluláceo, -cea, *n.f., a.* (*bot.*) convolvulus.

convólvulo, *n.m.* (*bot.*) convolvulus; (*entom.*) vine-borer, vine-fretter.

convoy, *n.m.* convoy, conduct; escort, guard; material under convoy; (*fig.*) cruetstand; (*coll.*) suite, retinue.

convoyante, *a.* convoying.

convoyar, *v.t.* to convoy, escort, guard.

convulsible, *a.* liable to convulsions.

convulsión, *n.f.* (*med.*) convulsion.

convulsionar, *v.t.* (*med.*) to produce convulsions.

convulsionario, -ria, *a.* (*med.*) convulsionary. — *n.m.pl.* (*hist.*) convulsionists.

convulsivamente, *adv.* convulsively.

convulsivo, -va, *a.* convulsive.

convulso, -sa, *a.* convulsed.

conyúdice, *n.m.* [CONJUEZ].

conyugable, *a.* marriageable.

conyugal, *a.* conjugal, connubial.

conyugalmente, *adv.* conjugally, connubially, matrimonially.

cónyuges, *n.m.pl.* married couple.

conyugicida, *n.m.f.* (*law*) murderer of husband or wife.

conyugicidio, *n.m.* (*law*) murder of husband or wife.

coñac, *n.m.* cognac, brandy.

cooperación, *n.f.* co-operation.

cooperador, -ra, *a.* co-operative. — *n.m.f.* co-operator.

cooperante, *a.* co-operating, co-operant, coactive.

cooperar, *v.t.* to co-operate, labour jointly; *cooperar a alguna cosa,* to concur in, contribute to something; *cooperar con otro,* to co-operate with another.

cooperario, *n.m.* co-operator.

cooperativamente, *adv.* co-operatively.

cooperativo, -va, *a.* co-operative. — *n.f.* co-operative society.

coopositor, -ra, *n.m.f.* competitor, rival (for a vacancy).

cooptación, *n.f.* co-optation.

coordenada, *n.f.* (*geom.*) co-ordinate.

coordinación, *n.f.* co-ordination, classification.

coordinadamente, *adv.* co-ordinately.

coordinado, -da, *a.* correlated; (*geom.*) co-ordinate. — *p.p.* [COORDINAR].

coordinador, -ra, *a.* co-ordinating.

coordinamiento, *n.m.* [COORDINACIÓN].

coordinar, *v.t.* to co-ordinate, classify, correlate.

copa, *n.f.* cup, vase, goblet, wine-glass; tree-top; crown of a hat; roof of an oven; gill; cupful, glassful; brazier, fire-pan. — *pl.* hearts, at cards; bosses of a bridle.

copado, -da, *a.* tufted (tree); cornered, surprised. — *n.f.* crested lark. — *p.p.* [COPAR].

copador, *n.m.* wooden hammer for copper or brass beating.

copaiba, *n.f.* copaiba tree and balsam.

copaína, *n.f.* principle extracted from copaiba.

copal, *n.m.* copal.

copaljocol, *n.m.* (*Mex.*) tree resembling a cherry tree.

copanete; cópano, *n.m.* small ship.

copar, *v.t.* to stake a sum equal to the amount in the bank (in games of chance); (*mil.*) to cut the retreat, capture, surprise; (*coll.*) to grab all the votes (in an election).

coparticipación, *n.f.* co-partnership, joint-participation.

copartícipe, *n.m.f.* (*law*) joint-sharer or participator.

copazo, *n.m.* large fleece of wool; large snowflake [COPO].

cope, *n.m.* thickest part of fishing-net.

copé, *n.m.* (*Am. Mer.*) native naphtha.

copear, *v.i.* to sell drinks by the glass; to tipple in a tavern.

copela, *n.f.* (*metal.*) cupel.

copelación, *n.f.* cupellation.

copelar, *v.t.* to cupel.

copeo, *n.m.* sale of drinks by the glass.

copera, *n.f.* cupboard, side-board, glass closet.

copernicano, -na, *a.* Copernican.

copero, *n.m.* (*obs.*) cup-bearer; sideboard, buffet.

copeta, *n.f.* small cup [COPA].

copete, *n.m.* small portion of flax, etc. [COPO] ready on distaff for spinning; toupee; crest, tuft; (*fig.*) top, summit; top of a shoe; fore-lock of a horse; crownwork of furniture; projecting top of ice-cream; (*fig.*) boldness, daring; *de alto copete,* aristocratic, of noble rank; *asir la ocasión por el copete,* to take advantage of an opportunity; *estar hasta el copete,* to have more than one can bear; *hombre de copete,* man of good standing and character; *tener copete,* to be very haughty, assume an air of authority.

copetón, *n.m.* (*Col.*) crested sparrow.

copetudo, -da, *a.* tufted; (*coll.*) haughty, proud. — *n.f.* lark; (*Cub.*) marigold.

copey, *n.m.* (*Am. Cent., Col., Ven.*) a tree used for making woodcut blocks.

copia, *n.f.* copiousness, plenty, abundance, fertility; copy, duplicate, imitation, transcript; counterpart; (*gram.*) list of nouns and verbs with the cases they govern; *copia al vivo,* facsimile; *copia verbal,* verbatim copy.

copiador, -ra, *a.* copying. — *n.m.f.* copyist, copier, transcriber. — *n.m.* (*com.*) letter-book; (*fig.*) imitator.

copiante, *n.m.f., a.* [COPIADOR].

copiar, *v.t.* to copy, duplicate, reproduce, imitate, draw after life; (*poet.*) to describe, depict; to ape, mimic; *copiar al pie de la letra,* to copy word for word; *copiar del natural,* to draw after life.

copilador, -ra, *a.* compiling. — *n.m.f.* compiler, collector.

copilar, *v.t.* to collect, compile.

copilla, *n.f.* cigar-lighter; chafing-dish.

copín, *n.m.* Asturian grain-measure of half a peck.

copina, *n.f.* (*Mex.*) skin taken off whole.

copinar, *v.t.* (*Mex.*) to remove a skin entire.

copiosamente, *adv.* copiously, abundantly, plentifully, largely.

copioso, -sa, *a.* copious, abundant, fluent, full, large, fruitful.

copismo, *n.m.* servile imitation.

copista, *n.m.f.* copyist, transcriber.

copita, *n.f.* small cup or glass [COPA].

copito, *n.m.* small fleece or snowflake [COPO].

copla, *n.f.* couplet, stanza; ballad, popular song, lampoon; pair, couple. — *pl.* (*fam.*) verses; *andar en coplas,* to be notorious; *coplas de ciego,* vulgar ballads; *echar coplas a uno,* to speak ill of someone.

coplear, *v.i.* to make couplets or ballads.

copleja, *n.f.* little ballad.

coplero, -ra, *n.m.f.* ballad-seller; (*fig.*) poetaster.

coplista, *n.m.f.* poetaster.

coplones, *n.m.pl.* low vile verses.

copo, *n.m.* small bundle of cotton, hemp, silk, etc. on distaff ready for spinning; flake of snow; bottom of purse-seine; fishing with purse-seine; cornering, surprise, grabbing; *poco a poco, hila la vieja el copo,* little strokes fell great oaks.

copón, *n.m.* large cup [COPA]; (*eccles.*) ciborium.

coposo, -sa, *a.* [COPADO].

copra, *n.f.* copra, dried kernel of the coconut.

coprófago, -ga, *a.* coprophagous.

coprolito, *n.m.* coprolite; (*med.*) intestinal calculus.

copropiedad, *n.f.* joint-property.

copropietario, -ria, *a.* owning jointly. — *n.m.f.* joint-proprietor.

cóptico, -ca, *a.* Coptic.

copto, -ta, *n.m.f., a.* Copt, Coptic.

copudo, -da, *a.* tufted, bushy, thick-topped (of trees).

cópula, *n.f.* joining, coupling of two things; copulation, carnal union; (*log.*) copula; (*arch.*) cupola.

copulación, *n.f.* copulation, carnal union.

copulador, -ra, *a.* copulatory.

copularse, *v.r.* to copulate.

copulativamente, *adv.* jointly.

copulativo, -va, *a.* joining; (*gram.*) copulative.

coque, *n.m.* coke.

coqueluche, *n.f.* whooping-cough.

coquera, *n.f.* head of top (toy); concavity in a stone; coke-scuttle.

coqueta, *a.* coquettish. — *n.f.* coquette, flirt; (*prov.*) blow with a ferrule; (*prov.*) small loaf.

coquetear, *v.i.* to coquet, flirt.

coqueteo, *n.m.;* **coquetería**, *n.f.;* **coquetismo**, *n.m.* coquetry, flirtation.
coqueto; coquetón, *a.* coquettish. — *n.m.* male flirt.
coquetonamente, *adv.* coquettishly.
coquí, *n.m.* (*Cub.*) insect of marshy lands.
coquimba, *n.m.* (*Am.*) kind of owl.
coquina, *n.f.* cockle; shell-fish.
coquinero, -ra, *n.m.f.* (*prov.*) cockle-gatherer or seller.
coquito, *n.m.* grimace to amuse children; (*Mex.*) turtledove; (*Chi., Ec.*) fruit of a palm-tree.
coráceo, -cea, *a.* [CORIÁCEO].
coracero, *n.m.* cuirassier; (*coll.*) poor cigar.
coracina, *n.f.* small breastplate.
coracora, *n.f.* (*Philip.*) coasting vessel.
coracha, *n.f.* (*Am.*) leather bag.
corada, *n.f.* (*prov.*) animal's viscera.
coraje, *n.m.* courage, fortitude, bravery, mettle; passion, anger.
corajina, *n.f.* (*fam.*) fit of anger.
corajudamente, *adv.* angrily.
corajudo, -da, *a.* passionate, angry.
coral, *a.* choral, of a choir. — *n.m.* coral. — *pl.* strings of coral; turkey's wattles; *fino como un coral*, astute, sharp. — *n.f.* (*Col., Ven.*) coral snake.
coralero, -ra, *n.m.f.* worker or dealer in corals.
coralífero, -ra, *a.* coralliferous.
coraliforme, *a.* coralliform.
coralígeno, -na, *a.* coralligenous.
coralillo, *n.m.* (*Am. Mer.*) coral-coloured snake.
coralina, *n.f.* coralline (sea-weed and polyzoa).
coralíneo, -nea; coralino, -na, *a.* coralline.
corambre, *n.f.* hides and skins of animals, pelts; skin bag for oil or wine; *alzar corambre*, to lift skins from the tanning-vats to dry.
corambrero, *n.m.* dealer in hides and skins.
Corán, *n.m.* Koran.
coránico, -ca, *a.* Koranic.
coranvobis, *n.m.* (*coll.*) a fat person who affects gravity.
coraza, *n.f.* cuirass; (*naut.*) armour-plating; turtle-shell.
coraznada, *n.f.* pith of pine-tree; fricassee of animals' hearts.
corazón, *n.m.* heart; will, mind; spirit, courage; affection, kindness, benevolence; middle, centre, sore; cam (in loom); pith; anything heart-shaped; *abrir el corazón a uno*, to encourage someone, *abrir su corazón*, to unbosom oneself; *anunciarle* or *darle* or *decirle a uno el corazón una cosa*, to have a presentiment; *atravesar el corazón, clavarle* or *clavársele a uno en el corazón*, to grieve one deeply; *blando de corazón*, tender-hearted; *buen corazón quebranta mala ventura*, set a stout heart to a steep brae; *cobrar* or *crecer corazón*, to take new heart or pluck up courage; *cubrírsele a uno el corazón*, to become very sad; *de corazón*, heartily, sincerely, unaffectedly; *dilatar* or *ensanchar el corazón*, to comfort, cheer up, be comforted; *encogérsele a uno el corazón*, to lose heart; *haber a corazón*, to resolve firmly; *hacer de tripas corazón*, to put a good face upon matters; *helársele a uno el corazón*, to be overcome (by shock, bad news, etc.); *llevar, tener* or *con el corazón en la(s) mano(s)*, to be very sincere, frank or open; to wear one's heart on one's sleeve; *meterse uno en el corazón a otro*, to declare one's love and

affection; *no caberle a uno el corazón en el pecho*, to be very anxious or vexed; to be big-hearted; *no tener corazón*, to be unmoved, insensible; *no tener uno corazón para hacer, decir*, etc., to have no heart or courage to do, say, etc.; *partir* or *quebrar una cosa el corazón*, to affect deeply; *partírsele a uno el corazón*, to be cut to the heart, break one's heart; *salirle a uno del corazón una cosa*, to speak sincerely, from the bottom of one's heart; *se me arranca el corazón al ver su miseria*, my heart bleeds at his misery; *si el corazón fuera de acero, no le venciera el dinero*, only a strong man can resist the temptation of wealth; *tener uno el corazón bien puesto*, to have one's heart in the right place; *tener uno mucho corazón*, to be very noble or bold; *tener uno un corazón de bronce*, to be hard-hearted; *tocarle a uno en el corazón*, to move one for the best.
corazonada, *n.f.* courage, impulse; presentiment, foreboding; (*coll.*) entrails, chitterlings.
corazoncico; corazoncito, *n.m.* little heart; (*coll.*) faint-hearted person.
corazoncillo, *n.m.* St. John's wort.
corbachada, *n.f.* blow with the *corbacho*.
corbacho, *n.m.* (*obs.*) pizzle, cowhide whip.
corbata, *n.f.* neck-tie, cravat; scarf, neckcloth knot or tassel attached to flagstaff; ribbon, insignia. — *n.m.* magistrate not brought up to the law; (*eccles. law*) layman.
corbatería, *n.f.* necktie-shop.
corbatero, -ra, *n.m.f.* maker or vendor of neck-ties.
corbatín, *n.m.* small neck-tie, bow-tie; stock, closely fitting neck-cloth; *irse* or *salirse por el corbatín*, said of a long-necked person.
corbatinero, -ra, *a.* relating to neck-ties. — *n.m.f.* [CORBATERO].
corbato, *n.m.* cooler, worm of a still.
corbatón, *n.m.* (*naut.*) small knee, bracket.
corbe, *n.m.* an ancient dry measure, by baskets.
corbeta, *n.f.* corvette; *corbeta de guerra*, sloop.
Córcega, *n.f.* Corsica.
corcel, *n.m.* horse, charger.
corcesca, *n.f.* ancient barbed spear.
corcino, *n.m.* small deer.
corconera, *n.f.* kind of blackish duck common in the Bay of Biscay.
corcova, *n.f.* hump, hunch, crooked back; protuberance.
corcovado, -da, *a.* hump-backed, hunchbacked; curved. — *n.m.f.* hunchback. — *p.p.* [CORCOVAR].
corcovar, *v.t.* to bend, curve.
corcovear, *v.i.* to curvet, cut capers.
corcoveo, *n.m.* curvet, curvetting.
corcoveta, *n.f.* small hump or hunch [CORCOVA]. — *n.m.f.* (*coll.*) crook-back, hunchback.
corcovo, *n.m.* curvet; (*coll.*) crookedness, unfair proceeding.
corcusido, -da, *a.* clumsily mended or sewn on. — *p.p.* [CORCUSIR].
corcusir, *v.t.* (*coll.*) to darn or patch clumsily.
corcha, *n.f.* cork; wine-cooler; beehive; (*naut.*) laying of a rope.
corchador, *n.m.* sailor laying a rope.
corchar, *v.t.* to lay a rope.
corche, *n.m.* cork-soled sandal or shoe.
corchea, *n.f.* quaver.

corchera, *n.f.* wine-cooler.

corcheta, *n.f.* eye of a hook or clasp.

corchete, *n.m.* clasp, hook and eye; locket, small lock; crotch, hook or clasp; (*mus.*, *print.*) brace, bracket; (*carp.*) bench-hook; (*coll.*) catchpole.

corcho, *n.m.* cork, cork bark; wine-cooler; stopper; beehive; cork box (for eatables); cork mat; cork-soled clog or sandal; float of fishing-line; *andar como el corcho sobre agua,* to be undecided, at the mercy of another's will; *flotar,* or *sobrenadar, como corcho en el agua,* to come through all difficulties; *tener cara de corcho,* to be brazen-faced, impudent.

corchoso, -sa, *a.* corky.

corchotaponero, -ra, *a.* appertaining to the manufacture of cork stoppers.

corda, *n.f.; estar el navío a la corda,* (*naut.*) to be close-hauled, lying-to.

cordado, -da, *a.* (*her.*) corded.

cordaje, *n.m.* cordage; (*naut.*) rigging.

cordal, *n.m.* double tooth, wisdom tooth; (*mus.*) string-bar (of instrument).

cordato, -ta, *a.* wise, prudent, judicious, discreet.

cordel, *n.m.* cord, thin rope, line; distance of five steps; (*Cub.*) land measure of about 1 sq. chain; *mozo de cordel,* porter; *apretar los cordeles,* to oblige someone to say or do something by violent means; *estar a cordel,* to be in a straight line.

cordelado, -da, *a.* corded (ribbons or garters).

cordelazo, *n.m.* stroke or lash with a cord.

cordelejo, *n.m.* small rope [CORDEL]; (*fig.*) fun, jest, joke; *dar cordelejo,* to chaff, banter.

cordelería, *n.f.* rope trade; cord-making; cord-making factory or shop; cordage; rope-walk; (*naut.*) rigging.

cordelero, -ra, *n.m.f.* rope-maker or seller. — *n.m.pl.* cordeliers.

cordelito, *n.m.* fine, thin rope or cord [CORDEL].

cordellate, *n.m.* grogram.

cordera, *n.f.* ewe lamb; (*fig.*) meek, gentle woman.

cordería, *n.f.* cordage.

corderica; corderilla; corderita, *n.f.* little ewe-lamb [CORDERA].

corderico; corderillo; corderito, *n.m.* young lamb [CORDERO].

corderillo, *n.m.* lambskin dressed with the fleece.

corderino, -na; corderuno, -na, *a.* of the lamb kind. — *n.f.* lamb's skin.

cordero, *n.m.* lamb; dressed lambskin; (*fig.*) meek, gentle, mild man; *cordero añal,* yearling lamb; *cordero de Dios,* the Lamb; *cordero pascual,* paschal lamb; *cordero recental,* suckling lamb; *tan presto va el cordero como el carnero,* lamb goes (to the slaughter) as much as the sheep.

corderuela, *n.f.* little ewe-lamb [CORDERA].

cordeta, *n.f.* (*prov.*) bast rope.

cordezuela, *n.f.* fine small rope [CUERDA].

cordíaco, -ca, *a.* [CARDÍACO].

cordial, *a.* cordial, hearty, affectionate, sincere; comforting, invigorating, reviving (of medicine). — *n.m.* cordial, tonic.

cordialidad, *n.f.* cordiality, heartiness; sincerity.

cordialmente, *adv.* cordially, heartily.

cordifoliado, -da, *a.* with heart-shaped leaves.

cordiforme, *a.* cordiform, heart-shaped.

cordila, *n.f.* spawn of a tunny-fish.

cordilo, *n.m.* lizard-like reptile.

cordilla, *n.f.* sheep's guts used as cat's meat.

cordillera, *n.f.* cordillera, chain or ridge of mountains.

cordillerano, -na, *a.* appertaining to a cordillera and its inhabitants. — *n.m.f., a.* inhabitant or native of a cordillera.

cordita, *n.f.* cordite.

corditis, *n.f.* inflammation of the vocal cords.

córdoba, *n.m.* (*Nic.*) monetary unit, peso.

cordobán, *n.m.* cordovan, cordwain, morocco leather, Spanish leather.

cordobana, *andar a la cordobana,* (*coll.*) to go naked.

cordobanero, -ra, *n.m.f.* cordoban tanner.

cordobés, -sa, *n.m.f., a.* of or belonging to Córdoba.

cordón, *n.m.* rope, cord, string, twine; twisted or plaited monk's girdle; (*mil.*) cordon. — *pl.* (*mil.*) aglet, ornamental shoulder-knot; rope strands; *cordón umbilical,* umbilical cord.

cordonazo, *n.m.* stroke with rope or cord; *cordonazo de San Francisco,* autumnal equinox.

cordoncico; cordoncito, *n.m.* thin cord [CORDÓN].

cordoncillo, *n.m.* the serrated edge of a coin [CORDÓN].

cordonería, *n.f.* cords, laces, etc. made by the lace-maker; lace or cord trade; lace- or cord-factory or shop.

cordonero, -ra, *n.m.f.* maker or seller of laces, fringes or ropes. — *n.m.* cordage-maker.

cordura, *n.f.* prudence, judgment, common-sense, sanity.

corea, *n.f.* dance accompanied by a chorus; (*med.*) chorea, St. Vitus' Dance.

coreado, -da, *a.* sung or played in chorus; choral; choric; *música coreada,* chorus, choral music. — *p.p.* [COREAR].

corear, *v.t.* to compose choral music; to play or sing in chorus.

corecico; corecillo, *n.m.* [CUERO], [CORE-ZUELO].

coreo, *n.m.* choree, trochee; connected harmony of choruses.

coreografía, *n.f.* choreography.

coreográfico, -ca, *a.* choreographic.

coreógrafo, *n.m.* choreographer.

corete, *n.m.* leather washer (under nails, nuts, etc.).

corezuelo, *n.m.* small pelt or hide [CUERO]; sucking-pig; crackling (of roasted sucking-pig).

cori, *n.m.* St. John's wort.

coriáceo, -cea, *a.* appertaining to leather, coriaceous.

coriámbico, -ca, *n.m., a.* choriambic.

coriambo, *n.m.* choriambus.

coriandro, *n.m.* coriander.

coribante, *n.m.* corybant, a priest of Cybele.

coribántico, -ca, *a.* corybantian, corybantic.

corifeo, *n.m.* coryphæus; (*fig.*) leader.

corimbifloro, -ra, *a.* (*bot.*) corymbiate.

corimbiforme, *a.* corymbiform.

corimbo, *n.m.* corymb.

corindón, *n.m.* corundum.

coríntico, -ca; corintio, -tia, *n.m.f., a.* Corinthian.

corista, *n.m.* chorister. — *n.m.f.* chorus singer.

corito, *a.* naked; (*fig.*) timid, pusillanimous.
— *n.m.* one who racks wine.

coriza, *n.f.* (*prov.*) sandal; clog; (*med.*) coryza.

corladura, *n.f.* vermeil (varnish), silver-gilt.

corlar; **corlear**, *v.t.* to put on vermeil varnish.

corma, *n.f.* stocks, fetters, shackles; trouble, uneasiness.

cormorán, *n.m.* cormorant.

cornac; **cornaca**, *n.m.* elephant-tamer.

cornada, *n.f.* thrust with a bull's horn; thrust with a foil.

cornadillo, *n.m.* small coin [CORNADO]; *emplear* or *poner su cornadillo*, to do one's bit.

cornado, *n.m.* old copper coin; *no vale un cornado*, (*coll.*) it is not worth a farthing.

cornadura, *n.f.* horns of an animal.

cornal; **cornil**, *n.m.* strap for yoking oxen by the horns.

cornalina; **cornelina**, *n.f.* cornelian.

cornalón, *a.* big-horned (bull).

cornamenta, *n.f.* horns of an animal.

cornamusa, *n.f.* brass horn or trumpet; bagpipe; (*naut.*) belaying cleat.

cornatillo, *n.m.* kind of olive.

córnea, *n.f.* cornea.

corneado, -da, *p.p.* [CORNEAR] butted.

corneador, -ra, *a.* butting (animal).

cornear, *v.i.* to butt with the horn.

cornecico; **cornecillo**; **cornecito**, *n.m.* small horn [CUERNO].

corneja, *n.f.* grey *or* hooded crow.

cornejal, *n.m.* place abounding in cornel or dogwood.

cornejalejo, *n.m.* pod.

cornejo, *n.m.* dogwood, cornel.

córneo, -nea, *a.* horny, cornesus, callous.

cornerina, *n.f.* cornelian.

cornero, *n.m.; cornero de pan*, crust of bread.

corneta, *n.f.* bugle, cornet; swine-herd's horn; (*obs.*) cornet, banderol; (*naut.*) broad pennant; (*obs., mil.*) cornet, troop of cavalry; head-dress of sisters of charity. — *n.m.* cornet-player, bugler; (*obs., mil.*) cornet-bearer; *corneta acústica*, ear-trumpet; hunting-horn; *corneta de posta*, postilion's or post-horn.

cornete, *n.m.* small horn [CUERNO]; (*anat.*) cartilage of nose. — *pl.* surgical instrument.

cornetilla, *n.f.; pimiento de cornetilla*, chilli.

cornetín, *n.m.* small bugle [CORNETA]; cornet-à-piston; player of such instrument.

cornezuelo, *n.m.* small horn [CUERNO]; (*bot.*) kind of olive; (*vet.*) instrument for bleeding horses; (*bot.*) ergot of rye.

corniabierto, -ta, *a.* having widespread horns.

cornial, *a.* horn-shaped.

corniapretado, -da, *a.* with close-set horns.

cornicabra, *n.f.* turpentine-tree; kind of olive; wild fig-tree.

cornidelantero, -ra, *a.* with horns pointing forward.

cornífero, -ra, *a.* (*geol.*) corniferous.

corniforme, *a.* corniform, horn-shaped.

cornigacho, -cha, *a.* with horns pointing slightly downwards.

cornígero, -ra, *a.* (*poet.*) horned, cornigerous.

cornija, *n.f.* (*arch.*) cornice.

cornijal, *n.m.* angle or corner of a building; (*eccles.*) purificator (at Mass).

cornijamento; **cornijamiento**; **cornijón**, *n.m.* entablature; corner of a street.

corniola, *n.f.* cornelian.

cornisa, *n.f.* cornice.

cornisamento; **cornisamiento**; **cornisón**, *n.m.* entablature.

corniveleto, -ta, *a.* having horns turned sharply upward.

cornizo; **corno**, *n.m.* cornelian cherry-tree.

cornizola, *n.f.* wild cherry.

Cornualla, *n.f.* Cornwall.

cornucopia, *n.f.* cornucopia; pier-glass with sconces.

cornudilla, *n.f.* hammer-fish.

cornudo, *a.* horned, cornuted. — *n.m.* (*coll.*) cuckold.

cornúpeta, *n.m.f., a.* (*poet., numis.*) butting (animal).

coro, *n.m.* choir; choir-loft; chorus; memory; unanimous assembly; (*poet.*) summer solstitial wind; *de coro*, by heart, by rote; *hablar* (*rezar*) *a coros*, to speak (pray) alternately; *hacer coro*, to second someone.

corocha, *n.f.* vine-fretter, vine-grub.

corografía, *n.f.* chorography.

corográficamente, *adv.* chorographically.

corográfico, -ca, *a.* chorographical.

corógrafo, -fa, *n.m.f.* chorographer.

coroideo, -dea, *a.* coroides.

coroides, *n.f.* (*anat.*) choroid.

corojal, *n.m.* plantation of *corojos*.

corojo, *n.m.* palm bearing an oily nut.

corolario, *n.m.* corollary, inference, deduction.

corolífero, -ra, *a.* corollate.

corología, *n.f.* chorology.

corona, *n.f.* crown, diadem, coronet; crown of the head; tonsure; various Spanish and foreign coins; chaplet (beads); rosary of seven decades; (*fig.*) royalty, regal power; monarchy, kingdom; honour, splendour; reward, glory; consummation, culmination; top of a height; (*arch., astron., bot.*) corona; (*eccles.*) corona, chandelier; (*fort.*) crown-work; (*naut.*) pendant (rope); crown of tooth; *corona del casco*, (*vet.*) cornet; *corona de rey* or *real*, (*bot.*) three-toothed globularia; *abrir la corona*, to tonsure; *ceñir(se) uno la corona*, to begin one's reign.

coronación, *n.f.* coronation; completion, crowning; end, finishing touch; (*arch.*) crowning, coping (of walls).

coronado, -da, *a.* crowned, perfectly finished. — *n.m.* tonsured priest. — *p.p.* [CORONAR].

coronador, -ra, *a.* crowning, finishing. — *n.m.f.* crowner, finisher.

coronal, *a.* belonging to the frontal bone. — *n.m.* frontal bone.

coronamente; **coronamiento**, *n.m.* (*arch.*) coping, cap; crowning, end of a work; (*naut.*) taffrail.

coronar, *v.t.* to crown, top, cap; to finish, complete, perfect; to decorate the top of a building; to crowd on a roof, height, etc.; to crown (at draughts). — *v.r.* to be crowned; *coronar con* or *de flores*, to crown with flowers; *coronar la fiesta*, to complete anything, put the finishing touch.

coronario, -ria, *a.* coronary, extremely refined (gold); (*bot.*) coronate; (*anat.*) coronary (arteries, veins). — *n.f.* crown-wheel of watch.

corondel, *n.m.* (*print.*) reglet, column-rule. — *pl.* watermark lines.

coronel, *n.m.* colonel; (*arch.*) cyma, top-moulding; (*her.*) crown.

coronela, *a.* of a colonel's flag, company, etc. — *n.f.* colonel's wife.

coronelía, *n.f.* colonelcy, colonelship.

corónide, *n.f.* end, crowning, consummation.

coroniforme, *a.* coronate.

coronilla; coronita, *n.f.* little crown [CORONA]; crown of the head; chaplet; ear of a bell; (*bot.*) coronilla; *coronilla de fraile,* French daisy; *andar* or *bailar de coronilla,* to take much trouble over something; *dar de coronilla,* to fall on one's head; *estar uno hasta la coronilla,* to be at the end of one's forbearance.

coronio, *n.m.* (*astron.*) coronium, element of sun.

coroza, *n.f.* dunce's cap; (*prov.*) straw cape.

corpachón; corpanchón, *n.m.* huge body [CUERPO]; bird's carcass.

corpazo, *n.m.* (*fam.*) huge body [CUERPO].

corpecico; corpecillo; corpecito, *n.m.* small body [CUERPO]; waistcoat; doublet.

corpiñejo, *n.m.* small waistcoat [CORPIÑO].

corpiñera, *n.f.* woman maker of *corpiños.*

corpiño, *n.m.* small body [CUERPO]; waistcoat, under-doublet, corset-cover.

corporación, *n.f.* corporation, body, community, guild.

corporal, *a.* corporal; *castigo corporal,* corporal punishment. — *n.m.* (*eccles.*) corporal (cloth).

corporalidad, *n.f.* corporality; corporeal thing.

corporalmente, *adv.* corporally, bodily.

corporativamente, *adv.* corporately.

corporativo, -va, *a.* corporative.

corporeidad, *n.f.* corporeity.

corporificación, *n.f.* materialization.

corporificar, *v.t.* to materialize; (*chem.*) to solidify (liquid).

corpóreo, -rea, *a.* corporeal, corporal.

corps, *n.m.* body, corps; *los guardias de corps,* Life Guards; *sumiller de corps,* Lord Chamberlain.

corpudo, -da, *a.* corpulent, bulky.

corpulencia, *n.f.* corpulence.

corpulento, -ta, *a.* corpulent, fat, fleshy.

corpus, *n.m.* Corpus Christi (day and procession).

corpuscular, *a.* corpuscular.

corpusculista, *n.m.* corpuscularian, atomist.

corpúsculo, *n.m.* corpuscle, atom, molecule.

corral, *n.m.* yard, enclosure; pen, fold, stockyard, poultry-yard; fish-pond; (*obs.*) open-air theatre; (*fig.*) blank left by students when taking down lectures; *corral de ovejas,* ruin, devastated building; *corral de madera,* timber-yard; *corral de vacas,* (*fam.*) dirty, ill-kept place; *hacer corrales,* to play truant.

corralero, -ra, *a.* appertaining to a corral. — *n.m.* keeper of a dung-yard. — *n.f.* (*prov.*) Andalusian song and dance; brazen-faced woman.

corralillo; corralito, *n.m.* small yard [CORRAL].

corraliza, *n.f.* yard, court.

corralón, *n.m.* large yard [CORRAL].

correa, *n.f.* leather strap or thong, leash; flexibility; patience, resistance; shoelace; (*arch.*) joist, purlin. — *pl.* duster made of thongs; *correa de transmisión* or *correa sin fin,* (*mech.*) belt, belting; *besar la correa,* to humble oneself to another; *tener correa,* to put up with chaff or sarcasm; to be strong for physical work.

correaje, *n.m.* belting; heap of leather straps.

correal, *n.m.* dressed reddish deerskin; *coser* or *labrar de correal,* to stitch with thongs.

correar, *v.t.* to draw out wool, prepare it for use.

correazo, *n.m.* blow with a leather strap.

correcalles, *n.m.f.* gadabout, idler, lounger.

corrección, *n.f.* correction; reprehension, amendment, emendation; correctness; proper demeanour.

correccional, *a.* correctional, corrective. — *n.m.* gaol, reformatory.

correccionalismo, *n.m.* treatment of delinquents in reformatories.

correccionalmente, *adv.* as a corrective, by way of correction.

correccionario, -ria, *n.m.f.* inmate of reformatory.

correctamente, *adv.* correctly.

correctivamente, *adv.* [CORRECCIONALMENTE].

correctivo, -va, *n.m.f.*, *a.* (*med.*) corrective, antidote.

correcto, -ta, *a.* exact, correct, conforming to rules; properly behaved. — *p.p. irreg.* [CORREGIR].

corrector, -ra, *a.* correcting, amending. — *n.m.f.* corrector, amender; proof-reader; superior in a convent of St. Francis of Paula.

corredentor, -ra, *n.m.f.* redeemer jointly with another.

corredera, *n.f.* race-ground; sliding panel; upper grinding-stone; wood-louse; cock-roach; street; (*naut.*) log, log-line; (*coll.*) procuress; (*print.*) track, slide, rail; (*mech.*) slide-valve; (*mech.*) tongue, rail, guide (of piston-rod, etc.); (*mint.*) milling machine; *echar la corredera,* (*naut.*) to heave the log.

corredizo, -za, *a.* easily untied; running (knot).

corredor, -ra, *a.* running much; (*orn.*) cursorial. — *n.m.* runner; corridor, gallery; (*fort.*) covered-way; (*mil.*) scout; (*mil.*) forager; (*com.*) broker; (*slang*) thief; (*slang*) catchpole. — *n.f.pl.* (*orn.*) Cursores; *corredor de cambios,* stock-broker, money-broker; *corredor de comercio, de lonja* or *de mercaderías,* (*com.*) agent or broker acting in commercial transactions as the stock-broker does in financial ones; *corredor(a) de oreja,* stock-broker; (*coll.*) tale-bearer; (*slang*) pimp, procurer, procuress.

corredorcillo, *n.m.* small corridor or gallery [CORREDOR].

corredura, *n.f.* overflow.

correduría, *n.f.* brokerage; broker's office.

correería, *n.f.* strap-maker's trade, shop or factory.

correero, -ra, *n.m.f.* strap-maker or vendor.

corregencia, *n.f.* co-regency.

corregente, *n.m.f.* co-regent.

corregibilidad, *n.f.* corrigibility.

corregible, *a.* corrigible.

corregidor, -ra, *a.* correcting. — *n.m.f.* corrector. — *n.m.* (*obs.*) corregidor, magistrate, mayor. — *n.f.* (*obs.*) magistrate's wife.

corregimiento, *n.m.* office or district of a corregidor or magistrate.

corregir, *v.t.* (*p.p.* **corregido** and **correcto;** *pres. indic.* **corrijo;** *pres. subj.* **corrija**) to correct, mend, amend; to admonish, reprehend; (*fig.*) to mitigate, temper; to rectify, set straight; to remove, destroy. — *v.r.* to mend, improve; *corregirse de un defecto,* to cure oneself of a defect.

corregüela; correhuela, *n.f.* small strap [CORREA]; child's play with a strap; (*bot.*) bindweed; *corregüela de buen cuero, de ruin mozo hace bueno,* a good belting improves a naughty child.

correinado, *n.m.* joint rule by two kings.

correinante, *a.* reigning jointly with another.

correjel, *n.m.* sole-leather.

correlación, *n.f.* correlation, analogy.

correlacionar, *v.t.* to correlate. — *v.r.* to be correlated.

correlativamente, *adv.* correlatively.

correlativo, -va; correlato, -ta, *a.* correlative.

correligionario, -ria, *a.* of the same religion or politics. — *n.m.f.* co-religionist; fellowmember of same (political) party.

correncia, *n.f.* (*coll.*) diarrhœa; (*coll.*) embarrassment, bashfulness.

correndilla, *n.f.* (*coll.*) short run.

correntía, *n.f.* irrigation of stubbly ground.

correntío, -tía, *a.* current, running; (*coll.*) light, unembarrassed, free. — *n.f.* (*fam.*) diarrhœa.

correntón, -na, *a.* gay, pleasant, fond of company, cheerful. — *n.m.f.* gadabout.

correntoso, -sa, *a.* (*Ám.*) swift, of strong current (rivers).

correo, *n.m.* messenger; postman; post; postoffice; mail; letters, correspondence; mailtrain; (*law*) accomplice; *correo de gabinete,* courier; *correo de malas nuevas,* (*coll.*) bearer of bad news.

correón, *n.m.* large leather strap [CORREA].

correosidad, *n.f.* ductility; flexibility.

correoso, -sa, *a.* ductile, flexible, easily bent or stretched; tough, hard to chew (bread).

correr, *v.i.* to run, speed, hasten, race; to glide, flow, stream; to run on, pass, slip away (time); to blow (winds); to extend, stretch; to count from (salary, etc.); to become due; to go on, continue; (*com.*) to pass through the proper channel; to be current, accepted; to solicit protection; to continue, be valid (for a period); to be worth, cost; (*naut.*) to sail with reduced canvas owing to strong wind; to be said, be common talk, rumoured; (*Mex.*) to run about carousing at night. — *v.t.* to tip over (scale); to race, gallop (a horse); to persecute, harass; to fight (bull); to pass, move; to turn (key); to push, draw aside, slide; to undo (knot); to run a risk, be exposed to; to travel in or over; to overrun; to auction; to sell in the street; (*com.*) to act as agent; (*coll.*) to snatch away; to shame, embarrass. — *v.r.* to file, move to the right or left; to slide; to gutter (candle); (*coll.*) to be too effusive or generous; to feel embarrassed; *a más* or *a todo correr,* at full speed; *a turbio correr,* however bad or unfortunate it may be; *correr a uno (alguna cosa),* to behove one, be incumbent on one (something); *correr el año,* the year is running on; *correr el pago,* to meet the payment; *corre la fama, el rumor* or *la voz,* it is said or ru-

moured; *corre el plazo,* (*com.*) the period of grace is elapsing; *correr la comparación,* to establish a comparison; *correr el cerrojo,* to bolt the door; *correr uno con* or *correr por uno alguna cosa,* to be in charge of, attend to something; *correr con uno,* to be on good terms with someone; *el que menos corre, vuela,* he gets what he wants while pretending indifference; *corre a mi cargo,* I am responsible for this; *correr con los gastos,* to bear the expenses; *correr en busca de uno,* to hasten in search of someone; *correr por mal camino,* to run on the wrong road; *correr un velo sobre lo pasado,* to draw a veil over the past, forget; *corre que corre,* to keep on running; *correr con desgracia,* to be unfortunate; *correr la voz,* to pass the word; to be divulged; *la línea corre . . . ,* the boundary line passes . . . ; *correr monte,* to hunt big game; *correr sangre,* to shed blood; *correr peligro,* to run the risk; *corre mal tiempo,* the times are evil; *corren las canales,* the water flows through the channels; *correr la cortina,* to draw the curtain; to pass over in silence; to discover; *correrla,* to go on the spree; *correr las horas* or *el tiempo,* time flies; *correr lanzas,* to joust; *correrlo todo,* to go through it all; *correr parejas,* to be alike (things); *correr prisa,* to be urgent; *corre como alma que lleva el diablo* or *como caballo desbocado, corre que se las pela,* he is running for his life; *correr a rienda suelta,* to ride at full speed; to give rein to one's passion; *correr fortuna,* (*naut.*) to sail before the wind; to pass through a storm; *corre el verso,* the verse runs smoothly; *quien más corre, menos anda,* the more haste, the less speed; *correr baquetas,* to run the gauntlet; *correr con armonía,* to live in peace; *correr ganado,* to capture stray cattle; *correr las amonestaciones,* to publish the banns of marriage; *correr sin freno,* to give oneself up to vice; *correr los negocios,* to transact business expeditiously; *correr en una dirección opuesta,* to run counter; *corre la moneda,* the money circulates; *correr las lágrimas,* to weep much; *correr el telón,* (*theat.*) to drop the curtain; *corre la tinta,* the ink is fluid; *corre viento del norte,* the wind blows from the north; *el monte corre a . . . ,* the mountain extends to . . . ; *correrse una vela,* to gutter (of a candle); *correr la palabra,* (*mil.*) to give the word; *correr la oficina,* to miss the office, play truant; *correr a bolina,* (*naut.*) to sail by the wind; *correr sobre un bajel,* (*naut.*) to bear down upon a vessel; *correr hacia la tierra,* (*naut.*) to stand in; *correr con la mar en popa,* (*naut.*) to scud before the sea; *correr los mares,* (*naut.*) to follow the sea; *correr a palo seco,* (*naut.*) to scud under bare poles; *correr tormenta* or *correr a dos puños,* (*naut.*) to run before the wind in a storm; *correr un viento forzado,* (*naut.*) to weather a storm.

correría, *n.f.* (*mil.*) hostile incursion, foray; leather strap; pleasure trip, excursion. — *pl.* youthful escapades; travels.

correspondencia, *n.f.* correspondence, mail; intercourse, friendship; fitness, consent, agreement; proportion, congruity, symmetry.

corresponder, *v.i.* to return (a favour, affection, regard, etc.); to fit, suit, agree, correspond, answer, belong to. — *v.r.* to correspond, keep up intimacy or intercourse by letter-writing; to respect and love reciprocally; *corresponder a los beneficios*, to return kindnesses; *corresponder con el bienhechor*, to be grateful to the benefactor; *corresponderse con un amigo*, to correspond with a friend; *a todos aquellos a quienes corresponda*, to all whom it may concern.

correspondiente, *a.* correspondent, agreeable, suitable, conformable; corresponding. — *n.m.f.* correspondent.

correspondientemente, *adv.* correspondently, correspondingly.

corresponsal, *a.* (*com.*) correspondent, agent. — *n.m.* correspondent, agent; correspondence clerk.

corresponsalía, *n.f.* office of a newspaper correspondent.

corretaje, *n.m.* broking; brokerage.

corretear, *v.t.* (*fam.*) to rove, ramble, walk the streets, jaunt, gad about.

correteo, *n.m.* gadding, roaming about.

corretero, -ra, *a.* gadding, idling about. — *n.m.f.* gadabout, idler.

correvedile; correveidile, *n.m.f.* (*coll.*) talebearer, mischief-maker; (*fig., coll.*) procurer, procuress, go-between.

correverás, *n.m.* spring or mechanical toy.

corrida, *n.f.* course, race, career, sprint, run; (*aer.*) taxying; *corrida de toros*, bull-fight; *corrida del tiempo*, flight of time; *de corrida*, fluently, easily.

corridamente, *adv.* fluently, easily, readily.

corrido, -da, *a.* exceeding in weight or measure; running, cursive (handwriting); (*fam.*) abashed, ashamed; (*fam.*) man of the world, expert, experienced, artful. — *n.m.* romance; shed built along the walls of a corral; *de corrido*, fluently, easily. — *p.p.* [CORRER].

corriente, *a.* running; instant, present (week, month, year or century); current; admitted, acknowledged generally; usual, ordinary; easy, fluent (style); common; middling (quality). — *n.f.* current (of water, etc.); (*fig.*) course, progression. — *adv.* all right, agreed; *al corriente*, punctually, regularly; *corriente de aire*, air draught; *corriente eléctrica*, electric current; *corriente y moliente*, very much as usual; *corriente alterna*, alternating current; *corriente continua*, continuous or direct current; *andar* or *estar corriente*, to suffer from diarrhœa; *dejarse llevar de*, or *irse con* or *tras la corriente*, to follow the crowd; *estar al corriente de una cosa*, to be acquainted with, be informed of something; *ir* or *navegar contra la corriente*, to go against the tide; *poner a uno al corriente de una cosa*, to acquaint, inform someone of something; *tomar la corriente desde la fuente*, to go to the source or root of a matter.

corrientemente, *adv.* easily, fluently.

corrigendo, -da, *n.m.f., a.* person in reformatory.

corrijo; corrija, *pres. indic.; pres. subj.* [CORREGIR].

corrillero, -ra, *a.* idling, roving. — *n.m.f.* vagabond, lounger, idler.

corrillo, *n.m.* coterie, clique, group of loungers.

corrimiento, *n.m.* running; melting; (*med.*) fluxion; (*fig.*) shyness, bashfulness; (*agric.*) blight (of vine blossoms).

corrincho, *n.m.* meeting of low people, rabble.

corrivación, *n.f.* impoundage (of water).

corro, *n.m.* circle or ring of spectators, etc.; round enclosure; children's round dance; *bailo bien, y echaisme del corro*, those most deserving of appreciation often get least; *hacer corro*, to clear the way, make room; *echar en corro*, to draw a bow at a venture; *escupir* or *meterse en corro*, to introduce oneself into a conversation; *hacer corro aparte*, to form or join another party.

corroborable, *a.* corroborable, confirmable.

corroboración, *n.f.* corroboration.

corroboradamente, *adv.* with corroboration, confirmatively.

corroborador, -ra, *a.* corroboratory. — *n.m.f.* corroborator.

corroborante, *a.* corroborating. — *n.m.* (*med.*) corroborative, corroborant.

corroborar, *v.t.* to corroborate, confirm; to fortify, strengthen. — *v.r.* to be corroborated, strengthened.

corroborativo, -va, *a.* corroborative, confirming.

corrobra, *n.f.* treat at conclusion of bargain.

corroer, *v.t.* to corrode; (*fig.*) to fret. — *v.r.* to become corroded.

corrompedor, -ra, *a.* corrupting. — *n.m.f.* corrupter.

corromper, *v.t.* (*p.p.* **corrompido** and **corrupto**) to alter, change (the form or shape); to corrupt, damage; (*fig.*) to seduce, pervert (a woman); to bribe, suborn; (*fig.*) to mar, falsify, vitiate; (*coll.*) to incommode, disturb, irritate; (*fam.*) to administer laxatives. — *v.i.* to stink, be corrupt. — *v.r.* to rot, become putrid; to become corrupt.

corrompidamente, *adv.* corruptly.

corroncho, *n.m.* (*Col.*) small fresh-water fish.

corrosal, *n.m.* custard-apple tree and fruit.

corrosible, *a.* easily corroded.

corrosión, *n.f.* corrosion, exulceration.

corrosivo, -va, *a.* corrosive; *sublimado corrosivo*, corrosive sublimate.

corroyente, *a.* corroding.

corrugación, *n.f.* corrugation.

corrugador, *n.m., a.* (*anat.*) corrugator.

corrulla, *n.f.* [CORULLA].

corrumpente, *a.* corrupting; (*coll.*) annoying, vexing.

corrupción, *n.f.* corruption, putrefaction, stench, pollution, filth; spurious passage in a writing; perversion of manners; corruptness, depravity, depravation.

corruptamente, *adv.* corruptly, viciously.

corruptela, *n.f.* corruption; depravation; (*law*) abuse.

corruptibilidad, *n.f.* corruptibility.

corruptible, *a.* corruptible.

corruptivo, -va, *a.* corruptive.

corrupto, -ta, *a.* corrupted, corrupt, defiled, perverse. — *p.p. irreg.* [CORROMPER].

corruptor, -ra, *a.* corrupting. — *n.m.f.* corrupter, misleader.

corrusco, *n.m.* (*coll.*) crust of bread.

corsario, *n.m., a.* corsair, privateer (man and ship); pirate.

corsé, *n.m.* corset, stays.

corsear, *v.i.* to cruise as a privateer.

corsetería, *n.f.* corset-factory or shop.

corsetero, -ra, *n.m.f.* corset-maker or seller.

corso, *n.m.* privateering cruise.

corso, -sa, *n.m.f.*, *a.* Corsican.

corta, *n.f.* felling of trees; (*W. Indies*) sugar-cane cutting.

cortaalambres, *n.m.* wire-cutter.

cortabolsas, *n.m.f.*, pickpocket, cutpurse.

cortacallos, *n.m.* corn-cutter.

cortacigarros, *n.m.* cigar-cutter.

cortacircuitos, *n.m.* (*elect.*) cut-out, circuit breaker.

cortacorriente, *n.m.* (*elect.*) contact-breaker.

cortadera, *n.f.* chisel for cutting hot iron; bee-keeper's knife; (*Arg., Chi.*) cyperaceous plant used in making rope and hats.

cortadillo, -lla, *a.* clipped (coin). — *n.m.* small drinking glass, tumbler; gill (liquid measure); *echar cortadillos,* (*fig.*) to speak affectedly; (*fig.*) to drink glasses of wine.

cortado, -da, *a.* cut; fit, exact, proportioned, adapted, accommodated; brief, laconic (style); (*her.*) parted in the middle. — *n.m.* caper, leap. — *p.p.* [CORTAR].

cortador, -ra, *a.* cutting. — *n.m.* cutter, (tailoring, etc.); butcher; incisor (tooth); cutter (tool).

cortadora, *n.f.* cutting board in a velvet loom.

cortadura, *n.f.* cut, cutting, abscission, slit, slash, incision; wound made by cutting, fissure; (*fort.*) parapet with embrasures and merlons; mountain pass; figure cut out of paper. — *pl.* shreds, cuttings.

cortafrío, *n.m.* cold chisel, cutting-iron.

cortafuego, *n.m.* (*agric.*) clearing left to prevent fire spreading; (*arch.*) fireproof wall between buildings.

cortalápices, *n.m.* pencil-sharpener.

cortamalla, *n.f.* pruning of agglomerated vine-branch.

cortamente, *adv.* sparingly, scantly, frugally; curtly, succinctly.

cortamiento, *n.m.* perturbation.

cortante, *a.* cutting, edged, sharp, biting. — *n.m.* butcher.

cortapapel, *n.m.* paper-cutter, paper-knife, letter opener.

cortapicos, *n.m.* earwig.

cortapicos y callares, (*coll.*) hold your tongue.

cortapiés, *n.m.* (*fencing*) thrust at the legs.

cortapisa, *n.f.* condition or restriction accompanying a gift; obstacle, impediment, hindrance; elegance in speaking.

cortaplumas, *n.m.* penknife.

cortapruebas, *n.m.* cutter for photographic prints.

cortapuros, *n.m.* cigar-cutter.

cortar, *v.t.* to cut, divide, shear, separate; to trim (a quill); to cut out (garments, etc.); to dilute (liquids); to cut (at cards); to detain, impede; to curtail, suppress; to cut honeycombs (from the hives); to cut away, trim, chip, pare off; to interrupt, cut in, suspend; to cut short; to engrave; to arbitrate, decide; to curdle; (*mil.*) to intercept. — *v.r.* to be perturbed; to be daunted, ashamed, confused; to chap; to curdle; to split, crack; to wear out in the folds (garments); (*geom.*) to intersect, cut each other; *aire que corta,* cutting, piercing wind; *cortar* (*un idioma, un verso*) *bien* or *mal,* to pronounce (a language, a verse) well or badly; *cortar las alas a uno,* (*fig.*) to take one down, clip one's wings; *cortar el agua,* to cut off the water; *cortar el hilo de la conversación,* to cut short the con-

versation; *cortar las libranzas,* to stop payment for goods received; *cortar el naipe,* to cut for deal (at cards); *cortar de raíz,* to eradicate; *cortar de vestir,* to cut and make clothes; (*coll.*) to censure; *cortar el vino con agua,* to dilute wine with water; *cortar las piernas,* to render (a thing) impossible; *cortar por el camino más corto,* to take a short cut; *cortar por lo sano,* to cut to the quick; *se corta la leche,* the milk is turning sour; *cortarse las uñas con alguno,* to pick a quarrel with someone.

cortarraíces, *n.m.* root-cutter.

cortavapor, *n.m.* cut-off of an engine.

cortavidrios, *n.m.* glazier's diamond.

cortaviento, *n.m.* wind-screen (of vehicles); (*aer.*) wind-shield.

corte, *n.m.* cut, cutting; cutting-edge; trimming (of quill); cut, fit (of garment, shoe, etc.); quantity of material needed for garment, etc.; (*mil.*) tailor's shop; exsection, abscission; notch, hack; felling of trees; arbitration; *corte de vestido,* dress- or suit-length; *un corte de cuentas,* non-payment of debts, defaulting.

corte, *n.f.* royal court; capital or city where the king resides; levee; suite, retinue; chancery; courtyard; stable; sheepfold. — *pl.* Cortes, legislative assembly of Spain; *la corte celestial,* paradise; *hacer la corte,* to court, woo.

cortedad, *n.f.* smallness, littleness, minuteness; (*fig.*) dullness, stupidity; pusillanimity, timidity, diffidence, bashfulness; *cortedad de medios,* lack of means.

cortejador, -ra, *a.* courting, wooing. — *n.m.f.* wooer.

cortejante, *a.* courting, wooing. — *n.m.* gallant, beau.

cortejar, *v.t.* to woo, make love; to court, pay homage; to accompany, escort, attend.

cortejo, *n.m.* court, homage, courtship, gift, present, gratification; gallant, beau; lover, sweetheart; paramour; cortège.

corteña, *n.f.* (*print.*) blank page.

cortes, *n.f.pl.* [CORTE].

cortés, *a.* courteous, polite, gentle, genteel, mild, civil, complaisant, gracious, courtly, mannerly.

cortesanamente, *adv.* courteously, politely.

cortesanazo, -za, *a.* affectedly polite, fulsome.

cortesanía, *n.f.* courtesy, civility, politeness, good manners, complaisance.

cortesano, -na, *a.* courtly, court-like; affable, courteous, obliging. — *n.m.* courtier; *dama cortesana,* courtesan.

cortesía, *n.f.* courtesy, civility, good manners, courteousness; obeisance; compliment; gift, present; favour, mercy, gratification; (*print.*) blank left between two chapters; (*obs.*) days of grace for payment of a bill of exchange; *hacer una cortesía,* to curtsey.

cortésmente, *adv.* courteously, civilly, politely, obligingly.

corteza, *n.f.* bark, peel, skin, rind, crust; outward appearance; (*met.*) rusticity, crustiness, boorishness; (*orn.*) widgeon.

cortezón, *n.m.* thick bark, rind, crust [CORTEZA].

cortezudo, -da, *a.* very barky or crusty; (*fig.*) rustic, boorish, unmannerly, unpolished.

cortezuela, *n.f.* thin bark, crust or rind [COR-TEZA].

cortical, *a.* cortical.

cortijada, *n.f.* houses round a farmhouse or grange.

cortijero, -ra, *n.m.f.* owner of a cortijo, farmer. — *n.f.* farmer's wife. — *n.m.* land agent or steward.

cortijo, *n.m.* farmhouse, grange; *alborotar el cortijo,* (*coll.*) to cause excitement.

cortil, *n.m.* courtyard.

cortina, *n.f.* curtain; shade, screen; (*fort.*) curtain; covering; lees, dregs; *cortina de muelle,* jetty; *correr la cortina,* to discover, decipher, detect; to hush up, pass over in silence; *dormir a cortinas verdes,* to sleep in the open air; *descorrer la cortina,* to draw the curtain; *a cortina corrida,* in secret, behind closed doors.

cortinaje, *n.m.* set of curtains for a house.

cortinal, *n.m.* allotment, croft.

cortinilla, *n.f.* net or lace curtain.

cortinón, *n.m.* large curtain [CORTINA] .

cortiña, *n.f.* (*prov.*) allotment, garden plot.

corto, -ta, *a.* short, narrow, small, little; brief; scanty; curt, laconic, concise; dull, stupid, weak-minded; pusillanimous; imperfect, defective; timid, shy, backward; *corto de genio,* diffident; short-tempered; *corto de oído,* hard of hearing; *corto de vista,* short-sighted; *a la corta o a la larga,* sooner or later; *corto en dar,* not over-generous; *quedarse corto,* to stop short, forget what one would say.

cortón, *n.m.* mole-cricket; mantis.

corúa, *n.f.* (*Cub.*) web-footed bird resembling the cormorant.

corulla, *n.f.* place for stowing cordage in galleys.

corundo, *n.m.* corundum.

coruña, *n.f.* coarse canvas.

coruñés, -sa, *n.m.f., a.* of or belonging to Corunna.

coruscación, *n.f.* (*phys.*) coruscation, flashing, brilliancy.

coruscante; corusco, -ca, *a.* (*poet.*) coruscant.

coruscar, *v.i.* (*poet.*) to shine, coruscate.

corva, *n.f.* back of the knee; (*vet.*) curb.

corvadura, *n.f.* curvature, crookedness, inflexion, gibbosity; (*arch.*) bend of an arch or vault.

corval, *a.* oblong-shaped (olive).

corvato, *n.m.* young crow or rook.

corvaza, *n.f.* (*vet.*) curb.

corvecito, *n.m.* small crow or rook [CUERVO].

corvejón, *n.m.* gambrel, hock, hough; spur of a cock; (*orn.*) cormorant.

corvejos, *n.m.pl.* hock-joint of quadrupeds.

corveta, *n.f.* curvet, leap or bound.

corvetear, *v.i.* to curvet, bound, leap.

corvídeo, -dea, *a.* (*orn.*) corvine.

córvidos, *n.m.pl.* corvus genus of birds.

corvillo, *n.m.* bill-hook, pruning-knife, paring-knife; small sickle for cutting velvet-pile; *miércoles corvillo,* Ash Wednesday.

corvina, *n.f.* kind of conger; white sea-bass.

corvinera, *n.f.* fishing-net for sea-bass.

corvino, -na, *a.* corvine, raven-like.

corvo, -va, *a.* bent, crooked, arched. — *n.m.* grappling-iron; (*ichth.*) kind of conger.

corzo, -za, *n.m.f.* roe-deer, fallow-deer.

corzuelo, *n.m.* wheat left by threshers.

cosa, *n.f.* thing, substance; matter, affair; (*law*) chattel, property; *cosa de entidad,* important, valuable thing; *cosa del otro jueves,* odd thing; out-of-date matter; *no ser cosa del otro jueves* or *mundo,* to be very insignificant or ordinary (action or saying); *cosa de mieles,* exquisite thing; *cosa de oír* or *de ver,* thing worth hearing or seeing; *cosa dura,* intolerable thing; *cosa no* or *nunca vista,* surprising, unheard-of thing; *cosa perdida* or *perdida cosa,* incorrigible, unreliable person; *¡cosa rara!,* how strange, how extraordinary! *cosa ridícula* or *de risa,* laughing-stock; *cada cosa en su tiempo, y los nabos en adviento,* everything at the proper time; *cada cosa para su cosa,* everything should be applied to its proper purpose; *como quien hace otra cosa* or *como quien tal cosa no hace,* dissembling, dissimulating; *como quien no quiere la cosa,* feigning indifference; *como si tal cosa,* as if nothing had happened; *corran las cosas como corrieren,* come what may; *cosa con cosa* or *quisicosa,* riddle, conundrum; *brava cosa,* (*iron.*) foolish or unreasonable thing; *fuerte cosa,* difficult, trying affair; *poquita cosa,* poor thing, weakling (bodily or mentally); *cosas del mundo,* ups and downs of life; *cosas de viento,* trifles; *a cosa hecha,* with certain success; *cosa de,* about, more or less; *ante todas cosas,* before everything; *cosas de . . . ,* doings or ways of . . . , just like . . . ; *cosa cumplida sólo en la otra vida,* there's no certainty in this life; *cosa hallada no es hurtada,* findings is keepings; *cosa mala nunca muere,* evil lives on (i.e. the good is forgotten); *cosas que van y vienen,* console yourself, that will pass; *dejando una cosa por otra,* changing the subject; *dejarlo como cosa perdida,* to give up as hopeless; *disponer uno sus cosas,* to put one's affairs in order (before dying); *el que no duda, no sabe cosa alguna,* don't take everything for granted; *es cosa de nunca acabar,* it's a never-ending business; *las cosas de palacio van despacio,* this affair is going very slowly; *muchas cosas a su madre,* kind regards to your mother; *ni cosa que lo valga,* nothing of the kind; *no es cosa,* it doesn't matter; *no hay tal cosa,* there's no such thing, it is not true; *no hacer cosa a derechas,* not to do anything right; *no hay cosa con cosa,* there's no order or method about it; *no hay cosa más barata que la que se compra,* gifts are often more expensive than purchases; *no ponérsele a uno cosa por delante,* to overcome all obstacles; *no sea cosa que,* lest; *no ser* or *valer cosa,* not to be worth a rush; *no tener uno cosa suya,* to be very generous, liberal; *¿qué cosa?* (*fam.*) what? what do you say? *quedarle a uno otra cosa en el cuerpo* or *estómago,* to say one thing and mean another; *quien las cosas mucho apura, no tiene vida segura,* mind your own business; *ser algo cosa de uno,* to be one's affair.

cosaco, -ca, *n.m.f., a.* Cossack. — *n.f.* Cossack dance.

cosaquería, *n.f.* brutal raid, incursion.

cosario, -ria, *a.* piratical; beaten, frequented (path, etc.). — *n.m.* carrier, messenger, courier; professional huntsman; (*obs.*) corsair, pirate.

coscarana, *n.f.* (*prov.*) cracknel.
coscarse, *v.r.* (*coll.*) to shrug the shoulders.
coscoja, *n.f.* oak inhabited by kermes insect; dried oak-leaf; ring on bridle-bit.
coscojal; coscojar, *n.m.* plantation of *coscojas*.
coscojo, *n.m.* kermes oak-gall; (*pl.*) chains of bridle-bit.
coscolina, *n.f.* (*Mex.*) harlot.
coscomate, *n.m.* (*Mex.*) corn barn.
coscón, -na, *n.m.f.*, *a.* crafty, sly (person).
coscoroba, *n.f.* (*Arg., Chi.*) small swan with a short neck.
coscorrón, *n.m.* contusion, blow, bruise (on the head).
coscorronera, *n.f.* [CHICHONERA].
cosecante, *n.m.* (*trig.*) cosecant.
cosecha, *n.f.* harvest, harvest-time; yield, crop; collection of immaterial things; *cosecha de vino*, vintage; *de su cosecha*, of one's own invention; *tras poca cosecha, ruin trigo*, troubles never come singly.
cosechar, *v.t.*, *v.i.* to reap, harvest.
cosechero, -ra, *n.m.f.* owner of the crop or harvest.
cosedizo, -za, *a.* which can be stitched or sewed.
coselete, *n.m.* corslet; pikeman; thorax (of insects).
coseno, *n.m.* (*trig.*) cosine; *coseno verso*, versed cosine.
coser, *v.t.* to sew, stitch, join, unite; (*naut.*) to lash, fix, seize, nail; to rivet (a boiler, etc.); *coserse la boca* or *los labios*, to remain silent; *coser a puñaladas*, (*coll.*) to stab repeatedly; *coser a zurcido*, to fine-draw, darn; *coser y cantar*, to offer no difficulties; *coserse unos a* or *con otros*, to stick close together (people); *máquina de coser*, sewing-machine.
cosera, *n.f.* (*prov.*) piece of land that can be irrigated all at once.
cosetada, *n.f.* race, quick run, sprint.
cosible, *a.* which can be sewed.
cosicosa, *n.f.* puzzle, riddle.
cosido, -da, *a.* sewed, sewn; attached. — *n.m.* needlework; action of sewing. — *p.p.* [COSER]; *cosido a*, devoted, wedded to; *cosido de la cama*, quilt and blankets stitched together.
cosidura, *n.f.* (*naut.*) kind of lashing.
cosmética, *n.f.* art of making cosmetics.
cosmético, *n.m.* cosmetic.
cósmico, -ca, *a.* cosmic.
cosmogonía, *n.f.* cosmogony.
cosmogónico, -ca, *a.* cosmogonic(al).
cosmografía, *n.f.* cosmography.
cosmográfico, -ca, *a.* cosmographical.
cosmógrafo, -fa, *n.m.f.* cosmographer.
cosmología, *n.f.* cosmology.
cosmológico, -ca, *a.* cosmological.
cosmólogo, -ga, *n.m.f.* cosmologist.
cosmopolita, *n.m.f.*, *a.* cosmopolite, cosmopolitan.
cosmopolitismo, *n.m.* cosmopolitism, cosmopolitanism.
cosmos, *n.m.* cosmos, universe.
coso, *n.m.* (*prov.*) high street; place for bullfights; timber-worm; *coso de flores*, battle of flowers.
cospe, *n.m.* hacking stroke (in timber-cutting).
cospel, *n.m.* planchet, coin-blank (in the mint).
cospillo, *n.m.* (*prov.*) olive lees, bagasse.
cosque, *n.m.* (*fam.*) [COSCORRÓN].
cosquilladizo, -za, *a.* touchy, peevish.

cosquillar; cosquillear, *v.t.* to tickle; to tease, irritate. — *v.r.* to be excited by curiosity, desire, suspicion; to be resentful, quarrelsome, touchy; to laugh, be amused.
cosquillas, *n.f.pl.* tickling, titillation; *buscarle a uno las cosquillas*, (*coll.*) to tease, irritate; *hacerle a uno cosquillas una cosa*, to be tickled by something; to excite desire or suspicion; *no sufrir cosquillas*, not to be able to stand jokes; *tener malas cosquillas*, (*coll.*) to be easily offended, ill-tempered.
cosquillejas, *n.f.pl.* light tickle or tickling [COSQUILLAS].
cosquilleo, *n.m.* tickling.
cosquilloso, -sa, *a.* ticklish; (*fig.*) susceptible, irritable, peevish.
costa, *n.f.* cost, charge, expense, price paid; costing; board wages; coast, shore; beach, seashore, seaboard; (*fig.*) labour, fatigue; shoemaker's boxwood polisher; (*pl.*) (*law*) costs; *a costa de*, at the expense of; *a mi costa*, at my expense; *a toda costa*, at all hazards, at all costs; *condenar en costas*, (*law*) to sentence a party to pay costs; *andar, ir* or *navegar costa a costa*, to coast, sail along the coast; *dar a la costa*, (*naut.*) to be blown towards the coast; *salir* or *ser condenado a costas*, to bear all the losses of an affair.
Costa del Marfil, *n.f.* Ivory Coast.
Costa de Oro, *n.f.* Gold Coast.
costado, *n.m.* side; flank of troops; side of a ship. — *pl.* race, lineage, succession of ancestors; *dolor de costado*, stitch in the side.
costal, *a.* (*anat.*) costal. — *n.m.* sack, large bag; brace of frame for making adobe walls; *ésa es harina de otro costal*, that is quite a different thing; *estar hecho un costal de huesos*, to be a bag of bones; *no ser uno costal*, not to be able to say everything at once; *no parecer costal de paja*, to be attractive to one of a different sex; *el costal de los pecados*, (*fam.*) the human body; *de costal vacío nunca buen bodigo*, poor men can give but poor presents; *vaciar el costal*, to unburden oneself.
costalada, *n.f.* fall on the ground.
costalazo, *n.m.* [COSTALADA]; *dar un costalazo*, to fall flat on the ground.
costalejo, *n.m.* small sack [COSTAL].
costalero, *n.m.* (*prov.*) porter.
costalgia, *n.f.* pain in the side.
costana, *n.f.* steep road or street; (*naut.*) frame.
costanera, *n.f.* slope. — *pl.* rafters.
costanero, -ra, *a.* coastal, coasting; inclining downwards; *buque costanero*, coaster.
costanilla, *n.f.* steep street; gentle slope.
costar, *v.i.* (*pres. indic.* cuesto; *pres. subj.* cueste) to cost, be bought for, be had at a price, be expensive; to cause loss or harm; *costar la torta un pan*, (*coll.*) to pay dear for one's whistle; *costarle a uno caro* (*cara*) *una cosa*, to pay dearly for a thing; *cueste lo que cueste*, at any price.
costarricense; costarriqueño, -na, *a.* Costa Rican.
coste, *n.m.* cost, expense, price; *a coste y costas*, at first cost, without profit.
costeado, -da, *a.* paid, paid for. — *p.p.* [COSTEAR(SE)].
costear, *v.t.* to pay the cost, bear all charges; (*naut.*) to coast. — *v.r.* to pay for itself, repay costs.

costeño, -na, *a.* coasting; sloping; *barco costeño,* small coasting boat.

costera, *n.f.* side of a bale of goods; outside quire of a ream of hand-made paper; slope, incline; coast; (*naut.*) salmon-fishing season.

costeramente, *adv.* coastward, coastwise.

costero, -ra, *a.* coastal, coasting; spoilt in manufacture and used as *costera* (paper). — *n.m.* wood nearest to the bark; (*min.*) side of a furnace; (*min.*) side face of a seam.

costezuela, *n.f.* slight declivity, slope [CUESTA].

costil, *a.* (*anat.*) costal.

costilla, *n.f.* rib; anything resembling a rib; (*carp.*) furring; part of an organ bellows; (*coll.*) property, support, wealth; chop, cutlet; (*coll.*) wife; rung of chair; stave of barrel. — *pl.* shoulders, back; (*mech.*) cramp-irons, chimney-ties; *costilla falsa,* false rib; *costilla flotante,* floating rib; *vivir a costillas de uno,* to be living at someone else's expense; *medirle a uno las costillas,* to cudgel a person.

costillaje; costillar, *n.m.* ribs and their place in the body.

costilludo, -da, *a.* (*coll.*) broad-shouldered.

costino, -na, *a.* belonging to the costmary plant; (*Chi.*) [COSTEÑO].

costo, *n.m.* cost, price, expense, charges; labour, fatigue; (*bot.*) alecost, costmary; *a costo y costas,* at cost price.

costosamente, *adv.* in a costly way, expensively, extravagantly.

costoso, -sa, *a.* dear, expensive, costly; (*fig.*) hard to obtain; (*fig.*) sad, grievous.

costra, *n.f.* crust; broken ship's biscuit; scab (on wounds); incrusted part of a wick; *costra de azúcar,* sugar crust (left in boilers); *costra láctea,* (*med.*) scald head, infantile eczema.

costrada, *n.f.* candied seed-cake.

costroso, -sa, *a.* crusty.

costumbre, *n.f.* custom, habit, fashion, usage, conventional manner; catamenia, menses. — *pl.* manners, customs, national habits; *de costumbre,* as usual; *según costumbre,* according to custom; *depravar las costumbres,* to corrupt morals; *la costumbre es otra* or *segunda naturaleza,* habit is second nature; *la costumbre hace ley,* custom has the force of law.

costumbrista, *n.m.f.* genre writer.

costura, *n.f.* seam; needlework, sewing, stitching; riveting; (*naut.*) splicing of a rope; (*surg.*) suture; (*mech.*) crease, ridge, joint; (*carp.*) joint; *sin costura,* seamless; *sentar las costuras,* to open and press seams (in tailoring); *sentar a uno las costuras,* to slap, chastise someone.

costurera, *n.f.* seamstress, dressmaker.

costurería, *n.f.* work-room (for sewing).

costurero, *n.m.* lady's work-box or table; (*prov.*) sewing-room.

costurón, *n.m.* (*contempt.*) thick seam; large scar; coarse suture [COSTURA].

cota, *n.f.* coat of mail (also *cota de malla*), tabard-coat, coat of arms; callous skin on boar's back; quota, share; figure indicating height above a datum line (on maps); (*Philip.*) rough earthwork raised by the Moslems.

cotana, *n.f.* mortise, mortise chisel.

cotangente, *n.f.* (*trig.*) cotangent.

cotanza, *n.f.* sort of medium-fine linen.

cotarrera, *n.f.* (*slang*) woman vagabond or tramp; (*coll.*) gossip, gadabout.

cotarro, *n.m.* charity-hut, casual ward; side of a pit; *alborotar el cotarro,* (*fig.*) to cause disturbance; *andar de cotarro en cotarro,* (*fig.*) to go sauntering about.

cotejar, *v.t.* to compare, confront, collate, confer.

cotejo, *n.m.* comparison, parallel, collation.

cotense, *n.m.* (*Mex.*) rough brown linen wrapper.

coterráneo, -nea, *a.* [CONTERRÁNEO].

cotí, *n.m.* tick, ticking (material).

cotidianamente, *adv.* daily.

cotidiano, -na, *a.* daily, every day, quotidian.

cotiledón, *n.m.* (*bot.*) cotyledon.

cotiliforme, *a.* (*bot.*) cotyliform.

cotiloide; cotiloideo, -dea, *a.* (*anat.*) cotyloid.

cotilla, *n.f.* stays, corsets; (*coll.*) backbiter, gossip.

cotillero, -ra, *n.m.f.* stay-maker, stay-seller.

cotillo, *n.m.* head, striking side of the hammer.

cotillón, *n.m.* cotillion (dance).

cotín, *n.m.* back stroke given to a ball.

cotiza, *n.f.* (*her.*) band of a shield; (*Ven.*) Indian sandal.

cotizable, *a.* quotable.

cotización, *n.f.* (*com.*) quotation, rate of exchange.

cotizado, -da, *a.* (*her.*) banded; (*com.*) quoted; priced, valued. — *p.p.* [COTIZAR].

cotizador, -ra, *n.m.f.* quoter, pricer, valuer.

cotizar, *v.t.* (*pret.* coticé; *pres. subj.* cotice) (*com.*) to quote, cry out current prices on the exchange.

coto, *n.m.* enclosed pasture-ground, landmark, boundary; rate, price; handbreadth; (*prov.*) territory, district; end, limit; price-fixing combine among traders; (*ichth.*) chub; billiard contest; (*obs. prov.*) fine, mulct; *coto redondo,* hamlet belonging to one owner; *coto de caza,* shooting preserve; *poner coto a,* to put a stop to; (*Am. Mer.*) goitre.

cotobelo, *n.m.* opening in branch of bridle.

cotomono, *n.m.* (*Per.*) (*zool.*) ursine howler.

cotón, *n.m.* printed cotton.

cotona, *n.f.* (*Am.*) coarse undervest; (*Mex.*) chamois jacket.

cotonada, *n.f.* cotton goods, calico prints.

cotoncillo, *n.m.* button of a maulstick.

cotonía, *n.f.* dimity.

cotorra, *n.f.* small parrot, parakeet; magpie; (*coll.*) talkative woman.

cotorrear, *v.i.* to chatter, gabble.

cotorreo, *n.m.* (*coll.*) chattering, gossiping.

cotorrera, *n.f.* hen-parrot; (*coll.*) talkative woman.

cotorrería, *n.f.* chattering of women.

cotorrón, -na, *a.* affecting youth (old people).

cototo (*Arg., Chi.*) *n.m.* bump, bruise.

cotral, *n.m.f.,* *a.* worn-out ox or cow.

cotudo, -da, *a.* cottony, hairy, fluffy; (*Am.*) suffering with goitre.

cotufa, *n.f.* Jerusalem artichoke; titbits, delicate food, dainties; *pedir cotufas en el golfo,* to ask for impossibilities.

cotufero, -ra, *n.m.f.* maker of delicacies.

cotundo (*Cub.*) *n.m.* a night bird.

coturno, *n.m.* cothurnus, buskin; *calzar el*

coturno, to use lofty, sublime language (in poetry); *de alto coturno*, of high category.

cotutela, *n.f.* joint-tutorship.

cotutor, -ra, *n.m.f.* joint-tutor.

cotuza, *n.f.* (*ES., Guat.*) agouti, agouty.

coulomb, *n.m.* (*phys.*) coulomb.

covacha, *n.f.* small cave.

covachuela, *n.f.* small grotto; hollow; (*coll.*) office of a Crown Minister.

covachuelista; covachuelo, *n.m.* (*coll.*) clerk in a *covachuela*.

covadera, *n.f.* (*Chi., Per.*) guano bed; (*Col.*) dell.

covalonga, *n.f.* (*Ven.*) plant of the Lauraceæ family used as a substitute for quinine.

covanilla, *n.f.*; **covanillo**, *n.m.* little grape basket [CUÉVANO].

covendedor, -ra, *n.m.f.* joint-vendor.

covezuela, *n.f.* small cave [CUEVA].

coxalgia, *n.f.* arthritic pain in the hip.

coxálgico, -ca, *n.m.f., a.* appertaining to or suffering from *coxalgia*.

coxcojilla; coxcojita, *n.f.* hopscotch; *a coxcox, a coxcojita*, lamely, haltingly.

coy, *n.m.* (*naut.*) hammock, cot.

coya, *n.f.* (*Per.*) queen, wife and sister of the Inca.

coyote, *n.m.* coyote.

coyunda, *n.f.* shoe-lace; strap for yoking oxen; (*fig.*) marriage tie; dominion, subjection.

coyuntura, *n.f.* (*anat.*) joint, conjuncture; articulation; (*fig.*) opportunity, occasion, nick of time.

coyuyo, *n.m.* (*Arg.*) large cicada.

coz, *n.f.* kick (as a horse); blow with the hind leg; recoil of a gun; flowing back of water; butt of a pistol; butt-end of log; heel of mast; (*coll.*) churlishness, unnecessary brusqueness; *a coces*, by dint of kicking; *andar a coz y bocado*, horse-play; *de hoz y de coz*, headlong; *soltar* or *tirar una coz*, to make a brusque or rude reply; *dar* or *tirar coces contra el aguijón*, (*fig.*) to kick against the pricks; *disparar* or *tirar coces*, to rebel, be insubordinate; *la coz de la yegua no hace mal al potro*, loving reprimands can only do good; *mandar a coces*, to command brusquely.

cozcojilla, cozcojita, *n.f.* [COXCOJILLA].

cozolmeca, *n.f.* (*Mex.*) plant of the sarsaparilla family.

crabrón, *n.m.* hornet.

crac, *n.m.* (*com.*) crash, failure, bankruptcy.

cran, *n.m.* (*print.*) nick of type.

craneal; craneano, -na, *a.* cranial.

cráneo, *n.m.* skull, cranium; *secársele a uno el cráneo* or *tener seco el cráneo*, to become or be mad.

craneología, *n.f.* craniology.

craneológico, -ca, *a.* craniological.

craneólogo, *n.m.* craniologist.

craneometría, *n.f.* craniometry.

craneométrico, -ca, *a.* craniometrical.

craneómetro, *n.m.* craniometer.

craneoscopia, *n.m.* cranioscopy.

craneotomía, *n.f.* craniotomy.

craniano, -na, *a.* cranial.

crápula, *n.f.* inebriation, intoxication, crapulence; low, dissolute people.

crapulosidad, *n.f.* crapulence.

crapuloso, -sa, *a.* crapulous, drunken, gluttonous, surfeited; dissolute, dissipated.

crasamente, *adv.* (*fig.*) crassly, grossly, rudely, ignorantly.

crascitar, *v.i.* to caw, croak.

crasicando, -da, *a.* (*zool.*) thick-tailed.

crasicaulo, -la, *a.* (*bot.*) thick-stemmed.

crasiento, -ta, *a.* greasy, oily; filthy.

crasitud, *n.f.* fatness, corpulence, obesity; (*coll.*) ignorance, stupidity.

craso, -sa, *a.* fat, greasy, oily, thick, unctuous; (*fig.*) crass, gross. — *n.m.* [CRASITUD].

cráter, *n.m.* crater.

cratícula, *n.f.* wicket in convent through which nuns receive the sacrament; confessional; (*phys.*) diffraction grating.

craza, *n.f.* crucible for melting precious metal.

crea, *n.f.* semi-fine cotton or linen stuff.

creable, *a.* creative, creatable.

creación, *n.f.* creation.

creado, -da, *p.p.* [CREAR] created, begotten, made.

creador, -ra, *a.* creative. — *n.m.f.* creator, maker, author. — *n.m.* God the Creator.

crear, *v.t.* to create, make, cause to exist, engender; to institute, establish; to appoint; to compose.

crébol, *n.m.* (*prov.*) holly tree.

crecedero, -ra, *a.* able to grow; that can be lengthened (children's clothes).

crecer, *v.i.* (*pres. indic.* **crezco**; *pres. subj.* **crezca**) to grow, increase, swell, bud forth, become larger, augment. — *v.r.* to swell with pride or authority; *crecer a palmos*, to grow very fast.

creces, *n.f.pl.* (*fig.*) augmentation, increase, excess; signs of growth; interest paid in kind by a farmer who borrows from the public granary; *con creces*, abundantly, amply.

crecida, *n.f.* swell of rivers, freshet.

crecidamente, *adv.* plentifully, abundantly, copiously.

crecidito, -ta, *a.* somewhat grown [CRECIDO].

crecido, -da, *a.* grown increased; (*obs.*) grave, important; swollen, large, great, big, numerous. — *p.p.* [CRECER]; *crecido de cuerpo*, tall.

crecidos, *n.m.pl.* increasing stitches in knitting.

creciente, *a.* growing, increasing; crescent; susceptible of increases. — *n.m.* (*her.*) half-moon with points upward. — *n.f.* freshet, swell (of waters); leaven; *creciente de la luna*, crescent, increasing moon; *creciente del mar*, (*naut.*) flow, flood-tide.

crecimiento, *n.m.* increase, increment; growth.

credencia, *n.f.* credence-table.

credencial, *a.* credential. — *n.f.pl.* credentials, credential letters.

credibilidad, *n.f.* credibility.

crédito, *n.m.* credit, credence, belief, faith; reputation, name, character; acquiescence, assent; trust, esteem, confidence; note, bill, order for payment; *créditos activos*, assets; *créditos pasivos*, liabilities; *dar a crédito*, to loan, give on credit; *dar crédito*, to believe, give credit; *sentar* or *tener sentado el crédito*, to enjoy a good reputation.

credo, *n.m.* creed, articles of faith; (*coll.*) convictions, opinions; *cada credo*, every moment; *en un credo*, in a trice; *con el credo en la boca*, in great risk or danger.

crédulamente, *adv.* credulously.

credulidad, *n.f.* credulity.

crédulo, -la, *a.* credulous.

creederas, *n.f.pl.* (*coll.*) credulity; *tener buenas, grandes, bravas, creederas,* to be very credulous.

creedero, -ra, *a.* credible.

creedor, -ra, *a.* credulous.

creencia, *n.f.* credence, credit; belief, creed.

creer, *v.t.* (*pret.* **él creyó**) to believe, give credit, think, consider probable. — *v.r.* to believe, consider, think oneself; *créamelo Vd.,* take my word for it; *no creo más de lo que veo* or *ver y creer,* to believe only what one sees; *creer a ojos cerrados,* to believe blindly, without examination; *creer a macha martillo,* to have implicit faith; *creer a puño cerrado,* to believe firmly; *ya lo creo,* of course, undoubtedly; *creer de su obligación,* to feel it incumbent upon one; *creerse de habladurías,* to be influenced by gossip; *creerse del aire,* to be credulous; *creer* or *creerse de ligero,* to accept on flimsy evidence; *creerse de uno,* to have faith in someone.

crehuela, *n.f.* crash, kind of linen.

creíble, *a.* credible, likely.

creíblemente, *adv.* credibly, probably.

crema, *n.f.* cream of milk; custard; cream of society; cold-cream; cosmetic; diæresis; liqueur.

cremación, *n.f.* cremation.

cremallera, *n.f.* (*mech.*) toothed bar, rack, ratch.

crematístico, -ca, *a.* chrematistic, appertaining to political economy. — *n.f.* chrematistics, political economy.

crematólogo, -ga, *n.m.f.* political economist.

crematología, *n.f.* political economy.

crematológico, -ca, *a.* relating to political economy.

crematorio, -ria, *a.* crematory. — *n.m.* cremator (furnace); crematorium.

cremento, *n.m.* increment.

cremómetro, *n.m.* creamometer.

crémor tártaro, *n.m.* cream of tartar.

cremoso, -sa, *a.* creamy.

crencha, *n.f.* parting of the hair in two; each of these parts.

creosota, *n.f.* creosote.

creosotar, *v.t.* to creosote.

crepitación, *n.f.* crepitation, crackling.

crepitante, *a.* crepitant, crepitating, crackling.

crepitar, *v.i.* to crepitate, crackle.

crepuscular, *a.* crepuscular, glimmering. — *n.m.pl.* crepuscular lepidoptera.

crepusculino, -na, *a.* crepuscular.

crepúsculo, *n.m.* crepuscule, twilight, dawn, dusk.

cresa, *n.f.* blow-fly, fly's egg; larva; egg of queen bee.

creso, *n.m.* Croesus, very wealthy man.

crespilla, *n.f.* agaric.

crespina, *n.f.* hair-net.

crespo, -pa, *a.* crisp, crispy; curled; (*bot.*) crisp-leaved; obscure, bombastic (of style); (*fig.*) angry, displeased, vexed; (*fig.*) elegant, graceful; haughty, conceited. — *n.m.* curl.

crespón, *n.m.* crape; crêpe.

cresta, *n.f.* comb, cock's comb; bird's crest; crest of a helmet; aigrette, tuft; top, brow, summit (of mountain); wave crest; *alzar* or *levantar la cresta,* to be elated with pride; *dar en la cresta,* to bring someone down a peg.

crestado, -da, *a.* crested, cristate.

crestería, *n.f.* (*arch.*) cresting; (*fort.*) battlement.

crestomatía, *n.f.* chrestomathy.

crestón, *n.m.* large comb or crest [CRESTA]; (*min.*) crop; crest of a helmet.

crestudo, -da, *a.* large-crested; (*fig.*) arrogant, conceited, presumptuous.

creta, *n.f.* chalk.

cretáceo, -cea, *a.* cretaceous, chalky.

cretense, *a.* Cretan.

crético, -ca, *a.* Cretan. — *n.m.* verse of three syllables.

cretinismo, *n.m.* cretinism, idiocy.

cretino, -na, *a.* cretinous. — *n.m.f.* cretin, idiot.

cretona, *n.f.* cretonne.

creyente, *a.* believing. — *n.m.f.* believer.

crezco; crezca, *pres. indic.; pres. subj.* [CRECER].

crezneja, *n.f.* plaited rope of bleached bassweed; braid of hair.

cría, *n.f.* brood of animals; act of nursing, rearing, breeding; suckling; child reared by a nurse.

criada, *n.f.* female servant, maid, maid-servant, handmaid; batlet; *salirle a uno la criada respondona,* to have the tables turned on one.

criadero, -ra, *a.* fruitful, prolific. — *n.m.* nursery (for plants or animals); fishhatchery; (*min.*) deposit of material, seam.

criadilla, *n.f.* testicle; lamb-fry; truffle; small loaf; potato.

criado, -da, *a.* educated, instructed, bred. — *n.m.* servant, menial, domestic, groom, valet. — *p.p.* [CRIAR].

criador, -ra, *a.* feeding, nourishing; fruitful, fertile, fecund. — *n.m.f.* creator, author; breeder, raiser. — *n.m.* God, the Creator. — *n.f.* wet-nurse.

criamiento, *n.m.* renovation and preservation.

criandera, *n.f.* (*Am.*) wet-nurse.

crianza, *n.f.* nursing; lactation; breeding, manners, education; *dar crianza,* to rear, bring up.

criar, *v.t.* to create, procreate, produce, give birth, give existence; to breed, suckle, nurse, rear, foster, nourish; to fatten animals; to instruct, educate; to invest with dignities, etc.; to treat (wine after fermentation); *estar criado,* to be able to look after oneself; *criar carnes,* to grow fat; *criar molleja,* to grow lazy; *Dios los cría y ellos se juntan,* birds of a feather flock together.

criatura, *n.f.* creature; fœtus; baby, infant, child; being, man; poor thing; henchman; *es una criatura,* he is but a child or a poor creature.

criba, *n.f.* sieve, riddle, screen; screening.

cribado, -da, *p.p.* [CRIBAR] screened, sifted. — *n.m.* screening, sifting.

cribador, -ra, *a.* sifting, screening. — *n.m.f.* sifter.

cribadura, *n.f.* screening.

cribar, *v.t.* to sift, pass through a sieve, screen, riddle.

cribero, -ra, *n.m.f.* maker or vendor of sieves.

cribo, *n.m.* sieve, riddle, screen.

criboso, -sa, *a.* (*anat.*) cribriform, cribrate; cribrose.

cric, *n.m.* screw-jack, lifting-jack.

crica, *n.f.* trench, fissure; (*anat.*) female pudenda.

cricoides, *n.m., a.* (*anat.*) cricoid.

cricquet, *n.m.* cricket.

crimen, *n.m.* crime, guilt, offence, misdemeanour; (*theol.*) mortal sin.

criminación, *n.f.* crimination.

criminal, *n.m.f., a.* criminal.

criminalidad, *n.f.* criminality, guiltiness.

criminalista, *n.m.* lawyer specializing in (or writer on) criminal law.

criminalizar, *v.t.* to transfer a case from civil to criminal court.

criminalmente, *adv.* criminally, guiltily.

criminar, *v.t.* to accuse, incriminate.

criminología, *n.f.* criminology.

criminosidad, *n.f.* criminality.

criminoso, -sa, *a.* criminal, guilty. — *n.m.f.* delinquent, criminal.

crimno, *n.m.* coarse flour of spelt and wheat.

crin, *n.f.* mane, horse-hair; *tenerse a las crines,* to hold on with might and main.

crinado, -da; crinito, -ta, *a.* crinite, maned; (*poet.*) long-haired.

crinífero, -ra, *a.* (*zool.*) mane-bearing.

criniforme, *a.* hairy, mane-like.

crinoideo, -dea, *a.* (*bot.*) crinoid, lily-shaped. — *n.m.pl.* Crinoidea.

crinolina, *n.f.* crinoline, horse-hair material.

crío, *n.m.* (*fam.*) nursing baby, nursling.

criolita, *n.f.* (*min.*) cryolite.

criollo, -lla, *n.m.f., a.* Creole.

cripta, *n.f.* crypt.

criptogámico, -ca, *a.* cryptogamic.

criptógamo, -ma, *a.* cryptogamous. — *n.m.f.* cryptogam.

criptografía, *n.f.* cryptography.

criptográficamente, *adv.* cryptically, by means of cryptography.

criptográfico, -ca, *a.* cryptographic.

criptógrafo, -fa, *n.m.f.* cryptographer.

criptograma, *n.f.* cryptogram.

criptotelegrafía, *n.f.* code telegraphy.

criptología, *n.f.* cryptology.

cris, *n.m.* creese, kris, Malayan dagger.

crisálida, *n.f.* pupa, chrysalis.

crisantemo, *n.m.* chrysanthemum.

criselefantino, -na, *a.* chryselephantine.

crisis, *n.f.* crisis, pitch, head, climax; criterion, judgment, decisive moment.

crisma, *n.m.* chrism. — *n.f.* head; *te quitaré* or *romperé la crisma,* (*coll.*) I'll break your bones.

crismera, *n.f.* chrismatory.

crisneja, *n.f.* [CRIZNEJA].

crisoberilo, *n.m.* chrysoberyl.

crisol, *n.m.* crucible, hearth of a furnace.

crisolada, *n.f.* quantity of molten metal in a crucible.

crisolar, *v.t.* to assay.

crisolito, *n.m.* chrysolite; *crisolito oriental,* yellow topaz.

crisopeya, *n.f.* alchemy.

crisoprasa, *n.f.* chrysoprase.

crispación, *n.f.; crispamiento,* *n.m.* [CRISPATURA].

crispante, *a.* twitching, convulsive.

crispar, *v.t.* to convulse, induce spasmodic contraction. — *v.r.* to twitch, contract convulsively; *crispársele los dedos* or *nervios,* to be annoyed, irritated, get angry; *crispársele los cabellos,* to be terrified; to be awed.

crispativo, -va, *a.* convulsive.

crispatura, *n.f.* (*med.*) convulsion, spasmodic contraction.

crispir, *v.t.* to marble.

crista, *n.f.* crest of a helmet.

cristal, *n.m.* crystal; glass, looking-glass; (*poet.*) water; fine woollen stuff; *cristal de roca,* rock crystal; *cristal hilado,* spun glass; *cristal tártaro,* crystallized cream of tartar.

cristalería, *n.f.* glass-works; glass-ware; glass store.

cristalero, -ra, *n.m.f.* glass-maker or -dealer. — *n.f.* glass-making machine.

cristalino, -na, *a.* crystalline, transparent; glassy, pellucid, bright. — *n.m.* (*anat.*) crystalline humour or lens.

cristalita, *n.f.* (*geol.*) crystallite.

cristalizable, *a.* crystallizable.

cristalización, *n.f.* crystallization.

cristalizador, -ra, *a.* crystallizing. — *n.m.* crystallizing pan.

cristalizante, *a.* crystallizing.

cristalizar, *v.t., v.i., v.r.* (*pret.* **cristalicé**; *pres. subj.* **cristalice**) to crystallize.

cristalografía, *n.f.* crystallography.

cristalográfico, -ca, *a.* crystallographic.

cristalógrafo, *n.m.* crystallographer.

cristel, *n.m.* clyster.

cristianamente, *adv.* in a Christian manner, christianly.

cristianar, *v.t.* (*coll.*) to baptize, christen.

cristiandad, *n.f.* Christianity, Christendom; observance of Christ's law; missionary's flock.

cristianesco, -ca, *a.* applied to Moorish forms which imitate the Christian style or manner.

cristianillo, -lla, *n.m.f.* (*contempt.*) nickname given to Spaniards by the Moors.

cristianísimo, -ma, *a. superl.* most Christian (applied to kings of France).

cristianismo, *n.m.* Christianism, Christianity; Christendom; baptism.

cristianizar, *v.t.* (*pret.* **cristianicé**; *pres. subj.* **cristianice**) to christianize.

cristiano, -na, *n.m.f., a.* Christian. — *n.m.* (*coll.*) brother, fellow-creature; living soul, person; (*coll.*) watered wine; *hablar* or *decir en cristiano,* to speak intelligibly.

cristífero, -ra, *a.* wearing the sign of the cross.

Cristina, *n.f.* Christina.

cristino, -na, *n.m.f., a.* partisan of Isabel II against the Pretender Don Carlos.

Cristo, *n.m.* Christ, Messiah, the Saviour; image or statue of Christ crucified; *¡Voto a Cristo!* Zounds! *haber la de Dios es Cristo,* to have a great quarrel; *ni por un cristo,* not for the world, not at all; *a mal cristo, mucha sangre,* bad works can be commended only by bad (i.e. vulgar) methods; *como a un santo cristo un par de pistolas,* quite inadequately or improperly; *donde Cristo dió las tres voces,* far away; *poner a uno como un cristo,* to beat, maltreat.

cristofué, *n.m.* (*Ven.*) a small bird.

cristus, *n.m.* Christ-cross-row, cross at the beginning of alphabet; the alphabet; *no saber el cristus,* to be very ignorant; *estar en el cristus,* to be at the rudiments of anything.

crisuela, *n.f.* dripping-pan of a lamp.

criterio, *n.m.* criterion, judgment, discernment.

crítica, *n.f.* criticism; critique, critical examination; censure, judgment; group of critics.

criticable, *a.* open to criticism, criticizable.
criticador, -ra, *a.* critical, criticizing. — *n.m.* critic, censurer, criticizer.
críticamente, *adv.* critically.
criticar, *v.t.* (*pret.* **critiqué**; *pres. subj.* **critique**) to criticize, judge; blame, find fault with, censure; *antes de criticar pon la mano en tu pecho*, look to yourself before finding fault with others.
criticastro, *n.m.* animadverter, criticaster, criticizer.
criticismo, *n.m.* criticism, critique; Kantian philosophy.
crítico, -ca, *a.* critical; decisive; (*med.*) indicating a crisis. — *n.m.* critic, criticizer; (*fam.*) one affected in style and language; censurer.
criticón, -na, *n.m.f., a.* [CRITICASTRO].
critiquizar, *v.t.* (*coll.*) to criticize, find fault, abuse, censure.
crizneja, *n.f.* rope of twisted twigs, or rushes; braid of hair.
croar, *v.i.* to croak (as a frog).
croata, *n.m.f., a.* Croat, Croatian.
crocante, *n.m.* almond cake.
crocino, -na, *a.* croceate, croceous. — *n.m.* (*pharm.*) ointment.
crocitar, *v.i.* [CRASCITAR].
crocodilo, *n.m.* crocodile.
croché, *n.m.* crochet.
cromático, -ca, *a.* chromatic. — *n.f.* chromatics.
cromatismo, *n.m.* (*opt.*) chromatic aberration.
cromato, *n.m.* (*chem.*) chromate.
cromatología, *n.f.* chromatics.
cromatoscópio, *n.m.* chromatoscope.
crómico, -ca, *a.* chromic.
cromita, *n.f.* (*min.*) chromite.
cromo, *n.m.* chrome, chromium; chromolithograph.
cromógeno, -na, *n.m.f., a.* (*biol.*) chromogen.
cromografía, *n.f.* vignette in colours.
cromógrafo, *n.m.* chromograph.
cromolitografía, *n.f.* chromo, chromolithograph; chromolithography.
cromolitografiar, *v.t.* to make chromolithographs.
cromolitográfico, -ca, *a.* chromolithographic.
cromolitógrafo, *n.m.* chromolithographer.
cromosfera, *n.f.* chromatosphere, chromosphere.
cromoso, -sa, *a.* chromic, chromous.
cromotipia, *n.f.* colour printing.
cromotipografía, *n.f.* chromotypography.
crónica, *n.f.* chronicle.
crónicamente, *adv.* chronically, habitually.
cronicidad, *n.f.*; **cronicismo**, *n.m.* (*med.*) chronic condition.
crónico, -ca, *a.* (*med.*) chronic.
cronicón, *n.m.* short chronicle.
cronista, *n.m.f.* chronicler.
cronografía, *n.f.* chronography.
cronográfico, -ca, *a.* chronographic.
cronógrafo, *n.m.* chronograph; chronographer.
cronograma, *n.f.* chronogram.
cronología, *n.f.* chronology.
cronológicamente, *adv.* chronologically.
cronológico, -ca, *a.* chronological.
cronologista, cronólogo, *n.m.* chronologist, chronologer.
cronometría, *n.f.* chronometry.
cronométrico, -ca, *a.* chronometrical.

cronómetro, *n.m.* chronometer.
cronoscopia, *n.m.* chronoscope.
croqueta, *n.f.* croquette, fritter.
croquis, *n.m.* hasty sketch, rough draft.
croscitar, *v.i.* to crow.
crótalo, *n.m.* (*poet.*) kind of castanet; rattlesnake.
crotón, *n.m.* (*bot.*) croton, castor-oil plant.
crotorar, *v.i.* to cry like a stork or crane.
cruce, *n.m.* crossing, cross-roads; *cruce de una vía*, railway crossing.
crucera, *n.f.* withers.
crucería, *n.f.* gothic architecture.
crucero, *n.m.* crucifer, cross-bearer; crossing of two roads; (*arch.*) transept; cross-vault; (*print.*) cross-bar of a chase; (*print.*) fold in sheet of paper; (*carp.*) beam; (*astron.*) cross, a constellation; (*naut.*) cruising station; cruiser; cruise; (*min.*) line or plane of cleavage; *crucero acorazado*, armoured cruiser.
cruceta, *n.f.* cross-piece; cross-stitch; (*naut.*) cross-trees.
crucial, *a.* crucial, in the form of a cross (incision).
cruciata, *n.f.* gentian.
cruciferario, *n.m.* cross-bearer, crucifer.
crucífero, -ra, *a.* (*poet.*) cruciferous, cross-shaped; (*bot.*) cruciate. — *n.m.* cross-bearer; crutched friar. — *n.f.pl.* (*bot.*) Cruciferae.
crucificado, -da, *p.p.* [CRUCIFICAR] crucified; *El Crucificado*, Jesus Christ.
crucificador, *n.m.* crucifier; (*fig.*) tormentor, tease.
crucificar, *v.t.* (*pret.* **crucifiqué**; *pres. subj.* **crucifique**) to crucify; (*coll.*) to vex, molest, torment.
crucifijo, *n.m.* crucifix.
crucifixión, *n.f.* crucifixion.
cruciforme, *a.* cruciform.
crucígero, -ra, *a.* (*poet.*) cruciferous.
crucillo, *n.m.* push-pin.
crudamente, *adv.* rudely, crudely, roughly.
crudelísimo, -ma, *a. superl.* [CRUEL] most cruel.
crudeza, *n.f.* crudeness, crudity, rawness, unripeness; hardness (of water); (*coll.*) rudeness; severity; cruelty; (*coll.*) vain boasting. — *pl.* undigested food.
crudo, -da, *a.* raw, uncooked, crude; pitiless, grievous, cruel; green, unripe; unfinished, rough; hard of digestion; (*coll.*) boastful; (*med.*) not mature; *agua cruda*, hard water; *lienzo crudo*, unbleached linen; *punto crudo*, critical moment or juncture; *tiempo crudo*, raw weather; *seda cruda*, raw silk; *cuero crudo*, untanned leather.
cruel, *a.* cruel, hard-hearted; insufferable, intolerable, intense, severe; fierce, violent, hard, oppressive; bloody, murderous, merciless, fiendish; *cruel con, para* or *para con*, cruel to, towards; *cruel de condición*, cruel by nature.
crueldad, *n.f.* cruelty, savageness, severity, hardness; barbarous action, outrage; inhumanity, mercilessness, ferociousness.
cruelisimamente, *adv.* very cruelly.
cruelísimo, -ma, *a. superl.* [CRUDELISIMO].
cruelmente, *adv.* cruelly, mercilessly.
cruentamente, *adv.* bloodily, with effusion of blood.
cruento, -ta, *a.* bloody, cruel, inhuman.

crujía, *n.f.* midship gangway; passage between sanctuary rails in a cathedral; large open corridor, hall or passage; aisle of a ward; *crujía de piezas,* suite of rooms in succession; (*obs.*) *pasar crujía* or *sufrir una crujía,* to run the gauntlet; to suffer great troubles.

crujidero, -ra, *a.* creaky, creaking, crackling, rustling.

crujido, -da, *p.p.* [CRUJIR] creaked, crackled. — *n.m.* creak, creaking; flaw in sword blade; *dar crujido,* to break, crack noisily.

crujidor, *n.m.* glass-cutter (tool).

crujiente, *a.* crackling, creaking, rustling.

crujir, *v.i.* to rustle, crackle, creak; to gnash; *allí será el llanto y el crujir de dientes,* there will be wailing and gnashing of teeth.

crúor, *n.m.* (*med., obs.*) colouring principle of blood; (*poet.*) blood; clot of gore; blood globule.

cruórico, -ca, *a.* appertaining to *crúor.*

crup, *n.m.* croup.

crupal, *a.* appertaining to croup.

crural, *a.* (*anat.*) crural, belonging to the thigh.

crustáceo, -cea, *a.* crustaceous, shelly. — *n.m., a.* (*zool.*) crustacean.

crústula, *n.f.* thin bark, skin or rind.

cruz, *n.f.* cross, rood; (*obs.*) instrument of torture; star; intersection of two lines; badge or insignia of knighthood, decoration; affliction, sorrow, trial of patience; toil, trouble, vexation; reverse of a coin; (*vet.*) withers; (*print.*) dagger, obelisk; top of tree-trunk where branches begin; (*astron.*) Southern Cross; (*naut.*) cross-tree.— *pl.* wings of a reel; *en cruz,* crosswise, with extended arms; *cruz y botón,* (*naut.*) frapping; *cruz del matrimonio,* matrimonial responsibilities; *adelante con la cruz,* to persist in one's resolution; *andar con las cruces a cuestas,* to pray earnestly for something; *detrás de la cruz está el diablo,* the devil (of vanity, etc.) is always behind one's good works (also applied to hypocrites); *entre la cruz y el agua bendita,* in grave danger; *estar uno por esta cruz de Dios,* not to have eaten, obtained or understood anything; *de la cruz a la fecha,* from beginning to end; *quedarse en cruz y en cuadro,* to be reduced to poverty and distress; *hacerle a uno la cruz,* to try to avoid or escape someone; *hacerse uno cruces* or *la cruz,* to be astonished, amazed; *llevar cruz y raya,* no more of this; *ser menester la cruz y los ciriales,* to need much diligence; *trasquilar a cruces,* to cut someone's hair badly.

cruzada, *n.f.* crusade; tribunal of the crusade; cross-roads.

cruzado, -da, *a.* cross-bred; crossed; crosswise, transverse, twilled. — *n.m.* cruzado; crusader; knight wearing the badge of a military order; manner of playing the guitar; (*obs.*) various coins; figure in dancing. — *p.p.* [CRUZAR]; *estarse con los brazos cruzados,* to be idle.

cruzamiento, *n.m.* cross-breeding; crossing, cross-roads; bestowal of a decoration.

cruzar, *v.t.* (*pret.* **crucé;** *pres. subj.* **cruce**) to cross, lay, place, pass across, go across; to bestow a decoration; (*naut.*) to cruise; to cross-breed; to twill. — *v.r.* to join a crusade; to cross each other; *cruzar la cara a alguno,* to hack someone's face; *cruzarse los*

negocios, to be overwhelmed with business; *cruzarse de caballero,* to be knighted; *cruzar por enfrente,* to cross in front; *cruzar los brazos,* to fold one's arms; *cruzarse de brazos,* to be idle; *cruzarse de palabras,* to quarrel; *cruzarse el saludo,* to greet each other in passing.

cu, *n.f.* the letter Q; *n.m.* (*Mex.*) ancient temple.

cuaderna, *n.f.* (*prov.*) fourth part of anything; (*naut.*) frame; double fours in backgammon.

cuadernal, *n.m.* (*naut.*) block, tackle.

cuadernillo, *n.m.* gathering of five sheets of paper, quinternion; clerical directory.

cuaderno, *n.m.* writing-book, note-book, exercise-book, ancient punishment for students; (*print.*) four sheets of paper placed within each other; (*coll.*) pack of cards; *cuaderno de bitácora,* log-book.

cuadra, *n.f.* hall, drawing-room, saloon; stable; croup (of horse); square; ward (in hospital, barracks, etc.); quarter of a ship; quarter of a mile; (*Am.*) block, group of houses.

cuadrada, *n.f.* (*mus.*) breve.

cuadradamente, *adv.* exactly, completely.

cuadradillo, *n.m.* gusset (of shirt); blank (of key, etc.); cube of sugar; square ruler.

cuadrado, -da, *a.* square, quadrate; perfect, without defect. — *p.p.* [CUADRAR]. — *n.m.* square, quadrate; clock (of stocking); square ruler; gusset of sleeve; (*arith.*) square number; die (for coining); (*print.*) quadrat, quad; *de cuadrado,* in front, opposite, face to face; perfectly, very well; *dejar* or *poner a uno de cuadrado,* to set forth one's intentions quite clearly.

cuadragenario, -ria, *n.m.f., a.* forty years old, quadragenarian.

cuadragésima, *n.f.* Lent, Quadragesima.

cuadragesimal, *a.* quadragesimal, lenten.

cuadragésimo, -ma, *a.* fortieth.

cuadral, *n.m.* (*arch.*) piece of timber making a diagonal with two others; (*carp.*) anglebrace, truss; shoulder-tie.

cuadrangular, *a.* quadrangular.

cuadrángulo, -la, *a.* quadrangular. — *n.m.* quadrangle.

cuadrantal, *a.* (*math.*) quadrantal.

cuadrante, *a.* squaring. — *n.m.* quadrant; fourth part of an inheritance; sun-dial; clock face, watch face; (*carp.*) cross-tie, angle-brace; ancient Roman copper coin; *hasta el último cuadrante,* to the last farthing.

cuadranura, *n.f.* radial crack in trees.

cuadrar, *v.t.* to square, form into a square; to multiply a number by itself; (*paint.*) to divide into squares. — *v.i.* to fit, suit, tally, correspond; to adjust, regulate; to please. — *v.r.* to assume a serious air; to stand at attention; (*equit.*) to stop short.

cuadratín, *n.m.* (*print.*) quadrat.

cuadratura, *n.f.* (*astron., math.*) quadrature; squaring, square; *la cuadratura del círculo,* the squaring of the circle, the impossible.

cuadrete, *n.m.* small square [CUADRO].

cuadricenal, *a.* done every forty years.

cuadrícula, *n.f.* checker-work, arrangement or pattern in squares.

cuadriculación, *n.f.* graticulation.

cuadriculado, -da, *a.* cross-section, squared (paper).

cuadricular, *a.* checkered; ruled in squares. — *v.t.* to copy by means of squares.
cuadrienal, *a.* quadrennial.
cuadrienio, *n.m.* quadrennium, time of four years.
cuadrífloro, -ra, *a.* (*bot.*) having four flowers.
cuadrifoliado, -da, *a.* (*bot.*) quadriphyllous.
cuadriforme, *a.* square-shaped.
cuadrifronte, *a.* four-faced.
cuadriga, *n.f.* quadriga, chariot drawn by four horses.
cuadril, *n.m.* haunch bone; (*vet.*) croup; hip, thigh.
cuadrilátero, -ra, *n.m.*, *a.* quadrilateral.
cuadriliteral; cuadrilítero, -ra, *a.* quadriliteral.
cuadrilongo, -ga, *a.* rectangular, oblong. — *n.m.* parallelogram, oblong; rectangle; square of infantry.
cuadriloquio, *n.m.* conversation between four persons.
cuadrilla, *n.f.* team of four or more persons; gang, herd, crew, troop; (*law*) band of more than three armed men; Inquisition patrol; quadrille.
cuadrillero, *n.m.* commander of an armed band; member of a *cuadrilla*; (*Philip.*) rural guard.
cuadrillo, *n.m.* Moorish dart.
cuadrimestre, *a.* lasting four months. — *n.m.* space of four months.
cuadrinieto, -ta, *n.m.f.* great-great-great-grandson or daughter.
cuadrinomio, *n.m.* (*alg.*) quadrinomial.
cuadripartición, *n.f.* quadripartition.
cuadripartido, -da, *a.* quadripartite, divided into four.
cuadriple, *a.* quadruple.
cuadriplicado, -da, quadrupled; quadruplicate(d). — *p.p.* [CUADRUPLICAR].
cuadriplicar, *v.t.* [CUADRUPLICAR] to quadruplicate.
cuadrivio, *n.m.* quadrivium; cross-roads, junction of four roads.
cuadríyugo, *n.m.* cart with four horses; quadriga.
cuadro, -dra, *a.* square; scene, tableau of a play; picture, painting; picture frame, window frame; square flower-bed; (*print.*) platen; (*mil.*) square of troops; (*mil.*) staff (of regiment); (*elec.*) switchboard; touching or imposing sight; vivid description; *cuadro de alimentación, distribución* or *de interruptores*, (*elec.*) feeder-switchboard, distribution-board; *cuadro de servicio*, (*railw.*) train schedule; *cuadros de costumbres*, writings on everyday life; *cuadros vivos*, tableaux vivants; *en cuadro*, squared; *estar* or *quedarse en cuadro*, to be friendless and penniless; (*mil.*) to be left with officers only (said of a body of troops having lost its soldiers).
cuadrupedal, *a.* quadrupedal, four-footed.
cuadrupedante, *a.* (*poet.*) quadrupedal.
cuadrúpede, cuadrúpedo, *n.m.*, *a.* quadruped.
cuádruple, *a.* quadruple, fourfold.
cuadruplicación, *n.f.* quadruplication.
cuadruplicar, *v.t.* to quadruplicate.
cuádruplo, -pla, *a.*, *n.m.* quadruple.
cuaga, *n.m.* (*zool.*) quagga.
cuaima, *n.f.* (*Ven.*) poisonous snake; (*fig.*) clever, dangerous, cruel person.

cuajada, *n.f.* curd (of milk).
cuajadillo, *n.m.* heavily embroidered silk.
cuajado, -da, *a.* coagulated, curdled; (*coll.*) immobile, paralyzed with astonishment; (*coll.*) fast asleep. — *n.m.* dish of meat, herbs, etc.; with eggs and sugar. — *p.p.* [CUAJAR]; *cuajado de gente*, packed with people.
cuajadura, *n.f.* coagulation, curdling.
cuajaleche, *n.m.* (*bot.*) lady's bed-straw; cheese rennet.
cuajamiento, *n.m.* coagulation.
cuajar, cuajarejo, *n.m.* abomasus, fourth stomach of a ruminant.
cuajar, *v.t.* to coagulate, concrete, curdle, cake; (*fig.*) to decorate, ornament profusely. — *v.i.* to obtain, attain; (*coll.*) to succeed, have the effect desired; to please, be liked. — *v.r.* to coagulate, curdle; (*coll.*) to fill, become crowded; *cuajarse la sangre de miedo*, to have the blood curdled with fear.
cuajarón, *n.m.* clot of blood.
cuajicote, *n.m.* (*Mex.*) carpenter bee.
cuajilote, *n.m.* (*Mex.*) bignoniaceous plant with edible fruit.
cuajiote, *n.m.* (*Cent. Am.*) a gum-producing tree.
cuajo, *n.m.* rennet; maw; curdling, coagulation; *arrancar de cuajo*, to tear up by the roots, eradicate; *tener buen* or *mucho cuajo*, to be dull and patient; *hierba de cuajo*, cheese rennet; *ensanchar el cuajo*, to exhort to patience; *volverse el cuajo*, to bring back the milk (infant).
cuakerismo, cuaquerismo, *n.m.* Quakerism.
cuákero, -ra, cuáquero, -ra, *n.m.f.* Quaker.
cual, *rel. pron.* (*pl.* **cuales**) (**cuál, cuáles** in interrogative and exclamatory sentences) which; (preceded by the article) which, who; such; such as, like; some. — *adv.* as. — *interj.* how then! *cada cual*, each one; *cuál más, cuál menos, todos hacen lo mismo*, they all more or less do the same; *a cúal más*, equally, on a par; *tal cual*, such as, exactly.
cualidad, *n.f.* quality.
cualitativo, -va, *a.* qualitative.
cualquier, *pron.* (*pl.* **cualesquier**) contraction of *cualquiera*, used only before a noun; *cualquier hombre*, any man.
cualquiera, *pron.* (*pl.* **cualesquiera**) any, anyone, someone, whoever, whichever, whosoever; *un hombre cualquiera*, any sort of man; *cualquiera que sea su mérito*, whatever may be his merit; *ser un cualquiera*, to be of no account.
cuan, *adv.* contraction of *cuanto* (not used before a verb) (**cuán** in interrogatory and exclamatory sentences) how, as.
cuando, *adv.* when, if, in case. — *conj.* though, although, even; sometimes, now and then; since, inasmuch as; *¿de cuándo acá?* since when? *de cuando en cuando*, from time to time, now and then; *el cuándo*, the critical moment; *¿hasta cuándo?* until when; *cuando más* or *cuando mucho*, at most, at best; *cuando menos*, at least; *cuando quiera*, when you please; whenever; *cuando no*, otherwise; *el cómo y el cuándo*, the how and when.
cuantía, *n.f.* amount, quantity; rank, distinction, importance; degree.
cuantiar, *v.t.* to value, estimate, appraise; to fix a price.

cuantidad   cuartogénito

cuantidad, *n.f.* quantity.
cuantimás, *adv.* (*coll.*) contraction of *cuanto y más.*
cuantiosamente, *adv.* copiously, in great quantity.
cuantioso, -sa, *a.* copious, numerous, rich.
cuantitativo, -va, *a.* quantitative.
cuanto, -ta, *a.* (**cuánto, -ta** in interrogatory and exclamatory sentences) as much as, as many as, all the, whatever. — *adv.* how much; how long; how far; as, the more; respecting; whilst; *cuanto* (*más*) *antes*, as soon as possible, at once; *cuanto más* (*que*), moreover, the more (because), all the more; *¿cuánto?* how much? *¿cuántos?* how many? *¿cuánto suma?* how much does it come to? *¿cuánto va?* how much do you bet? (*en*) *cuanto a*, with regard to; *en cuanto*, whilst, as soon as; *por cuanto*, inasmuch as; *¿a cuántos estamos?* what is the date today? *¡cuánto me alegro verle!* how pleased I am to see you!
cuaquerismo, cuáquero, *n.m.* [CUAKERISMO, CUÁKERO].
cuarango, *n.m.* Peruvian bark-tree.
cuarcífero, -ra, *a.* quartziferous.
cuarcita, *n.f.* quartzite.
cuarenta, *n.m.,* *a.* forty; fortieth; *las cuarenta*, points in card game of *tute*; *acusar las cuarenta*, to give a piece of one's mind.
cuarentavo, -va, *n.m.f.,* *a.* fortieth (part).
cuarentena, *n.f.* space of forty days, months or years; fortieth part; Lent; the number forty; (*naut.*) quarantine; (*met.*) suspension of assent; *hacer cuarentena*, to be in quarantine.
cuarentenal, *a.* relating to the number forty.
cuarentón, -na, *n.m.f.,* *a.* person forty years old.
cuaresma, *n.f.* Lent; collection of lenten sermons.
cuaresmal, *a.* lenten, used in Lent.
cuaresmario, *n.m.* collection of lenten sermons.
cuarta, *n.f.* fourth, fourth part, quarter; quart, sequence of four cards in piquet; quadrant; span of the hand; (*naut.*) point of the compass; quart measure; (*prov.*) guide mule; (*mus.*) fourth; (*mil.*) quarter-company of soldiers; (*Mex.*) riding whip.
cuartago, *n.m.* nag, pony, hack.
cuartal, *n.m.* kind of bread; quarter (dry measure).
cuartán, *n.m.* grain measure of about 1 bushel; oil measure of about 7 pints.
cuartana, *n.f.* (*med.*) quartan.
cuartanal, *a.* (*med.*) quartan, intermittent.
cuartanario, -ria, *a.* quartan. — *n.m.f.,* *a.* suffering from a quartan fever.
cuartar, *v.t.* to plough the ground the fourth time.
cuartazo, *n.m.* (*Mex.*) stroke with a whip. — *n.m.pl.* untidy, lazy and corpulent man.
cuartear, *v.t.* to quarter, divide into four parts; to bid a fourth more at sales; to make a fourth person at a game; to zig-zag up steep and bad roads; (*Mex.*) to whip. — *v.r.* to split into pieces, rift, crack.
cuartel, *n.m.* quarter, fourth part; district, ward; flower-bed; dwelling; home, tenement, habitation, lodging, barracks; (*her.*) quarter; (*mil.*) quarter, clemency; (*naut.*)

hatch; (*poet.*) quatrain; *cuartel de la salud*, safe place, shelter; *cuartel general*, (*mil.*) general headquarters; *cuartel maestre* (*general*), quartermaster-general; *estar de cuartel*, (*mil.*) to be on half-pay.
cuartelado, -da, *p.p.* (CUARTELAR) (*her.*) quartered. — *n.m.* (*her.*) quartering. — *n.f.* military revolt, coup d'état.
cuartelar, *v.t.* (*her.*) to quarter.
cuartelero, -ra, *a.* relating to barracks or quarters. — *n.m.* soldier appointed to keep rooms clean.
cuartelesco, -ca, *a.* relating to barracks; soldierly, military.
cuarteo, *n.m.* act of dodging, swerving, side-step; crack, rift, fissure.
cuartera, *n.f.* a grain measure used in Catalonia of about 2 bushels.
cuarterada, *n.f.* (*Bal. Is.*) a surface measure (about 75 square feet).
cuartero, -ra, *n.m.f.* (*prov.*) collector of the fourth of the crop of grain. — *n.f.* (in Catalonia) dry measure (about 2 bushels); surface measure (about 4,306 square yards); square timber (15' × 8" × 8").
cuarterola, *n.f.* quarter-cask; (*Chi.*) short cavalry carbine.
cuarterón, *n.m.* quartern, quarter of a pound; upper part of windows; panel of a door; quadroon.
cuarteta, *n.f.* (*poet.*) quatrain.
cuartete, cuarteto, *n.m.* (*poet.*) quatrain; (*mus.*) quartet.
cuartilla, *n.f.* grain or liquid measure, fourth part of an *arroba*, *cántara* or *fanega*; quarter of large sheet of paper; sheet of paper; (*print.*) sheet of copy; pastern of horses.
cuartillo, *n.m.* pint; fourth part of a peck; fourth part of a *real*; (*naut.*) dog watch; *andar a tres menos cuartillo*, to be hard up; to quarrel; *ir de cuartillo*, to go halves.
cuartilludo, -da, *a.* with long pasterns (horse).
cuartito, *n.m.* small room [CUARTO].
cuarto, -ta, *a.* fourth, fourth quarter; fourth part. — *n.m.* quarter, quadrant, fourth part; room, apartment, dwelling, abode, habitation, flat; copper coin worth four *maravedís*; crack in horses' hoofs; series of ancestors; quarter of the moon; quarter of an hour; quarter of animals or of criminals whose body has been quartered; service in the royal palace. — *n.m.pl.* (*coll.*) money, wealth; animal's well proportioned members; *cuarto de baño*, bathroom; *cuarto de costura*, sewing-room; *cuarto de dormir*, bedroom; *cuarto de conversión*, (*fenc.*, *mil.*) quarter-wheeling; *cuarto bajo*, ground floor; *cuarto creciente*, the first quarter of the moon; *cuarto principal*, first floor; *cuarto a cuarto*, in a miserable manner; *de tres al cuarto*, (*print.*) quarto; *tener* (*cuarto*) *cuartos*, to have money; *estar sin* or *no tener un cuarto*, to be penniless; *poner cuarto*, to take lodgings, to furnish apartments; *echar su cuarto a espadas*, to intervene in a conversation; *dar un cuarto al pregonero*, to tell or proclaim secrets; *de tres al cuarto*, of little moment; *el cuarto falso, de noche pasa*, crime and darkness go together; *caérsele* or *írsele a uno cada cuarto por su lado*, to be very untidy, ill-kept; *hacer* (*a uno*) *cuartos*, to quarter, carve up someone.
cuartogénito, -ta, *n.m.f.,* *a.* fourth-born child.

[271]

cuartón, *n.m.* quarter, large joist or girder; (*prov.*) measure of wine; oblong patch of farming land.

cuartuco, cuartucho, *n.m.* miserable little room.

cuarzo, *n.m.* quartz.

cuarzoso, -sa, *a.* quartzose.

cuasi, *adv.* almost.

cuasia, *n.f.* (*bot.*) quassia.

cuasicontrato, *n.m.* (*law*) quasi-contract.

cuasidelito, *n.m.* (*law*) quasi-crime.

cuasimodo, *n.m.* first Sunday after Easter, Low Sunday.

cuate, -ta, *n.m.f., a.* (*Mex.*) twin; *eso no tiene cuate,* (*Mex.*) that has no equal.

cuatequil, *n.m.* (*Mex.*) maize.

cuaterna, *n.f.* four points in the game of lotto.

cuaternario, -ria, *a.* quaternary.

cuaternidad, *n.f.* quaternary, quaternity.

cuaterno, -na, *a.* quaternary.

cuatezón, -na, *a.* (*Mex.*) hornless ox or sheep.

cuatí, *n.m.* (*Arg., Col.*) a monkey.

cuatralbo, -ba, *a.* with four white feet (horse); — *n.m.* (*obs.*) commander of four galleys.

cuatratuo, -tua, *n.m.f., a.* quadroon.

cuatreño, -ña, *a.* nearly four years old (cattle).

cuatrero, *n.m.* horse stealer, cattle stealer.

cuatriduano, -na, *a.* lasting four days.

cuatrienio, *n.m.* quadrennium.

cuatrilingüe, *a.* quadrilingual.

cuatrillo, *n.m.* game of cards.

cuatrillón, *n.m.* quadrillion.

cuatrimestre, *a.* lasting four months. — *n.m.* period of four months.

cuatrín, *n.m.* (*obs.*) small coin; (*coll.*) cash.

cuatrinca, *n.f.* union of four persons or things; four cards of a kind in bezique.

cuatrisílabo, -ba, *a.* quadrisyllabic. — *n.m.* quadrisyllable.

cuatro, *a.* four, fourth. — *n.m.* the figure 4; one casting the vote of, or speaking for, four persons; card with four marks; (*mus.*) quartet; (*Ven.*) four-stringed guitar; *las cuatro,* four o'clock; *más de cuatro personas,* many; (*coll.*) any number of people; *cuatro varas de paño entran en este vestido,* four yards of cloth are needed for this dress.

cuatrocentista, *n.m.f.* quattrocentist.

cuatrocientos, -tas, *a.* four hundred. — *n.m.* figure representing 400.

cuatrodoblar, *v.t.* to quadruple.

cuatropea, *n.f.* horse tax, duty on horse sales.

cuatropeado, *n.m.* step in dancing.

cuatrotanto, *n.m.* quadruple.

cuba, *n.f.* cask, tub, vat; tubful, vatful; (*coll.*) toper, hard drinker, drunkard; (*fig.*) big-bellied person; *cada cuba huele al vino que tiene,* a man's character may be judged by his actions; *calar las cubas,* to measure casks for duty, etc.; *estar hecho una cuba,* to be inebriated.

cubación, *n.f.* (*math.*) action of cubing.

cubano, -na, *n.m.f., a.* Cuban.

cubeba, *n.f.* (*bot.*) cubeb.

cubebina, *n.f.* (*chem.*) cubebin.

cubería, *n.f.* cooperage, cask-shop.

cubero, *n.m.* cooper; maker or vendor of casks; *a ojo de buen cubero,* near enough, good guess.

cubertura, *n.f.* act of covering oneself in the presence of the King (Spanish Grandee).

cubeta, *n.f.* small barrel, cask, keg, tub, pail, bucket, basin, tray [CUBA]; reservoir of mercury in barometer; base of harp; test-tube.

cubeto, *n.m.* small barrel, pail, tub, vessel [CUBO]; *todo saldrá del cubeto,* better times are bound to come.

cúbica, *n.f.* kind of woollen material.

cubicación, *n.f.* cubage, cubature.

cúbicamente, *adv.* cubically.

cubicar, *v.t.* to calculate the cubic contents of a solid; to cube.

cúbico, -ca, *a.* cubic, cubical.

cubículo, *n.m.* cubicle.

cubichete, *n.m.* (*naut.*) weather-boards; (*artill.*) gun apron.

cubierta, *n.f.* cover, covering; envelope; book cover; (*fig.*) pretence, pretext; casing, coat; (*arch.*) facing, roofing; deck of a ship; hood of a carriage; *cubierta del motor,* bonnet (of a car).

cubiertamente, *adv.* privately, secretly.

cubierto, -ta, *a.* covered; dark (wine). — *n.m.* cover, table service, place at table; dinner course; fixed-price meal; bread- or cake-tray; shelter, shed; roof; cover, covert. — *p.p. irreg.* [CUBRIR]; *camino cubierto,* (*mil.*) covered way; *ponerse a cubierto,* to shelter from danger.

cubil, *n.m.* lair of wild beasts; bed of river.

cubilar, *v.i.* to take shelter (sheep). — *n.m.* wild beast's lair; sheep-fold.

cubilete, *n.m.* copper pudding-basin or mould; food prepared therein; tumbler, mug, drinking cup; juggler's goblet; dice box; (*Col.*) top hat.

cubiletero, *n.m.* pudding basin or mould; juggler.

cubilote, *n.m.* cupola furnace.

cubilla, *n.f.* Spanish fly, blistering beetle.

cubillo, *n.m.* [CUBILLA]; (*theat.*) small box near the stage; water cooler.

cubismo, *n.m.* cubist school of painting.

cubista, *a.* follower of the cubist school.

cubital, *a.* cubital.

cúbito, *n.m.* (*anat.*) ulna.

cubo, *n.m.* wooden pail, tub, bucket, vat; mill-pond; barrel of a watch or clock; candlestick socket; (*math., geom.*) cube; (*fort.*) small tower; nave or hub of a wheel; bayonet socket; (*arch.*) dado, die; (*mech.*) tongue way, socket, shaft case.

cuboides, *n.m., a.* (*anat.*) cuboid.

cubrecadena, *n.m.* chain-cover (on bicycle).

cubrecama, *n.f.* bed-cover, coverlet, counter-pane.

cubrecorsé, *n.m.* camisole, corset cover.

cubremantel, *n.m.* fancy tablecloth.

cubrepán, *n.m.* fire-shovel used for cooking by shepherds.

cubrepiano, *n.m.* cloth cover for piano key-board.

cubrepiés, *n.m.* foot coverlet; counterpane.

cubreplatos, *n.m.* dish-cover; wire-net cover.

cubrición, *n.f.* covering, copulation (of animals).

cubriente, *a.* covering; copulating (animals).

cubrimiento, *n.m.* covering; roofing.

cubrir, *v.t.* (*p.p. irreg.* **cubierto**) to cover, overlay, spread over; to face, coat; to screen, protect, palliate; to envelop, shroud, cover up, hood, cloak, disguise; to compensate; to include, comprise; (*arch.*) to roof; (*mil.*) to cover a post; (*com.*) to meet a draft; to cover a shortage; to cover, pair (animals). — *v.r.* to insure oneself against loss; to put oneself into a position of defence; to hedge; to be well guarded (in fencing); to put on one's hat, be covered; *cubrir con un velo*, to conceal; *cubrir la cuenta*, to balance an account; *quien te cubre, te descubre*, the cloak that covers thee, reveals thy lack of merit; *cubrir la mesa*, to lay the table; *cubrírsele a uno el corazón*, to be deeply moved with grief; *cubrir los gastos*, to meet the expenses.

cuca, *n.f.* chufa; root tubercle of sedge; kind of caterpillar; (*coll.*) gambling woman; (*Chi.*) wading bird; *pl.* nuts; *cuca y matacán*, a card game; *mala cuca*, (*coll.*) wicked person.

cucador, -ra, *a.* winking.

cucadura, *n.f.;* **cucamiento**, *n.m.* wink; winking.

cucamonas, *n.f.pl.* (*fam.*) caresses, endearments.

cucaña, *n.f.* greasy pole; the sport itself; (*coll.*) something acquired with little trouble or at others' expense.

cucañero, -ra, *n.m.f.*, *a.* parasite, hanger-on.

cucar, *v.t.* to wink.

cucaracha, *n.f.* cockroach; cochineal insect; hazel-coloured snuff.

cucarachera, *n.f.* nest of cockroaches; cockroach trap; (*coll.*) good luck, lucky chance.

cucarda, *n.f.* cockade, badge.

cucarro, *n.m.* (*contempt.*) boy dressed up as friar.

cucarrón, *n.m.* (*Col.*) beetle.

cuclillas, *adv.;* **en cuclillas**, in a squatting position; *sentarse en cuclillas*, to squat.

cuclillo, *n.m.* cuckoo; (*fig.*) cuckold.

cuco, -ca, *a.* (*coll.*) small; prim, dainty; cunning, crafty, astute, alert for one's own convenience. — *n.m.f.* kind of caterpillar; gambler. — *n.m.* cuckoo; bogey, phantasm; card game; *¡qué cosa tan cuca!* what a sweet little thing!

cucú, *n.m.* call of the cuckoo.

cucubá, *n.m.* (*Cub.*) barking owl.

cuculí, *n.m.* (*Chi., Per.*) a handsome pigeon.

cuculla, *n.f.* cowl, old-fashioned hood.

cucuma, *n.f.* Colombian bread.

cucúrbita, *n.f.* retort for distilling.

cucurbitáceo, -cea, *a.* (*bot.*) cucurbitaceous.

cucurucho, *n.m.* roll or cone of paper, cornet.

cucha, *n.f.* (*Per.*) [LAGUNA].

cuchar, *n.f.* spoon; ancient corn measure; tax or duty on grain.

cuchara, *n.f.* spoon, ladle, dipper; (*mas.*) trowel; (*naut.*) pitch-ladle, scoop; (*mil.*) gunner's ladle; *dure lo que durare, como cuchara de pan*, make hay while the sun shines; *meter a uno con cuchara (de palo)*, to explain obscurely and minutely; *media cuchara*, person of mediocre capabilities; *meter uno su cuchara*, to intrude, put in one's oar.

cucharada, *n.f.* spoonful, ladleful; *meter su cucharada*, to join in others' conversation; to meddle.

cucharadita, *n.f.* teaspoonful.

cucharal, *n.m.* shepherd's leather bag for spoons.

cucharazo, *n.m.* stroke or blow with a spoon.

cucharero, -ra, *n.m.f.* maker or seller of spoons. — *n.m.* rack for spoons.

cuchareta, *n.f.* small spoon [CUCHARA]; (*prov.*)

kind of wheat; inflammation of liver in sheep; (*Am.*) flamingo.

cucharetear, *v.i.* (*coll.*) to stir with a spoon; *cucharetear en todo*, to busy oneself with others' business.

cucharetero, -ra, *n.m.f.* maker or seller of wooden spoons. — *n.m.* rack for spoons; petticoat fringe.

cucharica, cucharilla, cucharita, *n.f.* small spoon, tea- or coffee-spoon [CUCHARA].

cucharilla, *n.f.* (*min.*) scraper; liver disease in swine.

cucharón, *n.m.* soup spoon, large spoon; dipper, ladle [CUCHARA]; *despacharse uno con el cucharón*, to help oneself to the best or largest part; *tener el cucharón por el mango*, to direct, manage, have control.

cucharro, *n.m.* (*naut.*) harping.

cuchí, *n.m.* (*Per.*) hog.

cuchichear, *v.i.* to whisper.

cuchicheo, *n.m.* whisper, whispering.

cuchichero, -ra, *a.* whispering. — *n.m.f.* whisperer.

cuchichiar, *v.i.* to call like a partridge.

cuchilla, *n.f.* large kitchen knife; chopper; kind of poniard; (*poet.*) sword; blade; mountain ridge.

cuchillada, *n.f.* cut, slash; gash, wound. — *pl.* wrangles, quarrels; slashes made in garment to show the lining; *dar cuchillada*, to play to the gallery; *sanan cuchilladas, y no malas palabras*, slander has more lasting effects than a wound.

cuchillar, *a.* belonging to a knife.

cuchillazo, *n.m.* large knife [CUCHILLO]; wound, cut, slash.

cuchilleja, *n.f.* [CUCHILLA]; **cuchillejo**, *n.m.* small knife, paring knife [CUCHILLO].

cuchillera, *n.f.* knife case, scabbard.

cuchillería, *n.f.* cutler's shop, cutlery.

cuchillero, *n.m.* cutler; clamp, clasp.

cuchillo, *n.m.* knife; gore, triangular piece in a garment; triangular piece of ground; any object or place ending in a point or acute angle; right of governing; (*arch.*) gable frame. — *pl.* chief feathers of a hawk's wing; *vela de cuchillo*, (*naut.*) triangular sail; *cuchillo de madera*, paper knife; *cuchillo de monte*, hunter's cutlass; *cuchillo mangonero*, coarse, badly forged knife; *matar a uno con cuchillo de palo*, to mortify slowly and relentlessly; *pasar a cuchillo*, to put to the sword; *ser uno cuchillo de otro*, to be a thorn in someone's side.

cuchipanda, *n.f.* (*coll.*) banquet.

cuchitril, *n.m.* narrow hole; very small room, hut.

cucho, *n.m.* (*Chi.*) conical hat used by countrymen.

cuchuco, *n.m.* (*Col.*) onion soup with some pork.

cuchuchear, *v.i.* (*coll.*) to whisper; (*fig.*) to carry tales.

cuchufleta, *n.f.* joke, jest, fun.

cuchufletero, -ra, *a.* jesting, funny. — *n.m.f.* jester, joker.

cuchugo, *n.m.* (*Am.*) saddle bag.

cuchuña, *n.f.* (*Chi.*) small and very sweet water-melon.

cudria, *n.f.* flat, woven bass rope.

cudú, *n.m.* (*zool.*) koodoo.

cuébano, *n.m.* [CUÉVANO].

cuelga, *n.f.* cluster of grapes or other fruit; bunch (of onions, etc.); (*fam.*) birthday present.

cuelgacapas, *n.m.* cloak hanger, rack.

cuelgaplatos, *n.m.* wire plate-holder for wall decoration.

cuelgo, cuelgue, *pres. indic., pres. subj.* [COLGAR].

cuelmo, *n.m.* torch, firebrand.

cuelo, cuele, *pres. indic., pres. subj.* [COLAR].

cuelliangosta, -ta, *a.* thin-necked.

cuellicorto, -ta, *a.* short-necked.

cuelligrueso, -sa, *a.* thick-necked.

cuellierguido, -da, *a.* stiff-necked; conceited.

cuellilargo, -ga, *a.* long-necked.

cuello, *n.m.* neck, throat; neck of a vessel; collar (of garment); collar-band; neck-stock; small end of a candle; thinnest or tapering part of anything; collar of a beam in oil-mills; *levantar el cuello,* to recover one's health or fortune, be prosperous.

cuenca, *n.f.* wooden bowl; orbit, socket of the eye; deep valley; river basin.

cuenco, *n.m.* earthen bowl; (*prov.*) sifting basket; cavity, hollow.

cuenda, *n.f.* end of a skein of silk or thread; *madeja sin cuenda,* tangled business; *por la cuenda se devana la madeja,* the right way is the easiest way.

cuenta, *n.f.* calculation, computation, reckoning; narrative; account, count; statement, bill, note; number of threads in fabric; bead (of a rosary, etc.); reason, satisfaction; obligation, duty, care; answerableness; merit, consideration, importance; *cuenta corriente,* (*com.*) current account; *las cuentas del Gran Capitán,* account overcharged; *cuenta pendiente,* an unsettled account; *cuenta simulada,* pro forma account; *cuenta de venta,* (*com.*) account sales; *cuentas en participación,* joint-account; *a* or *en la cuenta de la vieja,* to count on one's fingers, by beads, etc.; *cuentas alegres* or *galanas,* vain hopes, deceptive calculations, castles in the air; *abrir* or *armar cuenta,* (*com.*) to open an account; *a cuentas viejas, barajas nuevas,* better to settle accounts without delay, thus avoiding disputes; *a esa cuenta,* at that rate; *a* or *por la cuenta,* apparently, as far as one can judge; *ajustar uno sus cuentas,* to go into the details of an affair; *correr por la misma cuenta,* to be in the same circumstances; *caer* or *dar en la cuenta,* to come to realize, to understand (after some difficulty); *con cuenta y razón,* exactly and precisely; punctually; *cubrir la cuenta,* to balance the account; *¡cuenta!* or *¡cuenta con la cuenta!* take care! *cuenta errada, que no valga,* (*com.*) errors and omissions excepted; *cuenta y razón conserva* or *sustenta amistad,* short reckonings make long friends; *danzar de cuenta,* to dance certain folk-dances; *dar cuenta,* to answer, give account; *dar cuenta de,* (*coll.*) to waste, destroy; *por cuenta y mitad,* joint-account; *dar uno buena* or *mala cuenta de su persona,* to give a good or bad account of oneself; *de cuenta,* of importance; *de cuenta y riesgo de uno,* on one's own responsibility; *echar la(s) cuenta(s),* to estimate, to go into accounts; *en resumidas cuentas,* (*coll.*) in short, in a word; at last; *echar la cuenta sin la huéspeda,* to reckon the advantages of a thing without its

inconveniences; *entrar en cuenta,* to be taken into account; *entrar uno en cuentas consigo,* to think matters over carefully; *girar la cuenta,* (*com.*) to make out and send the bill; *hacer(se) uno (la) cuenta,* to imagine, suppose; *haya buena cuenta, y blanca no parezca,* always keep accounts strictly; *la cuenta es cuenta,* business is business; *llevar la cuenta,* to keep accounts; *meter* or *poner en cuenta,* to add other reasons to those already known; *no hacer cuenta de una cosa,* not to appreciate something; *no querer uno cuentas con otro,* to wish to have no dealings with another; *no salirle a uno la cuenta,* to be disappointed in one's expectations; *no tener cuenta con una cosa,* to avoid being mixed up in something; *pedir cuenta,* to ask for an explanation; *perder la cuenta,* to lose count of; *por la cuenta,* by all accounts; *por mi cuenta,* in my opinion; *tener cuenta una cosa,* to be profitable, advantageous; *tener cuenta de,* to take care of; *tener en cuenta,* to keep in mind, consider; to take into account; *tomar cuentas,* to go carefully into accounts, etc.; *tomar en cuenta,* to accept on account; *tomar por su cuenta,* to take upon oneself; *tribunal de cuentas,* exchequer; *vamos* or *estemos a cuentas,* let us attend to this; *vivir a cuenta de otro,* to live at another's expense.

cuentacacao, *n.f.* (*Hond.*) a poisonous spider.

cuentacorrentista, *n.m.f.* one having a current account in a bank.

cuentadante, *n.m.f., a.* one having to render account of money held in trust.

cuentagotas, *n.m.* dropping-tube, dropping-bottle.

cuentahilos, *n.m.* thread-counter; linen-prover; weaver's glass.

cuentapasos, *n.m.* pedometer.

cuentecillo, *n.m.* little story [CUENTO].

cuentecita, cuentezuela, *n.f.* small account [CUENTA].

cuentero, -ra; cuentista, *a.* tale-telling. — *n.m.f.* tale-teller, informer, misrepresenter; story-teller, author, writer.

cuento, *n.m.* story, tale, narrative; fable, fairy-tale, fiction, lie, false report; million; butt-end of a pointed weapon; variance, disagreement between friends; prop, support; account, number; joint of the wing; *cuento de cuentos,* billion, a million millions; complicated story; *cuento de viejas,* old wives' tale, idle story; *cuento largo,* long story; *el cuento de nunca acabar,* a never-ending affair; *acabados son cuentos,* the matter is at an end; *a cuento,* seasonably, to the purpose; *andar en cuentos,* to fall out, disagree; *como digo* or *iba diciendo de mi cuento,* (*fam.*) as I was saying; *degollar el cuento,* to break the thread of a story; *dejarse* or *quitarse de cuentos,* to come to the main point; *despachurrar* or *destripar el cuento,* to interrupt the story; to frustrate; *en cuento de,* in place of; *en todo cuento,* in any case; *ese es el cuento,* that is the difficulty; *estar en el cuento,* to be well informed; *hablar en el cuento,* to speak to the point; *poner en cuentos,* to expose to risk or danger; *saber uno su cuento,* to know one's own business best; *ser mucho cuento,* to be very important; to need careful consideration; *sin cuento,* immeasurable; *traer a cuento,* to introduce into the subject; *va de* *cuento*, it is related or said; *venir a cuento*, to come opportunely; *venirle a uno con cuentos*, to worry someone with trifles.

cuento, cuente, *pres. indic., pres. subj.* [CONTAR]; *cuente usted conmigo*, you can rely upon me.

cuentón, -na, *a.* tale-telling, gossipy. — *n.m.f.* story-teller, tale-teller.

cuera, *n.f.* leather jacket.

cuerda, *n.f.* string, cord, rope, halter; fishing-line; cat-gut; fuse (for explosive); chain (of clock or watch); chain-gang; range of mountains, mountain-chain; (*mus.*) compass of a voice; (*PR.*) land measure (4,810 square yards); (*mus.*) string; (*geom.*) chord. — *pl.* human tendons; *cuerda falsa*, (*mus.*) string out of tune; *cuerda floja*, rope-dancer's tight rope; *cuerdas vocales*, vocal cords; *aflojar la cuerda* (*al arco*), to slacken, relax; to temper justice; *andar* or *bailar en la cuerda floja*, to vacillate, waver; *apretar hasta que salte la cuerda*, to try someone's patience to the utmost; *apretar la cuerda*, to treat with severity; *calar la cuerda*, to fire a musket; *dar cuerda al reloj*, to wind up a watch, clock, etc.; *dar cuerda a uno*, to turn the conversation into someone's favourite topic; *echar una cuerda*, (*surv.*) to measure roughly with only the line; *estar, tener* or *traer la cuerda tirante*, to be over-severe; *estirar las cuerdas*, to stretch one's legs, take a walk; *no ser una cosa de la cuerda de uno*, to be outside one's special aptitude; *no ser uno de la cuerda de otro*, not to be of someone's opinion; *por debajo de* or *bajo cuerda*, privately, in an underhand way; *tirar de la cuerda para todos o para ninguno*, to ask for equality of treatment.

cuerdamente, *adv.* prudently, advisedly.

cuerdecilla, cuerdecita, cuerdezuela, *n.f.* small cord [CUERDA].

cuerdero, *n.m.* (*mus.*) string-maker or -seller.

cuerdo, -da, *a.* prudent, discreet, judicious, sensible, in one's senses; *el cuerdo no ata el saber a estaca*, the wise man follows no one's opinions.

cuerezuelo, *n.m.* small skin or hide; skin of a roasted sucking-pig.

cuerna, *n.f.* stag or deer's horn; horn vessel; hunting-horn.

cuérnago, *n.m.* bed of a river; ditch, trench.

cuernecico, cuernecillo, cuernecito, *n.m.* small horn [CUERNO].

cuernezuelo, *n.m.* small horn [CUERNO]; instrument for bleeding horses.

cuerno, *n.m.* horn; feeler, antenna; (*mus.*) hunting-horn; horn of the moon; side; wing of an army or fleet; button of a manuscript roll; (*naut.*) outrigger. — *pl.* extremities of objects ending in a point. — *interj.* exclamation of surprise or admiration; *cuerno de abundancia*, horn of plenty; *cuerno de ciervo*, hart's horn; *cuerno de caza*, hunting-horn; *en los cuernos del toro*, in dire peril; *estar* (or *ponerse*) *de cuerno con uno*, to be (or get) angry with someone; *levantar, poner* or *subir hasta* or *sobre el cuerno* or *los cuernos de la luna*, to overpraise; *no valer un cuerno*, to be worth little or nothing; *obra a cuerno*, (*mil.*) horn-work; *poner los cuernos*, to cuckold; *saber a cuerno quemado*, to produce

a bad impression on the mind; *sobre cuernos, penitencia*, (*fam.*) to add insult to injury.

cuero, *n.m.* fell, pelt, rawhide; leather, tanned skin; goat-skin receptacle for wine, oil, etc.; toper, great drinker; *pl.* hangings or drapery of decorated leather; *cuero cabelludo*, scalp; *cuero exterior*, cuticle, epidermis; *cuero interior*, skin, cutis; *cuero en verde*, rawhide; *de cuero*, leathern; *de cuero ajeno, correas largas*, it's easy to give away others' property; *dejar a uno en cueros*, to ruin, leave penniless; *del cuero salen las correas*, the secondary matter is less important than the principal; *en cueros* (*vivos*), stark-naked; *entre cuero y carne*, between skin and flesh, (*fig.*) intimately; *estar hecho un cuero*, to be drunk; *poner un cuero y correas*, to do a favour and be out of pocket over it.

cuerpecito, cuerpezuelo, *n.m.* small body [CUERPO].

cuerpo, *n.m.* body, substance, matter; trunk, figure, build; bodice; corpse, dead body; corporation, public body; entire part of a building up to a cornice or entablature; volume, book; main portion of book; collection of laws, evidence, etc.; size; thickness (silk, woollens, cottons, etc.); strength of liquids; collective mass; (*mil.*) corps, division; (*print.*) size of letter; (*geom.*) body, solid; (*chem.*) body, element; *cuerpo de bomba*, barrel of hydraulic pump; *cuerpo de caballo*, (*mil.*) length of a horse's body; *cuerpo del cabrestante*, (*naut.*) barrel (of capstan); *¡cuerpo de Cristo* or *de Dios! ¡cuerpo de tal! ¡cuerpo de mí!* exclamations of annoyance; *cuerpo de(l) delito*, (*law*) corpus delicti; *cuerpo de ejército*, (*mil.*) army-corps; *cuerpo de guardia*, body of men on guard; guardroom; *cuerpo de iglesia*, nave, body of a church; *cuerpo de la batalla* or *del ejército*, (*mil.*) centre of an army; *cuerpo de reserva*, (*mil.*) reserve corps; *cuerpo facultativo*, the faculty, body of experts; *cuerpo glorioso*, (*theol.*) transfigured body of the blessed after the resurrection; (*fig., coll.*) one who seems exempt from material necessities for long periods; *cuerpo muerto*, (*naut.*) mooring-buoy; *cuerpo sin alma*, dull, dispirited person; *cuerpo tiroides*, (*anat.*) thyroid gland; *cuerpo volante*, (*mil.*) flying column; *a* or *en cuerpo*, without coat or wrap; *a cuerpo descubierto*, manifestly; without cover or shelter; *comer uno el cuerpo*, to waddle; *cuerpo a cuerpo*, hand to hand, in single combat; *dar con el cuerpo en tierra*, to fall down; *dar cuerpo*, to give body, consistence; *de cuerpo presente*, exposed to public view (of a dead body); *descubrir uno el cuerpo*, to be off one's guard; to take a risk; *echar el cuerpo fuera*, to avoid a difficulty or obligation; *en cuerpo de camisa*, without one's outer garments, in shirt-sleeves; *en cuerpo y en alma*, totally, leaving nothing; *falsear el cuerpo*, to move or twist the body to avoid a blow; *hacer del cuerpo*, to go to stool; *huir* or *hurtar el cuerpo*, to dodge a blow, a person or a difficulty; *no quedarse con nada en el cuerpo*, to deliver oneself of all one intended to say; *pedirle el cuerpo alguna cosa*, to desire something; *quedarse con una cosa en el cuerpo*, not telling the whole truth; *tomar cuerpo*, to increase, become bigger; *tratar a cuerpo de* rey or *tratar a qué quieres, cuerpo*, to feast like a king; *volverla al cuerpo*, to return insult for insult.

cuerria, *n.f.* (*prov.*) fenced circular space for ripening chestnuts.

cuerva, *n.f.* female jackdaw.

cuervo, *n.m.* raven; (*astron.*) southern constellation; *cuervo marino*, cormorant; *cuervo merendero*, jackdaw; *cría cuervos, y te sacarán los ojos*, to rear a snake in one's bosom; *venir el cuervo*, to receive repeated help.

cuesco, *n.m.* kernel; mill-stone; (*coll.*) noisy flatulence; (*min.*) dross, scoria.

cuesquillo, *n.m.* small fruit-stone; fruit-pip [CUESCO].

cuesta, *n.f.* hill, mount, sloping ground; *cuesta abajo*, downhill; *cuesta arriba*, uphill; painfully; *echarse de cuesta*, to lie down, go to bed; *a cuestas*, on one's shoulders or back; *hacérsele cuesta arriba una cosa*, to do something under great difficulties and with repugnance; *ir cuesta abajo*, to decline, depreciate; *lo mismo es a cuestas que al hombro*, it does not matter much how a thing is done, so long as it is done; *llevar a cuestas*, to support, sustain; *tener a cuestas*, to maintain someone at one's own cost; *tener la cuesta y las piedras*, to have all the advantage on one's side; *tomar a cuestas*, to undertake, be responsible for.

cuesta, cuestación, *n.f.* charitable appeal.

cuestecica, cuestecilla, cuestecita, *n.f.* easy slope [CUESTA].

cuestezuela, *n.f.* small hill; easy slope [CUESTA].

cuestión, *n.f.* question, enquiry; matter subject for argument or dispute; dispute, quarrel, riot; problem, business, affair; *cuestión batallona*, vexed and much debated important question; *cuestión candente*, burning question; *cuestión de gabinete*, state affair that may cause Cabinet crisis; serious matter; *agitarse una cuestión*, to be discussed heatedly; *desatar la cuestión*, to unravel the argument, solve the question.

cuestionable, *a.* questionable, doubtful.

cuestionador, -ra, *a.* questionary. — *n.m.f.* questioner.

cuestionar, *v.t.* to question, discuss, dispute, argue.

cuestionario, *n.m.* questionary, questionnaire.

cuesto; cueste, *pres. indic. ; pres. subj.* [COSTAR].

cuestor, *n.m.* quæstor; mendicant.

cuestuario, -ria; cuestuoso, -sa, *a.* lucrative, productive.

cuestura, *n.f.* quæstorship.

cuétano, *n.m.* (*ES.*) kind of caterpillar.

cueto, *n.m.* fortified lofty place; rocky place.

cueva, *n.f.* cave, grot, grotto; den; cellar; *cueva de ladrones*, nest of thieves; *cae en la cueva el que a otro lleva a ella*, the biter bit.

cuévano, *n.m.* grape-basket, hamper; small basket for carrying on the back.

cuevecita, *n.f.* small cave [CUEVA].

cuevero, *n.m.* cave-maker, grotto-maker.

cuezo; cueza, *pres. indic.; pres. subj.* [COCER]. — *n.m.f.* mortar-board; *meter el cuezo*, to interfere, meddle, intrude.

cuguardo, *n.m.* cougar.

cugujada, *n.f.* crested lark.

cugulla, *n.f.* cowl, monk's habit.

cuicacoche, *n.f.* (*Mex.*) a song bird.

cuida, *n.f.* big girl at school who looks after a child.

cuidado, -da, *p.p.* [CUIDAR] attended to, cared for. — *n.m.* care, carefulness, regard, heed, attention, solicitude; caution, apprehension, concern, anxiety, fear; custody, keeping, charge, trust; accuracy, exactness, nicety; *¡cuidado!* mind! stop! beware! *¡cuidado conmigo! ¡cuidado me llamo!* beware! I warn you! (as a threat); *cuidado de, a/c de*, care of; *cuidados ajenos matan al asno*, care killed the cat; *de cuidado*, dangerous; *estar de cuidado*, to be dangerously ill; *estar con cuidado*, to be uneasy in mind; *pierda Vd. o no pase Vd. cuidado*, don't worry; *salir de su cuidado una mujer*, to give birth felicitously.

cuidadosamente, *adv.* carefully, cautiously, mindfully, attentively, heedfully, providently, accurately.

cuidadoso, -sa, *a.* careful, solicitous, vigilant, mindful, heedful, painstaking, observing; *cuidadoso con* or *para con el enfermo*, solicitous for the patient; *cuidadoso del* or *por el resultado*, mindful of the result.

cuidante, *a.* taking care, careful, heedful, mindful, vigilant.

cuidar, *v.t.* to care, heed, mind, look after, keep, take care of, execute with care, tend, attend to, nurse, assist. — *v.r.* to take care of one's health; *cuidar de*, to look after; *cuidarse de*, to take notice of, pay attention to; *cuidar del número uno*, to look after one's own interests; *cuida tú de los cuartos, que los pesos se cuidan solos*, look after the pence, and the pounds will look after themselves.

cuido, *n.m.* (*prov.*) care, caretaking, minding.

cuija, *n.f.* (*Mex.*) small, thin lizard; (*fig.*) lean and ugly woman.

cuita, *n.f.* care, grief, affliction, trouble.

cuitadamente, *adv.* sorrowfully, afflictedly.

cuitado, -da, *a.* anxious, miserable, wretched; chicken-hearted.

cuitamiento, *n.m.* bashfulness, timidity.

cuja, *n.f.* bucket, holder (on saddle); bedstead.

cuje, *n.m.* (*Cub.*) stick placed horizontally on supports for hanging tobacco.

cují, *n.m.* (*Ven.*) aromatic myrrh tree.

culada, *n.f.* (*slang*) bumps-a-daisy. — *pl.* shocks and rollings of a ship.

culantrillo, *n.m.* maidenhair fern.

culantro, *n.m.* coriander.

culas, *n.f.pl.* (*coll.*) hoops (in croquet).

culata, *n.f.* butt-end of fire-arms; breech of a gun; breech-block; back part of anything; buttock, haunch (of animals); *dar de culata*, to move only the back portion of a carriage; *culata del cilindro*, head of the cylinder (of a car).

culatazo, *n.m.* blow with the butt-end of a fire-arm; recoil of a gun.

culazo, *n.m.* large buttocks [CULO]; [CULADA].

culcusido, *n.m.* (*coll.*) botch-work.

culebra, *n.f.* snake; worm (of a still); (*coll.*) trick, practical joke, fun; cunning, sagacious woman; (*coll.*) sudden disorder in peaceful gathering; *culebra de cascabel*, rattlesnake; *sabe más que las culebras*, he is very crafty; *hacer culebra*, to wriggle; *liársele a uno la culebra*, to find oneself suddenly in grave difficulties.

culebrazo, *n.m.* whipping given by jail prisoners to newcomers.

culebrear, *v.i.* to wriggle, move like a snake; (*naut.*) to bend a cable.

culebreo, *n.m.* wriggling, twisting.

culebrera, *n.f.* ring-tail blue hawk.

culebrilla, *n.f.* tetter, herpes; fissure in gun-barrel; (*bot.*) dragon-tree.

culebrina, *n.f.* (*mil.*) culverin; meteor following an undulating course.

culebrino, -na, *a.* snaky.

culebrón, *n.m.* large snake [CULEBRA]; (*coll.*) crafty fellow, double-dealer; (*coll.*) intriguing woman.

culera, *n.f.* stain of urine in swaddling-clothes; patch on seat of trousers.

culero, *n.m.* child's diaper; clout; pip, disease in birds.

culero, -ra, *a.* slothful, lazy.

culi, *n.m.* coolie.

culinario, -ria, *a.* culinary.

culinegro, -gra, *a.* black-bottomed. — *n.f.; dijo la sartén a la caldera ¡quítate allá, culinegra!* the pot called the kettle black.

culirroto, *a.* having torn seat (trousers).

culito, *n.m.* small breech [CULO].

culminación, *n.f.* (*astron.*) culmination; (*naut.*) high tide.

culminancia, *n.f.* (*poet.*) height, elevation, summit.

culminante, *a.* culminating; culminant; (*fig.*) supreme.

culminar, *v.i.* to culminate; (*naut.*) to be at high tide.

culo, *n.m.* buttocks, posteriors; breech, backside, anus; bottom of anything; haunch; croup of animals; *culo de mona,* ugly and ridiculous thing; *culo de plomo,* sedentary person; *culo de pollo,* rough, ill-mended part in stockings or clothes; *culo de vaso,* imitation precious stone; *dar con el culo, en las goteras,* to have squandered all one's money; *quien mucho se baja, el culo enseña,* humility can be carried too far; *ser el culo del fraile,* to have to bear other people's burdens.

culombio, *n.m.* (*elec.*) coulomb.

culón, -na, *a.* big-bottomed. — *n.m.* (*coll.*) invalided or retired soldier.

culote, *n.m.* metal end of projectiles.

culpa, *n.f.* fault, sin, offence, guilt, crime; failure, negligence; *culpa jurídica,* (*law*) fault, guilt; *culpa lata,* negligence, absence of the simplest precautions; *culpa leve,* omission, neglect; *culpa levísima,* slight inattention or mistake; *culpa no tiene quien hace lo que debe,* he who fulfils his duty cannot be held responsible for the consequences; *echar la culpa a uno,* to blame someone; *echar uno la culpa a otro,* to throw the blame on another; *tener la culpa de,* to be responsible for, be to blame for.

culpabilidad, *n.f.* culpability, guilt.

culpabilísimo, -ma, *a. superl.* [CULPABLE] extremely guilty, culpable in the highest degree.

culpable, *a.* culpable, faulty, blameable, condemnable, accusable, guilty. — *n.m.f.* (*law*) culprit, guilty person.

culpablemente, *adv.* culpably.

culpación, *n.f.* crimination, blame.

culpadamente, *adv.* culpably.

culpado, -da, *a.* guilty. — *n.m.f.* culprit. — *p.p.* [CULPAR].

culpar, *v.t.* to blame, impeach, accuse, condemn, reproach. — *v.r.* to blame, reproach oneself.

culpeo, *n.m.* (*Chi.*) large fox.

cultalatiniparla, *n.f.* (*coll.*) affected elegance of language.

cultamente, *adv.* neatly, genteelly; (*iron.*) affectedly; politely, in a cultured way.

cultedad, *n.f.* (*coll.*) affected elegance of style; (*fig.*) fustian.

culteranismo, *n.m.* high-flown style, fustian, cultism.

culterano, -na, *a.* relating to fustian, cultism. — *n.m.f.* cultist, cultorist.

cultero, -ra, *a.* (*fam.*) fustian [CULTERANO].

cultiparlar, *v.i.* to speak with affected elegance.

cultiparlista, *n.m.f.* talker of bombast.

cultipicaño, -ña, *a.* (*iron.*) knavish and affecting culture.

cultísimo, -ma, *a. superl.* [CULTO] highly civilized.

cultivable, *a.* cultivable, manurable, arable.

cultivación, *n.f.* cultivation, culture.

cultivador, -ra, *a.* cultivating. — *n.m.f.* cultivator, tiller, planter. — *n.m.* harrow.

cultivadora, *n.f.* cultivating machine.

cultivar, *v.t.* to cultivate, farm, husband; to manure, labour, till, improve, raise; (*fig.*) to preserve, keep up friendship; (*fig.*) to exercise (the memory, mind, etc.); to nurse a plant; (*fig.*) to study (arts, sciences, etc.); *tierra sin cultivar,* unimproved land.

cultivo, *n.m.* cultivation, farming, tillage; improvement, mind-culture; elegance of manners; (*bact.*) culture.

culto, -ta, *a.* pure, elegant, correct (language, style, etc.); affectedly elegant; cultured, educated, polished, civilized, enlightened, improved, cultivated. — *n.m.* cult; religion; worship, veneration, respect, adoration. — *adv.* in cultured style.

cultor, -ra, *a.* venerating, worshipping. — *n.m.f.* worshipper.

cultura, *n.f.* cultivation; culture; urbanity, politeness; improvement, elegance of style.

cultural, *a.* cultural.

culturar, *v.t.* to cultivate.

cuma, *n.f.* (*Am.*) godmother.

cumarú, *n.m.* (*Cent. Am.*) tonquin bean.

cumbarí, *n.m., a.* (*Arg.*) a very red chilli.

cumbé, *n.m.* Negro dance and tune.

cumbo, *n.m.* (*Hond., ES.*) calabash.

cumbre, *n.f.* top, summit, peak, crest; climax, acme, greatest height of favour or fortune.

cumbrera, *n.f.* (*arch.*) ridge-pole, tie-beam, roof-tree.

cúmel, *n.m.* kummel.

cumiche, *n.m.* (*Cent. Am.*) the younger, the baby of a family.

cumíneo, -nea, *a.* (*bot.*) cumin-like.

cuminol, *n.m.* (*chem.*) cumin-oil.

cúmplase, *n.m.* countersign, official confirmation of appointment; (*Am.*) presidential assent to Bills passed by parliament.

cumpleaños, *n.m.* birthday.

cumplefaltas, *n.m.* full deputy or substitute.

cumplidamente, *adv.* completely, entirely.

cumplidero, -ra, *a.* which must be fulfilled or accomplished; fit, convenient, suitable.

cumplido, -da, *a.* full, thorough, complete; ample, large, plentiful; accomplished, fulfilled; due; gifted, estimable, faultless;

polished, polite, civil, courteous. — *n.m.* attention, courtesy; formality; present. — *p.p.* [CUMPLIR]; *soldado cumplido*, soldier having served full time.

cumplidor, -ra, *a.* reliable, trustworthy. — *n.m.f.* one who executes a commission; executor, executive of a will.

cumplimentador, -ra, *a.* complimenting. — *n.m.f.* congratulator, one who compliments.

cumplimentar, *v.t.* to compliment, congratulate, extend a courtesy; to fulfil a social duty; (*law*) to carry out orders.

cumplimentero, -ra, *n.m.f., a.* (*coll.*) full of compliments, excessively courteous or formal, ceremonious (person).

cumplimiento, *n.m.* compliment, act of complimenting; courtesy, complaisance; ceremony, formality; accomplishment, performance, fulfilment; completion, perfection; lapse, expiration; complement; *al cumplimiento del plazo*, at the expiration of the time; *no se ande Vd. en cumplimientos*, do not stand upon ceremony; *de* or *por cumplimiento*, formally, ceremoniously, by etiquette.

cumplir, *v.t.* to execute, accomplish, realize, discharge, obey, fulfil; to provide, supply; to reach, attain (a certain age). — *v.i.* to do one's duty; to have served one's time in the army. — *v.i., v.r.* to fall due, mature; to be fit, convenient, advisable. — *v.r.* to become true, be realized; *cumple a Juan*, it is John's duty; *cumplir años* or *días*, to reach one's birthday; *cumplir a la letra*, to obey orders exactly; *cumplir con alguno*, to fulfil one's obligation to someone; *cumplir con todos*, to pay due respect to everyone; *cumplir de palabra*, to promise and not perform; *cumplir la palabra*, to keep one's word, promise and perform; *cumplir por cumplir*, just as a matter of form; *cumplir por su padre*, to act on his father's behalf; *cumplir una cita*, to keep an appointment; *cumple con todos, y fia de pocos*, do what best suits you without offending others.

cumquibus, *n.m.* (*coll.*) money, cash.

cumulador, -ra, *a.* accumulating.

cumular, *v.t.* accumulate.

cumulativamente, *adv.* (*law*) cumulatively.

cumulativo, -va, *a.* cumulative.

cúmulo, *n.m.* heap, pile; crowd, throng, multitude, quantity; cumulus (cloud).

cuna, *n.f.* cradle; (*prov.*) foundling-home; native soil, native land; family, lineage; origin, source; space between the horns of cattle; rope-bridge; (*naut.*) stocks; *de humilde cuna*, of humble birth; *de ilustre cuna*, of illustrious birth; *conocer a uno desde su cuna*, to know someone from early childhood; *lo que se aprende en la cuna, siempre dura*, what is learnt in childhood is never forgotten.

cunaguaro, *n.m.* (*Ven.*) a fierce, carnivorous beast.

cunar, *v.t.* to rock (a cradle).

cuncuna, *n.f.* (*Col.*) wild pigeon; (*Chi.*) caterpillar.

cundido, -da, *p.p.* [CUNDIR] spread, grown, expanded. — *n.m.* provision of oil, salt and vinegar given to shepherds; anything spread on a slice of bread.

cundidor, -ra, *a.* expanding, growing, spreading.

cundir, *v.i.* to spread (of oil and other liquids or news); to yield abundantly; to propagate, multiply, expand, grow.

cunear, *v.t.* to rock a cradle. — *v.r.* (*coll.*) to rock, swing oneself.

cuneiforme, *a.* cuneiform, wedge-shaped.

cuneo, *n.m.* rocking, swinging; rolling, pitching (of ships).

cunera, *n.f.* woman appointed to rock the royal children.

cunero, -ra, *n.m.f., a.* (*prov.*) foundling; maker or vendor of cradles; *diputado cunero*, (*coll.*) deputy elected by the influence of the Government.

cuneta, *n.f.* (*fort.*) small trench to drain dry moat; gutter, drain.

cuña, *n.f.* wedge; paving-stone; *meterse de cuña*, to insinuate oneself; *no hay peor cuña que la de la misma madera* or *del mismo palo*, there is no worse enemy than an alienated friend or relative or one in the same business.

cuñadía, *n.f.* kindred, relationship.

cuñado, -da, *n.m.f., a.* brother-in-law; sister-in-law.

cuñar, *v.t.* to wedge.

cuñete, *n.m.* keg, firkin.

cuño, *n.m.* die for coining money, etc.; impression made by the die; mark on gold, silver, etc.; triangular formation of troops.

cuociente, *n.m.* quotient.

cuodlibeto, *n.m.* quodlibet, thesis; paradox, argument, pungent saying, subtlety.

cuota, *n.f.* quota, fixed share; subscription, dues.

cuotidiano, -na, *a.* quotidian.

cupé, *n.m.* landau, coupé, cab.

cupido, *n.m.* cupid; (*fig.*) gallant, lover.

cupitel, *tirar de cupitel*, to throw the wood in the air (in Spanish bowling).

cuplé, *n.m.* cabaret song, ballad.

cupletista, *n.f.* ballad-singer.

cupo, *n.m.* quota, share, tax-rate.

cupón, *n.m.* coupon; dividend.

cupresino, -na, *a.* (*poet.*) belonging to the cypress-tree.

cúprico, -ca, *a.* cupric; of copper.

cuprífero, -ra, *a.* cupriferous.

cuprita, *n.f.* (*min.*) cuprite.

cuproso, -sa, *a.* cuprous, like copper.

cúpula, *n.f.* copula, dome, vault; turret of a warship; (*bot.*) cupule.

cupulado, -da; cupular, *a.* (*bot.*) cupular, cupulate.

cupulífero, -ra, *a.* (*bot.*) cupuliferous.

cupuliforme, *a.* cupulate.

cupulino, *n.m.* (*arch.*) lantern, small cupola.

cuquillo, *n.m.* cuckoo.

cura, *n.m.* parish priest, vicar, parson, clergyman, curate. — *n.f.* cure, healing; curing, preserving, pickling, seasoning; curacy, benefice, cure; *alargar la cura*, to prolong a matter unduly; *cura de almas*, cure of souls; *cura de misa y olla*, priest of little culture; *cúralo todo*, cure-all; *encarecer uno la cura*, to exaggerate one's performance in the hope of greater reward; *entrar, meterse* or *ponerse en cura*, to start a cure; *no se acuerda el cura de cuando fué sacristán*, those who rise in the world are apt to forget their beginnings; *no tener cura*, to be incurable; (*fig.*) to be incorrigible; *primera cura*, first aid; *tener cura*, to be curable; *cura económo*, (*eccles.*) locumtenens.

curabilidad, *n.f.* curability.

curable, *a.* curable, healable.

curaca, *n.m.* (*Am.*) governor, potentate, cacique.

curación, *n.f.* cure, healing.

curadero, *n.m.* bleachery.

curadillo, *n.m.* cod-fish, ling-fish.

curado, -da, *a.* (*fig.*) hardened, tanned, salted; cured; strengthened, restored to health. — *p.p.* [CURAR].

curador, -ra, *a.* curing; healing; curatorial. — *n.m.f.* overseer, caretaker; (*law*) guardian, curator, administrator; bleacher; curer, healer; curer (of food, etc.).

curaduría, *n.f.* guardianship.

curalle, *n.m.* purging physic given to falcons.

curandero, -ra, *n.m.f.* quack, medicaster.

curanto, *n.m.* (*Chi.*) dish made of meat, shell-fish, and vegetables, cooked on hot stones.

curar, *v.t.* to cure, heal, restore to health; to prescribe; to salt, cure, preserve; to bleach; to season (timber); (*fig.*) to soothe, console; to remedy an ill. — *v.i., v.r.* to be cured, recover from illness; (with *de*) to take care of; *curar al humo,* to smoke (meat, fish); *curarse en salud,* to guard against imaginary danger; *curarse las heridas,* to take revenge.

curare, *n.m.* (*bot.*) curare.

curarina, *n.f.* (*chem.*) curarine.

curasao, *n.m.* curaçao.

curatela, *n.f.* (*law*) guardianship.

curativo, -va, *a.* curative. — *n.f.* cure, healing.

curato, *n.m.* rectory, parsonage; parish; cure of souls.

curbaril, *n.m.* courbaril; locust-tree.

curculio, *n.m.* corn-weevil.

cúrcuma, *n.f.* (*bot.*) turmeric, curcuma.

curcumáceo, -cea, *a.* resembling turmeric.

curcumina, *n.f.* (*chem.*) curcumine, turmeric yellow.

curcusilla, *n.f.* coccyx.

curdo, -da, *n.m.f., a.* Kurd; (*coll.*) drunkard. — *n.f.* drunkenness.

cureña, *n.f.* gun-carriage; gun-stock in the rough; stay of a cross-bow; *a cureña rasa,* (*fort.*) without a parapet; (*coll.*) without shelter or defence.

cureñaje, *n.m.* collection of gun-carriages.

curesca, *n.f.* shear-wool, nap from cloth.

curí, *n.m.* (*Am.*) coniferous tree.

curia, *n.f.* ecclesiastical court; tribunal, bar, the legal profession; care, skill, careful attention; *curia romana,* Roman see.

curial, *a.* curial. — *n.m.* member of the Roman *curia;* subaltern clerk, officer of a court, attorney.

curialesco, -ca, *a.* clerical, priest-like.

curiana, *n.f.* cockroach.

curiara, *n.f.* (*Am.*) long, sailing canoe.

curibay, *n.m.* (*River Plate*) pine with highly purgative fruit.

curiel, *n.m.* (*Cub.*) rodent allied to the guinea-pig.

curiosamente, *adv.* curiously; diligently; neatly, carefully.

curiosear, *v.i.* to inquire, be curious, pry into other's affairs.

curiosidad, *n.f.* curiosity, inquisitiveness; object of curiosity; neatness, cleanliness; carefulness; rarity, curio.

curiosísimo, -ma, *a. superl.* [CURIOSO] extremely curious, rare.

curioso, -sa, *a.* curious, inquisitive, prying, meddlesome; neat, clean, attentive, careful; funny, odd, quaint, rare. — *n.m.f.* inquisitive person; *curioso por saber,* curious to know.

curiquingue, *n.m.* (*Ec., Per.*) bird resembling the vulture (the sacred bird of the Incas).

curricán, *n.m.* fishing-line used for streaming.

curro, -rra, *a.* pretty, elegant, delicate; showy, tawdry, loud.

curruca, *n.f.* linnet, warbler.

currutaco, -ca, *a.* ultra-fashionable, affectedly nice, elegant. — *n.m.* dandy, fop, bean. — *n.f.* belle.

cursadamente, *adv.* practically, in a practised manner.

cursado, -da, *a.* accustomed, experienced, exercised, practised; studied; frequented. — *p.p.* [CURSAR].

cursante, *a.* frequenting, assiduous, studious. — *n.m.f.* scholar, student.

cursar, *v.t.* to frequent a place; to follow courses of lectures, study; to do repeatedly; to transmit, expedite.

cursería, *n.f.* [CURSILERÍA].

cursi, *a.* vulgar, shoddy. — *n.m f.* shabby-genteel, pretentious person.

cursilería, *n.f.* pretentiousness, vulgarity.

cursilón, -na, *n.m.f., a.* very pretentious, vulgar, ridiculous (person) [CURSI].

cursillo, *n.m.* short course of lectures in a university.

cursivo, -va, *a.* cursive. — *n.m.f.* cursive writing; (*print.*) italic; *letra cursiva,* running hand.

curso, *n.m.* course, direction, progress, career; turn, run; route, travel; current; course of lectures; set of text-books; treatise; school session; mode of procedure; (*com.*) current rate; lapse; succession; circulation; diffusion. — *pl.* diarrhœa.

cursómetro, *n.m.* apparatus for measuring the velocity of trains.

cursor, *n.m.* (*mech.*) slider, slide.

curtación, *n.f.* (*astron.*) curtation.

curtidero, *n.m.* ground bark for tanning.

curtido, -da, *p.p.* [CURTIR] tanned, curried; weather-beaten; accustomed, expert. — *n.m.* bark for tanning. — *pl.* tanned leather.

curtidor, *n.m.* tanner, currier, leather-dresser.

curtiduría, *n.f.* tan-yard, tannery.

curtiente, *n.m., a.* tanning (material).

curtimbre, *n.f.* tanning; collection of tanned hides.

curtimiento, *n.m.* tanning.

curtir, *v.t.* to tan (leather, the complexion); (*fig.*) to inure, harden. — *v.r.* to brown in the sun; to be inured; *estar curtido en una cosa,* to be accustomed to or expert at something.

curto, -ta, *a.* (*prov.*) short; dock-tailed.

curú, *n.m.* (*Per.*) larvæ of the cloth moth.

curubo, *n.m.* (*Col.*) a climbing plant.

curuca, curuja, *n.f.* eagle-owl.

curucú, *n.m.* (*Cent. Am.*) a climbing bird.

curucurú, *n.m.* (*Am.*) disease caused by snake-bite.

curuguá, *n.m.* (*Am.*) a climbing plant.

curupay, *n.m.* (*River Plate*) tree of the mimosa genus.

cururo, *n.m.* (*Chi.*) kind of field rat.

cururú, *n.m.* Surinam toad (*Pipa*).

curva, *n.f.* curve, bend, curvature; (*geom.*)

curve-line; (*naut.*) knee; *curva de bao* (*naut.*), spur; *curva de nivel*, (*surv.*) contour-line.

curvatón, *n.m.* (*naut.*) small knee, bracket.

curvatura, curvidad, *n.f.* curvature.

curvicando, -da, *a.* curvicandate.

curvifoliado, -da, *a.* curvifoliate.

curvilíneo, -nea, *a.* curvilinear.

curvímetro, *n.m.* apparatus for measuring lines of a plan.

curvo, -va, *a.* curved, crooked, bent. — *n.m.* (*prov.*) enclosed pasture-ground.

cuscungo, *n.m.* (*Ec.*) small owl.

cuscurrear, *v.i.* to eat or pick crumbs to pass the time.

cuscurro, *n.m.* small crust or crumb of bread.

cuscuta, *n.f.* common dodder.

cuscús, *n.m.* [ALCUZCUZ].

cusir, *v.t.* (*coll.*) to sew or stitch badly, clumsily.

cusma, *n.f.* (*Per.*) coarse shirt worn by Indians.

cuspidado, -da, *a.* (*bot.*) cuspidate.

cúspide, *n.f.* cusp; apex, tip, top, summit, peak; sharp end; (*geom.*) vertex.

cuspídeo, -dea, *a.* (*bot.*) cuspidate.

custodia, *n.f.* custody, safe-keeping; guardianship; custodial, monstrance; tabernacle, shrine; guard, keeper, guardian, custodian.

custodiar, *v.t.* to keep, guard, take care of.

custodio, *n.m.* guard, keeper, watchman, custodian.

cusubé, *n.m.* (*Cub.*) sweetmeat made of yucca starch, water, sugar and eggs.

cusumbe, *n.m.* (*Ec.*); **cusumbo**, *n.m.* (*Col.*) coati.

cususa, *n.f.* (*Cent. Am.*) anisette.

cutache, *n.f.* (*Hond.*) a long knife.

cutama, *n.f.* (*Chi.*) dull and tedious person.

cutáneo, -nea, *a.* cutaneous, cuticular.

cúter, *n.m.* (*naut.*) cutter.

cutí, *n.m.* bed-ticking, crash.

cutícula, *n.f.* cuticle.

cuticular, *a.* cutaneous.

cutio, *n.m.* labour, work.

cutir, *v.t.* to knock, pound, strike, beat, hammer, dash against something.

cuto, -ta, *a.* (*ES.*) maimed, without the use of a limb.

cutral, *n.m.f.*, *a.* worn out (ox or cow).

cutre, *n.m.* (*coll.*) miserable, mean fellow.

cutusa, *n.f.* (*Col.*) kind of turtle-dove.

cuy, *n.m.* (*Cent. Am.*) guinea-pig.

cuyá, *n.m.* (*Cub.*) a lofty tree.

cuyabra, *n.f.* (*Col.*) a wooden bowl.

cuyamel, *n.m.* (*Hond.*) a fresh-water fish.

cuyo, -ya, *poss. & rel. pron.* whose, of whom, of which, whereof. — *n.m.* (*coll.*) beau, lover, sweetheart, wooer.

cuzcuz, *n.m.* [ALCUZCUZ].

cuz, cuz, *interj.* a call to dogs.

cuzco, *n.m.* small, cur dog.

cuzma, *n.f.* (*Per.*) a woollen sleeveless shirt used by Indians.

czar, czarina, *n.m.f.* tsar, tsarina.

czariano, -na, *a.* belonging to the tsar.

CH

Ch, ch, *n.f.* fourth letter and third consonant of the Spanish alphabet; is always sounded as *ch* in *church*.

cha, *n.f.* (*Philip.*, *Am.*) tea.

chabacanamente, *adv.* vulgarly; in a bungling way.

chabacanería, *n.f.* vulgarity; lack of taste or merit.

chabacano, *n.m.* (*Mex.*) a variety of apricot.

chabacano, -na, *a.* coarse, unpolished, vulgar.

chabela, *n.f.* (*Bol.*) beverage made of wine and chicha.

chabrana, *n.f.* jamb of door or window.

chacal, *n.m.* jackal.

chacalín, *n.m.* (*Hond.*) shrimp.

chacana, *n.f.* (*Ec.*) stretcher.

chacanear, *v.t.* (*Chi.*) to spur hard.

chacarero, -ra, *n.m.f.*, *a.* (*Am.*) farm labourer.

chacarero, *n.m.* (*Arg.*, *Ur.*) farm labourer.

chacarrachaca, *n.f.* (*fam.*) noisy altercation.

chacarrear, *v.i.* (*fam.*) to grumble.

chacina, *n.f.* dried salt pork for sausages; dried, corned beef.

chacó, *n.m.* shako.

chacolí, *n.m.* a light red wine from Biscay.

chacolotear, *v.i.* to clatter (loose horseshoe).

chacoloteo, *n.m.* clapping of a loose horseshoe.

chacón, *n.m.* (*Philip.*) a large lizard.

chacona, *n.f.* old Spanish dance and song, chaconne.

chaconada, *n.f.* jaconet.

chaconero, -ra, *n.m.f.*, *a.* composer or dancer of chaconnes.

chacota, *n.f.* noisy mirth; ridicule; *echar a chacota*, to carry off with a joke; *hacer chacota de*, to turn into ridicule.

chacotear, *v.i.* to scoff, indulge in noisy mirth.

chacoteo, *n.m.* mockery, ridicule; (*coll.*) rag, ragging.

chacotero, -ra, *a.* ludicrous, waggish. — *n.m.f.* mocker, wag.

chacra, *n.f.* (*Am.*) farm, ranch, plantation.

chacuaco, *n.m.* (*Mex.*) silver smelting furnace.

chacha, *n.f.* abbreviation of *muchacha*, little girl; (*coll.*) nursemaid.

chachal, *n.m.* (*Per.*) lead pencil.

chachalaca, *n.f.* (*Mex.*) a gallinaceous bird; (*fig.*) chatterbox.

cháchara, *n.f.* (*coll.*) chit-chat, idle talk, garrulity.

chacharear, *v.i.* (*coll.*) to chatter, prate, babble.

chacharero, -ra; chacharón, -na, *a.* talkative, garrulous. — *n.m.f.* prater, gabbler.

chacho, *n.m.* stake in ombre; word of affection to boys (abbreviation of *muchacho*).

chafador, -ra, *n.m.f.* flattener, leveller.

chafadura, *n.f.* flattening, levelling.

chafaldete, *n.m.* (*naut.*) clew-line.

chafaldita, *n.f.* (*coll.*) chaff, raillery, jest, banter.

chafalditero, -ra, *a.* (*fam.*) teasing, joking. — *n.m.f.* teaser, banterer.

chafalmejas, *n.m.f.* (*fam.*) dauber, bad painter.

chafalonía, *n.f.* old plate, broken articles of silver.

chafallar, *v.t.* (*coll.*) to botch, mend clumsily.

chafallo, *n.m.* coarse patch, botch.

chafallón, -na, *a.* botching. — *n.m.f.* botcher.

chafandín, *n.m.* vain feather-brained person.

chafar, *v.t.* to flatten, level; to crease, rumple, crumple clothing; (*coll.*) to cut someone short in a speech. — *v.r.* to become flat.

chafarotazo, *n.m.* blow and wound given by the *chafarote.*

chafarote, *n.m.* short, broad Turkish sword; (*coll.*) broadsword.

chafarrinada, *n.f.* blot, stain.

chafarrinar, *v.t.* to blot, stain.

chafarrinón, *n.m.* blot, stain; *echar un chafarrinón,* to disgrace one's family; to blot another's reputation.

chaflán, *n.m.* bevel, chamfer.

chaflanar, *v.t.* to form a bevel, cut a slope.

chagolla, *n.f.* (*Mex.*) counterfeit coin.

chagorra, *n.f.* (*Mex.*) woman of low class.

chagra, *n.m.* (*Ec.*) countryman.

chagrín, *n.m.* shagreen.

chagual, *n.m.* (*Arg., Chi., Per.*) a bromeliaceous plant.

chaguala, *n.f.* (*Am.*) ring that the Indians used to wear in their noses; (*Col.*) any old shoe; long scar in the face; (*Mex.*) slipper.

chagualón, *n.m.* (*Col.*) incense-tree.

cháguar, *n.m.* (*Am.*) Paraguayan sisal.

chaguarama, *n.m.* (*Cent. Am.*) a huge palm-tree.

chagüi, *n.m.* (*Ec.*) very common small bird resembling the European sparrow.

cháhuar, *a.* of reddish-brown colour (horse).

chai, *n.f.* (*slang*) girl; (*slang*) harlot, strumpet.

chaima, *a.* applied to an Indian tribe in north-west Venezuela.

chaira, *n.f.* shoemaker's knife; steel (to sharpen knives).

chajá, *n.m.* (*Arg.*) species of wading bird.

chajal, *n.m.* (*Ec.*) Indian servant in the vicarage.

chajuán, *n.m.* (*Col.*) sultry weather.

chal, *n.m.* shawl.

chala, *n.f.* (*Per.*) husk of maize.

chalado, -da, *a.* light-witted, addle-pated; enamoured, infatuated. — *p.p.* [CHALARSE].

chalán, -na, *a.* hawking; horsedealing. — *n.m.f.* hawker, huckster; dealer in cattle or horses. — *n.m.* (*Per.*) horse-breaker.

chalana, *n.f.* lighter, scow, wherry.

chalanear, *v.t.* to buy or sell dexterously; to deal in horses; (*Per.*) to break, train horses.

chalaneo, *n.m.* hawking, petty dealing; (*Per.*) horse training.

chalanería, *n.f.* huckstery, artifice in buying or selling.

chalanero, -ra; chalanesco, -ca, *a.* (*contempt.*) appertaining to hawkers, etc.

chalarse, *v.r.* to become infatuated, light-witted.

chalate, *n.m.* (*Mex.*) small and lean horse.

chalchal, *n.m.* (*River Plate*) coniferous tree.

chalchihuite, *n.m.* (*Mex.*) low grade emerald; (*ES., Guat.*) trifle, trash.

chaleco, *n.m.* waistcoat, vest; Turkish jacket.

chalequera, *n.f.* woman waistcoat-maker.

chalet, *n.m.* chalet, cottage in Swiss style.

chalí, *n.m.* mohair, delaine.

chalina, *n.f.* cravat, scarf.

chalón, *n.m.* (*Ur.*) shalloon.

chalona, *n.f.* (*Bol.*) dried and salted ewe meat; (*Per.*) dried and salted mutton.

chalote, *n.m.* shallot.

chalupa, *n.f.* sloop, shallop, launch, light vessel, long-boat; (*Mex.*) small canoe; (*Mex.*) corn pancake.

chalupero, *n.m.* boatman, canoe-man.

challulla, *n.f.* (*Per.*) a scaleless fresh-water fish.

chama, *n.f.* (*vulg.*) barter, exchange.

chamaco, *n.m.* (*Mex.*) boy, lad.

chamada, *n.f.* brushwood-fire; brushwood.

chamagoso, *a.* (*Mex.*) dirty, filthy; low, vulgar.

chamagua, *n.f.* (*Mex.*) ripening maize field.

chamal, *n.m.* (*Arg., Chi.*) cloth used by Araucanian Indians to cover the legs in trousers fashion.

chamanto, *n.m.* (*Chi.*) fine, striped mantle used by peasants.

chamar, *v.t.* (*vulg.*) to barter, exchange.

chámara, chamarasca, *n.f.* brushwood-fire; brushwood.

chamarilero, -ra; chamarillero, -ra, *n.m.f.* second-hand dealer; gambler.

chamarillón, -na, *n.m.f., a.* bad card-player.

chamariz, *n.m.* blue titmouse.

chamarón, *n.m.* long-tailed titmouse.

chamarra, *n.f.* garment of coarse frieze.

chamarreta, *n.f.* short loose jacket.

chamarro, *n.m.* (*Hond., Mex.*) coarse garment.

chamba, *n.f.* (*coll.*) fluke, chance.

chambado, *n.m.* (*Arg., Chi.*) drinking vessel made of horn.

chambelán, *n.m.* chamberlain.

chambelanía, *n.f.* chamberlainship.

chamberga, *n.f.* long, wide cassock; broad girdle; a Spanish dance; (*prov.*) very narrow ribbon.

chambergo, -ga, *a.* slouched, uncocked (hat).

chamberguilla, *n.f.* (*prov.*) very narrow ribbon.

chambilla, *n.f.* stone wall with an iron railing.

chambo, *n.m.* (*Mex.*) barter of grain and seeds.

chambón, -na, *a.* awkward, unhandy. — *n.m.f.* blunderer, duffer.

chambonada, *n.m.f.* awkwardness, blunder; (*fig.*) fluke, chance.

chambonear, *v.i.* to blunder.

chamborote, *a.* (*Ec.*) applied to white pepper; (*Ec.*) (*fig.*) long-nosed person.

chambra, *n.f.* dressing-jacket.

chamelote, *n.m.* camlet.

chamelotón, *n.m.* coarse camlet.

chamerluco, *n.m.* kind of close jacket with collar.

chamicado, -da, *a.* (*Chi., Per.*) said of a reserved and silent person; suffering from after-effects of drunkenness.

chamicero, -ra, *a.* belonging to scorched wood. — *n.f.* piece of forest where the wood has been scorched by fire.

chamiza, *n.f.* kind of wild cane used for thatching; (*prov.*) brushwood.

chamizo, *n.m.* half-burnt tree or log; thatched hut; (*coll.*) gambling den.

chamorra, *n.f.* shorn head.

chamorro, -rra, *a.* shorn, bald; *trigo chamorro,* beardless wheat. — *n.m.f.* bald-headed person.

champán, *n.m.* (*naut.*) sampan.

champaña, *n.m.* champagne.

champar, *v.t.* (*coll.*) to give someone a piece of one's mind; to reproach freely.

champear, *v.t.* (*Chi., Ec.*) to close a gap or flume with green sods or turf.

champola, *n.f.* (*Cub.*) refreshment made from custard-apple, sugar and ice.

champú, *n.m.* shampoo.

champurrado, *n.m.* (*Mex.*) chocolate made with cornflour.

[281]

champurrar, *v.t.* to mix drinks.

chamuchina, *n.f.* trifle, trash; (*Am.*) populace, rabble.

chamuscado, -da, *a.* tipsy, flustered with wine; vicious; scorched, singed. — *p.p.* [CHAMUSCAR].

chamuscar, *v.t.* (*pret.* **chamusqué**; *pres. subj.* **chamusque**) to singe, scorch. — *v.r.* to become singed, scorched.

chamusco, *n.m.* [CHAMUSQUINA].

chamuscón, *n.m.* large scorch or singe [CHAMUSCO].

chamusquina, *n.f.* scorching, singeing; (*fig.*) scolding, quarrelling, wrangling; *oler a chamusquina*, to go from words to blows.

chan, *n.m.* (*ES.*, *Guat.*) lime-leaved sage (*Chia*).

chanada, *n.f.* (*coll.*) trick, joke, fraud.

chanate, *n.m.* (*Mex.*) a blackbird.

chanca, *n.f.* heelless slipper; (*prov.*) clog; sabot.

chancaca, *n.f.* (*Cub.*, *Mex.*) sugar of the second crop; (*Ec.*) paste made of toasted maize ground with honey.

chancadora, *n.f.* (*Chi.*) crusher, grinder.

chancaquita, *n.f.* (*Am. Mer.*) cake of *chancaca*, with nuts, coconut, etc.

chancar, *v.t.* (*Chi.*) to crush; to masticate.

chancear, *v.i.*, *v.r.* to jest, joke, fool with.

chancero, -ra, *a.* jocose, sportive, merry.

chanciller, *n.m.* chancellor.

chancillería, *n.f.* chancery.

chancla, *n.f.* heelless slipper; old down-at-heel shoe; *en chancla*, in slippers; slipshod.

chancleta, *n.f.* heelless slipper; *en chancleta*, in slippers; slipshod. — *n.m.f.* inept person.

chancletear, *v.i.* to go slipshod or in slippers.

chancleteo, *n.m.* clatter of slippers.

chanclo, *n.m.* patten; clog; galosh, overshoe.

chancro, *n.m.* chancre.

chancuco, *n.m.* (*Col.*) contraband tobacco.

cháncharras máncharras, *n.f.pl.* (*coll.*) *andar en cháncharras máncharras*, to beat about the bush.

chanchería, *n.f.* (*Am.*) pork-butcher's shop.

chancho, -cha, *a.* (*Am.*) dirty, unclean. — *n.m.* hog.

chanchullero, -ra, *a.* tricky, sharp. — *n.m.f.* trickster, sharper.

chanchullo, *n.m.* (*coll.*) trickery, sharp practice.

chanfaina, *n.f.* ragout made of offal.

chanflón, -na, *a.* awkward, coarse, gawky. — *n.m.* (*obs.*) an old copper coin.

changa, *n.f.* (*Am.*) trade, occupation and service rendered by the *changador*.

changador, *n.m.* (*Am.*) porter, carrier.

changle, *n.m.* (*Chi.*) an edible parasite fungus growing on trees.

changote, *n.m.* oblong iron bar; (*min.*) bloom.

changüí, *n.m.* (*coll.*) hoax, trick; (*Cub.*) low class dance.

chantado, -da, *p.p.* [CHANTAR]. — *n.m.* (*prov.*) wall or fence of upright flagstones.

chantaje, *n.m.* blackmail.

chantajista, *n.m.f.* blackmailer.

chantar, *v.t.* to dress, put on; (*coll.*) to scold, rate; to pave or fence with flagstones.

chanto, *n.m.* (*prov.*) flagstone.

chantre, *n.m.* precentor, choir-master.

chantría, *n.f.* precentorship.

Chantung, *n.m.* Shantung.

chanza, *n.f.* joke, jest, fun; *hablar de chanza*, to speak jestingly.

chanzoneta, *n.f.* (*coll.*) joke, jest; ballad, chansonette, merry little song.

chanzonetero, *n.m.* writer of ballads, petty poet.

chapa, *n.f.* thin metal plate, escutcheon; wood veneer; foil, cap; rouge, artificial rosy spot on the cheek; flush; (*coll.*) judgment, good sense; (*pl.*) game of tossing up coins; *chapas de caoba*, mahogany veneers; *hombre de chapa*, man of ability and merit.

chapado, -da, *a.* plated, veneered. — *p.p.* [CHAPAR]; *chapado a la antigua*, old-fashioned, attached to old customs.

chapalear, *v.i.* to paddle, dabble, splash (in the water); to clatter.

chapaleo, *n.m.* splash, splashing.

chapaleta, *n.f.* valve (of hydraulic pump).

chapaleteo, *n.m.* lapping (of water on a beach).

chapapote, *n.m.* Trinidad asphalt.

chapar, *v.t.* to plate, coat, veneer; (*fig.*) to settle.

chaparra, *n.f.* kind of oak; (*obs.*) low-roofed coach; bramble bush.

chaparrada, *n.f.*; **chaparrón**, *n.m.* heavy shower of rain.

chaparral, *n.m.* plantation of evergreen oaks.

chaparrazo, *n.m.* (*Hond.*) violent shower of rain.

chaparrear, *v.i.* to shower, pour (rain).

chaparro, *n.m.* evergreen oak.

chaparrón, *n.m.* [CHAPARRADA].

chapatal, *n.m.* mire, muddy place.

chape, *n.m.* (*Col.*, *Chi.*) tress.

chapeado, -da, *p.p.* [CHAPEAR] adorned with metal plates; veneered.

chapeador, -ra, *n.m.f.* plater; veneerer.

chapear, *v.t.* to adorn with metal plates; to veneer, inlay; (*Cub.*) to clear ground with a machete. — *v.i.* to clatter (loose horseshoe).

chapecar, *v.t.* (*Chi.*) to braid, plait; (*Chi.*) to string onions, garlic, etc.

chapeo, *n.m.* hat.

chapera, *n.f.* inclined plank used instead of steps.

chapería, *n.f.* ornamentation of metal plates.

chaperón, *n.m.* ancient hood or cowl; (*arch.*) wooden support of gutter.

chapeta, *n.f.* small metal plate [CHAPA]; blush, red spot on the cheek.

chapetón, -na, *n.m.f.*, *a.* (*Am.*) Spaniard; Spanish. — *n.m.* (*Mex.*) silver plate on riding harness.

chapetonada, *n.f.* (*Per.*) illness affecting Europeans newly arrived in Peru.

chapín, *n.m.* clog with cork sole; tropical fish.

chapinazo, *n.m.* stroke or blow with a clog.

chapinería, *n.f.* shop where clogs are made or sold; art of making clogs.

chapinero, *n.m.* clog-maker or seller.

chápiro, *n.m.* (only used in anger) *¡Voto al chápiro! ¡Por vida del chápiro(verde)!* Zounds! Good gracious!

chapisca, *n.f.* (*CR.*) maize harvest.

chapitel, *n.m.* chapiter, head of a pillar; spire; jewel bearing of a magnetic needle.

chaple, *n.m.* graver, engraving-tool.

chapó, *n.m.* four- or six-handed billiard game.

chapodar, *v.t.* to lop, prune, trim (trees); (*fig.*) to curtail, cut down, cut out.

chapodo, *n.m.* pruned or trimmed branch.
chapola, *n.f.* (*Col.*) butterfly.
chapón, *n.m.* large ink-stain or blot.
chapona, *n.f.* woman's morning dress; (*Ur.*) coat, jacket.
chapote, *n.m.* (*Mex.*) black chewing-wax.
chapotear, *v.t.* to wet, damp with a sponge or cloth. — *v.i.* to paddle, dabble.
chapoteo, *n.m.* splash, splatter.
chapucear, *v.t.* to botch, bungle, cobble.
chapuceramente, *adv.* bunglingly, fumblingly, clumsily.
chapucería, *n.f.* botch-work, botchery; clumsy, bungling work; fib, lie.
chapucero, -ra, *a.* rough, clumsy, unpolished, bungling, rude, botchy. — *n.m.f.* bungler, botcher. — *n.m.* blacksmith; dealer in old iron.
chapul, *n.m.* (*Col.*) dragon-fly.
chapulín, *n.m.* (*Am.*) locust; large cicada.
chapurrado, -da, *p.p.* [CHAPURRAR] badly enunciated, gabbled, jabbered. — *n.m.* (*Cub.*) refreshment made of stewed plums, sugar and cloves.
chapurrar, *v.t.* to speak gibberish, speak a language badly; (*coll.*) to mix or shake various liquors together; to shake a cocktail.
chapurrear, *v.t.*, *v.i.* to jabber, speak gibberish.
chapuz, *n.m.* act of ducking; botch-work; (*naut.*) fish (for a spar, etc.); *dar chapuz*, to duck. — *pl.* chapuces, mast spars.
chapuza, *n.f.* botch-work.
chapuzamiento, *n.m.* botchy work.
chapuzar, *v.t.* (*pret.* chapucé; *pres. subj.* chapuce) to duck. — *v.i.*, *v.r.* to dive, duck.
chapuzón, *n.m.* (*coll.*) duck, ducking, diving.
chaqué, *n.m.* morning coat.
chaqueta, *n.f.* jacket.
chaquete, *n.m.* game resembling backgammon.
chaquetera, *n.f.* tailoress.
chaquetero, *n.m.* (*coll.*) turncoat.
chaquetilla, *n.f.* short jacket [CHAQUETA].
chaquetón, *n.m.* long jacket [CHAQUETA].
chaquira, *n.f.* (*Per.*) mock pearl or coloured glass bead; (*Col.*) bead.
charabán, *n.m.* charabanc.
charada, *n.f.* charade.
charadista, *n.m.f.* one good at charades.
charadrio, *n.m.* bittern.
charal, *n.m.* a fresh-water fish of the Mexican lakes.
charamusca, *n.f.* (*Mex.*) twisted candy; (*Per.*) brushwood.
charamusquero, *n.m.* (*Mex.*) seller of candy.
charanga, *n.f.* fanfare, flourish; military band.
charango, *n.m.* (*Per.*) kind of bandore or small guitar used by Indians.
charanguero, -ra, *a.* clumsy, artless, unpolished, bungling, botching. — *n.m.f.* botcher, bungler. — *n.m.* (*prov.*) pedlar, hawker; (*prov.*) ship used for coast trade, coaster.
charapa, *n.f.* (*Per.*) species of edible small tortoise.
charape, *n.m.* (*Mex.*) intoxicating beverage made with pulque, ear of maize, honey, clove and cinnamon.
charata, *n.f.* (*Arg.*) gallinaceous bird, kind of wood grouse.
charca, *n.f.* pool of water, pond, basin.

charcas, *n.m.pl.* Indians of the Inca empire.
charco, *n.m.* pond, small lake; *pasar el charco*, to cross the seas.
charla, *n.f.* chit-chat, chat, gossip, conversation, prattling; (*orn.*) chatterer, waxwing.
charlador, -ra, *a.* chattering, talkative. — *n.m.f.* gabbler, prater, chatterbox.
charladuría, *n.f.* garrulity, gossip, prattle.
charlante, *a.* talkative. — *n.m.f.* gabbler, chatterer.
charlar, *v.i.* (*coll.*) to prattle, babble, chatter, prate, gossip, gabble, jabber, clack, chat.
charlatán, -na, *a.* loquacious; in the manner of a charlatan; empirical. — *n.m.f.* prater, babbler; charlatan, quack, mountebank, humbug.
charlatanear, *v.i.* [CHARLAR].
charlatanería, *n.f.* garrulity, charlatanry, verbosity, quackery, humbug.
charlatanesco, -ca, *a.* charlatanish.
charlatanismo, *n.m.* charlatanry, quackery, charlatanism, empiricism.
charlear, *v.i.* to croak (like a frog).
charlotear, *v.i.* to chat, gossip.
charneca, *n.f.* mastic-tree, pistachio-tree.
charnecal, *n.m.* plantation of mastic-trees.
charnela, charneta, *n.f.* hinge, chape; hinge of a bivalve shell.
charol, *n.m.* varnish, japan, japan-work, lacquer; patent leather; *darse charol*, to brag, put on airs.
charolado, -da, *a.* lustrous, brilliant; varnished. — *p.p.* [CHAROLAR].
charolar, *v.t.* to varnish, japan, polish.
charolista, *n.m.* gilder, varnisher, japanner.
charpa, *n.f.* leathern belt with compartments for pistols and poniards.
charque, *n.m.* (*Arg.*, *Mex.*) jerked beef.
charquear, *v.t.* (*Am.*) to jerk beef.
charquecillo, *n.m.* (*Per.*) salted and dried conger eel.
charqui, *n.m.* (*Am.*) charqui, beef cut into strips and dried in the sun.
charquicán, *n.m.* (*Am.*) dish made of charqui, chili, potatoes, beans, etc.
charquillo, *n.m.* small pool, puddle [CHARCA].
charra, *n.f.* (*Hond.*) wide-brimmed hat with a low crown.
charrada, *n.f.* clownish speech or action; country dance; (*coll.*) tawdriness, tinsel, gaudiness.
charramente, *adv.* clownishly, gaudily, tastelessly.
charrán, *a.* rascally, knavish. — *n.m.* rogue, rascal.
charranada, *n.f.* knavish or roguish action.
charranear, *v.i.* to play the knave, be a rogue.
charranería, *n.f.* rascality, knavery, roguery.
charrasca, *n.f.*; charrasco, *n.m.* (*coll.*) trailing sword; clasp-knife.
charrería, *n.f.* tawdriness.
charrete, *n.f.* *charette*, a two-wheeled vehicle.
charretera, *n.f.* knee-strap, knee-buckle; epaulet; (*coll.*) shoulder-pad for carrying loads.
charro, -rra, *a.* relating to a peasant from Salamanca; (*fam.*) churlish, ill-bred, rustic; (*coll.*) tawdry, showy, gaudy. — *n.m.f.* peasant from Salamanca; churl, boor.
charrúa, *n.m.* Indian on the River Plate; small craft used as tugboat.
chasca, *n.f.* brushwood, lops.

[283]

chascar, *v.i.* to crack, crackle; to clack (with tongue).

chascarrillo, *n.m.* anecdote, tale; spicy anecdote.

chascás, *n.m.* lancer's helmet.

chasco, *n.m.* fun, joke, jest, trick; sham; disappointment, frustration; *dar chasco,* to disappoint; *dar un chasco,* to play a merry trick; *llevarse chasco,* to be disappointed.

chascón, -na, *a.* (*Chi.*) entangled, dishevelled.

chasconear, *v.t.* (*Chi.*) to entangle; to involve in difficulties; (*Chi.*) to pull out the hair.

chasis, *n.m.* frame for photographic plates; chassis.

chasponazo, *n.m.* abrasion made by a bullet grazing a solid object.

chasqueador, -ra, *a.* joking, fooling; whipping. — *n.m.f.* joker, hoaxer; whipper.

chasquear, *v.t.* to crack with a whip or lash; to disappoint, fool. — *v.i.* to crack, snap, crepitate. — *v.r.* to be deceived, disappointed.

chasqui, *n.m.* (*Per.*) postboy, messenger.

chasquido, *n.m.* crack (of whip, wood).

chatarra, *n.f.* (*prov.*) iron scoria; scrap iron or metal.

chatarrero, *n.m.* (*prov.*) *chatarra* dealer.

chatasca, *n.f.* (*River Plate*) [CHARQUICÁN].

chatedad, *n.f.* flatness, shallowness.

chato, -ta, *a.* flat, flattish; flat-nosed. — *n.m.* (*coll.*) glass tumbler. — *n.f.* bedpan. — *n.m.f.* flat-nosed person; *chata* or *embarcación chata,* flat-bottomed vessel.

chatón, *n.m.* large stone set in ring or brooch.

chatre, *a.* (*Ec.*) richly attired.

chaucha, *n.f.* (*Arg.*) small coin of silver or nickel; (*Arg.*) green bean; (*Chi.*) silver coin of low standard; (*Chi.*) new season potato left for seed.

chauche, *n.m.* paint made of red lead used for painting floors.

chaucera, *n.f.* (*Chi.*) purse.

chaúl, *n.m.* blue Chinese silk shawl.

chauvinismo, *n.m.* chauvinism, jingoism.

chauvinista, *n.m.f., a.* chauvinist, jingo.

chaval, -la, *n.m.f.* (*coll.*) lad, lass.

chavarí, *n.m.* kind of linen.

chavasca, *n.f.* brushwood.

chavea, *n.m.* lad, young boy.

chaveta, *n.f.* forelock, key, pin, pivot; *perder la chaveta,* to lose one's senses, become rattled.

chaya, *n.f.* (*Chi.*) jest, fun, tricks of carnival time.

chayo, *n.m.* (*Cub.*) shrub which secretes a kind of resin.

chayote, *n.m.* (*Mex.*) pear-shaped fruit of the *chayotera.*

chayotera, *n.f.* (*Cub.*) climbing plant of the Cucurbitaceæ family.

chaza, *n.f.* space between two portholes; place and mark where the ball stops (in *pelota*); *chazas corrientes,* handicap penalty in *pelota; hacer chazas,* (*equit.*) to hop on the hind feet.

chazador, *n.m.* player who stops the ball (in *pelota*); scorer, marker.

chazar, *v.t.* to stop the ball before it reaches the winning-point, or to mark the spot where the ball stops (in *pelota*).

che, *n.f.* name of the letter ch.

checo, -ca, *n.m.f., a.* Czech. — *n.m.* Czech language.

checoslovaco, -ca, *a.* Czechoslovak.

cheira, *n.f.* shoemaker's knife; table steel.

cheje, *n.m.* (*ES., Hond.*) link of a chain.

chelín, *n.m.* shilling.

chencha, *a.* (*Mex.*) lazy, indolent.

chepa, *n.f.* (*coll.*) hump, hunch.

chepica, *n.f.* (*Chi.*) gramma-grass.

cheque, *n.m.* cheque, draft.

chequén, *n.m.* (*Chi.*) kind of myrtle.

chercán, *n.m.* (*Chi.*) small bird resembling the nightingale.

chercha, *n.f.* (*Hond.*) noisy mirth; (*Ven.*) mockery, joke, jest.

cherchar, *v.i.* (*Cent. Am.*) to make fun, joke, jest.

chericles, *n.m.* (*Ec.*) climbing bird (species of parrot).

cherinol, *n.m.* (*slang*) leader of a band of robbers.

cherinola, *n.f.* (*slang*) meeting of robbers or ruffians.

cherna, *n.f.* Mediterranean sea-bass.

cherva, *n.f.* castor-oil plant.

chéster, *n.m.* English Cheshire cheese.

cheurón, *n.m.* (*her.*) chevron.

cheuronado, -da, *a.* (*her.*) chevroned.

cheuto, -ta, *a.* (*Chi.*) hare-lipped.

chía, *n.f.* (*obs.*) short black mourning mantle; (*obs.*) cowl; (*bot.*) lime-leaved sage; white medicinal earth.

chibalete, *n.m.* (*print.*) composing-frame.

chibcha, *a.* (*Col.*) applied to the aborigines of the plateau of Bogotá. — *n.m.* the Chibcha language.

chibera, *n.f.* (*Mex.*) coachman's whip.

chibolo, -la, *n.m.f.* (*Ec.*) thick, round and small body; bump, bruise.

chiborra, *n.f.* fool's bauble with an inflated bladder.

chibuquí, *n.m.* chibouk, Turkish pipe.

chica, *n.f.* (*Am. Mer.*) Negro dance; small bottle; (*Mex.*) small silver coin worth three centavos.

chicada, *n.f.* herd of sickly kids; childish action.

chicalé, *n.m.* (*Cent. Am.*) bird with beautiful plumage.

chicalote, *n.m.* argemone, prickly Mexican poppy.

chicle, *n.m.* (*Mex.*) chicle; chewing-gum.

chiclear, *v.i.* to masticate chewing-gum.

chico, -ca, *a.* small, tiny; young, childlike. — *n.m.* child, boy, lad; good fellow; (*fam.*) third of a pint. — *n.f.* little girl, lassie; good girl; servant girl; *chico con grande,* mixed (when arranging or selling various sizes); (*fig.*) without exception, all included, all told; *chico de cuerpo,* small in stature; *es un buen chico,* he is a decent chap.

chicolear, *v.i.* to joke or jest in gallantry, compliment a lady.

chicoleo, *n.m.* (*coll.*) joke or jest in gallantry.

chicoria, *n.f.* chicory.

chicoriáceo, -cea, *a.* appertaining to the chicory.

chicorro, *n.m.* (*fam.*) robust, bonny boy.

chicorrotico, -ca; chicorrotillo, -lla; chicorrotito, -ta; chicorrotín, -na, *a.* (*fam.*) tiny, very little, very small [CHICO].

chicote, -ta, *n.m.f.* fat, strong boy or girl. — *n.m.* (*coll.*) cigar; (*naut.*) end of a cable; (*Am.*) whip.

chicozapote, *n.m.* (*Mex.*) sapodilla.

chicuelo, -la, *n.m.f.,* *a.* [CHICO] little boy, little girl.

chicha, *n.f.* meat (used only in children's language); strong drink made from fermented maize; *calma chicha,* dead calm; *tener pocas chichas,* to be thin or weak.

chícharo, *n.m.* pea.

chicharra, *n.f.* cicada; toy making unpleasant noise; (*coll.*) chatterer; auger, gimlet; *cantar la chicharra,* to be scorching hot; *hablar como una chicharra,* (*coll.*) to be a chatterbox.

chicharrar, *v.t.* to overfry; to overheat.

chicharrero, -ra, *n.m.f.* maker or seller of *chicharra* (toy). — *n.m.* (*coll.*) hot place or climate.

chicharro, *n.m.* crackling.

chicharrón, *n.m.* crackling, fried lard left in the pan; over-roasted meat; (*coll.*) sun-burnt person.

chichear, *v.t., v.i.* to hiss.

chicheo, *n.m.* hissing.

chichería, *n.f.* (*Mex.*) tavern or shop where chicha is sold.

chichicuilote, *n.m.* (*Mex.*) wading bird akin to the curlew.

chichigua, *n.f.* (*Mex., vulg.*) wet nurse; (*Col.*) worthless trifle.

chichilasa, *n.f.* (*Mex.*) small and very harmful red ant.

chichilo, *n.m.* (*Bol.*) small yellow monkey.

chichimeco, -ca, *n.m.f., a.* (*Mex.*) Indian of the Chichimeca tribe.

chichisbeo, *n.m.* court paid to a lady; wooer; cicisbeo.

chicholo, *n.m.* (*River Plate*) sweet wrapped in corn husk.

chichón, *n.m.* bump on the head; bruise.

chichoncillo, *n.m.* small bump or bruise [CHICHÓN].

chichonera, *n.f.* wadded hood worn by children.

chichota, *n.f.; sin faltar chichota,* not a jot is wanting.

chifla, *n.f.* whistle; hiss, hissing in a public building; paring-knife.

chifladera, *n.f.* whistle.

chiflado, -da, *a., p.p.* [CHIFLAR]; (*coll.*) cracked, mentally unstable; *chiflado por,* infatuated, in love with.

chifladura, *n.f.* hissing; whistling; (*coll.*) craziness, crankiness, whim, fad, crotchet; hobby-horse.

chiflar, *v.t.* to hiss, mock, ridicule in public; (*fam.*) to tipple; to pare leather. — *v.i.* to whistle. — *v.r.* (*fam.*) to have a mental breakdown; to lose one's wits; to be infatuated, enamoured.

chiflato, *n.m.* whistle.

chifle, *n.m.* whistle, call; instrument to decoy birds; (*obs.*) priming-horn, powder-flask.

chiflete, chiflo, *n.m.* whistle.

chiflido, *n.m.* whistling.

chiflón, *n.m.* (*Am. Mer.*) air draught; (*Mex.*) water spout; (*Mex.*) caving in (roof, wall, etc.).

chigrero, *n.m.* (*Ec.*) pedlar, hawker.

chigua, *n.f.* (*Chi.*) basket from rope or bark and used domestically.

chigüil, *n.m.* (*Ec.*) dough made with maize, sugar, butter, eggs, cheese wrapped in green corn husk.

chigüiro, *n.m.* (*Ven.*) capybara, rodent allied to guinea-pig.

chihuahua, *n.m.* (*Ec.*) a kind of firework.

chilaba, *n.f.* galabieh, djellabah.

chilacayote, *n.m.* American or bottle gourd.

chilacoa, *n.f.* (*Col.*) woodcock.

chilanco, *n.m.* (*Cent. Am.*) pool left on the shore by a river.

chilaquil, *n.m.* (*Mex.*) maize omelet stewed with chilli sauce.

chilaquila, *n.f.* (*Guat.*) maize omelet stuffed with cheese, herbs and chilli.

chilar, *n.m.* (*Am.*) chilli orchard.

chilate, *n.m.* (*Cent. Am.*) beverage made with chilli, roasted maize and cacao.

chilatole, *n.m.* (*Mex.*) ear of corn cooked with chilli and pork meat.

chilco, *n.m.* (*Chi.*) wild fuchsia.

chilchote, *n.m.* (*Mex.*) species of very hot chilli.

chile, *n.m.* chilli, American red pepper.

chilenismo, *n.m.* phrase, idiom, colloquialism peculiar to Chileans.

chileno, -na, *n.m.f., a.* Chilean.

chilero, *n.m.* (*Mex.*) (*contempt.*) grocer.

chilindrina, *n.f.* (*coll.*) trifle; jest, joke, fun, anecdote; chaff, banter.

chilindrinero, -ra, *a.* (*fam.*) jesting, bantering. — *n.m.f.* jester, joker; chatterbox.

chilindrón, *n.m.* game at cards.

chilmote, *n.m.* (*Mex.*) sauce of chilli and tomato.

chilote, *n.m.* (*Mex.*) drink made with pulque and chilli.

chilpe, *n.m.* (*Ec.*) strip of agave leaf; (*Ec.*) dry leaf of maize; (*Chi.*) rag, tatter.

chiltipiquín, *n.m.* (*Mex.*) small hot chilli.

chiltuca, *n.f.* (*ES.*) highly poisonous spider.

chilla, *n.f.* call (decoy-instrument) for foxes, hares, etc.; thin board; (*Chi.*) species of small fox.

chillado, *n.m.* roof of shingles or thin boards; clap-boards.

chillador, -ra, *a.* screaming, shrieking. — *n.m.f.* screamer, shrieker.

chillar, *v.i.* to scream, shriek, mewl; to hiss, sizzle; to crackle, creak, squeak; (*hunt.*) to imitate birds' notes; (*art, fig.*) to be too bright, loud, or ill-matched (of colours); *chillarle a uno las orejas,* to feel one's ears ringing; *cuando la sartén chilla, algo hay en la villa,* there's no smoke without fire.

chilleras, *n.f.pl.* (*naut.*) shot-lockers for balls.

chillería, *n.f.* row, uproar, screeching, screaming.

chillido, *n.m.* squeak, shriek, shrill sound; *dar un chillido,* to utter a scream.

chillo, *n.m.* call, whistle (instrument).

chillón, *n.m.* lath nail; *chillón real,* spike.

chillón, -na, *a.* (*coll.*) bawling, shrieking, screaming; harsh, shrill, screechy; (*fig.*) loud, ill-matched (colours). — *n.m.f.* bawler, shrieker, screamer.

chimachima, chimango, *n.m.* (*Arg.*) beetle-eater.

chimbador, *n.m.* (*Per.*) expert in river crossing.

chimenea, *n.f.* chimney, flue; hearth, fireplace; kitchen-range, stove; *chimenea francesa,* fireplace; (*mil.*) nipple of a percussion rifle; *caerle a uno algo por la chimenea,* to have a windfall.

chimó, *n.m.* (*Ven.*) concoction of tobacco and hydrous carbonate of soda, chewed by the Indians.

chimpancé, *n.m.* chimpanzee.

china, *n.f.* pebble, small stone; porcelain, china; china-ware; china-root; china-silk or linen cloth; game of shutting hands and guessing which contains a pebble; (*fig., coll.*) money; (*Am. Mer.*) servant girl of Indian or mestizo blood; *poner chinas a uno,* to hinder, obstruct someone; *tocarle a uno la china,* to win; *tropezar en una china,* to drown oneself in a glass of water.

chinaca, *n.f.* (*Mex.*) beggars, poor people.

chinama, *n.f.* (*Guat.*) hut, hovel.

chinampa, *n.f.* (*Mex.*) small garden tract between the lagoons near Mexico City.

chinampero, -ra, *a.* (*Mex.*) tiller of a chinampa.

chinanta, *n.f.* (*Philip.*) a unit of weight (about 15 av. pounds).

chinapo, *n.m.* (*Mex.*) obsidian.

chinar, *v.t.* (*build.*) to pebble-dash.

chinarro, *n.m.* large pebble.

chinateado, *n.m.* stratum or layer of pebbles.

chinazo, *n.m.* large pebble [CHINA]; blow with a pebble.

chincol, *n.m.* (*Am. Mer.*) small sparrow-like bird with sweet song.

chincual, *n.m.* (*Mex.*) measles.

chinchar, *v.t.* (*coll.*) to vex, annoy.

chincharrazo, *n.m.* (*coll.*) blow with the flat of a sword.

chincharrero, *n.m.* place swarming with bugs; (*Am. Mer.*) fishing smack.

chinche, *n.f.* bed-bug; drawing-pin. — *n.m.f., a.* heavy, boring (person); *caer* or *morir como chinches,* to die like flies; *no haber más chinches que la manta llena,* it never rains but it pours; *tener uno de chinches la sangre,* to be extremely importunate.

chinchemolle, *n.m.* (*Chi.*) a loathsome insect.

chinchero, *n.m.* bug-trap made of twigs.

chinchilla, *n.f.* chinchilla.

chinchimén, *n.m.* (*Chi.*) species of sea-otter.

chinchín, *n.m.* (*Chi.*) an evergreen shrub; (*Cub.*) drizzling rain; (*Col.*) your health! (toast).

chinchintor, *n.m.* (*Hond.*) highly poisonous viper.

chinchona, *n.f.* (*Am.*) quinine.

chinchorrería, *n.f.* false report, alarming rumour.

chinchorrero, -ra, *n.m.f.* insidious tale-teller.

chinchorro, *n.m.* small rowing-boat; kind of fishing net; (*Ven.*) Indian hammock.

chinchoso, -sa, *a.* annoying, importunate, tiresome.

chiné, *a.* applied to a kind of embossed coloured cloth.

chinear, *v.t.* (*Cent. Am.*) to carry something or somebody in the arms or on the back.

chinela, *n.f.* slipper, patten, clog; galosh, overshoe.

chinelazo, *n.m.* blow with a slipper or clog.

chinelón, *n.m.* large slipper or clog [CHINELA]; (*Ven.*) peasant's shoe.

chinería, *n.f.* Chinese article.

chinero, *n.m.* china-closet.

chinesco, -ca, *a.* Chinese. — *n.m.pl.* (*mus.*) bell tree, instrument with small bells; *a la* chinesca, according to the Chinese custom; *sombras chinescas,* shadow pantomime.

chinga, *n.f.* (*Am.*) skunk; (*CR.*) sale by auction; (*CR.*) stub of a cigar or cigarette; (*Hond.*) jest, banter; (*Ven.*) drunkenness.

chingana, *n.f.* (*Am.*) low music-hall.

chingar, *v.t.* (*coll.*) to tipple; (*CR.*) to cut an animal's tail; (*ES.*) to importune, tire, bore. — *v.r.* to get drunk; (*Chi.*) to fail, miscarry; to be a failure.

chinguirito, *n.m.* (*Mex.*) rum from the lees of sugar.

chino, -na, *a.* Chinese. — *n.m.* Chinese man; hairless dog; (*Am.*) offspring of Indian and mestizo; (*Cub.*) offspring of negro and mulatto; (*Col.*) servant; newsboy; (*Am.*) endearing appellative; (*Chi.*) Indian; Chinese language. — *n.f.* Chinese woman; *engañar a uno como a un chino,* to deceive someone easily; *¿Somos chinos?* We are not easily deceived.

chipa, *n.m.* (*River Plate*) basket to gather fruit.

chipá, *n.m.* (*River Plate*) cake or loaf of maize or cassava.

chipaco, *n.m.* (*Arg.*) cake of bran.

chipé, *n.f.* (*slang*) truth, goodness; *de chipé,* first-class, excellent.

chipén, *n.f.* bustle, animation; *de chipén,* excellent.

chipichape, *n.m.* row, tumult; blow.

chipichipi, *n.m.* (*Mex.*) drizzle.

chipile, *n.m.* (*Mex.*) kind of cabbage.

chipilo, *n.m.* (*Bol.*) banana fritter.

chipirón, *n.m.* cuttle-fish.

chipojo, *n.m.* (*Cub.*) climbing, big, green lizard, also locally called chameleon.

chipolo, *n.m.* (*Col., Ec., Per.*) ombre, card game.

chipote, *n.m.* (*Cent. Am.*) cuff, slap, box.

Chipre, *n.f.* Cyprus.

chipriota, chipriote, *n.m.f., a.* Cyprian, Cypriot.

chiqueadores, *n.m.pl.* disks of tortoise shells formerly used as feminine ornament; home remedy for headache.

chiquear, *v.t.* (*Cub., Mex.*) to overindulge, fondle by word or writing.

chiqueo, *n.m.* (*Cub., Mex.*) indulgence, caress.

chiquero, *n.m.* pigsty; (*prov.*) hut for goats; enclosure for bulls.

chiquichaque, *n.m.* (*obs.*) sawer, sawyer; noise made when masticating strongly.

chiquiguite, *n.m.* (*Guat., Mex.*) wicker basket or hamper.

chiquilicuatro, *n.m.* (*coll.*) dabbler, meddler.

chiquillada, *n.f.* childish speech or action.

chiquillería, *n.f.* (*fam.*) crowd of children.

chiquillo, -lla, *n.m.f., a.* small child [CHICO].

chiquirín, *n.m.* (*Guat.*) cicada-like insect.

chiquirritico, -ca, very small, very little; tiny, wee.

chiquirritín, -na; chiquitín, -na, *a.* very little, tiny. — *n.m.f.* baby, infant.

chiquito, -ta, *a.* very little, small [CHICO]. — *n.m.f.* little boy or girl; *andarse en chiquitas,* to be evasive, to beat about the bush; *hacerse chiquito,* to dissemble or conceal one's knowledge or power; to affect modesty.

chira, *n.f.* (*CR.*) banana skin; (*Col.*) shred; (*ES.*) ulcer, sore.

chirapa, *n.f.* (*Bol.*) rag, tatter; (*Per.*) rain while the sun shines.

chirca, *n.f.* (*Cent. Am.*) a tree of the genus euphorbia.

chircal, *n.m.* (*Am.*) profusion of chirca trees.

chircate, *n.m.* (*Col.*) skirt of coarse stuff.

chiribico, *n.m.* (*Cub.*) a purple, elliptical fish with very small mouth and eyes.

chiribitas, *n.f.pl.* (*coll.*) motes in the eye.

chiribital, *n.m.* (*Col.*) untilled land.

chiribitil, *n.m.* crib; small room.

chiricatana, *n.f.* (*Ec.*) poncho of very coarse cloth.

chiricaya, *n.f.* (*Hond.*) sweet made with milk and eggs.

chirigaita, *n.f.* (*prov.*) kind of gourd or calabash.

chirigota, *n.f.* joke, fun.

chirigotero, -ra, *a.* jesting, fun-loving.

chiriguare, *n.m.* (*Ven.*) ravenous bird of prey.

chirigüe, *n.m.* (*Chi.*) a very common bird.

chirimbolos, *n.m.pl.* (*coll.*) pots and pans; odds and ends.

chirimía, *n.f.* kind of clarinet, flageolet. — *n.m.* chirimia-player.

chirimoya, *n.f.* cherimoya (an American fruit).

chirimoyo, *n.m.* (*Cent. Am.*) tree of the Anonaceous family.

chiringo, *n.m.* (*Mex.*) fragment, piece, bit.

chirinola, *n.f.* game resembling ninepins; (*fig.*) trifle; *estar de chirinola,* to be in good spirits.

chiripa, *n.f.* fluke (in billiards); (*coll.*) fortunate chance.

chiripá, *n.m.* (*Arg.*) cloth used by gauchos to cover the legs.

chiripear, *v.t.* to fluke at billiards.

chiripero, *n.m.* poor billiard-player who wins by flukes; lucky person.

chirivía, *n.f.* (*bot.*) parsnip; (*orn.*) wagtail.

chirivisco, *n.m.* (*Guat.*) dry brambly place.

chirla, *n.f.* mussel.

chirlador, -ra, *a.* prattling clamorously.

chirlar, *v.i.* to prattle, talk fast and loud.

chirlata, *n.f.* low-class gaming-den; (*naut.*) wedge, small piece of wood joined to another.

chirlatar, *v.t.* (*naut.*) to fix *chirlatas.*

chirle, *a.* (*coll.*) insipid tasteless. — *n.m.* sheep or goat dung.

chirlear, *v.i.* (*Ec.*) to chirp (applied only to the sound made by birds and their young at dawn).

chirlería, *n.f.* prattle, chat.

chirlo, *n.m.* long wound in the face and the scar it leaves.

chirlomirlo, *n.m.* low feeding value in food; refrain of a song.

chirmol, *n.m.* (*Ec.*) dish made with chilli, onions, tomatoes, etc.

chirola, *n.f.* (*Arg.*) unit of value and account in Bolivia; (*Chi.*) silver coin worth 20 centavos.

chirona, *n.f.* (*coll.*) prison.

chirote, *n.m.* (*Ec., Per.*) species of linnet easily domesticated.

chirraca, *n.f.* (*CR.*) resin from the chirraco tree.

chirraco, *n.m.* (*CR.*) tree secreting the chirraca resin.

chirriado, -da, *p.p.* [CHIRRIAR] sizzled; creaked; sung out of tune.

chirriador, -ra, *a.* sizzling; creaking; chirping, squeaking.

chirriar, *v.i.* to hiss, crepitate, sizzle, squeak, creak, chirp; (*coll.*) to sing out of time or tune.

chirrido, *n.m.* chirping, chattering (of birds and insects); any shrill disagreeable sound.

chirrío, *n.m.* creaking of carts and waggons; [CHIRRIDO].

chirrión, *n.m.* creaking tumbrel.

chirrionero, *n.m.* driver of a *chirrión.*

chirula, *n.f.* (*prov.*) pan-pipe.

chirulí, *n.m.* (*Ven.*) small bird so named from its call.

chirulio, *n.m.* (*Hond.*) dish made with beaten eggs, maize, chilli, fruit of the anatta tree and salt.

chirumbela, *n.f.* kind of clarinet, flageolet; (*Am.*) small cup or gourd for maté.

chirumen, *n.m.* (*coll.*) common sense.

chirusa, chiruza, *n.f.* (*Am.*) ignorant lass.

¡chis! *interj.* hush! silence!

chisa, *n.f.* (*Col.*) larva of a species of black-beetle.

chiscarra, *n.f.* very brittle limestone rock.

chiscón, *n.m.* hut, hovel.

chischás, *n.m.* sound of two swords in duelling.

chisgarabís, *n.m.* (*coll.*) dabbler; insignificant fellow.

chisguete, *n.m.* (*coll.*) small draught of wine; (*coll.*) spurt, squirt; *echar un chisguete,* to drink.

chisme, *n.m.* gossip's tale, misreport, misrepresentation; valueless lumber; trifle; *chisme de vecindad,* tittle-tattle.

chismear, *v.t.* to tell tales, tattle, report falsely.

chismería, *n.f.* tale-bearing, tittle-tattle.

chismero, -ra; chismoso, -sa, *a.* tattling, tale-bearing. — *n.m.f.* gossip, scandal-monger.

chismografía, *n.f.* (*coll.*) gossip, tattle.

chismoso, -sa, *a.* tale-bearing.

chispa, *n.f.* spark, ember, flake of fire; very small diamond; (*fig.*) any small particle; raindrop; penetration, acumen; brightness; (*coll.*) drunkenness; (*pl.*) (*slang*) gossip, scandals; *chispa eléctrica,* electric spark; *coger una chispa,* to get drunk; *echar chispas,* to be violently angry; *ser una chispa,* to be full of life; *tener chispa,* to be very witty; *¡chispas!* blazes!

chispazo, *n.m.* flying of a spark from the fire and damage it causes; (*coll.*) malicious tale.

chispeante, *a.* sparkling; (*fig.*) brilliant, witty.

chispear, *v.i.* to sparkle, scintillate, emit sparks; to glitter, glisten; to rain gently.

chispero, -ra, *a.* emitting sparks (firework, etc.). — *n.m.* smith who makes kitchen utensils; blacksmith; spark-catcher; (*coll.*) rough character of the Maravillas quarter (of Madrid).

chispo, -pa, *a.* (*fam.*) tipsy. — *n.m.* short drink.

chispoleto, -ta, *a.* vivacious, lively.

chisporrotear, *v.i.* to sizzle.

chisporroteo, *n.m.* sizzling, crackling, spluttering.

chisposo, -sa, *a.* sputtering, sparkling, emitting sparks.

chisquero, *n.m.* leather bag or pouch; cigarette lighter.

chistar, *v.i.* to mutter, mumble; *sin chistar ni mistar,* without uttering a word.

chiste, *n.m.* joke, fun, witty saying, facetiousness; *caer en el chiste*, to see through something; *dar en el chiste*, to hit the nail on the head, guess right.

chistera, *n.f.* narrow fish-basket; (*coll.*) silk hat.

chistosamente, *adv.* facetiously, wittily, gaily.

chistoso, -sa, *a.* gay, lively, humorous, facetious, witty.

chita, *n.f.* ankle bone of a sheep or bullock; game with such bones; *a la chita callando*, quietly, by stealth; *dar en la chita*, to hit the nail on the head; *no dársele a uno dos chitas de*, not to give two straws for; *no importar* or *valer una chita*, to be of little value; *tirar a dos chitas*, to cast one's eyes or make claims on two things at once.

chite, *n.m.* (*Col.*) shrub used in making carbon pencils.

chiticalla, *n.m.f.* (*coll.*) discreet person; secret.

chiticallando, *adv.; a la chiticallando*, quietly, noiselessly; discreetly; *ir* or *andar a la chiticallando*, to go on tip-toes, very stealthily.

chito, *n.m.* bone on which money is placed in the game of *chito; irse a chitos,* (*coll.*) to lead a fast life.

¡chito!, ¡chitón! *interj.* hush! hist! quietly! silence!

chitón, *n.m.* a Philippine mollusc.

chiva, *n.f.* (*Cent. Am.*) blanket, coverlet; (*Ven.*) fisherman's net bag; (*Am.*) goatee, imperial.

chivar, *v.t.* (*Am.*) to vex, annoy; to disturb, trouble; to deceive, cheat.

chivarras, *n.m.pl.* (*Mex.*) trousers of untanned kid.

chivarro, -rra, *n.m.f.* kid between 12 and 24 months old.

chivata, *n.f.* (*prov.*) shepherd's staff.

chivato, *n.m.* kid between 6 and 12 months old; (*Col.*) rogue, rascal.

chivetero, chivital, *n.m.* enclosure for kids.

chivicoyo, *n.m.* (*Mex.*) game bird of the gallinaceous family.

chivillo, *n.m.* (*Per.*) species of singing starling.

chivo, -va, *n.m.f.* kid. — *n.m.* well or tank for oil sediment.

¡cho! *interj.* whoa!

chocador, -ra, *a.* clashing, colliding.

chocante, *a.* provoking, irritating; shocking, offensive; (*Mex.*) vexing, annoying.

chocar, *v.i.* (*pret.* **choqué**; *pres. subj.* **choque**) (with *con*) to strike, knock, dash one thing against another, jostle, meet, fight, collide, clash, hit; (with *a*) to provoke, vex, shock, disgust; *chocarla;* (*fam.*) to shake hands.

chocarrear, *v.i., v.r.* to joke, jest, act the buffoon.

chocarrería, *n.f.* buffoonery, low jesting, vulgarity.

chocarrero, -ra, *a.* vulgar, coarse, obscene, ribald. — *n.m.f.* buffoon, low jester.

choclar, *v.i.* to drive the ball through the rings (in the game of *argolla*).

choclo, *n.m.* clog, overshoe, galosh; (*Am.*) green ear of maize; (*Per.*) cake of maize and sugar.

choclón, *n.m.* driving a ball through the rings (in *argolla*).

choco, *n.m.* small cuttle-fish.

chocolate, *n.m.* chocolate.

chocolatería, *n.f.* shop where chocolate is made or sold.

chocolatero, -ra, *a.* fond of chocolate. — *n.m.f.* maker or seller of chocolate; chocolate-pot.

chocoleo, *n.m.* gallantry, flattery.

chócolo, *n.m.* (*Col.*) clog, overshoe, galosh.

chocoyo, *n.m.* (*Guat.*) wagtail.

chocha, chochaperdiz, *n.f.* woodcock.

chochear, *v.i.* to dote.

chochera, chochez, *n.f.* dotage.

chocho, -cha, *a.* doting.

chocho, *n.m.* a sweetmeat; (*bot.*) lupin.

chófer, *n.m.* chauffeur.

chofes, *n.m.pl.* lungs; livers and lights.

chofeta, *n.f.* chafing-dish, fire-pan.

chofista, *n.m.* (*obs.*) poor student who lived upon offal.

cholgua, *n.f.* (*Chi.*) variety of mussel.

cholo, -la, *a.* (*Am.*) half-breed, mestizo; civilized Indian.

choloque, *n.m.* (*Am.*) tree whose fruit is used as soap.

cholla, *n.f.* (*coll.*) skull, head; (*fig.*) faculty, powers of the mind.

choncar, *n.m.* jackdaw.

chongo, *n.m.* (*Mex.*) chignon; (*Guat.*) curl, ringlet; (*Mex.*) joke, jest.

chonguearse, *v.r.* (*Mex.*) vulgarism for *chunguearse.*

chonta, *n.f.* (*Cent. Am., Per.*) hardwood palm-tree.

chontaduro, *n.m.* (*Ec.*) species of palm-tree.

chontal, *a.* (*Am.*) applied to an aboriginal of Central America with coarse and rude habits; (*fig.*) rude. — *n.m.* Indian of the Chontal tribe; the Chontal language.

chopa, *n.f.* (*ichth.*) sea-bream; (*naut.*) poop-house; top-gallant poop.

chopal, *n.m.; chopalera, chopera,* *n.f.* grove of black poplar-trees.

chope, *n.m.* (*Chi.*) farmer's implement to uproot bulbs, etc.; (*Chi.*) oyster tongs.

chopi, *n.m.* (*Arg.*) a thrush-like bird.

chopo, *n.m.* black poplar-tree; (*coll.*) musket.

choque, *n.m.* shock, clash, crash, collision; skirmish, slight engagement; (*fig.*) difference, contest, dispute; (*mech.*) impact.

choquezuela, *n.f.* knee-pan.

chorcha, *n.f.* woodcock.

chordón, *n.m.* raspberry jam.

choricería, *n.f.* pork-butcher's shop.

choricero, -ra, *n.m.f.* sausage-maker or -seller. — *n.f.* sausage-machine.

chorizo, *n.m.* pork sausage; acrobat's counterpoise.

chorlito, *n.m.* curlew, grey plover; red-shank; *cabeza de chorlito*, hare-brained person.

chorlo, *n.m.* basalt, schorl, tourmaline.

choro, *n.m.* (*Chi.*) kind of mussel.

chorote, *n.m.* (*Col.*) unglazed chocolate-pot; (*Cub.*) any thick drink; (*Ven.*) poor quality chocolate.

choroy, *n.m.* (*Chi.*) species of small parrot very harmful to agriculture.

chorrada, *n.f.* excess given in liquid measure.

chorreado, -da, *a.* (*obs.*) of a kind of satin; having striped skin (cattle). — *p.p.* [CHORREAR].

chorreadura, *n.f.* dripping, welling, spurting; stain left by dripping or spurting liquids.

chorrear, *v.i.* to fall, drop from a spout, out-pour, gush, drip; (*fig.*) to come gradually.

chorreo, *n.m.* dripping, spurting of liquids.

chorrera, *n.f.* spout, place from which liquids drop; mark left by running water; rapid (in river); ornament once appended to crosses of military orders; frill of a shirt.

chorretada, *n.f.* (*coll.*) water or other liquid running from a spout; squirt, jet; *hablar a chorretadas*, to speak fast.

chorrillo, *n.m.* continued action of receiving or expending anything; *sembrar a chorrillo,* (*agric.*) to sow grain in furrows; *irse por el chorrillo*, to go with the current; *tomar uno el chorrillo de hacer una cosa*, to accustom oneself to something.

chorro, *n.m.* spout of water; jet, spurt, stream; anything issuing, entering, etc.; *chorro de voz*, sonorous voice; *a chorros*, abundantly, copiously, fast; *estar or ser una cosa limpia como los chorros del oro*, to be very clean and pure; to be very bright, shiny, gleaming; *hablar a chorros*, to speak fluently; *soltar el chorro*, to laugh heartily.

chorroborro, *n.m.* (*coll., contempt.*) debris left by a flood; deluge.

chorrón, *n.m.* hackled or dressed hemp.

chortal, *n.m.* small pond fed by a spring at the bottom.

chotacabras, *n.f.* goatsucker; churn-owl.

chote, *n.m.* (*Cub.*) pear-shaped fruit with a large stone.

chotear, *v.i.* (*Cub.*) (*coll.*) to banter, gibe.

choteo, *n.m.* (*Cub.*) (*coll.*) chaffing, jeering.

chotis, *n.m.* schottische (dance).

choto, -ta, *n.m.f.* sucking kid; calf.

chotuno, -na, *a.* sucking (kid); poor, starved (goat or lamb); *oler a chotuno*, to smell like a goat.

chova, *n.f.* jay; chough; crow; jackdaw.

choz, *n.m.* suddenness, novelty, surprise, sensational happening.

choza, *n.f.* hut, poor cottage, hovel, cabin, shanty.

chozno, -na, *a.* (*fig.*) tender, green; delicate; recent. — *n.m.f.* great-great-great-grandson or -daughter.

chozo, *n.m.* small hut, cabin.

chozpar, *v.i.* to gambol, caper.

chozpo, *n.m.* caper, gambol.

chozpón, -na, *a.* frisky, capering.

chozuela, *n.f.* small hut or cottage [CHOZA].

chubasco, *n.m.* (*naut.*) squall; heavy shower.

chubascoso, -sa, *a.* gusty, showery, squally.

chuca, *n.f.* concave part of a knucklebone.

chucán, -na, *a.* (*Guat.*) scurrilous, vulgar.

chucanear, *v.i.* (*Guat.*) to jest, joke, make fun.

chucao, *n.m.* (*Chi.*) thrush-like forest bird.

chúcaro, -ra, *a.* (*Am.*) surly, wild (of un-tamed animals).

chucero, *n.m.* (*mil.*) pikeman; (*slang*) thief, robber.

chucua, *n.f.* (*Col.*) quagmire, bog.

chucuru, *n.m.* (*Ec.*) a weasel-like animal.

chucuto, -ta, *a.* (*Ven.*) docked, bobtailed.

chucha, *n.f.* female dog, bitch; (*Am.*) opossum. — *interj.* quiet! lie down! (to dogs).

chuchazo, *n.m.* (*Cub., Ven.*) lash with a cow-hide whip.

chuchear, *v.i.* to fowl with calls, gins and nets; to whisper.

chuchería, *n.f.* manner of fowling with calls, gins and nets; bauble, gewgaw, toy, pretty trifle; titbit, dainty morsel.

chuchero, -ra, *a.* ensnaring birds.

chucho, *n.m.* (*coll.*) dog; (*Arg.*) chill; malaria; intermittent fever; (*Cub., Ven.*) cowhide whip; (*Chi.*) small bird of prey whose screech is believed to be an ill omen; (*Am.*) a herring-like fish; (*Cub.*) goad, whip, skewer; (*Cub.*) a ray-fish; (*Col.*) dance-band instrument.

chuchoca, *n.f.* (*Am. Mer.*) dry potage of maize used for seasoning.

chuchumeco, *n.m.* contemptible little fellow; (*Mex.*) Chichimec.

chueca, *n.f.* tree stump; small ball used for hockey; game of hockey; soap-makers' paddle; (*coll.*) fun, trick; (*anat.*) condyle.

chueco, -ca, *a.* (*Am.*) bow-legged.

chuela, *n.f.* (*Chi.*) small axe, hatchet.

chueta, *n.m.f.* (*Balearic Is.*) descendant of converted Jews.

chufa, *n.f.* galingale, chufa; (*obs.*) empty boast; *echar chufas*, to hector, bully.

chufar, *v.i., v.r.* to mock, burlesque.

chufería, *n.f.* shop where orgeat of *chufas* is made or sold.

chufero, -ra, *n.m.f.* seller of *chufas*.

chufeta, *n.f.* jest, joke; chafing-dish, fire-pan.

chufla, chufleta, *n.f.* taunt, jeer, scoff, gibe; frivolous thing.

chufletear, *v.i.* to sneer, taunt, use sharp words.

chufletero, -ra, *a.* taunting, sneering. — *n.m.f.* taunter, sneerer.

chulada, *n.f.* funny speech or action; rude, uncivil word or action.

chulear, *v.t., v.r.* to jest, joke, ridicule; (*Mex.*) to court, woo.

chulería, *n.f.* pleasant manner of speaking and acting; reunion of *chulos*.

chulesco, -ca, *a.* appertaining to *chulos*.

chuleta, *n.f.* chop, cutlet; (*carp.*) chips for filling joints; filling; (*coll.*) slap, smack. — *pl.* side whiskers.

chulo, -la, *a.* roguish, joking; (*Am.*) pretty, nice, graceful. — *n.m.f.* punster, jester, merry fellow; lower-class native of Madrid loud in manners and dress. — *n.m.* butcher's assistant; bullfighter's assistant; pimp, bully; man kept by a woman.

chulla, *n.f.* (*prov.*) slice of meat.

chullo, -lla, *a.* (*Ec.*) odd, left of a pair; *un guante chullo*, an odd glove.

chumacera, *n.f.* (*naut.*) thole-pin, rowlock; (*mech.*) journal bearing.

chumbe, *n.m.* (*Col., Per.*) band, cord, belt to hold the dress at the waist.

chumbera, *n.f.* Indian pear, prickly pear.

chumbo, *n.m.* Indian fig, prickly pear.

chumpipe, *n.m.* (*Guat.*) turkey.

chuncho, *n.m.* (*Per.*) wild Indian tribesman; (*Per.*) marigold.

chunga, *n.f.* joke, jest, banter, fun; *estar de chunga*, to be merry, in good humour.

chungón, -na, *n.m.f.* jester, joker.

chunguearse, *v.r.* (*coll.*) to chaff, gibe, joke.

chunguero, -ra, *a.* fond of jokes. — *n.m.f.* joker, jester.

chuño, *n.m.* (*Am.*) starch of the potato.

chupa, *n.f.* (*obs.*) waistcoat, jacket; (*Philip.*) dry or liquid measure (about 2·7 gills); *poner a uno como chupa de dómine,* (*coll.*) to wipe the floor with a person.

chupable, *a.* chewable, suckable.

chupada, *n.f.* suck, suction.

chupaderito, chupadorcito, *n.m.* baby's teething-ring [CHUPADERO]; *andarse con chupaderitos* or *chupadorcitos,* to use ineffective means in difficult tasks; to send a boy on a man's errand.

chupadero, -ra, *a.* sucking, absorbent. — *n.m.* baby's teething-ring.

chupado, -da, *a.* sucked, absorbed; (*coll.*) lean, emaciated; (*print.*) tall, thin (letters). — *p.p.* [CHUPAR].

chupador, -ra, *a.* sucking, absorbing. — *n.m.f.* sucker, suckling. — *n.m.* baby's teething-ring; (*bot., zool.*) sucker.

chupadura, *n.f.* sucking, suction.

chupaflor, chupamirto, *n.m.* (*Ven., Mex.*) humming-bird.

chupalandero, *n.m.* (*prov.*) snail.

chupalla, *n.f.* (*Chi.*) medicinal plant of the Bromeliaceæ family.

chupar, *v.t., v.i.* to suck, draw, sip; to absorb moisture (of vegetables); (*coll.*) to sponge; to fool. — *v.r.* to become lean, emaciated; *chupar la sangre,* (*coll.*) to stick like a leech; *chuparse los dedos,* to eat with great eagerness and pleasure; to be overjoyed.

chupatintas, *n.m.* (*contempt.*) pen-pusher.

chupativo, -va, *a.* of a sucking nature, absorptive.

chupe, *n.m.* (*Chi., Per.*) popular hotchpotch dish.

chupeta, *n.f.* short waistcoat or jacket [CHUPA]; (*naut.*) round-house.

chupetada, *n.f.* suck, suction.

chupete, *n.m.* teat of feeding-bottle, dummy; (*coll.*) *ser una cosa de chupete,* to be delicious.

chupetear, *v.t.* to suck gently and fitfully.

chupeteo, *n.m.* gentle sucking.

chupetilla, *n.f.* (*naut.*) glass cover for hatchway.

chupetín, *n.m.* inner garment, doublet.

chupetón, *n.m.* strong suction.

chupón, -na, *a.* (*coll.*) absorbing, sucking, sponging. — *n.m.f.* sponger, blood-sucker, parasite. — *n.m.* (*bot.*) sucker; piston of suction-pump; down.

chuquiragua, *n.f.* (*Am.*) a febrifuge plant growing in the Andes.

chuquisa, *n.f.* (*Chi., Per.*) good-time girl.

churana, *n.f.* (*Am.*) Indian quiver.

churco, *n.m.* (*Chi.*) gigantic plant of the Oxalis genus.

churcha, *n.f.* (*Am.*) Indian name of the opossum.

churdón, *n.m.* raspberry (bush and fruit); raspberry jam.

churla, *n.f.;* **churlo,** *n.m.* bag in which spices are carried, seron.

churo, *n.m.* (*Ec.*) curl, ringlet; snail.

churra, *n.f.* small pin-tailed grouse.

churrasco, *n.m.* (*Am.*) braised meat.

churre, *n.m.* (*coll.*) thick, dirty oozing grease; anything resembling this.

churrería, *n.f.* shop where *churros* are made or sold.

churrero, -ra, *n.m.f.* maker or seller of *churros*.

churretada, *n.f.* quantity of dirty grease; many visible stains.

churrete, *n.m.* stain on face or hands.

churriana, *n.f.* (*vulg.*) strumpet.

churriburri, *n.m.* low fellow; rabble.

churriento, -ta, *a.* greasy.

churrigueresco, -ca, *a.* (*arch.*) after the style of José Churriguera, Ribera, and their followers of the 18th century; (*fig.*) overloaded, tawdry, loud.

churriguerismo, *n.m.* (*arch.*) overloading with unsuitable ornamentation.

churriguerista, *n.m.* architect adopting the extravagances of this style.

churro, -rra, *a.* applied to sheep with coarse wool. — *n.m.* kind of doughnut.

churrullero, *a.* prattling, gossipy. — *n.m.f.* prattler, tattler, gossip.

churrupear, *v.i.* to sip, drink in small draughts.

churruscar, *v.t., v.r.* to begin to scorch; to be scorched.

churrusco, *n.m.* over-toasted bread.

churumbela, *n.f.* wind-instrument resembling a flageolet; (*Am.*) small cup for maté.

churumen, *n.m.* (*coll.*) common sense.

churumo, *n.m.* juice, substance; *hay poco churumo,* there is little (judgment, money, etc.).

chus, *interj.* used for calling dogs; *no decir chus ni mus,* to say not a word.

chuscada, *n.f.* pleasantry, drollery, buffoonery, joke.

chuscamente, *adv.* amusingly, pleasantly.

chusco, -ca, *a.* pleasant, droll, merry, funny.

chusma, *n.f.* crew of galley-slaves; rabble, mob, crowd.

chuspa, *n.f.* (*Am.*) pouch, bag, game-bag.

chusque, *n.m.* (*Col.*) gramineous plant species of bamboo.

chute, *n.m.* (*Cent. Am.*) prick, goad, spur.

chuva, *n.f.* (*Per.*) species of monkey peculiar to S. America.

chuza, *n.f.* (*Mex.*) stroke at billiards knocking the five pins with one ball.

chuzar, *v.t.* (*Col.*) to prick, goad.

chuzazo, *n.m.* blow or stroke given with a pike.

chuznieto, -ta, *n.m.f.* (*Ec.*) great-great-great-grandson or daughter.

chuzo, *n.m.* lance, pike; (*Cub.*) whip made of twisted lengths of leather; *caer, llover* or *nevar chuzos,* to rain, snow or hail heavily; *a chuzos,* abundantly, impetuously; *echar chuzos,* to brag.

chuzón, -na, *a.* astute, shrewd; joking, bantering. — *n.m.f.* wag, punster, jester; artful person. — *n.m.* large pike or spear.

chuzonería, *n.f.* mockery, mimicry.

D

D, d, *n.f.* the fifth letter and fourth consonant of the Spanish alphabet; contraction for *Don, doctor.*

dable, *a.* easy, feasible, possible, practicable.

daca (contraction of *da acá*), give here, give me; *andar al daca y toma,* to argue.

dación, *n.f.* (*law*) giving up, delivery.

dactilado, -da, *a.* finger-shaped.

dactílico, -ca, *a.* dactylic.

dactiliforme, *a.* (*arch.*) palm-shaped.

dáctilo, *n.m.* dactyl.

dactilografía, *n.f.* dactylography, typewriting.

dactilografiar, *v.t.* to typewrite.

dactilográfico, -ca, *a.* relating to typewriting.

dactilógrafo, -fa, *n.m.f.* typist.

dactiloscopia, *n.f.* identification through the study of finger-prints.

dactiloscópico, -ca, *a.* relating to the study of finger-prints.

dádiva, *n.f.* gift, present, keepsake, grant, gratification; *acometer con dádivas*, to try to bribe someone; *dádiva ruineja, a su dueño semeja*, a man's actions betray his character; *dádivas quebrantan peñas*, a golden key unlocks all doors.

dadivosamente, *adv.* liberally, plentifully, bountifully.

dadivosidad, *n.f.* liberality, generosity, munificence.

dadivoso, -sa, *n.m.f.*, *a.* liberal, bountiful, munificent (person).

dado, -da, *p.p.* [DAR] given; *dado que*, provided, assuming that, so long as. — *n.m.* die (*pl.* dice); block; pivot-collar; (*naut.*) crossbar reinforcing chain-links; (*arch.*) dado; *dado falso*, cogged dice; *a mi no se ha de echar dado falso*, it won't do to throw loaded dice with me; *cargar los dados*, to load the dice; *conforme diere el dado*, it all depends on how things turn out; *correr el dado*, to be in good luck; *cuando te dieren el buen dado, échele la mano*, take advantage of the opportunity; *dar* or *echar dado falso*, to deceive; *estar una cosa como un dado*, to fit exactly; *a una vuelta de dado*, at the cast of the die; *lo mejor de los dados es no jugarlos*, risks are best avoided.

dador, -ra, *a.* giving. — *n.m.f.* donor, giver. — *n.m.* bearer of a letter; (*com.*) drawer of a bill of exchange.

daga, *n.f.* dagger; line of bricks in a kiln; *llegar a las dagas*, to reach the most difficult point.

dagón, *n.m.* large dagger [DAGA].

daguerrotipado, -da, *p.p.* [DAGUERROTIPAR] daguerrotyped. — *n.m.* daguerrotype.

daguerrotipar, *v.t.* to photograph by daguerreotype.

daguerrotipia, *n.f.* the art of daguerreotypes.

daguerrotipo, *n.m.* daguerreotype.

daguilla, *n.f.* (*prov.*) kind of hollow knitting-needle; (*Cub.*) lace-bark tree.

daifa, *n.f.* mistress, concubine.

dala, *n.f.* pump-dale of a ship.

¡dale! *interj.* *¡dale que dale!* a word expressing displeasure at another's obstinacy ('come along!', 'hurry up!').

dalia, *n.f.* dahlia.

dalmática, *n.f.* dalmatic, wide-sleeved tunic, deacon's vestment at mass.

daltoniano, -na, *n.m.f.*, *a.* colour-blind.

daltonismo, *n.m.* Daltonism, colour-blindness.

dallador, *n.m.* (*prov.*) mower, scytheman.

dallar, *v.t.* to mow.

dalle, *n.m.* scythe, sickle.

dama, *n.f.* lady, dame, noble woman; woman wooed or courted; mistress, concubine; king, at draughts; queen, at chess; principal actress; lady-in-waiting; an old Spanish dance; fallow deer; (*metal.*) crucible-door;

dama cortesana, courtesan; *dama* or *señora de honor*, lady-in-waiting; *dama de noche*, plant of the Solanacea family with flowers odorous at night; *dama joven*, (*theat.*) juvenile lead, ingénue; *primera dama*, (*theat.*) leading lady; *echar damas y galanes*, to indulge in certain amusements on New Year's Eve; *juego de damas*, game of draughts; *las damas al desdén, parecen bien*, true beauty is unadorned; *soplar la dama*, to huff a king at draughts; (*coll.*) to carry off a lady who was courted by another; *ser (una mujer) muy dama*, to be very ladylike, refined.

damaceno, -na; damasceno, -na, *n.m.f.*, *a.* Damascene. — *n.f.* damson plum.

damajuana, *n.f.* demijohn.

damascado, -da, *a.* damask-like.

damasco, *n.m.* damask; damson (tree and plum).

damasina, *n.f.* thin silk stuff resembling damask.

damasquillo, *n.m.* [DAMASINA]; (*prov.*) apricot.

damasquinado, -da, *p.p.* [DAMASQUINAR] damascened. — *n.m.* damascene work.

damasquinador, -ra, *n.m.f.*, *a.* one who or that which damascenes.

damasquinar, *v.t.* to inlay, damascene (steel).

damasquino, -na, *a.* damascened; *a la damasquina*, Damascus fashion.

damería, *n.f.* excessive scrupolosity; prudery.

damero, *n.m.* checker-board, draught-board.

damisela, *n.f.* young gentlewoman; (*coll.*) courtesan.

damnificado, -da, *n.m.f.*, *a.* damaged, injured, hurt (person). — *p.p.* [DAMNIFICAR]

damnificador, -ra, *a.* damaging, injuring. — *n.m.f.* damager, injurer.

damnificar, *v.t.* (*pret.* **damnifiqué**; *pres. subj.* **damnifique**) to hurt, damage, injure.

danchado, -da, *a.* (*her.*) dentate, indented.

dandismo, *n.m.* dandyism; dandyish deed or saying.

danés, -sa; dánico, -ca, *a.* Danish. — *n.m.f.* Dane. — *n.m.* Danish language.

dango, *n.m.* kind of eagle.

danta, *n.f.* tapir.

dante, *a.* giving.

dantellado, -da, *a.* (*her.*) dentated, serrated.

danubiano, -na, *a.* Danubian.

danza, *n.f.* dance, ball; set or number of dancers; entangled affair; (*Cub., PR.*) a slow dance and its tune; *danza de cintas*, maypole dance; *danza de espadas*, sword-dance; (*coll.*) quarrel, fight; *meterle a uno en la danza*, to involve someone in a dispute; *meterse en danza de espadas*, to mix in quarrels; *¿Por dónde va la danza?* Which way does the wind blow?

danzado, -da, *p.p.* [DANZAR] danced. — *n.m.* dance.

danzador, -ra, *a.* dancing. — *n.m.f.* dancer.

danzante, -ta, *n.m.f.* dancer; knowing, active person; fickle, airy person.

danzar, *v.t.* (*pret.* **dancé**; *pres. subj.* **dance**) to dance, whirl round; (*coll.*) to meddle with, interfere.

danzarín, -na, *n.m.f.* fine dancer; fickle, meddling person.

danzón, *n.m.* (*Cub.*) a slow dance and its tune.

dañable, *a.* prejudicial; condemnable.

dañado, -da, *a.* bad, wicked, eternally

damned; injured, damaged; (*Canary Is.*) leprous. — *n.m.* reprobate. — *p.p.* [DAÑAR].

dañador, -ra, *a.* damaging, harmful, injurious. — *n.m.f.* offender, one who harms.

dañar, *v.t.* to hurt, harm, damage, mar, weaken, spoil, impair, injure. — *v.r.* to spoil, become hurt, damaged, injured; *dañar* (*al próximo*) *en la honra*, to damage (one's neighbour's) honour; *dañarse del pecho*, to hurt one's chest.

dañino, -na, *a.* hurtful, harmful, noxious, mischievous, injurious (animals).

daño, *n.m.* damage, hurt, harm, prejudice, loss, injury, mischief, nuisance; *daños y perjuicios*, (*com.*) damages; *dar dinero a daño*, to put out money at interest; *daño emergente*, (*law*) damage resulting from retention of money; *a daño de uno*, at one's risk and expense; *en daño de una persona* or *cosa*, to the detriment or injury of a person or thing; *poco daño espanta, y mucho amansa*, a small loss frightens, a large one serves as a warning; *sin daño de barras*, without prejudice or danger to anyone.

dañosamente, *adv.* hurtfully, harmfully, mischievously.

dañoso, -sa, *a.* hurtful, harmful, mischievous.

dar, *v.t.* (*pres. indic.* **doy**; *pret.* **di**; *pres. subj.* **dé**) to give, bestow, distribute, hand, deliver; to confer; to afford, supply; to minister, administer, apply; to proffer, extend (as the hand); to suppose, consider, assume; to concede, admit (a proposition); to grant, allow, appoint; to suggest, inspire; to transfer; to represent (a play); to render (thanks); to yield, produce (fruits, crops, income, etc.); to explain, elucidate, impart, communicate; to emit (light, heat); to cause, excite (as pain, sorrow); to deal (cards); to exhibit, display, manifest; to show (as signals); to hit, beat, strike, knock; to strike the hours (of a clock); to declare, discover; to offer, entertain with (dance, etc.). — *v.i.* (*fig.*) to announce, foretell; to set in, come on (illness); to commit, incur (an error); to be situated, look out on; (with *en*) to persist in; to guess, hit (the mark); (with *de*) to fall down; to offer, serve (meals). — *v.r.* to give in, surrender; to happen, occur; to produce, yield (fruit, etc.); (with *por*) to devote oneself to; (with *por*) to think, consider oneself; (*hunt.*) to stop flying, fall (of birds); *a mal dar*, if the worst comes to the worst; *a quien dan en qué escoger, le dan en qué entender*, a choice is sometimes hard to make; *a quien dan no escoge*, beggars must not be choosers; *dar a*, to open upon, look out upon (of windows, rooms, houses); *dar un abrazo*, to embrace, greet; *dar el alma al diablo*, to be reckless; *dar de alta*, to inscribe on a register; to set free; to dismiss as cured (patient); *dar de baja*, to dismiss from the army; (*mil.*) to take note of an absence (from roll-call, etc.); *dar de barato*, to allow for peace and quietness' sake; *dar barreno*, to scuttle a ship; *dar de balde*, to give gratis; *dar a la bomba*, to pump; *dar una bofetada a*, to strike on the face; *dar bordos*, (*naut.*) to tack; *dar el beso al jarro*, to drink freely; *dar bien* or *mal* (*en el juego*), to have good or bad luck (at cards); *dar los buenos días*, to wish good day; *dar a bulto*, to give by the lump (or in bulk); *dar cabezadas*, to nod (through sleepiness); *dar*

calle, to clear the way; *dar una carcajada*, to guffaw, burst out laughing; *dar la cara por*, to go to the defence of; *dar las cartas*, to deal the cards; *dar caza*, to chase; *dar coces*, to kick (of animals); *dar coces contra el aguijón*, to kick against the pricks; *dar de codo* or *mano a*, to elbow away, despise, neglect; *dar del codo*, to nudge; *dar con*, to meet, find, come upon; *dar de comer*, to feed, sustain, maintain; *dar a conocer*, to make known; *dar a entender*, to explain; to insinuate, hint; *dar algo*, to bewitch, cast a spell; *dar algo bueno por*, to give anything for; *dar en blando*, to get easily, meet with no resistance; *dar en duro*, to encounter difficulties; *dar en ello*, to hit upon, realize; *dar contra*, to hit against; *dar crédito*, to accredit, believe; *dar a crédito*, to sell on credit; *dar un cuarto al pregonero*, to give confidential information to someone who cannot be trusted to keep it secret; *dar cuenta de*, to account for; *dar culadas*, (*naut.*) to strike repeatedly; *dar un chillido*, to scream; *dar que decir*, to give occasion to censure; *dar los días*, to congratulate on a birthday; *dar diente con diente*, to shiver with cold; *dé donde diere*, wildly, at random; *dar dinero a daño*, to lend money at interest; *dar un ejemplo*, to set an example; *dar en*, to persist in; to contract, acquire; to find out, guess; *dar en el blanco*, to hit the mark; *dar en cara*, to reproach; to stare in the face; *dar en qué entender*, to give trouble, worry, embarrassment; *dar en qué merecer*, to give sorrow, disgust; *dar* (*en*) *qué pensar*, to make one think, give one food for thought; *dar en rostro*, to reproach, cast in one's teeth; *dar la enhorabuena*, to congratulate; *dar de espaldas*, to fall on one's back; *dar el espíritu*, to die; *dar a la estampa*, to send to the press; *dar fiado*, to give credit; *dar fiador* or *fianza*, to find bail, give security; *dar fe*, to certify; *dar fondo*, (*naut.*) to cast anchor; (*coll.*) to offer advantages; *dar fruto*, to yield, bear fruit; *dar garrote*, to strangle; *dar gana*, to excite a desire, inspire with longing; *dar gemidos*, to groan; *dar golpe*, to astonish; *dar gracias*, to thank; *dar grima*, to strike with terror; *dar un grito*, to scream, cry; *dar guerra*, to wage war, torment; *dar gusto* (*pena*), to give pleasure (pain); *dar que hablar*, to cause commotion, talk or gossip; *dar que hacer*, to give trouble; *dar hasta sus entrañas*, to give one's life (for a cause); *dar higa*, to miss fire; *dar a interés*, to put out at interest; *darla de*, (*coll.*) to brag, pose as; *dar largas*, to prolong; procrastinate; *dar licencia*, to give leave; *dar a luz*, to be delivered, give birth to a child; to print, give out, publish; *dar en manías*, acquire mannerisms or manias; *dar de manos*, to fall forward on one's hands; *dar en manos de*, to fall into the power of; *dar la mano a*, to shake hands with; *dar margen*, to afford an opportunity; *dar memorias*, to give one's kind regards; *dar mascada*, to make somebody complete a half-finished task; *dar a merced*, to give up at discretion; *dar el naipe*, to be lucky at gambling with cards; *dar el nombre* or *el santo*, (*mil.*) to give the password; *dar las pascuas*, to wish someone a happy Christmas or Easter; *dar parte de*, to share with, to report; *dar el pésame*, to express condolence;

no dar pie con bola, not to do a thing right; *dar por bien empleado*, to consider worth while; *dar por concluida* or *hecha*, to consider finished, settled; *dar por concluso*, (*law*) to close the argument and await the judge's decision; *dar a uno por donde peca*, to touch someone's sore spot; *dar a uno por quito*, to release from an obligation; *dar en un precipicio*, to fall down a precipice; *dar poder*, to give power of attorney; *dar prestado*, to lend; *dar puntapiés*, to kick; *dar punto*, (*com.*) to fail, become insolvent; *dar de quilla*, (*naut.*) to careen; *dar un raspadillo a un bajel*, to scrape a ship's bottom; *dar mal rato*, to give someone a bad time; *dar razón de*, to give an account of; *dar la razón a*, to acknowledge someone's right; *dar rienda suelta a un caballo*, to let a horse go its own gait; *dar recados*, to greet absent friends; to invite visitors; *dar remolque a*, (*naut.*) to take in tow; *dar saltos*, to jump; *dar que sentir*, to hurt someone's feelings; *dar de sí*, to stretch, extend, give, have elasticity; to have good or bad results; *dar el sí*, to consent, to acquiesce; to marry; to grant; *dar sobre uno*, to attack someone furiously; *dar tras*, to follow, pursue relentlessly, persecute; *dar al traste*, to give up, lose, destroy; *dar de traste*, (*naut.*) to run aground; *dar treguas*, to grant a respite; *dar en vacío* or *en vago*, to fail in an attempt; *dar vez*, to give someone his turn; *dar un vistazo*, to glance; (*a*) *dar que van dando*, to return blow for blow, give as good as one takes; *dar voces*, to call, cry, scream; *dar voces al lobo*, to preach to the desert; *dar una vuelta*, to take a walk, stroll; *dar zapatetas*, to leap with joy; *ahí me las den todas*, other people's troubles don't worry me; *dar y tomar*, to argue, discuss; *andar en dares y tomares*, to contend, dispute; *donde las dan las toman*, they will be paid back in the same coin; *el dar y tener, seso ha menester*, giving and keeping needs brains; *el que luego da, da dos veces*, he gives twice who gives at once; *quien te da un hueso no te quiere ver muerto*, he who gives thee a bone does not wish to see thee dead; *dar con la carga en el suelo*, to let a burden fall through fatigue; *dar con quien lo entiende*, to find someone who understands; *dar contra un poste*, to strike against a post; *dar de palos*, to beat, cudgel; *dar (a la madera) de blanco*, to paint the wood white; *dar la bienvenida*, to welcome; *dar a cala* or *cata*, to sell on trial; *dar una cita*, to make an appointment; *dar aire a una cosa*, to impart animation, life to a thing; *lo mismo me da*, it's all the same to me; *dar de lado*, to slight, give the cold shoulder; *dar la lata*, to pester; *dar la casualidad de*, by coincidence; *me da rabia*, it annoys me greatly; *darse a*, to devote oneself to; *darse a buenas*, to yield, give in; *darse a conocer*, to make oneself known; *darse al diantre*, (*coll.*) to despair; *darse a entender*, to make oneself understood; *darse al estudio* or *a estudiar*, to give oneself up to study; *darse contra la pared*, to be in despair; *darse de baja*, to resign (from a club, etc.); *darse de cachetes*, to come to blows; *darse la mano con*, to be birds of a feather; *darse las manos*, to shake hands; *darse maña*, to contrive, manage ably; *darse a merced*, (*mil.*) to surrender uncondi-

tionally; to halt fatigued in a hunt; *darse una panzada*, (*coll.*) to have a surfeit; *darse a perros*, to become furious, enraged; *darse por*, to consider oneself; *darse prisa*, to make haste; *darse por buenos*, to make up a quarrel; *darse por entendido*, to show that one understands; to show one's appreciation or gratitude; *darse por sentido*, to take offence; *darse a la vela*, to set sail; *darse por vencido*, to surrender; *dársela a uno*, to hoax, disappoint someone; *dársele a uno algo (mucho, poco) de una cosa*, to care somewhat (much, little) about something; *dársele a uno tanto por lo que va como por lo que viene*, not to matter to one what happens; *no se me da nada* or *un bledo*, I don't care in the least.

dardabasí, *n.m.* hawk, kite.

dardada, *n.f.* blow with a dart.

dardo, *n.m.* dart; fresh-water fish; dart-fish, dace; (*fig.*) sarcasm; *dardo de pescador*, kind of harpoon, fizgig.

dares y tomares, *n.m.pl.* (*coll.*) give and take; (*coll.*) disputes, discussions, debates.

dársena, *n.f.* floating dock; inner harbour, basin.

dartros, *n.m.pl.* (*med.*) dartre.

darviniano, -na, *a.* Darwinian.

darvinismo, *n.m.* Darwinism.

darvinista, *n.m.f.* Darwinian, Darwinist.

dasímetro, *n.m.* baroscope.

dasocracia, *n.f.* science of forestry.

dasocrático, -ca, *a.* appertaining to forestry.

dasonomía, *n.f.* science of forestry.

dasonómico, -ca, *a.* appertaining to forestry.

data, *n.f.* date (time and place); item (of statement or account); outlet of a reservoir; kind of plum; *de buena* or *mala data*, well or badly; *larga data*, long ago, very ancient; *estar de mala data*, to be in a bad humour.

datar, *v.t.* to date; (*com.*) to credit on account. — *v.i.* to date, begin from.

datario, *n.m.* datary, papal official.

dátil, *n.m.* (*bot.*) date; (*zool.*) date-shell.

datilado, -da, *a.* date-like.

datilera, *n.f.* common date-palm.

datismo, *n.m.* (*rhet.*) redundant use of synonymous terms.

dativo, -va, *a.* (*law*) dative. — *n.m.* (*gram.*) dative.

dato, *n.m.* datum, fact or truth granted; document, testimony; foundation, basis; Oriental title of honour. — *pl.* data.

datura, *n.f.* thorn-apple.

daturina, *n.f.* (*chem.*) daturine.

dauco, *n.m.* wild carrot; carrot-like plant with petals used as toothpicks.

daudá, *n.f.* (*Chi.*) a medicinal plant.

davalar, *v.t.* (*naut.*) to drift.

davídico, -ca, *a.* appertaining to David, his poetry or style.

daza, *n.f.* lucerne; panic-grass.

de, *n.f.* name of the letter d. — *prep.* sign of possessive case; of; out of; made or composed of; from; by; with; at, for, on account of; concerning, about; between; on; in; to; *de balde*, gratis, freely; *de día*, by day; *de forma* or *manera que*, so that, in such a way that; *de fuerza*, forcibly, perforce, necessarily; *de golpe*, all at once, suddenly; *de intento*, on purpose; *¡desdichado de mí!* woe is me! *de noche*, by night; *el libro de Juan*,

John's book; *andar de prisa*, to walk quickly; *dibujo de pluma*, pen-and-ink drawing; *le dieron de palos*, they beat him with sticks; *es de Sevilla*, he is or comes from Sevilla; *salió del despacho*, he came out of or left the office; *la mesa de madera*, the wooden table; *el sombrero de fieltro*, the felt hat; *el libro de francés*, the French book; *¿de qué habla Vd.?* what are you talking about? *es un hombre de bien*, he is an upright man; *es un muchacho de talento*, he is a talented boy; *el mes de junio*, the month of June; *la ciudad de Toledo*, the city of Toledo; *vamos de París a Londres*, we are going from Paris to London; *es hora de trabajar*, it's time to work; *el bueno de Carlos*, that good fellow Charles; *el pícaro del muchacho*, the rogue of a boy; *hay que acabar de una vez*, it must be settled once for all; *de un trago se bebió la leche*, he drank the milk at one gulp; *¡pobre de mi amigo!* pity my poor friend! *recado de escribir*, writing-set; *cuarto de baño*, bathroom; *máquina de coser*, sewing-machine; *máquina de escribir*, typewriter; *cantaba de alegría*, she was singing for joy; *la señora del sombrero rojo*, the lady with the red hat; *de usted a mí*, between us; *bueno de comer*, good to eat; used by married woman before husband's surname, as *doña Inés Ruiz de González*, Mrs. Inez González (née Ruiz).

dé, *irreg. imper.* and *pres. subj.* [DAR].

dea, *n.f.* (*poet.*) goddess.

deambular, *v.i.* to walk, promenade.

deambulatorio, -ria, *a.* appertaining to walking. — *n.m.* (*arch.*) nave around main chapel.

deán, *n.m.* dean.

deanato, deanazgo, *n.m.* deanship.

debajo, *adv.* under, underneath, below; *debajo de*, beneath, under; (*fig.*) subject to, dependent on; *debajo de mano*, underhand, privately; *debajo de una mala capa hay un buen bebedor*, appearances are deceitful; *quedar debajo*, to get the worst of an affair.

debate, *n.m.* debate, altercation, discussion, expostulation, argument; battle, strife.

debatible, *a.* debatable.

debatir, *v.t.* to debate, argue, discuss; to combat.

debe, *n.m.* (*com.*) debtor, debtor-side, debit-side.

debelación, *n.f.* conquest, conquering in war.

debelador, -ra, *n.m.f.* conqueror, victor.

debelar, *v.t.* to conquer, subdue, vanquish.

deber, *n.m.* duty, obligation, debt. — *v.t.* to owe; to be obliged, have to, must, ought; *cumplir con* or *hacer su deber*, to fulfil one's duty; *es un deber de justicia*, it is a matter of justice; *debe de haber venido*, he must have come; *no deber nada* (*una cosa a otra*), not to be inferior in any way (one thing to another).

debidamente, *adv.* justly, duly, perfectly, exactly, properly.

debido, -da, *a.* due, just, exact, proper; owed. — *p.p.* [DEBER]; *como es debido*, as it should be, as is right and proper.

debiente, *a.* owing. — *n.m.f.* debtor.

débil, *a.* feeble, weak, insipid, faint, slight, poor, sickly, extenuated, debilitated, frail, fragile; (*fig.*) poor-spirited, pusillanimous.

debilidad, *n.f.* debility, weakness, languor, feebleness, pusillanimity.

debilitación, *n.f.* extenuation, debility, weakness.

debilitadamente, *adv.* weakly, in an extenuated fashion.

debilitar, *v.t.* to debilitate, extenuate, weaken, enfeeble, enervate. — *v.r.* to become weak, feeble.

débilmente, *adv.* weakly, feebly, faintly, lamely.

débito, *n.m.* debt; *débito conyugal*, conjugal duty.

debó, *n.m.* instrument used for scraping skins.

debut, *n.m.* debut, first performance.

debutante, *a.* beginning. — *n.m.f.* beginner, débutante.

debutar, *v.t.* to begin; to make one's first appearance or début.

decacordo, *n.m.* (*mus.*) decachord.

década, *n.f.* decade, group of ten; ten days or years; ten chapters.

decadario, -ria, *a.* decadal.

decadencia, *n.f.* decay, decline, fading, decadence; *ir en decadencia*, to be on the decline.

decadente, *a.* decaying, declining, decadent. — *n.m.f.* decadent.

decadentismo, *n.m.* (*Lit.*) principles, characteristics, etc., of decadents; decadence.

decadentista, *n.m.f., a.* decadent.

decaedro, *n.m.* decahedron.

decaer, *v.i.* (*pres. indic.* **decaigo**; *pres. subj.* **decaiga**) to decay, decline, fail, fade, languish; (*naut.*) to fall to leeward; *decaer de su prosperidad*, to decline in prosperity; *decaer en fuerzas*, to lose strength.

decagonal, *a.* decagonal.

decágono, *n.m.* decagon.

decagramo, *n.m.* decagram.

decaído, -da, *a.* faded, languid. — *p.p.* [DECAER].

decaimiento, *n.m.* (*obs.*) decay, decline, falling off, weakness.

decalco, *n.m.* transfer (of drawing); counter-tracing.

decalitro, *n.m.* decalitre.

decálogo, *n.m.* decalogue.

decalvación, *n.f.* shaving of the head.

decalvante, *a.* shaving (the head); (*med.*) producing baldness.

decalvar, *v.t.* to crop, shave the head as punishment.

decámetro, *n.m.* decametre.

decampar, *v.i.* (*mil.*) to decamp.

decanato, *n.m.* deanery, deanship.

decania, *n.f.* farm or parish church belonging to a monastery.

decano, *n.m.* senior member of a community or corporation; dean, doyen.

decantación, *n.f.* decantation, pouring off.

decantador, *n.m.* vessel for decanting liquids.

decantar, *v.t.* to cry up, puff, exaggerate, magnify; to decant, draw off liquor.

decapitación, *n.f.* decapitation, beheading.

decapitar, *v.t.* to decapitate, behead.

decápodo, -da, *a.* decapodal. — *n.m.pl.* Decapoda.

decárea, *n.f.* decare (1000 sq. metres).

decasílabo, -ba, *a.* decasyllabic.

decemnovenal, decemnovenario, *a.* lunar or Metonic (cycle).

decena, *n.f.* denary; number of ten; (*mus.*) tenth.

decenal, *a.* decennial.

decenar, *n.m.* crew of ten.

decenario, -ria, *a.* decennary, decennial. — *n.m.* decennary; rosary of ten beads.

decencia, *n.f.* decency, modesty; honesty, propriety; cleanliness, tidiness.

decenio, *n.m.* decennium, space of ten years.

deceno, -na, *a.* tenth, ordinal of ten.

decentar, *v.t.* (*pres. indic.* **deciento**; *pres. subj.* **deciente**) to begin the use of things; to begin to impair what had been preserved; to cut the first slice; to wound, injure, gall the body. — *v.r.* to have bed-sores.

decente, *a.* decent, just, honest, decorous, genteel, becoming, modest, reasonable, grave; convenient; tidy; well-behaved; of good quality.

decentemente, *adv.* decently, modestly, fairly, honourably; (*iron.*) excessively.

decenvir, decenviro, *n.m.* decemvir.

decenviral, *a.* decemviral.

decenvirato, *n.m.* decemvirate.

decepción, *n.f.* deception, humbug, illusion, disappointment.

decepcionar, *v.t.* to disillusion, disappoint.

deciárea, *n.f.* tenth of an acre (107·64 sq. ft.).

decible, *a.* expressible, that may be expressed.

decideras, *n.f.pl.* (*coll.*) verbosity.

decidero, -ra, *a.* that may be said without inconvenience or impropriety.

decididamente, *adv.* decidedly.

decidido, -da, *a.* decided, devoted, professed. — *p.p.* [DECIDIR].

decidir, *v.t.* to decide, determine, conclude, resolve. — *v.r.* to decide, to be determined; *decidir en un pleito,* (*law*) to give judgment.

decidor, -ra, *a.* witty. — *n.m.f.* fluent speaker, wit.

deciento; deciente, *pres. indic.; pres. subj.* [DECENTAR].

decigramo, *n.m.* decigram.

decilitro, *n.m.* decilitre.

décima, *n.f.* Spanish stanza of ten octosyllabic lines; tenth; tenth part, tithe.

decimal, *a.* decimal; belonging to tithes.

décimanovena, *n.f.* one of the registers of a pipe-organ.

decímetro, *n.m.* decimetre.

décimo, -ma, *a.* tenth. — *n.m.* tenth share of lottery ticket.

décimoctavo, -va, *a.* eighteenth.

décimocuarto, -ta, *a.* fourteenth.

décimonono, -na; décimonoveno, -na, *a.* nineteenth.

décimoquinto, -ta, *a.* fifteenth.

décimoséptimo, -ma, *a.* seventeenth.

décimosexto, -ta, *a.* sixteenth.

décimotercero, -ra; décimotercio, -cia, *a.* thirteenth.

deciocheno, -na, *a.* eighteenth.

decir, *v.t.* (*pres. part.* **diciendo**; *p.p.* **dicho**; *pres. indic.* **digo**; *pret.* **dije**; *fut.* **diré**; *pres. subj.* **diga**) to say, tell, speak, state, utter; to call, name; to assure, persuade, assert, affirm; to declare, depose; to bespeak; to correspond; to denote, indicate, show, be a sign of. — *n.m.* language; notable saying, witty remark; *como dijo el otro,* as someone or other said; *como quien no dice nada,* it's no light matter; *como si dijéramos,* so to speak (*expression used to modify a statement*); *decir*

a uno cuántas son cinco, to threaten, reproach, insult, scold someone; *decir bien,* to speak truthfully, gracefully or eloquently; *decir (bien* or *mal) con una cosa,* to go (well or badly) with something, suit, blend, harmonize; *decir de memoria,* to speak from memory; *decir entre* or *para sí* or *para su capote,* to say to oneself; *decir por decir,* to talk for talking's sake; *decir de repente,* to improvise; *decir de una hasta ciento,* to speak one's mind freely; to make many rash or inopportune remarks; *decirlo en broma,* to say it in fun; *decir en conciencia,* to speak conscientiously, honestly, candidly; *se dice,* it is said, rumoured; *decir de sí,* to affirm; *decir (de) nones,* to deny, not to confess; *decir los Jesuses,* to pray with a dying person; *decir una cosa por otra,* to say one thing instead of another; *decírselo a uno deletreado,* to explain very clearly; *decirse,* to declare (at cards); *decir y hacer,* to accomplish promptly; *decir de nuevo,* to repeat, tell over again; *decir (uno) su parecer,* to give one's opinion; *decir razones,* to argue; *es decir,* that is to say; that is, viz., namely; *por mejor decir,* more properly speaking; *¿lo he de decir cantado or rezado?* how many more times must I say it? *no decir uno malo ni bueno,* to vouchsafe no reply; *no digamos,* not quite but very nearly so; *no digo nada,* I needn't say more; *no tener que decir,* to be unable to reply (to an argument); *no es ambiciosa, que digamos,* (*iron.*) she is not ambitious—not much! *por más que V. diga,* whatever you may say; *por mejor decir,* better, rather; *el bien decir,* elegant style of language; *el decir de las gentes,* the opinion of the people; *es un decir,* it is a mere saying; *el qué dirán,* (undue) respect for public opinion, for what people may say; *ello dirá,* time will tell, we shall see presently; *¿qué quiere decir eso?* what does that mean? *quien dice de mí, mírese a sí,* look at the beam in your eye before you speak of the mote in mine; *quien dice lo que no debe, oye lo que no quiere,* rash speakers hear no good of themselves; *¡digo, digo!* say, listen! *dicho y hecho,* no sooner said than done; *dime con quién andas, y te diré quién eres,* a man is known by the company he keeps; *dizque=dicen que,* they say, it seems that.

decisión, *n.f.* decision, determination, resolution, issue; judgment, sentence, verdict.

decisivamente, *adv.* decisively.

decisivo, -va, *a.* decisive, conclusive, final, decretory.

decisorio, -ria, *a.* (*law*) decisive.

declamación, *n.f.* declamation, discourse, oration, harangue, speech, invective, oratory; delivery; manner of reciting.

declamador, -ra, *a.* declaiming, reciting. — *n.m.f.* declaimer, exclaimer, orator, reader, reciter.

declamar, *v.i.* to declaim, harangue, utter invective, recite in a loud voice, rant.

declamatorio, -ria, *a.* declamatory.

declarable, *a.* declarable.

declaración, *n.f.* declaration, interpretation, exposition, manifestation; account; overture, proposal; avowal; (*law*) deposition.

declaradamente, *adv.* declaredly, avowedly.

declarado, -da, *a.* manifest, clear, patent; declared. — *p.p.* [DECLARAR].

declarador, -ra, *a.* declaring, expounding. — *n.m.f.* declarer, expositor, expounder.

declarante, *a.* declaring. — *n.m.f.* (*law*) declarant; witness.

declarar, *v.t.* to declare, manifest, make known, exemplify, explain, expound; (*law*) to decide, find. — *v.i.* (*law*) to witness, depose. — *v.r.* to declare or explain one's opinion; (*coll.*) to make a declaration of love; *declarar en la causa,* to give evidence in the case; *declarar (a uno) por enemigo,* to declare (someone) as an enemy; *declarar sobre el caso,* to decide the case; *declararse contra alguno,* to come out openly against someone; *declararse por un partido,* to decide in favour of a party; *declararse a otro,* to confess, open one's heart to another.

declarativo, -va, *a.* declarative, assertive.

declaratorio, -ria, *a.* declaratory, explanatory.

declinabilidad, *n.f.* declinability.

declinable, *a.* (*gram.*) declinable.

declinación, *n.f.* (*gram.*) declension; decline, descent, decay, fall, falling; deviation; *declinación de la aguja* or *magnética,* declination of the needle or compass; *no saber uno las declinaciones,* to be completely ignorant.

declinado, -da, *a.* (*bot.*) declinate; declined. — *p.p.* [DECLINAR].

declinador, *n.m.* declinator.

declinante, *a.* declining, bending down.

declinar, *v.i.* to decline, sink, decay, lean downward or sideways; to degenerate, fail, fall off, abate, diminish; approach the end; (*naut.*) to vary from the true meridian. — *v.t.* to decline, reject; to challenge (a judge); to transfer to another tribunal; *va declinando el día,* the day is drawing to a close.

declinatoria, *n.f.* plea that questions the competency of a judge.

declinatorio, *n.m.* declinator (instrument).

declinómetro, *n.m.* declinometer.

declive, declivio, *n.m.* declivity, downward inclination, downhill, descent, slope, fall; *en declive,* slanting, sloping.

declividad, *n.f.* declivity.

decocción, *n.f.* decoction; (*surg.*) amputation.

decoctivo, -va, *a.* (*med.*) digestive.

decoloración, *n.f.* decoloration; discoloration.

decomisar, *v.t.* to confiscate, seize, forfeit.

decomiso, *n.m.* confiscation, forfeiture, seizure.

decoración, *n.f.* decoration, ornament; theatrical scenery; act of committing to memory.

decorado, -da, *a.* decorated. — *n.m.* decoration, ornamentation; thing committed to memory; stage equipment. — *p.p.* [DECORAR].

decorador, *n.m.* decorator.

decorar, *v.t.* to decorate, bestow a badge of honour, adorn, embellish, illustrate, exalt; to learn by heart, recite, repeat.

decorativo, -va, *a.* decorative.

decoro, *n.m.* honour, respect, reverence, gravity, circumspection; purity, honesty, integrity, decency, decorum, civility; (*arch.*) propriety, fitness.

decorosamente, *adv.* decently, decorously.

decoroso, -sa, *a.* decorous, decent.

decorticación, *n.f.* decortication.

decrecer, *v.i.* (*pres. indic.* **decrezco;** *pres. subj.* **decrezca**) to decrease.

decreciente, *a.* decreasing, diminishing.

decrecimiento, *n.m.* decrease.

decremento, *n.m.* decrement, decrease, diminution, declension, wane.

decrepitación, *n.f.* (*chem.*) decrepitation.

decrepitante, *a.* crackling.

decrepitar, *v.t., v.i.* to decrepitate, expose to great heat; to crackle.

decrépito, -ta, *a.* decrepit, worn with age.

decrepitud, *n.f.* decrepitude, old age, dotage.

decretal, *a.* decretal. — *n.f.pl.* decretals.

decretalista, *n.m.* decretist.

decretar, *v.t.* to decree, resolve, determine; (*law*) to give a decree in a suit.

decretero, *n.m.* (*obs.*) list of criminals and verdicts; collection of decrees.

decretista, *n.m.* decretist.

decreto, *n.m.* decree, decision, resolution; royal or official order; judicial decree.

decretorio, -ria, *a.* (*med.*) decretory, critical, determining.

decrezco; decrezca, *pres. indic.; pres. subj.* [DECRECER].

decumbente, *a.* recumbent, reclining.

decuplar, decuplicar, *v.t.* to decuple, multiply by ten.

décuplo, -pla, *a.* tenfold.

decuria, *n.f.* decury; assembly of ten students.

decuriato, *n.m.* student of a *decuria.*

decurión, *n.m.* decurion; monitor over ten pupils; commander set over a *decuria.*

decurionato, *n.m.* decurionate.

decurrencia, *n.f.* (*bot.*) decurrence.

decurrente, *a.* (*bot.*) decurrent.

decursas, *n.f.pl.* (*law*) arrears of rent.

decurso, *n.m.* course, lapse, succession of movement or time.

decusación, *n.f.* decussation, intersection.

decusado, -da, *a.* (*bot.*) decussated.

dechado, *n.m.* sample, pattern, standard design, example, model; sampler.

dedada, *n.f.* small portion, what can be taken up with a finger; *dedada de miel,* (*coll.*) sop, crumb of comfort.

dedal, *n.m.* thimble; leathern finger-stall.

dedalera, *n.f.* foxglove.

dédalo, *n.m.* confusion, labyrinth, entanglement.

dedeo, *n.m.* (*mus.*) fingers, skill in playing on a keyed instrument.

dedicación, *n.f.* dedication; consecration; inscription.

dedicante, *a.* dedicating.

dedicar, *v.t.* (*pret.* **dediqué;** *pres. subj.* **dedique**) to dedicate, devote, consecrate. — *v.r.* to apply oneself, devote oneself.

dedicativo, -va; dedicatorio, -ria, *a.* dedicative, dedicatory.

dedicatoria, *n.f.* dedication.

dedición, *n.f.* unconditional surrender (to ancient Rome).

dedignar, *v.t.* to disdain, scorn, despise.

dedil, *n.m.* finger-stall; (*slang*) ring.

dedillo, *n.m.* little finger [DEDO]; *saber una cosa al dedillo,* to have something at one's fingertips.

dedo, *n.m.* finger, toe; forty-eighth part of a *vara;* finger's breadth; very small distance; *dedo anular* or *médico,* ring-finger; *dedo cordial, de en medio* or *del corazón,* third and longest finger; *dedo índice mostrador* or *saludador,* index-finger, forefinger; *dedo* *pulgar* or *gordo*, thumb; *a dos dedos*, very near, on the point of; *alzar el dedo*, to raise one's hand in token of agreement or consent; *dedo auricular* or *meñique*, little finger; *estar a dos dedos de*, to be on the verge of; *antojársele a uno los dedos huéspedes*, to be exceedingly suspicious; *atar uno bien su dedo*, to take due precautions in one's own interest; *comerse uno los dedos por una cosa*, to be very much attached to something; *contar por los dedos*, to count on one's fingers; *chuparse uno los dedos*, to enjoy, relish greatly; *dar un dedo de la mano por*, to be ready to pay dearly for; *derribar con un dedo*, to knock down with one's little finger; *dos dedos del oído*, very clearly (of speaking); *ganar uno a dedos una cosa*, to attain something with much work; *ir al dedo malo*, to touch the sore spot; *los dedos de la mano no son iguales*, there are many distinctions between persons; *mamarse el dedo*, to pretend to be innocent or simple; *no mamarse el dedo*, to be wide-awake; *medir a dedos*, to examine or estimate something minutely; *meter a uno el dedo en la boca*, to demonstrate that a person is not so foolish as was thought; *meter a uno los dedos*, to pump someone; *meter a uno los dedos por los ojos*, to try to make someone believe the opposite of what he knows well; *morderse los dedos*, to feel frustrated; *no tener dos dedos de frente*, to be of little intelligence; *poner el dedo en la llaga*, to put one's finger on the spot; *poner los cinco dedos en la cara*, to slap in the face; *ponerse el dedo en la boca*, to keep silence, be discreet; *señalar a uno con el dedo*, to point one's finger at someone; *ser uno el dedo malo*, to be the scapegoat; *tener uno malos dedos para organista*, to be a square peg in a round hole; *poner bien los dedos*, to play an instrument skilfully; *tener los cinco dedos en la mano*, to be as brave or strong as anybody.

dedolar, *v.t.* (*surg.*) to make an oblique incision.

deducción, *n.f.* deduction, derivation, origin; consequence, inference, conclusion; (*log.*) deductive reasoning; (*mus.*) natural progression of sounds.

deducible, *a.* deducible, inferable.

deduciente, *a.* deducing, inferring.

deducir, *v.t.* (*pres. indic.* **deduzco;** *pret.* **deduje;** *pres. subj.* **deduzca**) to deduce, infer; (*law*) to allege (in pleading); (*com.*) to deduct, rebate, allow, discount, subtract; to devise; *deducir de* or *por lo dicho*, to infer from what has been said.

deductivo, -va, *a.* deductive.

defalcar, *v.t.* to defalcate.

defecación, *n.f.* (*chem.*) defecation, purification; (*med.*) dejection, excrement.

defecador, -ra, *a.* defecating, purifying. — *n.f.* defecator, second boiler (in sugar refining).

defecar, *v.t.* (*pret.* **defequé;** *pres. subj.* **defeque**) to defecate, purify, clarify; to go to stool.

defección, *n.f.* defection, desertion, apostasy, revolt.

defectible, *a.* faulty, defective, lacking.

defectivo, -va, *a.* defective, imperfect, lacking.

defecto, *n.m.* defect, fault, failing, blemish, imperfection; *a defecto*, (*law*) by default; *pl.*

(*print.*) sheets lacking or left over from an edition or issue.

defectuosamente, *adv.* defectively, deficiently, faultily.

defectuoso, -sa, *a.* defective, imperfect, faulty.

defendedero, -ra, *a.* defensible.

defendedor, -ra, *a.* defending. — *n.m.* defender, protector, keeper.

defender, *v.t.* (*pres. indic.* **defiendo;** *pres. subj.* **defienda**) to defend, shield, protect, guard; to justify, make good; to preserve, maintain, vindicate; to resist, oppose; (*law*) to uphold, plead for; to prohibit, forbid; to retard, prevent, delay. — *v.r.* to defend oneself, resist.

defendible, *a.* defendable, defensible.

defenecer, *v.t.* (*prov.*) to close an account.

defenecimiento, *n.m.* (*prov., com.*) settlement.

defensa, *n.f.* defence, safeguard, arms, guard; shelter, protection; vindication, justification, apology; lawyer who appears for the defence; plea of justification; *pl.* (*fort.*) defences, fortifications; (*naut.*) skids, fenders.

defensión, *n.f.* safeguard, defence.

defensiva, *n.f.* defensive; *estar* or *ponerse a la defensiva*, to be or stand on the defensive.

defensivo, -va, *a.* defensive, justificatory. — *n.m.* defence, safeguard, preservative; (*med.*) compress.

defensor, -ra, *a.* defending, protecting. — *n.m.f.* defender, conservator, protector, supporter; counsel for the defence.

defensoría, *n.f.* duty and office of a defender.

defensorio, *n.m.* plea, defence, apology, memoir, manifesto.

deferencia, *n.f.* deference, complaisance, condescension.

deferente, *a.* assenting, deferring, deferential.

deferido, -da, *p.p.* [DEFERIR] deferred; submitted; imparted.

deferir, *v.i.* (*pres. indic.* **defiero;** *pres. subj.* **defiera**) to defer, yield. — *v.t.* to invest someone with a share of power or jurisdiction; *deferir al parecer de otro*, to defer to another's opinion.

deficiencia, *n.f.* deficiency.

deficiente, *a.* defective, faulty, deficient.

déficit, *n.m.* deficit, deficiency, shortage.

defiendo; defienda, *pres. indic.; pres. subj.* [DEFENDER].

defiero; defiera, *pres. indic.; pres. subj.* [DEFERIR].

definible, *a.* definable.

definición, *n.f.* definition, decision, determination; *pl.* statutes of military orders.

definido, -da, *a.* definite; defined. — *n.m.* definition. — *p.p.* [DEFINIR].

definidor, -ra, *a.* defining. — *n.m.* definer; member of the government of a religious order.

definir, *v.t.* to define, describe, explain, interpret; to determine, decide, establish; (*paint.*) to put the finishing touches.

definitivamente, *adv.* definitely, definitively.

definitivo, -va, *a.* definite, determinate, conclusive; *en definitiva*, in conclusion, definitely.

definitorio, *n.m.* (*eccles.*) governing chapter; assembly of a religious order and place where chapter is held.

deflagración, *n.f.* deflagration, sudden burning.

deflagrador, -ra, *a.* bursting into flame suddenly. — *n.m.* (*phys.*, *min.*) deflagrator, igniter.

deflagrar, *v.i.* to deflagrate.

deflector, *n.m.* (*naut.*, *phys.*) deflector of compass.

deflegmación, *n.f.* (*med.*) expectoration; (*chem.*) rectification.

deflegmar, *v.i.* (*chem.*) rectify, separate water from spirituous liquids.

deflexión, *n.f.* deflexion, deflexure.

deflujo, *n.m.* recession of the moon from a planet; abundant deflexion.

defoliación, *n.f.* defoliation, shedding of leaves.

deformación, *n.f.* deformation, defacing, deformity.

deformador, -ra, *a.* deforming. — *n.m.f.* deformer, disfigurer.

deformatorio, -ria, *a.* deforming, disfiguring.

deforme, *a.* deformed, disfigured, ugly, hideous.

deformemente, *adv.* deformedly.

deformidad, *n.f.* deformity, hideousness, ugliness; (*fig.*) gross error, perversion, crime, excess.

defraudación, *n.f.* defrauding, fraud, deceit; usurpation; defaulting, defalcation.

defraudador, -ra, *a.* defrauding. — *n.m.f.* defrauder, defaulter, defalcator.

defraudar, *v.t.* to defraud, trick, rob, cheat; to frustrate; (*fig.*) to disturb or rob of sleep; to intercept light; to spoil taste; *defraudar en las esperanzas,* to disappoint one's hopes.

defuera, *adv.* externally, outwardly, on the outside; *por defuera,* outwardly.

defunción, *n.f.* death, decease, demise; (*obs.*) funeral.

degeneración, *n.f.* degeneration, degeneracy.

degenerado, -da, *a.* degenerate. — *p.p.* [DEGENERAR].

degenerante, *a.* degenerating.

degenerar, *v.i.* to degenerate, grow wild or base, fall from virtue or other desirable condition.

deglución, *n.f.* deglutition; swallowing.

deglutidor, -ra, *a.* swallowing.

deglutir, *v.t.*, *v.i.* to swallow.

degollación, *n.f.* decollation, beheading.

degolladero, *n.m.* throttle, windpipe; slaughterhouse, shambles; scaffold with block; (*obs.*) barrier in pit of theatre.

degollado, -da, *p.p.* [DEGOLLAR] beheaded. — *n.m.* low neck cut in a garment; sheath (of plough); (*build.*) joint.

degollador, -ra, *a.* beheading. — *n.m.* executioner, headsman.

degolladura, *n.f.* cutting of the throat; slender part of balustrade; low neck cut in a garment.

degollante, *a.* beheading; (*coll.*) presumptuous, overbearing, tiresome. — *n.m.f.* (*coll.*) bore.

degollar, *v.t.* (*pres. indic.* **degüello**; *pres. subj.* **degüelle**) to behead, decapitate, guillotine; to cut a garment low in the neck; (*fig.*) to destroy, ruin, annihilate; (*coll.*) to tease, importune, worry; *degollar algún cuento,* to interrupt a narrative; (*naut.*) to rend a sail with a knife in order to save the ship.

degollina, *n.f.* (*coll.*) slaughter, butchery.

degradación, *n.f.* degradation, degeneracy, humiliation, debasement, fall; (*paint.*) degradation, diminution; blending.

degradado, -da, *p.p.* [DEGRADAR] degraded.

degradante, *a.* degrading.

degradar, *v.t.* to degrade, debase, humiliate, deprive of place, dignity or honours; (*paint.*) to graduate light and shade. — *v.r.* to degrade oneself, demean oneself.

degu, *n.m.* (*Chi.*) rat.

degüello; degüelle, *pres. indic.*; *pres. subj.* [DEGOLLAR].

degüello, *n.m.* beheading, decollation; throat cutting; neck or narrow part (of dart, etc.); destruction, ruin; *tirar al degüello,* to endeavour to destroy or ruin a person; *entrar a degüello,* (*mil.*) to assault without giving quarter; *llevar a uno al degüello,* to place someone in imminent risk; *tocar a degüello,* to give the signal for a cavalry attack.

degustación, *n.f.* degustation, tasting.

dehesa, *n.f.* pasture-ground.

dehesar, *v.t.* to turn arable land into pasture-ground.

dehesero, *n.m.* keeper of pasture-ground.

dehiscencia, *n.f.* (*bot.*) dehiscence.

dehiscente, *a.* (*bot.*) dehiscent.

deicida, *n.m.f.*, *a.* slayer of Jesus.

deicidio, *n.m.* murder of Christ.

deidad, *n.f.* deity, divinity; god, goddess.

deificación, *n.f.* deification.

deificar, *v.t.* (*pret.* **deifiqué**; *pres. subj.* **deifique**) to deify; to exalt or praise extravagantly.

deífico, -ca, *a.* deific.

deiforme, *a.* deiform, godlike.

deípara, *a.* deiparous (the Virgin Mary).

deísmo, *n.m.* deism.

deísta, *a.* deistic. — *n.m.f.* deist.

deja, *n.f.* prominence between two fissures or notches.

dejación, *n.f.* abandonment, relinquishment, giving up; abdication, resignation; (*law*) assignment; *dejación de bienes,* assignment of one's property to one's creditors.

dejada, *n.f.* relinquishment.

dejadez, *n.f.* slovenliness, neglect, laziness, lassitude.

dejado, -da, *a.* slovenly, idle, indolent; low-spirited, depressed, dejected; *dejado de la mano de Dios,* god-forsaken; abandoned, deserted. — *p.p.* [DEJAR].

dejamiento, *n.m.* act of giving up, relinquishment; idleness, carelessness, languor, indolence; coolness, estrangement, indifference; abdication, resignation.

dejar, *v.t.* to leave, let, let go, relinquish; to quit; to come from, go from; to leave off, cease; to omit, leave out; to commit, entrust, give in charge; to permit, consent, allow; to fail, be absent; to deposit; to lay away; to desert, forsake, abandon; to give up, throw up; to produce, yield; to bequeath; to forbear, refrain or abstain from; to nominate, designate; to be lacking in respect or affection for. — *v.r.* to abandon, neglect oneself; to give oneself up to, devote oneself to; to relinquish, give up; *¡deja!* wait! leave it alone! *dejadle* (or *déjale*) *correr, que él parará,* let him go his own way; *¡déjame en paz!* leave me alone! *dejando burlas aparte,* joking apart; *dejar airoso a uno,* to contribute to someone's success; *dejar a todos iguales*, to make all lose equally; *dejar aparte*, to leave out part of a speech; *dejar atrás*, to surpass, excel; *dejar bien puesto el pabellón*, to carry out an undertaking with distinction and success; *dejar bien sentada una cosa*, to give a clear, precise explanation; *dejar buena impresión*, *memoria* or *recuerdo*, to leave a good impression or pleasant memory; *dejar caer*, to let go of, drop; *dejar cargado*, to debit; *dejar a uno con la palabra en la boca*, to turn away from one who is speaking; *dejar a uno con un palmo de narices*, to dash one's hopes to the ground; *dejar caer una cosa en la conversación*, to drop a hint casually; *dejar correr*, to allow, let pass, overlook; *dejar correr la pluma*, to write at great length; *dejar con la boca abierta*, to astonish, surprise; *dejar de*, to stop, leave off; *dejar de escribir*, to stop writing; *dejar Dios de su mano a uno*, to be thoroughly abandoned; *dejar en cueros*, to strip one of his property; *dejar dicho*, to leave word or orders; *dejar escrito* or *anotado*, to leave in writing; *dejar a oscuras* or *obscuras*, to deceive, leave in ignorance; *dejar feo a uno*, to slight, rebuff someone; *dejar fresco a alguno*, to frustrate, baffle; *dejar el alma* or *corazón en un sitio*, to leave one's heart behind; *dejar el campo libre*. to put no obstacles in the way; *dejar el miedo a un lado*, to have no fear at all; *dejar a uno para quienes*, to ignore purposely the actions of an ill-mannered person; *dejar en ayunas*, to leave in ignorance; *dejar en blanco*, to omit, pass over; to slight, rebuff; to disappoint; *dejar la acera*, to let pass (on the pavement); *dejar (a alguno) por loco*, to give (someone) up as mad; *dejar por decir*, to omit saying; *dejar por hacer*, to put off doing; *dejarle a gusto*, to leave someone completely at his ease; *dejarle como su madre le parió*, to strip someone of everything; *dejarle con qué comer*, to leave someone enough to live on; *dejarle corrido*, to shame, humiliate someone; *dejarle en su casa*, to accompany someone to his house; *dejarle frío* or *helado*, to surprise, astound; *dejarle mal a uno*, to let someone down; *dejarlo muy bien*, to leave well provided; *dejarlo de (su) cuenta*, to give up the responsibility; *(com.)* to refuse delivery (of goods); *dejarlo de su mano*, to abandon; *dejarlo para más adelante*, to leave for later on; *no dejar de tener*, not to be without, not to lack; *no dejar soldado con vida*, to give no quarter; *no dejar verde ni seco*, to destroy completely, leaving nothing; *dejar molido a uno*, to leave someone exhausted; *dejar a un lado*, to pass over; *dejar a uno a la luna*, to quit one's service suddenly; *dejar para mañana*, to delay, procrastinate; *dejar plantado*, to leave in the lurch; *dejar paso*, not to stand in the way; *dejarse caer por la popa*, *(naut.)* to drop astern; *dejarse (uno) caer*, to drop or fall down purposely; *(fig.)* to hint, insinuate; *(coll.)* to turn up unexpectedly; to give up, give in; *dejarse caer*, to shine brightly (sun); to make itself felt (heat); *dejarse uno correr*, to slide down; *dejarse uno decir*, to divulge, let out, be indiscreet; *dejarse llevar de una cosa*, to be carried away by something; *dejarse querer*, to let oneself be petted; *dejarse rogar*, to require pressing, defer con-

cession of something asked for; *dejarse vencer*, to submit to the opinion of another; *dejarse ver*, to be sociable, appear in public, at friend's homes, etc.; *dejarse de cuentos* or *historias*, to take no notice of trivialities; *dejarse de rodeos*, to come to the point, not to beat about the bush; *no me dejará mentir*, so-and-so will confirm what I say; *no dejarse ensillar*, not to allow oneself to be mastered.

dejativo, -va, *a.* lazy, indolent, languid.

deje, *n.m.* after-taste.

dejillo, *n.m.* slight taste after meals; particular accentuation on the endings of words.

dejo, *n.m.* end, termination; abandonment, relinquishment; *(fig.)* remains or effect of an action; laziness, carelessness, negligence.

del, of the (contraction of the preposition *de* and the article *el*).

delación, *n.f.* delation, accusation, denunciation.

delantal, *n.m.* apron; dash-board of a carriage.

delante, *adv.* before, in front, ahead; *delante de*, in the presence of, in front of, in the sight of; in preference to; *ir delante*, to precede, go ahead, in front.

delantera, *n.f.* front, fore end, fore part; front seats; fore part of a garment; front edge of book; lead, advance, advantage obtained over another; boundary line of town, village or estate; *coger* (or *tomar*) *a uno la delantera*, to get the start of a person. — *pl.* leather breeches.

delantero, -ra, *a.* foremost, first, front. — *n.m.* postilion; forward (in certain games).

delatable, *a.* accusable, blamable.

delatante, *a.* informing, accusing.

delatar, *v.t.* to inform against, denounce, accuse, impeach.

delator, -ra, *a.* accusing, denouncing. — *n.m.f.* accuser, informer, denouncer.

deleble, *a.* deletable, erasable.

delectación, *n.f.* delectation, pleasure, delight.

delegación, *n.f.* delegation, substitution; power conferred; proxy; delegate's office; assembly of delegates.

delegado, -da, *a.* delegated. — *n.m.f.* delegate, commissioner, deputy, minister, attorney, proxy. — *p.p.* [DELEGAR].

delegante, *a.* delegating; constituent.

delegar, *v.t.* (*pret.* **delegué;** *pres. subj.* **delegue**) to delegate, appoint as, substitute.

delegatorio, -ria, *a.* containing a delegation or commission, appertaining to such.

deleitable, *a.* delectable, agreeable, delightful.

deleitablemente, *adv.* delightfully.

deleitabilísimo, -ma, *a. superl.* [DELEITABLE] most enjoyable.

deleitación, *n.f.* delectation, delight, pleasure.

deleitamiento, *n.m.* delight, pleasure, enjoyment.

deleitante, *a.* delighting.

deleitar, *v.t.* to please, delight, content. — *v.r.* (with *de* or *en*) to delight in, have pleasure in; *deleitarse con la vista del mar*, to enjoy the sea-view.

deleite, *n.m.* delight, gratification, pleasure; lust, sensual gratification.

deleitosamente, *adv.* delightfully, pleasantly, cheerfully.

deleitoso, -sa, *a.* delightful, pleasing, agreeable.

deletéreo, -rea, *a.* deleterious, poisonous.

deletreador, -ra, *a.* spelling. — *n.m.f.* speller.

deletrear, *v.i.* to spell, read by spelling; to scrutinize, examine, decipher, interpret.

deletreo, *n.m.* spelling; teaching to read by spelling.

deleznable, *a.* slippery, smooth; frail, brittle, crumbly, fragile; (*fig.*) perishable.

délfico, -ca, *a.* Delphic, Delphian, of Delphi.

delfín, *n.m.* dolphin; dauphin.

delfina, *n.f.* (*chem.*) delphinine; dauphiness.

delfinidos, *n.m.pl.* (*ichth.*) delphinus.

delfino, *n.m.* (*bot.*) delphinium.

delgadamente, *adv.* thinly, delicately; acutely, sharply, finely.

delgadez, *n.f.* thinness, tenuity; slenderness, leanness, smallness; acuteness, ingenuity.

delgado, -da, *a.* thin, delicate, light, tenuous, exiguous, lean, slender, lank, gaunt; acute, sharp, ingenious; poor, exhausted (soil). — *n.m.* (*naut.*) dead-rising; *pl.* flanks of animals; loin (of beef, etc.).

delgaducho, -cha, *a.* rather thin, thinnish, lanky.

deliberación, *n.f.* deliberation, consideration, cogitation, reflection; resolution, determination.

deliberadamente, *adv.* deliberately, resolutely.

deliberante, *a.* deliberating, deliberative.

deliberar, *v.i.* to cogitate, weigh, ponder, consider, deliberate, discourse, consult. — *v.t.* to deliberate, think before choosing, determine after consideration.

deliberativo, -va, *a.* deliberative.

delicadamente, *adv.* delicately.

delicadez, *n.f.* delicacy, weakness of constitution, debility; frailty; prudery, squeamishness; touchiness; indolence, softness; [DELICADEZA].

delicadeza, *n.f.* considerateness; gentleness; refinement; daintiness, tenderness; scrupulosity; delicacy.

delicado, -da, *a.* considerate, refined, attentive, tender; weak, thin, ailing, delicate; frail, fragile; dainty, palatable, tasty; ticklish, risky, difficult; exquisite, beautiful; good-looking; subtle, ingenious, acute, sharp; suspicious, touchy, sensitive; fastidious; scrupulous.

delicia, *n.f.* delight, comfort, satisfaction; sensual pleasure.

deliciosamente, *adv.* delightfully, deliciously, daintily.

delicioso, -sa, *a.* delicious, pleasing, delightful.

delictivo, -va; delictuoso, -sa, *a.* unlawful, felonious.

delicuescencia, *n.f.* deliquescence.

delicuescente, *a.* deliquescent.

deligación, *n.f.* (*surg.*) art of bandaging; deligation, bandaging.

deligatorio, -ria, *a.* (*surg.*) relating to bandaging.

delimitación, *n.f.* delimitation.

delimitar, *v.t.* to delimit.

delincuencia, *n.f.* delinquency, offence, guilt. — **delincuente,** *n.m.f.* delinquent, culprit, offender.

delineación, *n.f.* delineation, draft, sketch, design.

delineador, -ra, *a.* delineating, delineatory. — *n.m.f.* delineator.

delineamento, delineamiento, *n.m.* delineation.

delineante, *a.* delineating, designing. — *n.m.f.* cartographer; designer; draughtsman.

delinear, *v.t.* to delineate, sketch, figure, describe; to draw, draft.

delinquimiento, *n.m.* delinquency, fault, transgression.

delinquir, *v.i.* (*pres. indic.* **delinco**; *pres. subj.* **delinca**) to offend, transgress.

deliquio, *n.m.* swoon, fainting-fit; ecstasy, rapture.

delirante, *a.* delirious, light-headed, raving.

delirar, *v.i.* to wander, rave, be delirious; to rant, talk nonsense; *delirar por la música,* to dote on music.

delirio, *n.m.* delirium; rant, nonsense; frenzy, rapture.

delito, *n.m.* transgression, crime, fault, delinquency; *delito flagrante,* or *in fraganti,* in the very act, red-handed.

delta, *n.f.* delta.

deltoideo, -dea, *a.* deltoid, triangular.

deltoides, *a.* deltaic, deltoid. — *n.m.* deltoid muscle.

deludir, *v.t.* to delude, deceive.

delusivo, -va, *a.* delusive, fallacious.

delusoriamente, *adv.* delusively, deceitfully, deceptively.

delusorio, -ria, *a.* deceitful, fallacious, deceptive.

demacración, *n.f.* (*med., vet.*) emaciation, marasmus.

demacrarse, *v.t.* to emaciate, debilitate. — *v.r.* to waste away.

demagogia, *n.f.* demagogy.

demagógico, -ca, *a.* demagogic.

demagogo, -ga, *a.* demagogic. — *n.m.f.* demagogue.

demanda, *n.f.* demand, petition, soliciting, supplication, request; alms-begging; image used in alms-begging; alms-collector; question; search, quest; intention, enterprise; desire, perseverance; defence; (*com.*) demand, order; (*law*) claim; *demandas y repuestas,* haggling; *contestar uno la demanda,* (*law*) to oppose the claim; *ir en demanda de una persona* or *cosa,* to look for a person or thing; *poner demanda,* to begin an action at law; to sue; *salir uno a la demanda,* (*law*) to oppose, defend (an action).

demandable, *a.* which may be demanded.

demandadero, -ra, *n.m.f.* messenger at a convent or prison.

demandado, -da, *n.m.f.* defendant, accused. — *p.p.* [DEMANDAR].

demandador, -ra, *a.* demanding. — *n.m.f.* asker, demander; alms-collector; (*law*) claimant, plaintiff.

demandante, *a.* [DEMANDADOR].

demandar, *v.t.* to demand, claim, solicit, ask, request; to covet, wish for, desire; (*law*) to enter an action.

demarcación, *n.f.* demarcation.

demarcador, -ra, *a.* demarcating, dividing. — *n.m.* boundary-surveyor.

demarcar, *v.t.* (*pret.* **demarqué**; *subj.* **demarque**) to survey, mark out bounds or limits; (*naut.*) to indicate the bearings by the compass.

demás, *a.; lo demás,* the rest, the remaining; *los, las demás,* the others; *y demás,* and others, etcetera. — *adv.* besides, moreover; *por demás,* uselessly, in vain; excessively; *por lo demás,* as for the rest, apart from this; *demás de esto,* besides this.

demasía, *n.f.* excess, superfluity; audacity, boldness; insolence, disrespect, rudeness; iniquity, wickedness, badness; (*min.*) space between two claims; *en demasía,* excessively.

demasiadamente, *adv.* excessively; too.

demasiado, -da, *a.* excessive, too much, more than enough. — *adv.* enough, too, excessively. — *p.p.* [DEMASIARSE].

demediar, *v.t.* to divide in halves; to wear a thing till it has lost half its value.

demencia, *n.f.* madness, insanity.

dementar, *v.t.* to send mad, render insane. — *v.r.* to become demented.

demente, *a.* demented, mad, insane, infatuated, distracted. — *n.m.f.* lunatic.

demérito, *n.m.* demerit, ill-desert; action of forfeiting esteem.

demeritorio, -ria, *a.* without merit, undeserving, demeritorious.

demisión, *n.f.* submission, humility.

democracia, *n.f.* democracy.

demócrata, *a.* democratic. — *n.m.f.* democrat.

democráticamente, *adv.* democratically.

democrático, -ca, *a.* democratic.

democratizar, *v.t., v.r.* to democratize.

demografía, *n.f.* demography.

demográfico, -ca, *a.* demographic.

demógrafo, *n.m.* demographer.

demoledor, -ra, *a.* demolishing. — *n.m.f.* demolisher.

demoler, *v.t.* (*pres. indic.* demuelo; *pres. subj.* demuela) to demolish, overthrow, raze, tear down, dismantle.

demolición, *n.f.* demolition, destruction.

demonche, *n.m.* (*coll.*) little devil.

demoníaco, -ca, *a.* demoniacal, devilish. — *n.m.f.* demoniac.

demonio, *n.m.* demon, devil, evil spirit; *¡demonio!* what the deuce! *estudiar* (*uno*) *con el demonio,* to be able but evil; *revestírsele a uno el demonio,* to be over-irritable or excitable; *ser el mismísimo demonio,* to be the very devil himself; *tener el demonio* or *los demonios en el cuerpo,* to be excessively restless or perverse.

demonólatra, *a.* worshipping demons.

demonolatría, *n.f.* demonolatry.

demonología, *n.f.* demonology.

demonomanía, *n.f.* demonomania.

demonomaníaco, -ca, *n.m.f., a.* (person) suffering from demonomania.

demontre, *n.m.* (*coll.*) demon. — *interj. ¡demontre!* the deuce!

demoñejo, demoñuelo, *n.m.* little demon, little devil, imp [DEMONIO].

demora, *n.f.* delay, procrastination; (*Am.*) period of eight months that the Indians were obliged to work in the mines; (*com.*) demurrage; (*naut.*) bearing; *sin demora,* without delay.

demorar, *v.t.* to delay, hinder, retard. — *v.i.* to tarry, linger, delay; to stop over, halt (on the way); (*naut.*) to bear; *la costa demora norte,* the coast bears north.

demóstenes, *n.m.* (*fig.*) eloquent speaker, orator.

demostrable, *a.* demonstrable, manifestable.

demostrablemente, *adv.* demonstrably.

demostración, *n.f.* demonstration, manifestation, proof, evidence, verification.

demostrador, -ra, *a.* demonstrating. — *n.m.f.* demonstrator.

demostrar, *v.t.* (*pres. indic.* demuestro; *pres. subj.* demuestre) to demonstrate, teach, prove, lay open, make evident.

demostrativamente, *adv.* demonstratively.

demostrativo, -va, *a.* demonstrative.

demudación, *n.f.* change, alteration.

demudar, *v.t.* to change, alter, vary; to cloak, disguise. — *v.r.* to become disturbed, change colour or expression suddenly.

demuelo; demuela, *pres. indic.; pres. subj.* [DEMOLER].

demuestro; demuestre, *pres. indic.; pres. subj.* [DEMOSTRAR].

demulcente, *n.m., a.* (*med.*) demulcent, emollient.

denario, -ria, *a.* denary, tenth. — *n.m.* denarius, denary.

dendriforme, *a.* dendriform.

dendrita, *n.f.* (*min.*) dendrite; fossil tree.

dendrítico, -ca, *a.* dendritic.

dendrografía, *n.f.* dendrology.

dendrográfico, -ca, *a.* relating to dendrology.

dendroide; dendroideo, -dea, *a.* dendroid.

denegación, *n.f.* denial, refusal.

denegar, *v.t.* (*pres. indic.* deniego; *pret.* denegué; *pres. subj.* deniegue) to deny, refuse.

denegatorio, -ria, *a.* negatory.

denegrecer, *v.t.* (*pres. indic.* denegrezco; *pres. subj.* denegrezca) to blacken, darken, obscure. — *v.r.* to become blackened, dark, obscured.

denegrido, -da, *a.* black, dark; blackened, darkened. — *p.p.* [DENEGRIR].

denegrir, *v.t.* [DENEGRECER].

denegué, *pret.* [DENEGAR].

dengoso, -sa, *a.* fastidious, over-nice.

dengue, *n.m.* fastidiousness, affectation, prudery; woman's cape with long points; (*med.*) dengue; influenza.

denguero, -ra, *a.* prudish, affected.

deniego; deniegue, *pres. indic.; pres. subj.* [DENEGAR].

denigración, *n.f.* denigration, stigma, disgrace.

denigrante, *a.* reviling, vilifying. — *n.m.f.* denigrator, reviler, traducer.

denigrar, *v.t.* to calumniate, defame, revile, vilify, traduce, censure; insult, affront.

denigrativamente, *adv.* injuriously, infamously.

denigrativo, -va, *a.* blackening, stigmatizing, disparaging.

denodadamente, *adv.* boldly, resolutely.

denodado, -da, *a.* bold, intrepid, audacious.

denominación, *n.f.* denomination.

denominadamente, *adv.* distinctly, definitely.

denominador, -ra, *a.* denominating. — *n.m.f.* denominator.

denominar, *v.t.* to denominate, give a name.

denominativo, -va, *a.* denominative.

denostadamente, *adv.* ignominiously, insultingly.

denostador, -ra, *a.* insulting, vilifying. — *n.m.* vilifier, railer, reviler.

denostar, *v.t.* (*pres. indic.* denuesto; *pres. subj.* denueste) to revile, abuse, insult with foul language.

denotación, *n.f.* designation, denotation.
denotar, *v.t.* to denote, signify; to explain.
denotativo, -va, *a.* denoting, denotative.
densamente, *adv.* densely, thickly, closely.
densidad, *n.f.* density, denseness, darkness, grossness, obscurity; thickness, closeness, compactness; (*phys.*) specific gravity.
densímetro, *n.m.* (*phys.*) densimeter.
denso, -sa, *a.* dense, thick, close, compact; (*fig.*) obscure, confused.
dentado, -da, *a.* dentate, dentated, denticulated, serrated, toothed, furnished with teeth; crenated, indented; cogged, pronged. — *p.p.* [DENTAR].
dentadura, *n.f.* set of teeth (natural or artificial).
dental, *a.* dental, dentary. — *n.m.f.* (*gram.*) dental. — *n.m.* ploughshare-bed; tooth of harrow.
dentar, *v.t.* (*pres. indic.* **diento**; *pres. subj.* **diente**) to tooth, furnish with teeth, clogs or prongs; to indent. — *v.i.* to teethe, cut teeth.
dentario, -ria, *a.* dental. — *n.f.* (*bot.*) toothwort.
dentecillo, *n.m.* small tooth [DIENTE].
dentejón, *n.m.* yoke (for oxen).
dentelaria, *n.f.* (*bot.*) plumbago.
dentelete, *n.m.* (*arch.*) dentil.
dentellada, *n.f.* gnashing of teeth; nip, pinch with the teeth; impression of teeth; *a dentelladas,* with the teeth; *dar* or *sacudir uno dentelladas a otro,* to answer someone peevishly, snappishly.
dentellado, -da, *a.* denticulated, dented, serrated, toothed; bitten or wounded with the teeth. — *p.p.* [DENTELLAR].
dentellar, *v.i.* to gnash, grind, snap; to chatter (teeth).
dentellear, *v.t.* to nibble.
dentellón, *n.m.* (*arch.*) moulding of cornice; piece of a door-lock; dentil.
dentera, *n.f.* tooth-edge, tingling pain in the teeth; (*fig.*) envy; longing; *dar dentera,* to set one's teeth on edge; to cause desire or longing, make one's mouth water.
dentezuelo, *n.m.* little tooth [DIENTE].
denticina, *n.f.* teething-powder.
dentición, *n.f.* dentition, teething.
denticulado, -da; denticular, *a.* denticular, denticulated.
dentículo, *n.m.* (*arch.*) denticle, dentil.
dentiforme, *a.* dentiform.
dentífrico, -ca, *a.* good for the teeth. — *n.m.* dentifrice.
dentina, *n.f.* dentine.
dentista, *n.m.f.* dentist.
dentivano, -na, *a.* having long and big teeth (of horses).
dentolingual, *a.* (*gram.*) dentilingual.
dentón, -na, *a.* with large, uneven teeth. — *n.m.* Mediterranean fish of the Sparus genus.
dentro, *adv.* within, inside; *de dentro,* interiorly, inwardly, inside; *hacia dentro,* toward the centre (or interior); *por de dentro,* in the interior; *dentro de poco,* shortly; *dentro del año,* in the course of the year; *dentro de casa,* in the house; *dentro o fuera,* (*coll.*) quickly! make up your mind! yes or no!
dentudo, -da, *a.* with large, uneven teeth.
denudación, *n.f.* denudation, nakedness, laying bare.

denudar, *v.t.* to strip, bare, denude. — *v.r.* to strip oneself, become bare, denuded
denuedo, *n.m.* boldness, courage, audacity, intrepidity.
denuesto; denueste, *pres. indic.; pres. subj.* [DENOSTAR].
denuesto, *n.m.* affront, insult.
denuncia, *n.f.* denunciation, arraignment, accusation; announcement, proclamation, declaration.
denunciable, *a.* fit to be denounced.
denunciación, *n.f.* denunciation, denouncement.
denunciador, -ra, *a.* denunciating, denouncing. — *n.m.f.* denunciator, denouncer, informer, accuser.
denunciante, *n.m.f., a.* [DENUNCIADOR].
denunciar, *v.t.* to advise, give notice; to denounce, denunciate; to prognosticate, foretell; to proclaim, make a solemn announcement; (*min.*) to register a claim.
denunciatorio, -ria, *a.* denunciatory.
denuncio, *n.m.* (*min.*) denouncement.
denutrición, *n.f.* denutrition.
deñarse, *v.r.* to deign, condescend.
deontología, *n.f.* deontology.
deparar, *v.t.* to offer, furnish, afford; to present, put forward.
departamental, *a.* departmental.
departamento, *n.m.* department; section, branch office; ministry; administrative division.
departidor, -ra, *a.* conversing, talking. — *n.m.f.* interlocutor, talker, conversationalist.
departir, *v.i.* to speak, converse, chat, talk, commune; *departir con un amigo,* to chat with a friend; *departir de* or *sobre la política,* to talk politics.
depauperación, *n.f.* (*med.*) debility, exhaustion.
depauperar, *v.t.* to impoverish; (*med.*) to debilitate, weaken, exhaust. — *v.r.* to become weak, debilitated.
dependencia, *n.f.* subordination, dependence, dependency; branch office; relation (by consanguinity or friendship); business, affair, agency; staff, employees. — *pl.* accessories; (*arch.*) outbuildings.
depender, *v.i.* (with *de*) to depend, be contingent on; to be dependent on, rely upon.
dependiente, *a.* dependent, depending. — *n.m.* dependant, clerk, employee, subordinate.
dependientemente, *adv.* dependently, subordinately, submissively.
depilar, *v.t.* (*med.*) to pull out or strip off (hair).
depleción, *n.f.* (*med.*) depletion.
depletivo, -va, *a.* (*med.*) depletive, depletory.
deplorable, *a.* deplorable, lamentable, mournful; hopeless, calamitous.
deplorablemente, *adv.* deplorably, mournfully, sorrowfully.
deplorar, *v.t.* to deplore, bewail, lament, bemoan, regret, mourn.
deponente, *a.* deposing, deponent. — *n.m.f.* deponent, deposer, (*law*) witness.
deponer, *v.t.* (*p.p.* **depuesto**; *pres. indic.* **depongo**; *pret.* **depuse**; *fut.* **depondré**; *pres. subj.* **deponga**) to depose, affirm, declare; to lay by, separate, put aside; to remove, take down. — *v.i.* to defecate;

deponer (*a alguno*) *de su cargo*, to depose, remove (someone) from office; *deponer en juicio*, (*law*) to depone, testify, make a deposition; *deponer las armas*, to lay down one's arms; *deponer la ira*, to calm down.

deponible, *a.* which may be deposed.

depopulador, -ra, *a.* depopulating, devastating. — *n.m.f.* depopulator, devastator.

deportación, *n.f.* deportation, transportation, banishment.

deportado, -da, *a.* deported. — *n.m.f.* banished person, exile; deportee. — *p.p.* [DEPORTAR].

deportar, *v.t.* to transport, banish, exile.

deporte, *n.m.* sport, diversion; amusement, pastime, recreation.

deportismo, *n.m.* inclination for outdoor sports; sportiveness, sport.

deportista, *a.* sporting. — *n.m.f.* sportsman, sportswoman.

deportivo, -va, *a.* sporting, sportive.

deposición, *n.f.* deposition, declaration, affirmation; deposition, removal, degradation; alvine evacuation; (*law*) testimony, the act of bearing witness on oath.

depositador, -ra, *a.* depositing, entrusting. — *n.m.f.* depositor, one who leaves anything in trust.

depositante, *a.* depositing, entrusting.

depositar, *v.t.* to deposit, place for safekeeping, give in trust; to impart, entrust, confide; to put a person judicially in a position where he is free to manifest his will; to enclose, contain; to place a corpse in a deposit until its interment; to lay aside, put away. — *v.r.* to settle, deposit (dregs, sediment).

depositaría, *n.f.* depository, repository; subtreasury; depositary; trustee; trusteeship.

depositario, -ria, *a.* relating to a depositor, depositary. — *n.m.f.* depositary, trustee, receiver.

depósito, *n.m.* deposit, trust; depositary; (*com.*) store, depot, warehouse; (*mech.*) chamber; (*med.*) abscess, tumour; (*min.*) alluvium; (*mil.*) depot; (*chem.*) precipitate, sediment, deposit; *depósito de agua*, tank, reservoir; *en depósito*, in bond.

depravación, *n.f.* depravation, depravity, corruption.

depravadamente, *adv.* depravedly pervertedly.

depravado, -da, *a.* bad, depraved, lewd, perverted.

depravador, -ra, *a.* depraving, corrupting. — *n.m.f.* depraver, corrupter.

depravar, *v.t.* to deprave, vitiate, corrupt, contaminate, spoil. — *v.r.* to become vitiated, depraved.

deprecación, *n.f.* petition, prayer; deprecation, conjuration.

deprecante, *a.* deprecating, pleading. — *n.m.f.* pleader, suppliant.

deprecar, *v.t.* (*pret.* **deprequé**; *pres. subj.* **depreque**) to entreat, implore, deprecate.

deprecativo, -va; **deprecatorio, -ria**, *a.* deprecative, deprecatory.

depreciación, *n.f.* depreciation.

depreciador, -ra, *a.* depreciating, depreciatory.

depreciar, *v.t.* to depreciate, undervalue, reduce the price.

depredación, *n.f.* depredation, plundering, laying waste, pillaging; malversation.

depredador, *n.m.* depredator, robber, destroyer.

depredar, *v.t.* to depredate, rob, pillage.

depresión, *n.f.* depression, abasement, pressing down; (*com.*) dullness, decline; *depresión de horizonte*, (*naut.*) dip of the horizon.

depresivo, -va, *a.* depressive.

depresor, -ra, *a.* depressing. — *n.m.f.* oppressor. — *n.m.* (*anat., surg.*) depressor.

deprimente, *a.* depressing; depressive.

deprimido, -da, *a.* (*med.*) depressed (pulse, etc.). — *p.p.* [DEPRIMIR].

deprimir, *v.t.* to depress, compress, flatten, press down; (*fig.*) to humble, sink, depreciate, belittle. — *v.r.* to become compressed or depressed; to appear, seem lower (line or surface).

depuesto, -ta, *p.p. irreg.* [DEPONER] deposed.

depurable, *a.* cleansable, purifiable.

depuración, *n.f.* depuration, purification.

depurador, -ra, *a.* depurating. — *n.m.f.* depurator.

depurar, *v.t.* to depurate, cleanse, purify, filter. — *v.r.* to become pure, filtered.

depurativo, -va, *a., n.m.* (*med.*) depurative, depurant.

depuratorio, -ria, *a.* depuratory, purifying.

depuse, *pret.* [DEPONER].

deputar, *v.t.* to depute.

deque, *adv.* (*coll.*) immediately, immediately that, since.

derecera, *n.f.* direct road, short cut.

derecha, *n.f.* right hand, right side; conservative party in politics; *¡ derecha !*, (*mil.*) right-about; *a* (*las*) *derechas*, right, well done; honestly, rightly, justly; *a tuertas o derechas*, right or wrong, inconsiderately.

derechamente, *adv.* directly, full, straight; straight on; (*fig.*) rightly, honestly, prudently, justly, expressly; formally, legally.

derechera, *n.f.* direct road, short cut.

derechero, *a.* just, honest, moderate. — *n.m.* clerk appointed to collect fees and taxes.

derechista, *n.m.f.* conservative person.

derecho, -cha, *a.* right, even, straight; direct; just, straightforward, legitimate, lawful, reasonable; right-hand; (*mech.*) standing, upright. — *adv.* straight, straight on, directly. — *n.m.* right, justice, equity; law; just claim, title; exemption, freedom, grant, privilege; road, path; right side of cloth; *pl.* fees, duties, tariff dues; *al derecho*, right, well done; honestly, justly; *cada uno alega en derecho de su dedo*, everyone is ready to defend his own business; *conforme a derecho*, *segun derecho*, according to law and justice; *de derecho*, by right; *derecho de gentes*, international law; *derecho de visita*, right of search; *estudiante de derecho*, law student; *hecho y derecho*, fully developed; true, certain; complete; without doubt; *no hay derecho*, it is not right; *perder uno de su derecho*, to give up one's rights for the sake of peace; *todo derecho*, straightforward; *usar uno de su derecho*, to exercise one's rights; *derecho civil* or *común*, civil law; *derecho consuetudinario* or *no escrito*, common law, law established by precedent and custom; *derecho criminal* or *penal*, criminal law; *derecho natural*, natural right; *derechos de* *aduana*, custom-house duties; *derechos consulares*, consular fees; *derechos de almacenaje* or *depósito*, warehouse dues, storage; *derechos de anclaje*, anchorage dues; *derechos de entrada*, import duties; *derechos de muelle*, wharfage, pierage; *derechos de puerto*, harbour or port dues; *derechos reales*, inheritance tax; *derechos de remolque*, towage.

derechuelo, *n.m.* first seam taught in sewing.

derechura, *n.f.* rectitude, right way; *en derechura*, by the most direct road; without delay, immediately.

derelicción, *n.f.* dereliction.

deriva, *n.f.* (*naut.*, *aer.*) deviation, drift, drifting.

derivable, *a.* derivable, deducible.

derivación, *n.f.* derivation, descent, deduction, inference; drawing off or turning aside from its proper course (water, etc.); (*elec.*) loss of current (through damp, etc.); *en derivación* (*elec.*) shunt.

derivado, -da, *n.m.f.*, *a.* (*math.*, *gram.*) derivative.

derivador, -ra, *a.* deriving. — *n.m.* (*phys.*) graduator (in telepathy).

derivar, *v.t.* to deduce; to guide, lead, conduct. — *v.i.* to derive, trace (from its origin); (*naut.*) to deflect; to emanate, proceed from. — *v.r.* (with *de*) to be derived, come from.

derivativo, -va, *a.* (*gram.*) derivative. — *n.m.*, *a.* (*med.*) counter-irritant.

dérmatoesqueleto, *n.m.* dermatoskeleton.

dermatoideo, -dea, *a.* dermatoid.

dermatología, *n.f.* dermatology.

dermatológico, -ca, *a.* appertaining to dermatology.

dermatólogo, *n.m.* dermatologist.

dermesto, *n.m.* larder beetle.

derogable, *a.* which may be derogated.

derogación, *n.f.* revocation, repeal, annulment, abolition; deterioration, diminution.

derogado, -da, *a.* annulled. — *p.p.* [DEROGAR].

derogador, -ra, *a.* abolishing, repealing.

derogar, *v.t.* (*pret.* **derogué;** *pres. subj.* **derogue**) to abolish, annul; to reform; to destroy; to remove; to repeal, revoke.

derogatorio, -ria, *a.* (*law*) annulling, repealing.

derrabar, *v.t.* to dock the tail.

derrama, *n.f.* assessment of taxes.

derramadamente, *adv.* profusely, lavishly; immoderately, irregularly; depravedly.

derramadero, *n.m.* dumping-place; weir; spillway.

derramado, -da, *a.* prodigal, wasteful; spilt, wasted. — *p.p.* [DERRAMAR].

derramador, -ra, *a.* prodigal, wasteful. — *n.m.f.* prodigal, waster, spendthrift.

derramamiento, *n.m.* effusion, spilling, shedding, overflow; dispersion, scattering, spreading; *derramamiento de lágrimas*, flood of tears; *derramamiento de sangre*, bloodshed, spilling of blood.

derramaplaceres, derramasolaces, *n.m.f.* kill-joy, wet blanket.

derramar, *v.t.* to pour; to publish, spread news; to spill, shed, waste, scatter; to apportion taxes. — *v.r.* to spread, fly abroad; to be scattered, overflow, run over, leak; to drain, empty; *derramar la hacienda*, to squander one's inheritance; *derramarse al*, *en* or *por el suelo*, to spill on the ground.

derrame, *n.m.* loss in measuring, leakage; (*arch.*) bevel, chamfer, splay (of window, etc.); declivity; effusion, discharge, overflow, shedding, waste; (*naut.*) draught from a sail; outlet of a ravine; *derrame de sangre*, loss of blood; *derrame cerebral*, cerebral hæmorrhage.

derramo, *n.m.* chamfer, splay, flare, bevel of a door or window.

derrape, *n.m.* (*naut.*, *aer.*) yawing.

derraspado, -da, *a.* beardless (of wheat).

derredor, *n.m.* circumference, circuit; *al* or *en derredor*, round about.

derrelicto, -ta, *a.* abandoned, forsaken. — *n.m.* (*naut.*) derelict. — *p.p. irreg.* [DERRELINQUIR].

derrelinquir, *v.t.* (*p.p.* **derrelicto;** *pres. indic.* **derrelinco;** *pres. subj.* **derrelinca**) to abandon, forsake.

derrenegar, *v.i.* (conjugated like NEGAR) (*coll.*) to hate, detest, loathe, abhor.

derrengado, -da, *a.* incurvated, bent, crooked; crippled, lame. — *n.f.* (*prov.*) step in dancing. — *p.p.* [DERRENGAR].

derrengadura, *n.f.* hip dislocation; lameness.

derrengar, *v.t.* (*pres. indic.* **derriengo;** *pres. subj.* **derriengue**) to cripple, sprain the hip, strain the spine, break the back; to bend, make crooked; (*prov.*) to knock the fruit off a tree. — *v.r.* to become bent, crooked.

derrengo, *n.m.* (*prov.*) stick with which fruits are knocked off.

derretido, -da, *a.* dissolved, melted, liquefied; (*fig.*) amorous, languishing, enamoured, deeply in love. — *n.m.* concrete. — *p.p.* [DERRETIR]; *plomo derretido*, molten lead.

derretimiento, *n.m.* thaw, liquefaction; (*fig.*) violent affection, consuming love.

derretir, *v.t.* (*pres. indic.* **derrito;** *pres. subj.* **derrita**) to liquefy, melt, fuse, smelt, found, cast, dissolve; (*coll.*) to change money into small coins; (*fig.*) to expend, consume, waste, exhaust. — *v.r.* to liquefy, fuse, melt, become liquid; (*fig.*) to be deeply in love, grow tender; to be full of impatience.

derribado, -da, *a.* demolished, ruined; having low buttocks (of horses). — *p.p.* [DERRIBAR].

derribador, -ra, *a.* demolishing, felling, knocking down. — *n.m.* cow-puncher.

derribar, *v.t.* to demolish, fell, overthrow, prostrate, throw, knock or tear down; to displace, depose; to ruin, destroy; to subject, subdue a passion. — *v.r.* to tumble down; to throw oneself on the ground; *derribar en* or *por tierra*, to bring to the ground.

derribo, *n.m.* demolition, pulling down; debris; ruins.

derriengo; derriengue, *pres. indic.; pres. subj.* [DERRENGAR].

derrito; derrita, *pres. indic.; pres. subj.* [DERRETIR].

derrocadero, *n.m.* precipice.

derrocamiento, *n.m.* throwing or falling headlong; overthrow, destruction, ruin.

derrocar, *v.t.* to precipitate, fling down from a rock; to pull down, fell, demolish; (*fig.*) to oust from or rob of fortune or happiness; *derrocar en* or *por tierra*, to fell to the ground.

derrochador, -ra, *a.* wasteful, squandering. — *n.m.f.* prodigal, spendthrift, squanderer.

derrochar, *v.t.* to dissipate, waste; to squander, destroy.

derroche, *n.m.* dissipation, waste, squandering, destruction.

derrostrarse, *v.r.* to injure one's face.

derrota, *n.f.* road, path, track; post-harvest pasture rights; (*naut.*) ship's course or tack; (*mil.*) defeat, overthrow, rout.

derrotadamente, *adv.* neglectfully, slovenly.

derrotar, *v.t.* to dissipate, break, tear, wear away; (*naut.*) to cause to deviate from the course; to destroy health or fortune; (*mil.*) to rout, defeat. — *v.r.* (*naut.*) to deviate from the course.

derrote, *n.m.* thrust of a bull's horn.

derrotero, *n.m.* (*naut.*) ship's course; navigation track; collection of sea-charts; (*fig.*) course, way, plan of life or conduct.

derrubiar, *v.t., v.r.* to undermine, erode, wash away (river banks); to break the bounds of a river.

derrubio, *n.m.* erosion, alluvion, alluvium.

derruir, *v.t.* (*pres. indic.* **derruyo**; *pres. subj.* **derruya**) to demolish, destroy, ruin, raze, tear down.

derrumbadero, *n.m.* precipice; craggy, steep ground; (*fig.*) thorny affair; danger.

derrumbamiento, *n.m.* precipitate fall; landslide, collapse.

derrumbar, *v.t.* to precipitate, throw down headlong. — *v.r.* to throw oneself headlong; to sink down, crumble away.

derrumbe, *n.m.* precipice; (*min.*) landslide, collapse.

derrumbo, *n.m.* precipice.

derviche, *n.m.* dervish.

desabarrancamiento, *n.m.* dragging out of ditch or difficulty.

desabarrancar, *v.t.* (conjugated like ABARRANCAR) to drag, draw out of a ditch; to disentangle, extricate.

desabastecer, *v.t.* (conjugated like ABASTECER) to prevent the supply of provisions; to leave unprovided with provisions.

desabastecimiento, *n.m.* stopping of supplies.

desabejar, *v.t.* to take bees from a hive.

desabillé, *n.m.* deshabille, undress, dressing-gown.

desabitar, *v.t.* (*naut.*) to unbitt.

desabollador, **-ra**, *a.* planishing, removing dents. — *n.m.* planisher (tool).

desabolladura, *n.f.* removal of dents or bruises.

desabollar, *v.t.* to remove dents or bruises (in metal).

desabonarse, *v.r.* to cease subscribing to something.

desabono, *n.m.* prejudice, calumny, injury; withdrawal of a subscription; *hablar en desabono de alguno*, to speak to the prejudice of another.

desabor, *n.m.* insipidity, tastelessness.

desabordarse, *v.r.* to get clear of a ship which has run foul of one's vessel.

desaborido, **-da**, *a.* tasteless, insipid; unsubstantial. — *n.m.f.*, *a.* (*coll.*) dull, inane (person).

desabotonar, *v.t.* to unbutton. — *v.i.* (*fig.*) to blow, bloom, blossom. — *v.r.* to become unbuttoned, unfastened; to undo one's buttons.

desabridamente, *adv.* bitterly, rudely, harshly; without taste or flavour.

desabrido, **-da**, *a.* tasteless, insipid; sour; kicking (cross-bow or gun); peevish, disgusted; bleak, sharp (weather); severe, hard (disposition). — *p.p.* [DESABRIR].

desabrigadamente, *adv.* without cover or shelter.

desabrigado, **-da**, *a.* lightly clothed; uncovered; shelterless; (*fig.*) abandoned, without support; (*naut.*) unsheltered, exposed (roadstead). — *p.p.* [DESABRIGAR].

desabrigar, *v.t.* (conjugated like ABRIGAR) to uncover, divest of covering, strip; to deprive of shelter. — *v.r.* to move from shelter; to uncover oneself.

desabrigo, *n.m.* nudity, nakedness; want of shelter; (*fig.*) destitution, want of protection.

desabrimiento, *n.m.* insipidity (in food); (*fig.*) rudeness, severity; despondency; recoil of fire-arms or crossbow.

desabrir, *v.t.* to impart bad taste (to food); (*fig.*) to vex, torment, harass, plague. — *v.r.* (with *con*) to become annoyed, vexed with.

desabrochamiento, *n.m.* unbuttoning, unfastening.

desabrochar, *v.t.* to unbutton, unfasten, unclasp, open, burst open. — *v.r.* to unbosom oneself, reveal in confidence, disclose; to undo one's buttons or fastenings.

desacaloramiento, *n.m.* cooling off.

desacalorarse, *v.r.* to take the fresh air; to grow less warm, cool off.

desacatadamente, *adv.* disrespectfully.

desacatado, **-da**, *a.* disrespectful. — *p.p.* [DESACATAR].

desacatador, **-ra**, *n.m.f.*, *a.* irreverent, disrespectful, uncivil (person).

desacatamiento, *n.m.* disrespect.

desacatar, *v.t.* to treat disrespectfully, desecrate, profane, dishonour.

desacatarrarse, *v.r.* to get rid of a cold.

desacato, *n.m.* disrespect, want of reverence, desecration, profanation; (*law*) contempt of court.

desacedar, *v.t.* to remove acidity.

desaceitado, **-da**, *a.* lacking oil, oilless, nongreasy. — *p.p.* [DESACEITAR].

desaceitar, *v.t.* to remove oil and grease (from wool).

desaceración, *n.f.* removing or wearing out of steel in a tool.

desacerar, *v.t.* wear out the steel (in a tool). — *v.r.* to lose its steel (tool).

desacerbar, *v.t.* to mitigate, assuage, sweeten, temper, take away sharpness and bitterness.

desacertadamente, *adv.* inconsiderately, wrongly, erroneously.

desacertado, **-da**, *a.* imprudent, inconsiderate, mistaken, wrong. — *p.p.* [DESACERTAR].

desacertar, *v.i.* (conjugated like ACERTAR) to err, be in error, commit a mistake.

desacidificación, *n.f.* (*chem.*) neutralization or removal of acid.

desacidificar, *v.t.* (*chem.*) to remove acid; to neutralize an acid. — *v.r.* to lose acid, become neutralized (from acid).

desacidular, *v.t.* to remove acid from a beverage.

desacierto, *n.m.* error, mistake, blunder.

desacobardar, *v.t.* to remove fear or cowardice; to inspire courage.

desacollar, *v.t.* (conjugated like ACOLLAR) to dig a hollow round vines.

desacomodadamente, *adv.* incommodiously, inconveniently.

desacomodado, -da, *a.* lacking the conveniences of one's station; uncomfortable; troublesome, inconvenient; disengaged, unemployed (servant). — *p.p.* [DESACOMODAR].

desacomodamiento, *n.m.* inconvenience, trouble; disengagement, unemployment.

desacomodar, *v.t.* to incommode, molest; to deprive of ease, convenience; to dismiss, discharge. — *v.r.* to lose one's place, be disengaged (servant).

desacomodo, *n.m.* discharge, loss of place or position.

desacompañamiento, *n.m.* lack of company or society, solitude, loneliness.

desacompañar, *v.t.* cease accompanying, avoid.

desaconsejadamente, *adv.* inconsiderately.

desaconsejado, -da, *n.m.f.*, *a.* inconsiderate, ill-advised, imprudent (person). — *p.p.* [DESACONSEJAR].

desaconsejar, *v.t.* to dissuade.

desacoplar, *v.t.* to unfasten, disconnect, uncouple.

desacordadamente, *adv.* discordantly, inconsiderately, unadvisedly.

desacordado, -da, *a.* untuned; discordant (painting).

desacordante, *a.* discordant.

desacordar, *v.t.* (conjugated like ACORDAR) (*mus.*) to untune. — *v.r.* to be forgetful, of short memory.

desacorde, *a.* incongruous, inharmonious; discordant, out of tune.

desacordonar, *v.t.* to undo, loosen (girdle); to untwist, untwine.

desacorralar, *v.t.* to bring a bull into the arena or open field; to let cattle out of the fold.

desacostumbradamente, *adv.* unusually.

desacostumbrado, -da, *a.* unusual, unaccustomed. — *p.p.* [DESACOSTUMBRAR].

desacostumbrar, *v.t.* to disaccustom. — *v.r.* to break oneself of, lose a habit.

desacotar, *v.t.* to lay open a pasture-ground, take down fences; to withdraw a prohibition; to play without rules (in boys' games); to relinquish a contract; to reject, refuse.

desacoto, *n.m.* withdrawal of a prohibition; taking fences from pasture-ground.

desacreditado, -da, *a.* discredited, disgraced. — *p.p.* [DESACREDITAR].

desacreditador, -ra, *n.m.f.*, *a.* discrediting (person or thing).

desacreditar, *v.t.* to discredit, to injure credit or reputation; to cry down, disparage. — *v.r.* to become discredited, lose one's reputation; to fall into disrepute.

desacuartelar, *v.t.* (*mil.*) to remove from barracks.

desacuerdo, *n.m.* disaccord, discordance, disagreement, disunion; error, mistake, blunder, inaccuracy, inexactness; forgetfulness, oblivion; mental derangement.

desacuerdo; desacuerde, *pres. indic.; pres. subj.* [DESACORDAR].

desacuñador, -ra, *a.* (*print.*) removing quoins; (*mint.*) removing dies. — *n.m.* unwedging.

desacuñar, *v.t.* (*print.*) to unwedge, remove the quoins; (*mint.*) to remove the die.

desaderezar, *v.t.* to ruffle, disarrange. — *v.r.* to become disarranged, untidy.

desadeudar, *v.t.* to clear, extricate from debt. — *v.r.* to pay one's debts.

desadoquinar, *v.t.* to remove paving-stones.

desadorar, *v.t.* to cease to worship or love.

desadormecer, *v.t.* (conjugated like ADORMECER) to wake, rouse from sleep; to free from numbness.

desadornado, -da, *a.* unadorned, undecorated, bare. — *p.p.* [DESADORNAR].

desadornar, *v.t.* to denude, lay bare, divest of ornaments.

desadorno, *n.m.* lack of ornaments.

desadujar, *v.t.* to undo the ropes from a sail.

desadvertidamente, *adv.* inadvertently, inconsiderately.

desadvertido, -da, *a.* inadvertent, heedless; unnoticed. — *p.p.* [DESADVERTIR].

desadvertimiento, *n.m.* inadvertence, heedlessness, thoughtlessness.

desadvertir, *v.t.* (conjugated like ADVERTIR) to give no heed to, not to notice.

desafear, *v.t.* to remove or diminish ugliness

desafección, *n.f.* disaffection.

desafectado, -da, *a.* unaffected.

desafecto, -ta, *a.* disaffected; opposed. — *n.m.* ill-will, hatred.

desaferramiento, *n.m.* weighing anchor.

desaferrar, *v.t.* to loosen anything fastened; to unfurl (sails); to unmoor, heave out, weigh anchor; to make one change his opinion.

desafiadero, *n.m.* duelling-ground.

desafiador, -ra, *a.* challenging; competing. — *n.m.f.* challenger; duellist; competitor, rival.

desafiar, *v.t.* to dare, defy, challenge; to rival, oppose; to compete, race, try one's strength against a rival.

desafición, *n.f.* disaffection.

desaficionadamente, *adv.* disaffectedly.

desaficionar, *v.t.* to disaffect, to alienate desire or affection. — *v.r.* to destroy one's desire, wish or affection.

desafijar, *v.t.* to disown or deny as a son.

desafilar, *v.t.* to blunt, dull (an edge, point). — *v.r.* to become blunt, dull.

desafinación, *n.f.* discordance, dissonance.

desafinadamente, *adv.* dissonantly, discordantly.

desafinado, -da, *a.* dissonant, out of tune, inharmonious. — *p.p.* [DESAFINAR].

desafinar, *v.i.*, *v.r.* (*mus.*) to be inharmonious, out of tune; (*fig.*) to speak irrelevantly.

desafío, *n.m.* challenge, duel; contest, struggle, combat, competition, rivalry, race.

desaforadamente, *adv.* excessively; irregularly, immoderately; lawlessly; outrageously, impudently.

desaforado, -da, *a.* disorderly, lawless; outrageous, impudent; (*fig.*) huge, very large. — *p.p.* [DESAFORAR].

desaforar, *v.t.* to encroach on one's rights, infringe one's privileges; (*mil.*) to cashier. — *v.r.* to be outrageous or disorderly.

desaforrar, *v.t.* to take off the lining.

desafortunadamente, *adv.* unlucky, unfortunately.

desafortunado, -da, *a.* unlucky, unfortunate.

desafrancesar, *v.t.*, *v.r.* to divest of frenchified ways and manners.

desafuero, *n.m.* excess, violence, outrage, injustice, infraction of the law.

desagarrar, *v.t.* (*coll.*) to loose, release.

desagitadera, *n.f.* instrument for removing honeycomb from the hive.

desagitar, *v.t.* to remove honeycombs from the hive.

desagraciado, -da, *a.* ungraceful, inelegant; deformed, disfigured. — *p.p.* [DESAGRACIAR].

desagraciar, *v.t.* to deform, disfigure, make ungraceful.

desagradable, *a.* disagreeable, unpleasant, uncomfortable.

desagradablemente, *adv.* disagreeably.

desagradar, *v.i.* to displease, offend. — *v.r.* to become offended.

desagradecer, *v.t.* (conjugated like AGRA-DECER) to be ungrateful.

desagradecidamente, *adv.* ungratefully.

desagradecido, -da, *a.* ungrateful. — *n.m.f.* ingrate. — *p.p.* [DESAGRADECER]; *desagradecido al beneficio*, ungrateful for the favour; *desagradecido con* or *para con su bienhechor*, ungrateful to his benefactor.

desagradecimiento, *n.m.* ingratitude.

desagrado, *n.m.* displeasure, discontent; *con desagrado*, ungraciously.

desagraviador, -ra, *a.* indemnifying. — *n.m.f.* indemnifier.

desagraviar, *v.t.* to give satisfaction, make amends, indemnify. — *v.r.* to indemnify oneself.

desagravio, *n.m.* vindication; compensation; damages.

desagregación, *n.f.* disintegration, separation.

desagregar, *v.t.* (conjugated like AGREGAR) to separate, disjoin, disintegrate. — *v.r.* to become disintegrated, separate.

desagriar, *v.t.* to neutralize acidity; (*fig.*) to sweeten, mollify; to appease.

desaguadero, *n.m.* channel, drain, outlet, waste-pipe; (*fig.*) drain of money.

desaguado, -da, *p.p.* [DESAGUAR] drained, emptied; squandered.

desaguador, -ra, *a.* draining, emptying. — *n.m.* water-pipe, small drain.

desaguamiento, *n.m.* drainage; outlet, waste-pipe, drain.

desaguar, *v.t.* to drain, draw off, empty; (*fig.*) to squander, waste. — *v.i.* to empty, flow into the sea. — *v.r.* to discharge by vomit or stool.

desaguazar, *v.t.* to drain.

desagüe, *n.m.* channel, outlet, drain, waste, drainage.

desaguisado, -da, *a.* lawless, illegal, unjust. — *n.m.* offence, injury, outrage, wrong.

desaherrojar, *v.t.* to unchain, unshackle. — *v.r.* to free oneself, become unchained.

desahijar, *v.t.* to wean, separate young from dams. — *v.r.* to swarm (bees).

desahitarse *v.r.* to relieve indigestion.

desahogadamente, *adv.* freely; impudently, unobstructedly, without embarrassment.

desahogado, -da, *a.* petulant, impudent, licentious, brazen-faced; free, clear, unencumbered; in comfortable circumstances; (*naut.*) having sea-room. — *p.p.* [DESAHOGAR].

desahogar, *v.t.* (conjugated like AHOGAR) to ease pain, alleviate distress. — *v.r.* to recover from fatigue or disease; to unbosom, disclose one's grief; to give a piece of one's mind; expostulate; to utter, vent one's feelings; to free oneself from debt.

desahogo, *n.m.* ease, alleviation; freedom, vent; laxity; *vivir con desahogo*, to live in comfortable circumstances.

desahuciadamente, *adv.* desperately, hopelessly.

desahuciado, -da, *a.* given over; past recovery; desperate, despaired of, hopeless; evicted. — *p.p.* [DESAHUCIAR].

desahuciar, *v.t.* to take away all hope from; to give up, give over, declare past recovery; to evict, dispossess a tenant. — *v.r.* to despair.

desahucio, *n.m.* eviction of a tenant.

desahumado, -da, *a.* smokeless, smoke-free; mild, faded, vapid; flat (of liquors). — *p.p.* [DESAHUMAR].

desahumar, *v.t.* to free from smoke, expel smoke.

desainadura, *n.f.* disease in horses caused by overwork.

desainar, *v.t.* to extenuate, lessen or diminish substance, remove the fat (of an animal). — *v.r.* to lose fat.

desairadamente, *adv.* gracelessly, clumsily.

desairado, -da, *a.* graceless; slighted, unrewarded, unsuccessful. — *p.p.* [DESAIRAR].

desairar, *v.t.* to slight, disregard, take no notice of, disrespect, rebuff.

desaire, *n.m.* slight, rebuff, disdain; awkwardness, disrespect; *tragarse un desaire*, to swallow an affront.

desaislarse, *v.r.* to cease to be isolated, leave one's seclusion.

desajustar, *v.t.* to mismatch, unfit, disarrange, disadjust. — *v.r.* to disagree, withdraw from an agreement; to get out of order.

desajuste, *n.m.* disarrangement; disagreement, breaking of a contract.

desalabanza, *n.f.* disparagement, vituperation.

desalabar, *v.t.* to dispraise, censure, depreciate, disparage.

desalabear, *v.t.* (*carp.*) to straighten, smooth, plane, level.

desalabeo, *n.m.* (*carp.*) planing, levelling, straightening.

desaladamente, *adv.* anxiously, swiftly, eagerly, hastily.

desalado, -da, *a.* anxious, eager; hasty, swift; unsalted. — *p.p.* [DESALAR].

desalar, *v.t.* to cut off the wings; to steep in order to free from salt, eliminate salt. — *v.r.* to run or walk swiftly; to be in great haste; (*fig.*) to long for, crave.

desalazón, *n.f.* (*chem.*) removal of salt from a liquid.

desalbardar, *v.t.* to take a packsaddle off (a beast of burden).

desalcoholizar, *v.t.* to remove the alcohol from a liquid.

desalentadamente, *adv.* without courage, faintly, feebly.

desalentador, -ra, *a.* dispiriting, discouraging.

desalentar, *v.t.* (conjugated like ALENTAR) to wind, put out of breath; (*fig.*) to discourage, dismay, damp. — *v.r.* to become discouraged.

desalfombrar, *v.t.* to take up carpets.

desalforjar, *v.t.* to take anything out of a saddlebag. — *v.r.* (*coll.*) to loosen one's garments, make oneself easy.

desalhajado, -da, *a.* denuded, dismantled, stripped. — *p.p.* [DESALHAJAR].

desalhajar, *v.t.* to dismantle, strip a room or chamber (of furniture, etc.).

desaliento; desaliente, *pres. indic.; pres. subj.* [DESALENTAR].

desaliento, *n.m.* dismay, depression of spirits, discouragement; faintness.

desalineación, *n.f.* bad alignment.

desalinear, *v.t.* (*mil.*) to break the line, put out of alignment.

desaliñadamente, *adv.* in a slovenly, uncleanly manner.

desaliñado, -da, *a.* disarranged, untidy, sloven. — *p.p.* [DESALIÑAR].

desaliñar, *v.t., v.r.* to disarrange, disorder, ruffle.

desaliño, *n.m.* slovenliness, dirtiness, neglect; disarray, negligence in dress, carelessness. — *pl.* (*obs.*) long diamond ear-rings.

desalisamiento, *n.m.* ruffling (of smooth hair); sorting (of paper, rags, etc.).

desalisar, *v.t.* to ruffle (hair); to sort (rags, etc. in paper-mill).

desalivación, *n.f.* salivation.

desalivar, *v.i.* to salivate.

desalmacenar, *v.t.* to remove from shop, warehouse or depot.

desalmadamente, *adv.* soullessly, inhumanly.

desalmado, -da, *a.* soulless, inhuman, merciless; impious, profligate. — *p.p.* [DESALMAR].

desalmamiento, *n.m.* inhumanity, impiety, profligacy, perversity.

desalmar, *v.t.* to weaken, deplete; to disturb. — *v.r.* to desire greatly, crave; to become weak, discouraged, anxious.

desalmenado, -da, *a.* stripped of turrets.

desalmidonar, *v.t.* to take the starch out of linen.

desalojamiento, *n.m.* dislodging.

desalojar, *v.t.* to dislodge, dispossess, evict, eject, oust. — *v.i.* to move, leave one's house or apartments.

desalquilado, -da, *a.* untenanted, unrented, vacant.

desalquilar, *v.t.* to give up (anything rented); to give notice to quit. — *v.r.* to become vacant, untenanted.

desalterar, *v.t.* to allay, assuage, settle, calm down.

desalucinación, *n.f.* dishallucination.

desalumbradamente, *adv.* blindly, erroneously.

desalumbrado, -da, *a.* dazzled, dazed, groping in the dark.

desalumbramiento, *n.m.* blindness, want of judgment, foresight or knowledge.

desamable, *a.* unlovable; unworthy of love.

desamador, -ra, *n.m.f., a.* (one) who does not love.

desamanerarse, *v.r.* to lose one's mannerisms or affectations.

desamar, *v.t.* to cease loving; to detest, hate.

desamarrar, *v.t.* (*naut.*) to unmoor, cast off; to untie, unbind, unlash; to separate. — *v.r.* to slip, become loose (knot, etc.).

desamarre, *n.m.* unmooring, untying.

desamasado, -da, *a.* dissolved, disunited.

desamazacotar, *v.t.* to remove the digressions from a literary work.

desamelgamiento, *n.m.* (*agric.*) fallowing.

desamelgar, *v.t.* (*agric.*) to vary the furrow; to fallow.

desamigado, -da, *a.* unfriendly, unconnected; estranged.

desamistarse, *v.r.* to fall out, quarrel.

desamoblar, *v.t.* [DESAMUEBLAR].

desamodorrar, *v.t., v.r.* to remove, lose sleepiness, drowsiness, lethargy.

desamoldar, *v.t.* to unmould; (*fig.*) to change the proportion of; to disfigure.

desamontonar, *v.t.* to undo a heap or pile; to sort out, separate a pile.

desamor, *n.m.* disregard, disaffection; enmity, hatred.

desamorado, -da, *a.* loveless, cold-hearted. — *p.p.* [DESAMORAR].

desamorar, *v.t.* to extinguish love. — *v.r.* to cease loving.

desamoroso, -sa, *a.* unloving, destitute of love or regard.

desamorrar, *v.t.* (*coll.*) to cheer up, make lively.

desamortizable, *a.* redeemable; that can be disentailed.

desamortización, *n.f.* disentail.

desamortizador, -ra, *n.m.f., a.* disentailing (person or thing).

desamortizar, *v.t.* (conjugated like AMORTIZAR) to disentail.

desamotinarse, *v.r.* to withdraw from mutiny.

desamparadamente, *adv.* helplessly, abandoned by all.

desamparado, -da, *p.p.* [DESAMPARAR] abandoned, forsaken, deserted.

desamparador, -ra, *a.* abandoning, deserting. — *n.m.f.* deserter.

desamparar, *v.t.* to forsake, abandon, desert; to quit, leave; (*law*) to relinquish; (*naut.*) to dismantle, dismast.

desamparo, *n.m.* abandonment, desertion; forlornness, helplessness; dereliction.

desamueblado, -da, *a.* unfurnished. — *p.p.* [DESAMUEBLAR].

desamueblar, *v.t.* to strip of furniture.

desamurar, *v.t.* to raise or free the tack of a sail.

desanclar, desancorar, *v.t.* to weigh anchor.

desandadura, *n.f.* turning back, retracing of one's steps.

desandar, *v.t.* (*pret.* desanduve) to turn back, retrace one's steps; *desandar lo andado*, to undo what has been done.

desandrajado, -da, *a.* ragged, tattered.

desangramiento, *n.m.* bleeding to excess.

desangrar, *v.t.* to bleed to excess; to empty a pond, etc.; to exhaust someone's means, make poor. — *v.r.* to lose much blood; to lose it all.

desanidar, *v.i.* to forsake the nest (of birds). — *v.t.* to dislodge from a post or place.

desanimadamente, *adv.* spiritlessly, without animation.

desanimado, -da, *a.* (*com.*) dull, flat.

desanimar, *v.t.* to dishearten, dispirit, discourage; to damp, pall, daunt. — *v.r.* to become jaded.

desánimo, *n.m.* discouragement, downheartedness.

desanublar, *v.t.* to clear, explain. — *v.r.* to clear up (weather).

desanudar, *v.t.* to loosen or untie a knot; (*fig.*) to extricate, disembroil, disentangle, make clear.

desañudadura, *n.f.* untying of a knot, disentanglement.

desañudar, *v.t.* to loosen, untie.

desaojadera, *n.f.* woman supposed to dispel the evil eye.

desaojar, *v.t.* to dispel, counteract the evil eye.

desapacibilidad, *n.f.* rudeness, peevishness, disagreeableness.

desapacible, *a.* sharp, rough, harsh; unpleasant, disagreeable.

desapaciblemente, *adv.* sharply, roughly, disagreeably.

desapadrinar, *v.t.* to disprove, contradict, disavow.

desaparear, *v.t.* to unmatch, disjoin, separate a pair.

desaparecer, *v.t.* (conjugated like APARECER) to remove out of sight; to hide, make disappear. — *v.i., v.r.* to disappear.

desaparecimiento, *n.m.* act of disappearing.

desaparejar, *v.t.* to unhitch, unharness; to unrig a ship.

desaparición, *n.f.* disappearance; (*astron.*) occultation.

desaparroquiar, *v.t.* to change one's parish. — *v.r.* (*com.*) to cease to be a customer at a shop.

desapasionadamente, *adv.* impartially, dispassionately.

desapasionarse, *v.r.* to root out love for a person or thing.

desapegar, *v.t.* to separate, disjoin. — *v.r.* to lose love or liking for a person or thing.

desapego, *n.m.* alienation of love or affection, coolness; impartiality, indifference, disinterestedness.

desapercibidamente, *adv.* inadvertently, carelessly, unpreparedly.

desapercibido, -da, *a.* unprovided; unprepared, careless.

desapercibimiento, *n.m.* unpreparedness.

desapestar, *v.t.* to disinfect.

desapiadadamente, *adv.* unmercifully, relentlessly; impiously [DESPIADADAMENTE].

desapiadado, -da, *a.* merciless, cruel, unrelenting [DESPIADADO].

desaplicación, *n.f.* want of application.

desaplicadamente, *adv.* indolently.

desaplicado, -da, *a.* indolent, neglectful, careless.

desaplomar, *v.t.* (*build.*) to put out of plumb.

desapoderado, -da, *a.* furious, impetuous, ungovernable. — *p.p.* [DESAPODERAR].

desapoderamiento, *n.m.* the act of ejecting from or depriving of; licentiousness, boundless liberty or licence.

desapoderar, *v.t.* to dispossess, rob of property; (*law*) to revoke a power of attorney.

desapolillar, *v.t.* to clear of moths. — *v.r.* (*coll.*) to take the air when the weather is cold or after a long confinement.

desaporcar, *v.t.* to take away from plants earth which had been heaped about them.

desaposentar, *v.t.* to turn out of lodgings; (*fig.*) to expel from one's mind.

desaposesionar, *v.t.* to dispossess.

desapoyar, *v.t.* to remove a foundation or support.

desapreciar, *v.t.* to depreciate, undervalue.

desaprecio, *n.m.* depreciation.

desaprender, *v.t.* to unlearn; to forget what one has learned.

desaprensar, *v.t.* to take the gloss off clothes.

desapretar, *v.t.* (conjugated like APRETAR) to slacken, loosen, loose; (*fig.*) to set at ease, free from anxiety.

desaprisionar, *v.t.* to release, set at liberty.

desaprobación, *n.f.* disapprobation, censure.

desaprobar, *v.t.* (conjugated like APROBAR) to disapprove, condemn, censure, blame, reprove.

desapropiamiento, *n.m.* renunciation or transfer (of property).

desapropio, *n.m.* alienation, transfer of property.

desaprovechadamente, *adv.* unprofitably, vainly, uselessly; lacking application.

desaprovechado, -da, *a.* unprofitable, useless; backward. — *p.p.* [DESAPROVECHAR].

desaprovechamiento, *n.m.* backwardness; waste; negligence.

desaprovechar, *v.t.* to waste, misspend; to turn to a bad use. — *v.i.* to be backward, make small or no progress; to lose one's time.

desapruebo; desapruebe, *pres. indic.; pres. subj.* [DESAPROBAR].

desapuntalar, *v.t.* to take away props or supports.

desapuntar, *v.t.* to unstitch, rip up; to lose one's aim (shooting).

desaquellarse, *v.r.* (*coll.*) to become disheartened.

desarbolado, -da, *a.* dismasted.

desarbolar, *v.t.* to unmast.

desarbolo, *n.m.* unmasting a ship or laying her up.

desarenar, *v.t.* to take away sand.

desareno, *n.m.* clearing a place of sand.

desarmado, -da, *a.* unarmed, defenceless, bare. — *p.p.* [DESARMAR].

desarmador, *n.m.* trigger of a gun.

desarmadura, *n.f.; ***desarmamiento,** *n.m.* disarming, disarmament.

desarmar, *v.t.* to disarm; to prohibit the carrying of arms; to disband a body of troops; to undo, dismount, take apart (machines, etc.); (*naut.*) to lay up; to make a bull butt in the air; to dismount (crossbow, cannon); (*fig.*) to pacify, disarm (wrath, etc.).

desarme, *n.m.* disarming, disarmament.

desarraigar, *v.t.* (conjugated like ARRAIGAR) to eradicate, root out; to extirpate, destroy, exterminate; to expel, banish.

desarraigo, *n.m.* eradication, expulsion.

desarrancarse, *v.r.* to desert, separate from a body or association.

desarrapado, -da, *a.* ragged.

desarrebozadamente, *adv.* frankly, clearly.

desarrebozar, *v.t.* to unmuffle; to discover; (*fig.*) to lay open, uncover, manifest.

desarrebujar, *v.t.* to disentangle, spread, unfold, uncover; (*fig.*) to explain, clear up.

desarregladamente, *adv.* disorderly, irregularly.

desarreglado, -da, *a.* immoderate, unrestrained, intemperate; lawless, unruly; extravagant, excessive. — *p.p.* [DESARREGLAR].

desarreglar, *v.t.* to discompose, derange, disorder, disarrange. — *v.r.* to lose one's regular habits.

desarreglo, *n.m.* disorder, disarrangement, confusion; irregularity, mismanagement; licence, licentiousness.

desarrendar, *v.t.* to break, give up the lease of; to unbridle a horse. — *v.r.* to shake off the bridle (a horse).

desarrimar, *v.t.* to remove, separate; to dissuade.

desarrimo, *n.m.* want of supports or props.

desarrollar, *v.t.* to unroll, uncoil, unspread, unfurl, unfold; (*fig.*) to develop; to expand, increase, promote, improve; (*fig.*) to explain; to work out; (*geom.*) to develop a surface; (*math.*) to expound and work a calculation. — *v.r.* to evolve, grow, develop (seeds, etc.).

desarrollo, *n.m.* development, unfolding, evolution, spread, expansion, increase.

desarropar, *v.t.* to uncover, undress.

desarrugar, *v.t.* (conjugated like ARRUGAR) to take out wrinkles, smooth out folds.

desarrumar, *v.t.* to unload a ship, discharge the cargo.

desarticulación, *n.f.* (*surg.*) disarticulation.

desarticular, *v.t.*, *v.r.* to disarticulate; to loose, disconnect (machine, etc.).

desartillar, *v.t.* to take the guns out of a ship or fortress.

desarzonar, *v.t.* to unhorse.

desasado, -da, *a.* without handles.

desaseadamente, *adv.* uncleanly, slovenly.

desasear, *v.t.* to make dirty or unclean; to discompose, disorder.

desasegurar, *v.t.* to loosen, unbrace, make unsteady; to lessen the security of anything. — *v.r.* to become uncertain; to cancel an insurance.

desasentar, *v.t.* (conjugated like SENTAR) to displace, move, remove. — *v.i.* (*fig.*) not to suit, not to set well. — *v.r.* to stand up.

desaseo, *n.m.* uncleanliness, dirtiness, carelessness, slovenliness, shabbiness.

desasimiento, *n.m.* loosening, letting loose; (*fig.*) lack of interest, disregard; alienation of affection.

desasimilación, *n.f.* (*physiol.*) katabolism.

desasir, *v.t.* (conjugated like ASIR) to loosen, let go of, give up. — *v.r.* to disengage oneself, free oneself; (*fig.*) to give away property; (*fig.*) to disregard.

desasnar, *v.t.* (*coll.*) to instruct, polish someone's manners. — *v.r.* to grow sharp, clever or polite.

desasociable, *a.* unsociable.

desasociar, *v.t.* to separate.

desasosegadamente, *adv.* uneasily.

desasosegado, -da, *a.* unquiet. — *p.p.* [DESASOSEGAR].

desasosegar, *v.t.*, *v.r.* (conjugated like SOSEGAR) to disquiet, disturb.

desasosiego, *n.m.* restlessness, uneasiness.

desastradamente, *adv.* wretchedly, disastrously.

desastrado, -da, *n.m.f.*, *a.* wretched, unfortunate, miserable; ragged, battered.

desastre, *n.m.* disaster, disgrace, misfortune, catastrophe.

desastrosamente, *adv.* wretchedly; disastrously.

desastroso, -sa, *a.* miserable, wretched.

desatacar, *v.t.* (conjugated like ATACAR) to loosen, untie, undo, unbutton, unclasp; to draw the ram-rod from a fire-arm; *desatacar*

la escopeta, to draw the charge from a gun. — *v.r.* to unfasten one's trousers.

desatadamente, *adv.* loosely, freely.

desatado, -da, *a.* loose, unbound, untied. — *p.p.* [DESATAR].

desatador, -ra, *n.m.f.* one who loosens, unfastens or unties; absolver.

desatadura, *n.f.;* **desatamiento**, *n.m.* untying, loosening.

desatancar, *v.t.* (*pret.* desatanqué; *pres. subj.* desatanque) to clear sewers of obstruction.

desatar, *v.t.* to loose, loosen, untie, unravel, unbind, unfasten, unhitch, undo (a knot), detach, separate; to solve; to dissolve, liquefy. — *v.r.* to give rein to one's tongue; to lose all reserve or fear; to break out, break loose (storm).

desatascar, *v.t.* (conjugated like ATASCAR) to draw out of the mire; to remove an obstruction from a conduit; (*fig.*) to extricate (someone) from difficulties.

desataviar, *v.t.* to strip of ornaments and decorations.

desatavío, *n.m.* uncleanliness, negligence in dress, disarray.

desate, *n.m.* loosing, loosening; glibness, excessive talk; *desate de vientre*, looseness of the bowels.

desatención, *n.f.* absent-mindedness, abstraction, inattention, disrespect, incivility.

desatender, *v.t.* (conjugated like ATENDER) to disregard, slight, contemn, neglect, take no notice of a person or a thing.

desatentadamente, *adv.* in disorderly fashion, confusedly; inconsiderately, unadvisedly.

desatentado, -da, *a.* inconsiderate, unadvised, thoughtless, careless, disordered; imprudent, heedless; excessive, rigorous. — *p.p.* [DESATENTAR].

desatentamente, *adv.* disrespectfully, uncivilly.

desatentar, *v.t.* (conjugated like ATENTAR) to perturb the mind, perplex, confuse, derange.

desatento, -ta, *a.* inattentive, careless; rude, unmannerly; heedless, thoughtless; discourteous, uncivil.

desaterrar, *v.t.* (*Am.*) to free a mine from debris; to remove earth or mud.

desatesorar, *v.t.* to remove or spend the treasure of.

desatiendo; **desatienda**, *pres. indic.; pres. subj.* [DESATENDER].

desatiento, *n.m.* lack of sense of touch; restlessness, uneasiness, worry.

desatierre, *n.m.* (*Am.*) (*min.*) dumping ground.

desatinadamente, *adv.* inconsiderately, extravagantly, wildly, indiscreetly, disproportionately; (*coll.*) crazily, helter-skelter.

desatinado, -da, *a.* extravagant, crazy, foolish, irregular, nonsensical, wild. — *p.p.* [DESATINAR].

desatino, *n.m.* idiot, fool, madcap.

desatinar, *v.i.* to do foolish things; to talk nonsense; to stagger, reel. — *v.t.* to confuse, bewilder, rattle; to disorder; to throw into a violent passion. — *v.r.* to get confused or bewildered; to lose one's bearings; to become deranged in one's mind.

desatino, *n.m.* lack of tact; extravagance, wildness, headiness, madness, nonsense; reeling; unwisdom, folly, error.

desatolondrar, *v.t.* to bring someone to his senses. — *v.r.* to recover one's senses.

desatollar, *v.t.* to pull out of the mud or mire.

desatontarse, *v.r.* to recover from stupefaction.

desatorar, *v.t.* (*naut.*) to unload a ship; (*min.*) to clear a gallery.

desatracar, *v.t.* (conjugated like ATRACAR) (*naut.*) to sheer off, bear away.

desatraer, *v.t.* (conjugated like TRAER) to separate, disjoin.

desatraillar, *v.t.* to uncouple hounds; to untie.

desatrampar, *v.t.* to clear a conduit; to sink a sewer.

desatrancar, *v.t.* (conjugated like ATRANCAR) to unbar (door, etc.), to clear a well, etc.

desatufarse, *v.r.* to go out of a hot room; to grow calm, allay one's passion; to regain one's self-control.

desaturdir, *v.t.* to rouse from a state of stupor or dizziness.

desautoridad, *n.f.* want of authority.

desautorización, *n.f.* withdrawal of authority.

desautorizadamente, *adv.* without authorization.

desautorizar, *v.t.* (conjugated like AUTORIZAR) to withdraw a power of attorney, etc.

desavahado, -da, *a.* uncovered; clear, free from fogs or vapours. — *p.p.* [DESAVAHAR].

desavahar, *v.t.* to expose to the air; to evaporate; to allow to cool; to air, ventilate. — *v.r.* to grow lively or sprightly.

desavecindado, -da, *a.* deserted, unpeopled. — *p.p.* [DESAVECINDARSE].

desavecindarse, *v.r.* to move, change one's domicile.

desavenencia, *n.f.* discord, disagreement, misintelligence, misunderstanding.

desavengo; desavenga, *pres. indic.; pres. subj.* [DESAVENIR].

desavenido, -da, *a.* discordant, disagreeing. — *p.p.* [DESAVENIR].

desavenir, *v.t.* (conjugated like VENIR) to discompose, disconcert, unsettle. — *v.r.* to disagree, to quarrel.

desaventajadamente, *adv.* disadvantageously, unprofitably.

desaventajado, -da, *a.* disadvantageous, unprofitable.

desaviar, *v.t.* to strip of necessaries or conveniences; to mislead, lead astray. — *v.r.* to go astray; to lose the means of acquiring necessaries.

desavío, *n.m.* the act of going astray; want of necessary means.

desavisado, -da, *a.* ill-advised, unadvised, misguided. — *p.p.* [DESAVISAR].

desavisar, *v.t.* to countermand; to contradict previous news or report.

desayudar, *v.t.* to refrain from assisting; to prevent from being aided.

desayunado, -da, *n.m.f., a.* one who has breakfasted. — *p.p.* [DESAYUNAR].

desayunarse, *v.r.* to have breakfast; (*fig.*) to get first intelligence of anything.

desayuno, *n.m.* light breakfast; having a light breakfast.

desazogar, *v.t.* (conjugated like AZOGAR) to take off the quicksilver from a looking-glass. — *v.r.* (*Per.*) to become restless.

desazón, *n.m.* insipidity, want of taste or flavour; disgust, displeasure; uneasiness, disquietude, restlessness; unfitness or unsuitability of soil.

desazonado, -da, *a.* ill-adapted, unfit for some purpose; ill-humoured, cross, peevish; poorly. — *p.p.* [DESAZONAR].

desazonar, *v.t.* to render tasteless; to disgust, vex, ruffle; to mortify. — *v.r.* to become indisposed in health.

desbabar, *v.i., v.r.* to drivel, slaver.

desbagar, *v.t.* (*pret.* **desbagué**; *pres. subj.* **desbague**) to extract flax-seed from the capsule.

desbalijamiento, *n.m.* (*vulg.*) plundering of a portmanteau.

desbalijar, *v.t.* to rob a portmanteau; (*vulg.*) to plunder.

desbancar, *v.t.* (*pret.* **desbanqué**; *pres. subj.* **desbanque**) to clear a room of benches; to break the bank (in gambling); to win all the money (at cards); to supplant someone in the friendship and affection of another; (*coll.*) to cut out.

desbandada, *n.f.* (*mil.*) disbandment; *a la desbandada*, in disorderly fashion, irregularly, helter-skelter; (*mil.*) rout.

desbandarse, *v.r.* (*mil.*) to disband, desert the colours.

desbarahustar, desbarajustar, *v.t.* to derange, discompose.

desbarahuste, desbarajuste, *n.m.* derangement, disorder, confused medley.

desbaratadamente, *adv.* confusedly, brokenly, dispersed, disorderly.

desbaratado, -da, *a.* (*coll.*) debauched, corrupted. — *p.p.* [DESBARATAR].

desbaratador, -ra, *n.m.f.* destroyer, confounder; debaucher; disturber.

desbaratamiento, *n.m.* perturbation, commotion, discomposure.

desbaratar, *v.t.* to destroy, defeat; to waste, misspend, dissipate, squander; (*fig.*) to cross, thwart, impede, prevent; to separate in pieces; (*mil.*) to rout, disperse; *desbaratar la paz*, to break the peace. — *v.i.* to speak foolishly, talk nonsense. — *v.r.* to be disordered in mind.

desbarate, desbarato, *n.m.* the act of routing or defeating; smash, breakage, destruction; waste, dissipation; *desbarate de vientre*, loose bowels.

desbarbado, -da, *a.* beardless (often in contemptuous sense). — *p.p.* [DESBARBAR].

desbarbar, *v.t.* (*coll.*) to shave; to trim; to cut off filaments.

desbarbillar, *v.t.* to prune the roots of young vines.

desbardar, *v.t.* to uncover a wall or fence; to remove thatch.

desbarrar, *v.i.* to throw, hurl, fling an iron bar (sport); (*fig.*) to rove, go beyond limits; to act foolishly, talk nonsense, exaggerate; to sneak, steal away; to waver.

desbarretar, *v.t.* to unbolt, unbar.

desbarrigado, -da, *a.* little-bellied. — *p.p.* [DESBARRIGAR].

desbarrigar, *v.t.* (*pret.* **desbarrigué**; *pres. subj.* **desbarrigue**) (*coll.*) to wound, rip open the belly.

desbarro, *n.m.* falling into error; nonsense, extravagance, madness, frenzy.

desbastador, *n.m.* chisel, hewer, paring-tool.

desbastadura, *n.f.* planing, trimming, polishing, hewing.

desbastar, *v.t* to plane, hew, dress, smooth, trim, polish; to waste, weaken, consume; (*fig.*) to educate and polish a coarse person.

desbaste, *n.m.* the act of polishing, trimming, hewing.

desbastecido, -da, *a.* unprovided.

desbautizarse, *v.r.* (*coll.*) to be irritated, fly into a passion; to fall and break one's head.

desbazadero, *n.m.* humid, slippery place.

desbeber, *v.i.* (*coll.*) to discharge urine.

desbecerrar, *v.t.* to wean calves.

desblanquecido, -da; desblanquiñado, -da, *a.* blanched, bleached.

desbocadamente, *adv.* impudently, ungovernedly.

desbocado, -da, *a.* wide-mouthed (cannon); broken-faced (tool); broken-lipped or edged (jar); open-mouthed, wild; broken-mouthed; runaway (horse); (*fig.*) foul-mouthed, indecent. — *p.p.* [DESBOCAR].

desbocamiento, *n.m.* impertinence, impudence; act of running away (of horses).

desbocar, *v.t.* (*pret.* **desboqué;** *pres. subj.* **desboque**) to break the brim of a jug, mug or other vessel. — *v.i.* to disembogue. — *v.r.* to be hard-mouthed; to use abusive language; to be wild; to run away (horse).

desbonetarse, *v.r.* (*coll.*) to take off the cap.

desboquillar, *v.t.* to break the mouth of a vessel; to break or remove the stem of a pipe, etc.; to break the nozzle of.

desbordamiento, *n.m.* inundation, overflowing.

desbordar, *v.i., v.r.* to overflow, run over, inundate; to lose self-control.

desbornizar, *v.t.* to take the cork from trees.

desborrar, *v.t.* to cut off loose threads; (*prov.*) to lop off branches.

desbotonar, *v.t.* (*Cub.*) to cut the buds of tobacco plants.

desbozar, *v.t.* to remove reliefs, carvings or mouldings.

desbragado, -da, *a.* (*contempt.*) unbreeched, very poor; shabby.

desbraguetado, -da, *a.* having the fore part of the breeches unbuttoned and open.

desbravador, *n.m.* mustang-breaker.

desbravar, desbravecer, *v.t.* to tame, break in (horses). — *v.i.* to moderate, diminish in strength, abate. — *v.r.* to moderate.

desbrazarse, *v.r.* to extend one's arms violently.

desbrevarse, *v.r.* to evaporate, lose body and strength (of wine).

desbridar, *v.t.* (*surg.*) to open up, sever the tissues of.

desbriznar, *v.t.* to divide into small parts; to chop or mince meat.

desbroce, *n.m.* trimmed leaves or branches; clearing of lands and trenches.

desbrozar, *v.t.* (*pret.* **desbrocé;** *pres. subj.* **desbroce**) to clear away rubbish.

desbrozo, *n.m.* the act of clearing away rubbish.

desbruar, *v.t.* (*text.*) to clean cloth; to remove grease.

desbrujar, *v.t.* to destroy gradually.

desbuchar, *v.t.* to disclose secrets; to tell all one knows; to ease the stomach.

desbulla, *n.f.* part of an oyster remaining on the shell.

desbullador, *n.m.* oyster-fork.

desbullar, *v.t.* to extract an oyster from its shell.

desca, *n.f.* (*naut.*) tar-pot.

descabal, *a.* imperfect, incomplete.

descabalar, *v.t.* to pilfer; to impair, damage, maim, chop off, cripple; to make incomplete.

descabalgadura, *n.f.* dismounting from a horse.

descabalgar, *v.i.* (conjugated like CABALGAR) to dismount from a horse. — *v.t.* to dismount an enemy gun.

descaballar, *v.t.* to take away the leaves and superfluous buds of plants.

descabelladamente, *adv.* without order or regularity.

descabellado, -da, *a.* dishevelled; disordered, disarranged; lavish; wild, disorderly, illogical, disproportionate; absurd. — *p.p.* [DESCABELLAR].

descabellamiento, *n.m.* absurdity.

descabellar, *v.t., v.r.* to undress the hair; to kill the bull by stabbing him in the cervix.

descabello, *n.m.* bull-killing.

descabestrar, *v.t.* to unhalter.

descabezado, -da, *a.* beheaded; (*fig.*) lightheaded, giddy, injudicious, imprudent. — *p.p.* [DESCABEZAR].

descabezamiento, *n.m.* beheading; perplexity, quandary, puzzling predicament.

descabezar, *v.t.* (*pret.* **descabecé;** *pres. subj.* **descabece**) to behead; to revoke (a municipal assessment); (*mil.*) to surmount, overcome; to begin; to poll, top, lop off; to get over the first obstacle; (*naut.*) to break a mast through its neck; *descabezar el sueño,* to take a nap; *descabezarse una vena,* to break a blood-vessel. — *v.i.* to terminate, abut on another property. — *v.r.* (*coll.*) to batter one's brains, be perplexed; to shed the grain (cereals).

descabritar, *v.t.* to wean goats.

descabullirse, *v.r.* to sneak off, steal away, scamper off; [ESCABULLIRSE].

descacilar, descafilar, *v.t.* to trim bricks.

descachar, *v.t.* (*Am.*) cut off the horns of an animal.

descachazar, *v.t.* (*Am.*) to remove the froth from boiling cane juice.

descaderar, *v.t.* to sprain a hip.

descadillar, *v.t.* to cut off the loose end of the warp.

descaecer, *v.i.* (conjugated like ACAECER) to decline, droop, languish, decay, grow less; (*naut.*) to edge away.

descaecido, -da, *p.p.* [DESCAECER], weak, feeble, languishing.

descaecimiento, descaimiento; *n.m.* weakness, debility, decay, despondency, languor.

descalabazarse, *v.r.* (*coll.*) to puzzle one's brains in vain.

descalabrado, -da, *a.* injured, wounded in the head. — *p.p.* [DESCALABRAR]; *salir descalabrado,* to be a loser in any matter.

descalabradura, *n.f.* contusion, wound in the head; loss, misfortune.

descalabrar, *v.t.* to hurt, injure (esp. the head); to cause a ship great damage; to attack one's character; to occasion the enemy losses. — *v.r.* to fall and break one's head.

descalabro, *n.m.* misfortune, great loss, calamity.

descalandrajar, *v.t.* to rend or tear clothes.

descalar, *v.t.* to unship the helm.

descalcador, *n.m.* (*naut.*) rave-hook; (*carp.*) claw.

descalcar, *v.t.* (conjugated like CALCAR) to extract oakum from seams.

descalce, *n.m.* (*agric.*) baring (root of a tree); undermining, unwedging.

descalcez, *n.f.* barefootedness.

descalostrado, -da, *a.* applied to a child after the colostrum stage.

descalzadero, *n.m.* (*prov.*) little door of a pigeon-house.

descalzado, -da, *a.* barefooted. — *p.p.* [DESCALZAR].

descalzador, *n.m.* bootjack; crowbar.

descalzamiento, *n.m.* pulling off one's boots; (*agric.*) baring.

descalzar, *v.t.* (conjugated like CALZAR) to pull off shoes and stockings; to remove any brake or impediment used to prevent movement of a wheel; to surmount an obstacle; to undermine; (*agric.*) to bare; to take away wedges or chocks. — *v.r.* to pull off one's shoes and stockings; to lose a shoe (of horses); *descalzarse los guantes*, to pull off one's gloves.

descalzo, -za, *a.* barefooted, discalced (applied to friars and nuns).

descamación, *n.f.* (*med.*) desquamation.

descambiar, *v.t.* to cancel an exchange or barter.

descaminadamente, *adv.* absurdly, unreasonably.

descaminado, -da, *p.p.* [DESCAMINAR] illadvised; misguided; *ir descaminado*, to deviate from rectitude or reason.

descaminar, *v.t.* to misguide, mislead; to seduce one from his duty; lead astray; to seize. — *v.r.* to go astray.

descamino, *n.m.* seizure of smuggled goods; the goods thus seized; leading or going astray; error, blindness.

descamisado, -da, *a.* poor; naked, shirtless. — *n.m.* (*coll.*) ragamuffin; (*polit.*) sansculotte.

descampado, -da, *a.* disengaged, free, open, clear; *en descampado*, in the open air.

descansadamente, *adv.* easily, without toil or fatigue.

descansadero, *n.m.* resting-place.

descansado, -da, *a.* rested, refreshed; *vida descansada*, quiet, easy life. — *p.p.* [DESCANSAR].

descansar, *v.i.* to rest from labour and fatigue; to pause; to trust in, rely on a person; to lean upon; to repose, sleep, lie down, lie at rest, lie up, lie fallow. — *v.t.* to help another in labour or alleviate his fatigue; to place or set down on a support or base.

descansillo, *n.m.* landing of a staircase.

descanso, *n.m.* peace, quiet, stillness, tranquillity, repose, rest, sleep; halt; ease, relief, help, aid; landing; (*mech.*) bench, seat, support, resting-place; (*mil.*) parade rest; halting-day for soldiers on a march; day of rest.

descantar, *v.t.* to clear of stones.

descantear, *v.t.* to smooth corners or angles; to splay, chamfer, edge.

descanterar, *v.t.* to take off the crust (usually of bread).

descantillar, descantonar, *v.t.* to pare off, break off part of a thing; to chip; to subtract; (*fig.*) to lessen.

descantillón, *n.m.* pattern, templet; rule.

descañar, *v.t.* to break the stem or branches of a tree, etc.

descañonar, *v.t.* to pluck out the feathers; to shave close; (*fig.*) to trick someone out of money.

descaperuzar, *v.t.* to take off the cowl or hood.

descaperuzarse, *v.r.* to uncover one's head.

descaperuzo, *n.m.* taking off the cowl, hood or hunting-cap.

descapillar, *v.t.* to take off the hood.

descapotable, *n.m.*, *a.* (*motor.*) convertible.

descaradamente, *adv.* impudently, saucily.

descarado, -da, *a.* impudent, barefaced, saucy, pert, petulant. — *p.p.* [DESCARARSE].

descararse, *v.r.* to behave insolently.

descarbonatar, descarburar, *v.t.* to decarbonize.

descarga, *n.f.* unburdening, unloading; (*mil.*) discharge, shooting, fire, round, volley; exoneration; (*arch.*) easing a wall of too great a weight; (*elec.*) discharge; *descarga de un buque*, unloading the cargo of a ship; *descarga de aduana*, customs clearance; *descarga cerrada*, volley.

descargadero, *n.m.* wharf, unloading-place.

descargador, *n.m.* discharger, unloader, stevedore, lighterman; (*artill.*) wad-hook.

descargadura, *n.f.* bones which a butcher removes from meat.

descargar, *v.t.* (conjugated like CARGAR) to discharge, unload, disburden, lighten, ease; to empty; to remove the flap and bones of meat; (*mil.*) to fire, discharge fire-arms; to unload a fire-arm; (*com.*) to unload a cargo; (*naut.*) to brace alee; to clear the sails or yards; (*elec.*) to discharge (as a battery); to lay on, inflict (as blows); (*law*) to acquit, clear of a criminal charge; to exonerate or liberate from an obligation or debt; *descargar la conciencia*, to confess or confide; *descargar la ira en alguno*, to vent one's anger upon someone. — *v.i.* to disgorge, disembogue; to burst, vent fury, strike with violence (as a storm). — *v.r.* (with *de*) to resign one's employment; to shirk duty by transferring it to another; (*law*) to clear or vindicate oneself from charges or accusations.

descargo, *n.m.* unloading, unburdening; exoneration, acquittal, discharge; (*law*) plea, answer to an impeachment; (*com.*) acquittance, receipt, release, discharge, voucher; *en descargo de mi conciencia*, for the satisfaction of my conscience.

descargue, *n.m.* unburdening, unloading; licence to discharge vessels.

descariñarse, *v.r.* to withdraw love or affection; to become cool.

descariño, *n.m.* coolness, indifference.

descarnadamente, *adv.* plainly, without trimmings; with effrontery.

descarnada (la), *n.f.* death.

descarnado, -da, *a.* thin, lean; bare, unadorned.

descarnador, *n.m.* (*dent.*) scraper; (*tan.*) hide scraper.

descarnadura, *n.f.* divesting of flesh.

descarnar, *v.t.* to divest of, clear from flesh; to corrode, wash away, abrade, denudate; (*fig.*) to take away part of a thing; (*tan.*) to flesh, scrape; (*fig.*) to examine minutely; (*fig.*) to remove from earthly things. — *v.r.* to lose flesh, become emaciated.

descaro, *n.m.* impudence, effrontery, barefacedness, sauciness, forwardness, assurance.

descarriamiento, *n.m.* going astray, sending astray; making anyone lose his way.

descarriar, *v.t.* to lead astray, mislead, misguide; to separate cattle. — *v.r.* to be separated, disjoined; to lead a dissipated life; (*fig.*) to deviate from justice or reason.

descarrilamiento, *n.m.* derailment.

descarrilar, *v.i.* to run off the rails (trains, tramways); to be derailed.

descarrío, *n.m.* going astray, losing one's way.

descartar, *v.t.* to discard, dismiss, put aside, lay aside, lay away, eject. — *v.r.* to discard (at cards); to excuse oneself; to shirk.

descarte, *n.m.* cards discarded from a hand; evasion, subterfuge, shirking.

descasamiento, *n.m.* annulment of marriage; repudiation, divorce.

descasar, *v.t.* to unmarry, divorce, declare a marriage null; to separate, disunite; (*print.*) to alter the position of the pages of a sheet.

descascar, *v.t.* (conjugated like CASCAR) to decorticate; (*fig.*) to bluster, brag; to mumble. — *v.r.* to break into pieces.

descascarador, **-ra**, *n.m.f.* huller, husker, shelter; *descascarador de café*, coffee-pulper.

descascarar, *v.t.* to peel, flay, decorticate. — *v.r.* to fall off, scale off, peel, shell off.

descaspar, *v.t.* to scrape the flesh from a hide; to remove dandruff from the head.

descasque, *n.m.* decortication (particularly of the cork-tree).

descastado, **-da**, *a.* showing little natural affection.

descastar, *v.t.* to exterminate (animals). — *v.r.* to lose natural affection.

descatolizar, *v.t.* to cause to abandon Catholicism (person or population).

descaudalado, **-da**, *a.* penniless, ruined.

descebar, *v.t.* to unprime fire-arms.

descendencia, *n.f.* descent, origin, extraction; offspring.

descendente, *a.* descending.

descender, *v.i.*, *v.t.* (*pres. indic.* **desciendo**; *pres. subj.* **descienda**) to descend, go down; to flow, run; to proceed from, be derived from; (*fig.*) to stoop, lower oneself; to decline in esteem.

descendiente, *a.* descending. — *n.m.* descendant, offspring.

descendimiento, *n.m.* descent, descension, lowering.

descensión, *n.f.* descent, descension.

descenso, *n.m.* descent; lowering; fall, degradation; (*med.*) hernia, rupture; prolapse of the womb; (*mech.*) *descenso del émbolo*, down-stroke of the piston.

descentrado, **-da**, *a.* out of the centre; out of plumb. — *p.p.* [DESCENTRAR].

descentralización, *n.f.* decentralization.

descentralizador, **-ra**, *a.* decentralizing. — *n.m.f.* decentralizer.

descentralizar, *v.t.* (conjugated like CENTRALIZAR) to decentralize; to grant local autonomy to.

descentrar, *v.t.* to make eccentric.

desceñidura, *n.f.* disjunction, ungirding, loosening.

desceñir, *v.t.* (conjugated like CEÑIR) to ungird, take off (girdle, belt, crown).

descepar, *v.t.* to pull up by the roots; to demolish, eradicate, extirpate; (*naut.*) to remove the anchor-stocks.

descerar, *v.t.* to take the empty combs from a beehive.

descercado, **-da**, *a.* open, unfortified, undefended. — *p.p.* [DESCERCAR].

descercador, *n.m.* one who forces the enemy to raise a siege.

descercar, *v.t.* to destroy, pull down a wall; to oblige the enemy to raise a siege.

descerezar, *v.t.* (*Am.*) to pulp the coffee berry.

descerrajado, **-da**, *a.* (*coll.*) corrupt, wicked, vicious, ill-disposed. — *p.p.* [DESCERRAJAR].

descerrajadura, *n.f.* forcing, wrenching off locks or bolts.

descerrajar, *v.t.* to force, wrench away a lock; (*coll.*) to discharge fire-arms.

descerrumarse, *v.r.* (*vet.*) to be wrenched, distorted at the joints.

descervigar, *v.t.* to twist the neck.

desciendo; descienda, *pres. indic.; pres. subj.* [DESCENDER].

descifrable, *a.* decipherable.

descifrador, **-ra**, *n.m.f.* decipherer.

descifrar, *v.t.* to decipher, interpret, translate; (*fig.*) to unfold, unravel.

descimbramiento, *n.m.* (*arch.*) removing the centring.

descimbrar, *v.t.* (*arch.*) to remove the centring.

descimentar, *v.t.* to demolish the foundations of a building.

descinchar, *v.t.* to ungirth a horse.

descinto, *p.p. irreg.* [DESCEÑIR].

desclavador, *n.m.* carpenter's chisel; nail-puller; claw-wrench.

desclavar, *v.t.* to unnail, draw out nails, unpeg; to remove gems from a jewel.

descoagulable, *adj.* redissoluble after coagulation.

descoagulación, *n.f.* solution, liquefaction of a clot or curd.

descoagulante, *a.* liquefying.

descoagular, *v.t.*, *v.r.* to dissolve, liquefy.

descobajar, *v.t.* to separate grapes from the stem.

descobijar, *v.t.* to uncover, undress.

descocadamente, *adv.* impudently, boldly, brazenly.

descocado, **-da**, *a.* (*coll.*) bold, impudent, free and forward. — *p.p.* [DESCOCAR].

descocar, *v.t.* (conjugated like CHOCAR) to clean, clear trees from insects. — *v.r.* (*coll.*) to be impudent, saucy.

descocedura, *n.f.* digestion.

descocer, *v.t.* (conjugated like COCER) to digest.

descoco, *n.m.* impudence, barefacedness, boldness, sauciness.

descodar, *v.t.* (*prov.*) to unstitch, rip.

descoger, *v.t.* (conjugated like COGER) to spread, extend, expand, unfold.

descogollar, *v.t.* to take out the heart from vegetables; to strip a tree of shoots.

descogotado, -da, *a.* with the neck exposed, low-necked. — *p.p.* [DESCOGOTAR].

descogotar, *v.t.* to knock or cut the horns off a stag.

descolar, *v.t.* (conjugated like COLAR) to dock, cut off the tail; (*carp.*) to unglue.

descolchar, *v.t.* (*naut.*) to untwist a cable.

descolgar, *v.t.* (conjugated like COLGAR) to unhang, let down, take down. — *v.r.* to come down gently; to slip down (by a rope, etc.); to descend; (with *con*) to make an unexpected remark or sally; to come on suddenly (as a cold snap).

descoligado, -da, *adj.* not belonging to a league; non-union.

descolmar, *v.t.* to strike off the corn in a measure; (*fig.*) to diminish.

descolmillar, *v.t.* to pull out or break the eye-teeth.

descolocado, -da, *a.* unemployed, workless.

descoloramiento, *n.m.* paleness, discoloration.

descolorar, *v.t.* to discolour, pale, bleach, fade. — *v.r.* to become discoloured or pale.

descolorido, -da, *a.* discoloured, pale, colourless, pallid. — *p.p.* [DESCOLORIR].

descolorimiento, *n.m.* paleness, discoloration.

descolorir, *v.t.* to discolour, pale, change the hue.

descolladamente, *adv.* loftily, haughtily.

descollamiento, *n.m.* [DESCUELLO].

descollar, *v.i.* (conjugated like ACOLLAR) to excel, surpass, exceed, outdo, overtop.

descombrar, *v.t.* to remove obstacles, disencumber, clear out.

descombro, *n.m.* disencumbrance.

descomedidamente, *adv.* rudely, unmannerly, coarsely, haughtily; excessively, immoderately.

descomedido, -da, *a.* excessive, disproportionate; haughty, lofty; overbearing, rude, insolent. — *p.p.* [DESCOMEDIRSE].

descomedimiento, *n.m.* rudeness, incivility.

descomedirse, *v.r.* to be rude or disrespectful; to forget oneself.

descomer, *v.i.* (*coll.*) to ease nature, defecate.

descomido; me descomida, *pres. indic.; pres. subj.* [DESCOMEDIRSE].

descomodidad, *n.f.* incommodity, discomfort, inconvenience.

descompadrar, *v.i.* to disagree, fall out. — *v.t.* to cause estrangement between friends.

descompás, *n.m.* excess, redundance; want of measure or proportion.

descompasadamente, *adv.* beyond measure.

descompasado, -da, *a.* excessive, extravagant, disproportionate; out of time or tune, beyond rule or measure. — *p.p.* [DESCOMPASARSE].

descompasarse, *v.r.* to exceed rule or measure; to transgress bounds and proportions; to insult; to be out of time or tune.

descompletar, *v.t.* to render incomplete.

descomponer, *v.t.* (conjugated like COMPONER) to discompose, upset, disturb, unsettle, disconcert; (*fig.*) to destroy harmony; to decompound; to disable; (*chem.*) to decompose; (*mech.*) to resolve forces. — *v.r.* to forget oneself, lose one's temper; to be out of gear, deranged; to be indisposed; to change for the worse (applied to the weather);

to decompose, spoil, rot; to mortify; to become stale, putrid or tainted.

descompongo; descomponga, *pres. indic.; pres. subj.* [DESCOMPONER].

descomposición, *n.f.* discomposure, disorder, confusion; disagreement; decomposition, corruption, mortification; (*chem.*) decomposition, analysis; (*mech.*) resolution of forces.

descompostura, *n.f.* forwardness, want of modesty; disrespectful conduct; impudence; disarrangement; disadjustment; slovenliness, uncleanliness, untidiness.

descompuestamente, *adv.* audaciously, impudently, insolently.

descompuesto, -ta, *a.* audacious, impudent, insolent; out of temper; out of order; immodest. — *p.p. irreg.* [DESCOMPONER].

descomulgado, -da, *a.* wicked, perverse, nefarious. — *p.p.* [DESCOMULGAR].

descomulgador, *n.m.* excommunicator.

descomulgar, *v.t.* (conjugated like COMULGAR) to excommunicate.

descomunal, *a.* uncommon, extraordinary, monstrous, enormous, huge, colossal.

descomunalmente, *adv.* uncommonly, extraordinarily, immoderately, disproportionately.

descomunión, *n.f.* excommunication.

desconcertadamente, *adv.* confusedly, in disorder, disconcertedly.

desconcertado, -da, *a.* slovenly, disorderly; disconnected; disconcerted, baffled. — *p.p.* [DESCONCERTAR].

desconcertador, -ra, *n.m.f.* disturber, disconcerter.

desconcertadura, *n.f.* discomposure, disturbance, confusion.

desconcertar, *v.t.* (conjugated like CONCERTAR) to discompose, confuse, disturb, baffle, thwart, confound; (*anat.*) to displace, dislocate, disjoint. — *v.r.* to disagree; to put out of joint; to be indisposed; to fall through; (*fig.*) to act or speak thoughtlessly or recklessly.

desconcierto, *n.m.* discomposure, disagreement, disorder, confusion; want of prudence; negligence, indolence; mismanagement, maladministration; (*fig.*) flux, looseness (of the bowels).

desconcierto; desconcierte, *pres. indic.; pres. subj.* [DESCONCERTAR].

desconcordia, *n.f.* discord; disagreement.

desconchado, *n.m.* part of wall that has lost its stucco; porcelain that has lost its glaze. — *p.p.* [DESCONCHAR].

desconchar, *v.t.* to strip of glaze, plaster, etc. — *v.r.* to strip off scales or shells.

desconchadura, *n.f.* removal of varnish, stucco, etc.; peeling, scaling.

desconectar, *v.t.* to disconnect, to throw out of gear (motor, steam-engine); to disconnect (the current).

desconfiadamente, *adv.* diffidently, distrustfully.

desconfiado, -da, *a.* diffident, distrustful; jealous. — *p.p.* [DESCONFIAR].

desconfianza, *n.f.* distrust, mistrust; diffidence, jealousy; suspicious fear.

desconfiar, *v.i.* (with *de*) to distrust, mistrust, discredit; to suspect, have no confidence in; to doubt; to have little hope.

desconformar, *v.t.* to dissent, disagree, differ in opinion. — *v.r.* to disagree, be in discord.

desconforme, *a.* discordant, disagreeing, unequal, unlike, contrary.

desconformidad, *n.f.* disagreement, nonconformity, inequality, dissimilitude; unlikeness, disparity; contrariety of opinion.

descongestión, *n.f.* removal of congestion.

descongestionar, *v.t.* to remove or diminish congestion.

descongojar, *v.t.* to relieve anguish, dismay, grief, sorrow.

desconocer, *v.t.* to fail to remember; to forget; to disown, disavow; to disregard, ignore; (*fig.*) to pretend to be unacquainted with; to be ungrateful; *desconocer el beneficio*, not to acknowledge a favour.

desconocidamente, *adv.* ignorantly, unknowingly; ungratefully.

desconocido, -da, *a.* unknown; fameless; nameless; ungrateful, unthankful. — *n.m.f.* stranger. — *p.p.* [DESCONOCER].

desconocimiento, *n.m.* ungratefulness, ingratitude; ignorance.

desconozco; desconozca, *pres. indic.; pres. subj.* [DESCONOCER].

desconsentir, *v.t.* (conjugated like CONSENTIR) to dissent, disagree.

desconsideradamente, *adv.* inconsiderately, rashly.

desconsiderado, -da, *a.* inconsiderate, imprudent, thoughtless, rash.

desconsiderar, *v.t.* to be inconsiderate, rash, reckless.

desconsolación, *n.f.* disconsolateness, grief, affliction.

desconsoladamente, *adv.* inconsolably, disconsolately.

desconsolado, -da, *a.* disconsolate, comfortless, sorrowful, melancholic. — *p.p.* [DESCONSOLAR].

desconsolar, *v.t.* (conjugated like CONSOLAR) to afflict, put in pain; to treat badly or rudely. — *v.r.* to become low-spirited or afflicted.

desconsuelo, *n.m.* affliction, trouble, mournfulness; (*med.*) disorder of the digestive organs.

desconsuelo; desconsuele, *pres. indic.; pres. subj.* [DESCONSOLAR].

descontagiar, *v.t.* to disinfect, purify.

descontar, *v.t.* (conjugated like CONTAR) to discount, deduct, allow, rebate; to abate, lessen, diminish; to detract from merit of someone; to take for granted. — *v.r.* to miscount.

descontentadizo, -za, *a.* discontented, displeased; squeamish, fastidious, particular, easily disgusted.

descontentamiento, *n.m.* discontent, displeasure, grief.

descontentar, *v.t.* to discontent, displease, dissatisfy.

descontento, -ta, *a.* discontent, dissatisfied, displeased; uneasy. — *n.m.* discontent, disgust, dissatisfaction, grumbling; uneasiness.

descontinuación, *n.f.* discontinuance, cessation.

descontinuar, *v.t.* to discontinue, leave off, cease, forbear, suspend.

descontinuo, -nua, *a.* discontinued, disjoined.

desconvenible, *a.* unsuitable; discordant, disagreeing, dissimilar.

desconveniencia, *n.f.* inconvenience, incommodity, disadvantage; discord; disproportion; dissimilitude.

desconveniente, *a.* inconvenient, discordant, incongruous.

desconvenir, *v.i.* (conjugated like CONVENIR) to disagree, be discordant, be unlike, be unsuited for.

desconversable, *a.* unsocial, retiring.

desconvidar, *v.t.* to retract, recall, revoke (an invitation, promise, etc.).

descopar, *v.t.* to lop the branches from a tree.

descorazonadamente, *adv.* dejectedly, spiritlessly, with dismay.

descorazonado, -da, *a.* disheartened, dejected, dispirited. — *p.p.* [DESCORAZONAR].

descorazonamiento, *n.m.* lowness of spirits, depression, dejection.

descorazonar, *v.t.* to tear out the heart; (*fig.*) to dishearten, discourage.

descorchador, *n.m.* uncorker; corkscrew.

descorchar, *v.t.* to decorticate (a cork-tree); to uncork (a bottle); to break open a chest, etc., to steal the contents; to break open a beehive to remove the honey.

descordar, *v.t.* to unstring (an instrument); to kill the bull by stabbing it in the cervix.

descorderar, *v.t.* to wean lambs.

descornar, *v.t.* to dishorn. — *v.r.* (*coll.*) to break one's skull by a fall.

descoronar, *v.t.* to take off the top or crown from anything.

descorrear, *v.i.* to shed off the skin which covers a deer's tenderlings.

descorregido, -da, *a.* incorrigible, incorrect, disarranged; inordinate.

descorrer, *v.t., v.i.* to move backward, run back; to flow (as liquids); *descorrer la cortina*, to draw the curtain.

descorrimiento, *n.m.* flow of any liquid.

descortés, *a.* impolite, uncivil, unmannerly, ill-bred, coarse, impudent, ill-behaved.

descortesía, *n.f.* discourtesy, impoliteness, incivility, churlishness.

descortesmente, *adv.* uncivilly, rudely, discourteously.

descortezador, *n.m.* one who strips off bark; decorticator.

descortezadura, *n.f.; descortezamiento, n.m.* decortication, excortication; bark taken off.

descortezar, *v.t.* (*pret.* descortecé; *pres. subj.* descortece) to strip (bark); to flay (skin); to take crust off bread; to hull or shell (fruit, etc.); (*fig.*) to polish, civilize. — *v.r.* (*coll.*) to become civilized and polite.

descortinar, *v.t.* to destroy the ramparts of a fort.

descosedura, *n.f.* ripping, unseaming.

descoser, *v.t.* to rip, unstitch, unseam; to disjoin, separate; (*naut.*) to unlash; *no descoser los labios*, to keep a profound silence. — *v.r.* to let one's tongue run on.

descosidamente, *adv.* excessively, immoderately.

descosido, -da, *a.* ripped, unseamed, unstitched; disjointed, disconnected; deranged. — *n.m.f.* babbler, idle talker, teller of secrets; heavy drinker; *comer* or *beber como un descosido*, to eat or drink immoderately. — *p.p.* [DESCOSER].

descostarse, *v.r.* to draw away from an object or a coast.

descostillar, *v.t.* to take out the ribs, break the ribs; to thumb someone on the ribs. — *v.r.* to fall violently on one's back.

descostrar, *v.t.* to take off the crust.

descotar, *v.t.* to remove a restriction from the use of a road, boundary or property. — *v.r.* to cut low in the neck (dress, etc.).

descote, *n.m.* décolleté, low-necked (dress).

descoyuntado, -da, *a.* disjointed, disconnected, out of gear. — *p.p.* [DESCOYUNTAR].

descoyuntamiento, *n.m.* dislocation, luxation; pain through over-exertion.

descoyuntar, *v.t.* dislocate, disjoint (bones); (*fig.*) to vex, molest, displease. — *v.r.* to experience a violent motion; *descoyuntarse de risa*, to split one's sides with laughter.

descrecencia, *n.f.* decrement, decreasing.

descrecer, *v.t.*, *v.i.* (conjugated like CRECER) to decrease, diminish, grow less; to fall, subside; to grow short (of days).

descrecimiento, *n.m.* decrease, diminution.

descrédito, *n.m.* discredit, loss of reputation.

descreer, *v.t.* to disbelieve; to deny credit, disown, abjure.

descreído, -da, *a.* incredulous, unbelieving. — *n.m.f.* unbeliever, infidel. — *p.p.* [DESCREER].

descreimiento, *n.m.* infidelity, unbelief, lack of religious faith.

descrestar, *v.t.* to take off the crest or comb; (*Am.*) (*coll.*) to impose upon; to sponge.

descriarse, *v.r.* to weaken, extenuate, pine with anxiety or desire.

describir, *v.t.* (*p.p.* **descrito, descripto**) to draw, delineate, describe; to relate minutely.

descripción, *n.f.* design, sketch, delineation; narration, relation, account, description, word-picture; (*law*) inventory, schedule.

descriptivo, -va, *a.* descriptive.

descripto, -ta, *a.* described. — *p.p. irreg.* [DESCRIBIR].

descriptor, -ra, *n.m.f.*, *a.* (person) describing, narrating.

descrismar, *v.t.* (*coll.*) to give a blow on the head; to remove the chrism. — *v.r.* to lose patience; to lose one's temper.

descristianar, *v.t.* to remove the chrism; (*fig.*) to give a blow.

descrito, -ta, *a.* described. — *p.p. irreg.* [DESCRIBIR].

descruzar, *v.t.* (conjugated like CRUZAR) to uncross.

descuadernar *v.t.* to unbind (books); to discompose, disconcert, disorder. — *v.r.* to get disjointed or loose.

descuadrillado, *n.m.* (*vet.*) sprain in the haunch.

descuadrillado, -da, *a.* separated from the ranks. — *p.p.* [DESCUADRILLAR].

descuadrillarse, *v.r.* to be sprained in the haunches (of animals).

descuajado, -da, *a.* dispirited, disheartened; liquefied. — *p.p.* [DESCUAJAR].

descuajar, *v.t.* to dissolve, liquefy; (*agric.*) to eradicate, grub up; (*fig.*) to dishearten, dispirit.

descuajaringarse, *v.r.* (*coll.*) to be broken down by excessive fatigue (used only hyperbolically).

descuaje, descuajo, *n.m.* (*agric.*) eradication, grubbing up of weeds; clearing ground of underbrush.

descuartelar, *v.t.* (*mil.*) to remove troops from winter quarters; (*naut.*) to unfurl sails.

descuartizamiento, *n.m.* quartering; breaking or cutting in pieces; carving.

descuartizar, *v.t.* (*pret.* **descuarticé**; *pres. subj.* **descuartice**) to quarter; to carve at table.

descubierta, *n.f.* crustless pie; (*mil.*) reconnaissance, reconnoitring; (*naut.*) scanning of the horizon at sunrise and sunset; *a la descubierta*, openly, clearly.

descubiertamente, *adv.* manifestly, openly.

descubierto, -ta, *a.* patent, manifest; bareheaded, unveiled; exposed. — *n.m.* solemn exposition of the Sacrament; discovery; overdraft, shortage, deficiency, deficit. — *p.p.* [DESCUBRIR]; *al descubierto*, openly, manifestly; *en descubierto*, (*com.*) overdrawn; *dejar en descubierto*, to leave others to pay a debt; *estar* or *quedar en descubierto*, to be a defaulter; to have overdrawn an account.

descubretalles, *n.m.* (*slang*) small fan.

descubridero, *n.m.* eminence commanding an extensive view; look-out post.

descubridor, -ra, *n.m.f.* discoverer, finder, descrier, searcher, seeker, investigator; (*mil.*) scout, spy; vessel on a voyage of discovery.

descubrimiento, *n.m.* discovery, find, disclosure; invention; country or thing discovered.

descubrir, *v.t.* (*p.p.* **descubierto**) to discover, disclose, show; to uncover, reveal, make visible, bring to light, expose to view; to communicate, make known; to find out; (*mil.*) to overlook (any position in a fortification); (*eccles.*) to expose the Sacrament to public worship; *descubrir el campo*, (*mil.*) to reconnoitre; *descubrir el cuerpo*, to expose any part of the body; *descubrir su pecho*, to unbosom oneself, tell secrets; *descubrir por la popa* or *proa*, (*naut.*) to descry astern, or ahead; *descubrir la tierra*, (*naut.*) to make the land; *descubrir una vía de agua*, (*naut.*) to discover a leak. — *v.r.* to uncover one's head, take off one's hat to anyone.

descuelgo; descuelgue, *pres. indic.; pres. subj.* [DESCOLGAR].

descuello; descuelle, *pres. indic.; pres. subj.* [DESCOLLAR].

descuello, *n.m.* excessive stature or height; (*fig.*) pre-eminence; superiority, loftiness, haughtiness.

descuento, *n.m.* discount; diminution, decrease; rebate, allowance, deduction.

descuernacabras, *n.m.* cold north wind.

descuerno, *n.m.* (*coll.*) slight, affront.

descuidadamente, *adv.* carelessly, negligently.

descuidado, -da, *a.* careless, negligent; thoughtless, heedless, forgetful, idle, unprepared, inattentive; unaware; slovenly, unclean. — *p.p.* [DESCUIDAR].

descuidar, *v.t.* to neglect, forget, overlook; to relieve from care; to divert the attention of. — *v.i.* to lack attention or diligence; to be careless or neglectful; not to trouble oneself.

— *v.r.* to be forgetful of duty; to put one-self at ease; *descuide Vd.*, put yourself at ease.
descuidero, *n.m.*, *a.* pickpocket.
descuido, *n.m.* carelessness, indolence, neglect, negligence, omission; forgetfulness, want of attention; absent-minded oversight; imprudence; immodesty; incivility, coldness, lack of esteem; *al descuido*, affectedly careless.
descuitado, -da, *a.* living without trouble and care.
descular, *v.t.* to break the bottom or end of anything (such as jar, etc.).
deschuponar, *v.t.* (*agric.*) to strip a tree of its shoots or suckers.
desdar, *v.t.* to turn in the opposite direction; to unwind.
desde, (*contr.* of *de, ex, de*) *prep.* since, after, from, as soon as; *desde allí*, thence, from there, from that time; *desde aquí*, hence, from here, from this place; *desde entonces*, from that time forward, ever since; *desde luego*, thereupon, immediately; certainly; *desde niño*, from one's childhood; *desde que*, since, ever since.
desdecir, *v.i.* (conjugated like DECIR) (with *de*) to degenerate, fall from its kind; to differ from, disagree with; to be unworthy of or unbecoming. — *v.r.* to retract, gainsay, recant.
desdén, *n.m.* disdain, contempt, neglect, slight, scorn; *al desdén*, affectedly careless.
desdeñador, -ra, *n.m.f.* scorner, disdainful person.
desdentado, -da, *a.* toothless. — *n.m.pl.* (*zool.*) edentata. — *p.p.* [DESDENTAR].
desdentar, *v.t.* to draw teeth.
desdeñable, *a.* contemptible, despicable.
desdeñadamente, *adv.* disdainfully, scornfully.
desdeñador, -ra, *n.m.f.*, *a.* scorner, disdainer.
desdeñar, *v.t.* to disdain, scorn; to exasperate, vex. — *v.r.* to be disdainful, reserved; to loathe doing or saying something.
desdeñosamente, *adv.* disdainfully, contemptuously.
desdeñoso, -sa, *a.* disdainful, contemptuous, fastidious.
desdevanar, *v.t.* to unwind or undo a clew.
desdibujado, -da, *a.* (*art*) badly drawn.
desdibujo, *n.m.* faulty sketch.
desdicha, *n.f.* misfortune, calamity; ill-luck; misery, poverty; unhappiness.
desdichadamente, *adv.* unfortunately, unhappily.
desdichado, -da, *a.* unfortunate, unlucky, unhappy, distressed, wretched, miserable, calamitous. — *n.m.f.* sorry creature, wretch; *es un desdichado*, (*coll.*) he is a pitiful creature, good-for-nothing, insignificant fellow.
desdicho, -cha, *p.p. irreg.* [DESDECIR].
desdigo; desdiga, *pres. indic.; pres. subj.* [DESDECIR].
desdinerar, *v.t.* to impoverish a country by exporting its currency.
desdoblar, *v.t.* to unfold, spread open.
desdonado, -da, *a.* graceless, insipid, foolish. — *p.p.* [DESDONAR].
desdonar, *v.t.* to take back a present.
desdorar, *v.t.* to take off the gilt; (*fig.*) to tarnish, sully someone's reputation.
desdoro, *n.m.* dishonour, blemish, blot, stigma.

deseable, *a.* desirable.
deseablemente, *adv.* desirously.
deseador, -ra, *n.m.f.* desirer, wisher.
desear, *v.t.* to desire, covet, wish for, long for.
desecación, *n.f.* exsiccation, desiccation.
desecamiento, *n.m.* desiccation, exsiccation.
desecante, *a.* drying. — *n.m.f.* (*chem.*) dryer, desiccator.
desecar, *v.t.*, *v.r.* (conjugated like SECAR) to dry, desiccate; to stop, detain; to drain.
desecativo, -va, *a.* desiccative, exsiccant. — *n.m.* healing plaster.
desechadamente, *adv.* vilely, despicably.
desechado, -da, *a.* refused, excluded, rejected; outcast. — *p.p.* [DESECHAR].
desechar, *v.t.* to refuse, reject, drive away, expel, exclude; to depreciate, undervalue; to lay aside, cast away, renounce, decline; to put aside sorrow, fear, etc.; to vote down; to unlock, unfasten (of keys); *lo que uno desecha, otro lo ruega*, one man's meat is another man's poison.
desecho, *n.m.* residue, remainder, surplus; refuse, débris, rubbish; offal; disregard, contempt; rejection.
desedificación, *n.f.* scandal, evil example.
desedificar, *v.t.* (conjugated like EDIFICAR) to set a bad example, scandalize.
desejecutar, *v.t.* (*law*) to raise a sequestration or seizure.
deselectrizar, *v.t.* (*elec.*) to discharge (battery, etc.).
deselladura, *n.f.* unsealing, taking off the seals.
desellar, *v.t.* to unseal, open (a letter).
desembalaje, *n.m.* unpacking, opening of bales.
desembalar, *v.t.* to unpack, open bales of goods.
desembaldosar, *v.t.* to unpave, take away tiles or flagstones.
desembanastar, *v.t.* to take out the contents of a basket; (*fig.*) to talk at random; (*coll.*) to draw the sword. — *v.r.* to break out, break loose (of penned animals); (*coll.*) to alight from a carriage.
desembarazadamente, *adv.* freely, without embarrassment.
desembarazado, -da, *a.* free, disengaged, clear, open, unrestrained; *modales desembarazados*, easy manners. — *p.p.* [DESEMBARAZAR].
desembarazar, *v.t.* (conjugated like EMBARAZAR) to disembarrass, ease, free, disengage; to remove an impediment, clear, extricate, disencumber, expedite. — *v.r.* to get out of difficulties; to overcome embarrassments.
desembarazo, *n.m.* disembarrassment, disencumbrance, freedom to act, liberty, ease; disengagement; extrication, forwardness.
desembarcadero, *n.m.* landing-place; quay, dock; platform.
desembarcado, -da, *p.p.* [DESEMBARCAR].
desembarcar, *v.t.* (conjugated like EMBARCAR) to unship, put on shore, unload; disembark. — *v.i.* to land, go on shore; to alight; (*naut.*) to cease being a member of a ship's crew; to end at a landing (of a staircase).
desembarco, *n.m.* disembarkation, unshipment; landing (of stairs); hostile landing.
desembargadamente, *adv.* freely, easily, without obstacle.

desembargador, *n.m.* chief magistrate and privy councillor in Portugal.

desembargar, *v.t.* (conjugated like EMBARCAR) to remove impediments, clear away obstructions; (*law*) to raise an embargo or sequestration.

desembargo, *n.m.* (*law*) raising an embargo.

desembarque, *n.m.* landing, disembarkation.

desembarrancar, *v.t.* to refloat a stranded ship.

desembarrar, *v.t.* to clear a thing from mud or clay.

desembaular, *v.t.* to empty a trunk, bag, etc.; (*fig.*) to speak one's mind freely.

desembebecerse, *v.r.* (conjugated like EMBEBECER) to recover the use of one's senses.

desembelesarse, *v.r.* to recover from amazement.

desembocadero, *n.m.;* **desembocadura,** *n.f.* mouth of a river, canal, etc.; exit, outlet.

desembocar, *v.i.* (conjugated like EMBOCAR) to disembogue, flow out at the mouth of a river; to end (at), lead (to); *desembocar la calle,* to go from one street into another.

desembojar, *v.t.* to remove cocoons of the silkworm from the southern-wood.

desembolsar, *v.t.* to empty a purse, disburse, expend, lay out.

desembolso, *n.m.* disbursement, expenditure.

desemborrachar, *v.t.* to make sober, cure of intoxication. — *v.r.* to grow sober.

desemboscarse, *v.r.* to get out of the woods; to get clear of an ambuscade.

desembotar, *v.t.* to remove dullness (from a tool, etc.); to sharpen one's wits.

desembozar, *v.t.* (conjugated like EMBOZAR) to unmuffle, uncover the face; (*fig.*) to show one's true colours.

desembozo, *n.m.* uncovering the face.

desembragar, *v.t.* (conjugated like EMBRAGAR) to unbind from the cable; (*mech.*) to ungear, disconnect; to declutch (the engine of a motor-car).

desembravecer, *v.t.* (conjugated like EMBRAVECER) to domesticate, tame.

desembravecimiento, *n.m.* taming, reclaiming from wildness.

desembrazar, *v.t.* (conjugated like ABRAZAR) to take something from the arms; to dart or throw weapons.

desembriagado, -da, *p.p.* ([DESEMBRIAGAR] recovered from intoxication.

desembriagar, *v.t.* (conjugated like EMBRIAGAR) to make sober, cure of intoxication. — *v.r.* to recover from drunkenness, grow sober.

desembridar, *v.t.* to unbridle a horse.

desembrollar, *v.t.* to unravel, clear, disentangle, extricate, disembroil.

desembuchar, *v.t.* to disgorge (said of birds); (*fig.*) to disclose one's secrets.

desemejante, *a.* dissimilar, unlike.

desemejantemente, *adv.* dissimilarly.

desemejanza, *n.f.* dissimilitude, unlikeness, dissimilarity.

desemejar, *v.i.* to be dissimilar or unlike. — *v.t.* to disfigure, deform.

desempacar, *v.t.* (conjugated like EMPACAR) to unpack. — *v.r.* to grow calm, be appeased.

desempachar, *v.t.* to disembarrass; to make the stomach disgorge undigested food. — *v.r.* to grow bold; to put in order, clear up.

desempacho, *n.m.* ease, forwardness.

desempalagar, *v.t.*, *v.r.* (conjugated like EMPALAGAR) to clean the palate, restore the appetite, remove nausea. — *v.t.* to clear a mill-stream of stagnant water.

desempañar, *v.t.* to clean a tarnished looking-glass; to remove swaddling-clothes from children.

desempapelar, *v.t.* to unwrap, unfold anything wrapped up in paper; to strip a wall of paper.

desempaquetar, *v.t.* to unpack, open a packet.

desemparejar, *v.t.* to unmatch, make things unequal or uneven. — *v.i.* to part, be separated.

desemparentado, -da, *a.* without relatives.

desemparvar, *v.t.* to gather threshed corn in heaps.

desempatar, *v.t.* to make unequal; to decide a tied election; to play, run, shoot, etc. off a tie.

desempedrar, *v.t.* (conjugated like EMPEDRAR) to unpave; (*fig.*) to frequent or haunt a place; to beat about a spot; *ir desempedrando la calle,* (*coll.*) to go very rapidly.

desempegar, *v.t.* (conjugated like PEGAR) to unglue; to take off pitch.

desempeñado, -da, *a.* free or clear of debt. — *p.p.* [DESEMPEÑAR].

desempeñar, *v.t.* to redeem, discharge from mortgage or pawn; to clear, disengage, free from debt; to discharge an office or a duty; to act (a part in a play); to free from obligation; to disengage from a difficulty. — *v.r.* to extricate oneself from debt; (*taurom.*) to disengage oneself from a bull's attack; (*naut.*) to stand off shore.

desempeño, *n.m.* redeeming a pledge; proof or confirmation of a statement; performance, fulfilment, discharge, completion; acting of a part.

desemperezar, *v.i.* (conjugated like EMPEREZAR) to shake off laziness.

desempernar, *v.t.* to take out bolts or spikes.

desempobrecerse, *v.r.* (conjugated like EMPOBRECER) to extricate oneself from poverty.

desempolvar, desempolvorar, *v.t.* to dust.

desempolvoradura, *n.f.* dusting.

desemponzoñar, *v.t.* to cure from the effects of poison; to free from poison.

desempotrar, *v.t.* to remove supports, stays or props.

desempulgadura, *n.f.* unbending of a bow.

desempulgar, *v.t.* (*pret.* **desempulgué;** *pres. subj.* **desempulgue**) to unbend a bow.

desenalbardar, *v.t.* to take off a packsaddle.

desenamorar, *v.t.* to destroy love or affection. — *v.r.* to lose love or affection.

desenastar, *v.t.* to take the handle from.

desencabalgar, *v.t.* (conjugated like CABALGAR) to dismount cannon.

desencabestradura, *n.f.* disentangling of a beast from the halter.

desencabestrar, *v.t.* to disentangle a beast from the halter.

desencadenar, *v.t.* to unchain; to free, liberate; (*fig.*) to dissolve all connexion. — *v.r.* to break loose; to become infuriated, lose self-control; to break out with fury (storm, rain, etc.).

desencajado, -da, *a.* looking very ill. — *p.p.* [DESENCAJAR].

desencajadura, *n.f.* unjointing, disconnexion.

desencajamiento, desencaje, *n.m.* disjointedness, luxation.

desencajar, *v.t.* to disjoint, unjoin, disconnect, put out of place or gear; to luxate; to disarticulate; to disfigure. — *v.r.* to change countenance, look ill, out of sorts, etc.; to get out of gear.

desencajonar, *v.t.* to unpack a box; (*taurom.*) to remove bulls from the travelling boxes.

desencalabrinar, *v.t.* to remove dizziness; to free from stupidity; to remove wrong impressions.

desencalcar, *v.t.* (conjugated like CALCAR) to loosen what was caked or stuck.

desencallar, *v.t.* to refloat a stranded ship.

desencaminar, *v.t.* to misguide, lead astray. — *v.r.* to lose one's way, go astray, deviate from virtue.

desencantamiento, *n.m.* disenchantment.

desencantar, *v.t.* to disenchant, disillusion, break a spell.

desencantaración, *n.f.* act and effect of drawing of lots.

desencantarar, *v.t.* to draw lots for a candidate; to withdraw a name on account of legal incapacity.

desencanto, *n.m.* disenchantment, disillusion.

desencapillar, *v.t.* (*naut.*) to unrig.

desencapotadura, *n.f.* act of stripping off a cloak.

desencapotar, *v.t.* to strip someone of a coat; (*coll.*) to uncover, reveal, make clear; to raise and keep up the head of a horse. — *v.r.* to put aside severity, assume a pleasing expression; *desencapotarse el cielo,* to clear up.

desencaprichar, *v.t.* to dissuade from error, cure of conceit. — *v.r.* to desist, yield, get over a whim; to give up a hobby or mania.

desencarcelar, *v.t.* to release, set at liberty.

desencarecer, *v.t.* (conjugated like CARECER) to lower the price.

desencarnar, *v.t.* to prevent dogs from eating game; (*fig.*) to lose an affection for anything.

desencastar, *v.t.* to cause a race to deteriorate; to cause to lose caste.

desencastillar, *v.t.* to expel, drive from a castle; to manifest, discover, reveal; (*fig.*) to deprive of power or favour.

desencepar, *v.t.* (*naut.*) to clear the anchor.

desencerrar, *v.t.* (conjugated like CERRAR) to free from confinement; to unclose, open, disclose.

desencintar, *v.t.* to loosen, untie, take off ribbons; to remove the kerb of a pavement.

desenclavar, *v.t.* to draw out nails; (*fig.*) to put someone violently out of his place.

desenclavijar, *v.t.* to take pins or pegs out of a musical instrument.

desencoger, *v.t.* (conjugated like COGER) to unfold. — *v.r.* to grow bold.

desencogimiento, *n.m.* freedom from perplexity, naturalness, ease.

desencoladura, *n.f.* ungluing.

desencolar, *v.t.*, *v.r.* to unglue.

desencolerizarse, *v.r.* to grow calm; to be appeased.

desenconar, *v.t.* to remove an inflammation; (*fig.*) to moderate one's passion; to make mild. — *v.r.* to become milder, be appeased, forget one's wrongs.

desencono, *n.m.* mitigating of anger or passion.

desencordar, *v.t.* (conjugated like ACORDAR) (*mus.*) to unstring; to loosen strings.

desencordelar, *v.t.* to loosen, untie, take away strings or cords.

desencorvar, *v.t.* to straighten, unbend, untwist, unwarp.

desencrespar, *v.t.* to uncurl.

desencrudecer, *v.t.* (conjugated like ENCRUDECER) to prepare silk or thread for dye; to clean fabrics.

desencuadernar, *v.t.* to unbind, remove binding.

desendemoniar, desendiablar, *v.t.* to exorcise, drive out an evil spirit.

desendiosar, *v.t.* to humble vanity.

desenfadaderas, *n.f.pl.* means of avoiding a difficulty; *tener desenfadaderas,* (*coll.*) to be able to get oneself out of difficulties.

desenfadado, -da, *a.* free, gay, joyful, unembarrassed; wide, spacious. — *p.p.* [DESENFADAR].

desenfadar, *v.t.* to abate, appease (anger or passion). — *v.r.* to calm down; to be entertained, amused.

desenfado, *n.m.* freedom, facility, ease, calmness; relaxation, diversion (of the spirit or mind).

desenfaldar, *v.t.* to let fall the train of a gown.

desenfangar, *v.t.* to clean, cleanse of mud or filth.

desenfardar, desenfardelar, *v.t.* to unpack bales of goods.

desenfilar, *v.t.* to cover from flank fire; to defilade.

desenfrailar, *v.i.* to leave the monastic life; (*coll.*) to come out from subjection; (*coll.*) to rest for a time (from business, etc.).

desenfrenadamente, *adv.* ungovernably, licentiously.

desenfrenado, -da, *a.* ungoverned, unbridled, licentious, outrageous, wanton. — *p.p.* [DESENFRENAR].

desenfrenamiento, *n.m.* unruliness, rashness; licentiousness; wantonness.

desenfrenar, *v.t.* to unbridle. — *v.r.* to fly into a violent passion; to give rein to one's passions and desires.

desenfreno, *n.m.* unruliness, wantonness; *desenfreno de vientre,* diarrhœa.

desenfundar, *v.t.* to take out of a bag, pillowcase, scabbard, etc.; *desenfundar la espada,* to draw the sword.

desenfurecerse, *v.r.* to grow calm, put aside anger.

desengalanar, *v.t.* to remove ornaments.

desenganchar, *v.t.* to unhook; to take down from a hook; to unharness; to uncouple; to disengage; to unhitch.

desenganche, *n.m.* taking out (horses from a carriage).

desengañadamente, *adv.* truly, clearly, ingenuously; (*fig.*) awkwardly, carelessly, scurvily.

desengañado, -da, *a.* undeceived, disabused; schooled by experience; (*obs.*) despicable, ill-executed. — *p.p.* [DESENGAÑAR].

desengañador, -ra, *n.m.f.* undeceiver.

desengañar, *v.t.* to undeceive, disabuse, set right; to discourage; to disillusion.

desengañilar, *v.t.* to free a person or animal clutched by the throat.

desengaño, *n.m.* detection of error; disillusion, undeceiving; censure, warning, reproof, reproach, upbraiding; (*coll.*) the naked truth. — *pl.* bitter lessons of experience.

desengarrafar, *v.t.* to disengage from claws or clutching fingers.

desengarzar, *v.t.* to loosen from clasps, links or hooks; (*jewel.*) to take out of a setting.

desengastar, *v.t.* to take a jewel from its setting.

desengomar, *v.t.* to ungum, unsize.

desengoznar, *v.t.* to disjoint, unhinge.

desengranar, *v.t.* to uncog, ungear, uncouple, disengage. — *v.r.* to get out of gear.

desengrane, *n.m.* disengaging of gear.

desengrasador, *n.m.* wringing machine; scourer; grease-rag.

desengrasar, *v.t.* to scour, take off the grease. — *v.i.* (*coll.*) to become thin, lose weight.

desengrase, *n.m.* removal of grease; scouring.

desengrilletar, *v.t.* (*naut.*) to knock off a coupling link of a chain.

desengrosar, *v.t.* (conjugated like ENGROSAR) to extenuate, debilitate, make lean; to thin or fine. — *v.i.* to grow thin.

desengrudamiento, *n.m.* rubbing off of cement or paste.

desengrudar, *v.t.* to scrape or rub off paste.

desengrueso; **desengruese**, *pres. indic.; pres. subj.* [DESENGROSAR].

desenhebrar, *v.t.* to unthread, unravel; (*fig.*) to explain.

desenhornar, *v.t.* to take out of the oven.

desenjaezar, *v.t.* (conjugated like ENJAEZAR) to unharness, unsaddle.

desenjalmar, *v.t.* to remove a packsaddle from mules or horses.

desenjaular, *v.t.* to uncage; (*slang*) to set free or move from jail.

desenjecutar, *v.t.* (*law*) to raise a sequestration or seizure.

desenlabonar, *v.t.* [DESLABONAR].

desenlace, *n.m.* (*theat.*) catastrophe (of a play or dramatic poem); dénouement; conclusion, end, unravelling.

desenladrillar, *v.t.* to take up bricks or tiles from a floor.

desenlazar, *v.t.* to unlace, untie, loose, unravel (a dramatic plot).

desenlodar, *v.t.* to remove, clean off mud.

desenlosar, *v.t.* to unpave, take up the flagstones of a floor.

desenlutar, *v.t.* to leave off mourning garments; to banish sorrow.

desenmallar, *v.t.* to take fish out of the net.

desenmarañar, *v.t.* to disentangle, separate, unravel (as the threads of a skein); (*fig.*) to extricate; to explain.

desenmascarar, *v.t.* to unmask; (*fig.*) to expose, lay bare, reveal.

desenmohecer, *v.t.* (conjugated like ENMOHECER) to clear from rust.

desenmudecer, *v.t.* (conjugated like ENMUDECER) to remove an impediment of speech. — *v.i.*, *v.r.* to break a long silence.

desenojar, *v.t.* to appease anger, allay passion. — *v.r.* to amuse or enjoy oneself; (*coll.*) to make friends.

desenojo, *n.m.* appeasement, getting over anger, reconciliation.

desenojoso, -sa, *a.* appeasing, reconciling.

desenredar, *v.t.* to disentangle, extricate,

clear, loose; (*fig.*) to put in order. — *v.r.* to extricate oneself from difficulties.

desenredo, *n.m.* disentanglement; (*poet.*) catastrophe, dénouement (of a play or poem).

desenrollar, *v.t.* to unroll, unwind.

desenronar, *v.t.* (*prov.*) to remove débris.

desenronquecer, *v.t.* to free from hoarseness.

desenroscar, *v.t.* (conjugated like ENROSCAR) to untwist.

desensabanar, *v.t.* (*coll.*) to change sheets.

desensamblar, *v.t.* (*carp.*) to disjoint, separate.

desensañar, *v.t.* to pacify, appease.

desensartar, *v.t.* to unthread, unstring (beads, etc.).

desensebar, *v.t.* to strip of fat. — *v.i.* to leave off work for a time; to change for a better job; to take away the taste of fat (with fruit, etc.).

desenseñar, *v.t.* to correct a wrong teaching or doctrine.

desensillar, *v.t.* to unsaddle.

desensoberbecerse, *v.r.* (conjugated like ENSOBERBECER) to moderate one's pride, be humbled.

desensortijado, -da, *a.* uncurled; dislocated, displaced.

desentablar, *v.t.* to rip up planks or boards; (*fig.*) to disturb, discompose, disarrange, confuse; to embroil; to break off a bargain; to interrupt friendly intercourse.

desentalingar, *v.t.* to free the chain of the anchor.

desentarimar, *v.t.* to remove a platform or stand.

desentarquinar, *v.t.* to clear out (a ditch, etc.).

desentenderse, *v.r.* (conjugated like ENTENDER) to feign not to understand; to pass by a thing without taking notice of it; to shirk.

desentendido, -da, *a.* unmindful, pretending ignorance; *hacerse el desentendido, darse por desentendido*, (*coll.*) to wink at, pretend not to have noticed a thing. — *p.p.* [DESENTENDERSE].

desenterrador, *n.m.* one who disinters or digs up.

desenterramiento, *n.m.* disinterment, exhumation; (*fig.*) unearthing, recollection.

desenterrar, *v.t.* (conjugated like ENTERRAR) to disinter, unbury, dig up, exhume, unearth; (*fig.*) to recall long-forgotten things; *desenterrar los muertos*, to slander the dead.

desentiendo; desentienda, *pres. indic.; pres. subj.* [DESENTENDERSE].

desentierramuertos, *n.m.* calumniator of the dead.

desentoldar, *v.t.* to take away an awning; (*fig.*) to strip of ornaments.

desentonación, *n.f.* dissonance, false tune.

desentonadamente, *adv.* unharmoniously.

desentonado, -da, *a.* out of tune, discordant, raucous. — *p.p.* [DESENTONAR].

desentonamiento, *n.m.* dissonance; exaggeration of tone (in the voice).

desentonar, *v.t.* to humble; to wound someone's pride. — *v.i.* (*mus.*) to be out of tune. — *v.r.* to be rude, uncouth, coarse in manner; to raise the voice in disrespect.

desentono, *n.m.* discord; harsh tone, rude tone, false note; (*fig.*) violent disrespect.

desentornillar, *v.t.* to unscrew.

desentorpecer, *v.t.* (conjugated like ENTOR-

PECER) to free from torpor, restore motion to torpid limbs. — *v.r.* to be freed from torpor; to become smart, pert, lively.

desentramparse, *v.r.* to get out of debt.

desentrañado, -da, *a.* disembowelled; (*fig.*) cruel, callous; without charity or humanity. — *p.p.* [DESENTRAÑAR].

desentrañamiento, *n.m.* giving away one's all.

desentrañar, *v.t.* to eviscerate, disembowel; (*fig.*) to penetrate into hidden or difficult matters; (*naut.*) to remove loops or twists from ropes. — *v.r.* (*fig.*) to give away one's fortune for love.

desentristecer, *v.t.* (conjugated like ENTRISTECER) to banish grief, sadness.

desentronizar, *v.t.* (conjugated like ENTRONIZAR) to dethrone.

desentumecer, desentumir, *v.t.* to restore motion to numbed limbs. — *v.r.* to be freed from numbness.

desenvainar, *v.t.* to unsheathe; (*coll.*) to expose to view; (*fig.*) to stretch out the claws or talons.

desenvelejar, *v.t.* to strip a vessel of sails.

desenvendar, *v.t.* to take off fillets or bands.

desenvenenar, *v.t.* to extract, remove or destroy poison.

desenvergar, *v.t.* (conjugated like ENVERGAR) to unbend a sail.

desenviolar, *v.t.* to purify a desecrated place.

desenvoltura, *n.f.* sprightliness, grace, ease; graceful and easy delivery in acting, etc.; assurance, impudence; lewd posture or gesture in women; effrontery, boldness, forwardness.

desenvolvedor, -ra, *n.m.f.* unfolder, investigator.

desenvolver, *v.t.* (conjugated like ENVOLVER) to unfold, unwrap, unroll; (*fig.*) to decipher, discover, unravel; (*fig.*) to develop (a theme); to evolve; to grow. — *v.r.* to be forward; behave with more assurance.

desenvolvimiento, *n.m.* unfolding, development, evolution.

desenvueltamente, *adv.* impudently; licentiously; expeditiously, in a free and easy way.

desenvuelto, -ta, *a.* forward, impudent; licentious; quick, expeditious, free and easy. — *p.p.* [DESENVOLVER].

desenzarzar, *v.t.* to disentangle from brambles; (*coll.*) to appease, reconcile.

deseo, *n.m.* desire, wish, mind, liking, lust, longing; *a medida del deseo*, according to one's wish; *coger a deseo*, to attain something vehemently desired; *tener deseo de*, *venir en deseo de*, to desire; *vienes a deseo*, *huélesme a poleo*, the welcome guest is well received.

deseoso, -sa, *a.* desirous, longing, greedy, eager.

desequido, -da, *a.* too dry.

desequilibrado, -da, *a.* foolish, senseless; unbalanced. — *n.m.f.* unbalanced person. — *p.p.* [DESEQUILIBRAR].

desequilibrar, *v.t.* to unbalance.

desequilibrio, *n.m.* unbalance; disorder; mental disorder.

deserción, *n.f.* desertion; (*law*) abandonment of a suit by the appellant.

deserrado, -da, *a.* free from error.

desertar, *v.t.* to desert; to quit company; (*law*) to abandon a cause. — *v.r.* (with *de*) to desert; *desertar a*, to go over to.

desertor, -ra, *n.m.f.* deserter; renegade.

deservicio, *n.m.* disservice; fault committed against a person who has a claim to service.

deservidor, *n.m.* he who fails in serving another.

deservir, *v.t.* (conjugated like SERVIR) to disserve, serve badly, not to perform one's duty.

desescamar, *v.t.* to scale, remove scales.

desescombrar, *v.t.* to remove rubbish.

deseslabonar, *v.t.* to cut the links of a chain.

desespaldar, *v.t.* to wound the shoulder.

desespaldillar, *v.t.* to wound in the shoulder-blade.

desesperación, *n.f.* despondency, despair, desperation; fury, passion, anger; *es una desesperación*, (*coll.*) it's intolerable.

desesperadamente, *adv.* despairingly, madly, desperately, hopelessly, furiously.

desesperado, -da, *a.* desperate, despairing, hopeless; furious, raving mad. — *n.m.f.* desperate, despairing person. — *p.p.* [DESESPERAR].

desesperante, *a.* causing despair, maddening.

desesperanza, *n.f.* despair; hopelessness; frenzy.

desesperanzar, *v.t.* (conjugated like ESPERANZAR) to deprive of hope; to discourage. — *v.r.* to lose hope, despair.

desesperar, *v.i.* to despair, lose hope. — *v.t.* to cause to despair, deprive of hope. — *v.r.* to despair utterly; to despond; to fret, be troubled; to be grievously vexed.

desespigar, *v.t.* (conjugated like ESPIGAR) to thresh grain.

desestancar, *v.t.* (conjugated like ESTANCAR) to abolish a monopoly.

desestañar, *v.t.* to remove tin from something, unsolder.

desesterar, *v.t.* to take up mats.

desestero, *n.m.* act of taking up mats and the time for doing it.

desestima, *n.f.* disesteem, disrespect; (*law*) rejection of a petition.

desestimación, *n.f.* disrespect, lack of esteem.

desestimador, -ra, *a.* contemning, despising. — *n.m.f.* contemner, despiser.

desestimar, *v.t.* to disregard, contemn, undervalue; to reject, deny.

desestivar, *v.t.* (*naut.*) to alter the stowage.

desfacedor, *n.m.* (*obs.*) destroyer; *desfacedor de tuertos* or *entuertos*, undoer of injuries.

desfacer, *v.t.* (*obs.*) [DESHACER].

desfacimiento, *n.m.* (*obs.*) destruction, undoing.

desfachatado, -da, *a.* (*coll.*) shameless, impudent, barefaced.

desfachatez, *n.f.* (*coll.*) impudence, effrontery, cheek.

desfajar, *v.t.* to ungird.

desfalcador, -ra, *a.* embezzling. — *n.m.f.* embezzler.

desfalcar, *v.t.* (*pret.* **desfalqué**; *pres. subj.* **desfalque**) to lop, cut off; to peculate, embezzle.

desfalco, *n.m.* diminution, diminishing, detracting; embezzlement, defalcation, peculation.

desfallecer, *v.i.* (conjugated like FALLECER) to pine, fall away; to swoon, faint. — *v.t.* to debilitate, weaken.

desfalleciente, *a.* pining, languishing.

[322]

desfallecimiento, *n.m.* languor; fainting; dejection of mind.

desfallezco; desfallezca, *pres. indic.; pres. subj.* [DESFALLECER].

desfavor, *n.m.* (*obs.*) [DISFAVOR].

desfavorable, *a.* unfavourable, contrary.

desfavorablemente, *adv.* unfavourably.

desfavorecedor, -ra, *n.m.f.* disfavourer, contemner.

desfavorecer, *v.t.* (conjugated like FAVORECER) to disfavour, discountenance; to despise, contemn; to injure, hurt; to contradict, oppose.

desfiguración, *n.f.; * **desfiguramiento,** *n.m.* deformation, disfiguration.

desfigurar, *v.t.* to disfigure, deform, misshape; to disguise (as the voice); (*fig.*) to darken, cloud; to misstate, misrepresent. — *v.r.* to become disfigured.

desfijar, *v.t.* to unsettle, remove, take off, pull off.

desfilachar, *v.t.* to ravel [DESHILACHAR].

desfilada, *n.f.* (*mil.*) single file.

desfiladero, *n.m.* defile, narrow passage; road skirting a precipice.

desfilar, *v.i.* (*mil.*) to defile, march by files, file past, file off; to march past in a review.

desfile, *n.m.* (*mil.*) defiling, march past.

desflaquecer, *v.t.* [ENFLAQUECER].

desflecar, *v.t.* (*pret.* **desflequé;** *pres. subj.* **desfleque**) to remove flakes from fabric.

desflegmación, *n.f.* (*chem.*) rectification, purification.

desflemar, *v.t.* (*chem.*) to rectify; to brag, boast.

desfloración, *n.f.* defloration.

desfloramiento, *n.m.* violation, rape.

desflorar, *v.t.* to pull up, cut off flowers; to deflower, violate; to tarnish, sully, stain; to write or speak superficially.

desflorecer, *v.i.* to lose the flower, wither.

desflorecimiento, *n.m.* falling of flowers.

desfogar, *v.t.* (*pret.* **desfogué;** *pres. subj.* **desfogue**) give vent to, emit fire; (*fig.*) to vent one's anger. — *v.i.* (*naut.*) to break in rain or wind (of a storm).

desfogonar, *v.t.* to widen or burst the vent of a cannon.

desfogue, *n.m.* venting or outburst of passion.

desfollonar, *v.t.* to strip off useless leaves or prune.

desfondar, *v.t.* to take the bottom off a vessel; (*naut.*) to break, pierce, penetrate the bottom of a ship; (*agric.*) to dig, plough deeply.

desformar, *v.t.* to disfigure, deform.

desfortalecer, *v.t.* to dismantle, demolish the works of a fortress.

desforzarse, *v.r.* to take revenge.

desfosforar, *v.t.* to dephosphorize.

desfrenar, *v.t.* to unbridle [DESENFRENAR].

desfrutar, *v.t.* to pick fruit while still green.

desgaire, *n.m.* graceless mien; slovenliness; gesture indicating scorn or contempt; *al desgaire,* affectedly careless.

desgajadura, *n.f.* disruption; tearing off the branches of a tree.

desgajar, *v.t.* to lop off the branches of trees; to break in pieces. — *v.r.* to be separated, disjointed, torn off; *desgajarse el cielo* or *las nubes,* to rain excessively.

desgaje, *n.m.* act of tearing off.

desgalgadero, *n.m.* rugged, precipitous place.

desgalgado, -da, *a.* precipitated; light; thin. — *p.p.* [DESGALGAR].

desgalgar, *v.t.* (*pret.* **desgalgué;** *pres. subj.* **desgalgue**) to precipitate, throw down headlong.

desgalichado, -da, *a.* (*coll.*) ungainly, ungraceful.

desgana, *n.f.* want of appetite; aversion, repugnance, reluctance.

desganar, *v.t.* to dissuade, disillusion. — *v.r.* to lose the appetite; to lose interest; to become reluctant or unwilling.

desganchar, *v.t.* to lop off the branches of trees.

desgañifarse, desgañitarse, *v.r.* (*coll.*) to shriek, scream, bawl.

desgarbado, -da, *a.* ungraceful, inelegant, ungainly.

desgarbo, *n.m.* clumsiness.

desgargantarse, *v.r.* (*coll.*) to scream oneself hoarse; to become hoarse from bawling or screaming.

desgargolar, *v.t.* to ripple (as flax or hemp); to take a board or stave from a groove.

desgaritar, *v.i., v.r.* (*naut.*) to lose the course. — *v.r.* (*fig.*) to give up a plan, design or undertaking; to go astray from a fold (of sheep), stray.

desgarradamente, *adv.* impudently; shamelessly, barefacedly.

desgarrado, -da, *a.* licentious, dissolute; shameless, impudent, bold. — *p.p.* [DESGARRAR].

desgarrador, -ra, *a.* tearing; heart-breaking, heart-rending. — *n.m.f.* tearer

desgarradura, *n.f.* rent, laceration, break.

desgarrar, *v.t.* to rend, tear, claw; to expectorate. — *v.r.* to withdraw from company, retire; to lead a licentious life.

desgarro, *n.m.* laceration, rent, break, breach; effrontery, impudence; looseness, criminal levity; fanfaronade, rodomontade, idle boasting, bragging.

desgarrón, *n.m.* large rent or hole [DESGARRO]; piece of cloth torn off.

desgastar, *v.t.* to consume, waste by degrees; to wear away, eat away, corrode, gnaw. — *v.r.* to ruin oneself, weaken oneself; to lose strength and vigour.

desgaste, *n.m.* slow waste, attrition; wear and tear; fraying.

desgatar, *v.t.* to root out the rest-harrow.

desgaznatarse, *v.r.* to shriek, scream.

desglosar, *v.t.* to blot out a note or comment; to separate sheets from a book or document.

desglose, *n.m.* act of blotting out a comment or gloss.

desgobernado, -da, *a.* ill-governed, ill-regulated; ungovernable. — *p.p.* [DESGOBERNAR].

desgobernadura, *n.f.* (*vet.*) placing a ligature on a vein of a horse's leg.

desgobernar, *v.t.* (conjugated like GOBERNAR) to disturb or overset the government; to misgovern; to dislocate, disjoint (as bones); (*vet.*) to place ligatures on the vein of a horse's leg; (*naut.*) to deviate, veer from the right course. — *v.r.* to make ridiculous motions in dancing.

desgobierno, *n.m.* mismanagement; misgovernment, misrule; maladministration of public affairs; (*vet.*) applying ligatures to a vein on a horse's leg.

desgolletar, *v.t.* to break the neck of a vessel; to loosen the collar; to give a décolleté cut to a woman's dress.

desgomar, *v.t.* to ungum, unsize (silk fabrics).

desgonzar, *v.t.* to unhinge.

desgorrarse, *v.r.* to pull off one's hat or cap.

desgoznar, *v.t.* to unhinge, disjoint. — *v.r.* to be dislocated, disjointed, torn in pieces; to distort the body with violent motions.

desgracia, *n.f.* misfortune, mishap; affliction, bereavement, sorrow, grief; enmity, unfriendly attitude; disgrace; lack of grace, ungracefulness; (*obs.*) illness, indisposition; unpleasantness, rudeness in manner or speech; *caer en desgracia,* (*coll.*) to be disgraced, out of favour; *correr con desgracia,* to be unfortunate in a design or undertaking; *hacerse sin desgracia (una cosa),* to be performed (something) without a hitch; *por desgracia,* unfortunately, unhappily.

desgraciadamente, *adv.* unfortunately, unhappily.

desgraciado, -da, *a.* unhappy, luckless, unfortunate, unlucky, miserable; out of favour, hapless; disagreeable, lacking grace; ungrateful; *estar uno desgraciado,* to be wrong, mistaken, unwise. — *n.m.f.* wretch, unfortunate or destitute person; *para los desgraciados se hizo la horca,* give a dog a bad name and hang him. — *p.p.* [DESGRACIAR].

desgraciar, *v.t.* to displease, disgust; to spoil, maim. — *v.r.* to fall out with someone; to degenerate; to lose one's former perfection; to become crippled; to die young, have an untimely end; to fail; to fall through (of a project).

desgramar, *v.t.* to pull up panic-grass by the root.

desgranador, -ra, *n.m.f.* sheller, thresher; flail.

desgranamiento, *n.m.* (*artill.*) grooves formed in the gun-barrel and venthole by the expanding force of powder.

desgranar, *v.t.* to shake out grain from ears of corn, etc.; to thresh, flail; to kill; to scatter about. — *v.r.* to scatter (of beads); to shed (of grain); (*mil.*) to wear away (applied to the vent or bore of fire-arms).

desgrane, *n.m.* shelling of grain; picking off of grapes.

desgranzar, *v.t.* to separate chaff from grain; (*art*) to give the first grinding to colours.

desgrasar, *v.t.* to remove grease.

desgrase, *n.m.* removal of grease.

desgravar, *v.t.* to reduce customs tariff.

desgreñar, *v.t.* to dishevel the hair; to discompose, disturb. — *v.r.* to quarrel, to pull each other's hair.

desguace, *n.m.* breaking up a ship.

desguarnecer, *v.t.* (conjugated like GUARNECER) to strip of trimmings; to dismantle, immobilize; to unharness; to disgarnish; to disarm.

desguarnezco; desguarnezca, *pres. indic.; pres. subj.* [DESGUARNECER].

desguarnir, *v.t.* (*naut.*) to remove rope, chain, etc. from a capstan or set of pulleys.

desguazar, *v.t.* to hew timber with an axe; (*naut.*) to break up; to take a ship to pieces.

desguince, *n.m.* knife which cuts rags in paper-mills; (*fenc.*) twist of the body to escape a thrust.

desguindar, *v.t.* (*naut.*) to lower anything that is hoisted, bring down from aloft. — *v.r.* to slide down by a rope.

desguinzar, *v.t.* to cut cloth or rags (in paper-mills).

deshabitado, -da, *a.* uninhabited, deserted, untenanted. — *p.p.* [DESHABITAR].

deshabitar, *v.t.* to leave, move out of a house; to depopulate, unpeople.

deshabituación, *n.f.* disuse, disusage, desuetude.

deshabituar, *v.t.* to disaccustom, disuse, destroy the force of habit.

deshacedor, *n.m.* undoer; *deshacedor de agravios,* righter of wrongs.

deshacer, *v.t.* (conjugated like HACER) to undo; to destroy; to untie, open, take apart; to cancel, efface, blot out; to lessen, diminish; to consume; to melt, liquefy; to cut up, divide; to rout an army, put to flight; to run through one's fortune; to violate an agreement; *deshacer agravios,* to revenge or redress (wrongs). — *v.r.* to be wasted, consumed, destroyed; to grieve, mourn; to disappear, vanish; to do anything with vehemence; to grow feeble; to become crippled; *deshacerse en lágrimas,* to burst into tears; *deshacerse como el humo,* to vanish like smoke; *deshacerse de,* to remove any hindrance to a project; to transfer, sell; *deshacerse de una cosa,* to give a thing away, get rid of a thing.

deshago; deshice; deshaga, *pres. indic.; pret.; pres. subj.* [DESHACER].

deshambrido, -da, *a.* famished, starving.

desharrapado, -da, *a.* shabby, ragged, in tatters.

desharrapamiento, *n.m.* misery, poverty.

deshebillar, *v.t.* to unbuckle.

deshebrar, *v.t.* to unthread; to separate into threads or filaments.

deshecha, *n.f.* simulation, evasion, shift; polite farewell; burden, refrain; step in a Spanish dance; *hacer la deshecha,* to dissemble, feign, pretend.

deshechizar, *v.t.* to disenchant, break a spell.

deshechizo, *n.m.* disenchantment, breaking of a magic spell.

deshecho, -cha, *a.* undone, destroyed, wasted; melted; in pieces; perfectly mixed (of colours); *borrasca deshecha,* violent tempest; *fuga deshecha,* precipitate flight. — *p.p.* [DESHACER].

deshelar, *v.t., v.r.* (conjugated like HELAR) to thaw; to melt.

desherbar, *v.t.* (conjugated like HERBAR) to extirpate herbs; to weed.

desheredación, *n.f.,* **desheredamiento,** *n.m.* disinheritance, disinheriting.

desheredar, *v.t.* to disinherit. — *v.r.* (*fig.*) to degenerate.

deshermanar, *v.t.* to destroy the conformity between two things which matched each other. — *v.r.* to violate brotherly love.

desherradura, *n.f.* (*vet.*) footsoreness; injury done to a horse's foot by being unshod.

desherrar, *v.t.* to unchain; rip off horses' shoes.

desherrumbrar, *v.t.* to clear a thing of rust.

deshidratar, *v.t., v.r.* to dehydrate, remove hydrogen.

deshielo, *n.m.* thaw.

deshielo; deshiele, *pres. indic.; pres. subj.* [DESHELAR].

deshijar, *v.t.* (*Cub.*) to remove suckers (from plants).

deshilachar, *v.t.* to ravel, uncord. — *v.r.* to fuzz.

deshiladiz, *n.m.* (*prov.*) silk refuse.

deshilado, -da, *a.* marching in file; *a la deshilada,* in file, one after another; deceitfully. — *n.m.* open work, drawn work, embroidery (in linen). — *p.p.* [DESHILAR].

deshiladura, *n.f.* ripping, ravelling out.

deshilar, *v.t.* to ravel; (*sew.*) to draw threads; to change a swarm of bees from one hive to another; to scrape lint; (*fig.*) to carve in thin strips. — *v.r.* to grow thin; to fuzz.

deshilo, *n.m.* obstructing the course of bees in order to get them into a new hive.

deshilvanado, -da, *a.* disjointed, disconnected; without sequence.

deshilvanar, *v.t.* to remove the tacking threads.

deshincadura, *n.f.* act of drawing out anything nailed or fixed.

deshincar, *v.t.* to draw a nail; to remove what is fixed.

deshinchadura, *n.f.* abating of a swelling.

deshinchar, *v.t.* to reduce a swelling; to let out air or fluid; (*fig.*) to appease anger or annoyance. — *v.r.* to contract, shrink, shrivel (applied to anything swollen or puffed out); (*coll.*) to abate presumption, assume more modest airs.

deshipotecar, *v.t.* to cancel a mortgage.

deshojador, *n.m.* stripper of leaves.

deshojar, *v.t.* to strip leaves; (*fig.*) to display rhetorical eloquence; to deprive of all hope.

deshoje, *n.m.* fall of leaves.

deshollejar, *v.t.* to pare, peel, strip, husk; to shell (beans, etc.); to skin (grapes).

deshollinador, *n.m.* chimney-sweeper; any appliance for sweeping chimneys; turk's-head; (*coll.*) one who examines closely.

deshollinar, *v.t.* to sweep chimneys; to clean anything dirty; (*coll.*) to examine attentively or curiously.

deshonestamente, *adv.* dishonestly, dishonourably, disgracefully; lewdly, immodestly.

deshonestar, *v.t.* (*obs.*) to dishonour; to disgrace. — *v.r.* to be insolent or saucy.

deshonestidad, *n.f.* immodesty; dishonesty; lewdness, libidinousness; lascivious or immodest action.

deshonesto, -ta, *a.* immodest, unchaste, lewd; dishonest.

deshonor, *n.m.* dishonour, disgrace; insult, injury, affront.

deshonorar, *v.t.* to dishonour, disgrace; to deprive of office or employment.

deshonra, *n.f.* dishonour, discredit, disgrace, infamy, obloquy, opprobrium; seduction or violation of a woman; *tener a deshonra alguna cosa,* to consider a thing unworthy.

deshonrabuenos, *n.m.f.* calumniator, libeller, slanderer; degenerate person.

deshonradamente, *adv.* dishonourably, shamefully, disgracefully.

deshonrador, -ra, *a.* dishonouring. — *n.m.f.* dishonourer, disgracer; violator.

deshonrar, *v.t., v.r.* to affront, insult, defame; to dishonour, disgrace; to scorn, despise; to seduce or ruin a pure woman.

deshonrible, *a.* (*coll.*) shameless, despicable.

deshonroso, -sa, *a.* indecent, dishonourable; low, mean.

deshora, *n.f.* unseasonable or inconvenient time; *a deshora(s),* unseasonably, at an untimely moment; suddenly, inopportunely.

deshorado, -da, *a.* untimely, unseasonable.

deshornar, *v.t.* to take out of the oven.

deshospedamiento, *n.m.* inhospitality.

deshuesar, *v.t.* to take out the bones of animals; to stone fruits.

deshumanizar, *v.t.* to render less human or life-like.

deshumano, -na, *a.* inhuman.

deshumedecer, *v.t.* (conjugated like HUMEDECER) to deprive of moisture, exsiccate. — *v.r.* to dry, grow dry.

desiderable, *a.* desirable.

desiderativo, -va, *a.* desirous.

desidia, *n.f.* idleness, negligence, indolence.

desidiosamente, *adv.* indolently, idly.

desidioso, -sa, *a.* negligent, idle, indolent.

desierto, -ta, *a.* deserted, solitary, desert, waste, lonely, lonesome, uninhabited. — *n.m.* desert, wilderness, waste; *predicar en desierto,* to preach to deaf ears.

designación, *n.f.* designation.

designar, *v.t.* to design, purpose, intend; to appoint, name, designate.

designativo, -va, *a.* designative.

designio, *n.m.* design, purpose, intention.

desigual, *a.* unequal, dissimilar, changeable, unlike, variable; uneven, unlevelled, craggy, broken; (*fig.*) mismated, mismatched; arduous, difficult, perilous; (*obs.*) abrupt, excessive, extreme.

desigualar, *v.t.* to make unequal or dissimilar; to mismatch. — *v.r.* to surpass, excel.

desigualdad, *n.f.* inequality, odds, difference, dissimilitude; inconstancy, levity, variableness; unevenness, cragginess, knottiness; (*math.*) sign of inequality ($<, >$).

desigualmente, *adv.* unequally, oddly.

desilusión, *n.f.* disappointment; disillusionment.

desilusionar, *v.t.* to disillusion, disenchant; to destroy a pet belief. — *v.r.* to be disabused, undeceived; to become disillusioned.

desimaginar, *v.t.* to blot out, obliterate from the mind.

desimanar, *v.t., v.r.* [DESIMANTAR].

desimantación, *n.f.* demagnetization.

desimantar, *v.t., v.r.* to demagnetize. — *v.r.* to lose magnetism, become demagnetized.

desimponer, *v.t.* (*print.*) to distribute the type from the forme.

desimpresionar, *v.t.* to undeceive.

desinclinar, *v.t.* to disincline.

desincorporación, *n.f.* disincorporation, end of corporate existence.

desincorporar, *v.t.* to separate what was hitherto united or incorporated. — *v.r.* to separate from a society.

desinencia, *n.f.* (*gram.*) termination, end; declension, inflection.

desinfección, *n.f.* disinfection; act of disinfecting or sterilizing.

desinfectador, *n.m.* disinfecting apparatus; disinfector.

desinfectante, *a.* antiseptic, disinfecting. — *n.m.* disinfectant, deodorizer.

desinfectar, *v.t., v.r.* to disinfect, sterilize, render antiseptic.

desinficionamiento, *n.m.* disinfection.

desinficionar, *v.t.* to disinfect, free from infection.

desinflamar, *v.t.* to cure or remove inflammation; to reduce a swelling.

desinflar, *v.t.* let out the air or fluid with which anything is inflated.

desinsaculación, *n.f.* act of drawing lots or names from an urn or ballot-box.

desinsacular, *v.t.* to draw lots.

desinsectar, *v.t.* to disinfest.

desintegrar, *v.t.* to disintegrate.

desinterés, *n.m.* disinterestedness, indifference to profit.

desinteresadamente, *adv.* disinterestedly, generously.

desinteresado, -da, *a.* disinterested, impartial.

desinteresarse, *v.r.* to lose interest in something.

desinvernar, *v.i.* (*mil.*) to leave winter quarters.

desirvo; desirva, *pres. indic.; pres. subj.* [DESERVIR].

desistencia, *n.f.;* **desistimiento,** *n.m.* desistance; the act of desisting.

desistir, *v.i.* to desist, leave, go back, abandon, cease, give up; to flinch; (*law*) to abdicate a right.

desjarretadera, *n.f.* knife in crescent form for hamstringing cattle.

desjarretar, *v.t.* to hough, hamstring; (*coll.*) to weaken, debilitate.

desjarrete, *n.m.* houghing, hocking, hamstringing.

desjugar, *v.t.* (conjugated like ENJUGAR) to extract juice from.

desjuntamiento, *n.m.* disjunction, separation.

desjuntar, *v.t., v.r.* to divide, part, separate, sever, disjoin.

desjurar, *v.t.* to forswear, retract an oath.

deslabonar, *v.t.* to unlink, disjoin; (*fig.*) to dismantle. — *v.r.* (*fig.*) to break from someone's company.

desladrillar, *v.t.* [DESENLADRILLAR].

deslamar, *v.t.* to clear of mud.

deslastrar, *v.t.* to unballast a ship.

deslatar, *v.t.* to remove the laths from.

deslavado, -da, *a.* impudent, barefaced. — *p.p.* [DESLAVAR].

deslavadura, *n.f.* washing, rinsing (superficially).

deslavar, deslavazar, *v.t.* to wash, wet superficially; to rinse; to take away the colour, force, vigour from.

deslazamiento, *n.m.* disjunction, dissolution.

deslazar, *v.t.* to unlace; to untie a knot.

desleal, *a.* disloyal; perfidious, faithless, traitorous.

deslealmente, *adv.* disloyally; treacherously.

deslealtad, *n.f.* disloyalty; treachery.

deslechar, *v.t.* (*prov.*) to remove dirt from silk-worms.

deslecho, *n.m.* (*prov.*) cleaning of silk-worms.

deslechugador, *n.m.* vine-dresser, pruner.

deslechugar, deslechuguillar, *v.t.* (*agric.*) to cut and prune branches of vines.

desleidura, *n.f.;* **desleimiento,** *n.m.* dilution; making thin or weak.

desleír, *v.t.* (*pres. indic.* **deslío;** *pret.* **él deslió;** *pres. subj.* **deslía**) to dilute; to dissolve; to make thin or weak.

deslendrar, *v.t.* to clear the hair of nits.

deslenguado, -da, *a.* loquacious, impudent, scurrilous, foul-mouthed. — *p.p.* [DESLENGUAR].

deslenguamiento, *n.m.* loquacity, gossip; impudence.

deslenguar, *v.t.* to cut out the tongue. — *v.r.* (*coll.*) to talk at random; to use abusive language.

desliar, *v.t.* to loose, untie, undo; to separate must from lees and dregs.

desligadura, *n.f.;* **desligamiento,** *n.m.* untying, disjoining, disjunction.

desligar, *v.t.* (conjugated like LIGAR) to loosen, untie, unbind; (*fig.*) to unravel, extricate, disentangle; to absolve from ecclesiastical censure; to excuse from an obligation; (*med.*) to unfasten bandages or ligatures; (*mus.*) to play or sing staccato; (*naut.*) to remove from a ship its knees or the futtock-timbers or the spikes holding them. — *v.r.* to get loose; to give way.

deslindable, *a.* limitable, surveyable, capable of demarcation.

deslindador, *n.m.* one who marks boundaries; land-surveyor.

deslindamiento, *n.m.* demarcation; survey of boundaries.

deslindar, *v.t.* to mark boundaries; (*fig.*) to define a thing, make something plain.

deslinde, *n.m.* demarcation.

desliñar, *v.t.* to clean fulled cloth before it goes to press.

deslío, *n.m.* separating must from lees.

desliz, *n.m.* slip; slipping; sliding; false step; frailty, failure, weakness, fault; (*min.*) mercury which escapes in smelting silver ore.

deslizable, *a.* that which can slip or slide.

deslizadero, *n.m.* slippery place.

deslizadero, -ra; deslizadizo, -za, *a.* slippery, slippy, lubricious.

deslizador, *n.m.* (*aer.*) glider.

deslizamiento, *n.m.* slip, slipping; sliding; skidding.

deslizar, *v.i.* (*pret.* **deslicé;** *pres. subj.* **deslice**) to slip, slide; to act or speak carelessly. — *v.r.* to shirk, evade; to slip away.

desloar, *v.t.* to scold, reproach.

deslomadura, *n.f.* act of breaking the back.

deslomar, *v.t.* to break the back, strain the loins.

deslucidamente, *adv.* ungracefully, inelegantly.

deslucido, -da, *a.* unadorned; ungraceful, inelegant; useless, fruitless; *quedar* or *salir deslucido,* to fail, be a failure. — *p.p.* [DESLUCIR].

deslucimiento, *n.m.* lack of brilliancy or smartness.

deslucir, *v.t.* (conjugated like LUCIR) to tarnish; to disparage or impair someone's reputation.

deslumbrador, -ra, *a.* dazzling, glaring, brilliant.

deslumbramiento, *n.m.* dazzle, glare, lustre; (*fig.*) hallucination; confusion of mind or sight.

deslumbrar, *v.t.* to dazzle; (*fig.*) to daze, leave doubtful or uncertain.

deslustración, *n.f.* tarnishing, sullying, dimming; removing polish.

deslustrador, -ra, *a.* tarnishing. — *n.m.f.* tarnisher.

deslustrar, *v.t.* to tarnish, dim, obscure; to soil or stain someone's reputation; to frost (glass, etc.).

deslustre, *n.m.* spot, stain; dimness, dullness; (*fig.*) disgrace, stigma, ignominy.

deslustroso, -sa, *a.* unbecoming, ugly.

desmadejamiento, *n.m.* languishing, languidness.

desmadejar, *v.t.* to enervate, produce languidness. — *v.r.* to languish, be enervated, be weak.

desmadrado, -da, *a.* motherless (animal).

desmadrar, *v.t.* to separate an animal from its mother.

desmajolar, *v.t.* to root up vines; untie the shoe-laces.

desmallador, *n.m.* one who breaks meshes of net or links of a chain; (*slang*) dagger.

desmalladura, *n.f.* breaking meshes of net or links of a chain.

desmallar, *v.t.* to destroy meshes of net or links of a chain.

desmamar, *v.t.* to wean.

desmamonar, *v.t.* to cut off the young shoots of vines or trees.

desmán, *n.m.* misfortune, disaster, mishap, calamity; excess in words or actions; misbehaviour; (*zool.*) musk-rat.

desmanarse, *v.r.* to stray from a flock or herd.

desmandado, -da, *a.* countermanded; impudent; lawless; disobedient. — *p.p.* [DESMANDAR].

desmandamiento, *n.m.* countermanding an order; disorder, irregularity; impertinent behaviour, sauciness.

desmandar, *v.t.* to countermand; to revoke a legacy; to repeal an ordinance. — *v.r.* to transgress the bounds of justice; to be impudent; to lose self-control; to stray from the flock; to go astray.

desmanear, *v.t.* to take off shackles (from horses, mules, etc.).

desmangar, *v.t.* to take off a handle.

desmanotado, -da, *a.* unhandy, awkward.

desmantecar, *v.t.* to take off the butter.

desmantelado, -da, *a.* dismantled, unfurnished, abandoned, ruinous, dilapidated. — *p.p.* [DESMANTELAR].

desmantelar, *v.t.* (*fort.*) to dismantle; to forsake, abandon, desert; (*naut.*) to unmast, unrig, disarm.

desmaña, *n.f.* idleness, laziness; clumsiness, awkwardness.

desmañado, -da, *a.* lazy, idle, indolent; clumsy, awkward, clownish.

desmarañar, *v.t.* to disentangle.

desmarcar, *v.t.* (conjugated like MARCAR) to remove, efface, obliterate marks.

desmarojar, *v.t.* to gather mistletoe from a tree.

desmarrido, -da, *a.* languid, tired, sad, dejected, exhausted.

desmatar, *v.t.* to eradicate, uproot (plants).

desmayadamente, *adv.* weakly, dejectedly.

desmayado, -da, *a.* pale, wan, dim, feeble; dismayed, appalled. — *p.p.* [DESMAYAR].

desmayar, *v.t.* to dismay, depress, discourage. — *v.i.* to be faint-hearted, dispirited, dejected, discouraged. — *v.r.* to faint, swoon.

desmayo, *n.m.* swoon, fainting-fit; decay of strength; dismay, discouragement; (*bot.*) weeping-willow.

desmazalado, -da, *a.* weak, spiritless, dejected, faint-hearted.

desmedidamente, *adv.* disproportionately, excessively.

desmedido, -da, *a.* disproportionate, excessive. — *p.p.* [DESMEDIRSE].

desmedirse, *v.r.* to forget oneself; to be impudent or saucy; to lose self-control.

desmedrar, *v.i.* to decrease, decay, deteriorate. — *v.t.* to impair.

desmedro, *n.m.* diminution, decay, detriment.

desmejora, *n.f.* deterioration, detriment, depreciation; diminution, loss.

desmejorar, *v.t.* to debase, make worse. — *v.r.* to decay, decline, get worse; to deteriorate.

desmelancolizar, *v.t.* to cheer up, enliven.

desmelar, *v.t.* to take honey from a hive.

desmelenar, *v.t.* to dishevel, disarrange the hair.

desmembración, *n.f.* dismemberment, division, amputation.

desmembrador, -ra, *n.m.f.* divider; one who dismembers.

desmembramiento, *n.m.* dismemberment.

desmembrar, *v.t.* (*pres. indic.* **desmiembro**; *pres. subj.* **desmiembre**) to dismember, tear asunder; to curtail; (*surg.*) to amputate; to separate, divide. — *v.r.* to separate, fall to pieces.

desmemoria, *n.f.* forgetfulness; loss of memory.

desmemoriado, -da, *n.m.f.*, *a.* forgetful (person). — *p.p.* [DESMEMORIARSE].

desmemoriarse, *v.r.* to forget, be forgetful, lose one's memory.

desmenguar, *v.t.* to lessen, diminish.

desmentida, *n.f.* the act of giving the lie.

desmentidor, -ra, *a.* that gives the lie; disproving. — *n.m.f.* contradictor, one who gives the lie or convicts of a falsehood.

desmentir, *v.t.* (conjugated like MENTIR) to give the lie; to convict of a falsehood; to counterfeit; to contradict, deny; (*fig.*) to dissemble, conceal, to do unworthy things. — *v.i.* to deviate from the right line.

desmenuzable, *a.* brittle, easily crumbled, crisp.

desmenuzador, -ra, *n.m.f.* scrutator, investigator; purifier; one who crumbles.

desmenuzar, *v.t.* (*pret.* **desmenucé**; *pres. subj.* **desmenuce**) to chip, shred, crumble, fritter; (*fig.*) to sift, examine minutely. — *v.r.* to crumble, fall into small pieces.

desmeollar, *v.t.* to remove the marrow from bones.

desmerecedor, -ra, *a.* unworthy, undeserving.

desmerecer, *v.t.* (conjugated like MERECER) to become unworthy or undeserving of. — *v.i.* to lose worth; to deteriorate; to compare unfavourably with.

desmerecimiento, *n.m.* demerit, unworthiness.

desmesura, *n.f.* excess, want of moderation.

desmesuradamente, *adv.* disproportionately, excessively.

desmesurado, -da, *a.* disproportionate, excessive; impolite, insolent. — *p.p.* [DESMESURAR].

desmesurar, *v.t.* to disorder, disarrange, discompose. — *v.r.* to act or talk with forwardness or impertinence.

desmiembro; desmiembre, *pres. indic.; pres. subj.* [DESMEMBRAR].

desmiento; desmiente, *pres. indic.; pres. subj.* [DESMENTIR].

desmigajar, *v.t., v.r.* to crumble.

desmigar, *v.t.* (*pret.* **desmigué;** *pres. subj.* **desmigue**) to crumble bread.

desmineralización, *n.f.* (*med.*) abnormal loss of mineral substances.

desmirriado, -da, *a.* (*coll.*) lean, extenuated, exhausted; melancholy.

desmocha, desmochadura, *n.f.;* **desmoche,** *n.m.* mutilation, lopping off, cutting off the top.

desmochar, *v.t.* to lop or cut off; to mutilate; to unhorn; to pollard (trees).

desmocho, *n.m.* heap of things lopped or cut off.

desmogar, *v.i.* to cast the horns (of deer).

desmogue, *n.m.* casting of the horns.

desmolado, -da, *a.* having no molar teeth.

desmoldamiento, desmolde, *n.m.* removal of a casting from the mould.

desmoldar, *v.t.* to remove from the mould.

desmonetización, *n.f.* demonetization; conversion of coin into bullion.

desmonetizar, *v.t.* to call in (money); to demonetize.

desmonta, *n.f.* clearing of trees and undergrowth; lumber left in a forest clearing.

desmontado, -da, *a.* unmounted, dismounted; (*mech.*) dismantled. — *p.p.* [DESMONTAR].

desmontador, -r ι, *n.m.f.* feller of wood; dismounter.

desmontadur ., *n.f.* felling of timber; clearing of undergrowth.

desmontar, *v.t.* to fell wood; to remove a heap of dirt or rubbish; to uncock fire-arms; to dismount (a troop of horse-soldiers); to dismount a cannon; to dismantle (machines, etc.); (*naut.*) *desmontar el timón,* to unhang the rudder. — *v.i., v.r.* to dismount (from horse, etc.).

desmonte, *n.m.* clearing a wood from trees; clearing, cleared ground.

desmoñar, *v.t.* (*coll.*) to undo or loosen the hair.

desmoralización, *n.f.* demoralization, corruption, depravity.

desmoralizado, -da, *a.* demoralized, depraved. — *p.p.* [DESMORALIZAR].

desmoralizar, *v.t.* (conjugated like MORALIZAR) to demoralize, corrupt, deprave. — *v.r.* to become demoralized; (*mil.*) to relax discipline, lose morale.

desmoronadizo, -za, *a.* easily crumbled, crumbly; lacking solidity or permanence.

desmoronar, *v.t.* to abrade, destroy gradually; (*fig.*) to cause to dwindle. — *v.r.* to moulder, crumble, fall, decay.

desmostar, *v.t.* to separate must from grapes. — *v.r.* to ferment.

desmotadera, *n.f.* woman who burls cloth; burling-iron.

desmotador, -ra, *a.* burling. — *n.m.f.* person who takes knots from cloth or wool. — *n.f.* instrument for burling cloth.

desmotar, *v.t.* to clear cloth of knots; to burl.

desmovilización, *n.f.* demobilization.

desmuelo, *n.m.* want or loss of molar teeth.

desmugrador, *n.m.* instrument for cleaning wool of grease.

desmugrar, *v.t.* to clean wool or cloth of grease.

desmullir, *v.t.* to disarrange or impair anything soft.

desmurador, *n.m.* (*prov.*) mouser (cat).

desmurar, *v.t.* (*prov.*) to exterminate rats or mice from a place.

desnarigado, -da, *a.* noseless. — *p.p.* [DESNARIGAR].

desnarigar, *v.t.* to cut off the nose.

desnatar, *v.t.* to skim milk; (*fig.*) to take the best part of something; (*min.*) to remove dross in smelting; *desnatar la hacienda,* to live on the fat of the land.

desnaturalización, *n.f.* expatriation; denationalization.

desnaturalizado, -da, *a.* unnatural; denaturalized. — *p.p.* [DESNATURALIZAR].

desnaturalizar, *v.t.* (conjugated like NATURALIZAR) to denaturalize, denationalize; to banish, expatriate, exile; to revoke the privileges of naturalization; to disfigure, pervert (facts, etc.). — *v.r.* to abandon one's country.

desnegamiento, *n.m.* denial; contradiction; retraction.

desnegar, *v.t.* (conjugated like NEGAR) to deny, gainsay, contradict. — *v.r.* to unsay, recant.

desnervar, desnerviar, *v.t.* [ENERVAR].

desnevado, -da, *a.* thawed, free from snow. — *p.p.* [DESNEVAR].

desnevar, *v.t.* (conjugated like NEVAR) to thaw, dissolve.

desnieve, *n.m.* thaw.

desnivel, *n.m.* unevenness; inequality; gradient, drop.

desnivelación, *n.f.* act and effect of making uneven.

desnivelar, *v.t.* to make uneven. — *v.r.* to become uneven or out of level.

desnucar, *v.t.* (*pret.* **desnuqué;** *pres. subj.* **desnuque**) to break the neck of. — *v.r.* to break one's neck.

desnudador, -ra, *a.* denuding. — *n.m.f.* one that denudes.

desnudamente, *adv.* nakedly; (*fig.*) clearly, manifestly, plainly.

desnudamiento, *n.m.* undressing.

desnudar, *v.t.* to strip, undress, denude; (*fig.*) discover, reveal; to fleece; (*naut.*) to unrig; *desnudar la espada,* to draw one's sword; *desnudar un santo para vestir a otro,* to rob Peter to pay Paul. — *v.r.* to undress, take off one's clothes; (*fig.*) to deprive oneself of; to rid oneself of.

desnudez, *n.f.* nudity, nakedness, bareness.

desnudo, -da, *a.* naked, nude, uncovered, bare; (*fig.*) ill-clothed; (*fig.*) apparent, plain, evident; (*fig.*) empty-handed; *desnudo nací, desnudo me hallo, ni pierdo ni gano,* naked I was born, and naked I am; I neither lose nor gain. — *n.m.* (*art*) nude.

desnutrición, *n.f.* (*med.*) malnutrition, underfeeding.

desobedecer, *v.t.* (conjugated like OBEDECER) to disobey; *desobedecer el timón,* (*naut.*) to fall off, deviate.

desobediencia, *n.f.* disobedience, lawlessness.

desobediente, *a.* disobedient.

desobedientemente, *adv.* disobediently.

desobligar, *v.t.* (conjugated like OBLIGAR) to

release from an obligation; to disoblige, offend; to alienate the good will of.

desobstrucción, *n.f.* removal of obstructions or obstacles.

desobstruente, *n.m., a.* (*med.*) deobstruent.

desobstruir, *v.t.* (conjugated like OBSTRUIR) (*med.*) to remove obstructions from.

desocasionado, -da, *a.* untimely, unseasonable.

desocupación, *n.f.* leisure, want of work.

desocupadamente, *adv.* freely, in a leisurely way.

desocupado, -da, *a.* idle, without occupation; empty, vacant. — *n.m.f.* unemployed. — *p.p.* [DESOCUPAR].

desocupar, *v.t.* to vacate; to evacuate; to empty. — *v.r.* free oneself from a business or occupation.

desodorante, *n.m., a.* deodorant.

desoír, *v.t.* to pretend not to hear; to pay no heed.

desojar, *v.t.* to break the eye of a needle. — *v.r.* to look intently, to strain the eyes.

desolación, *n.f.* desolation, destruction, extermination, havoc; (*fig.*) affliction, intense grief.

desolado, -da, *a.* desolate; disconsolate. — *p.p.* [DESOLAR].

desolar, *v.t.* (*pres. indic.* desuelo; *pres. subj.* desuele) to desolate, lay waste; to harass. — *v.r.* to suffer great sorrow.

desoldar, *v.t.* to unsolder. — *v.r.* to become unsoldered.

desolladamente, *adv.* (*coll.*) impudently, petulantly.

desolladero, *n.m.* abattoir, slaughterhouse.

desollado, -da, *a.* (*coll.*) forward, impudent, insolent. — *p.p.* [DESOLLAR].

desollador, -ra, *n.m.f.* flayer; extortioner. — *n.m.* butcher-bird.

desolladura, *n.f.* act or effect of flaying or skinning; excoriation; extortion.

desollar, *v.t.* (*pres. indic.* desuello; *pres. subj.* desuelle) to flay, skin, fleece, excoriate; *desollarle a uno vivo,* (*coll.*) to extort an immoderate price; to cause great harm; to speak ill of anyone.

desonce, *n.m.* discount of a certain number of ounces in each pound.

desonzar, *v.t.* to discount or deduct a certain number of ounces in each pound; (*fig.*) to defame, revile.

desopilar, *v.t., v.r.* to clear obstructions.

desopilativo, -va, *a.* (*med.*) deobstruent.

desopinar, *v.t.* to defame, impeach.

desoprimir, *v.t.* to free from oppression.

desorden, *n.m.* (formerly *n.f.*) disorder, confusion, irregularity, displacement, mess, misrule; licence, excess, lawlessness; turmoil, riot, disturbance.

desordenadamente, *adv.* in a disorderly or unruly way.

desordenado, -da, *a.* disordered, disorderly, irregular, lawless, licentious. — *p.p.* [DESORDENAR].

desordenamiento, *n.m.* disorder, tumult, lawlessness.

desordenar, *v.t.* to disorder, confound, disturb, confuse, throw into confusion, disarrange. — *v.r.* to be irregular, be out of order; to become unruly or unmanageable (as a horse).

desorejador, -ra, *n.m.f.* one who crops off the ears.

desorejamiento, *n.m.* cropping the ears.

desorejar, *v.t.* to crop the ears.

desorganización, *n.f.* disorganization.

desorganizadamente, *adv.* in a disorganized way.

desorganizador, -ra, *a.* disorganizing. — *n.m.f.* disorganizer.

desorganizar, *v.t.* (conjugated like ORGANIZAR) to disorganize; to break up, disperse; (*chem.*) to decompose; (*mil.*) to disband an army; to relax discipline. — *v.r.* to become disorganized; to disband, disperse.

desorientado, -da, *a.* disoriented, turned from the right direction. — *p.p.* [DESORIENTAR].

desorientar, *v.t., v.r.* to confuse, lead wrong, lead into error; to turn in the wrong direction; to lose one's way or bearings.

desorillar, *v.t.* to cut off the edge or border from cloth, paper, etc.

desortijado, -da, *a.* (*vet.*) sprained. — *p.p.* [DESORTIJAR].

desortijar, *v.t.* (*agric.*) to hoe or weed plants the first time.

desosado, -da, *p.p.* [DESOSAR]; **la desosada,** *n.f.* (*slang*) the tongue.

desosar, *v.t.* (*pres. indic.* deshueso; *pres. subj.* deshuese) to bone, unbone; to stone fruit.

desovar, *v.t.* to spawn.

desove, *n.m.* spawning; spawning season.

desovillar, *v.t.* to unwind; (*fig.*) to unclew, unravel, disentangle.

desoxidación, *n.f.* deoxidization.

desoxidante, *a.* deoxidizing. — *n.m.* deoxidizer.

desoxidar, *v.t.* to deoxidize.

desoxigenación, *n.f.* deoxygenation.

desoxigenar, *v.t., v.r.* to deoxygenate, deoxidize.

despabiladeras, *n.f.pl.* snuffers.

despabilado, -da, *a.* snuffed (of candles); (*fig.*) watchful, vigilant, lively, active, alert; —*p.p.* [DESPABILAR].

despabilador, -ra, *a.* snuffing (candles). — *n.m.f.* person who snuffs candles. — *n.m.* candle-snuffer.

despabiladura, *n.f.* snuff of the candle.

despabilar, *v.t.* to snuff a candle; to trim the wick; to finish off quickly; (*coll.*) to rob, plunder; to enliven, rouse; (*fig.*) to kill; *despabilar el ingenio,* to sharpen the wits; *despabilar los ojos,* to keep a sharp look-out. — *v.r.* to rouse oneself.

despacio, *adv.* slowly, leisurely, gently; little by little, continually; deliberately. — *interj.* softly! gently! carefully!

despacioso, -sa, *a.* slow, sluggish.

despacito, *adv.* (*coll.*) very gently, softly, leisurely, slowly. — *interj.* very slowly! tread carefully!

despachaderas, *n.f.pl.* (*coll.*) surly words in answer to a question; quickness, resourcefulness.

despachador, -ra, *n.m.f.* expeditor; (*Am.*) (*min.*) filler of trucks in an adit.

despachar, *v.t.* to dispatch; to facilitate, expedite; to send; to ship; to perform with dispatch; to attend to correspondence; to dismiss, discharge; (*com.*) to take papers for signature; to expend; (*coll.*) to attend on customers in a shop; *despachar un barco,* (*com.*) to clear a vessel; *despachar géneros* or *mercaderías en la aduana*, (*com.*) to clear goods at the custom-house; *despachar al otro mundo*, (*fig.*) to kill. — *v.r.* to accelerate, make haste; to give birth (a woman); to get rid of; (*coll.*) to say whatever comes to mind.

despacho, *n.m.* expedition, dispatch; shipping, shipment, sending; custom, application from buyers; sale of goods, trade, demand; office, counting-house; depot; cabinet, bureau; commission, patent, warrant; dispatch, official communication; expedient, determination; *despacho de aduana*, clearance; *despacho de billetes* or *boletos*, ticket-office; *despacho de coches, vapores, etc.*, depot, head office of coaches, steamships, etc.; *despacho de localidades*, box-office; *despacho telegráfico*, cablegram, telegram; *despacho universal*, department of a Minister of State; *tener buen despacho*, to be quick, energetic, prompt.

despachurrado, -da, *a.* smashed, squashed, crushed. — *p.p.* [DESPADURRAR].

despachurrar, *v.t.* (*coll.*) to crush, press together; to confound by a smart repartee; to make a jumble of a speech; *dejar a uno despachurrado*, (*coll.*) to leave one stupefied; *despachurrar un cuento*, (*coll.*) to interrupt a story and prevent its termination.

despajadura, *n.f.* winnowing; (*min.*) sifting refuse.

despajar, *v.t.* to winnow; (*min.*) to sieve refuse by hand to recover mineral.

despajo, *n.m.* winnowing grain.

despaldar, *v.t., v.r.* to dislocate or break the shoulder.

despaldillar, *v.t.* to dislocate shoulder or back of an animal; to stem raisins; to strip tobacco. — *v.r.* to dislocate one's shoulder.

despalmador, *n.m.* careening-place, dockyard; hoof-paring knife.

despalmar, *v.t.* (*naut.*) to grave, calk; to pare off a horse's hoof; to uproot grass or turf.

despampanador, *n.m.* pruner of vines.

despampanadura, *n.f.* pruning vines.

despampanar, *v.t.* to prune vines; (*coll.*) to astound, stun. — *v.i.* (*coll.*) to give vent to one's feelings. — *v.r.* (*coll.*) to injure oneself by falling.

despamplonar, *v.t.* to separate the shoots of plants. — *v.r.* (*fig.*) to sprain the hand.

despanado, *p.p.* [DESPANAR].

despanar, *v.i.* (*prov.*) to remove reaped corn from the fields.

despancar, *v.t.* (*Am.*) to husk maize.

despancijar, despanzurrar, *v.t.* (*coll.*) to burst the belly.

despapar, *v.i.* to carry the head too high (of a horse).

despapucho, *n.m.* (*Per.*) absurdity, nonsense.

desparecer, *v.i.* to disappear. — *v.r.* (*obs.*) to be unlike or dissimilar [DESAPARECER].

desparejar, *v.t.* to make unequal, uneven; to break a pair.

desparpajado, -da, *a.* pert, petulant; garrilous. — *p.p.* [DESPARPAJAR].

desparpajar, *v.t.* to undo in a disorderly way. — *v.i.* (*coll.*) to prattle, rant.

desparpajo, *n.m.* pertness of speech or action; (*Cent. Am.*) disorder, disturbance, turmoil.

desparramado, -da, *a.* scattered, spread, wide open. — *p.p.* [DESPARRAMAR].

desparramador, -ra, *n.m.f.* prodigal, waster, spendthrift; disperser; dilapidator.

desparramar, *v.t.* to spill, spread, scatter, disseminate; to lavish, squander. — *v.r.* to be dissipated; to amuse oneself, revel.

desparramo, *n.m.* (*Arg., Cub., Chi.*) spreading, scattering; squandering; (*Chi.*) disorder, disturbance.

despartidor, *n.m.* pacificator; one who divides or separates.

despartir, *v.t.* to part, divide; to conciliate.

desparvar, *v.t.* to remove the threshed corn from the threshing-floor to winnow it.

despasar, *v.t.* to unreeve a rope, etc.; to remove a cable, etc., from a windlass.

despatarrada, [*n.f.* the splits (in certain Spanish dances); (*coll.*) splits of the legs; *hacer la despatarrada*, to affect illness; to feign death.

despatarrado, -da, *p.p.* [DESPATARRAR].

despatarrar, *v.t.* to cause to open the legs wide; (*coll.*) to cause fear or amazement; *quedarse uno despatarrado*, to be thunderstruck. — *v.r.* (*coll.*) to straddle; to fall with split legs; to be stupefied.

despatillar, *v.t.* to cut grooves or mortises in wood; to break off the arm of an anchor. — *v.r.* (*coll.*) to shave off the whiskers.

despavesadura, *n.f.* snuffing (a candle, etc.).

despavesar, *v.t.* to snuff (a candle, etc.).

despavoridamente, *adv.* terrifiedly, aghast.

despavorido, -da, *a.* terrified, aghast. — *p.p.* [DESPAVORIR].

despavorir, *v.i., v.r.* (*defective, having only the tenses and persons containing the letter i*) to be terrified, frightened, aghast.

despeadura, *n.f.* (*vet.*) surbating, foundering, lameness (of horses).

despeamiento, *n.m.* (*vet.*) foundering.

despear, *v.t.* to founder (of horses). — *v.r.* to become lame through over-exertion.

despectivo, -va, *a.* depreciatory.

despechadamente, *adv.* angrily, spitefully.

despechar, *v.t.* to enrage, excite indignation; (*coll.*) to wean. — *v.r.* to fret, be peevish; to lose all hope, despair; to be spiteful.

despecho, *n.m.* spite, indignation, displeasure, wrath; dejection, despair; malevolence, ill-will, grudge; *a despecho*, in spite of; in defiance of.

despechugadura, *n.f.* cutting off the breast of a fowl; uncovering the breast.

despechugar, *v.t.* (conjugated like APECHUGAR) to cut off the breast (of a fowl). — *v.r.* (*coll.*) to show the breast; to walk bare-breasted.

despedazador, -ra, *a.* dissecting; lacerating, mangling. — *n.m.f.* dissector; tearer; lacerator, mangler.

despedazamiento, *n.m.* laceration, mangling; dissection, cutting to pieces.

despedazar, *v.t.* (conjugated like APEDAZAR) to cut into pieces, tear up; to claw, mangle, lacerate; (*fig.*) to torment, harrow. — *v.r.* to break or fall into pieces; *despedazarse de risa*, to burst out laughing.

despedida, *n.f.* leave-taking, farewell, parting; dismissal, discharge; the last stanza in popular songs.

despedido, -da, *p.p.* [DESPEDIR] dismissed, discharged; under notice to quit; thrown off.

despedimiento, *n.m.* farewell, leave.

despedir, *v.t.* (conjugated like PEDIR) to discharge, emit, dart, fling, throw off; to dismiss, discharge from an office; to escort a guest to the door; to see a person off on a journey; to dismiss (as from the mind). — *v.r.* (with *de*) to take leave, say good-bye; to quit; to renounce; to leave a service or occupation; *despedirse a la francesa*, to sneak away, take French leave.

despedregar, *v.t.* to clear a place of stones.

despegable, *a.* that may be unglued or disjointed.

despegadamente, *adv.* roughly, harshly, unconcernedly.

despegado, -da, *a.* unglued, unstuck; (*coll.*) rough, morose, sullen, unpleasant; sour of temper; unaffectionate. — *p.p.* [DESPEGAR].

despegador, -ra, *n.m.f.*, *a.* (person) that unglues or detaches.

despegadura, *n.f.* dissolving, detaching, separating, ungluing.

despegamiento, *n.m.* asperity, moroseness, aversion, displeasure, coldness.

despegar, *v.t.* (conjugated like PEGAR) to separate, detach, disjoin, unglue; *despegar los labios* or *la boca,* to speak; (*aer.*) to take off. — *v.r.* to come off; to grow displeased, indifferent; to withdraw one's affection.

despego, *n.m.* asperity, aversion; indifference, coldness.

despeinado, -da, *a.* dishevelled, unkempt. — *p.p.* [DESPEINAR].

despeinar, *v.t.* to entangle, disarrange the hair.

despejadamente, *adv.* readily, freely, expeditiously, smartly.

despejado, -da, *a.* sprightly, quick, smart, vivacious, dexterous; serene, cloudless; unobstructed, clear. — *p.p.* [DESPEJAR].

despejar, *v.t.* to remove (impediments); to clear; (*alg.*) to solve, find the value of. — *v.r.* (*obs.*) to amuse oneself; to become bright and smart; to abate (of fever); *despejarse el cielo, el día, el tiempo,* to clear up, become fine weather.

despejo, *n.m.* removing obstacles; smartness, sprightliness, briskness, vivacity; grace, ease; clear-sightedness.

despelotar, *v.t.* (*obs.*) to dishevel the hair.

despeluzamiento, *n.m.* entangling, dishevelling hair; making hair stand on end.

despeluzar, despeluznar, *v.t.* to entangle, dishevel the hair; to make the hair stand on end. — *v.r.* to become horror-struck.

despeluznante, *a.* making the hair stand on end; horrifying.

despellejadura, *n.f.* [DESOLLADURA].

despellejar, *v.t.* to skin, flay; (*fig.*) to backbite; *despellejar un conejo,* to skin a rabbit.

despenador, -ra, *n.m.f.*, *a.* (person or thing) that removes pain.

despenar, *v.t.* to relieve from pain; (*coll.*) to kill; (*Chi.*) to deprive of hope.

despendedor, -ra, *a.* spendthrift. — *n.m.f.* spendthrift, prodigal, lavisher, waster.

despender, *v.t.* to spend, expend; (*fig.*) to squander, waste.

despensa, *n.f.* pantry, larder; store of provisions; stewardship; marketing; contract for a yearly supply of fodder; (*naut.*) steward's room; (*Mex.*) strong room in gold or silver mines.

despensería, *n.f.* office of steward.

despensero, -ra, *n.m.f.* caterer; steward; dispenser.

despeñadamente, *adv.* precipitately, rashly.

despeñadero, -ra, *a.* steep, headlong, precipitous; (*fig.*) dangerous. — *n.m.* precipice, crag.

despeñadizo, -za, *a.* steep, precipitous; slippery.

despeñar, *v.t.* to precipitate, fling down a precipice. — *v.r.* to throw oneself headlong; to lead a riotous life.

despeño, despeñamiento, *n.m.* precipitate fall; loss of fortune, character or credit; diarrhœa.

despepitar, *v.t.* to remove the seeds from; to gin. — *v.r.* to give vent to one's tongue; to vociferate; to speak or act rashly or angrily; *despepitarse por una cosa,* to long or yearn for a thing.

despercudir, *v.t.* to cleanse of stains.

desperdiciadamente, *adv.* profusely, wastefully.

desperdiciado, -da, *a.* wasted, destroyed, squandered. — *p.p.* [DESPERDICIAR].

desperdiciador, -ra, *n.m.f.*, *a.* spendthrift, squanderer, lavisher.

desperdiciar, *v.t.* to misspend, squander, fling away; not to utilize, not avail oneself of, lose, miss (an opportunity, etc.).

desperdicio, *n.m.* prodigality, profusion, waste; (*usually pl.*) garbage, remains, refuse, offal.

desperdigar, *v.t.* to separate, disjoin; to scatter.

desperecerse, *v.r.* (*pres. indic.* **desperezco;** *pres. subj.* **desperezca**) to crave, long, desire eagerly.

desperezarse, *v.r.* to stretch one's limbs.

desperezo, *n.m.* stretching one's arms and legs.

desperfecto, *n.m.* deterioration, wear and tear; slight injury or damage, blemish, flaw.

desperfilar, *v.t.* (*art*) to soften the lines of a painting; (*mil.*) to camouflage. — *v.r.* to lose the posture of a profile.

despernada, *n.f.* motion in dancing.

despernado, -da, *a.* tired, weary, footsore. — *p.p.* [DESPERNAR].

despernar, *v.t.* (conjugated like APERNAR) to injure or cut off the legs, cripple, maim.

despertador, -ra, *a.* awakening, arousing. — *n.m.f.* awakener, person who arouses; (*slang*) knocker-up. — *n.m.* alarum; alarm-clock (*fig.*) hint, warning, stimulus, incentive.

despertamiento, *n.m.* awakening.

despertar, *v.t.*, *v.r.* (*p.p.* **despertado, despierto;** *pres. indic.* **despierto;** *pres. subj.* **despierte**) to wake; to excite, sharpen (as appetite); to enliven; to call to mind, remind, recall. — *v.i.* to awake from sleep; to revive.

despesar, *n.m.* displeasure, dislike, aversion.

despestañar, *v.t.* to pluck out the eyelashes. — *v.r.* to look fixedly at anything, inspect closely; to apply oneself attentively; (*Arg.*) to study hard, to cram.

despezar, *v.t.* (*arch.*) to arrange stones in a building; (*plumbing*) to taper; to level.

despezo, *n.m.* (*plumbing*) diminution (at one end of a tube, pipe, etc.). — *pl.* stones cut into shape for a building.

despezonar, *v.t.* to cut or break off the teat,

stalk, etc.; to divide, separate. — *v.r.* to break off (applied to the stalk of fruit, etc.).

despezuñarse, *v.r.* to become useless (the hoof); (*Col., P.R., Hond., Chi.*) to rush, to speed; (*Col., Chi., Hond., PR.*) to long for, be dying for.

despiadadamente, *adv.* unmercifully, pitilessly.

despiadado, -da, *a.* pitiless, cruel; impious, godless.

despicar, *v.t.* (conjugated like PICAR) to satisfy, gratify. — *v.r.* (with *de* or *con*) to take revenge on, get square with; (*Arg.*) to break the point of the beak (in cock-fighting).

despichar, *v.t.* (*prov.*) to pick grapes; to expel moisture; (*Col., Chi.*) to squash, smash, crush. — *v.i.* (*coll.*) to die.

despidida, *n.f.* (*prov.*) gutter.

despidiente, *n.m.* (*build.*) board placed between a hanging scaffold and the wall; *despidiente de agua,* (*arch.*) flashing.

despido, *n.m.* dispatch; discharge; dismissal.

despido; despida, *pres. indic.; pres. subj.* [DESPEDIR].

despierno; despierne, *pres. indic.; pres. subj.* [DESPERNAR].

despiertamente, *adv.* ingeniously, cleverly.

despierto, -ta, *a.* awake; watchful; vigilant; diligent; brisk, lively, sprightly, smart. — *p.p. irreg.* [DESPERTAR].

despiezo, *n.m.* (*arch.*) juncture, bonding of one stone with another.

despilarar, *v.t.* (*S. Am.*) (*min.*) to knock down the props.

despilfarradamente, *adv.* wastefully; slovenly.

despilfarrado, -da, *a.* ragged, tattered; prodigal, wasteful. — *p.p.* [DESPILFARRAR].

despilfarrador, -ra, *n.m.f.* squanderer, waster.

despilfarrar, *v.t., v.r.* to squander, waste, destroy.

despilfarro, *n.m.* slovenliness, uncleanliness; waste, lavishness, squandering, extravagance; mismanagement, misgovernment, maladministration.

desimpollar, *v.t.* to prune vines.

despinces, *n.m.pl.* tweezers.

despintar, *v.t.* to blot or efface; to disfigure; (*fig.*) to mislead. — *v.i.* to be unworthy of. — *v.r.* to mistake one card for another; to fade, lose colour, wash off; *no despintársele a uno una persona,* to have a lively recollection of a person.

despinte, *n.m.* (*Chi.*) mineral of inferior standard.

despinzadera, *n.f.* woman who burls cloth; burling-iron.

despinzar, *v.t.* (*pret.* despincé; *pres. subj.* despince) to burl, pick knots from cloth.

despinzas, *n.f.pl.* pincers, tweezers, burling-iron.

despiojador, *n.m.* delouser (method or instrument).

despiojar, *v.t.* to clean of lice, to louse; to relieve of misery.

despique, *n.m.* vengeance, revenge.

despistar, *v.t.* to put off the scent, turn from the right trail.

despitorrado, *a.* said of a fighting bull with a broken horn.

despizcar, *v.t.* (conjugated like PIZCAR) to cut into small pieces; to crush, triturate. — *v.r.* to make the utmost exertions.

desplacer, *n.m.* displeasure, disgust. — *v.t.* (conjugated like PLACER) to displease, disgust.

desplantación, *n.f.* uprooting.

desplantar, *v.t.* (*obs.*) to uproot; to deviate from the vertical. — *v.r.* to lose one's erect posture in fencing or dancing.

desplante, *n.m.* oblique posture in fencing or dancing; injudicious action or speech.

desplatar, *v.t.* to separate silver from.

desplate, *n.m.* the act of separating silver from other metals.

desplayar, *v.i.* to go out (ebb).

desplazamiento, *n.m.* (*naut.*) displacement (of a vessel).

desplazar, *v.t.* to displace; (*mil.*) to drive out the enemy (from a position, etc.); (*naut.*) to have a displacement of.

desplazco; desplazca, *pres. indic.; pres. subj.* [DESPLACER].

desplegadura, *n.f.* unfolding, spreading out; elucidation, explanation.

desplegar, *v.t.* (conjugated like PLEGAR) to unfold, display; to spread, lay out; (*mil.*) to deploy; (*fig.*) to elucidate, explain; *desplegar la bandera,* to unfurl the flag. — *v.r.* to unfold; *desplegarse en guerrilla,* to deploy troops in skirmishing order; (*fig.*) to be communicative, open up.

desplego, *n.m.* (*obs.*) ingenuousness, confidence.

despleguetear, *v.t.* to remove folds from tendrils (vines).

despliegue, *n.m.* unfurling, unfolding; (*mil.*) deploying into battle order.

desplomar, *v.t.* to put out of plumb, make a wall, etc., bulge out. — *v.r.* to get out of plumb; to collapse, tumble down.

desplome, *n.m.* bulging, sagging, lack of verticality; tumbling down, collapse; (*Per.*) old method of mining.

desplomo, *n.m.* tilt, jutting out, being out of plumb (of a wall).

desplumadura, *n.f.* deplumation.

desplumar, *v.t.* to pluck out (feathers); (*coll.*) to strip of property. — *v.r.* to moult.

despoblación, *n.f.* depopulation.

despoblado, *n.m.* desert, uninhabited place; (*law*) aggravating circumstance in a crime committed in *despoblado.* — *p.p.* [DESPOBLAR].

despoblador, *a.* depopulating.

despoblar, *v.t.* to depopulate; (*fig.*) to despoil, make desolate; (*min. law*) to furnish a mine with less than the proper complement of men. — *v.r.* to become deserted.

despojador, -ra, *a.* despoiling, spoiling. — *n.m.f.* despoiler, spoiler.

despojar, *v.t.* to strip, despoil of property; (*coll.*) to fleece; to dismiss, turn out of a place or employment; to deprive of. — *v.r.* (with *de*) to undress, strip; to relinquish, forsake.

despojo, *n.m.* spoliation; spoils, plunder; slough, serpent's skin; butcher's offal; (*Col.*) mineral hewn from a seam. — *pl.* giblets, pluck, chitterlings; remains, relics, leavings; debris; secondhand building materials; mortal remains, corpse.

despolarización, *n.f.* depolarization.

despolarizar, *v.t.* to depolarize.

despolvar, *v.t.* to remove dust.
despolvorear, *v.t.* to dust; to scatter, dissipate; (*Col., Chi.*) to sprinkle.
despopularizar, *v.t., v.r.* (conjugated like POPULARIZAR) to render or become unpopular.
desportillar, *v.t.* to break the neck (of a bottle, etc.); to chip off corners or edges; (*arch.*) to splay.
desposado, -da, *a.* newly married; handcuffed. — *p.p.* [DESPOSAR].
desposando, -da, *n.m.f.* person newly married or about to be married.
desposar, *v.t.* to marry, perform the marriage ceremony for. — *v.r.* to be betrothed or married.
desposeer, *v.t.* to dispossess, oust.
desposeimiento, *n.m.* dispossession.
desposorio, *n.m.* act of betrothal; (*usually pl.*) mutual promise to contract marriage.
despostar, *v.t.* (*Arg., Bol., Chi., Ec.*) to cut up (a carcass).
despostillar, *v.t.* (*Mex.*) [DESPORTILLAR].
déspota, *n.m.* despot, tyrant.
despóticamente, *adv.* despotically.
despótico, -ca, *a.* despotic, despotical.
despotismo, *n.m.* despotism, absolutism.
despotizar, *v.t.* (*Arg., Chi., Per.*) to govern, act or behave despotically.
despotricar, *v.i., v.r.* (*coll.*) to talk inconsiderately, rave.
despreciable, *a.* contemptible, despicable, abject, worthless, lowly, mean, paltry, insignificant.
despreciador, -ra, *a.* despising, scorning. — *n.m.f.* despiser, scorner, depreciator, contemner.
despreciar, *v.t.* to scorn, despise, depreciate, contemn; to reject, lay aside.
desprecio, *n.m.* disregard, scorn, contempt, dispraise, disdain, contumely.
desprender, *v.t.* to unfasten, loosen, disjoin, separate; to emit, give out. — *v.r.* (*usually* with *de*) to give way, fall down; to extricate oneself; to issue from, come out of; to be deduced, inferred from; to get rid of.
desprendido, -da, *a.* disinterested, generous; unfastened, loose. — *p.p.* [DESPRENDER].
desprendimiento, *n.m.* act of loosening; landslip; indifference; disinterestedness; (*art*) the descent from the cross.
desprensar, *v.t.* (*print.*) to remove from the press.
despreocupación, *n.f.* non-prejudice, freedom from bias, free thought.
despreocupado, -da, *a.* unprejudiced, without prepossessions; unconventional. — *p.p.* [DESPREOCUPAR].
despreocupar, *v.t.* to free from prejudice or bias. — *v.r.* to abandon a prejudice; to be set right; (with *de*) to ignore, pay no attention to; to discard.
desprestigiado, -da, *a.* of bad repute. — *p.p.* [DESPRESTIGIAR].
desprestigiar, *v.t.* to bring into disrepute, impair the reputation of. — *v.r.* to lose reputation or prestige.
desprestigio, *n.m.* loss of reputation or prestige.
desprevención, *n.f.* improvidence, want of caution.
desprevenidamente, *adv.* improvidently.

desprevenido, -da, *a.* unprovided, unprepared, improvident.
desproporción, *n.f.* disproportion, want of symmetry; disparity.
desproporcionadamente, *adv.* disproportionately.
desproporcionado, -da, *a.* disproportionate; unsymmetrical, disproportioned; unsuitable, unbecoming. — *p.p.* [DESPROPORCIONAR].
desproporcionar, *v.t.* to disproportion, mismatch.
despropositado, -da, *a.* absurd, ridiculous, odd.
despropósito, *n.m.* absurdity, oddity, nonsense.
desproveer, *v.t.* (*p.p.* **desproveído, desprovisto**) to deprive of provisions, or necessaries of life.
desproveidamente, *adv.* improvidently.
desprovisto, -ta, *a.* (with *de*) unprovided, unprepared. — *p.p. irreg.* [DESPROVEER].
despueble, *n.m.* depopulation.
despueblo; despueble, *pres. indic.; pres. subj.* [DESPOBLAR].
después, *adv.* after, posterior (in time, location, and order); afterwards, next, then, later; *después acá*, ever since; *después de*, after; next to; *después (de) que*, after.
despulir, *v.t.* to tarnish; to frost, grind (glass).
despulpado, *n.m.* extracting pulp, or stoning fruits.
despulpar, *v.t.* to stone (fruits).
despulsar, *v.t., v.r.* to be pulseless and powerless through sudden accident; (*obs.*) to be sorely vexed; (with *por*) to desire eagerly.
despumación, *n.f.* skimming (of liquids).
despumar, *v.t.* to skim liquids.
despuntador, *n.m.* (*Mex.*) mineral separator; (*Mex.*) geological hammer.
despuntadura, *n.f.* act of blunting.
despuntar, *v.t.* to blunt; to crop, cut off, wear out a point; to cut away the dry combs of a beehive; (*naut.*) to double a cape. — *v.i.* to bud, sprout; to show genius; to make progress in knowledge; to surpass, excel morally; to dawn, in phrases such as *despuntar el día, el alba, la aurora; al despuntar del día*, at break of day.
desquejar, *v.t.* to pluck up a shoot near the root of a plant.
desqueje, *n.m.* pulling up a shoot near the root.
desquerer, *v.t.* to lose affection or liking for, cease to love or like.
desquiciar, *v.t.* to unhinge, disjoint; to unsettle, disorder; to deprive of favour or affection; to undermine; to overthrow. — *v.r.* to become unhinged; to lose support; to falter (through lack of support).
desquijaramiento, *n.m.* act of breaking jaws.
desquijarar, *v.t.* to break the jaws; (*naut.*) to break the check of a block. — *v.r.* to dislocate the jawbone.
desquijerar, *v.t.* (*carp.*) to tenon.
desquilatar, *v.t.* to lower the standard of gold; (*fig.*) to diminish or debase the intrinsic value of anything.
desquitar, *v.t.* to retrieve a loss. — *v.r.* to win one's money back again; to retaliate, get even, get square.
desquite, *n.m.* compensation, recovery of a loss; retaliation, revenge, satisfaction.

desrabotar, *v.t.* to cut off the tails of lambs.

desramar, *v.t.* to strip of branches.

desrancharse, *v.r.* to withdraw from a mess (regimental, etc.).

desraspar, *v.t.* (*obs.*) to scrape; to erase; (*agric.*) to remove the stalk from crushed grapes.

desrastrojar, *v.t.* (*agric.*) to remove stubble.

desratizar, *v.t.* to clear a place of rats.

desrazonable, *a.* unreasonable; scatter-brained.

desregladamente, *adv.* in a disorderly way, irregularly.

desreglado, -da, *a.* disorderly, irregular.

desreglarse, *v.r.* to be irregular, ungovernable.

desreputación, *n.f.* (*coll.*) dishonour, disrepute.

desrizar, *v.t.* (conjugated like RIZAR) to uncurl; (*naut.*) to unfurl.

desroblar, *v.t.* to take out rivets, unclinch.

desroñar, *v.t.* (*prov.*) to lop off decayed branches.

destacamento, *n.m.* detachment, station; military post.

destacar, *v.t.* (conjugated like ATACAR) (*mil.*) to detach a body of troops. — *v.r.* (*paint.*) stand out clearly; (*fig.*) excel, stand out.

destaconar, *v.t.* to wear out the heels.

destajador, *n.m.* kind of smith's hammer.

destajamiento, *n.m.* (*obs.*) taking a new course (of a river, etc.).

destajar, *v.t.* to do task-work; to let out work by the job; to settle the conditions under which work is to be done; to cut (at cards); *quien destaja no baraja,* one thing at a time.

destajero, destajista, *n.m.* one who does job-work.

destajo, *n.m.* job, task-work; *a destajo,* by the job, piece-work; earnestly, diligently; *hablar a destajo,* to talk excessively.

destalonar, *v.t.* to deprive of talons or heels; to wear out the heels; to separate receipts, etc. from the counterfoils; (*vet.*) to level the hoofs of.

destallar, *v.t.* to prune useless branches.

destapada, *n.f.* pie without upper crust.

destapar, *v.t.* to uncover. — *v.r.* to be uncovered.

destapiar, *v.t.* to pull down mud walls.

destaponar, *v.t.* to uncork.

destarar, *v.t.* (*com.*) to diminish the tare allowed in weighing something.

destartalado, -da, *a.* huddled, jumbled; scantily and poorly furnished.

destazador, *n.m.* one who cuts up carcases.

destazar, *v.t.* to cut up carcases.

deste, desta, desto, (*obs.*) contraction of *de este, de esta, de esto.*

destechadura, *n.f.* unroofing.

destechar, *v.t.* to unroof.

destejar, *v.t.* to untile; (*fig.*) to leave defenceless.

destejer, *v.t.* to unweave, ravel, unknit, unbraid.

destellar, *v.t.* to emit sparks, scintillations, flashes.

destello, *n.m.* sparkle, flash, scintillation, brilliancy.

destempladamente, *adv.* intemperately.

destemplado, -da, *a.* inharmonious; incongruous; intemperate; out of tune. — *p.p.* [DESTEMPLAR].

destemplanza, *n.f.* changeable of weather; intemperance, disorder; excess, abuse; (*med.*) indisposition, distemper; (*fig.*) want of moderation in language or actions.

destemplar, *v.t.* to distemper, alter, derange, disconcert; to untune; to put to confusion. — *v.r.* to be ruffled; to be out of sorts; to become irregular or abnormal; to lose moderation; to act improperly or rashly; to get out of tune; to lose temper (of metals); (*Ec., Guat., Mex.*) to have the teeth on edge.

destemple, *n.m.* discordance, disharmony; being out of tune; discomposure, disorder; intemperance, lack of moderation; (*med.*) distemper, slight indisposition; untempering, lack of temper (in metals).

destentar, *v.t.* to lead out of temptation by means of persuasion.

desteñir, *v.t.* (conjugated like TEÑIR) to remove dye, to wash out.

desternillarse, *v.r.* to break one's cartilages; (*med.*) to break a tendon; *desternillarse de risa,* to split one's sides with laughter.

desterradero, *n.m.* remote, inconvenient or unfashionable part of a town.

desterrado, -da, *a.* exiled, outcast, banished. — *n.m.f.* exile, banished person. — *p.p.* [DESTERRAR].

desterrar, *v.t.* to banish, expel, drive away; to remove earth from the roots of; (*fig.*) to lay aside; *desterrar la tristeza,* to put sorrow aside.

desterronar, *v.t.* to break clods with a harrow or spade.

destetadera, *n.f.* pointed instrument placed on cow's teats to keep calves from sucking.

destetamiento, *n.m.* weaning.

destetar, *v.t.* to wean. — *v.r.* to wean oneself from evil habits; *destetarse uno con una cosa,* to have known of a thing from one's cradle.

destete, *n.m.* weaning.

desteto, *n.m.* number of weanings (applied to cattle); place where newly weaned mules are kept.

destiempo, *adv.; a destiempo,* unseasonably, untimely.

destiento, *n.m.* surprise, commotion.

destierre, *n.m.* cleaning ore.

destierro, *n.m.* exile, banishment; place of exile; (*fig.*) place remote from centre of town, etc.

destierro; destierre, *pres. indic.; pres. subj.* [DESTERRAR].

destilable, *a.* distillable.

destilación, *n.f.* distillation; flow of humours; filtration; *destilación seca,* destructive distillation.

destiladera, *n.f.* still, distillation vessel, alembic; (*Am.*) filter.

destilador, -ra, *a.* distilling. — *n.m.f.* distiller. — *n.m.* filtering-stone; alembic, still, retort.

destilar, *v.t.* to distil; to filter. — *v.i.* to distil, drop, fall in drops; to filter; *la llaga destilaba sangre,* blood was oozing from the wound.

destilatorio, -ria, *a.* distillatory, distilling. — *n.m.* distillery; still, alembic.

destinación, *n.f.* destination; assignment.

destinar, *v.t.* to destine; to appoint; to designate; to allot, assign; (*naut.*) to station ships.

destino, *n.m.* destiny, fate, fortune, doom; destination; profession, appointment, employment, office; (*naut.*) station; *con destino a,* bound for, going to.

destiño, *n.m.* piece of blackish or greenish dry honeycomb.

destiño; (él) **destiñó,** *pres. indic.; 3rd person sing. pret.* [DESTEÑIR].

destitución, *n.f.* dismissal from employment or office; destitution; dereliction; abandonment.

destituido, -da, *a.* destitute, forsaken, helpless. — *p.p.* [DESTITUIR].

destituir, *v.t.* (conjugated like HUIR) to deprive; to make destitute; to dismiss from office.

destocar, *v.t.* (conjugated like TOCAR) to uncoif; to pull off the cap or head-dress from.

destorcer, *v.t.* (conjugated like TORCER) to untwist, uncurl, untwine; (*fig.*) to rectify, straighten out. — *v.r.* (*naut.*) to deviate from the course; to drift.

destornillado, -da, *a.* reckless; (*fig., fam.*) with a screw loose. — *p.p.* [DESTORNILLAR].

destornillador, *n.m.* unscrewer; screwdriver, wrench, turnscrew.

destornillamiento, *n.m.* unscrewing; (*fig.*) rashness, wildness.

destornillar, *v.t.* to unscrew. — *v.r.* (*fig.*) to act rashly.

destoserse, *v.r.* to feign a cough, clear the throat.

destostarse, *v.r.* to remove or gradually lose sunburn.

destotro, -tra, *a.* (*obs.*) contraction of *de este otro, de esto otro, de esta otra.*

destrabar, *v.t.* to unfetter, unbind, untie, separate.

destraillar, *v.t.* to unleash dogs.

destral, *n.m.* small hatchet or axe.

destraleja, *n.f.* very small hatchet.

destralero, *n.m.* one who makes *destrales.*

destramar, *v.t.* to unweave, undo the warp; (*obs.*) to unravel or defeat a plot.

destre, *n.m.* measure of length used in Balearic Islands (about 14 ft.).

destrejar, *v.i.* to work with skill.

destrenzar, *v.t.* (conjugated like TRENZAR) to unbraid, undo a tress.

destreza, *n.f.* dexterity, address, skill, handiness, cunning, expertness, nimbleness, adroitness, mastery; (*obs.*) skill in fencing.

destrincar, *v.t., v.r.* (*naut.*) to loose, unlash.

destripacuentos, *n.m.f.* (*coll.*) constant interrupter of a speaker.

destripar, *v.t.* to disembowel, grit, eviscerate; to crush, smash; (*fig.*) to take the inside out of anything; (*coll.*) to interrupt and spoil (a story); *destripar una botella,* to crack a bottle.

destripaterrones, *n.m.* (*coll.*) harrower, day labourer; country bumpkin.

destrísimo, -ma, *a. superl.* very dexterous.

destriunfar, *v.t.* to draw out all the trumps (in games of cards).

destrizar, *v.t.* (conjugated like TRIZAR) to mince, crumble, break in pieces, tear in strips. — *v.r.* to become heartbroken, wear away with grief.

destrocar, *v.t.* (conjugated like TROCAR) to return a thing bartered.

destrón, *n.m.* blind man's guide.

destronamiento, *n.m.* dethronement.

destronar, *v.t.* to dethrone, overthrow.

destroncamiento, *n.m.* detruncation, lopping of trees; ruination.

destroncar, *v.t.* (conjugated like RONCAR) to detruncate, lop (a tree); to maim, mutilate; to ruin, destroy; to interrupt, cut short; *destroncar un discurso,* to interrupt a harangue; (*Chi., Mex.*) to uproot, extirpate plants.

destrozador, -ra, *n.m.f.* destroyer, mangler.

destrozar, *v.t.* (*pret.* **destrocé;** *pres. subj.* **destroce**) to destroy, shatter, mangle; to break or cut in pieces; (*mil.*) to annihilate an enemy; (*fig.*) to spend too much, squander, waste.

destrozo, *n.m.* destruction, ruin; rout, defeat; massacre.

destrozón, -na, *a.* destructive of clothes, shoes, etc.

destrucción, *n.f.* destruction, overthrow, ruin, havoc, loss, extinction.

destructibilidad, *n.f.* destructibility.

destructible, *a.* destructible.

destructivamente, *adv.* destructively.

destructivo, -va, *a.* destructive, wasteful, consumptive.

destructor, -ra, *a.* destructive, destroying. — *n.m.f.* destroyer, destructor, harasser; (*naut.*) torpedo-boat; destroyer.

destructorio, -ria, *a.* destroying.

destrueco, destrueque, *n.m.* mutual restitution of things bartered.

destrueco; destrueque, *pres. indic.; pres. subj.* [DESTROCAR].

destruible, *adj.* destructible.

destruidor, -ra, *a.* destroying. — *n.m.f.* destroyer, devastator.

destruir, *v.t.* (conjugated like HUIR) to destroy, ruin, harass, waste, exterminate, extirpate, overthrow; (*fig.*) to demolish (an argument, etc.); (*fig.*) to prevent from earning a living; (*fig.*) to squander, waste. — *v.r.* (*alg.*) to cancel.

destruyente, *a.* [DESTRUIR] destroying.

destuerzo; destuerza, *pres. indic.; pres. subj.* [DESTORCER].

destusar, *v.t.* (*Am.*) to husk maize.

desubstanciar, *v.t.* to enervate, deprive of strength.

desucación, *n.f.* act of extracting juice.

desudar, *v.t.* to wipe sweat off something.

desuelo; desuele, *pres. indic.; pres. subj.* [DESOLAR].

desuellacaras, *n.m.* (*coll.*) bad barber; (*fig.*) shameless person.

desuello, *n.m.* flaying, fleecing, skinning; (*fig.*) forwardness, impudence, insolence; extortion; *ser un desuello una cosa,* to be rated at or cost a very high price.

desuello; desuelle, *pres. indic.; pres. subj.* [DESOLLAR].

desuncir, *v.t.* (conjugated like UNCIR) to unyoke.

desunidamente, *adv.* separately, severally.

desunión, *n.f.* disunion, disjunction, separation; discord, dissension, feud.

desunir, *v.t.* to disunite, separate, part; (*fig.*) to occasion discord between. — *v.r.* to loosen, fall, or break apart; to come asunder, become separated.

desuñar, *v.t.* to tear off the nails; to pull out the roots of trees. — *v.r.* (*coll.*, *fig.*) to work one's fingers to the bone; to plunge into vice and dissipation.

desuñir, *v.t.* (*Arg.* and *prov.*) to unyoke.

desurcar, *v.t.* (conjugated like SURCAR) to remove or undo furrows.

desurdir, *v.t.* to unravel, unweave; to upset, stop, frustrate (a plot, etc.).

desusadamente, *adv.* unusually, out of use, contrary to custom.

desusado, -da, *a.* disused, old, obsolete, archaic, unfashionable. — *p.p.* [DESUSAR].

desusar, *v.t.* to disuse, discontinue the use of. — *v.r.* to become obsolete, fall into disuse.

desuso, *n.m.* disuse, obsoleteness, desuetude.

desustanciar, *v.t.* to deprive of strength or substance; to enervate.

desvahar, *v.t.* to trim off the withered or dead parts of a plant.

desvaído, -da, *a.* tall and graceless, gaunt; dull (of colours).

desvainadura, *n.f.* act of shelling beans.

desvainar, *v.t.* to husk, shell; to remove the outer integument.

desvalido, -da, *a.* helpless, destitute, unprotected.

desvalijador, *n.m.* highwayman.

desvalijamiento, *n.m.* stealing the contents of a valise, etc.

desvalijar, *v.t.* to take out the contents of a portmanteau, etc.; (*fig.*) to rob by fraud or gambling.

desvalimiento, *n.m.* dereliction, abandonment, want of favour or protection.

desvalor, *n.m.* (*obs.*) cowardice; lack of merit.

desvalorizar, *v.t.* to diminish the value of a thing.

desván, *n.m.* garret, loft; *desván gatero,* cockloft.

desvanecer, *v.t.* (*pres. indic.* **desvanezco;** *pres. subj.* **desvanezca**) to divide into imperceptible parts, disintegrate, spread; to cause to evanesce or disappear; to take away from the sight; to undo, remove (a doubt, etc.). — *v.r.* to pall, grow vapid, become insipid; to vanish, evaporate, evanesce; to become giddy, faint, swoon; to be puffed up with presumption or pride.

desvanecidamente, *adv.* vainly, haughtily.

desvanecimiento, *n.m.* pride, haughtiness, loftiness; giddiness, dizziness; faint, swoon.

desvaporizadero, *n.m.* place for evaporating.

desvarar, *v.t.*, *v.r.* to slip, slide; (*naut.*) to refloat.

desvariable, *a.* (*obs.*) variable, changeable, disorderly, irregular.

desvariadamente, *adv.* ravingly, foolishly.

desvariado, -da, *a.* delirious, raving; disorderly, irregular; nonsensical; long, luxuriant (applied to foliage). — *p.p.* [DESVARIAR].

desvariar, *v.t.*, *v.i.* to rave, rant; to dote; to make extravagant demands.

desvarío, *n.m.* delirium, raving, giddiness; extravagant action or speech, extravagancy; inequality; inconstancy, caprice, whim; (*obs.*) derangement, disunion.

desvedado, -da, *a.* unprohibited, free. — *p.p.* [DESVEDAR].

desvedar, *v.t.* to revoke a prohibition.

desveladamente, *adv.* watchfully, vigilantly.

desvelado, -da, *a.* watchful, vigilant, careful. — *p.p.* [DESVELAR].

desvelamiento, *n.m.* watchfulness.

desvelar, *v.t.* to keep awake. — *v.r.* to be watchful, vigilant or zealous; to go without sleep, wake, watch.

desvelo, *n.m.* watching, lack of sleep; vigilance, watchfulness; anxiety, uneasiness.

desvenar, *v.t.* to remove the veins from the flesh; to take mineral from the veins (of mines); to remove the fibres from tobacco leaves, etc.; to raise the bit of a bridle.

desvencijado, -da, *a.* rickety, loose-jointed. — *p.p.* [DESVENCIJAR].

desvencijar, *v.t.* to disunite, weaken, divide, break. — *v.r.* to be disjointed, to work loose; (*obs.*) to be ruptured.

desvendar, *v.t.* to unbandage, take off a bandage from.

desveno, *n.m.* arch of a bit (horse).

desventaja, *n.f.* disadvantage, damage, misfortune, loss, disfavour.

desventajosamente, *adv.* disadvantageously, unprofitably.

desventajoso, -sa, *a.* disadvantageous, unfavourable, unprofitable, detrimental.

desventar, *v.t.* to vent, let out the air.

desventura, *n.f.* misfortune, calamity, mischance, mishap; misery.

desventuradamente, *adv.* unhappily, unfortunately.

desventurado, -da, *a.* unfortunate, wretched, unlucky, unhappy, miserable; chicken-hearted, pusillanimous, timid. — *n.m.f.* unlucky person; coward.

desvergonzadamente, *adv.* impudently, shamelessly.

desvergonzado, -da, *a.* impudent; shameless; immodest. — *p.p.* [DESVERGONZARSE].

desvergonzarse, *v.r.* (conjugated like AVERGONZAR) to speak or act impudently or insolently.

desvergüenza, *n.f.* impudence, insolence, effrontery, assurance; shamelessness; shameless or insolent speech or action.

desvergüenzo; desvergüence, *pres. indic.; pres. subj.* [DESVERGONZAR].

desvestir, *v.t.*, *v.r.* (conjugated like VESTIR) to undress, strip, denude.

desvezar, *v.t.* (*prov.*) to cut the young shoots of vines.

desviación, *n.f.* deflection, aberration; oblique direction; (*med.*) change from the natural position of the bones; (*med.*) extravasation of fluids; (*elec.*) variation of the magnetic needle; extravasation of fluids; (*astron.*) deviation from the meridian; (*railw.*) shunting, side-tracking.

desviadero, *n.m.* (*railw.*) switch, siding, side-track.

desviado, -da, *a.* devious, askew. — *p.p.* [DESVIAR].

desviar, *v.t.* to divert, lead off, deflect, sway, avert; to turn aside; to dissuade; (*fenc.*) to ward off; (*railw.*) to switch. — *v.r.* to deviate, turn away, turn off, wander; to swerve.

desviejar, *v.t.* to separate the old ewes or rams from a flock.

desvío, *n.m.* deviation; deflection; aversion, dislike; (*build.*) steadying board in a suspended platform; (*Arg., Chi., PR.*) railway siding.

desvirar, *v.t.* to pare off the rough edges of a boot-sole; to trim the edges of a book; (*naut.*) to reverse the capstan.

desvirgar, *v.t.* to deflower (a woman).

desvirtuar, *v.t.* to lessen the value, strength or merit of; to detract from.

desvitrificar, *v.t.* to devitrify.

desvivirse, *v.r.* (with *por*) to love to excess; to desire anxiously; to long for, be dying to.

desvolvedor, *n.m.* nut-wrench.

desvolver, *v.t.* (conjugated like VOLVER) to alter the shape of; to plough, till land.

desvuelto, *p.p. irreg.* [DESVOLVER].

desyemar, *v.t.* to remove buds from a plant.

desyerbador, -ra, *a.* weeding, grubbing.

desyerbar, *v.t.* to weed, grub up.

deszocar, *v.t.* to hurt, wound or disable the foot.

deszumar, *v.t.* to extract juice from.

detalladamente, *adv.* in detail, by retail.

detallar, *v.t.* to detail, relate minutely, enumerate, particularize, to specify, to retail.

detalle, *n.m.* detail, enumeration, specification, particular; retail.

detallista, *n.m.f.* retailer.

detasa, *n.f.* (*railw.*) rebate of freight.

detective, *n.m.* detective.

detector, *n.m.* (*wire.*) detector.

detención, *n.f.* detention, arrest; delay, stop, halt, standstill, deadlock; (*naut.*) demurrage, embargo; arrest (of a ship).

detenedor, -ra, *n.m.f.* detainer, stopper, arrester; check, catch.

detener, *v.t.* (conjugated like TENER) to stop, detain, fix, keep; to arrest, put in gaol; to retain, keep; (*naut.*) to embargo. — *v.r.* to tarry, go slowly; to pause in order to consider a matter minutely.

detengo; detenga, *pres. indic.; pres. subj.* [DETENER].

detenidamente, *adv.* slowly, attentively; cautiously; in detail; dilatorily.

detenido, -da, *a.* sparing, niggardly, parsimonious; dilatory; thorough, careful, conscientious. — *p.p.* [DETENER].

detenimiento, *n.m.* [DETENCIÓN].

detentación, *n.f.* (*law*) withholding (of an estate, etc.) from its rightful owner.

detentador, *n.m.* (*law*) deforcer.

detentar, *v.t.* (*law*) to detain, retain, keep unlawfully.

detergente, *a.* (*med.*) detergent, detersive.

deterger, *v.t.* (*med.*) to cleanse an ulcer, wound, etc.

deterior, *a.* worse, of inferior quality.

deterioración, *n.f.* deterioration, detriment, damage.

deteriorar, *v.t.* to deteriorate, damage, spoil, wear out.

deterioro, *n.m.* deterioration, impairment, injury, damage, wear and tear.

determinable, *a.* determinable, ascertainable.

determinación, *n.f.* determination, resolution; conclusion or final decision; firmness, boldness, audacity.

determinadamente, *adv.* determinately; resolutely; definitely; expressly, especially.

determinado, -da, *a.* bold, firm, daring; specified, determinate, determinated; (*math.*) resolved, decided; fixed, resolute; definite, settled. — *p.p.* [DETERMINAR].

determinante, *a.* determinate, determinative. — *n.m.* (*gram.*) determining verb.

determinar, *v.t.* to determine; to limit; to specify; to distinguish; to appoint, assign (time, place, etc.); to decide, resolve; (*law*) to judge, define. — *v.r.* to make a resolution, resolve, determine.

determinativo, -va, *a.* determinative.

determinismo, *n.m.* (*phil.*) determinism.

determinista, *n.m., a.* (*phil.*) determinist.

detersión, *n.f.* (*med.*) cleansing, detersion.

detersivo, -va, *a.* detersive.

detersorio, -ria, *n.m., a.* detergent.

detestable, *a.* detestable, hateful, heinous, loathsome.

detestablemente, *adv.* detestably, hatefully.

detestación, *n.f.* detestation, horror, hatred, abomination, abhorrence.

detestar, *v.t.* to detest, hate, abhor, abominate, loathe.

detienebuey, *n.m.* (*bot.*) common rest-harrow.

detonación, *n.f.* detonation, report, noise.

detonar, *v.i.* to detonate, flash, explode.

detorsión, *n.f.* (*med.*) distortion.

detracción, *n.f.* detraction, defamation, slander, obloquy; withdrawal, taking away.

detractar, *v.t.* to detract, defame, slander.

detractor, -ra, *a.* detracting, slandering. — *n.m.* detractor, slanderer.

detraer, *v.t.* (conjugated like TRAER) to detract, remove, take away; to defame, slander, libel.

detrás, *adv.* behind, after, back, in the rear; *detrás de,* behind, at the back of; (*fig.*) in one's absence, behind one's back; *por detrás,* behind one's back, from behind.

detrimento, *n.m.* detriment, damage, loss, harm, injury; *con (sin) detrimento de,* with (without) detriment to.

detrítico, -ca, *a.* detrital, detritic.

detritus, *n.m.* detritus.

deuda, *n.f.* debt, fault, offence; indebtedness; public debt; *deudas activas,* assets; *deuda común,* death, nature's debt; *deuda consolidada,* funded debt; *deudas pasivas,* liabilities; *deuda pendiente,* unpaid balance; *sin deudas,* clear.

deudo, -da, *n.m.f.* relative, parent, kinsman, kindred, relation; kinship.

deudor, -ra, *a.* indebted. — *n.m.f.* debtor.

deuteronomio, *n.m.* Deuteronomy.

deutóxido, *n.m.* (*chem.*) dioxide.

devalar, *v.i.* (*naut.*) to drift, deviate from the course.

devanadera, *n.f.* reel, spool, bobbin, winding-frame; (*naut.*) log-reel; (*theat.*) revolving wing.

devanador, -ra, *a.* reeling, winding. — *n.m.* winder, quill, spool, reel; *devanador de lanzadera,* shuttle-winder.

devanar, *v.t.* to reel, spool, wind (yarn, etc.); *devanarse los sesos,* to cudgel one's brains.

devanear, *v.i.* to rave, dote, be delirious, talk nonsense.

devaneo, *n.m.* delirium, frenzy, giddiness; dissipation; idle or mad pursuit; alienation of mind; flirtation.

devantal, *n.m.* apron [DELANTAL].

devastación, *n.f.* devastation, destruction, waste, ruin.

devastador, -ra, *a.* devastating, destroying. — *n.m.f.* desolator, harasser, spoiler.

devastar, *v.t.* to desolate, waste, ruin, harass.

devengar, *v.t.* (conjugated like VENGAR) to obtain in exchange for labour or as fee, salary, interest, etc.; *derechos a devengar,* duties, rights, dues.

devoción, *n.f.* piety, godliness; prayer; ardent love, devotion, strong affection, strong attachment; (*theol.*) ready acceptance of God's will; *estar a la devoción de alguno,* to be at someone's disposal.

devocionario, *n.m.* prayer-book.

devocionero, -ra, *a.* devotional.

devolución, *n.f.* return, restitution; devolution; *devolución de derechos,* (*com.*) drawback; debenture.

devolutivo, -va, *a.* (*law*) restorable.

devolver, *v.t.* (conjugated like VOLVER) to restore (a thing to its original state); to return, refund, pay back (to the original possessor).

devoniano, -na, *a.* (*geol.*) devonian.

devorador, -ra, *a.* devouring, ravenous; intense. — *n.m.f.* devourer.

devorar, *v.t.* to devour, consume, swallow up.

devotamente, *adv.* devoutly, piously, devotedly.

devotería, *n.f.* bigotry.

devoto, -ta, *a.* devout, devotional, religious, godly, pious, exciting devotion; strongly attached, devoted.

devuelto, -ta, *a.* returned, restored. — *p.p. irreg.* [DEVOLVER].

devuelvo; devuelva, *pres. indic.; pres. subj.* [DEVOLVER].

dextro, *n.m.* area round a church.

deyección, *n.f.* (*geol.*) debris; (*med.*) dejection.

dezmable, *a.* tithable.

dezmar, *v.t.* [DIEZMAR].

dezmatorio, *n.m.* tithing; place in which tithes are collected.

dezmeño, -ña; dezmero, -ra, *a.* belonging to tithes. — *n.m.* payer or collector of tithes.

dezmería, *n.f.* tithe-land.

di, *pret. irreg.* [DAR]; *imperative irreg.* [DECIR].

día, *n.m.* day; daylight, sunshine; *a días,* at times; *buenos días,* good morning; *al día,* up to date; per day; *días ha,* a long time ago; *de día,* by day; *al otro día,* on the next day; *de día en día* or *de un día para otro,* from one day to another; *en su día,* at the proper time; *en días de Dios, en los días de la vida,* never; *dar los días,* to send birthday wishes; *entre día,* in the daytime; *tener días,* to be moody; to be old; *todo el santo día,* (*fam.*) the whole day long; *de hoy en ocho días,* this day week; *hombre de día;* or *entrado en días,* a quite elderly man; *los días de uno,* one's birthday; *no se van los días en balde,* age and experience count for much; *más días hay que longanizas,* there is no hurry or urgency; *ser del día,* to be in fashion; *llevarse el día en una cosa,* to be all day about a thing; *cada tercer día,* every other day; *en cuatro días,* very soon, very shortly; *un día sí y otro no,* every other day; *día de años* or *cumpleaños,* birthday; *día de ayuno,* fast-day; *día de besamanos,* court day; *días caniculares,* dog days; *día de carne,* nonfasting day; *día de cutio, día laborable,* work-day, working day; *día de descanso,* Sunday, rest-day; *día de fiesta* or *día festivo,* holiday; *días de gracia,* days of grace (in paying bills); *día de huelga,* day off (when no work is done); *día del juicio,* doomsday; *día de los difuntos,* All-Souls Day; *día de recibo,* at-home day; *día entre semana,* week-day;

día diado, appointed day; *uno que otro día,* some day or another; *el día menos pensado,* unexpectedly; *día de mucho, víspera de nada,* in luck to-day and out to-morrow; *día natural,* full day (from sunrise to sunset); *días y ollas,* patience and time work wonders; *día quebrado,* half-holiday; *día de trabajo, día útil* or *día laborable,* working day; *día de viernes,* lean day; *día de vigilia,* fast-day; *al buen día ábrele la puerta, y para el malo te apareja,* take good when it comes and be ready for evil; *al buen día, métele en casa,* take advantage of opportunities; *alcanzar a uno en días,* to outlive a person; *el día que te casas, o te curas o te matas,* marriage is killing or curing; *el día de hoy* or *hoy en día,* nowadays; *el mejor día,* some fine day; *mañana será otro día,* tomorrow is another day; there's no hurry; *abrir, despuntar* or *romper el día,* to dawn; *todo el santo día,* (*fam.*) the whole blessed day; *un día de vida es vida,* said when an expected misfortune does not come at once; *vivir al día,* to spend all one earns.

diabasa, *n.f.* (*geol.*) diorite.

diabetes, *n.m.* (*med.*) diabetes.

diabético, -ca, *a.* diabetic.

diabeto, *n.m.* automatic flushing cistern.

diabla, *n.f.* (*coll.*) she-devil; carding-machine; two-wheeled carriage; *a la diabla,* carelessly, rudely; *cosido a la diabla,* paper-bound (book).

diablazo, *n.m.* great devil.

diablear, *v.t.* (*coll.*) to lay diabolical plots, play pranks.

diablejo, *n.m.* little devil.

diablesa, *n.f.* (*coll.*) she-devil.

diablillo, *n.m.* little devil [DIABLO]; smart, clever fellow, a cute man.

diablito, *n.m.* (*Cub.*) person clowning at Twelfth Night.

diablo, *n.m.* devil, demon; fiend; (*fig.*) bad-tempered or ugly or cunning person; *ahí será el diablo,* there will be the devil to pay; *aquí hay mucho diablo,* (*coll.*) this is an awkward, dangerous or ticklish business; *andar* or *estar el diablo en Cantillana,* to make disturbances anywhere; *andar el diablo suelto,* the devil among the tailors; *dar al diablo,* to send to perdition; *dar que hacer al diablo,* to do an evil deed; *darse uno al diablo,* to become desperate; *el diablo harto de carne se metió fraile,* young sinner, old saint; *el diablo las carga,* unexpected trouble may arise; *¡el diablo que ...!* no one, the devil a bit ...; *el diablo sea sordo,* saving your presence; touch wood!; *diablo cojuelo,* artful, deceiving devil; *eso es el diablo,* (*coll.*) that is the difficulty; *no valer un diablo,* to be good for nothing; *como un diablo,* exceedingly, excessively; *ser (de) la piel del diablo,* to be a limb of the devil; *tras la cruz está el diablo,* behind the cross is the devil; *cuando el diablo reza, engañarte quiere,* beware of the devil as a monk; *dar de comer al diablo,* to slander; to use provocative language; *estar dado al diablo,* to be very infuriated; *guárdate del diablo,* take great care; *hablar con el diablo,* to be very astute; *llevarse una cosa el diablo,* to have ill success; *más que el diablo,* with great repugnance; *no sea al diablo que,* here's the rub; *tener uno el diablo en el cuerpo,* to be very astute; *tirar el diablo de la* *manta,* to let the cat out of the bag; *vaya el diablo por ruin,* let us have peace and good will.

diablotín, diabolín, *n.m.* sort of sweetmeat.

diablura, *n.f.* diabolical undertaking; devilishness, deviltry; wild prank, mischief.

diabólicamente, *adv.* diabolically, devilishly.

diabólico, -ca, *a.* diabolical, devilish.

diábolo, *n.m.* diabolo (game).

diacitrón, *n.m.* candied lemon-peel.

diacodión, *n.m.* syrup of poppy.

diaconado, diaconato, *n.m.* deaconship.

diaconal, *a.* diaconal.

diaconía, *n.f.* deaconry.

diaconisa, *n.f.* deaconess.

diácono, *n.m.* deacon.

diacrítico, -ca, *a.* (*gram.*) diacritic; (*med.*) diagnostic.

diacústica, *n.f.* diacoustics.

diacústico, -ca, *a.* diacoustic.

diadema, *n.f.* diadem, crown; halo.

diademado, -da, *a.* diademed.

diado, *a.; día diado,* appointed day.

diafanidad, *n.f.* transparency.

diáfano, -na, *a.* transparent, diaphanous.

diaforesis, *n.f.* (*med.*) perspiration.

diafragma, *n.m.* (*anat.*) diaphragm.

diafragmático, -ca, *a.* diaphragmatic.

diagnosis, *n.f.* (*med.*) diagnosis.

diagnosticar, *v.t.* (*pret.* **diagnostiqué**; *pres. subj.* **diagnostique**) (*med.*) to diagnose.

diagnóstico, -ca, *a.* (*med.*) diagnostic. — *n.m.* diagnosis.

diagonal, *a.* diagonal, oblique. — *n.f.* (*geom.*) diagonal.

diagonalmente, *adv.* diagonally, obliquely.

diágrafo, *n.m.* diagraph.

diagrama, *n.f.* diagram.

diálaga, *n.f.* (*min.*) diallage.

dialéctico, -ca, *n.f.* logic, dialectics; *n.m.* dialectician, logician. — *a.* dialectical, logical.

dialecto, *n.m.* dialect, variety of language; one of a group of languages descended from one parent stock.

dialogal, *a.* dialogical.

dialogar, *v.t.* to dialogize; to write in dialogue.

dialogístico, -ca, *a.* dialogic.

dialogizar, *v.i.* to dialogize.

diálogo, *n.m.* dialogue.

dialoguista, *n.m.* dialogist.

dialtea, *n.f.* marsh-mallow ointment.

diamantado, -da, *a.* diamond-like.

diamante, *n.m.* (*min.*) diamond; miner's lamp; *diamante en bruto,* rough diamond; (*fig., coll.*) rough diamond (person).

diamantino, -na, *a.* adamantine.

diamantista, *n.m.* diamond-cutter; jeweller.

diametral, *a.* diametrical.

diametralmente, *adv.* diametrically.

diámetro, *n.m.* diameter.

diana, *n.f.* (*mil.*) reveille; (*mil.*) bull's-eye, centre of a target; (*poét.*) moon.

dianche, diantre, *n.m.* (*coll.*) deuce, devil.

diapasón, *n.m.* diapason; pitch, accord; regular octave; *diapasón normal,* standard pitch; tuning fork.

diapente, *n.m.* (*mus.*) perfect fifth.

diaplejía, *n.f.* (*med.*) general paralysis.

diapositiva, *n.f.* diapositive, lantern-slide.

diaprea, *n.f.* kind of plum.

diaquilón, *n.m.* (*pharm.*) diachylon, plaster.

diariamente, *adv.* daily, every day.

diario, -ria, *a.* daily. — *n.m.* journal, diary; daily newspaper; daily household expenses; *libro diario,* (*com.*) day-book, journal; *diario de navegación,* (*naut.*) log-book.

diarista, *n.m.f.* journalist, diarist.

diarrea, *n.f.* diarrhœa.

diarreico, -ca, (*med.*) **diárrico, -ca,** *a.* diarrhœic.

diáspero, diaspro, *n.m.* jasper.

diástilo, *n.m.* (*arch.*) diastyle.

diatérmano, -na; diatérmico, -ca, *a.* diathermanous.

diatesarón, *n.m.* (*mus.*) diatessaron, the interval of a fourth.

diatómico, -ca, *a.* (*chem.*) diatomic.

diatónico, -ca, *a.* (*mus.*) diatonic.

diatriba, *n.f.* diatribe.

dibujador, -ra, *a.* delineating. — *n.m.f.* delineator, graver, designer.

dibujante, *a.* designing, sketching. — *n.m.* designer, draughtsman.

dibujar, *v.t.* to draw, sketch, design, paint, depict, outline, delineate; to describe, portray. — *v.r.* to appear, be revealed, take form, stand out.

dibujo, *n.m.* design, draft, drawing, sketch; description, delineation; *dibujo a pulso,* free-hand drawing; *dibujo del natural,* drawing from life or nature; *dibujo lineal,* instrumental drawing; *¡es un dibujo!* it's a picture!; *no meterse uno en dibujos,* to abstain from doing or saying more than is fitting.

dicacidad, *n.f.* pertness, banter, sauciness.

dicaz, *a.* keen, biting (of speech).

dicción, *n.f.* diction, style, expression.

diccionario, *n.m.* dictionary, lexicon.

diccionarista, *n.m.f.* lexicographer.

diciembre, *n.m.* December.

diciente, dicente, *a.* saying, talking.

dicotomía, *n.f.* dichotomy.

dicotómico, -ca; dicótomo, -ma, *a.* dichotomous.

dictado, *n.m.* dictation; title of dignity. — *pl.* dictates, promptings (of conscience, etc.); *escribir uno al dictado,* to write to another's dictation. — *p.p.* [DICTAR].

dictador, *n.m.* dictator.

dictadura, *n.f.* dictatorship, dictature.

dictamen, *n.m.* opinion, judgment, mind, sentiments; suggestion, insinuation, advice; *casarse uno con su dictamen,* to stick to one's opinions; *tomar dictamen de uno,* to take counsel of someone.

dictaminar, *v.i.* to express an opinion.

díctamo, *n.m.* (*bot.*) dittany; *díctamo blanco* or *real,* white paxinella; *díctamo crético,* marjoram; *díctamo bastardo,* bastard dittany.

dictar, *v.t.* to dictate; to command, prescribe, direct; (*fig.*) to inspire, prompt, suggest.

dictatorial, *a.* dictatorial.

dictatorialmente, *adv.* dictatorially.

dictatorio, -ria, *a.* dictatorial.

dicterio, *n.m.* taunt, keen reproach; insult.

dicha, *n.f.* happiness, felicity, fortune, good fortune, good luck; (*Chi.*) name of several weeds with prickly fruits or leaves; *por dicha* or *a dicha,* by chance; *nunca es tarde si la dicha es buena,* good luck is worth waiting for.

dicharachero, -ra, *a.* (*coll.*) addicted to using slang.

dicharacho, *n.m.* (*coll.*) low, vulgar or indecent expression.

dichero, -ra, *a.* (*prov.*, *coll.*) witty in conversation.

dicho, *n.m.* saying, proverb, saw; expression, sentence. — *p.p. irreg.* [DECIR]; *dicho y hecho,* no sooner said than done; *del dicho al hecho, hay gran trecho,* saying and doing are two very different things; *lo dicho, dicho,* I mean what I say; *tener una cosa por dicha,* to take a thing as having been said in earnest. — *pl.* statement of intention to marry made by both parties before a priest.

dichosamente, *adv.* happily, fortunately, luckily.

dichoso, -sa, *a.* happy, fortunate; lucky, prosperous, successful.

didáctica, *n.f.* didactics.

didácticamente, *adv.* didactically.

didáctico, -ca; didascálico, -ca, *a.* didactic.

diecinueve, *a.* nineteenth. — *n.m.* nineteen.

diecinueveavo, -va, *a.* nineteenth part.

dieciochavo -va; dieciocheno, -na, *a.* eighteenth. — *n.m.* a kind of cloth; old coin struck in Valencia.

dieciocho, *a.* eighteen.

dieciséis, *a.* sixteen.

dieciseisavo, -va; dieciseseno, -na, *a.* sixteenth.

diecisiete, *a.* seventeen.

diecisieteavo, -va, *a.* seventeenth.

diedro, -dra, *a.* (*geom.*) dihedral.

Diego, *n.m.* James.

dieléctrico, -ca, *a.* dielectric.

diente, *n.m.* tooth, fang, tusk; tooth (of a saw, comb, etc.); cog (of a wheel); prong (of a fork); tongue (of a buckle); clove (of garlic). — *pl.* indented edges of tools or ornaments, indentations; *diente de león,* dandelion; *diente de lobo,* spike, burnisher; *diente de perro,* sculptor's chisel; (*bot.*) dog-tooth violet; (*sew.*) sampler; *dar diente con diente,* to chatter with cold or fear (of teeth); *estar a diente,* to be hungry and fasting; *dientes postizos,* artificial teeth; *cuando pienses meter el diente en seguro, toparás en duro,* difficulties often crop up to prevent apparently certain success; *hincar el diente,* to misappropriate another's property; to calumniate another; *no haber para untar un diente, no llegar a un diente,* to have insufficient to eat; *tener buen diente,* to be a hearty eater; *a regaña dientes,* most unwillingly; *dientes de ajo,* cloves of garlic; *aguzar los dientes,* to whet the appetite; *ala:garle a uno una cosa los dientes,* to set one's teeth on edge; *antes* or *primero son mis dientes que mis parientes,* a man must study his own interests before those of others; *crujir de dientes, crujirle a uno los dientes,* to grind (or gnash) the teeth; *de dientes afuera,* insincerely; *enseñar* (*los*) *dientes,* to threaten, resist, oppose; *estar a diente,* to be hungry and have nothing to eat; *haberle nacido* or *salido a uno* (*los dientes*) *en una parte* or *haciendo una cosa,* to have lived in a place or been doing something since infancy; *hablar* or *decir entre dientes,* to mumble, speak indistinctly; to growl. mutter, grumble; *mostrar los dientes,* to oppose, growl at; *no entrarle a uno de los dientes adentro una persona* or *cosa,* not to be able to bear a person or thing; *pasar los dientes,* to set the teeth on edge with cold food; *quitar a uno los dientes,* to threaten

with severe punishment; *tomar* or *traer entre dientes,* to have a grudge against, speak ill of.

dientecico, dientecillo, dientecito, *n.m.* little tooth [DIENTE].

diento; diente, *pres. indic.; pres. subj.* [DENTAR].

diéresis, *n.f.* diæresis.

diesi, *n.f.* (*mus.*) diesis; (*mus.*) a sharp.

diestra, *n.f.* right hand; favour, support, protection; *juntar diestra con diestra,* to form a friendly alliance.

diestramente, *adv.* dexterously, cleverly, neatly.

diestro, -tra, *a.* right; expert, skilful, handy, dexterous, prudent; sagacious; sly, cunning, artful; favourable, propitious; *a diestro y a siniestro,* without order or discretion; recklessly; *a un diestro, un presto,* promptness is sometimes more important than skill; *de diestro a diestro, el más presto,* other things being equal, promptness wins the day. — *n.m.* skilful fencer; matador, bull-fighter; halter, bridle; *llevar del diestro,* to lead a beast by the halter or bridle; *esto va de diestro a diestro,* they are well matched.

dieta, *n.f.* diet, regimen; (*coll.*) fast, fasting; diet, legislative assembly; (*law*) day's journey of ten leagues; daily salary of judges and law officers; (*obs.*) daily fees paid to a doctor. — *pl.* (*naut.*) provisions for the sick and wounded; daily fees (*Cortes,* etc.).

dietario, *n.m.* day book; record of notable events.

dietético, -ca, *a.* dietetic. — *n.f.* dietetics.

diez, *n.m., a.* ten, tenth; *diez de bolos,* pin placed alone in front of ninepins; *a las diez,* at ten o'clock; *a las diez, en la cama estés, y si ser puede, a las nueve,* go early to bed.

diezmal, *a.* decimal, tenth.

diezmar, *v.t.* to decimate; to pay tithe; (*mil.*) to punish one in ten.

diezmero, *n.m.* one who pays or collects a tithe.

diezmesino, -na, *a.* ten-monthly; ten months old.

diezmilésimo, -ma, *a.* ten-thousandth (part).

diezmillonésimo, -ma, *a.* ten-thousand-millionth (part).

diezmillonésimo, -ma, *a.* ten-millionth (part).

diezmo, *n.m.* tithe; tenth part; duty of ten per cent.; decimation.

difamación, *n.f.* defamation, calumny, libelling.

difamador, -ra, *a.* defamatory. — *n.m.f.* defamer, libeller.

difamar, *v.t.* to defame, discredit, libel.

difamatorio, -ria, *a.* defamatory, libellous, scandalous, calumnious.

diferencia, *n.f.* difference, unlikeness, dissimilitude; controversy, contrariety, disagreement; *a diferencia,* with the difference; *partir la diferencia,* to split the difference.

diferenciación, *n.f.* differentiation.

diferencial, *a.* differential. — *n.f.* (*math., mec.*) differential.

diferenciar, *v.t.* to differentiate; to change or alter the use of. — *v.i.* to differ, dissent, disagree. — *v.r.* to be different; to distinguish oneself.

diferente, *a.* different, unlike, dissimilar.

diferentemente, *adv.* differently, diversely.

diferir, *v.t.* (*pres. indic.* **difiero**; *pres. subj.* **difiera**) to defer, delay, postpone; to adjourn, suspend, put off. — *v.i.* to differ, be different; (*naut.*) to remove the gaskets from a sail.

difícil, *a.* difficult, arduous, hard.

difícilmente *adv.* hardly, scarcely; with difficulty.

dificultad, *n.f.* difficulty, hardness; objection; obstacle; impediment; *herir (en) la dificultad*, to discover the difficulty; *quedar(se) la dificultad en pie*, to continue (of a difficulty).

dificultador, -ra, *a.* causing difficulty. — *n.m.f.* one who raises difficulties.

dificultar, *v.t.* to raise difficulties, render difficult; to impede. — *v.i.* to consider unlikely.

dificultosamente, *adv.* difficultly, with difficulty.

dificultoso, -sa, *a.* difficult, hard, laborious, painful; (*coll.*) ugly, deformed.

difidación, *n.f.* declaration of war; manifesto justifying such a declaration.

difidencia, *n.f.* distrust.

difidente, *a.* distrustful.

difiero; difiera, *pres. indic.; pres. subj.* [DIFERIR].

difilo, -la, *a.* (*bot.*) two-leafed.

difluir, *v.i.* to be diffused, spread out, shed.

difracción, *n.f.* (*opt.*) diffraction.

difrige, *n.m.* (*min.*) dross of smelted copper.

difteria, *n.f.* (*med.*) diphtheria.

diftérico, -ca, *a.* diphtheritic.

difteritis, *n.f.* (*med.*) diphtheritis.

difundido, -da, *a.* diffuse, scattered. — *p.p.* [DIFUNDIR].

difundir, *v.t., v.r.* (*p.p.* **difundido, difuso**) to diffuse, extend, outspread; to divulge, publish abroad; (*wire.*) to broadcast.

difunto, -ta, *a.* defunct, dead, deceased, late; decayed, withered. — *n.m.* dead person; corpse; *día de los difuntos*, All-Souls Day.

difusamente, *adv.* diffusely, diffusedly.

difusible, *a.* diffusible.

difusión, *n.f.* diffusion; dispersion; exuberance of style; (*wire.*) broadcasting.

difusivo, -va, *a.* diffusive.

difuso, -sa, *a.* diffuse, diffusive; wordy; widespread. — *p.p. irreg.* [DIFUNDIR].

difusor, -ra, *a.* diffusive; (*wire.*) broadcasting; diffuser (sugar manufacture).

digástrico, -ca, *a.* digastric.

digerible, *a.* digestible.

digerir, *v.t.* (*pres. indic.* **digiero**; *pres. subj.* **digiera**) to digest; to examine carefully; to be patient, bear, put up with; (*chem.*) to digest.

digestible, *a.* digestible.

digestión, *n.f.* digestion; (*med.*) infusion.

digestivo, -va, *a.* digestive. — *n.m.* (*surg.*) suppurative.

digesto, *n.m.* (*law*) digest.

digestor, *n.m.* digester (apparatus).

digiero; digiera, *pres. indic.; pres. subj.* [DIGERIR].

digitación, *n.f.* fingering.

digitado, -da, *a.* (*bot., zool.*) digitate.

digital, *a.* (*anat.*) digital. — *n.f.* (*bot.*) digitalis, foxglove.

digitalina, *n.f.* (*chem.*) digitalin.

digito, -ta, *a.* digital. — *n.m.* (*math., astron.*) digit.

dignación, *n.f.* condescension; accommodation.

dignamente, *adv.* with dignity; worthily, honourably, justly.

dignarse, *v.r.* to condescend, deign; vouchsafe.

dignatario, *n.m.* dignitary.

dignidad, *n.f.* rank, dignity, high office or position; honour, greatness; dignified bearing.

dignificante, *a.* (*theol.*) dignifying.

dignificar, *v.t.* to dignify.

digno, -na, *a.* meritorious, worthy, deserving; suitable, fitting, appropriate.

digo; diga, *pres. indic.; pres. subj.* [DECIR].

digresión, *n.f.* digression; deviation, divergence.

digresivamente, *adv.* digressively.

digresivo, -va, *a.* digressive.

dihueñe, dihueñi, *n.m.* (*Chi.*) edible fungus growing on trees.

dij, dije, *n.m.* amulet, charm; trinket; (*coll.*) person gorgeously attired; person of fine character. — *pl.* bravado, boasting, bragging, threats.

dije, *pret. irreg.* [DECIR].

dilaceración, *n.f.* tearing in pieces.

dilacerar, *v.t.* to lacerate, tear.

dilación, *n.f.* delay, procrastination.

dilapidación, *n.f.* dilapidation, squandering.

dilapidador, -ra, *a.* dilapidating. — *n.m.f.* dilapidator.

dilapidar, *v.t.* to dilapidate, squander.

dilatabilidad, *n.f.* (*phys.*) quality of dilatation.

dilatable, *a.* dilatable.

dilatación, *n.f.* dilatation, expansion, extension; prolongation; enlargement; prolixity, diffuseness; calmness, serenity in grief; *dilatación lineal*, linear expansion.

dilatadamente, *adv.* dilatedly; with delay or procrastination.

dilatado, -da, *a.* large, great, vast, extensive, spacious; prolix, drawn out. — *p.p.* [DILATAR].

dilatador, -ra, *a.* dilating, expanding; retarding, causing delay. — *n.m.f.* one who dilates or extends. — *n.m.* (*surg.*) dilator.

dilatar, *v.t.* to dilate, widen, enlarge, lengthen, expand; to swell out; (*fig.*) to retard, prolong, defer, protract; to cheer, comfort. — *v.r.* to be diffuse; to expatiate; to expand.

dilatativo, -va, *a.* dilative.

dilatoria, *n.f.* delay, waste of time; (*law*) time granted by a court to a debtor, etc.; *andar con dilatorias*, to deceive with false promises.

dilatorio, -ria, *a.* (*law*) dilatory, delaying, long.

dilección, *n.f.* dilection, love, affection.

dilecto, -ta, *a.* loved, beloved.

dilema, *n.m.* dilemma.

diligencia, *n.f.* diligence, industriousness, assiduity; activity, speed, briskness, haste; obligation, duty; (*coll.*) business, affair; stage-coach; (*law*) judicial formalities, procedure; *evacuar una diligencia*, to triumph over a difficulty; *hacer (la) diligencia*, to try, endeavour; to do an errand; *hacer uno sus diligencias*, to use all one's powers to achieve an object; *hacer las diligencias de cristiano*, to fulfil the ritual duties enjoined by the church; *la diligencia es madre de la buena ventura*, diligence is mother of good fortune.

diligenciar, *v.t.* to take the necessary steps, set into motion; (*law*) to carry out, take proceedings.

diligenciero, *n.m.* agent, attorney; (*law*) apparitor, summoner.

diligente, *a.* diligent, laborious, active, assiduous; prompt, ready, swift.

diligentemente, *adv.* diligently, assiduously.

dilogía, *n.f.* ambiguity, double sense.

dilucidación, *n.f.* elucidation, explanation.

dilucidador, -ra, *a.* elucidating. — *n.m.f.* elucidator.

dilucidar, *v.t.* to elucidate, explain.

dilucidario, *n.m.* explanatory writing.

dilución, *n.f.* dilution.

dilúculo, *n.m.* the sixth part of the night; dawn.

diluente, *a.* diluent.

diluir, *v.t.* (conjugated like HUIR) to dilute, weaken.

dilusivo, -va, *a.* delusive.

diluvial, *a.* (*geol.*) diluvial.

diluviano, -na, *a.* diluvian.

diluviar, *v. impers.* to rain like a deluge.

diluvio, *n.m.* deluge, inundation, flood; over-flow; (*coll.*) vast abundance.

dille, *n.m.* (*Chi.*) cicada.

dimanación, *n.f.* springing or issuing from; origin.

dimanante, *a.* springing from, originating.

dimanar, *v.i.* (with *de*) to spring from, flow; to originate in; to be due to; to follow from.

dimensión, *n.f.* dimension; extent, capacity, bulk, size, measure, magnitude.

dimensional, *a.* dimensional.

dimes, *n.m.pl.; andar en dimes y diretes,* to squabble, dispute about little things.

dimidiar, *v.t.* to divide into halves.

diminución, *n.f.* diminution, reduction, growing smaller; contraction; exhaustion; *ir en diminución,* to taper (as a pole); to be diminishing.

diminuir, *v.t.* (*obs.*) (conjugated like HUIR) to diminish.

diminutamente, *adv.* diminutively; minutely; by retail.

diminutivamente, *adv.* (*gram.*) diminutively.

diminutivo, -va, *a.* diminishing. — *n.m.* (*gram.*) diminutive.

diminuto, -ta, *a.* defective, faulty; small, minute, diminutive.

dimisión, *n.f.* resignation (of office, etc.).

dimisorias, *n.f.pl.* (*eccles.*) dimissory letter; (*coll.*) sack, unceremonious dismissal.

dimitir, *v.t.* to give up, relinquish, resign.

dimorfismo, *n.m.* (*min.*) dimorphism.

dimorfo, -fa, *a.* (*min.*) dimorphous.

din, *n.m.* (*coll.*) money.

dina, *n.f.* (*phys.*) dyne.

Dinamarca, *n.f.* Denmark.

dinamarqués, -esa, *a.* Danish. — *n.m.f.* Dane.

dinamia, *n.f.* dynam, foot-pound as unit of measurement.

dinámica, *n.f.* dynamics.

dinámico, -ca, *a.* dynamic.

dinamismo, *n.m.* dynamism.

dinamista, *a.* dynamistic. — *n.m.f.* dynamist.

dinamita, *n.f.* dynamite.

dinamitero, -ra, *n.m.f.* dynamiter.

dínamo, *n.f.* (*Am. n.m.*) dynamo.

dinamoeléctrico, -ca, *a.* dynamo-electric.

dinamométrico, -ca, *a.* dynamometric.

dinamómetro, *n.m.* dynamometer.

dinasta, *n.m.* dynast, sovereign, monarch.

dinastía, *n.f.* dynasty, sovereignty.

dinástico, -ca, *a.* dynastic.

dinastismo, *n.m.* loyalty to a dynasty.

dinerada, *n.f.* (*coll.*) large sum of money; an old silver coin.

dineral, *n.m.* large sum of money; (*obs.*) set of weights used for testing gold and silver coins; *dineral de quilates,* (*obs.*) set of weights used for valuing pearls and precious stones.

dinerillo, *n.m.* (*obs.*) small copper coin; (*coll.*) small sum of money.

dinero, *n.m.* coin, coinage; money, gold; standard of silver, 24 grains; ancient Spanish silver coin; small Peruvian silver coin; wealth, capital, fortune; *alzarse con el dinero,* to win money in gaming; *a pagar de mi dinero,* I vouch for the certainty of this; *acometer con dinero,* to attempt corruption or bribery; *a dinero contante, seco* or *efectivo,* in ready money, in cash; *dinero en mano,* ready money; *dinero llama dinero,* money makes money; *dinero olvidado, ni hace merced ni grado,* useful things are no longer so when not used; *dineros, y no consejos,* give me money, not good advice; *estar uno mal con su dinero,* to squander one's money; *estrujar el dinero,* to be mean in giving; *los dineros del sacristán, cantando se vienen y cantando se van,* lightly come, lightly go; *pasar uno el dinero,* to count one's money; *por mi dinero, papa le quiero,* I want full value for my money; *por dinero baila el perro, y por pan, si se lo dan,* money is a force even with those who have no need of it; *tener dinero* or *ser persona de dinero,* to be rich; *quien tiene dineros, pinta panderos,* with money one wants for nothing; *a dineros pagados, brazos quebrados,* don't pay for work in advance.

dineroso, -sa, *a.* moneyed, rich.

dineruelo, *n.m.* small coin; a little money, some money [DINERO].

dingo, *n.m.* (*zool.*) dingo.

dingolondango, *n.m.* (*coll.*) term of endear-ment, flattery, compliment.

dinosauro, *n.m.* dinosaur.

dintel, *n.m.* lintel, part of a door-frame.

dintelar, *v.t.* to provide with lintels.

dintorno, *n.m.* (*arch., art*) delineation.

diocesano, -na, *a.* diocesan. — *n.m.* diocesan bishop.

diócesi, diócesis, *n.f.* diocese.

dionisia, *n.f.* blood-stone; hematites.

dionisíaco, -ca, *a.* Bacchic.

dióptrica, *n.f.* dioptrics.

dióptrico, -ca, *a.* dioptric, dioptrical.

diorama, *n.m.* diorama.

diorita, *n.f.* (*min.*) diorite, greenstone.

Dios, *n.m.* God; god; idol; *¡a Dios!* or *¡anda con Dios!,* farewell, adieu, godspeed (other familiar expressions: *Dios con la colorada; a Dios, Madrid, que te quedas sin gente* (to someone of no importance); *a Dios, que esquilan* (to someone in a hurry); *a Dios, y veámonos* (having arranged a future meeting)); *¡oh santo Dios!* O gracious God!; *no lo quiera Dios* or *no lo plegue a Dios,* God forbid; *sea como Dios quiera,* God's will be done; *Dios le guarde,* God be with you; *la* or *las de Dios es Cristo,* turmoil, bedlam; *a Dios rogando y con el mazo dando,* praise the Lord and pass the ammunition; *a Dios y a dicha* or *a ventura,* at all events, at all risks; *a la* or *lo de Dios* (*es Cristo*), haphazard, without forethought; *alabado sea Dios* (salutation on entering), God be praised!; *a la buena de Dios*, without malice; *no lo quiera Dios*, God forbid; *amanecerá Dios, y medraremos*, it shall be done some other (more favourable) day; luck will turn; *aquel es rico, que está bien con Dios*, God's favour is true riches; *¡aquí de Dios!* God help me! I call God to witness!; *a quien Dios quiere, la casa le sabe*, everything prospers for the lucky man; *a quien madruga, Dios le ayuda*, fortune favours the diligent; *así Dios me salve*, so help me God; *así Dios te dé la gloria* or *te guarde*, prayer accompanying a request for alms, etc.; *¡bendito sea Dios!* exclamation denoting annoyance and resignation; *clamar a Dios*, to become despairing; *como Dios es servido*, unsatisfactorily, badly; *como Dios le da a uno a entender*, as well as he can in the circumstances; *miente más que da por Dios*, he is an awful liar; *no es Dios viejo*, hope on, hope ever; *no haber para uno más Dios ni Santa María que una cosa*, to be excessively devoted to something; *no servir a Dios ni al diablo*, to be useless, good for nothing; *plega* or *plegue a Dios*, please God; *poner uno a Dios por testigo*, to call God to witness; *por Dios*, for God's sake; *que de Dios goce* or *que Dios haya*, God rest his soul; *¡sabe Dios!* God knows!; *si no quisiera Dios*, would to God it may not happen; *si quisiera Dios*, would to God it may happen; *tomarse uno con Dios*, to persist in evil courses; *¡vale Dios!* by good luck; anyway, anyhow; *¡Válgame Dios!* bless me! *¡Válgate Dios!* God preserve you!; *como hay Dios*, as surely as God exists; *creer en Dios a macha martillo* or *a puño cerrado*, to be firm in the Christian faith; *cuando Dios amanece, para todos amanece*, God sends his rain on the just and the unjust; *dar a Dios a uno*, to administer the viaticum; *darse a Dios y a los santos*, to grieve or worry to excess; *de Dios*, abundantly; *de Dios venga el remedio*, the case is past human aid; *dejar Dios de su mano a uno*, to become a thorough reprobate; *digan, que de Dios dijeron*, I don't care what they may say; *de Dios viene el bien, y de las abejas, la miel*, everything good has its source in God; *después de Dios, la olla*, abundance of food is the best of temporal gifts; *Dios aprieta, pero no ahoga*, God often proves us, but never beyond our capacity; *Dios dará*, the Lord will provide; *Dios da el frío conforme la ropa*, God tempers the wind to the shorn lamb; *Dios delante*, with God's help; *Dios desavenga a quien nos mantenga*, some must profit by others' mischances; *Dios dijo lo que será*, I doubt the truth of that; *Dios dirá*, let it be as God wills; *Dios lo oiga, y el pecado sea sordo*, may it turn out well; *Dios los cría, y ellos se juntan*, birds of a feather flock together; *Dios mediante*, God willing; *Dios me entiende*, there's reason in what I say; *Dios me haga bien con esto*, I am content with this; *Dios mejorará sus horas*, bad luck will pass; *Dios nos asista* or *nos la depare buena* or *nos coja confesados* or *nos tenga de su mano*, God help us in this danger; *Dios sobre todo*, phrase expressing doubt about the success of an undertaking; *Dios te la depare buena*, may you succeed, though I doubt if you will;

donde Dios es servido, any indefinite place; *estar de Dios*, to be inevitable; *el hombre propone y Dios dispone*, man proposes, God disposes; *gozar uno de Dios*, to have died and gone to heaven; *hurtar de Dios, el medio*, to rob like a magpie; *irse uno mucho con Dios*, to leave in a rage; to be sent away summarily; to leave of one's own accord; *haber la de Dios es Cristo*, to have a great row; *llamar a Dios de tú*, to be too free and easy in one's manners; to have great merits; *llamar Dios a uno por un camino*, to have a natural aptitude for something; *maldita de Dios la cosa*, absolutely nothing; *¡vaya Vd. con Dios!* farewell, God be with you; *¡vaya con* or *por Dios!* God's will be done!; *venir Dios a ver a uno*, to take a sudden unexpected turn for the better (of events); *¡vive Dios! ¡voto a Dios! ¡voto a los ajenos de Dios!* damnation!; *Dios sufre los malos, pero no para siempre*, God bears with the wicked but not for ever; *Cada uno es como Dios le hizo, y aun peor muchas veces*, Each is as God made him, and oftentimes even worse; *Dios, que da la llaga, da la medicina*, God, who gives the wound, gives the cure.

diosa, *n.f.* goddess.

diostedé, *n.m.* (*S. Am.*) bird, similar to the toucan.

dipétalo, -la, *a.* (*bot.*) dipetalous.

diploma, *n.m.* diploma; patent, bull, licence; title, credential.

diplomacia, *n.f.* diplomacy, tact; (*coll.*) shrewdness.

diplomático, -ca, *a.* diplomatic, tactful; (*coll.*) astute. — *n.m.* diplomatist, diplomat. — *n.f.* diplomatics; diplomacy.

dipsomanía, *n.f.* dipsomania.

dipsómano, -na, *n.m.f.* dipsomaniac.

díptero, -ra, *a.* (*arch.*) having two wings or a double colonnade; (*ent.*) dipterous. — *n.m.pl.* (*ent.*) diptera.

díptica, *n.f.;* **díptico,** *n.m.* diptych.

diptongar, *v.t.* to diphthongize.

diptongo, *n.m.* diphthong.

diputación, *n.f.* deputation, committee; object of a deputation.

diputada, *n.f.* lady deputy or representative.

diputado, *n.m.* deputy, representative, delegate; (*com.*) assignee; *diputado a Cortes*, member of Spanish parliament, congressman; *diputado cunero*, (*pol., coll.*) carpetbagger. — *p.p.* [DIPUTAR]

diputador, -ra, *a.* constituent. — *n.m.f.* constituent.

diputar, *v.t.* to depute, commission, empower, delegate; to constitute, empower.

dique, *n.m.* dyke, dam, mole, mound, bank; (*fig.*) check, stop, bar; (*min.*) crop; *dique de construccion*, or *de carenar*, (*naut.*) dry dock; *dique flotante*, floating dock.

dirección, *n.f.* direction, course, aim, tendency; guiding, directing; government, administration; editorship; management, superintendence, executive board; guidance, order, command, prescription; route, way; turn, trend, relative position; address (for letters, etc.); office of director; *dirección general*, head office (government); *La Dirección*, the governing board.

directamente, *adv.* directly, in a direct manner.

directivo, -va, *a.* directive, managerial. — *n.f.* governing board, board of directors, management.

directo, -ta, *a.* direct; evident, apparent, open, clear; in a straight line.

director, -ra, *a.* directing, guiding. — *n.m.f.* director; manager; chief; editor; *director de escena,* stage manager; *director de orquestra,* conductor; *director espiritual,* confessor, religious director.

directoral, *a.* directoral.

directorial, *a.* pertaining to a directory.

directorio, -ria, *a.* directive, directorial. — *n.m.* directory, book of addresses; director- ate.

directriz, *n.f.* (*geom.*) directrix.

dirigente, *a.* directing, leading; ruling.

dirigible, *a.* dirigible; manageable. — *n.m.* dirigible, navigable balloon, airship.

dirigir, *v.t.* (*pres. indic.* **dirijo;** *pres. subj.* **dirija**) to direct, guide, conduct, govern, control, manage, regulate; to dedicate (a work); to address (a letter, etc.); (*mus.*) to conduct; to point (a gun); (*naut.*) to steer. — *v.r.* (with *a*) to address; to apply, resort to; to go towards; *dirigir la palabra* (*a*), to speak to, address.

dirimente, *a.* breaking off, dissolving.

dirimible, *a.* that may be dissolved, or broken off.

dirimir, *v.t.* to dissolve, separate, disjoin; to annul, declare void; to adjust, reconcile.

dirruir, *v.t.* (*obs.*) to ruin, destroy.

disanto, *n.m.* holy-day.

discantado, -da, *a.* (*Per.*) applicable to a Low Mass with music. — *p.p.* [DISCANTAR].

discantar, *v.t.* to chant, sing; to comment; to descant, discourse at length about; (*mus.*) to sing in counterpoint.

discante, *n.m.* treble; concert (especially of stringed instruments); small guitar.

disceptación, *n.f.* dispute, controversy.

disceptar, *v.i.* to dispute, argue.

discernidor, -ra, *a.* discerning. — *n.m.f.* dis- cerner.

discerniente, *a.* discerning.

discernimiento, *n.m.* discernment, judgment, insight, discrimination; (*law*) appointment of a guardian.

discernir, *v.t.* (*pres. indic.* **discierno;** *pres. subj.* **discierna**) to discern, distinguish, comprehend, discriminate, know, judge; (*law*) to appoint a guardian.

disciplina, *n.f.* discipline; education, instruc- tion; rule of conduct, order; systematic training; any art or science taught. — *pl.* instrument of chastisement; scourge, cat-o'- nine-tails; flagellation.

disciplinable, *a.* disciplinable, capable of instruction.

disciplinadamente, *adv.* with discipline.

disciplinado, -da, *a.* disciplined, trained; marbled, variegated (as flowers). — *p.p.* [DISCIPLINAR].

disciplinal, *a.* disciplinary.

disciplinante, *a.* disciplinary. — *n.m.* dis- ciplinant.

disciplinar, *v.t.* to discipline, instruct, train, bring up; (*mil.*) to drill; to correct, chastise. — *v.r.* to scourge oneself.

disciplinario, -ria, *a.* disciplinary.

disciplinazo, *n.m.* lash.

discipulado, *n.m.* number of scholars at one school; education, instruction.

discipular, *a.* pertaining to a disciple or pupil.

discípulo, -la, *n.m.f.* disciple; follower; scholar, pupil.

disco, *n.m.* disk; gramophone record; lens; quoit; circular plate (of glass, metal, etc.); solid wheel; discus; (*astron.*) disk; *disco de señales,* (*railw.*) signal disk, semaphore; *disco giratorio,* turntable (of a gramophone).

discóbolo, *n.m.* discobolus, discus-thrower.

discoidal; discoide; discoideo, -dea, *a.* disk-like, discoidal.

díscolo, -la, *a.* ungovernable; wayward.

discoloro, -ra, *a.* (*bot.*) having leaves of differently coloured sides.

disconforme, *a.* discordant, disagreeing.

disconformidad, *n.f.* disconformity; dis- agreement.

discontinuación, *n.f.* discontinuation.

discontinuar, *v.t.* to discontinue, suspend.

discontinuo, -nua, *a.* discontinuous.

disconveniencia, *n.f.* discord, disunion.

disconveniente, *a.* discordant; incongruous; inconvenient.

disconvenir, *v.i.* (conjugated like VENIR) to disagree; to be dissimilar.

discordancia, *n.f.* discordance, disagreement.

discordante, *a.* discordant, dissonant.

discordar, *v.i.* to disaccord, disagree; (*mus.*) to be out of tune.

discorde, *a.* discordant; (*mus.*) dissonant.

discordia, *n.f.* discord, disagreement, opposi- tion, contention, clash; *manzana de la dis- cordia,* apple of discord.

discoteca, *n.f.* gramophone record library.

discrasia, *n.f.* (*med.*) cacochymia.

discreción, *n.f.* discretion, sagacity, prudence, acuteness of mind; liberty of action and decision; *a discreción,* optional, at one's own free will; *darse, entregarse,* or *rendirse a dis- creción,* to surrender unconditionally; *jugar discreciones,* to play for love, without stakes.

discrecional, *a.* discretional, optional, dis- cretionary.

discrecionalmente, *adv.* optionally, dis- cretionally.

discrepancia, *n.f.* discrepancy.

discrepante, *a.* discrepant, differing.

discrepar, *v.i.* to differ, disagree.

discretamente, *adv.* discreetly.

discretear, *v.i.* to affect discretion.

discreteo, *n.m.* affected discretion.

discreto, -ta, *a.* discreet, circumspect, pru- dent; ingenious, sharp, witty; (*math.*) dis- crete; *a lo discreto,* at one's own free will. — *n.m.f.* (*eccles.*) counsellor to the Superior.

discrimen, *n.m.* hazard, risk, peril; differ- ence, diversity.

discriminar, *v.t.* (*Arg., Col.*) to discriminate.

disculpa, *n.f.* excuse, apology; exculpation.

disculpabilidad, *n.f.* excusability, pardon- ableness.

disculpable, *a.* excusable, pardonable.

disculpablemente, *adv.* excusably, pardon- ably.

disculpadamente, *adv.* excusably.

disculpar(se), *v.t., v.r.* to exculpate; to ex- cuse, palliate; to apologize.

discurrir, *v.i.* to gad, ramble, roam; to flow (of a river); to discourse upon (a subject); to reflect, think, reason. — *v.t.* to plan, invent, contrive, scheme; to infer, deduce, conjecture.

discursante, *n.m.f.* discourser; lecturer.

discursar, *v.t.* to conjecture, infer. — *v.i.* (with *sobre* or *acerca de*) to discourse on; to treat of; to lecture on.

discursear, *v.i.* (*coll.*, *iron.*) to harangue.

discursista, *n.m.f.* declaimer, great talker, argufier.

discursivo, -va, *a.* discursive; reflective, thoughtful, meditative.

discurso, *n.m.* discourse, reasoning, cogitation, ratiocination; speech, oration; lecture; dissertation, treatise; conversation, talk; duration, space of time.

discusión, *n.f.* discussion.

discutible, *a.* disputable; discussible.

discutidor, -ra, *a.* arguing. — *n.m.f.* arguer.

discutir, *v.t.*, *v.i.* to discuss, argue, debate.

disecación, disección, *n.f.* dissection, anatomy.

disecador, -ra, *n.m.f.* dissector, anatomist.

disecar, *v.t.* (conjugated like SECAR) to dissect; to practise taxidermy.

disecea, *n.f.* (*med.*) high-tone deafness.

disector, -ra, *n.m.f.* dissector, anatomist.

diseminación, *n.f.* dissemination; scattering, spreading, sowing.

diseminador, -ra, *a.* disseminating. — *n.m.f.* disseminator.

diseminar, *v.t.* to disseminate, propagate, spread, sow, scatter.

disensión, *n.f.* dissension; contention, contest, strife.

disenso, *n.m.* dissent, disagreement.

disentería, *n.f.* dysentery.

disentérico, -ca, *a.* dysenteric, dysenterical.

disentimiento, *n.m.* dissent, disagreement; dissension.

disentir, *v.i.* (conjugated like SENTIR) to dissent, disagree.

diseñador, -ra, *n.m.f.* designer, delineator.

diseñar, *v.t.* to draw, design; to sketch.

diseño, *n.m.* design, sketch, image, draft, plan, picture; pattern, model; delineation, description.

disertación, *n.f.* dissertation, discourse, disquisition.

disertador, -ra, *a.* discoursing, expounding. — *n.m.f.* discourser, expounder.

disertante, *a.* discoursing. — *n.m.f.* discourser.

disertar, *v.i.* (with *sobre* or *acerca de*) to discourse on, treat of, discuss.

diserto, -ta, *a.* eloquent, fluent.

disfamación, *n.f.* defamation.

disfamador, -ra, *a.* defaming. — *n.m.f.* defamer, detractor.

disfamar, *v.t.* to defame, discredit.

disfamatorio, -ria, *a.* defamatory, calumnious.

disfavor, *n.m.* disregard, want of favour, coldness.

disformar, *v.t.* to deform, misshape.

disforme, *a.* deformed; ugly; huge, monstrous.

disformidad, *n.f.* deformity; hugeness.

disfraz, *n.m.* mask, disguise; fancy dress; dissimulation.

disfrazar, *v.t.* (*pret.* **disfracé**; *pres. subj.* **disfrace**) to disguise, cloak, cover; to dissemble, misrepresent. — *v.r.* to masquerade, go in disguise; to travesty.

disfrutar, *v.t.* to benefit by; to have the benefit

of, to enjoy (good health, etc.); (*min.*) to work a mine. — *v.i.* to enjoy, to have.

disfrute, *n.m.* use, enjoyment, benefit.

disgregable, *a.* separable, segregable.

disgregación, *n.f.* separation, disjunction; disintegration.

disgregar, *v.t.* (conjugated like AGREGAR) to separate, disjoin, disperse.

disgregativo, -va, *a.* disjunctive.

disgustadamente, *adv.* disgustedly.

disgustado, -da, *a.* annoyed, vexed; sad, grief-stricken. — *p.p.* [DISGUSTAR].

disgustar, *v.t.* to displease; to dissatisfy; to offend (the taste, etc.); (*fig.*) to anger; *esto me disgusta*, I dislike this. — *v.r.* to be or become displeased or angry; to fall out, quarrel.

disgustillo, *n.m.* displeasure, slight unpleasantness [DISGUSTO].

disgusto, *n.m.* dissatisfaction; ill-humour; displeasure; quarrel; grief, sorrow; annoyance, vexation; *a disgusto*, against one's will, in spite of.

disidencia, *n.f.* dissidence, nonconformity.

disidente, *a.* dissident, nonconformist, schismatic. — *n.m.f.* dissenter, nonconformist.

disidir, *v.i.* to dissent, disagree.

disílabo, -ba, *a.* disyllabic.

disimetría, *n.f.* lack of symmetry.

disimétrico, -ca, *a.* unsymmetrical.

disímil, *a.* dissimilar, unlike.

disimilar, *a.* dissimilar.

disimilitud, *n.f.* unlikeness.

disimulable, *a.* that may be dissembled; excusable.

disimulación, *n.f.* dissimulation, dissembling, double-dealing, hypocrisy; reserve, reservedness.

disimuladamente, *adv.* dissemblingly, reservedly, underhand.

disimulado, -da, *a.* dissembling, reserved; sly, cunning, sullen. — *p.p.* [DISIMULAR]; *hacer la disimulada*, (*coll.*) to feign ignorance; *a lo disimulado* or *a la disimulada*, (*coll.*) feigning ignorance.

disimulador, -ra, *a.* dissembling. — *n.m.f.* dissembler.

disimular, *v.t.* to dissemble; to feign, pretend; to hide, conceal (feelings); to tolerate, overlook; to misrepresent; to pardon, forgive.

disimulo, *n.m.* dissimulation; reservedness; pretence, deceit; tolerance.

disipable, *a.* easily scattered; capable of being dissipated.

disipación, *n.f.* dissipation; dispersion, scattering; evanescence; waste, extravagance; separation of integral parts; resolution into vapour.

disipado, -da, *a.* dissipated; spendthrift, lavish, prodigal; dissolute, licentious. — *p.p.* [DISIPAR].

disipador, -ra, *a.* squandering, spendthrift. — *n.m.f.* spendthrift, prodigal.

disipar, *v.t.* to dissipate (as clouds); scatter, misspend; to drive away, put to flight. — *v.r.* to scatter, be dissipated, vanish; evaporate.

dislalia, *n.f.* (*path.*) dysphonia.

dislate, *n.m.* nonsense, absurdity.

dislocación, dislocadura, *n.f.* dislocation.

dislocar, *v.t.* (*pret.* **disloqué**; *pres. subj.* **disloque**) to dislocate, displace, disjoint. — *v.r.* to be dislocated.

dismembración, *n.f.* dismemberment.

disminución, *n.f.* diminution; (*vet.*) disease in horses' hoofs; *ir una cosa en disminución*, to dwindle, deteriorate; to taper.

disminuir, *v.t.* (conjugated like HUIR) to diminish, cut short, abridge, lessen, lower, decrease, reduce; to detract from. — *v.r.* to diminish, decrease.

disociación, *n.f.* disjunction, separation, dissociation.

disociar, *v.t.* to disjoin, separate, disconnect.

disolubilidad, *n.f.* dissolubility.

disoluble, *a.* dissoluble.

disolución, *n.f.* dissolution, disintegration; (*chem.*) solution; dissoluteness, dissipation; *disolución de sociedad*, (*com.*) dissolution of partnership.

disolutamente, *adv.* dissolutely, licentiously.

disolutivo, -va, *a.* dissolvent, licentiously.

disoluto, -ta, *a.* dissolute, loose, licentious.

disolvente, *a.* dissolvent. — *n.m.f.* dissolver.

disolver, *v.t.* (conjugated like ABSOLVER) to untie, loosen; to dissolve; to separate, disunite. — *v.r.* to dissolve, be melted.

disón, *n.m.* (*mus.*) discord.

disonancia, *n.f.* dissonance; (*mus.*) discord, harsh sound; disagreement.

disonante, *a.* dissonant, inharmonious; discordant, unsuitable.

disonar, *v.i.* (conjugated like SONAR) to disagree in sound, produce a discord, be inharmonious, to be discordant; to disagree.

dísono, -na, *a.* dissonant, inharmonious.

dispar, *a.* unlike, unequal, unmatched.

disparada, *n.f.* (*Arg., Mex.*) hasty start, sudden run or flight; *a la disparada*, at full speed, recklessly.

disparadamente, *adv.* hurriedly; blundering; nonsensically.

disparadero, *n.m.* [DISPARADOR].

disparador, *n.m.* shooter; trigger; ratchet-wheel in clockwork; (*naut.*) anchor-tripper; notch of a cross-bow; *poner a uno en el disparador*, to provoke someone until he loses his patience.

disparar, *v.t.*, to shoot, discharge, fire, let off; to cast or throw violently. — *v.i.* (*coll.*) to talk nonsense; to blunder. — *v.r.* to bolt (as a horse), to race (as a machine); to rush (towards); to go off (of a gun).

disparatado, -da, *a.* absurd, inconsistent, foolish. — *p.p.* [DISPARATAR].

disparatador, -ra, *a.* talking nonsense. — *n.m.f.* talker of nonsense.

disparatar, *v.i.* to act absurdly; to talk nonsense; to blunder.

disparate, *n.m.* nonsense, absurdity; blunder, mistake.

disparatón, *n.m.* very great blunder [DISPARATE].

disparatorio, *n.m.* nonsensical conversation, speech or writing.

disparejo, -ja, *a.* uneven.

disparidad, *n.f.* disparity, inequality.

disparo, *n.m.* discharge, explosion; shooting; nonsense, absurdity.

dispendio, *n.m.* excessive expense; excessive waste of time or fortune.

dispendiosamente, *adv.* expensively.

dispendioso, -sa, *a.* costly, expensive.

dispensa, *n.f.* dispensation, exemption, privilege; document granting a dispensation.

dispensable, *a.* dispensable; excusable.

dispensación, *n.f.* dispensation, exemption.

dispensador, -ra, *a.* dispensing; distributing. — *n.m.f.* dispenser, distributor; one who grants a dispensation.

dispensar, *v.t.* to dispense, exempt, excuse, dispense with; to deal out, grant, distribute; to acquit, absolve; to excuse, pardon.

dispensario, *n.m.* dispensary, surgery; pharmacopœia; laboratory.

dispepsia, *n.f.* dyspepsia.

dispéptico, -ca, *a.* dyspeptic.

dispersar, *v.t.* to disperse; (*mil.*) to scatter, rout, put to flight; to dissipate; (*mil.*) to deploy.

dispersión, *n.f.* dispersion.

dispersivo, -va, *a.* tending to scatter.

disperso, -sa, *a.* dispersed, separated; scattered.

dispertador, -ra, *a. obs.* [DESPERTADOR].

dispertar, *v.t., v.r. obs.* [DESPERTAR].

displacer, *v.t.* [DESPLACER].

displicencia, *n.f.* disagreeableness; lukewarmness in action.

displicente, *a.* disagreeable, unpleasing; peevish, fretful.

disponedor, -ra, *a.* disposing; distributing. — *n.m.f.* disposer, distributor.

disponente, *a.* disposing.

disponer, *v.t., v.i.* (conjugated like PONER) to arrange, order, settle, lay out, dispose, prepare; to resolve, direct, order, command; *disponer sus cosas*, to put one's affairs in order; *disponer las velas al viento*, to trim one's sails to the wind. — *v.r.* to prepare oneself, get ready; to make a will.

dispongo; disponga, *pres. indic.; pres. subj.* [DISPONER].

disponibilidad, *n.f.* availability, disposability.

disponible, *a.* disposable, free.

disposición, *n.f.* disposition, arrangement; disposal; aptitude, inclination, capacity, natural fitness; state of health; condition, circumstances; elegance of form; temper; ability; (*arch.*) proportion, symmetry, measure; resolution, command; specification, requirement; provision, proviso; dispatch of business; trim of a ship; *a la disposición de Vd.*, at your command, at your service; *estar en hallarse en disposición una persona o cosa*, to be fitted and ready for some purpose; *última disposición*, last will and testament.

dispositivamente, *adv.* dispositively, distributively.

dispositivo, -va, *a.* dispositive.

dispuesto, -ta, *a.* disposed, ready; comely; clever, bright. — *p.p. irreg.* [DISPONER]; *bien dispuesto*, well-disposed; well (in health); *mal dispuesto*, ill-disposed; indisposed, ill.

dispuse, *pret. irreg.* [DISPONER].

disputa, *n.f.* dispute, controversy; contest, conflict, contention; debate, argument; *sin disputa*, undoubtedly.

disputable, *a.* disputable, contestable, controvertible.

disputador, *a.* disputing. — *n.m.* disputant, disputer.

disputar, *v.t., v.i.* to dispute, controvert, contend, contest, argue, debate; to question; to fight for.

disputativamente, *adv.* disputingly.

disquisición, *n.f.* disquisition.

distancia, *n.f.* distance, remoteness, interval of time or space; range; difference, disparity; *a distancia,* far off, at a distance; *a respetable* or *respetuosa distancia,* at a respectful distance.

distanciar, *v.t., v.r.* to place at a distance; to put farther apart.

distante, *a.* distant, remote; (*naut.*) off.

distantemente, *adv.* distantly.

distar, *v.i.* to be distant, remote, far; to be different; *distar de,* to be far from; to be a specified distance from.

distender, *v.t.* (conjugated like TENDER) (*med.*) to distend, swell.

distensión, *n.f.* distension, expansion.

dístico, *n.m.* distich, couplet. — *a.* (*bot.*) distichous.

distinción, *n.f.* distinction; difference, diversity; prerogative, privilege; order, clearness, clarity, precision; honourable mark of superiority; *a distinción (de),* in contradiction from; *hacer uno distinción,* to form a right judgment of things, estimate them at their true worth; *persona de distinción,* person of discrimination.

distingo, *n.m.* (*log.*) distinction; restriction, qualification.

distinguible, *a.* distinguishable.

distinguido, -da, *a.* distinguished, conspicuous. — *p.p.* [DISTINGUIR].

distinguir, *v.t.* (conjugated like EXTINGUIR) to distinguish, discern, discriminate, differentiate, know, judge; to see clearly and at a distance; to show appreciation of; to clear up, explain; *no distinguir uno lo blanco de lo negro,* to be very ignorant and indiscriminating. — *v.r.* to distinguish oneself; to excel; (with *de*) to differ, be distinguished from.

distintamente, *adv.* distinctly; diversely.

distintivo, -va, *a.* distinctive. — *n.m.* distinctive mark (of rank); badge, attribute, characteristic feature.

distinto, -ta, *a.* distinct; different, diverse; clear, intelligible.

distracción, *n.f.* distraction, want of attention; heedlessness, absent-mindedness; amusement, sport, pastime; lack of constraint, licentiousness; *por distracción,* for amusement; through an oversight.

distraer, *v.t.* (conjugated like TRAER) to distract; to perplex, bewilder, confuse; to lead astray, seduce; to divert, amuse, entertain. — *v.r.* to muse, be absent-minded or inattentive; to amuse or enjoy oneself; to embezzle public funds.

distraídamente, *adv.* distractedly; licentiously.

distraído, -da, *a.* absent, inattentive, heedless; dissolute, licentious; (*Chi., Mex.*) slovenly, dirty, ragged.

distraigo; distraiga, *pres. indic.; pres. subj.* [DISTRAER].

distraimiento, *n.m.* distraction.

distraje, distrajo, *pret. irreg.* [DISTRAER].

distribución, *n.f.* distribution, apportionment, division, separation, collocation, arrangement; (*print.*) distribution of type; *caja* or *tablero de distribución,* switchboard; *tomar uno alguna cosa por distribución,* to persist in some piece of impertinent conduct.

distribuidor, -ra, *a.* distributing. — *n.m.* (*mech.*) distributor (motor, etc.); guide-ring

of a turbine; slide-valve; valve-gear. — *n.f.* (*agric.*) fertilizer distributor.

distribuir, *v.t.* (conjugated like HUIR) to distribute, divide, allot, deal, apportion; (*print.*) to distribute type.

distributivo, -va, *a.* distributive.

distributor, -ra, *a.* distributing. — *n.m.f.* distributor.

distribuyente, *a.* distributing, giving. — *n.m.f.* distributor.

distribuyo; distribuya, *pres. indic.; pres. subj.* [DISTRIBUIR].

distrito, *n.m.* district, region; ward, precinct; region.

disturbar, *v.t.* to disturb, interrupt.

disturbio, *n.m.* disturbance, interruption; outbreak, riot.

disuadir, *v.t.* to dissuade.

disuasión, *n.f.* dissuasion.

disuasivo, -va, *a.* dissuasive.

disuelto, -ta, *a.* dissolved, melted. — *p.p. irreg.* [DISOLVER].

disuelvo; disuelva, *pres. indic.; pres. subj.* [DISOLVER].

disyunción, *n.f.* disjunction, separation; (*gram.*) disjunctive particle.

disyunta, *n.f.* (*mus.*) (*obs.*) change of the voice.

disyuntivamente, *adv.* disjunctively, separately; singly.

disyuntivo, -va, *a.* disjunctive. — *n.f.* disjunctive proposition; dilemma.

disyuntor, *n.m.* (*elec.*) circuit-breaker.

dita, *n.f.* security, bond; surety, bondsman; (*Chi., Guat.*) debt, liability.

ditá, *n.f.* (*Philip.*) tree which yields ditamine.

ditaína, *n.f.* ditamine.

diteísmo, *n.m.* ditheism.

diteísta, *a.* ditheistic. — *n.m.f.* ditheist.

ditirámbico, -ca, *a.* dithyrambic.

ditirambo, *n.m.* dithyramb; (*fig.*) exaggerated eulogy.

dítono, *n.m.* (*mus.*) ditone.

diuca, *n.f.* (*Arg., Chi.*) small song bird; (*Arg., Chi.*) (*coll.*) teacher's pet pupil.

diurno, -na, *a.* diurnal. — *n.m.* diurnal, prayer-book. — *n.m.f.pl.* diurnal animals or plants.

diuturnidad, *n.f.* diuturnity, long duration.

diuturno, -na, *a.* diuturnal, lasting.

diva, *n.f.* (*poet.*) goddess; diva, great singer.

divagación, *n.f.* rambling, wandering, digression.

divagador, -ra, *a.* roaming; digressing. — *n.m.f.* rambler; digresser.

divagar, *v.i.* (conjugated like VAGAR) to ramble, roam; to digress.

diván, *n.m.* divan, low cushioned sofa; collection of Oriental poems.

divergencia, *n.f.* divergence, diversity (in opinion).

divergente, *a.* divergent; dissenting, opposed, contrary.

divergir, *v.i.* (*phys.*) to diverge; (*fig.*) to dissent.

diversamente, *adv.* diversely, differently.

diversidad, *n.f.* diversity, dissimilitude, unlikeness; variety, plenty, abundance.

diversificar, *v.t.* to diversify, vary.

diversiforme, *a.* diversiform, of varied forms.

diversión, *n.f.* diversion, sport, amusement, entertainment, merriment, fun; (*mil.*) diversion.

diversivo, -va, *a.* (*med.*) divertive.

diverso, -sa, *a.* diverse, different. — *pl.* various, several, sundry.

divertido, -da, *a.* amused, merry, festive; amusing, funny, entertaining; *andar uno divertido,* to pursue a hobby to the neglect of one's ordinary avocations; *andar* or *estar uno mal divertido,* to be addicted to vicious courses. — *p.p.* [DIVERTIR].

divertimiento, *n.m.* diversion, fun, merriment, sport, amusement, pastime, pleasure; momentary distraction (of the attention).

divertir, *v.t.* (conjugated like SENTIR) to divert, turn aside; to divert the mind; to amuse, entertain. — *v.r.* to amuse oneself; have a good time.

dividendo, *n.m.* dividend.

divididero, -ra, *a.* divisible, to be divided.

dividir, *v.t.* (*p.p.* **dividido**) to divide, separate, disjoin, disunite, cut, sever, split, cleave, part, parcel out. — *v.r.* to divide; to split; to be divided; (with *de*) part company with.

dividuo, -dua, *a.* (*law*) divisible.

divierto; divierta, *pres. indic.; pres. subj.* [DIVERTIR].

divieso, *n.m.* (*med.*) furuncle, boil.

divinal, *a.* (*poet.*) divine; excellent.

divinamente, *adv.* divinely, heavenly; admirably.

divinatorio, -ria, *a.* divinatory.

divinidad, *n.f.* divinity, deity, Godhead; godhead; (*fig.*) beautiful woman; *decir* or *hacer uno divinidades,* to say something opportunely or with extreme skill; *la Divinidad,* the Deity.

divinización, *n.f.* divinization.

divinizado, -da, *p.p.* [DIVINIZAR].

divinizar, *v.t.* (*pret.* **divinicé;** *pres. subj.* **divinice**) to deify; to sanctify; extol.

divino, -na, *a.* divine, heavenly, heaven-born, god-like; (*fig.*) excellent, most beautiful. — *n.m.f.* (*obs.*) diviner.

divirtió, (él) *3rd pers. sing., pret. irreg.* [DIVERTIR].

divisa, *n.f.* motto, badge, device, design; (*law*) portion of paternal estate devolving on a child; (*com.*) foreign currency.

divisar, *v.t.* to descry at a distance; to glimpse, to perceive indistinctly; (*her.*) to vary.

divisibilidad, *n.f.* divisibility.

divisible, *a.* divisible.

división, *n.f.* division, partition, separation; distribution; compartment, section, quarter; disunion, difference; hyphen.

divisional, *a.* divisional.

divisivo, -va, *a.* divisible, divisive.

diviso, -sa, *a.* divided, disunited. — *p.p. irreg.* [DIVIDIR].

divisor, -ra, *a.* dividing. — *n.m.* (*math.*) divisor. — *n.m.f.* divider, separator.

divisorio, -ria, *a.* dividing, divisionary. — *n.m.* (*print.*) copy-holder. — *n.f.* (*geol.*) divide.

divo, -va, *a.* (*poet.*) godlike, divine. — *n.m.f.* god, goddess; famous male singer, diva.

divorciar, *v.t.* to divorce; to separate, part, divide. — *v.r.* to be divorced, obtain a divorce.

divorcio, *n.m.* divorce; separation, rupture, disunion; breach of friendship.

divulgable, *a.* that which may be divulged.

divulgación, *n.f.* divulgation, publication.

divulgador, -ra, *a.* divulging. — *n.m.f.* divulger.

divulgar, *v.t.* (*pret.* **divulgué;** *pres. subj.* **divulgue**) to divulge, publish, report, give out, reveal; to popularize. — *v.r.* to be spread abroad.

diz, contraction of *dícese,* it is said.

dizque, contraction of *dícese que* or *dice que.* — *n.m.* objection; muttering; rumour.

do, *adv.* (*poet.*) where; *do quiera,* wherever. — *n.m.* (*mus.*) C, first note of the diatonic scale.

dobla, *n.f.* doubloon; (*coll.*) doubling a stake; (*Chi.*) right of one day's free mining granted by a mine owner; *jugar a la dobla,* to keep on doubling one's stake in gambling.

doblada, *n.f.* (*prov.*) (*ichth.*) gilt-head; (*Cub.*) tolling of a bell at sunset.

dobladamente, *adv.* doubly; deceitfully, artfully.

dobladilla, *n.f.* ancient card game; *a la dobladilla,* doubly, repeatedly.

dobladillo, *n.m.* hem; turn-up (of a trouser leg); strong yarn for knitting.

doblado, -da, *a.* strong robust, thick-set; double, twice; deceitful, dissembling. — *n.m.* measure of the fold in cloth; *tierra doblada,* broken, mountainous country. — *p.p.* [DOBLAR].

dobladura, *n.f.* fold, crease.

doblamiento, *n.m.* doubling, folding, bending.

doblar, *v.t.* to double; to fold; to crease; to bend, crook; to persuade someone to change his mind; *doblar un cabo* or *promontorio,* (*naut.*) to double a cape; *doblar la rodilla,* to bend the knee; *doblar la calle,* to turn the corner of a street; *doblemos la hoja,* let us change the subject. — *v.i.* to toll the passing-bell; *doblar a muerto,* to toll the passing-bell (funeral ringing); *bien pueden doblar por él,* I wouldn't give much for his chances of living. — *v.r.* to bend, bow, stoop; to submit, acquiesce.

doble, *a.* double, twofold, duplicate; thick, heavy (as cloth); thick-set, strong, robust; artful, deceitful; (*chem.*) binary; *al doble,* doubly. — *n.m.* fold, crease; double-dealing; toll of the passing-bell; step in a Spanish dance; *echar uno la doble,* (*coll.*) to bind an agreement, etc., so that it cannot be easily broken; *estar a tres dobles y un repique,* (*Chi., Per., PR.*) to be very poor.

doblegable, *a.* pliant, pliable, flexible; easily folded.

doblegadizo, -za, *a.* easily bent or folded.

doblegar, *v.t.* (*pret.* **doblegué;** *pres. subj.* **doblegue**) to bend, inflect, fold, twist; to make someone change his mind, to dissuade. — *v.r.* to bend; to yield, submit, acquiesce.

doblemente, *adv.* doubly; artfully, deceitfully.

doblero, *n.m.* (*prov.*) piece of timber; an 18th-century coin from Majorca.

doblescudo, *n.m.* (*bot.*) shield-fern; shepherd's purse.

doblete, *a.* of medium thickness. — *n.m.* doublet, imitation gem; stroke at billiards.

doblez, *n.m.* crease, ply, fold; fold mark. — *n.m.f.* duplicity, doubleness, double-dealing.

doblón, *n.m.* doubloon; *escupir uno doblones,* (*coll.*) to boast of being rich and powerful, be ostentatious of wealth.

doblonada, *n.f.* heap of doubloons or coins; *echar doblonadas,* (*coll.*) to brag of one's income.

doca, *n.f.* (*Chi.*) a trailing plant.
doce, *n.m.,* *a.* twelve, twelfth. — *n.f.pl., las doce,* twelve o'clock.
doceañista, *n.m.* party which proclaimed the Spanish Constitution of 1812.
docena, *n.f.* dozen; *la docena del fraile,* baker's dozen; *a docenas,* abundantly, in great quantities; *meterse en docena,* to interfere in a conversation of one's superiors; *no entrar en docena con otros,* not to be equal to or like others.
docenal, *a.* sold by dozens.
docenario, -ria, *a.* containing a dozen.
doceno, -na, *a.* twelfth. — *n.m., a.* kind of cloth with twelve hundred threads in the warp.
docente, *a.* educational; teaching; *centro docente,* teaching centre.
docientos, *a.* (*obs.*) two hundred.
dócil, *a.* docile, mild, gentle, yielding, tractable; obedient; flexible, governable; ductile, pliable, malleable.
docilidad, *n.f.* docility, meekness, gentleness; manageableness; tractableness.
dócilmente, *adv.* tractably, mildly, meekly.
docimástico, -ca, *a.* docimastic.
doctamente, *adv.* learnedly.
docto, -ta, *a.* learned.
doctor, -ra, *n.m.* doctor (of law, medicine, etc.); physician. — *n.f.* (*coll.*) doctor's *or* physician's wife; blue-stocking.
doctorado, *n.m.* doctorate, doctorship.
doctoral, *a.* doctoral. — *n.f.* canonry of that name in Spanish cathedrals. — *n.m.* canon of the *doctoral.*
doctoramiento, *n.m.* doctorate, doctorship.
doctorando, *n.m.* one about to take his doctor's degree.
doctorar, *v.t., v.r.* to confer a doctorate, dignify with the doctor's degree.
doctorcillo, *n.m.* (*coll.*) little doctor; quack [DOCTOR].
doctrina, *n.f.* doctrine; science, wisdom; preaching of the gospel; (*Am.*) curacy; Sunday school; catechism; *niños de la doctrina* [DOCTRINO].
doctrinador, -ra, *a.* instructing, teaching. — *n.m.f.* instructor, teacher.
doctrinal, *a.* doctrinal, relating to doctrine. — *n.m.* catechism.
doctrinante, *a.* instructing.
doctrinar, *v.t.* to teach, instruct.
doctrinario, -ria, *a.* doctrinarian. — *n.m.f.* doctrinaire.
doctrinero, *n.m.* teacher of Christian doctrine; (*Am.*) curate, parish priest.
doctrino, *n.m.* charity child; *parecer uno un doctrino,* to appear timid and spiritless.
documentación, *n.f.* documentation; documents.
documentado, -da, *a.* having the necessary documents or vouchers. — *p.p.* [DOCUMENTAR].
documental, *a.* documental, documentary.
documentalmente, *adv.* with proper documents.
documentar, *v.t.* to document, prove by documents; to teach, catechize.
documento, *n.m.* document, writing, record, voucher, deed, title, instrument, indenture; instruction, advice; (*com.*) collateral security.
dodecaedro, *n.m.* (*geom.*) dodecahedron.
dodecágono, *n.m.* (*geom.*) dodecagon.

dodecasílabo, -ba, *a.* with twelve syllables.
dogal, *n.m.* rope tied round the neck; hangman's halter; noose, slip-knot; *estar uno con el dogal a la garganta* or *al cuello,* to see no way of escape.
dogaresa, *n.f.* wife of the doge.
dogma, *n.m.* dogma.
dogmáticamente, *adv.* dogmatically.
dogmático, -ca, *a.* dogmatic. — *n.m.f.* dogmatist.
dogmatismo, *n.m.* dogmatism.
dogmatista, *n.m.* dogmatist.
dogmatizador, dogmatizante, *n.m.* dogmatizer, dogmatist.
dogmatizar, *v.t.* to dogmatize; to teach doctrines opposed to the Roman Catholic religion.
dogo, *n.m.* bulldog.
dogre, *n.m.* dogger, Dutch boat.
doladera, *a.* of a cooper's adze.
dolador, *n.m.* joiner; stone-cutter.
doladura, *n.f.* shavings, splinters, chips.
dolaje, *n.m.* wine absorbed by pipe-staves.
dolamas, *n.f.pl.* chronic complaints or indisposition (of persons).
dolames, *n.m.pl.* (*vet.*) chronic tumour or illness in horses.
dolar, *v.t.* to plane or smooth wood or stone.
dólar, *n.m.* dollar.
dolencia, *n.f.* ache, aching; disease, affliction; *dolencia larga y muerte encima,* long illness generally ends in death.
doler, *v.i.* (*pres. indic.* **duelo**; *pres. subj.* **duela**) to feel pain, ache, be in pain; to hurt; to cause regret or grief; to be unwilling to act. — *v.r.* (generally with *de*) to repent; to regret; to be moved by, take pity on, condole with; to feel sympathy for; to complain of; *ahí (le) duele,* that touches the spot; *a quien le duele, le duele,* the real pain is felt only by the sufferer.
doliente, *a.* aching, suffering; sorrowful; sick. — *n.m.* pall-bearer, mourner; patient, sick person.
dolo, *n.m.* fraud, deceit, imposition, trick, humbug; (*law*) premeditation; *dolo bueno,* (*law*) proper wise precautions; *dolo malo,* (*law*) chicanery; *poner dolo en una cosa,* to give a malicious interpretation to something.
dolobre, *n.m.* hammer for splitting stones.
dolomía, dolomita, *n.f.* (*min.*) dolomite.
dolomítico, -ca, *a.* dolomitic.
dolor, *n.m.* pain, aching, ache; grief, sorrow, affliction, anguish; contrition, repentance. — *pl.* throes of childbirth; *dolor de cabeza,* headache; *dolor de muelas,* toothache; *dolor de tripas,* griping; *dolor sordo,* dull continuous pain; *estar con dolores,* to be in labour; *dolor de mujer muerta dura hasta la puerta,* once widowed, twice wed.
dolora, *n.f.* short, sentimental philosophic poem.
dolorcillo, dolorcito, *n.m.* slight pain [DOLOR].
dolorido, -da, *a.* doleful, afflicted; aching, painful; sore, tender; heart-sick. — *n.m.f.* (*obs.*) chief mourner.
Dolorosa, *n.f.* Mater Dolorosa, Our Lady of Sorrows.
dolorosamente, *adv.* painfully; sorrowfully, miserably.
doloroso, -sa, *a.* painful; regrettable; pitiful,
dolosamente, *adv.* deceitfully.

doloso, -sa, *a.* deceitful; fraudulent.

dóllimo, *n.m.* (*Chi.*) freshwater mollusc.

dom, *n.m.* (*eccles.*) title of Carthusian and Benedictine monks.

doma, *n.f.* breaking in (a horse, etc.); subduing passions, vices, etc.

domable, *a.* tamable; conquerable.

domador, -ra, *n.m.f.* tamer, subduer; horse-breaker.

domadura, *n.f.* taming, subduing.

domar, *v.t.* to tame, break in; to subdue, conquer, overcome, master.

dombo, *n.m.* dome, cupola.

domeñar, *v.t.* to tame, domesticate; to master, subdue.

domesticable, *a.* tamable.

domésticamente, *adv.* domestically.

domesticar, *v.t.* (*pret.* **domestiqué;** *pres. subj.* **domestique**) to tame, domesticate, make gentle. — *v.r.* to grow tame.

domesticidad, *n.f.* domesticity; domestication.

doméstico, -ca, *a.* domestic; domesticated. — *n.m.f.* domestic, servant.

domestiquez, *n.m.* (*obs.*) tameness.

domiciliado, -da, *a.* domiciled, received as a denizen or citizen. — *p.p.* [DOMICILIAR].

domiciliario, *a.* domiciliary. — *n.m.* inhabitant, citizen.

domiciliar, *v.t.* to grant a domicile to. — *v.r.* to establish oneself in a domicile.

domicilio, *n.m.* habitation, abode, residence, domicile, home; *adquirir* or *contraer domicilio,* to acquire a domicile.

dominación, *n.f.* domination, power, authority, rule, command; (*mil.*) commanding ground. — *pl.* dominations, angelic beings.

dominador, -ra, *a.* dominating, controlling; overbearing. — *n.m.f.* dominator.

dominante, *a.* domineering, dictatorial, overbearing; prevailing, excelling, dominative; commanding, towering; (*mus.*) dominant.

dominar, *v.t.* to dominate, govern, rule, master, command; to repress, moderate (one's passions), correct (one's evil habits); to master (a subject, etc.). — *v.i.* to stand out, jut out (building, mountain, etc.). — *v.r.* to exercise self-control.

dominativo, -va, *a.* dominative.

dómine, *n.m.* teacher of Latin grammar; (*contempt.*) pompous fool.

dominada, *n.f.* Sunday festival.

domingo, *n.m.* Sunday; *domingo de Lázaro* or *de Pasión,* Passion Sunday; *domingo de Ramos,* Palm Sunday; *domingo de Resurrección,* Easter Sunday; *domingo de Cuasimodo,* Low Sunday; *salir con un domingo siete,* to put one's foot in it.

dominguejo, *n.m.* (*Am.*) insignificant person.

dominguero, -ra, *a.* belonging to Sunday, done or worn on Sunday; *sayo dominguero,* (*coll.*) Sunday best.

dominguillo, *n.m.* doll weighted so that it will always stand upright; (*obs.*) figure dressed as soldier placed in the bullring; *hacer a uno su dominguillo,* (*coll.*) to make one a laughing-stock; *traer a uno como* or *hecho un dominguillo,* to order someone to do several things at once in different places.

dominica, *n.f.* (*eccles.*) Sunday.

dominical, *a.* dominical; relating to feudal dues. — *n.f.* Sunday function in Spanish universities; *oración dominical,* the Lord's prayer.

dominicano, -na, *n.m.f., a.* Dominican.

dominicatura, *n.f.* (*prov.*) duty of vassalage.

dominico, -ca, *n.m.f.* friar of the order of St. Dominic; (*Cent. Am., Cub.*) kind of small banana; (*Cub.*) small bird.

dominio, *n.m.* dominion, territory, region; domination, rule, authority; domain; (*law*) fee; *dominio absoluto,* (*law*) fee simple; *dominio público,* public knowledge; (*law*) government property.

dómino, *n.m.* game of dominoes.

dominó, *n.m.* domino, hooded robe; game of dominoes.

domo, *n.m.* (*arch.*) dome, cupola.

dompedro, *n.m.* (*bot.*) morning-glory.

don, *n.m.* Mister (the Spanish title for a gentleman, used only before the Christian name); gift, present; faculty, dexterity, knack; gracefulness; ability; *don de acierto,* habitual dexterity, tact; *don de errar,* knack of doing things the wrong way; *don de gentes,* winning manners; *don de mando,* aptitude for command.

dona, *n.f.* (*obs.*) woman, lady; (*Chi.*) bequest. — *pl.* wedding presents given by bridegroom to bride.

donación, *n.f.* donation, gift, grant; cession of property; *donación piadosa,* pious gift.

donadío, *n.m.* (*prov.*) property derived from royal grants.

donado, -da, *n.m.f.* lay-brother, lay-sister.

donador, -ra, *a., n.m.f.* donating; donor, bestower.

donaire, *n.m.* grace, gentility, elegance; witty saying; graceful carriage; *hacer donaire de,* to laugh wittily at.

donairosamente, *adv.* facetiously; gracefully.

donairoso, -sa, *a.* pleasant, graceful, elegant; witty.

donante, *a.* giving. — *n.m.f.* donor, giver.

donar, *v.t.* to give, bestow, contribute.

donatario, -ria, *n.m.f.* donee, grantee.

donativo, *n.m.* donative, donation, gift.

doncel, *n.m.* king's page; chaste youth. — *a.* mellow, mild (of wine); *pino doncel,* timber of young pines without knots; *vino doncel,* wine of a mild flavour.

doncella, *n.f.* maid, virgin; lass, girl, damsel; lady's maid, waiting-maid; (*ichth.*) snake-fish; *la doncella honesta, el hacer algo es su fiesta,* an honest maid's holiday is to be busy; *quien adama a la doncella, el alma trae en pena,* the course of true love never runs smoothly.

doncelleja, *n.f.* little maid [DONCELLA].

doncellería, *n.f.* (*coll.*) maidenhead, virginity.

doncellez, *n.f.* virginity, maidenhood.

doncellica, doncellita, *n.f.* young girl [DONCELLA].

doncelluca, *n.f.* (*coll.*) old maid.

doncelluela, *n.f.* young maid [DONCELLA].

donde (interrogative **dónde**), *adv.* where, in what place, whither, wherein; (*Am.*) to or at the house of; *donde quiera,* anywhere; *donde hay gana, hay maña,* where there's a will, there's a way; *donde las dan, las toman,* as one sows, so must one reap; *donde no,* in the contrary case, otherwise; *a donde,* where, whereto; *¿dónde va a parar todo esto?* where is all this going to end? *¿hacia dónde?* whither, toward what place? *¿por dónde?* by what way? for what reason?

dondequiera, *adv.* anywhere; wherever; *por dondequiera,* everywhere.

dondiego, *n.m.* (*bot.*) jalap; *dondiego de noche,* (*bot.*) marvel of Peru; *dondiego de día,* (*bot.*) morning-glory.

dongón, *n.m.* (*Philip.*) tree of the Malvaceæ family (used in boat building).

donguindo, *n.m.* variety of pear-tree.

donillero, *n.m.* swindler, sharper, trickster, decoy, roper-in.

donjuán, *n.m.* [DONDIEGO].

donosamente, *adv.* gracefully, pleasingly.

donosidad, *n.f.* gracefulness; wittiness.

donoso, -sa, *a.* gay, witty, pleasant; graceful.

donosura, *n.f.* grace, gracefulness, elegance; wittiness.

doña, *n.f.* Miss, Mrs., title given to a lady (nowadays a married lady only), but used only before Christian name. — *pl.* (*obs.*) yearly present made to the workers in iron-mines.

doñear, *v.i.* (*coll.*) to womanize, to spend much time with women.

doñegal, doñigal, *n.m., a.* applied to a kind of fig.

doquier, doquiera, *adv.* wherever.

dorada, *n.f.* (*ichth.*) gilt-head, gilt-poll; (*astron.*) dorado; (*Cub.*) a poisonous fly.

doradilla, *n.f.* (*ichth.*) [DORADA]; (*bot.*) common ceterach.

doradillo, *n.m.* fine brass wire; satin-wood; (*orn.*) wagtail. — *a.* (*Arg., CR.*) applied to honey-coloured horses.

dorado, -da, *a.* gilt; *sopa dorada,* highly coloured soup. — *n.m.* act of gilding. — *p.p.* [DORAR].

dorador, *n.m.* gilder.

doradura, *n.f.* gilding.

doral, *n.m.* (*orn.*) fly-catcher.

dorar, *v.t.* to gild; to palliate, excuse; (*poet.*) to illumine.

dórico, -ca, (*arch.*) Doric.

dorio, -ria, *n.m.f., a.* Dorian.

dormán, *n.m.* dolman.

dormida, *n.f.* period of unbroken sleep; state of silk-worm when sloughing its skin; resting-place of animals; (*CR., Chi.*) bedroom.

dormidera, *n.f.* garden poppy; (*Cub.*) sensitive mimosa. — *pl.* sleepiness; *tiene buenas dormideras,* he sleeps well.

dormidero, -ra, *a.* sleepy, soporiferous, narcotic. — *n.m.* resting-place for cattle.

dormiente, *a.* sleeping, dormant.

dormilón, -ona, *n.m.f.* dull, sleepy person; (*Cent. Am., Cub.*) mimosa. — *n.f.pl.* screw earrings.

dormir, *v.i.* (*pres. indic.* **duermo;** *pret.* (**él**) **durmió;** *pres. subj.* **duerma**) to sleep; (*naut.*) to heel excessively; (*naut.*) applied to a sluggish magnetic needle; to be negligent; *dormir la mona* or *la zorra,* to sleep oneself sober; *dormir a pierna suelta,* to be fast asleep, to sleep soundly; *dormir como una piedra* or *un tronco,* to sleep like a top; *dormir con cortinas verdes,* to sleep in the open fields; *dormir sobre,* to sleep on (i.e. to consider maturely); *dormir al sereno,* to sleep in the open; *dormir la siesta,* to take a nap after dinner; *a* or *entre duerme y vela,* half-asleep; *durmiendo velando,* half-asleep; *no puede todo ser, dormir y guardar las eras,*

property needs vigilance; *mientras se duerme, todos son iguales,* while men are asleep they are all equal. — *v.r.* to fall asleep, be overcome with sleep; to become indolent.

dormirlas, *n.m.* hide-and-seek (game).

dormitar, *v.i.* to doze, nap.

dormitivo, *n.m.* dormitive.

dormitorio, *n.m.* bedroom; dormitory.

dornajo, *n.m.* trough, tray, pan, wooden bowl.

dornillo, *n.m.* [DORNAJO].

dorsal, *a.* dorsal.

dorso, *n.m.* spine, back; dorsum.

dos, *a.* two; second. — *n.m.* two; deuce. — *n.f.pl.* las dos, two o'clock; *dos de mayo,* the second of May; *a dos manos,* with both hands; *a dos por tres,* quickly and clearly; *en un dos por tres,* in a twinkling; *dos a dos,* two by two; *de dos en dos,* two by two, by couples; two abreast; *aquí para entre los dos,* between you and me; *decir las cosas dos por tres,* to say things emphasizing their truth and exactness.

dosalbo, -ba, *a.* having two white stockings (of horses).

dosañal, *a.* biennial.

doscientos, -tas, *a.* two hundred. — *n.m.f.pl.* two hundred.

dosel, *n.m.* canopy, dais; portière.

doselera, *n.f.* valance, drapery of a canopy.

dosificar, *v.t.* to measure out doses of medicine; to analyse.

dosis, *n.f.* dose, quantity.

dotación, *n.f.* dotation, endowment, foundation; settlement, dowry; equipment; (*mil.*) munition and garrison of a fortress; *dotación de un buque, de un avión, etc.,* complement of a crew; (*Cub.*) workmen employed on a plantation; *dotación de navíos,* fund appropriated to the repairing of ships.

dotado, -da, *a.* dowered, endowed, portioned; *dotado de,* endowed with. — *p.p.* [DOTAR].

dotador, -ra, *n.m.f.* endower, donor.

dotal, *a.* dotal.

dotar, *v.t.* to portion; to endow; to give a portion or dowry; (*fig.*) to endow with talents.

dote, *n.m.f.* dower, dowry; stock of counters; *constituir uno la dote,* to make a formal gift of a dowry. — *n.f.pl.* gifts, talents, natural blessings, endowments.

dovela, *n.f.* voussoir of an arch.

dovelaje, *n.m.* voussoirs for an arch.

dovelar, *v.t.* to hew a stone in curves for an arch.

doy, *1st pers. pres. indic.* [DAR].

dozavado, -da, *a.* twelve-sided; in twelve parts.

dozavo, -va, *n., a.* twelfth part.

draba, *n.f.* whitlow-grass.

dracma, *n.f.* drachm; drachma.

draconiano, -na, *a.* Draconian, severe, cruel.

dracúnculo, *n.m.* guinea-worm.

draga, *n.f.* dredge; (*naut.*) dredger.

dragado, -da, *a.* dredging. — *n.m.* action and effect of dredging. — *p.p.* [DRAGAR].

dragaminas, *n.m.* mine-sweeper.

dragante, *n.m.* (*bot.*) goat's thorn; (*naut.*) pillow of the bowsprit.

dragar, *v.t.* (*pret.* **dragué;** *pres. subj.* **drague**) (*naut.*) to dredge, deepen a channel.

drago, *n.m.* dragon-tree.

dragomán, *n.m.* dragoman.

dragón, *n.m.* dragon, fabulous monster; flying lizard; (*mil.*) dragoon; (*vet.*) white spots on the eyes of horses; *kind of* exhalation; (*astron.*) Draco; (*bot.*) dragon-tree; *dragón marino*, (*ichth.*) sea-dragon, weather fish.

dragona, *n.f.* female dragon; (*mil.*) shoulder-knot; (*Mex.*) cape, cloak; (*Chi., Mex.*) wrist-strap of a sword.

dragonazo, *n.m.* large dragon [DRAGÓN].

dragoncillo, *n.m.* little dragon; little dragoon [DRAGÓN]; (*obs.*) dragon, large-bore musket.

dragonear, *v.i.* (*Am.*) to pretend to be, to pose (as), to play (the).

dragontea, dragontía, *n.f.* (*bot.*) common dragon.

dragontino, -na, *a.* dragonish.

drama, *n.m.* drama, play.

dramática, *n.f.* dramatic art.

dramáticamente, *adv.* dramatically.

dramático, -ca, *a.* dramatic.

dramatismo, *n.m.* quality of being dramatic.

dramatización, *n.f.* dramatization.

dramatizar, *v.t.* (*pret.* **dramaticé**; *pres. subj.* **dramatice**) to dramatize.

dramaturgia, *n.f.* dramaturgy, dramatic art.

dramaturgo, -ga, *n.m.f.* dramatist, play-wright.

dramón, *n.m.* old-fashioned melodrama.

drástico, -ca, *a.* (*med.*) drastic.

drecera, *n.f.* straight row of houses, trees, etc.

drenaje, *n.m.* drainage.

dríada, dríade, *n.f.* dryad, wood-nymph.

dril, *n.m.* strong cloth, drill.

drino, *n.m.* green tree-snake.

driza, *n.f.* halyard.

drizar, *v.t.* (*naut.*) (*obs.*) to hoist up the yards.

droga, *n.f.* drug, medicine; (*fig.*) fib, strata-gem, artifice, deceit; nuisance; *es (una) droga, es mucha droga*, it's a nuisance; (*Chi., Mex., Per.*) debt; deceit, trick, bad debt.

droguería, *n.f.* druggist's shop; trade in drugs.

droguero, -ra, *n.m.f.* druggist; (*Chi., Mex., Per.*) cheat.

droguete, *n.m.* drugget.

droguista, *n.m.f.* druggist; (*fig.*) cheat, im-postor.

dromedario, *n.m.* dromedary.

dropacismo, *n.m.* (*med.*) depilatory.

drope, *n.m.* (*coll.*) vile, despicable man.

druida, *n.m.* druid.

druídico, -ca, *a.* druidic, druidical.

druidismo, *n.m.* druidism.

drupa, *n.f.* (*bot.*) drupe.

drusa, *n.f.* (*min.*) geode.

druso, -sa, *n.m.f., a.* Druse.

dúa, *n.f.* (*min., obs.*) gang of workmen.

dual, *a.* (*gram.*) dual. — *n.m.* incisor.

dualidad, *n.f.* duality.

dualismo, *n.m.* dualism.

dualista, *a.* dualistic. — *n.m.* dualist.

duba, *n.f.* (*prov.*) wall or enclosure of earth.

dubio, *n.m.* (*law*) doubt.

dubitable, *a.* doubtful, dubious.

dubitación, *n.f.* dubitation, doubt.

dubitativo, -va, *a.* doubtful, dubious.

ducado, *n.m.* duchy, dukedom; ducat.

ducal, *a.* ducal.

ducentésimo, -ma, *a.* two-hundredth.

dúctil, *a.* ductile, malleable; yielding.

ductilidad, *n.f.* ductility, malleability.

ductivo, -va, *a.* conducive.

ductor, *n.m.* guide, conductor; (*surg.*) probe.

ductriz, *n.f.* conductress.

ducha, *n.f.* shower-bath, douche; stripe in cloth.

ducho, -cha, *a.* dexterous, skilful.

duda, *n.f.* doubt, suspense, hesitation, irreso-lution; *sin duda (alguna)*, doubtless, no doubt.

dudable, *a.* doubtful, dubious.

dudar, *v.i.* to doubt, hesitate. — *v.t.* to give little credit to a report; *dudar de*, to distrust; *lo dudo*, I doubt it.

dudilla, *n.f.* slight doubt.

dudosamente, *adv.* doubtfully, dubiously.

dudoso, -sa, *a.* doubtful, dubious, uncertain, hesitating; hazardous.

duela, *n.f.* (*coop.*) stave.

duelaje, *n.m.* [DOLAJE].

duelista, *n.m.* duellist, fighter.

duelo, *n.m.* sorrow, affliction, grief, trouble; bereavement; assemblage of mourners; con-dolence, condolement; duel, combat. — *pl.* troubles, vexations. — *¿a dó vas, duelo? a do suelo*, sorrows never come singly; there is still some comfort left; *duelos y quebrantos*, giblets and offal; *no lloraré yo sus duelos*, he won't have to seek his troubles; *sin duelo*, abundantly.

duelo; duela, *pres. indic.; pres. subj.* [DOLER].

duena, *n.f.* (*obs.*) duenna.

duende, *n.m.* elf, fairy, ghost, goblin; *andar uno como un duende, parecer uno un duende*, to turn up in unexpected places; *tener uno duende*, to be uneasy in mind.

duendecillo, *n.m.* little fairy [DUENDE].

duendo, -da, *a.* domestic, tame.

dueña, *n.f.* married lady (*obs.*); chaperone, duenna; owner, mistress, proprietress, land-lady; *poner a uno como cual no digan dueñas*, to give someone a dressing-down.

dueñesco, -ca, *a.* (*coll.*) duenna-like.

dueño, *n.m.* owner, proprietor, landlord; master, mistress; *adonde no está el dueño, ahí está su dueño*, when the cat's away the mice will play; *dueño del arga-mandijo*, (*coll.*) person in command; *dueño de sí mismo*, self-controlled; *hacerse uno dueño de una cosa*, to make oneself master of something; to pretend rights or faculties not possessed by one; *ser uno (muy) dueño de hacer una cosa*, to have liberty to do some-thing; *ser dueño de*, to own, be master of; to be at liberty to do, etc.

duermevela, *n.m.* (*coll.*) dozing, light sleep.

duermo; duerma, *pres. indic.; pres. subj.* [DORMIR].

duerna, *n.f.; duerno*, *n.m.* trough.

duerno, *n.m.* (*print.*) double sheet of paper.

dueto, *n.m.* duo, duet.

dugo, *n.m.* (*Cent. Am.*) help.

dugongo, *n.m.* (*zool.*) dugong.

dula, *n.f.* common pasture-ground; *vete, or idos, a la dula*, (*coll.*), be off with you.

dulcamara, *n.f.* (*bot.*) bitter-sweet.

dulce, *a.* sweet, honeyed, sugared; gentle, soft, meek; mild; fresh (of water); pleasing, pleasant, agreeable; ductile (as metals). — *n.m.* sweetmeat, confection, bonbon, candied fruit, dried fruit; *dulce de almíbar*, preserves; *a nadie le amarga un dulce*, don't miss any-thing offered.

dulcecillo, -cilla; dulcecito, -cita, *a.* sweetish, rather sweet. — *n.m.f.* bonbon.

dulcedumbre, *n.f.* sweetness.

dulcémele, *n.m.* (*mus.*) dulcimer.

dulcemente, *adv.* sweetly, gently, delightfully.

dulcera, *n.f.* jam-jar; jar for jam or other preserves.

dulcería, *n.f.* sweet-shop.

dulcero, -ra, *a.* fond of sweets. — *n.m.f.* confectioner.

dulcificación, *n.f.* dulcification.

dulcificante, *a.* dulcifying, sweetening.

dulcificar, *v.t.* (*pret.* **dulcifiqué;** *pres. subj.* **dulcifique**) to sweeten, dulcify.

dulcinea, *n.f.* (*coll.*) sweetheart, beloved; (*fig.*) fantasy, ideal.

dulcísono, -na, *a.* sweet-toned.

dulero, *n.m.* herdsman.

dulzaina, *n.f.* (*mus.*) reed, flageolet, musical wind instrument; (*coll.*) quantity of defective sweetmeats.

dulzainero, *n.m.* flageolet-player.

dulzaino, -na, *a.* (*coll.*) too sweet or rich.

dulzamara, *n.f.* [DULCAMARA].

dulzarrón, -ona, *a.* (*coll.*) cloying, sickening, much too sweet.

dulzor, *n.m.;* **dulzura,** *n.f.* sweetness; gentleness; meekness; comfort, pleasure; forbearance; pleasing manner, kindliness.

dulzurar, *v.t.* (*chem.*) to dulcify, unsalt.

duna, *n.f.* dune.

dundo, -da, *a.* (*Cent. Am., Col.*) silly, stupid.

dúo, *n.m.* (*mus.*) duo, duet.

duodécimo, -ma, *a.* twelfth.

duodenal, *a.* duodenal.

duodenario, -ria, *a.* lasting twelve days.

duodeno, -na, *a.* twelfth. — *n.m.* (*anat.*) duodenum.

duomesino, -na, *a.* of two months.

dupla, *n.f.* extra dish given in colleges on special days.

duplex, dúplex, *a.* (*teleg.*) duplex.

dúplica, *n.f.* (*law*) rejoinder.

duplicación, *n.f.* duplication, doubling.

duplicadamente, *adv.* doubly.

duplicado, -da, *a.* duplicate; doubled. — *n.m.* duplicate; counterpart; *por duplicado,* in duplicate. — *p.p.* [DUPLICAR].

duplicador, -ra, *a.* duplicating. — *n.m.* duplicator (machine).

duplicar *v.t.* (*pret.* **dupliqué;** *pres. subj.* **duplique**) to duplicate, double; to repeat; (*law*) to answer a charge or pleading.

duplicatura, *n.f.* fold, crease.

dúplice, *a.* double.

duplicidad, *n.f.* duplicity, falseness, deceit.

duplo, *a., n.m.* double, twice as much.

duque, *n.m.* duke; (*coll.*) fold in mantillas.

duquecito, *n.m.* little duke; petty duke [DUQUE].

duquesa, *n.f.* duchess.

dura, *n.f.* duration, continuance.

durable, *a.* durable, lasting.

duración, *n.f.* duration, continuance; durability.

duraderamente, *adv.* durably, lastingly.

duradero, -ra, *a.* lasting, durable.

duramadre, duramáter, *n.f.* (*anat.*) dura mater.

duramente, *adv.* hardly, rigorously, harshly.

durando, *n.m.* kind of cloth formerly made in Spain.

durante, *adv.* during.

durar, *v.i.* to last, endure; to wear (of clothes).

duraznero, *n.m.* variety of peach-tree.

duraznillo, *n.m.* kind of peach-tree.

durazno, *n.m.* (*Arg., Chi.*) peach; peach-tree.

dureza, *n.f.* hardness, firmness, solidity; obstinacy, obduracy; steadiness, perseverance; sharpness, acerbity of temper; harshness, hardness of heart, cruelty; (*art*) crudeness; (*med.*) callosity, tumour; *dureza de estilo,* harshness of style; *dureza de oído,* dullness of hearing; *dureza de vientre,* costiveness.

durillo, -lla, *a.* rather hard, hardish [DURO]. — *n.m.* (*bot.*) common laurustinus; (*vet.*) callosity.

durmiente, *a.* sleeping, dormant. — *n.m.* (*arch.*) dormant, dormer; (*naut.*) clamp, shelf; (*Am.*) (*railw.*) cross-tie, sleeper, girder.

duro, -ra, *a.* hard, solid; unbearable, vexatious; unjust, oppressive; ill-natured, harsh, cruel; hard-hearted, unmerciful; stubborn, obstinate; avaricious, stingy; rude, harsh, rough; (*naut.*) stiff; (*art*) crude; (*mus.*) harsh, inharmonious; *a duro* or *de duro* (*obs.*), with difficulty; *a duras penas,* with difficulty, hardly, scarcely; *más da el duro que el desnudo,* even the miser has more to give than the pauper; *tomar las duras con* or *por las maduras,* to take the bad with the good, the inconveniences with the advantages. — *n.m.* dollar, five-peseta piece; (*Am.*) low, rough saddle; *duro y parejo, adv.* (*coll.*) (*Arg., Chi.*) with firmness and steadiness. — *adv.* hard, forcibly, violently.

duunvir(o), *n.m.* duumvir.

duunviral, *a.* duumviral.

duunvirato, *n.m.* duumvirate.

dux, *n.m.* doge.

E

E, e, *n.f.* sixth letter of the Spanish alphabet; used instead of *y* (and) when the following word begins with *i* or *hi*; e.g. *Juan e Ignacio; padre e hijo* (father and son). This rule does not apply at the beginning of interrogation or exclamation, or when the following word begins with the syllable *hie*; e.g. *y ¿Ignacio?*; *¡y Isidro también!* (and Isidro also!); *tigre y hiena,* (tiger and hyena).

¡ea! *interj.* come, let's go, let's see; exclamation denoting encouragement; *¡ea pues!,* well then, let us see.

ebanista, *n.m.* cabinet-maker.

ebanistería, *n.f.* cabinet-work; cabinet-maker's shop.

ébano, *n.m.* ebony, ebony-wood.

ebenáceo, -cea, *a.* (*bot.*) ebenaceous.

ebonita, *n.f.* ebonite.

ebriedad, *n.f.* ebriety.

ebrio, -ria, *a.* inebriated, tipsy, intoxicated.

ebrioso, -sa, *a.* intoxicated, drunken.

ebulición, ebullición, *n.f.* ebullition.

ebúrneo, -nea, *a.* (*poet.*) ivory-like, made of ivory.

eccehomo, *n.m.* Ecce Homo; (*coll.*) pitiable wretch.

eclampsia, *n.f.* (*med.*) spasm.

eclecticismo, *n.m.* eclecticism.

ecléctico, *n.m.f.*, *a.* eclectic.

eclesiásticamente, *adv.* ecclesiastically.

eclesiástico, -ca, *a.* ecclesiastical. — *n.m.* clergyman, priest; book of Ecclesiasticus.

eclesiastizar, *v.t.* to spiritualize (property).

eclímetro, *n.m.* (*surv.*) clinometer.

eclipsable, *a.* that may be eclipsed.

eclipsar, *v.t.* to eclipse; to outshine. — *v.r.* to vanish, disappear from society.

eclipse, *n.m.* eclipse.

eclíptica, *n.f.* ecliptic.

eclisa, *n.f.* (*railw.*) (*Am.*) fish-plate.

eco, *n.m.* echo; distant sound; repetition of words; *hacer eco,* to agree, fit, correspond; to become important or famous; to do something notable; *tener eco,* to be noised about.

ecoico, -ca, *a.* (*poet.*) relating to echoes.

economato, *n.m.* guardianship, trusteeship; co-operative shop.

economía, *n.f.* economy, prudent management; frugality, saving, thrift; scantiness, niggardliness; *economía animal,* animal economy; *economía política,* political economy.

económicamente, *adv.* economically.

económico, -ca, *a.* economical, economic; saving, thrifty; sparing, frugal; miserly, niggardly; cheap.

economista, *a.* economical. — *n.m.f.* economist.

economizar, *v.t.* (*pret.* **economicé;** *pres. subj.* **economice**) to economize; to save, spare.

ecónomo, *n.m.* trustee; curator, guardian; ecclesiastical administrator.

ectoplasma, *n.m.* ectoplasm.

ecuable, *a.* equitable; (*mech.*) uniform (motion).

ecuación, *n.f.* (*alg.*) equation; *ecuación de tiempo,* equation of time.

ecuador, ecuator (*obs.*) *n.m.* equator.

ecuanimidad, *n.f.* equanimity.

ecuatorial, *a.* equatorial. — *n.f.* equatorial telescope.

ecuatoriano, -na, *n.m.f.*, *a.* Ecuadorian.

ecuestre, *a.* equestrian.

ecuménico, -ca, *a.* œcumenical, universal.

ecuo, -cua, *a.* (*obs.*) just, right.

ecuóreo, -rea, *a.* (*poet.*) belonging to the sea.

eczema, *n.m.* (*med.*) eczema.

echacantos, *n.m.* (*coll.*) rattle-brained fellow.

echacorvear, *v.i.* (*coll.*) to procure, pimp.

echacorvería, *n.f.* (*coll.*) profession of a pimp or procurer.

echacuervos, *n.m.* (*coll.*) pimp, procurer; cheat, impostor.

echada, *n.f.* cast, throw; (*sport*) man's length on the ground; (*Arg., Mex.*) boast, bluff; lie, fib.

echadero, *n.m.* place of rest or repose.

echadillo, *n.m.* (*coll.*) foundling.

echadizo, -za, *a.* spying; subtly disseminated (as propaganda); foundling; rejected, discarded. — *n.m.f.* spy; (*coll.*) foundling; debris, garbage.

echado, -da, *n.m.f.* (*obs.*) foundling. — *n.m.* (*min.*) dip of a vein. — *a.* (*CR.*) indolent, lazy. — *p.p.* [ECHAR].

echador, -ra, *a.* throwing. — *n.m.f.* thrower.

echadura, *n.m.f.* brooding, hatching; winnowing; *echadura de pollos,* brood of chickens.

echamiento, *n.m.* cast, throw; throwing, expulsion, casting out; rejection; ejection.

echapellas, *n.m.* wool-soaker.

echaperros, *n.m.* beadle who drives dogs out of church.

echar, *v.t.* to cast, throw; to fling, dart, hurl, toss; to turn away, drive away; to cast away; to reject, eject, expel, throw out; to put in or into; to put on (as a cloak); to babble; to incline, recline; to deal out; to distribute; to throw into (a bag); to turn (as a key); to play (as a game); to lean toward; to impute, ascribe; to move, make room for, push; to deal cards; to tell a fortune (by cards); to couple animals sexually; to discharge; to dismiss; to lay or impose (as a law or tax); to emit (sparks); to pour out; *echar abajo, por tierra, por el suelo,* to throw; to demolish; *echar a fondo* or *pique,* (*naut.*) to sink a vessel; to ruin, wreck; *echar a la* or *en cara,* to throw in one's face; *echar al mundo,* to create; to bring forth; *echar a la calle,* to dismiss, discharge; *echar a la lotería, a una rifa,* to gamble in a lottery; *echar cartas,* to deal cards; to tell a fortune (by cards); *echar una carta,* to post a letter; *echar a la buena barba,* to toss a coin to decide who shall pay; *echar a patadas,* to kick out; *echar a perder,* to mar, spoil; *echar a mala parte* or *echar con cajas destempladas,* to dismiss one roughly or contemptuously; *echar bravatas,* to boast, to brag; *echar boca,* to sharpen; *echar aceite* or *leña al fuego,* to add fuel to the flames; *echar agua a un niño,* to baptize a child; *echar a galeras* or *a presidio,* to sentence to the galleys or gaol; *echar bendiciones,* to bless, shower blessings; *echar carnes,* to put on flesh; *echar carrillos,* to grow plump in the cheeks; *echar chufas,* to act the bully; *echar coche,* to set up a coach; *echar chispas (rayos, centellas, fuego),* to be very angry; *echar de menos a una persona* or *cosa,* to miss a person or a thing; *echar de ver,* to mark, perceive, notice; *echar cálculos* or *cuentas,* to do calculations, to reckon; *¿qué edad le echas?* how old do you think him?; *echar un bando,* to publish a law; *echar la comedia,* to perform a play; *echar un discurso, un sermón,* to give a lecture, a sermon; *echar coplas, refranes,* to sing, say proverbs; *echar ternos,* to swear; *echar de comer,* to give something to eat; *echar el bofe* or *los bofes,* to work very hard; to solicit anxiously; *echar el escandallo,* (*naut.*) to puff and blow; *echar en tierra,* (*naut.*) to land, disembark; *echar el ancla,* (*naut.*) to cast anchor; *echar el cuerpo fuera,* to withdraw from an affair; *echar la carga a otro,* to throw the blame on another; *echar la corredera,* (*naut.*) to heave the log; *echar el guante,* to throw down the glove; to arrest a person; *echar un guante,* to pass round the hat; *echar los hígados,* to be dead tired; *echar los hígados por,* (*coll.*) to yearn for; *echar por en medio, echar por la calle de en medio,* to rush recklessly; to take a final resolution; *echar toda la vela,* (*naut.*) to crowd sail; *echar maldiciones,* to curse; *echar el fallo,* to pass judgment; *echar el pecho al agua,* (*fig.*) to take the plunge; *echar las puertas abajo,* to hammer on a door; *echar hojas, flores,* to put forth, produce, leaves or flowers; *echar raíces,* to take root; (*fig.*) to become fixed in a place; *echar dientes (pelo, bigote, barba),* to begin to have (teeth, hair, etc.); *echar pelillos a la mar,* to be reconciled; *echar suertes*, to draw lots; *echar tierra a*, to bury; (*fig.*) to hush up; *echar falso*, to bluff at cards; *echar un solo, un tute*, to play a game of cards (solo, whist, etc.); *echar mano*, to give assistance; to lay hold of a thing; to make use of; *echar pie a tierra*, to disembark; to dismount (from a horse); *echarla de valiente, poeta, maestro*, to give oneself the airs of a hero, poet, master; *echar un remiendo a*, to put a patch on; *echar un remiendo a la vida*, to take some refreshment; *echarlo todo a rodar*, to make a mess of a business; to fly into a violent rage; *echar agua en el mar*, to carry coals to Newcastle; *echar ventosas*, to apply leeches or a cupping-glass; *echar la llave*, to lock a door; *echar tributos*, to impose a tax; *echar un censo*, to make a census; *echar el cuerpo atrás, a un lado*, to lean backward, lean aside; (*fig.*) to withdraw from an affair; *echar el asunto a pares* or *a nones*, to let the spin of a coin decide; *echar un bocado, un trago, un cigarro*, to eat, drink or smoke; *echarle a paseo*, to dismiss contemptuously; *echóse a mí*, he jumped at me. — *v.i.* to issue, emit, sprout, burst out (with the infinitive and *a*, it signifies the beginning of the action denoted by the verb, or the cause of it): *echar a reír*, to start laughing; *echar a llorar*, to burst out crying; *echar a correr*, to run away; *echar en saco roto*, to disregard advice; to forget; *echar por la iglesia, por médico, por abogado*, to go in for the church, medicine, law; *echar de baranda*, to exaggerate, boast; *echar en tierra*, (*naut.*) to land, disembark; *echar por*, to go by way of. — *v.r.* to lie, rest; to stretch oneself at full length; to sit (as a hen); to throw oneself down; to apply oneself to business; *echarse a la cama*, to lie down in bed fully clothed; *echarse al suelo*, to throw oneself on the floor; *echarse a morir*, to give up in despair; to worry oneself to death; *echarse a perder*, to spoil; to become stale; to be ruined, destroyed; to deteriorate in prestige; *echarse en brazos de*, to throw oneself in the arms of; to trust in; to resort to; *echarse sobre el ancla*, (*naut.*) to drag the anchor.

echazón, *n.f.* (*naut.*) jettison.

echona, *n.f.* (*Arg., Chi.*) sickle.

edad, *n.f.* age; epoch, era, time; *de cierta edad, de edad madura, de edad provecta*, of mature years; *mayor de edad*, of age; *mayor edad*, majority; *menor edad*, minority, infancy; *menor de edad*, a minor; *edad tierna*, tender years; *edad de piedra, bronce, hierro*, Stone, Bronze, Iron Age; *edad media*, the Middle Ages; *avanzado de edad*, advanced in years.

edecán, *n.f.* (*mil.*) aide-de-camp.

edema, *n.m.* (*med.*) œdema.

edén, *n.m.* Eden, paradise.

edición, *n.f.* edition, issue, publication; *edición príncipe*, first edition.

edicto, *n.m.* edict, proclamation.

edículo, *n.m.* small building; shrine, niche.

edificación, *n.f.* construction, art of building; edification.

edificador, -ra, *a.* constructing, building; edifying. — *n.m.f.* edifier; constructor, builder.

edificante, *a.* edifying.

edificar, *v.t.* (*pret.* **edifiqué**; *pres. subj.*

edifique) to construct, build; to edify, instruct.

edificativo, -va, *a.* exemplary, instructive, edifying.

edificatorio, -ria, *a.* edificatory.

edificio, *n.m.* edifice, structure, building.

edil, *n.m.* ædile; councillor.

edilidad, *n.f.* ædileship.

editar, *v.t.* to publish.

editor, *a.* publishing. — *n.m.* editor, publisher, bookseller; *editor responsable*, editor who accepts responsibility for.

editorial, *a.* editorial, publishing. — *n.m.* editorial. — *n.f.* publishing house.

edredón, *n.m.* eiderdown.

educable, *a.* educable.

educación, *n.f.* education; tuition, instruction, training; politeness, breeding; *educación física*, physical training.

educador, -ra, *a.* educating. — *n.m.f.* education(al)ist, instructor.

educando, -da, *n.m.f.* pupil, student.

educar, *v.t.* (*pret.* **eduqué**; *pres. subj.* **eduque**) to educate, instruct, train.

educativo, -va, *a.* educational.

educción, *n.f.* deduction; eduction.

educir, *v.t.* to educe, extract, bring out.

edulcoración, *n.f.* edulcoration.

edulcorar, *v.t.* (*chem.*) to sweeten.

efe, *n.f.* Spanish name of the letter *f*.

efectismo, *n.m.* (*art*) straining after effect.

efectista, *a.* (*art*) sensational.

efectivamente, *adv.* effectually, effectively; really, actually.

efectividad, *n.f.* effectiveness.

efectivo, -va, *a.* effective, effectual; true, certain, real, actual; permanent. — *n.m.* (*com.*) cash; *en efectivo*, in hard cash; *efectivo en caja*, cash in hand; *hacer efectiva una letra*, to cash a draft.

efecto, *n.m.* effect, operation; purpose, end, meaning; general intent. — *pl.* assets, effects, goods, chattels, merchandise; (*com.*) drafts; *con o en efecto*, in truth, indeed, in fact, actually; *efectos públicos*, public securities; *efectos a pagar*, bills payable; *efectos a recibir*, bills receivable; *surtir efecto*, to give a desired effect; *efectos en cartera*, securities in hand.

efectuación, *n.f.* effectuation, accomplishment.

efectuar, *v.t.* to effect, effectuate, accomplish, carry out.

efémera, *n.f.* (*med.*) ephemera, fever lasting one day.

efemérides, *n.f.pl.* ephemeris; journal of daily events.

efémero, *n.m.* (*bot.*) iris.

efervescencia, *n.f.* effervescence; ardour, fervour.

efervescente, *a.* effervescent.

efesino, -na; **efesio, -sia**, *n.m.f., a.* Ephesian.

efetá, *adv.* ephetha (in baptism).

eficacia, *n.f.* efficacy; efficiency.

eficaz, *a.* efficacious, effective.

eficazmente, *adv.* efficaciously, effectively, actively.

eficiencia, *n.f.* efficiency; effectiveness.

eficiente, *a.* efficient; effective.

eficientemente, *adv.* efficiently.

efigie, *n.f.* effigy, image.

efímera, *n.f.* (*med.*) ephemera; (*entom.*) ephemera, May-fly.

efímero, -ra, *a.* ephemeral, diurnal.
eflorecerse, *v.r.* (*chem.*) to effloresce.
eflorescencia, *n.f.* (*bot.*, *chem.*) efflorescence; (*med.*) eruption upon the face.
eflorescente, *a.* (*chem.*) efflorescent.
efluente, *adj.* effluent.
efluvio, *n.m.* effluvium; exhalation, emanation.
efod, *n.m.* ephod.
efugio, *n.m.* subterfuge, shift, evasion.
efundir, *v.t.* (*p.p.* **efundido, efuso**) to effuse, pour out, spill.
efusión, *n.f.* effusion, efflux; (*fig.*) confidential disclosure of sentiments.
efuso, -sa, *a.* effused. — *p.p. irreg.* [EFUNDIR].
égida, *n.f.* ægis; protection, defence.
egílope, *n.f.* (*bot.*) wild bastard oat.
egipcíaco, -ca; egipciano, -na; egipcio, -cia, *n.m.f.*, *a.* Egyptian.
egiptología, *n.f.* Egyptology.
egiptólogo, *n.m.* Egyptologist.
égira, *n.f.* hegira, hejira.
égloga, *n.f.* eclogue.
egoísmo, *n.m.* selfishness, egoism, self-love.
egoísta, *a.* selfish, egoistic. — *n.m.f.* egoist.
ególatra, *a.* egotistic.
egotismo, *n.m.* egotism.
egregiamente, *adv.* eminently, illustriously.
egregio, -gia, *a.* illustrious, eminent.
egrena, *n.f.* iron clamp.
egresión, *n.f.* egression.
egreso, *n.m.* expense, debit. — *pl.* discharge, release.
egrisador, *n.m.* box for diamond-dust.
egrisar, *v.t.* to cut diamonds.
eh! *interj.* ah! ha! here!
eirá, *n.m.* (*Arg.*, *Par.*) large fox.
eje, *n.m.* axis; axle-tree, axle; shaft, spindle, arbor; *eje auxiliar,* (*mech.*) countershaft; *eje conjugado,* (*geom.*) minor axis of an ellipse; *eje coordenado,* (*geom.*) co-ordinate axis; *eje de (las) abscisas,* (*geom.*) axis of abscissæ; *eje de (las) coordenadas,* (*geom.*) co-ordinate axis; *eje delantero,* front axle of a vehicle; *eje de ordenadas,* (*geom.*) axis of ordinates; *eje secundario,* (*mach.*) countershaft; *eje trasero,* rear axle of a vehicle; *eje terrestre* or *del mundo,* (*astron.*) axis of the earth; *partir* or *dividir a uno por el eje,* to spoil, make a mess of.
ejecución, *n.f.* execution, completion, fulfilment, performance; execution, capital punishment; (*law*) judicial writ; distraint, seizure; (*mus.*) technique.
ejecutable, *a.* executable, performable.
ejecutante, *a.* executing. — *n.m.* (*law*) one who forces another to pay by means of a distraint; (*mus.*) musician, performer.
ejecutar, *v.t.* to execute, perform, make, do, act; to pursue closely, dog the footsteps of; to oblige to pay; (*law*) to distrain, seize; to put to death, execute (a criminal).
ejecutivamente, *adv.* executively, promptly.
ejecutivo, -va, *a.* executive, executory.
ejecutor, -ra, *a.* executing. — *n.m.f.* executor; executer; officer of justice making distraints; *ejecutor de la justicia,* executioner.
ejecutoria, *n.f.* (*law*) writ or decree of execution; judgment; letters patent of nobility; executorship.
ejecutoría, *n.f.* office of an executive officer.
ejecutorial, *a.* (*law*) applied to the execution of the sentence of an ecclesiastical tribunal.

ejecutoriar, *v.t.* to confirm a judicial sentence; (*fig.*) to establish the truth of something.
ejecutorio, -ria, *a.* (*law*) executory.
ejemplar, *a.* exemplary. — *n.m.* pattern, model; precedent, example; prototype, specimen, sample; warning; copy of a book, etc.; *sin ejemplar,* without precedent; exceptional.
ejemplarmente, *adv.* exemplarily; edifyingly.
ejemplificación, *n.f.* exemplification.
ejemplificar, *v.t.* (*pret.* **ejemplifiqué;** *pres. subj.* **ejemplifique**) to exemplify, to illustrate.
ejemplo, *n.m.* example, instance, precedent; pattern, copy, exemplar; *dar ejemplo,* to set an example; *por ejemplo,* for instance; *sin ejemplo,* without precedent, unheard-of.
ejercer, *v.t.* (*pres. indic.* **ejerzo;** *pres. subj.* **ejerza**) to practise, exercise, perform, ply; to exert.
ejercicio, *n.m.* exercise, activity, exertion, training; practice; profession, employment, office, task; ministry; military drill; fiscal year; *ejercicio espiritual,* (*eccles.*) retreat; *el ejercicio hace maestro,* practice makes perfect; *hacer el ejercicio,* (*mil.*) drill.
ejercitación, *n.f.* exercise, practice.
ejercitante, *a.* exercising, training. — *n.m.f.* one in a spiritual retreat.
ejercitar, *v.t.* to exercise, practise (an art, profession, etc.); to train, drill, teach; to exercise a right; *ejercitar la paciencia,* to try the patience. — *v.r.* to make oneself skilful by practice.
ejército, *n.m.* army; *cuerpo de ejército,* army-corps.
ejido, *n.m.* common public land.
ejión, *n.m.* (*arch.*) corbel; purlin; bracket.
ejotes, *n.m.pl.* (*Mex.*, *Cent. Am.*) string beans.
el, *defin. art. m. sing.* the. — *pl.* **los.**
él, *pron. m. sing.* he. — *pl.* **ellos,** they; them (after prepositions only).
elaboración, *n.f.* elaboration.
elaborado, -da, *a.* elaborate; manufactured, fashioned. — *p.p.* [ELABORAR].
elaborador, -ra, *a.* elaborating; manufacturing. — *n.m.f.* manufacturer.
elaborar, *v.t.* to elaborate, finish with care; to manufacture.
elación, *n.f.* haughtiness, pride; elevation, grandeur; magnanimity, generosity; elevation of style.
elamí, *n.m.* (*mus.*) Phrygian mode as used in plain chant.
elástica, *n.f.* undershirt.
elásticamente, *adv.* elastically.
elasticidad, *n.f.* (*phys.*) elasticity, resiliency, springiness.
elástico, -ca, *a.* elastic. — *n.m.* elastic; elastic material. — *pl.* suspenders.
elaterio, *n.m.* (*bot.*) squirting cucumber.
elche, *n.m.* apostate, renegade (from Christianity).
ele, *n.f.* Spanish name of the letter *l.*
eléboro, elébor, *n.m.* hellebore.
elección, *n.f.* election; choice, selection.
electivo, -va, *a.* elective.
electo, -ta, *a.* elect, chosen. — *n.m.f.* person chosen, nominee. — *p.p. irreg.* [ELEGIR].
elector, -ra, *a.* electing. — *n.m.* elector.
electorado, *n.m.* electorate.
electoral, *a.* electoral.

electorero, *n.m.* (*polit.*) spoilsman.
electricidad, *n.f.* electricity.
electricista, *n.m.* electrician.
eléctrico, -ca, *a.* electric, electrical.
electrificación, *n.f.* electrification.
electrificar, *v.t.* to electrify.
electriz, *n.f.* electress.
electrizable, *a.* electrifiable.
electrización, *n.f.* electrization, electrification.
electrizador, -ra; electrizante, *a.* electrifying. — *n.m.f.* electrifier.
electrizar, *v.t.* (*pret.* **electricé;** *pres. subj.* **electrice**) to electrify; (*fig.*) to fill with enthusiasm, startle. — *v.r.* to become electrified, be charged with electricity; (*fig.*) to be electrified or thrilled.
electro, *n.m.* amber, electrum.
electrocución, *n.f.* electrocution.
electrocutar, *v.t.* to electrocute.
electrodinámica, *n.f.* electro-dynamics.
electrodinámico, -ca, *a.* electro-dynamic.
electrodo, *n.m.* electrode.
electroimán, *n.m.* electro-magnet.
electrólisis, *n.f.* electrolysis.
electrolítico, -ca, *a.* electrolytic.
electrólito, *n.m.* electrolyte.
electrolización, *n.f.* electrolization.
electrolizar, *v.t.* to electrolyze.
electromagnético, -ca, *a.* electro-magnetic.
electromagnetismo, *n.m.* electro-magnetism.
electrometría, *n.f.* electrometry.
electrométrico, -ca, *a.* electrometric.
electrómetro, *n.m.* electrometer.
electromotor, -ra, *a.* electro-motive. — *n.m.* electro-motor.
electromotriz, *a.* electro-motive; *fuerza electromotriz,* electro-motive force.
electrón, *n.m.* electron.
electronegativo, -va, *a.* electro-negative.
electropositivo, -va, *a.* electro-positive.
electroquímica, *n.f.* electro-chemistry.
electroquímico, -ca, *a.* electro-chemical.
electroscopio, *n.m.* electroscope.
electrotecnia, *n.f.* electro-technics.
electroterapia, *n.f.* electro-therapy, electro-therapeutics.
electrotipia, *n.f.* electrotyping.
electrotípico, -ca, *a.* electrotypic.
elefancía, elefantíasis, *n.f.* elephantiasis.
elefante, -ta, *n.m.f.* elephant.
elefantino, -na, *a.* elephantine.
elegancia, *n.f.* elegance, gracefulness, grace; neatness; beauty of style.
elegante, *a.* elegant, gallant, fine, nice, stylish, graceful, tasteful, dainty.
elegantemente, *adv.* elegantly, tastefully, gracefully.
elegía, *n.f.* elegy.
elegíaco, -ca, *a.* elegiac, mournful.
elegibilidad, *n.f.* eligibility.
elegible, *a.* eligible.
elegido, -da, *a.* elect, chosen. — *n.m.pl.* the elect, the blessed. — *p.p.* [ELEGIR].
elegir, *v.t.* (*p.p.* **elegido, electo;** *pres. indic.* **elijo;** *pres. subj.* **elija;** *pret.* 3rd *pers. sing.* (**él**) **eligió**) to elect, choose, select; to name, nominate; to prefer.
élego, -ga, *a.* mournful, plaintive.
elemental, elementar (*obs.*), *a.* elemental; elementary; fundamental, constitutive; obvious; *no hablemos más de esto, que es elemental,* don't let us discuss it any more for it is obvious.

elementalmente, *adv.* elementally.
elemento, *n.m.* element; (*elec.*) element; ingredient, constituent; first or constituent principle. — *pl.* elements, rudiments.
elemí, *n.m.* elemi, gum resin.
elenco, *n.m.* table, index, list, catalogue.
elevación, *n.f.* elevation; rise, ascent; height, eminence, highness, altitude, loftiness; exaltation, dignity; advancement; ecstasy, rapture; haughtiness, presumption, pride; (*arch.*) elevation (plan); *tirar por elevación,* (*artill.*) to fire with an elevation.
elevadamente, *adv.* with elevation, loftily.
elevado, -da, *a.* elevated; tall, high; sublime, majestic, grand, exalted. — *p.p.* [ELEVAR].
elevador, *n.m.* (*Am.*) lift, elevator, hoist.
elevamiento, *n.m.* elevation; ecstasy, rapture.
elevar, *v.t.* to raise, lift, elevate, hoist, heave; (*fig.*) to exalt. — *v.r.* to be elated, enraptured; to rise, soar, ascend.
elfo, *n.m.* elf.
elidir, *v.t.* to weaken, enervate, debilitate; (*gram.*) to elide.
elijable, *a.* (*pharm.*) capable of being seethed.
elijación, *n.f.* (*pharm.*) seething.
elijar, *v.t.* to seethe.
elijo; elija, *pres. indic.; pres. subj.* [ELEGIR].
eliminación, *n.f.* elimination.
eliminador, -ra, *a.* eliminating. — *n.m.f.* eliminator.
eliminar, *v.t.* to eliminate, strike out, leave out, remove.
elipse, *n.f.* (*geom.*) ellipse.
elipsis, *n.f.* (*gram.*) ellipsis.
elipsoidal, *a.* ellipsoidal.
elipsoide, *n.m.* ellipsoid.
elípticamente, *adv.* elliptically.
elipticidad, *n.f.* ellipticity.
elíptico, -ca, *a.* elliptic, elliptical.
eliseo, -sea; elisio, -sia, *a.* Elysian.
elisión, *n.f.* (*gram.*) elision.
elíxir, elixir, *n.m.* elixir.
elocución, *n.f.* elocution; effectiveness of diction.
elocuencia, *n.f.* eloquence.
elocuente, *a.* eloquent.
elocuentemente, *adv.* eloquently.
elogiador, -ra, *n.m.f., a.* eulogist, encomiast.
elogiar, *v.t.* to praise, laud, eulogize, extol.
elogio, *n.m.* eulogy, panegyric, praise.
elongación, *n.f.* elongation.
elote, *n.m.* (*Mex.*) ear of green corn; *pagar uno los elotes,* (*CR., Hond.*) (*coll.*) to get the blame, to be made the scapegoat.
elucidación, *n.f.* elucidation, explanation.
elucidar, *v.t.* to elucidate.
eludible, *a.* eludible, avoidable.
eludir, *v.t.* to elude, contrive to avoid.
ella, *pron. pers. f.* 3rd *pers. sing.* (*pl.* **ellas**) she; *ahora es ella,* now is the critical moment; *después será ella,* the rub will come later.
elle, *n.f.* Spanish name of the letter *ll.*
ello, *pron. neut.* it; *ello dirá,* we shall see; *ello es que,* the fact is that.
emaciación, *n.f.* emaciation.
emanación, *n.f.* emanation; effluvium.
emanante, *a.* emanating, emanant.
emanar, *v.i.* to emanate, proceed from; to follow, arise from.
emancipación, *n.f.* emancipation.
emancipador, -ra, *a.* emancipating. — *n.m.f.* emancipator.

emancipar, *v.t.* to emancipate. — *v.r.* to recover one's liberty.

emasculación, *n.f.* emasculation.

embabiamiento, *n.m.* (*coll.*) absentmindedness, woolgathering.

embachar, *v.t.* to pen sheep to be shorn.

embadurnador, **-ra**, *a.* daubing. — *n.m.f.* dauber.

embadurnar, *v.t.* to besmear, bedaub.

embaidor, **-ra**, *a.* swindling. — *n.m.f.* sharper, impostor, swindler.

embaimiento, *n.m.* delusion, illusion; deceit, imposture.

embair, *v.t.* *defective* (*only those moods and persons are used which have* i *in the termination*) to impose upon, deceive.

embajada, *n.f.* embassy, legation; errand, message; (*coll.*) impertinent suggestion or demand.

embajador, *n.m.* ambassador; *embajador cerca de*, ambassador to.

embajadora, **embajatriz**, *n.f.* ambassadress; ambassador's wife.

embalador, *n.m.* packer.

embalaje, *n.m.* packing; packing expenses.

embalar, *v.t.* to pack, bale.

embaldosado, **-da**, *a.*, *p.p.* [EMBALDOSAR] tiled. — *n.m.* tile-floor; pavement.

embaldosar, *v.t.* to floor with tiles.

embalijar, *v.t.* to pack into a valise.

embalsadero, *n.m.* pool of stagnant rainwater, morass, marsh, swamp.

embalsamador, **-ra**, *n.m.f.* embalmer.

embalsamamiento, *n.m.* embalming.

embalsamar, *v.t.* to embalm; to perfume.

embalsar, *v.t.* to put into a pool; to make a dam or pool; (*naut.*) to sling, hoist.

embalse, *n.m.* act of putting into a pond or on a raft; (*naut.*) slinging; artificial pond or pool.

embalumar, *v.t.* to load or fill with bulky things. — *v.r.* to burden oneself with business.

emballenador, **-ra**, *n.m.f.* corset-maker.

emballenar, *v.t.* to stiffen with whalebone.

emballestado, **-da**, *a.* (*vet.*) contracted (hoof). — *p.p.* [EMBALLESTARSE]. — *n.m.* contraction of the nerves in animals' feet.

emballestarse, *v.r.* to get ready to discharge a cross-bow.

embanastar, *v.t.* to put into a basket.

embancar, *v.i.* (*naut.*) to run aground. — *v.r.* (*Mex.*) to stick to the walls of the furnace.

embarazadamente, *adv.* perplexedly, awkwardly.

embarazado, **-da**, *a.* embarrassed, perplexed, hindered. — *n.f.* pregnant woman. — *p.p.* [EMBARAZAR].

embarazador, **-ra**, *a.* embarrassing. — *n.m.f.* embarrasser.

embarazar. *v.t.* (*pret.* **embaracé**; *pres. subj.* **embarace**) to embarrass, hinder, perplex; (*coll.*) to make pregnant.

embarazo, *n.m.* impediment; embarrassment, confusion; perplexity; pregnancy.

embarazosamente, *adv.* cumbersomely; awkwardly.

embarazoso, **-sa**, *a.* difficult, intricate, entangled, cumbersome; vexatious, embarrassing.

embarbascado, **-da**, *a.* difficult, intricate. — *p.p.* [EMBARBASCAR].

embarbascar, *v.t.* to stupefy fish by poison-ing the water; to perplex, confound, embarrass. — *v.r.* (*agric.*) to become foul, clogged or entangled among roots, etc. (plough, tools, etc.).

embarbecer, *v.i.* (*pres. indic.* **embarbezco**; *pres. subj.* **embarbezca**) to have a beard appearing.

embarbillar, *v.t.* to join planks or beams together.

embarcación, *n.f.* vessel, ship, craft; embarkation; *embarcación de alijo*, lighter; *embarcación menor*, small craft.

embarcadero, *n.m.* wharf, quay, pier; ferry; (*railw.*) goods station.

embarcador, **-ra**, *n.m.f.* shipper, loader.

embarcar, *v.t.* (*pret.* **embarqué**; *pres. subj.* **embarque**) to embark, ship; to engage, set out on an enterprise; *embarcar agua*, to ship a sea. — *v.r.* to embark.

embarco, *n.m.* embarkation, shipping of crew, passengers, etc.

embardar, *v.t.* to thatch.

embargador, **-ra**, *n.m.f.* sequestrator, one who lays an embargo.

embargante, *a.* arresting, impeding, restraining; *no embargante*, notwithstanding, nevertheless.

embargar, *v.t.* (*pret.* **embargué**; *pres. subj.* **embargue**) to arrest, lay under an embargo; (*law*) to distrain, seize; to impede, suspend, restrain.

embargo, *n.m.* indigestion; embargo, sequestration; (*law*) execution, seizure, attachment; *sin embargo*, notwithstanding, however.

embarnizador, *n.m.* varnisher.

embarnizadura, *n.f.* varnishing.

embarnizar, *v.t.* to varnish; (*fig.*) to adorn, embellish.

embarque, *n.m.* embarkation, shipment (of cargo, etc.).

embarradilla, *n.f.* (*Mex.*) small sweet pie.

embarrador, *n.m.* plasterer, dauber; (*fig.*) liar; mischief-maker.

embarradura, *n.f.* overlaying with plaster or mortar; smear, stain of mud.

embarrancar, *v.i.* (*naut.*) to run aground. — *v.r.* to be bogged, stuck in mud or mire.

embarrar, *v.t.* to bedaub; to besmear with mud; (*prov.*) to rough-cast with plaster. — *v.r.* to collect or mount upon trees (of birds).

embarrilador, *n.m.* packer in barrels.

embarrilar, *v.t.* to barrel, put in a barrel.

embarrotar, *v.t.* to bar; to strengthen with bars.

embarullador, **-ra**, *a.* muddling. — *n.m.f.* muddler.

embarullar, *v.t.* (*coll.*) to muddle, make a mess of.

embasamiento, *n.m.* (*arch.*) foundation.

embastar, *v.t.* to baste, to tack.

embaste, *n.m.* basting.

embastecer, *v.i.* (conjugated like ABASTECER) to become corpulent or fleshy. — *v.r.* to become gross or coarse.

embate, *n.m.* dashing of the sea; sudden, impetuous attack; (*naut.*) fresh breeze in summer; *embates de la fortuna*, sudden reverses of fortune.

embaucador, **-ra**, *a.* deceiving. — *n.m.* sharper, swindler, impostor.

embaucamiento, *n.m.* deception, humbug.

embaucar, *v.t.* (*pret.* **embauqué**; *pres. subj.* **embauque**) to deceive, delude, take in.

embaular, *v.t.* to pack in a trunk; (*coll.*) to cram with food.

embausamiento, *n.m.* amazement, astonishment.

embazador, *n.m.* person who dyes things brown; object which can be dyed brown.

embazadura, *n.f.* brown dye; (*fig.*) amazement, astonishment.

embazar, *v.t.* (*pret.* **embacé**; *pres. subj.* **embace**) to tinge or dye brown; (*fig.*) to embarrass, astonish, strike with amazement. — *v.i.* to be astonished, paralysed with amazement, dumbfounded. — *v.r.* to become tired, disgusted, satiated; to become ashamed.

embebecer, *v.t.* (*pres. indic.* **embebezco**; *pres. subj.* **embebezca**) to amuse. — *v.r.* to be struck with amazement.

embebecidamente, *adv.* amazedly.

embebecimiento, *n.m.* amazement.

embebedor, -ra, *a.* imbibing. — *n.m.f.* imbiber.

embeber, *v.t.* to imbibe, drink in, absorb; to soak, drench, saturate; (*fig.*) to introduce, insert, incorporate; to shrink, shorten, reduce, squeeze; to enclose, contain, include. — *v.i.* to shrink, contract. — *v.r.* to be enraptured; to be absorbed in thought; to learn thoroughly, master.

embecadura, *n.f.* (*arch.*) spandrel.

embelecador, -ra, *n.m.f.* impostor, sharper.

embelecar, *v.t.* (*pret.* **embelequé**; *pres. subj.* **embeleque**) to impose upon, deceive, humbug.

embeleco, *n.m.* fraud, imposition, humbug.

embeleñado, -da, *a.* enraptured, ravished; stupefied. — *p.p.* [EMBELEÑAR].

embeleñar, *v.t.* to stupefy, drug with henbane; to charm, fascinate.

embelesamiento, *n.m.* rapture, ecstasy.

embelesar, *v.t.* to charm, fascinate, enchant. — *v.r.* to be charmed, ravished, delighted.

embeleso, *n.m.* amazement, ravishment, fascination, ecstasy; charm.

embellaquecerse, *v.r.* to become a knave.

embellecer, *v.t.* (*pres. indic.* **embellezco**; *pres. subj.* **embellezca**) to embellish, adorn.

embellecimiento, *n.m.* act of embellishing.

embermejar, embermejecer, *v.t., v.r.* (*pres. indic.* **embermejezco**; *pres. subj.* **embermejezca**) to dye red; to put to shame, make blush. — *v.i.* to blush.

emberrenchinarse, emberrincharse, *v.r.* (*coll.*) to fly into a violent passion (as children).

embestida, *n.f.* assault, onset, attack; (*coll.*) detention by importunate solicitor.

embestidor, -ra, *a.* onrushing, attacking. — *n.m.f.* importunate solicitor or beggar.

embestidura, *n.f.* attack, assault, onset.

embestir, *v.t.* (*pres. indic.* **embisto**; *pres. subj.* **embista**) to assail, attack, rush against; (*coll.*) to importune with unreasonable demands; (*mil.*) to attack.

embetunar, *v.t.* to cover with pitch.

embicar, *v.t.* (*pret.* **embiqué**; *pres. subj.* **embique**) (*naut.*) to top. — *v.i.* (*Arg., Chi.*) to steer straight for the coast; *embicar las vergas*, to top the yards as a sign of mourning.

embijar, *v.t.* to paint with red-lead; (*Hond., Mex.*) to soil, smear, tarnish.

embisto; embista, *pres. indic.; pres. subj.* [EMBESTIR].

emblandecer, *v.t.* (*pres. indic.* **emblandezco**; *pres. subj.* **emblandezca**) to moisten, soften; (*fig.*) to mollify. — *v.r.* to be moved to pity.

emblanquecer, *v.t.* (*pres. indic.* **emblanquezco**; *pres. subj.* **emblanquezca**) to whiten, bleach. — *v.r.* to grow white; to become bleached.

emblanquecimiento, *n.m.* bleaching, whitening.

emblema, *n.m.* emblem, device, symbol.

emblemáticamente, *adv.* emblematically.

emblemático, -ca, *a.* emblematic.

embobamiento, *n.m.* astonishment, dumbfounded condition.

embobar, *v.t.* to amuse, entertain; to enchant, fascinate. — *v.r.* to be struck with astonishment, stand gaping.

embobecer, *v.t.* (*pres. indic.* **embobezco**; *pres. subj.* **embobezca**) to stupefy, stultify. — *v.r.* to become stupefied, foolish.

embobecimiento, *n.m.* stupefaction, stultification.

embocadero, embocador, *n.m.* mouth of a channel; *estar uno al embocadero*, to be on the verge of success.

embocado, -da, *a.* applied to wine which is between sweet and dry. — *p.p.* [EMBOCAR].

embocador, *n.m.* [EMBOCADERO].

embocadura, *n.f.* mouth or entrance of a narrow passage; mouthpiece of a bridle; mouthpiece of a musical instrument; mouth of a river; taste (of wine); (*arch.*) proscenium arch; *tener buena embocadura*, to have a good mouth (of a horse); *tomar la embocadura*, (*coll.*) to overcome the first difficulties.

embocar, *v.t.* (*pret.* **emboqué**; *pres. subj.* **emboque**) to put into the mouth; (*coll.*) to swallow in haste, cram food; to put through a narrow passage; (*coll.*) to hoax.

embochinchar, *v.t.* (*Am.*) to make a row.

embodegar, *v.t.* to store in a cellar (as wine).

embojar, *v.t.* to arrange branches for silk-worms.

embojo, *n.m.* branches placed for silk-worms.

embolada, *n.f.* piston-stroke.

embolar, *v.t.* to put balls on the tips of bulls' horns; to apply gilding size on; to shine, polish (shoes).

embolia, *n.f.* embolism.

embolismador, -ra, *a.* detracting. — *n.m.f.* detractor, reviler.

embolismal, *a.* intercalary.

embolismar, *v.t.* (*coll.*) to propagate malicious rumours, carry tales, gossip.

embolismo, *n.m.* embolism, intercalation, intercalary time; (*fig.*) maze, entanglement, confusion; (*coll.*) falsehood.

émbolo, *n.m.* (*mech.*) piston, plunger, forcer; embolus; *émbolo buzo*, plunger, sucker (of a pump).

embolsar, *v.t.* to put into a purse; to recover (a debt); to reimburse.

embolso, *n.m.* act of putting into a purse.

embonar, *v.t.* to make good, make firm, improve. repair; (*naut.*) to sheathe; (*Cub., Mex.*) to fit, suit; to be becoming.

embono, *n.m.* (*naut.*) sheathing.

emboñigar, *v.t.* to plaster with cow-dung.

emboque, *n.m.* passage through any narrow space (as of a ball through a hoop or hole, etc.); (*coll.*) deception, cheat, fraud.

emboquillar, *v.t.* to put a tip on a cigarette; (*min.*) to make the entrance of a shaft; to make a drill-hole for blasting.

embornal, *n.m.* (*naut.*) scupper-hole.

emborrachador, -ra, *a.* intoxicating. — *n.m.f.* one who makes drunk.

emborrachamiento, *n.m.* (*coll.*) drunkenness.

emborrachar, *v.t.* to intoxicate, inebriate. — *v.r.* to become intoxicated, get drunk.

emborrar, *v.t.* to pad, wad, stuff with hair, wool, etc.; to card wool a second time; (*fig., fam.*) to make someone swallow false information.

emborrascar, *v.t.* to provoke, enrage. — *v.r.* to become stormy (the weather); (*fig.*) to be spoiled, ruined (business); (*Arg., Hond., Mex.*) (*min.*) to be exhausted (seam).

emborrazamiento, *n.m.* act of larding a fowl.

emborrazar, *v.t.* (*pret.* **emborracé;** *pres. subj.* **emborrace**) to lard a fowl for roasting.

emborricarse, *v.r.* (*coll.*) to be stupefied; to be infatuated.

emborrizar, *v.t.* (*pret.* **emborricé;** *pres. subj.* **emborrice**) to give the first combing to wool.

emborronador, -ra, *a.* causing blots.

emborronar, *v.t.* to make blots; (*fig.*) to scribble.

emborrullarse, *v.r.* (*coll.*) to dispute noisily.

emboscada, *n.f.* ambuscade, ambush.

emboscadura, *n.f.* ambush.

emboscar, *v.t.* (*pret.* **embosqué;** *pres. subj.* **embosque**) (*mil.*) to place in ambush. — *v.r.* to retire into the depths of a forest; to lie in ambush; (*mil. slang*) to be a shirker, scrimshanker.

embosquecer, *v.i.* to become wooded.

embotado, -da, *a.* blunt, dull. — *p.p.* [EMBOTAR].

embotado, *n.m.* one who blunts the points or edges of swords.

embotadura, *n.f.* bluntness, dullness of weapons.

embotamiento, *n.m.* blunting of weapons or tools; bluntness, dullness; stupefaction.

embotar, *v.t.* to blunt, dull an edge or point; to place tobacco in a jar; (*fig.*) to enervate, debilitate; to stupefy. — *v.r.* to become dull; (*coll.*) to put on boots.

embotellador, -ra, *a.* bottling.—*n.m.f.* bottler.

embotellamiento, *n.m.* bottling.

embotellar, *v.t.* to bottle; (*naut.*) to block a channel by scuttling a ship.

embotijar, *v.t.* to place a tier of jars underneath a floor (against damp); to put into jars. — *v.r.* (*coll.*) to swell, expand; to be in a passion.

embovedado, -da, *a.* arched, vaulted. — *p.p.* [EMBOVEDAR].

embovedar, *v.t.* to arch, vault.

emboza, *n.f.* inequalities in the bottoms of barrels or casks.

embozadamente, *adv.* artfully, dissemblingly.

embozado, -da, *a.* muffled, with face hidden (especially by a cloak); involved. — *n.m.f.* one with muffled face. — *p.p.* [EMBOZAR].

embozar, *v.t.* (*pret.* **embocé;** *pres. subj.* **emboce**) to muffle the greater part of the face; (*fig.*) to dissemble, cloak; to muzzle. — *v.r.* to muffle oneself up.

embozo, *n.m.* part of a cloak or other garment covering the face; fold back in top part of sheet; (*fig.*) artfulness in expressing the thoughts; *quitarse uno el embozo,* to reveal one's secret intentions, to drop the mask.

embrace, *n.m.* curtain-clasp.

embracilado, -da, *a.* (*coll.*) carried about in the arms (of children).

embragar, *v.t.* (conjugated like BRAGAR) (*naut.*) to sling; to engage the clutch.

embrague, *n.m.* (*naut.*) act of slinging; clutch, coupling.

embravecer, *v.t.* (*pres. indic.* **embravezco;** *pres. subj.* **embravezca**) to irritate, enrage. — *v.i.* to become strong (of plants). — *v.r.* to become enraged or furious; (*naut.*) to swell, become extremely boisterous (of the sea).

embravecimiento, *n.m.* fury, rage, passion.

embrazadura, *n.f.* embracing; handle of a shield, etc.

embrazar, *v.t.* (*pret.* **embracé;** *pres. subj.* **embrace**) to clasp a shield. — *v.i.* (*mech.*) to put into gear.

embreado, *n.m.*; **embreadura,** *n.f.* (*naut.*) paying a ship with pitch, tarring.

embrear, *v.t.* (*naut.*) to pay with pitch.

embregarse, *v.r.* to quarrel, wrangle.

embreñarse, *v.r.* to hide oneself in a thicket or among brambles.

embriagado, -da, *a.* intoxicated, drunk. — *p.p.* [EMBRIAGAR].

embriagar, *v.t.* (*pret.* **embriagué;** *pres. subj.* **embriague**) to intoxicate, inebriate; (*fig.*) to transport, enrapture. — *v.r.* to become inebriated.

embriaguez, *n.f.* intoxication, inebriety, drunkenness; (*fig.*) rapture.

embridar, *v.t.* to bridle; to make horses carry their heads well.

embriología, *n.f.* embryology.

embriológico, -ca, *a.* embryological.

embriólogo, -ga, *n.m.f.* embryologist.

embrión, *n.m.* embryo; (*fig.*) embryo, germ of an idea; *en embrión,* in embryo.

embrionario, -ria, *a.* embryonic.

embroca, embrocación, *n.f.* (*pharm.*) embrocation.

embrocar, *v.t.* (*pret.* **embroqué;** *pres. subj.* **embroque**) to pour out of one vessel into another; to wind thread upon a bobbin; (*med.*) to apply embrocation; (*shoemaking*) to fasten with tacks to the last; (*tauro.*) to toss between the horns; (*Hond., Mex.*) to place upside down (vessel, plate, etc.).

embrochado, -da, *a.* embroidered.

embrochalar, *v.t.* to support a beam by a cross-piece or stay.

embrolla, *n.f.* (*coll.*) confusion, tangle; deception; involved situation.

embrolladamente, *adv.* in a tangled way.

embrollador, -ra, *a.* entangling; troublesome. — *n.m.f.* entangler; trouble-maker.

embrollar, *v.t.* to entangle, twist; to embroil.

embrollo, *n.m.* tangle, confusion, jumble; trickery, imposture; embroiling; (*fig.*) involved or difficult situation.

embrollón, -na, *n.m.f.* entangler; liar, impostor; tale-bearer, mischief-maker.

embrolloso, -sa, *a.* tangled.

embromado, -da, *a.* vexed, annoyed; *(naut.)* misty, hazy. — *p.p.* [EMBROMAR].

embromador, -ra, *n.m.f.*, *a.* banterer, chaffer, wheedler; one who is riotously merry.

embromar, *v.t.* to wheedle, cajole; to chaff, banter; *(Arg., Cub., Chi., PR.)* to annoy, vex; *(Chi., Mex.)* to detain, delay, waste time; *(Arg., Chi., PR.)* to injure, harm.

embroquelarse, *v.r.* to shield oneself.

embroquetar, *v.t.* to skewer the legs of fowls.

embrosquilar, *v.t.* *(prov.)* to put cattle into a fold.

embrujar, *v.t.* to bewitch.

embrutecer, *v.t.* *(pres. indic.* **embrutezco;** *pres. subj.* **embrutezca)** to make brutish, irrational. — *v.r.* to become brutish.

embrutecimiento, *n.m.* brutalization, brutishness.

embuchado, -da, *a.* stuffed with forcemeat. — *n.m.* pork sausage or salame; *(gambling)* large stake hidden under coins of small value. — *p.p.* [EMBUCHAR].

embuchar, *v.t.* to stuff with minced meat; to cram the crop of birds; *(coll.)* to swallow without chewing.

embudador, -ra, *n.m.f.* person using funnel for filling.

embudar, *v.t.* to put a funnel into the mouth of bottles, etc.; to trick, deceive, ensnare.

embudista, *n.m.* intriguer, deceiver, trickster.

embudo, *n.m.* funnel; water-closet basin; wax-candle mould; fraud, artifice, deceit, trick; *ley del embudo,* *(coll.)* law unevenly applied; one-sided contract.

embullar, *v.i.* *(Col., CR., Cub.)* to stir; to make noise.

embullarse, *v.r.* *(Cub.)* to make merry.

embullo, *n.m.* *(CR., Cub., PR.)* gaiety, revelry.

emburujar, *v.t.* *(coll.)* to jumble, muddle. — *v.r.* *(Col., Mex., PR., Ven.)* to wrap oneself up.

embuste, *n.m.* fiction, lie; trick, fraud, imposture. — *pl.* gewgaws, baubles, trinkets of little value.

embustear, *v.i.* to lie, tell lies habitually.

embustería, *n.f.* *(coll.)* deceit, imposture, trick.

embustero, -ra, *n.m.f.* liar; tale-teller, tale-bearer; impostor, cheat, trickster; dissembler, hypocrite; *(coll.)* cajoler.

embusteruelo, -la, *n.m.f.* little liar, fibber [EMBUSTERO].

embutidera, *n.f.* instrument for riveting tin-work.

embutido, -da, *p.p.* [EMBUTIR] inlaid. — *n.m.* inlaying, inlaid work; salame, sausage; *(Am.)* lace, insertion.

embutir, *v.t.* to inlay, make inlaying; to insert; to stuff, pack tightly; to force; *(coll.)* to cram, eat greedily; to make sausages; *(naut.)* to worm, wind spun-yarn round a cable.

eme, *n.f.* Spanish name of the letter *m.*

emendable, *a.* amendable, corrigible.

emendación, *n.f.* emendation; satisfaction, amends.

emendador, *n.m.* emendator.

emendar, *v.t.* [ENMENDAR].

emergencia, *n.f.* act of emerging; emergency, accident; *(opt.)* emergence.

emergente, *a.* emergent, issuing, resulting.

emerger, *v.i.* to emerge (from water).

emérito, -ta, *a.* retired, emeritus.

emersión, *n.f.* *(astron.)* emersion.

emético, -ca, *n.m.f.*, *a.* emetic. — *n.m.* tartar emetic.

emigración, *n.f.* emigration; migration; band of emigrants.

emigrado, -da, *n.m.f.*, *a.* emigré. — *p.p.* [EMIGRAR].

emigrante, *n.m.f.*, *a.* emigrant.

emigrar, *v.i.* to emigrate; migrate.

eminencia, *n.f.* eminence, prominence; height, hill.

eminencial, *a.* eminent.

eminencialmente, *adv.* eminently.

eminente, *a.* eminent, conspicuous, prominent; lofty, high.

eminentemente, *adv.* eminently.

eminentísimo, -ma, *a. superl.* most eminent.

emir, *n.m.* emir, ameer.

emisario, *n.m.* emissary; spy; *(obs.)* outlet, discharge; *(physiol.)* emunctory.

emisión, *n.f.* emission; *(wire.)* broadcast; issue of paper money, bonds, etc.; *nueva emisión,* *(com.)* new issue.

emisor, -ra, *a.* emitting; *(wire.)* broadcasting. — *n.f.* transmitting station. — *n.m.* *(wire.)* transmitter, broadcasting apparatus.

emitir, *v.t.* to emit, send forth, spread; to issue bonds, etc.; to utter, emit (an opinion, etc.); *(wire.)* to broadcast; to throw out, utter, declare.

emoción, *n.f.* emotion.

emocional, *a.* emotional.

emocionante, *a.* touching, thrilling.

emocionar, *v.t.* to arouse emotion in, excite.

emoliente, *n.m.*, *a.* emollient.

emolumento, *n.m.* emolument, fee, profit.

emotivo, -va, *a.* emotive.

empacar, *v.t.* *(pret.* **empaqué;** *pres. subj.* **empaque)** to pack up, put in bales. — *v.r.* to be stubborn, obstinate; to become peeved and sulky; *(Am.)* to balk (horse).

empacón, -ona, *a.* *(Arg., Per.)* obstinate, stubborn; balky (horse).

empachado, -da, *a.* awkward, timid, bashful; surfeited, glutted, overfed; *(naut.)* overloaded.

empachar, *v.t.* to impede, embarrass, disturb, perplex; to cram, surfeit, overload, encumber; to cause indigestion; to disguise. — *v.r.* to be ashamed, embarrassed; to overeat.

empacho, *n.m.* bashfulness, timidity, embarrassment; surfeit, indigestion; obstacle; *sin empacho,* without ceremony; unblushingly; unconcernedly.

empachoso, -sa, *a.* embarrassing; disgraceful.

empadronador, *n.m.* census-taker.

empadronamiento, *n.m.* census; list of persons liable to pay taxes.

empadronar, *v.t.* to take a census; to register names of tax-payers.

empajar, *v.t.* to cover or stuff with straw; *(Col., Chi.)* to thatch; *(Arg., Cub., PR.)* to cram, surfeit, overload with insubstantial food.

empalagamiento, *n.m.* cloying, surfeit.

empalagar, *v.t.* *(pret.* **empalagué;** *pres. subj.* **empalague)** to cloy, nauseate, surfeit; *(fig.)* to vex, bother.

empalago, *n.m.* disgust, surfeit.

empalagoso, -sa, *a.* cloying, over-sweet; (*fig.*) troublesome, wearisome.

empalamiento, *n.m.* impalement, impaling.

empalar, *v.t.* to impale; (*Chi.*) to persist, indulge in whims.

empaliada, *n.f.* (*prov.*) hangings of bunting.

empaliar, *v.t.* (*prov.*) to adorn with hangings.

empalicar, *v.t.* (*Chi.*) to inveigle, wheedle.

empalizada, *n.f.* palisade, pale-fence, stockade.

empalizar, *v.t.* to pale, palisade.

empalmadura, *n.f.* dovetailing; joint; coupling; splicing.

empalmar, *v.t.* to scarf, dovetail; to couple, join; to splice. — *v.i.* (*railw.*) to join, branch.

empalme, *n.m.* (*carp.*) scarf; join; connexion; (*railw.*) junction.

empalomado, *n.m.* (*hydro.*) loose-stone damming wall.

empalomar, *v.t.* to sew a bolt-rope to a sail.

empalletado, *n.m.* bulwark formed of sailors' hammocks.

empamparse, *v.r.* (*S. Am.*) to get lost in a pampa.

empanada, *n.f.* meat pie; *hacer una empanada*, to conceal an affair or involve it in fraudulent deception; *agua empanada*, muddy water.

empanadilla, *n.f.* small pie [EMPANADA]; moveable footstep in carriages.

empanado, -da, *a.* applied to room receiving light from another. — *p.p.* [EMPANAR].

empanar, *v.t.* to bake in paste; to sow grain. — *v.r.* (*agric.*) to be choked with too much seed.

empandar, *v.t.* to bend; to warp.

empandillar, *v.t.* (*coll.*) to cheat at cards.

empantanar, *v.t.* to submerge; to swamp; to bemire; (*fig.*) to embarrass; to obstruct.

empañadura, *n.f.* swaddling of children; stain; tarnishing.

empañar, *v.t.* to swaddle; to darken, dim, blur, tarnish; (with *en*) to imbibe; to be soaked; to absorb; to enter into the spirit of; (*coll.*) to be surfeited.

empañetar, *v.t.* (*Col., CR., Ec., Ven.*) to plaster walls, ceilings, etc.

empañicar, *v.t.* (*naut.*) to furl.

empapar, *v.t.* to soak, saturate, drench. — *v.r.* (with *en*) to imbibe; to be soaked; to absorb; to enter into the spirit of; (*coll.*) to be surfeited.

empapelado, -da, *p.p.* [EMPAPELAR]. — *n.m.* papering, paper-hanging; wall-paper; paper lining.

empapelador, *n.m.* one who wraps in paper; paper-hanger.

empapelar, *v.t.* to wrap in paper; to paper a wall; (*coll.*) to incriminate.

empapirotar, *v.t.* (*coll.*) to adorn carefully, deck nicely.

empapujar, *v.t.* (*coll.*) to make someone eat too much.

empaque, *n.m.* packing; air, mien, look, semblance, appearance; (*Chi., Per., PR.*) impudence, sauciness.

empaquetador, -ra, *n.m.f.* packer.

empaquetadura, *n.f.* packing, gasket.

empaquetar, *v.t.* to pack, bale, sack; (*fig.*) to stuff, pack in.

empara, *n.f.* (*law, prov.*) sequestration.

emparamado, -da, *a.* (*Am.*) frozen to death.

emparamarse, *v.r.* (*Am.*) to die from exposure to the cold (in the extreme South).

emparamentar, *v.t.* to adorn.

emparamento, emparamiento, *n.m.* (*law, prov.*) sequestration.

emparchar, *v.t.* to cover with plasters.

empardar, *v.t.* (*prov., Arg.*) to draw, tie.

emparedado, -da, *n.m.f.* recluse. — *n.m.* sandwich. — *p.p.* [EMPAREDAR].

emparedamiento, *n.m.* confinement, shutting up, immuring; religious retirement.

emparedar, *v.t.* to confine, shut up, immure.

emparejador, -ra, *n.m.f.* matcher, fitter.

emparejadura, *n.f.* equalization.

emparejamiento, *n.m.* matching, making equal.

emparejar, *v.t.* to level, make even, smooth; to match; to fit; to set ajar. — *v.i.* to overtake and go side by side; to be a match for something.

emparentado, -da, *a.* related by marriage. — *p.p.* [EMPARENTAR].

emparentar, *v.i.* to be related by marriage.

emparrado, -da, *p.p.* [EMPARRAR]. — *n.m.* vine arbour.

emparrar, *v.t.* to embower, form bowers of vine branches.

emparrillado, -da, *p.p.* [EMPARRILLAR]. — *n.m.* (*engin.*) grillage, piles used to give a foundation in soft soil.

emparrillar, *v.t.* to broil on a gridiron, grill.

emparvar, *v.t.* to heap up grains for threshing.

empastado, -da, *a.* bound in a stiff cover. — *p.p.* [EMPASTAR].

empastador, -ra, *a.* (*paint.*) that impastes. — *n.m.* paste-brush. — *n.m.f.* (*Am.*) book-binder.

empastar, *v.t.* to fill a tooth; to paste; (*paint.*) to impaste; to bind a book in a stiff cover; (*Arg., Chi., Guat., Mex.*) to turn into a meadow; (*Arg., Chi.*) to swell (of the belly of animals). — *v.r.* (*Chi.*) to become weed-grown (land)

empaste, *n.m.* filling of a tooth; binding of a book; (*art*) impasto.

empastelar, *v.t., v.r.* (*coll.*) to compound, compromise; (*print.*) to pie.

empatadera, *n.f.* (*coll.*) checking, impeding.

empatar, *v.t., v.r.* to equal; to be a tie (in voting); to tie, draw with; to hinder, obstruct; (*Col., CR., Mex., PR., Ven.*) to couple, join; to splice; *empatársela a uno*, to equal someone's performance.

empate, *n.m.* equality, equal number of votes, tie; hindrance, stop.

empavesada, *n.f.* bulwark formed of shields; (*naut.*) fringed cloth used to cover boat-seats, etc.

empavesado, -da, *a.* covered by a shield. — *n.m.* soldier covered by a shield; (*naut.*) dressing of a ship. — *p.p.* [EMPAVESAR].

empavesar, *v.t.* (*naut.*) to dress ships (with bunting, etc.).

empavonar, *v.t.* to blue iron or steel; (*Col., PR.*) to smear, grease.

empecatado, -da, *a.* incorrigible, evil-minded; unlucky.

empecé, *pret.* [EMPEZAR].

empecer, *v.t.* (*obs.*) (*pres. indic.* **empezco**; *pres. subj.* **empezca**) to hurt, injure, damage, offend. — *v.i.* to prevent.

empecimiento, *n.m.* damage; obstacle.

empecinado, *n.m.* dealer in pitch; (*Am.*) obstinate, stubborn man.

empecinarse, *v.r.* (*Am.*) to persist; to be stubborn.

empechar, *v.t.* (*obs.*) to prevent, hinder.

empedernido, -da, *a.* hard-hearted. — *p.p.* [EMPEDERNIR].

empedernir, *v.t.* defective (*only those tenses are used which have* i *in their termination*) to indurate, harden. — *v.r.* to become hardened, petrified; to become hard-hearted.

empedrado, -da, *a.* flecked with clouds; dappled (horses); pitted from smallpox. — *n.m.* stone pavement. — *p.p.* [EMPEDRAR].

empedrador, *n.m.* paver.

empedrar, *v.t.* to pave with stones.

empega, *n.f.* pitch; mark of pitch.

empegado, *n.m.* tarpaulin.

empegadura, *n.f.* coat of pitch.

empegar, *v.t.* (conjugated like PEGAR) to pitch, cover with pitch, mark with pitch.

empeguntar, *v.t.* to mark animals with pitch.

empeine, *n.m.* groin; instep; (*obs.*) hoof of a beast; tetter, ringworm; (*prov.*) cotton flower.

empeinoso, -sa, *a.* affected by ringworm.

empelar, *v.i.* to grow hair.

empelazgarse, *v.r.* (*coll.*) to be involved in a quarrel.

empelechar, *v.t.* to cover with marble; to join marble blocks.

empelotarse, *v.r.* to get into a wrangle; (*Col., Cub., Chi., Mex.*) to disrobe, to be left naked.

empeltre, *n.m.* slip for grafting.

empella, *n.f.* vamp of a shoe; (*Col., Chi., Mex.*) hog's fat.

empellar, *v.t.* to push, impel, jostle, shove.

empellejar, *v.t.* to cover or line with skins.

empellita, *n.f.* (*Cub.*) crackling (hog).

empellón, *n.m.* push, heavy blow; *a empellones,* rudely, with violence.

empenachado, -da, *a.* plumed.

empenachar, *v.t.* to adorn with plumes.

empenta, *n.f.* prop, stay, shore.

empeñadamente, *adv.* strenuously, hard, persistently.

empeñamiento, *n.m.* (*coll.*) obstinacy.

empeñar, *v.t.* to pawn, pledge; to compel, oblige. — *v.r.* to bind oneself; to persist; to encounter dangers with courage; to intercede, mediate; (*mil.*) to begin an action; (*naut.*) to hazard a ship; *empeñarse en algo,* to be bound, to persist in some undertaking.

empeñero, -ra, *n.m.f.* (*Mex.*) pawnbroker.

empeño, *n.m.* pledge, pawn; engagement, contract; earnest wish, longing; determination; boldness, firmness, constancy; favour, recommendation, protection; patron, supporter; (*Mex.*) pawnshop; *con empeño,* with great persistence or eagerness; *en empeño,* as guarantee, in pledge.

empeoramiento, *n.m.* deterioration; making matters worse; becoming worse.

empeorar, *v.t.* to impair, deteriorate. — *v.i., v.r.* to grow worse.

empequeñecer, *v.t.* (*pres. indic.* empequeñezco; *pres. subj.* empequeñezca) to diminish, make smaller; (*fig.*) to belittle. — *v.r.* to grow smaller.

emperador, *n.m.* emperor; (*Cub.*) sword-fish.

emperatriz, *n.f.* empress.

emperchado, *n.m.* fence of green stakes.

emperchar, *v.t.* to suspend on a perch.

emperelijar, *v.t.* (*coll.*) to ornament profusely, dress elaborately. — *v.r.* to be profusely adorned.

emperezar, *v.t.* to retard, delay, obstruct. — *v.i., v.r.* to be lazy, indolent.

empergaminado, -da, *a.* bound in parchment.

empergaminar, *v.t.* to bind books with parchment.

empernar, *v.t.* to nail; to fix with nails, bolts, etc.

empero, *conj.* yet, however; notwithstanding.

emperrarse, *v.r.* (with *en*) to be obstinate, stubborn about; to persist in.

empesador, *n.m.* broom of rushes for smoothing warp on a loom.

empetatar, *v.t.* (*Guat., Mex., Per.*) to cover with *petate* (sleeping mat).

empetro, *n.m.* crowberry.

empezar, *v.t.* (*pres. indic.* empiezo; *pres. subj.* empiece; *pret.* empecé) to begin, commence.

empicarse, *v.r.* to become too much attached to anything.

empicotadura, *n.f.* act of pillorying.

empicotar, *v.t.* to pillory, to picket.

empiedro; empiedre, *pres. indic.; pres. subj.* [EMPEDRAR].

empiezo; empiece, *pres. indic.; pres. subj.* [EMPEZAR].

empilonar, *v.t.* (*Cub.*) to stack tobacco leaves.

empinado, -da, *a.* elevated, steep, high; (*fig.*) stuck-up, conceited.

empinador, -ra, *n.m.f.* (*coll.*) toper.

empinadura, *n.f.;* **empinamiento,** *n.m.* elevation, exaltation, raising, erection.

empinar, *v.t.* to raise; to exalt; to incline; *empinar el codo,* (*coll.*) to crook the elbow, to drink too much. — *v.r.* to rise on the hind legs (of horses); to stand on tiptoe; to tower, rise high; (*aer.*) to zoom.

empingorotado, -da, *a.* haughty, stuck-up. — *n.m.* parvenu.

empingorotar, *v.t.* (*coll.*) to place an object on another.

empino, *n.m.* (*arch.*) summit of a curve.

empiolar, *v.t.* to hobble; sling dead animals by the feet, etc. [APIOLAR].

empíreo, *a.* empyreal; celestial, divine. — *n.m.* empyrean.

empíricamente, *adv.* empirically.

empírico, -ca, *a.* empiric, empirical. — *n.m.* quack, empyric.

empirismo, *n.m.* empiricism; quackery.

empizarrado, *n.m.* slate roof.

empizarrar, *v.t.* to slate, roof a building with slates.

emplastadura, *n.f.;* **emplastamiento,** *n.m.* plastering, affixing plasters; applying paint and cosmetics to the face.

emplastar, *v.t.* to apply plasters; to paint the face; (*coll.*) to stop, check, obstruct. — *v.r.* to get smeared.

emplastecer, *v.t.* (*pres. indic.* emplastezco; *pres. subj.* emplastezca) to level the surface before painting.

emplástico, -ca, *a.* gluey, sticky.

emplasto, *n.m.* plaster; *estar uno hecho un emplasto,* to be covered with plasters; (*coll.*) to be delicate and weak.

emplástrico, -ca, *a.* glutinous, sticky; (*med.*) suppurative.

emplazador, -ra, *n.m.f.* (*law*) summoner.
emplazamiento, *n.m.* (*law*) summons, citation; placing, siting.
emplazar, *v.t.* (*pret.* **emplacé;** *pres. subj.* **emplace**) to summon; to cite, cause to appear; to place, site. — *v.r.* to go into the centre of the ring (of the bull).
empleado, -da, *a.* employed. — *n.m.f.* employee; office-holder. — *p.p.* [EMPLEAR].
emplear, *v.t.* to employ; to appoint; to engage, hire; to give occupation to; to spend money or time; to invest. — *v.r.* to be employed; to follow business.
empleita, *n.f.* plaited strand of bass.
empleitero, -ra, *n.m.f.* one who plaits and sells bass matting.
emplenta, *n.f.* section of mud-wall pre-fabricated in one piece.
empleo, *n.m.* employ, employment; business, profession, calling, vocation; public station or office; investment; aim or object of desire; *apear a uno de un empleo,* to turn someone out of a post; *jurar un empleo,* to enter on a post after taking the usual oath; *suspender a uno del empleo,* to suspend someone for a time.
empleomanía, *n.f.* (*coll.*) craze or mania for public office.
emplomado, -da, *p.p.* [EMPLOMAR] leaded. — *n.m.* roof covered with lead.
emplomador, *n.m.* plumber.
emplomar, *v.t.* to lead, fit or line with lead; to put on lead seals.
emplumar, *v.t.* to feather; to adorn with plumes; to tar and feather; (*Ec., Ven.*) to send somebody to jail or exile; (*Col., Chi., Per., PR.*) to flee, escape; *que me emplumen si,* I'll be hanged if.
emplumarlas, (*Col.*) to run away, show a clean pair of heels.
emplumecer, *v.i.* (*pres. indic.* **emplumezco;** *pres. subj.* **emplumezca**) to fledge.
empobrecer, *v.t.* (*pres. indic.* **empobrezco;** *pres. subj.* **empobrezca**) to impoverish. — *v.i.* to become poor; to languish, fade.
empobrecimiento, *n.m.* impoverishment.
empodrecer, *v.i.* (*pres. indic.* **empodrezco;** *pres. subj.* **empodrezca**) to corrupt, putrefy.
empolvar, empolvorar, empolvorizar, *v.t.*, *v.r.* to powder; to cover with dust or powder.
empolvoramiento, *n.m.* covering with dust, powdering.
empollado, -da, *a.* hatched; confined, pent-up in the house. — *p.p.* [EMPOLLAR].
empollador, -ra, *a.* hatching, brooding. — *n.m.* incubator. — *n.m.f.* hatcher.
empolladura, *n.f.* pupa of bees; (*coll.*) swotting.
empollar, *v.t.* to hatch. — *v.i.* to breed (bees); (*fig.*) to brood; (*Am.*) to blister.
empollón, -ona, *a.* student who crams.
emponchado, -da, *a.* (*Arg., Chi., Per.*) wearing a poncho; (*Arg., Per.*) (*fig.*) suspicious.
emponzoñador, -ra, *a.* poisonous. — *n.m.f.* poisoner.
emponzoñamiento, *n.m.* poisoning.
emponzoñar, *v.t.* to poison; to taint, corrupt.
empopar, *v.t.* (*naut.*) to poop.
emporcar, *v.t.* (*pres. indic.* **empuerco;** *pret.* **emporqué;** *pres. subj.* **empuerque**) to soil, dirty, foul.
emporio, *n.m.* emporium, mart.

empotramiento, *n.m.* (*arch.*) embedding.
empotrar, *v.t.* (*arch.*) to embed in a wall; to mortise; to scarf; to put beehives in a pit; (*naut.*) to fasten cannon.
empotrerar, *v.t.* (*Am.*) to pasture (cattle, etc.).
empozar, *v.t.* (*pret.* **empocé;** *pres. subj.* **empoce**) to throw into a well; to soak flax. — *v.i.* (*Am.*) to stop flowing (water). — *v.r.* (*coll.*) to be pigeonholed.
empradizar, *v.t.* (*pret.* **empradicé;** *pres. subj.* **empradice**) to convert into a meadow; (*Col.*) to weed. — *v.r.* to become a meadow.
emprendedor, -ra, *a.* enterprising. — *n.m.f.* one who undertakes great deeds; enterpriser.
emprender, *v.t.* to undertake; to begin, venture, embark upon; *emprender a* or *con,* to address, accost; *emprenderla para un sitio,* to set out resolutely for a place.
empreñar, *v.t.* to beget.
empresa, *n.f.* enterprise, undertaking; symbol, motto, device; design, purpose, intention; commercial undertaking; management of a theatre.
empresario, *n.m.* one who undertakes anything; impresario; manager of a theatre; contractor.
empréstito, *n.m.* loan, something lent; *empréstito público,* government loan.
emprimado, -da, *p.p.* [EMPRIMAR]. — *n.m.* last combing of wool.
emprimar, *v.t.* to give the last combing to wool; (*paint.*) to prime; (*coll.*) to deceive.
empuchar, *v.t.* to put skeins of yarn into buck or lye.
empuerco; empuerque, *pres. indic.; pres. subj.* [EMPORCAR].
empujar, *v.t.* to push, force by violence, propel, impel, drive, push away, press forward, shove off.
empuje, empujo, *n.m.* impulse, impulsion, pushing, pressure; (*fig.*) energy; enterprise; (*engin.*) thrust.
empujón, *n.m.* push, shove; *a empujones,* with violence, rudely; by fits and starts.
empulgadura, *n.f.* stretching the cord of a cross-bow.
empulgar, *v.t.* to stretch the cord of a cross-bow.
empulgueras, *n.f.pl.* wings of a crossbow; thumbscrews; *apretar las empulgueras a uno,* to put the screw on someone.
empuntar, *v.t.* (*Col., prov.*) to guide, put on the right road. — *v.i.* (*Col.*) to go, leave.
empuntarlas, (*Col.*) to run away, show a clean pair of heels.
empuñador, -ra, *a.* grasping. — *n.m.f.* grasper, clutcher.
empuñadura, *n.f.* hilt of a sword; beginning of a story; *hasta la empuñadura,* (*coll., fig.*) which really goes home (of a reply in argument).
empuñar, *v.t.* to clutch, grasp, grip.
empuñidura, *n.f.* (*naut.*) earing.
empurrarse, *v.r.* (*CR., Guat., Hond.*) to become angry, fly into a violent passion.
emulación, *n.f.* emulation; jealousy, envy.
emulador, -ra, *a.* emulating. — *n.m.f.* emulator.
emular, *v.t.* to emulate, rival, contest with.
emulgente, *a.* (*anat.*) emulgent.
émulo, -la, *n.m.f.* competitor, rival, emulator.
emulsión. *n.f.* emulsion.

emulsivo, -va, *a.* emulsive, emulsifying.
emunción, *n.f.* (*med.*) excretion.
emundación, *n.f.* (*obs.*) cleansing.
emuntorio, *n.m.* (*anat.*) emunctory.
en, *prep.* in, into; at; on, upon; for; *en dos años,* in two years; *en la mesa,* on the table; *en adelante,* for the future; *convertir en gas,* to change into a gas; (before a gerund) on, upon, immediately after : *en diciendo esto,* on *or* immediately after saying this; *el domingo,* on Sunday; followed by an infinitive = *por: le conocí en el andar,* I knew him by his walk; *en* before adjectives gives them an adverbial signification: *en alto,* on high.
enaceitarse, *v.r.* to become oily or rancid.
enagua, *n.f.* (*usually pl.*) skirt; underskirt, petticoat.
enaguachar, *v.t.* to over-fill with water.
enaguazar, *v.t.* to flood, irrigate; to cover with water.
enagüillas, *n.f.pl.* short skirt or petticoat [ENAGUA]; kilt.
enajenable, *a.* alienable.
enajenación, *n.f.;* **enajenamiento,** *n.m.* alienation of property; absence of mind; rapture; *enajenación mental,* mental derangement.
enajenar, *v.t.* to alienate, transfer, or give away property; to transport, enrapture. — *v.r.* to become estranged; to be enravished, raptured.
enálage, *n.f.* (*gram.*) enallage.
enalbar, *v.t.* to bring iron or steel to white heat.
enalbardar, *v.t.* to lay a packsaddle upon beasts of burden; (*cooking*) to cover with batter.
enalmagrado, -da, *a.* coloured with ochre; (*fig.*) vile, despicable. — *p.p.* [ENALMAGRAR].
enalmagrar, *v.t.* to colour with ochre.
enaltecer, *v.t., v.r.* to exalt, praise.
enamarillecer, *v.i., v.r.* to turn yellow.
enamoradamente, *adv.* lovingly.
enamoradizo, -za, *a.* inclined to love.
enamorado, -da, *a.* in love; fond of love-making. — *n.m.f.* lover; sweetheart. — *p.p.* [ENAMORAR].
enamorador, -ra, *a.* courting, wooing; love-making. — *n.m.f.* wooer; love-maker.
enamoramiento, *n.m.* love, being in love; love-sickness.
enamorar, *v.t.* to excite or inspire love; to court, make love, woo. — *v.r.* (with *de*) to fall in love (with).
enamoricarse, *v.r.* (*coll.*) to be slightly in love.
enancarse, *v.r.* (*Arg., Mex., Per.*) to ride on the croup (of a horse).
enanchar, *v.t.* (*coll.*) to enlarge, widen.
enangostar, *v.t.* to narrow.
enanito, -ta, *a.* little, minute [ENANO]. — *n.m.f.* midget.
enano, -na, *a.* dwarfish, low, little, small. — *n.m.f.* dwarf.
enante, *n.m.* water-dropwart.
enarbolar, *v.t.* to hoist, raise high, hang out. — *v.r.* to rise on the hind legs; *enarbolar la bandera,* to hoist the colours.
enarcar, *v.t.* to hoop barrels; to arch. — *v.r.* (*Mex.*) to rise on the hind feet (horses).
enardecer, *v.t.* (*pres. indic.* **enardezco;** *pres. subj.* **enardezca**) to fire with passion, inflame, kindle. — *v.r.* to be kindled, inflamed.

enardecimiento, *n.m.* act of inflaming or state of being inflamed with passion.
enarenación, *n.f.* plastering a wall before painting it.
enarenar, *v.t.* to cover with sand; to gravel. — *v.r.* (*naut.*) to run on shore.
enarmonar, *v.t.* to raise, rear. — *v.r.* to rise on the hind feet.
enarmónico, -ca, *a.* enharmonic.
enastado, -da, *a.* horned. — *p.p.* [ENASTAR].
enastar, *v.t.* to fix a handle to a tool, etc.
encabalgamiento, *n.m.* gun-carriage.
encabalgar, *v.t.* (*pret.* **encabalgué;** *pres. subj.* **encabalgue**) to provide horses. — *v.i.* to rest upon, as a plank on a support.
encaballadura, *n.f.* (*build.*) imbrication.
encaballar, *v.t.* (*build.*) to overlap, imbricate (as tiles).
encabellecerse, *v.r.* to grow hair.
encabestrar, *v.t.* to put a halter on a beast; (*fig.*) to force to obey. — *v.r.* to be entangled in the halter.
encabezador, *n.m.* reaping machine.
encabezadura, *n.f.* scarfing.
encabezamiento, *n.m.* tax-list; census-taking; enrolment of taxable citizens; tax, tribute; head-line, heading; *encabezamiento de factura,* bill-head.
encabezar, encabezonar (*obs.*), *v.t.* to make up the tax-roll; to take a census of inhabitants; to put a heading or title to; to head, lead; to fortify wine with alcohol; (*carp.*) to scarf, join. — *v.r.* to compound for taxes; to compound a debt, etc.; to rest content with the lesser evil in order to avoid the greater.
encabillar, *v.t.* (*naut.*) to fasten, secure with spikes, pins or bolts.
encabriar, *v.t.* (*arch.*) to put rafters in their places.
encabritarse, *v.r.* to rise on the hind legs (horses); to pitch with an upward motion (ship, aeroplane, etc.).
encabullar, *v.t.* (*Cub., PR., Ven.*) to tie with sisal.
encachado, *n.m.* concrete lining of bridge or sewer.
encachar, *v.t.* to line with concrete; (*Chi.*) to lower the head before charging (bulls, goats, etc.).
encadenación, encadenadura, *n.f.;* **encadenamiento,** *n.m.* concatenation; chaining, linking, connexion.
encadenar, *v.t.* to chain, enchain, fetter, shackle; to subject, subjugate, enslave; to concatenate, link together (as ideas); to captivate, to paralyze.
encajador, *n.m.* one who encases, engraves or inserts; chasing or engraving tool.
encajadura, *n.f.* act of encasing, inserting, joining; socket, groove.
encajar, *v.t.* to encase, drive in, fit in, enclose, insert; (*mech.*) to gear; to thrust violently one into another; to fit closely (of a lid, etc.); (*carp.*) to rabbet, join; (*fig.*) to throw in a remark; to tell a story; to throw out a hint; to hurl a missile; to administer a reproof; to pass off (a spurious coin, etc.); to fire off; to introduce with cunning, impose upon, to pass off upon another, deceive; to administer; *encajar bien,* to be to the purpose, come to the point, be opportune. — *v.i.* to fit. — *v.r.* (*fig.*) to intrude.

encaje, *n.m.* act of fitting, adjusting; socket, cavity, groove; enchasing; joining together; lace; inlaid work, mosaic; *encajes de la cara,* aspect of the face.

encajerado, -da, *a.* (*naut.*) fouled (of a rope).

encajero, -ra, *n.m.* lace-maker.

encajetillar, *v.t.* to pack (cigarettes, tobacco).

encajonado, -da, *a.* flanked by steep inclines (of rivers). — *n.m.* (*arch.*) packed work; coffer-dam. — *p.p.* [ENCAJONAR].

encajonamiento, *n.m.* packing up in boxes or crates; narrowing of a river in a gorge.

encajonar, *v.t.* to pack up, box, crate. — *v.r.* to become narrow (river, etc.).

encalabozar, *v.t.* (*coll.*) to put into a prison.

encalabrinado, -da, *a.* headstrong, obstinate, stubborn. — *p.p.* [ENCALABRINAR].

encalabrinar, *v.t.* to affect the head with some unpleasant smell or vapour; to excite, irritate. — *v.r.* (*coll.*) to become headstrong, obstinate.

encalada, *n.f.* metal piece of harness.

encalador, *n.m.* lime-pit or vat for hides.

encaladura, *n.f.* whitewashing.

encalambrarse, *v.r.* (*Col., Chi., Mex., PR.*) to become numb.

encalamocar, *v.t., v.r.* (*Col., Ven.*) to become stupefied.

encalar, *v.t.* to whitewash; to lime; to place in a tube; to stow in a hold.

encalmadura, *n.f.* disease of horses caused by overheating.

encalmarse, *v.r.* (*vet.*) to be overheated; (*naut.*) to be becalmed.

encalostrarse, *v.r.* to become sick by sucking the first milk (of a child).

encalvecer, *v.i.* (*pres. indic.* **encalvezco;** *pres. subj.* **encalvezca**) to grow bald.

encalladero, *n.m.* (*naut.*) shoal, sand-bank.

encalladura, *n.f.* (*naut.*) grounding, stranding.

encallar, *v.i.* (*naut.*) to run aground; to hit against; (*fig.*) to be checked in an enterprise.

encallecer, *v.i.* (*pres. indic.* **encallezco;** *pres. subj.* **encallezca**) to get corns on the feet. — *v.r.* to become hardened or callous.

encallecido, -da, *a.* hardened; hard-hearted, callous. — *p.p.* [ENCALLECER].

encallejonar, *v.t., v.r.* to enter or put anything into a narrow street or passage.

encamación, *n.f.* (*min.*) struts and scaffolding which sustain galleries.

encamar, *v.t.* to lay down; (*min.*) to prop up. — *v.r.* to keep in bed; to lie, couch (said of game); to be lodged by rain, wind, etc. (as corn).

encamarar, *v.t.* to store grain.

encambijar, *v.t.* to conduct water by means of aqueducts.

encambrar, *v.t.* to put into a granary.

encambronar, *v.t.* to enclose with hedges; to strengthen with iron.

encaminadura, *n.f.;* **encaminamiento,** *n.m.* act of putting on the right road.

encaminar, *v.t.* to guide, put on the right road, show the way; to manage or direct a business affair; to forward. — *v.r.* (with *a*) to take the road to; to be on the way to; to be intended for, or to.

encamisada, *n.f.* (*mil.*) camisade; (*obs.*) masquerade by night.

encamisar, *v.t.* to put on a shirt. — *v.r.* to put a shirt over one's clothes for a camisade.

encamotarse, *v.r.* (*Arg., CR., Chi., Ec.*) to fall in love (with).

encampanado, -da, *a.* bell-shaped; *dejar a uno encampanado,* (*Mex., PR.*) to abandon one in peril.

encanalar, encanalizar, *v.t.* to convey through pipes or canals.

encanallarse, *v.r.* to associate with ruffians; to become a ruffian.

encanarse, *v.r.* to grow stupefied from fear or crying (of infants).

encanastar, *v.t.* to pack in baskets or hampers.

encancerarse, *v.r.* to be attacked with cancer.

encandecer, *v.t.* to heat to a white heat.

encandelar, *v.i.* to bud (of trees).

encandiladera, encandiladora, *n.f.* (*coll.*) procuress, bawd.

encandilado, -da, *a.* high-cocked (of hats). — *p.p.* [ENCANDILAR].

encandilar, *v.t.* to dazzle, bewilder, daze; (*coll.*) to stir the fire. — *v.r.* to be dazzled; to have bloodshot eyes.

encanecer, *v.i.* (*pres. indic.* **encanezco;** *pres. subj.* **encanezca**) to grow grey-haired; to grow mouldy; to grow old.

encanijamiento, *n.m.* weakness, meagreness, emaciation.

encanijar, *v.t.* to weaken a baby by giving it bad milk or nursing. — *v.r.* to pine, become emaciated.

encanillar, *v.t.* to wind silk, wool or linen on spools or bobbins.

encantación, *n.f.* enchantment; incantation, spell, charm.

encantado, -da, *a.* haunted; charmed, enchanted; absent-minded. — *p.p.* [ENCANTAR].

encantador, -ra, *a.* delightful, charming, enchanting. — *n.m.f.* enchanter, charmer, sorcerer; enchantress, sorceress.

encantamiento, *n.m.* enchantment; incantation.

encantar, *v.t.* to enchant, bewitch; to conjure, charm; to fascinate; to delight.

encantarar, *v.t.* to put into a jar or ballot-box.

encante, *n.m.* auction; market of second-hand frippery.

encanto, *n.m.* enchantment, charm, spell; fascination; delight.

encantorio, *n.m.* (*coll.*) enchantment.

encantusar, *v.t.* (*coll.*) to wheedle, coax.

encanutar, *v.t.* to flute, roll; to put into a tube.

encañada, *n.f.* gorge; (*U.S.A.*) notch.

encañado, -da, *n.m.f.* water-conduit; trellis of canes or reeds. — *p.p.* [ENCAÑAR].

encañador, -ra, *n.m.f.* spool-winder.

encañadura, *n.f.* strong rye-straw for stuffing straw-beds, packsaddle, etc.

encañar, *v.t.* to stake plants; to convey water through conduits; to drain; to wind silk. — *v.i.* to form or grow into stalk (of corn).

encañizada, *n.f.* weir made of canes, etc., for catching fish.

encañonar, *v.t.* to put into tubes or pipes; to plait, fold; to wind silk on cane quills. — *v.i.* to grow feathers, fledge (of birds); (*slang*) to hold someone under aim with a fire-arm.

encapacetado, -da, *a.* covered with a helmet.

encapachadura, *n.f.* number of frails of olives ready for pressing.

encapachar, *v.t.* to put into a frail or basket; to protect the shoots of grapes from the sun.

encapado, -da, *a.* cloaked, wearing a cloak.

encapazar, *v.t.* (*pret.* **encapacé;** *pres. subj.* **encapace**) to put into a basket [ENCAPACHAR].

encaperuzado, -da, *a.*, *p.p.* [ENCAPERUZARSE] hooded.

encaperuzarse, *v.r.* to cover one's head with a hood.

encapillado, *n.m.*; *lo encapillado,* (*coll.*) the clothes on one's back. — *p.p.* [ENCAPILLAR].

encapilladura, *n.f.* (*naut.*) act of rigging.

encapillar, *v.t.* (*naut.*) to rig the yards; (*min.*) to start a new gallery. — *v.r.* to put on clothes over the head; (*naut.*) to ship water (a vessel).

encapirotado, -da, *a.* wearing a cloak or hood.

encapotadura, *n.f.*; **encapotamiento,** *n.m.* scowl, frown.

encapotar, *v.t.*, *v.r.* to cloak; to veil, muffle. — *v.r.* (*fig.*) to scowl, frown; to become cloudy; to carry the head too low (of horses).

encapricharse, *v.r.* to indulge in whims or fancies; to become stubborn or obstinate; (*coll.*) to become enamoured, infatuated.

encapuchar, *v.t.* to cover with a hood.

encapuzar, *v.t.* (*pret.* **encapucé;** *pres. subj.* **encapuce**) to cover with a cowl.

encarado, -da, *a.* faced; haughty; *bien* or *mal encarado* with a good or bad face. — *p.p.* [ENCARAR].

encaramar, *v.t.*, *v.r.* to elevate, raise (oneself); to climb; to extol; to reach a high position.

encaramiento, *n.m.* act of pointing or aiming a gun.

encarar, *v.i.* to face, confront. — *v.t.* to aim, point, level fire-arms. — *v.r.* (with *con*) to face.

encaratulado, -da, *a.* masked, disguised. — *p.p.* [ENCARATULARSE].

encaratularse, *v.r.* to mask oneself.

encarcavinar, *v.t.* to put into a ditch; to infect with a pestilential smell.

encarcelación, *n.f.* incarceration.

encarcelar, *v.t.* to imprison; (*arch.*) to embed in mortar; (*carp.*) to clamp; (*naut.*) to woold.

encarecedor, -ra, *a.* praising. — *n.m.f.* praiser, extoller.

encarecer, *v.t.*, *v.i.*, *v.r.* (*pres. indic.* **encarezco;** *pres. subj.* **encarezca**) to raise the price; to overrate, overvalue; to enhance, exaggerate; to extol; to recommend.

encarecidamente, *adv.* highly, exceedingly; eagerly, earnestly.

encarecimiento, *n.m.* enhancement, augmentation; exaggeration; *con encarecimiento,* ardently, earnestly.

encargado, -da, *a.* in charge. — *n.m.f.* person in charge; agent, representative; *encargado de negocios,* chargé d'affaires. — *p.p.* [ENCARGAR].

encargar, *v.t.* (*pret.* **encargué;** *pres. subj.* **encargue**) to entrust to, put under the care of a person; to advise, warn; to order goods; to ask, request. — *v.r.* to take charge, see after.

encargo, *n.m.* charge, command, commission, request; office, place, employment; (*com.*) order; *como* (*hecho*) *de encargo,* as if made for it.

encariñar, *v.t.* to inspire love or affection. — *v.r.* (with *con*) to become fond of.

encarna, *n.f.* act of giving the entrails of dead game to the dogs.

encarnación, *n.f.* incarnation; (*art*) carnation, flesh-colour; adhesive cement.

encarnadino, -na, *a.* incarnadine.

encarnado, -da, *a.* incarnate; flesh-coloured. — *n.m.* flesh-colour. — *p.p.* [ENCARNAR].

encarnadura, *n.f.* natural state of flesh in a wound in regard to healing power; effect on flesh of an instrument that wounds it; *tener buena* or *mala encarnadura,* to heal speedily or slowly by nature.

encarnamiento, *n.m.* (*surg.*) incarnation.

encarnar, *v.i.* to become incarnate; to penetrate or lodge in the flesh; to granulate (of a wound); to make a strong impression on the mind. — *v.t.* to incarnate; to embody; to paint flesh-coloured; to feed the entrails of game to hounds; to bait a hook; to produce granulation (in a wound). — *v.r.* to unite, incorporate with one another.

encarnativo, -va, *a.* (*surg.*) incarnative.

encarne, *n.m.* first feed of entrails of game given to hounds.

encarnecer, *v.i.* (*pres. indic.* **encarnezco;** *pres. subj.* **encarnezca**) to grow fat and fleshy.

encarnizado, -da, *a.* blood- or flesh-coloured; bloodshot, inflamed; irate, furious; merciless. — *p.p.* [ENCARNIZAR].

encarnizamiento, *n.m.* act of fleshing hounds; cruelty, rage, fury.

encarnizar, *v.t.* (*pret.* **encarnicé;** *pres. subj.* **encarnice**) to flesh (animals); to provoke, irritate. — *v.r.* to be glutted with flesh; to become irritated, furious, cruel-minded; to show cruelty; to fight to the death; to engage in a bloody battle.

encaro, *n.m.* stare; (*prov.*) blunderbuss; aiming or levelling of a gun.

encarpetar, *v.t.* (*Arg., Chi., Ec., Per.*) to shelve an action, bill or resolution.

encarrilar; encarrillar, *v.t.* to direct, guide, put on the right road; to set right. — *v.r.* (*naut.*) to be fouled in the sheave of a block.

encarroñar, *v.t.* to infect, corrupt. — *v.r.* to become infected or corrupted.

encarrujado, -da, *a.* (*Mex.*) rugged, rough (ground).

encarrujar, *v.t.* to curl, coil, twist. — *v.r.* to become curled, wrinkled; to curl, twist, coil.

encartación, *n.f.* enrolment under a charter; recognition of vassalage; lands held under charter, particularly in Biscay.

encartamiento, *n.m.* outlawry, proscription; sentence against absent criminals; [ENCARTACIÓN].

encartar, *v.t.* to outlaw, ban, proscribe; to include, enrol, enter in a register; (*law*) to summon; to involve in an unpleasant affair; to serve (in card games). — *v.r.* to be unable to discard (in card games).

encarte, *n.m.* chance order in which cards remain at the end of a hand.

encartonador, -ra, *n.m.f.* book-binder.

encartonar, *v.t.* to bind (books) in boards.

encartuchar, *v.t.* (*Col., Chi., Ec., PR.*) to roll, wrap, coil.

encasar, *v.t.* to set a dislocated bone.

encascabelado, -da, *a.* adorned with bells.

encascotar, *v.t.* (*build.*) to cover with a layer of rubble.

encasillado, *n.m.* set of pigeonholes.

encasillar, *v.t.* to put in pigeonholes; to form a list of electoral candidates approved by the government.

encasquetar, *v.t.*, *v.r.* to clap on one's hat. — *v.t.* to put an idea into someone's head. — *v.r.* to persist, be headstrong; to get a notion.

encasquillar, *v.t.* (*Am.*) to shoe horses. — *v.r.* to jam (fire-arms); (*Cub.*) to be frightened.

encastar, *v.t.* to improve a breed of animals. — *v.i.* to breed.

encastillado, -da, *a.* fortified with castles; (*fig.*) haughty, lofty. — *p.p.* [ENCASTILLAR].

encastillador, -ra, *n.m.f.* scaffolder, spiderman; (*fig.*) headstrong person.

encastillamiento, *n.m.* act of building or of shutting up in a castle; (*fig.*) obstinacy in maintaining opinions.

encastillar, *v.t.* to fortify with castles. — *v.i.* to make the cell of the queen-bee. — *v.r.* to shut oneself up in a castle; (*fig.*) to adhere obstinately to one's opinion.

encastrar, *v.t.* (*mech.*) to embed.

encastre, *n.m.* groove; socket; fitting in.

encatarrado, -da, *a.* (*obs.*) having a cold.

encauchado, -da, *n.m.* (*Am.*) rubber poncho. — *p.p.* [ENCAUCHAR].

encauchar, *v.t.* to cover with rubber.

encausar, *v.t.* to prosecute, sue.

encauste, *n.m.* encaustic painting.

encáustico, -ca, *a.* encaustic.

encausto, *n.m.* enamelling, encaustic painting.

encauzamiento, *n.m.* act of making a channel.

encauzar, *v.t.* to channel; to conduct water through a channel; (*fig.*) to guide.

encavarse, *v.r.* to run to ground (animals), hide.

encebadamiento, *n.m.* (*vet.*) surfeit, repletion (of horses).

encebadar, *v.t.* (*vet.*) to surfeit with barley. — *v.r.* to be surfeited with barley and water (of horses).

encebollado, *n.m.* stew of beef and onions.

encefálico, -ca, *a.* encephalic.

encefalitis, *n.f.* encephalitis.

encéfalo, *n.m.* encephalon, brain.

encelamiento, *n.m.* jealousy.

encelar, *v.t.* to excite jealousy in, to make jealous. — *v.r.* to become jealous.

encella, *n.f.* cheese-mould.

encellar, *v.t.* to mould cheese or curds.

encenagado, -da, *a.* mixed or filled with mud. — *p.p.* [ENCENAGARSE].

encenagamiento, *n.m.* wallowing in mire; (*fig.*) wallowing in vice.

encenagarse, *v.r.* (*pret.* **encenagué**; *pres. subj.* **encenague**) to wallow in dirt, bemire oneself; (*fig.*) to indulge in vices.

encencerrado, -da, *a.* carrying a weatherbell.

encendedor, -ra, *a.* lighting. — *n.m.f.* lighter; *encendedor de bolsillo,* pocket lighter.

encender, *v.t.* (*pres. indic.* **enciendo**; *pres. subj.* **encienda**) to kindle, light, set fire to, heat; (*fig.*) to inflame; incite, inspire. — *v.r.* to take fire, be kindled; to blush; *encenderse en ira,* to burn with anger.

encendidamente, *adv.* ardently.

encendido, -da, *a.* inflamed. — *n.m.* (*motor*) ignition. — *p.p.* [ENCENDER]; *encendido de color,* high coloured.

encendimiento, *n.m.* kindling, lighting; incandescence, glow; ardour, eagerness.

encenizar, *v.t.* (*pret.* **encenicé**; *pres. subj.* **encenice**) to fill or cover with ashes.

encentador, -ra, *a.* using something for the first time.

encentadura, *n.f.*; **encentamiento,** *n.m.* broaching (a new topic); taking up (a fresh subject).

encentar, *v.t.* to broach (new topic), to take up (something new). — *v.r.* to develop bedsores.

encepador, *n.m.* gun-stocker.

encepadura, *n.f.* (*carp.*) tie-joint.

encepar, *v.t.* to put in the stocks; to stock a gun or anchor; (*carp.*) to join with ties. — *v.i.* to take root. — *v.r.* to foul the anchor.

encepe, *n.m.* (*agric.*) taking firm root.

encerado, -da, *a.* wax-coloured, like wax; thick; hard (as a boiled egg). — *n.m.* oilcloth, oilskin; window-blind; (*naut.*) tarpaulin; sticking-plaster; blackboard in schools. — *p.p.* [ENCERAR].

enceramiento, *n.m.* act and effect of waxing paper, cloth, etc.

encerar, *v.t.* to wax; to stain with wax; (*build.*) to thicken lime.

encerotar, *v.t.* to wax thread.

encerradero, *n.m.* sheepfold, pen.

encerrador, -ra, *a.* shutting or locking up. — *n.m.f.* shutter, locker. — *n.m.* penner of cattle in slaughterhouse.

encerradura, *n.f.*; **encerramiento,** *n.m.* locking up a thing; cloister, retreat; prison, dungeon, jail.

encerrar, *v.t.* (*pres. indic.* **encierro**; *pres. subj.* **encierre**) to lock up, shut up; (*fig.*) to confine; to include, embrace, contain, comprehend. — *v.r.* to be locked up; to be closeted, confined; (*fig.*) to live in seclusion.

encerrona, *n.f.* (*coll.*) voluntary retreat, spontaneous retirement; *hacer la encerrona,* (*coll.*) to go into retirement for a time.

encespedar, *v.t.* to turf.

encestar, *v.t.* to gather and put into a basket.

encía, *n.f.* gum (of the mouth).

encíclico, -ca, *a.* encyclic. — *n.f.* encyclical.

enciclopedia, *n.f.* encyclopædia.

enciclopédico, -ca, *a.* encyclopædian.

enciclopedista, *n.m.f.*, *a.* encyclopædist.

enciendo; encienda, *pres. indic.*; *pres. subj.* [ENCENDER].

encierra, *n.f.* (*Chi.*) locking up a drove in the abattoir; (*Chi.*) winter pasture.

encierro, *n.m.* act of enclosing or locking up; confinement; enclosure; cloister; religious retreat; solitary confinement; prison, lock-up; driving bulls into the penfold.

encierro; encierre, *pres. indic.*; *pres. subj.* [ENCERRAR].

encima, *adv.* above, over; besides, over and above; at the top, overhead; *encima de la mesa,* on (top of) the table; *por encima,* superficially; *por encima de,* over; in spite of, against the will of.

encimar, *v.t.* to place on top; to raise high; (*Col., Per.*) to give extra measure. — *v.r.* to rise above.

encime, *n.m.* (*Col.*) extra gift beyond what is stipulated.

encina, *n.f.* evergreen oak, holm-oak, ilex; wood of this tree.

encinal, encinar, *n.m.* evergreen oak forest.

encinta, *a.* pregnant.

encintado, *n.m.* kerb of a pavement.

encintar, *v.t.* to adorn with ribbons.

encismar, *v.t.* (*coll.*) to sow discord.

encisto, *n.m.* encysted tumour.

enclaustrado, -da, *a.* cloistered. — *p.p.* [ENCLAUSTRAR].

enclaustrar, *v.t.* to shut up in a convent or monastery.

enclavadura, *n.f.* (*carp.*) groove; embedding.

enclavar, *v.t.* to nail; to prick horses in shoeing; to pierce through; (*coll.*) to deceive.

enclavijar, *v.t.* to unite or join; to put pegs in a guitar, etc.

enclenque, *n.m.f.,* *a.* weak, feeble; sickly, ailing (person).

enclítico, -ca, *a.* (*gram.*) enclitic.

enclocar, encloquecer, encoclar, *v.i.,* *v.r.* to be or go broody (of poultry).

encobar, *v.i.,* *v.r.* to sit on eggs in order to hatch them.

encobijar, *v.t.* to cover, protect, shelter.

encobrado, -da, *a.* containing copper; copper-coloured.

encocorar, *v.t.* (*coll.*) to annoy.

encofrado, *n.m.* (*min.*) plank lining, timbering.

encofrar, *v.t.* (*min.*) to plank, timber.

encoger, *v.t.* (*pres. indic.* **encojo;** *pres. subj.* **encoja**) to contract, shorten, shrink; (*fig.*) to discourage, dispirit. — *v.r.* to be low-spirited, dismayed, bashful, to humble oneself; to shrink, contract; *encogerse de hombros,* to shrug one's shoulders.

encogidamente, *adv.* abjectly; bashfully; awkwardly.

encogido, -da, *a.* pusillanimous, timid, fearful, bashful. — *p.p.* [ENCOGER].

encogimiento, *n.m.* contraction, contracting, shrinkage; pusillanimity, want of resolution; bashfulness; awkwardness.

encohetar, *v.t.* to scourge, harass a beast with squibs. — *v.r.* (*CR.*) to become furious or enraged.

encojar, *v.t.* to cripple, lame. — *v.r.* to become lame; (*coll.*) to feign sickness.

encolado, *n.m.* (*Chi., Mex.*) dandy, fop, dude.

encoladura, *n.f.;* **encolamiento,** *n.m.* gluing; priming, sizing.

encolar, *v.t.* to glue; to clarify wine; to size.

encolerizar, *v.t.* (*pret.* **encolericé;** *pres. subj.* **encolerice**) to anger, irritate. — *v.r.* to become angry; to be in a rage.

encomendable, *a.* commendable.

encomendado, -da, *p.p.* [ENCOMENDAR]. — *n.m.* subordinate of a knight commander.

encomendamiento, *n.m.* commission, charge.

encomendar, *v.t.* (*pres. indic.* **encomiendo;** *pres. subj.* **encomiende**) to recommend, commend; to entrust; to bestow the rank of knight commander; (*obs.*) to praise. — *v.i.* to hold a knight-commandery. — *v.r.* to commit oneself to another's protection, to put oneself in another's hands; to send compliments to someone.

encomendero, *n.m.* agent; commissioner.

encomiador, -ra, *a.* praising. — *n.m.f.* praiser.

encomiar, *v.t.* to eulogize, praise, extol.

encomiasta, *n.m.* encomiast, panegyrist.

encomiástico, -ca, *a.* encomiastic.

encomienda, *n.f.* commission, charge; complimentary message; estate granted by Spanish kings; commandery in a military order; lands or rents belonging to a commandery; badge of a knight commander; patronage, protection, support; (*Arg., Col., Chi., Per.*) parcel-post. — *pl.* compliments, respects.

encomio, *n.m.* praise, encomium, eulogy.

encompadrar, *v.i.* (*coll.*) to contract relationship as godfather; to be friends.

enconamiento, *n.m.* inflammation, morbid swelling; infection; (*fig.*) anger.

enconar, *v.t.* to inflame, irritate, provoke; to increase inflammation; to infect. — *v.r.* to fester, rankle (of a wound).

enconcharse, *v.r.* to withdraw from society; to retire into one's shell.

encono, *n.m.* malevolence, rancour, ill-will; soreness; sore spot.

enconoso, -sa, *a.* hurtful, prejudicial, malevolent; liable to resentment.

encorrear, *v.t.* to oil wool that is to be carded.

encontradamente, *adv.* contrarily.

encontradizo, -za, *a.* which may be met on the way; *hacerse uno* (*el*) *encontradizo,* to seek a meeting with someone while making it appear a chance encounter.

encontrado, -da, *a.* opposite, in front; hostile; opposed. — *p.p.* [ENCONTRAR].

encontrar, *v.t., v.i.* (*pres. indic.* **encuentro;** *pres. subj.* **encuentre**) to meet, encounter; to find by chance. — *v.r.* to meet, encounter; to be, find oneself, feel in regard to health; to be opposed to one another; to conflict with; to find; (with *con*) to meet, come across; *¿cómo se encuentra Vd.?* how do you feel?

encontrón, *n.m.* collision, clash, push, shock.

encopetado, -da, *a.* presumptuous, presuming, haughty; of high social standing. — *n.m.* (*arch.*) cathetus. — *p.p.* [ENCOPETAR].

encopetar, *v.t.* to dress the hair high; (*fig.*) to become conceited.

encorachar, *v.t.* to put in a leather bag.

encorajar, *v.t.* to encourage; to inflame. — *v.r.* to be in a rage.

encorar, *v.t.* (*pres. indic.* **encuero;** *pres. subj.* **encuere**) to cover with leather; to cause wounds to granulate. — *v.i., v.r.* to heal, granulate (of wounds).

encorazado, -da, *a.* covered with a cuirass; covered with leather.

encorchadora, *n.f.* corking machine.

encorchar, *v.t.* to hive bees; to cork bottles.

encorchetar, *v.t.* to put on hooks or clasps; to hook or clasp.

encordar, *v.t.* (*pres. indic.* **encuerdo;** *pres. subj.* **encuerde**) to string musical instruments; to bind, lash with ropes.

encordelar, *v.t.* to string; to bind with cords or strings.

encordonado, -da, *a.* corded; adorned with cords. — *p.p.* [ENCORDONAR].

encordonar, *v.t.* to cord; to tie with string.

encorecer, *v.t.* (*pres. indic.* **encorezco;** *pres. subj.* **encorezca**) to cause the formation of skin over a wound. — *v.i., v.r.* [ENCORAR].

encoriación, *n.f.* skinning, healing a wound.

encornado, -da, *a.* horned.

encornadura, *n.f.* shape, position of horns.

encornudar, *v.i.* to begin to get horns. — *v.t.* to cuckold.

encorozar, *v.t.* to cover a criminal's head with a *coroza* or cone-shaped cap.

encorralar, *v.t.* to enclose, keep in a yard; to corral cattle.

encorrear, *v.t.* to tie up with straps.

encorsetar, *v.t., v.r.* to put on a corset.

encortinar, *v.t.* to provide with curtains, hang curtains in.

encorvada, *n.f.* bending, doubling the body; ungraceful way of dancing; *hacer uno la encorvada, (coll.)* to malinger.

encorvadura, *n.f.;* **encorvamiento,** *n.m.* bending; crookedness, curvature.

encorvar, *v.t.* to bend, curve, crook. — *v.r.* to bend, go crooked; to swerve; to warp; to have a leaning towards, to favour.

encostillado, *n.m. (min.)* timbering.

encostradura, *n.f.* incrustation, crust.

encostrar, *v.t.* to crust, incrust; to roughcast. — *v.r.* to become crusty; to develop a crust or scab.

encovadura, *n.f.* act of depositing in a cellar.

encovar, *v.t. (pres. indic.* **encuevo;** *pres. subj.* **encueve)** to put in a cellar; to guard, conceal, enclose, lock up, shut up. — *v.r.* to hide oneself.

encrasar, *v.t.* to fatten, thicken liquids; to manure land. — *v.r. (agric.)* to become more fertile.

encrespador, *n.m.* curling-iron, curling-tongs.

encrespadura, *n.f.* act of curling the hair.

encrespamiento, *n.m.* curling; standing on end (of the hair); roughness (of sea).

encrespar, *v.t.* to curl, frizzle, crimp; to make the hair stand on end; to ruffle (feathers, etc.). — *v.r.* to become rough (of the sea); to be agitated by an affair; to become entangled (business).

encrestado, -da, *a.* having a crest or comb; *(fig.)* haughty, lofty. — *p.p.* [ENCRESTARSE].

encrestarse, *v.r.* to stiffen the crest; to be proud, haughty.

encrucijada, *n.f.* cross-way, cross-road; ambush; opportunity to harm someone.

encrudecer, *v.t. (pres. indic.* **encrudezco;** *pres. subj.* **encrudezca)** to make anything look crude or raw; to exasperate, irritate. — *v.r.* to be enraged.

encrudecimiento, *n.m.* exasperation, irritation.

encruelecer, *v.t. (pres. indic.* **encruelezco;** *pres. subj.* **encruelezca)** to excite to cruelties. — *v.r.* to become cruel.

encuadernación, *n.f.* binding of books.

encuadernador, -ra, *n.m.f.* binder; book-binder.

encuadernar, *v.t.* to bind books; *(obs.)* to unite and arrange various things; *sin encuadernar,* unbound.

encuadrar, *v.t.* to enclose in a frame; to fit, adjust one thing inside another.

encuarte, *n.m.* extra horse to help a coach up-hill.

encubar, *v.t.* to put into casks, barrels, etc.

encubertar, *v.t. (pres. indic.* **encubierto;** *pres. subj.* **encubierte)** to overspread with cloth or silk, caparison, trap, adorn. — *v.r.* to cover oneself with armour as a defence.

encubierta, *n.f.* fraud, deceit.

encubiertamente, *adv.* hiddenly, secretly; deceitfully.

encubierto, -ta, *p.p. irreg.* [ENCUBRIR].

encubierto; encubierte, *pres. indic.; pres. subj.* [ENCUBERTAR].

encubridor, -ra, *a.* hiding, concealing. — *n.m.f.* concealer; procurer, bawd.

encubrimiento, *n.m.* concealment, hiding; *(law)* sheltering a criminal.

encubrir, *v.t.* to hide *(p.p.* **encubierto).**

encuentro, *n.m.* encounter, sudden meeting; shock, clash, collision; *(mil.)* encounter, fight; find, finding; *(arch.)* angle, nook, corner; joint of the wings in poultry next to the breast; point of shoulder-blades (in quadrupeds); *pl.* temples of a loom; *salirle a uno al encuentro,* to go out to receive someone arriving; to oppose someone; to anticipate, forestall.

encuentro; encuentre, *pres. indic.; pres. subj.* [ENCONTRAR].

encuerar, *v.t. (Cub., Mex.)* to undress, strip of clothes.

encuerdo; encuerde, *pres. indic.; pres. subj.* [ENCORDAR].

encuesta, *n.f.* inquiry, inquest.

encuitarse, *v.r.* to grieve.

enculatar, *v.t.* to cover a hive.

encumbrado, -da, *a.* high, elevated; lofty, stately.

encumbramiento, *n.m.* act of raising; height, eminence.

encumbrar, *v.t.* to raise, elevate; to climb a height. — *v.r.* to rise; to be proud; to have a high opinion of oneself.

encunar, *v.t.* to put (a child) in the cradle; *(taurom.)* to catch between the horns.

encureñado, -da, *a.* mounted on the carriage (of cannon).

encurtidos, *n.m.pl.* pickles.

encurtir, *v.t.* to pickle.

enchancletar, *v.t.* to go slipshod.

enchapado, -da, *p.p.* [ENCHAPAR]. — *n.m.* veneer; covering of metal plates.

enchapar, *v.i.* to veneer; to cover with metal plates.

enchapinado, -da, *a.* built or raised upon a vault or arch.

encharcada, *n.f.* pool, puddle.

encharcarse, *v.r.* to be inundated, covered with water, form puddles.

enchavetar, *v.t. (naut.)* to fasten with split pins *(chavetas).*

enchilada, *n.f. (Guat., Mex.)* pancake of maize with chilli.

enchilado, *n.m. (Cub.)* dish made of shellfish with chilli.

enchilar, *v.t. (CR., Hond., Mex.)* to season with chilli; *(Mex.)* to vex, pique; *(CR.)* to play practical jokes.

enchinar, *v.t. (Mex.)* to curl (the hair).

enchipar, *v.t. (Chi., Per.)* to cover sugar-loaves with straw.

enchiquerar, *v.t. (taurom.)* to shut the bull in the *chiquero; (coll.)* to imprison.

enchivarse, *v.r. (Col., Ec.)* to fly into a violent passion.

enchuecar, *v.t., v.r. (Chi., Mex.)* to bend, curve.

enchufar, *v.t., v.r.* to fit the end of one tube into another; to telescope. — *v.t. (elec.)* to plug in.

enchufe, *n.m.* socket, joint; telescoping; pipe-coupling, pipe-joint; *(elec.)* plug; *(fig.)* office obtained through nepotism.

ende, *adv. (obs.)* there; *por ende,* therefore; *facer ende al, (law)* to do the contrary of what was desired.

endeble, *a.* feeble, weak, frail; flimsy, flaccid; forceless.

endeblez, *n.f.* feebleness; flimsiness; flaccidity.

endécada, *n.f.* eleven years.

endecágono, *n.m.* hendecagon.

endecasílabo, -ba, *a.* hendecasyllable.

endecha, *n.f.* dirge, doleful ditty.

endechadera, *n.f.* paid mourning woman at funerals.

endechar, *v.t.* to sing funeral songs. — *v.r.* to grieve; to mourn.

endechoso, -sa, *a.* (*obs.*) mournful, doleful.

endehesar, *v.t.* to put cattle out to pasture.

endémico, -ca, *a.* endemic.

endemoniado, -da, *a.* devilish; demoniac; terribly bad, fiendish, perverse. — *p.p.* [ENDEMONIAR].

endemoniar, *v.t.* to demonize; (*coll.*) to irritate, provoke, enrage.

endentado, -da, *a.* (*her.*) serrated. — *p.p.* [ENDENTAR].

endentar, *v.t.* (*pres. indic.* **endiento;** *pres. subj.* **endiente**) to gear, engage; to join with a mortise.

endentecer, *v.i.* (*pres. indic.* **endentezco;** *pres. subj.* **endentezca**) to cut teeth, teethe.

endeñado, -da, *a.* (*prov.*) damaged, hurt.

enderezadamente, *adv.* rightly, directly, justly.

enderezado, -da, *a.* fit, appropriate. — *p.p.* [ENDEREZAR].

enderezador, -ra, *a.* managing well. — *n.m.f.* good manager; righter; straightener; *enderezador de entuertos* or *agravios,* righter, redresser.

enderezadura, *n.f.* straight, right road.

enderezamiento, *n.m.* straightening; guiding, directing, setting right.

enderezar, *v.t.* (*pret.* **enderecé;** *pres. subj.* **enderece**) to straighten, unbend; to rectify, right, set right; to erect, raise; to manage well; to address; to dedicate. — *v.i.* to take the direct road. — *v.r.* to straighten up; to prepare oneself for an undertaking; *enderezar el genio,* to break a bad temper.

endérmico, -ca, *a.* endermic.

endeudarse, *v.r.* to contract debts, get into debt.

endevotado, -da, *a.* pious; devoted, fond.

endiablada, *n.f.* boisterous masquerade.

endiabladamente, *adv.* devilishly; horribly, abominably.

endiablado, -da, *a.* devilish, diabolical; deformed, ugly; wicked, perverse. — *p.p.* [ENDIABLAR].

endiablar, *v.t.* to demonize; to corrupt, pervert. — *v.r.* to become furious, beside oneself.

endíadis, *n.f.* (*rhet.*) hendiadys.

endibia, *n.f.* (*bot.*) endive, chicory.

endilgador, -ra, *a.* (*coll.*) directing. — *n.m.f.* director, guide; (*coll.*) pander.

endilgar, *v.t.* (*coll.*) (*pret.* **endilgué;** *pres. subj.* **endilgue**) to direct, guide; to help; to thrust through; to deal a blow; to give an unpleasant surprise to.

endiosamiento, *n.m.* pride, loftiness, haughtiness; abstraction, ecstasy; deification.

endiosar, *v.t.* to deify, adore as a god. — *v.r.* to be devoutly abstracted; to be in a state of fervent devotion; (*fig.*) to be elated with pride.

enditarse, *v.r.* (*Chi.*) to contract debts.

endoblado, -da, *a.* applied to a lamb which sucks its own mother and another ewe.

endomingarse, *v.r.* (*coll.*) to wear one's Sunday best.

endorsar, endosar, *v.t.* (*com.*) to endorse (as a draft); to transfer.

endorso, endoso, *n.m.* (*com.*) endorsement.

endosador, endosante, *n.m.* endorser.

endosatario, -ria, *n.m.f.* (*com.*) endorsee.

endoselar, *v.t.* to make a dais; to provide with hangings or curtains.

endriago, *n.m.* fabulous monster.

endrino, -na, *a.* of a sloe colour. — *n.f.* sloe. — *n.m.* blackthorn, sloe-tree.

endrogarse, *v.r.* (*Chi., Mex., Per.*) to contract debts.

endulzadura, *n.f.;* **endulzamiento,** *n.m.* sweetening.

endulzar, endulzorar (*obs.*), *v.t.* (*pret.* **endulcé;** *pres. subj.* **endulce**) to sweeten; to soothe, soften, alleviate; (*art*) to tone down, soften.

endurador, -ra, *a.* parsimonious, miserly, niggardly. — *n.m.f.* miser.

endurar, *v.t.* to endure, suffer, bear; to put off, delay; to harden; to spare, economize.

endurecer, *v.t.* (*pres. indic.* **endurezco;** *pres. subj.* **endurezca**) to harden, toughen, stiffen; to exasperate, irritate; to inure, accustom to hardship. — *v.r.* to become cruel.

endurecidamente, *adv.* obstinately; harshly.

endurecido, -da, *a.* hardened; obdurate; hard, hardy; taught by experience. — *p.p.* [ENDURECER].

endurecimiento, *n.m.* hardness; hardening; obstinacy; tenacity, obdurateness; hardheartedness.

ene, *n.f.* Spanish name of the letter *n*; *ene de palo,* (*coll.*) gallows; *ser de ene una cosa,* (*coll.*) to be a necessary consequence, inevitable. — *a.* unknown or variable quantity : *eso costará ene pesetas,* that will cost *x* pesetas.

enea, *n.f.* (*bot.*) reed-mace, rush, cat-tail.

eneasílabo, -ba, *a.* of nine syllables.

enebral, *n.m.* plantation of juniper-trees.

enebrina, *n.f.* fruit of the juniper-tree.

enebro, *n.m.* common juniper.

enejar, *v.t.* to put on an axle (on a cart, etc.); to put anything on an axle.

eneldo, *n.m.* common dill.

enema, *n.f.* enema, injection, clyster.

enemiga, *n.f.* hatred, enmity, ill-will, malevolence, aversion.

enemigamente, *adv.* inimically, in a hostile way.

enemigo, -ga, *a.* (with *de*) inimical, unfriendly; adverse, hostile, contrary to. — *n.m.f.* enemy, foe, antagonist, fiend, devil; *enemigos pagados,* (*coll.*) servants; *ser enemigo de una cosa,* to dislike something; *quien tiene enemigos, no duerma,* the man with enemies can never rest; *al enemigo que huye, la puente de plata,* let an enemy who flees depart in peace; *¿quién es tu enemigo? El que es de tu oficio,* a man's colleague is often his worst enemy; *quien a su enemigo popa, a sus manos muere,* despise not thy enemy or he may slay thee; *de los enemigos los menos,* the fewer a man's enemies the better.

enemistad, *n.f.* hatred, enmity.

enemistar, *v.t.* to make an enemy of. — *v.r.* (with *con*) to become an enemy of; to fall out with.

éneo, -ea, *a.* (*poet.*) brazen, of brass.

energía, *n.f.* energy; mechanical power; *transmisión de energía,* power transmission.

enérgicamente, *adv.* energetically, expressively.

enérgico, -ca, *a.* vigorous, active, energetic, lively.

energúmeno, -na, *n.m.f.* energumen, person possessed by an evil spirit; (*fig.*) temperamental, violent, ill-tempered person.

enero, *n.m.* January; *de enero a enero, el dinero es del banquero,* (of gaming) the bank always wins; *alcalde del mes de enero,* a new broom sweeps clean.

enervación, *n.f.* enervation.

enervador, -ra, *a.* weakening, enervating.

enervamiento, *n.m.* enervation.

enervar, *v.t.* to enervate; to deprive of strength, weaken, debilitate. — *v.r.* to grow weak, become dull or effeminate.

enfadadizo, -za, *a.* irascible, peevish, irritable, waspish, easily offended.

enfadar, *v.t.* to offend, anger, vex, incense. — *v.r.* to become angry; to fret.

enfado, *n.m.* anger, vexation; drudgery, trouble.

enfadosamente, *adv.* vexatiously, offensively.

enfadoso, -sa, *a.* vexatious, annoying, troublesome.

enfaldar, *v.t.* to lop off the lower branches of trees. — *v.r.* to tuck up the skirts.

enfaldo, *n.m.* act of tucking up one's clothes.

enfangar, *v.t.* (*pret.* **enfangué;** *pres. subj.* **enfangue**) to soil with mud. — *v.r.* (*naut.*) to ground in the mud; (*coll.*) to be mixed up in shady business; (*fig.*) to indulge in sensuality.

enfardador, *n.m.* packer, one who packs bales, etc.

enfardar, *v.t.* to pack, bale; make packages.

enfardelador, *n.m.* packer.

enfardeladura, *n.f.* packing, baling.

enfardelar, *v.t.* to pack; to bale.

énfasis, *n.m.f.* emphasis.

enfáticamente, *adv.* emphatically.

enfático, -ca, *a.* emphatic.

enfebrecido, -da, *a.* slightly feverish.

enfermamente, *adv.* (*obs.*) weakly, feebly.

enfermar, *v.i.* to fall ill. — *v.t.* to make sick; (*fig.*) to weaken, enervate.

enfermedad, *n.f.* sickness, indisposition, illness, complaint, infirmity, distemper, malady; (*fig.*) moral or spiritual deterioration.

enfermería, *n.f.* infirmary; *estar en la enfermería,* (*coll.*) to be in the artisan's shop to be mended, to be dry-docked for repairs; *tomar uno enfermería,* to be considered an invalid.

enfermero, -ra, *n.m.f.* nurse (for the sick).

enfermizo, -za, *a.* sickly, infirm; unhealthy, morbose, unwholesome.

enfermo, -ma, *a.* diseased, sick, infirm, ill; (*fig.*) corrupted, tainted; unhealthy. — *n.m.f.* invalid, patient; *al enfermo que es de vida, el agua le es medicina,* a robust constitution is the best doctor; *apelar el enfermo,* (*coll.*) to make an unexpected recovery.

enfervorizar, *v.t.* to inflame, incite, heat. — *v.r.* to become fervid.

enfeudación, *n.f.* infeudation, enfeoffment.

enfeudar, *v.t.* to feoff, enfeoff, invest with a right or an estate.

enfielar, *v.t.* to counterpoise, balance.

enfiestarse, *v.r.* (*Col., Chi., Hond., Mex., Ven.*) to amuse oneself; to enjoy, take pleasure.

enfilar, *v.t.* to place in a row or line; to pierce or string in a line; (*mil.*) to enfilade; *enfilar el curso,* (*naut.*) to direct the course, to bear to.

enfisema, *n.m.* emphysema.

enfistolarse, *v.r.* to become a fistula.

enfiteusis, *n.m.f.* (*law*) emphyteusis.

enflaquecer, *v.t.* (*pres. indic.* **enflaquezco;** *pres. subj.* **enflaquezca**) to make thin or lean; to weaken. — *v.i., v.r.* to weaken; to become weak; to lose courage.

enflaquecidamente, *adv.* weakly, feebly, faintly, without strength.

enflaquecimiento, *n.m.* attenuation, thinness, loss of flesh, emaciation.

enflautado, -da, *a.* (*coll.*) inflated, turgid. — *n.f.* (*Hond., Per.*) blunder, absurdity. — *p.p.* [ENFLAUTAR].

enflautador, -ra, *n.m.f.* (*coll.*) deceiver; procurer.

enflautar, *v.t.* to blow, swell; (*coll.*) to procure; (*coll.*) to deceive, trick; to incite to do evil; (*Col., Mex.*) to put in a remark; to annoy, bother with an oft-repeated story.

enflechado, -da, *a.* ready to discharge (of a bent bow and arrow).

enfocar, *v.t.* (*phot.*) to focus; (*fig.*) focus, grasp.

enfoscado, -da, *n.m.f., a.* (*build.*) plaster covering holes. — *p.p.* [ENFOSCAR].

enfoscar, *v.t.* (*pret.* **enfosqué;** *pres. subj.* **enfosque**) (*build.*) to fill holes. — *v.r.* to be ill-humoured, uneasy, troubled, perplexed, gloomy; to be cloudy; to be immersed in business.

enfrailar, *v.t.* to make one a monk or friar. — *v.r.* to become a friar.

enfranquecer, *v.t.* to frank, to free, make free.

enfrascamiento, *n.m.* act of being entangled.

enfrascar, *v.t.* (*pret.* **enfrasqué;** *pres. subj.* **enfrasque**) to put liquid in a flask or bottle. — *v.r.* to be entangled or involved; to be deeply engaged in work.

enfrenador, -ra, *a.* bridling, restraining. — *n.m.f.* bridler; restrainer; one who puts on a bridle.

enfrenamiento, *n.m.* act of bridling a horse; checking, curbing.

enfrenar, *v.t.* to curb, restrain, bridle; to put on the brake.

enfrentar, *v.t.* to confront, put face to face; to face. — *v.r.* (with *con*) to face; to oppose.

enfrente, *adv.* opposite, facing, in front; *enfrente de,* opposite.

enfriadera, *n.f.* refrigerator; cooler.

enfriadero, enfriador, *n.m.* cooling-place; cold storage; refrigerator.

enfriamiento, *n.m.* act of cooling; refrigeration; cold, chill.

enfriar, *v.t.* to refrigerate; to cool. — *v.r.* to cool down, cool off; to become calm in mind; to grow cold.

enfrontar, *v.t., v.i.* to confront, face.

enfullar, *v.t.* (*coll.*) to cheat at cards.

enfundadura, *n.f.* casing; putting into cases.

enfundar, *v.t.* to case, put into a case (as a pillow); to sheathe; to stuff; to fill up.

enfurecer, *v.t.* (*pres. indic.* **enfurezco**; *pres. subj.* **enfurezca**) to enrage, irritate, madden, make furious. — *v.r.* (*fig.*) to rage; to grow boisterous or furious (of man or the elements).

enfurecimiento, *n.m.* fury.

enfurruñarse, *v.r.* (*coll.*) to grow angry, be in a pet.

enfurruscarse, *v.r.* (*coll.*) (*Chi.*) [ENFU-RRUÑARSE].

enfurtir, *v.t.* to full cloth; to felt.

engabanado, -da, *a.* wearing an overcoat.

engace, engarce, *n.m.* catenation, connexion.

engafar, *v.t.* to hook; to bend a cross-bow; to slip the safety-catch of a gun.

engaitador, -ra, *n.m.f.* (*coll.*) wheedler, coaxer; deceiver, swindler.

engaitar, *v.t.* (*coll.*) to coax, wheedle; to deceive, swindle.

engalanar, *v.t.* to deck, adorn; (*naut.*) to dress a ship.

engalgar, *v.t.* to pursue closely, not to lose sight of; to scotch a wheel; (*naut.*) to back an anchor.

engallado, -da, *a.* upright, erect; haughty.

engallador, *n.m.* martingale.

engalladura, *n.f.* ruddy spot in the yolk of an egg.

engallarse, *v.r.* to draw oneself up in a haughty manner, affect dignity; (*equit.*) to keep the head near the chest (as horses).

enganchador, *n.m.* hooker; (*mil.*) crimp, one who decoys others into military service.

enganchamiento, enganche, *n.m.* enlisting in the army; hooking; decoying.

enganchar, *v.t.* to clasp, hook, hitch; to connect, link, couple; *enganchar el caballo al coche*, to harness a horse to a carriage; to ensnare, entrap; to decoy into military service. — *v.r.* to enlist in the army; to engage; to be caught on a hook.

enganche, *n.m.* enlistment; hooking; decoying yoke, hook.

engandujo, *n.m.* twisted thread of a fringe.

engañabobos, *n.m.* (*coll.*) impostor, trickster; fooltrap.

engañadizo, -za, *a.* easily deceived.

engañado, -da, *a.* mistaken; deceived. — *p.p.* [ENGAÑAR].

engañador, -ra, *a.* deceiving. — *n.m.f.* deceiver, impostor, cheat; *el engañador engañado*, the biter bit.

engañapastores, *n.m.* wagtail.

engañar, *v.t.* to deceive, mislead, delude, cheat, impose upon, fool, hoax, mock, trick, swindle, gull, abuse; to while away (as time); *engañar el tiempo*, to kill time; *ser malo de engañar*, (*coll.*) to be sagacious, not easily deceived; *con el tomate voy engañando la carne*, I am making the meat tastier with tomato. — *v.r.* to be deceived; to make a mistake.

engañifa, *n.f.* (*coll.*) trick, deceit, fraudulent action.

engañifla, *n.f.* (*prov., Chi.*) [ENGAÑIFA].

engaño, *n.m.* fraud, imposition, deceit, falsehood; misunderstanding, misapprehension, mistake, misconception; lure, hoax; *deshacer un engaño*, to put one right after a deception; *llamarse uno a engaño*, to retract, revoke an agreement, contract, etc., alleging fraud.

engañosamente, *adv.* deceitfully, guilefully; mistakenly.

engañoso, -sa, *a.* false, deceitful, fraudulent, mendacious, artful, fallacious; (*prov.*) liar.

engarabatar, *v.t.* (*coll.*) to hook. — *v.r.* to become crooked.

engarabitar, *v.i.*, *v.r.* to ascend, climb, mount.

engaratusar, *v.t.* (*Guat., Hond., Mex.*) to inveigle, wheedle.

engarbarse, *v.r.* to perch on the highest branches of a tree (of birds).

engarbullar, *v.t.* (*coll.*) to make a mess of; to involve, entangle.

engarce, *n.m.* union or connection; hooking; chasing of jewellery.

engargantar, *v.t.* to put anything into the throat. — *v.i.* to thrust the foot into the stirrup; to interlock; to put into gear.

engargolar, *v.t.* to join pipes.

engaritar, *v.t.* to provide with sentry boxes, fortify; (*coll.*) to fool, deceive, trick.

engarrafador, *n.m.* grappler.

engarrafar, *v.t.* (*coll.*) to grapple, seize upon.

engarrotar, *v.t.* to garrotte; to squeeze hard. — *v.r.* (*Arg.*) to become numb with cold.

engarzador, -ra, *n.m.f.* one who links or enchains; stringer of beads.

engarzar, *v.t.* (*pret.* **engarcé**; *pres. subj.* **engarce**) to link, join; to hook; to curl; to set (as diamonds).

engastador, -ra, *a.* setting, encasing (of jewels). — *n.m.f.* setter, encloser.

engastar, *v.t.* to set (as diamonds); to encase.

engaste, *n.m.* encasing, setting of gems; pearl flat on one side.

engatado, -da, *a.* thievish (like a cat, etc.). — *n.m.f.* petty robber, pilferer; sharper. — *p.p.* [ENGATAR].

engatar, *v.t.* (*coll.*) to cheat, deceive; wheedle.

engatillado, -da, *a.* thick, high-necked (horses and bulls). — *p.p.* [ENGATILLAR].

engatillar, *v.t.* (*arch.*) to bind with a cramping-iron.

engatusador, -ra, *a.* (*coll.*) coaxing, wheedling. — *n.m.f.* coaxer, wheedler.

engatusamiento, *n.m.* (*coll.*) coaxing, wheedling.

engatusar, *v.t.* (*coll.*) to inveigle; to coax; to deceive.

engazador, -ra, *n.m.f.* [ENGARZADOR].

engazar, *v.t.* to dye cloth; to link; (*naut.*) to strap blocks.

engendrable, *a.* that may be engendered.

engendrador, -ra, *a.* generating. — *n.m.f.* engenderer, producer.

engendramiento, *n.m.* begetting, generating.

engendrar, *v.t.* to engender, beget, breed, generate; to produce, bear fruit; to create.

engendro, *n.m.* fœtus; shapeless embryo, monster, abortion; (*fig.*) abortive scheme; badly made thing; *mal engendro*, perverse youth.

engibar, *v.t.* to make crooked, gibbous; (*slang*) to receive stolen goods.

engina, *n.f.* (*obs.*) quinsy.

englandado, -da; englantado, -da, *a.* (*her.*) covered with acorns.

englobar, *v.t.* to enclose, include; to englobe.

engolado, -da, *a.* swallowed, gobbled; (*her.*) engouled; wearing a gorget.

engolfar, *v.t.* (*naut.*) to enter a gulf or deep

bay. — *v.r.* to be engaged in arduous affairs; to be absorbed in meditation.

engolillado, -da, *a.* wearing the *golilla.*

engolondrinarse, *v.r.* (*coll.*) to be elated with pride; to fall in love.

engolosinar, *v.t.* to allure. — *v.r.* to become fond of, have delight in.

engollar, *v.t.* to make a horse carry his head high by means of the bridle.

engolletado, -da, *a.* (*coll.*) haughty, conceited, puffed up. — *p.p.* [ENGOLLETARSE].

engolletarse, *v.r.* (*coll.*) to be conceited or haughty.

engomadura, *n.f.* first gumming; coat which bees lay over their hives before making wax.

engomar, *v.t.* to glue, gum, size.

engorar, *v.t.* to addle.

engorda, *n.f.* (*Chi., Mex.*) number of animals fattened at one time.

engordadero, *n.m.* sty to fatten hogs; time and food for fattening hogs.

engordador, -ra, *a.* fattening, pampering. — *n.m.f.* one who fattens or pampers.

engordar, *v.t.* to fatten, lard, make fat. — *v.i.* to grow fat; to grow rich; to increase in size (of waves).

engorde, *n.m.* fattening (hogs, etc.).

engorro, *n.m.* nuisance, embarrassment, obstacle.

engorroso, -sa, *a.* annoying, vexatious, troublesome, tiresome.

engoznar, *v.t.* to put hinges on; to hinge.

Engracia, *n.f.* Grace.

engranaje, *n.m.* (*mech.*) gearing, gear.

engranar, *v.i.* to gear, interlock, tooth, connect.

engrandar, *v.t.* to increase, make larger.

engrandecer, *v.t.* (*pres. indic.* **engrandezco;** *pres. subj.* **engrandezca**) to enlarge, aggrandize, augment; to extol, exalt; to exaggerate, magnify.

engrandecimiento, *n.m.* increase, enlargement; aggrandizement; exaggeration.

engranerar, *v.t.* to store grain in a granary.

engranujarse, *v.r.* to become covered with pimples; to become a vagabond, rogue.

engrapar, *v.t.* (*build., carp.*) to cramp, unite with cramp-irons.

engrasación, *n.f.* oiling, greasing, lubrication.

engrasador, *n.m.* oiler, lubricator.

engrasar, *v.t.* to oil, grease, lubricate; to dress cloth; (*prov.*) to manure; to stain with grease; to pickle. — *v.r.* (*Mex.*) to contract lead-poisoning.

engrase, *n.m.* greasing, lubrication; grease.

engredar, *v.t.* to full; to clay; to chalk; to cover with marl or fuller's earth.

engreído, -da, *a.* conceited, petulant; lofty, haughty. — *p.p.* [ENGREÍR].

engreimiento, *n.m.* vanity, presumption, conceit.

engreír, *v.t.* (*pres. indic.* **engrío;** *pres. subj.* **engría**) to encourage someone's pride, to make someone vain or conceited; to elate. — *v.r.* to become vain or conceited; (*Am.*) to become fond of.

engrescar, *v.t., v.r.* to cause a quarrel; to make someone join in merriment.

engrifar, *v.t.* to crisp, curl, crimp; to make the hair stand on end (from fright).

engrillar, *v.t.* to fetter; (*fig.*) to restrain; (*PR., Ven.*) to lower the head too much (horses).

engrillarse, *v.i.* to sprout (plants).

engrilletar, *v.t.* (*naut.*) to join two chains with shackles.

engringarse, *v.r.* (*coll.*) to follow foreign customs; to behave like foreigners.

engrosar, *v.t.* (*pres. indic.* **engrueso;** *pres. subj.* **engruese**) to enlarge, augment, swell; to increase the bulk or number; to thicken, expand, broaden, make strong, vigorous or fat. — *v.i., v.r.* to grow strong or corpulent; to increase in size or number.

engrudador, *n.m.* paster, gluer.

engrudamiento, *n.m.* pasting, gluing.

engrudar, *v.t.* to paste; to glue.

engrudo, *n.m.* paste, cement.

engruesar, *v.i.* [ENGROSAR].

engrueso; engruese, *pres. indic.; pres. subj.* [ENGROSAR].

engrumecerse, *v.r.* to clot; to curdle.

engualdar, *v.t.* to make like woad, or of the colour of woad.

engualdrapar, *v.t.* to caparison a horse with rich trappings.

enguantado, -da, *a.* wearing gloves. — *p.p.* [ENGUANTARSE].

enguantar, *v.t., v.r.* to put on gloves.

enguedejado, -da, *a.* wearing long hair.

enguijarrar, *v.t.* to pave with pebbles.

enguillar, *v.t.* (*naut.*) to wind a thin rope around a thicker one.

enguirnaldado, -da, *a.* garlanded, adorned with garlands. — *p.p.* [ENGUIRNALDAR].

enguirnaldar, *v.t.* to garland, adorn with garlands.

enguizgar, *v.t.* to stimulate, incite, set on, excite.

engullidor, -ra, *n.m.f.* devourer, gobbler.

engullir, *v.t.* to gorge, gobble, devour, glut.

engurrio, *n.m.* sadness, melancholy.

engurruñarse, *v.r.* (*coll.*) to become melancholy (of birds).

enharinar, *v.t.* to cover with flour.

enhastiar, *v.t.* to disgust, bore.

enhastillar, *v.t.* to put arrows in a quiver.

enhatijar, *v.t.* to cover the mouths of hives with matting for transportation.

enhebrar, *v.t.* to string, thread.

enhenar, *v.t.* to cover with hay, wrap up in hay.

enherbolar, *v.t.* to poison with herbs (heads of arrows, etc.).

enhestador, -ra, *n.m.f.* one who erects.

enhestadura, *n.f.;* **enhestamiento,** *n.m.* erection.

enhestar, *v.t.* (*pres. indic., p.p.* **enhiesto;** *pres. subj.* **enhieste**) to set upright; to raise; to erect. — *v.r.* to rise upright.

enhetradura, *n.f.* (*obs.*) entangling, entanglement of the hair.

enhielar, *v.t.* to mix with gall or bile.

enhiesto, -ta, *a.* erect, upright. — *p.p. irreg.* [ENHESTAR].

enhilado, -da, *a.* well-arranged, well-disposed, in good order, in line. — *p.p.* [ENHILAR].

enhilar, *v.t.* to thread; (*fig.*) to arrange, place in order; to direct. — *v.i.* to set out for.

enhorabuena, *n.f.* felicitation, congratulation. — *adv.* all right; well and good.

enhoramala, *adv.* in an evil hour; ¡ *véte enhoramala!* (*coll.*) away with you, go to blazes!

enhornar, *v.t.* to put into an oven; *al enhornar se hacen los panes tuertos,* as the twig is bent the tree is inclined.

enhorquetar, *v.t., v.r.* (*Arg., Cub., PR.*) to ride astride.

enhuecar, *v.t.* [AHUECAR].

enhuerar, *v.t.* to addle; to lay addled eggs.

enigma, *n.m.* enigma, riddle, obscure question.

enigmáticamente, *adv.* enigmatically.

enigmático, -ca, *a.* enigmatic, dark, obscure, ambiguous.

enigmatista, *n.m.* enigmatist.

enjabonadura, *n.f.* washing.

enjabonar, *v.t.* to wash with soap; to soap; (*coll.*) to apply soft-soap to; (*coll.*) to reprimand severely.

enjaezar, *v.t.* (*pret.* **enjaecé;** *pres. subj.* **enjaece**) to adorn, trap; to harness a horse.

enjagüe, *n.m.* adjudication required by the creditors of a ship.

enjalbegador, -ra, *n.m.f.* whitewasher.

enjalbegadura, *n.f.* whitewashing.

enjalbegar, *v.t.* to whitewash; (*fig.*) to paint (the face).

enjalma, *n.f.* kind of light packsaddle.

enjalmar, *v.t.* to packsaddle a horse; to make packsaddles.

enjalmero, *n.m.* packsaddle-maker.

enjambradera, *n.f.* queen-bee.

enjambradero, *n.m.* place where beehives are kept.

enjambrar, *v.t.* to gather a swarm of bees; to hive bees; to take a new swarm from a hive. — *v.i.* to produce abundantly. — *v.r.* to be filled with swarms (of bees).

enjambrazón, *n.f.* swarming of bees.

enjambre, *n.m.* swarm of bees; (*fig.*) crowd, multitude, bevy.

enjambrillo, *n.m.* little swarm [ENJAMBRE].

enjarciadura, *n.f.* act of rigging a ship.

enjarciar, *v.t.* to rig a ship; to put tackle aboard a ship.

enjardinar, *v.t.* to trim trees as in a garden.

enjaretado, *n.m.* grating, lattice-work.

enjaretar, *v.t.* to run a string through a hem; (*coll.*) to say or do something hurriedly and inconsiderately.

enjaular, *v.t.* to cage; (*coll.*) to imprison, confine.

enjebar, *v.t.* to steep in lye; to buck.

enjebe, *n.m.* lye; steeping in lye; bucking.

enjergar, *v.t.* (*coll.*) to start and direct a business; to set about a matter, bring a matter forward.

enjerido, -da, *a.* (*prov.*) benumbed with cold; budded. — *p.p.* [ENJERIR].

enjeridor, *n.m.* one who buds; grafting-knife.

enjerir, *v.t.* (*obs.*) to graft; to insert, include.

enjertación, *n.f.* budding; insertion; grafting; inoculation.

enjertal, *n.m.* nursery of grafted fruit-trees.

enjertar, *v.t.* to graft, inoculate.

enjerto, -ta, *n.m.* grafting; mixture. — *p.p. irreg.* [ENJERTAR].

enjorguinarse, *v.r.* to become a wizard or sorcerer.

enjoyar, *v.t.* to adorn with jewels; to adorn, embellish; to set with precious stones.

enjoyelado, -da, *a.* covered with jewels; (gold or silver) worked into jewels.

enjoyelador, *n.m.* jeweller, jewel-setter.

enjuagadientes, *n.m.* mouth-wash.

enjuagadura, *n.f.* rinsing the mouth.

enjuagar, *v.t.* (*pret.* **enjuagué;** *pres. subj.* **enjuague**) to rinse, (mouth, cups, etc.).

enjuagatorio, *n.m.* finger-bowl; act of rinsing; mouth-wash.

enjuague, *n.m.* [ENJUAGATORIO]; (*fig.*) plot, scheme.

enjugador, -ra, *n.m.f.* drier. — *n.m.* drum for drying or airing linen.

enjugar, *v.t.* (*pret.* **enjugué;** *pres. subj.* **enjugue**) to dry; to wipe off moisture. — *v.r.* to grow lean, dry up.

enjuiciamiento, *n.m.* (*law*) institution of legal proceedings.

enjuiciar, *v.t.* (*law*) to prosecute; to indict; to bring a suit or action; to pass judgment.

enjulio, enjullo, *n.m.* warp-rod; cloth-beam of a loom.

enjuncar, *v.t.* to fasten the sails with stops of grass rope; to ballast a ship.

enjundia, *n.f.* grease or fat of any animal; fat in the ovary of fowls; (*fig.*) force, substance.

enjundioso, -sa, *a.* substantial; fat, fatty.

enjunque, *n.m.* heavy ballast or cargo; kent-ledge.

enjuramiento, *n.m.* (*obs.*) legal oath.

enjurar, *v.t.* (*obs.*) to yield or transfer a right.

enjuta, *n.f.* (*arch.*) spandrel.

enjutar, *v.t.* (*build.*) to dry (plaster, etc.).

enjutez, *n.f.* dryness, aridity.

enjuto, -ta, *a.* lean; (*obs.*) sparing, mean; slender; dried; (*obs.*) austere; *pie enjuto,* without pains or labour. — *p.p. irreg.* [ENJUGAR]. — *n.m.pl.* brushwood; tit-bits to excite thirst.

enlabiador, -ra, *a.* wheedling. — *n.m.f.* wheedler, cajoler, seducer.

enlabiar, *v.t.* to cajole, wheedle, entice by soft words.

enlabio, *n.m.* enticement, alluring, enchantment by the power of speech.

enlace, *n.m.* coherence, connexion; lacing; liaison, link; interlocking; relationship; matrimony, wedding; affinity, kindred.

enlacé; enlace, *pret.; pres. subj.* [ENLAZAR].

enlaciar, *v.i., v.r.* to wither, to decay; to render languid or lax.

enladrillado, -da, *n.m.* brick pavement; brickwork. — *p.p.* [ENLADRILLAR].

enladrillador, *n.m.* bricklayer.

enladrilladura, *n.f.* brickwork.

enladrillar, *v.t.* to pave with bricks.

enlagunar, *v.t.* to flood, turn into a pond.

enlamar, *v.t.* to cover with slime.

enlanado, -da, *a.* covered or supplied with wool.

enlardar, *v.t.* to rub with grease, baste.

enlargues, *n.m.pl.* rope-ends.

enlatar, *v.t.* to cover with tin; (*Arg., Hond.*) to roof, etc., with battens; to can food, etc.

enlazable, *a.* that can be joined, fastened or bound.

enlazador, -ra, *n.m.f.* binder, uniter.

enlazadura, *n.f.; enlazamiento,* *n.m.* binding, uniting, connexion, coupling, linking; lacing.

enlazar, *v.t.* (*pret.* **enlacé;** *pres. subj.* **enlace**) to tie, bind; to link, relate; to lasso. — *v.r.* to become related by marriage; to be joined in wedlock; to interlock; to be joined or connected together.

enlechuguillado, -da, *a.* wearing a ruff round the neck.

enlegajar, *v.t.* to tie up papers into a docket.

enlejiar, *v.t.* to buck clothes; (*chem.*) to make into lye.

enlenzar, *v.t.* to strengthen something with adhesive strips of cloth.

enligarse, *v.r.* to be caught with bird-lime; to stick, adhere.

enlistonado, *n.m.* lath-work.

enlistonar, *v.t.* to lath.

enlizar, *v.t.* to provide a loom with leashes.

enlodadura, *n.f.* act of soiling, daubing or filling with mud.

enlodar, *v.t.* to soil with mud, bemire; to throw mud at; (*min.*) to stop up with clay; to lute.

enloquecedor, **-ra**, *a.* maddening.

enloquecer, *v.t.* (*pres. indic.* **enloquezco**; *pres. subj.* **enloquezca**) to render insane, to distract. — *v.i.*, *v.r.* to become mad, demented; to be annoyed, vexed; to be in despair; (*agric.*) to become barren (*trees*).

enloquecimiento, *n.m.* going mad; madness, insanity.

enlosado, *n.m.* flagging; flagged pavement. — *p.p.* [ENLOSAR].

enlosar, *v.t.* to lay a floor with flags or tiles.

enlozanarse, *v.r.* to make a show of vigour and strength.

enlucido, **-da**, *a.* covered with white plaster. — *n.m.* coat of plaster; plastering. — *p.p.* [ENLUCIR].

enlucidor, *n.m.* plasterer, whitener.

enlucimiento, *n.m.* pargeting; metal polishing, scouring of plate.

enlucir, *v.t.* (*pres. indic.* **enluzco**; *pres. subj.* **enluzca**) to parget, whitewash; to scour or polish plate.

enlustrecer, *v.t.* to brighten, polish, clean.

enlutar, *v.t.* to put into mourning; to veil; to darken; to put crape or mourning on.

enluzco; **enluzca**, *pres. indic.; pres. subj.* [ENLUCIR].

enllantar, *v.t.* to shoe, rim a wheel.

enllentecer, *v.t.* to soften, to blandish.

enmadejar, *v.t.* (*Chi.*) to reel.

enmachiembrar, *v.t.* to matchboard pieces of timber.

enmaderación, *n.f.; **enmaderamiento**, *n.m.* woodwork; wainscoting; covering of wood.

enmaderar, *v.t.* to roof with timber; to board or plank; to floor with boards.

enmagrecer, *v.t.*, *v.i.*, *v.r.* to grow lean, to lose fat.

enmalecerse, *v.r.* to be covered with weeds.

enmallarse, *v.r.* to be caught in the meshes of a net (of fish).

enmalletado, **-da**, *a.* fouled (of ropes).

enmangar, *v.t.* to put a handle on.

enmaniguarse, *v.r.* (*Cub.*) to revert to jungle; (*Cub.*) (*fig.*) to get used to the life of a countryman.

enmantar, *v.t.* to cover with a blanket. — *v.r.* to be melancholy (birds).

enmarañamiento, *n.m.* perplexity; entanglement; intricacy.

enmarañar, *v.t.* to perplex, entangle, involve in difficulties; to confound, puzzle; to tangle (as hair, etc.).

enmararse, *v.r.* to take sea-room.

enmaridar, *v.i.*, *v.r.* to take a husband, marry.

enmarillecerse, *v.r.* to become pale or yellow.

enmaromar, *v.t.* to tie with a rope.

enmascarar, *v.t.* to mask. — *v.r.* to masquerade, go in disguise.

enmasillar, *v.t.* (*carp.*) to fill; to glaze; to putty, cement (of glaziers).

enmatarse, *v.r.* to hide among vegetation.

enmelar, *v.t.* to sweeten; to bedaub with honey; to produce honey.

enmendación, *n.f.* emendation, correction.

enmendadamente, *adv.* accurately, exactly.

enmendador, **-na**, *n.m.f.* corrector, emendator, amender.

enmendadura, *n.f.; **enmendamiento**, *n.m.* [ENMIENDA].

enmendar, *v.t.* (*pres. indic.* **enmiendo**; *pres. subj.* **enmiende**) to correct, change, alter, improve, amend; to reform; to compensate; to repair; (*law*) to revise a sentence, etc. — *v.r.* to become better, mend, lead a new life.

enmienda, *n.f.* correction, emendation, amendment; (*obs.*) reward, premium; (*law*) satisfaction, indemnity, compensation; *poner enmienda*, to amend; *tomar enmienda*, to punish. — *n.pl.* fertilizer.

enmiendo; enmiende, *pres. indic.; pres. subj.* [ENMENDAR].

enmocecer, *v.i.* (*obs.*) to recover the vigour of youth.

enmohecer, *v.t.* (*pres. indic.* **enmohezco**; *pres. subj.* **enmohezca**) to mildew, mould, must; to rust. — *v.r.* to become mouldy; to rust.

enmohecido, **-da**, *a.* rusty, mildewed, mouldy, musty, spoiled with damp. — *p.p.* [ENMOHECER].

enmohecimiento, *n.m.* mustiness, mouldiness.

enmollecer, *v.t.* to soften, mollify, make tender.

enmonarse, *v.r.* (*Chi.*, *Per.*) to get drunk.

enmondar, *v.t.* to remove knots from cloth.

enmontadura, *n.f.* (*obs.*) elevation, erection.

enmontarse, *v.r.* (*Cent. Am.*) to become covered with weeds.

enmordazar, *v.t.* to gag, muzzle.

enmudecer, *v.t.* (*pres. indic.* **enmudezco**; *pres. subj.* **enmudezca**) to impose silence, hush. — *v.i.* to be silent; to become dumb.

enmugrar, *v.t.* (*Col.*, *Chi.*) to soil.

ennegrecer, *v.t.* (*pres. indic.* **ennegrezco**; *pres. subj.* **ennegrezca**) to obscure; to darken; to blacken.

ennegrecimiento, *n.m.* act of blackening, darkening, obscuring.

ennoblecedor, **-ra**, *a.* ennobling.

ennoblecer, *v.t.* (*pres. indic.* **ennoblezco**; *pres. subj.* **ennoblezca**) to ennoble; to adorn, embellish.

ennoblecimiento, *n.m.* ennoblement.

ennoviar, *v.i.* (*fam.*) to contract marriage.

ennudecer, *v.i.* [ANUDARSE].

enodio, *n.m.* fawn, young deer.

enojada, *n.f.* (*coll.*) fit of anger; getting angry.

enojadizo, **-za**, *a.* peevish, fretful, fractious, cross.

enojado, **-da**, *a.* angry, peevish, cross, fretful. — *p.p.* [ENOJAR].

enojante, *a.* vexing.

enojar, *v.t.* to irritate, fret, anger, vex; to offend, displease; to molest, annoy, tease. — *v.r.* to be angry, cross, displeased; to be offended, peevish, fretful; (*fig.*) to become boisterous, violent (of wind, etc.).

enojo, *n.m.* anger, passion, choler; trouble, suffering, annoyance; *crecido de enojo*, full of wrath; *ser en enojo con* (*obs.*), to be angry with.

enojosamente, *adv.* crossly, angrily; troublesomely.

enojoso, -sa, *a.* vexatious, troublesome; irritating.

enojuelo, *n.m.* slight peevishness [ENOJO].

enología, *n.f.* œnology, art of wine-making.

enológico, -ca, *a.* œnological.

enómetro, *n.m.* œnometer.

enorgullecer, *v.t.* (*pres. indic.* **enorgullezco;** *pres. subj.* **enorgullezca**) to make proud. — *v.r.* to be proud; to swell with pride.

enorgullecido, -da, *a.* haughty, arrogant, very proud. — *p.p.* [ENORGULLECER].

enorgullecimiento, *n.m.* haughtiness, arrogance.

enorme, *a.* huge, enormous; horrible, wicked, heinous.

enormemente, *adv.* enormously; horridly.

enormidad, *n.f.* enormousness, monstrousness, enormity; grievousness, horridness; atrocity; (*fig.*) absurdity, nonsense.

enormísimo, -ma, *a. superl.* most horrid.

enotecnia, *n.f.* technical knowledge of œnology.

enotécnico, -ca, *a.* relating to wine making.

enquiciar, *v.t.* to hinge, put on hinges; (*fig.*) to put in order; to make firm or stable.

enpuillotrar, *v.t.* to encourage someone's pride. — *v.r.* (*coll.*) to fall in love.

enquiridión, *n.m.* manual, handbook.

enquistado, -da, *a.* (*surg.*) cysted, encysted.

enrabiar, *v.t.* to enrage, anger.

enraizar, *v.i.* to take root.

enramada, *n.f.* bower, arbour; grove.

enramar, *v.t.* to embower or decorate with branches of trees. — *v.i.* to branch (of trees).

enramblar, *v.t.* to tenter cloth.

enrame, *n.m.* act of embowering.

enranciarse, *v.r.* to grow rancid, stale.

enrarecer, *v.t.* (*pres. indic.* **enrarezco;** *pres. subj.* **enrarezca**) to thin, rarefy, extenuate. — *v.r.* to become rare or in short supply.

enrarecimiento, *n.m.* rarefaction.

enrasar, *v.t.* (*build.*) to make even or level; to flush, smooth, plane.

enrase, *n.m.* (*build.*) levelling.

enrastrar, *v.t.* (*prov.*) to string silk cocoons.

enrayar, *v.t.* to fix spokes in a wheel.

enredadera, *a.* twining (plant). — *n.f.* climbing plant; bindweed, vine.

enredado, -da, *a.* matted, entangled, involved; (*naut.*) foul. — *p.p.* [ENREDAR].

enredador, -ra, *a.* climbing, entangling. — *n.m.f.* tell-tale, busybody, tattler, meddler; entangler.

enredamiento, *n.m.* (*obs.*) [ENREDO].

enredar, *v.t.* to perplex, confound, puzzle, involve in difficulties; to entangle, hamper; to lay snares for birds; to catch in snares, nets; to sow discord, to fumble. — *v.i.* to be frisky (of boys); — *v.r.* to become entangled, enmeshed; to foul the anchor; (*coll.*) to live in concubinage.

enredo, *n.m.* tangle, entanglement; perplexity, puzzle; mischief (of boys); intricacy; (*fig.*) falsehood, mischievous lie; (*fig.*) plot of a play. — *pl.* implements, tools of trade.

enredoso, -sa, *a.* entangled, intricate, full of snares, difficulties or knotty points.

enrehojar, *v.t.* to turn over, stir wax into sheets in order to bleach it.

enrejado, -da, *p.p.* [ENREJAR]. — *n.m.* trellis, lattice; open-work, grill-work; grating, railing.

enrejalar, *v.t.* to range bricks in criss-cross tiers.

enrejar, *v.t.* to surround with railing, grating, or lattice-work; to fix a grating to a window; to fence with railing or grating; to fix the share to a plough; to wound oxen or horse's feet with a ploughshare; (*Mex.*) to darn.

enrevesado, -da, *a.* frisky; difficult; nonsensical.

enriado, *n.m.* retting of flax or hemp.

enriador, -na, *n.m.f.* one who rets flax or hemp.

enriar, *v.t.* to ret hemp and flax, steep, submerge.

enrielar, *v.t.* to make ingots of gold or silver; (*Chi., Mex.*) to set on the rails (car, etc.); to guide in the right direction.

enripiar, *v.t.* (*build.*) to fill with rubble.

enriquecedor, -ra, *a.* enriching. — *n.m.f.* one who enriches.

enriquecer, *v.t.* (*pres. indic.* **enriquezco;** *pres. subj.* **enriquezca**) to enrich, to adorn. — *v.i.* to become rich.

enriscado, -da, *a.* full of cliffs; craggy, mountainous. — *p.p.* [ENRISCAR].

enriscamiento, *n.m.* act of raising; taking refuge amongst rocks.

enriscar, *v.t.* to raise, lift. — *v.r.* to take refuge amongst rocks.

enristrar, *v.t., v.i.* to couch the lance; (*fig.*) to go direct to a place; to string (onions, etc.); to overcome a difficulty.

enristre, *n.m.* act of couching a lance.

enrizamiento, *n.m.* curling.

enrizar, *v.t.* (*obs.*) to curl, turn into ringlets.

enrobrescido, -da, *a.* (*obs.*) hard or strong like an oak.

enrobustecer, *v.t.* to make robust.

enrocar, *v.t.* to castle the king at chess; to place flax or wool on the distaff.

enrodar, *v.t.* to break on the torture-wheel.

enrodelado, -da, *a.* armed with a shield.

enrodrigonar, *v.t.* to prop vines with stakes.

enrojar, enrojecer, *v.t.* (*pres. indic.* **enrojezco;** *pres. subj.* **enrojezca**) to redden; to make red-hot; to put to the blush. — *v.r., v.i.* to blush; to turn red.

enrojecido, -da, *a.* red; red-hot. — *p.p.* [ENROJECER].

enrollar, *v.t.* to wind, coil, roll, wrap.

enromar, *v.t.* to blunt, dull.

enrona, *n.f.* (*prov.*) refuse, rubbish, debris.

enronar, *v.t.* (*prov.*) to throw rubbish in a dump.

enronquecer, *v.t.* (*pres. indic.* **enronquezco;** *pres. subj.* **enronquezca**) to make hoarse. — *v.i., v.r.* to become hoarse.

enronquecimiento, *n.m.* hoarseness.

enroñar, *v.t.* to fill with scabs or scurf. — *v.r.* to become rusty.

enrosar, *v.t.* to tinge, dye, colour red.

enroscadamente, *adv.* curlingly.

enroscadura, *n.f.* convolution, sinuosity; curlicue, twist.

enroscar, *v.t.* (*pret.* **enrosqué;** *pres. subj.* **enrosque**) to twist, twine; to screw in. — *v.r.* to curl or twist itself; to coil.

enrostrar, *v.t.* (*Am.*) to upbraid, cast in one's teeth.

enrubiador, -ra, *a.* that turns the hair blond.

enrubiar, *v.t.* to dye the hair blond, bleach.

enrubio, *n.m.* act of dyeing blond; dye used for such a purpose; (*PR.*) tree with very hard wood.

enrudecer, *v.t.* (*pres. indic.* **enrudezco;** *pres. subj.* **enrudezca**) to make rude, coarse. — *v.i.* to become coarse, rough.

enruinecer, *v.i.* to become vile.

ensabanar, *v.t.* to wrap up in sheets; to cover a wall with plaster of Paris.

ensacador, -ra, *n.m.f.* sacker, bagger.

ensacar, *v.t.* (*pret.* **ensaqué;** *pres. subj.* **ensaque**) to sack, bag, enclose in a sack or bag.

ensaimada, *n.f.* kind of Bath-bun.

ensalada, *n.f.* salad; medley, hodge-podge.

ensaladera, *n.f.* salad dish or bowl.

ensaladilla, *n.f.* jewel made up of different precious stones; assortment of sweetmeats; Russian salad.

ensalmador, -ra, *n.m.f.* quack; bone-setter; one who pretends to cure by charms.

ensalmar, *v.t.* to set dislocated bones; to cure by spells; to enchant, bewitch, charm.

ensalmista, *n.m.* charlatan.

ensalmo, *n.m.* spell, enchantment, charm; (*como*) *por ensalmo,* with surprising speed, as if by magic.

ensalobrarse, *v.r.* to become salty (of water).

ensalzador, -ra, *a.* praising, extolling. — *n.m.f.* praiser, exalter, extoller.

ensalzamiento, *n.m.* praise, exaltation.

ensalzar, *v.t.* (*pret.* **ensalcé;** *pres. subj.* **ensalce**) to exalt, extol, magnify, praise. — *v.r.* to boast.

ensamblador, *n.m.* joiner, worker in wood.

ensambladura, *n.f.;* **ensamble,** *n.m.* joinery, joiner's trade; act of joining; joint.

ensamblaje, *n.m.* scarfing, joining, coupling.

ensamblar, *v.t.* to connect, join, couple; to scarf, dovetail, mortise.

ensamble, *n.m.* [ENSAMBLADURA].

ensancha, *n.f.* extension, enlargement; *dar ensanchas,* to give too much licence, or liberty.

ensanchador, -ra, *a.* stretching, expanding. — *n.m.* glove-stretcher; widener, stretcher, expander; reamer.

ensanchamiento, *n.m.* expansion, extension, stretch; dilation; enlarging, widening.

ensanchar, *v.t.* to stretch; to extend, enlarge, widen; *ensanchar el corazón,* to cheer up, raise one's spirits, unburden the mind. — *v.r.* to assume an air of importance; to expand, become larger.

ensanche, *n.m.* material turned in seams of garments; extension, enlargement, dilatation, widening, stretch; open ground reserved for new buildings.

ensandecer, *v.i.* to grow stupid, crazy; to become mad.

ensangrentamiento, *n.m.* covering with blood.

ensangrentar, *v.t.* (*pres. indic.* **ensangriento;** *pres. subj.* **ensangriente**) to stain with blood. — *v.r.* to become heated, irritated, vexed, in a dispute; to cover oneself with blood; to behave in a cruel way; *ensangrentarse con* or *contra uno,* to have murderous thoughts about someone.

ensañamiento, *n.m.* cruelty, ferocity; (*law*) aggravating circumstance.

ensañar, *v.t.* to irritate, enrage. — *v.r.* to gloat; to vent one's fury; (*law*) to be merciless.

ensarnecerse, *v.i.* to get the itch.

ensartar, *v.t.* to string (beads); to thread a needle; to link; to talk rigmarole; to make a string of observations; to detail the events of a long story.

ensay, *n.m.* (*mint*) trial, assay, proof.

ensayador, -ra, *n.m.f.* assayer; officer of a mint; rehearser.

ensayar, *v.t.* to try; rehearse, practise; to test; to assay precious metals. — *v.r.* to exercise oneself, train, practise.

ensaye, *n.m.* assay, trial, proof, test (of metals).

ensayista, *n.m.f.* essayist, essay-writer.

ensayo, *n.m.* test, assay; essay; examination, experiment, trial; preparatory practice, exercise; rehearsal of a play; (*com.*) sample; *ensayo general,* dress rehearsal.

ensebar, *v.t.* to grease, tallow.

enselvado, -da, *a.* wooded, full of trees. — *p.p.* [ENSELVAR].

enselvar, *v.t.* to place in ambush. — *v.r.* to retire to a forest; to become wooded.

ensenada, *n.f.* small bay, inlet, cove, creek.

ensenado, -da, *a.* having the form of a cove or inlet. — *p.p.* [ENSENAR].

ensenar, *v.t.* to put into one's bosom; (*naut.*) to embay. — *v.r.* (*naut.*) to become embayed (of a ship).

enseña, *n.f.* ensign, colours, standard.

enseñable, *a.* teachable.

enseñado, -da, *a.* accustomed; educated, trained. — *p.p.* [ENSEÑAR].

enseñador, -ra, *a.* teaching. — *n.m.f.* instructor, teacher.

enseñamiento, *n.m.;* **enseñanza,** *n.f.* doctrine; tuition, teaching; instruction, education.

enseñar, *v.t.* to train, teach, instruct; to point out, show the way, etc. — *v.r.* to school oneself; to become accustomed, inured.

enseño, *n.m.* (*coll.*) education.

enseñoreador, -ra, *n.m.f.* (*obs.*) person who domineers.

enseñorear, *v.t.* to domineer, lord over. — *v.r.* to possess oneself of a thing.

enserar, *v.t.* to cover with matting.

enseres, *n.m.pl.* fixtures; chattels; household goods; implements, articles; furniture.

enseriarse, *v.r.* (*Cub., Per., PR., Ven.*) to become serious.

ensiforme, *a.* ensiform, sword-shaped.

ensilaje, *n.m.* ensilage.

ensilar, *v.t.* to ensilage, preserve grain in pits.

ensilvecerse, *v.r.* to become a forest, wooded (field, etc.).

ensillado, -da, *a.* saddle-backed (horses). — *p.p.* [ENSILLAR].

ensilladura, *n.f.* act of saddling a horse; part of a horse or mule on which a saddle is placed.

ensillar, *v.t.* to saddle; (*obs.*) to raise, exalt; *aun no ensillamos, y ya cabalgamos,* you are in too much of a hurry.

ensimismado, -da, *a.* selfish; abstracted. — *p.p.* [ENSIMISMARSE].

ensimismarse, *v.r.* to become absorbed in thought, abstracted; (*Chi., Col.*) to be in love with oneself; to become vain.

ensoberbecer, *v.t.* (*pres. indic.* **ensoberbezco;** *pres. subj.* **ensoberbezca**) to make proud. — *v.r.* to become proud and haughty, to be arrogant; (*naut.*) to become rough (of the sea).

ensoberbecimiento, *n.m.* excessive haughtiness.

ensogar, *v.t.* to fasten with a rope; to line with rope (demijohn, etc.).

ensolerar, *v.t.* to fix stands, bases to beehives.

ensolver, *v.t. (p.p. irreg.* **ensuelto**; *pres. indic.* **ensuelvo**; *pres. subj.* **ensuelva**) to include, enclose; to abridge, contract; *(med.)* to resolve, dissipate.

ensombrecer, *v.t.* to darken; to make cloudy.

ensoñar, *v.t., v.i.* to have illusions, fantasy.

ensopar, *v.t.* to steep bread in wine, etc.; *(Arg., Hond., PR., Ven.)* to soak; to drench.

ensordecedor, -ra, *a.* deafening.

ensordecer, *v.t. (pres. indic.* **ensordezco**; *pres. subj.* **ensordezca**) to deafen. — *v.i.* to grow deaf; to become silent, observe silence.

ensordecimiento, *n.m.* deafness.

ensortijamiento, *n.m.* crimping, curling, crisping; kink, ringlet, curlicue; ringing (of animals).

ensortijar, *v.t.* to curl, to form rings or ringlets; to kink; to put on rings.

ensotarse, *v.r.* to hide oneself in a thicket.

ensuciador, -ra, *a.* staining, soiling. — *n.m.f.* defiler, stainer.

ensuciamiento, *n.m.* act or effect of staining, soiling or polluting.

ensuciar, *v.t.* to defile, pollute; to soil, smear, stain; *ensuciarla,* to make a mess of things, put one's foot in it. — *v.r.* to soil one's bed, clothes, etc.; *(coll.)* to be dishonest; to do something degrading; to let oneself be bribed.

ensuelto, -ta, *p.p. irreg.* [ENSOLVER].

ensuelvo; ensuelva, *pres. indic.; pres. subj.* [ENSOLVER].

ensueño, *n.m.* illusion, fantasy; dream.

entablación, *n.f.* act of flooring or boarding up; register in churches.

entablado, -da, *p.p.* [ENTABLAR]. — *n.m.* boarded or parquet floor; stage, dais.

entabladura, *n.f.* act of flooring or boarding up; planking.

entablamento, *n.m.* entablature.

entablar, *v.t.* to floor or cover with boards; to board up; to plank; to start, initiate, begin (a negotiation); to bring (a suit or action); to place the men on a chess-board; to make an entry in a church register; *(surg.)* to splint; *(Arg.)* to train cattle, horses, etc., to proceed in a drove. — *v.r.* to settle (as the wind); to establish oneself.

entable, *n.m.* position of chessmen; position, employment; business position.

entablillar, *v.t. (surg.)* to splint.

entalamado, -da, *a. (obs.)* hung with tapestry. — *p.p.* [ENTALAMAR].

entalamadura, *n.f.* awning of a cart, etc.

entalamar, *v.t. (obs.)* to cover with an awning.

entalegar, *v.t. (com.)* to put in a bag or sack; to save, hoard money.

entalingar, *v.t. (naut.)* to clinch the cable, fasten the cable to the anchor.

entallable, *a.* capable of being carved.

entallador, *n.m.* sculptor, cutter in wood or stone; engraver; carver.

entalladura, *n.f.; entallamiento,** *n.m.* sculpture, carving; *(carp.)* groove, mortise, notch.

entallar, *v.t.* to notch, make a cut in; to carve, sculpture, engrave. — *v.i.* to fit to the body (as a bodice).

entallecer, *v.i. (agric.)* to shoot, sprout.

entapizar, *v.t.* to hang or adorn with tapestry.

entarascar, *v.t. (coll.)* to overdress, cover with too many ornaments.

entarimado, -da, *p.p.* [ENTARIMAR]. — *n.m.* boarded or parqueted floor.

entarimar, *v.t.* to floor with boards.

entarquinamiento, *n.m.* fertilizing with slime.

entarquinar, *v.t.* to manure with slime; to cover with mud, bemire; to reclaim swamplands.

ente, *n.m.* being, entity; *(coll.)* ridiculous or remarkable person.

entecado, -da; enteco, -ca, *a. (prov.)* infirm, weak, languid.

entejar, *v.t. (Am.)* to tile roofs.

entelequia, *n.f. (phil.)* entelechy.

entelerido, -da, *a.* numb from cold; shivering from fright; *(CR., Hond., Ven.)* infirm, weak; lean.

entena, *n.f.* lateen yard.

entenada, *n.f.* stepdaughter.

entenado, *n.m.* stepson.

entenallas, *n.f.pl.* pincers; hand-vice.

entendederas, *n.f.pl. (coll.)* understanding, brain, wits.

entendedor, -ra, *n.m.f.* understander, one who understands; *al buen entendedor, pocas palabras,* a word to the wise.

entender, *v.t., v.i. (pres. indic.* **entiendo**; *pres. subj.* **entienda**) to understand, conceive, comprehend; to believe, conclude, infer; *entender de,* to be familiar with, skilled in; *entender en,* to be in charge of an affair; to be in a position to judge something; to have authority to inquire into; *no lo entenderá Galván,* it is an intricate matter; *ya te entiendo,* I've got your meaning. — *v.r.* to be understood; to be meant; to have some motive for doing a thing; to know what one is about; to agree, be agreed; to understand each other, come to an understanding; to have an understanding; *entenderse una cosa con uno,* to include, comprehend; *no se entiende eso conmigo,* this does not include me; *entenderse con una cosa,* to be skilled in something; *cada uno se entiende,* each puts his own meaning into what he says; *¿cómo se entiende?* or *¿qué se entiende?* what's the meaning of this, pray? — *n.m.* understanding, opinion; *a* (or *según*) *mi entender,* in my opinion.

entendidamente, *adv.* knowingly.

entendido, -da, *a.* able; instructed; prudent, knowing; *darse por entendido,* to take a hint; to take notice; to acknowledge a compliment or attention; *no darse por entendido,* to ignore. — *p.p.* [ENTENDER].

entendimiento, *n.m.* understanding, comprehension; mind, intellect; *de entendimiento,* very intelligent.

entenebrecer, *v.t.* to darken, obscure.

enterado, -da, *a.* informed. — *p.p.* [ENTERAR].

enteramente, *adv.* completely, fully, entirely; quite.

enterar, *v.t.* to report, inform, acquaint, advise, instruct, give intelligence; *(Arg., Chi.)* to adjust an account; *(Cub., CR., Hond., Mex.)* to pay, hand over money.

enterciar, *v.t. (Cub., Mex.)* to pack tobacco, etc., in bundles of 46 kilos.

entereza, *n.f.* entireness, entirety, completeness; rightness, integrity, rectitude, perfection; presence of mind; firmness, fortitude; haughtiness; *entereza virginal*, virginity.

entérico, -ca, *a.* enteric.

enterísimo, -ma, *a. superl.* most complete.

enterizo, -za, *a.* of one piece; whole.

enternecedor, -ra, *a.* touching, pitiful.

enternecer, *v.t.* (*pres. indic.* **enternezco;** *pres. subj.* **enternezca**) to soften, to make tender; to move to compassion. — *v.r.* to be moved to pity; to be affected.

enternecidamente, *adv.* compassionately.

enternecimiento, *n.m.* pity, compassion.

entero, -ra, *a.* entire, complete, whole, un-diminished; sound, perfect; upright, honest, just; robust, strong, vigorous; uncorrupted, pure; constant, firm; uncastrated; (*coll.*) strong, hard-wearing (of cloth); (*arith.*) integral. — *n.m.* (*arith.*) integer; (*Col., CR., Chi., Mex.*) payment, specially to public funds; *por entero*, full, entirely, completely; *caballo entero*, stallion; *números enteros*, whole numbers; *partir por entero*, to divide by com-pound division; (*coll.*) to divide something by taking all for oneself.

enterrador, *n.m.* sexton; grave-digger.

enterramiento, *n.m.* burial, funeral, inter-ment.

enterrar, *v.t.* (*pres. indic.* **entierro;** *pres. subj.* **entierre**) to inter, bury; to survive; (*Chi., Hond., PR.*) to drive in, force in (nails, etc.); *enterrar las vasijas en el lastre*, (*naut.*) to stow the casks in ballast; *enterrarse en vida*, to bury oneself, shun society; to enter a monastic order; *contigo me entierren*, my tastes are the same as yours.

enterronar, *v.t.* to cover with clods.

entesamiento, *n.m.* stretching, making taut.

entesar, *v.t.* to give force, vigour; to extend, stretch, tauten.

entestado, -da, *a.* stubborn, obstinate.

entibación, *n.f.* (*min.*) act and effect of prop-ping; pit-prop.

entibador, *n.m.* (*min.*) one who shores up mines.

entibar, *v.i.* to rest, lean upon. — *v.t.* (*min.*) to prop; to shore up mines.

entibiadero, *n.m.* room or bath for cooling anything.

entibiar, *v.t.* to make lukewarm; to cool; to temper; to moderate the passions. — *v.r.* to slacken, relax, languish; to cool down.

entibo, *n.m.* (*min.*) prop, stay, shore; founda-tion.

entidad, *n.f.* entity; value, moment, conse-quence, import, importance.

entiendo; entienda, *pres. indic.; pres. subj.* [ENTENDER].

entierro, *n.m.* funeral, burial, interment; grave, tomb, sepulchre; *Santo Entierro*, procession on Good Friday.

entierro; entierre, *pres. indic.; pres. subj.* [ENTERRAR].

entigrecerse, *v.r.* to become furious as a tiger.

entinar, *v.t.* to put in the dyeing-vat.

entintar, *v.t.* to stain with ink; to ink, ink in (a drawing, etc.); to tinge, dye.

entiznar, *v.t.* to stain; to defame.

entoldado, -da, *p.p.* [ENTOLDAR]. — *n.m.* tent; group of tents; covering with an awn-ing.

entoldamiento, *n.m.* covering with awnings.

entoldar, *v.t.* to adorn with hangings; to cover with an awning. — *v.r.* to swell with pride, to dress pompously or gorgeously; to grow cloudy or overcast.

entomizar, *v.t.* to tie bass cords around boards or laths so that the plaster may stick to them.

entomología, *n.f.* entomology.

entomológico, -ca, *a.* entomological.

entomólogo, *n.m.* entomologist.

entonación, *n.f.* intonation; modulation (of the voice); blowing the bellows of an organ; (*fig.*) pride, haughtiness, presumption.

entonadera, *n.f.* blow-lever of an organ.

entonado, -da, *a.* haughty, puffed with pride. — *p.p.* [ENTONAR]. — *n.m.* (*phot.*) process of toning.

entonador, -ra, *a.* singing in tune; (*phot.*) toning. — *n.m.f.* one who sings in tune; (*phot.*) one who or that which tones. — *n.m.* organ-blower.

entonamiento, *n.m.* intonation; arrogance, haughtiness.

entonar, *v.i.* to sing in tune. — *v.t.* to tune; to intone; to intonate; to tone prints; to strengthen the system; to blow the bellows of an organ; to harmonize colours. — *v.r.* to assume grand airs, look big.

entonatorio, *n.m.* book of sacred music.

entonces, *adv.* then; *en aquel entonces*, at that time, on that occasion.

entonelar, *v.t.* to barrel, put in casks or barrels.

entono, *n.m.* act of intoning; arrogance, haughtiness, pride.

entontecer, *v.t.* (*pres. indic.* **entontezco;** *pres. subj.* **entontezca**) to make foolish; to con-fuse. — *v.i., v.r.* to grow foolish, get stupid.

entontecimiento, *n.m.* act of becoming foolish or stupid; state of foolishness.

entorchado, *n.m.* twisted silk or gold or silver cord in embroideries; gold embroidery on the uniform of Spanish generals; bullion fringe. — *pl.* bass-strings.

entorchar, *v.t.* to make a torch by twisting candles; to make bullion fringe; (*mus.*) to cover a cord with wire.

entorilar, *v.t.* to stall the bull.

entornar, *v.t.* to set a door or window ajar; to half-close the eyes; to tilt, incline.

entornillar, *v.t.* to form a screw or spiral; to thread (as a screw).

entorpecer, *v.t., v.r.* (*pres. indic.* **entorpezco;** *pres. subj.* **entorpezca**) to benumb, to stupefy, to render torpid; to disturb, inter-rupt, obstruct, clog, delay.

entorpecimiento, *n.m.* stupefaction, numb-ness, torpor; delay, obstruction; stupidity, dullness.

entortadura, *n.f.* crookedness.

entortar, *v.t.* to make crooked, to bend; to pull out one eye.

entosigar, *v.t.* to poison.

entozoario, *n.m.* entozoan, internal parasite.

entrabar, *v.t.* (*prov., Col.*) to hinder, obstruct.

entrada, *n.f.* door, entrance, gate; entry, admission, admission ticket; avenue, drive; number of people in a theatre; intimacy, familiar access; beginning (of a book, speech, etc.); good hand at cards; commencement (of a season, etc.); entrée (course at dinner); (*naut.*) leak; (*min.*) shift; (*com.*) entry (in a book); cash receipts; capital invested in an

undertaking. — *derechos de entrada*, import
duty; *entrada de pavana*, (*coll.*) silly or tactless remark said in all gravity; *entrada llena*,
house full (of a theatre); *de primera entrada*,
at the first impulse; *entradas y salidas*, collusion; rights of entry. —*pl.* temples of the head.
entradero, *n.m.* (*prov.*) narrow entrance.
entrado, -da, *p.p.* [ENTRAR]; *entrado en años*,
advanced in years.
entrador, -ra, *a.* (*CR., Ven., Mex.*) fearless in
business, etc.; (*Chi.*) intrusive, interfering.
entramado, *n.m.* (*carp.*) framework.
entramar, *v.t.* to make framework.
entrambos, -bas, *a.pl.* both [AMBOS].
entrampar, *v.t.* to ensnare, entrap; to deceive,
trick, impose upon; (*coll.*) to entangle a business; encumber with debts. — *v.r.* (*coll.*) to
become indebted; (*fig.*) to be involved in
difficulties.
entrante, *a.* entering; coming; *el mes entrante*, next month; *ángulo entrante*, (*fort.*)
re-entering angle.
entraña, *n.f.* entrail; (*fig.*) heart, kindness,
affection; idiosyncrasy; (*coll.*) disposition;
(*fig.*) the inmost recess of anything; centre of
a city, heart of a country; *hacer las entrañas
a una criatura*, to give a child its first milk;
hacer las entrañas a uno, to influence someone
in his likes and dislikes; *hombre de buenas
entrañas*, good-natured man; *no tener
entrañas*, to be cruel; *entrañas mías*, my dear,
my love; *dar (hasta) las entrañas*, to give one's
very heart's blood; *esto me llega a las
entrañas*, that goes to my heart; *echar las
entrañas*, to be violently sick; *entrañas y
arquetas, a los amigos abiertas*, no secrets
between friends.
entrañable, *a.* most affectionate; deep, profound (affection, etc.).
entrañablemente, *adv.* deeply, dearly.
entrañar, *v.t.* to contain, carry within; to
penetrate to the core, know profoundly. —
v.r. to become intimate and familiar with.
entrañizar, *v.t.* (*obs.*) to love, be passionately
fond of.
entraño, -ña, *a.* (*obs.*) internal, interior.
entrapada, *n.f.* coarse crimson cloth.
entrapajar, *v.t.* to bandage with rags.
entrapar, *v.t.* (*obs.*) to powder the hair for a dry
shampoo; to manure with rags. — *v.r.* to
become filthy, clogged or matted, to be
covered with dust.
entrar, *v.i.* (with *a, en, por*) to go in or into,
enter, march in, come in; to flow into; to
attack; to be admitted one of, be counted
among; to be admitted in, to have free
access to; to join; to begin; to be credible or
understandable; to be overcome by fear,
etc.; to enter into an agreement; to attack;
to influence, convince. — *v.t.* to introduce,
put in; to invade, enter by force; to exercise
influence on, to win a trick at cards; to enroll
in a register; to make an entry in a book; to
advance a step in fencing; (*naut.*) to gain
upon a ship. — *v.r.* to enter, introduce
oneself into some place; to enter by stealth
or cunning, to break in; *entrar a* or *en*, to
begin; *a Juan no hay por donde entrarle*, one
cannot bring influence to bear on John;
entrar en un negocio, en una disputa or *casa*,
to go in or into, enter, march in, come in; *ni
entrar ni salir en una cosa*, to have nothing to

do with a matter; *entrar dentro de sí* or *en sí
mismo*, to think seriously over one's conduct;
entrar bien, to get on well; *entrar a servir*, to
enter a house as servant; *entró como Pedro
en su casa*, he came in as if the place belonged
to him; *entrar por fuerza*, to take forcible
possession of; *entrar en edad*, to be getting
on in years; *entrar de por medio*, to settle a
fray, to reconcile disputants; *entrar en
recelo*, to begin to suspect; *ahora entro yo*,
now *my* turn comes; *entrar a uno*, to prevail
upon someone; to show someone in; *entrar
en juego*, to come into play; *entrar la comida*,
to serve dinner; *entrar bien una cosa*, to come
opportunely; *entrar uno bien* or *mal en una
cosa*, to agree or not agree with what someone says or proposes; *no entrarle a uno una
cosa*, not to approve of something; to be
incapable of learning something; *entrarse
por un libro*, to be absorbed in a book.
entrazado, -da, *a.* (*Arg., Chi.*); *bien* or *mal
entrazado*, of good or bad disposition or
figure.
entre, *prep.* among, amongst, between,
amidst; *entre año*, in the course of the year;
entre dos y tres, between two and three;
entre dos luces, at dusk; *entre dos aguas*, in
a fix; wavering, irresolute; *entre que*, while;
entre hombres, among men; *estaba entre
niños*, he was amongst children; *entre tanto*,
in the interim, meanwhile; *entre manos*, in
hand; *traer una cosa entre manos*, to take
something in hand; *entre mí*, within myself;
entre bastidores, (lit. off stage) between ourselves; *entre bobos anda el juego*, it is in
capable hands; *entre duerme y vela*, between
sleeping and waking.
entreabierto, -ta, *a.* half-opened, ajar. — *p.p.
irreg.* [ENTREABRIR].
entreabrir, *v.t.* (*p.p. irreg.* **entreabierto**) to
half-open a door, to set it ajar.
entreacto, *n.m.* intermission, entr'acte; small
cigar.
entreancho, -cha, *a.* neither wide nor narrow.
entrecalle, *n.m.* (*arch.*) space or groove
between two mouldings.
entrecanal, *n.f.* (*arch.*) fillet between flutes.
entrecano, -na, *a.* greyish (of the hair).
entrecasco, *n.m.* [ENTRECORTEZA].
entrecava, *n.f.* very shallow digging.
entrecavar, *v.t.* to make a shallow excavation.
entrecejo, *n.m.* space between the eyebrows;
(*fig.*) frown, frowning.
entrecerca, *n.f.* space between enclosures.
entrecerrar, *v.t.* (*CR., Mex., ES.*) to set
ajar (door, window, etc.).
entreclaro, -ra, *a.* clear to a limited extent.
entrecogedura, *n.f.* act of catching.
entrecoger, *v.t.* to catch, to intercept; to
compel by arguments or threats.
entrecoro, *n.m.* chancel.
entrecortado, -da, *a.* intermittent, faltering
(sound or voice). — *p.p.* [ENTRECORTAR].
entrecortadura, *n.f.* a cut that does not sever.
entrecortar, *v.t.* to cut a thing without dividing it.
entrecorteza, *n.f.;* **entrecasco**, *n.m.* imperfection in timbers.
entrecriarse, *v.r.* to be reared among others
(of plants).
entrecruzar(se), *v.t.* to intercross; to interweave.

entrecubiertas, *n.f.pl.* (*naut.*) between decks.

entrecuesto, *n.m.* backbone.

entrechocarse, *v.r.* to collide with one another.

entredecir, *v.t.* (*obs.*) to interdict, prohibit.

entredicho, -cha, *p.p.* [ENTREDECIR]. — *n.m.* prohibition; (*eccles.*) interdict.

entredoble, *a.* of medium thickness.

entredós, *n.m.* (*sew.*) insertion; small wardrobe; (*print.*) long primer.

entrefino, -na, *a.* middling fine.

entrega, *n.f.* delivery, conveyance; fascicle, serial division of a book; (*mil.*) surrender.

entregadero, -ra, *a.* (*com.*) deliverable.

entregador, -ra, *a.* delivering. — *n.m.f.* deliverer; executor.

entregamiento, *n.m.* delivery.

entregar, *v.t.* (*pret.* **entregué;** *pres. subj.* **entregue**) to give up, deliver, hand over; (*com.*) to pay, transfer; (*arch.*) to introduce, insert, embed; *entregarla,* (*coll.*) to die; *a entregar,* (*com.*) to be supplied or delivered. — *v.r.* to give oneself up, surrender, submit; *entregarse a,* to abandon oneself to, or to devote oneself wholly to something; *entregarse a discreción,* (*mil.*) to surrender unconditionally; *entregarse de,* to receive, to take charge or possession of; *entregarse en brazos de uno,* to trust completely to someone.

entrejuntar, *v.t.* to join the panels of a door, etc. to the frame.

entrelazar, *v.t.* (conjugated like LAZAR) to interlace, interweave, braid, entwine.

entreliño, *n.m.* space between rows of trees, especially vines or olives.

entrelistado, -da, *a.* striped, variegated.

entrelucir, *v.i.* (*pres. indic.* **entreluzco;** *pres. subj.* **entreluzca**) to show through, glimmer, shine faintly.

entremedias, *adv.* in the meantime; betwixt, half-way; *entremedias de,* between, among.

entremés, *n.m.* (*theat.*) interlude, farce, entertainment; interval; (*us. pl.*) hors-d'œuvres.

entremesear, *v.t.* to act a part in a farce or interlude; to introduce jokes, etc. into a speech.

entremesista, *n.m.f.* writer of or player in farces or interludes.

entremeter, *v.t.* to insert, to place between; to change a child's napkins. — *v.r.* to obtrude, intrude; to meddle, intermeddle, interpose officiously; *entremeterse uno en una cosa* (*obs.*), to undertake something.

entremetido, -da, *a.* meddlesome, intrusive, officious. — *n.m.f.* meddler, intruder, intermeddler; busybody; go-between. — *p.p.* [ENTREMETER].

entremetimiento, *n.m.* intermeddling, intrusion, meddlesomeness, interposition.

entremezcladura, *n.f.* intermixture.

entremezclar, *v.t.* to intermingle, intermix, interweave.

entremiche, *n.m.* capstan, chock; bowsprit.

entremiso, *n.m.* long bench for cheesemaking.

entremorir, *v.i.* to flicker; to be dying away by degrees, to be nearly extinguished.

entrenador, -ra, *a.* training. — *n.m.* trainer.

entrenar, *v.t.*, *v.i.* to train (for sport, etc.).

entrencar, *v.t.* to put sections in a beehive.

entrenzar, *v.t.* to plait hair.

entreoír, *v.t.* (conjugated like OÍR) to hear indistinctly.

entreordinario, -ria, *a.* middling, between good and bad.

entrepalmadura, *n.f.* disease in hoofs of horses and mules.

entrepanes, *n.m.pl.* pieces of unsown ground between sown patches.

entrepañado, -da, *a.* composed of panels of doors.

entrepaño, *n.m.* space between pilasters, bay; pier; panel, shelf.

entreparecerse, *v.r.* to be transparent, to show through.

entrepaso, *n.m.* rack pace (horses).

entrepechuga, *n.f.* flesh within the wish-bone of birds.

entrepeines, *n.m.pl.* comb-wool.

entrepelado, -da, *a.* (*vet.*) pied; (*Arg., vet.*) variegated. — *p.p.* [ENTREPELAR].

entrepelar, *v.i.* to be of mixed colours (of horses).

entrepernar, *v.i.* to put the legs between those of others.

entrepiernas, *n.f.pl.* inner surface of the thighs; piece put into the fork of a pair of breeches; (*Chi.*) trunks (bathing-suit).

entrepiso, *n.m.* (*min.*) space between galleries.

entreponer, *v.t.* (conjugated like PONER) to interpose.

entrepretado, -da, *a.* with an injured breast or shoulder (of horses).

entrepuentes, *n.m.pl.* (*naut.*) between decks.

entrepunzadura, *n.f.* pricking pain of a tumour.

entrepunzar, *v.t.* to prick slightly.

entrerrenglón, *n.m.* interlineation.

entrerrenglonadura, *n.f.* interlineation, anything written between lines; interlineal note.

entrerrenglonar, *v.t.* to interline.

entresaca; entresacadura, *n.f.* thinning out (plants, trees); thinning out (hair).

entresacar, *v.t.* to pick or choose; to cull, sift, part; (*agric.*) to make a clearing; to thin out.

entresijo, *n.m.* mesentery; (*fig.*) anything occult, hidden; *tener muchos entresijos,* to be very difficult or complicated; (*fig.*) to be very cautious in one's dealings.

entresuelo, *n.m.* entresol, mezzanine.

entresurco, *n.m.* space between furrows.

entretalla; entretalladura, *n.f.* bas-relief.

entretallar, *v.t.* to carve in bas-relief; to cut, engrave; to make open-work on any material; to intercept. — *v.r.* to join.

entretanto, *adv.* meanwhile.

entretecho, *n.m.* (*Chi.*) attic, loft, garret.

entretejedor, -ra, *a.* interweaving.

entretejedura, *n.f.* intertexture.

entretejer, *v.t.* to intertwine, intermix, interweave; to variegate; to mix, mingle, insert.

entretejimiento, *n.m.* intertexture; interweaving; variegation.

entretela, *n.f.* (*sew.*) interlining; buckram.

entretelar, *v.t.* to insert an interlining, put buckram between lining and cloth.

entretención, *n.f.* (*Am.*) amusement, sport, pastime.

entretenedor, -ra, *a.* entertaining. — *n.m.f.* entertainer.

entretener, *v.t.* (conjugated like TENER) to amuse, please, divert, entertain; to keep in hope or expectation; to trifle with; to put off, protract, delay, postpone; to make less troublesome, allay pain. — *v.r.* to amuse oneself.

entretenida; *dar* (*con*) *la entretenida*, to give excuses, dismiss with vain promises.

entretenido, -da, *a.* pleasant, entertaining, amusing. — *n.m.* (*obs.*) aspirant to an office. — *p.p.* [ENTRETENER].

entretenimiento, *n.m.* sport, amusement, game, pastime, entertainment; delay, procrastination; (*obs.*) pay, allowance.

entretiempo, *n.m.* spring or autumn.

entreuntar, *v.t.* to anoint slightly.

entrevenarse, *v.r.* to diffuse through the veins.

entreventana, *n.f.* window-pier, wall space between windows.

entrever, *v.t.* (conjugated like VER) to see imperfectly, catch a glimpse of; to conjecture, suspect, guess.

entreverado, -da, *a.* intermingled, intermixed; interlined with fat and lean (of meat); (*Ven.*) dish of chitterlings of lamb and kid seasoned with salt and vinegar. — *p.p.* [ENTREVERAR].

entreverar, *v.t.* to intermix, intermingle. — *v.r.* (*Arg.*) inordinate mixture; (*Arg.*) hand to hand fight by cavalry troops.

entrevía, *n.f.* rail gauge.

entrevista, *n.f.* meeting, conference, interview.

entrevistar, *v.t., v.r.* to interview.

entreyacer, *v.i.* (*obs.*) to be in the middle.

entricado, -da, *a.* (*obs.*) perplexed, confused.

entricar, *v.t.* (*obs.*) to entangle.

entripado, -da, *a.* intestinal; contained in the intestines; ungutted (of a dead animal). — *n.m.* (*coll.*) dissembled anger or displeasure.

entristecer, *v.t.* (*pres. indic.* **entristezco;** *pres. subj.* **entristezca**) to grieve, sadden, afflict, make melancholy. — *v.r.* to grieve, grow sad.

entristecimiento, *n.m.* gloominess, sadness; fretting, mournfulness, dejection.

entrojar, *v.t.* to garner grain.

entrometer, *v.t.* [ENTREMETER].

entrometimiento, *n.m.* intermeddling; intrusion, meddlesomeness.

entronar, *v.t.* to enthrone.

entroncar, *v.i., v.r.* to be descended from the same stock; to be related to, have connexion with; (*Cub., Mex., PR.*) (*railw.*) to make a junction.

entronerar, *v.t.* to pocket a ball in billiards.

entronización, *n.f.* enthronement.

entronizar, *v.t.* (*pret.* **entronicé;** *pres. subj.* **entronice**) to enthrone, place on the throne; to exalt, raise to a distinguished rank or station. — *v.r.* to be elated or puffed up with pride.

entronque, *n.m.* cognation, blood-relationship; connexion; (*Cub., PR.*) railway junction.

entruchada, *n.f.;* **entruchado,** *n.m.* (*coll.*) plot, intrigue, underhand business.

entruchar, *v.t.* (*coll.*) to decoy, lure, entice.

entruchón, -ona, *n.m.f.* decoyer, plotter, schemer.

entrujar, *v.t.* to store up olives; (*coll.*) to put or keep in a purse.

entuerto, *n.m.* injustice, wrong, injury. — *pl.* after-pains.

entullecer, *v.t.* (*pres. indic.* **entullezco;** *pres. subj.* **entullezca**) to check, stop, paralyse. — *v.i.* to be crippled or maimed.

entumecer, *v.t.* (*pres. indic.* **entumezco;** *pres. subj.* **entumezca**) to benumb. — *v.r.* to swell, surge, rise high (of the sea).

entumecimiento, *n.m.* numbness, deadness, torpor; swelling.

entumirse, *v.r.* to become numb, torpid.

entunicar, *v.t.* to clothe with a tunic; to plaster a wall for fresco painting.

entupir, *v.t.* to tighten, compress, press; to block up, obstruct.

enturbiar, *v.t.* to make muddy or turbid; (*fig.*) to confound, obscure; to muddle; to derange. — *v.r.* to become muddy (of water); to get disordered or deranged.

entusiasmado, -da, *a.* enthusiastic, enthusiastical. — *p.p.* [ENTUSIASMAR].

entusiasmar, *v.t.* to enrapture, transport, make enthusiastic. — *v.r.* to become enthusiastic, to be enraptured.

entusiasmo, *n.m.* enthusiasm.

entusiasta, *a.* feeling enthusiastic; liable to enthusiasm. — *n.m.f.* enthusiast.

entusiástico, -ca, *a.* enthusiastic.

énula campana, *n.f.* (*bot.*) elecampane.

enumerable, *a.* numerable, enumerable.

enumeración, *n.f.* enumeration.

enumerar, *v.t.* to enumerate.

enunciación, *n.f.* enunciation, declaration.

enunciado, -da, *a.* that which is enunciated. — *n.m.* enunciation. — *p.p.* [ENUNCIAR].

enunciar, *v.t.* to enunciate, state.

enunciativo, -va, *a.* enunciative.

envainador, -ra, *a.* sheathing.

envainar, *v.t.* to sheathe (a sword, etc.).

envalentonamiento, *n.m.* emboldening.

envalentonar, *v.t.* to inspirit, make bold. — *v.r.* to turn bold, brag, strut.

envalijar, *v.t.* to pack in a portmanteau.

envanecer, *v.t.* (*pres. indic.* **envanezco;** *pres. subj.* **envanezca**) to make proud or vain. — *v.r.* to become conceited, proud, haughty or vain.

envanecimiento, *n.m.* conceit.

envarado, -da, *a.* stiff, deadened, benumbed. — *p.p.* [ENVARAR].

envaramiento, *n.m.* deadness, stiffness, numbness.

envarar, *v.t.* to benumb, stiffen, make torpid.

envaronar, *v.i.* to grow up strong, robust.

envasador, *n.m.* filler, packer; funnel.

envasar, *v.t.* to fill a vessel; to put into any container; to barrel, cask, bottle; to sack grain; (*fig.*) to drink liquor to excess; (*fig.*) to run through the body (with sword, etc.).

envase, *n.m.* bottling, filling; cask or vessel containing a liquid; (*com.*) packing.

envedijarse, *v.r.* to get entangled; (*coll.*) to quarrel, get into a scrimmage.

envegarse, *v.r.* (*Chi.*) to become a swamp.

envejecer, *v.t.* (*pres. indic.* **envejezco;** *pres. subj.* **envejezca**) to make old; to make to look old. — *v.i.* to grow old. — *v.r.* to become old or old-fashioned; to go out of use; to hold out a long time.

envejecido, -da, *a.* grown old; old-looking; old-fashioned; accustomed, habituated. — *p.p.* [ENVEJECER].

envejecimiento, *n.m.* age, oldness; ageing.

envenenador, -ra, *a.* poisonous. — *n.m.f.* poisoner.

envenenamiento, *n.m.* poisoning.

envenenar, *v.t.* to poison, envenom; (*fig.*) to put a bad interpretation on another's words or actions.

enverar, *v.i.* to look ripe.

enverdecer, *v.i.*, *v.r.* (*pres. indic.* **enverdezco;** *pres. subj.* **enverdezca**) to become green.

envergadura, *n.f.* wing-spread, wing-span (of birds); breadth of the sail along the yard; (*aer.*) wing-span, span.

envergar, *v.t.* to bend the sails.

envergues, *n.m.pl.* rope-bands.

envero, *n.m.* colour of ripe grapes, etc.

envés, *n.m.* back, shoulders; wrong side of anything, as cloth, etc.

envesado, *n.m.* fleshy part of hides.

envestidura, *n.f.* investiture (in an office, etc.).

envestir, *v.t.* (conjugated like VESTIR) to invest. — *v.r.* to introduce oneself.

enviada, *n.f.* consignment, shipment.

enviadizo, -za, *a.* missive.

enviado, -da, *p.p.* [ENVIAR]. — *n.m.* messenger; envoy; *enviado extraordinario,* envoy extraordinary.

enviador, -ra, *a.* sending. — *n.m.f.* sender.

enviajado, -da, *a.* (*arch.*) oblique, sloped.

enviar, *v.t.* to send, remit, dispatch; to transmit, forward, convey; *enviar a escardar,* to dismiss contemptuously or abruptly; *enviar a pasear* or *a paseo,* (*coll.*) to send anyone about his business; to dismiss contemptuously; *enviar a uno noramala,* (*coll.*) to send someone to the devil.

enviciar, *v.t.* to corrupt, make vicious, vitiate. — *v.i.* (*bot.*) to have luxurious foliage and little fruit. — *v.r.* (with *en*) to acquire bad habits; to acquire a habit.

envidador, *n.m.* challenger at cards.

envidar, *v.t.* to start bidding at cards.

envidia, *n.f.* envy; emulation; *comerse de envidia,* to be eaten up with jealousy.

envidiable, *a.* enviable.

envidiar, *v.t.* to envy, covet.

envidiosamente, *adv.* enviously.

envidioso, -sa, *a.* envious, jealous; invidious.

envilecedor, -ra, *a.* degrading, debasing.

envilecer, *v.t.* (*pres. indic.* **envilezco;** *pres. subj.* **envilezca**) to vilify, debase. — *v.r.* to degrade oneself.

envilecimiento, *n.m.* vilification, debasement.

envinado, -da, *a.* having the taste of (*or* for) wine.

envinagrar, *v.t.* to put vinegar into anything.

envinar, *v.t.* to mix wine with water.

envío, *n.m.* (*com.*) remittance; consignment of goods, shipment.

envión, *n.m.* push, shove.

envirotado, -da, *a.* full of airs, stuck-up.

enviscamiento, *n.m.* daubing with bird-lime; act of gluing.

enviscar, *v.t.* (*pres. indic.* **envisqué;** *pres. subj.* **envisque**) to daub with bird-lime; to glue; to incite, urge on; to irritate, anger. — *v.r.* to become stuck with bird-lime.

envisto; envista, *pres. indic.; pres. subj.* [ENVESTIR].

envite, *n.m.* stake at cards; invitation, polite offer; push, shove; *ahorrar* or *acortar envites,* to shorten discussion; *al primer*

envite, in the first place, at the start; at once, right off.

enviudar, *v.i.* to become a widower or widow.

envoltorio, *n.m.* bundle; fault, defective woof (in cloth).

envoltura, *n.f.* covering, wrapper, envelope.— *pl.* swaddling-clothes.

envolvedero; envolvedor, *n.m.* wrapper, envelope, cover, wrapping.

envolver, *v.t.* (*p.p.* **envuelto;** *pres. indic.* **envuelvo;** *pres. subj.* **envuelva**) to make up in a packet, bundle, envelop; to enwrap, lap or wrap round, wrap up; to muffle, swaddle; to convince by reasoning, floor an opponent in an argument; to imply, mean; to contain, embody; (*mil.*) to outflank, surround, envelop. — *v.r.* to be implicated in an affair; to be mixed with a crowd; to become entangled with women, live in concubinage.

envolvimiento, *n.m.* envelopment; wrapping.

envuelto, -ta, *a.* wrapped. — *n.m.* (*Mex.*) omelette made from maize. — *p.p. irreg.* [ENVOLVER].

enyerbarse, *v.r.* (*Am.*) to be overgrown with grass; (*Mex.*) to be poisoned.

enyesado, *n.m.* plaster-work.

enyesadura, *n.f.* plastering.

enyesar, *v.t.* to plaster; to chalk; to whitewash; to strengthen wine by adding gypsum.

enyugar, *v.t.* to yolk.

enzainarse, *v.r.* to look sideways, askance; (*coll.*) to become treacherous, false.

enzamarrado, -da, *a.* having a shepherd's jacket of undressed sheep-skin.

enzarzado, -da, *a.* tangled, matted (hair). — *p.p.* [ENZARZAR]. — *n.f.* (*obs., mil.*) strong entrenchment camouflaged with thornbushes.

enzarzar, *v.t.* to throw among brambles; to sow discord; to put branches for silkworms. — *v.r.* to be entangled among brambles; to squabble, wrangle; to become involved in difficulties.

enzootia, *n.f.* enzootic.

enzunchar, *v.t.* to bind with iron bands.

enzurdecer, *v.i.*, *v.r.* (*fam.*) to become left-handed.

enzurronar, *v.t.* to bag; (*coll.*) to enclose.

eñe, *n.f.* Spanish name of the letter Ñ.

eoceno, -na, *n.m.f.*, *a.* eocene.

¡epa! *int.* (*Hond., Mex., Ven.*) hello! (*naut.*) ahoy! (*Chi.*) hoy!

epactilla, *n.f.* ecclesiastical (devotional) calendar.

eperlano, *n.m.* (*ichth.*) smelt.

épica, *n.f.* epic poetry.

epicarpio, *n.m.* (*bot.*) epicarp.

epicedio, *n.m.* epicedium, elegy.

epiceno, -na, *a.* epicene.

epicentro, *n.m.* epicentre.

epicíclico, -ca, *a.* (*astron.*) epicyclic.

epiciclo, *n.m.* (*astron.*) epicycle.

epicicloide, *n.f.* (*geom.*) epicycloid.

épico, -ca, *a.* epic, heroic, narrative; *poema épico,* epopee.

epicráneo, *n.m.* epicranium.

epicureísmo, *n.m.* epicurism, epicureanism.

epicúreo, -rea, *a.* epicurean.

epidemia, *n.f.* epidemic.

epidemial; epidémico, -ca, *a.* epidemical, epidemic.

epidérmico, -ca, *a.* epidermic.

epidermis, *n.f.* epidermis, scarf-skin, cuticle;

tener la epidermis fina or *sensible,* to be ticklish; (*fig.*) to be touchy, peevish.

epidota, *n.f.;* **epidoto,** *n.m.* (*min.*) epidote.

epifanía, *n.f.* Epiphany; Twelfth Night.

epífisis, *n.f.* (*anat.*) epiphysis.

epifito, -ta, *a.* (*bot.*) epiphytic. — *n.f.* epiphyte.

epigástrico, -ca, *a.* epigastric.

epigastrio, *n.m.* epigastrium.

epiglotis, *n.f.* epiglottis.

epígrafe, *n.m.* epigraph, summary; title, heading, inscription; motto.

epigrafía, *n.f.* epigraphy.

epigráfico, -ca, *a.* epigraphic.

epigrafista, *n.m.f.* epigrapher.

epigrama, *n.m.f.* epigram; witticism; inscription.

epigramatario, -ria, *a.* epigrammatic.

epigramáticamente, *adv.* epigrammatically.

epigramático, -ca, *a.* epigrammatic.

epigramatista; epigramista, *n.m.* epigrammatist.

epilepsia, *n.f.* epilepsy.

epiléptico, -ca, *a.* epileptic, epileptical. — *n.m.f.* epileptic.

epilogación, *n.f.* [EPILOGO].

epilogal, *a.* compendious, summary.

epilogar, *v.t.* (*pret.* **epilogué;** *pres. subj.* **epilogue**) to recapitulate, sum up.

epilogismo, *n.m.* (*astron.*) epilogism, computation.

epílogo, *n.m.* epilogue, summing up; recapitulation.

epinicio, *n.m.* epinicion, triumphal ode.

epiplon, *n.m.* (*anat.*) omentum.

epiqueya, *n.f.* equitable interpretation of the law.

episcopado, *n.m.* bishopric, episcopate; episcopacy.

episcopal, *a.* episcopal.

episcopalismo, *n.m.* episcopalianism.

episcopologio, *n.m.* chronological list of bishops.

episódico, -ca, *a.* episodic, episodical.

episodio, *n.m.* episode, incidental narrative; digression.

epispástico, -ca, *a.* epispastic, blistering.

epistaxis, *n.f.* (*med.*) epistaxis, nosebleeding.

epístola, *n.f.* epistle, letter, poetic epistle; sub-diaconate.

epistolar, *a.* epistolary.

epistolario, *n.m.* epistolary; volume of letters.

epistolero, *n.m.* sub-deacon who sings the Epistle at Mass.

epístrofe, *n.f.* epistrophe.

epitafio, *n.m.* epitaph, epigraph.

epitalámico, -ca, *a.* epithalamic.

epitalamio, *n.m.* epithalamium, nuptial song.

epítema; epítima, *n.f.* (*med.*) epithem, lotion.

epíteto, *n.m.* (*gram.*) epithet.

epitimar, *v.t.* (*med.*) to apply an epithem to.

epítimo, *n.m.* (*bot.*) lesser dodder.

epitomadamente, *adv.* concisely.

epitomador, -ra, *a.* epitomizing. — *n.m.f.* epitomizer.

epitomar, *v.t.* to epitomize, abstract, summarize.

epítome, *n.m.* epitome, summary, compendium.

epizoario, -ria, *a.* (*zool.*) epizoic, epizoan.

epizootia, *n.f.* (*vet.*) epidemic influenza.

epizoótico, -ca, *a.* epizootic.

época, *n.f.* epoch, age, era; time; *formar* or *hacer época,* to be epoch-making.

epoda; epodo, *n.m.f.* epode.

epónimo, -ma, *a.* eponymous. — *n.m.* eponym.

epopeya, *n.f.* epopee, epic poem.

epsomita, *n.f.* Epsom salts.

epulón, *n.m.* great eater.

equiángulo, -la, *a.* equiangular.

equidad, *n.f.* equity, equitableness, right, honesty, conscientiousness, moderation; justice, impartiality.

equidiferencia, *n.f.* equidifference; arithmetical progression.

equidistancia, *n.f.* equidistance.

equidistante, *a.* equidistant.

equidistar, *v.i.* to be equidistant.

equidna, *n.m.* echidna.

equilátero, -ra, *a.* equilateral.

equilibrar, *v.t.* to balance, equilibrate; to counterpoise, counterbalance.

equilibre, *a.* balanced.

equilibrio, *n.m.* equilibrium, equipoise, equality of weight, counterbalance, counterpoise, balance; *equilibrio europeo,* European balance of power.

equilibrista, *n.m.* balancer, equilibrist.

equimosis, *n.m.* (*med.*) ecchymosis.

equino, -na, *a.* (*poet.*) equine. — *n.m.* (*zool., arch.*) echinus.

equinoccial, *a.* equinoctial.

equinoccio, *n.m.* equinox.

equinodermo, -ma, *n.m.f., a.* (*zool.*) echinoderm.

equipaje, *n.m.* luggage, baggage; equipment; provisions for a journey; (*naut.*) crew; (*mil.*) baggage-train.

equipal, *n.f.* (*Mex.*) wicker chair with seat and back of leather or woven palm.

equipar, *v.t.* to fit, equip, furnish, accoutre, gird.

equiparable, *a.* comparable, collatable.

equiparación, *n.f.* comparison, collation.

equiparar, *v.t.* to compare, collate.

equipo, *n.m.* act of equipping; (*mil.*) fitting out; accoutrement, equipment, trappings; team (in sporting events).

equipolencia, *n.f.* (*log.*) equipollence, equality of force or power.

equipolente, *a.* equivalent, equipollent.

equiponderante, *a.* equiponderant.

equiponderar, *v.i.* to equiponderate (statics).

equis, *n.f.* Spanish name of the letter X; (*Col., Per.*) small viper with deadly bite; *estar uno hecho una equis,* (*coll.*) to be too drunk to walk straight.

equitación, *n.f.* equitation, horsemanship, riding.

equitativamente, *adv.* equitably.

equitativo, -va, *a.* equitable, fair, reasonable, just.

equivalencia, *n.f.* equivalence, compensation.

equivalente, *a.* tantamount, equivalent; compensatory, compensative.

equivaler, *v.i.* (*pres. indic.* **equivalgo;** *pres. subj.* **equivalga**) to be of equal price or value; to be equivalent.

equivocación, *n.f.* blunder, misconception, misunderstanding, error, mistake.

equivocadamente, *adv.* mistakenly, by mistake.

equivocado, -da, *a.* mistaken. — *p.p.* [EQUI-
VOCAR].

equívocamente, *adv.* equivocally.

equivocar, *v.t.* (*pret.* **equivoqué**; *pres. subj.*
equivoque) to mistake. — *v.r.* to be mistaken; to make a mistake, blunder.

equívoco, -ca, *a.* ambiguous, equivocal. —
n.m. equivocation, quibble, pun.

equivoquista, *n.m.f.* quibbler, punster.

era, *n.f.* epoch, age, time; threshing-floor;
vegetable patch, garden-plot; *era común,
cristiana, vulgar* or *de Cristo,* Christian era;
era española, Cæsarian era beginning 38 B.C.

era, *imperf. ind.* [SER].

eraje, *n.m.* (*prov.*) virgin honey.

eral, *n.m.* two-year-old ox.

erar, *v.t.* to lay out a vegetable garden.

erario, *n.m.* exchequer, public treasury.

erbio, *n.m.* (*chem.*) erbium.

ere, *n.f.* Spanish name of the letter R.

erección, *n.f.* erectness, elevation; erection,
raising; foundation, establishment.

eréctil, *a.* erectile.

erectilidad, *n.f.* erectility.

erector, -ra, *a.* erecting. — *n.m.f.* erector,
founder.

eremita, *n.m.* hermit, recluse.

eremítico, -ca, *a.* solitary.

eremitorio, *n.m.* place with one or more
hermitages.

erg; ergio, *n.m.* erg, unit of energy.

ergástula; ergástulo, *n.m.* ergastulum, prison
for slaves.

ergotina, *n.f.* (*med.*) ergotine.

ergotismo, *n.m.* (*med.*) ergotism; (*phil.*)
sophistry.

ergotista, *a.* debating, arguing. — *n.m.f.*
sophist.

ergotizante, *a.* arguing.

ergotizar, *v.i.* to argue; to make a wrong use
of syllogistic argument.

erguimiento, *n.m.* straightening up.

erguir, *v.t.* (*pres. indic.* **irgo** or **yergo**; *pret.*
(él) **irguió**; *pres. subj.* **irga** or **yerga**; *pres.
part.* **irguiendo**) to raise up straight, erect.
— *v.r.* to straighten up; to stand or sit erect;
to swell with pride.

erial; eriazo, -za, *a.* unploughed, untilled.
— *n.m.* uncultivated land.

erica, *n.f.* heath, heather.

erigir, *v.t.* (*pres. indic.* **erijo**; *pres. subj.*
erija) to erect, raise, build; to found,
establish.

erina, *n.f.* (*surg.*) clip for holding open wound.

eringe, *n.f.* field eringo, sea-holly.

erinita, *n.f.* (*min.*) erinite.

erío, -ría, *a.* unploughed. — *n.m.* untilled land.

erisipela; erisípula, *n.f.* erysipelas.

erisipelar, *v.t., v.r.* to cause erysipelas.

erístico, -ca, *a.* eristic, disputatious.

eritreo, -ea, *n.m.f., a.* (*poet.*) the Red Sea.

erizado, -da, *a.* covered with bristles;
erizado de, bristling with (difficulties, etc.);
covered with, abounding in. — *p.p.* [ERIZAR].

erizamiento, *n.m.* setting on end, as the hair;
bristling up.

erizar, *v.t.* (*pret.* **ericé**; *pres. subj.* **erice**) to
set on end, bristle. — *v.r.* to bristle, stand on
end (the hair).

erizo, *n.m.* (*zool.*) hedgehog; (*bot.*) sea-
thistle; prickly husk of a chestnut, etc.;
(*mech.*) urchin, carding roller; sprocket-

wheel, rag-wheel, spur-toothed wheel; (*fort.*)
iron spikes set on top of a parapet; (*fig.*)
bad-tempered person; *erizo de mar* or
marino, sea-urchin; *al erizo, Dios le hizo,*
there are all sorts in the world.

erizón, *n.m.* kind of thistle.

ermar, *v.t.* (*obs.*) to destroy, lay waste.

ermita, *n.f.* hermitage.

ermitaño, -ña, *n.m.f.* hermit, recluse.

ermitorio, *n.m.* [EREMITORIO].

ermunio, *n.m.* (*obs.*) one exempt from tribute
and services.

erogación, *n.f.* distribution, division.

erogar, *v.t.* (*pret.* **erogué**; *pres. subj.* **erogue**)
to divide, distribute, apportion.

erogatorio, *n.m.* pipe through which liquor is
drawn.

erosión, *n.f.* erosion, wearing away.

erotema, *n.f.* (*rhet.*) interrogation.

eróticamente, *adv.* erotically.

erótico, -ca, *a.* erotical, erotic. — *n.f.* erotic
poetry.

erotismo, *n.m.* eroticism, sensuality.

erotomanía, *n.f.* erotomania, love-madness.

erotomaníaco, -ca, *n.m.f., a.* erotomaniac.

errabundo, -da, *a.* wandering, strolling about.

errada, *n.f.* miscue (in billiards).

erradamente, *adv.* erroneously, falsely, mistakenly.

erradicación, *n.f.* eradication, extirpation.

erradicar, *v.t.* to eradicate.

erradizo, -za, *a.* wandering to and fro.

errado, -da, *a.* erring, mistaken; erroneous.
— *p.p.* [ERRAR].

erraj, *n.m.* fuel made from the stones of olives.

errante, *a.* errant; roving, rambling, wandering; nomadic, excursive.

errar, *v.t.* (*pres. indic.* **yerro**; *pres. subj.*
yerre) to miss (target, etc.); to fail in one's
duty to; to offend. — *v.i.* to wander about
at random, to roam; to err. — *v.i., v.r.* to
be mistaken; to commit an error; *errar el
camino,* to take the wrong road; *después que
te erré, nunca bien te quise,* one generally
hates those one has wronged; *errar y porfiar,*
to persist in evil-doing.

errata, *n.f.* misprint, erratum, typographical
error; *erratas,* or *fe de erratas,* list or table of
errata.

errático, -ca, *a.* wandering, vagrant, vagabond; erratic, erratical.

errátil, *a.* wavering, varying, erratic.

erre, *n.f.* Spanish name of the letter RR;
hacer erres or *tropezar en las erres,* to be
drunk; *erre que erre,* pertinaciously,
obstinately.

erróneamente, *adv.* erroneously, mistakenly,
falsely.

erróneo, -nea, *a.* erroneous, mistaken, not
according to truth.

erronía, *n.f.* opposition, dislike, grudge,
hatred.

error, *n.m.* error, mistake; fault, defect; *error
clásico* or *craso,* gross error.

erso, -sa, *a.* Erse.

erubescencia, *n.f.* erubescence, blush.

eructación, *n.f.* eructation, belching.

eructar, *v.i.* to belch, eructate.

eructo, *n.m.* belching, eructation.

erudición, *n.f.* erudition, learning, knowledge,
letters.

eruditamente, *adv.* learnedly.

erudito, -ta, *a.* erudite, learned, lettered. — *n.m.f.* scholar, erudite person; *erudito a la violeta,* one having only superficial learning.

eruginoso, -sa, *a.* rusty, musty.

erupción, *n.f.* eruption, outbreak, bursting forth; (*med.*) rash, eruption.

eruptivo, -va, *a.* eruptive.

erutación, *n.f.* eructation, belching.

erutar, *v.i.* to eruct, belch [ERUCTAR].

eruto, *n.m.* [ERUTACIÓN].

ervato, *n.m.* sulphur wort.

ervilla, *n.f.* bitter vetch.

esa, *a.* that; **ésa,** *dem. pron.* (*fem.* form of ESE) that one, that person; *ésa es buena,* that's a good one; *ésa no la creo,* I can't believe that; *no venga con ésa,* tell it to the marines.

esbatimentar, *v.t.* (*art*) to delineate a shadow. — *v.i.* to cast a shadow.

esbatimento, *n.m.* (*art*) shadow.

esbeltez; esbelteza *n.f.* tall and elegant stature.

esbelto, -ta, *a.* tall, slim and well-shaped.

esbirro, *n.m.* bailiff, constable; hired ruffian, myrmidon.

esbozar, *v.t.* to sketch.

esbozo, *n.m.* sketch, outline; rough draft.

escabechado, -da, *a.* (*coll.*) having dyed hair or a painted face. — *p.p.* [ESCABECHAR].

escabechar, *v.t.* to pickle, steep, souse; (*fig.*) to dye the hair; (*coll.*) to stab and kill; (*coll.*) to plough in an examination.

escabeche, *n.m.* souse, pickle; pickled fish.

escabechina, *n.f.* ravage, destruction, havoc; (*coll.*) ploughing in an examination.

escabel, *n.m.* foot-stool; small seat; (*fig.*) stepping-stone.

escabiosa, *n.f.* field scabious.

escabioso, -sa, *a.* (*med.*) scabious.

escabro, *n.m.* roughness like mange upon the bark of trees; scab, itch or mange in sheep.

escabrosamente, *adv.* roughly, ruggedly.

escabrosidad, *n.f.* craggedness, cragginess; inequality, unevenness, roughness; hardness, asperity.

escabroso, -sa, *a.* rude, unpolished; cragged, craggy; crabbed, rugged, rough; difficult, risky, scabrous.

escabullimiento, *n.m.* evasion, slipping away.

escabullirse, *v.r.* to escape; to slip or sneak away.

escacado, -da, *a.* (*her.*) checkered.

escafandra, *n.m.* scaphander, diving-dress.

escafilar, *v.t.* to trim a brick or tile.

escafoides, *n.m.,* *a.* scaphoid (bone).

escala, *n.f.* step-ladder, ladder; scale; graduated rule or instrument; seaport, stopping place; (*mus.*) scale; (*mil.*) army list; *a escala vista,* openly; *escala franca,* free port; *escala de comercio,* seaport; *escala de viento,* (*naut.*) rope ladder; *hacer escala en,* to call at a seaport in the course of a voyage.

escalada, *n.f.* (*mil.*) escalade, scaling.

escalado, -da, *a.* cut open (fish, etc.) to be salted or cured. — *p.p.* [ESCALAR].

escalador, -ra, *a.* scaling, climbing. — *n.m.f.* climber, scaler, one who scales walls; (*slang*) cat burglar.

escalafón, *n.m.* army list.

escalamiento, *n.m.* (*mil.*) scaling.

escálamo, *n.m.* thole, thole-pin; rowlock.

escalar, *v.t.* to climb with ladders; to scale; to

enter surreptitiously; to open the sluice of a canal; (*fig.*) to rise by dubious means.

Escalda, *n.f.* Scheldt.

escaldada, *n.f.* (*coll.*) lewd woman, prostitute.

escaldado, -da, *a.* suspicious, cautious, wary. — *p.p.* [ESCALDAR].

escaldadura, *n.f.* scald.

escaldar, *v.t.* to scald, burn; to make red-hot. — *v.r.* to become chafed, made sore.

escaleno, *a.* (*geom.*) scalene.

escalentamiento, *n.m.* (*vet.*) inflammation of the feet.

escalentar, *v.t.* (*obs.*) to heat, warm; to inflame.

escalera, *n.f.* staircase; stair; sides of a cart; *escalera de caracol* or *de husillo,* winding stair; *escalera de mano,* ladder; *escalera de costado* or *escalera real,* (*naut.*) quarter-deck ladder; *escalera de servicio,* service stairs; *escalera excusada* or *falsa,* back stairs; *escalera de tijera* or *escalera doble,* step-ladder; *de escalera abajo,* (*fig.*) below-stairs (applied to servants, dependants, etc.).

escalereja; escalerilla, *n.f.* small ladder; step-ladder [ESCALERA]; (*mech.*) rack; *en escalerilla,* in degrees; applied to things grouped unequally as if in steps.

escalerón, *n.m.* large staircase [ESCALERA].

escaleta, *n.f.* jack for raising wheels of vehicles.

escalfado, -da, *a.* applied to badly plastered walls; poached (eggs). — *p.p.* [ESCALFAR].

escalfador, *n.m.* barber's water-heater; chafing-dish; paint remover (tool).

escalfar, *v.t.* to poach (eggs).

escalfarote, *n.m.* wide boot lined with hay.

escalfeta, *n.f.* small pan for live coals; chafing-dish; dish-heater.

escaliento; escaliente, *pres. indic.; pres. subj.* [ESCALENTAR].

escalinata, *n.f.* (*arch.*) perron, flight of steps.

escalio, *n.m.* waste land being put in cultivation.

escalmo, *n.m.* rowlock.

escalo, *n.m.* sapping a way into or out of a place.

escalofriado, -da, *a.* shivering, chilled.

escalofrío, *n.m.* shiver, chill, shivering; chills (of a fever).

escalón, *n.m.* step of a stair; stepping-stone; degree of dignity, grade; (*mil.*) echelon; *en escalones,* unevenly made or cut.

escalonar, *v.t.* (*mil.*) to form an echelon.

escaloña, *n.f.* shallot, scallion.

escalpar, *v.t.* to scalp.

escalpelo, *n.m.* scalpel, dissecting knife.

escalplo, *n.m.* currier or tanner's knife.

escama, *n.f.* scale; fish-scale; (*fig.*) grudge, resentment, sense of injury.

escamada, *n.f.* embroidery in shape of scales.

escamado, -da, *a.* scaled, scaly. — *n.m.* work wrought with the figure of scales. — *p.p.* [ESCAMAR].

escamadura, *n.f.* scaling (a fish); arousing suspicion; embroidery in shape of scales.

escamar, *v.t.* to scale fish; (*coll.*) to arouse anxiety or suspicion in. — *v.i.* to fashion in shape of scales. — *v.r.* to become uneasy or suspicious.

escamel, *n.m.* sword-maker's anvil.

escamochear, *v.i.* (*prov.*) to breed (bees).

escamocho, *n.m.* remnants of a meal; after-swarm of bees; *no arriendo sus escamochos*, he is very poor.

escamón, -ona, *a.* (*coll.*) suspicious by nature.

escamonda, *n.f.* act of pruning.

escamondadura, *n.f.* pruned branches.

escamondar, *v.t.* to prune or lop trees; to trim or clear a thing from superfluities; to clean, cleanse.

escamondo, *n.m.* pruning or clearing trees.

escamonea, *n.f.* (*bot.*) scammony.

escamoneado, -da, *a.* relating to scammony. — *p.p.* [ESCAMONEARSE].

escamonearse, *v.r.* (*coll.*) to become mistrustful, suspicious; to become offended.

escamoso, -sa *a.* scaly, squamous.

escamotar; escamotear, *v.t.* in jugglery, to palm, make disappear from the hands; to steal dexterously.

escamoteador, -ra, *a.* juggling; swindling. — *n.m.f.* juggler, prestidigitator, conjuror; cheat, swindler.

escamotear, *v.t.* [ESCAMOTAR].

escamoteo, *n.m.* jugglery, sleight of hand; swindling.

escampada, *n.f.* (*coll.*) bright interval (in a rainy day).

escampado, -da, *a.* open, clear. — *p.p.* [ESCAMPAR].

escampar, *v.i.* to stop raining; to clear up (of the sky); to leave off working. — *v.t.* to clear out a place; (*coll.*) *¡ya escampa!* he is forever babbling.

escampavía, *n.f.* (*naut.*) tender; revenue cutter.

escampo, *n.m.* clearing out a place; clearing up (of weather).

escamudo, -da, *a.* full of scales.

escamujar, *v.t.* to prune olive-trees, etc.

escamujo, *n.m.* lopped-off olive branch; time of pruning olive-trees.

escancia, *n.f.* pouring or serving wine.

escanciador, -ra, *a.* serving, pouring (wine). — *n.m.f.* cup-bearer.

escanciar, *v.t.* to serve, pour out wine. — *v.i.* to drink wine.

escanda, *n.f.* spelt-wheat.

escandalar, *n.m.* (*naut.*) compass-room (in a galley).

escandalera, *n.f.* (*coll.*) great hubbub.

escandalizador, -ra, *a.* scandalizing. — *n.m.f.* one who makes scandal.

escandalizar, *v.t.* (*pret.* **escandalicé;** *pres. subj.* **escandalice**) to scandalize. — *v.r.* to be scandalized; to be irritated.

escandalizativo, -va, *a.* scandalous.

escándalo, *n.m.* scandal; licentiousness; tumult, commotion; wonderment, astonishment.

escandalosa, *n.f.* gaff-sail; *echar la escandalosa,* (*coll.*) to make use of harsh words in a dispute.

escandalosamente, *adv.* scandalously, shamefully.

escandaloso, -sa, *a.* scandalous, disgraceful, offensive; shameful; turbulent.

escandallar, *v.t.* (*naut.*) to sound.

escandallo, *n.m.* (*naut.*) deep-sea lead; proof, trial, experiment.

escandecer, *v.t.* to irritate, provoke, put into a passion.

escandelar; escandelarete, *n.m.* (*naut.*) compass-room in a galley.

escandia, *n.f.* Cienfuegos wheat.

Escandinavia, *n.f.* Scandinavia.

escandinavo, -va, *n.m.f.,* *a.* Scandinavian.

escandio, *n.m.* (*chem.*) scandium.

escandir, *v.t.* to scan verses.

escanilla, *n.f.* (*prov.*) cradle.

escanillo, *n.m.* small backed bench [ESCAÑO].

escansión, *n.f.* scansion.

escantillar, *v.t.* (*arch.*) to measure from a point; to gauge; to cut out by templets; to trace lines on walls.

escantillón, *n.m.* gauge, templet, pattern, rule.

escaña, *n.f.* spelt-wheat.

escañero, *n.m.* seat-keeper.

escaño, *n.m.* bench with a back; (*naut.*) sheer-rail.

escañuelo, *n.m.* foot-stool.

escapada, *n.f.;* **escapamiento,** *n.m.* escape, flight; *en una escapada,* at full speed.

escapar, *v.t.* to drive a horse at great speed; to liberate from danger. — *v.i., v.r.* to escape; to flee, to run away; to make one's escape; *escapar en una tabla,* to have a narrow escape; *escapársele a uno una cosa,* not to notice something; *se me escapó el tren,* I just lost the train; *escapársele a uno la mano, la lengua, la risa,* to do or say something or laugh at the wrong moment.

escaparate, *n.m.* cabinet, wardrobe, cupboard, glass-case, press; shop-window.

escaparatico; escaparatillo, *n.m.* little cupboard, cabinet, or wardrobe [ESCAPARATE].

escapatoria, *n.f.* flying, escape, flight; (*coll.*) evasion, excuse, subterfuge.

escape, *n.m.* flight, flying, escape; evasion, subterfuge; escapement (of a watch); (*mech., engin.*) exhaust; *a* (*todo*) *escape,* at full speed, as swiftly as possible.

escapo, *n.m.* (*arch.*) shaft of a column; (*bot.*) stem.

escápula, *n.f.* (*anat.*) scapula, shoulder-blade.

escapular, *a.* (*anat.*) appertaining to the shoulder-blade. — *v.t.* (*naut.*) to double a cape, to clear a sand-bank, etc.

escapulario, *n.m.* scapulary.

escaque, *n.m.* square of a chessboard; (*her.*) quartering of a coat of arms. — *pl.* game of chess.

escaqueado, -da, *a.* checkered, of alternate colours.

escaquear, *v.t.* (*obs.*) to play chess or draughts.

escara, *n.f.* (*surg.*) scab, scar, scurf, slough.

escarabajear, *v.i.* to crawl to and fro like insects; to scribble, scrawl. — *v.t.* (*coll.*) to harass, worry, sting, give pain.

escarabajo, *n.m.* black-beetle; scarab; (*fig.*) short, ill-shaped person; (*fig.*) flaw in a cast. — *pl.* scrawl, badly-formed letters in writing.

escarabajuelo, *n.m.* vine-beetle [ESCARABAJO].

escarabídeo, -dea, *n.m.f., a.* scarabæid.

escaramucear, *v.i.* to skirmish.

escaramujo, *n.m.* dog-rose; hip, fruit of dog-rose; goose-barnacle.

escaramuza, *n.f.* skirmish, slight engagement; dispute, contention, contest, quarrel.

escaramuzador, -ra, *n.m.f.* skirmisher; disputer.

escaramuzar, *v.i.* to skirmish.

escarapela, *n.f.* badge, cockade; dispute ending in blows.

escarapelar, *v.i., v.r.* to wrangle, dispute, quarrel (said of women); (*Col., CR., Ven.*)

to peel, shell, husk; (*Col.*) to rumple; (*Mex., Per.*) to get goose-flesh.

escarbadero, *n.m.* place where boars, wolves, and other animals scratch the ground.

escarbadientes, *n.m.* tooth-pick.

escarbador, -ra, *a.* scraping, scratching. — *n.m.* scraper, scratcher.

escarbadura, *n.f.* scratching, effect of scratching.

escarbaorejas, *n.m.* ear-pick.

escarbar, *v.t.* to scrape or scratch the earth (as fowls); to poke the fire; to dig, dibble; to investigate, to inquire minutely; to use a tooth-pick or an ear-pick.

escarbo, *n.m.* scraping, scratching.

escarcela, *n.f.* game-bag; large pouch; cuisse, armour for the thigh; kind of head-dress for women.

escarceo, *n.m.* choppiness of sea. — *pl.* bounds and curvetting of horses.

escarcina, *n.f.* kind of cutlass.

escarcinazo, *n.m.* blow with a cutlass.

escarcuñar, *v.t.* (*prov.*) to pry into; to search, examine.

escarcha, *n.f.* white frost, rime; frost-work.

escarchada; escarchosa, *n.f.* ice-plant, marigold.

escarchado, -da, *a.* frosted. — *n.m.* gold or silver embroidery; icing upon cakes. — *p.p.* [ESCARCHAR].

escarchador, *n.m.* instrument for frosting cake.

escarchar, *v.i.* to freeze; to frost, be congealed. — *v.t.* to put icing on cakes; to dilute potter's clay.

escarcho, *n.m.* red gurnard.

escarda, *n.f.* weed-hook, grubbing-hoe; weeding.

escardadera, *n.f.* woman weeder; gardener's hoe.

escardador, -ra, *a.* weeding. — *n.m.f.* weeder. — *n.m.* weeding-hook.

escardadura, *n.f.;* **escardamiento,** *n.m.* weeding.

escardar; escardillar, *v.t.* to weed; (*fig.*) to weed out, separate good and bad, root out vice.

escardillo, *n.m.* (*prov.*) small weed-hook; gardener's hoe; thistle-down; *lo ha dicho el escardillo,* a little bird told me.

escariador, *n.m.* reamer; punch used by coppersmiths.

escariar, *v.t.* to ream.

escarificación, *n.f.* (*surg.*) scarification.

escarificador, *n.m.* (*agric.*) scarifier, harrow, cultivator; (*surg.*) scarificator.

escarificar, *v.t.* (*surg., agric.*) to scarify.

escarioso, -sa, *a.* (*bot.*) scarious.

escarizar, *v.t.* to clean a sore by taking away the scurf or scab.

escarlador, *n.m.* tool for polishing combs.

escarlata, *n.f.* red, scarlet; cloth of a scarlet colour; (*med.*) scarlet fever.

escarlatina, *n.f.* (*com.*) red or crimson woollen fabric; (*med.*) scarlet fever.

escarmenador, *n.m.* comb for wool, etc.

escarmenar, *v.t.* to comb wool, silk, etc.; to disentangle; to swindle gradually.

escarmentar, *v.i.* (*pres. indic.* **escarmiento;** *pres. subj.* **escarmiente**) to be tutored by experience; to take warning. — *v.t.* to correct severely; to inflict an exemplary punishment.

escarmiento, *n.m.* warning, caution; chastisement.

escarnecedor, -ra, *a.* scoffing, mocking. — *n.m.f.* scoffer, scorner, jeerer, mocker, giber.

escarnecer, *v.t.* (*pres. indic.* **escarnezco;** *pres. subj.* **escarnezca**) to mock, ridicule, jeer, scoff, gibe, laugh at.

escarnecidamente, *adv.* scornfully.

escarnecimiento, *n.m.* scoffing, derision.

escarnio, *n.m.* gibe, scoff, mock, jeer, ridicule.

escaro, *n.m.* scarus, a Mediterranean fish.

escaro, -ra, *a.* having crooked feet. — *n.m.f.* person with crooked feet.

escarola, *n.f.* endive; ruff, frill.

escarolado, -da, *a.* curled, frilled; shaped like endive. — *p.p.* [ESCAROLAR].

escarolar, *v.t.* to frill, ruffle.

escarolita, *n.f.* small endive.

escarótico, -ca, *a.* (*surg.*) caustic.

escarpa, *n.f.* declivity, bluff, slope, cliff; (*mil.*) scarp.

escarpado, -da, *a.* steep, craggy, sloped, rugged. — *p.p.* [ESCARPAR].

escarpadura, *n.f.* escarpment; bank, cliff, bluff, slope.

escarpar, *v.t.* to rasp works of sculpture; (*mil.*) to escarp, slope down; (*carp.*) to scarf.

escarpe, *n.m.* bluff, declivity; (*arch.*) scarf of a wall; (*carp.*) scarf-joint.

escarpelo, *n.m.* rasp; scalpel.

escarpia, *n.f.* tenter-hook, meat-hook; spike, clamp; *n.pl.* (*slang*) the ears.

escarpiador, *n.m.* clamp, fastener.

escarpiar, *v.t.* (*obs.*) to fasten with clamps.

escarpidor, *n.m.* large-toothed comb.

escarpín, *n.m.* woollen slipper; dancing pump; thin-soled shoe; sock.

escarpión, *adv.; en escarpión,* in the form of a tenter-hook.

escarramanchones, *adv.; a escarramanchones,* (*coll., prov.*) astride.

escarrancharse, *v.r.* (*Cub., Ven., prov.*) to spread the legs wide apart.

escarza, *n.f.* sore in the hoofs of horses.

escarzano, -na, *a.* (*arch.*); *arco escarzano,* arch less than a semicircle.

escarzar, *v.t.* to remove poor or dirty honeycombs from a hive.

escarzo, *n.m.* operation and time of removing honey from a hive; black comb without honey; floss silk; (*prov.*) fungus growing on trees.

escarzo, -za, *a.* (*prov.*) lame on account of sores in the hoof.

escasamente, *adv.* sparingly, scantily; with difficulty, hardly, scarcely.

escasear, *v.t.* to spare, live in a frugal manner; to give sparingly. — *v.i.* to grow less, decrease; to be scarce.

escasez, *n.f.* meanness; scarcity, lack, meagreness; poverty.

escaso, -sa, *a.* small, limited; little; sparing, parsimonious, niggardly; scarce, scanty; *escaso de bienes* or *medios,* anything but wealthy, hard up.

escatimado, -da, *a.* little, scanty. — *p.p.* [ESCATIMAR].

escatimar, *v.t.* to lessen, curtail, clip; to misconstrue (words, etc.).

escatimosamente, *adv.* maliciously, viciously.

escatimoso, -sa, *a.* malicious, cunning.

escatófago, -ga, a. scatophagous.
escatología, n.f. scatology; eschatology.
escatológico, -ca, a. scatologic; eschatological.
escaupil, n.m. (Mex.) padded garment used against arrows; (CR.) game bag.
escavanar, v.t. to loosen and weed the ground with a hoe.
escayola, n.f. stucco parget, scagliola.
escena, n.f. stage; scenery, scene; sight, view; display of passion; (fig.) acting, theatre; incident; estar en escena, to be on the stage (said of an actor); poner en escena, to stage.
escenario, n.m. stage; (cinema) scenario, script.
escénico, -ca, a. scenic, belonging to the stage.
escenita, n.f. short scene [ESCENA].
escenografía, n.f. scenography, art of perspective.
escenográfico, -ca, a. scenographic.
escenógrafo, n.m. scenographer.
escépticamente, adv. sceptically.
escepticismo, n.m. scepticism.
escéptico, -ca, n.m.f., a. sceptic.
esciagrafia, n.f. skiagraphy.
esciagráfico, -ca, a. skiagraphic.
esciágrafo, n.m. skiagraph.
escila, n.f. (bot.) squill; entre Escila y Caribdis, between Scylla and Charybdis.
escinco, n.m. (zool.) skink.
escindir, v.t. to divide, cut, sever, split.
esciolo, n.m. sciolist.
escirro, n.m. scirrhus.
escirroso, -sa, a. scirrhous.
escisión, n.f. division; schism.
escita, n.m.f., a.; escítico, -ca, a. Scythian.
esclarea, n.f. common clary.
esclarecedor, -ra, a. enlightening. — n.m.f. enlightener.
esclarecer, v.t. to illuminate, lighten; to ennoble, make illustrious; to elucidate; to make clear, enlighten. — v.i. to dawn.
esclarecidamente, adv. illustriously, conspicuously.
esclarecido, -da, a. noble, illustrious, honourable; eminent, conspicuous. — p.p. [ESCLARECER].
esclarecimiento, n.m. enlightening; dawn; illustriousness, merit, worth; ennoblement.
esclava, n.f. slave-bracelet.
esclavatura, n.f. (Arg., Chi., Per.) aggregate of slaves on a hacienda.
esclavillo, -illa; esclavito, -ita, n.m.f. little slave [ESCLAVO].
esclavina, n.f. cape worn by priests; pilgrim's cloak; tippet; cape of cloak.
esclavista, a. pro-slavery. — n.m.f. supporter of slavery.
esclavitud, n.f. slavery, bondage, servitude; slavishness; congregation, brotherhood; (fig.) servile subjection to passions.
esclavizar, v.t. (pret. esclavicé; pres. subj. esclavice) to enslave; to overwork, drive.
esclavo, -va, a. enslaved; docile, obedient; deeply enamoured. — n.m.f. captive, slave, helot; member of a brotherhood bound by vows; drudge; esclavo ladino, (obs.) one who has been more than a year in slavery; ser un esclavo, to be tied to a piece of work.
esclavón, -ona; esclavonio, -nia, n.m.f., a. Slav, Slavonic. — n.m. Slavonic language. — n.f. (Chi.) member of a brotherhood.
esclerosis, n.f. sclerosis.

esclerótica, n.f. sclerotic.
esclusa, n.f. sluice, lock, flood-gate.
escoa, n.f. bend of a ship's rib.
escoba, n.f. broom, besom; escoba nueva barre bien, new brooms sweep clean; escoba desatada, persona desalmada, a disorderly person is never of any use; la primera mujer escoba, la segunda señora, the second wife is treated better than the first; (bot.) yellow broom.
escobada, n.f. sweep, sweeping; dar una escobada, to sweep carelessly.
escobadera, n.f. woman sweeper.
escobajo, n.m. old broom; stalk of a bunch of grapes.
escobar, n.m. place where broom grows. — v.t. to sweep with a broom.
escobazar, v.t. to sprinkle water with a broom or aspergillum.
escobazo, n.m. stroke or blow with a broom; echar a uno a escobazos, to dismiss a person rudely; (coll.) to kick out; (Arg., Chi.) sweep, sweeping.
escobén, n.m. (naut.) hawse-hole.
escobera, n.f. (bot.) Spanish broom.
escobero, -ra, n.m.f. broom-maker or seller.
escobeta, n.f. small brush.
escobilla, n.f. brush; whisk, small broom; (bot.) bur of the teasel; (bot.) tamaric-leaved salt-wort; gold or silver sweepings.
escobillón, n.m. (artill.) swab, cannon-sponge.
escobina, n.f. chips or dust made in boring.
escobo, n.m. dense brushwood, briers, brambles.
escobón, n.m. large broom [ESCOBA]; Turk's head; scrubbing-brush; swab.
escocedura, n.f. burning pain.
escocer, v.i. (pres. indic. escuezo; pres. subj. escueza) to feel a sharp, burning pain; to chafe, smart. — v.t. to irritate, provoke, cause to smart. — v.r. to smart; to become red (face, etc.).
escocés, -esa, n.m.f., a. Scots, Scottish.
Escocia, n.f. Scotland.
escocia, n.f. (arch.) scotia; (com.) cod-fish.
escocimiento, n.m. smart pungent pain.
escoda, n.f. stone-cutter's hammer.
escodadero, n.m. place where deer rub their horns.
escodar, v.t. to hew or cut stones.
escofia; escofieta, n.f. coif, head-tire, net, head-dress of gauze, etc.
escofiar, v.t. to dress the head with a coif.
escofina, n.f. rasp, file; wood-rasp; wire brush.
escofinar, v.t. to rasp.
escofión, n.m. head-dress made of net-work.
escogedor, -ra, a. choosing. — n.m.f. selector, chooser.
escoger, v.t. (pres. indic. escojo; pres. subj. escoja) to select, choose, sort, pick out; to elect.
escogida, n.f. (Cub.) grading tobacco; (Cub.) place where the grading takes place.
escogidamente, adv. choicely, nicely.
escogido, -da, a. chosen, choice, select. — p.p. [ESCOGER].
escogimiento, n.m. selection; choosing; sorting, grading.
escolanía, n.f. boys' choir in a monastery.
escolano, n.m. pupil receiving free education in a monastery.
escolar, a. scholastic. — n.m. student, scholar.

escolásticamente, *adv.* scholastically.

escolasticismo, *n.m.* scholasticism.

escolástico, -da, *a.* scholastic, of or pertaining to schools. — *n.m.* schoolman; professor of scholastic philosophy.

escoliador, -ra; escoliasta, *n.m.f.* scholiast.

escoliar, *v.t.* to gloss, explain, comment.

escolimado, -da, *a.* (*coll.*) weak, delicate.

escolimoso, -sa, *a.* (*coll.*) difficult, fastidious fussy, hard to please.

escolio, *n.m.* scholium; gloss, commentary.

escoliosis, *n.f.* (*med.*) scoliosis.

escolopendra, *n.f.* (*entom.*) scolopendra, centipede; marine worm; (*bot.*) spleenwort, common hart's-tongue.

escolta, *n.f.* escort, convoy, guard.

escoltar, *v.t.* to escort, convoy, guard.

escollar, *v.i.* (*Arg., naut.*) to go aground on a reef or bank; (*Arg., Chi.*) to fail, fall through; run into difficulties.

escollera, *n.f.* breakwater, jetty; cliff.

escollo, *n.m.* reef, shelf of rock; difficulty, danger.

escombra, *n.f.* clearing, removal of obstacles.

escombrar, *v.t.* to remove rubbish; (*fig.*) to clear, to clean.

escombro, *n.m.* rubbish, fragments of building materials, debris; riprap; small raisin; (*ichth.*) mackerel.

escomerse, *v.r.* to become worn out by use.

esconce, *n.m.* corner, angle.

escondecucas, *n.m.* (*prov.*) game of hide-and-seek.

escondedero, *n.m.* hiding or lurking place.

esconder, *v.t.* to conceal, hide; to include, contain; to dissemble, disguise. — *v.r.* to be concealed, keep out of sight; to hide; to skulk.

escondidamente, *adv.* secretly, hiddenly, privately.

escondidas (a); escondidillas (a), *adv.* on the sly, privately, in a secret manner.

escondidas, *n.f.pl.* (*Arg., Col., Chi., Ec.*) game of hide-and-seek.

escondido, -da, *a.* hidden, concealed.

escondidos, *n.m.pl.* (*Per.*) game of hide-and-seek.

escondimiento, *n.m.* concealment.

escondite, *n.m.* hiding-place, lurking-place; *jugar al escondite*, to play hide-and-seek.

escondrijo, *n.m.* hiding or lurking-place.

escontrete, *n.m.* (*naut.*) prop, stay, shore.

esconzado, -da, *a.* angular, oblique.

escopa, *n.f.* stone-chisel.

escoperada; (*obs.*) escoperadura, *n.f.* gunwale.

escopero, *n.m.* (*naut.*) pitch-brush; swab.

escopeta, *n.f.* gun, fowling-piece, shot-gun; *escopeta de viento*, air-gun; *escopeta de dos cañones*, double-barrelled gun; *escopeta negra*, professional hunter; *a tiro de escopeta*, within gunshot; *aquí te quiero (ver), escopeta*, I am in a nice predicament.

escopetar, *v.t.* to excavate gold-mines.

escopetazo, *n.m.* gunshot; gunshot wound.

escopetear, *v.t.* to fire a gun repeatedly. — *v.r.* (*coll.*) to address alternate compliments or insults to one another.

escopeteo, *n.m.* gunfire.

escopetería, *n.f.* crowd armed with guns; repeated gunshots.

escopetero, *n.m.* musketeer, gunner; gunsmith, armourer.

escopetilla, *n.f.* small gun [ESCOPETA].

escopetón, *n.m.* large fowling-piece [ESCOPETA].

escopladura; escopleadura, *n.f.* mortisehole.

escoplear, *v.t.* to mortise, notch.

escoplillo; escoplito, *n.m.* small chisel [ESCOPLO].

escoplo, *n.m.* (*carp.*) chisel.

escopo, *n.m.* (*obs.*) scope, aim.

escora, *n.f.* (*naut.*) central line at extreme beam of a vessel; heel, inclination of sailing vessel; *navío de escora baja*, stiff ship; *escora lateral*, (*aer.*) rolling. — *pl.* shores, props.

escorar, *v.t.* to shore up, prop. — *v.i.* to list, heel. — *v.r.* (*Cub., Hond.*) to seek shelter or protection from the weather.

escorbútico, -ca, *a.* scorbutic, scorbutical.

escorbuto, *n.m.* scurvy.

escorchapín, *n.m.* ancient type of passageboat, ferry.

escorchar, *v.t.* to flay, skin.

escorche, *n.m.* (*obs.*) (*art*) foreshortening.

escordio, *n.m.* water germander.

escoria, *n.f.* dross, slag; (*fig.*) mean or worthless thing. — *pl.* volcanic ashes.

escoriáceo, -cea, *a.* scoriaceous.

escoriación, *n.f.* crust, scurf on a sore.

escorial, *n.m.* dumping place for dross; minedump; slag-heap.

escoriar, *v.t.* [EXCORIAR].

escorificación, *n.f.* (*chem.*) scorification.

escorificar, *v.t.* (*chem.*) to scorify; to reduce to slag.

escorodonia, *n.f.* wood sage.

escorpena; escorpina, *n.f.* (*ichth.*) grouper.

escorpioide, *n.f.* scorpion-grass.

escorpión, *n.m.* (*entom.*) scorpion; (*ichth.*) sea-scorpion, scorpion-fish; (*astron.*) Scorpio; cat-o'-nine-tails.

escorpiónideo, -dea, *a.* scorpion-like. — *n.m.pl.* Scorpionidea.

escorpiuro, *n.m.* caterpillar-plant.

escorrozo, *n.m.* (*coll.*) delight.

escorzado, -da, *p.p.* [ESCORZAR]. — *n.m.* (*art*) foreshortening.

escorzar, *v.t.* (*art*) to foreshorten.

escorzo, *n.m.* (*art*) foreshortening.

escorzón, *n.m.* toad.

escorzonera, *n.f.* viper's-grass.

escota, *n.f.* stone-cutter's hammer; (*naut.*) sheet; (*arch.*) scotia; *escotas mayores*, main sheets; *escotas de gavias*, topsail sheets; *escotas de las velas de estay*, staysail sheets; *escotas volantes*, flowing-sheets; *escotas de barlovento*, weather-sheets.

escotado, escotadura, *n.m.f.* low cut in the neck (of a dress); arm-hole in armour; large trap-door of a stage.

escotar, *v.t.* to cut a dress to the figure; to cut a bodice low in the neck; to club together, pay one's share, contribute to common expense; (*obs.*) to bail water out of a boat; to draw water from a river, etc., by trenching.

escote, *n.m.* low neck, *décolleté*; share, scot, quota; modesty-vest, tucker.

escotera, *n.f.* sheet-hole.

escotero, -ra, *a.* free, disengaged.

escotilla, *n.f.* hatchway; *escotilla mayor*, main hatchway; *escotilla de proa*, fore-hatch; *escotilla de popa*, aft hatchway.

escotillón, *n.m.* scuttle, trap-door; stage-trap.

escotín, *n.m.* topsail sheet.

escotismo, *n.m.* Scotism.

escotista, *n.m.* Scotist.

escoznete, *n.m.* (*prov.*) nut-pick.

escozor, *n.m.* smart, pungent pain; grief, affliction.

escriba, *n.m.* Hebrew scribe.

escribanía, *n.f.* office or employment of a notary; escritoire; portable writing-case; ornamental inkstand.

escribano, *n.m.* scrivener, actuary, notary public; clerk; penman; (*naut.*) purser; *escribano de número* or *del número*, one of a certain number of notaries public; *escribano de cámara*, clerk of a high court of justice; *escribano del agua*, (*entom.*) water-strider; *el mejor escribano echa un borrón*, even Homer sometimes nods; *por bueno o por malo, el escribano, de tu mano*, whatever you do, get the right man on your side.

escribido *p.p. reg.* [ESCRIBIR], used only in the idiom *leído y escribido*, half-educated person who gives himself the airs of a scholar.

escribiente, *n.m.* amanuensis, clerk; (*obs.*) author, writer.

escribir, *v.t.* (*p.p. irreg.* **escrito**) to write; to compose literary works. — *v.r.* to enrol oneself; to keep up an epistolary correspondence; *máquina de escribir*, typewriter; *escribir en la arena*, to bury in oblivion; *escribe antes que des, y recibe antes que escribas*, a proverb cautioning carefulness in business matters; *escribir muy tirado*, to write in great haste.

escriño, *n.m.* straw hamper; jewel-box, casket.

escrita, *n.f.* (*ichth.*) spotted skate.

escritillas, *n.f.pl.* lamb's testicles.

escrito, -ta, *p.p. irreg.* [ESCRIBIR]. — *n.m.* writing, manuscript; literary composition; examination paper; (*law*) writ; brief; *estaba escrito*, it was fated; *no hay nada escrito sobre eso*, courteous form of dissent from a definite statement; *por escrito*, in writing; *hablar por escrito*, to write what one means to say to another; *tomar por escrito*, to set down in writing.

escritor, -ra, *n.m.f.* writer, author, composer; copyist.

escritorcillo, -lla, *n.m.f.* petty writer, bad writer [ESCRITOR].

escritorio, *n.m.* counting-house; study, office, library; writing-desk; large chest of drawers; (*prov.*) warehouse (in Toledo).

escritorzuelo, -la, *n.m.f.* poor writer [ESCRITOR].

escritura, *n.f.* penmanship, handwriting, writing; art of writing; Scripture; deed, instrument, bond, contract, indenture; *escritura de seguro*, insurance policy.

escriturar, *v.t.* (*law*) to bind by deed; to indenture; to engage (as an artist). — *v.r.* to sign articles; *estar escriturado*, to be in articles.

escriturario, -ria, *a.* (*law*) scriptory, scriptorian; scriptural. — *n.m.f.* scripturist, one who explains the Scriptures.

escrófula, *n.f.* scrofula, king's evil.

escrofularia, *n.f.* figwort.

escrofuloso, -sa, *a.* scrofulous.

escrotal, *a.* scrotal.

escroto, *n.m.* scrotum.

escrupulillo, *n.m.* slight doubt, scruple, hesitation; jinglet, clapper of a small bell [ESCRÚPULO].

escrupulizar, *v.i.* to scruple, doubt, hesitate.

escrúpulo, *n.m.* scruple, hesitation, doubt; conscientiousness, scrupulosity; (*pharm.*) scruple (20 grains); (*astr.*) minute on a graduated sphere; *escrúpulo de Marigargajo* or *del padre Gargajo*, silly scruple; *escrúpulo de monja*, childish scruple.

escrupulosamente, *adv.* scrupulously; precisely, minutely.

escrupulosidad, *n.f.* scrupulosity, conscientiousness; preciseness, exactness, nicety.

escrupuloso, -sa, *a.* scrupulous, conscientious; hypercritical, squeamish; nice, precise, exact.

escrutador, -ra, *a.* examining, searching. — *n.m.f.* scrutator, examiner, searcher, inquirer; teller at an election.

escrutar, *v.t.* to count votes; to scrutinize.

escrutinio, *n.m.* investigation, scrutiny; close examination (of election returns, etc.).

escrutiñador, *n.m.* scrutator, censor.

escuadra, *n.f.* carpenter's square; triangle for geometrical drawing; knee, angle-iron, angle-tie; (*mil.*) squad; (*naut.*) squadron, fleet; *a escuadra*, square; *escuadra falsa*, bevel; *escuadra de agrimensor*, surveyor's cross; *escuadra sutil*, (*naut.*) scouting squadron; *fuera de escuadra*, off the square, oblique; *jefe de escuadra*, rear-admiral.

escuadración, *n.f.* squaring.

escuadrador, *n.m.* squaring-tool.

escuadrar, *v.t.* (*carp.*) to square.

escuadreo, *n.m.* squaring, quadrature of an area (for valuation, etc.).

escuadría, *n.f.* scantling of timber; (*obs.*) square, right-angled rule or measure.

escuadrilla, *n.f.* flight (of aircraft or small ships).

escuadro, *n.m.* (*ichth.*) spotted skate.

escuadrón, *n.m.* squadron, troop of horse; *escuadron volante*, flying column; (air-) squadron.

escuadronar, *v.t.* to form in squadrons, draw up troops in rank and file.

escuadroncillo; escuadroncete, *n.m.* small troop [ESCUADRÓN].

escuadronista, *n.m.* cavalry tactician.

escualidez, *n.f.* squalor, wretchedness.

escuálido, -da, *a.* weak, languid; squalid, filthy.

escualo, *n.m.* spotted dogfish; shark.

escualor, *n.m.* squalor, filthiness.

escuatina, *n.f.* sea-angel.

escucha, *n.f.* scout; vedette; advanced sentinel, sentry; (in convents) a chaperon; servant sleeping near her mistress; listening-in hole, listening-place; small window.

escuchador, -ra, *a.* hearing, listening. — *n.m.f.* listener.

escuchante, *a.* listening, hearkening.

escuchar, *v.t.* to hearken, hear, listen; to heed, mind. — *v.r.* to speak with affectation and self-complacency.

escudar, *v.t.* to protect, shield, defend, guard from danger. — *v.r.* to make use of some means of evading danger.

escuderaje, *n.m.* service of a squire, page or footman.

escuderear, *v.t.* to serve as a page or squire.

escudería, *n.f.* service of a page, squire or footman.

escuderil, *a.* belonging to a page or shield-bearer.

escuderilmente, *adv.* in the style of a page or shield-bearer.

escudero, *n.m.* page, squire, shield-bearer; gentleman of illustrious ancestry; shield-maker; henchman; footman; *escudero de a pie,* attendant in royal palace, groom of the chambers.

escuderón, *n.m.* conceited, pretentious person.

escudete, *n.m.* scutcheon; gusset; rain stain on olives; (*bot.*) white water-lily; *injertar de escudete,* shield-grafting.

escudilla, *n.f.* bowl, large cup, porringer.

escudillar, *v.t.* to pour into bowls; (*fig.*) to domineer.

escudillita, *n.f.* small bowl, porringer [ESCUDILLA].

escudillo; escudito, *n.m.* small shield [ESCUDO]; gold coin.

escudo, *n.m.* shield, buckler, escutcheon, coat of arms; coin; defence, protection; back of a wild boar; bandage used in bleeding; (*artill.*) shield of a gun; *escudo de bota,* backboard of a boat; *escudo de popa,* stern-scutcheon; *escudo vergeteado,* (*her.*) arms containing ten or more quarterings.

escudriñable, *a.* investigable.

escudriñador, -ra, *a.* prying, scrutinizing, searching. — *n.m.f.* prier, scrutator, one who inquires into others' secrets.

escudriñamiento, *n.m.* investigation, scrutiny.

escudriñar, *v.t.* to search, scrutinize, pry into; to examine.

escuela, *n.f.* school, place of instruction or learning; school-house, part of a university; college teaching, doctrine; (*art*) school; style; experience; *escuela primaria,* elementary school; *escuela secundaria,* secondary school; *escuela normal,* training college for teachers; *escuela superior,* high school, university, etc.; *escuela de Cristo,* religious community; *saber uno toda la escuela,* to know all the differences of a gymnastic exercise.

escuerzo, *n.m.* (*zool.*) toad; (*coll.*) flabby person.

escueto, -ta, *a.* disengaged, free from encumbrances; unadorned, plain, strict.

escueznar, *v.t.* (*prov.*) to extract the kernel from nuts.

escuezno, *n.m.* soft kernel of a nut.

escuezo; escueza, *pres. indic.; pres. subj.* [ESCOCER].

esculcar, *v.t.* to spy, to watch; (*Col., CR., Mex., PR.*) to search, inspect.

esculpidor, -ra, *n.m.f.* engraver.

esculpir, *v.t., v.i.* (*p.p. irreg.* **esculto**) to sculpture, engrave.

escultor, -ra, *n.m.f.* sculptor, sculptress, carver.

escultura, *n.f.* sculpture; carved work.

escultural, *a.* sculptural.

escullador, *n.m.* dipper for oil.

escullirse, *v.r.* to slip out, slip away, sneak off.

escuna, *n.f.* schooner.

escupidera, *n.f.* spittoon, cuspidor; (*Arg., Chi., Ec.*) chamber-pot.

escupidero, *n.m.* spitting-place; (*fig.*) situation in which one is exposed to being insulted or despised.

escupido, -da, *a.* very spit of; *Juana es escupida la madre,* Joan is the spit of her mother. — *n.m.* spittle. — *p.p.* [ESCUPIR].

escupidor, -ra, *n.m.f.* great spitter; (*Ec., PR.*) spittoon, cuspidor; (*Col.*) round plait or mat.

escupidura, *n.f.* spitting; spittle; fever sore, efflorescence.

escupir, *v.t., v.i.* to spit; to fling, dart, throw, cast away; to break out in the skin (as a rash); to dart, flash, throw off; to work out; to underrate, depreciate; *escupir en la cara,* to deride, ridicule; *escupir al cielo,* to act rashly; *escupir doblones,* to boast of one's wealth; *escupir sangre,* to boast of one's nobility; *escupir sangre en bacín de oro,* to have little happiness in the midst of wealth; *escupir las estopas,* (*naut.*) to work out the oakum from the seams; *no escupir alguna cosa,* not to despise, to be fond of a thing; *escupir a uno,* to scowl at someone.

escupitajo, *n.m.; ***escupitina,** *n.f.; ***escupitinajo,** *n.m.* (*coll.*) spit.

escurana, *n.f.* (*Col., Chi.*) obscurity, darkness.

escurar, *v.t.* to scour cloth before milling.

escurialense, *a.* belonging to or similar to the monastery of the Escorial.

escurreplatos, *n.m.* dish-draining rack.

escurribanda, *n.f.* (*coll.*) flight, escape; diarrhœa; whipping, spanking.

escurridero, *n.m.* drain-pipe in mines.

escurridizo, -za, *a.* slippery; difficult to hold or keep; *lazo escurridizo,* running knot; *hacerse escurridizo,* to escape, hurry away.

escurrido, -da, *a.* wearing tight-fitting skirts; having narrow hips (applied to women); (*Mex., PR.*) abashed, ashamed.

escurriduras; escurrimbres, *n.f.pl.* rinsings (as of wine); lees, dregs; *llegar uno a las escurriduras,* (*coll., fig.*) to have come to the end, dregs of something.

escurrimiento, *n.m.* dripping; running, sneaking away.

escurrir, *v.t.* to wring (as clothes); to drain a vessel. — *v.r., v.i.* to slip, drop, trickle, leak; to slide, glide, pass slowly; to slip out, escape, sneak away; *escurrir la bola* or *el bulto,* to take French leave.

escusalí, *n.m.* small apron.

escutas; escutillas, *n.f.pl.* (*naut.*) scuttles.

escuteliforme; escutiforme, *a.* (*bot.*) scutiform.

escutolaria, *n.f.* (*bot.*) scutellaria.

escuyer, *n.m.* purveyor of meat to the royal palace.

esdrújulo, -la, *a.* accented on the antepenultimate syllable; *verso esdrújulo,* line of verse ending with such a word. — *n.m.* word accented on the antepenultimate syllable.

ese, *n.f.* Spanish name of the letter S; link of a chain of the form of this letter; *andar* or *ir uno haciendo eses,* to walk unsteadily through drunkenness; *echar una ese (y un clavo),* to win over by means of favours.

ese, esa (*pl.* **esos, esas**)*, a.* that (just over there) (*pl.* those).

ése, ésa (*pl.* **ésos, ésas**)*, dem. pron. m.f.* that (one) (*pl.* those); the former; *ni por ésas (ni por esotras),* not at all, in no way; *eso mismo,* thus, exactly so.

esecilla, *n.f.* small link of a chain [ESE].

esencia, *n.f.* essence; being; *quinta esencia,* quintessence; *ser de esencia,* to be indispensably necessary.

esencial, *a.* essential.

esencialmente, *adv.* essentially, principally, naturally, materially.

esenciarse, *v.r.* (*obs.*) to become intimately united, become essential.

esenio, -ia, *n.m.f.* Essene.

esfacelo, *n.m.* gangrene.

esfenoides, *n.m.* sphenoid bone.

esfera, *n.f.* sphere, orb; clock-dial; condition, quality, state, rank; (*poet.*) heaven; *esfera armilar,* armillary sphere; *esfera celeste,* celestial sphere; *esfera de actividad,* sphere of activity; *fuera de mi esfera,* out of my power or reach; *quien espera en la esfera, muere en la rueda,* he who trusts in this world, fails.

esferal; esférico, -ca, *a.* spherical, globular.

esféricamente, *adv.* spherically.

esfericidad, *n.f.* sphericity, rotundity.

esferista, *n.m.* (*obs.*) astronomer.

esferoidal, *a.* spheroidal.

esferoide, *n.f.* spheroid.

esferómetro, *n.m.* spherometer.

esfinge, *n.f.* sphinx, fabulous monster. — *n.m.* hawk-moth.

esfíngido, -da, *a.* of the sphinx-moth or hawk-moth.

esfinter, *n.m.* sphincter.

esflorecer, *v.i.* (*chem.*) to effloresce.

esforrocinar, *v.t.* to remove the *esforrocinos* from a vine.

esforrocino, *n.m.* sprig shooting from the trunk of a vine.

esforzadamente, *adv.* vigorously, strenuously; valiantly.

esforzado, -da, *a.* vigorous, strong; valiant; enterprising. — *p.p.* [ESFORZAR].

esforzador, -ra, *n.m.f.,* *a.* encouraging, inciting (person).

esforzar, *v.t.,* *v.i.* (*pres. indic.* **esfuerzo;** *pret.* **esforcé;** *pres. subj.* **esfuerce**) to invigorate, strengthen; to exert, enforce, force; to encourage; to aid, abet. — *v.r.* to exert oneself, make efforts, try hard.

esfuerzo, *n.m.* spirit, courage, heart, vigour, manfulness; strong endeavour, effort, exertion; labouring, contention; confidence, faith; (*obs.*) help, aid; (*engin.*) stress; *esfuerzo cortante,* (*engin.*) shearing stress.

esfuerzo; esfuerce, *pres. indic.; pres. subj.* [ESFORZAR].

esfumado, -da, *a.* (*art*) sfumato; first (charcoal) sketch of a painting. — *p.p.* [ESFUMAR].

esfumar, *v.t.* (*art*) to stump, shade over pencilled outlines of a picture.

esfumino, *n.m.* (*art*) stump (for shading).

esgarrar, *v.t.,* *v.i.* to clear one's throat.

esgrafiado, *n.m.* (*art*) graffito.

esgrafiar, *v.t.* (*art*) to decorate with graffito.

esgrima, *n.f.* (art of) fencing; *maestro de esgrima,* fencing-master.

esgrimidor, *n.m.* fencer, fencing-master; *casa de esgrimidor,* house without furniture.

esgrimidura, *n.f.* (act of) fencing.

esgrimir, *v.t.* to practise the use of weapons, to fence; to fend off.

esgrimista, *n.m.f.* (*Arg., Chi., Per.*) fencer; fencing-master.

esguazable, *a.* fordable.

esguazar, *v.t.* to ford (a river).

esguazo, *n.m.* fording.

esgucio, *n.m.* (*arch.*) quarter-round moulding.

esguín, *n.m.* young salmon before entering the sea.

esguince, *n.m.* twist of the body to avoid a blow or fall; frown; twist or sprain of a joint.

esguízaro, -ra, *n.m.f.,* *a.* Swiss; *pobre esguízaro,* ragamuffin, wretch.

eslabón, *n.m.* link of a chain; table-steel; steel for striking fire with a flint; black scorpion; hard tumour on horses' legs; *eslabones de guimbalete,* (*naut.*) swivels.

eslabonador, *n.m.* chain-maker.

eslabonamiento, *n.m.* linking, uniting; connexion, concatenation.

eslabonar, *v.t.* to join, unite; to link, interlink, add one link to another; connect, concatenate.

eslavo, -va, *n.m.f.,* *a.* Slav; *lengua eslava,* the Slav language.

eslinga, *n.f.* (*naut.*) sling, span.

eslingar, *v.t.* (*naut.*) to sling up, hoist.

eslora; (*obs.*) **esloría,** *n.f.* length of a ship. — *pl.* beams running from stem to stern.

eslovaco, -ca, *n.m.f.,* *a.* Slovak, Slovakian.

esloveno, -na, *n.m.f.,* *a.* Slovene, Slovenian.

esmaltador, -ra, *n.m.f.* enameller.

esmaltadura, *n.f.* enamelling; enamel-work.

esmaltar, *v.t.* to enamel, variegate with colours inlaid; to adorn, embellish.

esmalte, *n.m.* enamel; enamel-work; smalt.

esmaltín, *n.m.* smalt.

esmaltina, *n.f.* smaltite.

esmaragdita, *n.f.* smaragdite.

esmarido, *n.m.* small sea-fish.

esmeradamente, *adv.* carefully, accurately, conscientiously.

esmerado, -da, *a.* careful, high-finished, executed with care. — *p.p.* [ESMERAR].

esmeralda, *n.f.* emerald.

esmeraldino, -na, *a.* emerald-like.

esmerar, *v.t.* to brighten, polish. — *v.r.* (with *con* or *en*) to do one's best, take great pains; to endeavour to attain eminence or excellence.

esmerejón, *n.m.* (*orn.*) merlin; (*obs.*) small cannon.

esmeril, *n.m.* emery; (*obs.*) small cannon.

esmerilar, *v.t.* to burnish, polish with emery

esmerilazo, *n.m.* shot from an *esmeril* (gun).

esmero, *n.m.* correctness, accuracy; careful attention, elaborate effort.

esmoladera, *n.f.* whetstone.

esmuciarse, *v.r.* (*prov.*) to slip from the hands.

esnón, *n.m.* spencer-mast, try-sail mast.

eso, *dem. pron. neut.* that. — *pl.* **esos;** *eso es,* that is it; *¿ no es eso ?* is not that so? *a eso de,* toward, about; *a eso de las cinco,* about five o'clock; *eso mismo,* the very thing.

esófago, *n.m.* œsophagus, gullet.

esotérico, -ca, *a.* esoteric; confidential, secret.

esotro, esotra, *dem. pron., a.* this or that other. — *pl.* **esotros, esotras,** those others.

espabiladeras, *n.f.pl.* snuffers.

espabilar, *v.t.* to snuff a candle.

espaciador, *n.m.* space-bar (of a typewriter).

espaciar, *v.t.* to space; (*print.*) to lead; to diffuse, dilate, expand, spread; to set apart, at a distance. — *v.r.* to grow gay, cheer up; to amuse oneself; to walk to and fro; to expatiate.

espacio, *n.m.* space; interval; delay, procrastination, slowness; distance between objects; room, place, capacity; (*print.*) lead; (*obs.*) diversion, recreation, pastime; *espacios imaginarios*, imaginary worlds; *espacio de tiempo*, length of time.

espaciosamente, *adv.* deliberately; spaciously.

espaciosidad, *n.f.* spaciousness, capacity.

espacioso, -sa, *a.* capacious, spacious, wide, ample, roomy, extensive, large; deliberate, slow.

espada, *n.f.* sword; blade, rapier; (*us. m.*) swordsman; (*cards*) suit of spades; (*ichth.*) swordfish; (*us.m.*) bullfighter who kills the bull with a sword; *espada blanca*, sword; *espada negra* or *de esgrima*, foil (used in fencing); *entrar con espada en mano*, to begin to do something violently; to enter sword in hand; *hombre de capa y espada*, man of no profession; *verse entre la espada y la pared*, to find oneself between Scylla and Charybdis; *sacar la espada por alguno*, to uphold someone's character or reputation; *ser buen espada*, to be skilled in polemic (or dialectic); *es una buena espada*, he is a good swordsman; *primer espada*, chief bullfighter; *espada ancha* or *de a caballo*, broadsword; *media espada*, bullfighter not of the first rank; second-rate performer of anything; *asentar la espada*, to put the point of the sword on the ground; *ceñir espada*, to be girt with a sword; to be a soldier by profession; *con la espada desnuda*, resolutely, prepared for anything; *llevar por la espada*, *meter a espada*, *pasar a espada*, (*obs.*) to put to the sword; *quedarse uno a espadas*, to be left with nothing; to be disappointed; *salir uno con su media espada*, to interrupt impertinently; *tirar uno de la espada*, to draw the sword; *comedia de capa y espada*, cloak-and-dagger play; *ser lo mismo que la espada de Bernardo, que ni pincha ni corta*, to be of no use.

espadachín, *n.m.* dexterous swordsman; (*slang*) bully.

espadadero, *n.m.* bench for braking flax or hemp.

espadado, -da, *a.* (*obs.*) armed with a sword. — *p.p.* [ESPADAR].

espadador, -ra, *n.m.f.* hemp-beater.

espadaña, *n.f.* (*bot.*) reed-mace; belfry.

espadañada, *n.f.* regurgitation; vomiting.

espadañal, *n.m.* place where reed-mace grows.

espadañar, *v.t.* to spread out the tail-feathers (of birds).

espadar, *v.t.* to brake, scutch, swingle (hemp, etc.).

espadarte, *n.m.* swordfish.

espadería, *n.f.* sword-cutler's shop.

espadero, *n.m.* sword-cutler, blade-smith.

espádice, *n.m.* (*bot.*) spadix.

espadilla, *n.f.* red insignia of the order of Santiago; large oar used as helm; ace of spades; swingle, hemp-brake; hair bodkin; (*bot.*) corn-flag, gladiolus.

espadillar, *v.t.* to brake, scutch, swingle.

espadillazo, *n.m.* adverse fortune at cards when loser holds the ace.

espadín, *n.m.* small dress sword; rapier.

espadita, *n.f.* small sword [ESPADA].

espadón, *n.m.* large sword, broadsword [ESPADA]; high ranking officer; eunuch.

espadrapo, *n.m.* [ESPARADRAPO].

espagírica, *n.f.* metallurgy.

espagírico, -ca, *a.* metallurgic.

espahí, *n.m.* spahi.

espalda, *n.f.* (*anat.*) back, shoulders; (*fort.*) shoulder of a bastion. — *pl.* back or back parts; (*mil.*) rearguard; *a espaldas* (*vueltas*), at one's back, in one's absence; treacherously, behind one's back; *echarse a las espaldas una cosa*, to abandon, forget designedly; *echarse uno sobre las espaldas*, to undertake, be responsible for something; *echar una cosa sobre las espaldas de uno*, to saddle someone with the responsibility of something; *espaldas de molinero*, broad, strong shoulders; *cargado de espaldas*, round-shouldered; *dar de espaldas*, to fall on one's back; *dar las espaldas*, to turn one's back, fly; *hablar por las espaldas de uno*, to say something behind someone's back; *espaldas vueltas, memorias muertas*, (*CR., Chi., Hond., PR.*) out of sight, out of mind; *hacer espaldas*, to suffer, bear, be prepared; *hacer espaldas a*, to protect, guard; *relucir la espalda*, to be very rich; *tener buenas espaldas*, to have great powers of resistance; *tener guardadas las espaldas*, to have more than adequate protection; *tener seguras las espaldas*, to be free from worry; *tirarle a uno de espaldas una cosa*, to give someone a surprise; *tornar*, or *volver, las espaldas*, to turn one's back on someone; to take to flight, to turn tail.

espaldar, *n.m.* backplate of a cuirass; back of a seat; espalier (in garden). — *pl.* tapestry, hangings against which chairs lean.

espaldarazo, *n.m.* accolade; light blow on the shoulders.

espaldarcete, *n.m.* palette in ancient armour.

espaldarón, *n.m.* backplate in armour.

espaldear, *v.t.* (*naut.*) to dash against the poop (of waves).

espalder, *n.m.* stroke, stern rower in a galley.

espaldera, *n.f.* wall to shelter trees; espalier; *a espaldera*, said of a wall-tree or wall-fruit.

espaldilla, *n.f.* shoulder-blade, scapula; back of waistcoat or jacket.

espalditendido, -da, *a.* (*coll.*) stretched on one's back.

espaldón, *n.m.* (*carp.*) tenon; (*fort.*) entrenchment, barrier; (*naut.*) hawse-piece.

espaldonarse, *v.r.* to take cover from the enemy's fire.

espaldudo, -da, *a.* broad-shouldered.

espalera, *n.f.* espalier, trellis-work.

espalmadura, *n.f.* parings of hoofs.

espalmar, *v.t.* to clean a ship's bottom.

espalto, *n.m.* dark-coloured paint; spalt; (*mil., obs.*) glacis.

espantable, *a.* frightful, horrid, terrible; awful.

espantablemente, *adv.* horribly, terribly, frightfully.

espantada, *n.f.* stampede, bolting; sudden fright, cold feet.

espantadizo, -za, *a.* timid, shy, skittish, easily frightened.

espantador, -ra, *a.* frightening, terrifying. — *n.m.f.* bugbear, frightener, one who terrifies.

espantajo, *n.m.* scarecrow; (*fig.*) anything causing needless fright; *espantajo de higuera*, guy, figure of fun.

espantalobos, *n.m.* bladder or bastard senna.

espantamoscas, *n.m.* fly-net; fly-flap.

espantanublados, *n.m.* (*coll.*) rainmaker; pesterer.

espantapájaros, *n.m.* scarecrow.

espantar, *v.t.* to frighten, scare, terrify, shock, daunt; to drive, chase away. — *v.r.* to become surprised, astonished; to marvel; *al espantado, la sombra le espanta,* the coward takes fright at a shadow; once bitten twice shy.

espantavillanos, *n.m.* (*coll.*) gaudy stuff or trinket.

espanto, *n.m.* fright, dread, terror; menace, threat; consternation, horror; surprise, wonder; hideousness, grimness; (*Col., CR., Hond., Mex., Ven.*) ghost, apparition; *estar curado de espanto,* to be cool from experience of danger, etc.

espantosamente, *adv.* dreadfully, frightfully; marvellously.

espantoso, -sa, *a.* fearful, dreadful, frightful, horrible; wonderful, marvellous.

España, *n.f.* Spain.

español, -la, *a.* Spanish; *a la española,* in the Spanish manner. — *n.m.* Spanish language. — *n.m.f.* Spaniard.

españolado, -da, *a.* Spanish-like; Hispanicized. — *p.p.* [ESPAÑOLAR].

españolar, *v.t.* to Hispanicize. — *v.r.* to adopt the customs and manners of Spain.

españoleta, *n.f.* ancient Spanish dance.

españolismo, *n.m.* love of *or* devotion to Spain, Hispanicism.

españolizar, *v.t., v.r.* [ESPAÑOLAR].

esparadrapo, *n.m.* court-plaster.

esparagón, *n.m.* grogram.

esparaván, *n.m.* (*vet.*) spavin; (*orn.*) sparrow-hawk; *esparaván huesoso,* bone-spavin.

esparavel, *n.m.* casting-net.

esparceta, *n.f.* sainfoin.

esparciata, *n.m.f., a.* Spartan.

esparcidamente, *adv.* distinctly, separately; gaily.

esparcido, -da, *a.* scattered; merry, festive, gay. — *p.p.* [ESPARCIR].

esparcidor, -ra, *a.* scattering, spreading. — *n.m.f.* scatterer, spreader.

esparcimiento, *n.m.* dissemination, scattering; amusement, outing, recreation, merriment; openness, frankness, generosity of mind.

esparcir, *v.t.* (*pres. indic.* **esparzo;** *pres. subj.* **esparza**) to spread abroad, divulge; to disseminate, scatter. — *v.r.* to amuse oneself; to make merry.

esparragado, *n.m.* dish of asparagus.

esparragador, -ra, *n.m.f.* asparagus-grower.

esparragamiento, *n.m.* cultivation of asparagus.

esparragar, *v.t.* to grow or gather asparagus; to cook with asparagus; *vete a esparragar,* (*coll.*) go to the devil!

espárrago, *n.m.* (*bot.*) asparagus; pole of an awning; (*min.*) peg-ladder; *anda* or *vete a freír espárragos,* be off with you! *solo como el espárrago,* as lonely as an asparagus-stalk.

esparraguera, *n.f.* asparagus plant; asparagus-bed; asparagus-plate.

esparraguero, -ra, *n.m.f.* asparagus-seller.

esparraguina, *n.f.* (*min.*) asparagine.

esparrancado, -da, *a.* wide-legged, straddle-legged; divaricated. — *p.p.* [ESPARRANCARSE].

esparrancarse, *v.r.* (*coll.*) to spread the legs wide apart.

esparsión, *n.f.* (*obs.*) dissemination, dispersion, scattering.

espartal, *n.m.* place where *esparto* grows.

espartano, -na, *n.m.f., a.* Spartan.

esparteína, *n.f.* genista alkaloid.

esparteña, *n.f.* rope-sole sandal.

espartería, *n.f.* shop where esparto-work is made or sold.

espartero, -ra, *n.m.f.* maker or seller of esparto-work.

espartilla, *n.f.* mop of esparto-grass.

espartizal, *n.m.* field on which esparto grass is growing.

esparto, *n.m.* esparto-grass.

espasmo, *n.m.* spasm.

espasmódicamente, *adv.* spasmodically.

espasmódico, -ca, *a.* spasmodic, convulsive.

espata, *n.f.* spathe.

espatarrada, *n.f.* (*coll.*) the splits.

espatarrarse, *v.r.* to slip and fall with legs wide open; to be stupefied.

espático, -ca, *a.* spathic.

espato, *n.m.* spar.

espátula, *n.f.* spatula; (*art*) palette-knife; (*zool.*) spoonbill.

espaviento, *n.m.* dread, fear, consternation.

espavorido, -da, *a.* frightened, terrified.

espay, *n.m.* [ESPAHÍ].

especería, *n.f.* grocer's shop, grocery, spicery.

especia, *n.f.* spice. — *pl.* medicinal drugs.

especial, *a.* special, particular; *en especial,* specially.

especialidad, *n.f.* speciality; particular knack, study, etc.

especialista, *n.m.f., a.* specialist.

especialización, *n.f.* specialization; specializing.

especializar, *v.t.* to specialize; to limit, confine. — *v.r.* (with *en*) to specialize in.

especialmente, *adv.* especially.

especiar, *v.t.* to spice.

especie, *n.f.* species, kind, class, sort; incident, event; matter, subject of discussion; affair, case, business; statement, piece of news; show, pretext; feint in fencing; (*phys.*) luminous rays diversely reflected; *en especie,* in kind, not in money; *escapársele a uno una especie,* (*coll.*) to drop a brick; *soltar uno una especie,* (*coll.*) to fly a kite.

especiería, *n.f.* grocery, grocer's shop.

especiero, *n.m.* grocer.

especificación, *n.f.* specification, minute enumeration.

especificadamente, *adv.* specifically.

especificar, *v.t.* (*pret.* **especifiqué;** *pres. subj.* **especifique**) to name, specify, particularize, itemize, go through minutely.

especificativo, -va, *a.* specifical, specifying.

específico, -ca, *a.* specific, specifical. — *n.m.* (*med.*) proprietary brand.

espécimen, *n.m.* specimen, sample.

especioso, -sa, *a.* beautiful, well-finished, neat; (*fig.*) specious, deceiving, plausible.

especiota, *n.f.* (*coll.*) hoax, faked news, cock-and-bull story.

espectable, *a.* (*obs.*) conspicuous, eminent.

espectacular, *a.* spectacular.

espectáculo, *n.m.* spectacle, show, pageant.

espectador, -ra, *a.* observing, looking-on. — *n.m.f.* spectator, looker-on.

espectro, *n.m.* spectre, phantom, ghost, hobgoblin; spectrum.

espectrografía, *n.f.* spectrography.
espectrógrafo, *n.m.* spectrograph.
espectroscopia, *n.f.* spectroscopy.
espectroscópico, -ca, *a.* spectroscopic.
espectroscopio, *n.m.* spectroscope.
especulación, *n.f.* speculation, contemplation; inspection; (*com.*) venture, speculation, scheme.
especulador, -ra, *a.* speculating. — *n.m.f.* speculator.
especular, *v.t.* to inspect, view, behold; to speculate on, meditate about. — *v.i.* to speculate; (*com.*) to speculate, gamble in stocks, share in commercial ventures, etc.
especulativa, *n.f.* understanding, speculative faculty.
especulativamente, *adv.* speculatively.
especulativo, -va, *a.* speculative; thoughtful.
espéculo, *n.m.* (*surg.*) speculum; (*law*) legal code compiled by Alfonso the Wise.
espejado, -da, *a.* mirror-like.
espejear, *v.i.* to shine or reflect as a mirror.
espejeo, *n.m.* mirage; illusion.
espejería, *n.f.* shop where mirrors are made and sold.
espejero, -ra, *n.m.f.* mirror-maker or seller.
espejico; espejillo; espejito, *n.m.* little mirror [ESPEJO].
espejismo, *n.m.* mirage; illusion.
espejo, *n.m.* looking-glass, mirror; (*naut.*) stern frame; *espejo de cuerpo entero,* full-length looking-glass; *espejo ustorio,* burning-glass; *espejo de popa,* (*naut.*) stern-frame; *limpio como un espejo,* as clean as a new penny; *no te verás en ese espejo,* you will not attain your object; *mirarse en una persona como en un espejo,* to love or admire someone very much.
espejuela, *n.f.* curve of the bit; *espejuela abierta,* snaffle.
espejuelo, *n.m.* small looking-glass [ESPEJO]; specular stone, selenite; leaf of mica; candied citron; lark mirror; (*vet.*) wart on pastern. — *pl.* spectacles, lenses, glasses.
espeleología, *n.f.* speleology.
espeleólogo, *n.m.* speleologist.
espelta, *n.f.* spelt.
espélteo, -ea, *a.* belonging to spelt.
espelunca, *n.f.* dark, gloomy cave.
espeluzar, *v.t.* [DESPELUZAR].
espeluznante, *a.* setting the hair on end with fear.
espeluznar, *v.t., v.r.* to dishevel the hair; to set the hair on end (from fright).
espeque, *n.m.* handspike; pump-brake; lever; *espeque de la bomba,* (*naut.*) pump-brake.
espera, *n.f.* expectation, expectance, expectancy; waiting, wait; stay, stop, pause; (*law*) respite, adjournment; (*mus.*) pause, rest; prudence, caution, steadiness, restraint; ancient piece of ordnance; (*carp.*) notch; *estar en espera,* to be in expectation of; *hombre de espera,* a cool, collected man; *cazar a espera,* to lie in wait for game; *compás de espera,* (*mus.*) a bar's rest.
esperable, *a.* that which may be expected or hoped for.
esperador, -ra, *a.* expectant, hoping.
esperantista, *n.m.f., a.* Esperantist.
esperanto, *n.m.* Esperanto.
esperanza, *n.f.* hope, expectancy; (*coll.*) prospect; *dar esperanza(s),* to give encourage-

ment; to be of promise; *no hay esperanza,* there is no chance; *áncora de la esperanza,* (*naut.*) sheet-anchor; *llenar la esperanza,* to fulfil one's hopes; *alimentarse de esperanzas,* to feed on false hopes; *más vale buena esperanza, que ruin posesión,* better a good hope than a bad certainty.
esperanzar, *v.t.* to give hope to.
esperar, *v.t.* to hope; to expect; to wait for, stay, await, look for; to fear; *espero la calentura,* I am afraid of the fever. — *v.i.* to wait; to hope; *quien espera desespera,* hope deferred maketh the heart sick; *esperar en,* to hope for favours from; *esperar sentado,* to hope against hope. — *v.r.* to stay, wait.
esperezarse, *v.r.* to stretch oneself.
esperezo, *n.m.* stretching one's arms and legs.
esperiego, *n.m.* sour-apple-tree.
esperma, *n.f.* sperm; *esperma de ballena,* spermaceti.
espermático, -ca, *a.* spermatic, seminal.
espermatorrea, *n.f.* spermatorrhœa.
espermatozoario, espermatozoide, *n.m.* spermatozoon.
espernada, *n.f.* end link of a chain.
espernancarse, *v.r.* (*Am., prov.*) to stretch the legs wide.
esperón, *n.m.* long wait [ESPERA]; (*naut.*) ram.
esperpento, *n.m.* (*coll.*) odd or ridiculous person; absurdity, nonsense.
esperriaca, *n.f.* (*prov.*) last pressing of grape-juice.
espesamiento, *n.m.* coagulation.
espesar, *v.t.* to thicken, inspissate, condense, coagulate, curdle, concrete; to mass, assemble; to make closer (as knitting). — *v.r.* to condense; to thicken; to become thicker.
espesativo, -va, *a.* thickening.
espeso, -sa, *a.* thick, dense, gross, crass; bulky, heavy, corpulent; frequent, often repeated; curdy; (*fig.*) dirty, slovenly; (*Ven.*) heavy, dull.
espesor, *n.m.* thickness; density, mass (of a solid, gas, etc.).
espesura, *n.f.* density, closeness, thickness; thicket, closely planted wood; abundant head of hair; (*fig.*) slovenliness, negligence in dress.
espetaperro (a), *adv.* at breakneck speed.
espetar, *v.t.* to skewer, spit; to run through, pierce; (*coll.*) to tell something that causes surprise or annoyance; *le espetó fuertes razones,* he gave him strong reasons. — *v.r.* to be stiff and stately, stuck up, inflated with pride; (*coll.*) to glue oneself to some position, dignity, etc.
espetera, *n.f.* kitchen-rack; dresser, kitchen utensils or furniture.
espetón, *n.m.* poker; spit; rake; iron prong; large pin; blow given with a spit; (*zool.*) sea-pike, spit-fish.
espía, *n.m.f.* spy; (*naut.*) warp; *espía del purgatorio,* feeble, languid person; *espía doble,* one who betrays the secrets of both sides.
espiar, *v.t.* to spy; to lurk, lie in wait for. — *v.i.* (*naut.*) to warp, move a ship by means of a warp.
espibia, *n.f.; espibio; espibión,* *n.m.* (*vet.*) dislocation or contraction in the nape of the neck of a horse.
espicacéltica, *n.f.* yellow valerian.
espicanardi; espicanardo, *n.f.* spikenard.

espicifloro, -ra, espiciforme, *a.* spicate.

espícula, *n.f.* spicule.

espicúleo, -lea, *a.* spiculate.

espichar, *v.t.* to prick. — *v.i.* (*coll.*) to give up the ghost; to die.

espiche, *n.m.* sharp-pointed weapon; meat-spit; spile, spigot.

espichón, *n.m.* wound with a pointed weapon.

espiga, *n.f.* spike or ear of grain; tenon, dowel, peg; pin, tongue, treenail, shank, stem; brad, headless nail; tang (of a sword, knife, chisel, etc.); fuse of a bomb or shell; mast-head; *espiga céltica,* valerian; *espiga de agua,* pond-weed; *quedarse a la espiga,* (*coll.*) to remain to the last, gather up others' fragments.

espigadera; espigadora, *n.f.* gleaner.

espigado, -da, *a.* (*agric.*) ripe, eared; tall, grown. — *p.p.* [ESPIGAR].

espigar, *v.t.* (*pret.* **espigué**; *pres. subj.* **espigue**) to glean; to make a tenon; (*prov.*) to give presents to a bride. — *v.i.* to ear (as wheat). — *v.r.* to grow tall, to grow up.

espigón, *n.m.* sting (as of bees); bearded spike; point of a sharp tool or dart; peak; ear of corn; breakwater, pier; top of a treeless hill; *ir con* or *llevar espigón,* to retire in indignation or annoyance.

espiguilla, *n.f.; espiguita,* *n.f.* spikelet; small edging of lace, tape, etc. [ESPIGA].

espilocho, *n.m.* (*obs.*) poor, destitute person.

espilorchería, *n.f.* (*vulg.*) sordid avarice.

espillador, *n.m.* (*slang*) gambler.

espín, *n.m.; puerco espín,* porcupine.

espina, *n.f.* thorn; spine, back-bone; fish-bone; splinter; doubt, scruple, suspicion; *espina blanca,* woolly-cotton thistle; *estar* or *quedarse uno en espinas* or *la espina,* or *quedarse en la espina de Santa Lucía,* to be on tenterhooks; to be exhausted, worn out; *dar mala espina a,* to arouse doubts, suspicions; *dejar a uno la espina en el dedo,* to fail to remedy entirely the harm that has been done; *sacar la espina,* to remove a grievance, etc.; *sacarse uno la espina,* to recoup a loss; *no saques espinas donde no hay espigas,* never work without hope of a result.

espinaca, *n.f.* spinach.

espinadura, *n.f.* pricking with a thorn.

espinal, *a.* spinal, dorsal.

espinar, *v.t.* to prick with thorns; to provoke, nettle, make uneasy; to surround trees with thorn-bushes, brambles or briers.

espinar, *n.m.* place full of thorn-bushes, brambles or briers; dangerous undertaking, arduous enterprise.

espinazo, *n.m.* spine, back-bone; *doblar el espinazo,* (*coll.*) to cringe in order to benefit.

espinel, *n.m.* fishing-line with many hooks.

espinela, *n.f.* (*poet.*) [DECIMA], octosyllabic ten-line stanza; spinel-ruby.

espíneo, -ea, *a.* made or full of thorns.

espinera, *n.f.* hawthorn.

espineta, *n.f.* spinet.

espingarda, *n.f.* small piece of ordnance (*obs.*); long Moorish musket.

espingardada, *n.f.* wound from an *espingarda.*

espinica; espinita; espinilla, *n.f.* small thorn [ESPINA].

espinilla, *n.f.* shin-bone; black-head, acne.

espinillera, *n.f.* greave, jambe (armour).

espino, *n.m* hawthorn; buckthorn; *espino blanco* or *majuelo,* hawthorn; *espino amarillo* common sea-buckthorn; *espino negro,* buck-thorn; *espino cerval,* purging buckthorn; *espino artificial,* barbed wire; *pasar por los espinos de Santa Lucía,* to be in great affliction.

espinosismo, *n.m.* Spinozism.

espinosista, *n.m.f.,* *a.* Spinozist.

espinoso, -sa, *a.* spiny, thorny; dangerous, arduous.

espinzar, *v.t.* (*prov.*) to burl.

espiocha, *n.f.* pickaxe.

espión, *n.m.* spy.

espionaje, *n.m.* espionage, spying.

espiote, *n.m.* (*obs.*) sharp-pointed weapon.

espira, *n.f.* helix, spiral line; whorl (of a shell); surbase of a column.

espiración, *n.f.* respiration.

espirador, -ra, *a.* breathing. — *n.m.f.* breather.

espiral, *a.* spiral, helical, winding. — *n.f.* spiral line; spiral spring of a watch.

espiralmente, *adv.* spirally.

espirante. *a.* respiring.

espirar, *v.i.* to breathe, exhale. — *v.t.* to breathe, exhale; to move, animate; to infuse a divine spirit in, inspire; (*poet.*) to blow (the wind) softly, mildly.

espirativo, -va, *a.* (*theol.*) that which inspires; that which can breathe.

espirea, *n.f.* spiræa.

espiritado, -da, *a.* (*coll.*) extremely thin.

espiritar, *v.t.* to demonize, possess with a devil; (*coll.*) to agitate, irritate. — *v.r.* (*coll.*) to be agitated, fret.

espiritillo, *n.m.* little spirit [ESPÍRITU].

espiritismo, *n.m.* spiritualism, spiritism.

espiritista, *n.m.f.,* *a.* spiritualist.

espiritosamente, *adv.* spiritedly, ardently.

espiritoso, -sa, *a.* lively, spirited, active, ardent; spirituous.

espíritu, *n.m.* spirit; soul; genius; courage, ardour; spiritus; alcoholic liquor; turn of mind, inclination; true sense or meaning; power of mind, strength, energy. — *pl.* demons, spirits, hobgoblins; (*chem.*) spirits, vapours, ether; *cobrar espíritu,* to take courage; *dar, despedir* or *exhalar el espíritu,* to give up the ghost, die; *levantar el espíritu,* to take new strength or courage; *el Espíritu Santo,* the Holy Ghost; *espíritu maligno,* the Evil One; *espíritu de la golosina,* very thin person.

espiritual, *a.* spiritual; ghostly.

espiritualidad, *n.f.* incorporeality; intellectual nature.

espiritualismo, *n.m.* spiritualism (as opposed to materialism).

espiritualista, *n.m.f.,* *a.* spiritualist.

espiritualización, *n.f.* spiritualization.

espiritualizar, *v.t.* to spiritualize, purify, refine the intellect.

espiritualmente, *adv.* spiritually.

espirituoso, -sa, *a.* spirituous; ardent; vivid, airy, lively.

espiritusanto, *n.m.* (*CR., Nic.*) large, white flower of a cactus.

espirómetro, *n.m.* spirometer.

espiroqueta, *n.f.* Spirochæta.

espita, *n.f.* measure of length (8 inches); tap, spout, stop-cock, faucet, spigot; (*coll.*) tippler, drunkard.

espitar, *v.t.* to put a faucet in; to tap.

espito, *n.m.* (*print.*) peel, hanger.

esplendente, *a.* (*poet.*) glittering, shining, resplendent.

esplender, *v.i.* (*poet.*) to shine, glitter.

espléndidamente, *adv.* splendidly, nobly, gloriously, brightly, magnificently.

esplendidez, *n.f.* splendour, magnificence, show, ostentation, grandeur; abundance; liberality.

espléndido, -da, *a.* splendid, magnificent, grand, large, costly, sumptuous, pompous; liberal; (*poet.*) resplendent.

esplendor, *n.m.* splendour, lustre, brilliancy, finery, glory, grandeur, magnificence; radiance, glitter, fulgency; nobleness, excellence, eminence.

esplendorosamente, *adv.* with splendour.

esplendoroso, -sa, *a.* splendid, radiant.

esplenético, -ca; esplénico, -ca, *a.* splenic.

espliego, *n.m.* lavender.

esplín, *n.m.* spleen, melancholy.

esplique, *n.m.* bird-snare.

espolada, *n.f.* prick with a spur; *espolada de vino*, (*coll.*) large draught of wine.

espolazo, *n.m.* violent prick with a spur.

espoleadura, *n.f.* wound made with a spur.

espolear, *v.t.* to spur; to instigate, incite, urge forward.

espoleta, *n.f.* fuse (of a bomb); wish-bone.

espolín, *n.m.* small spur [ESPUELA]; shuttle for brocading or flowering; silk brocade.

espolinado, -da, *a.* flowered, brocaded (of silks). — *p.p.* [ESPOLINAR].

espolinar, *v.t.* to brocade, to flower.

espolio, *n.m.* property left by a prelate.

espolique, *n.m.* running footman.

espolista, *n.m.* [ESPOLIQUE]; one who farms an *espolio*.

espolón, *n.m.* cock's spur; ridge, crag of a mountain; (*eng.*) mole, breakwater, jetty, groin; (*arch.*) spur, buttress; (*naut.*) ram of a man-of-war; beak of a galley; (*naut.*) fender-beam; chilblain on the heel; public walk; *tiene más espolones que un gallo*, he is very old.

espolonada, *n.f.* sudden onset of horsemen.

espolvorear, espolvorizar, *v.t.* to scatter powder on.

espondaico, -ca, *a.* spondaic.

espondeo, *n.m.* spondee.

espóndil, *n.m.* vertebra.

espóndilo, *n.m.* spondyl, vertebra.

esponja, *n.f.* sponge; (*coll.*) sponger.

esponjado, -da, *a.* spongy; (*coll.*) stuck-up. — *n.m.* meringue. — *p.p.* [ESPONJAR].

esponjadura, *n.f.* sponging; flaw in cast metal; (*Arg.*) arrogance.

esponjar, *v.t.* to soak, sponge, imbibe. — *v.r.* to swell; to be puffed up with pride; (*coll.*) to become glowing with health.

esponjera, *n.f.* sponge-holder.

esponjilla; esponjita; esponjuela, *n.f.* small sponge [ESPONJA].

esponjosidad, *n.f.* sponginess.

esponjoso, -sa, *a.* spongy, porous, fungous.

esponsales, *n.m.pl.* espousals, betrothal.

esponsalicio, -cia, *a.* nuptial, spousal.

espontáneamente, *adv.* spontaneously, voluntarily.

espontanearse, *v.r.* to avow or declare spontaneously.

espontaneidad, *n.f.* spontaneity, spontaneousness.

espontáneo, -nea, *a.* spontaneous; voluntary, willing.

espontón, *n.m.* spontoon, half-pike.

espontonada, *n.f.* salute or blow with a spontoon.

espora, *n.f.; esporo*, *n.m.* (*bot.*) spore.

esporádico, -ca, *a.* sporadic, isolated.

esportada, *n.f.* frailful, basketful.

esportear, *v.t.* to carry in frails, panniers or baskets.

esportilla, *n.f.* small frail [ESPUERTA].

esportillero, *n.m.* porter, carrier.

esportillo, *n.m.* pannier, frail, basket.

esportón, *n.m.* large pannier or frail [ESPUERTA].

esportonada, *n.f.* basketful.

espórtula, *n.f.* (*prov.*) court fees.

esposa, *n.f.* wife, spouse, consort, matron. — *pl.* manacles, handcuffs, fetters, shackles, chains.

esposo, *n.m.* husband, spouse, consort; (*Arg., Chi., Ec., Hond.*) episcopal ring.

espuela, *n.f.* spur, rowel; incitement, stimulus; *espuela de caballero*, larkspur; *calzar(se) la espuela*, to be dubbed a knight; *calzar espuela*, to be a knight; *correr la espuela*, to spur deeply; (*fig.*) to scold, mortify; *dar de (la) espuela*, to spur; *echar la espuela*, (*coll.*) to take the last drink at a festive gathering; *estar con las espuelas calzadas*, to be all ready for a journey; to be ready for business; *sentir la espuela*, to feel reproof, rebuke, etc.; *poner espuelas a*, to incite, spur on.

espuenda, *n.f.* (*prov.*) bank of a canal; fringe of a field.

espuerta, *n.f.* two-handled frail; *a espuertas*, abundantly.

espulgadero, *n.m.* place where beggars clean themselves from lice or fleas.

espulgador, -ra, *n.m.f.* one who cleans off lice or fleas.

espulgar, *v.t.* (*pret.* **espulgué**; *pres. subj.* **espulgue**) to delouse; (*fig.*) to examine closely.

espulgo, *n.m.* act of delousing.

espuma, *n.f.* foam, scum, lather, froth; *espuma de plata*, litharge of silver; *espuma de nitro*, saltpetre; *espuma de mar*, meerschaum; *espuma de la sal*, sea-froth; *crecer como (la) espuma*, to shoot up, grow (up).

espumadera, *n.f.* skimmer, colander.

espumador, -ra, *a.* skimming. — *n.m.f.* skimmer.

espumajear, *v.i.* to froth at the mouth.

espumajo, *n.m.* froth, spume, saliva.

espumajoso, -sa, *a.* foamy, frothy, spumous.

espumante, *a.* lathering, foaming, frothing; sparkling (of wine).

espumar, *v.t.* to skim, scum. — *v.i.* to froth, foam; (*fig.*) to grow up.

espumarajo, *n.m.* foam or froth from the mouth; *echar espumarajos por la boca*, to foam at the mouth with passion.

espumear, *v.t.* to raise foam on.

espumero, *n.m.* place where salt water crystallizes.

espumescente, *a.* spumescent.

espumilla, *n.f.* Oriental crape, gauzy fabric; (*Ec., Hond.*) meringue.

espumillón, *n.m.* heavy grogram.

espumosidad, *n.f.* frothiness, foaminess.

espumoso, -sa, *a.* spumy, frothy, spumous, foamy, nappy; sparkling (as wine).

espumuy, *n.f.* (*Guat.*) rock dove.

espundia, *n.f.* (*vet.*) cancerous ulcer, tumour.

espúreo, -rea; espurio, -ria, *a.* bastard, illegitimate; bogus, false, counterfeit, adulterated, not genuine, spurious.

espurrear; espurriar, *v.t.* to sprinkle, moisten with water held in the mouth.

espurrir, *v.t.* (*prov.*) to stretch out (as the feet).

esputar, *v.t.* to expectorate.

esputo, *n.m.* spittle, saliva; sputum.

esquebrajar, *v.t.* to split, cleave. — *v.r.* to become open, be split, full of chinks.

esqueje, *n.m.* (*agric.*) cutting, slip.

esquela, *n.f.* note, short letter; printed card; obituary notice; *esquela amatoria,* love letter.

esquelético, -ca, *a.* skeletal; very thin.

esqueleto, *n.m.* skeleton; framework; very thin person; works of a watch; (*Col., CR., Guat., Mex.*) form, application (with particulars to be filled in); (*Chi.*) rough draft of a speech, sermon, etc.; *en esqueleto,* unfinished.

esquelita, *n.f.* small note [ESQUELA].

esquema, *n.m.* scheme, diagram; outline, sketch; plan.

esquemáticamente, *adv.* schematically.

esquemático, -ca, *a.* schematic.

esquematismo, *n.m.* schematism.

esquena, *n.f.* spine, back-bone.

esquero, *n.m.* leather bag or pouch.

esquí, *n.m.* ski.

esquiador, -ra, *n.m.f.* skier.

esquiar, *v.i.* to ski.

esquiciado, -da, *a.* sketched, delineated. — *p.p.* [ESQUICIAR].

esquiciar, *v.t.* (*art*) to make a first sketch.

esquicio, *n.m.* sketch, outline.

esquifada, *n.f.* boat-load; vault of a cistern.

esquifar, *v.t.* to fit out a ship; to provide a boat with oars.

esquifazón, *n.f.* complement of oars and oarsmen on a galley, etc.

esquife, *n.m.* skiff, small boat; cylindrical vault.

esquila, *n.f.* small bell; cattle-bell; sheep-shearing; (*ichth.*) prawn; (*entom.*) water-spider; (*bot.*) squill.

esquilador, -ra, *n.m.f.* sheep-shearer, clipper.

esquilar, *v.t.* to shear, crop, clip; to fleece; *sin esquilar,* unshorn; *a Dios que esquilan,* phrase denoting great haste.

esquileo, *n.m.* shearing; shearing season; shearing place.

esquilimoso, -sa, *a.* (*coll.*) fastidious, over-nice.

esquilmar, *v.t.* to harvest; to impoverish; *esquilmar la tierra,* to impoverish the soil.

esquilmeño, -ña, *a.* (*prov.*) fruitful, productive.

esquilmo, *n.m.* harvest; produce of vines, cattle, etc.; (*Chi.*) stalk of grapes; (*Mex.*) profits of farming by-products.

esquilo, *n.m.* (*obs.*) shearing; (*prov.*) kind of squirrel.

esquilón, *n.m.* large cattle-bell.

esquimal, *n.m.f., a.* Eskimo.

esquina, *n.f.* corner, nook; edge, angle; *en la esquina de la calle,* at the corner of the street; *estar en esquina,* to be in disagreement; *las cuatro esquinas,* game of puss-in-the-corner; *darse contra* or *por las esquinas,* to wear oneself out without gaining success.

esquinado, -da, *a.* cornered, angled; unsociable. — *p.p.* [ESQUINAR].

esquinal, *n.m.* (*prov.*) corner-plate; angle-iron; iron knee.

esquinancia; esquinencia, *n.f.* quinsy.

esquinante; esquinanto, *n.m.* aromatic rush.

esquinar, *v.t.* to form a corner with; to square timber; to cause to quarrel. — *v.r.* to quarrel, become on bad terms.

esquinazo, *n.m.* (*coll.*) corner; (*Chi.*) serenade; *dar esquinazo a uno,* (*coll.*) to leave someone planted, leave in the lurch; to give the slip to someone.

esquinco, *n.m.* skink, lizard.

esquinela, *n.f.* greave, leg-armour.

esquinzador, *n.m.* rag-room in paper-mills; rag-engine.

esquinzar, *v.t.* to cut rags in paper-mills.

esquipar, *v.t.* (*obs.*) [ESQUIFAR].

esquiraza, *n.f.* ancient ship.

esquirla, *n.f.* splinter of a bone, glass, stone, etc.

esquirol, *n.m.* squirrel; (*prov.*) (*coll.*) strike-breaker, blackleg.

esquisto, *n.m.* schist; slate.

esquistoso, -ra, *a.* laminated; slaty.

esquitar, *v.t.* to pardon, remit a debt.

esquite, *n.m.* (*CR., Hond., Mex.*) popped corn.

esquivar, *v.t.* to avoid, elude, shun, evade, escape. — *v.r.* to withdraw; be reserved, coy.

esquivez, *n.f.* disdain, scorn, asperity, coldness, coyness.

esquivo, -va, *a.* elusive, evading; reserved, scornful, fastidious, shy, coy, cold.

esquizado, -da, *a.* mottled (as marble).

esquizofrenia, *n.f.* schizophrenia.

estabilidad, *n.f.* permanence, stability, firmness, duration, constancy, fixedness, consistence.

estabilísimo, -ma, *a. superl.* [ESTABLE] very stable, very firm.

estabilizador, -ra, *a.* giving stability. — *n.m.f.* stabilizer.

estabilizar, *v.t.* to stabilize (currency, etc.).

estable, *a.* permanent, stable, steady, fast, firm, durable, consistent.

establear, *v.t.* to tame, accustom to the stable.

establecedor, -ra, *a.* establishing. — *n.m.f.* founder, establisher, confirmer.

establecer, *v.t.* (*pres. indic.* **establezco;** *pres. subj.* **establezca**) to establish, fix securely, found; to decree, enact, constitute. — *v.r.* to establish or settle oneself in a place.

estableciente, *a.* establishing.

establecimiento, *n.m.* foundation, establishment, settlement; shop, store; institution; manufactory; law, statute, decree, ordinance.

Establecimientos del Estrecho, *n.m.pl.* Straits Settlements.

establemente, *adv.* firmly, stably.

establerizo (*obs.*); **establero,** *n.m.* hostler, groom; stableman.

establezco; establezca, *pres. indic.; pres. subj.* [ESTABLECER].

establo, *n.m.* stable; cattle-barn.

estabulación, *n.f.* stabling.

estaca, *n.f.* stake, pile, pole; cudgel, stick, bludgeon; grafting-twig; (*agr.*) cutting; (*carp.*) clamp-nail; (*Chi.*) partnership in a mine; *a estaca, a la estaca,* tied to a place, in durance; *estar a la estaca,* to be very poor and overworked; to have few resources or little liberty; *no dejar estaca en pared*, to destroy completely; *plantar*, or *clavar, estacas,* (*naut.*) to pitch in a head sea and make little progress.

estacada, *n.f.* palisade, stockade; paling, fence-work; pile-pier; place for a duel; (*prov.*) new plantation of olives; *dejar a uno en la estacada*, to leave someone in the lurch; *quedar(se) en la estacada*, to be vanquished, lose; to fail in an undertaking.

estacar, *v.t.* (*pret.* **estaqué;** *pres. subj.* **estaque**) to stake; to enclose, fence with stakes; to tie to a stake; (*Col., Chi., Hond., Ven.*) to sun-dry skins. — *v.r.* to remain stiff as a pole.

estacazo, *n.m.* blow with a stake.

estación, *n.f.* condition, state, position, situation; season of the year; hour, moment, time; railway station; telegraph or police station; stop, stay; devotional visit to a church; party of persons posted at some place; (*astron.*) stationary point; (*eccles.*) Stations of the Cross; *andar (las) estaciones*, to perform stationary prayers; to attend to one's business; *tornar a andar las estaciones*, to return to one's former evil habits; *vestir con la estación*, to dress according to the season.

estacional, *a.* seasonal; (*astron.*) stationary; *calenturas estacionales*, seasonal fevers.

estacionamiento, *n.m.* stationing; parking.

estacionario, -ria, *a.* stationary, fixed.

estacionarse, *v.r.* to remain stationary, take one's stand; to park (a car). — *v.t.* (*Arg.*) to mate sheep at certain seasons.

estacionero, -ra, *n.m.f., a.* (devotee) praying frequently at the stations in church.

estacón, *n.m.* large stake [ESTACA].

estacte, *n.m.* oil of myrrh.

estacha, *n.f.* tow-line, hawser; harpoon-rope for whaling.

estada, *n.f.* stay, sojourn, residence.

estadal, *n.m.* lineal measure (about 11 ft.); ornament or blessed ribbon worn round the neck; (*prov.*) length of wax taper.

estadero, *n.m.* (*obs.*) royal land-surveyor.

estadía, *n.f.* stay, detention; (*com., naut.*) demurrage; cost of such stay; (*art*) seating, session (model).

estadio, *n.m.* stadium, racecourse.

estadista, *n.m.* statistician; statist, statesman, politician.

estadística, *n.f.* statistics.

estadístico, -ca, *a.* statistical, statistic, political.

estadizo, -za, *a.* stagnant.

estado, *n.m.* state, nation, commonwealth; condition; footing, circumstances, rank, class, quality; condition (whether single, married or widowed); profession; account, statement, report; measure of length (2.17 yds.). — *pl.* estates, representative assembly; *estado de guerra* or *de sitio*, martial law; *estado general* or *llano*, commons, commonalty (as opposed to nobility); *estado honesto*, the condition of virginity; *estado libre*, free-state; *estado mayor*, (*mil.*) staff; *estado mayor general*, general staff; *hombre de estado*, statesman; *materias de estado*, state affairs; *poner a uno en estado*, to set one up in life; *caer de estado*, to lose status; *en estado de merecer*, (*coll.*) marriageable (of a girl);

estar en el estado de la inocencia, to have made no progress; *mudar estado*, to change one's profession or condition; *siete estados debajo de tierra*, deeply buried, very far hidden from sight.

estado, *p.p.* [ESTAR].

estadojo; estandorio; estadoño, *n.m.* (*prov.*) stake for supporting side-board of a cart.

Estados Unidos de América, *n.m.pl.* United States of America.

estafa, *n.f.* swindle, trick, deceit; stirrup.

estafador, -ra, *n.m.f.* impostor, swindler.

estafar, *v.t.* to swindle, deceive, defraud.

estafermo, *n.m.* wooden movable figure of an armed man, quintain; indolent, idle fellow.

estafero, *n.m.* (*obs.*) foot-boy, stable-boy.

estafeta, *n.f.* courier, post, express; post-office; diplomatic post-bag.

estafetero, *n.m.* post-master.

estafetil, *a.* belonging to a courier or post.

estafilococo, *n.m.* staphylococcus.

estafisagria, *n.f.* stavesacre, larkspur.

estagnación, *n.f.* (*neologism*) stagnation.

estala, *n.f.* stable; port of call.

estalación, *n.f.* class, rank, order (in cathedral churches, etc.).

estalactita, *n.f.* stalactite.

estalagmita, *n.f.* stalagmite.

estalingadura, *n.f.* bending a cable to an anchor.

estalingar, *v.t.* to bend a cable.

estallante, *a.* bursting, exploding.

estallar, *v.i.* to explode, burst; (*fig.*) to break out.

estallido; estallo, *n.m.* crack, crackling, crashing, snap, outburst; report (of fire-arms); *dar un estallido*, to make a great noise; *estar para dar un estallido*, to be in dread of some imminent danger.

estambor, *n.m.* stern-post.

estambrado, *n.m.* (*prov.*) worsted cloth.

estambrar, *v.t.* to spin worsted.

estambre, *n.m.* worsted, woollen yarn; stamen of flowers; *estambre de la vida*, (*poet.*) the thread of life.

Estambul, *n.m.* Istanbul.

estamenara, *n.f.* futtock.

estamento, *n.m.* each of the estates composing the Cortes in Aragon.

estameña, *n.f.* serge.

estameñete, *n.m.* light serge.

estamíneo, -nea, *a.* made of worsted.

estaminífero, -ra, *a.* staminate.

estampa, *n.f.* stamp, print, cut; engraving; portrait; printing press; impression, footprint; *dar una obra a la estampa*, to send a book to press; *estampas iluminadas*, coloured plates; *parecer una la estampa de la herejía*, (*coll.*) to be very ugly, or very badly dressed.

estampación, *n.f.* stamping; printing.

estampado, -da, *a.* stamped, figured (of cotton print, calico, etc.). — *n.m.* cotton print; stamping, impression; cloth-printing. — *p.p.* [ESTAMPAR].

estampador, *n.m.* stamper; stamp, puncheon; one who makes or sells prints.

estampar, *v.t.* to stamp, print, emboss; to imprint (as a kiss); to impress, leave an impression, fix (in the mind or memory).

estampería, *n.f.* office for printing or selling prints.

estampero, -ra, *n.m.f.* maker or seller of prints or stamps.

estampía, *n.f.; de estampía,* suddenly, in a rush.

estampida, *n.f.* [ESTAMPIDO]; (*Col., Guat., Mex., Ven.*) stampede; (*coll.*) *dar estampida,* to make a great noise resembling an explosion.

estampido, *n.m.* report of a gun; crack, crash, crashing; *dar un estampido,* to crash, make a noise.

estampilla, *n.f.* small print [ESTAMPA]; rubber stamp with facsimile of signature; impression of such a stamp; (*Am.*) postage stamp.

estampillado, -da, *n.m.f.* stamping. — *p.p.* [ESTAMPILLAR].

estampillar, *v.t.* to stamp.

estampita, *n.f.* small print or stamp [ESTAMPA].

estancación, *n.f.;* **estancamiento,** *n.m.* stagnation, stagnancy.

estancar, *v.t.* (*pret.* **estanqué;** *pres. subj.* **estanque**) to stanch, stop, check, stem a current; (*com.*) to corner, to monopolize; to put an embargo on goods. — *v.r.* be stagnant.

estancia, *n.f.* sojourn, stay, continuance in a place; dwelling, mansion, habitation; sitting-room; living-room; (*poet.*) stanza; (*Arg., Chi.*) hacienda, farm; (*Cub., Ven.*) country seat, villa.

estanciero, *n.m.* overseer on a farm, etc.; owner of a hacienda.

estanco, -ca, *a.* watertight, in good repair, seaworthy. — *n.m.* monopoly, forestalling; place where Government monopolized goods are sold; repository, archives, files; (*Ec.*) shop for the sale of spirits.

estandarte, *n.m.* standard, flag, banner, colours.

estangurria, *n.f.* strangury; catheter.

estanque, *n.m.* pond, basin, dam, reservoir.

estanquero, -ra, *n.m.f.* keeper of reservoirs; retailer of monopoly goods, tobacconist.

estanquillero, -ra, *n.m.f.* [ESTANQUERO].

estanquillo, *n.m.* cigar-store, tobacco-shop; (*Mex.*) small, poor shop; (*Ec.*) tavern.

estanquito, *n.m.* small pond or dam [ESTANQUE].

estantal, *n.m.* buttress.

estante, *a.* being, existing, extant; fixed, permanent. — *n.m.* shelf, stand; bookcase; (*prov.*) image-carrier in processions; (*print.*) cabinet; (*Am.*) wood-pile. — *pl.* props of the crossbeams.

estantería, *n.f.* shelving; bookcase.

estantigua, *n.f.* procession of phantoms, bugbears, hobgoblins; (*coll.*) tall, thin, badly dressed person, scarecrow, fright.

estantío, -tía, *a.* standing still, stationary; dull, slow, lifeless, spiritless.

estañador, *n.m.* tinner, tinman, pewterer.

estañadura, *n.f.* tinning.

estañar, *v.t.* to tin, cover with tin, blanch; to solder.

estañero, *n.m.* tinner; seller of tin-ware.

estaño, *n.m.* tin; iron plates covered with tin; (*obs.*) pond or pool of water.

estaquero, *n.m.* year-old buck or doe.

estaquilla; estaquita, *n.f.* (*shoe.*) peg; tack, tin-tack; spike, brad [ESTACA].

estaquillador, *n.m.* (*shoe.*) pegging-awl.

estaquillar, *v.t.* to peg, fasten with tacks.

estar, *v.i.* (*pres. indic.* **estoy;** *pret.* **estuve;**

pres. subj. **esté**) to be (temporarily, or in a place, state, or condition); to appertain to, concern; to fit (as a garment); *esa chaqueta le está ancha,* that jacket is loose on him; when followed by the present participle of a verb it is an auxiliary verb, denoting continuance of the action expressed by the principal verb, as *estar escribiendo,* to be writing; when followed by a reflexive verb, it may take the pronoun belonging to the principal verb, as *estarse muriendo,* instead of *estar muriéndose,* to be in a dying condition; *estar a,* to be (the day of the week or month that follows), as *estamos a lunes,* this is Monday; *estamos a cinco,* this is the fifth; *¿a cómo estamos?* or *¿a cuántos estamos?* what day of the month is it? *estar a,* to sell at: *las patatas están a tres pesetas,* potatoes are selling at three pesetas; *estar a cuentas,* to be on the point of doing accounts; *estar con,* to live with; to be talking to; to be ill with a disease; to be in a state of joy, etc.: *estar con Juan,* to be or live with John; to be engaged (in talk) with John; *estar de,* to be temporarily in the condition or doing the action indicated by the following noun, as *estoy de mudanza,* I am moving; *estoy de facción,* I am on sentry-go; *estoy de capitán,* I am acting as captain; *estar de buen* or *mal humor,* to be in a good (*or* bad) humour; *estar de pie* or *en pie* or *estar levantado,* to be standing; *estar de prisa,* to be in a hurry; *estar de casa, de obra, de viaje,* to be at home, at work, on a journey; *estar en* (a) to understand or comprehend: *estoy en lo que Vd. me dice,* I understand what you tell me; (b) to be of opinion: *estoy en que,* I am of opinion that; (c) to stand, to cost: *este vestido me está en veinte duros,* these clothes cost me twenty *duros;* (d) to depend on: *en eso está,* it depends on this; *¡dónde estamos!* what next!; *estar alerta,* to be on the watch, to be vigilant; *estar bien una cosa,* to suit, agree, fit; *estar por medio,* to interpose; *estar en grande,* to live in luxury; *¿está Vd.?* or *¿estamos?* do you understand? *estar con el pie en el aire,* to be unsettled; *estar a erre,* to be doing something with the utmost care; *estar a la capa,* (*naut.*) to lie to, to lie by; *estar a la capa con la trinquetilla y el estay mayor,* (*naut.*) to lie to under the fore- and main-stay sails; *estar a dos dedos de hacer una cosa,* to become almost decided to do something; *estar para,* to be about to: *estoy para partir,* I am about to start; *estar para una cosa,* to be ready for or disposed to do a thing; *no está para bromas,* he is not in a joking humour; *estar por,* to be for, in favour of; to continue to be (followed by infinitive); to have a mind to, wish to; to be going to; *estar por escribir,* to remain unwritten as yet; *estoy por el color blanco,* I am (all) for white; *estoy por romperle la cabeza,* I have a mind to break his head; *estoy por mi hermano,* I will answer for my brother; *está por partir,* he is going to start; *estar sobre sí,* to be cautious, to be conceited; *estar a todo,* to be ready for all eventualities; *estar a matar,* to be at daggers drawn; *estar de más* or *de sobra,* to be superfluous; *estar diciendo comedme,* to be very tempting (of food); *bien está* or *está bien,* interjection expressing either content or discontent;

están verdes or *no están maduras*, sour grapes! *está que bota*, he is full of indignation; *estar a la que salta*, to be always ready to seize an opportunity; *están al caer las cinco*, it is on the point of striking five; *está al caer tu ascenso*, you are on the point of being promoted; *estar a obscuras*, to be completely ignorant; *estar con uno*, to agree with some-one; *estar de gaita*, to be merry, high-spirited; *estar en una cosa*, to be expert at something; to be convinced of the truth of something; *estar en sí*, to be very sure of oneself; *estar uno en todo*, to be versatile; *estarle a uno bien empleada una cosa*, to serve a person right; *estar mal con uno*, not to get on well with someone; *estar uno para ello*, to be ready to do an accustomed job well; *estar por ver*, to remain to be seen; *estar sobre uno*, to importune someone; *estar sobre un negocio*, to conduct a business well; *estar viendo una cosa*, to foresee something as inevitable; *estaba visto* or *¡lo estaba viendo!* it was inevitable! — *v.r.* to stay, remain; to keep; to be detained or delayed; *estarse parado* or *quieto*, to stand still; *debo estarme aquí*, I must remain here; *María munca se está callada*, Mary is never silent; *estarse de más*, to be kicking one's heels.

estarcido, *n.m.* stencilled drawing; outline.

estarcir, *v.t.* to stencil, trace the outlines.

estarna, *n.f.* small partridge.

estatera, *n.f.* (*obs.*) balance; stater, ancient Greek coin.

estática, *n.f.* statics.

estátice, *n.m.* sea-lavender; *estátice común*, sea-gillyflower.

estático, -ca, *a.* static, statical.

estatua, *n.f.* statue; carved figure; *quedarse hecho una estatua*, to be paralysed with fright, etc.

estatuar, *v.t.* to adorn with statues.

estatuaria, *n.f.* statuary, sculpture.

estatuario, -ria, *a.* belonging to statuary. — *n.m.* statuary; sculptor.

estatúder, *n.m.* (*hist.*) stadholder.

estatuir, *v.t.* to establish, ordain, enact.

estatura, *n.f.* stature, height of a person.

estatutario, -ria, *a.* statutory.

estatuto, *n.m.* statute, law, ordinance. — *pl.* by-laws; *hacer estatutos*, to enact laws.

estay, *n.m.* (*naut.*) stay; *estay de galope*, top-mast-stay; *estay mayor*, mainstay; *estay del mastelero mayor*, maintop-stay; *estay de trinquete*, fore-stay.

este, *n.m.* east; east wind; *este cuarto* or *cuarta al nordeste*, east-by-north; *este* or *es nordeste*, east-north-east; *este cuarto al sudeste*, east-by-south; *este* or *es sudeste*, east-south-east.

este, esta, *a.* this (one); the latter. — *pl.* **estos, estas,** these.

éste, *m.;* **ésta,** *f., dem. pron.* this. — *pl.* **éstos,** *m.;* **éstas,** *f.* these; *ésta y nunca más*, this once is enough; *en éstas y en estotras*, in the meanwhile; *en esto*, at this time.

esté, *pres. subj.* [ESTAR].

esteárico, -ca, *a.* stearic; *bujías esteáricas*, stearin candles.

estearina, *n.f.* stearin.

esteatita, *n.f.* steatite, soap-stone.

esteatoma, *n.f.* fatty tumour.

esteba, *n.f.* prickly plant growing in swamps; stevedore's pole.

Esteban, *n.m.* Stephen.

estebar, *v.t.* to put cloth into the dye-kettle.

estegomia, *n.f.* mosquito (*stegomyia fasciata*).

estela, *n.f.* (*naut.*) wake, track of a ship; (*arch.*) stela.

estelar, *a.* sidereal, stellar.

estelaria, *n.f.* (*bot.*) silvery lady's mantle.

estelífero, -ra, *a.* (*poet.*) starry.

estelión, *n.m.* stellion; toad-stone.

estelionato, *n.m.* fraudulent conveyance.

estelón, *n.m.* toad-stone.

estemple, *n.m.* (*min.*) stemple.

estenocardia, *n.f.* (*med.*) angina pectoris.

estenografía, *n.f.* stenography, shorthand.

estenografiar, *v.t.* to write shorthand.

estenográficamente, *adv.* stenographically.

estenográfico, -ca, *a.* stenographic.

estenógrafo, -fa, *n.m.f.* stenographer.

estenordeste, *n.m.* east-north-east.

estentóreo, -ea, *a.* stentorian.

estepa, *n.f.* rock-rose; steppe, barren plain.

estepar, *n.m.* place filled with rock-roses.

estepilla, *n.f.* white-leaved rock-rose.

estera, *n.f.* mat, matting; *cargado de esteras*, (*coll.*) fed-up.

esteral, *n.m.* (*Arg.*) inlet, estuary.

esterar, *v.t.* to cover with mats or matting. — *v.i.* (*coll.*) to put on winter clothes before the proper time.

estercoladura, *n.f.;* **estercolamiento,** *n.m.* ejection of excrements; manuring.

estercolar, *v.t.* to dung, muck, manure. — *v.i.* to void the excrements.

estercolero, *n.m.* muck-collector; dunghill, muck-heap.

estercolizo, -za; estercoráceo, -cea, *a.* stercoraceous.

estercóreo, -ea, *a.* stercoral.

estercuelo, *n.m.* manuring.

estéreo, *n.m.* stere; measure of firewood.

estereografía, *n.f.* stereography.

estereográfico, -ca, *a.* stereographic.

estereógrafo, *n.m.* stereographer.

estereometría, *n.f.* stereometry.

estereométrico, -ca, *a.* stereometric.

estereómetro, *n.m.* stereometer.

estereoscopio, *n.m.* stereoscope.

estereotipa (*obs.*); **estereotipia,** *n.f.* stereo-typy, stereotyping; place where stereotypes are made.

estereotipador, *n.m.* stereotyper.

estereotipar, *v.t.* to stereotype; to print from stereotypes.

estereotípico, -ca, *a.* stereotypic.

estereotomía, *n.f.* stereotomy.

esterería, *n.f.* shop where mat-work is made and sold.

esterero, -ra, *n.m.f.* mat-maker, mat-seller.

estéril, *a.* barren, sterile; unproductive, fruitless.

esterilidad, *n.f.* sterility, unfruitfulness, barrenness; want of crops, scarcity.

esterilizador, -ra, *a.* sterilizing. — *n.m.f.* sterilizer.

esterilizar, *v.t.* to sterilize.

estérilmente, *adv.* barrenly, unfruitfully, meagrely.

esterilla, *n.f.* small mat; straw plait; narrow gold or silver braid [ESTERA]; (*CR., Chi., Ec.*) embroidery canvas; (*Arg.*) cane for backs and seats of chairs.

esterlín, *n.m.* fine glazed buckram.

esterlina, *a.* sterling (money); *libra esterlina,* pound sterling.

esternón, *n.m.* sternum, breastbone.

estero, *n.m.* land adjoining an estuary inundated by the tide; inlet, estuary; matting; covering with matting; time for putting on winter clothes; (*Arg.*) marshy land; (*Chi.*) rivulet, brook; (*Ven.*) pool, pond.

esterquilinio, *n.m.* dunghill, heap of dung.

estertor, *n.m.* death-rattle; noisy breathing.

estertoroso, -sa, *a.* stertorous.

estesudeste, *n.m.* east by south-east.

esteta, *n.m.f.* æsthetician; (*slang*) sodomite.

estética, *n.f.* æsthetics.

estéticamente, *adv.* æsthetically.

estético, -ca, *a.* æsthetic.

estetoscopia, *n.f.* stethoscopy.

estetoscopio, *n.m.* stethoscope.

esteva, *n.f.;* **estevón,** *n.m.* plough-handle; perch of a carriage.

estevado, -da, *a.* bow-legged.

estevón, *n.m.* [ESTEVA].

estezado, *n.m.* dressed deer-skin.

estiaje, *n.m.* low-watermark.

estiba, *n.f.* rammer; (*naut.*) stowage; place where wool is compressed.

estibador, *n.m.* stevedore, longshoreman.

estibar, *v.t.* to compress wool; to stow a cargo.

estibia, *n.f.* sprain in horse's neck.

estibina, *n.f.* (*min.*) stibine.

estibio, *n.m.* antimony, stibium.

estiércol, *n.m.* dung, excrement, manure; (*fig.*) filth, uncleanness.

estigio, -gia, *a.* Stygian; (*poet.*) infernal, hellish.

estigma, *n.m.* birth-mark; brand, stigma, mark of infamy (set on slave or criminal); affront; disgrace; (*R.C.*) stigmata.

estigmatizador, -ra, *a.* stigmatizing. — *n.m.f.* stigmatizer.

estigmatizar, *v.t.* to stigmatize, brand; to affront; (*R.C.*) to cause stigmata to appear.

estilar, *v.t., v.i.* to use, be in the habit of using; to draw up a document in regular form; (*Am., prov.*) to distil. — *v.r.* to be in fashion.

estilete, *n.m.* stiletto; (*surg.*) probe.

estilicidio, *n.m.* dripping, distillation.

estilista, *n.m.f.* stylist, master of style.

estilita, *a.* stylite.

estilo, *n.m.* stylus (writing instrument); gnomon or style of a dial; style; fashion, use, custom; *estilo antiguo,* old style; *estilo castizo,* correct style; *estilo familiar,* familiar style; *estilo nuevo,* new style; *por el* or *por ese estilo,* of that kind, like that.

estilóbato, *n.m.* stylobate, pedestal.

estilográfico, -ca, *a.* stylographic. — *n.f.* fountain pen.

estima, *n.f.* esteem, respect; (*naut.*) dead reckoning; *propasar la estima,* (*naut.*) to outrun the reckoning.

estimabilidad, *n.f.* estimableness; worthiness.

estimabilisimo, -ma, *a. superl.* [ESTIMABLE] most estimable.

estimable, *a.* estimable, worthy, excellent; computable.

estimación, *n.f.* esteem, estimation, regard; valuation, estimate, appraisement; *estimación propia,* self-esteem.

estimador, -ra, *a.* esteeming; estimating. — *n.m.f.* esteemer; estimator.

estimar, *v.t.* to respect, honour, regard,

esteem; to value, estimate, appraise; to form an opinion, judge; to look into; to acknowledge, thank.

estimativa, *n.f.* power of judging; instinct.

estimulante, *a.* stimulating, exciting. — *n.m.* stimulant, stimulator.

estimular, *v.t.* to stimulate; to sting, irritate, goad, excite; to encourage, incite.

estímulo, *n.m.* incitement; stimulus; stimulation; encouragement.

estinco, *n.m.* skink, kind of lizard.

estío, *n.m.* summer.

estiomenar, *v.t.* (*med.*) to corrode, mortify.

estiómeno, *n.m.* gangrene.

estipendiar, *v.t.* to give a stipend to.

estipendiario, *n.m.* stipendiary.

estipendio, *n.m.* stipend, salary, pay, fee, wages.

estípite, *n.m.* pilaster in form of a reversed pyramid.

estipticar, *v.t.* (*med.*) to apply a styptic to.

estipticidad, *n.f.* (*med.*) stypticity; costiveness.

estíptico, -ca; estítico, -ca, *a.* (*med.*) styptic, astringent; costive; (*fig.*) miserly, avaricious; hard to obtain.

estiptiquez, *n.f.* (*Arg., Col.*) costiveness; niggardliness.

estípula, *n.f.* stipule.

estipulación, *n.f.* stipulation, bargain, covenant, agreement.

estipulante, *a.* stipulating. — *n.m.f.* stipulator.

estipular, *v.t.* to contract, stipulate, settle terms, bargain, covenant.

estique, *n.m.* tool used by sculptors.

estira, *n.f.* knife used by curriers.

estiradamente, *adv.* scarcely; with difficulty; violently, forcibly.

estirado, -da, *a.* dilated, expanded, extended, stretched; (*fig.*) affectedly dignified, lofty, stiff, proud; drawn (of metals); *estirado en frío,* cold-drawn (of metals); niggardly. — *n.m.* stretching; drawing. — *p.p.* [ESTIRAR].

estirador, -ra, *n.m.* stretcher; drawing-frame.

estirajar; estirazar, *v.t.* (*coll.*) [ESTIRAR].

estirajón, *n.m.* (*coll.*) [ESTIRÓN].

estiramiento, *n.m.* stretching, pulling; drawing (of metals).

estirar, *v.t.* to draw, pull, tighten; to stretch out, extend, enlarge, dilate, lengthen; to draw metals; *estirar en frío,* to cold-draw; *estirar la pierna,* (*coll.*) to die. — *v.r.* to stretch, be extended; to grow haughty, put on airs; *estirar la barra,* to do one's utmost to attain something; to labour at the oars.

estirón, *n.m.* strong pull, stretch; haul or hauling, pluck; rapid growth; *dar uno un estirón,* (*coll.*) to shoot up, grow rapidly.

estirpe, *n,f,* race, origin, stock, pedigree.

estítico, -ca, *a.* [ESTIPTICO].

estivada, *n.f.* land cleared of brushwood ready for cultivation.

estival; estivo, -va, *a.* summerly, summer.

esto, *pron. dem. neut.* this; *a esto,* hereto, hereunto; *sobre esto,* hereon, hereupon; *con esto,* herewith; *en esto,* at this juncture; at once, right away; herein, hereinto; *por esto,* hereby; that is why; for this reason; *esto es,* that is, that is so.

estocada, *n.f.* stab, thrust, tilt, lunge; (*coll.*) *estocada de vino,* breath of a tipsy person; *estocada por cornada,* injury received in injuring another, tit for tat.

estocafís, *n.m.* (*com.*) stock-fish.

estofa, *n.f.* quilted silk stuff; (*fig.*) quality, condition; *de buena estofa,* of good quality; *de mi estofa,* of my class; *hombre de estofa,* a man of consideration.

estofado, -da, *a.* quilted; ornamented; stewed. — *n.m.* meat stew. — *p.p.* [ESTOFAR].

estofador, -ra, *n.m.f.* quilter.

estofar, *v.t.* to quilt; to paint relievos on a gilt ground; to size carvings before gilding; to stew meat.

estofo, *n.m.* quilting; painting on gilt; sizing.

estoicamente, *adv.* stoically.

estoicidad, *n.f.* imperturbability.

estoicismo, *n.m.* stoicism.

estoico, -ca, *a.* stoic, stoical. — *n.m.* stoic.

estola, *n.f.* stole; *derechos de estola,* surplice fees.

estolidez, *n.f.* stupidity, incapacity.

estólido, -da, *a.* stupid, foolish.

estolón, *n.m.* large stole [ESTOLA]; (*bot.*) stolon.

estoma, *n.m.* (*bot.*) stoma.

estomacal, *a.* stomachic.

estomagar, *v.t., v.i.* (*pret.* **estomagué;** *pres. subj.* **estomague**) to upset the stomach; (*coll.*) to bore, annoy, disgust; (*coll.*) to make angry, enrage; (*coll.*) to resent, remember with resentment.

estómago, *n.m.* stomach; (*coll.*) sponger; *de estómago,* constant, expectant; coarse; *hacer buen* or *mal estómago,* to cause pleasure or displeasure; *hacer estómago a una cosa,* to resolve to bear whatever may happen; *ladrar el estómago,* to be very hungry; *no retener nada en el estómago,* to be very communicative; *quedar a uno algo en el estómago,* not to divulge all one knows; *revolver el estómago,* to turn the stomach; *tener buen estómago,* to be very long-suffering, thick-skinned; to be morally unscrupulous; *no hay estómago que sea un palmo mayor que otro,* one stomach is of the same size as another.

estomaguero, *n.m.* stomacher.

estomatical, *a.* stomachic.

estomático, -ca, *a.* relating to the stomach.

estomaticón, *n.m.* stomach-plaster.

estonce; estonces, *adv.* (*obs.*) then, formerly, at that time.

estonio, -nia, *a.* Estonian.

estopa, *n.f.* tow; burlap; oakum.

estopada, *n.f.* quantity of tow for spinning; *si no fui avisada, tomé la estopada,* those who are not fitted for doing fine work must do coarse.

estopear, *v.t.* to calk with oakum.

estopeño, -ña, *a.* made of tow.

estopero, *n.m.* sucker of a pump.

estoperol, *n.m.* scupper-nail; tow wick; (*Am.*) upholstery nail.

estopilla, *n.f.* finest part of hemp or flax; yarn made from this; lawn, fine cloth; cotton cloth, cambric.

estopín, *n.m.* (*artill.*) priming-tube; quick-match.

estopón, *n.m.* coarse tow; cloth made from coarse tow yarns.

estopor, *n.m.* anchor-stopper.

estoposo, -sa, *a.* tow-like, filaceous.

estoque, *n.m.* rapier; sword-stick; (*bot.*) corn-flag; *estoque real,* royal sword of justice.

estoqueador, *n.m.* thruster; matador.

estoquear, *v.t.* to thrust with a rapier

estoqueo, *n.m.* thrusting, stabbing.

estoraque, *n.m.* officinal storax; gum of the storax-tree; sweet gum-tree; *estoraque líquido,* liquidambar.

estorbador, -ra, *a.* hindering, obstructing. — *n.m.f.* hinderer, obstructor.

estorbar, *v.t.* to hinder, obstruct, impede, hamper; to be in someone's way; *estorbarle a uno lo negro,* not to know how to read, not to be fond of reading.

estorbo, *n.m.* impediment, hindrance, obstruction, nuisance.

estorboso, -sa, *a.* hindering, in the way, obstructionist.

estorcer, *v.t.* (*obs.*) to liberate, evade.

estornija, *n.f.* linchpin-washer; (*prov.*) boy's game.

estornino, *n.m.* starling.

estornudar, *v.i.* to sneeze.

estornudo, *n.m.* sternutation, sneeze.

estornutatorio, *n.m.* sternutatory.

estotro, -tra, compound pronoun of *este, esto, esta* and *otro, otra,* this other.

estovar, *v.t.* to cook meat over a slow fire.

estoy, *pres. indic.* [ESTAR].

estrabismo, *n.m.* (*med.*) strabismus, squint.

estracilla, *n.f.* small rag; coarse brown paper; fine rag-paper.

estrada, *n.f.* causeway, paved road; *estrada encubierta,* (*mil.*) covert-way; *batir la estrada,* to reconnoitre.

estradiota, *n.f.* kind of lance; *a la estradiota,* riding with long stirrups and stiff legs.

estradiote, *n.m.* Albanian mercenary.

estrado, *n.m.* drawing-room; drawing-room furniture; dais for a throne; baker's table; lecturing platform. — *pl.* courtrooms, halls of justice; *hacer estrados,* (*law*) to hold a court.

estrafalariamente, *adv.* (*coll.*) carelessly, in a slovenly fashion; extravagantly, wildly, queerly.

estrafalario, -ria, *a.* (*coll.*) slovenly, uncleanly, or negligently dressed; queer, odd, eccentric; extravagant, wild.

estragadamente, *adv.* depravedly.

estragador, -ra, *a.* corrupting, destroying.

estragamiento, *n.m.* disorder, corruption, depravation; ravage, waste, ruin.

estragar, *v.t.* (*pret.* **estragué;** *pres. subj.* **estrague**) to vitiate, deprave, corrupt, spoil; to ravage; *estragar la cortesía,* to pay foolish compliments.

estrago, *n.m.* ravage, ruin, waste, havoc; destruction, carnage, damage; wickedness, corruption of morals, depravity.

estragón, *n.m.* tarragon wormwood.

estrambosidad, *n.f.* squinting.

estrambote, *n.m.* burden of a song.

estrambóticamente, *adv.* oddly, queerly.

estrambótico, -ca, *a.* eccentric, queer, odd, strange, irregular.

estramonio, *n.m.* common thorn-apple.

estrangol, *n.m.* inflammation in a horse's tongue.

estrangul, *n.m.* (*mus.*) mouthpiece.

estrangulación, *n.f.* choking; strangling; strangulation; (*hydrost.*) stoppage; (*engin.*) throttling, choke.

estrangulador, -ra, *a.* strangling. — *n.m.f.* strangler; (*engin.*) choke, strangler.

estrangular, *v.t.* to choke, strangle; (*med.*) to strangulate; (*engin.*) to throttle, choke.

estratagema, *n.f.* stratagem; artful deception, trick; craftiness; finesse; deceit.
estratega; estratego, *n.m.* strategist.
estrategia, *n.f.* strategy; (*fig.*) astuteness.
estratégicamente, *adv.* strategically.
estratégico, -ca, *a.* strategical. — *n.m.f.* strategist.
estratificación, *n.f.* stratification.
estratificar, *v.t.* to stratify, dispose in strata.
estratiforme, *a.* stratiform.
estratigrafía, *n.f.* stratigraphy.
estratigráfico, -ca, *a.* stratigraphical.
estrato, *n.m.* stratum, layer, bed; stratus (cloud).
estratosfera, *n.f.* stratosphere.
estrave, *n.m.* (*naut.*) stem-knee.
estraza, *n.f.* rag, fragment of cloth; *papel de estraza,* rough unbleached paper.
estrazar, *v.t.* (*obs.*) to tear, to rend into fragments.
estrechamente, *adv.* narrowly; hardly, nearly; tightly, fast, closely; intimately; punctually, exactly; rigorously, strictly; forcibly, strongly; penuriously, scantily.
estrechamiento, *n.m.* tightening, tightness; narrowing.
estrechar, *v.t.* to tighten; to compress, contract, constrict, reduce, curtail, narrow; to compel, constrain; to confine; obstruct, restrain; to press; to follow closely; *estrechar la mano,* to shake hands; to send kind regards or greetings to. — *v.r.* to become narrow; to bind oneself strictly; to reduce one's expenses; to become related or intimate with; to act in concert; *estrecharse uno con otro,* (*coll.*) to persuade in a friendly way to grant a request.
estrechez, *n.f.* narrowness; tightness; compactness, closeness; intimacy, close friendship; austere mode of living; penury, poverty; difficulty, embarrassment; *Pedro se halla en grande estrechez,* Peter's affairs are embarrassed.
estrecho, -cha, *a.* narrow; tight; intimate; austere, rigid; stingy, mean, miserly; mean-spirited, illiberal; punctual, exact; *estrecho de conciencia,* over-scrupulous, narrow-minded. — *n.m.* party game played at the Feast of the Epiphany; strait, channel; pass, narrow passage; peril, risk, danger, fix, predicament; *poner a uno en estrecho de hacer una cosa,* to force a person to do something; *al estrecho,* by force.
Estrecho de Magallanes, *n.m.* Magellan Strait.
estrechón, *n.m.* flapping of sails; pitching in a head sea.
estrechura, *n.f.* narrowness, straitness; austerity; danger, distress; predicament; narrow passage; straits; intimate familiarity.
estregadera, *n.f.* scrubbing-brush, mop.
estregadero, *n.m.* rubbing-post; place for washing clothes.
estregadura, *n.f.* friction, act of rubbing.
estregamiento, *n.m.* friction, rubbing.
estregar, *v.t.* (*pres. indic.* **estriego;** *pres. subj.* **estriegue;** *pret.* **estregué**) to rub, polish, scour; to scrape, scratch (as matches).
estregón, *n.m.* rough rubbing.
estrella, *n.f.* star; star-wheel; a kind of linen cloth; star or white mark on a horse's forehead; asterisk (*); lot, fate, destiny; (*fort.*)

star-traced fort; *estrella de mar,* starfish; *estrella de rabo,* comet; *estrellas errantes* or *erráticas,* planets; *estrella fija,* fixed star; *estrella fugaz,* shooting star; *estrella polar,* pole star; *con estrellas,* just after nightfall or before sunrise; *tener estrella* or *nacer con estrella,* to be lucky; *tomar la estrella,* to take the altitude of the pole star; *campar con su estrella,* to be very fortunate; *levantarse a las estrellas,* to become very much irritated, on one's dignity; *querer contar las estrellas,* to want to reach the moon; *poner por* or *sobre las estrellas,* to laud, extol, over-praise; *unos nacen con estrella, y otros nacen estrellados,* some are born lucky and some unlucky; *ver las estrellas,* (*coll.*) to see stars.
estrellada, *n.f.* (*bot.*) lady's mantle, great stitchwort.
estrelladera, *n.f.* (*cook.*) egg-slice, turnover.
estrelladero, *n.m.* confectioner's pan for cooking eggs, or making candied yolks.
estrellado, -da, *a.* starry; *caballo estrellado,* horse with a star on the forehead; *huevos estrellados,* fried eggs. — *p.p.* [ESTRELLAR].
estrellamar, *n.f.* (*bot.*) buckthorn plantain; (*ichth.*) starfish.
estrellar, *a.* stellated, starry.
estrellar, *v.t.* (*coll.*) to dash to pieces, break in a collision, shatter, shiver; to fry (eggs). — *v.r.* (with *contra*) to dash against, be shattered by, have a crash against; to fail, to come up against an insuperable obstacle; *estrellarse uno con otro,* to contradict flatly, fall out with.
estrellera, *n.f.* (*naut.*) burton.
estrellero, -ra, *a.* (horse) that throws up its head.
estrellica; estrellita; estrelluela, *n.f.* little star [ESTRELLA].
estrellón, *n.m.* large star [ESTRELLA], star-shaped piece in fireworks; (*Arg., Chi., Hond.*) impact, collision, clash.
estremecedor, -ra, *a.* frightful, terrifying.
estremecer, *v.t.* (*pres. indic.* **estremezco;** *pres. subj.* **estremezca**) to shake; to make tremble; to terrify. — *v.r.* to shake, tremble, shudder.
estremecimiento, *n.m.* trembling, quaking; shaking, shuddering.
estrena, *n.f.* love-offering, souvenir, present, handsel; (*obs.*) first use of a thing, inauguration, debut; tip.
estrenar, *v.t.* to use or do anything for the first time, to handsel; to begin, commence, inaugurate. — *v.r.* to begin to act in some capacity; to make one's debut; to perform a play for the first time.
estreno, *n.m.* first performance; debut; commencement, inauguration, handsel.
estrenque, *n.m.* stout rope of bass.
estrenuidad, *n.f.* vigour, energy; enterprise; strenuousness.
estrenuo, -nua, *a.* strong, agile, strenuous; enterprising.
estreñido, -da, *a.* constipated; niggardly. — *p.p.* [ESTREÑIR].
estreñimiento, *n.m.* costiveness, constipation.
estreñir, *v.t.* (*pres. indic.* **estriño;** *pres. subj.* **estriña**) to bind, make costive. — *v.r.* to be constipated, costive.
estrepada, *n.f.* (*naut.*) long, strong pull on a rope, etc.

estrépito, *n.m.* din, crash, clangor, clamour, deafening noise.

estrepitosamente, *adv.* clamorously, noisily.

estrepitoso, -sa, *a.* noisy, loud, clamorous; obstreperous, boisterous; (*mus.*) strepitoso.

estreptococia, *n.f.* infection by streptococcus.

estría, *n.f.* (*arch.*) fluting, stria, groove.

estriadura, *n.f.* (*arch.*) fluting, grooving.

estriar, *v.t.* (*arch.*) to flute. — *v.r.* to become grooved, striated.

estribación, *n.f.* (*arch.*) counter-fort; spur of a mountain range.

estribadero, *n.m.* prop, stay.

estribar, *v.i.* (with *en*) to rest on, to be based on, to lie in; (*fig.*) to depend on.

estribera, *n.f.* stirrup; (*Arg.*) stirrup strap.

estribería, *n.f.* place where stirrups are made or kept.

estriberón, *n.m.* stepping-stone; (*mil.*) temporary road.

estribillo, *n.m.* refrain of a song; tautology, needless repetition.

estribo, *n.m.* stirrup; brace, stay, stirrup-bolt; buttress, abutment; step or footboard of a coach; clasp of the felloes; cross-prop, main brace; bone of the ear; spur of a range; (*fig.*) rest, basis, support; *andar* or *estar sobre los estribos,* to go to work with great caution; *perder los estribos,* to lose one's head; to talk wildly.

estribor, *n.m.* starboard.

estricnina, *n.f.* strychnine.

estricote, *adv.; al estricote,* without rule or order; *tener a uno al estricote,* to lead someone a dance.

estrictamente, *adv.* strictly.

estricto, -ta, *a.* strict, exact, severe.

estridente, *a.* strident; (*poet.*) obstreperous.

estridor, *n.m.* strident noise, screech.

estriego; estriegue, *pres. indic.; pres. subj.* [ESTREGAR].

estrige, *n.f.* screech-owl.

estrígil, *n.m.* strigil.

estrillar, *v.t.* (*obs.*) to groom, currycomb horses, mules, etc.

estro, *n.m.* (*poet.*) afflatus, inspiration.

estrobilífero, -ra, *a.* cone-bearing.

estróbilo, *n.m.* cone.

estrobo, *n.m.* (*naut.*) loop of stout rope or cable; (*aer.*) grummet.

estrofa, *n.f.* strophe, stanza.

estronciana, *n.f.* strontia.

estroncianita, *n.f.* strontianite.

estroncio, *n.m.* strontium.

estropajear, *v.t.* to rub, scour a wall.

estropajeo, *n.m.* rubbing a wall.

estropajo, *n.m.* loofah; mop; dish-clout, swab; bundle of bass or esparto for scrubbing; worthless, trifling thing; *servir de estropajo,* to fill a menial office.

estropajosamente, *adv.* stutteringly, stammeringly.

estropajoso, -sa, *a.* (*coll.*) ragged, slovenly, despicable, low, mean; (*coll.*) tough (meat); (*coll.*) stuttering, stammering.

estropeado, -da, *a.* lame, crippled; damaged; fatigued. — *p.p.* [ESTROPEAR].

estropeamiento, *n.m.* maiming, laming, wounding.

estropear, *v.t.* to cripple, maim, mutilate; to damage or spoil by rough usage; to upset a plan, etc.; to mix mortar for the second time.

estropeo, *n.m.* rough usage; damage, injury; fatigue, tiredness.

estropicio, *n.m.* (*coll.*) breakage, crash (of crockery, etc.); needless turmoil.

estrovo, *n.m.* (*naut.*) strap for a block.

estructura, *n.f.* structure; (*fig.*) order, method.

estruendo, *n.m.* clamour, clangour, clatter, noise, din; confusion, turmoil; pomp, ostentation.

estruendosamente, *adv.* noisily.

estruendoso, -sa, *a.* noisy, clamorous.

estrujadura, *n.f.; estrujamiento,* *n.m.* pressure, pressing, squeezing, crushing, rumpling.

estrujar, *v.t.* to squeeze, press, crush, rumple, mash, jam, bruise.

estrujón, *n.m.* last pressing of grapes; crush, squeeze, pressure, jam.

estrupador, *n.m.; estrupar,* *v.t.; estrupo* (*obs.*), *n.m.* [ESTUPRADOR, ESTUPRAR, ESTUPRO].

estuación, *n.f.* flow of the tide.

estuante, *a.* hot, boiling, glowing.

estuario, *n.m.* estuary, inlet.

estucador, *n.m.* stucco-plasterer.

estucar, *v.t.* to stucco.

estuco, *n.m.* stucco; plaster, scagliola; *ser* or *parecer un estuco* or *de estuco,* to be stolid.

estucurú, *n.m.* (*CR.*) large owl.

estuche, *n.m.* box, casket; case (for jewellery, etc.); cabinet; etui, sheath (for scissors, etc.); in card games, certain combination of cards; small comb; clever, handy fellow; *mostrar el estuche,* to show one's teeth in anger; *estuche de habilidades,* very clever fellow; *ser un estuche,* to have skill in various things.

estudiador, -ra, *a.* (*coll.*) very studious.

estudiante, *n.m.* scholar, student; *estudiante de la tuna,* member of a strolling band of students; *estudiante pascuero* or *torreznero,* student who goes home often for festivities.

estudiantil, *a.* (*coll.*) student, of a student or scholar; collegial.

estudiantillo, *n.m.* young student [ESTUDIANTE].

estudiantina, *n.f.* students collectively; strolling band of students.

estudiantino, -na, *a.* (*coll.*) belonging to a scholar or student; *a la estudiantina,* (*coll.*) in the manner of students.

estudiantón, *n.m.* plodder [ESTUDIANTE].

estudiar, *v.t.* to study, acquire knowledge; to commit to memory; to attend the classes in a university; to copy a model, draw from nature.

estudio, *n.m.* learning, study; investigation; college, school; meditation, contemplation; studio; reading-room, library; *hacer estudio,* to make a special study, take care; *estudio general,* university; *juez de estudio(s),* vice-chancellor. — *pl.* letters, sciences; *estudios mayores,* studies formerly read at the higher university faculties; *dar estudios a uno,* to support someone during his studies.

estudiosamente, *adv.* studiously.

estudiosidad, *n.f.* studiousness, addiction or attention to study.

estudioso, -sa, *a.* studious; contemplative, reflective.

estufa, *n.f.* stove; hot-house; heater; sweating room; dry bath; drying chamber; small brazier; *criar en estufa,* (*fig.*) to mollycoddle.

estufador, *n.m.* stew-pan.

estufero; estufista, *n.m.* stove-maker *or* seller.

estufilla, *n.f.* small fur-muff; foot-warmer; chafing-dish.

estultamente, *adv.* foolishly, sillily.

estulticia, *n.f.* folly, foolishness, silliness.

estulto, -ta, *a.* foolish, silly.

estuosidad, *n.f.* excessive heat (as fever, sunstroke, etc.).

estuoso, -sa, *a.* hot, ardent, glowing.

estupefacción, *n.f.* stupefaction, numbness.

estupefactivo, -va, *a.* stupefying.

estupefacto, -ta, *a.* motionless, stupefied, petrified.

estupendamente, *adv.* stupendously, wonderfully.

estupendo, -da, *a.* stupendous, wondrous, wonderful, marvellous.

estúpidamente, *adv.* stupidly, foolishly.

estupidez, *n.f.* stupidity, stupidness.

estúpido, -da, *a.* dull, slow, stupid; insensible.

estupor, *n.m.* stupor; amazement, astonishment.

estuprador, *n.m.* ravisher, deflowerer, violator.

estuprar, *v.t.* (*law*) to ravish, violate, deflower.

estupro, *n.m.* (*law*) rape.

estuque, *n.m.* stucco.

estuquería, *n.f.* stuccoing; stucco-work.

estuquista, *n.m.* plasterer, stucco-worker.

esturar, *v.t.* to burn food; to scorch, toast.

esturgar, *v.t.* to polish pottery.

esturión, *n.m.* sturgeon.

estuve, estuvo, *pret.* [ESTAR].

ésula, *n.f.* leafy-branched spurge.

esviaje, *n.m.* (*arch.*) obliquity.

etalaje, *n.m.* tuyère of a blast-furnace.

etapa, *n.f.* ration given to troops in the field; stage, station, stop; epoch, period.

éter, *n.m.* (*poet.*) the sky; ether.

etéreo, -rea, *a.* ethereal; heavenly.

eterización, *n.f.* etherization.

eterizar, *v.t.* to anæsthetize with ether; to combine with ether.

eternal, *a.* eternal.

eternalmente, *adv.* eternally, everlastingly.

eternamente, *adv.* eternally, forever, everlastingly, evermore.

eternidad, *n.f.* eternity; (*fig.*) long time.

eternizar(se), *v.t., v.r.* (*pret.* **eternicé;** *pres. subj.* **eternice**) to eternize, perpetuate; to prolong indefinitely.

eterno, -na, *a.* eternal, endless, everlasting, never-ending; lasting, durable.

eteromancia, *n.f.* [HETEROMANCIA].

eteromanía, *n.f.* ether habit, etheromania.

eterómano, -na, *n.m.f., a.* etheromaniac.

etesio, *a.* etesian, recurring yearly (wind).

ética, *n.f.* ethics, morality, morals.

ético, -ca, *a.* moral, ethical; hectic, consumptive. — *n.m.f.* ethicist, moralist.

etileno, *n.m.* ethylene.

etílico, -ca, *a.* ethylic.

etilo, *n.m.* ethyl.

etimología, *n.f.* etymology.

etimológicamente, *adv.* etymologically.

etimológico, -ca, *a.* etymological.

etimologista, *n.m.* etymologist, etymologer.

etimologizar, *v.t.* to etymologize.

etimológico, -ca, *a.* etymological.

etimólogo, -ga, *n.m.f.* etymologist.

etiología, *n.f.* etiology.

etíope; etiópico, -ca; etiopio, -pia, *n.m.f., a.* Ethiopian.

etiópide, *n.f.* clary, Ethiopian mullein.

etiqueta, *n.f.* ceremony, etiquette, formality; (*com.*) label; *de etiqueta,* ceremonious, formal; *estar de etiqueta,* to have ceased to be on familiar terms; to be reserved, distant, cool; *traje* or *vestido de etiqueta,* full dress, evening dress.

etiquetero, -ra, *a.* formal, ceremonious, punctilious.

etites, *n.f.* eagle-stone.

etmoides, *n.m.* ethmoid bone.

étnico, -ca, *a.* ethnic.

etnografía, *n.f.* ethnography.

etnográfico, -ca, *a.* ethnographic.

etnógrafo, -fa, *n.m.f.* ethnographer.

etnología, *n.f.* ethnology.

etnológico, -ca, *a.* ethnologic(al).

etnólogo, -ga, *n.m.f.* ethnologist.

eubolia, *n.f.* propriety or discretion in speech.

eucalipto, *n.m.* eucalyptus.

eucaristía, *n.f.* eucharist.

eucarístico, -ca, *a.* eucharistic(al).

eucologio, *n.m.* (*eccles.*) euchologion, euchology.

eucrasia, *n.f.* eucrasy, sound health.

eucrático, -ca, *a.* eucrastic.

eudiometría, *n.m.* eudiometry.

eudiómetro, *n.m.* eudiometer.

eufemismo, *n.m.* euphemism.

eufonía, *n.f.* euphony.

eufónico, -ca, *a.* euphonic, euphonious.

euforbiáceo, -cea, *a.* euphorbiaceous.

euforbio, *n.m.* officinal spurge.

euforia, *n.f.* resistance to pain and disease; sense of feeling well.

eufrasia, *n.f.* (*bot.*) eyebright.

eugenesia, *n.f.* eugenics.

eunuco, *n.m.* eunuch.

eupepsia, *n.f.* eupepsy.

eupéptico, -ca, *a.* eupeptic, digestive.

euritmia, *n.f.* eurhythmy.

eurítmico, -ca, *a.* eurhythmic.

euro, *n.m.* (*poet.*) Eurus, east wind; *euro austro* or *noto,* south-east wind.

Europa, *n.f.* Europe.

europeizar, *v.t., v.r.* to europeanize.

europeo, -a, *a.* European.

euscalduna, *a.* said of the Basque language, Euskarian.

éuscaro, -ra; eusquero, -ra, *n.m.f., a.* Basque. — *n.m.* Basque language.

eutaxia, *n.f.* perfect health.

eutanasia, *n.f.* euthanasia.

eutrapelia; eutropelia, *n.f.* moderation in pleasures; harmless, innocent pastime, sport.

eutrapélico, -ca; eutropélico, -ca, *a.* moderate, temperate.

evacuación, *n.f.* evacuation; exhaustion.

evacuante, *a.* evacuant, evacuating.

evacuar, *v.t.* to empty, evacuate; to quit, leave, vacate; *evacuar un negocio* or *una diligencia,* to finish, transact a business; to do an errand.

evacuativo, -va; evacuatorio, -ria, *a.* evacuative, that which evacuates. — *n.m.* public convenience.

evadir, *v.t.* to escape, shirk, elude, evade. — *v.r.* to evade a difficulty; to slip away, escape, sneak away.

evagación, *n.f.* evagation, wandering (*obs.*); fancy, fantasy.

evaluación, *n.f.* evaluation.
evaluador, -ra, *a.* valuating.
evaluar, *v.t.* to evaluate.
evalúo, *n.m.* (*com.*) valuation, appraisement.
evanescente, *a.* (*poet.*) evanescent.
evangeliario, *n.m.* evangelistary.
evangélicamente, *adv.* evangelically.
evangélico, -ca, *a.* evangelical.
evangelio, *n.m.* gospel. — *pl.* Book of Hours; *decir* or *hablar el Evangelio,* to talk gospel truth; *evangelios abreviados* or *chicos,* proverbs; *ordenar* (*a uno*) *de evangelio,* (*eccles.*) to confer deacon's orders.
evangelismo, *n.m.* evangelism.
evangelista, *n.m.* evangelist; gospel-chanter, gospeller.
evangelistero, *n.m.* gospeller; (*obs.*) lectern.
evangelización, *n.f.* evangelization.
evangelizador, -ra, *a.* evangelizing. — *n.m.f.* evangelist.
evangelizar, *v.t.* (*pret.* **evangelicé;** *pres. subj.* **evangelice**) to evangelize.
evaporable, *a.* evaporable.
evaporación, *n.f.* evaporation.
evaporado, -da, *a.* evaporated. — *p.p.* [EVAPORAR].
evaporador, -ra, *a.* evaporating. — *n.m.f.* evaporator.
evaporar, *v.t.* to evaporate. — *v.r.* to vanish, evaporate.
evaporatorio, -ria, *a.* (*med.*) evaporative.
evaporizar, *v.t.,* *v.i.* (*pret.* **evaporicé;** *pres. subj.* **evaporice**) to vaporize.
evasión, evasiva, *n.f.* evasion; subterfuge; escape.
evasivamente, *adv.* evasively.
evasivo, -va, *a.* evasive, elusive, sophistical.
evección, *n.f.* (*astron.*) evection.
evento, *n.m.* unforeseen event, contingency; *a todo evento,* (prepared) for any eventuality.
eventual, *a.* eventual, fortuitous.
eventualidad, *n.f.* contingency.
eventualmente, *adv.* eventually.
eversión, *n.f.* eversion, destruction, desolation, ruin.
evicción, *n.f.* (*law*) eviction.
evidencia, *n.f.* evidence, manifestation, proof; obviousness, certainty; *evidencia por pruebas,* circumstantial evidence.
evidenciar, *v.t.* to prove, make clear, render evident.
evidente, *a.* evident, manifest, plain, obvious.
evidentemente, *adv.* plainly, evidently, manifestly.
evisceración, *n.f.* evisceration.
evitable, *a.* avoidable.
evitación, *n.f.* avoidance.
evitar, *v.t.* to elude, avoid; to spare, save; to shun, shirk, decline.
eviterno, -na, *a.* (*theol.*) imperishable, lasting.
evo, *n.m.* eternity, endless duration; (*poet.*) long time ago, age, aeon.
evocación, *n.f.* evocation, evoking.
evocar, *v.t.* (*pret.* **evoqué;** *pres. subj.* **evoque**) to call out, evoke.
evolución, *n.f.* evolution, gradual development, slow transformation; change of ideas, etc.; (*mil., naut.*) evolution, manœuvre.
evolucionar, *v.i.* to change one's conduct, etc.; to evolve; (*mil., naut.*) to perform evolutions or manœuvres.
evolucionismo, *n.m.* evolutionism, Darwinism.

evolucionista, *n.m.f.,* *a.* Darwinian, evolutionist.
evolutivo, -va, *a.* evolutionary.
exacción, *n.f.* exaction; impost, tax, contribution, levy.
exacerbación, *n.f.* exacerbation; exasperation.
exacerbar, *v.t.* to irritate, exasperate; to exacerbate.
exactamente, *adv.* exactly, accurately, minutely.
exactitud, *n.f.* exactness, accuracy; punctuality; correctness.
exacto, -ta, *a.* exact, precise, accurate; assiduous; punctual.
exactor, *n.m.* tax-gatherer.
exaedro, *n.m.* hexahedron.
exageración, *n.f.* exaggeration.
exagerador, -ra, *a.* exaggerating. — *n.m.f.* exaggerator.
exagerante, *a.* (*poet.*) exaggerating.
exagerar, *v.t.* to magnify, exaggerate, overstate.
exagerativamente, *adv.* exaggeratively, with exaggeration.
exagerativo, -va, *a.* exaggerating.
exagonal, *a.* hexagonal.
exágono, -na, *a.* hexagonal. — *n.m.* hexagon.
exaltación, *n.f.* exaltation, elevation; (*chem.*) sublimation.
exaltado, -da, *a.* ultra-radical in politics; hotheaded. — *p.p.* [EXALTAR].
exaltamiento, *n.m.* exaltation; ultra-radicalism.
exaltar, *v.t.* to elevate, exalt, lift; to extol, praise. — *v.r.* to be carried away by passion; *exaltarse la bilis* or *la cólera,* to become irritated.
examen, *n.m.* inquiry, search, investigation, inspection, examination; interrogatory; survey, exploration.
exámetro, *n.m.* hexameter.
examinador, -ra, *a.* examining. — *n.m.f.* examiner.
examinando, *n.m.* examinee, candidate.
examinante, *a.* examining.
examinar, *v.t.* to examine, to question; to inspect, go over; to inquire into, investigate; to review; to look up, look into, explore; to search, scan. — *v.r.* to sit an examination.
exangüe, *a.* bloodless, anæmic; (*fig.*) weak, without strength; (*fig.*) dead.
exanimación, *n.f.* exanimation.
exánime, *a.* spiritless, exanimous, weak, lifeless.
exápodo, -da, *a.* hexapod, six-footed. — *n.m.pl.* (*entom.*) Hexapoda.
exarca; exarco, *n.m.* exarch.
exarcado, *n.m.* exarchate, vice-royalty.
exasperación, *n.f.* exasperation.
exasperado, -da, *p.p.* [EXASPERAR]. — *a.* exasperated.
exasperador, -ra; exasperante, *a.* exasperating.
exasperar, *v.t.* to exasperate, irritate, acerbate, enrage, vex, offend.
exastilo, *n.m.* hexastyle.
excandecencia, *n.f.* anger, passion.
excandecer, *v.t.* (*pres. indic.* **excandezco;** *pres. subj.* **excandezca**) to enrage, provoke, irritate, send into a passion. — *v.r.* to become angry.

excarcelación, *n.f.* setting a prisoner free.

excarcelar, *v.t.* to set a prisoner free.

excava, *n.f.* pit around the root of a plant.

excavación, *n.f.* excavation.

excavar, *v.t.* to excavate, hollow out.

excedente, *a.* excessive, exceeding; temporarily out of service; redundant. — *n.m.* (*com.*) surplus.

exceder, *v.t.* to surpass, exceed; to overstep. — *v.i., v.r.* to go too far; to forget oneself; to overstep one's authority; *excederse uno a sí mismo*, to excel oneself.

excelencia, *n.f.* excellence, superiority, eminence, superior merit or value; excellency (title); *por excelencia*, par excellence.

excelente, *a.* excellent, exquisite, first-rate. — *n.m.* ancient gold coin; *excelente de la granada*, gold coin struck to celebrate the reconquest of Granada.

excelentemente, *adv.* excellently.

excelentísimo, -ma, *a. superl.* most excellent.

excelsamente, *adv.* sublimely.

excelsitud, *n.f.* excellent quality or feature.

excelso, -sa, *a.* elevated, sublime, lofty; *el Excelso*, the Most High.

excéntricamente, *adv.* eccentrically.

excentricidad, *n.f.* eccentricity.

excéntrico, -ca, *a.* eccentric, eccentrical; odd, queer, extravagant. — *n.f.* eccentric wheel.

excepción, *n.f.* exception; (*law*) demurrer, exception.

excepcional, *a.* exceptional, unusual, contrary to rule.

excepcionalmente, *adv.* exceptionally.

excepcionar, *v.t.* (*law*) to enter a demurrer; to except.

exceptivo, -va, *a.* exceptive.

excepto, *adv.* except, excepting, with the exception of.

exceptuación, *n.f.* exception, exclusion.

exceptuar, *v.t.* to except, exempt, leave out, exclude.

excerpta, *n.f.* compendium, digest, abstract.

excesivamente, *adv.* excessively.

excesivo, -va, *a.* excessive, immoderate.

exceso, *n.m.* excess; crime, enormity; (*com.*) surplus; *en exceso*, excessively; in excess; *exceso de equipaje* or *de peso*, excess luggage.

excisión, *n.f.* (*surg.*) excision.

excitabilidad, *n.f.* excitability.

excitable, *a.* excitable.

excitación, *n.f.* excitation, act of exciting; excitement.

excitador, *n.m.* (*elec.*) discharging rod.

excitante, *a.* exciting. — *n.m.* (*elec.*) exciter.

excitar, *v.t.* to excite, stimulate, move, rouse, stir up; (*elec.*) to energize. — *v.r.* to become excited.

excitativo, -va, *a.* exciting, stimulative.

exclamación, *n.f.* exclamation.

exclamar, *v.t.* to exclaim, clamour, cry out.

exclamativo, -va; exclamatorio, -ria, *a.* exclamatory.

exclaustración, *n.f.* (*eccles.*) secularization of monks or nuns.

exclaustrado, -da, *n.m.f.* (*eccles.*) secularized monk or nun. — *p.p.* [EXCLAUSTRAR].

exclaustrar, *v.t.* (*eccles.*) to secularize monks or nuns.

excluir, *v.t.* (*p.p.* excluido, excluso; *pres. indic.* excluyo; *pres. subj.* excluya) to exclude, shut out, eject; to debar, deny admission; to hinder from participation in.

exclusión, *n.f.* exclusion, denying admission, shutting out, ejection; rejection.

exclusiva, *n.f.* refusal; exclusion, rejection; special privilege, exclusive or sole right.

exclusivamente; exclusive, *adv.* exclusively.

exclusivismo, *n.m.* blind adherence to an idea, etc., exclusivism.

exclusivista, *a.* exclusive. — *n.m.f.* exclusivist.

exclusivo, -va, *a.* exclusive.

excluso, *p.p. irreg.* [EXCLUIR].

excogitable, *a.* imaginable, reasonable, conceivable.

excogitar, *v.t.* to excogitate, meditate; to invent, find, devise.

excomulgación, *n.f.* excommunication.

excomulgado, -da, *a.* excommunicated; (*coll.*) accursed, wicked, perverse. — *p.p.* [EXCOMULGAR].

excomulgador, *n.m.* excommunicator.

excomulgar, *v.t.* (conjugated like COMULGAR) to excommunicate; to anathematize; (*coll.*) to use abusive language to, to abuse.

excomunión, *n.f.* excommunication; document publishing sentence of excommunication; *excomunión a matacandelas*, solemn ceremony of excommunication; *excomunión mayor*, anathema, active and passive deprivation of the sacraments; *excomunión menor*, passive deprivation of the sacraments.

excoriación, *n.f.* excoriation, flaying.

excoriar, *v.t., v.r.* to excoriate, flay; to graze.

excrecencia, *n.f.* excrescence.

excreción, *n.f.* excretion.

excremental; excrementicio, -cia; excrementoso, -sa, *a.* excrementitious, excremental.

excrementar, *v.t.* to void excrement.

excremento, *n.m.* excrement; excretion.

excretar, *v.i.* to excrete; to eject excrement.

excreto, -ta, *a.* excreted, ejected.

excretorio, -ria, *a.* excretory, excretive.

excrex, *n.m.* (*pl.* excrez) (*law*) (*prov.*) increase of dower or portion.

exculpación, *n.f.* exculpation, exoneration.

exculpar, *v.t.* to exculpate, exonerate.

excursión, *n.f.* excursion, tour, trip; (*law*) [EXCUSIÓN].

excusa, *n.f.* excuse; (*law*) demurrer; *a excusas*, (*obs.*) dissemblingly; [EXCUSABARAJA].

excusabaraja, *n.f.* basket with a wickerwork cover.

excusable, *a.* excusable, pardonable.

excusación, *n.f.* excuse.

excusadamente, *adv.* unnecessarily.

excusado, -da, *a.* exempted, privileged; set apart; reserved; useless, superfluous, unnecessary; free from taxes. — *n.m.* water-closet, toilet-room; privilege of exemption from tithes; *pensar en lo excusado*, to hope for the impossible; *renta del excusado*, subsidy from the clergy; *meterse en la renta del excusado*, to meddle in other people's business. — *p.p.* [EXCUSAR].

excusador, -ra, *a.* excusing. — *n.m.f.* excuser. — *n.m.* substitute, deputy vicar.

excusalí, *n.m.* small apron.

excusaña, *n.m.* (*obs., mil.*) scout, spy, look-out; *a excusañas*, (*obs.*) hiddenly, secretly.

excusar, *v.t.* to excuse; to avoid, shun; to

hinder, obstruct, prevent; to exempt from taxes or obligations; (with infinitive) to be excused from, not to have to; *excusas venir, que ya no haces falta*, do not come, you are not needed. — *v.r.* to excuse oneself; to apologize; to send regrets; to decline or reject a request.

excusión, *n.f.* (*law*) stay of execution.

excuso, -sa, *a.* (*obs.*) [EXCUSADO].

exea, *n.m.* (*mil.*) scout.

execrable, *a.* execrable, accursed, detestable, hateful.

execrablemente, *adv.* execrably.

execración, *n.f.* execration, cursing; (*eccles.*) desecration.

execrador, -ra, *a.* execrating.

execrando, -da, *a.* execrable.

execrar, *v.t.* to execrate, curse, imprecate; to abhor, detest.

execratorio, -ria, *a.* execratory.

exégesis, *n.f.* exegesis.

exegeta, *n.m.* exegete.

exegético, -ca, *a.* exegetic, explanatory.

exención, *n.f.* exemption, immunity, privilege.

exentado, -da, *a.* exempt, exempted. — *p.p.* [EXENTAR].

exentamente, *adv.* freely; simply, frankly, clearly, sincerely.

exentar, *v.t.* to exempt; to excuse, absolve, acquit. — *v.r.* to excuse, exempt oneself.

exento, -ta, *a.* free, exempt; open, unobstructed, clear, isolated; freed, disengaged, privileged. — *n.m.* (*obs.*) subaltern officer. — *p.p. irreg.* [EXIMIR].

exequátur, *n.m.* exequatur.

exequias, *n.f.pl.* exequies, funeral rites, obsequies.

exequible, *a.* attainable.

exfoliación, *n.f.* exfoliation, scaling, peeling off.

exfoliador, *n.m.* (*Chi.*) writing-pad.

exfoliar, *v.t.* to exfoliate. — *v.r.* to scale off.

exhalación, *n.f.* exhalation; shooting star; bolt of lightning; effluvium, fume, vapour; (*fig.*) velocity, swiftness.

exhalador, -ra, *a.* exhaling. — *n.m.f.* exhaler.

exhalar, *v.t.* to exhale, breathe out, emit; *exhalar el espíritu*, to die. — *v.r.* (*fig.*) to chase, to long for, to pursue avidly.

exhauste, *n.m.* (*motor.*) exhaust.

exhausto, -ta, *a.* exhausted, totally drained.

exheredación, *n.f.* disinheritance.

exheredar, *v.t.* to disinherit.

exhibición, *n.f.* exhibition, exposition.

exhibir, *v.t.* to exhibit, expose, display, make manifest; (*law*) to produce documents.

exhortación, *n.f.* exhortation, admonition.

exhortador, -ra, *a.* exhorting. — *n.m.f.* exhorter, monitor.

exhortar, *v.t.* to exhort, admonish, warn.

exhortatorio, -ria, *a.* exhortatory.

exhorto, *n.m.* (*law*) letters requisitorial.

exhumación, *n.f.* exhumation, disinterment.

exhumar, *v.t.* to disinter, exhume.

exigencia, *n.f.* exigency, want; requirement; demand, exaction, pressing need.

exigente, *a.* exigent. — *n.m.f.* exacting person.

exigible; exigidero, -ra, *a.* exigible.

exigir, *v.t.* (*pres. indic.* **exijo**; *pres. subj.* **exija**) to demand, need, exact, require, desire, wish for; to urge.

exigüidad, *n.f.* exiguity, smallness.

exiguo, -gua, *a.* exiguous, small.

eximente, *a.* exempting; *circunstancia eximente*, exonerating circumstance.

eximio, -mia, *a.* eximious, famous, very eminent.

eximir, *v.t.* (*p.p.* **eximido, exento**) to exempt, clear from, free from; to excuse, privilege, except.

exinanición, *n.f.* inanition; want of vigour, debility.

exinanido, -da, *a.* debilitated, very weak, very feeble.

existencia, *n.f.* existence, life, being, state of being. — *pl.* (*com.*) stock-in-hand, goods; (*com.*) *en existencia*, in stock.

existente, *a.* existent, extant, existing; (*com.*) on hand.

existimación, *n.f.* estimation, opinion.

existimar, *v.t.* to form an opinion, hold an opinion, judge.

existir, *v.i.* to exist, be, have being.

éxito, *n.m.* end, termination, issue, accomplishment, result; success.

Éxodo, *n.m.* Exodus, second book of Moses.

exoneración, *n.f.* exoneration, disburdening.

exonerar, *v.t.* to exonerate, acquit.

exorable, *a.* exorable.

exorar, *v.t.* to beg, entreat.

exorbitancia, *n.f.* exorbitance.

exorbitante, *a.* exorbitant, excessive, enormous, extravagant.

exorbitantemente, *adv.* exorbitantly, extravagantly.

exorcismo, *n.m.* exorcism.

exorcista, *n.m.* exorciser, exorcist.

exorcizante, *a.* exorcizing. — *n.m.* exorciser.

exorcizar, *v.t.* (*pret.* **exorcicé**; *pres. subj.* **exorcice**) to exorcize, adjure, drive away by adjuration.

exordio, *n.m.* exordium, beginning, origin.

exornación, *n.f.* (*rhet.*) embellishment.

exornar, *v.t.* to embellish, adorn with rhetorical figures.

exortación, *n.f.* exhortation, admonition, monition.

exotérico, -ca, *a.* exoteric, public, common.

exótico, -ca, *a.* alien, foreign, extraneous; odd, bizarre.

expansibilidad, *n.f.* (*phys.*) expansibility.

expansible, *a.* (*phys.*) expansible.

expansión, *n.f.* (*phys.*) expansion; recreation.

expansivo, -va, *a.* expansive; (*fig.*) sociable, affable.

expatriación, *n.f.* expatriation.

expatriarse, *v.r.* to emigrate, become an exile.

expectable, *a.* conspicuous, eminent, illustrious.

expectación, *n.f.* expectance, expectation, anticipation, expectancy; Feast in honour of the Virgin (18 Dec.); *joven de expectación*, young man of promise; *hombre de expectación*, celebrated man.

expectante, *a.* expectant.

expectativa, *n.f.* expectation, hope, expectancy; (*law*) abeyance, expectancy.

expectoración, *n.f.* expectoration, sputum.

expectorante, *a.* expectorating. — *n.m.* (*med.*) expectorant.

expectorar, *v.t.* to expectorate, spit, spit out.

expedición, *n.f.* expedition, warlike enterprise; readiness, activity, haste, speed, despatch, nimbleness, freedom, facility; excursion, jaunt, journey; pontifical brevet or bull; (*com.*) despatch, shipment.

expedicionario, -ria, *a.* expeditionary.

expedicionero, *n.m.* despatcher of pontifical bulls.

expedido, -da, *a.* expeditious, prompt, nimble, quick. — *p.p.* [EXPEDIR].

expedidor, -ra, *n.m.f.* (*com.*) agent, forwarding merchant, shipper, despatcher, sender.

expediente, *n.m.* (*law*) proceedings, action; file of papers bearing on a case; despatch, course of business; provision, supply; means to an end, resource, expedient, measure; facility in the management of affairs; pretext, motive, reason; *cubrir uno el expediente*, to provide all the documents, etc. in a case; (*coll.*) to do the least possible in fulfilling an obligation; to commit a fraud while saving appearances; *dar expediente*, to expedite a business; *instruir uno un expediente*, to prepare a matter for speedy decision.

expedienteo, *n.m.* (*law*) procedure; (*coll.*) red tape.

expedir, *v.t.* (*pres. indic.* **expido**; *pres. subj.* **expida**) to facilitate, expedite; to issue; to draw up; to ship, forward, send, despatch.

expeditamente, *adv.* expeditiously, easily, expeditely.

expeditivo, -va, *a.* speedy, expeditious, quick.

expedito, -ta, *a.* speedy, expeditious, prompt, quick.

expelente, *a.* expellant.

expeler, *v.t.* (*p.p.* **expelido, expulso**) to expel, throw out, eject.

expendedor, -ra, *a.* spending. — *n.m.f.* dealer, seller, agent; *expendedor de moneda falsa*, (*law*) utterer, distributor of counterfeit money.

expendeduría, *n.f.* retail shop where tobacco or other monopolized goods are sold.

expender, *v.t.* to spend, lay out, expend; to sell by retail; (*law*) to pass counterfeit money; (*com.*) to sell on commission.

expendición, *n.f.* expending; selling by retail or on commission.

expendio, *n.m.* expense, outlay; consumption; (*Arg., Mex., Per.*) selling by retail; (*Mex.*) tobacconist.

expensar, *v.t.* (*Chi., Mex.*) (*law*) to pay the cost of.

expensas, *n.f.pl.* expenses, charges, costs; *a expensas*, to costs; *estar a expensas de otro*, to live at another's expense.

experiencia, *n.f.* experience; experiment, trial; *la experiencia es madre de la ciencia*, experience is the best master.

experimentado, -da, *a.* experienced, expert, conversant. — *p.p.* [EXPERIMENTAR].

experimentador, -ra, *n.m.f.* experimenter.

experimental, *a.* experimental.

experimentalmente, *adv.* experimentally.

experimentar, *v.t.* to experience, learn by practice; to test, try; to feel, suffer, undergo.

experimento, *n.m.* test, experiment, trial.

expertamente, *adv.* expertly, cunningly.

experto, -ta, *a.* expert, experienced. — *n.m.f.* expert.

expiación, *n.f.* atonement, expiation, reparation; purification.

expiar, *v.t.* to expiate, atone for a crime; to free from profanation, purify.

expiativo, -va, *a.* expiational.

expiatorio, -ria, *a.* expiatory.

expillo, *n.m.* common feverfew.

expiración, *n.f.* expiration.

expirante, *a.* expiring.

expirar, *v.i.* to die; to end, expire.

explanación, *n.f.* explanation, exposition, elucidation; (*railw.*) levelling.

explanada, *n.f.* esplanade; (*artill.*) platform; (*fort.*) glacis.

explanar, *v.t.* to level, grade; to explain, elucidate, clear up.

explayamiento, *n.m.* dwelling, dilating upon a subject; outing.

explayar, *v.t.* to dilate, extend, enlarge. — *v.r.* to dwell upon a subject; to be enlarged or extended; to enjoy an outing, have a good time; to open one's heart.

expletivo, -va, *a.* expletive.

explicable, *a.* explicable, explainable.

explicación, *n.f.* explanation, exposition, elucidation, interpretation.

explicadamente, *adv.* explicitly.

explicaderas, *n.f.pl.* (*coll.*) facility of explaining; *Juan tiene buenas explicaderas*, John explains a thing well.

explicador, -ra, *n.m.f.* explainer, commentator, glossarist.

explicar, *v.t.* (*pret.* **expliqué**; *pres. subj.* **explique**) to elucidate, explain, comment, expound, construe; *explicar el porque de una cosa*, to account for something. — *v.r.* to explain oneself, speak one's mind.

explicativo, -va, *a.* explicative, explicatory, exegetical.

explícitamente, *adv.* explicitly.

explícito, -ta, *n.f.pl.* explicit, clear, distinct, manifest.

exploración, *n.f.* exploration.

explorador, -ra, *a.* exploring. — *n.f.* explorator, explorer; boy scout.

explorar, *v.t.* to investigate, explore, search into, examine by trial; (*mil.*) to scout.

exploratorio, -ria, *a.* exploratory, exploring. — *n.m.* (*med.*) probe; catheter.

explosión, *n.f.* explosion; outburst; (*min.*) blast.

explosivo, -va, *a.* explosive. — *n.m.* (*gram.*) explosive.

explotable, *a.* exploitable; (*min.*) workable, minable.

explotación, *n.f.* exploitation; development; plant, works; operation, running (of factory, etc.); *la compañía ha instalado una magnífica explotación*, the company has established a splendid plant.

explotar, *v.t.* to exploit; to improve lands; to work or develop mines; to operate, run a business, etc.

expoliación, *n.f.* spoliation.

expoliador, -ra, *a.* spoliating. — *n.m.f.* spoliator.

expoliar, *v.t.* to spoliate, plunder, despoil.

exponencial, *a.* (*math.*) exponential.

exponente, *n.m.f.*, *a.* exponent; (*com.*) exhibitor. — *n.m.* (*alg., arith.*) exponent.

exponer, *v.t.* (conjugated like PONER) to expose, show, exhibit, lay open; to put in danger, jeopardize; to expound, disclose, explain; to abandon a child; to hazard, stake, risk. — *v.r.* to hazard, adventure, imperil oneself; to run a risk; to take a chance.

exportación, *n.f.* exportation, export; *derechos de exportación,* export duties.

exportador, -ra, *a.* exporting. — *n.m.f.* exporter.

exportar, *v.t.* to export.

exposición, *n.f.* explanation, interpretation, exposition, statement; risk, peril, jeopardy; (*drama*) exposition; claim, petition; exhibition, fair; (*arch.*) situation, orientation; public display; (*phot.*) exposure.

expositivo, -va, *a.* explanatory, expositive.

expósito, -ta, *a.* exposed; foundling. — *n.m.f.* foundling.

expositor, -ra, *a.* expounding; exhibiting. — *n.m.f.* explainer, expounder; exhibitor.

expremijo, *n.m.* cheese-vat.

expresado, -da, *a.* before-mentioned, cited, aforesaid.

expresamente, *adv.* expressly; clearly, plainly, in a direct fashion.

expresar, *v.t.* (*p.p.* **expresado, expreso**) to state, express, manifest, tell, utter; (*art*) to delineate, sketch, design.

expresión, *n.f.* expression; declaration, statement; expressiveness of face or gesture; utterance, phrase; gift, present; squeezing, expression, pressing out (of oils, etc.); *envió esta expresión,* he sent this present.

expresivamente, *adv.* expressively.

expresivo, -va, *a.* expressive; affectionate, kind, gracious.

expreso, -sa, *a.* expressed; clear, express; fast; *tren expreso,* express train. — *adv.* specially, expressly, on purpose. — *n.m.* express train; express messenger. — *p.p. irreg.* [EXPRESAR].

exprimidera, *n.f.;* **exprimidero,** *n.m.* squeezer.

exprimido, -da, *a.* squeezed, extenuated, dry. — *p.p.* [EXPRIMIR].

exprimir, *v.t.* to squeeze out, press out; (*fig.*) to express oneself clearly or vividly.

expropiación, *n.f.* expropriation, dispossession.

expropiar, *v.t.* to expropriate.

expuesto, -ta, *a.* exposed; liable; displayed; in danger. — *p.p. irreg.* [EXPONER].

expugnable, *a.* expugnable.

expugnación, *n.f.* (*mil.*) taking by storm.

expugnador, *n.m.* (*mil.*) assaulter, storm-trooper.

expugnar, *v.t.* (*mil.*) to take by storm, conquer, reduce by force of arms.

expulsar, *v.t.* (*p.p.* **expulsado, expulso**) to eject, expel, drive out, force away.

expulsión, *n.f.* expulsion, expelling, ejection, driving out.

expulsivo, -va, *a.* expulsive, expelling.

expulso, -sa, *a.* ejected, driven, expelled; outcast. — *p.p. irreg.* [EXPELER and EXPULSAR].

expulsor, -ra. *a.* expelling, ejecting. — *n.m.f.* expeller, ejector.

expurgación, *n.f.* expurgation, purification.

expurgar, *v.t.* (conjugated like PURGAR) to expurgate, purge away, expunge, purify, cleanse; to correct, mend, remove errors (from books, etc.).

expurgativo, -va, *a.* expurgatory.

expurgatorio, -ria, *a.* expurgatory. — *n.m.* index of the books prohibited by the Inquisition.

expurgo, *n.m.* expurgation, purification.

exquisitamente, *adv.* exquisitely.

exquisito, -ta, *a.* exquisite, delicious, excellent.

éxtasi; éxtasis, *n.m.* ecstasy; (*med.*) retardation of the normal rhythm of the pulse.

extasiarse, *v.r.* to be delighted, to be enraptured.

extático, -ca, *a.* ecstatic.

extemporal; extemporáneo, -nea, *a.* untimely; unpremeditated, extemporaneous.

extemporáneamente, *adv.* in an untimely way; extempore; without preparation.

extender, *v.t., v.r.* (*p.p.* **extendido, extenso;** *pres. indic.* **extiendo;** *pres. subj.* **extienda**) to extend, enlarge, widen, lengthen, spread, prolong, expand, dilate, stretch out, outspread, outstretch; to draw up (a document); to unfurl, unfold; to record (a message); (*com.*) to prolong, increase. — *v.r.* to extend; to stretch out; to become general or popular (as a fashion); to enlarge upon; to increase in bulk.

extendidamente, *adv.* extensively.

extendido, *a.* extended, stretched out; spacious; roomy, extensive; general, widely spread. — *p.p.* [EXTENDER].

extendimiento, *n.m.* (*obs.*) extension, dilatation.

extensamente, *adv.* extensively.

extensibilidad, *n.f.* extensibility.

extensión, *n.f.* extension; extent, duration; length; capacity; expanse, extensiveness; (*geom.*) space, dimension.

extensivamente, *adv.* extensively, amply, widely.

extensivo, -va, *a.* extensive, ample; extensible.

extenso, -sa, *a.* extensive, spacious; *por extenso,* at length, with full particulars. — *p.p. irreg.* [EXTENDER].

extensor, -ra, *a.* extending. — *n.m.* (*anat.*) extensor (muscle).

extenuación, *n.f.* attenuation; feebleness, wasting.

extenuado, -da, *a.* emaciated, attenuated; feeble, weak. — *p.p.* [EXTENUAR].

extenuar, *v.t.* to diminish, attenuate, weaken, wear away. — *v.r.* to languish, grow feeble, lose strength, decay.

extenuativo, -va, *a.* emaciating; weakening.

exterior, *a.* exterior; outward, external; foreign (trade, etc.); *lo exterior,* the outside; foreign affairs. — *n.m.* outside, exterior; personal appearance, aspect, deportment; foreign countries.

exterioridad, *n.f.* exteriority; demeanour; outwardness, outward appearance; pomp, ostentation, show, pageantry; outside, superficies.

exteriorizar, *v.t.* to externalize, make manifest. — *v.r.* to unbosom.

exteriormente, *adv.* externally, outwardly.

exterminador, -ra, *a.* exterminatory, exterminating. — *n.m.f.* exterminator.

exterminar, *v.t.* to exterminate, root out, tear up; to destroy; (*obs.*) to banish, expatriate.

exterminio, *n.m.* extermination, extirpation, destruction; banishment, expulsion.

externado, *n.m.* day-school.

externamente, *adv.* externally.

externo, -na, *a.* external; outward; exterior (angle, etc.). — *n.m.f.* day-pupil.

extiendo; extienda, *pres. indic.; pres. subj.* [EXTENDER].

extinción, *n.f.* extinction; suppression; quenching, extinguishing; extinguishment, obliteration.

extinguible, *a.* extinguishable.

extinguir, *v.t.* (*p.p.* **extinguido, extinto;** *pres. indic.* **extingo;** *pres. subj.* **extinga**) to extinguish, quench, put out; to destroy, suppress, extirpate.

extintivo, -va, *a.* (*law*) extinguishing.

extinto, -ta, *a.* extinguished; (*Arg., Chi.*) extinct, dead. — *p.p.* [EXTINGUIR].

extintor, *n.m.* fire-extinguisher.

extirpación, *n.f.* extirpation, eradication, extermination.

extirpador, -ra, *a.* extirpating. — *n.m.f.* extirpator. — *n.m.* (*agr.*) weed-extirpator, cultivator.

extirpar, *v.t.* to extirpate, root out, destroy, eradicate.

extorno, *n.m.* (*insurance*) rebate or refund for a no-claim clause.

extorsión, *n.f.* extortion; overcharge.

extra, *prep. prefix,* out, without, besides. — *a.* (*coll.*) extraordinary, remarkable; *extra de,* besides, in addition to. — *n.m.* tip, gratuity.

extracción, *n.f.* extraction; exportation; origin, descent; drawing numbers in a lottery; (*math.*) extraction (of root); *extracción de fondos,* (*com.*) secretion of effects.

extracta, *n.f.* (*law, prov.*) true copy, extract.

extractador, -ra, *a.* abstracting. — *n.m.f.* abstractor.

extractar, *v.t.* to abstract, epitomize, abridge.

extractivo, -va, *a.* extractive.

extracto, *n.m.* (*chem.*) extract; compendium, summary, abridgment, abstract; number drawn in a lottery; *extracto de Saturno,* white lead; *extracto tebaico,* aqueous extract of opium.

extractor, -ra, *a.* extracting. — *n.m.f.* extractor.

extradición, *n.f.* extradition.

extraente, *a.* extracting. — *n.m.f.* extractor.

extraer, *v.t.* (conjugated like TRAER) to extract, remove, draw out; to export; (*math.*) to extract (the root); (*law*) to draw a copy from any document.

extraigo; extraje, *pres. indic.; pret.* [EXTRAER].

extrajudicial, *a.* extrajudicial.

extrajudicialmente, *adv.* extrajudicially.

extralimitarse, *v.r.* to overstep one's power or authority.

extramuros, *adv.* outside the walls of a town, outside.

extranjería, *n.f.* alienship; *de extranjería,* foreign, strange, unexpected.

extranjerismo, *n.m.* fondness for foreign customs.

extranjerizar, *v.t.* to introduce foreign customs into a country. — *v.r.* to adopt foreign manners.

extranjero, -ra, *a.* foreign, exotic, outlandish. — *n.m.f.* alien, foreigner. — *n.m.* foreign countries; *está en el extranjero,* he is abroad.

extranjía, *n.f.* (*coll.*) alienship.

extranjis, *adv.; de extranjis,* (*coll.*) foreign, strange, unexpected; secretly, covertly.

extrañación, *n.f.;* **extrañamiento,** *n.m.* alienation, banishment, expulsion; exile, emigration.

extrañamente, *adv.* queerly, oddly.

extrañar, *v.t.* to banish, alienate; to wonder at; to cut, ignore (a person); to estrange; to miss, feel the lack of; to chide; (*Cent. Am., Ec., Mex., Per.*) to pine, long or yearn for something or somebody; *no hay que extrañar,* no wonder; *no he dormido bien, porque extrañaba la cama,* I did not sleep well on account of the strange bed. — *v.r.* to refuse, decline.

extrañeza, *n.f.* oddity, strangeness, singularity, irregularity, queerness; alienation, change of affection; wonderment, admiration, surprise.

extraño, -ña, *a.* queer, strange, odd; extraneous, foreign, outlandish; singular, rare; *es muy extraño,* it is very odd.

extraoficial, *a.* non-official.

extraordinariamente, *adv.* extraordinarily.

extraordinario, -ria, *a.* extraordinary, uncommon, rare, odd. — *n.m.* extra dish at dinner; special courier; (*newsp.*) special, extra.

extrarradio, *n.m.* suburb, outskirt.

extratémpora, *n.f.* dispensation to take holy orders.

extraterritorial, *a.* extra-territorial.

extraterritorialidad, *n.f.* extra-territoriality.

extravagancia, *n.f.* extravagance, irregularity, oddness; folly, freak.

extravagante, *a.* extravagant, eccentric; freakish, wild, odd, queer, out of the way, grotesque. — *n.f.pl.* (*eccles.*) extravagants.

extravagantemente, *adv.* extravagantly.

extravasarse, *v.r.* (*med.*) to extravasate, exude.

extravenado, -da, *a.* extravenate. — *p.p.* [EXTRAVENARSE].

extravenarse, *v.r.* to exude through the veins.

extraviado, -da, *a.* stray, strayed, gone astray; miscarried, mislaid, missing, of unsound mind; *los extraviados,* (*mil.*) the missing. — *p.p.* [EXTRAVIAR].

extraviar, *v.t.* to mislead, misguide; to mislay, misplace; to embezzle. — *v.r.* to go astray; lose one's way; to miscarry (as a letter); to err, deviate.

extravío, *n.m.* deviation; going astray, losing one's way; misplacement; misconduct; aberration, irregularity, disorder, frenzy.

extremadamente, *adv.* extremely.

extremadas, *n.f.pl.* time of making cheese.

extremado, -da, *a.* extreme; consummate (in good or bad sense). — *p.p.* [EXTREMAR].

extremamente, *adv.* extremely, exceedingly.

extremar, *v.t.* to carry to an extreme. — *v.r.* to take special pains, exert oneself to the utmost.

extremaunción, *n.f.* extreme unction.

extremeño, -ña, *n.m.f., a.* of Estremadura.

extremidad, *n.f.* extreme or remote part; end, extremity; brink, edge, border, brim. — *pl.* extremities (of animals).

extremista, *n.m.f., a.* extremist.

extremo, -ma, *a.* last, extreme; of the highest degree, greatest, utmost, excessive; terminal; furthest. — *n.m.* highest degree; extreme, utmost point; farthest end; apex; extremity; greatest care in doing a thing; *con extremo, en extremo,* or *por extremo,* extremely, in the utmost degree; *de extremo a extremo,* from one end to the other; from one extreme to another; *hacer extremos,* to go to extremes; to fondle, caress excessively; to express one's feelings extravagantly, be full of gush; *ir a extremo*, to move herds from one pasture to another according to the season; *ir*, or *pasar, de un extremo a otro*, to change one's opinions, etc., suddenly.

extremoso, -sa, *a.* extreme, vehement; impassioned, gushing, unbridled.

extrínsecamente, *adv.* extrinsically.

extrínseco, -ca, *a.* extrinsic, outward, external.

exuberancia, *n.f.* exuberance.

exuberante, *a.* exuberant, overabundant, luxuriant.

exuberar, *v.i.* (*obs.*) to be exuberant.

exudación, *n.f.* exudation, sweating.

exudar, *v.i.* to exude, ooze out.

exulceración, *n.f.* (*med.*) exulceration, ulceration.

exulcerar, *v.t.* (*med.*) to exulcerate, ulcerate. — *v.r.* to become ulcerated.

exultación, *n.f.* exultation, great joy.

exutorio, *n.m.* (*med.*) ulcer kept open.

exvoto, *n.m.* votive offering.

eyaculación, *n.f.* (*med.*) ejection, emission of secretions or of water.

eyacular, *v.t.* to eject secretions.

eyector, *n.m.* ejector (of a fire-arm).

F

F, f, *n.f.* seventh letter of the Spanish alphabet; formerly used instead of *h*, as *fablar*, for *hablar*. — (*mus.*) *forte, fuerte*, loud.

faba, *n.f.* (*obs., prov.*) bean.

fabada, *n.f.* Asturian stew made of pork and beans.

fabear, *v.t.* (*obs., prov.*) to vote with beans in secret ballot.

fabla, *n.f.* (*obs.*) talk, speech; fabliau.

fablador, -ra, *n.m.f.* (*obs.*) incessant talker.

fábrica, *n.f.* building, structure, edifice; works, factory; ecclesiastical funds for building; *de fábrica*, built of brick or stone and mortar; *pared de fábrica*, brick wall; *marca de fábrica*, trade-mark; *hombre de fábrica*, artful fellow; *mayordomo de fábrica*, churchwarden.

fabricación, *n.f.* construction; manufacturing; manufacture, make.

fabricador, -ra, *a.* fabricating; scheming, devising. — *n.m.f.* fabricator; schemer, inventor, contriver, deviser; (*naut.*) constructor.

fabricante, *a.* manufacturing. — *n.m.* fabricator, constructor, manufacturer.

fabricar, *v.t.* (*pret.* **fabriqué**; *pres. subj.* **fabrique**) to build, frame, construct; to fabricate, devise, contrive; to manufacture; *fabricar a juntas encontradas*, to construct with alternate courses of brick and hewn stone.

fabril, *a.* manufacturing; pertaining to factories or workmen.

fabriquero, *n.m.* manufacturer; charcoal-burner; churchwarden.

fabuco, *n.m.* (*bot.*) beech-mast.

fábula, *n.f.* fable, legend, fiction, fairy-tale, story; report, rumour, common talk; falsehood, lie; mythology; *está hecho la fábula del mundo*, he has become the laughing-stock of the world.

fabulador, *n.m.* fabulist, author of fables.

fabular, *v.t.* (*obs.*) to invent fables.

fabulilla; fabulita, *n.f.* little fable [FÁBULA].

fabulista, *n.m.* fabulist, writer of fables.

fabulosamente, *adv.* fabulously.

fabuloso, -sa, *a.* fabulous, legendary, feigned, romantic, fictitious; incredible, marvellous; excessive, extraordinary.

faca, *n.f.* jack-knife used by seamen.

facción, *n.f.* turbulent party, faction, uprising, tumult; (*mil.*) battle; (*mil.*) duty (as guard-duty, etc.); feature, countenance (*usually pl.*); *facción de testamento*, (*law*) faculty of testating.

faccionar, *v.t.* (*obs.*) to fashion, form.

faccionario, -ria, *a.* factionary.

faccioso, -sa, *a.* factious, unruly, turbulent, mutinous. — *n.m.f.* member of a faction, rebel; agitator; outlaw.

facer, *v.t.* (*obs.*) to make, do.

facería, *n.f.* (*prov.*) common pasture land.

faceta, *n.f.* facet of a gem; (*fig.*) facet.

faceto, -ta, *a.* (*Am.*) merry, lively, witty, gay.

facial, *a.* facial, belonging to the face; intuitive.

facialmente, *adv.* intuitively.

facie, *n.f.* face of a crystal.

fácil, *a.* easy, light, facile; of easy virtue; docile, compliant, handy, pliant; possible, probable; *es fácil que venga hoy*, it is possible he may come to-day; *fácil de* (with infinitive), easy to.

facilidad, *n.f.* ease, easiness, facility, ready compliance.

facilillo, -lla; facilito, -ta, *a.* rather easy [FÁCIL]; *facilillo es eso*, (*iron.*) easy enough that is!

facilitación, *n.f.* facilitation.

facilitar, *v.t.* to facilitate, expedite, make easy, free from difficulties; to deliver, supply.

facilitón, -ona, *n.m.f., a.* (*coll.*) (person) assuming everything to be easy.

fácilmente, *adv.* easily, without difficulty.

facineroso, *a.* wicked, atrocious, flagitious, villainous. — *n.m.f.* habitual criminal; highway robber; rascal, crook.

facistol, *n.m.* chorister's desk; lectern; (*obs.*) bishop's stall. — *a.* (*W. Ind., Ven.*) conceited, pedantic.

facón, *n.m.* (*Arg.*) gaucho's knife [FACA].

facoquero, -ra, *n.m.f.* wart-hog.

facsímile, *n.m.* facsimile.

factible, *a.* feasible, practicable.

facticio, -cia, *a.* artificial, factitious.

factor, *n.m.* factor; (*obs.*) performer, doer; (*mil.*) victualler; (*com.*) agent, factor, commissioner; (*railw.*) baggage-master; (*math.*) factor; (*fig.*) element, cause.

factoraje, *n.m.; factoría*, *n.f.* employment of a factor; factor's office; agency; factorage; factory, entrepot; commercial establishment in a colony.

factorial *a.* (*math.*) factorial.

factótum, *n.m.* factotum, man of all work; busybody.

factura, *n.f.* (*com.*) bill, invoice; (*art*) execution; *factura simulada*, pro-forma invoice.

facturar, *v.t.* (*com.*) to invoice, (*railw.*) register luggage; to remit goods by rail.

fácula, *n.f.* (*astron.*) facula, bright spot on the sun.

facultad, *n.f.* faculty; power, authority; faculty of a university; art, science; physiological power or ability; permission, licence.

— *pl.* wealth, fortune; *facultad mayor*, one of the university faculties of divinity, law, and medicine; *facultades del alma*, powers of the mind.

facultador, -ra, *n.m.f.* one who commissions or empowers.

facultar, *v.t.* to empower, commission, authorize.

facultativamente, *adv.* facultatively.

facultativo, -va, *a.* belonging to a faculty; facultative; optional. — *n.m.* physician or surgeon.

facundia, *n.f.* eloquence, fluency.

facundo, -da, *a.* eloquent, fluent.

facha, *n.f.* (*coll.*) appearance, look, aspect, face, mien; *facha a facha*, face to face; *vela en facha, ponerse en facha*, (*naut.*) lying to. — *n.m.f.* (*coll.*) gay sight, figure of fun; *ser un(a) facha*, to be ridiculous.

fachada, *n.f.* façade, front, face, frontage; frontispiece of a book; (*coll.*) figure, build (of a person); broad or fat face; *fachada de proa*, forefront of a ship; *hacer fachada a*, to face, front on.

fachado, -da, *a.* (*coll.*, with *bien* or *mal*) good-looking, unpleasant-looking.

fachear, *v.i.* (*naut.*) to be lying to.

fachenda, *n.f.* (*coll.*) vanity, conceit. — *n.m.* (*coll.*) vain, conceited fellow.

fachendear, *v.i.* (*coll.*) to brag, boast.

fachendista; fachendón, -ona; fachendoso, -sa, *n.m.f.*, *a.* conceited, vain, ostentatious.

fachinal, *n.m.* (*Arg.*) marshy land.

fachoso, -sa, *a.* (*coll.*) ugly-faced; ridiculous in appearance; (*Chi., Mex.*) conceited, vain.

fada, *n.f.* enchantress, fairy, witch; (*bot.*) small pippin apple.

faena, *n.f.* labour, toil, work, task; (*naut.*) work aboard ship, duty; (*Cub., Guat., Mex.*) overtime in a *hacienda*. — *pl.* business affairs.

faenero, *n.m.* (*Chi.*) farm labourer.

faetón, *n.m.* omnibus, char-à-banc; phaeton.

fagina, *n.f.* [FAJINA].

fagocito, *n.m.* (*biol.*) phagocyte.

fagot, *n.m.* bassoon, fagotto.

fagotista, *n.m.* bassoon-player.

faisán, *n.m.* pheasant.

faja, *n.f.* sash, belt, girdle; bandage, fillet, roller, band; swathing-band; border; (*geog.*) zone; (*arch.*) fascia, fillet, belt; newspaper wrapper; (*mil.*) general's sash or scarf; (*naut.*) reef-band.

fajadura, *n.f.* swathing, swaddling; (*naut.*) band of canvas, etc., lapped round a rope.

fajamiento, *n.m.* act of rolling or swathing.

fajar, *v.t.* to swathe, swaddle; to belt, band, girdle; (*Cub., Chi., Per.*) to beat, hit, slap; *fajar con*, (*coll.*) to fall on; to attack violently.

fajardo, *n.m.* meat pie, patty; vol-au-vent.

fajeado, -da, *a.* banded, fasciated.

fajero, *n.m.* swaddling-band made by crocheting.

fajín, *n.m.* small band or sash; general's sash.

fajina, *n.f.* faggot of brushwood; task, toil; work; (*mil.*) taps, retreat; (*agric.*) stook, shock, rick of sheaves; (*fort.*) fascine; *meter fajina*, (*coll.*) to talk at random.

fajinada, *n.f.* collection of faggots or stooks; fascine-work or revetment.

fajo, *n.m.* bundle, sheaf. — *pl.* swaddling-clothes.

fajón, *n.m.* (*arch.*) large band, roller, or sash; plaster border [FAJO].

fajuela, *n.f.* small bandage or roller [FAJA].

falacia, *n.f.* fraud, deceit; deceitfulness; treacherousness.

falange, *n.f.* (*mil.*) phalanx; (*anat.*) phalanx. — *pl.* phalanges.

falangia, *n.f.; falangio,** *n.m.* daddy-long-legs.

falárica, *n.f.* javelin.

falaris, *n.f.* (*orn.*) coot.

falaz, *a.* deceitful, treacherous.

falazmente, *adv.* deceitfully.

falbalá, *n.m.* flounce, furbelow; flap on the skirt of a coat.

falca, *n.f.* (*prov.*) small wedge; (*naut.*) wash-board.

falcado, -da, *a.* hooked, curvated. — *n.m.* shaped like a scythe; *carro falcado*, scythed chariot. — *p.p.* [FALCAR].

falcar, *v.t.* (*obs.*) to reap, to cut with hook or sickle; (*prov.*) to wedge.

falce, *n.f.* sickle, reaping-hook; falchion.

falcinelo, *n.m.* glossy ibis.

falcón, *n.m.* small cannon; (*obs.*) falcon.

falconete, *n.m.* falconet, small cannon.

falda, *n.f.* skirt, petticoat, train (*usually pl.*); armour from the waist downwards; lower slopes of a hill; lap; loin of beef, mutton, etc.; brim of a hat or a brazier; *pl.* women as opposed to men; *aficionado a las faldas*, fond of the ladies; *perrillo de falda*, lap-dog; *cortar las faldas*, (*obs.*) to punish a woman of bad character by cutting her skirts; (*fig.*) to back-bite.

faldamenta; faldamento, *n.m.* skirt, train, fold, flap.

faldar, *n.m.* tasset, tuille, in armour.

faldear, *v.t.* to skirt a hill.

faldellín, *n.m.* short skirt; underskirt.

faldero, -ra, *a.* belonging to the lap; fond of being among women; *perrillo faldero*, lap-dog.

faldeta, *n.f.* small skirt [FALDA]; (*theat.*) drop-curtain.

faldicorto, -ta, *a.* having short skirts.

faldillas, *n.f.pl.* skirts; coat-tails [FALDA].

faldistorio, *n.m.* bishop's seat.

faldón, *n.m.* hanging drapery; long flowing skirt; coat-tail; flap; shirt-tail; flap of a saddle; top mill-stone; (*arch.*) gable; tympanum; side walls and lintel of a chimney [FALDA]; *asirse*, or *agarrarse, a los faldones de alguno*, to seek someone's protection or patronage; *tener*, or *traer, uno el faldón levantado*, to have laid oneself open to blame, etc.

faldriquera, *n.f.* pocket, pouch.

falena, *n.f.* moth.

falencia, *n.f.* misstatement, mistake. — *n.m.f.* (*Arg., Chi., Hond.*) bankruptcy.

falibilidad, *n.f.* fallibility.

falible, *a.* fallible.

fálico, -ca, *a.* phallic.

falimiento, *n.m.* untruth, deception, falsehood, deceit.

falo, *n.m.* phallus, penis.

falondres, *adv.; de falondres*, (*naut., Cub., Ven.*) quickly, suddenly, briskly.

falordia, *n.f.* (*prov.*) story, fairy-tale.

falsa, *n.f.* (*prov.*) garret; guide-lines; (*mus.*) dissonance.

falsaamarra; falsamarra, *n.f.* (*naut.*) preventer-rope.

falsabraga, *n.f.* low rampart.

falsada, *n.f.* rapid flight of bird of prey soaring or swooping.

falsamente, *adv.* falsely, untruly, deceitfully.

falsario, -ria, *a.* falsifying, counterfeiting, forging. — *n.m.f.* forger, counterfeiter, falsifier.

falsarregla, *n.f.* bevel-square, bevel-rule; (*prov., Per., Ven.*) guide lines for writing.

falseable, *a.* falsifiable.

falseador, -ra, *a.* forging, counterfeiting, falsifying. — *n.m.f.* forger, falsifier, counterfeiter.

falsear, *v.t.* to falsify, forge, adulterate, counterfeit; to bevel; to penetrate armour; to pierce; *falsear el cuerpo*, to draw back the body to avoid a blow; *falsear los guardas*, to bribe the guards. — *v.i.* to slacken; to be out of tune (of a string).

falsedad, *n.f.* falsehood, falsity, untruth; deceit, guile, dissimulation; perfidy, duplicity.

falseo, *n.m.* bevelling.

falsete, *n.m.* spigot; small door; falsetto voice.

falsía, *n.f.* [FALSEDAD].

falsificación, *n.f.* falsification, forgery, counterfeit.

falsificador, -ra, *a.* forging, counterfeiting. — *n.m.f.* falsifier, counterfeiter, forger.

falsificar, *v.t.* (*pret.* **falsifiqué;** *pres. subj.* **falsifique**) to falsify, counterfeit, forge; to adulterate.

falsilla, *n.f.* guide-lines for writing.

falsío, *n.m.* (*prov.*) kind of stuffing or sausage.

falso, -sa, *a.* untrue, false, erroneous; incorrect; perfidious, treacherous, disloyal, false-hearted, deceitful, hypocritical; falsifying, lying; counterfeit, spurious, forged; vicious (of horses or mules); unreal, sham, artificial, mock; (*mech.*) temporary; unsubstantial; (*prov.*) cowardly, pusillanimous; spurious (of money); defective, false (of weights); *de* or *en falso*, falsely, deceitfully; *en* or *sobre falso*, without due security, safety or strength; *falso flete*, dead freight; *falso testimonio*, false testimony; slander, libel; imposture; *no levantarás falso testimonio*, thou shalt not bear false witness; *cerrar en falso la puerta*, to leave the door purposely slightly open. — *n.m.* (*sew.*) facing; padding of a garment.

falta, *n.f.* shortage, lack, deficiency, absence, want; fault; flaw, imperfection, blemish, defect; failure, misdoing, offence, faultiness; short-coming, failing; (*law*) default; deficiency in the weight of coin; stoppage of the catamenia in pregnant women; *a falta de*, in want of, for want of; *sin falta*, without fail; without fault; *hacer falta*, to be necessary; to be in want of; to disappoint; to be unpunctual; to be missing; to be missed; *él me hace mucha falta*, I miss him very much; *falta de aceptación*, non-acceptance; *falta de pago*, non-payment; *tiene cuatro faltas*, she is in the fifth month of her pregnancy; *acusar de falta*, to find fault with; *caer en falta*, to fail in one's duty; *a falta de hombres buenos, a mi padre hicieron alcalde*, the 'best of a bad lot' has been chosen; *a falta de pan, buenas son tortas*, or *a falta de*

polla, *pan y cebolla*, or *a falta de caldo, buena es la carne*, half a loaf is better than no bread; *tener más faltas que el caballo de Gonela* or *que un juego de pelota*, to be very imperfect; *falta de intención*, extenuating circumstances.

faltante, *a.* wanting, lacking.

faltar, *v.i.* to be wanting, to be deficient; to flinch, falter, fail; to be in want of, lack, need; to fall short; not to carry out one's engagement, not fulfil one's promise; to be missing or absent; to sin, offend; (*naut.*) to part, break, split, give way; to die; *faltar a*, to offend against; to be unfaithful; *faltar a la verdad*, to fail to speak the truth; *faltar al respeto a*, to be lacking in respect to; *faltar a su palabra*, to fail in, be untrue to one's word; *me faltan palabras para decir* or *expresar*, words fail me to tell; *me faltan tres peniques*, I need, or lack, or am short of three-pence; *faltar para*, (used impersonally) to lack; *faltar poco para*, to fall just short of, to be almost able to; *¡no faltaba más!* how absurd! what nonsense! the idea!

faltilla, *n.f.* slight fault or defect [FALTA].

falto, -ta, *a.* wanting, lacking; deficient, defective; scarce, short; mean, cowardly; devoid.

faltrero, -ra, *n.m.f.* pickpocket, petty thief.

faltriquera, *n.f.* pocket, pouch; *rascar(se) uno la faltriquera*, to spend money (unwillingly).

falúa, *n.f.* gig, small boat, tender.

falucho, *n.m.* felucca, vessel lateen-rigged; (*Arg.*) cocked hat.

falla, *n.f.* sort of head-covering worn by women; (*Col., Chi.*) failure, fault; defect, deficiency; (*geol.*) fault, dislocation, slide, break; (*Mex.*) baby's bonnet.

fallada, *n.f.* trumping (at cards).

fallanca, *n.f.* (*arch.*) flashing, run-off plate.

fallar, *v.t.* to ruff (at cards); (*law*) to judge, give sentence. — *v.i.* to fail, miss, be deficient or wanting; to break, give way; *falló la cosecha*, the harvest failed.

falleba, *n.f.* shutter-bolt.

fallecedero, -ra; fallecedor, -ra, *a.* that may fail or be deficient, perishable, exhaustible.

fallecer, *v.i.* (*pres. indic.* **fallezco;** *pres. subj.* **fallezca**) to die; to expire, run out, fail.

fallecimiento, *n.m.* death, decease, demise.

fallido, -da, *a.* frustrated, deceived, disappointed; bankrupt.

fallo, -lla, *a.* at cards, lacking a card of the suit played; *estoy fallo a bastos*, I have no clubs. — *n.m.* (*law*) judgment, sentence, decision; *echar el fallo*, to pass sentence; to declare a patient's case hopeless; *tengo fallo a espadas*, I have no spades (cards).

fama, *n.f.* fame, rumour, report; name, reputation, repute; glory; *correr fama*, to be spread (of news, etc.); *dar fama*, to inform; *quien la fama ha perdido, muerto está, aunque vivo*, he whose reputation is gone is done for; *cobra buena fama y échate a dormir*, get a reputation and you are a made man; *si quieres fama, no te dé el sol en la cama*, proverb in praise of diligence; *unos tienen la fama, y otros cardan la lana*, some do the work and others reap the reward.

famélico, -ca, *a.* hungry, ravenous.

familia, *n.f.* family; household; kin, clan;

religious order; domestic establishment; (*Chi.*) swarm (of bees); *cargar(se) de familia,* to fill (a house) with children or servants.

familiar, *a,* family, of the family; domestic; familiar, well-known, conversant; unceremonious, plain, home-like; frequent, common; agreeable, conformable; *estilo familiar,* easy or colloquial style. — *n.m.* domestic member of the household; servant, especially of the clergy; bosom friend; college-servant; officer of the Inquisition; familiar spirit, demon. — *n.m.pl.* attendants, suite; carriage with several seats.

familiarcito, *n.m.* servant boy, little servant; person who affects great intimacy [FAMILIAR].

familiaridad, *n.f.* familiarity, intimacy, acquaintance.

familiarizar, *v.t.* (*pret.* **familiaricé;** *pres. subj.* **familiarice**) to familiarize, make intimately known; to popularize. — *v.r.* to accustom, habituate oneself; to become familiar; *familiarizarse con el peligro,* to become familiar with danger.

familiarmente, *adv.* familiarly.

familiatura, *n.f.* position as familiar of the Inquisition; position of famulus.

famosamente, *adv.* famously, excellently.

famoso, -sa, *a.* celebrated, famous, noted, renowned, conspicuous, notorious; (*coll.*) great, remarkable, excellent.

fámula, *n.f.* (*coll.*) maid-servant.

famular, *a.* (*coll.*) domestic.

famulato; famulicio, *n.m.* service, servitude.

fámulo, *n.m.* famulus; (*coll.*) servant.

fanal, *n.m.* lighthouse; large lantern; bell-glass; candle-screen; (*obs., naut.*) poop-lantern of commodore's ship.

fanáticamente, *adv.* fanatically.

fanático, -ca, *a.* fanatic, fanatical.

fanatismo, *n.m.* fanaticism.

fanatizador, -ra, *a.* fanaticizing. — *n.m.f.* one who spreads fanaticism.

fanatizar, *v.t.* to fanaticize; to make fanatical.

fandango, *n.m.* fandango, a Spanish dance with castanets; music for this dance.

fandanguear, *v.t.* (*coll.*) to revel, carouse.

fandanguero, -ra, *n.m.f., a.* (person) fond of attending balls or dancing the fandango.

faneca, *n.f.* (*ichth.*) pout, whiting pout.

fanega, *n.f.* grain measure (about 1·5 bushels); *fanega de puño* or *de sembradura;* ground necessary to sow a *fanega* of seed; *fanega de tierra,* land measure (about 1·6 acres); *fanega de cacao,* about 116 pounds of cocoa.

fanegada, *n.f.* the same as *fanega de tierra; a fanegadas,* in great plenty, abundant.

fanerógamo, -ma, *a.* phanerogamic. — *n.f.pl.* phanerogams.

fanfarrear, *v.i.* to bully, brag, swagger.

fanfarria, *n.f.* (*coll.*) swagger, arrogance, bluster.

fanfarrón, -ona, *a.* (*coll.*) swaggering, boasting; bullying; showy; *trigo fanfarrón,* variety of wheat. — *n.m.* swaggering, boaster, bully.

fanfarronada, *n.f.* fanfaronade, boast, brag, rodomontade.

fanfarronazo, -za, *a.* very boastful.

fanfarronear, *v.i.* to brag, bully.

fanfarronería, *n.f.* fanfaronade, bragging.

fanfarronesca, *n.f.* swagger, fanfaronading.

fanfurriña, *n.f.* (*coll.*) fit of the sulks, pettishness.

fangal; fangar, *n.m.* fen, slough, marsh, swamp; bog, quagmire.

fango, *n.m.* mud, mire, silt, slush, slime, ooze.

fangoso, -sa, *a.* muddy, oozy, miry, slushy.

fano, *n.m.* (*obs.*) fane, temple.

fantaseador, -ra, *a.* fanciful, imaginative.

fantasear, *v.i.* to fancy, imagine.

fantasía, *n.f.* imagination, fantasy, fancy; (*naut.*) dead reckoning; conceit, humour, whim, caprice; (*coll.*) vanity, presumption; (*mus.*) fantasia. — *pl.* string of pearls; *de fantasía,* out of fashion (of clothes).

fantasioso, -sa, *a.* (*coll.*) vain, conceited.

fantasma, *n.m.* vision, ghost, spectre, phantom, apparition; vain, conceited person. — *n.f.* (*fig.*) scarecrow.

fantasmagoría, *n.f.* phantasmagoria, optical illusion.

fantasmagórico, -ca, *a.* phantasmagoric.

fantasmón, -ona, *n.m.f., a.* (*coll.*) supremely conceited (person) [FANTASMA].

fantásticamente, *adv.* fantastically.

fantástico, -ca, *a.* imaginary, fanciful, unreal, whimsical, fantastic; vain, presumptuous, conceited.

fantoche, *n.m.* puppet; puppet-show.

fañado, -da, *a.* one-year-old (beasts).

faquín, *n.m.* porter, carrier, labourer.

faquir, *n.m.* fakir.

fara, *n.f.* African serpent.

farachar, *v.t.* (*prov.*) to beat or clean hemp.

farad; faradio, *n.m.* (*elect.*) farad.

faradización, *n.f.* faradization.

faradizar, *v.t.* to faradize.

faralá, *n.m.* flounce, ruffle, frill.

farallón, *n.m.* headland, cliff; precipitous rock.

faramalla, *a.* (*coll.*) cajoling, deceiving. — *n.f.* (*coll.*) cajolery. — *n.m.f.* (*coll.*) cajoler; deceitful person.

faramallero, -ra; faramallón, -ona, *a.* (*coll.*) cajoling, deceiving; tattling, babbling. — *n.m.f.* deceiver; busybody.

farándula, *n.f.* profession of a low comedian; troupe of strolling players; (*coll.*) cajolement.

farandulero, -ra, *a.* cajoling, deceiving; tattling. — *n.m.f.* low class comedian; (*coll.*) cajoler; tattler, busybody.

farandúlico, -ca, *a.* relating to strolling players.

faraón, *n.m.* pharaoh; faro, card-game.

faraónico, *a.* pharaonic.

faraute, *n.m.* player who recites the prologue; pursuivant; messenger; (*coll.*) meddling fellow, busybody.

farda, *n.f.* ancient tax; bundle of clothing; (*carp.*) notch; *no pagar (la) farda,* not to be obsequious to someone from respect, fear, or interest.

fardacho, *n.m.* (*prov.*) lizard.

fardaje, *n.m.* dunnage; luggage, equipage.

fardar, *v.t.* to furnish, supply (with clothes).

fardel, *n.m.* bag, knapsack; parcel, bundle.

fardelillo; fardelejo, *n.m.* small bundle.

fardería, *n.f.* collection of packages, luggage.

fardo, *n.m.* bale, parcel, bundle, package; burden.

farellón, *n.m.* rocky headland, cliff.

farfalá, *n.f.* flounce, furbelow.

farfalloso, -sa, *a.* (*prov.*) stuttering, stammering. — *n.m.f.* stutterer, stammerer.

farfán, *n.m.* Christian of Spanish descent in Morocco.

farfante; farfantón, *n.m.* (*coll.*) boasting babbler.
farfantonada; farfantonería, *n.f.* idle boast.
fárfara, *n.f.* (*bot.*) coltsfoot; shell membrane (of an egg); *en fárfara,* immature, as an egg without a shell; (*fig.*) unfinished, half-done.
farfolla, *n.f.* husk of maize or millet.
farfulla, *n.f.* (*coll.*) gabble, gibberish, jabber. — *n.m.f.* (*coll.*) jabberer, gabbler.
farfulladamente, *adv.* hastily and carelessly.
farfullador, -ra, *a.* (*coll.*) stammering. — *n.m.f.* stammerer, mumbler, jabberer.
farfullar, *v.t.* (*coll.*) to talk hurriedly; to gabble, jabber; to act hurriedly.
farfullero, -ra, *a.* jabbering, chattering; hasty and confused in action.
fargallón, -ona, *a.* (*coll.*) careless, slovenly, untidy. — *n.m.f.* bungler, botcher.
farigola, *n.f.* (*prov.*) thyme.
farillón, *n.m.* steep cliff *or* rock; headland.
farináceo, -cea, *a.* farinaceous.
farinetas, *n.f.pl.* (*prov.*) kind of porridge; pap.
faringe, *n.f.* pharynx.
faríngeo, -gea, *a.* pharyngeal.
faringitis, *n.f.* pharyngitis.
fariña, *n.f.* (*Arg.*) coarse flour of manioc.
farisaicamente, *adv.* pharisaically.
farisaico, -ca, *a.* pharisaical, pharisaic.
farisaísmo; fariseísmo, *n.m.* pharisaism.
fariseo, *n.m.* pharisee; hypocrite; (*coll.*) tall, lean, ugly person.
farmacéutico, -ca, *a.* pharmaceutical. — *n.m.* pharmacist, druggist, apothecary.
farmacia, *n.f.* pharmacy; profession of druggist; chemist's shop.
farmacología, *n.f.* pharmacology.
farmacológico, -ca, *a.* pharmacological.
farmacólogo, *n.m.* pharmacologist.
farmacopea, *n.f.* pharmacopœia.
farmacopola, *n.m.* (*coll.*) apothecary, pharmaceutist, chemist, druggist.
farmacopólico, -ca, *a.* (*coll.*) pharmaceutical, pharmaceutic.
faro, *n.m.* lighthouse; (*fig.*) beacon; headlight.
farol, *n.m.* lantern, light; cresset; street-lamp; a feat in bullfighting; (*coll.*) conceited fellow; *faroles de señales,* (*naut.*) signal lanterns; *faroles de situación,* navigation lights; *adelante con los faroles,* go on bravely.
farola, *n.f.* large street lamp; beacon.
farolazo, *n.m.* blow given with a lantern; (*Cent. Am., Mex.*) drink.
farolear, *v.i.* (*coll.*) to give oneself airs, display conceit.
faroleo, *n.m.* showing off; bragging.
farolería, *n.f.* place where lanterns are made or sold; vulgar display; bragging, boast.
farolero, -ra, *a.* vain, conceited. — *n.m.f.* lantern-maker; lamplighter; (*coll.*) posing coxcomb.
farolico; farolito; farolillo, *n.m.* small lantern [FAROL]; *farolillo de jardín,* Indian heart-seed.
farolón, -ona, *a.* boasting, bragging. — *n.m.* (*coll.*) coxcomb, boaster; large lantern [FAROL].
farota, *n.f.* (*coll.*) brazen-faced woman.
farotón, -ona, *n.m.f., a.* (*coll.*) brazen-faced, cheeky, saucy (person).
farpa, *n.f.* pointed scallop on the edge of draperies.
farpado, -da, *a.* scalloped, notched.

farra, *n.f.* (*ichth.*) kind of salmon; (*Arg., Chi.*) spree, revelry, carousal.
farrago (*obs.*); **fárrago,** *n.m.* farrago, medley, confused mixture.
farraguista, *n.m.f.* person of confused ideas; pedantic scholar.
farrear, *v.i.* (*Arg., Chi.*) to go on the spree.
farro, *n.m.* peeled barley; spelt wheat.
farsa, *n.f.* farce; company of strolling players; badly constructed play; sham, humbug.
farsanta, *n.f.* actress who plays in farces.
farsante, *a.* hypocritical. — *n.m.f.* actor in farces; (*obs.*) pretender, deceiver.
farseto, *n.m.* quilted jacket.
farsista, *n.m.f.* writer of farces.
fartal; farte, *n.m.* (*prov.*) fruit tart.
fas, *adv.; por fas o por nefas,* (*coll.*) justly or unjustly.
fascal, *n.m.* (*prov.*) stook of 30 sheaves.
fasces, *n.f.pl.* fasces.
fasciculado, -da, *a.* fasciculate.
fascicular, *a.* fascicular.
fascículo, *n.m.* fascicle, part of a book.
fascinación, *n.f.* bewitching, spell-binding, fascination, enchantment; imposition, deceit.
fascinador, -ra, *a.* fascinating. — *n.m.f.* charmer.
fascinante, *a.* fascinating, charming.
fascinar, *v.t.* to fascinate, enchant, bewitch; to deceive, allure, impose upon.
fascismo, *n.m.* fascism.
fascista, *n.m.f., a.* fascist.
fase, *n.f.* phase, aspect, view.
faséolo, *n.m.* kidney bean.
fásoles, *n.m.pl.* French beans, kidney beans, haricots.
fastial, *n.m.* cope-stone.
fastidiar, *v.t.* to excite disgust in, sicken; to loathe; to disappoint; to bore, vex, annoy, bother, offend; to damage, harm, cause loss to. — *v.r.* to weary; to become vexed, bored, disgusted.
fastidio, *n.m.* squeamishness; loathing, dislike; fatigue, weariness, ennui, lassitude; bother, nuisance.
fastidiosamente, *adv.* squeamishly.
fastidioso, -sa, *a.* squeamish, sickening; fastidious; bothering, importunate, annoying, vexing; tedious, boring; vexed, angry.
fastigio, *n.m.* pinnacle, tip, apex; top, summit; pediment.
fasto, -ta, *a.* happy (day or event). — *n.m.* grandeur, splendour, pomp, pageantry, show. — *pl.* fasti; annals.
fastosamente; fastuosamente, *adv.* pompously, gaudily, magnificently.
fastoso, -sa; fastuoso, -sa, *a.* pompous, ostentatious; gaudy.
fatal, *a.* fatal, fated, ominous; deadly, destructive, mortal; unfortunate; (*law*) fixed, settled, unalterable (date for trying cause, etc.).
fatalidad, *n.f.* fatality, necessity; destiny; ill-luck, mischance, ill-fortune.
fatalismo, *n.m.* fatalism.
fatalista, *n.m.f., a.* fatalist, predestinarian.
fatalmente, *adv.* fatedly, fatefully; unavoidably; unluckily; awfully, badly.
fatídicamente, *adv.* fatidically.
fatídico, -ca, *a.* fatidical, oracular.
fatiga, *n.f.* lassitude, weariness, fatigue; hard labour, toil; hard breathing; anxiety, anguish, grief.

fatigadamente, *adv.* with difficulty, toilsomely.

fatigador, -ra, *a.* annoying; tiring.

fatigar, *v.t.* (*pret.* **fatigué;** *pres. subj.* **fatigue**) to tire, weary, fatigue; to annoy, vex, molest. — *v.r.* to tire, become tired out, weary, fatigued; *fatigar la selva,* (*poet.*) to employ oneself in hunting.

fatigosamente, *adv.* painfully, wearisomely, tediously.

fatigoso, -sa, *a.* troublesome, tiresome, wearisome; tiring; fatigued.

fatuidad, *n.f.* fatuity, foolishness; stupid speech or action, stupidity; vanity, conceit.

fatuo, -tua, *a.* fatuous, stupid; foppish, conceited. — *n.m. fuego fatuo,* will-o'-the-wisp, ignis fatuus.

fauces, *n.f.pl.* fauces, gullet.

fauna, *n.f.* fauna; treatise upon fauna.

fauno, *n.m.* faun.

fausto, -ta, *a.* happy, fortunate, prosperous, successful. — *n.m.* splendour, pageantry, pomp, ostentation; luxury, grandeur.

faustoso, -sa, *a.* pompous, ostentatious; luxurious.

fautor, -ra, *n.m.f.* helper, supporter, abetter, favourer, countenancer (chiefly in a bad sense).

fautoría, *n.f.* aid, help.

favila, *n.f.* (*poet.*) ashes of an extinguished fire.

favo, *n.m.* (*obs.*) honeycomb; (*med.*) ringworm.

favonio, *n.m.* (*poet.*) westerly wind, zephyr.

favor, *n.m.* favour; gift, grace, good turn, support, protection, countenance, aid, help, service, kindness granted; compliment; love-token; *a favor de,* in behalf of, on account of; by virtue of, by reason of; *a favor de obra,* denoting that something favours one's intent; *¡favor a la justicia!* or *¡favor al rey!* call for assistance to arrest criminals made by officers of justice; *tener uno a su favor a algo,* to use something as support or defence.

favorable, *a.* favourable, kind, propitious, friendly, advantageous.

favorablemente, *adv.* favourably.

favorcillo, *n.m.* small favour or service [FAVOR].

favorecedor, -ra, *a.* favouring, helping. — *n.m.f.* favourer, helper; client, customer; countenancer, friend, well-wisher.

favorecer, *v.t.* (*pres. indic.* **favorezco;** *pres. subj.* **favorezca**) to favour, befriend, protect, help, countenance; to flatter (as a portrait); to aid, abet. — *v.r.* (with *de*) to avail oneself (of help, support, etc.); to help one another.

favoreciente, *a.* favouring.

favoritismo, *n.m.* favouritism, nepotism.

favorito, -ta, *a.* beloved, favourite, darling, pet. — *n.m.f.* favourite.

fayado, *n.m.* (*prov.*) garret, lumber-room, attic.

fayanca, *n.f.* unsteady position of the body; *de fayanca,* carelessly; negligently.

fayanco, *n.m.* flat wicker basket.

faz, *n.f.* face; (*fig.*) face; (*arch.*) front; *faz a faz,* face to face; *a prima* or *primera faz,* at first sight; *en faz y en paz,* openly and peacefully.

fe, *n.f.* faith, belief in revealed religion, trust in God; faithfulness; promise given; testimonial, certificate; assertion, asseveration;

trust, credit; credence, confidence, testimony; *fe de erratas,* (*print.*) errata; *a fe,* in truth, in good earnest; *dar fe,* to attest, certify; *a fe mía* or *por mi fe,* upon my honour; *a buena fe,* certainly, without a doubt; *a la buena fe,* without deceit; *de buena fe,* bona fide, honestly and sincerely; *de mala fe,* in bad faith; craftily, deceitfully; *en fe,* consequently; *en fe de lo cual,* in witness whereof; *fe haciente,* authentic, bearing evident marks of truth; *a fe de bueno, de cristiano* or *de caballero,* upon my honour; *hacer fe,* to carry conviction; *prestar fe,* to assent to; *tener fe a,* to have faith in.

fealdad, *n.f.* ugliness; hideousness; deformity; (*fig.*) foulness, turpitude, dishonesty, depravity.

feamente, *adv.* uglily; deformedly; (*fig.*) indecorously; inordinately, brutally.

feazo, -za, *a.* very ugly, very deformed

febeo, -bea, *a.* (*poet.*) relating to Phœbus.

feblaje, *n.m.* light weight in a coin.

feble, *a.* feeble, faint, weak; (*jewel.*) deficient in weight or quality. — *n.m.* light coin.

feblemente, *adv.* feebly, weakly.

Febo, *n.m.* (*poet.*) Phœbus, the sun.

febrera, *n.f.* irrigation canal.

febrero, *n.m.* February.

febricitante, *a.* slightly feverish.

febrido, -da, *a.* (*obs.*) shining, refulgent.

febrífugo, -ga, *n.m., a.* febrifuge.

febril, *a.* febrile, feverish; (*fig.*) restless, anxious, uneasy, passionate.

fecal, *a.* (*med.*) fæcal.

fecí, *a.* relating to Fez. — *n.m.f.* native of Fez.

fécula, *n.f.* starch.

feculencia, *n.f.* dregs, lees.

feculento, -ta, *a.* dreggy, foul.

fecundable, *a.* capable of fecundation.

fecundación, *n.f.* fecundation, fertilization.

fecundamente, *adv.* fertilely, fruitfully.

fecundante, *a.* fecundating, fructifying.

fecundar, *v.t.* to fertilize, fecundate, impregnate, make fruitful.

fecundativo, -va, *a.* fecundating, fertilizing.

fecundidad, *n.f.* fecundity, fertility, productiveness, fruitfulness; abundance.

fecundizar, *v.t.* to fertilize, fecundate, fructify.

fecundo, -da, *a.* fecund, fertile, fruitful, prolific; copious, abundant.

fecha, *n.f.* date of a letter or writing; time or actual moment; *a estas fechas ya habrá llegado,* he will certainly have arrived by now; *esta carta ha tardado tres fechas,* this letter was three days in the post; *larga fecha,* old date, great age; *de la cruz a la fecha,* from the beginning to the end.

fechador, *n.m.* (*Chi., Mex.*) P.O. cancelling stamp.

fechar, *v.t.* to date (a letter, etc.).

fecho, -cha, *p.p. irreg.* (*obs.*) [FACER]; done, issued, or executed (in official documents).

fecho, *n.m.* (*obs.*) action, fact, exploit.

fechoría, *n.f.* bad action, misdeed.

federación, *n.f.* federation, confederation.

federal, *a.* federal. — *n.m.* federalist.

federalismo, *n.m.* federalism.

federar, *v.t., v.i.* to federate.

federativo, -va, *a.* federative.

Federico, *n.m.* Frederick.

féferes, *n.m.pl.* (*Col., CR., Cub., Ec., Mex.*)

household goods, implements, tools, trinkets.
fehaciente, *a.* (*law*) authentic.
felandrio, *n.m.* common water-hemlock.
feldespato, *n.m.* feldspar.
feldmariscal, *n.m.* field-marshal.
felice, *a.* (*poet.*) happy.
felicidad, *n.f.* felicity, happiness, blissfulness; success, prosperity.
felicitación, *n.f.* congratulation, felicitation.
felicitar, *v.t.* to congratulate, compliment, felicitate.
félidos, *n.m.pl.* (*zool.*) Felidæ.
feligrés, -sa, *n.m.f.* parishioner.
feligresía, *n.f.* parish; parishioners.
felino, -na, *a.* feline. — *n.m.f.* felid.
Felipe, *n.m.* Philip.
feliz, *a.* fortunate, happy, lucky, felicitous, prosperous.
felizmente, *adv.* fortunately, happily, luckily, felicitously.
felón, -ona, *n.m.f.*, *a.* felon, criminal.
felonía, *n.f.* treachery, disloyalty, felony.
felpa, *n.f.* plush; (*coll.*) reprimand; drubbing.
felpado, -da, *a.* plushy, shaggy, villous.
felpar, *v.t.* to cover with plush.
felpilla, *n.f.* chenille.
felposo, -sa, *a.* felted; plush-covered.
felpudo, -da, *a.* plushy; downy. — *n.m.* doormat.
felús, *n.m.* (*Morocco*) small change.
femenil, *a.* feminine, womanish.
femenilmente, *adv.* effeminately, womanishly.
femenino, -na, *a.* feminine; female; (*fig.*) weak, feeble; *género femenino,* feminine gender.
fementidamente, *adv.* falsely, unfaithfully, treacherously.
fementido, -da, *a.* false, unfaithful.
femineidad, *n.f.* femininity; (*for.*) belonging in law to a woman.
femíneo, -nea, *a.* feminine; effeminate.
feminismo, *n.m.* feminism.
feminista, *n.m.f.*, *a.* feminist.
femoral, *a.* femoral.
fémur, *n.m.* femur.
fenacitina, *n.f.* phenacetin.
fenda, *n.f.* crack, fissure in the grain or fibre of wood.
fendiente, *n.m.* gash, deep cut or wound.
fenecer, *v.t.* (*pres. indic.* **fenezco**; *pres. subj.* **fenezca**) to finish, terminate, close, conclude. — *v.i.* to die; to be at an end, terminate.
fenecimiento, *n.m.* close, finish, termination, end; settling of an account; death.
fenicar, *v.t.* to add carbolic acid to.
fenicio, -cia, *n.m.f.*, *a.* Phœnician.
fénico, *a.* carbolic.
fénix, *n.m.f.* phœnix; exquisite or unique thing; (*bot.*) kind of palm.
fenogreco, *n.m.* fenugreek.
fenol, *n.m.* phenol, carbolic acid.
fenomenal, *a.* phenomenal.
fenomenalismo, *n.m.* phenomenalism.
fenómeno, *n.m.* phenomenon.
feo, fea, *a.* ugly, homely, deformed, grim, hideous, haggard; causing horror or aversion; improper; serious, alarming. — *n.m.* slight, affront; *dejar feo a uno,* to affront, insult someone.
feote, -ta; feotón, -ona, *a.* very ugly [FEO].

feracidad, *n.f.* fecundity, fertility, fruitfulness.
feral, *a.* (*obs.*) cruel, bloodthirsty.
feraz, *a.* fruitful, fertile; copious, abundant, plentiful.
féretro, *n.m.* bier, coffin.
feria, *n.f.* bazaar, market, fair; (*eccles.*) any weekday (excepting Saturday or Sunday or a feast day); holiday, repose, rest. — *pl.* fairing, present bought at a fair; *ferias mayores,* Holy Week celebrations; *feria segunda, tercera, etc.,* Monday, Tuesday, etc.; *revolver la feria,* to brawl; to be the disturbing element in an affair; *cada uno cuenta de la feria según le va en ella,* everyone gives his own account of an event.
feriado, -da, *a.; día feriado,* (*law*) day in which the tribunals do not sit. — *p.p.* [FERIAR].
ferial, *a.* ferial. — *n.m.* market, fair.
feriante, *a.* attending a fair. — *n.m.f.* trader at fairs.
feriar, *v.t.* to sell, buy, trade, barter; to give fairings; to purchase at a fair. — *v.i.* to suspend work; to take a holiday.
ferino, -na, *a.* wild, savage, ferocious; *tos ferina,* whooping-cough.
fermentable, *a.* fermentable.
fermentación, *n.f.* fermentation.
fermentante, *a.* fermenting.
fermentar, *v.t.* to produce fermentation; (*fig.*) to rouse, excite, agitate. — *v.i., v.r.* to ferment; to become agitated.
fermentativo, -va, *a.* fermentative.
fermento, *n.m.* ferment, leaven, leavening; tumult.
fernambuco, *n.m.* Pernambuco wood.
fernandina, *n.f.* kind of linen.
Fernando, *n.m.* Ferdinand.
feroce, *a.* (*poet.*) ferocious.
ferocidad, *n.f.* ferocity, wildness, ferociousness, fierceness, savageness, fury.
feróstico, -ca, *a.* (*coll.*) irritable, wayward; (*coll.*) extremely ugly.
feroz, *a.* ferocious, savage, cruel, fell, fierce; (*fig.*) ravenous.
ferozmente, *adv.* ferociously.
ferra, *n.f.* variety of salmon.
ferrada, *n.f.* iron-knobbed club.
ferrado, -da, *a.* bound, shod, plated with iron. — *n.m.* (*prov.*) corn measure (about ¼ bushel); land measure (from 4 to 6 acres).
ferrar, *v.t.* to garnish with iron, strengthen with iron plates.
férreo, -rea, *a.* ferreous; iron, made of iron; harsh, stern, severe; *vía férrea,* railway.
ferrería, *n.f.* ironworks, foundry; forge.
ferreruelo, *n.m.* short cloak without cape.
ferrete, *n.m.* sulphate of copper used to colour glass; marking-iron.
ferretear, *v.t.* to fasten, work with iron.
ferretería, *n.f.* ironworks; hardware; hardware shop.
ferricianógeno, *n.m.* ferricyanogen.
ferricianuro, *n.m.* ferricyanide.
férrico, -ca, *a.* containing iron; ferric.
ferrífero, -ra, *a.* ferriferous, iron-bearing.
ferrificarse, *v.r.* to be converted into iron.
ferrizo, -za, *a.* ferreous, iron, of iron.
ferro, *n.m.* anchor.
ferrocarril, *n.m.* railway, railroad; *ferrocarril de sangre,* horse-tramway; *ferrocarril de cable,* cable-railway; *ferrocarril de cremallera,* rack-railway, mountain railway; *ferrocarril funi-*

cular, funicular, inclined cable-railway; *ferrocarril portátil*, portable railway; *ferrocarril de mina*, train-road; *ferrocarril aéreo*, elevated railway; *ferrocarril subterráneo*, underground railway.

ferrocarrilero, -ra, *n.m.f.*, *a.* (*Arg.*, *Col.*, *Ec.*) employee on a railway.

ferrolano, -na, *n.m.f.*, *a.* (native) of Ferrol.

ferrón, *n.m.* workman in ironworks; (*prov.*) iron manufacturer, ironmonger.

ferroso, -sa, *a.* ferrous.

ferrovía, *n.m.f.* railway, railroad.

ferrovial; ferroviario, -ria, *a.* pertaining to railways.

ferrugiento, -ta, *a.* containing iron.

ferrugíneo, -nea; ferruginoso, -sa, *a.* ferruginous.

fértil, *a.* fertile, fruitful, plentiful, copious.

fertilidad, *n.f.* fertility; copiousness, plenty.

fertilizante, *a.* fertilizing. — *n.m.* fertilizer.

fertilizador, -ra, *a.* fertilizing.

fertilizar, *v.t.* (*pret.* **fertilicé**; *pres. subj.* **fertilice**) to fertilize, enrich, fructify, make the soil fruitful.

fértilmente, *adv.* fertilely.

férula, *n.f.* ferule, cane; (*fig.*) rule, yoke, authority; (*bot.*) ferula; (*surg.*) splint.

feruláceo, -cea, *a.* ferulaceous.

ferventísimo, -ma, *a. superl.* very fervent, ardent or pious.

férvido, -da, *a.* fervid, ardent.

ferviente, *a.* fervent, ardent; warm in zeal.

fervor, *n.m.* violent heat; fervour, warmth; zeal, eagerness, fervidness, ardour, fervency.

fervorcillo, *n.m.* slight and brief fervour [FERVOR].

fervorín, *n.m.* short prayer.

fervorizar, *v.t.* to heat, inflame, incite.

fervorosamente, *adv.* fervently.

fervoroso, -sa, *a.* fervent; active, efficient, officious.

festejador, -ra, *a.* entertaining. — *n.m.f.* entertainer, host, hostess.

festejante, *a.* feasting, entertaining; wooing.

festejar, *v.t.* to entertain, feast; to make love to, woo, court; (*Mex.*) to whip, strike. — *v.r.* to amuse oneself.

festejo, *n.m.* entertainment, feast; obsequiousness; courtship. — *n.m.pl.* public rejoicing.

festero, *n.m.* director of church music.

festín, *n.m.* entertainment, feast, banquet.

festinación, *n.f.* speed, haste, hurry.

festinar, *v.t.* (*Col.*, *Hond.*, *Mex.*, *Ven.*, *Chi.*) to hasten, rush, hurry.

festival, *n.m.* festival (usually musical).

festivamente, *adv.* festively.

festividad, *n.f.* festivity; gaiety; rejoicing, merrymaking; holiday; witticism.

festivo, -va, *a.* gay, festive, joyful, light-hearted; festal, festival, pertaining to feasts; witty; *día festivo*, holiday.

festón, *n.m.* garland, wreath, festoon; edging.

festonar; festonear, *v.t.* to festoon; to border.

fetal, *a.* fœtal.

feticida, *n.m.f.* (*law*) one who procures an abortion.

feticidio, *n.m.* (*law*) fœticide, abortion.

fetiche, *n.m.* fetish, idol.

fetichismo, *n.m.* fetishism.

fetichista, *a.* fetishistic. — *n.m.f.* fetishist.

fetidez, *n.f.* fetidity, fetidness.

fétido, -da, *a.* fetid, stinking, foul.

feto, *n.m.* fœtus.

feúco, -ca; feúcho, -cha, *a.* (*coll.*) ugly, repulsive.

feudal, *a.* feudal.

feudalidad, *n.f.*; **feudalismo**, *n.m.* feudalism.

feudatario, -ria, *n.m.f.*, *a.* feudatory, feudary.

feudista, *n.m.f.* writer on feudal law.

feudo, *n.m.* fief, fee, feu, feud, feoff; feudal due; feudal privilege.

fez, *n.m.* fez, Turkish cap.

fiable, *a.* trustworthy, responsible.

fiado, -da, *a.* trustworthy (*obs.*); confident, trusting; on trust; *al fiado*, on credit; *dar fiado*, to give credit; *comprar al fiado*, to buy on credit; *en fiado*, upon bail. — *p.p.* [FIAR].

fiador, -ra, *n.m.f.* bondsman, guarantor, security, bail, surety. — *n.m.* cloak-fastener; (*mech.*) catch, stop, catch-bolt; locknut, paw, grip, trigger; safety-catch; tumbler of a lock, detent; (*falc.*) creance; (*coll.*) backside, rump; (*Chi.*, *Ec.*) chin-strap; *dar fiador* (or *salir fiador*) to procure or go surety.

fiambrar, *v.t.* to cook meat to be eaten cold.

fiambre, *a.* cold-served (as victuals). — *n.m.* cold meat, etc.; old joke or piece of news, chestnut.

fiambrera, *n.f.* lunch-basket; dinner-pail; nest of pots for keeping food hot; (*Arg.*) meat-safe; house refrigerator.

fianza, *n.f.* surety, bond, bail, guarantee, caution, security; pledge; suretyship; *fianza bancaria*, bank guarantee; *fianza de aduana*, custom-house bond; *dar fianza*, to give bail or pledge.

fiar, *v.t.* to guarantee, warrant, answer for; to sell upon trust; to go surety, bail; to give credit; to confide, commit, entrust. — *v.i.* to confide; to be sure of something; to give credit; *fiar el pecho*, to unbosom; *ser de fiar*, to be worthy of confidence; *yo lo fío*, I warrant it.

fiasco, *n.m.* failure, fiasco; *hacer fiasco*, to have a humiliating failure.

fiat, *n.m.* consent; (*law*) fiat.

fibra, *n.f.* fibre, filament, fibril; (*fig.*) vigour, energy, firmness; (*min.*) vein of ore.

fibrazón, *n.m.* all the ore-veins of a mine.

fibrilla, *n.f.* fibril.

fibrina, *n.f.* fibrin.

fibroideo, -dea, *a.* fibroid.

fibroso, -sa, *a.* fibrous.

ficción, *n.f.* fiction, invention; story, tale, fable.

fice, *n.m.* whiting.

ficticio, -cia, *a.* fictitious, fabulous.

ficto, -ta, *a.* feigned, artificial, counterfeited. — *p.p. irreg.* [FINGIR].

ficha, *n.f.* chip, counter, marker; domino (game); card-index; police dossier.

fichar, *v.t.* to file particulars in the police-record.

fichero, *n.m.* file, index.

fidedigno, -na, *a.* trustworthy, creditable.

fideero, -ra, *n.m.f.* maker of vermicelli, etc.

fideicomisario, *n.m.* trustee, fiduciary; fidei-commissary.

fideicomiso, *n.m.* trust; feoffment; fidei-commissum.

fideicomitente, *n.m.f.* fidei-commissor.

fidelidad, *n.f.* fidelity; honesty, honour, veracity, constancy, faith; punctiliousness; loyalty, fealty, faithful adherence.

fidelísimo, -ma, *a. superl.* [FIEL].

fideo, *n.m.* vermicelli, spaghetti, etc. (*usually pl.*); (*coll.*) very thin person.

fiduciario, -ria, *a.* fiduciary. — *n.m.f.* trustee, fiduciary.

fiebre, *n.f.* fever, (high) temperature; intense excitement; *fiebre amarilla,* yellow fever; *fiebre palúdica,* malaria; *fiebre perniciosa,* pernicious intermittent fever; *fiebre tifoidea,* typhoid fever; *limpiarse de fiebre,* to get rid of a fever; *declina la fiebre,* the fever abates; *recarga la fiebre,* the fever increases.

fiebrecilla, *n.f.* slight fever [FIEBRE].

fiel, *a.* honest, faithful, upright; loyal, devoted; true, right, exact; obedient, staunch (of Roman Catholics). — *n.m.* pointer or needle of a balance; public inspector, especially of weights and measures; pivot of a steelyard; pin of scissors; devout Christian; *fiel contraste,* official who weighs and stamps metals; *fiel de muelle,* wharfinger; *fiel de romana,* inspector of weights; *fiel medidor,* inspector of measures; *en fiel,* equal weight, even balance.

fielato; fielazgo, *n.m.* situation or office of the *fiel;* octroi, at a city's gates.

fieldad, *n.f.* public inspectorship; surety, guarantee, security.

fielmente, *adv.* faithfully.

fieltro, *n.m.* felt; greatcoat, hat, or rug made of felt.

fiemo, *n.m.* (*prov.*) dung, manure.

fiera, *n.f.* wild beast; fierce, savage person; shrewd or cunning person; (*coll.*) fiend, tiger (at games, etc.); *ser una fiera para* or *en una cosa,* to devote oneself wholeheartedly to something.

fierabrás, *n.m.* (*coll.*) bully, blusterer, rowdy; wayward, refractory child.

fieramente, *adv.* fiercely, savagely, ferociously; haughtily.

fiereza, *n.f.* cruelty, ferocity, fierceness; ugliness, deformity.

fiero, -ra, *a.* ferocious; bloodthirsty, cruel, fierce; rude, rough; deformed, ugly; terrible, furious; enormous, great, huge; savage, wild. — *n.m.pl.* menace, threat; *echar* or *hacer fieros,* to utter threats and menaces.

fierro, *n.m.* (*Am.*) iron; (*obs.*) fetter (*usually pl.*).

fiesta, *n.f.* feast, entertainment, merriment, feasting; festival, festivity, holiday; act of endearment, caress; holy day. — *pl.* fiestas, holidays, vacations; *hacer fiestas a uno,* to wheedle, caress; *hacer fiesta,* to take a holiday, leave one's work; *aguarse la fiesta,* to mar one's pleasure; *fiesta de consejo,* day on which a law court does not sit; *fiesta de guardar* or *de precepto,* day of obligation to hear mass; *fiesta de las Cabañuelas* or *de los Tabernáculos,* the Feast of Tabernacles; *fiesta de pólvora,* fireworks; (*fig.*) holiday, etc. quick in passing; *fiesta fija* or *inmoble,* fixed festival; *fiesta movible,* movable feast; *echar las fiestas,* to announce approaching festivals; (*obs.*) to utter insults and abuse; *estar de fiesta,* to be in good humour; *no estar para fiestas,* to be out of humour; *por modo de fiesta,* for fun; *guardar* or *sanctificar las fiestas,* to keep a feast-day sacred; *¡se acabó la fiesta!* that's enough of that! cut it out!; *tengamos la fiesta en paz,* don't let us have a bother.

fifiriche, *a.* (*CR., Mex.*) thin, frail, weak; fop, coxcomb.

figle, *n.m.* (*mus.*) ophicleide.

figón, *n.m.* eating-house, chop-house.

figonero, -ra, *n.m.f.* keeper of an eating-house.

figueral, *n.m.* plantation of fig-trees.

figulino, -na, *a.* made of terra-cotta.

figura, *n.f.* shape, form, figure; build, make; mien, countenance, face; picture, image, statue, cut (representing a figure); musical note, motive, theme; court-card. — *n.m.* stiffly pompous person; guy, figure of fun; *figura de proa,* figure-head of a ship; *figura de bulto,* high-relief figure; *figura de dicción,* grammatical inflexion; *figura de retórica,* figure of speech; *figura de tapiz,* guy, fright; *alzar* or *levantar figura,* to draw a horoscope; *hacer figura,* to make or cut a figure; *hacer figuras,* to make grimaces or ridiculous gestures; *genio y figura, hasta la sepultura,* what's bred in the bone will come out in the flesh; *tomar figura,* to copy, imitate.

figurable, *a.* imaginable.

figuración, *n.f.* figuration.

figuradamente, *adv.* figuratively.

figurado, -da, *a.* figurative; rhetorical, florid, ornate. — *p.p.* [FIGURAR].

figuranta, *n.f.* figurante, ballet-dancer.

figurante, *n.m.* figurant, dancer.

figurar, *v.t.* to shape, figure, fashion; to adorn with figures; to represent; to sketch, draw, design; to feign, pretend. — *v.i.* to cut a figure; take part in. — *v.r.* to fancy, imagine.

figurativamente, *adv.* figuratively.

figurativo, -va, *a.* figurative, typical; symbolical, emblematic.

figurería, *n.f.* grimace, affected gesture.

figurero, -ra, *a.* making figures. — *n.m.f.* (*coll.*) person who makes grimaces or affected gestures; maker of statuettes.

figurilla, figurita, *n.f.* (*coll.*) little insignificant person; (*art*) figurine, statuette [FIGURA].

figurín, *n.m.* fashion-plate; lay-figure; (*fig.*) dandy, dude.

figurón, *n.m.* (*coll.*) pretentious nobody; huge figure of ridiculous appearance [FIGURA]; *figurón de proa,* (*naut.*) figure-head.

fija, *n.f.* (*obs.*) door-hinge; (*build.*) pointing-trowel.

fijación, *n.f.* fixation, fixing; fastening; firmness, stability; billposting.

fijador, -ra, *a.* fixing, fastening; (*phot.*) fixing, fixative. — *n.m.f.* fixer; fastener. — *n.m.* (*build.*) pointer; (*carp.*) setter of doors and windows; (*phot., art*) fixing solution.

fijamente, *adv.* assuredly, firmly; fixedly, steadfastly; attentively, intensely.

fijante, *a.* (*artill.*) curving trajectory shot.

fijar, *v.t.* (*p.p.* **fijado, fijo**) to fix, fasten; to make fast, firm or stable; to determine, establish, settle, clinch; to fix (the eyes, the attention, etc.); to post (as bills); (*build.*) to point; (*carp.*) to set doors and windows; to fix (a date). — *v.r.* (with *en*) to fix or settle in a place; to rivet one's attention on something; to take notice of, pay attention to; to resolve, determine; *fijar las plantas,* to confirm oneself in an opinion.

fijeza, *n.f.* firmness, stability; steadfastness.

fijo, -ja, *a.* fixed, firm, secure; permanent, settled; (*mech.*) stationary; *de fijo,* surely, without doubt; *ésa es la fija,* that is certain;

ésta es la fija, this is the expected moment. — *p.p. irreg.* [FIJAR].

fil, *n.m.* (*obs.*) needle of a balance; equipoise, equilibration; *fil derecho*, leap-frog; *fil de roda*, (*naut.*) right ahead; *estar en un fil*, to be in line; to be equal.

fila, *n.f.* range, line, tier, row; (*mil.*) rank; *primera fila*, front rank; *en fila*, in a line; (*mil.*) abreast; *última fila*, rear rank; *en filas*, serving (army, navy, air, etc.).

filadiz, *n.m.* floss silk, ferret.

filamento, *n.m.* filament, fibre, thread.

filamentoso, -sa, *a.* filamentous.

filandria, *n.f.* filiform parasite worm.

filantropía, *n.f.* philanthropy.

filantrópicamente, *adv.* humanely, philanthropically.

filantrópico, -ca, *a.* philanthropical, philanthropic.

filántropo, -pa, *n.m.f.* philanthropist.

filar, *v.t.* to pay out a rope.

filarete, *n.m.* (*obs.*), (*naut.*) waist-netting.

filarmonía, *n.f.* love of harmony, passion for music.

filarmónico, -ca, *a.* philharmonic. — *n.m.f.* music-lover.

filástica, *n.f.* rope-yarn.

filatelia, *n.f.* philately.

filatélico, -ca, *a.* philatelic.

filatelista, *n.m.f.* philatelist.

filatería, *n.f.* verbosity, exuberance or superfluity of words.

filatero, -ra, *a.* verbose. — *n.m.f.* incessant talker.

filatura, *n.f.* spinning, art of spinning.

filbán, *n.m.* rough edge of a tool.

filderretor, *n.m.* superfine camlet.

filelí, *n.m.* fine cloth woven of silk and wool.

fileno, -na, *a.* (*coll.*) delicate, small; effeminate.

filera, *n.f.* fishing-net; spinneret of spiders.

filete, *n.m.* (*sew.*) narrow hem; (*arch.*) listel, fillet; welt of a shoe; small spit for roasting; fillet of beef or fish; (*print.*) ornamental line; (*mech.*) edge, ring, border, rim; snafflebit; thread of a screw; *gastar muchos filetes*, to use flowery language.

filetear, *v.t.* to fillet; to tool.

filetón, *n.m.* (*arch.*) large fillet or listel; heavy bullion for embroidering [FILETE].

filfa, *n.f.* (*coll.*) fib, fake, hoax.

filiación, *n.f.* filiation; relationship, connexion; regimental register; personal description.

filial, *a.* filial, befitting a son. — *n.f.* branch of a commercial house.

filialmente, *adv.* filially.

filiar, *v.t.* to register the pedigree and description of a person; to enrol a soldier. — *v.r.* to be enrolled as a soldier.

filibote, *n.m.* (*obs.*) fly-boat, light vessel.

filibusterismo, *n.m.* filibusterism.

filibustero, *n.m.* filibuster, freebooter; partisan fighting against Spanish colonialism.

filicida, *n.m.f.* (*law*) one who kills his child.

filicidio, *n.m.* (*law*) murder of one's child.

filiforme, *a.* filiform, thread-like.

filigrana, *n.f.* filigree, filigrane; spun work; watermark in paper; delicate, fanciful thing; something neatly made; (*Cub.*) wild shrub of the verbena family.

filili, *n.m.* (*coll.*) fineness, delicacy, neatness.

filipéndula, *n.f.* dropwort spiræa.

filipense, *n.m.f.*, *a.* Philippian.

filípica, *n.f.* philippic, invective, declamation.

filipichín, *n.m.* moreen.

Filipinas, *n.f.pl.* Philippines.

filipino, -na, *n.m.f.*, *a.* Filipino, native of, or relating to, the Philippine Islands.

filis, *n.f.* knack of doing a thing perfectly; trinket, charm.

filisteo, -tea, *n.m.f.*, *a.* Philistine. — *n.m.* (*coll.*) tall, massively built man.

filo, *n.m.* cutting edge; arris; ridge; dividing line; *filo del viento*, (*naut.*) direction of the wind; *filo rabioso*, rough, unpolished edge; *dar* (*un*) *filo*, to sharpen; *darse un filo a la lengua*, to back-bite; *embotar los filos*, to abate one's ardour; *herir por los mismos filos*, to hoist with his own petard; *pasar al filo de la espada*, to put to the sword; *por filo*, exactly, precisely.

filocartista, *n.m.f.* collector of postcards.

filófago, -ga, *a.* (*entom.*) phyllophagous.

filología, *n.f.* philology.

filológicamente, *adv.* philologically.

filológico, -ca, *a.* philological.

filólogo, -ga, *n.m.f.* philologist.

filomanía, *n.f.* (*bot.*) phyllomania.

filomela; filomena, *n.f.* nightingale.

filón, *n.m.* (*geol.*) vein, lodge, mineral layer.

filonio, *n.m.* (*pharm.*) electuary compounded with honey, opium, etc.

filopos, *n.m.pl.* fences of linen erected to direct game towards a particular place.

filoseda, *n.f.* cloth made of silk and wool or silk and cotton.

filoso, -sa, *a.* (*Arg.*, *CR.*, *Hond.*) sharp, keen edged.

filosofador, -ra, *a.* philosophizing. — *n.m.f.* philosophizer.

filosofal, *a.*; *piedra filosofal*, philosopher's stone.

filosofar, *v.i.* to philosophize; (*coll.*) to muse.

filosofastro, *n.m.* dilettante philosopher, philosophaster.

filosofía, *n.f.* philosophy; *filosofía natural*, physics *or* natural philosophy; *filosofía moral*, ethics *or* moral philosophy.

filosóficamente, *adv.* philosophically.

filosófico, -ca, *a.* philosophical, philosophic.

filosofismo, *n.m.* philosophism (in a deprecatory sense).

filosofista, *n.m.f.* philosophist, sophist.

filósofo, -fa, *a.* philosophic, philosophical. — *n.m.f.* philosopher.

filoxera, *n.f.* (*entom.*) phylloxera; (*coll.*) drunkenness.

filtración, *n.f.* filtration.

filtrador, *a.* filtering. — *n.m.f.* filterer. — *n.m.* filter.

filtrar, *v.t.* to filter, strain. — *v.i.* to percolate, filter. — *v.r.* to filter through; to leak out, disappear.

filtro, *n.m.* filter; philtre, love-potion; *filtro de vacío*, vacuum filter; *filtro prensa*, filter-press for refining sugar.

filván, *n.m.* wire-edge, burr.

fillós, *n.m.pl.* sort of fritters, pancakes.

fimbria, *n.f.* edge or border of a skirt.

fimo, *n.m.* dung, manure.

fimosis, *n.f.* phimosis.

fin, *n.m.f.* end, ending, conclusion; consummation, attainment. — *n.m.* end, object, purpose, goal; limit, boundary; *al fin*, at last;

dar fin, to die; to finish; *el fin del mundo*, at the back of beyond; *en fin, por fin*, finally, lastly; *en fin, veremos*, well, we shall see; *dar fin a*, to finish, conclude; *dar fin de una cosa*, to destroy a thing completely; *a fin de (que)*, in order that; *a fin de averiguar la verdad*, in order to find out the truth; *a fin de que no haya nuevas dilaciones*, so that there may be no further delay; *a fines del mes*, towards the end of the month; *por cualquier fin*, prompted by whatever motive; *al fin y al cabo, por fin y postre, al fin y a la postre*, finally; *al fin se canta la gloria*, you never know till the end; *sin fin*, innumerable, endless; *tornillo sin fin*, endless screw, worm drive; *cadena sin fin*, endless chain; *correa sin fin*, endless belt.

finado, -da, *a.* dead, deceased. — *n.m.f.* dead person; *Día de los finados*, All Souls' Day. — *p.p.* [FINAR].

final, *a.* ultimate; final; conclusive. — *n.m.* termination, end, conclusion; *por final*, in fine, ultimately, lastly; *Juicio final*, Last Judgment.

finalidad, *n.f.* finality; end pursued or attained.

finalizar, *v.t.* to conclude, finish. — *v.i.* to end, be finished or concluded.

finalmente, *adv.* finally, at last, in fine, lastly, ultimately.

finamente, *adv.* nicely, finely, delicately.

finamiento, *n.m.* decease, death.

financiero, -ra, *a.* financial. — *n.m.* financier.

finanza, *n.f.* (*obs.*) [FIANZA; RESCATE].

finar, *v.i.* to die. — *v.r.* to long (for, *por*).

finca, *n.f.* real estate, land or house property, tenement, building, house, real estate; *¡buena finca!* (*iron.*) person or thing unreliable.

fincabilidad, *n.f.* property (immovable).

fincar, *v.r., v.i.* (*pret.* **finqué;** *pres. subj.* **finque**) to buy real estate.

finchado, -da, *a.* (*coll.*) swelling with pride.

finchar, *v.r.* (*coll.*) to become proud or haughty.

finés, -esa, *a.* Finnic, Finnish. — *n.m.f.* Finn. — *n.m.* Finnish language.

fineta, *n.f.* compact and fine cotton cloth diagonally woven.

fineza, *n.f.* fineness, purity, goodness, perfection; friendly activity and zeal; expression of friendship or love, kindness; a favour; keepsake, friendly gift; delicacy, beauty.

fingidamente, *adv.* feignedly, fictitiously.

fingido, -da, *a.* feigned, dissembled, false. — *p.p.* [FINGIR]; *dientes fingidos*, (*coll.*) false or artificial teeth; *no te fíes de ése, que es muy fingido*, do not trust him, he is very deceitful.

fingidor, -ra, *a.* dissembler, simulator, feigner.

fingimiento, *n.m.* simulation, deceit, false appearance; pretence.

fingir, *v.t., v.r.* (*p.p.* **fingido, ficto;** *pres. indic.* **finjo;** *pres. subj.* **finja**) to feign, dissemble, pretend, counterfeit, sham, affect; to imagine, fancy.

finible, *a.* capable of being finished.

finiquitar, *v.t.* to settle and close an account; (*coll.*) to end, finish, settle.

finiquito, *n.m.* settlement of accounts, final receipt, discharge; adjustment, release, quittance; *dar finiquito*, to come to the end of one's money, etc.

finir, *v.i.* (*Col., Chi., Ven.*) to end, finish.

finítimo, -ma, *a.* bordering, near, contiguous (towns, fields, or lands).

finito, -ta, *a.* finite, limited, bounded.

finlandés, -esa, *a.* of Finland, Finnish. — *n.m.f.* Finn; Finnish language.

fino, -na, *a.* slender, subtle, thin; perfect, fine, pure; nice, delicate; true, affectionate; excellent, eminent; sharp (as a point); cunning, shrewd, sagacious, acute; courteous, urbane, of polished education and manners; (*naut.*) sharp; refined (as gold).

finquero, *n.m.* land-owner and planter in Rio Muni.

finta, *n.f.* ancient tax; feint in fencing.

finura, *n.f.* purity, delicacy, fineness; fine manners, urbanity, courtesy.

finústico, -ca, *a.* (*coll.*) alluding to a person who affects exaggerated courtesy.

fiñana, *n.m.* black-bearded wheat.

fío, *n.m.* (*Chi.*) small insectivorous bird of green and white plumage.

fique, *n.m.* (*Col., Mex., Ven.*) fibre of the agave.

firma, *n.f.* subscription, signature, sign-manual, hand (as hand and seal); (*com.*) firm, firm-name; act of signing; (*Aragon*) order or rescript of a tribunal for keeping possession; *buena firma*, a house of standing, solvent; *dar* (or *llevar*) *la firma*, to empower or be empowered to sign the firm-name; *media firma*, surname; *dar uno firma en blanco*, to give carte-blanche; *firma en blanco*, signature put to a blank document; (*fig.*) carte blanche; *mala firma*, firm in insolvent circumstances; *dar uno la firma a otro*, (*com.*) to empower another to represent one; *llevar uno la firma de otro*, (*com.*) to represent another's firm; *echar una firma*, to separate ashes from glowing embers.

firmal, *n.m.* piece of jewellery in the form of a clasp.

firmamento, *n.m.* firmament, sky, heaven.

firmán, *n.m.* firman.

firmante, *n.m.f.* signer, subscriber, supporter.

firmar, *v.t.* to sign, subscribe; (*obs.*) to attest, affirm. — *v.r.* to sign an assumed name; *no estar uno para firmar*, (*coll.*) to be drunk.

firme, *a.* firm, steady, unswerving, unshaken, unyielding, staunch, resolute, constant, consistent; compact, secure, hard, fast, solid, strong, stable. — *n.m.* bed, groundwork, foundation; ballast, or gravel bed on a road. — *adv.* firmly, strongly; *aguas firmes*, well or spring water; *de firme*, constantly, incessantly; solidly; violently; *en firme*, (*com.*) for settlement at a fixed date; *estar uno en lo firme*, to hold uncontrovertible opinions; *¡firmes!* (*mil.*) Stand to attention! Attention! *quedarse uno en* (*lo*) *firme*, (*coll.*) to be very thin; *tierra firme*, mainland.

firmemente, *adv.* firmly, strongly, immovably; steadily, faithfully, constantly.

firmeza, *n.f.* stability, firmness, hardness, constancy, solidity, steadiness, compactness, courage, resoluteness.

firmón, *n.m.* one who signs another's work.

firuletes, *n.m.pl.* (*Arg., Per.*) dress trimmings; ornaments; adornments.

fiscal, *a.* fiscal. — *n.m.* attorney-general; district attorney, prosecutor; (*coll.*) intermeddler, prier.

fiscalía, *n.f.* office and business of the fiscal.

fiscalización, *n.f.* discharge of a fiscal's duties.

fiscalizador, -ra, *a.* acting as a fiscal. — *n.* prier, censurer, fault-finder.

fiscalizar, *v.t.* (*pret.* **fiscalicé**; *pres. subj.* **fiscalice**) to act as a fiscal, to prosecute; to criticize, censure.

fisco, *n.m.* national treasury, exchequer; (*Ven.*) copper coin, the fourth part of a centavo.

fisga, *n.f.* harpoon; (*prov.*) · bread of spelt-wheat; spelt-wheat; chaff, banter, raillery; *hacer fisga de alguno,* to make fun of anyone.

fisgador, -ra, *n.m.f.* harpooner; banterer.

fisgar, *v.t.* to banter, chaff; to harpoon; to pry, peep, eavesdrop.

fisgón, -ona, *n.m.f.* chaffer, jester, banterer, buffoon; prier, peeper.

fisgonear, *v.t.* to pry habitually.

fisgoneo, *n.m.* habitual or frequent prying.

física, *n.f.* physics, natural philosophy; physic, medicine.

físicamente, *adv.* physically; corporeally; really, materially.

físico, -ca, *a.* natural, material; physical; (*Cub., Mex.*) pedantic, prudish. — *n.m.* physicist, naturalist; military or naval surgeon; physician; (*coll.*) physique, build, or constitution of a person.

fisiocracia, *n.f.* physiocracy; power of nature.

fisiócrata, *n.m.f.* physiocrat.

fisiología, *n.f.* physiology.

fisiológicamente, *adv.* physiologically.

fisiológico, -ca, *a.* physiological.

fisiologista, fisiólogo, *n.m.* physiologist.

fisonomía, fisonomía, *n.f.* physiognomy, lineaments, features.

fisioquímica, *n.f.* physio-chemistry.

fisioterapia, *n.f.* treatment of disease by natural agents; physiotherapy.

fisípedo, -da, *a.* fissiped.

fisonomía, *n.f.* [FISIONOMÍA].

fisonómico, -ca, *a.* physiognomical.

fisonomista, fisónomo, *n.m.* physiognomist.

fistol, *n.m.* crafty person; shrewd gambler; (*Mex.*) scarf pin.

fístola, fístula, *n.f.* water-pipe or conduit; (*mus.*) reed, pipe; (*surg.*) fistula.

fistular, *a.* fistular, fistulous.

fistuloso, -sa, *a.* fistulous.

fisura, *n.f.* fissure of bone, fracture; (*geol.*) cleft, fissure.

fitófago, -ga, *a.* phytophagous.

fitografía, *n.f.* phytography.

fitográfico, -ca, *a.* phytographic.

fitógrafo, *n.m.* phytographer.

fitología, *n.f.* phytology, botany.

fitotomía, *n.f.* phytotomy.

flabelación, *n.f.* agitation of the air, flabellation.

flabelado, -da, *a.* fan-shaped; like a fly-trap.

flabelicornio, *a.* having flabellate antennæ.

flabelífero, -ra, *a.* pertaining to a flabellum carrier.

flabeliforme, *a.* flabelliform.

flacamente, *adv.* languidly, weakly, feebly.

flaccidez, flacidez, *n.f.* flaccidity, laxity, limberness, want of tension.

fláccido, -da; flácido, -da, *a.* flaccid, limber, lax.

flaco, -ca, *a.* weak of resolution, frail; lank, lean, thin, flaccid, meagre; languid, feeble; *hacer un flaco servicio,* to do an ill turn; *flaco de memoria,* short of memory.

flacucho, -cha, *a.* rather thin or lank.

flacura, *n.f.* meagreness, leanness, weakness.

flagelación, *n.f.* flagellation, scourging.

flagelador, -ra, *n.m.f.* flagellator.

flagelante, *n.m.* flagellant; flagellating.

flagelar, *v.t.* to scourge, lash, flagellate, whip.

flagelo, *n.m.* lash, scourge, chastisement; flagellum.

flagicio, *n.m.* (*obs.*) heinous crime.

flagicioso, -sa, *a.* (*obs.*) deeply criminal.

flagrancia, *n.f.* flagrancy, flagrantness.

flagrante, *a.* flagrant, resplendent; now going on, actual; *en flagrante,* in the very act, red-handed.

flagrar, *v.i.* (*poet.*) to glow, burn, flame.

flama, *n.f.* flame, excessive ardour.

flamante, *a.* flaming, bright, resplendent; fresh, brand-new, spick and span.

flamear, *v.i.* to flame, blaze; (*naut.*) to flutter (sails), shiver; (*med.*) to burn alcohol, etc. in vessels to sterilize them.

flamenco, *n.m.* (*orn.*) flamingo.

flamenco, -ca, *a.* Flemish, relating to Flanders; Andalusian; gipsy-like; buxom; brazen. — *n.m.f.* Fleming; Andalusian gipsy.

flamenquilla, *n.f.* small dish or plate; (*bot.*) marigold.

flámeo, *n.m.* ancient bridal veil; flapping, fluttering.

flamero, *n.m.* torch-holder.

flamígero, -ra, *a.* (*poet.*) flammiferous, emitting flames.

flámula, *n.f.* (*naut.*) streamer, pennon; (*bot.*) virgin's bower (*clematis flammula*).

flan, flaón, *n.m.* baked custard.

flanco, *n.m.* side; (*mil., fort.*) flank, flanker; side of a ship.

Flandes, *n.m.pl.* Flanders; *¿estamos aquí o en Flandes?* is that a proper way to behave? *no hay más Flandes* (*obs.*), it's the very best of its kind.

flanero, *n.m.* flawn mould.

flanqueado, -da, *a.* having both flanks protected.

flanqueante, *a.* flanking.

flanquear, *v.t.* to flank, defend by lateral fortifications.

flanqueo, *n.m.* flank attack, outflanking.

flaquear, *v.i.* to slacken; to flag, weaken, grow feeble, lose vigour; to be disheartened; to sway, swag.

flaqueza, *n.f.* faintness, feebleness; thinness, leanness, lankness, meagreness, attenuation, want of flesh; foible, frailty, weakness; flagginess; molestation, importunity.

flato, *n.m.* flatus, windiness; gust of wind; (*Col., Mex., Ven.*) melancholy, sadness, gloom.

flatoso, flatuoso, -sa, *a.* flatuous, windy.

flatulencia, *n.f.* flatulency, windiness.

flatulento, -ta, *a.* flatulent, windy.

flauta, *n.f.* flute; *flauta travesera,* German flute; *y sonó la flauta,* it was a fluke.

flautado, -da, *a.* fluted, like a flute. — *n.m.* flute stop in an organ.

flauteado, *a.* flute-like (of the voice).

flautero, *n.m.* maker of flutes.

flautillo, *n.m.* flageolet, small flute.

flautín, *n.m.* octave flute, piccolo.

flautista, *n.m.f.* flute-player.

flautos, *n.m.pl.; pitos flautos,* frivolous pastimes; *cuando pitos, flautas* (or *flautos*); *cuando flautas* (or *flautos*), *pitos,* contrary to one's wishes or hopes.

flavo, -va, *a.* of a fallow or honey colour.

flébil, *a.* mournful, lamentable, deplorable, tearful.

flebitis, *n.f.* phlebitis.

flebotomía, *n.f.* phlebotomy, blood-letting.

flebotomiano, *n.m.* phlebotomist.

flebotomizar, *v.t.* to bleed, let blood.

fleco, *n.m.* purl, fringe, flounce; ravelled edge of cloth.

flecha, *n.f.* dart, arrow; (*fort.*) work two faces and two sides; (*naut.*) front piece of the cutwater; Sagitta, a northern constellation; *entrar de flecha,* to enter swiftly.

flechador, *n.m.* archer.

flechaduras, *n.f.pl.* ratlines.

flechar, *v.t.* to shoot an arrow or dart; to dart; to wound or kill with an arrow; (*Mex.*) to point out, without fear, in gambling; (*coll.*) to inspire sudden love. — *v.i.* to have a bow drawn ready to shoot.

flechaste, *n.m.* ratline.

flechazo, *n.m.* stroke with a dart or arrow; (*coll.*) sudden love, love at first sight.

flechera, *n.f.* (*Ven.*) long canoe.

flechería, *n.f.* shower of arrows.

flechero, *n.m.* archer, bowman; arrow-maker, fletcher.

flegmasía, *n.f.* inflammation.

fleje, *n.m.* hoop; strap; *flejes,* twigs for barrels; *flejes para aros,* hoop-poles; *flejes de hierro,* iron hoops.

flema, *n.f.* phlegm; coolness, apathy, dullness, sluggishness; *gastar flema,* proceed slowly; not to be easily rattled.

flemático, -ca, *a.* phlegmatic, slow, dull, sluggish, cold.

fleme, *n.f.* fleam.

flemón, *n.m.* phlegmon; gumboil.

flemonoso, -sa, *a.* phlegmonous.

flemoso, -sa, *a.* mucous, phlegmy.

flemudo, -da, *a.* (*prov.*) slow, dull, sluggish.

flequezuelo, *n.m.* narrow fringe.

flequillo, *n.m.* fringe, bang (hair).

Flesinga, *n.f.* Flushing.

fletador, *n.m.* freighter, charterer.

fletamento, fletamiento, *n.m.* charter, charterage, charter-party.

fletante, *a.; fletán, n.m.* (*Arg., Chi., Ec., Mex.*) person who hires out a ship or animal of burden.

fletar, *v.t.* to freight or charter a ship; to embark; (*Arg., Chi., Ec., Mex.*) to hire a beast of burden, cart or coach; (*Chi., Per.*) *le fletó una desvergüenza, una bofetada,* to burst out with offensive act or language; (*Chi., Guat.*) to rub, scrub; (*Cub., Mex.*) to get out, leave quickly; (*Arg.*) to gatecrash a party; *fletar redondo,* to set out and home freight.

flete, *n.m.* freight, freightage; *falso flete,* dead freight.

flexibilidad, *n.f.* flexibility, pliance, pliability, flexibleness, ductility; manageableness, mildness of temper.

flexible, *a.* flexible, pliant, ductile; manageable, docile; supple, lithe.

flexión, *n.f.* flexion, flexure.

flexor, -ra, *a.* (*anat.*) flexor; bender.

flexuoso, -sa, (*bot.*) flexuose.

flexura, *n.f.* plait, bend, ply, fold.

flibote, *n.m.* fly-boat.

flictena, *n.f.* small blister; (*elec.*) flex.

flin, *n.m.* polishing-stone.

flocadura, *n.f.* (*sew.*) fringe trimming.

flogístico, -ca, *a.* phlogistic.

flogisto, *n.m.* phlogiston.

flogosis, *n.f.* inflammation, phlegmasia.

flojamente, *adv.* slowly, laxly, carelessly.

flojear, *v.i.* to slacken, grow weak [FLAQUEAR].

flojedad, *n.f.* weakness, laxity, feebleness, laziness, sloth, slackness, negligence.

flojel, *n.m.* wool shorn from cloth; down, soft feathers.

flojera, *n.f.* (*coll.*) weakness.

flojo, -ja, *a.* lax, loose, slack; lazy, remiss, slothful, spiritless, cold, cool, negligent; flaccid, weak, feeble; (*Col.*) timid; *vino flojo,* thin, insipid wine; *seda floja,* soft, untwisted silk.

floqueado, -da, *a.* fringed.

flor, *n.f.* blossom, flower; bloom, prime; down of fresh fruits; (*chem.*) floss; film on the surface of liquors; maidenhood, virginity; grain of tanned leather; surface of the earth; complimentary remark to a lady. — *pl.* flowers or figures of rhetoric; cheating trick of gamblers; menstruation; the best of a kind; *flor de la harina,* superfine flour; *flor de la edad,* youth, bloom of youth; *a flor del agua,* level with the surface of the water; awash; *a flor de tierra,* flush with the ground; *flor del sol,* (*bot.*) sunflower; *flor de lis,* flower-de-luce, jacobea lily, amaryllis; *flor de oblón,* hops; *flor de cobre,* verdigris; *flor del cuclillo,* (*bot.*) ragged robin; *flor de viento,* (*naut.*) point of the compass; *flores de mano,* artificial flowers; *andarse a* (or *buscar*) *la flor del berro,* to give oneself up to pleasure; *andarse en flores,* to beat about the bush; *tener por flor,* to fall into a bad habit or custom; *entender a uno la flor,* to grasp somebody's intention; *ni de las flores de marzo, ni de la mujer sin empacho,* there is no more hope for a shameless woman than for the early flowers; *pasársela en flores,* to have a good time; *flor de la canela,* cassia buds; (*fig.*) something superfine; *flor de la maravilla,* kind of iris; (*coll.*) person who recovers quickly from an illness; *flor del viento,* (*naut.*) first puffs of wind after a calm; *flor de cantueso,* futile thing; *flor y nata,* flower, élite; *dar uno en la flor,* to acquire skill in something; *en flores,* without information; *decir* or *echar flores,* pay compliments; *flores blancas,* leucorrhœa.

floración, *n.f.* flowering, florescence.

florada, *n.f.* season of flowers best for beekeepers.

floral, *a.* floral.

florales, *a.pl.* floral feasts or games [JUEGOS FLORALES].

florar, *v.i.* to flower, blossom, bloom.

flordelisado, -da, *a.* (*her.*) fleurette; adorned with *fleur de lis.* — *p.p.* [FLORDELISAR].

flordelisar, *v.t.* (*her.*) to flourish with irises.

floreado, -da, *a.* flowered, figured goods; *pan floreado,* bread made of the finest flour. — *p.p.* [FLOREAR].

florear, *v.t.* to flower, adorn with flowers; to bolt flour; to brandish, flourish; (*mus.*) to flourish on the guitar; (*coll.*) to pay compliments; *florear del naipe,* (*coll.*) not to play fairly, to cheat at play; (*Arg., Chi., ES.*) to choose the best.

florecer, *v.i.* (*pres. indic.* **florezco;** *pres. subj.* **florezca**) to flower, blossom, bloom, bud;

to thrive, flourish, prosper. — *v.r.* to become mouldy.

florecica, -illa, -ita, *n.f.* floweret, floret.

floreciente, *a.* flourishing, blossoming, flowery; thriving, prosperous. — *p.a.* [FLORECER].

Florencia, *n.f.* Florence.

florentín; -tino, -tina, *n.m.f., a.* Florentine.

florentísimo, -ma, *a. superl.* very prosperous.

floreo, *n.m.* (*fenc.*) flourish of foils; (*fig.*) witty, but idle talk; (*mus.*) flourish on the guitar; cross-caper, in dancing; idle pastime.

florera, *n.f.* flower-girl.

florero, -ra, *a.* flatterer, complimenter. — *n.m.f.* florist; (*Col.*) cheater at cards.

florero, *n.m.* flower-pot; flower-vase; flower-stand; (*art*) flower-piece; (*fig.*) one who uses empty or florid language.

flores blancas, *n.f.pl.* leucorrhœa.

florescencia, *n.f.* (*bot.*) florescence, flowering, efflorescence.

floresta, *n.f.* forest, thicket, shrubbery; delightful rural place; collection of fine things.

florestero, *n.m.* forester.

floreta, *n.f.* leather border on the edge of a girth; (in paper-mills) pile, heap.

florete, *a.* (*com.*) first quality, superfine. — *n.m.* fencing foil.

floretear, *v.t.* to garnish with flowers.

floretista, *n.m.f.* expert fencer.

floricultor, -ra, *n.m.f.* floriculturist, cultivator of flowers.

floricultura, *n.f.* floriculture, cultivation of flowers.

floridamente, *adv.* elegantly, floridly, flourishingly.

floridez, *n.f.* abundance of flowers; floridity, floridness.

florido, -da, *a.* florid, flowery; full of flowers; elegant, choice, select; *dinero florido,* money which has been easily earned; *pascua florida,* Easter.

florífero, -ra; florígero, -ra, *a.* floriferous, flower-bearing.

florilegio, *n.m.* florilegium, anthology, selection of writings.

florín, *n.m.* florin, silver or gold coin.

floripondio, *n.m.* floripondio; magnolia.

florista, *n.m.f.* florist; maker or seller of artificial flowers.

florón, *n.m.* large flower [FLOR]; fleuron, rosette.

flósculo, *n.m.* (*bot.*) floscule, floret.

flota, *n.f.* fleet of merchant ships; naval squadron; fleet of aircraft.

flotable, *a.* floatable; navigable.

flotación, *n.f.* flotation, floating, flotage; friction, rubbing; (*naut.*) *línea de flotación,* water-line.

flotador, -ra, *a.* floater. — *n.m.* float.

flotadura, *n.f.; flotamiento,** *n.m.* flotation, flotage, floating; gentle friction.

flotante, *a.* floating; (*bot.*) rooted in the bed of a stream; *dique flotante,* floating dock; *deuda flotante,* floating debt.

flotar, *v.i.* to float on a liquid or in the air.

flote, *n.m.* floating; *a flote,* afloat; with knack of escaping happily.

flotilla, *n.f.* flotilla; small fleet.

fluatado, -da, *a.* fluorid, fluoric.

fluctuación, *n.f.* fluctuation; indetermination, wavering, irresolution, uncertainty.

fluctuante, *a.* fluctuating, fluctuant.

fluctuar, *v.i.* to fluctuate, float backward and forward, undulate, waver, oscillate; to be in danger; to vacillate, hesitate, be uncertain.

fluctuoso, -sa, *a.* fluctuant, wavering.

fluente, *a.* fluent, flowing.

fluidez, *n.f.* liquidity, fluidness, fluidity; *fluidez de estilo,* literary fluency.

fluidificación, *n.f.* liquefaction.

fluidificar, *v.t., v.r.* to convert or become converted into liquid; to liquefy.

fluido, -da, *a.* fluid, liquid, gaseous; fluent (as speech). — *n.m.* fluid, liquid or gas; (*med.*) fluid; *fluido eléctrico,* electric current.

fluir, *v.i.* (*pres. part.* **fluyendo**; *pres. indic.* **fluyo**; *pres. subj.* **fluya**) to flow, issue, run, ooze.

flujo, *n.m.* flow, flowing; (*naut.*) rising tide; (*med.*) flux, hæmorrhage; *flujo blanco,* the whites, leucorrhœa; *flujo de risa,* fit of laughter; *flujo de palabras,* flow of words, volubility; *flujo de reír,* habit of laughing to excess; *flujo de sangre,* hæmorrhage; *flujo de vientre,* diarrhœa.

fluor, *n.m.* fluorine.

fluorescencia, *n.f.* fluorescence.

fluorescente, *a.* fluorescent.

fluorhídrico, -ca, *a.* fluorhydric, hydrofluoric.

fluórico, -ca, *a.* (*chem.*) fluoric.

fluorina, fluorita, *n.f.* fluor (spar), fluorite.

fluvial, *a.* fluvial, fluviatic.

flux, *n.m.* flush, at cards; *hacer flux,* (*coll.*) to spend one's whole fortune and be in debt to everyone; (*Col.*) set of men's clothes.

fluxión, *n.f.* cold, catarrh.

foca, *n.f.* fur-bearing seal, phoca.

focal, *a.* focal.

foceifiza, *n.f.* kind of Arabic mosaic.

focino, *n.m.* goad for elephants.

foco, *n.m.* focus; centre of action, origin, source; (*chem.*) fire-box, furnace; (*med.*) core or centre of an abscess; (*mil.*) touch-hole of a gun; *foco de luz eléctrica,* spotlight, (*theatre*) spot.

fóculo, *n.m.* small fireplace.

focha, *n.f.* (*zool.*) rail; mud-hen.

fodolí, *a.* (*obs.*) meddlesome, intrusive.

fofadal, *n.m.* (*Arg.*) quagmire, quaking bog.

fofo, -fa, *a.* spongy, soft, bland.

fogaje, *n.m.* hearth-money; (*Arg., Mex.*) skin eruption, rash; (*Arg., Col., PR., Ven.*) sultry weather, scorching heat; (*Ec.*) bonfire, flash; (*PR.*) embarrassment, blush, vexation.

fogarada, *n.f.* blaze.

fogarear, *v.t.* (*prov.*) to burn with flame. — *v.r.* (*ES.*) to wilt or become diseased from excessive heat (vines).

fogaril, *n.m.* cresset; [FOGARÍN].

fogarín, *n.m.* common hearth for field hands.

fogarizar, *v.t.* to build bonfires.

fogata, *n.f.* bonfire, blaze; fougade.

fogón, *n.m.* hearth, fireside; vent or touch-hole of a gun; cooking-stove, kitchen-range; (*naut.*) caboose, cuddy, galley, cook-room.

fogonadura, *n.f.* (*naut.*) mast-hole, partner.

fogonazo, *n.m.* powder flash; flash in the pan.

fogonero, *n.m.* fireman, stoker.

fogosidad, *n.f.* excessive vivacity, fierceness, heat of temper; vehemence.

fogoso, -sa, *a.* vehement, fiery, ardent, choleric, hot-tempered, fervent, lively, impetuous; spirited (as a horse).

fogote, *n.m.* fagot, bundle of twigs; live coal.

fogueación, *n.f.* enumeration of hearths or fires.

foguear, *v.t.* to habituate to the discharge of fire-arms; (*artill.*) to scale a gun.

foguezuelo, *n.m.* small fire.

foja, *n.f.* (*law*) leaf of manuscript, folio; (*orn.*) coot, scoter.

fole, *n.m.* leather bag, especially of the bagpipe.

folgo, *n.m.* foot-warmer, foot-muff.

folía, *n.f.* kind of dance with castanets.

foliáceo, *a.* foliaceous.

foliación, *n.f.* foliation, act of numbering the pages of a book.

foliar, *v.t.* to page, number the pages, folio a book.

foliatura, *n.f.* numbering the pages of a book; numeration of the pages of a book.

foliculario, *n.m.* pamphleteer.

folículo, *n.m.* (*bot.*) follicle, pericarp; (*anat.*) follicle, membranous sac.

folijones, *n.m.pl.* ancient Castilian dance.

folio, *n.m.* folio, leaf of a book; size of a book-leaf; *de a folio*, (*coll.*) very bulky, very great, monumental (truth, fact, etc.); *libro en folio*, a folio book; *folio índico*, (*bot.*) Indian leaf; *al primer folio*, at first sight; *folio de Descartes*, (*geom.*) looped curve.

folión, *n.* light and popular music.

folklore, *n.m.* folklore.

folklórico, -ca, *a.* folkloristic.

folklorista, *n.m.f.* folklorist.

foluz, *n.f.* small ancient copper coin.

folla, *n.f.* irregular conflict in a tournament; variety show, medley; (*obs.*) olio.

follada, *n.f.* puff-paste patty.

follados, *n.m.pl.* ancient kind of trousers.

follaje, *n.m.* leafiness; frondage, foliage; gaudy ornament; leafage; superabundance of figures of rhetoric in a speech or writing; (*coll.*) fustian.

follar, *v.t.* to blow with bellows; to form in leaves. — *v.r.* (*vulg.*) to discharge wind without noise.

follero, folletero, *n.m.* maker or seller of bellows.

folleta, *n.f.* a wine measure (about a pint).

folletín, *n.m.* feuilleton, serial story in a newspaper.

folletinesco, -ca, *a.* (*coll.*) cheap, shoddy, superficial.

folletinista, *n.m.f.* writer of *folletines*.

folletista, *n.m.f.* pamphleteer.

folleto, *n.m.* pamphlet, booklet, tract; (*obs.*) small, handwritten newspaper.

follisca, *n.f.* (*Col., Ven.*) dispute, quarrel.

follón, -ona, *a.* indolent, inert, negligent, lazy, laggard, feeble, mean. — *n.m.* coward, rogue, conceited fellow, knave; (*vulg.*) wind voided without noise; noiseless rocket; (*obs.*) bud or branch of a tree.

follonería, *n.f.* (*obs.*) knavishness.

foma, *n.f.* a fungus.

fomentación, *n.f.* fomentation.

fomentador, -ra, *a.* fomenter.

fomentar, *v.t.* to impart warmth; (*med.*) to foment; to favour, protect, countenance, patronize, promote, encourage, excite, abet, instigate; (*agric.*) to improve.

fomento, *n.m.* fomentation; fuel, warmth;

(*med.*) lotion, fomentation; protection, patronage, encouragement, support, development, improvement; *Ministerio de Fomento*, Ministry of Public Works.

fonación, *n.f.* phonation, emission of the voice: pronunciation.

fonas, *n.f.pl.* (*sew., obs.*) gores, gussets.

fonda, *n.f.* inn, restaurant, tavern, lodging-house; eating-house.

fondable, *a.* fit for anchoring.

fondado, -da, *a.* (*coop.*) reinforced in the heads.

fondeadero, *n.m.* anchoring-ground; haven.

fondear, *v.t.* (*naut.*) to sound; to explore the depth of water; (*coll.*) to explore, sound; to examine closely; to search a ship. — *v.i.* to cast anchor.

fondeo, *n.m.* searching a ship; casting anchor.

fondillón, *n.m.* dregs and lees of a cask of liquor; old Alicante wine.

fondillos, *n.m.pl.* seat of trousers.

fondista, *n.m.f.* innkeeper, tavern-keeper.

fondo, *n.m.* depth; bottom; further end, rear part; (*art*) background; ground (of stuffs); extent of a man's capacity; thickness (of a diamond); quantity, stock, store (of virtues, vices. etc.); petticoat; (*Cub.*) boiler used in sugar mills; (*Mex.*) white underskirt; principal or essential part of a thing; disposition, nature (óf a person); capital, fund; (*mech.*) bottom, bed, plate, foundation; (*mil.*) space occupied by files of soldiers; (*coop.*) head; *agua, mar de fondo*, (*naut.*) swell; *fondo de amortización*, sinking fund; *fondo de reserva*, reserve fund; *dar fondo*, to cast anchor; *diez de fondo*, ten abreast; *echar a fondo*, to sink a vessel; *irse a fondo*, (*naut.*) to founder; *tirarse a fondo*, (*fenc.*) to thrust; *artículo de fondo*, leading article, editorial; *a fondo*, completely, perfectly, deeply; *hombre de fondo*, man of great talents; *sección de fondo*, editorial page. — *pl.* resources, funds, stocks; *fondos públicos* (or *del Erario*), public funds; *fondos vitalicios*, life-annuities; *estar en fondos*, to have money *or* ready cash; *limpiar los fondos*, to hog a ship's bottom.

fondón, *n.m.* ground of silk or velvet; brocade; (*min.*) fondon.

fondona, *n.f.*, *a.* old and inelegant (applied to a woman).

fonema, *n.m.* (*gram.*) phoneme, each of the simple sounds of the spoken language.

fonendoscopio, *n.m.* phonendoscope.

fonética, *n.f.* phonetics.

fonético, -ca, *a.* phonetic, relating to sounds.

fonetismo, *n.m.* phoneticism.

fonetista, *n.m.f.* phonetist.

fónico, -ca, *a.* phonic, acoustic.

fonil, *n.m.* funnel.

fonje, *a.* bland, soft, spongy.

fonografía, *n.f.* phonography.

fonográfico, -ca, *a.* phonographic.

fonógrafo, *n.m.* phonograph.

fonograma, *n.m.* phonogram.

fonolita, *n.f.* (*min.*) clinkstone, phonolite.

fonología, *n.f.* phonology.

fonsadera, *n.f.* personal service during war; ancient war-tax.

fonsado, *n.m.* (*fort.*) foss or ditch.

fonsario, *n.m.* (*obs.*) foss or ditch surrounding a fort.

fontal, *a.* fontal; (*obs.*) original, main, chief, principal.

fontana, *n.f.* (*poet.*) fountain, spring, water-jet.

fontanal, *a.* fontanel. — *n.m.* source or spring of water; place abounding in springs.

fontanar, *n.m.* spring of water.

fontanela, *n.f.* (*anat.*) fontanel; (*surg.*) seton-needle.

fontanería, *n.f.* hydraulic engineering; water-works.

fontanero, -ra, *a.* hydraulic engineer.

fontegí, *n.m.* variety of wheat.

fontezuela, *n.f.* small fountain.

fontículo, *n.m.* (*surg.*) fonticulus, issue.

foque, *n.m.* (*naut.*) jib; *foque mayor* (or *foque de caza*), standing jib; *foque segundo,* fore-stay-sail; *botalón de foque,* jib-boom; *petifoque,* fore-stay-gallant-sail; *contra-foque,* standing-jib.

forajido, -da, *n.m.f.,* *a.* highwayman, outlaw; robbing; villainous, wicked.

foral, *a.* belonging to the statute law; *bienes forales,* leasehold estate.

foralmente, *adv.* judicially, in the manner of courts.

foramen, *n.m.* hole in the under stone of a mill.

foráneo, -nea, *a.* alien, foreign.

forastería, *n.f.* inn for strangers.

forastero, -ra, *a.* strange; exotic. — *n.m.f.* stranger, guest, visitor (of a town).

forcejar, forcejear, *v.i.* to struggle, strive, labour, contend, contest.

forcejo, *n.m.* struggle, struggling, labouring, striving, strife, contention.

forcejón, *n.m.* push, violent effort, struggle.

forcejudo, -da, *a.* strong, robust, of great strength.

fórceps, *n.m.* forceps.

forcina, *n.f.* swelling of a tree; (*obs.*) trident.

forchina, *n.f.* fork-like weapon; (*obs.*) fork.

forense, *a.* (*law*) forensic; alien.

forero, -ra, *a.* conformable to the statute law of a country. — *n.m.* owner of leasehold estate; lessee.

forestal, *a.* forestal.

forfícula, *n.f.* earwig.

forillo, *n.m.* backcloth in theatrical scenery.

forja, *n.f.* smelting-furnace; chafery; smithy; bloomery; forge, forging; (*mas.*) mortar.

forjador, *n.m.* forger; iron-master, smith, blacksmith; gold-beater.

forjadura, *n.f.* forging; forgery, falsification; trap, snare, injury.

forjar, *v.t.* to hammer or stamp metal into shape; to forge; to falsify, counterfeit; to form, frame, fabricate; to invent, concoct (as a falsehood).

forlón, *n.m.* old kind of chaise with four seats.

forma, *n.f.* shape, form, figure, cast; established practice, ritual, ceremony, manner of doing something; make, frame, fashion, method, order, regularity; pattern, mould, matrix; form or cast of writing; (*print.*) forme, format, size of a book; (*eccles.*) unleavened bread (for the communion of the lay brothers); hatter's block; shoemaker's last; cheese-vat. — *pl.* build, figure (of persons); *en forma,* truly, certainly; seriously, in earnest; *de forma que,* in such a manner that; *en forma* (or *en debida forma*), in due form, correctly; *tener buenas formas,* to be of fine figure; to be polite; *dar forma,* to regulate or arrange that which was disordered; *hombre de forma,* grave, serious man; *tomar forma,* to materialize, to develop.

formable, *a.* that which may be formed.

formación, *n.f.* formation, forming; shape, figure, form; education, schooling; (*geol.*) formation, system; twisted cord for gold embroidery; (*mil.*) array of troops.

formador, -ra, *n.m.f., a.* former, one that forms, fashions or shapes.

formaje, *n.m.* cheese-vat; (*obs.*) cheese.

formal, *a.* regular, formal, methodical; genuine, proper; grave, steady serious, sedate; reliable, truthful.

formalidad, *n.f.* formality; propriety; exactness; seriousness, gravity, solemnity; ceremony; requirement, requisite; established practice; legal precedent; *con formalidad,* properly, respectably, with propriety.

formalismo, *n.m.* formalism; rigorous method; adhesion to routine, red-tape.

formalista, *n.m.f., a.* formalist.

formalizar, *v.t.* (*prct.* **formalicé;** *pres. subj.* **formalice**) to formalize; to execute, legalize (a deed, etc.). — *v.r.* to grow formal, to become serious or earnest; affect gravity.

formalmente, *adv.* formally, according to form or rule; seriously.

formar, *v.t.* to shape, fashion, form, make up, frame, cut out; to model, mould; to conceive, devise, form (as ideas); to constitute (as a corporation); to draw up; (*mil.*) to combine, arrange. — *v.i.* to adjust the edges of embroidery work; to educate, train, develop (as the mind or the body); — *v.r.* to take shape, grow, develop; to join a procession, march, etc.; *formar concepto,* to form a judgment; *formar queja,* to complain.

formativo, -va, *a.* formative.

formatriz, *a.* forming. — *n.m.* former, producer, maker.

formejar, *v.t.* to clear the ship; to trim the hold.

formero *n.m.* (*arch.*) side arch of a vault.

formiato, *n.m.* formic.

formicante, *a.* (*med.*) formicant (pulse).

formicarios, formicidos, *n.m.pl.* hymenoptera which carry a sting (bees, wasps, etc.).

fórmico, *n.m.* (*chem.*) formic (acid or ether); hard tumour.

formidable, *a.* formidable, tremendous, dreadful, terrific; uncommonly large.

formidablemente, *adv.* formidably.

formidoloso, -sa, *a.* timid, timorous, fearful; dreadful, horrible, frightful.

formillón, *n.m.* hat-block, hat-form.

formón, *n.m.* firmer-chisel, paring-chisel; punch; *formón de punta corriente,* skewchisel; punching-press for cutting wafers.

fórmula, *n.f.* formula: (*med.*) recipe; (*eccles.*) profession of faith.

formular, *v.t.* to formulate; to prescribe (medicine); to express, state.

formulario, *n.m.* formulary, book of rules or formulas.

formulismo, *n.m.* formulism; red-tape.

formulista, *a.* formulist, formulistic.

fornáceo, -cea, *a.* (*poet.*) like a furnace.

fornecer, *v.t.* (*obs.*) to furnish, to provide.

fornecino, -na, *a.* (*obs.*) bastard, illegitimate.

fornelo, *n.m.* portable little oven or furnace.

fornicación, *n.f.* fornication.

fornicador, -ra, *n.m.f., a.* fornicator.

fornicar, *v.i.* to fornicate.
fornicario, -ria, *a.* relating or addicted to fornication.
fornicio, *n.m.* fornication.
fornido, -da, *a.* robust, lusty, stout, corpulent.
fornitura, *n f.* (*print.*) types cast to complete sorts. — *pl.* (*mil.*) leather straps worn by soldiers.
foro, *n.m.* forum; court of justice; bar, legal profession; leasehold; rental; back (in stage scenery); *por tal foro,* on such conditions.
forrado, *a.* lined, doubled. — *p.p.* [FORRAR]; *tonto forrado en lo mismo,* a thorough fool.
forraje, *n.m.* fodder, forage; foraging; (*coll.*) abundance of things of little value.
forrajeador, *n.m.* forager; fodderer.
forrajear, *v.t.* to forage, collect forage or fodder.
forrajera, *n.f.* shako guard.
forrar, *v.t.* to line (as clothes); (*naut.*) to sheathe, to fur; to cover with a case (as a book or an umbrella).
forro, *n.m.* backing, lining, inside, doubling; (*naut.*) planking, furring, sheathing; cover of a book; *forro de cabos,* (*naut.*) service, serving ropes; *forro sobrepuesto de cable,* (*naut.*) keckling, rounding; *ni por el forro,* (*coll.*) not the foggiest idea; *forro interior de un buque,* ceiling or foot-waling of a ship.
fortachón, -ona, *a.* (*coll.*) powerfully strong [FUERTE].
fortalecedor, -ra, *n.m.f.* fortifier, fortifying.
fortalecer, *v.t.* (*pres. indic.* **fortalezco;** *pres. subj.* **fortalezca**) to fortify, strengthen, corroborate; to fortify a place; to encourage, aid, support.
fortalecimiento, *n.m.* fortifying, strengthening; fortification, defences of a place.
fortaleza, *n.f.* firmness, fortitude; courage, valour; vigour, strength, force, nerve, manhood; fortress, stronghold, fortified place. — *pl.* flaw in a sword blade.
¡forte! *interj.* (*naut.*) avast! — *a.* (*mus.*) loud.
fortepiano, *n.m.* (*obs.*) pianoforte.
fortezuelo, -la, *a.* not very strong. — *n.m.* small fort [FUERTE].
fortificable, *a.* fortifiable.
fortificación, *n.f.* fortification; works raised for the defence of a place; military architecture; *fortificación de campaña,* field-fortification.
fortificador, *n.m.* fortifier.
fortificante, *a.* fortifying.
fortificar, *v.t.* (*pret.* **fortifiqué;** *pres. subj.* **fortifique**) to strengthen, fortify, corroborate, invigorate; (*mil.*) to fortify a place.
fortín, *n.m.* fortlet, small fort.
fortitud, *n.f.* (*poet.*) [FORTALEZA].
fortuitamente, *adv.* fortuitously.
fortuito, -ta, *a.* fortuitous, accidental, unexpected.
fortuna, *n.f.* fortune, chance, fate; success, good luck; capital, wealth; (at sea or on land) tempest, storm; *por fortuna,* luckily; *probar fortuna,* to take one's chances; *fortuna de la Mancha,* eggs and bacon; *al hombre osado la fortuna le da la mano,* fortune favours the brave; *soplar la fortuna a uno,* to be lucky; *fortuna te dé Dios, hijo, que el saber, poco te vale,* better luck than knowledge.
fortunón, *n.m.* (*coll.*) great fortune, immense riches; [FORTUNA].

forúnculo, furúnculo, *n.m.* (*med.*) boil.
forzadamente, *adv.* forcibly, violently, forcefully.
forzado, -da, *a.* forced, compelled, constrained. — *n.m.* criminal sentenced to the galleys. — *p.p.* [FORZAR].
forzador, *n.m.* ravisher; forcer.
forzal, *n.m.* solid part of a comb.
forzamento, forzamiento, *n.m.* act of forcing.
forzar, *v.t.* (*pres. indic.* **fuerzo;** *pret.* **forcé;** *pres. subj.* **fuerce**) to force, break in (as a door), overpower by strength; to constrain, compel, urge, enforce; to ravish; to subdue by force.
forzosa, *n.f.* decisive move at the game of draughts; compulsion; *hacer a uno la forzosa,* (*coll.*) to compel one to do something against his will.
forzosamente, *adv.* forcibly, necessarily; forcedly, violently.
forzoso, -sa, *a.* indispensable, necessary, requisite, needful, obligatory.
forzudamente, *adv.* with great power and strength.
forzudo, -da, *a.* strong, potent, vigorous, stout, lusty, able-bodied.
fosa, *n.f.* grave, burial, sepulture; (*anat.*) fossa; (*obs.*) pit, hole, grave, foss.
fosar, *v.t.* to make a pit, dig a trench, ditch or foss.
fosca, *n.f.* haze; (*prov.*) thicket, jungle, thick grove.
fosco, -ca, *a.* frowning; dark; swarthy.
fosfático, -ca, *a.* phosphatic.
fosfato, *n.m.* phosphate.
fosfito, *n.m.* phosphite.
fosforado, -da, *a.* phosphated.
fosforera, *n.f.* match-box.
fosforero, -ra, *n.m.f.* seller of matches.
fosforescencia, *n.f.* phosphorescence.
fosforescente, *a.* phosphorescent.
fosforescer, fosforecer, *v.i.* (*pres. indic.* **fosforezco;** *pres. subj.* **fosforezca**) to phosphoresce, shed a phosphorescent light.
fosfórico, -ca, *a.* phosphoric.
fosforita, *n.f.* phosphorite.
fósforo, *n.m.* phosphorus; friction match; morning star.
fosforoscopio, *n.m.* phosphoroscope.
fosforoso, -sa, *a.* phosphorous.
fosfuro, *n.m.* phosphide.
fósil, *a.* fossil, petrified; (*coll.*) old, antiquated. — *n.m.* fossil, petrifaction, organic remains.
fosilífero, -ra, *a.* fossiliferous.
fosilización, *n.f.* fossilization.
fosilizarse, *v.r.* to fossilize, become fossilized, petrified.
foso, *n.m.* pit, hole in the ground; (*theat.*) cellar under the stage; (*fort.*) moat, ditch, foss.
fotocopia, *n.f.* photocopy.
fotogénico, -ca, *a.* photogenic.
fotograbado, *n.m.* photogravure.
fotografía, *n.f.* photography; photograph.
fotografiar, *v.t.* to photograph.
fotográficamente, *adv.* photographically.
fotográfico, -ca, *a.* photographic.
fotógrafo, *n.m.* photographer.
fotolitografía, *n.f.* photo-lithography; photolithograph.
fotolitográficamente, *adv.* photo-lithographically.
fotolitográfico, -ca, *a.* photo-lithographic.

fotometría, *n.f.* photometry.
fotométrico, -ca, *a.* photometric.
fotómetro, *n.m.* photometer.
fotosfera, *n.f.* photosphere.
fototipia, *n.f.* phototypy.
fototipografía, *n.f.* photo-typography.
fototipográfico, -ca, *a.* photo-typographic.
fótula, *n.f.* (*prov.*) flying cockroach.
fotuto, *n.m.* (*Col., Cub.*) whistle; trumpet, horn.
fovila, *n.f.* (*bot.*) fovilla.
foya, *n.f.* (*prov.*) oven full of charcoal.
frac, *n.m.* dress-coat; swallow-tailed coat.
fracasado, -da, *a.* (*coll.*) applied to a person who has failed to make good.
fracasar, *v.i.* (*naut.*) to crumble, to break in pieces (ships); to fail in an undertaking; to be abortive, fall through, come to naught, be lost or destroyed.
fracaso, *n.m.* destruction, downfall, ruin, unfortunate event, calamity, abortiveness, failure.
fracción, *n.f.* fraction, breaking into parts; broken part.
fraccionamiento, *n.m.* division into fractions.
fraccionar, *v.t.* to divide into fractions.
fraccionario, -ria, *a.* fractional; *número fraccionario,* mixed number.
fractura, *n.f.* fracture, breach, separation of parts, breaking, breakage; (*surg.*) fracture.
fracturar, *v.t.* to fracture, break, rupture.
fraga, *n.f.* species of raspberry; thicket of brambles; waste wood.
fragancia, *n.f.* fragrance, scent, aroma, perfume, sweet odour; good name, repute for virtues; commission of a crime.
fragante, *a.* fragrant, odoriferous; flagrant, notorious; *en fragante* or *en flagrante,* in the act itself.
fragaria, *n.f.* strawberry.
fragata, *n.f.* frigate; *fragata de aviso,* packet-boat; *fragata ligera,* light fast-sailing vessel.
frágil, *a.* fragile, brittle, frangible, weak, frail, perishable, breakable.
fragilidad, *n.f.* fragility, frangibility, brittleness; folly, frailty, sinfulness.
frágilmente, *adv.* frailly.
fragmentar, *v.t.* to reduce to fragments.
fragmento, *n.m.* fragment, piece, bit, small part.
fragor, *n.m.* clamour, noise, crash.
fragoroso, -sa, *a.* (*poet.*) noisy, obstreperous.
fragosidad, *n.f.* unevenness, roughness of the road; imperviousness of a forest; craggedness, cragginess.
fragoso, -sa, *a.* craggy, uneven, rough; full of brambles and briers; noisy.
fragancia, fragrancia, *n.f.* fragrance, sweetness of smell.
fragrante, fragante, *a.* fragrant.
fragua, *n.f.* forge, as for iron.
fraguador, -ra, *a.* scheming, planning an intrigue; forging.
fraguar, *v.t.* to forge; to plan, plot, contrive, brew, hatch. — *v.i.* (*mas.*) to set hard (of concrete, etc.).
fragura, *n.f.* roughness of the road; imperviousness of a forest.
frailada, *n.f.* (*coll.*) rude or unbecoming action of a monk.
fraile, *n.m.* friar, monk, brother; (*arch.*) hood over a hearth; fold at bottom of a skirt; (*print.*) friar, badly inked spot; fold in a leaf;

(*Cub.*) bagasse of a sugar-cane; upright post of a flood-gate; *fraile de misa y olla,* friar who assists only at the altar and in the choir; *fraile que pide para Dios, pide para dos,* charity benefits the giver as well as the receiver.
frailear, *v.t.* to prune a tree close to the trunk.
frailecico, -cillo, *n.m.* little friar; wedge securing the spindle of a silk-reel; (*orn.*) lapwing.
frailecito, *n.m.* husk of the broad bean fashioned by children, as a game, like a monk's cowl.
frailengo, -ga; fraileño, -ña, *a.* monkish, of monks or friars.
frailería, *n.f.* (*coll.*) assembly of friars.
frailero, -ra, *a.* friary; (*coll.*) very fond of friars.
frailesco, -ca, *a.* (*coll.*) monkish.
frailía, *n.f.* monkishness, monastic life; regular clergy.
frailote, *n.m.* big and coarse friar.
frailuco, *n.m.* despicable friar.
frailuno, -na, *a.* (*coll.*) friary.
frambuesa, *n.f.* raspberry.
frambueso, *n.m.* raspberry-bush.
frámea, *n.f.* javelin, dart.
francachela, *n.f.* (*coll.*) a plentiful and splendid repast.
francalete, *n.m.* leather strap with a buckle.
francamente, *adv.* frankly, openly, freely, nakedly.
francés, -esa, *a.* French. — *n.m.f.* Frenchman, Frenchwoman.
francés, *n.m.* the French language; *mal francés,* venereal disease; *despedirse a la francesa,* (*coll.*) to take French leave; *a la francesa,* after the French fashion.
francesilla, *n.f.* common yard crowfoot (*Ranunculus asiaticus*).
Francia, *n.f.* France.
Francisca, *n.f.* Frances.
Francisco, *n.m.* Francis.
franciscano, -na, *a.* Franciscan; grey-coloured.
francisco, -ca, *a.* Franciscan.
francmasón, *n.m.* Freemason, mason.
francmasonería, *n.f.* Freemasonry.
franco, *n.m.* franc, French coin; fair-time, when merchandise is sold free of duty. — *pl.* **francos,** Franks, Oriental appellation given to western Europeans.
franco, -ca, *a.* open, frank, generous, open-hearted, liberal, bountiful; privileged, exempt; clear, free, disengaged; plain, ingenuous, fair, sincere; (*com.*) post free, duty free; *franco de porte,* post-paid; *puerto franco,* free port; *franco a bordo,* free on board, f.o.b.; (in compound words) French, as *franco-americano,* Franco-American; *lengua franca,* lingua franca.
francolín, *n.m.* francolin.
francote, -ta, *a.* (*coll.*) frank, plain-spoken.
franchipán, *n.m.* frangipane, a perfume.
franchote, -ta; franchute, -ta, *n.m.f.* (*contempt.*)Frenchy.
franela, *n.f.* flannel.
frange, *n.m.* (*her.*) division of the field of a shield.
frangente, *a.* frangent, fracturing. — *n.m.* accident, disaster, mishap.
frangible, *a.* brittle, frangible, breakable.
frangollar, *v.t.* (*coll.*) to do a thing hurriedly and carelessly; (*obs.*) to grind corn coarsely.

frangollo, *n.m.* pottage of wheat and milk; (*Am.*) poorly made stew; (*coll.*) disorder, confusion.

frangote, *n.m.* bale of goods.

frángula, *n.f.* berry-bearing alder (*Rhamnus frangula*).

franja, *n.f.* (*sew.*) fringe, trimming, band, border, braid, stripe.

franjar, franjear, *v.t.* (*sew.*) to trim with bands, braids, or stripes; to border.

franjón, *n.m.* wide braid trimming.

franjuela, *n.f.* narrow braid trimming.

franqueamiento, *n.m.* manumission.

franquear, *v.t.* to prepay postage on letters, etc.; to exempt, grant immunity from, enfranchise; to open, extricate, disengage, clear from impediments; to gratify, make liberal grants or gifts; to free a slave. — *v.r.* to fall in with the wishes of others; to become liberal; to unbosom oneself; to be ready for sailing.

franqueo, *n.m.* franking (of letters, etc.), postage; liberating a slave.

franqueza, *n.f.* liberty, freeness, freedom, exemption, enfranchisement; sincerity, frankness, open-heartedness, generosity; ingenuousness.

franquía, *n.f.* sea-room, offing; *en franquía,* ready to sail; (*coll.*) in readiness.

franquicia, *n.f.* exemption from taxes, franchise, grant, privilege.

frasca, *n.f.* dry leaves or small branches.

frasco, *n.m.* flask, bottle, vial, gallipot; powder-flask.

frase, *n.f.* phrase; epigram, idiom; style of a writer; *frase hecha,* proverb, saying, saw; *frase musical,* phrase; *gastar frases y rodeos,* (*coll.*) to beat about the bush; *frase sacramental,* standard form; *hacer frases,* to speak much saying little.

frasear, *v.t.* to phrase; to employ idioms or epigrams; (*mus.*) to phrase, give expression.

fraseología, *n.f.* phraseology, style of a writer; verbosity, pomposity.

frasquera, *n.f.* bottle-case, liquor-case; *frasquera de fuego,* (*naut.*) fire-case or fire-chest.

frasquerilla, -ita, *n.f.* small bottle-case.

frasqueta, *n.f.* frisket of a printing-press.

frasqueta, *n.f.; frasquillo, -ito,* *n.m.* small flask.

fratás, *n.m.* plastering trowel.

fratasar, *v.t.* to trowel, smooth with the trowel.

fraterna, *n.f.* severe reprimand, lecture, lesson.

fraternal, *a.* fraternal, brotherly.

fraternalmente, *adv.* fraternally.

fraternidad, *n.f.* fraternity, brotherhood.

fraternizar, *v.i.* (*pret.* **fraternicé;** *pres. subj.* **fraternice**) to fraternize.

fraterno, -na, *a.* fraternal, brotherly.

frates, *n.m.* (square) wooden trowel.

fratricida, *n.m.f.* fratricide, murderer of a brother.

fratricidio, *n.m.* fratricide, murder of a brother.

fraude, *n.m.* fraud, deceit, trick, cheat, imposture, artifice, gull, craft; (*law*) bribery.

fraudulencia, *n.f.* fraudulence, trickiness, deceitfulness.

fraudulentamente, *adv.* fraudulently, knavishness.

fraudulento, -ta, *a.* fraudulent, deceitful, knavish, artful.

fraustina, *n.f.* wooden head for fashioning ladies' head-dresses.

fraxinela, *n.f.* white dittany.

fray, *n.m.* (abbrev. of *fraile*) brother, used as an appellation before the names of clergy of certain religious orders; *fray modesto nunca fué prior,* the timid and faint-hearted never gets to the top.

frazada, *n.f.* blanket.

frazadero, *n.m.* maker of blankets.

frazadilla, *n.f.* small or light blanket.

frecuencia, *n.f.* frequency.

frecuentación, *n.f.* frequentation, frequenting, visiting.

frecuentador, -ra, *a.* frequenter.

frecuentar, *v.t.* to frequent, haunt, visit often; to repeat.

frecuentativo, -va, *a.* frequentative.

frecuente, *a.* frequent.

frecuentemente, *adv.* frequently, often, commonly, oftentimes.

fregadero, *n.m.* scullery, sink.

fregado, *n.m.* act of scouring or scrubbing; (*coll.*) complicated affair; *mujer de buen fregado,* buxom girl; (sometimes) prostitute. — *a.* (*Arg., Chi.*) silly, obtrusive, vexatious; (*Col.*) stubborn; (*Mex.*) artful, roguish; *servir uno lo mismo para un fregado que para un barrido,* to be Jack of all trades.

fregado, -da, *a., p.p.* [FREGAR].

fregador, *n.m.* sink, scrubbing-board; dishclout, mop, scrubbing brush.

fregadura, *n.f.* rubbing, scrubbing, scouring.

fregajo, *n.m.* mop, swab.

fregamiento, *n.m.* friction, rubbing.

fregar, *v.t.* (*pres. indic.* **friego;** *pret.* **fregué;** *pres. subj.* **friegue**) to rub, mop, scrub, scour, swab; (*Am.*) to annoy, to tease.

fregatina, *n.f.* (*Chi.*) bother.

fregatriz, fregona, *n.f.* kitchen-maid, scrubbing girl.

fregonil, *a.* (*coll.*) wench-like.

fregonzuela, *n.f.* little kitchen-girl.

freidura, *n.f.* frying or dressing in a pan.

freila, *n.f.* lay-sister of a military order.

freile, *n.m.* knight or priest of a military order.

freír, *v.t.* (*p.p.* **freído, frito;** *pres. part.* **friendo;** *pres. indic.* **frío;** *pret.* **él frió;** *pres. subj.* **fría**) to fry or dress in a frying-pan; *freírse de calor,* to be excessively hot; *freírsela a alguno,* (*coll.*) to deceive one premeditatedly; *al freír de los huevos lo verás,* the proof of the pudding is in the eating; *al freír será el reír, y al pagar será el llorar,* the feast is good until the reckoning comes.

freje, *n.m.* (*prov.*) osier hoop.

fréjol, *n.m.* French bean, kidney bean.

frelo, -la, *a.* (*prov.*) delicate, weakly, sickly.

frémito, *n.m.* roar.

frenar, *v.t.* to bridle, to govern by the bridle; to apply the brake to, to brake.

frenería, *n.f.* bridle-making; harness-shop.

frenero, *n.m.* bridle-maker or seller; (*railw.*) brakeman.

frenesí, *n.m.* frenzy, fury, madness, distraction, folly.

frenéticamente, *adv.* frantically, frenziedly, madly.

frenético, -ca, *a.* mad, frantic, distracted, furious, frenzied, insane, lunatic.

frenillar, *v.t.* to bridle the oars.

frenillo, *n.m.* (*anat.*) frenum; (*naut.*) bridle, fox, ratline; (*Cent. Am., Cub.*) string or stay of a kite; *no tener frenillo en la lengua,* to be outspoken.

freno, *n.m.* bridle or bit of the bridle; brake (for wheel); (*mech.*) check, stop, brake; control, curb, restrain; *morder el freno,* to chafe at the bridle; *correr sin freno,* to run headlong into vice; *meter en freno,* to control, limit; *trocar los frenos,* to do or say things in inverted order; *tirar del freno,* to curb, restrain; *freno automático* or *freno al vacío,* vacuum brake; *beber el freno,* to bite the bridle.

frenología, *n.f.* phrenology.

frenológico, -ca, *a.* phrenological.

frenólogo, *n.m.* phrenologist.

frenópata, *n.m.* phrenopathist, alienist.

frenopatía, *n.f.* phrenopathy, alienism.

frental, *a.* frontal, of the forehead.

frente, *n.f.* forehead; mien, countenance; intellect. — *n.m.* (*mil.*) front rank; face of a bastion; blank space at the beginning of a document. — *n.m.f.* front, fore part, face, façade; obverse (of coins, etc.). — *adv.* in front, opposite, across the way; *frente a frente,* face to face; *de frente,* (*mil.*) facing; abreast; *a frente,* straight ahead; *enfrente, en frente,* or *frente por frente,* directly opposite; *al frente,* carried forward; *del frente,* brought forward; *arrugar la frente,* to show signs of anger or annoyance; *traerlo escrito en la frente,* to have it written on one's face; *frente de batalla,* the firing line; *navegar de frente,* to sail abreast.

frentero, *n.m.* pad to protect a child's forehead.

freo, *n.m.* narrow channel, strait; (*prov.*) gorge, canyon, ravine.

fresa, *n.f.* strawberry, strawberry plant; (*mech.*) drill, bit, milling tool.

fresada, *n.f.* dish formerly made of flour, milk and butter.

fresadora, *n.f.* milling machine.

fresal, *n.m.* strawberry patch.

fresar, *v.t.* to mill, to drill, to machine; (*prov.*) to mix flour and water before kneading. — *v.i.* (*obs*). to grumble, growl, snarl.

fresca, *n.f.* air, fresh air; early morning freshness; (*coll.*) piece of one's mind, biting remark; *salir con la fresca,* to go out while the air is fresh; *tomar la fresca,* to take the air; *decir cuatro frescas a uno,* to rebuke one without mincing words.

frescachón, -ona, *a.* robust, ruddy; *viento frescachón,* brisk wind.

frescal, *a.* not entirely fresh, but preserved with salt (of fish).

frescales, *n.m.f.* (*coll.*) outspoken person.

frescamente, *adv.* freshly, recently, lately; coolly, bluntly, resolutely, dispassionately.

fresco, -ca, *a.* fresh, cool; newly come, recent; latest; just made, finished or gathered; serene, calm; buxom, plump, ruddy; (*coll.*) forward, bold; *dinero fresco,* ready money; *viento fresco,* fresh breeze; *quedarse fresco,* (*coll.*) to be disappointed; *agua fresca,* cool water.

fresco, *n.m.* cool temperature, coolness, refreshing air; (*art*) fresco painting; (*Cent. Am., Mex., Per.*) pine-apple juice.

frescón, -ona, *a.* (*obs.*) very fresh, blooming.

frescor, *n.m.* cool, refreshing air; (*art*) fleshcolour.

frescote, -ta, *a.* (*coll.*) ruddy, youthful, healthy, strong.

frescura, *n.f.* coolness, freshness, gentle cold; luxuriant verdure or foliage; cheek, nerve, insolence; cheeky reply, piece of insolence; tranquillity, serenity, coolness of mind; carelessness, indolence, negligence.

fresero, -ra, *n.m.f.* strawberry vendor. — *n.f.* strawberry plant.

fresita, *n.f.* service-berry.

fresnal, *n.m.* belonging to the ash-tree.

fresneda, *n.f.* plantation of ash-trees.

fresnillo, *n.m.* white fraxinella.

fresno, *n.m.* ash-tree; ash wood; *fresno húngaro,* Hungarian ash; *fresno americano,* white ash; *fresno florido,* flowering ash.

fresón, *n.m.* Chili strawberry.

fresquecito, -ita; fresquillo, -lla, *a.* coolish; nice and fresh. — *n.m.f.* cool breeze.

fresquera, *n.f.* meat-safe; cool spot.

fresquería, *n.f.* (*Am.*) ice-cream saloon.

fresquero, -ra, *n.m.f.* vendor of fresh fish.

fresquilla, *n.f.* kind of peach.

fresquista, *n.m.f.* fresco painter.

fresquito, -ta, *a.* cool, coolish.

fresquito, *n.m.* cool, fresh air. — *adv.* just now, freshly made, recently.

freszar, *v.i.* (*obs.*) [FREZAR].

frey, *n.m.* (abbrev. of *freile*); used as an appellation before the names of knights and clergymen belonging to a military order. — [FRAY].

frez, *n.f.* dung, excrement.

freza, *n.f.* dung, excrement; trail of fish in spawning; spawning; roe, spawn; time in which silk-worms eat; ground dug up or hollow left by the rooting or scratching of a pig or other animal.

frezada, *n.f.* blanket; *de frezada* (or *frezadilla*), in deshabille.

frezar, *v.i.* (*pret.* **frecé;** *pres. subj.* **frece**) to eject excrements (of animals); to eject the droppings of grubs from hives. — *v.t.* to clean bee-hives; to nibble the leaves of mulberry-trees (silk-worms); to spawn; to rub in order to spawn; to root (of hogs); to scratch the earth (of dogs).

friabilidad, *n.f.* friability, brittleness.

friable, *a.* friable, fragile, brittle.

frialdad, *n.f.* frigidity, coldness; unconcern, lukewarmness, coolness, indifference; dullness, insipidity; want of affection; (*med.*) impotence, frigidity.

fríamente, *adv.* coldly, frigidly, coolly; flatly.

friático, -ca, *a.* foolish, graceless, silly; chilly.

fricación, *n.f.* friction, frication.

fricandó, *n.m.* fricandeau, Scotch collop.

fricar, *v.t.* to rub, scour.

fricasé, *n.m.* fricassee.

fricativo, -va, *a.* fricative.

fricción, *n.f.* friction, rubbing; embrocation, liniment.

friccionar, *v.t.* to rub.

friega, *n.f.* friction, rubbing with flesh-brush, etc.; (*Col., CR.*) bother, annoyance, nuisance; (*Chi.*) sound beating, flogging.

friego; friegue, *pres. indic.; pres. subj.* [FREGAR].

friera, *n.f.* chilblain.

frigidez, *n.f.* frigidity, coldness.

frígido, -da, *a.* (*poet.*) cold, frigid.

frigio, -gia, *a.* Phrygian.

frigorífico, -ca, *a.* frigorific, refrigerating, freezing, refrigerative. — *n.m.* refrigerator.
friísimo, -ma, *a. superl.* extremely cold.
fríjol, *n.m.* kidney-bean.
frijolar, *n.m.* plot of land sown with beans.
fringa, *n.f.* (*Hond.*) travelling rug; cloak with sleeves.
fringilago, *n.m.* titmouse.
frío, fría, *a.* cold, frigid, chilly; impotent; iced (as water); passionless, indifferent, heartless, unmoved, unsympathetic; graceless, dull, ineffective, witless.
frío, *n.m.* cold, coldness, chilliness, frigidity; fresh, cool air; *Dios da el frío conforme a la ropa,* God tempers the wind to the shorn lamb; *no entrarle a uno frío ni calor,* or *no darle frío ni calentura,* to be quite indifferent.
friolento, -ta; friolero, -ra, *a.* chilly; very sensitive to cold.
friolera, *n.f.* trifle, bauble, gewgaw, insignificant speech or action.
frisa, *n.f.* frieze; palisade; (*naut.*) lining or packing; (*León*) shawl of peasant women; (*Arg., Chi.*) nap (plush, etc.).
frisado, *n.m.* silk plush or shag. — *p.p.* [FRISAR].
frisador, -ra, *n.m.f.* frizzler.
frisadura, *n.f.* frizzling, shagging.
frisar, *v.t.* to frizzle or frizz cloth, raise the nap; to rub; (*naut.*) to line, pack. — *v.i.* to be like, assimilate, resemble; (*fig.*) to be near, approach.
friso, *n.m.* frieze; wainscot, dado, mop-board.
frísol, *n.m.* kidney-bean.
frisón, -ona, *n.m.f.,* *a.* a Frisian.
frisón, *n.m.* large draught-horse.
frisuelo, *n.m.* kidney-bean. — *pl.* **frisuelos,** fritters.
frita, *n.f.* frit; slag.
fritada, *n.f.* fry; dish of anything fried.
fritilaria, *n.f.* fritillary.
fritillas, *n.f.pl.* fritters, pancakes.
frito, -ta, *p.p. irreg.* [FREÍR]; fried; *si están fritas o no están fritas,* with or without reason, come what may.
frito, *n.m.* fry; anything fried.
fritura, *n.f.* fry, fritter.
friura, *n.f.* (*prov.*) frigidity, cold.
frívolamente, *adv.* frivolously, triflingly, without weight.
frivolidad, *n.f.* frivolity, frivolousness, triflingness, frothiness, emptiness.
frivolité, *n.f.* tatting, fancy work.
frívolo, -la, *a.* frivolous, vain, trifling, slight, empty, light, frothy, futile.
friz, *n.f.* flower of the beech-tree.
froga, *n.f.* (*obs.*) brickwork, masonry.
fronda, *n.f.* leaf of a plant; frond; (*surg.*) sling-shaped bandage. — *pl.* **frondas,** foliage, frondage, verdure.
fronde, *n.m.* (*bot.*) frond, fern, leaf.
frondescencia, *n.f.* leafing process, frondescence.
frondífero, -ra, *a.* frondiferous, leaf-bearing.
frondio, -dia, *a.* (*Col.*) peevish, disagreeable; (*Mex.*) dirty, untidy.
frondosidad, *n.f.* frondage, luxuriant growth, foliage.
frondoso, -sa, *a.* leafy, luxuriant.
frontal, *a.* frontal, relating to the forehead. — *n.m.* frontal, altar hanging; frontlet; chisel; (*Col., Ec., Mex.*) headstall of a bridle.

frontalera, *n.f.* brow-band (of a bridle); browpad under a yoke; (*eccles.*) trimmings of an altar frontal; place where frontals are kept.
frontera, *n.f.* frontier, boundary, border, confine, limit; (*arch.*) façade; binder of a frail-basket; side of a soft-brick mould.
fronterizo, -za, *a.* limitary; frontier; fronting, opposite, over against.
frontero, -ra, *a.* placed in front, opposite.
frontero, *n.m.* governor or commander of frontier forces; frontlet or brow-pad for children. — *adv.* in front.
frontil, *n.m.* yoke-pad for draught-oxen.
frontino, -na, *a.* animal marked in the face.
frontis, *n.m.* (*arch.*) frontispiece, façade.
frontispicio, *n.m.* front; frontispiece; façade; (*coll.*) face, visage.
frontón, *n.m.* main wall of a hand-ball court; fives-court; (*arch.*) pediment; (*min.*) part of the wall of the seam; cliff on the coast.
frontudo, -da, *a.* broad-faced.
frontura, *n.f.* front of a stocking-frame.
frotación, frotadura, *n.f.* friction, rubbing.
frotador, -ra, *n.m.f.* one who or that which rubs; kind of brush used by hatters.
frotamiento, *n.m.* rubbing, friction.
frotante, *a.* rubbing.
frotar, *v.t.* to rub, stroke gently.
frote, *n.m.* friction, rubbing; attrition.
fructíferamente, *adv.* fruitfully.
fructífero, -ra, *a.* fructiferous, frugiferous, fruit-bearing, fruitful.
fructificación, *n.f.* fructification, fertilization.
fructificador, -ra, *a.* fertilizing.
fructificar, *v.i.* (*pret.* **fructifiqué**; *pres. subj.* **fructifique**) to fructify, bear or yield fruit, produce; (*fig.*) to profit or give profit; to benefit, edify, promote morality or piety.
fructuario, -ria, *a.* usufructuary.
fructuosamente, *adv.* fruitfully, profitably.
fructuoso, -sa, *a.* fruitful, useful, fructuous, profitable.
fruente, *a.* enjoying.
frugal, *a.* frugal, parsimonious, thrifty, sparing.
frugalidad, *n.f.* frugality, parsimony, thrift, economy.
frugalmente, *adv.* frugally, thriftily, sparingly.
frugífero, -ra, *a.* (*poet.*) fruit-bearing.
frugívoro, -ra, *a.* frugivorous, herbivorous, feeding on fruit.
fruición, *n.f.* satisfaction, enjoyment, fruition, taste, relish, gratification.
fruir, *v.i.* (conjugated like HUIR) to enjoy, live happily.
fruitivo, -va, *a.* fruitive, enjoyable.
frumentario, -ria; frumenticio, -cia, *a.* cereal, frumentaceous.
frunce, *n.m.* (*sew.*) shirr, shirring, gather; plait.
fruncido, -da, *a.* shirred, gathered; contracted. — *p.p.* [FRUNCIR]; *fruncido de boca,* hare-lipped.
fruncidor, *n.m.* (*sew.*) gatherer, plaiter, folder.
fruncimiento, *n.m.* shirring, gathering; (*coll.*) fiction, deceit, imposture.
fruncir, *v.t.* (*pres. indic.* **frunzo**; *pres. subj.* **frunza**) (*sew.*) to gather, shirr; to contract, reduce; to pucker; to conceal or twist the truth. — *v.r.* to affect modesty and composure; *fruncir las cejas,* to knit the eye-

brows; *fruncir los labios*, to pucker or curl the lips.

fruslera, *n.f.* brass turnings or clippings.

fruslería, *n.f.* bauble, trifle, titbit; *(coll.)* frivolity.

fruslero, -ra, *a.* trifling, futile, insignificant, frivolous. — *n.m.* rolling-pin.

frustración, *n.f.* frustration.

frustráneo, -nea, *a.* useless, nugatory.

frustrar, *v.t.* to disappoint, frustrate, baulk, thwart, elude, mock, defeat, prevent, deprive, annul. — *v.r.* to fail, miscarry, fall through.

frustratorio, -ria, *a.* frustrative, defeating.

fruta, *n.f.* fruit, fruitage; result, consequence; *fruta nueva*, anything new; *fruta de sartén*, pancake, fritter; *fruta del tiempo*, fruit eaten in season; *(fig.)* anything seasonal or recurrent; *uno come la fruta aceda, y otro tiene la dentera,* one calls the tune and another has to pay the piper.

frutaje, *n.m. (art)* painting of fruits and flowers.

frutal, *a.* fruitful, fruit-bearing. — *n.m.* fruit-tree.

frutar, *v.i.* to bear or yield fruit.

frutecer, *v.i. (poet.)* to start to bear or yield fruit.

frutería, *n.f.* fruit-store; office of providing fruit for the royal palace.

frutero, -ra, *n.m.f.* fruiterer; fruit-basket, fruit-dish.

frutero, *n.m.* napkin or doily over a fruit-dish; *(art)* painting representing fruit; ornamental piece of artificial fruit.

frútice, *n.m.* perennial shrub.

fruticoso, -sa, *a. (bot.)* fruticose, frutescent; shrubby.

fruticultura, *n.f.* art and science of cultivating fruit trees and plants.

frutilla, *n.f.* small fruit; *(Am.)* strawberry; bead of a rosary.

frutillar, *n.m. (Am.)* strawberry-bed.

fruto, *n.m.* fruit, useful produce of the earth; product of man's intellect or labour; profit, benefice, advantage. — *pl.* **frutos**, *(com.)* produce, commodities; *dar fruto*, to yield fruit; *fruto de bendición*, child lawfully begotten.

fu, *interj.* of disgust; sound imitating the snarling of a cat; *ni fu ni fa (coll.)*, neither good nor bad, indifferent.

fúcar, *n.m.* rich, opulent man; nabob.

fucilar, *v.i.* to flash, glisten.

fucilazo, *n.m.* fulguration, heat lightning.

fuco, *n.m.* fucus, bladder-wrack, olive sea-weeds.

fucsia, *n.f.* fuchsia.

fucsina, *n.f.* fuchsine.

fucha, *interj. (Mex.)* exclamation of approval for neatness.

fuego, *n.m.* fire, blaze, conflagration; watch-fire, bonfire, beacon-fire; *(coll.)* vigour, animation, force, life; hearth, fire-place; eruption in the skin; firing of fire-arms; ardour, heat of an action; *(vet.)* cautery; *fuego de San Antón*, erysipelas; *fuego de San Telmo*, corposant; *esa aldea tiene cincuenta fuegos,* that village contains fifty hearths (i.e. houses); *fuego fatuo*, jack-o'-lantern, will-o'-the-wisp, ignis fatuus; *dar fuego a un navío,* (naut.) to bream a ship; *fuegos*, light-house; *dar fuego a los tablones*, (naut.) to heat

planks for the purpose of bending them; *fuego Griego*, Greek or wild fire; *hacer fuego*, *(mil.)* to fire; *tocar a fuego*, to give an alarm of fire; *pegar fuego*, to set on fire; *levantar fuego*, to arouse a quarrel or dissension; *fuegos artificiales*, fireworks; *meter fuego*, to promote, set on foot; *fuego graneado*, *(mil.)* successive or incessant firing; *a fuego y sangre*, with fire and sword; *huir del fuego y dar en las brasas*, to escape the frying-pan and fall into the fire; *si el fuego está cerca de la estopa, llega el diablo y sopla*, proverb warning against excessive familiarity between men and women.

¡fuego! ¡fuego de Dios! *interj.* bless me ! *¡fuego!* Fire ! (military command to shoot).

fueguecillo, -cito, -zuelo, *n.m.* small fire.

fuellar, *n.m.* bright talcum ornament on wax tapers.

fuelle, *n.m.* bellows; blower; *(car.)* hood, top; clouds over mountains; *(coll.)* tale-bearer; *(sew.)* pucker in clothes; *(prov.)* goat-skin bag used in the transport of flour.

fuente, *n.f.* fountain, fount, waterspout, jet; spring of water; platter, dish; primal source, originating cause; *(surg.)* seton, small ulcer, issue; *beber en buenas fuentes*, to be well-informed.

fuentecica, -cilla, -cita, -zuela, *n.f.* small fountain.

fuer, *n.m., contr.* [FUERO]. — *adv., a fuer de*, as a, in the manner of; *a fuer de caballero*, as a gentleman.

fuera, *adv.* without, out, not in, away, outside, off; over and above; *de fuera* (or *por fuera*), outside, exteriorly; *fuera de sí*, deranged, aghast; *fuera de*, out of, forth, besides, in addition to; *fuera de esto*, short of this; aside from this; *fuera de eso*, moreover, besides; *hacia fuera*, outward; *fuera de que*, besides, over and above; *fuera de propósito*, inopportunely, untimely; *fuera de quicio*, unhinged; out of order, out of joint; *estar fuera*, not to be at home.

¡fuera! *interj.* away, clear the way, get off, put him out !

fuerarropa (hacer), *interj.* command used in the galleys for the oarsmen to undress.

fuercecilla, *n.f.* little strength.

fuerista, *n.m.f.* expert in statute law.

fuero, *n.m.* statute-law; privilege of exemption; judicial power, jurisdiction; compilation of laws; *fuero de la conciencia, fuero interior* (or *fuero interno*), the tribunal of conscience, heart of hearts; *fuero mixto*, canon and civil laws; *a fuero*, according to law, use and custom; *de fuero*, of right, by right of law.

fuerte, *a.* potent, strong, able, vigorous, lusty, hardy, stout, hale, healthy; fast, secure, impregnable; efficacious, cogent, powerful, forcible, compact, firm, hard, substantial, solid, not malleable; tough, heavy, thick; active, intense; loud; surpassing, proficient, determined, manly, unswerving; having excess of weight; excessive; grave, terrible. — *n.m.* fortification, fort, fortress, hold, entrenchment; forte, strong point; *(mus.)* forte, loud; coin having excess of weight; *hacerse fuerte*, to entrench, defend oneself; *agua fuerte*, aqua fortis. — *adv.* hard, strongly, abundantly, copiously, excessively.

fuertecico, -cito, -cillo, -zuelo, *n.m.* small fortress, blockhouse.

fuertemente, *adv.* lustily, strongly, firmly, vehemently, fast, forcibly.

fuerza, *n.f.* strength, force, might, stress, cogency, vigour; constancy, manliness, courage, valour, fortitude; staunchness, efficacy, firmness, toughness, solidity; constraint, coercion, compulsion, violence; mental power, virtue, efficiency; rape, defloration; (*mech.*) power; resistency; (*phys.*) energy, force, moment, agency, impulsive weight; (*fort.*) fortress, a strong place; strongest part of a thing; natural power, proneness, strong propensity; the part of a sword next to the hilt; stiffening piece in garments. — *pl.* **fuerzas,** soldiers, armies; *fuerzas de mar y de tierra,* naval and land forces; *fuerza de agua,* water power; *fuerza animal* (or *de sangre*), animal power; *fuerza mayor,* (*law, com.*) superior force, force majeure; *a viva fuerza,* with great resolution, by main force; *hacer fuerza de remos,* to pull hard with the oars; *fuerza de vapor,* steam power; *fuerza de inercia,* vis inertiæ; *fuerza electromotriz,* electro-motive force; *a fuerza de,* by dint of, by force of; *por fuerza* (or *de por fuerza*), by force, violently, forcibly, necessarily; *hacer fuerza de velas,* to crowd sail, to carry a press of sail; to make a strenuous effort; *sacar fuerzas de flaqueza,* to bring strength out of weakness; *de grado o por fuerza,* willingly or unwillingly; *a viva fuerza,* with great resolution, by main force.

fuerzo; fuerce, *pres. indic.; pres. subj.* [FORZAR].

fuetazo, *n.m.* (*Am.*) stroke with a whip.

fuete, *n.m.* (*Am.*) whip.

fufar, *v.i.* to make a spitting noise (of an angry cat).

fufu, *n.m.* (*Col., Cub., PR.*) pounded mass of yam, plantain, etc.

fuga, *n.f.* escape, flight, runaway elopement; escape of gas, leak, leakage, issue; (*mus.*) fugue; *fuga precipitada,* stampede; *fuga de risa,* fit of laughter.

fugacidad, *n.f.* fugacity, fugitiveness, volatility, fugaciousness, brevity.

fugado, -da, *a.* fugato, written in the style of a fugue.

fugar, *v.t.* (*obs.*) to cause to fly or escape. — *v.r.* (*pret.* **me fugué;** *pres. subj.* **me fugue**) to escape, fly, run away.

fugaz; (*poet.*) **fúgido, -da,** *a.* fugacious, volatile, apt to fly away; running away, fugitive; brief, fleeting, decaying, perishable; *estrella fugaz,* shooting star.

fugazmente, *adv.* fleetingly.

fugitivo, -va, *a.* fugitive, runaway; unsteady, brief, perishable, unstable.

fuguillas, *n.m.* (*coll.*) short-tempered man.

fuina, *n.f.* marten.

fulanito, -ita, *n.m.f.* little master, little miss.

fulano, -na, *n.m.f.* such a one; so-and-so; *Fulano de tal,* John Doe; *Fulano, Sutano, Mengano,* Tom, Dick and Harry.

fular, *n.m.* foulard.

fulcro, *n.m.* fulcrum.

fulero, -ra, *a.* (*coll.*) rough, unpolished; clumsy; (*prov.*) deceitful.

fulgecer, *v.i.* (*poet.*) to shine, be resplendent.

fulgente, *a.* refulgent, brilliant.

fúlgido, -da, *a.* bright, resplendent.

fulgor, *n.m.* fulgency, resplendence, brilliancy.

fulguración, *n.f.* flash, flashing; (*med.*) lightning stroke.

fulgurante, *a.* resplendent, shining.

fulgurar, *v.i.* to fulgurate, flash, shine with brilliancy.

fulguroso, -sa, *a.* fulgorous.

fúlica, *n.f.* fulica, coot.

fulidor, *n.m.* (*slang*) thief who uses children to open doors for him.

fuliginoso, -sa, *a.* fuliginous, dark, sooty, obscure, smutty.

fulminación, *n.f.* fulmination, thundering.

fulminado, -da, *a.* struck by lightning. — *p.p.* [FULMINAR].

fulminador, -ra, *a.* thunderer; fulminator.

fulminante, *a.* fulminating, fulminant, fulminatory, thundering; explosive, exploding; (*med.*) violent, deadly. — *n.m.* percussion cap.

fulminar, *v.t.* to fulminate; to cause to explode; to emit lightning; to throw out as an object of terror; to express wrath; to issue ecclesiastical censures, excommunications, etc.

fulminato, *n.m.* (*chem.*) fulminate.

fulminatriz, *a.* fulminating.

fulmíneo, -nea, *a.* (*poet.*) fulmineous.

fulmínico, *a.* fulminic (acid).

fulminoso, -sa, *a.* fulminatory, thundering, striking awe.

fulleresco, -ca, *a.* belonging to sharpers.

fullería, *n.f.* cheating at play; cunning arts used to deceive.

fullero, -ra, *n.m.f.* sharper, cheater at play; (*Col.*) tale-bearer, informer.

fullona, *n.f.* (*coll.*) dispute, quarrel, wrangle.

fumable, *a.* smokeable, good to smoke.

fumada, *n.f.* puff, whiff of smoke.

fumadero, *n.m.* smoking-room.

fumador, -ra, *n.m.f.* smoker.

fumante, *a.* smoking, fuming.

fumar, *v.i.* to smoke; to disperse in vapours. — *v.r.* (*coll.*) to spend, waste one's money; to dodge one's duty; *fumarse la clase* or *la oficina,* to play truant.

fumarada, *n.f.* puff, whiff or blast of smoke; pipeful of tobacco.

fumaria, *n.f.* fumitory.

fumarola, *n.f.* fumarole.

fumífero, -ra, *a.* (*poet.*) smoking, emitting smoke.

fumífugo, -ga, *a.* smoke-dispersing.

fumigación, *n.f.* fumigation.

fumigador, *n.m.* fumigator.

fumigar, *v.t.* (*pret.* **fumigué;** *pres. subj.* **fumigue**) to fumigate, smoke, fume, purify or medicate by vapours.

fumigatorio, -ria, *a.* fumigatory. — *n.m.* perfuming pan.

fumista, *n.m.* stove-maker; seller of stoves.

fumistería, *n.f.* shop or works where stoves are sold or repaired.

fumívoro, -ra, *a.* smoke-consuming.

fumorola, *n.f.* smoke-emitting cavity [FUMAROLA].

fumosidad, *n.f.* smokiness.

fumoso, -sa, *a.* fumy, smoky, full of smoke or fumes.

funámbulo, -la, *n.m.f.* funambulist, tight-rope walker, rope-dancer.

función, *n.f.* function, working, operation; vital action; discharge of a duty, office, or employment; entertainment, feast, festival, social party, solemnity; public demonstration, religious ceremony; engagement, fight, battle.

funcional, *a.* functional.

funcionar, *v.i.* to work, perform, operate, act, function.

funcionario, *n.m.* functionary, civil servant.

funche, *n.m.* (*Cub., Mex., PR.*) porridge made of maize flour.

funda, *n.f.* case, sheath, covering, cover, envelope, wrapper, slip; *funda de almohada,* pillow-case.

fundación, *n.f.* foundation, founding or establishment; origin, beginning, rise; building, raising, erection; endowment, endowed institution; ground-work.

fundadamente, *adv.* fundamentally, with good foundation.

fundador, -ra, *a.* founder.

fundago, *n.m.* (*obs.*) warehouse, magazine.

fundamental, *a.* fundamental, cardinal, essential, principal; *hueso fundamental,* (*anat.*) the sacrum; the sphenoid bone; *acorde fundamental,* (*mus.*) chord in root (or basic) position.

fundamentalmente, *adv.* fundamentally.

fundamentar, *v.t.* to found, lay a basis, establish on a basis; to ground, set firm, base.

fundamento, *n.m.* foundation, ground, ground-work, basis; leading or basic proposition; cause, reason, principle; root, origin, source; (*weav.*) weft, woof.

fundar, *v.t.* to found, raise, erect, build, put up; to endow, establish, institute; to start, set up, originate; to base, ground. — *v.r.* to base one's opinion on or upon; *fundarse en algo,* to take as a principle.

fundente, *a.* fusing, melting, smelting. — *n.m.* (*chem.*) flux; (*med.*) dissolvent.

fundería, *n.f.* foundry.

fundible, *a.* fusible.

fundíbulo, *n.m.* ballista, catapult.

fundición, *n.f.* fusion, fuse, blow-out; melting of metals, casting; foundry, smeltery; cast-iron; (*print.*) fount, set of types.

fundidor, *n.m.* founder, melter, smelter.

fundir, *v.t.* to fuse, melt metals; to smelt; to cast, found; to unmake in order to make anew. — *v.r.* to fuse, blend, combine, unite; (*elec.*) to fuse, blow; (*Am.*) to come to ruin.

fundo, *n.m.* rural property.

fúnebre, *a.* mournful, sad, lamentable; funeral, funereal, mourning; dark, lugubrious.

fúnebremente, *adv.* mournfully, sorrowfully, lamentably.

funeral, *a.* funeral, funereal. — *n.m.* funeral, obsequies.

funerala, (a la) *adv.* (*mil.*) with inverted arms.

funeraria, *n.f.* business of a funeral undertaker.

funerario, -ria, *a.* funeral, funereal.

funéreo, -rea, *a.* (*poet.*) mournful, sad, funereal.

funestamente, *adv.* sadly, dolefully.

funestar, *v.t.* to blot, stain, tarnish, profane; (*obs.*) to sadden, make sad.

funesto, -ta, *a.* funest, doleful, lamentable; untoward; sad, mournful, dismal.

fungible, *a.* consumable, fungible.

fungiforme, *a.* fungiform.

fungir, *v.i.* (*Am.*) to affect importance; (*Mex.*) to be employed.

fungita, *n.f.* fungite.

fungívero, -ra, *a.* fungiverous.

fungo, *n.m.* (*surg.*) fungus.

fungón, *n.m.* (*coll.*) great snuff-taker.

fungosidad, *n.f.* fungosity, excrescence.

fungoso, -sa, *a.* fungous, excrescent, spongy.

funicular, *a.* funicular; *ferrocarril funicular,* funicular railway.

funículo, *n.m.* funicle, funiculus.

fuñador, *n.m.* (*slang*) quarrelsome.

fuñar, *v.i.* (*slang*) to stir up quarrels.

fuñicar, *v.i.* to do a job clumsily.

fuñique, *a.* awkward; timorous, pusillanimous.

furente, *a.* (*poet.*) furious, frantic, raging, transported by passion.

furgón, *n.m.* transport wagon; baggage-car, freight-car, express-car, box-car; van.

furia, *n.f.* fury, rage; fit of madness; hurry, velocity, vigour; zeal, ardour; a furious woman, a virago; *a toda furia,* with the utmost speed.

furibundo, -da; (*poet.*) **furiente,** *a.* furious, frantic, enraged, raging.

furiosamente, *adv.* furiously.

furioso, -sa, *a.* furious, frantic, frenetic, mad, fierce, violent, raging; excessive, very great.

furo, -ra, *a.* shy, reserved, unsociable; (*prov.*) ferocious, fierce, wild, untamed.

furo, *n.m.* orifice of the sugar mould; (*prov.*) *hacer furo,* to conceal a thing with the intention of keeping it.

furor, *n.m.* fury, madness, choler, franticness, frenzy, anger, rage; (*poet.*) enthusiasm, exaltation of fancy; *furor uterino,* nymphomania.

furriel, furrier, *n.m.* quartermaster; clerk of the king's mews.

furriela, furriera, *n.f.* place of keeper of the keys of the king's palace.

furris, *a.* (*Mex., Ven.*) bad, contemptible; badly made.

furruco, *n.m.* (*Ven.*) kind of rustic drum.

furrusca, *n.f.* (*Col.*) quarrel, brawl.

furtivamente, *adv.* by stealth, clandestinely.

furtivo, -va, *a.* furtive, clandestine.

furuminga, *n.f.* (*Chi.*) tangle, jumble.

furúnculo, *n.m.* furuncle, boil.

furunculoso, -sa, *a.* furunculose.

fusa, *n.f.* demi-semiquaver.

fusado, -da; fuselado, -da, *a.* (*her.*) charged with fusils or spindles.

fusca, *n.f.* dark-coloured duck.

fuscar, *v.t.* (*obs.*) to obscure.

fusco, -ca, *a.* fuscous, brown, dark.

fuselaje, *n.m.* (*aer.*) fuselage.

fusentes, *a.pl.* of the receding tide of the Guadalquivir river.

fusibilidad, *n.f.* fusibility, flexibility.

fusible, fúsil, *a.* fusible.

fusiforme, *a.* fusiform, spindle-shaped.

fusil, *n.m.* rifle, gun, musket; *fusil de aguja,* needle-gun; *fusil de percusión* (or *de platón*), musket; *fusil de chispa,* flint-lock, musket; *fusil rayado,* rifle gun; *fusil de retrocarga,* breech-loader.

fusilamiento, *n.m.* shooting by musketry.

fusilar, *v.t.* to shoot (malefactors); to kill by shooting; (*coll.*) to plagiarize.

fusilazo, *n.m.* musket-shot, rifle-shot, blow with a gun.

fusilería, *n.f.* musketry; body of fusiliers or musketeers.

fusilero, *n.m.* fusilier, musketeer.

fusión, *n.f.* fusion, liquation, melting; alliance, union, liquefaction.

fusionar, *v.t.* to unite, bring together, merge.

fusionista, *a.* fusionist.

fusique, *n.m.* bottle-shaped snuff-box.

fuslina, *n.f.* smelting-works.

fusor, *n.m.* smelting ladle or vessel.

fusta, *n.f.* brushwood; woollen stuff or cord; whip-lash; lateen-rigged lighter.

fustán, *n.m.* fustian; (*Am.*) petticoat.

fustanero, *n.m.* fustian manufacturer.

fuste, *n.m.* wood, timber; tree and bows of a saddle; (*poet.*) saddle; shaft of a lance; substance, importance; foundation of anything not material; (*arch.*) fust, shaft of a column; *hombre de fuste,* man of weight and importance.

fustero, -ra, *a.* pertaining to timber, foundation, etc.

fustero, *n.m.* (*obs.*) turner, carpenter.

fustete, *n.m.* Venetian sumach or its wood; fustic, yellow-wood.

fustigante, *a.* fustigating.

fustigar, *v.t.* (*pret.* **fustigué;** *pres. subj.* **fustigue**) to whip, lash, fustigate.

fustina, *n.f.* place for fusing metals.

futbol, *n.m.* football.

futbolista, *n.m.* footballer.

futesa, *n.f.* trifle, bagatelle, bauble, gewgaw.

fútil, *a.* futile, worthless, trifling, flimsy.

futilidad, *n.f.* futility, weakness, groundlessness.

futre, *n.m.* (*Ec., Bol., Chi., Arg.*) coxcomb, fop.

futura, *n.f.* acquired right to an office or employment before its vacancy; (*coll.*) betrothed, intended bride; survivorship, survival.

futuro, -ra, *a.* future, forthcoming, next.

futuro, *n.m.* (*gram.*) future tense; the future, futurity; (*coll.*) betrothed, future husband; *en lo futuro,* for the future.

G

G, g, eighth letter of the Spanish alphabet.

gabacho, -cha, *a.* applied to the natives of some places at the foot of the Pyrenees; used also in derision of the French.

gabacho, *n.m.* (*coll.*) a Frenchified person; Spanish language full of Gallicisms.

gabán, *n.m.* great-coat, overcoat.

gabarda, *n.f.* wild rose.

gabardina, *n.f.* gabardine; weatherproof coat, mackintosh.

gabarra, *n.f.* (*naut.*) lighter, barge, gabbart.

gabarrero, *n.m.* lighterman; dealer in wood and timber.

gabarro, *n.m.* flaw or defect in cloth or stone; error or mistake in accounts; defect discovered in goods after they have been bought; drudgery, burdensome charge, obligation; (*vet.*) morbid swelling on the pastern of horses; pip, a horny pellicule on the tongue of fowls; (*mas., art*) badigeon, filling.

gabarrón, *n.m.* large barge.

gabasa, *n.f.* prostitute.

gábata, *n.f.* bowl, small basin for mess on galleys.

gabazo, *n.m.* bagasse, bruised sugar-cane.

gabela, *n.f.* gable, tax, excise, impost; duty, heavy service.

gabinete, *n.m.* cabinet; reception-room, sitting-room, private parlour, library, study; ladies' boudoir, dressing-room; *gabinete de lectura,* reading-room; *gabinete de física y química,* laboratory; *de gabinete,* applied to one whose knowledge is purely theoretical.

gablete, *n.m.* gable.

gabón, *n.m.* powder magazine.

gabote, *n.m.* (*prov.*) shuttlecock.

gabrieles, *n.m.pl.* (*coll.*) cooked chickpeas.

gacel, gacela, *n.m.f.* gazelle, antelope.

gaceta, *n.f.* gazette, newspaper, official publication; *mentir más que la gaceta,* to be an inveterate liar.

gacetera, *n.f.* woman who sells newspapers.

gacetero, *n.m.* gazetteer, news-writer; seller of newspapers.

gacetilla, *n.f.* personal news column; town talk, gossip; newsmonger; newspaper squib.

gacetillero, *n.m.* editor of a *gacetilla,* newspaper reporter, paragrapher, poor writer, penny-a-liner.

gacetista, *n.m.f.* one who delights in reading newspapers; newsmonger, gossip.

gacha, *n.f.* very thin watery mass; (*Cub.*) unglazed crock; (*Col., Ven.*) earthen bowl. — *pl.* **gachas,** porridge; pap; (*prov.*) caresses, pettings; *hacerse unas gachas,* to be too soft or affectionate; *¡ánimo a las gachas!* cheer up! courage!

gaché, *n.m.* (*prov.*) beau; 'feller,' guy.

gacheta, *n.f.* spring lever of a latch; tooth of a latch; sticking paste.

gacho, -cha, *a.* curvated, turned down, bent downward; having horns curved downwards (cattle); slouching (as hats); *a gachas,* (*coll.*) on all fours.

gachón, -ona, *n.m.f., a.* (*coll.*) graceful, attractive, sweet, bright; (*prov.*) spoiled, petted child.

gachonada, gachonería, *n.f.* (*coll.*) gracefulness, brightness; (*prov.*) fondness, caress, endearment.

gachumbo, *n.m.* (*Am.*) shell of various fruits, from which cups and other vessels are made.

gachupín, cachupín, *n.m.* (*Mex.*) name given to native of Spain.

gaditano, -na, *n.m.f., a.* of or belonging to Cádiz.

gaélico, -ca, *a.* Gaelic.

gafa, *n.f.* gaffle, hook for bending a cross-bow. — *pl.* **gafas,** (*naut.*) can-hooks, grapple-hooks; spectacles; spectacle-bows.

gafar, *v.t.* to hook, claw, to catch with a hook or with the nails; to clench, fasten, joint, repair broken objects with a *gafa*.

gafedad, *n.f.* (*med.*) contraction of the nerves; claw-hand; kind of leprosy.

gafete, *n.m.* clasp, hook and eye.

gafo, -fa, *a.* suffering from claw-hand or leprosy; (*Per.*) paralytic, tremulous.

gago, -ga, *a.* (*Per., PR., Ven.*) stammerer, stutterer.

gaguear, *v.i.* (*Cub., Chi., Per., PR., Ven.*) to stutter.

gaita, *n.f.* flageolet; hurdy-gurdy; *gaita gallega,* bagpipe; hornpipe; *(coll.)* the neck; *estar de gaita, (coll.)* to be very merry; *ándese la gaita por el lugar,* do as you like, I am quite indifferent.

gaitería, *n.f.* gay and gaudy dress.

gaitero, -ra, *a. (coll.)* unbecomingly sportive and gay; *(coll.)* gaudy, showy, flamboyant.

gaitero, *n.m.* piper, one who plays the bagpipes.

gaje, *n.m.* salary, pay, wages; gage (in a duel). — *pl.* **gajes,** perquisites, fees; *gajes del oficio,* (*joc.*) cares of office.

gajo, *n.m.* branch of a tree; pyramidal raceme of any fruit; part of a bunch of grapes torn off; each division of an orange, pomegranate, etc.; spur of a mountain, ridge; prong of pitchforks, etc.

gajoso, -sa, *a.* composed of *gajos;* branching, spreading.

gala, *n.f.* gala, full, or court dress; *día de gala,* court-day, holiday; graceful, pleasing address; parade, ostentation; choicest part of a thing; *(Antilles, Mex.)* present or premium as a reward of merit. — *pl.* **galas,** regalia, finery, trapping, paraphernalia; *galas de novia,* bridal trousseau; *de gala,* full-dress uniform; *hacer gala,* to glory in having done anything; *hacer gala del sambenito,* to glory in one's wickedness; *llevar la gala,* to deserve applause, etc.; *la gala del nadador es saber guardar la ropa,* the chief thing is not to suffer loss.

galabardera, *n.f. (bot.)* wild rose.

galactita, galactite, *n.f.* fuller's earth, alumina.

galactómetro, *n.m.* galactometer, lactometer.

galafate, *n.m.* artful thief, cunning rogue; porter who carries burdens.

galaico, -ca, *a.* Galician.

galamero, -ra, *a.* sweet-toothed.

galán, *n.m.* (contr. of *galano*), spruce, well-made man; courtier, gallant; wooer, lover; ladies' man; *(theat.) primer galán,* leading man; *segundo galán,* walking gentleman; *galán joven,* juvenile lead; *galán de noche,* night-smelling cestrum.

galanamente, *adv.* gallantly, elegantly.

galancete, *n.m.* spruce little man, a spark; *(theat.)* juvenile.

galanga, *n.f.* officinal galingale.

galano, -na, *a.* gallant, fine, gay, genteel, splendidly dressed; elegant, ingenious, sprightly, lively; *(Cub.)* parti-coloured (beasts); dissolute.

galante, *a.* gallant, elegant, handsome, courtly, polished; brave, liberal, generous; facetious, witty; flirtatious (of women).

galanteador, *n.m.* wooer, lover; flatterer.

galantear, *v.t.* to court, woo, pay attention; solicit favour; *(obs.)* to ornament, deck.

galantemente, *adv.* gallantly, civilly.

galanteo, *n.m.* gallantry, courtship, wooing, intrigue.

galantería, *n.f.* gallantry, courtesy, politeness; elegance, grace; compliment to a lady; generosity, liberality, munificence.

galanto, *n.m. (bot.)* snowdrop.

galanura, *n.f.* prettiness, showiness, gorgeousness, gracefulness, elegance; pretty dress or ornament.

galapagar, *n.m.* place where tortoises abound.

galápago, *n.m.* fresh-water tortoise; *(agric.)* bed of a ploughshare; *(arm.)* frame for boring guns; mould for convex tiles; *(found.)* pig of lead or tin; *(mas.)* small centering-frame; *(surg.)* funda; *(sad.)* English saddle; *(mil.)* shed formed with shields joined together; mantelet, cat-castle, sow; *(vet.)* scratch; *(Hond., Ven.)* sidesaddle.

galapaguera, *n.f.* aquarium for tortoises.

galapo, *n.m.* (rope-making) laying-top.

galardón, *n.m.* guerdon, reward, recompense, prize.

galardonador, -ra, *n.m.f.* remunerator, rewarder.

galardonar, *v.t.* to reward, recompense, requite.

galato, *n.m.* gallate.

galatites, *n.f.* fuller's earth.

galaxia, *n.f.* soap-stone, steatite; galaxy, the Milky Way.

galayo, *n.m. (prov.)* cliff.

galbana, *n.f.* sloth, laziness, indolence.

galbanado, -da, *a.* of the colour of galbanum.

galbanero, -ra, *a. (coll.)* lazy, indolent.

gálbano, *n.m.* galbanum.

galbanoso, -sa, *a.* indolent, lazy, shiftless.

gálbula, *n.m.* nut of the cypress-tree.

galdrope, *n.m.* wheel-rope.

galdrufa, *n.f. (prov.)* top, a child's plaything.

gálea, *n.f.* galea, ancient morion or helmet.

galeato, -ta, *a.* said of the preface to a work defending itself against possible objections.

galeaza, *n.f.* galleass.

galega, *n.f.* common goat's-rue.

galénico, -ca, *a.* galenic, galenical.

galeno, -na, *a.* moderate, soft wind. — *n.m. (coll.)* physician; medico.

gáleo, *n.m.* sword-fish.

galeón, *n.m.* galleon.

galeota, *n.f.* galliot.

galeote, *n.m.* galley-slave.

galera, *n.f.* van, wagon; galley; house of correction for women; extra line of beds in a hospital ward; smooth plane, organ-builder's plane; line cutting off the quotient in division; furnace for distilling sulphur; subterranean gallery; *(Hond., Mex.)* shed, hut; *(Arg., Chi., Ur.)* silk hat, slouch-hat. — *pl.* **galeras,** punishment of rowing on board of galleys; *azotes y galeras, (met.)* ordinary food never varied; *estar en galeras, (met.)* to be in distress.

galerada, *n.f.* car-load, van-load; *(print.)* galley-proof; galley of type.

galerero, *n.m.* wagoner, van-driver.

galería, *n.f.* gallery, corridor, lobby; narrow covered passage across a moat; art museum; collection of paintings; *(theat.)* gallery; *(min.)* gallery, heading, driftway; *galería de popa,* stern-gallery, balcony.

galerilla, *n.f.* small gallery.

galerín, *n.m. (print.)* wooden galley.

galerita, *n.f.* crested lark.

galerna, *n.f.;* **galerno,** *n.m.* stormy north-west wind in Spain.

galerón, *n.m. (Col., Ven.)* popular air and dance.

Gales, *n.m.* Wales.

galés, -esa, *n.m.f., a.* Welsh, Welshman.

galés, *n.m.* Welsh language.

galfarro, *n.m. (obs.)* magistrate; rogue, loafer, idler; swindler; *(prov.)* hawk.

galga, *n.f.* boulder; greyhound bitch; stone wheel that grinds olives; kind of itch; drag, brake scotch, hub-brake; bier for poor people; (*naut.*) back of an anchor. — *pl.* **galgas,** long ribbons for tying women's shoes.

galgo, *n.m.* greyhound; *el que nos vendió el galgo,* the very man we spoke of; *vete a espulgar un galgo,* go to the devil.

galgo, -ga, *a.* (*Am.*) hungry, eager, anxious.

galgueño, -ña, *a.* resembling or concerning a greyhound.

gálgulo, *n.m.* (*orn.*) roller.

galianos, *n.m.pl.* shepherd's meal.

galibar, *v.t.* (*naut.*) to trace, mould.

gálibo, *n.m.* model of a ship; templet; gauge for the load of an open freight-car.

galicado, -da, *a.* somewhat Frenchified.

galicano, -na, *a.* Gallican; *iglesia galicana,* Gallican church.

galicista, *n.m.f.* one who makes frequent use of Gallicisms.

galicismo, *n.m.* Gallicism.

gálico, *n.m.* venereal disease, syphilis.

galicoso, -sa, *a.* (*coll.*) infected with syphilis.

galilea, *n.f.* galilee porch or chapel.

galileo, -lea, *a.* Galilean, of Galilee. — *n.m.f.* disrespectful name applied to the Saviour or to Christians.

galillo, *n.m.* uvula, hanging palate; (*coll.*) windpipe, throat.

galimatias, *n.m.* (*coll.*) gibberish, confused speech; galimatias, confused or intricate matter.

galio, *n.m.* bed-straw, cheese-rennet; (*chem.*) gallium.

galiopsis, *n.m.* common hedge-nettle.

galiparla, *n.f.* Spanish language mixed with French words.

galiparlista, *n.m.f.* Gallicizer.

galizabra, *n.f.* lateen-rigged vessel.

galo, -la, *n.m.f.,* *a.* Gallic, native of Gaul.

galocha, *n.f.* galosh, clog, patten, wooden overshoe.

galón, *n.m.* galloon, tape, trimming, braid, lace; binding-stripe; bullion, gold or silver galloons used on uniforms; gallon, liquid measure. — *pl.* **galones,** sheer rails.

galonazo, *n.m.* large galloon; excessive ornament.

galoneador, -ra, *n.m.f.* binder with braid or galloons.

galoneadura, *n.f.* trimming, garnishing with galloons, etc.

galonear, *v.t.* to bind, trim with galloons, adorn with lace.

galonero, *n.m.* braid or galloon maker.

galonista, *n.m.* (*coll.*) pupil of a military college wearing corporal stripes as a reward.

galop, *n.m.* galop, Hungarian dance.

galopada, *n.f.* race at the gallop.

galopar, *v.i.* to gallop.

galope, *n.m.* gallop; haste, speed; *a galope* (or *de galope*), hurriedly, speedily, gallopingly.

galopeado, -da, *a.* (*coll.*) hastily done. — *p.p.* [GALOPEAR].

galopeado, *n.m.* (*coll.*) whipping, flogging.

galopear, *v.i.* to gallop.

galopillo, *n.m.* scullion, kitchen-boy.

galopín, *n.m.* ragamuffin; shrewd fellow; rogue, rascal; clever knave; cabin-boy, swabber; scullion.

galopinada, *n.f.* roguish act, knavery.

galopo, *n.m.* rascal, rogue.

galpito, *n.m.* weak or sickly chicken.

galpón, *n.m.* (*Arg., Ur.*) a large shed.

galucha, *n.f.* (*Col., CR., Cub., PR., Ven.*) gallop; haste, speed.

galuchar, *v.i.* (*Col., CR., Cub., PR., Ven.*) to gallop.

Galván; *no lo entenderá Galván,* (*coll.*) said of something intricate, difficult.

galvánico, -ca, *a.* galvanic.

galvanismo, *n.m.* galvanism.

galvanización, *n.f.* galvanization.

galvanizar, *v.t.* (*pret.* **galvanicé;** *pres. subj.* **galvanice**) to galvanize; to electroplate; to rouse into life or activity.

galvanómetro, *n.m.* galvanometer.

galvanoplastia, galvanoplástica, *n.f.* galvanoplasty, electrotypy.

galladura, *n.f.* cicatricle, tread of an egg.

gallar, *v.t.* to tread (as a cock).

gallarda, *n.f.* Spanish dance and music; (*print.*) type of a size between minion and brevier.

gallardamente, *adv.* elegantly, gracefully, gallantly.

gallardear, *v.i.* to do anything with grace or elegance.

gallardete, *n.m.* pennant, streamer.

gallardetón, *n.m.* broad pennant.

gallardía, *n.f.* graceful air and deportment; gracefulness, elegance, genteelness; briskness, activity; nobleness, magnanimity, bravery, gallantry.

gallardo, -da, *a.* graceful, gay, elegant, genteel; high-spirited, generous, great of mind, magnanimous; gallant, bold, daring, brave; lively.

gallareta, *n.f.* widgeon.

gallarín, *n.m.* (*obs.*) excessive gain or loss; *salir al gallarín,* to suffer a loss or disgrace.

gallarón, *n.m.* kind of bustard.

gallaruza, *n.f.* hooded garment, coarse country garment.

gallear, *v.t.* to tread (as cocks). — *v.i.* to surpass, excel; to raise the voice in anger; to assume an air of importance; to crow, bully; (*found.*) to have flaws.

gallegada, *n.f.* number of *gallegos* assembled together; Galician dance and its tune; peculiar action or speech of a *gallego.*

gallego, -ga, *n.m.f.,* *a.* language spoken in Galicia; Galician; (*Arg., Bol., PR., Cub.*) Spaniard (immigrant).

gallego, *n.m.* the north-west wind in Castile.

galleo, *n.m.* flaw in a casting.

gallera, *n.f.* (*Philip.*) cock-pit.

gallería, *n.f.* (*Cub.*) cock-pit.

galleta, *n.f.* ship-biscuit, hard-tack; small vessel or pan; (*coll.*) blow on the face with the palm of the hand; a kind of anthracite coal; (*Arg., Chi.*) bread made of grit and bran; (*Arg.*) small gourd for mate.

galletica, *n.f.* small cracker or biscuit.

gallillo, *n.m.* uvula.

gallina, *n.f.* hen. — *n.m.f.* coward, chicken-hearted person; *hijo de la gallina blanca,* lucky person; *gallina ciega,* blind-man's-buff, hoodman's blind; *gallina clueca,* brood-hen; *gallina de Guinea,* guinea-hen; *acostarse con las gallinas,* (*coll.*) to go to bed very early; *gallina en corral ajeno,* a fish out of water; *viva la gallina, aunque sea con su pepita,* long live the hen, pip and all; *aldeana es la gallina y cómela el de Sevilla,* nothing should be despised however humble; *tan contenta va una gallina con un pollo como otra con ocho*, an only child is as dear to its mother as are many children.

gallináceo, -cea, *a.* gallinaceous.

gallinaza, *n.f.* hen-dung; carrion, buzzard, kite, vulture, caracara.

gallinería, *n.f.* poulterer's shop; (*obs.*) hen-coop, hen-house; (*coll.*) cowardice, pusillanimity.

gallinero, -ra, *a.* (*falc.*) preying or feeding upon fowls. — *n.m.f.* poulterer, poultry-dealer.

gallinero, *n.m.* poultry-yard, hen-coop, hen-roost, hen-house; basket for carrying poultry; (*coll.*) ladies' club, or meeting place; family circle; (*theat.*) gallery.

gallineta, *n.f.* sand-piper; ruffed grouse; (*Arg., Col., Chi., Ven.*) guinea-hen.

gallipato, *n.m.* an amphibious lizard.

gallipava, *n.f.* large variety of hen.

gallipavo, *n.m.* turkey; (*coll.*) false, unpleasant note in singing.

gallipollo, *n.m.* cockerel.

gallipuente, *n.m.* bridge without rails.

gallito, *n.m.* small cock; beau, coxcomb, cock-of-the-walk. — *pl.* **gallitos,** shaggy-leaved toad-flax.

gallo, *n.m.* cock, rooster; *gallo inglés* (or *de pelea*), game-cock; dory, sea-fish; (*fig.*) leader, chief, boss; float of cork for fishing; wall-board of the roof; false note in singing; *salir con una pata de gallo*, to give foolish or irrelevant answer; *alzar* (or *levantar*) *el gallo*, to speak loud and arrogantly; *al primer gallo* (*obs.*), in the middle of the night, at the first cock-crow; *hacerse* (or *ser*) *el gallo*, to become the ruler in any meeting, body, etc.; *en menos que canta un gallo*, in a moment; *tener mucho gallo*, to be very arrogant and proud; *al gallo que canta, le aprietan la garganta*, strangle the cock that crows (*i.e.* be careful that secrets are kept); *ir a escucha gallo*, to proceed carefully and attentively; *cada gallo canta en su muladar*, everyone is master in his own house; *el que solo come su gallo, solo ensilla su caballo*, he who is selfish in prosperity can expect no help in adversity or need; *escarbó el gallo, y descubrió el cuchillo*, inquisitive people hear no good of themselves; *daca el gallo, toma el gallo, quedan las plumas en la mano*, too much attention may ruin any business; *engreído como gallo de cortijo*, as proud as a fighting-cock.

gallobosque, *n.m.* wood-grouse.

gallocresta, *n.f.* annual clary sage.

gallofa, *n.f.* food given to pilgrims; idle tale; salad and pottage; (*prov.*) French roll; directory of divine service.

gallofear, *v.i.* to saunter about and live upon alms; loaf, loiter.

gallofero, -ra; gallofo, -fa, *a.* idle, lazy, vagabond. — *n.m.f.* tramp.

gallón, *n.m.* green sod, turf; (*arch.*) echinus. — *pl.* **gallones,** festoons; (*naut.*) the last bow-frame.

gallonada, *n.f.* wall made of sods.

gallote, -ta, *a.* (*CR., Mex.*) forward, free; resolute, daring.

galludo, *n.f.* tope, dogfish.

gama, *n.f.* (*zool.*) doe; (*mus.*) gamut; (*fig.*) the whole range or extent (of colours).

gamalote, *n.m.* arrow-grass.

gamarra, *n.f.* martingale, check, strap.

gamarza, *n.f.* wild Syrian rue.

gamba, *n.f.* Mediterranean shrimp.

gambaj, gambax, *n.m.* acton, quilted woollen jacket.

gámbalo, *n.m.* kind of linen cloth.

gambalúa, *n.f.* (*coll.*) tall, ill-shaped man, without spirit; loafer.

gámbaro, *n.m.* kind of crawfish.

gamberro, -rra, *a.* libertine, dissolute; (*prov.*) *n.f.* prostitute, strumpet.

gambesina, *n.f.*; **gambesón,** *n.m.* short quilted jacket.

gambeta, *n.f.* cross-caper, prance; prancing (of a horse); affected tone or language; (*Arg., Bol.*) dodge, twist; dodging.

gambetear, *v.i.* to caper; to prance (horse).

gambeto, *n.m.* quilted great-coat; cap for a new-born child.

gambito, *n.m.* gambit, an opening in chess.

gamboa, *n.f.* variety of quince.

gambota, *n.f.* (*naut.*) counter-timber, arched timber.

gamella, *n.f.* bow of the yoke for oxen and mules; large wooden trough or tub; wash-tub; mound made as a boundary line; camlet; (*obs.*) she-camel.

gamelleja, *n.f.* small trough or tub; small yoke.

gamellón, *n.m.* large yoke; large tub; trough in which grapes are trodden.

gamezno, *n.m.* little young fallow-deer.

gamo, *n.m.* buck of the fallow-deer; (*coll.*) restless person.

gamón, *n.m.* asphodel.

gamonal, *n.m.* place where asphodels flourish; (*Am.*) manager of a party machine.

gamonito, *n.m.* shoot, tiller, sucket; young asphodel.

gamonoso, -sa, *a.* abounding in asphodels.

gamuno, -na, *a.* applied to the skins of deer.

gamuza, *n.f.* chamois, antelope.

gamuzado, -da, *a.* chamois-colour.

gamuzón, *n.m.* large chamois.

gana, *n.f.* appetite, hunger; desire, inclination, list, mind; *de buena gana*, with pleasure, willingly, voluntarily; *de mala gana*, unwillingly, with reluctance, with dislike; *tener ganas de*, to have a desire to; *donde hay gana, hay maña*, where there's a will, there's a way.

ganable, *a.* gainable.

ganadería, *n.f.* cattle-raising; cattle-ranch; stock farm; livestock; cattle brand.

ganadero, -ra, *a.* belonging to cattle. — *n.m.f.* grazier, owner of cattle; stock-farmer; dealer in cattle; drover.

ganado, *n.m.* livestock, cattle, flock, drove, herd; collection of bees; (*coll.*) collection of persons; *ganado mayor*, cattle (including horses and mules); *ganado menor*, sheep; *ganado de pata hendida*, oxen, cows, sheep, goats; hogs, pigs; (*coll.*) gang, rabble; *ganado moreno* (or *de cerda*), swine, hogs, pigs.

ganado, -da, *a., p.p.* [GANAR]; *entre ruin ganado poco hay que escoger*, poor choice is little choice; *quien tiene ganado, no desea mal año*, only self-interest desires bad weather; *correr ganado* (*obs.*), to round up cattle.

ganador, -ra, *n.m.f.* gainer, winner.

ganancia, *n.f.* gain, profit, advantage, gainfulness, lucre; (*Chi., Guat., Mex.*) tip, gratuity; *andar de ganancia*, to pursue a thing successfully; *hijo de ganancia*, bastard; *ganancias y pérdidas*, profit and loss; *ganancia líquida*, net profit.

ganancial, *a.* lucrative; *bienes gananciales*, property acquired during marriage.

ganancioso, -sa, *a.* lucrative, gainful, profitable.

ganapán, *n.m.* porter; drudge; (*coll.*) rude, coarse man.

ganapierde, *n.m.f.* mode of playing draughts, etc., where he who loses all his men wins the game.

ganar, *v.t.* to gain, win; to profit, clear, make; to win over, deserve, conquer; to earn, attain, acquire, obtain; (*fig.*) to surpass; *ganar de barlovento*, to get to windward; *ganar las albricias*, to be early with good news; *ganar la vida*, to gain one's livelihood; *ganar el cielo con rosario ajeno*, to rob Peter to pay Paul. — *v.i.* to thrive.

ganchero, *n.m.* (*prov.*) conductor of a raft of timber.

ganchillo, -ito, *n.m.* little hook or crotch.

gancho, *n.m.* hook, crook, crotch; shepherd's crook, sheep-hook; (*coll.*) allurer, roper-in; (*fig.*) pimp, procurer, pander; (*coll.*) attractiveness, especially of a woman; (*Col., CR., Hond., Mex., Per.*) hair-pin; (*Ec.*) lady's saddle.

ganchoso, -sa, *a.* hooked, curved.

ganchuelo, *n.m.* little hook or crotch.

gándara, *n.f.* low, rough, uncultivated ground; jungle.

gandaya, *n.f.* laziness, idleness; kind of coif; *ir por la gandaya* or *andar* (or *buscar*, or *correr*) *la gandaya*, to gad, loaf, lounge.

gandido, -da, *a.* (*Col., CR., Cub., Mex., Ven.*) gluttonous, sweet-toothed.

gandinga, *n.f.* (*min.*) small, cleaned ore; (*Cub., PR.*) liver stew.

gandir, *v.t.* (*obs.*) to eat.

gandujado, *n.m.* accordion plaiting. — *p.p.* [GANDUJAR].

gandujar, *v.i.* (*sew.*) to bend, plait, shirr, fold.

gandul, -la, *n.m.f.*, *a.* (*coll.*) idler, lounger, loafer, vagabond, vagrant, tramp. — *n.m.* Moorish soldier of Granada.

gandulear, *v.i.* to loaf, lounge, gad, be idle.

gandulería, *n.f.* idleness, laziness, lounging.

ganeta, *n.f.* genet.

ganforro, -ra, *n.m.f.*, *a.* (*coll.*) rogue, rascal, vagabond.

ganga, *n.f.* little pin-tailed grouse; (*Cub.*) wading bird of the family of curlews; (*min.*) gangue, vein-stone; (*coll.*) bargain, anything valuable acquired with little labour; *andar a caza de gangas*, to spend one's time looking for easy jobs or bargains; *¡buena ganga es ésa!* (*iron.*) that's a fine reward for your trouble!

gangarilla, *n.f.* company of strolling players.

ganglio, *n.m.* ganglion.

gangocho, *n.m.* (*Cent. Am., Chi., Mex.*) burlap.

gangoso, -sa, *a.* snuffling, speaking with a twang.

gangrena, *n.f.* gangrene, mortification.

gangrenarse, *v.r.* to become gangrenous or mortified.

gangrenoso, -sa, *a.* gangrenous.

ganguear, *v.i.* to snuffle, speak with a twang.

ganguero, -ra, *a.* (*coll.*) cinch-seeking, running after easy bargains or jobs.

gánguil, *n.m.* fishing-barge; dump-scow.

ganil, *n.m.* calcareous rock.

ganoso, -sa, *a.* desirous, wishing, longing.

gansada, *n.f.* (*coll.*) stupidity.

gansarón, *n.m.* gosling; (*fig.*) lanky, gawky man.

ganso, -sa, *n.m.f.* gander, goose; (*fig.*) tall, thin person; (*fig.*) slow, lazy person; (*fig.*) bumpkin, ninny; *ganso bravo*, wild goose. — *pl.* **gansos,** goose's giblets.

ganta, *n.f.* (*Philip.*) measure of capacity for cereals and liquids (= 5 pints).

Gante, *n.m.* Ghent.

gante, *n.m.* linen manufactured in Ghent.

gantés, *n.m.f.*, *a.* from or relating to Ghent.

ganzúa, *n.f.* picklock, false key, skeleton key; burglar; (*coll.*) pumper, wheedler; (*slang*) executioner.

gañán, *n.m.* day-labourer; farm hand, teamster, rustic.

gañanía, *n.f.* gang of labourers; lodge for the same.

gañido, *n.m.* yelping or howling. — *p.p.* [GAÑIR].

gañiles, *n.m.pl.* cartilaginous larynx of animals; gills of the tunny-fish.

gañir, *v.i.* to yelp or howl; to croak, cackle, crow; (*coll.*) to talk hoarsely.

gañón, gañote, *n.m.* (*coll.*) throat; (*prov.*) kind of fritters.

gaón, *n.m.* substitute for the oar in Indian vessels.

garabatada, *n.f.* hooking.

garabatear, *v.t.* to hook, catch with a hook; to scribble, scrawl; (*coll.*) to beat about the bush.

garabateo *n.m.* hooking; scribbling, scrawling.

garabatillo, *n.m.* small hook.

garabato, *n.m.* pot-hook; grapple, grapnel, creeper, claw-bar, hand bale-hook; meathook or gambrel; muzzle; scribble, scrawl; (*Cub., Chi., PR.*) gallows, gibbet; winning ways in a woman; *mozo de garabato*, thief. — *pl.* **garabatos,** scrawling letters or characters; pot-hooks; (*fig.*) excessive or extravagant hand-gestures.

garabatoso, -sa, *a.* full of scrawls; elegant, charming, attractive.

garabito, *n.m.* market-stall, cover spread over a market-stall.

garaje, *n.m.* garage.

garama, *n.f.* (*Morocco*) tax; collective fines levied from a tribe; (*coll.*) presents, gifts.

garambaina, *n.f.* flamboyancy in dress or ornamentation; (*coll.*) ridiculous affectation or mannerism; (*coll.*) illegible scrawl.

garambullo, *n.m.* (*Mex.*) a cactaceous plant.

garandumba, *n.f.* (*Am.*) a lighter for carrying goods by river.

garante, *a.* responsible. — *n.m.f.* warranter, guarantor, surety; bondsman, bail.

garantía, *n.f.* warranty, guaranty, security, surety bond; endorsement, collateral; bail.

garantir, *v.t.* to guarantee.

garantizar, *v.t.* (*pret.* **garanticé**; *pres. subj.* **garantice**) to guarantee, warrant; to endorse, answer for, vouch for, secure.

garañón, *n.m.* stallion jackass; male breeding-camel; (*Chi., Mex.*) stallion horse.

garapacho, *n.m.* shell of a tortoise, crab, crawfish, etc.; (*Cub.*) meat cooked in the shell of crustaceans.

garapiña, *n.f.* congealed particles of any liquid; scalloped galloon or lace; (*Mex., Cub.*) pineapple juice.

garapiñado, -da, *a.* candied, sugar-coated; (*jewel.*) frosted; *almendras garapiñadas,* sugar-almonds, pralines.

garapiñar, *v.t.* to freeze, clot (syrup, cream, etc.); to candy.

garapiñera, *n.f.* ice-cream freezer, winecooler, refrigerator.

garapita, *n.f.* net for small fishes.

garapito, *n.m.* small insect, water-skipper.

garapullo, *n.m.* paper dart; shuttlecock.

garatura, *n.f.* (*tan.*) scraper.

garatusa, *n.f.* a card game; (*coll.*) caress, cajolery, act of endearment; (*fenc.*) composite attack.

garay, *n.m.* (*Philip.*) ancient sail-boat.

garba, *n.f.* (*prov.*) hairy bastard vetch; (*prov.*) sheaf, as of wheat.

garbanzal, *n.m.* ground sown with chick-peas.

garbanzo, *n.m.* gram, chick-pea.

garbanzuelo, *n.m.* small chick-pea; disease in horse's hock.

garbar, *v.t.* (*prov.*) to sheaf or sheave.

garbear, *v.t.* to sheaf (*prov.*); to rob, plunder, lay hold of. — *v.i.* to affect an air of dignity and grandeur.

garbeña, *n.f.* common heath.

garbera, *n.f.* (*prov.*) shock of sheaves.

garbías, *n.m.pl.* omelet of herbs, cheese and flour.

garbillador, -ra, *a.* sifter; riddler; garbler.

garbillar, *v.t.* to sift grain; (*min.*) to riddle; to garble.

garbillo, *n.m.* coarse sieve for grain; (*min.*) riddle; riddled ore.

garbín, *n.m.* coif made of net-work.

garbino, *n.m.* south-west wind.

garbo, *n.m.* gracefulness, gentility, elegant carriage, gentlemanly deportment, jauntiness; grace; (*fig.*) clever knack of doing things; (*fig.*) frankness, generosity, disinterestedness.

gárboli, *n.m.* (*Cub.*) game of hide-and-seek.

garbón, *n.m.* male partridge.

garbosamente, *adv.* nattily, generously, gallantly, nobly, liberally.

garboso, -sa, *a.* natty, spruce, genteel, graceful, comely, elegant, sprightly, gallant; generous, liberal, munificent.

garbullo, *n.m.* garboil, mêlée of children, multitude, crowd.

garcero, -ra, *a.* heron-hawk.

garceta, *n.f.* little egret; side locks of hair. — *pl.* **garcetas,** tenderlings, the first horns of a deer.

gardenia, *n.f.* gardenia.

gardingo, *n.m.* Visigoth official.

garduja, *n.f.* barren stone in quicksilver mines.

garduña, *n.f.* marten (*Mustela martes*).

garduño, -ña, *n.m.f.* (*coll.*) filcher, petty thief.

garete, *n.m.; (naut.) ir* or *irse al garete,* adrift.

garfa, *n.f.* claw of a beast or bird; hand (in contempt); ancient tax; *echar la garfa,* to claw or seize anything with the nails.

garfada, garfiada, *n.f.* clawing or seizing with the nails.

garfear, *v.i.* to hook, seize with a hook.

garfio, *n.m.* hook, drag-hook; gaff.

gargajeada, *n.f.;* **gargajeo,** *n.m.* ejecting phlegm.

gargajear, *v.i.* to expectorate.

gargajiento, -ta; gargajoso, -sa, *a.* continually expectorating.

gargajo, *n.m.* phlegm.

garganchón, *n.m.* windpipe, gullet.

garganta, *n.f.* throat, gullet; singing-voice; instep; gorge, canyon, ravine; shaft of a column or balustrade; sheath of a plough; (*mech.*) collar, neck, throat, gullet, waist, groove of a sheave; *tener buena garganta,* to be a good singer; *tener el agua a la garganta,* to be in imminent danger; *seca la garganta, ni gruñe ni canta,* you can do nothing with a dry throat.

gargantada, *n.f.* liquid or blood ejected violently from the throat.

gargantear, *v.i.* to quaver, warble; (*naut.*) to strap a dead-eye.

garganteo, *n.m.* quavering, warbling.

gargantil, *n.m.* cut in basins formerly used by barbers.

gargantilla, *n.f.* necklace worn by women; each of the beads of a necklace; (*Philip.*) water-jug.

gárgara, *n.f.* gargling.

gargarismo, *n.m.* gargle; gargling.

gargarizar, *v.i.* to gargle.

gárgaro, *n.m.* (*Cub., Ven.*) the game of hide-and-seek.

gargavero, *n.m.* [GARGÜERO]; pan-pipe.

gárgol, *a.* empty, addled (eggs). — *n.m.* groove, furrow, channel, mortise.

gárgola, *n.f.* gargoyle; linseed.

gargüero, garguero, *n.m.* gullet; windpipe.

garibaldina, *n.f.* garibaldi, loose blouse for women or children.

garifalte, *n.m.* gerfalcon.

gariofilea, *n.f.* common avens, herb-bennet.

garita, *n.f.* sentry-box; porter's lodge; water-closet, privy.

garitear, *v.i.* (*coll.*) to gamble.

garitero, *n.m.* master of a gaming-house; gamester, gambler; (*slang*) fence.

garito, *n.m.* gaming-house, gambling-den; profits of gaming.

garla, *n.f.* (*coll.*) talk, chatter.

garlador, -ra, *a.* (*coll.*) babbler, prattler.

garlante, *a.* (*coll.*) babbling, prattling.

garlar, *v.i.* (*coll.*) to babble, prattle, chatter.

garlito, *n.m.* fish-trap; snare, trap, gin; *caer en el garlito,* (*coll.*) to fall into a trap; *coger en el garlito,* to detect a person in wrong-doing.

garlocha, *n.f.* goad-stick, ox-goad.

garlopa, *n.f.* jack-plane, long-plane.

garma, *n.f.* (*prov.*) steep slope.

garnacha, *n.f.* judge's robe; variety of purple grape, and the wine made from it; company of strolling players.

garniel, *n.m.* muleteer's girdle; (*Ec., Mex.*) leather bag or case.

garoso, -sa, *a.* (*Col., Ven.*) greedy, gluttonous.

garra, *n.f.* claw of a wild beast, talon of a bird of prey, clutch, fang; (*mech.*) catch hook, claw, clutch, fang; (*fig.*) human hand; (*Arg., Mex.*) the four corners of a hide; (*Col., Arg., CR., Chi.*) hardened and wrinkled piece of rawhide; (*Col.*) leather bag; *echarle a uno la garra,* (*coll.*) to grasp, arrest, imprison anyone; *sacar de las garras de,* to free from; *caer en las garras de,* to fall into the clutches of.

garrafa, *n.f.* carafe, decanter.

garrafal, *a.* said of large and sweet cherries; (*fig.*) great, huge, vast.

garrafilla, *n.f.* small carafe, cooler for liquids.

garrafiñar, *v.t.* (*coll.*) to snatch away.

garrafón, *n.m.* large carafe; demijohn, carboy.

garrama, *n.f.* tax paid by Mohammedans; (*coll.*) fraud, robbery.

garramar, *v.t.* to rob, plunder, pillage.

garrancha, *n.f.* (*coll.*) sword; (*Col.*) hook; (*bot.*) spathe.

garrancho, *n.m.* branch broken off a tree, splinter.

garrapata, *n.f.* sheep-tick; (*mil.*) disabled horse; short person.

garrapatear, *v.i.* to scribble, scrawl.

garrapatero, *n.m.* (*Col., Ec., Ven.*) South American tick-bird.

garrapatilla, *n.f.* small tick.

garrapato, *n.m.* pot-hook, scrawl.

garrar, garrear, *v.i.* to drag; *el ancla garra,* the anchor drags.

garrasí, *n.m.* (*Ven.*) plainsman's breeches.

garridamente, *adv.* (*obs.*) gracefully, neatly.

garrideza, *n.f.* (*obs.*) elegance.

garrido, -da, *a.* handsome, neat, graceful.

garroba, *n.f.* carob-bean.

garrobal, *n.m.* plantation of carob-trees.

garrobilla, *n.f.* chips of carob-trees for tanning hides.

garrobo, *n.m.* (*CR., Hond.*) tropical lizard.

garrocha, *n.f.* alpenstock; goad-stick, javelin; spear used by bullfighters on horseback.

garrochada, *n.f.;* **garrochazo,** *n.m.* prick or blow with a goad-stick.

garrocheador, *n.m.* goader, pricker.

garrochear, *v.t.* to prick, to goad.

garrochón, *n.m.* spear or goad-stick used by bullfighters on horseback.

garrofa, *n.f.* carob-bean.

garrofal, *n.m.* plantation of carob-trees.

garrón, *n.m.* spur of birds; talon of a bird of prey; paw of a rabbit, etc.; *tener garrones,* (*coll.*) to be experienced, not easily deceived; *al garrón,* (*PR.*) disreputably dressed.

garrotal, *n.m.* plantation of olive-trees, made with cuttings.

garrotazo, *n.m.* blow with cudgel.

garrote, *n.m.* club, bludgeon, stick, truncheon, cudgel; tourniquet; (*naut.*) turning fid; garrotte (strangling, Spanish form of capital punishment); (*prov.*) hazel basket or pannier; *dar garrote,* to execute by strangling.

garrotear, *v.t.* (*Am.*) [APALEAR].

garrotillo, *n.m.* croup, diphtheria of the larynx.

garrotín, *n.m.* gipsy dance.

garrubia, *n.f.* carob-bean.

garrucha, *n.f.* pulley; *garrucha combinada,* sheave, block; *garrucha fija,* fast pulley; *garrucha movible,* movable pulley; *garrucha simple,* single pulley.

garrucho, *n.m.* (*naut.*) cringle, mast-hoop.

garruchuela, *n.f.* small pulley.

garrudo, -da, *a.* strong, brawny, sinewy.

garrulador, -ra, *n.m.f., a.* garrulous person; talkative, loquacious.

garrular, *v.i.* to babble, chatter.

garrulería, *n.f.* prattle, chatter.

garrulidad, *n.f.* garrulity.

gárrulo, -la, *a.* chirping as birds; chattering, prattling, garrulous.

garúa, *n.f.* (*Am.*) (*naut.*) drizzle.

garuar, *v.i.* (*Am.*) to drizzle.

garujo, *n.m.* concrete.

garulla, *n.f.* loose grapes; (*coll.*) rabble; little rogue, urchin.

garullada, *n.f.* gang of rogues.

garvín, *n.m.* net-headdress formerly worn by women.

garza, *n.f.* heron; *garza real,* purple heron.

garzo, -za, *a.* blue-eyed. — *n.m.* agaric, mushroom.

garzón, *n.m.* lad, boy; stripling; adjutant in the lifeguards; (*obs.*) wooer, lover.

garzonear, *v.t.* (*obs.*) to woo, court.

garzonía, *n.f.* (*obs.*) wooing, sowing wild oats.

garzota, *n.f.* night-heron; plumage, aigrette; crest of a helmet.

garzul, *n.m.* (*prov.*) species of wheat.

gas, *n.m.* gas; vapour, emanation, fume; *gas del alumbrado,* gaslight; *gas pobre,* producer gas.

gasa, *n.f.* gauze, muslin, very fine cloth.

gascón, -ona; gasconés, -esa, *a.* Gascon.

gasconada, *n.f.* gasconade, boast, bravado.

gaseiforme, *a.* gasiform, gaseous.

gaseosa, *n.f.* soda water.

gaseoso, -sa, *a.* gaseous.

gasífero, -ra, *a.* gas-conducting.

gasificable, *a.* convertible into gas.

gasificación, *n.f.* gasification.

gasificar, *v.t.* to gasify, convert into gas.

gasista, *n.m.* gas fitter.

gasógeno, *n.m.* gazogene; mixture of benzene and alcohol.

gasoleno, *n.m.;* **gasolina,** *n.f.* petrol.

gasolinera, *n.f.* boat with petrol engine.

gasometría, *n.f.* gasometry.

gasómetro, *n.m.* gasometer; gas-meter.

gasón, *n.m.* large clods of unbroken earth; sod.

gastable, *a.* that may be wasted or spent.

gastadero, *n.m.* (*coll.*) place where anything is wasted or spent; wasting, spending; waster, spender.

gastado, -da, *a.* worn-out, useless. — *p.p.* [GASTAR].

gastador, -ra, *a.* wasteful, lavish, extravagant. — *n.m.f.* spender, waster, spendthrift; prodigal; (*mil.*) pioneer, sapper; criminal sentenced to hard labour.

gastamiento, *n.m.* consumption of anything, wearing out.

gastar, *v.t.* to spend, expend, disburse, lay out money; to have or wear habitually; to waste, consume, use, fret, wear out; to own, disport, keep (as carriages, etc.); to digest; to plunder, pillage, sack; *gastarlas,* (*coll.*) to act, behave, conduct oneself. — *v.r.* to grow old or useless; to be wasted, consumed, worn out; to fray; *gastar coche,* to keep a carriage; *gastar bromas,* to crack jokes.

gasterópodo, -da, *a.* gasteropod.

gasto, *n.m.* expenditure, expense, outlay, disbursement, charge, consumption, cost; wear and tear, use, waste, consuming, spending. —*pl.* **gastos,** charges, disbursements; *gastos de oficina,* office expenses; *gastos de explotación,* working expenses.

gastoso, -sa, *a.* wasteful, lavish, extravagant.

gastricismo, *n.m.* generic denomination for several gastric conditions of the stomach.

gástrico, -ca, *a.* gastric.

gastronomía, *n.f.* gastronomy, epicurism.

gastronómico, -ca, *a.* gastronomic.

gastrónomo, -ma, *n.m.f.* epicure, gastronomer, judge of good eating.

gata, *n.f.* she-cat, puss; (*coll.*) a woman native of Madrid; (*bot.*) rest-harrow, cammock; (*mil.*) cat-castle; (*naut.*) cat-head; *gata del ancla*, (*naut.*) cat-tackle; *a gatas*, on all-fours.

gatada, *n.f.* cat-trick; wounding with claws, clawing; turn of a hare when closely pursued; (*coll.*) artful dodge, scurvy trick.

gatafura, *n.f.* cake of herbs and sour milk.

gatallón, *n.m.* (*coll.*) rogue, cheat, scamp.

gatatumba, *n.f.* (*coll.*) affected civility or submission; dissembling, pretence.

gatazo, *n.m.* large cat; (*coll.*) artful trick, cheat, deception, clumsy joke.

gateado, -da, *a.* feline, catlike. — *n.m.* American striped wood employed in rich furniture. — *p.p.* [GATEAR].

gateamiento, *n.m.* scratching; clambering; going on all-fours.

gatear, *v.i.* to climb up, clamber; to go upon all-fours. — *v.t.* (*coll.*) to scratch or claw; (*coll.*) to steal, rob.

gatera, *n.f.* cat's hole; (*bot.*) common catmint; (*Bol., Ec., Per.*) saleswoman, especially greengrocer.

gatería, *n.f.* number of cats together; (*coll.*) rabble, gang of roughs or ill-bred boys; cringing servility.

gatero, -ra, *a.* frequented by cats.

gatesco, -ca, *a.* (*coll.*) feline, catlike.

gatica, -illa, -ita, *n.f.* little she-cat, pussy.

gaticida, *n.m.* (*coll.*) cat-killer.

gatico, -ito, *n.m.* kitten, pussy.

gatillazo, *n.m.* noise made by a trigger at firing.

gatillo, *n.m.* pelican, dentist's forceps; trigger of a gun; nape of a bull or ox; (*arch.*) cramp-iron; (*coll.*) juvenile petty thief; (*Chi.*) horse's mane.

gato, *n.m.* cat, tom-cat; money-bag, money kept in a bag; (*coll.*) pickpocket, petty thief, filcher; shrewd fellow; (*artill.*) gun-searcher; (*mech.*) jack, lifting-jack, screw-jack; cramp-iron; (*coop.*) hopping tongs; (*coll.*) native of Madrid; (*Arg.*) popular dance and its music; (*Per.*) open market; *gato de algalia*, civet-cat; *gato cornaquí*, (*naut.*) jack-screw; *gato montés*, mountain cat; *dar* (or *vender*) *gato por liebre*, (*coll.*) to cheat, misrepresent; *ata el gato*, rich and miserly person; *el gato maullador, nunca buen cazador*, great talkers are little actors; *el gato escaldado, del agua fría ha miedo*, a burnt child dreads the fire; *buscar tres pies al gato*, to look for three feet on a cat, to expect an impossibility; *no hay para venderme el gato por la liebre*, there's no selling me a cat for a hare; *de noche todos los gatos son pardos*, by night all cats are grey; *gato con guantes no caza ratones*, a gloved cat is no mouser; *buscar el gato en el garbanzal*, to take much trouble over a difficult matter; *correr como gato por ascuas*, to go like a cat on hot bricks; *echarle a uno el gato a las barbas*, to insult, outrage a person; *hasta los gatos quieren zapatos*, everyone's claims are greater than his deserts; *llevar el gato al agua*, to accomplish a difficult task.

gatuna, gatuña, *n.f.* rest-harrow, cammock (*Ononis arvensis*).

gatunero, *n.m.* (*prov.*) seller of smuggled meat.

gatuno, -na, *a.* catlike, feline.

gatuperio, *n.m.* hotch-potch; (*coll.*) fraud, snare, intrigue.

gauchada, *n.f.* (*Am.*) artifice; action of a gaucho.

gauchaje, *n.m.* (*Arg., Chi.*) assembly of gauchos.

gaucho, -cha, *n.m.f.* herdsman or Indian of the pampas; (*Arg., Chi., Ur.*) skilled horseman; (*fig.*) rustic, rude man, man of the people.

gaudeamus, *n.m.* (*coll.*) feast, entertainment, merrymaking.

gavanza, *n.f.*, flower of the dog-rose.

gavanzo, *n.m.* dog-rose.

gavera, *n.f.* (*Col., Mex., Ven.*) tile or brick mould; (*Per.*) form or mould for mud wails; (*Col.*) wood mould for sugar.

gaveta, *n.f.*, drawer, till, locker.

gavetilla, *n.f.*, small desk drawer.

gavia, *n.f.* main-topsail; top (in galleys); ditch for draining or as a boundary; mad man's cage; (*orn.*) gull, sea-gull; (*min.*) gang of basket passers. — *pl.* **gavias**, topsail of the main- and fore-mast.

gaviero, *n.m.* top-man, mast-man.

gavieta, *n.f.* scuttle; bowsprit bee.

gaviete, *n.m.* davit in a long-boat.

gavilán *n.m.* sparrow-hawk; fine hair-stroke in penmanship; either side of the nib of a pen; (*naut.*) iron hook; (*arm.*) quillon of a sword; brad or pin of a goad-stick; (*Cent. Am., Cub., Chi., Mex., PR.*) ingrowing nail, especially on the big toe. — *pl.* **gavilanes**, tholes; thistle flowers.

gavilancillo, *n.m.* young hawk; incurvated point of an artichoke leaf.

gavilla, *n.f.* sheaf of grain; bundle of vine-shoots; (*fig.*) gang of suspicious persons.

gavillero, *n.m.* place where sheaves are collected.

gavina, *n.f.* sea-gull.

gavión, *n.m.* (*mil.*) gabion; (*coll.*) large hat.

gaviota, *n.f.* gull, sea-gull.

gavitel, *n.m.* small buoy.

gavota, *n.f.* gavotte.

gaya, *n.f.* stripe on material; badge given to victors in Olympic games; magpie; (*slang*) harlot.

gayado, -da, *a.* motley, striped. — *p.p.* [GAYAR].

gayadura, *n.f.* garniture, trimming of various colours.

gayar, *v.t.* to trim with ribbons of various colours.

gayata, *n.f.* (*prov.*) crook, sheep-hook.

gayo, *n.m.* (*orn.*) jay.

gayo, -ya, *a.* gay, festive, merry; showy; *gaya ciencia* (or *doctrina*) poesy, minstrelsy.

gayola, *n.f.* (*naut.*) cage; (*coll.*) jail; (*prov.*) hut in vineyards.

gayomba, *n.f.* white single-seed broom (*Spartium monospermum*).

gayuba, *n.f.* red-berried arbutus.

gayubal, *n.m.* place where *gayubas* abound.

gaza, *n.f.* loop of a bow; (*naut.*) strap. loop, collar, noose, splice, stay.

gazafatón, gazapatón, *n.m.* nonsense, foolish talk, balderdash.

gazapa, *n.f.* (*coll.*) lie, fib, falsehood.

gazapela, *n.f.* clamorous wrangling.

gazapera, *n.f.* rabbit-warren; (*coll.*) wrangle, quarrel; (*coll.*) unlawful hiding-place or den.

gazapico, -illo, -ito, *n.m.* small rabbit, bunny.

gazapina, *n.f.* (*coll.*) assembly of ruffians; wrangling, quarrelling, disorder, confusion.

gazapo, *n.m.* cony, young rabbit; (*coll.*) great lie, dissembling villain; (*coll.*) blunder, mistake.

gazapón, *n.m.* gaming-house, gambling-den.

gazmiar, *v.t.* to steal and eat tit-bits. — *v.r.* (*coll.*) to complain, resent.

gazmoñada, gazmoñería, *n.f.* hypocrisy, prudery, false devoutness.

gazmoñero, -ra; gazmoño, -na, *a.* prude, priggish, dissembling, hypocritical.

gaznápiro, -ra, *n.m.f.,* *a.* churlish, simpleton, booby.

gaznar, *v.i.* to croak, caw, cackle.

gaznatada, *n.f.* violent blow on the windpipe; (*Mex., Hond., PR., Ven.*) cuff.

gaznate, *n.m.* throat, windpipe, gorge; kind of fritters; (*Mex.*) sweet made of pineapple and coconut; *a gaznate tendido* (or *a todo gaznate*), at the top of one's lungs.

gaznatón, *n.m.* blow on the throat; pancake, fritter.

gazofia, *n.f.* offal, refuse.

gazpachero, *n.m.* (*prov.*) maker of *gazpacho*; one who carries dinner to workmen.

gazpacho, *n.m.* Andalusian dish made of bread, oil, vinegar, onions and garlic; crumbs of bread fried in a pan.

gazuza, *n.f.* (*coll.*) keen appetite, violent hunger.

ge, *n.f.* Spanish name of the letter G.

geato, *n.m.* (*chem.*) geate, humate.

gecónidos, *n.m.pl.* family of saurian reptiles (stellion, star-lizard).

geico, -ca, *a.* (*chem.*) geic, humic.

gelatina, *n.f.* gelatine.

gelatinoso, -sa, *a.* gelatinous, glutinous.

gelatinudo, -da, *a.* (*Am.*) gelatinous; phlegmatic, lazy, indolent.

gelfe, *n.m.* individual of a tribe of Senegal.

gélido, -da, *a.* (*poet.*) gelid, frigid.

gema, *n.f.* gem; (*bot.*) bud; (*carp.*) slab, flitch; *sal gema,* rock-salt.

gemación, *n.f.* (*bot., zool.*) gemmation.

gemebundo, -da, *a.* groaning, moaning, howling.

gemela, *n.f.* Arabian jasmine.

gemelo, -la, *n.m.f.* twin. — *n.m.pl.* **gemelos,** binoculars; opera glass, field or marine glass; sleeve-buttons, pair of studs; (*astron.*) Gemini.

gemido, *n.m.* groan, lamentation, moan; howl. — *p.p.* [GEMIR].

gemidor, -ra, *a.* groaning, moaning, wailing.

geminación, *n.f.* rhetorical form of speech in which a word is repeated.

geminar, *v.t.* (*obs.*) to repeat, duplicate.

géminis, *n.m.* (*astron.*) Gemini; (*pharm.*) kind of plaster.

gemíparo, -ra, *a.* reproducing by the development of gemmæ.

gemiquear, *v.i.* (*prov., Chi.*) to whine.

gemir, *v.i.* (*pres. indic.* **gimo**; *pres. subj.* **gima**; *pret.* **gemí, gemiste, gimió**) to groan, grieve, moan; to grunt; to howl; to roar, whistle (of sea or wind).

genciana, *n.f.* gentian.

gencianáceo, -cea; gencianeo, -nea, *a.* gentianaceous.

gendarme, *n.m.* gendarme.

gendarmería, *n.f.* gendarmerie, police force.

genealogía, *n.f.* genealogy, lineage.

genealógico, -ca, *a.* genealogical.

genealogista, *n.m.* genealogist.

genearca, *n.m.* (*obs.*) head or chief of a family or race.

geneático, -ca, *a.* genethliacal.

geneo, *n.m.* Peruvian banana.

generable, *a.* generable, that may be begotten or produced.

generación, *n.f.* generation; race, progeny, offspring; age; succession, lineage.

generador, -ra, *a.* generator; generating. — *n.m.* (*mech., elec.*) generator. — *n.f.* (*math.*) generatrix. — *n.m.pl.* **generadores,** genital organs.

general, *a.* general; customary, common, prevalent, usual; *en general, por lo general,* generally, in general. — *n.m.* general (officer); superior of a religious order; lecture-hall of a university; (*prov.*) customhouse.

generala, *n.f.* the general (a roll of the drum); wife of a general; (*naut.*) signal to join convoy.

generalato, *n.m.* generalship.

generalero, *n.m.* (*prov.*) customs-house officer.

generalidad, *n.f.* generality, great majority; (*prov.*) community, corporation; *La Generalidad,* the autonomous government of Catalonia. — *pl.* **generalidades,** (*prov.*) customs duties; generalities, general principles, lack of precision, vagueness.

generalísimo, *n.m.* generalissimo, commander-in-chief.

generalización, *n.f.* generalization.

generalizar, *v.t.* (*pret.* **generalicé**; *pres. subj.* **generalice**) to become general, usual, or popular. — *v.r.* to be divulged, spread.

generalmente, *adv.* generally.

generante, *a.* (*obs.*) generating, engendering.

generar, *v.t.* to generate, produce.

generativo, -va, *a.* generative.

generatriz, *n.f.,* *a.* (*geom.*) generatrix.

genéricamente, *adv.* generically.

genérico, -ca, *a.* generic.

género, *n.m.* genus; class, species; way, manner, kind, sort, style or mode of doing anything; (*gram.*) gender; cloth, stuff, material, goods. — *pl.* **generos,** goods, merchandise, wares, produce, commodities; (*art*) *de género,* genre; *género humano,* human nature, mankind.

generosamente, *adv.* generously.

generosidad, *n.f.* hereditary nobility; generosity, unselfishness, magnanimity; liberality, frankness, munificence; valour, fortitude.

generoso, -sa, *a.* noble, generous, magnanimous, honourable, free-hearted, unselfish, frank, liberal, munificent, open-handed; excellent, fine, choice (of wines); vigorous.

génesis, *n.m.* Book of Genesis. — *n.f.* origin, beginning, cause.

genetlíaca, *n.f.* genethliacs, astrology.

genetlíaco, -ca, *a.* genethliacal.

gengibre, *n.m.* ginger [JENGIBRE].

genial, *a.* genial, pleasant, cheerful; in character, individual; of genius; *días geniales,* festivals.

genialidad, *n.f.* disposition of a person produced by his natural temper.

genialmente, *adv.* genially.

geniazo, *n.m.* strong temper.

geniculado, -da, *a.* geniculate, bent like a knee.

genio, *n.m.* genius; creative intellect; humour, inclination, temper, disposition, peculiar character, nature; representative type, embodiment; genie, spirit; *genio del mal,* evil spirit; *mal genio,* bad or ill temper; *corto de genio,* diffident; *genio y figura, hasta la sepultura,* what's bred in the bone will come out in the flesh.

genipa, *n.f.* wormwood.

genista, *n.f.* genista.

genital, *a.* genital.

genitales, *n.m.pl.* genitals.

genitivo, -va, *a.* generative. — *n.m.* genitive or possessive case.

genitura, *n.f.* (*obs.*) generation, procreation; horoscope; (*obs.*) seed, generating matter.

genízaro, -ra, *a.* (modern spelling **jenízaro**) composed of different species; (*Mex.*) half-breed. — *n.m.* janizary.

genol, *n.m.* (*naut.*) futtock.

genolí, *n.m.* yellow paste made of sandarach, used by painters.

Génova, *n.f.* Genoa.

genovés, -sa, *n.m.f., a.* Genoese.

gentalla (*obs.*), **gentualla,** *n.f.* rabble, mob.

gente, *n.f.* people, folk, crowd, number of persons, army, troops; gang; retinue; clan, race, genus, nation; (*coll.*) a family; (*Col., Chi., PR.*) the best people; crew of a ship; *gente baja* (or *del gordillo*), rabble, mob; *gente de bien* (or *de buen proceder*), honest people; *gente común* (or *vulgar*), common folk; *gente del bronce,* merry set of people; *gente menuda,* children; *gente de trato,* tradesmen, dealers; *de gente en gente,* from one to another, from generation to generation; *gente de pelo* (or *de pelusa*), people of property; *gente fina,* refined (or well-educated) persons; *gente principal,* the nobility or gentry; *gente de paz,* friend, friends (reply to a sentry); *gente de modo* (or *de traza*), well-behaved people; *gente de la vida airada* (or *del hampa*), debauched set of people; *gente de la cuchilla,* butchers; *gente de la garra,* thieves; *gente de capa parda,* villagers, rustics, country-people; *gente de razón,* educated people, white men (as contrasted with American Indians); *ahogarse de gente,* to be suffocated by the crowd; *ande yo caliente y ríase la gente,* comfort is preferable to fine appearances; *gente loca, coméis de mi rabo y no de mi boca,* proverb condemning those who judge ill of others in their absence.

gentecilla, *n.f.* (*contempt.*) mob, rabble.

gentil, *a.* genteel, elegant, graceful, handsome; excellent, exquisite; *gentil necedad,* a pretty piece of foolishness. — *n.m.* gentile, pagan, heathen.

gentileza, *n.f.* gentility, gracefulness, elegance, refinement, exquisiteness; sprightliness, easiness; nattiness; ostentation, pageantry; politeness, civility, courtesy, genteelness; naturalness, grace.

gentilhombre, *n.m.* a fine fellow; my good man; gentleman, the servant who waits about the person of a man of rank; person sent to the king with important dispatches; *gentilhombre de cámara,* lord of the bedchamber; *gentilhombre de manga,* nobleman who attends the princes of Spain when they are children; *gentilhombre de placer,* (*coll.*) buffoon.

gentilicio, -cia, *a.* gentilitious, peculiar to a nation, national, tribal; hereditary; *adjetivo gentilicio,* (*gram.*) adjective denoting nationality.

gentílico, -ca, *a.* heathen, gentile, pagan, heathenish, Hellenic.

gentilidad, *n.f.* gentilism, heathenism, paganism; body of heathens or gentiles.

gentilismo, *n.m.* gentilism, heathenism, paganism.

gentilizar, *v.i.* to gentilize, observe the rites of gentiles or heathens. — *v.t.* to make gentile, paganize.

gentilmente, *adv.* gently, genteelly; heathenishly.

gentío, *n.m.* crowd, multitude.

gentualla, gentuza, *n.f.* rabble, mob; people of no account.

genués, *a.* (*obs.*) Genoese.

genuflexión, *n.f.* genuflexion, bending of the knee.

genuino, -na, *a.* genuine, pure, real, legitimate, natural, good.

geocéntrico, *a.* geocentric.

geoda, *n.f.* geode.

geodesia, *n.f.* geodesy.

geodésico, -ca, *a.* geodesic, geodetic.

geodesta, *n.m.* geodesist; professor of geodesy.

geófago, -ga, *n.m.f., a.* geophagous, earth-eating.

geofísica, *n.f.* geophysics.

geogenia, *n.f.* geogeny.

geogénico, -ca, *a.* geogenic.

geognosia, *n.f.* geognosy.

geognosta, *n.m.* geognost, geologist.

geognóstico, -ca, *a.* geognostic.

geogonía, *n.f.* geogeny.

geogónico, -ca, *a.* geogenic.

geografía, *n.f.* geography.

geográficamente, *adv.* geographically.

geográfico, -ca, *a.* geographical.

geógrafo, *n.m.f.* geographer.

geoide, *n.m.* theoretical form of the earth according to geodesy.

geología, *n.f.* geology.

geológico, -ca, *a.* geological.

geólogo, *n.m.* geologist.

geomancia, *n.f.* geomancy.

geomántico, -ca, *a.* geomantic.

geómetra, *n.m.* geometer, geometrician.

geometral, *a.* geometrical, geometric.

geometría, *n.f.* geometry; *geometría del espacio,* solid geometry.

geométricamente, *adv.* geometrically.

geométrico, -ca, *a.* geometrical, geometric.

geomorfía, *n.f.* geomorphy.

geonomía, *n.f.* geonomy.

geonómico, -ca, *a.* geonomic.

geoponía, geopónica, *n.f.* geoponics, agriculture; gardening.

geopónico, -ca, *a.* geoponic, agricultural.

geórgica, *n.f.* georgic, poem upon husbandry.

geranáceo, -cea; geranico, -ca, *a.* geraniaceous.

geranio, *n.m.* (*bot.*) crane's bill; geranium.

gerbo, *n.m.* jerboa (modern spelling **jerbo**).

gerencia, *n.f.* (*com.*) managership, management.

gerente, *n.m.* (*com.*) manager.
gericaya, *n.f.* (*Mex.*) custard.
gerifalco, gerifalte, *n.m.* (*orn.*) gerfalcon.
germanesco, -ca, *a.* belonging to the jargon of thieves.
germanía, *n.f.* jargon or cant of thieves, etc.; slang; concubinage; faction in Valencia during the days of Charles V.
germánico, -ca, *a.* Germanic, German; of Germany.
germanio, *n.m.* (*chem.*) germanium.
germanismo, *n.m.* germanism, a German idiom employed in another language.
germano, -na, *a.* Germanic, German; of Germany; (*obs.*) pure, genuine.
germen, *n.m.* germ, bud, shoot, sprout, first bud, gem; source, spring, origin; (*bot.*) germen.
germinación, *n.f.* germination.
germinal, *n.m., a.* germinal; Germinal, the seventh month of the French republican year.
germinar, *v.i.* to germinate, bud.
germinativo, -va, *a.* germinative.
gerundense, *a.* of or belonging to Gerona.
gerundiada, *n.f.* (*coll.*) bombastic, pompous, and unmeaning expression.
gerundiano, -na, *a.* (*coll.*) pompous, high sounding, empty (style or phrase).
gerundio, *n.m.* gerund, verbal noun; (*coll.*) pompous and bombastic preacher or lecturer, gerund-grinder.
gesolreút, *n.m.* mixolydian mode (in plainchant).
gesta, *n.f.pl.* **gestas,** actions, feats, achievements.
gestación, *n.f.* (*med.*) gestation; exercise among the Romans for the health.
gestatorio, -ria, *a.* gestatory, portable; *silla gestatoria,* papal chair.
gestear, *v.i.* to gesticulate, make grimaces, play tricks, grin.
gestero, -ra, *a.* gesticulator.
gesticulación, *n.f.* gesticulation, grimacing.
gesticular, *v.i.* to gesticulate, make grimaces. — *a.* gesticulatory, relating to facial expressions.
gestión, *n.f.* conduct, exertion, effort, action, measure, step; negotiation, agency, management.
gestionar, *v.t.* to procure, deal, promote, manage, negotiate; to take steps, to attain or carry out.
gesto, *n.m.* face, visage; aspect, appearance; gesture, grimace, likeness, resemblance. — *pl.* **gestos,** (*obs.*) feats, deeds; *estar de buen gesto,* to be in good humour; *hacer gestos,* to ogle, make wry faces or grimaces, to gesticulate; *ponerse a gesto,* (*obs.*) to set oneself off for the purpose of pleasing; *poner gesto,* to show annoyance or anger in one's face.
gestor, *n.m.* (*com.*) superintendent, manager, agent, proxy, promoter, representative, attorney.
gestudo, -da, *a.* (*coll.*) ill-humoured, cross.
giba, *n.f.* hump, crooked back, hunch, gibbosity; (*coll.*) nuisance, annoyance; importunity.
gibado, -da, *a.* crooked, humpbacked. — *p.p.* [GIBAR].
gibar, *v.t.* (*coll.*) to molest, annoy, vex.
gibelino, -na, *a.* Ghibelline.
gibosidad, *n.f.* hump, gibbosity.

giboso, -sa, *a.* gibbous, crook-backed, humpbacked.
gibraltareño, -ña, *a.* of or belonging to Gibraltar [JIBRALTAREÑO; JIBRALTAR].
gícama, *n.f.* (*Mex.*) an edible root.
giga, *n.f.* (*mus.*) jig.
giganta, *n.f.* giantess; (*bot.*) sunflower, acanthus.
gigantazo, -za, *n.m.f.* huge giant.
gigante, *a.* gigantic, huge. — *n.m.* giant; one superior in courage, talents or virtues.
gigantea, *n.f.* (*bot.*) sunflower.
giganteo, -tea; gigantesco, -ca, *a.* gigantic, giantlike; surpassing, excelling.
gigantez, *n.f.* gigantism, tallness.
gigantilla, *n.f.* large-headed figure.
gigantismo, *n.m.* (*med.*) gigantism.
gigantón, -ona, *n.m.f.* enormous giant. — *n.m.pl.* **gigantones,** gigantic figures of pasteboard; *echar a alguno los gigantones,* (*coll.*) to make unwittingly a wounding remark.
gigote, *n.m.* dish of minced meat steeped in lard; (*fig.*) *hacer gigote,* to cut into very small pieces.
gijonense; gijonés, -esa, *a.* of or belonging to Gijón.
gil, *n.m.* individual of a factious band formed in the fifteenth century in Santander.
gilvo, -va, *a.* honey-coloured or pinky.
gimelga, *n.f.* (*naut.*) fish, paunch.
gimnasia, *n.f.* gymnastics.
gimnasio, *n.m.* gymnasium; school, academy.
gimnasta, *n.m.f.* gymnast, athlete.
gimnástica, *n.f.* gymnastics.
gimnástico, -ca; gímnico, -ca, *a.* gymnastic, gymnastical.
gimnosofista, *n.m.* gymnosophist; Indian philosopher.
gimnoto, *n.m.* (*zool.*) gymnotus.
gimo; gima; él gimió, *pres. indic.; pres. subj.; pret.* [GEMIR].
gimotear, *v.i.* (*contempt.*) to be always crying or moaning.
gimoteo, *n.n.* frequent crying or moaning; whining.
ginandra, *a.* (*bot.*) gynandrian, gynandrous.
Ginebra, *n.f.* Geneva.
ginebra, *n.f.* Moorish rattle; gin (liquor); bedlam; disorder, confusion; game at cards.
ginebrada, *n.f.* sort of puff-paste tart.
ginebrés, -esa; ginebrino, -na, *a.* Genevan, relating to Geneva.
gineceo, *n.m.* gynæceum.
ginecocracia, *n.f.* gynæcocracy; gynarchy.
ginecología, *n.f.* gynæcology.
ginesta, *n.f.* genista.
gineta, *n.f.* genet, a kind of weasel.
gingidio, *n.m.* wild spinach.
gingival, *a.* pertaining to the gums.
gingivitis, *n.f.* inflammation of the gums.
gira, *n.f.* picnic, outing; outdoor banquet among friends, public rejoicing; *a la gira,* a way of mooring ships.
girada, *n.f.* gyration, pirouette.
girado, *n.m.* (*com.*) drawee.
girador, girante, *n.m.* (*com.*) drawer.
giralda, *n.f.* vane or weather-cock in the form of a statue; vane of this name on the spire of Seville cathedral tower; name of this tower.
giraldete, *n.m.* rochet, surplice without sleeves.

giraldilla, *n.f.* small vane or weather-cock; popular dance in Asturias.

girándula, *n.f.* girandole.

girar, *v.i.* to revolve, rotate, gyrate, wheel round; (*mech.*) turn round, spin, turn, wheel; (*com.*) to draw (bills, cheques, etc.); *girar contra* (or *a cargo de*), to draw on.

girasol, *n.m.* sunflower, helianthus.

giratorio, -ria, *a.* revolving, rotary, rotatory, gyrating, turning.

girel, *n.m.* caparison, horse's trappings

girifalte, *n.m.* gerfalcon.

girino, *n.m.* whirligig beetle; (*obs.*) embryo of a frog.

giro, *n.m.* gyre, gyration, circumgyration, turn, revolution, rotation, course or turn of affairs; trend, bias; tendency, bend; bravado; menace; turn of a sentence; (*com.*) exchange, draft, circulation, bulk of business; speciality or line of business; *tomar otro giro*, to take another shape, to change one's mind; *giro regular de los negocios,* (*coll.*) fair run of business; *giro postal,* postal order.

giro, -ra, *n.m.f.* (*Arg., Chi.*) black and white cock.

girola, *n.f.* nave which encompasses the presbytery in Roman and Gothic architecture.

girómetro, *n.m.* revolution counter.

girondino, -na, *n.m.f.* Girondist, Girondin.

giróvago, -ga, *a.* vagabond. — *n.m.f.* wandering monk or nun.

gis, *n.m.* crayon.

gitanada, *n.f.* mean, contemptible trick; wheedling, blandishment, caress, flattery.

gitanamente, *adv.* in a sly, winning manner.

gitanear, *v.i.* to flatter, wheedle, cajole, caress, entice with soft words.

gitanería, *n.f.* wheedling, flattery, cajolery

gitanesco, -ca, *a.* gipsy-like, gipsy.

gitanillo, -lla, *n.m.f.* little gipsy.

gitanismo, *n.m.* gipsyism, gipsy life.

gitano, -na, *a.* gipsy-like; gipsy; artful, sly, hoydenish, honey-mouthed. — *n.m.f.* gipsy.

glabro, -bra, *a.* bald; beardless.

glacial, *a.* glacial; frosty; freezing.

glacialmente, *adv.* glacially.

glaciar, *n.m.* glacier.

glacis, *n.m.* (*fort.*) glacis.

gladiador, gladiator, *n.m.* gladiator.

gladiatorio, -ria, *a.* gladiatorial, gladiatory.

gladio, gladíolo, *n.m.* gladiolus.

glande, *n.m.* glans penis.

glandífero, -ra; glandígero, -ra, *a.* (*poet., bot.*) glandiferous.

glándula, *n.f.* (*anat., bot.*) gland; *glándula pineal,* pineal body; *glándula pituitaria,* pituitary gland.

glandular, *a.* glandular.

glandulilla, *n.f.* glandule, small gland.

glanduloso, -sa, *a.* glandulous, glandular.

glasé, *n.m.* glacé, glacé silk.

glaseado, -da, *a.* glossy, glacé-like, embroidered, variegated.

glasear, *v.t.* to calender (paper).

glasto, *n.m.* woad, dyer's woad.

glauberita, *n.f.* glauberite.

glaucio, *n.m.* celandine.

glauco, -ca, *a.* (*bot.*) sea-green, pale bluish green. — *n.m.* (*zool.*) glaucus.

glaucoma, *n.m.* glaucoma.

gleba, *n.f.* lump or clod turned up by the plough; glebe, fief, heritage.

gleboso, -sa, *a.* (*prov.*) glebous, turfy.

glera, *n.f.* gravel pit; place full of gravel and pebbles.

glicerina, *n.f.* glycerine.

gliconio, *n.m.* kind of Latin verse.

glíptica, *n.f.* glyptics, stone engraving.

gliptografía, *n.f.* glyptography.

global, *a.* global.

globiforme, *a.* globe-shaped, spherical.

globo, *n.m.* globe, sphere, ball, orb; the earth; globular lamp-shade; *globo celeste,* celestial globe; *globo aerostático,* aerostat, balloon; *en globo,* in a nutshell, summarily, without details; (*com.*) in bulk, in the lump; *globo terrestre* (or *terráqueo*), terrestrial globe; *globo de fuego,* shooting-star, meteor; *globo cautivo,* observation balloon; *globo dirigible,* dirigible, airship.

globoso, -sa, *a.* globose, spherical, globy.

globular, *a.* globular, global, globate, spherical.

globulariáceo, -cea, *a.* globularia.

glóbulo, *n.m.* globulet, little globule; homœopathic pill.

globuloso, -sa, *a.* globular.

glomerula, *n.f.* glomerule, flower-cluster.

gloria, *n.f.* paradise; the divine presence or its manifestations; the felicity of heaven; glory, fame, honour, renown; majesty, splendour, magnificence, brilliance; heavenly state, bliss, blessedness, exaltation, beatitude, boast, pride, illustriousness; gossamer, transparent gauze, tissue; kind of cream tart or pie; (*art*) opening in the sky representing angels, splendours, etc. — *n.m.* (*eccles.*) gloria, doxology; (*theat.*) curtain calls; *con las glorias se olvidan las memorias,* those who succeed are apt to forget friends and favours; *estar en la gloria,* to be very happy; *estar en sus glorias,* to be in one's element; *gloria vana, florece y no grana,* the world's glory is soon over.

gloriarse, *v.r.* to glory, boast in, be proud of, take a delight in.

glorieta, *n.f.* summer-house, bower, arbour; circle or square at intersection of streets.

glorificación, *n.f.* glorification, giving glory; praise.

glorificador, -ra, *a.* glorifier. — *n.m.* God.

glorificante, *n.m.f., a.* glorifying; glorifier.

glorificar, *v.t.* (*pret.* **glorifiqué;** *pres. subj.* **glorifique**) to glorify, worship, adore; to praise, extol, honour, laud, to exalt. — *v.r.* to glory, boast in, be proud of, take a delight in anything.

gloriosamente, *adv.* gloriously.

glorioso, -sa, *a.* glorious, excellent, illustrious, exalted, celebrated, honourable; enjoying the bliss of heaven, blessed; boastful, ostentatious, proud.

glosa, *n.f.* gloss, scholium; comment, commentary; marginal or footnote; (*com., law*) explanatory annotation in accounts; (*poet.*) kind of rondel; (*mus.*) variation of a theme.

glosador, -ra, *n.m.f.* commentator, glosser, glossist; (*com.*) auditor.

glosar, *v.t.* to gloss, annotate, interpret, explain by comments; (*poet.*) to compose *glosas*; (*com.*) to audit accounts; (*mus.*) to vary a theme; (*fig.*) to interpret or construe with a sinister intention, a word, act, or proposition.

glosario, *n.m.* glossary; special lexicon.
glose, *n.m.* glossing, commentating.
glosilla, *n.f.* short gloss, comment, or note; (*print.*) minion type (7-point).
glositis, *n.f.* (*med.*) glossitis.
glosopeda, *n.f.* foot-and-mouth disease.
glótico, -ca, *a.* (*zool.*) glottic, relating to the glottis.
glotis, *n.f.* (*anat.*) glottis.
glotón, -ona, *a.* gluttonous. — *n.m.f.* glutton, gormandizer.
glotonamente, *adv.* gluttonously.
glotonazo, -za, *n.m.f.* great glutton, voracious eater, gormandizer.
glotoncillo, -illa, *n.m.f.* little glutton.
glotonear, *v.i.* to act the glutton, devour food, over-indulge, gormandize.
glotonería, (*obs.*) **glotonía,** *n.f.* gluttony.
gloxínea, *n.f.* (*Col.*) gloxinia.
glucina, *n.f.* (*chem.*) glucina.
glucinio, *n.m.* (*chem.*) glucinum, beryllium.
glucómetro, *n.m.* (*chem.*) glucometer, hydrometer for determining the quantity of sugar in a liquid.
glucosa, *n.f.* glucose.
glucósido, *n.m.* (*chem.*) glucoside.
glucosuria, *n.f.* diabetes.
gluma, *n.f.* (*bot.*) glume.
gluten, *n.m.* gluten; gliadin, glutin; glue.
glúteo, -tea, *a.* gluteal.
glutinosidad, *n.f.* glutin, viscosity.
glutinoso, -sa, *a.* glutinous, viscous, mucous.
gneis, *n.m.* gneiss.
gnetáceo, -cea, *a.* (*bot.*) gnetaceous.
gnómico, -ca, *a.* gnomic, sententious.
gnomo, *n.m.* gnome, dwarf.
gnomon, *n.m.* gnomon, azimuth dial; *gnomon movible,* bevel square.
gnomónica, *n.f.* gnomonics.
gnomónico, -ca, *a.* gnomonic, gnomonical.
gnosticismo, *n.m.* gnosticism.
gnóstico, *n.m.,* *a.* gnostic.
goa, *n.f.* pig-iron bloom.
gobernación, *n.f.* government; *Ministerio de la Gobernación,* Home Office.
gobernador, -ra, *a.* governing. — *n.m.* governor, master, ruler. — *n.f.* governor's wife; female ruler.
gobernadorcillo, *n.m.* (*Philip.*) justice of the peace.
gobernalle, *n.m.* rudder, helm.
gobernante, *n.m.f.,* *a.* governing; (*coll.*) person assuming the management of a thing.
gobernar, *v.t.* (*pres. indic.* **gobierno;** *pres. subj.* **gobierne**) to govern, rule; to lead, head, command, control, regulate, manage; (*naut.*) to steer, helm, bear, head; to direct, guide. — *v.i.* to obey the helm (the ship).
gobernativo, -va, *a.* administrative, relating to government.
gobernoso, -sa, *a.* (*coll.*) methodical, systematic, loving good order.
gobierna, *n.f.* weather-vane.
gobierno, *n.m.* government, public administration, executive power; ministers composing a cabinet; district or province under a governor; office, dignity, and term of a governor; guidance, control, conduct, direction, management; (*naut.*) helm, rudder, steering, conning; *para su gobierno,* for your guidance; *mujer de gobierno,* housekeeper;

sirva de gobierno, let this be a warning; *gobierno de casa,* household.
gobierno; gobierne, *pres. indic.; pres. subj.* [GOBERNAR].
gobio, *n.m.* (*ichth.*) gudgeon.
goce, *n.m.* enjoyment, fruition; possession.
gocete, *n.m.* armpit guards in ancient armour.
gociano, -na, *n.m.f.,* *a.* a native of Gotland (Sweden).
gocha, *n.f.* (*coll.*) sow.
gocho, *n.m.* (*coll.*) pig, hog.
godeño, -ña, *a.* (*slang*) rich, renowned.
godesco, -ca; godible, *a.* joyful, cheerful.
godo, -da, *n.m.f.,* *a.* Gothic; Goth; (*Arg., Chi.*) (*contempt.*) Spaniard; (*Col.*) conservative.
gofio, *n.m.* (*Arg., Bol., Cub., Ec., PR.*) roasted maize; (*Ven.*) sweet made of yucca, pineapple and ginger.
gofo, -fa, *a.* stupid, ignorant, rude; (*art*) dwarf figure.
gofrador, *n.m.* leaf-marker, florist's tool; one who uses this tool.
gofrar, *v.t.* to goffer.
gol, *n.m.* (*sport*) goal.
gola, *n.f.* gullet, throat, œsophagus; (*mil.*) gorget, crescent-shaped insignia of duty; gorget in ancient armour; (*fort.*) gorge; (*arch.*) gula, gorge, cyma, cymatium, ogee moulding.
goldre, *n.m.* quiver for shafts and arrows.
goleta, *n.f.* schooner.
golf, *n.m.* golf.
golfán, *n.m.* water-lily.
golfín, *n.m.* dolphin; member of a band of thieves.
golfo, *n.m.* gulf; sea, main; (*poet.*) gulf, abyss; faro, a game of cards; ragamuffin, tramp.
goliardesco, -ca, *a.* goliardic.
goliardo, -da, *a.* immoderate, exceeding proper bounds (eating, drinking, passions, etc.).
golilla, *n.f.* (*sew.*) gorget, ruff; collar worn by some magistrates in Spain; (*build.*) jointpipe; (*mech.*) rim of a pipe. — *n.m.* (*coll.*) magistrate wearing a *golilla;* (*Bol.*) gaucho's scarf; (*Chi.*) hub washer; *ajustar a uno la golilla,* (*coll.*) to make someone do his duty; (*fig.*) to execute a criminal; *levantar la golilla,* to become passionate; *bajar la golilla,* to be pacified.
golillero, -ra, *n.m.f.* collar-maker.
golmajo, -ja, *n.m.f.* (*prov.*) gormandizer.
golondrina, *n.f.* swallow; flying gurnard; swallowfish; (*prov.*) small passenger boat; (*CR., Hond.*) herb of the Euphorbiaceæ family; (*Chi.*) pantechnicon; *golondrina de mar,* tern; *una golondrina no hace verano,* one swallow does not make a summer.
golondrinera, *n.f.* swallow-wort, celandine.
golondrino, *n.m.* male swallow; (*mil.*) deserter; tubfish; large tumour in the armpit.
golondro, *n.m.* (*coll.*) desire, longing; *campar de golondro,* (*coll.*) to live at another's expense; *andar en golondros,* (*coll.*) to feed on vain hopes.
golosamente, *adv.* daintily, with relish.
golosear, *v.i.* to look for and eat titbits, dainties, or sweetmeats; to taste and relish nice things.
golosina, *n.f.* dainty, delicacy, sweet morsel,

titbit; sweet tooth, daintiness; desire, cupidity.

golosinar, golosinear, golosmear, *v.i.* to look for and eat titbits, dainties or sweetmeats; to taste and relish nice things.

goloso, -sa, *n.m.f., a.* one who has a sweet tooth, fond of dainties, niceties, or sweetmeats; *tornillo de rosca golosa,* screw nail.

golpazo, *n.m.* great blow, stroke, or knock.

golpe, *n.m.* blow, stroke, knock, dash; clash, shock; hurt, wound; act, push, action; abundance; crowd, throng of people; sudden mishap, fit, or accident; heart-beat; spring bolt of a lock; (*sew.*) passementerie trimming; pocket-flap (of a coat); witty sally or remark; (*fenc.*) movement of attack; surprise, admiration; timely and fitting action; (*mech.*) stroke, travel, throw; with gardeners, hole for planting, also number of cuts planted in one hole; (*mus.*) action of striking a string, key, etc.; (*naut.*) sweep; (*Mex.*) sledge hammer; *golpe de arco,* bowing of a violin; *golpe de remo,* stroke in rowing; *golpe de mar,* (*naut.*) surge, a heavy sea; *golpe de fortuna,* a fortunate event; *de golpe,* plump, all at once; *golpe de música,* beat of music; *golpe de reloj,* tick of the watch or clock; *de golpe y zumbido* (or *porrazo*), unexpectedly, unawares; *golpe de estado,* coup d'état; *a golpes,* once, all at once; *errar el golpe,* to fail in any attempt; *darse golpes de pecho,* to beat one's breast; *dar golpe en bola,* to come safely out of a difficult enterprise; *el golpe de la sartén, si no duele, tizna bien;* slander, even where it hurts not, leaves a stain; *un solo golpe no derriba un roble,* Rome was not built in a day; *golpe de gracia,* finishing stroke, coup de grâce.

golpeadero, *n.m.* place for beating iron, etc.; repeated strokes.

golpeador, -ra, *n.m.f., a.* striker, beater.

golpeadura, *n.f.* percussion; act of beating, hammering, or striking.

golpear, *v.t.* to beat, strike, hit, knock, hammer, give blows; to bruise; to tick (as a watch); to knock, pound (as a piston).

golpeo, *n.m.* repeated striking or beating.

golpete, *n.m.* door-catch (to keep it open).

golpeteo, *n.m.* lively and continued striking; constant hammering.

gollería, golloría, *n.f.* dainty, delicious morsel; (*coll.*) pernicketiness, superfluity, excess.

gollete, *n.m.* throttle, upper part of the throat; neck of a bottle; neck-band of some religious habits; *estar hasta el gollete,* (*coll.*) to be full, to be in difficulties, to have lost patience.

gollizo, gollizno, *n.m.* gorge, ravine, narrow pass.

goma, *n.f.* gum, rubber; elastic band; *goma adragante* (*alquitira,* or *tragacanto*), gum tragacanth; *goma arábiga,* gum-arabic; *goma elástica,* india-rubber; *goma laca,* lac; (*surg.*) gumma, a kind of syphilitic tumour. — *pl.* **gomas,** (*Am.*) galoshes.

gomecillo, *n.m.* (*coll.*) blind person's guide.

gomer, *n.m., a.* member of the Gomara, a Berber tribe in North Africa.

gomero, -ra, *a.* pertaining or related to rubber; (*Arg.*) rubber merchant.

gomia, *n.f.* bugbear, bogy, monster; (*coll.*)

glutton, voracious eater; *gomia del caudal,* spendthrift.

gomífero, -ra, *a.* gummiferous.

gomorresina, *n.f.* gum-resin.

gomosidad, *n.f.* gumminess, viscosity.

gomoso, -sa, *a.* gummy, productive of gum; full of viscous humours.

gomoso, *n.m.* dandy; (*coll.*) fop, coxcomb.

gonagra, *n.f.* gout which attacks the knees.

gonce, *n.m.* hinge.

góndola, [*n.f.* gondola; omnibus, stage, carry-all; the car of an airship or balloon.

gondolero, *n.m.* gondolier.

gonela, *n.f.* a tunic or outer garment of silk or leather, sleeveless, and reaching to the calf of the leg, worn over the armour; skirt formerly worn by ladies in Aragon.

gonete, *n.m.* dress formerly worn by women.

gonfalón, *n.m.* banner, gonfalon, pennant.

gonfalonier, gonfaloniero, *n.m.* standard-bearer.

gongorino, -na, *a.* (*poet.*) gongoresque, euphuistic, pompous, lofty (of style).

gongorismo, *n.m.* (*poet.*) Gongorism, euphuism, pedantic and high-flown language.

gongorista, *n.f.* (*poet.*) Gongorist, euphuist.

gongorizar, *v.t.* to affect a lofty, Gongoristic style.

goniometría, *n.f.* goniometry.

goniométrico, -ca, *a.* goniometric.

goniómetro, *n.m.* goniometer.

gonococo, *n.m.* gonococcus.

gonorrea, *n.f.* gonorrhœa, urethritis.

gonorréico, -ca, *a.* gonorrhœal.

gorbión, gurbión, *n.m.* coarse twisted silk; heavy yarn silk cloth; spurge gum resin.

gordal, *a.* fat, big, fleshy.

gordana, *n.f.* fat, lard; oil extracted from the testicles of oxen.

gordico, -ica; -illo, -illa; -ito, -ita, *n.m.f.* not very fat, rather plump.

gordiflón, -ona; gordinflón, -ona, *n.m.f.*(*coll.*) chubby, flabby person.

gordo, -da, *a.* fat, corpulent, full-fed, plump, fleshy, obese, stout; oily, greasy, fat, rich; coarse, thick; great, large, big; *tocino gordo,* fat pork; *lienzo gordo,* coarse linen; *mentira gorda,* gross falsehood; *hablar gordo,* to speak thickly.

gordo, *n.m.* fat, suet, lard; first prize (in a lottery, etc.). — *n.f.* (*Mex.*) thick maize omelet.

gordolobo, *n.m.* (*bot.*) great mullein.

gordón, -na; gordote, -ta, *a.* (*coll.*) very fat and corpulent.

gordozo, -za, *a.* very fat and big.

gordura, *n.f.* grease, fat; fatness, corpulence.

gorfe, *n.m.* deep hole in a river forming a whirlpool or eddy.

gorga, *n.f.* hawks' food; (*prov.*) whirlpool.

gorgojarse, *v.r.* to be destroyed by insects (of corn).

gorgojo, *n.m.* grub, mite, weevil; (*coll.*) dwarfish person.

gorgojoso, -sa, *a.* full of grubs or weevils.

gorgón, *n.m.* (*Col.*) kind of concrete used for building; parr, a young salmon.

gorgona, *n.f.* gorgonia, sea-fan, a zoophyte; (*Am.*) whirlpool near the island of this name, off the S.W. coast of Colombia.

gorgorán, *n.m.* sort of silk grogram.

gorgorear, *v.i.* (*prov.*) (*Chi.*) to cry like a turkey-cock [GORGORITEAR].

gorgorita, *n.f.* rain bubble. — *pl.* **gorgoritas,** trilling, shakes, quavers.

gorgoritear, *v.i.* (*coll.*) to warble, trill, quiver; gargle.

gorgoritos, *n.m.pl.* (*coll.*) trill, shake, quiver.

górgoro, *n.m.* (*Mex.*) bubble.

gorgorotada, *n.f.* quantity of liquid swallowed at once.

gorgoteo, *n.m.* gurgle, gurgling sound.

gorgotero, *n.m.* pedlar, hawker.

gorguera, *n.f.* gorgeret, ruff; (*arm.*) gorget, neck-armour; (*bot.*) involucre.

gorguerán, *n.f.* (*obs.*) kind of grogram [GORGORÁN].

gorguz, *n.m.* javelin, shaft; (*Mex.*) goad stick.

gorigori, *n.m.* (*coll.*) dirge.

gorila, *n.m.* gorilla.

gorja, *n.f.* throat, throttle; *estar uno de gorja,* (*coll.*) rejoicing, merry-making.

gorjal, *n.m.* collar of a doublet; (*arm.*) gorget.

gorjeador, -ra, *n.m.f.* warbler, modulator.

gorjear, *v.i.* to warble, chirp, twitter, trill, quaver, sing (of persons and birds); (*Am.*) to mock, laugh at. — *v.r.* to gurgle, crow, begin to speak (of a baby).

gorjeo, *n.m.* warble, chirp, twitter, trilling, quaver; child's chatter, gabble.

gormar, *v.t.* to vomit; (*fig.*) to return what belongs to another.

gorra, *n.f.* cap, bonnet, headgear, hunting-cap; (*mil.*) bearskin, cap; (*coll.*) intrusion at feasts without invitation; (*Col.*) (*fig.*) sponging; *gorra de señora,* lady's hat or bonnet. — *n.m.* parasite, sponger; *de gorra,* (*coll.*) at other people's expense; *duro de gorra,* disinclined (or slow) to salute, waiting for another to salute first.

gorrada, gorretada, *n.f.* salute with a cap.

gorrero, -ra, *n.m.f.* cap maker or seller; sponger, parasite.

gorrería, *n.f.* cap and bonnet shop, and factory.

gorreta, *n.f.* small bonnet or cap.

gorrete, *n.m.* small cap.

gorrín, gorrino, *n.m.* small pig, sucking pig; (*fig.*) slovenly person.

gorrinada, gorrinería, *n.f.* (*coll.*) dirty, hoggish action; pigsty.

gorrinera, *n.f.* pigsty, pig's pen.

gorrión, *n.m.* sparrow.

gorrionera, *n.f.* (*coll.*) den of rogues.

gorrista, *n.m.f.* parasite, sponger.

gorro, *n.m.* cap, coif; *gorro de dormir,* night-cap; *gorro frigio,* Phrygian cap; cap of liberty.

gorrón, -ona, *a.* sponger, parasite. — *n.m.* libertine.

gorrón, *n.m.* round, smooth pebble; (*mech.*) journal, spindle, pivot, or gudgeon of a gate or door; pillow, swing-block; unhealthy silk-worm.

gorrona, *n.f.* prostitute. — *a. pasa gorrona,* large-size raisin.

gorronal, *n.m.* place full of pebbles or coarse gravel.

gorullo, *n.m.* lump, ball (as wool).

gorupo, *n.m.* (*naut.*) granny's bend.

gosipino, -na, *a.* of a cottony surface.

gota, *n.f.* drop of liquid; (*med.*) gout; (*arch.*) gutta; kind of topaz; *gota a gota,* drop by drop; *gota serena,* (*med.*) amaurosis; *gota coral* (or *caduca*), (*med.*) epilepsy, falling-sickness; *gotas amargas,* bitters; *no ver gota,* to see nothing; *gota a gota, la mar se apoca,*

however slowly, the end comes at last; *no quedar gota de sangre en el cuerpo* (or *en las venas*), to be half-dead with fear; *sudar la gota gorda,* to make superhuman efforts; *una y otra gota apagan la sed,* many drops quench much thirst. — *pl.* **gotas,** drops of rum or brandy added to coffee.

goteado, -da, *a.* guttated, sprinkled, spotted, speckled. — *p.p.* [GOTEAR].

gotear, *v.i.* to drop, drip, dribble, leak; (*fig.*) to measure by drops, to give by driblets.

gotera, *n.f.* leak, leakage, drip, dripping; (*arch.*) gutter, valley; valance of a canopy or tester; (*agric.*) disease in trees caused by infiltration; chronic ailing; *la gotera cava la piedra,* many drops wear the hardest stone. — *pl.* **goteras,** (*Am.*) suburbs, environs.

gotero, *n.m.* (*Mex., PR.*) dropper (for counting or measuring drops).

goterón, *n.m.* large raindrop; (*arch.*) throating.

gótico, -ca, *a.* Gothic; *letra gótica,* Gothic characters; (*fig.*) noble, illustrious. — *n.m.* Gothic language.

gotón, -ona, *n.m.f.*, *a.* Goth.

gotoso, -sa, *a.* gouty.

goyesco, -ca, *a.* in the style of the Spanish painter Goya.

gozante, *a.* enjoying.

gozar, *v.t.* (*pret.* **gocé;** *pres. subj.* **goce**) to enjoy, to have possession or fruition of. — *v.r.* to rejoice. — *v.i.* (with the preposition *de*) to enjoy, to have; *gozar de una posición holgada,* to enjoy comfortable circumstances.

gozne, *n.m.* hinge.

gozo, *n.m.* joy, pleasure, satisfaction, glee, merriment, mirth, gladness, cheerfulness; sudden blaze of dry chips of wood. — *pl.* **gozos,** couplets with a refrain, in praise of the Blessed Virgin or the saints; *no caber de gozo* (or *saltar de gozo*), to be in high spirits, to be very merry; ¡*el gozo en el pozo!* all my illusions have vanished!

gozosamente, *adv.* joyfully, cheerfully.

gozoso, -sa, *a.* joyful, cheerful, content, glad, festive, mirthful, merry.

gozque, *n.m.* cur.

gozquejo, *n.m.* small cur.

grabado, -da, *a.* engraved, carved out. — *p.p.* [GRABAR].

grabado, *n.m.* engraving; art of engraving; print, cut, picture, illustration; *grabado en madera,* wood-cut; *grabado al humo,* half-tone plate or process, mezzotint; *grabado al agua fuerte,* etching; *grabado al agua tinta,* aquatint; *grabado al barniz blando,* soft-ground etching; *grabado a puntos,* stipple engraving; *grabado en fondo* or *en hueco,* punch or die sinking.

grabador, -ra, *n.m.f.* engraver, carver, cutter, chiseller, sinker; *grabador en matrices,* (*print.*) form-cutter.

grabadura, *n.f.* act of engraving, sculpture.

grabar, *v.t.* to engrave, to grave, cut, carve; (*fig.*) impress upon the mind; *grabar en blanco* or *relieve,* to emboss.

grabazón, *n.f.* overlay with engraved ornament.

gracejada, *n.f.* (*Am. Cent., Mex.*) clownish joke, buffoonery, jest (in bad taste).

gracejar, *v.i.* to jest, joke, write or speak wittily.

gracejo, *n.m.* graceful, cheerful, witty way of speaking.

gracia, *n.f.* grace, gracefulness, elegance of mien or manner, gentility; (*theol.*) divine grace; by extension: free gift, benefaction, kindness, grant, concession; cleverness; condescension, graciousness; courtesy, pleasing manners, benevolence; mercy, pardon; witty saying or expression; remission of a debt; comicalness; mirth, jest, joke; (*coll.*) name of a person; brightness, cuteness of a child. — *pl.* **gracias,** thanks; (*myth.*) the Three Graces; *gracias,* thank you; *dar gracias,* to thank or to give thanks; *¡gracias a Dios!* thank God! *la gracia de Dios,* (*coll.*) bread; sunshine; *¿cómo es la gracia de Vd.?* pray, what is your name?; *caer en gracia,* to please, to be liked; *de gracia,* gratis, for nothing; *caer de la gracia de alguno,* to lose one's favour, to be disliked; *decir dos gracias,* to tell home-truths; *en gracia de,* for the sake of; *golpe de gracia,* finishing stroke; *ella tiene muchas gracias,* she has many accomplishments; *¡qué gracia!* what a wonder! a fine thing! *más vale caer en gracia, que ser gracioso,* fortune can do more than merit; *no está gracia en casa,* (or *no está de gracia* or *no está para gracias*), he is ill-humoured; *Ministerio de Gracia y Justicia,* Ministry of Justice.

graciable, *a.* good-natured, affable; easily granted or obtained.

grácil, *a.* gracile, slender, small.

graciola, *n.f.* hedge hyssop.

graciosamente, *adv.* graciously, gracefully, gratefully, kindly; gratuitously.

graciosidad, *n.f.* gracefulness, beauty, perfection, wit, elegance, excellence, dignity of manners.

gracioso, -sa, *a.* graceful, pleasing, accomplished; title of dignity of English monarchs; witty, funny, entertaining; liberal, benevolent, gracious; ridiculous, extravagant; gratuitous, free.

graciosa, *n.f.* soubrette, chambermaid.

gracioso, *n.m.* low comedian, fool.

grada, *n.f.* step of a staircase; gradin (as of an amphitheatre); stand or gallery having gradins; super-altar; (*in convents*) locutory; (*agric.*) harrow, brake; *grada de construcción,* (*naut.*) stocks for shipbuilding; *grada de cota,* bush-harrow; *grada de dientes,* harrow with teeth; *grada de astillero* (or *de dique*), (*naut.*) one of the steps in a dry-dock. — *pl.* **gradas,** (*arch.*) perron, gradatory; bar (in law); seats of an amphitheatre.

gradación, *n.f.* gradation; (*mus.*) gradation, chords rising step by step to a climax; (*rhet.*) climax.

gradado, -da, *a.* having gradins or steps. — *p.p.* [GRADAR].

gradar, *v.t.* to harrow, break with the harrow.

gradería, *n.f.* series of seats, gradins or super-altars.

gradiente, *n.m.* (*meteor.*) gradient. — *n.f.* (*Arg., Chi., Ec.*) slope, declinity, gradient.

gradilla, *n.f.* small seat or step; tile or brick mould; small step-ladder.

gradinar, *v.t.* to chisel with a gradine.

gradino, *n.m.* gradine, sculptor's chisel.

gradilo, *n.m.* gladiolus, corn-flag.

grado, *n.m.* step of a staircase; degree of kindred, order of lineage; (*mil.*) rank; degree, academical title; (*com.*) grade, class,

graduation of value or quality; (*math., geog.*) degree; (*law*) stage of proceedings; (*gram.*) degree of comparison; (*fig.*) will, pleasure; *de grado* (or *de su grado*), willingly, with pleasure; *mal de mi, tu, su,* etc. *grado,* unwillingly; *grado de longitud* (or *latitud*), degree of longitude or latitude; *de grado en grado,* gradually, by degrees, in regular progression; *grado de calor,* degree of heat; *en grado superlativo,* in the highest degree; *ni grado ni gracias,* no praise is due to me; *no pidas de grado lo que puedes tomar por fuerza,* don't ask as a favour what you can take by force. — *pl.* **grados,** minor orders.

gradoso, -sa, *a.* (*obs.*) pleasing, pleasant.

graduable, *a.* that may be graduated.

graduación, *n.f.* graduation; admission to a degree; (*mil.*) rank, condition, quality; (*math.*) scale of degrees; degree of alcoholic strength.

graduado, -da, *a.* (*mil.*) brevet; graduated.

graduado, -da, *n.m.f.* graduate. — *p.p.* [GRADUAR].

graduador, *n.m.* graduator, gauger.

gradual, *a.* gradual, proceeding by degrees. — *n.m.* (*eccles.*) response sung at mass between the epistle and the gospel.

gradualmente, *adv.* gradually, by degrees.

graduando, -da, *n.m.f.* candidate for academical degrees.

graduar, *v.t.* to gauge, measure, compare, classify; to give military rank; to graduate, dignify with an academical degree; to divide into degrees; (*com.*) to gauge, calculate, appraise. — *v.r.* to graduate, to take an academic degree.

gráficamente, *adv.* graphically.

gráfico, -ca, *a.* graphic, graphical; clear, vivid. — *n.m.f.* graph, diagram.

grafila, *n.f.* milled edge of coin.

grafio, *n.m.* graver for graffito or scratch-work.

grafioles, *n.m.pl.* biscuits in the form of an S.

grafito, *n.m.* graphite, plumbago.

grafolita, *n.f.* grapholite.

grafología, *n.f.* graphology.

grafólogo, *n.m.* graphologist.

grafomanía, *n.f.* graphomania, mania for writing.

grafómetro, *n.m.f.* (*surv.*) graphometer, circumferentor.

gragea, *n.f.* small coloured bonbon.

graja, *n.f.* female jackdaw; jay.

grajal, *a.* belonging to crows, ravens, or magpies.

grajear, *v.i.* to caw, as crows; to chatter, as magpies.

grajero, -ra, *a.* applied to rookeries.

grajo, *n.m.* jackdaw; (*Col., Cub., Ec., Per., PR.*) odour of unwashed people.

grajuelo, *n.m.* small jackdaw.

gralario, -ria, *a.* grallatory, wading (of birds).

grama, *n.f.* (*bot.*) creeping cynodon; couch-grass, dog's grass, grama-grass.

gramal, *n.m.* place where couch-grass or dog's grass grows.

gramalote, *n.m.* (*Col., Ec., Per.*) fodder crop.

gramalla, *n.f.* long scarlet gown worn in ancient times by the magistrates of Catalonia and Aragon; coat of mail.

gramallera, *n.f.* (*prov.*) pot-hanger.

gramar, *v.t.* (*prov.*) to knead the dough of bread.

gramática, *n.f.* grammar; study of the Latin language; *gramática parda,* (*coll.*) shrewdness, strength of natural reason.

gramatical, *a.* grammatical.

gramaticalmente, *adv.* grammatically.

gramático, -ca, *a.* grammatical. — *n.m.* grammarian.

gramatiquería, *n.f.* (*contempt.*) pedantic point of grammar.

gramil, *n.m.* joiner's marking-gauge.

gramilla, *n.f.* bed of the hemp-brake.

gramíneo, -nea, *a.* (*bot.*) graminaceous, grassy.

graminívoro, -ra, *a.* graminivorous, grass-eating, living on grass.

gramo, *n.m.* gramme, gram, unit of weight in the metrical system.

gramófono, *n.m.* gramophone; (*Am.*) phonograph.

gramómetro, *n.m.* (*print.*) type-gauge.

gramoso, -sa, *a.* pertaining to (ground) where couch-grass grows, belonging to couch-grass.

grampa, *n.f.* staple, clamp, cramp, hook for carrying weights.

gran, *a.* (*contr.* of GRANDE, used only in *sing.* and before *m.* or *f.* nouns), large, big, grand, great, e.g. *gran casa,* large house; *gran palacio,* grand palace; *gran filósofo,* great philosopher.

grana, *n.f.* small seed of some plants; the time when corn, flax etc., form their seed; cochineal; kermes dye; kermes; kermes-berry; scarlet grain; scarlet colour; fine scarlet cloth; fresh red colour of the lips and cheeks; *grana del paraíso,* grain of paradise, cardamom; *ponerse como una grana,* (*coll.*) to blush up to one's eyes; *poner a uno como una grana,* put someone to the blush.

granada, *n.f.* pomegranate; hand-grenade, grenade, shell.

granadera, *n.f.* grenadier's pouch.

granadero, *n.m.* grenadier; (*coll.*) very tall person.

granadilla, *n.f.* passion-flower, granadilla.

granadillo, *n.m.* West India red ebony.

granadina, *n.f.* silk cloth with open work; variety of Cante flamenco peculiar to Granada; refreshing beverage made of pomegranate.

granadino, -na, *n.m.f.*, *a.* native of or belonging to Granada (Spain) or Colombia (formerly New Granada). — *n.m.* flower of the pomegranate-tree.

granado, *n.m.* pomegranate-tree.

granado, -da, *a.* large, remarkable, notable, principal, illustrious; select, choice; full of seed, seedy; (*fig.*) seasoned, expert. — *p.p.* [GRANAR].

granador, *n.m.* granulating sieve for gunpowder; spot destined for this operation.

granaje, *n.m.* granulating powder.

granalla, *n.f.* granulation, granulated metal.

granar, *v.i.* to seed, kern, ear out.

granate, *n.m.* garnet, precious stone.

granático, -ca, *a.* deep red, garnet.

granatín, *n.m.* kind of ancient cloth.

granazón, *n.f.* seeding, shedding the seed.

Gran Bretaña, *n.f.* Great Britain.

grancé, *a.* madder-coloured.

grancolombiano, -na, *a.* pertaining to Greater Colombia (now *Colombia, Venezuela, and Ecuador*).

grande, *a.* large, big, extensive, huge; grand, great, principal. — *n.m.* grandee.

grandecico, -ica; -illo, -illa; -ito, -ita, *a.* (*prov.*) growing rather big, pretty large, fairly big.

grandemente, *adv.* greatly; very well; extremely; grandly.

grandevo, -va, *a.* (*poet.*) of advanced age.

grandeza, *n.f.* greatness, bigness; grandeur, magnificence, grandness, nobleness; grandeeship; body or assembly of grandees; size, magnitude.

grandezuelo, -la, *a.* pretty large or big.

grandilocuencia, *n.f.* grandiloquence.

grandilocuente; grandílocuo, -cua, *a.* grandiloquent.

grandillón, -ona, *a.* excessively large and big.

grandiosamente, *adv.* magnificently.

grandiosidad, *n.f.* greatness, grandeur; magnificence, abundance.

grandioso, -sa, *a.* grandiose; grand, great, magnificent, splendid.

grandor, *n.m.* size, tallness, bigness, magnitude, greatness, extensiveness.

grandote, -ta, *a.* (*coll.*) big, bulky.

grandullón, -ona, *a.* overgrown, large in proportion to age.

graneado, -da, *a.* grained, spotted, granulous; (*Per.*) select, choice. — *p.p.* [GRANEAR].

graneador, *n.m.* granulating sieve for gunpowder; place where gunpowder is sifted; tool for stipple-graver.

granear, *v.t.* to sow or shed grain in the earth; to engrave, stipple, grain a lithographic stone.

granel (a), *adv.* in a heap; (*com.*) in bulk, in abundance.

granelar, *v.t.* to grain leather.

graneo, *n.m.* act of shedding or sowing seed; stippling.

granero, *n.m.* granary, barn, grange, corn-loft; fruitful, grain-producing country.

granero, -ra, *a.* pertaining to El Grao (port of Valencia). — *n.m.f.* a native or inhabitant of El Grao.

granete, *n.m.* marking awl, countersink, punch.

granévano, *n.m.* goat's-thorn.

granguardia, *n.f.* grand-guard; advanced guard.

granico, *n.m.* granule, small grain.

granífero, -ra, *a.* bearing grains as seeds.

granilla, *n.f.* rough nap on cloth.

granillero, -ra, *a.* (*prov.*) (of hogs) that feed on fallen acorns.

granillo, *n.m.* granule, small grain; gain or profit frequently obtained; pimple on the rump of canaries and linnets.

granilloso, -sa, *a.* granulous, granular.

granítico, -ca, *a.* granitic, formed of granite.

granito, *n.m.* small grain; small pimple; (*min.*) granite; (*pharm.*) granule; small egg of a silk-worm.

granívoro, -ra, *a.* granivorous, eating grain, living upon grain.

granizada, *n.f.* heavy fall of hail, hailstorm; multitude of things which fall in abundance; (*Arg., Chi.*) iced drink.

granizado, -da, *a.* destroyed by hail. — *p.p.* [GRANIZAR].

granizado, *n.m.* water-ice.

granizar, *v.i.* (*pres. subj.* **granice**) to hail. *v.i., v.t.* to pour, or throw down with violence.

granizo, *n.m.* hail; hailstorm; cloud or web in the eyes.

granja, *n.f.* grange, farm, farmhouse, country house; *granja modelo*, model farm; *ir de granja*, to go into the country for recreation.

granjear, *v.t.* to gain, earn, profit; *granjear a barlovento*, to gain to windward. — *v.r.* to get, obtain, conciliate, win (as the goodwill of another).

granjeo, *n.m.* act of getting or acquiring; gain, profit, advantage, advancement in interest, influence, etc.

granjería, *n.f.* gain, profit, advantage.

granjero, **-ra**, *n.m.f.* farmer, husbandman, granger, cattle-rancher; dealer in profitable commodities; (*obs.*) broker.

grano, *n.m.* grain, cereal; seed; grain of sand, wood, or fibrous matter, minute particle; (*pharm.*) grain (20 = an English scruple, 24 = a Spanish one); (*artill.*) blushing (or bouching) of a cannon; pimple, pustule on the skin; unit of weight for precious stones, used also to describe the fineness of gold. — *pl.* **granos**, (*com.*) cereals, corn; *granos del paraíso* or *amomo*, (*bot.*) grain of paradise; *ir al grano*, (*coll.*) to come to the point; (*iron.*) *¡ahí es un grano de anís!* that's an important matter!; *apartar el grano de la paja*, to separate the important from the trivial; *con su grano de sal*, with a grain of salt, with due caution; *grano a grano, allega para tu año* (or *grano a grano, hinche la gallina el papo*, or *un grano no hace granero, pero ayuda a su compañero*), many a mickle makes a muckle.

granoso, **-sa**, *a.* granulous, grainy, granular, granulated (as leather).

granuja, *n.f.* loose berries of grapes; grapestone; group of roving boys. — *n.m.* (*coll.*) little rogue, waif, gamin, urchin.

granujado, **-da**, *a.* full of pimples, stones or seeds.

granujiento, **-ta**, *a.* full of pimples.

granujo, *n.m.* (*coll.*) pimple or tumour in the flesh.

granujoso, **-sa**, *a.* full of pimples.

gránula, *n.f.* spore of cryptogamous plants.

granulación, *n.f.* granulation.

granulador, **-ra**, *n.m.f.* granulating machine.

granular, *v.t.* to granulate, reduce to grains. — *v.r.* to be covered with granules or pimples.

granular, *a.* granular, full of pimples.

gránulo, *n.m.* granule, granula; pellet.

granulosidad, *n.f.* granularity.

granuloso, **-sa**, *a.* granulous, granular.

granza, *n.f.* (*bot.*) madder; garancin. — *pl.* **granzas**, siftings, chaff; refuse, dross of metals.

granzón, *n.m.* screenings of ore. — *pl.* **granzones**, lumps of straw left uneaten by cattle.

granzoso, **-sa**, *a.* full of chaff, refuse or screenings.

grañón, *n.m.* pap made of boiled semolina; boiled grain of wheat.

grao, *n.m.* landing place; shore.

grapa, *n.f.* clamp, clasp, clutch, cramp-iron; (*carp.*) holdfast; mangy ulcers in the joints of horses.

grapón, *n.m.* (*mech.*) brace, hook, ram, iron dog, large cramp-iron.

graptolita, *n.f.* (*min.*) dendrite.

grasa, *n.f.* grease, fat, suet, kitchen-stuff; lubricating oil; *grasa de ballena*, whale-oil, blubber; train-oil; *grasa de pescado*, fish-oil; gum of juniper-trees; grease of clothes; pounce; (*naut.*) slush; (*min.*) slag of metals; base of an ointment or pomade.

grasera, *n.f.* ointment-jar, vessel for fat or grease; oil-sump; slush-tub; dripping-pan.

grasería, *n.f.* tallow-chandler's shop.

grasero, *n.m.* (*min.*) slag-dumper.

graseza, *n.f.* fattiness.

grasiento, **-ta**, *a.* greasy, oily; filthy, grimy.

grasilla, *n.f.* pounce; (*bot.*) juniper-resin.

graso, **-sa**, *a.* fat, oily, unctuous, lardy.

graso, *n.m.* fattiness.

grasones, *n.m.pl.* dish made of flour, milk of almonds, sugar and cinnamon.

grasoso, **-sa**, *a.* greasy, oily, filthy.

grasura, *n.f.* fat, suet, tallow.

grata, *n.f.* burnisher, smoothing chisel, wire brush.

gratamente, *adv.* graciously, gratefully, kindly, benevolently.

gratar, *v.t.* to brush or burnish plate.

gratificación, *n.f.* reward, recompense, gratuity, fee, tip, gratification; allowance to officers for expenses; indulgence.

gratificador, **-ra**, *n.m.f.*, *a.* gratifier, rewarder; one who fees or tips.

gratificar, *v.t.* (*pret.* **gratifiqué**; *pres. subj.* **gratifique**) to reward, requite, recompense; to tip, fee; to gratify; please, indulge, delight.

grátil, *n.m.* head or edge of a sail; luff, leech.

gratis, *adv.* gratis, free, for nothing.

gratisdato, **-ta**, *a.* gratuitous, given away.

gratitud, *n.f.* gratitude, gratefulness.

grato, **-ta**, *a.* graceful, pleasing, pleasant, luscious; acceptable; grateful; gratuitous; *su grata*, (*com.*) your favour.

gratonada, *n.f.* chicken ragout or fricassee.

gratuitamente, *adv.* gratuitously.

gratuito, **-ta**, *a.* gratuitous, gratis; unfounded, uncalled for.

gratulación, *n.f.* congratulation; (*obs.*) anxiety to oblige.

gratular, *v.t.* to congratulate. — *v.r.* to rejoice.

gratulatorio, **-ria**, *a.* congratulatory.

grava, *n.f.* gravel, coarse sand.

gravamen, *n.m.* charge, obligation, hardship, load, inconvenience, nuisance; encumbrance, burden; (*law*) mortgage, lien.

gravar, *v.t.* to burden, oppress, fatigue, molest; (*law*) to encumber a piece of property.

gravativo, **-va**, *a.* grievous, injurious, burdensome.

grave, *a.* weighty, ponderous, heavy; grave, important, momentous, of weight, of great consequence, grievous, serious; troublesome; dangerous; mortal, deadly; great, huge, vast; circumspect, formal, haughty, lofty; vexatious; arduous, difficult; (*mus.*) low, bass; (*gram.*) said of a word when the stress falls on the penultimate syllable; *delito grave*, (*law*) heinous crime; *enfermedad grave*, dangerous disease; *ponerse grave*, to assume an air of importance.

gravear, *v.i.* to weigh, gravitate, sink.

gravedad, *n.f.* gravity; weight, heaviness; composure, circumspection, graveness, seriousness, sobriety of behaviour; gravity, enormity, atrociousness; dangerousness; vanity, pride.

gravedoso, -sa, *a.* haughty, self-important, vain.

gravemente, *adv.* gravely, seriously, dangerously.

gravidez, *n.f.* pregnancy.

grávido, -da, *a.* (*poet.*) gravid, pregnant; full, abundant.

gravímetro, *n.m.* gravimeter.

gravitación, *n.f.* gravitation.

gravitar, *v.i.* to gravitate, weigh down, incline towards one side.

gravoso, -sa, *a.* grievous, offensive, afflictive, painful, onerous; unbearable.

graznador, -ra, *a.* croaking, cawing, cackling.

graznar, *v.i.* to croak, caw, cackle.

graznido, *n.m.* croak, caw, cackle, croaking.

greba, *n.f.* (*arm.*) greave(s) or jamb.

greca, *n.f.* Grecian fret.

greciano, -na, *a.* Greek, Grecian.

grecismo, *n.m.* Græcism.

grecizante, *a.* grecianizing, hellenizing.

grecizar, *v.t.,* *v.i.* to græcize, hellenize.

greco, -ca, *a.* Grecian; *a la greca,* in Grecian style. — *n.m.f.* Greek.

grecolatino, -na, *a.* Græco-Latin.

grecorromano, -na, *a.* Græco-Roman.

greda, *n.f.* marl, fuller's earth.

gredal, *n.m.* marl-pit. — *a.* marly (plot or field).

gredoso, -sa, *a.* marly.

grefier, *n.m.* keeper of the rolls in the royal house; official assistant in the ceremony of the imposition of the Golden Fleece.

gregal, *n.m.* north-east wind in the Mediterranean. — *a.* gregarious, going in flocks.

gregario, -ria, *a.* gregarian; servile.

gregoriano, -na, *a.* Gregorian.

gregorillo, *n.m.* neckcloth formerly worn by women.

gregorito, *n.m.* (*Mex.*) disappointment; practical joke.

greguería, *n.f.* outcry, confused clamour, hubbub; whimsical, personified metaphor.

gregüescos, *n.m.pl.* Grecian wide breeches.

greguisco, -ca, *a.* Grecian, Greek.

greguizar, *v.t.* to græcize, grecianize, talk Greek, convert into Greek.

gremial, *a.* belonging to a guild or trade union. — *n.m.* member of a guild; (*eccles.*) bishop's lap-cloth.

gremio, *n.m.* (*obs.*) lap; body; society, company, guild, corporation, fraternity; trade-union; *gremio de la iglesia,* pale of the church; *gremio de una universidad,* academic senate.

grenchudo, -da, *a.* having long mane (as a lion).

greña, *n.f.* entangled or matted hair; anything entangled; *andar a la greña,* to pull one another by the hair; to squabble, argue; (*prov., Mex.*) heap of grain laid to be threshed; (*prov.*) first leaves of a vine-shoot.

greñudo, -da, *a.* entangled (of hair); dishevelled.

greñudo, *n.m.* shy horse.

greñuela, *n.f.* (*prov.*) first shoots of a year old vine.

gres, *n.m.* pottery, material consisting of clay and quartzose sand; pottery made of this material refractory to heat and acids.

gresca, *n.f.* carousal, revelling, clatter; wrangle, quarrel.

greuge, *n.m.* (*obs.*) complaints formerly made in the Cortes of Aragon.

grey, *n.f.* flock, herd; congregation of the faithful people; race, nation.

grial, *n.m.* grail, legendary holy chalice of the Last Supper.

griego, -ga, *a.* Greek, Grecian. — *n.m.* the Greek language; (*coll.*) gibberish; nonsense; *hablar en griego,* to talk gibberish; (*coll.*) cheating, gambler.

griesco, griesgo, *n.m.* (*obs.*) encounter, battle, conflict.

grieta, *n.f.* crevice, crack, cleft; chink, fissure, cranny, flaw; split, vein, shake, rent; scratch or fissure in the skin; *grieta(s) en las manos,* chapped hands.

grietado, -da, *a.* fissured, cleft, showing flaws.

grietarse, *v.r.* to crack, split, cranny; to part in clefts or fissures; to become chapped.

grietecilla, *n.f.* small fissure, crevice or scratch.

grietoso, -sa, *a.* crannied, flawy.

grifa, *n.f.* (*print.*) italics.

grifado, -da, *a.* italicized.

grifalto, *n.m.* small culverin.

grifo, -fa, *a.* (*print.*) italic **;** (*Am.*) kinky, curly, entangled (hair).

grifo, *n.m.* griffin, a fabulous animal; (*Am.*) child of a Negro and an Indian; (*mech.*) faucet, stop-cock, tap; *grifos,* frizzled hair.

grifón, *n.m.* faucet or spigot (of fountains, etc.).

grigallo, *n.m.* (*orn.*) variety of francolin.

gril, *n.m.* grilse, a young salmon when it first returns from the sea, usually in its second year.

griliforme, *a.* (*zool.*) shaped like a cricket.

grilla, *n.f.* female cricket **;** *ésa es grilla,* (*coll.*) that's a cock-and-bull story.

grillar, *v.i.* (*obs.*) to chirp (of crickets). — *v.r.* to shoot, to sprout.

grillera, *n.f.* cricket-cage.

grillero, *n.m.* he who puts on and takes off the irons of prisoners.

grillete, *n.m.* shackle, fetter.

grillo, *n.m.* (*entom.*) cricket; (*bot.*) shoot, sprout. — *pl.* **grillos,** fetters, irons, gyves, shackles or chains for the feet; any impediment which prevents motion; *andar a grillos,* to waste time in useless pursuits.

grima, *n.f.* fright, horror, revulsion, grimness.

grimazo, *n.m.* grotesque posture or contortion.

grímpola, *n.f.* (*naut.*) vane, weather-cock; pennant, streamer; *huso de la grímpola,* spindle of a vane.

grinalde, *n.m.* ancient form of grenade.

gringo, *n.m.* [*corrup.* GRIEGO]; *hablar en gringo,* to talk gibberish; (*Am.*) (*contempt.*) nickname given to foreigners, especially English and Americans.

gringuele, *n.m.* (*Cub.*) an edible tiliaceous plant.

griñón, *n.m.* wimple worn by nuns; apricot ingrafted in a peach-tree.

gripal, *a.* relating to influenza.

gripe, *n.f.* grippe, influenza.

gripo, *n.m.* (*obs.*) merchant ship.

gris, *a.* grizzled, grey; (*fig.*) gloomy, languid. — *n.m.* miniver, Siberian squirrel and its fur; (*coll.*) cold, sharp weather.

grisalla, *n.f.* (*art*) grisaille.

grisáceo, -cea; gríseo, -sea, *a.* greyish, grizzly.

grisar, *v.t.* to polish diamonds.

griseta, *n.f.* flowered silk stuff; disease of trees; French grisette.

grisma, *n.f.* (*Chi., Guat., Hond.*) fragment, mite, crumb.

grisón, -ona, *a.* of or pertaining to the Swiss Canton Grisons. — *n.m.f.* native or inhabitant of the Grisons. — *n.m.* the Romansch language.

grisú, *n.m.* (*min.*) fire-damp.

grita, *n.f.* clamour, outcry, hubbub, uproar, shouting, vociferation, hallo; *grita foral,* (*law*) summons, citation (used in Aragon).

gritador, -ra, *n.m.f.* clamourer; bawler.

gritar, *v.i.* to shout, cry out, clamour, clatter, hallo, exclaim, whoop, hoot; to talk very loud; to bawl; to shriek.

gritería, *n.f.* outcry, shouting, clamour, screaming; hooting, tumult, hurly-burly, hullabaloo, hue and cry.

grito, *n.m.* cry, scream, howl, shriek, hoot, whoop, shout; *a voz en grito,* at the top of one's voice; *alzar* (or *levantar*) *el grito,* to talk loud and haughtily; *hablar a gritos,* to shout; *estar en un grito,* to be in continual pain; *a grito herido,* in a loud voice, clamorously.

gritón, -na, *a.* (*coll.*) vociferous, clamorous.

gro, *n.m.* grogram, twilled silk fabric.

groenlandés, -esa, *n.m.f., a.* Greenlander.

groera, *n.f.* (*naut.*) ropehole.

gromo, *n.m.* (*prov.*) leafy bud, young shoot.

gropos, *n.m.pl.* cotton put in inkstands or inkhorns.

gros, *n.m.* ancient coin of small value.

grosamente, *adv.* grossly.

grosca, *n.f.* kind of venomous serpent.

grosella, *n.f.* berry of the red currant; *grosella blanca,* gooseberry.

grosellero, *n.m.* currant bush.

groseramente, *adv.* grossly, coarsely, rudely; bunglingly, in an unmannerly way.

grosería, *n.f.* grossness, rudeness, ill-breeding, ill manners; discourtesy; clownishness, coarseness, clumsiness, shameless word or action.

grosero, -ra, *a.* gross, coarse, rough; plain, homely, home-spun, not fine, not elegant; rude, discourteous, unpolished, clownish, churlish, uncivil; brutal, rough; indecent, indelicate, smutty; fat, thick, bulky.

grosezuelo, -la, *a.* rather stout.

grosísimo, -ma, *a. superl.* [GRUESO] exceedingly stout, very bulky.

groso, *n.m.*, coarse snuff badly powdered.

grosor, *n.m.* thickness, bulk, size, density, closeness, compactness.

grosularia, *n.f.* (*min.*) grossular.

grosularieo, -a, *a.* (*bot.*) grossulaceous.

grosularina, grosulina, *n.f.* (*chem.*) grossulin.

grosura, *n.f.* fat, suet, tallow; meat diet, in opposition to fasting; *día de grosura.* Saturday (formerly so called in Castile).

grotescamente, *adv.* grotesquely.

grotesco, -ca, *a.* grotesque, ridiculous, laughable, extravagant, uncouth, farcical.

grúa, *n.f.* crane, derrick, gin, hoisting machine; ancient military machine; (*naut.*) bend; *grúa de la cuaderna maestra,* midship bend; *a la grúa,* in and out; *grúa corredera,* travelling crane; *grúa flotante,* floating crane; *grúa fija,* stationary crane; *grúa de caballete,* gantry crane.

gruero, -ra, *a.* trained to pursue cranes (birds of prey).

gruesa, *n.f.* gross, twelve dozen; (*eccles.*) chief part of a prebend; (*naut.*) bottomry.

gruesamente, *adv.* grossly, coarsely, wholesale; in bulk.

grueso, -sa, *a.* bulky, corpulent, thick, fat, fleshy, full-fed, gross, plump; great, big, large; strong, solid, firm; plain, home-spun, coarse, not fine; compact, dense; (*fig.*) heavy, dull, stupid, dim, slow.

grueso, *n.m.* bulk, thickness, depth, corpulence, density; main part, main body (of an army); down stroke (in penmanship); *en grueso,* (*com.*) in gross, by the gross, in bulk, wholesale.

gruir, *v.i.* to cry (of a crane).

grujidor, *n.m.* small bar used by glaziers for trimming glass.

grujir, *v.t.* to trim or pare ragged edges with a *grujidor.*

grulla, *n.f.* (*orn.*) crane; an ancien war-engine.

grullada, *n.f.* (*coll.*) gang or crowd of idlers; (*coll.*) patrol of constables or police officers.

grullero, -ra, *a.* applied to falcons or birds of prey in chase of cranes.

grullo, *a.* (*Mex.*) applied to an ash-coloured horse. — *n.m.* (*Arg., Cub., Mex., Ven.*) 1-dollar coin; (*Arg.*) stallion.

grumete, *n.m.* cabin-boy, ship-boy, younker; (*slang*) cat burglar.

grumillo, *n.m.* small grume, clot or curd.

grumo, *n.m.* grume, clot; *grumo de leche,* curd; cluster, bunch; bud of trees; tip of a fowl's wing.

grumoso, -sa, *a.* grumous, clotty.

gruñido, *n.m.* grunt (of a hog); growl (as of a dog); grumpiness, maundering of a discontented person. — *p.p.* [GRUÑIR].

gruñidor, -ra, *n.m.f.* grunter, growler, grumbler, mutterer, murmurer.

gruñimiento, *n.m.* grunting, muttering, growling, grumbling.

gruñir, *v.i.* to grunt like a hog; to creak (as doors, hinges, etc.); (*fig.*) to grumble, growl, snarl; *mamar y gruñir,* (*coll.*) to be discontented with everything.

gruñón, -ona, *n.m.f.* (*coll.*) growler, grunter, grumbler.

grupa, *n.f.* croup, rump of a horse; *cargar la grupa,* to pass a horse's tail through the crupper; *volver grupas,* to turn back, to retreat.

grupada, *n.f.* squall, burst of wind and rain; leap of a horse.

grupera, *n.f.* pillion (of a horse, motor-cycle); crupper.

grupo, *n.m.* group, assemblage; clump, cluster.

gruta, *n.f.* cavern, cavity between rocks; grotto, grot; *gruta de fieras,* menagerie. — *pl.* **grutas,** crypts, vaults, subterranean galleries.

grutesco, -ca, *a.* (*art*) grotesque, bizarre.

¡gua! *interj.* (*Bol., Col., Per., Ven.*) gracious! now, now!

guabá, *n.f.* (*Am. Cent., Ec.*) fruit of the guamotree.

guaba, *n.m.* (*West Ind.*) small hairy spider allied to the tarantula.

guabairo, *n.m.* (*Cub.*) a nocturnal insectivorous bird.

guabán, *n.m.* (*Cub.*) wild tree with poisonous seeds; its wood is used for tool handles.

guabico, *n.m.* (*Cub.*) tree of the Anonaceous family; its wood is fine and hard.

guabina, *n.f.* (*Col., Ven.*) fresh-water fish; (*Col.*) popular peasant melody.

guabirá, *n.m.* (*Arg.*) big tree with smooth and white trunk.

guabiyú, *n.m.* (*Arg.*) tree of the myrtle family with medicinal properties.

guabo, *n.m.* (*CR., Ec.*) [GUAMO].

guabul, *n.m.* (*Hond.*) refreshing drink made of ripe bananas cooked and dissolved in water.

guaca, *n.f.* (*Bol., Per.*) Indian grave; buried or hidden treasure; (*CR., Cub.*) pit where green fruit is kept for maturing; (*Bol., CR., Cub., Mex.*) money box.

guacal, *n.m.* (*Am.*) kind of gourd tree; vessel made of this; (*W. Ind., Col., Mex., Ven.*) oblong hamper for carrying fruit.

guacalote, *n.m.* (*Cub.*) climbing plant.

guacamaya, (*Cent. Am., Col., Mex.*) **guacamayo,** *n.m.* macao, macaw.

guacamole, *n.m.* (*Cub.*) salad of alligator pear.

guacamote, *n.m.* (*Mex.*) manioc, cassava (erroneously called yucca).

guacia, *n.f.* acacia; acacin, gum-arabic.

guácima, *n.f.* (*W. Ind., Col., CR.*) lofty wild tree (balsa wood).

guaco, *n.m.* (*bot.*) guaco, birthwort; (*orn.*) curassow.

guachapear, *v.t.* (*coll.*) to paddle, dabble, and splatter in water; (*coll.*) to make a botch of a thing. — *v.i.* to clap, as horses' shoes when loose; to clatter.

guachapelí, *n.m.* (*Am. Cent., Ec., Ven.*) leguminous tree similar to the acacia, with strong wood used by shipwrights.

guáchara, *n.f.* (*Cub., PR.*) fib, lie.

guacharaca, *n.f.* (*Col., Ven.*) [CHACHALACA].

guácharo, -ra, *a.* sickly, dropsical; (*obs.*) crying, whining.

guácharo, *n.m.* birdling, especially of a sparrow; (*orn.*) oil-bird, great goat-sucker.

guachinango, -ga, *n.m.f., a.* (*Cub., Mex.*) (*ichth.*) braize; (*Cub., PR.*) nickname given to the Mexicans; (*Cub., Mex., PR.*) crafty person.

guacho, -cha, *n.m.f., a.* (*Am.*) orphan, foundling; solitary, forlorn; (*Arg., Chi.*) wild plant or tree; bastard; (*Ec.*) furrow.

guacho, *n.m.* nestling of a sparrow.

guadafiones, *n.m.pl.* hopple, fetter-lock.

guadamací, guadamacil, *n.m.* embossed or printed leather.

guadamacilería, *n.f.* manufacture of embossed leather.

guadamacilero, *n.m.* manufacturer of embossed leather.

guadamecí, guadamecil, *n.m.* embossed or printed leather; *guadamecí brocado,* gilt or silvered embossed leather.

guadameco, *n.m.* ornament formerly worn by women.

guadaña, *n.f.* scythe, knife; (*fig.*) death, the Reaper.

guadañador, *n.m.* mowing machine.

guadañar, *v.t.* to scythe, mow.

guadañero, *n.m.* scythe-man; (*Cub.*) owner of a *guadaño.*

guadañil, *n.m.* mower of hay.

guadaño, *n.m.* (*Cádiz, Cub., Mex.*) small transport vessel equipped with an awning, used in seaports.

guadapero, *n.m.* wild common pear; boy who carries victuals to reapers or mowers.

guadarnés, *n.m.* harness-room; harness-keeper; officer of the king's mews.

guadijeño, *n.m.* poniard, stiletto, knife. — *a.* belonging to Guadix.

guadramaña, *n.f.* (*obs.*) trick, fraud; imposition.

guádua, *n.f.* (*Col., Ec., Ven.*) bamboo-cane.

guadual, *n.m.* (*Col., Ec., Ven.*) plantation of bamboo-canes.

guagua, *n.f.* trivial thing; (*Cub., Mex.*) insect that destroys fruit-trees; (*Arg., Bol., Chi., Ec., Per.*) baby; (*Cub.*) omnibus, streetcar; *de guagua,* free, gratis.

guaguasí, *n.m.* (*Cub.*) wild tree the resin of which is used as a purge.

guagüero, -ra, *n.m.f.* (*Cub.*) bargain driver; dead-head.

guaicán, *n.m.* (*ichth.*) remora.

guaicurú, *n.m.* (*Arg., Chi.*) a medicinal plant.

guaina, *n.m.* (*Arg., Bol., Chi.*) boy, youth.

guainambí, *n.m.* (*Mex.*) humming-bird.

guaira, *n.f.* (*Am.*) smelting furnace; (*naut.*) leg of mutton, triangular sail; (*Am. Cent.*) Indian flute.

guairo, *n.m.* (*Am.*) small two-masted coaster.

guaita, *n.f.* night watch, sentinel.

guajacón, *n.m.* (*Cub.*) small fresh-water fish.

guajalote, guajolote, *n.m.* (*Mex.*) turkey.

guajamón, -ona, *a.* (*Cub.*) orange-coloured.

guájar, *n.m.f.; * **guájaras,** *n.f.pl.* fastnesses, roughest part of a mountain.

guaje, *n.m.* (*Mex., Hond.*) calabash for learning to swim; (*Mex.*) kind of acacia; (*Hond., Mex.*) fool, ninny.

guájete por guájete, tit for tat.

guajira, *n.f.* (*Cub.*) popular song.

guajiro, -ra, *a.* (*Cub.*) rustic, rural; rude, boorish; (*Am. Cent.*) kind of flute with several tubes used by Indians. — *n.m.f.* white countryman or woman in Cuba.

¡gualá! *interj.* certainly! (*lit.* by Allah!)

gualatina, *n.f.* dish made of boiled apples, milk of almonds, spice, etc.

gualda, *n.f.* (*bot.*) weld, wild woad, dyer's woad, reseda; *cara de gualda,* pale face.

gualdado, -da, *a.* weld-coloured, yellowish.

gualdera, *n.f.* (*artill.*) trail, bracket; (*carp.*) stringboard; (*naut.*) whelp, check.

gualdo, -da, *a.* weld, yellow or gold colour.

gualdón, *n.m.* (*bot.*) base-rocket.

gualdrapa, *n.f.* horse-trappings, sumpter-cloth, housing foot-cloth; (*coll.*) tatter, rag hanging from clothes.

gualdrapazo, *n.m.* (*naut.*) flap of a sail; jerk.

gualdrapear, *v.t.* to place things head to tail. — *v.i.* (*naut.*) to flap (as sails).

gualdrapeo, *n.m.* flapping of sails.

gualdrapero, *n.m.* ragamuffin, ragged fellow.

gualdrín, *n.m.* weather-strip.

guama, *n.f.* (*Col., Ven.*) fruit of the *guamo*; (*Col.*) guamo-tree.

guamá, *n.m.* a West Indian tree much used for shade.

guamo, *n.m.* tall tree of the Leguminosæ family planted to shade the coffee plant.

guampa, *n.f.* (*Arg.*) drinking horn; (*Arg., Ur.*) horn.

guanabá, *n.m.* (*Cub.*) wading bird.

guanábana, *n.f.* (*bot.*) bullock's heart, custard-apple.

guanábano, *n.m.* fruit-tree of the Anona family (custard-apple).

guanaco, *n.m.* (*Chi.*) guanaco, kind of llama or alpaca; (*Cent. Am., Arg.*) gawk, gump.

guanajo, *n.m.* (*Cub.*) turkey; (*coll.*) simpleton.

guanche, *n.m.f., a.* ancient inhabitant of the Canaries.

guando, *n.m.* (*Am.*) litter, stretcher.

guandú, *n.m.* (*CR., Cub., Hond.*) a leguminous shrub.

guanera, *n.f.* place abounding in guano.

guangoche, *n.m.* (*Cent. Am., Mex.*) burlap.

guangocho, -cha, *a.* (*Mex.*) broad, loose; comfortable; (*Hond.*) burlap, and anything made of burlap.

guanín, *n.m.* (*W. Ind., Col.*) base gold made by Indians; jewel made with this gold.

guanina, *n.f.* (*Cub.*) leguminous plant.

guano, *n.m.* (*Cub.*) palm-tree; palm-tree leaves used for thatching; (*Am.*) guano.

guanquí, *n.m.* (*Chi.*) dioscorea plant allied to the yam.

guantada, *n.f.;* **guantazo,** *n.m.* slap or blow with the open hand.

guante, *n.m.* glove; collection for charity. — *pl.* **guantes,** extra pay, fee, or tip; *guantes de cabritilla,* kid gloves; *guantes de ante,* buff gloves; *adobar los guantes,* to regale, remunerate a person; *echar el guante,* to catch, lay hold on, challenge; (*coll.*) to seize, grasp; to imprison; *echar un guante,* to make a collection for charity; *salvo el guante,* (*coll.*) excuse my glove; *arrojar el guante,* to fling down the gauntlet; *poner a uno como un guante,* to render someone as pliable as a glove; (*coll.*) to abuse one; *calzarse* (or *descalzarse*) *los guantes,* to put on (or take off) one's gloves.

guantelete, *n.m.* gauntlet.

guantería, *n.f.* glover's shop or trade.

guantero, *n.m.* glover, glove maker.

guañir, *v.i.* (*prov.*) to grunt like pigs.

guao, *n.m.* (*Mex., Cub., Ec.*) a terebinthine tree whose seeds are used to feed hogs; the wood is used for charcoal; (*W. Ind.*) guaco (*Mikania amara*) said to cure snake-bites.

guapamente, *adv.* (*coll.*) bravely, courageously, dashingly.

guapear, *v.i.* (*coll.*) to be dashing; (*coll.*) to take a pride in fine dress; (*Chi.*) to brag, boast.

guapetón, -na, *a.* brave, daring, resolute.

guapeza, *n.f.* (*coll.*) bravery, courage; ostentation in dress.

guapinal, *n.m.* (*Am.*) resin-yielding tree.

guapo, -pa, *a.* (*coll.*) pretty, handsome; (*Am.*) stout, courageous, valiant, bold, resolute, daring, enterprising; spruce, neat, elegant, ostentatious, vain; gay, sprightly.

guapo, *n.m.* gallant, beau, sweetheart; bully.

guapote, -ta, *a.* (*coll.*) good-natured and good-looking person.

guaquero, *n.m.* vessel for drinking *chicha* found in ancient Peruvian tombs.

guara, *n.f.* (*Cub.*) tree resembling very closely the chestnut tree; (*Hond.*) macao or macaw; (*Chi.*) ridiculous affection; tawdry ornaments of dress.

guará, *n.m.* (*Am.*) kind of wolf of the pampas.

guaraca, *n.f.* (*Col., Chi., Ec., Per.*) sling; whip.

guaracha, *n.f.* (*Cub., PR.*) kind of Spanish clog-dance.

guarache, *n.m.* (*Mex.*) sandal.

guaraguao, *n.m.* (*Cub., PR.*) predatory bird.

guaraná, *n.f.* (*bot.*) (*Am. Cent., Bol., Par.*) guarana, paullinia; paste and stimulating drink made from its seeds.

guarango, *n.m.* (*Ec., Per.*) shrub used for dyeing; species of prosopis. — *a.* (*Arg., Chi., Ur.*) uncivil, impudent, insolent.

guaraní, *a.* guaranis. — *n.m.* Guarani.

guarapo, *n.m.* (*Am.*) juice of the sugar-cane, fermented cane-liquor.

guarapón, *n.m.* (*Arg., Chi., Per.*) wide-brimmed hat.

guarda, *n.m.f.* guard, keeper. — *n.f.* custody, trust, wardship, guard, safe-keeping, observance of a law or ordinance; outside rib or guard of a fan; nun who accompanies men through convents; fly-leaf, blank sheet; ward of a lock or of a key; (*mech.*) guard-plate, shoe; sheath of a pruning-knife; *guarda de la aduana,* officer of the customs-house; *guardainfantes,* (*naut.*) capstan whelps; *guardacadenas,* (*naut.*) laths of the chain-whales; *guarda de coto,* gamekeeper.

¡guarda! *interj.* take care! beware! look out!

guardabanderas, *n.m.* (*naut.*) yeoman of signals.

guardabarrera, *n.m.f.* (*railw.*) gate-keeper.

guardabarros, *n.m.* mudguard.

guardabosque, *n.m.* keeper of a forest, game-keeper.

guardabrazo, *n.m.* (*arm.*) brassard.

guardabrisa, *n.f.* glass shade for candles; (*motor.*) windscreen.

guardacabras, *n.m.* goat-herd.

guardacalada, *n.f.* window or opening in roof of a house.

guardacantón, *n.m.* spur-stone, paving-stone, check-stone.

guardacartuchos, *n.m.* (*naut.*) cartridge-case.

guardacostas, *n.m.* revenue cutter; coast-guard ship.

guardacuños, *n.m.* keeper of the dies in the mint.

guardadamas, *n.m.* officer who escorts court ladies.

guardadamente, *adv.* guardedly.

guardado, -da, *a.* guarded, reserved. — *p.p.* [GUARDAR].

guardador, -ra, *n.m.f.* very careful, watchful, and provident man; law-abiding person; miser; faithful keeper; (*mil.*) keeper of the spoils.

guardafrenos, *n.m.* (*railw.*) brakeman.

guardafuego, *n.m.* (*naut.*) breaming board; screen for a chimney.

guardaguas, *n.m.* (*naut.*) spurn-water; (*carp.*) flashing-board; (*motor.*) mudguard, splash leather.

guardagujas, *n.m.* pointsman.

guardahúmo, *n.m.* fire-screen, (*naut.*) smoke-sail.

guardainfante, *n.m.* farthingale, lady's hoop; (*naut.*) capstan whelps.

guardajoyas, *n.m.* keeper of the crown jewels; place where the crown jewels are kept.

guardalado, *n.m.* battlement of a bridge.

guardalmacén, *n.m.* store-keeper.

guardalobo, *n.m.* (*bot.*) poet's cassia.

guardamalleta, *n.f.* pelmet; valance.

guardamancebo, *n.m.* (*naut.*) man-rope.
guardamangel, *n.m.* larder in a mansion or palace.
guardamangier, *n.m.* officer in charge of victuals and staff payroll in the royal palace.
guardamano, *n.f.* guard of a sword.
guardamateriales, *n.m.* buyer of bullion and other necessaries for a mint.
guardamecha, *n.f.* (*naut.*) match-tub.
guardamigo, *n.m.* prop placed under the chin of criminals while they are flogged.
guardamonte, *n.m.* guard of a gunlock; forester, keeper of a forest.
guardamuebles, *n.m.* store-room for furniture; keeper of the furniture of a palace.
guardamujer, *n.f.* maid of honour.
guardapapo, *n.m.* (*arm.*) gorget.
guardapelo, *n.m.* locket.
guardapesca, *n.m.* fishery protection vessel.
guardapiés, *n.m.* skirt.
guardapolvo, *n.m.* dust-guard, dust wrapper, cover; dust-coat; duster, case, cap, lid; inner lid of a watch; tongue (of a shoe); projection over a window or door to carry off the water; the dust-guard of a carriage or railway car.
guardapuerta, *n.f.* storm-door; door-screen, door-curtain.
guardar, *v.t.* to keep, guard, protect, watch over, defend, take care of; preserve from damage; to respect, observe; to store, lay up, retain, reserve, lay by, conserve, keep back, maintain; to hold for another; to fulfil one's duty; to be upon one's guard, to avoid, abstain from, guard against; to be sparing, to be chary of spending; *guardar batideros,* to anticipate and avoid difficulties; *guardársela a alguno,* to delay vengeance for a favourable opportunity; *guardar cama,* to keep one's bed; *guardar rencor,* to bear a grudge; *quien guarda, halla,* the saver has always money. — *v.r.* to guard (against), avoid, beware (used with the prep. *de*).
guardarraya, *n.f.* boundary.
guardarrío, *n.m.* (*orn.*) kingfisher.
guardarropa, *n.f.* cloak-room, coat-room. — *n.m.f.* keeper of a wardrobe; wardrobe, clothes-press; (*theat.*) property-man (or woman); (*bot.*) lavender-cotton.
guardarropía, *n.f.* (*theat.*) props, property; *de guardarropía,* make believe, pretend.
guardarruedas, *n.m.* fender to protect the lintel of a house against the wheels of carriages.
guardasilla, *n.f.* moulding of wood fixed to a wall to prevent damage by the back of chairs.
guardasol, *n.m.* sunshade, parasol.
guardatimón, *n.m.* (*naut.*) stern-chaser.
guardavajilla, *n.f.* room for keeping the royal plate or table-service.
guardavela, *n.m.* small purchase rope to secure the sails.
guardavía, *n.m.* (*railw.*) signalman, line-keeper.
guardería, *n.f.* keepership; day-nursery.
guardesa, *n.f.* female-keeper; *guarda's* wife.
guardia, *n.f.* guard, body of armed men to watch by way of defence; (*naut.*) watch; turn of persons in watching or of officers on duty; defence, custody, protection, watch, assistance; (*fenc.*) guard. — *n.m.* soldier belonging to the guards, guardsman; *cuerpo de guardia,* guard-room; *guardia de estribor,*

starboard watch; *guardia de babor,* larboard watch; *guardia del tope,* masthead look-out; (*mil.*) *estar de guardia,* to be on duty; *estar en guardia,* to be on one's guard, alert; *mudar la guardia,* to relieve the guard; *montar la guardia,* to mount guard; *salir de guardia,* to come off guard; *guardia marina,* midshipman; *guardia civil, n.f.* body of rural police in Spain. — *n.m.* a member of this body; *guardia municipal, n.f.* city police. — *n.m.* policeman; *en guardia,* (*fenc.*) on guard.
guardián, -ana, *n.m.f.* keeper, guardian, warden, watchman.
guardián, *n.m.* local superior of convents of the order of St. Francis; (*naut.*) boatswain's mate; quarterman; gunner's yeoman; (*naut.*) strong hawser.
guardianía, *n.f.* guardianship of a convent and the district assigned to it.
guardilla, *n.f.* garret, skylight, attic; (*sew.*) guard, welt; each of the two extreme thick teeth of a comb.
guardillón, *n.m.* loft, air space under a roof.
guardín, *n.m.* tiller-rope, tiller-chain; portlanyard.
guardoso, -sa, *a.* frugal, parsimonious; niggardly, stingy.
guarecer, *v.t.* (*pres. indic.* **guarezco;** *pres. subj.* **guarezca**) to shelter, guard, aid, succour, assist, protect, preserve; to cure. — *v.i.* (*obs.*) to recover, grow well. — *v.r.* to take refuge or shelter.
guarén, *n.m.* (*Chi.*) water-rat.
guarentigio, -gia, *a.* applied to a contract containing a warranty clause.
guaria, *n.f.* (*CR.*) an indigenous orchid.
guariao, *n.m.* (*Cub.*) large bird with dark plumage spotted with white.
guaricha, *n.f.* (*Col., Ec., Ven.*) female, woman; (*Ec.*) soldier's moll.
guarida, *n.f.* den, cave, or couch of a wild beast; shelter, lurking-place, cover, haunt; protection; (*obs.*) aid.
guarimán, *n.m.* (*Am.*) tree of the magnolia family, with aromatic bark used as spice.
guarín, *n.m.* sucking pig, last pig of a litter.
guarisapo, *n.m.* (*Chi.*) tadpole.
guarismo, *n.m.* (*arith.*) figure, digit, cipher, combination of figures or numerals.
guaritoto, *n.m.* (*Ven.*) euphorbiaceous shrub used as hæmostatic.
guarne, *n.m.* turn of a cable or tackle.
guarnecedor, -ra, *a.* garnisher, furnisher, trimmer.
guarnecer, *v.t.* (*pres. indic.* **guarnezco;** *pres. subj.* **guarnezca**) to garnish, adorn, embellish, beautify, decorate, furbish, dress, deck, array; (*sew.*) to trim, bind, edge, face, border, line, welt; to provide, furnish; to accoutre, equip; (*build.*) to plaster; (*jewel.*) set in gold, silver, etc.; (*arm.*) to put a guard on a sword; to harness horses or mules; (*mil.*) to garrison.
guarnecido, *n.m.* (*build.*) plastering, stucco-work. — *p.p.* [GUARNECER].
guarnés, *n.m.* harness-room.
guarnición, *n.f.* (*sew.*) trimming, binding, edging, valance, welt, flounce, furbelow, garniture, garnish, ornamental hem, lace, or border; (*mech.*) packing; (*jewel.*) setting; (*mil.*) garrison; (*arm.*) guard of a sword. — *pl.* **guarniciones,** gears or traces of mules and horses; harness; ancient steel armour.

guarnicionar, *v.t.* to garrison.

guarnicionería, *n.f.* shop of a harness-maker.

guarnicionero, *n.m.* harness-maker.

guarniel, *n.m.* leather pouch with divisions used by carriers; (*Mex.*) powder-flask.

guarnigón, *n.m.* young quail.

guarnimiento, *n.m.* lines or ropes for reeving.

guarnir, *v.t.* to garnish, adorn, embellish, decorate, beautify, furbish, deck, dress, array; (*naut.*) to reeve; to rig.

guaro, *n.m.* small, very talkative parrot; (*Cent. Am.*) sugar-cane fire-water.

guarra, *n.f.* sow.

guarrillo, *n.m.* small pig.

guarro, *n.m.* hog, pig. — *n.m.*, *a.* dirty, filthy (person).

¡guarte! *interj.* [*contr. of* GUÁRDATE]; take care! beware! look out!

guaruba, *n.f.* (*Am.*) red-necked parrot; howling monkey.

guarumo, *n.m.* (*Cent. Am.*, *Col.*, *Ec.*, *Mex.*, *Ven.*) tree of the Artocarpus family.

guarura, *n.f.* (*Ven.*) a very large snail whose shell is used as a horn.

guasa, *n.f.* (*coll.*) jest, fun, joke; satire, irony; dullness; (*Cub.*) jewfish.

guasanga, *n.f.* (*Cent. Am.*, *Col.*, *Cub.*, *Mex.*) noisy mirth.

guasanguero, -ra, *a.* (*Cent. Am.*, *Col.*, *Cub.*, *Mex.*) jolly, merry, noisy.

guasasa, *n.f.* (*Cub.*) swarm of mosquitoes in humid and gloomy places.

guasca, *n.f.* (*Am.*, *W. Ind.*) cord, thong, whip; (*Col.*) fibrous bark; *dar guasca*, to whip, scourge.

guasería, *n.f.* (*Arg.*, *Chi.*) dullness, rudeness.

guaso -sa, *a.* (*Chi.*) rustic, rural; (*Arg.*, *Chi.*, *Cub.*, *Ec.*) coarse, uncouth, churlish, uncivil.

guasón, -ona, *a.* (*coll.*) waggish, leg-pulling.

guasquear, *v.t.* (*Am.*) to whip, scourge.

guataca, *n.f.* (*Cub.*) spade; (*coll.*) large ear.

guatacare, *n.m.* (*Ven.*) tree of the genus *Borago*, with flexible and resistant wood.

guataquear, *v.t.* (*Cub.*) to spade, clear ground with the spade.

guate, *n.m.* (*CR.*, *Hond.*) corn stalks used for fodder.

guatemalteco, -ca, *n.m.f.*, *a.* native or inhabitant of the Republic of Guatemala; belonging or relating to Guatemala.

guateque, *n.m.* (*Am.*) country dance.

guatusa, *n.f.* (*CR.*, *Ec.*, *Hond.*) edible rodent akin to the spotted cavy.

guau, *n.m.* bow-wow, the bark of a dog.

¡guay! *interj.* alas! alack!

guaya, *n.f.* grief, sorrow, affliction.

guayaba, *n.f.* fruit of the guava-tree; (*W. Ind.*, *Col.*, *ES.*) (*coll.*) lie, fraud; *jalea de guayaba*, guava jelly; *pasta de guayaba*, guava sweet-meat; *casquitos de guayaba*, guava preserve.

guayabal, *n.m.* orchard of guava trees.

guayabera, *n.f.* (*Cub.*) short coat made of light material, worn by countryman.

guayabo, *n.m.* the guava tree.

guayaca, *n.f.* (*Arg.*, *Bol.*, *Chi.*) bag, sack.

guayacán, guayaco, *n.m.* lignum-vitæ tree, guaiacum.

guayacana, *n.f.* date-plum.

guayacol, *n.m.* (*chem.*) guaiacol.

guayadero, *n.m.* (*obs.*) place or room set aside for crying or expressing grief and sorrow, esp. at funerals.

guayado, -da, *a.* (*Cub.*, *Cent. Am.*) applied to songs with the refrain *¡guay!* or *¡ay, amor!*

guayapil, guayapín, *n.m.* (*Am.*) loose Indian dress.

guayaquil, *a.* pertaining to Guayaquil (Ecuador). — *n.m.* cacao of Guayaquil.

guayaquileño, -ña, *n.m.f.*, *a.* native or inhabitant of Guayaquil (Ecuador); relating to Guayaquil.

guayo, *n.m.* (*Chi.*) tree of the Rosaceæ family with reddish and hard wood.

guayuco, *n.m.* (*Col.*, *Ven.*) loin-cloth used by the Indians.

guayusa, *n.f.* (*Ec.*) plant used as a substitute for tea or maté.

guazapa, *n.f.* (*Guat.*, *Hond.*) teetotum.

guazubirá, *n.m.* (*Arg.*) wild deer.

gubán, *n.m.* (*Philip.*) large clinker-built canoe.

gubernamental, *a.* governmental.

gubernativamente, *adv.* by act of the government.

gubernativo, -va, *a.* administrative, governmental, gubernatorial.

gubia, *n.f.* (*carp.*) gouge, centering-chisel; (*artill.*) vent-searcher.

gubilete, *n.m.* (*obs.*) kind of vase.

guedeja, *n.f.* long lock of hair; forelock; lion's mane.

güeldo, *n.m.* shrimps, clams, etc., used as bait.

güelfo, -fa, *n.m.f.*, *a.* Guelph.

guelte, gueltre, *n.m.* money, cash; wealth.

güepil, güipil, *n.m.* (*Mex.*) sack of rich cloth, worn by Indian women.

güermeces, *n.m.* morbid swelling in the throat of birds of prey.

guerra, *n.f.* war, warfare; hostility, strife, dissension, struggle, fight, conflict, opposition; *guerra galana*, war carried out by small detachments and with very slight losses, skirmish; *guerra guerreada*, experienced warfare; *guerra a muerte*, war without quarter, relentless war; *guerra de bolas*, *guerra de palos*, two different games of billiards; *tener la guerra declarada*, to be at daggers drawn; *armar en guerra*, to fit or equip a ship for war; *dar guerra*, to cause annoyance; *hacer (la) guerra*, to war, to wage war; *el que tonto va a la guerra, tonto viene de ella*, travelling benefits only the intelligent and not the foolish.

guerreador, -ra, *n.m.f.* warrior, fighter.

guerreante, *n.m.f.*, *a.* warrior, warring.

guerrear, *v.i.* to war, wage war, fight; be in a state of hostility; (*fig.*) to oppose, resist, argue.

guerrera, *n.f.* (*mil.*) coat (uniform).

guerreramente, *adv.* in a warlike way.

guerrero, -ra, *a.* martial, warlike; (*coll.*) mischievous, troublesome, vexatious.

guerrero, *n.m.* warrior, fighter, soldier, military man.

guerrilla, *n.f.* band or body of partisans, skirmishers, light horsemen; skirmish, light engagement; game of cards.

guerrillear, *v.i.* to engage in guerrilla warfare.

guerrillero, *n.m.* guerrilla fighter; commander of skirmishers.

guía, *n.m.f.* guide, conductor, cicerone, director, leader, adviser, regulator. — *n.m.* sergeant or corporal who attends to dressing the line. — *n.f.* guide, guide-sign; guide-book; (*com.*) custom-house permit, cocket;

young shoot left on a vine or tree for training others; young shoot or sucker of a vine; (*mech.*) guide, rule, guide-bar, guide-pin, guide-screw, guide-tube, etc.; (*naut.*) guy, leader, span, hauling-line, preventer-rope; (*pyr.*) fuse; (*min.*) leader; handle-bar of a bicycle; guard of a fan; leader, foremost horse; *guia de forasteros*, vade-mecum of a town. — *pl.* **guias,** guide-lines; jeweller's tool to guide 'drills; reins for controlling the leader horses; *a guías*, driving four-in-hand.

guiabara, *n.f.* (*Cub.*) wild tree of the Polygonaceæ family.

guiadera, *n.f.* guide or conductor in mills. — *pl.* **guiaderas,** upright guides in oil-mills, mine-lifts, etc.

guiado, -da, *a.* guided; having a guide or a permit. — *p.p.* [GUIAR].

guiador, -ra, *n.m.f.* guide, director, leader.

guiar, *v.t.* to guide, lead, conduct, show the way; to advise, counsel, teach, direct; to drive; to pilot; (*agric.*) to train a plant. — *v.r.* to be led or to go by; to follow; *guiar el agua a su molino*, to bring grist to one's mill.

guiguí, *n.m.* (*Philip.*) flying squirrel.

guija. *n.f.* pebble, cobble-stone; (*bot.*) blue vetch. — *pl.* **guijas,** (*coll.*) strength, force, vigour; *ser de pocas guijas* or *tener poca guijas*, to be very weak.

guijarral, *n.m.* heap of pebbles, place abounding in pebbles.

guijarrazo, *n.m.* blow with a pebble or a cobble.

guijarreño, -ña, *a.* pebbly, gravelly; (*coll.*) hardy, strong (a person).

guijarrillo, -ito, *n.m.* small pebble.

guijarro, *n.m.* small boulder, cobble-stone.

guijarroso, -sa, *a.* full of cobbles, pebbly.

guijeño, -ña, *a.* belonging to or resembling pebbles; (*coll.*) hard, relentless, difficult.

guijo, *n.m.* gravel for roads.

guijón, *n.m.* caries, rottenness in the teeth.

guijoso, -sa, *a.* gravelly, pebbly.

guilalo, *n.m.* (*Philip.*) coasting vessel with sails of matting.

guilla, *n.f.* plentiful harvest.

guillame, *n.m.* joiner's rabbet-plane.

guilledín, *n.m.* gelding.

Guillelmo, Guillén, Guillermo, *n.m.*William.

guillemote, *n.m.* puffin.

guillote, *n.m.·* husbandman who enjoys the produce of a farm; (*naut.*) treenail, iron pin; vagrant, sponger, idle fellow; novice at gambling; simpleton.

guillotina, *n.f.* guillotine; cardboard-cutting machine; (*parl.*) rule by which a government closes a debate; *de guillotina*, said of sash windows.

guillotinar, *v.t.* to guillotine.

guimbalete, *n.m.* pump brake, pump handle.

guimbarda, *n.f.* ancient dance; (*carp.*) grooving plane.

guinchar, *v.t.* to prick, goad, wound.

guincho, *n.m.* goad, pike; (*Cub.*) sea-bird of prey of the Falconides family.

guinda, *n.f.* berry of the mazard; height of the masts (and top-masts).

guindado, -da, *a.* hoisted, set up; garnished with mazard-berries. — *p.p.* [GUINDAR].

guindajos, *n.m.pl.* (*Cub.*) hangings, fringes, tassels.

guindal, *n.m.* mazard-tree, cherry-tree.

guindalera, *n.f.* plantation of mazard-trees, cherry orchard.

guindaleta, *n.f.* crank-rope; fulcrum of a balance.

guindaleza, *n.f.* hawser.

guindamaina, *n.f.* salute by dipping the flag.

guindar, *v.t.* to raise, hoist, hang, lift on high; (*coll.*) to obtain or win against competition from others; (*coll.*) to hang a person. — *v.i.*, *v.r.* to be suspended, to hang from or on anything.

guindaste, *n.m.* (*mech.*) horse, frame; (*naut.*) timber-head tackle.

guindilla, *n.f.* pod of the Cayenne or red pepper.

guindillo de Indias, *n.m.* shrub of the Capsicum family; red pepper.

guindo, *n.m.* kind of cherry-tree; mazard-tree; *guindo griego*, large mazard cherry-tree; *don Guindo*, (*joc.*) coxcomb.

guindola, *n.f.* (*naut.*) triangular hanging stage; lifebuoy; (*naut.*) float of the log.

guinea, *n.f.* guinea, English gold coin.

guineo, -a, *a.* Guinea, of Guinea; *gallina guinea*, guinea-hen.

guineo, *n.m.* negro dance; (*Cub.*) banana.

guinga, guingans, *n.f.* gingham.

guinja, *n.f.*; **guinjo,** *n.m.* jujube.

guiñada, guiñadura, *n.f.* wink; (*naut.*) yaw, lurch.

guiñador -ra, *n.m.f.* winker.

guiñapiento, -ta; guiñaposo, -sa, *a.* ragged, tattered, torn.

guiñapo, *n.m.* tatter, rag; ragamuffin, tatterdemalion, ragged fellow; (*Chi.*) ground maize used for brewing *Chicha*.

guiñar, *v.t.* to wink; to make eyes at; (*naut.*) to yaw, lurch, steer unsteadily.

guiño, *n.m.* wink.

guión, *n.m.* cross, standard carried before prelates, communities and corporations; royal standard; gonfalon in processions; master of ceremonies; leader of a dance; explanatory text or reference table; hyphen; subtitles (of a film); (*mil.*) guidon; (*naut.*) loom of an oar; (*mus.*) mark of repetition, repeat; script of a film or radio feature.

guionaje, *n.m.* office of guide or conductor.

guipar, *v.t.* (*vulg.*) to see.

guipuzcoano, -na, *a.* native of or belonging to the province of Guipuzcoa; one of the eight principal Basque dialects.

güira, *n.f.* (*Am.*) calabash-tree.

guirigay, *n.m.* (*coll.*) gibberish; jargon.

guirindola, *n.f.* breast, frill (of a shirt).

guirlache, *n.m.* roast almond caramel.

guirnalda, (*obs.*) **guirlanda,** *n.f.* garland, wreath; (*naut.*) puddening; (*mil.*) light ball.

guirnaldeta, *n.f.* small garland.

güiro, *n.m.* (*Arg., Bol., Per.*) green Indian corn stalk; (*obs.*) bottle-gourd, fruit of the calabash-tree; (*Cub.*) (*obs.*) gourd used as an instrument to accompany dance music.

guiropa, *n.f.* meat dish with potatoes, etc.

guirre, *n.m.* (*Canaries*) vulture.

guisa, *n.f.* mode, manner, species; *a guisa de*, as, like, in the manner of.

guisado, *n.m.* stew, made-up dish; ragout, fricassee; remarkable action.

guisado, -da, *a.; estar uno mal guisado*, to be discontented. — *p.p.* [GUISAR].

guisador, -ra; guisandero, -ra, *n.m.f., a.* a cook; one who cooks.

guisantal, *n.m.* patch planted with peas.

guisante, *n.m.* pea; *guisante de olor* (or *oloroso*), sweet-pea.

guisar, *v.t.* to cure meat, cook or dress victuals; (*coll.*) to arrange, prepare, adjust.

guisaso, *n.m.* (*Cub.*) generic name given to several wild herbaceous plants with prickly or spinous fruit.

guiso, *n.m.* cooked dish; seasoning, condiment.

guisopillo, *n.m.* small water-sprinkler.

guisote, *n.m.* dish of meat dressed, poorly cooked.

guita, *n.f.* packthread, hemp, twine; (*coll.*) money.

guitar, *v.t.* to sew with packthread.

guitarra, *n.f.* guitar; (*mas.*) muller for pulverizing gypsum; *ser buena guitarra,* (*coll.*) to be very artful; *está bien* (or *mal*) *templada la guitarra,* he is good- (or ill-) humoured; *pegar como guitarra en un entierro,* to be very unfitting, out-of-place.

guitarrazo, *n.m.* blow with a guitar.

guitarrear, *v.i.* to strum the guitar.

guitarrero, -ra, *n.m.f.* guitar-maker; player on the guitar.

guitarresco, -ca, *a.* (*coll.*) belonging to the guitar.

guitarrillo, -lla, *n.m.f.* small guitar with four strings.

guitarrista, *n.m.f.* player on the guitar.

guitarro, *n.m.* small four-string guitar.

guitarrón, *n.m.* large guitar; (*coll.*) acute knave.

guitero, -ra, *n.m.f.* twine-maker.

guito, -ta, *a.* (*Ar.*) treacherous, vicious (as a mule).

guitón, -na, *n.m.f.* mendicant, vagrant, vagabond, tramp. — *n.m.* ancient coin.

guitonear, *v.i.* to loiter, loaf, idle about, lead a vagabond life.

guitonería, *n.f.* idleness; vagabond life.

guizazo, *n.m.* (*Cub.*) a weed.

guizgar, *v.t.* to excite, invite.

guizque, *n.m.* boat-hook; (*prov.*) sting of a wasp.

guja, *n.f.* halbert, voulge.

gula, *n.f.* gluttony, inordinate eating and drinking.

gules, *n.m.pl.* (*her.*) gules, red (colour).

guloso, -sa, *a.* gluttonous, greedy.

gulusmear, *v.i.* (*coll.*) to eat delicacies.

gullería, *n.f.* delicacy; *pedir gullerías,* to wish or look for something unreasonable.

gulloría, *n.f.* kind of lark.

gumamela, *n.f.* (*Philip.*) plant belonging to the Malvaceæ family.

gúmena, *n.f.* anchor-cable.

gumeneta, *n.f.* small cable.

gumía, *n.f.* dagger or poniard used by the Moors.

gumífero, -ra, *a.* gum-producing, gummiferous.

gura, *n.f.* (*Philip.*) crested wild pigeon.

gurbia, *n.f.* (*Am.*) [GUBIA].

gurbión, *n.m.* coarse twisted silk; silk stuff; gum-resin extracted from spurge.

gurdo, -da, *a.* silly, simple nonsensical.

gurrar, *v.i.* (*naut.*) to get clear of another ship; to retrograde, fall back.

gurriato, *n.m.* nestling sparrow.

gurrufero, *n.m.* (*coll.*) deformed and vicious nag.

gurrullada, *n.f.* (*coll.*) gang, crowd of people.

gurrumina, *n.f.* (*coll.*) uxoriousness, unbecoming submission to a wife; (*Arg., Cub., Guat., Mex.*) trifle; (*Hond.*) sly (person).

gurrumino, -na, *n.m., a.* mean, base, despicable; (*coll.*) henpecked husband; (*Bol., Per.*) coward, faint-hearted; (*Mex., prov.*) small child.

gurullo, *n.m.* (*prov.*) lump, knot.

gurullón, *n.m.* knot of wool in cloths.

gurumete, *n.m.* ship's boy [GRUMETE].

gurupa, *n.f.* croup of a horse [GRUPA].

gurupera, *n.f.* crupper [GRUPERA].

gurupetín, *n.m.* small crupper.

gurvio, -via, *a.* curved, arched, incurvated (of tools).

gusanear, *v.i.* to itch.

gusanera, *n.f.* place where worms or microbes are bred; (*coll.*) ruling passion.

gusanico, -ito, *n.m.* small worm or maggot.

gusaniento, -ta, *a.* grubby, full of vermin, maggoty, worm-eaten.

gusanillo, *n.m.* small worm or grub; gold, silver, or silk twist; twist-stitch embroidery; (*mech.*) bit of a gimlet or auger.

gusano, *n.m.* worm, maggot, grub, caterpillar, thread-worm, pin-worm; (*fig.*) meek, dejected person; distemper among sheep; *gusano de seda,* silk-worm; *gusano de luz,* glow-worm, firefly; *gusano de la conciencia,* remorse, worm of conscience; *gusano de San Antón,* grey grub; *gusano revoltón,* vine inch-worm.

gusarapiento, -ta, *a.* wormy, grubby; corrupted.

gusarapillo, -ito, *n.m.* small water-worm.

gusarapo, *n.m.* water-worm.

gusil, *n.m.* Russian harp.

gustable, *a.* tastable, gustable.

gustadura, *n.f.* gustation, tasting.

gustar, *v.t.* to taste; to try, experience, experiment. — *v.i.* to please; to be agreeable, satisfy, be liked, cause enjoyment; *gustar de,* to desire, like, love, enjoy, relish, be pleased with.

gustativo, -va, *a.* lingual (gustatory nerve).

gustazo, *n.m.* (*coll.*) great pleasure.

gustillo, *n.m.* peculiar savour, flavour, or relish.

gusto, *n.m.* taste and sense; flavour, savour, season, relish; sensation of tasting, gust; caprice, fancy, whim, diversion; election, choice; discernment; pleasure, delight, contentment, gratification, complacence; liking, mind; one's own will and determination; taste, intellectual relish or discernment. — *pl.* **gustos,** sensual pleasures, evil habits, vices; *de buen gusto,* in good taste; *artículo* (or *cosa*) *de gusto,* tasty, fancy article; *el gusto del día,* prevalent taste or fashion; *con mucho gusto,* with great pleasure; *dar gusto,* to gratify; *al gusto dañado* (or *estragado*) *lo dulce le es amargo,* to the soured taste all is bitter; *de gustos no hay nada escrito,* there's no law about tastes; *más vale un gusto que cien panderos,* a whim is more attractive than many solid benefits; *sobre gustos no hay disputa,* there's no accounting for tastes.

gustosamente, *adv.* tastefully, fain, gladly, acceptably.

gustoso, -sa, *a.* savoury, gustable, dainty, pleasing to the taste; pleasing, entertaining, pleasant; tasty; cheerful, merry, content, blithe, joyful; ready, willing.

gutagamba, *n.f.* indigenous tree from India (*Garcinia Hanburii*).

gutapercha, *n.f.* gutta-percha; caoutchouc, india-rubber.

gutiámbar, *n.m.* gamboge, the yellow gum-resin of the *gutagamba* tree.

gutifero, -ra, *a.* guttiferous, gum-yielding.

gutiforme, *a.* guttiform.

gutural, *a.* guttural.

guturalmente, *adv.* gutturally.

guturoso, -sa, *a.* (*bot.*) throated; throaty.

guzla, *n.f.* one-string rebec.

guzmán, *n.m.* nobleman who formerly served as midshipman or cadet.

guzpatarra, *n.f.* ancient game played by boys.

H

H, h, *n.f.* ninth letter of the Spanish alphabet, named *hache*. It is no longer aspirated, except by the common people in Andalusia, Extremadura, and in some parts of Spanish-America; and in a few words indicated below.

ha, *3rd pers. sing. pres. indic.* [HABER].

¡ha! *interj.* ah, alas; (*naut.*) haul away.

haba, *n.f.* bean plant, bean; *haba común caballar,* horse-bean; *haba de las Indias,* sweet-pea; *haba marina,* navel-wort, kidney-wort; *haba de San Ignacio,* St. Ignatius's bean; *haba de perro,* dog's bane; tumour in the palate of horses; (*min.*) prill. — *pl.* **habas,** white and black balls used in secret ballots; *son habas contadas,* this is perfectly clear; that is a sure thing; *echar las habas,* to practise sorcery, divination by lots, etc.

habado, -da, *a.* (*vet.*) having a tumour called *haba*; dappled (as a horse).

habanera, *n.f.* slow Cuban dance and song.

habanero, -ra, *a.* Havanese, of Havana.

habano, -na, *a.* of Havana (tobacco).

habano, *n.m.* Havana cigar.

habar, *n.m.* bean-field.

habascón, *n.m.* (*Am.*) parsnip-like root.

háber, *n.m.* doctor of the law among the Jews; title inferior to rabbi.

haber, *v.t.* (*pres. indic.* **he;** *pret.* **hube;** *fut.* **habré;** *pres. subj.* **haya**) to have, own, possess; to get, catch, lay hands on, take, recover (*haber* is less used as an active verb than as an auxiliary and an impersonal); *el ladrón no pudo ser habido,* the thief could not be apprehended; *el niño lee cuantos libros puede haber,* the boy reads as many books as he can get; *más vale saber que haber,* wisdom is more precious than rubies. — *v. auxil.* to have; *haber sido,* to have been; (with *de* and an infinitive) to have to: *he de escribir,* I have to write, I must write; *habremos de cantar,* we shall have to sing; also denotes that a thing will normally happen: *el jefe ha de venir mañana,* the chief will come tomorrow. — *v. impers.* (in this sense *haber* has two inflections in the 3rd pers. sing. pres. indic., i.e., *ha* and *hay;* *ha* signifies lapse of time, otherwise *hay* is used) to happen, occur, befall; to be, exist; *tres*

años ha, three years ago; *no hay pan,* there is no bread; *no hay tal,* there is no such thing; *hay que,* it is necessary, one must, it is imperative; *no hay de que,* don't mention it. — *v.r.* to behave, act, conduct oneself, become, pretend; *haber la de San Quintín,* (*coll.*) to have a great row; *no haber tal,* not to be certain; to be no such thing; *no hay más que pedir,* it is perfect, one couldn't expect more; *habérselas con alguno,* to contend, dispute, face, have it out with someone.

haber, *n.m.* property, income, fortune, assets (gen. used in *pl.* **haberes**); (in book-keeping), credit, Cr.

haberío, *n.m.* beast of burden; livestock.

habichuela, *n.f.* French-bean, kidney-bean; *habichuelas verdes,* string beans.

habiente, *a.* (*law*) having, possessing.

hábil, *a.* capable, intelligent, learned, able; agile, active, ready; clever, skilful, expert, dexterous, cunning, knowing; (*law*) fit, apt, handy, qualified; (*law*) *día hábil,* lawful day.

habilidad, *n.f.* ability, ableness, dexterity, expertness, cleverness, mastery, talent, knowledge, skill; quickness, nimbleness, speed; instinct; cunning. — *pl.* **habilidades,** accomplishments.

habiloso, -sa, *a.* accomplished, clever.

habilitación, *n.f.* habilitation, qualification; equipment, outfit; office of a paymaster; *habilitación de bandera,* concession to a foreign vessel to engage in the coasting trade.

habilitado, -da, *a.* habilitated, qualified.

habilitado, *n.m.* paymaster; (*law*) deputy of a judicial secretary. — *p.p.* [HABILITAR].

habilitador, -ra, *n.m.f.* qualifier; outfitter; one who makes able or fit.

habilitar, *v.t.* to qualify, enable; to provide, supply, fit out, furnish means, equip.

hábilmente, *adv.* dexterously, ably, cleverly, knowingly.

habiloso, *a.* (*Chi.*) [HABILIDOSO].

habilla, *n.f.* (*Cub., Hond.*) tree of the Euphorbiaceous family.

habitable, *a.* habitable.

habitación, *n.f.* dwelling, residence, habitation, abode, lodging; room, suite of rooms, chamber, apartments; habitat.

habitáculo, *n.m.* small dwelling, residence, abode.

habitador, -ra, *n.m.f.* inhabitant, resident, dweller, abider.

habitante, *a.* inhabiting. — *n.m.* inhabitant, habitant, dweller, resident.

habitar, *v.t.* to inhabit, live, dwell, reside, lodge.

hábito, *n.m.* dress, habit, habiliment, garment; custom, habit, habitude, customariness; robes of the military orders; *caballero del hábito de Santiago,* knight of the military order of Saint James; *el hábito no hace al monje,* it's not the cowl that makes the monk; *tomar el hábito,* (*eccles.*) to profess, to take vows. — *pl.* **hábitos,** dress of ecclesiastics; *ahorcar* (or *colgar*) *los hábitos,* (*coll.*) to throw off the cowl.

habituación, *n.f.* habituation, accustoming.

habitual, *a.* habitual, usual, accustomed, customary, inveterate, frequent, common.

habitualmente, *adv.* habitually, customarily, usually, by habit.

habituar, *v.t.* to accustom, habituate, inure. — *v.r.* to become accustomed; to accustom oneself.

habitud, *n.f.* habitude, respect, relation.

habiz, *n.m.* donation, in trust, of immovable property to a religious Mohammedan institution.

habla, *n.f.* speech, language, idiom, dialect; argument, discourse, address; conversation, talk; *estar en habla*, to talk about a matter; *negar* (or *quitar*) *el habla*, to refuse to speak to a person; *estar sin habla* or *perder el habla*, to be speechless; *al habla*, (*naut.*, usu. with the verbs *estar*, *ponerse* and *pasar*) within speaking distance; *ponerse al habla*, (*coll.*) to speak over the telephone.

hablado, -da, *a.; bien hablado*, well-spoken, polite; *mal hablado*, ill-spoken, uncouth. — *p.p.* [HABLAR].

hablador, -ra, *n.m.f.* talker, gabbler, prattler, chatterer, chatterbox; gossiper.

habladorcillo, -lla, *n.m.f.* affected babbler.

habladuría, *n.f.* impertinent speech; gossip, empty talk.

hablanchín, -ina; hablantín, -ina, *a.* (*coll.*) talkative (person).

hablante, *a.* speaking, talking.

hablar, *v.i.* to speak; to talk, commune, converse, reason; to advise, admonish; to harangue, address, make a speech; (*naut.*) to hail a ship. — *v.t.* to speak a language; to utter, give expression to. — *v.r.* to speak to each other; *hablar de*, to discuss, refer to, talk about, mention; *hablar con*, to speak with, to court, woo; *hablar a*, to address, speak to; *hablar Dios a alguno*, to be inspired; *hablar de chanza*, to talk in jest; *hablar de hilván*, to speak too rapidly and confusedly; *hablar de vicio*, to be loquacious; *hablar de* (or *en*) *bóveda*, to speak pompously, boastfully; *hablar danzante*, to stammer; *hablar de cabeza*, (*coll.*) to talk through one's hat; *hablar a bulto*, (or *a tiento*), to talk at random; *hablar con el dedo*, to speak with authority; *hablar de talanquera*, to find fault with an absent person; *hablar desde la talanquera*, to speak with impunity; *hablar de burlas* (or *de chanza*) to mock, jeer; *hablar por alguien*, to speak for, to intercede; *hablar disparates* (or *necedades*), to talk nonsense; *hablar al aire*, to talk vaguely, in the air; *hablar al alma*, to speak things that touch the quick; *hablar atinadamente*, to talk to the purpose; *hablar al caso*, to speak to the point; *hablar a destajo*, to talk at random; *hablar en plata* (or *hablar claro*), to speak clearly, without ambiguity; *hablar en Vascuence*, to speak broken Spanish; *hablar en cadencia*, to speak in a singsong tone; *hablar en romance*, to speak out, speak plainly; *hablar alto*, to talk loud; *hablar gordo*, to brag; *hablar por hablar*, to talk for the sake of talking; *hablar por demás*, to talk to no effect; *hablar por boca de ganso*, to speak by hearsay; *hablar entre dientes*, to mutter, mumble; *hablar de veras*, to talk in earnest; *hablar paso* (or *quedo*) to talk low; *hablar de la mar*, to talk on an endless subject; *hablar por los codos*, to talk incessantly, to chatter; *hablar con los ojos*, to look in a speaking manner; *ese retrato está hablando*, that is a speaking likeness; *hablen cartas y callen barbas*, let there

be fewer words and more action; *habló el buey y dijo 'mu'*, when fools speak they speak nonsense; *hablar a tontas y a locas*, to talk without rhyme or reason; *quien mucho habla, mucho yerra*, great talkers make great mistakes.

hablilla, *n.f.* rumour, gossip, report, little tale; babbling, foolish talk.

hablista, *n.m.f.* elegant speaker or writer, scholarly writer.

hablistán, *n.m.f.*, *a.* (*coll.*) prattler, chatterer.

habón, *n.m.* wheal; whelk; large bean.

haca, *n.f.* pony, pad, small horse; *¡qué haca morena!* to what good (*or* purpose)?

hacán, *n.m.* learned man or doctor among the Jews.

hacanea, *n.f.* nag, small horse.

hacecico, -illo, -ito, *n.m.* small sheaf; fascicle; *hacecillo de rayos luminosos*, shaft of light.

hacedero, -ra, *a.* feasible, practicable.

Hacedor, *n.m.* the Creator.

hacedor, *n.m.* steward, manager of a farm.

hacendado, -da, *a.* landed, owning a real estate. — *p.p.* [HACENDAR].

hacendado, *n.m.* landholder, farmer, planter; (*Arg.*) rancher.

hacendar, *v.t.* to transfer or make over the property of an estate. — *v.r.* to purchase real estate.

hacendeja, *n.f.* small farm.

hacendera, *n.f.* public work, at which all the neighbourhood must assist.

hacendero, -ra, *a.* industrious, laborious, sedulous. — *n.m.* workman employed in the Almadén mines.

hacendilla, -duela, *n.f.* small farm.

hacendista, *n.m.f.* economist; financier

hacendoso, -sa, *a.* assiduous, diligent.

hacer, *v.t.* (*p.p.* **hecho**; *pres. indic.* **yo hago**, **él hace**; *pret.* **yo hice, él hizo**; *fut.* **haré**; *pres. subj.* **haga**) to create, make, manufacture, produce, construct, build, shape, fashion, form; to raise, to devise, conceive, invent, contrive, compose, utter, deliver; to shed; to cast, project (a shadow); to prepare, arrange, dispose, make up, pack (a trunk, valise); to draw, design, paint, carve; to cook, dress (a dish); to practise, do, carry out, execute, effect; to complete, make up a number, to be equal to, amount to, complete; to occasion, cause, accomplish, impart, turn out; to earn, gain; to inure, habituate, accustom; to perform, act; to recruit, convoke, assemble; to order, compel, force, induce; to suppose, think; *hacer estimación* (or *aprecio*), to esteem or prize; *hacer mofa*. to mock; *hacer ánimo*, to mean, to purpose; *hacer pedazos*, to tear into pieces; *hacer señas*, to motion; *hacer daño*, to hurt; *hacer fuego*, to fire; *yo hacía a Juan en París*, I thought John was in Paris; *le hacíamos muy rico*, we supposed he was very rich; *hacer con* (or *de*), to provide, supply, furnish. — *v.i.* to matter, signify, fit the case; *eso no hace al caso*, this has nothing to do with the case; to agree, accord, match; (with *de*) to act as; to be pertinent, or to the purpose; (with *por* or *para* and an infinitive), to endeavour, try, make an effort; (with *el* or *del*), to represent, feign, counterfeit, appear what is not in reality; (with *como que* or *como si*), to act as if. — *v.r.* to grow, become, develop, reach maturity or perfection; to move, shift, recede, draw aside; to be converted, transformed; to inflict upon oneself (as a wound, a scratch); to come by, acquire; *hacerse a,* to become accustomed or inured to. — *v. impers.* of the state of the weather or a lapse of time, to be; as: *hace calor,* it is warm; *hacía mal tiempo,* the weather was bad; *ayer hizo un mes,* it was a month ago yesterday; *hace un año,* it is now a year; *se hace tarde,* it is getting late; *hacer un papel,* to play a part, a role; *hacer hacer,* to cause to be made, to order a thing to be made; *hacer diligencia,* to try, endeavour, take measures; *hacer buen tercio,* to do a good turn to one; *hacer presente,* to remind one; *hacer ver,* to show, demonstrate; *hacer venir,* to order an article to be brought or sent; *no hacer caso,* not to mind, to pay no attention; *hacer antesala,* to dance attendance, to be kept waiting; *hacer la vista gorda,* to wink at, connive at; *hacer alarde,* to muster, to boast of; *hacer añicos,* to break into fragments; *hacer a uno perder los estribos,* to make anyone lose his temper; *hacer cara* (or *hacer frente*), to face, resist, oppose; *hacer bancarrota,* to fail, become bankrupt; *hacer chacota de,* to ridicule, to turn into ridicule; *hacer del cuerpo,* to go to stool; *hacer de tripas corazón,* to pluck up courage or heart; *hacer fiesta,* to take a holiday; *hacer fiestas,* to fondle, endear, pat, caress, cajole, fawn; *hacer gasto,* to spend; *hacer juego,* to be well matched; *hacer por la vida,* to eat something; *hacer limosna,* to give alms; *hacer la barba,* to shave, to be shaved; (*Mex.*) to flatter; *hacer la cuenta sin la huéspeda,* to reckon without one's host; *hacer las amistades,* to make it up; *hacer memoria,* to recollect, remember; *hacer un seguro,* to effect an insurance; *hacer mal de ojo,* (*coll.*) to fascinate; *hacer milagros,* to do wonders; *hacer morisquetas,* to play pranks; *hacer por hacer,* to act to no purpose; *hacer papel,* to cut a figure; *hacer que hacemos,* to affect doing some business; *estar una cosa por hacer,* something yet to be made, done, or acted upon; *hacer saber,* to acquaint, to make known; *hacer agua,* (*naut.*) to leak, spring a leak; *hacer agua la boca,* to make one's mouth water; *hacer su agosto,* to make hay while the sun shines; *hacer vela* (or *hacerse a la vela*), (*naut.*) to set sail; *hacer fuerza de vela,* (*naut.*) to crowd sail; *hacer almanaques,* to be pensive, silent, musing; *hacer aguas,* to make water; *hacer pensar,* to give cause to think or suspect; *hacer calceta,* (or *malla*) to knit; *hacer honor a,* to honour (a bill, etc.); *hacer cuerpo presente,* to be present at a function but take no part; *hacer estrados,* to give a hearing (of judges, etc.); *hacer derrota,* (*naut.*) to stand on the course; *hacer cabeza,* (*naut.*) to head; *hacer avergonzar,* to put to the blush; *hacer diligencia,* to do one's best; *hacer su casa,* to aggrandize one's family; *no hacer alto,* not to mind, to overlook; *no haga Vd. caso,* don't bother; *hacer aire,* to blow (of the wind); *hacer aire a,* to vex, plague; *hacer correrías,* to make incursions; *hacer bajar las orejas,* to humble; *hacer a dos palos,* to benefit from two sources at once; *hacer orejas de mercader,* to turn a deaf ear; *hacer costilla(s),* to suffer, bear with patience; *hacer espaldas,* to endure; *hacer gente,* to raise soldiers; *hacer honras,* to honour, esteem; *hacer plaza,* to sell by retail; *hacer las cosas por arte de birlibirloque,* to do things by hocus-pocus; *comida hecha, compañía deshecha,* when the favour has been given, the favoured disappears; *haz bien y guárdate,* do kind deeds, but be on your guard; *no hace tanto la zorra en un año como paga en una hora,* the criminal receives full retribution at the last; *lo que no se hace a la boda, no se hace a toda hora,* if a person refuses to grant favours at favourable times he will never grant them at all; *haces mal, espera otro tal,* as a man sows, so shall he also reap; *no hacemos moneda falsa,* we are not having a private conversation; *algo hemos* (or *se ha*) *de hacer, para blanca ser,* one's faults take much dissimulating; *no la hagas y no la temas,* he who does no wrong need have no fear; *no me hagas hablar,* don't make me say what I shall be sorry for; *hacer de una pulga un elefante,* to make a mountain out of a molehill; *hacer las cosas a troche y moche,* to do things at random; *hacerse de miel,* to be sweet, lenient, or obliging; *hágame Vd. el favor,* please, pray; *hacerse tortilla,* to fall down flat; *hacerse chiquito,* to pretend to be modest; to conceal one's knowledge; *hacerse de rogar,* to like to be coaxed; *hacerse olvidadizo,* to feign forgetfulness; *hacerse rico,* to become rich; *hacerse lugar,* to gain a reputation; *hacerse una zarpa,* to get very wet; *hacerse las narices,* to receive an unexpected blow in the face; *hacerse unas gachas,* to be over-affectionate; *hacerse con una cosa,* to obtain a thing rightly or wrongly; *hacerse de nuevas,* to feign ignorance.

hacera, *n.f.* side-walk.

hacezuelo, *n.m.* small faggot.

hacia, *prep.* toward, in a direction; near to, about; *hacia adelante,* forward; *hacia atrás,* backward; *hacia acá,* hither; *hacia allá,* thither; *hacia casa, hacia su país,* homeward; *hacia donde,* whither, toward which, to what place, where; *hacia el cielo,* heavenward; *hacia popa,* (*naut.*) abaft; *hacia proa,* (*naut.*) afore; *hacia el mar,* seaward.

hacienda, *n.f.* landed property, plantation, farm, ranch; estate, fortune, wealth; finance. — *pl.* **haciendas,** domestic work, household duties; *real hacienda,* exchequer; *Ministro de Hacienda,* Chancellor of the Exchequer; *hacienda pública,* public treasury; finances; *haciendas apalabradas,* goods already bespoken; *hacienda de beneficio,* (*Mex., min.*) reduction works; *hacienda, tu dueño te vea* or *hacienda de sobrino, quémala el fuego y llévala el río,* proverb satirizing the carelessness or bad faith of guardians; *quien da su hacienda antes de la muerte, merece que le den con un mazo en la frente,* proverb warning against giving away one's property during one's lifetime.

hacina, *n.f.* stack, rick; pile, heap.

hacinador, -ra, *n.m.f.* stack-maker; accumulator.

hacinamiento, *n.m.* accumulation, heaping or hoarding up; acervation, heaping together.

hacinar, *v.t.* to stack or pile up sheaves; to hoard; to cumulate; to coacervate.

hacha, *n.f.* axe or hatchet; large taper with four wicks; *hacha de viento,* flambeau, torch;

(*naut.*) link; *paje de hacha*, link-boy; *hacha de armas*, battle-axe, twibill; ancient Spanish dance.

hachazo, *n.m.* blow or stroke with an axe; (*taurom.*) side blow from a bull's horn which inflicts no wound; (*Col.*) sudden bound of a horse.

hache, *n.f.* name of the letter H; *llámele usted hache*, it is the same thing.

hachear, *v.t.* to cut with an axe; to hew. — *v.i.* to strike with an axe.

hachero, *n.m.* candlestick; axeman; woodman, wood-cutter, lumberman; (*prov.*) carpenter.

hacheta, *n.f.* small axe or hatchet; small torch or link.

hachich, *n.m.* hashish, hasheesh.

hacho, *n.m.* firebrand, torch; beacon hill.

hachón, *n.m.* large torch or firebrand; cresset.

hachote, *n.m.* large axe.

hachuela, *n.f.* small hatchet or axe; hand axe, adze.

hada, *n.f.* fairy; (*obs.*) fate, fortune-teller, witch.

hadar, *v.t.* to divine, foretell future events; to enchant.

hado, *n.m.* fate, destiny, inevitable doom.

hafiz, *n.m.* guardian, keeper; overseer, supervisor.

hagiografía, *n.f.* (*eccles.*) hagiography.

hagiógrafo, *n.m.* hagiographer.

hago; haga, *pres. indic.; pres. subj.* [HACER].

haitano, -na, *a.* Haytian.

¡hala! *interj.* (*naut.*) pull! haul!

halacabuyas; halacuerdas, *n.m.* apprentice sailor; (*coll.*) fresh-water sailor.

halagador, -ra, *n.m.f.* cajoler, flatterer.

halagar, *v.t.* (*pret.* **halagué;** *pres. subj.* **halague**) to cajole, flatter, dandle, coax, coy, allure, wheedle, hug, fondle, treat with tenderness.

halago, *n.m.* cajolery, flattery, caress, adulation, cooing.

halagüeñamente, *adv.* endearingly, flatteringly.

halagüeño, -ña, *a.* endearing, attractive, alluring, fawning, flattering, honey-mouthed, meek, gentle.

halar, *v.t.* (*naut.*) to haul, pull, tow. — *v.i.* to pull ahead.

halcón, *n.m.* falcon, trained hawk.

halconado, -da, *a.* falcon-like, hawk-like.

halconcico, -illo, -ito, *n.m.* jashawk.

halconear, *v.t.* (*coll.*) to inveigle, allure men (as harlots).

halconera, *n.f.* place where falcons are kept.

halconería, *n.f.* falconry.

halconero, -ra, *a.* lascivious, lewd (woman). — *n.m.* falconer, hawk trainer.

halda, *n.f.* skirt; (*prov.*) lapful; packing-bag; *poner haldas en cinta*, (*coll.*) prepared and ready for anything; *de haldas o de mangas*, (*coll.*) in any way, justly or unjustly, with good or ill will.

haldada, *n.f.* skirtful of anything.

haldear, *v.i.* to run along with the skirts flying loose.

haldica, -illa, -ita, *n.f.* small skirt.

haldudo, -da, *a.* full-skirted, with flying skirts.

haleche, *n.m.* anchovy; horse-mackerel.

halía, *n.f.* sea-nymph; name of a moth and of an African plant.

haliéntica, *n.f.* angling, the art of fishing.

halieto, *n.m.* sea-eagle.

halinatrón, *n.m.* native soda.

hálito, *n.m.* breath; vapour, effluvium; (*poet.*) soft air.

halo, halón, *n.m.* (*astron.*) halo.

halófilo, -la, *a.* growing in salty earth.

halógeno, -na, *a.* (*chem.*) halogen.

halografía, *n.f.* (*chem.*) halography.

haloideo, -a, *a.* (*chem.*) haloid.

haloque, *n.m.* ancient boat.

halotecnia, *n.f.* the science of extracting industrial salts.

haloza, *n.f.* wooden shoe.

halterio, *n.m.* ancient dumb-bell; halter of the diptera.

hallado, -da, *a.* found; *bien hallado*, welcome, easy, contented; *mal hallado*, uneasy, constrained. — *p.p.* [HALLAR].

hallador, -ra, *n.m.f.* finder, discoverer.

hallar, *v.t.* to find, come across, hit upon, meet with, perceive by chance, fall upon; to find out after searching; to remark, observe, compare, note, verify; to discover, invent, excogitate; to catch, detect; to solve, understand, interpret, comprehend, decipher. — *v.r.* to happen to be (in a place); to reside; to be pleased or content; to feel (as to comfort or health), to fare.

hallazgo, *n.m.* act of finding or recovering anything lost; thing found, treasure trove; reward for finding anything lost.

hallulla, *n.f.;* **hallullo,** *n.m.* cake baked on or under cinders; (*Chi.*) fine bread.

hamaca, *n.f.* hammock; hammock-carriage.

hámago, *n.m.* a yellow, flexible substance found in a honeycomb; (*coll.*) squeamishness, nausea.

hamaquear, *v.t.* (*S. Am.*) to rock, shake, swing; (*Cub.*, *coll.*) to vex, importune, bother.

hamaquero, *n.m.* hammock-maker; hammock-bearer; hammock-hook.

hambre, *n.f.* hunger, appetite; scarcity and dearth of provisions (especially of wheat), famine; greediness, eagerness, longing, desire; *acosado de hambre*, pinched with hunger; *muerto de hambre*, starved with hunger; *hambre de tres semanas*, affected fastidiousness, dislike for certain dishes, etc.; *tener hambre estudiantina*, to be as hungry as a hunter; *a la hambre no hay mal pan* or *a buen hambre no hay pan duro, ni falta salsa a ninguno*, hunger is the best sauce; *hambre y esperar hacen rabiar*, hunger and waiting are intolerable; *ni con toda hambre al arca, ni con toda sed al cántaro*, prudence and abstinence are necessary on occasions; *la mejor salsa del mundo es la hambre*, hunger is the best sauce; *si quieres cedo engordar, come con hambre y bebe a vagar*, eat when hungry, drink slowly and get fat.

hambrear, *v.t.* to cause hunger, starve, famish; to subdue by famine. — *v.i.* to hunger, to be hungry.

hambrientamente, *adv.* hungrily.

hambriento, -ta, *a.* hungry, starved, greedy, ravenous; longing, eager, vehemently desirous; (*Col.*) mean, stingy.

hambrón, -ona, *n.m.f.* (*coll.*) hungry person.

hamez, *n.f.* distemper in falcons which makes them lose their feathers.

hamo, *n.m.* fish-hook.

hampa, *n.f.* life of a company of vagabonds formerly in Andalusia; underworld.

hampesco, -ca, *a.* vagabond, villainous; vainglorious.

hampo, hampón, *n.m.* rowdy, bully. — *a.* bold; licentious.

hanega, *n.f.* a dry measure (about 1·6 bush.) [FANEGA].

hanegada, *n.f.* land sown with a *fanega* of corn.

hanquilla, *n.f.* kind of boat.

hanseático, -ca, *a.* Hanseatic.

¡hao! *interj.* (*obs.*) halloo!

haragán, -ana, *n.m.f.*, *a.* idler, loiterer, lingerer, lounger, loafer; idle, lazy person. — *a.* idle, inactive, indolent, slothful.

haraganamente, *adv.* idly, lazily, slothfully, indolently.

haraganazo, -za, *a.* very idle.

haraganear, *v.i.* to lead an idle life, be lazy, to play truant; to lounge, idle, loiter, loaf.

haraganería, *n.f.* idleness, laziness, sluggishness, inactivity, slothfulness.

harapiento, -ta; haraposo, -sa, *a.* ragged, tattered.

harapo, *n.m.* tatter, rag; *andar* (or *estar*) *hecho un harapo,* to go about in rags.

harca, [aspirated *h*], *n.f.* (*Morocco*) military expedition of conscripted troops; band of rebels.

harem, harén, *n.m.* harem, seraglio.

harija, *n.f.* mill-dust.

harina, *n.f.* flour, meal; farina; breadstuffs; powder, dust; *cerner, cerner y sacar poca harina,* to work hard to no purpose; *donde no hay harina, todo es mohina,* poverty often brings discord in its train; *hacer buena* (or *mala*) *harina,* to do good (or ill); *ser harina de otro costal,* to be quite another matter.

harinado, *n.m.* flour dissolved in water.

harinero, -ra, *a.* made of or belonging to flour.

harinero, *n.m.* meal-man, flour-dealer; flour-chest.

harinoso, -sa, *a.* mealy, farinaceous.

harma, *n.f.* wild rue [ALHARMA].

harmonía (modern spelling, ARMONÍA), *n.f.* harmony.

harnerico, -illo, -ito, *n.m.* small sieve.

harnero, *n.m.* sieve, sifter, bolt; *estar hecho un harnero,* to be covered with wounds.

harneruelo, *n.m.* the central piece of a wooden ceiling.

harón, -ona, *a.* slow, inactive, sluggish; balky.

haronear, *v.i.* to dawdle, move sluggishly; to be tardy or slow; to balk, stop short (of a horse).

haronía, *n.f.* sluggishness, laziness, idleness.

harpa, *n.f.* harp [ARPA].

harpado, -da, *a.* serrated, toothed [ARPADO].

harpía, *n.f.* harpy [ARPÍA].

harpillera, *n.f.* burlap, sack cloth.

hartada, *n.f.* satiety, glutting.

hartar, *v.t.*, *v.r.*, *v.i.* (*p.p.* **hartado, harto**) to glut, stuff, gorge; to sate, satiate, gratify desire; to satisfy, cloy, fill to excess.

hartazgo, hartazón, *n.m.* satiety, glut, fill.

harto, -ta, *a.* satiate, satiated, glutted, full of satiety; sufficient, full, complete. — *p.p. irreg.* [HARTAR].

harto, *adv.* enough.

hartura, *n.f.* satiety, fullness beyond desire or pleasure, glut, fill; plethora, superabundance; full gratification of a desire.

hasta, *prep.* till, until; up to, down to; as far as; *hasta no más,* to the utmost; *hasta ahora, hasta aquí,* hitherto; *hasta luego, hasta la vista,* (or *hasta después*), good-bye, until we meet again; *¿hasta cuándo?* when shall I see you next? *hasta los tuétanos,* to the quick. — *conj.* also, even.

hastial, *n.m.* (*arch.*) gable-wall; coarse, rude man; (*min.*) side face of a gallery.

hastiar, *v.t.* to loathe, disgust; to cloy, sate.

hastío, *n.m.* loathing, disgust; tedium, wearisomeness, abhorring.

hataca, *n.f.* large wooden ladle; rolling-pin.

hatajar, *v.t.* to divide cattle into flocks or herds.

hatajo, *n.m.* small herd or flock; (*coll.*) lot, collection; *hatajo de disparates,* lot of nonsense.

hatear, *v.i.* to collect one's clothes, etc., for travelling; to supply shepherds with provisions.

hatería, *n.f.* allowance of provisions and clothes for shepherds.

hatero, -ra, *a.* applied to the animals that carry the shepherd's baggage.

hatero, *n.m.* carrier of provisions to shepherds; (*Cub.*) cowboy, herder of cattle.

hatijo, *n.m.* covering of straw or feather-grass over beehives.

hatillo, *n.m.* small bundle; a few clothes; *echar el hatillo al mar,* (*coll.*) to lose one's temper; *coger* (or *tomar su* or *el*) *hatillo,* (*coll.*) to pack off, go away.

hato, *n.m.* herd of cattle; flock of sheep; (*Cub., Ven.*) cattle-ranch; shepherds' lodge; provisions for shepherds; clothes, wearing apparel; assemblage, collection, abundance; heap, lot, cluster, gang, band or crowd of suspicious people.

Haváy, *n.f.* Hawaii.

haxix, *n.m.* hashish.

hay, *impers. irreg.* there is, there are [HABER].

haya, *n.f.* beech-tree; 3rd *pers. pres. subj.* of HABER.

Haya, La, *n.f.* The Hague.

hayal, hayedo, *n.m.* beech forest.

hayo, *n.m.* (*Col.*) coca; coca leaves prepared for chewing.

hayuco, *n.m.* beech mast, fruit of the beech.

haz, *n.m.* faggot, bundle, bunch; (*agric.*) gavel, sheaf; beam (light or radio); (*mil.*) file of soldiers, also troops arranged in divisions.— *n.f.* face, visage; (*arch., obs.*) facing, façade; right side or outside of cloth.—*pl.* **haces,** fasces; *sobre la haz de la tierra,* upon the face of the earth; *a sobre haz,* apparently, at first view; *ser de dos haces,* to be double-faced; *en haz y en paz,* by common consent and agreement. — *imperative irreg.* [HACER].

haza, *n.f.* piece of cultivable land.

hazaleja, *n.f.* towel.

hazaña, *n.f.* exploit, achievement, heroic feat; *las grandes hazañas para los grandes hombres están guardadas,* great deeds are reserved for great men.

hazañería, *n.f.* affected show of fear or surprise.

hazañero, -ra, *a.* prudish, affectedly grave, fearful or alarmed.

hazañosamente, *adv.* valorously.

hazañoso, -sa, *a.* valiant, courageous, heroic.

hazcona, *n.f.* dart.

hazmerreír, *n.m.* ridiculous person, laughing-stock, gazing-stock.

hazteallá, *n.m.* roughness of behaviour.

he, *adv.* generally followed by the adverbs *aquí* or *allí*, sometimes preceded by conjunctive pronouns *me, te, la, le, lo, las, los; he aquí,* here is; *heme aquí,* here I am; *helos allí,* there they are. — *interj.* exclamation calling attention, etc.

hebdómada, *n.f.* hebdomad, week, seven days; seven years.

hebdomadario, -ria, *a.* weekly. — *n.m.f.* (*eccles.*) hebdomadary.

hebe, *n.f.* age of puberty; down, soft hair; name of a moth.

hebén, *a.* of white grapes like muscatels; insignificant, of no account.

hebilla, *n.f.* buckle, clasp.

hebillaje, *n.m.* set of buckles.

hebillero, -ra, *n.m.f.* buckle maker or seller.

hebilleta, hebilluela, *n.f.* small buckle; *no faltar hebilleta,* to be complete.

hebillón, *n.m.* large buckle.

hebra, *n.f.* fibre, thread, filament; staple; grain (of wood); needleful of thread; pistil of the blossom of saffron; (*min.*) vein, layer, stratum. — *pl.* **hebras,** (*poet.*) hair; *ser* (or *estar*) *de buena hebra,* to be strong and robust; *cortar la hebra,* to cut the thread of life.

hebraico, -ca, *a.* Hebrew.

hebraísmo, *n.m.* Hebraism.

hebraísta, *n.m.* Hebraist, Hebrew scholar.

hebraizante, *n.m.* Hebraist.

hebreo, -rea, *a.* Hebraic, Judaical. — *n.m.f.* Hebrew.

hebreo, *n.m.* Hebrew language; (*pej.*) trader, pawnbroker; usurer.

hebrero, *n.m.* œsophagus of ruminants; (*obs.*) February.

hebrica, -illa, -ita, *n.f.* small needleful of thread.

Hébridas, *n.f.pl.* Hebrides.

hebroso, -sa, *a.* fibrous, filaceous.

hecatombe, *n.f.* hecatomb.

hectárea, *n.f.* hectare, measure of surface.

héctico, -ca, *a.* consumptive, hectic.

hectiquez, *n.f.* phthisis.

hectógrafo, *n.m.* hectograph, copygraph.

hectolitro, *n.m.* hectolitre.

hecha, *n.f.* (*obs.*) date; (*obs.*) action, act, feat; irrigation tax; *de esta hecha,* from this time.

hechiceresco, -ca, *a.* relating to witchcraft.

hechicería, *n.f.* witchcraft, witchery, enchantment; charmingness, fascination.

hechicero, -ra, *n.m.f., a.* witch, wizard; hag; charmer, enchanter, bewitcher; entrancing, charming, bewitching, fascinating; *niña hechicera,* (*poet.*) charming girl.

hechizar, *v.t.* (*pret.* **hechicé;** *pres. subj.* **hechice**) to bewitch, enchant, entrance; to charm, fascinate.

hechizo, *n.m.* bewitchment, fascination; trance, enchantment; entertainment, delight, bliss.

hechizo, -za, *a.* artificial, fictitious, imitated, adapted, feigned; made to order; portable, easily mounted.

hecho, -cha, *p.p. irreg.* [HACER]. — *a.* perfect, made, done; ready-made, finished; fully matured, ripe or developed; accustomed, inured, used; *hecho un león,* like a lion, furiously angry; *a lo hecho pecho,* we must

make the best of what we have done; *de hecho y de derecho,* (*law*) by act and right, de facto and de jure. — *n.m.* action, act, feat; fact, event, incident; subject or matter discussed; (*law*) point litigated; *a hecho,* indiscriminately, incessantly; *de hecho,* in fact, actually, effectually; *hecho a machete,* roughly made; *hecho de encargo,* made to order; *hecho un Adán,* in rags and tatters; *estar hecho una ascua,* to be burning with anger; *estar hecho una sopa de agua,* to be wet to the skin; *estar hecho un cartón,* to be as thin as a lath; *estar hecho un pollo de agua,* to be covered with perspiration; *estar hecho un costal de huesos,* to be nothing but skin and bones; *en hecho de verdad,* in truth; *hecho y derecho,* perfect, absolute, complete; right; *bien hecho,* well done, all right; *mal hecho,* that's wrong; *tiempo hecho,* settled weather; *a nuevos hechos, nuevos consejos,* circumstances alter cases; *a lo hecho no hay remedio, y a lo por hacer consejo,* prevention is not for the past, but the future; *Hechos de los Apóstoles,* the Acts of the Apostles

hechura, *n.f.* making, make, form, cut, shape, fashion, figure or form given to a thing; effigy, statue; build of a person, workmanship; work done and price paid for it; creature, henchman; *no tener hechura,* to be impracticable, or not feasible.

hedentina, *n.f.* stench, stink, fetidness.

heder, *v.i.* (*pres. indic.* **hiedo;** *pres. subj.* **hieda**) to stink, to emit an offensive smell; to vex, annoy, bore, fatigue, be intolerable.

hediondamente, *adv.* stinkingly.

hediondez, *n.f.* strong stench or stink; fetidness.

hediondo, -da, *a.* fetid, mephitical, stinking; annoying, wearisome, intolerable; dirty, repulsive; lewd, obscene. — *n.m.* wild Syrian rue.

hedor, *n.m.* stench, stink, fetor.

hegemonía, *n.f.* (*pol.*) hegemony, supremacy.

héjira, *n.f.* Hegira, Mohammedan epoch.

hejotes, ejotes, *n.m.pl.* (*Am. Cent., Mex.*) string-beans.

helable, *a.* congealable.

helada, *n.f.* frost; nip; *helada blanca,* hoarfrost.

heladería, *n.f.* (*Col., Chi.*) ice-cream shop.

heladero, *n.m.* (*Chi.*) ice-cream seller or maker.

heladizo, -za, *a.* easily congealed.

helado, -da, *a.* gelid, frigid; frozen, congealed, frost-bitten, glacial, icy; cold, chilly in affection, indifferent; astonished, astounded.

helado, *n.m.* ice-cream, water-ice; (*prov.*) pink sugar.

helamiento, *n.m.* congelation, frostiness.

helar, *v.t., v.i.* (*pres. indic.* **hielo;** *pres. subj.* **hiele**) to congeal, to ice, turn to ice, freeze; to dispirit, discourage, dissuade; to chill, astound, astonish, amaze. — *v.r.* to freeze, to be frozen; to congeal, nip, glaciate; to be coagulated; to grow motionless, be stupefied, dispirited; *se me heló la sangre,* my blood curdled.

¡hele (or **hétele**) **aquí!** *interj.* behold, look here.

helechal, *n.m.* fern field.

helecho, *n.m.* fern.

helena, *n.f.* (*naut.*) St. Elmo's fire; Castor and Pollux.

helénico, -ca, a. Hellenic, Greek.
helenio, n.m. sneeze-weed.
helenismo, n.m. Hellenism; Greek idiom.
helenista, n.m.f. Hellenist.
helenístico, -ca, a. Hellenistic.
heleno, -na, n.m.f., a. Hellenic, Greek.
helera, n.f. pip, disease in fowls.
helero, n.m. snow-cap on mountains; glacier.
helgado, -da, a. jag-toothed.
helgadura, n.f. space between or irregularity of the teeth.
helíaco, -ca, a. (astron.) heliacal rising or setting of a star.
hélice, n.f. constellation of Ursa Major; (geom.) helix, helical line; spiral; (anat.) the rim or fold of the external ear; (arch.) the small volute under the abacus; (naut., aer.) screw propeller.
helicoidal, a. helicoidal, spiral.
helicoide, n.m. (geom.) helicoid.
helicónides, n.f.pl. the Muses.
helio, n.m. helium.
heliocéntrico, -ca, a. heliocentric.
heliograbado, n.m. heliogravure.
heliógrafo, n.m. heliograph.
heliograma, n.m. heliogram.
heliómetro, n.m. heliometer.
helioscopio, n.m. helioscope.
heliosis, n.f. sunstroke.
helióstata, helióstato, n.m. heliostat.
helioterapia, n.f. heliotherapy.
heliotropio, heliotropo, n.m. (bot.) turnsole, heliotrope; (min.) bloodstone; (astr.) heliotrope, an instrument.
helminto, -ta, a. helminthic.
helminto, n.m. helminth, worm.
helvecio, -cia, a. Helvetian, Swiss.
helvético, -ca, n.m.f., a. Helvetic, Swiss (used of persons).
hemacrimo, -ma, a. (zool.) cold-blooded.
hematemesis, n.f. (med.) hæmatemesis.
hematites, n.f. hæmatite.
hematometro, n.m. (med.) hæmatinometer.
hematosis, n.f. hæmatosis.
hematuria, n.f. hæmaturia, blood in the urine.
hembra, n.f. female of animals or plants; (coll. or vulg.) woman; eye of a hook; (mech.) female plug or screw; hembra del timón, (naut.) gudgeon of the rudder.
hembraje, n.m. (S. Am.) female cattle of a herd (as a whole).
hembrear, v.i. to be inclined to females (of males); to beget or produce females only or chiefly.
hembrica, -illa, -ita, n.f. little female.
hembrilla, n.f. (mech.) small female socket, plug, clasp, nut, staple, etc.; ring or eye-bolt.
hemeroteca, n.f. public library of newspapers and periodicals.
hemiciclo, n.m. semicircle; central space of the Spanish parliament.
hemicránea, n.f. megrim.
hemina, n.f. liquid and surface measure.
hemiplejía, n.f. (med.) hemiplegia.
hemíptero, -ra, a. hemipterous. — n.m.pl. hemiptera; bugs.
hemisférico, -ca, a. hemispheric, hemispherical.
hemisferio, n.m. hemisphere.
hemisferoidal, a. hemispheroidal.
hemistiquio, n.m. (poet.) hemistich.

hemofilia, n.f. hæmophilia.
hemoglobina, n.f. hæmoglobin.
hemopatía, n.f. illness of the blood.
hemoptisis, n.f. hæmoptysis.
hemorragia, n.f. hæmorrhage, flux of blood.
hemorrágico, -ca, a. hæmorrhagic.
hemorroida, hemorroide, n.f. (med.) piles, hæmorrhoids.
hemorroidal, a. hæmorrhoidal.
hemorroisa, n.f. woman suffering from an abnormal discharge of blood.
hemorroo, n.m. African viper.
hemostático, -ca, a. hæmostatic.
henal, n.m. hayloft.
henar, n.m. meadow of hay.
henchidor, -ra, n.m.f. filler, satiator.
henchidura, n.f. repletion, fill, filling.
henchimiento, n.m. abundance, repletion. — pl. (naut.) filling timbers.
henchir, v.t. (pres. part. hinchiendo; pres. indic. hincho; pret. él hinchió; pres. subj. hincha) to fill up, blow, cram, stuff, fill, to farce; to sow discord; to produce mischief. — v.r. to fill oneself; henchirse de lepra, to be covered with leprosy.
hendedor, -ra, n.m.f. divider, splitter, cleaver.
hendedura, n.f. fissure, crack, rent, chink, cleft, crevice, cranny, cut.
hender, v.t. (pres. indic. hiendo; pres. subj. hienda) to chink, crack, break, flaw, fissure, cleave, split; to go through; to move swiftly on the water or through the air; to elbow or open a passage through a crowd.
hendible, a. fissile, cleavable.
hendido, -da, a. crannied, full of chinks, cleft. — p.p. [HENDER].
hendidura, n.f. fissure, crack, cranny.
hendiente, n.m. down-stroke of a sword.
hendija, n.f. (Am.) [REHENDIJA].
hendrija, n.f. small fissure, crack.
henequén, n.m. (Mex.) Mexican agave; henequen, sisal hemp.
hénide, n.f. (poet.) nymph of the meadows.
henil, n.m. hayloft, barn.
heno, n.m. hay.
henojil, n.m. garter.
heñir, v.t. to knead dough; hay mucho que heñir, (coll.) there is much to do.
hepática, n.f. liverwort; liverleaf.
hepático, -ca, a. (med.) hepatic, hepatical.
heptacordo, n.m. heptachord.
heptagonal; heptágono, -na, a. heptagonal.
heptarquía, n.f. heptarchy.
heptasílabo, -ba, a. containing seven syllables.
heptateuco, n.m. heptateuch.
heráldica, n.f. heraldry.
heráldico, -ca, a. heraldic.
heraldo, n.m. herald; harbinger; king-at-arms.
herbáceo, -cea, a. herby, herbaceous.
herbajar, herbajear, v.t. to put flocks to graze, pasture. — v.i. to pasture, graze, browse.
herbaje, n.m. herbage, grass, pasture, feeding; pasturage fee; coarse cloth used by sailors.
herbajero, n.m. one who rents or lets meadows or pastures.
herbar, v.t. to dress skins with herbs.
herbario, -ria, a. herbal.
herbario, n.m. herbalist, herbarian; herbarium.
herbaza, n.f. large weed.
herbazal, n.m. herbous place; pasture-ground.

herbecer, *v.i.* to begin to grow (of herbs or grass).

herbero, *n.m.* œsophagus of a ruminant.

herbívoro, -ra, *a.* herbivorous.

herbolado, -da, *a.* poisoned with juice of plants (as daggers, darts, etc.).

herbolario, *n.m.* herbist, herbman, one who sells herbs; (*coll.*) nonsensical, stupid, crazy madcap.

herborización, *n.f.* herborization, botanizing.

herborizador, herborizante, *n.m.* herbalist, herborist, herborizer.

herborizar, *v.i.* to herborize, botanize, go searching for herbs and plants.

herboso, -sa, *a.* herbous, herby, grassy.

herciano, -na, *a.* (*phys.*) hertzian.

hercúleo, -ea, *a.* herculean; very strong.

Hércules, *n.m.* Hercules; (*astron.*) northern constellation; kind of giant beetle.

heredad, *n.f.* country place, farm, property.

heredado, -da, *a.* landed, owning real estate. — *n.m.f.* heir to property. — *p.p.* [HEREDAR].

heredamiento, *n.m.* landed property, lands, tenements.

heredar, *v.t.* to inherit; to leave property to another; to institute as heir; to possess the disposition or temperament of the progenitors; *quien lo hereda no lo hurta,* a chip of the old block.

heredero, -ra, *n.m.f.* heir, heiress, inheritor; possessing the same propensities as his predecessors; *heredero forzoso,* general heir; *heredero presunto,* heir-presumptive.

heredípeta, *n.m.f.* legacy-seeker.

hereditario, -ria, *a.* hereditary; entailed.

hereje, *n.m.f.* heretic; *cara de hereje,* impudent, shameless, insolent.

herejía, *n.f.* heresy; gross error; injurious expression; *la estampa de la herejía,* (*coll.*) a hideous face.

herejote, -ta, *n.m.f.* (*coll.*) great heretic.

herén, *n.m.* vetch.

herencia, *n.f.* inheritance, hereditament, heritage, heirship, heirdom.

heresiarca, *n.m.* heresiarch, leader of heresy.

heretical, *a.* heretical.

hereticar, *v.i.* (*obs.*) to defend heresies.

herético, -ca, *a.* heretical.

heria, *n.f.* (*slang*) life of vagrancy.

herida, *n.f.* wound; stab; affliction; injury, mischief, outrage; (*falcon.*) place where the game perches when pursued by the hawk; *renovar la herida,* (*fig.*) to open a wound; *tocar en la herida,* to touch on a sore spot.

herido, -da, *a.* wounded; *a grito herido,* with loud cries; *mal herido,* dangerously wounded; *a pendón herido,* urgently, with great speed. — *p.p.* [HERIR].

heridor, -ra, *a.* stabber, wounder, striker.

herimiento, *n.m.* (*obs.*) act of wounding; (*gram.*) (*obs.*) synalepha, elision.

herir, *v.t.* (*pres. part.* **hiriendo;** *pres. indic.* **hiero,** *pret.* **él hirió;** *pres. subj.* **hiera**) to wound, stab; to harm, hurt, cause mischief; to collide, dash against; to shine upon, to irradiate; to knock, strike, rap; to finger or pluck the keys or strings of a musical instrument; to affect, touch, move; to offend the senses; to pique, irritate; *herir las letras,* to pronounce the letters; *herir el casco,* to hull a ship.

hermafrodita, hermafrodito, *n.m., a.* hermaphrodite, androgyne.

hermafroditismo, *n.m.* hermaphroditism.

hermana, *n.f.* sister.

hermanable, *a.* fraternal, brotherly.

hermanablemente, *adv.* fraternally.

hermanado, -da, *a.* mated, matched. — *p.p.* [HERMANAR].

hermanal, *a.* brotherly.

hermanamiento, *n.m.* mating, matching, joining.

hermanar, *v.t.* to mate, match, suit, proportion, fellow, pair, harmonize; to own for a brother. — *v.i.* to fraternize, join, match, agree, unite. — *v.r.* to love one another as brothers.

hermanastro, -tra, *n.m.f.* step-brother, step-sister.

hermanazgo, *n.m.* fraternity, brotherhood.

hermandad, *n.f.* fraternity, brotherhood, confraternity; conformity, resemblance; amity, friendship; *la Santa Hermandad,* rural Spanish police and judicial organization instituted in the fifteenth century.

hermandarse, *v.r.* to join a religious brotherhood.

hermandino, *n.m.* (*hist.*) fellow of a rebellious movement in Galicia.

hermanear, *v.t.* to treat as a brother.

hermanecer *v.i.* to have a little brother just born.

hermanita, *n.f.* little sister.

hermanito, *n.m.* little brother.

hermano, *n.m.* brother; mate, companion, twin; matched (speaking of objects); suitable, kindred, germane, akin, similar; (*fig.*) *hermano carnal,* brother by the same father and mother; *hermano de padre,* brother by the same father, but not the same mother; *hermano uterino,* brother by the same mother, but not the same father; *hermano de leche,* foster-brother; *medio hermano,* half-brother, step-brother; *hermano político,* brother-in-law. — *pl.* **hermanos,** members of the same religious confraternity; lay-brothers of a religious order.

hermanuco, *n.m.* lay-brother (used contemptuously).

hermenéutica, *n.f.* (*eccles.*) hermeneutics.

hermenéutico, -ca, *a.* hermeneutic.

herméticamente, *adv.* hermetically.

hermético, -ca, *a.* hermetical, air-proof, air-tight; (*fig.*) impenetrable, close.

hermodátil, *n.m.* colchicum.

hermosamente, *adv.* beautifully, handsomely, lovely; perfectly, properly.

hermoseador, -ra, *a.* beautifier.

hermosear, *v.t.* to beautify, embellish, accomplish, adorn, add beauty.

hermoso, -sa, *a.* beautiful, handsome, graceful, lovely, comely, goodly, neat, fair, beauteous, fine.

hermosura, *n.f.* beauty, handsomeness, fineness, fairness, loveliness, freshness; harmony of lines and proportions; belle, beauty.

hernia, *n.f.* hernia, rupture.

herniario, -ria, *a.* hernial.

hernioso, -sa, *a.* herniated.

hernista, *n.m.* specialist in herniotomy.

héroe, *n.m.* hero, champion.

heroicamente, *adv.* heroically.

heroicidad, *n.f.* heroic action.

heroico, -ca, *a.* heroic, heroical; *a la heroica,* in the manner of heroic times.

heroína, *n.f.* heroine.

heroísmo, *n.m.* heroism.

herpe, *n.m.f.* herpes, tetter.

herpético, -ca, *a.* herpetic.

herpil, *n.m.* bag of esparto netting with wide meshes for carrying melons, straw, etc.

herrada, *a.* applied to water in which red-hot iron has been cooled; *una herrada no es caldera*, phrase excusing a slight mistake. — *n.f.* wooden pail *or* bucket.

herradero, *n.m.* branding cattle; place where cattle are branded; season for branding.

herrador, *n.m.* farrier, horse-shoer, smith.

herradora, *n.f.* (*coll.*) farrier's wife.

herradura, *n.f.* horse-shoe; anything shaped like a horse-shoe; *se asienta la herradura*, the shoe pinches; *herradura de la muerte*, certain signs of approaching death; *mostrar las herraduras*, to show a clean pair of heels.

herraj (modern, ERRAJ)

herraje, *n.m.* iron-work, pieces of iron used for ornament and strength.

herramental, *n.m., a.* tool-bag; tool-chest.

herramienta, *n.f.* tool, implement, instrument; set of tools or instruments; (*coll.*) horns of a beast; (*coll.*) teeth, grinders.

herrar, *v.t.* (*pres. indic.* **hierro**, *pres. subj.* **hierre**) to shoe horses; to brand cattle; to garnish or bind with iron.

herrén, *n.m.* maslin, mixed grain for horses.

herrenal, herreñal, *n.m.* piece of ground in which maslin is sown.

herrera, *n.f.* (*coll.*) blacksmith's wife.

herrería, *n.f.* iron-works; smith's shop, smithy; forge; smith's trade, smithery; clamour, confused noise.

herrerico, herrerillo, *n.m.* small bird.

herrero, *n.m.* smith; *herrero de grueso*, iron-worker;(*Chi.*) [HERRADOR].

herrerón, *n.m.* bad, clumsy smith.

herreruelo, *n.m.* (*orn.*) wagtail; (*hist.*) a German horseman.

herrete, *n.m.* tip, ferrule, aiguillete.

herretear, *v.t.* to tip a string or ribbon.

herrezuelo, *n.m.* light piece of iron.

herrial, *a.* applied to large black grapes.

herrín, *n.m.* rust of iron.

herrón, *n.m.* quoit; washer; iron prop for young trees; (*Col.*) point of a spinning top.

herronada, *n.f.* violent blow with a quoit, etc.; blow from a bird's beak.

herrugiento, -ta, *a.* rusty.

herrumbre, *n.f.* rust of iron; irony taste.

herrumbroso, -sa, *a.* rusty, drossy, scaly.

hertziano, -na, *a.* (*phys.*) Hertzian.

hervencia, *n.f.* boiling to death (medieval punishment).

herventar, *v.t.* to boil anything.

hervidero, *n.m.* ebullition, boiling; small spring whence water bubbles out; phlegmy rattling in the chest; multitude, crowd, great number or quantity.

hervidor, *n.m.* kettle; boiler (domestic).

herviente, *a.* boiling, seething.

hervir, *v.i.* to boil, seethe; to become choppy (the sea); to bubble, effervesce, be fervent, vehement; to surge (as a crowd); *hervir el garbanzuelo*, to be too solicitous. (conjugated like SENTIR).

hervor, *n.m.* ebullition, boiling; fervour, heat, vigour; fret; noise and movement of waters;

hervor de la sangre, rash; *alzar* (or *levantar*) *el hervor*, to begin to boil.

hervoroso, -sa, *a.* fiery, ardent, impetuous.

hesitación, *n.f.* hesitation, doubt, perplexity, hesitancy.

hespéride; hespérido, -da, *a.* relating to the Pleiades; (*poet.*) western. — *pl.* **hespérides**, Hesperides.

hesperidio, -dia, *a.* hesperidium.

Héspero, *n.m.* (*astron.*) the planet Venus; evening star.

heteo, -a, *n.m.f., a.* Hittite.

hetera, *n.f.* hetæra.

heteróclito, -ta, *a.* (*gram.*) heteroclite; irregular, abnormal.

heterodoxia, *n.f.* heterodoxy, misbelief.

heterodoxo, -xa, *a.* heterodox.

heterogeneidad, *n.f.* heterogeneousness, heterogeneity.

heterogéneo, -nea, *a.* heterogeneous.

heteromancia, *n.f.* divination by the flight of birds.

heterónomo, -ma, *a.* heteronomous.

heterópsido, -da, *a.* in a state of alkaline earth, lustreless (metals).

hético, -ca, *a.* hectical, consumptive.

hetiquez, *n.f.* phthisis, consumption.

hexacordo, *n.m.* hexachord.

hexaedro, *n.m.* hexahedron, a cube.

hexagonal; hexágono, -na, *a.* hexagonal.

hexágono, *n.m.* hexagon.

hexámetro, *n.m.* hexameter.

hexápeda, *n.f.* toise, old French measure of length (about 6½ ft.) [TOESA].

hexasílabo, -ba, *a.* containing six syllables.

hez, *n.f.* scum, lee, bottom, sediment, dregs of liquors; dross of metals; grains of malt; *la hez del pueblo*, the scum of the people. — *pl.* **heces**, fæces, excrement.

hi, *n.m.* [HIJO], son, used only in the compound word *hidalgo* with its derivations and the vulgar phrases *hi de puta*, *hi de perro*.

híadas, híades, *n.f.pl.* (*astron.*) Hyades, Hyads.

hialino, -na, *a.* hyaline, transparent.

hialitis, *n.f.* (*med.*) hyalitis.

hialoideo, -dea, *a.* vitreous, glass-like.

hialoides, *n.f.* hyaloid membrane.

hialurgia, *n.f.* glass-making.

hiante, *a.* of a verse with a hiatus.

hiato, *n.m.* hiatus, pause, cacophony.

hibernal; hibernizo, -za, *a.* hibernal, wintry.

hibernés, -esa, *a.* Hibernian, Irish.

hibierno, *n.m.* (*obs.*) winter.

hibridación, *n.f.* hybridization, hybridism.

híbrido, -da, *a.* hybridous, hybrid.

hicaco, *n.m.* (*W. Ind.*) tree of the rosaceous family.

hice; hiciera, *preterit perfect indic.; imperfect subj.* [HACER].

hicoteca, *n.f.* hiccatee, a fresh-water tortoise of the Antilles.

hidalgamente, *adv.* nobly, gentlemanly.

hidalgarse, *v.r.* to affect the nobleman.

hidalgo, -ga, *a.* noble, illustrious, excellent, exalted. — *n.m.f.* hidalgo, generous or noble man or woman; *hidalgo de bragueta*, one entitled to nobility from being the father of seven successive sons; *hidalgo de cuatro costados*, one descended from noble ancestors on both sides; *el hidalgo de Guadalajara, lo que dice a la noche, no cumple a la mañana,* proverb satirizing those who break their word; *hidalgo honrado, antes roto que remendado*, better poverty than dishonest gain.

hidalgón, -ona; -gote, -ta, *n.m.f.* old ceremonious hidalgo.

hidalguejo, -ja; -guelo, -la; -guete, -ta; -guillo, -lla, *n.m.f.* petty hidalgo.

hidalguez, hidalguía, *n.f.* nobility; rights of an *hidalgo;* nobleness, liberality.

hidatídico, -ca, *a.* (*med.*) hydatic.

hidra, *n.f.* poisonous serpent; hydra, freshwater polyp; (*fig.*) seditions, plots.

hidrácido, *n.m.* hydracid.

hidragogo, *n.m., a.* (*med.*) hydragogue.

hidrargirido, -da, *a.* resembling mercury.

hidrargirio, hidrargiro, *n.m.* mercury (hydrargyrum).

hidratado, -da, *a.* hydrate(d).

hidratar, *v.t.* to hydrate.

hidrato, *n.m.* hydrate.

hidráulica, *n.f.* hydraulics.

hidráulico, -ca, *a.* hydraulical, hydraulic.

hidráulico, *n.m.* expert in hydraulics.

hidria, *n.f.* ancient jar or pitcher.

hidroavión, *n.m.* hydroplane; seaplane; *hidroavión de flotadores,* flying-boat.

hidrobiología, *n.f.* biology of living matter in the waters.

hidrocarburo, *n.m.* hydrocarbon, hydrocarburet.

hidrocéfalo, *n.m.* hydrocephalus.

hidroclorato, *n.m.* hydrochlorate.

hidroclórico, -ca, *a.* hydrochloric.

hidrodinámica, *n.f.* hydrodynamics.

hidrodinámico, -ca, *a.* hydrodynamic.

hidroeléctrico, -ca, *a.* hydro-electric.

hidroesfera, *n.f.* hydrosphere.

hidrófana, *n.f.* (*min.*) hydrophane.

hidrofilacio, *n.m.* great cavern full of water.

hidrófilo, -la, *a.* water-loving; absorbent (cotton).

hidrofobia, *n.f.* hydrophobia; rabies.

hidrófobo, -ba, *a.* suffering from hydrophobia.

hidrogala, *n.m.* mixture of milk and water.

hidrógeno, *n.m.* hydrogen.

hidrogogía, *n.f.* science of canal making.

hidrografía, *n.f.* hydrography.

hidrográfico, -ca, *a.* hydrographical.

hidrógrafo, *n.m.* hydrographer.

hidrología, *n.f.* hydrology.

hidrológico, -ca, *a.* hydrologic.

hidromancía, *n.f.* hydromancy.

hidromántico, -ca, *a.* hydromantic.

hidromel, hidromiel, *n.m.* hydromel, mead, metheglin.

hidrometeoro, *n.m.* hydrometeor.

hidrómetra, *n.m.f.* expert in hydrometry.

hidrometría, *n.f.* hydrometry.

hidrómetro, *n.m.* hydrometer.

hidrópata, *n.m.f.* hydropath.

hidropatía, *n.f.* hydropathy, hydrotherapy.

hidropático, -ca, *a.* hydropathic.

hidropesía, *n.f.* dropsy.

hidrópico, -ca, *a.* hydropic, hydropical, dropsical.

hidroplano, *n.m.* hydroplane.

hidroscopio, *n.m.* hydroscope.

hidrostática, *n.f.* hydrostatics.

hidrostáticamente, *adv.* hydrostatically.

hidrostático, -ca, *a.* hydrostatical.

hidrosulfúrico, -ca, *a.* hydrosulphuric, sulphydric.

hidrotecnia, *n.f.* hydraulic engineering; science of constructing hydraulic machines.

hidroterapia, *n.f.* hydrotherapy.

hidroterápico, -ca, *a.* hydrotherapeutic.

hiedra, *n.f.* ivy; *hiedra terrestre,* ground ivy.

hiel, *n.f.* gall, bile; bitterness, asperity; *echar la hiel,* (*coll.*) to labour excessively; *no tener hiel,* (*coll.*) to be meek and gentle; *poca hiel hace amarga mucha miel,* a small fly corrupts much ointment; *quien te dió la hiel, te dará la miel,* spare the rod and spoil the child; *estar hecho de hieles,* to be as bitter as gall; *dar a beber hieles,* to make one wretched.

hiel de la tierra, *n.f.* (*bot.*) fumitory, earthsmoke.

hielo, *n.m.* frost, ice; congelation; coolness, indifference; astonishment, stupefaction; *punto de hielo,* freezing-point; *estar hecho un hielo,* to be very cold.

hiemal, *a.* wintry, hibernal.

hiena, *n.f.* hyena.

hienda, *n.f.* dung; *quien hienaa echa en la coladera, hienda saca de ella,* ill-gotten gains never prosper.

hiendo; hienda, *pres. indic.; pres. subj.* [HENDER].

hieracio, *n.m.* (*bot.*) hawkweed.

hierático, -ca, *a.* hierarchical, sacerdotal.

hierba, *n.f.* grass, weed, herb; food for cattle, herbage. — *pl.* **hierbas,** poison given in food; (among the members of a religious order) greens, garden-stuff; (speaking of cattle, horses, etc.) age; years; grass, pasturage; *otras hierbas,* (*joc.*) and so forth; *crecer como la mala hierba,* to grow apace (i.e., like weeds); *haber pisado buena* (or *mala*) *hierba,* to have had great (*or* small) success; *sentir crecer* (or *nacer*) *la hierba,* (*coll.*) to know one's onions; *la mala hierba crece mucho,* ill weeds grow apace (said jocularly of a boy who grows quickly).

hierbabuena, *n.f.* peppermint, mint.

hierbatero, *n.m.* (*Chi.*) retailer of fodder, grass, etc.

hiero; él hirió, *pres. indic.; pret.* [HERIR]

hierofanta, -te, *n.m.* hierophant.

hieroglífico, -ca (modern, JEROGLÍFICO), *a.* hieroglyphical, emblematical.

hieroscopia, *n.f.* haruspicy.

hierosolimitano, -na (modern, JEROSOLIMITANO), *a.* native of or belonging to Jerusalem.

hierrezuelo, *n.m.* small piece of iron.

hierro, *n.m.* iron; brand or mark made by or with a hot iron; iron head of a shaft, arrow, or dart; any pointed weapon, as a sword or goad. — *pl.* **hierros,** fetters, shackles, handcuffs; (*naut.*) bilboes; *hierro albo,* red-hot iron; *hierro colado* (or *fundido*), cast-iron; *hierro forjado,* forged iron; *hierro de fragua,* wrought iron; *hierro cuadrillado,* square iron; *hierro laminado,* (or *en planchas*), sheet-iron; *hierro varilla,* round iron; *es de hierro,* he is indefatigable, he is as firm (*or* hardy) as steel; *machacar* (or *majar*) *en hierro frío,* to labour in vain; *echarle a uno hierros,* to put someone in irons; *me ha puesto un hierro,* he has put me deeply in his debt.

hierro; yo hierre, *pres. indic.; pres. subj.* [HERRAR].

hiervo; él hirvió; hierva, *pres. indic.; pret.; pres. subj.* [HERVIR].

higa, *n.f.* amulet, charm hung about a baby's neck; method of pointing derisively at a person; ridicule, derision; *dar higa la escopeta,* to hang fire; *dar higas,* to despise; *no dar por una cosa dos higas,* not to value a thing at all; *mear claro y dar una higa al médico,* the healthy man needs no physician.

higadilla, *n.f.;* **higadillo,** *n.m.* small liver; liver of birds, fishes and other small animals.

hígado, *n.m.* liver. — *pl.* **hígados,** *(coll.)* courage, bravery, valour; *echar los hígados,* to be very tired or fatigued; *echar los hígados por alguna cosa, (coll.)* to desire anxiously; *malos hígados, (coll.)* ill-will; *hasta los hígados,* to the heart; *lo que es bueno para el hígado, es malo para el bazo,* what is one man's meat is another man's poison; *querer comer a uno los hígados,* to desire vengeance on another.

higate, *n.m.* pottage of figs, pork, etc.

higiene, *n.f.* hygiene.

higiénicamente, *adv.* hygienically.

higiénico, -ca, *a.* hygienic.

higienista, *n.m.f.* hygienist.

higienizar, *v.t.* to preserve health, make sanitary.

higo, *n.m. (bot.)* fig; venereal excrescence; *higo chumbo* (or *de pala*) prickly pear; *pan de higos,* fig-cake; *de higos a brevas,* once in a while; *no dársele un higo,* not to care a fig.

higrometría, *n.m.* hygrometry.

higrométrico, -ca, *a.* hygrometric.

higrómetro, *n.m.* hygrometer.

higroscopia, *n.f.* hygroscopy, hygrometry.

higroscopio, *n.m.* hygroscope.

higuera, *n.f.* fig-tree; *higuera infernal,* castor-oil plant; *higuera chumba (nopal,* or *de Indias)* Indian fig-tree, prickly-pear cactus; *sal de higuera,* Epsom salts.

higueral, *n.m.* plantation of fig-trees.

higuerón, *n.m.* large tree in tropical America.

higuito, *n.m.* small fig.

hija, *n.f.* daughter; *hija política,* daughter-in-law; *hija enlodada, ni viuda ni casada,* give a dog a bad name and hang him.

hijadalgo, *n.f.* well-born girl or woman.

hijastro, -tra, *n.m.f.* step-child.

hijear, *v.i. (Cub.)* to adopt (children).

hijito, -ta, *n.m.f.* little child, little dear.

hijo, *n.m.* son; *hijo político,* son-in-law.

hijo, *n.m.·* son, child, scion; son or native of a place; young of all animals; *(bot.)* shoot, sucker; *(fig.)* child, issue, anything which is the product or effect of another; bud or root of the horns of animals; fruit, result; junior (after a person's name); *Alejandro Dumas Hijo,* Alexandre Dumas the Younger; *hijo adoptivo,* adopted child; *hijo bastardo, hijo natural, hijo de ganancia,* or *hijo de su madre, (coll.)* bastard; *hijo de bendición,* legitimate child; *hijo de familia,* minor; *hijo de la piedra,* foundling; *hijo del agua,* good sailor, good swimmer; *hijo de leche,* foster-child; *al hijo del rico no le toques el vestido,* the rich youth is frequently unbearable; *buscar un hijo prieto en Salamanca,* to look for a person among many similar to him; *cada hijo de vecino,* any mother's son; *como mi hijo entre fraile, mas que no me quiera nadie,* everyone wants his own way, i.e., is disinclined to be dissuaded; *echar al hijo,* to abandon one's child; *el hijo borde y la mula cada día se mudan,* low-born folk can never be relied upon; *el hijo de la cabra, de una hora a otra bala,* the low-born man sooner or later gives himself away; *el hijo de la gata ratones mata* and *el hijo del asno, dos veces rebuzna al día,* like father, like son; *el hijo del bueno pasa malo y bueno,* a sound upbringing helps one to bear both prosperity and adversity; *hijo no tener, y nombre le poner,* to count one's chickens before they're hatched; *cada uno es hijo de sus obras,* everyone is the son of his own works.

hijodalgo, *n.m.* man of noble descent [HIDALGO].

hijuela, *n.f.* little daughter; *(eccles.)* pall, chalice cover; *(sew.)* gore, or piece for widening a garment; small drain; small mattress put between others, to make the bed even; estate of a deceased person; rural postman; *(law)* schedule given to an heir of his share in the partition of the estate; side-road; bundle of kindling wood; palm seed; leader for fish-hooks.

hijuelo, -la, *n.m.f.* young child; *(bot.)* shoot, sucker.

hila, *n.f.* row, line; thin gut; spinning; *hila de agua,* measure of water for irrigation. — *pl. (surg.)* lint; *hilas raspadas,* scraped lint; *a la hila,* in a row, single file.

hilacha, *n.f.;* **hilacho,** *n.m.* filament or thread ravelled out of cloth.

hilachoso, -sa, *a.* filamentous.

hilada, *n.f.* row, line; *(arch.)* course, horizontal range; layer.

hiladillo, *n.m.* ferret silk; narrow ribbon or tape.

hilado, *n.m.* spinning; spinstry; yarn, thread. — *p.p.* [HILAR].

hilador, -ra, *n.m.f.* silk-spinner.

hilandera, *n.f.* woman spinner, spinster.

hilandería, *n.f.* spinnery, spinning-mill; spinstry.

hilandero, -ra, *n.m.f.* spinner.

hilandero, *n.m.* spinning-room, spinnery.

hilanderilla, *n.f.* spinning girl, little spinster.

hilanderuelo, -la, *n.m.f.* spinning boy or girl.

hilar, *v.t.* to spin; to argue, discuss, infer, deduce; to spin a cocoon (of silk-worms); *hilar delgado,* to handle a subject in too subtle and nice a manner; to be exceedingly careful; to split hairs.

hilaracha, *n.f.* filament, loose thread.

hilarante, *a. (chem.)* laughing (gas).

hilaridad, *n.f.* hilarity, laughter, jollity.

hilatura, *n.f.* the art of spinning (wool, cotton, silk, etc.).

hilaza, *n.f.* yarn; fibre; uneven thread.

hilera, *n.f.* row, line, range, tier, file; *(metal.)* wire-drawer; fine thread or yarn; *(arch.)* ridge-pole; slit or catch of a spindle; *(mil.)* file; *hilera de tirar alambre,* wire plate.

hilero, *n.m.* ripples; thread of a river; current.

hilete, *n.m.* small thread.

hilo, *n.m.* thread, yarn; clothes of linen or hemp as distinguished from wool, cotton, etc.; fibre, filament; wire; slender thread formed by falling liquids; edge of a sword or razor; (*min.*) seam; fine thread of spiders or silk-worms; series, continuation; *hilo de palomar, hilo bramante* or (*de*) *acarreto*, packthread, twine; *hilo de velas* (or *volatín*) sailmaker's yarn; *hilo de una corriente*, (*naut.*) thread of a current; *hilo de perlas*, number of pearls strung on a thread; *a hilo*, successively, one after another; *al hilo*, (*sew.*) along the thread; *de hilo*, directly, instantly; *ir al hilo del mundo* (or *de la gente*), to go with the stream, follow popular opinion; *cortar el hilo de la vida*, to kill, deprive of life; *cortar el hilo del discurso*, to interrupt the thread of the discourse; *estar colgado* (or *pendiente*) *de un hilo*, to be in great peril, *or* hanging by a thread; *más tonto que un hilo de uvas*, (*prov.*) as foolish as a goose; *por el hilo se saca el ovillo*, by the thread is discovered the ball, you can recognize a thing by a sample of it; *tomar el hilo*, to continue an interrupted discourse, take up the thread of a story.

hilván, *n.m.* (*sew.*) tacking, basting; *hablar de hilván*, (*coll.*) to speak very fast.

hilvanar, *v.t.* (*sew.*) to tack, baste; (*fig.*) to string together, co-ordinate; to act in a hurry.

himen, *n.m.* (*anat.*) hymen.

himeneo, *n.m.* marriage, matrimony; epithalamium.

himenófilo, *n.m.* filmy fern, lace fern.

himenópteros, *n.m.pl.* (*entom.*) hymenoptera.

himnario, *n.m.* hymnary.

himno, *n.m.* (*poet., mus.*) hymn.

himnología, *n.f.* hymnology.

himplar, *v.i.* to roar or bellow (of the panther and ounce).

hin, *n.m.* whinny, neigh.

hincadura, *n.f.* thrusting into; prick.

hincapié, *n.m.; hacer hincapié*, to dig in one's toes; to stand one's ground.

hincar, *v.t.* (*pret.* **hinqué**; *pres. subj.* **hinque**) to thrust in, drive into, nail one thing to another; *hincar la rodilla*, to kneel down; to plant; *hincar el diente*, to bite; to censure, to calumniate.

hincón, *n.m.* ferry-post, hitching-post.

hincha, *n.f.* (*coll.*) hatred, displeasure, enmity.

hinchadamente, *adv.* haughtily, loftily.

hinchado, -da, *a.* swollen, tumefied, swelled, vain, arrogant, presumptuous; inflated, turgid, high-flown (of style). — *p.p.* [HINCHAR].

hinchar, *v.t.* to inflate, swell with wind. — *v.r.* to swell; to grow arrogant, be elated.

hinchazón, *n.m.* swelling, tumefaction; ostentation, pride, vanity; inflation; euphuism.

hiniesta, *n.f.* genista, Spanish broom [RETAMA].

hinnible, *a.* capable of neighing.

hinojal, *n.m.* fennel bed.

hinojo, *n.m.* knee; (*bot.*) fennel; *hinojo marino*, (*bot.*) samphire; *de hinojos*, on bended knees.

hinque, *n.m.* children's game.

hintero, *n.m.* baker's kneading table.

hiño; yo hiña, *pres. indic.; pres. subj.* [HEÑIR].

hioides, *a.* (*anat.*) hyoid.

hipar, *v.i.* to hiccup; to whimper; desire eagerly, be anxious; to be overfatigued; to pant, snuffle (of dogs on the scent).

hipear, *v.i.* to hiccup.

hipérbola, *n.f.* hyperbola.

hipérbole, *n.f.* hyperbole.

hiperbólicamente, *adv.* hyperbolically.

hiperbólico, -ca, *a.* hyperbolical.

hiperbolizar, *v.i.* to use hyperboles.

hiperboloide, *n.f.* hyperboloid.

hiperbóreo, -rea, *a.* hyperborean.

hipercrítico, -ca, *a.* hypercritical, censorious.

hiperdulía, *n.f.* (*eccles.*) hyperdulia.

hiperemia, hiperhemia, *n.f.* hyperæmia, congestion of blood.

hiperémico, -ca, *a.* hyperæmic, congested.

hipericineos, -nas, *n.m.f.pl.* Hypericaceæ.

hipérico, *n.m.* (*bot.*) hypericum.

hipertrofia, *n.f.* hypertrophy.

hipertrofiarse, *v.r.* to hypertrophy.

hipertrófico, -ca, *a.* hypertrophic.

hípico, -ca, *a.* equine, relating to horses.

hipido [aspirated *h*], *n.m.* action and effect of hiccuping.

hipil, *n.m.* (*Am.*) loose garment worn by Indians.

hipismo, *n.m.* relating to the breeding and training of horses.

hipnal, *n.m.* kind of asp said by the ancients to cause sleep.

hipnosis, *n.f.* hypnosis.

hipnótico, -ca, *n.m., a.* hypnotic.

hipnotismo, *n.m.* hypnotism, mesmerism.

hipnotizar, *v.t.* to hypnotize.

hipo, *n.m.* hiccup; wish, desire, anxiety; anger, fury, displeasure.

hipocampo, *n.m.* hippocampus, sea-horse.

hipocausto, *n.m.* hypocaust.

hipocicloide, *n.f.* hypocycloid.

hipocondría, *n.f.* hypochondria, melancholy.

hipocondríaco, -ca, *a.* hypochondriac, melancholy.

hipocóndrico, -ca, *a.* hypochondriac, hypochondriacal, melancholy, fanciful.

hipocondrio, *n.m.* (*anat.*) hypochondrium.

hipocrás, *n.m.* hippocras, medicated wine.

hipocrático, -ca, *a.* Hippocratic.

hipocrénides, *n.f.pl.* (*poet.*) the Muses.

hipocresía, *n.f.* hypocrisy, dissimulation.

hipócrita, *a.* hypocritical, dissembling, insincere. — *n.m.f.* hypocrite, dissembler.

hipócritamente, *adv.* hypocritically.

hipocritilla, *n.f.* sly hypocrite.

hipocritón, -ona, *a.* extremely hypocritical or dissembling.

hipodérmico, -ca, *a.* hypodermic.

hipódromo, *n.m.* hippodrome, race-course.

hipófisis, *n.f.* (*path.*) hypophysis.

hipofosfito, *n.m.* hypophosphite.

hipogástrico, -ca, *a.* hypogastric.

hipogastrio, *n.m.* hypogastrium.

hipogénico, -ca, *a.* (*geol.*) hypogene.

hipogloso, -sa, *a.* (*zool.*) hypoglossal.

hipogrifo, *n.m.* hippogriff.

hipómanes, *n.m.* vaginal discharge from the mare when in heat.

hipomoclio, hipomoclion, *n.m.* fulcrum of a lever.

hiponitrato, *n.m.* subnitrate.

hiponítrico, -ca, *a.* hyponitrous.

hipopótamo, *n.m.* hippopotamus.

hiposo, -sa, *a.* having hiccups.

hipóstasis, *n.f.* (*theol.*) hypostasis.

hipostáticamente, *adv.* hypostatically.

hipostático, -ca, *a.* hypostatical.

hiposulfato, *n.m.* (*chem.*) a salt of hyposulphuric acid with an element or radical.

hiposulfito, *n.m.* (*chem.*) hyposulphite.
hiposulfuroso, *a.* (*chem.*) hyposulphurous.
hipoteca, *n.f.* mortgage, pledge; (*law*) hypothec, hypothecation.
hipotecable, *a.* mortgageable.
hipotecar, *v.t.* (*pret.* **hipotequé;** *pres. subj.* **hipoteque**) to hypothecate, pledge, mortgage.
hipotecario, -ria, *a.* belonging to a mortgage; hypothecary.
hipotenusa, *n.f.* hypotenuse.
hipótesis, *n.f.* hypothesis, supposition.
hipotético, -ca, *a.* hypothetic, hypothetical, conditional.
hipsometría, *n.f.* hypsometry.
hipsométrico, *a.* hypsometric.
hipsómetro, *n.m.* hypsometer.
hirco, *n.m.* wild goat.
hirma, *n.f.* selvedge, edge of cloth.
hirsuto, -ta, *a.* hirsute, hairy, bristly; (*poet.*) rough, rugged.
hirundinaria, *n.f.* common celandine, swallow-wort.
hirviente, *a.* boiling, seething, ebullient.
hisca, *n.f.* bird-lime.
hiscal, *n.m.* esparto rope of three strands.
hisopada, *n.f.* water sprinkled with an aspergill.
hisopear, *v.t.* to sprinkle holy water with an aspergill.
hiscpillo, *n.m.* small aspergill; piece of soft linen used in the sick-room to wash and refresh the mouth; (*bot.*) winter-savory.
hisopo, *n.m.* hyssop; (*eccles.*) aspergill, asperges, sprinkler; *hisopo húmedo,* grease collected in washing fleeces of wool.
hispalense, *a.* native of or belonging to Seville.
hispánico, -ca, *a.* Hispanic.
hispanismo, *n.m.* Hispanicism.
hispanista, *n.m.f.* Spanish scholar.
hispano, -na, *a.* Spanish. — *n.m.f.* (*poet.*) Spaniard.
Hispanoamérica, *n.f.* Spanish America.
hispanoamericanismo, *n.m.* doctrine propounding the spiritual union of all Spanish-American nations.
hispanoamericano,-na, *a.* Spanish-American.
hispanófilo, -a, *a.* Hispanophile.
híspido, -da, *a.* bristly, hirsute.
hispir, *v.t., v.i.* to swell, make, or become spongy; to rarefy.
histérico, -ca, *a.* hysteric, hysterical.
histérico, *n.m.* hysterics.
histerismo, *n.m.* hysteria.
histerología, *n.f.* (*rhet.*) hysteron-proteron.
histerotomía, *n.m.* hysterotomy.
histología, *n.f.* histology.
histológico, -ca, *a.* histological.
histólogo, *n.m.* histologist.
historia, *n.f.* history; tale, story; (*coll.*) tale, tattle; (*art*) history-piece; *dejar de historias,* to come to the point; *picar en historia,* to gain importance; *meterse en historias,* to meddle unjustifiably; *historia sagrada,* the Old and New Testaments; *historia antigua,* ancient history; *historia de la edad media,* mediæval history; *historia moderna,* modern history.
historiado, -da, *a.* (*coll.*) excessively adorned; (*art*) well-composed figure-painting; *libro historiado,* book illustrated with plates.
historiador, -ra, *n.m.f.* historian, historiographer, chronicler.

historial, *a.* historic, historical.
historialmente, *adv.* historically.
historiar, *v.t.* to relate, to chronicle, to record in history; (*art*) to represent historical events in paintings or tapestry.
históricamente, *adv.* historically.
histórico, -ca, *a.* historical, historic.
historieta, *n.f.* short story or tale, short novel or anecdote.
historiógrafo, *n.m.* historiographer, historian.
historión, *n.m.* tedious, long-winded story.
histrión, *n.m.* actor, player; juggler, buffoon.
histriónico, -ca, *a.* histrionic, histrionical.
histrionisa, *n.f.* actress, danseuse.
histrionismo, *n.m.* histrionism; theatrical profession.
hita, *n.f.* headless nail, brad, wire-nail; sign-post.
hito, -ta, *a.* adjoining (used only for a house or a street); firm, fixed; black (horse).
hito, *n.m.* landmark, sign-post; hob and quoits; milestone; (*artill.*) target; *a hito,* fixedly, firmly; *mirar de hito en hito,* to fix the eyes on an object, to stare; *dar en el hito,* to hit the nail on the head, to see the point; *mudar de hito,* to change one's methods; *tener la suya sobre el hito,* not to give in, to refuse to acknowledge defeat.
hitón, *n.m.* large square nail without head.
hizo (**él**), *pret.* [HACER].
hobachón, -ona, *a.* sluggish, fat, and lazy. — *n.m.f.* (*Col.*) a shy horse.
hocicada, *n.f.* blow with or on the nose.
hocicar, *v.t.* to root (as hogs). — *v.i.* to fall headlong with the face to the ground; to knock one's face against an object; (*coll.*) to get into difficulties; (*naut.*) to pitch.
hocico, *n.m.* snout, muzzle, muffle; pouting; (*coll.*) the face; (*coll.*) thick-lipped mouth of a man; *meter el hocico en todo,* to stick one's nose into other people's business, to meddle in everything; *poner tanto hocico,* (*coll.*) to pout; *caer, dar de hocicos,* (*coll.*) fall flat on the face, bang the face against; *estar con* (or *de*) *hocico,* to be ill-humoured, sulky, at variance.
hocicudo, -da; hocicón, -ona, *a.* long-snouted; blubber-lipped, flap-mouthed.
hocino, *n.m.* (*agric.*) bill, bill-hook; glen, dell; narrow gorge or canyon. — *pl.* fertile spots in glens and dells.
hociquillo, -ito, *n.m.* little snout.
hogañazo, hogaño, *adv.* (*coll.*) this present year; in this epoch.
hogar, *n.m.* hearth, fire-place; house, residence, home.
hogaza, *n.f.* large loaf of bread; *a quien cuece y amasa, no le hurtes hogaza,* never try to sell a musty loaf to a baker; *pues tenemos hogazas, no busquemos tortas,* we have loaves already, let us not look for cakes.
hoguera, *n.f.* bonfire, large fire, blaze.
hoja, *n.f.* leaf (of trees and plants, of a book, of a door); petal; leaf, foil, sheet, or thin plate of metal; blade of a sword or knife; by extension a sword; sheet of paper; veneer; window shutter; half of each of the principal parts of a garment; ground cultivated one year, and lying at rest for another; scale of metals; scale-armour; *hoja de servicios,* (*mil.*) certificate setting forth the rank and services of a military officer; *hoja de lata,* tin-plate; *hoja de tocino,* side of a hog; *hoja de estaño,*

tinfoil; *hoja volante*, fly-sheet, handbill, supplement, extra; *doblemos la hoja*, no more of that, let us change the subject; *volver la hoja*, to turn over a new leaf; *no se mueve la hoja en el árbol sin la voluntad del Señor*, nothing is without its purpose; *ser tentado de la hoja*, to be fond of a thing; *ser todo hoja y no tener fruto*, to be all words and no deeds; *hoja toledana*, Toledo blade. — *pl.*
hojas, (*arch.*) leaf ornaments, foliation; years of age (of wine); *hojas de las puertas*, (*naut.*) port-lids.

hojalata, *n.f.* tin-plate.

hojalatería, *n.f.* tin-plate, tin-ware; tinshop.

hojalatero, *n.m.* tinman, tinsmith.

hojaldrado, *a.* resembling puff-pastry, lamellar, foliated. — *p.p.* [HOJALDRAR].

hojaldrar, *v.t.* to make puff-pastry.

hojaldre, *n.m.f.* puff-pastry; *quitar la hojaldre al pastel*, (*coll.*) to detect any fraud, to discover a plot.

hojaldrista, *n.m.f.* puff-pastry baker.

hojarasca, *n.f.* withered leaves; frondage, redundancy, trash, excessive foliage.

hojear, *v.t.* to turn the leaves of a book; to skim, glance at a book. — *v.i.* to exfoliate, scale off.

hojica, -illa, -ita, *n.f.* small leaf.

hojoso, -sa; hojudo, -da, *a.* leafy, fronded.

hojuela, *n.f.* small leaf, leaflet; pancake; gold or silver flat thread for embroidery; skins of pressed olives.

¡hola! *interj.* hello, ho! ho! (*naut.*) hoy! ahoy!

holán, holán batista, *n.m.* cambric; batiste.

Holanda, *n.f.* Holland.

holanda, *n.f.* fine Dutch linen, cambric.

holandés, -esa, *a.* Dutch, Hollandish.

holandeta, holandilla, *n.f.* brown holland; *tabaco holandilla*, tobacco of poor quality.

holgachón, -ona, *a.* (*coll.*) fond of ease and little work.

holgadamente, *adv.* widely, amply, fully, loosely, easily; quietly, carelessly.

holgado, -da, *a.* loose, lax, easy; large, commodious; disengaged, at leisure; well off.

holganza, *n.f.* repose, rest, leisure, ease, quiet; diversion, recreation, amusement, entertainment.

holgar, *v.i.* (*pres. indic.* **huelgo**; *pres. subj.* **huelgue**) to rest; to quit work; to be idle; to be needless or useless; to take pleasure or satisfaction in. — *v.r.* to sport; to dally, trifle, idle, amuse oneself.

holgazán, -ana, *a.* idle, lazy, slothful, inactive, indolent. — *n.m.f.* idler, loiterer, vagabond, lounger.

holgazanear, *v.i.* to idle; to lead an idle life; to be lazy; to loiter, lounge.

holgazanería, *n.f.* idleness, laziness, sluggishness, slothfulness, inactivity, indolence.

holgorio [aspirated *h*], *n.m.* (*coll.*) boisterous frolic or spree, mirth, jollity.

holgueta, *n.f.* (*coll.*) feast, merry-making.

holgura, *n.f.* frolic, spree, merry-making; width, breadth; ease, repose; laxity, looseness; (*mech.*) play.

holocausto, *n.m.* holocaust, burnt sacrifice.

hológrafo, -fa, *a.* holographic, holograph.

holómetro, *n.m.* holometer; pantometer.

holosérico, -ca, *a.* cloth of pure silk.

holostérico, *a.*; *barómetro holostérico*, aneroid barometer.

holladura, *n.f.* trampling; duty paid for the run of cattle.

hollar, *v.t.* (*pres. indic.* **huello**; *pres. subj.* **huelle**) to tread upon, trample under foot; to humble, pull down, depress.

hollejo, *n.m.* grapeskin; bean pod, peel, husk.

hollejuelo, *n.m.* small pod or rind.

hollí, *n.m.* (*Mex.*) resinous liquor mixed with chocolate.

hollín, *n.m.* soot, lampblack.

holliniento, -ta, *a.* fuliginous, sooty.

homarrache, *n.m.* clown, buffoon, merry-Andrew.

hombracho, *n.m.* well-built man.

hombrachón, *n.m.* tall, well-built man.

hombrada, *n.f.* manly action; impulse.

hombradía, *n.f.* manliness.

hombrazo, *n.m.* large man.

hombre, *n.m.* man; mankind; (*vulg.*) husband; ombre, game at cards; *hombre bueno*, (*law*) arbiter, arbitrator, referee; *hombre de buena capa*, well-dressed man; *hombre de bien*, honest man; *hombre de bigotes*, grave and determined man; *hombre de pro* (or *de provecho*), worthy, useful man; *hombre de asiento*, prudent man; *hombre de corazón*, courageous man; *hombre de burlas*, empty jester; *hombre de dinero*, moneyed man; *hombre de copete*, man of consequence; *hombre de negocios*, business man; *hombre seco*, thin and spare man; *ser muy hombre*, to be a man of spirit and courage; *hombre lleno* (or *de buenas letras*), worthy man; *hombre de su palabra*, man of his word; *hombre de cabeza*, talented man; *hombre de calzas atacadas*, strict, old-fashioned man; *hombre de capricho*, fanciful, whimsical man; *hombre de chapa*, man of ability and merit; *hombre de días*, old man; *hombre hecho* (or *hecho y derecho*), grown man; *hombre sin dolo*, plain-speaking man; *hombre de pelo en pecho*, a brave, bold man; *¡hombre!* an exclamation of surprise; *¡hombre al agua!* man overboard! *hombre de armas tomar*, a resolute man; *buen hombre, pero mal sastre*, an honest fellow, but with no ability; *al hombre vergonzoso el diablo le llevó a palacio*, proverb describing the difficulty of accustoming oneself to high society; *anda el hombre a trote por ganar su capote*, proverb describing the care which some take to attain insignificant ends; *de hombres es errar; de bestias, perseverar en el error*, stubbornness is a quality of beasts, not of men; *el hombre en la plaza, y la mujer en la casa*, the man's place is at his work, and the woman's in the home; *el hombre pone* (or *propone*) *y Dios dispone*, man proposes and God disposes; *hombre bellaco, tres barbas o cuatro*, the cunning man has many disguises; *hombre enamorado nunca casa con sobrado*, men in love are great spenders; *hombre honrado, antes muerto que injuriado*, prefer honour to life; *hombre pobre, todo es trazas*, poverty can find a way; *hombre prevenido vale por dos*, forewarned is forearmed; *no hay hombre sin hombre*, there's nothing like help for getting on, or union is strength; *ser hombre muy llegado a las horas de comer*, to be ready to perform things useful to oneself; *debajo de ser hombre puedo venir a ser papa*, any man may become a pope.

hombrear, *v.i.* to shoulder, push with the

shoulder; to act too old for one's years. — *v.i.*, *v.r.* to vie with one another.

hombrecico, -cito, -cillo, -zuelo, *n.m.* little man; youth.

hombrecillos, *n.m.pl.* (*bot.*) hops.

hombrera, *n.f.* (*arm.*) pauldron.

hombría de bien, *n.f.* honesty, probity.

hombrillo, *n.m.* (*sew.*) gusset; yoke of a shirt.

hombro, *n.m.* shoulder; *hombro con hombro,* shoulder to shoulder; *encogerse de hombros,* to shrug the shoulders; *llevar en hombros,* to support, protect; *a hombro* (or *sobre los hombros*), on the shoulders; *arrimar el hombro,* to work with a will, to lend a hand; *echar al hombro,* to shoulder, to become responsible for; *mirar sobre el hombro,* to look contemptuously upon.

hombrón, *n.m.* big, lusty man; man of great talent or courage.

hombronazo, *n.m.* huge, strong man.

hombruno, -na, *a.* mannish (of a woman).

homenaje, *n.m.* homage; obeisance; fealty, respect, veneration.

homeópata, *n.m.f.* homœopath(ist).

homeopatía, *n.f.* (*med.*) homœopathy.

homeopático, -ca, *a.* homœopathic.

homérico, -ca, *a.* Homeric.

homicida, *a.* homicidal. — *n.m.f.* murderer, murderess.

homicidio, *n.m.* murder; ancient tribute.

homiliario, *n.m.* collection of homilies.

homilía, *n.f.* homily.

homilista, *n.m.f.* author or writer of homilies.

hominal, *a.* (*nat. hist.*) relating to man.

hominicaco, *n.m.* (*coll.*) paltry fellow; whipper-snapper.

homocéntrico, -ca, *a.* homocentric.

homofonía, *n.f.* homophony.

homófono, -na, *a.* homophonous.

homogeneidad, *n.f.* homogeneity, homogeneousness.

homogéneo, -nea, *a.* homogeneous.

homógrafo, -fa, *a.* homonymous.

homologación, *n.f.* (*law*) homologation.

homologar, *v.t.* (*law*) to homologate.

homólogo, -ga, *a.* (*geom.*) homologous; (*log.*) synonymous.

homonimia, *n.f.* homonymy.

homónimo, -ma, *a.* homonymous, equivocal; namesake.

honda, *n.f.* sling; *honda y precinta,* (*naut.*) parbuckle.

hondable, *a.* (*naut.*) soundable.

hondamente, *adv.* deeply, profoundly, with deep insight.

hondarras, *n.f.pl.* dregs, lees, sediment.

hondazo, *n.m.* cast or throw with a sling.

hondear, *v.t.* (*naut.*) to sound; to unload a vessel.

hondero, *n.m.* slinger.

hondica, -illa, -ita, *n.f.* small sling.

hondijo, *n.m.* sling.

hondillos, *n.m.pl.* any of the pieces which form the seats of breeches or drawers.

hondo, -da, *a.* profound, deep; low. — *n.m.* bottom.

hondón, *n.m.* bottom; dell, glen; broken ground, deep hole; foot-piece of a stirrup; eye of a needle.

hondonada, *n.f.* dale, ravine, glen, combe.

hondura, *n.f.* depth, profundity; *meterse en honduras,* to go beyond one's depth.

hondureño, -na, *a.* of or relating to Honduras. — *n.m.f.* native of Honduras.

honestamente, *adv.* virtuously; modestly.

honestar, *v.t.* to honour, dignify; to excuse, palliate.

honestidad, *n.f.* modesty, moderation, purity, decency, honourableness, decorousness, composure, urbanity.

honesto, -ta, *a.* decent, decorous; chaste, pure, virtuous; reasonable, just, honourable; *mujer de estado honesto,* spinster.

hongo, *n.m.* mushroom, fungus; slouch hat, Derby hat.

hongoso, -sa, *a.* (*prov.*) fungous, spongy.

honor, *n.m.* honour; reputation, fame, celebrity; chastity in women. — *pl.* **honores,** dignity, rank, employment; honours, privileges, marks of respect; honorary title or position.

honorable, *a.* honourable, illustrious, noble.

honorablemente, *adv.* honourably, creditably.

honorario, -ria, *a.* honorary.

honorario, *n.m.* salary, stipend, professional fees, honorarium.

honoríficamente, *adv.* honourably.

honorífico, -ca, *a.* honorary, creditable, honourable.

honra, *n.f.* honour, respect, reverence; celebrity, reputation, glory, fame; chastity in women, purity; mark of respect, favour conferred or received; *de honra y provecho,* (*coll.*) with good solid qualities, wearing well. — *pl.* **honras,** obsequies.

honradamente, *adv.* honourably, reputably, honestly.

honradez, *n.f.* honesty, probity, fairness, integrity, faithfulness.

honrado, -da, *a.* honest, honourable, just, reputable, upright, fair. — *p.p.* [HONRAR].

honrador, -ra, *a.* honourer.

honramiento, *n.m.* honouring.

honrar, *v.t.* to honour, reverence, respect; to caress, fondle, cajole; to dignify, glorify, exalt; to praise, applaud; to grace, adorn, do credit; (*com.*) to pay a draft. — *v.r.* to deem it an honour.

honrilla, *n.f.* keen sense of honour or duty, punctiliousness (generally in the phrase *la negra honrilla*), some small point of honour or sense of shame.

honrosamente, *adv.* honourably, honestly, creditably.

honroso, -sa, *a.* honourable, decent, decorous, creditable, just, honest, jealous of one's honour.

hontanal, hontanar, *n.m.* place abounding in springs.

hontanales, *n.m.pl.* feats of the ancients held at fountains.

hopa, *n.f.* long cassock; sack for those who are executed for crime.

hopalanda, *n.f.* gown worn by students.

hopear, *v.i.* to wag the tail (applied to foxes).

hopo, *n.m.* bushy tail (as of a fox); *seguir el hopo,* to dog, pursue closely; *sudar el hopo,* to cost much trouble to attain; *volver el hopo,* to run away, escape.

hoque, *n.m.* treat to close a bargain.

hora, *n.f.* hour; time, season for doing anything; death; way made in an hour, a league. — *pl.* **horas,** (*eccles.*) book of devotions; canonical hours; *hora menguada,* fatal, or unhappy hour; *a la hora de ésta* (or *a la hora de ahora*), (*coll.*) at this moment; *a última hora*, at the last moment; *a poco de hora*, soon afterwards; *a la hora*, in the nick of time; *a buena hora*, at a seasonable time; *en hora buena*, it is well; *por hora*, each hour; *por horas*, by instants; *dar la hora*, to strike (of a clock); *vete en hora mala*, (*coll.*) begone, get out of my sight; ¿ *qué hora es* ? (in some places, ¿*qué horas son* ?), what time is it? *hora de la modorra*, time near daybreak, early morning; *hora suprema*, hour of death, one's last hour; *antes de la hora, gran denuedo; venidos al punto, mucho miedo*, great talkers are small doèrs; *a tal hora te amanezca*, said to a person arriving late for an appointment; *de hora a hora, Dios mejora*, Heaven sends help when the time comes; *en chica hora Dios obra*, God's power knows no limit; *no ver la hora de una cosa*, to await some happening eagerly; *tener sus horas contadas*, to have one's days numbered; (*llegar*) *a la hora undécima*, at the eleventh hour.

hora, *adv.* now, at this time, at present.

horaciano, -na, *a.* Horatian; in the style and manner of Horace.

horadable, *a.* capable of being pierced.

horadación, *n.f.* perforation; boring, piercing, tunnelling.

horadado, *n.m.* silk-worm's cocoon bored through. — *p.p.* [HORADAR].

horadador, -ra, *n.m.f., a.* perforator, borer, burrower.

horadar, *v.t.* to perforate, burrow, bore, pierce.

horado, *n.m.* hole bored through; cavern, grotto, niche, cavity.

horambre, *n.m.* hole in the millstone.

horario, -ria, *a.* horary, horal.

horario, *n.m.* hour-hand (of a clock or watch); railway timetable.

horca, *n.f.* gallows, gibbet; (*agric.*) hay-fork, pitch-fork; forked prop for trees or vines; yoke for dogs or hogs; rope or string of onions or garlic; *señor de horca y cuchillo*, lord of the manor (i.e., lord invested with civil and criminal jurisdiction within his estate); *pasar por las horcas caudinas*, to be compelled to do something against one's will; *mostrar la horca antes que el lugar*, to meet troubles half-way.

horcado, -da, *a.* forked, forky.

horcadura, *n.f.* fork of a tree.

horcajadas or **horcajadillas (a)**, *adv.* astride, astraddle.

horcajadura, *n.f.* crotch formed by the two thighs.

horcajo, *n.m.* yoke or collar for mules; in oil-mills, the Y-shaped division of the beam; fork or confluence of two streams; point of union of two mountains or hills.

horcate, *n.m.* hame, collar of a horse.

horco, *n.m.* rope or string of onions or garlic.

horcón, *n.m.* forked pole to support the branches of fruit-trees.

horchata, *n.f.* orgeat; *horchata de chufas*, water-ice made of *chufas*.

horchatería, *n.f.* place where *horchata* is made and sold.

horchatero, -ra, *n.m.f.* maker or seller of *horchata*.

horda, *n.f.* horde, clan, tribe.

hordiate, *n.m.* pearl-barley; barley-water.

hordeína, *n.f.* hordein; finest barley-bran.

horizontal, *n.m.f., a.* horizontal.

horizontalidad, *n.f.* horizontality.

horizontalmente, *adv.* horizontally, flatly.

horizonte, *n.m.* horizon.

horma, *n.f.* mould, model; shoemaker's last, hatter's block; drystone wall; (*Cub., Per.*) mould for sugar-loaf; *hallar la horma de su zapato*, to meet one's wishes; (*iron.*) to meet one's match.

hormaza, *n.f.* drystone wall.

hormazo, *n.m.* blow with a last or block; heap of stones; (*prov.*) house and garden.

hormero, *n.m.* last-maker.

hormiga, *n.f.* ant, pismire, emmet; (*med.*) itch, cutaneous eruption; *hormiga león*, ant-lion; *por su mal nacieron alas a la hormiga*, it was a bad day for the ant when she got wings.

hormigo, *n.m.* sifted ash used in smelting quicksilver. — *pl.* **hormigos**, sweetmeat of mashed nuts, honey, etc.; coarse parts of flour or ill-ground wheat.

hormigón, *n.m.* concrete; (*vet.*) disease of cattle; (*bot.*) disease of some plants; *hormigón hidráulico*, beton, hydraulic mortar; *hormigón armado*, reinforced concrete.

hormigonera, *n.f.* concrete mixer.

hormigoso, -sa, *a.* formic, formicate, formicine, formican; damaged by ants.

hormigueamiento, *n.m.* formication, itching.

hormiguear, *v.i.* to itch; to swarm, run about like ants.

hormigüela, *n.f.* small ant.

hormigueo, *n.m.* formication, itching.

hormiguero, *n.m.* anti-hill or hillock, formicarium; swarm of people or little animals; (*orn.*) wryneck; (*slang*) petty thief; (*slang*) cheater at dice. — *pl.* **hormigueros**, piles of weeds covered with earth and burned to serve as manure.

hormiguero, -ra, *a.* relating to the *hormiga* or itch.

hormiguita, *n.f.* small ant.

hormiguillar, *v.t.* (*min.*) to mix grains of silver with salt.

hormiguillo, *n.m.* (*vet.*) distemper which affects horses' hoofs; people ranged in a line who pass materials or loads from hand to hand; (*Mex.*) spicy syrup; almond sweetmeat; (*min.*) amalgamating mixture.

hormilla, *n.f.* small last; button-mould.

hormón, *n.m.* hormone.

hormonal, *a.* relating to hormone.

hornabeque, *n.m.* (*fort.*) hornwork.

hornablenda, *n.f.* hornblende.

hornacero, *n.m.* person who tends crucibles with silver and gold in the furnace.

hornacina, *n.f.* vaulted niche.

hornacho, *n.m.* shaft of a mine; excavation formed in a hill, as a sand-pit, etc.; furnace for casting statues.

hornachuela, *n.f.* cave, hut, hole in a wall.

hornada, *n.f.* batch, bread baked at one time.

hornaguear, *v.t.* to dig for coal.

hornaguera, *n.f.* pit-coal, hard coal.

hornaguero, -ra, *a.* wide, spacious; coaly.

hornaje, *n.m.* (*prov.*) fee for baking bread.

hornaza, *n.f.* small furnace of the silversmith, etc.; (*art*) light yellow colour; yellow glazing.

hornazo, *n.m.* Easter cake ornamented with eggs; present given to Lenten preacher.

hornear, *v.i.* to carry on the trade of a baker.
hornería, *n.f.* trade of a baker.
hornero, -ra, *n.m.f.* baker. — *n.m.* (*Arg., Bol.*) oven-bird.
hornija, *n.f.* brushwood for heating the oven.
hornijero, *n.m.* person who supplies the oven with fuel.
hornilla, *n.f.* grated chamber in a masonry kitchen-range; stew-hole; pigeon-hole for nesting; nest-pan.
hornillo, *n.m.* portable furnace, range or stove; (*min.*) blast-hole; (*mil.*) fougade; *hornillo de atanor,* athanor, self-feeding furnace.
hornito, *n.m.* (*Mex.*) mud-volcano.
horno, *n.m.* oven, kiln, furnace; cavity in which bees lodge; *horno de ladrillo,* brick-kiln; *horno de reverbero* (or *boliche*) Spanish furnace; *horno castellano,* Castilian furnace; *alto horno,* blast furnace; *horno de manga,* cupola furnace; *horno de copela,* cupelling or cupellation furnace; *horno de calcinación,* calcining furnace; *calentarse el horno,* to grow warm in argument; *no está el horno para bollos,* there is no chance (*or* opportunity) of doing something.
horometría, *n.f.* horometry.
horón, *n.m.* large round hamper or frail.
horópter, horóptero, *n.m.* horopter; a straight line through the point where the optical axes meet.
horóscopo, *n.m.* horoscope.
horqueta, *n.f.* forked pole; (*naut.*) outrigger.
horquilla, *n.f.* forked pole, pitchfork, croom; hairpin; double-pointed tack; upper extremity of the sternum; wish-bone; disease which causes the hair to split; (*surg.*) fourchette; (*mil.*) fork-rest; (*vet.*) frog of a horse's foot; (*naut.*) rowlock. — *pl.* (*naut.*) crutches, curbs; *horquillas de dar fuego,* breaming forks.
horrendamente, *adv.* dreadfully.
horrendo, -da, *a.* dreadful, hideous, horrible, vast, fearful, awful, grim.
hórreo, *n.m.* kind of granary.
horrero, *n.m.* keeper of a granary.
horribilidad, *n.f.* horribleness, dreadfulness.
horribilísimo, *a.* most horrible.
horrible, *a.* horrid, awful, hideous, dreadful, horrible, heinous.
horriblemente, *adv.* horribly, heinously, horridly, formidably.
horridez, *n.f.* horridness, dreadfulness.
hórrido, -da, *a.* horrid, horrible, hideous.
horrífico, -ca, *a.* (*poet.*) horrific, awful.
horripilante, *a.* horrifying, harrowing.
horripilar, *v.t.* to make one's hair stand on end with fright; to horripilate; to inspire horror. — *v.r.* to feel horripilation.
horro, -ra, *a.* enfranchised; free, disengaged; sterile, barren (of ewes, mares, etc.).
horror, *n.m.* horror, consternation, fright; dread, hate, abhorrence; enormity, horridness, grimness, hideousness, frightfulness.
horrorizar, *v.t.* to cause horror, terrify. — *v.r.* to be terrified.
horrorosamente, *adv.* horribly.
horroroso, -sa, *a.* horrible, horrid, hideous, dreadful, frightful, shocking, offensive.
horrura, *n.f.* filth, dirt, scoria, dross; (*obs.*) terror, horror.
hortaliza, *n.f.* garden stuff, vegetables.
hortatorio, -ria, *a.* hortatory.
hortecillo, *n.m.* small garden.

hortelana, *n.f.* gardener's wife.
hortelano, -na, *a.* relating to gardens.
hortelano, *n.m.* gardener, horticulturist; (*orn.*) ortolan.
hortense, *a.* relating to gardens.
hortensia, *n.f.* hydrangea.
hortera, *n.f.* wooden bowl. — *n.m.* (in Madrid) shop-boy.
hortícola, *a.* horticultural.
horticultor, -ra, *n.m.f.* horticulturist.
horticultura, *n.f.* horticulture, gardening.
horuelo, *n.m.* (*prov.*) common meeting-place for young people.
hosco, -ca, *a.* dark-coloured (as a mulatto); sullen, gloomy; boastful, arrogant, vainglorious.
hoscoso, -sa, *a.* unsmooth, rough.
hospedado, -da, *a.* of a house receiving guests and strangers.
hospedador, -ra, *n.m.f.* one who entertains guests and strangers.
hospedaje, *n.m.* lodging; price paid for lodging, reception of guests and strangers.
hospedamiento, *n.m.* lodging; reception of guests.
hospedar, *v.t.* to lodge, give lodging, harbour. — *v.i., v.r.* to lodge or take lodgings; to stop at, reside.
hospedería, *n.f.* hospice; hostel in universities; hostelry, inn; spare room, guest room; lodging.
hospedero, -ra, *n.m.f.* host; innkeeper, hospitaller, hosteller.
hospiciano, -na, *n.m.f.* poor person who lives in a house of charity.
hospicio, *n.m.* hospice; poor-house; house of correction; orphan asylum.
hospital, *n.m.* hospital, infirmary; *hospital de sangre,* field hospital. — *a.* (*obs.*) hospitable.
hospitalario, -ria, *n.m.f., a.* hospitaller, hospitable.
hospitalero, -ra, *n.m.f.* manager of a hospital; hospitaller; hospitable person.
hospitalidad, *n.f.* hospitality, hospitage; hospitableness; time spent in a hospital.
hospitalito, *n,m.* small hospital.
hospitalmente, *adv.* hospitably.
hostal, *n.m.* hostelry, inn.
hostalero, *n.m.* (*obs.*) inn- or tavern-keeper, host.
hoste, *n.m.* (*obs.*) host; army, enemy.
hostelero, -ra, *n.m.f.* innkeeper, tavernkeeper.
hostería, *n.f.* inn, tavern, hostelry.
hostia, *n.f.* host; victim; (*eccles.*) wafer, host; sugar wafer.
hostiario, *n.m.* (*eccles.*) wafer-box.
hostiero, *n.m.* one who prepares the host.
hostigador, -ra, *a.* harasser, chastiser.
hostigamiento, *n.m.* chastisement, vexation, molestation.
hostigar, *v.t.* (*pret.* **hostigué;** *pres. subj.* **hostigue**) to lash, scourge, chastise; to vex, molest, trouble, harass, gall; to bore, tire.
hostigo, *n.m.* lash; weather-beaten wall; beating rain and winds against a wall.
hostil, *a.* hostile, adverse, inimical.
hostilidad, *n.f.* hostility, enmity, antagonism; armed aggression.
hostilizar, *v.t.* (*pret.* **hostilicé;** *pres. subj.* **hostilice**) to commit hostilities; to attack, skirmish.

hostilmente, *adv.* hostilely.

hotel, *n.m.* hotel; villa, mansion, house standing in its grounds.

hotentote, -ta, *n.m.f., a.* Hottentot.

hoy, *adv.* today; now, the present time; nowadays; *hoy día* or *hoy en día*, nowadays; *hoy por hoy*, this very day; *de hoy en adelante* or *de hoy más*, henceforward, in future; *de hoy a mañana*, before tomorrow; when you least expect it; *antes hoy que mañana*, the sooner the better; *hoy por ti y mañana por mí*, thou today and I tomorrow.

hoya, *n.f.* hole, cavity, pit; pitfall; the grave; dale, glen, valley; basin; (*Per.*) bed (of a river).

hoyada, *n.f.* low dale, lowest part of a field.

hoyanca, *n.f.* (*coll.*) potter's field in cemeteries.

hoyito, *n.m.* small hole, cavity, pit, excavation.

hoyo, *n.m.* hole, pit, excavation; indention, dent, hollow; pock-mark; the grave.

hoyoso, -sa, *a.* pitted, full of holes.

hoyuela, *n.f.* hollow in the neck under Adam's apple.

hoyuelo, *n.m.* little hole; dimple; a boy's game.

hoz, *n.f.* sickle, reaping-hook; defile, ravine, narrow pass; *de hoz y de coz*, (*coll.*) headlong; *la hoz en el haza, y el hombre en la casa*, the work waiting and the workmen idling.

hozadero, *n.m.* place where hogs root.

hozadura, *n.f.* rooting (as hogs).

hozar, *v.t.* to root (as hogs).

huaca, *n.f.* (*Bol., Per.*) ancient Indian tomb.

huacal, *n.m.* crate; (*Mex., Col., Ven.*) hurdle-basket.

huacatay, *n.f.* (*Am.*) kind of mint.

huaco, *n.m.* idol found in *huacas*.

huachache, *n.m.* (*Per.*) a mosquito.

huaico, *n.m.* (*Per.*) avalanche of enormous rocks from the Andes.

huairuro, *n.m.* (*Per.*) a kind of kidney bean used as an ornament.

huango, *n.m.* (*Ec.*) hairdressing of Indian women, pigtail.

huaquero, *n.m.* (*Per.*) pitcher found in *huacas*.

huasca, *n.f.* (*Per.*) whip, lash.

huayno, *n.m.* (*Per.*) Indian dance.

hucha, *n.f.* large chest; money box; toy bank; savings.

huchear, *v.t.* to hoot, shout, cry out, call; to urge, set, sick (dogs).

huchohó, *interj.* word used to call birds (as falcons).

huebra, *n.f.* ground ploughed in one day by a yoke of oxen; pair of mules with a ploughman hired or let out for a day's work.

huebrero, *n.m.* day-labourer who ploughs with a pair of mules; one who lets out mules by the day.

hueca, *n.f.* notch of a spindle.

hueco, -ca, *a.* hollow, empty, concave; vain, ostentatious; resonant, inflated, soft, spongy (as ground or wool); *voz hueca*, sonorous and hollow; *se ha puesto muy hueco*, he has become very vain.

hueco, *n.m.* gap, hollow, hole, break, void; (*coll.*) office or post vacant; interval of time or space; notch or nick of wheel.

huecograbado, *n.m.* photogravure for rotary presses.

huecú, *n.m.* (*Chi.*) deep slough covered with grass.

huélfago, *n.m.* difficulty of breathing in beasts.

huelga, *n.f.* rest, repose, leisure, relaxation from work; strike; recreation, merry-making; (*agric.*) lying fallow; (*mech.*) windage.

huelgo, *n.m.* breath, respiration; (*mech.*) windage; room, space; *tomar huelgo*, to take breath.

huelgo; huelgue, *pres. indic.; pres. subj.* [HOLGAR].

huelguista, *n.m.* striker.

huella, *n.f.* track, footstep, footprint; tread; trampling; stair-tread, tread-board; impression; trace, vestige, trail.

huello, *n.m.* step (of an animal); tread, trodden path; lower part of an animal's hoof.

huello; huelle, *pres. indic.; pres. subj.* [HOLLAR].

huemul, *n.m.* (*Arg., Chi.*) the Andes deer.

huequecito, *n.m.* small cavity or space.

huerco, *n.m.* (*obs., poet.*) hell; Hades, underworld; (*fig.*) weeper, whiner, unhappy fellow.

huérfago, *n.m.* (*vet.*) difficulty of breathing in animals.

huerfanito, -ta, *n.m.f.* little orphan.

huérfano, -na, *n.m.f., a.* orphan.

huero, -ra, *a.* empty, void; addle, addled; (*Mex.*) fair, blonde.

huerta, *n.f.* large vegetable (or kitchen) garden; orchard; irrigated or irrigable land (the *huerta* is always larger than the *huerto*).

huertezuela, *n.f.* small kitchen garden.

huertezuelo, *n.m.* small orchard.

huerto, *n.m.* orchard, fruit and vegetable garden.

huesa, *n.f.* grave, sepulchre, sepulture.

huesarrón, *n.m.* large bone.

huesecico, -ito *n.m.* little bone.

huesera, *n.f.* (*Chi.*) [OSARIO].

huesillo, *n.m.* (*prov., Am. Mer.*) peach dried in the sun.

hueso, *n.m.* bone; stone; core; part of a limestone which remains unburnt in the kiln; drudgery, drudge; *a hueso*, (*mas.*) dry stone; *la sin hueso*, (*coll.*) the tongue; *soltar la sin hueso*, to talk too much; *estar con lo huesos en punto*, to stand up; *el hueso y la carne duélense de su sangre*, flesh and blood will not see itself insulted; *estar en los huesos*, to be exceedingly thin or weak, nothing but a skeleton; *mondar los huesos*, to eat up every scrap; *no dejar a uno hueso sano*, not to leave a person a leg to stand upon; *no estar con sus huesos*, to care little about one's health; *quien te da un hueso, no te quiere ver muerto*, he who shares his food with you loves you indeed; *roerle a uno los huesos*, to grumble at someone; *dar un hueso que roer*, to set a difficult and unprofitable task; *a otro perro con ese hueso*, tell that to the marines.

huesoso, -sa, *a.* bony, osseous.

huésped, -da, *n.m.f.* guest, lodger; host, innkeeper, tavern-keeper; stranger; *ser huésped en su casa*, to stay at home little; *huésped con sol, ha honor* (said of travellers), the earliest to arrive gets the warmest bed; *iránse los huéspedes y comeremos el gallo*, when the guests are gone we'll get to business (i.e., the unpleasant business).

hueste, *n.f.* host, army in campaign; partisan. — *pl.* **huestes,** hosts, armies.

huesudo, -da, *a.* bony, having large bones.

hueva, *n.f.* spawn of fishes, roe.

huevar, *v.i.* to begin to lay eggs.

huevecico, -illo, -ito, -zuelo, *n.f.* small egg.
huevera, *n.f.* ovarium of birds; egg-stand, egg-cup.
huevero, -ra, *n.m.f.* dealer in eggs.
huevo, *n.m.* egg; (*shoe.*) hollow piece of wood for shaping the sole; *huevo de Colón* (or *de juanelo*), something which appears difficult to do, but when tried is found to be easy; *huevos de faltriquera,* candied yolks of eggs; *huevos pasados por agua,* soft-boiled eggs; *huevos estrellados,* fried eggs; *huevos escalfados,* poached eggs; *huevos moles,* yolks of eggs, made up with pounded almonds and sugar; *huevos hilados,* thread-like sweetmeat made of eggs and sugar; *huevos y torreznos,* collops and eggs; *huevos revueltos,* scrambled or buttered eggs; *sórbete* (or *chúpate*) *ese huevo,* (*coll.*) put that in your pipe and smoke it; *cacarear, y no poner huevo,* to promise much and perform little; *parece que está empollando huevos,* he seems to be quite a hermit; *parecerse como un huevo a una castaña,* to be as unlike as possible; *un huevo y ése, huero,* only one son, and he an invalid.
hugonote, -ta, *n.m.f., a.* Huguenot.
huida, *n.f.* flight, escape; outlet. — *pl.* **huidas,** evasions, subterfuges.
huidero, *n.m.* cover, shelter; labourer in quick-silver-mines.
huidizo, -za, *a.* fugitive, fleeing.
huila, *a.* (*Mex.*) crippled, invalid.
huiliento, *a.* (*Chi.*) ragged.
huillín, *n.m.* (*Chi.*) kind of otter.
huincha, *n.f.* (*Chi.*) hair-ribbon.
huir, *v.i., v.r.* (*pres. part.* **huyendo;** *pres. indic.* **huyo;** *pret.* **él huyó;** *pres. subj.* **huya**) to flee, escape, get off, elope, run away; to flit away, give the slip, slip away; with words denoting time, pass rapidly, fly; to disappear, scatter; to avoid, shun; *huir del fuego, y dar en las brasas,* out of the frying pan into the fire.
hule, *n.m.* india-rubber; oilcloth, oilskin.
hulero, *n.m.* rubber-gatherer.
hulla, *n.f.* pit-coal, bituminous or soft coal; *hulla blanca,* hydraulic power.
hullero, -ra, *a.* containing or pertaining to soft coal.
hullera, *n.f.* colliery.
humada, *n.f.* smoke-signal.
humanamente, *adv.* humanely, kindly, mercifully; humanly; *eso humanamente no se puede hacer,* that cannot possibly be done.
humanar, *v.t.* to humanize, soften. — *v.r.* to become man (applied to the Son of God); to become humane, meek, familiar; to be lowered, humbled.
humanidad, *n.f.* humanity, humankind, mankind; human weakness; benevolence, benignity, kindness, tenderness; (*coll.*) corpulence, fleshiness. — *pl.* **humanidades,** humanities.
humanismo, *n.m.* humanism.
humanista, *n.m.f.* humanist.
humanístico, -ca, *a.* humanistic.
humanitario, -ria, *a.* humanitarian, philanthropic.
humanitarismo, *n.m.* humaneness, humanity.
humanizar, *v.t., v.r.* (*pret.* **humanicé;** *pres. subj.* **humanice**) to humanize, soften.
humano, -na, *a.* human; humane, kind, benevolent, merciful; *en lo humano,* as regards human power or agency.

humano, *n.m.* man, human being.
humarazo, *n.m.* dense smoke.
humareda, *n.f.* great deal of smoke; perplexity, confusion.
humazga, *n.f.* hearth-money, fumage.
humazo, *n.m.* dense smoke; *humazo de narices,* (*fig.*) displeasure, vexation.
humeante, *a.* smoky, fuming.
humear, *v.i.* to smoke, emit smoke, fumes, or vapours. — *v.t.* (*Am.*) to fumigate.
humectación, *n.f.* humectation, dampening; (*med.*) action of fomentations.
humectante, *a.* (*med.*) moistening.
humectar, *v.t.* (*med.*) to moisten, wet.
humedad, *n.f.* humidity, moisture, dampness, moistness.
humedal, *n.m.* humid soil, marsh.
humedecer, *v.t.* (*pres. indic.* **humedezco;** *pres. subj.* **humedezca**) to moisten, wet, soak, steep, humectate, dampen.
húmedo, -da, *a.* humid, wet, moist, watery, damp.
humera [aspirated *h*], *n.f.* (*coll.*) drunkenness, orgy, carousal.
humeral, *a.* (*anat.*) humeral. — *n.m.* humeral veil.
húmero, *n.m.* (*anat.*) humerus.
humero, *n.m.* smoke-pipe, chimney-flue, flue, shaft of a chimney.
húmido, -da, *a.* (*poet.*) damp.
humildad, *n.f.* humility, modesty, meekness; submission; meanness, lowliness.
humilde, *a.* humble, modest, submissive, meek; (*fig.*) low, base, ignoble.
humildemente, *adv.* humbly, submissively; modestly, meekly.
humillación, *n.f.* humiliation, submission; self-contempt, mortification; obsequiousness, abjectness, humbling.
humilladero, *n.m.* roadside chapel or shrine.
humillador, -ra, *n.m.f., a.* humiliator.
humillante, *a.* humiliating, humbling, unbecoming, indecorous, degrading.
humillar, *v.t.* to humiliate, humble, lower; to bend, bow; to crush, subdue, depreciate, degrade, bring down from a position of pride. — *v.r.* to humble oneself.
humillo, *n.m.* thin smoke or vapour; vanity, petty pride; disease of sucking pigs.
humita, *n.f.* (*Arg., Chi., Per.*) cake of maize and sugar.
humo, *n.m.* smoke; vapour, steam, fume; black silk. — *pl.* **humos,** families or houses in a town or village; (*fig.*) vanity, haughtiness, petty pride, presumption; *a humo de pajas,* lightly, without reflection; *bajarle a uno los humos,* to tame one's pride; *irse todo en humo,* to vanish into smoke, end in smoke; *subirse el humo a las narices,* to be irritated or annoyed.
humor, *n.m.* humour, blitheness, disposition; (*med.*) humour; *buen humor,* good nature, jovial disposition; *mal humor,* ill-temper; *estar de buen humor,* to be in good humour, to be gay; *seguirle a uno el humor,* to humour someone, follow his whims; *remover humores,* to disturb the peace.
humorada, *n.f.* pleasant joke, witty saying; sprightliness.
humorado, -da, *a.* full of humours; well or ill disposed.
humoral, *a.* humoral.

humorcico, -illo, -ito, *n.m.* little temper.
humorista, *n.m.f.* humorist; (*med.*) humoralist.
humorístico, -ca, *a.* merry, humorous, facetious.
humorosidad, *n.f.* copiousness of humours.
humoroso, -sa, *a.* watery, containing fluid.
humoso, -sa, *a.* smoky, fumy.
humus, *n.m.* vegetable mould; humus.
hundible, *a.* sinkable, submersible, destructible.
hundimiento, *n.m.* submersion, immersion, sinking; downfall, collapse, cave-in.
hundir, *v.t.* to submerge, immerse, sink; to pull down, bear down, destroy, ruin; to beat down, overwhelm, crush, stave in; to refute, confound. — *v.r.* to sink, fall down, collapse, crumble; (*coll.*) to hide, lie low; not to be found; to have dissension or strife.
hungarina, *n.f.* a loose coat hanging down to the knees and without sleeves.
húngaro, -ra, *a.* Hungarian.
Hungría, *n.f.* Hungary.
huno, -na, *a.* Hunnish.
hupe, *n.f.* punk, touchwood.
hura, *n.f.* carbuncle on the head.
huracán, *n.m.* hurricane, cyclone, violent storm.
hurañamente, *adv.* intractable.
hurañía, *n.f.* shyness, wildness (of animals).
huraño, -ña, *a.* shy, diffident; intractable.
hurera, *n.f.* hole; ferret-hole.
hurgar, *v.t.* (*pret.* **hurgué;** *pres. subj.* **hurgue**) to stir, poke; to stir up, excite; *peor es hurgallo,* let well alone.
hurgón, *n.m.* poker, fire-rake; (*coll.*) thrust in fencing.
hurgonada, *n.f.* poking the fire; (*coll.*) thrust with a sword.
hurgonazo, *n.m.* blow with a poker; (*coll.*) thrust with a sword.
hurgonear, *v.t.* to poke the fire; (*coll.*) to make thrusts with a poker or a sword.
hurgonero, *n.m.* fire-poker.
hurguete, *a.* (*Arg., Chi.*) prying.
hurí, *n.f.* houri.
hurón, -ona, *n.m.f.* ferret; (*coll.*) ferreter, prier. — *a.* unsociable, shy, loveless, disdainful, intractable.
huronear, *v.i.* to hunt with a ferret; (*coll.*) to pry, ferret out secrets.
huronera, *n.f.* ferret-hole; (*coll.*) lurking-place; small dark-room.
huronero, *n.m.* ferret-keeper.
¡hurra! *interj.* hurrah!
hurraca, *n.f.* magpie.
hurtable, *a.* that may be stolen.
hurtadillas (a), *adv.* by stealth, slyly, artfully, unbeknown, privately, in a secret way.
hurtadineros, *n.m.* (*prov.*) money-box, toy bank.
hurtador, -ra, *n.m.f.* robber, thief.
hurtagua, *n.f.* kind of watering-pot.
hurtamano (de), *adv.* without pity or consideration.
hurtar, *v.t.* to steal, rob, make away with; to eat away land (of the sea or a river); to cheat in weight or measure; to plagiarize; to alienate, separate; *hurtar el cuerpo,* to flee. — *v.r.* to withdraw, hide, move away, abscond.
hurto, *n.m.* theft, robbery, stealing; the thing stolen; (*min.*) driftway, heading; *a hurto,* by stealth.

husada, *n.f.* spindleful of yarn.
husaño, *n.m.* large spindle.
húsar, *n.m.* hussar.
husero, *n.m.* beam of an antler.
husillo, *n.m.* small spindle; (*mill.*) wheel-spindle or shaft; screw-pin. — *pl.* **husillos,** drains, small channels for draining fens.
husita, *n.m.* Hussite.
husma, *n.f.; andar a la husma,* (*coll.*) to examine in a prying way; to try to discover secrets.
husmeador, -ra, *n.m.f.* scenter, smeller, prier.
husmeadorcillo, -lla, *n.m.f.* little smeller; little prier.
husmear, *v.t.* to scent, smell, get wind of; (*coll.*) to pry, peep, nose about. — *v.i.* to smell high (of meat).
husmeo, *n.m.* scenting, smelling; prying.
husmo, *n.m.* high smell of meat; *estar al husmo,* (*coll.*) to be upon the scent; to watch for a favourable opportunity.
huso, *n.m.* spindle, cop tube, bobbin; drum of a windlass; (*aer.*) fuselage.
huta, *n.f.* hut, huntsman's blind.
hutía, *n.f.* Cuban rat.
¡huy! *interj.* of surprise, astonishment, or grief.
huyuyo, -ya, *a.* (*Cub.*) intractable, shy, diffident.

I

I, i, tenth letter of the Spanish alphabet; (*num.*) one.
ib, *n.m.* (*Mex.*) small kidney-shaped bean.
ibayaú, *n.m.* night bird of the pampas.
ibérico, -ca; iberio, -ria, *a.* Iberian.
ibero, -ra, *n.m.f., a.* native of or belonging to Iberia.
iberoamericano, -na, *n.m.f., a.* Ibero-American; Latin-American.
íbice, *n.m.* ibex, kind of goat.
ibis, *n.f.* ibis, wading bird.
ibón, *n.m.* lake or basin on the slopes of the Pyrenees.
icaco, *n.m.* West Indian cocoa-plum.
icástico, -ca, *a.* natural, without disguise or ornament.
icipo, *n.m.* (*Arg.*) a creeping plant used for thatching and rope-making.
icnografía, *n.f.* (*arch.*) ichnography, ground-plan; ground-plot.
icnográfico, -ca, *a.* (*arch.*) ichnographical.
iconoclasta, *n.m.f., a.* iconoclast, iconoclastic.
iconografía, *n.f.,* iconography.
iconográfico, -ca, *a.* iconographical.
iconólatra, *n.m.* iconolater.
iconología, *n.f.* (*art*) iconology.
iconómaco, *a.* iconoclastic.
iconostasio, *n.m.* (*eccles.*) iconostasis.
icor, *n.m.* (*surg.*) gleet, ichor, watery humour.
icoroso, -sa, *a.* ichorous, serous.
icosaedro, *n.m.* icosahedron.
ictericia, *n.f.* jaundice.
ictericiado, -da; ictérico, -ca, *a.* icterical, jaundiced.
ictíneo, *n.m.* submarine vessel.
ictiófago, -ga, *a.* fish-eating. — *n.m.f.* ichthyophagist.
ictiología, *n.f.* ichthyology.
ictiológico, -ca, *a.* ichthyologist.

ictiosauro, *n.m.* ichthyosaurus.
ictiosis, *n.f.* ichthyosis.
ichal, *n.m.* (*Per.*) place where icho grows.
icho, ichú, *n.m.* (*Per.*) the grass of the Andes.
ida, *n.f.* departure, outgoing; impetuosity, rash proceeding; trail of game; (*fenc.*) sally; *ida del humo,* departure never to return; *idas,* frequent visits; *darse dos idas y venidas,* to talk a matter over very quickly; *en dos idas y venidas,* (*coll.*) in a jiffy; *ida y vuelta,* out and home, round trip, excursion; return ticket; *¡la ida del cuervo!* he's off, good riddance.
idea, *n.f.* idea, notion, conception; contrivance, intention, design, plan, scheme, project; model, example; thread of a discourse; talent, genius; impression; conceit, fancy, judgment, opinion; brief outline, suggestion.
ideal, *a.* ideal, mental, intellectual, notional, imaginary. — *n.m.* an ideal.
idealidad, *n.f.* ideality, ideal.
idealismo, *n.m.* idealism.
idealista, *n.m.f.*, *a.* idealist; idealistic.
idealizar, *v.t.* (*pret.* **idealicé;** *pres. subj.* **idealice**) to idealize.
idealmente, *adv.* ideally, intellectually.
idear, *v.t.* to form or conceive an idea; to plan, think, invent, contrive, imagine, meditate.
ideático, -a, *a.* (*Am.*) whimsical, capricious.
idénticamente, *adv.* identically.
idéntico, -ca, *a.* identic, identical, congenerous, the same.
identidad, *n.f.* identity, sameness, identicalness.
identificación, *n.f.* identification.
identificar, *v.t.* (*pret.* **identifiqué;** *pres. subj.* **identifique**) to identify. — *v.r.* to identify oneself with.
ideografía, *n.f.* ideography.
ideográfico, -ca, *a.* ideographic.
ideología, *n.f.* ideology.
ideológico, -ca, *a.* ideological.
ideólogo, *n.m.* ideologist.
idílico, -ca, *a.* idyllic.
idilio, *n.m.* (*poet.*) idyll, pastoral poem.
idioma, *n.m.* language, dialect, idiom, parlance.
idiomático, -ca, *a.* idiomatic, proper to a language.
idiosincrasia, *n.f.* idiosyncrasy.
idiosincrásico, -ca, *a.* idiosyncratic.
idiota, *a.* idiotic, foolish, nonsensical. — *n.m.f.* idiot, fool.
idiotez, *n.f.* idiotism, silliness, idiocy, ignorance.
idiótico, -ca, *a.* idiotic.
idiotismo, *n.m.* idiocy, folly, imbecility; idiom, idiotism.
idólatra, *a.* idolatrous; heathen, paganish. — *n.m.f.* idolater; (*coll.*) ardent lover.
idolatradamente, *adv.* idolatrously.
idolatrar, *v.t.* to idolatrize; to idolize, love with great fondness.
idolatría, *n.f.* idolatry; inordinate love.
idolátrico, -ca, *a.* idolatrous, heathenish.
ídolo, *n.m.* idol; (*coll.*) person or thing extravagantly loved, idol.
idolología, *n.f.* science dealing with idols.
idoneidad, *n.f.* aptitude, fitness, capacity.
idóneo, -nea, *a.* fit, convenient, proper, meet.
idos, idus, *n.m.pl.* ides.

iglesia, *n.f.* church, temple; ecclesiastical state; clergy, chapter; diocese; right of immunity enjoyed in churches; *iglesia, o mar, o casa real,* the church, the sea, or the royal service (i.e., for the man who would get on in the world); *llevar a una mujer a la iglesia,* to marry a woman; *iglesia fría,* church where a malefactor does not enjoy protection against the law; *iglesia me llamo,* expression of a delinquent seeking the immunity of the church; *iglesia oriental,* Greek church.
ignaro, -ra, *a.* ignorant, unlearned.
ignavia, *n.f.* idleness, laziness, carelessness.
igneo, -nea, *a.* igneous, fiery.
ignición, *n.f.* ignition, setting on fire.
ignícola, *n.m.* fire-worshipper.
ignífero, -ra, *a.* igniferous.
igniscencia, *n.f.* incandescence.
ignito, -ta, *a.* ignited, inflamed, red-hot.
ignívomo, -ma, *a.* (*poet.*) vomiting fire.
ignoble, *a.* ignoble.
ignografía, *n.f.* (*arch.*) ichnography.
ignominia, *n.f.* ignominy, infamy, disgrace, opprobrium.
ignominiosamente, *adv.* ignominiously, opprobriously, disgracefully.
ignominioso, -sa, *a.* ignominious, opprobrious, disgraceful, reproachful.
ignorado, -da, *a.* unknown, occult, fameless. — *p.p.* [IGNORAR].
ignorancia, *n.f.* ignorance.
ignorante, *a.* ignorant, stupid; unaware, not knowing. — *n.m.* ignoramus.
ignorantemente, *adv.* ignorantly.
ignorantón, -ona, *a.* grossly ignorant.
ignorar, *v.t.* to be ignorant of, not to know.
ignoto, -ta, *a.* unknown, undiscovered.
igorrote, *n.m.* (*Philip.*) name of a savage tribe of the island of Luzón, and of their language.
igual, *a.* equal, similar, alike; level, flat, even; fellow, coequal; firm, constant, determined, unchangeable, consistent, uniform, equable. — *n.m.* the sign of equality (=); *en igual de,* instead of, in lieu of; *al igual,* equally; *no tiene igual,* he has not his like; *sin igual,* not to be equalled, matchless; *por igual* (or *por un igual*) equally, with equality; *me es igual,* it is all the same to me.
iguala, *n.f.* agreement, convention, stipulation, contract, commutation; equalling, equalizing; (*mas.*) level; stipend, gratuity on agreement; *a la iguala,* equally; *tiene iguala con,* he serves for a fixed sum.
igualación, *n.f.* equalling, equalizing, equalization; levelling; agreement, stipulation, contract; matching; (*carp.*) counter-gauge; (*math., obs.*) equation.
igualado, -da, *a.* equalled (said of birds with even plumage); *está igualado con,* he gets a fixed sum; *dejar a uno igualado,* to give someone a good drubbing. — *p.p.* [IGUALAR].
igualador, -ra, *n.m.f.* equalizer, leveller, evener.
igualamiento, *n.m.* equalizing, equalization, levelling.
igualar, *v.t.* to equalize, mate, match, pair; to size, adjust, face; to fit; to hold in equal estimation; to smooth, even; to level, flatten, make even (as roads or fields); to agree upon, to adjust differences; to put a fair price upon. — *v.i.* to be equal. — *v.r.* to place

oneself upon a level with others; *igualar la sangre*, (*coll.*) to bleed a second time.

igualdad, *n.f.* equality, similitude; conformity, consimilitude, likeness; regularity, uniformity; evenness, levelness; *igualdad de ánimo*, constancy, equanimity, equability.

igualmente, *adv.* equally, uniformly, equably, evenly; likewise; constantly.

iguana, *n.f.* iguana, kind of lizard.

iguanodonte, *n.m.* iguanodon.

igüedo, *n.m.* buck.

ijada, *n.f.* flank (of an animal); pain in the side; colic; *tener su ijada*, (*met.*) to have a weak side or point.

ijadear, *v.i.* to pant, palpitate.

ijar, *n.m.* flank; *caballo de pocos ijares*, light-flanked horse.

ijujú, *n.m.* shout of joy.

ilación, *n.f.* inference, illation, conclusion.

ilapso, *n.m.* trance, ecstasy.

ilativo, -va, *a.* illative.

ilécebra, *n.f.* cajolery, flattery.

ilegal, *a.* illegal, unlawful.

ilegalidad, *n.f.* illegality, unlawfulness.

ilegalmente, *adv.* illegally, lawlessly, unlawfully.

ilegible, *a.* illegible.

ilegítimamente, *adv.* illegitimately, foully.

ilegitimidad, *n.f.* illegitimacy.

ilegítimo, -ma, *a.* illegal, unlawful; illegitimate, unlawfully begotten.

íleo, *n.m.* (*med.*) ileus, iliac passion.

íleon, *n.m.* (*anat.*) ileum.

ileso, -sa, *a.* unhurt, unharmed, sound.

ilíaco, -ca, *a.* iliac, relating to the ilium; belonging or relating to Ilium or Troy.

iliberal, *a.* illiberal.

ilicíneo, -nea, *a.* (*bot.*) ilicaceous.

ilícitamente, *adv.* illicitly, forbiddenly.

ilícito, -ta, *a.* illicit, unlawful.

ilimitado, -da, *a.* unlimited, boundless, limitless; unconditional.

ilion, *n.m.* (*anat.*) ilium.

ilíquido, -da, *a.* unliquidated.

iliterato, *a.* illiterate, unlearned.

ilógico, -ca, *a.* illogical.

ilota, *n.m.f.* helot; one deprived of civil rights.

ilotismo, *n.m.* helotism, serfdom.

iludir, *v.t.* to elude.

iluminación, *n.f.* illumination, lighting; painting in tempera; intellectual or spiritual enlightenment.

iluminado, -da, *a.* illuminate, enlightened; *estampas iluminadas*, coloured plates. — *n.m.pl.* illuminati; visionaries. — *p.p.* [ILUMINAR].

iluminador, -ra, *a.* lighter. — *n.m.f.* (*art*) illuminator.

iluminar, *v.t.* to illuminate, illumine, fill or supply with light, light; to colour, illumine books; to adorn with lamps or bonfires; to infuse grace; to enlighten; to render transparent.

iluminativo, -va, *a.* illuminative.

ilusión, *n.f.* illusion, hallucination; hopeful anticipation; smart and witty irony.

ilusionar, *v.t.* to cause illusion, fascinate. — *v.r.* to suffer illusions.

ilusivo, -va, *a.* delusive, illusive, false, deceitful.

iluso, -sa, *a.* deluded, deceived, beguiled; ridiculed.

ilusoriamente, *adv.* illusively.

ilusorio, -ria, *a.* delusive, illusory, deceptive; (*law*) null, void, nugatory.

ilustración, *n.f.* illustration, explanation, elucidation, exposition, explication; learning, enlightenment. — *pl.* **ilustraciones,** (*print.*) illustrations, engravings.

ilustrado, -da, *a.* wise, intelligent; learned, well informed.

ilustrador, *n.m.f.* illustrator, explainer.

ilustrar, *v.t.* to illustrate, clear up, enlighten, explain, elucidate; to aggrandize, ennoble, make illustrious; (*theol.*) to inspire, infuse supernatural light; to provide printed matter with plates or engravings; to teach, educate, civilize. — *v.r.* to acquire knowledge, to learn; to become illustrious.

ilustrativo, -va, *a.* illustrative.

ilustre, *a.* illustrious, noble, celebrated, conspicuous, glorious, honourable, magnificent.

ilustremente, *adv.* illustriously, greatly.

ilustrísimo, -ma, *a.* very illustrious; title given to bishops.

imadas, *n.f.pl.* (*naut.*) ways, sliding planks.

imagen, *n.f.* image, figure, imagery, statue, effigy; appearance, show, conception, fancy; (*rhet.*) image (metaphor, simile); (*opt.*) spectrum.

imagencita, -cilla, *n.f.* little image.

imaginable, *a.* imaginable, contrivable, conceivable.

imaginación, *n.f.* imagination, fancy; imagining, conception, image; conceit, fantasy.

imaginar, *v.i.* to imagine, fancy, image; to form erroneous suppositions. — *v.t.* to suppose, imagine, scheme, contrive, conceive. — *v.r.* to fancy, imagine, suppose.

imaginaria, *n.f.* reserve guard; (*mil.*) night guard in the dormitories of the barracks.

imaginariamente, *adv.* in a visionary manner.

imaginario, -ria, *a.* imaginary, fancied, visionary. — *n.f.* (*math.*) imaginary.

imaginativa, *n.f.* imagination, common sense.

imaginativo, -va, *a.* imaginative, fantastic, fanciful.

imaginería, *n.f.* imagery; fancy embroidery in colours; (*art*) statuary.

imaginero, *n.m.* painter or sculptor of religious images.

imán, *n.m.* loadstone, magnet; charm, attraction; *imán artificial*, electro-magnet; imam, Mohammedan priest.

imanación, *n.f.* magnetization.

imanar, *v.t.* to magnetize.

imantación, *n.f.* magnetization.

imantar, *v.t.* to magnetize.

imbécil, *a.* imbecile, simple, silly, feeble, weak.

imbecilidad, *n.f.* imbecility, simplicity, silliness, debility, weakness.

imbele, *a.* (*poet.*) feeble, weak; unfit for war.

imberbe, *n.m.* beardless youth.

imbibición, *n.f.* imbibition.

imbornal, *n.m.* (*naut.*) scupper-hole; house drains.

imborrable, *a.* indelible.

imbricación, *n.f.* imbrication.

imbricado, -da, *a.* imbricated.

imbuir, *v.t.* (*pres. indic.* **imbuyo**; *pres. subj.* **imbuya**) to imbue, infuse, instruct, persuade.

imbunche, *n.m.* (*Chi.*) Araucanian witch who kidnapped children six months old to change them into monsters; (*Chi.*) ugly and fat child; imbroglio; perplexing or confused state of affairs.

imbursación, *n.f.* (*prov.*) putting into a sack.

imbursar, *v.t.* (*prov.*) to sack, bag.

imitable, *a.* imitable.

imitación, *n.f.* imitation, copying; copy; *a imitación de,* after, in imitation of.

imitado, -da, *a.* copied, imitated, mock, artificial, not genuine. — *p.p.* [IMITAR].

imitador, -ra, *n.m.f.* imitator, follower.

imitante, *a.* imitator.

imitar, *v.t.* to imitate, ape, counterfeit, copy, follow.

imitativo, -va, *a.* imitative (as arts).

imoscapo, *n.m.* (*arch.*) apophyge.

impacción, *n.f.* impact, collision.

impaciencia, *n.f.* impatience, eagerness, hastiness; restlessness, peevishness, vehemence of temper, passionateness.

impacientar, *v.t.* to vex, irritate, make one lose patience. — *v.r.* to lose patience, become impatient.

impaciente, *a.* impatient, fidgety, restless, peevish.

impacientemente, *adv.* impatiently, longingly, peevishly, eagerly, ardently.

impacto, *n.m.* impact.

impagable, *a.* that cannot be paid back.

impalpabilidad, *n.f.* impalpability.

impalpable, *a.* impalpable.

impar, *a.* dissimilar, odd, uneven, unequal. — *n.m.f.* an odd number, thing, person, etc.

imparcial, *a.* impartial, equitable, unbiassed, disinterested, just, unprejudiced.

imparcialidad, *n.f.* impartiality, equitableness, indifference, justice.

imparcialmente, *adv.* impartially, equitably, justly, honestly.

imparidad, *n.f.* inequality, dissimilarity, imparity.

impartible, *a.* indivisible.

impartir, *v.t.t.* to grant, impart; (*law*) to demand or require assistance.

impasable, *a.* impassable.

impasibilidad, *n.f.* indifference, impassiveness.

impasible, *a.* indifferent, unfeeling, insensitive to pain.

impastar, *v.t.* to reduce to paste.

impávidamente, *adv.* intrepidly, undauntedly.

impavidez, *n.f.* intrepidity, courage, boldness.

impávido, -da, *a.* dauntless, intrepid, undaunted.

impecabilidad, *n.f.* impeccability.

impecable, *a.* impeccable.

impedido, -da, *a.* invalid, disabled, sick, valetudinarian, crippled, without use of the limbs.

impedidor, -ra, *n.m.f.* obstructor.

impediente, *a.* hindering, obstructing.

impedimento, *n.m.* impediment, obstacle, hindrance, obstruction, let, cumbrance, shackles, clog, cumbersomeness, impeachment.

impedir, *v.t.* (*pres. indic.* impido; *pres. subj.* impida) to impede, hinder, obstruct, prevent, preclude, deprive; to constrain, restrain, counteract; (*poet.*) to suspend.

impeditivo, -va, *a.* impeding, hindering, impeditive.

impelente, *a.* forcing, impelling, propelling.

impeler, *v.t.* to push, impel, propel, press on, drive, drift; to urge, spur, incite; move, stimulate.

impender, *v.t.* to spend, invest.

impenetrabilidad, *n.f.* impenetrability.

impenetrable, *a.* impenetrable, impervious; incomprehensible; fathomless.

impenitencia, *n.f.* impenitence.

impenitente, *a.* impenitent, obdurate, hard-hearted.

impensa, *n.f.* (*law*) expense.

impensadamente, *adv.* unexpectedly.

impensado, -da, *a.* unexpected, unforeseen, fortuitous.

imperante, *a.* commanding; (*astrol.*) ruling.

imperar, *v.i.* to rule as emperor, to command, reign.

imperativamente, *adv.* imperatively, authoritatively.

imperativo, -va, *a.* imperative, commanding. — *n.m.* (*gram.*) imperative mood; *tomar la imperativa,* to assume authority.

imperatoria, *n.f.* (*bot.*) masterwort.

imperatorio, -ria, *a.* imperial, royal, eminent, noble.

imperceptible, *a.* imperceptible.

imperceptiblemente, *adv.* imperceptibly.

imperdible, *a.* that cannot be lost. — *n.m.* safety-pin.

imperdonable, *a.* unpardonable, irremissible.

imperecedero, -ra, *a.* imperishable.

imperfección, *n.f.* imperfection, fault, flaw, blemish, slight failure.

imperfectamente, *adv.* imperfectly, faultily, inadequately, lamely.

imperfecto, -ta, *a.* imperfect, defective, faulty, crippled, broken. — *n.m.* (*gram.*) imperfect tense.

imperforación, *n.f.* (*med.*) imperforation.

imperial, *a.* imperial; kind of small black plum. — *n.f.* coach top; top seats on a stage-coach; (*naut.*) poop-royal.

imperialismo, *n.m.* imperialism, government by empire.

imperialista, *n.m.f.* imperialist.

impericia, *n.f.* unskilfulness, want of experience or knowledge.

imperio, *n.m.* empire, dominion, command, sway; dignity of an emperor; imperial state or nation; kind of linen made in Germany.

imperiosamente, *adv.* imperiously, masterly, in a lordly manner.

imperiosidad, *n.f.* imperiousness.

imperioso, -sa, *a.* imperious, commanding, arrogant, haughty; powerful, overbearing, magisterial.

imperitamente, *adv.* unskilfully, ignorantly.

imperito, -ta, *a.* unlearned, unskilled.

impermeabilidad, *n.f.* impermeability.

impermeable, *a.* impermeable, water-tight, waterproof, impervious. — *n.m.* waterproof garment, mackintosh.

impermutable, *a.* unexchangeable.

imperscrutable, *a.* inscrutable.

impersonal, *a.* impersonal; *verbo impersonal,* impersonal verb; *en* (or *por*) *impersonal,* impersonally.

impersonalizar, *v.t.* to use verbs impersonally.

impersonalmente, *adv.* impersonally.

impersuasible, *a.* not susceptible of persuasion.

impertérrito, -ta, *a.* intrepid, unterrified, dauntless.

impertinencia, *n.f.* impertinence, folly, nonsense; troublesomeness, intrusion; peevishness; meticulousness.

impertinente, *a.* impertinent, intrusive, importunate, meddling, obnoxious; peevish, fretful.

impertinentemente, *adv.* impertinently.

imperturbabilidad, *n.f.* imperturbability.

imperturbable, *a.* imperturbable.

imperturbablemente, *adv.* imperturbably.

impetra, *n.f.* diploma, licence, permission; bull granting dubious benefices.

impetrable, *a.* (*law*) impetrable, possible to be obtained.

impetración, *n.f.* impetration.

impetrado, -da, *a.* impetrate, impetrated, granted. — *p.p.* [IMPETRAR].

impetrador, -ra, *n.m.f.* one who impetrates.

impetrante, *a.* impetrating. — *n.m.* (*law*) grantee; impetrator.

impetrar, *v.t.* to entreat, impetrate, obtain by petition or entreaty.

ímpetu, *n.m.* impetus, impetuosity, fit, impulse, sally, start.

impetuosamente, *adv.* impetuously, vehemently, violently.

impetuosidad, *n.f.* impetuosity, vehemence.

impetuoso, -sa, *a.* impetuous, fierce, violent, forcible, vehement, excitable, passionate.

impíamente, *adv.* impiously.

impiedad, *n.f.* impiety; irreligion, impiousness.

impiedoso, -sa, *a.* impious, irreligious.

impiísimo, -ma, *a.* very impious.

impío, -pía, *a.* impious, irreligious, wicked, profane, godless.

impla, *n.f.* wimple; material for wimples.

implacabilidad, *n.f.* implacability.

implacable, *a.* implacable; inexorable.

implacablemente, *adv.* implacably.

implantación, *n.f.* implantation.

implantar, *v.t.* to implant, inculcate.

implantón, *n.m.* (*prov.*) piece of timber.

implaticable, *a.* intractable; averse to conversation.

implicación, *n.f.* implication; contradiction; complicity.

implicado, -da, *a.* entangled, implicated; implicit. — *p.p.* [IMPLICAR].

implicante, *a.* implicating.

implicar, *v.t.* (*pret.* **impliqué;** *pres. subj.* **implique**) to implicate, involve, entangle, embarrass. — *v.i.* to oppose, prevent, contradict.

implicatorio, -ria, *a.* implicative; contradictory.

implícitamente, *adv.* implicitly.

implícito, -ta, *a.* implicit, inferred.

imploración, *n.f.* entreaty, imploration, act of imploring.

implorar, *v.t.* to implore, crave, entreat, ask eagerly, beg, solicit, call upon.

implume, *a.* unfeathered.

impolítica, *n.f.* incivility, discourtesy, clownishness, rudeness, coarseness.

impolíticamente, *adv.* (*coll.*) impolitically; unwisely.

impolítico, -ca, *a.* impolitic, indiscreet, imprudent; impolite, rude, coarse, unpolished.

impoluto, -ta, *a.* unpolluted, pure, stainless, clean.

imponderabilidad, *n.f.* imponderability.

imponderable, *a.* inexpressible, unutterable, imponderable.

imponedor, *n.m.* imposer, assessor.

imponente, *a.* imposing.

imponer, *v.t.* (conjugated like PONER) to impose or lay (tax, duty, burden, penalty); to advise, give notice, acquaint, instruct; to charge or impute falsely; to infuse respect or fear; (*print.*) to impose, arrange type.

imponible, *a.* taxable, dutiable.

impopular, *a.* unpopular.

impopularidad, *n.f.* unpopularity.

importable, *a.* (*com.*) importable.

importación, *n.f.* (*com.*) importation.

importador, *n.m.* importer.

importancia, *n.f.* importance, import, consequence, moment, concern; significance, urgency; considerableness.

importante, *a.* important, momentous, weighty, material, considerable, significant, urgent.

importantemente, *adv.* importantly, usefully, materially, essentially.

importar, *v.i.* to be of moment, be important or convenient; to concern, matter; *no importa,* no matter, it doesn't matter; *¿qué importa?* what does it matter? what of that? — *v.t.* to be a consequence of; (*com.*) to import; to amount to.

importe, *n.m.* (*com.*) amount, gross amount, value; *importe medio,* average amount.

importunación, *n.f.* importunity.

importunadamente, *adv.* importunately.

importunador, -ra, *n.m.f.* importunator, importuner, pesterer.

importunamente, *adv.* importunely, unseasonably.

importunar, *v.t.* to importune, pester, vex, harass, tease.

importunidad, *n.f.* importunity, importunacy.

importuno, -na, *a.* importune, importunate, unseasonable; troublesome, heavy, vexatious, annoying, pestering.

imposibilidad, *n.f.* impossibility, impracticability, impracticableness.

imposibilitado, -da, *a.* helpless, without means, poor; disabled, weakened, unfit for service.

imposibilitar, *v.t.* to render unable, make impossible.

imposible, *a.* impossible, impracticable, unfeasible; extremely difficult; *los imposibles,* a Spanish dance; *imposible de toda imposibilidad,* (*coll.*) altogether impossible.

imposiblemente, *adv.* impossibly.

imposición, *n.f.* imposition, act of imposing anything; act of laying, putting or setting upon; tax, charge, or duty imposed; (*print.*) imposition.

imposta, *n.f.* (*arch.*) impost; springer; fascia.

impostor, -ra, *n.m.f.* impostor.

impostura, *n.f.* imposture, false imputation or charge; fiction, deceit, cheat, fraud.

impotable, *a.* undrinkable, not potable.

impotencia, *n.f.* impotence, inability, weakness, incapacity.

impotente, *a.* impotent, weak, feeble; frigid; without power of propagation.

impracticable, *a.* impracticable, impossible, unfeasible, impassable.

imprecación, *n.f.* imprecation, curse.

imprecar, v.t. to imprecate, curse.
imprecatorio, -ria, a. imprecatory.
impregnable, a. impregnable, invincible.
impregnación, n.f. impregnation.
impregnar, v.t. to impregnate, saturate. — v.r. to be impregnated.
impremeditación, n.f. unpremeditation, absence of plan.
impremeditado, -da, a. unpremeditated, unforeseen.
imprenta, n.f. printing; printing-office; print; press; press in general.
imprescindible, a. that which cannot be put aside or done without, indispensable.
imprescriptible, a. imprescriptible.
impresentable, a. that which does not deserve to be recommended or presented.
impresión, n.f. impression, impress, stamping, stamp; print, printing, press-work, edition, issue; influence, moral or physical effect; footprint; image fixed in the mind.
impresionable, a. emotional, impressionable.
impresionar, v.t. to impress, to fix on the mind or memory; to affect, influence; (phot.) to effect chemical changes on a plate by exposure to light; to record (upon a cylinder, disk, tape, etc. for sound-reproduction).
impresionismo, n.m. (art) impressionism.
impreso, -sa, a. printed, stamped. — n.m. pamphlet, printed matter, print. — p.p. irreg. [IMPRIMIR].
impresor, n.m. printer.
impresora, n.f. wife of a printer; female proprietor of a printing office.
imprestable, a. that cannot be lent.
imprevisión, n.f. imprevision, improvidence.
imprevisto, -ta, a. unforeseen, unexpected, unprovided for. — m.pl. unforeseen expenses.
imprimación, n.f. (art) priming; stuff for priming.
imprimadera, n.f. (art) priming tool.
imprimador, n.m. (art) one who primes.
imprimar, v.t. (art) to prime.
imprimir, v.t. (p.p. **impreso**) to print, have printed, stamp, imprint, impress; fix in the mind.
improbabilidad, n.f. improbability, unlikelihood.
improbable, a. improbable, unlikely.
improbablemente, adv. improbably.
improbar, v.t. to disapprove, dislike, censure.
improbidad, n.f. improbity, dishonesty.
improbo, -ba, a. dishonest, corrupt, wicked; laborious, painful.
improcedencia, n.f. unrighteousness.
improcedente, a. contrary to law, unrighteous.
improductivo, -va, a. unproductive, unfruitful, barren, unprofitable, useless.
impronta, n.f. (art) cast; stereotype plate.
impronunciable, a. unpronounceable.
improperar, v.t. to upbraid, gibe, taunt.
improperio, n.m. contemptuous reproach, injurious censure; (eccles.) versicles sung during Good Friday service.
impropiamente, adv. improperly.
impropiedad, n.f. impropriety, unfitness, inappropriateness.
impropio, -pia, a. inappropriate, unsuited, improper, unfit; unqualified, unbecoming.
improporción, n.f. disproportion.
improporcionado, -da, a. disproportionate.

improrrogable, a. that which cannot be prorogued.
impróspero, -ra, a. unfortunate, unprosperous, unhappy.
impróvidamente, adv. improvidently.
improvidencia, n.f. improvidence.
impróvido, -da, a. improvident, thoughtless.
improvisación, n.f. improvisation.
improvisamente, adv. unexpectedly, suddenly, improvidently.
improvisar, v.t. to improvise, extemporize, speak extempore.
improviso, -sa; improvisto, -ta, a. unexpected, unforeseen; de improviso or a la improvista, unexpectedly, all of a sudden.
imprudencia, n.f. imprudence, indiscretion, recklessness.
imprudente, a. imprudent, indiscreet, improvident.
imprudentemente, adv. imprudently.
impúber; impúbero, -ra, a. impuberal.
impudencia, n.f. impudence, shamelessness, immodesty.
impudente, a. impudent, shameless.
impúdicamente, adv. lewdly, impudently.
impudicia, impudicicia, n.f. immodesty, unchastity, lewdness, incontinence, lustfulness, impudicity.
impúdico, -ca, a. immodest, unchaste, lewd, lustful, obscene; impudent, shameless.
impuesto, n.m. tax, duty, imposition.
impuesto, -ta, a. imposed; informed; estar (or quedar) impuesto de una cosa, to be well informed about something. — p.p. irreg. [IMPONER].
impugnable, a. impugnable.
impugnación, n.f. opposition, contradiction, refutation, impugnment.
impugnador, -ra, n.m.f. impugner, objector.
impugnar, v.t. to impugn, contradict, oppose, confute.
impugnativo, -va, a. impugning.
impulsar, v.t. to impel, urge on; (mech.) to drive, force, move.
impulsión, n.f. impulsion, impulse; momentum, impetus; influence, motive.
impulsivo, -va, a. impulsive.
impulso, n.m. impulsion; impulse.
impulsor, -ra, n.m.f. impeller, propeller.
impune, a. unpunished.
impunemente, adv. with impunity.
impunidad, n.f. impunity, freedom from punishment.
impuramente, adv. obscenely, impurely.
impureza, n.f. impurity, dishonesty, adulteration; pollution, unchastity; obscenity, foulness.
impurificación, n.f. impuration, defilement.
impurificar, v.t. to defile, render impure; to adulterate.
impuro, -ra, a. impure, foul, defiled; adulterated.
imputabilidad, n.f. imputableness.
imputable, a. imputable, chargeable.
imputación, n.f. imputation, attribution, accusation.
imputador, -ra, n.m.f. imputer.
imputar, v.t. to impute, accuse, charge, attribute; to charge upon; (com.) to credit on account.
inabarcable, a. not capable of being embraced or envisaged.

inacabable, *a.* interminable, unending, endless.

inaccesibilidad, *n.f.* inaccessibility.

inaccesible, *a.* inaccessible, unapproachable.

inaccesiblemente, *adv.* inaccessibly.

inacción, *n.f.* inaction, inactivity, rest, cessation from labour.

inaceptable, *a.* unacceptable.

inactividad, *a.* inactivity.

inactivo, -va, *a.* inactive.

inadaptable, *a.* unadaptable.

inadecuado, -da, *a.* inadequate.

inadmisible, *a.* inadmissible.

inadoptable, *a.* unadoptable.

inadvertencia, *n.f.* inadvertence, carelessness, inattention, heedlessness, oversight.

inadvertidamente, *adv.* inadvertently.

inadvertido, -da, *a.* inadvertent, inconsiderate, careless; unseen, unnoticed.

inafectado, -da, *a.* natural, unaffected.

inagotable, *a.* inexhaustible, exhaustless; unexhausted; never-failing.

inaguantable, *a.* insupportable, intolerable.

inajenable, inalienable, *a.* inalienable.

inalámbrico, -ca, *a.* wireless (communication).

inalterabilidad, *n.f.* immutability, stability, inalterability.

inalterable, *a.* inalterable.

inalterablemente, *adv.* unalterably.

inalterado, -da, *a.* unchanged, stable.

inamisible, *a.* inamissible.

inamovible, *a.* immovable.

inamovibilidad, *n.f.* immovability.

inanalizable, *a.* that bears no analysis.

inane, *a.* empty, void, inane.

inanición, *n.f.* (*med.*) inanition, extreme weakness.

inanidad, *n.f.* emptiness; inanity; uselessness.

inanimado, -da, *a.* inanimate, lifeless.

inapagable, *a.* inextinguishable, unquenchable.

inapeable, *a.* incomprehensible, inconceivable; obstinate, stubborn.

inapelable, *a.* without appeal.

inapetencia, *n.f.* inappetence, inappetency, want of appetite or desire for food.

inapetente, *a.* having no appetite; inappetent.

inaplacable, *a.* unappeasable.

inaplicable, *a.* inapplicable.

inaplicación, *n.f.* indolence, inapplication.

inaplicado, -da, *a.* indolent, careless, inactive.

inapreciable, *a.* inestimable, invaluable, inappreciable.

inarmónico, -ca, *a.* inharmonious.

inarticulado, -da, *a.* inarticulate.

inasequible, *a.* unattainable, which cannot be followed.

inasimilable, *a.* unassimilable.

inatacable, *a.* (*coll.*) that cannot be attacked.

inaudible, *a.* inaudible.

inaudito, -ta, *a.* unheard of, strange, most extraordinary; monstrous.

inauguración, *n.f.* inauguration, commencement; inaugural ceremony; (*obs.*) coronation, investiture; auguration, augury.

inaugural, *a.* inaugural.

inaugurar, *v.t.* to inaugurate; to divine by the flight of birds.

inaveriguable, *a.* that cannot be ascertained.

inca, *n.m.* (*Per.*) inca, king, prince, royalty in old Peru; gold coin.

incaico, -ca, *a.* belonging or relating to an inca.

incalculable, *a.* incalculable.

incalificable, *a.* unqualifiable, downright.

incalmable, *a.* that cannot be calmed or subdued.

incandescencia, *n.f.* incandescence.

incandescente, *a.* incandescent.

incansable, *a.* indefatigable, unwearied.

incansablemente, *adv.* indefatigably.

incantable, *a.* that cannot be sung.

incapacidad, *n.f.* incapacity, inability, incapability, incapableness, unfitness, incompetence.

incapacitar, *v.t.* to incapacitate, render incapable, disable.

incapaz, *a.* incapable, unable, unfit, incompetent; *incapaz de sacramentos*, very weak and silly.

incasable, *a.* unmarriageable; opposed to marriage.

incautación, *n.f.* (*law*) attachment of property.

incautamente, *adv.* unwarily, incautiously.

incautarse, *v.r.* (*law*) to attach property.

incauto, -ta, *a.* incautious, unwary, heedless.

incendiar, *v.t.* to set on fire, to commit arson.

incendiario,-ria, *n.m.f.* incendiary; firebrand; inflaming passions or factions, promoting quarrels.

incendio, *n.f.* fire, conflagration, burning; combustion; broil.

incensación, *n.f.* perfuming with incense, thurification.

incensar, *v.t.* (*pres. indic.* **incienso**; *pres. subj.* **inciense**) to perfume, cense, offer incense; to bestow fulsome praise or adulation.

incensario, *n.m.* incensory, thurible.

incensurable, *a.* unblamable, not culpable.

incentivo, *n.m.* incentive, incitement, spur; encouragement.

incertidumbre, *n.f.* incertitude, uncertainty, doubtfulness, hesitancy, fluctuation.

incertísimo, -ma, *a.* extremely doubtful.

incesable, *a.* incessant, unceasing.

incesablemente, *adv.* incessantly, without intermission.

incesante, *a.* incessant, unceasing, continual, uninterrupted.

incesantemente, *adv.* incessantly, continually.

incesto, *n.m.* incest.

incestuosamente, *adv.* incestuously.

incestuoso, -sa, *a.* incestuous.

incidencia, *n.f.* incidence, incidency, accident, casualty; *ángulo de incidencia*, angle of incidence.

incidental, *a.* incidental, dependent, subsidiary.

incidentalmente, *adv.* incidentally.

incidente, *a.* casual, incidental, incident, chance, accidental. — *n.m.* incident, accident, casualty, occurrence. — *pl.* (*com.*) appurtenances; *incidentes de comercio*, lease and good-will.

incidentemente, *adv.* incidentally.

incidir, *v.i.* to fall into (as an error); to fall upon, meet with.

incienso, *n.m.* incense; reverence, veneration; flattery.

inciertamente, *adv.* uncertainly.

incierto, -ta, *a.* untrue, false, unreal; uncertain, doubtful; unstable, inconstant; unknown.

incinerable, *a.* to be incinerated; applied to bank bills which are incinerated when withdrawn.

incineración, *n.f.* incineration, cremation.

incinerar, *v.t.* to incinerate, cremate.

incipiente, *a.* beginning, incipient, inceptive, inchoative.

incircunciso, -sa, *a.* uncircumcised.

incircunscripto, -ta, *a.* uncircumscribed.

incisión, *n.f.* incision, cut, gash, notch, wound with a sharp instrument.

incisivo, -va, *a.* incisive, keen, sharp, cutting; *dientes incisivos,* incisors, cutting teeth.

inciso, -sa, *a.* incised, cut. — *n.m.* (*gram.*) clause; comma.

incisorio, -ria, *a.* (*surg.*) incisory.

incitación, *n.f.* incitation, incitement.

incitador, -ra, *n.m.f.* instigator, inciter, exciter.

incitamento, incitamiento, *n.m.* incitement, impulse, incentive.

incitante, *a.* inciting, exciting.

incitar, *v.t.* to incite, excite, spur, stimulate, instigate.

incitativa, *n.f.* writ from a superior to a lower court urging that justice be administered.

incitativo, -va, *a.* incentive, inciting, incensive; (*law*) stimulating.

incitativo, *n.m.* incitement.

incivil, *a.* uncivil, unpolished, incivil.

incivilidad, *n.f.* incivility, rudeness, coarseness, grossness.

incivilmente, *adv.* uncivilly, rudely.

inclasificable, *a.* unclassifiable.

inclemencia, *n.f.* inclemency, severity, rigour, harshness, unmercifulness; roughness of the weather; *a la inclemencia,* openly, without shelter.

inclemente, *a.* inclement, unmerciful, cruel.

inclinación, *n.f.* inclination, propensity; tendency, bent; fancy, liking, preference, affection, predilection, inclination, fondness; (*geom.*) inclination; bow (of the head); (*mech.*) tilt, fall, bend, pitch; (*min.*) hade, underlay, dip; (*rail.*) gradient; declivity, slope, descent; *inclinación de la aguja magnética,* dip of the needle, magnetic dip.

inclinado, -da, *a.* inclined, slanting, sloping; affected, disposed, minded. — *p.p.* [INCLINAR].

inclinador, -ra, *n.m.f.* one who inclines.

inclinante, *a.* inclining, bending, drawing nigh to.

inclinar, *v.t.* to incline, bend; to tilt, tip over; to induce, influence, persuade. — *v.i.* to resemble, be like. — *v.r.* to incline, bend to, lean, sway, slope; to be favourably disposed to; to stoop, bow; (*naut.*) to heel.

inclito, -ta, *a.* famous, renowned, conspicuous, illustrious.

incluir, *v.t.* (*p.p.* incluido, incluso; *pres. indic.* incluyo; *pres. subj.* incluya) to include, comprise; to enclose; to comprehend, contain.

inclusa, *n.f.* foundling asylum.

inclusero, -ra, *n.m.f., a.* foundling.

inclusión, *n.f.* inclusion; easy access; familiar intercourse.

inclusivamente; inclusive, *adv.* inclusively.

inclusivo, -va, *a.* inclusive.

incluso, -sa, *a.* enclosed; including, included (in this sense it is used as an adv.). — *p.p. irreg.* [INCLUIR].

incluyente, *a.* including, enclosing.

incoado, -da, *a.* inchoate, begun, commenced. — *p.p.* [INCOAR].

incoagulable, *a.* incoagulable, uncoagulable.

incoar, *v.t.* (only the *infin.* and *p.p.* are used); (*law*) to commence, begin, inchoate.

incoativo, -va, *a.* inchoative, inceptive.

incobrable, *a.* irrecoverable, irretrievable; (*com.*) uncollectable.

incoercible, *a.* incoercible.

incógnita, *n.f.* (*math.*) unknown quantity.

incógnito, -ta, *a.* unknown; *de incógnito,* incog., incognito; hiddenly, clandestinely.

incognoscible, *a.* incognizable.

incoherencia, *n.f.* incoherence.

incoherente, *a.* incoherent, inconsistent.

íncola, *n.m.* inhabitant, resident.

incoloro, -ra, *a.* colourless.

incólume, *a.* sound, safe, unharmed.

incolumidad, *n.f.* security, safety.

incombinable, *a.* uncombinable.

incombustibilidad, *n.f.* incombustibility.

incombustible, *a.* incombustible, fireproof.

incomerciable, *a.* contraband, unlawful, prohibited; unsaleable, unmarketable.

incómodamente, *adv.* incommodiously, uncomfortably.

incomodar, *v.t.* to incommode, disturb, inconvenience, trouble. — *v.r.* to be vexed or angered; to be disturbed.

incomodidad, *n.f.* incommodiousness, inconvenience; nuisance, annoyance; vexation, anger.

incómodo, -da, *a.* incommodious, inconvenient, uncomfortable, troublesome, unhandy, cumbersome.

incomparable, *a.* incomparable, matchless.

incomparablemente, *adv.* incomparably.

incomparado, -da, *a.* incomparable, matchless.

incompartible, *a.* indivisible.

incompasible; incompasivo, -va, *a.* uncompassionate, pitiless.

incompatibilidad, *n.f.* incompatibility, contrariety; inconsistency, uncongeniality, discordance.

incompatible, *a.* incompatible, inconsistent, uncongenial.

incompensable, *a.* incompensable.

incompetencia, *n.f.* incompetency, unfitness, inability.

incompetente, *a.* incompetent, incapable, unfit; (*law*) unqualified.

incomplejo, -ja, *a.* uncomplicated, simple.

incompletamente, *adv.* incompletely.

incompleto, -ta, *a.* incomplete.

incomplexo, -xa, *a.* disunited, disconnected, disjointed, non-adherent.

incomponible, *a.* unrepairable, unmendable.

incomportable, *a.* intolerable, unbearable.

incomposibilidad, *n.f.* incompossibility.

incomposible, *a.* incompossible.

incomposición, *n.f.* want of proportion.

incomprehensibilidad, incomprensibilidad, *n.f.* incomprehensibility.

incomprehensible, incomprensible, *a.* incomprehensible.

incomprensiblemente, *adv*. inconceivably, incomprehensibly.
incomprimible, *a*. incompressible.
incomunicabilidad, *n.f*. incommunicability.
incomunicable, *a*. incommunicable.
incomunicado, -da, *a*. with no means of communication with the outside world; in solitary confinement.
incomunicar, *v.t*. (*pret*. **incomuniqué**; *pres. subj*. **incomunique**) to deprive of intercourse or communication; to isolate.
inconcebible, *a*. inconceivable.
inconciliable, *a*. irreconcilable.
inconcino, -na, *a*. disordered, disarranged.
inconcusamente, *adv*. certainly, indubitably.
inconcuso, -sa, *a*. incontrovertible, incontestable.
incondicional, *a*. unconditional, absolute, unrestricted.
incondicionalmente, *adv*. unconditionally.
inconducente, *a*. unconducive, incongruous.
inconexión, *n.f*. incoherency, incongruity, inconnexion.
inconexo, -xa, *a*. unconnected, incoherent, inconsequential, independent.
inconfesable, *a*. matter which for its disgraceful character cannot be confessed.
inconfeso, -sa, *a*. unconfessed.
inconfidencia, *n.f*. distrust, mistrust, diffidence, disloyalty, want of fidelity.
incongruamente, *adv*. incongruously.
incongruencia, *n.f*. incongruence, unsuitableness, want of proportion.
incongruente, *a*. incongruous, incongruent.
incongruentemente, *adv*. incongruously, incompatibly.
incongruo, -grua, *a*. incongruous, disproportionate, unsuitable.
inconjugable, *a*. inconjugable.
inconmensurabilidad, *n.f*. incommensurability.
inconmensurable, *a*. incommensurable, immeasurable.
inconmutabilidad, *n.f*. immutability, unchangeableness.
inconmutable, *a*. immutable; that cannot be commuted.
inconquistable, *a*. unconquerable, impregnable, inexpugnable; invincible; incorruptible (of persons).
inconsciente, *a*. unconscious, unknowing, ignorant.
inconscientemente, *adv*. unconsciously, unknowingly, unwittingly.
inconsecuencia, *n.f*. inconsequence, inconsistency.
inconsecuente, *a*. inconsequent, inconsequential, inconsistent.
inconservable, *a*. unpreservable.
inconsideración, *n.f*. inconsiderateness, thoughtlessness, inattention, inadvertency.
inconsideradamente, *adv*. inconsiderately, thoughtlessly.
inconsiderado, -da, *a*. inconsiderate, thoughtless, inattentive.
inconsiguiente, *a*. inconsequent, inconsistent, contradictory.
inconsistencia, *n.f*. inconsistency, self-contradiction, unsubstantiality, incoherence, incongruity, unsteadiness, unstableness.
inconsistente, *a*. inconsistent, unsubstantial, unstable, unsteady, incongruous, absurd.

inconsolable, *a*. inconsolable.
inconsolablemente, *adv*. inconsolably.
inconstancia, *n.f*. inconstancy, fickleness, unsteadiness, levity, lightness, frailty.
inconstante, *a*. inconstant, changeable, mutable, unsteady, variable, fickle.
inconstantemente, *adv*. inconstantly, unsteadily, giddily.
inconstitucional, *a*. unconstitutional.
inconstruible, *a*. that cannot be construed or constructed; whimsical, variable.
inconsútil, *a*. seamless, having no seam.
incontable, *a*. innumerable.
incontaminado, -da, *a*. undefiled, uncontaminated.
incontestable, *a*. incontestable, indisputable, incontrovertible.
incontestablemente, *adv*. incontestably.
incontinencia, *n.f*. incontinence, incontinency; unchastity, lewdness.
incontinente, *a*. incontinent; unchaste.
incontinentemente, *adv*. incontinently, unchastely.
incontinenti, *adv*. at once, straightway, immediately.
incontrastable, *a*. insurmountable, irresistible, invincible, insuperable; unanswerable, undeniable; inconvincible, incontrovertible, unshakable.
incontratable, *a*. untractable, stubborn.
incontrovertible, *a*. incontrovertible, indisputable.
inconvencible, *a*. inconvincible.
inconvenible, *a*. inconvenient; discordant, inconsistent.
inconveniencia, *n.f*. inconvenience, incommodity, trouble; incongruence, unfitness, unsuitableness; unlikeliness; impropriety.
inconveniente, *a*. inconvenient, incommodious, unsuitable, troublesome, unbecoming, improper. — *n.m*. difficulty, obstacle, obstruction, objection, impediment.
inconversable, *a*. unsociable, incommunicative, surly, grouchy.
inconvertible, *a*. inconvertible.
incordio, *n.m*. (*med.*) bubo; (*vulg.*) nuisance.
incorporación, *n.f*. incorporation.
incorporal, *a*. incorporeal.
incorporalmente, *adv*. incorporeally, incorporally.
incorporar, *v.t*. to incorporate, unite, embody; to raise or to make a patient sit up in his bed; to mix. — *v.r*. to incorporate, mingle, join; to sit up (in bed); to form a corporation; (*naut.*) to sail in company.
incorporeidad, *n.f*. incorporeity, incorporeality, immateriality.
incorpóreo, -rea, *a*. incorporeal, immaterial, unbodied.
incorporo, *n.m*. incorporation.
incorrección, *n.f*. incorrectness, inaccuracy.
incorrectamente, *adv*. inaccurately.
incorrecto, -ta, *a*. incorrect, inaccurate.
incorregibilidad, *n.f*. incorrigibleness, hopeless depravity.
incorregible, *a*. incorrigible, froward.
incorrupción, *n.f*. incorruption, incorruptness, purity, integrity, honesty.
incorruptamente, *adv*. incorruptly.
incorruptibilidad, *n.f*. incorruptibility.
incorruptible, *a*. incorruptible.

incorrupto, -ta, *a.* incorrupt, uncorrupt, uncorrupted; honest, chaste, pure.

incrasante, *a.* incrassating, inspissating.

incrasar, *v.t.* to inspissate, thicken, incrassate.

increado, -da, *a.* uncreated, increate.

incredibilidad, *n.f.* incredibility, incredibleness.

incredulidad, *n.f.* incredulity, incredulousness.

incrédulo, -la, *a.* incredulous. — *n.m.f.* unbeliever, miscreant.

increíble, *a.* incredible, unbelievable.

increíblemente, *adv.* incredibly.

incremento, *n.m.* increment, increase.

increpación, *n.f.* increpation, reprehension, chiding, reproach.

increpador, -ra, *n.m.f.* chider, rebuker, scolder.

increpante, *a.* chiding, scolding.

increpar, *v.t.* to chide, reprehend, reproach, scold, rebuke.

incriminación, *n.f.* incrimination.

incriminar, *v.t.* to incriminate; to exaggerate a fault or defect.

incristalizable, *a.* uncrystallizable.

incruento, -ta, *a.* bloodless.

incrustación, *n.f.* incrustation; scale in boilers; (*geol.*) sinter; (*art*) inlaying.

incrustar, *v.t.* to incrust, incrustate; to enchase, inlay.

incuartación, *n.f.* (*chem.*) quartation.

incubación, *n.f.* incubation, hatching; (*med.*) incubation; (*fig.*) secret planning or plotting.

incubadora, *n.f.* incubator.

incubar, *v.t.* to incubate, hatch.

incubo, *n.m.* incubus, male demon; (*obs.*) nightmare.

incuestionable, *a.* unquestionable.

inculcación, *n.f.* inculcation, enforcing; (*print.*) binding or wedging in a form.

inculcar, *v.t.* (*pret.* **inculqué**; *pres. subj.* **inculque**) to inculcate, impress, teach, enforce; to make one thing tight against another; (*print.*) to lock up types. — *v.r.* to be obstinate.

inculpabilidad, *n.f.* inculpableness, blamelessness.

inculpable, *a.* inculpable, blameless.

inculpablemente, *adv.* inculpably.

inculpación, *n.f.* inculpation.

inculpadamente, *adv.* faultlessly.

inculpar, *v.t.* to accuse, inculpate, blame.

incultamente, *adv.* rudely, without culture.

incultivable, *a.* inarable, uncultivable, incapable of cultivation.

inculto, -ta, *a.* incult, uncultivated, untilled, unimproved; uncivilized, unpolished, uncultured, unrefined (style of writing), clownish, clumsy.

incultura, *n.f.* inculture.

incumbencia, *n.f.* incumbency; obligation, duty, concern; *no es de la incumbencia de Vd.,* it doesn't concern you.

incumbir, *v.i.* to concern, pertain, relate.

incumplido, -da, *a.* unfulfilled.

incunable, *n.m.,* *a.* (*print.*) incunabula.

incurable, *a.* incurable, hopeless, irremediable, immedicable.

incuria, *n.f.* negligence, carelessness, inaccuracy, indolence.

incurioso, -sa, *a.* negligent, careless, incurious, inattentive, indolent.

incurrimiento, *n.m.* act of incurring.

incurrir, *v.i.* (*p.p.* **incurrido, incurso**) (followed by *en*), to incur, become liable, deserve, bring upon oneself.

incursión, *n.f.* (*mil.*) incursion.

incurso, -sa, *p.p. irreg.* [INCURRIR].

incusar, *v.t.* to accuse, impute, charge.

incuso, -sa, *a.* incuse (as some coins).

indagación, *n.f.* investigation, search, inquiry, examination, inquest.

indagador, -ra, *n.m.f.* investigator, inquirer, examiner.

indagar, *v.t.* (*pret.* **indagué**; *pres. subj.* **indague**) to investigate, search, inquire, examine into.

indagatoria, *n.f.* (*law*) investigatory.

indebidamente, *adv.* unduly, illegally.

indebido, -da, *a.* undue, illegal, unlawful.

indecencia, *n.f.* indecency, indecorum, obscenity; nuisance.

indecente, *a.* indecent, obscene, dishonest, unbecoming, fulsome, foul.

indecentemente, *adv.* indecently.

indecible, *a.* inexpressible, unutterable.

indeciblemente, *adv.* inexpressibly.

indecisamente, *adv.* irresolutely.

indecisión, *n.f.* irresolution, indecision, hesitation, hesitancy.

indeciso, -sa, *a.* irresolute, indecisive, undecided, hesitating.

indeclinable, *a.* unavoidable; (*law*) undeclinable; (*gram.*) indeclinable.

indecoro, *n.m.* indecorum, indecorousness, indecency.

indecorosamente, *adv.* indecorously, indecently.

indecoroso, -sa, *a.* indecorous, indecent, unbecoming.

indefectibilidad, *n.f.* indefectibility.

indefectible, *a.* indefectible, unfailing.

indefectiblemente, *adv.* indefectibly.

indefendible, indefensable, indefensible, *a.* indefensible.

indefenso, -sa, *a.* defenceless, indefensive.

indeficiente, *a.* indefectible, unfailing.

indefinible, *a.* indefinable.

indefinidamente, *adv.* indefinitely.

indefinido, -da, *a.* indefinite, indeterminate, vague; undefined, not limited.

indehiscente, *a.* (*bot.*) indehiscent.

indeleble, *a.* indelible, ineffaceable.

indeleblemente, *adv.* indelibly.

indeliberación, *n.f.* indetermination, inadvertency, unpremeditation, indeliberation.

indeliberadamente, *adv.* indeliberately.

indeliberado, -da, *a.* indeliberate, indeliberated, unpremeditated.

indemne, *a.* undamaged, unhurt.

indemnidad, *n.f.* bond of indemnity.

indemnizable, *a.* indemnifiable.

indemnización, *n.f.* indemnification, reimbursement.

indemnizar, *v.t.* (*pret.* **indemnicé**; *pres. subj.* **indemnice**) to indemnify, compensate, make good, secure against loss.

indemostrable, *a.* indemonstrable.

independencia, *n.f.* independence.

independiente, *a.* independent, uncontrolled, free; *independiente de eso,* besides that.

independientemente, *adv.* independently.

indescifrable, *a.* undecipherable.

indescribible, indescriptible, *a.* indescribable.

indeseable, *a.* undesirable (alien).

indesignable, *a.* that cannot be designed or designated.

indestructibilidad, *n.f.* indestructibility.

indestructible, *a.* indestructible, imperishable.

indeterminable, *a.* indeterminable, irresolute, undecided.

indeterminación, *n.f.* indetermination, irresolution, hesitancy.

indeterminadamente, *adv.* indeterminately.

indeterminado, -da, *a.* indeterminate; undetermined, loose, irresolute, hesitating; pusillanimous, chicken-hearted; (*gram.*) indefinite.

indevoción, *n.f.* want of devotion.

indevoto, -ta, *a.* not devout, irreligious.

índex, *n.m.* (*obs.*) hand of watch or clock [ÍNDICE].

indezuelo, -la, *n.m.f.* little Indian.

india, *n.f.* (*coll.*) great wealth or plenty.

indiana, *n.f.* printed calico, chintz.

indianista, *n.m.f.* Indianist.

indiano, -na, *a.* native or resident of America or the West Indies; Indian, East Indian, belonging to India.

indiano, *n.m.* nabob, one who returns rich from America; *indiano de hilo negro,* (*coll.*) skinflint, miser.

Indias, *n.f.pl.* Indies; *Indias Occidentales,* West Indies; *Indias Orientales,* East Indies.

indicación, *n.f.* manifestation, prediction, warning, hint; indication, mark, sign, token, symptom.

indicador, *n.m.* indicator, pointer, gauge, recorder, index, detector, register; forefinger.

indicante, *a.* indicating. — *n.m.* (*med.*) indicant.

indicar, *v.t.* (*pret.* **indiqué;** *pres. subj.* **indique**) to indicate, suggest, point out, hint, show.

indicativo, -va, *a.* indicative, pointing.

indicativo, *n.m.* (*gram.*) indicative.

indicción, *n.f.* convening of a synod, council, etc.; indiction; manner of computing time.

índice, *n.m.* index, mark, indication, sign; hand of a watch or clock; index, table of contents of a book; pointer on a sundial; forefinger; *índice expurgatorio,* catalogue of books prohibited by the Inquisition.

indiciado, -da, *a.* suspicious, suspected of a crime or vice. — *n.m.f.* suspicious character. — *p.p.* [INDICIAR].

indiciador, -ra, *n.m.f.* informer, one who suspects another.

indiciar, *v.t.* (*law*) to give reasons to suspect or surmise; to indicate offenders to the magistrates; to indicate.

indicio, *n.m.* indication, mark, sign, token; (*chem.*) trace; *indicios vehementes,* (*law*) circumstantial evidence.

índico, -ca, *a.* East Indian.

indiferencia, *n.f.* indifference, incuriosity; unconcern, neglect, coldness, lukewarmness, listlessness, neutrality.

indiferente, *a.* indifferent, neutral; unconcerned, regardless, inattentive; lukewarm, cool, listless, frigid; *eso es indiferente,* (*coll.*) that is immaterial, that makes no difference.

indiferentemente, *adv.* indifferently, impartially, coolly.

indiferentismo, *n.m.* indifferentism.

indígena, *a.* indigenous, native. — *n.m.f.* native.

indigencia, *n.f.* indigence, want, poverty, need, penury.

indigente, *a.* indigent, necessitous, needy, poor.

indigerible, indigestible, *a.* indigestible.

indigestión, *n.f.* indigestion; ill-nature, ill-temper.

indigesto, -ta, *a.* indigestible; confused, not methodized, disordered; surly, harsh, ill-tempered.

indignación, *n.f.* indignation, anger.

indignado, -da, *a.* provoked, teased, indignant, angry. — *p.p.* [INDIGNAR].

indignamente, *adv.* unworthily, unsuitably.

indignante, *a.* indignant, irritating.

indignar, *v.t.* to irritate, anger, provoke. — *v.r.* to become angry or indignant.

indignidad, *n.f.* indignity, unworthy action, meanness; passion, indignation.

indigno, -na, *a.* unworthy, undeserving; unbecoming, incongruous, unsuitable; disgraceful, mean, vile, despicable.

índigo, *n.m.* indigo (plant and dye).

indiligencia, *n.f.* indiligence, carelessness.

indio, -dia, *a.* Indian; blue, azure. — *n.m.f.* Indian. — *n.m.* (*chem.*) indium.

indirecta, *n.f.* innuendo, hint, cue, surmise; *indirecta del padre Cobos,* broad hint.

indirectamente; indirecte, *adv.* indirectly, obliquely.

indirecto, -ta, *a.* indirect, oblique.

indisciplina, *n.f.* want of discipline, insubordination.

indisciplinable, *a.* indisciplinable.

indisciplinado, -da, *a.* lax, undisciplined.

indiscreción, *n.f.* indiscretion, imprudence, rashness, inconsideration, folly.

indiscretamente, *adv.* indiscreetly.

indiscreto, -ta, *a.* indiscreet, imprudent, incautious, foolish; injudicious, inconsiderate.

indisculpable, *a.* inexcusable.

indiscutible, *a.* unquestionable, beyond discussion or question.

indisoluble, *a.* indissoluble, indissolvable.

indisolublemente, *adv.* indissolubly.

indispensable, *a.* inexcusable; indispensable.

indispensablemente, *adv.* indispensably, necessarily.

indisponer, *v.t.* to disable, indispose, render unfit; to disincline, prejudice against; to make ill. — *v.r.* to be indisposed; to grow ill; to fall out with a person; to be fretful, cross, peevish.

indisponible, *a.* (*law*) that cannot be bequeathed.

indisposición, *n.f.* indisposition, disinclination, dislike; slight disorder in health.

indisposicioncilla, *n.f.* slight indisposition.

indispuesto, -ta, *a.* indisposed; at variance. — *p.p. irreg.* [INDISPONER].

indisputable, *a.* indisputable, incontrovertible.

indisputablemente, *adv.* indisputably.

indistinción, *n.f.* indistinction, indiscrimination.

indistinguible, *a.* undistinguishable, indistinguishable.

indistintamente, *adv.* indistinctly, indiscriminately.

indistinto, -ta, *a.* indistinct, indiscriminate, confused, vague, not clear.

individuación, *n.f.* individuation.

individual, *a.* individual, peculiar.

individualidad, *n.f.* individuality.

individualismo, *n.m.* individualism.

individualista, *a.* individualistic. — *n.m.f.* individualist.

individualizar, *v.t.* (*pret.* **individualicé;** *pres. subj.* **individualice**) to individualize.

individualmente, *adv.* individually, inseparably.

individuar, *v.t.* to individuate, distinguish, individualize, particularize, specify individually.

individuo, -dua, *a.* individual, indivisible, inseparable. — *n.m.f.* a person *or* one's person (*coll.*); member, associate, fellow.

indivisamente, *adv.* indivisibly.

indivisibilidad, *n.f.* indivisibility.

indivisible, *a.* indivisible.

indivisiblemente, *adv.* inseparably, indivisibly.

indivisión, *n.f.* entirety, completeness.

indiviso, -sa, *a.* undivided, individuate.

indo, -da, *a.* Indian.

indócil, *a.* indocile, unteachable; forward, headstrong, unruly; inflexible, brittle.

indocilidad, *n.f.* indocility, stubbornness of temper, inflexibility.

indócilmente, *adv.* inflexibly.

indoctamente, *adv.* ignorantly.

indocto, -ta, *a.* ignorant, uninstructed, unlearned, uneducated.

indocumentado, -da, *a.* lacking the documents for identification.

indoeuropeo, -ea; indogermánico, -ca, *a.* Indo-European.

índole, *n.f.* disposition, temper, inclination, idiosyncracy, humour.

indolencia, *n.f.* indolence, indifference, insensibility, laziness; kind, sort, nature.

indolente, *a.* indolent, indifferent.

indolentemente, *adv.* indolently, inertly.

indomable, *a.* untamable, indomitable, unmanageable; inflexible, unconquerable.

indomado, -da, *a.* untamed.

indomesticable, *a.* untamable.

indoméstico, -ca, *a.* untamed, intractable, fierce.

indómito, -ta, *a.* untamed, ungoverned, wild.

indostánico, -ca, *a.* Hindu.

indotación, *n.f.* (*law*) lack of dowry.

indotado, -da, *a.* unendowed; portionless.

indubitable, *a.* indubitable, unquestioned, irrefutable, unquestionable.

indubitablemente, *adv.* undoubtedly, indubitably, unquestionably.

inducción, *n.f.* inducement, persuasion; (*log.*) induction; (*elect.*) induction; *por inducción,* inductively.

inducidor, -ra, *n.m.f.* inducer, persuader.

inducimiento, *n.m.* inducement, motive.

inducir, *v.t.* (*pres. indic.* **induzco;** *pret.* **induje;** *pres. subj.* **induzca**) to induce, persuade, influence, attract; (*elect.*) to induce.

indúctil, *a.* not ductile.

inductivo, -va, *a.* inductive.

inductor, -ra, *a.* (*elect.*) inductive.

inductor, *n.m.* inductor.

indudable, *a.* indubitable, certain.

indulgencia, *n.f.* indulgence, forbearance, leniency, clemency, tenderness, grace, forgiveness; (*ecc.*) indulgence.

indulgente, *a.* indulgent, lenient, forbearing, mild, gentle, kind.

indulgentemente, *adv.* indulgently.

indultar, *v.t.* to pardon, forgive; to free, exempt.

indultario, *n.m.* one who by virtue of a pontifical privilege can dispense ecclesiastical benefices.

indulto, *n.m.* pardon, forgiveness, amnesty; indult, exemption, privilege.

indumentaria, *n.f.* study of ancient apparel; dress, clothes, clothing.

indumento, *n.m.* wearing apparel.

induración, *n.f.* (*med.*) induration.

industria, *n.f.* industry, diligence, assiduity, ingenuity, subtlety, acuteness; manufacturing; trade; productive labour; *de industria,* designedly, purposely, intentionally; *caballero de industria,* man who lives by his wits; confidence man; share pusher, etc.

industrial, *a.* industrial, manufacturing. — *n.m.* manufacturer, industrialist.

industrialismo, *n.m.* industrialism.

industriar, *v.t., v.r.* to instruct, coach, train; to find means, find a way, manage things well.

industriosamente, *adv.* industriously; (*obs.*) designedly.

industrioso, -sa, *a.* industrious, skilful, ingenious, dexterous; painstaking, laborious, assiduous.

inedia, *n.f.* fast, abstinence from food.

inédito, -ta, *a.* unpublished, unedited, inedited.

inefabilidad, *n.f.* ineffability, unspeakableness.

inefable, *a.* ineffable, unspeakable, unutterable.

inefablemente, *adv.* ineffably.

ineficacia, *n.f.* inefficacy, ineffectualness, inefficiency.

ineficaz, *a.* inefficacious, ineffectual, ineffective, inefficient.

ineficazmente, *adv.* inefficaciously.

inelegancia, *n.f.* inelegance.

inelegante, *a.* inelegant.

ineluctable, *a.* ineluctable, irresistible.

ineludible, *a.* inevitable, unavoidable.

inenarrable, *a.* inexplicable, inexpressible.

ineptamente, *adv.* unfitly, ineptly.

ineptitud, *n.f.* ineptitude, incompetency, inability, unfitness.

inepto, -ta, *a.* inept, incapable, incompetent, useless, unfit; foolish.

inequívoco, -ca, *a.* unequivocal, unmistakable.

inercia, *n.f.* inertia; inertness, inactivity, indolence, dullness.

inerme, *a.* disarmed, defenceless.

inerrable, *a.* inerrable, unmistakable; infallible.

inerrante, *a.* fixed (of stars).

inerte, *a.* inert, slow, dull, sluggish; unskilful; paralytic, paralyzed, senseless.

inerudito, -ta, *a.* unlearned, inerudite.

inescrutable, *a.* inscrutable, unsearchable.

inescudriñable, *a.* inscrutable.

inesperadamente, *adv.* unexpectedly, suddenly.
inesperado, -da, *a.* unexpected, unforeseen.
inestimabilidad, *n.f.* inestimableness.
inestimable, *a.* inestimable, invaluable.
inestimado, -da, *a.* (*law*) unestimated, not rated, unappraised, unvalued.
inevitable, *a.* inevitable, unavoidable, fatal.
inevitablemente, *adv.* inevitably.
inexactamente, *adv.* inexactly.
inexactitud, *n.f.* inaccuracy, inexactness.
inexacto, -ta, *a.* inexact, inaccurate.
inexcusable, *a.* inexcusable; indispensable, inevitable; excuseless.
inexcusablemente, *adv.* inexcusably.
inexhausto, -ta, *a.* unexhausted, unemptied, unspent; full, abundant, plentiful.
inexistente, *a.* inexistent, non-existent.
inexorable, *a.* inexorable, hard-hearted, relentless.
inexperiencia, *n.f.* inexperience.
inexperto, -ta, *a.* unskilful, inexperienced, inexpert.
inexpiable, *a.* inexpiable.
inexplicable, *a.* inexplicable, unexplainable.
inexplorado, -da, *a.* unexplored.
inexpugnable, *a.* inexpugnable, impregnable; firm, constant, obstinate, stubborn.
inextinguible, *a.* inextinguishable, unquenchable; perpetual.
inextricable, *a.* inextricable.
infacundo, -da, *a.* ineloquent.
infalibilidad, *n.f.* infallibility.
infalible, *a.* infallible.
infaliblemente, *adv.* infallibly.
infamable, *a.* calumnious, capable of infamy.
infamación, *n.f.* slander, calumny, defamation.
infamador, -ra, *n.m.f.* defamer, libeller.
infamante, *a.* defaming; opprobrious.
infamar, *v.t.* to defame, dishonour, disgrace.
infamativo, -va, *a.* that which defames.
infamatorio, -ria, *a.* defamatory, libellous, foul-spoken.
infame, *a.* infamous, vile, despicable, damnable.
infamemente, *adv.* infamously, vilely.
infamia, *n.f.* infamy, dishonour, disgrace; meanness, baseness.
infancia, *n.f.* infancy; beginning, commencement.
infando, -da, *a.* unmentionable, so abominable as not to be expressed.
infanta, *n.f.* female child under seven years of age; daughter of the King of Spain other than the heir-apparent; wife of an infante.
infantado, *n.m.* territory assigned to a prince of the royal blood of Spain.
infante, *n.m.* infant, male child under seven years of age; infante, son of the King of Spain, except the heir-apparent to the crown; infantry soldier. — *pl.* **infantes,** choristers.
infantería, *n.f.* infantry, foot-soldiers.
infanticida, *n.m.f.* infanticide, child murderer.
infanticidio, *n.m.* infanticide, child-murder.
infantil, *a.* infantile, infantine, childlike.
infanzón, *n.m.* ancient nobleman.
infanzonado, -da, *a.* pertaining to an *infanzón.*
infanzonazgo, *n.m.* territory of an *infanzón.*
infanzonía, *n.f.* ancient nobility.
infartación, *n.f.* (*med.*) infarction.

infarto, *n.m.* (*med.*) infarct.
infatigable, *a.* indefatigable, unwearied.
infatigablemente, *adv.* indefatigably.
infatuación, *n.f.* infatuation, vanity.
infatuar, *v.t.* to infatuate. — *v.r.* to become infatuated, stupid, conceited.
infaustamente, *adv.* unluckily.
infausto, -ta, *a.* unlucky, unhappy, unfortunate, accursed.
infebril, *a.* fever-free.
infección, *n.f.* infection, contagion.
infeccioso, -sa, *a.* infectious, contagious.
infectar, *v.t.* to infect, spread contagion; to corrupt, vitiate, pervert. — *v.r.* to catch infection.
infectivo, -va, *a.* infective, infectious.
infecto, -ta, *a.* infected, tainted, corrupt.
infecundidad, *n.f.* infecundity, sterility, infertility.
infecundo, -da, *a.* infecund, barren, unfruitful, infertile, sterile.
infelice, *a.* (*poet.*) unhappy, unfortunate, luckless, miserable.
infelicidad, *n.f.* misfortune, calamity, disgrace, misery, unhappiness.
infeliz, *a.* unhappy, unfortunate, luckless, miserable; *es un infeliz,* (*coll.*) he is a poor devil, a good-natured fool.
infelizmente, *adv.* unhappily, unluckily, unfortunately.
inferencia, *n.f.* inference, illation.
inferior, *a.* inferior; lower; subject, subordinate; (*com.*) low, common, poor in quality.
inferioridad, *n.f.* inferiority, lower position.
inferir, *v.t.* (*pres. indic.* **infiero;** *pres. subj.* **infiera**) to infer, draw conclusions, deduce; to inflict (a wound); to collect, gather; to offer (as affront). — *v.r.* to follow, to be consequential.
infernáculo, *n.m.* boyish game, hop-scotch.
infernal, *a.* infernal, hellish; extremely hurtful; (*coll.*) annoying, vexatious; *máquina infernal,* infernal machine; *piedra infernal,* lapis infernalis, nitrate of silver in sticks.
infernalmente, *adv.* (*coll.*) hellishly, infernally.
infernar, *v.t.* (*pres. indic.* **infierno;** *pres. subj.* **infierne**) to damn; to irritate, vex, provoke.
inferno, -na, *a.* (*poet.*) infernal.
ínfero, -ra, *a.* (*bot., poet.*) inferior.
infestación, *n.f.* infestation; annoyance.
infestar, *v.t.* to infest, overrun, harass; to infect, fill with stench.
infesto, -ta, *a.* (*poet.*) prejudicial, dangerous.
infeudación, *n.f.* enfeoffment.
infeudar, *v.t.* to enfeoff.
inficionar, *v.t.* to infect, spread contagion; to poison, corrupt, pervert, defile, taint, vitiate.
infidelidad, *n.f.* infidelity, unfaithfulness, treachery, deceit, faithlessness; unbelief, want of faith, disbelief in Christianity, miscreance; whole body of infidels.
infidelísimo, -ma, *a. superl.* most unfaithful.
infidencia, *n.f.* unfaithfulness, faithlessness; treason; (*law*) misfeasance.
infidente, *a.* unfaithful.
infiel, *n.m.f., a.* unfaithful, infidel; faithless, disloyal; godless; pagan; unbeliever; inaccurate, inexact.
infielmente, *adv.* unfaithfully.
infierno, *n.m.* hell; limbo; place or state of extreme torment, evil, or misery; refectory

or eating-room in some convents; (*chem.*) large retort; cave of a baking machine; tank in oil-mills; ¡ *vete al infierno!* go to blazes!

infigurable, *a.* that which cannot be represented by any figure.

infiltración, *n.f.* infiltration, percolation.

infiltrar, *v.t., v.r.* to infiltrate, percolate, filter; to imbue, infuse.

ínfimo, -ma, *a.* lowest, lowermost, undermost, least; vilest, most abject; (*com.*) most inferior in quality.

infinidad, *n.f.* infinity, infiniteness, boundlessness, immensity; endless number.

infinitamente, *adv.* infinitely, immensely.

infinitesimal, *a.* infinitesimal.

infinitésimo, -ma, *a.* (*coll.*) infinitely small.

infinitivo, *n.m.* (*gram.*) infinitive.

infinito, -ta, *a.* infinite, unbounded, immense, limitless; numberless, excessive. — *adv.* infinitely, immensely.

infinitud, *n.f.* infinitude.

infirmar, *v.t.* (*law*) to invalidate, make null and void; (*obs.*) to weaken, shake.

inflación, *n.f.* inflation; swelling, distension; conceit, vanity, haughtiness, vaingloriousness.

inflamable, *a.* inflammable, combustive; phlogistic.

inflamación, *n.f.* inflammation, ignition, combustion; blaze; (*med.*) inflammation.

inflamar, *v.t.* to inflame, kindle, burn, set on fire; to excite the passions. — *v.r.* to become ignited, red-hot; to blaze; (*med.*) to become inflamed.

inflamatorio, -ria, *a.* inflammatory.

inflar, *v.t.* to inflate, blow up, puff, distend; to elate, puff up with pride. — *v.r.* to swell; to strut.

inflativo, -va, *a.* that which inflates.

inflexibilidad, *n.f.* inflexibility, stiffness, rigidity; inflexibleness, obstinacy, inexorability.

inflexible, *a.* inflexible, unbending; immovable; contumacious, inexorable.

inflexiblemente, *adv.* inflexibly, inexorably, invariably.

inflexión, *n.f.* inflexion, bending, warping; accent, modulation; (*opt.*) diffraction.

infligir, *v.t.* to inflict, impose, condemn.

inflorescencia, *n.f.* (*bot.*) inflorescence.

influencia, *n.f.* influence, prestige, credit, consequence, efficient power; inspiration of divine grace.

influente, *a.* influencing, influential.

influir, *v.t.* (*pres. indic.* **influyo;** *pres. subj.* **influya**) to influence; to modify; to prevail upon, persuade, induce; to inspire with grace; to interfere.

influjo, *n.m.* influx, influence, power, credit; rising tide.

influyente, *a.* influencing, influential.

infolio, *n.m.* book in folio form.

inforciado, *n.m.* second part of the digest or pandects of Justinian.

información, *n.f.* information, account, report; intelligence given, inquiries; inquiry, investigation; judicial inquiry and process; (*law*) brief.

informador, -ra, *s.* informer, reporter.

informal, *a.* irregular; improper, unrespectable, unreliable; unconventional.

informalidad, *n.f.* unconventionality; breach of etiquette, indecency, impropriety.

informante, *a.* informing, instructing. — *n.m.* informant, informer, detective.

informar, *v.t.* to inform, advise, instruct, communicate, state, supply with news, report, acquaint; to animate, give form to, shape, substantiate. — *v.i.* (*law*) to plead. — *v.r.* to inquire, investigate, find out, get information.

informativo, -va, *a.* instructive; animative, informative.

informe, *a.* shapeless, formless, irregular, out of shape. — *n.m.* information; report, account, statement, advice; reference; (*law*) plea, pleading, brief.

informidad, *n.f.* shapelessness.

infortificable, *a.* that cannot be fortified.

infortuna, *n.f.* sinistrous influence of the stars.

infortunado, -da, *a.* unfortunate, unlucky, unhappy.

infortunio, *n.m.* misfortune, ill-luck, calamity, mischance; misery; fatality.

infosura, *n.f.* a disease of horses.

infracción, *n.f.* infraction, breach, infringement, contravention, violation of a compact; misdemeanour, trespass.

infracto, -ta, *a.* steady, not easily moved.

infractor, -ra, *n.m.f.* infractor, breaker, violator, transgressor.

infrangible, *a.* infrangible; inviolable.

infranqueable, *a.* insurmountable; inextricable.

infrascripto, -ta; infrascrito, -ta, *a.* undersigned; hereafter mentioned.

infrecuente, *a.* unusual, infrequent.

infringir, *v.t.* (*pres. indic.* **infrinjo;** *pres. subj.* **infrinja**) to infringe, violate, break.

infructífero, -ra; infrugífero, -ra, *a.* unfruitful, unproductive, unprofitable, useless.

infructuosamente, *adv.* unfruitfully, fruitlessly, uselessly.

infructuosidad, *n.f.* unfruitfulness, unproductiveness, uselessness.

infructuoso, -sa, *a.* fruitless, unproductive, unprofitable, gainless, abortive, unsuccessful.

ínfulas, *n.f.pl.* (*eccles.*) infula (head-dress); ribbon of a bishop's mitre; haughtiness, conceit, boasting, ostentation, presumption.

infumable, *a.* unsmokable (tobacco).

infundadamente, *adv.* groundlessly, without reason or cause.

infundado, -da, *a.* groundless, baseless.

infundibie, *a.* infusible.

infundibuliforme, *a.* (*bot.*) funnel-shaped.

infundir, *v.t.* (*p.p.* **infundido, infuso**) to infuse, inspire with; to imbue, instil.

infurción, infulción, *n.f.* ancient ground-lease.

infurcioniego, -ga, *a.* subject to ground-lease.

infurtir, *v.t.* to full or mill clothes.

infusibilidad, *n.f.* infusibility.

infusible, *a.* infusible.

infusión, *n.f.* infusion; inspiration; (*eccles.*) baptism by sprinkling; *estar en infusión para una cosa,* to be about to obtain what one wishes.

infuso, -sa, *a.* infused (as the grace of God). — *p.p. irreg.* [INFUNDIR].

infusorio, -ria, *a.* infusorian. — *pl.* infusoria.

ingenerable, *a.* ingenerable.

ingeniar, *v.t.* to conceive, contrive, devise, work out. — *v.r.* to endeavour to find out;

to manage skilfully; to find means to obtain or do anything.

ingeniatura, *n.f.* (*coll.*) ingenuity, subtlety, acuteness, skilful management; (*Am.*) engineering.

ingeniería, *n.f.* engineering.

ingeniero, *n.m.* engineer; *ingeniero naval* (*de la armada* or *de marina*), naval engineer; *ingeniero militar*, military engineer; *ingeniero civil*, any engineer who is not a naval or military engineer; *ingeniero de caminos, canales y puertos*, civil engineer; *ingeniero agrónomo*, agricultural engineer; *ingeniero mecánico*, mechanical engineer; *ingeniero de minas*, mining engineer; *ingeniero químico* (or *industrial*), chemical engineer; *ingeniero de montes*, forest engineer; *ingeniero electricista*, electrical engineer; *ingeniero hidráulico*, hydraulic engineer.

ingenio, *n.m.* talent; mind, creative or inventive faculty; cleverness, skill, smartness; talented person, original genius; device, contrivance; engine, machine, mechanical apparatus; plough-cutter, plough-press, tool used by bookbinders; *ingenio de azúcar*, sugar-works, sugar-mill, sugar-plantation; *ingenio de pólvora*, powder-mill.

ingeniosamente, *adv.* ingeniously.

ingeniosidad, *n.f.* ingenuity, ingeniousness, invention.

ingenioso, -sa, *a.* clever, talented, ingenious, inventive; cleverly made.

ingénito, -ta, *a.* unbegotten; innate, inborn, ingenerate.

ingente, *a.* very large, huge, prodigious.

ingenuamente, *adv.* candidly, ingenuously.

ingenuidad, *n.f.* ingenuousness, candour, frankness, openness, open-heartedness.

ingenuo, -nua, *a.* ingenuous, open, fair, open-hearted, candid; (*law*) ingenuous, free-born.

ingerencia, *n.f.* interference, intermeddling.

ingeridor *n.m.* grafting-knife.

ingeridura, *n.f.* grafting, place of grafting.

ingerir, *v.t.* (*pres. indic.* **ingiero;** *pres. subj.* **ingiera**) to feed or inject orally; (*agric.*) to graft. — *v.r.* to interfere, intermeddle.

ingerto, -ta, *a.* grafted, ingrafted. — *p.p.* [INGERIR].

ingina, *n.f.* jaw-bone.

Inglaterra, *n.f.* England.

ingle, *n.f.* groin, part next the thigh.

inglés, -esa, *a.* English; *a la inglesa*, in the English fashion.

inglés, *n.m.* Englishman; the English language.

inglesa, *n.f.* English woman.

inglesar, *v.t.*, *v.r.* to anglicize.

inglesismo, *n.m.* anglicism.

inglete, *n.m.* diagonal; angle of 45°.

inglosable, *a.* admitting no gloss or comment.

ingobernable, *a.* ungovernable, unmanageable, unruly.

ingratamente, *adv.* ungratefully.

ingratitud, *n.f.* ingratitude; ungratefulness, unthankfulness.

ingrato, -ta, *a.* ungrateful, unthankful; thankless, ingrate; harsh, disagreeable, unpleasing.

ingrediente, *n.m.* ingredient.

ingresar, *v.i.* to enter; to come in (of money, etc.); to join, become a member.

ingreso, *n.m.* ingress, entrance; commencement; (*com.*) entry, money received; (*eccles.*) surplice-fees; *derecho de ingreso*, entrance fee. — *pl.* **ingresos,** revenue, receipts, earnings.

íngrimo, -ma, *a.* (*Am.*) entirely alone.

inguinal; inguinario, -ria, *a.* inguinal, belonging to the groin.

ingurgitación, *n.f.* ingurgitation; introduction of fluids by a tube.

ingurgitar, *v.t.* to ingurgitate, swallow. — *v.r.* to get filled (of a cavity).

ingustable, *a.* unsavoury, unpalatable, tasteless.

inhábil, *a.* unable, incapable, awkward, clumsy, incompetent; unfit, unskilful; unqualified, disqualified.

inhabilidad, *n.f.* inability, incompetency, incapacity, unskilfulness, unfitness.

inhabilitación, *n.f.* disabling, disqualifying; disqualification; disability.

inhabilitar, *v.t.* to disqualify; to disable, render unfit. — *v.r.* to lose a right; to become disabled.

inhabitable, *a.* uninhabitable.

inhabitado, -da, *a.* uninhabited.

inhabituado, -da, *a.* unhabituated, unaccustomed.

inhalación, *n.f.* inhalation.

inhalador, -ra, *a.* inhaler.

inhalar, *v.t.* to inhale.

inhartable, *a.* insatiable.

inherencia, *n.f.* inherence, inherency.

inherente, *a.* inherent.

inhestar, *v.t.* to erect, set upright.

inhibición, *n.f.* (*law*) inhibition, prohibition.

inhibir, *v.t.* (*law*) to inhibit, prohibit an inferior court from proceeding further.

inhibitorio, -ria, *a.* inhibitory, prohibitory.

inhiesto, -ta, *a.* steep.

inhonestamente, *adv.* immodestly, dishonestly.

inhonestidad, *n.f.* immodesty, indecency, dishonesty.

inhonesto, -ta, *a.* immodest, indecent, dishonest.

inhospedable; inhospitable; inhospital; inhospitalario, -ria, *a.* inhospitable, reluctant to entertain guests; (*fig.*) affording no shelter, desolate.

inhospitalidad, *n.f.* inhospitableness, want of courtesy to guests.

inhumanamente, *adv.* inhumanly.

inhumanidad, *n.f.* inhumanity, cruelty.

inhumano, -na, *a.* inhuman, savage, cruel.

inhumar, *v.t.* to bury, inhume, inter.

iniciación, *n.f.* initiation, introduction.

inicial, *a.* initial, elementary; *iniciales* or *letras iniciales*, initials.

iniciador, -ra, *a.* initiator, starter.

iniciar, *v.t.* to initiate; to commence, begin, start. — *v.r.* to be initiated; (*eccles.*) to receive first orders.

iniciativa, *n.f.* initiative, the right of proposing laws, etc.; *tomar la iniciativa*, to be first in doing or saying something.

iniciativo, -va, *a.* initiating, initiatory.

inicuamente, *adv.* iniquitously.

inicuo, -cua, *a.* iniquitous, wicked, unjust.

inimaginable, *a.* unimaginable, inconceivable.

inimicísimo, -ma, *a.* *superl.* very inimical.

inimitable, *a.* inimitable, above imitation or copying.

ininteligible, *a.* unintelligible.

iniquidad, *n.f.* iniquity, injustice, unrighteousness.

iniquísimo, -ma, *a. superl.* most iniquitous, wicked, unjust.

injertar, *v.t.* (*p.p.* injertado, injerto) to ingraft, graft, inoculate.

injertera, *n.f.* orchard of grafted trees.

injerto, *n.m.* graft, grafting, tree ingrafted. — *p.p. irreg.* [INJERTAR].

injuria, *n. f.* injury, offence, wrong, insult, outrage, affront; reproachful or contumelious language; annoyance, contumely, hardship, damage, mischief, harm; *aquél que dice injurias cerca está de perdonar,* he that hurls insults is ready to grant forgiveness.

injuriado, -da, *a.* injured, wronged. — *p.p.* [INJURAR].

injuriador, -ra, *n.m.f.* aggressor, injurer, wrongdoer.

injuriante, *a.* injuring, offending, injurer.

injuriar, *v.t.* to injure, insult, outrage, wrong, annoy, offend, harm, hurt.

injuriosamente, *adv.* injuriously, offensively, hurtfully.

injurioso, -sa, *a.* injurious, outrageous, offensive, insulting, opprobrious, hurtful.

injustamente, *adv.* unjustly

injusticia, *n.f.* injustice, iniquity, wrong.

injustificable, *a.* unjustifiable.

injustificadamente, *adv.* unjustifiably.

injustificado, -da, *a.* unjustified.

injusto, -ta, *a.* unjust, wrongful.

inlegible, *a.* illegible.

inllevable, *a.* insupportable, unbearable.

inmaculadamente, *adv.* immaculately.

inmaculado, -da, *a.* immaculate, holy, spotless, stainless, pure.

inmadurez, *n.f.* immaturity.

inmaleable, *a.* unmalleable.

inmanejable, *a.* unruly, unmanageable.

inmanente, *a.* immanent, inherent.

inmarcesible, *a.* unfading, unwithering.

inmaterial, *a.* immaterial, incorporeal.

inmaterialidad, *n.f.* immateriality.

inmaturo, -ra, *a.* immature.

inmediación, *n.f.* contiguity, contact. — *pl.* **inmediaciones,** environs, suburbs, outskirts.

inmediatamente, *adv.* contiguously; immediately, forthwith.

inmediato, -ta, *a.* contiguous, nigh, close, adjoining, hard by, next; *darle a uno por las inmediatas,* to give an unanswerable rejoinder; to hit a person's weakest (*or* sorest) spot; *llegar a las inmediatas,* to reach the vital point (*or* the hardest part) of a contest.

inmedicable, *a.* incurable, irremediable.

inmejorable, *a.* unimprovable, unsurpassable.

inmemorable, *a.* immemorable, immemorial.

inmemorablemente, *adv.* immemorably.

inmemorial, *a.* immemorial.

inmensamente, *adv.* immensely, infinitely, hugely.

inmensidad, *n.f.* immensity, vastness, unbounded greatness; infinity; great multitude or number.

inmenso, -sa, *a.* immense, unlimited, unbounded, infinite; countless.

inmensurable, *a.* immeasurable, measureless.

inmerecidamente, *adv.* undeservedly.

inmerecido, -da, *a.* unmerited, undeserved.

inmergir, *v.t.* (*neol.*) to submerge, souse; (*astron.*) to disappear in the shadow of or behind another heavenly body; [SUMERGIR].

inméritamente, *adv.* unmeritedly.

inmérito, -ta, *a.* undeserved, unmerited.

inmeritorio, -ria, *a.* immeritorious, undeserving.

inmersión, *n.f.* immersion.

inmigración, *n.f.* immigration.

inmigrante, *n.m.* immigrant.

inmigrar, *v.i.* to immigrate.

inminencia, *n.f.* imminence, nearness.

inminente, *a.* imminent, impending, near, at hand.

inmiscible, *a.* immiscible.

inmiscuir, *v.t.* to mix. — *v.r.* to interfere in, to intermeddle.

inmoble, *a.* unmovable, immovable, fixed, unaffected; motionless; constant, unshakable.

inmoderación, *n.f.* immoderation, immoderateness; excess.

inmoderadamente, *adv.* immoderately.

inmoderado, -da, *a.* immoderate, excessive.

inmodestamente, *adv.* immodestly.

inmodestia, *n.f.* immodesty, indecency, indelicacy.

inmodesto, -ta, *a.* immodest, indelicate.

inmolación, *n.f.* immolation, sacrifice.

inmolador, -ra, *n.m.f.* immolator.

inmolar, *v.t.* to immolate, sacrifice.

inmoral, *a.* immoral; licentious.

inmoralidad, *n.f.* immorality, licentiousness, vice, corruption.

inmorigerado, -da, *a.* not self-controlled, of bad habits.

inmortal, *a.* immortal; endless.

inmortalidad, *n.f.* immortality.

inmortalizar, *v.t.* to immortalize, perpetuate.

inmortalmente, *adv.* immortally.

inmortificación, *n.f.* immortification, licentiousness.

inmortificado, -da, *a.* unmortified.

inmotivado, -da, *a.* without reason or cause.

inmoto, -ta, *a.* motionless.

inmovible, *a.* immovable.

inmóvil, *a.* motionless; immovable, fixed, set; constant, unshaken.

inmovilidad, *n.f.* immobility, fixedness; firmness, constancy.

inmudable, *a.* immutable.

inmueble, *a.* (*law*) immovable (property). — *n.m.* (*law*) immovable.

inmundicia, *n.f.* filth, dirt, garbage; nastiness, filthiness, dirtiness; impurity, lewdness.

inmundo, -da, *a.* unclean, filthy, dirty; unchaste, obscene.

inmune, *a.* free, exempt; immune.

inmunidad, *n.f.* immunity, privilege, exemption, freedom, franchise; liberty.

inmunización, *n.f.* immunization.

inmunizar, *v.t.* to immunize.

inmutabilidad, *n.f.* immutability.

inmutable, *a.* immutable, unchangeable, invariable, unalterable.

inmutación, *n.f.* change, alteration.

inmutar, *v.t.* to change, alter. — *v.r.* to start, wince, flinch, lose one's calm.

inmutativo, -va, *a.* that which changes or causes alterations.

innato, -ta, *a.* innate, inborn, natural.

innavegable, *a.* innavigable, unseaworthy.

innecesario, -ria, *a.* unnecessary.

innegable, *a.* undeniable, incontestable, incontrovertible.

innoble, *a.* ignoble, of mean birth.

innocuo, -cua, *a.* innocuous, harmless.

innominado, -da, *a.* nameless; *hueso innominado,* innominate bone.

innovación, *n.f.* innovation.

innovador, -ra, *n.m.f.* innovator.

innovamiento, *n.m.* innovation.

innovar, *v.t.* to innovate.

innumerabilidad, *n.f.* innumerability, innumerableness.

innumerable, *a.* innumerable, numberless, countless.

innumerablemente, *adv.* innumerably.

innúmero, -ra, *a.* numberless, countless.

innutrición, *n.f.* want of nourishment.

inobediencia, *n.f.* disobedience.

inobediente, *a.* disobedient; unmanageable.

inobservable, *a.* unobservable, inobservable.

inobservancia, *n.f.* inadvertency, neglect, inobservance.

inobservante, *a.* inobservant.

inocencia, *n.f.* innocence, guilelessness; harmlessness, innocuousness; guiltless simplicity, sincerity, candour.

inocentada, *n.f.* (*coll.*) naïve or silly speech or action; booby trap, practical joke.

inocente, *a.* innocent, pure, candid; innocuous, harmless; guiltless; lamblike, simple, easily duped; *día de inocentes,* Holy Innocents' Day (28 Dec.).

inocentemente, *adv.* innocently, guiltlessly, harmlessly, innocuously.

inocentón, -ona, *a.* very simple and credulous.

inoculación, *n.f.* inoculation; vaccination.

inoculador, *n.m.* inoculator.

inocular, *v.t.* to inoculate; to contaminate, pervert.

inodoro, -ra, *a.* inodorous, odourless.

inodoro, *n.m.* deodorizer in water-closets.

inofensivo, -va, *a.* inoffensive.

inoficioso, -sa, *a.* (*law*) inofficious (will); (*Am.*) inefficient, useless.

inojeta, *n.f.* top of a boot.

inolvidable, *a.* unforgettable, not to be forgotten.

inoperable, *a.* (*med.*) inoperable.

inopia, *n.f.* indigence, poverty, penury.

inopinable, *a.* indisputable, incontrovertible, unthought of, unforeseeable.

inopinadamente, *adv.* unexpectedly.

inopinado, -da, *a.* unexpected, unforeseen.

inoportunamente, *adv.* inopportunely.

inoportunidad, *n.f.* inopportuneness, unseasonableness, inconvenience.

inoportuno, -na, *a.* inopportune.

inordenadamente, *adv.* inordinately.

inordenado, -da; inordinado, -da, *a.* inordinate, irregular, disorderly.

inorgánico, -ca, *a.* inorganic.

inoxidable, *a.* inoxidizable, rustless.

inquebrantable, *a.* inviolable, irrevocable.

inquietador, -ra, *n.m.f.* disturber.

inquietamente, *adv.* disquieted, uneasily.

inquietar, *v.t.* to disquiet, trouble, disturb; to molest, vex, tease, harass; to stir up or excite disturbances. — *v.r.* to become uneasy or restless, to fret, worry.

inquieto, -ta, *a.* restless, turbulent; noisy, troublesome, clamorous; anxious, solicitous, fidgety, uneasy, inquiet.

inquietud, *n.f.* inquietude, restlessness, uneasiness, vexation, anxiety.

inquilinato, *n.m.* lease, leasehold; *impuesto de inquilinato,* municipal rates.

inquilinaje, *n.m.* (*Chi.*) leasehold.

inquilino, -na, *n.m.f.* tenant, inmate, lodger; (*law*) lessee.

inquina, *n.f.* (*coll.*) aversion, hatred.

inquinamento, *n.m.* infection.

inquinar, *v.t.* to contaminate, pollute.

inquiridor, -ra, *n.m.f.* inquirer, inquisitor, investigator.

inquirir, *v.t.* (*pres. indic.* **inquiero;** *pres. subj.* **inquiera**) to inquire, look into, search, investigate, examine, explore.

inquisición, *n.f.* inquest, examination, inquiry; (*eccles.*) Inquisition; Holy Office.

inquisidor, -ra, *n.m.f.* inquirer, examiner.

inquisidor, *n.m.* (*eccles.*) inquisitor.

inquisitivo, -va, *a.* (*obs.*) inquisitive, curious.

inquisitorial, *a.* inquisitorial, inquisitorious.

insabible, *a.* that can never be known.

insaciabilidad, *n.f.* insatiableness, greediness.

insaciable, *a.* insatiable, greedy, craving.

insaciablemente, *adv.* insatiably.

insaculación, *n.f.* (*law*) balloting for names.

insaculador, *n.m.* (*law*) balloter.

insacular, *v.t.* to ballot, vote by ballot.

insalivación, *n.f.* insalivation.

insalivar, *v.t.* to insalivate, mix with saliva.

insalubre, *a.* insalubrious, unhealthy.

insalubridad, *n.f.* insalubrity, unhealthfulness.

insanable, *a.* incurable, irremediable.

insania, *n.f.* insanity.

insano, -na, *a.* insane, mad, crazy.

inscribir, *v.t.* (*p.p.* **inscrito, inscripto**) to inscribe, register, record, book; (*geom.*) to inscribe; (*law*) to record (deeds).

inscripción, *n.f.* inscription; record, register, entry; registration; government bond.

inscripto, -ta; inscrito, -ta, *p.p. irreg.* [INSCRIBIR].

insculpir, *v.t.* to engrave, sculpture.

insecable, *a.* (*coll.*) that cannot be dried, divided or cut.

insección, *n.f.* incision, cut, sharp wound.

insecticida, *n.f.* insecticide. — *a.* insecticidal.

insectil, *a.* insectile.

insectívoro, -ra, *a.* insectivorous.

insecto, *n.m.* insect.

insectólogo, -ga, *n.m.f.* entomologist.

inseguridad, *n.f.* insecurity, uncertainty.

inseguro, -ra, *a.* insecure, unsafe, uncertain, dubious.

insembrado, -da, *a.* unsowed, unsown.

insenescencia, *n.f.* quality of not becoming old, agelessness.

insensatamente, *adv.* madly, stupidly.

insensatez, *n.f.* nonsense, stupidity, folly.

insensato, -ta, *a.* insensate, nonsensical, meaningless; stupid, mad, fatuous.

insensibilidad, *n.f.* insensibility, unconsciousness; hard-heartedness.

insensible, *a.* insensible, senseless, unconscious; hard, callous, stupid; imperceptible, obdurate, unfeeling, cold-hearted, loveless.

insensiblemente, *adv.* insensibly.

inseparabilidad, *n.f.* inseparableness, inseparability.

inseparable, *a.* inseparable.
inseparablemente, *adv.* inseparably.
insepulto, -ta, *a.* unburied, uninterred, graveless.
inserción, *n.f.* insertion, engrafting.
inserir, *v.t.* to insert, graft.
insertar, *v.t.* (*p.p.* **insertado, inserto**) to insert, introduce. — *v.r.* (*zool., bot.*) to be inserted or attached.
inserto, -ta, *a.* inserted. — *p.p. irreg.* [INSERTAR].
inservible, *a.* unserviceable, useless.
insidia, *n.f.* ambush, snare, contrivance.
insidiador, -ra, *n.m.f.* plotter, waylayer.
insidiar, *v.t.* to plot against, waylay, ambush.
insidiosamente, *adv.* insidiously, guilefully.
insidioso, -sa, *a.* insidious, circumventive, sly, guileful.
insigne, *a.* notable, remarkable, flagrant, noted.
insignemente, *adv.* notably, signally, conspicuously.
insignia, *n.f.* decoration, device, medal, badge, standard; (*naut.*) pennant. — *pl.* insignia.
insignificación, insignificancia, *n.f.* insignificance.
insignificante, *a.* insignificant, unimportant.
insignificativo, -va, *a.* insignificant; insignificative.
insinceridad, *n.f.* insincerity, hypocrisy, deceit.
insinuación, *n.f.* insinuation, innuendo, hint, indirect suggestion; (*law*) exhibition of a public instrument before a judge; (*rhet.*) kind of exordium.
insinuante, *a.* insinuant, insinuating.
insinuar, *v.t.* to insinuate, hint, touch lightly on, suggest. — *v.r.* to insinuate, ingratiate, wheedle; to creep in, get in, steal into (the mind); to grow (on one, as a habit, etc.).
insípidamente, *adv.* insipidly, without taste, without spirit; dully.
insipidez, *n.f.* insipidity, insipidness.
insípido, -da, *a.* insipid, tasteless, unsavoury, spiritless, vapid, flat.
insipiencia, *n.f.* ignorance, lack of judgment, taste or knowledge.
insipiente, *a.* ignorant, uninformed, insipient.
insistencia, *n.f.* persistence, steadiness, constancy, obstinacy.
insistir, *v.i.* to insist on, persist in; to dwell upon.
ínsito, -ta, *a.* engrafted, inborn.
insociabilidad, *n.f.* unsociability, unsociableness.
insociable, insocial, *a.* unsociable.
insolación, *n.f.* sun-stroke, heat-stroke.
insolar, *v.t.* to insolate, to expose to the sun. — *v.r.* to become overheated in the sun.
insoldable, *a.* that cannot be soldered.
insolencia, *n.f.* insolence, impudence, pertness, effrontery, frowardness, barefacedness.
insolentar, *v.t.* to make bold. — *v.r.* to become insolent.
insolente, *n.m.f., a.* insolent, impudent, froward, haughty; (*obs.*) unusual, uncommon, unaccustomed; barefaced, shameless (person).
insolentemente, *adv.* insolently, haughtily, insultingly.
insólito, -ta, unusual, unaccustomed.
insolubilidad, *n.f.* insolubility.

insoluble, *a.* indissoluble, insoluble; fast, strong; unsolvable.
insolvencia, *n.f.* insolvency.
insolvente, *a.* insolvent.
insomne, *a.* insomnious, sleepless.
insomnio, *n.m.* insomnia, sleeplessness, watchfulness, wakefulness.
insondable, *a.* unfathomable, fathomless; inscrutable, unsearchable; abysmal.
insonoro, -ra, *a.* insonorous, not clear.
insoportable, *a.* insupportable, intolerable.
insostenible, *a.* indefensible.
inspección, *n.f.* inspection, survey; superintendence; control; inspector's office.
inspeccionar, *v.t.* to inspect, examine, oversee.
inspector, -ra, *n.m.f.* inspector, examiner; supervisor, superintendent, controller, overseer, surveyor.
inspiración, *n.f.* inspiration; (*med.*) inhalation.
inspirador, -ra, *n.m.f., a.* inspirer.
inspirante, *a.* inspiring.
inspirar, *v.t.* to inspire, inhale; to infuse into the mind, animate; to instil, infuse (an emotion in or into); (*poet.*) to blow.
inspirativo, -va, *a.* inspiratory.
instabilidad, *n.f.* instability, inconstancy, fickleness, mutability, giddiness, fragility.
instable, *a.* unstable, inconstant, changing, mutable, fickle.
instalación, *n.f.* installation, instalment; settling; induction (of a soldier); plant, works, factory; system (as of gas pipes, etc.); *instalación eléctrica,* electric plant; *instalación de gas,* gas-fittings.
instalar, *v.t.* to install, place, set up; (*law*) to install; to induct.
instancia, *n.f.* instance or instancy; memorial, petition; prosecution or process of a suit; pressing argument; *de primera instancia,* instantly, on the first impulse; in the first place, in the first instance.
instantáneamente, *adv.* instantly, instantaneously.
instantáneo, -nea, *a.* instantaneous. — *n.f.* snapshot.
instante, *a.* instant, urgent, pressing. — *n.m.* instant, moment; *al instante,* immediately; *por instantes,* incessantly, continually, at every moment.
instantemente, *adv.* instantly.
instar, *v.t.* to press, urge; to prove the fallacy of an argument in debate. — *v.i.* to be urgent, urge promptness.
instauración, *n.f.* instauration, restoration.
instaurar, *v.t.* to renew, re-establish, restore.
instaurativo, -va, *a.* restorative.
instigación, *n.f.* instigation, incitement, encouragement, impulse.
instigador, -ra, *n.m.f.* instigator, abetter.
instigar, *v.t.* (*pret.* **instigué;** *pres. subj.* **instigue**) to instigate, provoke, incite, urge.
instilación, *n.f.* instillation.
instilar, *v.t.* to instil; (*fig.*) infuse, insinuate.
instintivamente, *adv.* instinctively.
instintivo, -va, *a.* instinctive.
instinto, *n.m.* instinct, natural desire or tendency; divine inspiration, encouragement, impulse; *por instinto,* instinctively.
institución, *n.f.* institution, establishment, settlement; (*obs.*) education, instruction; collation or bestowal of a benefice; *institu-*

ción de crédito, (*com.*) bank. — *pl.* institutes of any science.

instituente, *a.* instituting; founding.

instituidor, -ra, *n.m.f.* institutor, founder.

instituir, *v.t.* (*pres. indic.* **instituyo**; *pres. subj.* **instituya**) to institute, establish, found; (*obs.*) to instruct, teach; to appoint, nominate; (*obs.*) to resolve, determine.

instituta, *n.f.* (*law*) the *Institutions* of Justinian.

instituto, *n.m.* institution, established law; institute; institution of learning; design, object, end; school; *instituto de segunda enseñanza* or *general y técnico*, high school; *instituto armado*, any armed body for the defence of country or established order.

institutor, -ra, *n.m.f.* institutor; professor, teacher.

institutriz, *n.f.* governess, instructress.

instituyente, *a.* institutor; founder.

instrucción, *n.f.* instruction, tuition, teaching; education; lesson; knowledge; lore, learning; (*law*) court proceedings; *instrucción primaria*, elementary education; *instrucción pública*, public education. — *pl.* **instrucciones**, instructions, directions, orders.

instructivamente, *adv.* instructively.

instructivo, -va, *a.* instructive.

instructor, *n.m.* instructor, teacher.

instructora, *n.f.* woman teacher.

instruir, *v.t.* (*pres. indic.* **instruyo**; *pres. subj.* **instruya**) to instruct, teach, train, coach; (*mil.*) to drill, train; to inform, report, advise; (*law*) to instruct, to model a cause according to established rules; to put in legal form.

instrumentación, *n.f.* instrumentation, orchestration.

instrumental, *a.* instrumental; (*law*) belonging to legal instruments; set of scientific implements for surgical operations; *causa instrumental*, (*law*) test case.

instrumentalmente, *adv.* instrumentally.

instrumentar, *v.t.* to orchestrate.

instrumentista, *n.m.f.* instrumentalist; maker of musical or surgical instruments, etc.

instrumento, *n.m.* instrument, tool, implement, appliance, utensil; engine, apparatus, machine; (*fig.*) agent or means of doing anything; (*law*) instrument, indenture, deed; *instrumento de cuerda*, stringed instrument; *instrumento de viento*, wind instrument; *instrumento de percusión*, percussion instrument.

insuave, *a.* unpleasant, disagreeable.

insubordinación, *n.f.* insubordination, disorder, rebelliousness.

insubordinado, -da, *a.* insubordinate, rebellious, resisting authority. — *p.p.* [INSUBORDINAR].

insubordinar, *v.t.* to incite to resist authority. — *v.r.* to rebel against authority.

insubsistencia, *n.f.* instability, inconstancy.

insubsistente, *a.* unable to subsist, instable; groundless, baseless.

insubstancial, *a.* unsubstantial, inane, pointless.

insubstancialidad, *n.f.* insubstantiality, inanity.

insubstancialmente, *adv.* insubstantially, inanely.

insudar, *v.i.* to toil, drudge, work hard.

insuficiencia, *n.f.* insufficiency, inadequateness.

insuficiente, *a.* insufficient, inadequate.

insuficientemente, *adv.* insufficiently.

insuflación, *n.f.* insufflation.

insuflar, *v.t.* to insufflate; to prompt, suggest.

insufrible, *a.* intolerable, insufferable, unbearable, insupportable.

insufriblemente, *adv.* insufferably.

ínsula, *n.f.* small isle, island; a petty state (allusion to Sancho Panza's government).

insular; **insulano, -na**, *a.* insular.

insulina, *n.f.* (*med.*) insulin.

insulsamente, *adv.* insipidly.

insulsez, *n.f.* insipidity, flatness, tastelessness.

insulso, -sa, *a.* insipid, tasteless; (*fig.*) dull, flat, cold, heavy.

insultada, *n.f.* (*Am.*) insult.

insultador, -ra, *n.m.f.*, *a.* insulter.

insultante, *a.* insulting, insulter.

insultar, *v.t.* to insult. — *v.r.* (*coll.*) to have a fit; meet with an accident.

insulto, *n.m.* insult, affront; outrage, assault; sudden fit of illness.

insumable, *a.* incalculable, innumerable.

insume, *a.* costly, expensive.

insumergible, *a.* unsinkable.

insumiso, -sa, *a.* disobedient, rebellious.

insuperable, *a.* insuperable, insurmountable.

insupurable, *a.* that cannot suppurate.

insurgente, *a.* insurgent. — *n.m.* rebel.

insurrección, *n.f.* insurrection, rebellion.

insurreccionar, *v.t.* to promote an insurrection. — *v.r.* to rebel.

insurrecto, -ta, *n.m.f.*, *a.* insurgent, rebel.

insustancial, *a.* unsubstantial, inane, pointless.

intáctil, *a.* intangible, intactible.

intacto, -ta, *a.* untouched, intact, whole, entire, unmingled, pure.

intachable, *a.* uncensurable, irreproachable, unexceptionable, blameless.

intangible, *a.* intangible; not to be touched.

integérrimo, -ma, *a.* upright, very sincere.

integración, *n.f.* integration.

integral, *a.* integral, whole.

integralmente, *adv.* integrally, wholly.

íntegramente, *adv.* entirely, wholly.

integrante, *a.* integral, integrant.

integrar, *v.t.* to integrate, make up a whole; (*com.*) to reimburse.

integridad, *n.f.* integrality, wholeness, completeness; confidence, honour, integrity, honesty, uprightness; virginity, maidenhead.

íntegro, -ra, *a.* integral, entire, complete; upright, candid, just, disinterested, honest.

integumento, *n.m.* integument; (*fig.*) disguise, fiction, fable.

intelección, *n.f.* intellection, act of understanding.

intelectiva, *n.f.* intellect, the power of understanding.

intelectivo, -va, *a.* intellective, having power to understand.

intelecto, *n.m.* intellect, understanding.

intelectual, *a.* intellectual, mental, ideal.

intelectualmente, *adv.* intellectually, mentally, ideally.

inteligencia, *n.f.* intellect, mind, spirit; intelligence, knowledge, comprehension, understanding, ability, skill, experience; sense, meaning; *en* (*la*) *inteligencia*, on the understanding, suppositively.

inteligenciado, -da, *a.* instructed, informed.

inteligente, *a.* intelligent, skilful, talented, learned, clever, knowing.
inteligibilidad, *n.f.* intelligibility, capacity for being understood.
inteligible, *a.* intelligible, perspicuous, conceivable.
inteligiblemente, *adv.* intelligibly.
intemperancia, *n.f.* intemperance, excess.
intemperante, *a.* intemperate.
intemperie, *n.f.* rough weather; *a la intemperie*, in the open air, outdoors, unsheltered.
intempesta, *a.* (*poet.*); *noche intempesta*, the dead of night.
intempestivamente, *adv.* unseasonably, inopportunely.
intempestivo, -va, *a.* unseasonable, inopportune.
intención, *n.f.* intention, design, purpose; viciousness of animals; meaning, mind, view; caution, discretion; *hombre de intención*, dissembler; *segunda intención*, afterthought, double meaning, double dealing; *cura de primera intención*, first aid to the injured.
intencionadamente, *adv.* designedly, intentionally.
intencionado, -da, *a.* inclined, disposed (gen. used with the adv. *bien*, well, *mal*, badly, *mejor*, better, or *peor*, worse).
intencional, *a.* intentional, designed.
intencionalmente, *adv.* intentionally.
intendencia, *n.f.* administration, management; place, employment, or district of an *intendente*.
intendenta, *n.f.* wife of an *intendente*.
intendente, *n.m.* intendant, sub-treasurer of the government; *intendente de marina*, commandant of a navy-yard.
intensamente, *adv.* intensively.
intensidad, *n.f.* intensity; vehemence.
intensión, *n.f.* intenseness, vehemence, ardency; earnestness.
intensivo, -va; intenso, -sa, *a.* intense, intensive, vehement, lively, ardent.
intentar, *v.t.* to try, attempt, endeavour; to intend, purpose, mean, design; (*law*) to enter an action, commence a lawsuit.
intento, *n.m.* intent, purpose, design; *de intento*, purposely, designedly, knowingly.
intentona, *n.f.* (*coll.*) rash attempt, ill-advised action.
inter, *adv.* meanwhile. — *n.m.* (*Per.*) substitute curate.
interandino, -na, *a.* relating to matters on both sides of the Andes.
intercadencia, *n.f.* unreliability, falling-off, unevenness, inconstancy; (*med.*) intermission or inequality of the pulse.
intercadente, *a.* changeable, variable.
intercadentemente, *adv.* changeably.
intercalación, *n.f.* intercalation, insertion.
intercalar, *a.* intercalary.
intercalar, *v.t.* to insert, intercalate.
intercambiable, *a.* interchangeable.
intercambio, *n.m.* interchange.
interceder, *v.i.* to intercede, mediate, entreat for another; to interpose, place between.
interceptación, *n.f.* interception, stoppage.
interceptar, *v.t.* to intercept, cut off, obstruct.
intercesión, *n.f.* intercession, mediation.
intercesor, -ra, *n.m.f.* intercessor, interceder.

intercesorio, -ria, *a.* intercessory.
interciso, -sa, *a.* cut by half, in the middle; *día interciso*, half-holiday.
interclusión, *n.f.* interclusion.
intercolumnio, *n.m.* intercolumniation.
intercontinental, *a.* intercontinental.
intercostal, *a.* (*anat.*) intercostal.
intercurrencia, *n.f.* (*path.*) intercurrence.
intercurrente, *a.* intercurrent, intervening.
intercutáneo, -nea, *a.* intercutaneous.
interdecir, *v.t.* (conjugated like DECIR) to interdict, prohibit.
interdental, *a.* interdental.
interdicción, *n.f.* interdiction, prohibition; interdict.
interdicto, *n.m.* prohibition, interdiction; (*law*) judgment of summary possession.
interdigital, *a.* interdigital.
interés, *n.m.* interest, gain, profit; share, concern, concernment, advantage; attraction, desire, inclination, inducement; (*com.*) interest, premium, money paid for the use of money; (*poet.*) pathos, dramatic interest; *interés compuesto*, compound interest; *dar a interés*, to put at interest; *llevar interés*, to bear interest; *por interés*, *lo más feo hermoso es*, self-interest throws all things awry. — *pl.* **intereses**, money matters, business affairs; *intereses creados*, vested interests.
interesable, *a.* avaricious, mercenary.
interesado, -da, *a.* interested, concerned; selfish, avaricious, mercenary. — *n.m.f.* associate, partner. — *p.p.* [INTERESAR].
interesante, *a.* interesting, attractive, convenient, useful; *estado interesante*, (*coll.*) pregnancy.
interesar, *v.i.*, *v.r.* to be concerned or interested in. — *v.t.* to invest; to give an interest; to interest, concern, attract.
interesencia, *n.f.* presence, attendance.
interesente, *a.* present; concurring.
interesillo, *n.m.* slight interest.
interestelar, *a.* interstellar, intersideral.
interfecto, -ta, *n.m.f.* (*law*) victim (of murder).
interferencia, *n.f.* (*phys.*) interference.
interfoliar, *v.t.* to interleave (a book).
ínterin, *n.m.* interim, office pro tempore; *en el ínterin*, in the meantime. — *adv.* meanwhile.
interinamente, *adv.* in the interim, meantime, provisionally, pro tem.
interinato, *n.m.* (*Arg., Chi.*) [INTERINIDAD].
interinidad, *n.f.* interim; temporary post.
interino, -na, *a.* provisional, temporary; pro tempore.
interior, *a.* interior, internal, inward, inside, inner. — *n.m.* the inside, inner part, interior; mind, soul; middle compartment of coaches which have three. — *pl.* **interiores**, entrails, intestines.
interioridad, *n.f.* inside, inward part; act of concealment. — *pl.* **interioridades**, family secrets.
interiormente, *adv.* internally, inwardly, interiorly.
interjección, *n.f.* (*gram.*) interjection.
interlínea, *n.f.* (*print.*) lead, space, line.
interlineación, *n.f.* interlineation; (*print.*) leading.
interlineal, *a.* interlineal.
interlinear, *v.t.* to write between lines; (*print.*) to lead, to space.

interlocución, *n.f.* interlocution, dialogue, interchange of speech.

interlocutor, -ra, *n.m.f.* interlocutor; speaker; collocutor, colloquist.

interlocutoriamente, *adv.* (*law*) intermediately.

interlocutorio, -ria, *a.* (*law*) interlocutory, intermediate.

intérlope, *a.* interloping.

interludio, *n.m.* (*mus.*) interlude.

interlunio, *n.m.* interlunar period.

intermaxilar, *a.* intermaxillary.

intermediar, *v.t.* to interpose, mediate, come between, be in the middle.

intermediario, -ria, *n.m.f.* (*law*) mediator, intermediary; middleman. — *a.* intermediary.

intermedio, -dia, *a.* intermediate, intervening, interposed.

intermedio, *n.m.* interval, intermedium; interim; intermission; (*theat.*) farce, interlude.

interminable, *a.* interminable, endless.

intermisión, *n.f.* intermission, interruption, forbearance.

intermitencia, *n.f.* (*med.*) intermission.

intermitente, *a.* intermittent.

intermitir, *v.t.* to intermit, discontinue.

internación, *n.f.* importation; *derechos de internación,* importation duties.

internacional, *a.* international; *derecho internacional,* international law.

internacionalismo, *n.m.* internationalism.

internacionalista, *n.m.f.,* *a.* internationalist.

internacionalizar, *v.t.* to internationalize.

internado, -da, *n.m.f.* boarding-school system; state of being a boarder; body of boarders.

internamente, *adv.* internally.

internar, *v.t.* to penetrate into the interior of a country. — *v.i.* to pierce, go through. — *v.r.* to insinuate, probe; to go deeply into (a subject); to worm oneself into another's confidence.

interno, -na, *a.* interior, internal, inward. — *n.m.f.* boarder, resident pupil.

internodio, *n.m.* (*bot.*) internode.

internuncio, *n.m.* spokesman; interlocutor; (*eccles.*) internuncio.

interpelación, *n.f.* interpellation, summons.

interpelar, *v.t.* to appeal to, implore the aid of; to interpellate; (*law*) to summon, cite.

interplanetario, -ria, *a.* interplanetary.

interpolación, *n.f.* interpolation.

interpoladamente, *adv.* in an interpolating manner.

interpolar, *v.t.* to interpolate, intermix, intermit; to interpose, interrupt; to stop or pause briefly in (address, etc.).

interponer, *v.t.* (conjugated like PONER) to interpose, place between; (*law*) to present a petition to a court; to appoint as a mediator. — *v.r.* to go between, interpose.

interposición, *n.f.* interposition, interference, mediation, meddling.

interprender, *v.t.* (*mil.*) to take by surprise.

interpresa, *n.f.* (*mil.*) taking by surprise.

interpretable, *a.* interpretable.

interpretación, *n.f.* interpretation, translation, explanation, elucidation, exposition, commentary, construction, deciphering; *interpretación de lenguas,* translation bureau in the State Department of Spain.

interpretador, -ra, *n.m.f.* interpreter, translator.

interpretante, *a.* interpreting. — *n.m.f.* translator.

interpretar, *v.t.* to interpret, explain, translate, expound, decipher, construe; (*theat.*) to act a part; to attribute, understand in a special sense.

interpretativamente, *adv.* interpretatively.

interpretativo, -va, *a.* interpretative.

intérprete, *n.m.f.* interpreter, expounder, translator; indication, sign.

interpuesto, -ta, *a.* interposed, intervening, placed between, mediate. — *p.p. irreg.* [INTERPONER].

interregno, *n.m.* interreign, interregnum.

interrogación, *n.f.* interrogation, question, inquiry; (*print.*) question mark.

interrogante, *a.* interrogative; mark of interrogation. — *n.m.f.* interrogator; *punto interrogante,* question mark.

interrogar, *v.t.* (*pret.* **interrogué**; *pres. subj.* **interrogue**) to question, interrogate.

interrogativamente, *adv.* interrogatively.

interrogativo, -va, *a.* interrogative.

interrogatorio, *n.m.* interrogatory; crossexamination.

interrumpidamente, *adv.* interruptedly.

interrumpido, -da, *a.* interrupted, broken. — *p.p.* [INTERRUMPIR].

interrumpir, *v.t.* to interrupt, hinder, obstruct, shut off, cut off, cut short, discontinue, break.

interrupción, *n.f.* interruption, interpellation, discontinuance, obstruction, stoppage, check, break, hindrance.

interruptor, *n.m.* (*elect.*) switch, interrupter; circuit-breaker; *interruptor bipolar,* two-pole switch; *interruptor de aceite,* oil-break switch; *interruptor de dos (tres) direcciones,* two- (three-) way switch.

intersecarse, *v. rec.* (*geom.*) to intersect one another.

intersección, *n.f.* (*geom.*) intersection.

intersideral, *a.* interstellar.

intersticio, *n.m.* interstice; interval; (*eccles.*) obligatory lapse of time between the reception of two orders in the priestly office.

intertropical, *a.* intertropical.

interusurio, *n.m.* interest allowed to a woman for the delay in repaying or returning her marriage dowry.

intervalo, *n.m.* interval, stretch, interlapse; *claro (or lúcido) intervalo,* remission of madness, lucid intervals.

intervención, *n.f.* intervention, supervision, superintendence, mediation, interposition; auditing accounts; (*law*) intervention.

intervenir, *v.i.* to intervene, mediate, intermediate; to occur, happen. — *v.t.* to audit accounts; to offer to pay a draft or a promissory note for a third party; to control, regulate; to supervise, superintend; (*surg.*) to operate, perform an operation.

interventor, -ra, *n.m.f.* comptroller, supervisor, inspector, superintendent, auditor.

intervertebral, *a.* invertebral.

intervocálico, -ca, *a.* intervocalic, occurring between vowels.

interyacente, *a.* interjacent, intervening, lying between.

intestado, -da, *a.* intestate.

intestinal, *a.* intestinal.
intestino, -na, *a.* intestine, internal; civil, domestic.
intestino, *n.m.* intestine; gut; bowels.
íntima, intimación, *n.f.* intimation, hint.
intimamente, *adv.* intimately.
intimar, *v.t.* to intimate, indicate, make known, suggest, hint. — *v.r.* to pierce, penetrate; to gain the affections, insinuate oneself, become intimate.
intimatorio, -ria, *a.* (*law*) intimating.
intimidación, *n.f.* intimidation.
intimidad, *n.f.* intimacy, inwardness, close friendship, familiarity or connexion.
intimidar, *v.t.* to intimidate, daunt, frighten.
íntimo, -ma, *a.* internal, innermost; intimate, familiar, conversant, closely acquainted.
intitular, *v.t.* to prefix a title to a book or writing, to entitle; to confer a title. — *v.r.* to use a title.
intitulata, *n.f.* title prefixed to a book or other writing.
intocable, *a.* untouchable.
intolerabilidad, *n.f.* intolerableness.
intolerable, *a.* intolerable, insufferable.
intolerancia, *n.f.* intolerance.
intolerante, *a.* intolerant.
intonso, -sa, *a.* (*poet.*) unshorn; ignorant, unpolished; (book) bound with uncut leaves.
intorsión, *n.f.* (*bot.*) intortion.
intoxicación, *n.f.* poisoning, intoxication.
intoxicar, *v.t.* (*pret.* **intoxiqué;** *pres. subj.* **intoxique**) (*med.*) to poison.
intradós, *n.m.* (*arch.*) intrados.
intraducible, *a.* untranslatable.
intramuros, *adv.* within the city, within the walls.
intranquilo, -la, *a.* uneasy, restless.
intransferible, *a.* not transferable.
intransigente, *a.* intransigent, irreconcilable.
intransitable, *a.* impassable, impenetrable.
intransitivo, -va, *a.* (*gram.*) intransitive.
intransmisible, *a.* untransmissible.
intransmutabilidad, *n.f.* intransmutability.
intransmutable, *a.* intransmutable.
intratable, *a.* intractable, ungovernable, unruly, unmanageable; unsociable, rude; impassable.
intrépidamente, *adv.* intrepidly, fearlessly.
intrepidez, *n.f.* intrepidity, courage, boldness, dauntlessness, fearlessness, hardiness, temerity.
intrépido, -da, *a.* intrepid, daring, fearless, dauntless, courageous, gallant, hardy.
intriga, *n.f.* intrigue; entanglement, embroilment; (complicated) plot of a play.
intrigante, *n.m.* intriguer.
intrigar, *v.i.* (*pret.* **intrigué;** *pres. subj.* **intrigue**) to intrigue, plot, scheme. — *v.t.* to perplex, puzzle, make anxious.
intrincable, *a.* intricate, perplexed, easily entangled.
intrincación, *n.f.* intricacy.
intrincadamente, *adv.* intricately.
intrincado, -da, *a.* intricate, entangled, knotty, perplexed, obscure. — *p.p.* [INTRINCAR].
intrincamiento, *n.m.* intricacy.
intrincar, *v.t.* (*pret.* **intrinqué;** *pres. subj.* **intrinque**) to perplex, entangle, involve, knot, obscure, confound.
intríngulis, *n.m.* (*coll.*) crafty intention, hidden motive; mystery, enigma.

intrínsecamente, *adv.* intrinsically, essentially.
intrínseco, -ca, *a.* intrinsic, intrinsical, essential, internal.
introducción, *n.f.* introduction, access, intercourse; preface, foreword to a book; (*mus.*) introduction.
introducir, *v.t.* (*pres. indic.* **introduzco;** *pret.* **introduje;** *pres. subj.* **introduzca**) to introduce, put in, conduct, usher in, thrust, insert; to make known, bring to notice; to start; to present (a person). — *v.r.* to insinuate; to find one's way, get into; to interfere.
introductivo, -va, *a.* introductory, introductive.
introductor, -ra, *n.m.f.* introducer; introductor.
introductorio, -ria, *a.* (*law*) introductory.
introito, *n.m.* beginning of an oration; (*eccles.*) introit; (*theat.*) prologue.
intromisión, *n.f.* intromission, insertion; intermeddling.
introversión, *n.f.* introversion.
introverso, -sa, *a.* introverted, self-contemplating.
intrusamente, *adv.* intrusively.
intrusarse, *v.r.* to obtrude, intrude.
intrusión, *n.f.* intrusion, obtrusion.
intruso, -sa, *a.* intruded, intrusive, obtrusive.
intruso, *n.m.* intruder, obtruder, squatter.
intubación. *n.f.* (*med.*) intubation, tracheotomy.
intuición, *n.f.* intuition.
intuitivamente, *adv.* intuitively.
intuitivo, -va, *a.* intuitive, evident.
intuito, *n.m.* view, look, glance; *por intuito,* (*adv.*) in consideration *or* by reason of.
intumescencia, *n.f.* intumescence, swelling.
intumescente, *a.* intumescent, swollen.
intususcepción, *n.f.* (*med.*) intussusception.
inulto, -ta, *a.* (*poet.*) unrevenged, unpunished.
inundación, *n.f.* inundation, overflow, flood, deluge; confluence; multitude.
inundante, *a.* inundating; inundant.
inundar, *v.t.* to inundate, overflow, deluge, flood; to overrun with numbers.
inurbanamente, *adv.* incivilly, uncivilly.
inurbanidad, *n.f.* incivility, inurbanity.
inurbano, -na, *a.* uncivil, rude, unpolished, inurbane.
inusitadamente, *adv.* unusually.
inusitado, -da, *a.* unusual, not now in use.
inútil, *a.* useless, unserviceable, inutile, frivolous, fruitless, unnecessary, needless, idle.
inutilidad, *n.f.* inutility, uselessness, unprofitableness, needlessness.
inutilizar, *v.t.* (*pret.* **inutilicé;** *pres. subj.* **inutilice**) to render useless; to disable, spoil.
inútilmente, *adv.* uselessly, idly.
invadeable, *a.* unfordable.
invadir, *v.t.* to invade; to encroach upon.
invaginación, *n.f.* (*med.*) invagination.
invaginar, *v.t.* to invaginate.
invalidación, *n.f.* invalidation, invalidity.
inválidamente, *adv.* invalidly.
invalidar, *v.t.* to invalidate, nullify, irritate, deprive of force or efficiency.
inválido, -da, *a.* invalid; crippled; feeble, forceless, weak; null, void.
inválido, *n.m.* (*mil.*) invalid; *conceder inválidos,* to give pensions to veteran soldiers.
invariabilidad, *n.f.* invariability.

invariable, *a.* invariable, constant.
invariablemente, *adv.* invariably.
invariación, *n.f.* immutability, invariableness.
invariadamente, *adv.* unvariedly.
invariado, -da, *a.* unvaried, constant.
invasión, *n.f.* invasion, inroad, attack.
invasor, -ra, *n.m.f.* invader.
invectiva, *n.f.* invective, harsh censure.
invencible, *a.* invincible, insuperable, unconquerable.
invenciblemente, *adv.* invincibly.
invención, *n.f.* invention, discovery, finding, contrivance, fiction, artifice; *hacer invenciones*, to make wry faces; *vivir de invenciones*, to live by trickery; *invención de la Santa Cruz*, feast of the Invention of the Cross (3 May).
invencionero, -ra, *n.m.f.* inventor; plotter; trifler, trickster; gesticulator, mimic; boaster.
invendible, *a.* unsaleable, unmarketable.
inventar, *v.t.* to invent, discover, find out, excogitate; to concoct, contrive, fabricate.
inventariar, *v.t.* to inventory, register; to commemorate a person's doings.
inventario, *n.m.* inventory, catalogue, stock.
inventiva, *n.f.* inventiveness; creativeness.
inventivo, -va, *a.* inventive, quick at contrivances or expedients.
invento, *n.m.* invention, discovery.
inventor, -ra, *n.m.f.* inventor, framer, contriver; fibber, story-teller, fabricator.
inverecundo, -da, *a.* shameless, impudent.
inverisímil, *a.* unlikely, improbable.
inverisimilitud, *n.f.* improbability, unlikelihood.
invernáculo, *n.m.* green-house, hot-house, conservatory.
invernada, *n.f.* winter season.
invernadero, *n.m.* winter-quarters; hot-house, conservatory.
invernal, *a.* hibernal, wintry.
invernar, *v.i.* (*pres. indic.* **invierno**; *pres. subj.* **invierne**) to winter.
invernizo, -za, *a.* winterly, hibernal.
inverosímil, *a.* unlikely, improbable.
inverosimilitud, *n.f.* improbability, unlikelihood.
inversamente, *adv.* inversely; contrariwise.
inversión, *n.f.* inversion; (*com.*) investment.
inverso, -sa, *a.* inverse, inverted. — *p.p. irreg.* [INVERTIR]; *a* (or *por*) *la inversa*, the other way round, contrariwise.
invertebrado, -da, *a.* invertebrate. — *n.m.pl.* the invertebrata.
invertir, *v.t.* (*p.p.* **invertido, inverso**; *pres. part.* **invirtiendo**; *pres. indic.* **invierto**; *pret.* él **invirtió**; *pres. subj.* **invierta**) to invert, reverse; (*com.*) to invest.
investidura, *n.f.* investiture.
investigable, *a.* investigable.
investigación, *n.f.* investigation, research; inquest.
investigador, -ra, *n.m.f.* investigator.
investigar, *v.t.* (*pret.* **investigué**; *pres. subj.* **investigue**) to investigate, ascertain, examine, inquire, research.
investir, *v.t.* to invest, confer.
inveteradamente, *adv.* inveterately.
inveterado, -da, *a.* inveterate, old, chronic, obstinate. — *p.p.* [INVETERARSE].
inveterarse, *v.r.* to become antiquated, old, chronic.
invictamente, *adv.* unconquerably, valiantly.

invicto, -ta, *a.* invincible, unconquered.
invierno, *n.m.* winter; rainy season (in the tropics).
invigilar, *v.i.* to watch carefully.
inviolabilidad, *n.f.* inviolability, inviolableness.
inviolable, *a.* inviolable; inviolate.
inviolablemente, *adv.* inviolably; infallibly.
inviolado, -da, *a.* inviolate, unhurt, uninjured.
invisibilidad, *n.f.* invisibility.
invisible, *a.* invisible; *en un invisible*, (*coll.*) in less than no time.
invisiblemente, *adv.* invisibly.
invitación, *n.f.* invitation.
invitador, -ra, *n.m.f.* inviter, one who invites.
invitar, *v.t.* to invite; to excite, stimulate, entice; to treat.
invitatorio, *n.m.* (*eccles.*) invitatory.
invocación, *n.f.* invocation.
invocador, -ra, *n.m.f.* invoker.
invocar, *v.t.* (*pret.* **invoqué**; *pres. subj.* **invoque**) to invoke, implore.
invocatorio, -ria, *a.* invocatory.
involución, *n.f.* involution.
involucrar, *v.t.* to introduce as a digression; to wrap up, cover, involve; to introduce foreign matter; to mingle, upset, confuse.
involucro, *n.m.* (*bot.*) involucre.
involuntariamente, *adv.* involuntarily.
involuntariedad, *n.f.* involuntariness.
involuntario, -ria, *a.* involuntary.
involuta, *n.f.* (*arch.*) volute.
invulnerabilidad, *n.f.* invulnerability.
invulnerable, *a.* invulnerable.
inyección, *n.f.* injection; liquid injected.
inyectar, *v.t.* to inject.
inyector, *n.m.* (*mech.*) injector.
ion, *n.m.* (*chem.*) ion.
ipecacuana, *n.f.* ipecacuanha; *ipecacuana de las Antillas*, wild ipecac.
ipil, *n.m.* (*Cent. Am.*) outer garment worn by half-breed women; (*Philip.*) hardwood tree.
ir, *v.i.* (*pres. part.* **yendo**; *p.p.* **ido**; *pres. indic.* **voy**; *imperf.* **iba**; *pret.* **fuí**; *pres. subj.* **vaya**) to go, move, walk; to fit, suit, be becoming; to consist, depend on, to bet, lay a wager; to import, concern, interest, affect, involve; to differ; be distant; to conduct, lead; to act, proceed; (with *pres. part.*) to become, grow; (with *past part.*) to be (*passive sense*); (with *por*) to go to look for; (with *contra* or *fuera de*) to persevere in, act in a contrary manner to. — *v.r.* to go, go away, go off, leave, depart; to exhale, evaporate; to ooze, leak; to break to pieces; to grow old; to discharge wind; *ir con tiento*, to go softly; *ir a pie*, to walk; *ir a caballo*, to ride on horseback; *ir a medias*, to go halves; *ir en coche*, to drive; *ir en alcance*, (*print.*) to divide the copy for setting; *ir adelante*, to go on, go forward; *ir en demanda de*, to be on the look-out for; *van cinco duros a que llego antes*, I bet you I get there first; *nada me va en ello*, it is no concern of mine; *ir agua arriba* (or *ir contra la corriente*), to go up stream; *ir por justicia*, to go to law; *ir chitacallando* (or *a puntillas*), to go upon tiptoe; *ir de máscara*, to wear a mask; *ir mejorando*, to be recovering little by little; *ir en pos de*, to follow; *ir a campo travieso* (or *traviesa*), to take a short cut; *ir al amor del agua*, (*fig.*) to swim with the tide; *ir (por) delante*, to go ahead; *ir a una*, to act with

one accord (*or* in unity); *ir de capa caída*, to be crestfallen; *ir de manga*, to conspire; *ir de campo*, to go for a picnic; *ir con espigón*, to retire in indignation; *a gran ir*, (or *a más ir*), at the greatest speed; *ir* (or *irse*) *a pique* (or *por ojo*), (*naut.*) to founder; *ir separadamente*, to go asunder; *ir sobre seguro*, to go upon sure grounds; *ir tras la corriente*, to go down stream; *se mete en lo que no le va*, he meddles in what does not concern him; *¿quién va allá?* who goes there? *vaya Vd. con Dios*, farewell; *vaya Vd. a paseo*, (*coll.*) get along with you; *¡vaya!* come, come! stop now; dear me!, to be sure!; *allá se va*, it's all the same; *ni va ni viene*, he has no mind of his own; *vaya Vd. al cielo* (or *al rollo*), go to Jericho; *mucho va de Pedro a Pedro*, no two men are alike; *a donde fueres, haz lo que vieres*, in Rome do as the Romans do; *por la calle de 'después' se va a la casa de 'nunca,'* procrastination is the thief of time; *írsele a uno el alma por una cosa*, to long for something; *írsele a uno la mula*, to speak carelessly or without reflection; *irse de boca*, to speak thoughtlessly; *no hay que irse atrás*, you mustn't flinch (*or* look back); *irse los ojos tras de alguien* (*or algo*), to gaze longingly at someone (*or* something); *irse a la mano*, to restrain oneself; *irse a leva y monte*, to escape, retire; *irse con Dios* (or *con la madre de Dios*), to absent oneself; *írsele a uno la cabeza*, (*fig.*) to lose one's head; *irse por sus pies*, to escape, run away; *írsele a uno la lengua*, to give rein to one's tongue; *irse los pies*, to stumble, slip; *irse de la memoria*, to escape one's memory.

ira, *n.f.* ire, anger, passion, indignation, wrath, choler, fury, rage; violence of the elements; *¡ira de Dios!* Lord deliver us! *a ira de Dios no hay cosa fuerte*, nothing can withstand the wrath of God; *ira de hermanos, ira de diablos*, no quarrels are so fierce as those between brothers.

iracundia, *n.f.* irascibility, ire, irascibleness.

iracundo, -da, *a.* passionate, ireful; (*poet.*) enraged, furious (the elements).

iranio, -nia, *a.* Iranian.

irascible, *a.* irascible, choleric, impetuous.

iribú, *n.m.* (*Arg.*) bird of prey.

iridáceo, -cea, *a.* iridaceous, iris-like.

íride, *n.f.* (*bot.*) iris.

irídeo, -dea, *a.* irideous.

iridio, *n.m.* iridium.

iridiscente, *a.* iridescent, rainbow-hued.

iris, *n.m.* iris, rainbow; (*opt.*) iris; *iris de paz*, mediator, peace-maker; (*min.*) opal; prism.

irisado, -da, *a.* rainbow-hued.

irisar, *v.i.* to iridesce.

Irlanda, *n.f.* Ireland.

irlanda, *n.f.* cotton and woollen cloth; fine Irish linen.

irlandés, -esa, *a.* Irish. — *n.m.* Irishman; Irish language. — *n.f.* Irish woman.

ironía, *n.f.* (*rhet.*) irony.

irónicamente, *adv.* ironically.

irónico, -ca, *a.* ironical.

iroqués, -esa, *a.* Iroquois.

irupé, *n.m.* (*Arg., Bol.*) a plant.

irracional, *a.* irrational, absurd; (*math.*) irrational. — *n.m.* brute, animal.

irracionalidad, *n.f.* irrationality, absurdity.

irracionalmente, *adv.* irrationally, absurdly.

irradiación, *n.f.* irradiation, radiation, irradiance, illumination, intellectual light.

irradiar, *v.t.* to irradiate, illuminate, emit beams of light.

irrazonable, *a.* unreasonable.

irrealizable, *a.* unrealizable.

irrebatible, *a.* indisputable.

irreconciliable, *a.* irreconcilable.

irreconciliablemente, *adv.* irreconcilably.

irrecuperable, *a.* irrecoverable, irretrievable.

irrecusable, *a.* unimpeachable.

irredento, -ta, *a.* irredent.

irredentista, *n.m.f.* irredentist.

irredimible, *a.* irredeemable.

irreducible, *a.* irreducible; stubborn, obstinate.

irreflexión, *n.f.* rashness, indiscretion.

irreflexivo, -va, *a.* inconsiderate, indiscreet, unreflecting.

irreformable, *a.* not to be reformed or reclaimed.

irrefragable, *a.* irrefragable, irrefutable.

irrefragablemente, *adv.* irrefragably.

irrefrenable, *a.* unmanageable.

irregular, *a.* irregular, abnormal, disorderly, unmethodical.

irregularidad, *n.f.* irregularity, unevenness, misgovernment, disorder, abnormality.

irregularmente, *adv.* irregularly.

irreligión, *n.f.* irreligion, impiety, unbelief.

irreligiosamente, *adv.* irreligiously.

irreligiosidad, *n.f.* irreligiousness, impiety.

irreligioso, -sa, *a.* irreligious, impious.

irremediable, *a.* irremediable, incurable: helpless.

irremediablemente, *adv.* irremediably, helplessly, irrecoverably.

irremisible, *a.* irremissible, unpardonable.

irremisiblemente, *adv.* unpardonably, irremissibly.

irremunerado, -da, *a.* unremunerated.

irreparable, *a.* irreparable, irretrievable.

irreparablemente, *adv.* irreparably, irretrievably, irrecoverably.

irreprensible, *a.* irreprehensible, irreproachable, irreprovable.

irreprensiblemente, *adv.* irreprehensibly, irreproachably.

irresistible, *a.* irresistible.

irresistiblemente, *adv.* irresistibly.

irresoluble, *a.* indeterminable, indissoluble; irresolute, inconstant.

irresolución, *n.f.* irresolution, hesitation, want of firmness.

irresolutamente, *adv.* irresolutely.

irresoluto, -ta; irresuelto, -ta, *a.* irresolute, hesitating, wavering.

irrespetuoso, -sa, *a.* disrespectful.

irrespirable, *a.* irrespirable, not fit to be breathed.

irresponsabilidad, *n.f.* irresponsibility.

irresponsable, *a.* irresponsible.

irreverencia, *n.f.* irreverence, disrespect.

irreverente, *a.* irreverent.

irreverentemente, *adv.* irreverently.

irrevocabilidad, *n.f.* irrevocability.

irrevocable, *a.* irrevocable, irreversible.

irrevocablemente, *adv.* irrevocably.

irrigación, *n.f.* (*med.*) irrigation.

irrigador, *n.m.* (*med.*) irrigator.

irrigar, *v.t.* (*med.*) to irrigate.

irrisible, *a.* risible, laughable.

irrisión, *n.f.* derision; ridicule, mockery.
irrisoriamente, *adv.* laughingly, derisively.
irrisorio, -ria, *a.* derisive, risible.
irritabilidad, *n.f.* irritability.
irritable, *a.* irritable, easily provoked; (*law*) that can be annulled.
irritación, *n.f.* irritation, commotion, agitation; (*law*) invalidation, abrogation.
irritador, -ra, *n.m.f.* irritator, stimulator.
irritamente, *adv.* (*law*) invalidly, vainly.
irritamiento, *n.m.* irritation, anger, agitation.
irritante, *a.* irritative, irritant, stimulating; (*law*) annulling or making void.
irritante, *n.m.* (*med.*) stimulant, irritant.
irritar, *v.t.* to irritate, exasperate, nettle, offend, anger; (*med.*) to irritate; (*law*) to annul, render void.
írrito, -ta, *a.* (*law*) null, void.
irrogar, *v.t.* (*pret.* **irrogué;** *pres. subj.* **irrogue**) to cause to occasion (damage).
irrompible, *a.* unbreakable.
irruir, *v.t.* to invade, enter by force; to assail.
irrumpir, *v.i.* to burst in; to invade suddenly.
irrupción, *n.f.* irruption, inroad, invasion.
Isabel, *n.f.* Elizabeth.
isabelino, -na, *a.* stamped with the bust of Isabella II (*coin*). — *n.m.f.,* *a.* partisan of Queen Isabella; concerning any of the queens of Spain or England bearing the name of Isabel (Elizabeth); light bay (horse).
isagoge, *n.f.* introduction, exordium.
isagógico, -ca, *a.* isagogic, introductive, introductory.
isatis, *n.m.* the Arctic fox (*Alopex lagopus*).
iscofonía, *n.f.* (*med.*) defect of the voice.
isla, *n.f.* isle, island; block (of houses); *en isla,* insulated.—*Isla de Francia,* Mauritius; *Isla de Pascua,* Easter Island; *Islas Baleares,* Balearic Islands; *Islas de Barlovento,* Windward Islands; *Islas Malvinas,* Falkland Islands; *Islas Vírgenes,* Virgin Islands.
islam, *n.m.* Islam.
islámico, -ca, *a.* Islamic.
islamismo, *n.m.* Mohammedanism.
islán, *n.m.* ancient lace veil.
islandés, -esa; islándico, -ca, *a.* Icelandic.
Islandia, *n.f.* Iceland.
isleño, -ña, *n.m.f.* islander; (*Cub.*) native of the Canary Islands.
isleo, *n.m.* small island.
isleta, -ita, -illa, *n.f.* small isle, islet, holm.
islilla, *n.f.* (*anat.*) flank; collar-bone.
islote, *n.m.* small barren island.
ismaelita, *n.m.f., a.* Ishmaelite, Arab.
isobárico, -ca, *a.* isobaric.
isocronismo, *n.m.* isochronism.
isócrono, *a.* isochronal.
isógono, -na, *a.* (*phys.*) isogonic.
isomería, *n.f.* (*chem.*) isomerism.
isómero, -ra; isomérico, -ca, *a.* isomeric.
isomorfismo, *n.m.* (*min.*) isomorphism.
isomorfo, -fa, *a.* isomorphous, isomorphic.
isoperímetro, -tra, *a.* isoperimetrical.
isoquímeno, -na, *a.* (*meteor.*) isocheimal.
isósceles, *a.* isosceles.
isotermo, -ma, *a.* (*phys.*) isothermal.
isótero, -ra, *a.* (*meteor.*) isotheral.
isquion, *n.m.* (*anat.*) ischium.
israelita, *n.m.f.* Israelite, Jew, Jewess.
israelítico, -ca, *a.* Israelitish, Jewish.
istacayota, *n.f.* (*Mex.*) a variety of pumpkin.
istmeño, -ña, *a.* native of an isthmus.

ístmico, -ca, *a.* isthmian.
istmo, *n.m.* isthmus.
istriar, *v.t.* (*arch.*) to flute.
isuate, *n.m.* (*Mex.*) kind of palm, the bark of which is used to make mattresses.
italianismo, *n.m.* Italianism.
italianizar, *v.t.* to Italianize.
italiano, *a.* Italian. — *n.m.* Italian language.
itálico, -ca, *a.* Italic; *letra itálica,* (*print.*) italics.
italo, -la, *a.* (*poet.*) Italian.
itamo, *n.m.* (*Cub.*) wild plant (*euphorbia tithimaloides*).
ítem, *n.m.* item, new article.
ítem; ítem más, *adv.* (*L.*) also, moreover.
iterable, *a.* iterable.
iteración, *n.f.* iteration, repetition.
iterar, *v.t.* to iterate, repeat.
iterativo, -va, *a.* iterative, repeating, redoubling.
itinerario, -ria, *a.* itinerary.
itinerario, *n.m.* itinerary, route; railway guide, time-table.
itria, *n.f.* (*min.*) yttria.
itrio, *n.m.* yttrium.
iva, *n.f.* (*bot.*) musky bugle.
iza, *n.f.* (*naut.*) hoisting, lifting up.
izaga, *n.f.* place abounding in rushes and reeds.
izar, *v.t.* (*naut.*) to hoist, heave, haul up, raise on high.
izquierda, *n.f.* the left hand; (*polit.*) the Left (Spanish Liberal party).
izquierdear, *v.i.* (*coll.*) to degenerate, grow wild.
izquierdo, -da, *a.* left-handed; left; sinister; crooked. — *n.m.f.* left-handed person; *a la izquierda,* to the left, on the left.

J

J, j, eleventh letter of the Spanish alphabet; its name in Spanish is *jota.*
jaba, *n.f.* (*Cub.*) basket made of yarey leaves; (*Am. Cent.*) light wooden box for transporting crockery.
jabalcón, jabalón, *n.m.* (*arch.*) bracket, purlin, tie-beam.
jabalconar, *v.t.* to frame a roof with tie-beams.
jabalí, *n.m.* (*zool.*) wild boar.
jabalina, *n.f.* sow of a wild boar; javelin.
jabardear, *v.t.* to swarm (of bees).
jabardillo, *n.m.* noisy swarm of insects or birds; (*coll.*) noisy crowd.
jabardo, *n.m.* small swarm of bees; (*coll.*) noisy crowd, mob, rabble.
jabato, *n.m.* young wild boar.
jábeca, jábega, *n.f.* sweep-net; fishing smack; drag-net; an old-fashioned oven for the distillation of mercury in Almaden.
jabegote, *n.m.* man who draws the sweep-net.
jabeguero, -ra, *a.* pertaining to sweep-net fishing. — *n.m..* sweep-net fisherman.
jabeque, *n.m.* (*naut.*) xebec; (*coll.*) knife wound in the face.
jabera, *n.f.* Andalusian popular song in ⅜ tempo.
jabí, *n.m.* small wild apple; small kind of grape; (*Cent. Am.*) (*bot.*) breakax.

jabillo, *n.m.* (*Cent. Am.*) (*bot.*) tree of the spurge family.
jabín, *n.m.* (*Mex.*) [JABÍ].
jabladera, *n.f.* crozer; a cooper's tool for making the *croze*.
jable, *n.m.* (*coop.*) croze.
jabón, *n.m.* soap; *jabón de Palencia*, batlet; *jabón duro* (or *de piedra* or *de Castilla*) Castile soap; *dar un jabón*, to reprimand severely.
jabonado, -da, *a.* soaped, cleansed with soap. — *n.m.* wash, washing. — *p.p.* [JABONAR].
jabonadura, *n.f.* washing. — *pl.* suds, soap-suds, lather; *echarle* (or *darle*) *a uno una jabonadura*, (*coll.*) to reprimand.
jabonar, *v.t.* to soap, cleanse; (*coll.*) to reprimand severely.
jaboncillo, *n.m.* soapstone, steatite; toilet soap; (*bot.*) soap-tree.
jabonera, *n.f.* soap-dish; woman who sells soap; (*bot.*) soapwort.
jabonería, *n.f.* soap-manufactory, soap-shop.
jabonero, *n.m.* soap-maker or seller.
jabonete de olor, *n.m.* toilet soap.
jabonoso, -sa, *a.* soapy, saponaceous.
jaborandi, *n.m.* (*Brazil*) (*bot.*) jaborandi.
jabuco, *n.m.* (*Cub.*) large straw basket.
jaca, *n.f.* nag, pony, cob, jennet, bidet, tit.
jacal, *n.m.* (*Mex.*) Indian hut, wigwam.
jacamar, *n.m.* (*orn.*) jacamar.
jacana, *n.f.* (*orn.*) tropical wading bird.
jácara, *n.f.* merry ballad; type of popular song and dance; roisterers singing and shouting in the streets; (*coll.*) molestation, vexation; story, tale, idle talk, prattle; lie, fable, vainglorious fiction.
jacaranda, *n.f.* (*bot.*) jacaranda.
jacarandina, jacarandana, *n.f.* slang, vulgar language; assembly of ruffians and thieves.
jacarandoso, -sa, *a.* (*coll.*) blithe, merry, gay.
jacarear, *v.i.* to sing *jácaras*; (*coll.*) to sing in the streets at night-time; to taunt with offensive remarks; to be vexatious, troublesome.
jacarero, *n.m.* ballad singer; wag or merry droll, facetious person.
jacarilla, *n.f. dim.* [JÁCARA].
jácaro, -ra, *a.* belonging to singers of *jácaras*. — *n.m.* boaster, bully; *a lo jácaro*, boastfully, braggingly.
jácena, *n.f.* (*arch.*) girder.
jacerina, *n.f.* coat of mail.
jacilla, *n.f.* mark which a thing leaves upon the ground.
jacinto, *n.m.* (*bot., min.*) hyacinth; *jacinto de Ceilán*, zircon; *jacinto de Compostela*, red crystallized quartz; *jacinto occidental*, topaz; *jacinto oriental*, ruby.
jacio, *n.m.* (*naut.*) dead calm.
jaco, *n.m.* nag, pony, jade; coat of mail; short jacket, formerly used by soldiers.
jacobinismo, *n.m.* Jacobinism.
jacobino, *n.m.* Jacobin; bloody revolutionist, jacobin.
Jacobo, *n.m.* James.
jactancia, *n.f.* boasting, arrogance, ostentation.
jactanciosamente, *adv.* boastingly, arrogantly.
jactancioso, -sa, *a.* boastful, arrogant, vainglorious, ostentatious.
jactarse, *v.r.* to vaunt, boast, glory, brag, display, flourish.

jaculatoria, *n.f.* ejaculation, short prayer.
jaculatorio, -ria, *a.* short and fervent.
jachalí, *n.m.* (*bot.*) custard-apple tree.
jada, *n.f.* (*agric., prov.*) hoe; spade.
jade, *n.m.* (*min.*) jade, axestone.
jadeante, *a.* panting, out of breath.
jadear, *v.i.* to pant, heave, palpitate.
jadeo, *n.m.* panting, palpitation.
jadiar, *v.t.* (*prov.*) to dig up with a spade; to hoe.
jaecero, -ra, *n.m.f.* harness-maker.
jaén, *n.m.* kind of large white grape.
jaez, *n.m.* harness; trappings; manner or quality. — *pl.* trappings.
jafético, -ca, *a.* Japhetic, Indo-European.
jagua, *n.f.* (*bot.*) inaja-palm and fruit.
jaguar, jaguarete, *n.m.* (*zool.*) jaguar.
jaguarzo, *n.m.* (*bot.*) helianthemum.
jaguay, *n.m.* (*Cub.*) tree of yellow wood.
jagüey, *n.m.* (*S. Am.*) large pool or basin; (*Cub.*) (*bot.*) liana.
jaharrar, *v.t.* to plaster.
jaharro, *n.m.* (*mas.*) plaster, plastering.
jahuei, *n.m.* (*Arg., Bol., Chi.*) [JAGÜEY].
jaiba, *n.f.* (*Cub.*) (*ichth.*) crab.
Jaime, *n.m.* James.
jaique, *n.m.* Moorish cape with a hood.
jaira, *n.f.* bezel of a plane-bit.
jairar, *v.t.* to bevel leather.
jaire, *n.m.* bevel cut.
¡ja, ja, ja! *interj.* ha! ha! (denoting laughter).
jalapa, *n.f.* (*bot.*) jalapa; jalap.
jalbegar, *v.t.* to whiten, whitewash; to paint to excess.
jalbegue, *n.m.* whitewash, whitewashing.
jaldado, -da; jaldo, -da; jalde, *a.* bright yellow, crocus-coloured.
jaldre, *n.m.* yellow peculiar to birds.
jalea, *n.f.* jelly; *hacerse una jalea*, (*fig.*) to love with excessive fervour; *jalea del agro*, conserve of citron; *jalea de guayaba*, guava jelly.
jaleador, -ra, *a.* one who encourages hounds or dancers.
jalear, *v.t.* to encourage hounds to follow the chase; to encourage dancers by clapping hands; to make the voice quaver.
jaleco, *n.m.* Turkish jacket.
jaleo, *n.m.* clapping of hands to encourage dancers; Andalusian dance; (*coll.*) uproar, scuffle.
jaletina, *n.f.* calf's-foot jelly; gelatine.
jalifa, *n.m.* supreme authority in Spanish Morocco (delegate of the Sultan).
jalma, *n.f.* kind of packsaddle.
jalmería, *n.f.* packsaddler's trade.
jalmero, *n.m.* maker of packsaddles.
jalón, *n.m.* levelling pole, rod, or staff; (*Mex.*) a drink.
jaloque, *n.m.* south-east wind.
jallulo, *n.m.* (*prov.*) bread toasted on hot embers.
jamar, *v.t.* (*prov.*) to eat.
jamás, *adv.* never, at no time; *jamás, por jamás* (or *nunca jamás*) never, nevermore; *para siempre jamás*, (*coll.*) for ever and ever.
jamba, *n.f.* (*arch.*) door-jamb, window-post.
jambaje, *n.m.* door- or window-case.
jámbico, -ca, *a.* iambic.
jamelgo, *n.m.* (*coll.*) jade, sorry nag.
jamerdana, *n.f.* sewer of a slaughterhouse.
jamerdar, *v.t.* to clean the guts of animals; (*coll.*) to wash hastily.
jamete, *n.m.* rich silk-stuff.
jamón, *n.m.* ham, leg of ham.

jamona, *n.f., a.* (*coll.*) buxom middle-aged woman; *doncella jamona,* old maid.

jámparo, *n.m.* (*Col.*) small boat or canoe.

jamuga, jamugas, *n,f.* mule-chair.

jándalo, -la, *a.* nickname given to Andalusians and those who give the *h* a strong guttural sound.

jangada, *n.f.* (*coll.*) silly remark or idea; (*naut.*) raft, float.

jangua, *n.f.* small armed vessel.

jansenismo, *n.m.* Jansenism.

jansenista, *n.m.f.* Jansenist.

Japón, *n.m.* Japan.

japón, -ona; japonense, japonés, -esa, *a.* Japanese.

japuta, *n.f.* an edible Mediterranean fish of the Acanthopterygii order.

jaque, *n.m.* check, in chess; braggart, boaster; saddle-bag; smooth combing of the hair; *jaque mate,* checkmate; *¡jaque de aquí!* out of it! away from here! *tener a uno en jaque,* to hold anyone by a threat.

jaquear, *v.t.* to give check at chess.

jaqueca, *n.f.* migraine, hemicrania.

jaquel, *n.m.* (*her.*) square; chess-board.

jaquelado, -da, *a.* checkered.

jaquero, *n.m.* fine-toothed comb.

jaqueta, *n.f.* jacket, short, loose coat.

jaquetilla, *n.f.* small *jaqueta.*

jaquetón, *n.m.* large, wide coat; swaggerer, boaster.

jáquima, *n.f.* headstall of a halter.

jaquimazo, *n.m.* stroke with the headstall of a halter; (*coll.*) displeasure; disappointment; bad, spiteful turn.

jara, *n.f.* (*bot.*) cistus, rock-rose; kind of dart or arrow.

jarabe, *n.m.* syrup; sickly-sweet drink; *ser todo jarabe de pico,* to be full of empty talk; lip service.

jarabear, *v.t.* to prescribe syrups very often. — *v.r.* to take syrups frequently.

jaracolito, *n.m.* (*Per.*) popular Indian dance.

jaragua, *n.f.* (*Cub.*) hardwood tree (Phialanthius).

jaraíz, *n.m.* pit for pressing grapes.

jaral, *n.m.* bramble, brake; intricate or puzzling point.

jaramago, *n.m.* (*bot.*) hedge-mustard.

jarameño, -ña, *a.* reared on the banks of the Jarama (cattle).

jaramugo, *n.m.* small or young fish used as bait.

jarana, *n.f.* (*coll.*) carousal, revelry, romping; (*coll.*) scuffle, quarrel, outcry; *no querer meterse en jaranas,* not to want to get into scrapes; (*Hond.*) debt.

jaranear, *v.i.* (*coll.*) to jest; to carouse.

jaranero, -ra, *a.* fond of jests or sprees, jolly.

jarano, *n.m.* Mexican sombrero.

jarapote, *n.m.* (*prov.*) drug habit.

jarapotear, *v.t.* (*prov.*) to stuff or fill with drugs.

jarazo, *n.m.* blow or wound with a dart.

jarcia, *n.f.* accoutrements; heap of things; (*naut.*) tackle, rigging and cordage, fishing-tackle, shrouds.

jardín, *n.m.* flower-garden; spot which disfigures an emerald; (*naut.*) privy.

jardincito, jardinito, *n.m.* small garden.

jardinera, *n.f.* flower-stand, jardinière; basket carriage; open tramcar.

jardinería, *n.f.* gardening.

jardinero, -ra, *n.m.f.* gardener.

jareta, *n.f.* (*sew.*) fold or tuck for gathering; (*naut.*) netting, harpings.

jaretera, *n.f.* garter.

jarife, *n.m.* Moorish title of honour.

jarifo, -fa, *a.* showy, spruce, nobby, natty, fully-dressed, adorned.

jaro, -ra, *a.* resembling a wild boar.

jarocho, *n.m.* (*prov.*) rough, stout countryman; (*Mex.*) countryman of Veracruz.

jaropar, jaropear, *v.t.* (*coll.*) to stuff with syrups or drugs.

jarope, *n.m.* syrup; (*coll.*) nasty draught or potion; bitter beverage.

jaropeo, *n.m.* (*coll.*) drug habit.

jaroso, -sa, *a.* full of brambles.

jarra, *n.f.* earthen jar; Aragonese order of chivalry; *en jarra* (or *de jarras*), akimbo.

jarrear, *v.i.* (*coll.*) to use a wine jar often; to drink often.

jarrero, *n.m.* vendor or maker of jars.

jarreta, -illa, -ita, *n.f.* small jar; (*naut.*) gratings.

jarrete, *n.m.* hock; gambrel; calf; *tener bravos jarretes,* to have strong hams.

jarretera, *n.f.* garter; Order of the Garter.

jarrito, *n.m.* small jug or pitcher.

jarro, *n.m.* pitcher, jug, pot, ewer; (*prov.*) chatterer; *echar un jarro de agua* (*fría*), to throw cold water on a project, etc.

jarrón, *n.m.* large jar, urn, flower-vase.

jarros (a), *adv.* hard, with great force.

Jartum, *n.m.* Khartoum.

jaspe, *n.m.* (*min.*) jasper.

jaspeado, -da, *a.* spotted, marbled, mottled, variegated; *p.p.* [JASPEAR].

jaspeadura, *n.f.* marbling.

jaspear, *v.t.* to marble, paint in imitation of jasper, vein, speckle.

jastial, *n.m.* (*arch.*) façade of an edifice.

jateo, -tea, *a.* fox-hunter (dogs).

jato, -ta, *n.m.f.* calf.

¡jau! *interj.* to incite animals, especially bulls.

Jauja, *n.f.* a mythical country of the ideal happiness; *¿Estamos aquí o en Jauja?* Where do you think we are? Be very careful with your words.

jaula, *n.f.* cage; cell for insane persons; (*min.*) miner's cage.

jaulón, *n.m.* large bird-cage, aviary.

jauría, *n.f.* pack of hounds.

jauto, -ta, *a.* (*prov.*) insipid, flat, tasteless.

javanés, -esa; javo, -va, *a.* Javan, Javanese.

javia, javio, *n.m.* (*bot.*) sand-box tree.

jayán, -ana, *n.m.f.* tall, robust person.

jayanazo, *n.m.* huge fellow.

jazmín, *n.m.* (*bot.*) jessamine, jasmine.

jazmineo, -a, *a.* (*bot.*) jasminaceous.

jazminorro, *n.m.* (*bot.*) yellow jasmine.

¡je, je, je! *interj.* he! he! (denoting laughter).

jea, *n.f.* ancient duty on Moorish goods.

jebe, *n.m.* rock-alum; (*S. Am.*) india-rubber.

jedive, *n.m.* khedive, viceroy of Egypt.

jeera, *n.f.* drained, marshy ground.

jefatura, *n.f.* dignity and office of a chief.

jefe, -fa, *n.m.f.* chief, head, superior, leader; (*mil.*) commanding officer above the rank of captain and below that of brigadier; *jefe de escuadra,* (*naut.*) rear-admiral; *jefe político,* governor of a province; *jefe de las caballerizas,* master of the horse.

jeja, *n.f.* (*prov.*) white wheat.

jeito, *n.m.* fishing-net used in the Bay of Biscay.

jején, *n.m.* (*Cub.*) gnat, gall-midge.

jema, *n.f.* badly squared part of a beam.

jemal, *a.* having the length of a *jeme.*

jeme, *n.m.* distance from the end of the thumb to the end of the forefinger when both are extended; (*coll.*) woman's face.

jemoso, -sa, *a.* badly squared (of a beam).

jenabe, jenable, *n.m.* mustard.

jengibre, *n.m.* ginger.

jeniquén, *n.m.* henequen, sisal hemp.

jenízaro, -ra, *n.m.f., a.* cross-breed; (*Mex.*) of Chinese and Indian parents; janizary.

jeque, *n.m.* Moorish old man or chief; (*prov.*) portmanteau.

jera, *n.f.* ground which can be ploughed in a day with a pair of oxen; present, gift.

jerapellina, *n.f.* old ragged garment.

jerarca, *n.m.* (*eccles.*) hierarch.

jerarquía, *n.f.* hierarchy; important rank.

jerárquico, -ca, *a.* hierarchical.

jerbo, *n.m.* jerboa (*Dipus Ægyptius*).

jeremiada, *n.f.* jeremiad.

Jeremías, *n.m.f.* Jeremiah, whiner.

jeremiqueo, *n.m.* (*Cub., Chi., PR.*) persistent supplication; whining.

jerez, *n.m.* sherry wine.

jerezano, -na, *n.m.f., a.* of or belonging to Jerez.

jerga, *n.f.* coarse frieze; jargon, gibberish; straw bed; *estar* (*dejar* or *poner*) *una cosa en jerga,* to be begun, but not finished.

jergón, *n.m.* straw bed; misfit clothes; Kidderminster carpeting; (*coll.*) paunch, belly; (*coll.*) ill-shaped person; (*jewel.*) zircon.

jerguilla, *n.f.* silk or worsted serge.

jericoplear, *v.t.* (*Guat., Hond.*) to disturb, to annoy.

jerife, *n.m.* descendant of Mohammed's daughter Fatima; (*hist.*) the chief authority of Mecca; a member of the reigning dynasty of Morocco.

jerifiano, -na, *a.* pertaining to the *jerife*; *Su Majestad Jerifiana,* His Majesty the Sultan of Morocco.

jerigonza, *n.f.* (*coll.*) jargon, gibberish, slang; strange and ridiculous action; *andar en jerigonzas,* to cavil, quibble.

jeringa, *n.f.* syringe; sausage-stuffer.

jeringar, *v.t.* (*pret.* **jeringué**; *pres. subj.* **jeringue**) to syringe, inject; (*coll.*) to vex, annoy, tease.

jeringazo, *n.m.* syringing, injecting; clyster, injection.

jeringuilla, *n.f.* hypodermic syringe; (*bot.*) syringa, mock orange.

jeroglífico, *n.m.* hieroglyph.

jeroglífico, -ca, *a.* hieroglyphical.

jerosolimitano, -na, *a.* native of Jerusalem.

jerpa, *n.f.* sterile shoot of a vine.

jerricote, *n.m.* pottage of almonds, sugar, sage and ginger.

jerviguilla, jervilla, *n.f.* kind of short boot.

jesnato, -ta, *a.* child dedicated to Jesus when born.

Jesucristo, *n.m.* Jesus Christ.

jesuita, *n.m.* Jesuit; (*coll.*) hypocrite.

jesuíticamente, *adv.* Jesuitically.

jesuítico, -ca, *a.* Jesuitical.

jesuitismo, *n.m.* Jesuitism.

Jesús, *n.m.* Jesus; *en un decir Jesús,* in an instant; *¡Jesús mil veces!* good God! *no saber ni el Jesús,* not to know even the alphabet; *decir los Jesuses,* to assist dying people; *morir sin decir Jesús,* to die very suddenly.

jesusear, *v.i.* to repeat often the name of Jesus.

jeta, *n.f.* thick, heavy lips; blubber-lip; hog's snout; (*coll.*) person's face; (*mech.*) faucet, cock.

jetar, *v.t.* (*prov.*) to dilute, dissolve, liquefy.

jeto, *n.m.* (*prov.*) empty beehive rubbed with honey to attract bees.

jetudo, -da, *a.* thick-lipped.

¡ji, ji, ji! *interj.* denoting laughter, he! he!

jíbaro, *n.m.* (*Am.*) countryman, rustic.

jíbaro, -ra, *a.* (*Am.*) rustic, rude, run wild; (*Mex.*) of cross-breed.

jibia, *n.f.* (*zool.*) cuttle-fish.

jibión, *n.m.* cuttle-fish bone.

jibraltareño, -ña, *a.* of or from Gibraltar.

jícara, *n.f.* chocolate cup; gourd-tree.

jicarazo, *n.m.* large chocolate cup; blow with such a cup; *dar un jicarazo,* (*coll.*) to give poison to a person.

jicarón, *n.m.* large chocolate cup.

jicotea, *n.f.* (*Am.*) tortoise; mud-turtle.

jifa, *n.f.* refuse of slaughtered beasts.

jiferada, *n.f.* stroke with a butcher's knife.

jifería, *n.f.* slaughtering.

jifero, -ra, *a.* belonging to the slaughterhouse.

jifero, *n.m.* butcher's knife; butcher.

jifia, *n.f.* (*ichth.*) xiphias, sword-fish.

jiga, *n.f.* jig (dance and tune).

jigote, *n.m.* hash, broth; minced meat.

jiguilete, *n.m.* indigo-plant.

jijallar, *n.m.* bramble-patch, broom-patch.

jijallo, *n.m.* (*bot.*) prickly broom.

jijene, *n.m.* (*S. Am.*) sand-fly.

jijona, *n.f.* variety of flinty wheat; *turrón de Jijona,* sweet-almond paste.

jilguero, *n.m.* (*orn.*) linnet.

jilmaestre, *n.m.* artillery officer in charge of horses, mules, etc.

jilocopo, *n.m.* carpenter bee (*xylocopa*).

jilote, *n.m.* (*Mex.*) ear of green corn.

jimagua, *n.m.f.* (*Cub.*) twin.

jimelga, *n.f.* (*naut.*) fish of a mast.

jimenzar, *v.t.* to ripple flax or hemp.

jinestada, *n.f.* sauce made of milk, dates, etc.

jineta, *n.f.* art of horsemanship; short lance used in olden times; ancient tribute on cattle; sergeant's shoulder-knot; *andar a la jineta,* to go at a short trot; *cabalzar a la jineta,* to ride with very short stirrups; *tener los cascos a la jineta,* to be hare-brained, wild, giddy.

jineta, *n.m.* (*zool.*) genet, small mammal allied to the civet.

jinete, *n.m.* trooper, cavalry-man; horseman, cavalier, rider, equestrian; pure-breed horse.

jinetear, *v.t.* (*Guat., Hond., Mex.*) to tame wild horses by riding them; *v.i.* to ride on horseback for show.

jinglar, *v.i.* to swing, vibrate, oscillate.

jingoismo, *n.m.* jingoism.

jingoista, *n.m.f., a.* jingoist(-ic).

jinjol, *n.m.* jujube.

jipa, *n.f.* (*Col.*) [JIPIJAPA].

jipato, -ta, (*Cub.*) pale, sickly; full, replete with eating.

jipe, *n.m.* (*Mex.*) [JIPIJAPA].

jipijapa, *n.f.* very fine woven straw.

jiquilete, *n.m.* (*bot.*) indigo-tree.

jira, *n.f.* strip, slip of cloth; picnic, outing.

jirafa, *n.f.* (*zool.*) giraffe.

jirapliega, *n.f.* purgative confection.

jirasal, *n.f.* (*bot.*) fruit of the lac-tree.

jirel, *n.m.* rich trappings, caparison for a horse.

jíride, *n.f.* fetid iris, gladdon (*Iris fœtidissima*).

jirofina, *n.f.* kind of sauce or gravy.

jiroflé, *n.m.* clove-tree.

jirón, *n.m.* (*sew.*) facing of a skirt; piece torn from clothing; pennant, pointed banner; small part of any whole; long street.

jironado, -da, *a.* torn into or garnished with strips or tatters.

jirpear, *v.t.* to dig about vines.

jisca, *n.f.* cylindrical sugar-cane.

jiste, *n.m.* yeast, barm, leaven; froth of beer.

jitar, *v.t.* (*prov.*) to emit, vomit, turn out, throw out.

¡jo! *interj.* whoa!

jobo, *n.m.* (*Am.*) tree of the terebinth family.

jocó, *n.m.* jocko, ape.

jocosamente, *adv.* jocosely, jocularly, waggishly, humorously, ludicrously, good-humouredly.

jocoserio, -ria, *a.* jocoserious.

jocosidad, *n.f.* jocularity, jocoseness, jocosity, waggery.

jocoso, -sa, *a.* jocose, jocular, waggish, humorous, comical, facetious.

jocoyote, *n.m.* (*Am.*) youngest child, pet.

jocundidad, *n.f.* joviality.

jocundo, -da, *a.* jovial, jolly.

jofaina, *n.f.* wash-basin, wash-bowl.

jojoto, *n.m.* (*Ven.*) maize cooked in milk.

jolgorio, *n.m.* [HOLGORIO].

jolito, *n.m.* rest, leisure; (*naut.*) calm.

joloano, -na, *a.* of or belonging to Sulu islands (*Philip.*).

jónico, -ca; jonio, -nia, *a.* of or belonging to Ionia; *orden jónico*, (*arch.*) Ionic order.

jónico, *n.m.* ionic foot in poetry.

jonja, *n.f.* (*Chi.*) mockery, sneer, flout.

jonjabar, *v.t.* (*coll.*) to inveigle, wheedle.

¡jopo! *interj.* (*coll.*) out of here! be off!

jora, *n.f.* (*S. Am.*) maize prepared for making chicha.

jorcar, *v.t.* (*prov.*) to winnow grain.

jorco, *n.m.* (*prov.*) licentious feast and dance.

jordán, *n.m.* anything which purifies, revives, or gives fresh bloom.

jorfe, *n.m.* dry stone wall; steep rock; tor.

Jorge, *n.m.* George.

jorguín, *n.m.* wizard, sorcerer; soot, condensed smoke.

jorguina, jorjina, *n.f.* witch, sorceress.

jorguinería, *n.f.* witchcraft, spell.

jornada, *n.f.* one-day march; working day; stage, journey, trip, travel; king's stay in a royal country residence; (*mil.*) expedition; occasion, opportunity, circumstance; passage through life, passage from life to eternity; span of life; act of a play; (*print.*) number of sheets printed off in a day; *a grandes* (or *a largas*) *jornadas*, by forced marches; *al fin de la jornada*, (*fig.*) at the end, at last.

jornal, *n.m.* day-work, journey-work, day-wages; *a jornal*, by the day; (*com.*) journal, diary.

jornalero, *n.m.* day-labourer, journeyman.

joroba, *n.f.* hump; (*coll.*) importunity, annoyance, nuisance, worry.

jorobado, -da, *a.* crooked, gibbous, hump-backed, or crook-backed. — *n.m.f.* hunchback. — *p.p.* [JOROBAR].

jorobar, *v.t.* (*coll.*) to importune, worry, harass, tease, annoy.

jorrar, *v.t.* to haul a sweep-scine.

jorro, *n.m.* (*Cub.*) bad tobacco; *red de jorro*, sweep-seine.

josa, *n.f.* plot of land planted with vines and fruit-trees.

José, *n.m.* Joseph.

jostrado, -da, *a.* round-headed shaft or dart.

jota, name of the letter *j*; iota, jot, tittle; Aragonese and Valencian dance and tune; pottage of greens and spices; (*Chi., Per.*) Indian sandal; *no saber una jota*, to be very ignorant of anything; *sin faltar una jota*, not a jot missing.

jote, *n.m.* Chilean vulture of the turkey-buzzard family.

joule, *n.m.* (*phys.*) joule.

jovada, *n.f.* (*prov.*) ground tilled by a pair of mules in one day.

joven, *a.* young, youthful, juvenile. — *n.m.f.* youth, stripling; young man; young woman; young person.

jovenado, *n.m.* (*eccles.*) juniorate.

jovenzuelo, -la, *n.m.f.* youngster.

jovial, *a.* Jovian; jovial, gay, merry, cheerful, blithe.

jovialidad, *n.f.* joviality, jollity, mirth, merriment, gaiety.

joya, *n.f.* jewel, gem; piece of jewellery; a valued person or thing; present, gift; (*arch., art*) astragal. — *pl.* **joyas,** jewels, trinkets; wedding outfit.

joyante, *a.* extremely glossy (of silk).

joyel, *n.m.* small jewel, valuable trinket.

joyelero, *n.m.* jewel-case, jewel-box.

joyera, *n.f.* woman who keeps a jeweller's shop.

joyería, *n.f.* jeweller's shop.

joyero, *n.m.* jeweller; jewel-casket; (*Arg., Chi., PR.*) goldsmith.

joyita, *n.f.* small jewel.

joyo, *n.m.* (*bot.*) bearded darnel, darnel-grass.

joyón, *n.m.* large jewel.

joyuela, *n.f.* jewel of small value.

juaguarzo, *n.m.* (*bot.*) Montpellier rock-rose.

Juan, *n.m.* John; *buen Juan* (or *Juan de buena alma*), poor, silly fellow; *Juan Lanas*, simpleton, pliant fellow; *hacer San Juan*, to leave one's salaried post before the allotted time.

juanete, *n.m.* bunion; prominent cheek-bone; (*naut.*) top-gallant sail; *juanete mayor*, main-top-gallant sail; *juanete de sobremesana*, mizen-top-gallant sail.

juanetero, *n.m.* marine in care of the top-gallant sails.

juanetudo, -da, *a.* having bunions.

juanillo, *n.m.* (*Chi., Per.*) gratuity, tip.

juarda, *n.f.* stain in cloth due to faulty scouring.

juardoso, -sa, *a.* stained, spotted (cloth).

juay, *n.m.* (*Mex.*) knife.

jubete, *n.m.* doublet covered with mail.

jubetería, *n.f.* shop where *jubetes* are sold.

jubetero, *n.m.* maker and seller of *jubetes*.

jubilación, *n.f.* pensioning off or superannuating; retirement; exemption from office or duty, with reduced pay; reduced salary thus paid, pension.

jubilar, *v.t.* to pension off; to superannuate; to

exempt from duty, with reduced pay; to place on the retired list; (*coll.*) to lay aside as useless. — *v.r.*, *v.i.* to become a pensioner; to be retired. — *v.i.* to jubilate, rejoice.

jubileo, *n.m.* jubilee, public festivity; (*eccles.*) concession of plenary indulgence; *por jubileo*, rarely, happening seldom.

júbilo, *n.m.* glee, joy, merriment, rejoicing, mirth, festivity, hilarity.

jubiloso, -ca, *a.* gleeful, merry, joyful, gay.

jubo, *n.m.* (*Cub.*) small snake.

jubón, *n.m.* doublet, jacket; waist in female dress; *jubón de azotes*, (*coll.*) public whipping.

juboncito, *n.m.* small jacket, doublet or waist.

jubonero, *n.m.* maker of jackets, doublets or waists.

júcaro, *n.m.* a West-Indian hardwood tree.

judaico, -ca, *a.* Judaical, Jewish.

judaísmo, *n.m.* Judaism.

judaizante, *n.m.f.*, *a.* Judaizing, Judaizer.

judaizar, *v.t.* to Judaize.

Judas, *n.m.* an impostor, traitor; silk-worm that does not spin; effigy of Judas burnt in the streets during Holy Week.

judería, *n.f.* Jewry, Jewish quarter; tax on Jews.

judía, *n.f.* French bean, kidney-bean; *judía de careta*, small spotted French beans; Jewess.

judiada, *n.f.* inhuman action; usurious profit.

judicante, *n.m.* (*prov.*) judge appointed to try impeachment cases.

judicatura, *n.f.* judicature; dignity of a judge.

judiega, *n.f.* inferior kind of olives.

judihuela, *n.f.* small French bean.

judihuelo, -la, *n.m.f.* young Jew or Jewess.

judío, -día, *a.* Jewish, Hebrew; (*pejorative*) usurious. — *n.m.* Jew; *judío de señal*, converted Jew, wearing a distinguishing badge.

judión, *n.m.* large variety of French beans.

juego, *n.m.* play, amusement, sport, diversion, game; gambling, gaming; hand of cards; game of cards; set, suit, suite; movement, play, working (of a mechanism); (*car.*) running gear of a vehicle; disposition, ability, cunning, artfulness; (*mech.*) play, free space, clearance; *juego de cartas* (or *de naipes*), card game; *juego de azar* (or *de suerte*), game of chance; *juego de bochas*, bowling alley; *juego de palabras*, pun, quibble; *juego de manos*, juggling feat, legerdemain; *juego de suerte y ventura*, game of chance; *juego de bolos*, ninepins; *juego de pelota*, handball game, fives; fives-court; *juego de prendas*, forfeits; *juego de niños*, play-game, child's play; *juego de cajones*, nest of boxes or drawers; *juego de habitaciones*, suite of rooms; *juego de velas* (*naut.*) set of sails; *juego de té* (or *de café*), tea-set, coffee-set; *por juego* (or *por modo de juego*), in jest, in joke, in fun; *tener juego*, (*naut.*) to be under way; not to be firm or steady; *conocer el juego*, to know anyone's designs; *entrar en juego*, to come in play; *juego limpio*, fair play; *hacer juego*, to match, to suit, to fit; *juego de manos, juego de villanos*, proverb warning against excessive familiarity in playing with strangers. — *pl.* **juegos,** public feasts, exhibitions, or rejoicings.

juego; juegue, pres. indic.; pres. subj. [JUGAR].

jueguecico, -illo, -ito, *n.m.* little game, bit of play.

juerga, *n.f.* (*coll.*) spree, carousal.

juerguista, *n.m.f.*, *a.* (*coll.*) reveller; carousing.

jueves, *n.m.* Thursday; *cosa del otro jueves*, something very unusual, seldom seen; *jueves de comadres*, Thursday before Lent; *jueves de compadres*, second Thursday before Lent; *jueves Santo* (or *jueves de la cena*) Maundy Thursday.

juez, *n.m.* judge, justice; juror, juryman; expert, connoisseur, critic; *juez árbitro*, arbitrator, umpire; *juez de hecho*, lay judge; *juez de paz*, justice of the peace; *juez de primera instancia*, judge of the primary court of claims.

jugada, *n.f.* play, act of playing, throw, stroke, move; ill turn, wicked trick.

jugadera, *n.f.* shuttle for network.

jugador, -ra, *n.m.f.* player; gamester, gambler; *jugador de manos*, juggler, prestidigitator.

jugar, *v.t.*, *v.i.* (*pres. indic.* **juego;** *pret.* **jugué;** *pres. subj.* **juegue**) to play, sport, frolic, toy, trifle, romp, gambol; to make a move in a game; to game, gamble; to wield, handle; to make use of weapons; to move a part of the body; to intervene; to move on joints or hinges; to exercise; to take an active part in an affair; to mock, make game of; *jugar a cara o cruz*, to bet on the toss of a coin; *jugar al alza*, (*com.*) to bull the market; *jugar en* (or *a*) *la bolsa*, to dabble in stocks; *jugar a castillo o león*, to toss up; *jugar al desquite*, to double the stake; *jugar grueso*, to play for big stakes; *jugar hasta la camisa*, to stake the shirt on one's back, to play to the last penny; *jugar a la baja*, to bear the market; *ni juega, ni da de barato*, he is indifferent, he has no strong opinions.

jugarreta, *n.f.* (*coll.*) bad play; bad turn, nasty trick.

juglándeo, -dea, *a.* (*bot.*) juglandaceous. — *n.f.* the walnut family.

juglar, *n.m.* juggler, mountebank, mimic, buffoon; minstrel.

juglara, juglaresa, *n.f.* female buffoon or mimic.

juglaresco, -ca, *a.* of jugglers or minstrels.

juglaría, juglería, *n.f.* jugglery, buffoonery, mimicry; minstrelsy.

jugo, *n.m.* sap, juice; marrow, pith, substance.

jugosidad, *n.f.* sappiness, succulence, juiciness.

jugoso, -sa, *a.* sappy, juicy, succulent.

juguete, *n.m.* toy, plaything, gewgaw, trinket; jest, joke; carol; (*theat.*) comedietta; *por juguete*, jestingly.

juguetería, *n.f.* toy-shop, toy-trade.

juguetear, *v.i.* to toy, frolic, sport, gambol, dally, wanton, play tricks.

juguetón, -ona, *a.* playful, frolicsome, playsome.

juicio, *n.m.* judgment; act of judging, decision reached; criterion, sense, opinion, notion, report; wisdom, prudence; forecast of yearly events by astrologers; (*law*) trial; *pedir en juicio*, to sue at law; *asentar el juicio*, to begin to be judicious; *tener mucho juicio*, to be sedate, steady, well-behaved; *no estar en su juicio*, to be out of one's senses; *no tener juicio*, to be wild, to be a harum-scarum fellow; *tener el juicio en los calcañares* (or *en los talones*), to conduct oneself imprudently.

juiciosamente, *adv.* judiciously, wisely, considerately.

juicioso, -sa, *a.* judicious, wise, prudent, mature, clear-sighted.

julepe, *n.m.* (*pharm.*) julep; game of cards; (*coll.*) reprimand, punishment; (*S. Am.*) scare, fright, shock.

julepear, *v.t.* (*Arg.*) to alarm, to scare; (*Mex.*) to torment, to annoy.

juliano, -na, *a.* Julian.

julio, *n.m.* the month of July; (*elec.*) joule, watt-second.

julo, *n.m.* bell-mule, bell-cow.

jumenta, *n.f.* she-ass, jenny.

jumental, jumentil, *a.* belonging to the ass.

jumentillo, -illa; -ito, -ita, *n.m.f.* little ass, small beast of burden.

jumento, *n.m.* ass; beast of burden; stupid person.

juncáceas, *n.f.pl.* (*bot.*) Juncaceæ.

juncada, *n.f.* kind of fritter; (*vet.*) medicine for the glanders.

juncago, *n.m.* (*bot.*) bastard rush.

juncal, *a.* of or resembling rushes.

juncar, *n.m.* ground full of rushes.

júnceo, -cea, *a.* rush-like. — *n.f.pl.* (*bot.*) rush family.

juncia, *n.f.* (*bot.*) cyperus, sedge; *juncia olorosa,* galangal; *vender juncia,* to boast, brag.

junciana, *n.f.* (*coll.*) brag, boast.

junciera, *n.f.* earthenware vessel with perforated lid, for aromatic roots.

juncino, -na, *a.* rushy; made of rushes.

junco, *n.m.* (*bot.*) rush; *junco de Indias,* rattan; *junco florido,* flowering rush; *junco oloroso,* camel grass; (*naut.*) Chinese junk.

juncoso, -sa, *a.* rushy; juncous.

junio, *n.m.* the month of June.

júnior, *n.m.* (*eccles.*) junior.

junípero, *n.m.* (*bot.*) juniper.

junquera, *n.f.* (*bot.*) rush.

junqueral, *n.m.* ground full of rushes.

junquillo, *n.m.* (*bot.*) jonquil; reed, rattan; (*arch.*) round moulding.

junta, *n.f.* junta, board; junto, meeting, congress, conference, council, convention, tribunal, assembly, sitting; whole, entirety; fraternity, union, conjunction, junction; concession; (*carp.*) joint, joining, seam; (*mech.*) coupling; (*build.*) coursing joint; *junta de médicos,* (*med.*) consultation; *junta de comercio,* board of trade; *junta de accionistas,* stockholders' meeting; *junta de sanidad,* board of health; *junta directiva,* managing board, executive board; *junta de acreedores,* (*com.*) meeting of creditors.

juntamente, *adv.* jointly, together, at the same time, conjunctively.

juntar, *v.t.* (*p.p.* **juntado; junto**) to join, attach, connect, couple, unite; to amass, collect, heap, gather; to associate, assemble, congregate; (of doors, windows) to push to, leave ajar; (*carp.*) to join, clamp, fit. — *v.r.* to join, meet, assemble, concur; to be closely united; to copulate; *juntar meriendas,* (*coll.*) to join interests; (with *con*) to associate with.

juntera, *n.f.* (*carp.*) jointing-plane.

junterilla, *n.f.* (*carp.*) small joiner's plane.

junto, -ta, *a.* united, annexed, joined, conjoined, together. — *p.p. irreg.* [JUNTAR].

junto, *adv.* near, close to, at hand, near at hand; at the same time; *por junto* (or *de por junto*), in the bulk, by the lump, wholesale; *en junto* together, in all; *todo junto,* altogether; *junto a,* next to, by; *todo junto, como al perro los palos,* all at once, like sticks on a dog.

juntura, *n.f.* juncture, joining, joint, articulation, seam; (*naut.*) scarf; (*bot.*) knuckle.

jupa, *n.f.* (*CR.*) round pumpkin.

Júpiter, *n.m.* (*astron.*) Jupiter; (*alch.*) tin.

jura, *n.f.* oath; act of taking or administering an oath.

jurado, *n.m.* jury; juror, juryman.

jurador, -ra, *n.m.f.* swearer, profane swearer.

juraduría, *n.f.* office of a juror.

juramentar, *v.t.* to swear, to put to an oath. — *v.r.* to bind oneself by an oath, be sworn in.

juramento, *n.m.* oath; act of swearing; curse, imprecation; *juramento asertorio,* declaratory oath; *juramento falso,* perjury.

jurar, *v.t.* to swear, make oath, promise upon oath, attest solemnly; *v.i.* to swear profanely.

jurásico, -ca, *a.* Jurassic.

juratoria, *n.f.* Gospel tablet for administering the oath.

juratorio, *a.* juratory; *caución juratoria, fianza juratoria,* juratory security, release on oath. — *n.m.* instrument setting forth the oaths taken by Aragonese magistrates.

jurdía, *n.f.* kind of fishing net.

jurel, *n.m.* (*ichth.*) jurel, carangoid sea-fish.

jurero, *n.m.* (*Chi., Ec.*) false witness.

jurguina, jurgina, *n.f.* witch, sorceress.

jurídicamente, *adv.* lawfully, legally, juridically.

jurídico, -ca, *a.* lawful, legal, juridical.

jurisconsulto, *n.m.* jurisconsult; jurist, lawyer; civilian, professor of civil law.

jurisdicción, *n.f.* jurisdiction; power, authority, boundary, territory.

jurisdiccional, *a.* jurisdictional; *n.f.pl. aguas jurisdiccionales* (or *mar jurisdiccional*), territorial waters.

jurisperito, *n.m.* professor of jurisprudence.

jurisprudencia, *n.f.* jurisprudence, law, science of law; laws of a country.

jurisprudente, *n.m.* professor of jurisprudence.

jurista, *n.m.* jurist, lawyer; pensioner.

juro, *n.m.* right of perpetual property; annuity, pension; *de juro,* certainly.

jusbarba, *n.f.* (*bot.*) field myrtle.

jusello, *n.m.* pottage of broth, cheese and eggs.

jusi, *n.m.* (*Philip.*) striped thin gauze.

justa, *n.f.* joust, tournament; competition, contest.

justador, *n.m.* tilter, jouster.

justamente, *adv.* justly, just, exactly; precisely, fairly, equitably.

justar, *v.i.* to joust, tilt, tourney.

justicia, *n.f.* justice, equity; right, fairness; judge, court of justice; punishment, retribution; (*coll.*) execution (of a criminal). — *n.m.* justice, magistrate, tribunal; *de justicia,* according to justice, duly, meritedly; *ir por justicia, pedir justicia,* to go to law; *la justicia,* the police, the authorities, the officers of the law.

justiciero, -ra, *a.* strictly just; one who administers justice rigidly.

justificable, *a.* justifiable.

justificación, *n.f.* justification, defence, maintenance, support; equity; production of evidence to sustain a claim; sanctification by grace; (*print.*) adjustment, justifying.

justificadamente, *adv.* justly, correctly, justifiably.

justificado, -da, *a.* equal; justified. — *p.p.* [JUSTIFICAR].

justificador, *n.m.* justifier, justificator; (*print.*) dressing-stick, justifier.

justificante, *a.* justifying; justificative.

justificar, *v.t.* (*pret.* **justifiqué;** *pres. subj.* **justifique**) to justify, free from sin, to render just; (*law*) to prove or establish a claim before a court; to absolve, exculpate; (*print.*) to justify, adjust; to rectify, arrange, adjust, regulate exactly. — *v.r.* to vindicate one's character; to clear oneself from imputed guilt; to justify one's conduct.

justificativo, -va, *a.* justificative, justifying, justificatory.

justillo, *n.m.* waistcoat, jerkin; corset-cover.

justipreciador, *n.m.* appraiser.

justipreciar, *v.t.* to appraise, set value to.

justiprecio, *n.m.* appraisement, valuation.

justo, -ta, *a.* just, equitable, right, rightful, lawful, fair, above-board; correct, exact, punctual, strict; pious, good, faithful, honourable, honest, upright; tight, fit, close, flush.

justo, *n.m.* just and pious man. — *adv.* tightly, straitly; *al justo,* fitly, duly; completely, punctually; *en justos y en verenjustos,* (*coll.*) rightly or wrongly; *pagar justos por pecadores,* the innocent very often have to pay for the guilty.

juta, *n.f.* (*S. Am.*) kind of goose.

jutía, *n.f.* (*Cub.*) edible kind of rat.

juvenil, *a.* juvenile, young, youthful; girlish.

juventud, *n.f.* youthfulness, youth, juvenility; young people.

juvia, *n.f.* (*bot.*) Brazil-nut tree.

juzgado, *n.m.* tribunal, court of justice; judicature.

juzgamundos, *n.m.f.* (*coll.*) fault-finder.

juzgante, *a.* judging.

juzgar, *v.t., v.i.* (*pret.* **juzgué;** *pres. subj.* **juzgue**) to judge, pass sentence upon, give judgment; to form or give an opinion; to opine, hold, find.

K

K, k, twelfth letter of the Spanish alphabet; (*chem.*) symbol of potassium; words which are begun with *k* are properly spelled with *qu* if the following letter is *e* or *i*, and with *c* before *a, o,* or *u.*

ka, *n.f.* name of the letter *k.*

kadi, *n.m.* Turkish judge.

kalenda, *n.f.* kalends.

kan, *n.m.* khan, Tatar chief or prince.

kantiano, -na, *a.* Kantian.

kantismo, *n.m.* Kantism.

kepis, *n.m.* (*mil.*) small shako [QUEPIS].

keralila, *n.f.* (*Mex.*) horny flint.

kermes, *n.m.* kermes.

kiliárea, *n.f.* measure of about 24 acres.

kilo, *n.m.* (*com.*) kilogramme.

kilográmetro, *n.m.* kilogrammetre.

kilogramo, *n.m.* kilogram(me).

kilolitro, *n.m.* kilolitre (1,000 litres).

kilométrico, -ca, *a.* kilometric.

kilómetro, *n.m.* kilometre (1,000 metres), about five-eighths of a mile.

kilovatio, *n.m.* kilowatt, 1,000 watts.

kimono, *n.m.* (*Cub.*) [QUIMONO].

kiosco, *n.m.* kiosk, small pavilion, news-stand, refreshment-stand [QUIOSCO].

kirie, *n.m.* (*eccles.*) kyrie (eleison).

kirieleisón, *n.m.* kyrie eleison; (*coll.*) funeral chant.

Krausismo, *n.m.* philosophical doctrine of Karl Christian Krause.

Krausista, *a.* pertaining to or characteristic of the philosophy of Krause.

kurdo, -da, *a.* Kurdish, Kurd [CURDO].

L

L, l, thirteenth letter of the Spanish alphabet.

la, *def. art. fem. sing.* the

la, *pron. pers. acc. fem. sing.* her, it.

la, *n.m.* (*mus.*) la, sixth sound of the scale (A).

lábaro, *n.m.* labarum.

labe, *n.f.* stain, spot.

laberíntico, -ca, *a.* labyrinthine.

laberinto, *n.m.* labyrinth, maze; great uncertainty, difficulty; intricate matter; (*anat.*) labyrinth of the ear.

labia, *n.f.* (*coll.*) gift of the gab.

labiado, -da, *a.* (*bot.*) labiate.

labial, *a.* labial.

labiérnago, *n.m.* (*bot.*) shrub with lanceolate, shining leaves.

labihendido, -da, *a.* hare-lipped.

lábil, *a.* (*chem., phys., etc.*) labile; slippery; fragile, weak, frail.

labio, *n.m.* lip; mouth; edge, brim; *labio hendido,* hare-lip; *morderse los labios,* to restrain oneself with difficulty from speech or laughter; *no descoser* (or *despegar*) *los labios,* to be silent, not to reply; *sellar el labio* (or *los labios*), to be dumb *or* silent.

labor, *n.f.* labour, task, toil, work; design, scroll-work; (*sew.*) needlework, embroidery, fancy-work; trimming; (with the definite article *la*) school for young girls to learn sewing; thousand tiles or bricks; cultivation, husbandry, tillage; egg of a silk-worm. — *pl.* **labores,** figures raised upon a ground; diaper; (*min.*) works, working; *ir a la labor,* to go to school (said of girls); *campo de labor,* cultivated field; *meter en labor* (*agric.*) to prepare for sowing.

laborable, *a.* tillable, workable; *día laborable,* (*com.*) workday.

laborador, *n.m.* tiller, farmer; worker.

laborante, *a.* tilling, working. — *n.m.* (*Cub.*) conspirator.

laborantismo, *n.m.* (*Cub.*) (*polit.*) secret plotting to free the island.

laborar, *v.t.* to till, to work; to intrigue, plot.

laboratorio, *n.m.* laboratory.

laborcico, -ca, -illa, -ita, *n.f.* pretty needle-work.

laborear, *v.t.* to work; (*naut.*) to reeve, run.

laboreo, *n.m.* culture, labour; (*naut.*) reeving, running; (*min.*) works, working.

laborera, *a.* clever, skilful (of a workwoman).

laborero, *n.m.* (*Chi.*) foreman or overseer in mines.

laboriosamente, *adv.* industriously; laboriously.

laboriosidad, *n.f.* industriousness, industry, assiduity.

laborioso, -sa, *a.* assiduous, industrious; laborious, painful, tiresome, wearisome.

labra, *n.f.* stone, metal or wood cutting or carving.

labrada, *n.f.* land ploughed and fallowed.

labradero, -ra, *a.* workable, arable, capable of labour.

labradío, día, *a.* tillable (of land).

labrado, -da, *a.* wrought, worked, figured; hewn; tilled; (*com.*) manufactured. — *n.m.pl.* cultivated lands.

labrador, -ra, *a.* industrious, laborious. — *n.m.f.* labourer, farm-hand, tiller, ploughman; grower, farmer, husbandman, husbandwoman; rustic, peasant; *labrador de capa negra, poco medra*, the farmer who lives in ease reaps little.

labradoresco, -ca, *a.* relating to a farmer; rustic, clownish.

labradorita, *n.f.* (*min.*) labradorite.

labrandera, *n.f.* seamstress, embroiderer.

labrante, *n.m.* stonecutter, sculptor.

labrantín, *n.m.* petty farmer.

labrantío. -tía, *a.* arable, tillable.

labranza, *n.f.* tillage, cultivation, farming, ploughing, husbandry; farm-land.

labrar, *v.t.* to work, labour, elaborate, work out, fabricate, manufacture, produce; to till, plough, cultivate; to cut, dress, carve stone, wood, silver, etc.; to build, erect, construct buildings; to make designs in fabrics, stones, arms, etc.; to do needlework, embroider; to form, cause, bring about. — *v.i.* to make a strong impression on the mind.

labrero,-ra, *a.* applied to fishing nets for sharks.

labriego, *n.m.* rustic, farm-hand, peasant.

labro, *n.m.* upper lip of insects.

labrusca, *n.f.* wild grape-vine.

laburno, *n.m.* (*bot.*) laburnum.

laca, *n.f.* lac, gum-lac; red colour, lake; lacquer, japan; *laca en palillos*, stick-lac; *laca en grano*, seed-lac; *laca en tablillas*, shellac.

lacayo, *n.m.* lackey, groom, footman; knot of ribbons worn by women.

lacayuelo, *n.m.* foot-boy, groom; (*slang*) tiger.

lacayuno, -na, *a.* belonging to a lackey.

lacear, *v.t.* to lace, trim, tie with bows; to trap game or drive it within shot.

lacedemón; lacedemonio, -ia, *a.* Lacedemonian.

laceración, *n.f.* laceration, tearing.

lacerado, -da, *a.* unfortunate, unhappy; leprous. — *p.p.* [LACERAR].

lacerar, *v.t.* to mangle, tear in pieces, lacerate; (*fig.*) to hurt, damage.

laceria, *n.f.* misery, poverty, trouble, wretchedness; drudgery, weariness, fatigue, labour.

lacería, *n.f.* set of bows and ribbons.

lacerioso, -sa, *a.* miserable, wretched; scrofulous.

lacero, *n.m.* expert with the lasso; poacher.

lacertoso, *a.* muscular, athletic.

lacinia, *n.f.* (*bot.*) lacinia, slender lobe.

laciniado, -da, *a.* (*bot.*) laciniate, slashed.

lacio, -cia, *a.* faded, dried up, withered; flaccid, languid; straight (as hair).

lacónicamente, *adv.* laconically, concisely.

lacónico, -ca, *a.* laconic, brief, concise.

laconismo, *n.m.* laconism, conciseness, brevity, concise or laconic style.

lacra, *n.f.* mark or trace left by illness, defect, fault; vice, viciousness, wickedness.

lacrar, *v.t.* to injure or impair the health; to cause pecuniary damage; to seal with sealing-wax.

lacre, *n.m.* sealing-wax.

lacrimal, *a.* lachrymal.

lacrimatorio, -ria, *n.m.f.*, *a.* lachrymatory.

lacrimógeno, -na, *n.m.f.*, *a.* tear-gas, tear-shell.

lacrimosamente, *adv.* tearfully, lachrymosely.

lacrimoso, -sa, *a.* weeping, tearful, lachrymose.

lactación, *n.f.* act of suckling.

lactancia, *n.f.* lactation, period of suckling.

lactante, *n.m.* feeding on milk.

lactar, *v.t.* to nurse, give suck, feed with milk. — *v.i.* to suckle; to feed on milk.

lactario, -ria, *a.* lactary, lacteous, lactescent.

lactato, *n.m.* (*chem.*) lactate.

lácteo, -tea, *a.* lacteous, milky, lacteal, lactean, lactescent; *vía láctea* (*astron.*) galaxy, Milky Way.

lactescente, *a.* lactescent.

lacticíneo, -nea, *a.* lacteous.

lacticinio, *n.m.* milk or any food prepared with milk.

láctico, -ca, *a.* (*chem.*) lactic, lactic acid.

lactífero, -ra; lactífico, -ca, *a.* lactiferous.

lactina, lactosa, *n.f.* (*chem.*) lactose, lactin, milk sugar.

lactómetro, *n.m.* lactometer.

lactucario, *n.m.* (*pharm.*) lactucarium.

lactumen, *n.m.* (*med.*) lactumen, milk-scall.

lacunario, *n.m.* (*arch.*) lacunar.

lacustre, *a.* lacustrian, lacustrine, marshy.

lacha, *n.f.* (*ichth.*) anchovy; shame.

lada, *n.f.* (*bot.*) cistus.

ládano, *n.m.* ladanum, gum ladanum.

ladeado, -da, *a.* turned to one side, crooked, inclined, tilted, lopsided. — *p.p.* [LADEAR].

ladear, *v.i.*, *v.r.* to tilt, tip, turn on one side, sway. — *v.i.* to skirt; to be even with; to deviate. — *v.r.* to incline to an opinion or party; (*Chi.*) to fall in love.

ladeo, *n.m.* inclination or motion to one side.

ladera, *n.f.* declivity, slope, hillside. — *pl.* **laderas**, rails or staves of a truck; cheeks of a gun-carriage.

ladería, *n.f.* small dale on the slope of a mountain.

ladero, -ra, *a.* lateral.

ladi, *n.f.* lady, woman of social standing.

ladierno, *n.m.* (*bot.*) buckthorn.

ladilla, *n.f.* crab-louse; (*bot.*) common barley.

ladillo, *n.m.* shifting panel placed in the sides of coaches.

ladinamente, *adv.* sideways; artfully, sagaciously.

ladino, -na, *a.* (*obs.*) versed in languages; sagacious, cunning, crafty; linguistic; *esclavo ladino*, (*Am.*) slave who has served one year.

lado, *n.m.* side (of a body or object); direction or position (right or left); border, margin, edge, verge; party, interest, faction; (*mil.*) flank; mat for the side of carts, etc.; bend, course, manner; mode of proceeding. — *pl.* **lados**, patrons, advisers; *al lado*, just by, near at hand; *de lado*, incidentally, sideways;

a un lado, aside; clear the way; *lado a lado*, side by side; *echar a un lado*, to finish, bring to an end; *mirar de lado* (or *de medio lado*) to look with scorn upon; to steal a glance at.

ladón, *n.m.* (*bot.*) cistus.

ladra, *n.f.* barking; cry of hounds after the game.

ladrador, -ra, *n.m.f.* barker; useless talker.

ladrante, *a.* barking.

ladrar, *v.i.* to bark, howl, or cry like a dog; (*coll.*) to use empty threats; to clamour, to vociferate; to upbraid; *ladrar el estómago*, to be very hungry.

ladrear, *v.i.* to bark frequently and uselessly.

ladrería, *n.f.* lazaretto.

ladrido, *n.m.* barking, bow-wow; vociferation, outcry; calumny, slander.

ladrillado, *n.m.* brick floor.

ladrillador, *n.m.* bricklayer.

ladrillal, ladrillar, *n.m.* brick-yard.

ladrillar, *v.t.* to lay bricks.

ladrillazo, *n.m.* blow with a brickbat.

ladrillejo, *n.m.* little brick; boy's amusement of knocking at doors with bricks.

ladrillero, *n.m.* brick-maker; brick seller.

ladrillo, *n.m.* brick, tile; *ladrillo de chocolate*, cake of chocolate.

ladrilloso, -sa, *a.* bricky, made of brick.

ladrón, -ona, *n.m.f.* thief, robber, highwayman, cut-purse; *hacer del ladrón fiel*, to confide in a doubtful confidant; *piensa el ladrón que todos son de su condición*, the villain thinks all are like him; *por un ladrón pierden ciento en el mesón*, a thief causes many innocent men to be suspected; *el buen ladrón* (the good thief) St. Dimas *or* Dysmas.

ladrón, *n.m.* lock, sluice-gate; snuff of a candle that makes it melt.

ladronamente, *adv.* thievishly, dissemblingly.

ladroncillo, *n.m.* petty thief, filcher; *ladroncillo de agujeta, después sube a barjuleta*, a young thief becomes in time a big criminal.

ladronera, *n.f.* nest of rogues, den of robbers; extortion, filching; money-box; sluice-gate in a mill.

ladronería, *n.f.* larceny, robbery, theft.

ladronesca, *n.f.* set of thieves.

ladronesco, -ca, *a.* (*coll.*) belonging to thieves, thievish.

ladronicio, *n.m.* larceny, theft, robbery.

ladronzuelo, -la, *n.m.f.* petty thief, young filcher, pickpocket.

lagaña, *n.f.* blearedness, slimy moisture running from the eyes.

lagañoso, -sa, *a.* blear-eyed.

lagar, *n.m.* wine-press.

lagarada, *n.f.* wine-pressful.

lagarejo, *n.m.* small winepress.

lagarero, *n.m.* wine-presser; olive-presser.

lagareta, *n.f.* small wine-press; puddle, pool.

lagarta, *n.f.* female lizard; (*coll.*) sly, cunning woman.

lagartera, *n.f.* lizard-hole.

lagartero, -ra, *a.* lizard-catcher.

lagartija, *n.f.* eft, newt, small lizard.

lagartijero, -ra, *a.* eft-catcher.

lagartillo, *n.m.* small lizard.

lagarto, *n.m.* lizard; (*anat.*) large muscle of the arm; (*coll.*) sly, artful person.

lago, *n.m.* lake; *lago de leones*, den of lions; *Lago Salado*, Salt Lake.

lagostín, *n.m.* (*obs.*) crayfish.

lagotear, *v.i.* (*coll.*) to flatter, wheedle, cajole.

lagotería, *n.f.* (*coll.*) flattery, adulation.

lagotero, -ra, *a.* (*coll.*) flattering, soothing, wheedling, honey-mouthed.

lágrima, *n.f.* tear; drop of any liquid; drop-like exudation from a tree; wine that drips from the grape without pressure; (*bot.*) gromwell; *lágrima de David* (or *de Job*), (*bot.*) Job's-tears; *lágrimas de S. Pedro* (or *de Moisés*) pebbles, stones thrown at any person; *lágrimas de Batavia* (or *de Holanda*), Prince Rupert's drops, glass globules; *deshacerse en lágrimas*, to burst into tears, weep freely; *lo que no va en lágrimas va en suspiros*, one thing compensates for another; *llorar lágrimas de sangre* (or *llorar a lágrima viva*), to feel the keenest grief.

lagrimable, *a.* lachrymable, lamentable, worthy of tears.

lagrimal, *a.* lachrymal. — *n.m.* lachrymal caruncle near corner of the eye.

lagrimar, lagrimear, *v.i.* to weep, shed tears.

lagrimeo, *n.m.* shedding tears.

lagrimón, *n.m.* large tear.

lagrimoso, -sa, *a.* tearful, lachrymose; watery (eyes), (*bot.*) exuding.

laguer, *n.m.* (*Cub.*) lager beer.

laguna, *n.f.* pond, small lake, lagoon, basin; hiatus, lacuna, gap in a book or writing; uneven country.

lagunajo, *n.m.* puddle, pool, plashet.

lagunar, *n.m.* (*arch.*) lacunar.

lagunero, -ra, *a.* belonging to a lagoon.

lagunoso, -sa, *a.* marshy, fenny, swampy.

laical, *a.* laical, laic.

laicalizar, *v.t.* (*Chi.*) [SECULARIZAR].

laicismo, *n.m.* secularism.

laico, -ca, *a.* laic, laicist.

lairén, *a.* kind of grapes and vines.

laja, *n.f.* flag-stone, slab; (*naut.*) rock at the entrance of a port; (*Col.*) thin cord made of sisal.

lama, *n.f.* mud, slime, surface foam on water, ooze; seaweed; lama (gold or silver cloth); fine sand used for mortar; dust of ores in mines. — *n.m.f.* lama, Tibetan monk or nun.

lamaísmo, *n.m.* Lamaism.

lamaísta, *n.m.f.* Lamaist.

lambel, *n.m.* (*her.*) lambel, label.

lambrequines, *n.m.pl.* (*her.*) mantelets.

lambrija, *n.f.* worm bred in the human body; (*coll.*) meagre, slender person.

lamedal, *n.m.* musty, miry place.

lamedero, *n.m.* salt-lick.

lamedor, -ra, *n.m.f.* licker; (*pharm.*) syrup; wheedling; *dar lamedor*, to feign a losing game in order to ensure greater success.

lamedura, *n.f.* act of licking.

lamelar, *v.t.* to roll copper into sheets.

lameliforme, *a.* lamelliform, in thin layers.

lamentable, *a.* lamentable, deplorable.

lamentablemente, *adv.* lamentably.

lamentación, *n.f.* lamentation, wail, groaning.

lamentador, -ra, *n.m.f.* lamenter, weeper, mourner, complainer.

lamentar, *v.t.* to lament, regret, mourn, bewail, moan. — *v.i., v.r.* to lament, grieve, wail; to complain, cry.

lamento, *n.m.* lamentation, lament, moan, wail, mourning, cry.

lamentoso, *a.* lamentable, mournful.
lameplatos, *n.m.* (*coll.*) glutton, gorger; (*coll.*) one who feeds on leavings.
lamer, *v.t.* to lick, lap; to touch slightly.
lamerón, -ona, *a.* (*coll.*) fond of dainties or sweets.
lamia, *n.f.* lamia, a fabulous monster; shark.
lamido, -da, *a.* thin, weak; clean, scrubbed (of persons); affected, dandified. — *p.p.* [LAMER].
lamiente, *a.* licking, licker.
lamín, *n.m.* (*prov.*) dainty tit-bit.
lámina, *n.f.* plate, sheet, lamina, flake, engraved copper-plate; print, engraving, picture, illustration, plate.
laminado, -da, *a.* lamellated, laminated.
laminador, *n.m.* rolling-press, plate-roller.
laminar, *v.t.* to roll or beat metal into sheets; (*prov.*) to lick, to guzzle dainties.
laminar, *a.* laminar, lamellar; in sheets.
laminera, *n.f.* (*prov.*) bee leading its companions.
laminero, -ra, *a.* fond of sweets. — *n.m.f.* manufacturer of metal plates; one who makes shrines for relics.
laminoso, -sa, *a.* laminose.
lamiscar, *v.t.* (*coll.*) to lick with haste and great eagerness.
lamoso, -sa, *a.* oozy, slimy, muddy.
lampa, *n.f.* (*Chi., Per., agric.*) shovel for grain.
lampacear, *v.t.* (*naut.*) to swab.
lampar, *v.i., v.r.* to be eager for anything; to crave, long for.
lámpara, *n.f.* lamp, light, luminous body; oil-spot, grease spot or stain; bough placed at the door on festivals or rejoicings; blow-lamp; miner's safety lamp; *atizar la lámpara,* (*coll.*) to refill the glasses.
lamparería, *n.f.* lamp-factory, lamp-store.
lamparero, -ra, *n.m.f.* lamp-maker or -seller; lamp-lighter.
lamparilla, *n.f.* small lamp; night-light; sort of camlet; (*bot.*) aspen, trembling poplar.
lamparín, *n.m.* lamp-holder, lamp-case.
lamparista, *n.m.f.* lamp-maker or -seller; lamp-lighter.
lamparón, *n.m.* large grease-spot; king's evil; (*vet.*) disease of horses.
lamparanoso, -sa, *a.* scrofulous.
lampatán, *n.m.* Chinese plant.
lampazo, *n.m.* (*bot.*) burdock; (*naut.*) swab, mop; *pl.* **lampazos,** pimples.
lampiño, -ña, *a.* beardless.
lampión, *n.m.* large lantern.
lampo, *n.m.* (*poet.*) light, splendour.
lampote, *n.m.* (*Philip.*) cotton cloth.
lamprea, *n.f.* (*ichth.*) sea-lamprey.
lamprear, *v.t.* to dress or season with wine and sour gravy.
lamprehuela, lampreílla, *n.f.* small lamprey, river lamprey.
lámpsana, *n.f.* (*bot.*) common nipplewort.
lampuga, *n.f.* (*ichth.*) yellow mackerel.
lampuso, -sa, *a.* (*Cub., PR.*) impudent, bare-faced.
lana, *n.f.* wool, fleece; hair of some animals; woollen manufacture in general; *a costa de Lanas,* at another man's expense; *perro de lanas,* poodle; *lana peladiza,* glover's wool; *lana en rama,* uncombed wool; *ir por lana y volver trasquilado,* to go for wool and come back shorn; *lavar la lana,* to enquire min-

utely into the conduct of a person suspected of doing wrong; *cardarle a uno la lana,* to reprimand severely; *aunque vestido de lana, no soy borrego,* I'm not such a fool as I look.
lanada, *n.f.* (*artill.*) sponge.
lanado, -da, *a.* (*bot.*) lanate, wool-like.
lanar, *a.* woolly (of sheep); wool-bearing.
lanaria, *n.f.* (*bot.*) soapwort.
lancán, *n.m.* (*Philip.*) barge.
lance, *n.m.* cast, throw; casting of a fish-net; catch in a net; critical moment; chance, casualty, accident, occurrence; incident, episode (of a play or novel); quarrel, dispute; transaction; move in a game; skill of a player; event; missile shot from a bow; (bullfight) flourish with the cape; *lance de honor,* duel; *a pocos lances,* in a short time; *de lance,* cheap, at bargain price; *tener pocos lances,* to be uninteresting; *echar buen lance,* to attain one's desires or aims; *jugar el lance,* to handle a delicate matter.
lanceado, -da, *a.* (*bot.*) lanceolate.
lancear, *v.t.* to wound with a lance.
lancéola, *n.f.* (*bot.*) rib-grass plantain.
lanceolado, -da, *a.* (*bot.*) lanceolate.
lancera, *n.f.* lance-rack in an armoury.
lancero, *n.m.* pikeman, lancer; maker of pikes. — *pl.* lancers (music and dance).
lanceta, *n.f.* (*surg.*) lancet; (*vet.*) fleam; potter's knife.
lancetada, *n.f.;* **lancetazo,** *n.m.* opening or wounding with a lancet.
lancetero, *n.m.* case for carrying lancets.
lancinante, *a.* lancinating.
lancita, *n.f.* small lance.
lancurdia, *n.f.* small trout.
lancha, *n.f.* flagstone, slab; (*naut.*) boat, gig; lighter, launch; snare for partridges; *lancha de socorro,* life-boat; *lancha cañonera,* gun-boat; *lancha de pescar,* fishing smack.
lanchada, *n.f.* lighter-load.
lanchaje, *n.m.* (*com.*) ferriage; lighterage.
lanchar, *n.m.* flagstone quarry.
lanchazo, *n.m.* blow with a flagstone.
lanchero, *n.m.* bargeman, boatman, oarsman.
lanchón, *n.m.* (*naut.*) lighter, barge, scow.
lanchonero, *n.m.* lighterman, bargeman.
landgrave, *n.m.* landgrave.
landgraviato, *n.m.* landgraviate.
landó, *n.m.* (*car.*) landau.
landre, *n.f.* swelling of the glands; acorn; purse concealed in the clothes.
landrecilla, *n.f.* round lump among the glands.
landrero, -ra, *a.* niggardly (beggar).
landrilla, *n.f.* (*vet.*) tongue-worm.
lanería, *n.f.* shop where wool is sold.
lanero, -ra, *a.* woollen. — *n.m.* dealer in wool; warehouse for wool; African falcon.
langa, *n.f.* small dry codfish.
langaruto, -ta, *a.* (*coll.*) tall, lank, ill-shaped.
langor, *n.m.* languor, faintness.
langosta, *n.f.* (*ent.*) locust; (*ichth.*) spiny lobster.
langostera, *n.f.* name of a fishing-net.
langostín, or **langostino,** *n.m.* (*ichth.*) craw-fish or crayfish.
langostón, *n.m.* (*ent.*) green grasshopper.
languidamente, *adv.* languidly, languishingly.
languidecer, *v.i.* to languish.
languidez, languideza, *n.f.* languishment,

languidness, languor, weakness, weariness, faintness.

lánguido, -da, *a.* languid, faint, weak, languishing, feeble, heartless.

lanífero, -ra, *a.* (*poet.*) laniferous, woolly.

lanificación, *n.f.;* **lanificio,** *n.m.* woollen manufacturing; woollen goods.

lanilla, *n.f.* nap of cloth; down; swan skin, fine flannel; (*naut.*) bunting.

lanío, -nía, *a.* woolly.

lanosidad, *n.f.* (*bot.*) down of leaves, fruit, etc.

lanoso, -sa, *a.* woolly.

lansquenete, *n.m.* (*hist.*) German foot-soldier.

lantaca, *n.f.* (*Philip.*) small culverin.

lantano, *n.m.* (*chem.*) lanthanum.

lanteja, *n.f.* lentil.

lantejuela, *n.f.* spangle; scurf left by a sore.

lanudo, -da, *a.* woolly, fleecy.

lanuginoso, -sa, *a.* (*bot.*) lanuginous, downy, covered with soft hair.

lanza, *n.f.* lance, spear, pike; nozzle; pikeman; pole of a coach or waggon; free-lance; *a punta de lanza,* with all one's might; *echar la lanza,* to impugn, contradict, distrust; *echar lanzas en la mar,* to strive in vain; *romper lanzas,* to remove hindrances; *no haber* (or *no quedar*) *lanza enhiesta,* to rout the enemy; *romper lanzas con,* to break a lance with, have a contest with; *ser una lanza,* (*Am.*) to be clever, expert; *nunca la lanza embotó la pluma, ni la pluma la lanza,* the lance never yet blunted the pen, nor the pen the lance; *lanza en ristre,* ready for action. — *pl.* **lanzas,** duty formerly paid by the nobility in lieu of military service.

lanzada, *n.f.* blow or stroke with a lance; *a moro muerto gran lanzada,* even hares can insult a dead lion.

lanzadera, *n.f.* shuttle, weaver's instrument.

lanzado, -da, *a.* (*naut.*) raking, overhanging. — *p.p.* [LANZAR].

lanzador, -ra, *n.m.f.* thrower, ejecter.

lanzafuego, *n.m.* (*artill.*) linstock, match-staff.

lanzallamas, *n.m.* (*mil.*) flame-thrower.

lanzamiento, *n.m.* launching, casting, or throwing; jaculation; (*law*) dispossessing, ejectment; (*naut.*) flaring of bows and knuckle timbers; rake of the stem and stern-post. — *pl.* **lanzamientos,** length of a ship from stem to stern-post.

lanzar, *v.t.* (*pret.* **lancé;** *pres. subj.* **lance**) to lance, dart, throw, hurl, launch, fling; (*law*) to dispossess, eject; to throw up, vomit, spout, let loose. — *v.r.* to rush upon, dart upon; to launch forth; (*com.*) to engage or embark in.

lanzatorpedos, *n.m.* (*naut.*) torpedo tube.

lanzazo, *n.m.* blow or stroke with a lance.

lanzón, *n.m.* short and thick goad.

lanzuela, *n.f.* small lance or spear.

laña, *n.f.* brace, clamp, cramp, cramp-iron; green coconut.

lañar, *v.t.* to cramp, clamp; (*prov.*) to open and gut fish.

lapa, *n.f.* vegetable film on the surface of a liquid; barnacle; (*bot.*) goose-grass, cleavers.

lapachar, *n.m.* swamp, marsh, morass.

lapacho, *n.m.* (*S. Am.*) hard-wood tree of the Bignonia family.

lápade, *n.f.* acorn shell-fish, barnacle.

lapaza, *n.f.* (*prov.*) rough panic-grass.

lapicero, *n.m.* pencil-case; pencil-holder.

lápida, *n.f.* tablet, memorial stone; *lápida mortuoria,* grave-stone.

lapidación, *n.f.* lapidation, stoning to death.

lapidar, *v.t.* to stone, stone to death.

lapidaria, *n.f.* lapidary's profession.

lapidario, -ria, *a.* lapidary.

lapidario, *n.m.* lapidary.

lapídeo, -dea, *a.* lapidose, stony.

lapidificación, *n.f.* petrification, lapidification.

lapidificar, *v.t.* (*chem.*) lapidify.

lapidoso, -sa, *a.* lapidose, stony.

lapilla, *n.f.* (*bot.*) hound's-tongue.

lapislázuli, *n.m.* lapis-lazuli.

lápiz, *n.m.* black-lead, graphite, plumbago; lead pencil, crayon; *lápiz rojo* (or *encarnado*), red ochre; (*coll.*) censor's blue pencil.

lapizar, *n.m.* black-lead mine.

lapizar, *v.t.* to pencil; to draw with chalk or pencil.

lapo, *n.m.* (*coll.*) blow with a cane, or flat of a sword; (*Arg., Chi., Mex.*) slap in the face, buffet.

lapón, -ona, *n.m.f., a.* Lapp, Laplander.

lapso, *n.m.* lapse or course of time; fall, lapse, slip.

lar, *n.m.* Lar, tutelar god (usually *pl.* **lares**); hearth, fireplace; furnace; (*fig.*) home.

larario, *n.m.* lararium.

lardar, lardear, *v.t.* to baste meat on the spit; to scald with boiling oil.

lardero (jueves), *n.m.* Thursday before Lent.

lardo, *n.m.* lard, fat of animals.

lardón, *n.m.* (*print.*) marginal addition; also a piece of paper clinging to the frisket and preventing the impression of some part of a sheet.

lardoso, -sa, *a.* greasy, oily, smearing.

larga, *n.f.* (*shoe.*) lengthening piece put to a last; longest billiard-cue; *dar largas,* to delay, procrastinate.

largamente, *adv.* largely, copiously; frankly, liberally; completely; for a long time.

largar, *v.t.* (*pret.* **largué;** *pres. subj.* **largue**) to loosen, slacken, to shed; to set free, let go; to heave (a sigh); to give (a slap, etc.); (*naut.*) to set sail, to ease a rope; *toda vela larga,* (*naut.*) all sails out; *largar las velas,* (*naut.*) to set sail. — *v.r.* (*coll.*) to go off, leave, quit, pack away; (*naut.*) to set sail.

largo, -ga, *a.* long, extended, prolonged; prompt, expeditious; liberal, generous, large, free; protracted, lasting, continued; abundant, copious, excessive; (*coll.*) astute, shrewd, cunning. — *pl.* many, quite a number. — *n.m.* length; (*mus.*) largo. — *adv.* largely, profusely. — *interj.* ¡largo! or ¡largo de ahí! away! begone! *largo de lengua,* over free with the tongue; *de largo a largo,* from one end to the other; *largo de uñas,* light-fingered; *pasar de largo,* to pass without stopping; *navegar a lo largo de la costa,* (*naut.*) to navigate along the coast; *a la larga,* at length, in the long run, slowly; *a la corta* (or *a la larga*), sooner or later; *largos años,* many years, long life; *a lo largo,* at a distance; *gastar largo y tendido,* to spend lavishly; *ése es cuento largo,* that is a long story.

largomira, *n.m.* telescope.

largor, *n.m.* length.

largueado, -da, *a.* striped.

larguero, *n.m.* (*carp.*) jamb-post; bolster, stringer; (*aer.*) longeron; (*aer.*) spar.

largueza, *n.f.* length, largeness, width, extent; liberality, generosity, munificence, frankness.

larguirucho, -cha, *a.* (*coll.*) tall and thin.

larguito, -ta, *a.* not very long.

largura, *n.f.* length, stretch, extent.

lárice, *n.m.* (*bot.*) larch-tree.

laricino, -na, *a.* belonging to the larch-tree.

larije, *a.* kind of red grapes.

laringa, *n.f.* larch-turpentine; Venice turpentine.

laringe, *n.f.* (*anat.*) larynx.

laríngeo, -gea, *a.* laryngeal.

laringitis, *n.f.* (*med.*) laryngitis.

laringología, *n.f.* laryngology.

laringoscopia, *n.f.* laryngoscopy.

laringoscopio, *n.m.* laryngoscope.

laringotomía, *n.f.* (*surg.*) laryngotomy.

laro, *n.m.* larus, gull, sea-gull.

larva, *n.f.* (*obs.*) mask; (*entom.*) larva, grub; (*obs.*) larvas, hobgoblins; lemures.

larvado, -da, *a.* (*med.*) larvate, masked.

larval, *a.* of a larva; mask-like; frightful, ghastly.

las, *def. art. f.pl.* the; *pers. pron. f.pl.* (in the accusative case), them.

lasaña, *n.f.* a leaf-shaped fritter.

lasca, *n.f.* chip from a stone.

lascar, *v.t.* (*naut.*) to ease away, slacken, pay out; (*Mex.*) to hurt, bruise, mangle.

láscar, *n.m.* lascar, Indian seaman or gunner.

lascivamente, *adv.* lasciviously, lustfully.

lascivia, *n.f.* lasciviousness, lewdness, luxury, lust.

lascivo, -va, *a.* lascivious, lewd, lustful, libidinous; merry, sportive; luxuriant, exuberant.

láser, *n.m.* benzoin.

laserpicio, *n.m.* (*bot.*) laserwort.

lasitud, *n.f.* lassitude, weariness, faintness.

laso, -sa, *a.* weary, tired, exhausted; lax, flaccid; silk or hemp untwisted.

lastar, *v.t.* to pay, answer, or suffer for another.

lástima, *n.f.* sympathy, compassion, pity, condolence, grief; pitiful object; plaint, lamentation, tale of woe; *es lástima,* it is a pity.

lastimadura, *n.f.* sore, hurt.

lastimar, *v.t.* to hurt, injure, damage, wound, offend; to pity, sympathize. — *v.r.* to grieve, regret, be sorry for; to complain.

lastimeramente, *adv.* sadly, sorrowfully.

lastimero, -ra, *a.* doleful, mournful, miserable, moving, grievous; injurious, hurtful.

lastimosamente, *adv.* pitifully, grievously, miserably, lamentably.

lastimoso, -sa, *a.* doleful, sad.

lasto, *n.m.* receipt given to one who has paid on behalf of another.

lastra, *n.f.* flagstone, slab; boat, lighter.

lastrar, *v.t.* (*naut., rail.*) to ballast.

lastre, *n.m.* ballast, lastage; stone slat; (*fig.*) weight, motive, judgment.

lastrón, *n.m.* large stone slat.

lasún, *n.m.* (*ichth.*) loach.

lata, *n.f.* small log; tin-plate or tinned iron-plate; tin can; lath, ledge, batten; (*coll.*) annoyance, nuisance; (*coll.*) protracted and tedious visit or performance; *hoja de lata,* tin-plate.

latamente, *adv.* largely, amply.

latania, *n.f.* (*bot.*) latania palm.

latastro, *n.m.* (*arch.*) plinth of a pillar.

lataz, *n.f.* (*zool.*) sea-otter.

latebra, *n.f.* cave, den, hiding-place.

latebroso, -sa, *a.* hiding, furtive, secretive.

latente, *a.* latent, dormant; concealed, obscure, hidden.

lateral, *a.* lateral.

lateralmente, *adv.* laterally.

laticaude, *a.* (*zool.*) long-tailed.

latido, *n.m.* palpitation, pant, pulsation, beat or throb of the heart; howling of a dog. — *p.p.* [LATIR].

latiente, *a.* palpitating, fluttering.

latifundio, *n.m.* vast rural property.

latifundista, *n.m.f.* owner of one or more *latifundios.*

latigadera, *n.f.* strap or thong for lashing the yoke.

latigazo, *n.m.* lash, whipping; crack of a whip; jerk; (*fig.*) harsh reproof; unintentional offence.

látigo, *n.m.* whip; lashing cord for weighing objects with a steelyard; cinch-strap; long plume round a hat.

latiguear, *v.i.* to smack, crack, ply, lash with a whip.

latiguera, *n.f.* cinch-strap.

latiguero, *n.m.* maker or seller of whips.

latiguillo, *n.m.* small whip; (*theat.*) mannerism.

latín, *n.m.* Latin; Latin tongue; *saber mucho latín,* to be very cunning.

latinajo, *n.m.* (*coll.*) Latin jargon.

latinamente, *adv.* in Latin, Latinly.

latinar, latinear, *v.i.* to speak or write Latin; to use Latin phrases often.

latinidad, *n.f.* Latinity, the Latin tongue.

latinismo, *n.m.* Latinism.

latinizar, *v.t.* to Latinize. — *v.i.* to use words borrowed from the Latin.

latino, -na, *a.* Latin; the Western Catholic Church; *vela latina,* lateen sail. — *n.m.f.* Latinist; native of Latium.

latipinado, -da, *a.* (*zool.*) latipennate, broad-finned; broad-winged.

latir, *v.i.* to palpitate, pulsate, throb, beat; to yelp, howl, bark.

latitud, *n.f.* breadth, width, latitude, stretch, extent; (*geog., astron.*) latitude.

latitudinal, *a.* latitudinal.

latitudinario, -ria, *a.* (*theol.*) latitudinarian, liberal.

latitudinarismo, *n.m.* (*theol.*) latitudinarianism.

lato, -ta, *a.* large, diffuse, extensive.

latón, *n.m.* brass; *latón en hojas* (or *planchas*), latten brass, sheet brass.

latonería, *n.f.* working in brass, brass-trade; braziery, brass-works; brass-ware.

latonero, *n.m.* brazier, worker in brass.

latoso, -sa, *a.* vexing, annoying; tedious, tiresome.

latría, *n.f.* worship of God.

latrina, *n.f.* latrine, privy.

latrocinio, *n.m.* frequent and systematic robbery.

latvio, -a, *n.m.f., a.* Latvian.

laucha, *n.f.* (*Arg., Ur., Bol., Chi.*) small mouse.

laúd, *n.m.* (*mus.*) lute; (*naut.*) craft, catboat; striped turtle.

lauda, *n.f.* tombstone.

laudable, *a.* laudable, praiseworthy.

laudablemente, *adv.* laudably.

láudano, *n.m.* (*pharm.*) laudanum; mixture of white wine, opium, saffron, etc.

laudar, *v.t.* (*obs.*) to praise; (*law*) to render a decision as an arbitrator or umpire.

laudatorio, -ria, *a.* laudatory, acclamatory, full of praise. — *n.f.* laudatory, panegyric.

laude, *n.f.* inscribed tombstone. — *pl.* **laudes,** (*eccles.*) lauds; *a laudes,* frequently, continually; *tocar a laudes,* to blow one's own trumpet.

laudemio, *n.m.* (*law*) dues paid to the lord of the manor on transfers of his landed property.

laudo, *n.m.* (*law*) finding of an arbitrator or umpire.

launa, *n.f.* lamina, thin plate of metal; schistose clay for roofing houses.

lauráceo, -cea, *a.* laurel-like; (*bot.*) lauraceous, laurineous.

láurea, *n.f.* laurel wreath.

laureado, -da, *a.* laureate. — *p.p.* [LAUREAR].

laureando, *n.m.* scholar about to graduate.

laurear, *v.t.* to crown with laurel; to honour, reward; to confer a degree.

lauredal, *n.m.* plantation of laurel-trees.

laurel, *n.m.* (*bot.*) laurel; laurel wreath, honour, distinction, reward; *laurel cerezo,* (*bot.*) cherry-laurel.

laurente, *n.m.* workman in paper-mills.

lauréola, *n.f.* laurel wreath; diadem; *lauréola hembra,* (*bot.*) mezereon daphne; *lauréola macho,* spurge laurel.

laurífero, -ra, *a.* (*poet.*) lauriferous.

lauríneo, -nea, *a.* (*bot.*) laurineous.

laurino, -na, *a.* belonging to laurel.

lauro, *n.m.* (*bot.*) laurus; glory, honour, fame, triumph.

lauroceraso, laurorreal, *n.m.* cherry-laurel.

lautamente, *adv.* splendidly.

lauto, -ta, *a.* rich, wealthy, opulent.

lava, *n.f.* lava; (*min.*) washing of metals.

lavabo, *n.m.* wash-stand; lavatory.

lavacaras, *n.m.* (*coll.*) flatterer.

lavación, *n.f.* (*pharm.*) lotion, wash.

lavadero, *n.m.* washing-place, laundry; lavatory; (*tan.*) vat or pit for washing hides; (*min.*) buddling tank; (*Am.*) placer, place where gold deposits are washed.

lavado, *n.m.* wash, washing; laundry-work; (*art*) aquarelle in a single tint.

lavador, -ra, *a.* washer, cleaner.

lavador, *n.m.* (*artill.*) burnisher; *n.f. lavadora mecánica,* washing machine.

lavadura, *n.f.* wash, washing, lavation; composition for dressing glove-leather; slops.

lavaje, *n.m.* washing of wools.

lavajo, *n.m.* pool where cattle go to drink; morass.

lavamanos, *n.m.* fitted wash-stand; lavatory.

lavamiento, *n.m.* washing, ablution.

lavanco, *n.m.* kind of wild duck.

lavandera, *n.f.* laundress, washerwoman.

lavandero, *n.m.* launderer, one who washes.

lavaplatos, *n.m.f.* dish-washer.

lavar, *v.t.* to wash, lave, launder, scour, rinse, cleanse; (*mas.*) to whitewash, calcimine; (*art*) to paint in water-colours; to purify, clear from blemish.

lavativa, *n.f.* clyster, injection, enema; syringe; (*fig.*) vexation, annoyance, bore.

lavatorio, *n.m.* lavation, washing; lavatory, wash-stand; (*pharm.*) lotion; (*eccles.*) maundy, feet-washing on Maundy Thursday; part of the Mass; tablet containing the appropriate prayers.

lavazas, *n.f.pl.* foul water, slops.

lave, *n.m.* washing, of ores in mines.

lavotear, *v.t., v.r.* (*coll.*) to wash hurriedly and poorly.

lavoteo, *n.m.* washing hurriedly and poorly performed.

laxación, *n.f.* loosening, laxation, slackening.

laxamiento, *n.m.* laxation, laxity, laxness, loosening.

laxante, *a.* loosening, softening. — *n.m.* (*med.*) laxative.

laxar, *v.t.* to loosen, soften.

laxativo, -va, *n.m.f., a.* laxative, lenitive.

laxidad, laxitud, *n.f.* laxity, laxness.

laxo, -xa, *a.* lax, slack.

lay, *n.m.* (*poet.*) lay, ballad.

laya, *n.f.* (*agric.*) fork; quality, nature, kind, class.

layador, *n.m.* spadesman.

layar, *v.t.* (*agric.*) to fork, turn up with a *laya.*

lazada, *n.f.* bow-knot; (*sew.*) bow; true-lover's knot.

lazador, *n.m.* lassoer.

lazar, *v.t.* to lasso, capture with a lasso.

lazareto, *n.m.* lazaretto, lazaret; pest-house.

lazarillo, *n.m.* blind person's guide.

lazarino, -na, *a.* leprous, lazar-like, lazarly. — *n.m.f.* lazar, leper.

lázaro, *n.m.* lazar.

lazo, *n.m.* (*sew.*) bow, loop, true-lover's knot; bond, chain, tie, lasso, slip-knot; snare (for game); trap, scheme (for persons); (*arch.*) knot or ornament; *roer el lazo,* to escape from a difficulty or danger. — *pl.* (*danc.*) figures.

lazulita, *n.f.* lazulite, lapis-lazuli.

le, *pers. pron. dative sing.* (*m.* or *f.*) to him, to her, to it. — *acc. masc. sing.* him.

leal, *a.* loyal, true, faithful.

lealmente, *adv.* loyally, faithfuliy.

lealtad, *n.f.* loyalty, fidelity, fealty; gentleness, attachment.

lebeche, *n.m.* a south-east wind in the Mediterranean.

lebeni, *n.m.* Moorish drink prepared with sour milk.

lebrada, *n.f.* fricassee of hare.

lebratico, -illo, -ito; lebrato, lebratón, *n.m.* young hare, leveret.

lebrel, *n.m.* greyhound.

lebrela, *n.f.* greyhound bitch.

lebrero, -ra, *a.* good at hunting hares.

lebrillo, *n.m.* glazed earthenware tub.

lebrón, *n.m.* large hare; (*coll.*) coward, poltroon.

lebroncillo, *n.m.* young hare.

lebruno, -na, *a.* leporine, of the hare kind.

lección, *n.f.* lesson; tuition; reading; lecture; lection; admonition, warning, example; *dar la lección,* to say a lesson before a teacher; *dar lección,* to give a lesson to a scholar; *dar una lección,* to teach someone a lesson, reprimand him; *tomar lección,* to take a lesson from a teacher; *tomar la lección,* to hear a lesson from a scholar.

leccionario, *n.m.* (*eccles.*) lectionary.

leccioncita, *n.f.* short lecture or lesson.

leccionista, *n.m.f.* private tutor.
lectisternio, *n.m.* banquet of the heathen gods.
lectivo, -va, *a.* lecture times in universities.
lector, -ra, *n.m.f.* reader; teacher, lecturer; (*eccles.*) instructor in the Gospel.
lectorado, *n.m.* (*eccles.*) lectorate.
lectoral, *n.f.* (*eccles.*) prebend. — *n.m.* prebendary, holder of a *lectoral*.
lectoría, *n.f.* (*eccles.*) lectureship.
lectura, *n.f.* reading, perusal; lecture; (*print.*) pica.
lecturita, *n.f.* (*print.*) small pica.
lecha, lechaza, *n.f.* seminal fluid of fishes; each of the two sacs which contain it, roe.
lechada, *n.f.* grout, slate and lime, whitewash; pulp for making paper; lime-water.
lechal, *a.* sucking; (*bot.*) lactiferous, milky. — *n.m.* (*bot.*) milky juice of plants.
lechar, *a.* nursing; promoting the secretion of milk in female mammals.
leche, *n.f.* milk; (*bot.*) milky juice; *vaca de leche,* milch cow; *cochinillo de leche,* sucking pig; *leche de gallina* or *de pájaro,* (*bot.*) common star of Bethlehem; *leche de canela,* oil of cinnamon dissolved in wine; *leche de tierra,* magnesia; *hermano de leche,* foster-brother; *estar con la leche en los labios,* to lack experience; *estar en leche,* to be immature; (*naut.*) to be calm (said of the sea); *leche crema,* custard; *leche quemada,* sweetmeat made of simmered milk; *mamar una cosa en la leche,* to imbibe something in infancy; *lo que en la leche se mama, en la mortaja se derrama,* habits acquired in childhood disappear only at death.
lechecillas, *n.f.pl.* sweetbread; livers and lights.
lechera, *a.* milch (applied to animals). — *n.f.* milkmaid, dairymaid; milk-can; milk-pot, milk-ewer.
lechería, *n.f.* cow-house, dairy, lactary.
lechero, -ra, *a.* milky.
lechero, *n.m.* milkman.
lecherón, *n.m.* (*prov.*) milk-pail, milk-vessel; flannel wrap for new-born infants.
lechetrezna, *n.f.* (*bot.*) spurge.
lechigada, *n.f.* breed, litter; gang of ruffians; company of persons working or living together.
lechiguana, *n.f.* (*Arg., Bol.*) a kind of wasp (*Nectarina mellifica*).
lechín, *n.m.* variety of olive-tree and the olive it yields; (*vet.*) tumour in horses.
lechino, *n.m.* (*vet.*) tent; small tumour in horses.
lecho, *n.m.* bed, couch; litter; bed of a river; bottom of the sea or lake; row, tier, layer, foundation, stratum, base; *lecho de lobo,* haunt of a wolf.
lechón, *n.m.* (sucking) pig; (*coll.*) dirty fellow.
lechona, *n.f.* female sucking pig; (*coll.*) dirty woman.
lechoncico, -illo, -ito, *n.m.* sucking pig; very young pig.
lechoso, -sa, *a.* (*bot.*) having a milky juice. — *n.m.* (*S. Am.*) papaw-tree. — *n.f.* papaw.
lechuga, *n.f.* (*bot.*) lettuce; (*sew.*) frill.
lechugado, -da, *a.* resembling lettuce.
lechuguero, -ra, *n.m.* retailer of lettuce.
lechuguilla, *n.f.* wild lettuce; frill, ruff.
lechuguina, *n.f.* (*coll.*) modish young lady.

lechuguino, *n.m.* lettuce sprout; plot of small lettuces; (*coll.*) dandy, dude.
lechuza, *n.f.* (*orn.*) owl, barn-owl; (*fig.*) an old and ugly woman, a hag.
lechuzo, -za, *a.* (*fig.*) owlish; suckling (of a mule colt).
lechuzo, *n.m.* bill-collector or server of summonses.
ledamente, *adv.* (*poet.*) merrily, gaily, cheerfully.
ledo, -da, *a.* (*poet.*) gay, merry, cheerful, glad, joyful.
leedor, -ra, *n.m.f.* reader, peruser.
leer, *v.t.* to read; to peruse; to instruct, lecture; to read or divine someone's thoughts; *leer para sí,* to read to oneself; *leer cátedra,* to occupy a University chair; *leer a uno la cartilla,* to reprimand a person.
lega, *n.f.* (*eccles.*) lay-sister.
legacía, *n.f.* legateship; message entrusted to a legate; province or duration of a legateship.
legación, *n.f.* legation, legateship; embassy.
legado, *n.m.* (*law*) legacy; deputy, ambassador, legate; commander of a Roman legion; *legado a látere,* Pope's legate.
legador, *n.m.* labourer who ties the feet of sheep for shearing them.
legadura, *n.f.* tie; binding cord or strap.
legajo, *n.m.* file, docket, bundle of papers.
legal, *a.* legal, lawful, legitimate, constitutional; true, faithful, loyal.
legalidad, *n.f.* legality, lawfulness, legitimateness; fidelity, punctuality.
legalización, *n.f.* legalization, attestation, notary's certificate.
legalizar, *v.t.* to legalize, authorize, make lawful.
legalmente, *adv.* legally, lawfully; faithfully.
legamente, *adv.* ignorantly.
légamo, *n.m.* slime, mud, clay left by water.
legamoso, -sa, *a.* slimy, oozy, greasy.
legaña, *n.f.* gummy secretion, bleariness of the eyes.
legañoso, -sa, *a.* blear-eyed.
legar, *v.t.* (*pret.* **legué;** *pres. subj.* **legue**) to depute; to send a legate; (*law*) to bequeath.
legatorio, -ria, *n.m.f.* (*law*) legatee.
legenda, *n.f.* (*eccles.*) legend, history of saints.
legendario, -ria, *a.* legendary.
legendario, *n.m.* legendary, book of legends.
legible, *a.* legible, readable.
legión, *n.f.* legion, multitude.
legionario, -ria, *a.* legionary.
legislación, *n.f.* legislation.
legislador, -ra, *n.m.f., a.* legislator, lawmaker.
legislar, *v.t.* to legislate, enact laws; to criticize, censure.
legislativo, -va, *a.* legislative, law-making, law-giving.
legislatura, *n.f.* term of legislature.
legisperito, *n.m.* professor of laws.
legista, *n.m.f.* legist; professor of laws; student of laws.
legítima, *n.f.* (*law*) legitime.
legitimación, *n.f.* legitimation.
legítimamente, *adv.* legitimately, lawfully.
legitimar, *v.t.* to legitimate, legalize; to prove, establish in evidence.
legitimidad, *n.f.* legitimacy, legality, lawfulness.
legitimista, *n.m.f., a.* legitimist.

legítimo, -ma, *a.* legitimate, legal, lawful, genuine, authentic, true, certain.

lego, -ga, *a.* laical, lay, laic; illiterate, ignorant.

lego, *n.m.* layman; lay-brother, lay-friar.

legón, *n.m.* (*agric.*) hoe.

legra, *n.f.* (*surg.*) periosteotome.

legración, legradura, *n.f.* (*surg.*) periosteotomy.

legrar, *v.t.* (*surg.*) perform periosteotomy.

legrón, *n.m.* veterinary's periosteotomy.

legua, *n.f.* league, measure of distance (equal to 3½ miles); *a legua, a la legua, a leguas, de muchas leguas, de cien leguas, desde media legua,* very far, at a great distance; *por doquiera hay su legua de mal camino,* everything has its difficulties.

leguario, *n.m.* (*Bol., Chi.*) a post or stone marking the distances on a road.

leguario, -ria, *a.* relating to a *legua.*

leguleyo, *n.m.* petty lawyer, pettifogger.

legumbre, *n.f.* pulse, legume; garden-stuff, vegetable, produce.

leguminoso, -sa, *a.* (*bot.*) leguminous.

leíble, *a.* legible, readable.

Leiden, Leiden; (*phys.*) *botella de Leiden,* Leiden jar.

leído, -da, *a.* well-read, book-learned. — *p.p.* [LEER]; *leído y escribido,* (*coll.*) one who affects learning.

leila, *n.f.* nocturnal Moorish dance.

leima, *n.m.* (*mus.*) limma.

lejanía, *n.f.* distance, remoteness.

lejano, -na, *a.* distant, remote, far.

lejas, *a.pl.*; far away; *de lejas tierras,* from far away lands.

lejía, *n.f.* bleaching-liquid; buck, lye; (*coll.*) severe reprimand, reproof.

lejío, *n.m.* (among dyers), lye.

lejitos, *adv.* rather distant.

lejos, *adv.* far, far away, far off. — *n.m.* perspective, distant view, background; resemblance, similarity; *a lo lejos, de lejos, de muy lejos, desde lejos,* at a great distance; *buen lejos,* looking best at a distance.

lejuelos, *adv.* at a little distance.

lelilí, *n.m.* Moorish war-whoop.

lelo, -la, *a.* stupid, dull, ignorant, crazy. — *n.m.f.* ninny.

lema, *n.m.* lemma, argument, theme, text, motto, device.

lemanita, *n.f.* (*min.*) jade.

lemnáceo, -a, *a.* (*bot.*) lemnaceous.

lemniscata, *n.f.* (*math.*) lemniscate.

lemosín, -ina, *a.* Languedocian. — *n.m.* Languedocian; Provençal, *langue d'oc,* language of the troubadours.

lémur, *n.m.* (*zool.*) lemur. — *pl.* lemurs; lemures.

len, *a.* soft, untwisted; flossy (of thread or silk).

lena, *n.f.* spirit, vigour.

lencera, *n.f.* woman who deals in linen; linen-draper's wife.

lencería, *n.f.* linen goods; linen-draper's shop; linen-hall; linen-room; linen-trade.

lencero, -ra, *n.m.f.* linen-draper, linen merchant.

lendel, *n.m.* track, or circle described by a mill-horse.

lendrera, *n.f.* fine comb for removing nits.

lendrero, *n.m.* place full of nits.

lendroso, -sa, *a.* nitty, full of nits.

lene, *a.* soft, mild, bland; sweet, pleasant, kind; light, not weighty or heavy, of small consideration.

lengua, *n.f.* (*anat.*) tongue; speech, discourse, language; idiom; advice, information; clapper of a bell; *lengua de tierra,* strip of land running out into the sea; *lengua del agua,* at the edge of the water; *irse la lengua,* to give rein to one's tongue; *andar en lenguas,* to be much talked of; *mala lengua,* slanderer, backbiter; *con la lengua de un palmo,* or *con un palmo de lengua,* with great longing or fatigue; *lengua de buey,* (*bot.*) bugloss, alkanet; *lengua canina* or *de perro,* (*bot.*) hound's-tongue; *lengua de vaca,* (*bot.*) sanseviera, fibre-plant; *lengua cerval,* (*bot.*) hart's tongue; *de lengua en lengua,* from mouth to mouth; *hacerse lenguas,* to speak in praise; *tomar lengua* (or *lenguas*), to seek information; *no morderse la lengua,* not to mince words; *tener en* (*el pico de*) *la lengua,* to have at the tip of one's tongue; *poner la lengua en,* to speak ill of; *tener la lengua gorda,* to be tipsy; *tener mala lengua,* to be a blasphemer, backbiter, etc.; *trabarse la lengua,* to stammer, be unable to speak (through illness, accident, etc.); *buscar la lengua,* to incite (or provoke) to dispute (or strife); *no dice más la lengua que lo que siente el corazón,* the tongue says no more than the heart feels; *pegársele a uno la lengua al paladar,* to be unable to speak for one's emotions; *quien tiene lengua* (or *quien lengua ha*) *a Roma va,* he who wants to know should ask.

lenguado, *n.m.* (*ichth.*) sole, flounder.

lenguaje, *n.m.* language, idiom, speech; parlance; tongue, vernacular; style; *lenguaje bajo,* loose language.

lenguaraz, *a.* languaged, free-tongued, talkative, fluent, voluble, forward, petulant.

lenguaz, *a.* garrulous, talkative, loquacious.

lengüecica, -illa, -ita, *n.f.* small tongue.

lengüeta, *n.f.* small tongue; (*anat.*) epiglottis; languet, barb; (*mus.*) languette; needle of a balance; (*mech.*) feather, wedge, tongue, awl, bore; bit; bookbinder's cutting-knife; (*arch.*) buttress; moulding; catch of a trap or snare.

lengüetada, *n.f.* act of licking.

lengüetería, *n.f.* reed-work of an organ.

lengüezuela, *n.f.* small tongue.

lenguón, -ona, *a.* (*CR., Ec., Mex.*) [LENGUARAZ].

lenidad, *n.f.* lenity, mildness, favour.

lenificar, *v.t.* to lenify, soften.

lenificativo, -va, *a.* mollifying, softening.

lenitivo, -va, *a.* lenitive, assuasive, lenient, mitigant. — *n.m.* emollient; mitigator, lenient.

lenocinio, *n.m.* pimping, pandering.

lentamente, *adv.* slowly, heavily, lazily, lingeringly.

lente, *n.m.f.* (*opt.*) lens; quizzing glass; lorgnette; monocle. — *n.m.pl.* pince-nez.

lentecer, *v.i.* to grow soft or tender.

lenteja, *n.f.* (*bot.*) lentil; disc of a pendulum; *lenteja de agua* (*bot.*) gibbous duck-weed.

lentejuela, *n.f.* spangle.

lenticular, *a.* lenticular, lentil-shaped.

lentiscal, *n.m.* thicket of mastic-trees.

lentisco, *n.m.* (*bot.*) mastic-tree, lentisk.

lentitud, *n.f.* slowness, sluggishness, coldness.

lento, -ta, *a.* slow, sluggish, tardy, heavy, long,

lingering; (*pharm.*) glutinous; (*mus.*) slowly; (*mil.*) slow march.

lentor, *n.m.* (*obs.*) flexibility of trees or shrubs; (*med.*) viscidity, tenacity (of blood, etc.).

lenzuelo, *n.m.* (*agric.*) sheet for carrying straw.

leña, *n.f.* fire-wood, kindling-wood; (*coll.*) drubbing, beating; *llevar leña al monte*, to carry coals to Newcastle; *echar leña al fuego*, to foment discord; *del árbol caído todos hacen leña*, of a fallen tree, all make firewood, i.e. anyone will kick a man when he's down.

leñador, -ra, *n.m.* woodman (-woman), wood-cutter; dealer in firewood.

leñame, *n.m.* wood; provision of fire wood.

leñar, *v.t.* (*prov.*) to cut wood.

leñazgo, *n.m.* pile of timber.

leñera, *n.f.* wood-shed, wood-bin.

leñero, *n.m.* timber-merchant, wood-dealer; log-man.

leño, *n.m.* log; (*naut.*) ancient galley; (*poet.* & *fig.*) ship, vessel; (*coll.*) dull, thick-witted person.

leñoso, -sa, *a.* woody, ligneous.

Leo, *n.m.* (*astron.*) Leo, a constellation; sign of the zodiac.

león, *n.m.* (*zool.*) lion; (*ent.*) dragon-fly, ant-lion; (*zool.*) boa; brave and commanding man; cruel and irritable man; (*Chi.*) puma, the cougar *Felis concolor*; children's game similar to chess; (*naut.*) figure-head; (*astron.*) Leo; *león marino*, sea lion.

leona, *n.f.* lioness; brave, determined woman.

leonado, -da, *a.* lion-coloured, tawny.

leoncico, -illo, -ito, *n.m.* whelp of a lion.

leonera, *n.f.* cage or den of lions; (*coll.*) gambling-den; menagerie; lumber room.

leonero, *n.m.* keeper of lions; master of a gambling house.

leonés, -esa, *a.* of or belonging to Leon.

leónica, *n.f.* (*vet.*) vein under the tongue.

leonina, *n.f.* (*med.*) leontiasis.

leonino, -na, *a.* leonine; (*law*) one-sided, un-fair; (*poet.*) leonine (verse).

leontina, *n.f.* (*jewel.*) watch-chain.

leopardo, *n.m.* leopard, panther.

leopoldina, *n.f.* (*jewel.*) fob-chain; (*mil.*) Spanish helmet.

Lepe (saber más que), to be very smart and shrewd.

lépero, -ra, *n.m.f., a.* (*Mex.*) low, base, wretched (of persons).

lepidia, *n.f.* (*Chi.*) indigestion.

lepidio, *n.m.* (*bot.*) pepper-grass.

lepidóptero, -ra, *a.* (*ent.*) lepidopterous. — *n.m.pl.* lepidoptera.

lepisma, *n.f.* (*ent.*) lepisma; bristle-tail, silver-fish.

leporino, -na, *a.* like a hare; *labio leporino*, hare-lip.

lepra, *n.f.* leprosy.

leprosidad, *n.f.* leprosy, leprousness.

leproso, -sa, *a.* leprous. — *n.m.f.* leper.

lercha, *n.f.* reed for hanging fishes and birds.

lerda, *n.f.* (*vet.*) tumour in a horse's pastern.

lerdamente, *adv.* slowly, heavily, obtusely.

lerdo, -da, *a.* slow, heavy; dull, obtuse.

lerdón, *n.m.* (*vet.*) tumour in a horse's pastern.

les, *pers. pron. dat. m.f.pl.* to them, them (in-direct object); *les vi pasar,* I saw them pass by; *les hablé,* I spoke to them.

lesbio, -bia, *a.* Lesbian, of Lesbos.

lesión, *n.f.* hurt, damage, wound; injury, wrong.

lesivo, -va, *a.* prejudicial, injurious.

lesna, *n.f.* awl.

lesnordeste, *n.m.* (*naut.*) east-north-east wind.

leso, -sa, *a.* wounded, hurt, damaged; per-verted; *lesa majestad,* lese-majesty, high treason.

leste, *n.m.* (*naut.*) east wind, east.

lessueste, *n.m.* (*naut.*) east-south-east wind.

letal, *a.* mortal, deadly, destructive, lethal.

letame, *n.m.* mud for fertilizing.

letanía, *n.f.* (*eccles.*) litany; (*coll.*) long list of things. — *pl.* supplicatory procession.

letárgico, -ca, *a.* lethargic, lethargical.

letargo, *n.m.* lethargy, drowsiness.

letargoso, -sa, *a.* deadening, causing lethargy.

leteo, -a, *a.* (*poet.*) Lethean.

leticia, *n.f.* (*obs.*) joy, mirth.

letífero, -ra, *a.* deadly, death-bringing.

letificante, *a.* exhilarating.

letificar, *v.t.* to rejoice, make merry; to ani-mate, cheer.

letífico, -ca, *a.* cheering, bringing joy.

letra, *n.f.* letter, character of the alphabet; hand, penmanship, chirography; (*print.*) type; inscription, motto; literal meaning of a phrase; arithmetical character; figure; (*poet.*) kind of rondeau; words of any song. — *pl.* **letras,** letters, learning; the learned profes-sions; *letra de cambio,* (*com.*) bill of exchange; *letra abierta,* (*com.*) open credit; *tener mucha letra,* to be very artful and cunning; *a la letra,* literally, punctually, entirely; *letra por letra,* entirely, omitting nothing; *seguir las letras,* to devote oneself to study; *atarse a la letra,* to be bound to the letter (*or* literal interpretation) of something; *mantas letras tiene un no como un sí,* nay has as many letters as yea; *letras humanas, litterae humaniores,* humanities; *letras sagradas,* sacred studies, the Scriptures; *tener las letras gordas,* to be dull or ignorant in book-learning; *la letra con sangre entra,* it's with blood that letters enter, spare the rod and spoil the child.

letrada, *n.f.* (*coll.*) lawyer's wife.

letrado, -da, *a.* learned, erudite, lettered; (*coll.*) vain, presumptuous; *a lo letrado,* as a lawyer.

letrado, *n.m.* lawyer, advocate, counsellor.

letrero, *n.m.* sign, label, placard, poster.

letrilla, *n.f.* small letter; (*mus.*) rondelet.

letrina, *n.f.* privy, water-closet, latrine.

letrón, *n.m.* large letter.

letrones, *n.m.pl.* placards posted at the doors of churches with the names of newly ex-communicated persons.

letuario, *n.m.* kind of jam.

leucina, *n.f.* (*chem.*) leucin.

leucocito, *n.m.* leucocyte, white blood-corpuscle.

leucorrea, *n.f.* (*med.*) leucorrhœa; whites.

leudar, *v.t.* to leaven. — *v.r.* to yeast.

leudo, -da, *a.* fermented, leavened (bread).

leva, *n.f.* (*naut.*) act of weighing anchor; (*mil.*) levy, press; (*naut.*) swell of the sea; (*mech.*) lever, cog, tooth, cam, tappet; *hay mar de leva,* there is a swell in the offing. — *pl.* **levas,** tricks, artful devices.

levada, *n.f.* moving silk-worm; (*fenc.*) salute or flourish with the foil.

levadero, -ra, *a.* to be collected or deman-ded.

levadizo, -za, *a.* that can be lifted or raised, as a draw-bridge.

levador, *n.m.* in paper-mills, piler; (*mech.*) cam, cog, tooth.

levadura, *n.f.* ferment, leaven, yeast, barm; (*carp.*) sawed-off plank.

levantadamente, *adv.* highly, loftily.

levantado, -da, *a.* raised, elevated, lofty. — *p.p.* [LEVANTAR].

levantador, -ra, *n.m.f.* one who raises or lifts up; disturber, rioter.

levantamiento, *n.m.* elevation, raising; sublimity; insurrection, revolt, uprising; (*prov.*) settlement of accounts.

levantar, *v.t.* to raise, lift, lift up, heave up, get up, hang up, hold up, set upright, mount, pick up; to rouse, excite, stir up; to aggrandize, elevate, promote; to build up, raise, erect a building; to impute, or attribute falsely; to start game; (*mil.*) to levy, press for service; to cut cards; to utter loudly, raise the voice; to increase, enlarge; to begin; to cause, occasion. — *v.r.* to rise, get up, stand up; to be above, higher than; to start suddenly (of game); to rise up in arms, rebel; *levantar un plano, mapa,* etc., to draw the sketch of a place, to survey; *levantar falso testimonio,* to accuse falsely, to bear false witness; *levantar la casa,* to remove house; *levantar caballo,* to gallop a horse; *levantar la cabeza,* to retrieve one's fortune, to take courage; *levantar la cerviz,* to exalt, extol oneself; *levantar la mesa,* to clear the table; *levantar el pensamiento,* to conceive a noble idea; *levantarse con algo,* to take unlawful possession of anything; *levantarse las piedras contra uno,* to be unfortunate, unpopular; *levantar el cerco,* to raise the blockade; *levantar fuego,* to make a disturbance; *levantar los talones,* to take to one's heels.

levante, *n.m.* Levant, east; east wind; (*Chi.*) compensation paid to a landowner for timber cut on his property; (*min.*) operation of cleaning the ducts of quicksilver furnaces; *estar de levante,* to be ready to depart.

levantín; levantino, -na, *a.* Levantine.

levantisco, -ca, *a.* turbulent, restless; Levantine.

levar, *v.t.* (*naut.*) to weigh anchor. — *v.r.* to set sail.

leve, *a.* light; of little weight; trifling.

levedad, *n.f.* lightness, levity; inconstancy.

levemente, *adv.* lightly, gently; venially.

leviatán, *n.m.* leviathan.

levigación, *n.f.* levigation, elutriation.

levigar, *v.t.* to levigate, elutriate, free from grit.

levirato, *n.m.* levirate, Mosaic marriage.

levita, *n.m.* Levite; deacon. — *n.f.* frockcoat; *gente de levita,* middle classes; *señor de levita,* respectable man.

levítico, -ca, *a.* Levitical, priestly.

levítico, *n.m.* book of Leviticus; (*coll.*) ceremonial used at a festival.

levitón, *n.m.* great-coat, like a frock-coat.

léxico, lexicón, *n.m.* lexicon, dictionary; glossary, vocabulary.

lexicografía, *n.f.* lexicography.

lexicográfico, -ca, *a.* lexicographic.

lexicógrafo, *n.m.* lexicographer, dictionary maker.

lexicología, *n.f.* lexicology.

lexicológico, -ca, *a.* lexicological.

lexicólogo, *n.m.* lexicologist.

ley, *n.f.* law, enactment, ordinance, decree, statute; rule of action; religion, the Scriptures; legal standard of quality, weight, or measure; loyalty, faithful attachment; precept, rules, and regulations; principle or universal property. — *pl.* **leyes,** study and profession of the law; body or collection of laws; *a la ley,* with propriety and neatness; *de buena ley,* sterling; *a toda ley,* perfectly, according to rule; *ley antigua,* law of Moses; *ley escrita,* revealed laws, decalogue; *a ley de caballero* (or *de cristiano*), on the word of a gentleman (*or* a Christian); *ley del embudo,* severity for others, indulgence for ourselves; *ley de la trampa,* trickery, fraud; *echar la ley,* to judge very severely; *venir contra la ley,* to break the law; *hecha la ley, hecha la trampa,* the law was made to be broken; *ley caldaria,* hot-water ordeal; *de mala ley,* disreputable; crooked; low, base; *allá van leyes, do quieren reyes,* the powerful man is a law unto himself.

leyenda, *n.f.* reading; legend; superscription, inscription, motto, device.

leyente, *a.* reading, reader.

lezda, *n.f.* ancient tax on merchandise.

lezna, *n.f.* awl.

lía, *n.f.* plaited bass-rope; sediment, lees, dregs, settlings; *estar hecho una lía,* (*coll.*) to be tipsy.

liar, *v.t.* to tie, bind, faggot, bundle, do up; (*coll.*) to embroil, draw into an entanglement. — *v.r.* to contract an alliance; to enter into concubinage; *liarlas,* (*coll.*) to escape, clear off; to die.

liásico, -ca, *a.* (*geol.*) liassic.

liaza, *n.f.* collection of hoops used by coopers.

libación, *n.f.* libation, pouring wine or oil on the ground (sacrifice offering).

libamen, libamiento, *n.m.* offering in ancient sacrifices.

libán, *n.m.* rope made of esparto.

libar, *v.t.* to suck, sip, extract the juice; to taste; to perform a libation.

libatorio, *n.m.* libatory cup.

libelar, *v.t.* (*law*) to petition.

libelático, -ca, *a.* renegade (of persecuted early Christians).

libelista, *n.m.f.* author of a libel.

libelo, *n.m.* libel, defamatory writing, lampoon; (*law*) petition; *libelo de repudio,* written repudiation of a wife by her husband; (*coll.*) discarding, abandoning, giving up.

libélula, *n.f.* libellula, dragon-fly.

liber, *n.m.* (*bot.*) bast, liber, inner bark.

liberación, *n.f.* liberation; (*law*) quittance.

liberal, *a.* liberal, generous, free, open, munificent, open-hearted; quick, brisk, active; (*polit.*) liberal, advanced; liberal (arts).

liberalidad, *n.f.* liberality, generosity, largeness, munificence, open-heartedness.

liberalismo, *n.m.* Liberalism; Liberal party.

liberalizar, *v.t.* to liberalize.

liberalmente, *adv.* liberally, expeditiously, generously, freely.

libérrimo, -ma, *a. superl.* most free.

libertad, *n.f.* liberty, freedom; exemption, immunity, privilege; licence, relaxation of restraint, assumed familiarity; independence, unconventionality; freedom, address, agility; ransom; *libertad de cultos*, freedom of worship; *libertad de comercio*, free-trade; *libertad provisional*, liberation on bail; *libertad de estado*, the single state, single blessedness.

libertadamente, *adv.* freely, impudently.

libertado, -da, *a.* audacious, free, ungoverned; libertine, impudent; idle, disengaged. — *p.p.* [LIBERTAR].

libertador, -ra, *n.m.f.* deliverer, liberator.

libertar, *v.t.* to free, set at liberty, liberate; to exempt, excuse; to rid from, clear from; to acquit.

liberticida, *n.m.* liberticide.

libertinaje, *n.m.* libertinism, licentiousness, libertinage, licence, irreligion.

libertino, -na, *n.m.f.* child of a freed slave. — *a.* libertine, dissolute, licentious, lewd, irreligious.

liberto, -ta, *n.m.f.* freed or emancipated slave.

libídine, *n.f.* lewdness, lust.

libidinosamente, *adv.* libidinously.

libidinoso, -sa, *a.* libidinous, lewd, lustful.

libio, -bia, *n.m.f.*, *a.* Libyan.

libra, *n.f.* pound, ancient weight; coin, varying in value; (*astron.*) Libra; *libra esterlina*, pound sterling; *libra medicinal*, pound troy; (*Cub.*) tobacco of superior quality.

libración, *n.f.* libration.

libraco, libracho, *n.m.* (*coll.*) old, trashy book or pamphlet.

librado, *n.m.* (*com.*) drawee. — *p.p.* [LIBRAR].

librador, -ra, *n.m.f.* deliverer; (*com.*) drawer of a cheque or draft; store-keeper of the king's stables; grocer's scoop.

libramiento, *n.m.* delivery, delivering; warrant, order of payment.

librancista, *n.m.f.* (*com.*) holder of a draft or warrant.

libranza, *n.f.* (*com.*) draft, bill of exchange; *libranza postal*, money order.

librar, *v.t.* to free, preserve, deliver, extricate, exempt; to expedite, despatch; to pass (sentence); to engage (battle); to issue (a decree); (*com.*) to draw. — *v.i.* to receive a visitor in the locutory (of nuns); to give birth (of humans); (*surg.*) to extrude the afterbirth. — *v.r.* to escape, be free from, avoid, get rid of; *librar en*, to depend on; *a bien* (or *buen*) *librar*, the best that could possibly happen.

libratorio, *n.m.* locutory.

librazo, *n.m.* blow with a book.

libre, *a.* free, uncumbered, unrestrained; unembarrassed, disengaged, vacant; independent; exempt, privileged; clear, open, unobstructed; guiltless, innocent; libertine, loose, licentious; single, unmarried; rash, bold, forward, thoughtless; impudent; isolated, alone; *libre de gastos*, free of charge; *libre cambio*, free trade; (*com.*) *libre de derechos*, duty free; (*com.*) *libre a bordo* (or *l.a.b.*), free on board (*or* f.o.b.); *entrada libre*, free admission; *libre pensador*, freethinker.

librea, *n.f.* livery, uniform.

librear, *v.t.* to weigh or sell by pounds.

librecambio, *n.m.* free-trade.

librecambista, *n.m.f.* free-trader.

librejo, *n.m.* little book; worthless book.

libremente, *adv.* freely; boldly.

librepensador, -ra, *a.* freethinker.

librepensamiento, *n.m.* freethought.

librería, *n.f.* book-shop, bookseller's shop; book-trade; library; large collection of books.

libreril, *a.* relating to the book-trade.

librero, *n.m.* bookseller.

libreta, *n.f.* troy pound; loaf of bread weighing one pound; note-book; memorandum book; small blank book; pass-book.

librete, *n.m.* small book; foot-stove.

libretín, *n.m.* small book; booklet.

libreto, *n.m.* (*mus.*) libretto.

librillo, *n.m.* earthen tub; small book of cigarette paper; *librillo de cera*, kind of wax taper; *librillo de oro*, gold-leaf-book.

libro, *n.m.* book; (*mus.*) libretto; (*zool.*) omasum, third stomach of a ruminant; (*fig.*) tax, impost; *libro becerro*, doomsday-book; *libro de caja*, cash-book; *libro borrador*, (*book-keeping*) diary, journal; *libro de facturas*, invoice-book; *libro de asiento* or *libro de cuentas*, account-book; *libro en blanco*, book of blank paper; *libro diario*, journal; *libro de memoria*, memorandum book; *libro mayor*, ledger; *libro verde*, (*coll.*) book for notes about places and persons; also the compiler of such memoranda; *libro talonario*, receipt-book, cheque-book; *libro de las cuarenta hojas*, (*coll.*) pack of cards; *ahorcar los libros*, to give up one's studies; *hablar como un libro*, to talk like a book (i.e. fluently); *no hay libro tan malo que no tenga algo bueno*, there's no book so bad but has some good points; *libro cerrado no saca letrado*, books do no good except when studied.

librote, *n.m.* large book.

licantropía, *n.f.* (*med.*) lycanthropy.

licántropo, *n.m.* lycanthrope.

liceísta, *n.m.f.* member of a lyceum.

licencia, *n.f.* permission, leave, licence, liberty; (*poet.*) licence; leave of absence, (*mil.*) furlough; licentiousness, wantonness, looseness; degree of licentiate; *licencia absoluta*, (*mil.*) discharge.

licenciadillo, *n.m.* (*coll.*) ridiculous little man in clerical robes.

licenciado, -da, *a.* licensed; presuming knowledge. — *n.m.* bachelor, licentiate; (*coll.*) any university scholar; (*coll.*) title given to lawyers; (*mil.*) discharged soldier. — *p.p.* [LICENCIAR].

licenciamiento, *n.m.* act of taking the degree of licentiate; (*mil.*) discharge of soldiers.

licenciar, *v.t.* to permit, allow; to license; to licentiate; to confer a degree; (*mil.*) to discharge. — *v.r.* to become dissolute; to obtain a degree of bachelor or licentiate.

licenciatura, *n.f.* degree of licentiate; act of receiving it.

licenciosamente, *adv.* licentiously.

licencioso, -sa, *a.* licentious, dissolute.

liceo, *n.m.* lyceum; literary society; public school; (*Chi.*) secondary school.

lición, *n.f.* (*Col., Mex.*) lesson.

licitación, *n.f.* bid at auction.

licitador, *n.m.* bidder at auction.

licitamente, *adv.* lawfully, justly, licitly.

licitante, *a.* bidder or buyer at auction.

licitar, *v.t.* to bid at auction.

lícito, -ta, *a.* licit, lawful; just.

licnobio, -bia, *n.m.f.* one accustomed to be up late at night, lychnobite; one who turns night into day.

licopodio, *n.m.* (*bot.*) lycopodium.
licor, *n.m.* liquor, strong drink, spirits; liquid.
licorera, *n.f.* liquor-case, bottle-case.
licorista, *n.m.f.* liquor distiller or dealer.
licoroso, -sa, *a.* generous, spirituous (wine).
licuable, *a.* liquable, liquefiable.
licuación, *n.f.* liquefaction, melting.
licuante, *a.* liquefying, dissolving, melting.
licuar, *v.t.* to liquefy, dissolve, melt.
licuefacción, *n.f.* liquefaction.
licuefacer, *v.t., v.r.* to liquefy.
licuefactible, *a.* liquefiable.
lichera, *n.f.* woollen bed-cover.
lid, *n.f.* conflict, contest, fight; dispute, argument.
lidia, *n.f.* battle, fight, contest; bull-fight.
lidiadero, -ra, *a.* in fighting condition.
lidiador, -ra, *n.m.f.* combatant, fighter; arguer.
lidiar, *v.i.* to fight, combat, contend; (*fig.*) to deal with annoying, vexing persons. — *v.t.* to run or fight bulls.
lidio, *n.m.f., a.* Lydian.
liebrastón, liebratico, liebratón, *n.m.* young hare, leveret.
liebre, *n.f.* hare; (*coll.*) coward, poltroon; *coger una liebre,* to fall flat ; *comer liebre,* to be chicken-hearted. — *pl.* (*naut.*) racks, ribs; dead-eyes; *donde no se piensa, salta la liebre* (or *donde menos se piensa, salta la liebre*), the hare jumps up where one least expects it.
liebrecica, -illa, -ita; liebrezuela, *n.f.* young or small hare.
liebrecilla, *n.f.* (*bot.*) blue-bottle.
liencecico, -illo, -ito, *n.m.* (*prov.*) little linen cloth.
liendre, *n.f.* nit, egg of a louse; *cascar a uno las liendres,* (*coll.*) to give one a severe drubbing.
lientera, lientería, *n.f.* (*med.*) lientery.
lientérico, -ca, *a.* lienteric.
liento, -ta, *a.* damp, moist.
lienza, *n.f.* narrow strip of cloth.
lienzo, *n.m.* linen, hemp or cotton cloth; (*art*) canvas; (*arch.*) face or front of a building; (*fort.*) curtain; stretch of a wall.
liga, *n.f.* garter; alliance, combination, league, confederacy, coalition; (*coll.*) friendship; mistletoe; bird-lime; alloy for gold and silver.
ligación, *n.f.* ligation, tying, binding; union, mixture.
ligada, *n.f.* tying, binding; ligature. — *pl.* **ligadas,** (*print.*) ligatures.
ligado, *n.m.* (*mus.*) legato; tie.
ligado, -da, *a.* tied, bound, leagued, confederate. — *p.p.* [LIGAR].
ligadura, *n.f.* ligature, ligation; binding; subjection; (*mus.*) ligature, suspension, tie; (*naut.*) seizing, lashing.
ligamaza, *n.f.* viscid matter surrounding the seeds of some fruits or plants.
ligamen, *n.m.* spell causing impotency.
ligamento, *n.m.* bond, chain, tie, entanglement; (*anat.*) ligament.
ligamentoso, -sa, *a.* ligamentous, ligamental.
ligamiento, *n.m.* union, concord; uniting, tying, binding.
ligar, *v.t.* (*pret.* **ligué;** *pres. subj.* **ligue**) to tie, fasten, bind; to alloy gold or silver; to league, coalesce, confederate; to join, knit together, knit; to render impotent by spells. — *v.i.* to combine cards of the same suit. —

v.r. to league, be confederate; to bind or compromise oneself.
ligazón, *n.f.* union, contexture, tie, bond, attachment, fastening, connexion, ligament; (*naut.*) futtock-timbers.
ligeramente, *adv.* swiftly, lightly, easily; (*fig.*) giddily; slightly.
ligereza, *n.f.* lightness, celerity, swiftness, fleetness, nimbleness, agility; levity; inconstancy, flirtation, fickleness.
ligero, -ra, *a.* light (i.e. not heavy), thin; swift, active, nimble, gay, airy; (*fig.*) giddy, unsteady, trifling; easily interrupted or disturbed; easily digested; *ligero de dedos,* light-fingered; *a la ligera,* lightly, expeditiously; *de ligero,* rashly, easily, without reflection; *ligero de cascos,* feather-brained.
ligeruelo, -la, *a.* early (*of grapes*).
ligio, -gia, *a.* liege, bound by feudal tenure.
lignario, -ria, *a.* ligneous.
lignito, *n.m.* (*min.*) lignite.
ligón, *n.m.* kind of hoe with a long handle.
ligua, *n.f.* (*Philip.*) battle-axe.
liguano, -na, *a.* (*Chi.*) applied to a kind of sheep with thick and heavy wool.
liguilla, *n.f.* narrow ribbon or garter.
ligula, *n.f.* (*bot.*) ligule.
ligur; ligurino, -na, *n.m.f., a.* Ligurian.
ligustre, ligustro, *n.f.* (*bot.*) privet-flower, privet.
ligustrino, -na, *a.* relating to privet.
lija, *n.f.* (*ichth.*) dog-fish; skin of the dog-fish, shark-skin; sand-paper.
lijar, *v.t.* to polish, smooth, sand-paper.
lila, *n.f.;* **lilac,** *n.f.* lilac-tree, lilac-flower, lilac colour; (*coll.*) silly, foolish (person).
lilaila, *n.f.* thin woollen stuff; bunting; (*coll.*) impertinence, prank, trick, wile, artifice.
liliáceo, -cea, *a.* (*bot.*) liliaceous.
lililí, *n.m.* warwhoop of the Moors.
liliputiense, *n.m.f., a.* Lilliputian.
lima, *n.f.* (*bot.*) sweet lime, lime-tree; file; correction, correctness, polish, finish; (*arch.*) channel in a roof.
limadura, *n.f.* filing, limature. — *pl.* filings.
limalla, *n.f.* filings.
limar, *v.t.* to file, polish; (*fig.*) to gnaw, corrode; to put the finishing touches to (a literary work).
limatón, *n.m.* coarse round file, rasp.
limaza, *n.f.* snail.
limazo, *n.m.* viscosity, sliminess.
limbo, *n.m.* limbo; hem, edge; (*astron.*) limb, border of sun or moon; protractor; the graduated arc of a sextant, theodolite, etc.
limeño, -ña, *n.m.f., a.* native of Lima.
limera, *n.f.* (*naut.*) helmport, rudder-hole; woman file-seller or lime-seller.
limero, *n.m.* man who sells files or limes; (*bot.*) sweet lime-tree.
limeta, *n.f.* vial, small flask or bottle.
limiste, *n.m.* cloth of Segovia wool.
limitación, *n.f.* limitation, modification, restriction; limit, district.
limitadamente, *adv.* in a limited way, finitely.
limitado, -da, *a.* limited, scanty; short-witted. — *p.p.* [LIMITAR].
limitáneo, -nea, *a.* limitary, limitaneous, bounding.
limitar, *v.t.* to limit, bound, set bounds, narrow, fix or establish limits, restrain, constrict, circumscribe; to reduce expense.

límite, *n.m.* limit, bound, boundary, confine, border.

limítrofe, *a.* limiting, bounding, conterminous.

limo, *n.m.* slime, mud.

limón, *n.m.* lemon; lemon-tree; shaft, thill.

limonada, *n.f.* lemonade; *limonada purgante*, citrate of magnesia; *limonada de vino*, wine lemonade, sangaree.

limonado, -da, *a.* lemon-coloured.

limonar, *n.m.* plantation of lime-trees or lemon-trees; (*Guat.*) lemon-tree.

limoncillo, *n.m.* small lemon.

limonera, *n.f.* woman lemon-seller; shaft (in horse carriages), thill.

limonero, *n.m.* (*bot.*) lemon-tree; dealer in lemons.

limonero, -ra, *a.* said of a shaft horse.

limosidad, *n.f.* sliminess; foul matter in the teeth, tartar.

limosna, *n.f.* alms, charity.

limosnera, *n.f.* alms-bag, alms-box.

limosnero, *n.m.* almoner; (*Am.*) beggar.

limosnero, -ra, *a.* charitable.

limoso, -sa, *a.* slimy, muddy.

limpia, *n.f.* cleansing, cleaning; dredging.

limpiabarros, *n.m.* foot-scraper.

limpiabotas, *n.m.* shoe-black, boot-black.

limpiachimeneas, *n.m.* chimney-sweeper.

limpiadera, *n.f.* clothes-brush; comb-brush; plough-cleaner.

limpiadientes, *n.m.* toothpick.

limpiador, -ra, *n.m.f.* cleaner, cleanser, scourer.

limpiadura, *n.f.* cleaning, cleansing. — *pl.* **limpiaduras**, dirt, scourings, waste, refuse, rubbish.

limpiamente, *adv.* cleanly, neatly, purely, faithfully, sincerely.

limpiamiento, *n.m.* act of cleaning.

limpiaplumas, *n.m.* penwiper.

limpiar, *v.t.* to clean, scour, cleanse, purify; (*fig.*) to steal; to win from (at gambling). — *v.r.* to clean oneself; *limpiar las faldriqueras* (or *la faltriquera*), to pick the pockets.

limpiaúñas, *n.m.* nail-cleaner.

limpidez, *n.f.* (*poet.*) limpidity.

límpido, -da, *a.* (*poet.*) limpid, crystal-clear.

limpieza, *n.f.* cleanness, cleanliness, neatness, purity; limpidity; chastity, integrity, honesty, rectitude, disinterestedness; *limpieza de bolsa*, emptiness of the purse, penury; *limpieza de corazón*, rectitude, purity of intention.

limpio, -pia, *a.* clean, limpid, neat, elegant, pure, unmingled, free, clear, stainless, spotless; immaculate, untarnished; *en limpio*, clearly, in substance; *jugar limpio*, to deal fairly, act uprightly; *juego limpio*, fair play; *poner en limpio*, to make a fair copy; *costa limpia*, (*naut.*) clear coast.

limpión, *n.m.* act of cleaning; (*prov.*) streetsweeper.

linaje, *n.m.* lineage, race, offspring, progeny, family, house, kin, generation, extraction; (*fig.*) class, condition; *linaje humano*, mankind.

linajista, *n.m.f.* genealogist, maker of pedigrees.

linajudo, -da, *n.m.f.* one who is of (or who boasts of his) good family or descent.

lináloe, *n.m.* (*bot.*) aloe.

linao, *n.m.* (*Chi.*) kind of hand-ball game (pelota).

linar, *n.m.* flax-field.

linaria, *n.f.* (*bot.*) wild flax, yellow toad-flax.

linaza, *n.f.* linseed, flax-seed.

lince, *n.m.* (*zool.*) lynx, ounce; (*fig.*) very sharp person. — *a.* sharp-sighted, acute, observant.

lincear, *v.t.* (*coll.*) to observe something not easily seen.

línceo, *n.m.* lyncean; (*poet.*) sharp, keen.

lincurio, *n.m.* semi-precious stone.

linchamiento, *n.m.* lynching.

linchar, *v.t.* to lynch.

linches, *n.m.pl.* (*Mex.*) fibre saddle-bags.

lindamente, *adv.* neatly, elegantly, prettily.

lindante, *a.* coterminous, bordering, contiguous.

lindar, *v.i.* to be contiguous, border.

linde, *n.m.f.* landmark, boundary, limit.

lindero, -ra, *a.* contiguous, bordering.

lindero, *n.m.* limit, boundary.

lindeza, lindura, *n.f.* elegance, prettiness, neatness. — *pl.* (*iron.*) insults.

lindo, -da, *a.* neat, handsome, pretty, nice, fine, genteel, complete, perfect; *de lo lindo*, perfectly, wonderfully, greatly.

lindo, *n.m.* (*coll.*) beau, coxcomb, minion.

lindón, *n.m.* frame or bar for hanging asparagus, etc.

lindura, *n.f.* [LINDEZA].

línea, *n.f.* line; lineage, progeny; equator; boundary, limit; class, order; (*fort.*) trench; (*mil.*) file, rank; figure, waistline; line, twelfth part of an inch; *línea de agua* or *de flotación*, (*naut.*) Plimsoll line; *línea de colimación* or *de fe*, (*surv.*) line of colimation; *línea equinoccial*, equator; *línea férrea*, railway.

lineal, *a.* lineal, composed of lines.

lineamento, lineamiento, *n.m.* lineament, feature.

linear, *v.t.* to draw lines; to sketch, limn.

líneo, -nea, *a.* (*bot.*) linaceous.

linfa, *n.f.* lymph; (*poet.*) water.

linfático, -ca, *a.* lymphatic.

linfatismo, *n.m.* (*path.*) morbid state by excess of lymph.

lingote, *n.m.* (*min.*) ingot, pig; *lingotes de cobre*, copper pigs.

lingual, *a.* lingual.

lingue, *n.m.* (*Chi.*) tree of the genus Laurus.

linguete, *n.m.* (*naut.*) pawl of the capstan, ratchet.

lingüista, *n.m.f.* linguist.

lingüística, *n.f.* linguistics.

lingüístico, -ca, *a.* linguistic.

linimento, linimiento, *n.m.* (*med.*) liniment.

linio, *n.m.* row of plants.

lino, *n.m.* (*bot.*) flax; linen; canvas, sail-cloth; (*poet.*) sail.

linóleo, *n.m.* linoleum.

linón, *n.m.* lawn (fabric).

linotipia, *n.f.* linotype.

lintel, *n.m.* lintel.

linterna, *n.f.* lantern; (electric) torch; (*mech.*) lantern-wheel; (*naut.*) lighthouse; (*arch.*) lantern; *linterna sorda* (or *secreta*), dark lantern; *linterna mágica*, magic lantern.

linternazo, *n.m.* blow with a lantern or any other instrument.

linternero, *n.m.* lantern-maker.

linternón *n.m.* large lantern; (*naut.*) poop-lantern.

liño, *n.m.* row of plants or trees; ridge between furrows.

liñuelo, *n.m.* strand of a rope or cord.
lío, *n.m.* bundle, parcel, pack; (*coll.*) muddle, scrape; intrigue, liaison.
liorna, *n.f.* (*coll.*) uproar, confusion, hubbub.
lipemanía, *n.f.* (*med.*) melancholia.
lipemaníaco, *a.* (*med.*) melancholic.
lipes, lipis, *n.f.* blue vitriol, copper sulphate.
lipiria, *n.f.* (*med.*) continuous or remittent fever.
lipoideo, *a.* greasy.
lipotimia, *n.f.* (*med.*) lipothymy; faint, swoon.
liquefacción, *n.f.* liquefaction.
liquen, *n.m.* (*bot.*) lichen.
liquidable, *a.* liquefiable; (*com.*) adjustable.
liquidación, *n.f.* liquefaction; liquidation, settlement; balance; disposal of a merchant's remaining goods at reduced prices; sale.
liquidador, -ra, *a.* liquefying; *n.m.f.* liquefier; liquidator.
liquidámbar, *n.m.* liquidambar.
liquidamente, *adv.* in a liquid state or manner.
liquidar, *v.t.* to liquefy, melt, dissolve; *liquidar a plazos,* to pay by instalments; *liquidar cuentas,* to liquidate debts (or accounts). — *v.r.* to liquefy, liquate, become or grow liquid.
liquidez, *n.f.* liquidness, fluidity.
líquido, *n.m.* liquid; (*com.*) balance, net profit; *líquido imponible,* amount of assessment for tax collection. — *n.f.* (*gram.*) liquid consonant, i.e. L or R.
líquido, -da, *a.* liquid, fluid, fluent; evident, clear; neat; (*com.*) net.
lira, *n.f.* lyre; lyric poem or poetry; the Italian monetary unit; (*astron.*) Lyra.
lirado, -da, *a.* shaped like a lyre.
liria, *n.f.* bird-lime.
lírico, -ca, *a.* lyric, lyrical.
lirio, *n.m.* (*bot.*) iris; lily.
lirismo, *n.m.* lyricism; effusiveness.
lirón, *n.m.* (*zool.*) dormouse; (*naut.*) jack-screw; (*coll.*) sleepy head; (*bot.*) water plantain (*Alisma plantago*).
lirondo, -da, *a.* pure, clean, neat; *mondo y lirondo,* (*coll.*) pure, unmixed.
lis, *n.f.* fleur-de-lis, lily, iris.
lisa, *n.f.* polishing stone; (*ichth.*) river fish.
lisamente, *adv.* smoothly, plainly; *lisa y llanamente,* frankly and openly.
lisbonés, -esa; lisbonense, *n.m.f., a.* native of Lisbon.
lisera, *n.f.* berm.
lisiado, -da, *a.* lamed, injured, hurt. — *p.p.* [LISIAR].
lisiar, *v.t.* to lame, hurt, injure, maim, cripple.
lisimaquia, *n.f.* (*bot.*) loosestrife.
liso, -sa, *a.* plain, even, flat, smooth; clear, evident; *hombre liso,* plain-dealing man; *liso y llano,* clear and evident.
lisol, *n.m.* lysol.
lisonja, *n.f.* adulation, flattery; fawning, coaxing; (*her.*) lozenge.
lisonjeador, -ra, *n.m.f.* flatterer.
lisonjear, *v.t.* to flatter, compliment, coax, wheedle, fawn, please, delight; *lisonjear el oído,* to tickle the ear, flatter.
lisonjeramente, *adv.* flatteringly, fawningly.
lisonjero, -ra, *n.m.f.* fawner, flatterer. — *a.* parasitical, wheedling, fawning, flattering; complimentary, pleasing, agreeable.
lista, *n.f.* slip of paper, shred of linen, list, strip of cloth, selvage; list, catalogue; (*law*)

docket; (*mil.*) roll, muster; (*naut.*) muster-book; bill (of expenses, charges, etc.); *pasar lista,* to call over, muster, review; *lista de correos,* poste restante; *lista de platos,* menu, bill of fare; *lista civil,* civil list.
listadillo, *n.m.* (*Am.*) striped gingham.
listado, -da; listeado, -da, *a.* striped, listed.
listel, *n.m.* (*arch.*) fillet, listel, tringle.
listo, -ta, *a.* ready, prompt, active, diligent, clever.
listón, *n.m.* ribbon, ferret; (*carp.*) lath, cleat; (*arch.*) fillet, listel.
listonado, -da, *a.* (*carp.*) made of laths.
listonar, *v.t.* (*carp.*) to batten, lath.
listonería, *n.f.* parcel of ribbons, tapes, etc.; ribbon-shop; ribbon factory.
listonero, -ra, *n.m.f.* ribbon-maker.
listura, *n.f.* smartness, quickness.
lisura, *n.f.* smoothness, evenness, glibness, flatness; candour, sincerity; (*Am.*) impudent or shameless behaviour.
lita, *n.f.* tongue-worm in dogs.
litación, *n.f.* sacrificing.
litar, *v.t.* to sacrifice to the Deity.
litarge, litargirio, *n.m.* litharge.
lite, *n.m.* lawsuit, trial.
litera, *n.f.* litter; (*naut.*) berth.
literal, *a.* literal.
literalista, *n.m.f.* literalist, one who adheres to the letter.
literalmente, *adv.* literally.
literario, -ria, *a.* literary.
literato, *n.m.* literary man. — *pl.* **literati,** learned men.
literato, -ta, *a.* learned, lettered, literary, literate, versed in letters.
literatura, *n.f.* literature, learning, literary skill.
literero, *n.m.* one who makes or drives a litter.
litería, *n.f.* royal official in charge of the litters.
lítico, -ca, *a.* (*med.*) lithic, of the stone.
litigación, *n.f.* litigation, lawsuit.
litigante, *n.m.f., a.* litigating, litigant, party in a lawsuit.
litigar, *v.t.* (*pret.* **litigué;** *pres. subj.* **litigue**) to litigate, go to law, contend, dispute.
litigio, *n.m.* litigation, lawsuit, contest, dispute.
litigioso, -sa, *a.* litigious, contentious.
litina, *n.f.* (*chem.*) oxide of lithium.
litio, *n.m.* (*chem.*) lithium.
litis, *n.f.* lawsuit.
litisconsorte, *n.m.f.* associate in a lawsuit.
litiscontestación, *n.f.* (*law*) answer to a juridical command.
litisexpensas, *n.pl.* (*law*) costs of lawsuit.
litispendencia, *n.f.* state of a lawsuit under judgment.
litocálamo, *n.m.* petrified or fossil reed.
litoclasa, *n.f.* (*geol.*) fissure.
litocola, *n.f.* lithocolla, lapidary's cement.
litófago, -ga, *a.* rock-consuming, rock-boring (molluscs).
litófito, *n.m.* lithophyte; coral.
litografía, *n.f.* lithography.
litografiar, *v.t.* to lithograph.
litográfico, -ca, *a.* lithographic.
litógrafo, *n.m.* lithographist.
litología, *n.f.* lithology.
litológico, -ca, *a.* lithological.
litólogo, *n.m.* lithologist.
litoral, *a.* littoral. — *n.m.* coast, shore.
litontrípico, -ca, *n.m.f., a.* lithontriptic.

litote, *n.f.* (*rhet.*) litotes.
litotomía, *n.f.* lithotomy.
litotomista, *n.m.f.* lithotomist.
litre, *n.m.* (*Chi.*) tree of the terebinth family; illness produced by the shade of this tree.
litro, *n.m.* litre.
lituano, -na, *n.m.f., a.* Lithuanian.
lituo, *n.m.* lituus, augur's staff; ancient musical instrument.
liturgia, *n.f.* liturgy, form of prayers, form of celebrating the Mass.
litúrgico, -ca, *a.* liturgic, liturgical, of or belonging to the liturgy.
liudo, -da, *a.* (*Col., Chi.*) fermented, leavened.
livianamente, *adv.* licentiously, lightly, superficially.
liviandad, *n.f.* lightness, want of weight; levity, incontinence, frivolity; lewdness, libidinousness, imprudence.
liviano, -na, *a.* light, of little weight; imprudent, incontinent, libidinous, unchaste, unsteady; *n.m.* leading jackass.
livianos, *n.m.pl.* lungs.
lividez, *n.f.* lividity, lividness.
lívido, -da, *a.* livid, black and blue.
livor, *n.m.* livid colour; (*fig.*) malignity, perversity; envy, hatred.
lixiviar, *v.t.* (*chem.*) to lixiviate.
liza, *n.f.* (*ichth.*) skate; lists for jousts.
lizo, *n.m.* skein of silk, warp-thread, heddle.
lizón, *n.m.* (*bot.*) water-plantain.
lo, *pers. pron. acc. masc. sing.* him, it; *indef. adj.* and *pron.* the.
loa, *n.f.* praise; (*naut.*) lee; prologue of a play; short dramatic panegyric.
loable, *a.* laudable, praiseworthy.
loablemente, *adv.* laudably, commendably.
loador, -ra, *n.m.f.* praiser, lauder.
loam, *n.m.* (*min.*) loam.
loán, *n.m.* (*Philip.*) land measure (11 perches).
loanda, *n.f.* kind of scurvy.
loar, *v.t.* to praise, approve, eulogize.
loba, *n.f.* she-wolf; clergyman's gown, student's gown; ridge between furrows. — *n.m.* morbid swelling on horses.
lobado, -da, *a.* morbid swelling on horses; (*zool., bot.*) lobate.
lobanillo, *n.m.* wen; callous excrescence.
lobato, *n.m.* young wolf, wolf cub.
lobera, *n.f.* (*obs.*) narrow door or passage; thicket.
lobero, -ra, *a.* relating to wolves; wolfish.
lobezno, *n.m.* young wolf, wolf cub.
lobina, *n.f.* (*ichth.*) striped bass.
lobo, *n.m.* wolf; (*anat., bot.*) lobe; (*ichth.*) loach; (*coll.*) thief; (*fam.*) intoxication, drunkenness; instrument for defending walls; (*text.*) picking-process, picking-machine (cotton); (*Mex.*) half-breed; *coger* (or *pillar*) *un lobo,* (*fam.*) to be tipsy; *desollar* (or *dormir*) *el lobo,* to sleep off a drunken bout; *quien con lobos anda a aullar se enseña,* he who touches pitch is defiled; *lobos de una camada,* persons in league together; *son lobos de la misma camada,* they are chips of the same block; *del lobo un pelo, y ése de la frente,* take from a stingy person anything he will give you; *de lo contado come el lobo,* there's many a slip 'twixt cup and lip; *el lobo está en la conseja,* an intruder is present; *esperar del lobo carne,* to hope for favours from those unlikely to give them; *muda el lobo los dientes,*

y no las mientes, the wolf grows older, but remains always a wolf; *ver las orejas del lobo,* to find oneself in the greatest danger.
lobo, -ba, *a.* (*Chi.*) shy, unsociable.
loboso, -sa, *a.* full of wolves.
lóbrego, -ga, *a.* murky, obscure, lugubrious, gloomy, sad, dark.
lobreguecer, *v.i.* to grow dark, be dark. — *v.t.* to make dark.
lobreguez, *n.f.* obscurity, darkness.
lóbulo, *n.m.* lobe, lobule.
lobuno, -na, *a.* wolfish.
locación, *n.f.* (*law*) lease; *locación y conducción,* agreement to let.
locador, -ra; locatario, -ria, *n.m.f.* (*Ven.*) landlord; lessor.
local, *a.* local. — *n.m.* place, premises, site.
localidad, *n.f.* locality, location; seat (theatre, etc.).
localización, *n.f.* localization.
localizar, *v.t.* (conjugated like ALZAR) to localize.
localmente, *adv.* locally.
locamente, *adv.* madly, immoderately, extravagantly, fondly, foolishly.
locarias, *n.m.* (*coll.*) madcap, wild or hot-brained fellow.
locativo, -va, *n.m.f., a.* (*gram.*) locative.
locazo, -za, *a.* very mad.
loción, *n.f.* lotion, wash; lavation, washing.
loco, -ca, *n.m.f., a.* madman, madwoman, fool, insane, crazy, or crackbrained person; plentiful, abundant, fertile, excessive; *estar loco,* to be very angry, out of one's mind with joy or excitement; *cada loco con su tema,* everyone has his craze; *el loco, por la pena es cuerdo,* even the madman feels the sting of the whip; *más sabe el loco en su casa que el cuerdo en la ajena,* everyone is the best judge of his own business; *al loco y al aire, darles calle,* avoid disputes with hasty persons; *a palabras locas, orejas sordas,* a silly question deserves no answer; *a tontas y a locas,* inconsiderately, without reflection.
locomoción, *n.f.* (*phys.*) locomotion.
locomotor, -ra, *a.* locomotive. — *n.f.* locomotive, railway engine.
locomotriz, *n.f.* locomotive.
locomóvil, *a.* portable, movable.
locro, *n.m.* (*Am.*) kind of stew.
locuacidad, *n.f.* loquacity, talkativeness, flippancy, garrulity.
locuaz, *a.* loquacious, talkative, garrulous.
locuazmente, *adv.* with loquacity, flippantly.
locución, *n.f.* locution, manner of speech, idiom, phrase.
locuela, *n.f.* particular individual manner of speaking.
locuelo, -la, *n.m.f.* madcap, giddy youth.
locura, *n.f.* madness, lunacy, insanity; frenzy, fury, craziness, folly, absurdity; *hacer locuras,* to act absurdly or foolishly; *si la locura fuese dolores, en cada casa habría voces,* everyone acts imprudently at times.
locutor, -ra, *n.m.f.* radio announcer or speaker.
locutorio, *n.m.* locutory parlour, place in convents and monasteries for receiving visits; (*teleph.*) private call box.
locha, *n.f.; loche,** *n.m.* (*ichth.*) loach.
lodachar, lodazal, lodazar, *n.m.* muddy place, quagmire, bog.

lodo, *n.m.* mud, mire; gore; *poner a uno de lodo,* to offend, insult someone; *salir del lodo y caer en el arroyo,* to be out of the frying-pan and into the fire.

lodoño, *n.m.* (*bot.*) European nettle-tree.

lodoso, -sa, *a.* muddy, miry.

lof, lo, *n.m.* (*naut.*) luff, weather side of a ship; *amura del lof,* (*naut.*) weather tack; *no más de lof,* (*naut.*) not nearer.

logarítmico, -ca, *a.* (*math.*) logarithmic, logarithmical.

logaritmo, *n.m.* logarithm.

logia, *n.f.* (Freemasons') lodge.

lógica, *n.f.* logic, dialectics.

logical, *a.* logical.

lógicamente, *adv.* logically.

lógico, -ca, *a.* logical.

lógico, *n.m.* logician, dialectician, professor of logic.

logística, *n.f.* logistics, algebra.

logogrifo, *n.m.* logogryph, riddle.

logomaquia, *n.f.* logomachy, dispute about words.

lograr, *v.t.* to gain, obtain, attain, procure, compass, possess, enjoy, succeed, avail oneself of, hit upon, do well, manage. — *v.r.* to reap the benefit of one's efforts.

logrear, *v.i.* to borrow or lend on interest.

logrería, *n.f.* dealing in interest, usury.

logrero, -ra, *n.m.f.* lender at interest, usurer; profiteer.

logro, *n.m.* gain, benefit, profit; attainment of purpose; interest, usury; *dar a logro,* to put out money at usury.

loica, *n.f.* (*Chi.*) singing bird.

loma, *n.f.* small hill, hillock, rising ground, slope.

lombarda, *n.f.* lombard gun; (*bot.*) red cabbage.

lombardada, *n.f.* shot from a lombard gun.

lombardear, *v.t.* to discharge lombard guns.

lombardería, *n.f.* park of lombard guns.

lombardero, *n.m.* soldier appointed to lombard guns.

lombárdico, -ca; lombardo, -da, *a.* belonging to Lombardy.

lombardo, -da, *a.* Lombard; bank that advances money on goods delivered for sale; fighting bull of light hazel colour.

lombriguera, *n.f.* hole made by worms; (*bot.*) southern-wood.

lombriz, *n.f.* earth-worm, intestinal worm; *lombriz solitaria,* tapeworm.

lombrizal, *a.* vermiform.

lomear, *v.i.* to jerk the loins in a circular manner (of horses).

lomento, *n.m.* (*bot.*) loment.

lomera, *n.f.* main strap of harness; (*arch.*) ridge of a roof; (*bookbinding*) backing.

lomiancho, -cha, *a.* strong, broad-backed.

lomica, *n.f.* very small hill.

lomillo, *n.m.* small loin; (*sew.*) cross-stitch, kind of needlework; cantle. — *pl.* pads of a packsaddle.

lominhiesto, -ta, *a.* with high loins; presumptuous, arrogant, stiff-necked.

lomo, *n.m.* loin, back, chine; back of book or cutting tool; double (of a cloth, leather, etc.); crease; ridge between furrows. — *pl.* **lomos,** ribs, loins; *jugar de lomo,* to be idle and in good health or condition; *llevar* (or *traer*) *a lomo,* to carry on the back.

lomoso, -sa, *a.* belonging to the loins.

lomudo, -da, *a.* broad-backed.

lona, *n.f.* canvas.

loncha, *n.f.* slab, flag-stone, thin flat stone; long slice of meat.

londinense, *a.* of or belonging to London. — *n.m.f.* Londoner.

Londres, *n.m.* London.

londrina, *n.f.* kind of woollen cloth; woollen cloth from London.

londrino, -na, *a.* in the London fashion.

londro, *n.m.* galley-like vessel.

loneta, *n.f.* ravens-duck, sail-cloth.

longa, *n.f.* (*mus.*) long (two breves).

longanimidad, *n.f.* longanimity, forbearance.

longánimo, -ma, *a.* forbearing, generous, magnanimous.

longaniza, *n.f.* kind of long sausage; choice pork sausage.

longar, *a.* long (honey-comb).

longazo, -za, *a.* very long.

longevidad, *n.f.* longevity.

longevo, -va, *a.* longeval, long-lived.

longincuo, -cua, *a.* distant, remote.

longitud, *n.f.* length; longitude.

longitudinal, *a.* longitudinal.

longitudinalmente, *adv.* longitudinally, lengthwise.

longuera, *n.f.* long, narrow strip of land.

longuetas, *n.f.pl.* (*surg.*) bandages.

lonja, *n.f.* exchange, meeting-place of merchants; store-room for wool; warehouse, saleroom; grocer's shop; slice of meat; portico; leather strap in falconry.

lonjero, *n.m.* grocer.

lonjeta, *n.f.* small slice; small strap; pergola, lawn, arbour.

lonjista, *n.m.f.* grocer.

lontananza, *n.f.* distance, background.

loor, *n.m.* (*poet.*) praise.

lopigia, *n.f.* baldness, alopecia.

loquear, *v.i.* to act the fool, talk nonsense; to rejoice, revel, exult, frolic.

loquera, *n.f.* madhouse.

loquero, -ra, *n.m.f.* keeper or physician of a madhouse.

loquesca, *n.f.* frantic behaviour of mad people.

loquesto, -ta, *a.* crazy; funny, jesting.

loquillo, -lla; -to, -ta, *a.* wild, frisky.

loquios, *n.m.pl.* (*med.*) lochia, loches.

lora, *n.f.* (*Col., CR., Hond., Per.*) parrot; (*Chi.*) female parrot.

lorantáceo, -cea, *a.* (*bot.*) lauraceous.

lord, *n.m.* (*pl.* **lores**) lord, ruler, master; owner; nobleman, peer of the realm; title of honour conferred on certain official personages.

lorenzana, *n.f.* kind of linen.

loriga, *n.f.* cuirass, coat of mail, lorica; naveband.

lorigado, -da, *a.* loricate, armed with a coat of mail.

loriguillo, *n.m.* shrub used by dyers.

loro, -ra, *a.* tawny; wan, pale; black and blue.

loro, *n.m.* parrot; (*bot.*) Portugal (or cherry) laurel.

loronés, -esa, *n.m.f.,* *a.* belonging or pertaining to Lorraine; native or inhabitant of Lorraine.

los, *def. art. masc. pl.* the; *pers. pron. masc. acc. pl.* them.

losa, *n.f.* flagstone; painter's block; rat-trap; grave-stone; grave.

losado, *n.m.* tiled floor.

losado, -da, *a., p.p.* [LOSAR].

losange, *n.m.* lozenge, rhomb.

losar, *v.t.* to tile.

loseta, losilla, *n.f.* small trap or snare; *coger en la loseta* (or *losilla*) to deceive by guile.

losica, losita, *n.f.* small flagstone.

lota, *n.f.* (*prov.*) fish sold by auction; place where this auction is held.

lote, *n.m.* lot, chance, fortune.

lotería, *n.f.* lottery; raffle; lotto, a game.

lotero, -ra, *n.m.f.* lottery-ticket-seller.

loto, *n.m.* lotus, lotus-tree, lotus-flower.

lotófago, -ga, *a.* lotus-eating.

loxodromia, *n.f.* (*naut.*) loxodrome.

loxodrómico, -ca, *a.* (*naut.*) loxodromic.

loza, *n.f.* fine earthenware, delft, porcelain; *ande la loza,* (*coll.*) noisy mirth.

lozanamente, *adv.* luxuriantly.

lozanear, *v.i.* to look vigorous and lusty, affect ostentation and pomp.

lozanía, *n.f.* luxuriance, exuberant growth; elegance; lustiness, vigour.

lozano, -na, *a.* luxuriant; lusty, sprightly.

lúa, *n.f.* esparto glove for cleaning horses; (*naut.*) lee; (*prov.*) saffron bag; *tomar por la lúa,* (*naut.*) to bring to the lee.

lubricación, *n.f.* lubrication.

lubricán, *n.m.* dawn of day.

lubricar, lubrificar, *v.t.* (conjugated like BUSCAR) to lubricate.

lubricativo, -va, *a.* lubricant, lubricative.

lubricidad, *n.f.* lubricity; slipperiness; lewdness.

lúbrico, -ca, *a.* slippery, lubricious; lewd.

lucencia, *n.f.* (*obs.*) brightness, lucidity.

lucentísimo, -ma, *a. superl.,* brightest.

lucentor, *n.m.* make-up formerly used by women.

lucera, *n.f.* skylight.

lucerna, *n.f.* glow-worm; chandelier, lamp.

lucérnula, *n.f.* (*bot.*) lucern, sainfoin.

lucero, *n.m.* morning-star, Venus, day-star, Lucifer; bright star, brightness, splendour; part of a window where the light enters; star on a horse's forehead. — *pl.* luceros, (*poet.*) eyes.

lucidamente, *adv.* lucidly, clearly, splendidly, brightly.

lucidar, *v.t.* to copy on transparent paper.

lúcido, -da, *a.* lucid, shining, lucific; gay, magnificent, splendid, graceful. — *p.p.* [LUCIR].

lucidura, *n.f.* (*coll.*) whiteness, whitewashing.

luciente, *a.* shining, luminous, bright, lucid.

luciérnaga, *n.f.* glow-worm, fire-fly.

lucifer, *n.m.* Lucifer, Satan; a proud and bad man; morning star.

luciferino, -na, *a.* Luciferian.

lucífero, -ra, *a.* (*poet.*) resplendent, shining, luciferous.

lucifero, *n.m.* morning star.

lucífugo, -ga, *a.* that which shuns the light.

lucillo, *n.m.* tomb, sarcophagus.

lucimiento, *n.m.* lucidity, clearness, brightness; splendour, lustre, applause; *quedar con lucimiento,* to enjoy complete success.

lucio, -cia, *a.* lucid, clear, bright.

lucio, *n.m.* (*ichth.*) pike, luce.

lucir, *v.t., v.i.* (*pres. indic.* **luzco,** *pres. subj.* **luzca**) to emit light, shine, gleam, glow, glitter, illuminate, lighten, enlighten, out-

shine, exceed in brilliance; (*coll.*) to display, sport, show off. — *v.r.* to be brilliant, shine; to dress to advantage; to show off; to be very successful, to do splendidly.

lucrarse, *v.r.* to derive profit from a business.

lucrativo, -va, *a.* lucrative, profitable, productive of gain.

lucro, *n.m.* gain, profit, lucre; *lucros y daños,* (*com.*) profit and loss.

lucroso, -sa, *a.* lucrative, gainful, profitable.

luctuosa, *n.f.* feudal death tax.

luctuosamente, *adv.* mournfully, sorrowfully.

luctuoso, -sa, *a.* sad, mournful.

lucubración, *n.f.* lucubration, nocturnal study.

lucubrar, *v.i.* to lucubrate.

lúcuma, *n.f.* fruit of the lúcumo tree.

lúcumo, *n.m.* (*Chi., Per.*) lucuma, the Chicle tree (*Achras zapota*).

lucha, *n.f.* struggle, strife, battle, contest, wrestle; dispute, argument.

luchador, -ra, *n.m.f.* wrestler.

luchar, *v.t.* to wrestle, struggle; fight, contend; discuss, debate, wrangle.

lucharniego, -ga, *a.* applied to dogs used for catching hares at night.

luche, *n.m.* (*Chi.*) edible seaweed.

luchillo, *n.m.* (*naut.*) goring, goring-cloth.

ludia, *n.f.* (*prov.*) ferment, yeast.

ludiar, *v.t., v.r.* (*prov.*) to ferment.

ludibrio, *n.m.* mockery, scorn, derision.

ludimiento, *n.m.* friction, rubbing.

ludión, *n.m.* (*phys.*) Cartesian devil.

ludir, *v.i.* to rub, waste by friction; to collide.

lúe, *n.f.* infection.

luego, *adv., conj.* immediately, outright, soon, presently, by-and-bye; *con tres luegos,* quickly, instantly; *de luego,* very promptly; *desde luego,* naturally, certainly; at once, instantly; *hasta luego,* good-bye for the present; so long.

luello, *n.m.* (*prov.*) bad seed growing among grain or corn.

luengo, -ga, *a.* long, dilated; *en luengo,* finally, in the end.

lugano, *n.m.* (*orn.*) linnet.

lugar, *n.m.* place, spot, position, site, situation; room, space; village, small place, hamlet, small town; time, occasion, opportunity, leisure; employment, seat, dignity, office; convenience; cause, reason, motive; text, authority; *lugares comunes,* commonplaces; *lugar pasajero,* thoroughfare; *en lugar de,* instead of; in lieu of; *no ha lugar,* (*law*) the petition is not granted; *en primer lugar,* in the first place; *tener lugar,* to have time enough; *hacer lugar,* to make room, leave a place free; *quien en ruin lugar hace viña, a cuestas saca la vendimia,* little good comes from ploughing sterile ground (or from helping thankless people); *lugar excusado,* privy-house, water-closet; *en su lugar, descanso,* (*mil.*) stand at ease.

lugarcico, -cillo, -cito, -ejo, -ete, -illo, *n.m.* hamlet, small village.

lugarejo, *n.m.* small village.

lugareño, -na, *n.m.f., a.* one belonging to a village, villager.

lugarón, lugarote, *n.m.* large, ugly or straggling village.

lugartenencia, *n.f.* lieutenancy.

lugarteniente, *n.m.* deputy, substitute, delegate, lieutenant.

lugre, *n.m.* (*naut.*) lugger, small vessel.
lúgubre, *a.* mournful, lugubrious, gloomy, sad, melancholy, dismal.
luir, *v.i.* (*naut.*) to gall, be galled or fretted, wear away by friction.
luisa, *n.f.* (*bot.*) lemon verbena or aloysia.
lujación, *n.f.* (*surg.*) luxation.
lujar, *v.t.* (*Cub.*) to rub. — *v.r.* (*surg.*) to luxate, dislocate.
lujo, *n.m.* profuseness, extravagance, superfluity, excess; luxury, finery.
lujoso, -sa, *a.* profuse, lavish, fond of show, showy, sumptuous.
lujuria, *n.f.* lust, lubricity, excess, profuseness, luxury, lavishness.
lujuriante, *a.* lusting; luxuriant, exuberant.
lujuriar, *v.i.* to lust, be luxurious or libidinous; to couple (of animals).
lujuriosamente, *adv.* lustfully, voluptuously, luxuriously.
lujurioso, -sa, *a.* lustful, voluptuous, lewd, luxurious, libidinous.
luliano, -na, *n.m.f.*, *a.* Lullian.
lulismo, *n.m.* system of Ramón Lull.
luma, *n.f.* (*Chi.*) tree of the Myrtaceous family with very hard wood, used for horse-wagon axles.
lumaquela, *n.f.* fire-marble.
lumbago, *n.m.* (*med.*) lumbago.
lumbar, *a.* lumbar, lumbal.
lumbrada, lumbrerada, *n.f.* great fire, fierce conflagration.
lumbre, *n.f.* fire, something burning, spark, light, splendour, brightness, lucidity, clearness; skylight; hammer of a flint-lock; forepart of a horse-shoe; *lumbre del agua*, level (*or* surface) of the water; *a lumbre de pajas*, (*coll.*) very swiftly; *ni por lumbre*, not at all, by no means; *es la lumbre de mis ojos*, she is the light of my eyes (i.e. is very dear to me). — *pl.* **lumbres**, tinder-box, hammer of a gunlock, fore-part of horse-shoes.
lumbrera, *n.f.* luminary; skylight; light shaft; eminent and distinguished person; vent, port-hole.
lumen, *n.m.* (*phys.*) unit of light, lumen.
luminar, *n.m.* luminary; light as distinct from shade.
luminaria, *n.f.* illumination, festival light, light burning before the Blessed Sacrament. — *pl.* **luminarias**, money paid for festival illuminations.
lumínico, *n.m.* (*phys.*) light.
luminiscencia, *n.f.* luminescence.
luminiscente, *a.* luminescent.
luminosamente, *adv.* luminously, luciferously.
luminoso, -sa, *a.* luminous, lucid, shining.
lumpo jibado, *n.m.* (*ichth.*) lump (a suctorial fish).
luna, *n.f.* moon; glass plate for mirrors; (*prov.*) open court; *ladrar a la luna*, to rage uselessly against a person; *estar de buena* (or *mala*) *luna*, to be in a good (*or* bad) humour; *quedarse a la luna de Valencia*, to be baulked (*or* left in the cold); *tener lunas*, to be affected by the changes of the moon; *media luna*, crescent moon; crescent; (*fig.*) Islam, Mohammedanism; Turkish Empire; *luna de miel*, honeymoon.
lunación, *n.f.* lunation, revolution of the moon.

lunada, *n.f.* (*obs.*) ham, gammon.
lunado, -da, *a.* lunated, formed like a half-moon.
lunanco, -ca, *a.* of animals with one quarter higher than the other.
lunar, *n.m.* mole, spot, discoloration, flaw, patch, stain, blemish. — *a.* lunar, lunary.
lunarejo, -ja, *a.* (*Arg., Col., Per.*) person with moles.
lunaria, *n.f.* (*bot.*) moonwort, honesty.
lunario, -ria, *a.* lunarian.
lunario, *n.m.* calendar.
lunático, -ca, *a.* lunatic, moonstruck, mad.
lunecilla, *n.f.* crescent, crescent-shaped jewel.
lunes, *n.m.* Monday.
luneta, *n.f.* eyeglass, lens; crescent (adornment for women's hair or boys' shoes); telescope; (*arch.*) lunette; saddler's knife.
lunfardo, *n.m.* (*Arg.*) thief, filcher; pimp; thieves' Latin.
lunisolar, *a.* (*astr.*) lunisolar.
lunista, *n.m.* lunatic, madman.
lúnula, *n.f.* half-moon-shaped geometrical figure, lune; (*opt.*) meniscus.
lupanar, *n.m.* brothel.
lupanario, -ria, *a.* belonging to a brothel.
lupia, *n.f.* (*med.*) encysted tumour, wen.
lupino, -na, *a.* wolfish.
lupino, *n.m.* (*bot.*) lupin.
lúpulo, *n.m.* (*bot.*) hops.
lupus, *n.m.* (*med.*) lupus.
luquete, *n.m.* zest, slice of orange dropped into wine; match, firebrand.
luquetera, *n.f.* match-girl.
lurte, *n.m.* iceberg; avalanche, landslide.
lusitanismo, *n.m.* Lusitanism, Portuguese idiom.
lusitano, -na, *a.* Lusitanian; Portuguese.
lustración, *n.f.* lustration, purification by water; lustrum.
lustrador, *n.m.* hot-press, mangler; polisher.
lustral, *a.* lustral.
lustrar, *v.t.* to expiate, purify; to illustrate, make brilliant, polish, lustre, gloss; to wander.
lustre, *n.m.* gloss, glaze, polish, lustre, fineness; brightness, clearness, nobleness, splendour, brilliancy, glory; shoe-polish.
lústrico, -ca, *a.* (*poet.*) belonging to a lustre.
lustrina, *n.f.* lustring; (*Chi.*) shoeblacking.
lustro, *n.m.* lustrum, period of five years; lamp, chandelier.
lustrosamente, *adv.* brilliantly, splendidly, glitteringly.
lustroso, -sa, *a.* bright, brilliant, lustrous, shining, golden, glossy.
lutación, *n.f.* (*chem.*) lutation.
lútea, *n.f.* (*orn.*) oriole; cazique.
lúten, *n.m.* (*chem.*) lute.
lúteo, -tea, *a.* muddy, miry.
luteranismo, *n.m.* Lutheranism.
luterano, -na, *n.m.f.*, *a.* Lutheran.
Lutero, *n.m.* Luther.
luto, *n.m.* mourning, condolence, sorrow, grief, affliction. — *n.m.pl.* **lutos**, mourning, mourning clothes.
lutocar, *n.m.* (*Chi.*) small cart used for collecting rubbish.
luz, *n.f.* light, clearness, clarity; lamp, candle, taper; day, daylight; brightness; notice, hint, information; knowledge; inspiration; luminary, prominent man; lustre, splendour;

lighthouse; (*pict.*) light and shade. — *pl.*
luces, windows, lanterns, loopholes; culture,
learning, knowledge, enlightenment; *a primera luz*, at dawn; *a buena luz*, carefully,
after examination; *a dos luces*, ambiguously;
a todas luces, anyway, everywhere; *dar luz*,
to light, lighten; *dar a luz*, to give birth to;
to be delivered (of a child); *sacar a luz*, to
publish, give to the world; *echar luz*, to
recover health and strength, to give light to
the understanding; *entre dos luces*, at twilight,
at dawn; *primera luz*, light which comes to a
room from outside; *luz de luz*, borrowed (*or*
reflected) light; *luz de la razón*, intuitive
reason; *hacer dos luces*, to light up both sides
at once; *salir a luz*, to appear, come out,
come to light, be discovered; to leak out.
luzbel, *n.m.* Lucifer, Satan.
luzco ; yo luzca, *pres. indic.; pres. subj.* [LUCIR].

LL

Ll, ll, the fourteenth letter of the Spanish
alphabet; its name is *elle*.
llábana, *n.f.* (*prov.*) smooth and slippery flagstone.
llaca, *n.f.* (*Arg., Chi.*) a kind of opossum.
llaga, *n.f.* wound, sore; prick, thorn; ulcer;
seam or crack in a wall; tormenting thoughts;
la mala llaga sana; la mala fama mata, give a
dog a bad name and hang him; *sanan llagas,
y no malas palabras*, evil tongues wound more
deeply than blows.
llagador, -ra, *n.m.f.*, *a.* wounder, one who
wounds.
llagar, *v.t.* (*pret.* **llagué;** *pres. subj.* **llague**) to
wound, injure, hurt.
llaguita, -illa, *n.f.* slight ulcer or wound.
llama, *n.f.* flame, blaze; violent passion;
marshy ground. — *n.m.f.* (*zool.*) llama.
llamada, *n.f.* call, act of calling; knock;
marginal note; motion or sign to call attention; (*mil.*) beat of the drum; (*mil.*) chamade;
(*print.*) reference mark, index-mark; (*com.*)
entry; *última llamada*, last peal.
llamadera, *n.f.* goad-stick.
llamador, -ra, *n.m.f.* caller, one who calls;
beadle, messenger; knocker of a door.
llamamiento, *n.m.* calling, call, act of calling,
convening, convention, convocation; vocation, inspiration; attraction of humours to one
part of the body.
llamar, *v.t.* to call, call upon, cite, summon,
invoke, appeal to; to name, denominate; to
incline, attract, excite; to knock (at a door).
— *v.i.* to knock or ring at the door; to excite
thirst. — *v.r.* to be called, named, to have a
name; *llamar a Cortes*, to summon parliament; *el viento llama a popa*, (*naut.*) the wind
veers aft; *el viento llama a proa*, (*naut.*) the
wind hauls forward; *llamar por los nombres*,
to call the role; *llamarse andana* (or *antana*),
to deny forcibly what one has said or
offered.
llamarada, *n.f.* blaze of fire, flash; flush, sudden blush; sudden burst of wit.
llamarón, *n.m.* (*Col., CR., Chi.*) [LLAMARADA].
llamativo, -va, *a.* exciting thirst; showy.
llamazar, *n.m.* marsh, swamp.
llambria, *n.f.* steep face of a rock.

llana, *n.f.* trowel; page of a book; plain, flat or
level ground.
llanada, *n.f.* plain, tract of level ground.
llanamente, *adv.* ingenuously, simply, sincerely, plainly, clearly, flatly.
llanca, *n.f.* (*Chi.*) bluish-green copper ore.
llanero, -ra, *n.m.f.* (*Am.*) dweller on a plain.
llaneza, *n.f.* plainness, sincerity, simplicity;
familiarity; uncultivated style; (*obs.*) evenness, equality.
llano, -na, *a.* plain, even, level, flat, smooth,
easy, unobstructed; meek, affable, gentle,
homely; frank, open, honest, simple, rough,
without ornament, plain; clear, evident, discernible; castrated; (*gram.*) (of a word)
accented on the penultimate syllable; (of a
line of verse) ending with a *palabra llana; a
la llana*, simply, sincerely, candidly; *de llano*
(or *de llano en llano*), clearly, openly; *aquél va
más sano, que anda por el llano*, the safest way
is the best.
llano, *n.m.* level field, even ground.
llanque, *n.m.* (*Per.*) sandal made of untanned
leather.
llanta, *n.f.* tyre, hoop, band of a wheel; (*mot.*)
rim (sometimes tyre); kind of cabbage.
llantén, *n.m.* (*bot.*) plantain, rib grass; *llantén
de agua*, water plantain, alisura.
llantería, *n.f.* (*Chi.*) a general weeping.
llanto, *n.m.* flood of tears, weeping; *anegarse en
llanto*, to weep copiously.
llanura, *n.f.* evenness, flatness, level; equality;
plain, stretch of level ground, prairie.
llapa, *n.f.* (*min.*) quicksilver for amalgamation.
llapar, *v.t.* to add more quicksilver in the extraction of metals.
llar, *n.m.* (*prov.*) hearth, range. — *f.pl.* **llares,**
pot-hook, pot-hanger.
llatar, *n.m.* (*prov.*) fence with posts and railings.
llaullau, *n.m.* (*Chi.*) edible mushroom.
llave, *n.f.* key; spanner, wrench; cock; faucet,
spigot; spout, tap, lock of a gun; knuckle-
duster; introduction to knowledge; explanation of a difficulty; bolt, pin, tightening wedge,
cotter; clock winder; (*arch.*) keystone; (*naut.*)
knee; (*print.*) brace; tuning-key; (*mus.*) clef,
key; piston of musical instruments; *debajo de
llave*, under lock and key; *llave maestra*, pass-
key, master key; *llaves de la Iglesia*, spiritual
authority; *echar la llave*, to lock; *debajo de
siete llaves*, (kept) very securely; *falsear la
llave*, to get a false key; *llave de la mano*,
breadth of the palm of a man's hand; *llave
del pie*, distance from heel to instep; *recoger
las llaves*, to be the last person left (at a
meeting, etc.); *torcer la llave*, to turn the key
in the lock; *tras llave*, locked up; *las llaves en
la cinta y el perro en la cocina*, (said of persons) careless, with an appearance of carefulness; *llave inglesa*, adjustable spanner.
llavero, -ra, *n.m.f.* keeper of the keys; key-
ring; (*prov.*) housekeeper.
llavín, *n.m.* latch key.
lleco, -ca, *a.* virgin, uncultivated, not broken
up (of land).
llega, *n.f.* (*prov.*) gathering, collecting; joining, uniting; juncture.
llegada, *n.f.* arrival, coming.
llegar, *v.i.* (*pret.* **llegué;** *pres. subj.* **llegue**) to
arrive, come, reach, attain, go as far as; to
continue, last; to be enough, suffice; to

amount, rise, ascend. — *v.t.*, *v.r.* to approach, bring near; to join, unite, gather, collect; to go to some neighbouring place; *llegar a afirmar que* . . ., to go so far as to affirm that . . .; *llegar a las manos*, to fight, come to blows; *llegar de arribada*, (*naut.*) to put into port through heavy weather; *llegar a oír*, to hear; *llegar al poder*, to come into power; *llegar a saber*, to find out, be informed of; *llegar y besar*, to get one's object very quickly; *el que primero llega, ése la calza*, the most diligent person commonly wins; *no llegar*, to fall short, not to reach, be inferior; *no llegar la camisa al cuerpo*, to be terrified and anxious.

lleira, *n.f.* (*prov.*) place full of pebbles or gravel.

lleivún, *n.m.* (*Chi.*) plant of the bulrush family.

llena, *n.f.* alluvion, overflow, flood.

lenamente, *adv.* fully, copiously.

llenar, *v.t.* to fill, stuff; satisfy, content; to occupy a public place (as an incumbent); to make up a number; to fecundate, fertilize; *v.i. llenar* (*la luna*), to be full moon; *llenar a uno de vituperios*, to vituperate a person. — *v.r.* to feed gluttonously; to be irritated after long suffering; to be packed, crowded.

llenero, -ra, *a.* (*law*) full, complete, absolute.

lleno, *n.m.* fill, glut, plenty, abundance; perfection, completeness; fullness (of the moon); (*theat.*) full house.

lleno, -na, *a.* full, replete, complete; learned; *de lleno* (or *de lleno en lleno*), entirely, totally; *lleno de bote en bote*, brimful.

llenura, *n.f.* fullness, plenty, copiousness, abundance.

lleta, *n.f.* sprout, stalk of plants bearing fruit.

lleudar, *v.t.* to leaven, ferment bread with leaven.

lleulle, *a.* (*Chi.*) inept, incompetent.

lleva, llevada, *n.f.* carriage, transport, means of carrying.

llevadero, -ra, *a.* tolerable, bearable, light.

llevador, -ra, *n.m.f.*, *a.* carrier, conductor.

llevar, *v.t.* to carry, convey, transport, take, take away, carry away, have with one, bear, wear; to exact, demand, charge, set, ask a price; to gain, obtain; to produce; to exceed, excel; to suffer, endure, stand; (*com.*) to keep (books); to lead, guide, conduct, manage (a horse); to dismember, cut off; to fetch away, fetch off; to have spent or devoted (so much time); to induce, bring to an opinion; to introduce; to be (by so many years) older (than another); to be reprimanded, suffer (chastisement); *llevar al crédito*, (*com.*) to bring to the credit; *llevar un golpe*, to get a blow; *llevar adelante*, to pursue (a thing) diligently; *llevar a lomo*, to carry on one's back; *llevar a cabo*, to accomplish, carry out; *llevar a mal*, to take a thing badly; *llevar la carga*, to be burdened with anxiety; *llevar y conllevar*, to bear and forbear; *llevar el compás*, to beat time; *llevar calabazas*, to fail in an examination; *llevar consigo*, to carry with, have (persons) with (one), be attached to, be a consequence of; *llevar una caída* (or *un golpe*) to get a fall (or a blow); *llevar hierro a Vizcaya*, to bring coals to Newcastle; *llevar recado*, to take a message; *llevar por cortesanía*, to be polite or courteous; *llevar a cuestas*, to carry on one's back or shoulders, be burdened with other's affairs; *llevar estudiado*, to study beforehand; *llevar lo mejor*, (or *peor*) to be getting the best (or worst) of a thing; *llevar los juanetes viados*, (*naut.*) to have the topgallant sails set; *llevar la suya adelante*, to carry one's point; *llevar la proa al noroeste*, (*naut.*) to stand to the north-west; *llevar las velas al buen viento*, (*naut.*) to fill the sails; *llevar las velas llenas*, (*naut.*) to keep the sails full. — *v.r.* to allow oneself to be led away by passion; *llevarse el día*, to carry the day; *llevarse bien* (or *mal*), to be on good (or bad) terms; *llevarse chasco*, to be disappointed; *no llevarlas todas consigo*, to be suspicious.

lloica, *n.f.* (*orn.*) (*Chi.*) robin redbreast.

lloradera, *n.f.* woman hired to weep or mourn at funerals. — *a.* easily weeping.

llorado, *n.m.* (*Col., Ven.*) popular song of the Llaneros.

llorador, -ra, *n.m.f.* one who weeps.

lloraduelos, *n.m.* (*coll.*) weeper, moaner.

llorar, *v.t.*, *v.i.* to weep, cry, mourn, lament, bewail; to affect distress or poverty; (*fig.*) to drip, fall drop by drop; *llorar con un ojo*, to shed crocodile tears; *llorar la aurora*, (*poet.*) to drop dew at dawn; *quien bien te quiere te hará llorar*, he loves thee well that makes thee weep.

lloriquear, *v.t.* to be constantly crying.

lloro, *n.m.* act of weeping or crying.

llorón, *n.m.* weeper, mourner, shedder of tears.

llorón, -ona, *a.* crying with small cause; *sauce llorón*, (*bot.*) weeping willow.

lloronas, *n.f.pl.* weepers, mourners.

llorosamente, *adv.* weepingly.

lloroso, -sa, *a.* sorrowful, mournful, tearful.

llosa, *n.f.* (*prov.*) enclosed estate.

llovediza, *a.* leaky; *agua llovediza*, rainwater.

llover, *v. impers.* (*pres. indic.* **llueve**; *pres. subj.* **llueva**) to rain, shower, pour, come down as rain; to abound, come in plenty. — *v.r.* to leak (said of roofs); *llover a cántaros* (or *a chorros*), to rain bucketsful; *llover chuzos*, to rain cats and dogs; *llover sobre mojado*, to come one after another (of troubles, etc.); *a secas y sin llover*, without preparation or warning; *llueva o no*, rain or shine.

llovido, *n.m.* stowaway. — *a.*, *p.p.* [LLOVER]; *como llovido*, unexpectedly.

llovioso, -sa, *a.* rainy.

llovizna, *n.f.* mist, drizzle.

lloviznar, *v. impers.* to drizzle.

llueca, *n.f.* brooding hen.

lluqui, *a.* (*Ec.*) left-handed.

lluvia, *n.f.* rain, storm, shower, water; abundance, copiousness.

lluvioso, -sa, *a.* rainy, wet, showery.

M

M, m, the fifteenth letter of the Spanish alphabet; *m* is never doubled in Spanish; abbreviations: *majestad* (majesty); *merced* (grace); *mano* (hand); in recipes stands for *manípulus* (handful); its name is *eme*.

mabinga, *n.f.* (*Cub., Mex.*) tobacco of an inferior quality.

mabita, *n.f.* (*Ven.*) unlucky person.

mabolo, *n.m.* (*Philip.*) a tree of the Ebenaceæ.

maca, *n.f.* bruise in fruit; spot, stain; fraud, trick, deceit; aphæresis of *Hamaca* (hammock).

Macabeos, Libro(s) de los, Book(s) of Maccabees.

macabro, -bra, *a.* macabre, ugly, hideous, gruesome.

macaco, -ca, *n.m.f.* monkey; (*Hond.*) small coin of the value of 1 peso; (*Cub., Chi.*) ugly, ill-shaped, squat; (*Mex.*) hobgoblin, bogie.

macadam, macadán, *n.m.* macadam.

macadamizar, *v.t.* to macadamize.

macagua, *n.f.* (*Ven.*) a poisonous snake; (*Cub.*) macaw-tree; (*orn.*) South American bird of prey.

macagüita, *n.f.* (*Ven.*) a thorny palm-tree.

macana, *n.f.* (*Mex.*) ancient wooden weapon; (*Col.*) a palm-tree; (*Cub.*) cudgel, club; (*Arg.*) blunder; fib, joke.

macanazo, *n.m.* blow with a *macana*.

macano, *n.m.* (*Chi.*) dark colour used to dye wool.

macanudo, -da, *a.* (*coll.*) fine, excellent, dandy, first rate.

macareno, -na, *a.* (*coll.*) bragging, boasting; gaudily dressed.

macarrón, *n.m.* macaroni; macaroon.

macarronea, *n.f.* macaronics; kind of burlesque poetry.

macarrones, *n.m.pl.* macaroni; (*naut.*) awning-stanchions.

macarrónico, -ca, *a.* macaronic.

macarronismo, *n.m.* macaronic style of poetry.

macarse, *v.r.* to rot, be spoiled by a bruise or fall (of fruit).

macaurel, *n.f.* (*Ven.*) a non-poisonous snake.

macazúchil, *n.m.* (*Mex.*) a plant of the Piperaceæ family used to flavour chocolate.

maceador, *n.m.* beater, hammerer, mauler.

macear, *v.t.* to beat or drive with a mallet; to knock, hammer in; to maul. — *v.i.* to harp on a subject.

macelo, *n.m.* slaughterhouse, abattoir.

maceración, *n.f.;* **maceramiento,** *n.m.* maceration, steeping, infusion, mortification, corporeal severity.

macerar, *v.t.* to macerate, soak, steep, soften; to mortify, harass, ill-treat; (*chem.*) to digest, bruise in order to extract juice from plants.

macerina, *n.f.* kind of saucer.

macero, *n.m.* mace-bearer.

maceta, *n.f.* small mace, mallet or maul; stone-cutter's hammer; flower-pot, flower-vase; handle of a stick or tool; two-clawed hammer; haunch of mutton; (*naut.*) maul, mallet. — *pl.* **macetas,** beetles or mallets used in oakum-making.

macia, *n.f.* [MACIS].

macicez, *n.f.* (*prov.*) solidity, compactness.

macilento, -ta, *a.* lean, extenuated, withered.

macillo, *n.m.* hammer of a piano.

macis, macia, *n.f.* mace, kind of spice.

macizamente, *adv.* firmly, solidly.

macizar, *v.t.* to fill up, stop up, close an opening or passage; to form into a compact body; to support a proposition by arguments.

macizo, -za, *a.* compact, close, massive, solid, firm; certain.

macizo, *n.m.* massiveness, bulk; (*build.*) solid wall; flower-bed; (*motor.*) solid tyre.

macla, *n.f.* (*bot.*) water-caltrops; wooden flail.

macle, *n.m.* (*her.*) mascle.

macolla, *n.f.* bunch, cluster.

macón, *n.m.* dry brown honeycomb.

macona, *n.f.* basket without handles, hamper.

macrocefalía, *n.f.* macrocephalism.

macrocéfalo, -la, *a.* macrocephalous.

macrocosmo, *n.m.* macrocosm.

macsura, *n.f.* reserved precinct in a mosque.

macuache, *n.m.* (*Mex.*) ignorant; illiterate Indian.

macuba, *n.f.* Martinique tobacco.

macuca, *n.f.* (*bot.*) kind of wild pear.

mácula, *n.f.* stain, spot, blemish; (*ast.*) macula.

macular, *v.t.* (*print.*) to mackle; to stain, spot, mark, with infamy.

maculatura, *n.f.* (*print.*) spoiled sheet.

maculoso, -sa, *a.* full of spots, stains, or blemishes.

macún, macuñ, *n.m.* (*Chi.*) poncho.

macuquero, *n.m.* unlawful worker of abandoned mines.

macuquino, -na, *a.* cut, clipped, edgeless (of coin).

macurije, *n.m.* (*Cub.*) medicinal tree (*Cupania oppositifolia*).

macuteno, *n.m.* (*Mex.*) petty thief.

macuto, *n.m.* (*Ven.*) bag made of palm leaves.

macha, *n.f.* (*Chi.*) a mollusc.

machaca, *n.m.f.* (*coll.*) bore, tiresome person.

machacadera, *n.f.* instrument for pounding, crushing or breaking.

machacador, -ra, *n.m.f.* pounder, crusher, beetler, bruiser, mauler.

machacante, *n.m.* (*mil.*) orderly of a sergeant.

machacar, *v.t., v.i.* (*pret.* **machaqué,** *pres. subj.* **machaque**) to pound or break into small pieces, crush, bruise, contuse; (*coll.*) to harp on a subject, to brood upon, insist upon; *machacar en hierro frío,* to beat on cold iron, to pursue a matter uselessly.

machacón, -ona, *a.* heavy, importunate, monotonous.

machada, *n.f.* flock of he-goats; (*coll.*) stupidity.

machado, *n.m.* hatchet. — *a., p.p.* [MACHAR].

machaje, *n.m.* (*Arg., Chi.*) a herd of male animals.

machango, *a.* (*Cub.*) coarse, unpolished person.

machaqueo, *n.m.* pounding, crushing.

machar, *v.t.* to pound; *a macha martillo,* firmly, strongly, solidly; *creer en Dios a macha martillo,* to believe in God firmly and sincerely.

machear, *v.i.* to beget more males than females (of animals).

machera, *n.f.* cork-tree plantation.

machetazo, *n.m.* blow or stroke with a cutlass (machete).

machete, *n.m.* machete, machet; matchet; cutlass, chopping-knife.

machetear, *v.t.* to wound with a cutlass; (*Col.*) to wrangle.

machetero, *n.m.* one who clears away bushes with a cutlass; (*S. Am.*) (*coll.*) sabre rattler; ignorant military chief.

machi, *n.m.f.* (*Chi.*) a quack doctor.

máchica, *n.f. (Per.)* roast Indian meal.

machihembrado, *n.m. (carp.)* match-board.

machihembrar, *v.t. (carp.)* to dovetail, join up, tenon.

machina, *n.f.* big crane, derrick; pile-driver.

machinete, *n.m. (prov.)* chopping-knife.

macho, *n.m.* male animal or plant; part of any instrument which enters into another; tap, tool for cutting female screw-threads; male screw; hook to catch hold in an eye; bolt (of a lock); *(arch.)* spur, buttress, abutment; *(mech.)* sledge hammer; block in which an anvil is fixed; mould for bells; square anvil; ignorant fellow; *machos del timón, (naut.)* rudder-pintles.

macho, *a.* male, masculine, robust, vigorous.

machón, *n.m. (arch.)* spur, buttress; arched pillar; piece of timber 18 feet long.

machorra, *n.f. (prov.)* barren ewe; barren woman.

machota, *n.f.* maul, mallet.

machote, *n.m. (Mex.)* boundary stone.

machucadura, *n.f.;* **machucamiento,** *n.m.* pounding, bruising.

machucar, *v.t. (pret.* **machuqué;** *pres. subj.* **machuque)** to pound, bruise.

machucho, -cha, *a.* mature, ripe (of age or understanding), judicious.

machuelo, *n.m.* small he-mule; heart of an onion, clove of garlic.

machuno, -na, *a.* mannish, masculine.

madama, *n.f.* madam.

madamisela, *n.f.* affected young lady.

madeja, *n.f.* hank, skein, worsted; lock of hair; *(coll.)* weak, lazy person; *madeja sin cuenda,* confused, disordered, irregular person or thing; *hacer madeja,* to be ropy (of liquors).

madejeta, -ica, -illa, -ita, *n.f.* small skein.

madera, *n.m.* madeira wine. — *n.f.* timber, wood; lumber; horny part of a hoof; *madera del aire,* horn of animals; *madera de sierra,* lumber; *a media madera,* scarfed (of timbers); *descubrir la madera (coll.)* to manifest any unknown vice or defect; *no holgar la madera,* to work incessantly; *ser de* (or *tener*) *mala madera,* to be lazy.

maderada, *n.f.* lumber floated downstream.

maderaje, maderamen, *n.m.* timber necessary for a building; wooden framework.

maderar, *v.t.* to plank.

maderería, *n.f.* timber-yard, lumber-yard.

maderero, *n.m.* timber-merchant, lumber-dealer, wood-monger, carpenter.

maderico, -ilto, -ito, *n.m.* small piece of timber.

maderista, *n.m. (prov.)* conductor of a raft or float.

madero, *n.m.* beam, large piece of timber; *(coll.)* stupid person; *(fig.)* ship, vessel.

madia, *n.f.* oily plant of Chile (*Madia sativa*).

madrastra, *n.f.* step-mother; something disagreeable.

madraza, *n.f. (coll.)* very fond mother.

madre, *n.f.* mother; title of nuns; dam; matron in a hospital; basis, origin, foundation; matrix, womb; bed of a river; sewer, sink; lees, scum or other substance concreted in liquid; *(coll.)* old woman; *(naut.)* gallows-beam; *(carp.)* main piece, spindle; *madre de leche,* wet-nurse; *mal de madre, madre pía,*

daño cría, spare the rod and spoil the child; *salir de madre,* to exceed one's regular custom or allowance; *sacar de madre,* to worry, cause to lose patience; *irse con su madre gallega,* to go to seek one's fortune; *madre de la rueda de timón, (naut.)* barrel of the steering-wheel; *madre política,* mother-in-law; *no es la madre del cordero,* that's not the real reason.

madrearse, *v.r.* to become, to turn ropy (applied to wines or liquors).

madrecita, *n.f.* an endearing expression for 'mother.'

madrecilla, *n.f.* ovarium of birds.

madreclavo, *n.m.* clove of two years' growth.

madreperla, *n.f.* mother-of-pearl, pearl-oyster.

madrépora, *n.f.* madrepore, white coral.

madrero, -ra, *a. (coll.)* fondling, caressing a mother; attached to one's mother.

madreselva, *n.f. (bot.)* honeysuckle.

madrigada, *a.* twice married (of a woman).

madrigado, -da, *a.* bull that has been a sire; *(fig.)* practical, experienced.

madrigal, *n.m.* madrigal.

madrigaleja, *n.f.;* **madrigalete,** *n.m.* short madrigal.

madriguera, *n.f.* burrow, holes made by rabbits or conies; den, lurking-place.

madrileño, -ña, *n.m.f., a.* (native or inhabitant) of Madrid.

madrilla, *n.f. (ichth.) (prov.)* small river-fish.

madrillera, *n.f. (prov.)* instrument for catching small fish.

madrina, *n.f.* godmother; bridesmaid; protectress, patroness; prop, stanchion; straps or cords yoking two horses; *(Ven.)* small herd; *a la madrina, que eso ya me lo sabía,* tell me another, that's old news.

madrona, *n.f. (coll.)* mother who spoils her children; main irrigating ditch; *(bot.)* clandestine toothwort.

madroncillo, *n.m.* strawberry.

madroñal, *n.m.;* **madroñera,** *n.f.* plantation of madroño-trees.

madroñero, *n.m. (bot.)* madroño-tree.

madroñito, *n.m.* small madroño-tree.

madroño, *n.m.* madroño-tree; silk tassel.

madrugada, *n.f.* dawn, early morning; early rising; *de madrugada,* very early.

madrugador, -ra, *n.m.f.* early riser.

madrugar, *v.i. (pret.* **madrugué;** *pres. subj.* **madrugue)** to rise early; to contrive, premeditate, anticipate, be beforehand.

madrugón *n.m.* act of early rising; early riser.

maduración, *n.f.* ripeness, maturity.

maduradero, *n.m.* place for ripening fruits.

madurador, -ra, *n.m.f.* that which matures or ripens.

maduramente, *adv.* maturely, prudently, considerably.

madurante, *a.* maturing, ripening.

madurar, *v.t.* to ripen, mature, mellow; *(med.)* to maturate. — *v.i.* to ripen, grow ripe, reach mature years; *(med.)* to suppurate perfectly. — *v.r.* to ripen, grow ripe.

madurativo, -va, *a.* maturative.

madurativo, *n.m.* something that matures; *(med.)* maturant; means employed to make a person grant a request.

madurez, *n.f.* maturity, mellowness, ripeness; prudence, wisdom.

madurillo, -lla, *a.* beginning to ripen.

maduro, -ra, *a.* ripe, mellow, mature, perfect, full-grown; judicious, prudent; of age.

maese, *n.m.* (*obs.*) master.

maesillas, *n.f.pl.* cords used in making passementerie to raise or lower the skeins.

maestra, *n.f.* mistress, schoolmistress; master's wife; one who or that which instructs; queen-bee; (*build.*) guide-line.

maestral, *a.* relating to a grand master of a military order; north-west (wind). — *n.m.* cell of the queen-bee.

maestralizar, *v.i.* (*naut.*) to decline to north-west.

maestramente, *adv.* dexterously, skilfully.

maestrante, *n.m.* member of a *maestranza.*

maestranza, *n.f.* society of noblemen in Spain for practising equestrian exercises; dock-yard, naval storehouse, arsenal, armoury.

maestrazgo, *n.m.* dignity or jurisdiction of the grand-master of a military order.

maestrazo, *n.m.* great master.

maestre, *n.m.* master of a military order; (*naut.*) master of a merchant-ship, ship-master; (*obs.*) master, doctor; *maestre de plata,* (*naut.*) supercargo on board the royal Spanish galleons; *maestre de raciones,* (*naut.*) purser.

maestrear, *v.i.* (*coll.*) to domineer, act the master, act as an expert. — *v.t.* to lop (vines); to level the surface of a wall; to direct, instruct.

maestreescuela, maestrescuela, *n.m.* cathedral dignitary whose duty was to teach divinity; chancellor of a university.

maestresala, *n.m.* chief waiter and taster at a nobleman's table.

maestrescolia, *n.f.* dignity of a *maestrescuela.*

maestría, *n.f.* mastership, mastery, complete knowledge; dignity or degree of a master; (*obs.*) mastership of a vessel; (*obs.*) stratagem.

maestril, *n.m.* queen cell (of beehives).

maestrillo, *n.m.* insignificant schoolmaster.

maestro, *n.m.* master, teacher, expert, skilled exponent, professor, title of respect or dignity in monastic orders; (*mus.*) composer; (*naut.*) mainmast; *maestro de armas* (or *de esgrima*), fencing-master; *maestro de capilla,* choir-master; *maestro de obras,* builder, contractor; *maestro de llagas,* surgeon; *al maestro, cuchillada,* to teach a person his own trade; *el maestro ciruela, que no sabe leer y pone escuela,* expression ridiculing a person for presuming to instruct in matters of which he is ignorant.

maestro, -tra, *a.* masterly, principal, first, main; learned, trained; *pared maestra,* main wall.

magancear, *v.i.* (*Col., Chi.*) to lead an idle life; to loiter, lounge.

magancés, *a.* traitorous, injurious, crooked.

maganel, *n.m.* (*mil.*) battering-ram.

maganto, -ta, *a.* spiritless, dull, languid, faint.

magaña, *n.f.* honeycomb, flaw in the bore of a gun; (*coll.*) cunning trick.

magarza, *n.f.* (*bot.*) downy chamomile.

magarzuela, *n.f.* (*bot.*) stinking chamomile.

magdalena, *n.f.* kind of biscuit; magdalen, a repentant woman.

magdaleón, *n.m.* (*pharm.*) roll of plaster.

magia, *n.f.* magic, necromancy, black art; *magia blanca* or *natural,* white magic; *magia negra,* black magic, black art.

mágicamente, *adv.* magically.

mágico, -ca, *a.* magic, magical, necromantic.

mágico, -ca, *n.m.f.* magician, one who professes magic.

magín, *n.m.* fancy, imagination; *se le ha metido en el magín,* he has taken it into his head.

magisterial, *a.* magisterial.

magisterio, *n.m.* mastery, mastership; academic degree; title or rank of a master; body of teachers; seriousness, affected gravity, mock solemnity; magistery; (*chem.*) precipitate.

magistrado, *n.m.* magistrate; magistracy; court, tribunal.

magistral, *a.* magisterial, masterly, oracular; (*med.*) magistral, magistralia. — *n.m.* title of a Roman Catholic prebendary; *canónigo magistral,* priest who enjoys the *magistral.*

magistralmente, *adv.* magisterially, in a masterly way.

magistratura, *n.f.* magistracy, judicature, judgeship.

magnánimamente, *adv.* magnanimously, bravely, generously.

magnanimidad, *n.f.* magnanimity, fortitude, greatness of mind, generosity.

magnánimo, -ma, *a.* magnanimous, heroic, generous, honourable.

magnate, *n.m.* magnate, person of rank or wealth, grandee.

magnesia, *n.f.* (*chem.*) magnesia.

magnesiano, -na, *a.* magnesian.

magnésico, -ca, *a.* magnesic.

magnesio, *n.m.* magnesium.

magnesita, *n.f.* meerschaum.

magnético, -ca, *a.* magnetic, attractive.

magnetismo, *n.m.* magnetism; hypnotism.

magnetización, *n.f.* magnetization.

magnetizador, -ra, *n.m.f.* magnetizer; hypnotizer, mesmerizer.

magnetizar, *v.t.* (conjugated like ALZAR) to touch with a magnet, make magnetic; to hypnotize.

magneto, *n.f.* magneto.

magníficamente, *adv.* magnificently, nobly, loftily.

magnificar, *v.t.* (*pret.* **magnifiqué;** *pres. subj.* **magnifique**) to magnify, extol, exalt.

magníficat, *n.m.* the hymn of the Blessed Virgin Mary; *criticar* (or *corregir*) *el magníficat,* to criticize without reason or judgment.

magnificencia, *n.f.* magnificence, splendour, grandeur, gorgeousness.

magnífico, -ca, *a.* magnificent, splendid, grand, costly, gaudy.

magnitud, *n.f.* magnitude, size, bulk; greatness, grandeur.

magno, -na, *a.* great (used as an epithet, as *Alejandro el Magno,* Alexander the Great).

magnolia, *n.f.* (*bot.*) magnolia.

mago, -ga, *n.m.f.* Magus, Eastern philosopher or sage, magician, necromancer; *los reyes magos,* the Magi.

magosto, *n.m.* bonfire to roast chestnuts.

magra, *n.f.* rasher, slice of ham.

magrez, *n.f.* thinness, leanness.

magrica, -illa, -ita, *n.f.* small rasher.

magro, -gra, *a.* meagre, lean.

magro, *n.m.* (*coll.*) lean slice of pork.

magrujo, -ja, *a.* meagre.

magrura, *n.f.* leanness, thinness.

magua, *n.f.* (*Cub.*) joke.
maguer, maguera, *conj.* although.
magüeto, -ta, *n.m.f.* young steer or heifer.
maguey, *n.m.* (*bot.*) American agave.
maguillo, *n.m.* wild apple-tree.
magujo, *n.m.* (*naut.*) rave-hook.
magulla, magulladura, *n.f.* bruise, hurt, contusion.
magullado, -da, *a.* bruised, worn out. — *p.p.* [MAGULLAR].
magullamiento, *n.m.* bruising, contusion.
magullar, *v.t.* to mangle, bruise.
maharrana, *n.f.* (*prov.*) fresh bacon.
maherir, *v.t.* to convene, anticipate.
Mahoma, *n.m.* Mohammed.
mahometano, -na, *n.m.f.,* *a.* Mahometan, Mohammedan.
mahometismo, *n.m.* Mohammedanism.
mahometista, *n.m.* Mohammedan.
mahometizar, *v.i.* to profess Islam.
mahón, *n.m.* nankin, nankeen, kind of light cotton cloth.
mahona, *n.f.* Turkish transport vessel.
mahozmedín, *n.m.* gold maravedi.
maicena, *n.f.* maize flour finely ground.
maicero, *n.m.* (*Cub.*) seller of maize.
maicillo, *n.m.* (*Am. Mer.*) plant of the Gramineæ order similar to millet.
maído, *n.m.* mewing, mew.
maimón, *n.m.* monkey; *pl.* Andalusian soup made with olive oil.
maimona, *n.f.* beam of a horse-mill.
maimonetes, *n.m.pl.* (*naut.*) belaying-pins.
maitencito, *n.m.* (*Chi.*) children's game resembling blind-man's-buff.
maitinante, *n.m.* one who attends matins.
maitinario, *n.m.* book containing matins.
maitines, *n.m.pl.* matins.
maíz, *n.m.* (*bot.*) maize, Indian corn.
maizal, *n.m.* Indian corn plantation, maize-field.
majá, *n.m.* (*Cub.*) a large non-poisonous snake.
majada, *n.f.* sheep-cote, sheep-fold; animals' dung; (*obs.*) inn.
majadal, *n.m.* land used for a sheep-fold; good pasture ground.
majadear, *v.i.* to take shelter in the night (of sheep); to manure.
majadería, *n.f.* absurdity, insolence, nonsense.
majaderillo, -ito, *n.m.* bobbin for lace.
majadero, -ra, *a.* dull, foolish, silly, doltish, sottish.
majadero, *n.m.* gawk, bore; pestle, pounder. — *pl.* **majaderos,** bobbins for making lace.
majaderón, *n.m.* great gawk, fool or bore.
majador, -ra, *n.m.f.* pounder, bruiser.
majadura, *n.f.* pounding, bruising.
majagranzas, *n.m.* (*coll.*) stupid, ignorant fellow.
majagua, *n.f.* (*Cub., Am. Mer.*) tree of the linden family; cordage made from it.
majagüero, *n.m.* (*Cub.*) maker or seller of majagua cordage.
majal, *n.m.* school of fishes.
majano, *n.m.* heap of stones as landmark.
majar, *v.t.* to pound, pulverize, break in a mortar; (*fig.*) to vex, importune, molest.
majarrana, *n.f.* (*prov.*) fresh pork.
majenca, *n.f.* (*prov.*) digging of vines.
majencar, *v.t.* to dig about vines.
majencia, *n.f.* (*prov.*) spruceness, fineness in dress.

majestad, *n.f.* majesty, royalty, dignity, grandeur, gravity, loftiness; power, sovereignty, kingship, elevation.
majestuosamente, *adv.* majestically, in kingly fashion.
majestuosidad, *n.f.* majesty, dignity.
majestuoso, -sa, *a.* majestic, majestical, august, grand, stately, lofty, pompous, grave, solemn.
majeza, *n.f.* (*coll.*) gaudiness; spruceness.
majo, -ja, *n.m.f.* beau *or* belle, young man-about-town, gallant. — *a.* gallant, spruce, fine, gay.
majolar, *v.t.* (*obs.*) to put straps to the shoes. — *n.m.* white hawthorn-grove.
majuela, *n.f.* fruit of the white hawthorn; shoe-lace made of leather.
majuelo, *n.m.* vine newly planted; white hawthorn.
mal, *a.* (apocope of *malo,* used solely before a masculine noun) evil, harm, injury, wrong, hurt, mischief; illness, disease, complaint; fault, imperfection, trespass. — *adv.* badly, ill, injuriously, wickedly, wrongly; *anda mal,* he is a bad walker; *mal avenidos,* on bad terms; *de mal en peor,* worse and worse; *del mal el menos,* the lesser of two evils; *echar a mal,* despise, depreciate, lose, waste; *hacer mal,* to break in (a horse); *hacérsele a uno de mal una cosa,* to be a nuisance (to undertake something); *haces mal, espera otro tal,* those who do ill, must expect ill in return; *mal caduco,* epilepsy; *mal de ánimo,* heart-sore; *mal de mi* (or *tu,* or *su*) *grado,* in spite of me (or you, him, her), unwillingly; *mal de muchos, consuelo de tontos,* that other people are injured also is a fool's consolation (the contrary opinion is expressed thus: *mal de muchos, consuelo de todos*); *mal de ojo,* evil eye; *mal de ojos,* eyesore; *mal francés,* venereal disease; *mal largo, muerte al cabo,* it will soon be over; *más mal hay en la aldehuela del que se suena,* it's worse than it seems; *no haría mal a un gato,* he wouldn't hurt a fly; *no hay mal que por bien no venga,* every cloud has a silver lining; *no hay mayor mal que el descontento de cada cual,* discontent is the worst of evils; *el mal llama a otro,* one ill brings another; *mal por mal,* for want of something better; *mal que bien,* by hook or by crook (or with good or ill will); *mal que le pese,* in spite of him; *parar en mal,* come to a bad end (or an unfortunate conclusion); *poco mal y bien quejada,* making mountains out of molehills; *el mal ajeno de pelo cuelga,* the troubles of others hang by a hair; *bien vengas mal si vienes solo,* welcome, evil, if thou comest alone (or troubles never come singly); *mal hecho,* badly done, badly finished, unjust; *el mal, para quien le fuere a buscar,* anyone can find trouble by looking for it; *en mal de muerte, no hay médico que acierte,* even the doctor cannot cure a mortal illness; *estar tocado del mal de la rabia,* to be dominated by a ruling passion; *quien escucha, su mal oye,* listeners hear no good of themselves; *quien canta, sus males espanta,* a light heart drives away trouble.
mala, *n.f.* mail, post, mail-bag; deuce of spades; manille.
malabarista, *n.m.f.* juggler; (*Chi.*) sly thief, confidence man.
Malaca, *n.f.* Malay Peninsula.

malacate, *n.m.* (*Mex.*, *min.*) kind of capstan or windlass.

malacia, *n.f.* (*med.*) depraved appetite.

malaconsejado, -da, *a.* ill-advised.

malacostumbrado, -da, *a.* having bad habits; spoiled.

malacuenda, *n.f.* sacking, coarse cloth; oakum, tow.

malagana, *n.f.* (*coll.*) faintness, dizziness.

malagaña, *n.f.* (*prov.*) pole set up to catch bees swarming.

malagueña, *n.f.* popular song of Malaga.

malagueño, -ña, *n.m.f.*, *a.* (inhabitant) of Malaga.

malagueta, *n.f.* grains of paradise.

malamente, *adv.* badly, evilly, wickedly, poorly, wrongly.

malandante, *a.* unhappy, unfortunate.

malandanza, *n.f.* misfortune, calamity.

malandar, *n.m.* wild hog.

malandrín, *n.m.* rascal, scoundrel. — *a.* perverse, malign.

malanga, *n.f.* Cuban edible root, arum.

malaquita, malaquites, *n.f.* (*min.*) malachite.

malar, *a.* (*anat.*) malar.

Malasia, *n.f.* Malay Archipelago.

malatía, *n.f.* leprosy; (*obs.*) malady, disease, disorder, distemper.

malato, -ta, *a.* leprous; (*obs.*) diseased, disordered.

malato, *n.m.* (*chem.*) malate.

malavenido, -da, *n.m.f.*, *a.* quarrelsome person, sower of discord.

malaventura, *n.f.* calamity, misfortune.

malaventurado, -da, *n.m.f.* unfortunate, ill-fated, luckless.

malaventuranza, *n.f.* infelicity, unhappiness.

malayo, *n.m.f.*, *a.* Malay, Malayan.

malbaratador, -ra, *n.m.f.* spendthrift, prodigal.

malbaratar, *v.t.* to misspend, squander, lavish; to undersell.

malbaratillo, *n.m.* cheap second-hand shop.

malcarado, -da, *a.* grim-faced, foul-faced.

malcasado, -da, *a.* adulterous; unfaithful, undutiful (spouse). — *p.p.* [MALCASAR].

malcasar, *v.t.* to mismate, make anyone marry against his or her will. — *v.i.*, *v.r.* to contract an unsuitable or unfortunate marriage.

malcaso, *n.m.* treason, turpitude, crime.

malcocinado, *n.m.* entrails of an animal; tripe-shop.

malcomer, *v.t.* to eat poorly.

malcomido, -da, *a.* hungry, without good food.

malcontento, *n.m.* malcontent, grumbler; a card game.

malcontento, -ta, *a.* discontented.

malcorte, *n.m.* transgressing of wood-cutting laws.

malcriado, -da, *a.* ill-bred, unmannerly, clownish, impolite, spoiled (of children).

malcriar, *v.t.* to spoil (a child).

maldad, *n.f.* wickedness, iniquity, corruption, abomination, guilt, mischievousness, criminality.

maldadoso, -sa, *a.* wicked, ill-disposed.

maldecido, -da, *a.*, *p.p.* wicked, depraved.

maldecidor, -ra, *n.m.f.* swearer; calumniator, detractor.

maldecimiento, *n.m.* backbiting, calumny, censure.

maldecir, *v.t.* (conjugated like DECIR except: *p.p.* **maldecido**, *fut.* **maldeciré**; *conditional* **maldeciría**, *imperative sing.* **maldice**) to curse, accurse, damn, execrate. —*v.i.* to slander, detract, speak ill; to defame, backbite.

maldiciente, *n.m.f.*, *a.* cursing, curser; defamer.

maldición, *n.f.* malediction, execration, imprecation, curse; divine chastisement, damnation.

maldicho, -cha, *a.* accursed, calumniated. — *p.p. irreg. obs.* [MALDECIR].

maldispuesto, -ta, *a.* indisposed; reluctant, unwilling.

maldita, *n.f.* (*coll.*) tongue; *soltar la maldita*, (*coll.*) to give rein to one's tongue, to speak one's mind.

maldito, -ta, *a.* perverse, wicked; accursed, damned, confounded; chastised by Divine justice; (*coll.*) none, not one. — *p.p. obs.* [MALDECIR]; *maldito lo que me importa*, devil a bit do I care.

maleabilidad, *n.f.* malleability, malleableness.

maleable, *a.* malleable.

maleador, -ra, *n.m.f.* rogue, villain, corrupter.

maleante, *n.m.* corrupter, injurer. — *a.* corrupting.

malear, *v.t.*, *v.r.* to pervert, corrupt, injure, harm.

malecón, *n.m.* dyke, mound, embankment, jetty, breakwater, pier, mole.

maledicencia, *n.f.* slander, obloquy, calumny.

maleficencia, *n.f.* mischievousness, mischief-making, wrong-doing.

maleficiador, -ra, *n.m.f.* adulterator, corrupter.

maleficiar, *v.t.* to hurt, injure, harm, adulterate, corrupt, vitiate; to bewitch, harm by witchcraft.

maleficio, *n.m.* hurt, damage, injury; witchcraft, enchantment, charm, spell.

maléfico, -ca, *a.* mischievous; malicious; injuring others by witchcraft.

malejo, -ja, *a.* rather bad [MALO].

malentrada, *n.f.* tax, fee.

malestar, *n.m.* malaise, uneasiness.

maleta, *n.f.* portmanteau, valise, hand-bag; (*vulg.*) prostitute; *hacer la maleta*, to pack, prepare for a journey.

maletero, *n.m.* saddler, portmanteau-maker, harness-maker.

maletía, *n.f.* (*obs.*) malice; injury to health.

maletica, -illa, -ita, *n.f.* small portmanteau, hand-bag.

maletón, *n.m.* large portmanteau or satchel.

malevo, -va, *a.* (*Arg.*, *Bol.*) [MALEVOLO].

malevolencia, *n.f.* malevolence, ill-will, ill-nature, malignity.

malévolo, -la, *a.* malevolent, malignant, mischievous, hateful.

maleza, *n.f.* overgrowth of weeds; ground covered with brambles; brake, thicket, coppice; (*Arg.*, *Chi.*) pus, rotten substance.

malgastador, -ra, *n.m.f.* squanderer, spendthrift.

malgastar, *v.t.* to misspend, squander, lavish, lose, waste, throw away (money, time, patience, etc.).

malgenioso, -sa, *a.* (*Chi.*, *Mex.*) wrathful, enraged.

malhablado, -da, *a.* bold, impudent; foul-mouthed.

malhadado, -da, *a.* unfortunate, wretched.

malhecho, *n.m.* flagitious action; evil deed, misdeed.

malhecho, -cha, *a.* ill-shaped, deformed.

malhechor, -ra, *n.m.f.* malefactor, (habitual) offender, misdoer.

malherido, -da, *a.*, *p.p.* dangerously wounded.

malherir, *v.t.* to wound badly.

malhojo, *n.m.* refuse of plants; worthless remains, rubbish.

malhumorado, -da, *a.* ill-humoured, peevish.

malicia, *n.f.* malice, perversity, malignity, wickedness, mischievousness; apprehension, suspicion; artifice, cunning, guile; shrewdness, sharpness; hypocrisy, dissimulation; rancour, animosity.

maliciar, *v.t.* to corrupt, adulterate; to injure, harm; to put a malicious construction on a matter; to speak maliciously.

maliciosamente, *adv.* maliciously.

malicioso, -sa, *a.* malicious, suspicious, mischievous, knavish, wicked.

malignamente, *adv.* malignantly, hatefully, mischievously, malevolently.

malignante, *n.m.f.*, *a.* maligner.

malignar, *v.t.* to vitiate, corrupt, deprave. — *v.r.* to become sore; to grow worse.

malignidad, *n.f.* malignity, malice, perverseness, mischievousness, hatred.

maligno, -na, *a.* malignant, perverse, malicious, ill-disposed, hateful, wicked.

malilla, *n.f.* manille; *(coll.)* malicious person.

malintencionado, -da, *a.* evil-disposed.

malmandado, -da, *a.* *(coll.)* disobedient, obstinate.

malmeter, *v.i.* *(coll.)* to incline, induce to evil; to breed quarrels, estrange friends; to waste, misspend.

malmirado, -da, *a.* impolite, indiscreet; disliked.

malo, -la, *a.* bad, evil, not good, wicked; naughty, mischievous; vicious, obnoxious, perverse, imperfect, defective, licentious, dissolute; artful, crafty, cunning; sickly, disordered, ill, sick; difficult, disagreeable; worn out, used up; *estar malo,* to be ill; *ser malo,* to be wicked; *por malas o por buenas,* willy-nilly; *de malas,* deceitfully; *a malas,* in enmity; *a las malas,* with evil intentions; *el malo, para mal hacer, achaques no ha menester,* the wicked man can always find a pretext for his evil deeds; *el malo siempre piensa engaño,* like suspects like; *más vale malo conocido que bueno por conocer,* better to take an indifferent person known to you than one you know nothing about.

malo, *interj.* bad! so much the worse! — *n.m.* devil, evil one.

maloca, *n.f.* *(S. Am.)* invasion of Indian lands.

malogrado, -da, *a.* unfortunate, lamented (often said of one who has died). — *p.p.* [MALOGRAR].

malogramiento, *n.m.* disappointment, failure.

malograr, *v.t.* to disappoint, disconcert; to miss, lose; *(com.)* to spoil, waste. — *v.r.* to be disappointed; to fail of success, fall through, come to naught, to have an untimely end.

malogro, *n.m.* disappointment, miscarriage, failure, untimely end.

maloja, *n.f.* *(Cub.)* maize-leaves and stalks, used for fodder.

malojal, *n.m.* *(Ven.)* plantation of *maloja.*

malojero, *n.m.* *(Cub.)* seller of *maloja.*

malojo, *n.m.* *(Ven.)* [MALOJA].

malón, *n.m.* *(S. Am.)* sudden attack by Indians.

maloquear, *v.i.* *(S. Am.)* to raid settled territory (by Indians).

malordenado, -da, *a.* badly contrived, ill-arranged.

malparado, -da, *a.* ill-conditioned, impaired, useless. — *p.p.* [MALPARAR].

malparar, *v.t.* to ill-treat, impair, damage, hurt, blemish.

malparida, *n.f.* woman who has miscarried.

malparir, *v.i.* to miscarry.

malparto, *n.m.* miscarriage.

malquerencia, *n.f.* ill-will, hatred.

malquerer, *v.t.* to abhor, hate; to bear ill-will.

malquistar, *v.t.* to excite quarrels, estrange friends; to create prejudice against. — *v.r.* to incur hatred; make oneself unpopular.

malquisto, -ta, *a.* hated, detested, abhorred.

malrotador, -ra, *n.m.f.* squanderer, spendthrift.

malrotar, *v.t.* to lavish, misspend, squander, waste.

malsano, -na, *a.* sickly, unhealthy, infirm, unwholesome, noxious, insalubrious.

malsín, *n.m.* talebearer, mischief-maker, backbiter.

malsinar, *v.t.* to inform against someone through malice.

malsindad, malsinería, *n.f.* malicious information.

malsonante, *a.* offensive to pious ears.

malsufrido, -da, *a.* impatient, unresigned.

malta, *n.f.* malt; *fiebre de Malta,* Malta fever.

maltés, -esa, *n.m.f.*, *a.* Maltese.

maltrabaja, *n.m.f.* *(coll.)* idler, lounger.

maltraer, *v.t.* to treat ill.

maltratamiento, *n.m.* ill-treatment, ill usage, affliction.

maltratar, *v.t.* to abuse, treat ill, maltreat, misuse, spoil, destroy.

maltrato, *n.m.* ill-treatment.

maltrecho, -cha, *a.* ill-treated, misused, in bad condition; damaged; badly off, battered.

maluco, -ca, *a.* of or from the Moluccas Isles; native or inhabitant of Moluccas.

malucho, -cha, *a.* *(coll.)* sickly, ailing.

malva, *n.f.* *(bot.)* mallow; *como una malva,* good, obedient, meek; *haber nacido en las malvas,* to be of humble birth.

malváceo, -cea, *a.* *(bot.)* malvaceous.

malvadamente, *adv.* wickedly, naughtily, mischievously, lewdly.

malvado, -da, *a.* malicious, wicked, vicious, nefarious, insolent.

malvar, *v.t.* to corrupt, vitiate or defile.

malvar, *n.m.* place covered with mallows.

malvasía, *n.f.* malmsey (grape or wine).

malvavisco, *n.m.* *(bot.)* marsh-mallow.

malvender, *v.t.* to sell at a loss, to sacrifice.

malversación, *n.f.* misapplication or maladministration of money; malversation.

malversador, -ra, *n.m.f.* one who misapplies property or funds.

malversar, *v.t.* to misapply, apply (money) to wrong purposes.

Malvinas, *n.f.pl.* Falkland Islands.

malvis, malviz, *n.m.* (*orn.*) red-wing.

malla, *n.f.* mesh of a net; (*naut.*) net-work; coat of mail; *hacer malla,* to knit.

mallar, *v.i.* to make net-work; *v.t.* to arm with a coat of mail.

mallero, *n.m.* armourer, maker of coats of mail.

mallete, *n.m.* gavel, mallet. — *pl.* (*naut.*) partners.

mallo, *n.m.* mall, pall-mall; game of bowls; mallet; game of croquet.

mallorquín, -ina, *n.m.f., a.* of or belonging to Majorca.

mama, mamá, *n.f.* ma, mamma; teat, nipple.

mamacallos, *n.m.* (*coll.*) simpleton, dolt.

mamacona, *n.f.* (*Per., Bol., Col.*) religious virgin among the Incas.

mamada, *n.f.* (*coll.*) suck, time taken by a child in sucking.

mamadera, *n.f.* breast-pump.

mamador, -ra, *n.m.f.* sucker, one who sucks.

mamaluco, *n.m.* (*coll.*) dolt, simpleton, fool.

mamancia, *n.f.* (*coll.*) childishness, silliness.

mamancona, *n.f.* (*Chi.*) an old and fat woman.

mamandurria, *n.f.* (*S. Am.*) (*coll.*) sinecure.

mamante, *a.* sucking; *piante ni mamante* (with *quedar* and a negative) not one, none.

mamantón, -ona, *a.* sucking (of animals).

mamar, *v.t.* to suck, draw milk; (*coll.*) to cram and devour victuals; to acquire as a child; (*coll.*) to get, obtain.

mamario, -ria, *a.* mammary.

mamarrachada, *n.f.* collection of ridiculous figures; foolish speech or action.

mamarrachista, *n.m.f.* dauber, bad painter.

mamarracho, *n.m.* ill-drawn figure; grotesque ornament; daub.

mambla, *n.f.* rounded hillock.

mameluco, *n.m.* Mameluke, Egyptian soldier; dolt, ignorant person (used contemptuously); children's night-dress.

mamellado, -da, *a.* mamillated.

mamíferos, *n.m.pl.* mammalia.

mamila, *n.f.* part of a woman's breast round the nipple; mamilla of a man.

mamilar, *a.* mamillary.

mamilas, *n.f.pl.* papillæ in the roof of the mouth.

mamola, *n.f.* chuck under the chin.

mamón, -ona, *n.m.f.* sucking animal; child that sucks overmuch; milksop. — *pl.* **mamones,** tender quills of birds; suckers, young twigs.

mamoncillo, *n.m.* (*W. Ind.*) honey-berry.

mamoso, -sa, *a.* sucking. — *n.m.* a variety of panic grass.

mamotreto, *n.m.* memorandum book; (*coll.*) bulky book; bundle of papers.

mampara, *n.f.* screen.

mamparar, *v.t.* (*vulg.*) to shelter, protect.

mamparos, *n.m.pl.* (*naut.*) bulkheads, partitions in a ship.

mamperlán, mampernal, *n.m.* wooden guard on steps of a staircase while building.

mamporro, *n.m.* (*coll.*) slight thump, cuff, tap.

mampostear, *v.t.* to raise rubble-work, cement with mortar.

mampostería, *n.f.* rubble-work; covered battery; collection of alms for certain hospitals.

mampostero, *n.m.* mason, stone mason; collector of alms.

mampresar, *v.t.* to begin to break horses.

mampuesta, *n.f.* (*build.*) course, row of bricks.

mampuesto, *n.m.* materials for raising masonry; (*Am.*) rest or support for a firearm in taking aim; parapet; *de mampuesto,* set apart, extra.

mamujar, *v.t.* to suck capriciously or irregularly (of babies).

mamullar, *v.t.* to eat or chew as if sucking; (*coll.*) to mumble, mutter.

mamut, *n.m.* mammoth.

man, *n.f.* (apocope of *mano*), hand; *a man salva,* easily, without risk or danger; *man a mano,* instantly; *buena man derecha,* fortune, good luck.

maná, *n.m.* manna; gum obtained from ash-trees; almond-tart; kind of sugar-plum.

manada, *n.f.* flock, herd, drove; handful; cluster; crowd, fry, multitude; *a manadas,* in troops, in crowds.

manadero, *n.m.* source, spring; shepherd, herdsman.

manadero, -ra, *a.* springing, issuing.

manadilla, *n.f.* small flock.

manante, *a.* issuing, proceeding.

manantial, *n.m.* source, spring, origin, fount, principle, head. — *a.* flowing, running (of water); *agua manantial,* spring-water.

manar, *v.i.* to spring from, distil from, proceed, issue, arise; (*fig.*) abound.

manare, *n.m.* (*Ven.*) sieve for yucca starch.

manatí, manato, *n.m.* (*ichth.*) manatee, manatus, sea-cow; whip made of sea-cow's hide.

manaza, *n.f.* large hand.

mancamiento, *n.m.* want, defect, privation, lack, deficiency, maimedness.

mancar, *v.t.* (*pret.* **manqué;** *pres. subj.* **manque**) to maim, render useless, cripple, lame, disable (a man) for business.

manceba, *n.f.* mistress, concubine.

mancebete, *n.m.* youth, young fellow.

mancebía, *n.f.* brothel, bawdy-house.

mancebico, -illo, -ito, *n.m.* little young man.

mancebo, -ba, *n.m.f.* youth, girl, young person; shop-assistant, clerk, journeyman, hired workman; bachelor.

máncer, *n.m.* prostitute's son.

mancera, *n.f.* plough-tail, plough-handle.

mancerina, *n.f.* saucer with holder for chocolate cup.

mancilla, *n.f.* (*obs.*) wound, sore; spot, stain, blemish; (*obs.*) commiseration.

mancillar, *v.t.* to spot, stain.

mancipar, *v.t.* to enslave, subject.

manco, -ca, *a.* handless, one-handed; armless; maimed, defective, imperfect, faulty. — *n.m.f.* armless, handless or one-handed person; *no ser manco* (or *no ser cojo ni manco*), to be unscrupulous.

mancomún, *n.m.* concurrence; *de mancomún* (or *mancomunadamente*), jointly, by common consent.

mancomunar, *v.t.* to unite, associate; (*law*) to make several persons pay the costs of a lawsuit. — *v.r.* to act together, join in an act.

mancomunidad, *n.f.* union, conjunction, fellowship.

mancornar, *v.t.* (*pres. indic.* **mancuerno;** *pres. subj.* **mancuerne**) to twist the neck of (a steer, etc.) and hold down on the ground with the horns downwards; to join, couple, tie two head of cattle by the horns.

mancuerda, *n.f.* each turn of the rack bars (torture).

mancuerna, *n.f.* pair tied together; thong for tying two steers; (*Cub.*) tobacco stem with two leaves; (*Philip.*) pair of convicts chained together.

mancha, *n.f.* spot, stain, blot, blemish, discoloration, stigma; ground covered with weeds; dishonour, disgrace; (*astron.*) spot on the sun or other heavenly body; *no es mancha de judío,* (*coll.*) it is only a trifling thing; *no temas mancha que sale con el agua,* things easily remedied are little to be feared.

manchadizo, -za, *a.* easily stained or soiled.

manchado, -da, *a.* spotted, speckled. — *p.p.* [MANCHAR].

manchar, *v.t.* to stain, spot, soil, corrupt, contaminate, daub, darken, cloud, defile, tarnish; (*art*) to speckle; daub; *manchar papel,* to scribble, write much to no purpose.

manchega, *n.f.* parti-coloured garter.

manchego, -ga, *n.m.f., a.* of or belonging to La Mancha.

manchica, -illa, -ita, -uela, *n.f.* small stain or spot.

manchón, *n.m.* large stain or spot; thick patch of vegetation.

manda, *n.f.* offer, proposal; legacy, bequest, donation.

mandadero, -ra, *n.m.f.* porter, messenger, errand-boy, errand-girl.

mandado, *n.m.* mandate, precept, order, command; errand, message; notice, advertisement.

mandamiento, *n.m.* mandate, precept, command, order; (*eccles.*) commandment, article of the decalogue; (*law*) writ, mandate. — *pl.* **mandamientos,** (*coll.*) the five fingers of the hand; the Ten Commandments.

mandante, *a.* commanding; (*law*) constituent, mandator.

mandar, *v.t.* to command, order, enact, give orders, direct, decree, ordain; to head, lead; to leave, will, bequeath; to send, transmit, forward; to offer, promise; *mandar hacer,* to have (a thing) made, bespeak. — *v.r.* to have free use of one's limbs; to communicate with (said of rooms in buildings); to go from room to room; *mandar a alguno a puntapiés* (*a puntillazos* or *a zapatazos*), to have complete ascendancy over anyone; *mandar a coces,* to command harshly.

mandarín, *n.m.* mandarin; (*coll.*) petty officer.

mandarria, *n.f.* (*naut.*) iron maul, sledgehammer.

mandatario, *n.m.* (*law*) attorney, agent; mandatory.

mandato, *n.m.* mandate, precept, instruction, order, injunction, ordinance; charge, trust, commission; ceremony of washing of the feet on Maundy Thursday; (*law*) mandate, contract of bailment.

mande, *interj.* at your service; (*naut.*) holla!

mandí, *n.m.* (*Arg.*) an edible fish (*silurus bagol*).

mandíbula, *n.f.* jaw-bone; jaw; mandible.

mandibular, *a.* (*med.*) mandibular, belonging to the jaw.

mandil, *n.m.* leather or coarse cloth or apron; fine-meshed net; freemason's apron.

mandilar, *v.t.* to wipe (a horse) with a coarse cloth.

mandilejo, *n.m.* small apron, ragged cloth or apron.

mandilete, *n.m.* (*artil.*) door of the port-hole of a battery.

mandilón, *n.m.* (*coll.*) coward, mean fellow.

mandioca, *n.f.* tapioca, manioc, cassava.

mando, *n.m.* command, authority, power, rule, dominion.

mandoble, *n.m.* two-handed blow with a sword; severe reprimand.

mandón, -ona, *a.* imperious, domineering. — *n.m.f.* imperious, domineering person. — *n.m.* (*S. Am.*) foreman, boss.

mandrachero, *n.m.* proprietor of a gaming-house.

mandracho, *n.m.* gambling-house.

mandrágora, *n.f.* (*bot.*) mandrake.

mandria, *n.m., a.* coward, poltroon.

mandriez, *n.f.* (*obs.*) debility, weakness.

mandril, *n.m.* (*zool.*) baboon; (*mech.*) mandrel, chuck, spindle of a lathe.

mandrón, *n.m.* stone ball used as missile.

manducación, *n.f.* (*coll.*) manducation, act of eating, chewing.

manducar, *v.t.* (*pret.* **manduqué;** *pres. subj.* **manduque**) (*coll.*) to eat, chew.

manducatoria, *n.f.* (*coll.*) dining-room, refectory; eatables, food.

manea, *n.f.* shackles, fetters, fetterlock.

manear, *v.t.* to chain, fetter, shackle, hobble (a horse).

manecica, -ita, *n.f.* small hand.

manecilla, *n.f.* small hand; mark, index; (*print.*) fist (☞); plough-handle; book clasp; hand of clock or watch; tendril of vines.

manejable, *a.* manageable, tractable.

manejado, -da, *a.* (*art*) handled. — *p.p.* [MANEJAR].

manejar, *v.t.* to manage, master, wield, move with the hand, conduct, govern, drive, ride, train; to handle, contrive, hand, manage, carry on. — *v.r.* to know how to conduct oneself; to have oneself in hand.

manejo, *n.m.* employment of the hands, handling; management, administration, conduct; horsemanship, manège; cunning, intrigue, stratagem, trick, device; *manejo doméstico,* household.

maneota, *n.f.* shackles, fetters, hobbles.

manera, *n.f.* manner, form, figure; guise, style, way, method, mode, kind; deportment, behaviour; (*obs.*) pocket-hole, opening in women's cloaks; (*art*) manner, style; forepart of breeches. — *pl.* (*obs.*) moral habits, behaviour, conduct; *a manera,* in the style of; *de* (or *por*) *manera que,* in such a way, so that; *en gran manera,* greatly, highly; *sobre manera,* extremely, exceedingly.

manero, -ra, *a.* tame (of hawks, etc.).

manes, *n.m.pl.* manes, the spirits of the dead; the shade of a deceased.

manezuela, *n.f.* small hand; buckle, book clasp.

manfla, *n.f.* (*prov.*) old sow; (*coll.*) concubine.

manga, *n.f.* sleeve; arm of axletree; cloak-bag, portmanteau; hose; whirlwind, water spout; line of troops; piquet; kind of mango; fishing-net; (*naut.*) extreme breadth (of a ship); wind sail; bag used for straining liquids; (*Mex.*) kind of cloak; poncho; (*eccles.*) case for covering a cross; (*bot.*) variety of mango; (*Arg., Cub., Chi.*) guide-rails for enclosing or shipping horses, cattle, etc.; *manga* *de ángel*, woman's wide sleeve; *manga de agua*, water spout; *en mangas de camisa*, in one's shirt sleeves; *tener manga ancha*, to be broadminded; *andar manga por hombro*, to be careless in domestic matters; *buenas son mangas después de pascua*, useful things are welcome whenever they come; *echar de manga*, to make use of someone unknown to himself; *entra por la manga, y sale por el cabezón*, phrase used of those who abuse the kindness or generosity of those who have helped them; *traer una cosa en la manga*, to have something at hand.

mangachapuy, *n.m.* (*Philip.*) a dipterad tree.
mangajarro, *n.m.* (*coll.*) long, ill-shaped sleeve.
mangana, *n.f.* lasso, lariat.
manganear, *v.t.* (*Am.*) to lasso.
manganeo, *n.m.* (*Am.*) rodeo.
manganesa, manganesia, *n.f.* peroxide of manganese.
manganeso, *n.m.* (*min.*) manganese.
manganilla, *n.f.* sleight of hand; trick, stratagem; (*prov.*) pole for gathering acorns.
mangla, *n.f.* (*Sierra Morena*) gum exuding from certain plants.
manglar, *n.m.* plantation of mangrove trees.
mangle, *n.m.* (*bot.*) mangrove-tree.
mango, *n.m.* handle, haft, heft, helve; tiller; (*bot.*) Indian mango-tree; *mango de pluma*, penholder; *mango de escoba*, broomstick.
mangonada, *n.f.* push with the arm.
mangonear, *v.i.* (*coll.*) to loaf, loiter, wander about, rove idly; to intermeddle, pry.
mangoneo, *n.m.* prying, intermeddling.
mangorrero, -ra, *a.* wandering, roving, rambling; hafted (of a knife); worthless, useless.
mangosta, *n.f.* (*zool.*) mongoose, mungoose.
mangote, *n.m.* (*coll.*) large, wide sleeve; oversleeve.
mangual, *n.m.* war flail, morning star.
manguardia, *n.f.* (*Mex.*) buttress of a bridge.
manguera, *n.f.* hose, tube for conveying liquids; (*naut.*) tarred canvas, wind sail; waterspout; (*Arg.*) large corral; *manguera de desinflar*, (*aer.*) deflating sleeve; *manguera de inflar*, (*aer.*) inflating sleeve.
manguero, *n.m.* horseman gamekeeper (*obs.*); fireman.
mangueta, *n.f.* jamb of a glass-door; pipe for clysters; lever; neck of a water-closet hopper.
manguilla, manguita, *n.f.* small sleeve.
manguitero, *n.m.* muff-maker, muff-seller; leather-dresser.
manguito, *n.m.* muff; closely-fitting sleeve; wristlet; large coffee cake; oversleeve; (*mech.*) bush, coupler, collar, sleeve.
maní, *n.m.* (*Am.*) peanut.
manía, *n.f.* mania, frenzy, madness; whim, fad; extravagance, inordinate desires.
maníaco, -ca, *n.m.f.*, *a.* maniacal, mad, frantic.
manialbo, -ba, *a.* white-footed (of a horse).
maniatar, *v.t.* to manacle, handcuff.
maniático, -ca, *a.* maniacal.
manicomio, *n.m.* asylum, madhouse.
manicordio, *n.m.* manichord, clavichord.
manicorto, -ta, *a.* illiberal, parsimonious.
manicuro, -ra, *n.m.f.* manicure.
manida, *n.f.* mansion, abode, resort, nest, place of shelter, lair (of thieves).

manido, -da, *a.* hidden, concealed; high (of game, etc.). — *p.p.* [MANIR].
manifacero, -ra, *a.* intriguing, meddlesome, intrusive.
manifactura, *n.f.* make, manufacture, form in which a thing is made.
manifestable, *a.* manifestable, ostensible, easily discovered.
manifestación, *n.f.* manifestation, declaration, statement, public demonstration; (*law, prov.*) writ resembling habeas corpus.
manifestador, -ra, *n.m.f.* discoverer, publisher.
manifestar, *v.t.* (*pres. indic.* **manifiesto**; *pres. subj.* **manifieste**; *p.p.* **manifestado, manifiesto**), to discover, manifest, expose, exhibit, declare; *manifestar una herida*, to probe a wound.
manifiestamente, *adv.* manifestly, overtly.
manifiesto, *n.m.* exposition of the Blessed Sacrament; manifesto, public declaration; (*com.*) manifest; *poner de manifiesto*, to manifest, make public, expose, display.
manifiesto, -ta, *a.* manifest, plain, open, clear, overt, obvious. — *p.p. irreg.* [MANIFESTAR].
manigua, *n.f.* (*Cub.*) thicket, jungle.
manigueta, *n.f.* haft, handle. — *pl.* **maniguetas**; (*naut.*) kevels.
maniguetones, *n.m.pl.* (*naut.*) snatch-cleats.
manija, *n.f.* haft, handle; shackles, handcuffs; ring, brace, clamp, clasp.
manijero, *n.m.* (*prov.*) manager, foreman.
manilargo, -ga, *a.* long-handed, pugilistic; generous.
manilense; manileño, -ña, *n.m.f.*, *a.* of or belonging to Manila.
maniluvio, *n.m.* bath for the hands.
manilla, *n.f.* small hand; bracelet; book-clasp; manacle, handcuff.
maniobra, *n.f.* handiwork; handling; trick, stratagem, artifice; (*naut.*) working of a ship; gear, rigging, tackle; (*mil.*) manœuvre, evolution of troops; *pl.* (*railw.*) shunting, switch-engine work; *maniobras altas* (or *bajas*), upper (or lower) rigging; *maniobras de carena*, careening gears; *maniobras de combate*, preventive rigging.
maniobrar, *v.i.* to work with the hands; (*naut.*) to work a ship; (*met.*) to seek to effect something; (*mil.*) to manœuvre troops.
maniobrero, -ra, *a.* manœuvring (of troops).
maniobrista, *n.m.* (*naut.*) skilled naval tactician.
maniota, *n.f.* fetterlock, manacles, shackles.
manipulación, *n.f.* manipulation.
manipulador, *n.m.* (*teleg.*) circuit key for morse.
manipulante, *n.m.* (*coll.*) administrator, negotiator.
manipular, *v.t.* (*coll.*) to work, manipulate, handle, manage one's business; to meddle with everything.
manípulo, *n.m.* (*eccles.*) maniple; standard; division of the Roman army; (*med.*) handful.
maniqueísmo, *n.m.* Manichæism.
maniqueo, -ea, *a.* Manichæan.
maniquete, *n.m.* black lace; mitten.
maniquí, *n.m.* manikin, puppet, figure; subservient person.
manir, *v.t.* defect., to keep meat till it becomes soft; to mellow. — *v.r.* to become tender or mellow (of meat).

manirroto, -ta, *a.* extravagant, lavish, wasteful.
manirrotura, *n.f.* extravagance, superfluous generosity.
manita, *n.f.* hour-hand of a watch or clock.
manivacío, -cía, *a.* (*coll.*) empty-handed, idle, lazy.
manivela, *n.f.* (*mech.*) crank; crankshaft; *manivela de arranque,* (*motor.*) starting handle, crank.
manjar, *n.m.* food, victuals; morsel, delicacy; (*fig.*) recreation, entertainment; (*obs.*) suit of cards; *manjar blanco,* dish made of chicken mixed with sugar, milk and rice; blancmange; *manjar de ángeles,* dish of milk and sugar.
manjarejo, *n.m.* savoury dish, tit-bit.
manjelín, *n.m.* weight used for diamonds (254 milligrammes); carat.
manjolar, *v.t.* to carry a hawk.
manjorrada, *n.f.* excessive eating, abundance of victuals.
manjúa, *n.f.* (*prov.* and *Cub.*) a variety of sardine.
manlevar, *v.t.* (*obs.*) to contract; to burden oneself with debts.
manlieva, *n.f.* tax levied in haste, and collected from house to house.
manlieve, *n.m.* confidence trick, fraud.
mano, *n.f.* hand; side, direction; forefoot of a quadruped; trotter (of sheep, pig, etc.); proboscis, elephant's trunk; hand of a clock; pestle; quire of paper; musical scale; command, power, workmanship; reprimand, censure; finishing stroke; cylindrical stone for grinding cocoa; first hand at cards; round of any game; coat (of paint, varnish, etc.); manner of acting; band of reapers or harvesters; possession; scheme of action; handiwork, handicraft; aid, help, protection, favour; *a mano,* at hand; with the hand, studiously; *a la mano,* at hand, near at hand; *estar a mano,* to be square, quits; *de mano* secretly, underhandedly; *mano de gato,* correction by a superior hand, ladies' make-up; *lo tengo de buena mano,* I have it on good authority; *mano a mano,* in company, familiarly; *¡manos a la obra!* (naut.) bear a hand! *manos de carnero,* sheep's trotters; *mano de Judas,* kind of candle-snuffer; *manos de vaca,* cow's heels; *manos libres,* emoluments annexed to an office; *manos limpias,* honesty, integrity, fairness; *manos muertas,* mortmain, unalienable estate; *a dos manos,* willingly, readily; *a manos llenas,* liberally, copiously, abundantly; *abrir la mano,* to be open to receive gifts, to give liberally, to be generous; *abrir la mano al caballo,* to give a horse rein; *alzar la mano a uno,* to raise one's hand threateningly; *asentar la mano,* to chastise, correct; *atar las manos a uno,* to tie a person's hand, impede one; *bajo mano,* in an underhand way, secretively; *buenas manos,* dexterity, skill; *cantar en la mano,* to be very astute; *cerrar la mano,* to be stingy, mean; *comerse las manos tras una cosa,* to eat up something greedily; *como con* (or *por*) *la mano,* very lightly, very easily; *con franca* (or *larga*) *mano,* liberally, abundantly; *estar con las manos en la masa,* to be in the act of doing something; *con mano pesada,* harshly, rigorously; *correr por mano de,* to be in the hands of; *cruzar las manos* (or *cruzarse de manos*), to be calm, quiet; *dar de mano,* to stop, leave

(one's work); *dar de manos,* to fall on one's hands; *dar en manos de,* to fall into the power of; *dar la última mano,* to give the finishing touches; *darse la mano,* to help mutually, to be near or related; *de buena mano, buen dado,* fear nothing from a good fellow; *dejado de la mano de Dios,* caring for nothing and nobody; *dejar de la mano,* to abandon; *de la mano y pluma,* a genuine autograph; *de manos a boca,* suddenly, unexpectedly; *de ruin mano, ruin dado,* the poor man cannot but give poor gifts; *descargar la mano sobre,* to chastise, bear heavily upon; *de una mano a otra,* in a very short time; *echar mano a la bolsa,* to take out some money; *ensuciar(se) las manos,* to soil one's hands (by crime); *estar (una cosa) en la mano,* to be easy, evident; *hablar de manos,* to talk with many gestures; *ir a la mano a,* to restrain, moderate; *la mano cuerda no hace todo lo que dice la lengua,* the wise man does less than he says; *las manos en la rueca, y los ojos en la puerta,* to be thinking of one thing and doing another; *llevar la mano blanda,* to treat kindly; *manos besa el hombre que quisiera ver cortadas,* to flatter one whom one secretly dislikes; *manos blancas no ofenden,* woman's spite can do no harm to man; *mano sobre mano,* lazily, indolently; *manos y vida componen villa,* time and labour can accomplish much; *meter la mano en el pecho* (or *seno*), to consider, ruminate, reflect; *no darse manos a una cosa,* to be unable, with effort, to accomplish something; *pasar la mano por el cerro,* to caress, fondle; *por debajo de mano,* in an underhand way; *quedarse soplando las manos,* to be ashamed (at having mismanaged an affair, etc.); *sentar la mano a,* to beat, lay hands on; *ser a las manos con,* to come to blows with; *ser sus pies y sus manos,* to be one's chief support in distress; *si a mano viene,* perhaps; *sin levantar mano,* without intermission; *tener mano con,* to have influence with; *tener mano en,* to intervene in; *tener muchas manos,* to have great skill or courage; *traer entre manos,* to handle, manage; *untar las manos,* to bribe; *venir a uno a la mano,* to come to someone without being solicited; *venir (unos) a las manos,* to fight, come to blows; *venir con las manos en el seno,* to be indolent, lazy; *venir con sus manos lavadas,* to wish to enjoy the fruits of another's labours; *vivir de* (or *por*) *sus manos,* to live by one's own efforts (or work).
manobra, *n.f.* (*prov.*) raw material.
manobre, *n.m.* (*prov.*) hodman, hod-carrier.
manobrero, *n.m.* cleaner of fountains or aqueducts.
manojear, *v.t.* (*Cub., Chi.*) to tie tobacco leaves in small bundles.
manojico, -illo, -ito, *n.m.* small bundle, small faggot.
manojo, *n.m.* faggot, bundle of twigs or herbs; bunch (of keys, etc.); handful; *a manojos,* abundantly.
manola, *n.f.* common girl from Madrid.
manolo, -la, *n.m.f.* low-class madrilenian; one loud in dress or habits.
manométrico, -ca, *a.* manometric.
manómetro, *n.m.* manometer.
manopla, *n.f.* gauntlet; coachman's whip; (*Chi.*) knuckle-duster; *tela de manoplas,* silk ornamented with large flowers.

manosear, *v.t.* to feel, touch, handle; to paw, rumple (clothes).

manoseo, *n.m.* handling.

manota, *n.f.* large, ugly hand.

manotada, *n.f.;* **manotazo,** *n.m.* cuff, slap, blow with the hand.

manotear, *v.t.* to cuff, buffet, strike with the hand. — *v.i.* to wring the hands, gesticulate.

manoteo, *n.m.* slap, blow with the hand; gesticulation with the hands.

manquear, *v.i.* to affect the cripple, pretend to be maimed.

manquedad, manquera, *n.f.* lack of one or both arms or hands; (*fig.*) lameness, maim, fault, defect, imperfection.

manquillo, -illa; -ito, -ita, *a.* handless; somewhat faulty or imperfect; diminutive [MAN-co].

mansalva (a), *adv.* without risk or danger; in a cowardly manner.

mansamente, *adv.* meekly, slowly, quietly, gently.

mansedumbre, *n.f.* meekness, mildness, gentleness, peaceableness, manageableness, tameness.

mansejón, -ona, *a.* very tame.

manseque, *n.m.* (*Chi.*) children's dance.

mansera, *n.m.* (*Cub.*) vat for the sugar-cane juice.

mansico, -ica; -ito, -ita, *a.* very tame, meek, mild.

mansión, *n.f.* stay, sojourn, residence; habitation, abode, mansion, home.

manso, -sa, *a.* tame, meek, mild, tractable, docile, gentle, soft, quiet, lamblike; *a lumbre mansa*, by a mild light.

manso, *n.m.* manor, manor-house; manse; bell-wether.

manta, *n.f.* rug, blanket; travelling rug; men's shawl; horse blanket; (*Mex.*) coarse cotton shirting; tapestry; (*mil.*) mantelet; threshing, drubbing; tossing in a blanket; quill feathers of birds of prey; (*Am.*) bag of agave for carrying ore; card game; *manta de algodón*, wadding; *manta blanca*, bleached cotton; *manta prieta*, unbleached cotton; *a manta (de Dios)*, (*coll.*) plentifully, copiously.

mantaterilla, *n.f.* coarse hempen cloth for horse blankets.

manteador, -ra, *n.m.f.* tosser, one who tosses in a blanket.

manteamiento, *n.m.* tossing in a blanket.

mantear, *v.t.* to toss in a blanket. — *v.i.* (*prov.*) to gad about (of women).

manteca, *n.f.* lard, grease, fat; pomatum; butter; pulpy part of fruits; (*joc.*) money; *manteca de cacao*, cocoa butter.

mantecada, *n.f.* buttered toast; a kind of cake.

mantecado, *n.m.* butter-cake; French ice-cream.

mantecón, *n.m.* milksop; sweet-toothed person.

mantecoso, -sa, *a.* buttery, made of butter, mellow.

manteísta, *n.m.* day student in a seminary.

mantel, *n.m.* table-cloth; altar-cloth; covering; *levantar los manteles*, to clear the table; *levantarse de los manteles*, to rise from table.

mantelería, *n.f.* table-linen.

manteleta, *n.f.* mantelet, small scarf or mantle, lady's shawl.

mantelete, *n.m.* (*eccles.*) mantelet; bishop's mantle; (*fort.*) movable parapet; (*her.*) mantling.

mantelo, *n.m.* very wide apron.

mantellina, *n.f.* mantilla.

mantenedor, *n.m.* president of a tournament or jousts.

mantenencia, *n.f.* maintenance, aliment, support.

mantener, *v.t.* (conjugated like TENER) to maintain, support, lift up, hold up, keep up; to nourish, feed, support life; to continue; to persevere, pursue, persist; to be the first challenger; to defend, sustain an opinion. — *v.r.* to maintain oneself; to continue living in a place; to remain in the same condition; to nourish, gain nourishment; *mantenerse en lo dicho*, to abide by what one has said; *mantenerse a la mar*, to keep the sea; *mantenerse firme*, to stand firm, hold one's ground.

mantengo; mantenga, *pres. indic.; pres. subj.* [MANTENER].

manteniente, *n.m.* (*obs.*) violent blow with both hands; *a manteniente*, with all one's might, firmly.

mantenimiento, *n.m.* maintenance, sustenance, subsistence, necessaries of life, livelihood, living; ration, allowance.

manteo, *n.m.* long cloak or mantle; woollen skirt; tossing in a blanket.

mantequera, *n.f.* churn; butter-dish; butter-woman, dairymaid.

mantequero, *n.m.* butterman, butter-seller.

mantequilla, *n.f.* butter; butter-cake.

mantera, *n.f.* mantle-maker.

mantero, -ra, *n.m.f.* one who sells or makes blankets.

mantés, -esa, *n.m.f., a.* (*coll.*) rogue, scoundrel.

mantilla, *n.f.* mantilla, headcover for women; housing, horsecloth; (*print.*) blanket; birthday present from one prince to another; slip, infant's frock. — *pl.* **mantillas,** swaddling-clothes; *estar en mantillas*, to be in a state of infancy; *haber salido de mantillas*, to be out of leading-strings.

mantilleja, *n.f.* small mantilla.

mantillo, *n.m.* (*agric.*) humus; rotten, fermented manure.

mantillón, -ona, *a.* (*prov.*) dirty, slovenly.

mantisa, *n.f.* (*math.*) mantissa.

manto, *n.m.* silken veil, mantle, large mantilla, kirtle, cloak, robe; mantelpiece; (*min.*) vein; stratum, layer; *debajo de mi manto, al rey mato*, a man's thoughts are his own.

mantón, *n.m.* large cloak, kind of shawl, trimming on women's jackets; (*Cub.*) mantilla.

mantudo, -da, *a.* having drooping wings.

mantuve, *pret. irreg.* [MANTENER].

manuable, *a.* tractable, manageable, easily handled, handy.

manual, *a.* manual, handy, easily handled, tractable, pliant, light, prompt; domestic, home-made. — *n.m.* manual, journal, note-book, account-book; (*eccles.*) ritual. — *pl.* **manuales;** (*eccles.*) choir-fees.

manualmente, *adv.* manually.

manubrio, *n.m.* handle of an instrument or tool; crank; manubrium.

manucodiata, *n.f.* (*orn.*) bird of paradise.

Manuel, *n.m.* Emmanuel.

Manuela, *n.f.* Emma.

manuela, *n.f.* open hackney-carriage (in Madrid).

manuella, *n.f.* (*naut.*) capstan bar, handspike.

manufactura, *n.f.* manufacture, mechanical work.

manufacturar, *v.t.* to manufacture.

manufacturero, -ra, *a.* manufacturing.

manumisión, *n.f.* manumission.

manumiso, -sa, *a.* emancipated; free, disengaged. — *p.p. irreg.* [MANUMITIR].

manumisor, *n.m.* (*law*) liberator.

manumitir, *v.t.* (*p.p.* **manumitido, manumiso**) to manumit, emancipate.

manuscribir, *v.t.* to write by hand.

manuscrito, -ta, *a.* manuscript, not printed.

manuscrito, *n.m.* manuscript.

manutención, *n.f.* maintaining, maintenance, support, protection, conservation.

manutener, *v.t.* (*law*) to support, maintain.

manutigio, *n.m.* a gentle friction with the hand.

manutisa, *n.f.* (*bot.*) sweet-william pink.

manvacío, -a, *a.* (*coll.*) empty-handed.

manzana, *n.f.* (*bot.*) apple; pommel, knob; block of houses between two streets; cypress nut; (*Arg., Chi.*) square; *sano como una manzana,* as healthy as can be; *la manzana podrida pierde a su compañía,* evil communications corrupt good manners.

manzanal, manzanar, *n.m.* orchard, apple-orchard.

manzanil, *a.* like an apple.

manzanilla, *n.f.* (*bot.*) common chamomile; small ball or knob; kind of olive; lower part of the chin; pad of some animals' feet; small apple; white sherry wine.

manzanillo, *n.m.* (*bot.*) common manchineel, poison tree.

manzanillo, -ito, *n.m.* little apple-tree.

manzanita, *n.f.* little apple.

manzano, *n.m.* (*bot.*) apple-tree.

maña, *n.f.* handiness, skill, knack, dexterity, craftiness, contrivance, cleverness, expertness, cunning, faculty, ability, craft, artifice; tact, care; evil habit or custom; bundle of hemp or flax when reaped; *darse maña,* to manage, contrive, bring about; *más vale maña que fuerza,* a smooth tongue does more than force; *el que malas mañas ha, tarde o nunca las perderá,* bad habits are difficult, or impossible, to uproot.

mañana, *n.f.* morning, forenoon, morrow. — *n.m.* the near future. — *adv.* to-morrow; soon, immediately; expression of negation; in time to come, by and by; *de mañana,* in the morning; *de gran mañana, muy de mañana,* very early; *tomar la mañana,* to drink an aperitif before breakfast; *mañana será otro día,* to-morrow may bring better luck.

mañanear, *v.i.* to rise very early.

mañanica, *n.f.* break of day.

mañear, *v.t., v.i.* to act with craft and skill to attain one's end.

mañería, *n.f.* (*obs.*) sterility; cunning; feudal right of inheriting from those who died without legitimate issue.

mañero, -ra, *a.* clever, dexterous, skilful, artful; meek, tractable; handy, easy.

maño, -ña, *n.m.f.* (*Arg., Chi.*) brother, sister (term of endearment).

mañoco, *n.m.* tapioca; (*Ven.*) Indian corn meal.

mañosamente, *adv.* dexterously, neatly, handily, cleverly, subtly, maliciously, craftily.

mañoso, -sa, *a.* dexterous, neat, handy, clever; crafty, malicious, subtle.

mañuela, *n.f.* mean trick, low cunning. — *pl.* **mañuelas,** artful, cunning person.

mapa, *n.m.* map. — *n.f.* something of outstanding excellence; *no estar en el mapa,* to be extraordinary; *llevarse la mapa,* to excel.

mapache, *n.m.* (*zool.*) raccoon.

mapalia, *n.f.* sheep-cot, sheep-fold.

mapamundi, *n.m.* map of the world.

mapanare, *n.f.* (*Ven.*) a highly poisonous snake.

mapurite, *n.m.* (*zool.*) skunk.

maque, *n.m.* (*Mex.*) sumac lacquer.

maquear, *v.t.* to lacquer with *maque.*

maqueta, *n.f.* a clay or plaster model of a building made to scale.

maqui, *n.m.* (*Chi.*) kind of ginger.

maquiavélico, -ca, *a.* Machiavellian.

maquiavelismo, *n.m.* Machiavellism.

maquiavelista, *n.m.f.* Machiavellian.

maquila, *n.f.* toll-corn, toll in general; corn-measure; (*Cent. Am.*) unit of weight (about 125 lb.).

maquilandero, *n.m.* (*prov.*) measure with which corn is tolled.

maquilar, *v.t.* to measure and take dues for grinding corn; to clip, retrench, cut off.

maquilero, maquilón, *n.m.* one who measures or takes dues for grinding corn.

maquillaje, *n.m.* make-up.

máquina, *n.f.* machine, engine; great number, abundance, multitude, concourse; vast structure; theatrical contrivance effecting change of scenery, etc.; intrigue, machination, contrivance; supernatural agency in a poem, etc.; fancy project; locomotive; *máquina de vapor,* steam engine; *máquina compuesta,* compound engine; *máquina de coser,* sewing machine; *máquina de escribir,* typewriter; *máquina neumática,* air pump; *máquina de arbolar,* (*naut.*) sheers, sheer-hulk.

maquinación, *n.f.* machination, contrivance, artifice.

maquinador, -ra, *n.m.f.* contriver, schemer, plotter, machinator.

maquinal, *a.* mechanical.

maquinalmente, *adv.* mechanically.

maquinante, *a.* planning, contriving, machinating.

maquinar, *v.t.* to machinate, plan, hatch, contrive, compass, conspire.

maquinaria, *n.f.* machinery; engineering, mechanics.

maquinete, *n.m.* (*prov.*) chopping-knife.

maquinica, *n.f.* mechanics.

maquinista, *n.m.f.* machinist, mechanic, engine-driver.

mar, *n.m.f.* sea, large lake, sheet of water; swell of the sea; large number or quantity; *alta mar* (or *mar ancha*), main sea, high sea; *mar alta,* rough sea; *de mar a mar,* copiously, excessively, in the extreme of fashion; *baja mar,* (*naut.*) low water, ebb-tide; *mar llena* (or *plena mar*), high water; *mar de través,* (*naut.*) sea on the beam; *mar gruesa,* a heavy sea; *mar de leva,* high swelling sea; *correr con la mar en popa,* (*naut.*) to scud before the sea; *hablar de la mar,* to attempt something inexhaustible or impossible; *do va la mar,* *vayan las arenas*, better to venture little when one has lost much; *hacerse a la mar*, to put out to sea; *ir con la proa a la mar*, (naut.) to head the sea; *mantener dos señales de mar enfilados*, (naut.) to keep two seamarks in line; *mar de fondo*, swell; *mar bonanza*, calm sea; *mar jurisdiccional* or *territorial*, territorial waters; *correr los mares*, to follow the seas; *meter el mar en un pozo*, to attempt the impossible; *quien no se arriesga* (or *se aventura*), *no pasa la mar*, faint heart never won fair lady.

marabú, *n.m.* (*zool.*) marabou.

maraca, *n.m.* (*Chi.*, *Per.*) game played with three dice marked with sun, diamond, heart, star, moon and anchor; (*fig.*, *Chi.*) harlot, prostitute.

maracá, *n.m.* (*Arg.*) Guarani musical instrument consisting of a dry gourd in which some pebbles are placed.

maracure, *n.m.* (*bot.*) curare plant.

maragato, *n.m.* native of Astorga (Spain).

maranata, *n.f.* maranatha, anathema.

maraña, *n.f.* place full of brambles or briers; jungle, tangle, entanglement of a skein; refuse of silk; perplexity, puzzle; plot of a play; imposition, fraud; (*vulg.*) prostitute.

marañado, -da, *a.* entangled, perplexed.

marañero, -ra; marañoso, -sa, *a.* entangling, ensnaring, perplexing.

marañón, *n.m.* (*Cub.*, *Cent. Am.*) tree producing a gum resembling gum arabic; cashew-tree; cashew-nut.

marasmo, *n.m.* (*med.*) marasmus, wasting, consumption.

maravedí, *n.m.* an old Spanish coin.

maravilla, *n.f.* marvel, wonder, prodigy; admiration; (*bot.*) heliotrope; marigold; *a maravilla*, marvellously; *a las mil maravillas*, unusually well; *por maravilla*, very seldom.

maravillar, *v.t.* to admire, regard with wonder. — *v.r.* to marvel; to be astonished, struck with wonder.

maravillosamente, *adv.* wonderfully, marvellously, miraculously.

maravilloso, -sa, *a.* wonderful, marvellous, astonishing, admirable, miraculous, monstrous, strange.

marbete, *n.m.* stamp, label, manufacturer's mark, tag, ticket, luggage receipt; fillet, border.

marca, *n.f.* mark, measure, weight; landmark; lighthouse; brand, impress, stamp, manufacturer's mark; kind, quality; standard (of size); gauge or rule for measuring; marker, stencil, label, tag, ticket; (*geog.*) march, frontier region or province; (*vulg.*) prostitute; *marca de fábrica*, trade-mark; *de marca*, excellent of its kind; *de más de marca* (or *de marca mayor*), very superior; *palos de marca*, buoys.

marcación, *n.f.* (*naut.*) bearing; taking a ship's bearings.

marcador, *n.m.*, *a.* marker; assay master; index; bookmark.

marcar, *v.t.* (*pret.* **marqué**; *pres. subj.* **marque**) to brand, stamp, impress, mark, mark out; to note, observe, designate; to embroider initials; (*naut.*) to take bearings; *marcar el compás*, (*mus.*) to beat time, keep time. — *v.r.* to determine a ship's bearings.

marcear, *v.t.* to shear (animals). — *v.i.* to be rough, March-like (of the weather).

marceo, *n.m.* trimming honeycombs in spring.

marcescente, *a.* (*bot.*) marcescent, withering.

marcial, *n.m.* aromatic powder for dressing gloves. — *a.* martial, war-like; unceremonious, frank; (*pharm.*) chalybeate.

marcialidad, *n.f.* freedom, frankness; martialism.

marco, *n.m.* door-case, window-case; picture-frame; branding-iron; model, archetype; mark, gold and silver weight; standard (of weight); scantling and length of timber; mark (German coin).

márcola, *n.f.* pruning-hook.

marconigrama, *n.m.* marconigram, wireless telegram.

marcha, *n.f.* march; signal to move; progress, course, turn, run; working order; marching tune; (*mus.*) march, two-step; movement of a watch; (*prov.*) bonfire; (*naut.*) speed, headway; *a largas marchas*, with celerity, speedily; *sobre la marcha*, immediately, on the spot; *batir* (or *tocar*) *la marcha*, to strike up a march; *doblar las marchas*, to get through an unusual amount; *a marchas forzadas*, (*mil.*) forced marches.

marchamar, *v.t.* to mark goods at the customs-house.

marchamero, *n.m.* customs-house marker.

marchamo, *n.m.* mark made by the customs officials.

marchante, *a.* mercantile, commercial, trading. — *n.m.* shopkeeper, dealer; (*Am.*) customer.

marchapié, *n.m.* foot-board; (*naut.*) horse, foot-rope.

marchar, *v.i.*, *v.r.* to go, go away, go off, depart; to march, walk slowly; to progress, proceed, go ahead; to work, go, function (of mechanism); (*naut.*) to make headway; (*mil.*) to march.

marchazo, *n.m.* boaster, bragger.

marchitable, *a.* perishable, apt to wither.

marchitamiento, *n.m.* fading, withering.

marchitar, *v.t.* to wither, cause to fade, deprive of vigour, wear away. — *v.r.* to wither, fade, decay, shrivel, fall away, dry up; to pine away, grow lean.

marchitez, marchitura, *n.f.* withering, fading.

marchito, -ta, *a.* faded, withered, decayed.

marchoso, *a.* swaggering.

marea, *n.f.* tide; beach, seashore; surf; soft sea breeze; collection of dirt; dew, mizzle; *marea creciente*, flood-tide; *marea menguante*, ebb-tide; *ir contra marea*, to sail against the tide; *mareas vivas*, spring-tides; *la marea mengua*, the tide ebbs; *la marea crece*, the tide comes up.

mareado, -da, *a.* sea-sick, queer, unwell. — *p.p.* [MAREAR].

mareaje, *n.m.* navigating of a ship, seamanship; course of a ship.

mareamiento, *n.m.* sea-sickness.

mareante, *a.* skilled in navigation.

marear *v.t.* to work, navigate (a ship); (*naut.*) to trim (sails); to sell goods by auction; (*coll.*) to vex, bother, importune, worry. — *v.r.* to be sea-sick; to be damaged at sea.

marejada, *n.f.* swell, head-sea, surf; (*fig.*) commotion, excitement.

mare mágnum, *n.m.* (*Lat.*) abundance, magnitude; commotion, disorder.

mareo, *n.m.* sea-sickness; (*coll.*) botheration.

marero, *n.m.,* *a.* sea-breeze.
mareta, *n.f.* (*naut.*) slight disturbance of the sea, surge; growing or decreasing excitement.
maretazo, *n.m.* surge of the sea.
márfaga, *n.f.* (*prov.*) rug, bed coverlet, straw bed.
márfega, *n.f.* (*prov.*) sack of straw, rude mattress.
marfil, *n.m.* ivory; *marfil vegetal,* ivory nut.
marfileño, -ña, *a.* (*poet.*) resembling or belonging to ivory.
marfuz, *a.* repudiated, rejected; deceitful.
marga, marega, *n.f.* marl, loam; coarse cloth; burlap.
margajita, *n.f.* (*min.*) white pyrites.
margal, *n.m.* marl-pit.
margar, *v.t.* to manure with marl.
margarina, *n.f.* margarine.
margarita, *n.f.* pearl; (*bot.*) common daisy; (*naut.*) messenger-rope; periwinkle.
margen, *n.m.f.* margin, border, edge, verge, fringe; marginal note; margin of a book; *a la margen,* marginally; *dar margen,* to give cause, occasion, opportunity; *andarse por las márgenes,* to beat about the bush; *margen de seguridad,* safety margin.
margenar, marginar, *v.t.* to make marginal annotations; to leave a margin on paper.
marginado, -da, *a.* marginated, having a margin.
marginar, *v.t.* [MARGENAR].
margoso, -sa, *a.* marly, loamy.
margrave, *n.m.* margrave.
margraviato, *n.m.* margraviate.
marguera, *n.f.* marl-pit.
María, *n.f.* Mary; (*coll.*) white wax taper; ancient silver coin.
marial, *a.* of books in praise of the Blessed Virgin Mary.
mariano, -na, *a.* (*eccles.*) Marian.
marica, *n.f.* (*orn.*) magpie; thin asparagus; knave of diamonds. — *n.m.* milksop; (*coll.*) sissy; *¿De cuándo acá Marica con guantes?* since when has this happened? *Buscar a Marica por Rabena, o al bachiller en Salamanca,* to look for a needle in a haystack.
maricangalla, *n.f.* (*naut.*) driver, spanker.
Maricastaña, *n.f.* a proverbial character signifying remote times; *en tiempos de Maricastaña,* in the days of yore; long, long ago.
maricón, *n.m.* (*coll.*) pansy, homosexual, sodomite.
maridable, *a.* conjugal, matrimonial, connubial, marital.
maridablemente, *adv.* conjugally.
maridaje, *n.m.* marriage, intimate connexion, conjugal union.
maridanza, *n.f.* (*prov.*) treatment of a wife.
maridar, *v.t.* to unite, join. — *v.i.* to marry, live as man and wife.
maridillo, *n.m.* sorry, pitiful husband; kind of brazier.
marido, *n.m.* husband, married man.
marimacho, *n.m.* virago, masculine woman.
marimanta, *n.f.* bugbear, phantom, hobgoblin.
marimba, *n.f.* African drum; (*Am.*) xylophone.
marimoña, *n.f.* (*bot.*) common yard crowfoot.
marimorena, *n.f.* (*coll.*) dispute, quarrel.
marina, *n.f.* shore, sea coast; (*art*) sea-piece; navy, marine, nautical art, seamanship, sea

affairs; *marina de guerra,* the navy; *marina mercante,* merchant marine.
marinaje, *n.m.* seamanship, body of sailors.
marinar, *v.t.* to marinate, to salt (fish); to man (a ship taken from the enemy).
marinear, *v.i.* to be a mariner.
marinerado, -da, *a.* manned, equipped.
marinería, *n.f.* seamanship, profession of sailors, body of seamen; *me ha salido mal esta marinería,* (*coll.*) that speculation has turned out badly for me.
marinero, *n.m.* mariner, sailor, seaman; *a lo marinero,* in a seamanlike manner.
marinero, -ra, *a.* ready to sail, seaworthy, sea-going.
marinesco, -ca, *a.* nautical; *a la marinesca* (or *marinera*), in a seamanlike manner.
marino, *n.m.* mariner, seaman, seafaring man.
marino, -na, *a.* marine, nautical, of the sea.
marión, marón, *n.m.* (*ichth.*) sturgeon.
mariona, *n.f.* Spanish dance.
marioneta, *n.f.* puppet.
maripérez, *n.f.* servant-girl.
mariposa, *n.f.* butterfly; rushlight, night-light.
mariposear, *v.i.* (*fig.*) to flit like a butterfly; to be capricious.
mariposica, -illa, -ita, *n.f.* small butterfly.
mariquita, *n.f.* ladybird, ladyfly; (*fig.*) effeminate man.
marisabidilla, *n.f.* (*coll.*) blue-stocking.
mariscal, *n.m.* marshal; blacksmith, farrier; *mariscal de campo,* general commanding a division.
mariscala, *n.f.* marshal's wife.
mariscalato, *n.m.; **mariscalía,** *n.f.* marshalship, dignity or office of marshal.
mariscar, *v.t.* (conjugated like BUSCAR) to gather shell-fish.
marisco, *n.m.* shell-fish.
marisma, *n.f.* marsh, swamp, morass.
marital, *a.* marital.
maritata, *n.f.* (*Chi.*) trough lined with leather used to wash rich minerals.
marítimo, -ma, *a.* maritime, marine.
maritornes, *n.f.* (*coll.*) coarse, unfeminine, ungainly servant-girl.
marjal, *n.m.* fen, marsh, moor, moorland, marshy ground; a measure of land (5,650 sq. ft.).
marjoleto, *n.m.* (*bot.*) white hawthorn.
marlota, *n.f.* kind of Moorish gown.
marmita, *n.f.* stew-pot, saucepan, porridge-saucepan.
marmitón, *n.m.* scullion, dish-washer.
mármol, *n.m.* marble, marble sculpture; (*print.*) imposing-stone.
marmolejo, *n.m.* small pillar or marble column.
marmoleño, -ña, *a.* marbly, made of marble, resembling marble.
marmolería, *n.f.* marble work; marble works.
marmolillo, *n.m.* fender stone; (*fig.*) unfeeling person.
marmolista, *n.m.* sculptor, worker in marble.
marmoración, *n.f.* marbling.
marmóreo, -rea; **marmoroso, -sa,** *a.* marble, marbled, made of marble, marmorean.
marmosa, *n.f.* (*zool.*) marmose.
marmosete, *n.m.* (*print.*) vignette.
marmota, *n.f.* (*zool.*) marmot; (*fig.*) sleepy-head.
marmotear, *v.i.* (*prov.*) to jabber.

maro, *n.m.* (*bot.*) germander, marum.

marojo, *n.m.* (*bot.*) red-berried mistletoe.

maroma, *n.f.* rope, cord, cable; *andar en la maroma,* to have the support, backing; to engage in a perilous undertaking.

marón, *n.m.* (*ichth.*) sturgeon.

marqués, *n.m.* marquis, marquess.

marquesa, *n.f.* marchioness.

marquesado, *n.m.* marquisate.

marquesica, -illa, -ita, *n.f.* little marchioness.

marquesico, -illo, -ito, *n.m.* little marquis.

marquesina, *n.f.* marquee, awning.

marquesita, *n.f.* (*min.*) marcasite.

marquesota, *n.f.* high white collar worn by men (18th cent.).

marquesote, *n.m.* contemptible marquis (term of contempt); (*Mex.*) caramel, burnt sugar; (*Hond.*) sweet cake.

marqueta, *n.f.* crude cake of wax.

marquetería, *n.f.* cabinet-manufactory; marquetry, inlaid work.

marquida, marquisa, *n.f.* (*vulg.*) prostitute.

marquilla, *n.f.* demy (paper).

marquista, *n.m.* (*prov.*) wholesale dealer in sherry.

marra, *n.f.* want, deficiency, lack, defect; kind of pickaxe; opening in a row of vines.

márraga, *n.f.* coarse grogram, ticking.

marrajo, *n.m.* (*ichth.*) white shark.

marrajo,-ja, *a.* sly, cunning, artful, crafty, wily.

marramao, marramáu, *n.m.* miaow.

marrana, *n.f.* sow; (*coll.*) dirty woman.

marranada, *n.f.* hoggish action, filthiness, brutishness.

marranalla, *n.f.* rabble.

marrancho, *n.m.* pig, hog; dirty man.

marraneta, *n.f.* young sow.

marranillo, *n.m.* little pig.

marrano, *n.m.* pig, hog; dirty man; woodwork supporting a floor, etc.; drum of a waterwheel; board to equalize pressure in oil mills.

marrano, -na, *a.* dirty; (*obs.*) cursed, excommunicated; (*pejorative*) Jewish.

marraqueta, *n.f.* (*Chi.*) loaf of bread resembling biscuits.

marrar, *v.i.* to deviate from truth or justice; to fail, miss.

marras, *adv.* (*coll.*) long ago, long since.

marrasquíno, *n.m.* maraschino.

marrazo, *n.m.* mattock.

márrega, *n.f.*; **marregón,** *n.m.* straw bed.

marrido, -da, *a.* (*obs.*) melancholy.

marrillo, *n.m.* (*prov.*) short, thick stick.

marro, *n.m.* kind of quoits; twisting aside of pursued game to avoid capture; disappointment, failure; crooked bat; fault, failure, miss.

marrojar, *v.t.* to lop branches off trees.

marrón, *n.m.* quoit(stone); (*Am.*) maroon.

marrón, *a.* brown.

marroquí; marroquín, -ina, *n.m.f.*, *a.* Moroccan.

marrotar, *v.t.* to waste, misspend.

marrubio, *n.m.* (*bot.*) white horehound.

marrueco, -ca, *n.m.f.*, *a.* Moroccan.

Marruecos, *n.m.* Morocco.

marrullería, *n.f.* cunning, craft; artful tricks; wheedle, cajolery.

marrullero, -ra, *a.* crafty, cunning, deceiving, wheedling, coaxing.

Marsella, *n.f.* Marseilles.

marsellés, *n.m.* kind of short jacket.

marsellés,-esa, *a.* of or belonging to Marseilles.

marsellesa, *n.f.* Marseillaise (French national anthem).

marsopa, marsopla, *n.f.* porpoise.

marsupial, *a.* (*zool.*) marsupial; *n.m.pl.* marsupials.

marta, *n.f.* pine marten; Martha, a proper name. — *pl.* **martas,** dressed marten skins; *muera Marta y muera harta,* said of one who pleases only himself; *allá se lo haya Marta con sus pollos,* one should mind one's own business.

martagón, -ona, *n.m.f.* (*coll.*) cunning, artful person.

martagón, *n.m.* (*bot.*) wild lily.

martajar, *v.t.* (*Mex.*) to pound (corn).

marte, *n.m.* (*astr.*) Mars; iron.

martelo, *n.m.* jealousy, immoderate passion.

martellina, *n.f.* marteline, millstone hammer.

martes, *n.m.* Tuesday; *martes de carnaval, martes de carnestolendas,* Shrove Tuesday.

martillada, *n.f.* hammer-stroke.

martillador, -ra, *n.m.f.* hammerer, hammer-man.

martillar, *v.t.* to hammer, malleate; to spur (a horse).

martillazo, *n.m.* hammer-stroke.

martillejo, *n.m.* smith's hammer; little hammer.

martilleo, *n.m.* hammering; clatter.

martillero, *n.m.* (*Chi.*) owner or manager of an auction mart.

martillito, *n.m.* small hammer.

martillo, *n.m.* hammer; claw-hammer, tuning hammer; persevering person; auction mart; (*anat.*) malleus; (*com.*) hardware shop; (*ichth.*) hammer-headed shark; *a martillo,* with hammer-strokes; *de martillo,* wrought metal; *a macha martillo,* strongly made.

Martín, San, *n.m.* hog-killing season; *llegarle a uno su San Martín,* to pay for one's sins.

martín del río, *n.m.* (*orn.*) [MARTINETE].

martín pescador, *n.m.* (*orn.*) kingfisher.

martinete, *n.m.* (*orn.*) bird of the heron family; hammer in copper-works; copper-mill; drop-hammer; pile-driver; hammer of a pianoforte.

martingala, *n.f.* martingale; ancient kind of breeches worn under the armour; stake in the game of *monte.*

martinico, *n.m.* (*coll.*) ghost.

martiniega, *n.f.* tax payable on St. Martin's Day.

mártir, *n.m.* martyr.

martirio, *n.m.* martyrdom; torture; grief.

martirizador, -ra, *n.m.f.* persecutor, torturer.

martirizar, *v.t.* (*pret.* **martiricé;** *pres. subj.* **martirice**) to martyr, martyrize; to inflict great sufferings.

martirologio, *n.m.* martyrology, register of martyrs.

marucho, *n.m.* (*Chi.*) a castrated cock, capon.

marullo, *n.m.* swell of (waves).

marxismo, *n.m.* Marxism.

marxista, *n.m.f.*, *a.* Marxist, Marxian.

marzadga, *n.f.* tax payable in March.

marzal, *a.* belonging to the month of March.

marzo, *n.m.* month of March.

mas, *conj.* but, yet; *mas que,* although; *mas si,* perhaps, if. — *n.m.* (*prov.*) farm-house.

más, *adv.* more, besides, moreover. — *n.m.* (*math.*) plus; *a más, a más de,* besides; *a lo más,* at most; *de más,* over, overmuch, extra;

a más correr, with the utmost speed; *a más tardar*, at latest; *a más y mejor*, greatly, highly, at best, excellently; *de más a más*, still more and more; *en más*, more, above, over; *por más que*, however much; *más bien*, rather; *los más*, the largest number; *más claro, el agua*, as plain as a pikestaff; *sin más acá ni más allá*, without any reason; *sin más ni más*, heedlessly, without more ado; *más hace el que quiere que el que puede*, where there's a will there's a way; *más puede maña que fuerza*, brain can do more than brawn; *más vale doblarse que quebrarse*, better to bow than to break.

masa, *n.f.* dough; mortar; mass of metal; (*phys.*) mass; volume, lump, whole mass; (*obs.*) league, coalition; union, aggregation; (*prov.*) farm-house; (*mil.*) arrears of pay; condition, nature, disposition.

masada, *n.f.* country-house, farm-house.

masadero, *n.m.* farmer.

masaje, *n.m.* massage.

mascabado, -da, *a.* raw, unrefined (of sugar).

mascada, *n.f.* (*Mex.*) silk handkerchief.

mascador, -ra, *n.m.f.* chewer, masticator.

mascadura, *n.f.* mastication, manducation.

mascar, *v.t.* (conjugated like BUSCAR) to masticate, chew; (*coll.*) to mumble, pronounce or talk indistinctly.

máscara, *n.m.f.* masker, mummer, masquerader, person in a mask; mask, disguise, fancy-dress masquerade; pretence, subterfuge; (*surg.*) bandage.

mascarada, *n.f.* masquerade, mummery.

mascarero, *n.m.* dealer in masks.

mascarilla, *n.f.* small mask; death-mask, mould of a person's face; *quitarse la mascarilla*, to throw off the mask, declare one's sentiments boldly.

mascarón, *n.m.* large, ugly mask; hideous form; ridiculously solemn person.

mascujar, *v.i.* (*coll.*) to masticate with difficulty; to pronounce with difficulty.

masculillo, *n.m.* children's game.

masculinidad, *n.f.* (*law*) masculinity, manhood.

masculino, -na, *a.* masculine, male, virile.

mascullar, *v.t.* (*coll.*) to falter in speaking.

masecoral, masejicomar, *n.m.* sleight of hand, legerdemain.

masera, *n.f.* kneading-trough; cloth for covering the dough.

masería, masía, *n.f.* farm-house.

masetero, *n.m.* masseter, muscle of the lower jaw.

masilla, *n.f.* little mass; putty.

masita, *n.f.* (*mil.*) pittance for purchasing shoes.

maslo, *n.m.* root of the tail of quadrupeds.

masón, *n.m.* mess given to fowls; large mass; freemason.

masonería, *n.f.* freemasonry.

masónico, -ca, *a.* Masonic.

masora, *n.f.* Masorah.

masovero, *n.m.* farmer.

masque, *adv.* (*Mex.*) no matter, let it be.

mastelerillo, *n.m.* (*naut.*) topgallant and royal mast.

mastelero, *n.m.* (*naut.*) top-mast; *masteleros de respeto*, spare top-masts.

masticación, *n.f.* mastication.

masticar, *v.t.* (conjugated like BUSCAR) to chew, masticate; to ruminate, mediate.

masticatorio, -ria, *a.* masticatory.

mastigador, *n.m.* horse's bit.

mástil, *n.m.* mast, top-mast; bed-post, loom-post; trunk, stem; wide breeches worn by Indians; handle or neck of a violin, guitar, etc.; *mástil de barrena*, shank of an auger.

mastín, *n.m.* mastiff, bull-dog, large dog; clumsy fellow, clown.

mastina, *n.f.* mastiff, bitch.

mastinazo, *n.m.* large mastiff.

mastinillo, *n.m.* little mastiff.

mástique, *n.m.* mastic; mastic tree.

masto, *n.m.* stock into which a scion is grafted; (*prov.*) male bird.

mastodonte, *n.m.* mastodon.

mastoides, *a.* mastoid.

mastranto, mastranzo, *n.m.* (*bot.*) round-leaved mint.

mastuerzo, *n.m.* (*bot.*) common cress; simpleton, dolt.

masturbación, *n.f.* masturbation.

mata, *n.f.* plant, bush, shrub; blade, sprig; orchard, copse, coppice; lock of matted hair; white metal; young evergreen oak; a game of cards; matte, an impure metallic product; *de mala mata, nunca buena zarza* (or *caza*), an evil tree brings forth evil fruit; *saltar de la mata*, to come out from concealment; *seguir hasta la mata*, to follow to the bitter end.

matacabras, *n.m.* the north wind, especially when it is strong and cold.

matacallos, *n.m.* (*Chi., Ec.*) plant used for treating the corns or callousness of the feet.

matacán, *n.m.* dog-poison; old hare; (*bot.*) dog-bane; nux vomica; pebble, stone; deuce of clubs (in cards); troublesome or painful business; (*fort.*) machicolation gallery.

matacandelas, *n.m.* candle extinguisher, snuffer.

matacandil, *n.m.* (*prov.*) lobster.

matacía, *n.f.* (*prov.*) havoc, slaughter (of animals for food).

matachín, *n.m.* merry-andrew; jack-pudding; grotesque dance; slaughterman, butcher; laughing-stock; (*coll.*) a bully.

matadero, *n.m.* slaughterhouse; drudgery.

matador, *n.m.* slayer, murderer; card in the game of ombre; matador (bullfighter who kills the bull).

matador, -ra, *a.* killer, killing; mortal; murderous, homicidal.

matadora, *n.f.* murderess.

matadura, *n.f.* (*vet.*) harness-sore; gall; foolish, troublesome person.

matafuego, *n.m.* fire-engine, fire extinguisher, fireman.

matagallina, *n.f.* (*bot.*) flax-leaved daphne.

matahambre, *n.m.* (*Cub.*) marzipan; (*Arg.*) big portion of meat.

matahombres, *n.m.* black beetle with yellow stripes; oil beetle; Spanish fly, blister-fly.

matajudío, *n.m.* (*ichth.*) mullet.

matalahuga, matalahuva, *n.f.* (*bot.*) anise; aniseed.

matalobos, *n.m.* (*bot.*) wolf's-bane, aconite.

matalón, matalote, *n.m.* worn-out horse.

matalotaje, *n.m.* (*naut.*) ship's stores; heap of things jumbled together.

matanza, *n.f.* action of slaughtering; cattle to

be slaughtered; massacre, butchery, slaughter; (*coll.*) obstinacy, eagerness of pursuit.

matapalo, *n.m.* (*Am.*) tree yielding rubber and also a fibre for sackcloth.

mataperrada, *n.f.* boy's mischievous prank.

mataperros, *n.m.* (*coll.*) street urchin.

matapiojos, *n.m.* (*Col.*, *Chi.*) dragon fly.

matapolvo, *n.m.* light rain.

matapulgas, *n.f.* (*bot.*) round-leaved mint.

matar, *v.t.* to kill, slay, put to death, execute, murder, destroy; (*carp.*) to bevel, round; to put out (a light); to extinguish (a fire); to slake (lime); to spot (cards); to worry, vex, molest; to make a horse's back sore (of harness); (*art*) to subdue, tone down (a colour); to mat (metal); *matar el polvo*, to lay the dust; *estar a matar con uno*, to be at daggers drawn; *matar a pesadumbres*, (*coll.*) to break one's heart; *¡que me maten!* (*coll.*) I'll be flayed alive if it's not so! *matar de un golpe*, to kill with a blow on the head, etc.; *matar de hambre*, to famish, starve; *matar a uno a preguntas*, to ply a person with questions; *a mata caballo*, in the utmost hurry; *mátalas callando*, hypocrite, sly dog. — *v.r.* to commit suicide; to make great exertions; to be extremely troubled at the failure of something; to be saddle-galled (of horses); *matarse con otro*, to be at daggers drawn; *matarse por una cosa*, to do one's utmost to attain or accomplish something.

matarife, *n.m.* (*prov.*) slaughterman.

matarrata, *n.f.* game of cards.

matasanos, *n.m.* quack, charlatan; empiric.

matasapo, *n.m.* (*Chi.*) children's game.

matasellos, *n.m.* post-office cancellation stamp.

matasiete, *n.m.* bully, braggart, boaster.

mate, *n.m.* mate, checkmate; gold or silver painter's size; rough ore; (*bot.*) maté, Brazilian holly; Paraguay tea; vessel in which maté is made; gourd, vessel; *dar mate*, (*coll.*) to checkmate, to ridicule, laugh at; (*Mex.*) *entrar a mates*, to understand by signs.

mate, *a.* mat, dull, lustreless.

matear, *v.i.*, *v.r.* to shoot up, grow up (of wheat, etc.).

matemática, matemáticas, *n.f.* mathematics.

matemáticamente, *adv.* mathematically.

matemático, *n.m.* mathematician.

matemático, -ca, *a.* mathematical.

materia, *n.f.* matter, materials; subject-matter, cause, occasion, question considered, point discussed; copy for writing; (*med.*) matter, pus; *en materia de*, as regards; *primera materia*, raw material; *entrar en materia*, to plunge into a subject.

material, *a.* material, substantial; (*fig.*) rude, uncouth, ungenteel. — *n.m.* ingredient, stuff, materials; (*print.*) copy; *material rodante*, (*rail.*) rolling-stock.

materialidad, *n.f.* materiality, corporeity; coarseness, rudeness, incivility; literalness; outward appearance.

materialismo, *n.m.* materialism.

materialista, *n.m.f.* materialist.

materializar, *v.t.* to materialize; *v.r.* to become materialistic.

materialmente, *adv.* materially, corporeally.

maternal, *a.* maternal.

maternalmente, *adv.* maternally.

maternidad, *n.f.* maternity; *casa de maternidad*, maternity hospital.

materno, -na, *a.* maternal, motherly.

matero, -ra, *a.*, *n.* (*S. Am.*) maté drinker.

matigüelo, matihuelo, *n.m.* tumbler (a toy).

matinal, *a.* (*poet.*) matutinal, morning.

matiné, *n.m.* matinée.

matiz, *n.m.* shade of colour; tint, hue, shade; blending of colours.

matizado, -da, *a.* variegated. — *p.p.* [MATIZAR].

matizar, *v.t.* (conjugated like ALZAR) to embellish, adorn, variegate, mix colours with effect; to give a fine shade (of tone or meaning).

mato, *n.m.* brake, coppice.

matojo, *n.m.* bush; (*bot.*) glasswort; (*Cub.*) shoot, sucker, tiller.

matón, *n.m.* bully; noisy, quarrelsome fellow.

matorral, *n.m.* bushy or brambly place, thicket.

matoso, -sa, *a.* bushy, covered with bushes.

matraca, *n.f.* wooden rattle; (*coll.*) jest, contemptuous joke; coxcomb; *dar matraca*, to banter.

matraquear, *v.t.* to jest, mock, scoff, ridicule.

matraquista, *n.m.f.* wag, jester, punster.

matraz, *n.m.* (*chem.*) matrass, apothecaries' vessel.

matrería, *n.f.* cunning, sagacity, knowingness.

matrero, -ra, *a.* cunning, knowing, sagacious.

matrero, *n.m.* artful knave, cunning soldier.

matriarcado, *n.m.* matriarchate.

matricaria, *n.f.* (*bot.*) common feverfew.

matricida, *n.m.f.* matricide, murderer of one's mother.

matricidio, *n.m.* matricide, murder of a mother.

matrícula, *n.f.* register, list; matriculation; registration number (of a car, etc.); enrolment; *matrícula de mar*, mariner's register.

matriculado, -da, *a.* matriculate, matriculated. — *p.p.* [MATRICULAR].

matriculador, *n.m.* one who matriculates.

matricular, *v.t.* to matriculate, register, enrol; enter on a list.

matricularse, *v.r.* to register; to enter (a contest, etc.).

matrimonial, *a.* matrimonial, connubial, nuptial.

matrimonialmente, *adv.* matrimonially.

matrimoniar, *v.t.* (*joc.*) to marry.

matrimonio, *n.m.* marriage, matrimony; (*coll.*) married couple, husband or wife; *matrimonio ni señorío no quieren furia ni brío*, marry in haste, repent at leisure; *matrimonio rato*, legal marriage not consummated.

matriz, *n.f.* matrix, womb; (*mech.*) mould, matrix; die; nut, female screw; original draft of a writing; metropolitan or mother church; counterpart of a cheque-book; (*geol.*) matrix. — *a.* first, principal, chief; *lengua matriz*, mother tongue.

matrona, *n.f.* matron; midwife.

matronal, *a.* matronal.

matronaza, *n.f.* plump, respectable matron.

maturrango, -ga, *n.m.f.* (*S. Am.*) bad horseman; (*Chi.*) clumsy, rough person.

matusalén, *a.* old as Methuselah.

matute, *n.m.* smuggling, smuggled goods, contraband; gambling den.

matutear, *v.t.* to smuggle.

matutero, *n.m.f.* smuggler, contrabandist.

matutinal; matutino, -na, *a.* morning, belonging to the morning.

maula, *n.f.* frippery, rubbish, trifling thing;

something found in the street; drink-money; deceitful trickery; cunning, craft. — *n.m.f.* (*coll.*) cheat, bad payer; *buena maula*, (*coll.*) good-for-nothing fellow; hussy.

maulería, *n.f.* shop where remnants are sold; craft, cunning.

maulero, *n.m.* seller of remnants; impostor, swindler, cheat.

maulón, *n.m.* great cheat.

maullador, -ra, *a.* mewing, miauling (of a cat).

maullar, *v.i.* to miaow (of a cat).

maullido, maúllo, *n.m.* miaow.

mauraca, *n.f.* (*prov.*) roasting chestnuts over coals.

mauseolo, mausoleo, *n.m.* mausoleum.

máuser, *n.m.* Mauser rifle; *máuser español*, improved Mauser rifle manufactured in Spain.

mavorcio, -a, *a.* (*poet.*) belonging to war.

maxilar, *a.* maxillary.

máxima, *n.f.* maxim, axiom, sentence, apothegm, idea, thought; (*mus.*) large (four breves).

máximamente, *adv.* chiefly, principally.

máxime, *adv.* principally.

máximo, -ma, *a. superl.* chief, principal, very great.

máximum, *n.m.* maximum, extreme limit.

maya, *n.f.* (*bot.*) common daisy; may-queen; Maya (Yucatan Indian).

mayador, -ra, *n.m.f.* mewer. — *a.* mewing.

mayal, *n.m.* flail; lever in oil-mills.

mayar, *v.i.* to mew.

mayeto, *n.m.* mallet for paper-beating.

mayo, *n.m.* May; maypole; Mayday festivity.

mayólica, *n.f.* majolica ware.

mayonesa, *n.f.* mayonnaise.

mayor, *a. compar.* greater, greatest; larger, older, elder, eldest, senior; of age; main, principal; (*eccles.*) high (altar, mass); (*mus.*) major; (*math.*) sign >. — *n.m.* mayor, chief of a community, principal, superior; (*mil.*) major; (*naut.*) mainsail. — *n.f.* (*log.*) first proposition in a syllogism. — *pl.* **mayores**, ancestors, forefathers; superiors; *mayor* (or *mayor de edad*), of age; *ganado mayor*, cattle and larger beasts of burden; *por mayor*, wholesale, in the lump; summarily; *alzarse* (or *levantarse*) *a mayores*, to become proud, haughty; *papel de marca mayor*, royal paper.

mayora, *n.f.* mayoress.

mayoral, *n.m.* head shepherd, leader, overseer, steward; stage-driver.

mayoralía, *n.f.* flock, herd; herdsman's wages.

mayorana, *n.f.* (*bot.*) sweet marjoram.

mayorazga, *n.f.* woman, or wife of a person, having an entailed estate.

mayorazgo, *n.m.* right of succession vested in the first-born son of a family; first-born son with right of primogeniture; family estate falling to the first-born son; entailed estate.

mayorazguillo, -guito, *n.m.* small entailed estate.

mayorazguista, *n.m.* (*law*) author treating of entails.

mayordoma, *n.f.* steward's wife.

mayordomear, *v.t.* to manage or administer an estate.

mayordomía, *n.f.* administration, stewardship, controllership.

mayordomo, *n.m.* butler, steward, majordomo, superintendent, overseer, chief of servants.

mayoría, *n.f.* superiority, advantage, excellence; majority, largest part or proportion; full age, coming of age; major's commission.

mayoridad, *n.f.* superiority.

mayorista, *n.m.* student of the highest class in a grammar-school; wholesale merchant; wholesale trade.

mayormente, *adv.* principally, chiefly.

mayúscula, *n.f.*, *a.* capital, capital letter, large letter.

mayúsculo, -la, *a.* large, good-sized; important, prominent.

maza, *n.f.* war club, iron-shod stick; pile driver, drop hammer, mace; nave or hub of a wheel; drumstick of a bass drum; thick end of a billiard cue; roller of a sugar cane mill; something noisy tied to a dog's tail; engine; clog; beetle for flax or hemp; (*fig.*) importunate or troublesome fellow; pestle; something absurd; *la maza y la mona*, two close companions; *maza de Fraga*, martinet, authoritative person; *la maza de Fraga saca polvo debajo del agua*, importunity can work miracles.

mazacote, *n.m.* kali, barilla; concrete; dry, hard mass; (*coll.*) peevish person; (*Am.*) antimony.

mazada, *n.f.* blow with a mallet; offensive expression.

mazagatos, *n.m.* dispute, noise, contention.

mazamorra, *n.f.* bread-dust; bits, scraps; broken biscuit; (*Per.*) pap made of Indian corn with sugar or honey; (*Col.*) a thick corn soup; (*Arg.*) divided maize boiled with milk; (*naut.*) mess made of broken tack.

mazaneta, *n.f.* apple-shaped ornament in jewels.

mazapán, *n.m.* marzipan, marchpane.

mazar, *v.t.* (*prov.*) to churn (milk).

mazarí, *n.m.* tile-shaped brick.

mazarota, *n.f.* (*metal.*) deadhead.

mazmodina, *n.f.* a gold coin of the Spanish Moors.

mazmorra, *n.f.* dungeon.

maznar, *v.t.* to squeeze, press gently; to soften; to disjoin.

mazo, *n.m.* mallet, wooden hammer; bundle of things tied together; (*prov.*) clapper of a bell; importunate or troublesome person; *mazo de llaves*, bunch of keys.

mazonería, *n.f.* masonry, brickwork; relief-work.

mazorca, *n.f.* spindle full of thread; ear of corn; female spike of maize; (*Chi.*) a clique forming a despotic government.

mazorral, *a.* rude, uncouth, clownish; (*print.*) solid.

mazorralmente, *adv.* clownishly, rudely.

mazote, *n.m.* cement, mortar; blockhead.

mazotear, *v.t.* to strike with a club or mallet.

me, *pron. acc. dat.* me, to me.

mea, *n.f.* word used by children wishing to make water.

meada, *n.f.* quantity of urine passed; urine stain or marks.

meadero, *n.m.* place for making water.

meaja, *n.f.* ancient coin; embryo in white of egg; (*law*) execution dues.

meajuela, *n.f.* small piece attached to the bits of a bridle.

meandro, *n.m.* meander; (*arch.*) maze scroll-work; intricate ornamentation.

meaperros, *n.m.* (*bot.*) stinking goose-foot.

mear, *v.i.* to urinate, make water.

meato, *n.m.* (*med.*) passage, conduit, pore; (*anat.*) meatus.

meauca, *n.f.* (*orn.*) a kind of sea gull.

meca, *n.f.; casa de meca,* house of noise and confusion; *andar de ceca en meca,* to go from pillar to post, wander about.

mecánica, *n.f.* mechanics; (*coll.*) mean action; (*mil.*) management of soldiers' affairs.

mecánicamente, *adv.* mechanically; meanly, sordidly.

mecánico, -ca, *a.* mechanical; machine-made or operated; power-driven; mean, servile. — *n.m.* mechanic, craftsman, artisan; motor-car driver.

mecanismo, *n.m.* mechanism, mechanical action.

mecanografía, *n.f.* the art of typewriting.

mecanografiar, *v.t.* to typewrite, type.

mecanográfico, -ca, *a.* typewritten; relating to typewriting.

mecanógrafo, -fa, *n.m.f.* typist.

mecapal, *n.f.* (*Mex.*) leather band with ropes used by porters.

mecate, *n.m.* (*Mex., Hond., Philip.*) maguey-rope.

mecatito, *n.m.* small cord, string, twine.

mecedero, mecedor, *n.m.* stirrer.

mecedor, -ra, *n.m.f.* rocker; rocking-chair.

mecedura, *n.f.* act of rocking.

mecenas, *n.m.* a patron of art or literature.

mecer, *v.t.* to stir, mix, agitate, jumble, shake, dandle; rock.

mecereón, *n.m.* (*bot.*) mezereon.

meco, -ca, *a.* (*Mex.*) blackish red, copper-coloured.—*n.m.f.* (*Mex.*) wild Indian.

meconio, *n.m.* meconium of children; poppy juice.

mecha, *n.f.* wick, fuse, match, match-rope; roll of lint; bacon for larding; lock of hair; bundle of threads; *alargar la mecha,* to augment a salary, extend time for credit.

mechar, *v.t.* to lard, force, stuff.

mechazo, *n.m.* (*min.*) fizzle of a blast fuse.

mechera, *n.f.* larding-pin; shoplifter.

mechero, *n.m.* tube for lamp-wick; candle-stick-socket; lamp burner; gas burner; cigar-ette lighter.

mechinal, *n.m.* columbarium; putlog hole.

mechita, *n.f.* small wick, small match.

mechoacán, *n.m.* (*bot.*) bindweed.

mechón, *n.m.* large match, lock, wick or bundle of threads.

mechoso, -sa, *a.* full of wicks or matches.

medalla, *n.f.* medal; (*sculpt.*) round or oval target; (*coll.*) gold coin.

medallón, *n.m.* medallion, locket; round or oval bas-relief.

médano, medaño, *n.m.* sand-bank, mound of sand.

medero, *n.m.* (*prov.*) collection of vine-shoots.

media, *n.f.* stocking, sock; *media diferencial,* arithmetical mean; *media proporcional,* geo-metrical mean, mean proportional.

mediacaña, *n.f.* (*arch.*) fluted moulding; picture moulding; (*carp.*) gouge; half-round file; curling tongs.

mediación, *n.f.* mediation, interposition, intervention, intercession; (*mus.*) double-bar; nearest distance of one thing from another.

mediado, -da, *a.* half, half-content; *pedir sobrado por salir con lo mediado,* ask for twice what you expect to receive.

mediador, *n.m.; ***mediadora,** *n.f.* mediator, intercessor.

mediados (a), *adv.* in or about the middle of.

mediana, *n.f.* long billiard cue; top of a fish-ing rod; (*geom.*) median.

medianamente, *adv.* moderately, middlingly, meanly.

medianejo, -ja, *a.* (*coll.*) worse than mediocre.

medianería, *n.f.* moiety; partition-wall; bounds or limits of contiguous things.

medianero, -ra, *a.* intermediate, partitioning; interceding, mediating, mediatory.

medianero, *n.m.* mediator, go-between; owner of a house having a common wall.

medianía, medianidad, *n.f.* moderation, moderateness; mediocrity, middle state, mean.

medianil, *a.* (*agric.*) middle-piece of ground; (*print.*) crossbar of a chase.

medianista, *n.m.* student of the fourth class in grammar schools.

mediano, -na, *a.* moderate, mediocre, mid-dling.

medianoche, *n.f.* midnight; small meat pie.

mediante, *adv.* by virtue of, by means of. — *a.* mediating, intervening.

mediar, *v.i.* to be at the middle, come to the middle; to intercede, mediate, intervene; *si no mediara su respeto,* but for the respect due to him.

mediatamente, *adv.* mediately.

mediatizar, *v.t.* to mediatize.

mediato, -ta, *a.* mediate.

mediator, *n.m.* ombre, a card game.

médica, *n.f.* doctor's wife; female physician.

medicable, *a.* curable, medicable.

medicación, *n.f.* medical treatment, medica-tion.

medicamento, *n.m.* medicament, medicine, physic.

medicar, *v.t.* (conjugated like BUSCAR) to cure by medicine, administer medicine.

medicastro, *n.m.* quack, empiric.

medicina, *n.f.* physic, medicine; art of heal-ing.

medicinal, *a.* medicinal, healing.

medicinante, *n.m.* medical student who prac-tises before taking his final degree.

medicinar, *v.t.* to medicine, administer medi-cines, apply medicaments.

medición, *n.f.* measurement, mensuration.

médico, *n.m.* physician, bachelor of medicine.

médico, -ca, *a.* medical, medicinal.

medicucho, *n.m.* quack, charlatan; indiffer-ent physician.

medida, *n.f.* measure, gauge, standard, mea-surement, mensuration, height, length, or breadth measured; proportion, correspon-dence, relation; means; moderation, pru-dence; measuring stick or rule; *a medida de,* according to; *a medida de su paladar,* to his heart's content; *a medida que,* according as, in proportion; *llenar* (or *henchir*) *las medidas,* to express a candid opinion; *tomar sus medidas,* to take the measure (of a task, etc.); *llenarse la medida,* to drain a cup of sorrow.

medidamente, *adv.* moderately.

medidor, -ra, *n.m.f.* measurer; *n.m.* (*Am.*) meter for gas, water or electricity.

mediera, *n.f.* girl or woman stocking-maker.

mediero, *n.m.* hosier, stocking-dealer, stocking-maker; co-partner in farming or ranch.

medieval, medioeval, *a.* medieval.

medio, -dia, *a.* half, part; *medio borracho,* tipsy; *medio día,* noon, midday; *media noche,* midnight; *a medio nao,* (*naut.*) midships; *a medias,* by halves; *ir a medias,* to go halves.

medio, *n.m.* middle, centre; measure, expedient, method, way, means, instrument, medium; twin. — *pl.* **medios,** means, income, revenue, fortune; *a medias,* fairly, half, half and half; *atrasado de medios,* of small (*or* diminished) means; *de medio a medio,* half and half, in the middle; *en medio,* in the middle, midway, nevertheless, notwithstanding; *echar por en medio,* to take a way right out of a difficulty; *de por medio,* half, half and half; *estar de por medio,* to intervene, interpose; *quitar de en medio,* to remove, take out of the way.

mediocre, *a.* middling, mean, mediocre, moderate.

mediocridad, *n.f.* mediocrity, middle state, small degree.

mediodía, *n.m.* noon, midday, noonday, noontide; meridian; south, south wind.

mediopaño, *n.m.* thin woollen cloth.

mediquillo, *n.m.* (*Philip.*) medicine man.

medir, *v.t.* (*pres. indic.* **mido**; *pres. subj.* **mida**; *pret.* **él midió**) to measure, ascertain or determine measure; to compare, estimate, examine. — *v.r.* to be moderate, restrained; to act prudently; *medir el suelo,* (*coll.*) to fall flat on the ground.

meditabundo, -da, *a.* pensive, thoughtful, musing.

meditación, *n.f.* meditation, cogitation, contemplation, deep thought.

meditar, *v.t.* to meditate, contemplate, consider, cogitate, muse.

meditativo, -va, *a.* meditative.

mediterráneo, -nea, *a.* mediterranean, midland, encircled with land.

médium, *n.m.* spiritualistic medium.

medo, -da, *n.m.f.,* *a.* Mede.

medra, *n.f.* proficiency, progress, improvement, melioration.

medrar, *v.i.* to thrive, prosper, improve, grow rich, get on in the world.

medriñaque, *n.m.* (*Philip.*) stuff for lining and stiffening women's skirts; short skirt.

medros, *n.m.pl.* progress, improvement.

medrosamente, *adv.* timorously, faintly, fearfully.

medroso, -sa, *a.* fearful, timorous, fainthearted, cowardly, terrible, inspiring fear.

medula, médula, *n.f.* marrow, medulla, substance, essence.

medular, *a.* medullar, medullary.

meduloso, -sa, *a.* full of marrow, marrowish.

medusa, *n.f.* (*ichth.*) medusa, jellyfish.

mefítico, -ca, *a.* mephitic, mephitical.

megáfono, *n.m.* megaphone.

megalítico, -ca, *a.* megalithic.

megalito, *n.m.* megalith.

megalomanía, *n.f.* megalomania.

megalómano, -na, *a.* megalomaniac.

mégano, *n.m.* dune.

mego, -ga, *a.* gentle, peaceful, mild, meek.

megohmio, *n.m.* (*elec.*) megohm.

mehala, *n.f.* (*Morocco*) corps of regular troops.

mejana, *n.f.* islet in the middle of a river.

mejicanismo, *n.m.* phrase or word peculiar to Mexico.

mejicano, *n.m.* Mexican.

Méjico, *n.m.* Mexico.

mejido, -da, *a.* beaten up with sugar and water (of eggs).

mejilla, *n.f.* cheek.

mejillón, mijillón, *n.m.* sea mussel.

mejor, *a.* *comp.* of *bueno,* better; best. — *adv. comp.* of *bien,* more exactly, rather; *a lo mejor,* probably, in all probability; *mejor que mejor,* much better; *lo mejor,* the best; *el mejor día,* some fine day; *tanto mejor,* so much the better; *llevar lo mejor,* to get the best of something; *mejor postor,* highest bidder; *mejor dicho,* rather, more exactly.

mejora, *n.f.* improvement, melioration, addition, growth; appeal to a superior court; higher bid; (*law*) special bequest to a lawful heir.

mejorable, *a.* improvable.

mejoramiento, *n.m.* improvement, melioration.

mejorana, *n.f.* sweet marjoram.

mejorar, *v.t.* to improve, meliorate, heighten cultivate, mend; to outbid, bid above; (*law*) to leave to an heir a special bequest. — *v.i.* to recover, get well. — *v.r.* to grow better, improve.

mejoría, *n.f.* improvement, mending, bettering, melioration; repairs; advantage, superiority.

mejunje, *n.m.* medical mixture, stuff.

melada, *n.f.* toast dipped in honey.

melado, -da, *a.* honey-coloured. — *p.p.* [MELAR]. — *n.m.* cane-juice syrup; honey-cake.

meladucha, *n.f.* coarse, mealy apple.

meladura, *n.f.* (*Am.*) treacle; concentrated syrup.

melampo, *n.m.* (*theat.*) prompter's candle with shade.

melancolía, *n.f.* melancholia, melancholy, gloom, gloominess, low spirits, depression.

melancólico, -ca, *a.* melancholic, sad, gloomy, cloudy, mournful, fanciful, hypochondriacal.

melancolizar, *v.t.* (conjugated like ALZAR) to affect with melancholy, dispirit, make gloomy or dejected.

melandro, *n.m.* (*zool.*) badger.

melanesio, -sia, *n.m.f.,* *a.* Melanesian.

melanita, *n.f.* (*min.*) melanite.

melanosis, *n.f.* (*med.*) melanosis, black cancer.

melapia, *n.f.* kind of pippin.

melar, *v.t.* to reboil juice (in sugar making); to deposit honey (said of bees).

melaza, *n.f.* (*prov.*) dregs of honey; molasses.

melcocha, *n.f.* molasses; honey-cake.

melcochero, *n.m.* honey-cake-maker.

melele, *a.* foolish, silly.

melena, *n.f.* dishevelled hair; fore-top (of a horse's mane); covering put on foreheads of oxen; (*med.*) melaena, intestinal hæmorrhage; *traer a la melena,* to compel one against his will.

melenera, *n.f.* crown of oxen's head; fleecy skin put under a yoke.

melenudo, -da, *a.* hairy, with bushy hair.

melera, *n.f.* state of melons spoiled by rain or hail; (*bot.*) alkanet, bugloss.

melero, *n.m.* dealer in honey; place for preservation of honey.

melesa, *n.f.* candle-wood.

melgacho, *n.m.* dog-fish.

melgar, *n.m.* patch of wild alfalfa.

melgarejo, *n.m.* helmsman's post.

mélico, -ca, *a.* lyrical, melic.

melífero, -ra, *a.* (*poet.*) honey-producing.

melificado, -da, *a.* mellifluous. — *p.p.* [ME-LIFICAR].

melificar, *v.t., v.i.* to make honey (of bees).

melifluamente, *adv.* mellifluently.

melifluidad, *n.f.* mellifluence, delicacy, suavity.

melifluo, -flua, *a.* mellifluous, mellifluent, honey-mouthed, flowing with honey.

meliloto, *n.m.* bird's foot trefoil; melilot.

melindre, *n.f.* honey fritters; lady-finger; prudery, affectedness, over-nicety, fastidiousness.

melindrear, *v.i.* to act the prude.

melindrero, -ra, *a.* prudish, affectedly grave, fastidious.

melindroso, -sa, *a.* prudish, precise, finical, over-nice, over-formal, fastidious, dainty, particular.

melinita, *n.f.* melinite.

melisa, *n.f.* bee balm (*Melissa officinalis*).

melocotón, *n.m.* peach, peach-tree.

melocotonero, *n.m.* peach-tree; vendor of peaches.

melodía, *n.f.* melody, melodiousness, sweetness of sound.

melodiosamente, *adv.* melodiously, harmoniously.

melodioso, -sa, *a.* melodious, musical, harmonious.

melodrama, *n.m.* melodrama.

melodramático, -ca, *a.* melodramatic.

meloe, *n.m.* meloe, oil-beetle.

melografía, *n.f.* art of writing music.

meloja, *n.f.* metheglin, mead.

melojo, *n.m.* a variety of white oak.

melomanía, *n.f.* melomania, music-mania.

melón, *n.m.* melon, musk-melon; *catar el melón,* to sound, pump; *decentar el melón,* to run risk of loss, be in for it; *el melón y el casamiento ha de ser acertamiento,* choose a wife and a melon with great care.

melonar, *n.m.* field or bed of melons.

meloncillo, *n.m.* a kind of mongoose.

melonero, -ra, *n.m.f.* rearer of melons, melonseller.

melosidad, *n.f.* honey-sweetness, lusciousness; meekness, gentleness.

meloso, -sa, *a.* mellow, honeyed, gentle, mild, pleasing.

melote, *n.m.* dregs of molasses; (*prov.*) honey preserves.

melsa, *n.f.* (*prov.*) phlegm, slowness.

mella, *n.f.* hollow, crack, notch in edged tools; dent, indentation; gap, empty space; *hacer mella,* to leave an impression on someone's mind.

mellado, -da, *a.* notched, hacked; toothless, wanting teeth. — *p.p.* [MELLAR].

mellar, *v.t.* to hack, notch, cut in small grooves; to deprive of lustre; *mellar la honra,* to wound one's honour.

melliza, *n.f.* kind of sausage made with honey.

mellizo, -za, *a.* twin.

mellón, *n.m.* handful of straw used as a torch.

membrado, -da, *a.* (*her.*) membered.

membrana, *n.f.* membrane, thin skin, caul.

membranáceo, -cea, *a.* membranaceous.

membranoso, -sa, *a.* membraneous, filmy.

membrete, *n.m.* short note, annotation, memorandum, card of invitation; address; letter-head; heading.

membrilla, *n.f.* quince-bud.

membrillar, *n.m.* plantation of quince-trees.

membrillero, *n.m.* quince-tree.

membrillo, *n.m.* quince; quince-tree; *crecerá el membrillo, y mudará el pelillo,* time improves many things.

membrudamente, *adv.* robustly, strongly.

membrudo, -da, *a.* strong, robust, corpulent; membered.

memela, *n.f.* (*Hond.*) omelet of maize and sugar wrapped with fresh leaves of banana; (*Mex.*) thin omelet of maize.

memo, -ma, *a.* silly, foolish; *hacer memo,* to pretend not to understand.

memorable; memorando, -da, *a.* memorable, notable, famous.

memorablemente, *adv.* memorably.

memorándum, *n.m.* memorandum, note-book; diplomatic note.

memorar, *v.t.* to remember, record, mention.

memoratísimo, -ma, *a. superl.* worthy of eternal memory.

memoria, *n.f.* memory, recollection, reminiscence; fame, glory; memorial, memoir, record, dissertation; anniversary; bill, account; memorandum; codicil; *encomendar a la memoria,* to commit to memory, learn by heart; *hacer memoria,* to put in mind; *de memoria,* by heart; *hablar de memoria,* to talk at random; *huirse de la memoria,* to slip one's memory; *recorrer la memoria,* to ransack one's memory, endeavour to remember. — *pl.* **memorias,** compliments, expressions of civility; memoirs; memorandum-book; rings used as reminders.

memorial, *n.m.* memorial; brief; memorandum book.

memorialista, *n.m.* amanuensis.

memorión, *n.m.* strong memory.

memorioso, -sa, *a.* retentive (of the memory); mindful.

mena, *n.f.* (*naut.*) girt of cordage; (*ichth.*) small sea-fish; ball-gauge; (*min.*) ore; (*Philip.*) size and shape of a cigar.

ménade, *n.f.* bacchante; frenzied woman.

menador, -ra, *n.m.f.* (*prov.*) winder (of silk).

menaje, *n.m.* furniture, movables, house-stuff.

menar, *v.t.* (*prov.*) to wind (silk); (*coll.*) to contemplate.

mención, *n.f.* mention, recital, account.

mencionar, *v.t.* to mention, name.

mendicación, *n.f.* begging, asking charity.

mendicante, *a.* mendicant, begging. — *n.m.* mendicant, beggar.

mendicidad, *n.f.* mendicity, mendicancy, beggary.

mendigante, -ta, *n.m.f.* mendicant, beggar.

mendigar, *v.t.* (*pret.* **mendigué;** *pres. subj.* **mendigue**) to ask charity, beg, mendicate, live upon alms; crave, entreat.

mendigo, *n.m.* beggar.

mendiguez, *n.f.* beggary, indigence, mendicancy.

mendosamente, *adv.* falsely, erroneously.

mendoso, -sa, *a.* false, mendacious.

mendrugo, *n.m.* broken bread given to beggars.

mendruguillo, *n.m.* crumb of bread.

meneador, -ra, *n.m.f.* mover, manager, director.

menear, *v.t.* to move from place to place; to stir, shake; to wag, waggle; to direct, manage. — *v.r.* to be active, brisk; to stir oneself; to wriggle, waddle; *menear las manos,* to work expertly; to fight; *será mejor no menear el arroz, aunque se pegue,* better not stir the rice, even though it sticks.

meneo, *n.m.* shake, shaking; wriggling, waddling; (*obs.*) trade, business; (*coll.*) drubbing, beating.

menester, *n.m.* need, necessity, want, wanting; employment, business, office, occupation, implement. — *pl.* **menesteres,** bodily necessities; implements, tools of trade; *haber* (or *ser) menester,* to be wanting, necessary; *ser menester la cruz y los ciriales,* much diligence and care are necessary; *todo es menester: migar y sorber,* not the smallest detail should be omitted.

menesteroso, -sa, *a.* needy, necessitous.

menestra, *n.f.* pottage; vegetable soup served in barracks and jails.

menestral, *n.m.* mechanic, tradesman, handicraftsman, workman.

menestrete, *n.m.* (*naut.*) nail puller.

menfita, *n.m.f.,* *a.* native of Memphis; *n.f.* (*min.*) onyx.

mengajo, *n.m.* (*prov.*) rag, tatter.

mengano, -na, *n.m.f.* such a one, so-and-so (used with *fulano* or *zutano* in a sense of Tom, Dick and Harry).

mengua, *n.f.* diminution, waning, decrease; decay, decline; poverty, need, indigence; disgrace.

menguadamente, *adv.* ignominiously.

menguado, -da, *a.* coward, mean-spirited fellow; fool; avaricious man; decrease, narrowing of stockings in knitting.

menguado, -da, *a.* impaired, diminished, stunted; cowardly, weak-spirited; *hora menguada,* fatal moment. — *p.p.* [MENGUAR].

menguante, *n.f.* ebb-tide, low water, neap-tide; decline, decay; decrease of the moon.

menguar, *v.i.* to decline, decay, fall off; to be deficient; to decrease; to narrow stockings.

mengue, *n.m.* (*coll.*) deuce, devil.

meniantes, *n.m.* (*bot.*) marsh-trefoil.

menina, *n.f.* young lady-in-waiting.

meningitis, *n.f.* (*med.*) meningitis.

menino, *n.m.* royal page; (*prov.*) affected little boy.

menique, *n.m.* little finger. — *a.* of the little finger.

menisco, *n.m.* (*phys.*) meniscus.

menologio, *n.m.* menology.

menopausia, *n.f.* (*med.*) menopause, change of life in women.

menor, *n.m.f.* minor; minorite, Franciscan friar or nun; (*log.*) minor premise; (*mus.*) minor; (*arch.*) small block. — *pl.* **menores,** minor orders.

menor, *a. compar.* of *pequeño;* less, smaller, minor, younger; *menor edad,* minority, under age; *por menor,* in small parts, minutely, by retail.

Menorca, *n.f.* Minorca.

menorete (al), *a.* (*coll.*) at least.

menoría, *n.f.* inferiority, subordination; under age.

menorquín, -ina, *a.* of or belonging to Minorca.

menos, *adv.,* less, except, with the exception of; least, but, barring; (*arith.*) the minus sign (—); *a lo menos* (or *por lo menos*), at least, however; *ni más ni menos,* exactly, neither more nor less; *poco más o menos,* roughly, more or less; *venir a menos,* to decay, grow worse; *a menos que,* unless.

menoscabador, -ra, *n.m.f.* detractor, lessener.

menoscabar, *v.t.* to lessen, impair, make worse, reduce, deteriorate; to defame.

menoscabo, *n.m.* deterioration, diminution, loss.

menoscuenta, *n.f.* discount.

menospreciable, *a.* despicable, contemptible.

menospreciador, -ra, *n.m.f.* contemner, despiser.

menospreciar, *v.t.* to undervalue, underrate; to despise, contemn, overlook, neglect, make light of.

menosprecio, *n.m.* contempt, scorn; undervaluing; neglect, contumely.

mensaje, *n.m.* message, errand, dispatch; petition; official communication.

mensajería, *n.f.* carrier van; steamship line.

mensajero, -ra, *n.m.f.* messenger; (*naut.*) bull's-eye traveller; secretary-bird; *mensajero frío, tarda mucho y vuelve vacío,* take pains with a piece of business or it may turn out badly.

menstruación, *n.f.* menstruation.

menstrual, *a.* menstrual.

menstruar, *v.i.* to menstruate.

menstruo, *n.m.* menses; (*chem.*) menstruum.

menstruo, -rua, *a.* menstruous, monthly, menstrual.

mensual, *a.* monthly.

mensualidad, *n.f.* monthly salary, month's pay.

mensualmente, *adv.* monthly.

ménsula, *n.f.* (*arch.*) bracket; rest for the elbows.

mensura, *n.f.* measure.

mensurabilidad, *n.f.* mensurability.

mensurador, -ra, *n.m.f.* meter, measurer.

mensural, *a.* measuring.

menta, *n.f.* (*bot.*) mint; peppermint.

mentado, -da, *a.* famous, renowned, celebrated. — *p.p.* [MENTAR].

mental, *a.* mental, intellectual, ideal.

mentalmente, *adv.* mentally, intellectually, ideally.

mentar, *v.t.* to mention, record.

mente, *n.f.* mind, understanding, will, disposition, intellect; sense, meaning; *de buena mente,* with good will; *tener en la mente,* to have in one's mind, to consider carefully.

mentecatería, *n.f.* folly, absurdity, nonsense.

mentecatez, *n.f.* silliness, foolishness.

mentecato, -ta, *a.* silly, foolish, stupid, crackbrained. — *n.m.f.* fool.

mentidero, *n.m.* (*coll.*) tattling corner.

mentir, *v.t., v.i.* (*pres. indic.* **miento;** *pret.* él **mintió;** *pres. subj.* **mienta**) to lie, equivocate, prevaricate, be misleading, utter untruths; to disappoint, deceive, frustrate; to gainsay, retract; to falsify; to fail to keep one's word or promise; *mentir sin suelo,* to lie

brazenly; *el mentir pide memoria*, a good liar
needs a good memory; *miente más que departe*
(or *habla*), he will lie as soon as look at you;
quien siempre me miente, nunca me engaña, the
liar is never believed, not even when he
speaks the truth.

mentira, *n.f.* lie, untruth, falsehood, mendacity; error, mistake in writing; (*coll.*)
white spot on the nails; *coger en mentira*, to
catch out in a lie; *decir mentira por sacar
verdad*, to feign knowledge to draw out
another person; *la mentira no tiene pies*, (or
la mentira presto es vencida), the liar is soon
found out; *parece mentira*, it hardly seems
possible.

mentirilla, *n.f.* falsehood told in jest; *de
mentirillas*, in jest.

mentirón, *n.m.* great lie.

mentirosamente, *adv.* falsely, lyingly, deceitfully.

mentirosito, -ta, *a.* somewhat false or deceitful; (*coll.*) little fibber.

mentiroso, -sa, *a.* lying, mendacious, erroneous, equivocal, incorrect; deceptive, deceitful; full of errors or misprints; *más presto se
coge al mentiroso que al cojo*, the liar is easily
found out.

mentís, *n.m.* 'you lie!' — an abusive word.

mentol, *n.m.* (*pharm.*) menthol.

mentón, *n.m.* (*anat.*) the chin.

mentor, *n.m.* guide, counsellor, mentor.

menudamente, *adv.* minutely, particularly.

menudear, *v.t.* to repeat, detail minutely. —
v.i. to relate little things; (*com.*) to sell by
retail.

menudencia, *n.f.* trifle, littleness, minuteness,
minute accuracy. — *pl.* **menudencias**,
small matters; offal of young pigs; pork
sausages.

menudeo, *n.m.* act of repeating minutely;
retail.

menudero, -ra, *n.m.f.* dealer in tripes, giblets,
etc.

menudico, -ica; -ito, -ita, *a.* somewhat small.

menudillo, *n.m.* extremities of animals. —
pl. **menudillos**, giblets of fowls.

menudo, -da, *a.* small, minute, slender;
valueless, worthless, trifling, mean, miserable,
vulgar, common. — *adv. a menudo*, repeatedly,
frequently, continually, often; *por menudo*,
minutely, by retail.

menudo, *n.m.* intestines, viscera; tithe of
minor produce and fruits; copper coin,
small change.

menura, *n.f.* lyre-bird.

meñique, *a.* relating to the little finger of the
hand; very small.

meollada, *n.f.* (*prov.*) fry of animals' brains.

meollar, *n.m.* (*naut.*) spun yarn.

meollo, *n.m.* marrow; judgment, understanding; crumb of bread; substance, essential
part; brains.

meón, -ona, *a.* continually making water.

meona, *n.f.* (*coll.*) newly-born girl-child.

meple, *n.m.* (*bot.*) maple; *meple moteado*,
bird's-eye maple.

mequetrefe, *n.m.* insignificant fellow, coxcomb, jackanapes.

meramente, *adv.* merely, solely.

merar, *v.t.* to mix liquors; to mix wine with
water.

merca, *n.f.* (*coll.*) purchase.

mercachifle, *n.m.* pedlar, hawker.

mercadantesco, -ca, *a.* mercantile.

mercadear, *v.i.* to traffic, trade.

mercader, mercadante, *n.m.* dealer, trader,
shopkeeper.

mercadera, *n.f.* shopkeeper's wife, tradeswoman.

mercadería, *n.f.* merchandise, commodity;
trade, trading; goods.

mercado, *n.m.* market, mart, market-place;
poder vender en un buen mercado, to be very
astute and cunning.

mercaduría, *n.f.* merchandise, trade.

mercal, *n.m.* ancient Spanish copper coin.

mercancía, *n.f.* trade, traffic; merchandise,
goods.

mercante, *n.m.*, *a.* dealer, trader; trading,
mercantile, commercial.

mercantil, *a.* commercial, mercantile, merchant-like.

mercantilismo, *n.m.* mercantilism, commer-
cialism.

mercantilmente, *adv.* in a commercial or
mercantile manner.

merced, *n.f.* wages; gift, favour, grace, mercy;
will, pleasure; grant, favour; courteous
appellation given to untitled persons, as
vuestra (or *vuesa*) *merced*, your honour, your
grace, your worship, sir; religious and
military order founded by James I the
Conqueror and St. Pedro Nolasco; *estar a
merced de otro*, to be at another's expense;
hágame Vd. la merced, do me the favour; *no
estoy hoy para mercedes*, I am not in a generous mood; *entre merced y señoría*, medium,
neither very good nor very bad; *merced a*,
thanks to; *muchas mercedes*, many thanks.

mercenario, *n.m.* day-labourer, mercenary,
hireling.

mercenario, -ria, *a.* mercenary, hired, hireling; said of a military member, a friar or
nun in the order of *la Merced*.

mercería, *n.f.* haberdasher's trade; (*S. Am.*)
dry-goods store.

mercero, *n.m.* mercer, haberdasher.

merculino, -na; mercurino, -na, (*obs.*) *a.*
belonging to Wednesday.

mercurial, *a.*, *n.m.* mercurial; (*bot.*) mercury,
allgood.

mercúrico, -ca, *a.* mercuric.

mercurio, *n.m.* mercury, quicksilver; (*astron.*)
Mercury.

mercurioso, -sa, *a.* mercurous.

merchante, *n.m.*, *a.* merchant; jobber.

merdellón, -ona, *a.* (*coll.*) slovenly, dirty,
unclean (of a servant).

merdoso, -sa, *a.* nasty, filthy.

mere, *adv.* merely.

merecedor, -ra, *n.m.f.* one deserving reward
or punishment.

merecer, *v.t.*, *v.i.* (*pres. indic.* **merezco**;
pres. subj. **merezca**) to deserve, merit, owe,
be indebted for; to do anything deserving
reward or reproof; *merecer el trabajo*, to be
worth the trouble.

merecidamente, *adv.* worthily, meritoriously, condignly.

merecido, -da, *a.* meritorious, worthy, condign. — *p.p.* [MERECER].

merecido, *n.m.* condign punishment.

merecimiento, *n.m.* merit, desert.

merendar, *v.i.* (*pres. indic.* **meriendo**; *pres.*

subj. **meriende**) to have lunch, to take a collation; to pry into another's work or writings. — *v.t.* to take a collation, have lunch; to anticipate, be in advance of.

merendero, -ra, *a.* picking up seeds (of birds). — *n.m.* lunch-room, tea-garden.

merendilla, *n.f.* light lunch.

merendona, *n.f.* magnificent or abundant collation.

merengue, *n.m.* kiss, meringue; sugar-plum; (*Am.*) slender or delicate person.

meretricio, -cia, *a.* meretricious, lustful.

meretricio, *n.m.* carnal sin.

meretriz, *n.f.* strumpet.

merey, *n.f.* cashew-tree.

merezco; merezca, *pres. indic.; pres. subj.* [MERECER.]

mergo, *n.m.* (*orn.*) diver.

meridiana, *n.f.* meridional line; *a la meridiana,* at midday, noon.

meridiano, -na, *a.* meridional (section, cut); meridian; *n.m.* meridian.

meridional, *a.* southern, southernly, meridional.

merienda, *n.f.* luncheon, collation; (*coll.*) humpback.

meriendo; meriende, *pres. indic.; pres. subj.* [MERENDAR.]

merino, *n.m.* shepherd of merino sheep; merino wool; merino cloth; royal judge; superintendent of sheepwalks.

merino, -na, *a.* applied to sheep with thick, curled hair.

meritísimo, -ma, *a. sup.* of *mérito,* most worthy.

mérito, *n.m.* merit, deserts, virtue, excellence.

meritoriamente, *adv.* meritoriously.

meritorio, -ria, *a.* meritorious; employee who begins with a small or no salary; emeritus.

merla, *n.f.* blackbird.

merlín, *n.m.* (*naut.*) marline; magician; *saber más que Merlín,* to be very shrewd or knowing.

merlón, *n.m.* (*fort.*) merlon.

merluza, *n.f.* cod, hake.

merma, *n.f.* waste, leakage; decrease.

mermar, *v.i.* to waste, diminish, lessen, dwindle; wear away, shrink. — *v.t.* to take away, reduce.

mermelada, *n.f.* jam, preserves; *brava mermelada,* (*com.*) a fine hodge-podge.

mero, -ra, *a.* mere, pure, simple, naked; (*Mex.*) proper, same.

mero, *n.m.* kind of halibut; a variety of Mediterranean sea bass.

merodeador, *n.m.* marauder, pillager.

merodear, *v.i.* to pillage, maraud.

merodeo, *n.m.* act of pillaging.

merodista, *n.m.* pillager, marauder.

mes, *n.m.* month; menses, courses; monthly wages; *al mes,* by the month (*or* in a month's time); *caer en el mes del obispo,* to arrive opportunely; *cuando un mes demedia, a otro semeja,* as one month ends, so the next begins (of weather); *meses mayores,* last months of pregnancy; months immediately preceding harvest.

mesa, *n.f.* table; table-land, plateau; landing of a staircase; (*print.*) case of type; fare, viands; set, rubber of cards; truck-table; flat (of a sword, etc.); communion table; executive board; business section of a public office; rents of cathedrals, churches, prelates, or dignitaries in Spain; billiard table; billiard game; facet of a crystal, cut diamond or other gem; *mesa de cambios,* bank; *mesas de guarnición,* (*naut.*) channels; *mesa franca,* open table; *media mesa,* servants' table; *mesa de milanos,* scanty table; *mesa redonda,* table d'hôte; round table; *levantar* (or *alzar*) *la mesa,* to clear the table; *a mesa puesta,* without trouble or expense; *sentarse a mesa puesta,* to live at others' expense; *tener buena mesa,* to keep a good table; *dar la mesa,* to invite to share one's table; *estar a mesa y mantel de,* to share meals daily with; *ni mesa que se ande, ni piedra en el escarpe,* avoid all that is uncertain and unstable; *ni mesa sin pan, ni ejército sin capitán,* the principal item is essential; *mesa de Ampère,* Ampère's stand.

mesada, *n.f.* monthly pay, allowance, wages, stipend.

mesadura, *n.f.* tearing the hair.

mesana, *n.f.* (*naut.*) mizen-mast.

mesar, *v.t.* to pluck off the hair with the hands.

mescal, mexcal, *n.m.* (*Mex.*) liquor made of *maguey.*

mescolanza, *n.f.* medley; mess, jumble.

meseguería, *n.f.* guard over fruits; money paid for watching the harvest.

meseguero, *n.m.* keeper of harvested grain; (*prov.*) guard of vineyard.

meseguero, -ra, *a.* of or relating to harvested grain or fruits.

mesentérico, -ca, *a.* mesenteric.

mesenterio, *n.m.* mesentery.

mesero, *n.m.* journeyman paid by the month.

meseta, *n.f.* staircase-landing; table-land, plateau; (*naut.*) backstay-stool; *la meseta central,* (*coll.*) Madrid.

mesiánico, -ca, *a.* Messianic.

mesianismo, *n.m.* Messianism.

Mesías, *n.m.* Messiah.

mesiazgo, *n.m.* dignity of Messiah.

mesilla, *n.f.* small table; sideboard; screw; board wages; mock reproof; staircase-landing; (*arch.*) window sill.

mesillo, *n.m.* first menses after parturition.

mesino, -na, *n.m.f., a.* native or inhabitant of Metz.

mesita, *n.f.* small table, stand.

mesmedad, *n.f.; por su misma mesmedad,* by the very fact.

mesmerismo, *n.m.* mesmerism.

mesmo, -ma, *a.* [MISMO.]

mesnada, *n.f.* armed retinue; association, group.

mesnadería, *n.f.* payment of a *mesnada.*

mesnadero, *n.m.* commander of a *mesnada.*

mesón, *n.m.* inn, hostelry.

mesonaje, *n.m.* street full of numerous inns.

mesoncillo, *n.m.* little inn.

mesonero, -ra, *n.m.f.* inn-keeper, publican, landlord or landlady; host or hostess.

mesonero, -ra, *a.* waiting, serving in an inn.

mesonista, *n.m.* waiter in an inn.

mesta, *n.f.* body of cattle- or sheep-owners.

mestal, *n.m.* piece of barren, uncultivated ground.

mestizar, *v.t.* to cross breeds of animals.

mestizo, -za, *a.* mongrel, hybridous.

mesto, *n.m.* prickly oak.

mestura, *n.f.* (*prov.*) meslin, mixed grain.

mesura, *n.f.* grave deportment, serious countenance; civility, politeness, moderation, measure.

mesuradamente, *adv.* gently, prudently, measurably.

mesurado, -da, *a.* moderate, circumspect, regular, temperate, regulated, modest. — — *p.p.* [MESURAR].

mesurar, *v.t.* to act with reserve, assume a serious countenance. — *v.r.* to behave with prudence and modesty.

meta, *n.f.* boundary, limit; goal.

metabolismo, *n.m.* metabolism; (*rhet.*) pleonasm.

metafísica, *n.f.* metaphysics.

metafísicamente, *adv.* metaphysically.

metafísico, -ca, *a.* metaphysical, abstract, obscure.

metafísico, *n.m.* metaphysician, ontologist.

metáfora, *n.f.* metaphor.

metafóricamente, *adv.* metaphorically, figuratively.

metafórico, ca, *a.* metaphorical.

metaforizar, *v.t.* (*pret.* **metaforicé**; *pres. subj.* **metaforice**) to use metaphors.

metal, *n.m.* metal; brass, latten; sound, tone or compass of the voice; quality, nature, condition; (*mus.*) brass instruments.

metalario, metálico, metalista, *n.m.* metal-worker, metal-dealer, metallist, metallurgist.

metalescente, *a.* of metallic lustre.

metálico, -ca, *a.* metallic; medallic.

metálico, *n.m.* bullion; specie, hard cash; *metálico en caja,* (*com.*) cash in hand.

metalífero, -ra, *a.* (*poet.*) metalliferous.

metalizar, *v.t.* (conjugated like ALZAR) to give a body metallic properties. — *v.r.* to be converted into metal; to be controlled by love of money, to become mercenary.

metalografía, *n.f.* metallography.

metaloide, *n.m.* metalloid.

metalurgia, *n.f.* metallurgy.

metalúrgico, -ca, *a.* relating to metallurgy, metallurgic, metallurgical.

metalúrgico, *n.m.* metallurgist.

metalla, *n.f.* small pieces of gold leaf for mending.

metamorfosear, *v.t.* to metamorphose, transform.

metamorfóseos, metamorfosi, metamorfosis, *n.f.* metamorphosis, transformation.

metano, *n.m.* (*chem.*) methane.

metaplasmo, *n.m.* (*gram., biol.*) metaplasm.

metástasis, *n.f.* (*med.*) metastasis.

metate, *n.m.* (*Mex.*) curved stone on which the women grind maize or cocoa.

metátesis, *n.f.* (*rhet.*) metathesis.

metedor, -ra, *n.m.f.* smuggler; he who puts one thing into another.

meteduría, *n.f.* smuggling.

metempsícosis, metempsicosis, *n.f.* metempsychosis.

metemuertos, *n.m.* (*theat.*) stage hand; busybody, meddler.

meteórico, -ca, *a.* meteoric, meteorous.

meteorista, *n.m.* meteorologist.

meteorito, *n.m.* meteorite.

meteorización, *n.f.* influence of atmospheric phenomena on the soil.

meteoro, *n.m.* meteor.

meteorología, *n.f.* meteorology.

meteorológico, -ca, *a.* meteorological.

meteorologista, *n.m.f.* meteorologist.

meter, *v.t.* to place, put in, include, insert, introduce; to smuggle; to urge, move, occasion, engage; to induce, prevail upon, impose upon, deceive; to cause (as fear); to tell (as fibs); to stake; to cram down (*or* together), heap together, put close together; to compress, narrow, straighten, reduce; (*coll.*) to eat; (*naut.*) to take in (sail); *meter a fuego y sangre,* to put to fire and sword; *meter a voces,* to put one off with shouts; *meter bulla,* to make a noise; *meter el cuezo,* to introduce oneself without ceremony; *meter en calor,* to incite, excite; *meter la nariz en todas partes,* to be a busybody; *meter paz,* to reconcile two disputants; *meter prisa,* to urge, hasten; *meter zizaña,* to sow discord, breed disturbances; *no me meto en nada,* I have neither part nor lot in it; *meter la pata,* to put one's foot in it. — *v.r.* **meterse,** to meddle, interfere, intermeddle; to be on familiar terms; to choose (a profession, etc.); to plunge into vice; to be led astray; to empty into the sea (of rivers); to attack, sword in hand; *meterse a sabio,* to affect learning; *meterse con alguno,* to pick a quarrel; *meterse donde no le llaman,* to poke one's nose into something, to meddle; *meterse en sí mismo,* to follow one's own opinion; *meterse en todo,* to be Jack of all trades; *meterse en vidas ajenas,* to dive into others' affairs.

metesillas y sacamuertos, *n.m.* (*theat.*) stage hand.

meticuloso, -sa, *a.* meticulous.

metido, *n.m.* strong lye.

metido, -da, *n.m., a.* placed into, put into, engaged, deceived; blow with the fist on the throat; (*sew.*) material for letting out (in seams), clout; *n.f.* lecture, dressing down; *estar muy metido en un negocio,* to be deeply involved (*or* engaged) in an affair; *estar muy metido con,* to be very intimate with.

metileno, *n.m.* (*chem.*) methylene.

metilo, *n.m.* (*chem.*) methyl.

metimiento, *n.m.* introduction, insertion.

metódicamente, *adv.* methodically, in an orderly way.

metódico, -ca, *a.* methodical, formal.

metodismo, *n.m.* systematic method; (*eccles.*) Methodism.

metodista, *n.m f.* Methodist; one given to method and order.

método, *n.m.* method, manner, mode, order, form, custom.

metonimia, *n.f.* metonymy.

metonímico, -ca, *a.* metonymical.

metoposcopia, *n.f.* metoposcopy.

metralla, *n.f.* grape-shot, canister-shot.

metrallar, *v.t.* to attack with grape-shot.

metreta, *n.f.* a Greek and Roman liquid measure.

métrica, *n.f.* metrical art, prosody; poesy.

metricador, *n.m.* versifier.

métricamente, *adv.* metrically.

metricar, *v.t.* to versify, make verses.

métrico, -ca, *a.* metrical, composed in verse.

metrificar, *v.t., v.i.* to compose verses.

metro, *n.m.* metre, unit of length; (*poet.*) metre; apocope of *metropolitano.*

metrología, *n.f.* metrology.

metromanía, *n.f.* metromania, rhyming-madness.

metrónomo, *n.m.* (*mus.*) metronome.

metrópoli, *n.f.* metropolis, chief city of a country; archiepiscopal church.

metropolitano, *n.m.* metropolitan; archbishop; underground or elevated railway.

metropolitano, -na, *a.* metropolitan.

meya, *n.f.* maia, spider-crab.

mezcal, *n.m.* (*Am.*) kind of maguey; pulque.

mezcla, *n.f.* mixture, commixture, composition, compound, medley; mortar; mixed cloth.

mezcladamente, *adv.* in a mixed or promiscuous manner.

mezcladillos, *n.m.pl.* a kind of confectionery.

mezclado, -da, *a.* mixed, medley, mingled. — *p.p.* [MEZCLAR].

mezclador, -ra, *n.m.f.* one who mixes, mingles or compounds; (*obs.*) tattler, busybody.

mezcladura, *n.f.; mezclamiento,* *n.m.* mixture, mixing, medley.

mezclar, *v.t.* to mix, commix, mingle, unite; to blend; to spread false reports, excite disturbances, sow discord. — *v.r.* to mix, mingle, be united; to intermarry; to meddle in anything; to take part.

mezclilla, *n.f.* mixed cloth, grey; (*coll.*) pepper and salt cloth.

mezcolanza, *n.f.* bad mixture of colours; (*coll.*) medley, hotch-potch, mishmash, jumble.

mezquinamente, *adv.* miserably, avariciously.

mezquinidad, *a.* poverty, penury, indigence; covetousness, avarice, meanness.

mezquino, -na, *a.* poor, indigent, penurious, diminutive; avaricious, covetous, niggardly, paltry, mean; lean, miserable, petty, minute, puny.

mezquita, *n.f.* mosque.

mezquital, *n.m.* clump of mesquite shrubs.

mezquite, *n.m.* Mexican shrub.

mí, *pers. pron.* oblique cases *sing.* *m.f.* of *yo,* used only after a *prep.,* me.

mi, mis, *poss. pron.* apocope of **mío, mía, míos, mías;** only used before a noun.

mi, *n.m.* (*mus.*) E, third note of the scale.

mía, *n.f.* a contingent of Moroccan troops (100 foot and 100 horse) in Spanish service.

miaja, *n.f.* crumb; mouthful; small copper coin.

miar, *v.i.* to mew (as a cat).

miasma, *n.f.* (*pl.* **miasmata**) miasma.

miasmático, -ca, *a.* miasmatic.

miau, *n.m.* mew of a cat.

mica, *n.f.* mica; female monkey; (*Guat.*) flirt.

micáceo, -cea, *a.* mica-like.

micción, *n.f.* micturition.

micer, *n.m.* Mister, ancient title of respect in Aragon.

mico, *n.m.* monkey, long-tailed ape; (*coll.*) libidinist; *dejar a uno hecho un mico,* to leave someone ashamed of himself; *hacer mico,* to miss an appointment.

micología, *n.f.* mycology, the science of fungi.

micra, *n.f.* micron, the millionth of a metre.

microbio, *n.m.* microbe.

microbiología, *n.f.* microbiology, bacteriology.

microcefalia, *n.f.* microcephaly.

microcéfalo, -la, *a.* microcephalic.

microcosmo, *n.m.* microcosm, little world; man.

micrófono, *n.m.* microphone.

micrografía, *n.f.* micrography.

micrómetro, *n.m.* micrometer.

micromilímetro, *n.m.* one thousandth of a millimetre.

microorganismo, *n.m.* micro-organism.

microscópico, -ca, *a.* microscopic, microscopical.

microscopio, *n.m.* microscope.

micuré, *n.m.* (*Par.*) kind of opossum.

michino, *n.m.* kitten, pussy.

micho, -cha, *n.m.f.* puss.

mida, *n.f.* mida, bean-fly.

midió (**él**), *pret. 3rd pers. sing.* [MEDIR].

mido; mida, *pres. indic.; pres. subj.* [MEDIR].

miedo, *n.m.* fear, apprehension, dread; *al que de miedo se muere, de cagajones le hacen la sepultura,* proverb encouraging one to rise above one's difficulties; *al que mal vive, el miedo le sigue,* conscience doth make cowards of us all; *miedo ha Payo, que reza,* the worst of men calls on God in trouble; *mucho miedo y poca vergüenza,* he fears the punishment but not the crime.

miedoso, -sa, *a.* fearful, timorous, easily afraid.

miel, *n.m.* honey; molasses, cane juice; *miel de caña,* molasses; *hacerse de miel,* to be sickly sweet in one's manner; *no hay miel sin hiel,* trouble always succeeds pleasure in the end; *quien anda entre la miel, algo se le pega,* he who touches pitch becomes defiled; *no es la miel para la boca del asno,* honey is not for the ass's mouth; *miel sobre hojuelas,* added lustre; *dejar a uno con la miel en los abios,* to deprive someone of a thing which he was just beginning to enjoy; *miel en la boca, y guarda la bolsa,* if you do not give, reply courteously; *quedarse a media miel,* to lose something one had just begun to enjoy. *haceos miel y paparos han moscas,* make yourself honey and the flies will swarm to you.

mielga, *n.f.* (*bot.*) wild lucerne; rake; strip of ground; (*ichth.*) a kind of dog-fish; four-pronged pitchfork.

mielgo, *n.m.* twin.

miembro, *n.m.* member; limb; heading, clause; branch; part of a whole.

mienta, *n.f.* (*bot.*) mint.

miente, *n.f.* (*obs.*) mind, inclination, will; thought, idea; *parar mientes,* to consider, reflect.

miento, mienta, *pres. indic., pres. subj.* [MENTIR].

miento, miente, *pres. indic., pres. subj.* [MENTAR].

mientras, mientra, mientre (*obs.*), *adv., conj.* in the meantime, in the meanwhile, whilst, as long as; when; *mientras tanto,* meanwhile; *mientras en mi casa estoy, rey soy,* a man's house is his castle; *mientras más,* the more.

miera, *n.f.* juniper oil, resin.

miércoles, *n.m.* Wednesday; *miércoles de ceniza* or (*coll.*) *miércoles de corvillo,* Ash Wednesday.

mierda, *n.f.* excrement, fæces; dirt, grease.

mierdacruz, *n.f.* (*bot.*) ciliate sparrow-wort.

mierla, *n.f.* (*orn., obs.*) blackbird.

mies, *n.f.* wheat, corn; crop; harvest time; (*fig.*) multitude converted or ripe for conversion; *pl.* grain fields.

miga, *n.f.* crumb, fragment; soft part of bread;

scrap, particle, bit; marrow, substance; *hacer buenas* (or *malas*) *migas*, (*coll.*) to agree (or disagree) readily with anyone; *helársele a uno las migas*, to lose an opportunity through carelessness; *pl.* fried crumbs.

migaja, *n.f.* particle, scrap, bit, crumb; (*coll.*) little or nothing, nothing; *no tiene migaja de juicio*, he has not a grain of sense. — *pl.* **migajas**, offal, leavings, broken meat.

migajada; migajica, -illa, -ita, -uela, *n.f.* small particle.

migajón, *n.m.* crumb, marrow, core; pith and substance.

migar, *v.t.* (conjugated like APAGAR) to crumble, crumb, break into small particles.

migración, *n.f.* migration.

migraña, *n.f.* megrim, headache.

migratorio, -ria, *a.* migrating, migratory.

Miguel, *n.m.* Michael.

miguelete, *n.m.* mountain fusilier in Catalonia; member of the Basque militia.

miguero, -ra, *a.* crumby, relating to crumbs fried in a pan; *lucero miguero*, (*coll.*) morning star.

mijar, *n.m.* millet-field.

mijediega, *n.f.* (*bot.*) shrubby trefoil.

mijero, *n.m.* milestone; (*obs.*) mile.

mijo, *n.m.* (*bot.*) millet, panic grass.

mil, *n.m.* thousand; one thousandth; *las mil y quinientas*, (*coll.*) lentils; *sala de mil y quinientas*, ancient supreme court of appeal in Spain.

miladi, *n.f.* milady.

milagrero, -ra, *n.m.f.* miracle-monger; person who calls everything a miracle.

milagro, *n.m.* miracle, wonder, marvel, supernatural sign, portent; commemorative offering; *vivir de milagro*, to keep oneself with great difficulty; *vida y milagros*, (*coll.*) life, character and behaviour; *hágase el milagro, y hágalo el diablo*, if the work is good, what matter who does it?

milagrón, *n.m.* (*coll.*) dread, astonishment; extreme.

milagrosamente, *adv.* miraculously, marvellously.

milagroso, -sa, *a.* miraculous, marvellous, admirable.

milamores, *n.f.* kind of valerian.

milán, *n.m.* linen cloth made in Milan.

milano, *n.m.* (*orn.*) kite, glede, bird of prey; a flying fish; bur or down of the thistle; *mesa de milanos*, poor table for hungry folk.

milcao, *n.m.* (*Chi.*) national dish based on potatoes.

mildeu, *n.m.* mildew.

milenario, *n.m.* millenary; millennium; space of a thousand years; one who expects the millennium.

milengrana, *n.f.* (*bot.*) rupture-wort.

mileno, -na, *a.* of cloth with warp of a thousand threads.

milenrama, *n.f.* (*bot.*) milfoil, yarrow.

milépora, *n.f.* millepore.

milésimo, -ma, *a.* thousandth, millesimal, thousandth part, ordinal of a thousand.

milhojas, *n.f.* (*bot.*) milfoil, yarrow.

miliamperio, *n.m.* (*elec.*) milliampere.

miliar, *a.* miliary.

miliárea, *n.f.* milliare.

milicia, *n.f.* warfare, art and science of war; militia, soldiery.

miliciano, *n.m.* militia-man.

miliciano, -na, *a.* military.

miligramo, *n.m.* milligram.

mililitro, *n.m.* millilitre.

milímetro, *n.m.* millimetre.

militante, *a.* militant, military.

militar, *n.m.* soldier, military man. — *pl.* **militares**, military, soldiery. — *a.* military, warlike, soldierly, martial. — *v.i.* to serve in the army, be a soldier, bear arms; (*fig.*) to militate, combat, go against, stand for.

militara, *n.f.* (*coll.*) wife, widow or daughter of a soldier.

militarismo, *n.m.* militarism, military spirit.

militarista, *a.* militarist.

militarización, *n.f.* militarization.

militarizar, *v.t.* to militarize.

militarmente, *adv.* militarily, in military style.

militarón, *n.m.* military man deeply versed in the science of warfare.

milmillonésimo, -ma, *a.* billionth (thousand-millionth).

milo, *n.m.* (*prov.*) earthworm.

miloca, *n.f.* a kind of owl.

milocha, *n.f.* kite (children's toy).

milonga, *n.f.* (*Arg., Bol.*) popular dance.

milonguero, -ra, *a.* (*Arg., Bol.*) dancing the *milonga*.

milord (*pl.* **milores**), *n.m.* milord; my lord.

milpa, *n.f.* (*Cent. Am., Mex.*) cornfield.

milpiés, *n.m.* cochineal insect.

milla, *n.f.* mile; (*naut.*) mile (nautical).

millar, *n.m.* thousand; (*in plural*) huge number; certain quantity of cocoa (varies between 3½ and 4 lb.).

millarada, *n.f.* several thousands; *echar millaradas*, to brag of riches; *a millaradas*, innumerable times.

millo, *n.m.* (*prov.*) maize.

millón, *n.m.* million, huge number. — *pl.* **millones**, certain ancient customs duties in Spain; *sala de millones*. board of excise, regulating these duties.

millonario, *n.m.* very rich person; millionaire.

millonésimo, -ma, *a.* millionth.

mimado, -da, *a.* spoiled, humoured.

mimador, *n.m.* coaxer.

mimar, *v.t.* to coax, wheedle, fondle, flatter, caress, indulge, humour, pet; to spoil a child.

mimbral, *n.m.* osier-plantation.

mimbre, *n.m.* osier-twig, willow-twig.

mimbrear, *v.t.*, *v.r.* to sway, bend (in the breeze).

mimbreño, -ña, *a.* osier-like.

mimbrera, *n.m.* osier.

mimbreral, *n.m.* osier-plantation.

mimbroso, -sa, *a.* made of osiers.

mimesis, *n.f.* mimesis, burlesque.

mímica, *n.f.* pantomime, language of signs.

mímico, -ca, *a.* mimic.

mimo, *n.m.* buffoon, merry-andrew, mimic; fondness, indulgence; prudery, delicacy.

mimología, *n.f.* mimology.

mimosa, *n.f.* mimosa.

mimoso, -sa, *a.* delicate, soft, fond, foolish. tender, nice.

mina, *n.f.* mine, underground passage or conduit; mine under a fortress; spring, source, sinecure; much money; profitable business; (*coll.*) cinch, snap; ancient Greek coin and weight; (*mil., naut.*) mine; *encontrar una mina*, (*coll.*) to discover a gold-mine, find a way of getting rich quickly;

volar la mina, to make known a secret (*or* one's secret intentions).

minador, -ra, *n.m.f.* miner, sapper; mining engineer; (*naut.*) minelayer.

minal, *a.* belonging to a mine.

minar, *v.t.* to mine, dig mines; sap, undermine; to exert oneself unusually to attain some end; to consume, ruin, destroy; to work hard.

minarete, *n.m.* minaret.

minera, *n.f.* mine containing metals.

mineraje, *n.m.* labour of mining.

mineral, *a.* mineral. — *n.m.* mineral, ore; mine containing minerals; spring of water, fountain-head, source; *mineral bruto*, raw ore; *mineral virgen*, native ore.

mineralización, *n.f.* mineralization.

mineralogía, *n.f.* mineralogy.

mineralógico, -ca, *a.* mineralogical.

mineralogista, *n.m.f.* mineralogist.

minería, *n.f.* art of mining; body of miners.

minero, *n.m.* mine; miner; source, origin.

mingaco, *n.m.* (*Chi.*) communal work done by neighbours.

mingitorio, -ria, *n.m.,* *a.* upright urinal.

mingo, *n.m.* red or object ball in billiards.

mingón, *n.m.* (*joc.*) great coward.

mingos, *n.m.pl.* (*prov.*) small stockings.

minguito, *n.m.* quarter-loaf.

miniar, *v.t.* to paint in miniature, miniate.

miniatura, *n.f.* miniature.

miniaturista, *n.m.f.* miniature-painter.

mínima, *n.f.* (*mus.*) minim.

mínimo, -ma, *a.* least, smallest.

minino, mino, *n.m.* word used for calling a cat.

minio, *n.m.* minium, red lead, lead oxide.

ministerial, *a.* ministerial.

ministerialmente, *adv.* ministerially.

ministerio, *n.m.* ministry, office, employment, labour, public place.

ministra, *n.f.* minister's wife; prelatess of Trinitarian nuns.

ministrador, -ra, *n.m.f.* one who ministers.

ministrante, *a.* serving, ministrating.

ministrar, *v.t.,* *v.i.* to minister, serve an office, perform public functions; to supply, furnish.

ministril, *n.m.* apparitor, tipstaff, petty officer of justice; minstrel, flute player; a professional musician who played wind or string instruments.

ministro, *n.m.* minister, agent; minister of state; petty officer of justice; head of a religious community; *Ministro de Fomento*, Minister of Public Works; *Ministro de Gracia y Justicia*, Home Secretary; *Ministro de Hacienda*, Chancellor of the Exchequer.

minoración, *n.f.* minoration.

minorar, *v.t.* to lessen, reduce, clip, diminish. — *v.r.* to lower, fall; to decrease, diminish.

minorativo, -va, *a.* lessening, decreasing; (*med.*) laxative.

minoría, *n.f.* minority, smaller number.

minoridad, *n.f.* minority, nonage.

minotauro, *n.m.* Minotaur.

minucia, *n.f.* minuteness, smallness, mite, atom, thing of small value; small tithe; (*in plural*) minutiæ.

minuciosidad, *n.f.* minute explanation; trifle.

minucioso, -sa, *a.* over-exact, over-nice, minutely cautious.

minué, *n.m.* minuet.

minueta, *n.f.* shipwright's boat.

minúscula, *n.f.,* *a.* small; lower-case, small letter.

minúsculo, -a, *a.* very small, tiny; of very little importance.

minuta, *n.f.* minute, first draft, heads of a contract; memorandum, collection of brief notes; lawyer's bill; list of employees, roll; *libro de minutas*, minute-book, memorandum-book, commonplace book.

minutar, *v.t.* to make notes or a first draft.

minutario, *n.m.* minute-book.

minutero, *n.m.* minute-hand of a clock or watch.

minutía, *n.f.* (*bot.*) pink, carnation.

minutisa, *n.f.* (*bot.*) sweet-william pink.

minuto, *n.m.* minute, moment of time, sixtieth part of a degree or of an hour.

minuto, -ta, *a.* minute, small, little, fine.

miñón, *n.m.* light infantry, rural guard; minion; scoriæ of iron ore.

miñona, *n.f.* (*print.*) minion type, 7-point type.

miñosa, *n.f.* (*prov.*) intestinal worm.

mio, *n.m.* puss, pet name for a cat.

mío, mía; míos, mías, *pron. pers. poss.* my, mine; *es muy mío*, he is a great friend; *de mío*, by myself, of my own accord; *soy mío*, I am my own master.

miodinia, *n.f.* (*med.*) myodinia, muscular pain.

miografía, *n.f.* myography.

miología, *n.f.* myology.

miope, *n.m.f.* myope. — *a.* myopic, near-sighted.

miopía, *n.f.* myopia, short-sightedness.

miosis, *n.f.* (*med.*) myosis.

miosota, *n.f.* (*bot.*) forget-me-not.

mira, *n.f.* sight, (of firearms and mathematical instruments); levelling-rod; watch-tower; care, vigilance; design, expectation, purpose, intention; view; (*build.*) rule; *estar a la mira*, to be on the look-out, on the watch; *a la mira y a la maravilla*, phrase denoting excellence.

¡mira! *interj.* look! lo! behold! take care!

mirabel, *n.m.* (*bot.*) cypress goose-foot; sunflower.

mirada, *n.f.* glance, gaze, look, view.

miradero, *n.m.* watch-tower, view-point, lookout, observation; cynosure.

mirado, -da, *a.* (when preceded by *muy, tan, mas, menos*) considerate, prudent, thoughtful, moderate, circumspect; (when preceded by *bien, mal, mejor, peor*) considered, reputed. — *p.p.* [MIRAR].

mirador, -ra, *n.m.f.* spectator, looker-on.

mirador, *n.m.* balcony, gallery, view-point, belvedere, oriel.

miradura, *n.f.* act of looking.

miraguano, *n.m.* (*bot.*) fan palm.

miramiento, *n.m.* awe, reverence, dread; reflection, consideration, expectation, prudence, circumspection, civility, respect; attendance, courtesy.

miranda, *n.f.* height, elevated position, grand view.

mirante, *a.* one who looks.

mirar, *v.t.* to look, gaze, glance, look at, behold, look on, look upon, look towards, spy, observe, watch; to respect, appreciate, esteem, have regard for; to have in view, aim at, take notice, notice; to attend to, protect; to think, consider, meditate, respect; to take care; to enquire; to contemplate, view, survey, observe, scan, watch, see; to front, face, overlook; to attend, protect; *mirar alrededor*, to look round about; *mirar con malos ojos*, to look askance, to look with the evil eye; *mirar de hito en hito*, to look at steadfastly; *mirar de reojo*, to look askance; *mirar de través*, to squint; *mirar por*, to look after, take care of; *mirar por encima*, to examine slightly; *miren si es parda*, phrase warning one against a liar or exaggerator; *mirar sobre el hombro*, to cast a contemptuous look or frown; *antes que ates, mira que desates*, look before you leap; *quien adelante no mira, atrás se queda*, he who does not look forward remains behind; *quien más mira, menos ve*, he who suspects most, sees least; *mirarse a los pies*, to examine one's own failings; *mirarse en (ello)*, to reflect seriously; *mirarse las uñas*, to be idle.

mirasol, *n.m.* (*bot.*) sunflower.

miriagramo, *n.m.* myriagram.

miriámetro, *n.m.* myriametre.

miriápodo, miriópodo, *n.m., a.* myriapod, centipede.

mirífico, -ca, *a.* (*poet.*) marvellous, admirable, wonderful.

mirilla, *n.f.* spy-hole, peep-hole; target of a levelling rod.

miriñaque, *n.m.* trinket, bauble, gewgaw; manilla grass-cloth; hoop-skirt, crinoline.

mirística, *n.f.* nutmeg tree.

mirla, *n.f.* blackbird.

mirlamiento, *n.m.* air of importance, affected gravity.

mirlarse, *v.r.* to assume an air of importance; to affect gravity.

mirlo, *n.m.* blackbird; (*coll.*) air of importance, affected gravity.

mirón, -ona, *n.m.f.* spectator, looker-on, bystander; prier, busybody, gazer.

mirra, *n.f.* myrrh.

mirrado, -da, *a.* myrrhic, composed of myrrh, scented with myrrh.

mirrauste, *n.m.* (*cook.*) timbale of pigeons; pigeon-sauce.

mirrino, -na, *a.* myrrhic.

mirtáceo, -a, *a.* myrtaceous; *n.f.pl.* myrtaceæ.

mirtidano, *n.m.* myrtle sprout.

mirtiforme, *a.* myrtiform.

mirtino, -na, *a.* resembling myrtle.

mirto, *n.m.* myrtle.

miruello, miruella, *n.m.f.* (*prov.*) blackbird.

misa, *n.f.* mass, music of a mass; *misa del gallo*, midnight mass; *misa mayor*, high mass; *misa rezada*, low mass; *por oír misa y dar cebada, nunca se perdió jornada*, few have suffered through adherence to duty or devotion; *no saber de la misa la media*, to know nothing; *la misa, dígala el cura*, do not meddle in what you do not understand.

misacantano, *n.m.* celebrant (of a first mass).

misal, *n.m.* missal, mass-book; (*print.*) two-line pica.

misantropía, *n.f.* misanthropy.

misantrópico, -ca, *a.* misanthropic, hating mankind.

misántropo, *n.m.* misanthropist.

misar, *v.i.* (*coll.*) to say or hear mass.

misario, *n.m.* acolyte.

miscelánea, *n.f.* miscellany, medley, mixture.

misceláneo, -a, *a.* miscellaneous, mixed.

miscible, *a.* miscible.

miserable, *a.* miserable, wretched, unhappy, hapless, lamentable; exhausted, dejected; covetous, avaricious, niggardly, miserly; *n.m.* wretch, miserable person.

miserablemente, míseramente, *adv.* miserably, unhappily, covetously, sordidly, meanly.

miserear, *v.i.* to act penuriously.

miserere, *n.m.* solemn Lenten service; *cólico miserere*, iliac passion.

miseria, *n.f.* misery, miserableness, wretchedness, forlornness, calamity, oppression, need, penury, straitness, poverty; covetousness, niggardliness, avariciousness, stinginess, hardness, meanness; trifle, small matter.

misericordia, *n.f.* mercy, mercifulness, pity, clemency, loving kindness, compassionateness; misericord seat of a choir-stall; small, straight dagger for the *coup de grâce*.

misericordiosamente, *adv.* piously, clemently, mercifully.

misericordioso, -sa, *a.* pious, humane, compassionate, merciful.

misero, -ra, *a.* (*coll.*) mass-loving, fond of saying masses.

mísero, -ra, *a.* miserable, hapless, luckless, wretched.

misérrimo, -ma, *a. superl.* very wretched, most wretched, most miserable.

misión, *n.f.* mission, missionary journey, missionary address or sermon; embassy, legation; commission; expense, costs, charges; money and victuals allowed to reapers for harvesting.

misionar, *v.i.* to preach missions; to reprimand.

misionario, *n.m.* messenger, agent, missionary. — *pl.* **misionarios,** a body of persons sent on a diplomatic mission.

misionero, *n.m.* missionary.

Misisipí, *n.m.* Mississippi.

misivo, -va, *n.f., a.* missive, short letter, note.

mismamente, *adv.* (*coll.*) exactly, precisely.

mismísimo, -ma, *a. superl.* very same, self-same, identical.

mismo, -ma, *a.* same, similar, selfsame, equal, like; *yo mismo*, myself; *él mismo*, himself, etc.; *así mismo*, likewise; *lo mismo*, the same thing; *por lo mismo*, for the same reason; *lo mismo da*, it makes no difference to me.

misoginia, *n.f.* misogyny, hatred of women.

misógino, -a. misogynic.

misquio, *n.m.* kind of marble.

mistagógico, -ca, *a.* mystagogic.

mistagogo, *n.m.* mystagogue, teacher of mystical doctrines.

mistar, *v.i.* to speak, mumble, make a noise with the mouth.

mistela, *n.f.* refreshing beverage made of aniseed, water, sugar and cinnamon; (*Col.*) a popular highly intoxicating liquor.

misterio, *n.m.* mystery, enigma, mysteriousness, abstruseness; secrecy; *hablar de misterio*, to speak in a mysterious or enigmatic fashion; *no ser sin misterio*, not to be without a meaning.

misteriosamente, *adv.* mysteriously, secretly.

misterioso, -sa, *a.* mysterious, dark, obscure, mystic, mystical, enigmatical.

mística, *n.f.* study of the contemplative life.

místicamente, *adv.* mystically, spiritually, emblematically.

misticismo, *n.m.* mysticism.
místico, -ca, *a.* mystic, mystical, spiritual, emblematical.
místico, *n.m.* mystic, contemplative, writer on mystical theology; (*naut.*) small coasting vessel in the Mediterranean.
misticón, *n.m.* great mystic; (*coll.*) affectedly mystical.
mistilíneo, -nea, *a.* (*geom.*) mixtilinear.
mistión, misto [MIXTIÓN] [MIXTO].
misturera, *n.f.* (*Am.*) flower-girl.
mita, *n.f.* (*Am.*) enforced service of Indians; tax paid by the Indians of Peru.
mitad, *n.f.* half, moiety; centre, middle; (*coll.*) husband or wife; *mitad y mitad,* in equal parts; *mi cara mitad,* my better half; *por mitades,* by halves; *cuenta y mitad,* (*com.*) joint account; *mentir por la mitad de la barba,* to tell lies unashamedly.
mitadenco, *a.* (*law*) lease paid half in products, half in cash.
mitayo, *n.m.* (*Am.*) Indian serving his *mita;* Indian in charge of the accounts of the *mita.*
mítico, -ca, *a.* mythical.
mitigación, *n.f.* mitigation, extenuation, moderation.
mitigador, *n.m.* mitigator, mollifier.
mitigante, *a.* mitigating, mitigant, allaying.
mitigar, *v.t.* (*pret.* **mitigué;** *pres. subj.* **mitigue**) to mitigate, soften, mollify, lull, allay, soothe; quench, assuage.
mitigativo, -va; mitigatorio, -ria, *a.* lenitive, mitigant, mitigative.
mitin, *n.m.* meeting, assembly.
mito, *n.m.* myth.
mitología, *n.f.* mythology.
mitológico, -ca, *a.* mythological.
mitológico, mitologista, mitólogo, *n.m.* mythologist.
mitón, *n.m.* mitt; lace glove with half fingers only.
mitote, *n.m.* (*Am.*) Indian dance; (*Mex.*) riot, uproar, confusion, disturbance; fastidiousness, affectedness; (*Cent. Am.*) household festival.
mitotero, -ra, *a.* (*Am.*) finical, fastidious; jolly, rollicking.
mitra, *n.f.* mitre; bishopric.
mitrado, *a.* mitred. — *p.p.* [MITRAR].
mitrar, *v.i.* (*coll.*) to obtain a bishopric.
mitridato, *n.m.* mithridate, antidote.
mítulo, *n.m.* mytilus, mussel.
mixtamente, *adv.* (*law*) belonging to both civil and ecclesiastical courts.
mixtela, *n.f.* refreshing beverage [MISTELA].
mixtifori, *n.m.* (*coll.*) medley, hotchpotch.
mixtión, *n.f.* mixture, commixture.
mixto, -ta, *a.* mixed, mingled, of cross breed, mongrel. — *n.m.* sulphur match; (*artill.*) explosive compound.
mixtura, *n.f.* mixture, compound, meslin; mixed corn.
mixturar, *v.t.* to mix, mingle.
mixturero, -ra, *a.* mixing, one who mixes.
miz, *n.m.* pussy.
mizcal, *n.m.* (*Morocco*) small coin (about 1½*d.*).
mízcalo, *n.m.* a kind of mushroom.
mnemónica, mnemotecnia, *n.f.* mnemonics.
moaré, *n.m.* (*text.*) moiré.
mobiliario, -ria, *a.* movable (of furniture, etc.); unregistered bonds or securities.

mobiliario, *n.m.* furniture, fitment, household goods and chattels.
moblaje, *n.m.* household furniture.
moblar, *v.t.* to furnish, decorate with furniture.
mocadero, mocador, *n.m.* pocket handkerchief.
mocarro, *n.m.* mucus.
mocasín, -ina, *n.m.f.* moccasin.
mocear, *v.t.* to act like a boy; to revel, act the rake.
mocedad, *n.f.* youth, youthfulness; light or careless living; frolic.
mocero, *a.* lascivious.
mocetón, -ona, *n.m.f.* strapping young person.
moción, *n.f.* motion, movement; inclination, tendency; proposition; divine inspiration.
mocionar, *v.t.* (*Arg., Hond.*) to present a motion.
mocito, -ta, *a.* juvenile, youthful. — *n.m.f.* very young person.
moco, *n.m.* mucus, mucous matter; snuff or gutter of a candle; iron-slag; glutinous matter; (*naut.*) martingale boom, dolphin striker; (*bot.*) love-lies-bleeding; *a moco de candil,* by candlelight; *escoger a moco de candil,* to examine with great care; *moco de pavo,* turkey's crest, trifle, worthless matter; *llorar a moco tendido,* (*coll.*) to weep copiously; *no sabe quitarse los mocos,* he can't even blow his nose; *quitar a uno los mocos,* to knock off one's nose with a blow.
mococoa, *n.f.* (*Col., Bol.*) bad humour, ill temper.
mocora, *n.f.* (*Ec.*) small plant the fibre of which is used for hammocks and hats.
mocosidad, *n.f.* mucosity, viscosity.
mocoso, -sa, *a.* mucky, snivelly; despicable, worthless; thoughtless, ignorant. — *n.m.f.* ignorant or inexperienced person.
mocosuelo, -la, *n.m.f.* ignorant, inexperienced young person; child.
mochada, *n.f.* butt, stroke with the head of a horned animal.
mochar, *v.t.* to butt, thrust or push with the head.
mochazo, *n.m.* blow with the butt-end of a musket.
mocheta, *n.f.* (*arch.*) quoin; corner-stone; thick edge of tools.
mochete, *n.m.* sparrow-hawk.
mochil, *n.m.* farmer's boy.
mochila, *n.f.* caparison, cover for a horse; knapsack, haversack; soldier's provisions for some days; *hacer mochila,* to provide for a journey.
mochilero, *n.m.* baggage-carrier.
mochín, *n.m.* executioner.
mocho, -cha, *a.* dishonoured; cropped, lopped, shorn; mutilated, maimed; (*Mex.*) (*coll.*) hypocritical.
mocho, *n.m.* butt-end.
mochuelo, *n.m.* red owl; *cargar con el mochuelo,* to get the worst part of an undertaking.
moda, *n.f.* fashion, custom, mode, form, style; *estar de moda,* to be in fashion; *a la última moda,* in the latest fashion.
modal, *a.* fashionable; (*log.*) modal.
modales, *n.m.pl.* manners, customs.
modelar, *v.t.* to model, shape, form.
modelo, *n.m.* model, pattern, standard, copy, rule, paragon.

moderación, *n.f.* moderation, temperance, abstemiousness, frugality, continence; circumspection.

moderadamente, *adv.* moderately, temperately, reasonably, measurably.

moderado, -da, *a.* moderate, temperate, abstemious, considerate, gentle; (*pol.*) conservative.

modeador, -ra, *n.m.f.* moderator, one who moderates.

moderante, *n.m.f.* moderator, presiding officer.

moderar, *v.t.* to moderate, regulate, curb, adjust, repress, restrain. — *v.r.* to become moderate, refrain from excesses, calm down.

moderativo, -va, *a.* moderating.

moderatorio, -ria, *a.* that which moderates.

modernamente, *adv.* recently, newly, freshly, lately.

modernismo, *n.m.* modernism.

modernista, *n.m.f.* modernist.

modernizar, *v.t.* (*pret.* **modernicé;** *pres. subj.* **modernice**) to modernize.

moderno, -na, *a.* late, recent, modern, new, novel.

modestamente, *adv.* modestly, meekly, honestly.

modestia, *n.f.* modesty, decency, chastity, meekness, comeliness, coyness, humility.

modesto, -ta, *a.* modest, chaste, decent, pure, maidenly, unpretending, unassuming.

módicamente, *adv.* moderately, sparingly, meanly.

modicidad, *n.f.* moderateness, cheapness.

módico, -ca, *a.* moderate-priced.

modificable, *a.* modifiable.

modificación, *n.f.* modification, act of modifying.

modificador, -ra, *n.m.f.* modifier.

modificar, *v.t.* (*pret.* **modifiqué;** *pres. subj.* **modifique**) to modify, moderate, change, alter, qualify.

modificativo, -va, *a.* modificative, that which modifies.

modificatorio, -ria, *a.* modificatory.

modillón, *n.m.* (*arch.*) bracket.

modio, *n.m.* Roman dry measure.

modismo, *n.m.* idiom, peculiar phraseology.

modista, *n.m.f.* fashion-monger; person fond of dress or fashion; modiste, dressmaker, seamstress; *modista de sombreros,* milliner.

modistilla, *n.f.* (*coll.*) young inexperienced dressmaker or milliner; seamstress.

modo, *n.m.* mode, manner, form, sort, method; moderation; civility, urbanity; temperance; (*gram.*) mood; (*mus.*) key, mode; *a modo,* after a similar manner; *de modo que,* so that; *sobre modo,* extremely.

modorra, *n.f.* drowsiness, sleepiness, heaviness; dawn, approach of day; softness of pulp; (*vet.*) sturdy.

modorrar, *v.t.* to make heavy or drowsy. — *v.r.* to become flabby.

modorrilla, *n.f.* third night-watch.

modorro, -rra, *a.* drowsy, sleepy, heavy; stupid, dull.

modoso, -sa, *a.* temperate, well-behaved.

modrego, *n.m.* dunce, dolt, awkward fellow.

modulación, *n.f.* modulation.

modulador, -ra, *n.m.f.* modulator.

modular, *v.i.* to modulate.

módulo, *n.m.* (*arch.*) module; (*mus.*) modulation; (*numis.*) size of coins, etc.; (*math.*) modulus; (*hydr.*) unit of measure of running water.

modurria, *n.f.* (*obs.*) folly.

moeda, *n.f.* moidore, a Portuguese gold coin.

mofa, *n.f.* mockery, jest, scoff, sneer, ridicule.

mofador, -ra, *n.m.f.* scoffer, scorner, jester, jeerer, mocker.

mofadura, *n.f.* jest, scoff, scorn, jeer.

mofante, *a.* sneering, mocking, scoffing.

mofar, *v.t., v.i.* to jeer, scoff, deride, mock, ridicule. — *v.r.* to sneer, scoff, behave with contempt.

mofeta, *n.f.* mofette; mephitis; (*zool.*) mephitis, skunk; polecat.

moflete, *n.m.* chubby-cheek, fat-cheek.

mofletudo, -da, *a.* with chubby cheeks.

moflón, *n.m.* Siberian sheep.

mogate, *n.m.* varnish, glazing; *a medio mogate,* (*coll.*) carelessly, heedlessly.

mogol, -la, *n.m.f.* Mongol.

mogólico, -ca, *a.* Mongolian.

mogollón, *n.m.* hanger-on, parasite, sponger; *comer de mogollón,* to sponge upon others.

mogón, -ona, *a.* beast with one horn missing or broken.

mogote, *n.m.* hillock, hummock; rick or stack of corn; brocket's antler.

mogrollo, *n.m.* parasite, sponger; rustic, clown.

mohada, *n.f.* humectation, wetting.

moharra, *n.f.* head of a spear.

moharrache, moharracho, *n.m.* merry-andrew, jester, clown.

mohatra, *n.f.* sham sale; sharp practice in buying and selling, fraud.

mohatrar, *v.t.* to make a sharp or fraudulent sale.

mohatrero, -ra, *n.m.f.;* **mohatrón,** *n.m.* extortioner, trickster, swindler.

mohecer, *v.t.* to moss, cover with moss, mildew.

moheda, *n.f.* mountain covered with bramble and underbrush.

mohín, *n.m.* grimace, gesture.

mohina, *n.f.* animosity, grudge against someone.

mohino, -na, *a.* fretful, peevish; mournful, sad; black (of horses, mules, etc.); applied to a mule begotten by a stallion and a she-ass.

mohino, *n.m.* one playing alone against several others.

moho, *n.m.* (*bot.*) moss; mould, rust, verdigris, mouldiness; bluntness; *no criar moho* or *no dejar criar moho a,* to use continually; to spend quickly.

mohoso, -sa, *a.* mouldy, mildewed, musty, rusty, mossy.

Moisés, *n.m.* Moses.

mojada, *n.f.* wetting, moistening, humectation; sop, bread moistened in liquid; (*coll.*) stab.

mojador, -ra, *n.m.f.* wetter, moistener.

mojadura, *n.f.* wetting, moistening, drenching.

mojama, *n.f.* dry, salted tunny-fish.

mojar, *v.t., v.r.* to wet, damp, moisten; to meddle, interfere. — *v.i.* to be immersed in any business.

mojarra, *n.f.* a sea fish; (*Am.*) broad and short knife.

mojarrilla, *n.m.* (*coll.*) punster, jester, jolly person.

moje, *n.m.* broth, gravy.

mojel, *n.m.* (*naut.*) braided cord for the anchor.

mojí, *n.m.* sponge-cake; pie.

mojicón, *n.m.* blow with a fist in the face; kind of sweetmeat, sponge-cake or pie.

mojiganga, *n.f.* morris dance, masquerade, masque, mummery.

mojigatería, mojigatez, *n.f.* hypocrisy, religious fanaticism, bigotry.

mojigato, -ta, *n.m.f.* dissembler, hypocrite, fanatic, bigot. — *a.* deceitful, hypocritical, affectedly humble, bigoted, prude.

mojón, *n.m.* landmark; pile, heap; milestone; wine-sampler; kind of game; solid excrement.

mojona, *n.f.* retail wine-duty; survey of land, setting up of landmarks.

mojonera, *n.f.* landmark.

mojonero, *n.m.* gauger.

mola, *n.f.* (*med.*) mole, a kind of tumour in the womb; salted flour used in sacrifices.

molada, *n.f.* colours ground together.

molar, *a.* molar.

molcajete, *n.m.* (*Mex.*) mortar.

moldar, *v.t.* to mould.

molde, *n.m.* mould, matrix, pattern mould, block, model, form; (*print.*) forme ready for printing; (*fig.*) well, perfectly, masterly; *de molde,* printed, in print; fitting, to the purpose.

moldeador, *n.m.* moulder, cast-maker.

moldear, *v.t.* to cast, mould, make moulds.

moldura, *n.f.* moulding.

moldurar, *v.t.* to make a moulding.

mole, *a.* soft, mild. — *n.f.* vast size, mass, lump; massiveness; mole, breakwater; (*Mex.*) fricasse of meat or turkey with chilli sauce.

molécula, *n.f.* molecule, particle, atom.

molecular, *a.* molecular.

moledera, *n.f.* grinding stone; (*coll.*) botheration.

moledero, -ra, *a.* which is to be ground.

moledor, -ra, *n.m.f.* grinder; powdering-mill; copper, pot; crushing cylinder in a sugar mill; (*coll.*) bore, worrying person.

moledura, *n.f.* grinding.

molejón, *n.m.* (*Cub.*) a ridge of rock near the surface of the water.

molendero, *n.m.* miller, grinder; chocolate manufacturer.

moleña, *a., n.* rock from which upper mill-stones are made.

moler, *v.t.* (*pres. indic.* **muelo;** *pres. subj.* **muela**) grind, pulverize, mill; (*Cub.*) to crush the sugar cane; (*fig.*) to worry, weary, overtire; (*fig.*) to vex; to waste, consume; to masticate, chew; *moler a azotes,* to whip, lash; *moler a palos,* to whip, beat, flog.

molero, *n.m.* maker or seller of millstones.

molestador, -ra, *n.m.f.* disturber, vexer, molester.

molestamente, *adv.* troublesomely, uncomfortably, vexatiously, grievously.

molestar, *v.t.* to worry, vex, disturb, trouble, tease, hurt, grate, annoy.

molestia, *n.f.* injury, hardship, grievance, trouble, nuisance, molestation, annoyance, bother; discomfort.

molesto, -ta, *a.* annoying, bothersome, uncomfortable, grievous, vexatious, oppressive, heavy.

moleta, *n.f.* muller; polisher; (*print.*) ink-grinder.

molibdeno, *n.m.* molybdenum.

molicie, *n.f.* softness; effeminacy.

molido, -da, *a.* ground; flogged; fatigued. — *p.p.* [MOLER].

molienda, *n.f.* milling, grinding; grist; mill; weariness, fatigue, lassitude; quantity of sugar-cane, corn, olives or chocolate to be ground together; the mill; season for grinding sugar-cane or olives.

moliente, *a.* grinder, grinding; *moliente y corriente,* right, exactly, justly.

molificable, *a.* mollifiable.

molificación, *n.f.* mollification.

molificador, *n.m.* mollifier.

molificar, *v.t.* (*pret.* **molifiqué;** *pres. subj.* **molifique**) to mollify, mitigate, soften.

molificativo, -va, *a.* mollifying, lenitive.

molimiento, *n.m.* grinding, pounding, beating up; (*fig.*) fatigue, lassitude, weariness.

molinar, *n.m.* place where there are mills.

molinejo, *n.m.* small mill.

molinera, *n.f.* miller's wife, mill-woman.

molinería, *n.f.* collection of mills, mill industry.

molinero, *n.m.* miller, grinder.

molinero, -ra, *a.* that which is to be ground or pounded; that which belongs to a mill.

molinete, *n.m.* windlass; turnstile; little mill; pin-wheel; friction-roller; ventilating wheel; an old-fashioned dance; moulinet, swing of sabre.

molinillo, *n.m.* hand-mill, churn-staff; coffee-mill.

molinillo, molinito, *n.m.* small mill.

molinismo, *n.m.* Molinism.

molinista, *n.m.f.* Molinist.

molino, *n.m.* mill; restless, bustling fellow; (*coll.*) mouth; *molino de agua,* water-mill; *molino de aserrar,* sawing-mill; *molino de estampar,* stamping-mill; *molino de herrería,* forge-mill; *molino de mano,* hand-mill; *molino de sangre,* mill turned by men or animals; *molino de viento,* windmill; *empatársele a uno el molino,* to meet with difficulties; *ir al molino,* to conspire against someone.

molitivo, -va, *a.* mollient.

mololoa, *n.f.* (*Hond.*) noisy conversation.

molondro, molondrón, *n.m.* mean, ignorant fellow, poltroon.

moloso, *n.m.* (*poet.*) molossus.

moltura, *n.f.* grinding.

molusco, *n.m.* mollusc.

moly, *n.m.* great yellow garlic.

molla, *n.f.* crumb of bread; lean meat.

mollar, *a.* soft, tender, pulpous, boneless, fleshy; flexible; (*coll.*) credulous; useful.

molle, *n.m.* (*Am.*) sacred tree of the Incas (*Schinus molle*).

mollear, *v.i.* to grow soft and pliable, soften, yield easily.

molledo, *n.m.* fleshy part of a limb; crumby part of bread.

molleja, *n.f.* gland; gizzard; maw; sweetbread.

mollejilla, mollejuela, *n.f.* small gland.

mollejón, *n.m.* grindstone; large gland; big, corpulent person.

mollejuela, *n.f.* sweetbread.

mollentar, *v.t.* to mollify.

mollera, *n.f.* crown, top of the head; (*fig.*) judgment, intelligence, brains; *cerrado de mollera,* rude, ignorant; *duro de mollera,* obstinate.

mollero, *n.m.* fleshy part of the arm.

molleta, *n.f.* biscuit; brown bread. — *pl.* snuffers.

mollete, *n.m.* manchet, French roll; fleshy part of the arm. — *pl.* **molletes,** plump cheeks.

molletero, -ra, *n.m.f.* baker of rolls.

molletudo, -da, *a.* chubby-cheeked.

mollina, mollizna, *n.f.* mist, drizzle.

molliznar, molliznear, *v.i.* to drizzle, fall in small drops.

moma, *n.f.* (*Mex.*) blind man's buff.

momentáneamente, *adv.* momentarily.

momentáneo, -nea, *a.* momentary, of short duration; immediately, prompt.

momento, *n.m.* moment; minute; (*mech.*) weight, momentum; consequence, importance; *al momento,* immediately, in a moment; *por momentos,* continually, successively.

momería, *n.f.* mummery.

momia, *n.f.* mummy.

momio, -mia, *a.* meagre, lean. — *n.m.* (*fig.*) extra allowance.

momificar, *v.t.* to mummify. — *v.r.* to resemble a mummy.

momo, *n.m.* buffoonery, low jesting, grimacing.

mona, *n.f.* female monkey; mimic, imitator; (at cards) old maid; (*joc.*) drunkenness, drunkard; instrument for copying pictures; (*prov.*) Easter cake; iron plate worn on the right leg by *picadores* (bullfighting); *dormir la mona,* to sleep off the effects of a drunken bout; *aunque la mona se vista de seda, mona se queda,* a hog in disguise is still a hog for all that.

monacal, *a.* monastic, monkish, belonging to monks.

monacalmente, *adv.* monastically.

monacato, *n.m.* monachism, monkhood.

monacillo, *n.m.* acolyte.

monacordio, *n.m.* spinet.

monada, *n.f.* grimace, wry face, monkey trick; flattery, fawning; a pretty, sweet little thing.

mónada, *n.f.* monad.

monago, monaguillo, *n.m.* choir-boy, server.

monaquismo, *n.m.* monachism.

monarca, *n.m.* monarch, king, lord, sovereign.

monarquía, *n.f.* monarchy; kingdom.

monárquico, -ca, *a.* monarchical, kingly, kinglike.

monasterial, *a.* monastic.

monasterio, *n.m.* monastery, convent, cloister, religious house.

monásticamente, *adv.* monastically.

monástico, -ca, *a.* monastic, monkish.

monda, *n.f.* pruning of trees, pruning season.

mondadiente, mondadientes, *n.m.* tooth-pick.

mondador, -ra, *n.m.f.* cleaner, purifier.

mondadura, *n.f.* cleaning, cleansing. — *pl* paring, peeling.

mondaoídos, mondaorejas, *n.m.* ear-pick.

mondar, *v.t.* to clean, cleanse, free from filth; to husk, decorticate, peel; (*fig.*) to deprive

of money, fleece; **to cut the hair; to trim,** prune (trees).

mondejo, *n.m.* belly of a pig or sheep stuffed with mincemeat.

mondo, -da, *a.* neat, clean, pure, unadulterated; *mondo y lirondo,* (*coll.*) pure, without admixture.

mondón, *n.m.* barkless tree-trunk.

mondonga, *n.f.* kitchen-wench.

mondongo, *n.m.* tripe, black-pudding.

mondonguería, *n.f.* place or shop where tripe is sold.

mondonguero, -ra, *n.m.f.* seller or cooker of tripe.

monear, *v.i.* to act ridiculously or preposterously.

moneda, *n.f.* money, coinage, change; specie; *moneda corriente,* currency; *casa de moneda,* mint; *moneda de vellón,* inferior coin, copper coin; *moneda sonante,* specie, hard cash; *moneda suelta,* small change; *correr la moneda,* to pass money; *no hacemos moneda falsa,* no secrets here! *pagar en buena moneda,* to give entire satisfaction; *pagar en la misma moneda,* to pay one in his own coin; *ser moneda corriente,* to be commonly allowed or admitted.

monedaje, *n.m.* coinage; seigniorage.

monedar, monedear, *v.t.* to coin.

monedería, *n.f.* mint, mintage.

monedero, *n.m.* officer of the mint, coiner, moneyer; *monedero falso,* counterfeiter.

monedilla, monedita, *n.f.* small coin.

monería, *n.f.* grimace; pretty ways (of children), mimicry; trifle, gewgaw, bauble.

monesco, -ca, *a.* apish, monkeyish.

monetario, *n.m.* cabinet of ancient coins.

monetario, -ria, *a.* monetary, financial.

monfí, *n.m.* a Moorish highwayman.

monforte, *n.m.* strong cloth.

monicaco, monicongo, *n.m.* conceited, careless person.

monición, *n.f.* admonition; publication of banns.

monigote, *n.m.* lay-brother; person unskilled in his profession; (*fig.*) puppet; grotesque figure.

monillo, *n.m.* waist, bodice, corset.

monipodio, *n.m.* meeting or agreement arranged for an unlawful purpose.

monís, *n.f.* (*prov.*) kind of fritters; small, neat thing. — *pl.* **monises,** money.

monismo, *n.m.* (*philos.*) monism.

monista, *n.m.f.* monist.

mónita, *n.f.* artifice, cunning, suavity.

monitor, *n.m.* monitor.

monitoria, *n.f.* ecclesiastical monition.

monitorio, -ria, *a.* monitory, admonitory.

monja, *n.f.* nun, religious, female recluse. — *pl.* sparks thrown off from burning paper.

monje, *n.m.* monk, religious, male recluse, anchorite; (*orn.*) brown peacock.

monjecico, -cillo, -cito, *n.m.* little monk.

monjía, *n.f.* prebend (of a monk in a convent).

monjil, *n.m.* habit of a nun; mourning-dress, widow's weeds. — *a.* relating or belonging to nuns, nun-like.

monjío, *n.m.* nunship; taking of the veil.

monjita, *n.f.* little nun; (*Arg.*) small bird of the Pampas.

mono, -na, *a.* (*coll.*) nice, pretty, neat; funny, *estar de monos (dos o más personas),* to be on bad terms; *quedarse hecho un mono*, to be ashamed.

mono, *n.m.* monkey, ape; mimic; nincompoop; overalls; *monosabio*, a kind of horse-boy at the service of a picador (bullfighting).

monobloque, *a.* (*eng.*) in block, in one piece.

monocerote, monoceronte, *n.m.* unicorn.

monociclo, *a.* monocycle.

monocilíndrico, -ca, *a.* having a single cylinder.

monocordio, *n.m.* monochord, one-stringed instrument.

monocromata, *n.f.* monochrome, painting in one colour.

monocromático, -ca, *a.* monochromatic.

monocromo, -ma, *a.* monochrome.

monóculo, -la, *a.* monoculous, monocular, one-eyed.

monóculo, *n.m.* monocle.

monodía, *n.f.* (*mus.*) monody.

monogamia, *n.f.* monogamy.

monógamo, *n.m.* monogamous.

monografía, *n.f.* monograph.

monográfico, -ca, *a.* monographic.

monograma, *n.m.* monogram.

monolítico, -ca, *a.* monolithic.

monolito, *n.m.* monolith.

monologar, *v.i.* to monologize, to soliloquize.

monólogo, *n.m.* monologue; soliloquy.

monomanía, *n.f.* monomania.

monomaquia, *n.f.* monomachy; duel.

monona, *n.f.* (*coll.*) graceful, pretty girl.

monopastos, *n.m.* one-wheeled pulley.

monoplano, *n.m.* (*aer.*) monoplane.

monopolio, *n.m.* monopoly.

monopolista, *n.m.f.* monopolist, monopolizer, forestaller.

monopolizar, *v.t.* (conjugated like ALZAR) to monopolize, forestall.

monosilábico, -ca, *a.* monosyllabled, monosyllabic.

monosílabo, -ba, *n.m.f., a.* monosyllable.

monote, *n.m.* one dumbfounded.

monoteísmo, *n.m.* monotheism.

monoteísta, *n.m.f., a.* monotheist, monotheistic.

monotonía, *n.f.* monotony, uniformity.

monótono, -na, *a.* monotonous, monotonical.

monóxilo, *n.m.* a boat formed of a single log hollowed out.

monseñor, *n.m.* title of honour given to certain prelates; Monseigneur, Monsignor.

monserga, *n.m.* (*coll.*) gabble, gibberish.

monstruo, *n.m.* monster, prodigy, huge or unnatural being.

monstruosamente, *adv.* monstrously.

monstruosidad, *n.f.* monstrosity; monstrous, excessive ugliness.

monstruoso, -sa, *a.* monstrous, enormous, huge, shocking, hideous, extraordinary.

monta, *n.f.* amount, sum; value, price, worth; signal for cavalry to mount; mounting, raising.

montacargas, *n.f.* hoist, winch, windlass, goods-lift.

montadero, *n.m.* one who mounts; mounting-block.

montado, -da, *a.* ready for mounting; mounted, set (e.g. of gems). — *n.m.* trooper or horseman. — *p.p.* [MONTAR].

montador, *n.m.* one who mounts; mounting-block, horse-block; (*elec., motor., etc.*) installer, fitter.

montadura, *n.f.* trooper's accoutrements; mounting; (*jewel.*) setting.

montaje, *n.m.* setting up, installing; assembling; (*artill.*) act of mounting. — *pl.* (*artill.*) mountings.

montanera, *n.f.* oak forest; feeding of pigs with acorns.

montanero, *n.m.* forester, forest-keeper.

montano, -na, *a.* mountainous.

montantada, *n.f.* boasting, ostentation; multitude, crowd.

montante, *n.m.* broadsword; (*carp., mech.*) upright, standard; post, strut, jamb; (*min.*) stempel; (*arch.*) transom; (*com.*) amount, footing. — *n.f.* (*naut.*) flood-tide.

montantear, *v.i.* to wield the broadsword; (*fig.*) to vaunt, boast, brag; to intermeddle.

montantero, *n.m.* broadsword fighter.

montaña, *n.f.* mountain, mount; (*Chi., Per.*) waste or unoccupied land covered with trees. — *pl.* **montañas**, highlands.

montañés, -esa, *a.* of mountains, mountainous, inhabiting mountains. — *n.m.f.* mountaineer, highlander; native of the province of Santander.

montañeta, montañuela, *n.f.* small mountain.

montañoso, -sa, *a.* mountainous, hilly.

montar, *v.i.* to mount, rise to the top, go on horseback; to amount to, be worth; to be of moment. — *v.t.* to ride, straddle a horse; (*jewel.*) to set diamonds, etc.; to impose a fine for trespassing livestock, etc.; to cock (a gun); (*naut.*) to double (a cape); to take command (of a ship); to hang (the rudder); to cover (a horse, etc.); to mount, set (a machine); to wind (a clock, etc.); (*mil.*) to mount guard; to carry or be equipped with (guns, etc.); — *v.r.* to get into a passion, rage, etc.; *montar en cuidado*, to be careful, on one's guard; *montar en pelo*, to mount an animal barebacked; *montar la brecha*, (*mil.*) to mount the breach.

montaraz, *n.m.* mountaineer, mountainguard, forester. — *a.* mountainous; wild, untamed, haggard.

montaraza, *n.f.* (*prov.*) forester's wife.

montazgar, *v.t.* to levy or collect toll on cattle.

montazgo, *n.m.* toll on cattle.

monte, *n.m.* mountain, mount, hill; wood, forest, woodland; difficulty, obstruction; bushy head of hair; pool (in cards); a game of cards; talon, cards left in the pack after dealing; *monte alto*, lofty wood or grove; *monte bajo*, copse, thicket; *monte de piedad*, pawnbroker's shop; *monte pío* or *montepío*, fund for widows and orphans; *andar a monte*, to lurk, skulk, be absent for unknown motives; *montes de oro* (or *montes y maravillas*), exaggerated promises (or expectations).

montea, *n.f.* hewing of stone; (*arch.*) working drawing; plan or profile of a building; versed sine of an arch; beating a wood for game; stone-cutting.

montear, *v.t.* to beat a wood; to draw the plan of a building; (*arch.*) to vault, arch.

montecillo, *n.m.* small wood; hillock, hummock.

montepío, *n.m.* (see MONTE).

montera, *n.f.* cloth cap; sky-light; condenser of a still; hunter's wife; (*naut.*) skysail.

monterería, *n.f.* cap-factory, cap-store.

monterero, *n.m.* seller or maker of *monteras*.

montería, *n.f.* hunting, hunt, chase.

montero, *n.m.* huntsman, hunter; beater (hunting).

monterrey, *n.m.* (*cook.*) meat pie.

monteruca, *n.f.* ugly cap.

montés, -esa, *a.* wild, bred or found in mountain or forest.

montesa, *n.f.* a Spanish military order.

montescos, *n.m.pl.; haber Montescos y Capeletes,* to have great disputes or contentions.

montesino, -na, *a.* montigenous, bred in mountain or forest.

montículo, *n.m.* monticle, mound.

monto, *n.m.* sum of money; (*com.*) amount (principal plus interest).

montón, *n.m.* heap, pile, crowd, mass, cluster; *ser uno del montón,* a dirty, lazy fellow; *a montones,* abundantly, by heaps.

montonera, *n.f.* (*S. Am.*) group of mounted revolutionaries; large crowd; (*Col.*) rick.

montonero, *n.m.* (*Am.*) bushwhacker, guerrilla.

montuno -na, *a.* montigenous, highland, rustic.

montuosidad, *n.f.* (*prov.*) mountainousness.

montuoso, -sa, *a.* mountainous, hilly, well-wooded.

montura, *n.f.* saddle-horse, riding-horse mount; saddle, trappings of horses; (*jewel.*) setting.

monuelo, *n.m.* fop; coxcomb.

monumental, *a.* monumental.

monumento, *n.m.* monument, erection, ancient building.

monzón, *n.m.* monsoon.

moña, *n.f.* doll, puppet; badge on a bull's neck; dressmaker's lay figure; peevishness, fretfulness; (*coll.*) drunkenness; ribbons for the head.

moño, *n.m.* tuft of hair (*or* feathers); chignon, top-knot; *ponérsele a uno una cosa en el moño,* to take a capricious resolution.

moñón, -ona; moñudo, -da, *a.* crested, topped; (*Col.*) sulky, sullen, morose.

moquear, *v.i.* to snivel; to run (the nose).

moquero, *n.m.* pocket-handkerchief.

moqueta, *n.f.* moquette.

moquete, *n.m.* blow on the face or nose.

moquetear, *v.i.* to discharge violently from the nose, blow the nose often. — *v.t.* to give blows in the face.

moquillo, *n.m.* little mucus; pip (in fowls); distemper (of dogs and cats).

moquita, *n.f.* running from the nose.

mor, *n.m.* aphæresis of *amor*; *por mor de,* (*coll.*) for the love of.

mora, *n.f.* delay; (*bot.*) mulberry, blackberry.

morabito, *n.m.* Mohammedan hermit.

moracho, -cha, *n.m.f., a.* kind of light purple.

morada, *n.f.* abode, habitation, lodging, residence, mansion, home; continuance, stay, sojourn.

morado, -da, *a.* mulberry-coloured, violet, purple.

morador, *n.m., a.* dweller, lodger, inhabitant, resident.

moraga, *n.f.; morago,* *n.m.* handful, bunch, gleaner's bundle.

moral, *n.m.* (*bot.*) mulberry-tree, blackberry bush, bramble. — *n.f.* morals, ethics, morality. — *a.* moral.

moraleja, *n.f.* brief moral observation, maxim, lesson.

moralidad, *n.f.* morality, moral virtue.

moralista, *n.m.f.* moralist.

moralización, *n.f.* moralization.

moralizador, -ra, *n.m.f.* moralizer, commentator, critic.

moralizar, *v.t., v.i.* (*pret.* **moralicé;** *pres. subj.* **moralice**) to moralize, speak or write on morals.

moralmente, *adv.* morally; practically.

morar, *v.i.* to dwell, lodge, reside, live, inhabit, remain, continue.

moratoria, *n.f.* (*law., com.*) moratorium, extension of time, delay.

morbidez, *n.f.* (*art.*) softness, mellowness of tint.

mórbido, -da, *a.* morbid, diseased; morbose; (*art.*) soft, mellow.

morbífico, -ca, *a.* morbific, causing disease.

morbo, *n.m.* disease, distemper, disorder, infirmity; *morbo comicial,* epilepsy; *morbo gálico,* venereal disease; *morbo regio,* jaundice.

morbosidad, *n.f.* morbosity.

morboso, -sa, *a.* morbid, diseased.

morcella, *n.f.* spark from a lamp.

morciguillo, *n.m.* (*orn.*) bat.

morcilla, *n.f.* black pudding; (*theat.*) stale gag.

morcillero, -ra, *n.m.f.* maker of black puddings; (*theat.*) gagger.

morcillo, -lla, *a.* reddish-black (of horses).

morcillo, *n.m.* fleshy or muscular part of the arm.

morcón, *n.m.* large black pudding; large sausage; (*coll.*) short, plump fellow; sloven person.

mordacidad, *n.f.* mordacity; asperity, roughness, acrimony; sarcastic language.

mordacilla, *n.f.* small gag.

mordante, *n.m.* (*print.*) guide, container.

mordaz, *a.* corrosive, biting, keen, nipping; sarcastic; acrimonious, satirical.

mordaza, *n.f.* gag; pincers, nippers, tongs; muzzle; holder, clamp, stopper; (*railw.*) fish-plate.

mordazmente, *adv.* acrimoniously, nippingly.

mordedor, -ra, *n.m.f.* biter, backbiter.

mordedura, *n.f.* bite; mordication.

mordente, *n.m.* (*mus.*) mordent.

morder, *v.t.* (*pres. indic.* **muerdo;** *pres. subj.* **muerda**) to bite, nip, seize with the teeth, gnaw, nibble, eat, wear away; to grip, grasp, clutch; to be sharp, pungent, rough; to etch, corrode; to carp at, taunt, find fault with, satirize; to revile, back-bite; (*naut.*) to bite (of an anchor), hold fast in the ground; *no morderse los labios,* (*coll.*) not to mince matters; *morderse los dedos,* to be irritated, desire revenge; *morderse la lengua,* to refrain from speech; *morder la tierra,* to bite the dust.

mordicación, *n.f.* mordication, smarting, stinging.

mordicante, *a.* biting, pungent, mordicant, acrid, corrosive.

mordicar, *v.t.* (*pret.* **mordiqué;** *pres. subj.* **mordique**) to nibble, gnaw, sting, smart.

mordicativo, -va, *a.* biting, gnawing, stinging, mordicant.

mordido, -da, *a.* diminished, wasted away. — *p.p.* [MORDER].

mordido, *n.m.* bit, mouthful.

mordiente, *n.m.* (*art.*) gold size; (*engr.*) aqua fortis, nitric acid. — *a.* biting.

mordihuí, *n.m.* weevil.

mordimiento, *n.m.* bite, biting, mordication.

mordiscar, *v.t.* (*pret.* **mordisqué;** *pres. subj.* **mordisque**) to nibble, gnaw, have a bite.

mordisco, mordiscón, *n.m.* bite, biting; bit, piece bitten off.

morel de sal, *n.m.* (*art*) purple-red for fresco painting.

morena, *n.f.* brown bread; (*bot.*) frog-bit; (*agric.*) rick of newly-mown grain; (*ichth.*) muræna; (*geol.*) moraine.

morenilla, morenita, *n.f.* brunette.

morenillo, *n.m.* compound of charcoal and vinegar for curing sheep.

moreno, -na, *a.* brown, dark-brown, dark, tawny, swarthy; (*Cub.*)Negro, mulatto; *sobre ello morena,* to be determined come what may, at all costs.

morera, *n.f.* (*bot.*) white mulberry-tree.

moreral, *n.m.* plantation of white mulberry-trees.

morería, *n.f.* Moorish quarter; Moorish land.

moreta, *n.f.* kind of sauce.

moretón, *n.m.* (*coll.*) bruise.

morfa, *n.f.* fungus disease of orange and lemon trees.

Morfeo, *n.m.* (*myth.*) Morpheus.

morfina, *n.f.* (*pharm.*) morphine.

morfinismo, *n.m.* (*med.*) morphinism.

morfinómano, -na, *n.m.f.,* *a.* morphinist, drug fiend.

morfología, *n.f.* morphology.

morfológico, -ca, *a.* morphologic(al).

morga, *n.f.* juice oozing from a heap of olives before pressing.

morganático, -ca, *a.* morganatic.

moribundo, -da, *a.* dying, near death.

moriche, *n.m.* a tropical palm-tree.

moriego, -ga, *a.* Moorish.

morigeración, *n.f.* morigeration, obedience, obsequiousness, temperance, moderation.

morigerado, -da, *a.* temperate, abstemious.

morigerar, *v.t.* to moderate, restrain one's passions.

morillo, *n.m.* little Moor; andiron, firedog.

morir, *v.i.* (*p.p.* **muerto;** *pres. part.* **muriendo;** *pres. indic.* **muero;** *pres. subj.* **muera;** *pret.* **él murió**) to die, expire, perish, be lost, end, finish, go out; to hanker, desire excessively; *morir al mundo,* to be dead to the world; *morir como chinches,* to die in great numbers; *morir de pesadumbre* (or *pena*), to die of a broken heart; *morir vestido,* to die suddenly, to meet a violent death. — *v.r.* to go out, be extinguished or quenched (as fire or light); to be benumbed (of a limb); *morirse de tristeza,* to die of a broken heart; *morirse por,* to be very fond of.

morisco, -ca, *n.m.f.* Morisco. — *a.* Moorish, moresque.

morisma, *n.f.* multitude of Moors.

morisqueta, *n.f.* Moorish trick; (*coll.*) deception, trick, fraud; (*Philip.*) boiled rice without salt; (*Col.*) face, grimace.

morlaco, -ca, *a.* affecting ignorance.

morlés, *n.m.* kind of linen, lawn; *morlés de morlés,* all of a piece.

mormón, -ona, *n.m.f.* Mormon.

mormonismo, *n.m.* Mormonism.

mormullo, mormureo, *n.m.* murmur.

moro, -ra, *n.m.f.,* *a.* Moorish, Moor; (*coll.*) not watered (wine); a black horse with a white patch on the forefront; Mohammedan; *a más moros, más ganancia,* the greater the peril, the greater the glory; *haber moros y cristianos,* to have a great dispute; *moro de paz,* peaceful person; *hay moros en la costa,* the coast is not clear; *moros van, moros vienen,* said of one who is almost drunk.

morocada, *n.f.* butt of a ram.

morocho, -cha, *a.* (*S. Am.*) fresh, vigorous (of persons).

morón, *n.m.* hill, hillock, mound.

moroncho, -cha; morondo, -da, *a.* bald, leafless, hairless.

morondanga, *n.f.* (*coll.*) medley, hodgepodge.

morosamente, *adv.* sluggishly, tardily, slowly.

morosidad, *n.f.* tardiness, slowness, delay.

moroso, -sa, *a.* tardy, slow, heavy, laggard.

morquera, *n.f.* Spanish thyme.

morra, *n.f.* crown, top of head; mora, a game; *andar a la morra,* to come to blows.

morrada, *n.f.* butting with the head.

morral, *n.m.* horse-bag; game-bag; rustic, clown; (*naut.*) boom-sail.

morralla, *n.f.* heap of rubbish, medley; small fry, little fish.

morrillo, *n.m.* pebble; fat of the nape of a sheep.

morriña, *n.f.* murrain; (*coll.*) sadness, melancholy, homesickness, blues.

morrión, *n.m.* (*mil.*) morion; vertigo (in hawks).

morro, *n.m.* something round; overhanging lip, snout, muffle; headland, head, bluff; peak; pebble; *andar al morro,* to come to blows; *jugar al morro con uno,* to deceive.

morro, -rra, *a.* purring.

morrocotudo, -da, *a.* (*coll.*) strong, stout; very important or difficult.

morrocoyo, morrocoy, *n.m.* (*Cub.*) boxturtle.

morrón, *n.m.* knotted flag; large sweet pepper; (*aer., coll.*) crash.

morroncho, -cha, *a.* mild, meek, tame.

morrongo, -ga; morroño, -ña, *n.m.f.* (*coll.*) cat.

morrudo, -da, *a.* blubber-lipped, flap-mouthed.

morsa, *n.f.* walrus, morse.

mortadela, *n.f.* Bologna sausage.

mortaja, *n.f.* shroud, winding-sheet, graveclothes; mortise; (*S. Am.*) cigarette paper.

mortal, *a.* mortal, fatal, deadly, destructive, implacable; at death's door. — *n.m.* mortal, human being.

mortalidad, *n.f.* mortality; death rate.

mortalmente, *adv.* mortally.

mortandad, *n.f.* mortality; butchery, massacre.

mortecino, -na, *a.* dying a natural death; on the point of dying; weak, exhausted; pale, deathly; *hacer la mortecina,* to sham death.

morterada, *n.f.* food or sauce prepared in a mortar; (*artill.*) stones or grape-shot fired from a mortar.

mortecete; morterico, -illo, -ito, *n.m.* small

mortar; gun for firing salutes; maroon; broad candlestick.

mortero, *n.m.* mortar, cement; short wax taper; nether mill-stone; *mortero de brújula,* inner compass-box.

morteruelo, *n.m.* small mortar; a toy for boys; fricassee of hog's liver.

morticinio, *n.m.* carrion, carcass.

mortífero, -ria, *a.* mortiferous, fatal.

mortificación, *n.f.* mortification; humiliation, vexation, trouble; gangrene.

mortificar, *v.t. (pret.* **mortifiqué;** *pres. subj.* **mortifique)** to mortify, to subdue passions; to disgust, afflict, vex, humiliate. — *v.r.* to gangrene, mortify; to conquer one's passions; to practise bodily mortifications.

mortuorio, *n.m.* funeral, burial.

mortuorio, -ria, *a.* belonging to the dead; *casa mortuoria,* house of the deceased.

morucho, *n.m.* young bull with horns tipped.

morueco, *n.m.* ram, male sheep.

moruno, -na, *a.* Moorish.

moruro, *n.m.* Cuban acacia.

morusa, *n.f. (coll.)* cash, money.

mosaico, *n.m.* Mosaic; mosaic.

mosaísmo, *n.m.* Mosaic law.

mosca, *n.f.* fly; impertinent intruder; tuft of hair under the lip; cash, specie, money in hand; vexation, trouble. — *pl.* **moscas,** sparks; *mosca de burro,* horse-fly; *mosca muerta,* one who feigns meekness; *papar moscas,* to gape with astonishment; *moscas blancas,* falling snowflakes; *pasar el tiempo en cazar moscas,* to waste time in idleness; *picar la mosca,* to be alarmed, disquieted; *cazar moscas,* to pursue vain ends; *más moscas se cogen con miel que no con hiel,* a smooth tongue does more than harsh words; *soltar* (or *aflojar*) *la mosca,* to be forced to give or spend money.

moscarda, *n.f.* gad-fly, horse-fly; bees' eggs.

moscardear, *v.i.* to lay eggs (of bees).

moscardón, *n.m.* botfly; horse bot; bumble-bee; hornet, drone; (*fig.*) importunate man, sly fellow.

moscareta, *n.f. (orn.)* fly-catcher.

moscatel, *a.* muscatel. — *n.m.* muscatel (grape, wine or vineyard).

mosco, *n.m.* gnat, mosquito.

moscón, *n.m.* large fly; hanger-on.

moscorrofio, *n.m.* (*Col., Hond.*) particularly ugly person.

moscovita, *a.* Muscovite, Russian.

Moscou, *n.f.* Moscow.

mosén, *n.m.* sir; title given to clergymen in Aragon and Catalonia.

mosqueado, -da, *a.* spotted, painted, brindled.

mosqueador, *n.m.* fly-flap; (*coll.*) tail of a horse or cow.

mosquear, *v.t.* to flap, catch flies; to retort, make a repartee; to flog, whip. — *v.r.* to become angry or vexed, repel embarrassments, show resentment.

mosqueo, *n.m.* fly-catching.

mosquero, *n.m.* fly-trap, fly-flap; (*Cub., Chi.*) swarm of flies.

mosquerola, mosqueruela, *n.f.* Muscadine pear.

mosqueta, *n.f.* white musk-rose.

mosquetazo, *n.m.* musket-shot.

mosquete, *n.m.* musket.

mosquetería, *n.f.* body of musketeers.

mosqueteril, *a.* (*coll.*) of or belonging to musketeers; (*theat.*) (*coll.*) belonging to the crowd in the pit.

mosquetero, *n.m.* musketeer, foot-soldier; (*coll.*) spectator standing in the pit of a theatre.

mosquetón, *n.m.* a short cavalry carbine.

mosquil; mosquino, -na, *a.* belonging to flies.

mosquita, *n.f. (orn.)* small bird of Sardinia.

mosquitero, -ra, *n.m.f.* mosquito net.

mosquito, *n.m.* gnat; mosquito; tippler.

mostacero, -ra, *n.m.f.* mustard pot.

mostacilla, *n.f.* sparrow-shot; small bead.

mostacho, *n.m.* moustache; spot on the face; (*naut.*) bowsprit shrouds.

mostachón, *n.m.* kind of cake.

mostachoso, -sa, *a.* wearing moustaches.

mostagán, *n.m.* (*coll.*) wine.

mostajo, *n.m.* (*bot.*) white beam-tree.

mostaza, *n.f.* mustard, mustard-seed; grape-shot; *hacer la mostaza,* to draw blood from the nose with a blow; *subir la mostaza a las narices,* to be very much irritated.

mostazo, *n.m.* (*bot.*) mustard-plant; strong must.

mostear, *v.i.* to yield must; to put must into vats; to mix must with old wine.

mostela, *n.f. (agric.)* gavel, sheaf.

mostelera, *n.f.* place where sheaves are laid up.

mostellar, *n.m.* white beam-tree.

mostillo, *n.m.* must-cake; sauce made of must and mustard.

mosto, *n.m.* stum, must, new wine; *mosto agustín,* must cake cooked with flour, fine spices, and various fruit.

mostrable, *a.* that can be shown.

mostrado, -da, *a.* accustomed, habituated, inured.

mostrador, -ra, *n.m.f.* demonstrator.

mostrador, *n.m.* counter; dial (of a clock or watch).

mostrar, *v.t. (pres. indic.* **muestro;** *pres. subj.* **muestre)** to show, exhibit, view, point out, place before; to establish, prove, expound, explain, demonstrate; to feign, dissemble; *mostrar las suelas de los zapatos,* to show a clean pair of heels, run away. — *v.r.* to show oneself, appear.

mostrenco, -ca, *a.* strayed, vagabond, home-less, unowned, masterless, vagrant; dull, ignorant, stupid; bulky, fat; *bienes mostrencos,* goods which have no known owner.

mota, *n.f.* small knot on cloth; thread speck, mite, mote, small particle; slight, defect, fault; bank of earth, mound, hummock; (*Arg., Bol.*) tightly curled lock of hair.

motacila, *n.f. (orn.)* wagtail.

mote, *n.m.* motto, sentence, device, nickname; (*S. Am.*) stewed corn.

motear, *v.t.* to speckle, mark with spots.

motejador, -ra, *n.m.f.* mocker, scoffer, censurer.

motejar, *v.t.* to censure, ridicule, nickname, chaff.

motete, *n.m.* (*mus.*) motet; (*fig.*) nickname; affront, abuse.

motil, *n.m.* farmer's boy.

motilar, *v.t.* to crop, cut the hair.

motilón, *a.* having little hair. — *n.m.* lay brother.

motín

motín, *n.m.* mutiny, riot, insurrection.
motivar, *v.t.* to assign a reason or motive; to cause.
motivo, *n.m.* motive, cause, occasion, reason; (*mus.*) motif, theme; *con motivo de*, owing to, in order to, by reason of.
motivo, -va, *a.* motive, moving, causing motion.
moto, *n.m.* guide-post, landmark.
motocicleta, *n.f.* motor-cycle.
motociclista, *n.m.f.* motor-cyclist.
motolita, *n.f.* (*orn.*) wagtail.
motolito, -ta, *a.* ignorant, easily deceived.
motón, *n.m.* (*naut.*) block, pulley.
motonave, *n.f.* motor-ship, motor-boat.
motonería, *n.f.* (*naut.*) pulley-blocks.
motonero, *n.m.* pulley-block maker.
motor, *n.m.* mover, author, impeller, contriver; motor; *motor bipolar*, two-pole motor; *motor de cilindros convergentes*, V-motor, V-engine; *motor de combustión interna*, internal-combustion engine; *motor diesel*, diesel-engine; *motor propulsor*, (*aer.*) pusher engine; *motor tractor*, tractor; *el primer motor*, God.
motor, -ra, *a.* motor, motive.
motorismo, *n.m.* motorism.
motorista, *n.m.f.* motorist, driver.
motril, *n.* apprentice in a shop.
motriz, *a.* motive, motory, moving.
movedizo, -za, *a.* movable, easily moved, variable, inconstant, shifting; shaky, unsteady; *genio movedizo*, versatile genius.
movedor, -ra, *n.m.f., a.* mover, motor, exciter, occasioner.
movedura, *n.f.* movement, miscarriage.
mover, *v.t.* (*pres. indic.* **muevo;** *pres. subj.* **mueva**) to move, to make move, stir; incite, persuade; drive, impel, propel; induce, excite, inspire, promote, occasion; to shake, wag; to prevail upon; to touch, affect with emotion. — *v.i.* to sprout, bud; (*arch.*) to spring an arch; (*med.*) to miscarry. — *v.r.* to move, walk forward, stir.
movible, *a.* movable, mobile, locomotive; loose, changeable, fickle.
moviente, *a.* moving, motor, motive.
móvil, *a.* movable, mobile, shaky, unsteady, portable. — *n.m.* motive, mover, motor; moving body.
movilidad, *n.f.* mobility, movableness, fickleness, inconstancy, unsteadiness.
movilización, *n.f.* mobilization.
movilizar, *v.t.* (*pret.* **movilicé;** *pres. subj.* **movilice**) (*mil.*) to mobilize.
movimiento, *n.m.* move, movement, motion, moving; commotion, revolt, sedition, rising, tumult, disturbance; life, liveliness, animation; (*mech.*) motion; (*astron.*) clock error; earthquake; (*com.*) lively trade, traffic; (*mus.*) tempo, time; *juguete de movimiento*, mechanical toy; *en movimiento*, going, working; *movimiento alternativo*, reciprocating motion; *movimiento continuo* or *perpetuo*, perpetual movement; *movimiento oratorio*, oratorical gesture.
moxa, *n.f.* (*surg.*) moxa; cautery.
moyana, *n.f.* a large culverin; (*coll.*) lie, falsehood; dog biscuit.
moyo, *n.m.* liquid measure of about 57 gallons.
moyuelo, *n.m.* very fine bran.
moza, *n.f.* girl, maid, lass, young woman,

maid-servant; concubine, mistress; cloth pounder; last or conquering game; *moza de cámara*, chambermaid; *moza de fortuna*, prostitute; *a la moza, con el moco, y al mozo, con el bozo*, refrain which advocates the marrying of a young man early; *bien parece la moza lozana cabe la barba cana*, refrain urging that husbands should be older than their wives; *como la moza del abad, que no cuece y tiene pan*, refrain directed at those who wish to eat without working.
mozalbete, mozalbillo, *n.m.* lad, beardless youth.
mozallón, *n.m.* young, robust labourer.
mozárabe, *a.* Mozarabic. — *n.m.f.* Mozarab, Christian who lived among the Moors in Spain.
mozo, -za, *a.* young, youthful, single, unmarried.
mozo, *n.m.* youth, young man, lad, bachelor; manservant, waiter, porter; *mozo de paja y cebada*, ostler; *mozo de cordel* or *de cuerda*, railway- or street-porter; *al mozo amañado, la mujer al lado*, if a young man is industrious, marry him early lest he grow vicious; *el mozo y el gallo, un año*, change servants often; *mozo bueno, mozo malo, quince días después del año*, familiarity often changes opinions; *mozo de quince años, tiene papo y no tiene manos*, growing boys eat much and work little.
mozuela, *n.f.* very young girl.
mozuelo, *n.m.* very young man.
mu, *n.f.* sleep, repose; term bidding children to be silent; *vamos a la mu*, go to sleep. — *n.m.* bellowing of bulls, lowing of cattle.
muaré, *n.m.* moiré, watered silk.
mucamo, -ma, *n.m.f.* (*S. Am.*) servant.
muceta, *n.f.* (*eccles.*) mozetta.
mucilaginoso, -sa, *a.* mucilaginous, slimy.
mucílago, mucilago, *n.m.* mucilage, slime.
mucosidad, *n.f.* mucosity.
mucoso, -sa, *a.* mucous, viscous.
múcura, *n.m.* (*Ven.*) pitcher, ewer, gurglet; (*Col.*) blockhead.
muchacha, *n.f.* girl, lass, young woman.
muchachada, *n.f.* boyish trick, girlish trick.
muchachear, *v.i.* to act or play childishly.
muchachería, *n.f.* boyish trick; crowd of noisy boys.
muchachez, *n.f.* childhood, puerility.
muchacho, *n.m.* boy, lad, young man.
muchedumbre, *n.f.* multitude, crowd, large number, plenty, abundance.
mucho, -cha, *a.* much, large in quantity, many in number, plentiful, abundant; *no ha mucho*, not long since; *no es mucho*, it is no wonder; *muchos pocos hacen un mucho*, many a mickle makes a muckle. — *adv.* much, greatly, excessively, exceedingly, by far, often, long; *ni mucho menos*, far from it, nor anything like it.
muda, *n.f.* change, alteration; mute letter; change of linen; mew; moulting-time; roost of birds of prey; cosmetic.
mudable, *a.* changeable, variable, mutable, fickle.
mudamente, *adv.* silently, tacitly, mutely.
mudanza, *n.f.* alteration, removal; change, mutation, commutation, inconstancy, levity; figure in dancing, motion.
mudar, *v.t.* to change, remove, deviate, vary, alter; to mew, moult, shed feathers. — *v.r.*

to change, shift, dress in fresh clothes; to move into another house, change quarters.

muday, *n.m.* (*Chi.*) a drink made of maize or barley.

mudéjar, *n.m.f.*, *a.* Mohammedan subject of Christian sovereigns.

mudenco, -ca, *n.m.*, *a.* (*CR., Hond.*) stammerer.

mudez, *n.f.* dumbness.

mudo, -da, *a.* dumb, silent, still, mute.

mué, *n.m.* moiré.

mueblaje, *n.m.* furniture.

mueble, *n.m.* piece of furniture. — *n.m.pl.* **muebles,** furniture, movable goods.

mueblería, *n.f.* furniture factory or store.

mueblista, *n.m.f.* maker or seller of furniture.

mueca, *n.f.* grimace, wry face, grin.

muecín, *n.m.* muezzin.

muela, *n.f.* runner, upper mill-stone; milldam; grindstone, whetstone; grinder, molar tooth; hill, hillock; track, circle; *haberle salido a uno la muela del juicio,* to have cut one's wisdom teeth, learned prudence; *al que le duele la muela, que se la saque,* if your tooth hurts you, have it out (phrase excusing oneself from interference); *entre dos muelas cordales, nunca pongas tus pulgares,* never put your thumbs between two back teeth (i.e. never ask for trouble).

muellaje, *n.m.* dues paid on entering a port.

muelle, *n.m.* spring, regulator, watch spring; (*jewel.*) chatelaine; (*naut.*) pier, mole, jetty, wharf, quay. — *a.* tender, soft, delicate; luxurious, licentious.

muellemente, *adv.* softly, gently, tenderly, delicately.

muérdago, *n.m.* (*bot.*) mistletoe.

muérgano, *n.m.* (*Col.*) worthless or contemptible person or thing.

muergo, *n.m.* sprat, a mollusc.

muermo, *n.m.* (*vet.*) glanders.

muermoso, -sa, *a.* glandered, suffering from *muermo.*

muero; muera, *pres. indic.; pres. subj.* [MORIR].

muerte, *n.f.* death, decease, mortality; murder, homicide, assassination; severe affliction; havoc, destruction, ruin; skeleton representing death; *acusar a muerte,* to accuse of a capital crime; *a muerte o a vida,* a matter of life or death; *muerte chiquita,* (*coll.*) nervous shiver; *de mala muerte,* of little worth; *de muerte,* implacably, ferociously; *estar a la muerte,* to be at death's door; *muerte no venga, que achaque no tenga,* excuses can always be found for disagreeable tasks; *ser una muerte,* to be extremely annoying, unbearable; *para todo hay remedio, si no es para la muerte,* there's a remedy for everything but death; *hasta la muerte todo es vida,* nobody's dying till he's dead.

muerto *n.m.* dead body, dead man, corpse; *contarle a uno con los muertos,* to leave out of one's reckoning; *desenterrar los muertos,* to speak ill of the dead; *a muertos e idos, no hay amigos,* out of sight, out of mind; *echarle a uno el muerto,* to blame someone.

muerto, -ta, *p.p.* irregular of MORIR and MATAR. — *a.* dead, extinguished, lifeless, languid, faded.

muesca, *n.f.* groove, indentation, hack, notch, nick, mortise, dovetail scarf.

muestra, *n.f.* shop sign; pattern, sample; end of a piece of cloth; specimen, model, design; sign, proof, indication, demonstration; (*mil.*) muster-roll; *por la muestra se conoce el paño,* one can tell quality by a sample, you can judge a person by one of his acts.

muestrario, *n.m.* collection of samples; specimen-book.

muestro; muestre, *pres. indic.; pres. subj.* [MOSTRAR].

muevo; mueva, *pres. indic.; pres. subj.* [MOVER].

mufla, *n.f.* muffle oven. — *pl.* **muflas,** thick winter gloves.

muftí, *n.m.* mufti.

muga, *n.f.* boundary, landmark.

mugido, *n.m.* bellow of a bull or ox.

mugiente, *a.* bellowing, roaring, lowing.

mugir, *v.i.* (*pres. indic.* **mujo;** *pres. subj.* **muja**) to bellow, roar, low.

mugre, *n.f.* grime, dirt, filth, grease.

mugriento, -ta, *a.* greasy, grimy, dirty, filthy.

mugrón, *n.m.* sprig, shoot, sucker, tiller.

muguete, *n.m.* lily of the valley.

muharra, *n.f.* steel point of lance or spear.

muir, *v.t.* (*prov.*) to milk.

mujalata, *n.f.* (*Morocco*) farming partnership between a Moroccan and a Christian or a Jew.

mujer, *n.f.* woman, wife, mate; *tomar mujer,* to take a wife, marry; *mujer de su casa,* good housekeeper; *mujer de bigotes,* commanding woman; *mujer de gobierno,* housewife; *a la mujer barbuda, de lejos la saluda,* beware of manly women; *a la mujer casada, el marido le basta,* it is enough for a married woman if she pleases her husband; *a la mujer casta, Dios le basta,* Heaven guards the pure woman; *la mujer algarera, nunca hace larga tela,* the woman who talks much, accomplishes little; *la mujer buena, de la casa vacía hace llena,* the careful housewife fills the larder; *la mujer y el vidrio siempre están en peligro,* woman is as easily broken as glass (referring to loss of honour); *la primera mujer, escoba, y la segunda, señora,* a second wife is better treated than a first; *mujer, viento y ventura, pronto se mudan,* woman, wind and luck are fickle things; *el consejo de la mujer es poco y el que no le toma es loco,* women's counsel may be of little worth yet everyone but a fool takes it; *la mujer y la gallina, por andar se pierden aína,* women and hens soon get lost through gadding about.

mujeracha, *n.f.* large, coarse woman.

mujercilla, *n.f.* little woman, worthless woman; prostitute.

mujerengo, *a.* (*Cent. Am., Arg.*) effeminate.

mujeriego, -ga, *a.* feminine, womanly, womanish; fond of women, philandering; *montar a la mujeriega,* to ride side-saddle.

mujeriego, *n.m.* woman-kind.

mujeril, *a.* womanly, womanish, feminine; effeminate.

mujerilmente, *adv.* effeminately.

mujerío, *n.m.* assembly of women.

mujerona, *n.f.* matron, stout or lusty woman.

mujerzuela, *n.f.* worthless woman; prostitute.

mújol, *n.m.* (*ichth.*) mullet.

mula, *n.f.* she-mule; ancient Roman shoe worn now by the Pope on ceremonial occasions; *írsele a uno la mula,* to slip out (of an unseemly expression); *quien endura, caballero va en buena mula*, economy brings riches.

mulada, *n.f.* (*Am.*) drove of mules.

muladar, *n.m.* dungheap; anything filthy or infectious.

muladí, *a.* Spanish convert to Islam.

mulante, *n.m.* muleteer, mule-boy.

mular, *a.* belonging to mules.

mulata, *n.f.* crustacean very common in the Bay of Biscay.

mulatero, *n.m.* muleteer, mule-driver.

mulato, -ta, *a.* mulatto, tawny; (*Am.*) silver mineral of a dark green colour.

muleque, *n.m.* (*Cub.*) young slave, newly arrived from Africa.

mulero, *n.m.* mule-boy.

muleta, *n.f.* young she-mule; prop, support, crutch; snack; bull-fighters' red flag.

muletada, *n.f.* herd of mules.

muletero, *n.m.* muleteer, mule-driver.

muletilla, *n.f.* senseless word; cross-handle cane; (*min.*) crutch; phrase often repeated in talking; wand, rod.

muleto, *n.m.* young he-mule.

muletón, *n.m.* swanskin.

mulilla, *n.f.* small mule.

mulo, *n.m.* mule.

mulquía, *n.f.* (*Morocco*) (*law*) title deed.

mulso, -sa, *a.* sweetened with honey or sugar.

multa, *n.f.* mulct, fine, forfeit.

multar, *v.t.* to mulct, fine.

multicolor, *a.* many-coloured.

multifloro, -ra, *a.* (*bot.*) multiflorous.

multiforme, *a.* multiform.

multilátero, -ra, *a.* multilateral.

multimillonario, -ria, *n.m.f.*, *a.* multimillionaire.

multíparo, -ra, *a.* multiparous.

multiplicable, *a.* multiplicable.

múltiple, *a.* multiple, manifold.

multiplicación, *n.f.* multiplication.

multiplicador, -ra, *n.m.f.* multiplier, multiplicator.

multiplicando, *n.m.* (*arith.*) multiplicand.

multiplicar, *v.t.*, *v.r.* (*pret.* **multipliqué**; *pres. subj.* **multiplique**) to multiply, increase, reproduce.

multíplice, *a.* multiple.

multiplicidad, *n.f.* multiplicity.

múltiplo, -pla, *a.* multiple.

multitubular, *a.* multitubular.

multitud, *n.f.* multitude, crowd, huge number.

mulla, *n.f.* digging round vines.

mullidor, -ra, *n.m.f.* bruiser, mollifier.

mullir, *v.t.* to pound, beat up, knead, fluff, soften, mollify; to dig around (vines and trees); *mullir la cama*, to beat up the bed; *mullírselas a*, to chastise, mortify.

mulló, *n.m.* (*ichth.*) surmullet; (*Am.*) glass bead.

mundanal, *a.* worldly, mundane.

mundanalidad, *n.f.* worldliness.

mundanear, *v.i.* to give excessive attention to worldly things.

mundano, -na, *a.* mundane, worldly.

mundial, *a.* universal, world-wide.

mundificar, *v.t.* (*pret.* **mundifiqué**; *pres. subj.* **mundifique**) to cleanse, make clean.

mundificativo, -va, *a.* mundificative, mundatory, cleansing.

mundillo, *n.m.* warming-pan; arched cloth dryer; (*bot.*) viburnum; cushion for lacemaking.

mundinovi, mundinuevo, *n.m.* raree-show.

mundo, *n.m.* world, earth, sphere, globe; (*coll.*) great crowd, quantity or multitude; social life; dissipated life, worldly desires or habits; *echar al mundo*, to create, give birth to; *echarse al mundo*, to plunge into dissipation; *no ser de este mundo*, to live retired from the world; *medio mundo*, many people; *hacer mundo nuevo*, to introduce changes or novelties; *tener mundo* (or *tener mucho mundo*), to be acute, sharp; *ver mundo*, to travel; *desterrar del mundo*, to banish from society; *anda el mundo al revés*, the world is sadly changed; *en este mundo cansado, ni hay bien cumplido ni mal acabado*, everything is changeable and uncertain in this world; *aunque se hunda el mundo*, even if the world comes to an end; *no cabe en este mundo*, he is too big for his boots; *todo el mundo es país* (or *es uno*), it's the same the world over, there is evil everywhere.

munición, *n.f.* munition, ammunition; warlike stores; charge of fire-arms; small shot, birdshot; *municiones de boca*, provisions, victuals; *municiones de guerra*, war stores; *de munición*, supplied by the government; done hurriedly.

municionar, *v.t.* to store, supply with ammunition.

municipal, *a.* municipal. — *n.m.* policeman.

municipalidad, *n.f.* municipality, municipal government.

munícipe, *n.m.* citizen, denizen.

municipio, *n.m.* city, township.

munificencia, *n.f.* munificence, liberality.

munificentísimo, -ma, *a.* most munificent.

munífico, -ca, *a.* munificent, liberal.

munitoria, *n.f.* art of fortification.

muñeca, *n.f.* (*anat.*) wrist; doll, puppet; pounce bag; rubber or polishing bag; bundle of medicaments; dressmaker's figure. — *pl.* **muñecas**, screws (in the mint).

muñeco, *n.m.* puppet, manikin, boy doll, effeminate fellow.

muñeira, *n.f.* popular dance of Galicia.

muñequear, *v.t.* to play with the wrist in fencing.

muñequera, *n.f.* wrist watch strap.

muñequería, *n.f.* effeminacy in dress; overdressing.

muñequilla, *n.f.* (*Chi.*) young ear of corn.

muñidor, *n.m.* beadle, apparitor, messenger.

muñir, *v.t.* to summon, call, convoke.

muñón, *n.m.* stump of an amputated arm or leg; (*mech.*) journal, gudgeon, pivot; (*artill.*) trunnion.

muñonera, *n.f.* trunnion plate; (*mech.*) gudgeon socket, journal box, bearing.

murajes, *n.m.pl.* (*bot.*) medicinal herb.

mural, *a.* mural, belonging to walls.

muralla, *n.f.* wall, rampart.

murallón, *n.m.* (*fort.*) a very strong wall.

murar, *v.t.* to wall, surround with a wall or rampart.

murciélago, *n.m.* (*orn.*) bat.

murciglero, *n.m.* (*slang*) thief prowling at night.

murena, *n.f.* (*ichth.*) kind of eel, muræna (*morena*).

murete, *n.m.* small wall.

murga, *n.f.* lees of olives; street band.

murgón, *n.m.* (*ichth.*) parr, smolt.

muriático, -ca, *a.* (*chem.*) muriatic.

muriato, *n.m.* (*chem.*) muriate.

múrice, *n.m.* murex, shell-fish; (*poet.*) purple.

murmujear, *v.i.* (*coll.*) to mutter, murmur.

murmullo, *n.m.* mutter, murmur; whisper; whispering; (*poet.*) ripple, purl; rustle.

murmuración, *n.f.* backbiting, gossiping, slander.

murmurador, -ra, *n.m.f.* murmurer, backbiter; detractor.

murmurante, *a.* murmuring, purling.

murmurar, *v.i.* to murmur, ripple, flow gently, purl (as streams); to rustle (as leaves); to grudge, grumble, mutter; to backbite, gossip; to whisper.

murmurio, *n.m.* murmuring of a stream.

muro, *n.m.* (*build.*) wall; (*fort.*) rampart.

murria, *n.f.* melancholy, reverie; fit of blues, surliness, spleen; (*pharm.*) an astringent lotion.

murrio, -rria, *a.* sad, melancholy, sullen, surly, sulky.

murtilla, murtina, *n.f.* (*bot.*) Chilean myrtus; its berry; liquor made from this.

murtón, *n.m.* myrtle-berry.

murucuya, *n.f.* (*bot.*) purple passion-flower.

mus, *n.m.* game of cards.

musa, *n.f.* muse, goddess of poetry; poetry. — *pl.* the fine arts.

musaraña, *n.f.* fetid shrew-mouse; any small animal, vermin or insect; (*coll.*) ridiculous stuffed figure; (*coll.*) floating speck in the eye; *pensar en las musarañas,* to be absent-minded.

muscicapa, *n.f.* (*orn.*) fly-catcher.

musco, *n.m.* moss; musk rat.

musco, -ca, *a.* musk-colour, dark brown.

muscular, *a.* muscular, strong, vigorous, powerful.

musculatura, *n.f.* musculature.

músculo, *n.m.* muscle; (*zool.*) huge whale.

musculoso, -sa, *a.* muscular, brawny.

muselina, *n.f.* muslin, fine cotton.

museo, *n.m.* museum.

muserola, *n.f.* noseband of a bridle.

musgaño, *n.m.* shrew-mouse.

musgo, *n.m.* moss.

musgo, -ga, *a.* dark brown.

musgoso, -sa, *a.* mossy, moss-covered.

música, *n.f.* music, harmony, melody; body of performing musicians, band; *dar música a un sordo,* to try to persuade an intractable person; *no entender la música,* to feign deafness to what one wishes not to hear; *donde hay música no puede haber cosa mala,* where there's music there can't be mischief.

musical, *a.* musical.

musicalmente, *adv.* musically.

músico, -ca, *n.m.f.* musician. — *a.* musical, harmonious.

musicógrafo, -fa, *n.m.f.* writer of music.

musiquero, *n.m.* music cabinet.

musitar, *v.i.* to mutter, mumble, whisper.

muslera, *n.f.* cuisse, thigh-armour.

muslime; muslímico, -ca, *a.* Moslem, Mohammedan.

muslo, *n.m.* (*anat.*) thigh.

musmón, *n.m.* (*zool.*) an hybrid animal product of the cross of a sheep with a goat.

musquerola, *n.f.* muscadine pear.

mustaco, *n.m.* cake made of flour, must, butter, etc.

mustela, *n.m.* (*ichth.*) a selachian fish.

mustiamente, *adv.* sadly, glumly, in a melancholy way.

mustio, -tia, *a.* sad; parched, withered; musty.

musulmán, -ana, *n.m.f.* Mussulman.

muta, *n.f.* pack of hounds.

mutabilidad, *n.f.* mutability, fickleness.

mutación, *n.f.* mutation, change; (*theat.*) change of scene; unseasonable weather.

mutilación, *n.f.* mutilation, maimedness.

mutilar, *v.t.* to mutilate, cripple, maim; dock, mangle; to reduce, cut short; to mar, deface.

mutis, *n.m.* (*theat.*) exit of an actor.

mutismo, *n.m.* mutism, muteness.

mutual, *a.* mutual, reciprocal.

mutualidad, *n.f.* mutuality; (*com.*) system of mutual insurance or help.

mútuamente, *adv.* mutually.

mutuante, *n.m.f.* lender, loaner.

mutuatario, -ria, *a.* (*law*) mutuary.

mutún, *n.m.* (*Bol.*) bird similar to a turkey.

mutuo, -tua, *a.* mutual, reciprocal, commutual.

mutuo, *n.m.* (*law*) loan.

muy, *adv.* very, greatly; most; *muy de mañana,* very early; *muy mucho,* (*coll.*) very much; *soy muy de Vd.,* I am entirely at your service; *muy Señor mío,* dear sir (in letters).

muz, *n.m.* (*naut.*) extremity of the cutwater.

N

N, n, sixteenth letter of the Spanish alphabet, its name *ene*; symbol for an unknown proper name, *el Señor N* (so-and-so, Mister X); for *norte* (north), and *número* (number).

naba, *n.f.* Swedish turnip.

nabab, *n.m.* nabob.

nabal, nabar, *n.m.* turnip-field. — *a.* belonging to turnips.

nabería, *n.f.* turnip-pottage, heap of turnips.

nabí, *n.m.* Moorish prophet.

nabicol, *n.m.* (*bot.*) kind of turnip.

nabina, *n.f.* rape and turnip-seed.

nabiza, *n.f.* (*bot.*) lateral branches of turnip-roots; turnip rootlets.

nabla, *n.f.* ancient musical instrument, kind of psaltery.

nabo, *n.m.* rape, colewort.

naborí, *n.m.f.* (*Am.*) free Indian servant.

naboría, *n.f.* (*Am.*) allotment of Indian servants (during the Spanish conquest).

nácar, *n.m.* mother-of-pearl, pearl-colour.

nácara, *n.f.* kettledrum of Spanish cavalry.

nacarado, -da, *a.* set with mother-of-pearl, pearl-colour.

nacáreo, -rea; nacarino, -na, *a.* set with mother-of-pearl, of pearl-colour.

nacarón, *n.m.* mother-of-pearl of low quality.

nacascolo, *n.m.* (*Cent. Am.*) dividivi, a tree yielding dyeing and tanning products.

nacatamal, *n.m.* (*Hond.*) tamale stuffed with pork.

nacatete, *n.m.* (*Mex.*) a very young cockerel.

nacencia, *n.f.* tumour, outgrowth.

nacer, *v.i.* (*pres. indic.* **nazco**; *pres. subj.*

nazca) to be born, come into the world; to bud, flower, blossom, shoot, grow; to take rise or beginning; to rise, start up, appear on the horizon; to spring, rise, flow, have its source (as a stream, river, etc.); to begin, originate, start, issue; to be reared; to infer. — *v.r.* to be propagated by natural means (of plants, etc.); to fray near a seam (as clothes); *nacer de cabeza*, to be born to misery; *nacer de pies* (or *en buena hora*), to be born lucky; *nacer tarde*, to be wanting in intelligence or experience; *no le pesa de haber nacido*, he is very proud of his talents; *no con quien naces, sino con quien paces*, a man is known by the company he keeps; *quien antes nace, antes pace*, the eldest son is wont to get the lion's share.

nacido, -da, *a.* born, proper, fit, apt; *bien* or *mal nacido*, well or ill bred. — *p.p.* [NACER].

nacido, *n.m.* living man; pimple, pustule, tumour, abscess.

naciente, *a.* growing; (*her.*) naissant. — *n.m.* Orient, East.

nacimiento, *n.m.* birth, nativity; beginning, origin; growing (of plants); descent, lineage; head, source (of a river); physical or moral cause; scene representing the Nativity, the Crib; *de nacimiento*, from birth.

nación, *n.f.* nation; (*coll.*) birth, issue; (*Am.*) race, tribe; *de nación*, native of.

nacional, *a.* national; native; domestic. — *n.m.* native; militiaman.

nacionalidad, *n.f.* nationality, national manners and customs.

nacionalismo, *n.m.* nationalism, love of one's country.

nacionalista, *n.m.f.*, *a.* nationalist(ic).

nacionalización, *n.f.* nationalization.

nacionalizar, *v.t.* to nationalize.

nacionalmente, *adv.* nationally.

naco, *n.m.* (*Arg., Bol.*) piece of black chewing tobacco.

nada, *n.f. pron.* nothing, nothingness, naught; nonentity; very little. — *adv.* in no degree, by no means, not at all; *nada de ello*, not at all, by no means, far from it; *en una nada*, in an instant; *enfadarse por nada*, to be annoyed by a mere trifle; *nada entre dos platos*, great show and no reality; *nada menos*, nothing less; *más vale algo que nada*, half a loaf is better than no bread.

nadaderas, *n.f.pl.* corks or bladders for learning to swim.

nadadero, *n.m.* swimming-place.

nadador, -ra, *n.m.f.* swimmer.

nadar, *v.i.* to swim, float; to be plentiful, abound; *se me nadan los pies en los zapatos*, my shoes are very loose.

nadie, *indef. pron.* nobody, no one, none.

nadir, *n.m.* (*astr.*) nadir.

nádir, *n.m.*, (*Morocco*) administrator or trustee of a charitable institution.

nado (a), *adv.* afloat, with great difficulty; *salir a nado*, to save oneself by swimming; *echarse a nado*, to hazard, undertake boldly.

nafa, *n.f.* orange-flower water (used solely in the phrase *agua de nafa*).

nafta, *n.f.* naphtha.

naftalina, *n.f.* naphthaline.

naftol, *n.m.* naphthol.

nagual, *n.m.* (*Mex.*) sorcerer, conjurer, wizard; (*Hond.*) pet animal.

naguapate, *n.m.* (*Hond.*) a cruciate plant used to cure venereal diseases.

naguas, *n.f.pl.* under-petticoat.

naguatlato, -ta, *a.* (*Mex.*) Indian interpreter.

nagüela, *n.f.* (*obs.*) thatched cottage, hovel.

naife, *n.m.* diamond of the first water.

naipe, *n.m.* playing-card; pack of cards; *dar el naipe para una cosa*, to be very clever; *dar a uno el naipe*, to have good luck at cards; *estar como el naipe*, to be very thin; *tener el naipe*, to have good luck, to have the deal.

naire, *n.m.* elephant-keeper.

nalca, *n.f.* (*Chi.*) edible leaf stalk.

nalga, *n.f.* buttock, rump.

nalgada, *n.f.* leg, ham; blow on or with the rump.

nalgatorio, *n.m.* seat, posteriors.

nalgón, -ona, *a.* (*Hond.*) [NALGUDO].

nalgudo, -da, *a.* with round fleshy posteriors.

nalguear, *v.i.* to shake the posteriors in walking.

nalguilla, *n.f.* thick part of the hub of a wheel.

nambí, *n.m.f.* (*Arg.*) horse or mare with drooping ears.

nambimba, *n.f.* (*Mex.*) dish made of maize boiled with honey, cocoa and chilli.

nambira, *n.f.* (*Hond.*) half of a dried gourd used as a drinking vessel, etc.

nana, *n.f.* (*coll.*) grandma; lullaby; (*Mex.*) child's nurse, nanny.

nanacate, *n.m.* (*Mex.*) (*bot.*) mushroom.

nance, *n.m.* (*Hond.*) (*bot.*) a shrub and its fragrant fruit (in Cuba called *nancer*).

nancear, *v.i.* (*Hond.*) to catch; to fit, have room, reach.

nandú, *n.m.* American ostrich.

nango, -ga, *a.* (*Mex.*) foreign; silly, foolish, stupid.

nanjea, *n.f.* (*Philip.*) a tree largely used in making cabinets and musical instruments.

nanquín, *n.m.* nankeen.

nansa, *n.f.* fish-pond; fish trap.

nansu, nanzu, *n.m.* (*Cub., Chi.*) a kind of cotton cloth.

nao, *n.f.* (*poet.*) ship, vessel.

naonato, -ta, *a.* born on board ship.

napea, *n.f.* (*myth.*) wood-nymph.

napelo, *n.m.* (*bot.*) monk's-hood, wolf's-bane

Nápoles, *n.m.* Naples.

napolitana, *n.f.* a combination of cards in some games (ace, two and three same suit; the four aces, or three aces and knight of *copas*).

napolitano, -na, *a.* Neapolitan, of or belonging to Naples.

naque, *n.m.* two strolling comedians.

naranja, *n.f.* orange, fruit of the orange-tree; cannon ball of the size of an orange; *media naranja*, (*arch.*) cupola; well-mated spouse.

naranjada, *n.f.* orange-water, orangeade; (*fig.*) rude speech or action.

naranjado, -da, *a.* orange-coloured.

naranjal, *n.m.* orangery, orange-grove.

naranjazo, *n.m.* blow with an orange.

naranjera, *n.f.* orange-woman.

naranjero, *n.m.* orange-seller; orange-tree.

naranjero, -ra, *n.m.f.* orange-seller. — *a.* applied to artillery carrying balls the size of oranges.

naranjillo, *n.m.* (*Ec.*) plant of edible fruit (*Solanum quitoense*).

naranjita, naranjilla, *n.f.* small orange to preserve.

naranjo, *n.m.* orange-tree; (*coll.*) booby, noodle.

narcisismo, *n.m.* narcissism.

narciso, *n.m.* (*bot.*) narcissus, daffodil; fop, coxcomb.

narcosis, *n.f.* (*path.*) narcosis.

narcótico, -ca, *n.m.f.*, *a.* narcotic, narcotical.

narcotina, *n.f.* (*chem.*) narcotine.

narcotismo, *n.m.* narcotism, narcosis.

narcotizar, *v.t.*, *v.r.* (*pret.* **narcoticé**; *pres. subj.* **narcotice**) to give a narcotic.

nardino, -na, *a.* made of spikenard.

nardo, *n.m.* spikenard; common tuberose.

narguile, *n.m.* narghile, hookah.

narigada, *n.f.* (*Arg., Chi., Ec.*) portion of snuff.

narigón, *n.m.* large nose; (*Cub.*) hole made in a tree-trunk for dragging it.

narigón, -ona ; narigudo, -da, *a.* having a long and large nose.

nariguera, *n.f.* nose pendant (Indians).

narigueta, nariguita, *n.f.* small nose.

nariz, *n.f.* nose, nostril, snout; sense of smell; bouquet (of wine); socket of a door knocker; nozzle; tube of an alembic; projecting point of a bridge; (*naut.*) cutwater: *caballete de la nariz,* bridge of the nose; *hinchar las narices,* to be exceedingly annoyed; *torcer las narices,* to be disgusted at something said, to turn up one's nose at a thing; *nariz chata* (or *remachada*), pug-nose, snub nose; *dar en las narices,* to smell or perceive something from a distance; *no ver más allá de sus narices,* to be dull, not to see beyond one's nose; *meter la nariz en todas partes,* to be a busybody; *ser hombre de buenas narices,* to be cautious, provident, prudent; *tener largas narices,* to be keen-scented; *tener narices de perro perdiguero,* to be keen-scented; to foresee the future.

narizudo, -da, *a.* large-nosed.

narra, *n.m.* (*bot.*) a Philippine tree.

narrable, *a.* capable of being narrated.

narración, *n.f.* narration, relation, account, chronicle.

narrador, *n.m.*, *a.* narrator.

narrar, *v.t.* to narrate, relate, tell; to recite.

narrativa, *n.f.* narrative, relation, history; account, art or talent of relating.

narrativo, -va; narratorio, -ria, *a.* narrative, narratory.

narria, *n.f.* sledge; sled; heavy or fat woman.

narval, *n.m.* (*ichth.*) narwhal; sea-unicorn.

nasa, *n.f.* fike, fish trap, fishing basket; round, narrow net; big jar.

nasal, *a.* nasal.

nasalmente, *adv.* nasally.

nasardo, *n.m.* nasard (register of an organ).

nata, *n.f.* cream; main part of a thing, prime or choice part; (*Am.*) skim, scum. — *pl.* **natas,** whipped cream with sugar; *ser la nata de,* to be the cream (i.e., best part) of.

natación, *n.f.* swimming, natation.

natal, *a.* natal, native. — *n.m.* birth, birthday.

natalicio, -cia, *n.m.f.*, *a.* natal; nativity, birthday.

natátil, *a.* swimming, natatory.

natatorio, -ria, *a.* natatory, relating to swimming.

natatorio, *n.m.* place prepared for swimming.

naterón, *n.m.* second curds after the first cheese has been made.

natilla, *n.f.* first cream of milk.

natillas, *n.f.pl.* custard.

**natío, *n.m.*, *a.* (*prov.*) birth; sprouting (of plants); *oro natío,* native gold.

natividad, *n.f.* nativity; Yuletide, Christmas.

nativo, -va, *a.* native, natal; fit, proper, apt; vernacular.

natral, *n.m.* (*Chi.*) land planted with *natris.*

natri, *n.m.* (*Chi.*) medicinal plant (*Solanum crispum*).

natrón, *n.m.* (*chem.*) natron.

natura, *n.f.* nature; genital parts; (*mus.*) major scale.

natural, *n.m.* genius, temper, disposition; native, inhabitant from birth. — *a.* natural, native, ingenuous; regular, usual, common; pure, unadulterated; artless, spontaneous; *al natural,* without affectation or art.

naturaleza, *n.f.* nature, instinct, order, disposition, inclination, temperament, genius, property; sex, species, kind; brute instinct; naturalization.

naturalidad, *n.f.* naturalness, ingenuity, candour, birthright.

naturalismo, *n.m.* naturalism, exaggerated or thorough-going realism.

naturalista, *n.m.f.* naturalist.

naturalización, *n.f.* naturalization.

naturalizar, *v.t.* (*pret.* **naturalicé**; *pres. subj.* **naturalice**), to naturalize. — *v.r.* to be accustomed.

naturalmente, *adv.* naturally, natively, by nature, humanly; plainly, ingenuously, frankly.

naufragante, *a.* wrecking, sinking, perishing.

naufragar, *v.i.* (*pret.* **naufragué**; *pres. subj.* **naufrague**) to be stranded, shipwrecked; to suffer shipwreck; to fail, be unsuccessful, fall through.

naufragio, *n.m.* shipwreck; heavy loss, calamity, disappointment, miscarriage.

náufrago, -ga, *a.* relating to shipwreck; wrecked. — *n.m.f.* shipwrecked person, survivor of a wreck.

naumaquia, *n.f.* naumachy.

náusea, *n.f.* nauseousness, nausea; (*fig*). squeamishness.

nauseabundo, -da, *a.* nauseous, loathsome, exciting nausea.

nausear, *v.i.* to nauseate, loathe, become squeamish, suffer nausea.

nauseativo, -va, *a.* nauseous.

nauseoso, -sa, *a.* nauseous, loathsome.

nauta, *n.m.* mariner.

náutica, *n.f.* navigation.

náutico, -ca, *a.* nautical.

nautilo, *n.m.* nautilus.

nava, *n.f.* low-lying, level piece of ground surrounded by mountains.

navacero, -ra, *n.m.f.* gardener who cultivates the sandy soil close to the shores of Andalusia.

navaja, *n.f.* razor; clasp-knife, folding-knife ; wild boar's tusk; backbiter's tongue; *navajas de gallo,* cockspurs.

navajada, *n.f.; ***navajazo,** *n.m.* thrust or gash with a knife.

navajero, *n.m.* razor-case; shaving-towel.

navajita, *n.f.* small clasp-knife.

navajo, *n.m.* fool; plain.

navajón, *n.m.* large knife, kind of poniard.

naval, *a.* naval.

navarro, -rra, *n.m.f.*, *a.* Navarrese.

navazo, *n.m.* kitchen garden on a sandy shore.

nave, *n.f.* ship, vessel; nave of a church, aisle; *nave aérea,* airship; *nave de San Pedro,* Roman Catholic Church.

navecica, -illa, -ita, *n.f.* small vessel, incense-boat.

navegable, *a.* navigable.

navegabilidad, *n.f.* seaworthiness.

navegación, *n.f.* navigation, art of navigating, passage by water, time of a sea voyage; *navegación aérea,* aerial navigation, aviation; *navegación costera,* coasting trade; *navegación de altura,* deep-sea navigation.

navegador, *n.m.* navigator, sailor, seaman.

navegador, -ra, *a.* navigating.

navegante, *n.m.f.,* *a.* navigator, navigating.

navegar, *v.i.* (*pret.* **navegué;** *pres. subj.* **navegue**) to navigate, sail; travel.

naveta, *n.f.* incense-boat, thurible, vessel for incense; small drawer.

navícula, *n.f.* small ship; (*bot.*) navicula, microscopic algæ.

navicular, *a.* (*anat.*) navicular.

navichuelo, *n.m.* small vessel.

navidad, *n.f.* nativity; Christmas; *tiene muchas navidades,* he is very old.

navideño, -ña, *a.* belonging to the time of nativity.

naviero, *n.m.* ship-owner.

naviero, -a, *a.* shipping.

navío, *n.m.* ship, vessel, large ship, ship of war; a three-masted, three-decked vessel; *navío pesado,* bad sailor; *navío de tres puentes,* three-decker; *navío a palo seco,* (*naut.*) a ship under bare poles.

náyada, náyade, *n.f.* naïad, water-nymph.

nayuribe, *n.f.* an amarantaceous herb.

nazareno, -na, *a.* Nazarene, native of Nazareth.

nazareno, *n.m.* Holy Week pilgrim dressed in a long robe and accompanying the *pasos* in Spanish towns.

nazareo, -rea, *a.* Nazarite.

nazco ; nazca, *pres. indic. ; pres. subj.* [NACER].

názula, *n.f.* second curds.

nébeda, *n.f.* (*bot.*) lesser calamint, catmint.

nebladura, *n.f.* damage caused to crops by mist.

neblí, *n.m.* (*orn.*) falcon.

neblina, *n.f.* mist, drizzle; obscurity, confusion.

nebrina, *n.f.* juniper-berry.

nebulón, *n.m.* hypocrite.

nebulosidad, *n.f.* nebulosity.

nebuloso, -sa, *a.* misty, cloudy, nebulous.

necear, *v.i.* to talk nonsense, play the fool.

necedad, *n.f.* stupidity, foolish ignorance, idiocy, gross ignorance, foppery, folly.

necesaria, *n.f.* privy, water-closet.

necesariamente, *adv.* necessarily, indispensably, consequently.

necesario, -ria, *a.* necessary, needful, requisite.

neceser, *n.m.* dressing case; toilet case; *neceser de costura,* work basket.

necesidad, *n.f.* necessity, need, want; emergency; *la necesidad carece de ley,* necessity knows no law; *la necesidad hace a la vieja trotar,* necessity is the mother of invention; *la necesidad hace maestro,* necessity brings perfection; *la necesidad tiene cara de hereje,* phrase implying that things done of necessity are to be avoided.

necesitado, -da, *a.* necessitous, poor, needy; compelled, necessitated. — *p.p.* [NECESITAR].

necesitado, *n.m.f.* poor or needy person.

necesitar, *v.t.* to necessitate, compel, constrain. — *v.i.* to need, want, lack.

neciamente, *adv.* stupidly, ignorantly, foolishly.

necio, -cia, *a.* ignorant, stupid, foolish, idiotic, imprudent, injudicious. — *n.m.f.* fool; *más sabe el necio en su casa que el cuerdo en la ajena,* even a fool knows his own business best; *a cada necio agrada su porrada,* a fool is content with his folly.

necrología, *n.f.* necrology.

necrológico, -ca, *a.* necrological.

necrologio, *n.m.* necrology, mortuary.

necromancía, *n.f.* necromancy, magic, black art.

necrópolis, *n.m.* necropolis.

necropsia, necroscopia, *n.f.* post-mortem examination.

necrosis, *n.f.* (*surg., path.*) necrobiosis.

néctar, *n.m.* nectar; exquisite drink.

nectáreo, -rea, *a.* nectareal, nectarean.

nectarífero, -ra, *a.* nectar-bearing.

neerlandés, -esa, *n.m.f.,* *a.* Dutch, Flemish.

nefalista, *n.m.f.* total abstainer; prohibitionist.

nefandamente, *adv.* basely, nefariously, abominably.

nefando, -da, *a.* base, abominable.

nefario, -ria, *a.* nefarious, abominable.

nefas, por fas o por, *adv.* justly or unjustly.

nefasto, -ta, *a.* ill-omened, fatal.

nefrítico, -ca, *a.* nephritic.

nefritis, *n.f.* nephritis.

negable, *a.* which may be denied.

negación, *n.f.* negation, denial; want, privation; (*gram.*) negative particle.

negado, -da, *a.* incapable, unfit, inapt; early Christian who abjured, a recanter.

negador, -ra, *n.m.f.* denier, disclaimer.

negante, *a.* denying, disclaiming.

negar, *v.t.* (*pres. indic.* **niego;** *pret.* **negué;** *pres. subj.* **niegue**) to deny, contradict, refuse, gainsay; to forbid, prohibit; to disregard, disown, disclaim, oppose, hinder; to hide, conceal, dissemble; *negar de plano,* to deny flatly; *negar los oídos,* to refuse a hearing. — *v.r.* to decline; to refuse to see people who call; *negarse a sí mismo,* to govern one's passions, exercise self-control.

negativa, *n.f.* negation, repulse, negative, refusal.

negativamente, *adv.* negatively.

negativo, -va, *a.* negative; (*law*) pleading not guilty.

negligencia, *n.f.* negligence, neglect, heedlessness, idleness, forgetfulness.

negligente, *a.* negligent, careless, heedless, absent, listless, thoughtless.

negligentemente, *adv.* negligently, listlessly, heedlessly, giddily, loosely.

negociabilidad, *n.f.* negotiability.

negociable, *a.* negotiable.

negociación, *n.f.* negotiation, management, commerce.

negociado, *n.m.* employment; department, section (of administrations); (*Chi.*) illicit transaction, shop, store.

negociador, *n.m.* negotiator; man of business or agent.

negociante, *n.m., a.* trader, dealer; negotiating, dealing, trading.

negociar, *v.i.* to trade, buy and sell goods; to negotiate bills of exchange; to engage in political negotiations.

negocio, *n.m.* occupation, employment, business, management; trade, negotiation, commerce; affair; enterprise; proceeds, profit; treaty, agency. — *pl.* business, commercial affairs.

negocioso, -sa, *a.* diligent, careful, prompt, business-like.

negozuelo, *n.m.* insignificant affair or business.

negra, *n.f.* Negro (girl or woman); (*fenc.*) foil; (*mus.*) crotchet, quarter note.

negrada, *n.f.* (*Cub.*) crowd or gathering of Negroes.

negral, *a.* blackish.

negrear, *v.i.* to grow black, appear black.

negrecer, *v.i.* (*pres. indic.* **negrezco;** *pres. subj.* **negrezca**) to blacken, become black.

negrero, *n.m.* slave-dealer; (*fig.*) harsh and cruel employer.

negreta, *n.f.* (*orn.*) coot.

negrilla, *n.f.* little Negro; (*ichth.*) black conger-eel.

negrillera, *n.f.* plantation of black poplars.

negrillo, *n.m.* young Negro, little Negro; (*bot.*) black poplar; (*min.*) black silver ore, stephanite; (*Arg., Bol.*) a black and yellow linnet.

negrito, *n.m.* young or little Negro; (*coll.*) dearest; (*Cub.*) small bird resembling a canary in size and song.

negro, -gra, *a.* black, jet-black, blackish; murky, gloomy, dismal, melancholy; unfortunate, wretched; (*her.*) sable.

negro, -gra, *n.m.f.* Negro, black (person); (*Am.coll.*) sweetheart, dear. *n.m.* black (colour); *negro de humo,* lampblack; *negro de hueso,* boneblack; *negro de marfil,* ivory-black; *negro de plomo,* ochre black; *negro de platino,* platinum black, *negro animal,* boneblack.

negroide, *s., a.* Negroid.

negror, *n.m.;* **negrura,** *n.f.* blackness.

negruzco, -ca, *a.* blackish, dark brown.

neguijón, *n.m.* caries, rottenness of the teeth.

neguilla, *n.f.* (*bot.*) fennel-flower, love-in-a-mist; age mark in horses' teeth; obstinate denial.

neguillón, *n.m.* (*bot.*) campion, corn-rose.

nema, *n.f.* seal, sealing of a letter.

nemoroso, -sa, *a.* woody, nemorous.

nene, nena, *n.m.f.* (*coll.*) infant, baby.

neneque, *n.m.* a helpless and weak person.

nenúfar, *n.m.* (*bot.*) white water-lily.

neocelandés, -esa, *n.m.f., a.* native of New Zealand.

neófito, *n.m.* neophyte, convert; novice, beginner.

neolatino, -na, *a.* Neo-Latin, Romance.

neolítico, -ca, *a.* neolithic.

neología, *n.f.* neology.

neológico, -ca, *a.* neological.

neologismo, *n.m.* neologism.

neólogo, *n.m.* neologist, word-coiner.

neón, *n.m.* (*chem.*) neon.

neoplasma, *n.m.* (*med.*) neoplasm.

neotérico, -ca, *a.* neoteric.

neoyorkino, -na, *n.m.f., a.* native of New York.

nepente, *n.m.* nepenthe.

nepotismo, *n.m.* nepotism; favouritism towards relatives.

neptuniano, -na, *a.* (*geol.*) Neptunian.

neptuno, *n.m.* (*astron.*) Neptune; (*poet.*) sea.

nequáquam, *adv.* (*coll.*) by no means, certainly not.

nequicia, *n.f.* perversity.

nereida, *n.f.* nereid, sea-nymph.

nerita, *n.f.* (*zool.*) a gasteropod mollusc.

nerón, *n.m.* (*fig.*) cruel, inhuman, unfeeling person.

nervado, -da, *a.* nervate, nerved.

nervadura, *n.f.* (*arch.*) nervure, rib; (*carp.*) feather; (*min.*) leader; (*bot.*) nervation, nervure.

nérveo, -a, *a.* nerval.

nervezuelo, *n.m.* nervule.

nervino, -na, *a.* nervine, nerve-strengthening.

nervio, *n.m.* nerve; energy, vigour; tendon; string of a musical instrument; (*bookbind.*) rib, fillet; (*naut.*) span-rope, stay; rib, reinforcement, strength; main part of anything; *nervio maestro,* tendon; *nervio óptico,* optic nerve; *nervio vago,* vagus pneumogastric nerve.

nerviosidad, *n.f.* nervousness.

nervioso, -sa, *a.* nervous; vigorous; (*bot.*) nerved.

nerviosamente, *adv.* nervously.

nerviosidad, *n.f.* strength, nervousness; vigour; efficacy; flexibility.

nerviosismo, *n.m.* neurosis.

nervoso, -sa; nervudo, -da, *a.* nervous; strong, vigorous, robust.

nesciencia, *n.f.* ignorance, nescience, want of knowledge.

nesciente, *a.* ignorant, foolish.

nescientemente, *adv.* ignorantly.

nesga, *n.f.* (*sew.*) gore; triangular piece.

néspera, *n.f.* medlar.

netezuelo, -la, *n.m.f.* little grandchild.

neto, -ta, *a.* neat, pure, clean, unadulterated, genuine; (*com.*) net; (*Chi.*) green, unripe fruit; *producto neto,* net produce; *peso neto,* net weight; *en neto,* purely.

neto, *n.m.* (*arch.*) naked pedestal of a column.

neuma, *n.m.* (*mus.*) neume. — *n.m.f.* (*rhet.*) affirmative or negative expression by signs or nods.

neumático, -ca, *a.* pneumatic. — *n.f.* pneumatics. — *n.m.* tyre (car, bicycle, etc.).

neumonía, *n.f.* pneumonia, inflammation of the lungs.

neumónico, -ca, *a.* pneumonic.

neuralgia, *n.f.* (*med.*) neuralgia.

neurálgico, -ca, *a.* neuralgic.

neurastenia, *n.f.* neurasthenia.

neurasténico, -ca, *a.* neurasthenic.

neurítico, -ca, *a.* neurotic.

neuroesqueleto, *n.m.* (*zool.*) endoskeleton.

neurología, *n.f.* neurology.

neurólogo, *n.m.* neurologist.

neuropatía, *n.f.* neuropathology.

neurosis, *a.* neurosis.

neurótico, -ca, *a.* neurotic.

neurotomía, *n.f.* (*anat.*) neurotomy.

neutral, *a.* neutral, neuter, indifferent.

neutralidad, *n.f.* neutrality, indifference.

neutralizar, *v.t.* (*pret.* **neutralicé;** *pres. subj.* **neutralice**) to neutralize.

neutralmente, *adv.* neutrally, indifferently.

neutro, -tra, *a.* neutral, neuter.

nevada, *n.f.* fall of snow.

nevadilla, *n.f.* whitlow-wort; whittle-wort.

nevado, -da, *a.* snow-covered; snowy, white as snow. — *n.m.f.* snow-capped mountain.

nevar, *v. impers. (pres. indic.* **nieva;** *pres. subj.* **nieve)** to snow. — *v.t.* to make white as snow.

nevasca, nevisca, *n.f.* fall of snow, snow-storm.

nevatilla, *n.f.* (*orn.*) wagtail.

nevazón, *n.f.* (*Arg., Chi., Ec.*) [NEVADA].

nevera, *n.f.* woman ice-seller; ice-box, refrigerator; very cold place.

nevería, *n.f.* ice-house, place where ice is sold.

nevero, *n.m.* ice-seller; place of perpetual snow.

nevisca, *n.f.* gentle fall of snow.

neviscar, *v.i.* to snow lightly.

nevoso, -sa, *a.* snowy, abounding with snow.

nexo, *n.m.* nexus, knot, string, tie, union.

ni, *conj.* neither, nor; *ni por semejas* (or *ni por sombra*), nothing of the sort (*or* not at all); *ni tanto ni tan poco,* neither too much nor too little; *ni siquiera,* not even; *no dice ni sí ni no,* he is neither for nor against, he is indifferent.

niara, *n.f.* straw-rick, haystack.

nicaragüense; nicaragüeño, -ña, *a.* Nicaraguan.

nicle, *n.f.* kind of agate.

nicociana, *n.f.* tobacco.

nicotina, *n.f.* nicotine.

nicotismo, *n.m.* nicotinism.

nictagíneo, -a, *a.* (*bot.*) nyctaginaceous, nyctitropic.

nictalopia, *n.f.* (*med.*) day-blindness.

nicho, *n.m.* niche, recess, hole, corner; suitable position.

nidada, *n.f.* nest, nestful, brood, covey.

nidal, *n.m.* nest; nest-egg, basis; foundation; motive; haunt.

nidificación, *n.f.* nidification.

nidificar, *v.i.* (conjugated like BUSCAR) to nest, build a nest

nido, *n.m.* nest, eyry; home, habitation, residence, abode; haunt; den; *en los nidos de antaño, no hay pájaros hogaño,* in last year's nests, there are none of this year's birds.

niebla, *n.f.* fog, mist, haze, damp; destroying mildew; mental obscurity; (game) very small shot.

niego, *a.* new-born (of a falcon).

niel, *n.m.* niello work; embossment, relief, raised work.

nielar, *v.t.* to emboss, form with a protuberance, carve in relief, engrave, enamel.

niéspera, *n.f.* (*bot.*) medlar.

nieta, *n.f.* granddaughter, grandchild.

nietastro, -tra, *a.* step-grandson or step-granddaughter.

nieto, *n.m.* grandson, grandchild, descendant.

nieva; nieve, *pres. indic.; pres. subj.* [NEVAR].

nieve, *n.f.* snow; snowy weather; fall of snow; (*poet.*) extreme whiteness.

nigromancia, *n.f.* necromancy.

nigromante, *n.m.* necromancer.

nigromántico, -ca, *a.* necromantic.

nigua, *n.f.* chigoe, jigger flea.

nihilismo, *n.m.* nihilism.

nihilista, *n.m.f.* nihilist.

nilad, *n.m.* (*Philip.*) shrub of the rubiaceous family.

nimbo, *n.m.* halo, nimbus.

nimiamente, *adv.* excessively; minutely.

nimiedad, *n.f.* excess, superfluity; extravagant nicety, niceness; frugality, sparingness.

nimio, -mia, *a.* excessive, too much, prolix; stingy.

ninfa, *n.f.* nymph; kell, chrysalis, pupa; young lady.

ninfea, *n.f.* (*bot.*) water-lily.

ninfo, *n.m.* (*coll.*) fop, beau, affected creature.

ninfomana, *n.f.* nymphomaniac.

ninfomanía, *n.f.* nymphomania.

ninguno, -na, *a.* (shortened to **ningún** before singular masculine nouns) none, not one, not any.

niña, *n.f.* pupil, apple of the eye; girl, female child; *niña de los ojos,* darling; *tocar en las niñas de los ojos,* (*met.*) to touch someone in his most vulnerable spot.

niñada, *n.f.* puerility, childishness.

niñato, *n.m.* calf in belly of a cow which has been killed.

niñear, *v.i.* to behave childishly.

niñera, *n.f.* nursemaid.

niñería, *n.f.* puerility; bauble, gewgaw, trifle, plaything.

niñero, -ra, *n.m.f., a.* one fond of children, dandler.

niñeta, *n.f.* small pupil of the eye.

niñez, *n.f.* childhood, infancy, cradle.

niñita, *n.f.* babe, infant.

niño, *n.m.* child, infant; inexperienced person; (*prov.*) a single person; (*Cub.*) respectful mode of address of a servant to his master; *desde niño,* from infancy; *no es niño,* (*iron.*) he is no child; *como niño con zapatos nuevos,* (as pleased) as a child with a new toy; *los niños lo saben,* all the world knows it; *los niños y los locos dicen las verdades,* there's many a true word spoken by a child or a fool; *ni al niño el bollo, ni al santo el voto,* all that is promised should be performed.

niño, -ña, *a.* childish, child-like, puerile.

niobio, *n.m.* (*chem.*) niobium.

nioto, *n.m.* dogfish or small shark.

nipa, *n.f.* nipa, a S.E. Asian palm; the leaves of this tree; beverage made from the sap of this.

nipis, *n.m.* (*Philip.*) fine cloth woven from the fibre of abaca.

nipón, -ona, *a.* Japanese.

nipos, *n.m.pl.* (*coll.*) money.

níquel, *n.m.* (*chem.*) nickel.

niquelado, -da, *n.m., a.* nickel-plating; nickel-plated. — *p.p.* [NIQUELAR].

niquelar, *v.t.* to cover with nickel.

niquelina, *n.f.* nickelite.

niquiscocio, *n.m.* (*coll.*) trifle.

níspero, *n.m.* (*bot.*) medlar-tree.

níspola, *n.f.* fruit of the medlar-tree.

nítido, -da, *a.* (*poet.*) bright, shining, lustrous.

nito, *n.m.* (*Philip.*) a fibrous fern or brake.

nitral, *n.m.* place where nitre is formed; nitre-bed.

nitrato, *n.m.* (*chem.*) nitrate.

nitrería, *n.f.* saltpetre works.

nítrico, -ca, *a.* nitric.

nitrito, *n.m.* nitrite.

nitro, *n.m.* nitre, saltpetre.

nitrobencina, *n.f.* nitrobenzene.

nitrocelulosa, *n.f.* nitrocellulose.

nitrogenar, *v.t.* to nitrogenize.
nitrógeno, *n.m.* nitrogen.
nitroglicerina, *n.f.* nitroglycerine.
nitroso, -sa, *a.* nitrous.
nivel, *n.m.* level, flat surface; levelness; water-mark; (*surv.*) level; (*build.*) plummet; *a nivel,* perfectly level.
nivelación, *n.f.* levelling, grading.
nivelador, *n.m.* (*surv.*) leveller.
nivelar, *v.t.* to level; to grade; to make even; to put on a basis of equity.
níveo, -vea, *a.* (*poet.*) snowy, like snow.
nivoso, *a.* snowy.
no, *adv.* no, not, nay; *decir que no,* to give a flat denial; *no obstante,* nevertheless, notwithstanding; *por sí o por no,* at any rate; *sin faltar un sí ni un no,* without a jot lacking; *¿ a que no ?* (*coll.*) I bet that isn't so; I bet you won't; *no, que no,* most certainly not; *no bien,* no sooner; *no más,* only.
nobiliario, *n.m.* nobiliary.
nobilísimo, -ma, *a. superl.* [NOBLE]; most noble.
noble, *a.* noble, eminent, conspicuous, illustrious, high-born, honourable, respectable, generous. — *n.m.* nobleman, noble; an ancient gold coin.
noblemente, *adv.* nobly, magnanimously.
nobleza, *n.f.* nobleness, nobility; gentility; dignity, greatness, generousness, magnanimity, worth; a fine damask silk.
noca, *n.f.* variety of crab.
nocente, *a.* noxious; guilty.
noción, *n.f.* notion, idea, acceptation; element, rudiment (usually in *pl.*).
nocional, *a.* notional.
nocivamente, *adv.* mischievously, harmfully, hurtfully.
nocivo, -va, *a.* noxious, hurtful, mischievous, malignant.
noctambulismo, *n.m.* somnambulism.
noctámbulo, *n.m.* somnambulist.
noctiluca, *n.f.* glow-worm.
nocturnal, *a.* nocturnal, nightly, done by night.
nocturnamente, *adv.* nocturnally, during the night.
nocturnidad, *n.f.* (*law*) increased liability resulting from committing a crime by night.
nocturno, -na, *a.* nocturnal, nightly, during the night; (*fig.*) lonely and sad.
nocturno, *n.m.* (*eccles.*) nocturn; (*astr.*) evening star; (*mus.*) nocturne; (*zool.*) nocturnæ.
noche, *n.f.* night; (*poet.*) death; (*fig.*) obscurity, ignorance; *primera noche,* nightfall, evening; *de la noche a la mañana,* suddenly, unexpectedly; *buenas noches,* good night; *noche buena,* Christmas Eve; *noche toledana,* restless night; *anoche* (or *ayer noche*) last night; *hacerse de noche,* night is falling, it is growing dark; *quedarse a buenas noches,* (*Mex.*) to be left in the dark about a matter, to be disappointed; *de noche todos los gatos son pardos,* in bad light everything looks dark (i.e. it is easy to swindle or deceive); *hacer noche una cosa,* to steal something; *la noche es capa de pecadores,* night is the malefactor's friend.
nochebuena, *n.f.* Christmas Eve.
nochebueno, *n.m.* large Christmas cake; yule log.
nochecita, *n.f.* (*Am.*) twilight, nightfall.
nochizo, *n.m.* (*bot.*) wild hazel-tree.

nodación, *n.f.* (*surg.*) impediment caused by a node.
nodal, *a.* nodal.
nodo, *n.m.* knot; node.
nodriza, *n.f.* wet-nurse.
nódulo, *n.m.* nodule.
nogada, *n.f.* sauce of pounded walnuts and spice.
nogal, *n.m.* walnut-tree, walnut-wood.
noguera, *n.f.* walnut-tree.
noguerado, -da, *a.* of walnut colour.
nogueral, *n.m.* walnut-plantation.
noguerela, *n.f.* a medicinal plant of the euphorbia genus.
noguerón, *n.m.* large walnut-tree.
noli, *n.m.* (*Col.*) a kind of tinder obtained from lichen.
nolición, *n.f.* (*phil.*) unwillingness.
noli me tángere, *n.m.* (*bot.*) touch-me-not.
nómada, nómade, *a.* nomad, nomadic.
nombradamente, *adv.* expressly mentioned.
nombradía, *n.f.* fame, reputation, credit, renown.
nombrador, *n.m.* nominator, elector, appointer.
nombramiento, *n.m.* nomination, naming, appointment, creation, commission, brevet.
nombrar, *v.t.* to name, mention by name, nominate, elect, appoint.
nombre, *n.m.* name, title; watchword; credit; fame, reputation; nickname; (*gram.*) noun, substantive; (*mil.*) countersign; *nombre de bautismo* (or *de pila*), Christian name; *poner nombre,* to fix a price; *hacer nombre de Dios,* to begin something; *en el nombre,* for heaven's sake.
nomenclador, *n.m.* nomenclator, gazetteer, vocabulary, glossary.
nomenclátor, *n.m.* nomenclator.
nomenclatura, *n.f.* nomenclature, terminology; catalogue.
nomeolvides, *n.f.* (*bot.*) forget-me-not.
nómina, *n.f.* catalogue, alphabetical list; pay-roll.
nominación, *n.f.* nomination, appointment.
nominador, -ra, *n.m.f.* nominator, appointer.
nominal, *a.* nominal, titular.
nominalismo, *n.m.* (*Philip.*) nominalism.
nominalista, *n.m.f.*, *a.* nominalist.
nominalmente, *adv.* nominally.
nominar, *v.t.* to name.
nominativo, *a.* (*com.*) personal, registered (as bonds, shares, etc.); *n.m.* (*gram.*) nominative. — *pl.* **nominativos,** elements, rudiments.
nominilla, *n.f.* pay warrant, voucher.
nómino, *n.m.* nominee, person appointed or nominated.
nomología, *n.f.* nomology.
nomparell, *n.f.* (*print.*) nonpareil, a small type.
non, *a.* odd, uneven. — *n.m.pl.* odd number; *quedar de non,* to be odd man out; *ha dicho nones,* he has said no, refused; *andar de nones,* to be idle; *estar de non,* to serve for nothing; *pares y nones,* (*coll.*) even or odd.
nona, *n.f.* none, last of the canonical hours.
nonada, *n.f.* trifle, nothingness.
nonagenario, -ria, *a.* nonagenarian.
nonagésimo, -ma, *a.* ninetieth, nonagesimal.
nonagonal, *a.* nine-sided.
nonágono, *n.m.* nonagon.
nonato, -ta, *a.* not naturally born, extracted by Cæsarean section.

nones, pares y, (*coll.*) even or odd.
nonio, *n.m.* (*math.*) nonius, sliding gauge; vernier.
nono, -na, *a.* ninth.
non plus ultra, (*Lat.*) utmost; nonpareil; (*print.*) pearl, a small type.
nonuplo, -pla, *a.* nonuple, nine-fold.
nopal, *n.m.* (*bot.*) nopal, cochineal fig-tree.
nopalera, *n.f.* cochineal plantation.
noque, *n.m.* tanning vat; heap or basket of bruised olives.
noquero, *n.m.* currier, leather-dresser.
norabuena, *n.f.* congratulation. — *adv.* well and good.
noramala, *adv.* in an evil hour.
noray, *n.m.* (*naut.*) mooring.
nordestal, *a.* north-easterly.
nordeste, *n.m.* north-east.
nordestear, *v.i.* (*naut.*) to be north-easting.
nórdico, *n.m.* nordic.
nordovestear, *v.i.* (*naut.*) to decline to north-west.
noria, *n.f.* engine or wheel for drawing water; draw-well, deep well.
norial, *a.* relating to a *noria*.
norma, *n.f.* square (builder's or joiner's); norm, model, guide, standard, pattern, gauge.
normal, *a.* normal, usual, regular, model, standard; (*geom.*) *línea normal,* perpendicular line; *escuela normal,* normal school.
normalidad, *n.f.* normality.
normalizer, *v.t.* to normalize; to standardize.
Normandía, *n.f.* Normandy.
normando, -da, *n.m.f.,* *a.* Norman (from Normandy).
normano, -na, *n.m.f.* Norman, Northman.
nornordeste, *n.m.* north-north-east.
nornoroeste, nornorueste, *n.m.* north-north-west.
noroeste, *n.m.* north-west.
noroestear, *v.i.* (*naut.*) to decline to the north-west (the compass).
nortada, *n.f.* north gale, norther.
norte, *n.m.* north, north-wind; pole-star; rule, law, guide, clue, direction.
norteamericano, -na, *n.m.f.,* *a.* North American, inhabitant of the United States.
nortear, *v.t.* (*naut.*) to stand or steer to the northward. — *v.i.* to decline to the north.
norteño, -ña, *a.* of or from the north, especially from the north of Spain.
Noruega, *n.f.* Norway.
noruego, -ga, *n.m.f.,* *a.* Norse, Norwegian, Norseman.
nos, *pers. pron.,* *m.f.pl.* us; (in authoritative style) I.
nosocomio, *n.m.* (*med.*) hospital.
nosogenia, *n.f.* (*med.*) nosogenia.
nosografía, *n.f.* (*med.*) nosography.
nosología, *n.f.* nosology.
nosológico, -ca, *a.* nosological.
nosotros, -tras, *pers. pron.,* *m.f.pl.* we, us, ourselves; (in literary style) I.
nostalgia, *n.f.* nostalgia, homesickness.
nostramo, *n.m.* (*naut.*) master, title given by sailors to the boatswain.
nota, *n.f.* note, sign, mark, token, imputation, reproach, stigma, censure; notice, critique; repute, renown, fame; annotation, memorandum; (*mus.*) musical note; single sound; style, manner of writing; official communication from one state to another; (*com.*)

account, bill, schedule, statement; mark (in examinations). — *pl.* **notas,** notary's minutes.
notabilidad, *n.f.* notability.
notabilísimo, -ma, *a. superl.* most notable.
notable, *a.* notable, remarkable, conspicuous; noticeable, noteworthy; eminent, distinguished, very great.
notablemente, *adv.* notably, observably, noticeably.
notación, *n.f.* note, annotation; (*math., mus.*) notation.
notar, *v.t.* to note, notice, mark; observe, remark, heed, mind, expound; comment, annotate; to dictate; to censure, criticize, find fault; to reprehend; to cause loss of reputation, to defame.
notaria, *n.f.* profession or office of notary.
notariado, *n.m.* notary's title or profession.
notarial, *a.* notarial.
notariato, *n.m.* title or practice of a notary.
notario, *n.m.* notary; amanuensis.
noticia, *n.f.* notice, knowledge, information; note, light; news (in this sense, usually in the plural), intelligence, tidings; (*com.*) advice; *noticia remota,* vague remembrance.
noticiar, *v.t.* to give notice, notify, inform, make known, communicate.
noticiero, *n.m.* news-monger, news-agent, reporter; (*S. Am.*) bulletin of current news (broadcast).
notición, *n.m.* (*coll.*) great or sensational news.
noticioso, -sa, *a.* informed, knowing, learned, instructed.
notificación, *n.f.* notification, intimation, official notice.
notificado, -da, *a.* (*law*) notified.
notificar, *v.t.* (*pret.* **notifiqué**; *pres. subj.* **notifique**) to notify, make known, intimate, inform, announce.
notita, *n.f.* short note, memorandum.
noto, -ta, *a.* known, notorious; bastard, illegitimate.
noto, *n.m.* Notus, south wind.
notomía, *n.f.* (*obs.*) skeleton; anatomy.
notoriamente, *adv.* notoriously, manifestly, glaringly.
notoriedad, *n.f.* notoriety, notoriousness.
notorio, -ria, *a.* notorious, generally known.
notro, *n.m.* (*Chi.*) tree of the Proteaceæ family.
nova, *n.f.* (*astron.*) nova, a new star.
novación, *n.f.* (*law*) novation.
novador, -ra, *n.m.f.* innovator.
noval, *a.* newly broken up (of land); fruit produced in such land.
novar, *v.t.* (*law*) to renew by novation.
novatada, *n.f.* ragging (in colleges, schools, etc.).
novato, -ta, *a.* (*coll.*) new, commencing. — *n.m.f.* novice, beginner, tyro.
novator, -ra, *n.m.f.* innovator.
novecientos, -tas, *a.* nine hundred.
novedad, *n.f.* novelty, fad, change; innovation, newness, modernness; surprise, recent occurrence, latest news; trouble, danger; *estar* (or *quedar*) *sin novedad,* to be in a good state of health; *no haber novedad,* to have no special news; *sin novedad,* as usual; well, safe.
novedoso, -sa, *a.* (*Arg., Chi., Mex.*) [NOVELERO].

novel, *a.* new, inexperienced.

novela, *n.f.* novel, fiction tale, story; falsehood, fictitious statement; (*law*) novel.

novelador, -ra, *n.m.f.* novelist.

novelar, *v.i.* to compose or publish novels, novelize, tell stories.

novelería, *n.f.* narration of fiction; love of novels, fads or novelties.

novelero, -ra, *a.* fond of fiction; new-fangled; inconstant, wavering. — *n.m.f.* (*slang*) newsmonger, gossip.

novelesco, -ca, *a.* novelistic.

novelista, *n.m.f.* novelist.

novena, *n.f.* (*eccles.*) novena.

novenario, *n.m.* (*eccles.*) novenary.

noveno, -na, *a.* ninth, ninthly. — *n.m.* ninth part of tithes.

noventa, *n.m.* ninety.

noventavo, -va, *a.* ninetieth part.

noventón, -ona, *n.m.f.* nonagenarian.

novia, *n.f.* bride, woman betrothed, fiancée, sweetheart; *sacar la novia por el vicario*, to get one's sweetheart her liberty.

noviazgo, *n.m.* engagement, betrothal.

noviciado, *n.m.* novitiate, apprenticeship.

novicio, *n.m.* novice, probationer, apprentice, tyro, raw hand.

novicio, -cia, *a.* probationary.

noviciote, *n.m.* (*coll.*) big, overgrown novice.

noviembre, *n.m.* November.

novilunio, *n.m.* new moon.

novilla, *n.f.* young heifer.

novillada, *n.f.* drove of young bulls; bull-fight with young animals.

novillejo, -eja, *n.m.f.* young bull or heifer.

novillero, *n.m.* stable or herdsman for young cattle; pasture ground for weaned calves; young bullfighter learning the profession; truant, idler.

novillo, *n.m.* young bull or ox; (*fam.*) cuckold; *hacer novillos*, (*coll.*) to play truant.

novio, -via, *n.m.f.* person betrothed, lover, sweetheart, bridegroom or bride; one new to some dignity or state.

novísimo, -ma, *a. superl.* newest, most recent, latest; *Novísima Recopilación*, code of laws promulgated in Spain, July 15, 1805.

noyó, *n.m.* noyau, a cordial.

nubada, nubarrada, *n.f.* shower of rain; plenty, abundance.

nubado, -da; nubarrado, -da, *a.* clouded.

nubarrón, *n.m.* large threatening cloud.

nube, *n.f.* cloud, shadow; crowd, swarm, multitude; (*med.*) film on the eye; nebula; cloud or shade in precious stones; *por las nubes* (or *en* or *sobre* or *a las nubes*), very high (of praise *or* of price); *como caído de las nubes,* heaven-sent, unexpected.

nubecita, *n.f.* small cloud.

nubífero, -ra, *a.* (*poet.*) cloud-bringing.

núbil, *a.* nubile, marriageable.

nubilidad, *n.f.* nubility.

nubiloso, -sa, *a.* (*poet.*) cloudy, nubilous.

nublado, *n.m.* large cloud; dread, apprehension; gloominess.

nublado, -da, *a.* cloudy, nebulous. — *p.p.* [NUBLAR].

nublar, nublarse, *v.t., v.r.* [ANUBLAR] to cloud, cloud over, be clouded.

nublo, -bla, *a.* cloudy.

nubloso, -sa, *a.* cloudy, dark, overcast; gloomy, ill-fated.

nuca, *n.f.* (*anat.*) nucha, nape of the neck.

núcleo, *n.m.* nucleus, kernel, stone of fruit, centre of development.

nuco, *n.m.* (*Chi.*) a kind of owl.

nuche, *n.m.* (*S. Am., ent.*) gadfly, horsefly.

nudamente, *adv.* nakedly, plainly.

nudillo, *n.m.* knuckle, finger-joint; nodule; (*build.*) plug, dowel; small knot in stocking seam.

nudo, *n.m.* knot, knuckle, joint; knag; tie, bond, union; intricacy, difficulty, tangle; (*bot.*) node, snag; (*med.*) node, tumour; knotty point; (*naut.*) knot of the log line, nautical mile; crisis of a drama; *nudo gordiano,* Gordian knot; *nudo en la garganta,* lump in the throat, great emotion; *quien no da nudo, pierde punto,* the longest way round is the shortest way home.

nudo, -da, *a.* nude, naked.

nudoso, -sa, *a.* knotty, nodous, knotted.

nuecero, -ra, *n.m.f.* walnut-seller.

nuégado, *n.m.pl.* kind of sweet paste.

nuera, *n.f.* daughter-in-law.

nuestramo, -ma, *n.m.f. contr. of nuestro amo,* our master, *nuestra ama,* our mistress; (*Am.*) the Eucharist.

nuestro, -tra, *poss. pron.* our, ours; (in literary or authoritative style) my, mine.

nueva, *n.f.* news, tidings; *dormiré, dormiré, buenas nuevas hallaré,* phrase rebuking those who trust to good fortune turning up; *las malas nuevas siempre son ciertas,* ill news is always true.

Nueva Escocia, *n.f.* Nova Scotia.

Nueva Gales del Sur, *n.f.* New South Wales.

nuevamente, *adv.* newly, recently, freshly.

Nueva Orleans, *n.f.* New Orleans.

Nueva York, *n.f.* New York.

Nueva Zelandia, *n.f.* New Zealand.

nueve, *n.m., a.* nine, ninth.

nuevecito, -ta, *a.* quite new, quite fresh.

nuevo, -va, *a.* new, novel, modern, fresh; newly arrived; renovated, repaired; unfamiliar; *de nuevo,* recently, of late; *¿qué hay de nuevo?* what's the news? *nuevo flamante,* brand new, spick and span.

nuez, *n.f.* walnut; Adam's apple; nut or kernel of coconuts, cocoa, etc.; notch of a cross-bow; (*mus.*) ferrule of a bow; *apretar a uno la nuez,* to throttle, cause to choke.

nueza, *n.f.* (*bot.*) briony.

nugatorio, -ria, *a.* nugatory, deceitful, futile.

nulamente, *adv.* invalidly, ineffectually.

nulidad, *n.f.* nullity, want of force or efficacy; defeasance; inability, incompetence.

nulo, -la, *a.* null, void of effect, incapable.

numen, *n.m.* divinity, deity, genius, talent; (*poet.*) inspiration.

numerable, *a.* numerable.

numeración, *n.f.* numeration.

numerador, *n.m.* enumerator; numberer; numbering machine; (*arith.*) numerator.

numeral, *a.* numeral.

numerar, *v.t.* to number, enumerate, numerate, reckon, cipher, calculate, to page.

numerario, -ria, *a.* numerary.

numerario, *n.m.* coin, hard cash, specie.

numéricamente, *adv.* numerically, individually.

numérico, -ca, *a.* numerical, numeral, individual.

número, *n.m.* number, cipher, character,

figure; poetical or musical measure, rhythm, harmony; quantity, multitude, aggregation; *pl.* the Book of Numbers; *de número*, one of a fixed number; *sin número*, numberless, innumerable.

numerosamente, *adv.* numerously.

numerosidad, *n.f.* numerousness.

numeroso, -sa, *a.* numerous, containing many; melodious, harmonious.

numismática, *n.f.* numismatics.

numismático, -ca, *a.* numismatic. — *n.m.f.* collector of coins, numismatist.

numo, *n.m.* money, coin.

numulario, *n.m.* trade in money; banker, money broker.

nunca, *adv.* never, at no time; *nunca jamás*, never, never more; *nunca mucho costó poco*, nothing worth much was ever bought for little; *nunca es tarde para arrepentirse*, it's never too late to mend.

nunciatura, *n.f.* nunciature.

nuncio, *n.m.* nuncio, ambassador, messenger; (*fig.*) forerunner, harbinger.

nuncupativo, -va, *a.* nuncupative.

nuncupatorio, -ria, *a.* nuncupatory.

nuño, *n.m.* (*Chi.*) a plant of the Iridaceæ family.

nupcial, *a.* nuptial, hymeneal.

nupcialidad, *n.f.* marriage rate.

nupcias, *n.f.pl.* nuptials, wedding.

nutación, *n.f.* (*astr.*) nutation.

nutra, nutria, *n.f.* otter, otter-fur.

nutricio, -cia, *a.* nutritious, nourishing, nutritive.

nutrición, *n.f.* nutrition, nourishing; (*pharm.*) preparation of medicines.

nutrido, -da, *a.* (*fig.*) (with *de*) full of; abounding.

nutrimental, *a.* nutrimental, nourishing.

nutrimento, *n.m.* nutriment, nourishment, aliment, food, nutrition.

nutrir, *v.t.* to nourish, fatten, feed; (*fig.*) to foment; support, encourage.

nutritivo, -va, *a.* nutritive, nourishing.

nutriz, *n.f.* nurse.

nutual, *a.* ecclesiastical living or civil post which can be terminated at will of the patron.

Ñ

Ñ, ñ, seventeenth letter of the Spanish alphabet.

ña, *n.f.* (*Am.*) proprietress, landlady.

ñacanina, *n.f.* (*Arg.*) a large poisonous snake.

ñaco, *n.m.* (*Chi.*) porridge or pap.

ñacurutú, *n.m.* (*Arg.*, *Ur.*) a kind of barn owl (*Bubo cassirostris*).

ñagaza, *n.f.* bird-call, decoy-call.

ñame, *n.m.* yam.

ñandú, *n.m.* American ostrich.

ñandubay, *n.m.* (*Am.*) a kind of mimosa with a very hard red wood.

ñandutí, *n.m.* (*Arg.*, *Par.*) hand-made cloth used for underwear.

ñangotarse, *v.r.* (*PR.*) to be in a squatting position.

ñangué, *n.m.* (*Cub.*) (*bot.*) stramonium.

ñaña, *n.f.* (*Chi.*) children's nurse; (*Arg.*) elder sister.

ñáñigo, -ga, *a.* (*Cub.*) member of a secret society of negroes.

ñaño, -ña, *a.* (*Col.*) spoiled child; (*Per.*) very

close friend; (*Chi.*) elder brother (or sister).

ñapa, *n.f.* (*Am.*) allowance; *de ñapa*, to boot.

ñapango, -ga, *a.* (*Col.*) mestizo, half-breed; mulatto.

ñapinda, *n.m.* (*Arg.*) (*bot.*) mimosa.

ñapo, *n.m.* (*Chi.*) jonquil; reed; rattan.

ñaque, *n.m.* useless trifles, odds and ends.

ñaruso, -sa, *a.* (*Ec.*) pock-marked.

ñato, -ta, *a.* (*Am.*) flat-nosed.

ñeque, *a.* (*CR.*) energetic, strong, brave. — *n.m.* (*Chi.*, *Per.*) energy, vim.

ñipe, *n.m.* (*Chi.*) shrub used for dyeing.

ñiqueñaque, *n.m.* (*coll.*) whipper-snapper, an expression of depreciation; good-for-nothing; trash.

ñire, *n.m.* (*Chi.*) (*bot.*) a very tall tree.

ñisñil, *n.m.* (*Chi.*) (*bot.*) a rush used for basket-making.

ño, *n.m.* (*Am.*) landlord, proprietor, owner, boss.

ñocios, *n.m.pl.* kind of sweetmeat.

ñocha, *n.f.* (*Chi.*) a kind of brome-grass.

ñongo, -ga, *a.* (*Chi.*) (*coll.*) lazy, good-for-nothing. — *n.m.pl.* (*Col.*) loaded dice.

ñonería, *n.f.* sentimental drivel.

ñoñez, *n.f.* sloppiness; drivel.

ñoño, -ña, *a.* feeble-minded; sentimental, sloppy; (*obs.*) doting.

ñorbo, *n.m.* (*Ec.*, *Per.*) (*bot.*) passion flower.

ñu, *n.m.* gnu.

ñublado, *n.m.*; **ñublar**, *v.t.*; **ñublo**, *n.m.* [NUBLADO] [NUBLAR] [NUBLO].

ñudo, *n.m.* [NUDO].

ñuñu, *n.m.* (*Chi.*) iridaceous plant with edible fruit.

ñuto, -ta, *a.* (*Ec.*) anything reduced to fine powder.

O

O, o, eighteenth letter of the Spanish alphabet. — *conj.* or, either; *o sea*, that is, in other words. — *interj.* Oh!

oasis, *n.m.* oasis.

obcecación, *n.f.* obduracy; obfuscation; blindness.

obcecadamente, *adv.* blindly.

obcecado, -da, *a.* blind; obdurate.

obcecar, *v.t.* (*pret.* **obcequé**; *pres. subj.* **obceque**) to blind, darken, obscure.

obduración, *n.f.* obduracy, obstinacy.

obedecedor, -ra, *n.m.f.* obeyer.

obedecer, *v.t.* (*pres. indic.* **obedezco**; *pres. subj.* **obedezca**) to obey, yield to, submit to; to respond; to be due, arise (from); *obedecer al tiempo*, to act according to circumstances.

obedecimiento, *n.m.* obedience.

obediencia, *n.f.* obedience, submission, docility, obsequiousness, flexibility, pliancy.

obediencial, *a.* obediential.

obediente, *a.* obedient, submissive, obsequious, compliant.

obedientemente, *adv.* obediently.

obelisco, *n.m.* obelisk; (*print.*) dagger, the mark †.

obenques, *n.m.pl.* (*naut.*) shrouds.

obertura, *n.f.* (*mus.*) overture.

obesidad, *n.f.* obesity, corpulence.

obeso, -sa, *a.* obese, fat.

óbice, *n.m.* obstacle, impediment, opposition, hindrance.

obispado, *n.m.* bishopric, episcopate.

obispal, *a.* episcopal.

obispalía, *n.f.* bishop's palace; bishopric, diocese.

obispar, *v.i.* to obtain a bishopric, be made a bishop; (*univ.*) to rag a freshman.

obispillo, *n.m.* boy-bishop; little bishop; large black pudding; rump of a fowl; (*univ.*) freshman.

obispo, *n.m.* bishop.

óbito, *n.m.* (*law*) death, decease, demise.

obituario, *n.m.* obituary.

obiubi, *n.m.* (*Ven.*) a black monkey.

objeción, *n.f.* objection, opposition, exception.

objetar, *v.t.* to object, oppose, remonstrate.

objetivamente, *adv.* objectively.

objetivo, -va, *a.* objective.

objetivo, *n.m.* (*opt.*) objective, eyepiece.

objeto, *n.m.* object, aim, end, design.

oblación, *n.f.* oblation, offering, gift.

oblada, *n.f.* (*eccles.*) funeral offering of bread; *quien lleva las obladas, que taña las campanas,* he who takes the profit, should do the work.

oblata, *n.f.* (*eccles.*) contribution for church expenses; oblate.

oblato, *n.m.* lay monk, oblate.

oblea, *n.f.* wafer for sealing letters.

obleera, *n.f.* wafer-holder, wafer-case.

oblicuamente, *adv.* obliquely.

oblicuángulo, *n.m.* oblique-angled.

oblicuar, *v.t.,* *v.i.* to cant, slant; (*mil.*) to move forwards obliquely.

oblicuidad, *n.f.* obliquity, slant, cant, bias, deviation.

oblicuo, -cua, *a.* oblique, slanting, bias, traverse, inclined.

obligación, *n.f.* obligation, contract, duty, bond, debenture. — *pl.* **obligaciones,** engagements, obligations; (*com.*) liabilities.

obligacionista, *n.m.f.* (*com.*) bondholder.

obligado, *n.m.* public contractor; (*law*) obligee; (*mus.*) obligato.

obligante, *a.* obligating, imposing.

obligar, *v.t.* (*pret.* **obligué;** *pres. subj.* **obligue**) to oblige, compel, bind, necessitate, constrain; to place under an obligation. — *v.r.* to bind oneself.

obligatorio, -ria, *a.* obligatory, binding.

obliteración, *n.f.* obliteration.

obliterar, *v.t.* to obliterate.

oblongo, -ga, *a.* oblong.

obnoxio, -xia, *a.* obnoxious.

oboe, *n.m.* oboe, hautboy; oboe-player.

óbolo, *n.m.* obolus; mite; (*pharm.*) obole.

obra, *n.f.* work, writings, volume, book; repairs; construction, fabric, building; virtue; power, means, influence, agency; employment, labour, toil; repairs in a house; (*metal.*) hearth of a blast furnace; *obra de,* about, more or less; *obras pías,* charitable funds; *obra de retacitos,* patchwork; *obra de romanos,* task of great difficulty; *obra de taracea,* checkered work; *obras muertas,* (*naut.*) upper-works; *obra prima,* shoe-making; *dar obra,* to give employment; *hacer mala obra,* to do a bad turn; *poner por obra,* to set to work; *obra de común, obra de ningún,* what is anybody's work is nobody's work; *obra empezada, medio acabada,* well begun is half done; *obra saca obra,* one piece of work makes another; *obra hecha, venta* (or *dinero*) *espera,* work brings profit with it; *seca está*

la obra, work's a dry job (phrase requesting drink); *tomar una obra,* to take on work.

obrada, *n.f.* day's work; land measure (varies between 1 and 1½ acres).

obrador, -ra, *n.m.f.* workman, workwoman; artificer, mechanic; workshop.

obradura, *n.f.* oil produced by an oil-mill at each pressing.

obraje, *n.m.* manufacture, handiwork, something made by art; manufactory, workshop.

obrajero, *n.m.* foreman, overseer, quarterman, superintendent.

obrante, *a.* acting, working.

obrar, *v.t.* to work, make, construct, build, manufacture, operate, execute, perform, put into practice. — *v.i.* to be in the hands of; to ease nature; *obrar conforme a derecho,* to act according to law; *obró mal con su hermano,* he dealt badly with his brother.

obrepción, *n.f.* (*law*) obreption.

obrepticio, -cia, *a.* (*law*) obreptitious.

obrería, *n.f.* workman's task; money for the repairs of a church.

obrerismo, *n.m.* (*polit., econ.*) labour; the working class.

obrero, -ra, *n.m.f.* worker, workman, day-labourer; missionary; churchwarden. — *a.* working.

obrita, *n.f.* small work, booklet.

obrizo, -za, *a.* pure, refined (of gold).

obscenamente, *adv.* obscenely.

obscenidad, *n.f.* obscenity, lewdness.

obsceno, -na, *a.* obscene, lewd, lustful.

obscuramente, *adv.* obscurely, darkly; confusedly, faintly; modestly, humbly.

obscurantismo, *n.m.* obscurantism.

obscurantista, *n.m.f.,* *a.* obscurantist.

obscuras (a), *adv.* obscurely, darkly.

obscurecer, *v.t.* (*pres. indic.* **obscurezco;** *pres. subj.* **obscurezca**) to darken, obscure; to cloud, confuse, impair lustre; to denigrate; (*art*) to use deep shades. — *v. impers.* to grow dark. — *v.r.* to disappear, be lost; to cloud over.

obscurecimiento, *n.m.* obscuration.

obscuridad, *n.f.* obscurity, darkness, gloominess, cloudiness; obscurity of meaning; insignificance.

obscuro, -ra, *a.* obscure, dark, gloomy; (*art*) heavily shaded; unintelligible, confused, abstruse, little known, unknown. — *adv. a obscuras,* in the dark.

obsecuente, *a.* submissive, obedient.

obsequiante, *a.* gallant, courtly.

obsequiar, *v.t.* to treat, entertain; to wait upon, court, woo, serve, obey, pay attentions, make presents.

obsequias, *n.f.pl.* funeral rites; the ceremony of burial.

obsequio, *n.m.* civility, attention, complaisance, treat, courtesy; present, gift; *en obsequio de,* for the sake of, from respect to.

obsequiosamente, *adv.* obligingly, flatteringly, gallantly.

obsequioso, -sa, *a.* obedient, attentive, compliant, obliging.

observable, *a.* observable, noticeable.

observación, *n.f.* observation, note, remark.

observador, -ra, *n.m.f.* observer, remarker. — *a.* observant, watchful.

observancia, *n.f.* observance, respect, regard, reverence; attentiveness, obedience; *poner* *en observancia*, to execute punctually.

observante, *a.* observant, observing, respectful; obedient; (*eccles.*) observantine, Observant Friars.

observar, *v.t.* to observe, examine, scrutinize, remark, regard with attention; to mind, notice, heed, obey, keep, follow, abide by; to look into, pry, watch; (*naut., astron.*) to make an observation.

observatorio, *n.m.* observatory.

obsesión, *n.f.* obsession.

obseso, -sa, *a.* beset, obsessed, tempted.

obsidiana, *n.f.* (*geol.*) obsidian.

obsidional, *a.* (*mil.*) obsidional, pertaining to a siege.

obsoleto, -ta, *a.* (*obs.*) obsolete, out of use.

obstáculo, *n.m.* obstacle, impediment, obstruction, clog, check, hindrance.

obstante, *a.* withstanding; *no obstante*, nevertheless, notwithstanding.

obstar, *v.i.* withstand, hinder, obstruct; *v. imp.* to oppose.

obstetricia, *n.f.* (*med.*) obstetrics, midwifery.

obstinación, *n.f.* obstinacy, obduracy, stubbornness.

obstinadamente, *adv.* obstinately, stubbornly, inflexibly.

obstinado, -da, *a.* obstinate, opinionated, headstrong, obdurate.

obstinarse, *v.r.* to be obstinate.

obstrucción, *n.f.* (*med.*) obstruction, stoppage.

obstruccionista, *n.m.f.*, *a.* obstructionist.

obstructivo, -va, *a.* obstructive, obstruent.

obstruir, *v.t.* (conjugated like CONSTRUIR) to obstruct, block up; stop up, choke, check, bar, hinder. — *v.r.* to be obstructed or choked.

obtemperar, *v.t.* to obey, assent.

obtención, *n.f.* attainment, obtainment.

obtener, *v.t.* (conjugated like TENER) to obtain, attain, procure; to preserve, maintain.

obtento, *n.m.* (*eccles.*) prebend, benefice.

obtentor, *a.* (*eccles.*) one who obtains a prebend.

obtestación, *n.f.* (*rhet.*) supplication, entreaty; obtestation.

obturación, *n.f.* stopping, obturation.

obturador, -triz, *a.* stopping-up, plugging.

obturador, *n.m.* stopper, plug; (*surg.*) obturator; (*phot.*) shutter.

obturar, *v.t.* (*surg.*) to plug, stop up, obturate.

obtusángulo, -la, *a.* obtuse-angled, obtuse-angular.

obtuso, -sa, *a.* obtuse, blunt; dull.

obué, *n.m.* oboe, hautboy; oboe-player.

obús, *n.m.* howitzer; shell; core of tyre-valve.

obusera, *a.* gun-boat.

obvención, *n.f.* casual profit, perquisite.

obviar, *v.t.* to obviate, prevent, remove. — *v.i.* to oppose, hinder.

obvio, -via, *a.* obvious, palpable, evident.

obyecto, *n.m.* objection, reply.

oca, *n.f.* goose; (*bot.*) oxalis; royal goose (a game); (*Bol., Chi., Per.*) [ARRACACHA].

ocal, *n.m.* kind of apple or pear; cocoon formed by two silk-worms; coarse kind of silk.

ocarina, *n.f.* ocarina.

ocasión, *n.f.* occasion, chance, opportunity, juncture; danger, risk; convenience; *de ocasión*, second-hand; *asir la ocasión por la melena* (or *por los cabellos*), (*coll.*) to take time by the forelock; *por ocasión*, by chance, by hazard, by accident; *la ocasión hace al ladrón*, opportunity makes the thief; *quien quita la ocasión, quita el pecado*, no temptation, no sin; *a la ocasión la pintan calva*, opportunities should not be lost.

ocasionado, -da, *a.* provoking, perilous; insolent, vexatious.

ocasionador, -ra, *n.m.f.* occasioner.

ocasional, *a.* occasional, chance, casual.

ocasionalmente, *adv.* occasionally.

ocasionar, *v.t.* to cause, occasion; to excite, move; to jeopardize, endanger.

ocaso, *n.m.* occident, setting of sun, etc.; (*fig.*) decadence, ending; West.

occidental, *a.* occidental, western; (*astron.*) applied to any planet setting after the sun.

occidente, *n.m.* occident, west.

occiduo, -dua, *a.* occidental.

occipital, *a.* (*anat.*) occipital.

occipucio, *n.m.* occiput.

occisión, *n.f.* killing, murder.

occiso, -sa, *a.* murdered, killed.

oceánico, -ca, *a.* oceanic.

oceánidas, *n.f.pl.* (*myth.*) oceanids, ocean-nymphs.

océano, *n.m.* ocean, sea, vast expanse.

oceanografía, *n.f.* oceanography.

oceanográfico, -ca, *a.* oceanographic(al).

ocelado, -da, *a.* having ocelli.

ocelo, *n.m.* (*biol.*) ocellus.

ocelote, *n.m.* ocelot, tiger-cat, leopard-cat.

ocena, *n.f.* (*med.*) disease of the nasal mucous membrane.

ociar, *v.i.* (*obs.*) to loiter, idle, be at leisure.

ocio, *n.m.* idleness, leisure, pastime, diversion.

ociosamente, *adv.* idly, uselessly.

ociosear, *v.i.* (*Arg., Chi.*) to be idle.

ociosidad, *n.f.* idleness, laziness, leisure; *la ociosidad es madre de todos los vicios*, idleness is mother of all the vices.

ocioso, -sa, *a.* idle, lazy, fruitless, useless.

oclocracia, *n.f.* ochlocracy.

ocluir, *v.t.* (conjugated like INCLUIR) (*med.*) to occlude, close, shut up.

oclusión, *n.f.* occlusion.

ocosial, *n.m.* (*Per.*) lowland, morass.

ocotal, *n.m.* (*Mex.*) grove of ocotes.

ocote, *n.m.* (*Mex.*) torch-pine.

ocotillo, *n.m.* (*Mex.*) resinous tree (*Fouquieria splendens*).

ocozoal, *n.m.* (*Mex.*) the Mexican rattlesnake.

ocozol, *n.m.* (*bot.*) sweet-gum, liquidambar tree.

ocre, *n.m.* ochre.

octacordio, *n.m.* octachord.

octaedro, *n.m.* (*geom.*) octahedron.

octagonal, *a.* octagonal, eight-sided and angled.

octágono, *n.m.* (*geom.*) octagon. — *a.* eight-sided, octagonal.

octangular, *a.* octangular.

octante, *n.m.* (*naut.*) octant.

octava, *n.f.* (*eccles.*) octave; eight days; (*mus.*) octave; (*poet.*) eight-line stanza.

octavar, *v.i.* (*mus.*) to form octaves on stringed instruments; to deduct the eighth part.

octavario, *n.m.* eight-days' festival.

octavilla, *n.f.* the eighth part of a sheet of paper; old tax on food and beverages; (*poet.*) stanza of eight lines of octosyllabic verse.

octavín, *n.m.* piccolo.

octavo, *n.m.* eighth.
octavo, -va, *a.* octave, octonary, eighth.
octogenario, -ria, *a.* octogenary.
octogésimo, -ma, *a.* eightieth.
octópodo, -da, *a.* octopod, having eight feet.
octosilábico, -ca, *a.* octosyllabic.
octóstilo, *a.* (*arch.*) with eight columns.
octubre, *n.m.* October.
óctuplo, -pla, *a.* octuple, eight-fold.
ocuje, *a.* (*Cub.*) hypocritical.
ocular, *a.* ocular; *testigo ocular*, eye-witness; *dientes oculares*, eye-teeth. — *n.m.* eye-glass, eye-piece.
ocularmente, *adv.* ocularly.
oculista, *n.m.f.* oculist, eye-specialist.
ocultación, *n.f.* concealment, hiding; (*astron.*) occultation; (*law*) withholding facts.
ocultador, -ra, *n.m.f.* hider, concealer.
ocultamente, *adv.* secretly, hiddenly.
ocultar, *v.t.* to hide, conceal, disguise, cloak, hoodwink, secrete, mask; to withhold, keep secret.
ocultismo, *n.m.* occultism.
ocultista, *n.m.f.*, *a.* occultist.
oculto, -ta, *a.* hidden, occult, secret, clandestine, concealed.
ocumo, *n.m.* (*Ven.*) a common plant of edible roots (*Xanthosoma sagittæfolium*).
ocupación, *n.f.* occupation, concern, business, employment, pursuit, office, action; (*rhet.*) prolepsis.
ocupada, *a.* (*coll.*) pregnant, with child.
ocupador, *n.m.* occupier, possessor, occupant.
ocupante, *n.m.*, *a.* occupant, occupying.
ocupar, *v.t.* to occupy, take possession of; to busy, give work, employ; to fill, hold (an employment); to live in, inhabit (a house); to fill a space; to disturb, obstruct, interrupt; to preoccupy, engage the attention. — *v.r.* to occupy oneself with; follow business.
ocurrencia, *n.f.* occurrence, accident, incident, occasion; idea occurring to the mind; witty saying; *ocurrencia de acreedores*, meeting of creditors (*obs.*, now *concurso de acreedores*).
ocurrente, *a.* occurring; humorous, or funny, original, witty, bright.
ocurrir, *v.i.* to occur, happen; to anticipate, meet; (*law*) to have recourse to; to obviate; to apply to; to strike (of an idea).
ocurso, *n.m.* (*Mex.*) petition, claim.
ochava, *n.f.* eighth part; (*eccles.*) octave; *ochavas del molinete*, (*naut.*) whelps of the windlass.
ochavado, -da, *a.* octagonal, eight-sided.
ochavar, *v.t.* to form an octagon.
ochavo, *n.m.* something octagonal in shape; (*obs.*) small coin worth two maravedis.
ochavón, -ona, *a.* (*Cub.*) offspring of a white and a quadroon.
ochenta, *n.m.*, *a.* eighty; eightieth.
ochetón, -ona, *a.* eighty years old, octogenarian.
ocho, *n.m.*, *a.* eight. — *n.m.* figure eight; card with eight spots; *las ocho*, eight o'clock.
ochocientos, -tas, *a.* eight-hundred.
ochosén, *n.m.* small ancient coin of Aragon.
oda, *n.f.* ode.
odalisca, *n.f.* odalisque.
odeón, *n.m.* odeon, odeum.
odiar, *v.t.* to hate, detest, abhor.
odio, *n.m.* hatred, odium, detestation, abhorrence.

odiosamente, *adv.* odiously, hatefully.
odiosidad, *n.f.* hatefulness, odiousness, odium.
odioso, -sa, *a.* odious, hateful, detestable.
odisea, *n.f.* Odyssey; (*fig.*) long voyage with adventures and vicissitudes.
odómetro, *n.m.* hodometer.
odontalgia, *n.f.* odontalgia, toothache.
odontálgico, *n.m.* odontalgic.
odontoideo, -a, *a.* (*anat.*) toothlike, odontoid.
odontología, *n.f.* (*med.*) odontology.
odontólogo, -ga, *n.m.f.*, *a.* odontologist.
odontorrea, *n.f.* (*med.*) odontorrhagia, bleeding of the gums.
odorante, *a.* odorous, fragrant.
odorífero, -ra, *a.* odoriferous, fragrant, perfumed.
odorífico, -ca, *a.* [ODORÍFERO].
odre, *n.m.* wine-skin, leather-bottle; (*joc.*) drunkard.
odrería, *n.f.* leather-bottle factory *or* shop.
odrezuelo, *n.m.* small leather-bottle.
odrina, *n.f.* ox-skin bag for wine.
oesnorueste, *n.m.* west-north-west.
oessudueste, *n.m.* west-south-west.
oeste, *n.m.* west, west wind; *oeste cuarta al norte* (or *sur*), west by north (or south).
ofendedor, -ra, *n.m.f.* offender.
ofender, *v.t.* to offend, harm, insult, injure, make angry. — *v.r.* to take offence, be vexed, displeased.
ofensa, *n.f.* offence, sin, transgression, injury, insult, crime, attack.
ofensión, *n.f.* offence, grievance, injury.
ofensiva, *n.f.* offensive.
ofensivamente, *adv.* offensively, injuriously.
ofensivo, -va, *a.* offensive; displeasing, disgusting; attacking.
ofensor, -ra, *n.m.f.* offender.
oferente, *n.m.* offerer.
oferta, *n.f.* offer, offering, gift; promise; (*com.*) offer, tender, supply; *oferta y demanda*, (*com.*) supply and demand.
ofertorio, *n.m.* offertory.
oficial, *n.m.* tradesman, journeyman, artificer; commissioned officer below major; clerk; hangman, executioner; butcher; *oficial de la sala*, (*law*) actuary in criminal causes; *oficial mayor*, (*law*) chief clerk. — *a.* official, public.
oficiala, *n.f.* workwoman, forewoman, saleswoman.
oficialía, *n.f.* clerk's place in an office; artist's work-room.
oficialidad, *n.f.* body of officers.
oficialmente, *adv.* officially.
oficiar, *v.t.* to officiate, minister; *oficiar de*, to act as.
oficina, *n.f.* office, work-shop, counting-house; bureau; laboratory.
oficinal, *a.* (*med.*, *pharm.*) officinal.
oficinesco, -ca, *a.* departmental; (*coll.*) red-tape.
oficinista, *n.m.f.* office clerk, employee.
oficio, *n.m.* office, work, occupation, employ, employment, profession, ministry, trade, craft, business; function, operation; official letter; service, benefit. — *pl.* (*eccles.*) office, service (especially in Holy Week); *de oficio*, officially; *estar sin oficio ni beneficio*, to be of no occupation; *hacer buenos oficios*, to give one's good offices; *Santo Oficio*, Holy Office (i.e., Inquisition); *tomarlo por oficio*,

to do something frequently; *quien tiene oficio, tiene beneficio*, work brings its own reward; *oficio que no da de comer a su dueño no vale dos habas*, a trade that doesn't feed its master is useless; *oficios mudan costumbres*, offices change habits.

oficionario, *n.m.* canonical office-book.

oficiosamente, *adv.* officiously.

oficiosidad, *n.f.* officiousness, diligence, alacrity.

oficioso, -sa, *a.* diligent, useful, fruitful, accommodating, compliant; officious, meddling, forward.

ofidio, -dia, *a.* (*zool.*) ophidian.

ofiómaco, *n.m.* kind of locust.

ofita, *n.f.* (*min.*) ophite.

ofrecedor, *n.m.* offerer.

ofrecer, *v.t.* (*pres. indic.* **ofrezco**; *pres. subj.* **ofrezca**) to offer, present, hold out, promise, propose; to manifest, exhibit; to dedicate, consecrate; (*com.*) to bid. — *v.r.* to present itself, come to mind; to occur; to volunteer.

ofreciente, *a.* offering.

ofrecimiento, *n.m.* offer, promise, offering.

ofrenda, *n.f.* offering, gift, oblation.

ofrendar, *v.t.* to make offerings; to make contributions.

oftalmía, *n.f.* ophthalmia.

oftálmico, -ca, *a.* ophthalmic.

oftalmología, *n.f.* ophthalmology.

oftalmografía, *n.f.* ophthalmography.

oftalmoscopia, *n.f.* ophthalmoscopy.

ofuscación, *n.f.*; **ofuscamiento**, *n.m.* obfuscation, dazzle, haziness of sight; confusion of mind.

ofuscar, *v.t.* (*pret.* **ofusqué**; *pres. subj.* **ofusque**) to obfuscate, darken, dazzle, confuse, render obscure; *ofuscar la razón*, to disturb the mind.

ogaño, *adv.* (*coll.*) this present year; these days.

ogro, *n.m.* ogre, fabulous monster; (*fig.*) a cruel person.

¡oh! *interj.* oh!

ohm, ohmio, *n.m.* (*elec.*) ohm.

óhmico, -ca, *a.* (*elec.*) ohmic.

oíble, *a.* audible, that may be heard.

oída, *n.f.* hearing.

oídas, de (or **por**), *adv.* by hearsay.

oídio, *n.m.* (*bot.*) oidium.

oído, *n.m.* ear, organ or sense of hearing; (*artill.*) vent, priming-hole, touchhole; *dolor de oídos*, ear-ache; *lisonjear* (or *regalar*) *el oído*, to please, flatter; *tener buen oído*, to have a quick ear; *tocar de oído*, to play by ear; *negar los oídos* (or *no dar oídos*), to refuse to listen; *hacer* (or *tener*) *oídos de mercader*, to turn a deaf ear.

oidor, -ra, *n.m.f.* hearer; judge.

oidoría, *n.f.* office or dignity of an *oidor*.

oír, *v.t.* (*pres. part.* **oyendo**; *pres. indic.* **oigo**; *pret.* **él oyó**; *pres. subj.* **oiga**) to hear, listen; to understand, comprehend; to attend (as lectures), be present at; *¡oiga!* Hear! Listen! *¿oyes?* or *¿oye Vd.?* do you hear? or I say!; *oye, oye*, hear, hear; *oír, ver y callar*, mind your own business; *como quien oye llover*, indifferently.

oíslo, *n.m.f.* (*coll.*) husband or wife, person beloved.

ojal, *n.m.* button-hole; (*min.*) loop.

¡ojalá! *interj.* God grant, would to God.

ojaladera, *n.f.* button-hole-maker.

ojalador, -ra, *n.m.f.* button-hole-maker.

ojaladura, *n.f.* set of button-holes.

ojalar, *v.t.* to make button-holes.

ojalatero, *n.m.*, *a.* (*coll.*) stay-at-home patriot (during a war).

ojanco, *n.m.* (*Cub.*, *PR.*) pink fish with large eyes (*Mesoprion ojanco*).

ojaranzo, *n.m.* (*bot.*) common hornbeam; witch-hazel.

ojeada, *n.f.* glance, look, glimpse, view, ogle.

ojeador, *n.m.* beater, one who starts game.

ojeadura, *n.f.* glazing of clothes.

ojear, *v.t.* to eye, view attentively, look, stare at, glance at; to start game.

ojeo, *n.m.* starting of game, hallooing.

ojera, *n.f.* ring under the eye; eye-cup.

ojeriza, *n.f.* spite, grudge, ill-will.

ojeroso, -sa; **ojerudo, -da**, *a.* sunken, hollow-eyed, having rings round the eyes.

ojete, *n.m.* eyelet-hole; (*coll.*) anus.

ojeteador, *n.m.* eyeleteer, stiletto.

ojetear, *v.t.* to make eyelet-holes.

ojetera, *n.f.* piece of whalebone sown near eyelet-hole; eyelet-maker.

ojialegre, *a.* with sparkling eyes.

ojienjuto, -ta, *a.* dry-eyed.

ojimel, ojimiel, *n.m.* (*pharm.*) oxymel.

ojimoreno, -na, *a.* brown-eyed.

ojinegro, -gra, *a.* black-eyed.

ojito, *n.m.* small eye.

ojiva, *n.f.* (*arch.*) ogive.

ojival, *a.* ogival.

ojizaino, -na, *a.* (*coll.*) squint-eyed; moon-eyed.

ojizarco, -ca, *a.* (*coll.*) blue-eyed.

ojo, *n.m.* eye, sight, ocular knowledge; socket; bow of a key, key-hole; water-spring, geyser; mesh of a net, eye (of a needle); drop of oil or grease; head formed on liquors; (*arch.*) span of a bridge; perforation, hole; care, attention, notice, look; lather; eye or face of type; eye or hollow in bread or cheese; opening in the centre of a winding staircase; reference mark; perception, a shrewd eye. — *pl.* **ojos**, dearest, darling; *ojo de pollo* (or *de gallo*) colour of certain wines; (*prov.*) corn between the toes; *ojo alerta*, look sharp!; *ojo de buey*, (*bot.*) ox-eye; (*coll.*) doubloon (16 gold dollars); *a ojo*, by the lump; *a los ojos de*, in presence of; *a ojos vistas*, publicly, visibly; *abrir tanto ojo*, to stare with joy; *avivar el ojo*, to be on one's guard; *a ojos cerrados* or *a cierra ojos*, without hesitation; *cerrar los ojos a*, to be present at someone's death; *clavar los ojos en*, to gaze fixedly at; *comer con los ojos*, to devour with one's gaze; *como los ojos de la cara*, as dear as one's own eyes; *con el ojo tan largo*, with great attention (or care); *costar un ojo*, to be excessively dear; *dar de ojos*, to fall, fall into an error, meet somebody; *dar en los ojos*, to be absolutely clear, clear at first sight; *despabilar(se) los ojos*, to live with care and prudence; *dormir con los ojos abiertos*, (*met.*) to sleep with one's eyes open; *de medio ojo*, lurkingly, hiddenly; *echar el ojo*, to gaze at, desire; *en un abrir y cerrar de ojos*, in the twinkling of an eye; *entrar por el ojo*, to please; *estar con cien ojos*, to have continual suspicions; *estimar sobre los ojos*, to prize very highly; *hablar con los ojos*, to make one's meaning clear by a look; *hacer del ojo*, to wink; *hacerse ojos*, to look with sharp eyes; *empeñado hasta los ojos*, to be deeply in debt;

llevar los ojos, to attract attention; *llorar con un ojo*, to shed crocodile tears; *más ven cuatro ojos que dos*, two heads are better than one; *mal de ojo*, fascination, enchantment; *mal de ojos*, eyesore; *mentir el ojo*, to be mistaken; *mirar con otros ojos*, to look at very differently; *¡mucho ojo!* take care! *no pegar el ojo*, not to sleep a wink; *no saber donde tiene los ojos*, to be ignorant of the most elementary facts; *ojo a la margen*, look out! pay attention! *niña del ojo*, pupil of the eye; *niñas de los ojos*, apple of the eye; *ojos que no ven, corazón que no quiebra* (also *llora*), what the eye cannot see the heart cannot grieve for; *pasar los ojos por*, to cast one's eyes over; *quebrar los ojos a*, to disgust, displease; *sacar los ojos a uno*, to importune one to do something; *saltar a los ojos*, to be abundantly clear; *tener ojo a*, to pay attention to; *traer entre ojos*, to be annoyed with.

ojoche, *n.m.* (*CR.*) a tree the fruit of which serves as food for cattle.

ojota, *n.f.* (*Am.*) Indian woman's sandal.

ojuelo, *n.m.* small eye. — *pl.* **ojuelos,** sparkling eyes; spectacles.

ola, *n.f.* wave, billow; *ola de marea*, tidal wave.

olaje, *n.m.* succession of waves, surge, motion of the waves.

ole, *n.m.* Andalusian dance; **¡olé!** *interj.* bravo!

oleáceo, -cea, *a.* oleaceous; *n.f.pl.* Oleaceæ.

oleada, *n.f.* surge, swell of the sea; surging of a crowd; abundant oil-crop.

oleaginosidad, *n.f.* oleaginousness, oiliness.

oleaginoso, -sa, *a.* oleaginous, oily.

oleaje, *n.m.* surge, succession of waves.

oleandro, *n.m.* (*bot.*) oleander.

olear, *v.t.* to administer extreme unction.

oleastro, *n.m.* (*bot.*) oleaster.

oleato, *n.m.* oleate.

oleaza, *n.f.* (*prov.*) refuse of oil-extraction.

oledero, -ra, *a.* odorous, fragrant.

oledor, -ra, *n.m.f.* smeller, one who smells.

oleína, *n.f.* olein, oily substance.

óleo, *n.m.* oil; anointing, extreme unction; holy oil; *al óleo*, in oils; *cuadro* (or *pintura*) *al óleo*, oil-painting.

oleografía, *n.f.* oleography.

oleómetro, *n.m.* oleometer.

oleosidad, *n.f.* oleosity, oiliness.

oleoso, -sa, *a.* oily, oleaginous.

oler, *v.t.* (*pres. indic.* **huelo;** *pres. subj.* **huela**) to smell, sniff, snuff, scent; to discover, search, find out; to pry. — *v.i.* to smell, strike the nostrils, smack; *no oler bien*, to be suspicious (said of a thing); *huele a hereje*, he smells of heresy.

olfacción, *n.f.* smelling, olfaction.

olfatear, *v.t.* to smell, scent, sniff, snuff.

olfato, *n.m.* smell, odour, scent, sense of smell.

olfatorio, -ria, *a.* olfactory.

olíbano, *n.m.* (*bot.*) gum-resin; incense.

oliente, *a.* smelling, odorous.

oliera, *n.f.* vessel for holy oil.

oligarca, *n.m.* oligarch.

oligarquía, *n.f.* oligarchy.

oligárquico, -ca, *a.* oligarchical.

olimpiada, *n.f.* Olympiad, Olympic games.

olímpico, -ca, *a.* Olympic.

olimpo, *n.m.* Olympus; height, eminence; (*poet.*) heaven.

olingo, *n.m.* a Central-American monkey.

olio, *n.m.* oil.

oliscar, *v.t.* to smell, sniff, scent; to examine, investigate, ascertain. — *v.i.* to be tainted, to be *or* smell 'high'; to smell strongly.

oliva, *n.f.* olive, olive-tree; owl; (*fig.*) peace.

olivar, *n.m.* olive-grove. — *v.t.* to prune, lop off superfluous branches, etc.

olivarda, *n.f.* (*orn.*) green goshawk; (*bot.*) elecampane.

olivarse, *v.r.* to form bubbles when baking (bread).

olivera, *n.f.* olive-tree.

olivífero, -ra, *a.* (*poet.*) olive-producing.

olivillo, *n.f.* (*bot.*) a variety of terebinth.

olivino, *n.m.* (*min.*) olivin, peridot.

olivo, *n.m.* olive-tree; *olivo y aceituno, todo es uno*, a distinction without a difference.

olmeda, *n.f.;* **olmedo,** *n.m.* elm-grove.

olmo, *n.m.* elm-tree.

ológrafo, -fa, *a.* holograph.

olomina, *n.f.* (*CR.*) small fresh-water fish (not edible).

olopopo, *n.m.* (*CR.*) a very big owl.

olor, *n.m.* odour, scent, fragrance, stink, stench; hope, offer, promise; suspicion; reputation, fame.

oloroso, -sa, *a.* odoriferous, fragrant, perfumed.

olvidadizo, -za, *a.* forgetful, oblivious, short of memory.

olvidado, -da, *a.* forgotten, forlorn forsaken.

olvidar, *v.t.* to forget, omit, neglect.

olvido, *n.m.* forgetfulness, oversight; carelessness, heedlessness, neglect, oblivion; *echar al* (or *en*) *olvido*, to cast into oblivion; *poner en olvido*, to forget.

olla, *n.f.* stewpot; dish of boiled meat and vegetables; whirlpool; *olla carnicera*, boiler, large kettle; *olla podrida*, a wellknown Spanish dish; *a olla que hierve, ninguna mosca se atreve*, few will attempt a feat known to be risky; *no hay olla tan fea que no tenga su cobertera*, no person so bad but has his good points; *olla de fuego*, (*artill.*) stinkpot; *olla de grillos*, great confusion, pandemonium.

ollao, *n.m.* (*naut.*) eyelet-hole.

ollar, *a.* soft (stone). — *n.m.* horse's nostril.

ollaza, *n.f.* large pot.

ollería, *n.f.* pottery; crockery-shop.

ollero, *n.m.* potter; earthenware dealer.

olleta, *n.f.* (*Ven.*) a dish made with maize; (*Col.*) chocolate jug.

ollita, *n.f.* small pot.

olluco, *n.m.* (*Per.*) plant with edible tubercle.

ombligada, *n.f.* (*tannery*) part of a skin corresponding to the navel.

ombligo, *n.m.* navel, navel-string; umbilical cord; centre, middle; *ombligo de Venus*, (*bot.*) Venus' navelwort.

ombliguero, *n.m.* bandage for baby's navel.

ombría, *n.f.* shade, shady place.

ombú, *n.m.* South-American tree.

omega, *n.f.* omega; last, end.

omental, *a.* belonging to the omentum.

omento, *n.m.* (*anat.*) omentum.

ominar, *v.t.* to augur, foretell, foretoken.

ominoso, -sa, *a.* ominous, foreboding ill.

omisión, *n.f.* omission, carelessness, neglect, negligence, heedlessness.

omiso, -sa, *a.* neglectful, heedless, remiss, careless. — *p.p.* [OMITIR].

omitir, *v.t.* (*p.p.* **omitido, omiso**) to omit, neglect, drop, leave out.

ómnibus, *n.m.* omnibus; slow, stopping train.
omnímodamente, *adv.* entirely, by all means.
omnímodo, -da, *a.* entire, total.
omnipotencia, *n.f.* omnipotence.
omnipotente, *a.* omnipotent, almighty.
omnipotentemente, *adv.* omnipotently.
omnipresencia, *n.f.* omnipresence.
omnisapiente, *a.* omniscient.
omnisciencia, *n.f.* omniscience.
omniscio, -cia, *a.* omniscient.
omnívoro, -ra, *a.* omnivorous.
omóplato, *n.m.* (*anat.*) omoplate, shoulder-blade.
onagra, *n.f.* (*bot.*) evening primrose.
onagro, *n.m.* onager, wild ass; ancient weapon like a cross-bow.
onanismo, *n.m.* onanism.
once, *n.m.,* *a.* eleven, eleventh; figure eleven; football team; *las once,* eleven o'clock; *tomar las once,* (*coll.*) to have elevenses.
oncear, *v.t.* to weigh out by ounces.
oncejera, *n.f.* small snare for catching birds.
oncejo, *n.m.* (*orn.*) swift, black-martin, martlet.
oncemil, *n.m.* (*slang*) coat of mail.
onceno, -na, *a.* eleventh.
onda, *n.f.* wave, undulation, ripple; flicker, reverberation of light; fluctuation, agitation; (*sew.*) scallop. — *pl.* the sea; *onda etérea,* ether wave; *onda sonora,* sound wave.
ondeado, *n.m.* scalloping.
ondeante, *a.* undulating, waving.
ondear, *v.i.* to undulate, fluctuate. — *v.r.* to swing, sway.
ondeo, *n.m.* undulating, waving.
ondina, *n.f.* undine, water-sprite.
ondisonante, *a.* (*poet.*) billowy.
ondulación, *n.f.* undulation; *ondulación permanente,* permanent wave.
ondulado, -da, *p.p.* undulated, rippled; scalloped, wavy.
ondulante, *a.* waving, undulating.
ondular, *v.t.* to undulate, wave.
onerario, -ria, *a.* said of ancient cargo boats.
onerosamente, *adv.* onerously.
oneroso, -sa, *a.* burdensome, onerous.
onfacino, *n.m.,a.* oil extracted from green olives.
onfacomeli, *n.m.* (*pharm.*) oxymel.
ónice, ónique, ónix, *n.m.* (*min.*) onyx.
onocrótalo, *n.m.* white pelican.
onomástico, -ca, *n.m.f., a.* onomastic.
onomatopeya, *n.f.* onomatopoeia.
onomatopéyico, -ca, *a.* onomatopoeic.
onoquiles, *n.f.* (*bot.*) dyer's bugloss, alkanet.
onoto, *n.m.* (*Ven.*) arnotto tree.
ontogenia, *n.f.* (*biol.*) ontogenesis.
ontogénico, -ca, *a.* ontogenetic.
ontología, *n.f.* ontology.
ontológico, -ca, *a.* ontologic, ontological.
ontologista, *n.m.f.* ontologist.
ontólogo, *n.m.* ontologist.
onza, *n.f.* ounce; (*zool.*) ounce, lynx; *por onzas,* sparingly; *onza de oro,* Spanish doubloon.
onzavo, *n.m.* eleventh part.
onzavo, -va, *a.* eleventh.
oolítico, -ca, *a.* oolitic.
oolito, *n.m.* (*geol.*) oolite.
opa, *n.f.* (*Col., Per.*) dumb, silly, foolish; (*prov.*) a hole left in a wall on removing the scaffolding.
opacamente, *adv.* obscurely, darkly.
opacidad, *n.f.* opacity, darkness, cloudiness.
opaco, -ca, *a.* opaque; dark, gloomy.

opalino, -na, *a.* opaline, opalescent.
ópalo, *n.m.* (*min.*) opal.
opción, *n.f.* option, choice, right.
ópera, *n.f.* opera, musical drama.
operable, *a.* capable of operating, operable, practicable.
operación, *n.f.* operation, working, action; (*chem.*) process; (*com.*) transaction; venture. — *pl.* operaciones, (*com.*) business.
operador, *n.m.* surgical-operator; (*min.*) prospector.
operante, *a.* operating, operative.
operar, *v.i.* to operate, act, work; (*com.*) to speculate. — *v.t.* (*surg.*) to operate.
operario, -ria, *n.m.f.* operator, labourer, working man, hand.
operario, *n.m.* priest who assists sick or dying persons.
operativo, -va, *a.* operative.
operatorio, -ria, *a.* operative; (*med.*) relating to operations.
opérculo, *n.m.* operculum, lid, cover.
opereta, *n.f.* operetta.
operista, *n.m.f.* opera-singer.
operístico, -ca, *a.* operatic.
operoso, -sa, *a.* laborious, wearisome.
opiado, -da; opiato, -ta, *a.* opiate, narcotic, anodyne.
opiata, *n.f.* opiate.
opilación, *n.f.* oppilation, obstruction; amenorrhœa.
opilar, *v.t.* to oppilate, obstruct. — *v.r.* to suffer from amenorrhœa.
opilativo, -va, *a.* obstructive, oppilative.
opimo, -ma, *a.* rich, fruitful, abundant.
opinable, *a.* disputable, problematical, questionable.
opinante, *a.* arguing. — *n.m.f.* arguer.
opinar, *v.i.* to argue, opine, judge.
opinativo, -va, *a.* opinionative, opinionated.
opinión, *n.f.* opinion, judgment, character, reputation, sentiment, estimate; *hacer opinión,* to form an opinion; *casarse con su opinión,* to be wedded to one's own opinion.
opio, *n.m.* opium.
opíparamente, *adv.* splendidly.
opíparo, -ra, *a.* sumptuous, splendid.
opobálsamo, *n.m.* opobalsam, balm of Gilead.
oponer, *v.t., v.r.* (conjugated like PONER) to oppose, contradict, object; to hinder, bar, resist, withstand; to act against, dispute, controvert, be contrary, be adverse; to front, face, be opposite to; to compete.
oponible, *a.* opposable.
opopónaca, opopónace, *n.f.* (*bot.*) rough parsnip.
opopónaco, opopánax, *n.m.* opoponax.
oporto, *n.m.* port wine.
oportunamente, *adv.* opportunely.
oportunidad, *n.f.* opportunity, convenience.
oportunismo, *n.m.* (*polit.*) opportunism.
oportunista, *n.m.f., a.* (*polit.*) opportunist.
oportuno, -na, *a.* opportune, convenient.
oposición, *n.f.* opposition, resistance, antagonism, counter-view, contrariety, competition.
opositor, -ra, *n.m.f.* opposer, opponent, competitor.
opresión, *n.f.* oppression, coercion, pressure, hardship, severity.
opresivamente, *adv.* oppressively, overwhelmingly.

opresivo, -va, *a.* oppressive, overwhelming, cruel.

opresor, *n.m.* oppressor, extortioner.

oprimir, *v.t.* (*p.p.* **oprimido, opreso**) to oppress, overpower, overbear, subdue; to press, crush, squeeze; to weigh down, lie heavy upon.

oprobiar, *v.t.* to defame, revile.

oprobio, *n.m.* opprobrium, infamy, ignominy.

oprobioso, -sa, *a.* opprobrious, reproachful, disgraceful.

optación, *n.f.* (*rhet.*) optation.

optante, *a.* one who chooses.

optar, *v.t.* to choose; to take up (an appointment, etc.).

optativo, *n.m.* (*gram.*) optative.

óptica, *n.f.* optics; stereoscope.

óptico, -ca, *a.* optic, optical, visual.

óptico, *n.m.* optician.

óptimamente, *adv.* eminently, excellently, perfectly.

optimismo, *n.m.* optimism.

optimista, *n.m.f.* optimist.

óptimo, -ma, *a.* best, eminently good.

optómetro, *n.m.* optometer.

opuestamente, *adv.* oppositely, contrarily.

opuesto, -ta, *a.* opposed; (*bot.*) opposite, contrary, adverse. — *p.p. irreg.* [OPONER].

opugnación, *n.f.* opposition.

opugnador, *n.m.* oppugner, opposer.

opugnar, *v.t.* to oppugn, attack, oppose, resist, contradict.

opulencia, *n.f.* opulence, wealth, affluence.

opulentamente, *adv.* opulently.

opulento, -ta, *a.* opulent, wealthy, rich, affluent.

opúsculo, *n.m.* opuscule, tract, short treatise, booklet, essay.

oquedad, *n.f.* hollow, cavity.

oquedal, *n.m.* plantation of lofty trees.

oqueruela, *n.f.* tangled, knotted thread; kink in a sewing thread.

ora, *conj.* whether, either, now; *ora . . . ora . . .,* now . . . now . . .: *tomando ora la espada, ora la pluma,* taking now the sword and now the pen.

oración, *n.f.* oration, harangue, speech; prayer, supplication; (*gram.*) sentence; *partes de la oración,* (*gram.*) parts of speech; *oración de perro no va al cielo,* an ungracious request is seldom granted; *la oración breve sube al cielo,* a brief request is most likely to be granted. — *pl.* first part of catechism; the angelus.

oracional, *n.m.* prayer-book.

oracionero, *n.m.* one who goes from door to door praying.

oráculo, *n.m.* oracle.

orador, *n.m.* orator, preacher, public speaker.

oral, *a.* oral, verbal, vocal. — *n.m.* (*prov.*) soft breeze.

orangután, *n.m.* (*zool.*) orang-outang.

orante, *a.* praying.

orar, *v.t., v.i.* to harangue; to ask, request; pray.

orate, *n.m.f.* lunatic, madman; *casa de orates,* lunatic asylum.

oratoria, *n.f.* oratory, eloquence.

oratoriamente, *adv.* oratorically.

oratorio, -ria, *a.* oratorial, rhetorical, oratorical.

oratorio, *n.m.* oratory; (*mus.*) oratorio; (*eccles.*) congregation of presbyters founded by St. Philip Neri.

orbe, *n.m.* orb, sphere; the earth; celestial body; (*ichth.*) globe-fish.

orbicular, *a.* orbicular, circular.

orbicularmente, *adv.* orbicularly.

órbita, *n.f.* (*astron.*) orbit; (*anat.*) cavity of the eye.

orbital, *a.* relating to the orbit.

orca, *n.f.* (*ichth.*) grampus, orca.

orcaneta, *n.f.* (*bot.*) dyer's bugloss, alkanet.

orcina, *n.f.* (*chem.*) orcein.

orco, *n.m.* (*ichth.*) grampus; (*poet.*) hell.

orchilla, *n.f.* (*Ec.*) (*bot.*) archil, orchil.

órdago, *n.m.* move in a game of cards; *de órdago,* (*coll.*) first class, excellent.

ordalías, *n.f.pl.* ordeal, trial by ordeal.

orden, *n.m.* order, regularity, method, system, régime, course, series, rotation; group, class; religious fraternity. — *pl.* sacrament of ordination; clerical office. — *n.f.* command, mandate; precept; order of knighthood; (*com.*) order; *en orden,* in an orderly manner; *por su orden,* in turn, successively; *a la orden,* (*com.*) to order; *a la orden de,* to the order of; *orden del día,* (*mil.*) order of the day; *orden de batalla,* battle array.

ordenación, *n.f.* disposition, array, methodical arrangement; clerical ordination; edict, ordinance; auditor's office.

ordenada, *n.f.* (*geom.*) ordinate.

ordenadamente, *adv.* in an orderly way, methodically.

ordenador, -ra, *n.m.f.* ordainer, orderer, disposer, regulator, auditor.

ordenamiento, *n.m.* ordaining, regulating; ordinance, edict.

ordenancista, *n.m.f.* disciplinarian, martinet.

ordenando, ordenante, *n.m.* ordinand.

ordenanza, *n.f.* method, order; command; ordination; law, statute, ordinance. — *n.m.* (*mil.*) orderly.

ordenar, *v.t.* to class, arrange, assort, put in order; to enact, ordain, enact; command; to regulate, direct; to confer holy orders. — *v.r.* to be ordained.

ordeñadero, *n.m.* milk-pail.

ordeñador, -ra, *n.m.f.* milker.

ordeñar, *v.t.* to suck; to milk; to pick olives.

ordinal, *a.* ordinal, ritual.

ordinariamente, *adv.* frequently, ordinarily, customarily; rudely.

ordinariez, *n.f.* rude manners, grossness, want of politeness.

ordinario, -ria, *a.* ordinary, customary, common, usual, plain, familiar; mean, coarse, vulgar.

ordinario, *n.m.* ordinary; ecclesiastical judge; daily household expense; bishop; regular mail or post; carrier, muleteer; *de ordinario,* regularly, commonly.

ordinativo, -va, *a.* ordering, regulating, ordinative.

orea, oréada, oréade, *n.f.* oread, woodnymph.

oreante, *a.* cooling, airing, refreshing.

orear, *v.t.* to cool, refresh, dry, expose to the air, aerate, ventilate. — *v.r.* to go out for an airing.

orégano, *n.m.* (*bot.*) wild marjoram.

oreja, *n.f.* ear, auricle; hearing; tale-teller, flatterer; flap of a shoe; (*mech.*) lug, flange; (*naut.*) fluke (of an anchor); *oreja de zapato,* shoe-flap; *oreja de abad,* (*bot.*) Venus' navelwort; *oreja de ratón*, (*bot.*) mouse-ear; *oreja de oso*, (*bot.*) primrose; *oreja marina*, (*conch.*) gasteropod; *oreja de mercader*, (*coll.*) deaf ear; *con las orejas caídas*, crestfallen, dejected; *apearse por las orejas*, to give an absurd answer; *bajar las orejas*, to yield, humble oneself; *calentar a uno las orejas*, to chide (*or* reprove) severely; *ver las orejas al lobo*, to be in great peril.

orejano, -na, *a.* unbranded (calf).

orejeado, -da, *a.* informed, advised, instructed, warned.

orejear, *v.i.* to shake the ears (an animal); (*fig.*) to act reluctantly; to whisper.

orejera, *n.f.* covering for the ears, ear-cap, oreillette; mould-board of a plough.

orejeta, *n.f.* small ear or lug.

orejita, *n.f.* small ear.

orejón, *n.m.* pull of the ear; slice of dried fruit; hind part of a plough; (*fort.*) orillon; (*Per.*) nobleman, privileged noble; Inca; name given to several South American tribes; (*Col.*) dweller on the savanna of Bogotá; (*fig.*) countryman, clown.

orejudo, -da, *a.* flap-eared, long-eared.

oreo, *n.m.* breeze, fresh air.

orfanato, *n.m.* orphanage.

orfandad, *n.f.* orphanage; orphan's pension.

orfebre, *n.m.* goldsmith, silversmith.

orfebrería, *n.f.* gold or silver work.

orfeón, *n.m.* choral society.

orfeonista, *n.m.f.* member of a choral society.

órfico, -ca, *a.* orphic.

orfo, *n.m.* (*ichth.*) orfe.

organdí, *n.m.* organdie.

organero, *n.m.* organ-maker, organ-builder.

orgánicamente, *adv.* organically.

orgánico, -ca, *a.* organic, organical; harmonious.

organico, -illo, -ito, *n.m.* small-organ, chamber-organ, barrel-organ.

organismo, *n.m.* organism; organization; association.

organista, *n.m.f.* (*mus.*) organist.

organizable, *a.* organizable.

organización, *n.f.* organization; construction; order, arrangement.

organizado, -da, *a.* organized, constituted.

organizador, -ra, *n.m.f.,* *a.* organizer.

organizar, *v.t.* (*pret.* **organicé;** *pres. subj.* **organice**) to organize, constitute; to tune an organ.

órgano, *n.m.* (*mus.*) organ, pipe organ; pipe refrigerator; (*physiol.*) medium, instrument, agency.

orgasmo, *n.m.* orgasm.

orgia, orgía, *n.f.* orgy, mad revel.

orgullo, *n.m.* pride, haughtiness, loftiness.

orgullosamente, *adv.* proudly, haughtily.

orgulloso, -sa, *a.* proud, haughty, lofty.

orientación, *n.f.* orientation, situation; finding the cardinal points, finding one's way.

oriental, *a.* oriental, eastern. — *n.m.* Oriental.

orientalista, *n.m.f.* orientalist.

orientar, *v.t.* to orientate, give the right direction, give the proper aspect, put right, set right, turn something eastward. — *v.r.* to find one's bearings; to consider the course to be taken.

oriente, *n.m.* orient, east; east wind; lustre (of pearls); source, origin; youth.

orificación, *n.f.* (*dent.*) gold filling.

orificar, *v.t.* (*dent.*) to fill with gold.

orífice, *n.m.* goldsmith.

orificia, *n.m.* goldsmith's art or profession.

orificio, *n.m.* orifice, mouth, hole, aperture; anus; (*artill.*) vent-hole.

oriflama, *n.f.* oriflamme; flag, banner.

origen, *n.m.* origin, motive, source, fount, genesis, cause; native country; family, extraction, lineage; beginning.

original, *a.* original, primitive, new, first, novel, odd, quaint. — *n.m.* original, first copy or draft, manuscript; archetype; odd person; person represented in a portrait.

originalidad, *n.f.* (*coll.*) originality.

originalmente, *adv.* originally.

originar, *v.t.* to originate, create, invent, bring into existence. — *v.r.* to originate, descend, cause, occasion, spring from, arise.

originariamente, *adv.* primarily, originally, radically.

originario, -ria, *a.* originary, primary, primitive; native, descendant; derived.

orilla, *n.f.* limit, extent, border, margin; edge, selvedge; sidewalk; river-bank, shore, water's edge; fresh breeze; *a la orilla*, on the brink; *salir a la orilla*, to overcome difficulties; *nadar, nadar, y a la orilla ahogar*, to lose at the last moment something one has worked for.

orillar, *v.t.,* *v.i.* to approach the shore; to border; to leave a selvedge on cloth; to conclude, arrange; to surmount; (*sew.*) to border. — *v.r.* to reach the shore.

orillo, *n.m.* selvedge.

orín, *n.m.* rust; taint, stain, defect. — *pl.* urine.

orina, *n.f.* urine.

orinal, *n.m.* chamber-pot; urinal.

orinar, *v.i.* to urinate, make water.

oriniento, -ta, *a.* rusty, mouldy.

orinque, *n.m.* (*naut.*) buoy-rope.

oriol, *n.m.* golden thrush, oriole.

orión, *n.m.* (*astron.*) Orion.

oriundo, -da, *a.* originating, derived from; native of, coming from.

orla, *n.f.* list, selvedge, border, fringe, trimming; (*her.*) orle; (*typ.*) ornamental border.

orlador, -ra, *n.m.f.* borderer.

orladura, *n.f.* border, edging, list.

orlar, *v.t.* to border, edge, garnish.

orlo, *n.m.* Alpine oboe; organ-stop; plinth.

ormesí, *n.m.* kind of silk stuff.

ormino, *n.m.* (*bot.*) annual clary sage.

ornabeque, *n.m.* (*fort.*) hornwork.

ornadamente, *adv.* ornamentally.

ornado, -da, *a.* ornate.

ornamentación, *n.f.* ornamentation.

ornamental, *a.* ornamental.

ornamentar, *v.t.* to ornament, embellish, adorn, bedeck.

ornamento, *n.m.* ornament, decoration, embellishment, adornment, accomplishment. — *pl.* **ornamentos,** (*eccl.*) vestments; (*arch.*) frets, mouldings; moral qualities.

ornar, *v.t.* to adorn, embellish, garnish.

ornato, *n.m.* dress, apparel, decoration, ornament, embellishment.

ornitología, *n.f.* ornithology.

ornitológico, -ca, *a.* ornithological.

ornitólogo, *n.m.* ornithologist.

oro, *n.m.* gold; gold colour; money, riches, wealth; gold ornaments or trinkets. — *pl.* **oros,** diamonds (in cards); *de oro*, golden; *oro batido*, leaf gold; *oro en bruto*, (*or oro* *virgen,* or *oro en pasta*) bullion; *oro en libritos,* gold-leaf; *oro en polvo,* gold-dust; *oro mate,* gold size; *de oro y azul,* splendidly attired; *oro es lo que oro vale,* money is not everything; *no es oro todo lo que reluce,* all is not gold that glitters; *oro majado luce,* tried friends are best; *oros son triunfos,* diamonds are trumps; (*fig.*) self-interest governs the business; *poner a uno de oro y azul,* to give a dressing-down, severe reprimand.

orobanca, *n.f.* (*bot.*) broom rape.

orobias, *n.m.* fine incense.

orografía, *n.f.* orography.

orográfico, -ca, *a.* orographic.

orología, *n.f.* orology.

orondo, -da, *a.* pompous, showy; hollow.

oropel, *n.m.* pinchbeck, tinsel, leaf-brass, glitter.

oropelero, *n.m.* gold-foil-worker.

oropéndola, *n.f.* loriot; golden oriole.

oropesa, *n.f.* woolly sage.

oropimente, *n.m.* (*min.*) orpiment.

oroya, *n.f.* (*Am.*) hanging basket for carrying passengers over rope bridges.

orozuz, *n.m.* liquorice.

orquesta, orquestra, *n.f.* orchestra; (*theat.*) place for the orchestra; *butaca de orquesta,* first row of stalls.

orquestación, *n.f.* orchestration.

orquestar, *v.t.* to orchestrate.

orquídeas, *n.f.pl.* orchids.

orquídeo, -dea, *a.* orchidaceous.

orquitis, *n.f.* (*med.*) orchitis.

orre, en, *adv.* loose, in bulk.

ortega, *n.f.* hazel-grouse.

ortiga, *n.f.* nettle; *ser como unas ortigas,* to be thoroughly cross.

ortivo, -va, *a.* (*astr.*) oriental, eastern, ortive.

orto, *n.m.* rising of the sun or a star.

ortodoxia, *n.f.* orthodoxy.

ortodoxo, -xa, *a.* orthodox.

ortodromia, *n.f.* (*naut.*) orthodromy.

ortogonal; ortogonio, -nia, *a.* orthogonal, rectangular.

ortografía, *n.f.* orthography.

ortográficamente, *adv.* orthographically.

ortográfico, -ca, *a.* orthographical.

ortógrafo, *n.m.* orthographer.

ortología, *n.f.* orthoepy, art of correct pronunciation.

ortológico, -ca, *a.* orthoepic.

ortólogo, -ga, *n.m.f.* orthoepist.

ortopedia, *n.f.* (*med.*) orthopædy.

ortopédico, -ca, *a.* orthopædic.

ortopedista, *n.m.f.* orthopædist.

ortóptero, -ra, *a.* orthopterous.—*pl.* orthoptera.

ortosa, *n.f.* (*min.*) orthoclase.

oruga, *n.f.* (*bot.*) rocket; salad made with rocket and called *oruga de azúcar* or *miel;* (*ent.*) caterpillar.

orujo, *n.m.* skin of pressed grapes, olives, cotton seed, etc.

orvalle, *n.m.* (*bot.*) annual clary sage.

orvietano, *n.m.* orvietan.

orza, *n.f.* gallipot, preserve-jar; (*naut.*) luff; (*yachting*) lead stabilizer.

orzada, *n.f.* (*naut.*) luffing, hauling.

orzaderas, *n.f.pl.* (*naut.*) leeboards.

orzaga, *n.f.* (*bot.*) orache.

orzar, *v.i.* (*naut.*) to luff.

orzaya, *n.f.* children's nurse.

orzoyo, *n.m.* silk yarn forming the pile of velvet.

orzuelo, *n.m.* (*med.*) sty; snare, trap (for animals).

orzura, *n.f.* (*chem.*) minium.

os, *pron. pers. dative and accusative of* VOS *and* VOSOTROS: you, to you.

osa, *n.f.* she-bear; *osa mayor,* (*astron.*) Ursa Major, dipper; *osa menor,* Ursa Minor.

osadamente, *adv.* boldly, daringly.

osadía, *n.f.* resolution, boldness, hardiness, audacity.

osado, -da, *a.* daring, high-spirited, audacious, bold. — *p.p.* [OSAR].

osambre, *n.m.;* **osamenta,** *n.f.* skeleton.

osar, *v.i.* to dare, outdare, venture.

osar, osario, *n.m.* ossuary, charnel-house.

oscilación, *n.f.* oscillation, vibration.

oscilador, *n.m.* (*phys.*) oscillator; oscillation valve.

oscilante, *a.* oscillating, vibrating.

oscilar, *v.i.* to oscillate, vibrate, waver.

oscilatorio, -ria, *a.* oscillatory.

oscitancia, *n.f.* carelessness, heedlessness.

ósculo, *n.m.* kiss.

oscuramente, *adv.* darkly.

oscuras (a), *adv.* darkly; in the dark.

oscurecer, *v.t., v.i.* (conjugated like NACER) to darken, grow dark.

oscurecimiento, *n.m.* darkening, darkness.

oscuridad, *n.f.* darkness, obscurity.

oscuro, -ra, *a.* dark, obscure.

osecico, osecillo, osezuelo, *n.m.* little bone.

oseína, *n.f.* (*chem.*) ossein.

óseo, -sea, *a.* osseous, bony.

osera, *n.f.* den of bears.

osero, *n.m.* charnel-house.

osezno, *n.m.* bear whelp, bear cub.

osificación, *n.f.* ossification.

osificado, -da, *a.* ossified. — *p.p.* [OSIFICARSE].

osificarse, *v.r.* (conjugated like BUSCAR) to ossify, become ossified.

osífico, -ca, *a.* ossific.

osífraga, *n.f.;* **osífrago,** *n.m.* osprey, ossifrage.

osmio, *n.m.* (*min.*) osmium.

oso, *n.m.* bear; *oso hormiguero,* ant-eater; *oso colmenero,* bear that robs bee-hives; *oso blanco,* polar bear; *oso marino,* fur seal; *hacer el oso,* (*coll.*) to woo without inhibition; to make a fool of oneself.

ososo, -sa, *a.* osseous, bony.

osta, *n.f.* (*naut.*) lateen brace.

ostaga, *n.f.* (*naut.*) tie, runner.

ostensible, *a.* ostensible, apparent.

ostensiblemente, *adv.* ostensibly.

ostención, *n.f.* show, manifestation.

ostensivo, -va, *a.* ostensive, showy.

ostentación, *n.f.* ostentation, appearance; parade, display, show.

ostentador, -ra, *n.m.f.* boaster, ostentatious person.

ostentar, *v.t.* to demonstrate, show, exhibit; to brag, boast, be fond of shows.

ostentativo, -va, *a.* ostentatious.

ostento, *n.m.* show, spectacle; ostent, prodigy, portent.

ostentosamente, *adv.* ostentatiously, boastfully.

ostentoso, -sa, *a.* sumptuous, ostentatious.

osteolito, *n.m.* a fossil bone.

osteología, *n.f.* osteology.

osteomielitis, *n.f.* (*path.*) inflammation of bone and medulla.

ostiario, *n.m.* (*eccl.*) ostiary, door-keeper.

ostión, *n.m.* large oyster.
ostra, *n.f.* oyster.
ostraceo, -cea, *a.* ostraceous.
ostracismo, *n.m.* ostracism.
ostracita, *n.f.* (*palæont.*) ostracite.
ostral, *n.m.f.* oyster-bed.
ostrera, *n.f.* oyster-bed; oyster-woman.
ostrero, *n.m.* oyster-dealer.
ostrero, -ra, *a.* ostraceous.
ostricultura, *n.f.* oyster-culture, oyster-farming.
ostrífero, -ra, *a.* ostriferous, oyster-producing.
ostro, *n.m.* large, coarse oyster; south wind; purple-yielding mollusc; Sidonian purple.
ostrogodo, -da, *n.m.f.,* *a.* Ostrogothic, Ostrogoth.
ostrón, *n.m.* large oyster.
ostugo, *n.m.* piece, bit; corner.
osudo, -da, *a.* bony.
osuno, -na, *a.* bearlike, bearish.
otalgia, *n.f.* (*med.*) earache.
otario, -ria, *a.* (*Arg.*) silly, foolish, stupid.
oteador, *n.m.* spy, secret observer.
otear, *v.t.* to examine, pry into, observe, inspect.
otero, *n.m.* hill, height, hillock, knoll.
oteruelo, *n.m.* little height, hillock, mound.
otitis, *n.f.* otitis, inflammation of the ear.
oto, *n.m.* bustard.
otoba, *n.f.* (*S. Am.*) a variety of nutmeg tree.
otología, *n.f.* (*med.*) otology.
otólogo, *n.m.* otologist.
otomana, *n.f.* ottoman, divan.
otomano, -na, *a.* Ottoman.
otoñada, *n.f.* autumn season, pasturage.
otoñal, *a.* autumnal.
otoñar, *v.i.* to spend the autumn; to grow in autumn. — *v.r.* to be tempered, seasoned.
otoño, *n.m.* autumn; aftermath.
otorgador, -ra, *n.m.f.* consenter; (*law*) grantor, stipulator.
otorgamiento, *n.m.* grant, licence, contract.
otorgante, *n.m.f.,* *a.* granter, authorizer, maker of a deed.
otorgar, *v.t.* (*pret.* **otorgué;** *pres. subj.* **otorgue**) to grant, consent, agree to, condescend; (*law*) to execute, declare, stipulate; *otorgar de cabeza,* to nod one's assent; *quien calla otorga,* silence gives consent.
otorgo, *n.m.* marriage contract.
otorrinolaringología, *n.f.* (*path.*) the study of the diseases of ear, nose and larynx.
otoscopia, *n.f.* otoscopy.
otoscopio, *n.m.* otoscope.
otramente, *adv.* otherwise, differently.
otro, -tra, *a.* other, another; *otros tantos,* as many more; *otro que tal,* (*coll.*) another such.
otrora, *adv.* at some other time.
otrosí, *adv.* besides, moreover. — *n.m.* (*law*) every petition made after the principal.
ova, *n.f.* seawrack, laver.
ovación, *n.f.* ovation.
ovado, -da, *a.* rounded, ovate; fecundated.
oval, *a.* oval.
ovalado, -da, *a.* egg-shaped, oval-shaped.
óvalo, *n.m.* oval.
ovante, *a.* victorious, triumphant.
ovar, *v.i.* to lay eggs.
ovario, *n.m.* ovary; ovarium; (*arch.*) egg ornament.
ovas, *n.f.pl.* (*prov.*) roe.
ovecico, *n.m.* small egg.

oveja, *n.f.* ewe, female sheep; *cada oveja con su pareja,* birds of a feather flock together; *encomendar las ovejas al lobo,* to leave one's business in unscrupulous hands; *oveja chiquita, cada año es corderita,* small persons hide well their ages; *oveja que bala, bocado pierde,* he who is distracted, loses the prize; *quien tiene ovejas tiene pellejas,* there's no rose without its thorn.
ovejero, -ra, *n.m.f.* shepherd, shepherdess.
ovejuela, *n.f.* young ewe.
ovejuno, -na, *a.* relating to ewes.
overa, *n.f.* ovary of birds.
overo, -ra, *a.* egg-coloured, speckled, blossom-coloured (horse); bulging eyes.
ovezuelo, *n.m.* small egg.
óvidos, *n.m.pl.* (*zool.*) ovidæ.
oviducto, *n.m.* (*anat.*) oviduct.
ovil, *n.m.* sheep-cot.
ovillar, *v.i.* to hank, wind, clew. — *v.r.* to contract into a ball.
ovillejo, *n.m.* small clew or ball; kind of verse.
ovillo, *n.m.* clew; wound or entangled thread.
ovíparo, -ra, *a.* oviparous.
ovoide, *a.* ovoid.
óvolo, *n.m.* (*arch.*) ovolo.
ovoso, -sa, *a.* full of roe.
ovovivíparo, -ra, *a.* ovoviviparous.
ovulación, *n.f.* (*biol.*) ovulation.
óvulo, *n.m.* (*biol.*) ovule.
¡ox! *interj.* shoo! (used to scare birds).
oxalato, *n.m.* (*chem.*) oxalate.
oxálico, *a.* oxalic.
oxalídeo, -a, *a.* (*bot.*) oxalis.
oxalme, *n.m.* acidulated brine.
oxear, *v.t.* to shoo (birds).
oxiacanta, *n.f.* (*bot.*) hawthorn, whitehorn.
oxidable, *a.* (*chem.*) oxidizable.
oxidación, *n.f.* oxidation.
oxidante, *a.* oxidant.
oxidar, *v.t.* to oxidate, oxidize. — *v.r.* to absorb oxygen.
óxido, *n.m.* oxide.
oxigenable, *a.* (*chem.*) oxygenizable.
oxigenar, *v.t.* to oxygenate.
oxígeno, *n.m.* oxygen.
oximel, oximiel, *n.m.* oxymel.
oxipétalo, *n.m.* a Brazilian vine.
oxizacre, *n.m.* bitter-sweet beverage.
¡oxte! *interj.* keep off, begone; *sin decir oxte ni moxte,* (*coll.*) without so much as a by-your-leave.
oyente, *a.* hearing. — *n.m.* listener, hearer.
ozona, *n.f.;* **ozono,** *n.m.* ozone.
ozonómetro, *n.m.* (*chem.*) ozonometer.

P

P, p, nineteenth letter of the Spanish alphabet.
pabellón, *n.m.* pavilion, field-bed, bell tent, tent-like curtain; dais; bed canopy; summer-house; (*naut.*) national colours, flag; bell of a wind instrument; (*mil.*) stack (of arms); (*anat.*) external ear, pinna.
pábilo, pabilo, *n.m.* wick, snuff of a candle.
pabilón, *n.m.* bunch of silk, wool or oakum hanging from the distaff.
pablar, *v.i.* (*coll.*): *ni hablar, ni pablar,* to say never a word.
Pablo, *n.m.* Paul.

pábulo, *n.m.* pabulum, nourishment, food; (*fig.*) nutriment of a physical, mental or spiritual kind.

paca, *n.f.* spotted cavy; bundle, bale of goods.

pacana, *n.f.* pecan-tree; pecan nut.

pacato, -ta, *a.* pacific, gentle, quiet, tranquil, mild.

pacay (*pl.* **pacayes** or **pacaes**) *n.m.* (*Am.*) a large fruit tree, guamo.

pacaya, *n.f.* (*C.R., Hond.*) shrub with palm leaves.

pacayar, *n.m.* (*Per.*) plantation of *pacayes*.

pacedero, -ra, *a.* pasturable, fit for pasture.

pacedura, *n.f.* pasture-ground.

paceño, -ña, *a.* (*Bol.*) of or belonging to the town of La Paz.

pacer, *v.i.* (conjugated like NACER) to pasture, feed, graze. — *v.t.* to nibble, gnaw, eat away.

paciencia, *n.f.* patience, endurance, forbearance; *paciencia y barajar*, (*fig.*) have patience and shuffle the cards.

paciente, *a.* patient, forbearing; (*fig.*) consenting. — *n.m.* patient, sufferer, sick person.

pacientemente, *adv.* patiently, tolerantly.

pacienzudo, -da, *a.* patient, tolerant.

pacificación, *n.f.* pacification.

pacificador, -ra, *n.m.f.* pacificator, pacifier, peacemaker.

pacíficamente, *adv.* pacifically.

pacificar, *v.t.* (*pret.* **pacifiqué**; *pres. subj.* **pacifique**) to pacify, appease, reconcile. — *v.i.* to seek peace. — *v.r.* to become quiet or calm.

pacífico, -ca, *a.* pacific, peaceful, tranquil, undisturbed, gentle, mild.

pacifismo, *n.m.* pacifism.

pacifista, *n.m.f.,* *a.* pacifist.

paco, *n.m.* (*zool.,* *min.*) paco; alpaca; a Moroccan sniper; (*Chi.*) a policeman.

pacón, *n.m.* (*Hond.*) soapbark.

pacotilla, *n.f.* (*naut.*) venture; small stock of goods; *de pacotilla*, poor in quality.

pactar, *v.t.* to covenant, contract, stipulate.

pacto, *n.m.* contract, covenant, agreement, pact.

pacú, *n.m.* (*Arg.*) a large river fish.

pacul, *n.m.* (*Philip.*) wild plantain.

pachamanca, *n.f.* (*Per.*) barbecue.

pachocha, *n.f.* (*Chi.*) [PACHORRA].

pachón, *n.m.* peaceful, quiet man; pointer (-dog).

pachona, *n.f.* pointer-bitch.

pachorra, *n.f.* sluggishness, slowness, phlegm; *tener pachorra*, to be phlegmatic in disposition.

pachorrudo, -da, *a.* sluggish, tardy, phlegmatic, slow.

pachulí, *n.m.* patchouli plant and perfume.

padecer, *v.t.* (*pres. indic.* **padezco**; *pres. subj.* **padezca**) to suffer, feel deeply, be liable to, put up with; to be hurt, injured.

padecimiento, *n.m.* suffering, sufferance.

padilla, *n.f.* small frying-pan; small oven.

padrastro, *n.m.* step-father; obstacle, impediment; (*fig.*) unnatural father; (*fig.*) hang-nail.

padrazo, *n.m.* (*coll.*) indulgent parent.

padre, *n.m.* father, ancestor; a priest, the superior of a convent; stallion, sire; male animal; author, source, origin. — *pl.* **padres,** father and mother; ancestors; elders, senators, the leading men (of a city, etc.); *padre de familia*, householder; *padre nuestro*, the Lord's prayer; *Padre Santo* (or *Santo Padre*), Pope; *para quien es padre, bástale madre*, he who is of little worth cannot aspire to much; *de padre cojo, hijo renco*, like father, like son; *de padre santo, hijo diablo*, good education can do little against an evil nature; *no ahorrarse con nadie, ni con su padre*, to care only for one's own interests; *quien padre tiene alcalde, seguro va a juicio*, with powerful friends one can safely go to law; *sin padre ni madre, ni perro que me ladre*, with no friends, totally independent; *sobre padre no hay compadre*, blood is thicker than water.

padrear, *v.i.* to resemble one's father; to breed, be kept for procreation.

padrenuestro, *n.m.* Lord's Prayer.

padrina, *n.f.* godmother.

padrinazgo, *n.m.* (baptismal) sponsorship; patronage.

padrino, *n.m.* godfather; second in a duel; groomsman; assistant; protector.

padrón, *n.m.* poll, census, tax-list; mark of infamy; pattern, model; (*coll.*) indulgent parent.

paella, *n.f.* dish of rice with hashed meat, etc.

¡paf! *interj.* noise of something falling.

paflón, *n.m.* (*arch.*) soffit.

paga, *n.f.* fee, payment; amends, satisfaction; sum or fine paid; monthly pay, wages, salary; requital of love or friendship; *buena* (or *mala*) *paga*, one who pays promptly (or tardily).

pagadero, -ra, *a.* payable, easily paid.

pagadero, *n.m.* time and place of payment.

pagado, -da, *a.* paid; satisfied; conceited. — *p.p.* [PAGAR].

pagador, -ra, *n.m.f.* payer, paymaster; paying teller (bank); *el buen pagador es señor de lo ajeno*, phrase recommending prompt payment; *al buen pagador no le duelen prendas*, pledges don't worry the man who pays up promptly.

pagaduría, *n.f.* paymaster's office, disbursement office.

pagamento, pagamiento, *n.m.* payment.

paganismo, *n.m.* paganism.

pagano, -na, *n.m.f.* pagan, paynim, heathen; (*coll.*) one who pays his share.

pagano, -na, *a.* pagan, paganish, heathenish.

pagar, *v.t.* (*pret.* **pagué**; *pres. subj.* **pague**) to pay, acquit, atone, make amends; to please, give pleasure; to requite, reward. — *v.r.* to be pleased (with oneself); *paga lo que debes, sabrás lo que tienes*, pay your debts, and your money is your own; *pagar en anticipación*, to pay in advance; *pagar un delito*, to suffer for a fault; *pagar una visita*, to return a visit; *pagar en buena moneda*, to give satisfaction; *pagar en la misma moneda*, to return like for like; *pagar con el pellejo*, to die; *pagar el pato*, to suffer for another's misconduct; *estar uno muy pagado de sí mismo*, to have a great opinion of oneself.

pagaré, *n.m.* note of hand, promissory note, I.O.U.

pagaya, *n.f.* (*Philip.*) single-bladed paddle.

página, *n.f.* page of a book, folio; a record; an episode.

paginación, *n.f.* pagination, paging.

paginar, *v.t.* to page, number the pages, paginate.

pago, *n.m.* payment, discharge, disbursement,

requital, reward; lot of land; vineyard district; *en pago*, in return, as a recompense; *suspender el pago*, (*com.*) to stop payment; *pronto pago*, prompt payment.

pago, -ga, *a.* (*coll.*) paid.

pagoda, *n.f.* pagoda; idol.

pagote, *n.m.* (*coll.*) one charged with (*or* suffering for) the faults of others, scapegoat.

pagro, *n.m.* (*ichth.*) braize.

paguro, *n.m.* small crab.

paico, *n.m.* (*Am.*) saltwort.

paidología, *n.f.* pædeutics, the science of education.

paila, *n.f.* large pan, boiler, caldron, kettle; (*Cub.*) evaporator, sugar pan.

pailebot, pailebote, *n.m.* (*naut.*) small schooner without main topsail; pilot's boat.

pailón, *n.m.* large copper.

painel, *n.m.* (*carp.*) panel.

paipai, *n.m.* (*Philip.*) large fan made of palm.

pairar, *v.i.* (*naut.*) to bring to, lie to.

pairo (al), *adv.* lying to with all sail set.

país, *n.m.* country, nation, region, land, territory; (*art*) landscape; paper, cloth, etc. forming the cover of a hand fan.

paisaje, *n.m.* landscape; countryside.

paisajista, *n.m.* landscape-painter.

paisana, *n.f.* country woman; kind of country dance.

paisanaje, *n.m.* peasantry; condition of coming from the same country as another.

paisano, -na, *a.* of the same country.

paisano, *n.m.* fellow countryman, compatriot; (*Mex.*) nickname for Spaniards.

Países Bajos, *n.m.pl.* Low Countries.

paisista, *n.m.f.* landscape-painter.

paja, *n.f.* straw; beard of grain; chaff; blade of grass; trash; *¡pajas!* ditto! *quitar la paja*, to be first to drink from a wine-flask; *a lumbre de pajas*, in a trice, speedily; *echar pajas*, to draw lots with straws; *en un quítame allá esas pajas*, in a twinkling; *por quítame allá esas pajas*, to quarrel about a straw; *no dormirse en las pajas*, to be very vigilant.

pajada, *n.f.* moist straw with bran.

pajado, -da, *a.* pale, straw-coloured.

pajar, *n.m.* barn, straw-rick, straw-loft.

pájara, *n.f.* hen-bird; artful woman; paper kite; *pájara pinta*, game of forfeits.

pajarear, *v.t.* to go bird catching; to loiter about.

pajarel, *n.m.* (*orn.*) linnet.

pajarera, *n.f.* aviary; large bird cage.

pajarería, *n.f.* large number of little birds; bird-market.

pajarero, -ra, *a.* merry, gay, cheerful; showy, gaudy, loud.

pajarero, *n.m.* bird-catcher, bird-fancier.

pajarete, *n.m.* sherry wine liqueur.

pajarico, -ca; -ito, -ita, *n.m.f.* little bird.

pajaril (hacer), *adv.* (*naut.*) passarado.

pajarilla, *n.f.* (*bot.*) columbine; spleen.

pajarillo, *n.m.* small bird.

pájaro, *n.m.* bird; decoy partridge; sly fellow; *chico pájaro para tan gran jaula*, a poor man in a large house; *matar dos pájaros de una pedrada* (*or de un tiro*), to kill two birds with one stone; *más vale pájaro en mano, que buitre volando*, a bird in the hand is worth two in the bush; *pájaro viejo no cae en el lazo*, old birds are not caught with chaff.

pajarota, pajarotada, *n.f.* idle rumour, hoax.

pajarote, *n.m.* large ugly bird.

pajarraco, *n.m.* large bird; (*coll.*) cunning fellow, sharper.

pajaza, *n.f.* stalks of horses' fodder left uneaten.

pajazo, *n.m.* prick of stubble in a horse's eye.

paje, *n.m.* page, valet; cabin boy; a clip used by women to prevent their skirts touching the ground; kind of dressing table with a high mirror; *paje de hacha*, link-boy.

pajear, *v.i.* (*coll.*) to feed well; to behave.

pajecillo, *n.m.* little page; (*prov.*) washstand.

pajel, *n.m.* red sea-bream.

pajera, *n.f.* straw-loft.

pajero, *n.m.* straw-dealer.

pajica, pajilla, *n.f.* cigar made of maize-leaf.

pajizo, -za, *a.* made of straw, thatched with straw; straw-coloured.

pajo, *n.m.* mango from the Philippines.

pajón, *n.m.* coarse straw.

pajonal, *n.m.* (*Am.*) field with tall grass.

pajoso, -sa, *a.* made of (*or* full of) straw.

pajote, *n.m.* straw interwoven with bulrush.

pajucero, *n.m.* (*prov.*) place where straw is deposited to rot.

pajuela, *n.f.* sulphur match; short straw.

pajuelera, *n.f.* match-girl.

pajuelero, *n.m.* match-maker.

pajulí, *n.m.* (*PR.*) cashew; cashew nut.

pajuncio, *n.m.* booby, ninny, fool.

pajuz, pajuzo, *n.m.* (*prov.*) rotting straw.

pala, *n.f.* wooden shovel, scoop, slice, fire-shovel; beetle for pounding clothes; dustpan; racket (for ball games); upper (of a shoe); leaf of a hinge; top of an epaulet; flat surface of the teeth; baker's peel; battledore; blade of an oar, hoe, spade; (*fig.*, *coll.*) craft, cunning, dexterity, cleverness, artifice; *meter su media pala*, (*coll.*) to put in one's oar, have something to do with a matter.

palabra, *n.f.* word, affirmation, confirmation, promise, offer; (*mil.*) pass-word; turn (to speak). — *pl.* **palabras**, superstitious words, text, quotation; (*eccl.*) formula of the sacraments. *¡palabra!* I say! *de palabra*, orally, by word of mouth; *atravesar una palabra con*, to exchange a few words with; *palabra de matrimonio*, promise of marriage; *beber las palabras a*, to drink in someone's words; *dar palabra y mano*, to contract matrimony; *dejarle a uno con la palabra en la boca*, to turn a cold shoulder upon someone; *esa palabra está gozando de Dios*, he is very complacent; *faltar a la palabra*, to break one's word; *medir las palabras*, to choose one's words carefully; *no hay palabra mal dicha si no fuese mal entendida*, evil interpretations are more common than evil words; *no tiene más que una palabra*, he is very sincere; *no tiene palabra*, he is very untrustworthy; *palabras mayores*, offensive words; *palabras de santo, uñas de gato*, soft words and hypocritical intentions; *palabra y piedra suelta no tienen vuelta*, stray words are dangerous things; *a media palabra*, at the slightest hint; *empeñar la palabra*, to pledge one's word; *no tener palabras*, to explain oneself badly or insufficiently; *tener la palabra*, to have the floor (in debates, etc.); *a palabras locas, orejas sordas*, turn a deaf ear to a fool; *quitarle a uno las palabras de la boca*, to take the words from someone's mouth; *tratar mal de palabra a uno*, to insult, abuse; *volverle a uno las palabras al cuerpo*, to make one eat one's words; *palabras y plumas el viento las lleva*, promises are soon forgotten (*or* broken).

palabrada, *n.f.* low, scurrilous language.

palabreja, *n.f.* silly, superfluous word.

palabrería, *n.f.* long senseless speech, string of words, wordiness.

palabrero, -ra, *a.* talkative, loquacious.

palabrimujer, *n.m.* (*coll.*) man with an effeminate voice.

palabrista, *n.m.f.* loquacious person, chatter-box.

palabrita, *n.f.* short word; word charged with meaning.

palabrota, *n.f.* offensive word; coarse expression.

palaciego, *n.m.* courtier.

palaciego, -ga, *a.* of or belonging to the palace.

palacio, *n.m.* palace, royal residence; splendid mansion, castle; *de mozo, a palacio; de viejo, a beato,* youth seeks glory but virtue comes with old age; *echar a palacio una cosa,* to take no account of a thing; *hacer palacio,* to make public; *estar embargado para palacio,* to allege urgent business as an excuse.

palacra, palacrana, *n.f.* gold nugget.

palada, *n.f.* shovelful; (*naut.*) stroke of an oar.

paladar, *n.m.* palate, roof of the mouth, taste, relish; longing, desire.

paladear, *v.t.* to taste, relish; to rub the palate of a new-born baby. — *v.i.* to desire suck. — *v.r.* to relish, taste.

paladeo, *n.m.* tasting, relishing.

paladial, *a.* (*gram.*) palatal.

paladín, *n.m.* paladin, knight, champion.

paladinamente, *adv.* publicly, clearly.

paladino, -na, *a.* manifest, public, clear, apparent.

paladio, *n.m.* (*min.*) palladium.

paladión, *n.m.* palladium, safeguard.

palado, -da, *a.* (*her.*) pale, paled.

palafito, *n.m.* primitive house or dwelling built upon stakes in a lake.

palafrén, *n.m.* palfrey, groom's horse.

palafrenero, *n.m.* groom, ostler, stable-boy.

palahierro, *n.m.* bushing of the spindle of the upper millstone.

palamallo, *n.m.* pall-mall.

palamenta, *n.f.* oars of a row galley; (*naut.*) set of oars.

palanca, *n.f.* lever, bar, brake, crowbar, cowl-staff; (*naut.*) stay-rope; (*naut.*) garnet-tackle; (*fort.*) outer fortification, palisade; (*fig.*) favouritism, influence.

palancada, *n.f.* stroke with a lever.

palancana, palangana, *n.f.* basin, wash-hand basin.

palanganero, *n.m.* portable wash-stand.

palangre, *n.m.* fishing line with several fish-hooks.

palanquera, *n.f.* enclosure with stakes or poles.

palanquero, *n.m.* pile-driver; blower of bellows.

palanqueta, *n.f.* (*artill.*) bar-shot or crossbar shot; (*Cub.*) sweetmeat with sugar-cane sirup; small lever; dumb-bell.

palanquín, *n.m.* heavy porter; palanquin; (*naut.*) double-tackle, clew-garnet.

Palas, *n.m.* (*astron.*) Pallas, the second asteroid.

palastro, *n.m.* iron plate; sheet-iron.

palatina, *n.f.* tippet, women's boa.

palatinado, *n.m.* palatinate.

palatino, -na, *a.* palatial; palatine; (*anat.*) palatal.

palatino, *n.m.* palatine.

palay, *n.m.* (*Philip.*) unhusked rice.

palazo, *n.m.* blow with a stick or shovel.

palazón, *n.m.* (*naut.*) masting; timber used in the construction of a house.

palca, *n.f.* (*Bol.*) cross-road.

palco, *n.m.* theatre-box; *palco escénico,* the stage.

paleador, *n.m.* stoker, shoveller.

palear, *v.t.* to pound, beat.

palenque, *n.m.* palisade, paling, enclosure; (*theat.*) passage from pit to stage.

paleografía, *n.f.* palæography.

paleográfico, -ca, *a.* palæographic.

paleógrafo, *n.m.* palæographer.

paleolítico, -ca, *a.* palæolithic.

paleólogo, *n.m.* palæologist.

paleontográfico, -ca, *a.* palæontographic.

paleontología, *n.f.* palæontology.

paleozoico, -ca, *a.* palæozoic.

palería, *n.f.* draining of low, wet lands.

palero, *n.m.* shoveller, ditcher, drainer, pioneer; shovel-maker.

palestina, *n.f.* (*print.*) two-line small pica.

palestino, -na, *n.m.f.,* *a.* Palestinian.

palestra, *n.f.* palæstra, gymnasium; competition, tournament; art of wrestling.

paléstrico, -ca, *a.* palæstric, palæstrical.

palestrita, *n.m.* athlete, wrestler.

paleta, *n.f.* fire-shovel; palette; iron ladle; small shovel, trowel; (*anat.*) shoulder-blade; (*mech., naut., aer.*) blade of a screw-propeller; (*hydr.*) paddle board; *de paleta,* opportunely; *en dos paletas,* briefly, shortly.

paletada, *n.f.* trowelful of mortar.

paletazo, *n.m.* thrust with a bull's horn.

paletear, *v.t.* to row ineffectively.

paletilla, *n.f.* little fire-shovel; shoulder-blade; cartilage of the sternum or xiphoid; short candlestick.

paleto, *n.m.* fallow-deer; (*fig.*) bumpkin.

paletó, *n.m.* paletot.

paletón, *n.m.* bit, part of a key.

paletoque, *n.m.* dress like a scapulary; defensive jacket.

palhuén, *n.m.* (*Chi.*) papilionaceous thorny shrub.

palia, *n.f.* altar-cloth; veil before the tabernacle; pall, square piece of linen covering the chalice.

paliación, *n.f.* palliation, extenuation.

paliadamente, *adv.* dissemblingly.

paliar, *v.t.* to palliate, excuse, extenuate.

paliativo, -va; paliatorio, -ria, *a.* palliative, mitigating.

palidecer, *v.i.* (*pres. indic.* **palidezco**; *pres. subj.* **palidezca**) to grow pale.

palidez, *n.f.* paleness, wanness, pallor, ghastliness.

pálido, -da, *a.* pallid, pale, ghastly.

palillero, *n.m.* toothpick-case; maker or seller of toothpicks.

palillo, *n.m.* small stick; knitting-needle case; rolling-pin; trigger (of a gun); bobbin (for lace); toothpick; tobacco stem; drum-stick; (*coll.*) table-talk, chit-chat. — *pl.* **palillos,**

castanets; knitting needles; rudiments, first principles; trifles; small pins (5) put on the centre of the billiard table in certain games.

palimpsesto, *n.m.* palimpsest.

palingenesia, *n.f.* palingenesia, new birth, regeneration.

palinodia, *n.f.* palinode, recantation.

palio, *n.m.* cloak, short mantle; pall, canopy; dais.

palique, *n.m.* (*coll.*) small talk, chit-chat.

palisandro, *n.m.* rosewood.

palito, *n.m.* little stick.

palitoque, palitroque, *n.m.* rough, ill-shaped stick.

paliza, *n.f.* cudgelling, caning.

palizada, *n.f.* palisade, stockade; paling.

palma, *n.f.* (*bot.*) palm-tree, palm-bud; palm leaf; palmetto; palm of the hand; ferula; (*vet.*) under-part of the hoof; emblem of victory or martyrdom; pre-eminence. — *pl.* applause; *andar en palmas,* to be generally applauded; *ganar* (or *llevarse*) *la palma,* to carry the day; *como* (*por*) *la palma de la mano,* very easily.

palmacristi, *n.f.* (*bot.*) castor-oil palm or plant.

palmada, *n.f.* slap, clap. — *pl.* **palmadas,** hand-clapping, applause; *darse una palmada en la frente,* to make efforts to remember a thing.

palmadica, -illa, -ita, *n.f.* slight slap with the palm of the hand; kind of dance.

palmar, *a.* measuring of *palmo* (8¼ in.); relating to palms; obvious, clear, evident. — *n.m.* palm-grove; fuller's thistle.

palmario, -ria, *a.* clear, obvious, evident.

palmatoria, *n.f.* ferule; small candlestick.

palmeado, -da, *a.* palmiped, web-footed, palmated; (*bot.*) palmate.

palmear, *v.t.* to slap with the open hand. — *v.i.* clap hands, applaud.

palmejar, *n.m.* (*naut.*) thick stuff.

palmeo, *n.m.* measuring by *palmos.*

palmera, *n.f.* palm-tree.

palmero, *n.m.* palmer, pilgrim; keeper of palms.

palmeta, *n.f.* ferule; slap on the palm; *ganar la palmeta,* to get ahead of.

palmetazo, *n.m.* blow with a ferule.

palmiche, *n.m.* fruit of the Cuban palm-tree; (*Cub.*) a light cloth for men's suits.

palmífero, -ra, *a.* (*poet.*) palmiferous.

palmilla, *n.f.* blue woollen cloth; inner sole of a shoe.

palmípedo, -da, *n.m.f., a.* (*orn.*) palmiped.

palmitieso, -sa, *a.* flat-hoofed (horse).

palmito, *n.m.* (*Cub.*) bud shooting from a palm-tree; (*bot.*) dwarf fan-palm, palmetto; its root; (*fig., coll.*) woman's face *or* figure.

palmo, *n.m.* palm, span, measure of length (8¼ inches); hand-breadth (3 inches); game of span-farthing; *palmo a palmo,* inch by inch; *crecer a palmos,* to shoot up, grow very quickly; *dejar a uno con un palmo de narices,* to disappoint one of success; *tener medido a palmos,* to know a place thoroughly.

palmotear, *v.i.* to applaud.

palmoteo, *n.m.* clapping of hands, applause; beating with a ferule.

palo, *n.m.* stick, cudgel; timber, wood, log; whack, blow with a stick; execution on the gallows; suit at cards; pedicle, stalk of fruit; hook of a letter; (*her.*) pale; (*naut.*) mast. —

pl. **palos,** blows, cudgelling; billiard pins; *palo de Campeche* (or *de tinte*), logwood; *palo dulce,* liquorice; *palo de marca,* (*naut.*) buoy; *palo santo,* lignum vitæ; *de tal palo, tal astilla,* like father, like son (*or* a chip of the old block); *dar palo,* to turn out contrarily to one's hopes; *dar de palos,* to thrash, drub; *estar del mismo palo,* to be in the same condition, etc.; *no se dan palos de balde,* nothing is done without labour (*or* except for self-interest); *palo compuesto no parece palo,* a stick dressed up does not look like a stick.

paloma, *n.f.* (*orn.*) pigeon, dove; meek and mild person; *paloma buchona,* pouter; *paloma brava* (or *silvestre*), rock dove; *paloma torcaz,* ring-dove; *paloma zorita,* wood-pigeon.

palomadura, *n.f.* (*naut.*) boltrope tie.

palomar, *n.m.* pigeon-house, dovecot; hard-twisted twine; *si al palomar no le falta cebo, no le faltarán palomas,* if the pigeon-house doesn't lack food, it won't lack pigeons.

palomariego, -ga, *a.* domestic (of pigeons).

palomear, *v.i.* to shoot or breed pigeons.

palomera, *n.f.* small dovecot; bleak place.

palomería, *n.f.* pigeon-shooting.

palomero, *n.m.* dealer in doves or pigeons.

palometa, *n.f.* (*Am.*) edible fish.

palomilla, *n.f.* young pigeon; little butterfly; grain moth; journal bearing; wall bracket; (*print.*) galley rack; (*bot.*) common fumitory; horse's back; chrysalis; peak of a pack-saddle; milk-white horse.

palomina, *n.f.* pigeon dung; (*bot.*) fumitory.

palomino, *n.m.* young pigeon.

palomo, *n.m.* cock-pigeon.

palón, *n.m.* (*her.*) guidon.

palor, *n.m.* pallor, paleness.

palotada, *n.f.* stroke with a drum-stick; *no dar palotada,* to do or say nothing right.

palote, *n.m.* stick, drum-stick, ruler; down-stroke in penmanship.

paloteado, *n.m.* rustic dance; scuffle, dispute.

palotear, *v.i.* to clash, scuffle; dispute loudly, wrangle.

paloteo, *n.m.* fight with sticks.

palpable, *a.* palpable, clear; obvious, evident, perceptible.

palpablemente, *adv.* palpably, evidently.

palpadura, *n.f.;* **palpamiento,** *n.m.* (*med.*) feeling, touching, palpation, palpability, palpableness.

palpallén, *n.m.* (*Chi.*) a flower-bearing shrub.

palpar, *v.t.* to touch, feel; to grope in the dark; to see as self-evident; (*med.*) to palpate; (*fig.*) to know positively.

pálpebra, *n.f.* eye-lid.

palpitación, *n.f.* palpitation, panting, heaving, throbbing.

palpitante, *a.* vibrating, palpitating.

palpitar, *v.i.* to palpitate, pant, flutter, beat, throb, quiver, thrill.

palpos, *n.m.pl.* (*zool.*) palps, palpi.

palqui, *n.m.* (*Am.*) medicinal shrub of the solanaceous family.

palta, *n.f.* alligator-pear.

palúdico, -ca, *a.* paludal, malarial.

paludoso, -sa, *a.* marshy, swampy.

palurdo, -da, *a.* rustic, boorish.

palurdo, *n.m.* country bumpkin.

palustre, *a.* marshy, boggy, fenny. — *n.m.* trowel.

pallaco, *n.m.* (*Chi.*) pay-dirt recovered from a derelict mine.

pallador, *n.m.* (*Am.*) minstrel, roving singer.

pallar, *v.t.* (*Per.*) to extract the richest part from minerals. — *n.m.* Peruvian bean.

pallete, *n.m.* (*naut.*) fender.

pallón, *n.m.* button of gold, assay of gold by cupellation.

pamandabuán, *n.m.* (*Philip.*) snake boat, a large dugout.

pambil, *n.m.* (*Ec.*) a small palm-tree.

pamela, *n.f.* Leghorn hat.

pamema, *n.f.* (*coll.*) trifle, bagatelle.

pampa, *n.f.* (*Am.*) pampas, extensive plain.

pámpana, *n.f.* vine-leaf.

pampanada, *n.f.* juice of vine-shoots.

pampanaje, *n.m.* abundance of vine-shoots; (*fig.*) empty words.

pampanilla, *n.f.* trunks, loin-cloth.

pámpano, *n.m.* vine-branch, tendril.

pampanoso, -sa, *a.* abounding in grapes, tendrils or foliage.

pampeano, -na, *n.m.f., a.* (*Am.*) of or from the pampas.

pampear, *v.i.* (*Am.*) to travel over the pampas.

pampero, *n.m.* pampero, a violent wind.

pampero, -ra, *n.m.f.* (*Am.*) dweller on the pampas.

pampirolada, *n.f.* garlic sauce; (*coll.*) silly thing.

pamplina, *n.f.* (*bot.*) duck-weed, chickweed, pimpernel; (*coll.*) trifle, frivolity.

pamporcino, *n.m.* (*bot.*) sow-bread, cyclamen.

pamposado, -da, *a.* lazy, idle, cowardly.

pampringada, *n.f.* (*coll.*) frivolity, frivolous thing.

pan, *n.m.* bread, loaf; food; piecrust; wheat; wafer; gold- or silver-leaf. — *pl.* **panes,** cereals; *pan ázimo,* unleavened bread; *pan de la boda,* wedding celebrations, wedding presents; *pan de azúcar,* loaf sugar; *pan de jabón,* cake of soap; *pan de oro,* gold leaf; *pan de cera virgen,* cake of white wax; *pan bazo* (or *casero*), household bread; *pan y quesillo,* (*bot.*) shepherd's purse; *pan tierno,* fresh bread; *pan duro,* stale bread; *buscar pan de trastrigo,* to ask inopportunely, ask for trouble, ask for it; *al que come bien el pan, es pecado darle ajo,* never give much to him who wants but little; *a pan duro, diente agudo,* hard tasks require much labour; *a quien no le sobra pan, no críe can,* a man cannot live beyond his means; *comer el pan de los niños,* to be very old and in the way; *comer pan con corteza,* to be grown-up and independent; *con su pan se lo coma,* let him do as he likes (i.e., for all the speaker cares); *contigo, pan y cebolla,* love in a cottage; *¡el pan de cada día!* sufficient unto the day! *el pan, pan y el vino, vino,* call a spade a spade! *engañar el pan,* to eat something pleasant with one's bread; *no come pan,* it does no harm; *no le comerán el pan las gallinas,* he will arrive very late; *repartir como pan bendito,* to distribute in tiny portions; *los duelos con pan son menos,* bread makes one's troubles less; *el pan comido y la compañía deshecha,* once the bread is eaten, one's friends go (i.e., their friendship is cupboard-love).

pana, *n.f.* velveteen, corduroy; (*naut.*) limber-board.

pánace, *n.f.* (*bot.*) opopanax.

panacea, *n.f.* panacea, catholicon.

panadear, *v.t.* to bake bread for sale.

panadeo, *n.m.* baking bread.

panadera, *n.f.* baker's wife.

panadería, *n.f.* baker's shop, bakehouse.

panadero, -ra, *n.m.f.* baker, baker's wife.

panaderos, *n.m.pl.* kind of dance.

panadizo, panarizo, *n.m.* whitlow; (*coll.*) pale and sickly person.

panado, -da, *a.* (bread) soaked in water for sick persons.

panal, *n.m.* honeycomb; hornet's nest; sponge sugar.

panamá, *n.m.* Panama hat.

panameño, -ña, *n.m.f., a.* Panamanian.

panamericanismo, *n.m.* Pan-Americanism.

panamericano, -na, *a.* pan-American.

panarra, *n.m.* simpleton, blockhead, dolt.

panatela, *n.f.* sponge-cake.

panática, *n.f.* (*naut.*) provision of bread.

panca, *n.f.* (*Am.*) corn husk; (*Philip.*) a fishing boat.

pancada, *n.f.* wholesale disposal of goods.

pancarpia, *n.f.* garland.

pancera, *n.f.* stomach-armour.

pancilla, *n.f.* (*print.*) roman.

pancista, *a.* (*coll.*) (*polit.*) one who sits on the fence.

panco, *n.m.* (*Philip.*) coasting vessel.

páncreas, *n.m.* (*anat.*) pancreas.

pancreático, -ca, *a.* pancreatic.

pancreatina, *n.f.* pancreatin.

pancho, *n.m.* (*ichth.*) spawn of the sea bream; (*coll.*) paunch, belly.

panda, *n.f.* cloister gallery.

pandear, *v.i.* to bend, bulge out, warp, belly.

pandectas, *n.f.pl.* (*law*) pandects; (*com.*) index-book.

pandemonio, *n.m.* pandemonium.

pandeo, *n.m.* bulge.

panderada, *n.f.* number of tambourines; stroke with a tambourine; (*coll.*) silly proposition, nonsense.

panderazo, *n.m.* blow with a tambourine.

pandereta, *n.f.* tambourine.

panderete, *n.m.* small tambourine.

panderetear, *v.i.* to play on the tambourine.

pandereteo, *n.m.* beating of the tambourine; merriment.

panderetero, *n.m.* one who beats the tambourine, tambourine-maker.

pandero, *n.m.* tambourine; paper-kite; (*coll.*) silly person.

pandiculación, *n.f.* (*met.*) pandiculation, gaping.

pandilla, *n.f.* party, league; gang, faction; picnic.

pandillero, pandillista, *n.m.* author and fomenter of plots and factions; leader or member of a gang.

pando, -da, *a.* bulgy; slow-moving.

pandorga, *n.f.* (*coll.*) fat, bulky woman; (*prov.*) kite.

panecico, -illo, -ito, *n.m.* small loaf of bread, French roll.

panegerizar, *v.t., v.i.* to panegyrize, to extol.

panegírico, -ca, *a.* panegyrical.

panegírico, *n.m.* panegyric, eulogy.

panegirista, *n.m.f.* panegyrist, encomiast, eulogist.

panel, *n.m.* (*art, elec.*) panel.
panela, *n.f.* maize-cake; brown sugar; (*her.*) panel; (*Col., Hond.*) unrefined brown sugar.
panera, *n.f.* pannier, bread-basket; granary.
panero, *n.m.* baker's basket.
paneslavismo, *n.m.* Pan-Slavism.
panetela, *n.f.* panada; (*Am.*) sponge-cake; cigar.
panetería, *n.f.* pantry of the royal palace.
panetero, *n.m.* pantler.
pánfilo, *n.m.* slow, heavy person; parlour game.
pangelín, *n.m.* angelin tree.
pangue, *n.m.* (*Chi., Per.*) a herb with edible leaves (*Gunnera scabra*).
paniaguado, *n.m.* comrade, close friend; employee, servant, protégé.
pánico, -ca, *a.* panic, panicky.
pánico, *n.m.* panic, fright.
panículo, *n.m.* panicle, pellicle, membrane.
paniego, -ga, *a.* eating or yielding much bread; (*prov.*) bag of coarse cloth.
panificación, *n.f.* panification.
panificar, *v.t.* (conjugated like BUSCAR) to bake bread; to convert pasture into arable land.
panilla, *n.f.* small measure of oil.
panizo, *n.m.* panic-grass; Indian corn; (*Am.*) mineral bed.
panocha, panoja, *n.f.* (*bot.*) panicle; bunch of anchovies.
panoplia, *n.f.* panoply; collection of arms.
panóptico, -ca, *n.m., a.* panopticon.
panorama, *n.m.* panorama.
panorámico, -ca, *a.* panoramic.
panormitano, -na, *n.m.f., a.* native of Palermo.
panoso, -sa, *a.* mealy.
panque, *n.m.* (*Chi.*) plant used in tanning leather.
pantalán, *n.m.* (*Philip.*) a pier made of wood or bamboo.
pantalón, *n.m.* (usually *pl.*) pair of trousers.
pantalla, *n.f.* sconce; lamp-shade; screen; shelter; (*fig.*) pall, cover; person or object that obstructs the view; *pantalla de chimenea*, fire-screen.
pantanal, *n.m.* swampy, marshy ground.
pantano, *n.m.* stagnant pool, marsh, fen, moor, swamp, morass; reservoir, dam; (*fig.*) hindrance, difficulty, obstacle.
pantanoso, -sa, *a.* swampy, boggy, marshy, fenny; full of difficulties.
pantasana, *n.f.* fishing seine.
panteísmo, *n.m.* pantheism.
panteísta, *n.m.f.* pantheist.
panteístico, -ca, *a.* pantheistic.
panteón, *n.m.* pantheon, mausoleum.
pantera, *n.f.* (*zool.*) panther; (*min.*) yellow agate.
pantógrafo, *n.m.* pantograph.
pantómetra, *n.f.* pantometer.
pantomima, *n.f.* pantomime, dumb show.
pantomímico, -ca, *a.* pantomimic, pantomimical.
pantomimo, *n.m.* pantomimist, mimic.
pantoque, *n.m.* (*naut.*) bilge or flat of the ship.
pantorrilla, *n.f.* calf of the leg.
pantorrillera, *n.f.* padded stocking.
pantorrilludo, -da, *a.* with large or thick calves.
pantuflazo, *n.m.* blow given with a slipper.

pantuflo, *n.m.*; pantufla, *n.f.* slipper; babouche.
panuco, *n.m.* (*Chi.*) a handful of toasted flour as a meal.
panucho, *n.m.* (*Mex.*) omelet of corn-meal crust with meat.
panudo, *a.* (*Cub.*) firm, not over-ripe alligator pear.
panul, *n.m.* (*Chi.*) celery.
panza, *n.f.* belly, paunch; belly of a vase; rumen of ruminants.
panzada, *n.f.* bellyful (*coll.*); push with the belly.
panzón, -ona, *n.m.f.* large-bellied person.
panzudo, -da, *a.* big-bellied.
pañal, *n.m.* napkin, (*coll.*) nappy, (*Am.*) diaper; shirt-tail. — *pl.* (*fig.*) infancy; *estar en pañales*, to know little of anything.
pañalón, *n.m.* (*coll.*) one whose shirt-tails are always hanging out.
pañería, *n.f.* draper's shop.
pañero, *n.m.* woollen-draper, clothier.
pañetes, *n.m.pl.* inferior or light cloth; (*Col.*) plastering. — *pl.* fisherman's trunks; linen attached to the crucifix below the waist.
pañil, *n.m.* (*Chi.*) small tree with yellow flowers and vulnerary leaves (*Buddleia globosa*).
pañito, pañizuelo, *n.m.* small cloth; (*Mex.*) small handkerchief.
paño, *n.m.* cloth, woollen stuff; kitchen clout; tapestry, drapery, hanging; red colour of a bloodshot eye; livid spot; spot on glass, crystals or precious stones; small plot of land; (*sew.*) breadth; (*naut.*) sail-cloth; *ser del mismo paño*, to be of the same material (or origin); *paño de lágrimas*, one who sympathises; *paño de mesa*, tablecloth; *al paño*, peeping; (*theat.*) off-stage, without; *paños menores*, deshabille, underclothes; *paños calientes*, insufficient means; *paños lucen en palacio, que no hijosdalgo*, fine feathers make fine birds(*iron.*); *tender el paño del púlpito*, to talk tediously and at length.
pañol, *n.m.* (*naut.*) store-room in a ship; *pañol de proa*, boatswain's store-room; *pañol de pólvora*, magazine.
pañolería, *n.f.* handkerchief shop or factory.
pañolero de Santabárbara, *n.m.* (*naut.*) gunner's yeoman.
pañoleta, *n.f.* triangular shawl.
pañolón, *n.m.* large square shawl.
pañoso, -sa, *a.* ragged, tattered.
pañosa, *n.f.* (*coll.*) cloak.
pañuelo, *n.m.* handkerchief, neckcloth, kerchief, shawl.
papa, *n.m.* pope; (*coll.*) papa. — *n.f.* (*coll.*) food, grub; fib, hoax; (*Am.*) potato; *no ocupa más pies de tierra el cuerpo del Papa que el del sacristán*, the Pope takes up no more space in his grave than the sacristan; (*Per.*) lump of native silver; (*orn.*) goldfinch.
papá, *n.m.* papa, daddy.
papacho, *n.m.* (*Mex.*) cuddle, caress.
papada, *n.f.* double chin, dewlap.
papadilla, *n.f.* fleshy part under the chin.
papado, *n.m.* popedom, pontificate, papacy.
papafigo, *n.m.* (*orn.*) Epicurean warbler, beccafico.
papagayo, -ya, *n.m.f.* parrot; (*ichth.*) rock bass; (*bot.*) three-coloured amaranth; white arum; (*Ec.*) a highly poisonous snake; (*Cent. Am.*) violent north-east wind.

papahigo, *n.m.* winter cap; (*naut.*) course, lower sail.

papahuevos, *n.m.* simpleton, duffer.

papal, *a.* papal, papistical; *zapatos papales*, overshoes, clogs.

papalina, *n.f.* cap with ear-flaps; coif; drunken fit.

papalmente, *adv.* pontifically, in a papal manner.

papalote, *n.m.* (*Mex.*) a sort of kite.

papamoscas, *n.m.* (*orn.*) fly-catcher; (*met.*) ninny.

papanatas, *n.m.* ninny, simpleton, dolt.

papandujo, -ja, *a.* (*coll.*) too soft, over-ripe.

papar, *v.t.* to eat, swallow without chewing; to gape; to pay little attention to important matters; *papar moscas*, to gape.

páparo, *n.m.* ancient Indian of Panama; *a.* clown, churl, gawk.

paparrabias, *n.m.f.* (*coll.*) testy, fretful, peevish person.

paparrasolla, *n.f.* hobgoblin.

paparrucha, *n.f.* silliness; humbug, hoax, fake.

papasal, *n.m.* boy's game; bagatelle, trifle.

papaya, *n.f.* papaw, fruit of the *papayo*.

papayo, *n.m.* (*bot.*) papaw-tree.

papazgo, *n.m.* popedom, pontificate.

papel, *n.m.* paper, sheet of paper, letter; writing, discourse, treatise; pamphlet, tract; role, part in a play; actor, actress; bill, document; deed, obligation; *hacer (el) papel*, to cut a figure, cut a dash, play a part; *papel avitelado*, vellum paper; *papel esmeril*, emery paper; *papel de estraza*, brown paper; *papel de fumar*, cigarette paper; *papel pintado*, wallpaper; *papel de lija*, sandpaper; *papel jaspeado*, marbled paper; *papel majado*, papier mâché; *papeles mojados*, worthless documents; *papel marquilla*, card paper; *papel moneda*, paper currency; *papel sellado*, stamped paper; *papel secante* (or *chupón*), blotting-paper; *papel de tornasol* (or *reactivo*), litmus paper; *papel de seda*, tissue paper; *papel viejo*, waste paper; *papel volante*, small pamphlet; *mano de papel*, quire of paper; *pliego de papel*, sheet of paper; *resma de papel*, ream of paper.

papelear, *v.i.* to search through papers; (*coll.*) to cut a figure.

papeleo, *n.m.* turning over of old papers.

papelera, *n.f.* number of written papers; writing desk.

papelería, *n.f.* untidy heap of papers; paper-trade; stationery.

papelero, -ra, *a.* boastful, ostentatious. — *n.m.f.* paper-maker, stationer.

papeleta, *n.f.* slip of paper, ticket, check, card; paper-bag.

papelillo, *n.m.* scrap of paper; cigarette.

papelina, *n.f.* small wine-glass; poplin; (*coll.*) drunken fit.

papelista, *n.m.f.* scribbler; paper-maker, stationer; keeper of documents.

papelito, *n.m.* small paper; curl-paper.

papelón, *n.m.* large piece of paper; prolix writing; poster, bill; paper board; pamphlet; boaster; (*Cub.*) raw sugar.

papelón, -ona, *a.* (*coll.*) boastful, ostentatious.

papelonear, *v.i.* (*coll.*) to boast, pretend.

papelote, papelucho, *n.m.* insignificant writing, scurrilous article.

papera, *n.f.* mumps; goitre.

papero, *n.m.* pot in which pap is made.

papialbillo, *n.m.* (*zool.*) weasel.

papila, *n.f.* (*med.*) papilla.

papilar, *a.* papillary, papillous, papillose.

papilla, *n.f.* pap; guile, deceit, trick.

papillote, *n.m.* papillote, a curl-paper.

papión, *n.m.* a large American monkey.

papiro, *n.m.* (*bot.*) Egyptian papyrus.

papirolada, *n.f.* (*coll.*) garlic sauce; frivolity.

papirotada, *n.f.* fillip; rap.

papirote, *n.m.* fillip.

papisa, *n.f.*; only in *la papisa Juana*, Pope Joan.

papismo, *n.m.* papism.

papista, *n.m.f.* papist.

papo, *n.m.* second or double-chin; dewlap, lower part of an animal's neck, external throat; thistledown; food given to a bird of prey; fowl's gizzard; puff in garments; *hablar de papo*, to speak idly or presumptuously; *estar en papo de buitre*, to be in someone's firm grip; *hablar papo a papo*, to speak bluntly, plainly.

papudo, -da, *a.* double-chinned.

papujado, -da, *a.* swollen, full-gorged (of birds); (*fig.*) thick; elevated, puffed up.

paquear, *v.t.* to snipe Spanish soldiers (in Morocco).

paquebote, *n.m.* packet-boat, steamer.

paquete, *n.m.* packet, parcel, bundle; (*coll.*) dandy; (*naut.*) packet-boat; (*print.*) a typographic composition containing approx. 1000 letters.

paquetería, *n.f.* (*com.*) shop; retail trade.

paquidermo, *n.m.* (*zool.*) pachyderm.

par, *a.* equal, even, alike, level; on a par; homologous, corresponding. — *adv.* near. — *n.m.* pair, couple; peer of the realm; handle of a bell; (*elec.*) cell; (*arch.*) angle rafter; team of horses, mules, etc.; (*mech.*) couple. — *f.pl.* placenta; *sin par*, singular, matchless; *a la par*, jointly; (*com.*) at par; *ir a la par*, to go halves; *pares y nones*, odd or even; *a pares*, by pairs, by twos; *de par en par*, wide open, openly, without hindrance; *par de torsión*, *par motor* (*elec. & motor.*) torque.

para, *prep.* for, to, towards, in order to, wherefore, to the end (that); *tengo para mí*, I really believe; *¿para qué?* wherefore?; *leer para sí*, to read to oneself; *para conmigo*, in relation to myself, compared with me; *para entre los dos*, between us both; *para siempre*, for ever; *para siempre jamás*, for ever and ever; *decir para su capote*, to say to oneself; *sin qué ni para qué*, without rhyme or reason.

paraba, *n.f.* (*Bol.*) kind of parrot.

parabién, *n.m.* congratulation, felicitation, compliment.

paraboidal, *a.* (*geom.*) paraboliform.

parábola, *n.f.* parable; (*geom.*) parabola.

parabolano, *n.m.* a priest of the orthodox primitive church; one who uses parables; hoaxer.

parabólico, -ca, *a.* parabolical.

paraboloide, *n.m.* paraboloid.

parabrisas, *n.m.* (*motor-car*) wind-screen.

paraca, *n.m.* (*Am.*) a strong breeze from the Pacific.

paracaídas, *n.m.* parachute.

paracaidista, *n.m.* parachutist.

paracleto, paráclito, *n.m.* Paraclete, Holy Ghost.

paracronismo, *n.m.* parachronism.

parachispas, *n.m.* (*elec.*) suppressor.
parachoques, *n.m.* (motor-car) bumper.
parada, *n.f.* halt, halting, stay, stop, suspension, pause; relay of horses and place where the change is made; dam; stall, fold for cattle; (*fenc.*) parry; bet, stake; (*mil.*) parade, review; taxi-rank; stake in gambling; *parada en firme* (or *en seco*), dead stop; *doblar la parada,* to double the stake; *llamar de parada,* to hold (game) at bay.
paradera, *n.f.* sluice, flood-gate; fishing net.
paradero, *n.m.* halting-place; station, depot, terminus, landing; end, term, limit; address, whereabouts; *no saber el paradero de alguno,* not to know what has become of a person.
paradeta, -illa, *n.f.* short-stop, in dancing. — *pl.* kind of a dance.
paradigma, *n.m.* paradigm, example, instance.
paradina, *n.f.* round enclosure, corral for sheep.
paradisíaco, -ca, *a.* paradisical.
paradislero, *n.m.* hunter waiting for his game; news-monger.
parado, -da, *a.* indolent, careless, inactive, slow, remiss, cold; unoccupied, not busy; stopped (of a clock); closed; (*Am.*) standing up.
paradoja, *n.f.* paradox.
paradójico, -ca; paradojo, -ja, *a.* paradoxical.
parador, -ora, *n.m.f.* horse or mare easily brought to a halt; inn, tavern, hostelry; heavy better.
parafernales (bienes), *n.m.pl.* (*law*) paraphernalia.
parafina, *n.f.* paraffin.
parafrasear, *v.t.* to paraphrase.
paráfrasis, *n.f.* paraphrase.
parafraste, *n.m.* paraphrast, expounder.
parafrásticamente, *adv.* paraphrastically.
parafrástico, -ca, *a.* paraphrastic, paraphrastical.
paragonar, *v.t.* to compare, be or have equal.
parágrafo, *n.m.* (*obs.*) paragraph.
paragranizo, *n.m.* (*agric.*) cover to protect plants from hail.
paraguas, *n.m.* umbrella.
paraguatán, *n.m.* (*Cent. Am.*) a tree of the Rubia genus.
paraguay, *n.m.* (*orn.*) kind of parrot.
paraguayano, -na; -guayo, -ya, *a.* of Paraguay.
paragüería, *n.f.* umbrella shop.
paragüero, -ra, *n.m.f.* maker or seller of umbrellas.
parahuso, *n.m.* jeweller's bow.
paraíso, *n.m.* paradise, heaven; (*theat.*) gallery; *paraíso de bobos,* fool's paradise.
paraje, *n.m.* place, spot, residence; condition, disposition.
paral, *n.m.* scaffolding prop or pole; (*naut.*) launching-trough.
paraláctico, -ca, *a.* parallactic.
paralaje, *n.f.* (*astron.*) parallax.
paralelepípedo, *n.m.* (*geom.*) parallelepiped.
paralelismo, *n.m.* parallelism.
paralelizar, *v.t.* to parallel, compare.
paralelo, -la, *a.* parallel.
paralelo, *n.m.* parallel, comparison.
paralelogramo, *n.m.* parallelogram.
Paralipómenos, *n.m.pl.* the Books of Chronicles.
parálisis, *n.f.* paralysis.

paralítico, -ca, *a.* paralytic, palsied.
paralización, *n.f.* paralysation; (*com.*) stagnation.
paralizado, -da, *a.* (*com.*) dull, stagnant, flat.
paralizar, *v.t.* (*pret.* **paralicé;** *pres. subj.* **paralice**) to palsy, paralyse; to stop, impede.
paralogismo, *n.m.* (*log.*) paralogism, false reasoning.
paralogizar, *v.t.* to paralogize.
paramentar, *v.t.* to embellish, adorn, bedeck.
paramento, *n.m.* hanging, ornament, embellishment; caparison, trappings; (*arch.*) facing; *paramentos sacerdotales,* (*eccl.*) robes and ornaments.
paramera, *n.f.* desert, bleak land, moorland, moor.
parámetro, *n.m.* (*geom.*) parameter.
páramo, *n.m.* desert, wilderness; (*fig.*) exceedingly cold spot.
parancero, *n.m.* bird-catcher.
parangón, *n.m.* paragon, comparison, model.
parangona, *n.f.* (*print.*) paragon type.
parangonar, *v.t.* to paragon, match, compare.
paraninfico, -ca, *a.* (*arch.*) having statues of nymphs.
paraninfo, *n.m.* best man at a wedding; paranymph; harbinger of felicity; college hall.
paranomasia, *n.f.* paranomasia.
paranza, *n.f.* hut or blind for huntsmen.
parao, *n.m.* (*Philip.*) passenger vessel.
parapara, *n.f.* fruit of the *paraparo.*
paraparo, *n.m.* (*Ven.*) soapbark tree.
parapetar, *v.t.* (*fort.*) to construct a parapet. — *v.r.* to shelter behind a parapet.
parapeto, *n.m.* (*fort.*) parapet, breastwork; railing on a bridge, quay, etc.
parapoco, *n.m.f.* (*coll.*) timid person; numskull.
parar, *n.m.* lansquenet. — *v.i.* to stop, halt, finish, desist, reach, land at, get to; to come to the possession of, devolve; to fall out, happen; to become, end in; to live, lodge, reside; to be changed (into); — *v.t.* to stop, detain, restrain, check; to get ready, prepare; to prevent, place, fix, end; to stake (at cards). — *v.r.* to stop, halt, cease; to discontinue, come to an end; to waver, desist, stop before an obstacle; (*Am.*) to stand up; *parar mientes,* to consider carefully; *sin parar,* instantly, without delay; *no pararse en pelillos,* not to stop at trifles.
pararrayo, *n.m.* lightning conductor.
parasceve, *n.f.* Good Friday.
paraselene, *n.f.* (*astron.*) mock-moon.
parasemo, *n.f.* figure-head of a galley.
parasismo, *n.m.* paroxysm.
parasítico, -ca, *a.* parasitic.
parásito, *n.m.* parasite, sponger, toad-eater.
parásito, -ta, *n.m.f.,* *a.* parasite, parasitic.
parasol, *n.m.* parasol, sunshade.
parástade, *n.m.* (*arch.*) anta, pilaster.
parata, *n.f.* artificial land terrace.
paratifoidea, *n.f.* paratyphoid.
paraulata, *n.f.* (*Ven.*) a bird like the thrush.
parausar, *v.t.* to drill (metals).
parauso, *n.m.* jeweller's bow drill.
parca, *n.f.* one of the Parcæ or fates; (*poet.*) death.
parcamente, *adv.* sparingly, parsimoniously.
parce, *n.m.* certificate given to grammar-students.
parcela, *n.f.* small part, particle, parcel of land.

parcelar, *v.t.* to parcel out, partition, measure (land).

parcelario, -ria, *a.* in small parts or portions.

parcial, *a.* partial, incomplete, partisan, one-sided, biased, prejudiced.

parcialidad, *n.f.* partiality, prejudice, bias; friendship, familiar intercourse.

parcialmente, *adv.* partially, in part.

parcidad, *n.f.* parsimony, frugality.

parcionero, *n.m.* partner, participant.

parcísimo, -ma, *a. superl.* [PARCO].

parco, -ca, *a.* sparing, scanty; moderate, parsimonious, sober.

parcha, *n.f.* (*Am.*) any plant of the Passiflora genus.

parchazo, *n.m.* large plaster; (*met.*) deception, jest; (*naut.*) flapping of a sail.

parche, *n.m.* plaster, sticking-plaster; drum-cover; drum-head; drum; (*shoe*) patch; botch; parchment cover; *pegar un parche,* (*coll.*) to play a mean trick.

pardal, *a.* clownish, rustic, cunning. — *n.m.* (*orn.*) sparrow, linnet; (*zool.*) kind of giraffe; old name for a leopard; (*bot.*) aconite, wolf's-bane; (*coll.*) crafty fellow.

pardear, *v.i.* to grow brownish, dusky, dark, grey.

¡pardiez! *interj.* heavens! by Jove! good gracious!

pardillo, *n.m.* linnet; kind of grape and wine made from it.

pardillo, -lla, *a.* greyish, brown (cloth).

pardo, -da, *a.* grey, brown, dark, dusky; cloudy. — *n.m.f.* (*Cub.*, *PR.*) mulatto, Negro; (*zool.*) leopard.

pardusco, -ca, *a.* dark grey, grizzly.

parear, *v.t.* to mate, match, pair, couple.

parecer, *v.i.* (*pres. indic.* **parezco;** *pres. subj.* **parezca**) to appear, seem, look; to judge; to show up, turn up; *al parecer,* as it seems, to all appearance; *me parece,* I think; *por el bien parecer,* to save appearances; *un diablo se parece a otro,* one devil is much like another. — *v.r.* to look alike, to resemble, be like; to assimilate, conform to. — *n.m.* opinion, advice, counsel; countenance, appearance, look, mien, air.

parecido, -da, *a.* resembling, like. — *n.m.* resemblance, likeness. — *p.p.* found [PARECER].

pareciente, *a.* similar, apparent.

pared, *n.f.* wall; wall-calendar; close field of barley; *entre cuatro paredes,* retired, confined; *las paredes oyen,* walls have ears; *darse contra una pared,* to be obstinate in one's anger; *darse contra* (or *por*) *las paredes,* to wear oneself out without achieving one's object; *pegado a la pared,* ashamed, confused.

paredaño, -ña, *a.* having a wall between.

paredón, *n.m.* thick wall, standing wall.

pareja, *n.f.* pair, couple, team, span, brace, match; coupling; dancing partner; *por parejas,* two by two; *cada oveja con su pareja,* like with like.

parejo, -ja, *a.* equal, similar, even; *por parejo,* on equal terms, on a par.

parejura, *n.f.* equality, similarity, similitude.

paremiología, *n.f.* treatise on proverbs.

parénesis, *n.f.* precept, warning, monition, exhortation.

parenético, -ca, *a.* admonitory.

parentela, *n.f.* parentage, kindred, kinsfolk, relations.

parentesco, *n.m.* cognation, kindred, relationship; union, bond, tie.

paréntesis, *n.m.* parenthesis; *entre* (or *por*) *paréntesis,* by-the-bye.

pareo, *n.m.* pairing, coupling, matching.

parergon, *n.m.* additional ornament.

pares, *n.f.pl.* (*anat.*) placenta.

paresa, *n.f.* peeress.

parezco; parezca, *pres. indic.; pres. subj.* [PARECER].

pargo, *n.m.* (*ichth.*) braize, porgy.

parhelia, *n.f.;* **parhelio,** *n.m.* parhelion, mock sun.

parhilera, *n.f.* (*arch.*) ridgepole, ridgepiece.

paria, *n.f.* pariah, outcast; low caste.

parición, *n.f.* calving-time.

parida, *n.f.* woman lately delivered of a child.

paridad, *n.f.* parity, equality, comparison.

paridera, *a.* fruitful, prolific. — *n.f.* parturition; time and place where cattle bring forth their young.

pariente, -ta, *n.m.f.* relative, kinsman, kinswoman; (*coll.*) something resembling another; (*coll.*) appellation given by husband and wife to each other.

parietal, *a.* (*anat.*) parietal; relating to walls.

parietaria, *n.f.* (*bot.*) pellitory.

parificar, *v.t.* (conjugated like BUSCAR) to exemplify.

parihuela, *n.f.* barrow, litter, stretcher.

parima, *n.f.* (*Arg.*) large heron of the pampas.

parir, *v.i. & v.t.* to bring forth, give birth, bear; to be productive; to lay eggs, spawn; to explain, clear up; to cause, produce; to publish; *poner a parir,* to oblige someone to do something against his will.

parisiena, *n.f.* (*print.*) five-point type.

parisiense, *n.m.f.,* *a.* Parisian.

paritario, -ria, *a.* applied to organizations in which managers and workers meet on equal terms.

parla, *n.f.* loquacity, gossip, easy delivery.

parlador, -ra, *n.m.f.* chattering person.

parladuría, *n.f.* loquacity, impertinent speech.

parlaembalde, *n.m.f.* (*coll.*) chatterbox.

parlamental, *a.* parliamentary.

parlamentar, parlamentear (*obs.*), *v.i.* to talk, converse; to treat, parley.

parlamentario, *n.m.* member of parliament; (*mil.*) flag of truce.

parlamentario, -ria, *a.* parliamentary, parliamentarian.

parlamento, *n.m.* parliament, legislative body; (*theat.*) public speech, harangue; (*mil.*) flag of truce, parley.

parlanchín, -ina, *n.m.f., a.* chatterer, jabberer.

parlante, *a.* speaking, talking.

parlar, *v.i.* to chatter, babble; *parlar en balde,* to talk nonsense.

parlatorio, *n.m.* converse, parley; parlour.

parlería, *n.f.* loquacity, garrulity, gossip, tale, jest.

parlero, -ra, *a.* loquacious, talkative, garrulous.

parlero, *n.m.* tale-teller, tattler; (*poet.*) purling brook, rill; expressive (eyes); chirping (birds); interesting talk.

parleta, *n.f.* (*coll.*) conversation on trifles.

parlotear, *v.i.* to chatter, prattle, gossip, prate.

parloteo, *n.m.* prattle, talk.

Parnaso, *n.m.* (*poet.*) Parnassus, Helicon; collection of poems; company of poets.

paro, *n.m.* (*orn.*) titmouse; coal-tit; lock-out,

suspension of work; *paro forzoso,* want of work, unemployment.

parodia, *n.f.* parody.

parodiar, *v.t.* to parody.

paródico, -ca, *a.* parodistic.

parola, *n.f.* (*coll.*) eloquence, volubility, fluency; chat, chatter, idle talk.

pároli, *n.m.* triple stakes.

parónimo, -ma, *a.* paronymous, cognate, alike.

paronomasia, *n.f.* paronomasia.

parótida, *n.f.* parotid gland; mumps; tumour of parotid glands.

paroxismal, *a.* paroxysmal.

paroxismo, *n.m.* paroxysm.

parpadear, *v.i.* to blink; to wink.

párpado, *n.m.* eyelid.

parpalla, *n.f.* milled copper piece.

parpar, *v.i.* to quack (as a duck).

parque, *n.m.* park, paddock; car park; (*artill.*) park; (*Col.*) armoury; ammunition dump; equipment; *parque de artillería,* train of artillery; *parque de ingenieros,* camp and field-equipage; *parque zoológico,* zoological garden.

parquedad, *n.f.* parsimony.

parra, *n.f.* vine raised on stakes or nailed to a wall; honey jar.

párrafo, *n.m.* paragraph, paragraph mark.

parragón, *n.m.* standard silver for essayers.

parral, *n.m.* vine abounding in shoots; large earthen jar.

parranda, *n.f.* revel, carousal.

parrar, *v.i.* to extend, spread out in branches.

parricida, *n.m.f.* parricide, slayer of father or mother.

parricidio, *n.m.* parricide, murder of father or mother.

parrilla, *n.f.* two-handled jar. — *pl.* **parrillas,** grid-iron, toaster, grate.

parriza, *n.f.* wild vine.

parro, *n.m.* duck.

párroco, *n.m.* rector or vicar of a parish; parish priest.

parroquia, *n.f.* parish, parish church; rector's jurisdiction; clergy; customers.

parroquial, *a.* parochial. — *n.f.* parochial church.

parroquialidad, *n.f.* parochial right.

parroquiano, -na, *a.* belonging to a parishioner.

parroquiano, *n.m.* parishioner; (*com.*) customer.

parsi, *n.m.,* *a.* Parsee.

parsimonia, *n.f.* parsimony, frugality, economy, husbandry.

parsimonioso, -sa, *a.* economic; sober, moderate, prudent.

parte, *n.f.* part, portion, share, lot; spot, location; side, place; character in a play; (*law*) party, interest. — *n.m.* royal or official message or messenger; special dispatch, urgent message; return, report. — *f.pl.* **partes,** parts, talents, endowments, ability; party, faction; the genitals; *en parte,* partly, in part; *parte por parte,* part by part, distinctly; *por todas partes,* on all hands; *de parte,* by command, by order; *a partes,* or *en partes,* by parts or in parts; *de parte a parte,* from side to side; *dar parte,* to give an account, inform; *dar parte sin novedad,* to report that nothing has happened; *hacer uno de su parte,* to do what one can towards an end; *hacer las partes,* to do something for a person in his name; *ir a la parte,* to share, go halves; *meterse a parte,* to be on someone's side; *no ser parte en,* to have no influence in; *por todas partes se va a Roma,* all roads lead to Rome; *de ocho días a esta parte,* within these last eight days; *echar una cosa a buena* (or *mala*) *parte,* to take a thing in a good (or bad) sense; *parte de la oración,* part of speech; *partes pudendas, púdicas* or *vergonzosas,* genitals, privy parts.

partear, *v.t.* to assist, deliver (in childbirth).

partenogénesis, *n.f.* parthenogenesis.

partera, *n.f.* midwife.

partería, *n.f.* midwifery, obstetrics.

partero, *n.m.* accoucheur, obstetrician, male nurse in childbirth.

parterre, *n.m.* garden, lawn.

partesana, *n.f.* partisan, kind of halberd.

partible, *a.* divisible, separable.

partición, *n.f.* partition, division, distribution, separation, lot.

particionero, -ra, *a.* participant.

participación, *n.f.* participation; communication; (*com.*) co-partnership; *cuenta en participación,* joint account.

participante, *a.* participant, sharing.

participar, *v.t.,* *v.i.* to inform, give notice; to participate, share, partake.

partícipe, *a.* participant, sharing; *n.m.* partner.

participial, *a.* (*gram.*) participial.

participio, *n.m.* participle.

partícula, *n.f.* particle, small part; molecule.

particular, *a.* particular, special, peculiar; odd; individual. — *n.m.* individual, private person; peculiar or particular matter or subject; *en particular,* particularly.

particularidad, *n.f.* particularity, peculiarity; intimacy, friendship.

particularizar, *v.t.* to detail, particularize. — *v.r.* to be characterized by; to be particular.

particularmente, *adv.* particularly, especially; privately.

partida, *n.f.* departure; charge, entry, item in an account, record, annotation; party of soldiers; game; parcel, lot; death, decease; (*mil.*) squad; guerrilla; factious band; (*com.*) shipment, lot, consignment; crew, gang. — *pl.* **partidas,** parts, accomplishments, talents; *¡buena partida!* excellent conduct; *partida doble,* (*com.*) double entry; *partida simple,* single entry; *partida serrana,* disloyal behaviour; *las siete partidas,* the laws of Castile compiled by King Alfonso X.

partidamente, *adv.* distinctly, separately.

partidario, *n.m.* partisan; adherent, follower; party-man; district physician; guerrilla.

partidario, -ria, *a.* with the charge of a certain district; adhering, following.

partido, -da, *a.* (*her.*) party, parted, or *parti per pale;* free, liberal, munificent.

partido, *n.m.* party; advantage, profit, utility; favour, interest, protection; game, match, contest; odds in a game; agreement, treaty; district; *mujer del partido,* strumpet, woman of the town; *tomar partido,* to resolve, embrace a resolution; to engage, join, enlist.

partidor, *n.m.* parter, divider, cleaver; (*arith.*) divisor.

partija, *n.f.* partition.

partimento, partimiento, *n.m.* partition.

partir, *v.t.* to part, divide, share, split, distribute; to cleave, cut, sever, disunite; to break violently; to attack in combat; to resolve; (*arith.*) to divide. — *v.i.* to part, leave, depart, march, set out. — *v.r.* to be divided in opinion; *partir las amarras,* (*naut.*) to part the cable; *partir mano,* to abandon, desist; *partir abierto,* to uncover a beehive for swarming; *partirse el alma,* to die broken-hearted.

partitivo, -va, *a.* (*gram.*) partitive.

partitura, *n.f.* (*mus.*) score.

parto, *n.m.* childbirth, parturition; newborn child; natural production; literary composition; expected and important future event.

parturienta, parturiente, *a.* parturient.

párulis, *n.m.* (*med.*) gumboil.

parva, *n.f.* unthreshed corn in heaps; multitude, great quantity; light breakfast (of farm labourers); *salirse de la parva,* to withdraw from anything.

parvada, *n.f.* place for unthreshed corn.

parvedad, parvidad, *n.f.* minuteness, littleness; snack, bite of food.

parvo, -va, *a.* small, little.

parvulez, *n.f.* smallness, small size.

parvulico, -ica; -illo, -illa; -ito, -ita, *a.* very little.

párvulo, -la, *a.* very small, innocent, humble, lowly. — *n.m.f.* child.

pasa, *n.f.* raisin; (*obs.*) migration of birds; (*naut.*) channel; (*Am.*) woolly hair.

pasabalas, *n.m.* (*mil.*) ball calibre gauge.

pasacaballo, *n.m.* horse ferry-boat.

pasacalle, *n.m.* street-music, lively march.

pasada, *n.f.* passage; step, pace; malicious action; game; trick; competency, livelihood; *dar pasada,* to permit, tolerate; *de pasada,* on the way, in passing; hastily, cursorily; *mala pasada,* (*coll.*) bad turn.

pasadera, *n.f.* stepping-stone; (*naut.*) spun-yarn, furling line, sea gasket.

pasaderamente, *adv.* passably.

pasadero, -ra, *a.* supportable, sufferable; passable, fairly good.

pasadillo, *n.m.* embroidery with design on both sides.

pasadizo, *n.m.* narrow passage, covered way; alley; corridor, hall, aisle.

pasado, -da, *a.* past, spent, gone through; hale, old.

pasado, *n.m.* past time; deserter from the army. — *pl.* **pasados,** ancestors; *lo pasado, pasado,* let bygones be bygones.

pasador, *n.m.* smuggler; sharp arrow; one who carries a thing from place to place; brooch; bolt of a lock; clock-peg; linch-pin; sieve; window-fastener; pin; hatpin or bodkin; cotter; colander; (*naut.*) marline spike. — *pl.* **pasadores,** cord-straps.

pasadura, *n.f.* passage; fit of crying (children).

pasagonzalo, *n.m.* (*coll.*) slight, sharp blow.

pasahilo, *n.m.* thread-guide.

pasaje, *n.m.* passage, road, way; passage money; journey, voyage; (*naut.*) narrow; strait; accident, event, piece of business; (*mus.*) modulation (of key or voice); passage of a book.

pasajeramente, *adv.* transiently, going along, without stopping.

pasajero, -ra, *a.* transient, transitory. — *n.m.f.* passenger, traveller.

pasamanar, *v.t.* to make ribbons, lace, etc.

pasamanera, *n.f.* lace-woman, lace-maker.

pasamanería, *n.f.* lace-trade, lace-making; fancy trimming, passementerie.

pasamanero, *n.m.* lace-maker, ribbon-maker.

pasamano, *n.m.* balustrade; banister; edging of clothes; (*naut.*) gangway.

pasamiento, *n.m.* passage, transit.

pasante, *n.m.* doctor's or lawyer's assistant; student teacher; (*her.*) passant; game of cards.

pasantía, *n.f.* student's profession (law or medicine).

pasapán, *n.m.* (*coll.*) throat, gullet.

pasapasa, *n.m.* legerdemain, hocus-pocus.

pasaporte, *n.m.* passport; (*mil.*) furlough.

pasar, *v.i.* to pass, move, be in motion, go, travel; to make way; to ascend, be promoted; to pass away, elapse, be spent, die; to pass, become current (as money); to happen, turn out; to be marketable; to live; to manage to exist; to last, endure; to pass (at cards). — *v.t.* to pass; to send, carry or convey from place to place; to present, handle; to pierce, penetrate, go through; to smuggle; to advance, promote; to change for the better or worse; to exceed, pass beyond; to distance, outdo, outrun, outstrip; to stroke, rub; to swallow (food or drink); to terminate, stop; to walk the hospitals; to study or rehearse (a lesson, play, etc.); to pass, spend (as time); to undergo, bear, suffer; to omit, pass in silence, overlook, dissemble; to percolate, strain, clarify; to draw up, handle (a legal matter). — *v.r.* to cease, finish; to surpass, exceed; to be out of season, spoiled (of fruit, etc.); to go over to another party; to shut badly; to slip from one's memory; to burn out (as a fire); to graduate (university, etc.); to pass in vain (of an opportunity); to blot (of paper); *v. impers.* to pass, happen, turn out; *pasar a cuchillo,* to kill, put to the sword; *pasar de largo,* to pass without stopping or reflecting; *pasar al frente,* to carry forward; *pasar a la vuelta,* to carry over; *pasar el dinero,* to count over one's money; *pasar el tiempo,* to loiter, pass the time idly; *pasar muestra* (or *revista*), to muster, review; *pasar por las armas,* to shoot a soldier; *pasar por alto,* to overlook, take no notice of; *pasar uno por,* to experience; *pasar en claro,* to omit mentioning; *pasar por encima,* to overcome; *ir pasando,* to be about the same; *pasar por agua* (*un huevo*), to boil (an egg); *pasar el peine a un caballo,* to curry a horse; *pasar un cabo,* (*naut.*) to reeve a rope; *un buen pasar,* a competency; *¿cómo lo pasa Vd.?* how are you? *pasarlo cómodamente,* to be fairly well off, get along pretty well; *pasar por cierto,* to be taken as certain; *pasarse con poco,* to get on with little; *pasarse de bueno,* to be too good; *pasarse de cortés,* to be too polite; *pasársela en flores,* to be in clover.

pasatiempo, *n.m.* pastime, amusement, diversion.

pasavante, *n.m.* (*naut.*) gangway; safe-conduct, permit.

pasavolante, *n.m.* inconsiderate or hasty action or speech.

pasavoleo, *n.m.* ball passing the line (game of *pelota*).

pascana, *n.f.* (*Arg., Bol., Ec., Per.*) inn; a halt during a long journey.

pascar, *v.i.* (*Bol.*) to encamp.

pascua, *n.f.* passover; (*coll.*) church festival extending over several days (Twelfth-night, Pentecost, Easter, and Christmas); *decir los nombres de las pascuas,* to use injurious language; *¡felices Pascuas!* a happy Christmas; *hacer pascua,* to begin to eat meat after Lent; *santas pascuas,* be it so! *or* there's no other way! *estar como una pascua,* to be as merry as a cricket.

pascual, *a.* paschal, relating to Easter.

pascuilla, *n.f.* Low Sunday.

pase, *n.m.* permit, pass, passport; (*fenc.*) venue, thrust.

paseadero, *n.m.* avenue, public walk.

paseador, -ra, *n.m.f.* walker.

paseante, *n.m.f., a.* walker, goer; walking; *paseante en corte,* one without office or employment.

pasear, *v.t., v.i.* to walk, exercise, take the air, move slowly, bring out for a walk, take for a walk. — *v.r.* to walk, take a walk; to loiter, wander idly; *pasear la calle,* to court a lady in the street; *pasear las calles,* to be whipped through the streets.

paseata, *n.f.* walk, airing, drive.

paseo, *n.m.* walk; gait; public avenue; drive; ride; ramble; parade; *¡Váyase Vd. a paseo!* get along with you!

pasera, *n.f.* (*prov.*) place where raisins are dried.

pasibilidad, *n.f.* passibleness, susceptibility.

pasible, *a.* passible, capable of suffering.

pasicorto, -ta, *a.* short-stepped.

pasiego, -ga, *n.m.f.* highlander of Santander.

pasiflora, *n.f.* passion-flower.

pasilargo, -ga, *a.* long-stepped.

pasillo, *n.m.* short step; corridor, passage; basting stitch.

pasión, *n.f.* passion, susceptibility, anger, emotion, affection, inclination, fondness; *pasión de ánimo.* broken heart.

pasionaria, *n.f.* passion-flower.

pasionario, *n.m.* (*eccl.*) Passion-book.

pasionero, *n.m.* chorister who sings the Passion.

pasito, *adv.* gently, softly. — *n.m.* short step; *pasito a pasito,* very gently.

pasitrote, *a.* short trot of a horse.

pasivamente, *adv.* passively.

pasivo, -va, *a.* passive, unresisting, not acting; pension, retirement; (*gram.*) passive.

pasmado, -da, *a.* chilled, stunned.

pasmar, *v.t.* to cause a spasm; to benumb, stun, stupefy, chill, deaden. — *v.i.* to wonder, marvel. — *v.r.* to suffer spasms, be spasmodic; to be astonished, wonder.

pasmarota, pasmarotada, *n.f.* (*coll.*) feigned spasm; motiveless admiration.

pasmo, *n.m.* spasm, convulsion; astonishment, amazement; object of admiration; (*med.*) tetanus, lockjaw.

pasmosamente, *adv.* wonderfully, astonishingly.

pasmoso, -sa, *a.* marvellous, wonderful.

paso, -sa, *a.* dried (fruit). — *p.p. irreg.* [PASAR].

paso, *n.m.* pace, footstep, step; gait, walk; act of passing; flight of steps; passage, passport, pass, licence; lobby, narrow entrance, pass; progress, improvement, advance; diligence; death, decease; image or sculptured group carried about the streets for Holy Week; (*geog.*) strait; (*mech.*) pitch; (*theat.*) curtain-

raiser, sketch; passage in a writing. — *pl.* **pasos,** conduct, steps, proceedings; basting stitches; *paso a paso,* step by step, slowly; *paso de garganta,* (*mus.*) trill, quaver; *más que de paso,* in a hurry; *paso de tortuga,* snail's pace; *a buen paso,* at a good rate; *a cada paso,* at every step, frequently; *al paso,* without delay; *al paso que,* at the same time that, whilst; *a dos pasos,* very near; *a pocos pasos,* at a short distance; *a ese paso,* at that rate; *a paso de buey,* very slowly; *andar en malos pasos,* to follow evil ways; *dar paso,* to clear the way; *apretar el paso,* to hasten; *vista de paso,* cursory view; *de paso,* passing; *salir del paso,* to get out of a difficulty; *salir de su paso,* to change one's habits; *alargar el paso,* to lengthen one's stride, go more quickly; *a paso llano,* regularly, smoothly; *cada paso es un gazapo* (or *un tropiezo*), he stumbles (*or* makes mistakes) at every step; *ceder el paso,* to allow another to pass before one; *cerrar el paso,* to get in the way, obstruct; *coger al paso,* to take a pawn in passing (in chess); *más que de paso,* hurriedly, violently; *no poder dar* (*un*) *paso,* not to be able to walk a step; *paso entre paso,* slowly, little by little; *por sus pasos contados,* in its regular order (*or* course); *salirle a uno al paso,* to accost, greet someone; stop him in his tracks; *seguir los pasos de uno,* to observe someone very closely.

paso, *adv.* softly, gently.

paspié, *n.m.* kind of dance.

pasquín, *n.m.* pasquinade, lampoon.

pasquinada, *n.f.* pasquinade.

pasquinar, *v.t.* to satirize, lampoon, ridicule.

pássim, *adv.* passim, here and there.

pasta, *n.f.* paste; batter; pastry; soup-paste; noodles; bullion, mass of gold or silver; pie-crust; board-binding; paste-board covered with leather, roan leather; pulp in paper-making; *buena pasta,* excessive mildness; *media pasta,* half-leather binding; *buena pasta,* (*fig.*) good disposition.

pastar, *v.i.* to pasture, graze. — *v.t.* to lead cattle to graze.

paste, *n.m.* (CR., *Hond.*) a cucurbitaceous plant used as a sponge when dry.

pasteca, *n.f.* (*naut.*) snatch-block.

pastel, *n.m.* pie, tart, cake, pastry; (*bot.*) woad; (*print.*) pie; type for recasting; (*art*) pastel; trick in card-dealing; plot, secret meeting.

pastelear, *v.i.* (*coll.*) to trim politically.

pastelera, *n.f.* pastry-cook's wife.

pastelería, *n.f.* pastry-cook's shop; pastry, pies.

pastelero, *n.m.* pastry-cook.

pastelillo, -ito, *n.m.* little pie or tart; patty.

pastelón, *n.m.* large pie; pigeon or meat pie.

pasterización, *n.f.* pasteurization.

pasterizar, *v.t.* to pasteurize.

pastero, *n.m.* one who throws the mass of crushed olives into baskets.

pastilla, *n.f.* cake, tablet; lozenge, pastille.

pastinaca, *n.f.* (*bot.*) parsnip; (*zool.*) sting-ray.

pasto, *n.m.* pasture, pasture-ground; food, aliment, nourishment; *a pasto,* abundantly, plentifully; *pasto espiritual,* spiritual food.

pastor, *n.m.* shepherd; pastor, clergyman.

pastora, *n.f.* shepherdess.

pastoral, *a.* pastoral, rural, rustic. — *n.f.* pastoral poem.

pastoralmente, *adv.* pastorally, rustically.

pastorear, *v.t.* to lead to pasture, graze, pasture; to feed souls with sound doctrine.

pastorela, *n.f.* (*mus. & poet.*) pastoral, rustic melody.

pastoreo, *n.m.* pasturing, tending flocks.

pastoría, *n.f.* pastoral or rural life; body of shepherds.

pastoril; pastoricio, -cia, *a.* pastoral.

pastorilmente, *adv.* pastorally, rustically.

pastosidad, *n.f.* mellowness, softness.

pastoso, -sa, *a.* soft, mellow, doughy, clammy.

pastura, *n.f.* pasture, pasture-ground; fodder.

pasturaje, *n.m.* pasturage; duty for grazing of cattle.

pata, *n.f.* foot and leg of animals, paw; flap; pocket flap; female duck; (*coll.*) human leg or foot; leg of a piece of furniture; *pata de cabra,* crowbar; (shoe) heel burnisher; nail puller; unforeseen hindrance; *pata de gallo,* ridiculous saying, bull; crow's foot, wrinkle near the eye; stupidity, silliness; *a la pata coja,* hopscotch; *a pata(s),* on foot; *a pata llana,* plainly, without affectation; *patas arriba,* heels over head, upside down; *pata es la traviesa,* tit for tat; the biter bit; *quedar* (or *salir*) *pata(s),* to be a tie; *a cuatro patas,* on all fours; *meter la pata,* to interfere, meddle.

patabán, *n.m.* (*Cub.*) mangrove (variety of *Rhizophora mangel*).

pataca, *n.f.* Jerusalem artichoke; small copper coin.

pataco, -ca, *a.* boorish, churlish.

patacón, *n.m.* dollar, patacoon; copper coin of about one penny.

patache, *n.m.* (*naut.*) advice-boat.

patada, *n.f.* kick, blow with the foot, step, pace, track, footmark; *no dar pie ni patada,* to take not the slightest trouble.

patadión, *n.m.* (*Philip.*) cloth for skirts.

patagón, -ona, *n.m.f.,* *a.* from or of Patagonia, Patagonian.

patagorrillo, *n.m.* hash of pork liver and lights.

patagua, *n.f.* Chile linden, whitewood.

pataje, *n.m.* (*naut.*) patache, tender, advice-boat.

patalear, *v.i.* to kick violently; to stamp the foot; to patter.

pataleo, *n.m.* act of stamping the foot.

pataleta, *n.f.* (*coll.*) fainting-fit (usually feigned); ridiculous speech or action; absurd enterprise.

pataletilla, *n.f.* kind of dance.

patán, -ana, *a.* clownish, churlish, boorish. — *n.m.f.* countryman or countrywoman; bumpkin, churl.

patana, *n.f.* (*Cub.*) thorny cactaceous plant (*Harrisia eriphora*).

patanco, *n.m.* (*Cub.*) wild plant with poisonous prickles.

patanería, *n.f.* clownishness, churlishness, boorishness, rudeness, rusticity.

patao, *n.m.* (*Cub.*) edible fish (*Gerres patao*).

patarata, *n.f.* fiction, idle tale; affected concern.

pataratero, -ra, *a.* of fictitious appearance.

patarráez, *n.m.* (*naut.*) preventer-shroud.

patasca, *n.f.* (*Arg.*) dish made of pork and maize; (*Per.*) dispute, angry argument.

patata, *n.f.* potato.

patatal, *n.m.* potato-field.

patatero, -ra, *n.m.f.,* *a.* potato-seller, potato-eater.

patatús, *n.m.* (*coll.*) swoon, fainting-fit.

patay, *n.m.* (*Am.*) dry paste made from carob beans.

pate, *n.m.* (*Hond.*) a tree with bitter and caustic bark used in medicine.

pateadura, *n.f.* kicking, stamping; (*coll.*) severe reprimand, dressing down.

pateamiento, *n.m.* kicking, act of kicking.

patear, *v.t., v.i.* (*coll.*) to kick, stamp; to be irritated, vexed; to be very angry.

patena, *n.f.* paten; patina; large medal.

patentado, -da, *a.* patented.

patentar, *v.t.* to secure by patent.

patente, *a.* patent, evident, manifest, clear, palpable. — *n.f.* patent, warrant, commission; *patente de sanidad,* (*naut.*) bill of health; *patente de corso,* letters of marque.

patentemente, *adv.* openly, obviously, clearly, visibly.

patentizar, *v.t.* (*pret.* **patenticé;** *pres. subj.* **patentice**) to render evident.

pateo, *n.m.* (*coll.*) kicking; stamping of feet.

pátera, *n.f.* goblet.

paternal, *a.* paternal, fatherly.

paternalmente, *adv.* paternally, in a fatherly way.

paternidad, *n.f.* paternity, fatherhood.

paterno, -na, *a.* paternal, fatherly.

paternóster, *n.m.* paternoster, Lord's prayer; (*fig., coll.*) tight knot.

pateta, *n.f.* (*coll.*) lame person; (*coll.*) Devil, deuce, Old Nick; *se lo llevó pateta,* Old Nick took charge.

patéticamente, *adv.* pathetically.

patético, -ca, *a.* pathetic, moving, plaintive, passionate.

patiabierto, -ta, *a.* (*coll.*) straddling; bowlegged.

patialbillo, *n.m.* weasel.

patiblanco, -ca, *a.* white-footed.

patibulario, -ria, *a.* harrowing.

patíbulo, *n.m.* gallows, scaffold.

patica, *n.f.* small foot.

patico, -ito, *n.m.* gosling, young goose.

paticojo, -ja, *a.* (*coll.*) lame, crippled.

patiestevado, -da, *a.* bow-legged.

patihendido, -da, *a.* cloven-footed.

patilla, *n.f.* small foot; (*naut.*) rudder spike; trigger; whiskers; chape of a buckle; pocket flap; manner of playing on the guitar; (*carp.*) tenon; (*Venez.*) water-melon. — *pl.* **patillas,** side whiskers; (*coll.*) the devil.

patín, *n.m.* small court or yard; (*orn.*) goosander; skate; *patín de ruedas,* roller skate.

pátina, *n.f.* patina.

patinadero, *n.m.* skating rink; skating place.

patinador, -ra, *n.m.f.* skater.

patinar, *v.i.* to skate; (*motor.*) to skid.

patinejo, -illo, *n.m.* small skate.

patio, *n.m.* court, courtyard; (*theat.*) the ground floor; hall of college, university, etc.; *estar a patio,* to be a student not provided for by the foundation.

patita, *n.f.* small foot, leg (of animals), paw; *echar de patitas,* to turn away; *poner de patitas en la calle,* to discharge, turn on the street.

patitieso, -sa, *a.* (*coll.*) deprived of sense and feeling; stiff, stately, starchy; benumbed, stupefied, surprised.

patituerto, -ta, *a.* crooked-legged; (*coll.*) ill-disposed, perverse.

patizambo, -ba, *a.* bandy-legged.

pato, -ta, *n.m.f.* (*orn.*) duck; *estar hecho un pato*, to get a ducking; *pagar el pato*, to suffer undeserved punishment.

patochada, *n.f.* blunder, nonsense.

patogenia, *n.f.* (*med.*) pathogenesis.

patojo, -ja, *a.* waddling like a duck.

patología, *n.f.* pathology.

patológico, -ca, *a.* pathologic.

patólogo, *n.m.* pathologist.

patón, -ona, *a.* large-footed, clumsy-footed.

patón, *n.m.* clumsy foot.

patraña, *n.f.* fabulous story, cock-and-bull story.

patrañuela, *n.f.* insignificant tale.

patria, *n.f.* native land, fatherland; native or proper place; heaven.

patriarca, *n.m.* patriarch, founder of a religious order; *vive como un patriarca*, he enjoys all the conveniences of life.

patriarcado, *n.m.* patriarchate.

patriarcal, *a.* patriarchal.

patriarcalmente, *a.* patriarchally.

patriciado, *n.m.* dignity of a patrician.

patricio, -cia, *a.* native, national; patrician.

patricio, *n.m.* patrician, noble.

patrimonial, *a.* patrimonial.

patrimonialidad, *n.f.* birthright, right of patrimony.

patrimonio, *n.m.* patrimony.

patrio, -ria, *a.* native; paternal.

patriota, *n.m.f.* patriot.

patriotería, *n.f.* (*coll.*) jingoism.

patriótico, -ca, *a.* patriotic, beneficent.

patriotismo, *n.m.* patriotism.

patrística, *n.f.* patristics.

patrístico, -ca, *a.* patristic.

patrocinar, *v.t.* to favour, patronize, protect, countenance.

patrocinio, *n.m.* protection, patronage, favour.

patrología, *n.f.* patrology.

patrón, -ona, *n.m.f.* patron or patroness, protector; boss, master; host, landlord, landlady; patron saint; sample, standard, pattern, model, copy; (*naut.*) skipper.

patrona, *n.f.* ship next in importance to the commodore's.

patronado, -da, *a.* having a patron (of churches, etc.).

patronato, patronazgo, *n.m.* patronage, patronship; foundation of a charitable establishment.

patronear, *v.t.* to be commander of a trading vessel.

patronía, *n.f.* mastership of a vessel.

patronímico, *n.m.*, *a.* patronymic.

patrono, *n.m.* patron, protector, defender; tutelary; lord of the manor; employer.

patrulla, *n.f.* patrol; gang, band, squad; crowd of people going about the streets.

patrullar, *v.t.*, *v.i.* to patrol, go the rounds.

patudo, -da, *a.* (*coll.*) club-footed, having large feet or paws.

patulea, *n.f.* band of disorderly soldiers; rabble.

patullar, *v.i.* to trample, run through muddy places; go through thick and thin; (*coll.*) to prattle.

paturro, *a.* (*Col.*) small; chubby.

paují, paujil, *n.m.* (*Per.*) guan, a S. American gallinacean.

paúl, paular, *n.m.* low, damp place, bog.

paulatinamente, *adv.* gently, slowly, little by little.

paulatino, -na, *a.* slow, slowly, by degrees.

paulina, *n.f.* decree of excommunication, interdict, reproof, objurgation; (*coll.*) anonymous letter.

paulinia, *n.f.* (*Am.*) a shrub (*Paullinia Cupana*).

paulonia, *n.f.* (*bot.*) paulownia.

pauperismo, *n.m.* pauperism, abject poverty.

paupérrimo, -ma, *a. superl.* very poor.

pausa, *n.f.* pause, stop, intermission; at repose, rest; delay, suspense; *a pausas*, at leisure.

pausadamente, *adv.* slowly, deliberately.

pausado, -da, *a.* slow, deliberate; calm, quiet. — *adv.* slowly.

pausar, *v.i.* to pause, cease, hesitate, forbear from action.

pauta, *n.f.* rule, pattern, guide, example model; ruled paper.

pautada, *n.f.* ruled music-paper.

pautador, *n.m.* marker of lines on paper.

pautar, *v.t.* to draw lines with a *pauta;* to prescribe, give rules.

pava, *n.f.* turkey-hen, pea-hen; large furnace bellows; (*Am.*) joke; (*Ven.*) large hat; (*Col.*) kind of guan; *pelar la pava*, to flirt, court.

pavada, *n.f.* flock of turkeys; a childish game.

pavana, *n.f.* pavan; *pasos de pavana*, grave, solemn step, stately gait.

pavería, *n.f.* place for rearing turkeys.

pavero, -ra, *n.m.f.* feeder or seller of turkeys; *n.m.* broad-brimmed hat; *n.f.* (*Arg., Bol.*) kettle.

pavés, *n.m.* kind of large shield.

pavesa, *n.f.* embers, hot cinders; snuff of the candle; remains, relic; *estar hecho una pavesa*, to be very weak; *ser una pavesa*, to be very mild or gentle. — *pl.* **pavesas,** ashes.

pavesadas, *n.f.pl.* (*naut.*) waistcloths.

pavesear, *v.i.* to flicker, flutter.

pavezno, *n.m.* young turkey.

pavía, *n.f.* clingstone peach (fruit and tree).

pávido, -da, *a.* (*poet.*) timid, fearful.

pavilla, -ita, *n.f.* little turkey-hen.

pavillo, -ito, *n.m.* little turkey.

pavimentación, *n.f.* paving.

pavimentar, *v.t.* to pave.

pavimento, *n.m.* pavement, tiled floor.

paviota, *n.f.* seagull, mew.

pavipollo, *n.m.* young turkey.

pavito real, *n.m.* pea-chick.

pavo, *n.m.* (*orn.*) turkey; *pavo real*, peacock; (*ichth.*) peacock-fish. — *a.* (*coll.*) peacock-like, foppish.

pavón, *n.m.* peacock.

pavonada, *n.f.* strut, short walk, affected walk.

pavonar, *v.t.* to give a bluish colour (to iron or steel).

pavonazo, *n.m.* crimson, purple pigment.

pavoncillo, -ito, *n.m.* little peacock.

pavonear, *v.i.* to flutter, strut, flaunt; (*coll.*) to beguile with false hopes.

pavor, *n.m.* fear, terror, dread.

pavorde, *n.m.* provost of a cathedral; divinity professor.

pavordear, *v.i.* to swarm (of bees).

pavordía, *n.f.* office and dignity of a provost.

pavorido, -da, *a.* intimidated, terror-struck.

pavorosamente, *adv.* awfully, fearfully.

pavoroso, -sa, *a.* awful, dreadful, fearful.

pavura, *n.f.* dread, terror, fear.

paya, *n.f.* improvised song, calypso.

payacate, *n.m.* (*Mex.*) large handkerchief.

payada, *n.f.* (*Arg., Chi.*) song of the payador.

payador, *n.m.* (*Am.*) minstrel who accompanies himself with a guitar.

Payagua, *n.m.* Indian of Paraguay.

payasada, *n.f.* clownish joke or action.

payaso, *n.m.* mountebank, tumbler, clown.

payés, -esa, *n.m.f.* Catalan or Balearic countryman (-woman).

payo, paya, *n.m. f., a.* clown, churl, hoyden, rough country girl.

payuelas, *n.f.pl.* chicken-pox.

paz, *n.f.* peace, tranquillity, ease; peace of mind; respite from war, truce, armistice; peaceful disposition; equality of luck; salute, kiss, kiss of peace; ceremony of the mass. — *interj.* hush! *bandera de paz,* flag of truce; *gente de paz,* friend (answer to the challenge of a sentry); *en paz,* quits, clear; *a la paz de Dios,* God be with you; *paz y pan,* peace and bread (i.e. public tranquillity); *vaya en paz, vaya con la paz de Dios,* go in peace (polite formula of leave-taking).

pazguato, -ta, *n.m.f.* dolt, fool, simple person.

pazote, *n.m.* saltwort.

pazpuerca, *a. & n.f.* (*coll.*) dirty, slovenly woman.

pe, *n.m.* name of the letter *p*; *de pe a pa,* from beginning to end, throughout, entirely.

pea, *n.f.* intoxication, drunkenness.

peaje, *n.m.* bridge-toll, ferriage.

peajero, *n.m.* toll-gatherer.

peal, *n.m.* sock, stocking-foot, legging; worthless person.

peana, peaña, *n.f.* pedestal, base of a statue; (*mech.*) ground plate; step before an altar.

peatón, *n.m.* walker, pedestrian; rural postman; messenger.

peazgo, *n.m.* bridge-toll.

pebete, *n.m.* perfume; aromatic burning-stick; (*coll.*) stench, evil odour; tube for fireworks; punk, touchwood; (*Ur., Arg.*) young boy.

pebetero, *n.m.* censer.

pebrada, pebre, *n.f.* sauce made of pepper, garlic and vinegar.

peca, *n.f.* speck, freckle, spot.

pecable, *a.* peccable, sinful.

pecadazo, *n.m.* heinous or terrible sin.

pecadillo, *n.m.* peccadillo, slight fault.

pecado, *n.m.* sin; excess, extravagance; (*coll.*) devil; *pecado mortal,* deadly sin; *estar hecho un pecado,* to be unfortunate, unsuccessful; *a pecado nuevo, penitencia nueva,* for every sin a fresh penance.

pecador, -ra, *n.m.f.* sinner; *pecador de mí,* poor wretch that I am! poor me!

pecadora, *n.f.* (*coll.*) prostitute.

pecadorazo, -za, *n.m.f.* great sinner.

pecaminoso, -sa, *a.* sinful.

pecante, *a.* peccant; excessive.

pecar, *v.i.* (*pret.* **pequé;** *pres. subj.* **peque**) to sin; to be wanting in what is right; to violate laws, commit excesses; to brag, boast; to have a strong propensity; (*med.*) predominate; to deserve or occasion punishment; *darle por donde peca,* to reproach one with an undeniable fault.

pece, *n.f.* clay for making mud walls; ridge between furrows; *el pece, para quien lo merece,* let the best man have the prize.

pececico, -illo, -ito, *n.m.* small fish.

peceño, -ña, *a.* pitch-coloured (said of horses); tasting of pitch.

pecera, *n.f.* fish bowl; aquarium.

pecezuela, *n.f.* small piece.

pecezuelo, *n.m.* small foot; small fish.

peciento, -ta, *a.* of a pitchy colour.

peciluengo, -ga, *a.* long-stalked (fruit).

pecina, *n.f.* piscina; slime.

pecinal, *n.m.* slimy pool.

pecio, *n.m.* (*law*) jetsam, flotsam, ligan, wreckage.

pécora, *n.f.* sheep, head of sheep; (*coll.*) crafty, evil woman, cunning rogue.

pecorea, *n.f.* marauding; idle strolling, loitering.

pecorear, *v.t.* to steal cattle. — *v.i.* to loot, maraud (by soldiers).

pecoso, -sa, *a.* freckly, freckled.

pectiniforme, *a.* (*zool.*) pectiniform.

pectoral, *a.* pectoral. — *n.m.* cross worn by bishops on the breast; breastplate.

pecuario, -ria, *a.* of or pertaining to cattle.

peculado, *n.m.* peculation; peculation of public funds.

peculiar, *a.* peculiar, appropriate, special.

peculiaridad, *n.f.* peculiarity.

peculiarmente, *adv.* peculiarly.

peculio, *n.m.* stock of money; (*law*) peculium.

pecunia, *n.f.* (*coll.*) hard cash, specie.

pecuniariamente, *adv.* in ready money.

pecuniario, -ria, *a.* pecuniary.

pecha, *n.f.* (*obs.*) tax, impost, tribute.

pechada, *n.f.* (*Am.*) blow on the chest.

pechar, *v.i.* to pay taxes.

peche, *n.m.* pilgrim's shell.

pechera, *n.f.* stomacher; breast; shirt-frill; chest protector; (*saddl.*) breast strap; (*coll.*) bosom.

pechería, *n.f.* paying tax, toll or duty.

pechero, -ra, *n.m.f.* commoner, one liable to taxation.

pechero, *n.m.* bib.

pechiblanco, -ca, *a.* white-breasted.

pechico, *n.m.* small breast, teat.

pechicolorado, *n.m.* robin-redbreast.

pechigonga, *n.f.* a game of cards.

pechina, *n.f.* pilgrim's shell; (*arch.*) triangle formed by arches.

pechirrojo, *n.m.* robin-redbreast.

pechisacado, -da, *a.* haughty, arrogant.

pecho, *n.m.* breast, chest, bosom; (*anat.*) thorax; (*fig.*) valour, fortitude, courage; conscience, heart; (*mus.*) quality and power of the voice; slope, gradient; ancient tax; confidence, regard, esteem; *dar el pecho,* to suckle; *criar a los pechos,* to educate, instruct; *echarse a pechos,* to drink copiously, greedily; *echar el pecho al agua,* to undertake a risky matter with confidence; *entre pecho y espalda,* in the stomach; *hombre de pecho,* firm, spirited man; *hombre de pelo en pecho,* daring man; *no caber una cosa en el pecho,* not to be able to restrain oneself (*or* to keep silence); *pecho por el suelo* (*or* *pecho por tierra*), very humbly (*or* submissively); *tener pecho,* to be persevering, patient, firm; *poner a los pechos una pistola,* to hold one up with a pistol; *tomar a pechos,* to take to heart; *a pecho descubierto,* unarmed, defenceless.

pechuelo, *n.m.* small breast.

pechuga, *n.f.* breast of a fowl; (*coll.*) bosom.

pechugón, *n.m.* blow on the breast.

pechuguera, *n f.* cough, hoarseness.

pedacico, -illo, -ito, *n.m.* small bit, small piece; *a pedacicos,* piecemeal.

pedagogía, *n.f.* pedagogy.

pedagógico, -ca, *a.* pedagogical.

pedagogo, *n.m.* pedagogue, schoolmaster; educator; mentor.

pedaje, *n.m.* bridge-toll.

pedal, *n.m.* (*mus.*) pedal; (*mech.*) treadle, pedal.

pedáneo, *a.* (*law*) petty, inferior.

pedante, *n.m.* pedant; schoolmaster.

pedantear, *v.i.* to pedantize, play the pedant.

pedantería, *n.f.* pedantry, show of learning.

pedantesco, -ca, *a.* pedantic.

pedantismo, *n.m.* pedantry.

pedantón, *n.m.* great pedant.

pedazo, *n.m.* piece, bit, part, fragment, lump; *pedazo de alcornoque* (or *de animal*), foolish, brutish person; *pedazo del alma,* my love, my dear; *a* (or *en*) *pedazos,* in bits, in fragments; *estar hecho pedazos,* to be broken in pieces; *morirse por sus pedazos,* to languish for a person.

pedazuelo, *n.m.* small piece, small bit.

pederasta, *n.m.* pederast, sodomite.

pederastia, *n.f.* pederasty.

pedernal, *n.m.* flint; extreme hardness.

pedernalino, -na, *a.* (*poet.*) flinty, hard.

pedestal, *n.m.* pedestal, foundation; base, support.

pedestre, *a.* pedestrian; low, vulgar, common.

pediatría, *n.f.* science of children's diseases.

pedicoj, *n.m.* hopping, jumping on one foot.

pedicular, *a.* pedicular, lousy.

pedículo, *n.m.* louse; (*bot.*) peduncle; (*med.*) pedicel.

pedicuro, *n.m.* chiropodist.

pedido, *n.m.* demand, call; contribution demanded by the king; (*com.*) order.

pedidor, -ra, *n.m.f.* petitioner, craver.

pedidura, *n.m.f.* begging, craving, petitioning.

pedigón, *n.m.* craver, insatiable asker, importuner.

pedigüeño, -ña, *a.* craving, importuning.

pediluvio, *n.m.* (*med.*) pediluvium, foot-bath.

pedimento, *n.m.* petition; (*law*) claim, bill; *a pedimento de,* at the request of.

pedir, *v.t.* (*pres. indic.* **pido;** *pret.* **el pidió;** *pres. subj.* **pida**) to petition, beg, solicit, supplicate; ask, ask for; crave, demand, call for, claim, inquire after, wish for; *pedir cuentas,* to ask for the accounts; *pedir cuenta a,* to call to account; *pedir limosna,* to beg, ask alms; *a pedir de boca,* adequately, according to desire; *pedírselo a uno el cuerpo,* to long for; *pedir justicia* (or *en juicio*), to bring an action against; *pedir sobrado por salir con lo mediado,* ask for twice as much as you expect to get; *pedir la palabra,* to ask for the floor, ask leave to speak (in debates, etc.).

pedo, *n.m.* (*vulg.*) fart; *pedo de lobo,* (*bot.*) puff-ball.

pedómetro, *n.m.* pedometer.

pedorrear, *v.i.* to discharge wind; (*fig.*) to sing very badly.

pedorreras, *n.f.* kind of light breeches; flatulency.

pedorrero, -ra; pedorro, -rra, *a.* flatulent.

pedorreta, *n.f.* (*slang*) raspberry.

pedrada, *n.f.* blow, cast, throw, or casting of a stone; lapidation; cockade bow; smart repartee, taunt, sneer; *como pedrada en ojo de boticario,* apropos, fitting.

pedrea, *n.f.* lapidation, stone-throwing; hail-storm.

pedrecita, *n.f.* small stone.

pedregal, *n.m.* stony place or ground.

pedregoso, -sa, *a.* stony, abounding in stones; (*med.*) afflicted with the gravel.

pedrejón, *n.m.* large, loose stone.

pedreñal, *n.m.* blunderbuss, firelock.

pedrera, *n.f.* quarry, stone-pit.

pedrería, *n.f.* collection of jewels.

pedrero, *n.m.* stone-cutter; (*artill.*) stone mortar; slinger; lapidary; (*prov.*) foundling.

pedrezuela, *n.f.* small stone.

pedriscal, *n.m.* stony place.

pedrisco, *n.m.* hailstone; shower of stones; heap of loose stones.

pedriza, *n.f.* quarry; heap of loose stones.

pedro, *n.m.* (*slang*) kind of rough dress, night burglar's dress; (*slang*) lock; Peter, a proper name; *como Pedro por su casa,* with entire freedom (or plainness).

pedrojiménez, *n.m.* a kind of grape from Jerez; wine made with these grapes.

pedrusco, *n.m.* (*coll.*) rough piece of stone.

pedunculado, -da, *a.* (*bot.*) peduncled.

pedunculillo, *n.m.* pedicel.

pedúnculo, *n.m.* peduncle.

peer, *v.i.* to break wind.

pega, *n.f.* art of cementing or joining; pitch, varnish; leather tanning; (*min.*) firing of a blast; jest, joke, trick, sham; (*orn.*) magpie; (*ichth.*) remora; *ser de la pega,* to be one of the gang; *saber a la pega,* to develop bad habits; *pega de patadas,* a good kicking.

pegadillo, *n.m.* little patch, sticking-plaster; (*coll.*) bore, nuisance.

pegadizo, -za, *a.* clammy, glutinous, viscous; contagious, catching; clinging, importunate.

pegado, *n.m.* patch, sticking-plaster, cataplasm.

pegador, -ra, *n.m.f.* bill-sticker, paper-hanger; (*min.*) blaster.

pegadura, *n.f.* pitching, daubing with pitch; sticking to.

pegajoso, -sa, *a.* sticky, glutinous; catching, contagious; adhesive; attractive, alluring.

pegamiento, *n.m.* act of cementing.

pegante, *a.* viscous, glutinous.

pegar, *v.t.* (*pret.* **pegué;** *pres. subj.* **pegue**) to join, close, unite; to clap on; to dash violently together; to punish, beat, chastise; to infect, communicate a disease. — *v.i.* to root, take root (of plants); to make an impression on the mind; to catch (fire); to communicate (vices, habits, etc.); to cleave, cling; to join, be contiguous; to say or do something disagreeable; to begin to take effect. — *v.r.* to intrude; to adhere, stick; to insinuate, steal upon the mind, to be affected with (a passion); *pegar un petardo,* to borrow money and not return it; *pegar fuego,* to set fire; *pegar la boca a la pared,* to keep one's sorrow to oneself; *no pegar los ojos,* not to sleep; *pegar mangas,* to intermeddle; *pegar tumbos,* (*naut.*) to founder; *no pega,* (*coll.*) it is an absurdity.

pegáseo, -sea, *a.* (*poet.*) belonging to Pegasus.

Pegásides, *n.f.pl.* the Muses.

Pegaso, *n.m.* (*myth., astron.*) Pegasus.

pegata, *n.f.* (*coll.*) trick, fraud, imposition.

pegatista, *n.m.* sponger, indigent person.

pegmatita, *n.f.* (*min.*) pegmatite.

pego, *n.m.* trick, fraudulent card-game.

pegollo, *n.m.* (*prov.*) pillar, post.
pegote, *n.m.* plaster made of pitch; coarse patch; fricassee with thick sauce; sponger, toady, sycophant.
pegotear, *v.i.* (*coll., fig.*) to sponge.
pegual, *n.m.* (*Am.*) strap with rings.
peguera, *n.f.* pit where pinewood is burnt to obtain pitch; place where sheep are marked with pitch.
peguero, *n.m.* one who makes or deals in pitch.
pegujal, pegujar, *n.m.* peculium; small dead or live stock.
pegujalero, pegujarero, *n.m.* small farmer, grazier.
pegujón, *n.m.* pellet or ball of wool or hair.
pegunta, *n.f.* mark on cattle, sheep, etc.
peguntar, *v.t.* to mark cattle, etc. with pitch.
peinada, *n.f.* combing, dressing hair.
peinado, -da, *a.* combed, curled, dressed.
peinado, *n.m.* hair dressed, combed and curled; effeminate, dressy person.
peinador, *n.m.* hairdresser; combing-gown, hairdresser's cloth or sheet.
peinadura, *n.f.* act of combing the hair; combing, hair pulled out with a comb.
peinar, *v.t.* to comb, dress the hair; to comb wool; to rub slightly, touch; to excavate, eat away (a rock); (*poet.*) to move, divide gently, skim; to correct (the style); *no peinar canas,* to be young; *no peinarse (una mujer) para uno,* not to be for the man who wants her.
peinazo, *n.m.* cross-piece of a door or window-frame.
peine, *n.m.* comb; hemp-comb; weaver's reed; comb of the loom; wool-card; rack; *a sobre peine,* slightly imperfect.
peinería, *n.f.* comb-shop, comb-factory.
peinero, -ra, *n.m.f.* comb-maker, comb-seller.
peineta, *n.f.* large curved comb.
peje, *n.m.* fish; crafty fellow; *peje araña,* (*ichth.*) stingbull; *peje diablo,* (*ichth.*) grouper.
pejegallo, *n.m.* large fish from Chile.
pejemuller, *n.f.* mermaid.
pejepalo, *n.m.* stockfish.
pejerrey, *n.m.* a variety of mackerel.
pejesapo, *n.m.* toad-fish.
pejiguera, *n.f.* (*coll.*) difficulty, embarrassment; too much ado about nothing.
pel, *n.f.* (*obs.*) hide, pelt, skin.
pela, *n.f.* peeling; shelling; plucking.
pelada, *n.f.* pelt, stripped skin of a sheep; (*med.*) pelada.
peladera, *n.f.* shedding of the hair; (*med.*) alopecia.
peladero, *n.m.* scalding-house, scalding-vessel; (*fig., coll.*) sharper's den; (*Am.*) barren spot.
peladilla, *n.f.* sugared almond; small pebble, whitish stone.
peladillo, *n.m.* clingstone peach (fruit and tree). — *pl.* **peladillos,** wool.
pelado, -da, *a.* plumed, bared, decorticated; hairless; shrubless fields or mountains; *letra pelada,* clearly formed letter; *ser un pelado,* to be a nobody. — *n.m.* penniless person.
pelador, *n.m.* plucker.
peladura, *n.f.* plucking, decortication.
pelafustán, pelagallos, pelagatos, *n.m.* ragamuffin, vagabond; vagrant.
pelágico, -ca, *a.* pelagic.
pelagra, *n.f.* pellagra, a cutaneous disease.
pelaire, *n.m.* wool-dresser.

pelairía, *n.f.* wool-comber's trade.
pelaje, *n.m.* nature and quality of hair and wool; quality of clothes; (*fig.*) character, disposition.
pelambrar, *v.t.* to flesh hides.
pelambre, *n.m.* hides put into lime-pits; want of hair.
pelambrera, *n.f.* quantity of hair; shedding of hair; place where hides are macerated in lime-pits.
pelambrero, *n.m.* tanner.
pelamesa, *n.f.* scuffle in which hair is torn out; shock-head of hair.
pelámide, *n.f.* young brood of tunny-fish.
pelandusca, *n.f.* strumpet.
pelantrín, *n.m.* small farmer.
pelar, *v.t.* to pull out the hair, pluck or strip the feathers; to divest of bark, shell; to blanch, boil, scald; to rob, fleece; *duro de pelar,* difficult to achieve. — *v.r.* to shed or cast the hair; *pelárselas,* to desire or execute a thing with vigour and efficiency; *pelarse de fino,* to be very cunning.
pelarruecas, *n.f.* poor woman who lives by spinning.
pelásgico, -ca, *a.* Pelasgic.
pelasgo, -ga, *n.m.f., a.* Pelasgian.
pelaza, *n.f.* chopped or beaten straw; quarrel, affray; caterwauling; *dejar a uno en la pelaza,* to leave one in the lurch.
pelazga, *n.f.* quarrel, scuffle.
peldaño, *n.m.* single step of a flight of stairs.
pelea, *n.f.* battle, engagement, fight, quarrel, conflict, dispute; struggle, toil, fatigue.
peleador, *n.m.* fighter, combatant.
peleante, *a.* combating, fighting.
pelear, *v.t.* to fight, combat, quarrel, dispute, contend, toil, labour. — *v.r.* to scuffle, come to blows; *pelear hasta con los dientes,* to fight tooth and nail.
pelechar, *v.t.* to grow a new coat (of hair or feathers); to fledge, shed feathers; (*coll.*) to improve one's fortune or health.
pelele, *n.m.* scarecrow; stuffed figure; (*fig.*) insignificant man.
pelendengue, *n.m.* frivolous foppery.
peleón, *n.m., a.* strong, common wine.
peleona, *n.f.* quarrel, scuffle, dispute.
pelete, *n.m.* one who punts (at cards); poor man; *en pelete,* nakedly.
peletería, *n.f.* trade of furrier or skinner; (*Cub.*) leather goods, and shop; fellmonger.
peletero, *n.m.* currier, skin-dealer.
pelgar, *n.m.* ragamuffin, blackguard.
peliagudo, -da, *a.* downy, furry; (*coll.*) arduous; ingenious, skilful, dexterous.
peliblanco, -ca, *a.* having white hair.
peliblando, -da, *a.* having soft, fine hair.
pelicabra, *n.f.* satyr.
pelícano, *n.m.* pelican.
pelicano, -na, *a.* grey-haired, hoary.
pelicorto, -ta, *a.* short-haired.
película, *n.f.* pellicle; photographic or cinematographic film.
pelicular, *a.* pellicular, in the form of a pellicle.
peliforra, *n.f.* (*coll.*) harlot, whore.
peligrar, *v.i.* to be in danger, peril or risk.
peligro, *n.m.* danger, risk, hazard, jeopardy, peril; *correr peligro,* to be in peril.
peligrosamente, *adv.* perilously, hazardously, dangerously.

peligroso, -sa, *a.* dangerous, perilous, hazardous.

pelilargo, -ga, *a.* long-haired.

pelillo, *n.m.* short tender hair; trifle, slight trouble; *pelillos a la mar,* honour bright; *echar pelillos a la mar,* not to bear malice; *no tener pelillos en la lengua,* to speak out one's mind; *reparar en pelillos,* to take offence at trifles.

pelilloso, -sa, *a.* cavilling.

pelinegro, -gra, *a.* black-haired.

pelirrojo, -ja, *a.* red-haired, red-skinned.

pelirrubio, -bia, *a.* fair-haired, flaxen-haired.

pelitieso, -sa, *a.* with strong, bushy hair.

pelitre, *n.m.* (*bot.*) pellitory of Spain.

pelitrique, *n.m.* trifle, fiddling matter.

pelmacería, *n.f.* heaviness, slowness.

pelmazo, *n.m.* anything squashed flat; food lying heavy on the stomach; (*fig.*) slow, heavy person.

pelo, *n.m.* hair, down, soft fibre, slender thread; hair's breadth; pubescence (of fruit); nap, pile (of cloth); (*com.*) raw silk; grain in wood; colour of animal's coat; hair-spring of a watch or fire-arms; flaw in a jewel or crystal; split in metal, horse's hoof, etc.; abscess in a woman's breast; splinter; trifle; kiss (in billiards); *contra pelo* (or *a contrapelo*), against the grain, unseasonable; *al* (or *a*) *pelo,* timely, to the purpose; *a medios pelos,* to be half-seas over; *del lobo un pelo y ése de la frente,* take anything you can get from a miser; *de pelo en pecho,* strong, robust, courageous; *en pelo,* barebacked, naked; *estar con el pelo de la dehesa,* to be boorish, clownish; *largo como pelo de huevo,* wretched, sordid, mean; *gente de pelo,* rich people; *ser capaz de contarle los pelos al diablo,* he is capable of finding out anything; *pelo arriba,* against the grain; *no tener pelo de tonto,* to be bright, clever, quick; *tener pelos en el corazón,* to be courageous and energetic; *ser de buen pelo,* (*iron.*) to be ill-disposed; *venir a pelo,* to come to the point; *tener pelos,* to be intricate; *tomar el pelo,* to make fun of, pull one's leg.

pelón, -ona, *a.* (*coll.*) hairless, bald. — *n.m.f.* poor, needy man or woman.

pelona, pelonía, *n.f.* baldness.

pelonería, *n.f.* (*coll.*) poverty, indigence, want.

peloponense, *a.* Peloponnesian.

pelosilla, *n.f.* (*bot.*) hawkweed, mouse-ear.

peloso, -sa, *a.* hairy.

pelota, *n.f.* ball; cannon ball; anything round; ball game; (*Am.*) punt made of leather; *juego de pelota,* game of *pelota* (a kind of racquets); *jugar a la pelota con alguno,* to send someone on a fruitless errand; *sacar pelotas de una alcuza,* to be very ingenious; *rechazar la pelota,* to rebut a charge; *no tocar pelota,* not to get at the root of a difficulty; *en pelota,* quite naked; (*coll.*) penniless.

pelotari, *n.m.f.* professional player of *pelota.*

pelotazo, *n.m.* blow or stroke with a ball.

pelote, *n.m.* goat's hair.

pelotear, *v.i.* to play at ball; to argue, dispute; (*Am.*) to cross a river with the leather-punt. — *v.t.* to examine (an account). — *v.r.* to quarrel, dispute; to snowball one another.

pelotera, *n.f.* quarrel, battle, dispute, contention.

pelotería, *n.f.* heap of balls; heap of goat's hair.

pelotero, *n.m.* ball-maker.

pelotilla, *n.f.* small ball; small ball of wax and pieces of glass fastened to a scourge; *hacer pelotillas,* to pick the nose.

pelotón, *n.m.* large ball; tight bundle of hair; (*mil.*) platoon; small crowd of people.

pelta, *n.f.* ancient buckler.

peltiforme, *a.* shield-shaped.

peltre, *n.m.* pewter.

peltrero, *n.m.* pewterer, pewter-worker.

pelú, *n.m.* (*Chi.*) a leguminous tree with hard rich wood.

peluca, *n.f.* wig, periwig, peruke; (*coll.*) very severe reproof.

pelucón, *n.m.,* large bushy wig.

pelucona, *n.f.* (*coll.*) double doubloon.

peludo, -da, *a.* hairy, hirsute, covered with hair.

peludo, *n.m.* oval bass-mat; (*River Plate*) armadillo.

peluquera, *n.f.* hair-cutter's wife; female wig-maker; hairdresser.

peluquería, *n.f.* hairdresser's establishment.

peluquero, *n.m.* wig-maker; hairdresser, hair-cutter.

peluquín, *n.m.* bag-wig, top-wig.

pelusa, *n.f.* down of fruit or plants; floss, fuz, nap; *gente de pelusa,* (*joc.*) the wealthy.

pella, *n.f.* pellet, ball; parcel; mass of crude ore; fleece; lump; lard (of pigs); head of cauliflower; unpaid loan; lump of amalgamated silver; (*orn.*) heron.

pellada, *n.f.* pat, dab, gentle blow; trowelful; *no dar pellada en una cosa,* to hold up something.

pelleja, *n.f.* animal's hide or skin; (*fig.*) strumpet.

pellejería, *n.f.* house, shop, street or district where skins are dressed and sold.

pellejero, *n.m.* fellmonger, leather dresser, skinner.

pellejina, *n.f.* small skin.

pellejo, *n.m.* skin, hide, pelt; rind of fruit; (*joc.*) tippler, drunkard; *pagar con el pellejo,* to pay the penalty with one's life; *no caber en el pellejo,* to be very fat; *mudar el pellejo,* to change manners and customs; *no quisiera estar en su pellejo,* I wouldn't be in his shoes.

pellejudo, -da, *a.* having a great quantity of skin.

pellejuela, *n.f.* small hide or skin.

pellejuelo, *n.m.* small skin.

pelleta, *n.f.* skin, hide.

pellica, *n.f.* coverlet of fine furs; small dressed skin.

pellico, *n.m.* shepherd's jacket; dress made of skins or furs.

pelliza, *n.f.* pelisse, fur-cloak; (*mil.*) dolman.

pellizcar, *v.t.* (*pret.* **pellizqué**; *subj.* **pellizque**) to pinch, squeeze, grip, wound artfully; to pilfer; to take very little food. — *v.r.* to prick oneself; to long for anything.

pellizco, *n.m.* pinch, nip, small bit or piece; act of pinching; remorse, disquietude; *pellizco de monja,* lozenge, sugar-plum or cookie.

pello, *n.m.* fine fur jacket.

pellón, pellote, *n.m.* long robe of skin or fur; (*Am.*) fur riding-cloak.

pelluzgón, *n.m.* handful of hair or wool; *tener la barba a pelluzgones,* to have an uneven beard.

pena, *n.f.* punishment, penalty, chastisement, correction; pain, affliction, grief, sorrow, trouble; uneasiness, anxiety; hardship, difficulty, labour, toil; necklace; (*obs.*) pen feather, quill feather; *a duras penas,* with great difficulty, scarcely, hardly; *ni pena ni gloria,* without pain or pleasure; indifferently; *pasar la pena negra,* to suffer greatly; *valer la pena,* to be worth the trouble; *pasar las penas del purgatorio,* to be in terrible and continual trouble.

penable, *a.* punishable.

penachera, *n.f.* tuft, plume, ornament.

penacho, *n.m.* tuft on birds' heads; plume, ornament of feathers; (*fig.*) presumption, loftiness, haughtiness, pride.

penachudo, -da, *a.* crested, tufted, plumed.

penadamente, *adv.* painfully.

penadilla, *n.f.* narrow-mouthed vessel; blister, pustule.

penado, -da, *a.* punished, chastised, suffered; painful; narrow-mouthed (of vessels).

penal, *a.* penal, judicial.

penalidad, *n.f.* suffering; calamity, trouble, hardship; (*law*) penalty.

péname, *n.m.* (*prov.*) condolence.

penante, *a.* suffering; love-sick, love-lorn; difficult, arduous, laborious. — *n.m.* lover, gallant.

penar, *v.i.* to suffer pain; to agonize, crave; to linger. — *v.t.* to chastise, punish. — *v.r.* to mourn, grieve.

penates, *n.m.pl.* penates, household gods.

penca, *n.f.* fleshy leaf or joint of some plants; cowhide for flogging criminals; *hacerse de pencas,* not to give what is asked.

pencazo, *n.m.* lash with a cowhide.

penco, *n.m.* (*coll.*) raw-boned horse, jade, sorry nag.

pencudo, -da, *a.* with pulpy leaves or joints.

pendanga, *n.f.* (*coll.*) common prostitute.

pendejo, *n.m.* short hairs over the groin, etc.; (*fam.*) coward; (*Am.*) (*coll.*) fool.

pendencia, *n.f.* quarrel, affray, dispute, feud, jangling, contention.

pendenciar, *v.i.* to wrangle, quarrel.

pendenciero, -ra, *a.* quarrelsome, wrangling.

pender, *v.i.* to hang, dangle; depend; be pending.

pendiente, *a.* pendent, hanging; clinging; pending; *cuenta pendiente,* (*com.*) unsettled account. — *n.m.* ear-ring, pendant. — *n.f.* declivity, slope; grade, gradient; dip or pitch.

pendil, *n.m.* mantle worn by women; *tomar el pendil,* to go away, disappear.

pendingue, *n.m.* French leave.

pendol, *n.m.* (*naut.*) boot-topping.

péndola, *n.f.* pen; pendulum.

pendolaje, *n.m.* plunder of a captured vessel.

pendolero, -ra, *a.* hanging, pendent.

pendolista, *n.m.* penman.

pendón, *n.m.* standard, banner; (*bot.*) tiller, shoot; (*her.*) pennon; (*coll.*) tall, awkward woman. — *pl.* **pendones,** reins of the leading mule; *a pendón herido,* with all speed and diligence.

pendoncito, *n.m.* small pennon.

pendonista, *n.m.f., a.* standard bearer (in a procession).

péndulo, -la, *a.* pendent, hanging, pendulous.

péndulo, *n.m.* pendulum; *péndulo sidéreo,* standard clock, chronometer.

pene, *n.m.* penis.

peneque, *n.m.* (*coll.*) drunkard.

penetrabilidad, *n.f.* penetrability.

penetrable, *a.* penetrable.

penetración, *n.f.* penetration, acuteness, sagacity, intelligence.

penetrador, *n.m.* discerner.

penetral, *a.* (*poet.*) interior part, innermost recess.

penetrante, *a.* penetrating, penetrant; heart-rending; clear-sighted, keen.

penetrar, *v.t.* to penetrate, pierce; pass through, to force in; to permeate; to fathom, comprehend.

penetrativo, -va, *a.* penetrative, penetrant.

penígero, -ra, *a.* (*poet.*) winged, feathered.

península, *n.f.* peninsula.

peninsular, *a.* peninsular.

penique, *n.m.* penny.

penisla, *n.f.* peninsula.

penitencia, *n.f.* penance, penitence, penalty, mulct, fine; *hacer penitencia,* (*coll.*) to take pot-luck.

penitenciado, -da, *a.* punished. — *n.m.f.* convict sentenced by the Inquisition.

penitencial, *a.* penitential.

penitenciar, *v.t.* to impose a penance.

penitenciaría, *n.f.* penitentiary (tribunal).

penitenciario, *n.m.* penitentiary.

penitenta, *n.f.* female penitent.

penitente, *n.m.f., a.* penitent, repentant, contrite.

penol, *n.m.* yard-arm.

penosamente, *adv.* painfully, grievously.

penoso, -sa, *a.* painful, grievous, laborious, tormenting, distressing.

penoso, *n.m.* affected creature, fop.

pensado, -da, *a.* deliberate, premeditated; *de pensado* (or *de caso pensado*), on purpose, designedly; *bien pensado,* wise, proper; *mal pensado,* unwise, foolish.

pensador, -ra, *n.m.f.* thinker. — *a.* thoughtful, meditative.

pensamiento, *n.m.* mind, thought, idea; meditation, contemplation, cogitation, design; resolution; promptitude, swiftness; suspicion, surmise; project, scheme, plan; (*art*) first sketch or outline; (*bot.*) heartsease, pansy; *ni por pensamiento,* not even a thought of it; *en un pensamiento,* in a trice; *encontrarse en los pensamientos,* said of two people who think of the same thing at once.

pensar, *v.t., v.i.* (*pres. indic.* **pienso;** *pres. subj.* **piense**) to think, consider, imagine, fancy, muse, cogitate, reflect, meditate; to mean, intend; to weigh maturely; to feed cattle; *sin pensar,* unexpectedly, thoughtlessly; *pensar en lo excusado,* to attempt something impossible; *uno piensa el bayo, otro quien le ensilla,* the bay thinks one thing, but the person who saddles him thinks another.

pensativamente, *adv.* pensively, thoughtfully, moodily.

pensativo, -va, *a.* pensive, thoughtful, cogitative, ruminative.

penseque, *n.m.* careless or thoughtless error.

pensil, *a.* pensile, hanging. — *n.m.* lovely garden.

pensilvano, -na, *a. & n.* Pennsylvanian.

pensión, *n.f.* pension, annuity, scholarship, reward, gift of money; boarding-house, small hotel; board; labour, toil; encumbrance, trouble, painful duty.

pensionado, -da, *n.m.f.* pensioner, pensionary, scholarship-holder.

pensionar, *v.t.* to confer a pension, award; a grant of money; to impose annual charges.

pensionario, *n.m.* pensionary; city recorder.

pensionista, *n.m.f.* pensioner; boarder.

pentacordio, *n.m.* pentachord.

pentadecágono, *n.m.,* *a.* pentadecagon, fifteen-sided polygon.

pentaedro, *n.m.* pentahedron.

pentagloto, -ta, *a.* written in five languages.

pentagonal, *a.* pentagonal.

pentágono, *n.m.* pentagon.

pentagrama, *n.m.* musical staff.

pentámetro, *n.m.* pentameter.

pentasílabo, -ba, *a.* five-syllabled.

pentateuco, *n.m.* Pentateuch.

pentecostés, *n.m.* Whitsuntide.

penúltimo, -ma, *a.* penultimate.

penumbra, *n.f.* penumbra.

penuria, *n.f.* penury, poverty, indigence, need.

peña, *n.f.* rock, large stone; body of friends; club; *por peñas,* a long time.

peñascal, *n.m.* rocky hill or mountain.

peñasco, *n.m.* large rock; strong silk stuff.

peñascoso, -sa, *a.* rocky, mountainous.

peñol, *n.m.* (*obs.*) large rock.

peñol, *n.m.* yard-arm; (*obs.*) large rock.

péñola, *n.f.* (*poet.*) pen.

peñón, *n.m.* large rock, rocky mountain.

peón, *n.m.* pedestrian; day-labourer; hodman; metrical foot of four syllables; footsoldier; gig, top, spinning-top, humming top; pawn (in chess), piece (in draughts); (*mech.*) spindle, axle.

peonada, *n.f.* labourer's day's work; gang of labourers.

peonaje, *n.m.* crowd of people on foot; party of day-labourers.

peonería, *n.f.* day's ploughing.

peonía, *n.f.* peony; (*mil.*) land given to a soldier.

peonza, *n.f.* top, whipping-top, gig; noisy little fellow; *a peonza,* (*coll.*) on foot.

peor, *a.,* *adv. comp.* of MALO and MAL, worse; *peor que peor,* worse and worse; *tanto peor,* so much the worse.

peoría, *n.f.* detriment, deterioration.

peormente, *adv.* worse.

pepinar, *n.m.* cucumber-field.

pepinillos, *n.m.pl.* gherkins, pickled cucumbers.

pepino, *n.m.* cucumber; *no dársele un pepino,* not to give a straw for something.

pepita, *n.f.* seed of fruit; pip, distemper (in fowls); grain of pure gold; *no tener pepita,* not to mince matters.

pepitoria, *n.f.* fricassee of giblets, livers and lights; medley; (*Mex.*) peanut butter.

pepitoso, -sa, *a.* abounding in grains or seeds; having the pip (of fowls).

peplo, *n.m.* peplum.

pepón, *n.m.* water-melon.

pepona, *n.f.* large paper doll.

pepónide, *n.f.* pepo (melon, pumpkin, etc.).

pepsina, *n.f.* pepsin.

peptona, *n.f.* peptone.

pequén, *n.m.* (*Chi.*) a bird of prey.

pequeñamente, *adv.* little, in a small quantity or degree; not much.

pequeñez, *n.f.* smallness of size, littleness, minuteness; youth, tender age; trifle, trifling matter; lowness of mind, pusillanimity.

pequeño, -ña, *a.* little, small, minute; young, of tender age; (*fig.*) abject, humble, low-spirited.

pequeñuelo, -la, *a.* very little or young. — *n.m.f.* babe, infant.

pequín, *n.m.* Chinese silk stuff.

pera, *n.f.* pear; small tuft of hair on the chin; (*coll.*) sinecure; *dar para peras,* to threaten to strike; *escoger como entre peras,* to choose very carefully; *pedir peras al olmo,* to expect the impossible; *partir peras con alguno,* to treat someone familiarly; *poner las peras a cuarto* (or *a ocho*), to make one act against his will.

perada, *n.f.* pear-juice conserve, pear jam.

peraile, *n.m.* (*obs.*) wool-comber.

peral, *n.m.* (*bot.*) pear-tree.

peraleda, *n.f.* pear-orchard.

peralejo, *n.m.* (*bot.*) kind of white poplar.

peraltar, *v.t.* (*arch.*) to stilt an arch or vault; (*railw.*) to raise, elevate.

peralte, *n.m.* super-elevation of the outer rail in a curve.

perantón, *n.m.* (*bot.*) marvel-plant; (*fig.*) very tall person.

peraza, *n.f.* fruit of an engrafted pear-tree.

perca, *n.f.* (*ichth.*) perch.

percal, *n.m.* percale.

percalina, *n.f.* glazed calico; book muslin.

percance, *n.m.* perquisite; mischance, misfortune.

percarburo, *n.m.* (*chem.*) percarbide.

percatar, *v.i., v.r.* to think, consider carefully, take care, be on one's guard.

percebe, *n.m.* goose barnacle.

percepción, *n.f.* perception, notion, feeling, idea.

perceptibilidad, *n.f.* perceptibility.

perceptibile, *a.* perceptible, perceivable.

perceptiblemente, *adv.* perceivably, perceptibly.

perceptivo, -va, *a.* perceptive.

percibir, *v.t.* to perceive; to comprehend; to receive, collect.

percibo, *n.m.* act of perceiving or receiving.

perclorato, *n.m.* perchlorate.

perclórico, -ca, *a.* perchloric.

percloruro, *n.m.* perchloride.

percocería, *n.f.* filigree or silver work.

percuciente, *a.* percutient, striking.

percudir, *v.t.* to tarnish, stain, soil.

percusión, *n.f.* percussion, collision.

percusor, *n.m.* striker, one who strikes; (*artill.*) percussion hammer.

percutir, *v.t.* to percuss, strike, beat.

percha, *n.f.* perch, pole, staff; snare for catching partridges; fowler's string; coat-hanger; hat-rack; (*naut.*) spar, rough tree; head rail; (*ichth.*) perch; *estar en percha,* (*fig.*) to be in the bag.

perchador, -ra, *n.m.f.* napper, one raising nap on cloth.

perchar, *v.t.* to raise the nap on cloth.

perchón, *n.m.* principal vine-shoot.

perchonar, *v.i.* to leave several important shoots on a vine-stock; to lay snares for catching game.

perdedero, *n.m.* occasion or motive of losing.

perdedor, -ra, *n.m.f.* loser.

perder, *v.t.* (*pres. indic.* **pierdo;** *pres. subj.* **pierda**) to lose, forfeit, squander, lavish, misspend, miss, ruin, spoil, mar, damage; to let slip (an opportunity); to wager, bet; to fall (of the tide). — *v.i.* to lose; to fade, lose colour. — *v.r.* to go astray, be lost, be spoiled, to be shipwrecked; *perder el habla,* to become speechless; *perder los estribos,* to lose patience; *perder cuidado,* to set one's mind at rest; *perder terreno,* to lose ground; *tener qué perder,* to be a person of credit, to be able to afford to lose; *no pierde por delgado sino gordo y mal hilado,* quality is more important than size or quantity; *de la mano a la boca se pierde la sopa,* there's many a slip 'twixt cup and lip; *no se perderá,* said of an intelligent person who lets no chance pass; *perderse de risa,* to be convulsed with laughter; *perderse de vista,* to surpass oneself; *lo que hoy se pierde se gana mañana,* what's lost to-day may be won to-morrow.

perdición, *n.f.* perdition, destruction; eternal death, damnation; ruin, loss; excessive love; prodigality, extravagance.

pérdida, *n.f.* losing; loss, damage, privation, detriment, waste; *de pérdida,* in a perilous manner.

perdidamente, *adv.* desperately.

perdidizo, -za, *a.* lost designedly or on purpose; *hacerse perdidizo,* to lose (at cards) intentionally; *hacerse el perdidizo,* to sneak away, disappear.

perdido, -da, *a.* lost, strayed; misguided; dissolute, profligate; *mujer perdida,* prostitute; *pan perdido,* vagrant; *perdido por uno, perdido por todo,* in for a penny, in for a pound; *perdido por,* passionately in love, crazy.

perdidoso, -sa, *a.* sustaining loss.

perdigana, *n.f.* young partridge.

perdigar, *v.t.* (conjugated like APAGAR) to broil partridges slightly; to brown meat; to dispose, prepare.

perdigón, *n.m.* young partridge; decoy partridge; shot; squanderer, reckless gambler. — *pl.* **perdigones,** small shot, hail-shot.

perdigonada, *n.f.* shot or wound with bird shot.

perdigonera, *n.f.* shot pouch.

perdiguero, -ra, *a.* setting, pointing (of a dog).

perdiguero, *n.m.* poulterer, partridge-dealer.

perdimiento, *n.m.* loss.

perdiz, *n.m.* partridge; *perdiz o no comerla,* neck or nothing; *perdices en campo raso,* things hard to obtain.

perdón, *n.m.* pardon, forgiveness; absolution, mercy, grace; remission; drop of hot oil, wax, etc.; *con perdón,* under your favour, by your leave.

perdonable, *a.* pardonable, forgivable.

perdonador, *n.m.* pardoner, excuser.

perdonar, *v.t.* to forgive, pardon; to spare, exempt, excuse; to remit (a debt); *perdone Vd.* (or *perdone*), excuse me.

perdonavidas, *n.m.* (*coll.*) bully, hector.

perdulario, -ria, *a.* careless of one's interest; licentious, vicious.

perdurable, *a.* perpetual, continual, everlasting.

perdurablemente, *adv.* perpetually, eternally.

perdurar, *v.i.* to last long.

perecear, *v.t.* to protract, delay, put off.

perecedero, -ra, *a.* perishable, decaying, fading.

perecedero, *n.m.* great want, misery.

perecer, *v.i.* (*pres. indic.* **perezco;** *pres. subj.* **perezca**) to perish, die, be destroyed; to suffer damage, harm, fatigue; to be extremely poor. — *v.r.* to crave, desire greatly, to be greatly moved, to die of love; *perecer(se) de risa,* to be convulsed with laughter.

perecido, -da, *a.* dying with anxiety; lost, undone. — *p.p.* [PERECER].

pereciente, *a.* perishing.

perecimiento, *n.m.* decay, decline, loss; shipwreck.

pereda, *n.f.* orchard of pear trees.

peregrina, *n.f.* (*Cub.*) a shrub of the Euphorbia genus.

peregrinación, *n.f.* peregrination, pilgrimage; course of life.

peregrinaje, *n.m.* pilgrimage.

peregrinamente, *adv.* rarely, curiously.

peregrinante, *a.* sojourning, travelling.

peregrinar, *v.i.* to peregrinate, go on a pilgrimage; to exist in this mortal life.

peregrinidad, *n.f.* strangeness, wonderfulness.

peregrino, -na, *a.* peregrine, foreign; migratory, going on a pilgrimage; strange, wonderful; handsome, perfect.

peregrino, *n.m.* pilgrim, palmer.

perejil, *n.m.* parsley; (*fig.*) showy apparel.

perejila, *n.f.* a card game.

perejilón, *n.m.* creeping crowfoot.

perendeca, *n.f.* low wench, hussy, whore.

perendengues, *n.m.pl.* ear-pendants; women's gaudy dress; small coin minted by Philip IV.

perengano, -na, *n.m.f.* so-and-so.

perennal, *a.* perennial, perpetual.

perenne, *a.* perennial, perpetual.

perennemente, perennalmente, *adv.* perennially, perpetually.

perennidad, *n.f.* continuity, perenniality.

perentoriamente, *adv.* peremptorily.

perentoriedad, *n.f.* peremptoriness; great urgency.

perentorio, -ria, *a.* peremptory, decisive, absolute; urgent.

perero, *n.m.* fruit-parer.

pereza, *n.f.* laziness, tardiness, idleness, negligence, carelessness, sloth, slowness of movement, difficulty in rising from a seat.

perezco; perezca, *pres. indic.; pres. subj.* [PERECER].

perezosamente, *adv.* lazily, slothfully, idly.

perezoso, -sa, *a.* lazy, indolent, idle, slothful. — *n.m.* (*zool.*) sloth.

perfección, *n.f.* perfection, great virtue, superior excellence, faultlessness, beauty, grace, completeness, accomplishment.

perfeccionador, *n.m.* perfecter.

perfeccionamiento, *n.m.* improving, perfecting, finishing, completion.

perfeccionar, *v.t.* to perfect, finish, heighten, complete.

perfectamente, *adv.* perfectly, completely.

perfectibilidad, *n.f.* perfectibility.

perfectivo, -va, *a.* perfective.

perfecto, -ta, *a.* perfect, complete, accomplished, accurate, consummate, faultless.

perfecto, *n.m.* perfect tense.

perficiente, *a.* that which perfects.

pérfidamente, *adv.* perfidiously.

perfidia, *n.f.* perfidy, treachery.

pérfido, -da, *a.* perfidious, treacherous, disloyal.

perfil, *n.m.* profile, outline, side-view, contour; section (of a plan); delicate tracery.

perfilado, -da, *a.* elongated; outlined; *n.m.* (*eng.*) structural shape.

perfiladura, *n.f.* art of drawing profiles, sketching of outlines.

perfilar, *v.t.* to draw profiles, sketch outlines. — *v.r.* to turn sideways; to dress in an elaborate way.

perfoliada, perfoliata, *n.f.* (*bot.*) hare's-ear.

perfoliado, -da, *a.* (*bot.*) perfoliated.

perfolla, *n.f.* (*prov.*) corn husk; shucks.

perforación, *n.f.* perforation.

perforado, -da, *a.* perforated. — *p.p.* [PER-FORAR].

perforador, -ra, *a.* perforating.

perforadora, *n.f.* drill, rock drill.

perforar, *v.t.* to perforate, pierce.

perfumadero, perfumador, *n.m.* perfumer; perfuming-pan, vessel in which perfumes are kept.

perfumar, *v.t.* to perfume, fumigate.

perfume, *n.m.* scent; perfume, fragrance, odour.

perfumería, *n.f.* perfumer's shop.

perfumero, -ra, *n.m.f.* perfumer.

perfumista, *n.m.* perfumer, dealer in perfumes.

perfunctoriamente, *adv.* perfunctorily, superficially.

perfunctorio, -ria, *a.* perfunctory.

perfusión, *n.f.* affusion, sprinkling.

pergal, *n.m.* leather paring for sandal straps.

pergaminero, *n.m.* parchment-maker.

pergamino, *n.m.* parchment, vellum; formal writing, diploma.

pergeñar, *v.t.* (*coll.*) to dispose or perform skilfully.

pergeño, *n.m.* (*coll.*) skill, dexterity.

pérgola, *n.f.* roof garden.

peri, *n.f.* (*myth.*) peri, beautiful fairy.

periancio, periantio, *n.m.* (*bot.*) perianth.

pericardio, *n.m.* (*anat.*) pericardium.

pericarpio, *n.m.* (*bot.*) pericarp.

pericia, *n.f.* skill, knowledge, practical experience.

pericial, *a.* expert.

perico, *n.m.* kind of small parrot, parakeet; woman's curls; horseman (queen) of clubs in the game of *truque*; (*naut.*) mizzen topgallant sail; large fan; *dim.* of Pedro (Peter); *¿De cuándo acá Perico con guantes?* Heavens! How unusual!; *perico de los palotes*, John Jones (any unimportant person).

pericón, -ona, *a.* fit for all uses. — *n.m.* large fan; horseman (queen) of clubs in the game of *quinolas*; (*Arg.*) quadrille dance.

pericona, *n.f.* shaft-mule.

pericote, *n.m.* (*Am.*) large field rat.

pericráneo, *n.m.* (*anat.*) pericranium.

peridoto, *n.m.* (*min.*) chrysolite.

periferia, *n.f.* periphery.

periférico, -ca, *a.* peripheric, circumferential.

perifollo, *n.m.* common chervil. — *pl.* ribbons, tawdry ornaments or dress.

perifonear, *v.t.* to broadcast music, talks or news.

perifonía, *n.f.* the art of constructing, installing or using transmitting apparatus.

perífono, *n.m.* microphone, mike.

perifrasear, *v.i.* to periphrase, use circumlocutions.

perífrasi, perífrasis, *n.f.* periphrasis.

perifrástico, -ca, *a.* periphrastic, periphrastical, round about, circumlocutory.

perigallo, *n.m.* skin hanging from the chin; kind of ribbon; (*coll.*) tall, thin man; sling; (*naut.*) navel-line; topping lift.

perigeo, *n.m.* (*astron.*) perigeum.

perigonio, *n.m.* (*bot.*) perianth.

perihelio, *n.m.* (*astron.*) perihelion.

perilustre, *a.* very illustrious.

perilla, *n.f.* small pear; pear-shaped ornament; pommel, knob; small tuft of hair on the chin; *de perilla*, to the purpose.

perillán, -ana, *a.* artful, knavish, vagrant.

perillán, *n.m.* huckster, sly fellow, clever person.

perillo, *n.m.* gingerbread nut.

perímetro, *n.m.* perimeter.

perínclito, -ta, *a.* great, famous, renowned.

perineo, *n.m.* (*anat.*) perinœum.

perinola, *n.f.* four-faced dice, teetotum; neat little woman.

períoca, *n.f.* synopsis, summary of a book.

periódicamente, *adv.* periodically.

periódico, -ca, *a.* periodic, periodical.

periódico, *n.m.* newspaper; periodical, journal

periodismo, *n.m.* journalism.

periodista, *n.m.* journalist.

periodístico, -ca, *a.* journalistic.

período, *n.m.* period, space of time; (*rhet.*) sentence, clause; (*mus.*) period, phrase; menstruation; (*elec.*) cycle.

periostio, *n.m.* (*anat.*) periosteum.

peripatético, -ca, *n.m.f.,* *a.* peripatetic; (*fig.*, *coll.*) ridiculous or extravagant opinion.

peripecia, *n.f.* peripeteia.

periplo, *n.m.* periplus, circumnavigation.

peripuesto, -ta, *a.* (*coll.*) very gay, elegant or spruce.

periquete, *n.m.* jiffy, instant, trice.

periquillo, *n.m.* sugar-plum.

periquito, *n.m.* (*naut.*) stay-sail; (*orn.*) parroquet, small parrot.

periscios, *n.m.pl.* (*geog.*) periscii.

periscópico, -ca, *a.* periscopic.

periscopio, *n.m.* periscope.

perispermo, *n.m.* (*bot.*) perisperm.

perista, *n.m.* (*slang*) fence.

peristáltico, -ca, *a.* peristaltic.

per ístam (quedarse), to be foiled *or* ignorant.

peristilo, *n.m.* (*arch.*) peristyle, colonnade.

perita, *n.f.* small pear.

perito, *m.* connoisseur, critical person, skilful workman.

perito, -ta, *a.* skilful, able, experienced.

perjudicador, -ra, *n.m.f.* injurer.

perjudicar, *v.t.* (*pret.* **perjudiqué;** *subj.* **perjudique**) to damage, hurt, injure, impair.

perjudicial, *a.* pernicious, hurtful, mischievous.

perjudicialmente, *adv.* mischievously; harmfully, injuriously.

perjuicio, *n.m.* detriment, damage, injury, mischief, grievance.

perjurador, -ra, *n.m.f.* perjurer, forswearer.

perjurar, *v.i.* to swear, swear falsely or profanely; commit perjury. — *v.r.* to perjure oneself.

perjurio, *n.m.* perjury, false swearing.

perjuro, -ra, *n.m.f.*, *a.* forswearer, perjurer; perjured, foresworn.

perla, *n.f.* pearl; (*fig.*) anything precious or bright; (*print.*) pearl. — *pl.* **perlas,** fine teeth; *de perlas,* much to the purpose, eminently fine.

perlada, *a.* pearled (barley).

perlático, -ca, *a.* paralytic, palsied.

perlería, *n.f.* collection of pearls.

perlesía, *n.f.* paralysis, palsy.

perlino, -na, *a.* (*poet.*) pearl-coloured.

perlita, *n.f.* small pearl; (*geol.*) phonolite, clinkstone.

perlongar, *v.i.* (*naut.*) to coast, sail along the coast; to pay out a cable.

permaná, *n.m.* (*Bol.*) first-class chicha (beverage made of maize).

permanecer, *v.i.* (*pres. indic.* **permanezco**; *pres. subj.* **permanezca**) to last, persist, endure; to stay, remain.

permaneciente, *a.* permanent, persisting.

permanencia, *n.f.* permanency, perseverance, duration, consistency, constancy.

permanente, *a.* permanent, lasting, durable, constant.

permanentemente, *adv.* permanently.

permeabilidad, *n.f.* permeability.

permeable, *a.* permeable.

pérmico, *a.* (*geol.*) permian.

permisible, *a.* permissible.

permisión, *n.f.* permission, concession, grant, leave.

permisivamente, *adv.* permissively.

permisivo, -va, *a.* permissive.

permiso, *n.m.* permission, leave, allowance, liberty, licence; difference in weight of coin.

permitente, *a.* that grants or permits.

permitidero, -ra, *a.* that may be permitted.

permitidor, *n.m.* permitter, granter.

permitir, *v.t.* to permit, allow, grant; to suffer, consent, agree to, give leave.

permuta, permutación, *n.f.* permutation.

permutador, *n.m.* permuter.

permutante, *a.* permutant, exchanging.

permutar, *v.t.* to permute, exchange, commute, barter.

perna, *n.f.* flat shell-fish.

pernada, *n.f.* kick, violent movement of the leg; (*naut.*) leg.

pernaza, *n.f.* thick or big leg.

perneador, *a.* strong-legged.

pernear, *v.i.* to kick, shake the legs; (*fig., coll.*) to fret, be worried or vexed. — *v.t.* (*prov.*) to sell pigs at market.

perneo, *n.m.* (*prov.*) public sale of pigs.

pernera, *n.f.* trousers leg.

pernería, *n.f.* (*naut.*) collection of pins or bolts.

pernetas (en), *adv.* bare-legged.

pernete, *n.m.* (*naut.*) small pin, bolt, or peg.

perniabierto, -ta, *a.* bandy-legged.

perniciosamente, *adv.* perniciously, hurtfully, mischievously.

pernicioso, -sa, *a.* pernicious, mischievous, destructive.

pernigón, *n.m.* Genoese preserved plum.

pernil, *n.m.* ham; leg of pork; leg of a pair of trousers.

pernio, *n.m.* door-hinge, window-hinge.

perniquebrar, *v.t.* to break the legs.

pernituerto, -ta, *a.* crook-legged.

perno, *n.m.* spike, large nail; bolt; hook of a hinge; (*mech.*) joint-pin, crank-pin.

pernoctar, *v.i.* to pass the night.

pero, *n.m.* kind of apple or apple-tree; fault, defect. — *conj.* but, yet, nevertheless.

perogrullada, *n.f.* (*coll.*) platitude of no importance; evident truth, truism.

perol, *n.m.* boiler, copper, kettle.

peroné, *n.m.* (*anat.*) fibula, perone.

peroración, *n.f.* peroration.

perorar, *v.i.* to deliver a speech or oration; to declaim; to urge.

perorata, *n.f.* harangue, speech.

peróxido, *n.m.* peroxide.

perpendicular, *n.f.*, *a.* perpendicular.

perpendicularmente, *adv.* perpendicularly.

perpendículo, *n.m.* plumb, plummet; pendulum; altitude of a triangle.

perpetración, *n.f.* perpetration.

perpetrador, *n.m.* perpetrator, aggressor.

perpetrar, *v.t.* to perpetrate, commit (a crime).

perpetua, *n.f.* (*bot.*) immortelle.

perpetuación, *n.f.* perpetuation.

perpetuamente, *adv.* for ever, everlastingly, perpetually.

perpetuar, *v.t.* to perpetuate. — *v.r.* to continue unceasingly.

perpetuidad, *n.f.* perpetuity, duration.

perpetuo, -tua, *a.* perpetual, everlasting.

perplejamente, *adv.* perplexedly, confusedly.

perplejidad, *n.f.* perplexity, irresolution, embarrassment, hesitation.

perplejo, -ja, *a.* doubtful, perplexed, uncertain.

perpunte, *n.m.* quilted under-waistcoat.

perquirir, *v.t.* to seek diligently.

perra, *n.f.* bitch; (*coll.*) drunkenness; coin.

perrada, *n.f.* pack of dogs; (*fig.*) perfidy, treachery, base action.

perramente, *adv.* (*fig.*) badly, very ill.

perrazo, *n.m.* large dog.

perrengue, *n.m.* short-tempered *or* surly person; (*fig.*) negro.

perrera, *n.f.* kennel; drudgery, toil; (*coll.*) child's fit of temper; fatiguing and unprofitable work.

perrería, *n.f.* pack of dogs; nest of rogues; vexation; bad word.

perrero, *n.m.* kennel-keeper; dog-fancier; beadle who expels dogs from church.

perrezno, -na, *n.m.f.* whelp, puppy.

perrico, *n.m.* little dog.

perrillo, *n.m.* little dog; trigger of a gun; piece of horse's bridle; *perrillo de falda,* lap dog.

perrito, *n.m.* puppy, little dog.

perro, *n.m.* dog; (*fig.*) obstinate or persevering person; (*fig.*) damage, deception, loss; ignominious name; *perro de aguas* (or *de lanas*), water spaniel; *perro cobrador,* retriever; *perro de muestra,* pointer; *perro de presa,* bull-dog; *perro chico,* coin (5 centimos); *perro gordo,* coin (10 centimos); *perro de ajeo,* setting dog; *perro viejo,* cautious man. *A otro perro con ese hueso,* try that on someone else; *a perro viejo no hay 'tus, tus,'* it's no good trying to wheedle an old dog; *vióse el perro en bragas de cerro, y no conoció su compañero,* the dog found himself in hempen breeches, and didn't know his old companion.

perroquete, *n.m.* topmast.

perruna, *n.f.* dog-bread, dog-cake.

perruno, -na, *a.* doggish, currish, canine.

persa, persiano, -na, *n.m.f.*, *a.* Persian.

persecución, *n.f.* persecution, pursuit; importunity.

persecutorio, -ria, *a.* of persecution, persecutory.

perseguidor, *n.m.* persecutor, pursuer.

perseguimiento, *n.m.* persecution.

perseguir, *v.t.* (conjugated like SEGUIR) to pursue; to dun, beset, importune; to persecute, harass.

perseo, *n.m.* (*astron.*) Perseus.

persevante, *n.m.* pursuivant at arms.

perseverancia, *n.f.* perseverance, constancy.

perseverante, *a.* perseverant, persevering.

perseverantemente, *adv.* constantly, perseverantly.

perseverar, *v.i.* to persist, persevere, abide.

persiana, *n.f.* silk stuff; venetian blind.

persicaria, *n.f.* (*bot.*) spotted snakeweed, lady's thumb.

pérsico, pérsigo, *n.m.* peach tree and its fruit.

pérsico, -ca, *n.m.f.*, *a.* Persian.

persignarse, *v.r.* to make the sign of the cross.

persigo; persiga, *pres. indic.; pres. subj.* [PERSEGUIR].

persistencia, *n.f.* persistence, steadiness, perseverance, obstinacy.

persistente, *a.* permanent, firm, persistent.

persistir, *v.t.*, *v.i.* to persist, persevere.

persona, *n.f.* person, personage, human being, individual; *en persona,* (or *por su persona*), personally, in person.

personado, *n.m.* (*eccles.*) benefice without jurisdiction.

personaje, *n.m.* personage, character; important person.

personal, *a.* personal, particular, private. — *n.m.* personal tax; outward appearance, air; personnel.

personalidad, *n.f.* personality, individuality; (*law*) legal person.

personalizar, *v.t.* (conjugated like ALZAR), to personify, personalize. — *v.r.* to appear as a party at law.

personalmente, *adv.* personally, in person.

personarse, *v.r.* to appear personally; to meet on business; (*law*) to take part as an interested party.

personería, *n.f.* agent's charge, solicitorship.

personero, -ra, *n.m.f.* deputy, agent, attorney, trustee.

personificar, *v.t.* (*pret.* **personifiqué;** *pres. subj.* **personifique**) to personify, to personalize.

personilla, *n.f.* mannikin, ridiculous little person.

perspectiva, *n.f.* perspective; view, vista, prospect, outlook, appearance.

perspicacia, perspicacidad, *n.f.* perspicacity, perspicaciousness, clear-sightedness, acumen, sagacity.

perspicaz, *a.* perspicacious, quick-sighted; acute, sagacious.

perspicazmente, *adv.* perspicaciously.

perspicuamente, *adv.* perspicuously.

perspicuidad, *n.f.* perspicuity, transparency, clearness.

perspicuo, -cua, *a.* perspicuous, clear, transparent.

persuadidor, -ra, *n.m.f.* persuader.

persuadir, *v.t.* to persuade, act upon, influence, induce. — *v.r.* to be persuaded, convinced.

persuasible, *a.* persuasible, persuadible.

persuasión, *n.f.* persuasion, inducement, judgment, opinion.

persuasiva, *n.f.* persuasiveness, persuasion.

persuasivamente, *adv.* persuasively.

persuasivo, -va, *a.* persuasive, moving.

persuasor, -ra, *n.m.f.* persuader, inducer.

pertenecer, *v.i.* (*pres. indic.* **pertenezco;** *pres. subj.* **pertenezca**) to appertain, concern, belong; to become, behave; to relate, pertain.

pertenecido, *n.m.* dependence.

perteneciente, *a.* belonging, appertaining; apt, ready, fit.

pertenencia, *n.f.* ownership, proprietorship, possession; tenure, holding; appurtenance, dependence, accessory, appendage; (*min.*) claim (2½ acres).

pértica, *n.f.* (*geom.*) perch.

pértiga, pertigal, *n.f.* long rod or pole.

pértigo, *n.m.* pole of waggon or cart.

pertiguería, *n.f.* verger's office.

pertiguero, *n.m.* verger.

pertinacia, *n.f.* pertinacy, obstinacy, doggedness, stubbornness.

pertinaz, *a.* pertinacious, obstinate, opinionated.

pertinazmente, *adv.* pertinaciously.

pertinente, *a.* pertinent, apt, appropriate, relevant, to the purpose; (*law*) concerning, pertaining.

pertinentemente, *adv.* pertinently, opportunely, congruously.

pertrechar, *v.t.* to supply with stores, equip; prepare, dispose, arrange. — *v.r.* to be equipped for defence.

pertrechos, *n.m.* defence equipment; equipment.

perturbable, *a.* capable of being perturbed.

perturbación, *n.f.* perturbation, confusion, agitation, excitement.

perturbadamente, *adv.* confusedly.

perturbador, -ra, *n.m.f.* perturbator, perturber, disturber.

perturbar, *v.t.* to perturb, disturb, unsettle; to agitate, confuse; interrupt.

peruano, -na, *n.m.f.*, *a.* Peruvian, of Peru.

peruétano, *n.m.* wild pear-tree.

perulero, -ra, *n.m.f.*, *a.* Peruvian, of Peru.

perulero, *n.m.* (*fig.*) moneyed person; narrow-bottomed pitcher.

peruviano, -na, *a.* Peruvian; of or from Peru; *corteza peruviana,* Peruvian bark, cinchona.

perversamente, *adv.* perversely, wickedly.

perversidad, *n.f.* perversity, malignity, perverseness, wickedness.

perversión, *n.f.* perversion, corruption, depravation, perverseness, perverting.

perverso, -sa, *a.* perverse, mischievous, depraved, wicked.

pervertidor, -ra, *n.m.f.* perverter, corrupter.

pervertimiento, *n.m.* perversion, perverting.

pervertir, *v.t.* (conjugated like VERTIR) to pervert, distort, garble, misrepresent; corrupt, turn from the right path; seduce, mislead, debase. — *v.r.* to become corrupted, depraved.

pervigilio, *n.m.* sleeplessness, wakefulness.

pervulgar, *v.t.* to divulge; to promulgate.

pesa, *n.f.* weight; clock weight; counterweight; *pesa de la romana,* weight of a steelyard; *pesas y medidas,* weights and measures.

pesacartas, *n.m.* letter-scale.

pesada, *n.f.* quantity weighed at once.

pesadamente, *adv.* heavily, weightily, ponderously; cumbrously; sorrowfully, grievously; slowly, tardily.

pesadez, *n.f.* heaviness, gravity, weight; sluggishness, slowness; corpulence, obesity; drowsiness; abundance, excess; peevishness, troublesomeness; pain, fatigue.

pesadilla, *n.f.* nightmare.

pesado, -da, *a.* peevish, fretful; cumbersome, ponderous, massive, heavy, cumbrous; dull, vexatious, tedious, fastidious, tiresome; offensive; slow, lazy, tardy, clumsy; deep, profound (of sleep); corpulent, fat, gross; hard; insufferable; importunate; *día pesado,* boring day, gloomy day.

pesado, *n.m.* bore, tease.

pesador, -ra, *n.m.f.* weigher.

pesadumbre, *n.f.* grief, heaviness, weightiness, gravity; trouble, pain, displeasure; affliction, sorrow, regret, unpleasantness.

pesalicores, *n.m.* hydrometer, areometer.

pésame, *n.m.* expression of condolence; sympathy.

pésamedello, *n.m.* old Spanish song and dance.

pesante, *a.* that which weighs, weighing. — *n.m.* half-drachm weight.

pesantez, *n.f.* heaviness, gravity, weight.

pesar (a p. de), *adv.* in spite of; notwithstanding.

pesar, *v.i.* to weigh; to be weighty, important, valuable; to preponderate, prevail; to repent; to cause sorrow or regret. — *v.t.* to weigh; to examine, consider, ponder. — *n.m.* sorrow, repentance, grief, regret, concern; *mal que le pese,* whether you like it or not; *pese a quien pese,* whatever anybody says; *a pesar de,* in spite of, notwithstanding.

pesario, *n.m.* (*surg.*) pessary.

pesaroso, -sa, *a.* sad, sorrowful; restless.

pesca, *n.f.* fishing; fishery, angling; haul, fish caught.

pescada, *n.f.* hake.

pescadería, *n.f.* fish-market.

pescadero, *n.m.* fish-monger.

pescadilla, *n.f.* small hake.

pescado, *n.m.* fish (when caught); salted cod.

pescador, *n.m.* fisherman, angler; *anillo del Pescador,* the Pope's seal.

pescadora, *n.f.* fishwoman, fishwife.

pescante, *n.m.* jib of a crane or derrick; boom; driving-seat; coach-box; (*naut.*) davit; fish davit; (*theat.*) trap-door.

pescar, *v.t.* (*pret.* **pesqué**; *pres. subj.* **pesque**) to fish, catch fish, angle, trawl; to get one's way; to pick up, find; to surprise, catch in the act; *pescar un bulto,* to lay hold on someone.

péscola, *n.f.* beginning of a furrow.

pescozada, *n.f.;* **pescozón,** *n.m.* slap on neck.

pescozudo, -da, *a.* thick-necked.

pescuezo, *n.m.* neck; (*fig.*) stiff-neckedness, haughtiness, pride.

pescuño, *n.m.* wedge of the coulter.

pesebre, *n.m.* crib, rack, manger.

pesebrejo, *n.m.* small manger; alveolus of horses' teeth.

pesebrera, *n.f.* row of mangers.

pesebrón, *n.m.* boot of a coach.

peseta, *n.f.* Spanish monetary unit equivalent to about 2d. at par.

pésete, pesia, *n.m.,* *interj.* kind of imprecation, or execration.

pesgua, *n.f.* (*Ven.*) evergreen tree with aromatic leaves.

pesillo, *n.m.* small scales for weighing coin.

pésimamente, *adv.* very badly.

pesimismo, *n.m.* pessimism.

pesimista, *n.m.f.* pessimist.

pésimo, -ma, *a.* very bad.

pesita, *n.f.* small weight.

peso, *n.m.* weight, heaviness, load, gravity; balance, scales; moment, consequence, importance; Spanish-American monetary unit; charge, burden of an enterprise; place where victuals are sold wholesale; *en peso,* suspended in the air, totally, entirely; *de peso,* of due weight; *a peso de oro,* of its weight in gold; *de su peso,* of itself, naturally; *peso muerto,* dead weight; *peso específico,* specific gravity; *peso seco,* dry weight.

pésol, *n.m.* kind of pea.

pespuntador, -ra, *n.m.f.* (*sew.*) back-stitcher.

pespuntar, *v.t.* to back-stitch.

pespunte, *n.m.* back-stitching.

pesquera, *n.f.* fishery, fishing grounds.

pesquería, *n.f.* fisherman's trade, act of fishing, fishery.

pesquis, *n.m.* cleverness, acumen.

pesquisa, *n.f.* inquiry, examination, investigation, search.

pesquisante, *a.* investigating, inquiring.

pesquisar, *v.t.* to inquire, search, investigate.

pesquisidor, -ra, *n.m.f.* examiner, inquirer, searcher.

pestaña, *n.f.* eyelash; end of a piece of linen; edging, fringe; (*mech.*) flange, rib, rim; (*bot.*) hairs.

pestañear, *v.i.* to wink, blink, flutter the eyelashes.

pestañeo, *n.m.* winking, blinking, moving of the eyelids.

peste, *n.f.* pest, plague, pestilence; corruption; epidemic, contagion; foul smell; (*fig.*, *coll.*) plenty, abundance; great plenty, superabundance. — *pl.* **pestes,** words of wrath or menace.

pestíferamente, *adv.* pestiferously, pestilently.

pestífero, -ra, *a.* pestiferous, noxious, foul.

pestilencia, *n.f.* pest, plague, pestilence; foulness, stench.

pestilencial, *a.* pestiferous, pestilential; contagious, infectious; destructive.

pestilencioso, -sa, *a.* pestilential.

pestilente, *a.* pestilent, pernicious, contagious, noxious, foul.

pestillo, *n.m.* bolt, door-latch; bolt of a lock.

pestiño, *n.m.* sweet fritter.

pestorejo, *n.m.* back of the neck.

pestorejón, *n.m.* blow on the back of the neck.

pesuña, *n.f.* foot of cloven-hoofed animals.

pesuño, *n.m.* each half of a cloven hoof.

petaca, *n.f.* tobacco-pouch; cigar-case; (*Am.*) leather-covered trunk or chest.

petalismo, *n.m.* (*polit.*) banishment.

pétalo, *n.m.* petal.

petanque, *n.m.* (*min.*) native silver.

petaquilla, *n.f.* small leather trunk.

petaquita, *n.f.* (*Col.*) climbing rose tree.

petar, *v.t.* to gratify, please, content.

petardear, *v.t.,* (*mil.*) to beat down with petards; (*fig.*) to cheat, deceive, gull, trick.

petardero, *n.m.* petardeer; (*fig.*) impostor, cheat, swindler, trickster.

petardista, *n.m.f.* deceiver, cheat, swindler, impostor.

petardo, *n.m.* petard, bomb; (*fig.*) fraud, cheat, gull, trick.

petate, *n.m.* palm-mat; swindler, impostor; luggage, baggage (of sailors, soldiers or convicts); good-for-nothing fellow; *liar el petate,* (*coll.*) to pack up and begone; (*fig.*) to die.

petenera, *n.f.* popular Andalusian song.

petequia, *n.f.* (*med.*) petechiæ.

petequial, *a.* petechial.

petera, *n.f.* wrangle, fit of temper (of children).

peteretes, *n.m.pl.* titbits, sweets.

peticano, peticanón, *n.m.* (*print.*) petitcanon type, 26 points.

petición, *n.f.* petition; demand, request, claim; (*law*) petition, prayer.

peticionario, *n.m.* petitioner.

petifoque, *n.m.* (*naut.*) outer jib.

petigrís, *n.m.* trade name of the pelt of squirrels.

petillo, *n.m.* small stomacher; jewel.

petimetra, *n.f.* stylish, affected lady.

petimetre, *n.m.* petit-maître, fop, coxcomb, beau.

petirrojo, *n.m.* robin-redbreast.

petiso, -sa, *a.* (*Arg., Ur., Chi.*) small, chubby.

petitoria, *n.f.* petition.

petitorio, -ria, *a.* petitory, petitionary.

peto, *n.m.* breastplate, stomacher; (*fenc.*) plastron; (*Cub.*) a large edible fish; the underpart of the shell of tortoises and turtles.

petra, *n.f.* (*Chi.*) a tree of the genus Myrtus with white flowers.

petral, *n.m.* breast-leather.

petrarquista, *n.m.f., a.* a follower of Petrarch.

petrel, *n.m.* (*orn.*) petrel.

pétreo, -rea, *a.* stony, hard, rocky.

petrificación, *n.f.* petrification.

petrificante, *a.* petrifying.

petrificar, *v.t.* (*pret.* **petrifiqué;** *pres. subj.* **petrifique**) to petrify, change to stone. — *v.r.* to petrify, turn to stone, become stone.

petrífico, -ca, *a.* petrific.

petrografía, *n.f.* petrography.

petróleo, *n.m.* petroleum.

petrolero, -ra, *n.m.f.* petroleum-seller; incendiary, pétroleur; ultraradical.

petrolífero, -ra, *a.* oil-bearing.

petulancia, *n.f.* petulance, insolence, flippancy, pertness.

petulante, *a.* petulant, flippant, insolent, pert, pettish.

petulantemente, *adv.* petulantly, pertly.

petunia, *n.f.* petunia.

peucédano, *n.m.* sulphurwort.

pez, *n.m.* fish [*cf.* PESCADO], catch, haul. — *n.f.* pitch, tar; *pez griega,* colophony; *pez rubia,* rosin.

pezolada, *n.f.* end-threads.

pezón, *n.m.* leaf stalk, stem of fruits; flower stalk; teat, nipple, dug; arm of an axle-tree; end of a spindle; cape or point of land.

pezonera, *n.f.* linchpin; nipple-shield.

pezpalo, *n.m.* (*com.*) stockfish.

pezpita, *n.f.;* **pezpítalo,** *n.m.* wagtail.

pezuelo, *n.m.* beginning of cloth in weaving.

pezuña, *n.f.* foot of cloven-hoofed animals.

piache, *tarde piache,* too late.

pïada, *n.f.* chirping of birds, puling of chickens.

pïador, -ra, *n.m.f.* puler, chirper.

piadosamente, *adv.* piously, clemently, mercifully.

piadoso, -sa, *a.* pious, clement, godly, merciful.

piafar, *v.i.* to stamp, paw (horses).

piale, *n.m.* (*S. Am.*) casting the lasso.

piamáter, *n.f.* (*anat.*) pia mater.

piamente, *adv.* piously.

piamontés, -esa, *n.m.f., a.* Piedmontese.

pian, piano, *adv.* gently, softly, slowly.

pianino, *n.m.* upright piano.

pianista, *n.m.f.* pianist. — *n.m.* pianoforte dealer.

piano, pianoforte, *n.m.* pianoforte; *piano de cola,* grand piano; *piano vertical,* upright piano.

pianola, *n.f.* pianola.

piante, *a.* puling, chirping.

piar, *v.i.* to pule, chirp, whine; (*coll.*) to whine, cry.

piara, *n.f.* herd of swine, drove of mares, or mules.

piariego, -ga, *a.* owner of a herd of swine, or a drove of mares or mules.

piastra, *n.f.* piastre.

pica, *n.f.* pike, long lance; bull-fighter's goad; stone-cutter's hammer; a measure of depth (12¾ ft.); (*med.*) pica; *poner una pica en Flandes,* to achieve a triumph.

picacureba, *n.f.* Brazilian pigeon.

picacho, *n.m.* top, summit, peak.

picada, *n.f.* puncture, pricking; bite (of insects, snakes, etc.).

picadero, *n.m.* riding-school; (*naut.*) stocks, boat skid; stamping ground of a stag in mating time.

picadillo, picado, *n.m.* minced meat, hash.

picado, -da, *a.* (*sew.*) pinked; pitted (with smallpox); smitten (with love); (*aer.*) dive, diving; *bombardeo en picado,* dive bombing.

picador, *n.m.* riding-master; horse-breaker; horseman armed with a goad (in bullfights); chopping-block; pinking-iron; file-cutter.

picadura, *n.f.* pricking, puncture, pinking; bite, sting; cut, slash; cut tobacco.

picaflor, *n.m.* humming-bird.

picajón, -ona; picajoso, -sa, *a.* easily offended, peevish.

picamaderos, *n.m.* woodpecker.

picana, *n.f.* (*Am.*) goad.

picanear, *v.t.* (*Am.*) to goad.

picante, *a.* pricking, piercing, stinging; pungent, hot, acrid; high-seasoned; offensive. — *n.m.* piquancy, pungency, acrimony; keen satire.

picantemente, *adv.* piquantly.

picaño, *n.m.* patch on a shoe.

picaño, -ña, *a.* roguish, deceitful, vagrant, lazy.

picapedrero, *m.* stone-cutter.

picapica, *n.f.* dust, leaves or floss of certain American trees which produce intense smarting of the skin.

picapleitos, *n.m.* (*coll.*) litigious person; pettifogging lawyer.

picaporte, *n.m.* picklock; spring latch, catch bolt; latch-key; (*Am.*) door-knocker.

picaposte, *n.m.* woodpecker.

picapuerco, *n.m.* an insectivorous bird.

picar, *v.t.* (*pret.* **piqué**; *pres. subj.* **pique**) to prick, pierce, puncture; sting, bite (as insects and some reptiles); to bite (fish); to itch; to pink, perforate; to peck (birds); pick, nibble; to harass; to tame (a horse); to hash, mince, chop; to spur, goad; excite, incite, pursue, stimulate; to vex, provoke, pique; to scorch (of the sun); (*art*) to stipple; to roughen with a pointed tool; (*aer.*) to dive; (*mil.*) to harass a retreating enemy. — *v.r.* to be vexed, offended; to be damaged, moth-eaten; to be sour (as wine), be stale, begin to rot (as fruit); to become choppy (of the sea); *picar el pez*, (*coll.*) to ensnare; *picar en poeta*, to be something of a poet; *picar la bomba*, (*naut.*) to work the pump; *picar muy alto*, to be over-ambitious.

picaramente, *adv.* knavishly, roguishly.

picaraza, *n.f.* (*orn.*) magpie.

picarazo, -za, *n.m.f.*, *a.* great rogue.

picardear, *v.i.* to play the knave; to make mischief.

picardía, *n.f.* knavery, roguery, malice, deceit, wantonness, lewdness; meeting of rogues. — *pl.* **picardías**, offensive words.

picardihuela, *n.f.* prank, roguish trick.

picaresca, *n.f.* meeting of knaves, rogues' den, knavery.

picaresco, -ca; picaril, *a.* roguish, knavish.

pícaro, -ra, *a.* knavish, roguish, low, vile, mischievous, malicious, crafty, sly. — *n.m.f.* rogue, knave, rascal; *pícaro de cocina*, scullion, kitchen-boy.

picarón, *n.m.* great rogue, villain.

picarona, *n.f.* jade.

picaronazo, -za, *a.* very knavish, villainous.

picarote, *a.* subtle, crafty.

picatoste, *n.m.* buttered toast, fried bread with bacon.

picaza, *n.f.* magpie; mattock; *picaza marina*, flamingo.

picazo, *n.m.* blow, stroke; sting; young magpie. — *a.* black and white (horse).

picazón, *n.m.* itching, peevishness, fretfulness.

picazuroba, *n.f.* (*Cent. Am.*) bird of the Gallinaceous genus.

picea, *n.f.* (*bot.*) spruce.

piceo, -cea, *a.* piceous, pitchy, tarry.

pico, *n.m.* beak, bill; (*coll.*) mouth; twibill; pick, pickaxe; nib; dock-spade; (*orn.*) woodpecker; spout of a jar; top, summit, peak; loquacity, talkativeness, garrulity; small balance of an account; short time; corner or cock of a hat; (*orn.*) woodpecker; (*Philip.*) measure of weight of about 140 lb.; *de pico*, words, not deeds; *las tres y pico*, (*coll.*) a few minutes past three; *pico de oro*, very eloquent man; *pico verde*, green woodpecker; *callar el pico*, to hold one's tongue; *tener mucho pico*, to chatter about secrets; *andar a picos pardos*, to go on the spree.

picofeo, *n.m.* (*Col.*) toucan.

picolete, *n.m.* bolt staple.

picón, -ona, *a.* having the upper teeth projecting over the lower ones (horses, mules, etc.).

picón, *n.m.* jest; small charcoal; small freshwater fish; broken rice.

piconero, *n.m.* maker of small charcoal; picador, horseman bull-fighter.

picor, *n.m.* sharp, pungent taste; itching.

picoso, -sa, *a.* pitted with smallpox.

picota, *n.f.* pillory; (*naut.*) cheek of a pump; (*fig.*) peak, point, top, spire; children's game.

picotada, *n.f.; picotazo*, *n.m.* stroke with a bird's beak or an insect bite; the mark left.

picote, *n.m.* coarse stuff made of goat's-hair; glossy silk stuff.

picoteado, -da, *a.* peaked; many-pointed.

picotear, *v.t.* to strike with the beak. — *v.i.* to gossip; to toss the head (of horses). — *v.r.* to quarrel, wrangle.

picotería, *n.f.* gossip, loquacity, volubility.

picotero, -ra, *a.* wrangling; chattering, prattling.

picotillo, *n.m.* inferior goat's-hair cloth.

picotín, *n.m.* a dry measure of capacity, the fourth part of a *cuartal* (about 3 pints).

picrato, *n.m.* (*chem.*) picrate.

pícrico, *a.* picric.

pictografía, *n.f.* pictography.

pictórico, -ca, *a.* pictorial.

picuda, *n.f.* (*Cub.*) a fish (*Sphyræna picuda*).

picudilla, *n.f.* kind of olive; insectivorous bird.

picudo, -da, *a.* beaked, pointed; chattering, prattling.

pichagua, *n.f.* (*Ven.*) fruit of the *pichagüero* tree.

pichagüero, *n.m.* (*Ven.*) kind of pumpkin.

pichana, *n.f.* (*Arg., Chi.*) broom.

pichanga, *n.f.* (*Col.*) broom.

pichel, *n.m.* pewter tankard; mug; pitcher.

pichelería, *n.f.* tankard factory.

pichelero, *n.m.* tankard maker.

pichelete, *n.m.* small mug or tankard.

pichi, *n.m.* (*Chi.*) a medicinal shrub.

pichihuén, *n.m.* (*Am.*) a fish of the Acanthopterygii order.

pichoa, *n.f.* (*Chi.*) a Euphorbiaceous cathartic plant.

pichola, *n.f.* Galician wine measure (about 1 pint).

pichón, *n.m.* young pigeon; (*fig.*) darling, dearest; (*coll.*) duck.

pidén, *n.f.* (*Chi.*) a bird resembling the coot with a melodious song.

pidientero, *n.m.* beggar.

pidón, *n.m.* persistent asker.

pie, *n.m.* foot, leg; support, stand, base; basis, foundation, footing; trunk of trees and plants; lees, sediment; warped yarn; foot-measure; (*poet.*) foot of verse; last player (at cards); (*theat.*) cue; occasion, cause, motive, opportunity; first colour given in dyeing; custom, use, rule; foot of a stocking; *pie derecho*, (*naut.*) stanchion; *pie de roda*, (*naut.*) forefoot, forepart of the keel; *pie de cabra*, crowbar; *a pie enjuto*, without pain or labour; *a pie firme*, steadfastly, without stirring; *a los pies de Vd.*, at your service (to a lady); *de pie(s) a cabeza*, up and down, from head to foot; *dar pie*, to give occasion; *echar el pie atrás*, to flinch; *echar el pie adelante a alguno*, to outdo anyone; *haber nacido de pies*, to be born lucky; *soldados de a pie*, infantry; *no tiene pies ni cabeza*, it has neither rime nor reason.

piecezuela, *n.f.* little piece.

piecezuelo, *n.m.* little foot.

piedad, *n.f.* piety, godliness, mercy, pity, charity.

piedra, *n.f.* stone; hail; (*med.*) gravel; block; cobblestone; memorial stone; gunflint; foot-stone; place where foundlings are left; *piedra de amolar* (or *afilar*), whetstone, grindstone; *piedra fundamental,* head-stone; *piedra imán,* magnet; *piedra infernal,* silver nitrate; *piedra lipis,* copper sulphate; *piedra pómez,* pumice-stone; *piedra sepulcral,* gravestone, headstone; *piedra de toque,* touchstone; *piedra movediza, nunca moho la cobija,* a rolling stone gathers no moss.

piedrezuela, *n.f.* little stone, pebble.

piel, *n.f.* skin, epidermis, hide, pelt; leather, fur; peel or skin of fruits; *piel de gallina,* goose-flesh.

piélago, *n.m.* high sea, ocean; great abundance.

pienso, *n.m.* fodder; *ni por pienso,* not a bit, absolutely not.

pienso, piense, *pres. indic., pres. subj.* [PEN-SAR].

pierdo, pierda, *pres. indic., pres. subj.* [PERDER].

Piérides, *n.f.pl.* (*poet.*) the Muses.

pierio, -ria, *a.* (*poet.*) pierian.

pierna, *n.f.* leg, limb; leg of meat or fowl; leg of a pair of compasses; honey jar; unequal selvedge of cloth; downstroke of a letter; cheek of a printing-press; (*mech.*) shank, fork; section, part, leg; lobe (of a walnut); *en piernas,* bare-legged; *a pierna suelta* (or *a pierna tendida*), at one's ease, carelessly. *Nadie tienda más la pierna de cuanto fuere larga la sábana,* let no one stretch his feet beyond the length of his sheet.

piernitendido, -da, *a.* with extended legs.

pietismo, *n.m.* pietism.

pietista, *n.m.f., a.* pietist.

pieza, *n.f.* piece, fragment, bit; coin; distance; quarry, game; article of furniture; room (of a house); part (of a machine, etc.); member (of a structure); piece or roll of cloth; length of time; piece of work; (*theat.*) play; piece or man in the games of draughts, chess, etc.; (*her.*) division of a shield; piece of ordnance; buffoon, jester, wag; sly trick; *¡buena pieza!* a fine fellow!

piezgo, *n.m.* foot of a hide or skin; dressed wine-skin.

pífano, *n.m.* (*mus.*) fife; fifer.

pifia, *n.f.* miscue at billiards; error, blunder.

pifiar, *v.i.* to breathe audibly in playing the flute. — *v.t.* to make a miscue.

pigargo, *n.m.* pygarg, osprey; ringtail hawk.

pigmento, *n.m.* pigment.

pigmeo, -mea, *n.m.f., a.* dwarf, pigmy; dwarfish.

pignorar, *v.t.* to pledge, hypothecate.

pigre, *a.* lazy, indolent, slothful.

pigricia, *n.f.* idleness, laziness.

pigro, -gra, *a.* negligent, lazy, careless.

pihua, *n.f.* sandal.

pihuela, *n.f.* lash, leash; obstruction, impediment, hindrance. — *pl.* **pihuelas,** fetters, shackles.

pijama, *n.m.* pyjamas.

pijibay, *n.m.* (*CR., Hond.*) a tropical palm.

pijije, *n.m.* (*CR., Guat., ES.*) edible aquatic bird.

pijojo, *n.m.* (*Cub.*) a wild tree with hard, yellow wood.

pijota, *n.f.* (*ichth.*) hake, codling.

pijote, *n.m.* (*naut.*) swivel-gun.

pila, *n.f.* cattle trough; holy water basin; baptismal font; shorn wool belonging to one owner; pile, heap; parish; (*arch.*) buttress, pile; (*elect.*) battery.

pilada, *n.f.* pile of mortar; heap, pile; cloth fulled.

pilapila, *n.f.* (*Chi.*) medicinal plant of the Malva genus.

pilar, *v.t.* to hull grain by pounding or crushing.

pilar, *n.m.* pillar, column, post; milestone; basin of a fountain; spur, support, abutment; pedestal; bed-post; arbor of a press.

pilarejo, pilarito, *n.m.* small pillar.

pilastra, *n.f.* (*arch.*) pilaster, square column.

pilatero, *n.m.* worker employed fulling cloth.

pilca, *n.f.* (*Am.*) wall made of stone and mud.

pilche, *n.m.* (*Per.*) wooden cup or bowl.

píldora, *n.f.* pellet, pill; (*fig., coll.*) bad news, affliction; *dorar la píldora,* (*met.*) to gild a bitter pill.

píleo, *n.m.* pileus; cardinal's red hat.

pileta, pilica, *n.f. dim.* [PILA].

pilífero, -ra, *a.* (*bot.*) piliferous, hairy.

pilme, *n.m.* (*Chi.*) a coleopterous insect of the genus cantharides.

pilo, *n.m.* (*Chi.*) medicinal shrub used as an emetic.

pilón, *n.m.* watering-trough; basin of a fountain; drop of a steelyard; counterpoise in an olive-press; heap of grapes ready to be pressed; pounding-mortar; loaf (of sugar); frontispiece of temples in ancient Egypt; heap of mortar; *pilón de azúcar,* loaf sugar.

pilonero, -ra, *n.m.f.* newsmonger.

pilongo, -ga, *a.* peeled and dried (chestnut); thin, meagre, lean.

pilórico, -ca, *a.* (*anat.*) pyloric.

píloro, *n.m.* (*anat.*) pylorus.

piloso, -sa, *a.* pilous, hairy.

pilotaje, *n.m.* (*naut.*) pilotage; pile-work, piling.

pilotar, *v.t.* to pilot a ship, a motor-car, a plane, etc.

pilote, *n.m.* (*eng.*) pile.

pilotín, *n.m.* pilot's mate, second pilot.

piloto, *n.m.* pilot, sailing-master, navigator, mate.

pilpil, *n.m.* (*Chi.*) creeping plant (*Lardizabala*).

pilpilén, *n.m.* (*Chi.*) wading bird (*Hæmatocus palliatus*).

piltraca, piltrafa, *n.f.* skinny piece of flesh. — *pl.* **piltrafas,** scraps of food, etc.

pilvén, *n.m.* (*Chi.*) fresh-water fish.

pilla, *n.f.* pillage, plunder.

pillada, *n.f.* knavish trick.

pillador, -ra, *n.m.f.* plunderer, pillager.

pillaje, *n.m.* pillage, plunder, foray, marauder.

pillar, *v.t.* to pillage, rifle, plunder, foray; (*coll.*) to find out, catch out; to catch, grasp, lay hold upon.

pillastre, pillastro, pillastrón, *n.m.* roguish fellow, rascal.

pillear, *v.t.* (*coll.*) to play the rascal.

pillería, *n.f.* crowd of rogues or vagabonds; knavish trick.

pillo, -lla, *n.m.f., a.* vagabond, rascal, scamp, sly, shrewd person; loafer; blackguard, petty thief.

pilluelo, *n.m.* little rogue.

pimental, *n.m.* pepper-bearing ground.

pimentero, *n.m.* pepper-box; (*bot.*) pepper-plant.

pimentón, *n.m.* ground pepper; cayenne pepper.

pimienta, *n.f.* (black) pepper.

pimiento, *n.m.* capsicum; cayenne pepper.

pímpido, *n.m.* (*ichth.*) kind of dog-fish.

pimpín, *n.m.* child's game.

pimpina, *n.f.* (*Ven.*) large earthenware bottle.

pimpinela, *n.f.* (*bot.*) burnet, pimpernel.

pimpleo, -plea, *a.* belonging to the Muses.

pimplón, *n.m.* (*prov.*) waterfall, cascade.

pimpollar, *n.m.* nursery (of plants).

pimpollecer, *v.i.* to sprout, bud.

pimpollejo, -illo, -ito, *n.m.* small bud, sprout, shoot, sucker.

pimpollo, *n.m.* sucker, sprout, shoot, rosebud; spruce young fellow.

pimpollón, *n.m.* large sprout, shoot or sucker.

pimpolludo, -da, *a.* full of sprouts or buds.

pina, *n.f.* cone-shaped landmark; jaunt; felloe of a wheel.

pinabete, *n.m.* spruce fir, fir-wood.

pinacate, *n.m.* (*Mex.*) black beetle.

pinacoteca, *n.f.* picture-gallery.

pináculo, *n.m.* pinnacle, top, acme, summit.

pinada, *a.* (*bot.*) pinnate, pinnated.

pinar, pinarejo, *n.m.* pine-forest, pine-grove.

pinariego, -ga, *a.* belonging to pines.

pinastro, *n.m.* wild pine.

pinatífido, -da, *a.* (*bot.*) pinnatifid.

pinaza, *n.f.* pinnace, small vessel.

pincarrascal, *n.m.* grove of small branched pines.

pincarrasco, *n.m.* maritime pine, pin-oak.

pincel, *n.m.* artist's brush; (*fig.*) painter; work painted, painting; second feather in a martin's wing.

pincelada, *n.f.* pencil-stroke, stroke with a brush; *dar la última pincelada,* to give the finishing touch.

pincelero, *n.m.* brush-maker, pencil-maker; brush-box.

pincelillo, -ito, *n.m.* fine brush; camel-hair brush.

pincelote, *n.m.* large pencil or brush.

pincerna, *n.m.f.* cupbearer.

pinchadura, *n.f.* puncture, pricking.

pinchar, *v.t.* to prick, wound, puncture, pierce.

pinchaúvas, *n.m.* despicable person.

pinchazo, *n.m.* puncture; prick, stab.

pinche, *n.m.* scullion, kitchen-boy.

pincho, *n.m.* thorn, prickle of plants; skewer, goad.

pindárico, -ca, *a.* Pindaric.

pindonga, *n.f.* gadding, gossiping woman.

pindonguear, *v.i.* (*coll.*) to gad about.

pineda, *n.f.* braid for garters; pine grove.

pinga, *n.f.* (*Philip.*) yoke, bamboo for carrying loads.

pingajo, *n.m.* rag, tatter, patch hanging from clothes.

pinganitos (en), *adv.* (*coll.*) in a prosperous state.

pingar, *v.i.* to drip, to fall in drops.

pingo, *n.m.* rag. — *pl.* **pingos,** worthless clothes, duds; *ir* (*andar* or *estar*) *de pingo,* to gad about.

pingorotudo, -da, *a.* (*coll.*) puffed up; lofty.

pingüe, *a.* pinguid, fat, oily, greasy; rich, plentiful, abundant.

pingüedinoso, -sa, *a.* fatty, pinguid.

pingüino, *n.m.* penguin.

pinguosidad, *n.f.* fatness.

pinífero, -ra, *a.* (*poet.*) piniferous.

pinillo, *n.m.* (*bot.*) germander.

pinjante, *n.m.* (*arch.*) moulding of eaves; pendant.

pino, -na, *a.* very perpendicular, steep.

pino, *n.m.* (*bot.*) pine; child's (or convalescent's) first step; (*poet.*) ship.

pinocha, *n.f.* pine-leaf, pine-needle.

pinocho, *n.m.* pine-cone.

pinol, *n.m.* (*Am.*) cereal meal.

pinola, *n.f.* (*naut.*) spindle.

pinole, *n.m.* (*Mex.*) aromatic powder to mix with chocolate.

pinoso, -sa, *a.* belonging to or producing pines.

pinta, *n.f.* spot, mark, stain, blemish, scar; drop; pint; outward appearance; marks or lines on playing cards. — *pl.* **pintas,** spots on the skin (in fevers), rash; basset, a card game.

pintacilgo, *n.m.* goldfinch.

pintada, *n.f.* guinea-hen.

pintadera, *n.f.* instrument for ornamenting bread.

pintadillo, *n.m.* goldfinch.

pintado, -da, *a.* painted, mottled. — *p.p.* [PINTAR]; *venir pintado,* to fit exactly.

pintamonas, *n.m.* (*coll.*) nickname for a bad painter.

pintar, *v.t.* to picture, paint, colour; to stain (as glass); to describe, fancy, imagine; to dapple; to exaggerate. — *v.i.* to begin to ripen; to show, give signs of. — *v.r.* to make up one's face; *el pintar como el querer,* the wish is father to the thought.

pintarrajar, pintarrajear, *v.t.* (*coll.*) to daub.

pintarrajo, *n.m.* (*coll.*) daub, bad painting.

pintarrojo, *n.m.* linnet.

pintica, -illa, -ita, *n.f.* little dot, little spot.

pintiparado, -da, *a.* perfectly like, closely resembling, apposite, fit.

pintiparar, *v.t.* to compare.

pintojo, -ja, *a.* spotted, mottled, stained.

pintor, -ra, *n.m.f.* painter; *pintor de brocha gorda,* house painter; (*fig.*) dauber.

pintorcillo, *n.m.* bad painter, dauber.

pintorescamente, *adv.* picturesquely.

pintoresco, -ca, *a.* picturesque.

pintorrear, *v.t.* to daub, paint badly.

pintorzuelo, *n.m.* wretched painter.

pintura, *n.f.* painting, picture; colour, pigment, paint; lively description; caper (horses).

pinturero, *n.m.* vain person, self-admirer.

pínula, *n.f.* sight of an optical instrument.

pinzas, *n.f.pl.* pincers, nippers; forceps, tweezers; claws of lobsters, etc.; burling-iron.

pinzón, *n.m.* chaffinch.

pinzote, *n.m.* (*naut.*) whip-staff.

piña, *n.f.* pine-cone, pine-nut, pineapple; pool (in billiards); (*naut.*) wall-knot; gathering, cluster; (*min.*) virgin silver treated with mercury; (*Philip.*) fabric made with the fibres of pineapple leaf.

piñata, *n.f.* pot; suspended balloon filled with sweets at a fancy dress ball.

piñón, *n.m.* pine-nut, pine-kernel; (*bot.*) nut-pine; (*mech.*) pinion; spring catch of a gun; extreme point of a bird's wing.

piñonata, *n.f.* conserve of shredded almonds.

piñonate, *n.m.* pine-nut paste.
piñoncico, -illo, -ito, *n.m.* small pine kernel; pinion.
piñonear, *v.i.* to click (as a gun being cocked); to call (of a male partridge in rut).
piñoneo, *n.m.* cry of partridges in rut.
piñuela, *n.f.* figured silk; cypress nut, cypress fruit; (*Ec.*) American agave.
pío, pía, *a.* pious, devout, religious, holy; mild, merciful; pied, piebald (horse).
pío, *n.m.* chirping, cheep; anxious desire.
piocha, *n.f.* trinket for women's headdress; flower made of feathers.
piojento, -ta, *a.* lousy.
piojería, *n.f.* lousiness; (*fig.*) misery, poverty.
piojillo, *n.m.* small louse infesting birds.
piojo, *n.m.* louse; *piojo pegadizo,* (*coll.*) crab louse; (*fig.*) importunate person.
piojoso, -sa, *a.* lousy; miserable, stingy; mean.
piojuelo, *n.m.* small louse.
piola, *n.f.* (*naut.*) housing, house-line.
pionía, *n.f.* bucare seeds used as an ornament.
piorno, *n.m.* (*bot.*) white single-seed broom; hairy Cytisus.
pipa, *n.f.* cask, butt, hogshead; tobacco-pipe; pip of fruit; reed of a clarion; (*artill.*) fuse.
pipar, *v.i.* to smoke a tobacco-pipe.
pipería, *n.f.* collection of pipes, barrels, etc.
pipeta, *n.f.* pipette.
pipí, *n.m.* (*orn.*) pit-pit, honey creeper.
pipián, *n.m.* (*Am.*) Indian fricassee.
pipiar, *v.i.* to chirp.
pipiolo, *n.m.* novice, beginner.
pipirigallo, *n.m.* (*bot.*) sainfoin.
pipirijaina, *n.f.* (*coll.*) band of strolling players.
pipiripao, *n.m.* (*coll.*) splendid feast.
pipiritaña, pipitaña, *n.f.* green-cane flute.
pipo, *n.m.* (*orn.*) fly-catcher.
piporro, *n.m.* bassoon.
pipote, *n.m.* keg.
pique, *n.m.* pique, offence, resentment; term in a card game (piquet); chigoe, jigger flea; (*naut.*) sharp-cut cliff; (*naut.*) crutch; *echar a pique a,* (*naut.*) to sink (*v.t.*); *estar a pique,* to be on the point of, in danger of; *irse a pique,* (*naut.*) to founder.
piqué, *n.m.* (*com.*) quilting, cotton-fabric.
piquera, *n.f.* cock-hole; entrance-hole in a hive; outlet of a smelting furnace; lamp-burner.
piquero, *n.m.* pikeman; (*Chi., Per.*) (*orn.*) tern.
piqueta, *n.f.* pickaxe, mattock; mason's hammer.
piquete, *n.m.* prick, scratch, cut; small hole in clothes; stake, picket; (*mil.*) piquet, small party of soldiers.
piquetero, *n.m.* (*min.*) pick or mattock carrier.
piquetilla, *n.f.* bricklayer's hammer.
piquituerto, *n.m.* (*orn.*) cross-bill.
pira, *n.f.* funeral pyre, pile, stake.
piragua, *n.f.* (*naut.*) pirogue, canoe; vine.
piragüero, *n.m.* canoeist.
piramidal, *a.* pyramidal.
piramidalmente, *adv.* pyramidally.
pirámide, *n.f.* pyramid.
pirata, *n.m.* pirate, corsair; cruel wretch.
piratear, *v.i.* to pirate, cruise, rob at sea.
piratería, *n.f.* piracy, robbery.
pirático, -ca, *a.* piratic, piratical.
pirausta, *n.f.* fabulous firefly.
pirca, *n.f.* (*Am.*) kind of dry-stone wall.

pircar, *v.t.* (*Am.*) to fence with *pirca.*
pirco, *n.m.* (*Chi.*) kind of succotash.
pirenaico, -ca, *a.* Pyrenean.
pírico, -ca, *a.* pyrotechnic.
piriforme, *a.* pear-shaped.
pirineo, -a, *a.* Pyrenean.
Pirineos, *n.m.pl.* Pyrenees.
pirita, pirites, *n.f.* (*min.*) pyrites.
pirofilacio, *n.m.* subterraneous fire.
pirogálico, -ca, *a.* pyrogallic.
pirólatra, *n.m.* pyrolater, fire-worshipper.
pirolatría, *n.f.* pyrolatry, fire-worship.
piromancia, *n.f.* pyromancy.
piromántico, -ca, *a.* pyromantic.
pirómetro, *n.m.* pyrometer.
piropear, *v.t.* (*coll.*) to compliment, flatter.
piropo, *n.m.* precious stone, carbuncle; pyrope; (*coll.*) flattery, compliment.
piróscafo, *n.m.* steamboat.
piroscopio, *n.m.* pyrometer.
pirosis, *n.f.* (*med.*) pyrosis.
pirotecnia, *n.f.* pyrotechnics.
pirotécnico, -ca, *a.* pyrotechnical.
piroxilina, *n.f.* gun-cotton.
pirquén (al), (*Chi.*) at will, without restrictions or method (said of the right to work a leased mine).
pirquinear, *v.i.* (*Chi.*) to work *al pirquén.*
pírrico, -ca, *a.* Pyrrhic.
pirrónico, -ca, *n.m.f., a.* pyrrhonic, sceptic, unbeliever.
pirronismo, *n.m.* pyrrhonism.
pirueta, *n.f.* pirouette, gyration.
pirulé, *n.m.* (*Cub., PR.*) caramel bonbon.
pisa, *n.f.* tread, act of treading; portion of olives or grapes obtained in one pressing; kick.
pisada, *n.f.* footstep, footprint; stepping on one's foot; *seguir las pisadas,* to follow the footsteps (or example).
pisador, -ra, *n.m.f., a.* treader of grapes; prancing horse; (*poet.*) charger, high-stepper.
pisadura, *n.f.* act of treading.
pisapapeles, *n.m.* paper-weight.
pisar, *v.t.* to tread on, trample; to ram down; to beat, step on; to press; to cover (birds); to strike (the keyboard of a piano).
pisasfalto, *n.m.* mixture of bitumen and pitch.
pisaúvas, *n.m.* treader of grapes.
pisaverde, *n.m.* (*coll.*) fox, coxcomb, popinjay.
piscator, *n.m.* yearly almanac.
piscatorio, -ria, *a.* piscatory.
piscicultor, -ra, *n.m.f.* pisciculturist.
piscicultura, *n.f.* pisciculture, fish-culture.
pisciforme, *a.* pisciform, fish-shaped.
piscina, *n.f.* fishpond; (*eccl.*) piscina; swimming-pool.
piscis, *n.m.* (*astron.*) pisces, zodiacal sign.
piscívoro, -ra, *a.* piscivorous.
pisco, *n.m.* (*Chi., Per.*) first-quality anisette made in Pisco (Peru).
piscolabis, *n.m.* (*coll.*) snack, bite; light meal.
piso, *n.m.* tread; pavement; flooring; floor, story; loft; flat, apartment; *piso bajo,* ground floor.
pisón, *n.m.* rammer.
pisonear, *v.t.* to ram.
pisotear, *v.t.* to tread, trample under foot.
pisoteo, *n.m.* treading under foot, trampling.
pista, *n.f.* trace, track, scent; clue; race-track, circus-track.
pistacho, *n.m.* pistachio nut.
pistadero, *n.m.* pestle for pounding.

pistar, *v.t.* to pound with a pestle.
pistero, *n.m.* feeding-cup.
pistilo, *n.m.* (*bot.*) pistil.
pisto, *n.m.* chicken broth for the sick; dish of tomatoes and red pepper.
pistola, *n.f.* pistol.
pistolera, *n.f.* holster.
pistolero, *n.m.* gunman, armed gangster.
pistoletazo, *n.m.* pistol-shot.
pistolete, *n.m.* pistolet, pocket-pistol.
pistón, *n.m.* piston, embolus; percussion-cap; piston of a brass instrument.
pistoresa, *n.f.* short dagger.
pistraje, pistraque, *n.m.* unpleasant beverage.
pistura, *n.f.* pounding, pestling.
pita, *n.f.* agave, agave-thread; word for calling hens; boys' game.
pitaco, *n.m.* stem of aloe-plant.
pitada, *n.f.* blast or blow of whistle; nonsense, foolish talk.
pitagórico, *n.m.,* *a.* Pythagorean.
pitahaya, *n.f.* tree-cactus.
pitancería, *n.f.* distribution of allowances; office of such distribution.
pitanciero, *n.m.* distributor of allowances, purveyor, steward.
pitanga, *n.f.* (*Arg.*) tree with edible fruit (*Eugenia specialis*).
pitanza, *n.f.* daily allowance, pittance, alms; (*coll.*) daily food; price, salary, stipend.
pitaña, *n.f.* secretion in the eyes.
pitañoso, -sa, *a.* blear-eyed.
pitar, *v.i.* to pipe, blow a whistle. — *v.t.* to discharge a debt; to distribute allowances.
pitarra, *n.f.* blearedness.
pitarroso, -sa, *a.* blear-eyed.
pitecántropo, *n.m.* pithecanthrope.
pitezna, *n.f.* bolt for stocks; spring of a trap.
pitido, *n.m.* whistling of a pipe or of birds.
pitihue, *n.m.* (*Chi.*) variety of woodpecker.
pitillera, *n.f.* a woman cigarette-maker; cigarette-case.
pitillo, *n.m.* cigarette.
pítima, *n.f.* (*pharm.*) plaster; (*coll.*) drunkenness.
pitío, *n.m.* whistling of a pipe or of birds.
pitipié, *n.m.* (*math.*) line divided by degrees, scale.
pitirre, *n.m.* (*Cub.*) grey kingbird.
pito, *n.m.* pipe, whistle, fife, fifer; boy's game; (*orn.*) woodpecker; cat-call; *no vale un pito,* it's not worth a straw; *no me importa,* or *no se me da un pito,* I don't care a straw; *no tocar pitos en,* to have no part in.
pitoflero, -ra, *n.m.f.* (*coll.*) musician of no account; gossip.
pitoitoy, *n.m.* (*Am.*) a wading-bird.
pitón, *n.m.* python; tenderling; protuberance, lump, prominence; sprig, shoot; nozzle, spout; sprout; antler, horn.
pitonisa, *n.f.* pythoness; witch, sorceress.
pitora, *n.f.* (*Col.*) a highly poisonous snake.
pitorra, *n.f.* woodcock.
pitorrearse, *v.r.* to make fun of someone.
pitpit, *n.m.* (*orn.*) pit-pit.
pituita, *n.f.* pituita, mucus.
pituitario, -ria; pituitoso, -sa, *a.* pituitous, pituitary.
pituso, -sa, *a.* small, graceful, pretty (of children).
piular, *v.i.* to chirp, pule, pipe.
piune, *n.m.* (*Chi.*) small medicinal tree.

piuquén, *n.m.* (*Chi.*) a large bird similar to the wild turkey.
piure, *n.m.* (*Chi.*) an edible mollusc.
píxide, *n.f.* (*eccles.*) pyx, ciborium.
pizarra, *n.f.* (*min.*) slate, shale; slate (for writing); blackboard.
pizarral, *n.m.* slate quarry.
pizarreño, -ña, *a.* slate-coloured.
pizarrero, *n.m.* slater, slate-cutter, roofer.
pizarrín, *n.m.* slate pencil.
pizca, *n.f.* (*coll.*) mite, jot, whit; *ni pizca,* not a jot, nothing at all.
pizcar, *v.t.* to pinch; (*Mex.*) to glean maize.
pizco, *n.m.* pinch.
pizmiento, -ta, *a.* pitch-coloured.
pizote, *n.m.* (*CR., Guat., Hond.*) a plantigrade resembling the squirrel.
pizpereta, pizpireta, *a.* sharp, brisk, lively (woman).
pizpirigaña, *n.f.* boy's game.
pizpita, *n.f.;* **pizpitillo,** *n.m.* wagtail.
placa, *n.f.* small coin circulating in the Low Countries during the Spanish rule; (*Mex.*) baggage check; star, insignia of an order; (*phot.*) dry plate; (*art*) plaque; *placa de asiento,* railway chair; *placa giratoria,* turntable.
placabilidad, *n.f.* placability.
placable, *a.* placable, easily soothed.
placarte, *n.m.* placard, poster.
placativo, -va, *a.* placable.
placear, *v.t.* to publish, post up, proclaim; to sell at retail (provisions).
placel, *n.m.* (*naut.*) sand-bank.
pláceme, *n.m.* expression of congratulation.
placenta, *n.f.* (*anat., bot.*) placenta, after-birth.
placenteramente, *adv.* joyfully, pleasantly.
placentero, -ra, *a.* joyful, pleasant, merry, gay, mirthful.
placer, *defect. v.t.* (*pres. indic.* **plazco;** *pres. subj.* **plazca,** él **plegue** *or* **plazca;** *pret.* él **plugo** *or* **plació**) to please, content, gratify, humour.
placer, *n.m.* pleasure, content, complaisance, rejoicing, amusement, consent, will; (*naut.*) sand-bank; (*Am.*) pearl-fishing.
placero, -ra, *a.* pertaining to the market-place. — *n.m.f.* marketer, seller at a market; gadabout, idler.
placeta, placetilla, placetuela, *n.f.* small square or public place.
placibilidad, *n.f.* agreeableness.
placible, *a.* placid, agreeable, pleasant.
plácidamente, *adv.* placidly, quietly, easily, mildly.
placidez, *n.f.* placidness, placidity.
plácido, -da, *a.* placid, easy, quiet, calm.
placiente, *a.* pleasing, mild, agreeable, pleasant.
plafón, *n.m.* (*arch.*) soffit of an architrave.
plaga, *n.f.* plague, scourge, affliction, calamity, misery, vexatious matter; scourge, epidemic; abundance, plenty, super-abundance, glut in the market; climate, country; zone; (*naut.*) cardinal point.
plagado, -da, *a.* full of defects.
plagar, *v.t.* (*pret.* **plagué;** *pres. subj.* **plague**) to plague, infest. — *v.r.* to be overrun with.
plagiar, *v.t.* to plagiarize; (*Am.*) to kidnap.
plagiario, -ria, *n.m.f., a.* plagiary, plagiarist.
plagio, *n.m.* plagiarism; (*Am.*) kidnapping, abduction.

plan, *n.m.* plan, draft, project, outline, scheme, design; slab; tier; description, specification; schedule; plane, level; (*naut.*) floor-timber.

plana, *n.f.* trowel; (*print.*) page; copy; plane, level ground; *plana mayor*, (*mil.*) staff; *enmendar la plana*, to point out a mistake, find fault, to outdo a person.

planada, *n.f.* level ground, plain.

planador, *n.m.* planisher.

plancha, *n.f.* iron, smoothing-iron, sad-iron; cramp iron; sheet, slab, plate; tailor's goose; injudicious action or speech; (paper making) mould; cloth plate of a sewing machine; horizontal suspension (in gymnastics); (*naut.*) gangway, gang-board; *plancha de agua*, (*naut.*) floating stage; *plancha de viento*, (*naut.*) hanging stage; *plancha de blindaje*, armour plate.

planchada, *n.f.* (*naut.*) framing or apron of a gun.

planchado, *n.m.* ironing; linen ironed.

planchadora, *n.f.* ironer.

planchar, *v.t.* to iron (linen); to press clothes.

planchear, *v.t.* to plate, sheathe, cover with metal.

plancheta, *n.f.* (*surv.*) plane table.

planchón, *n.m.* large plate.

planchuela, *n.f.* small plate; fluting-iron.

planeador, *n.m.* (*aer.*) glider.

planear, *v.t.* (*aer.*) to glide; to form, draw a plan.

planeo, *n.m.* (*aer.*) gliding.

planeta, *n.f.* (*astron.*) planet; (*eccl.*) planeta.

planetario, -ria, *a.* planetary.

planetario, *n.m.* planetarium.

planetícola, *n.m.f.* inhabitant of a planet other than the earth.

planga, *n.f.* kind of eagle.

planicie, *n.f.* plane, surface.

planimetría, *n.f.* planimetry.

planímetro, *n.m.* planimeter.

planisferio, *n.m.* planisphere.

plano, -na, *a.* plain, level, flat, smooth, even.

plano, *n.m.* plan, design, draft; (*geom.*) plane; ground-plot; delineation, projection; (*aer.*) flap, wing; flat of a sword, etc.; *de plano*, openly, plainly, clearly; *plano de nivel*, datum plane; *plano inclinado*, inclined plane.

planta, *n.f.* sole of the foot; (*bot.*) plant; nursery for plants, plantation; plan or site of a building; project; (*fenc., danc.*) position of the feet; disposition; (*eng.*) plan, horizontal projection, top view; *planta baja*, ground floor; *buena planta*, fine physique; *echar plantas*, to boast, brag.

plantación, *n.f.* plantation, planting.

plantador, -ra, *n.m.f.* planter (person or machine).

plantaina, *n.f.* (*bot.*) plantain.

plantaje, *n.m.* collection of plants.

plantar, *v.t.* to plant, bed; set up, place, fix; set, put, found, establish; to strike (a blow); to jilt; (*coll.*) to leave in the lurch. — *v.r.* to stop short, jib; stand firm; to reach; arrive; in some games, to stand pat; *plantar en la calle*, to throw into the street; *plantar en la cárcel*, to clap into prison.

plantario, *n.m.* nursery, ground for rearing plants.

planteamiento, *n.m.* putting a plan into execution.

plantear, *v.t.* to plan, trace, try, attempt; to act upon, execute, establish; to state (a problem, argument, etc.).

plantel, *n.m.* nursery; training-school; educational institution.

plantífero, -ra, *a.* (*poet.*) plantiferous.

plantificar, *v.t.* (*pret.* **plantifiqué;** *pres. subj.* **plantifique**) to plant, land (a blow); to put into execution.

plantígrado, -da, *a.* plantigrade.

plantilla, *n.f.* young plant; first sole of a shoe; vamp; mould; model, pattern; (*mech.*) template, templet; (*med.*) plaster for the feet; plate of a gun-lock; (*astron.*) celestial configuration; (*Cub., PR.*) lady-finger; (*com.*) established (staff, civil service, etc.).

plantillar, *v.t.* to vamp, sole (shoes, etc.).

plantío, *n.m.* plantation, nursery for trees, garden-bed.

plantío, -tía, *a.* planted, ready to be planted.

plantista, *n.m.* bully, bravado, hector; landscape-gardener.

plantón, *n.m.* scion, sprout, shoot; (*coll.*) long wait; watchman, door-keeper; (*mil.*) sentry doing long guard as a punishment; *estar de plantón*, to be in a place for a very long time; *llevar un plantón*, to dance attendance.

planudo, -da, *a.* (*naut.*) drawing little water, flat-bottomed.

plañidera, *n.f.* hired mourner; weeper.

plañidero, -ra, *a.* mourning, moaning, weeping.

plañido, *n.m.* lamentation, crying, moan.

plañir, *v.i.* (*pres. part.* **plañendo;** *pret.* **él plañó**) to grieve, bewail, lament.

plaqué, *n.m.* plated metal, plate, plating.

plaquín, *n.m.* hauberk, loose coat of mail.

plasma, *n.m.* (*biol.*) plasma.

plasmador, -ra, *n.m.f.* moulder, former, creator.

plasmante, *a.* moulding, moulder.

plasmar, *v.t.* to mould, shape.

plasta, *n.f.* paste, soft clay; anything soft, flattened or poorly done.

plaste, *n.m.* size or filler made of thin glue and plaster of Paris.

plastecer, *v.t.* (*pres. indic.* **plastezco;** *pres. subj.* **plastezca**) to size, besmear with size.

plastecido, *n.m.* (*art*) sizing, act of sizing.

plástica, *n.f.* art of modelling, moulding.

plasticidad, *n.f.* plasticity.

plástico, -ca, *a.* plastic, soft, fictile.

plastrón, *n.m.* (*fenc.*) plastron; leather apron; large cravat.

plata, *n.f.* silver; wrought silver, plate; silver coin, money; (*her.*) white; *como una plata*, very bright or neat; *en plata*, briefly, in a word; *plata agria*, stephanite; *plata alemana*, German silver; *plata córnea*, cerargyrite; *plata labrada*, silverware; *plata virgen*, native silver; *plata roja*, pyrargyrite.

plataforma, *n.f.* platform, terrace; (*mach.*) index-plate, division plate; (*naut.*) orlop.

platal, *n.m.* great wealth, riches.

platanal, platanar, *n.m.* plane-tree plantation.

platanero, -ra, *a.* (*Cub.*) very stormy, hurricane-like.

plátano, *n.m.* banana; (*bot.*) plane-tree; plantain-tree and its fruit; *plátano falso*, sycamore maple.

platazo, *n.m.* platter, blow with a plate or dish; dishful.

platea, *n.f.* (*theat.*) orchestra, pit; *asiento or*

butaca de platea, (*theat.*) stall, fauteuil.
plateado, -da, *a.* silvered, silver-plated.
plateador, *n.m.* plater, silverer.
plateadura, *n.f.* silvering, silver-plating.
platear, *v.t.* to silver, plate with silver.
platel, *n.m.* platter, tray.
plateresco, -ca, *a.* (*arch.*) plateresque.
platería, *n.f.* silversmith's shop or trade.
platero, *n.m.* silversmith, plate-worker, jeweller; *platero de oro,* goldsmith.
plática, *n.f.* speech, address, short sermon or lecture, colloquy, discourse, talk; conversation, chat.
platicar, *v.t.* (*pret.* **platiqué;** *pres. subj.* **platique**) to talk, converse, chat.
platija, *n.f.* (*ichth.*) kind of plaice, flounder.
platilla, *n.f.* Silesian linen.
platillo, *n.m.* saucer, small dish; balance-pan; beef stew; meat dish in convents; valve of a chain pump; (cards) kitty; (*mus.*) cymbal; (*fig.*) small-talk, backbiting.
platina, *n.f.* slide of microscope; plate of air-pump; (*print.*) platen, bedplate; imposing table; (*min.*) ore of platinum.
platinado, *n.m.* action and effect of plating.
platinar, *v.t.* to plate, to coat with a layer of platinum.
platinífero, -ra, *a.* platiniferous, platinum bearing.
platino, *n.m.* platinum.
plato, *n.m.* dish, plate; daily fare; balance-pan; (*arch.*) metope; *plato de segunda mesa,* second-hand, makeshift; *platos lisos* (*llanos* or *trincheros*), dining-plates; *nada entre dos platos,* much ado about nothing.
platónicamente, *adv.* platonically.
platónico, -ca, *a.* platonic.
platonismo, *n.m.* Platonism.
plausibilidad, *n.f.* plausibility, speciousness.
plausible, *a.* plausible, specious.
plausiblemente, *adv.* plausibly, speciously.
plauso, *n.m.* applause.
plaustro, *n.m.* (*poet.*) carriage, cart.
playa, *n.f.* shore, beach, strand, sea-coast.
playado, -da, *a.* with a shore or beach.
playazo, *n.m.* wide or extensive shore.
playeras, *n.f.pl.* a popular Andalusian song.
playero, -ra, *n.m.f.* fisherman or fisherwoman.
playón, *n.m.* large shore or beach.
playuela, *n.f.* small shore or beach.
plaza, *n.f.* square, place, market-place; (*com.*) emporium, market; fortified place or town; room, space; office, public post, position, employment; character, reputation, fame; *¡plaza!* make way! *plaza de armas,* garrison, parade ground; *plaza fuerte,* stronghold, fortress; *sentar plaza,* to enlist; *pasar plaza,* to gain a false reputation; *sacar a plaza,* to publish, make public; *plaza de toros,* bull-ring.
plazo, *n.m.* term; duration, time, space of time; day of payment; credit; instalment; writ; dwelling-ground.
plazoleta, plazuela, *n.f.* small square or place.
ple, *n.m.* hand-ball game.
pleamar, *n.f.* highwater, high tide.
plébano, *n.m.* curate of a parish.
plebe, *n.f.* populace, common people.
plebeyo, -ya, *a.* plebeian. — *n.m.f.* commoner, plebeian.
plebiscitario, -ria, *a.* plebiscitary.
plebiscito, *n.m.* plebiscite.

pleca, *n.f.* (*print.*) rule, straight line.
plectro, *n.m.* plectrum; ((*poet.*) inspiration.
plegable, *a.* pliable, folding.
plegadamente, *adv.* confusedly.
plegadera, *n.f.* folder.
plegadizo, -za, *a.* pliable, folding.
plegado, -da, *n.m.f.,* *a.* plaiting, folding.
plegador, -ra, *n.m.f.* plaiter, folder, folding-machine; beam of a silk loom. — *a.* folding.
plegadura, *n.f.* fold, crease, plait, doubling, folding, plaiting.
plegar, *v.t.* (*pres. indic.* **pliego;** *pret.* **plegué;** *pres. subj.* **pliegue**) to fold, double, plait; to purse, crimp, gather, pucker, crimple, do up; to turn the warp on the beam (silk loom); to please; *plega* (or *plegue*) *a Dios,* please God, God grant.
plegaria, *n.f.* public prayer, supplication; the angelus bell, the noon prayers.
pleguete, *n.m.* small tendril of vines.
pleistoceno, *a.* (*geol.*) pleistocene.
pleita, *n.f.* plaited strand of bass.
pleiteador, -ra, *n.m.f.* pleader; wrangler.
pleiteante, *n.m.f.,* *a.* litigating, litigant, pleader.
pleitear, *v.t.* to plead, contend, litigate.
pleitista, *n.m.* pettifogger.
pleito, *n.m.* dispute, controversy, contest; debate, contention, strife; lawsuit, litigation, judicial contest; *ver el pleito,* to try a cause.
plenamar, *n.f.* high water.
plenamente, *adv.* fully, completely.
plenariamente, *adv.* plenarily, completely, fully.
plenario, -ria, *a.* (*law*) plenary; *indulgencia plenaria,* plenary indulgence.
plenilunio, *n.m.* full moon.
plenipotencia, *n.f.* plenipotence.
plenipotenciario, -ria, *n.m.f.,* *a.* plenipotentiary.
plenitud, *n.f.* plenitude, fullness, abundance.
pleno, -na, *a.* full, complete; joint session.
pleonasmo, *n.m.* pleonasm.
pleonástico, -ca, *a.* pleonastic.
plepa, *n.f.* (*coll.*) bother; person, animal or thing full of defects or flaws.
plesímetro, *n.m.* (*med.*) pleximeter.
plesiosauro, *n.m.* (*palæont.*) plesiosaurus.
pletina, *n.f.* small iron plate.
plétora, *n.f.* plethora, super-abundance.
pletórico, -ca, *a.* plethoric.
pleuresía, pleuritis, *n.f.* pleurisy.
pleurítico, -ca, *a.* pleuritic, pleuritical.
pleurodinia, *n.f.* (*med.*) pleurodynia, pain in the side.
plexo, *n.m.* (*anat.*) plexus; network of veins, fibres, or nerves.
Pléyadas, *n.f.* (*astron.*) Pleiades.
plica, *n.f.* sealed will, etc.; matted hair, plica.
pliego, *n.m.* sheet of paper; folded paper; bundle of letters in one cover; *pliego de condiciones,* specifications, tender, bid.
pliego, pliegue, *pres. indic.,* *pres. subj.* [PLEGAR].
pliegue, *n.m.* fold, plait, crease; (*sew.*) gather.
plieguecillo, *n.m.* half sheet of standard *pliego* (435 mm × 315 mm).
plinto, *n.m.* plinth.
plioceno, *a.* (*geol.*) pliocene.
plomada, *n.f.* blacklead pencil; plumb, plummet; (*naut.*) lead; apron of a cannon; fishing-net sinker; scourge with lead balls, cat-o'-nine-tails.

plomar, *v.t.* to put a lead seal on a diploma.
plomazón, *n.m.* gilding cushion.
plombagina, *n.f.* plumbago, graphite.
plomería, *n.f.* plumber's trade; lead roofing; storehouse of leaden goods.
plomero, *n.m.* plumber.
plomizo, -za, *a.* leaden.
plomo, *n.m.* lead, ball or piece of lead; plumb, plummet, bob; bullet; (*coll.*) bore, tiresome person; *andar con pies de plomo,* to proceed with great caution; *a plomo,* true plumb; *caer a plomo,* to fall flat down.
plomoso, -sa, *a.* leaden.
pluma, *n.f.* feather, quill pen; penmanship; writer, author; down; *buena pluma,* skilful penman; *pluma de agua,* running water; *a vuela pluma,* written in haste; *pluma viva,* eiderdown; *pluma estilográfica,* fountain-pen; *dejar correr la pluma,* to scribble away, write at great length.
plumada, *n.f.* dash, stroke, flourish with the pen.
plumado, -da, *a.* feathered, feathery, plumy.
plumaje, *n.m.* plume, plumage.
plumajería, *n.f.* feather-trade.
plumajero, *n.m.* feather-seller, feather-dealer.
plumario, *n.m.* painter of birds; plume-maker.
plumazo, *n.m.* feather mattress, feather pillow.
plumazón, *n.m.* plumage.
plúmbeo, -bea; plúmbico, -ca, *a.* leaden.
plumeado, *n.m.* (*art*) lines in miniature painting.
plumear, *v.t.* (*art*) to shade, darken.
plúmeo, -mea, *a.* plumigerous, feathered, plumed.
plumería, *n.f.* feather-trade, plumagery.
plumerilla, *n.f.* (*River Plate*) red flowered mimosa.
plumero, *n.m.* plume, bunch of feathers; feather-duster; box for feathers or plumes.
plumífero, -ra, *a.* (*poet.*) feathered.
plumista, *n.m.* quill-driver; petty notary; plume-maker.
plumita, *n.f.* small pen, small feather.
plumón, *n.m.* soft, downy feathers; feather bed.
plumoso, -sa, *a.* feathered, plumy.
plúmula, *n.f.* (*bot.*) plumule.
plural, *a.* (*gram.*) plural.
pluralidad, *n.f.* plurality, majority, multitude; *a pluralidad de votos,* by a majority.
pluralizar, *v.t.* (conjugated like ALZAR) to pluralize.
plus, *n.m.* extra pay for soldiers; bonus; extra.
pluscuamperfecto, *n.m.* (*gram.*) pluperfect.
plus ultra, *Lat.* more beyond; *ser el non plus ultra,* to be transcendent.
plúteo, *n.m.* drawer, shelf, bookshelf.
plutocracia, *n.f.* plutocracy.
plutócrata, *n.m.f.* plutocrat.
plutocrático, -ca, *a.* plutocratic.
Plutón, *n.m.* (*astron.*) Pluto.
plutónico, -ca, *a.* (*geol.*) plutonic.
plutonismo, *n.m.* (*geol.*) plutonism.
pluvia, *n.f.* (*poet.*) rain.
pluvial, *n.m.* (*eccles.*) pluvial, cope.
pluvímetro, pluviómetro, *n.m.* (*phys.*) pluviometer.
pluvioso, -sa, *a.* rainy, wet.
poa, *n.f.* (*naut.*) bowline bridle.
pobeda, *n.f.* poplar plantation.

población, *n.f.* population; town, city, village, large place.
poblacho, poblachón, *n.m.* ugly village.
poblado, *n.m.* town, village, settlement.
poblador, -ra, *n.m.f.* founder, populator.
poblano, -na, *a.* (*Am.*) belonging to a village.
poblar, *v.t.,* *v.i.* (*pres. indic.* **pueblo;** *pres. subj.* **pueble**) to people, found, populate; to breed fast; to occupy, fill; to bud, leaf.
poblazo, *n.m.* large, ugly village.
poblezuelo, *n.m.* small village.
pobo, *n.m.* white poplar.
pobre, *a.* poor, necessitous, indigent, needy, pitiable; barren, dry; humble, modest; paltry, insignificant, trifling; wretched, unhappy. — *n.m.* poor person, beggar, pauper.
pobrecico, -ica; -illo, -illa; -ito, -ita, *n.m.f., a.* poor little thing.
pobremente, *adv.* poorly, miserably, wretchedly.
pobrería, pobretería, *n.f.* poverty; beggars, paupers, wretched people.
pobrero, *n.m.* distributor of alms.
pobreta, *n.f.* prostitute, strumpet.
pobrete, -ta, *n.m.f.* poor, unfortunate person.
pobretear, *v.i.* to pretend poverty.
pobretón, -ona, *a.* very poor.
pobreza, *n.f.* poverty, indigence, need, want; necessity; sterility, barrenness, poorness; vow of poverty; lowness of spirit; heap of useless trifles.
pobrezuelo, -la, *n.m.f.* poor man or woman. — *a.* rather poor.
pobrismo, *n.m.* poor people, beggars, pauperism.
pocero, *n.m.* well-sinker; sewer-man.
pocilga, *n.f.* pigsty, dirty place.
pocillo, *n.m.* vessel sunk in the ground in oil mills; chocolate cup.
pócima, *n.f.* disagreeable drink, potion, draught; medicinal tea.
poción, *n.f.* potion; drink, draught.
poco, -ca, *a.* little, scanty, limited, small, not much, few, some. — *adv.* little, briefly, shortly, in a short time. — *n.m.* little piece, bit, small part, small proportion, small quantity; *a poco,* immediately, shortly afterwards; *de poco tiempo acá,* latterly; *poco a poco,* gently, softly, little by little, carefully!; *poco antes,* shortly before; *poco después,* shortly afterwards; *tener en poco,* to set little value on; *lo que cuesta poco, se estima en menos,* what costs little is valued less.
póculo, *n.m.* drinking-cup.
pocho, -cha, *a.* discoloured, faded.
poda, *n.f.* pruning of trees, pruning season.
podadera, *n.f.* pruning-knife, pruning-hook, hedging-bill.
podador, -ra, *n.m.f.* pruner of trees or vines.
podagra, *n.f.* gout in the feet.
podar, *v.t.* to prune trees; to head, lop, trim.
podazón, *n.f.* pruning-season.
podenco, *n.m.* hound.
poder, *n.m.* power, might, authority; dominion, ability, command, influence; vigour, strength, force, mastery, faculty; power of attorney; military strength; proxy, possession, tenure. — *pl.* **poderes,** power, written authority. — *v.i.* (*pres. part.* **pudiendo;** *pres. indic.* **puedo;** *pres. subj.* **pueda;** *pret.* **pude;** *fut. indic.* **podré**) to be able, may, can; to

have force; to be given power; to act. — *v. impers.* to be possible or contingent; *a poder de,* by force; *a más no poder,* to the utmost; *no poder ver a,* to hate the very sight of; *no poder más,* to be exhausted, unable to do more.

poderdante, *n.m.f. (law)* constituent.

poderhabiente, *n.m.* attorney.

poderío, *n.m.* power, might, authority, jurisdiction, dominion; wealth, riches.

poderosamente, *adv.* powerfully, mightily.

poderoso, -sa, *a.* powerful, potent, mighty; rich, wealthy, eminent; effective, efficacious, excellent; able, forcible.

podio, *n.m. (arch.)* podium.

podómetro, *n.m.* podometer.

podón, *n.m.* mattock, hoe, bill-hook.

podre, *n.m.f.* pus; corrupted matter.

podrecer, *v.t., v.i.* to putrefy, grow rotten.

podrecimiento, *n.m.* rottenness, putrefaction.

podredumbre, *n.f.* pus; putrid matter; decay, corruption; grief.

podrir, *v.t., v.i., v.r.,* variant of **pudrir,** used only in infin. and past part.

poema, *n.m.* poem, long metrical composition.

poesía, *n.f.* poetry, poesy, metrical composition. — *pl.* **poesías,** poetical works.

poeta, *n.m.* poet.

poetastro, *n.m.* poetaster.

poética, *n.f.* poetry, poetics.

poéticamente, *adv.* poetically.

poético, -ca, *a.* poetic, poetical.

poetisa, *n.f.* poetess.

poetizar, *v.i. (pret.* **poeticé;** *pres. subj.* **poetice)** to poetize, write poems. — *v.t.* to versify.

poíno, *n.m.* gantry, stilling.

polaco, -ca, *n.m.f., a.* Pole, Polish.

polacra, *n.f. (naut.)* polacre.

polaina, *n.f.* leggings.

polar, *a.* polar.

polaridad, *n.f.* polarity.

polarización, *n.f.* polarization.

polarizar, *v.t. (pret.* **polaricé;** *pres. subj.* **polarice)** to polarize.

polca, *n.f.* polka.

polcar, *v.i.* to dance the polka.

polea, *n.f.* pulley; tackle-block, block-pulley; *polea loca,* loose pulley; *polea motriz,* driving-pulley.

poleadas, *n.f.pl.* kind of pap.

poleame, *n.m.* collection of pulleys or masts, tackle.

polémica, *n.f.* polemics; science of fortification; literary controversy, dispute.

polémico, -ca, *a.* polemical, polemic.

polemista, *n.m.f.* polemicist, controversialist.

polemizar, *v.i.* to polemize.

polemonio, *n.m. (bot.)* Jacob's ladder.

polen, *n.m.* pollen.

polenta, *n.f.* polenta, a kind of porridge made of corn meal.

poleo, *n.m. (bot.)* penny-royal; strutting gait; pompous style; strong cold wind.

poliandria, *n.f. (bot.)* polyandria.

poliantea, *n.f.* polyanthea, budget of news.

poliarquía, *n.f.* polyarchy.

poliárquico, -ca, *a.* relating to polyarchy.

policarpo, *n.m. (bot.)* polycarpous.

pólice, *n.m.* thumb.

policía, *n.f.* police; good breeding, politeness, neatness, cleanliness. *n.m.* policeman.

policitación, *n.f.* pollicitation; *(law)* a promise not yet accepted.

policlínica, *n.f. (med.)* consulting institution; clinic; policlinic.

policromo, -ma, *a.* polychromatic.

polichinela, *n.m.f.* buffoon.

polidor, *n.m. (slang)* seller of stolen goods.

poliédrico, -ca, *a.* polyhedral, polyhedric.

poliedro, *n.m.* polyhedron.

polifásica, *n.f. (elec.)* multiphase.

polifonía, *n.f.* polyphony.

polifónico, -ca, *a.* polyphonic.

polígala, *n.f.* milkwort.

poligamia, *n.f.* polygamy.

polígamo, -ma, *n.m.f., a.* polygamist, polygamous.

polígloto, -ta, *a.* polyglot. — *n.m.f.* linguist.

poligonal, *n.f. (surv.)* broken line. — *a. (geom.)* polygonal.

polígono, *n.m.* polygon; *(artill.)* range for firing practice.

poligrafía, *n.f.* polygraphy, writing in cipher, interpreting of ciphers.

polígrafo, *n.m.* polygraph.

polihedro, *n.m.* polyhedron.

polilla, *n.f.* moth; consumer, waster.

polímita, *a.* made of many-coloured threads.

polimorfo, -fa, *a. (chem.)* polymorphous.

polín, *n.m.* wooden roller.

polinización, *n.f. (bot.)* pollination.

polinomio, *n.m. (alg.)* polynomial.

poliorcética, *n.f. (mil.)* the twin sciences of fortification and siegecraft.

polipétalo, -la, *a. (bot.)* polypetalous.

pólipo, *n.m. (med.)* polypus; *(zool.)* polyp; octopus, poulpe.

polipodio, *n.m.* fern.

polisílabo, *n.m.* polysyllable.

polisílabo, -ba, *a.* polysyllabic.

polisinodia, *n.f.* multiplicity of synods or councils.

polisón, *n.m.* bustle; pad, cushion or framework.

polispasto, *n.m.* burton, hoisting tackle.

polispermo, -ma, *a. (bot.)* polyspermous.

polista, *n.m. (Philip.)* Indian serving in communal works; polo player.

politécnico, -ca, *a.* polytechnic.

politeísmo, *n.m.* polytheism.

politeísta, *n.m.f.* polytheist.

política, *n.f.* policy, politics; civility, politeness.

políticamente, *adv.* politically, civilly.

politicastro, *n.m.* politicaster.

político, -ca, *a.* political, politic; polite, courteous; *padre político,* father-in-law; *madre política,* mother-in-law, etc.

politicón, -ona, *a.* exceedingly polite and ceremonious.

politiquear, *v.i.* to affect the politician.

polivalvo, -va, *a.* multivalve.

póliza, *n.f. (com.)* policy; check, draft, scrip; custom-house permit; pay-bill; entrance ticket; insurance policy; lampoon; excise stamp.

polizón, *n.m.* vagrant; sponger, parasite; stowaway.

polizonte, *n.m. (coll.)* policeman, detective.

polo, *n.m. (geom., astron.)* pole; pole of the magnetic needle; polo (game); *(Philip.)* personal service of forty days in the year to the community, levied from the Indians;

foundation, support; Andalusian song; *polo ártico*, North Pole.

polonés, -esa, *a.* Polish.

polonesa, *n.f.* polonaise.

Polonia, *n.f.* Poland.

poltrón, -ona, *a.* idle, lubberly, lazy; easy, comfortable, commodious; *silla poltrona*, elbow-chair, easy chair.

poltrón, *n.m.* coward, poltroon.

poltronería, *n.f.* idleness, laziness, sluggishness, indolence.

poltronizarse, *v.r.* to become lazy.

polución, *n.f.* (*med.*) pollution.

poluto, -ta, *a.* polluted, contaminated, defiled, filthy, unclean.

polvareda, *n.f.* cloud of dust; altercation, dispute, debate.

polvera, *n.f.* powder-box.

polvificar, *v.t.* (*pret.* **polvifiqué;** *pres. subj.* **polvifique**) (*coll.*) to pulverize.

polvo, *n.m.* dust, powder; pinch of snuff. — *pl.* **polvos,** toilet powder; *limpio de polvo y paja*, free from all charges; *polvos para dientes*, tooth-powder; *sacudir el polvo*, to beat.

pólvora, *n.f.* powder, gunpowder; fireworks; vivacity, liveliness, briskness; bad temper, irritability; *gastar la pólvora en salvas*, to throw one's money away, to work to no purpose; *ser una pólvora*, to be as quick as lightning.

polvoreamiento, *n.m.* pulverization, powdering.

polvorear, *v.t.* to powder, sprinkle with powder.

polvorero, -ra, *a.* (*Col.*) [POLVORISTA].

polvoriento, -ta, *a.* dusty, full of dust.

polvorín, *n.m.* very fine powder; powder-flask, priming-horn; powder magazine.

polvorista, *n.m.* maker of gunpowder; firework-maker.

polvorización, *n.f.* pulverization.

polvorizar, *v.t.* (*pret.* **polvoricé;** *pres. subj.* **polvorice**) to pulverize.

polvoroso, -sa, *a.* dusty, covered with dust.

polla, *n.f.* pullet, chicken, young hen; (*coll.*) pretty girl; pool (at cards); (*orn.*) fulica, coot.

pollada, *n.f.* brood, flock; hatch, covey; (*mil.*) grape-shot.

pollancón, -ona, *n.m.f., a.* large chicken; (*coll.*) overgrown youth.

pollastre, -tra, *n.m.f.* pullet.

pollazón, *n.m.* hatch, brood, hatching and rearing fowls.

pollera, *n.f.* chicken-rearer, hen-coop; go-cart; hooped skirt; (*Am.*) skirt; (*astron.*) Pleiades.

pollería, *n.f.* poultry-shop, poultry-market; group of young people.

pollero, *n.m.* fowl-yard, poulterer.

pollerón, *n.m.* (*Arg.*) riding-skirt.

pollina, *n.f.* young she-ass.

pollinarmente, *adv.* (*coll.*) stupidly.

pollino, *n.m.* ass, young ass, donkey; stupid fellow.

pollito, -ta, *n.m.f.* chick, chicken; (*coll.*) boy or girl. — *a.* of tender age.

pollo, *n.m.* chicken, nestling, young bee; (*coll.*) young man; artful fellow.

polluelo, -la, *n.m.f.* chick, small chicken.

poma, *n.f.* apple; perfume-box; smelling-bottle; pomander box.

pomada, *n.f.* pomatum, pomade.

pomar, *n.m.* orchard, apple-orchard.

pomarada, *n.f.* apple plantation.

pomarrosa, *n.f.* rose apple.

pómez, *n.m.* pumice; *piedra pomez*, pumice-stone.

pomo, *n.m.* pip fruit; pommel; flask, flagon, smelling-bottle; nosegay; pomum; pomander box.

pomol, *n.m.* (*Mex.*) a corn-flour omelet for breakfast.

pompa, *n.f.* pomp, pageantry, splendour, grandeur, parade, stateliness, ostentation, procession; inflation of clothes; expanded tail of a peacock; (*naut.*) pump; bubble.

pompearse, *v.r.* to appear with pomp and ostentation; to strut.

pompo, -pa, *a.* (*Col.*) obtuse, blunt; flat-nosed.

pompón, *n.m.* (*mil.*) pompon.

pomposamente, *adv.* pompously, magnificently.

pomposo, -sa, *a.* pompous, ostentatious, majestic, magnificent, splendid, inflated, swelled.

pómulo, *n.m.* cheekbone.

ponasí, *n.m.* (*Cub.*) poisonous shrub with deep-red flowers (*Hamelia patens*).

poncí, poncidre, poncil, *n.m., a.* kind of bitter citron or lemon.

ponchada, *n.f.* quantity of punch.

ponche, *n.m.* punch.

ponchera, *n.f.* punch-bowl.

poncho, -cha, *a.* soft, lazy, listless.

poncho, *n.m.* military cloak; (*Am.*) travelling cloak or blanket, poncho.

ponderable, *a.* measurable, ponderable; wonderful, important.

ponderación, *n.f.* pondering, considering, weighing mentally; exaggeration, heightening.

ponderador, -ra, *n.m.f.* ponderer; one who exaggerates.

ponderal, *a.* ponderal, relating to weight.

ponderar, *v.t.* to ponder, consider, weigh; to exaggerate, heighten.

ponderativo, -va, *a.* exaggerating, hyperbolical.

ponderosamente, *adv.* attentively, carefully.

ponderosidad, *n.f.* ponderousness, ponderosity, weightiness.

ponderoso, -sa, *a.* ponderous, grave, weighty; cautious, circumspect.

ponedero, -ra, *a.* laying eggs, layer; capable of being laid.

ponedero, *n.m.* nest; nest-egg.

ponedor, -ra, *n.m.f.* wagerer, better, outbidder; egg-laying, egg-layer; horse trained to rear.

ponencia, *n.f.* office, report or decision of a chairman or umpire.

ponente, *n.m., a.* referee, arbitrator; chairman of a committee of inquiry.

poner, *v.t.* (*past. part.* **puesto;** *pres. indic.* **pongo;** *pres. subj.* **ponga;** *pret.* **puse;** *fut. indic.* **pondré**) to put, place, set, lay (as the table); to leave to one's judgment or action; arrange, dispose, appoint, place in charge; to wager; to take part, contribute; to assume, suppose; to adduce; to agree; to leave; to bring forth, lay eggs; to cause (fear, etc.); to name, nickname, call; to join, add; to impose, enjoin, compel, oblige, enforce; to write, set down, put down; to treat badly; to cause to become (red, angry, etc.). — *v.r.* to apply oneself, start, begin, set about; to arrive, get to a place; to oppose, object; to don, put on, dress, adorn oneself; to undergo a change, become, grow, get; to set (of sun, moon, etc.); *al poner del sol* (or *al ponerse el sol*), at sunset; *poner el grito en el cielo*, to complain bitterly; *poner en ridículo*, to make a fool of; *poner sobre las estrellas*, to laud to the skies; *poner cariño a*, to take a fancy to; *poner casa*, to set up house; *poner como un trapo*, to scold severely; *poner colorado*, to put to the blush; *ponerse colorado*, to blush; *poner complacencia en*, to take pleasure in; *poner peros* (or *defectos*), to find fault; *poner de vuelta y media*, to humiliate; *poner coto a*, to put a stop (or limit); *ponerse en jarras* (or *asas*), to set one's arms akimbo; *poner en (tanto)*, to bid (so much); *poner en duda*, to question, doubt; *poner miedo a*, to make afraid; *poner pies en pared*, to persist obstinately; *ponerse moreno*, to get sunburnt; *poner en claro* (or *manifiesto*), to make clear; *poner por escrito*, to set down in writing; *ponérsele a uno*, to take a fancy to someone; *ponerse en la razón*, to listen to reason; *poner en relieve*, to carve in relief, describe graphically; *poner de patitas en la calle*, to discharge, send about one's business; *poner de vuelta y media*, to abuse, scold soundly; *poner fuego a*, to set on fire; *poner las gavias en facha*, (*naut.*) to lay the topsails aback; *poner las vergas en cruz*, (*naut.*) to square the yards; *poner los ojos en*, to set one's heart upon; *poner los ojos en blanco*, to turn up the whites of one's eyes; *poner en limpio*, to make a clean copy of; *poner nombres a*, to call names; *poner lengua en*, to speak abusively of; *poner mar de por medio*, to put the ocean between one (and one's pursuers); *ponerse en caso de*, to put oneself in the place of; *poner pies en polvorosa*, to take to one's heels; *ponerse hueco*, to give oneself airs; *ponerse flaco*, to get very thin; *poner una pica en Flandes*, to achieve a difficult task; *poner una carta*, to write a letter; *poner unos renglones*, to drop a few lines; *poner un bajel a nado*, to launch a ship.

pongo, *n.m.* (*zool.*) orang-outang; (*Bol., Per.*) Indian servant; (*Ec., Per.*) narrow and dangerous ford.

poniente, *n.m.* west; west wind.

ponimiento, *n.m.* act of putting (on).

ponleví, *n.m.* high heel, high-heeled shoe.

ponqué, *n.m.* (*Cub., Ven.*) cake made of flour, butter, eggs, and sugar.

pontazgo, pontaje, *n.m.* bridge-toll, pontage.

pontear, *v.t.* to erect bridges.

pontezuelo, -la, *n.m.f.* small bridge.

pontificado, *n.m.* pontificate, papacy, popedom.

pontifical, *a.* pontifical, papal. — *n.m.* pontifical (book), pontifical robe; parochial tithes.

pontificalmente, *adv.* pontifically.

pontificar, *v.i.* (conjugated like BUSCAR) to pontificate, govern as pontiff.

pontífice, *n.m.* pope, pontiff; archbishop.

pontificio, -cia, *a.* pontifical.

pontín, *n.m.* (*Philip.*) coasting vessel.

ponto, *n.m.* (*poet.*) sea.

pontón, *n.m.* (*mil.*) pontoon; (*naut.*) mudscow, dredge; hulk serving as store-ship, hospital or prison ship; log bridge.

pontonero, *n.m.* pontoneer.

ponzoña, *n.f.* poison, venom, toxin.

ponzoñosamente, *adv.* poisonously.

ponzoñoso, -sa, *a.* poisonous, venomous, toxic; noxious, corrupting.

popa, *n.f.* (*naut.*) poop, stern; prosperity; *a popa, de popa*, aft, abaft; *viento en popa*, (*naut.*) before the wind.

popamiento, *n.m.* despising; cajoling.

popar, *v.t.* to contemn, despise; to flatter, caress, fawn.

popel, *a.* sternmost.

popelina, *n.f.* a very thin cotton tissue.

popés, popeses, *n.m.pl.* stays at the mizenmast.

popocho, -cha, *a.* (*Col.*) very full, replete, sated, gorged.

popote, *n.m.* (*Mex.*) Indian straw for brooms.

población, *n.f.* population.

populachería, *n.f.* clap-trap, cheap talk.

populachero, -ra, *a.* vulgar, common.

populacho, *n.m.* populace; crowd, rabble, mob.

popular, *a.* popular, plebeian.

popularidad, *n.f.* popularity.

popularizar, *v.t.* (*pret.* **popularicé;** *pres. subj.* **popularice**) to popularize, make popular. — *v.r.* to become popular.

populazo, *n.m.* populace, rabble, mob.

populeón, *n.m.* white poplar ointment.

populoso, -sa, *a.* populous, full of people.

popusa, *n.f.* (*ES., Guat.*) maize omelet stuffed with cheese and meat.

poquedad, *n.f.* littleness, paucity; cowardice, pusillanimity; imbecility; trifle, mite.

poquillo, -lla, *a.* little, small, trifling.

poquísimo, -ma, *a. superl.* very little, very small.

poquitico, -ica; -illo, -illa; -ito, -ita; poquitín, *a.* very little, very small.

poquito, -ta, *a.* very little, weak, diminutive; *a poquitos*, in tiny portions; *de poquito*, pusillanimous; *poquito a poco*, gently, slowly.

por, *prep.* for, for the sake of, on behalf of, on account of; by; about; through, between; because, as; per; *por mí*, on my behalf; *por otra parte*, on the other hand; *por ahí*, about that, very nearly; *por la mañana*, in the morning; *por mayor*, wholesale; *por Navidad*, about Christmas; *cuentas por cobrar*, bills to be collected; *por barba*, per head; *por carta de más*, excessively; *por carta de menos*, insufficiently; *por cé o por bé*, by hook or by crook; *por cuanto*, whereas; *por debajo de mano*, furtively, in an underhand manner; *por mejor decir*, to speak more exactly; *por tanto*, wherefore; *por acá o por allá*, here or there; *por ahora*, for the present; *por cierto*, indeed; *de por sí*, by itself, by oneself; *por demás*, overmuch, excessive; *por encima*, slightly, superficially; *por ende*, for that reason; *por entre*, through; *por más que* (or *por mucho que*), however much; *por buenas*, by fair means; *por malas*, by foul means; *por donde fueres, haz como vieres*, when in Rome do as the Romans do; *¿por dónde va la danza?* (*met.*) which way does the wind blow? *por el bien parecer*, for appearances' sake; *por si acaso*, if by any chance; *por completo*, completely; *por supuesto*, of course; *por junto*, in the aggregate, in the sum; *por más que Vd. diga*, whatever you say *or* say what you will; *estar por*, to be on the point of; to feel like, be inclined to.

porca, *n.f.* earth between furrows.

porcachón, -ona, *a.* (*coll.*) very dirty, hoggish.

porcal, *a.* kind of large plum.

porcelana, *n.f.* porcelain, China ware; (*jewel.*) enamel.

porcelanita, *n.f.* porcellanite.

porcentaje, *n.m.* percentage.

porcino, *n.m.* young pig; bruise, bump; *pan porcino*, (*bot.*) sow-bread.

porción, *n.f.* part, portion, lot, dose; (*com.*) allowance, share, allotment, pittance.

porcioncica, -lla, -ta, *n.m.f.* small portion.

porcionero, -ra, *a.* apportioning, participating.

porcionista, *n.m.f.* holder of a share or portion; boarder in college.

porcipelo, *n.m.* (*coll.*) bristle.

porcuno, -na, *a.* hoggish, porcine.

porchada, *n.f.* stretcher in paper-factories.

porche, *n.m.* covered walk, porch, portico.

pordiosear, *v.i.* to beg, ask charity.

pordiosería, *n.f.* beggary, asking alms.

pordiosero, -ra, *n.m.f.* beggar.

porfía, *n.f.* tussle, dispute, obstinate quarrel; obstinacy, stubbornness, importunity; *a porfía*, emulously, in competition.

porfiadamente, *adv.* pertinaciously, obstinately, contentiously.

porfiado, -da, *a.* obstinate, stubborn.

porfiador, -ra, *n.m.f.* contender, brawler, wrangler, persistent person.

porfiar, *v.i.* to contend, wrangle, persist, importune, insist.

porfídico, -ca, *a.* porphyritic.

pórfido, *n.m.* porphyry, jasper.

porfirizar, *v.t.* (*pharm.*) to pound, reduce to powder.

porfolio, *n.m.* portfolio, album.

porgadero, *n.m.* (*prov.*) sieve, riddle.

pormenor, *n.m.* detail, minute account, particular.

pormenorizar, *v.t.* to detail, itemize, give in detail.

pornagrafía, *n.f.* pornography; obscene writing, drawing, or painting.

pornográfico, -ca, *a.* pornographic.

pornógrafo, *n.m.* pornographer, obscene writer or artist.

poro, *n.m.* pore, interstice.

pororó, *n.m.* (*Am.*) toasted corn.

pororoca, *n.f.* (*Arg.*) breaking wave of a spring tide; tide rip.

porosidad, *n.f.* porosity, porousness.

poroso, -sa, *a.* porous.

poroto, *n.m.* (*Am.*) a variety of French bean; dish, course prepared with *porotos*.

porque, *conj.* because, for the reason that, as, in order that.

¿por qué? *interr.* why? wherefore? for what reason?

porqué, *n.m.* why, reason, cause, motive; (*coll.*) allowance, portion, pittance.

porquera, *n.f.* wild boar's lair.

porquería, *n.f.* nastiness, uncleanliness; filth, rudeness, hoggishness; nuisance, dirty trick or action; trifle.

porqueriza, *n.f.* pigsty.

porquerizo, porquero, *n.m.* swineherd.

porquerón, *n.m.* catchpoll, bumbailiff.

porqueta, *n.f.* woodlouse; cochineal insect.

porquezuelo, -la, *n.m.f.* young pig; nasty, dirty person, slovenly person.

porra, *n.f.* club, bludgeon, heavy-headed stick; maul; last player in children's games; (*coll.*). stupid, dull person; (*coll.*) boast, vanity, presumption.

porrada, *n.f.* blow with a club, etc.; (*coll.*) foolishness, nonsense ; abundance, copiousness, affluence.

porrazo, *n.m.* blow, knock, fall.

porrear, *v.i.* (*coll.*) to insist, persist, be importunate.

porrería, *n.f.* (*coll.*) obstinacy, tediousness, stupidity.

porreta, *n.f.* green leaf of leeks, garlic or onions; *en porreta* (*coll.*) stark naked.

porrilla, *n.f.* forging hammer; small club-headed stick; (*vet.*) osseous tumour in joints.

porrillo (a), *adv.* (*coll.*) abundantly, freely, copiously.

porrina, *n.f.* field of green corn.

porrino, *n.m.* tender leek-plant.

porrizo, *n.m.* leek-bed, leek-plot.

porro, -rra, *a.* dull, ignorant, heavy, stupid.

porro, *n.m.* leek.

porrón, *n.m.* earthen jug, pitcher; wine bottle with long spout.

porrón, -ona, *a.* (*coll.*) heavy, slow, sluggish.

porrudo, *n.m.* (*prov.*) shepherd's crook.

porta, *n.f.* (*artill.*) door of a porthole; (*football*) goal; (*naut.*) porthole.

portaaguja, *n.f.* needle-holder.

portabandera, *n.f.* flag-pole socket.

portacaja, *n.f.* loom carrier; (*mil.*) drumsash or strap.

portacarabina, *n.f.* scabbard or sheath for the carbine of a horseman.

portacartas, *n.m.* mail-bag; postman.

portachuelo, *n.m.* opening between two mountains.

portada, *n.f.* porch, façade, portal; title page, frontispiece; division of the warp.

portadera, *n.f.* chest.

portado, -da, *a.;* *bien portado*, well dressed or behaved; *mal portado*, poorly dressed, badly behaved. — *p.p.* [PORTAR].

portador, -ra, *n.m.f.* bearer, porter, carrier; (*com.*) holder, bearer.

portador, *n.m.* waiter's tray.

portaestandarte, *n.m.* standard-bearer, colour-sergeant.

portafusil, *n.m.* musket-sling.

portaguión, *n.m.* standard-bearer in cavalry.

portal, *n.m.* porch, entry, entrance, vestibule; portico, piazza; town-gate.

portalápiz, *n.m.* pencil holder.

portalazo, *n.m.* large door or porch.

portalejo, *n.m.* portico, little porch.

portaleña, *n.f.* (*fort., naut.*) embrasure; plank for doors.

portalero, *n.m.* octroi officer.

portalibros, *n.m.* book-strap, school satchel.

portalón, *n.m.* gangway.

portamantas, *n.m.* rug-strap.

portamanteo, *n.m.* portmanteau.

portamira, *n.m.* (*surv.*) rodman.

portamonedas, *n.m.* pocket-book, purse.

portaneumáticos, *n.m.* (*motor.*) tyre holder.

portante, *n.m.* gait in which a horse raises the

legs of one side simultaneously; *tomar el portante, (coll.)* to go away.

portantillo, *n.m.* tiny, rapid steps, pattering steps (especially of a chicken).

portanuevas, *n.m.f.* newsmonger.

portanveces, *n.m.* (*prov.*) coadjutor, locum.

portañola, *n.f.* porthole.

portañuela, *n.f.* fly of trousers.

portaobjetos, *n.m.* slide of a microscope.

portaparaguas, *n.m.* umbrella stand.

portapaz, *n.m.f.*(*eccles.*) pax.

portaplacas, *n.m.* plate-holder (in photography).

portapliegos, *n.m.* portfolio, document-case.

portaplumas, *n.m.* pen-holder.

portarse, *v.t.* to behave, comport oneself, act. — *v.i.* (*naut.*) to fill (of the sails).

portátil, *a.* portable, easily carried.

portavasos, *n.m.* glass rack.

portaventanero, *n.m.* carpenter specializing in doors and window making.

portaviandas, *n.m.* lunch basket; dinner pail.

portavoz, *n.m.* megaphone, speaking trumpet; spokesman.

portazgo, *n.m.* toll, turnpike-duty.

portazguero, *n.m.* toll-collector, toll-gatherer.

portazo, *n.m.* bang of a door; slamming a door in one's face.

porte, *n.m.* portage, porterage; carriage, freight, postage; (*naut.*) burden or tonnage; gait, port, deportment; conduct, demeanour, behaviour; nobility, illustrious descent; size, capacity; *porte franco,* post free or prepaid.

portear, *v.t.* to carry, heave. — *v.i.* to shut a door or window violently. — *v.r.* to migrate (of birds).

portento, *n.m.* prodigy, portent, wonder.

portentoso, -sa, *a.* prodigious, marvellous, portentous.

porteño, -ña, *a.* of or from Buenos Aires.

porteo, *n.m.* portage, cartage, transport of merchandise.

porterejo, *n.m.* little porter.

portería, *n.f.* porter's lodge, conciergerie; employment of a porter; (*naut.*) all the portholes in a ship.

portero, -ra, *a.* half-fired brick. — *n.m.f.* porter, gate-keeper, janitor; concierge; (*sport*) goal-keeper; *portero de estrados,* usher of a court.

portezuela, *n.f.* little door; carriage door; flap, pocket-flap; (*Mex.*) narrow pass between hills.

pórtico, *n.m.* portico, porch; hall, lobby.

portier, *n.m.* portière, door-curtain.

portilla, *n.f.* track or path across a person's land; (*naut.*) porthole.

portillo, *n.m.* aperture, opening, passage, breach, gap; gate, wicket; means to an end; pass between mountains; chip (in crockery, etc.); octroi gate of a town.

portón, *n.m.* inner door of a house.

portorriqueño, -ña, *a.* Puerto-Rican.

portugués, *n.m.* Portuguese language.

portugués, -esa, *n.m.f., a.* Portuguese.

portuguesada, *n.f.* exaggeration, talking big.

portulano, *n.m.* set of charts of ports and harbours.

porvenir, *n.m.* future, time to come.

¡porvida! *interj.* for the love of!

pos, en, *adv.* after, behind, in pursuit of.

posa, *n.f.* passing bell; (*eccles.*) halt to sing a response. — *pl.* **posas,** buttocks.

posada, *n.f.* home, dwelling; lodging-house,

inn, small hotel; lodging; *posada con asistencia,* board and lodging.

posadera, *n.f.* hostess, landlady.

posaderas, *n.f.pl.* buttocks.

posadero, *n.m.* inn-keeper, host; rope seat.

posante, *a.* reposing; (*naut.*) smooth-sailing.

posar, *v.i.* to lodge, board; to rest, repose; to sit upon; to perch, light. — *v.t.* to lay down a load, to rest. — *v.r.* to settle (of a liquid).

posaverga, *n.f.* (*naut.*) yard prop; spare mast or yard.

posca, *n.f.* mixture of vinegar and water.

posdata, *n.f.* postscript.

poseedor, -ra, *n.m.f.* possessor, owner, holder.

poseer, *v.t.* (*p.p.* **poseído, poseso;** *pres. part.* **poseyendo;** *pret.* **él poseyó**) to possess, own, have, hold; master (an art, language, etc.).

poseído, -da, *a.* possessed; possessed of an evil spirit. — *p.p.* [POSEER].

posesión, *n.f.* possession, dominion, holding, tenure, tenancy; farm, land, real estate; the state of being possessed or under psychical or supernatural influence. — *pl.* **posesiones,** lands, real estate, wealth, property.

posesional, *a.* including or belonging to possession; *acto posesional,* (*law*) act of possession.

posesionarse, *v.r.* to take possession.

posesionero, *n.m.* cattle-keeper who owns pasturage.

posesivo, -va, *a.* (*gram.*) possessive.

poseso, -sa, *a.* possessed; possessed of an evil spirit. — *p.p. irreg.* [POSEER].

posesor, -ra, *n.m.f.* possessor, owner, holder.

posesorio, -ria, *a.* possessory.

poseyente, *a.* possessing, possessive.

posfecha, *n.f.* post-dating, post-date.

posfechar, *v.t.* to post date.

posibilidad, *n.f.* possibility, likelihood, feasibility; wealth, means, property.

posibilista, *n.m.* (*polit.*) possibilist, aiming at reforms that are practicable.

posibilitar, *v.t.* to render possible, facilitate.

posible, *a.* possible, feasible. — *n.m.pl.* **posibles,** wealth, substance, capital, income, means; best of one's ability.

posiblemente, *adv.* possibly.

posición, *n.f.* position, situation, posture, pose, attitude; placing, placement; location, situation, status, standing; (*law*) questions and answers of a cross-examination; (*mil.*) strong point.

positivamente, *adv.* positively, absolutely, certainly, by all means.

positivismo, *n.m.* positivism; positiveness.

positivista, *n.m.f.* positivist.

positivo, -va, *a.* positive, sure, certain; true, indubitable, real; absolute; matter-of-fact; *de positivo,* certainly, without doubt.

pósito, *n.m.* public granary; (*econ.*) brotherhood.

positura, *n.f.* posture, disposition, state.

posma, *n.f.* sluggishness, dullness, sloth.

poso, *n.m.* sediment, settlement, lees, dregs; repose, rest.

posó, *n.m.* (*Philip.*) chignon, hair knot.

posón, *n.m.* round matted stool.

pospelo (a), *adv.* reluctantly, against the grain.

pospierna, *n.f.* horse's flank.

posponer, *v.t.* (conjugated like PONER) to place

one thing behind or after another; to sub-ordinate; to postpone, put off, delay.
pospositivo, -va, *a.* suffixed, postpositive.
pospuesto, -ta, *p.p. irreg.* [POSPONER].
posta, *n.f.* post-house, stage-house, post-horses, relay, post; slug of lead; slice, piece of meat or fish; memorial tablet; stake (at cards). —*n.m.* one who travels post; *a posta,* designedly, intentionally; *correr la posta* (or *ir en posta*), to travel by post.
postal, *a.* postal. —*n.f.* post-card; (*Am.*) *casilla postal,* letter-box; *giro postal,* postal order.
postdiluviano, -na, *a.* postdiluvian.
poste, *n.m.* post, pillar; school punishment; *oler el poste,* to smell a rat, to scent danger.
postear, *v.i.* to travel by post.
postelero, *n.m.* (*naut.*) skid.
postema, *n.f.* abscess, tumour; bore, tedious person; boredom.
postemero, *n.m.* (*surg.*) large lancet.
postergación, *n.f.* deferring, leaving behind, postponement; disregard of seniority.
postergar, *v.t.* (*pret.* **postergué;** *pres. subj.* **postergue**) to leave behind, postpone, defer; to disregard or ignore the right of seniority (office, employment, etc.).
posteridad, *n.f.* posterity.
posterior, *a.* posterior, hinder, later, rear.
posterioridad, *n.f.* posteriority.
posteriormente, *adv.* lastly, subsequently.
posteta, *n.f.* (*print.*) number of printed sheets stitched together.
postfijo, -ja, *a.* (*gram.*) suffix.
postigo, *n.m.* wicket; (*fort.*) sally-port; postern, small gate; peep-window, shutter.
postila, *n.f.* postil, annotation, marginal note.
postilación, *n.f.* act of making annotations or marginal notes.
postilador, *n.m.* annotator.
postilar, *v.t.* to postillate, gloss, annotate, comment.
postilla, *n.f.* scab on wounds.
postillón, *n.m.* postilion, driver, post-boy.
postilloso, -sa, *a.* pustulous, scabby.
postín, *n.m.* airs, ostentation, conceit; *darse postín,* to put on airs.
postiza, *n.f.* upper works on galleys for an additional tier of oars.
postizo, -za, *a.* artificial, false, not natural; *dientes postizos,* dentures, artificial teeth; *pelo postizo,* false hair.
postizo, *n.m.* toupet, switch.
postmeridiano, -na, *a.* postmeridian, after-noon.
postor, *n.m.* bidder.
postración, *n.f.* prostration; kneeling; humilia-tion, dejection, depression, complete ex-haustion.
postrado, -da, *a.* prostrate, prostrated; prone, procumbent. — *p.p.* [POSTRAR].
postrador, -ra, *n.m.f.* one who prostrates himself; foot-stool in choir.
postrar, *v.t.* to prostrate, humble; to demolish, overthrow; to debilitate, weaken, exhaust. — *v.r.* to prostrate oneself, lie prone, kneel down, be completely exhausted.
postre, *a.* last in order; *a la postre,* at last, in the long run; *por fin y postre,* (*coll.*) finally.
postre, *n.m.* dessert.
postremo, -ma, *a.* last.

postrer, (apocope of POSTRERO and used only before a masculine, singular noun).
postreramente, *adv.* ultimately, lastly.
postrero, -ra, *a.* (shortened form, **postrer**) last in order, hindermost.
postrimeramente, *adv.* finally, at last.
postrimería, *n.f.* (*theol.*) last years of life.
postrimero, -ra, *a.* last in order; hindmost; (shortened form **postrimer,** used before a masculine, singular noun).
póstula, postulación, *n.f.* postulation, peti-tion, request.
postulado, *n.m.* postulate.
postulanta, *n.f.* woman seeking admission to a religious community.
postulante, *n.m.f.* postulant.
postular, *v.t.* to elect; to postulate; to solicit eagerly.
póstumo, -ma, *a.* posthumous.
postura, *n.f.* posture, position, situation; atti-tude; (*com.*) bid; bet, wager; egg-laying, eggs laid; planting trees, trees planted; tree or plant transplanted; assize of provisions; agreement, convention.
potable, *a.* potable, drinkable.
potación, *n.f.* potation, beverage, drinking.
potador, -ra, *n.m.f.* inspector of weights and measures.
potaje, *n.m.* pottage, boiled food; dressed vege-table, porridge; mixed drink; useless medley.
potajería, *n.f.* heap of dry pulse; vegetable store.
potajier, *n.m.* keeper of the vegetables in the royal palace.
potala, *n.f.* stone anchor; small slow vessel.
potar, *v.t.* to equalize weights and measures; to drink.
potasa, *n.f.* potash.
potásico, -ca, *a.* potassic.
potasio, *n.m.* (*min.*) potassium.
pote, *n.m.* pot, gallipot, jar, jug; flower-pot; standard weight or measure; *a pote,* abun-dantly.
potecillo, -ito, *n.m.* little pot or jar.
potencia, *n.f.* power, ability, potency, author-ity; dominion, kingdom, nation, state; force, strength, power of generation; possibility; faculty; (*min.*) thickness of a vein of ore; (*artill.*) reach. — *pl.* **potencias,** mental powers (memory, judgment, will).
potencial, *a.* potential, virtual, possible.
potencialidad, *n.f.* potentiality, virtuality.
potencialmente, *adv.* potentially, virtually.
potentado, *n.m.* potentate, sovereign, mon-arch.
potente, *a.* potent, mighty, powerful; strong, vigorous; (*coll.*) great, bulky, huge.
potentemente, *adv.* powerfully, potently.
potentísimo, -ma, *a. superl.* most powerful.
poterna, *n.f.* (*mil.*) postern, sally-port.
potestad, *n.f.* power, dominion; jurisdiction, command; potentate. — *pl.* **potestades,** angelic powers.
potestativo, -va, *a.* (*law*) facultative.
potingue, *n.m.* (*coll.*) potion, concoction.
potísimo, -ma, *a.* most special.
potista, *n.m.f.* (*coll.*) tippler, drunkard.
potoco, -ca, *a.* (*Chi.*) short, fat, stout.
potorrillo, *n.m.* (*Ec.*) shrub with pretty red flower.
potosí, *n.m.* (*Am.*) (*fig.*) untold riches; *valer*

un Potosí, (fig.) above, beyond or without price, priceless.

potra, *n.f. (coll.)* rupture, hernia; filly; *tener potra,* to have good luck.

potrada, *n.f.* troop of young mares at pasture.

potranca, *n.f.* filly, young mare.

potrear, *v.t. (coll.)* to vex, tease, molest, annoy.

potrera, *n.f.* hempen head-stall.

potrero, *n.m. (coll.)* surgeon who cures ruptures; herdsman of colts; pasture-ground; *(Am.)* cattle-farm.

potrico, -illo, *n.m.* small colt.

potril, *n.m., a.* pasture for foals.

potrilla, *n.f. (fig., coll.)* nickname given to old persons affecting youthful habits.

potro, -tra, *a.* colt, filly, foal; wooden horse, rack; shoeing frame; pit in the ground for breaking open a beehive; something that torments or molests; obstetrical chair; *estar en un potro,* to be on the rack (i.e. in suspense).

potroso, -sa, *a.* having a rupture; *(coll.)* fortunate, lucky.

poya, *n.f.* fee for baking in a public oven; hemp bagasse.

poyal, *n.m.* striped cover for benches; stone seat.

poyar, *v.i.* to pay the *poya.*

poyata, *n.f.* shelf, cupboard.

poyo, *n.m.* stone seat or bench; judge's fee.

poza, *n.f.* tank, pond; pool for retting hemp.

pozal, *n.m.* bucket, pail; coping of a well.

pozanco, *n.m.* pool in a river bank.

pozero, *n.m.* well-digger.

pozo, *n.m.* well; deep hole in a river; eddy, whirlpool; anything complete, deep or full; *(min.)* pit, shaft; *(naut.)* hold; *es un pozo de ciencias,* he is deeply learned; *pozo artesiano,* artesian well; *pozo negro,* cesspool.

pozol, pozole, *n.m. (CR., Hond.)* boiled barley, beans and meat; *(Mex.)* beverage made of barley and sugar.

pozuela, *n.f.* small pond, puddle.

pozuelo, *n.m.* small well or pit; vessel sunk in the ground to collect oil, etc.

práctica, *n.f.* practice; habit, custom, use; experience, exercise; manner, method, mode; learning of a profession under a master.

practicable, *a.* practicable, feasible.

practicador, -ra, *n.m.f.* practiser, practitioner.

practicaje, *n.m. (naut.)* pilotage.

prácticamente, *adv.* practically.

practicante, *n.m.* practiser, practitioner; hospital intern; hospital nurse; assistant chemist. — *a.* practising.

practicar, *v.t. (pret.* **practiqué;** *pres. subj.* **practique)** to practise, perform, do, execute; to learn (a profession); *practicar investigaciones,* to make inquiries.

práctico, -ca, *a.* practical, skilful, experienced.

práctico, *n.m.* practiser, practitioner; *(naut.)* pilot.

practicón, -ona, *n.m.f. (coll.)* one with great practical knowledge.

pradeño, -ña, *a.* relating to meadows.

pradera, pradería, *n.f.* country full of meadows and pasture-ground; meadow, prairie, mead, pasture-land.

praderoso, -sa; pradial, *a.* relating to meadows.

prado, *n.m.* lawn, field, meadow, pasture ground, paddock; city walk (Madrid, etc.);

prado de guadaña, meadow mown annually.

pragmática, *n.f.* pragmatic, royal ordinance, rescript, decree.

pragmático, -ca, *a.* pragmatic, pragmatical. — *n.m.* commentator upon national laws.

pragmatismo, *n.m.* pragmatism.

pragmatista, *n.m.f., a.* pragmatist(ic).

prasio, *n.m. (min.)* prase.

prasma, *n.m. (min.)* dark green agate.

pravedad, *n.f.* perversity, iniquity, depravity.

praviana, *n.f.* an Asturian popular song.

pravo, -va, *a.* depraved, perverse, wicked.

pre, *n.m.* soldier's daily pay.

preámbulo, *n.m.* preamble, preface, exordium; *(coll.)* circumlocution, evasion.

prebenda, *n.f.* prebend, sinecure, canonry, benefice.

prebendado, *n.m.* prebendary.

prebendar, *v.t.* to confer a prebend or benefice.

prebostal, *a.* provostal.

prebostazgo, *n.m.* provostship.

preboste, *n.m.* provost.

precariamente, *adv.* precariously.

precario, -ria, *a.* precarious, uncertain.

precaución, *n.f.* precaution, guard, vigilance.

precaucionarse, *v.r.* to be cautious.

precautelar, *v.t.* to caution, forewarn.

precaver, *v.t.* to obviate, prevent. — *v.r.* to be on one's guard.

precavido, -da, *a.* sagacious, cautious, guarded.

precedencia, *n.f.* precedence, priority; precession, preference; superiority, primacy.

precedente, *a.* precedent, preceding, foregoing. — *n.m.* precedent.

preceder, *v.t.* to precede, go before; excel, be superior.

preceptista, *n.m., a.* one who gives precepts.

preceptivamente, *adv.* preceptively.

preceptivo, -va, *a.* preceptive, didactic.

precepto, *n.m.* precept; order, mandate, rule; injunction, commandment.

preceptor, *n.m.* preceptor, teacher, master.

preceptora, *n.f.* schoolmistress.

preceptuar, *v.t.* to issue precepts.

preces, *n.f.pl.* prayers; devotions; supplication.

percesión, *n.f. (astron.)* precession; *(rhet.)* reticence.

preciado, -da, *a.* valued, appraised, esteemed, priced; excellent, valuable, magnificent, precious; boastful, vain.

preciador, -ra, *n.m.f.* appraiser.

preciar, *v.t.* to value, price, appraise, appreciate. — *v.r.* to boast, brag, glory.

precinta, *n.f.* wooden or iron bands for securing the corners of boxes; *(naut.)* parcelling.

precintar, *v.t.* to strap, hoop, bind corners of boxes; to seal; *(naut.)* to parcel the seams.

precinto, *n.m.* strapping, sealed strap.

precio, *n.m.* price; cost, value; premium, reward; esteem, estimation; *tener en precio,* to esteem; *precio fijo,* fixed prices, no reductions.

preciosa, *n.f. (eccles.)* allowance to prebendaries.

preciosamente, *adv.* preciously, richly.

preciosidad, *n.f.* worth, value; preciousness, excellence; beautiful object.

precioso, -sa, *a.* precious, valuable, excellent; witty, merry.

precipicio, *n.m.* precipice, chasm; ruin, destruction; great fall.
precipitación, *n.f.* (*chem.*) precipitation; precipitancy, rash haste.
precipitadamente, *adv.* precipitately, hastily.
precipitadero, *n.m.* precipice, steep cliff.
precipitado, -da, *a.* precipitate, abrupt, hasty. — *n.m.* (*chem.*) precipitate; *precipitado blanco,* calomel; *precipitado rojo,* red precipitate.
precipitante, *n.m.* (*chem.*) precipitant.
precipitar, *v.t.* to precipitate, cast headlong; hasten; to expose to ruin; (*chem.*) to cause precipitation. — *v.r.* to act precipitately, hurry, hasten.
precípite, *a.* in danger of falling.
precipitosamente, *adv.* precipitately, hastily.
precipitoso, -sa, *a.* steep, slippery; precipitous; rash, inconsiderate.
precipuamente, *adv.* principally, chiefly.
precipuo, -pua, *a.* principal, chief.
precisamente, *adv.* precisely, nicely, exactly; inevitably, indispensably, necessarily; just so.
precisar, *v.t.* to oblige, compel; to state precisely, set forth; to fix, arrange.
precisión, *n.f.* necessity; obligation, compulsion; exactness, preciseness, precision, accuracy.
preciso, -sa, *a.* necessary; requisite, needful; punctual, accurate, precise, exact; distinct, clear; concise.
precitado, -da, *a.* fore-cited, above-quoted, aforesaid.
precito, -ta, *a.* damned, condemned to hell.
preclaramente, *adv.* illustriously, with distinction.
preclaro, -ra, *a.* illustrious, eminent, famous.
precocidad, *n.f.* precocity, forwardness.
precognición, *n.f.* precognition.
precolombino, -na, *a.* pre-Columbian.
preconcebir, *v.t.* to preconceive.
preconización, *n.f.* preconization, eulogy.
preconizador, *n.m.* extoller, eulogiser.
preconizar, *v.t.* (*pret.* **preconicé;** *pres. subj.* **preconice**) to preconize, proclaim, praise, eulogize.
preconocer, *v.t.* (conjugated like CONOCER) to foreknow, foretell.
precoz, *a.* precocious, forward.
precursor, -ra, *a.* preceding. — *n.m.f.* precursor, harbinger, forerunner, herald.
predecesor, -ra, *n.m.f.* predecessor, antecessor, forerunner.
predecir, *v.t.* (conjugated like DECIR) to foretell, predict, anticipate.
predefinición, *n.f.* (*theol.*) predetermination.
predefinir, *v.t.* (*theol.*) to predetermine.
predestinación, *n.f.* predestination, preordination.
predestinado, *n.m.* predestinate.
predestinado, -da, *a.* foreordained.
predestinante, *a.* predestinator.
predestinar, *v.t.* to predestine, predestinate, foreordain.
predeterminación, *n.f.* predetermination, foreordination.
predeterminar, *v.t.* to anticipate, predetermine, foreordain.
predial, *a.* predial.
prédica, *n.f.* sermon, preaching.
predicable, *a.* fit or able to be preached; (*log.*) predicable.
predicación, *n.f.* preaching, sermon.

predicadera, *n.f.* pulpit. — *pl.* **predicaderas,** (*coll.*) facility for preaching.
predicado, *n.m.* (*log.*) predicate.
predicador, -ra, *n.m.f.* preacher, orator, homilist.
predicamental, *a.* (*phil.*) predicamental.
predicamento, *n.m.* predicament, position, station, standing.
predicante, *n.m.* sectarian preacher.
predicar, *v.t.* (*pret.* **prediqué;** *pres. subj.* **predique**) to preach; to rebuke vice; to praise highly; to publish, make clear, make evident; *bien predica quien bien vive,* he who practises is the successful preacher.
predicción, *n.f.* prediction.
predicho, -cha, *a.,* *p.p. irreg.* [PREDECIR].
predigo; prediga; predije, *pres. indic.; pres. subj.; pret.* [PREDECIR].
predilección, *n.f.* predilection.
predilecto, -ta, *a.* darling, favourite, preferred.
predio, *n.m.* landed property, farm; *predio rústico,* piece of arable ground; *predio urbano,* town or country dwelling-house.
predisponer, *v.t.* (conjugated like PONER) to predispose.
predisposición, *n.f.* predisposition, propensity, inclination.
predispuesto, -ta, *a.* predisponent, predisposed, biased, inclined.
predominación, *n.f.* predominance, superiority.
predominante, *a.* predominant, prevailing.
predominar, *v.t.* to predominate, overrule, overpower; to exceed in height, overlook; to prevail (of a wind); to control, compel.
predominio, *n.m.* predominance, superiority.
preeminencia, *n.f.* pre-eminence, mastery.
preeminente, *a.* pre-eminent, superior.
preexcelso, -sa, *a.* illustrious, great, eminent.
preexistencia, *n.f.* pre-existence.
preexistente, *a.* pre-existent.
preexistir, *v.i.* to pre-exist.
prefacio, *n.m.* preface, prologue.
prefación, *n.f.* preface, introduction, prologue.
prefecto, *n.m.* prefect, president, chairman.
prefectura, *n.f.* prefecture.
preferencia, *n.f.* preference, choice.
preferente, *a.* preferring; preferential; preferable.
preferentemente, *adv.* preferably.
preferible, *a.* preferable.
preferiblemente, *adv.* preferably.
preferir, *v.t.* (*pres. part.* **prefiriendo;** *pres. indic.* **prefiero;** *pres. subj.* **prefiera;** *pret.* **prefirió**) to prefer.
prefiguración, *n.f.* prefiguration.
prefigurar, *v.t.* to prefigure, foretoken.
prefijar, *v.t.* to prefix, determine, pre-designate.
prefijo, -ja, *a.,* *p.p. irreg.* [PREFIJAR], prefixed.
prefijo, *n.m.* (*gram.*) prefix.
prefinición, *n.f.* act of prefining, fixing a time-limit.
prefinir, *v.t.* to fix a time-limit.
prefulgente, *a.* resplendent, lucid, bright.
pregón, *n.m.* publication by crier, cry.
pregonar, *v.t.* to cry or proclaim publicly; cry about the streets, make publicly known.
pregoneo, *n.m.* cry of street hawkers; crying of goods.

pregonería, *n.f.* office of common crier.
pregonero, *n.m.* town crier; one who tells secrets; auctioneer.
pregonero, -ra, *a.* praising, proclaiming.
pregunta, *n.f.* question; query, inquiry; catechism; *absolver las preguntas,* to answer under oath; *estar a la cuarta pregunta,* to be penniless, hard up.
preguntador, -ra, *n.m.f.* questioner, interrogator, examiner, inquirer.
preguntante, *a.* inquiring.
preguntar, *v.t.* to question, ask, inquire, demand.
preguntón, -ona, *n.m.f.* inquisitive person.
prehistoria, *n.f.* prehistory.
prehistórico, -ca, *a.* prehistoric.
preinserto, -ta, *a.* previously-inserted.
prejudicial, *a.* (*law*) requiring judicial decision.
prejudicio, prejuicio, *n.m.* prejudice, bias.
prejuzgar, *v.t.* (conjugated like JUZGAR) to prejudge.
prelacía, *n.f.* prelacy, prelature.
prelación, *n.f.* preference.
prelada, *n.f.* abbess of a convent, mother superior, prelatess.
prelado, *n.m.* prelate.
prelaticio, -cia, *a.* prelatic.
prelatura, *n.f.* prelacy, prelature.
preliminar, *a.* preliminary, proemial. — *n.m.* preliminary protocol.
prelucir, *v.i.* (conjugated like LUCIR) to sparkle, shine forth.
preludiar, *v.i.* (*mus.*) to play a prelude.
preludio, *n.m.* prelude; flourish, introduction.
prelusión, *n.f.* prelude, prelusion, prologue.
prematuramente, *adv.* prematurely.
prematuro, -ra, *a.* premature, precocious, unripe, unseasoned; (*law*) impuberal.
premeditación, *n.f.* premeditation, forethought.
premeditadamente, *adv.* premeditatedly, with malice aforethought.
premeditar, *v.t.* to consider carefully, premeditate.
premiador, -ra, *n.m.f.* rewarder.
premiar, *v.t.* to reward, remunerate, requite.
premio, *n.m.* reward; recompense, remuneration; prize; premium, interest.
premiosamente, *adv.* tightly, by force.
premioso, -sa, *a.* tight, close; troublesome, burdensome; pinching; rigid, strict; slow in speaking or writing.
premisa, *n.f.* (*log.*) premise; (*fig.*) mark, indication.
premiso, -sa, *a.* premised; (*law*) precedent.
premoción, *n.f.* predisposition (a scholastic term).
premonitorio, -ria, *a.* premonitory.
premoriencia, *n.f.* (*law*) prior death, predeceased.
premorir, *v.i.* (*law*) to die before another.
premura, *n.f.* narrowness; hurry, haste; pressure, urgency.
prenda, *n.f.* pledge, pawn, security; present, gift, token of love or friendship; person or thing greatly loved; piece of jewelry; garments. — *pl.* **prendas,** endowments, talents, accomplishments; children, family, pledges of affection; game of forfeits.
prendado, *a.* smitten (with love); *ser muy*

prendado, to be very accomplished; *estar prendado,* to be taken up with.
prendador, *n.m.* pledger, pawner.
prendamiento, *n.m.* pledging, pawning.
prendar, *v.t.* to take pledges, lend on pledge; to please, charm. — *v.r.* to take a fancy to anything.
prendedero, *n.m.* hook; fillet, brooch.
prendedor, *n.m.* catcher, breast-pin, shawl-pin.
prender, *v.t.* (*p.p.* **prendido, preso**) to grasp, catch, seize; to pin; to imprison, capture; to couple, copulate; to set off, adorn. — *v.i.* to take root; to take fire. — *v.r.* to make an elaborate toilet.
prendería, *n.f.* second-hand shop; pawnbroker's shop; frippery.
prendero, -ra, *n.m.f.* second-hand dealer; broker, pawnbroker; fripper.
prendido, *n.m.* women's garment (especially for the head); pattern or piece of bone-lace.
prendimiento, *n.m.* seizure, capture.
prenoción, *n.f.* (*phil.*) prenotion, first knowledge.
prenombre, *n.m.* prenomen.
prenotar, *v.t.* to note in advance.
prensa, *n.f.* (*mech.*) press; vice, clamp, mill; journalism; printing press; press, newspapers; (*photo.*) printing-frame; *prensa de lagar,* wine-press; *prensa de paños,* clothes-press; *dar a la prensa,* to publish; *prensa periódica,* the press.
prensado, *n.m.* lustre remaining on stuff.
prensador, -ra, *n.m.f.* presser.
prensadura, *n.f.* pressure.
prensar, *v.t.* to press; to calender.
prensero, *n.m.* (*Col.*) worker in a sugar mill.
prensil, *a.* prehensile.
prensista, *n.m.* (*print.*) pressman.
prensor, -ra, *a.* (*zool.*) psittacine, of the parrot family. — *n.f.pl.* **prensoras,** Psittaci, the parrot family.
prenunciar, *v.t.* to prognosticate, foretell.
prenuncio, *n.m.* prognostication, prediction.
preñado, -da, *a.* full; pregnant, enceinte; bulging out.
preñado, *n.m.* pregnancy, gestation.
preñez, *n.f.* pregnancy, gestation; conception; (*fig.*) confusion, difficulty, obscurity; impending danger.
preocupación, *n.f.* preoccupation; prepossession, bias, prejudice, preconception; worry.
preocupadamente, *adv.* in a prejudiced or preoccupied way.
preocupado, -da, *a.* preoccupied, worried; prepossessed, prejudiced.
preocupar, *v.t.* to preoccupy, prejudice, prepossess. — *v.r.* to be biased or prejudiced; to worry.
preopinante, *n.m.f., a.* last speaker, previous speaker (in a debate).
preordinación, *n.f.* (*theol.*) pre-ordination.
preordinadamente, *adv.* in a manner foreordained.
preordinar, *v.t.* (*theol.*) to foreordain.
preparación, *n.f.* preparation.
preparado, -da, *a.* prepared. — *n.m.* preparation, compound; (*pharm.*) medicine.
preparamiento, *n.m.* preparation; compound; medicine.

preparar, *v.t.* to prepare, make ready. — *v.r.* to be prepared, ready; to make preparations.

preparativo, -va, *a.* preparative, qualifying.

preparativo, *n.m.* thing prepared, preparation.

preparatorio, -ria, *a.* preparatory, introductory.

preponderancia, *n.f.* preponderance, overbalancing, sway.

preponderante, *a.* preponderant, overwhelming.

preponderar, *v.i.* to preponderate, outweigh, overbalance, overpower, prevail.

preponer, *v.t.* (conjugated like PONER) to prepose, put before, prefer.

preposición, *n.f.* (*gram.*) preposition.

prepósito, *n.m.* president, chairman; provost.

prepositura, *n.f.* dignity of a provost.

preposteración, *n.f.* inversion of a regular order.

prepósteramente, *adv.* preposterously.

preposterar, *v.t.* to transpose, reverse, invert, disarrange.

prepóstero, -ra, *a.* preposterous, absurd.

prepotencia, *n.f.* preponderance; (*biol.*) prepotency.

prepotente, *a.* very powerful.

prepucio, *n.m.* (*anat.*) prepuce, foreskin.

prepuesto, -ta, *a.* preferred. — *p.p. irreg.* [PREPONER].

prerrafaelista, *a.* (*art*) pre-Raphaelite.

prerrogativa, *n.f.* prerogative, privilege.

presa, *n.f.* capture, seizure; prize, spoils, booty; catch, hold, prey; mole, dam, dike, bank; trench, conduit, drain; slice, morsel, bit; fang, tusk, claw; bird killed by a bird of prey; fish weir, stake work; *presa de caldo,* meat juice, beef tea.

presada, *n.f.* dam, reservoir, storage water (in mills).

presado, -da, *a.* pale-green (colour).

presagiar, *v.t.* to presage, foretell, forebode.

presagio, *n.m.* presage, omen, token.

presagioso, -sa; présago, -ga, *a.* ominous, presaging, divining, guessing.

presbicia, *n.f.* (*med.*) presbyopia, far-sightedness.

présbita, présbite, *n.m.f., a.* presbyope, presbyte, far-sighted, presbyopic.

presbiterado, *n.m.* presbytership, priesthood.

presbiteral, *a.* sacerdotal.

presbiterianismo, *n.m.* Presbyterianism.

presbiteriano, -na, *a.* Presbyterian.

presbiteriato, *n.m.* rank of a presbyter.

presbiterio, *n.m.* presbytery, chancel.

presbítero, *n.m.* presbyter, priest.

presciencia, *n.f.* prescience, foreknowledge.

prescindible, *a.* capable of abstraction or omission.

prescindir, *v.t.* to prescind, abstract, omit, do without; *prescindiendo de eso,* leaving that out of the question.

prescribir, *v.t., v.i.* (*p.p.* **prescripto, prescrito**) to prescribe, determine; to acquire a right by possession.

prescripción, *n.f.* prescription.

prescriptible, *a.* prescriptible.

prescripto, -ta; prescrito, -ta, *p.p. irreg.* [PRESCRIBIR].

presea, *n.f.* jewel, gem, ornament of value.

presencia, *n.f.* presence, coexistence; build, physique, figure; ostentation, show; *buena presencia,* fine figure of a man or woman; *presencia de ánimo,* presence of mind.

presencial, *a.* relating to actual presence; *testigo presencial,* (*law*) eyewitness.

presenciar, *v.t.* to witness, be present at, attend.

presentación, *n.f.* presentation, presentment, exhibition, display; personal introduction; *a presentación,* (*com.*) at sight.

presentado, *n.m., a.* student of divinity; presentee.

presentador, -ra, *n.m.f.* presenter; bearer.

presentalla, *n.f.* gift offered to the saints, votive offering.

presentáneo, -a, *a.* quick-acting.

presentar, *v.t.* to present, exhibit to view; offer, give; lay before, display; to introduce; (*eccles.*) to offer as candidate. — *v.r.* to present oneself, offer one's services; (*mil.*) to enlist as a volunteer.

presente, *n.m.* present, keepsake, gift. — *a.* present, face to face, actual, instant, current; *al presente* or *de presente,* at present, now; *hacer presente,* to consider as present; *tener presente,* to bear in mind; *mejorando lo presente,* present company excepted.

presentemente, *adv.* presently, at present, now.

presentero, *n.m.* (*ecc.*) presenter, one who offers himself as a candidate.

presentillo, *n.m.* small gift.

presentimiento, *n.m.* presentiment, misgiving, foreboding.

presentir, *v.t.* (conjugated like SENTIR) to foresee, forebode, have a presentiment; to suspect.

presepio, *n.m.* stable, manger.

presera, *n.f.* goose-grass, cleavers.

presero, *n.m.* dam-keeper, dike-keeper.

preservación, *n.f.* preservation, conservation.

preservador, -ra, *n.m.f., a.* preserver.

preservar, *v.t.* to save, preserve, guard, keep.

preservativamente, *adv.* preservatively.

preservativo, -va, *a.* preservative.

preservativo, *n.m.* preservative, preventive.

presidario, presidiario, *n.m.* convict; (*coll.*) jail-bird.

presidencia, *n.f.* presidentship, presidency, chairmanship; presidential term.

presidencial, *a.* presidential.

presidencialismo, *n.m.* political system in which the executive power is vested in the President of the Republic.

presidenta, *n.f.* president's wife; moderatrix; woman chairman; woman president.

presidente, *n.m.* president; chairman; speaker (of a parliamentary body); presiding officer or judge.

presidiar, *v.t.* to garrison.

presidiario [PRESIDARIO].

presidio, *n.m.* garrison; garrisoned fortress; penitentiary; punishment by hard labour; (*fig.*) help, aid.

presidir, *v.t.* to preside; to govern, sway, determine.

presilla, *n.f.* small piece of string for fastening; loop, shank, eye; (*sew.*) buttonhole stitching; a kind of linen.

presión, *n.f.* pressure.

preso, -sa, *n.m.f.* prisoner. — *a., p.p. irreg.* [PRENDER]; *preso por uno, preso por ciento,* in for a penny, in for a pound.

prest, *n.m.* (*mil.*) daily pay allowed to soldiers.

presta, *n.f.* (*bot.*) mint.

prestación, *n.f.* (*law*) act of granting or lending, loan; rent, tax, contribution.

prestadizo, -za, *a.* that may be lent or borrowed.

prestado, -da, *a.* lent. — *p.p.* [PRESTAR]; *de prestado,* for a short time; *dar prestado,* to lend; *pedir* (or *tomar*) *prestado,* to borrow.

prestador, -ra, *n.m.f.* lender.

prestamente, *adv.* speedily, promptly, quickly.

prestamera, *n.f.* (*eccles.*) kind of benefice.

prestamería, *n.f.* (*eccles.*) dignity of a sinecure.

prestamero, *n.m.* incumbent of a *prestamera.*

prestamista, *n.m.* lender; pawnbroker, money-lender.

préstamo, *n.m.* loan.

prestancia, *n.f.* excellence.

prestante, *a.* excellent.

prestar, *v.t.* to lend, loan; to credit, give credit; to help, aid, assist; to give, communicate; to pay (attention). — *v.i.* to expand, extend; to be useful, to contribute towards an object. — *v.r.* to offer oneself, to agree; *prestar paciencia a,* to deal patiently with.

prestatario, -ria, *a.* borrowing.

preste, *n.m.* celebrant at High Mass; *Preste Juan,* Prester John.

presteza, *n.f.* quickness, haste, speed, promptitude, nimbleness.

prestidigitación, *n.f.* juggling, sleight of hand, legerdemain.

prestidigitador, *n.m.* juggler; prestidigitator.

prestigiador, *n.m.* juggler; cheat, impostor.

prestigio, *n.m.* fame, prestige; conjuring imposture, juggling; prejudice, prepossession; spell, fascination.

prestigioso, -sa, *a.* prestigious; eminent, distinguished, famous.

presto, -ta, *a.* quick, swift, prompt, diligent; ready, disposed.

presto, *adv.* soon, quickly; *de presto,* promptly, swiftly.

presumible, *a.* presumable, supposable.

presumido, -da, *a.* presumptuous, arrogant.

presumir, *v.t.* to presume, assume, take for granted, suppose, conjecture; *es de presumir,* that may be presumed. — *v.i.* to presume, boast.

presunción, *n.f.* presumption, conjecture, supposition; presumptuousness, vanity.

presuntamente, *adv.* presumptively.

presuntivamente, *adv.* conjecturally.

presuntivo, -va, *a.* presumptive, supposed.

presunto, -ta, *a.* (*p.p. obs.* PRESUMIR) presumed; *presunto heredero,* heir-presumptive.

presuntuosamente, *adv.* presumptuously, arrogantly.

presuntuoso, -sa, *a.* presumptuous, vain, arrogant, conceited.

presuponer, *v.t.* (conjugated like PONER) to presuppose; estimate.

presuposición, *n.f.* presupposition.

presupuesto, *n.m.* motive, pretext, pretence; calculation, estimate; budget.

presupuesto, -ta, *a., p.p. irreg.* [PRESUPONER].

presura, *n.f.* hurry, haste; promptitude; oppression, pressure, anxiety; persistency, eagerness.

presurosamente, *adv.* hastily, promptly.

presuroso, -sa, *a.* hasty, prompt, quick; nimble.

pretal, *n.m.* breastplate, poitrel, breast leather.

pretender, *v.t.* to try, attempt, endeavour; claim, pretend, solicit, seek; to aspire to; (*Col.*) to be in love with; to court.

pretendido, -da, *a.* pretended.

pretendiente, -ta, *n.m.f.* pretender; solicitant, candidate; office-hunter; (*Col.*) suitor.

pretensión, *n.f.* pretension, solicitation, claim.

pretenso, -sa, variant of **pretendido.**

pretensor, -ra, *n.m.f.* pretender, claimant.

preterición, *n.f.* omission; (*rhet., law*) preterition.

preterir, *v.t.* (*law*) to omit (lawful) heirs from a will. (conjugated like SENTIR)

pretérito, -ta, *a.* preterit, past; (*gram.*) preterit.

pretermisión, *n.f.* preterition, pretermission.

pretermitir, *v.t.* to omit, pretermit, pass over.

preternatural, *a.* preternatural.

preternaturalizar, *v.t.* to pervert, render preternatural.

preternaturalmente, *adv.* preternaturally.

pretextar, *v.t.* to make an excuse or a pretence; to urge a pretext.

pretexto, *n.m.* pretext, pretence, mask, cover; *bajo ningún pretexto,* on no consideration.

pretil, *n.m.* railing, battlement, breastwork.

pretina, *n.f.* girdle, waistband, belt.

pretinazo, *n.m.* blow with a girdle.

pretinero, *n.m.* maker of girdles.

pretinilla, *n.f.* lady's belt or girdle.

pretor, *n.m.* prætor; blackness of the waters where tunny fish abound.

pretoría, *n.f.* prætorship.

pretorial, pretoriano, -na, *a.* prætorian.

pretoriense, *a.* belonging to the prætor's residence.

pretorio, *n.m.* prætorium.

pretorio, -ria, *a.* prætorian.

pretura, *n.f.* prætorship.

prevalecer, *v.i.* (*pres. indic.* **prevalezco**; *pres. subj.* **prevalezca**) to prevail, predominate; to take root; to outshine, surpass.

prevaleciente, *a.* prevalent, prevailing.

prevalente, *a.* prevalent.

prevalerse, *v.r.* to avail oneself, make use.

prevaricación, *n.f.* transgression, betrayal of a trust.

prevaricador, -ra, *n.m.f.* transgressor, betrayer, turn-coat.

prevaricar, *v.t.* (*pret.* **prevariqué,** *pres. subj.* **prevarique**) to transgress; to betray, play false. — *v.i.* to fail in one's word or duty.

prevaricato, *n.m.* (*law*) prevarication.

prevención, *n.f.* disposition, preparation; supply of provisions; foresight, forethought; monition, advice, warning, intimation, instruction; prepossession; prevention; sustenance, subsistence; prejudice, preoccupation; police station; (*mil.*) guard-room, cell; (*law*) prevenience of a judge in the knowledge of a case.

prevenidamente, *adv.* previously, beforehand.

prevenido, -da, *a.* prepared, provided; careful, cautious, provident.

preveniente, *a.* predisposing, prevenient, foreseeing.

prevenir, *v.t.* (conjugated like VENIR), to foresee, pre-arrange, prepare, prevent; to advise; to provide, make ready, forestall; to hinder, impede, avoid; to supervene; to prepossess, predispose; to preoccupy. — *v.r.* to be predisposed; to be prepared, ready or on guard; *prevenírsele a uno*, to occur to one.

preventivamente, *adv.* preventively.

preventivo, -va, *a.* preventive.

prever, *v.t.* (conjugated like VER) to foresee, anticipate.

previamente, *adv.* previously.

previo, -via, *a.* previous, antecedent, prior.

previsión, *n.f.* foresight, prescience.

previsor, -ra, *a.* provident, prudent.

previsto, -ta, *a., p.p. irreg.* [PREVER].

prez, *n.m.* honour, fame, distinction, glory.

priesa, *n.f.* haste, hurry.

prieto, -ta, *a.* blackish, dark; close-fisted, mean; tight, compressed; illiberal, narrow-minded.

prima, *n.f.* morning; (*eccles.*) prime; (*mus.*) treble chord of stringed instruments; female cousin; (*eccles.*) first tonsure; (*com.*) bounty, insurance premium; (*mil.*) first quarter of the night.

primacía, *n.f.* priority, precedence; primacy, primateship.

primacial, *a.* primatial, relating to primacy.

primada, *n.f.* (*coll.*) playing one for a sucker; sponging trick.

primado, *n.m.* primeness; primate.

primado, -da, *a.* primary, primatial.

primal, -la, *a.* yearling.

primal, *n.m.* lace; silk cord.

primamente, *adv.* neatly, finely, elegantly.

primariamente, *adv.* principally, chiefly, primarily.

primario, -ria, *a.* principal, primary; (*elec.*) primary circuit. — *n.m.* professor who lectures at dawn.

primate, *n.m.* distinguished person, worthy fellow; (*zool.*) one of the primates.

primavera, *n.f.* spring season; kind of flowered silk; (*bot.*) primrose.

primaveral, *a.* spring, vernal.

primazgo, *n.m.* cousinship.

primearse, *v.r.* to treat each other as cousins.

primer, *a.* (apocope of PRIMERO); *primer galán*, (*theat.*) lead; *primer ministro*, prime minister; *primer movimiento*, first movement.

primeramente, *adv.* first, mainly, primarily, principally, in the first place.

primerizo, -za, *a.* first; firstling, first produced or brought forth. — *n.f.* woman who has borne her first child.

primero, -ra, *a.* (shortened form, **primer**) first, prior, former; chief, principal, leading, superior, surpassing. — *adv.* first, rather, sooner; *primera cura*, first aid; *primera dama*, (*theat.*) leading lady; *de primero*, at first, at the beginning, *de buenas a primeras*, suddenly, all at once; *de primera*, (*com.*) of superior or highest quality.

primevo, -va, *a.* primeval, original.

primicerio, -ria, *a.* principal, first in a line.

primicerio, *n.m.* precentor, chanter.

primicia, *n.f.* first-fruits; offering of the first-fruits.

primicial, *a.* primitial.

primichón, *n.m.* skein of fine, soft silk.

primigenio, -nia, *a.* primigenial.

primilla, *n.f.* (*coll.*) pardon of a first offence.

primitivamente, *adv.* originally.

primitivo, -va, *a.* primitive, original, primeval.

primo, -ma, *a.* first; great, excellent, superior;

skilful; *materia prima*, raw material. — *n.m.f.* cousin; (*coll.*) simpleton, dupe.

primogénito, -ta, *n.m.f., a.* primogenital, first-born.

primogenitura, *n.m.f.* primogeniture.

primor, *n.m.* beauty, dexterity, ability, accuracy, exquisiteness, excellence; nicety.

primordial, *a.* primordial, original, primal.

primorear, *v.i.* to perform neatly and elegantly.

primorosamente, *adv.* finely, excellently, handsomely, nicely, neatly.

primoroso, -sa, *a.* neat, elegant, excellent, graceful, dexterous, exquisite, fine.

prímula, *n.f.* (*bot.*) primula.

princesa, *n.f.* princess; princesse (gown).

principada, *n.f.* undue assumption of authority.

principado, *n.m.* princedom, principality, primacy, pre-eminence. — *pl.* **principados,** princedoms.

principal, *a.* principal, main, chief, capital; essential, important; illustrious, notable, renowned, celebrated. — *n.m.* (*com.*) stock, principal, capital; first floor of a house; head of a commercial establishment; (*law*) constituent; (*mil.*) main guard.

principalía, *n.f.* (*Philip.*) board of town officials, sort of municipal council.

principalidad, *n.f.* principalness; nobility.

principalmente, *adv.* principally, mainly.

príncipe, *n.m.* prince, sovereign, ruler; leader, chief; young queen-bee; *edición príncipe*, editio princeps.

principela, *n.f.* a sort of light camlet.

principiador, -ra, *n.m.f.* beginner.

principiante, -ta, *n.m.f.* beginner, learner, apprentice, novice.

principiar, *v.t.* to begin, commence, start.

principio, *n.m.* element, principle; beginning, commencement, start; motive, source, origin; fountain, issue; (*cook.*) entrée; axiom, tenet, basis; (*chem.*) principle. — *pl.* **principios,** introductory matter in a book, prelims; *al principio* or *a los principios*, at the beginning; *del principio al fin*, from start to end; *en principio*, essentially.

principote, *n.m.* one who affects haughtiness or ostentation or makes a pretentious display.

pringada, *n.f.* toasted bread in gravy.

pringamoza, *n.f.* (*Cub., Col., Hond.*) nettle.

pringar, *v.t.* (*pret.* **pringué**; *pres. subj.* **pringue**) to dip in grease; to baste (meat); to spatter, stain with grease; to ill-treat, wound; to interfere, meddle; to stain one's reputation; to scald with boiling fat; to share in a business. — *v.r.* to obtain an unlawful advantage from a trust committed to one's charge.

pringón, -na, *a.* nasty, greasy, dirty.

pringón, *n.m.* begreasing oneself; grease stain.

pringoso, -sa, *a.* greasy, fat.

pringote, *n.m.* mixture of viands.

pringue, *n.m.f.* grease, lard, fat; greasiness, oiliness, fattiness; grease spot in clothes.

prionodonte, *n.m.* (*Am.*) giant armadillo.

prior, *n.m.* prior; one having precedence; (*prov.*) rector, parson, curate. — *a.* prior, preceding.

priora, *n.f.* prioress.

prioral, *a.* belonging to a prior or prioress.

priorato, priorazgo, *n.m.* priorship.

prioridad, *n.f.* priority, precedence.

prioste, *n.m.* steward of a confraternity.

prisa, *n.f.* promptness, celerity, hurry, haste, speed, despatch; urgency; skirmish, surprise, hot fight; *a toda prisa*, with the greatest haste; *darse prisa*, to hurry; *estar de prisa*, to be hurried, pressed for time.

prisco, *n.m.* kind of peach.

prisión, *n.f.* seizure, capture, apprehension; imprisonment; prisoner; gaol; bond, tie. — *pl.* **prisiones,** chains, shackles, fetters.

prisionero, *n.m.* (*mil.*) prisoner; one captivated by affection or passion.

prisma, *n.m.* prism.

prismático, -ca, *a.* prismatic.

prismáticos, *n.m.pl.* field-glasses.

priste, *n.m.* saw-fish.

prístino, -na, *a.* pristine, first, original.

prisuelo, *n.m.* muzzle for ferrets.

privación, *n.f.* privation, want; deprivation, loss, lack; degradation.

privada, *n.f.* privy, water-closet; filth thrown into the street.

privadamente, *adv.* privately, privily; separately.

privadero, *n.m.* nightman, cesspool-cleaner.

privado, -da, *a.* deprived, despoiled; privy, secret, personal, private; particular.

privado, *n.m.* favourite, court minion.

privanza, *n.f.* favour at court, protection.

privar, *v.t.* to deprive, despoil, dispossess; to interdict, prohibit, debar; to degrade; to daze, stun. — *v.i.* to enjoy the protection of a magnate; prevail; to be in favour or in vogue. — *v.r.* to deprive oneself; *privarse de juicio*, to become insane.

privativamente, *adv.* privatively, solely.

privativo, -va, *a.* privative; exclusive, special, peculiar, particular.

privilegiadamente, *adv.* in a privileged manner.

privilegiar, *v.t.* to privilege, favour; to grant privilege.

privilegiativo, -va, *a.* containing a privilege.

privilegio, *n.m.* privilege; immunity, grant, exemption, concession; grace, franchise; faculty; patent, copyright.

pro, *n.m.f.* profit, benefit, advantage; *buena pro*, much good may it do you; *en pro de*, in favour of, for the good (*or* benefit) of; *hombre de pro*, worthy man.

proa, *n.f.* (*naut.*) bow, prow; foreship, foredeck, steerage.

proal, *a.* belonging to the prow.

probabilidad, *n.f.* probability, likelihood.

probabilísimo, -ma, *a.* most probable.

probabilismo, *n.m.* (*theol.*) probabiliorism, probabilism.

probabilista, *n.m.* (*theol.*) probabilist.

probable, *a.* probable; provable, credible, likely.

probablemente, *adv.* probably, in a likely manner.

probación, *n.f.* proof; probation time; trial.

probado, -da, *a.* proved, tried.

probador, -ra, *n.m.f.* taster, sampler, trier.

probadura, *n.f.* trial, tasting, sampling.

probanza, *n.f.* proof, evidence.

probar, *v.t.* (*pres. indic.* **pruebo;** *pres. subj.* **pruebe**) to try, examine, taste, test, experiment; to sample (wine, etc.); to attempt, endeavour; to prove, give evidence, make good, justify. — *v.i.* to suit, fit, agree; *probar ventura*, to try one's luck. — *v.r.* to try on (a coat, etc.).

probatorio, -ria, *a.* probatory, probationary. — *n.f.* time allowed for producing evidence.

probatura, *n.f.* (*coll.*) trial, experiment, test.

probeta, *n.f.* manometer, pressure gauge; (*artill.*) powder prover; (*chem.*) test-glass; specimen; (*phot.*) developing tray.

probidad, *n.f.* probity, honesty, integrity.

problema, *n.m.* problem; proposition.

problemáticamente, *adv.* problematically.

problemático, -ca, *a.* problematical.

probo, -ba, *a.* upright, honest.

procacidad, *n.f.* procacity, petulance, insolence.

procaz, *a.* petulant, impudent, saucy, bold, insolent.

procedencia, *n.f.* derivation, origin, place of sailing or departure.

procedente, *a.* (*naut.*) having sailed, set out; (*law*) according to law, rules, or practice.

proceder, *v.i.* to proceed, issue, emanate; to follow, prosecute; to behave, conduct oneself; to be in conformity with the law, rules, or practice; to carry on judicial proceedings. — *n.m.* conduct, behaviour, action, management.

procedimiento, *n.m.* proceeding, procedure; method, process of manufacture.

procela, *n.f.* (*poet.*) storm, tempest.

proceloso, -sa, *a.* procellous, tempestuous, stormy.

prócer, *a.* tall, high, elevated, lofty. — *n.m.* grandee, person of exalted station, one high in office. — *pl.* **próceres,** the grandees and high nobility of Spain.

procerato, *n.m.* high station or rank.

proceridad, *n.f.* procerity, tallness; height of stature, eminence, elevation; vigour, growth.

procesado, -da, *a.* (*law*) indicted, prosecuted.

procesal, *a.* belonging to a lawsuit.

procesar, *v.t.* (*law*) to indict, accuse, sue, prosecute.

procesión, *n.f.* procession, parade, pageant, train.

procesional, *a.* processional.

procesionalmente, *adv.* processionally.

proceso, *n.m.* process, lawsuit; records of a lawsuit; progress; lapse of time.

procinto, *n.m.* (*mil.*) ready, prepared.

proción, *n.m.* (*astron.*) procyon.

proclama, *n.f.* proclamation, publication, address, marriage banns.

proclamación, *n.f.* proclamation; acclamation, applause.

proclamar, *v.t.* to proclaim; to praise publicly; to promulgate; to acclaim, cheer.

proclive, *a.* proclivous, inclined, disposed.

proclividad, *n.f.* proclivity, propensity to evil.

procomún, procomunal, *n.m.* public utility.

procónsul, *n.m.* proconsul.

proconsulado, *n.m.* proconsulship.

proconsular, *a.* proconsular.

procreación, *n.f.* procreation, generation.

procreador, -ra, *n.m.f.* procreator, begetter, generator.

procreante, *a.* procreating.

procrear, *v.t.* to procreate, generate, beget, produce.

procura, *n.f.* power of attorney.

procuración, *n.f.* care, diligence, careful

management; procurement; power of attorney.

procurador, -ra, *n.m.f.* procurer, obtainer.
procurador, *n.m.* attorney; solicitor; proctor; *procurador síndico general,* attorney general; (in certain towns) town clerk.
procuradora, *n.f.* manageress of a nunnery.
procuraduría, *n.f.* attorney's office; proctorship.
procurante, *a.* solicitant.
procurar, *v.t.* to solicit, try, endeavour; procure, manage, transact for another; get, gather, obtain, secure; to act as an attorney; *procurar camino,* to find a way.
procurrente, *n.m.* cape, headland, promontory, peninsula.
prodición, *n.f.* prodition, treason, treachery.
prodigalidad, *n.f.* prodigality, profusion, waste, lavishness, extravagance; plenty, abundance.
pródigamente, *adv.* prodigally, lavishly, profusely.
prodigar, *v.t.* (*pret.* **prodigué;** *pres. subj.* **prodigue**) to waste, be lavish of, squander, misspend.
prodigiador, *n.m.* soothsayer, foreteller.
prodigio, *n.m.* prodigy, portent, monster; wonder, marvel.
prodigiosamente, *adv.* prodigiously, marvellously; charmingly, beautifully.
prodigiosidad, *n.f.* prodigiousness, portentousness.
prodigioso, -sa, *a.* prodigious, marvellous, monstrous, exquisite, excellent.
pródigo, -ga, *a.* prodigal, wasteful, lavish; liberal, generous, unstinted.
proditorio, -ria, *a.* treacherous.
pródromo, *n.m.* (*med.*) prodrome, prodromus, a symptom of approaching disease.
producción, *n.f.* production; growth, product, produce, yield; crop, delivery.
producente, *a.* generating, producing.
producibilidad, *n.f.* (*phil.*) productiveness.
producible, *a.* (*phil.*) producible.
producidor, -ra, *n.m.f.* producer, procreator.
producir, *v.t.* (*p.p.* **producido, producto;** *pres. ind.* **produzco;** *pres. subj.* **produzca;** *pret.* **produje**) to produce, bring forth; to generate, create; to publish; to yield, bring, bring in; to occasion, cause; to exhibit, produce as evidence; *v.r.* to explain oneself.
productible, *a.* productile.
productivo, -va, *a.* productive, constitutive, profitable, fruitful.
producto, *n.m.* product, production, proceed, produce, fruit, growth; (*com.*) *producto neto,* net produce. — *p.p. irreg.* [PRODUCIR].
proejar, *v.i.* to row against the wind or current.
proel, *n.m.* (*naut.*) fore part of a ship; seaman at prow; bow hand. — *a.* (*naut.*) fore.
proemial, *a.* proemial, preliminary, introductory.
proemio, *n.m.* proem, introduction, preface.
proeza, *n.f.* prowess, bravery, valour.
profanación, *n.f.* profanation, desecration.
profanador, -ra, *n.m.f.* profaner, polluter, violator.
profanamente, *adv.* profanely.
profanamiento, *n.m.* profanation.
profanar, *v.t.* to profane, violate, defile, desecrate, pollute; to disgrace, dishonour, abuse.

profanidad, *n.f.* profanity, profaneness.
profano, -na, *a.* profane, irreverent, worldly, secular, irreligious; immodest, unchaste; unfamiliar, ignorant.
profecía, *n.f.* prophecy, prediction. — *pl.* **profecías,** the Prophets.
proferente, *a.* pronouncing, uttering.
proferir, *v.t.* (*pres. part.* **profiriendo;** *pres. indic.* **profiero;** *pres. subj.* **profiera;** *pret.* **él profirió**) to pronounce, express, name, utter.
profesante, *n.m.f., a.* professor; professing.
profesar, *v.t.* to profess, declare openly; to teach, exercise; to entertain, harbour (friendship); to sustain, avow; to join a religious house.
profesión, *n.f.* profession, calling, occupation; assurance, declaration, avowal.
profesional, *a.* professional.
profeso, -sa, *a.* professed (monk or nun).
profesor, -ra, *n.m.f.* professor, lecturer, teacher, instructor.
profesorado, *n.m.* professorship; professorial or teaching body.
profeta, *n.m.* prophet, foreteller.
proféticamente, *adv.* prophetically.
profético, -ca, *a.* prophetic, prophetical.
profetisa, *n.f.* prophetess.
profetizador, -ra, *n.m.f.* prophesier, foreteller.
profetizante, *a.* prophesying, foretelling.
profetizar, *v.t.* (conjugated like ALZAR) to prophesy, predict, foretell.
proficiente, *a.* proficient, making progress, advanced.
proficuo, -cua, *a.* advantageous, profitable, useful.
profiláctica, *n.f.* (*med.*) prophylactic, preventive, preservative.
profiláctico, -ca, *a.* prophylactic, preventive.
profilaxis, *n.f.* (*med.*) prophylaxis.
prófugo, -ga, *a.* fugitive from justice. — *n.m.* shirker from military service.
profundamente, *adv.* profoundly, deeply, acutely, highly.
profundidad, *n.f.* profundity, depth, concavity; height; excellence, grandeur, intensity, impenetrability.
profundizar, *v.t.* (conjugated like ALZAR) to deepen, make deep or profound; (*fig.*) to fathom, penetrate, explore.
profundo, -da, *a.* profound, deep; dense, intense, thick; great, tall, high; abstruse, recondite. — *n.m.* profundity; (*poet.*) the sea, the deep; (*poet.*) hell.
profusamente, *adv.* profusely, lavishly, prodigally, extravagantly.
profusión, *n.f.* profusion, prodigality, lavishness, abundance, extravagance.
profuso, -sa, *a.* profuse, plentiful, prodigal, lavish, extravagant.
progenie, progenitura, *n.f.* progeny, race, offspring, issue.
progenitor, *n.m.* progenitor, ancestor, forefather.
prognato, -ta, *n.m.f., a.* prognathous, heavy-jawed.
progne, *n.f.* (*poet.*) swallow.
prognosis, *n.f.* (weather) forecast.
programa, *n.m.* programme; plan; prospectus; scheme, order; play-bill; proclamation, public notice.
progresar, *v.i.* to improve, advance, progress.

progresión, *n.f.* progression, progressiveness, progress.

progresista, *n.m.* progressionist.

progresivamente, *adv.* progressively, onward, forward.

progresivo, -va, *a.* progressive.

progreso, *n.m.* progress, growth, advancement, forwardness.

prohibente, *a.* prohibiting.

prohibición, *n.f.* prohibition, interdict.

prohibir, *v.t.* to prohibit, interdict, forbid, restrain.

prohibitivo, -va, *a.* prohibitory, forbidding.

prohibitorio, -ria, *a.* prohibitory.

prohijación, *n.f.;* **prohijamiento,** *n.m.* adoption.

prohijador, *n.m.* adopter.

prohijar, *v.t.* to adopt.

prohombre, *n.m.* head man, top man, notable; master of a guild.

proís, *n.m.* (*naut.*) hitching post; tying or fastening place or object; mooring berth.

prójima, *n.f.* (*coll.*) insignificant or contemptible woman.

prójimo *n.m.* fellow-creature; (biblical language) neighbour.

prolapso, *n.m.* (*med.*) prolapsus, prolapsion, descent.

prole, *n.f.* issue, progeny, offspring, race, fruit.

prolegómenos *n.m. pl.* prolegomena.

proletariado, *n.m.* proletariat, lower classes.

proletario, -ria, *n.m.f., a.* proletary, proletarian, labourer, very poor person.

prolífico, -ca, *a.* prolific, fruitful, productive.

prolijamente, *a.* prolixly, tediously.

prolijidad, *n.f.* prolixity, tediousness, minute attention to trifles.

prolijo, -ja, *a.* prolix; over-careful, over-nice; impertinent, tedious, troublesome.

prologar, *v.t.* to write a preface or prologue.

prólogo, *n.m.* prologue, introduction, preface.

prologuista, *n.m.* prologue-writer.

prolonga, *n.f.* (*artill.*) prolonge.

prolongación, *n.f.* prolongation, lengthening, extension, continuation.

prolongadamente, *adv.* tardily, extendedly, protractedly.

prolongado, -da, *a.* prolonged, extended, protracted.

prolongador, -ra, *n.m.f.* one who prolongs or delays.

prolongamiento, *n.m.* prolongation.

prolongar, *v.t.* (*pret.* **prolongué;** *pres. subj.* **prolongue**) to protract, prolong, lengthen out, continue, extend; *prolongar un plazo,* (*com.*) to grant an extension of time; *prolongarse a la costa,* (*naut.*) to coast.

proloquio, *n.m.* maxim, axiom, apothegm.

prolusión, *n.f.* prolusion, prelude.

promediar, *v.t.* to divide into equal parts; (*com.*) to average. — *v.i.* to mediate.

promedio, *n.m.* middle, average, mean.

promesa, *n.f.* promise, offer; pious vow or offering.

prometedor, -ra, *n.m.f.* promiser.

prometer, *v.t.* to promise, offer, bid; to assure. — *v.i.* to give indications or signs. — *v.r.* to flatter oneself; to expect confidently; to become betrothed, promise marriage; to devote oneself to the service of God.

prometido, *n.m.* promise, offer; outbidding, overbidding.

prometido, -da, *n.m.f., a.* betrothed.

prometiente, *a.* promising, assuring.

prometimiento, *n.m.* promise, offer.

prominencia, *n.f.* prominence, protuberance; knoll.

prominente, *a.* prominent, protuberant, jutting out.

promiscuamente, *adv.* promiscuously.

promiscuar, *v.i.* to eat meat with fish on fasting-days.

promiscuo, -cua, *a.* promiscuous.

promisión. *n.f.* promise; *tierra de promisión,* land of promise.

promisorio, -ria, *a.* promissory.

promoción, *n.f.* promotion, advancement, preferment.

promontorio, *n.m.* promontory, foreland, headland, cape; anything bulky and unwieldy.

promotor, -ra, *n.m.f.* promoter, advancer, forwarder, furtherer; *promotor fiscal,* district attorney; *promotor de la fe,* devil's advocate.

promovedor, -ra, *n.m.f.* promoter.

promover, *v.t.* to forward, promote, advance, further, help; to prefer, exalt, raise.

promulgación, *n.f.* promulgation.

promulgador, -ra, *n.m.f.* promulgator, disseminator.

promulgar, *v.t.* (*pret.* **promulgué;** *pres. subj.* **promulgue**) to promulgate, publish, proclaim.

prono, -na, *a.* prone; propense, inclined, disposed, bent.

pronombre, *n.m.* (*gram.*) pronoun.

pronominal, *a.* pronominal.

pronosticación, *n.f.* prognostication.

pronosticador, -ra, *n.m.f.* foreteller, prognosticator.

pronosticar, *v.t.* (*pret.* **pronostiqué;** *pres. subj.* **pronostique**) to foretell, prognosticate, predict, augur.

pronóstico, *n.m.* prognostic, prediction, divination, omen; almanac; (*med.*) prognosis.

prontamente, *adv.* promptly, quickly, nimbly.

prontitud, *n.f.* promptitude, promptness; readiness; activity, speed, swiftness, celerity, diligence; dispatch; repartee.

pronto, -ta, *a.* prompt, ready, hasty, quick, fast; forward, expedient. — *adv.* promptly, quickly, soon, early, expediently. — *n.m.* movement, sudden emotion; *al pronto,* at first; *de pronto,* suddenly, without thinking; *por el* (or *lo*) *pronto,* provisionally.

prontuario, *n.m.* memorandum book; compendium of rules.

prónuba, *n.f.* (*poet.*) bridesmaid.

pronunciación, *n.f.* pronunciation, utterance, enunciation, articulation.

pronunciador, -ra, *n.m.f.* publisher; pronouncer, propagator.

pronunciamiento, *n.m.* (*law*) pronouncement of a sentence; military revolution, sedition.

pronunciar, *v.t.* to pronounce, utter, articulate, enunciate; to deliver, make (a speech); to pronounce judgment and pass sentence. — *v.r.* to rise in insurrection; to rebel.

propagación, *n.f.* propagation, offspring; spreading, diffusion, increase, extension, dissemination.

propagador, -ra, *n.m.f.* propagator.

propaganda, *n.f.* propaganda.

propagandista, *n.m.* propagandist.

propagar, *v.t.* (*pret.* propagué; *pres. subj.* propague) to propagate, diffuse, extend, generate, spread, disseminate, circulate.

propagativo, -va, *a.* that which propagates.

propalador, -ra, *n.m.f.* divulger.

propalar, *v.t.* to publish, divulge.

propao, *n.m.* (*naut.*) breastwork, bulkhead.

propartida, *n.f.* time preceding departure.

propasar, *v.t.* to exceed, transgress. — *v.r.* to lack good breeding, take undue liberties; to exceed one's authority.

propender, *v.i.* (*p.p.* propendido, propenso) to tend, be inclined, aim.

propensamente, *adv.* with propension, inclination.

propensión, *n.f.* propension, propensity, inclination, tendency, proclivity, bent.

propenso, -sa, *a.* propense, inclined, disposed, minded, bent on, prone towards.

propiamente, *adv.* properly, fittingly.

propiciación, *n.f.* propitiation, atonement.

propiciador, -ra, *n.m.f.* propitiator.

propiciamente, *adv.* propitiously.

propiciar, *v.t.* to propitiate, conciliate.

propiciatorio, *a.* propitiatory. — *n.m.* mercy-seat.

propicio, *n.m.* propitious, favourable.

propiedad, *n.f.* property, dominion, possession, right of property, landed estate; ownership, proprietorship; copyright; fitness, meetness; expediency, habit, custom, inclination, propensity; (*art*) naturalness, close imitation.

propietariamente, *adv.* with the right of property.

propietario, -ria, *n.m.f.* proprietor, or proprietress; owner, landlord or landlady.

propina, *n.f.* tip, gratuity, drink-money, perquisite.

propinar, *v.t.* to treat, invite to drink; to prescribe medicines; (*iron.*) to dress down.

propincuidad, *n.f.* propinquity, proximity, nearness.

propincuo, -cua, *a.* near, contiguous.

propio, -pia, *a.* one's own; proper, private; suitable, fit, convenient, adapted; peculiar, characteristic; exact, precise; natural, genuine, original; same, veritable.

propio, *n.m.* express messenger, postman; *al propio*, properly. — *pl.* propios, public lands or estates.

proponedor, -ra, *n.m.f.* proposer, offerer, proponent.

proponente, *n.m.f.*, *a.* proposer, proposing.

proponer, *v.t.* (conjugated like PONER) to propose, propound, hold out, represent; to resolve, determine, mean; to present or name (as candidate). — *v.r.* to plan, purpose, resolve.

proporción, *n.f.* proportion; symmetry; aptitude; similarity; chance, opportunity, occasion; *a proporción*, conformably, proportionally, as fast as.

proporcionable, *a.* proportionable.

proporcionablemente, proporcionadamente, *adv.* proportionably, in proportion.

proporcionado, -da, *a.* proportionate, regular, fit, harmonious.

proporcional, *a.* proportional.

proporcionalidad, *n.f.* proportionableness, proportionality.

proporcionalmente, *adv.* proportionally.

proporcionar, *v.t.* to proportion; to adapt, adjust; to furnish, afford, grant, supply, provide.

proposición, *n.f.* proposition; proposal, overture, scheme.

propósito, *n.m.* purpose, design, intention; purport, scope, object, aim, end; subject-matter; *a propósito*, fit, apposite, knowingly, for the purpose; by the by; *de propósito*, purposely, on purpose; *fuera de propósito*, untimely, out of the question.

propuesta, *n.f.* proposal, proposition, offer; nomination, tender; representation.

propuesto, -ta, *a.*, *p.p. irreg.* [PROPONER].

propugnáculo, *n.m.* fortress; (*fig.*) bulwark.

propulsa, propulsión, *n.f.* repelling (an enemy).

propulsar, *v.t.* to repulse; to push.

propulsor, -ra, *n.m.f.*, *a.* propeller; pusher (of engines).

prora, *n.f.* (*poet.*) prow.

prorrata, *n.f.* quota, apportionment; *a prorrata*, (*com.*) in due proportion.

prorratear, *v.t.* to divide, apportion.

prorrateo, *n.m.* distribution, average, division into shares, pro rata.

prórroga, prorrogación, *n.f.* prorogation, prolongation, respite, extension, renewal.

prorrogable, *a.* capable of prorogation.

prorrogar, *v.t.* (*pret.* prorrogué; *pres. subj.* prorrogue) to prorogue, put off, adjourn, extend, defer.

prorrumpir, *v.i.* to break forth, burst (into shouts, cries, etc.).

prosa, *n.f.* prose; (*coll.*) tedious talk.

prosador, *n.m.* prose-writer; (*coll.*) sarcastic or tedious speaker.

prosaico, -ca, *a.* prosaic, prosy, tedious, dull.

prosaísmo, *n.m.* prosaism, prosaicism.

prosapia, *n.f.* race, line, family, ancestry, lineage.

proscenio, *n.m.* proscenium.

proscribir, *v.t.* (*p.p.* proscripto, proscrito) to outlaw, proscribe; to interdict; to forbid.

proscripción, *n.f.* proscription, banishment.

proscripto, -ta, *n.m.f.*, *a.* outlaw. — *p.p.* [PROSCRIBIR].

proscriptor, *n.m.* proscriber.

prosecución, *n.f.* prosecution, pursuit.

proseguible, *a.* pursuable.

proseguimiento, *n.m.* prosecution.

proseguir, *v.t.* (conjugated like SEGUIR) to pursue, continue, follow; prosecute, proceed.

proselitismo, *n.m.* proselytism.

prosélito, *n.m.* proselyte, convert.

prosificación, *n.f.* turning poetry into prose.

prosificador, -ra, *n.m.f.*, *a.* one that turns poetry into prose.

prosificar, *v.t.* to turn poetry into prose.

prosista, *n.m.* prose-writer.

prosita, *n.f.* short piece or essay in prose.

prosodia, *n.f.* prosody.

prosódico, -ca, *a.* prosodical.

prosopopeya, *n.f.* prosopopœia; (*coll.*) pompousness.

prospecto, *n.m.* prospectus, announcement.

prósperamente, *adv.* prosperously, luckily, fortunately.

prosperar, *v.t.* to prosper, make happy, favour. — *v.i.* to prosper, thrive, be prosperous.

prosperidad, *n.f.* prosperity, success, good fortune.

próspero, -ra, *a.* prosperous, successful, fortunate.

próstata, *n.f.* prostate gland.

prostático, -ca, *a.* prostatic.

prosternación, *n.f.* profound reverence, humiliation.

prosternarse, *v.r.* to prostrate oneself, fall in adoration.

próstilo, *n.m.* (*arch.*) prostyle.

prostitución, *n.f.* prostitution.

prostituir, *v.t.* (*pres. part.* **prostituyendo;** *pres. indic.* **prostituyo;** *pres. subj.* **prostituya**) to prostitute, corrupt, debase. — *v.r.* to hack, turn prostitute.

prostituta, *n.f.* prostitute, harlot.

prostituto, -ta, *a.* prostituted. — *p.p.* [PROSTITUIR].

protagonista, *n.m.f.* protagonist, hero, heroine; leader; principal actor or actress in a play.

prótasis, *n.f.* protasis.

protección, *n.f.* protection, support, favour.

proteccionismo, *n.m.* (*polit.*) protectionism.

proteccionista, *n.m.* (*polit.*) protectionist.

protector, *n.m.* protector, defender, guardian.

protectora, *n.f.* protectress.

protectorado, *n.m.* protectorate.

protectoría, *n.f.* protectorship, protectorate.

protectorio, -ria, *a.* of or belonging to a protector.

protectriz, *n.f.* protectress.

proteger, *v.t.* (*pres. indic.* **protejo;** *pres. subj.* **proteja**) to defend, favour, protect.

protegido, -da, *n.m.f.* person favoured or protected; protégé, *or* protégée.

proteico, -ca, *a.* proteiform.

proteína, *n.f.* protein.

proteo, *n.m.* a fickle person.

protervamente, *adv.* forwardly, arrogantly, perversely.

protervia, protervidad, *n.f.* protervity, arrogance.

protervo, -va, *a.* stubborn, peevish, forward, wanton.

prótesis, *n.f.* (*surg. and gram.*) prosthesis.

protesta, *n.f.* protest, protestation, solemn promise.

protestación, *n.f.* protestation; threat, menace, solemn declaration.

protestante, *n.m.f.,* *a.* protestant; protesting.

protestantismo, *n.m.* Protestantism.

protestar, *v.t.* to protest; to assure, asseverate; to menace; to declare publicly; *protestar una letra,* to protest a bill of exchange.

protestativo, -va, *a.* that which protests.

protesto, *n.m.* protest of a bill.

protético, -ca, *a.* prosthetic, prefixed.

protoalbéitar, *n.m.* principal veterinary surgeon.

protoalbeiterato, *n.m.* veterinary examining board.

protocloruro, *n.m.* (*chem.*) protochloride.

protocolar, protocolizar, *v.t.* to place on the register; to protocol, record.

protocolo, *n.m.* protocol, registry, judicial record.

protomártir, *n.m.* protomartyr.

protomedicato, *n.m.* board of royal physicians; office of royal physician.

protomédico, *n.m.* royal physician.

protón, *n.m.* (*elec.*) proton.

protonotario, *n.m.* first notary.

protoplasma, *n.m.* protoplasm.

prototipo, *n.m.* prototype, original; model.

protráctil, *a.* protractile.

protuberancia, *n.f.* protuberance.

protutor, *n.m.* (*law*) guardian.

provecto, -ta, *a.* advanced in years, learning, or experience; mature.

provecho, *n.m.* profit, advantage, utility, benefit, gain; improvement, progress, proficiency, advancement; *hombre de provecho,* useful man; *buen provecho,* good appetite, may it profit you greatly.

provechosamente, *adv.* profitably, usefully, advantageously.

provechoso, -sa, *a.* profitable, beneficial, useful, lucrative, advantageous; good (as for the health).

proveedor, -ra, *n.m.f.* purveyor, furnisher, contractor.

proveeduría, *n.f.* store-house; purveyor's office.

proveer, *v.t.* (*p.p.* **proveído, provisto;** *pres. part.* **proveyendo;** *pret.* **él proveyó**) to provide, furnish, get ready, supply with provisions, stock; to dispatch; to decree; to maintain, minister; to transact; to adjust, dispose; to confer dignity. — *v.r.* to ease oneself.

proveído, *n.m.* (*law*) judgment, decree, sentence.

proveimiento, *n.m.* providing, provisioning, supply.

provena, *n.f.* layer of vine.

proveniente, *a.* proceeding, originating.

provenir, *v.i.* to arise, proceed, originate.

provento, *n.m.* product, rent, revenue.

provenzal, *n.m.f.,* *a.* of or belonging to Provence.

proverbiador, *n.m.* collection of proverbs, memorandum-book.

proverbial, *a.* proverbial.

proverbialmente, *adv.* proverbially.

proverbio, *n.m.* proverb, saying; omen, prediction. — *pl.* **Proverbios,** Book of Proverbs.

proverbista, *n.m.f.* (*coll.*) one using proverbs freely.

próvidamente, *adv.* providently, carefully.

providencia, *n.f.* providence, foresight, forethought; providing, disposition; (*law*) sentence, judgment, decision.

providencial, *a.* providential.

providencialmente, *adv.* providentially.

providenciar, *v.t.* to command, ordain, take steps; to decide a case, pronounce judgment.

providente, *a.* provident, careful.

próvido, -da, *a.* provident, careful.

provincia, *n.f.* province; provincial court.

provincial, *n.m.,* *a.* provincial; (*eccles.*) the provincial of an order, etc.

provincialismo, *n.m.* provincialism.

provinciano, -na, *n.m.f.,* *a.* provincialist; native of Biscay.

provisión, *n.f.* provision, supply, stock; food; (*obs.*) writ, decree or sentence passed by Spanish tribunals; (*com.*) remittance of funds.

provisional, *a.* provisional.

provisionalmente, *adv.* provisionally.

proviso (al), *adv.* on the spot, immediately.

provisor, -ra, *n.m.f.* provider; vicar-general.

provisorato, *n.m.* office of provider.

provisoría, *n.f.* college (*or* convent) pantry; office of a *provisor.*

provisorio, -ria, *a.* provisional, temporary.
provisto, -ta, *a., p.p. irreg.* [PROVEER].
provocación, *n.f.* provocation, irritation; incitement.
provocador, -ra, *n.m.f.* provoker, inciter.
provocante, *a.* provoking.
provocar, *v.t.* (*pret.* **provoqué;** *pres. subj.* **provoque**) to provoke, rouse, nettle, excite, anger, offend; to facilitate, promote; to vomit.
provocativamente, *adv.* provocatively.
provocativo, -va, *a.* provocative, exciting, provoking, irritating, quarrelsome.
próximamente, *adv.* nearly, soon, immediately.
proximidad, *n.f.* proximity, vicinity, nearness; relative, kindred.
próximo, -ma, *a.* next, nearest, neighbouring, proximate.
proyección, *n.f.* projection, plan; (*artill.*) projectile motion; (*phot.*) slide.
proyectar, *v.t.* to project, contrive, plan, scheme, map out; to devise; to shoot out, throw out, extend. — *v.r.* to be thrown (as a shadow).
proyectil, *n.m.* projectile, missile.
proyectista, *n.m.* projector, schemer.
proyecto, -ta, *a.* projected, in perspective; planned.
proyecto, *n.m.* project, design, scheme, plan.
proyector, -ra, *n.m.f., a.* searchlight; projector; projecting.
proyectura, *n.f.* projecture; (*arch.*) jut, projection, corbelling.
prudencia, *n.f.* prudence, counsel, temperance, moderation.
prudencial, *a.* prudential.
prudencialmente, *adv.* prudentially.
prudente, *a.* prudent, judicious, circumspect, heedful.
prudentemente, *adv.* prudently, judiciously, circumspectly, discreetly.
prueba, *n.f.* proof, reason, argument; sample, sign, mark, token, indication, attempt, experiment, trial, essay; temptation; taste, relish; (*law*) evidence; (*tailor.*) trial, fit; (*math.*) check; (*print.*) proof, proof sheet; *a prueba de bomba,* bomb-proof; *a prueba de fuego,* fire-proof; *tomar a prueba,* to take on trial.
pruebo; pruebe, *pres. indic.; pres. subj.* [PROBAR].
prurito, *n.m.* (*med.*) prurience, itching; appetite, strong desire.
prusiano, -na, *n.m.f., a.* Prussian.
prusiato, *n.m.* (*chem.*) prussiate.
prúsico, -ca, *a.* (*chem.*) prussic.
psicología, *n.f.* psychology.
psicológico, -ca, *a.* psychological.
psicólogo, *n.m.* psychologist.
psicópata, *n.m.f.* psychopath.
psicopatía, *n.f.* psychopathy.
psicosis, *n.f.* psychosis.
psicoterapia, *n.f.* psychotherapy.
psiquiatra, psiquíatra, *n.m.f.* psychiatrist.
psiquiatría, *n.f.* psychiatry.
psíquico, -ca, *a.* psychical, psychological.
psitacosis, *n.f.* (*med.*) psittacosis.
¡pu!, *interj.* phew! exclamation at bad smell.
púa, *n.f.* point, prickle, prong, fork, tine; tooth of a comb; wire tooth of a weaving card or reed; engrafted shoot, graft, scion; spine or

quill of a hedgehog, etc.; point of a spinning top; (*mus.*) plectrum; cause of grief or sorrow; (*coll.*) cunning, wily person.
púado, *n.m.* teeth of a comb, set of prongs, etc.
púar, *v.t.* to indent, make teeth or prongs.
púber, -ra; púbero, -ra, *a.* pubescent.
pubertad, *n.f.* puberty.
pubes, pubis, *n.m.* (*anat.*) pubes.
pubescencia, *n.f.* pubescence, puberty.
pubescente, *a.* pubescent.
pubescer, *v.i.* to attain the age of puberty.
pública, *n.f.* (*univ.*) public debate before graduating.
publicación, *n.f.* publication, proclamation.
publicador, -ra, *n.m.f.* publisher, proclaimer.
públicamente, *adv.* publicly, openly.
publicano, *n.m.* publican, Roman tax-gatherer.
publicar, *v.t.* (*pret.* **publiqué;** *pres. subj.* **publique**) to publish, proclaim, print or issue a book, pamphlet, etc.; to reveal, announce, lay open, disclose; (*eccles.*) to publish the banns.
publicata, *n.f.* certificate of publication.
publicidad, *n.f.* publicity, notoriety.
publicista, *n.m.* journalist.
público, -ca, *a.* public, notorious, general, common, vulgar.
público, *n.m.* public; *en público,* publicly.
pucelana, *n.f.* volcanic ash.
pucia, *n.f.* closed pharmaceutical vessel.
puchada, *n.f.* cataplasm; pigs' food, swill.
pucherazo, *n.m.* (*polit.*) falsifying of an election.
puchero, *n.m.* glazed earthen pot; dinner, food; olla, a Spanish dish of meat and vegetables; grimace, wry face; *hacer pucheros,* (*coll.*) to pout (children).
puches, *n.f.pl.* kind of pap.
pucho, *n.m.* cigar stump; (*fig.*) left-over trifle.
puchusco, *n.m.* (*Chi.*) [PUCHO].
pude, *pret. indic.* [PODER].
pudelación, *n.f.* puddling.
pudelador, *n.m.* puddler.
pudelar, *v.t.* to puddle.
pudendo, -da, *a.* shameful, immodest; obscene. — *n.m.* the male organ.
pudibundo, -da, *a.* (*joc.*) shamefaced, modest.
púdicamente, *adv.* timidly, shamefacedly.
pudicicia, *n.f.* pudicity, chastity, modesty.
púdico, -ca, *a.* chaste, modest, maidenly.
pudiente, *a.* powerful, rich, wealthy, opulent.
pudín, *n.m.* pudding.
pudor, *n.m.* bashfulness, modesty.
pudorosamente, *adv.* bashfully, shamefacedly.
pudoroso, -sa, *a.* bashful, shamefaced, modest, shy.
pudrición, *n.f.* rottenness, putrefaction.
pudridero, *n.m.* rotting place; chamber with vaults for interment of bodies that are later transferred to mausoleums; fermenting pit.
pudridor, *n.m.* steeping-vat for making paper.
pudrigorio, *n.m.* (*coll.*) sickly, infirm man.
pudrimiento, *n.m.* rottenness, putrefaction.
pudrir, *v.t.* to rot, corrupt, decay, molest, consume, vex, worry. — *v.i.* to have died, to be buried. — *v.r.* to be broken-hearted, die of grief. (*p.p.* **podrido**)
pudú, *n.m.* (*Chi.*) variety of goat.
puebla, *n.f.* seed sown in gardens.

pueblada, n.f. (Am.) mob; uprising.
pueble, n.m. (min.) working gang.
puebleño, -ña, n.m.f., a. (Col.) (contemp.) villager, rustic; boor.
pueblerino, -a, a. belonging to a village, rustic.
pueblo, n.m. town, village; settlement; nation; population, populace; common people; working classes.
pueblo; pueble, pres. indic.; pres. subj. [POBLAR].
puedo; pueda, pres. indic.; pres. subj. [PODER].
puelche, n.m. (Chi.) a native of the eastern side of the Andes.
puente, n.m.f. bridge; (carp.) transom, lintel, cross-beam; (naut.) bridge; gun-carrying deck; (mus.) bridge of a stringed instrument; puente giratorio, turn-table; puente colgante, suspension bridge; puente levadizo, draw-bridge; puente volante, flying bridge.
puentecilla, n.f. small bridge of a stringed instrument.
puentezuela, n.f. small bridge.
puerca, n.f. sow; (entom.) millepede; wood-louse; ring of hinge; (med.) scrofulous swelling; slut.
puercada, n.f. (Cent. Am., PR.) foul action.
puercamente, adv. dirtily, filthily.
puerco, -ca, a. nasty, filthy, dirty, foul; coarse, mean, rude, lewd, dishonest.
puerco, n.m. hog; wild boar; ill-bred man; puerco espín, porcupine; a cada puerco viene su San Martín, every pig comes to his Martinmas (i.e., end).
puericia, n.f. boyhood.
pueril, a. childish, boyish, puerile; (astron.) first (quadrant).
puerilidad, n.f. puerility, boyishness, childishness; trifle.
puerilmente, adv. puerilely, childishly, boyishly.
puérpera, n.f. woman in childbed.
puerperal, a. puerperal.
puerperio, n.m. childbirth.
puerquezuela, n.f. slut, wench.
puerquezuelo, n.m. little pig.
puerro, n.m. leek.
puerta, n.f. door, doorway, gate; entrance; entrance-toll, octroi, duty; a puerta cerrada, secretly; puerta de dos hojas, folding-door; llamar a la puerta, to knock at the door; poner puertas al campo, to put gates to an open field; donde una puerta se cierra otra se abre, where one gate shuts another opens; puerta abierta al santo tienta, opportunity makes the thief.
puertaventana, n.f. window shutter.
puertezuela, n.f. small door.
puertezuelo, n.m. small port.
puerto, n.m. port, harbour, haven; mountain-pass; (fig.) asylum, shelter, refuge; river-dam; puerto habilitado, port of entry.
Puerto España, n.m. Port of Spain.
Puerto Príncipe, n.m. Port-au-Prince.
puertorriqueño, -ña, n.m.f., a. of or from Puerto Rico.
pues, conj. then, therefore, inasmuch as, since, because, for; surely, certainly. — interj. well, well then; therefore; ¿y pues? and what of that? pues sí, why, yes! yes, indeed! ¿pues y qué? well, what then? — adv. yes; so; certainly; exactly.
puesta, n.f. stake at cards; resigning a hand (at cards); (astron.) setting; puesta del sol, sunset.

puesto, n.m. place, space, spot; shop, stall, booth; breeding-stall; employment, post; office, dignity; condition, state; (mil.) barracks; cover. — a., put, placed, set. — p.p. irreg. [PONER].
puesto que, conj. since, inasmuch as, although.
¡puf!, interj. faugh! phew!
púgil, n.m. prize-fighter, boxer, bruiser, pugilist.
pugilato, n.m. pugilism, boxing.
pugna, n.f. battle, combat, conflict, struggle.
pugnacidad, n.f. pugnacity, quarrelsomeness.
pugnante, a. fighting, opposing; enemy, foe.
pugnar, v.i. to fight, combat, struggle, contend; to solicit; to rival; to importune.
pugnaz, a. pugnacious, quarrelsome.
puja, n.f. outbidding, overbidding; higher bid.
pujador, -ra, n.m.f. outbidder.
pujame, pujamen, n.m. (naut.) foot of a sail.
pujamiento, n.m. flow of blood or humours.
pujante, a. powerful, strong.
pujanza, n.f. power, might, strength.
pujar, v.t. to outbid; to push through, push ahead; to strive earnestly. — v.i. to falter; (coll.) to pout.
pujavante, n.m. butteris, hoof parer.
pujo, n.m. violent desire, eagerness; pujo de reír, irresistible impulse to laugh; a pujos, slowly, with difficulty.
pulcritud, n.f. pulchritude, refinement, neatness.
pulcro, -cra, a. beautiful, graceful; neat, tidy.
pulchinela, n.m. punchinello.
pulga, n.f. flea; small playing top; tener malas pulgas, to be irritable, ill-tempered.
pulgada, n.f. inch.
pulgar, n.m. thumb; shoot left on vines.
pulgarada, n.f. fillip, pinch; inch.
pulgón, n.m. vine-fretter, vine-grub, green fly, aphis.
pulgoso, -sa, a. pulicose, pulicene, abounding with fleas.
pulguera, n.f. place abounding with fleas; (bot.) fleawort.
pulguilla, pulguita, n.f. little flea. — pl. pulguillas, (coll.) restive, peevish person.
pulicán, n.m. dentist's forceps.
pulicaria, n.f. (bot.) fleawort.
pulidamente, adv. neatly, sprucely, cleanly, nicely.
pulidero, n.m. polisher, glosser, burnisher.
pulidez, n.f. neatness, cleanliness.
pulido, -da, a. neat, nice, cleanly.
pulidor, n.m. polisher, furbisher, polishing instrument.
pulimentar, v.t. to polish, gloss, burnish; make bright.
pulimento, n.m. polish, glossiness, gloss.
pulir, v.t. to burnish, polish, adorn, furbish; to beautify; to make polite. — v.r. to become polished or elegant; to deck oneself.
pulmón, n.m. lung.
pulmonar, a. pulmonary.
pulmonaria, n.f. (bot.) lungwort.
pulmonía, n.f. pneumonia.
pulmoníaco, -ca, a. pulmonary, pulmonic, pneumonic.
pulpa, n.f. pulp, flesh.
pulpejo, n.m. fleshy prominence of some organs of the body, as the ball of the thumb or lobe of the ear.

pulpería, *n.f.* (*Am.*) grocer's shop.
pulpero, *n.m.* (*Am.*) grocer; catcher of cuttle-fish.
pulpeta, *n.f.* slice of stuffed meat.
pulpetón, *n.m.* large slice of stuffed meat.
púlpito, *n.m.* pulpit; office of a preacher.
pulpo, *n.m.* (*ichth.*) cuttle-fish, octopus.
pulposo, -sa, *a.* pulpy, pulpous, fleshy.
pulque, *n.m.* (*Am.*) pulque, fermented juice of the agave.
pulque curado, *n.m.* (*Am.*) pulque prepared with pineapple and sugar.
pulquería, *n.f.* (*Am.*) shop where pulque is sold.
pulsación, *n.f.* pulsation, pulse, beating.
pulsada, *n.f.* pulsation, throbbing.
pulsador, -ra, *n.m.f.* one who feels the pulse.
pulsante, *a.* feeling the pulse; pulsating.
pulsar, *v.t.* to touch lightly; (*fig.*) explore, sound, examine; to feel the pulse. — *v.i.* to pulsate, beat.
pulsátil, pulsativo, -va, *a.* pulsing, beating.
pulsatila, *n.f.* the pasque-flower.
pulsear, *v.i.* to test the strength in the wrist of two persons by grasping hands and resting the elbows on a table.
pulsera, *n.f.* bracelet; (*surg.*) wrist bandage; side lock of hair; *reloj de pulsera,* wrist-watch.
pulsímetro, *n.m.* (*hydrost.*) pulsometer; (*med.*) pulsimeter, sphygmograph.
pulsión, *n.f.* (*phys.*) pulsion.
pulsista, *n.m.,* *a.* specialist in cardio-vascular diseases.
pulso, *n.m.* pulse, wrist; steadiness of the hand; pulse-beat; tact, care; *a pulso,* with the strength of the hand; *tomar el pulso,* to feel the pulse.
pultáceo, -cea, *a.* pultaceous, soft; (*med.*) rotten or gangrened.
pululante, *a.* pullulating.
pulular, *v.i.* to pullulate, germ, bud, swarm; to multiply rapidly; to swarm; to be lively.
pulverizable, *a.* pulverizable.
pulverización, *n.f.* pulverization.
pulverizador, *n.m.* crushing-machine; atomizer, spray.
pulverizar, *v.t.* (*pret.* **pulvericé;** *pres. subj.* **pulverice**) to pulverize, grind; to atomize, spray.
pulverulento, -ta, *a.* pulverulent, dusty.
pulla, *n.f.* loose, obscene, coarse expression; repartee, witty saying; hint; *echar pullas,* to hint, make innuendoes.
¡pum! *interj.* bang!
puma, *n.m.* puma, the cougar.
pumita, *n.f.* pumice-stone.
puna, *n.f.* (*Am.*) puna, bleak, arid table-land.
punción, *n.f.* (*surg.*) puncture.
puncha, *n.f.* thorn, prickle, sharp point.
punchar, *v.t.* to prick, puncture.
pundonor, *n.m.* point of honour, punctiliousness.
pundonorcillo, *n.m.* punctilio.
pundonorosamente, *adv.* punctiliously.
pundonoroso, -sa, *a.* punctilious.
pungente, *a.* pungent.
pungimiento, *n.m.* punching, pricking.
pungir, *v.t.* (*pres. indic.* **punjo;** *pres. subj.* **punja**) to punch, prick; to hurt the mind or heart (passions, etc.).

pungitivo, -va, *a.* punching, pricking.
punible, *a.* punishable.
punición, *n.f.* punishment, chastisement.
púnico, -ca, *a.* Punic, Carthaginian.
punitivo, -va, *a.* punitive.
punta, *n.f.* point, tip, extremity, nib, sharp end; prong, thorn; top, head, summit, apex; (*her.*) lower part of a shield; prong or tine of an antler; headland, promontory, cape; (*print.*) bodkin; coulter; touch, turn, trace, suggestion; small part; stub of a cigar; pointing of game by a dog; tartness, sourish taste; *hacer punta,* to excel, surpass; *estar de punta,* to be on bad terms; *tener puntas de loco,* to be slightly 'touched' in the head; *punta de París,* wire nail; *punta seca,* point of dividers; *de punta en blanco,* in full regalia, Sunday best; *punta de diamante,* glazier's diamond. — *pl.* **puntas,** bonelace, point lace; horns of a bull; head of a river; *de puntas,* on tiptoe, softly.
puntación, *n.f.* punctuation.
puntada, *n.f.* stitch; careless word, hint.
puntador, *n.m.* noter, observer; prompter.
puntal, *n.m.* stanchion, prop, support, stay; fulcrum; (*naut.*) depth of hold.
puntapié, *n.m.* kick; *dar un puntapié,* to dismiss one with contempt.
puntar, *v.t.* to mark with points.
puntear, *v.t.* (*art*) to stipple; to play on the guitar; to mark, punctuate; to sew, stitch. — *v.i.* (*naut.*) to tack.
puntel, *n.m.* blow-pipe, glass-blower's rod.
puntera, *n.f.* toe-cap (of a boot, shoe or stocking); (*coll.*) kick.
puntería, *n.f.* aim, pointing of fire-arms.
puntero, *n.m.* farrier's punch; chisel; graver, style.
puntero, -ra, *a.* good shot.
puntiagudo, -da, *a.* sharp-pointed.
puntilla, *n.f.* small point; narrow lace edging; brad, joiner's nail; carpenter's tracing point; *de puntillas,* gently, on tiptoe; *ponerse de puntillas,* to persist obstinately in one's opinion.
puntillazo, *n.m.* kick.
puntillero, *n.m.* bull-fighter who kills the bull.
puntillo, *n.m.* small point; punctilio.
puntillón, *n.m.* kick.
puntilloso, -sa, *a.* ticklish, punctilious.
punto, *n.m.* point in time or space; subject of consideration; state, degree; full stop (in writing); dot; close of a lecture; end, design; detail, particular; instant, moment, chance, opportunity, nick of time; stop, rest; recess; stitch; tumbler of gunlock; pen-nib; hole in stockings; mesh of a net; knitting; point in lace; punch-hole in straps; polka dot in fabrics; smallest part of a thing; point of honour, punctilio; twelfth part of a line; gist, substance, pith; end, object, aim; condition, stage; *punto en boca,* silence; *punto menos de,* rather less than; *a buen punto,* opportunely; *punto y coma,* semi-colon; *al punto,* instantly; *estar a punto de,* to be about to; *hacer punto,* to stop; to knit; *en punto,* precisely, punctually; *hasta cierto punto,* to a certain extent; *por punto general,* as a rule. — *pl.* **puntos,** stitches to close a wound; points on dice or cards; mesh (of a net); *por puntos,* from one moment to another.
puntoso, -sa, *a.* acuminated; over-punctilious.

puntuación, *n.f.* punctuation.
puntual, *a.* punctual, exact, punctilious, prompt, certain, sure; convenient.
puntualidad, *n.f.* punctuality, preciseness.
puntualizar, *v.t.* (*pret.* **puntualicé;** *pres. subj.* **puntualice**) to imprint on the mind; to finish, complete; to describe minutely.
puntualmente, *adv.* punctually, exactly, faithfully, accurately.
puntuar, *v.t.* to punctuate, point.
puntura, *n.f.* puncture; (*print.*) register point.
punzada, *n.f.* prick, puncture, sting, sharp pain; compunction.
punzador, -ra, *n.m.f.* pricker, wounder.
punzadura, *n.f.* puncture, prick.
punzante, *a.* pricking, pointed.
punzar, *v.t.* (*pret.* **puncé;** *pres. subj.* **punce**) to punch, perforate, bore; to sting, prick, cause pain; to grieve, cause compunction.
punzó, *n.m.* very bright scarlet red colour.
punzón, *n.m.* punch, puncheon, puncher; graver; point, bodkin, pick, awl; countersink, counterdie; type mould; young horn of a deer.
punzonería, *n.f.* collection of moulds for type-making.
puñada, *n.f.* cuff, punch, box, blow with the fist.
puñado, *n.m.* handful; a few; *a puñados,* plentifully.
puñal, *n.m.* poniard, dagger.
puñalada, *n.f.* poniard-stab; stab of grief.
puñalejo, *n.m.* small poniard.
puñalero, *n.m.* maker or seller of poniards.
puñera, *n.f.* flour measure (about a third of a peck).
puñetazo, *n.m.* blow with the closed fist.
puñete, *n.m.* blow with the fist; bracelet.
puñetero, *a.* (*vulg.*) damned, cursed.
puño, *n.m.* fist, handful, grasp; scantiness; wrist-band; mittens, cuff; haft, hilt of a sword; (*naut.*) corner of a sail; handle, head of a cane; *ser como un puño,* to be close-fisted; *apretar los puños,* to exert the utmost efforts; *a puños cerrados,* with might and main.
pupa, *n.f.* pimple, pustule; childish word to express pain.
pupila, *n.f.* eyeball, pupil; orphan girl, ward.
pupilaje, *n.m.* pupilage, wardship; board and lodging; boarding-house.
pupilar, *a.* pupillary; pertaining to the eyeball.
pupilero, -ra, *n.m.f.* master or mistress of a boarding-house.
pupilo, *n.m.* pupil, scholar, ward; boarder.
pupitre, *n.m.* writing-desk; school-desk.
puposo, -sa, *a.* pustulous.
puramente, *adv.* purely, chastely, merely, entirely, genuinely; (*law*) without qualification, exception, restriction, or time limit.
puré, *n.m.* purée soup.
pureza, *n.f.* purity, chastity, innocence; genuineness, excellence.
purga, *n.f.* purge, cathartic; draining impurities, or molasses.
purgable, *a.* purgeable, that may be purged.
purgación, *n.f.* (*law*) purgation; (*med.*) catamenia; gonorrhœa.
purgador, -ra, *n.m.f.* purger, one who purges.
purgante, *n.m., a.* purgative, laxative, cathartic.

purgar, *v.t.* (*pret.* **purgué;** *pres. subj.* **purgue**) to purge, purify, cleanse, evacuate; to clarify, refine; to expiate, atone; to drain molasses; to undergo the pains of purgatory. — *v.r.* to clear oneself of guilt; to take a purge.
purgativo, -va, *a.* purgative, cathartic.
purgatorio, *n.m.* purgatory.
puridad, *n.f.* purity; *en puridad,* clearly, openly, without concealment; in secret.
purificación, *n.f.* purification, cleansing.
purificadero, -ra, *a.* cleansing, purifying.
purificador, -ra, *n.m.f.* purifier, purger; purificatory.
purificar, *v.t.* (*pret.* **purifiqué;** *pres. subj.* **purifique**) to purify, cleanse, clean, clarify, refine. — *v.r.* to be purified.
purificatorio, -ria, *a.* purificatory, purificative.
Purísima, La, *n.f.* the Holy Virgin.
purismo, *n.m.* purism.
purista, *n.m.* purist.
puritanismo, *n.m.* puritanism.
puritano, -na, *n.m.f., a.* puritan, puritanical.
puro, -ra, *a.* pure, clear, free; modest, chaste; clean, neat; innocent; incorrupt, sterling, unmixed, unalloyed, solid (gold, silver, etc.); genuine, unsullied, unblemished, spotless; only, absolute; *a puro,* by dint of; *de puro,* extremely.
puro, *n.m.* cigar.
púrpura, *n.f.* murex; purple shell; cloth dyed with purple; (*fig.*) imperial or regal power; dignity of a cardinal; (*poet.*) blood; (*med.*) a morbid condition characterized by hæmorrhage, etc.
purpurado, -da, *n.m.* cardinal.
purpurante, *a.* giving a purple colour.
purpurar, *v.t.* to purple, redden; to dress in purple.
purpúreo, -rea, *a.* purple.
purpurina, *n.f.* (*chem.*) purpurin.
purpurino, -na, *a.* purplish.
purrela, *n.f.* worthless wine.
purriela, *n.f.* (*coll.*) despicable or valueless object.
purulencia, *n.f.* purulence, purulency.
purulento, -ta, *a.* purulent.
pus, *n.m.* pus; gleet.
pusilánime, *a.* pusillanimous, faint-hearted.
pusilánimemente, *adv.* pusillanimously, timorously.
pusilanimidad, *n.f.* pusillanimity.
pústula, *n.f.* pustule, pimple.
puta, *n.f.* prostitute, whore, harlot.
putaísmo, putanismo, *n.m.* whoredom, harlotry.
putañear, *v.i.* (*coll.*) to harlot, whore.
putañero, *n.m.* whoremonger.
putativo, -va, *a.* putative, reputed.
putería, *n.f.* (*vulg.*) prostitute's life or habits; harlotry; brothel.
putero, *n.m.* whoremonger.
putesco, -ca, *a.* relating to whores.
puto, *n.m.* catamite, sodomite; *a puto el postre,* the devil take the hindmost.
putput, *n.m.* hoopoe.
putrefacción, *n.f.* putrefaction, corruptness.
putrefactivo, -va, *a.* putrefactive.
putrefacto, -ta, *a.* putrefied, putrid, decayed, rotten.
putridez, *n.f.* putridity, rottenness.
pútrido, -da, *a.* rotten, putrid, decayed.

putuela, *n.f.* very degraded prostitute.
puya, *n.f.* (*Chi.*) a plant of the genus Bromeliaceæ.
puyo, *n.m.* (*Arg.*) kind of poncho made of coarse wool.
puzol, *n.m.;* **puzolana,** *n.f.* pozzolana.

Q

Q, q, the twentieth letter of the Spanish alphabet, always followed by (mute) *u*; occurs only in the syllables *que* and *qui*.
que, *rel. pron.* that, who, whom, which, what; *conj.* that, than, whether, because, as, when.
¿qué? *interrog. pron.* what?
¡qué! *interj.* what! *no hay de qué,* don't mention it, not at all; *pues ¿y qué?* well, what then? *¿qué es eso?* or *¿qué hay?* or *¿qué pasa?* what is the matter; *¿qué es del libro?* where is the book? *sin qué ni para qué,* without motive or cause.
quebracho, *n.m.* (*Am.*) medicinal bark used in cases of fever.
quebrada, *n.f.* ravine, gorge; (*Am.*) brook; (*com.*) failure.
quebradero, *n.m.* breaker; *quebradero de cabeza,* worry.
quebradillo, *n.m.* wooden shoe-heel; (*danc.*) flexure of the body.
quebradizo, -za, *a.* brittle, fragile; infirm, sickly, frail.
quebrado, -da, *a.* broken, weakened, enervated, debilitated; (*com.*) bankrupt; rolling, uneven (ground); ruptured.
quebrado, *n.m.* (*arith.*) fraction; bankrupt; ruptured person; (*Cub.*) tobacco leaf full of holes.
quebrador, -ra, *n.m.f.* breaker; delinquent.
quebradura, *n.f.* breaking, cleaving, splitting, gap, slit; (*med.*) fracture, rupture, hernia.
quebraja, *n.f.* crack, flaw, fissure, split.
quebrajar, *v.t.* to crack; to split.
quebrajoso, -sa, brittle, fragile; full of cracks.
quebramiento, *n.m.* fracture, rupture.
quebrantable, *a.* breakable, frangible, brittle.
quebrantador, -ra, *n.m.f.* breaker; debilitator; violator; crusher, bruiser, crushing machine.
quebrantadura, *n.f.* fracture, rupture.
quebrantahuesos, *n.m.* (*orn.*) osprey; bore, tease.
quebrantamiento, *n.m.* fracture, rupture, fatigue, weariness; law-breaking; burglary; (*law*) to abscond, to break bail; crash, smash.
quebrantanueces, *n.m.* (*orn.*) nutcracker.
quebrantaolas, *n.m.* breakwater; mooring buoy.
quebrantar, *v.t.* to break, crack, crash, pound, crush, grind, mash, smash; to move to pity; to revoke, cancel a will; to vex; to fatigue; to transgress (laws); to violate (contracts); to debilitate, weaken, diminish; (*law*) to annul, repeal.
quebrantaterrones, *n.m.* (*coll.*) clodhopper.
quebranto, *n.m.* weakness, lassitude; commiseration, pity; breaking, crushing; (*com.*) great loss; heavy damage; grief, affliction.
quebrar, *v.t.* to break, smash, crush, burst open; to twist, double, bend; to intercept, interrupt, hinder; to cast asunder; to trans-

gress (laws); to conquer, overcome; to moderate, temper; to diminish (friendship, etc.). — *v.i.* (*com.*) to fail, become bankrupt, suspend payment. — *v.r.* to be ruptured; broken; *quebrar amistad,* to break off an acquaintance; *quebrar por lo más delgado,* the weakest goes to the wall.
queche, *n.f.* ketch.
quechemarín, *n.m.* coasting lugger.
quechol, *n.m.* (*Mex.*) flamingo.
queda, *n.f.* curfew, curfew bell.
quedada, *n.f.* sojourn, stay, residence.
quedar, *v.i.* to stay, stop in a place; continue, linger, be left, remain, tarry; to hold, subsist, last; to agree, arrange; to decide, resolve; to be reputed, considered; to act, be appointed. — *v.r.* to stay, remain; to diminish, slacken, abate; to retain, keep; *quede,* (*print.*) stet, let stand; *quedar en hacer una cosa,* to agree to do a thing; *quedar por,* to become surety for; *quedar atrás,* to be left behind, beaten by others; *no quedar por corta ni mal echada,* to leave no stone unturned; *quedar limpio,* to be absolutely without money; *quedarse a obscuras,* to lose what one had; *quedarse frío,* to have the contrary happen of what one desired; *quedarse fresco,* to experience the failure of one's wishes; *quedarse muerto,* to be dumbfounded; *quedarse in albis* (or *quedarse en blanco*), to fail to achieve what one wished; *quedársele a uno en el tintero,* to forget to write or say something.
quedito, -ta, *a., adv.* soft, easy, gentle.
quedo, -da, *a.* quiet, still, noiseless, easy, gentle.
quedo, *adv.* gently, softly, in a low voice. — *interj.,* stop! be quiet!
quehacer, *n.m.* business, occupation, affairs.
queja, *n.f.* murmur, complaint, grumbling; resentment, grudge; moan; *más vale buena queja que mala paga,* better a good grievance than bad pay.
quejarse, *v.r.* to murmur, grumble; complain, clamour; lament, regret.
quejicoso, -sa, *a.* plaintive, querulous.
quejido, *n.m.* complaint, moan; *dar quejidos,* to groan.
quejigal, *n.m.* muricated oak plantation.
quejigo, *n.m.* muricated oak.
quejigueta, *n.f.* shrub of the *Quercus* genus, common in Spain.
quejita, *n.f.* murmur, slight complaint.
quejosamente, *adv.* querulously, complainingly.
quejoso, -sa, *a.* plaintive, querulous, complaining.
quejumbre, *n.f.* grumble, growl.
quejumbroso, -sa, *a.* plaintive, complaining, growling, grumbling.
quema, *n.f.* burn; fire, combustion, conflagration.
quemadero, *n.m.* place where criminals were burnt.
quemadero, -ra, *a.* apt to be burnt.
quemado, -da, *a.* burnt; angry, irritated. — *n.m.* burn forest or thicket.
quemador, -ra, *n.m.f.* burner; incendiary.
quemador, *n.m.* gas-burner.
quemadura, *n.f.* burn, scald, mark or hurt by fire; (*agric.*) brand, smut upon plants.
quemajoso, -sa, *a.* pricking, burning.
quemar, *v.t.* to burn; scald; to kindle, fire,

parch, dry, scorch; to vex, irritate; to sell at a low price. — *v.i.* to be very hot, burning. — *v.r.* to burn, be consumed; to heat oneself; to fret, worry, be impatient; to be near, almost to attain a desired object; *quemarse las cejas*, to study much; *a quema ropa*, very near, quite close, unexpectedly.

quemazón, *n.f.* burn, combustion, conflagration; act of burning; excessive heat; itching; eagerness, covetousness; offensive remark; (*Cub.*) bargain sale.

quena, *n.f.* (*Am.*) kind of Indian flute.

quepis, *n.m.* kepi, forage cap.

quepo; **quepa**, *pres. indic.; pres. subj.* [CABER].

querella, *n.f.* complaint, fray; petition in a court of justice; (*law*) contesting a will; quarrel, dispute; plaint.

querellador, -ra, *n.m.f.* complainant.

querellante, *a.* murmuring, complaining. — *n.m.f.* complainant.

querellarse, *v.r.* to bewail, lament; to complain; (*law*) to make an accusation; to contest a will.

querellosamente, *adv.* plaintively.

querelloso, -sa, *a.* querulous.

querencia, *n.f.* homing instinct; affection, fondness.

querencioso, -sa, *a.* affectionate; frequented by beasts.

querer, *v.t.* (*pres. indic.* **quiero**; *pres. subj.* **quiera**; *pret.* **quise**; *fut. indic.* **querré**) to want, will, wish, desire; to like, love, cherish; to command, order; to be willing, determine, resolve; to endeavour, attempt; to agree, conform; to give occasion; to cause; to accept a challenge in certain card games. — *v. impers.* to be going to. — *n.m.* will, desire; love, affection; *¿qué quiere ser eso?* what is all this about? *sin querer*, unwillingly, undesignedly; *querer más*, to prefer; *querer decir*, to signify, mean; *como Vd. quiera*, as you like; *como quiera que*, anyhow, whereas, inasmuch as; *cuando quiera*, at any time; *donde quiera*, anywhere; *quien bien quiere, bien obedece*, love brings obedience; *quien bien te quiere, te hará llorar*, the true friend will reprove and not flatter; *quien todo lo quiere, todo lo pierde*, grasp all, lose all; *si quieres vivir sano, hazte viejo temprano*, a little care brings a long life; *a quien lo quiere celeste, que le cueste*, every prize means work; *quien más tiene, más quiere*, the ambitious man is never satisfied.

querido, -da, *n.m.f.* dear, darling, sweetheart; lover, paramour, mistress. — *a.* dear, beloved; desired, wished for. — *p.p.* [QUERER].

queriente, *a.* willing, loving.

quermes, *n.m.* (*ent.*) kermes.

querub, querube, querubín, *n.m.* cherub.

querva, *n.f.* (*bot.*) Palma Christi oil, castor-oil.

quesadilla, *n.f.* kind of sweetmeat; cheese-cake.

quesear, *v.i.* to make cheese.

quesera, *n.f.* dairy, dairy-maid; cheese-board, cheese-vat; cheese dish.

quesería, *n.f.* cheese-season; cheese-room, dairy.

quesero, *n.m.* cheese-maker, cheesemonger.

quesero, -ra, *a.* caseous, cheesy.

queso, *n.m.* cheese; *algo es queso, pues se da por peso*, never despise small things; *queso de*

bola, Dutch cheese; *queso de cerdo*, head-cheese; *queso helado*, ice-cream brick.

quetro, *n.m.* (*Chi.*) a duck with featherless wings.

quevedos, *n.m.pl.* eye-glasses, pince-nez.

¡quiá! *interj.* no, indeed!

quicial, *n.m.; quicialera*, *n.f.* side-post.

quicio, *n.m.* hook-hinge; support, prop; *sacar de quicio*, to unhinge, exasperate; *fuera de quicio*, unhinged, furious.

quiché, *n.m.f., a.* (*Guat.*) Indian tribe and language.

quichua, *n.m.f., a.* (*Per.*) Indian tribe and language.

quid, *n.m.* gist, pith, main point.

quidam (un), *n.m.* (*coll.*) a certain person; a nobody.

quiebra, *n.f.* crack, fracture; failure, bankruptcy; loss, damage; gaping hole, fissure.

quiebrahacha, *n.m.* (*Cub.*) (*bot.*) breakaxe.

quiebro, *n.m.* (*mus.*) trill; movement of the body.

quiebro; **quiebre**, *pres. indic.; pres. subj.* [QUEBRAR].

quien, *pron. rel.* (*pl.* **quienes**) who, which, whoever, whichever (*interr.* **quién**).

quienquiera, *pron. rel.* (*pl.* **quienesquiera**) whosoever, whoever, whomsoever, whichever.

quiero; **quiera**, *pres. indic.; pres. subj.* [QUERER].

quietación, *n.f.* quieting, appeasing.

quietador, -ra, *n.m.f.* quieter, appeaser.

quietamente, *adv.* quietly, calmly.

quietar, *v.t.* to quiet, appease. — *v.r.* to become quiet.

quiete, *n.m.* repose, quiet.

quietismo, *n.m.* Quietism.

quietista, *n.m.f., a.* Quietist.

quieto, -ta, *a.* quiet, still, pacific, peaceable, moderate, orderly, virtuous, silent, steady, undisturbed.

quietud, *n.f.* quietude, quietness, quiet, tranquillity, repose, rest.

quijada, *n.f.* jaw, jawbone.

quijal, quijar, *n.m.* grinder, back-tooth; jaw.

quijarudo, -da, *a.* large-jawed.

quijera, *n.f.* cheeks of a cross-bow; each of the two straps of the noseband.

quijero, *n.m.* sloping bank of a flume.

quijo, *n.m.* (*Am.*) silver or gold ore.

quijones, *n.m.pl.* (*bot.*) dill.

quijongo, *n.m.* (*CR.*) a one-string Indian musical instrument.

quijotada, *n.f.* quixotic enterprise.

quijote, *n.m.* thigh-armour, cuisse; upper part of the haunch (of horses); (*fig.*) one who engages in quixotic deeds.

quijotería, *n.f.* quixotry, quixotism.

quijotescamente, *adv.* quixotically.

quijotesco, -ca, *a.* quixotic.

quijotismo, *n.m.* quixotism.

quila, *n.f.* (*Am.*) a variety of very strong bamboo.

quilatador, *n.m.* assayer of gold or silver.

quilatar, *v.t.* to assay gold or silver.

quilate, *n.m.* carat; an ancient coin; degree of perfection.

quilatera, *n.f.* (*jewel.*) pearl sieve.

quilco, *n.m.* (*Chi.*) large basket or hamper.

quilífero, -ra, *a.* (*zool.*) chyliferous.

quilificación, *n.f.* chylification.

quilificar, v.t. to chylify, make chyle.
quilo, n.m. kilogramme.
quilo, n.m. (zool.) chyle; *sudar el quilo,* to work hard.
quilogramo, n.m. kilogramme.
quilombo, n.m. (Ven.) cabin, rustic shanty; (Arg., Chi.) brothel, bawdy house.
quilómetro, n.m. kilometre.
quiloso, -sa, a. chylous, chylaceous.
quilquil, n.m. (Chi.) an arboreous fern.
quiltro, n.m. (Chi.) cur.
quilla, n.f. keel of a ship; (orn.) breastbone.
quillango, n.m. (Arg.) patch-work made of furs used by the Indians as a blanket.
quillay, n.m. (Arg., Chi.) soapbark tree.
quillotrar, v.t. to incite, urge, excite; to woo, enamour; to attract; to think over, consider; to adorn, deck; to complain, whine.
quillotro, -tra, n.m.f. incitement, urging; sign, indication; lovemaking, love affair; puzzling situation; dear friend, or lover.
quimera, n.f. dispute, quarrel, scuffle; chimera, whim, fancy.
quimérico, -ca; quimerino, -na, a. chimerical, fantastic, unreal.
quimerista, n.m. brawler, wrangler; visionary man.
quimerizar, v.i. (conjugated like ALZAR) to fill the head with fantastic ideas.
química, n.f. chemistry.
químicamente, adv. chemically.
químico, -ca, a. chemical.
químico, n.m. chemist.
quimificar, v.t. (zool.) to convert into chyme.
quimo, n.m. chyme.
quimón, n.m. chintz, printed cotton.
quimono, n.m. kimono.
quina, n.f. cinchona, Peruvian or Jesuits' bark; throw of dice, fives.
quinado, -da, a. applied to medicinal wine prepared with *quina* (Peruvian bark).
quinal, n.m. (naut.) preventer shroud.
quinario, -ria, a. consisting of five.
quincalla, n.f. hardware, small wares, fancy goods.
quincallería, n.f. ironmongery, hardware trade, fancy store.
quince, a. fifteen, fifteenth; a card game.
quincena, n.f. fortnight; fortnightly (pay); (mus.) fifteenth (interval and organ stop); preventive arrest of 15 days.
quincenal, a.; **quincenalmente,** adv. fortnightly.
quincenario, a. fortnightly. — n.m.f. one who serves one or more *quincenas* in prison.
quinceno, -na, a. fifteenth. — n. mule fifteen months old.
quincuagenario, -ria, a. fiftieth. — n.m.f. person fifty years old.
quincuagésima, n.f. Quinquagesima Sunday.
quincuagésimo, -ma, a. fiftieth.
quincha, n.f. (Per.) kind of wall made of clay and canes.
quinchamalí, n.m. (Chi.) medicinal plant (*Quinchimalium chilense*).
quindécima, n.f. fifteenth part.
quindécimo, -ma, a. fifteenth.
quindenio, n.m. period of fifteen years.
quinete, n.m. kind of camlet.
quinfa, n.f. (Col.) Indian sandal (shoe).
quingentésimo, -ma, a. five-hundredth.
quingombó, n.m. (bot.) gumbo, okra.

quingos, n.m. (Am.) zigzag.
quinientos, -tas, a. five hundred.
quinina, n.f. quinine.
quinismo, n.m. effects of the use or abuse of quinine; cinchonism.
quino, n.m. cinchona-tree; (chem.) quinine.
quinoa, n.f. (Am.) species of goosefoot.
quínolas, n.f.pl. four of a kind, a card game.
quinqué, n.m. paraffin table lamp.
quinquefolio, n.m. (bot.) cinquefoil.
quinquenal, a. quinquennial.
quinquenervia, n.f. (bot.) rib-grass plantain.
quinquenio, n.m. quinquennium, lustrum.
quinquillería, n.f. hardware.
quinquillero, n.m. hawker, pedlar.
quinta, n.f. country-house, country-seat, villa; (mil.) draft; drawing lots; quint (in piquet); (mus.) fifth.
quintador, -ra, n.m.f. (mil.) one who draws lots in fives.
quintaesencia, n.f. quintessence.
quintal, n.m. quintal, hundred-weight; *quintal métrico,* metric quintal (100 kgs.).
quintalada, n.f. (naut.) primage (2½% on the freight).
quintaleño, -ña; quintalero, -ra, a. capable of holding a quintal.
quintana, n.f. country house; fever occurring every fifth day.
quintante, n.m. quintant, an instrument used in navigation and astronomy divided into 72° instead of the 60° of the sextant.
quintañón, -na, a. centenarian.
quintar, v.t. to draw one out of five; to draw lots for soldiers; to draft men for service. — v.i. to reach the fifth day (of the moon).
quintería, n.f. farm; grange.
quinterno, n.m. five sheets of paper; five numbers drawn.
quintero, n.m. farmer, overseer; farm-hand.
quinteto, n.m. (mus.) quintet.
quintilla, n.f. five-lined stanza; *andar en quintillas con,* to oppose obstinately.
quintillo, n.m. ombre, card game with five players.
quinto, -ta, a. fifth.
quinto, n.m. fifth; one-fifth; share of pasture-ground; duty of 20 per cent.; (mil.) conscript.
quintral, n.m. (Chi.) kind of mistletoe with red berries; (Chi.) disease of water-melons and beans.
quintuplicar, v.t. (conjugated like BUSCAR) to quintuple.
quíntuplo, -pla, a. quintuple, fivefold.
quinua, n.f. (Am.) quinoa.
quiñón, n.m. share of partnership or profit; (Philip.) land measure (approx. 2 acres).
quiñonero, n.m. part-owner, shareholder.
quiosco, n.m. kiosk, pavilion, summer-house.
quipo, n.m. quipu, a contrivance of coloured threads and knots used by primitive Peruvians as writing.
quique, n.m. (Chi.) a kind of weasel (*Galictis vitatta*); (Arg.) a ferret.
quiquiriquí, n.m. cock-a-doodle-do; (coll.) cock of the walk.
quiragra, n.f. chiragra, gout in the hand.
quirófano, n.m. operating theatre.
quirógrafo, -n.m., a. chirograph; chirographic.
quiromancia, n.f. chiromancy, palmistry.
quiromántico, -ca, n.m.f., a. palmster, chiromancer.

quirópteros, *n.m.pl.* bats, Cheiroptera.
quiroteca, *n.f.* (*coll.*) glove.
quirquincho, *n.m.* (*Am.*) a kind of armadillo.
quirúrgico, -ca, *a.* surgical.
quirurgo, *n.m.* (*coll.*) surgeon.
quisa, *n.f.* (*Mex.*) kind of black pepper; (*Bol.*) toasted banana.
quise, *pret.* [QUERER].
quisicosa, *n.f.* (*coll.*) enigma, riddle, puzzle.
quisquemenil, *n.m.* (*Am.*) short cloak.
quisquilla, *n.f.* bickering; finickiness; (*ichth.*) shrimp.
quisquilloso, -sa, *a.* fastidious, precise; touchy, peevish.
quiste, *n.m.* (*surg.*) cyst.
quisto, *a.;* bien quisto, well-received, popular; mal quisto, unpopular, hated.
quita, *n.f.* (*law*) acquittance, discharge, release (from debt). — *interj.* God forbid! ¡quita de ahí! away with you! out of my sight! de quita y pon, removable, adjustable.
quitación, *n.f.* salary, income, wages, pay.
quitador, -ra, *n.m.f.* remover, taker away.
quitamanchas, *n.m.* clothes-cleaner.
quitameriendas, *n.f.pl.* meadow-saffron.
quitamiento, *n.m.* acquittance.
quitamotas, *n.m.f.* (*coll.*) servile flatterer.
quitanieve, *n.m.* snow-plough.
quitanza, *n.f.* (*law*) quittance; (*com.*) receipt in full, discharge.
quitapelillos, *n.m.f.* (*coll.*) flatterer, fawner.
quitapesares, *n.m.f.* comfort, consolation.
quitapón, *n.m.* ornament of the headstall of mules.
quitar, *v.t.* to remove, take off, take away; take out, release, free; separate, extract, subtract; to hinder, disturb; to prohibit, forbid; to rob, usurp, strip; to suppress; to abrogate, annul; (*fenc.*) to parry. — *v.r.* to abstain, refrain; to withdraw, retire; to get rid of; to quit, move away; ¡quítate de ahí! get out of that! sin quitar ni poner, literally, without omissions or exaggerations; quíteselo de la cabeza, get that idea out of your head; quitar las barbas, to get shaved.
quitasol, *n.m.* parasol, sunshade.
quite, *n.m.* hindrance, impediment, obstacle; (*fenc.*) parry; dodge.
quiteño, -ña, *a.* of or belonging to Quito (Ecuador).
quito, -ta, *a.* quits.
quitrín, *n.m.* (*Cub.*) gig, light chaise.
quizá, quizás, *adv.* perhaps, maybe.

R

R, r, *n.f.* r, the twenty-first letter of the Spanish alphabet. (*N.B.* rr is a single letter in the Spanish alphabet.)
raba, *n.f.* bait for pilchards.
rabada, *n.f.* hind quarter, rump.
rabadán, *n.m.* chief shepherd.
rabadilla, *n.f.* rump, croup; coccyx.
rabanal, *n.m.* ground sown with radishes.
rabanero, -ra, *n.m.f.* (*coll.*) shameless woman; radish-seller. — *a.* (*coll.*) very short (skirt); forward.
rabanete, *n.m.* small radish.
rabanillo, *n.m.* wild radish; sour taste of wine; (*coll.*) sourish temper; (*coll.*) ardent desire to do something.

rabaniza, *n.f.* radish seed.
rábano, *n.m.* (*bot.*) radish; tomar el rábano por las hojas, to misinterpret, misconstrue.
rabazuz, *n.m.* liquorice juice.
rabear, *v.i.* to wag the tail.
rabel, *n.m.* (*mus.*) rebec; (*vulg.*) breech, backside.
rabeo, *n.m.* wagging of the tail.
rabera, *n.f.* tail, hind part; chaff, remains; handle of a cross-bow.
raberón, *n.m.* top of a felled tree.
rabí, *n.m.* rabbi.
rabia, *n.f.* hydrophobia, rabies; rage, fury; espumar de rabia, to foam with rage, be in a raging temper; de rabia mató la perra, an angry man will wreak vengeance on anything.
rabiar, *v.i.* to suffer from hydrophobia; to rage, be furious; to suffer dreadful pain; rabiar por, to long for; rabiar de hambre, to be famished.
rabiatar, *v.t.* to tie by the tail.
rabiazorras, *n.m.* east wind.
rabicán; rabicano, -na, *a.* white-tailed (of a horse).
rabicorto, -ta, *a.* short-tailed; docked.
rábido, -da, *a.* rabid, mad.
rabieta, *n.f.* (*coll.*) fretting, impatience, fit of temper.
rabihorcado, *n.m.* (*orn.*) frigate bird.
rabil, *n.m.* (*prov.*) crank; (*prov.*) wheat husker.
rabilargo, -ga, *a.* long-tailed.
rabilargo, *n.m.* blue crow.
rabillo, *n.m.* mildew; darnel; little tail, stem.
rabínico, -ca, *a.* rabbinical.
rabinista, *n.m.* rabbinist.
rabino, *n.m.* rabbi.
rabión, *n.m.* rapids.
rabiosamente, *adv.* furiously, madly, outrageously.
rabioso, -sa, *a.* rabid, mad, furious, raging, fierce.
rabisalsera, *a.* (*coll.*) sprightly, petulant, impudent, pert, smart, forward.
rabiza, *n.f.* point of a fishing-rod; rope-end; point, end of a shoal; tail of a block.
rabo, *n.m.* tail of animals; hind part; train; rabo de gallo, (naut.) stern timbers; rabo entre piernas, crestfallen; mirar con el rabo del ojo, to look askance; falta el rabo por desollar, the worst has yet to be done; aun le ha de sudar el rabo, with (however) great difficulty; de rabo de puerco, nunca buen virote, you can't make a silk purse from a sow's ear; volver de rabo, to turn out differently from one's expectations.
rabón, -na, *a.* docked, bob-tailed, short-tailed.
rabona, *n.f.* (*Am.*) woman camp-follower.
raboseada, raboseadura, *n.f.* splashing; chafing, fraying.
rabosear, *v.t.* to spatter, fray, fret, chafe.
raboso, -sa, *a.* ragged, tattered.
rabotada, *n.f.* insolent answer.
rabotear, *v.t.* to crop the tail.
raboteo, *n.m.* cutting of sheep's tails.
rabudo, -da, *a.* long-tailed, thick-tailed.
rábula, *n.f.* pettifogger, ignorant lawyer.
racamenta, *n.f.; racamento,** *n.m.* (*naut.*) parral, parrel; cranse-iron.
racel, *n.m.* (*naut.*) run, rising of a ship.
racial, *a.* racial.
racima, *n.f.* raceme, grapes left on vines.
racimado, -da, *a.* in clusters or racemes.

racimar, *v.t.* (*prov.*) to pick a *racima*.
racimo, *n.m.* bunch of grapes, cluster, raceme.
racimoso, -sa, *a.* full of grapes; racemose.
raciocinación, *n.f.* ratiocination, reasoning.
raciocinar, *v.i.* to argue, reason.
ración, *n.f.* ration, pittance, allowance, supply; prebend in a cathedral; *poner a ración,* to keep on short commons.
racionabilidad, *n.f.* rationality.
racional, *a.* rational, reasonable. — *n.m.* (*eccles.*) rationale, pectoral, breastplate.
racionalidad, *n.f.* rationality.
racionalismo, *n.m.* rationalism.
racionalmente, *adv.* rationally.
racionar, *v.t.* to ration, issue rations.
racionero, *n.m.* distributor of rations; prebendary.
racionista, *n.m.f.* one who receives daily allowances; (*theat.*) utility man.
racha, *n.f.* gust of wind; streak of luck; flaw; (*min.*) piece of wood for shoring.
rada, *n.f.* (*naut.*) road, anchoring-ground, roadstead.
radal, *n.m.* (*Chi.*) a medicinal tree of the proteaceæ family.
radiación, *n.f.* radiation.
radiactividad, *n.f.* radioactivity.
radiactivo, -va, *a.* radioactive.
radiado, -da, *a.* (*bot.*) radiated. — *n.m., a.* (*zool.*) radiate.
radiador, *n.m.* radiator (heating and motor).
radial, *a.* (*anat.*) radial.
radiante, *a.* radiant, brilliant, shining.
radiantemente, *adv.* radiantly, flamingly.
radiar, *v.i.* to radiate.
radicación, *n.f.* radication, taking root; (*fig.*) long established use or practice.
radical, *a.* radical, original, fundamental, primitive; relating to the root. — *n.m.* (*math.*) radical (the sign √); (*gram.*) root; (*polit.*) radical; (*chem.*) radical.
radicalismo, *n.m.* (*polit.*) radicalism.
radicalmente, *adv.* radically.
radicar, *v.i.* (*pret.* **radiqué**; *pres. subj.* **radique**) to take root, be in such a place. — *v.r.* to radicate, take root; to settle, establish oneself.
radicoso, -sa, *a.* radical.
radícula, *n.f.* (*bot.*) radicle.
radífero, *a.* radium-bearing.
radio, *n.m.* radius, circuit, distance; (*chem.*) radium; *n.f.* (*wire.*) radio receiver.
radioactividad, *n.f.* radioactivity.
radioactivo, -va, *a.* radioactive.
radiodifusión, *n.f.* broadcasting.
radiodifusora, radioemisora, *n.f.* broadcasting station.
radioescucha, *n.m.f.* radio-listener.
radiofonía, *n.f.* radiophony.
radiografía, *n.f.* radiography.
radiografiar, *v.t.* to radiograph.
radiograma, *n.m.* radiogram.
radiología, *n.f.* radiology.
radiólogo, *n.m.* radiologist.
radiómetro, *n.m.* radiometer.
radiorreceptor, *n.m.* radio-receiver.
radiorrevista, *n.f.* radio magazine.
radioscopia, *n.f.* radioscopy.
radioso, -sa, *a.* radiant, diffusing light rays.
radiotelefonía, *n.f.* radiotelephony.
radiotelegrafía, *n.f.* radiotelegraphy.
radiotelegrafista, *n.m.* wireless operator.

radioterapia, *n.f.* radiotherapy.
radiotransmisor, *n.m.* radio-transmitter.
radioyente, *n.m.f.* listener.
radiumterapia, *n.f.* radiotherapy.
raedera, *n.f.* scraper, raker.
raedizo, -za, *a.* easily scraped.
raedor, -ra, *a.* scraper, eraser.
raedura, *n.f.* scrapings, filings, parings, erasure.
raer, *v.t.* (*pres. part.* **rayendo**; *pres. indic.* **raigo**; *pres. subj.* **raiga**; *pret.* **él rayó**) to scrape, grate, erase; to fret, fray, rub off, abrade; to blot out; to lay aside; to efface (a habit).
rafa, *n.f.* (*arch.*) buttress; irrigating trench or ditch, small opening in a canal; ; (*vet.*) crack in the toe of hoofs; (*min.*) cut in a rock to anchor a supporting arch.
ráfaga, *n.f.* gust of wind; flash of light; blast; small distant cloud; burst (of gunfire).
rafe, *n.m.* (*arch.*) eaves; (*anat., bot.*) raphe.
rafear, *v.t.* to support with buttresses.
rafia, *n.f.* (*bot.*) raffia.
rahez, *a.* low, vile.
raíble, *a.* that may be scraped or scratched.
raiceja, -cilla, -cita, *n.f.* rootlet, radicle.
raído, -da, *a.* scraped; worn out; frayed, threadbare; (*fig.*) impudent, shameless.
raigal, *a.* relating to the root. — *n.m.* foot of a tree.
raigambre, *n.f.* mass of roots united.
raigón, *n.m.* large, strong root; stump or root of back tooth.
rail, *n.m.* rail.
raimiento, *n.m.* scraping; impudence, shamelessness.
raíz, *n.f.* (*pl.* **raíces**) root; radix; base, foundation, origin; *a raíz,* close to the root; *cortar de raíz,* to nip in the bud; *de raíces,* from the root; *bienes raíces,* landed property; *echar raíces,* to take root, become fixed or settled.
raja, *n.f.* chink, crevice, cranny; fissure, opening, split, rent, gap; portion, part, share; slice (as of fruit); split; coarse cloth; *a raja tabla,* courageously, forthrightly; *hacer rajas,* to divide; *sacar raja,* (*coll.*) to get what one desires, or a part of it.
rajá, *n.m.* rajah.
rajable, *a.* easily split.
rajabroqueles, *n.m.* (*coll.*) bully, brawler.
rajadillo, *n.m.* frangipane; sugared almonds.
rajadizo, -za, *a.* fissile, easily split.
rajador, *n.m.* wood-splitter.
rajadura, *n.f.* cleft, chink, fissure, split, crack.
rajante, *a.* splintering.
rajar, *v.t.* to split, cleave, crack, rend. — *v.i.* to boast, chatter.
rajeta, *n.f.* sort of coarse cloth.
rajuela, *n.f.* small fissure, crack; thin rough stone of low quality.
ralea, *n.f.* race, breed, stock, quality, genus, species; prey (of predatory birds).
ralear, *v.i.* to thin, become thin or sparse.
raleón, -na, *a.* predatory (of birds of prey).
raleza, *n.f.* thinness, rarity, liquidity.
ralo, -la, *a.* thin, rare, sparse.
ralladura, *n.f.; ra llador,** *n.m.* grater.
ralladura, *n.f.* mark left by the grater, gratings.
rallar, *v.t.* to grate; to vex, molest.
rallo, *n.m.* grater, rasp, scraper.
rallón, *n.m.* arrow with crosshead.
rama, *n.f.* (*bot.*) branch, shoot, sprig, twig, bough; rack in cloth-mills; (*print.*) chase;

de rama en rama, always changing, varying; *en rama*, raw material, crude, in leaf (of tobacco); *andarse por las ramas*, to beat about the bush; *asirse a las ramas*, to make frivolous excuses.

ramada, *n.f.;* **ramaje,** *n.m.* arbour, mass of branches.

ramal, *n.m.* strand of a rope, rope-end; halter; branch, division; (*railw.*) branch; (*min.*) shaft, gallery.

ramalazo, *n.m.* lash, marks of lashes; blow or stroke with a rope; spot on the face or body caused by acute pain, sudden grief.

ramalla, *n.f.* twigs, brushwood.

rambla, *n.f.* sandy beach, sandy ground, dry ravine or river-bed; (*text.*) tenter or tentering machine; (in Barcelona) avenue.

ramblazo, *n.m.* gravelly torrent-bed.

rameado, -da, *a.* with ramiform formation.

rameal ; rámeo, -a, *a.* belonging to branches.

ramera, *n.f.* prostitute, whore, harlot.

ramería, *n.f.* brothel; prostitution.

ramero, -ra, *a.* hopping from branch to branch.

rameruela, *n.f.* little whore.

ramial, *n.m.* ramie plantation.

ramificación, *n.f.* ramification, branching off.

ramificarse, *v.r.* to ramify, branch off.

ramilla, -ita, *n.f.* small sprig or shoot, twig.

ramillete, *n.m.* bunch of flowers, nosegay, posy; umbel, cluster; pyramid of fruit; collection of choice objects; table centre-piece.

ramilletera, *n.f.* flower-girl.

ramilletero, *n.m.* flower-vase; flower-seller.

ramillo, -ito, *n.m.* small branch, sprig, twig.

ramina, *n.f.* ramie yarn.

ramio, *n.m.* (*bot.*) ramie.

ramiza, *n.f.* collection of lopped branches.

ramo, *n.m.* branch, bough; antler; a trace of illness; branch of trade, business, concern; part of a whole; cluster, bouquet; line of goods; section, division, department; *Domingo de Ramos*, Palm Sunday.

ramojo, *n.m.* small lopped branch, brushwood.

ramón, *n.m.* top of branches, browse, browsing.

ramonear, *v.i.* to cut or lop branches; to browse.

ramoneo, *n.m.* cutting or lopping branches.

ramoso, -sa, *a.* branchy, ramous.

rampa, *n.f.* ramp; hand-rail; acclivity; gradient; (*mil.*) slope of a glacis.

rampante, *a.* (*her.*) rampant.

rampiñete, *n.m.* (*artill.*) vent-gimlet.

ramplón, -na, *a.* coarse, vulgar, gross, rude, unpolished, heavy. — *n.m.* calk of a shoe.

rampojo, *n.m.* rape, grape-stalk; (*mil.*) caltrop.

rampollo, *n.m.* branch, cutting, slip of a plant.

rana, *n.f.* frog; *no ser rana*, to be able, skilled; *cuando la rana críe pelos*, a very long time, never; *rana marina* (or *pescadora*), (*ichth.*) angler. — *pl.* **ranas,** frog tongue, ranula.

ranacuajo, *n.m.* [RENACUAJO].

rancajada, *n.f.* uprooting plants, sprouts, etc.

rancajado, -da, *a.* wounded by a splinter.

rancajo, *n.m.* splinter in the flesh.

ranciarse, *v.r.* to grow rancid, stale.

rancidez, *n.f.* rancidity, rankness, ranciness.

rancio, -cia, *a.* rank, rancid, stale, strong-scented; choice, ripe (of wine).

rancio, *n.m.* rancidity, rankness; greasiness.

rancioso, -sa, *a.* rancid, rank, sour.

rancheadero, *n.m.* place containing huts.

ranchear, *v.i.* to build huts.

ranchería, *n.f.* group of labourers' huts; hamlet, settlement, cluster of small houses; horde.

ranchero, *n.m.* mess-steward; small farmer; (*Mex.*) rancher.

rancho, *n.m.* mess, mess-room; hut; hamlet; camp; (*Am.*) cattle ranch; clan; (*coll.*) friendly meeting; gang; *asentar el rancho*, to stop in a place to rest or to have a meal; *hacer rancho*, to make room.

randa, *n.f.* lace, net-work.

randado, -da, *a.* lace, lace-adorned.

randera, *n.f.* lace-worker.

rangífero, *n.m.* reindeer.

rango, *n.m.* rank, class, position.

rangua, *n.f.* spindle-box, shaft-socket.

ranilla, *n.f.* frog of a horse's hoof; disease in the bowels of cattle.

ranina, *n.f.pl.* (*anat.*) ranine veins.

ránula, *n.f.* (*med., vet.*) ranula.

ranúnculo, *n.m.* ranunculus; crowfoot, buttercup.

ranura, *n.f.* groove, rabbet, chamfer.

ranzal, *n.m.* an old-fashioned linen cloth.

raña, *n.f.* hook frame for catching octopuses; lowland.

raño, *n.m.* oyster-tongs; (*ichth.*) kind of pike-perch.

rapa, *n.f.* flower of the olive tree.

rapacejo, *n.m.* border, edging; child, urchin.

rapacería, *n.f.* childish prank.

rapacidad, *n.f.* rapacity, robbery.

rapador, -ra, *n.m.f.* (*coll.*) scraper, barber; plunderer.

rapadura, *n.f.* shaving, hair-cutting; plundering.

rapagón, *n.m.* beardless youth.

rapamiento, *n.m.* act of shaving or erasing.

rapante, *a.* snatching, robbing; shaving; (*her.*) rampant.

rapapiés, *n.m.* kind of running squib; chaser.

rapapolvo, *n.m.* (*coll.*) sharp reproof.

rapar, *v.t.* to shave, skin, peel; to crop (the hair); (*fig.*) to plunder, rob.

rapasa, *n.f.* wax-stone.

rapavelas, *n.m.* (*vulg., contempt.*) sacristan, acolyte, etc.

rapaz, -za, *n.m.f.* boy, girl. — *a.* rapacious, thievish.

rapazada, *n.f.* childish speech or action.

rapazuelo, -la, *n.m.f.* little boy, little girl.

rapé, *n.m.* rappee, snuff.

rape, *n.m.* (*coll.*) shaving; *al rape*, cropped.

rápidamente, *adv.* rapidly.

rapidez, *n.f.* rapidity, celerity, velocity.

rápido, -da, *a.* rapid, quick, swift. — *n.m.pl.* **rápidos,** rapids.

rapiego, -ga, *a.* rapacious (of birds).

rapingancho, *n.m.* (*Per., Col.*) omelet with cheese.

rapiña, *n.f.* rapine, robbery, spoliation; *ave de rapiña*, bird of prey.

rapiñador, -ra, *n.m.f.* plunderer, robber.

rapiñar, *v.t.* (*coll.*) to plunder, rob.

rapista, *n.m.* (*coll.*) barber, shaver, scraper.

rapo, *n.m.* round-rooted turnip.

rapónchigo, *n.m.* (*bot.*) rampion, bellflower.

raposa, *n.f.* vixen; cunning, artful person.

raposear, *v.i.* to be fox-like, use cunning artifices.

raposera, *n.f.* fox-hole.

raposería, *n.f.* artful kindness.
raposino, -na, *a.* vulpine, foxy.
raposo, *n.m.* dog-fox.
raposuno, -na, *a.* vulpine, foxy.
rapsoda, *n.m.* rhapsode.
rapsodia, *n.f.* rhapsody.
rapsodista, *n.m.* rhapsodist.
rapta, *n.f., a.* abducted, ravished (woman).
raptar, *v.t.* to carry off a woman by force.
rapto, *n.m.* rapine, robbery; rape, ravishment, abduction; rapture, ecstasy, trance, swoon.
raptor, *n.m.* ravisher, abductor.
raque, *n.m.* wrecker, plundering wrecks.
raquear, *v.i.* to plunder wrecks.
Raquel, *n.f.* Rachel.
raquero, *n.m.* (*naut.*) wrecker; dock-thief.
raquero, -ra, *a.* piratical.
raqueta, *n.f.* racket; battledore and shuttlecock; badminton; tennis.
raquetero, *n.m.* racket-maker, racket-seller.
raquis, *n.m.* (*anat.*) rachis, the spinal column; (*bot.*) stalk.
raquítico, -ca, *a.* rickety; rachitic; (*fig.*) niggardly, flimsy, feeble.
raquitis, *n.f.; * **raquitismo**, *n.m.* (*med.*) rachitis, rickets.
rara, *n.f.* (*Am.*) a destructive bird.
raramente, *adv.* seldom, rarely; ridiculously, oddly.
rarefacción, *n.f.* rarefaction.
rarefacer, *v.t.* (conjugated like HACER) to rarefy.
rarefacto, -ta, *p.p. irreg.* [RAREFACER].
rareza, *n.f.* rarity, rareness; curio, curiosity, oddity; uncommonness, infrequency; fad, freakishness, queerness.
raridad, *n.f.* rarity, oddity, subtlety.
rarificar, *v.t.* (*pret.* **rarifiqué**; *pres. subj.* **rarifique**) to rarefy, make thin, dilute. — *v.r.* to rarefy, become thin.
rarificativo, -va, *a.* rare, active, with power of rarefying.
raro, -ra, *a.* rare, thin, rarefied, porous, having little density; scarce, uncommon, queer, odd; extravagant; extraordinary; excellent, superb, precious, choice; *rara vez*, seldom.
ras, *n.m.* level; *ras en ras, ras con ras*, on an equal footing, on a par.
rasa, *n.f.* tease in textiles; plateau, table-land.
rasadura, *n.f.* levelling with a strickle.
rasamente, *adv.* openly, publicly, clearly.
rasante, *a.* levelling. — *n.f.* grading line.
rasar, *v.t.* to rase, graze, skim; to level with a strickle. — *v.r.* to clear up (the sky).
rascacielos, *n.m.* skyscraper.
rascadera, *n.f.* scraper, curry-comb.
rascador, *n.m.* scraper, scaler, scratcher, rasp; bodkin, hat-pin; huller, sheller.
rascadura, *n.f.* scraping, scratching, rasping; scratch.
rascalino, *n.m.* (*bot.*) dodder.
rascamiento, *n.m.* act of scratching or scraping.
rascamoño, *n.m.* head-pin, hatpin, bodkin.
rascar, *v.t.* (*pret.* **rasqué**; *pres. subj.* **rasque**) to scrape, scratch, rasp; (*Col.*) to itch.
rascatripas, *n.m.f.* (*facet.*) gut-scraper, indifferent fiddler.
rascazón, *n.f.* pricking, tickling, itching.
rascle, *n.m.* fishing net used in coral fishing.
rascón, -na, *a.* sour, sharp, acrid, tart.
rascón, *n.m.* water-rail; marsh-hen.

rasel, *n.m.* entrance and run of a ship.
rasero, *n.m.* strickle, strike.
rasete, *n.m.* satinet, sateen.
rasgado, -da, *a.* rent, open, torn; *ojos rasgados*, almond eyes; *boca rasgada*, wide mouth.
rasgador, -ra, *a.* tearer, cleaver, scratcher, ripper.
rasgadura, *n.f.* rent, ripping.
rasgar, *v.t.* (*pret.* **rasgué**; *pres. subj.* **rasgue**) to tear, cut apart, rend, lacerate, rip.
rasgo, *n.m.* dash, stroke, scroll, flourish, line elegantly drawn; fine action, deed or feat; happy expression or saying; stroke (of wit, etc.). — *pl.* **rasgos**, features.
rasgón, *n.m.* rent, rag, rip, laceration, tatter, tear.
rasgueado, *n.m.* act of making flourishes (on the guitar).
rasguear *v.i.* to make flourishes. — *v.t.* to play flourishes (on the guitar, etc.); to play the guitar with strokes of the tips of the fingers.
rasgueo, *n.m.* lines elegantly drawn; art of making flourishes.
rasguillo, *n.m.* small dash (of a pen).
rasguñar, *v.t.* to scratch, scrape; to sketch, outline.
rasguño, *n.m.* scratch, nip, scar; outline, sketch.
rasilla, *n.f.* serge; fine flooring tile.
raso, -sa, *a.* clear, plain, flat, unobstructed, open; *al raso*, in the open air; *tiempo raso*, fine weather; *cielo raso*, clear sky; flat ceiling; *soldado raso*, private soldier. — *n.m.* satin.
raspa, *n.f.* rasp, coarse file; (*carp.*) wood-rasp, scraper, grater; grape-stalk; fruit-rind; fish-bone; hair on a pen-nib; beard of ear of wheat; (*Am.*) (*coll.*) lecture, sermon, dressing down.
raspador, *n.m.* rasp, grater, scraper; eraser.
raspadura, *n.f.* erasure, rasping, filing, scraping, paring, abrasion; (*Cub.*) pan sugar.
raspajo, *n.m.* grape-stalk.
raspamiento, *n.m.* act of rasping or filing.
raspante, *a.* rasping, rough (wine).
raspar, *v.t.* to erase, rub off, scrape, rasp, pare; to prick, bite, sting; to steal, carry away.
raspear, *v.i.* to sputter, scratch (of a pen).
raspilla, *n.f.* (*bot.*) forget-me-not.
raspón, (*Col.*) large straw hat of peasants; (*Chi.*) severe reprimand.
rasqueta, *n.f.* (*naut.*) scraper; (horse grooming) curry-comb.
rastel, *n.m.* bar, lattice, railing.
rastra, *n.f.* sled, sledge; dray, brake; (*agric.*) harrow; dragging along; track, trail; string of dried fruit; reaping-machine; (*naut.*) drag, grapnel; *a la rastra, a rastra*, or *a rastras*, dragging; (*fig.*) unwillingly, by force.
rastracueros, *n.m.* (*Am.*) a person who makes a fortune in the hide business.
rastrallar, *v.t.* to crack with a whip.
rastreador, -ra, *n.m.f.* tracker.
rastrear, *v.t.* to trace, scent, nose, track, trail; (*agric.*) to harrow, rake; to drag (fishing); to sell carcases by wholesale; to investigate, inquire into, fathom; to skim the ground. — *v.i.* to float in the air near the ground; (*aer.*) to fly very low.
rastreo, *n.m.* dragging in the sea.
rastrero, -ra, *a.* creeping, trailing; dragging; skimming the ground; scenting; low, abject, base, grovelling; cringing.

rastrero, *n.m.* employee in a slaughterhouse.
rastrillada, *n.f.* rakeful.
rastrillador, -ra, *n.m.f.* hackler, hatcheller, flax-dresser; raker.
rastrillar, *v.t.* to hackle, hatchel, comb, dress flax; to rake.
rastrillazo, *n.m.* blow from a rake.
rastrilleo, *n.m.* hackling, raking.
rastrillo, *n.m.* hackle, flax-comb; *(agric.)* rake; ward of a key; ward of a lock; *(artill.)* hammer of a gunlock; rack (of a manger); *(fort.)* portcullis.
rastro, *n.m.* scent, trail; slaughterhouse; track, print, trace, sign, vestige, token, relic; *(agric.)* harrow, rake; (in Madrid) market of knick-knacks.
rastrojera, *n.f.* stubble-ground.
rastrojo, *n.m.* stubble.
rasura, *n.f.* shaving, scraping, filing.
rasuración, *n.f.* shaving.
rasurar, *v.t., v.r.* to shave.
rata, *n.f.* rat; female rat.
ratafía, *n.f.* ratafia.
ratania, *n.f.* (*Per.*) a shrub.
rataplán, *n.m.* rataplan, drum-beat; rub-a-dub.
ratear, *v.t.* to lessen, abate, divide proportionally; to filch. — *v.i.* to creep, trail along the ground.
rateo, *n.m.* proportional distribution, apportionment.
rateramente, *adv.* meanly, vilely.
ratería, *n.f.* larceny; petty dishonesty; meanness.
ratero, -ra, *a.* creeping, flying low, skimming the ground (of birds); thievish; vile, despicable, mean.
ratero, *n.m.* petty thief, pickpocket.
rateruelo, *n.m.* little pilferer.
ratificación, *n.f.* ratification, confirmation.
ratificar, *v.t.* (*pret.* **ratifiqué;** *pres. subj.* **ratifique**) to ratify, approve, confirm.
ratificatorio, -ria, *a.* ratificative, confirming.
ratigar, *v.t.* to secure the load on a cart with a rope.
rátigo, *n.m.* truck-load, cart-load.
ratihabición, *n.f.* (*law*) ratification.
ratimago, *n.m.* (*prov.*) trick, cunning.
ratina, *n.f.* ratteen.
ratito, *n.m.* short time, little while.
rato, *n.m.* short time; while, little while; *buen rato,* fair, considerable time; *mal rato,* bad, unpleasant time; *a ratos perdidos,* in leisure hours; *de rato en rato* (or *a ratos*), occasionally, from time to time; *pasar el rato,* to pass the time, to while the time away.
rato, -ta, *a.* (*law*) firm, valid, conclusive.
ratón, *n.m.* mouse; *ratones, arriba; que todo lo blanco no es harina,* all is not gold that glitters; *ratón que no sabe más que un horado, presto es cazado,* the man of one expedient only is soon beaten.
ratona, *n.f.* female mouse.
ratonar, *v.t.* to gnaw. — *v.r.* to become sick from eating mice (of cats).
ratonera, *n.f.* mouse-trap; mouse-hole; *caer en la ratonera,* to fall into a trap.
ratonero, -ra, *n.m.f.* ratter. — *a.* mousy.
rauco, -ca, *a.* (*poet.*) raucous, hoarse, husky.
raudal, *n.m.* torrent, rapid stream, rapids; *(fig.)* abundance, plenty.
raudamente, *adv.* rapidly.

raudo, -da, *a.* rapid, swift, precipitate, impetuous.
raulí, *n.m.* (*Chi.*) a tree of the cupuliferous family.
rauta, *n.f.* (*coll.*) road, way, route.
raya, *n.f.* stroke, dash, streak, stripe; mark, score; term, limit, line, boundary, frontier; parting of the hair; spiral groove of a rifle. — *n.m.* (*ichth.*) ray, skate; *a raya,* within proper bounds or limits; *tener a raya,* to keep within bounds (or at bay); *pasar de (la) raya,* to exceed bounds; *hacer raya,* to be eminent, brilliant; *tres en raya,* a children's game.
rayado, *n.m.* stripes, ruling.
rayado, -da, *a.* streaky, variegated; ruled, striped; (*artill.*) rifled, grooved.
rayano, -na, *a.* neighbouring, contiguous.
rayar, *v.t.* to form, mark, draw (lines); to rule, stripe, streak, variegate; to rifle, striate; to underline, underscore; to expunge, strike out, scratch out. — *v.i.* to surpass, excel; to border on; to begin, appear.
rayo, *n.m.* beam, ray of light, straight line; spoke (of a wheel); radius; fire-arms; brilliant or lively genius; thunderbolt; lightning flash; sudden havoc, misfortune, scourge; *¡rayo!* or *¡rayos!* fury! *echar rayos,* to be wroth; *allá darás, rayo, en casa de Tamayo,* there you are, thunderbolt, fall on that man's house (i.e., not mine).
rayoso, -sa, *a.* full of lines or rays.
rayuela, *n.f.* small lines; game of drawing lines.
rayuelo, *n.m.* kind of snipe.
raza, *n.f.* race, lineage, clan, family; cleft in a horse's hoof; lightly woven stripe in fabrics; ray of light; crack, fissure.
razado, -da, *a.* lightly-woven (of stripes).
rázago, *n.m.* coarse cloth, sackcloth, burlap.
razón, *n.f.* reason, reasoning faculty, ratiocination, reasonableness, moderation; equity, right, justice; argument, consideration, explanation; motive, cause, occasion; (*math.*) ratio, account, calculation; mode, method, order; *razón comercial,* (*com.*) firm, partnership; *envolver en razones a, alcanzar de razones a,* to vanquish in a dispute; *dar razón,* to inform; *dar la razón,* to approve, agree with; *razón de pie de banco,* (*coll.*) futile allegation; *a razón de,* at the rate of; *en razón,* with regard to; *perder la razón,* to lose one's reason; *ponerse en la razón,* to be reasonable; *por razón,* consequently; *ponerse a razones con,* to have an altercation with; *tomar razón,* to register.
razonable, *a.* reasonable, fair, just, moderate.
razonablemente, *adv.* reasonably, moderately.
razonado, -da, *a.* rational, judicious, prudent; detailed, itemized.
razonador, -ra, *n.m.f.* reasoner.
razonamiento, *n.m.* reasoning, argument.
razonante, *a.* reasoning, reasoner.
razonar, *v.i.* to discourse, reason, argue, converse, talk. — *v.t.* to itemize, vouch, attest.
razzia, *n.f.* foraging expedition, raid, plundering, ravaging.
re, *n.m.* (*mus.*) re, second note of scale; D.
rea, *n.f.* female charged with the commission of a crime.
reacción, *n.f.* reaction; revulsion, rebound; resistance, opposition.

reaccionar, *v.i.* to react.
reaccionario, -ria, *n.m.f., a.* reactionary.
reacio, -cia, *a.* stubborn, obstinate.
reactivo, *n.m.* reagent.
reagravación, *n.f.* reaggravation.
reagravar, *v.t.* to aggravate anew.
reagudo, -da, *a.* very acute.
real, *a.* real, actual, positive, genuine, certain, true; fair, open; royal, king-like, kingly, magnificent, splendid, grand; noble, handsome. — *n.m.* camp, encampment, king's tent; former Spanish silver coin; fair ground; ship of the line; royal galley; *real sitio,* royal country-seat; *real hacienda,* Exchequer, Treasury; *real de minas,* (*Mex.*) town near silver mines; *con mi real y mi pala,* with my person and property; *sentar los reales,* to fix the king's tent, to pitch a camp; *alzar* (or *levantar*) *los reales,* to strike camp, to give up house-keeping.
realce, *n.m.* raised work, embossment; splendour, lustre; (*art*) high light.
realdad, *n.f.* royal office, sovereignty.
realegrarse, *v.r.* to be extremely glad.
realejo, *n.m.* chamber organ.
realengo, -ga, *a.* royal, kingly; unappropriated (land).
realera, *n.f.* (*api.*) queen-cell.
realete, *n.m.* small coin of the kingdom of Valencia.
realeza, *n.f.* royalty, regal dignity.
realidad, *n.f.* reality, fact; sincerity, truth; *en realidad,* really, truly.
realillo, -ito, *n.m.* small real.
realismo, *n.m.* royalism; (*art*) realism.
realista, *n.m.f., a.* royalist; realist.
realizable, *a.* realizable; (*com.*) saleable.
realización, *n.f.* realization, fulfilment; (*com.*) sale.
realizar, *v.t.* (*pret.* **realicé**; *pres. subj.* **realice**) to realize, perform, fulfil; (*com.*) to sell, turn into cash.
realmente, *adv.* really, truly, effectually.
realzar, *v.t.* (conjugated like **ALZAR**) to raise, elevate; to emboss; to aggrandize, heighten, make prominent; (*art*) to heighten the colours of.
reanimar, *v.t.* to re-animate, cheer, comfort; revive, encourage.
reanudar, *v.t.* to renew, resume.
reaparecer, *v.i.* to reappear.
reaparición, *n.f.* reappearance, reappearing.
reapretar, *v.t.* to press again, to squeeze.
rearar, *v.t.* to plough again.
reaseguro, *n.m.* (*com.*) reinsurance.
reasumir, *v.t.* (*p.p.* **reasumido, reasunto**) to resume, reassume, retake.
reasunción, *n.f.* reassumption, resumption.
reata, *n.f.* rope to tie horses in single file; drove of horses or mules thus tied; leading mule drawing a cart; (*Mex.*) any rope; *de reata,* in single file.
reatadura, *n.f.* act of retying, tying animals in single file.
reatar, *v.t.* to tie one beast to another; to retie, tie tightly; to follow blindly others' opinions.
reato, *n.m.* (*eccles.*) obligation of atonement.
reavivar, *v.t.* to revive, re-encourage; to heighten colours.
rebaba, *n.f.* (*mech.*) burr, fin, mould mark.
rebaja, *n.f.* abatement, deduction, diminution; (*com.*) drawback, rebate, discount.

rebajado, -da, *n.m.f.* discharged soldier.
rebajamiento, *n.m.* curtailment, abatement, abasement.
rebajar, *v.t.* to diminish, lessen, abate; rebate, reduce, dock; to allow discount; to underbid; (*carp.*) to shave off, cut down; (*art*) to weaken a high light or colour. — *v.r.* to humble oneself, stoop down; to commit low actions; (*mil.*) to be discharged, mustered out.
rebajo, *n.m.* (*carp.*) rabbet; groove in timber or stone.
rebalaje, *n.m.* windings in a river, current, flow of water.
rebalsa, *n.f.* stagnation; stagnant water; puddle, pool, pond; stagnation of fluid in some part of the body.
rebalsar, *v.t.* to dam water to form a pool; to stop, detain.
rebanada, *n.f.* slice.
rebanar, *v.t.* to slice, cut up, divide.
rebañadera, *n.f.* drag, drag-hook, grapnel.
rebañadura, *n.f.* (*coll.*) gleaning, picking up.
rebañego, -ga, *a.* gregarious.
rebaño, *n.m.* flock of sheep, herd of cattle, fold, drove; heap, crowd; assembly, congregation.
rebañuelo, *n.m.* small flock.
rebasadero, *n.m.* (*naut.*) pass.
rebasar, *v.t.* to sail past; to trespass, go beyond, exceed.
rebate, *n.m.* dispute, contention.
rebatible, *a.* refutable, rebuttable.
rebatimiento, *n.m.* repulsion, refutation.
rebatiña, *n.f.; andar a la rebatiña,* to grab and snatch things from one another.
rebatir, *v.t.* to rebate, rebut; repel, resist, ward off, drive back; refute, repress, object; to settle accounts; (*fenc.*) to ward off a thrust.
rebato, *n.m.* (*mil.*) surprise, surprise attack; alarm, alarm-bell; call to arms; excitement, commotion; *tocar a rebato,* alarm bell; *de rebato,* suddenly.
rebautización, *n.f.* rebaptism.
rebautizar, *v.t.* (conjugated like **BAUTIZAR**) to rebaptize, baptize a second time.
rebeco, *n.f.* (*zool.*) chamois.
rebelarse, *v.r.* to rebel, revolt, mutiny, resist.
rebelde, *n.m.* rebel; (*law*) defaulter. — *a.* rebellious, stubborn, unmanageable.
rebeldía, *n.f.* rebelliousness, contumacy, obstinacy, stubbornness, disobedience; (*law*) default, non-appearance; *en rebeldía,* by default.
rebelión, *n.f.* rebellion, insurrection, revolt.
rebelón, -na, *a.* restive, stubborn (of a horse).
rebencazo, *n.m.* blow with a ratline.
rebenque, *n.m.* (*naut.*) ratline; cross rope; (*Am.*) riding whip.
rebién, *adv.* (*coll.*) very well.
rebina, rebinadura, *n.f.* third ploughing.
rebisabuela, *n.f.* great-great-grandmother.
rebisabuelo, *n.m.* great-great-grandfather.
rebisnieta, *n.f.* great-great-grand-daughter.
rebisnieto, *n.m.* great-great-grandson.
reblandecer, *v.t.* (*pres. indic.* **reblandezco**; *pres. subj.* **reblandezca**) to make soft or tender.
rebocillo, rebociño, *n.m.* shawl.
rebolisco, *n.m.* (*Cub.*) commotion without motive.
rebollar, rebolledo, *n.m.* thicket of oak saplings.

rebollidura, *n.f.* (*gunn.*) honeycomb, flaw in a gun.

rebollo, *n.m.* Turkey oak; tree-trunk.

rebolludo, -da, *a.* thick-set; *diamante rebolludo,* rough diamond.

rebombar, *v.i.* to resound, make a loud report.

reborde, *n.m.* rim, flange, collar, border.

rebosadero, *n.m.* place of overflowing.

rebosadura, *n.f.; rebosamiento, n.m.* overflow, exudation.

rebosar, *v.t.* to overflow, abound, be plenty; to run over, teem; to unbosom oneself.

rebotadera, *n.f.* nap-raiser.

rebotador, -ra, *n.m.f.* one who rebounds.

rebotadura, *n.f.* rebounding.

rebotar, *v.i.* to rebound (of a ball). — *v.t.* to cause to rebound; to clinch a spike or nail; to raise the nap; to repel; (*coll.*) to exasperate, vex. — *v.r.* to retract, change one's views; to change or turn colour.

rebote, *n.m.* rebound, rebounding, resilience; (*Col.*) indigestion; *de rebote,* indirectly, on a second mission.

rebotica, *n.f.* room behind a chemist's shop.

rebotín, *n.m.* second growth of mulberry leaves.

rebozar, *v.t.* (*pret.* **rebocé**; *pres. subj.* **reboce**) (*cook.*) to dip in, to cover meat with batter, baste; to muffle. — *v.r.* to be muffled in a cloak.

rebozo, *n.m.* muffling; muffler; woman's shawl; pretext; *de rebozo,* secretly, hiddenly; *sin rebozo,* openly, frankly.

rebramar, *v.i.* to bellow (*or* low) repeatedly.

rebramo, *n.m.* belling of stags.

rebudiar, *v.i.* to snuffle, grunt (wild boar).

rebufar, *v.i.* to blow or snort repeatedly.

rebufo, *n.m.* (*artill.*) muzzle-blast.

rebujado, -da, *a.* tangled, entangled.

rebujal, *n.m.* number of cattle above fifty in a flock; small piece of arable ground.

rebujiña, *n.f.* (*coll.*) wrangle, scuffle.

rebujo, *n.m.* muffler, wrapper, thick veil; clumsy bundle; portion of tithe paid in money.

rebullicio, *n.m.* great tumult or clamour.

rebullir, *v.i., v.r.* (conjugated like BULLIR) to begin to move, stir.

reburujar, *v.t.* (*coll.*) to wrap, pack in bundles.

reburujón, *n.m.* clumsy bundle.

rebusca, *n.f.* research, searching; gleaning; refuse, remains.

rebuscador, -ra, *n.m.f.* gleaner; researcher.

rebuscar, *v.t.* (conjugated like BUSCAR) to glean grapes; to inquire carefully, search diligently.

rebusco, *n.m.* research; gleaning.

rebutir, *v.t.* (*prov.*) to stuff, fill up.

rebuznador, -ra, *n.m.f.* brayer.

rebuznar, *v.i.* to bray.

rebuzno, *n.m.* braying of an ass.

recabar, *v.t.* to obtain by entreaty.

recadero, -ra, *n.m.f.* porter, messenger.

recado, *n.m.* errand, message; greeting, regards, compliments, complimentary message; present, gift; voucher; outfit; tool, implement; daily supply of provisions; abundance, plenty; (*Am.*) saddle and trappings; *llevar recado,* to be reproved *or* punished; *recado de escribir,* writing materials.

recaer, *v.i.* (conjugated like CAER) to fall back, relapse, devolve; to behove.

recaída, *n.f.* relapse; second fall or offence.

recaigo; recaiga, *pres. indic.; pres. subj.* [RECAER].

recalada, *n.f.* landfall; act of descrying the land.

recalar, *v.t.* to soak, drench, saturate (slowly). — *v.i.* to sight or reach land, make a landfall.

recalcadamente, *adv.* closely, contiguously; vehemently.

recalcar, *v.t.* (*pret.* **recalqué**; *pres. subj.* **recalque**) to cram, pack, press, push, squeeze, stuff; to repeat, reiterate, emphasize. — *v.i.* (*naut.*) to heel, list. — *v.r.* to lean back; to harp on a subject.

recalcitrante, *a.* recalcitrant, obstinate.

recalcitrar, *v.i.* to wince (as a horse); to offer resistance; to recede, go back; to oppose, resist.

recalentamiento, *n.m.* excandescence; reheating, overheating; (*engin.*) superheating.

recalentar, *v.t.* (conjugated like CALENTAR) to heat again, rekindle, overheat; to excite; (*eng.*) to superheat. — *v.r.* to become overheated.

recalmón, *n.m.* (*naut.*) lull of the wind.

recalvastro, -tra, *a.* bald-headed.

recalzar, *v.t.* (conjugated like CALZAR) (*agric.*) to drill; (*arch.*) to reinforce the foundation of a building; (*art*) to colour a drawing.

recalzo, *n.m.* repairing, strengthening a foundation; outer felloe of a cart-wheel.

recalzón, *n.m.* outer felloe of a wheel.

recamado, *n.m.* raised work (embroidery).

recamador, -ra, *n.m.f.* embroiderer.

recamar, *v.t.* to embroider with raised work.

recámara, *n.f.* wardrobe, household furniture; dressing-room, boudoir; (*Mex.*) bedroom; (*min.*) explosives store; (*gunn.*) chamber (of a gun); (*coll.*) caution, reserve.

recambiar, *v.t.* to rechange, re-exchange; (*com.*) to redraw.

recambio, *n.m.* re-exchange, fresh barter.

recamo, *n.m.* embroidery of raised work.

recancanilla, *n.f.* children's play, hobbling; (*coll.*) emphasis.

recantación, *n.f.* recantation, retraction.

recantón, *n.m.* corner-stone.

recapacitar, *v.t.* to recall to mind.

recapitulación, *n.f.* recapitulation.

recapitular, *v.t.* to sum up, recapitulate.

recarga, *n.f.* second charge of fire-arms.

recargar, *v.t.* (*pret.* **recargué**; *pres. subj.* **recargue**) to recharge; to overload, surcharge; to renew an attack; (*law*) to increase a sentence; (*med.*) increase in temperature.

recargo, *n.m.* new charge or accusation; additional payment or tax, surcharge; overload; increase of fever; (*law*) increase of a sentence.

recata, *n.f.* tasting again.

recatadamente, *adv.* cautiously; modestly, prudently; cunningly.

recatado, -da, *a.* prudent, circumspect; honest, coy, shy; modest, candid.

recatar, *v.t.* to secrete, conceal; to taste again. — *v.r.* to take care.

recato. *n.m.* prudence, circumspection, caution; privacy, secrecy; modesty, bashfulness, coyness; virtue, honour.

recatonazo, *n.m.* stroke with the butt of a lance.

recaudación, *n.f.* collection of taxes; recovery of debts; collector's office.

recaudador, *n.m.* tax-gatherer, collector.

recaudamiento, *n.m.* collection of taxes; collector's office or district.

recaudar, *v.t.* to collect rents or taxes; to put in custody; to obtain.

recaudo, *n.m.* collection of rents or taxes; supply, provision; precaution, caution, care; *(law)* surety, security, bail, bond; *a buen recaudo,* well guarded, under custody.

recavar, *v.t.* to dig a second time.

recazo, *n.m.* guard of sword; back of knife-blade.

recebar, *v.t.* to spread gravel.

recebo, *n.m.* sand or gravel for a road.

recelador, *a.* shy (horse).

recelar, *v.t.* to doubt, mistrust, suspect, fear; to excite a mare sexually. — *v.r.* to fear, be afraid or suspicious.

recelo, *n.m.* fear, foreboding, gloomy imagining, suspicion.

receloso, -sa, *a.* suspicious, mistrustful, fearful.

recentadura, *n.f.* leaven for fermenting dough.

recental, *a.* suckling (lamb or calf).

recentar, *v.t.* to put leaven into dough. — *v.r.* to renew.

receñir, *v.t.* (conjugated like CEÑIR) to regird.

recepción, *n.f.* reception, receiving, acceptation, admission; *(law)* cross-examination.

recepta, *n.f.* record of fines.

receptáculo, *n.m.* receptacle; asylum, refuge, shelter.

receptador, *n.m.* receiver of stolen goods; abettor.

receptar, *v.t.* to receive stolen goods; to abet; to hide, shelter. — *v.r.* to take refuge.

receptivo, -va, *a.* receptive.

recepto, *n.m.* asylum, shelter, place of refuge.

receptor, -ra, *a.* receiving, recipient.

receptor, *n.m.* receiver; abettor, secretary; *(elec., law)* receiver.

receptoría, *n.f.* receiver's office; receivership; power of delegate judge.

recercador, *n.m.* chaser (of jewellery).

recercar, *v.t.* to fence, fence again.

recésit, *n.m.* vacation, recess.

receso, *n.m.* recess, withdrawal, retirement, recession; *(astr.)* deviation.

receta, *n.f.* prescription, recipe, formula; memorandum of orders; schedule; *(com.)* amount brought forward.

recetador, *n.m.* prescriber of medicines.

recetar, *v.t.* to prescribe (medicines).

recetario, *n.m.* register of physicians' prescriptions; dispensatory, pharmacopœia; apothecary's file.

recetor, *n.m.* receiver, treasurer.

recetoría, *n.f.* treasury, sub-treasury.

recial, *n.m.* rapid (in rivers).

reciamente, *adv.* strongly, forcibly, stoutly.

recibí, *n.m.* payment received, receipt.

recibidero, -ra, *a.* receivable.

recibidor, *n.m.* receiver; vestibule; hall.

recibiente, *a.* receiving.

recibimiento, *n.m.* reception, receipt; entertainment, hospitality, greeting, welcome; ante-chamber, vestibule, hall; social reception.

recibir, *v.t.* to receive, let in, take in, get, accept, admit; to take charge of; to greet, meet, welcome; to receive calls; to experience (an injury); face (an attack). — *v.r.* [to] graduate, be admitted to practise a profession; *recibir a cuenta,* to receive on account; *recibirse de abogado,* to be called to the bar.

recibo, *n.m.* *(com.)* receipt; discharge, acquittance; reception; *acusar recibo,* *(com.)* to acknowledge receipt; *estar de recibo,* to be at home to callers; *de recibo,* fit for service; *pieza de recibo,* drawing-room.

recidiva, *n.f.* relapse.

recién, *adv.* (shortened form of *reciente,* used only before past participles) recently, just, lately.

reciente, *a.* recent, new, fresh, modern, just made.

recientemente, *adv.* recently, lately, newly.

recinchar, *v.t.* to gird, bind with a girdle.

recinto, *n.m.* precinct, district; ambit; enclosure.

recio, -cia, *a.* stout, robust, strong, vigorous; rude, coarse, uncouth; swift, impetuous; arduous, grievous; hard to bear; rigorous, severe (weather). — *adv.* strongly, stoutly, rapidly, vehemently; *hablar recio,* to talk loudly; *de recio,* strongly, violently.

récipe, *n.m.* prescription; *(coll.)* displeasure, offence.

recipiente, *n.m.* *(chem.)* recipient, receiver; *(phys.)* bell of an air pump.

reciprocación, *n.f.* reciprocation, mutuality.

recíprocamente, *adv.* reciprocally, mutually, conversely.

reciprocar, *v.t.* (*pret.* **reciproqué** ; *pres. subj.* **reciproque**) to reciprocate. — *v.r.* to correspond mutually.

reciprocidad, *n.f.* reciprocity.

recíproco, -ca, *a.* reciprocal, mutual.

recisión, *n.f.* rescission, abrogation.

recitación, *n.f.* recitation, recital.

recitado, *n.m.* recitative.

recitador, -ra, *n.m.f.* reciter.

recitar, *v.t.* to recite; to rehearse.

recitativo, -va, *a.* recitative.

reciura, *n.f.* strength, force, rigour (of weather).

recizalla, *n.f.* second clippings.

reclamación, *n.f.* reclamation; objection, remonstrance; *(com.)* complaint, claim.

reclamante, *n.m., a.* claimant.

reclamar, *v.t.* to claim, reclaim, demand; to decoy (birds); *(naut.)* to hoist a sail. — *v.i.* to oppose, contradict.

reclame, *n.m.* sheave hole in a topmast head.

reclamo, *n.m.* reclamation; decoy-bird; lure; allurement, enticement; call; *(print.)* catchword; *(naut.)* tie-block.

recle, *n.m.* *(eccles.)* vacation from choir duties.

reclinación, *n.f.* reclining.

reclinar, *v.t., v.r.* to lean back, recline.

reclinatorio, *n.m.* couch, thing to lean upon; praying-desk, prie-Dieu.

recluir, *v.t.* (conjugated like INCLUIR) to shut up, seclude.

reclusión, *n.f.* reclusion, closeness; recess, seclusion; *reclusión perpetua,* life imprisonment.

recluso, -sa, *n.m.f., a.* recluse.

reclusorio, *n.m.* recess, place of retirement.

recluta, *n.f.* recruiting, supply; *(Arg.)* gathering of cattle. — *n.m.* recruit.

reclutador, *n.m.* recruiting-officer.

reclutamiento, *n.m.* recruiting.

reclutar, *v.t.* to recruit; *(Arg.)* to gather cattle.

recobrar, *v.t.* to recover. — *v.r.* to recuperate, regain strength, recover from an illness; *recobrar tiempo perdido,* to make up for lost time.

recobro, *n.m.* recovery.

recocer, *v.t.* (conjugated like COCER) to boil again, boil too much; to reburn; to reheat; to anneal. — *v.r.* to be consumed with rage.

recocido, -da, *a.* over-boiled; skilful, clever; over-ripe, dried-up. — *n.m.f.* annealing; reheating; overcooking. — *p.p.* [RECOCER].

recocina, *n.f.* pantry.

recocho, -cha, *a.* over-boiled, over-done.

recodadero, *n.m.* elbow-chair.

recodar, *v.i., v.r.* to lean upon with the elbow; to wind, turn (of roads).

recodo, *n.m.* corner, jutting angle; turn; elbow; winding, bend.

recogeabuelos, *n.m.* comb to hold the straggly ends of hair at the nape.

recogedero, *n.m.* store-room; instrument for picking up articles, dust-pan.

recogedor, *n.m.* gatherer, gleaner; shelterer.

recoger, *v.t.* (*pres. indic.* **recojo**; *pres. subj.* **recoja**) to retake; gather, hoard, collect, pick, take in, receive; to suspend, retire, withdraw; to shrink, shorten; contract, pucker, tuck; to glean, cull; to reform, retrench; to shelter, protect; to lock up. — *v.r.* to take shelter; to retire; to collect oneself; to reform; to abstract oneself from worldly thoughts and cares; to go home.

recogida, *n.f.* withdrawal, retirement; harvesting; woman inmate of house of correction; (*com.*) withdrawal.

recogidamente, *adv.* in retirement, devoutly.

recogido, -da, *a.* retired, secluded; contracted.

recogimiento, *n.m.* collection, assemblage; retreat; house of correction for women.

recolección, *n.f.* collection, compilation; abridgement, summary; crop, gathering, harvest; recollection or collection of money or taxes; retirement, abstraction.

recolectar, *v.t.* to gather in, harvest, collect, hoard.

recoleto, -ta, *n.m.f., a.* (*eccles.*) belonging to an order of strict life.

recomendable, *a.* commendable, laudable.

recomendablemente, *adv.* laudably.

recomendación, *n.f.* recommendation; request; praise, eulogy; authority, merit; *carta de recomendación,* letter of introduction; *recomendación del alma,* prayers for the dying.

recomendar, *v.t.* (*pres. indic.* **recomiendo**; *pres. subj.* **recomiende**) commend, recommend; to entrust; to ask, request.

recomendatorio, -ria, *a.* recommendatory.

recompensa, *n.f.* compensation, remuneration, recompense, reward; *en recompensa,* in return.

recompensable, *a.* deserving reward.

recompensación, *n.f.* recompense, reward.

recompensar, *v.t.* to recompense, reward, gratify.

recomponer, *v.t.* (conjugated like COMPONER) to recompose, readjust; to mend, repair.

recompuesto, -ta, *a., p.p. irreg.* [RECOMPONER].

reconcentración, *n.f.; reconcentramiento,* *n.m.* act of concentrating; concentration.

reconcentrar, *v.t.* to introduce; to concentre, concentrate; to dissemble. — *v.r.* to concentrate one's mind.

reconciliable, *a.* reconcilable.

reconciliación, *n.f.* reconciliation, reconcilement.

reconciliador, -ra, *n.m.f.* reconciler.

reconciliar, *v.t.* to reconcile, accommodate; (*eccles.*) to hear a short additional confession; to reconsecrate. — *v.r.* to confess one's sins; to be reconciled.

reconcomerse, *v.r.* to scratch one's back often.

reconcomio, *n.m.* itching; craving, eager desire; fear, apprehension, suspicion, misgiving.

reconditez, *n.f.* (*coll.*) reconditeness.

recóndito, -ta, *a.* recondite, secret, hidden, concealed, abstruse.

reconducción, *n.f.* renewal of a lease.

reconducir, *v.t.* (conjugated like CONDUCIR) to renew a lease or contract.

reconocedor, -ra, *n.m.f.* examiner.

reconocer, *v.t.* (conjugated like CONOCER) to recognize; to acknowledge; to comprehend, conceive; to ascertain, scrutinize, examine closely; to consider; to confess, own; (*mil.*) to reconnoitre; to scout; (*polit.*) to recognize a government, etc. — *v.r.* to repent, confess one's guilt; to judge oneself justly.

reconocidamente, *adv.* gratefully, confessedly.

reconocido, -da, *n.m.f., a.* grateful, obliged; acknowledged, confessed. — *p.p.* [RECONOCER].

reconociente, *a.* recognizing.

reconocimiento, *n.m.* recognition; recognizance; gratitude, acknowledgement; confession, owning; submission, subjection; examination, inquiry, inspection, survey; (*mil.*) reconnoitring; (*surv.*) reconnaissance.

reconquista, *n.f.* reconquest.

reconquistar, *v.t.* to reconquer.

reconstitución, *n.f.* reconstitution.

reconstituir, *v.t.* (conjugated like CONSTITUIR) to reconstitute.

reconstituyente, *a.* (*med.*) corroborant, tonic.

reconstrucción, *n.f.* reconstruction.

reconstruir, *v.t.* to reconstruct, rebuild.

recontamiento, *n.m.* narration.

recontar, *v.t.* (conjugated like CONTAR) to recount, relate.

recontento, -ta, *a.* very pleased, greatly delighted. — *n.m.* deep satisfaction.

reconvalecer, *v.i.* (conjugated like OBEDECER) to recover from sickness.

reconvención, *n.f.* charge, accusation, expostulation, reproach, recrimination.

reconvenir, *v.t.* (conjugated like VENIR) to reproach; to reprimand; (*law*) to countercharge.

recopilación, *n.f.* compendium, summary, abridgement; compilation, collection of extracts from books; (*law*) digest.

recopilador, *n.m.* compiler, collector, abridger.

recopilar, *v.t.* to collect, abridge, compile.

recoquín, *n.m.* short chubby fellow.

record, *n.m.* record (in sports).

recordable, *a.* worthy of record.

recordación, *n.f.* remembrance, recollection.

recordador, -ra, *n.m.f.* recorder.

recordante, *a.* recording, reminding.

recordar, *v.t.* (*pres. indic.* **recuerdo**; *pres. subj.* **recuerde**) to remind. — *v.i.* to awaken. — *v.r.* to hit upon, remember.

recordativo, -va, *a.* reminding.
recordativo, *n.m.* reminder, remembrancer.
recorrer, *v.t.* to run over, examine, survey; (*mech.*) to travel, pass over; to traverse; to read over, peruse; to repair, mend, overhaul, refit; (*print.*) to run over, readjust. — *v.i.* to recur, have recourse to.
recorrido, *n.m.* run, sweep; (*mech.*) distance travelled; (*motor.*) mileage; refit.
recortado, -da, *a., p.p.* (*bot.*) incised. — *n.m.* figure cut out.
recortador, -ra, *n.m.f.* cutter-out.
recortadura, *n.f.* clipping.—*pl.* **recortaduras,** cuttings.
recortar, *v.t.* to cut away, shorten, pare off, trim, clip; to cut out; (*art*) to delineate, outline.
recorte, *n.m.* outline, profile, cutting, clipping. — *pl.* **recortes,** parings, clippings; remnants.
recorvar, *v.t.* to bend, arch, curve.
recoser, *v.t.* to sew again; to mend linen.
recosido, *n.m.* mending.
recostadero, *n.m.* resting-place.
recostar, *v.t.* to recline, lean against. — *v.r.* to go to rest, repose, recline; to lean back or against.
recova, *n.f.* dealing in eggs, poultry, etc., for resale; poultry market; (*prov.*) shed; pack of hounds.
recoveco, *n.m.* turning, winding; (*fig.*) artifice, simulation.
recovero, *n.m.* huckster; poultry-dealer.
recre, *n.m.* (*eccles.*) choristers' vacation.
recreación, *n.f.* recreation, amusement, diversion, relief.
recrear, *v.t.* to delight, amuse, recreate, gladden. — *v.r.* to amuse or divert oneself.
recreativo, -va, *a.* recreative, diverting, amusing.
recrecer, *v.t.* (conjugated like CRECER) to augment, increase. — *v.i.* to grow again, be overgrown; to happen, occur. — *v.r.* to recover one's spirits.
recrecimiento, *n.m.* increase, growth.
recreído, -da, *a.* intractable, having recovered its native wildness (of a hawk).
recrementicio, -cia, *a.* recrementitious.
recremento, *n.m.* (*physiol.*) recrement.
recreo, *n.m.* recreation, amusement; place of amusement.
recría, *n.f.* repasturing (colts, etc.).
recriar, *v.t.* to improve herds with new pastures; to reanimate, give new strength; to redeem (mankind) by the atonement of Christ.
recriminación, *n.f.* recrimination, mutual accusation.
recriminar, *v.t.* to recriminate.
recrudecer, *v.t., v.r.* (conjugated like CRECER) to recrudesce, recur.
recrudecimiento, *n.m.* recrudescence.
recrujir, *v.i.* to squeak.
rectamente, *adv.* rightly, honestly, justly.
rectangular, *a.* rectangular.
rectángulo, -la, *a.* rectangular, rectangled.
rectángulo, *n.m.* rectangle.
rectificable, *a.* rectifiable.
rectificación, *n.f.* rectification.
rectificador, *n.m., a.* rectifier.
rectificar, *v.t.* (*pret.* **rectifiqué;** *pres. subj.* **rectifique**) to rectify, correct, amend, make right.

rectificativo, -va, *a.* that which rectifies.
rectilíneo, -nea, *a.* rectilinear, rectilineal.
rectitud, *n.f.* rectitude, uprightness, rightness, straightness; accuracy, exactitude.
recto, -ta, *a.* straight; erect; right, just, upright, fair, honest; literal; (*trig.*) right (cylinder, section, sine, angle, etc.).
recto, *n.m.* (*zool.*) rectum; (*geom.*) right angle.
rector, -ra, *n.m.f.* principal, superior, rector, ruler, governor; (*eccles.*) rector (of a parish).
rectorado, *n.m.* rectorship.
rectoral, *n.f.* rectory, rector's house. — *a.* rectorial.
rectorar, *v.i.* to attain the office of rector.
rectoría, *n.f.* rectory; rectorship.
recua, *n.f.* drove, herd; multitude.
recuadro, *n.m.* (*arch.*) square compartment.
recuaje, *n.m.* tribute, duty for the passing of cattle.
recuarta, *n.f.* an additional fourth string for the *vihuela.*
recudimento, recudimiento, *n.m.* power to collect rents, rates or taxes.
recudir, *v.t.* to pay money, dues, etc. — *v.i.* to rebound, set out again, revert.
recuelo, *n.m.* strong lye for steeping very dirty clothes; reboiled coffee sold cheaply.
recuento, *n.m.* inventory; muster; recension.
recuerdo, *n.m.* remembrance, hint, memory, recognition; keepsake, memento; memorandum. — *pl.* **recuerdos,** compliments, regards.
recuerdo; recuerde, *pres. indic.; pres. subj.* [RECORDAR].
recuero, *n.m.* muleteer, mule-driver.
recuesta, *n.f.* request, intimation; (*obs.*) duel; *a toda recuesta,* at all events.
recuestar, *v.t.* to demand, ask, request.
recuesto, *n.m.* declivity, gradual descent.
recuesto; recueste, *pres. indic.; pres. subj.* [RECOSTAR].
recuezo; recueza, *pres. indic.; pres. subj.* [RECOCER].
reculada, *n.f.* (*naut.*) falling astern; falling back, retrograding, recoil, recoiling.
recular, *v.i.* to fall back, retrograde, recoil; (*naut.*) to fall astern; (*coll.*) to give up, yield, turn back.
reculo, -la, *a.* tailless (of poultry).
reculones, (a), *adv.* (*coll.*) in a retrograde fashion; going backwards.
recuñar, *v.t.* (*min.*) to wedge, break with wedges.
recuperable, *a.* recoverable.
recuperación, *n.f.* recovery, recuperative, act of recovering.
recuperador, -ra, *n.m.f., a.* rescuer, redeemer.
recuperar, *v.t.* to recover, regain, retrieve, recuperate. — *v.r.* to recover from sickness, gather strength.
recuperativo, -va, *a.* that which recovers.
recura, *n.f.* comb-saw.
recurar, *v.t.* to make or open the teeth (of combs).
recurrente, *a.* recurrent.
recurrir, *v.i.* to apply to, resort to, revert.
recurso, *n.m.* recourse, resource, reversion, return; petition, memorial; (*law*) appeal. — *pl.* **recursos,** means; *sin recurso,* definitively, without possibility of appeal.
recusable, *a.* refusable, exceptionable.

recusación, *n.f.* (*law*) challenge, recusation.

recusante, *a.* refusing, recusant.

recusar, *v.t.* to decline; (*law*) to challenge.

rechazador, -ra, *n.m.f.* repeller, contradictor; buffer.

rechazamiento, *n.m.* repulsion.

rechazar, *v.t.* (*pret.* **rechacé;** *pres. subj.* **rechace**) to repel, repulse, drive back, reject; to contradict, impugn.

rechazo, *n.m.* rebound, rebuff, recoil, rejection.

rechifla, *n.f.* whistle, whistling (in derision); ridicule, mockery.

rechiflar, *v.t.* to whistle, ridicule, mock, make cat-calls.

rechinador, -ra, *a.;* **rechinamiento,** *n.m.;* **rechinante,** *a.* creaking, squeaking, grating.

rechinar, *v.i.* to creak, squeak, grate; to gnash the teeth; to do something reluctantly.

rechoncho, -cha, *a.* (*coll.*) chubby.

rechupete, (de), *a.* (*coll.*) exquisite.

red, *n.f.* net, net-work, netting; luggage-rack; railing, grating; fraud, snare; railway system, telephone, telegraph, etc.; *red de araña,* cobweb; *caer en la red,* to fall into the trap; *echar* (or *tender*) *la red,* to cast or set the net; (*fig.*) to prepare a snare, trap, etc.

redacción, *n.f.* editing, wording; editorial staff; editorial office.

redactar, *v.t.* to compile, compose, write, edit, draw up.

redactor, -ra, *n.m.f.* compiler; editor; reporter, journalist.

redada, *n.f.* casting of a net; netful, haul, catch.

redar, *v.t.* to cast a net.

redargución, *n.f.* retort, refutation.

redargüir, *v.t.* (conjugated like ARGÜIR) to reargue, retort; (*law*) to impugn.

redaya, *n.f.* net for fishing in rivers.

redecilla, *n.f.* small net, bag-net; mesh; hair net; (*anat.*) reticulum, the second stomach of ruminants.

rededor, *n.m.* surroundings, environs; *al rededor,* round about.

redel, *n.m.* (*naut.*) loof-frame.

redención, *n.f.* redemption, recovery; salvation, ransom.

redentor, -ra, *n.m.f.* redeemer.

redero, -ra, *a.* reticular, retiform, reticulated.

redero, *n.m.* net-maker; one who catches with nets.

redescuento, *n.m.* (*com.*) rediscount.

redhibición, *n.f.* (*law*) redhibition.

redhibir, *v.t.* to use the right of redhibition.

redhibitorio, -ria, *a.* redhibitory.

redición, *n.f.* reiteration, repetition.

redicho, -cha, *a.* speaking with affectation.

rediezmar, *v.t.* to tithe a second time.

rediezmo, *n.m.* extra tithe.

redil, *n.m.* sheepfold.

redimible, *a.* redeemable.

redimir, *v.t.* to redeem, ransom, rescue; to relieve, liberate, set free; (*com.*) to pay off.

redingote, *n.m.* redingote, great-coat.

rédito, *n.m.* (*com.*) rent, interest, revenue, proceeds, profit, yield.

redituable, reditual, *a.* rent-producing.

redituar, *v.t.* to yield, produce.

redivivo, -va, *a.* redivivous, revived, restored.

redoblado, -da, *a.* redoubled; double-lined; (*mil.*) double (step); stocky, heavy-built.

redobladura, *n.f.;* **redoblamiento,** *n.m.* redoubling, reduplication.

redoblante, *n.m.,* *a.* drum, drumming, drummer.

redoblar, *v.t.* to redouble; to rivet, clinch; to repeat often. — *v.i.* to roll a drum.

redoble, *n.m.* (*mil., mus.*) redoubling; roll of a drum.

redoblegar, *v.t.* (conjugated like DOBLEGAR) to redouble.

redoblón, *n.m.* rivet, clinch-nail.

redolente, *a.* smarting, aching.

redolino, *n.m.* wheel for drawing lots.

redolor, *n.m.* dull ache or pain left after an illness or injury.

redoma, *n.f.* phial, flask; (*chem.*) balloon.

redomado, -da, *a.* sly, artful, crafty, cunning.

redomazo, *n.m.* blow with a phial.

redomón, -na, *a.* (*Am.*) half broken-in horse or mule.

redonda, *n.f.* district, neighbourhood; (*naut.*) square sail; pasture-ground; (*mus.*) semibreve; *a la redonda,* roundabout.

redondamente, *adv.* roundly; clearly, plainly, decidedly.

redondeador, *n.m.* rounding-tool.

redondear, *v.t.* to round, make round; to settle, perfect. — *v.r.* (*coll.*) to clear debts and charges; to acquire estate or possessions.

redondel, *n.m.* circle; bull-ring; circular mat; round cloak; (*mech.*) flange.

redondete, *a.* circular, roundish.

redondez, *n.f.* roundness, rotundity; *redondez de la tierra,* face of the earth.

redondilla, *n.f.* stanza of four octosyllables, rhyming *abba*.

redondo, -da, *a.* round, circular, spherical, rotund, cylindrical; decided, determined; (*print.*) Roman; in good circumstances; turned to pasture; *en redondo,* all around; *negocio redondo,* profitable deal. — *n.m.* species, hard cash; anything in the form of globe, orb, disk, etc.

redondón, *n.m.* large sphere or circle.

redopelo, redropelo, *n.m.* against the grain; scuffle, fray; *al redopelo,* against the grain, against reason; *traer al redopelo,* to drag about.

redor, *n.m.* round mat; *en redor* (*poet.*) round about.

redro, *adv.* (*coll.*) backward, behind; yearly ring formed upon the horns of animals of the genus *Ovis* and *Capra.*

redrojo, redruejo, redrojuelo, *n.m.* aftervintage grapes, after-fruit; (*coll.*) small, weak child.

reducción, *n.f.* reduction, decrease, diminution, contraction; alteration; shrinkage, condensation; retrenchment; exchange; conquest; (*com.*) rebate; (*Am.*) settlement of Indians converted to Christianity.

reducible, *a.* reducible.

reducidamente, *adv.* sparingly, narrowly.

reducido, -da, *a.* reduced, diminished; close, narrow.

reducimiento, *n.m.* reduction.

reducir, *v.t.* (*pres. indic.* **reduzco;** *pret.* **reduje;** *pres. subj.* **reduzca**) to reduce; to decrease, diminish, retrench, lessen, shorten; to cause to shrink, contract; to resolve; to abridge, condense; to turn into a liquid; to barter, exchange, convert; to divide into small parts; to contain, comprehend, confine, include; to persuade, reclaim, bring into submission. — *v.r.* to take to an ordered life.

reducto, *n.m.* redoubt.

reductor, -ra, *a.* reducing. — *n.m.* (*eng.*) reducer.

redundancia, *n.f.* superfluity, excess, redundancy; overflowing.

redundante, *a.* redundant, superfluous.

redundantemente, *adv.* redundantly.

redundar, *v.i.* to redound, be redundant; to overflow.

reduplicación, *n.f.* reduplication.

reduplicado, -da, *a.* reduplicated.

reduplicar, *v.t.* (conjugated like DUPLICAR) to redouble, reduplicate; to reiterate.

reedificable, *a.* capable of rebuilding.

reedificación, *n.f.* rebuilding.

reedificador, -ra, *n.m.f.* rebuilder.

reedificar, *v.t.* (conjugated like EDIFICAR) to rebuild.

reeditar, *v.t.* to reprint.

reelección, *n.f.* re-election.

reelecto, -ta, *p.p. irreg.* [REELEGIR].

reelegible, *a.* re-eligible.

reelegir, *v.t.* (*p.p.* **reelegido, reelecto;** *pres. part.* **reeligiendo;** *pres. indic.* **reelijo;** *pret.* **él reeligió;** *pres. subj.* **reelija**) to re-elect.

reembarcar, *v.t.*, *v.r.* (conjugated like EMBARCAR) to re-embark, re-ship.

reembarco, reembarque, *n.m.* re-embarkation, reshipment.

reembargar, *v.t.* (conjugated like EMBARGAR) to seize or embargo a second time.

reembolsar, *v.t.* to reimburse, repay, refund. — *v.r.* to recover money lent.

reembolso, *n.m.* reimbursement, refunding.

reempacar, *v.t.* (conjugated like EMPACAR) to re-pack.

reemplazar, *v.t.* to replace, substitute, supersede.

reemplazo, *n.m.* replacement, substitution; call-up of yearly draft; *de reemplazo,* officer on active service but without command.

reemprender, *v.t.* to undertake again.

reencarnación, *n.f.* reincarnation.

reencarnar, *v.i.*, *v.r.* to be reincarnated.

reencuentro, *n.m.* skirmish, collision.

reenganchar, *v.t.*, *v.r.* to re-enlist; (*mech.*) to recouple.

reenganchamiento, reenganche, *n.m.* re-enlisting; premium given at re-enlistment.

reengendrador, *n.m.* regenerator.

reengendrar, *v.t.* to reproduce, regenerate; to renew, revive.

reensayar, *v.t.* to re-examine; to rehearse anew.

reensaye, *n.m.* re-assay.

reensayo, *n.m.* (*theat.*) second rehearsal.

reenvasar, *v.t.* (*com.*) to refill, repack.

reenviar, *v.t.* to forward.

reexaminación, *n.f.* re-examination.

reexaminar, *v.t.* to re-examine.

reexpedición, *n.f.* forwarding.

reexpedir, *v.t.* to forward.

reexportación, *n.f.* re-exportation.

reexportar, *v.t.* to re-export.

refacción, *n.f.* refection, repast; retribution, reparation; allowance; boot allowance; (*Cub.*) financing a sugar or tobacco plantation.

refaccionar, *v.t.* (*Cub.*) to finance a sugar or tobacco plantation.

refaccionista, *n.m.* (*Cub.*) financial backer.

refajo, *n.m.* flannel underskirt.

refalsado, -da, *a.* false, deceitful.

refección, *n.f.* refection, light meal; repairs.

refectorio, *n.m.* refectory (in convents).

referencia, *n.f.* reference; relation; narrative, testimonial.

referendario, *n.m.* countersigner.

referendum, *n.m.* referendum.

referente, *a.* referring, relating.

referible, *a.* that may be referred.

referir, *v.t.* (*pres. part.* **refiriendo;** *pres. indic.* **refiero;** *pret.* **él refirió;** *pres. subj.* **refiera**) to refer, relate, report, direct, submit. — *v.r.* to refer, allude, relate, have relation.

refertero, -ra, *a.* quarrelsome, wrangling.

refigurar, *v.t.* to refigure.

refilón, (de), *adv.* askance, obliquely.

refinación, *n.f.* refinement, refining.

refinadera, *n.f.* stone roller for refining chocolate.

refinado, -da, *a.* refined, polished; artful, subtle; fine, nice.

refinador, *n.m.* refiner.

refinadura, *n.f.* refining, refinement.

refinamiento, *n.m.* refining, refinement; exactness, niceness, nicety.

refinar, *v.t.* to refine, polish, purify; to make refined, polite, polished; to make perfect.

refinería, *n.f.* refinery, distillery.

refino, -na, *a.* refined, fine.

refino, *n.m.* refining; high-class grocery.

refirmar, *v.t.* to strengthen; to ratify, confirm.

refitolero, -ra, *n.m.f.* refectioner; (*coll.*) meddler, busybody; (*Cub.*) snob, officious person.

reflectante, *a.* reflecting.

reflectar, *v.i.* to reflect.

reflector, -ra, *a.* reflecting, reflective. — *n.m.* reflector, searchlight; (*motor.*) head-lights.

refleja, *n.f.* reflection, observation, remark.

reflejar, *v.i.* (*opt.*) to reflect. — *v.t.* to think, ponder, consider, reflect. — *v.r.* to be reflected.

reflejo, -ja, *a.* reflected, reflex; (*gram.*) reflexive; meditative.

reflejo, *n.m.* reflex, light reflected.

reflexible, *a.* reflectible.

reflexión, *n.f.* reflection; meditation, consideration, thought.

reflexionar, *v.i.* to think, consider, meditate.

reflexivamente, *adv.* reflectively, reflexively.

reflexivo, -va, *a.* reflexive, reflective; cogitative, considerate.

reflorecer, *v.i.* (conjugated like FLORECER) to reflourish, blossom again; to become fine or flourishing once more.

refluente, *a.* refluent; flowing back.

refluir, *v.i.* (conjugated like FLUIR) to re-flow, flow back; to redound.

reflujo, *n.m.* reflux; ebb, ebb-tide.

refocilación, *n.f.* reinvigoration; recreation.

refocilar, *v.t.* to strengthen, revive, reinvigorate; to brace up. — *v.r.* to be reinvigorated, strengthened.

refocilo, *n.m.* reinvigoration; healthy pleasure.

reforma, *n.f.* reform, reformation; alteration, amendment, correction, improvement; (*eccles.*) Reformation.

reformable, *a.* reformable.
reformación, *n.f.* reformation, reform.
reformado, -da, *a.* reformed.
reformador, -ra, *n.m.f.,* *a.* reformer, corrector, mender.
reformar, *v.t.* to reform, amend, correct, mend, alter, change, improve; to reduce, lessen, diminish; to re-form, reorganize, reconstruct, reconstitute. — *v.r.* to reform; to mend.
reformatorio, -ria, *a.* corrective. — *n.m.* reformatory.
reformista, *n.m.f.* reformer, reformist.
reforzada, *n.f.* narrow tape.
reforzado, -da, *a.* strengthened, reinforced. — *p.p.* [REFORZAR].
reforzar, *v.t.* (conjugated like FORZAR) to strengthen, reinforce, fortify; to encourage, animate, cheer.
refracción, *n.f.* refraction.
refractar, *v.t.* to refract. — *v.r.* to be refracted.
refractario, -ria, *a.* refractory; obstinate, rebellious, disobedient.
refracto, -ta, *a.* (*opt.*) refracted.
refrán, *n.m.* proverb, adage, saying.
refranero, *n.m.* collection of proverbs.
refregadura, *n.f.* rubbing, friction.
refregamiento, *n.m.* friction, rubbing.
refregar, *v.t.* (conjugated like FREGAR) to rub, fray; (*coll.*) to reprove, scold.
refregón, *n.m.* rubbing, chafing, fraying, friction; abrasion, attrition.
refreír, *v.t.* to fry thoroughly.
refrenable, *a.* capable of being restrained.
refrenamiento, *n.m.* refrainment, restraint, curb, check.
refrenar, *v.t.* to refrain, restrain (a horse); to curb, check.
refrendación, *n.f.* legalization, authentication.
refrendar, *v.t.* to legalize, authenticate, countersign.
refrendario, *n.m.* counter-signer.
refrendata, *n.f.* counter-signature.
refrendo, *n.m.* legalization, authentication.
refrescador, -ra, *a.* refreshing, refrigerating.
refrescadura, *n.f.* refreshing.
refrescamiento, *n.m.* refreshment.
refrescante, *a.* cooling, refreshing.
refrescar, *v.t.* (*pret.* **refresqué**; *pres. subj.* **refresque**) to refresh, freshen, cool; to take up again, renew. — *v.i.* to get cool (of weather); to take the air. — *v.r.* to cool off; *refrescar los víveres,* to take in fresh provisions.
refresco, *n.m.* refreshment; cooling drink, ices, etc.; light luncheon; *de refresco,* again, once more.
refriega, *n.f.* skirmish, fray, affray, encounter, strife, scuffle.
refrigeración, *n.f.* cooling, refrigeration.
refrigerador, -ra, *a.* refrigeration, freezing, cooling.
refrigerador, *n.m.* refrigerator, freezer, cooler; ice box.
refrigerante, *a.* refrigerant, refrigerative. — *n.m.* refrigerator, cooling-chamber; (*med.*) cooler.
refrigerar, *v.t.* to cool, refrigerate.
refrigerativo, -va, *a.* refrigerative, refrigerant.
refrigerio, *n.m.* refrigeration, coolness; refreshment, refection; comfort, consolation.

refringente, *a.* refracting, refractive.
refringir, *v.t.,* *v.r.* to refract.
refrito, -ta, *p.p. irreg.* [REFREÍR].
refuerzo, *n.m.* reinforcement; backing, bracing; welt of a shoe; succour, aid.
refugiar, *v.t.* to shelter. — *v.r.* to take refuge.
refugio, *n.m.* refuge, shelter, retreat, asylum, harbourage.
refulgencia, *n.f.* refulgence, splendour.
refulgente, *a.* refulgent.
refulgir, *v.i.* to shine, to emit or reflect rays of light.
refundición, *n.f.* (*metal.*) recasting; (*fig.*) recasting, reworking.
refundir, *v.t.* (*metal.*) to recast, remelt; reconstruct, re-arrange, adapt. — *v.i.* to redound.
refunfuñador, -ra, *n.m.f.* grumbler, growler.
refunfuñadura, *n.f.* grumbling, growling.
refunfuñar, *v.i.* to snort, mutter, grumble, snarl, growl.
refunfuño, *n.m.* grumbling, growling, snort, snarl.
refutación, *n.f.* refutation.
refutable, *a.* refutable.
refutador, -ra, *n.m.f.* refuter.
refutar, *v.t.* to refute, confute.
refutatorio, -ria, *a.* refutatory.
regadera, *n.f.* watering-pot, sprinkler; irrigation-trench, canal.
regadero, *n.m.* ditch for irrigation.
regadío, -día, *a.* irrigated.
regadío, *n.m.* irrigated land.
regadizo, -za, *a.* irrigable, that can be watered.
regador, -ra, *n.m.f.,* *a.* one who irrigates or waters; comb maker's gauge.
regadura, *n.f.* irrigation.
regaifa, *n.f.* large cake, Easter cake; grooved stone of an oil-mill.
regajal, regajo, *n.m.* puddle, pool, rill.
regala, *n.f.* (*naut.*) gunwale, gunnel.
regalada, *n.f.* king's stables; king's horses.
regaladamente, *adv.* delicately, daintily, pleasantly.
regalado, -da, *a.* delicate, dainty, sweet, suave. — *p.p.* [REGALAR].
regalador, -ra, *n.m.f.* generous person, liberal entertainer; stick for cleaning wine-skins.
regalamiento, *n.m.* regalement.
regalar, *v.t.* to give, present, favour, make a gift or present; treat, regale, entertain, refresh; to fondle, caress, cajole, cherish, make much of; to gratify, cheer, delight; *el que regala, bien vende, si el que recibe bien entiende,* a favour given is a favour received. — *v.r.* to feast, regale; to fare sumptuously.
regalejo, *n.m.* small gift.
regalero, *n.m.* royal purveyor of fruit and flowers.
regalia, *n.f.* regalia, royal rights; exemption, privilege; (*Cub.*) cigar of superior quality. — *pl.* **regalías,** perquisites.
regaliolo, *n.m.* small present; muff.
regaliolo, *n.m.* wren.
regalismo, *n.m.* regalism.
regalista, *n.m.,* *a.* regalist.
regalito, *n.m.* small present.
regaliz, *n.m.;* **regaliza,** *n.f.* liquorice.
regalo, *n.m.* present, gift, keepsake, largesse; gratification, pleasure; regalement; convenience, comfort; luxury.
regalón, -na, *a.* (*coll.*) delicate, ease-loving; pampered, spoiled.

regamiento, *n.m.* irrigation.

reganar, *v.t.* to regain.

regante, *n.m., a.* (*p.a.* of REGAR) irrigant.

regañada, *n.f.* (*prov.*) kind of sweet cake.

regañadientes, (a), *adv.* reluctantly, grumblingly.

regañado, -da, *a.* frowning (said of a kind of plums and bread). — *p.p.* [REGAÑAR].

regañador, -ra, *n.m.f.* grumbler, growler, snarler.

regañamiento, *n.m.* grumbling, growling, snarl.

regañar, *v.i.* to grumble, murmur, growl, snarl; to fall out, quarrel, be peevish, quarrelsome; to crack, split open; to yelp, howl; to have domestic quarrels. — *v.t.* to chide, scold, reprehend.

regañir, *v.i.* to yelp, howl.

regaño, *n.m.* stern or sour aspect; gesture of annoyance; reprimand; (*fig.*) scorched bread.

regañón, -na, *n.m.f., a.* snarling, growling; snarler, murmurer, grumbler; north-west wind.

regar, *v.t.* (*pres. indic.* **riego**; *pret.* **regué**; *pres. subj.* **riegue**) to water, wash, irrigate; to sprinkle with water, to rain heavily; to moisten the larvæ cocoons (of bees).

regata, *n.f.* small channel of water for irrigation; (*naut.*) regatta.

regate, *n.m.* quick movement to avoid a blow; evasion, escape.

regatear, *v.t., v.i.* to wriggle, escape, move sideways; (*naut.*) to compete in a regatta, to rival in sailing; to refuse the execution of something; to haggle, drive a bargain after long discussion; to retail provisions.

regateo, *n.m.* haggling, bartering.

regatería, *n.f.* huckster's shop.

regatero, -ra, *n.m.f., a.* hawker, haggler.

regato, *n.m.* small rivulet.

regatón, -na, *n.m.f.* huckster; haggler; socket, ferrule. — *a.* retailing.

regatonear, *v.i.* to huckster, buy wholesale and sell at retail.

regatonería, *n.f.* huckster's shop; retail sale.

regazar, *v.t.* (*pret.* **regacé**; *pres. subj.* **regace**) to tuck up.

regazo, *n.m.* lap; (*fig.*) affectionate reception.

regencia, *n.f.* regency, ruling, governing, regentship.

regeneración, *n.f.* regeneration.

regenerador, -ra, *n.m.f.* regenerator. — *a.* regenerating.

regenerar, *v.t.* to regenerate, reproduce.

regenerativo, -va, *a.* which regenerates.

regenta, *n.f.* regent's wife; woman professor.

regentar, *v.t.* to govern, rule; to exercise lordship or superiority.

regente, *n.m.* regent; director, manager; schoolmaster in holy orders; president of a court of justice; professor in Spanish universities; (*print.*) foreman. — *a.* ruling.

regentear, *v.i.* to domineer, rule; to be a pedant.

regiamente, *adv.* royally, in a kingly manner.

regicida, *n.m.* murderer of a king, regicide.

regicidio, *n.m.* murder of a king, regicide.

regidor, *n.m.* magistrate, alderman, director, governor, prefect.

regidora, *n.m.f.* alderman's wife, governor's wife.

regidoría, regiduría, *n.f.* governorship.

régimen, *n.m.* regimen; management, system, conduct, regime, rule; (*gram.*) government of parts of speech; (*med.*) regimen, treatment.

regimentar, *v.t.* to organize into a regiment several battalions or companies.

regimiento, *n.m.* administration, government; council-board; (*mil.*) regiment; (*naut.*) pilot's sailing book.

regio, -gia, *a.* royal, regal, kingly; sumptuous, magnificent, stately.

región, *n.f.* region; tract of ground, space.

regional, *a.* regional, of a region or district.

regionalismo, *n.m.* belief in regional autonomy; attachment to a region, regionalism.

regionalista, *a.* relating to regional autonomy; attached to a particular region; regionalist.

regir, *v.t.* (*pres. part.* **rigiendo**; *pres. indic.* **rijo**; *pret.* **él rigió**; *pres. subj.* **rija**) to rule, govern, direct; to manage, conduct, command, lead. — *v.i.* (*naut.*) to obey the helm; to be in force.

registrador, *n.m.* register, registrar, recorder; searcher; controller; toll-gatherer.

registrar, *v.t.* to survey, inspect, search, examine, investigate; to register, record; to place a mark in a book; (*min.*) to prospect. — *v.r.* to be registered or matriculated; *no registrar,* (*prov.*) to do something carelessly.

registro, *n.m.* searching, examining; register; entry of goods, certificate of entry; census; enrolling office; register of a stove, etc.; regulator (of a clock or watch); (*print.*) correspondence of pages; prier, over-curious person; marker of a book; stop of an organ; air hole; *tocar* (or *echar*) *todos los registros,* to do one's utmost.

regitivo, -va, *a.* ruling, governing.

regla, *n.f.* rule, ruler; statute, law, maxim, precept; canon, fundamental principle; measure, moderation; order; catamenia; *a regla,* prudently, regularly; *en regla,* duly; *salir de regla,* to exceed the bounds of what is right (or proper).

regladamente, *adv.* regularly, in an orderly way.

reglado, -da, *a.* regulated, temperate.

reglamentación, *n.f.* regulation.

reglamentar, *v.t.* to regulate.

reglamentario, -ria, *a.* relating to regulations.

reglamento, *n.m.* regulation, ordinance, order, by-law.

reglar, *v.t.* to rule, draw lines with a ruler; to regulate, measure. — *v.r.* to reform, amend. — *a.* regular.

reglero, *n.m.* ruler for drawing lines.

regleta, *n.f.* (*print.*) reglet; lead.

regletear, *v.t.* (*print.*) to lead.

reglón, *n.m.* mason's level.

regnícola, *n.f.* native of a kingdom; writer on topics of his own country.

regocijadamente, *adv.* merrily, joyfully.

regocijado, -da, *a.* joyful, merry, festive, rejoicing.

regocijador, -ra, *n.m.f.* rejoicer, cheerer, gladdener.

regocijar, *v.t.* to gladden, cheer, rejoice, delight, exult, exhilarate.

regocijo, *n.m.* pleasure, joy, hilarity, mirth, merriment; rejoicing, satisfaction, exhilaration.

regodearse, *v.r.* (*coll.*) to rejoice, be merry,

be delighted; to trifle, dally, play the fool,
jest, joke; to cloak a desire, assume a reluctant air.

regodeo, *n.m.* joy, merriment, mirth; jest,
joke, diversion, dalliance.

regojo, *n.m.* crumb of bread; puny boy.

regojuelo, *n.m.* very small crumb of bread.

regoldano, -na, *a.* said of the wild chestnut.

regoldar, *v.i.* (*ind.* **regüeldo;** *subj.* **regüelde**)
to belch, eruct; to brag, boast.

regoldo, *n.m.* wild chestnut tree.

regolfar, *v.i.*, *v.r.* to flow back.

regolfo, *n.m.* reflux, whirlpool; gulf, bay, arm
of the sea.

regona, *n.f.* large irrigating canal.

regordete, -ta, *a.* (*coll.*) chubby, plump, short
and stout.

regostarse, *v.r.* to delight, dally, take pleasure.

regosto, *n.m.* craving for more.

regraciar, *v.t.* to thank, show gratitude.

regresar, *v.i.* to return, regress; (*law*) to
recover possession of a benefice.

regresión, *n.f.* regression, regress, return.

regresivo, -va, *a.* regressive.

regreso, *n.m.* return; (*law*) retaking possession
of a benefice.

regruñir, *v.i.* to growl, snarl.

reguardarse, *v.r.* to take care of oneself.

regüeldo, *n.m.* eructation, belching; boast,
brag.

reguera, *n.f.* irrigating canal; moorings.

reguero, *n.m.* small rivulet; spot, mark of a
liquid.

regulación, *n.f.* regulation, computation,
comparison, adjustment.

regulador, -ra, *a.* regulating, governing. —
n.m. (*mech.*) regulator, governor; throttle of
a locomotive; controller of an electric car;
regulador de fuerza centrífuga, ball governor;
(*mus.*) the sign < or >.

regular, *v.t.* to regulate, adjust, set in order,
compare, methodize. — *a.* regular, orderly,
moderate, sober, frequent, common, probable, convenient, likely; *por lo regular*,
commonly.

regularidad, *n.f.* regularity, punctuality,
order, orderliness, custom, common use;
discipline.

regularizar, *v.t.* (conjugated like ALZAR) to
regularize, systematize, subject to rules.

regularmente, *adv.* regularly, in an orderly
way; as a rule; ordinarily, generally, naturally.

régulo, *n.m.* sovereign of a small state; basilisk; (*orn.*) kinglet, golden-crested wren.

regurgitación, *n.f.* (*med.*) regurgitation.

regurgitar, *v.i.* to regurgitate, overflow.

rehabilitación, *n.f.* rehabilitation.

rehabilitar, *v.t.* to reinstate, restore, rehabilitate; to refit, repair.

rehacer, *v.t.* (conjugated like HACER) to mend,
repair, remake; to add new strength; to
increase the quantity or weight of. — *v.r.* to
regain new strength; (*mil.*) to rally, reorganize.

rehacimiento, *n.m.* renovation, renewal;
recuperation.

rehago; rehaga, *pres. indic.; pres. subj.* [RE-
HACER].

rehala, *n.f.* drove of sheep.

rehalero, *n.m.* driver of a *rehala*.

rehartar, *v.t.* to satiate, surfeit.

reharto, -ta, *a.* surfeited.

rehecho, -cha, *a.* renovated, renewed, done
over again; thick-set.

rehelear, *v.i.* to grieve, to become sad.

rehén, *n.m.* hostage.

rehenchidura, *n.f.* stuffing, refilling.

rehenchimiento, *n.m.* act of stuffing.

rehenchir, *v.t.* to fill or stuff again.

rehendija, rendija, *n.f.* cleft, crevice.

reherir, *v.t.* to repel, repulse.

reherrar, *v.t.* to re-shoe (a horse).

rehervir, *v.t.* (conjugated like HERVIR) to boil
again. — *v.i.* (*fig.*) to be blinded by passion;
to be inflamed with love. — *v.r.* to ferment,
become sour.

rehiladillo, *n.m.* ribbon.

rehilandera, *n.f.* pinwheel.

rehilar, *v.t.* to twist over-much. — *v.i.* to
stagger, reel; to whiz, whir.

rehilete, rehilero, *n.m.* kind of shuttlecock;
dart; (*fig.*) malicious hint.

rehilo, *n.m.* shivering, shaking.

rehogar, *v.t.* (*pret.* **rehogué;** *pres. subj.*
rehogue) to dress meat with a slow fire.

rehollar, *v.t.* to trample under foot, tread
upon.

rehoya, *n.f.; **rehoyo,** *n.m.* deep hole or pit.

rehoyar, *v.t.* to dig holes again.

rehuida, *n.f.* flight.

rehuir, *v.r.*, *v.t.*, *v.i.* (conjugated like HUIR) to
withdraw; *v.t.* to reject, decline, refuse,
condemn; *v.i.* to return, run back (of
game).

rehumedecer, *v.t.*, *v.r.* to dampen well.

rehundir, *v.t.* to sink; to remelt; to deepen; to
lavish, dissipate, waste.

rehurtarse, *v.r.* to feint (said of animals).

rehurto, *n.m.* feint, dodge; shrug.

rehusar, *v.t.* to decline, deny, refuse, abrogate,
reject.

reidero, -ra, *a.* inclined to laugh, laughable.

reidor, -ra, *n.m.f.*, *a.* laughter; jolly, hilarious
(person).

reimportación, *n.f.* reimportation.

reimportar, *v.t.* to reimport.

reimpresión, *n.f.* reimpression, reissue, reprint.

reimpreso, -sa, *p.p.* [REIMPRIMIR].

reimprimir, *v.t.* (*p.p.* **reimpreso**) to reprint.

reina, *n.f.* queen; queen-bee; queen at chess;
superior or excellent woman or female
animal; hop-scotch.

reinado, *n.m.* reign.

reinal, *n.m.* strong hemp cord.

reinante, *a.* reigning; prevailing, fashionable;
excelling.

reinar, *v.i.* to govern, reign, command; to
predominate, prevail.

reincidencia, *n.f.* reiteration, repetition of an
offence; backsliding.

reincidente, *a.* reiterating, relapsing, backsliding.

reincidir, *v.i.* to relapse into vice, backslide;
to reiterate.

reincorporación, *n.f.* renewing, reincorpora-
tion.

reincorporar, *v.t.* to reincorporate, re-
embody.

reingresar, *v.i.* to re-enter.

reino, *n.m.* kingdom, reign; kingdom (natural
history).

reinstalación, *n.f.* reinstalment.

reinstalar, *v.t.* to reinstall.
reintegrable, *a.* (*com.*) reimbursable, payable.
reintegración, *n.f.* reintegration, devolution, restitution, reimbursement.
reintegrar, *v.t.* to reintegrate, restore; to repay, reimburse, refund. — *v.r.* to be reintegrated, restored; to recover, collect.
reintegro, *n.m.* reintegration.
reír, *v.i.* (*pres. part.* **riendo**; *pres. indic.* **río**; *pret.* **él rió**; *pres. subj.* **ría**) to laugh; smile, giggle, titter; sneer; *reír a carcajadas*, to laugh loudly, guffaw. — *v.r.* to laugh at, scoff, make jest of; to begin to tear or be threadbare (of cloth); *reírse por nada*, to giggle.
reiteración, *n.f.* reiteration, repetition.
reiteradamente, *adv.* repeatedly.
reiterar, *v.t.* to reiterate, repeat.
reiterativo, -va, *a.* reiterative.
reivindicable, *a.* (*law*) recoverable.
reivindicación, *n.f.* (*law*) recovery, replevin.
reivindicar, *v.t.* (conjugated like VINDICAR) (*law*) to recover, regain possession of.
reivindicatorio, -ria, *a.* (*law*) replevisable.
reja, *n.f.* ploughshare, coulter; ploughing, tillage; grate, grating, railing.
rejacar, *v.t.* to plough across for clearing weeds.
rejada, *n.f.* paddle of a plough.
rejado, *n.m.* grate, grating, grid, railing.
rejal, *n.m.* pile of bricks laid in a cross.
rejalgar, *n.m.* (*min.*) realgar.
rejazo, *n.m.* stroke with a ploughshare.
rejería, *n.f.* iron-grating factory.
rejero, *n.m.* bar-maker, grate-maker.
rejilla, *n.f.* lattice (e.g., in a confessional); small grating; cane back or seat of a chair; foot-brasier.
rejo, *n.m.* iron spike; iron rim; goad-stick; insect's sting; hob for quoits; strength, vigour; (*bot.*) caulicle.
rejón, *n.m.* dagger, poniard; lance, spear; broad knife.
rejonazo, *n.m.* dagger-thrust.
rejoncillo, *n.m.* small lance or spear.
rejoneador, *n.m.* bull-fighter who uses the *rejón*.
rejonear, *v.t.* to thrust a *rejón* into a bull.
rejoneo, *n.m.* fighting bulls with the *rejón*.
rejuela, *n.f.* small grate; foot-stove, foot-brasier.
rejuvenecer, *v.i., v.r.* (conjugated like MERECER) to rejuvenate.
relabrar, *v.t.* to re-cut (precious stones).
relación, *n.f.* relation, report, account, narrative, memoir, narration; correspondence, coherence; analogy; proportion; connexion, dealing, intercourse; (*law*) brief; (*mil.*) return, report; (*theat.*) long speech; *relación de ciego*, something read in a monotonous voice. — *pl.* **relaciones**, relations, connexions; acquaintance, intercourse; courting; *relación jurada*, sworn statement; *tener relaciones con*, to be acquainted with; to be betrothed to.
relacionar, *v.t.* to report, relate, narrate; to connect, put in connexion; make acquainted. — *v.r.* to get acquainted, make connexions; to be related.
relacionero, *n.m.* narrator, reporter, relater; ballad-singer.
relai, *n.m.* (*wire.*) relay.

relajación, *n.f.* relaxation, dilatation, extension; slackening; laxity, looseness; licence, lewdness; diminution, mitigation of a penalty; (*law*) release from an oath or vow; (*law*) delivery of a criminal by the ecclesiastical judge to the secular; release (from an oath); (*med.*) hernia, rupture.
relajadamente, *adv.* licentiously, dissolutely.
relajador, -ra, *a.* relaxing, remitting.
relajamiento, *n.m.* relaxation, laxity, slackness.
relajante, *a.* laxative, relaxing, loosening.
relajar, *v.t.* to relax, slacken, loosen; to remit; to release (from an oath, promise, duty, etc.); to deliver to the criminal tribunal; to weaken; to ease, divert, amuse. — *v.r.* to be relaxed, loosened, weakened; to grow vicious or corrupted; to be ruptured.
relamer, *v.t.* to relick. — *v.r.* to lick one's lips; to relish; to boast, brag; to use make-up.
relamido, -da, *a.* affected, prim, over-fine, over-nice.
relámpago, *n.m.* lightning-flash, fulguration; quick person or action; (*vet.*) blemish in the eyes of horses.
relampagueante, *a.* lightning, flashing.
relampaguear, *v.i.* to lighten, sparkle, flash, gleam.
relampagueo, *n.m.* lightning, flashing.
relance, *n.m.* repeated casting of a net; chance, fortuitous event; repeated attempt; series of chances.
relancina, *n.f.* (*Ec.*) chance; chance event.
relanzar, *v.t.* (*pret.* **relancé**; *pres. subj.* **relance**) to repulse, repel.
relapso, -sa, *a.* relapsed.
relatador, -ra, *n.m.f.* relater, narrator.
relatante, *a.* reporting, narrating.
relatar, *v.t.* to relate, narrate, report.
relativamente, *adv.* relatively, comparatively.
relatividad, *n.f.* relativity.
relativismo, *n.m.* relativism.
relativista, *n.m., a.* relativist.
relativo, -va, *a.* relative, comparative.
relato, *n.m.* statement, narration, narrative, report, account.
relator, *n.m.* relater, teller, narrator; reporter; (*law*) relator.
relatoría, *n.f.* reporter's office; (*law*) office of a *relator*.
relavar, *v.t.* to re-wash.
relave, *n.m.* second washing of metals. — *pl.* **relaves**, washings, sweepings.
relazar, *v.t.* to tie many times.
relé, *n.m.* (*elec.*) relay.
releer, *v.t.* (conjugated like LEER) to reread.
relegación, *n.f.* relegation, exile, banishment.
relegar, *v.t.* (*pret.* **relegué**; *pres. subj.* **relegue**) to relegate, banish, exile.
relej, releje, *n.m.* wheel rut, track; (*artill.*) narrow chamber; (*arch.*) tapering of a wall; burr in a cutting tool.
relejar, *v.i.* (*arch.*) to taper, slope.
relente, *n.m.* night dew; (*coll.*) assurance, slyness.
relentecer, *v.i., v.r.* (conjugated like LENTECER) to soften or be softened by the falling of dew.
relevación, *n.f.* raising, lifting up; relevation, liberation; relief, alleviation; (*law*) remission, pardon; exemption, release.
relevante, *a.* excellent, eminent.

relevar, v.t. to emboss, bring into relief; to disburden, forgive, release, exonerate; to pardon, acquit; to aggrandize, exalt; (mil.) to relieve, substitute. — v.i. (art) to stand out in relief.

relevo, n.m. (mil.) relief.

relicario, n.m. reliquary; locket; shrine.

relictos, n.m.pl. (law) estate.

relieve, n.m. relief, relievo, raised work, embossment. — pl. **relieves,** offal, scraps, bits, leavings; bajo relieve, bas-relief; relief; medio relieve, demi-relief.

religa, n.f. (jewel.) second alloy.

religación, n.f. religation; binding, tying.

religar, v.t. (pret. **religué;** pres. subj. **religue)** to bind, solder, realloy.

religión, n.f. religion, worship; faith, belief, creed; devotion, piety; religious system; entrar en religión, to become a monk or nun.

religionario, religionista, n.m. religionist, sectary; Protestant.

religiosamente, adv. religiously, piously; moderately; punctually, exactly.

religiosidad, n.f. religiousness, religiosity, sanctity, piety; punctuality.

religioso, -sa, a. religious, devout, pious, godly; punctual, scrupulous, exact, strict; moderate; bound by monastic vows.

relimar, v.t. (mech.) to re-file.

relimpiar, v.t. to clean again.

relimpio, -pia, a. (coll.) very clean, very neat.

relinchador, -ra, a. neighing, crying, whinnying.

relinchante, a. neighing, whinnying.

relinchar, v.i. to whinny, neigh.

relincho, relinchido, n.m. neigh, neighing; sh ut of triumph.

relindo, -da, a. very neat; very fine.

relinga, n.f. (naut.) bolt-rope.

relingar, v.t. (naut.) to sew on bolt-ropes. — v.i. (naut.) to rustle.

reliquia, n.f. relic, residue, remains; trace, track, vestige; habitual or regular complaint.

reliquiario, n.m. reliquary; locket; shrine.

reliz, n.m. (Mex.) landslide.

reloco, -ca, a. (coll.) raving mad.

reloj, n.m. clock, watch, timepiece; reloj de arena, hour-glass; reloj de agua, clepsydra; reloj de sol, sun-dial; reloj de repetición, repeater; reloj de bolsillo, pocket watch; reloj de longitudes, chronometer; reloj de pulsera, wrist watch; reloj despertador, alarm clock; reloj desconcertado, irregular, uncertain person; estar como un reloj, (coll.) to be as regular as clockwork.

relojera, n.f. clock-case; watch-case, watch-stand; watchmaker's wife; (Am.) watch pocket.

relojería, n.f. clock-making; art of clock-making; watchmaker's shop.

relojero, n.m. watchmaker, clockmaker.

reluciente, a. lucent, relucent, shining, glittering, clear, bright.

relucir, v.i. (conjugated like LUCIR) to shine, glisten, glitter, glow; to be brilliant, excel.

reluchar, v.i. to struggle, wrestle, strive.

relumbrante, a. resplendent.

relumbrar, v.i. to sparkle, shine, glitter, glisten, glare.

relumbre, n.m. lustre.

relumbrón, n.m. lustre, brightness, fleeting idea or sound; tinsel, flash.

rellanar, v.t. to relevel. — v.r. to stretch at full length.

rellano, n.m. landing (of a staircase).

rellenar, v.t. to refill, replenish; to feed plentifully, stuff; cram, fill up. — v.r. to be more than sated.

relleno, n.m. forcemeat, stuffing; filling, repletion; padding, wadding; (mech.) packing, gasket.

relleno, -na, a. satiated, stuffed, crop-sick.

remachado, -da, a. clinched, riveted; flat-nosed; remachado alternado, staggered riveting; remachado de cadena, chain riveting.

remachar, v.t. to flatten; to rivet, clinch; to affirm, secure, make sure.

remache, n.m. flattening, securing, clinching; rivet.

remachón, n.m. buttress.

remador, n.m. rower.

remadura, n.f. rowing.

remaldecir, v.t. (conjugated like MALDECIR) to curse the cursers.

remallar, v.t. to mend a net or coat of mail.

remamiento, n.m. rowing, act of rowing.

remandar, v.t. to order several times.

remanecer, v.i. (pres. indic. **remanezco;** pres. subj. **remanezca)** to appear, occur, reappear suddenly.

remaneciente, a. reappearing.

remanente, n.m. remainder, remnant, residue. — a. residual (magnetism).

remanezco; remanezca, pres. indic.; pres. subj. [REMANECER].

remangadura, n.f. (prov.) act of tucking up.

remangar, v.t. (pret. **remangué;** pres. subj. **remangue)** to tuck up (the sleeves, etc.). — v.r. to be determined.

remango, n.m. tucking up.

remansarse, v.r. to eddy, stop flowing.

remanso, n.m. back-water, dead water, stagnant water; tardiness, slowness.

remante, n.m. rower, rowing.

remar, v.i. to row, paddle; to struggle, toil.

remarcar, v.t. (conjugated like MARCAR) to mark again.

rematada, n.f. (vulg.) decayed strumpet.

rematadamente, adv. totally, entirely.

rematado, -da, a. ended, terminated; utterly ruined, totally lost; condemned; knocked down (at auction); loco rematado, stark mad; rematado a galeras, condemned to the galleys. — p.p. [REMATAR].

rematamiento, n.m. end, conclusion, termination.

rematante, n.m. highest bidder.

rematar, v.t. to close, end, finish, terminate; to adjudge, knock down (in auctions); to kill at one shot; (sew.) to finish a seam; to give the coup de grâce. — v.i. to be at an end. — v.r. to be utterly ruined; rematar al mejor postor, to knock down to the highest bidder; rematar un ajuste, to strike a bargain.

remate, n.m. end, termination, finish, conclusion, expiration; edge, hem, border; (com.) auction, public sale; best bidding; artificial flowers on an altar; (print.) vignette; abutment; (arch.) pinnacle; remate de cuentas, closing of accounts; de remate, utterly, irremediably; por remate, finally.

remecedor, n.m. olive-beater.

remecer, v.t. (conjugated like MECER) to rock, swing, move to and fro.

remedable, *a.* imitable.
remedador, -ra, *n.m.f.* imitator, mimic.
remedamiento, *n.m.* copy, imitation.
remedar, *v.t.* to copy, imitate, mimic; to gesticulate; to mock; to follow others.
remediable, *a.* remediable.
remediador, -ra, *n.m.f., a.* curer, healer; mender; comforter, helper.
remediar, *v.t.* to remedy; repair, mend; to help, support, assist; to free, liberate; to repair damage; to avoid; *lo que no se puede remediar, se ha de aguantar,* what can't be cured must be endured.
remedición, *n.f.* act of re-measuring.
remedio, *n.m.* remedy, reparation, help; correction, amendment; cure; refuge, resource; action at law; *no encontrarse una cosa para un remedio,* to be impossible to find something; *no hay más remedio; no tiene remedio,* there's no help for it; *sin remedio,* without fail.
remedión, *n.m.* (*theat.*) makeshift performance.
remedir, *v.t.* to re-measure.
remedo, *n.m.* imitation, copy; mockery.
remellado, -da, *a.* dented, jagged.
remellar, *v.t.* to unhair hides.
remellón, -ona, *a.* dented, jagged.
remembración, *n.f.* remembrance.
remembrar, *v.t.* to remember.
rememorar, *v.t.* to recall, remember.
rememorativo, -va, *a.* that reminds, recalls, remembers.
remendado, -da, *a.* patched, mended; spotted, tabby. — *p.p.* [REMENDAR].
remendar, *v.t.* (*pres. indic.* **remiendo;** *pres. subj.* **remiende**) to patch, mend, adjust, correct, repair; (*sew.*) to piece, stitch, darn.
remendón, -na, *n.m.f.* botcher, patcher; cobbler.
remeneo, *n.m.* rapid movements in dancing, etc.
rementir, *v.i.* (conjugated like MENTIR) to lie often.
remera, *n.f.* flight feather (of birds).
remero, *n.m.* rower, paddler, oarsman.
remesa, *n.f.* (*com.*) sending of goods, remittance of money, shipment.
remesar, *v.t.* to pull out the hair; (*com.*) to send, remit, ship.
remesón, *n.m.* plucking out of hair, hair pulled out; stopping a horse in full gallop; (*fenc.*) closing in, *corps-à-corps.*
remeter, *v.t.* to put in, put back.
remezón, *n.m.* (*Am.*) slight earthquake.
remiche, *n.m.* space between benches in galleys.
remiel, *n.m.* second extract of soft sugar from the cane.
remiendo, *n.m.* patch, clout; repair, mending-piece, darning; amendment; addition; (*print.*) job-work; brindle; *a remiendos,* by piecemeal, by patchwork; *ser remiendo del mismo paño,* to be of the same origin; *echar un remiendo a la vida,* to take a light meal; *no hay mejor remiendo que el del mismo paño,* if you want a thing done, do it yourself.
remiendo; remiende, *pres. indic.; pres. subj.* [REMENDAR].
remilgadamente, *adv.* with affected nicety, prudishly, squeamishly.
remilgado, -da, *a.* affectedly nice or grave;

squeamish, prudish, fastidious. — *p.p.* [REMILGARSE].
remilgarse, *v.r.* (*pret.* **me remilgué;** *pres. subj.* **me remilgue**) to be affectedly nice, squeamish, prudish.
remilgo, *n.m.* affected niceness or gravity; prudery, squeamishness.
reminiscencia, *n.f.* reminiscence, recollection, memory.
remirado, -da, *a.* cautious, prudent.
remirar, *v.t.* to review, revise. — *v.r.* to do a thing with great care; to inspect or consider with pleasure; to examine oneself.
remisamente, *adv.* remissly, carelessly.
remisible, *a.* remissible.
remisión, *n.f.* act of sending; remission, abatement; remitting, remitment; forgiveness, grace, indolence; relaxation, abatement.
remisivamente, *adv.* with remission.
remisivo, -va, *a.* remitting, remissory, remissive.
remiso, -sa, *a.* remiss, indolent, careless, slack, slow.
remisoria, *n.f.* (*law*) reference of a case to another tribunal.
remisorio, -ria, *a.* remissory, having power to forgive.
remitir, *v.t.* to remit, send, forward, transmit; pardon, forgive; to suspend, give up, forego; to put off, defer; to relax, lessen tension; (*law*) to transfer to another court. — *v.i., v.r.* to slacken, grow less tense. — *v.r.* to refer to another's judgment, submit; to quote, cite.
remo, *n.m.* oar; long, hard labour; *al remo,* rowing; *a remo y sin sueldo,* labouring in vain; *a remo y vela,* very expeditiously, very diligently; *condenado al remo,* condemned to the galleys. — *pl.* **remos,** arms and legs, hind and forelegs; wings of a bird.
remoción, *n.f.* removal, removing.
remojadero, *n.m.* steeping-tub.
remojar, *v.t.* to steep, imbrue, drench, wet much, soak again; *remojar la palabra,* (*coll.*) to wet one's whistle.
remojo, *n.m.* steeping or soaking; *echar (un negocio) en remojo,* to allow (affairs, business, etc.) to ripen.
remolacha, *n.f.* beetroot; sugar beet.
remolar, *n.m.* master-carpenter, oar-maker; oar-shop.
remolcador, *n.m.* (*naut.*) tug.
remolcar, *v.t.* (*pret.* **remolqué;** *pres. subj.* **remolque**) (*naut.*) to tow, take in tow; to haul.
remoler, *v.t.* (conjugated like MOLER) to re-grind, grind excessively.
remolida, *n.f.* regrinding of sugar cane.
remolimiento, *n.m.* act of regrinding.
remolinante, *a.* whirling, making gyrations.
remolinar, *v.i.* to make gyrations; to whirl, spin, rotate. — *v.r.* to whirl round; to crowd, throng, swarm.
remolinear, *v.t.* to whirl about; to whirl, gyrate, spin.
remolino, *n.m.* whirl, whirlwind; whirlpool, vortex; maelstrom, eddy; overhanging lock of hair; crowd, throng; commotion, disturbance.
remolón, -na, *a.* soft, indolent, lazy.
remolón, *n.m.* upper tusk of boar; horse's sharp tooth.

remolonear, *v.i.,* *v.r.* to be idle; to lag, loiter; refuse to stir, skulk; to shirk work.

remolque, *n.m.* (*naut.*) towage, act of towing; towline, trackage; *a remolque,* towing, in tow; *dar remolque,* to tow.

remondar, *v.t.* to clean (plants) a second time; to take away what is useless.

remono, -na, *a.* (*coll.*) very neat, very pretty.

remonta, *n.f.* collection of cavalry horses; remount, remounting cavalry; (*shoe.*) repairing, resoleing, vamping; stuffing a horse saddle.

remontamiento, *n.m.* remounting cavalry.

remontar, *v.t.* to frighten away, oblige to withdraw (as game); to remount, supply remounts; to repair (saddles); (*shoe.*) to repair, resole, revamp. — *v.r.* (*fig.*) to tower, soar; to conceive great ideas; to take refuge in the mountains (fugitive slaves).

remonte, *n.m.* remounting, repairing; soaring, flight; sublimity of conceptions.

remontista, *n.m.* commissioner for the purchase of cavalry horses.

remoque, *n.m.* (*coll.*) sarcastic word.

remoquete, *n.m.* thump of the fist; witty expression; (*coll.*) gallantry, courtship; epigram; satire.

rémora, *n.f.* (*ichth.*) sucking fish, remora; hindrance, obstacle, cause of delay.

remordedor, -ra, *a.* causing remorse.

remorder, *v.t.* (conjugated like MORDER) to bite repeatedly; to sting, fret, cause remorse, make uneasy. — *v.r.* to show concern, remorse, worry, regret.

remordimiento, *n.m.* remorse, uneasiness, compunction, regret.

remosquearse, *v.r.* (*print.*) to be smeared or blurred; to show suspicion of surroundings.

remostar, *v.t.* to put must into old wine. — *v.r.* to grow sweet and must-like (of wine).

remostecerse, *v.r.* [REMOSTARSE].

remosto, *n.m.* putting of must into old wine.

remotamente, *adv.* remotely, at a distance, vaguely, confusedly, in an unlikely way.

remoto, -ta, *a.* remote, far off, distant, unlike, unlikely, alien, foreign.

remover, *v.t.* (conjugated like MOVER) to move, remove, shift; change, alter, transfer; to dismiss, displace.

removimiento, *n.m.* removal; revulsion, fermentation; dismissal.

remozadura, *n.f.;* **remozamiento,** *n.m.* appearing or becoming young.

remozar, *v.t.* (*pret.* **remocé**; *pres. subj.* **remoce**). — *v.t.* to rejuvenate. — *v.r.* to be rejuvenated.

rempujar, *v.t.* to push out of place, jostle; impel, carry away; to approach game.

rempujo, *n.m.* push, thrust, pressure, impulse; (*naut.*) sailmaker's palm.

rempujón, *n.m.* impulse, push, thrust.

remuda, *n.f.* exchange, re-exchange; relay of horses; change of clothes.

remudamiento, *n.m.* removal, exchange; change of clothing.

remudar, *v.t.* to remove, move again, change again, exchange, replace.

remuerdo; remuerda, *pres. indic.; pres. subj.* [REMORDER].

remuevo; remueva, *pres. indic.; pres. subj.* [REMOVER].

remugar, *v.t.* (*prov.*) to ruminate.

remullir, *v.t.* to soften; to mollify.

remunerable, *a.* remunerable, rewardable.

remuneración, *n.f.* remuneration; recompense, reward, consideration; gratuity.

remunerador, -ra, *n.m.f.* remunerator.

remunerar, *v.t.* to remunerate, reward, recompense.

remuneratorio, -ria, *a.* remuneratory.

remusgar, *v.i.* (*pret.* **remusgué**; *pres. subj.* **remusgue**) to suspect, presume.

remusgo, *n.m.* chill wind or atmosphere.

remusguillo, *n.m.* coolish place.

renacentista, *n.m., a.* scholar of, relating to, the Renaissance.

renacer, *v.i.* (conjugated like NACER) to be born again, spring up again, grow again; to receive grace from baptism.

renaciente, *a.* renascent, springing up anew.

renacimiento, *n.m.* regeneration, new birth; renascence; Renaissance.

renacuajo, *n.m.* frogs' spawn, tadpole; (*fig.*) little shapeless man.

renadío, *n.m.* second crop.

renal, *a.* (*anat.*) renal.

renazco; renazca, *pres. indic.; pres. subj.* [RENACER].

rencilla, *n.f.* slight grudge after a quarrel; slight feeling of rancour; heart-burning.

rencilloso, -sa, *a.* peevish, quarrelsome, touchy.

rencionar, *v.t.* to occasion heart-burnings, quarrels or rancour.

renco, -ca, *a.* lame, with a dislocated hip.

rencor, *n.m.* rancour, animosity, grudge.

rencorosamente, *adv.* rancorously.

rencoroso, -sa, *a.* rancorous, spiteful.

renda, *n.f.* second dressing of vines.

rendaje, *n.m.* set of reins and bridles of horses.

rendajo, *n.m.* mocking-bird, mimic [ARRENDAJO].

rendar, *v.t.* to dress vines a second time.

rendición, *n.f.* rendition, surrender, yielding; rent, yield, product, profit.

rendidamente, *adv.* humbly, compliantly, submissively.

rendido, -da, *a.* obsequious, devoted; fatigued, exhausted, worn-out.

rendija, *n.f.* crevice, fissure, cleft, crack.

rendimiento, *n.m.* rendition; weariness; faintness, fatigue; submission, obsequiousness; efficiency; yield, produce, rent, income.

rendir, *v.t.* (*pres. part.* **rindiendo**; *pres. indic.* **rindo**; *pres. subj.* **rinda**; *pret.* **él rindió**) to subdue, subject, conquer, overcome, render, surrender; yield, produce; to throw up, vomit; to give up, deliver, return, give back, restore; (*naut.*) to come to the end of a voyage or cruise; (*mil.*) to give up the post, to commit it to another; (*naut.*) to spring a mast or yard. — *v.r.* to be tired, fatigued, worn out; to yield, submit, surrender, give up, give way; *rendir la guardia,* hand over the guard; *rendir marea,* to stem the tide; *rendir las armas,* to surrender; *rendir gracias,* to give thanks; *rendir obsequios,* to fête; *rendir el alma a Dios,* to die.

renegado, *n.m.* renegade, apostate, wicked person; ombre.

renegador, -ra, *n.m.f.* swearer, blasphemer, apostate.

renegar, *v.t.* (conjugated like NEGAR) to disown, deny; to abhor, detest. — *v.i.* to apostatize; to blaspheme, curse, swear.

renegón, -na, *n.m.f.* inveterate swearer.

renegrear, *v.i.* to blacken intensely.

renegrido, -da, *a.* deeply livid (said of bruises).

rengífero, *n.m.* reindeer.

renglón, *n.m.* (written or printed) line; part of one's revenue or expenses; (*com.*) line of business; *dejar entre renglones,* to neglect, forget; *leer entre rengones,* (*fig.*) to read between the lines. — *pl.* **renglones,** lines, writings.

renglonadura, *n.f.* ruling (of paper).

rengo, -ga, *a.* lame, hurt in the back; *dar con la de rengo,* (*fam.*) to disappoint, disillusion; *hacer la de rengo,* to escape work by feigning illness.

renguear, *v.i.* (*Arg., Col., Chi., Ec., Per.*) [RENQUEAR].

reniego, *n.m.* execration, blasphemy, curse.

renitencia, *n.f.* resistance, opposition.

renitente, *a.* renitent, repugnant.

reno, *n.m.* reindeer.

renombrado, -da, *a.* renowned, celebrated, famous.

renombre, *n.m.* surname, family name; fame, renown, glory.

renovable, *a.* renewable, replaceable.

renovación, *n.f.* renovation, renewal; change, reform.

renovador, -ra, *n.m.f.* renovator; reformer.

renovar, *v.t.* (*pres. indic.* **renuevo;** *pres. subj.* **renueve**) to renovate; replace, renew, reform; to reiterate, republish; *renovar la memoria,* to refresh the memory. — *v.r.* to recollect oneself, reform.

renovero, -ra, *n.m.f.* usurer, fripper.

renquear, *v.i.* to limp, halt.

renta, *n.f.* rent, rental; revenue; tax; profit, income; *rentas públicas,* state revenues; *señalar rentas,* to assign a revenue.

rentado, -da, *a.* living on an income.

rentar, *v.t.* to yield, produce, bring in.

rentera, *n.f.* renter's wife.

rentería, *n.f.* productive land.

rentero, *n.m.* renter, farmer, lessee.

rentilla, *n.f.* small rent; game of cards, game of dice.

rentista, *n.m.* financier, bondholder, annuitant.

rentístico, -ca, *a.* financial.

rento, *n.m.* annual rent, rental.

rentoso, -sa, *a.* producing income.

rentoy, *n.m.* game of cards.

renuencia, *n.f.* reluctance, unwillingness.

renuente, *a.* unwilling, reluctant.

renuevo, *n.m.* shoot, sprout; nursery of plants; renovation, renewal.

renuncia, *n.f.* renunciation, resignation, abjurement.

renunciable, *a.* that can be renounced or resigned; transferable.

renunciación, *n.f.* renunciation.

renunciamiento, *n.m.* renouncement.

renunciante, *n.m.f., a.* renouncer, renouncing, abjurer.

renunciar, *v.t.* to renounce, resign; abrogate, disown, reject, refuse, leave, forego, waive, give up; abandon, relinquish, depreciate.

renunciatario, *n.m.* one to whom anything is resigned.

renuncio, *n.m.* revoke (at cards); (*coll.*) error, mistake, contradiction, untruth.

renvalsar, *v.t.* to shave off (doors and windows).

renvalso, *n.m.* rebate in a door-panel to fit the frame.

reñidero, *n.m.* cock-pit.

reñido, -da, *a.* at variance with another.

reñidor, -ra, *n.m.f.* quarreller, scold.

reñir, *v.t., v.i.* (*pres. part.* **riñendo;** *pres. indic.* **riño;** *pret.* **él riñó;** *pres. subj.* **riña**) to quarrel, wrangle, dispute; to reprimand, reprove, scold, reproach; to fall out, fight; to discuss, argue.

reo, *n.m.f.* criminal, offender, culprit, defendant in a lawsuit; (*ichth.*) ray trout.

reojo, *n.m.; mirar de reojo,* to look obliquely, askance; to look with contempt or disfavour.

reorganización, *n.f.* reorganization.

reorganizar, *v.t.* (conjugated like ORGANIZAR) to reorganize.

reóstato, *n.m.* (*elec.*) rheostat.

repacer, *v.t.* (conjugated like PACER) to consume all the grass (beasts).

repagar, *v.t.* (conjugated like PAGAR) to repay; to overpay.

repajo, *n.m.* enclosure for pasture.

repantigarse, repanchigarse, *v.r.* to lean back at full length.

repapilarse, *v.r.* to eat to excess.

reparable, *a.* reparable, remediable; noticeable, remarkable.

reparación, *n.f.* reparation, repair; restoration, mending; satisfaction, amends, atonement, indemnity, compensation.

reparada, *n.f.* sudden bound of a horse.

reparado, -da, *a.* repaired; provided; squint-eyed.

reparador, -ra, *n.m.f.* repairer; observer; fault-finder.

reparamiento, *n.m.* repair, recovery.

reparar, *v.t.* to repair, restore, refit; to consider, heed, observe, remark, notice; to contemplate, reflect; to expiate; to make amends, give satisfaction; to defend, guard, help, protect; to suspend, detain; to parry; to give the final touch to. — *v.i.* to stop, halt. — *v.r.* to forbear, refrain; (*Mex.*) to rear (of horses).

reparativo, -va, *a.* reparative.

reparo, *n.m.* repair, reparation, restoration, recovery; careful inspection; remark, observation, advice, notice, warning; consideration, reflection; difficulty, objection, doubt; inconvenience; defence, protection, help, support; poultice to strengthen the stomach; (*fenc.*) parry.

reparón, *n.m.* (*coll.*) great doubt or difficulty.

reparón, -na, *n.m.f.* carper, fault-finder. — *a.* carping, cavilling, fault-finding.

repartible, *a.* distributable.

repartición, *n.f.* partition, distribution, division.

repartidamente, *adv.* in various parts or divisions.

repartidero, -ra, *a.* parting, distributing.

repartidor, -ra, *n.m.f.* distributor; assessor of taxes.

repartimiento, *n.m.* partition, division, distribution; apportionment; assessment, allotment of lands made by Spaniards on the conquest of America.

repartir, *v.t.* to divide, distribute; apportion, assess, allot.

reparto, *n.m.* (*theat.*) cast.

repasadera, *n.f.* smoothing plane.

repasadora, *n.f.* woman-carder of wool.

repasar, *v.t.*, *v.i.* to pass again, repass; revise, review, go through; to repeat; to scan, peruse, glance over; to air (clothes); to sew again, mend (clothes); to clean dyed wool for carding; (*min.*) to mix and pound mercury with silver ore.

repasata, *n.f.* reprehension, chiding, censure.

repaso, *n.m.* revision, re-examination; final inspection, finishing; (*coll.*) reprimand, chastisement; (*min.*) remixing mercury with silver ore.

repastar, *v.t.* to feed or pasture a second time; to re-knead (flour, clay, etc.), adding water, flour, etc.

repasto, *n.m.* increase of feed (beasts).

repatriación, *n.f.* repatriation, return to one's country.

repatriar, *v.t.*, *v.i.*, *v.r.* to return to one's country.

repechar, *v.i.* to mount a slope, go uphill.

repecho, *n.m.* short steep incline; *a repecho*, (*adv.*) uphill.

repelada, *n.f.* salad of herbs.

repeladura, *n.f.* re-stripping.

repelar, *v.t.* to pull out the hair; to nip the tops of grass; to nibble, browse; to put a horse to his speed; (*fig.*) to clip, crop, lop off.

repelente, *a.* repelling, refuting, rejecting.

repeler, *v.t.* to repel, repulse, refute, reject.

repelo, *n.m.* that which goes against the grain; cross fibre; slight scuffle or dispute; aversion, repugnance.

repelón, *n.m.* pulling out the hair; small part torn from anything; loose thread in stockings; slight fall; bolting of a horse; *a repelones*, piecemeal; little by little; *de repelón*, by the way; in haste; *ser más viejo que el repelón*, to be old as the hills.

repeloso, -sa, *a.* of a bad grain (wood); peevish, touchy; rigid, punctilious.

repellar, *v.t.* (*build.*) to dub out.

repensar, *v.t.* (conjugated like PENSAR) to reconsider, think over, reflect.

repente, *n.m.* sudden movement; unexpected event; *de repente*, suddenly.

repentinamente, *adv.* suddenly.

repentino, -na, *a.* sudden, unexpected, unforeseen; abrupt, unpremeditated, extemporaneous.

repentista, *n.m.* improviser, extemporizer.

repentizar, *v.i.* (conjugated like ALZAR) to perform (music) at sight.

repentón, *n.m.* unexpected event or incident.

repeor, *a.*, *adv.* much worse.

repercudida, *n.f.* rebound, repercussion.

repercudir, *v.i.* to rebound.

repercusión, *n.f.* repercussion, reverberation.

repercusivo, -va, *a.* (*med.*) repercussive.

repercutir, *v.i.* to rebound; reverberate, re-echo; drive back, reflect.—*v.t.* (*med.*) to repel.

repertorio, *n.m.* repertory, repertoire.

repesar, *v.t.* to weigh again.

repeso, *n.m.* re-weighing; weighing office.

repetición, *n.f.* repetition, reiteration; dissertation, thesis; (*mus.*) repeat; repeater (clock or watch); (*art*) replica; (*law*) action for recovering damages.

repetidamente, *adv.* repeatedly.

repetidor, -ra, *n.m.f.* repeater.

repetir, *v.t.* (*pres. part.* **repitiendo**; *pres. indic.* **repito**; *pres. subj.* **repita**; *pret.* **él repitió**) to repeat, reiterate, try again, use again, do again; to rehearse, recite; to echo; (*law*) to demand one's rights. — *v.i.* to 'repeat' (of taste); to read a thesis at a university. — *v.r.* to repeat oneself.

repicar, *v.t.*, *v.i.* (conjugated like PICAR) to hash, mince, chop; to chime, ring a peal; to repique (in piquet); *a buen salvo está el que repica*, the bellringer's berth is safe. — *v.r.* to glory, boast, flatter oneself.

repicotear, *v.t.* to pink; to indent.

repinaldo, *n.m.* large apple.

repinarse, *v.r.* to soar, elevate.

repintar, *v.t.* to repaint. — *v.r.* to paint oneself; (*print.*) to set off, mackle, double.

repique, *n.m.* chopping, cutting, mincing; chime, peal; altercation, dispute.

repiquete, *n.m.* chime, festive peal; opportunity, chance; (*naut.*) short tack.

repiquetear, *v.t.* to chime, ring a merry peal. — *v.r.* to bicker, quarrel, wrangle.

repiqueteo, *n.m.* ringing merry peals.

repisa, *n.f.* mantelpiece; shelf; pedestal, bracket, console.

repisar, *v.t.* to tamp; (*fig.*) to commit something to memory.

repiso, *n.m.* second press wine.

repitiente, *a.* repeating.

repizcar, *v.t.* (*pret.* **repizqué**; *pres. subj.* **repizque**) to pinch.

repizco, *n.m.* pinch, pinching.

replantación, *n.f.* replanting.

replantar, *v.t.* to replant.

replantear, *v.t.* (*arch.*) to lay out the ground-plan.

repleción, *n.f.* repletion.

replegar, *v.t.* (conjugated like PLEGAR) to redouble, replait, refold. — *v.r.* (*mil.*) to fall back, retreat in order and according to plan.

repleto, -ta, *a.* a replete, very full.

réplica, *n.f.* reply, answer, repartee, objection; (*art*) replica.

replicador, -ra, *n.m.f.* disputant, replier.

replicante, *n.m.f.*, *a.* replier, disputant; replying.

replicar, *v.i.* (*pret.* **repliqué**; *pres. subj.* **replique**) to answer, retort; to contradict, impugn, argue; (*law*) to respond.

replicato, *n.m.* (*law*) answer, reply; objection.

replicón, -na, *a.* (*coll.*) replier, disputer, argufier.

repliegue, *n.m.* doubling; folding; fold, crease; (*mil.*) withdrawal, retreat.

repo, *n.m.* (*Chi.*) verbenaceous shrub.

repoblación, *n.f.* repopulation.

repoblar, *v.t.* (conjugated like POBLAR) to repeople, repopulate.

repodrir, *v.t.* to rot excessively.

repollar, *v.i.* to form head (cabbage, lettuce, etc.).

repollo, *n.m.* white cabbage; round head (of a plant).

repolludo, -da, *a.* cabbage-headed, round-headed; (*fig.*) short chubby fellow.

reponer, *v.t.* (conjugated like PONER) to replace, reinstate, reinstall; to refill; to answer, reply; to restore. — *v.r.* to recover (health or property); to become fair (weather); to become serene, pacify.

reportación, *n.f.* moderation, forbearance, serenity, calm.

reportado, -da, *a.* moderate, forbearing, temperate.

reportaje, *n.m.* (*newsp.*) report, reporting.

reportamiento, *n.m.* forbearance, restraint.

reportar, *v.t.* to moderate, refrain, restrain, check, forbear; to get, gain, obtain, reach, attain; to carry, bring. — *v.r.* to forbear, refrain, compose, control oneself.

reporte, *n.m.* report, news, information, notice; gossip; lithographic proof.

reporterismo, *n.m.* (*newsp.*) office of a reporter; reporters collectively.

reportero, -ra, *n.m.f.* reporter.

reportista, *n.m.* highly skilled lithographer.

reportorio, *n.m.* almanac, calendar.

reposadamente, *adv.* peaceably, quietly.

reposadero, *n.m.* trough for receiving molten metal.

reposado, -da, *a.* peaceful, quiet.

reposar, *v.i.* to rest, repose; lie down, have a nap; to stay undisturbed; to lean; to lie in the grave; *reposar la comida,* to rest after a meal. — *v.r.* to settle (of liquid).

reposición, *n.f.* act of restoring; reposition, replacement; recovery of health.

repositorio, *n.m.* repository.

reposo, *n.m.* rest, repose; tranquillity, sleep.

repostada, *n.f.* (*Am.*) discourteous answer.

repostarse, *v.r.* (*Am.*) to lay in stock.

repostería, *n.f.* larder, pantry, still-room; plate-room; butlership; confectionery, pastry-shop.

repostero, *n.m.* king's butler; pastrycook; ornamental cloth with the coat of arms.

repregunta, *n.f.* (*law*) second question or demand; cross-examination.

repreguntar, *v.t.* (*law*) to question repeatedly, cross-examine.

reprender, reprehender, *v.t.* to reprehend, reprimand; scold, censure, blame, reprove; chide, correct.

reprendiente, *a.* censuring, reprimanding.

reprensible, reprehensible, *a.* reprehensible.

reprensión, reprehensión, *n.f.* reprehension, censure, reprimand, blame, reproof, scolding.

reprensor, -ra, *n.m.f.* reprehender, censurer, reprover.

represa, *n.f.* dam, dyke, sluice, lock, basin; restriction, act of stopping or retaining; (*naut.*) recapture.

represalia, *n.f.* reprisal.

represar, *v.t.* to retake, recapture; to stop, detain, retain; to repress; to bank, dam, dyke; restrain, check.

representable, *a.* representable, that may be represented.

representación, *n.f.* representation; description, statement; image, idea, figure; address, petition, memorial; power, dignity, authority; performance, production; remonstrance; (*law*) right of succession; *representación proporcional,* proportional representation.

representador, -ra, *n.m.f.* representative; actor, player.

representante, *a.* representing another. — *n.m.* player, comedian; representer, representative; deputy.

representar, *v.t.* to represent, set forth, manifest, make to appear, express; to perform, play on the stage; to be agent or deputy of; to symbolise, stand for. — *v.r.* to imagine, conceive.

representativo, -va, *a.* representative.

represión, *n.f.* repression, control, check.

represivo, -va, *a.* repressive, restrictive.

reprimenda, *n.f.* reprimand.

reprimir, *v.t.*, *v.r.* to refrain, repress, curb; check, restrain, control.

reprobable, *a.* reprehensible.

reprobación, *n.f.* reproof, reprobation.

reprobado, -da, *a.* reprobate; failed in an examination.

reprobador, -ra, *n.m.f.* reprover, condemner.

reprobar, *v.t.* (conjugated like PROBAR) to reject, reprobate, damn, condemn; to reprove, rebuke, upbraid.

reprobatorio, -ria, *a.* reprobative, objurgatory.

réprobo, -ba, *n.m.f., a.* reprobate, wicked.

reprochar, *v.t., v.r.* to reproach, blame, impute; to challenge witnesses, to exclude, reject.

reproche, *n.m.* reproach, reproof; rebuff, rebuke.

reproducción, *n.f.* reproduction.

reproducir, *v.t.* (conjugated like PRODUCIR) to reproduce.

reproductible, *a.* reproducible.

reproductividad, *n.f.* reproductiveness.

reproductivo, -va, *a.* reproduction.

reproductor, -ra, *n.m.f.* reproducing, reproducer; stallion, ram, bull, etc., kept for breeding purposes.

repromisión, *n.f.* repeated promise.

repropiarse, *v.r.* to disobey, get unruly (horses).

repropio, -pia, *a.* restive, unruly, refractory (horses).

reprueba, *n.f.* new proof.

reps, *n.m.* rep or reps (cloth).

reptar, *v.i.* to crawl (as a reptile).

reptil, *n.m., a.* reptile.

república, *n.f.* republic, commonwealth.

republicanismo, *n.m.* republicanism.

republicano, -na, *n.m.f., a.* republican.

repúblico, *n.m.* patriot; statesman, eminent man.

repudiable, *a.* repudiable.

repudiación, *n.f.* repudiation, rejection, divorce.

repudiar, *v.t.* to disclaim, reject, repudiate; put away, disavow, renounce, disown, divorce (one's wife).

repudio, *n.m.* repudiation, divorce.

repudrir, *v.t.* to decay, rot greatly. — *v.r.* (*coll.*) to pine away.

repuesto, -ta, *p.p. irreg.* [REPONER]. — *a.* retired, secluded, hidden.

repuesto, *n.m.* depository, store, stock; sideboard, cupboard; pantry, larder; money staked in the game of ombre; *de repuesto,* extra, spare.

repugnancia, *n.f.* repugnance, reluctance, resistance; aversion, loathing; opposition, contradiction, contrariety.

repugnante, *a.* repugnant, reluctant, loathsome.

repugnar, *v.t.* to oppose, contradict, repugn; withstand; to act with reluctance.

repujado, *n.m.* repoussé, repoussage.

repujar, *v.t.* to emboss (metal, leather, etc.).

repulgado, -da, *a.* affected.

repulgar, *v.t.* (*pret.* **repulgué**; *pres. subj.* **repulgue**) to border, hem; to put an edging on pastry.

repulgo, *n.m.* hem; border or fringe of a pie; (*coll.*) ridiculous scruple.

repulido, -da, *a.* neat, prim, spruce.

repulir, *v.t.* to repolish. — *v.t., v.r.* to dress affectedly.

repulsa, *n.f.* repulse, refusal, rebuke, countercheck.

repulsar, *v.t.* to refuse, reject, repel, decline.

repulsión, *n.f.* repulsion.

repulsivo, -va, *a.* repulsive, repulsory.

repullo, *n.m.* jerk, leap, bound, bounce, start, shock; small dart or arrow.

repunta, *n.f.* point, cape, headland; mark of displeasure; (*coll.*) dispute, disagreement.

repuntar, *v.i.* to begin to ebb or rise (the tide). — *v.r.* to be on the turn (of wine); (*coll.*) to be soured, displeased with one another.

repunte, *n.m.* turn (of tide).

repurgar, *v.t.* (conjugated like PURGAR) to clean or purify again.

reputación, *n.f.* reputation, repute, credit, renown, fame, character.

reputante, *n.m.* appraiser.

reputar, *v.t.* to repute; to estimate, appraise.

requebrador, *n.m.* suitor, lover, wooer, gallant.

requebrar, *v.t.* (conjugated like QUEBRAR) to court, woo, make love, dally, flatter, wheedle; to break again.

requemado, -da, *a.* sunburnt, browncoloured. — *n.m.* black fabric used for mourning.

requemar, *v.t.* to burn a second time; to roast to excess, overcook; to parch plants; to smart, bite, sting; to inflame (blood). — *v.r.* to burn with passion, to be deeply in love.

requemazón, *n.f.* pungency, bitter taste.

requeridor, *n.m.* summons server; suitor.

requerimiento, *n.m.* request, requisition; summons, intimation.

requerir, *v.t.* (*pres. part.* **requiriendo**; *past part.* **requerido, requisito**; *pres. indic.* **requiero**; *pret.* **él requirió**; *pres. subj.* **requiera**) to notify, intimate; to investigate, examine, research into; to require, need, request; to be on one's guard; to court, woo, make love; to persuade, induce.

requesón, *n.m.* second curds; cottage cheese.

requeté, *n.m.* member of the Carlist regiments in Spanish Civil War.

requetebién, *adv.* (*coll.*) very good (or well); well done.

requiebro, *n.m.* endearing expressions, lovetale; compliment, flattery; well crushed ore.

réquiem, *n.m.* requiem; *misa de réquiem*, requiem mass.

requilorios, *n.m.pl.* (*coll.*) subterfuges, circumlocution; useless ceremony.

requintador, -ra, *n.m.f.* outbidder.

requintar, *v.t.* to outbid by a fifth part; (*mus.*) to raise or lower the pitch by five tones; to exceed, surpass.

requinto, *n.m.* second fifth subtracted from a quantity; rise of a fifth in bidding; (*mus.*) treble clarinet; small guitar; treble clarinet player.

requisa, *n.f.* night or morning visit (of a gaoler, etc.); round, tour of inspection; (*mil.*) requisition.

requisar, *v.t.* to inspect, make the rounds; (*mil.*) to requisition.

requisición, *n.f.* requisition, levy.

requisito, -ta, *p.p. irreg.* [REQUERIR].

requisito, *n.m.* requisite, requirement.

requisitoria, *n.f.* (*law*) requisition.

requisitorio, -ria, *a.* requisitory.

res, *n.f.* head of cattle, beast; *a la res vieja alíviale la reja*, old folk must be given light burdens.

resaber, *v.t.* (conjugated like SABER) to know very well.

resabiar, *v.t.* to cause to contract vices or bad habits. — *v.r.* to contract bad habits; to become vicious, learn vices; to be dissatisfied; to relish.

resabido, -da, *a.* very learned, affecting learning.

resabio, *n.m.* bad habit, vicious habit; unpleasant after-taste.

resabioso, -sa, *a.* (*Am.*) ill-tempered.

resaca, *n.f.* (*naut.*) undertow; (*com.*) redraft.

resacar, *v.t.* (*naut.*) to underrun, haul; (*com.*) to redraw.

resalado, -da, *a.* (*coll.*) very charming or graceful.

resalir, *v.i.* (conjugated like SALIR) to jut out, project.

resaltar, *v.i.* to jut out, project; to be evident, appear; to get loose; to result; to rebound.

resalte, *n.m.* protuberance, prominence, projection.

resalto, *n.m.* rebound, resilience; prominence, projection; (*railw.*) super-elevation of curves.

resaludar, *v.t.* to return a salute.

resalutación, *n.f.* return of a salute.

resalvo, *n.m.* tiller, sapling.

resallar, *v.t.* to weed again.

resanar, *v.t.* to regild defective spots.

resarcimiento, *n.m.* compensation, reparation, indemnity.

resarcir, *v.t.* (*pres. indic.* **resarzo**; *pres. subj.* **resarza**) to compensate, recompense, reward, indemnify, make amends to.

resbaladero, -ra, *a.* slippery, elusive.

resbaladero, *n.m.* slippery place.

resbaladizo, -za, *a.* slippery; glib; elusive; alluring, tempting; *memoria resbaladiza*, treacherous memory.

resbalador, -ra, *n.m.f.* slider; backslider.

resbaladura, *n.f.* slip, slide, slippery track; backsliding.

resbalamiento, *n.m.* slip; *resbalamiento de ala*, (*aer.*) side-slip; *resbalamiento de cola*, (*aer.*) tail slide.

resbalante, *a.* slider, slipping.

resbalar, *v.i., v.r.* to slip, slide, glide; to err, go astray; to fail to keep an engagement.

resbalo, *n.m.* (*Am.*) steep incline.

resbalón, *n.m.* slip; error, fault, offence; *de resbalón*, erroneously.

resbaloso, -sa, *a.* slippery.

rescaldar, *v.t.* to scorch, scald.

rescaño, *n.m.* leavings, fragments, scraps.

rescatar, *v.t.* to ransom; redeem, recover, extricate; to barter, exchange; to commute; (*Am.*) to buy ore in the mine.

rescate, *n.m.* ransom; redemption; ransommoney; barter; permutation, exchange.

rescatín, *n.m.* (*Am.*) buyer of ore from Indians.

rescaza, *n.f.* (*ichth.*) grouper.

rescindir, *v.t.* to rescind, annul, cancel.

rescisión, *n.f.* recission, annulment, cancellation.

rescisorio, -ria, *a.* rescissory, rescinding.

rescoldera, *n.f.* heartburn.

rescoldo, *n.m.* cinders, embers, hot ashes; scruple, doubt, apprehension.

rescontrar, *v.t.* to offset, set off (accountancy).

rescripto, *n.m.* order, rescript, mandate.

rescriptorio, -ria, *a.* rescriptive.

resecación, *n.f.* exsiccation, desiccation.

resecar, *v.t.* (conjugated like SECAR) to dry again, dry thoroughly, desiccate.

resección, *n.f.* (*surg.*) resection.

reseco, -ca, *a.* too dry, very lean.

reseco, *n.m.* exsiccation; dry part of a honeycomb.

reseda, *n.m.* reseda, mignonette; woad.

resegar, *v.t.* (conjugated like SEGAR) to mow again.

reseguir, *v.t.* to put an edge to swords.

resellante, *a.* recoining, restamping.

resellar, *v.t.* to recoin. — *v.r.* (*polit.*) to cross the floor.

resello, *n.m.* recoinage; surcharge (stamps, etc.).

resembrar, *v.t.* to resow.

resentido, -da, *a.* angry, resentful, displeased.

resentimiento, *n.m.* crack, cleft, flaw; resentment, grudge.

resentirse, *v.r.* (conjugated like SENTIR) to begin to give way, fail, get out of order; to resent, express displeasure; to be offended or hurt.

reseña, *n.f.* review, succinct description; signal; muster of troops, review of soldiers; distinguishing mark on the body.

reseñar, *v.t.* (*mil.*) to review; to sketch, outline; to give a brief description.

resequido, -da, *a.* dried up.

reserva, *n.f.* reserve; secret; exception, reservation; reservedness, circumspection, prudence, modesty; *reserva mental*, mental reservation; *de reserva*, extra, spare; *sin reserva*, without reserve.

reservación, *n.f.* reservation.

reservadamente, *adv.* secretly, reservedly.

reservado, -da, *a.* close, reserved, cautious, circumspect; (*coll.*) confidential; private. — *n.m.* (*eccles.*) ciborium.

reservar, *v.t.* to reserve; to exempt; to postpone, defer; to limit, restrain; to separate, set aside, keep back; to hide, conceal; to shut up. — *v.r.* to act cautiously; to beware; to bide one's time.

reservativo, -va, *a.* reserved.

reservatorio, *n.m.* reservoir for water; greenhouse, hot-house, conservatory.

reservista, *n.m.* (*mil.*) reservist.

resfriado, *n.m.* cold, chill.

resfriador, *n.m.* refrigerator.

resfriadura, *n.f.* cold in horses.

resfriamiento, *n.m.* refrigeration.

resfriante, *a.* cooling, refrigerating.

resfriar, *v.t.* to cool, make cold; to moderate ardour, fervour, etc. — *v.i.* to begin to be cold. — *v.r.* to catch cold; to proceed with coolness.

resfrío, *n.m.* cold, chill.

resguardar, *v.t.* to defend, preserve, protect, harbour. — *v.r.* to be on one's guard; to take shelter; to protect oneself.

resguardo, *n.m.* guard, preservation, safety; defence, shelter, protection; (*com.*) security, surety, collateral security; watchfulness; body of customs officials; preventive service; (*naut.*) sea room, wide berth.

resí, *adv.* yes, yes.

residencia, *n.f.* residence, lodging, hostel, home; mansion; (*law*) impeachment.

residenciado, -da, *a.* resident, residentiary.

residencial, *a.* residential, residentiary.

residenciar, *v.t.* to call a public officer to account; to impeach.

residente, *a.* resident, residing, residentiary. — *n.m.* resident, minister at a foreign court.

residentemente, *adv.* assiduously, constantly.

residir, *v.i.* to reside, live, dwell, lodge; to be present; to be lodged as a right; to inhere.

residual, *a.* residual.

residuo, *n.m.* residue, remainder; (*chem.*) residuum; (*arith.*) difference. — *pl.* **residuos,** by-products, leavings, fragments, scraps.

resiembra, *n.f.* (*agric.*) resowing.

resigna, *n.f.* (*eccles.*) resignation.

resignación, *n.f.* resignation, submission, abnegation.

resignadamente, *adv.* resignedly.

resignante, *a.* resigning.

resignar, *v.t.* to resign, yield up, give up, abrogate. — *v.r.* to resign, submit.

resignatorio, *n.m.* resignee.

resina, *n.f.* resin, rosin.

resinar, *v.t.* to tap trees for resin.

resinero, -ra, *a.* resinous.

resinífero, -ra, *a.* resin-bearing.

resinoso, -sa, *a.* resinous.

resisa, *n.f.* eighth part taken as duty.

resisar, *v.t.* to diminish further things taxed.

resistencia, *n.f.* resistance, opposition, defence; (*mech., elec.*) resistance; *resistencia de materiales*, strength of materials.

resistente, *a.* resisting, repelling.

resistero, *n.m.* hottest part of the day; heat produced by reflection of the sun's rays; place where such heat is felt.

resistible, *a.* resistible.

resistidor, -ra, *n.m.f.* resister, opponent.

resistir, *v.t., v.i.* to oppose, resist; to reject; to repel, contradict; to endure, tolerate; to weather (a storm). — *v.r.* to struggle, contend.

resma, *n.f.* ream of paper.

resmilla, *n.f.* four quires of paper.

resobrar, *v.r.* to be considerably over and above.

resobrino, -na, *n.m.f.* son or daughter of a nephew or niece.

resol, *n.m.* glare of the sun.

resolano, *n.m.* place exposed to the sun.

resoluble, *a.* resolvable, resoluble.

resolución, *n.f.* resolution, deliberation, determination, decision; solution; activity, promptitude, courage, firmness, boldness; (*law*) lapse, nullification; (*med.*) resolution (inflammation, etc.); *en resolución*, in short, in a word.

resolutivamente, *adv.* resolutely.

resolutivo, -va, *a.* analytical. — *n.m.* (*med.*) resolutive.

resoluto, -ta, *a.* resolute, audacious, bold; prompt, brief, compendious; dexterous.

resolutoriamente, *adv.* resolutely.

resolutorio, -ria, *a.* resolute, prompt.

resolvente, *a.* resolvent, resolving.

resolver, *v.t.* (conjugated like VOLVER) (*p.p.* **resuelto;** *pres. ind.* **resuelvo;** *pres. subj.* **resuelva**) to resolve, decide, determine; to solve, unriddle; to sum up, reduce to small compass; to find out; to decree; to analyse; to dissolve; to dissipate; to destroy, undo; to divide up into parts. — *v.r.* to determine, resolve; to be included, comprised.

resollar, *v.i.* (*pres. indic.* **resuello;** *pres. subj.* **resuelle**) to respire, breathe heavily; to take breath; (*coll.*) to show up; to break silence.

resonación, *n.f.* resounding, noise of repercussion.

resonancia, *n.f.* resonance, repercussion of sound; consonance, harmony; (*fig.*) news, events, personal qualities noised abroad.

resonante, *a.* resounding, resonant.

resonar, *v.i.* (conjugated like SONAR) to resound; to clatter, chink; to be echoed back.

resoplar, *v.i.* to breathe audibly; to snort.

resoplido, resoplo, *n.m.* audible breathing, blowing of the nose, snorting.

resorber, *v.t.* to reabsorb; to sip again.

resorte, *n.m.* spring; (*fig.*) cause, means, medium.

respailar, *v.i.* (*coll.*) to skedaddle.

respaldar, *n.m.* back (of seat). — *v.t.* to endorse; to back; to guarantee; — *v.r.* to lean (against); to get backing; (*vet.*) to dislocate the backbone.

respaldo, *n.m.* back, back part; leaning-stock; endorsement.

respectar, *v.i. defect.* to regard, concern.

respectivamente, respective, *adv.* respectively, proportionally.

respectivo, -va, *a.* respective, relative.

respecto, *n.m.* relation, proportion; respect, relativeness; *respecto a* (or *de*), considering; with regard to; *al respecto*, respectively, relatively.

résped, *n.m.* tongue of a snake; wasp or bee's sting; (*fig.*) viper's tongue.

respetabilidad, *n.f.* respectability.

respetable, *a.* respectable, considerable; worthy; honourable, reliable.

respetador, -ra, *n.m.f.* respecter, venerator.

respetar, *v.t.* to respect, revere, venerate, honour. — *v.i. defect.* respectar.

respeto, *n.m.* respect, observance, regard, attention, consideration, veneration; *de respeto,* for ceremony's sake; (*com.*) *respeto a,* with regard to; *cabos de respeto,* (*naut.*) spare rigging; *velas de respeto,* (*naut.*) spare sails; *campar por su respeto,* to be one's own master.

respetosamente, *adv.* respectfully.

respetoso, -sa, *a.* respectable; respectful, dutiful.

respetuosamente, *adv.* respectfully.

respetuoso, -sa, *a.* respectful, obsequious, dutiful, ceremonious.

réspice, *n.m.* (*coll.*) retort; short, sharp reproof.

respigador, -ra, *n.m.f.* gleaner.

respigar, *v.t.* (*pret.* **respigué;** *pres. subj.* **respigue**) to glean.

respigón, *n.m.* hangnail; sore on a horse's foot.

respingar, *v.i.* (*pret.* **respingué;** *pres. subj.* **respingue**) to kick; to wince (of beasts); to obey reluctantly; (*coll.*) to misfit (of garments).

respingo, *n.m.* kick, jerk; reluctance, peevishness, unwillingness.

respingona, *a.* turned up, retroussé (nose).

respingoso, -sa, *a.* kicking, wincing.

respirable, *a.* respirable.

respiración, *n.f.* respiration, breathing, expiration, vent.

respiradero, *n.m.* vent, breathing-hole; respiratory organ; (*surg.*) cupping-glass; (*arch.*) air passage; air hole; ventilator; (*arch.*) femerell, louver; repose, rest.

respirante, *a.* respiring, exhaling, breathing.

respirar, *v.i.* to breathe, respire, exhale; to rest, take rest; to open the lips, speak; to get breath; to spread odours; *sin respirar,* quickly, without drawing breath; *no tener por donde respirar,* to have no satisfactory answer; *respirar por la herida,* to speak ill of someone who has done one wrong.

respiratorio, -ria, *a.* respiratory, serving for breathing.

respiro, *n.m.* respite, delay; cessation, stoppage; act of breathing; moment of rest; (*com.*) extension, extra time.

resplandecencia, *n.f.* resplendency, splendour, fame, lustre, glory.

resplandecer, *v.i.* (conjugated like MERECER) to gleam, glitter, shine, be brilliant, glow; to be eminent, conspicuous.

resplandeciente, *a.* gleaming, glittering, shining, resplendent, luminous.

resplandecimiento, resplandor, *n.m.* light, splendour, brilliancy, brightness, radiance; glare; (*obs., poet.*) ancient make-up for women.

resplandina, *n.f.* (*coll.*) sternness, severe reproof.

respondedor, -ra, *n.m.f.* answerer.

responder, *v.t., v.i.* to reply, answer; to acknowledge; to produce, yield; to account, be responsible; to re-echo; to correspond, answer to.

respondiente, *a.* respondent, answering.

respondón, -na, *a.* (*coll.*) given to answering back; saucy, pert.

responsabilidad, *n.f.* responsibility, accountableness, liability.

responsable, *a.* responsible, accountable, liable, answerable.

responsar, responsear, *v.i.* to pray or repeat a responsory.

responso, *n.m.* (*eccles.*) responsory for the dead.

responsorio, *n.m.* response.

respuesta, *n.f.* reply, answer, response, report; sound echoed back; refutation; *respuesta aguda* (or *picante*), repartee.

resquebradura, resquebrajadura, *n.f.* crack, cleft, flaw, split.

resquebrajar, *v.i.* to split, crack.

resquebrajo, *n.m.* cleft, crack.

resquebrajoso, -sa, *a.* brittle, fragile.

resquebrar, *v.i.* to split, crack, burst, begin to open.

resquemar, *v.t., v.i.* to burn the tongue.

resquemo, *n.m.,* **resquemazón,** *n.f.* pungency; (*fig.*) burning passion; pricking of the conscience.

resquicio, *n.m.* chink, cleft, crack, slit, crevice; chance, opportunity.

resta, *n.f.* (*arith.*) subtraction; rest, residue, remainder.

restablecedor, -ra, *n.m.f., a.* restorer.

restablecer, *v.t.* (conjugated like ESTABLECER) to restore, re-establish, reinstate. — *v.r.* to recover from illness, mend, get better, improve in health.

restablecimiento, *n.m.* restoration, re-establishment.

restablezco; restablezca, *pres. indic.; pres. subj.* [RESTABLECER].

restallar, *v.i.* to smack, crackle, crack (as a whip).

restante, *n.m.f., a.* remainder, residue, remaining.

restañadero, *n.m.* inlet; estuary.

restañadura, *n.f.* tinning, retinning, re-covering with tin.

restañar, *v.t.* to stanch, stop blood; to re-tin, re-cover with tin. — *v.r.* to restagnate.

restañasangre, *n.f.* bloodstone.

restaño, *n.m.* cloth of gold or silver; stagnation.

restar, *v.t.* (*arith.*) to subtract, find the residue; to return a ball (in tennis, etc.). — *v.i.* to remain, be left, be due.

restauración, *n.f.* restoration, redintegration.

restaurador, -ra, *n.m.f.* restorer.

restaurante, *n.m.* restorer, re-establisher. — *a.* restoring.

restaurar, *v.t.* to restore, retrieve; renew, repair.

restaurativo, -va, *a.* restorative.

restinga, *n.f.* sandbank, ridge of rocks in the sea.

restingar, *n.m.* locality full of ridges or sandbanks.

restitución, *n.f.* restitution, restoring.

restituíble, *a.* restorable, which may be restored.

restituidor, -ra, *n.m.f.* restorer, re-establisher.

restituir, *v.t.* (conjugated like ATRIBUIR) to restore, give up, give back, lay down; to re-establish. — *v.r.* to return to the place of departure.

restitutivo, -va; restitutorio, -ria, *a.* relating to restitution; (*law*) restitutive.

resto, *n.m.* remainder, residue, balance, rest, limit for stakes at cards; rebound of a ball (in tennis); player who returns the service-ball (tennis). — *pl. restos mortales,* remains, a dead body; *a resto abierto,* unlimited; *echar el resto,* to stake one's all; to do the very best.

restregadura, restregamiento, *n.m.* hard rubbing.

restregar, *v.t.* (conjugated like CONFESAR) to scrub.

restregón, *n.m.* scrubbing, hard rubbing.

restribar, *v.i.* to lean heavily.

restricción, *n.f.* restriction, limitation, modification.

restrictivamente, *adv.* restrictively.

restrictivo, -va, *a.* restrictive, restringent.

restricto, -ta, *a.* limited; restricted.

restringa, *n.f.* (*naut.*) shoal, bar; submerged rocks.

restringente, *n.m.* restrainer, restringent. — *a.* restraining.

restringible, *a.* restrainable, limitable.

restringir, *v.t.* (*pres. indic.* **restrinjo;** *pres. subj.* **restrinja**) to restrain, restrict; to limit, constrain, confine; to contract, astringe.

restriñente, *a.* restringent, binding.

restriñidor, -ra, *n.m.f.* restringent, restrainer, binder.

restriñimiento, *n.m.* restriction, costiveness.

restriñir, *v.t.* to restrain; to bind, make costive, astringe.

restrojo, *n.m.* stubble field.

resucitador, -ra, *n.m.f.* restorer, reviver.

resucitar, *v.t.* to resuscitate, revive; to renew, modernize, renovate. — *v.i.* to return to life.

resudación, *n.f.* slight perspiration.

resudar, *v.i.* to perspire, transude slightly.

resudor, *n.m.* slight perspiration.

resueltamente, *adv.* resolutely.

resuelto, -ta, *a.* resolute, audacious, bold; determined, quick, prompt, diligent; confident, constant.

resuello, *n.m.* breathing, respiration; *sin resuello,* panting, breathless; *meter el resuello,* intimidate.

resulta, *n.f.* result, consequence, effect; resolution; vacancy of a post, etc.

resultado, *n.m.* result, issue, consequence, effect, outcome; *resultado, nada entre dos platos,* it all ended in smoke.

resultancia, *n.f.* result, resultance.

resultante, *a.* resulting, proceeding, following. — *n.f.* (*mech.*) resultant (force, velocity, etc.).

resultar, *v.i.* to follow, result, proceed; to conduce; to redound; (*coll.*) to work well (or badly); to work out, succeed.

resumen, *n.m.* abridgment, summary, extract, résumé, recapitulation, compendium; (*law*) brief; *en resumen,* in short, briefly, summing up.

resumidamente, *adv.* briefly, summarily, compendiously.

resumir, *v.t.* to abridge, conclude, resume, repeat. — *v.r.* to be included; to convert; to absorb.

resunción, *n.f.* summary, abridgment; repetition.

resurgimiento, *n.m.* reappearance; (*hist.*) risorgimento.

resurgir, *v.i.* to reappear, arise, spring up.

resurrección, *n.f.* resurrection, revival, resuscitation.

resurtida, *n.f.* rebound, repercussion.

resurtir, *v.i.* to rebound, spring back.

retablo, *n.m.* (*eccles.*) retable, altar-piece, reredos.

retacar, *v.t.* to hit a billiard-ball twice (with the cue).

retacería, *n.f.* collection of remnants of cloth.

retaco, *n.m.* light fowling-piece; short cue; short, thick person.

retador, *n.m.* challenger.

retaguardia, *n.f.* rearguard; *picar la retaguardia,* to harass the retreating enemy.

retahila, *n.f.* file, range, series, string.

retajar, *v.t.* to cut round; to circumcise.

retal, *n.m.* clipping, remnant, piece.

retallar, *v.i.* to shoot or sprout anew. — *v.t.* to regrave, retouch a graving; (*arch.*) to form projecting ledges or juts in a wall.

retallecer, *v.i.* to re-sprout.

retallo, *n.m.* new sprout; (*arch.*) jut.

retama, *n.f.* (*bot.*) genista; broom; *retama negra (or de escobas),* furze, whin; *retama de tintes,* dyer's-broom, dyeweed.

retamal, retamar, *n.m.* land covered with broom; broom or gorse bush.

retamero, -ra, *a.* relating to broom or gorse.

retamilla, *n.f.* (*Mex.*) a shrub.

retamo, *n.m.* (*Arg., Col., Chi.*) [RETAMA].

retamón, *n.m.* (*bot.*) purging broom.

retar, *v.t.* to challenge; to impeach; to reprehend.

retardación, *n.f.* retardation, detention; delay; loitering.

retardar, *v.t., v.r.* to retard, defer, delay, detain, slacken.

retardo, *n.m.* delay, retardment, protraction, procrastination.

retasa, *n.f.* second valuation or assessment.

retasación, *n.f.* second valuation.

retasar, *v.t.* to value a second time, re-assess, re-appraise.

retazar, *v.t.* to tear in pieces.

retazo, *n.m.* piece, remnant, cutting, fragment, portion.

retejador, *n.m.* retiler.

retejar, *v.t.* to re-tile, repair a roof; (*coll.*) to provide with clothes.

retejer, *v.t.* to weave closely.

retejo, *n.m.* retiling, repairing of a roof.

retemblar, *v.i.* (conjugated like TEMBLAR) to vibrate, tremble repeatedly, shake, quiver.

retén, *n.m.* stock, store, reserve; (*mil.*) reserve corps; (*mech.*) ratchet, catch.

retención, *n.f.* retention, suspension, keeping back, stagnation.

retener, *v.t.* (conjugated like TENER) to guard, preserve; to catch, keep, hold; to detain, arrest; to retain, withhold, suspend, keep back.

retenida, *n.f.* (*naut.*) preventer rope; *retenida de costado,* (*aer.*) side guy wire; *retenida de guiñada,* (*aer.*) yaw guy; *retenida de proa,* (*naut.*) headfast.

retenidamente, *adv.* retentively.

retentar, *v.t.* to threaten with a relapse.

retentiva, *n.f.* retentiveness, memory.

retentivo, -va, *a.* retentive, retaining.

reteñir, *v.t.* (conjugated like TEÑIR) to dye over again. — *v.i.* to tingle.

retesamiento, *n.m.* coagulation, hardness; rebracing, tightening harder.

retesarse, *v.r.* to become stiff, hard.

reteso, *n.m.* stiffness, distension; rebracing, retightening; brow of a hill.

reticencia, *n.f.* reticence.

reticular, *a.* reticular, reticulate, netted.

retín, *n.m.* tinkling, jingle, clink; (*coll.*) sarcastic speech.

retina, *n.f.* retina.

retinte, *n.m.* second dye; tingling sound.

retintín, *n.m.* jingle, tingling, clink; sarcastic tone of voice.

retinto, -ta, *a.* dark, obscure; almost black (of animals). — *p.p. irreg.* [RETEÑIR].

retiñir, *v.i.* to tingle, resound, jingle, tinkle, ring, clink.

retiración, *n.f.* (*print.*) printing the back of a sheet; forme for backing.

retirada, *n.f.* retreat, retirement, withdrawal; place of safety; water closet; step in an ancient Spanish dance; land left dry by a changing river; *tocar la retirada,* (*mil.*) to sound the retreat.

retiradamente, *adv.* secretly, retiredly.

retirado, -da, *a.* retreated, retired, isolated; cloistered, solitary; pensioned; remote, distant. — *n.m. oficial retirado,* officer on half-pay

retiramiento, *n.m.* retirement.

retirar, *v.t.* to retire, withdraw; revoke, retreat; draw aside, put away; reserve, conceal; (*com.*) to withdraw, call in; (*print.*) to back. — *v.r.* to withdraw, retreat, go back, recede; take refuge, retire from active life; to raise a blockade or siege; to abandon a post.

retiro, *n.m.* retreat; recess, refuge, asylum; retirement, obscurity, privacy, private life; (*mil.*) condition and salary of a retired officer; (*eccles.*) retreat.

reto, *n.m.* challenge, menace, threat.

retobado, -da, *a.* (*Am.*) given to grumbling; obstinate, unruly; (*Arg., Per.*) cunning, wily.

retobar, *v.t.* (*Arg.*) to cover with hides; (*Chi.*) to pack in hides or burlap. — *v.r.* (*Arg.*) to become surly.

retobo, *n.m.* (*Col., Hond.*) refuse, useless thing; (*Chi.*) burlap; oilcloth; (*Arg.*) packing in hides.

retocador, *n.m.* retoucher (photographs).

retocar, *v.t.* (conjugated like TOCAR) to retouch, touch up, mend; to finish.

retoñar, retoñecer, *v.i.* to sprout again, shoot again; reappear.

retoño, *n.m.* sprout, shoot, sucker, tiller.

retoque, *n.m.* retouch; finishing stroke; repeated pulsation; paralytic stroke; slight attack of a disease.

rétor, *n.m.* teacher or writer on rhetoric.

retor, *n.m.* twilled cotton fabric.

retorcedura, *n.f.* twisting, wreathing.

retorcer, *v.t.* (conjugated like TORCER) to wring, twist; contort, convolve; to retort, reargue; to distort, twist, misconstrue. — *v.r.* to wring, writhe, squirm.

retorcido, *n.m., a.* twisted; sweetmeat; tutti-frutti.

retorcimiento, *n.m.* twisting, wreathing, contortion.

retórica, *n.f.* rhetoric. — *pl.* **retóricas,** (*coll.*) sophistries, quibbles, subtleties.

retóricamente, *adv.* rhetorically.

retórico, -ca, *a.* rhetorical, oratorical.

retórico, *n.m.* rhetorician.

retornamiento, *n.m.* return.

retornante, *a.* a returning.

retornar, *v.i.* to return, come back; to retrograde, recede. — *v.t.* to restore, give back, requite, return; to contort, twist, turn; to cause to go back.

retorno, *n.m.* return, requital, repayment; coming back, home trip; traffic, exchange, barter; (*naut.*) leading block.

retorsión, *n.f.* retortion, retort.

retorsivo, -va, *a.* bending back, retorting.

retorta, *n.f.* (*chem.*) retort; twilled linen fabric.

retortero, *n.m.* twirl, rotation; *andar al retortero,* to hover about; *traer al retortero,* (*coll.*) to twist one round, deceive with false hopes.

retortijar, *v.t.* to twist, curl.

retortijón, *n.m.* twisting, contortion, curlicue; *retortijón de tripas,* griping, cramp.

retostado, -da, *a.* brown-coloured.

retostar, *v.t.* (conjugated like TOSTAR) to retoast, toast brown.

retozador, -ra, *n.m.f.* frisker. — *a.* frisky, frolicsome, pranky.

retozadura, *n.f.* friskiness.

retozar, *v.i.* (*pret.* **retocé;** *pres. subj.* **retoce**) to frisk, skip, sport, romp, frolic, gambol, play. — *v.t.* to tickle, make merry; to titillate;

to become inflamed (passions); *retozar con el verde*, to indulge in high jinks.

retozo, *n.m.* friskiness, frisk, gambol, prank, frolic, romping, wantonness, gaiety; *retozo de la risa*, giggle, titter.

retozón, -na, *a.* wanton, rompish.

retracción, *n.f.* retraction, drawing back.

retractable, *a.* retractable.

retractación, *n.f.* retractation.

retractar, *v.t.* to retract, recant, withdraw; (*law*) to redeem. — *v.r.* to go back upon one's word.

retráctil, *a.* retractile.

retracto, *n.m.* (*law*) retraction, right of redemption.

retraducir, *v.t.* to retranslate, to translate back into the original language.

retraer, *v.t.* (conjugated like TRAER) to retract, retrieve, reclaim; (*law*) to redeem; to keep from, dissuade. — *v.r.* to take refuge, flee; to withdraw from, shun; to retire, keep aloof; to live a retired life.

retraído, *n.m.* refugee; lover of solitude.

retraimiento, *n.m.* retreat, asylum, refuge; seclusion, privacy; sanctum, private room.

retranca, *n.f.* large crupper; (*Col., Mex., Cub.*) brake.

retranquear, *v.t.* (*arch.*) to carve figures round columns.

retranquero, *n.m.* (*Col., Mex., Cub.*) brakeman.

retransmisión, *n.f.* (*wire.*) relay.

retransmitir, *v.t.* to relay, to broadcast signals or a programme received from another station.

retrasar, *v.t.* to delay, defer, put off, set back. — *v.i.* to retrograde, go back, decline. — *v.r.* to be backward, late, behind time.

retraso, *n.m.* delay, slowness, backwardness.

retratable, *a.* retractable.

retratación, *n.f.* retractation, recantation.

retratador, -ra, *n.m.f.* portrait painter; photographer.

retratar, *v.t.* to portray, limn, draw portraits; to imitate, copy; to paint; to describe; to photograph. — *v.r.* to be depicted; to sit for a portrait or photograph.

retratería, *n.f.* (*Guat., Urug.*) photographer's studio.

retratista, *n.m.* portrait painter, limner, photographer.

retrato, *n.m.* portrait, picture, likeness; photograph, effigy; resemblance, copy, imitation; personal description.

retrayente, *n.m.f., a.* retracter, recanter; (*law*) redeemer.

retrechar, *v.i.* to back, move backward.

retrechería, *n.f.* (*coll.*) evasion, cunning.

retrechero, -ra, *n.m.f., a.* charming, winsome, bewitching; cunningly evasive.

retrepado, -da, *a.* slanting backward.

retreparse, *v.r.* to lean back, recline in a chair.

retreta, *n.f.* (*mil.*) tattoo; retreat; (*Col.*) open-air concert by a military band.

retrete, *n.m.* closet, private room; alcove, boudoir; water-closet.

retribución, *n.f.* retribution, reward, recompense, consideration, tip, fee.

retribuir, *v.t.* (conjugated like HUIR) to retribute, recompense, reward, tip, fee.

retribuyente, *a.* retributive, retributory.

retrillar, *v.t.* (*agric.*) to thresh again.

retroacción, *n.f.* retroaction.

retroactivamente, *adv.* retroactively.

retroactividad, *n.f.* retroactivity.

retroactivo, -va, *a.* retroactive.

retrobar, *v.t.* (*Chi.*) to reproach; to scold, chide.

retrobón, -na, *n.m.f., a.* (*Chi.*) growler, grumbler.

retrocarga, *n.f.* breech-loading (of fire-arms).

retroceder, *v.i.* to retrocede, recede, retrograde, go backward, draw back, fall back; to grow worse.

retrocesión, *n.f.; retroceso*, *n.m.* retrocession, receding; motion backward.

retroceso, *n.m.* backward motion; (*med.*) aggravation; (billiards) screw.

retrogradación, *n.f.* (*astron.*) retrogradation, retrogression.

retrogradar, *v.i.* (*astron.*) to retrograde; to recede.

retrógrado, -da, *a.* retrograde, retrogressive; (*polit.*) reactionary.

retronar, *v.i.* (conjugated like TRONAR) to make a thundering noise.

retrónica, *n.f.* (*vulg., facet.*) rhetoric.

retrospectivamente, *adv.* retrospectively.

retrospectivo, -va, *a.* retrospective.

retrotracción, *n.f.* (*law*) antedating.

retrotraer, *v.t.* (conjugated like TRAER) to date back, antedate.

retrovendendo, *n.m.* (*law*) reversion sale.

retrovender, *v.t.* (*law*) to sell back to the first vendor.

retrovendición, *n.f.* selling back to the vendor.

retrucar, *v.i.* (*pret.* **retruqué**; *pres. subj.* **retruque**) in billiards, to kiss, hit again (of a rebounding ball).

retruco, *n.m.* kiss (billiards).

retruécano, *n.m.* pun, play upon words, quibble; antithesis, contrast.

retruque, *n.m.* kiss (of a rebounding ball).

retuerto, -ta, *a.* twisted. — *p.p. irreg.* [RETORCER].

retumbante, *a.* sonorous, resonant; pompous, bombastic, high-flown.

retumbar, *v.i.* to jingle, clink, resound, sound loudly.

retumbo, *n.m.* resonance, echo, loud noise.

retundir, *v.t.* (*build.*) to even (a wall); (*med.*) to repel.

reuma, *n.m.* rheumatism. — *n.f.* rheum.

reumático, -ca, *a.* rheumatic.

reumatismo, *n.m.* rheumatism.

reunión, *n.f.* union, reunion; meeting, gathering, circle, assembly, congregation.

reunir, *v.t.* to congregate, gather, unite; reunite; to reconcile. — *v.r.* to join, assemble, unite, meet.

reuntar, *v.t.* to oil again, grease again.

revacunación, *n.f.* revaccination.

revacunar, *v.t.* to revaccinate.

reválida, *n.f.* final university examination.

revalidación, *n.f.* confirmation, ratification.

revalidar, *v.t.* to ratify, confirm. — *v.r.* to be admitted into a faculty.

revancha, *n.f.* revenge; *en revancha*, in return, in exchange.

revecero, -ra, *n.m.f.* farmhand tending oxen.

reveedor, *n.m.* revisor, censor, inspector.

revejecer, *v.i.* (conjugated like ENVEJECER) to grow prematurely old.

revejecido, -da; revejido, -da, *a.* prematurely old.
revelación, *n.f.* revelation, disclosure.
revelado, *n.m.* (*phot.*) development.
revelador, -ra, *n.m.f.* revealer; (*phot.*) developer.
revelamiento, *n.m.* revelation; (*phot.*) development.
revelante, *a.* revealing.
revelar, *v.t.* to reveal, disclose, lay bare, divulge, manifest, make known, communicate; (*phot.*) to develop.
reveler, *v.t.* (*med.*) to cause revulsion.
revellín, *n.m.* (*fort.*) ravelin.
revenar, *v.i.* to sprout (plants, trees, etc.).
revendedor, *n.m.* retailer, hawker, huckster, pedlar; tout, spiv reselling tickets.
revender, *v.t.* to retail; peddle, huckster; to re-sell.
revenimiento, *n.m.* (*min.*) caving in (galleries).
revenirse, *v.r.* (conjugated like VENIR) to be gradually consumed; to grow sour, ferment (as wine and preserves); to shrink, waste away; to exude; to yield, assent, concede.
reveno, *n.m.* sprout, shoot.
reventa, *n.f.* retail, resale, second sale.
reventadero, *n.m.* rough piece of ground; painful work, drudgery.
reventar, *v.i.* (*pres. indic.* **reviento**; *pres. subj.* **reviente**) to burst; to blow up, blow out; crack, break; to splash (of waves); to break loose (as a passion); to shoot, grow, sprout, blossom; to crave, long for; to drudge. — *v.t.* to vex, annoy, harass, molest; to burst; to break; to crush, smash, ruin; to tire, fatigue, exhaust; to wind a horse; *reventar de risa,* to split one's sides with laughing.
reventazón, *n.f.* disruption, rupture; bursting; blow-out; (*naut.*) breaker, dashing of the waves.
reventón, *a.* bursting; bulging. — *n.m.* burst, blow-out, explosion, disruption; steep declivity; (*fig.*) toil, drudgery, fatigue.
rever, *v.t.* (conjugated like VER) to revise, review, overlook, re-survey; (*law*) to retry.
reverberación, *n.f.* reverberation; (*chem.*) calcination in a reverberatory furnace.
reverberar, *v.i.* to reverberate, reflect.
reverbero, *n.m.* reverberation; reflector; street lamp; (*Arg., Cub., Ec., Hond.*) cooking stove, spirit stove.
reverdecer, *v.i.* (conjugated like VERDECER) to sprout again, grow green again, reverdure; to acquire new vigour.
reverdeciente, *a.* growing fresh and green again.
reverencia, *n.f.* reverence, homage, veneration, respect, honour, observance; courtesy, obeisance; (*eccles.*) reverence (title of honour).
reverenciable, *a.* worthy of reverence, reverend.
reverenciador, -ra, *n.m.f.* reverencer.
reverencial, *a.* reverential.
reverenciar, *v.t.* to reverence, venerate; to hallow; to revere, respect.
reverendísimo, -ma, *a. superl.* Most Reverend (cardinal, archbishop, nuncio).
reverendo, -da, *a.* reverend, worthy of reverence.
reverente, *a.* reverent, respectful.

reversibilidad, *n.f.* revertibility, reversibility.
reversible, *a.* (*law*) revertible; (*phys.*) reversible.
reversión, *n.f.* (*law*) reversion, return.
reverso, *n.m.* reverse (of coins); back side, rear side; *el reverso de la medalla,* the opposite, diametrically different.
reverter, *v.i.* (conjugated like VERTER) to overflow.
revertir, *v.i.* (*law*) to revert.
revés, *n.m.* back part, reverse, wrong side; box, slap, stroke with the back of the hand; misfortune, misadventure, disappointment; (*fenc.*) reverse; (*Cub.*) worm attacking the tobacco plant; *al revés,* on the contrary, contrariwise; *de revés,* diagonally; *al revés me las calcé,* I did it the wrong way round.
revesa, *n.f.* eddy, backwater.
revesado, -da, *a.* intractable, stubborn, obstinate; complicated; laborious; obscure; difficult, entangled; (*fig.*) wayward, mischievous.
revesar, *v.t.* to vomit.
revesino, *n.m.* reversi, a card game; *cortar el revesino,* to thwart.
revestido, *n.m.* (*arch.*) facing.
revestimiento, *n.m.* (*build.*) revetment.
revestir, *v.t.* (conjugated like VESTIR) to dress, clothe, vest, revest; to repair; (*build.*) to revet. — *v.r.* to be invested with; to be swayed away; to be haughty, lofty, proud.
revezar, *v.i.* to alternate, work in rotation, come in by turn.
revezo, *n.m.* alternacy, turn; relay; gang.
reviejo, *n.m.* withered branch of a tree.
reviejo, -ja, *a.* very old.
revientacaballo, *n.m.* (*Cub.*) dog's-bane.
reviernes, *n.m.* each of the first seven Fridays after Easter.
revindicar, *v.t.* (conjugated like VINDICAR) to claim.
revirado, -da, *a.* (*bot.*) twisted.
revirar, *v.t.* (*naut.*) to change the direction of a vessel; to veer again, retack.
revisada, *n.f.* (*Chi.*) [REVISION].
revisar, *v.t.* to revise, review, examine; *revisar las cuentas,* to audit accounts.
revisión, *n.f.* (*mil.*) revision, reviewing, revisal, revise; (*law*) new trial or hearing.
revisita, *n.f.* revision, reinspection.
revisor, *n.m.* reviser, reviewer, censor, corrector, overseer; inspector.
revisoría, *n.f.* office of censor or reviser.
revista, *n.f.* review, magazine, journal; revision, revisal, revise; re-inspection, re-examination; (*mil.*) parade, muster, review; (*law*) new trial; (*theat.*) revue; *suplicar en revista,* (*law*) to present a bill of review; to appeal.
revistar, *v.t.* to revise (a lawsuit); to review, inspect (troops).
revistero, -ra, *n.m.f.* (*newsp.*) reporter.
revisto, -ta, *a., p.p. irreg.* [REVER].
revividero, *n.m.* place for rearing silk-worms.
revivificable, *a.* revivable.
revivificar, *v.t.* (conjugated like BUSCAR) to revivificate, revivify.
revivir, *v.i.* to revive, return to life.
revocable, *a.* revocable, reversible.
revocablemente, *adv.* in a revocable manner.
revocación, *n.f.* revocation, abrogation.
revocador, -ra, *n.m.f.* one who revokes; plasterer, whitewasher.

revocadura, *n.f.* plaster, whitewash; edge of the canvas covered by the frame.

revocante, *n.m.f.*, *a.* revoker.

revocar, *v.t.* (*pret.* **revoqué**; *pres. subj.* **revoque**) to revoke, recall, repeal, annul, abolish, abrogate, reverse, cancel; countermand; to plaster, whitewash, dress, repaint (a wall).

revocatorio, -ria, *a.* revocatory, recalling.

revoco, *n.m.* drawing back; plaster, whitewash; cover of broom for charcoal baskets.

revolante, *a.* fluttering, hovering.

revolar, *v.i.* (conjugated like VOLAR) to take a second flight; to fly again, fly around, hover, flutter.

revolcadero, *n.m.* weltering-place, wallowing-place.

revolcado, *n.m.* (*Guat.*) a dish made of fried bread, tomato, chile and other condiments.

revolcadura, *n.f.* weltering, wallowing.

revolcar, *v.t.* (conjugated like VOLCAR) to tread upon, trample upon, knock down; (*coll.*) to floor (an opponent). — *v.r.* to wallow, welter; to be stubborn.

revolcón, *n.m.* wallowing, rolling.

revolear, *v.i.* to fly precipitately, fly around. — *v.t.* (*Arg.*) to hurl, fling (the lasso).

revolotear, *v.i.* to flutter, fly around, hover. — *v.t.* to pitch, hurl.

revoloteo, *n.m.* fluttering, hovering.

revoltijo, revoltillo, *n.m.* parcel of things jumbled together; mass, medley, mess, jumble; plait or braid of tripes of sheep, etc.; (*Cub.*) a peasant's dish; *revoltillo de huevos*, scrambled eggs.

revoltón, *n.m.* vine-grub, vine-fretter.

revoltoso, -sa, *a.* turbulent, seditious, prankish, mischievous.

revoltura, *n.f.* (*min.*) mixture of fluxes.

revolución, *n.f.* revolution; (*astron., mech.*) revolving, gyration, turn; rebellion, disturbance, revolt, sedition, commotion.

revolucionar, *v.t.* to revolutionize. — *v.r.* to rise, break into a disturbance.

revolucionario, -ria, *n.m.f.*, *a.* revolutionary, revolutionist.

revolvedero, *n.m.* wallowing place for beasts.

revolvedor, -ra, *n.m.f.* revolter, disturber, seditious or turbulent person; (*Cub.*) revolving cauldron used in sugar mills.

revólver, *n.m.* revolver, pistol.

revolver, *v.t.* (*pres. indic.* **revuelvo**; *pres. subj.* **revuelva**) to revolve, gyrate, turn up, turn over, turn round; to wrap up; to return, retrace, revert; to stir, shift, shake; to excite commotion; to turn over in the mind, excogitate; to turn swiftly (as a horse); to estrange, create bad feeling; *revolver la feria*, to create a disturbance; *revolver a uno con otro*, to set two people against each other. — *v.r.* to move to and fro; to change (of the weather).

revolvimiento, *n.m.* revolution, perturbation, commotion.

revoque, *n.m.* whitewashing, whitewash, plaster.

revotarse, *v.r.* to take a new ballot, reconsider a ballot.

revuelco, *n.m.* rolling, wallowing.

revuelo, *n.m.* second flight of a bird; gyration; irregular motion; disturbance; *de revuelo*, promptly, speedily.

revuelta, *n.f.* return; second turn; contention, dissension; deviation, winding; revolution, revolt, sedition; change, commutation.

revueltamente, *adv.* pell-mell, higgledy-piggledy, upside down, confusedly.

revuelto, -ta, *a.* easily turned (horse); intricate, difficult; restless, mischievous, boisterous. — *p.p. irreg.* [REVOLVER].

revuelvepiedras, *n.m.* (*orn.*) turnstone.

revulsión, *n.f.* (*med.*) revulsion of humours.

revulsivo, -va; revulsorio, -ria, *a.* (*med.*) revulsory, revulsive.

rey, *n.m.* king, monarch, sovereign; king-bee; king in cards or chess; step in a Spanish dance; chief among men or beasts; *rey de armas*, (*her.*) king at arms; *debajo de mi manto, al rey mando*, when under my cloak I have no superior; *más vale migaja de rey, que merced de señor*, a king's crumb is better than a lord's bounty; (*día de*) *los Reyes*, Epiphany, Twelfth Night; *allá van leyes, do quieren reyes*, laws are made at the will of kings; *al que no tiene, el rey le hace libre*, if one hasn't the money, one can't pay; *con el rey en el cuerpo*, excessively overbearing; *a rey muerto, rey puesto*, things lost are soon replaced; *cual es el rey, tal la grey*, like king, like people; *ni quito ni pongo rey*, I have no part nor lot in the matter; *no conocer al rey por la moneda*, to be very poor; *no temer rey ni roque*, to fear nobody.

reyerta, *n.f.* difference, dispute, quarrel, wrangle.

reyezuelo, *n.m.* petty king; (*orn.*) kinglet.

rezado, *n.m.* prayer, divine service.

rezador, -ra, *n.m.f.* one who prays often.

rezagado, -da, *n.m.f.* straggler, one left behind, laggard, tramp.

rezagante, *n.m.* straggler, laggard.

rezagar, *v.t.* (*pret.* **rezagué**; *pres. subj.* **rezague**) to leave behind, put off, defer; to outstrip; to dally. — *v.r.* to straggle, remain behind, lag.

rezago, *n.m.* remainder, residue, balance.

rezar, *v.t.* (*pret.* **recé**; *pres. subj.* **rece**) to pray, read or say prayers; to say mass; to recite, quote; (*coll.*) to predict, announce; *v.i.* to grumble; to mutter; *rezar con*, to concern, behove.

rezno, *n.m.* the larva of the bot-fly; gadfly.

rezo, *n.m.* prayer, act of praying; devotions; divine office.

rezón, *n.m.* (*naut.*) grappling-iron, grapnel.

rezongador, -ra, *n.m.f.* grumbler, mutterer, growler.

rezongar, *v.i.* (*pret.* **rezongué**; *pres. subj.* **rezongue**) to murmur, mutter, grumble, growl.

rezonglón, -na; rezongón, -na, *n.m.f.*, *a.* grumbler, growler.

rezumadero, *n.m.* dripping-place; cesspool.

rezumarse, *v.r.* to run gently, leak, ooze, percolate; (*coll.*) to transpire.

ría, *n.f.* mouth of a river, estuary.

riacho, riachuelo, riatillo, *n.m.* rivulet, streamlet.

riada, *n.f.* inundation, flood, overflow.

riba, *n.f.* sloping bank, embankment.

ribaldería, *n.f.* ribaldry, wickedness, coarse abuse.

ribaldo, -da, *n.m.f.*, *a.* ribald, wicked, obscene; ruffian, coarse person.

ribazo, *n.m.* sloping ditch or bank, mound, hillock.

ribera, *n.f.* shore, bank, strand, beach.

ribereño, -ña, *a.* riparian.

riberiego, -ga, *a.* grazing on the banks of rivers.

ribero, *n.m.* bank of a dam, river-wall; levee.

ribes, *n.f.* currant-bush.

ribete, *n.m.* ribbon or tape sewn on edge of a cloth; border, seam, fringe; binding, galloon; between gamblers, interest charged for a loan. — *pl.* **ribetes,** (*fig.*) traces, signs; embellishment to a tale.

ribeteador, -ra, *n.m.f.*, *a.* (*sew.*) binder.

ribetear, *v.t.* to hem, border, fringe.

ricacho, -cha, *a.* (*coll.*) very rich.

ricadueña, ricafembra, ricahembra, *n.f.* lady, nobleman's wife or daughter.

ricamente, *adv.* richly, opulently, splendidly.

ricazo, -za, *a.* opulent, enormously rich.

ricial, *a.* growing again, green, new (pasture).

ricino, *n.m.* (*bot.*) Palma Christi, castor-oil plant.

rico, -ca, *a.* rich, opulent, wealthy; delicious, agreeable to the taste; delicate, exquisite, choice, select; abundant, plentiful; *rico o pinjado,* neck or nothing.

ricohombre, ricohome, *n.m.* grandee, peer of the ancient nobility of Castile.

ridículamente, *adv.* ridiculously, contemptibly.

ridiculez, *n.f.* ridicule; folly, extravagance, eccentricity, oddity; extreme sensibility.

ridiculizar, *v.t.* (conjugated like ALZAR) to ridicule, laugh at, burlesque, deride, mock at.

ridículo, -la, *a.* ridiculous; ludicrous, contemptible, despicable, laughable, eccentric, odd, queer, outlandish; absurd, strange.

ridículo, *n.m.* ridicule, mockery; hand-bag, reticule.

riego, *n.m.* irrigation.

riego ; riegue, *pres. indic.; pres. subj.* [REGAR].

riel, *n.m.* ingot; rail.

rielado, -da, *a.* reduced to ingots.

rielar, *v.i.* to shimmer, glimmer.

rielera, *n.f.* ingot-mould.

rienda, *n.f.* rein of a bridle; moderation, restraint. — *pl.* **riendas,** reins, ribbons; direction, government; *a rienda suelta,* loose-reined, swiftly, violently; *soltar la rienda,* to overstep the bounds, to give oneself to vice, to let oneself go; *tener las riendas,* to hold back a horse.

riente, *a.* smiling, laughing.

riesgo, *n.m.* danger, risk, peril, hazard, jeopardy.

rifa, *n.f.* scuffle, contest, dispute, wrangle; raffle, lottery.

rifador, *n.m.* raffler; disputer.

rifadura, *n.f.* splitting a sail.

rifar, *v.t.* to raffle. — *v.r.* to split a sail. — *v.i.* to quarrel, dispute.

rifeño, -ña, *n.m.f.*, *a.* from the Riff (in Morocco).

rifirrafe, *n.m.* hasty words; squabble.

rifle, *n.m.* rifle.

riflero, *n.m.* (*Arg., Chi.*) rifleman.

rigente, *a.* (*poet.*) rigid, rigescent.

rígidamente, *adv.* rigidly.

rigidez, *n.f.* rigidity, asperity, sternness; *rigidez cadavérica,* rigor mortis, the stiffening of the body following death.

rígido, -da, *a.* rigid, stiff; harsh, rigorous, severe, inflexible.

rigodón, *n.m.* rigadoon.

rigor, *n.m.* rigour; (*med.*) rigidity; inflexibility, precision, strictness, harshness, sternness, severity, vehemence, cruelty; (*med.*) chill, muscular rigidity; *ser de rigor,* to be indispensable; *en rigor,* to be precise.

rigorismo, *n.m.* rigorousness, austerity, severity.

rigorista, *n.m.f.*, *a.* rigorist.

rigorosamente, rigurosamente, *adv.* rigorously, severely, scrupulously, strictly.

rigüe, *n.m.* (*Hond.*) omelet made of the ears of green corn.

riguridad, *n.f.* (*Chi.*) rigor; sternness; (*med.*) rigidity.

rigurosidad, *n.f.* rigour, severity.

riguroso, -sa; rigoroso, -sa, *a.* rigorous, rigid, severe, harsh, austere, strict, exact, scrupulous.

rija, *n.f.* lachrymal fistula; quarrel, dispute, scuffle.

rijador, -ra, *a.* quarrelsome, litigious.

rijo, *n.m.* lust, sensuality.

rijo ; rija, *pres. indic.; pres. subj.* [REGIR].

rijoso, -sa, *a.* quarrelsome; restless at the sight of the female (horses); lustful, lewd.

rima, *n.f.* (*poet.*) rime, rhyme; heap, pile; *rima imperfecta,* (*poet.*) assonance.

rimado, -da, *a.* versified, rimed.

rimador, -ra, *n.m.f.* rhymer, versifier.

rimar, *v.t.*, *v.i.* to rhyme, compose verses.

rimbombancia, *n.f.* resonance, great noise; bombast, ostentation.

rimbombante, *a.* resounding; bombastic, highfalutin.

rimbombar, *v.i.* to resound, echo.

rimbombe, rimbombo, *n.m.* repercussion of sound.

rimero, *n.m.* heap, pile.

rimú, *n.m.* (*Chi.*) a plant of the Oxalis genus.

Rin, *n.m.* Rhine.

rincón, *n.m.* inside corner, angle, nook; remote place, private place, lurking-place; (*coll.*) dwelling house.

rinconada, *n.f.* corner.

rinconcillo, *n.m.* small corner.

rinconera, *n.f.* corner-table, corner-cupboard.

rinconera, -ra, *a.* transverse, athwart (honeycomb).

rindo, rinda, el rindió, *pres. indic., pres. subj., pret.* [RENDIR].

ringla, *n.f.; ringle,* *n.m.; ringlera,* *n.f.* row, file, line, tier, series.

ringlero, *n.m.* line for writing.

ringorrango, *n.m.* (*coll.*) flourish of the pen; frill, frippery, extravagant affectation in dress.

rinoceronte, *n.m.* rhinoceros.

rinoplastia, *n.f.* (*surg.*) rhinoplasty.

riña, *n.f.* quarrel, scuffle, dispute, fray; *riña de por San Juan, paz para todo el año,* bitter enemies make firm friends.

riño ; riña ; él riñó, *pres. indic.; pres. subj.; pret.* [REÑIR].

riñón, *n.m.* kidney; (*arch.*) spandrel; (*min.*) nodule, kidney ore; central point of a country; *tener cubierto el riñón,* to be rich.

riñonada, *n.f.* dish of kidneys.

río, *n.m.* river, stream, flood; *a río revuelto,* in confusion, in disorder; *a río revuelto, ganancia de pescadores,* much profit may be reaped from confusion; *cuando el río suena, agua lleva*, all rumours have some foundation; *no crece el río con agua limpia*, riches honestly come by come slowly.

río, yo ría, *v.i. pres. indic., pres. subj.* REIR.

riolada, *n.f.* assembly, collection, concourse, affluence.

rioplatense, *a.* of or from the River Plate.

riostra, *n.f.* (*arch.*) brace, truss, strut, spur.

riostrar, *v.t.* to brace, stay.

ripia, *n.f.* shingle for roofing.

ripiar, *v.t.* to fill up chinks of a wall.

ripio, *n.m.* remainder, residue; rubbish, debris; word used to fill up a line of verse; useless word; verbiage; *no perder ripio*, to miss no chance; *dar ripio a la mano*, to give easily and abundantly.

riqueza, *n.f.* riches, opulence, wealth; excellence, abundance; fertility, fruitfulness; gorgeousness.

risa, *n.f.* laugh, laughter; pleasant emotion; sneer, ridicule; *caerse de risa*, to split one's sides with laughing; *comerse de risa*, to repress, contain one's laughter; *morirse de risa*, to laugh heartily; *retozar la risa*, to try to restrain one's laughter.

risada, *n.f.* horse-laugh, burst of laughter.

riscal, *n.m.* cliffy, craggy place.

risco, *n.m.* steep rock; honey fritter.

riscoso, -sa, *a.* steep, rocky, craggy.

risibilidad, *n.f.* risibility.

risible, *a.* risible, ludicrous, laughable.

risiblemente, *adv.* laughably.

risica, -illa, -ita, *n.f.* feigned laugh, giggle, titter.

riso, *n.m.* (*poet.*) gentle laugh.

risotada, *n.f.* loud laugh, horse-laugh.

ríspido, -da, *a.* rough, rugged, harsh.

ristra, *n.f.* string of onions or garlic; row, file; string.

ristre, *n.m.* lance-rest.

ristrel, *n.m.* (*arch.*) wooden moulding.

risueño, -ña, *a.* smiling, pleasing, agreeable.

¡rita! *interj.* word used to call sheep.

rítmico, -ca, *a.* rhythmical.

ritmo, *n.m.* rhythm.

rito, *n.m.* rite, ceremony.

ritual, *n.m., a.* ritual, ceremonial.

ritualidad, *n.f.* ritualism.

ritualismo, *n.m.* ritualism.

ritualista, *n.m.f., a.* ritualist.

rival, *n.m.* rival, competitor.

rivalidad, *n.f.* rivalry, emulation, competition.

rivalizar, *v.i.* (*pret.* **rivalicé**; *pres. subj.* **rivalice**) to vie with, rival, compete.

rivera, *n.f.* brook, stream.

riza, *n.f.* stubble; destruction, desolation, ravage.

rizado, *n.m.* crimp, frizzle.

rizador, *n.m.* curling-iron; (*sew.*) **ruffler.**

rizar, *v.t.* (*pret.* **ricé**; *pres. subj.* **rice**) to curl, plait, frizzle, to flute, corrugate, crinkle; to ripple (of water). — *v.r.* to curl naturally.

rizo, *n.m.* (*aer.*) loop, looping the loop.

rizo, -za, *a.* naturally curled.

rizo, *n.m.* curling, curl, frizzle, ringlet, crimpling; cut velvet; *tomar rizos*, to take in reefs.

rizófago, -ga, *a.* (*zool.*) root-eating.

rizoma, *n.m.* (*bot.*) rhizome.

rizoso, -sa, *a.* naturally curly.

ro, ro, *interj.* used as a lullaby.

roa, *n.f.* (*naut.*) stem.

roán, *n.m.* Rouen linen.

roano, -na, *a.* sorrel, roan (horse).

rob, *n.m.* (*pharm.*) rob; fruit jelly.

robada, *n.f.* a land measure ($\frac{1}{4}$ acre).

robadera, *n.f.* (*agric.*) levelling harrow.

robado, -da, *a.* robbed.

robador, -ra, *n.m.f.* robber, thief.

robaliza, *n.f.* female of the *róbalo.*

róbalo, robalo, *n.m.* haddock.

robar, *v.t.* to rob, plunder, steal, despoil, pillage, thieve, rifle, strip; purloin, abduct; to sweep away; to eat away (as land by a river); in some card games, to draw; to take the honeycomb after removing the bees.

robellón, *n.m.* an edible mushroom.

robezo, *n.m.* wild goat.

robín, *n.m.* rust of metal.

robinia, *n.f.* locust-tree.

robla, *n.f.* ancient pasturage fee.

robladero, -ra, *a.* made to be riveted.

robladura, *n.f.* clinching, riveting.

roblar, *v.t.* to clinch, rivet, make strong.

roble, *n.m.* oak-tree, oak-wood; (*fig.*) very strong person or thing.

robleda, *n.f.* oak-grove.

robledal, robledo, *n.m.* plantation of oak-trees.

roblizo, -za, *a.* oaken; hard, strong.

roblón, *n.m.* rivet; ridge of tiles.

robo, *n.m.* theft, robbery, plunder; cards drawn; drawing of cards; a grain measure (6 gallons 2 pints).

roboración, *n.f.* corroboration, strengthening.

roborante, *a.* corroborant; (*med.*) roborant.

roborar, *v.t.* to corroborate; confirm, strengthen, give strength.

roborativo, -va, *a.* corroborative.

robra, *n.f.* treat or tip given at the conclusion of a deal; (*law*) deed.

robre, *n.m.* oak.

robredo, *n.m.* oak grove or wood.

robustamente, *adv.* robustly.

robustecer, *v.t.* (conjugated like MERECER) to make strong, robust.

robustez, *n.f.* robustness, hardiness, lustiness, strength.

robusto, -ta, *a.* robust, strong, vigorous, hale.

roca, *n.f.* rock, cliff, stone, boulder.

rocada, *n.f.* quantity of wool or cotton wound on the distaff.

rocadero, *n.m.* distaff-knob.

rocador, *n.m.* distaff-head.

rocalla, *n.f.* chippings of stone; riprap; glass beads.

rocalloso, -sa, *a.* rocky.

rocambola, *n.f.* (*bot.*) leek.

rocambor, *n.m.* (*Am.*) card game, kind of ombre.

roce, *n.m.* friction, rubbing, attrition; familiarity, intercourse.

rociada, *n.f.* sprinkling, aspersion, scattering; shower of missiles; (*naut.*) spray, squall; dew on plants; dew-drenched herbs given to animals as medicine; slander, aspersion; rough rebuke.

rociado, -da, *a.* dewy, bedewed.

rociador, *n.m.* sprinkler, sprayer.

rociadura, *n.f.* sprinkling.

rociadera, *n.f.* watering can, sprinkler.

rociamiento, *n.m.* sprinkling, bedewing.

rociar, *v.i.* to fall in dew. — *v.t.* to sprinkle,

strew, scatter; to slander; to gratify a gambler for money lent.

rocín, *n.m.* hack, jade; working horse; coarse, ignorant man, lout, clown; *ir de rocín en rocín,* to go from bad to worse.

rocinal, *a.* belonging to a hack.

rocinante, *m.* sorry hack.

rocino, *n.m.* hack, jade.

rocío, *n.m.* dew; spray, sprinkling; slight shower, drizzle, mizzle, spoondrift.

roción, *n.m.* (*naut.*) breaker (sea).

rococó, *a.* rococo.

rocote, *n.m.* (*Am.*) kind of capsicum; pepper.

rocha, *n.f.* ground clear of brambles.

rochela, *n.f.* (*Col., Ven.*) disorder, great noise.

rocho, *n.m.* roc, a fabulous bird.

roda, *n.f.* (*naut.*) stem.

rodaballo, *n.m.* (*ichth.*) turbot, flounder.

rodada, *n.f.* rut, cart-track, wheel-track.

rodadero, -ra, *a.* rolling or wheeling easily.

rodadizo, -za, *a.* easily rolled round.

rodado, -da, *a.* dapple, dappled, roan (of horses); round, fluent, easy (period); (*min.*) scattered fragments of ore; (*Arg., Chi.*) vehicle; *venir rodado,* to attain an end by chance.

rodador, *n.m.* roller; a S. American mosquito; sunfish.

rodador, -ra, *a.* rolling, rolling down.

rodadura, *n.f.* rolling; rut; tread of a wheel.

rodaja, *n.f.* small wheel or disk; rowel of a spur; castor; jagging iron; bookbinder's tool.

rodaje, *n.m.* wheelworks, set of wheels; tax on vehicles.

rodal, *n.m.* place, spot, seat.

rodalán, *n.m.* (*Chi.*) plant of the Anagraceæ family.

Ródano, *n.m.* Rhone.

rodante, *a.* rolling.

rodapelo, *n.m.* rubbing against the grain; (*coll.*) scuffle, affray.

rodapié, *n.m.* mopboard; foot rail; fringe, dado, skirting.

rodaplancha, *n.f.* main ward of a key.

rodar, *v.i.* (*pres. indic.* **ruedo;** *pres. subj.* **ruede**) to roll, revolve, gyrate, rotate, wheel; to wander about; to run on wheels; to be tossed about, go about; to lose a job; to abound; to follow, succeed one another; (*cinema*) to shoot a scene, to film; to project a film; *¡ruede la bola!* let things alone.

Rodas, *n.f.* Rhodes.

rodeabrazo, (a), *adv.* swinging the arm for a throw.

rodeado, -da, *a.* surrounded, encircled.

rodeador, -ra, *n.m.f.* roller, wrapper, that which surrounds.

rodear, *v.i.* to encompass, go round, encircle, enclose, environ, girdle; to lose a job; happen by chance. — *v.t.* to wrap up, girdle, circle, compass; (*mil.*) to invest; to turn round, whirl about; to drive, impel; (*Arg., Col., Cub., Chi., Mex.*) to round up, gather cattle in a rodeo; to make a detour; to take the longer road.

rodela, *n.f.* round shield, buckler.

rodelero, *n.m.* soldier bearing a buckler.

rodenal, *n.m.* spinney of red pines.

**rodeno, *n.m.,* *a.* red, reddish (earth, rock, etc.); kind of porous stone.

rodeo, *n.m.* winding, turn; roundabout course,

method or way; round up, rodeo; enclosure for cattle, stockyard, corral; protraction, delay, tedious method; evasion, subterfuge, circumlocution; cattle-market.

rodeón, *n.m.* complete winding or rolling round.

rodera, *n.f.* rut, cart-track.

rodero, -ra, *a.* relating to wheels.

rodero, *n.m.* collector of pasturage fee.

Rodesia, *n.f.* Rhodesia.

rodete, *n.m.* roundlet of platted hair; padded ring for carrying loads on the head; ward of a lock; circle iron of a carriage; drum for an endless belt; horizontal water wheel.

rodezno, *n.m.* cogwheel; (*hyd.*) turbine.

rodezuela, *n.f.* tiny wheel.

ródico, -ca, *a.* (*chem.*) rhœadic.

rodilla, *n.f.* knee; ward in a lock; clout, dusting cloth; *de rodillas,* on one's knees; *a media rodilla,* on one knee; *hincar* (or *doblar*) *las rodillas,* to kneel down.

rodillada, *n.f.* push with the knee; kneeling position.

rodillazo, *n.m.* push with the knee.

rodillera, *n.f.* knee-cap, knee-guard, knee-patch; bagging of trousers at the knee; injury of the knees of horses.

rodillo, *n.m.* roll, roller, cylinder; rolling-pin, rolling-stone; road-roller, clod-crusher; (*print.*) inking-roller.

rodilludo, -da, *a.* having large knees.

rodio, *n.m.* (*chem.*) rhodium.

rodo, *n.m.* roller.

rododafne, *n.f.* rosebay, daphne.

rododendro, *n.m.* rhododendron.

rodomiel, *n.m.* rose-juice with honey.

rodrigar, *v.t.* (*pret.* **rodrigué;** *pres. subj.* **rodrigue**) to prop up vines.

rodrigazón, *n.m.* time for propping vines.

rodrigón, *n.m.* vine-prop; (*coll.*) old servant who waits upon ladies.

roedor, -ra, *n.m.f., a.* gnawer; detractor; *gusano roedor,* remorse. — *pl.* **roedores,** rodents.

roedura, *n.f.* gnawing, corrosion.

roela, *n.f.* button of crude silver or gold.

roer, *v.t.* (*defect.*) (*pres. part.* **royendo;** *pres. indic.* **roo;** *pret.* **él royó;** *pres. subj.* **roa**) to gnaw, corrode, eat away, fret away; to detract, backbite; to harass, molest.

roete, *n.m.* medicinal pomegranate wine.

rogación, *n.f.* request, petition. — *pl.* **rogaciones,** litany, rogation.

rogador, -ra, *n.m.f.* supplicant, petitioner.

rogar, *v.t.* (*pres. indic.* **ruego;** *pret.* **rogué;** *pres. subj.* **ruegue**) to pray, implore, entreat, request, beg; to court, crave.

rogativa, *n.f.* supplication, prayer; (*eccles.*) rogation.

rogativo, -va, *a.* supplicatory.

rogatorio, -ria, *a.* rogatory.

rogo, *n.m.* fire, pyre.

roído, -da, *a.* gnawed, corroded; penurious, despicable.

rojal, *a.* reddish, ruddy (earth, plants, etc.).

rojear, *v.i.* to redden; to blush.

rojete, *n.m.* rouge.

rojez, rojeza, *n.f.* redness.

rojizo, -za, *a.* reddish, ruby, rubicund.

rojo, -ja, *a.* red, ruby, ruddy, reddish, crimson; (*polit.*) red, revolutionary; *rojo alambrado,* bright red; *al rojo,* at (or to) red heat.

rojura, *n.f.* redness, ruddiness.

rol, *n.m.* roll, catalogue, list; (*naut.*) muster-roll.

rolar, *v.i.* (*naut.*) to veer around.

roldana, *n.f.* (*naut.*) sheave; pulley-wheel; caster.

rolde, *n.m.* (*prov.*) circle, knot of persons.

rolla, *n.f.* collar of draught-horse; (*Col.*) nurse.

rollar, *v.t.* to roll; to wrap; to twist.

rollete, *n.m.* small roller.

rollizo, -za, *a.* plump, robust, round.

rollizo, *n.m.* log.

rollo, *n.m.* roller, rouleau; rolling-pin; log; yoke-pad; column of stone, round stone, round pillar; (*law*) roll.

rollón, *n.m.* fine bran.

rollona, *n.f.* (*coll.*) nurse.

Roma, *n.f.* Rome. *Cuando a Roma fueres, haz como vieres*, do in Rome as the Romans do.

romadizarse, *v.r.* to catch cold, have a catarrh, hay-fever.

romadizo, *n.m.* catarrh, hay-fever.

romana, *n.f.* steelyard; *hacer romana*, to balance, equipoise; *venir a la romana*, to be just weight.

romanador, *n.m.* weigh-master.

romanar, *v.t.* to weigh with a steelyard.

romance, *a.* Romanic, Romance. — *n.m.* Spanish language; romance, tale of chivalry; historic ballad, short lyric poem; poem in octosyllabic metre with alternate assonance; *hablar en romance*, to speak out, speak plainly; *en buen romance*, quite clearly. — *pl.* **romances**, excuses; babble, prattle.

romancear, *v.t.* to translate into the vulgar language; to periphrase.

romancero, *n.m.* collection of ballads or romances; romancer.

romancero, -ra, *a.* singing or composing romances or ballads; using evasions or subterfuges.

romancillo, *n.m.* short romance.

romancista, *n.m.* author who writes in the vernacular.

romancito, *n.m.* short romance.

romanear, *v.t.* to weigh with a steelyard; to shift part of the stowage. — *v.i.* to outweigh, preponderate.

romaneo, *n.m.* weighing with steelyard; (*naut.*) arranging the stowage.

romanero, *n.m.* weigh-master.

romanesco, *a.* Roman; novelistic.

romanía, (de), *adv.* crestfallen.

románico, -ca, *a.* Romanesque.

romanilla, *n.f.* (*Ven.*) dining-room screen.

romanillo, -lla, *a.* round-hand.

romanista, *n.m.* someone versed in Roman law.

romanizar, *v.t.* to Romanize, to Latinize. — *v.r.* to become Romanized or Latinized.

romano, -na, *a.* Roman, relating to Rome; tabby (cat); large peach; (*print.*) roman type; *a la romana*, in the Roman fashion.

románticamente, *adv.* romantically.

romanticismo, *n.m.* romanticism.

romántico, -ca, *a.* romantic.

romanza, *n.f.* (*mus.*) romance, romanza.

romanzar, *v.t.* to translate into the vernacular.

romanzón, *n.m.* long and tedious romance.

romaza, *n.f.* (*bot.*) sorrel.

rombal, *a.* rhombic.

rombo, *n.m.* rhomb; lozenge, diamond.

romboedro, *n.m.* (*geom.*) rhombohedron.

romboidal, *a.* rhomboidal.

romboide, *n.m.* (*geom.*) rhomboid.

romera, *n.f.* (*bot.*) rosemary-leaved cistus.

romeraje, *n.m.* pilgrimage.

romeral, *n.m.* place full of rosemary.

romería, *n.f.* pilgrimage; picnic, excursion.

romero, *n.m.* palmer, pilgrim; (*bot.*) rosemary; (*ichth.*) pilot-fish; whiting.

romí, romín, *n.m.* bastard-saffron.

romo, -ma, *a.* obtuse, blunt; flat-nosed. — *n.m.f.* henny.

rompecabezas, *n.m.* sling-shot; (*coll.*) difficult problem; jigsaw puzzle.

rompecoches, *n.m.* everlasting prunella.

rompedera, *n.f.* chisel for cutting hot iron; powder screen.

rompedero, -ra, *a.* brittle, easily broken.

rompedor, -ra, *n.m.f.* breaker, destroyer, crusher.

rompedura, *n.f.* fracture, rupture, break.

rompegalas, *n.m.* (*coll.*) slovenly person.

rompehielos, *n.m.* icebreaker (ship).

rompenueces, *n.m.* (*Am.*) nut-cracker.

rompeolas, *n.m.* breakwater, jetty, mole.

romper, *v.t.*, *v.i.*, *v.r.* (*pres. part.* **rompiendo**, *p.p.* **roto**), to break, force apart, cut asunder, dash, fracture, crash, smash, tear; to wear out; to penetrate, pierce; to begin, start; to dawn (the day); to plough land for the first time; to rout, defeat; to quarrel, fall out; to interrupt; to exceed; to break out, spring up; to infringe, violate; to resolve, determine; to sprout, bloom; *romper con alguno*, to fall out with someone; *de rompe y rasga*, open, free, undaunted. — *v.r.* to break; to acquire ease of manner; *romperse el alma*, to fall and hurt badly; to break one's neck.

rompesacos, *n.m.* long-spiked hardgrass.

rompesquinas, *n.m.* bully, corner loafer.

rompezargüelles, *n.m.* (*Am.*) an aromatic and medicinal plant.

rompible, *a.* breakable.

rompido, *n.m.* ground newly broken (*obs. p.p.* of ROMPER).

rompiente, *n.m.* (*naut.*) surge, surf, breakers; reef, shoal.

rompimiento, *n.m.* rupture, fracture, breaking, crack, cleft; first ploughing of land; break, dispute, rupture; dues paid to the parish for reopening a grave; (*theat.*) open drop scene; (*art*) opening in the background of a painting; (*min.*) drift, driftway.

rompopo, *n.m.* (*Hond.*) refreshing drink.

ron, *n.m.* rum.

ronca, *n.f.* threat, menace, brag, boast; kind of halberd; cry of a buck at rutting time; *echar roncas*, (*coll.*) to menace, threaten.

roncador, -ra, *n.m.f.* snorer; (*ichth.*) little bass.

roncadora, *n.f.* (*Arg., Bol., Ec.*) spur with large wheel.

roncamente, *adv.* hoarsely, vulgarly, coarsely.

roncar, *v.i.* (*pret.* **ronqué**; *pres. subj.* **ronque**) to snore; to roar; to cry in rutting time (buck); to brag, boast; to threaten.

ronce, *n.m.* blandiloquence, flattery.

roncear, *v.i.* to defer, protract, lag, use evasions; to wheedle; (*naut.*) to sail slowly.

roncería, *n.f.* sloth, laziness, tardiness; flattery; (*naut.*) sluggish sailing.

roncero, -ra, *a.* slothful, tardy; growling, snarling; wheedling, flattering.

ronco, -ca, *a.* hoarse, husky rough-voiced.

ronco, *n.m.* (*Cub.*) a fish of the Caribbean Sea.

roncón, *n.m.* drone of a bagpipe. — *a.* (*Col., Ven.*) bullying, boasting.

roncha, *n.f.* weal; bruise; loss of money by fraud; round slice.

ronchar, *v.t.* to chew something hard. — *v.i.* to make weals.

ronchón, *n.m.* large swelling.

ronda, *n.f.* round, night-patrol, beat; first three cards in a hand; clear space between a town and the ramparts; round of drinks; *coger la ronda a uno,* to catch someone in the act (of crime, etc.).

rondador, *n.m.* watchman, night-guard; roundsman, night wanderer; (*Ec.*) musical instrument (reed).

rondalla, *n.f.* fable, story.

rondar, *v.t., v.i.* to go round to prevent disorders; to serenade; to haunt, hover round; to impend, threaten; (*mil.*) to make the round of inspection.

rondel, *n.m.* (*poet.*) rondel.

rondeña, *n.f.* popular song and dance of Ronda.

rondí, rondiz, *n.m.* face or table of a precious stone.

rondín, *n.m.* corporal's rounds; watchmen in an arsenal.

rondó, *n.m.* rondo.

rondón, (de), *adv.* rashly, abruptly, intrepidly.

ronfea, *n.f.* broad and long sword.

rongigata, *n.f.* pinwheel.

ronquear, *v.i.* to be hoarse with cold.

ronquedad, *n.f.* hoarseness, roughness of voice.

ronquera, *n.f.* hoarseness.

ronquido, *n.m.* harsh, rough sound; snore.

ronquillo, -illa; -ito, -ita, *a.* slightly hoarse.

ronrón, *n.m.* (*Hond.*) kind of black scarab; child's toy.

ronronear, *v.i.* to purr (of a cat).

ronroneo, *n.m.* purr.

ronza, *n.f.* (*naut.*) to leeward.

ronzal, *n.m.* halter; (*naut.*) purchase rope.

ronzar, *v.t.* (*naut.*) to rouse; to haul; to chew hard things; to crunch.

roña, *n.f.* scab, mange, manginess; (*coll.*) craft; cunning, fraud; nastiness, filth, dirt; bark of pine-trees; rust; moral infection; (*coll.*) niggardly person.

roñada, *n.f.* (*naut.*) garland.

roñal, *n.m.* (*prov.*) bark depot or storage place.

roñería, *n.f.* craft, cunning; niggardliness, parsimony.

roñoso, -sa, *a.* scabby, leprous, diseased; dirty, nasty, filthy; crafty, wily; rusty; (*coll.*) mean, niggardly, parsimonious.

ropa, *n.f.* dry goods; cloth, clothes, wearing apparel; stuff, fabric; costume, dress; wardrobe, outfit, garments; robe or gown of office; *ropa blanca,* linen; *ropa de cámara,* morning gown; *ropa usada,* worn-out clothes, old clothes; *ropa vieja,* boiled and dressed meat; *a quema ropa,* point-blank; off one's guard; *palpar* (or *tentar*) *la ropa,* to be near death; *no tocar a la ropa,* to do no injury whatever; *tentarse la ropa,* to hesitate, be at a loss; *a toca ropa,* very near; *acomodar de ropa limpia a,* (*iron.*) to soil, dirty; *de poca ropa,* badly dressed *or* unworthy of great esteem; *nadar y guardar la ropa,* to proceed very cautiously.

ropaje, *n.m.* wearing apparel, clothes; robe, vestments; gown; garb; drapery.

ropavejería, *n.f.* frippery, old-clothes shop.

ropavejero, *n.m.* fripper, old-clothes man.

ropería, *n.f.* clothes-store; wardrobe, wardrobe-keeper.

ropero, *n.m.* vestiary, wardrobe-keeper; salesman; wardrobe, locker.

ropeta, *n.f.* short garment.

ropilla, *n.f.* doublet; *dar una ropilla* (*fig., coll.*) to give a friendly reproof.

ropón, *n.m.* loose over-gown; (*Chi.*) lady's riding habit.

roque, *n.m.* rook (in chess); *ni rey ni roque,* not a soul.

roqueda, *n.f.* rocky place.

roquedo, *n.m.* rock, boulder.

roqueño, -ña, *a.* rocky, full of rocks; hard, flinty.

roquero, -ra, *a.* rocky, situated on rocks.

roqués, *n.m.* black falcon.

roqueta, *n.f.* turret in a fortress.

roquete, *n.m.* (*eccles.*) rochet; barbed spearhead; (*artill.*) ramrod, rammer.

rorcual, *n.m.* rorqual (whale).

rorro, *n.m.* sucking-child.

ros, *n.m.* (*mil.*) Spanish shako.

rosa, *n.f.* rose; rose-colour; rose diamond; rosy appearance; rose-window; rosette; flower of saffron; *rosa náutica* or *rosa de los vientos,* rose of a mariner's compass.

rosáceo, -cea, *a.* rosaceous. — *n.f.pl.* **rosáceas,** Rosaceæ.

rosada, *n.f.* hoar-frost, rime.

rosado, -da, *a.* rosy, crimsoned, flushed; relating to or made up of roses; *agua rosada,* rose-water; *miel rosada,* honey of roses.

rosal, *n.m.* (*bot.*) rose-bush; *rosal castellano,* red rose; *rosal de cien hojas,* cabbage-rose; *rosal perruno,* dog-rose.

rosariero, *n.m.* maker and seller of rosaries.

rosario, *n.m.* rosary; prayers of a rosary; chain pump; (*coll.*) backbone; *acabar como el rosario de la aurora,* to break up in disorder.

rosbif, *n.m.* roast-beef.

rosca, *n.f.* screw and nut; screw-thread; twist, spiral, line or motion; circular badge of Spanish students; (*naut.*) flake of a cable; (*Chi.*) yoke-pad; *rosca de pan,* twisted loaf; *hacer la rosca* (*del galgo*) to lie down anywhere for a nap; *hacerle la rosca a,* flatter, wheedle.

roscar, *v.t.* to cut a screw-thread.

roscón, *n.m.* large screw; large loaf of round bread.

róseo, -sea, *a.* rosy, roseate.

roséola, *n.f.* (*med.*) roseola, German measles.

rosero, -ra, *n.m.f.* collector of saffron-flowers; (*Ec.*) dessert on Corpus Christi day.

roseta, *n.f.* shoe-tassel; rosette; bloom of the cheeks; hose or watering-pot rose; rose-shaped jewel.

rosetón, *n.m.* (*arch.*) rose-window; rosette.

rosicler, *n.m.* bright rose colour; rich ore; ruby silver.

rosillo, -illa, *a.* clear red; roan (horse).

rosmarino, -na, *a.* light red. — *n.m.* (*bot.*) rosemary.

rosmaro, *n.m.* manatee, sea-cow.

roso, -sa, *a.* red, rosy; threadbare; *a roso y velloso,* without distinction.

rosoli, *n.m.* Rosolio.

rosones, *n.m.pl.* worms in animals.

rosqueado, -da, *a.* twisted.

rosquete, *n.m.* ring-shaped fritter.

rosquilla, *n.f.* sweet ring-shaped fritter; vine-fretter; *no saber a rosquillas,* to have caused great pain.

rostrado, -da, *a.* rostrated.

rostral, *a.* rostral (column).

rostrico, rostrillo, *n.m.* veil, head-dress; small seed-pearl.

rostrituerto, -ta, *a.* showing anger in one's face.

rostro, *n.m.* rostrum; beak or prow of a war-galley; bird's beak; countenance, human face; *a rostro firme,* resolutely; *rostro a rostro,* face to face; *dar en rostro a uno alguna cosa,* to reproach one with something; *hacer rostro,* to face, resist; *más vale rostro bermejo, que corazón negro,* better be over-frank than over-secretive.

rota, *n.f.* (*mil.*) rout, defeat; (*naut.*) course; (*eccles.*) Rota; (*bot.*) rattan; *de rota* (*batida*), of a sudden; with total ruin.

rotación, *n.f.* rotation, revolution, circular motion; *rotación de cultivos,* rotation of crops.

rotamente, *adv.* barefacedly, impudently.

rotante, *a.* rolling, revolving.

rotar, *v.i.* to roll, revolve on an axis.

rotativo, -va, *a.* rotary. — *n.f.* rotary printing press; (*fig.*) the press.

rotatorio, -ria, *a.* rotatory.

roten, *n.m.* (*bot.*) rattan; rattan cane.

rotería, *n.f.* (*Chi.*) rabble.

roto, -ta, *a.* broken, destroyed, shattered, torn, chipped, pierced, battered; ragged; leaky; lewd, debauched, intemperate; (*Chi.*) individual of the lower orders; (*Arg., Per.*) contemptuous adjective applied to Chileans; (*Ec.*) half-breed of Spanish and Indian; (*Mex.*) common fop, low coxcomb. — *p.p. irreg.* [ROMPER]; *ser peor lo roto que lo descosido,* to be the greater of two evils.

rotonda, *n.f.* rotunda; back part of a coach.

rotoso, -sa *a.* (*Arg., Chi.*) torn; ragged, in tatters.

rótula, *n.f.* (*anat.*) rotula, knee-pan; (*pharm.*) troche, lozenge.

rotulación, *n.f.* labelling.

rotulador, -ra, *a.* labeller.

rotular, *v.t.* to label, inscribe, letter, title, ticket, mark, stamp, endorse.

rotulata, *n.f.* label, title, mark; collection of labels.

rótulo, *n.m.* label; show-bill, placard, poster; mark, inscription, lettering, heading, title; school rota.

rotunda, *n.f.* rotunda, round building.

rotundamente, *adv.* circularly; explicitly, categorically, roundly, positively.

rotundidad, *n.f.* roundness, rotundity, sphericity.

rotundo, -da, *a.* round, circular, rotund, spherical; plain, peremptory; full, sonorous.

rotura, *n.f.* rupture, fracture, breakage, crack; hernia; (*agric.*) breaking up ground; (*vet.*) plaster applied to wounds or hernias.

roturación, *n.f.* (*agric.*) breaking new ground.

roturar, *v.t.* (*agric.*) to break new ground.

roya, *n.f.* (*bot.*) rust, red blight, mildew.

royo, -ya, *a.* red.

roza, *n.f.* stubbing; clearing, grubbing up; ground cleared of briers.

rozadero, *n.m.* stubbing-place; (*mech.*) bearing-plate.

rozado, -da, *a.* stubbed, cleared; chilled, frappé (of a beverage).

rozador, -ra, *n.m.f.* stubber, weeder.

rozadura, *n.f.* friction; attrition; chafing, abrasion; gall; clashing, clash; (*bot.*) punk-knot.

rozagante, *a.* showy; haughty, arrogant, pompous, lofty; strapping.

rozamiento, *n.m.* friction; rubbing, clashing; disagreement.

rozar, *v.t.* (*pret.* **rocé;** *pres. subj.* **roce**) to stub up, clear the ground, grub up; to graze, scrape, browse, nibble; to gall, chafe. — *v.i.* to graze, rub. — *v.r.* to cut, strike; to treat familiarly; to stammer, falter; to have a resemblance or connexion; (*naut.*) to fret, gall.

roznar, *v.t.* to bray; to crack with the teeth, crunch.

roznido, *n.m.* braying; crunching noise.

rozno, *n.m.* little ass.

rozo, *n.m.* stubbing, weeding; chip of wood; brushwood.

rozón, *n.m.* short, broad and thick scythe.

rúa, *n.f.* village street; highroad.

ruán, *n.m.* printed cotton cloth made in Rouen (France).

ruana, *n.f.* (*Col., Ven.*) square and heavy poncho.

ruano, -na, *a.* prancing; round, circular; sorrel-coloured, roan (horse).

ruante, *a.* walking through the streets.

ruar, *v.i.* to ride or walk through the streets; to flirt, court in the street.

rubefacción, *n.f.* rubefaction.

rubefaciente, *a.* rubefying, rubefacient.

Rubén, *n.m.* Reuben.

rúbeo, -bea, *a.* ruby, reddish, ruddy.

rubéola, *n.f.* rubeola, German measles.

rubeta, *n.f.* toad.

rubí, *n.m.* ruby; red colour, redness of the lips.

rubia, *n.f.* (*bot.*) madder; (*ichth.*) small red river-fish.

rubial, *n.m.* madder-field. — *a.* reddish.

rubicán, *a.* applied to a horse or mare of white and reddish colour.

rubicela, *n.f.* reddish topaz.

rubicundez, *n.f.* blush, red colour; rubicundity, rubescence.

rubicundo, -da, *a.* red, rubicund; blonde, golden-red; rosy with health.

rubiera, *n.f.* (*Ven.*) mischief, tomfoolery; (*PR.*) merry-making, carousal.

rubificar, *v.t.* to rubefy, make red.

rubín, rubinejo, *n.m.* ruby.

rubio, -bia, *a.* red, reddish, ruddy; blonde, fair, golden.

rubio, *n.m.* (*ichth.*) red gurnard.

rubión, *a.* reddish (wheat).

rublo, *n.m.* rouble.

rubor, *n.m.* blush, flush; bashfulness, shame.

ruborizar, *v.t.* to make somebody blush. — *v.r.* to blush, to flush.

ruborosamente, *adv.* blushingly, bashfully.

ruboroso, -sa, *a.* shameful, bashful.

rúbrica, *n.f.* red mark; (*eccles.*) rubric; flourish to a signature; *de rúbrica,* (*coll.*) according to rule (*or* custom).

rubricante, *a.* signing, attesting; (*obs.*) junior minister.

rubricar, *v.t.* (*pret.* **rubriqué**; *pres. subj.* **rubrique**) to endorse, subscribe, sign, sign and seal.

rubriquista, *n.m.* rubrician.

rubro, -ra, *a.* red, reddish. — *n.m.* (*Am.*) rubric, title, chapter-heading.

ruc, *n.m.* roc, a fabulous bird.

ruca, *n.f.* (*Arg., Chi.*) Indian hut, cabin.

rucio, -cia, *a.* silver-grey (of horses); (*Col.*) grey-haired, hoary.

ruco, -ca, *a.* (*Cent. Am.*) old, worthless (especially norses).

ruchique, *n.m.* (*Hond.*) wooden saucer.

rucho, *n.m.* donkey.

ruda, *n.f.* (*bot.*) rue.

rudamente, *adv.* roughly, rudely.

rudeza, *n.f.* roughness, asperity, rudeness, grossness, coarseness.

rudimental, *a.* rudimental, rudimentary, embryonic, undeveloped, elementary, elemental.

rudimentario, -ria, *a.* rudimentary.

rudimento, *n.m.* beginning, rudiment, embryo, germ; vestige, element. — *pl.* **rudimentos**, rudiments, elements.

rudo, -da, *a.* rough, rude, unpolished; gross, churlish, coarse; hard, severe; stupid.

rueca, *n.f.* distaff; twist, winding; (*naut.*) fish of a mast or yard.

rueda, *n.f.* wheel; castor, roller; (*ichth.*) sunfish; peacock's spread tail; circle of people; crowd; round slice; turn, succession, time; wheel (for torture); hoop for a skirt; three-handed billiard game; *hacer la rueda a*, to coax, cajole, flatter; *clavar la rueda de la fortuna*, to make one's fortunes secure; *tragárselas como ruedas de molino*, to be excessively credulous; *rueda catalina*, Catherine wheel; *rueda de andar*, treadmill; *rueda de presos*, identification parade.

ruedecica, -cilla, -cita, -zuela, *n.f.* small wheel; caster, roller.

ruedo, *n.m.* rotation, turn; circumference; circuit; edge of a wheel or disc; bull-ring; selvage, border; bass-mat, plat; skirt-lining; *a todo ruedo*, at all events.

ruedo; ruede, *pres. indic.; pres. subj.* [RODAR].

ruego, *n.m.* prayer, request, petition, entreaty, supplication.

ruego, ruegue, *pres. indic., pres. subj.* [ROGAR].

ruejo, *n.m.* mill-wheel; ground-roller.

ruello, *n.m.* (*prov.*) ground-roller.

rufián, *n.m.* ruffian; pimp, procurer, pander.

rufiana, *n.f.* bawd, procuress.

rufiancete, rufiancillo, *n.m.* little pimp.

rufianear, *v.t.* to pander, pimp.

rufianería, *n.f.* ruffianism.

rufianesco, -ca, *a.* ruffianly, ruffianish. — *n.f.* ruffians collectively.

rufo, -fa, *a.* carroty, red-haired; frizzed, curled.

ruga, *n.f.* wrinkle; corrugation; fault.

rugar, *v.t.* to wrinkle.

rugible, *a.* capable of roaring.

rugido, *n.m.* roar; rumbling (of bowels).

rugiente, *a.* bellowing, roaring.

ruginoso, -sa, *a.* rusty, covered with rust.

rugir, *v.i.* (*pres. indic.* **rujo**; *pres. subj.* **ruja**) to roar, bawl, bellow, halloo, howl. — *v. impers.* to be whispered about, leak out, transpire.

rugosidad, *n.f.* rugosity.

rugoso, -sa, *a.* rugose; corrugated.

ruibarbo, *n.m.* rhubarb.

ruido, *n.m.* noise; clamour, din, clatter, outcry, murmur; report, rumour; difference, dispute; lawsuit.

ruidosamente, *adv.* noisily; loudly.

ruidoso, -sa, *a.* noisy, clamorous, loud, obstreperous.

ruin, *a.* vile, despicable, mean; wicked, low, base, malicious; poor, worthless, wretched, humble; little, puny; avaricious, covetous; insidious, treacherous, infamous; vicious (of animals). — *n.m.* small nerve in the tip of a cat's tail; *un ruin ido, otro venido*, one ill coming after another; *ruin sea quien por ruin se tiene*, wretched be he that holds himself so.

ruina, *n.f.* ruin, fall, overthrow, downfall, destruction, decline. — *pl.* **ruinas**, ruins, debris.

ruinar, *v.t., v.r.* to ruin, destroy.

ruindad, *n.f.* meanness, malice, baseness, humility, covetousness.

ruinmente, *adv.* basely, meanly.

ruinoso, -sa, *a.* ruinous, worthless, destructive, baneful.

ruipóntico, *n.m.* kind of rhubarb, pie-plant.

ruiseñor, *n.m.* (*orn.*) nightingale.

rujiada, *n.m.* (*prov.*) heavy shower; (*fig.*) reprimand.

rular, *v.i.* (*vulg.*) to roll.

ruleta, *n.f.* roulette.

rulo, *n.m.* ball, bowl; stone in oil-mills, road-roller; (*Chi.*) unwatered land.

ruló, *n.m.* (*print.*) inking roller; brayer.

ruma, *n.f.* (*Arg., Chi., Ec.*) heap, pile, mass.

rumano, -na, *n., a.* Rumanian.

rumba, *n.m.* (*Am.*) rumba.

rumbada, *n.f.* wale of a row galley.

rumbar, *v.i.* (*prov.*) to be pompous, magnificent; (*Col.*) to buzz, to hum; (*Chi.*) to find one's bearings. — *v.t.* (*Hond.*) to throw, cast, fling.

rumbatela, *n.f.* (*Cub., Mex.*) feast, splendid repast, revel.

rumbático, -ca, *a.* pompous, splendid, liberal.

rumbeador, *n.m.* (*Arg.*) guide.

rumbear, *v.i.* (*Arg.*) to find one's bearings; (*Cub.*) to carouse, revel.

rumbo, *n.m.* course, direction, bearing; road, route, way; (*coll.*) pomp, ostentation, show; generosity, liberality; (*naut.*) scuttle; (*her.*) rustre; (*Guat.*) revel, carousal; (*Col.*) small humming bird; *abatir el rumbo*, to fall to leeward; *con rumbo a*, in the direction of, heading for; *hacer rumbo a*, to sail for.

rumbón, -na, *a.* (*coll.*) liberal; pompous, magnificent.

rumbosamente, *adv.* (*coll.*) grandly, liberally, pompously.

rumboso, -sa, *a.* pompous, splendid, liberal, magnificent.

rumí, *a.* appellative given to the Christians by the Moors.

rumia, *n.f.* rumination, chewing the cud.

rumiador, -ra, *n.m.f., a.* ruminator, ruminant.

rumiadura, *n.f.* rumination.

rumiante, *a.* ruminant; reflecting, musing. — *n.m.pl.* **rumiantes**, Ruminantia.

rumiar, *v.t.* to ruminate; to meditate, muse.

rumión, -na, *a.* greatly ruminating.

rumo, *n.m.* first hoop of a cask.

rumor, *n.m.* rumour, report, murmur, hearsay; sound of voices.

rumoroso, -sa, *a.* causing rumours.

rumpiata, *n.f.* (*Chi.*) a shrub of the Sapindaceæ family.

runa, *n.f.* rune, runic character.

runcho, *n.m.* (*Col.*) a kind of opossum.

rundún, *n.m.* (*Arg.*) a very small hummingbird; (*Arg.*) a child's toy.

runfla, runflada, *n.f.* series, number, succession of things.

rúnico, -ca; runo, -na, *a.* runic.

runrún, *n.m.* (*coll.*) rumour, report; (*Arg., Chi.*) rattle; horn call; (*Chi.*) a wading-bird.

ruña, ruñadera, *n.f.* croze.

ruñar, *v.t.* to croze.

rupia, *n.f.* rupee; (*med.*) rupia.

rupicabra, *n.f.* chamois-goat.

ruptura, *n.f.* rupture.

rural, *a.* rural, rustic, of the country.

ruralmente, *adv.* rurally.

rurrupata, *n.f.* (*Chi.*) lullaby.

rus, *n.m.* (*bot.*) sumach.

rusco, -ca, *a.* rude, froward, peevish.

rusco, *n.m.* (*bot.*) butcher's-broom.

rusel, *n.m.* a kind of woollen serge.

Rusia, *n.f.* Russia; (*Cub.*) coarse canvas used for hammocks; *piel de Rusia*, Russian leather.

rusiente, *a.* reddish, becoming red-hot.

ruso, -sa, *n.m.f., a.* Russian.

rústica, (en), paper-covered, unbound (of a book).

rusticación, *n.f.* rustication.

rustical, *a.* rustic, rural, wild.

rústicamente, *adv.* rustically, rudely.

rusticano, -na, *a.* wild (of plants).

rusticar, *v.t.* (*pret.* **rustiqué**; *pres. subj.* **rustique**) to rusticate.

rusticidad, *n.f.* rusticity, rudeness, clumsiness.

rústico, -ca, *n.m.f.* rustic, peasant. — *a.* rustic, rural, coarse, clumsy; clownish, unmannerly.

rustiquez, rustiqueza, *n.f.* rusticity.

rustir, *v.t.* to toast; to fry; (*Ven.*) to bear, endure.

ruta, *n.f.* route, itinerary.

rutenio, *n.m.* (*chem.*) ruthenium.

rutilante, *a.* brilliant, flashing.

rutilar, *v.i.* (*poet.*) to radiate, shine, glitter, twinkle.

rútilo, -la, *a.* shining, sparkling.

rutina, *n.f.* routine, custom, habit, rut.

rutinario, -ria, *n.m.f., a.* routine; one who acts by routine.

rutinero, -ra, *a.* of routine, routinist.

ruzafa, *n.f.* garden, park.

S

S, s, twenty-second letter of the Spanish alphabet.

sábado, *n.m.* Saturday; sabbath.

sabalar, *n.m.* net for catching shad.

saballera, *n.f.* fire-grate of a furnace; a kind of fishing net.

sabalero, *n.m.* shad-fisher.

sábalo, *n.m.* (*ichth.*) shad.

sábana, *n.f.* sheet of a bed; altar-cloth; *pegársele a uno las sábanas*, to rise late.

sabana, *n.f.* (*Am.*) savanna, treeless large plain, stretch of level ground.

sabandija, *n.f.* grub, insect, vermin; (*fig.*) small, deformed person.

sabanero, *n.m.* (*Am.*) herdsman of the *sabanas;* dweller on the *sabanas;* bird resembling the starling; *n.f.* (*Ven.*) savanna snake.

sabanilla, *n.f.* small sheet; napkin; kerchief; altar-cloth; (*Chi.*) bedspread, coverlet.

sabañón, *n.m.* chilblain; *comer como un sabañón*, to devour, eat greedily.

sabara, *n.f.* (*Ven.*) very light fog.

sabatario, -ria, *a.* sabbatarian.

sabático, -ca, *a.* sabbatical.

sabatina, *n.f.* divine service of Saturday; (*Chi.*) flogging, drubbing.

sabatino, -na, *a.* sabbatine.

sabedor, -ra, *n.m.f.* learned person, one who knows.

saber, *v.t.* (*pres. indic.* **sé**; *pret.* **supe**; *fut. indic.* **sabré**; *pres. subj.* **sepa**) to know, be cognisant of; to be able, have ability, be learned, be knowing; to experience; to master; to be acquainted with. — *v.i.* to taste of; to be very sagacious; to resemble; to look alike; to control oneself; *saber al dedillo*, to have at one's finger tips, *or* to know A from Z; *saber de buena tinta*, to know on good authority; *saber a qué atenerse*, to know how to go on; *saber mucho latín*, to be very prudent and sagacious; *saber con puntualidad*, to know exactly; *saber de qué pie cojea uno*, to know a person's weak points; *el que las sabe, las tañe*, let a man speak only of what he understands; *más vale saber que haber*, knowledge is better than wealth; *no saber cuántas son cinco*, to be a great fool; *a saber*, to wit, that is to say; *no saber de sí*, to have no time to attend even to one's own concerns; *no saber lo que tiene*, not to know one's own wealth.

saber, *n.m.* learning, knowledge, lore.

sabiamente, *adv.* wisely, knowingly, sagely.

sabicú, *n.m.* (*Cub.*) (*bot.*) sabicu, horseflesh mahogany.

sabidilla, *n.f.* blue-stocking.

sabidillo, -lla, *n.m.f., a.* little pedant, know-all.

sabido, -da, *a.* well-informed, learned.

sabiduría, *n.f.* learning, knowledge, sapience, wisdom.

sabiendas, (a), *adv.* knowingly, wittingly, consciously.

sabiente, *a.* sapient, knowing.

sabihondez, *n.f.* (*coll.*) deceptive sagacity, affectation of knowledge.

sabihondo, -da, *n.m.f., a.* sciolist, one who claims to have great learning; know-all.

sabina, *n.f.* (*bot.*) savin.

sabinar, *n.m.* clump of savins.

sabio, -bia, *a.* sage, wise, learned, sapient, knowing, cunning. — *n.m.f.* sage, wise person; scholar, learned person; scientist.

sablazo, *n.m.* sabre-stroke; (*coll.*) borrowing or sponging.

sable, *n.m.* sabre, cutlass; (*Cub.*) a long, flat silvery fish. — *a.* (*her.*) sable, black.

sablista, *n.m.* sponger, one who asks small loans.

sablón, *n.m.* coarse sand.

saboga, *n.f.* shad.

sabogal, *n.m.* shad-catching net.

saboneta, *n.f.* hunting-case watch, hunter.

sabor, *n.m.* relish, savour, smack, flavour, taste; pleasure, dash, zest; *a sabor*, at pleasure; *sabor local*, local colour. — *pl.* **sabores**, round knobs on a horse's bit.

saboreamiento, *n.m.* relish, relishing.

saborear, *v.t.* to flavour; to give a zest; to wheedle, cajole; to interest. — *v.r.* to be delighted, glad, pleased; to relish, enjoy, find delicious.

saboreo, *n.m.* relish, flavour, zest.

saborete, *n.m.* slight flavour or taste.

sabotaje, *n.m.* sabotage.

sabotear, *v.t.* to sabotage.

saboyana, *n.f.* open skirt; paste or pie.

saboyano, -na, *n.m.f., a.* Savoyard.

sabrosamente, *adv.* pleasantly, deliciously.

sabroso, -sa, *a.* savoury, palatable, tasty; delicious, delightful, pleasant; salted, saltish.

sabucal, sabugal, *n.m.* clump of elders.

sabuco, sabugo, *n.m.* eldertree [SAÚCO].

sabueso, *n.m.* hound; (*fig.*) investigator, detective.

sábulo, *n.m.* gravel, coarse sand.

sabuloso, -sa, *a.* sabulous, sandy, gritty, gravelly.

saca, *n.f.* sack, bag; exportation; extraction, drawing out; mail-bag; authorized copy of a bill of sale; *estar de saca,* to be on sale, (*coll.*) to be ready for marriage (said of women).

sacabalas, *n.m.* bullet-extractor.

sacabocado(s), *n.m.* hollow punch.

sacabotas, *n.m.* boot-jack.

sacabrocas, *n.m.* tack-drawer, pincers.

sacabuche, *n.m.* (*mus.*) sackbut; sackbut-player; (*naut.*) hand pump; nincompoop.

sacacorchos, *n.m.* corkscrew.

sacada, *n.f.* district separated from a province.

sacadilla, *n.f.* a restricted battue.

sacadinero(s), *n.m.* (*coll.*) catch-penny.

sacador, -ra, *n.m.f.* extractor, drawer; (*print.*) delivery table.

sacadura, *n.f.* sloping cut; (*Chi.*) taking out, extracting.

sacafilásticas, *n.f.* (*artill.*) gun-spike, priming-wire.

sacaliña, *n.f.* trick, cunning.

sacamanchas, *n.m.* cleaner, one who takes spots out of clothes.

sacamantas, *n.m.* (*coll.*) tax-collector.

sacamiento, *n.m.* taking out, drawing out.

sacamolero, sacamuelas, *n.m.* tooth-drawer, dentist.

sacanabo, *n.m.* (*artill.*) bomb extractor (from mortar).

sacanete, *n.m.* lansquenet; a card game.

sacapelotas, *n.m.* bullet-screw.

sacapotras, *n.m.* bad surgeon.

sacar, *v.t.* (*pret.* **saqué;** *pres. subj.* **saque**) to take out, pull out, pick out, bring out, bring forth, draw out; extract, remove, eradicate, extort; to imitate, copy; to dispossess; to exclude; to manufacture, invent, produce; to deduce; to free, place in safety; to investigate, discover; to interpret, solve; to get, obtain, attain; to manifest, exhibit, show; to excite passion or anger; to ballot, elect by ballot, draw lots; to win at play; to name, quote, cite; *sacar a luz,* to exhibit, print, publish, bring out; *sacar a la vergüenza,* to place in the pillory, to bring shame upon; *sacar apodos,* to call nicknames; *sacar agua,* to draw water; *sacar en claro* (or *en limpio*), to clear up all doubts, come to a conclusion; *sacar la cara,* to be an interested party; *sacar la espina,* to remove the root of an evil; *sacar fruto,* to reap the fruits of one's labours; *sacar de madre,* to make one lose patience; *sacar de pañales,* to relieve one's misery;

sacar de pila, to stand sponsor; *sacar el pecho,* to stand up and defend.

sacarímetro, *n.m.* saccharimeter.

sacarina, *n.f.* saccharine.

sacarino, -na, *a.* saccharine.

sacasebo, *n.m.* (*Cub.*) fodder plant.

sacasillas, *n.m.* (*theat.*) stage hand; (*fig.*) busybody.

sacatapón, *n.m.* corkscrew.

sacate, *n.m.* (*Mex.*) grass, herb, hay.

sacatinta, *n.m.* (*Cent. Am.*) shrub giving a dye.

sacatrapos, *n.m.* (*artill.*) wad hook, wormer.

sacaxquihuite, *n.m.* (*Mex.*) sapindaceous plant of the lowlands (*Cupania*).

sacayán, *n.m.* (*Philip.*) small boat.

sacerdocio, *n.m.* priesthood, ministry.

sacerdotal, *a.* sacerdotal.

sacerdote, *n.m.* priest, clergyman.

sacerdotisa, *n.f.* priestess.

saciable, *a.* satiable, that may be satisfied.

saciar, *v.t.* to satiate, cloy; to gratify desire.

saciedad, *n.f.* satiety.

saciña, *n.f.* (*bot.*) kind of willow.

sacio, -a, *a.* satiate, satiated.

saco, *n.m.* sack, bag; sackful, bagful; coarse stuff or dress; heap; pillage, plunder; (*Am.*) man's coat; Roman sagum; in the game of pelota, *saque*; (*naut.*) bay, cove, small bay; *a saco,* sacking, pillaging; *saco de noche,* valise, hand-bag.

sácope, *n.m.* (*Philip.*) subject, liegeman.

sacra, *n.f.* tablet standing on the altar, sacring tablet.

sacramentado, -da, *a.* (*eccles.*) transubstantiated; sacramented, having received the sacraments.

sacramental, *a.* sacramental.

sacramentalmente, *adv.* sacramentally.

sacramentar, *v.t.* to administer the sacraments. — *v.r.* to transubstantiate.

sacramentario, -ria, *a.* sacramentarian.

sacramente, *adv.* in a sacred way.

sacramento, *n.m.* sacrament; *hacer sacramento,* to make a mystery; *incapaz de sacramentos,* an absolute fool.

sacratísimo, -ma, *a. superl.* [SAGRADO].

sacre, *n.m.* (*orn.*) saker; (*artill.*) small cannon.

sacrificadero, *n.m.* place of sacrifice.

sacrificador, *n.m.* sacrificer.

sacrificante, *a.* sacrificing, sacrificatory.

sacrificar, *v.t.* (*pret.* **sacrifiqué;** *pres. subj.* **sacrifique**) to sacrifice. — *v.r.* to submit, conform to, yield.

sacrificatorio, -ria, *a.* sacrificatory.

sacrificio, *n.m.* sacrifice, offering; submission, obsequiousness, compliance.

sacrílegamente *adv.* sacrilegiously.

sacrilegio, *n.m.* sacrilege.

sacrílego, -ga, *a.* sacrilegious.

sacrismoche, -cho, *n.m.* (*coll.*) man in a ragged black coat.

sacrista, sacristán, *n.m.* sacristan, sexton, clerk; hoop-skirt; *ser gran sacristán,* to be very sagacious, cunning, sly.

sacristana, *n.f.* sexton's wife; nun in charge of the sacristy.

sacristanía, *n.f.* sexton's office.

sacristía, *n.f.* sacristy, vestry; sacristan's office.

sacro, -cra, *a.* sacred, holy; *fuego sacro,* erysipelas.

sacrosanto, -ta, *a.* sacred, sacrosanct, consecrated, very holy.

sacuara, *n.f.* (*Per.*) sapling of cane or reed.

sacudida, *n.f.* shaking, jerk, shake; *de sacudida*, resulting from.

sacudidamente, *adv.* rejectingly.

sacudido, -da, *a.* harsh, indocile, intractable; determined; unembarrassed.

sacudidor, *n.m.* shaker; beater; duster.

sacudidura, *n.f.* shaking, dusting, cleaning.

sacudimiento, *n.m.* shake, shock, jerk, jolt; rejecting, shaking off.

sacudión, *n.m.* rapid dusting or shaking.

sacudir, *v.t.* to shake, jolt, shock, jerk; to beat, drub; to dart, throw, discharge, shake off; *sacudir el polvo*, to strike or beat severely; *sacudir el yugo*, to throw off the yoke, become independent.

sachadura, *n.f.* hoeing, weeding, turning up the ground.

sachaguasca, *n.f.* (*Arg.*) a climbing plant of the Bignonia family.

sachar, *v.t.* to weed, hoe.

sacho, *n.m.* hoe, weeder; (*Chi.*) wooden frame loaded with stones used as an anchor.

saduceo, *n.m.* Sadducee.

saeta, *n.f.* arrow, shaft, dart; bud of a vine; hand of a clock; cock of a sundial; magnetic needle; song addressed to the Virgin in Holy Week processions; (*astr.*) Sagitta; *echar saetas*, to utter pious ejaculations.

saetada, *n.f.*; **saetazo**, *n.m.* throw or wound of an arrow.

saetear, *v.t.* to kill with arrows.

saetera, *n.f.* loophole; small grated window in prisons.

saetero, -ra, *a.* relating to arrows.

saetero, *n.m.* archer, bowman.

saetí, *n.m.* kind of sateen.

saetía, *n.f.* (*naut.*) settee; loophole; (*Cub.*) a graminaceous plant used for pasture.

saetilla, *n.f.* small arrow; hand of a watch; devotional verse; (*bot.*) sagittaria.

saetín, *n.m.* mill-trough, mill-run, sluice; flume; pin, peg, tack; drag-net; tenter-hook; sateen.

saetón, *n.m.* dart for shooting rabbits.

sáfico, -ca, *a.* (*poet.*) sapphic.

safio, *n.m.* (*Cub.*) a kind of conger eel.

saga, *n.f.* witch; saga.

sagacidad, *n.f.* sagacity, penetration.

sagapeno, *n.m.* sagapenum (gum).

sagatí, *n.m.* a light fabric of silk and cotton.

sagaz, *a.* sagacious, quick of scent (said of dogs), discerning, far-sighted, far-seeing, keen-witted.

sagazmente, *adv.* sagaciously.

sagita, *n.f.* (*geom.*) sagitta, segment.

sagital, *a.* sagittal, sagittated.

sagitaria, *n.f.* (*bot.*) sagittaria, arrowhead.

sagitario, *n.m.* (*astr.*) Sagittarius; archer, dartman.

sago, *n.m.* loose greatcoat.

ságoma, *n.f.* (*arch.*) reglet, rule.

sagradamente, *adv.* sacredly, religiously, inviolably.

sagrado, -da, *a.* sacred, consecrated; holy, venerable; (*obs.*) cursed, execrable.

sagrado, *n.m.* asylum, haven, safe place.

sagrario, *n.m.* tabernacle; sanctuary; ciborium.

sagú, *n.m.* sago-palm tree; (*Cent. Am., Cub.*) herbaceous plant of the Canna family; sago.

saguaipe, *n.m.* (*Arg.*) a parasitic worm.

ságula, *n.f.* an open sleeve used by native women.

sahárico, -ca, *a.* of or from the Sahara desert.

sahina, *n.f.* sorghum.

sahornarse, *v.r.* to be excoriated, chafe.

sahorno, *n.m.* chafe, chafing, excoriation.

sahumado, -da, *a.* fumigated; improved, bettered; select, apposite; (*Am.*) tipsy, slightly intoxicated.

sahumador, *n.m.* perfumer; perfume-jar.

sahumadura, *n.f.* fumigation; perfuming.

sahumar, *v.t.* to fume, smoke, fumigate; to perfume.

sahumerio, sahumo, *n.m.* smoke, fume, steam, vapour; fumigation; aromatics burnt as perfumes.

sai, *n.m.* (*Am.*) a monkey.

saimiri, *n.m.* squirrel monkey.

sain, *n.m.* grease, dirt on clothes; fat, fatness; sardine fat used as lamp-oil.

sainar, *v.t.* to fatten (animals).

sainete, *n.m.* kind of burlesque, one-act farce; zest, flavour, relish; something choice; high-flavoured sauce; tit-bit, delicacy; elegance, good taste.

sainetear, *v.i.* to act a farce.

sainetero, *n.m.* writer of farces.

sainetesco, -ca, *a.* comical, burlesque.

saíno, *n.m.* (*Am.*) a kind of boar.

saja, sajadura, *n.f.* scarification.

sajador, *n.m.* scarifier; bleeder.

sajar, *v.t.* to scarify.

sajelar, *v.t.* to sift and clean clay.

sajón, -na, *n.m.f., a.* Saxon.

sajumaya, *n.f.* (*Cub.*) a deadly disease attacking pigs.

sajuriana, *n.f.* (*Chi., Per.*) ancient popular dance.

sal, *n.f.* salt; wit, wisdom; grace, winning manners; facetiousness; *sal de la Higuera*, Epsom salts; *sal gema*, mineral salt; *echar en sal*, to keep for another occasion; *hacerse sal y agua*, to disperse, be spent (of wealth, etc.); *no alcanzar la sal al agua*, to have insufficient means to keep one; *con su sal y pimienta*, maliciously.

sala, *n.f.* hall, drawing-room, parlour, entertaining room; tribunal; court of justice; *hacer sala*, to form a quorum; *sala de batalla*, sorting room (post-office); *sala de justicia*, court of justice; *sala del crimen*, criminal court.

salab, *n.m.* (*Philip.*) a shrub of the Sapindaceæ family.

salabardo, *n.m.* landing net.

salacidad, *n.f.* salacity, lechery.

salacot, *n.m.* (*Philip.*) sun-helmet.

saladamente, *adv.* saltily; wittily, facetiously.

saladar, *n.m.* salt-marsh.

saladería, *n.f.* (*Arg.*) meat salting factory.

saladero, *n.m.* salting-place; salting tub.

saladillo, *n.m.* fresh bacon half-salted.

salado, -da, *a.* salted, salty, brackish, briny; facetious, witty; winsome, graceful; (*CR., PR.*) hapless; (*Arg., Chi.*) dear, costly. — *p.p.* [SALAR].

salado, *n.m.* saltwort; saline land.

salador, -ra, *n.m.f.* salter, curer, salting-place.

saladura, *n.f.* salting, curing; pickled or salted meat, fish, etc.; saltness.

salamanca, *n.m.* (*Chi.*) natural cave; (*Arg.*) a kind of salamander; (*Philip.*) legerdemain.

salamandra, *n.f.* salamander, fire-sprite.
salamanquesa, *n.f.* star-lizard; stellion.
salangana, *n.f.* (*Philip.*) swift swallow.
salar, *v.t.* to salt, season with salt; to preserve, corn, cure, brine.
salariar, *v.t.* to pay a salary.
salario, *n.m.* salary, wages, hire, stipend, pay.
salaz, *a.* salacious, lustful.
salazón, *n.f.* seasoning, salting; salted meats or fish.
salbadera, *n.f.* sand-box.
salbanda, *n.f.* (*min.*) argillaceous layer.
salce, *n.m.* willow.
salceda, *n.f.;* **salcedo,** *n.m.* willow-plantation.
salcereta, *n.f.* dice-box.
salcochar, *v.t.* to cook, boil with water and salt.
salcocho, *n.m.* (*Am.*) food partly cooked with water and salt only.
salchicha, *n.f.* small sausage; (*mil.*) saucisse; (*fort.*) long fascine; (*mil.*) French sausage balloon.
salchichería, *n.f.* sausage-shop.
salchichero, -ra, *n.m.f.* sausage-maker, sausage-seller.
salchichón, *n.m.* large sausage; (*fort.*) large fascine.
saldar, *v.t.* to liquidate a debt; to hold a sale.
saldista, *n.m.* second-hand dealer.
saldo, *n.m.* (*com.*) balance; conclusion or settlement of an account, liquidation; bargain-sale.
saldré, *fut. indic.* [SALIR].
saledizo, *a.* jutting, salient. — *n.m.* [SALIDIZO].
salegar, *n.m.* salt-lick.
salema, *n.f.* (*ichth.*) gilt-head.
salep, *n.m.* salep.
salera, *n.f.* salt-lick; salt-mine.
salero, *n.m.* salt-mine; salt-cellar, salt-pan, salt-magazine; wit, gracefulness, winning ways.
saleroso, -sa, *a.* (*coll.*) witty, winsome, winning, graceful.
saleta, *n.f.* small hall; royal antechamber; court of appeal.
salga, *n.f.* (*hist.*) salt tax in Aragon.
salgar, *v.t.* to give salt (to cattle).
salgo; salga, *pres. indic.; pres. subj.* [SALIR].
salguera, *n.f.;* **salguero,** *n.m.* osier, willow.
salicilato, *n.m.* (*chem.*) salicylate.
salicílico, -ca, *a.* salicylic.
salicina, *n.f.* (*chem.*) salicin.
sálico, -ca, *a.* Salic.
salicor, *n.m.* (*bot.*) fleshy-leaved saltwort.
salida, *n.f.* start, departure, setting out, outset; exit, loophole, outlet; egress, result, issue, conclusion; (*mil.*) sally; (*naut.*) headway; projection, prominence; (*com.*) salableness; expenditure, outlay; subterfuge, pretext; *estar de salida,* to be ready for sailing; *salida de teatro,* lady's evening cloak.
salidizo, *n.m.* (*arch.*) projection, corbel.
salido, -da, *a.* gone out, departed; prominent, projecting; in heat (of female animals).
saliente, *a.* jutting out, projecting, salient.
salífero, -ra, *a.* (*chem.*) saliferous.
salificable, *a.* salifiable.
salín, *n.m.* salt magazine.
salina, *n.f.* salt-pit, salt-work, salt-mine.
salinero, *n.m.* salter, salt-maker; dealer in salt.
salino, -na, *a.* saline.
salir, *v.i.* (*pres. indic.* **salgo;** *pres. subj.* **salga;**

fut. indic. **saldré**) to go out, depart, leave, quit, retire, desist; to appear, shoot, spring, grow; to come out, come forth, come off; to set out, march out, go away, proceed, issue; to occur, happen; to end, be over (as a season); to lead to, open to; to escape, get out, get over, extricate oneself; to stand out, jut out, project; to disappear, come off (as a stain); to rise (as the sun, the stars, etc.); to do (well, badly, etc.); to cost; to start (in a game, etc.); to dispose of, sell out; (*theat.*) to enter, appear; to result, be the outcome; to be drawn, elected (in a ballot, etc.); to do something unexpectedly; to resemble; (*naut.*) to pass another vessel in sailing; *salir a la mar,* to put to sea; *salir al encuentro de,* to go to meet; *salir a luz,* to be published; *salir a nado,* to save oneself by swimming; *salir de un puesto,* to throw up a post; *salir con las manos en la cabeza,* to come away with a flea in one's ear; *salir limpio de polvo y paja,* to come out of it without a scratch; *salga lo que saliere,* come what may; *salir con,* to obtain; *salir con bien,* to be successful; *salir de su padre,* to be released from the paternal sway; *salir de alguno,* to get rid of someone; *salir de sus casillas,* to lose one's temper. — *v.r.* to drop, leak, overflow; *salirse con la suya,* to get one's own way.
salisipan, *n.m.* (*Philip.*) a swift boat.
salitrado, -da, *a.* impregnated with saltpetre.
salitral, *a.* nitrous. — *n.m.* saltpetre bed, salt-petre works.
salitre, *n.m.* saltpetre.
salitrería, *n.f.* saltpetre work.
salitrero, -ra, *n.m.f.* saltpetre dealer, saltpetre refiner.
salitroso, -sa, *a.* nitrous, salinitrous.
saliva, *n.f.* saliva, spittle.
salivación, *n.f.* salivation.
salivadera, *n.f.* (*Arg., Chi.*) spittoon.
salival, *a.* salivous, salivary.
salivar, *v.i.* to spit, salivate.
salivera, *n.f.* round knob on a bridle.
salivoso, -sa, *a.* salivous.
salma, *n.f.* ton-weight.
salmantino, -na, *n.m.f.,* *a.* native of or relating to Salamanca.
salmear, salmodiar, *v.t.* to sing psalms.
salmerón, *n.m.,* *a.* fanfaron wheat.
salmista, *n.m.* psalmist, psalm-singer.
salmo, *n.m.* psalm.
salmodia, *n.f.* psalmody; psalter.
salmodiar, *v.t.* to singsong, to pray with monotonous cadence.
salmón, *n.m.* (*ichth.*) salmon; *salmón pequeño,* samlet; *salmón zancado,* kelt.
salmonado, -da, *a.* tasting like salmon.
salmonera, *n.f.* salmon net.
salmonete, *n.m.* (*ichth.*) red mullet.
salmorejo, *n.m.* rabbit sauce.
salmuera, *n.f.* brine; pickle.
salmuerarse, *v.r.* to become sick from eating too much salt (of cattle).
salobral, *a.* salty, briny. — *n.m.* brine, briny ground.
salobre, *a.* brackish, saltish, briny.
salobreño, -ña, *a.* saltish, brackish.
salobridad, *n.f.* brackishness, saltiness.
saloma, *n.f.* (*naut.*) shanty.
salomar, *v.i.* to sing shanties.
salón, *n.m.* saloon, salon, drawing-room, large

hall; assembly room; salted and smoked meat or fish.

saloncillo, *n.m.* small salon; special room, rest room; lady's room.

salpa, *n.f.* (*ichth.*) big-head, gilt-head.

salpicadura, *n.f.* spattering, dab, splash.

salpicar, *v.t.* (*pret.* **salpiqué**; *pres. subj.* **salpique**) to bespatter or splash with dirt; (*coll.*) to pass rapidly from subject to subject.

salpicón, *n.m.* bespattering, splashing; salmagundi; (*Ec.*) a cooling drink made from fruit juices.

salpimentar, *v.t.* (*pres. indic.* **salpimiento**; *pres. subj.* **salpimiente**) to season with pepper and salt.

salpimienta, *n.f.* mixture of pepper and salt.

salpresar, *v.t.* (*p.p.* **salpresado, salpreso**) to season, preserve with salt.

salpullido, *n.m.* rash, eruption.

salpullir, *v.t.* to break out in a rash.

salsa, *n.f.* sauce, condiment, dressing, gravy; *salsa de San Bernardo*, (*coll.*) hunger.

salsedumbre, *n.f.* saltness.

salsera, *n.f.* saucer, tureen, gravy-dish.

salserilla, *n.f.* small saucer; dice-box.

salsero, *n.m.* Spanish thyme.

salsifí, *n.m.* (*bot.*) salsify; goat's-beard.

saltabanco, saltabancos, *n.m.* mountebank, quack, jester.

saltabardales, *n.m.* (*coll.*) wild youth.

saltabarrancos, *n.m.* (*Col.*) noisy fellow.

saltacaballo, *n.m.* (*arch.*) overlapping.

saltación, *n.f.* leaping, hopping; dancing, dance.

saltacharquillos, *n.m.* person with a mincing gait.

saltadero, *n.m.* leaping-place; artificial fountain.

saltadizo, -za, *a.* breaking, snapping.

saltador, -ra, *n.m.f.* jumper, leaper, hopper, springer.

saltaembarca, *n.f.* kind of rustic dress.

saltamontes, *n.m.* grasshopper, locust.

saltanejoso, *a.* (*Cub.*) undulating (ground).

saltante, *a.* salient; jumping, leaping, springing; (*Chi.*) outstanding.

saltaojos, *n.m.* kind of peony.

saltaparedes, *n.m.* (*coll.*) wild youth.

saltar, *v.i.* to jump, leap; frisk, skip, hop; to bound, rebound; to dash out; to burst, crack, snap, break into pieces; to fly asunder; to come off (as a button); to be obvious, clear; to come to the mind; (*naut.*) to chop about, change, shift (of the wind); *saltar en tierra*, to disembark, land; *saltar de gozo*, to be highly delighted; *saltarse la tapa de los sesos*, to blow out one's brains. — *v.t.* to leap over, jump over; to cover the female of an animal.

saltarelo, *n.m.* saltarello, an ancient dance.

saltarén, *n.m.* tune on the guitar; grasshopper.

saltarín, -na, *n.m.f.* dancer; restless young person.

saltarregla, *n.f.* bevel square; sliding-rule.

saltaterandate, *n.m.* kind of embroidery.

saltatrás, *n.m.* half-breed.

saltatriz, *n.f.* woman rope-dancer, ballet-girl.

saltatumbas, *n.m.* (*contempt.*) clergyman who makes a living from funerals.

salteador, *n.m.* footpad, highwayman.

salteadora, *n.f.* female footpad; woman living with highwaymen.

salteamiento, *n.m.* assault, attack, highway robbery.

saltear, *v.t.* to assault, attack, hold up, rob on the highway; to pass rapidly from one thing to another; to forestall; take by surprise.

salteo, *n.m.* highway assault, robbery.

salterio, *n.m.* psalter; rosary; psaltery.

saltero, *n.m.* highlander.

saltico, -illo, -ito, *n.m.* little hop; *a saltillos*, hopping.

saltimbanco, saltimbanqui, *n.m.* mountebank; quack; trifler.

salto, *n.m.* leap, jump, spring, bound; distance leaped; jerk; leaping-place; sudden change, transition; (*obs.*) plunder, assault; omission, gap, skip, hiatus; high promotion with omission of intervening stages; *salto de mata*, flight from fear of punishment; *a saltos*, by hops; *de salto*, suddenly; *de un salto*, at one bound; *por salto*, irregularly, by turns; *a saltos y corcovos*, (*coll.*) by fits and starts; *salto mortal*, somerset, summersault; *dar un salto*, to give a jump, leap over; *a gran salto, gran quebranto*, pride goes before a fall; *salto de agua*, waterfall; *salto de trucha*, tumbling; *más vale salto de mata, que ruego de hombres buenos*, better an escape from death than good men's prayers.

saltón, *n.m.* grasshopper.

saltón, -na, *a.* hopping or leaping much; (*Col., Chi.*) half-cooked or boiled food; projecting; *ojos saltones*, goggle-eyes.

salubérrimo, -ma, *a. superl.* most salubrious.

salubre, *a.* healthful.

salubridad, *n.f.* salubrity, healthfulness, wholesomeness, salutariness.

salud, *n.f.* health; prosperity, welfare; good condition; salvation; public weal; ¡*salud!* good luck! good health! *en sana salud*, in perfect health; *gastar salud*, to have good health.

saludable, *a.* salutary, healthful, salubrious, wholesome.

saludablemente, *adv.* healthily, salubriously.

saludador, -ra, *n.m.* greeter, saluter; quack.

saludar, *v.t.* to greet, hail, salute, welcome; to proclaim; to fire a salute; to apply nostrums; (*naut.*) to dip the flag.

saludo, *n.m.* salute, salutation, greeting, bow; *saludo a la voz*, (*naut.*) cheers, hurrahs.

salumbre, *n.f.* flower of salt.

salutación, *n.f.* salutation, greeting, salute; exordium of a sermon; Ave Maria.

salutíferamente, *adv.* salubriously.

salutífero, -ra, *a.* healthful, salubrious.

salva, *n.f.* pregustation; salute (of fire-arms), salvo; round (of applause); ordeal; oath, solemn promise, assurance; salver, tray.

salvación, *n.f.* salvation, deliverance.

salvachia, *n.f.* (*naut.*) salvage strap.

salvadera, *n.f.* sand-box for writing; (*Cub.*) a tree of the spurge family.

salvado, *n.m.* bran.

salvador, -ra, *n.m.f.* saviour, rescuer, redeemer; *El Salvador*, Our Saviour, Our Redeemer.

salvadoreño, -ña, *n.m.f., a.* from El Salvador.

salvaguardia, *n.m.* safeguard, security, protection; watchman, guard. — *n.f.* passport; safe-conduct.

salvajada, *n.f.* rude behaviour, brutal action.

salvaje, *a.* savage, barbarous, ferocious; wild (of plants, beasts or country); rough, ignorant. — *n.m.* savage.

salvajería, *n.f.* savageness; brutal action.
salvajez, *n.f.* savageness.
salvajina, *n.f.* wild beast; multitude of wild beasts; collection of wild beast's skins.
salvajino, -na, *a.* savage, wild, untamed; gamey (of meat).
salvajismo, *n.m.* barbarism, savagery, savagedom.
salvamano, (a), *adv.* without danger, in the manner of a coward.
salvamanteles, *n.m.* table-mat.
salvamente, *adv.* safely, securely.
salvamento, salvamiento, *n.m.* salvage; safety, place of safety; salvation.
salvar, *v.t.* (*p.p.* **salvado, salvo**) to save, free from danger; (*naut.*) to salve; to avoid (a danger); to clear (an obstacle); to prove legally the innocence of somebody; to go over, pass over, jump over; to excuse, make allowance for; to remove hindrances, to avoid, overcome. — *v.i.* to taste the food before serving the king or noblemen. — *v.r.* to escape from danger; to gain salvation.
salvavidas, *n.m.* (*naut.*) lifebuoy, life-preserver; (*railw.*) cow-catcher.
salve, *interj.*, *n.f.* hail!; ¡*salve!* God bless you.
salvedad, *n.f.* reservation, exception, excuse.
salvia, *n.f.* (*bot.*) sage, salvia.
salvilla, *n.f.* salver, tray; waiter; glass-rock; (*Chi.*) cruet-stand.
salvo, -va, *a.* saved, excepted, omitted. — *p.p. irreg.* (*obs.*) [SALVAR]; *a salvo,* without injury; *en salvo,* in security, at liberty; *salvo el guante,* pardon the glove; *en salvo está el que repica,* the bell-ringer's berth is a safe one.
salvoconducto, *n.m.* pass, passport, safe-conduct; licence, permission.
salvohonor, *n.m.* (*coll.*) buttocks, breeches.
salladura, *n.f.* weeding; stowage of logs and planks.
sallar, *v.t.* to weed, to clear the ground; to stow logs and planks.
sallete, *n.m.* weeder, weeding tool.
sámago, *n.m.* alburnum, alburn, sap-wood.
samán, *n.m.* rain-tree.
samaritano, -na, *n.m.f.*, *a.* Samaritan.
samaruco, *n.m.* (*Chi.*) game bag.
samaruguera, *n.f.* fishing net across streams.
sambenitar, *v.t.* to make infamous; to dishonour publicly.
sambenito, *n.m.* garment worn by penitent convicts of the Inquisition; sanbenito; placard in churches with names of penitents; note of infamy, disgrace.
samblaje, *n.m.* joinery.
sambrano, *n.m.* (*Hond.*) a medicinal leguminous root.
sambuca, *n.f.* (*mus.*) sambuca, sambuke.
sambumbia, *n.f.* (*Cub.*) drink made from cane juice, water and chilli; (*Mex.*) drink made from pine-apple, water and sugar; (*Col.*) (*fig.*) anything reduced to small pieces.
sambumbiería, *n.f.* (*Cub., Mex.*) place where sambumbia is made and sold.
samfusco, *n.m.* marjoram.
samotana, *n.f.* (*CR., Hond.*) merrymaking; bustle, din, clamour.
sampa, *n.f.* (*Arg.*) a ramose shrub growing in saltpetrous lands.
sampaguita, *n.f.* tropical flower resembling the jasmine.

sampsuco, *n.m.* marjoram.
samuga, *n.f.* mule-chair.
samuro, *n.m.* (*Col., Ven.*) turkey-buzzard, turkey-vulture.
san, *a.* (contraction of SANTO) Saint (before masculine proper nouns except Tomás or Tomé, Toribio, and Domingo).
sanable, *a.* healable, curable.
sanador, -ra, *n.m.f.* healer, curer.
sanalotodo, *n.m.* panacea, cure-all, general remedy.
sanamente, *adv.* naturally; sanely; sincerely.
sanar, *v.t.* to heal, cure, restore. — *v.i.* to heal, recover.
sanativo, -va, *a.* sanative, curative.
sanatorio, *n.m.* sanatorium.
sanción, *n.f.* sanction, ratification.
sancionar, *v.t.* to sanction; to authorize, ratify.
sanco, *n.m.* (*Arg., Chi.*) kind of porridge; (*Chi.*) thick mud.
sancochar, *v.t.* to parboil.
sancocho, *n.m.* half-cooked meal; (*Am.*) stew of meat, yucca, banana, etc.
sanctasanctórum, *n.m.* sanctuary, holiest of holies.
sanctus, *n.m.* sanctus (in the Mass).
sandalia, *n.f.* sandal.
sandalino, -na, of or belonging to sandalwood; tinctured with sanders.
sándalo, *n.m.* (*bot.*) bergamot mint; sandal wood, sanders; *ser como el sándalo, que perfuma el hacha que le hiere,* to return good for evil.
sandáraca, *n.f.* sandarach; (*min.*) realgar.
sandez, *n.f.* folly, simplicity, inanity.
sandía, *n.f.* water-melon.
sandialahuén, *n.m.* (*Chi.*) a medicinal verbenaceous plant.
sandiar, *n.m.* water-melon patch.
sandiego, *n.m.* (*Cub.*) a species of amaranth.
sandilla, *n.f.* (*Chi.*) a verbenaceous plant with a fruit resembling a small water-melon.
sandio, -dia, *a.* foolish, inane, nonsensical.
sandunga, *n.f.* elegance, gracefulness; winsomeness; (*Chi., PR.*) carousal, revelry.
sandunguero, -ra, *a.* (*coll.*) winsome, graceful.
saneado, -da, *a.* free, clear, unencumbered.
saneamiento, *n.m.* (*law*) surety, guarantee, security, bail; indemnification, reparation; drainage; improvement (of land).
sanear, *v.t.* (*law*) to indemnify; to give security; to drain, improve (lands).
sanedrín, *n.m.* Sanhedrin.
sanfrancia, *n.f.* (*coll.*) dispute, quarrel.
sangley, *n., a.* (*Philip.*) Chinese or Japanese trader.
sangradera, *n.f.* lancet; basin for blood-letting; lock, sluice, drain.
sangrador, *n.m.* phlebotomist, blood-letter; fissure, opening, outlet.
sangradura, *n.f.* (*surg.*) bleeding; bend of the arm opposite the elbow; draining, drainage.
sangrar, *v.t.* to bleed, let blood; to drain; (*coll.*) to extort, borrow; (*print.*) to indent. — *v.i.* to bleed. — *v.r.* to be bled.
sangraza, *n.f.* corrupt blood.
sangre, *n.f.* blood, gore; race, kindred, family; *beber la sangre a uno,* to thirst for someone's blood; *de la sangre azul,* blue blood, of the nobility; *a sangre fría,* in cold blood; *a sangre y fuego,* utterly, (*or* to the death *or* by fire and

sword); *la sangre se hereda, y la virtud se aquista*, blood is inherited, but virtue is acquired; *bullirle a uno la sangre*, to have warm blood in one's veins; *chupar la sangre*, (*fig.*) to be a blood-sucker; *escupir sangre en bacín de oro*, to be rich and discontented; *hacer sangre*, to draw blood; *no llegará la sangre al río* (*coll.*) it's not such a terrible matter; *tener la sangre caliente*, to be hasty in action; *verter sangre*, (*coll.*) to be rosy-red; *sangre ligera* (*Am.*) pleasant disposition; *sangre pesada*, (*Am.*) unpleasant disposition.

sangría, *n.f.* bleeding, blood-letting; drain, drainage; pelfering; inside of the arm; present made to a person who bleeds; drink made of red wine and lemon-juice; (*print.*) indenting a line; (*metal.*) tapping a furnace.

sangrientamente, *adv.* bloodily, cruelly.

sangriento, -ta, *a.* bloody, cruel, sanguinary, bloodthirsty, blood-stained.

sanguaraña, *n.f.* (*Per.*) a popular dance; *pl.* **sanguaranas** (*Ec., Per.*) circumlocution, evasion, subterfuge.

sanguaza, *n.f.* corrupt blood; reddish fluid of fruits and vegetables.

sangüeño, *n.m.* dogberry tree, wild cornel.

sangüesa, *n.f.* (*bot.*) raspberry.

sangüeso, *n.m.* raspberry-bush.

sanguífero, -ra, *a.* (*med.*) sanguiferous.

sanguificación, *n.f.* (*med.*) sanguification.

sanguificar, *v.t.* (conjugated like BUSCAR) to sanguify, make blood.

sanguijuela, *n.f.* leech; (*coll.*) cheat, sharper.

sanguinaria, *n.f.* knot-grass, blood-wort; blood-stone.

sanguinariamente, *adv.* sanguinarily.

sanguinario, -ria, *a.* sanguinary, cruel, bloody, bloodthirsty.

sanguíneo, -nea; sanguino, -na, *a.* sanguine, red, ruddy, sanguineous.

sanguinolento, -ta, *a.* bloody.

sanguinoso, -sa, *a.* bloody, sanguinary, cruel.

sanguiñuelo, *n.m.* dogberry tree, wild cornel.

sanguisorba, *n.f.* great burnet.

sanícula, *n.f.* sanicle.

sanidad, *n.f.* soundness, health, sanity, vigour, healthfulness; *carta de sanidad*, bill of health; *casa de sanidad*, health office; *sanidad marítima*, quarantine officers.

sanie sanies, *n.f.* sanies.

sanioso, -sa, *a.* sanious.

sanitario, -ria, *a.* hygienic; sanitary, health-giving, healthy, conducive to health.

sanjacado, sanjacato, *n.m.* Turkish provincial district, sanjak.

sanjuanada, *n.f.* picnic on St. John's Day.

sanjuanero, -ra, *a.* ripe on St. John's Day (of fruits).

sanmiguelada, *n.f.* Michaelmas-tide.

sanmigueleño, -ña, *a.* ripe at Michaelmas.

sano, -na, *a.* sound, salutary, healthy, wholesome, sane; harmless, safe; entire, complete; sure, secure; honest, good; wise, steady, discreet; *sano y salvo*, safe and sound.

sánscrito, *n.m.* Sanskrit.

sansimonismo, *n.m.* St. Simonism.

sansón, *n.m.* (*fig.*) very strong man.

santa, *n.f.* female saint.

santabárbara, *n.f.* (*naut.*) magazine, powder-room.

Santa Elena, *n.f.* St. Helena.

santamente, *adv.* saintly; piously, religiously; plainly, simply.

Santelmo, *n.m.* St. Elmo's fire.

santero, -ra, *n.m.f.* caretaker of a sanctuary; alms-begging. — *a.* over-devout to the saints.

Santiago, *n.m.* St. James.

santiago, *n.m.* war-cry of the Spaniards on engaging with Moors; middling sort of linen made in Santiago (Spain).

santiagueño, -ña, *a.* ripe on St. James' Day (of fruits); of or from Santiago del Estero (*Arg.*).

santiaguero, -ra, *n.m.f., a.* of Santiago (Cuba).

santiagués, -sa, *n.m.f., a.* of Santiago (Galicia).

santiaguino, -na, *n.m.f., a.* of Santiago (Chile).

santiamén, (en un), *n.m.* (*coll.*) instant, moment, twinkling of an eye, jiffy.

santico, -ca, *n.m.f.* good child; little image of a saint.

santidad, *n.f.* sanctity, saintliness, piety, holiness, godliness; *Su Santidad*, his Holiness (the Pope).

santificación, *n.f.* sanctification, making holy; *santificación de las fiestas*, keeping of holy days.

santificador, *n.m.* sanctifier.

santificante, *a.* blessing, sanctifying.

santificar, *v.t.* (*pert.* **santifiqué**, *pres. subj.* **santifique**), to sanctify, hallow, consecrate, dedicate; to bless, praise, to keep holy days. — *v.t., v.r.* to justify, acquit, clear.

santiguada, *n.f.* sign of the cross.

santiguador, -ra, *n.m.f.* healer by signing with the cross.

santiguamiento, *n.m.* act of crossing, blessing by crossing.

santiguar, *v.t.* to bless, heal by blessing; (*coll.*) to slap, chastise. — *v.r.* to cross oneself, bless oneself.

santimonia, *n.f.* sanctity, sanctimony, holiness; (*bot.*) corn, marigold, chrysanthemum.

santísimo, -ma, *a. superl.* most holy. — *n.m.* *El Santísimo*, the holy sacrament.

santo, -ta, *a.* holy, pious, just, blessed; saintly, virtuous, sacred; consecrated; inviolable; (*coll.*) plain, artless, simple. — *n.m.f.* saint, image of a saint, saint's day; *santo y bueno*, well and good; well, well; *todo el santo día*, the whole day long; *santo varón*, holy man; simpleton, hypocrite; *dar el santo*, (*mil.*) to give the watchword; *rogar el santo hasta pasar el tranco*, to be devout till one's end is gained; *alzarse con el santo y la limosna*, to make away with everything; *comerse los santos*, to be excessively devout; *dar con el santo en la tierra*, (*coll.*) to let something fall; *encomendarse a buen santo*, to be very fortunate in an enterprise; *desnudar a un santo para vestir a otro*, to rob Peter to pay Paul.

santol, *n.m.* sandal-tree.

santón, *n.m.* hypocrite, false saint; elder; Mohammedan hermit, dervish.

santónico, -ca, *n.m.* (*med.*) santonica.

santonina, *n.f.* (*chem.*) santonine.

santoral, *n.m.* church-choir book; collection of lives of the saints.

santuario, *n.m.* sanctuary; (*Col.*) treasure.

santucho, -cha, *n.m.f.* (*coll.*) hypocrite.

santurrón, -na, *n.m.f., a.* (*coll.*) hypocrite, zealot.

santurronería, *n.f.* hypocrisy, sanctimony.

saña, *n.f.* anger, passion, rage, fury.

sañosamente, *adv.* furiously, angrily.
sañoso, -sa, *a.* furious, enraged.
sañudamente, *adv.* furiously.
sañudo, -da, *a.* furious, enraged, angry.
sao, *n.m.* laburnum; (*Cub.*) small savanna with some trees or shrubs.
sapajú, *n.m.* sapajou, S. American monkey.
sapán, *n.m.* (*Philip.*) sapan-wood; sapan-tree.
sapenco, *n.m.* a kind of snail.
sápido, -da, *a.* high-flavoured, savoury.
sapiencia, *n.f.* wisdom; the Book of Wisdom.
sapiencial, *a.* belonging to wisdom. — *n.m.pl.* sapiential books.
sapiente, *a.* wise, learned.
sapillo, *n.m.* little toad; small tumour.
sapina, *n.f.* glasswort.
sapino, *n.m.* fir-tree.
sapo, *n.m.* toad; (*Arg., Chi.*) children's play; (*Chi.*) flaw in a precious stone; (*Chi.*) fluke in billiards; (*Cub.*) small river fish.
saponáceo, -cea, *a.* saponaceous.
saponaria, *n.f.* (*bot.*) common soapwort.
saponia, *n.f.* (*chem.*) saponin.
saponificación, *n.f.* saponification.
saponificar, *v.t.* (*pret.* saponifiqué; *pres. subj.* saponifique) to saponify. — *v.r.* to become saponified.
saporífero, -ra, *a.* saporific.
sapotina, *n.f.* (*Ec.*) hydrosilicate of magnesia and alumina used in the manufacture of porcelain.
saque, *n.m.* playing a ball on the rebound; striker, player-out.
saqueador, -ra, *n.m.f.* ransacker, free-booter.
saqueamiento, saqueo, *n.m.* pillage, sack, plunder, foray.
saquear, *v.t.* to ransack, plunder, pillage.
saquera, *n.f.* packing-needle.
saquería, *n.f.* manufacture of sacks; collection of sacks.
saquero, -ra, *n.m.f.* sack-maker.
saquete, *n.m.* cartridge bag.
saquilada, *n.f.* small quantity of grain for grinding.
saraguate, *n.m.* (*Cent. Am.*) a kind of monkey.
saragüete, *n.m.* informal or family dance.
sarampión, *n.m.* measles.
sarandí, *n.m.* (*Arg.*) a shrub of the euphorbiaceæ family.
sarangasti, *n.m.* (*naut.*) pitch-gum.
sarao, *n.m.* dancing party or entertainment, informal dance.
sarape, *n.m.* (*Mex.*) a blanket or shawl.
sarapia, *n.f.* tonka-bean.
sarapico, *n.m.* curlew.
sarasa, *n.m.* effeminate man, sissy.
saraviado, -da, *a.* (*Col., Ven.*) spotted, piebald.
sarazo, *a.* (*Col., Cub., Mex., Ven.*) applied to ripening wheat.
sarcasmo, *n.m.* sarcasm.
sarcásticamente, *adv.* sarcastically.
sarcástico, -ca, *a.* sarcastic, taunting, jeering.
sarcia, *n.f.* load, burden.
sarcocola, *n.f.* resinous gum.
sarcófago, *n.m.* tomb, grave, sarcophagus.
sarda, *n.f.* horse mackerel.
sardana, *n.f.* national Catalonian dance.
sardesco, -ca, *a.* (*coll.*) rude, stubborn.
sardesco, *n.m.* pony, small ass.
sardina, *n.f.* sardine, pilchard; *la última sardina de la banasta*, (*coll.*) the very last;

como sardinas en banasta or *en barril*, packed like sardines.
sardinal, *n.m.* sardine net.
sardinel, *n.m.* brickwork having the bricks set on edge.
sardinero, -ra, *n.m.f.* sardine-dealer. — *a.* belonging to sardines.
sardineta, *n.f.* small sardine; sprat; part of cheese that overtops the cheese-vat; (*naut.*) knittle, lanyard; fillip with the wet finger. — *pl.* sardinetas, (*mil.*) chevrons on uniforms.
sardio, sardo, *n.m.* sardius, sard.
sardo, -da, *n.m.f., a.* Sardinian; red, black and white (cattle).
sardonia, *n.f.* (*bot.*) crowfoot, spearwort.
sardónica, sardónice, *n.f.* sardonyx.
sardónicamente, *adv.* sardonically.
sardónico, -ca, *a.* sardonic; insincere, affected (of laughter).
sarga, *n.f.* serge, twill; fabric painted in distemper or oil, like tapestry; (*bot.*) willow, osier.
sargadilla, *n.f.* soda-ash plant.
sargado, -da, *a.* serge-like.
sargal, *n.m.* osier-bed.
sargazo, *n.m.* gulf-weed.
sargenta, *n.f.* sergeant's halberd; sergeant's wife.
sargentear, *v.t.* to perform a sergeant's duties, take command; (*coll.*) to act overbearingly.
sargentería, *n.f.* body of sergeants, sergeant's drill.
sargentía, *n.f.* sergeant's office, sergeantship.
sargento, *n.m.* sergeant; *sargento primero*, sergeant-major.
sargentona, *n.m.* big, coarse woman.
sargo, *n.m.* sheep's head.
sargueta, *n.f.* thin serge.
sarilla, *n.f.* marjoram.
sarmentar, *v.t.* to gather pruned vine-shoots.
sarmentera, *n.f.* place for pruned vine-shoots.
sarmentillo, *n.m.* slender vine-shoot.
sarmentoso, -sa, *a.* full of vine-shoots.
sarmiento, *n.m.* vine-shoot, runner.
sarna, *n.f.* itch, mange; *más viejo que la sarna*, as old as Methuselah.
sarnazo, *n.m.* malignant itch.
sarnoso, -sa, *a.* itchy, mangy, scabby.
sarpullido, *n.m.* flea-bite; rash, eruption.
sarpullir, *v.i.* to be flea-bitten; to have a rash. — *v.r.* to be full of flea-bites, to have an all-over rash.
sarracénico, -ca, *a.* Saracenic.
sarraceno, -na, *n.m.f.* Saracen.
sarracina, *n.f.* fight, scuffle, contest.
sarria, *n.f.* rope net; large frail.
sarrillo, *n.m.* death-rattle; (*bot.*) arum.
sarro, *n.m.* (*med.*) incrustation, sediment, foulness; scale.
sarroso, -sa, *a.* encrusted.
sarta, *n.f.* string (of pearls, etc.), file, line, row, series.
sartal, *n.m.* string. — *a.* stringed.
sartén, *n.f.* frying-pan; *dijo la sartén a la caldera, 'quítate allá, culinegra,'* the pot called the kettle black.
sartenada, *n.f.* contents of a frying-pan.
sartenazo, *n.m.* blow with a frying-pan; (*coll.*) hard blow.
sarteneja, *n.f.* small frying-pan; (*Ec.*) fissures made by drought.

sasafrás, *n.m.* sassafras.

sastra, sastresa, *n.f.* tailor's wife; tailoress.

sastre, *n.m.* tailor; *sastre remendón,* old-clothes mender; *buen sastre,* person who knows what he is talking about (contrary: *corto sastre*); *entre sastres no se pagan hechuras,* there is honour among thieves; *no es mal sastre el que conoce el paño,* a good tailor knows his cloth.

sastrería, *n.f.* tailoring, tailor's trade; tailor's shop.

Satán, Satanás, *n.m.* Satan.

satánicamente, *adv.* satanically.

satánico, -ca, *a.* satanic, devilish.

satélite, *n.m.* satellite; (*coll.*) bailiff, sheriff, constable; henchman, follower; sycophant.

satén, satín, *n.m.* satin.

satinador, -ra, *n.m.f.* glazer, burnisher; polishing tool.

satinar, *v.t.* to glaze, gloss, calender, polish, burnish.

sátira, *n.f.* satire, sharp epigram; (*coll.*) witty woman.

satíricamente, *adv.* satirically.

satírico, -ca, *a.* satirical, censorious.

satírico, *n.m.* satirist.

satirio, *n.m.* kind of water-rat.

satirión, *n.m.* orchis.

satirizante, *a.* satirizing.

satirizar, *v.t.* (*pret.* **satiricé;** *pres. subj.* **satirice**) to satirize, libel, lampoon.

sátiro, *n.m.* satyr, sylvan god; lewd fellow.

satisfacción, *n.f.* satisfaction, atonement, recompense, amends; complacence, presumption; excuse, apology; gratification, pleasure, fulfilment; conceit, confidence; settlement; *a satisfacción,* fully, satisfactorily, without ceremony.

satisfacer, *v.t.* (conjugated like HACER) to satisfy, pay in full; to content, please, gratify, humour; to make amends, atone, expiate; to sate, satiate, allay, indulge; to reward; to repay, indemnify; to answer, reply; to explain, solve, free from perplexity or suspense; to humour a caprice; to convince; (*com.*) to honour (a bill, draft, etc.). — *v.r.* to take satisfaction, be satisfied, be revenged.

satisfaciente, *a.* satisfying, satisfactory.

satisfactoriamente, *adv.* satisfactorily.

satisfactorio, -ria, *a.* satisfactory.

satisfago, satisfaga, *pres. indic., pres. subj.* [SATISFACER].

satisfecho, -cha, *a.* satisfied, confident, complacent, arrogant, conceited. — *p.p. irreg.* [SATISFACER].

satisfice, satisfizo, *pret.* [SATISFACER].

sativo, -va, *a.* sown, cultivated.

sátrapa, *n.m.* satrap; sly fellow.

satrapía, *n.f.* satrapy.

saturable, *a.* saturable.

saturación, *n.f.* saturation.

saturar, *v.t.* to saturate, imbibe, impregnate; to glut, fill, satiate.

saturnal, *a.* saturnalian. — *n.f.* saturnalia.

saturnino, -na, *a.* saturnine, melancholy, grave, gloomy, morose; (*med.*) pertaining to lead-poisoning.

saturno, *n.m.* (*astr.*) Saturn; (*alch.*) lead.

sauale, *n.m.* (*Philip.*) reed used for awnings.

sauce, *n.m.* willow; *sauce llorón,* weeping-willow.

sauceda, saucedal, *n.m.;* **saucera,** *n.f.* willow-plantation.

saucillo, *n.m.* knot-grass.

saúco, *n.m.* elder-tree; second hoof of horses.

sauquillo, *n.m.* dwarf elder.

sausería, *n.f.* palace larder.

sausier, *n.m.* head of a palace larder.

sautor, *n.m.* (*her.*) saltire.

sauz, *n.m.* willow.

sauzal, *n.m.* willow-plantation.

sauzgatillo, *n.m.* Agnus Castus tree.

savia, *n.f.* sap, juice of plants; (*fig.*) vital fluid, strength, vigour.

saxátil, *a.* growing among rocks.

saxífraga, saxifragia, *n.f.* saxifrage.

saxófono, *n.m.* saxophone.

saxoso, -sa, *a.* stony.

saya, *n.f.* dress skirt; ancient tunic worn by men; upper petticoat; dowry given by the Queen of Spain to her maids when marrying.

sayal, *n.m.* sackcloth, serge, coarse cloth; *so el sayal, hay ál,* appearances are deceitful; *no es todo el sayal alforjas,* there are exceptions to everything.

sayalería, *n.f.* trade of coarse cloth weaving.

sayalero, *n.m.* weaver of *sayal.*

sayalesco, -ca, *a.* made of *sayal* cloth.

sayalete, *n.m.* light, thin stuff.

sayama, *n.f.* (*Ec.*) kind of snake.

sayo, *n.m.* loose coat, smock-frock, clown's dress; *decir para su sayo,* to laugh in one's sleeve.

sayón, *n.m.* ugly, corpulent fellow; executioner.

sayuela, *n.f.* kind of fig-tree; woollen shift; (*Cub.*) petticoat.

sayuelo, *n.m.* small dress; slit sleeves worn by peasant women of León.

sazón, *n.f.* maturity, ripeness; seasoning, taste, relish, flavouring; season; opportunity, occasion; *a la sazón,* then, at that time; *en sazón,* opportunely, seasonably.

sazonadamente, *adv.* seasonably, maturely.

sazonado, -da, *a.* seasoned, mature, mellow, ripe; witty; apposite, pertinent.

sazonador, -ra, *n.m.f.* seasoner.

sazonar, *v.t.* to season; to mature, come to maturity. — *v.r.* to ripen, mature.

se, *pron. m.f., s. and pl.* himself, herself, yourself, yourselves, themselves, oneself. Used as reflexive, as personal conjunctive for *le, les* before another governed pronoun of the third person, and as giving a passive sense to a verb: *morirse,* to die; *reírse,* to laugh.

sé, *pres. indic.* [SABER].

sebáceo, -cea, *a.* sebaceous.

sebe, *n.f.* wattle, fence.

sebera, *n.f.* (*Chi.*) leather bag to carry tallow.

sebestén, *n.m.* sebesten (tree or fruit).

sebillo, *n.m.* tallow; suet-paste; toilet-soap.

sebiya, *n.f.* (*Cub.*) wading bird.

sebo, *n.m.* tallow, candle-grease, suet, fat.

seboro, *n.m.* (*Bol.*) fresh-water crab.

seboso, -sa, *a.* fat, greasy, tallowy, unctuous.

sebucán, *n.m.* (*Ven.*) manioc strainer.

seca, *n.f.* drought, dry season; dry sandbank; (*med.*) infarction of a gland. — *pl.* **secas,** sands, rocks; *a secas,* alone, singly.

secadal, *n.m.* barren ground.

secadero, *n.m.* drying shed, drying floor; drier; fruit-drier.

secadero, -ra, *a.* good for drying (especially fruit or tobacco).

secadillo, *n.m.* kind of dry almond biscuit.

secador, *n.m.* (*Arg.*) drier; drying shed, room or floor for clothes.

secamente, *adv.* drily, plainly; morosely, harshly, peevishly.

secamiento, *n.m.* desiccation, act of drying.

secano, *n.m.* unirrigated land; dry sandbank; anything very dry.

secansa, *n.f.* game of cards.

secante, *n.m.* drier, drying oil; blotting-paper. — *n.f.* (*geom.*) secant. — *a.* siccative, exsiccative.

secar, *v.t.* (*pret.* **sequé**; *pres. subj.* **seque**) to dry, parch, exsiccate, desiccate; to wipe; to vex, tease, bore, annoy. — *v.r.* to dry, grow dry, become parched or dried up; to decay; to be very thirsty.

secaral, *n.m.* dryness, drought.

secatura, *n.f.* insipidity, flatness, vapidness, dullness; coolness, indifference.

sección, *n.f.* section, division, portion; act of cutting; (*mil.*) platoon.

seccionado, -da, *a.* sectional, in sections.

seccionar, *v.t.* to section.

secesión, *n.f.* secession, separation.

secesionista, *n.m.f.*, *a.* secessionist.

seceso, *n.m.* excrement, stool.

seco, -ca, *a.* dry, dried up, barren, arid, juiceless, sapless, withered, parched; meagre, lean, lank; bare, mere, plain, unadorned, unvarnished; curt, rude, unsociable; indifferent, cold, lukewarm; thin and spare; *golpe seco,* sharp, quick blow; *en seco,* high and dry.

secreción, *n.f.* (*med.*) secretion; segregation.

secreta, *n.f.* private examination preceding the graduation of licentiates; (*eccles.*) secret; secret investigation; privy, closet.

secretamente, *adv.* secretly, clandestinely.

secretar, *v.t.* (*physiol.*) to secrete, separate.

secretaria, *n.f.* lady secretary; secretary's wife.

secretaría, *n.f.* secretary's office, secretaryship.

secretario, *n.m.* secretary; clerk, amanuensis, scribe.

secretear, *v.i.* (*coll.*) to speak in private, whisper.

secreteo, *n.m.* (*coll.*) whispering.

secretista, *n.m.* naturalist; dealer in secrets.

secreto, -ta, *a.* secret, private, hidden, occult, dark, obscure, clandestine, confidential.

secreto, *n.m.* secrecy; secret arcanum, secret knowledge, dissimulation, caution; silence; secret drawer; concealment; darkness; *de secreto, en secreto,* secretly, privately; *echar un secreto en la calle,* to make a secret public.

secretorio, -ria, *a.* (*med.*) secretory.

secta, *n.f.* sect; doctrine of a sect; heresy.

sectador, -ra, *n.m.f.* sectarist.

sectario, -ria, *n.m.f.*, *a.* sectarian, sectary.

sectarismo, *n.m.* sectarianism.

sector, *n.m.*, *a.* (*geom.*) sector.

secua, *n.f.* (*Cub.*) a cucurbitaceous plant.

secuaz, *n.m.f.*, *a.* follower; sequacious, following, attendant.

secuela, *n.f.* sequel, continuation; result.

secuencia, *n.f.* (*eccles.*) sequence.

secuestrable, *a.* sequestrable.

secuestración, *n.f.* sequestration.

secuestrador, *n.m.* sequestrator.

secuestrar, *v.t.* to sequester, sequestrate; to kidnap, abduct.

secuestro, *n.m.* sequestration; embargo; kid-napping, abduction; (*surg.*) sequestrum; (*obs.*) umpire, referee.

sécula seculórum, *adv.* for ever and ever, world without end.

secular, *a.* secular; lay; centenary, centennial.

secularidad, *n.f.* secularity.

secularización, *n.f.* secularization.

secularizar, *v.t.* (conjugated like ALZAR) to secularize.

secundar, *v.t.* to second; to assist, aid, favour.

secundariamente, *adv.* secondarily.

secundario, -ria, *a.* secondary; high (school); subordinate, accessory, second-rate, subsidiary. — *n.m.* (watch) seconds hand.

secundinas, *n.f.pl.* afterbirth, secundines.

secura, *n.f.* dryness, drought.

sed, *n.f.* thirst; drought; eagerness; anxiety, longing; *tener sed,* to be thirsty; *no dar una sed de agua,* not to give the least help.

seda, *n.f.* silk; wild boar's bristles; *ser (como) una seda,* to be of a sweet temper.

sedadera, *n.f.* hackle for dressing flax.

sedal, *n.m.* angling line; (*vet.*) rowel; (*surg.*) seton.

sedar, *v.t.* to mitigate, allay, appease, quiet, soothe.

sedativo, -va, *a.* (*med.*) sedative.

sede, *n.f.* (*eccles.*) see; *Santa Sede,* Holy See, Papacy.

sedear, *v.t.* to clean jewels with a brush.

sedentario, -ria, *a.* sedentary.

sedeña, *n.f.* flaxen tow.

sedeño, -ña, *a.* silky, silken, silk-like; made of hair.

sedera, *n.f.* brush made of bristles.

sedería, *n.f.* silks, silk stuff, silk mercer's shop.

sedero, *n.m.* silk-mercer.

sedero, -ra, *a.* silk, silken.

sedición, *n.f.* sedition, insurrection, mutiny.

sediciosamente, *adv.* seditiously, factiously, mutinously.

sedicioso, -sa, *a.* seditious, factious, mutinous.

sediento, -ta, *a.* thirsty, dry; desirous, eager, longing.

sedimentación, *n.f.* sedimentation.

sedimentar, *v.t.*, *v.i.* to settle; to deposit (as dregs).

sedimentario, -ria, *a.* sedimentary.

sedimento, *n.m.* sediment, settlings, dregs; fæces; sinter.

sedoso, -sa, *a.* silky, silk-like, silken.

seducción, *n.f.* seduction, deceiving, abuse.

seducir, *v.t.* (*pres. indic.* **seduzco,** *pret.* **seduje,** *pres. subj.* **seduzca**) to seduce; to deceive, mislead, corrupt, entice, lead astray; to captivate, charm.

seductivo, -va, *a.* seductive, enticing.

seductor, -ra, *n.m.f.* seducer, corrupter, deceiver; charming, delightful person. — *a.* seductive, fascinating.

sefardí, sefardita, *n.m.f.*, *a.* sephardi, a Spanish or Portuguese Jew; sephardic.

segable, *a.* fit to be reaped.

segada, *n.f.* harvest.

segadera, *n.f.* reaping-hook, sickle.

segadero, -ra, *a.* fit for reaping.

segador, -ra, *n.m.f.* mower, reaper, harvester, sickleman. — *n.f.* mowing machine.

segar, *v.t.* (*pres. indic.* **siego,** *pret.* **segué,** *pres. subj.* **siegue**) to reap, mow, crop, harvest; to cut down, cut off.

segazón, *n.f.* harvest season, reaping.

seglar, *a.* worldly; secular, lay. — *n.m.* layman.
seglarmente, *adv.* secularly.
segmento, *n.m.* segment.
segregación, *n.f.* segregation, separation.
segregar, *v.t.* (*pret.* **segregué,** *pres. subj.* **segregue**) to segregate, set apart; (*med.*) to secrete.
segregativo, -va, *a.* segregative.
segrí, *n.m.* heavy, raised silk stuff.
segueta, *n.f.* fretsaw.
seguetear, *v.i.* to use a fretsaw.
seguida, *n.f.* following, continuation, succession; *de seguida,* successively, uninterruptedly; *en seguida,* forthwith, immediately.
seguidamente, *adv.* successively, immediately.
seguidero, *n.m.* guide-lines for writing.
seguidilla, *n.f.* (*poet.*) stanza of four or seven lines; *pl.* **seguidillas,** a merry Spanish tune and dance; (*coll.*) diarrhœa.
seguido, -da, *a.* continued, successive; straight, direct.
seguido, *n.m.* narrowing of a stocking at the foot.
seguidor, -ra, *n.m.f.* follower; *n.m.* guide rules for writing.
seguimiento, *n.m.* pursuit, chase, hunt; continuation, prosecution, endeavour.
seguir, *v.t.* (*pres. part.* **siguiendo**; *pres. indic.* **sigo**; *pres. subj.* **siga**; *pret.* **él siguió**) to follow, pursue, come after, accompany; to proceed, continue, go on; to exercise, practise (profession, etc.); to dog, follow closely, hound; to copy, imitate; to carry out orders; to conform to, agree; to bring, institute (as a lawsuit; *seguirle los pasos a uno,* to keep one's eye on a person's actions. — *v.r.* to follow, ensue; to succeed; to issue, spring from.
según, *prep.* according to, as; it depends; *según y como* (or *según y conforme*), just as; it depends; *según derecho,* according to law.
segunda, *n.f.* (*mus.*) second; double meaning; double turn of a key.
segundar, *v.t.* to repeat. — *v.i.* to be second.
segundario, -ria, *a.* secondary.
segundero, -ra, *a.* (*agric.*) said of a second crop in the same year. — *n.m.* seconds hand of a watch.
segundilla, *n.f.* call bell in convents.
segundillo, *n.m.* second portion of bread distributed in some monasteries; (*mus.*) accidental.
segundo, -da, *a.* second; favourable; *de segunda mano,* at second hand; *en segundo lugar,* secondly.
segundo, *n.m.* second (of time or of a degree).
segundogénito, -ta, *n.m.f.,* *a.* second-born.
segundón, *n.m.* second or younger son.
segur, *n.f.* axe, sickle.
segurador, *n.m.* security, surety, bondsman.
seguramente, *adv.* securely, certainly, surely, fast, safely.
segurar, *v.t.* [ASEGURAR].
segureja, *n.f.* small hatchet.
seguridad, *n.f.* security, surety, certainty; confidence, safety; fastness, custody; corroboration.
seguro, -ra, *a.* secure, safe, assured, easy, sure, positive, certain, constant, firm; staunch, strong, steady; unfailing, infallible, unfaltering.
seguro, *n.m.* permission, warrant, permit, licence; insurance; certainty, confidence,

assurance; (*mech.*) pawl, click, stop, ratchet; (*com.*) insurance, assurance; tumbler of a lock; *al seguro,* securely; *a buen seguro,* indubitably; *de seguro,* assuredly; *sobre seguro,* without risk; *compañía de seguros,* insurance company; *seguro contra accidentes, incendio, etc.,* accident, fire, etc., insurance; *seguro sobre la vida,* life insurance; *irse del seguro,* (*coll.*) to throw wisdom overboard.
segurón, *n.m.* large axe or hatchet.
seis, *n.m., a.* six; six-spotted card, dice, etc.; the sixth of the month; (*PR.*) popular dance, kind of *zapateado.* — *f.pl.* **las seis,** six o'clock.
seisavado, -da, *a.* hexagonal.
seisavo, *n.m.* sixth part; hexagon. — *a.* sixth.
seiscientos, -tas, *a.* six hundred, six hundredth.
seise, *n.m.* one of the six choirboys who sing and dance in some cathedrals.
seiseno, -na, *a.* sixth.
seisillo, *n.m.* sextolet.
séismico, *a.* seismic.
seje, *n.m.* (*Am.*) a kind of palm-tree.
selección, *n.f.* selection, choice; *selección natural,* natural selection.
selectas, *n.f.pl.* analects.
selecto, -ta, *a.* select, choice, excellent.
selenio, *n.m.* selenium.
selenita, *n.f.* selenite. — *n.m.f* inhabitant of the moon.
selenitoso, -sa, *a.* selenitic.
seleniuro, *n.m.* (*chem.*) selenide.
selenografía, *n.f.* selenographia.
selfinducción, *n.f.* (*elec.*) (incorrect but commonly used) self-induction (*autoinducción*).
selva, *n.f.* forest, wood, woodland, thicket.
selvático, -ca, *a.* forest-born, wild, rustic, sylvan.
selvatiquez, *n.f.* rusticity, wildness.
selvicultura, *n.f.* forestry, silviculture.
selvoso, -sa, *a.* woody, sylvan, belonging to forests.
sellador, *n.m.* sealer.
selladura, *n.f.* sealing.
sellar, *v.t.* to stamp, seal; to conclude, finish; to close up, cover; *sellar los labios,* to silence; to keep silent.
sello, *n.m.* stamp, seal, signet; stamp office; (*pharm.*) wafer; *echar* (or *poner*) *el sello a,* to carry to perfection; *sello de aduana,* cocket; *sello de correo,* postage stamp; *sello de Salomón,* Solomon's seal.
semafórico, -ca, *a.* semaphoric.
semáforo, *n.m.* semaphore.
semana, *n.f.* week; week's wages; *entre semana,* one day in a week, other than the first and last; *semana santa,* Holy Week; *la semana que no tenga viernes,* a phrase expressing impossibility.
semanal, *a.* weekly, hebdomadal.
semanalmente, *adv.* weekly.
semanario, -ria, *a.* weekly. — *n.m.f.* weekly publication; set of seven razors.
semanería, *n.f.* work done in the course of a week.
semanero, -ra, *n.m.f.* one who is engaged by the week, one having weekly functions.
semántica, *n.f.* semantics, semasiology.
semántico, -ca, *a.* semantic.
semasiología, *n.f.* semasiology, semantics.
semblante, *n.m.* face, feature, phase, aspect,

countenance, expression, look, mien; *hacer semblante*, to pretend, feign.

semblanza, *n.f.* biographical sketch.

sembradera, *n.f.* sowing machine, sower, seeder.

sembradío, -día, *a.* ready for sowing seed; arable land.

sembrado, *n.m.* corn-field; sown ground.

sembrador, *n.m.* sower.

sembradura, *n.f.* sowing, seeding.

sembrar, *v.t.* (*pres. indic.* **siembro;** *pres. subj.* **siembre**) to sow; to seed; to scatter, propagate, disseminate, spread; to give cause; *quien bien siembra, bien coge,* he who sows well, reaps well; *como sembráredes, cogéredes,* as you sow, so shall you reap.

semeja, *n.f.* resemblance, likeness; mark, sign.

semejable, *a.* resembling, similar, like.

semejablemente, *adv.* similarly, in a like manner.

semejado, -da, *a.* like, resembling.

semejante, *a.* similar, like, resembling, alike, akin. — *n.m.* fellow-creature; likeness, resemblance; *por semejante,* equally, similarly.

semejantemente, *adv.* likewise, similarly.

semejanza, *n.f.* resemblance, similarity, semblance, likeness, conformity, similitude.

semejar, *v.i.* to resemble, be like.

semen, *n.m.* semen, sperm, seed.

semencera, *n.f.* sowing, seeding.

semencontra, *n.m.* (*pharm.*) vermifuge.

semental, *a.* seminal, germinal. — *n.m.* stallion, stud horse.

sementera, *n.f.* sowing, seeding; seed sown; seed-field, seed-bed, seed plot, any land sown; seed-time; origin, beginning, cause.

sementero, *n.m.* seed-bag; seed-bed; seed-plot.

sementino, -na, *a.* belonging to seed or seed-time.

semestral, *a.;* **semestralmente,** *adv.* half-yearly.

semestre, *n.m.* space of six months; six-months' pay. — *a.* semi-annual.

semibreve, *n.f.* (*mus.*) semibreve.

semicabrón, semicapro, *n.m.* satyr, half-goat.

semicilindro, *n.m.* half cylinder.

semicircular, *a.* semicircular.

semicírculo, *n.m.* semicircle.

semicopado, -da, *a.* syncopated.

semicorchea, *n.f.* semiquaver.

semidea, *n.f.* (*poet.*) demigoddess.

semideo, *n.m.* (*poet.*) demigod.

semidiáfano, -na, *a.* semi-diaphanous.

semidiámetro, *n.m.* semidiameter, radius.

semidifunto, -ta, *a.* half-dead, almost dead.

semidiós, -sa, *n.m.f.* demigod, demigoddess.

semiditono, *n.m.* demi-ditone.

semidoble, *n.m., a.* semidouble.

semidormido, -da, *a.* half-asleep, sleepy.

semieje, *n.m.* (*geom.*) semiaxis; (*motor.*) half axle-tree.

semiesfera, *n.f.* hemisphere.

semiesférico, -ca, *a.* hemispherical.

semiflúido, -da, *a.* semifluid.

semiforme, *a.* half-formed, undeveloped.

semifusa, *n.f.* double demisemiquaver.

semigola, *n.f.* (*fort.*) demi-gorge.

semihombre, *n.m.* half-man, pigmy.

semilunar, *a.* semilunar.

semilunio, *n.m.* half-moon.

semilla, *n.f.* seed; cause, origin.

semillero, *n.m.* seed-bed, seed-plot, nursery; (*fig.*) hotbed.

seminal, *a.* seminal, radical, germinal, spermatic.

seminario, *n.m.* seed-plot, nursery; seminary; beginning, root, origin.

seminarista, *n.m.* seminarist, theological student.

semínima, *n.f.* crotchet.

semipedal, *a.* of half a foot long.

semiplena, *n.f.* (*law*) imperfect evidence.

semiplenamente, *adv.* (*law*) half proved.

semirrecto, -ta, *a.* (*geom.*) of forty-five degrees.

semirrubio, -bia, *a.* nearly blonde.

semis, *n.m.* half a Roman pound.

semita, *n.m.f., a.* Semite.

semítico, -ca, *a.* Semitic.

semitono, *n.m.* semitone.

semitransparente, *a.* almost transparent.

semivivo, -va, *a.* half-alive.

semivocal, *n.f.* semivowel. — *a.* semivocalic.

sémola, *n.f.* groats, grits; semolina.

semoviente, *a.* (*law*) self-moving.

sempiterna, *n.f.* everlasting (a kind of cloth).

sempiternamente, *adv.* eternally.

sempiterno, -na, *a.* everlasting, sempiternal.

sen, sena, *n.f.* senna.

sena, *n.f.* six spots (on dice). — *pl.* **senas,** double sixes (on dice).

senado, *n.m.* senate; senate-house, town-hall; audience.

senadoconsulto, *n.m.* senatus-consultum, senatorial decree.

senador, *n.m.* senator.

senaduría, *n.f.* senatorship.

senara, *n.f.* piece of ground assigned to servants as part of their wages.

senario, *n.m.* (*poet.*) senarius.

senario, -ria, *a.* senary.

senatorio, -ria, *a.* senatorial.

sencillamente, *adv.* simply, ingenuously, plainly, candidly.

sencillez, *n.f.* simplicity, artlessness, candour; plainness.

sencillo, -lla, *a.* simple, ingenuous, plain, artless, candid, guileless; unmixed, single; harmless; of less value (coins); unadorned, natural; slender, slight, of thin body (fabrics).

senda, *n.f.* path, footpath, way.

sendar, *v.t.* to walk on a path; to make a path.

senderear, *v.t.* to guide on a footpath; to make a path.

sendero, *n.m.* path, footpath, by-way.

sendos, -das, *a.pl.* either, each of two, one for each, respective; (*incorr.*) good, strong; *sendos golpes,* heavy blows.

senectud, *n.f.* old age, senescence.

senescal, *n.m.* seneschal.

senescalía, *n.f.* office of a seneschal.

senil, *a.* senile. — *n.m.* (*astron.*) fourth quadrant.

seno, *n.m.* bosom, breast, chest; lap; womb; hole, cavity; (*surg.*) sinus; gulf, bay; innermost recess; security, refuge; (*math.*) sine; deceit; (*arch.*) spandrel; (*naut.*) curvature of a sail or line; *seno recto,* (*trig.*) sine; *seno segundo,* (*trig.*) cosine.

senojil, *n.m.* garter.

sensación, *n.f.* sensation, feeling, emotion.

sensacional, *a.* sensational.

sensatamente, *adv.* wisely, prudently.

sensatez, *n.f.* sense, sensibleness, good sense, prudence, judgment.

sensato, -ta, *a.* sensible, reasonable, prudent, wise, judicious.

sensibilidad, *n.f.* sensibility, sensitiveness, quickness of perception.

sensibilizar (*pret.* **sensibilicé;** *subj.* **sensibilice**), *v.t.* (*phot.*) to sensitize.

sensible, *a.* sensible, sensitive, perceptiole; grievous, lamentable, regrettable; (*phot.*) sensitized. — *n.f.* (*mus.*) seventh note.

sensiblemente, *adv.* sensibly.

sensiblería, *n.f.* exaggerated sentimentality.

sensitiva, *n.f.* sensitive plant, mimosa.

sensitivo, -va, *a.* sensitive, sensible, sensual.

sensorio, -ria, *a.* sensorial, sensory.

sensorio, *n.m.* sensorium (called also *sensorio común*).

sensual, *a.* sensuous; sensual, lewd, lustful.

sensualidad, *n.f.* sensuality, lewdness, lust.

sensualismo, *n.m.* sensualism, sensuality; (*phil.*) sensationalism.

sensualista, *n.m.f.* sensualist, sensationalist. — *a.* sensualistic.

sensualmente, *adv.* sensually, carnally.

sentada, *n.f.* sitting.

sentadero, *n.m.* any place or thing where one can sit.

sentadillas, (a), *adv.* side-saddlewise.

sentado, -da, *a.* seated, sitting down; sedate, judicious; grave, prudent, settled, steady, firm; (*bot.*) sessile; (*med.*) *pulso sentado,* pulse quiet, steady, firm. — *p.p.* [SENTAR].

sentar, *v.t.* (*pres. indic.* **siento;** *pres. subj.* **siente**) to become, fit, suit; to set up, establish; to seat. — *v.i.* to become, suit, fit, agree with; to please, be agreeable. — *v.r.* to sink, settle, subside; to sit down; to settle down; to squat.

sentencia, *n.f.* sentence, verdict, decision, judgment; penalty; opinion, dogma, axiom, maxim; (*com.*) award; *fulminar* or *pronunciar la sentencia,* to pass judgment, publish the sentence.

sentenciador, -ra, *n.m.f., a.* one who passes judgment.

sentenciar, *v.t.* to sentence, condemn, pass judgment; to decide, determine.

sentención, *n.m.* severe or excessive sentence.

sentenciosamente, *adv.* sententiously.

sentencioso, -sa, *a.* sententious, axiomatic, pithy.

sentenzuela, *n.f.* light sentence.

senticar, *n.m.* brambly place.

sentidamente, *adv.* feelingly, painfully, regretfully.

sentido, -da, *a.* sensitive, feeling; experienced, felt; relaxed, cracked, cloven, split; touchy, susceptible, easily offended; *darse por sentido,* to show resentment; *estar sentido,* to be slightly put out.

sentido, *n.m.* sense, reason, feeling, understanding; meaning, acceptation, significance, import, construction; (*geom.*) course, direction; *sentido común,* common sense; *costar un sentido,* to be exceedingly high-priced; *perder el sentido,* to faint; *poner sus cinco sentidos en uno,* to pay someone the greatest attention; *sin sentido,* senseless, foolish, nonsensical.

sentimental, *a.* sentimental, emotional, pathetic, affecting.

sentimentalismo, *n.m.* sentimentalism.

sentimentalmente, *adv.* sentimentally.

sentimiento, *n.m.* sentiment, perception, feeling, emotion, sensation; resentment, grief, sorrow, pain; judgment; concern, regret.

sentina, *n.f.* (*naut.*) bilge; drain, sink, well; place of iniquity.

sentir, *v.t.* (*pres. part.* **sintiendo;** *pres. indic.* **siento;** *pres. subj.* **sienta;** *pret.* **él sintió**) to feel, perceive; to hear; to judge, to endure, suffer; to regret, grieve, mourn, be sorry; to taste; to form an opinion; to foreknow, foresee. — *v.r.* to be affected, moved; to complain; to crack; to be in a ruinous condition; to resent, be sensible; to feel (well, bad, sad); (*naut.*) to spring (yard or mast). — *n.m.* feeling, judgment, opinion.

seña, *n.f.* sign, mark, token; signal, motion, nod; (*mil.*) password, watchword. — *pl.* **señas,** address; *señas mortales,* unmistakable signs; *por (más) señas,* as a stronger proof; *por señas,* by signs.

señal, *n.f.* sign, mark, token, trace, track, vestige; handsel, earnest-money, pledge; (*med.*) symptom, indication; signal; landmark; reminder, book-mark; stump, scar; footstep; prognostic, image, representation; prodigy, wonder; (*teleg., wire.*) warning, call; *en señal,* in proof; *señal de peligro,* distress or danger signal; *código de señales,* signal code; *ni señal,* not a vestige, not a trace.

señaladamente, *adv.* especially, signally, namely, remarkably.

señalado, -da, *a.* famous, celebrated, noted.

señalamiento, *n.m.* assignation, appointment, date.

señalar, *v.t.* to stamp, mark out; to indicate, show, signalize, make signals, point out, make known; to fix, determine; to sign; to mark with a wound (especially in the face); (*fenc.*) to make a feint; to mark the points (at card games). — *v.r.* to excel, distinguish oneself.

señaleja, *n.f.* little sign or mark.

señera, *n.f.* ancient pendant or banner.

señero, -ra, *a.* solitary; nonpareil, alone, unique.

señolear, *v.i.* to catch birds with a lure.

señor, *n.m.* sir; lord, owner, master; Mr.; God, our Lord; the Eucharist; *quedar señor del campo,* to be master of the situation; *el Señor,* the Lord; our Lord (Jesus Christ); *nuestro Señor,* our Lord; *ministro del Señor,* a clergyman; *casa del Señor,* a church; *sirve a señor y sabrás de dolor,* put not your trust in princes.

señora, *n.f.* lady, mistress, owner, madam, dame, gentlewoman; *nuestra Señora,* our Lady (the Virgin).

señoraje, señoreaje, *n.m.* seigniorage.

señoreador, -ra, *n.m.f.* domineering person.

señoreaje, *n.m.* seigniorage.

señoreante, *a.* domineering (person).

señorear, *v.t.* to master, domineer, lord, rule despotically, excel; to tower over, overtop; to control one's passions; (*coll.*) to lord it over. — *v.r.* to play the lord.

señoría, *n.f.* lordship, seigniory; dominion; government of a particular state; senate; prince.

señorial, *a.* manorial.

señoril, *a.* lordly, noble; genteel.

señorilmente, *adv.* nobly, majestically.

señorío, *n.m.* seigniory, dominion; lordship; imperiousness; gravity, dignity of mien; manor; freedom and self-control in action.

señorita, *n.f.* girl, young lady, young mistress; Miss; (*coll.*) mistress of the house.

señoritingo, *n.m.* (*contempt.*) little master, youth of no account.

señorito, *n.m.* lordling, young lord, young master; (*coll.*) master of the house.

señorón, -na, *n.m.f.* great lord or lady.

señuelo, *n.m.* lure, enticement; bait; decoy; *caer en el señuelo*, to fall into the trap.

seo, *n.f.* cathedral church.

seo, seor, seora, *n.m.f.* (contraction of **señor, señora**) (*coll.*) lord, sir; madam, lady.

sepa, *pres. subj.* [SABER].

sépalo, *n.m.* sepal.

sepancuantos, *n.m.* (*coll.*) spanking; scolding, punishment.

separable, *a.* separable.

separación, *n.f.* (*law*) separation; segregation, dissociation, disseverance, abstraction; parting; deposition, discharge, dismissal; (*pol.*) secession.

separadamente, *adv.* separately.

separador, -ra, *n.m.f.* separator, divider.

separante, *a.* separating.

separar, *v.t.* to separate, cut, divide, part; to disjoin; to disconnect; segregate, detach, dissever; to lay aside, set apart; to remove, take off; to divorce; to depose, dismiss, discharge. — *v.r.* to part, come apart, be disjoined, be disunited, withdraw; to resign, to drop all intercourse; (*com.*) to dissolve; (*law*) to waive a right.

separatismo, *n.m.* separatism; (*pol.*) secessionism.

separatista, *n.m.f.*, *a.* separatist; secessionist.

separativo, -va, *a.* separatory.

sepe, *n.m.* (*Bol.*) white ant.

sepedón, *n.m.* seps; a lizard of the Scincidæ family.

sepelio, *n.m.* interment, burial.

sepia, *n.f.* (*ichth.*) cuttle-fish; (*art*) sepia.

septena, *n.f.* septenary.

septenario, *n.m.* septenary, heptate.

septenario, -ria, *a.* septenary.

septenio, *n.m.* space of seven years.

septentrión, *n.m.* septentrion; north wind; (*astr.*) Great Bear.

septentrional, *a.* septentrional, northern, northerly.

septeto, *n.m.* (*mus.*) septet.

séptico, -ca, *a.* septic.

septiembre, *n.m.* September.

séptima, *n.f.* (*mus.*) seventh; sequence of seven cards in piquet.

séptimo, -ma, *a.* seventh.

septuagenario, -ria, *a.* septuagenary, seventy years of age.

septuagésima, *n.f.* third Sunday before Lent.

septuagésimo, -ma, *a.* seventieth, septuagesimal.

septuplicar, *v.t.* (conjugated like BUSCAR), to multiply by seven.

séptuplo, -pla, *a.* septuple, sevenfold.

sepulcral, *a.* sepulchral; monumental.

sepulcro, *n.m.* sepulchre, tomb, grave.

sepultador, *n.m.* burier, grave-digger.

sepultar, *v.t.* to inter, bury, entomb; to conceal, hide.

sepulto, -ta, *p.part. irreg. of* SEPELIR and SEPULTAR, buried.

sepultura, *n.f.* sepulture, interment; tomb, grave; *dar sepultura*, to inter.

sepulturero, *n.m.* grave-digger, sexton.

sequedad, *n.f.* aridity, dryness; sterility, barrenness; asperity, gruffness, surliness; lack of irrigation.

sequedal, sequeral, *n.m.* dry, barren soil.

sequero, *n.m.* dry, arid, unirrigated land.

sequeroso, -sa, *a.* dry, moistureless.

sequete, *n.m.* dry crust; dry bread or biscuit; stale; curt, harsh answer; harshness; violent shock; stroke, blow.

sequía, *n.f.* dryness, drought; (*obs. and prov.*) thirst.

sequillo, *n.m.* rusk, kind of biscuit.

sequío, *n.m.* unirrigated arable ground.

séquito, *n.m.* retinue, suite, train; popularity.

sequizo, -za, *a.* dry (fruits); dryish.

ser, substantive verb; auxiliary verb by which the passive is formed, and *v.i.* (*pres. part.* **siendo**; *pres. indic.* **soy**; *imperf.* **era**; *pret.* **fuí**; *pres. subj.* **sea**) to be, exist; to belong; to happen, fall out; to be worth; *un si es no es*, somewhat; *soy con Vd.*, I agree with you (or I'll be with you in a moment); *soy de Vd.*, I am, yours truly (in letters); *ser para todo*, to be fit for everything; *sea lo que fuere*, be that as it may; *si yo fuera que Vd.*, if I were you; *lo que fuere, sonará*, wait and see; *ser para menos*, to be less capable than another; *érase que se era*, once upon a time.

ser, *n.m.* life, being, existence; essence, nature, substance, entity; value.

sera, *n.f.* large pannier or basket, frail.

serado, seraje, *n.m.* number of panniers or baskets.

seráficamente, *adv.* seraphically.

seráfico, -ca, *a.* seraphic, angelic; (*coll.*) poor, humble; *hacer la seráfica*, to affect virtue or modesty.

serafín, *n.m.* seraph, angel; extremely beautiful person.

serafina, *n.f.* kind of swanskin.

seraje, *n.m.* [SERADO].

serba, *n.f.* fruit of the service-tree.

serbal, serbo, *n.m.* service-tree.

serena, *n.f.* evening dew; serenade.

serenamente, *adv.* serenely, calmly, composedly, coolly, quietly.

serenar, *v.t.*, *v.i.*, *v.r.* to grow clear, clear up, become serene (of the weather); to settle, become clear (of liquids); pacify, tranquillize; to cool water in the night air.

serenata, *n.f.* (*mus.*) serenade.

serenero, *n.m.* nightrail, night-wrap; (*Arg.*) a kerchief worn by peasant women.

serení, *n.m.* (*naut.*) jolly-boat; yawl.

serenidad, *n.f.* serenity, clearness, calmness, tranquillity, placidity; serene highness (title).

serenísimo, -ma, *a.* most serene (title of princes).

sereno, -na, *a.* serene, calm, fair, cloudless, quiet, peaceful, clear, unruffled, placid.

sereno, *n.m.* night watch, watchman; night dew; *al sereno*, *a la serena*, in the night air.

sergas, *n.f.pl.* exploits, achievements.

sergenta, *n.f.* lay sister of the order of Santiago.

seriamente, *adv.* seriously; gravely; in earnest, once and for all.

sericícula, *a.* sericultural.

sericultor, -ra, *n., a.* sericulturist; sericultural.

sericultura, *n.f.* silk culture, sericulture.

sérico, -ca, *a.* silken.

serie, *n.f.* series, order, gradation, succession, suite, sequence; (*manufact.*) mass production.

seriedad, *n.f.* seriousness, gravity; sternness, severity; sincerity; plainness; earnestness, soberness.

serijo, serillo, *n.m.* small basket, small frail.

seringa, *n.f.* (*Am.*) rubber-tree.

serio, -ria, *a.* serious, grave, important, dignified, weighty; majestic, solemn, grand; stern, severe; earnest, sober; plain, true.

sermón, *n.m.* sermon, homily; (*fig.*) reprehension, censure.

sermonario, -ria, *a.* relating to a sermon.

sermonario, *n.m.* collection of sermons.

sermonear, *v.t.* to reprimand, reprove, censure, sermonize.

sermoneo, *n.m.* reproof, reprimand, lecture.

serna, *n.f.* cultivated field.

seroja, *n.f.; serojo, n.m.* withered leaf; brushwood.

serón, *n.m.* hamper, crate; frail, pannier; seron, seroon; *serón caminero,* horse-pannier.

seronero, *n.m.* trail-maker; frail-seller.

serosidad, *n.f.* (*med.*) serosity, serousness.

seroso, -sa, *a.* serous, thin, watery.

serpa, *n.f.* provine, layer, runner.

serpear, *v.i.* to meander; crawl, creep, wind, wriggle, squirm.

serpentaria, *n.f.* snake-root; *serpentaria virginiana,* Virginia snake-root.

serpentario, *n.m.* (*orn.*) secretary bird; (*astron.*) Ophiuchus.

serpentear, *v.i.* to serpentine, meander, wriggle, squirm.

serpentín, *n.m.* (*min.*) serpentine; cock, musket lock; (*chem.*) distilling worm; (*artill.*) a twenty-four pounder.

serpentina, *n.f.* cock of a gun; culverin; (*min.*) serpentine.

serpentinamente, *adv.* in a serpentine manner.

serpentino, -na, *a.* serpentine, resembling a serpent, serpent-like, snake-like; slanderous, poisoned tongue; serpentine marble; sinuous, wriggling, zigzag.

serpentón, *n.m.* large serpent; (*mus.*) serpent.

serpezuela, *n.f.* little serpent.

serpiente, *n.f.* serpent, snake; devil, Satan; (*astron.*) Serpens; *serpiente de cascabel,* rattlesnake.

serpiginoso, -sa, *a.* (*med.*) serpiginous.

serpigo, *n.m.* ring-worm, tetter.

serpol, *n.m.* wild thyme.

serpollar, *v.i.* to shoot, sprout.

serpollo, *n.m.* shoot, sprout, sucker, sapling.

serradizo, -za, *a.* fit to be sawn.

serrado, -da, *a.* dentated, serrate. — *p.p.* [SERRAR].

serrador, *n.m.* sawer, sawyer.

serraduras, *n.f.pl.* sawdust.

serrallo, *n.m.* seraglio, harem; brothel.

serrana, *n.f.* (*poet.*) bucolic poem.

serranía, *n.f.* ridge of mountains, mountainous country.

serraniego, -ga, *n.m.f., a.* mountaineer, highlander.

serranil, *n.m.* kind of knife or poniard.

serranilla, *n.f.* poem in popular style on a rustic subject.

serrano, -na, *n.m.f., a.* mountaineer, highlander.

serrar, *v.t.* (*pres. indic.* **sierro;** *pres. subj.* **sierre**) to saw.

serrátil, *a.* (*med.*) irregular (of pulse).

serratilla, *n.f.* small mountain chain.

serrato, -ta, *a.* (*anat.*) denticulated, serrated.

serreta, *n.f.* small saw; nose band used in breaking mules; rank chevron of auxiliary army corps.

serretazo, *n.m.* sudden pulling of reins (horses or mules).

serrezuela, *n.f.* small saw.

serrijón, *n.m.* short mountain chain.

serrín, *n.m.* sawdust.

serrino, -na, *a.* belonging to or like a saw; (*med.*) irregular (of pulse).

serrucho, *n.m.* hand-saw; *serrucho braguero,* pit-saw; (*Cub.*) saw-fish.

serum, *n.m.* (*med.*) serum.

servador, *n.m.* (*poet.*) guard, defender.

servato, *n.m.* hog-fennel, sulphur-weed.

serventia, *n.f.* (*Cub.*) path with right of way.

servible, *a.* serviceable, adaptable.

serviciador, *n.m.* collector of sheepwalk dues.

servicial, *a.* obliging, diligent, friendly, compliant, obsequious, accommodating. — *n.m.* (*coll.*) clyster.

servicialmente, *adv.* serviceably, obsequiously.

serviciar, *v.t.* to collect dues (sheepwalk, donations to the state, etc.).

servicio, *n.m.* service; condition of a servant; help, servants; benefit, utility, advantage, usefulness, favour, good turn, kind office; (*eccles.*) divine service; money voluntarily offered to the king or nation; cover, course; tea, coffee or dinner set; close-stool; *a buen servicio mal galardón,* for good service bad reward.

servidero, -ra, *a.* fit for service, useful; requiring personal attention.

servidor, *n.m.* servant, waiter; wooer, gallant; privy-pan; *servidor de Vd.,* at your service.

servidora, *n.f.* maid, female servant.

servidumbre, *n.f.* attendance, servitude, serfdom; service, help, servants; inexcusable obligation; *servidumbre de luces,* (*law*) ancient lights; *servidumbre de paso,* (*law*) right of way.

servil, *a.* servile, fawning, grovelling, menial, slavish; abject, mean, low, vile; (*Span. hist.*) partisan of absolute monarchy.

servilidad, *n.f.* servility, meanness.

servilismo, *n.m.* servility, servileness; (*Span. hist.*) absolutism.

servilmente, *adv.* servilely, slavishly, basely, indecently.

servilla, *n.f.* (*shoe*) pump.

servilleta, *n.f.* napkin, serviette; *doblar la servilleta,* (*coll.*) to die.

servilletero, *n.m.* serviette-ring.

servio, -via, *n.m.f.* Serbian.

serviola, *n.f.* cat-head, anchor beam.

servir, *v.t.* (*pres. part.* **sirviendo;** *pres. indic.* **sirvo;** *pres. subj.* **sirva;** *pret. él sirvió*) to serve, be employed, hold a position; to do a duty, favour, etc.; to wait at table; to court, pay attention; to dress or serve food. — *v.i.* to serve, be in another's service; to be a sailor or soldier; to follow suit (at cards); to serve (at tennis, etc.); to heat the oven or kiln (baker), potter; to agree; to be useful, fit; to answer the purpose; to hold an employment; to perform another's functions; to act as a substitute; to wait at table; to administer. — *v.r.* to deign, condescend, be pleased; to help oneself (as at table); *para servir a Vd.*, at your service; *sirva de aviso*, let this be a warning; *servirse de*, to employ, make use of; *no servir uno para descalzar a otro*, (*fig.*) to be unworthy to black a person's boots (*or* lace a person's shoes); *sírvase venir*, please come.

sesada, *n.f.* fried brains.

sésamo, *n.m.* sesame.

sesear, *v.i.* to pronounce *c* before *e* and *i* as *s*.

sesenta, *n.*, *a.* sixty, sixtieth.

sesentavo, -va, *a.* sixtieth.

sesentén, *n.*, *a.* plank of timber (usually 12 m. long, 60 cm. wide and 40 cm. thick).

sesentón, -na, *a.* sexagenarian.

seseo, *n.m.* pronouncing *c* before *e*, *i* like *s*.

sesera, *n.f.* brain, brain-pan.

sesga, *n.f.* (*sew.*) goring.

sesgadamente, *adv.* slopingly, slantwise, askew, on the bias.

sesgado, -da, *a.* sloping, slanting, oblique, biased, askew, bevelled.

sesgadura, *n.f.* slope, obliquity, bias.

sesgamente, *adv.* obliquely.

sesgar, *v.t.* (*pret.* **sesgué**; *pres. subj.* **sesgue**) to slope, slant; to bevel; to give an oblique direction.

sesgo, *n.m.* slope, slant, obliqueness; bias; medium, mean.

sesgo, -ga, *a.* sloped, slanting, oblique, biased; unruffled, calm, placid, serene; grave, severe, stern; *al sesgo*, slopingly, obliquely.

sesí, *n.m.* (*Cub., PR.*) a fish resembling the porgy.

sesil, *a.* sessile.

sesión, *n.f.* session, sitting, meeting; consultation, conference.

sesmo, *n.m.* division, administrative unit of territory.

seso, *n.m.* brain; wisdom, understanding, prudence, talent; stone, brick or iron under a pot to keep it steady on the fireplace; *no tener seso*, to have no common-sense; *devanarse los sesos*, to rack one's brains; *tener los sesos en los calcañales*, to have very little sense or judgment; *el dar y tener, seso ha menester*, in matters of money, excess is easy in both directions; *levantarse la tapa de los sesos*, to blow out one's brains.

sesquidoble, *a.* two and a half times.

sesquipedal, *a.* sesquipedalian.

sesteadero, *n.m.* resting-place for cattle.

sestear, *v.i.* to take a siesta, nap, rest.

sestercio, *n.m.* sesterce, sestertius.

sesudamente, *adv.* maturely, wisely, prudently.

sesudo, -da, *a.* judicious, prudent, wise, discreet.

seta, *n.f.* bristle; mushroom, kind of fungus; snuff of a candle.

sete, *n.m.* office in a mint.

setecientos, -tas, *a.* seven hundred.

setena, *n.f.* seventh, sevenfold; *pagar con las setenas*, to suffer excessive punishment.

setenta, *a.* seventy, seventieth.

setentón, -na, *a.* septuagenarian.

setentrión, *n.m.* septentrion, north.

setica, *n.f.* (*Per.*) a tree of the Artocarpeous group.

setiembre, *n.m.* September.

seto, *n.m.* fence, defence, enclosure, hedge; (*PR.*) wall; *seto vivo*, quickset hedge.

setuní, *n.m.* (*hist.*) rich oriental cloth; (*arch.*) arabesque work.

seudo, *a.* pseudo-, false.

seudónimo, -ma, *a.* pseudonymous. — *n.m.* pseudonym, nom-de-plume.

severamente, *adv.* severely, sternly, harshly.

severidad, *n.f.* severity, harshness, strictness, rigour, acerbity, gravity, seriousness.

severo, -ra, *a.* severe, rigorous; rigid, harsh, serious, grave; exact, strict.

sevicia, *n.f.* fierceness, excessive cruelty.

seviche, *n.m.* (*Ec., Per.*) dish made of fish cooked with orange juice.

sevillanas, *n.f.pl.* Sevillan air and dance.

sevillano, -na, *n.m.f.*, *a.* Sevillan, of Seville.

sexagenario, -ria, *a.* sexagenary, sixty years old.

sexagésima, *n.f.* Sexagesima, second Sunday before Ash Wednesday.

sexagésimo, -ma, *a.* sixtieth, sexagesimal.

sexagonal, *a.* hexagonal.

sexángulo, *n.m.* sexangle.

sexángulo, -la, *a.* sexangular.

sexenio, *n.m.* space of six years.

sexma, *n.f.* small coin; sixth part of a yard.

sexmero, *n.m.* chief district officer.

sexmo, *n.m.* administrative district.

sexo, *n.m.* sex; *bello sexo*, fair sex.

sexta, *n.f.* (*eccles.*) sext; sequence of six cards at piquet; (*mus.*) sixth; ancient Roman division of the day; afternoon.

sextante, *n.m.* sextant; ancient Roman copper coin, sextans.

sextil, *a.* (*astrol.*) sextile.

sexto, -ta, *a.* sixth.

sexto, *n.m.* book of canonical decrees.

sextuplicar, *v.t.* (conjugated like BUSCAR) to sextuple.

séxtuplo, -pla, *a.* sixfold.

sexual, *a.* sexual; genital, generative.

si, *n.m.* (*mus.*) ti, B or si, seventh note of the diatonic scale. — *conj.* if, although, provided that, when, unless, whether; *si bien*, although; *si acaso*, (or *por si acaso*), if by chance, should it happen that; *¡si no lo quiero!* certainly I don't want it; *si tal*, certainly; *¡si será verdad!* I wonder if it be true; *un si es no es*, a trifle, somewhat.

sí, *adv.* yes, yea, indeed, certainly. — *pron.* (reflexive form of the personal pronoun of the third person, in both genders and numbers) himself, herself, yourself, itself, oneself, themselves; *de por sí*, apart, separately; *de sí*, spontaneously; *por sí o por no*, in any case. — *n.m.* yea; assent, consent, permission; *dar el sí*, to say yes; to accept a marriage proposal.

sialismo, *n.m.* (*med.*) salivation.

siampán, *n.m.* sapan-tree, sapan-wood.

sibarita, *n.m.* sybarite, voluptuary, epicure.

sibarítico, -ca, *a.* Sybaritic.

sibaritismo, *n.m.* sybaritism.

sibil, *n.m.* cave, underground cellar, vault.

sibila, *n.f.* prophetess, sibyl.

sibilante, *a.* sibilant, hissing.

sibilino, -na, *a.* sibylline.
sibucao, *n.m.* (*Philip.*) sapan-tree.
sicario, *n.m.* bravo, hired assassin.
siciliano, -na, *n.m.f.*, *a.* Sicilian.
siclo, *n.m.* shekel, an ancient Jewish weight and coin.
sicofanta, *n.m.* sycophant, flatterer, parasite.
sicómoro, *n.m.* (*bot.*) sycamore; plane tree, cotton-wood, sycamore maple.
sideral; sidéreo, -rea, *a.* sidereal, astral, starry.
siderita, siderosa, *n.m.* (*min.*) siderite; (*bot.*) ironwort.
siderurgia, *n.f.* manufacture of iron and steel.
siderúrgico, -ca, *a.* relating to the iron and steel industry.
sidra, *n.f.* cider.
sidrería, *n.f.* cider shop.
siega, *n.f.* harvest, mowing, reaping-time.
siego ; siegue, *pres. indic.; pres. subj.* [SEGAR].
siembra, *n.f.* sowing, seed-time, cornfield, sown field.
siembro ; siembre, *pres. indic.; pres. subj.* [SEMBRAR].
siempre, *adv.* ever, always, at all times.
siempreviva, *n.f.* (*bot.*) everlasting flower, immortelle; *siempreviva menor,* stone-crop; *siempreviva mayor,* houseleek.
sien, *n.f.* temple.
siento ; siente, *pres. indic.; pres. subj.* [SENTAR].
siento ; sienta; él sintió, *pres. indic.; pres. subj.; pret.,* of SENTIR.
sierpe, *n.f.* serpent, snake; shrew, peevish or spiteful woman; ugly person; anything that wriggles; (*bot.*) sucker.
sierpecilla, *n.f.* small serpent; *pl.* **sierpecillas,** winding sky-rocket.
sierra, *n.f.* saw; mountain-ridge, mountain-range; (*ichth.*) saw-fish; *sierra abrazadera,* frame-saw; *sierra de cinta,* band-saw; *sierra de mano,* framing-saw; *sierra de punta,* key-hole-saw; *sierra de trasdós,* tenon-saw.
sierrecilla, *n.f.* small saw.
sierro ; sierre, *pres. indic.; pres. subj.* [SERRAR].
siervo, -va, *n.m.f.* slave, servant, serf; *siervo de Dios,* servant of God, member of a religious order; (*coll.*) poor devil.
sieso, *n.m.* anus.
siesta, *n.f.* siesta, after-dinner nap; hottest part of the day.
siete, *n.m.*, *a.* seven, seventh; v-shaped tear in a garment; *hablar más que siete,* to talk nineteen to the dozen.
sieteañal, *a.* septennial.
sietecolores, *n.m.* (*Chi.*) sylph, a small multicoloured bird.
sietecueros, *n.m.* (*Col., Chi., Ec., Hond.*) tumour in the heel; (*CR., Cub., Per.*) whitlow.
sieteenrama, *n.f.* (*bot.*) tormentil.
sietemesino, -na, *a.* born seven months after conception; (*coll.*) puny and conceited youth.
sieteñal, *a.* septennial.
sifilis, *n.f.* syphilis.
sifilítico, -ca, *a.* syphilitic.
sifón, *n.m.* syphon.
sifosis, *n.f.* hunch, crooked back.
sifué, *n.m.* surcingle.
sigilación, *n.f.* impression, mark, seal, stamp.
sigilar, *v.t.* to seal; to conceal, keep secret.
sigilo, *n.m.* sigil, seal; secret; reserve, concealment; *sigilo profesional,* professional secrecy

(lawyers, doctors); *sigilo sacramental,* seal of confession.
sigilosamente, *adv.* secretly, silently.
sigilosidad, *n.f.* quality of silence.
sigiloso, -sa, *a.* silent, reserved, keeping a secret.
sigla, *n.f.* abbreviation in initials ; press-mark.
siglo, *n.m.* century, epoch, age, very long time; worldly intercourse; *por los siglos de los siglos,* for ever and ever; *por el siglo de mi padre* (or *madre*), on my oath, on my honour; *el siglo de cobre,* the Bronze Age; *el siglo de hierro,* the Iron Age; *el siglo de plata,* the Silver Age; *el siglo de oro,* the Golden Age.
signáculo, *n.m.* signet, seal.
signar, *v.t.* to sign, mark with a seal. — *v.r.* to make the sign of the cross.
signatario, -ria, *a.* signing.
signatura, *n.f.* sign, mark, signature in printing.
significación, *n.f.* significance; meaning, signification.
significado, *a.* well known, important, reputable. — *n.m.* significance.
significador, -ra, *n.m.f.*, *a.* signifier; that signifies.
significante, *a.* significant, expressive.
significar, *v.t.* (*pret.* **signifiqué,** *pres. subj.* **signifique**) to signify, denote, mean; to declare; to indicate, express, represent, make known. — *v.i.* to import, be worth.
significativamente, *adv.* significatively.
significativo, -va, *a.* significative, expressive.
signo, *n.m.* sign, mark; signet; sign of the zodiac; fate, destiny; type, emblem; motion, gesture, nod; benediction, sign of the cross; (*mus.*) character.
sigo ; siga, *pres. indic.; pres. subj.* [SEGUIR].
sigua, *n.f.* (*Cub.*) a tree resembling the ash-tree.
siguapa, *n.f.* (*CR., Cub.*) small nocturnal bird of prey.
síguemepollo, *n.m.* ribbon adornment hanging down the back.
siguiente, *a.* following, successive, next.
sijú, *n.m.* a nocturnal bird of prey of the West Indies.
sil, *n.m.* yellow ochre.
sílaba, *n.f.* syllable.
silabar, *v.t.* to syllable.
silabario, *n.m.* spelling-book.
silabear, *v.i.* to syllabize, syllabify.
silabeo, *n.m.* act of forming syllables.
silábico, -ca, *a.* syllabic.
sílabo, *n.m.* syllabus, index, summary.
silanga, *n.f.* (*Philip.*) a long and narrow inlet.
silba, *n.f.* (*theat.*) hissing, booing.
silbador, -ra, *n.m.f.* whistler, hisser.
silbar, *v.i.* to whistle, whiz. — *v.t.* to hiss, catcall.
silbato, *n.m.* whistle; small crack letting out a liquid or air in with a whiz.
silbido, silbo, *n.m.* whistle, whistling; hiss, whiz, sibilation.
silbón, *n.m.* a kind of hissing widgeon.
silboso, -sa, *a.* (*poet.*) whistling, hissing.
silenciario, -ria, *a.* observing silence, silent place.
silenciero, *n.m.* silentiary.
silencio, *n.m.* silence, stillness, repose, secrecy; reservedness, taciturnity; prudence; (*mus.*) rest; *perpetuo silencio,* (*law*) forever hold his peace. — *interj.* hush! silence!

silenciosamente, *adv.* silently, gently, softly.
silencioso, -sa, *a.* silent, solitary, mute, still, noiseless.
silepsis, *n.f.* (*gram.*) syllepsis.
silería, *n.f.* group of silos.
silero, *n.m.* (*agric.*) silo.
silfide, *n.f.*, **silfo,** *n.m.* sylph.
silguero, *n.m.* linnet.
silicato, -ta, *a.* silicate.
silice, *n.f.* (*chem.*) silica.
silicio, *n.m.* silicon.
silicua, *n.f.* siliqua; carat; (*bot.*) pod.
silo, *n.m.* silo; subterranean granary; cavern, dark place.
silogismo, *n.m.* syllogism; *silogismo cornuto,* horn of a dilemma.
silogístico, -ca, *a.* syllogistic, syllogistical.
silogizar, *v.i.* (conjugated like ALZAR) to syllogize, argue, reason.
silueta, *n.f.* silhouette.
silúrico, -ca, *a.* Silurian.
siluro, *n.m.* catfish; self-propelling torpedo.
silva, *n.f.* a Spanish verse; miscellany, anthology.
silvestre, *a.* wild, rustic, savage; uncultivated.
silvicultor, *n.m.* silviculturist, forester.
silvicultura, *n.f.* forestry.
silla, *n.f.* chair, seat; diocese, see; saddle; *silla de manos,* sedan chair; *silla de posta,* post-chaise; *silla de columpio,* rocking-chair; *silla giratoria,* revolving-chair; *silla plegadiza,* folding-chair, camp-stool; *silla poltrona,* arm-chair, easy chair; *silla volante,* jig; *de silla a silla,* tête-à-tête, in private; *pegárse¡e a uno la silla,* to stay too long (on a visit, etc.); *quien fué a Sevilla, perdió su silla,* the absentee loses his job; *silla de la reina,* chair made by two persons' hands and wrists; (*Arg., Col., CR., Chi.*) *silla de manos =* silla de la reina.
sillar, *n.m.* square hewn stone; back of a horse.
sillarejo, *n.m.* small ashlar.
sillera, *n.f.* place for sedan-chairs.
sillería, *n.f.* set of chairs or seats; shop where chairs are made or sold; choir-stalls; ashlar masonry.
sillero, *n.m.* saddler; chair-maker.
silleta, *n.f.* small chair; side-saddle; bed-pan; stone on which chocolate is ground. — *pl.* **silletas,** mule chairs.
silletazo, *n.m.* blow with a chair.
silletero, *n.m.* chair-man; chair-maker, chair-seller.
sillico, *n.m.* basin of a close-stool.
sillín, *n.m.* light riding saddle; harness saddle; elaborate mule chair; cycle seat.
sillita, *n.f.* small chair.
sillón, *n.m.* arm-chair; large elbow-chair; easy chair; sidesaddle for ladies.
sima, *n.f.* abyss, chasm, gulf; deep cave.
simado, -da, *a.* deep (of lands).
simarruba, *n.f.* (*Arg., Col., CR.*) a medicinal tree of the rutaceæ family.
simbiosis, *n.f.* symbiosis.
simbol, *n.m.* (*Arg.*) pampas-grass.
simbólicamente, *adv.* symbolically, typically, hieroglyphically.
simbólico, -ca, *a.* symbolical, analogous, emblematic.
simbolismo, *n.m.* symbolism.
simbolización, *n.f.* symbolization.

simbolizar, *v.i.* (conjugated like ALZAR) to symbolize, figure, typify, represent.
símbolo, *n.m.* symbol, type, emblem, representation, figure; mark, device, sign; creed, belief, articles of faith.
simetría, *n.f.* symmetry, harmony, proportion.
simétricamente, *adv.* symmetrically.
simétrico, -ca, *a.* symmetrical, proportionate.
simia, *n.f.* female ape.
simiente, *n.f.* seed, germ; semen, sperm.
simiesco, -ca, *a.* simian.
símil, *n.m.* similarity, resemblance; comparison; simile. — *a.* similar, like, alike, resembling.
similar, *a.* similar, homogeneous, resembling.
similicadencia, *n.f.* (*rhet.*) rhyming cadences.
similitud, *n.f.* similitude, resemblance.
similitudinario, -ria, *a.* similar, similitudinary.
similor, *n.m.* pinchbeck, similor.
simio, *n.m.* male ape.
simón, -na, *n.m.f.*, *a.* hack; cab; Madrid cabby.
simonía, *n.f.* simony.
simoníaco, -ca; simoniático, -ca, *a.* simoniacal.
simpa, *n.f.* (*Arg., Per.*) braid; plait; braided hair, tress.
simpatía, *n.f.* sympathy, fellow-feeling, congeniality; similarity.
simpáticamente, *adv.* sympathetically.
simpático, -ca, *a.* congenial, sympathetic; analogous; *gran simpático,* (*anat.*) sympathetic system.
simpatizar, *v.i.* (conjugated like ALZAR) to sympathize; to be congenial.
simple, *a.* simple, natural, plain, single; pure, mere, naked, artless; ingenuous; silly, crazy, idiotic, foolish; gentle, mild; insipid, tasteless; brief; informal; extra-judicial. — *n.m.* (*pharm.*) simple.
simplemente, *adv.* simply, plainly; sillily; absolutely, merely.
simpleza, *n.f.* simpleness, fatuity; (*obs.*) foolishness, rusticity, rudeness.
simplicidad, *n.f.* simplicity, simpleness, plainness, silliness; artlessness, candour.
simplificación, *n.f.* simplification.
simplificar, *v.t.* (*pret.* **simplifiqué;** *pres. subj.* **simplifique**) to simplify.
simplista, *n.m.* simplist, herbalist. — *a.* oversimplifying.
simplón, -na, *n.m.f.* great simpleton.
simulación, *n.f.* simulation, feigning, subterfuge.
simulacro, *n.m.* simulacrum, image, idol; (*mil.*) sham battle.
simuladamente, *adv.* feigningly, dissemblingly.
simulador, -ra, *n.m.f.* simulator, feigner, dissembler.
simular, *v.t.* to simulate; to counterfeit; to imitate, feign; to put on.
simultáneamente, *adv.* simultaneously.
simultaneidad, *n.f.* simultaneity.
simultáneo, -nea, *a.* simultaneous.
simún, *n.m.* simoom, sirocco.
sin, *prep.* without, besides; *sin embargo,* however, notwithstanding, nevertheless; *sin pies ni cabeza,* without order; *sin un cuarto,* penniless; *sin ambajes ni rodajes,* without ifs and ands; *sin comerlo ni beberlo,* undeservedly;

sin decir agua va, without giving warning; *sin decir oxte ni moxte*, without so much as a 'by your leave'; *sin más acá ni más allá* (or *sin más ni más*), without more ado; *si no puedes lo que quieres, quiere lo que puedes*, if you can't get what you want, make the best of what you can get; *sin por qué*, without cause; *sin qué ni por qué* (or *sin ton ni son*), without rhyme or reason; *sin quitar ni poner*, the naked truth.

sinagoga, *n.f.* synagogue.

sinalagmático, -ca, *a.* (*law*) synallagmatic, mutually obligatory.

sinamay, *n.m.* (*Philip.*) the finest fabric made from abaca fibre.

sinamayera, *n.f.* (*Philip.*) woman who sells *sinamay* or other fabrics.

sinapismo, *n.m.* sinapism; poultice; (*coll.*) nuisance, bore.

sincerador, -ra, *n.m.f.* exculpator, excuser.

sinceramente, *adv.* sincerely, frankly, heartily, cordially.

sincerar, *v.t., v.r.* to exculpate, justify, excuse, vindicate.

sinceridad, *n.f.* sincerity, purity, frankness, cordiality, good will.

sincero, -ra, *a.* sincere, ingenuous, honest, pure.

síncopa, *n.f.* syncope; syncopation.

sincopal, *n.m.* syncope. — *a.* (*med.*) syncopal.

sincopar, *v.t.* to syncopate; to abridge.

síncope, *n.f.* fainting-fit.

sincopizar, *v.t., v.r.* (conjugated like ALZAR) to cause a swoon or fainting-fit.

sincresis, *n.f.* (*med.*) syncresis, fusion, mixture.

sincrónico, -ca, *a.* synchronous, synchronistic.

sincronismo, *n.m.* synchronism.

sindéresis, *n.f.* discretion; good judgment.

sindicado, *n.m.* syndicate; body of trustees.

sindicador, -ra, *n.m.f.* informer, prosecutor.

sindicadura, *n.f.* office of a syndic.

sindical, *a.* of a syndic.

sindicar, *v.t.* (*pret.* **sindiqué**; *pres. subj.* **sindique**) to inform, accuse, lodge an information; to syndicate.

sindicato, *n.m.* syndicate; trade union.

sindicatura, *n.f.* syndic's office.

síndico, *n.m.* receiver; syndic, recorder, assignee; alms-house treasurer.

sinécdoque, sinédoque, *n.f.* (*rhet.*) synecdoche.

sinecura, *n.f.* sinecure.

sinedrio, *n.m.* Sanhedrin.

sinéresis, *n.f.* (*gram.*) synæresis.

sinfín, *n.m.* no end, great number; a great many.

sínfito, *n.m.* (*bot.*) comfrey.

sinfonía, *n.f.* symphony; concert.

sinfónico, -ca, *a.* symphonic.

sinfonista, *n.m.* symphonist, player in an orchestra.

singa, *n.f.* sculling.

singar, *v.i.* to scull over the stern.

singladura, *n.f.* (*naut.*) day's run.

singlar, *v.i.* to sail over a fixed course.

single, *a.* single rope.

singlón, *n.m.* any of the timbers placed over the keel, futtock.

singular, *a.* singular, single, individual, particular; strange, extraordinary, extravagant; unique; excellent; (*gram.*) singular.

singularidad, *n.f.* singularity, notability, oddity.

singularizar, *v.t.* (conjugated like ALZAR) to singularize, distinguish, particularize. — *v.r.* to distinguish oneself, be singular.

singularmente, *adv.* singularly.

singulto, *n.m.* sob; hiccough, singultus.

sinhueso, *n.f.* (*coll.*) tongue.

sínico, -ca, *a.* Chinese.

siniestra, *n.f.* left hand.

siniestramente, *adv.* in a sinister manner.

siniestro, -tra, *a.* sinister, left (side); unlucky, unhappy, inauspicious; froward, vicious.

siniestro, *n.m.* perverseness, depravity, evil habit; shipwreck; disaster; damage, loss at sea. — *n.f.* left hand; left-hand side.

sinistrórsum, *a.* from right to left.

sinnúmero, *n.m.* innumerable quantity, huge number.

sino, *conj.* if not, but, except, besides; solely, only, otherwise. — *n.m.* fate, destiny.

sinoble, *a.* (*her.*) vert.

sinocal; sinoco, -ca, *a.* (*med.*) synochal.

sinodal, *a.* synodic, synodal.

sinodático, *n.m.* tax paid to the bishop.

sinódico, -ca, *a.* synodal, synodical; (*astron.*) synodic.

sínodo, *n.m.* synod; conjunction of the heavenly bodies.

sinonimia, *n.f.* synonymy.

sinónimo, -ma, *a.* synonymous.

sinónimo, *n.m.* synonym.

sinople, *a.* (*her.*) sinople, green.

sinopsis, *n.f.* synopsis, epitome, summary.

sinóptico, -ca, *a.* synoptic, synoptical.

sinrazón, *n.f.* wrong, injury, injustice.

sinsabor, *n.m.* displeasure, disgust; pain, uneasiness, unpleasantness, offensiveness.

sinsonte, *n.m.* mocking-bird.

sintáctico, -ca, *a.* syntactic, syntactical.

sintaxis, *n.f.* (*gram.*) syntax.

síntesis, *n.f.* synthesis.

sintéticamente, *adv.* synthetically.

sintético, -ca, *a.* synthetical.

sintetizar, *v.t.* (conjugated like ALZAR) to synthesize.

síntoma, *n.m.* symptom; token, sign, indication.

sintomáticamente, *adv.* symptomatically.

sintomático, -ca, *a.* symptomatic(al).

sintonización, *n.f.* (*wire.*) tuning.

sintonizador, *n.m.* (*wire.*) tuner.

sintonizar, *v.t.* (*wire.*) to tune in.

sinuosidad, *n.f.* sinuosity, sinuousness.

sinuoso, -sa, *a.* sinuous, sinuate, wavy.

sinvergüencería, *n.f.* (*coll.*) shamelessness, brazenness.

sinvergüenza, *n.m., a.* scoundrel; brazen; caitiff; (*Col.*) coward.

sinvergüenzada, *n.f.* (*Col.*) base action.

sionismo, *n.m.* Zionism.

sionista, *n., a.* Zionist.

sipedón, *n.m.* seps, a serpent-lizard.

siquier, siquiera, *conj., adv.* though, although, at least, scarcely, whether, or, or even, otherwise; *ni siquiera*, not even; *siquiera un poquito*, ever so little; *ni siquiera*, not even.

sirena, *n.f.* syren, mermaid; siren, foghorn.

sirga, *n.f.* tow-line, tow-rope; line for hauling seines; *a la sirga*, tracking from the shore.

sirgadura, *n.f.* trackage.

sirgar, *v.t.* to track, tow (a boat).

sirgo, *n.m.* twisted silk, silken stuff.
sirguero, *n.m.* linnet.
siríaco, -ca, *a.* Syrian.
sirio, *n.m.* (*astron.*)Sirius.
sirle, *n.f.* sheep's dung, goat's dung.
siroco, *n.m.* sirocco.
sirria, *n.f.* sheep-dung.
sirte, *n.f.* moving sandbank; hidden rock; danger, peril.
sirvienta, *n.f.* female servant, servant-girl, maid.
sirviente, *n.m.,* *a.* servant, serving-man; menial, serving, being a servant.
sirvo; sirva; él sirvió, *pres. indic.; pres. subj.; pret.* [SERVIR].
sisa, *n.f.* pilfering, petty theft; size used by gilders; excise; (*tailor.*) clippings; (*sew.*) dart.
sisador, -ra, *n.m.f.* filcher, pilferer, petty thief; cutter, sizer.
sisallo, *n.m.* saltwort.
sisar, *v.t.* to filch, pilfer; to cut, curtail; to size for gilding; to excise; (*sew.*) to take in.
sisear, *v.i.* to hiss.
siseo, *n.m.* hiss, hissing.
sisero, *n.m.* exciseman, excise-collector.
sisimbrio, *n.m.* water-radish, hedge-mustard.
sisitoté, *n.m.* tropical song bird.
sísmico, -ca, *a.* seismic.
sismógrafo, *n.m.* seismograph.
sismología, *n.f.* seismology.
sismológico, -ca, *a.* seismological.
sismómetro, *n.m.* seismometer.
sisón, *n.m.* filcher, pilferer, petty thief; (*orn.*) godwit or moor-cock.
sistema, *n.m.* system.
sistemáticamente, *adv.* systematically.
sistemático, -ca, *a.* systematic, methodical.
sistematizar, *v.t.* (conjugated like ALZAR) to systematize.
sístilo, *n.m.* (*arch.*) systyle.
sístole, *n.f.* (*physiol. and rhet.*) systole.
sistólico, -ca, *a.* (*physiol.*) systolic.
sistro, *n.m.* (*mus.*) sistrum.
sitiador, *n.m.* besieger.
sitial, *n.m.* president's chair, seat of honour; stool, backless seat; bench, form.
sitiar, *v.t.* to besiege, lay siege; to close all avenues, deprive of means; to compass, hem in, surround.
sitibundo, -da, *a.* (*poet.*) thirsty.
sitiero, *n.m.* (*Cuba*) petty farmer.
sitio, *n.m.* place, spot, seat; station, stand; location, situation, site; blockade, siege; country house, country-seat; (*Cuba*) cattle-farm; *real sitio,* king's residence; *dejar en el sitio,* to kill one outright; *quedar en el sitio,* to die on the spot.
sito, -ta, *a.* situated, lying; located, assigned.
situación, *n.f.* situation; position; site, location; condition, state, standing; appointment, assignment; (*naut.*) bearing; *situación activa,* active service, position or office; *situación pasiva,* position of a retired or redundant person.
situado, *n.m.* allowance, pay, kind of annuity.
situado, -da, *a.* situate, situated, placed, located, lying. — *p.p.* [SITUAR].
situar, *v.t.* to situate, station, locate, put, place; (*com.*) to remit or place funds. — *v.r.* to be situated, placed, established, stationed; to settle.
síu, *n.m.* (*Chi.*) kind of linnet.

so, *prep.* below, under; *so capa* (or *color*), under colour (*or* pretext); *so pena de,* under penalty of, on pain of.
¡so! *interj.* whoa! stop! (said to horses).
soasar, *v.t.* to half roast, cook insufficiently, underdo.
soata, *n.f.* (*Ven.*) kind of squash.
soba, *n.f.* rumpling, beating up, kneading, making soft; massage, manipulation.
sobacal, *a.* axillary.
sobaco, *n.m.* armpit, arm-hole; (*bot.*) axil.
sobadero, *a.* that may be handled. — *n.m.* place where hides are tanned.
sobado, *n.m.* drubbing, beating, violent handling; (*CR.*) molasses made of inferior honey.
sobadura, *n.f.* kneading, rubbing.
sobajadura, *n.f.* kneading; scrubbing, friction.
sobajamiento, *n.m.* friction, rubbing.
sobajanero, *n.m.* (*coll.*) errand-boy.
sobajar, *v.t.* to squeeze, scrub, rub hard.
sobanda, *n.f.* end of a cask.
sobaquera, *n.f.* arm-hole, opening in clothes under the armpit.
sobaquina, *n.f.* smell of the armpit.
sobar, *v.t.* to pummel, box, handle roughly; to soften, squeeze; to massage, knead, manipulate; to paw.
sobarba, *n.f.* noseband of a bridle.
sobarbada, *n.f.* sudden check; jerk; reprimand, scolding.
sobarcar, *v.t.* (*pret.* **sobarqué,** *pres. subj.* **sobarque**) to draw up (clothes) to the arm-holes; to carry under the arm.
sobeo, *n.m.* leather thong for tying the yoke to the pole.
soberanamente, *adv.* sovereignly, supremely, exceedingly, most.
soberanear, *v.i.* to domineer, lord it.
soberanía, *n.f.* sovereignty, pride, majesty, dominion, rule, sway.
soberano, -na, *a.* sovereign, supreme, royal, superior, pre-eminent. — *n.m.f.* sovereign, lord, ruler, king or queen, liege-lord.
soberbia, *n.f.* excessive pride, haughtiness; pomp, arrogance, loftiness, magnificence, presumption; passion, anger.
soberbiamente, *adv.* proudly, superbly, haughtily, arrogantly.
soberbio, -bia, *a.* overproud, haughty, arrogant; elated, lofty, superb; fiery, mettlesome (horses); passionate; eminent, sublime.
soberbiosamente, *adv.* haughtily.
sobina, *n.f.* peg, wooden pin.
sobón, *n.m.* (*coll.*) lazy, cunning fellow.
sobón, -na, *a.* over-loving, over-fond.
sobordo, *n.m.* (*naut.*) check of a cargo with its manifest.
sobornación, *n.f.* subornation.
sobornador, -ra, *n.m.f.* briber, suborner, corrupter.
sobornal, *n.m.* overload.
sobornar, *v.t.* to bribe, corrupt, suborn.
soborno, *n.m.* subornation, bribe; incitement, inducement; (*Arg., Bol., Chi.*) overload.
sobra, *n.f.* overplus, surplus, excess; left over, leaving; terrible offence or injury. — *pl.* **sobras,** offal, broken victuals; *de sobra,* over and above, superfluously; *estar de sobra,* (*coll.*) to be one too many.
sobradamente, *adv.* superabundantly, excessively, more than enough.
sobradar, *v.t.* to erect a loft in a building.

sobradillo, *n.m.* cockloft, penthouse.
sobrado, *n.m.* attic, garret; (*Chi.*) leavings; (*Arg.*) shelf in a kitchen. — *adv.* over and above.
sobrado, -da, *a.* abundant, excessive; rich, wealthy; bold, audacious; licentious.
sobrancero, -ra, *a.* disengaged, unemployed; (*Cub.*) overplus, surplus.
sobrante, *n.m.* residue, overplus, surplus, superfluity; wealthy, rich.
sobrante, *a.* left-over, remaining.
sobrar, *v.t.* to exceed, surpass. — *v.i.* to have overmuch; to be over and above, be left, remain; (*coll.*) *estar de más,* to be intrusive.
sobrasada, *n.f.* a sausage speciality of Majorca.
sobrasar, *v.t.* to add fuel under a pot, etc.
sobre, *prep., adv.* on, upon, over, above; (*in compounds*) super; to, towards, near; about, nearly; after, since; (*naut.*) off; *estar sobre sí,* to be self-possessed, on guard; *ir sobre alguno,* to go in pursuit of someone; *sobre manera,* excessively; *sobre que,* besides, moreover; *sobre poco más o menos,* more or less, just about; *sobre cuernos, penitencia,* adding insult to injury.
sobre, *n.m.* envelope; superscription, address; *sobre monedero,* envelope coin container.
sobreabundancia, *n.f.* superabundance.
sobreabundante, *a.* superabundant, luxuriant.
sobreabundantemente, *adv.* superabundantly.
sobreabundar, *v.i.* to superabound, be superabundant, be exuberant.
sobreaguar, *v.i.* to float on water.
sobreagudo, *n.m.* (*mus.*) highest treble.
sobrealiento, *n.m.* difficult breathing.
sobrealimentación, *n.f.* overfeeding.
sobrealimentar, *v.t.* to overfeed.
sobrealzar, *v.t.* (conjugated like ALZAR) to extol, laud highly, over-praise.
sobreañadir, *v.t.* to superadd, superinduce.
sobreañal, *a.* more than a year old (of beasts).
sobreasada, *n.f.* [SOBRASADA].
sobreasar, *v.t.* to roast again.
sobrebarato, -ta, *a.* extra cheap.
sobreboya, *n.f.* (*naut.*) marking buoy.
sobrecaja, *n.f.* outer case.
sobrecalza, *n.f.* leggings.
sobrecama, *n.f.* quilt, coverlet, bedspread.
sobrecaña, a tumour on a horse's leg.
sobrecarga, *n.f.* surcharge, overburden; additional trouble or grief; overload; packing strap.
sobrecargado, -da, *a.* overloaded.
sobrecargar, *v.t.* (conjugated like CARGAR) to overload, surcharge, overburden, overweight, overtask; (*com.*) to overcharge.
sobrecargo, *n.m.* supercargo.
sobrecarta, *n.f.* envelope, cover of a letter; (*law*) second decree or warrant repeating a former order.
sobrecebadera, *n.f.* (*naut.*) sprit topsail.
sobrecédula, *n.f.* second royal decree.
sobreceja, *n.f.* part of the forehead above the eyebrows.
sobrecejo, *n.m.* supercilious aspect, frown.
sobreceño, *n.m.* frown.
sobrecercar, *v.t.* (*sew.*) to welt.
sobrecerco, *n.m.* (*sew.*) welt.
sobrecincho, -cha, *n.m.f.* surcingle.
sobrecoger, *v.t.* (conjugated like COGER) to

surprise, overtake. — *v.r.* to become timorous or apprehensive.
sobrecogimiento, *n.m.* astonishment, fearfulness, apprehension.
sobrecomida, *n.f.* dessert.
sobrecopa, *n.f.* lid of a cup.
sobrecoser, *v.t.* (*sew.*) to whipstitch, fell.
sobrecrecer, *v.i.* (conjugated like CRECER) to outgrow, grow on top.
sobrecreciente, *a.* outgrowing, growing on top.
sobrecruces, *n.m.pl.* (*carp.*) cross-joints.
sobrecubierta, *n.f.* coverlet, second cover; (*naut.*) upper deck.
sobrecuello, *n.m.* collar.
sobredicho, -cha, *a.* above-mentioned, aforesaid.
sobredorar, *v.t.* to gild metals, especially silver; to re-gild; (*met.*) to palliate.
sobreedificar, *v.t.* (conjugated like EDIFICAR) to super-erect; to build over anything.
sobreempeine, *n.m.* covering for the instep.
sobreentender, *v.t., v.r.* [SOBRENTENDER].
sobreestadías, *n.f.pl.* (*com.*) extra lay days.
sobreexcitación, *n.f.* over-excitement.
sobreexcitar, *v.t.* to over-excite.
sobrefalda, *n.f.* overskirt.
sobrefaz, *n.f.* superficies, surface, outside; (*fort.*) face prolonged.
sobrefino, -na, *a.* superfine, overfine.
sobreflor, *n.f.* flower growing within another.
sobrefusión, *n.f.* (*phys., chem.*) superfusion.
sobreguarda, *n.m.* second guard.
sobrehaz, *n.f.* surface; outside cover.
sobreherido, -da, *a.* slightly wounded.
sobrehilar, *v.t.* (*sew.*) to overcast.
sobrehueso, *n.m.* (*vet.*) splint; encumbrance, burden.
sobrehumano, -na, *a.* superhuman.
sobrehusa, *n.f.* stew of fried fish.
sobrejalma, *n.f.* cover of a packsaddle.
sobrejuanete, *n.m.* (*naut.*) royal.
sobrellave, *n.f.* double key. — *n.m.* keeper of double keys in royal palace.
sobrellenar, *v.t.* to overfill, overflow, glut.
sobrelleno, -na, *a.* overfull, superabundant.
sobrellevar, *v.t.* to ease another's burden; to carry, bear, endure, undergo; to overlook, be lenient.
sobremanera, *adv.* beyond measure, excessively.
sobremano, *n.m.* bony tumour on fore-hoofs.
sobremesa, *n.f.* table cloth; dessert; *de sobremesa,* after dinner.
sobremesana, *n.f.* mizen topsail.
sobremuñonera, *n.f.* (*artill.*) clamp, capsquare.
sobrenadar, *v.i.* to float, overfloat.
sobrenatural, *a.* supernatural.
sobrenaturalmente, *adv.* supernaturally.
sobrenombre, *n.m.* surname; nickname.
sobrentender, *v.t.* (conjugated like ENTENDER) to understand, read between the lines.
sobrepaga, *n.f.* increase of pay, additional pay.
sobrepaño, *n.m.* upper cloth, wrapper.
sobreparto, *n.m.* (*med.*) confinement.
sobrepeine, *adv.* slightly, briefly. — *n.m.* hair-trimming.
sobrepelliz, *n.f.* surplice.
sobrepeso, *n.m.* overweight.
sobrepié, *n.m.* bony tumour on rear hoofs.
sobreplán, *n.m.* (*naut.*) rider.

sobreponer, *v.t.* (conjugated like PONER) to add (one thing to another), put over, superimpose, overlap. — *v.r.* to raise oneself, exalt oneself; to overcome, master, overpower.

sobreprecio, *n.m.* extra price.

sobrepuerta, *n.f.* cornice; portière, door-curtain; pelmet.

sobrepuesto, *n.m.* honeycomb formed after the hive is full.

sobrepuesto, -ta, *a.* superposed. — *p.p.* irreg. [SOBREPONER].

sobrepuja, *n.f.* outbidding.

sobrepujamiento, *n.m.* surpassing, excelling.

sobrepujante, *a.* surpassing, excelling.

sobrepujanza, *n.f.* great strength, exceeding vigour.

sobrepujar, *v.t.* to surpass, exceed, excel.

sobrequilla, *n.f.* keelson.

sobrerronda, *n.f.* (*mil.*) counter-round.

sobreropa, *n.f.* overcoat, overalls.

sobresaliente, *a.* surpassing, excelling, excellent. — *n.m.* officer in command of a picket; substitute; (*theat.*) understudy; (*bullfight.*) second in command of the 'cuadrilla.'

sobresalir, *v.i.* (conjugated like SALIR) to excel, be prominent, stand out; to surpass, outvie, exceed, overtop, overreach; to overhang, protrude.

sobresaltar, *v.t.* to assail, assault, attack, surprise; to frighten, startle, terrify. — *v.i.* to be striking, noticeable. — *v.r.* to be surprised, frightened, startled.

sobresalto, *n.m.* surprise, sudden fear, sudden assault; *de sobresalto,* unexpectedly, unawares, suddenly.

sobresanar, *v.t.* to heal superficially; to palliate, screen.

sobresano, *adv.* superficially healed, feignedly, affectedly. — *n.m.* (*naut.*) tabling, beach-lining.

sobrescribir, *v.t.* to superscribe; to direct, address (a letter).

sobrescrito, *n.m.* direction, address (of a letter).

sobredrújulo, -la, *a.* accented on any syllable before the antepenultimate.

sobreseer, *v.i.* to supersede; to relinquish; to stay, desist; (*law*) to stay a judgment, charge, etc.

sobreseguro, *adv.* safely, without risk.

sobreseimiento, *n.m.* suspension, omission, discontinuance; (*law*) stay of proceedings.

sobresello, *n.m.* second seal, double seal.

sobresembrar, *v.t.* to sow over again.

sobreseñal, *n.f.* knight's device.

sobresolar, *v.t.* to resole; to pave anew.

sobrestante, *n.m.* overseer, controller, foreman, inspector, supervisor.

sobresueldo, *n.m.* addition to pay.

sobresuelo, *n.m.* re-laid pavement.

sobretarde, *n.f.* close of the evening.

sobretodo, *n.m.* greatcoat, overcoat. — *adv.* above everything; especially.

sobreveedor, *n.m.* chief supervisor, overseer.

sobrevenida, *n.f.* supervention.

sobrevenir, *v.i.* (conjugated like VENIR) to fall out, take place, happen, supervene, come upon.

sobreverterse, *v.r.* to run over, overflow.

sobrevesta, sobreveste, *n.f.* greatcoat, surtout.

sobrevestir, *v.t.* (conjugated like VESTIR) to put on a surtout or a greatcoat.

sobrevidriera, *n.f.* wire netting before a window; window of double glass.

sobrevienta, *n.f.* violent gust of wind; (*fig.*) onslaught, impetuous fury; surprise.

sobreviento, *n.m.* gust of wind; *estar a sobreviento,* to have the wind of.

sobrevista, *n.f.* beaver of a helmet.

sobreviviente, *n.m.f.,* *a.* survivor, surviving.

sobrevivir, *v.i.* to outlive, survive.

sobrexceder, *v.t.* to surpass, exceed, excel.

sobrexcedente, *a.* surpassing, excelling.

sobrexcitación, *n.f.* overexcitement; overexcitation.

sobrexcitar, *v.t.* to overexcite.

sobriamente, *adv.* soberly, frugally, temperately, abstemiously.

sobriedad, *n.f.* sobriety, abstemiousness, abstinence, frugality.

sobrina, *n.f.* niece.

sobrinazgo, *n.m.* relationship of a nephew or niece.

sobrino, *n.m.* nephew.

sobrio, -ria, *a.* sober, frugal, temperate.

soca, *n.f.* (*Am.*) ratoon of the sugar cane; (*Bol.*) bud of rice-plant.

socaire, *n.m.* (*naut.*) slatch; shelter; lee, lee-gauge.

socairero, *n.m.* (*naut.*) skulker, lurker.

socaliña, *n.f.* cunning, artifice, trick.

socaliñar, *v.t.* to extort by cunning.

socaliñero, -ra, *n.m.f.* cheat, trickster.

socalzar, *v.t.* (conjugated like CALZAR) (*arch.*) to underpin, underset.

socapa, *n.f.* pretext, pretence; *a socapa,* on pretence, under colour; cautiously.

socapar, *v.t.* (*Bol., Ec., Mex.*) to hide, conceal; palliate another's faults and sins.

socarra, *n.f.* singe, singeing, half-roasting; cunning, craft.

socarrar, *v.t.* to singe, scorch, half-roast.

socarrén, *n.m.* eave, gable end.

socarrena, *n.f.* hollow, cavity, interval, space between rafters.

socarrina, *n.f.* (*coll.*) scorching, singeing.

socarrón, -na, *a.* cunning, crafty, sly.

socarronamente, *adv.* slyly, cunningly, craftily.

socarronería, *n.f.* craft, cunning, artfulness, slyness.

socava, socavación, *n.f.* undermining; rooting or digging round trees.

socavar, *v.t.* to excavate, undermine.

socavón, *n.m.* cave, cavern; (*min.*) adit, tunnel.

socaz, *n.m.* outlet of a mill.

sociabilidad, *n.f.* sociability, sociableness, civility.

sociable, *a.* sociable, courteous.

sociablemente, *adv.* sociably, companionably.

social, *a.* social, companionable.

socialismo, *n.m.* socialism.

socialista, *n.m.f.* socialist.

socialización, *n.f.* socialization, nationalization.

socializar, *v.t.* to socialize, nationalize.

sociedad, *n.f.* society, social intercourse, friendship, familiarity, friendly intercourse; partnership; corporation, association, company; *sociedad anónima,* stock company; *sociedad en comandita,* limited society.

socio, *n.m.* comrade, partner, fellow (of a society, etc.), member; (*coll.*) confederate.

sociología, *n.f.* sociology.

sociológico, -ca, *a.* sociological.
sociólogo, -ga, *n.m.f.* sociologist.
socolar, *v.t.* (*Ec., Hond.*) to clear land.
socolor, *n.m.* pretence, pretext, colour.
socollada, *n.f.* (*naut.*) flapping; jerking, pitching.
soconusco, *n.m.* (*Mex.*) cocoa from Soconusco.
socoro, *n.m.* place under the choir.
socorredor, -ra, *n.m.f.* succourer, assister, helper.
socorrer, *v.t.* to succour, help, favour, aid, assist; to pay money on account.
socorrido, -da, *a.* furnished, well supplied; (*coll.*) handy, useful.
socorro, *n.m.* succour, aid, support, relief, assistance, help; part payment on account.
socrático, -ca, *a.* Socratic.
socrocio, *n.m.* (*pharm.*) saffron poultice.
socucho, *n.m.* (*Am.*) small room, den, garret.
sochantre, *n.m.* (*eccles.*) choir master.
soda, *n.f.* (*bot.*) soda-ash, kelp.
sódico, -ca, *a.* (*chem.*) sodic.
sodio, *n.m.* (*min.*) sodium.
sodomía, *n.f.* sodomy.
sodomita, *n.m.*, *a.* sodomite.
sodomítico, -ca, *a.* of or belonging to sodomy.
soez, *a.* vile, base, coarse, mean.
soezmente, *adv.* meanly, basely, vilely.
sofá, *n.m.* sofa.
sofaldar, *v.t.* to raise up, lift up, tuck up, truss up.
sofaldo, *n.m.* tucking up, trussing-up (of clothes).
sofí, *n.m.* sofi, shah.
sofión, *n.m.* hoot; reprimand, reproof, censure.
sofisma, *n.m.* sophism.
sofista, *n.m.* sophist, sophister, quibbler.
sofistería, *n.f.* sophistry, fallacy.
sofisticación, *n.f.* sophistication, adulteration.
sofísticamente, *adv.* sophistically, fallaciously.
sofisticar, *v.t.* (conjugated like BUSCAR) to sophisticate, adulterate, vitiate, falsify.
sofístico, -ca, *a.* sophistical, fallacious.
sofito, *n.m.* (*arch.*) soffit.
soflama, *n.f.* subtle flame; glow, blush; artful speech; flimflam.
soflamar, *v.t.* to raise a blush; to speak artfully or deceitfully; to swindle, cheat. — *v.r.* to get scorched.
soflamero, *n.m.* sophist; trickster.
sofocación, *n.f.* suffocation, choking, smothering.
sofocante, *a.* suffocating, stifling, oppressive, close.
sofocar, *v.t.* (*pret.* **sofoqué**; *pres. subj.* **sofoque**) to suffocate, stifle, choke, smother; to put out, extinguish, quench; (*fig.*) to harass, oppress; to molest, importune, provoke; to raise a blush.
sofoco, *n.m.* suffocation; (*fig.*) chagrin, vexation.
sofocón, *n.m.* (*coll.*) irritation, chagrin.
sofreír, *v.t.* (conjugated like FREÍR) to fry slightly.
sofrenada, *n.f.* sudden check with the bridle; severe or rude reproof.
sofrenar, *v.t.* to check (a horse); (*fig.*) to reprove rudely or severely; (*fig.*) to check, control (a passion).
sofrenazo, *n.m.* violent pull of the bridle; severe or rude reproof.

sofrito, -ta, *a.*, *p.p. irreg.* [SOFREÍR].
soga, *n.f.* rope, cord; (*Col.*) lasso; halter; a variable measure of land; face of a brick; *dar soga a,* to make fun of; *quebrar la soga,* to fail to keep one's promise; *quien no trae soga, de sed se ahoga,* always be prepared; *siempre quiebra la soga por lo más delgado,* the weakest goes to the wall; *con la soga a la garganta,* in imminent danger; *arrojar la soga tras el caldero,* to throw the rope after the bucket; *no se ha de mentar la soga en casa del ahorcado,* don't speak of a halter in the house of a man that has been hanged.
soguear, *v.t.* to measure with a rope.
soguería, *n.f.* rope-walk; rope-yard; collection of ropes.
soguero, *n.m.* rope-maker.
soguica, -illa, -ita, *n.f.* small rope; small braid of hair.
soja, *n.f.* soy(a)bean.
sojuzgador, *n.m.* subduer, conqueror.
sojuzgar, *v.t.* (*pret.* **sojuzgué**; *pres. subj.* **sojuzgue**) to subjugate, conquer, subdue.
sol, *n.m.* sun, sunlight, day; old lace; (*Per.*) sol, dollar; (*mus.*) sol, G, fifth note of the scale; *puesta del sol,* sunset; *quemadura del sol,* sunburn; *rayo del sol,* sunbeam; *reloj de sol,* sundial; *al salir el sol* (or *al sol naciente*), at daybreak; *al sol puesto,* at nightfall; *de sol a sol,* from sunrise to sunset; *el sol sale,* the sun rises; *el sol se pone,* the sun sets; *tomar el sol,* to sun oneself, walk in the sun; *aun hay sol en las bardas,* there's still hope; *arrimarse al sol que más calienta,* to fawn on influential men; *jugar al sol antes que salga,* to gamble away a day's pay in advance; *morir sin sol, sin luz y sin moscas,* to die deserted by all; *no dejar a sol ni a sombra a uno,* to importune someone by night and by day; *sol que mucho madruga, poco dura,* fires lit early soon burn out; *tomar el sol,* to take the altitude of the sun.
solacear, *v.t.* to solace, console, comfort.
solada, *n.f.* floor; seat; site; dregs, sediment, lees.
solado, *n.m.* tile floor, pavement.
solador, *n.m.* tiler, paver.
soladura, *n.f.* paving; paving materials.
solamente, *adv.* only, solely, merely.
solampiar, *v.t.* (*Arg.*) to eat alone and hastily.
solana, *n.f.* strong sunshine, sun-gallery, open gallery, sun-bath, sunny place.
solanera, *n.f.* sun-bath; hot, sunny place; sunburn.
solano, *n.m.* hot easterly wind; (*bot.*) nightshade.
solapa, *n.f.* lapel; pretext, pretence, colour; (*vet.*) cavity inside a small wound.
solapadamente, *adv.* deceitfully.
solapado, -da, *a.* cunning, artful, crafty.
solapadura, *n.f.* overlap; *obra de solapadura,* clinker work.
solapar, *v.t.*, *v.i.* to overlap; to cloak, conceal, hide under false pretences.
solape, solapo, *n.m.* lapel; pretence; *a solapo,* (*coll.*) sneakingly.
solar, *n.m.* lot, ground-plot; manor house, ancestral dwelling; position or site of an ancestral dwelling. — *a.* solar. — *v.t.* (*pres. indic.* **suelo**; *pres. subj.* **suele**) to floor, pave; to sole (shoes).
solariego, -ga, *a.* manorial, ancestral; belong-

ing to a noble family; held by full legal tenure.

solas, a mis (tus, sus, *etc.***),** *adv.* all by myself (thyself, himself, etc.).

solaz, *n.m.* solace, comfort, consolation; relaxation, enjoyment; *a solaz,* pleasantly, agreeably.

solazar, *v.t.* (*pret.* **solacé;** *pres. subj.* **solace**) to solace, comfort, cheer, amuse; *v.r.* to be comforted, enjoy oneself.

solazo, *n.m.* (*coll.*) scorching sun.

solazoso, -sa, *a.* comforting, delectable, enjoyable.

soldada, *n.f.* wages, service-pay, salary.

soldadero, -ra, *a.* stipendiary, receiving wages.

soldadesca, *n.f.* soldiery, soldiership; shamfight; undisciplined troops.

soldadesco, -ca, *a.* soldierly, soldier-like, martial, military.

soldado, *n.m.* soldier; *soldado raso,* private soldier.

soldador, *n.m.* solderer; soldering-iron.

soldadura, *n.f.* soldering, solder; welding; amending, correction; *soldadura autógena,* welding.

soldán, *n.m.* sultan.

soldar, *v.t.* (*pres. indic.* **sueldo;** *pres. subj.* **suelde**) to solder, weld; (*fig.*) to mend, amend, correct.

solear, *v.t.* to sun.

solecismo, *n.m.* solecism.

soledad, *n.f.* solitude, seclusion, solitariness, lonesomeness, loneliness; homesickness; desert, lonely place; orphanage; (*mus.*) Andalusian dance, song or air.

solejar, *n.m.* place exposed to the sun.

solemne, *a.* solemn, famous, celebrated, impressive, grand, high; formal; (*coll.*) confirmed, downright; *un solemne bobo,* a great booby.

solemnemente, *adv.* solemnly.

solemnidad, *n.f.* solemnity, solemnness; religious pomp, ceremony; impressiveness. — *pl.* **solemnidades,** formalities.

solemnizador, -ra, *n.m.f.* solemnizer, one who solemnizes.

solemnizar, *v.t.* (*pret.* **solemnicé;** *pres. subj.* **solemnice**) to solemnize, perform solemnly; to celebrate; to praise, extol, laud.

solenoide, *n.m.* (*elect.*) solenoid.

sóleo, *n.m.* (*anat.*) soleus.

soler, *v.i.* (a defective verb of which only the present indicative **suelo** and the imperfect tense, **solía,** are used, always followed by an infinitive) to accustom, be used to, be in the habit of, be apt to, be wont.

soler, *n.m.* (*naut.*) under-flooring.

solera, *n.f.* entablature, cross-beam, rib, lintel, plinth; lower millstone, flat stone, stone slab; wine-lees.

solercia, *n.f.* industry; shrewdness; talents, abilities.

solería, *n.f.* pavement, floor; a bale of skins for shoe-soles.

solero, *n.m.* lower millstone.

solerte, *a.* shrewd, sagacious, cunning.

soleta, *n.f.* additional sole; (*coll.*) brazen woman; (*Mex.*) iced cake; *apretar* (or *picar*) *de soleta* (or *tomar soleta*), to turn away.

soletar, soletear, *v.t.* to resole, refoot (stockings).

soletero, -ra, *n.m.f.* vamper, refooter, resoler.

solevantado, -da, *a.* unquiet, perturbed, agitated, excited, restless.

solevantamiento, *n.m.* revolt, insurrection, uprising, upheaval.

solevantar, *v.t.* to raise, agitate, excite commotion, upheave, uplift; to induce, incite.

solfa, *n.f.* sol-fa; solfeggio; solmization; musical annotation, notes; (*coll.*) sound beating, drubbing; music, harmony; *tocar la solfa a,* to flog, beat, cudgel; *estar en solfa,* to be artistically arranged (*or* to appear ridiculous); *poner en solfa,* to arrange artistically (*or* to make to appear ridiculous).

solfeador, *n.m.* music-master; songster; solfaist.

solfear, *v.i.* (*mus.*) to sol-fa; (*coll.*) to cudgel, flog.

solfeo, *n.m.* sol-fa; melody; beating, flogging, drubbing.

solfista, *n.m.f.* sol-faist, musician.

solicitación, *n.f.* solicitation; importunity; inducement, temptation.

solicitado, -da, *a.* in brisk demand.

solicitador, -ra, *n.m.f.* solicitor, agent.

solícitamente, *adv.* solicitously, diligently.

solicitante, *a.* solicitor.

solicitar, *v.t.* to solicit; to entreat; to importune, urge; to court, woo; to seek, search; *solicitar permiso,* to ask leave; *solicitar un puesto,* to apply for a post.

solícito, -ta, *a.* solicitous, anxious, diligent, careful.

solicitud, *n.f.* solicitude, anxiety; importunity; diligence; petition, application; (*com.*) demand.

sólidamente, *adv.* solidly, firmly.

solidar, *v.t.* to harden, make firm, make solid, consolidate; to establish.

solidariamente, *adv.* conjointly; (*law*) in solidum, for the whole.

solidaridad, *n.f.* solidarity.

solidario, -ria, *a.* (*law*) jointly and severally liable.

solidarizar, *v.t.* solidarize.

solideo, *n.m.* (*eccles.*) calotte.

solidez, *n.f.* solidity, firmness, strength; integrity.

solidificación, *n.f.* solidification.

solidificar, *v.t., v.r.* (conjugated like BUSCAR) to solidify.

sólido, -da, *a.* solid, firm, compact, consistent.

sólido, *n.m.* solid, compact body.

soliloquiar, *v.i.* to soliloquize.

soliloquio, *n.m.* soliloquy, monologue.

solimán, *n.m.* corrosive sublimate.

solio, *n.m.* canopied throne.

solípedo, -da, *a.* soliped.

solista, *n.m.f.* soloist.

solitaria, *n.f.* post-chaise; tapeworm.

solitariamente, *adv.* solitarily, lonesomely.

solitario, -ria, *a.* solitary, lonely, lonesome, retired, isolated, secluded.

solitario, *n.m.* hermit, recluse, solitary; solitaire (game); solitaire diamond.

sólito, -ta, *a.* wont, accustomed.

solitud, *n.f.* (*poet.*) solitude, loneliness, loneness; lonely place.

soliviadura, *n.f.* raising or lifting slightly.

soliviantar, *v.t.* to induce, incite, instigate, rouse.

soliviar, *v.t.* to raise up, prop up, lift up

slightly. — *v.r.* to raise oneself, get up a little.

solivio, *n.m.* rising a little, raising slightly.

solo, -la, *a.* alone, single; only, solitary, lonely. lonesome; *a solas,* alone, unaided; *a mis solas, a sus solas, etc.,* all by myself, himself, etc.

solo, *n.m.* (*mus.*) solo; lone hand in certain games (cards); a card game.

sólo, *adv.* only, solely.

solomillo, solomo, *n.m.* loin, chine, sirloin (of pork).

solsticial, *a.* solstitial.

solsticio, *n.m.* solstice.

soltadizo, -za, *a.* easily untied; cleverly loosened.

soltador, -ra, *n.m.f.* one that unties, loosens.

soltar, *v.t.* (*pres. indic.* **suelto;** *pres. subj.* **suelte**) to loosen, unfasten, untie; to turn on (water); to discharge, let go, set free; to solve; to cast off; to explain; to burst out (into laughter, tears, etc.); to utter; to give (a slap, kick, etc.); *soltar la deuda,* to forgive a debt; *soltar la palabra,* to absolve one from a promise. — *v.r.* to get loose; to come off; to get handy, clever; to lose restraint; to lose all modesty.

soltera, *n.f.* spinster, old maid, unmarried woman.

soltería, *n.f.* celibacy, bachelorhood.

soltero, *n.m.* bachelor, unmarried man.

soltero, -ra, *a.* unmarried, single.

solterón, *n.m.* old bachelor.

solterona, *n.f.* old maid.

soltura, *n.f.* freedom; release; laxity; easiness; activity, agility; fluency; looseness, licentiousness; (*law*) order issued by a judge releasing a prisoner.

solubilidad, *n.f.* solubility, solubleness.

soluble, *a.* soluble, solvable.

solución, *n.f.* solution; resolution; loosening, untying; dissolution; dénouement, climax or end of a drama; satisfaction.

solucionar, *v.t.* to solve; to overcome (a difficulty).

solutivo, -va, *a.* (*med.*) solutive, dissolving.

solvencia, *n.f.* solvency.

solventar, *v.t.* to settle debts; to solve.

solvente, *a.* solvent, dissolvent, unbinding.

solver, *v.t.* (*obs.*) (*p.p.* **suelto;** *pres. indic.* **suelvo;** *pres. subj.* **suelva**) to solve, find out; to loosen, untie.

sollado, *n.m.* orlop.

sollamar, *v.t.* to single, scorch, burn slightly.

sollastre, *n.m.* scullion, kitchen boy; cunning knave.

sollastría, *n.f.* scullery.

sollo, *n.m.* sturgeon, pike.

sollozar, *v.i.* (*pret.* **sollocé;** *pres. subj.* **solloce**) to sob.

sollozo, *n.m.* sob; (*Mex.*) huckleberry.

soma, *n.f.* coarse flour.

somanta, *n.f.* beating, drubbing.

somatar, *v.t.* (*Mex., Hond.*) to misspend, waste, squander.

somatén, *n.m.* armed body of citizens; alarmbell; (*coll.*) tumult, hubbub; ¡*somatén!* Catalan war cry.

somatología, *n.f.* somatology.

somatológico, -ca, *a.* somatological.

sombra, *n.f.* shade, shadow, darkness; ghost, spirit; protection, shelter, favour; similitude,

resemblance; (*Arg., Chi., Hond.*) guide lines for writing; appearance, vestige, sign; (*astron.*) umbra; (*art*) shade, shading; umber; *mirarse a la sombra,* to have a good opinion of oneself; *ni por sombra,* by no means; *hacer sombra,* to shade; to outshine; to protect; *no ser ni su sombra,* to be but the shadow of one's former self; *tener buena sombra,* to be pleasing, popular; *tener mala sombra,* to exert a bad influence, to be unpopular, disagreeable; *poner a la sombra,* (*fam.*) to imprison.

sombraje, *n.m.* branch-covered hut or screen.

sombrajo, *n.m.* shed, hut; shadow cast by a person preventing the light from reaching another.

sombrar, *v.t.* to astonish.

sombreado, *n.m.* (*art*) shading.

sombrear, *v.t.* (*art*) to shade.

sombrerazo, *n.m.* large hat; blow with a hat; doffing the hat.

sombrerera, *n.f.* hat-box; milliner; a medicinal plant.

sombrerería, *n.f.* hat-shop, hat-factory.

sombrerero, *n.m.* hatter, hat-maker.

sombrerete, -ico, *n.m.* small hat; (*mech.*) cap, bonnet, cowl; spark catcher of a locomotive; (*arch.*) calotte.

sombrerillo, *n.m.* alms basket in prisons; navel-wort.

sombrero, *n.m.* hat; sounding-board; pulpit canopy; *sombrero de cabrestante,* (*naut.*) capstan drum; *sombrero apuntado,* cocked hat; *sombrero de tres picos,* three-cornered hat; *sombrero de copa,* silk hat, tall hat; *sombrero de muelles* (or *clac*), opera hat; *sombrero gacho,* slouch hat; *sombrero de jipijapa,* Panama hat; *sombrero de pelo,* (*Arg., Chi.*) silk hat, tall hat; *sombrero jarano,* Mexican hat; *sombrero jíbaro,* Cuban and Puerto Rican hat; *sombrero del patrón,* (*naut.*) hat money, primage.

sombría, *n.f.* shady place.

sombrilla, *n.f.* parasol, sunshade; slight shade.

sombrío, -bría, *a.* shady, gloomy, hazy, sombre; dark, murky, overcast; taciturn, sulky, sullen; (*art*) shaded.

sombroso, -sa, *a.* shady, shadowy.

someramente, *adv.* superficially.

somero, -ra, *a.* superficial, shallow. — *n.f.* (*print.*) sleeper of the old printing press.

someter, *v.t.* to submit, subject, subdue. — *v.r.* to humble oneself; to submit, acquiesce, comply.

sometimiento, *n.m.* submission, subduing, subjection.

somnambulismo, *n.m.* somnambulism.

somnámbulo, -la, *n.m.f.* somnambulist.

somnífero, -ra, *a.* somniferous, soporiferous, inducing sleep.

somnílocuo, -cua, *a.* somniloquous, talking in sleep.

somnolencia, *n.f.* somnolence, sleepiness, drowsiness.

somo, *n.m.* summit, peak.

somonte, (de), *a.* coarse, rough, shaggy.

somorgujador, *n.m.* diver.

somorgujar, *v.t., v.i., v.r.* to dive, duck.

somorgujo, somorgujón, somormujo, *n.m.* (*orn.*) dun-diver; *a lo somorgujo* or *a somormujo,* under water, privately.

sompesar, *v.t.* to weigh, heft.

sompopo, *n.m.* (*Hond.*) yellow ant; (*Hond.*) a dish of meat cooked with butter.

son, *n.m.* sound, noise; tale, report; manner, guise, mode; reason, pretext; ¿ *a qué son ?* why? for what reason?; *a son de,* at the sound of; *en son de,* like, as, in the guise of; *sin ton y sin son,* without rhyme or reason; *bailar a cualquier son,* to be easily moved; *bailar uno al son que le tocan,* to adapt oneself to any circumstances; *bailar sin son,* to be very eager; *no venir el son con la castañeta,* to produce disproportionately small results; *quedarse al son de buenas noches,* to be foiled in one's intentions.

sonable, *a.* sonorous, sounding, loud; celebrated, famous.

sonada, *n.f.* tune; (*obs.*) sonata.

sonadera, *n.f.* blowing the nose.

sonadero, *n.m.* handkerchief.

sonado, -da, *a.* wiped; blown; bruited about; celebrated, famous.

sonador, *n.m.* handkerchief.

sonador, -ra, *n.m.f., a.* one who makes a noise.

sonaja, *n.f.* timbrel; jingles.

sonajero, *n.m.; ***sonajuela,** *n.f.* small timbrel; baby's rattle.

sonambulismo, *n.m.* somnambulism.

sonámbulo, -la, *n.m.f.* somnambulist.

sonante, *a.* sounding, sonorous.

sonar, *v.t.* (*pres. indic.* **sueno;** *pres. subj.* **suene**) to sound, ring; to pronounce, enunciate; to allude, refer; to please or displease. — *v.i.* to sound. clink, jingle, tinkle, ring, make a noise; to have a familiar ring. — *v. impers.* to spread rumours; to be rumoured, reported. — *v.r.* to blow the nose; *lo que me suena, me suena,* I take the obvious interpretation of the words.

sonata, *n.f.* sonata.

sonatina, *n.f.* sonatina.

soncle, *n.m.* (*Mex.*) a measure for firewood (400 logs).

sonda, *n.f.* sounding; lead, sounder, plummet; sound, probe; annular borer; diamond drill; (*surg.*) catheter; (*artill.*) proof stick.

sondable, *a.* which may be sounded.

sondaleza, *n.f.* lead-line, sounding line.

sondar, sondear, *v.t.* to sound; to sift, explore, examine, try, fathom; *sondar la bomba,* (*naut.*) to sound the pump.

sondeo, *n.m.* sounding, exploring, fathoming; (*min.*) boring.

sonecillo, *n.m.* very slight sound; little tune.

sonetico, *n.m.* sound made by tapping with the fingers.

sonetillo, *n.m.* a sonnet of verses of eight or less syllables.

sonetista, *n.m.* sonnet writer.

soneto, *n.m.* sonnet.

sonido, *n.m.* sound, noise; report, rumour; fame; pronunciation; literal meaning. — *sonido timpánico,* tympanic resonance.

sonochada, *n.f.* evening watch.

sonochar, *v.i.* to keep watch during the first hours of the night.

sonómetro, *n.m.* sonometer.

sonoramente, *adv.* sonorously; harmoniously.

sonoridad, *n.f.* sonorousness, sonority.

sonoro, -ra; sonoroso, -sa, *a.* sonorous, soniferous, harmonious; sounding, loud, clear; (*phon.*) voiced.

sonreír, *v.i., v.r.* (conjugated like REÍR) to smile; flatter; look pleasant.

sonrisa, *n.f.; ***sonriso,** *n.m.* smile.

sonrodarse, *v.r.* to stick in the mud.

sonrojar, sonrojear, *v.t.* to make flush, put to the blush. — *v.r.* to blush, flush.

sonrojo, *n.m.* blush; word which causes a blush.

sonrosar, sonrosear, *v.t.* to dye rose-red. — *v.r.* to blush.

sonroseo, *n.m.* blush.

sonsaca, *n.f.* wheedling; enticement; petty theft, pilfering.

sonsacador, -ra, *n.m.f.* wheedler, enticer, coaxer; petty thief.

sonsacamiento, *n.m.* wheedling, extortion.

sonsacar, *v.t.* (conjugated like SACAR) to pilfer; to obtain by guile; to entice, allure.

sonsaque, *n.m.* petty theft; wheedling; enticement.

sonsonete, *n.m.* sing-song voice; rhythmical tapping sound; (*fig.*) derisory smile or laugh.

sonto, -ta, *a.* (*Guat., Hond.*) with cropped ears (of horses).

soñador, -ra, *n.m.f.* dreamer, visionary.

soñante, *a.* dreaming.

soñar, *v.t.* (*pres. indic.* **sueño;** *pres. subj.* **sueñe**) to dream, indulge in reveries; *ni soñarlo,* I couldn't dream of it; *soñar despierto,* to indulge in daydreams. — *v.i.* (with *con*) to desire anxiously, dream of.

soñarrera, *n.f.* dreaming, heavy sleep; drowsiness.

soñera, *n.f.* sleepiness, drowsiness.

soñolencia, *n.f.* sleepiness, drowsiness, somnolence.

soñolientamente, *adv.* sleepily, heavily, drowsily.

soñoliento, -ta, *a.* heavy, sleepy, drowsy, soporiferous; lazy, dull, sluggish.

sopa, *n.f.* soup; sop; *sopa de gato,* thin soup; *caerse la sopa en la miel,* to succeed beyond one's expectations; *hecho una sopa,* wet through, wet to the skin; *a la sopa boba,* (*coll.*) living at others' expense.

sopaipa, *n.f.* fritter steeped in honey.

sopalancar, *v.t.* to raise with a lever.

sopalanda, *n.f.* student's gown.

sopanda, *n.f.* brace; lintel, joist, cross-beam.

sopapear, *v.t.* to slap; to vilify, abuse.

sopapo, *n.m.* chuck under the chin; slap; (*mech.*) sucker, pump-valve.

sopar, sopear, *v.t.* to sop, steep (bread); to trample, tread upon; to maltreat, to domineer.

sopeña, *n.f.* rock-formed cavity.

sopera, *n.f.* soup-tureen.

sopero, *n.m.* soup-plate; soup lover.

sopesar, *v.t.* to heft, try the weight.

sopetear, *v.t.* to sop, steep (bread); to abuse, maltreat, use bad language to.

sopeteo, *n.m.* sopping, dipping (bread).

sopetón, *n.m.* toasted bread in oil; cuff, slap, box on the ear; *de sopetón, adv.* suddenly.

sopicaldo, *n.m.* watery soup.

sopista, *n.m.f.* person living upon charity.

sopita, *n.f.* light soup.

¡ sopla !, *interj.* gracious me! what a thing!

sopladero, *n.m.* draught, air-hole from subterraneous passages.

soplado, -da, *a.* blown; affected, spruce; conceited.

soplador, *n.m.* ventilator, air-fan.

soplador, -ra, *n.m.f.* blower, exciter, inflamer; (*Ec.*) prompter.

sopladura, *n.f.* blowing.

soplamocos, *n.m.* slap, blow.

soplar, *v.t., v.i.* to blow, blow out, inflate, fill with air; to fan; to rob, steal; to suggest, prompt, inspire; to huff (at draughts); to tipple; to denounce, accuse. — *v.r.* to be affected in dress; to eat and drink heavily; *soplársela a alguno,* to deceive.

soplete, *n.m.* blow-pipe; soldering-pipe.

soplico, *n.m.* slight blast, puff.

soplido, *n.m.* blowing.

soplillo, *n.m.* crape; gauze, chiffon; any thin, light stuff; blowing-fan; light sponge-cake.

soplo, *n.m.* blowing, blast; gust, puff, breath; information, denunciation; hint, tip; moment, instant.

soplón, -ona, *n.m.f., a.* informer, tale-teller; (*Cent. Am.*) prompter.

sopón, *n.m.* one living on charity soup.

soponcio, *n.m.* grief; fainting-fit, swoon.

sopor, *n.m.* heaviness, lethargic sleep.

soporífero, -ra, *a.* soporific, soporiferous.

soporífico, -ca, *a.* soporific, opiate, narcotic.

soporoso, -sa, *a.* soporiferous.

soportable, *a.* tolerable, supportable, bearable, endurable.

soportador, -ra, *n.m.f., a.* supporter.

soportal, *n.m.* portico.

soportar, *v.t.* to tolerate, suffer, bear, endure, support, abide; support, carry.

soporte, *n.m.* support, stand, base, bracket, bearing, rest, hanger.

soprano, *n.m.f.* soprano.

sopuntar, *v.t.* to underscore a word or letter with dots.

sor, *n.f.* (*eccles.*) sister.

sora, *n.f.* (*Per.*) mash prepared from maize to make *chicha*.

sorba, *n.f.* sorb-apple.

sorbedor, *n.m.* sipper.

sorber, *v.t.* to sip, sup, suck; to imbibe, soak, absorb; to swallow.

sorbete, *n.m.* sherbet.

sorbetera, *n.f.* ice-cream freezer; (*coll.*) tall hat.

sorbetón, *n.m.* large draught of liquor.

sorbible, *a.* that can be sipped.

sorbito, *n.m.* little sip.

sorbo, *n.m.* sip, sup, swallow, gulp, draught; absorption, sipping; (*bot.*) sorb-tree.

sorda, *n.f.* woodcock; (*naut.*) stream-cable.

sordamente, *adv.* secretly, silently.

sordera, sordedad (*obs.*), **sordez,** *n.f.* deafness.

sórdidamente, *adv.* sordidly, dirtily.

sordidez, *n.f.* sordidness, nastiness; covetousness, avarice.

sórdido, -da, *a.* sordid, dirty; nasty, licentious, indecent, impure, scandalous.

sordina, *n.f.* mute, sordine; damper of a piano; *a la sordina,* privately, secretly, on the quiet.

sordino, *n.m.* kit, small fiddle.

sordo, -da, *a.* deaf; still, quiet, silent, noiseless; muffled, stifled; voiceless, unvoiced; unmoved; (*math.*) irrational; *a la sorda* (or *a lo sordo* or *a sordas*), noiselessly, imperceptibly; *sordo como una tapia,* as deaf as a post; *no hay peor sordo que el que no quiere oir,* there are none so deaf as those who won't hear.

sordomudez, *n.f.* deafness and dumbness.

sordomudo, -da, *n.m.f., a.* deaf-mute.

sordón, *n.m.* old kind of fagotto, double curtall.

sorgo, *n.m.* sorghum.

sorna, *n.f.* slowness, laziness, sluggishness; a feigned sloth; malice.

soro, *n.m.* year-old hawk.

soroche, *n.m.* (*Am.*) mountain sickness; (*Bol., Chi.*) (*min.*) galena.

soroque, *n.f.* matrix of ores.

sorprendente, *a.* surprising, astonishing, extraordinary, rare, strange.

sorprender, *v.t.* to surprise, astonish, amaze, overtake; to come upon, take unawares.

sorpresa, *n.f.* surprise, deceit; perplexity, confusion; astonishment, amazement, consternation.

sorra, *n.f.* coarse ballast; side of a tunny fish.

sorregar, *v.t.* (conjugated like REGAR) to water accidentally a plot of land, by deviation or overflow from a neighbouring one.

sorriego, *n.m.* overflow *or* overflowing of an irrigation channel.

sorrostrada, *n.f.* insolence; bluntness.

sorteable, *a.* that which can be cast lots for.

sorteador, *n.m.* one who casts lots; skilful bullfighter.

sorteamiento, *n.m.* casting lots.

sortear, *v.i.* to draw lots, cast lots, raffle; to fight bulls with skill and dexterity; to elude a conflict, risk, etc.

sorteo, *n.m.* casting lots, drawing lots, raffle.

sortiaria, *n.f.* fortune-telling by cards.

sortija, *n.f.* ring, finger-ring; buckle, hoop; curl of hair.

sortijero, *n.m.* jewel-case.

sortijita, sortijuela, *n.f.* little ring; ringlet.

sortilegio, *n.m.* sortilege, sorcery.

sortílego, -ga, *n.m.f., a.* sorcerer, fortuneteller, conjurer.

sosa, *n.f.* glass-wort, kelp, soda-ash; (*chem.*) soda.

sosal, *n.m.* soda-bearing field.

sosamente, *adv.* insipidly, tastelessly.

sosegadamente, *adv.* quietly, peacefully, calmly.

sosegado, -da, *a.* quiet, peaceful, calm, pacific.

sosegador, -ra, *n.m.f.* pacifier, appeaser.

sosegar, *v.t.* (*pres. indic.* **sosiego**; *pret.* **sosegué**; *pres. subj.* **sosiegue**) to appease, calm, pacify, silence, quiet, lull, put to sleep. — *v.i., v.r.* to rest, repose, be calm.

sosera, sosería, sosez, *n.f.* insipidity, tastelessness; nonsense.

sosero, -ra, *a.* yielding soda.

sosiega, *n.f.* rest after work; night-cap.

sosiego, *n.m.* tranquillity, calmness, peacefulness.

soslayar, *v.t.* to place obliquely; to sidestep (a difficulty).

soslayo, *adv.* obliquely; *al soslayo* (or *de soslayo*), askew, sidewise, askance, on the slant.

soso, -sa, *a.* insipid, unsalted, tasteless, unsavoury; vapid, senseless, foolish; dull, inane, uninteresting.

sospecha, *n.f.* suspicion, jealousy, mistrust.

sospechar, *v.t.* to suspect, conjecture, mistrust.

sospechosamente, *adv.* suspiciously.

sospechoso, -sa, *a.* suspicious, suspected, mistrustful.

sospesar, *v.t.* to try the weight of.

sosquín, *n.m.* treacherous blow.

sostén, *n.m.* support; maintenance, sustenance; steadiness; brassière; steadiness of a ship against wind.

sostenedor, -ra, *n.m.f.* supporter.

sostener, *v.t.* (conjugated like TENER) to sustain, keep, maintain, support, affirm; to

suffer, tolerate, endure, bear; to countenance; to defend. — *v.r.* to support oneself, maintain oneself.
sostenido, -da, *a.* supported, sustained.
sostenido, *n.m.* (*mus.*) sharp.
sosteniente, *a.* sustaining, supporting.
sostenimiento, *n.m.* sustenance, maintenance; support.
sostituir, *v.t.* (*obs.*) [SUSTITUIR].
sota, *n.f.* jack, knave (at cards); jade, hussy. — *n.m.* substitute, deputy.
sotabanco, *n.m.* (*arch.*) pediment of an arch over a cornice; attic, garret.
sotabraga, *n.f.* (*mil.*) axletree band, yoke hoop.
sotacola, *n.f.* crupper.
sotacoro, *n.m.* place under the choir.
sotalugo, *n.m.* second hoop of a cask.
sotana, *n.f.* cassock; (*coll.*) flogging, beating, drubbing.
sotanear, *v.t.* (*coll.*) to beat, chastise; to reprimand severely.
sotaní, *n.m.* short skirt without pleats.
sótano, *n.m.* underground cellar.
sotaventarse, *v.r.* to fall to leeward.
sotavento, *n.m.* leeward, lee.
sotayuda, *n.m.* assistant steward in the royal palace.
sote, *n.m.* (*Col.*) small jigger flea.
sotechado, *n.m.* covered place, roofed place, shed.
soteño, -ña, *a.* produced in forests.
soterramiento, *n.m.* burial underground.
soterraño, -ña, *a.* subterraneous, underground.
soterrar, *v.t.* (*pres. indic.* **sotierro**; *pres. subj.* **sotierre**) to bury; (*fig.*) to hide, conceal; put underground.
sotil, sotileza [SUTIL, SUTILEZA].
sotillo, *n.m.* little grove.
soto, *n.m.* thicket, grove, brake. — *prep.* under, beneath, below.
sotoministro, *n.m.* assistant steward (in some convents).
sotreta, *n.f.* (*Arg., Bol.*) person or animal full of defects.
sotrozo, *n.m.* linch-pin, axle-pin; (*mech.*) key; foot-hook staff.
sotuer, *n.m.* (*her.*) saltire.
sotuto, *n.m.* (*Bol.*) an insect of the order Diptera which bores through the human skin.
soviet, *n.m.* soviet.
soviético, -ca, *a.* sovietic.
sovoz, (a), *adv.* in a low tone, sotto voce.
soy, *1st pers. sing. pres. indic.* [SER].
soya, *n.f.* soya bean, soybean.
su, *pron. poss. 3rd pers. m. & f. sing.* (*pl.* **sus**) his, her, its, one's, their.
suasorio, -ria, *a.* suasive, suasory.
suave, *a.* smooth, soft, mellow, delicate; mild, meek, docile, easy, tranquil, unruffled, quiet, gentle, tractable.
suavemente, *adv.* gently, kindly, mildly, softly, sweetly.
suavidad, *n.f.* softness, smoothness; suavity, sweetness; delicacy, kindness, gentleness, meekness; easiness; mellowness; levity, forbearance.
suavizador, *n.m.* razor-strop.
suavizador, -ra, *a.* mollifying, softening, smoothing.
suavizar, *v.t.* (*pret.* **suavicé**; *pres. subj.* **suavice**) to soften, mollify, ease, mitigate,

smooth, mellow; to temper; to strop.
subácido, -da, *a.* sub-acid.
subalcaide, *n.m.* deputy-warden.
subalternante, *a.* subalternant.
subalternar, *v.t.* to subject, subdue.
subalterno, -na, *a.* subaltern, inferior subordinate.
subalterno, *n.m.* subordinate; subaltern, junior officer.
subarrendador, -ra, *n.m.f.* sub-tenant, sub-renter, under-letter.
subarrendamiento, *n.m.* subrenting, subletting.
subarrendar, *v.t.* (conjugated like ARRENDAR) to under-let, sublease.
subarrendatorio, -ria, *n.m.f.* subrenter, under-tenant.
subarriendo, *n.m.* subrenting, sublease, underlease.
subasta, subastación, *n.f.* judicial sale, public sale, auction; *sacar a pública subasta,* to sell at auction.
subastador, *n.m.* auctioneer.
subastar, *v.t.* to sell by auction.
subcinericio, -cia, *a.* baked under ashes.
subclase, *n.f.* (*bot., zool.*) subclass.
subclavio, -via, *a.* (*anat.*) subclavian.
subcolector, *n.m.* subcollector.
subcomendador, *n.m.* deputy-commander.
subconciencia, *n.f.* subconsciousness.
subcutáneo, -nea, *a.* subcutaneous.
subdelegable, *a.* that may be subdelegated.
subdelegación, *n.f.* subdelegation.
subdelegado, *n.m.* subdelegate.
subdelegar, *v.t.* (conjugated like DELEGAR) to subdelegate.
subdiaconado, subdiaconato, *n.m.* subdeaconship.
subdiácono, *n.m.* subdeacon.
subdirector, *n.m.* assistant manager.
subdistinción, *n.f.* subdistinction.
subdistinguir, *v.t.* (conjugated like DISTINGUIR) to make a subdistinction.
súbdito, -ta, *a.* subject, inferior.
súbdito, *n.m.* subject.
subdividir, *v.t.* to subdivide.
subdivisible, *a.* subdivisible.
subdivisión, *n.f.* subdivision.
subduplo, -pla, *a.* subduple.
subejecutor, *n.m.* deputy executor, subagent.
subentender, *v.t.* (conjugated like ENTENDER) to understand something implied. — *v.r.* to be understood, to be implied.
subérico, -ca, *a.* suberic.
suberina, *n.f.* suberin.
suberoso, -sa, *a.* suberose, corky.
subfiador, *n.m.* second surety, co-surety.
subforo, *n.m.* agreement of sub-lease.
subgénero, *n.m.* (*biol.*) subgenus.
subgobernador, -ra, *n.m.f., a.* vicegovernor, lieutenant-governor.
subida, *n.f.* ascension, going up, rising, mounting; elevation, ascent; acclivity; enhancement; rise of price; aggravation of an illness.
subidero, -ra, *a.* rising, mounting, climbing.
subidero, *n.m.* ladder; up-grade, uphill road; mounting-block.
subido, -da, *a.* mounted, raised; high, high-priced; strong; loud (of colour); strongly scented; finest, most excellent.
subidor, *n.m.* porter; lift, elevator.
subiente, *a.* rising, ascending. — *n.m.* leaf-

ornaments around a rising column or pilaster.
subilla, *n.f.* awl.
subimiento, *n.m.* rising, ascending, climbing.
subinquilino, *n.m.* subtenant.
subinspector, *n.m.* subinspector, assistant inspector.
subintendente, *n.m.* subintendant.
subintración, *n.f.* (*med.*) subingression; immediate succession.
subintrar, *v.t.* (*med.*) to fracture or displace part of the cranium; to suffer one paroxysm of fever after another.
subir, *v.t.* to raise, lift up; to take up, bring up; to set up, build up, erect; to straighten, set straight; (*com.*) to advance, raise the price of. — *v.i.* to mount, climb, rise, ascend, come up, go up; (*com.*) to amount to; to swell, grow; to be promoted; to climb to the twigs and boughs (silk-worms); to increase in intensity; (*mus.*) to raise the voice or pitch. — *v.r.* to go up, to climb; to rise; *subirse a las bovedillas,* (*coll.*) to be violently irritated; *subirse el vino a la cabeza,* to get tipsy.
súbitamente, subitáneamente, *adv.* suddenly, of a sudden.
subitáneo, -nea, *a.* sudden, unexpected.
súbito, -ta, *a.* sudden, hasty, unexpected, unforeseen.
súbito, *adv.* unexpectedly, suddenly; *de súbito,* unexpectedly, suddenly.
subjefe, *n.m.* second in command; assistant chief.
subjetivamente, *adv.* subjectively.
subjetividad, *n.f.* subjectivity.
subjetivismo, *n.m.* subjectivism.
subjetivo, -va, *a.* subjective.
subjuntivo, *n.m.* subjunctive.
sublevación, *n.f.;* **sublevamiento,** *n.m.* insurrection, sedition, revolt.
sublevar, *v.t.* to excite, rouse to rebellion. — *v.r.* to revolt.
sublimación, *n.f.* (*chem.*) sublimation.
sublimado, *n.m.* sublimate; *sublimado corrosivo,* corrosive sublimate.
sublimar, *v.t.* to elevate, exalt, heighten; to sublime; (*chem.*) to sublimate.
sublimatorio, -ria, *a.* sublimatory.
sublime, *a.* sublime, exalted, eminent, majestic, grand, lofty; *La Sublime Puerta,* Sublime Porte.
sublimemente, *adv.* sublimely, loftily.
sublimidad, *n.f.* sublimity, loftiness, grandeur.
sublingual, *a.* sublingual, subglossal.
sublunar, *a.* sublunar, sublunary; terrestrial, earthly.
submarino, *n.m.* submarine.
submarino, -na, *a.* submarine.
submúltiplo, -pla, *n.m.f.,* *a.* (*math.*) submultiple.
suboficial, *n.m.* warrant officer; (*mar.*) petty officer.
subordinación, *n.f.* subordination, subjection.
subordinadamente, *adv.* subordinately, subserviently.
subordinar, *v.t.* to subordinate, subject.
subpolar, *a.* subpolar, under or near the pole.
subprefecto, *n.m.* sub-prefect, deputy prefect.
subprefectura, *n.f.* sub-prefecture.
subrayar, *v.t.* to underline, underscore; to emphasize.
subrepción, *n.f.* subreption; underhand proceeding.

subrepticiamente, *adv.* surreptitiously.
subrepticio, -cia, *a.* surreptitious, fraudulent; clandestine, stealthy.
subrigadier, *n.m.* sub-brigadier.
subrogación, *n.f.* subrogation, surrogation, substitution.
subrogar, *v.t.* (conjugated like ROGAR) to subrogate, substitute.
subsanable, *a.* excusable; reparable, surmountable.
subsanar, *v.t.* to excuse, exculpate; to mend, amend, repair, correct.
subscribir, *v.t., v.r.* (*p.p.* subscripto, subscrito) to subscribe (to); accede, agree to.
subscripción, *n.f.* subscription.
subscripto, -ta; subscrito, -ta, *a., p.p. irreg.* [SUBSCRIBIR].
subscriptor, -ra, *n.m.f.* subscriber.
subsecretario, *n.m.* under-secretary, assistant secretary.
subsecuente, *a.* subsequent.
subseguir, *v.i., v.r.* (conjugated like SEGUIR) to follow next.
subséstuplo, -pla, *a.* subsextuple.
subsidiariamente, *adv.* subsidiarily.
subsidiario, -ria, *a.* subsidiary, auxiliary; ancillary.
subsidio, *n.m.* subsidy; aid; war-tax.
subsiguiente, *a.* subsequent, succeeding.
subsistencia, *n.f.* subsistence, permanence, stability; livelihood, living, competence.
subsistente, *a.* subsistent, subsisting.
subsistir, *v.i.* to subsist, last; exist, live; to have means of livelihood.
subsolano, *n.m.* easterly wind.
substancia, *n.f.* substance, being, essence; support; nutrition, nourishment, sustenance, pabulum; nutritious juice or extract; property, wealth; gist, meaning; value, importance; (*coll.*) judgment, sense; *substancia blanca,* white matter (of the brain and spinal cord); *substancia gris,* grey matter; *en substancia,* shortly, briefly.
substanciación, *n.f.* substantiation.
substancial, *a.* substantial, solid, firm; essential, real, material; nutritive, nutritious, nourishing.
substancialmente, *adv.* substantially.
substanciar, *v.t.* to substantiate, verify, prove; to abridge, extract the substance, epitomize; (*law*) to try a case.
substancioso, -sa, *a.* nutritious, nutritive, nourishing, juicy; substantial.
substantivadamente, *adv.* (*gram.*) substantively.
substantivar, *v.t.* to use as a substantive.
substantivo, *n.m.* substantive, noun.
substantivo, -va, *a.* substantive.
substitución, *n.f.* substitution, replacement.
substituidor, -ra, *a.* substituting.
substituir, *v.t.* (*pres. part.* substituyendo; *p.p.* substituido, substituto; *pres. indic.* substituyo; *pres. subj.* substituya; *pret.* él substituyó) to substitute.
substituto, *n.m.* substitute.
substituto, -ta, *a., p.p. irreg.* [SUBSTITUIR].
substituyente, *a.* substituting.
substracción, *n.f.* subtraction, deducting.
substraendo, *n.m.* subtrahend.
substraer, *v.t.* (conjugated like TRAER) to subtract, deduct, take away, remove. — *v.r.* to withdraw oneself, retire, elude.

subsuelo, *n.m.* subsoil, under-soil.
subtangente, *n.f.* subtangent.
subtender, *v.t.* (conjugated like TENDER) (*geom.*) to subtend.
subteniente, *n.m.* sub-lieutenant, second lieutenant.
subtensa, *n.f.* (*geom.*) subtense (chord).
subtenso, -sa, *a.*, *p.p. irreg.* [SUBTENDER].
subterfugio, *n.m.* subterfuge, evasion, trick.
subterráneamente, *adv.* subterraneously.
subterráneo, -nea, *a.* subterraneous, subterranean, underground.
subterráneo, *n.m.* subterranean cave, cellar, vault; subterrane.
subtítulo, *n.m.* subtitle.
suburbano, -na, *a.* suburban. — *n.m.f.* resident in the suburbs.
suburbio, *n.m.* suburb, outskirt.
subvención, *n.f.* subvention, aid, subsidy, grant.
subvencionar, *v.t.* to grant a subvention, subsidize.
subvenir, *v.t.* (conjugated like VENIR) to succour, aid, assist, subvene; to supply, provide, furnish, defray.
subversión, *n.f.* subversion, overthrow.
subversivo, -va, *a.* subversive, destructive.
subversor, -ra, *n.*, *a.* subverter, overturner.
subvertir, *v.t.* (conjugated like VERTIR) to subvert, ruin, destroy.
subyacente, *a.* underlying.
subyugación, *n.f.* subjugation, subjection.
subyugador, -ra, *n.m.f.* subjugator.
subyugar, *v.t.* (*pret.* subyugué; *pres. subj.* subyugue) to subjugate, overcome, subdue, subject.
succino, *n.m.* succinite, yellow amber.
succión, *n.f.* sucking, suction.
sucedáneo, -nea, *a.* succedaneous. — *n.m.* succedaneum.
suceder, *v.i.* to succeed, follow, take the place, inherit, be the successor. — *v. impers.* to happen, befall, chance, come about, fall out; *suceda lo que sucediere*, come what may.
sucedido, *n.m.* event, happening.
sucediente, *a.* succeeding, following.
sucesible, *a.* capable of succession.
sucesión, *n.f.* succession, series, issue, concatenation, offspring, children; (*law*) estate.
sucesivamente, *adv.* successively.
sucesivo, -va, *a.* successive, consecutive, next, next in order; *en lo sucesivo*, in process of time, hereafter.
suceso, *n.m.* event, occurrence; happening, incident; issue, outcome, result; course of time.
sucesor, -ra, *n.m.f.* succeeder, successor.
suciamente, *adv.* nastily, dirtily, filthily, foully.
suciedad, *n.f.* nastiness, dirtiness, filthiness, obscenity.
sucintamente, *adv.* succinctly, briefly.
sucintarse, *v.r.* to be precise, brief.
sucinto, -ta, *a.* brief, succinct; tucked up; compendious, concise.
sucio, -cia, *a.* dirty, nasty, filthy; foul, grimy, unclean, soiled; obscene, unchaste; dark, obscure; uncivil, unpolished, rude; untidy.
suco, *n.m.* sap, juice; (*Bol., Chi., Ven.*) muddy land.
sucotrino, *a.* Socotrine (of aloes).
sucre, *n.m.* Ecuadorean monetary unit.

súcubo, *n.m.*, *a.* succubus.
sucucho, *n.m.* ship's store-room; (*Am.*) small room, den, hiding-place.
súcula, *n.f.* windlass, winch.
suculencia, *n.f.* succulence, juiciness.
suculentamente, *adv.* succulently.
suculento, -ta, *a.* succulent, juicy.
sucumbir, *v.i.* to succumb, submit, surrender, yield, sink; to perish, die; (*law*) to lose a lawsuit.
sucursal, *a.* subsidiary, ancillary. — *n.f.* (*com.*) branch of a business house.
suche, *n.m.* (*Ec., Per.*) a tree of the Apocynaceæ family; (*Arg.*) mud; (*Chi.*) minor employee. — *a.* (*Ven.*) green, unripe, sour.
súchel, súchil, *n.m.* (*Cub., Mex.*) the suche-tree.
sud, *n.m.* south; south wind.
sudadero, *n.m.* handkerchief; horse's back-cloth; sweating-place, sudatory, sweating-bath; moist ground.
Sudáfrica, *n.f.* South Africa.
sudafricano, -na, *n.m.f.*, *a.* South African.
Sudamérica, *n.f.* South America.
sudamericano, -na, *n.m.f.*, *a.* South American.
sudante, *a.* sweating.
sudar, *v.t.* to sweat, perspire; to exude, ooze; to distil; to toil, labour; to give with reluctance; *hacer sudar la prensa*, to print a great deal.
sudario, *n.m.* handkerchief; sudarium; cloth put on the face of the dead.
sudatorio, -ria, *a.* sudorific.
sudeste, *n.m.* south-east; south-east wind.
sudoeste, *n.m.* south-west; south-west wind.
sudor, *n.m.* perspiration, sweat; labour, drudgery, toil; gum distilling from trees.
sudoriento, -ta, *a.* sweated, perspiring.
sudorífero, -ra, *a.* sudorific.
sudoroso, -sa, *a.* sweating, perspiring freely.
sudoso, -sa, *a.* sweaty, covered with sweat.
sudsudeste, *n.m.* south-south-east.
sudsudoeste, *n.m.* south-south-west.
sudueste, *n.m.* south-west.
Suecia, *n.f.* Sweden.
sueco, -ca, *a.* Swedish. — *n.m.f.* Swede; *hacerse el sueco*, to pretend not to hear.
suegra, *n.f.* mother-in-law; hard crust of bread; *suegra, ni aun de azúcar es buena*, even the best mothers-in-law are hard to get on with.
suegro, *n.m.* father-in-law.
suela, *n.f.* sole, sole-leather; (*arch.*) base; tip of a billiard-cue; (*ichth.*) sole; horizontal rafter supporting partition walls. — *pl.* **suelas**, sandals; *pícaro de siete suelas*, consummate rascal; *no llegarle a la suela del zapato*, to be very inferior to someone.
suelda, *n.f.* comfrey.
sueldo, *n.m.* soldier's pay; wages, salary, earnings, stipend; sou or sol; ancient copper coin of Castile; *sueldo de oro*, Byzantine coin.
sueldo; suelde, *pres. indic.; pres. subj.* [SOLDAR].
suelo, *n.m.* ground, pavement, surface, floor; soil; bottom; terra firma, earth, world; ground-plot; (*fig.*) terminus, end; (*vet.*) sole, horse's hoof; rest (of a stirrup); lees, dregs, settlings. — *pl.* **suelos**, leavings of grain; *suelo natal*, native soil, native country; *dar en el suelo con*, to throw to the ground and break; *venirse al suelo*, to fall to the ground;

sin suelo, to excess; *medir el suelo*, to measure one's length on the ground; *por los suelos*, prostrate, cast down, in a state of depreciation; *no dejar caer en el suelo*, not to let a thing pass unnoticed; *no salir del suelo* (or *no vérsele en el suelo*), (*coll.*) to be very short of stature.

suelta, *n.f.* loosening, freeing; relay of oxen, and place where oxen are changed; fetters.

sueltamente, *adv.* loosely, lightly, freely, spontaneously, expeditiously; laxly, licentiously.

suelto, -ta, *a.* loose, light, free, easy, disengaged, expeditious, swift; daring, bold; fluent, voluble; single (copy); blank (verse). — *p.p. irreg.* [SOLTAR]; *suelto de lengua*, outspoken.

suelto, *n.m.* loose piece of metal; small change; editorial paragraph; newspaper item or paragraph.

suelto; suelte, *pres. indic.; pres. subj.* [SOLTAR].

suelvo; suelva, *pres. indic.; pres. subj.* [SOLVER].

sueno; suene, *pres. indic.; pres. subj.* [SONAR].

sueño; sueñe, *pres. indic.; pres. subj.* [SOÑAR].

sueño, *n.m.* sleep, sleeping; dream, vision; any fantastic idea without foundation, imagining; sleepiness, drowsiness; event of short duration; a licentious dance of the 18th cent.; *no dormir sueño*, to be unable to sleep; *guardar el sueño*, to keep someone from being wakened; *tener sueño*, to be sleepy; *caerse de sueño*, to be overcome with sleep; *conciliar el sueño*, to coax sleep; *descabezar el sueño*, to have a brief nap; *entre sueños*, half-asleep; *ni por sueños*, never, by no means.

suero, *n.m.* whey; serum (of blood).

sueroso, -sa, *a.* serous.

suerte, *n.f.* chance, lot, luck, fate, doom, destiny, hazard; fortune, good luck; kind, sort, species; way, mode, manner; bullfighter's manœuvre; piece of ground enclosed by bounds or landmarks; original stock, lineage; (*mil.*) draft; trick, juggle, feat; (*Arg.*) meat; (*Per.*) lottery ticket. — *pl.* **suertes,** tricks; *correr bien* (*o mal*) *la suerte a uno*, to have good (or ill) luck; *de suerte que*, so that, in such a way that; *caerle* (or *tocarle*) *a uno la suerte*, to fall to one's lot; *entrar en suerte*, to go in for a raffle or sweepstake; *echar suertes*, to draw lots; *por suerte*, luckily, by chance.

suertero, *n.m.* (*Per.*) seller of lottery tickets.

sueste, *n.m.* south-east.

suevo, -va, *a.* Swabian.

sufí, *n.m., a.* sufi, Persian mystic.

suficiencia, *n.f.* sufficiency; ability, capacity; *a suficiencia*, sufficiently, enough.

suficiente, *a.* sufficient, enough; fit, apt, capable, qualified, competent.

suficientemente, *adv.* sufficiently.

sufijo, *n.m.* (*gram.*) suffix, affix.

sufijo, -ja, *a.* suffixed, affixed.

sufocación, *n.f.* suffocation.

sufocador, -ra, *n.m.f.* suffocater, choker.

sufocante, *a.* suffocating.

sufocar, *v.t.* (*pret.* **sufoqué;** *pres. subj.* **sufoque**) to choke, suffocate, smother.

sufra, *n.f.* ridge-band of a harness.

sufragáneo, -nea, *n.m., a.* suffragan.

sufragar, *v.t.* (*pret.* **sufragué;** *pres. subj.* **sufrague**) to favour, assist, aid; to defray,

make good (*Arg., Chi., Ec.*) to vote for; to give the vote to.

sufragio, *n.m.* vote, voice, suffrage; favour, assistance, aid, support; (*eccles.*) suffrage.

sufrible, *a.* sufferable, bearable, tolerable.

sufridera, *n.f.* smith's puncher.

sufridero, -ra, *a.* supportable, tolerable.

sufrido, -da, *a.* bearing, consenting, enduring, long-suffering, accommodating; cuckold by tacit consent; not prone to show the dirt (of colours). — *p.p.* [SUFRIR]; *mal sufrido*, impatient, rude, severe.

sufridor, -ra, *n.m.f.* sufferer, endurer.

sufriente, *a.* enduring, bearing, suffering, tolerating.

sufrimiento, *n.m.* patience, tolerance, endurance, sufferance.

sufrir, *v.t.* to suffer, endure, sustain, bear up; to undergo (as a change); tolerate, put up with, abide; to comport; to resist; to permit; to meet with (as a reverse); to do penance. — *v.i.* to be in pain, to suffer.

sufumigación, *n.f.* suffumigation.

sufusión, *n.f.* suffusion.

sugerente, *a.* suggesting.

sugerir, *v.t.* (*pres. part.* **sugiriendo;** *pres. indic.* **sugiero;** *pret.* **él sugirió;** *pres. subj.* **sugiera**) to hint, inspire, insinuate, suggest; to instigate, prompt.

sugestible, *a.* suggestible.

sugestión, *n.f.* suggestion, intimation, hint; temptation.

sugestionar, *v.t.* to suggest.

suicida, *n.m.f.* suicide (person).

suicidarse, *v.r.* to commit suicide.

suicidio, *n.m.* suicide (act).

suita, *n.f.* (*Hond.*) a grass plant used as fodder and for thatching.

suite, *n.m.* dwarf palm.

Suiza, *n.f.* Switzerland.

suiza, *n.f.* ancient military sport; (*coll.*) brawl, row.

suizo, -za, *n.m.f., a.* Swiss.

sujeción, *n.f.* subjection; coercion, control; subordination, obedience; surrendering, submitting; connexion.

sujetar, *v.t.* (*p.p.* **sujetado, sujeto**) to subdue, subject, overcome, conquer; hold down, hold fast, fasten, catch, grasp. — *v.r.* to subject or constrain oneself; to submit.

sujeto, -ta, *a.* subject, exposed, liable; amenable; chargeable. — *p.p. irreg.* [SUJETAR].

sujeto, *n.m.* subject, topic, matter, theme; individual, person, fellow.

sulfatar, *v.t.* to steep in copper sulphate.

sulfato, *n.m.* sulphate.

sulfhidrato, *n.m., a.* hydrosulphate.

sulfhídrico, *n.m., a.* sulphydric.

sulfito, *n.m.* sulphite.

sulfonal, *n.m.* sulphonal.

sulfurar, *v.t.* to sulphurize, sulphurate; to anger, irritate, enrage. — *v.t.* to become furious with anger.

sulfúreo, -rea, *a.* sulphurous.

sulfúrico, -ca, *a.* sulphuric.

sulfuro, *n.m.* (*chem.*) sulphide.

sulfuroso, -sa, *a.* sulphurous.

sultán, *n.m.* sultan.

sultana, *n.f.* sultana; Turkish admiral's ship.

sultanía, *n.f.* sultanate.

suma, *n.f.* sum, aggregate; addition, total; quantity, amount, number; summing-up, substance, conclusion; abridgment, compendium; *suma y sigue* (or *suma a la vuelta*), carried forward; *suma del frente* (or *suma de la vuelta*), brought forward; *en suma*, in short, finally.

sumaca, *n.f.* (*Am.*) smack, small coasting vessel.

sumamente, *adv.* chiefly, extremely, highly, mightily.

sumando, *n.m.* (*math.*) addend.

sumar, *v.t.* to sum, add; cast up, tot up, amount to; to recapitulate, make a summary.

sumaria, *n.f.* indictment.

sumariamente, *adv.* (*law*) summarily.

sumario, -ria, *a.* summary, compendious, cursory, plain, brief.

sumario, *n.m.* summary, abstract, abridgment, compendium; (*law*) indictment.

sumarísimo, -ma, *n., a.* (*law*) swift, expeditious; *consejo sumarísimo,* drum-head court-martial.

sumergible, *a.* submergible, sinkable. — *n.m.* submarine.

sumergimiento, *n.m.* submersion, sinking.

sumergir, *v.t., v.r.* (*pres. indic.* **sumerjo;** *pres. subj.* **sumerja**) to submerge, immerse, sink; to dive, duck, plunge; (*fig.*) to overwhelm, plunge.

sumersión, *n.f.* submersion, immersion.

sumidad, *n.f.* top, summit, apex, height, extremity, crest.

sumidero, *n.m.* sewer, sink, drain, gutter, gully; (*min.*) sump.

sumiller, *n.m.* chamberlain; *sumiller de corps,* lord chamberlain; *sumiller de cortina,* royal chaplain.

sumillería, *n.f.* lord chamberlain's office.

suministración, *n.f.* provision, supply.

suministrador, -ra, *n.m.f.* provider, purveyor, supplier.

suministrar, *v.t.* to minister, provide, furnish, supply, afford, purvey.

suministro, *n.m.* provision, furnishing, supply.

sumir, *v.t.* to sink, depress, overwhelm; to receive the elements at Mass. — *v.r.* to sink, be sunk (as the cheeks for want of teeth).

sumisamente, *adv.* submissively, low.

sumisión, *n.f.* submission, obsequiousness, acquiescence, obedience, compliance; (*law*) renunciation.

sumiso, -sa, *a.* submissive, resigned, humble, compliant, meek.

sumista, *n.m.* abridger, computer, rapid adder.

sumo, -ma, *a.* highest, loftiest, greatest, most elevated, excessive; *a lo sumo,* at most; *de sumo,* totally, fully; *Sumo Pontífice,* Pontifex Maximus (in ancient Rome); the Pope.

sumoscapo, *n.m.* top of the shaft of a column.

súmula(s), *n.f.* (*pl.*) compendium of the elements of logic.

sumulista, *n.m.* teacher or student of logic.

sunción, *n.f.* partaking of the Eucharist.

sundín, *n.m.* (*Arg.*) merry gathering, dancing of criollos.

sunsún, *n.m.* (*Cub.*) humming-bird.

suntuario, -ria, *a.* sumptuary.

suntuosamente, *adv.* sumptuously.

suntuosidad, *n.f.* sumptuosity, sumptuousness, magnificence, gorgeousness, luxuriance.

suntuoso, -sa, *a.* sumptuous, expensive, gorgeous, luxurious.

supedáneo, *n.m.* pedestal of a crucifix.

supeditación, *n.f.* trampling underfoot; subjection, tyranny, oppression.

supeditar, *v.t.* to trample, overpower, subdue, subject.

superable, *a.* superable, conquerable.

superabundancia, *n.f.* superabundance, overflow.

superabundante, *a.* superabundant, luxuriant, excessive.

superabundantemente, *adv.* superabundantly, excessively.

superabundar, *v.i.* to superabound, overflow.

superádito, -ta, *a.* superadded.

superante, *a.* surpassing, surmounting, exceeding.

superar, *v.t.* to surpass, excel, exceed; overcome, overpower, conquer.

superávit, *n.m.* (*com.*) surplus, residue.

superchería, *n.f.* cunning, wile, fraud, deceit, trickery, swindle, craft, guile, cozenage.

superchero, -ra, *a.* wily, cunning, deceitful, fraudulent, crafty.

superdominante, *a.* (*mus.*) submediant.

supereminencia, *n.f.* supereminence.

supereminente, *a.* supereminent.

superentender, *v.t.* (conjugated like ENTENDER) to superintend, inspect, oversee, supervise.

supererogación, *n.f.* supererogation.

supererogatorio, -ria, *a.* supererogatory.

superfetación, *n.f.* superfetation, superimpregnation.

superficial, *a.* surface, superficial; shallow, frivolous, vapid.

superficialidad, *n.f.* superficiality.

superficialmente, *adv.* superficially.

superficiario, -ria, *a.* (*law*) superficiary.

superficie, *n.f.* superficies, surface, area; *superficie alabeada,* warped surface; *superficie de calefacción,* heating surface; *superficie de rodadura,* tread of a wheel; *superficie desarrollable,* developable surface; *superficie reglada,* ruled surface.

superficionario, -ria, *a.* lease-holder.

superfino, -na, *a.* superfine, extra fine.

superfluamente, *adv.* superfluously.

superfluidad, *n.f.* superfluity, superabundance.

superfluo, -flua, *a.* superfluous, needless.

superfosfato, *n.m.* superphosphate.

superhombre, *n.m.* superman.

superhumeral, *n.m.* ephod, superhumeral.

superintendencia, *n.f.* superintendence, supervision.

superintendente, *n.m.f.* superintendent; supervisor, overseer; manager, inspector; controller, comptroller.

superior, *a.* superior, surpassing; upper, higher; greater, better, finer, grander, paramount. — *n.m.* superior.

superiora, *n.f.* mother superior.

superiorato, *n.m.* office of a superior; term of office.

superioridad, *n.f.* superiority, pre-eminence.

superiormente, *adv.* in a masterly or superior way.

superlativamente, *adv.* superlatively.

superlativo, -va, *a.* superlative; *en grado superlativo,* in the highest degree.

superlativo, *n.m.* superlative degree.

superno, -na, *a.* supreme, highest, supernal.

supernumerario, -ria, *a.* supernumerary.

superponer, *v.t.* to superpose.

superposición, *n.f.* superposing, superposition.
superstición, *n.f.* superstition.
supersticiosamente, *adv.* superstitiously.
supersticioso, -sa, *a.* superstitious.
supérstite, *a.* surviving.
supersubstancial, *a.* supersubstantial.
supervacáneo, -nea, *a.* superfluous.
superveniencia, *n.f.* supervention.
supervivencia, *n.f.* survivorship, survivance, survival.
superviviente, *n., a.* survivor.
supia, *n.f.* (*Bol.*) liquor of inferior quality.
supinador, *n.m.* supinator muscle.
supino, -na, *a.* supine, indolent, ignorant.
supino, *n.m.* (*gram.*) supine.
suplantación, *n.f.* supplanting.
suplantador, -ra, *n.m.f.* supplanter.
suplantar, *v.t.* to supplant, displace; to falsify, forge, alter fraudulently.
suplefaltas, *n.m.* (*coll.*) scapegoat.
suplemental, *a.* supplemental.
suplementario, -ria, *a.* supplementary.
suplemento, *n.m.* supplement, supplying, supply.
suplente, *a.* assistant; replacing, substituting. — *n.m.* substitute.
supletorio, -ria, *a.* suppletory, supplemental.
súplica, *n.f.* petition, supplication, request, memorial; *a súplica,* by request.
suplicación, *n.f.* request, petition, supplication; rolled waffle; (*law*) appeal to a high court against its own decision; *a suplicación,* on petition, by request.
suplicacionero, -ra, *n.m.* waffle seller.
suplicante, *a.* supplicant, supplicatory, petitioning. — *n.m.f.* memorialist, petitioner, supplicant, suitor.
suplicar, *v.t.* (*pret.* **supliqué**; *pres. subj.* **suplique**) to entreat, supplicate, beg, request, petition, implore, pray, crave; (*law*) to appeal; *suplicar de la sentencia,* to appeal against the sentence.
suplicatoria, *n.f.;* **suplicatorio,** *n.m.* (*law*) letters rogatory.
suplicio, *n.m.* punishment, torment, torture; capital punishment; place of execution.
suplidor, -ra, *n.m.f.* substitute, deputy.
suplir, *v.t.* to supply, afford, provide, furnish, fill up; to act as substitute; to excuse, overlook; (*gram.*) to imply, supply in one's own mind.
suponedor, -ra, *n.m.f.* supposer.
suponer, *v.t.* (conjugated like PONER) to suppose, surmise, assume; to take for granted; to imagine, fancy. — *v.i.* to have authority or weight.
suportación, *n.f.* toleration, endurance.
suportar, *v.t.* to bear, endure, tolerate, put up with.
suposición, *n.f.* supposition, surmise; distinction, authority; imposture, falsehood.
suposticio, -cia, *a.* supposititious, feigned, supposed, assumed, spurious.
supositorio, *n.m.* suppository.
suprema, *n.f.* Supreme Council of the Inquisition.
supremacía, *n.f.* supremacy.
supremamente, *adv.* supremely, ultimately.
supremo, -ma, *a.* supreme, highest, most excellent, excessive, paramount; final, last.
supresión, *n.f.* suppression, omission, extinction.

supresivo, -va, *a.* suppressive.
supreso, -sa, *a., p.p. irreg.* [SUPRIMIR].
suprimir, *v.t.* (*p.p.* **suprimido, supreso**) to suppress, abolish, cut out, keep back, omit, extinguish; (*math.*) to cancel.
suprior, -ra, *n.m.f.* sub-prior, sub-prioress.
supriorato, *n.m.* office of sub-prior or sub-prioress.
supuesto, *n.m.* supposition, assumption, hypothesis.
supuesto, -ta, *a.* supposititious, suppositive, supposed. — *p.p. irreg.* [SUPONER]; *por supuesto,* of course; *supuesto que,* granting that, since.
supuración, *n.f.* suppuration.
supurante, *a.* suppurating.
supurar, *v.i.* to suppurate. — *v.t.* (*obs.*) to waste, consume; to dissipate.
supurativo, -va; supuratorio, -ria, *a.* suppurative, suppurating.
suputación, *n.f.* computation, calculation, reckoning.
suputar, *v.t.* to compute, calculate, reckon.
sur, *n.m.* south; south wind.
sural, *a.* (*anat.*) sural.
Suramérica, *n.f.* South America.
surcador, -ra, *n.m.f.* ploughman, plougher.
surcar, *v.t.* (*pret.* **surqué**; *pres. subj.* **surque**) to furrow, plough; to flute; to cut through; to cleave through water or air (as a boat or an aeroplane); *surcar los mares,* (*poet.*) to plough the waves.
surco, *n.m.* furrow, rut, groove, hollow track; wrinkle, line.
surculado, -da, *a.* having only one stem.
súrculo, *n.m.* stem without branches.
surculoso, -sa, *a.* having only one stem.
surgente, *a.* surging, salient.
surgidero, *n.m.* port, road, anchoring-place.
surgidor, *n.m.* one who anchors.
surgir, *v.i.* (*p.p.* **surgido, surto;** *pres. indic.* **surjo;** *pres. subj.* **surja**) to surge; to spout, spurt; to issue, appear, come out; (*naut.*) to anchor.
suri, *n.m.* (*Arg.*) ostrich.
suripanta, *n.f.* (*obs.*) chorus-girl; (*contempt.*) slut, hussy.
sursudoeste, *n.m.* south-south-west; south-south-west wind.
surtida, *n.f.* sally, sortie; back-door; sally-port; (*naut.*) slipway.
surtidero, *n.m.* conduit, outlet; jet, fountain; *surtidero de agua,* reservoir.
surtido, *n.m.* supply, assortment, stock; *de surtido,* in stock, in common use.
surtidor, -ra, *n.m.f.* caterer, purveyor.
surtidor, *n.m.* water-spout, jet of water, fountain.
surtimiento, *n.m.* supply, assortment, stock.
surtir, *v.t.* (*p.p.* **surtido, surto**) to furnish, supply, provide, accommodate, stock, fit out. — *v.i.* to spout, spurt; *surtir efecto,* to have the desired effect.
surto, -ta, *a.* anchored; calm, quiet, becalmed. — *p.p. irreg.* [SURGIR].
súrtuba, *n.f.* (*CR.*) an edible giant fern.
surubí, *n.m.* (*Arg., Bol.*) a big river-fish.
surumbiar, *v.t.* (*Arg.*) to punish, to whip, to beat.
surumpe, *n.m.* (*Per.*) inflammation of the eyes, snow-blindness.
surupí, *n.m.* (*Bol.*) [SURUMPE].

sus, *pron. poss. pl. of* SU.

¡sus!, *interj.* Hurry up! Cheer up!

suscepción, *n.f.* susception; (*eccles.*) receiving holy orders.

susceptibilidad, *n.f.* susceptibility.

susceptible, *a.* susceptible.

susceptivo, -va, *a.* susceptible, susceptive; sensitive, touchy.

suscitar, *v.t.* to stir up, excite, rouse, promote.

suscitación, *n.f.* excitation.

suscribir, *v.t., v.r. (p.p.* **suscripto, suscrito**) to subscribe; to sign; to accede, agree to.

suscripción, *n.f.* subscription.

suscriptor, -ra, *n.m.f.* subscriber.

suscripto, -ta; suscrito, -ta, *a., p.p. irreg.* [SUSCRIBIR].

susidio, *n.m.* anxiety, uneasiness.

suso, *adv.* above.

susodicho, -cha, *a.* aforementioned, aforesaid.

suspendedor, -ra, *n.m.f.* suspender, hanger.

suspender, *v.t. (p.p.* **suspendido, suspenso**) to suspend, to hang up; to delay, stop; to dally, interrupt; to hoist; to surprise, amaze, astonish; to adjourn; *suspender los pagos,* to stop payment. — *v.r.* to rear (of a horse).

suspensión, *n.f.* suspension, detention; interruption, pause; amazement, admiration; privation; hesitation, suspense, uncertainty, indetermination; *suspensión de armas,* cessation of hostilities; *suspensión de pagos,* (*com.*) suspension of payment; *suspensión de garantías,* suspension of the constitution.

suspensivo, -va, *a.* suspensive. — *n.m.pl.* **suspensivos,** (*print.*) leaders (. . . . .), dots.

suspenso, -sa, *a., p.p. irreg.* [SUSPENDER] hung; suspended; bewildered.

suspensorio, -ria, *a.* suspensory.

suspensorio, *n.m.* suspensory bandage, truss, brace.

suspicacia, *n.f.* suspiciousness, mistrust.

suspicaz, *a.* suspicious, mistrustful.

suspicazmente, *adv.* suspiciously.

suspirado, -da, *a.* expected, longed for, desired.

suspirador, *n.m.* one who frequently sighs.

suspirar, *v.i.* to sigh, groan; to crave, long for, desire greatly.

suspiro, *n.m.* sigh; suspiration, breath; glass whistle with high pitch; kind of meringue; (*mus.*) short pause; (*Chi.*) pansy, heartsease; (*Arg.*) name given to several climbing plants.

suspiroso, -sa, *a.* breathing with difficulty.

sustancia, *n.f.* substance, being, essence; nutriment, support; *en sustancia,* summarily, briefly.

sustancial, *a.* substantial.

sustancialmente, *adv.* substantially.

sustanciar, *v.t.* to substantiate.

sustancioso, -sa, *a.* substantial; nutritive.

sustantivar, *v.t.* to use as a substantive.

sustantivo, *n.m.* (*gram.*) substantive.

sustenido, *n.m.* a step in Spanish dancing; (*mus.*) sharp.

sustentable, *a.* sustainable, defensible.

sustentación, *n.f.* sustentation, support, sustenance.

sustentáculo, *n.m.* stay, prop, support.

sustentador, -ra, *n.m.f.* sustainer.

sustentamiento, *n.m.* substance, sustenance.

sustentante, *a.* sustaining. — *n.m.* supporter, defender.

sustentar, *v.t.* to nourish, feed, support, sustain, maintain; assert, defend, advocate.

sustento, *n.m.* sustenance, maintenance, support, food.

sustitución, *n.f.* substitution.

sustituidor, -ra, *n.m.f.* one that substitutes.

sustituir, *v.t.* to substitute.

sustituto, *n.m.* substitute, delegate, surrogate.

sustituto, -ta, *a., p.p. irreg.* [SUSTITUIR].

susto, *n.m.* fright, terror, shock, scare.

sustracción, *n.f.* subtraction; privation; concealment.

sustraendo, *n.m.* subtrahend.

sustraer, *v.t.* (conjugated like TRAER) to subtract; to steal, to take feloniously. — *v.r.* to steal away, withdraw, give the slip.

susurración, *n.f.* susurration, whisper, whispering.

susurrador, -ra, *n.m.f.* whisperer.

susurrante, *a.* whispering, murmuring.

susurrar, *v.i.* to whisper; (*poet.*) to purl (of a stream); to rustle (of trees); to murmur, make a gentle noise; to leak out (of a secret). — *v.r.* to be whispered, bruited about.

susurro, *n.m.* whisper, murmur, rustle, purl, humming.

susurrón, -ona, *a.* whispering, murmuring. — *n.m.f.* grumbler, malcontent.

sutás, *n.m.* soutache, a narrow ornamental braid.

sute, *a.* (*Col., Ven.*) sickly, weak, thin. — *n.m.* (*Col.*) sucking pig; (*Hond.*) avocado, alligator pear.

sutil, *a.* slender, thin; subtle, acute, cunning, keen; volatile, light, airy.

sutileza, sutilidad, *n.f.* subtlety, fineness, thinness, slenderness; sagacity, cunning, artifice; acumen; nicety; perspicacity; *sutileza de manos,* sleight of hand.

sutilización, *n.f.* subtilization.

sutilizador, -ra, *n.m.f.* one who subtilizes, subtilizer.

sutilizar, *v.t.* (*pret.* **sutilicé;** *pres. subj.* **sutilice**) to subtilize; to refine, make thin; to make minute distinctions; to polish, file. — *v.i.* to talk subtleties, talk ingeniously.

sutilmente, *adv.* subtly, subtilely, pointedly; finely, nicely, delicately.

sutorio, -ria, *a.* belonging to the shoe-making trade.

sutura, *n.f.* seam, suture.

suversión, *n.f.* subversion, destruction, ruin.

suversivo, -va, *a.* subversive.

suyo, -ya, *pron. poss. 3rd person, m. f.* (*pl.* **suyos, suyas**), his, hers, theirs, one's; his own, her own, its own, one's own, their own; *los suyos,* his (or her, or their) family, friends, people, supporters, etc.; *de suyo,* spontaneously; *una de las suyas,* one of his (or her) pranks; *salirse con la suya,* to carry one's point.

suyru, *n.m.* (*Per.*) long robe used by the Incas.

suyuntu, *n.m.* (*Am.*) [ZOPILOTE].

T

T, t, *n.f.* the twenty-third letter of the Spanish alphabet.

¡ta!, *interj.* beware! take care! stay! *ta, ta,* tut-tut.

taba, *n.f.* bone of the knee-pan.

tabacal, *n.m.* tobacco plantation.

tabacalero, -ra, *a.* tobacco, of tobacco.

tabacalero, *n.m.* tobacco-grower, tobacco-dealer.

tabaco, *n.m.* tobacco, snuff; dry rot of interior of certain tree trunks; *a mal dar, tomar tabaco,* to seek consolation in misfortunes; *acabársele a uno el tabaco,* (*Arg.*) to be left penniless.

tabacoso, -sa, *n.m.f., a.* one who uses tobacco or snuff freely; tree attacked by dry rot. — *a.* snuffy.

tabalada, *n.f.* (*coll.*) heavy fall.

tabalario, *n.m.* (*coll.*) breech, buttocks, posteriors.

tabalear, *v.t.* to rock to and fro. — *v.i.* to drum with the fingers upon a table.

tabaleo, *n.m.* rocking, swinging; drumming with the fingers on a table.

tabanazo, *n.m.* (*coll.*) blow, slap.

tabanco, *n.m.* market stall; (*Mex.*) cock-loft.

tábano, *n.m.* gadfly, horse-fly.

tabanque, *n.m.* treadle of a potter's wheel.

tabaola, *n.f.* clamour, hubbub.

tabaque, *n.m.* basket (for fruit, sewing, etc.); large tack.

tabaquera, *n.f.* snuff-box, pipe-case, tobacco-case, cigar-case; pipe-bowl; (*Arg., Chi.*) tobacco-pouch.

tabaquería, *n.f.* tobacco-and-snuff shop, tobacconist.

tabaquero, *n.m.* tobacconist, cigar-maker.

tabaquismo, *n.m.* nicotism.

tabaquista, *n.m.f.* one taking much tobacco or snuff; tobacco expert.

tabardete, tabardillo, *n.m.* a fever; sunstroke; *tabardillo pintado,* spotted fever.

tabardo, *n.m.* tabard.

tabasco, *n.m.* (*Mex.*) popular name of a kind of banana (*Musa Sapientum*).

tabellar, *v.t.* to fold cloth in pieces, leaving the selvage visible; to mark fabrics with the trade-mark.

taberna, *n.f.* tavern, public house, wine-shop, drinking saloon, bar-room.

tabernáculo, *n.m.* tabernacle.

tabernario, -ria, *a.* (*coll.*) relating to a tavern; low, vile, vulgar.

tabernera, *n.f.* innkeeper's wife, barmaid.

tabernero, *n.m.* innkeeper, tavern-keeper, bar-keeper.

tabes, *n.m.* tabes; consumption; *tabes dorsal,* tabes dorsalis, locomotor ataxia.

tabí, *n.m.* tabby, moreen, watered fabric.

tabica, *n.f.* lintel, panel, covering board.

tabicar, *v.t.* (conjugated like BUSCAR) to wall up, close up, shut up.

tabicón, *n.m.* thick wall.

tábido, -da, *a.* tabid, wasted; putrid, corrupted.

tabinete, *n.m.* tabinet (fabric).

tabique, *n.m.* thin wall, partition-wall.

tabiquería, *n.f.* set of partition walls.

tabla, *n.f.* board, plank; seat, bench; slab; tablet, plate; chest; butcher's block; list, index, catalogue; box-pleat; (*art*) panel; (*jewel.*) flat diamond; table of contents, of logarithms, of prices, etc.; meat-stall; (*mus.*) sounding-board; bed of a river; full breadth gore of a skirt; largest face of a piece of timber; smooth, flat part of the body (as of the thigh or chest); bed or patch in a garden; strip of land between a row of trees; revenue office

at the frontier; (*chess and draughts*) draw. —*pl.* **tablas,** stage, boards; astronomical tables; tables of the decalogue; *escapar en una tabla,* to escape miraculously; *tablas reales,* backgammon tables; *tabla de sembrado,* field of corn; *a la tabla del mundo,* before the world, in public; *a raja tabla,* energetically; *hacer(se) tablas,* to be undecided.

tablachina, *n.f.* kind of buckler.

tablacho, *n.m.* flood-gate, sluice-gate.

tablada, *n.f.* (*Arg.*) slaughterhouse corral.

tablado, *n.m.* stage, scaffold, platform; flooring; boards of a bedstead; boards of the stage; *sacar al tablado,* to publish, make known.

tablaje, *n.m.* planking, pile of boards; gaming-house.

tablajería, *n.f.* gaming, gambling; hire of the gaming-table; butcher's shop.

tablajero, *n.m.* scaffold-maker; stage carpenter; collector of taxes; gambler; keeper of a gaming house; (*prov., iron.*) assistant resident surgeon in a hospital; butcher.

tablar, *n.m.* division of gardens into plots; set of garden plots.

tablazo, *n.m.* stroke with a board; shallow arm of a river or sea; sheet of water; (*Am.*) sea-floor deposit.

tablazón, *n.f.* boards, planks, platform; planking, flooring; decks and sheathing of a ship; lumber; *tablazón de la cubierta,* (*naut.*) deck planks.

tablear, *v.t.* to divide a garden into beds; to plank, saw into boards; to hammer iron into plates; (*sew.*) to make box-pleats.

tablero, *n.m.* board; kneading-board; panel; gambling-house, gambling-table; money-table; shop-counter; timber for sawing up; dog-nail; stock of a cross-bow; chess-board; (*tail.*) cutting-table; blackboard; (*Mex.*) backgammon board; planking of a bridge; skirts of a coat; compartment; *tablero contador,* abacus; *tablero de cocina,* dresser; *tablero de distribución,* (*elect.*) switch-board.

tableta, *n.f.* tablet; memorandum; writing-pad; lozenge, pastille; clapper; *estar en tabletas,* to be in suspense.

tableteado, *n.m.* noise made by boards when trodden upon; noise made by clappers.

tabletear, *v.i.* to move boards; to rattle clappers.

tablica, -ita, *n.f.* small board, small table, tablet.

tablilla, *n.f.* tablet, slab; notice-board; (*surg.*) splint; *tablilla de mesón,* sign of an inn; kind of cake; *por tablilla,* indirectly.

tablón, *n.m.* plank, thick board; beam; *tablón de aparadura,* (*naut.*) garboard strake.

tabloncillo, *n.m.* flooring-board; last row of seats in a bull-ring.

tabloza, *n.f.* painter's palette.

tabo, *n.m.* (*Philip.*) cup made from coconut shell.

tabor, *n.m.* a unit of Moroccan troops in the Spanish Army.

tabora, *n.f.* (*prov.*) stagnant pool.

tabú, *n.m.* taboo.

tabuco, *n.m.* hut, hovel; narrow room.

tabular, *a.* tabular.

tabuquillo, -quito, *n.m.* shack, shanty.

taburete, *n.m.* stool, armless chair. — *pl.* **taburetes,** (*theat.*) benches in the pit.

taca, *n.f.* cupboard, small pantry; (*prov.*) stain;

(*min.*) plates of the crucible; (*Chi.*) an edible mollusc.

tacaco, *n.m.* (*CR.*) a plant of the Cucurbitaceous family.

tácada, *n.f.* stroke at billiards; (*naut.*) wedges.

tacamaca, *n.f.* balsam-poplar.

tacana, *n.m.* rich grey silver ore.

tacañamente, *adv.* sordidly, in a niggardly or miserly way.

tacañear, *v.i.* to act the miser.

tacañería, *n.f.* niggardliness, meanness, closeness; narrow-mindedness; (*obs.*) cunning, low craft.

tacaño, -ña, *a.* stingy, sordid, mean, close, niggardly, parsimonious; (*obs.*) malicious, cunning, artful.

tacar, *v.t.* to mark (the face of a person). — *v.i.* to have one's turn at billiards.

tacazo, *n.m.* stroke with a cue.

taceta, *n.f.* copper basin used in oil-mills.

tacica, -illa, -ita, *n.f.* small cup.

tácitamente, *adv.* tacitly; silently, secretly.

tácito, -ta, *a.* tacit, silent; implied, inferred.

taciturnidad, *n.f.* taciturnity, silence.

taciturno, -na, *a.* taciturn, silent, reserved, melancholy.

taclobo, *n.m.* (*Philip.*) a shell-fish.

taco, *n.m.* (*artill.*) wad, wadding, stopper, rammer; plug, peg, bung; (*coll.*) volley of oaths; billiard-cue; almanac, pad; popgun; (*coll.*) snack, light meal; (*coll.*) draught of wine; tangle, confusion, intrigue; (*Cub.*) dandy, fop, coxcomb; *echar tacos*, (*coll.*) to speak in a rage.

tacón, *n.m.* heel-piece of a shoe.

taconazo, *n.m.* stamp with a heel.

taconear, *v.i.* to drum with the heels; (*fig.*) to strut loftily.

taconeo, *n.m.* drumming, stamping made with the heels.

tacotal, *n.m.* (*CR.*) a dense thicket; (*Hond.*) marsh, quagmire.

táctica, *n.f.* tactics; orderly array.

táctico, *n.m.* tactician.

táctico, -ca, *a.* tactical.

táctil, *a.* tactile.

tacto, *n.m.* touch, touching, feeling; tact; dexterity, handiness.

tacuacín, *n.m.* (*Cent. Am.*) opossum.

tacuará, *n.f.* (*Arg.*) a kind of hard bamboo.

tacurú, *n.m.* (*Arg.*) a small variety of black ant.

tacuacha, *n.f.* (*Cub.*) skilful trick.

tacuache, *n.m.* (*Cub., Mex.*) a nocturnal, insectivorous mammalian quadruped.

tacha, *n.f.* fault, defect, blemish, flaw, imperfection; spot, stain; fissure, crack; large tack; *poner tacha*, to make objections.

tachar, *v.t.* to censure, tax, blame, accuse, reprehend, find fault; to cross out, efface, scratch out; *tachar testigos*, (*law*) to challenge a witness.

tachero, *n.m.* (*Cub.*) one who works the *tacho* ; (*Am.*) tinman, tinsmith.

tachigual, *n.m.* (*Mex.*) a cheap cotton cloth.

tacho, *n.m.* (*Cub.*) sugar-boiler, evaporator, pan; (*Per.*) earthen jar for heating water; (*Arg., Chi.*) a big metal vessel with two handles.

tachón, *n.m.* scratch, erasure, effacement; ornamental nail; erasing line; (*sew.*) trimming.

tachonar, *v.t.* (*sew.*) to trim; to adorn with gilt tacks; to spot.

tachonería, *n.f.* ornamental work with gilt nails.

tachoso, -sa, *a.* defective, faulty.

tachuela, *n.f.* tack, small nail.

tael, *n.m.* (*Philip.*) tael (coin and weight).

tafanario, *n.m.* (*coll.*) breech, buttocks.

tafetán, *n.m.* taffeta, thin silk; *tafetán inglés*, court-plaster. — *pl.* **tafetanes**, flags, colours, standard, ensign.

tafia, *n.f.* (*Ven.*) tafia, molasses rum.

tafilete, *n.m.* tafilet or 'filali' leather (goatskins).

tafiletear, *v.t.* to ornament with tafilet leather.

tafiletería, *n.f.* art of dressing tafilet leather.

tafurea, *n.f.* flat-bottomed boat for transporting horses.

tagalo, -la, *n.m., a.* (*Philip.*) Tagalog language.

tagarino, -na, *n.m.f.* Moor who lived among Christians.

tagarnina, *n.f.* (*bot.*) golden thistle; (*coll.*) bad cigar.

tagarote, *n.m.* hobby, sparrow-hawk; quill-driver, scrivener; tall, awkward person; (*coll.*) noble but impoverished sponger, has-been.

tagarotear, *v.t.* (*coll.*) to write with a flourish.

tagua, *n.f.* (*Ec.*) tagua, ivory nut; (*Chi.*) a bird similar to the coot.

taguán, *n.m.* (*Philip.*) flying squirrel.

taha, *n.f.* region, district.

tahalí, *n.m.* shoulder-belt; baldric.

taharal, *n.m.* tamarisk-plantation.

**taheño, -a.m.* red-bearded; (*Chi.*) of the colour of weak coffee.

tahona, *n.f.* crushing-mill; bakehouse, bakery, baker's shop.

tahonero, *n.m.* miller; baker.

tahulla, *n.f.* (*prov.*) a measure of land (about ¼ acre).

tahur, -ra, *n.m.f.* gambler, gamester, cardsharper. — *a.* given to gambling.

tahurería, *n.f.* gambling; gaming-house; cheating at cards.

taifa, *n.f.* party, faction; (*coll.*) assemblage of rogues or foolish people.

taima, *n.f.* (*Chi.*) slyness, artfulness.

taimado, -da, *a.* crafty, sly, cunning.

taita, *n.m.* (*coll.*) daddy; brothel-keeper (male); (*Am.*) a form of address for an old negro; (*Ven.*) family name for the head of the household; (*Arg., Chi.*) child's name for father or as a term of courteous address; *taita cura*, reverend father.

taja, *n.f.* cut, incision, dissection; tally; tree of a packsaddle.

tajada, *n.f.* cut, slice, sliver; hoarseness; drinking bout, orgy; *tener una buena tajada*, to have a lucrative post.

tajadera, *n.f.* chopping-knife; (*mech.*) gouge, round chisel. — *pl.* **tajaderas**, sluice of a mill dam.

tajadero, *n.m.* chopping-block, trencher.

tajadilla, *n.f.* small slice; dish of lights.

tajado, -da, *a.* cut, notched; steep, sheer, perpendicular; (*her.*) said of a shield divided diagonally.

tajador, -ra, *n.m.f.* cutter, chopper; cutting edge.

tajadura, *n.f.* cut, notch; cutting, chopping; section.

tajalán, -ana, *a.* (*Cub.*) idle, lazy, indolent.

tajamar, *n.m.* cutwater, stem.

tajante, *a.* cutting.

tajaplumas, *n.m.* penknife.

tajar, *v.t.* to cut, chop, hew, hack, cleave, cut off; sharpen, trim.

tajea, *n.f.* channel, water-course; drain.

tajo, *n.m.* cut, notch, incision; steep cliff, gorge; chopping-board, chopping-block; cutting, reaping, digging; cutting a quill; trench, cut or opening in a mountain; cutting edge.

tajón, *n.m.* chopping-block, butcher's block; (*prov.*) vein of white earth in a limestone quarry.

tajú, *n.m.* (*Philip.*) Indian brew of tea, ginger and sugar.

tajuela, *n.f.;* **tajuelo,** *n.m.* rustic seat, low stool.

tal, *pl.* **tales,** *a.* such, as, so; a similar, such a; as much, so much, so great; *¿ qué tal ?* (*coll.*) how are you? how goes it? *el tal* (or *la tal*), that person, such a one; *otro que tal*, another (of the same ilk); *tal cual vez*, sometimes; *tal cual es*, such as he (*or* it) is; *tal palo, tal astilla*, like father, like son. — *pron.* such, such a one, such a thing; *tal para cual*, two of a kind; *tal por cual*, person of little account or importance; *no hay tal*, there is no such thing. — *adv.* thus, so, in such manner; *con tal que*, provided that.

tala, *n.f.* felling of trees; havoc, destruction, ruin, desolation; tip-cat (boys' game); cat (in the game); (*Arg.*) a large urticaceous tree.

talabarte, *n.m.* sword-belt.

talabartería, *n.f.* saddlery.

talabartero, *n.m.* belt-maker.

talador, -ra. *n.m.f.* destroyer, one who lays waste.

taladrador, -ra, *n.m.f.* penetrator, borer, piercer; drilling-machine.

taladrar, *v.t.* to bore, drill, perforate, penetrate, pierce, tap, worm; to comprehend a difficult point.

taladrilla, *n.f.* insect that attacks olive trees.

taladro, *n.m.* drill, gimlet, borer, auger; auger-hole; blasting charge.

talaje, *n.m.* (*Chi.*) pasturage and duty paid for it.

talamera, *n.f.* tree used for snaring birds.

talamete, *n.m.* (*naut.*) fore-deck planking.

tálamo, *n.m.* bride-chamber; bridal bed; (*bot.*) receptacle.

talán, *n.m.* ding-dong, the sound of a bell.

talanquera, *n.f.* parapet, defence, breastwork, place of safety; *hablar desde la talanquera*, to speak with security.

talante, *n.m.* manner, mode; aspect, appearance, mien, countenance; pleasure, desire, disposition, will; *estar de buen* (or *mal*) *talante*, to be in a pleasant (*or* unpleasant) humour.

talar, *v.t.* to fell (trees); to lay waste, desolate; to prune.

talar, *a.* full length, reaching the heels (said of clothes).

talco, *n.m.* talc; tinsel.

talcoso, -sa, *a.* talcoid, talcose.

talcualillo, -lla, *a.* (*coll.*) fair, not bad; somewhat better in health.

talega, *n.f.* bag, small sack, money-bag; bag of 1000 silver dollars; bagful; diaper.

talego, *n.m.* coarse bag, sack; clumsy, dumpy fellow; *tener talego*, to have money.

taleguilla, *n.f.* small bag; bullfighter's breeches; *taleguilla de la sal*, (*coll.*) daily expenditure.

talento, *n.m.* talent, genius, ability; understanding, intellect.

talentoso, -sa, *a.* talented, able, ingenious.

tálero, *n.m.* thaler.

talio, *n.m.* thallium.

talión, *n.m.* talion, retaliation, requital.

talionar, *v.t.* to requite, retaliate.

talismán, *n.m.* talisman, amulet, charm.

talma, *n.f.* long cape or cloak.

talmente, *adv.* (*coll.*) likewise, in the same way.

talmud, *n.m.* Talmud.

talmúdico, -ca, *a.* Talmudical.

talmudista, *n.m.* Talmudist.

talón, *n.m.* heel, heelpiece; heel of the hoof; heel of a violin bow; (*com.*) cheque, counterfoil, etc., detached from its book; coupon; (*naut.*) heel of the keel; *apretar* (or *levantar*) *los talones*, to take to one's heels.

talonario, -ria, *a.* taken from counterfoil book. — *n.m.* counterfoil book, cheque- or stub-book.

talonear, *v.i.* to be nimble, walk quickly.

talonera, *n.f.* (*Chi.*) spur support.

talonesco, -ca, *a.* (*coll.*) relating to the heels.

talque, *n.m.* kind of earth or refractory clay.

talqueza, *n.f.* (*CR.*) grass used for thatching.

talquina, *n.f.* (*Chi.*) treason, ambush, artful trick.

taltuza, *n.f.* (*CR.*) a large rat.

talud, *n.m.* (*arch.*) talus, batter, side slope.

taludín, *n.m.* (*Guat.*) a kind of alligator.

talvina, *n.f.* almond-meal porridge.

talla, *n.f.* raised work, carved work, sculpture; price on a criminal's head; (*jewel.*) cut, cutting; gurglet earthen jug; ransom, subsidy; round of a card game; instrument for measuring height; (*naut.*) purchase-block; size, stature; mark, measure; (*surg.*) operation for the stone; *a media talla*, carelessly, perfunctorily; *media talla*, half-relief; *poner talla*, to offer a reward for the capture of a criminal.

tallado, -da, *a.* cut, carved, engraved, chopped; *bien* (or *mal*) *tallado*, of a good (or bad) figure. — *n.m.* carving.

tallador, *n.m.* carver, engraver, die-sinker; (*Am.*) dealer (in a game); croupier.

talladura, *n.f.* engraving.

tallar, *v.t.* to cut, chop, carve, engrave; (*jewel.*) to cut, polish; to tax; to estimate, value, prize, appraise; (*gaming*) to form a bank. — *v.i.* to deal (at cards). — *n.m.* forest ready for cutting. — *a.* ready for cutting.

tallarín, *n.m.* noodle (for soup).

tallarola, *n.f.* knife for cutting velvet pile.

talle, *n.m.* shape, size; figure, form; waist; cut, fit of clothes; disposition, manners.

tallecer, *v.i.* (conjugated like MERECER) to sprout, shoot.

taller, *n.m.* workshop, factory, laboratory, mill; studio, atelier; *taller de reparaciones*, repair shop, (*motor.*) service station.

tallista, *n.m.* engraver, carver in wood.

tallo, *n.m.* stem, stalk, shoot, sprout; pumpkin, melon, etc., candied; (*Col.*) cabbage, broccoli; (*Chi.*) blessed thistle, holy thistle.

talludo, -da, *a.* grown into long stalks; grown up; slender, tall; overgrown; habit-ridden.

tamagás, *n.m.* (*Am.*) a highly poisonous snake.

tamango, *n.m.* (*Chi.*) sheepskin cover for the feet; (*Arg.*) coarse shoe worn by the gauchos.

tamañamente, *adv.* as great as.

tamañico, -ica; -illo, -illa; -ito, -ita, a. very small; abashed, ashamed.

tamaño, n.m. size, stature, magnitude, bulk, shape; *hombre de tamaño,* a man of great gifts.

tamaño, -ña, a. so large, so small (said in denoting the size by a motion of the hand).

tamañuelo, -la, a. small, little.

támara, n.f. palm-tree or -field of Canary Islands. — n.f.pl. **támaras,** dates in a bunch; chips, faggots of waste wood.

tamarao, n.m. (*Philip.*) a kind of small buffalo.

tamarindo, n.m. tamarind-tree, tamarind-fruit.

tamarisco, tamariz, n.m. tamarisk.

tamba, n.m. (*Ec.*) loin-cloth.

tambalco, n.m. staggering, reeling, tottering.

tambalear, v.i.; **tambalearse,** v.r. to stagger, totter, reel, waver, sway.

tambaleo, n.m. stagger, tottering movement.

tambalisa, n.f. (*Cub.*) a leguminous plant with yellow flowers.

tambanillo n.m. (*arch.*) tympanum.

tambarillo, n.m. chest with an arched cover.

tambarria, n.f. (*Col., Ec., Hond., Per.*) carouse; (*Chi.*) low tavern.

tambero, -ra, n.m.f. (*Per.*) innkeeper. — a. (*Arg.*) tame, gentle (of cattle).

tambesco, n.m. (*prov.*) swing.

también, adv. also, too, likewise, moreover, as well, even; *también hay bulas para difuntos,* there's a cure for everything.

tambo, n.m. (*Col., Chi., Ec., Per.*) roadside lodging-house, hostelry; (*Arg.*) cow-shed.

tambobón, n.m. (*Philip.*) stone granary to store rice.

tambocha, n.f. (*Col.*) a poisonous ant.

tambor, n.m. drum; drummer; chestnut roaster; coffee roaster; small room; tambour frame; (*mech.*) band pulley, cylinder, rope-barrel; (*fort., arch.*) tambour; (*jewel.*) barrel; screen; thole; (*naut.*) capstan-drum; paddle-box; (*anat.*) tympanum, eardrum; *tambor mayor,* drum-major; *a tambor* (or *con tambor batiente*), beating the drum.

tambora, n.f. bass drum.

tamborete, n.m. timbrel; (*naut.*) cap of the masthead.

tamboril, n.m. tabour, timbrel.

tamborilada, n.f. (*coll.*) fall onto the backside; slap on the head or shoulders.

tamborilazo, n.m. [TAMBORILADA].

tamborilear, v.i. to beat the tabour. — v.t. to praise, extol; (*print.*) to plane, level (*types*).

tamborileo, n.m. the beating of a drum.

tamborilero, n.m. tabourer.

tamborilete, n.m. taboret; (*print.*) planer.

tamborín, tamborino, n.m. tabour.

tamborón, n.m. large bass-drum.

tambre, n.m. (*Col.*) dam; water-wheel.

tameme, n.m. (*Chi., Mex., Per.*) Indian porter, carrier.

Támesis, n.m. Thames.

tamiz, n.m. fine sieve, sifter, tamis; *pasar por tamiz,* to sift.

tamizar, v.t. (*pret.* tamicé; *pres. subj.* tamice) to sift.

tamo, n.m. wool-down, linen-down; corn-dust, chaff, winnowings; dust collected or gathered under beds, etc.

tamojo, n.m. salt-wort.

tampoco, adv. neither, not either.

tamujal, n.m. buckthorn thicket.

tamujo, n.m. buckthorn.

tan, n.m. sound of the tambourine. —adv. (contraction of TANTO) so, so much, as much, as well.

tanaceto, n.m. tansy.

tanate, n.m. (*Mex., Hond., CR.*) bale made of hide or palm-leaf; (*Cent. Am.*) bundle, parcel.

tanatero, n.m. (*Mex.*) carrier in the mines.

tanato, n.m. tannate.

tanda, n.f. turn, rotation; task; gang, relay, or shift of workmen; set, batch; each game of billiards; number of persons or animals employed; (*theat.*) (*Chi.*) separate division of a performance.

tándem, n.m. tandem bicycle, a cycle for two; carriage with two horses, one behind the other.

tandeo, n.m. distribution of irrigating water by turns.

tangán, n.m. (*Ec.*) square board hung from the ceiling for storing food.

tanganillas, (en), adv. waveringly.

tanganillo, n.m. small prop or stay.

tángano, n.m. hob, a boy's game; stick used in this game.

tangente, n.m., a. tangent; *escapar, escaparse, irse* or *salir por la tangente,* to escape by a subterfuge, to befog the issue.

Tánger, n.m. Tangier.

tangerino, -na, n.m.f., a. Tangerine.

tangible, a. tangible, tactile.

tangidera, n.f. stern-fast, cable.

tango, n.m. tango, popular dance; (*Hond.*) Indian drum, tom-tom.

tangón, n.m. outrigger.

tanguillo, n.m. (*prov.*) top (toy).

tánico, -ca, a. tannic.

tanino, n.m. tannin.

tanor, -ra, n.m.f., a. (*Philip.*) Indian compelled to serve in Spanish households.

tanoría, n.f. (*Philip.*) obligatory and unpaid domestic service for the Spaniards.

tanque, n.m. (*Am.*) tank, pool, pond; (*api.*) bee-glue; (*mil.*) tank.

tanta, n.f. (*Per.*) bread made of maize.

tantalato, n.m. tantalate.

tantalio, n.m. tantalum.

tantarantán, n.m. tantarara, rub-a-dub-dub, double drum-beat.

tanteador, n.m. calculator, measurer, marker.

tantear, v.t. to try, calculate, reckon, proportion, measure, mark; to sound, scrutinize, consider closely; to estimate roughly, tot up; to examine; (*art*) to sketch, outline. — v.i. to keep the score. — v.r. to agree to pay the price.

tanteo, n.m. estimate, approximate calculation; trial; outlines of a picture; number of points in a game; valuation.

tantico, tantillo, n.m. (*coll.*) small sum, small quantity; a little, a little bit.

tanto, -ta, a. so much, as much, so great, as great, very great. — pl. **tantos, tantas,** many; as many, so many.

tanto, n.m. certain sum, certain quantity; copy of a writing; counter, mark, point; (*com.*) rate. — dem. pron. that; *por tanto,* therefore; *por lo tanto,* for that reason, on that ground. — adv. so, so much, so greatly, in such a way; so long, as long; often; *al tanto,* for the same price; *tanto mejor* (or *peor*), so much the better (or worse); *en tanto* (or *entre*

tanto), in the meantime; *algún tanto*, somewhat, trifle, little, few; *tanto más o menos*,
so much more or less; *tanto uno como otro*,
both one and the other; *tanto por ciento*,
percentage; *tanto por tanto*, at the same price;
en su tanto, proportionably; *tanto vales cuanto
tienes*, you are worth as much as you have.

tanza, *n.f. (prov.)* fishing-line.

tañedor, -ra, *n.m.f.* player on a musical
instrument.

tañente, *a.* playing on a musical instrument.

tañer, *v.t.* to play a musical instrument; to
ring a bell.

tañido, *n.m.* tune, sound, clink, ring.

tañimiento, *n.m.* playing on an instrument.

tao, *n.m.* badge of the orders of St. Antony and
St. John.

tapa, *n.f.* cover, cap, lid; horny part of a hoof;
heel of a shoe; *(motor.)* cylinder head; board
case, book cover; knuckle of veal; facing of
a lapel; snacks served with drinks; *(Philip.)*
jerked beef; *(Hond.)* common thorn apple;
tapa de los sesos, top of a skull.

tapabalazo, *n.m.* shot-plug.

tapaboca, *n.f. (coll.)* slap on the mouth;
muffler; silencer; interruption; *(artill.)* tampion.

tapaculo, *n.m.* fruit of the dog-rose; *(Chi.)*
small bird; *(Cub.)* fish resembling the sole.

tapachiche, *n.m (CR.)* a kind of locust with
red wings.

tapada, *n.f.* veiled woman.

tapadera, *n.f.* cover, lid; *(Mex.)* leather cover
of a stirrup.

tapadero, *n.m.* stopper, cover; leather guard
worn in front of the stirrup in California.

tapadillo, *n.m.* concealment of a woman's face;
flute-stop of an organ; *de tapadillo*, secretly.

tapadizo, *n.m.* cover, shed.

tapado, -da, *a. (Arg., Chi.)* horse without any
patches; *n.m. (Col., Hond.)* meal prepared
with bananas and meat; *(Arg., Chi.)* overcoat for women or children; *(Arg.)* buried
treasure.

tapador, -ra, *a.* coverer.

tapador, *n.m.* plug, stopper; cover, lid.

tapadura, *n.f.* stopping, covering.

tapafunda, *n.f.* holster-flap.

tapagujeros, *n.m. (coll.)* makeshift, poor
substitute; clumsy mason.

tapajuntas, *n.m.* door strip covering joint with
wall; corner angle protecting plaster.

tápalo, *n.m. (Mex.)* woman's shawl.

tapamiento, *n.m.* stopping, covering.

tápana, *n.f. (bot.)* caper.

tapanca, *n.f. (Chi., Ec.)* horse trappings.

tapanco, *n.m. (Philip.)* boat tilt or awning made
of bamboo.

tapaojo, *n.m. (Col., Ven.)* blinkers for horses.

tapapiés, *n.m.* long, silken skirt.

tapar, *v.t.* to stop up, obstruct, cover, occlude;
to hide, conceal; to hoodwink, dissemble. —
v.r. to cover the track of the fore feet with
the track of the hind feet (horses).

tápara, *n.f. (bot.)* caper; *(Ven.)* gourd for drink.

taparo, *n.m.* gourd-tree.

taparrabo, *n.m.* loin cloth; bathing trunks.

tapayagua, *n.f. (Hond., Mex.)* drizzle.

tapera, *n.f. (Bol., Par.)* deserted and ruined
village; *(Cent. Am.)* abandoned and tumble-
down house.

taperujarse, *v.r. (coll.)* to cover up one's face.

taperujo, *n.m. (coll.)* ill-shaped stopper; clumsy
manner of covering the face.

tapetado, -da, *a.* dark brown.

tapete, *n.m.* rug, small carpet, small cover;
tapete verde, card-table.

tapetí, *n.m. (Arg.)* a rodent resembling a rabbit.

tapia, *n.f.* mud wall; adobe wall; wall fence;
wall measure (50 sq. ft.).

tapiador, *n.m.* mud-wall builder.

tapial, *n.m.* mould for making mud-walls.

tapiar, *v.t.* to wall up, stop up with a mud
wall; to stop a passage; to obstruct a view.

tapicería, *n.f.* tapestry; art of making tapestry;
upholstery; tapestry-shop.

tapicero, *n.m.* tapestry-worker; carpet-mon-
ger; upholsterer. — *tapicero mayor*, tapestry
keeper in the royal palace.

tapido, -da, *a.* closely woven.

tapioca, *n.f.* tapioca.

tapir, *n.m.* tapir.

tapis, *n.m. (Philip.)* sash used by women.

tapiscar, *v.t. (CR., Hond.)* to gather and thresh
maize.

tapiz, *n.m.* tapestry.

tapizar, *v.t. (pret.* **tapicé**; *pres. subj.* **tapice***)* to
hang with tapestry.

tapón, *n.m.* cork, stopper; plug, bung; *(surg.)*
tampon; *tapón de cuba, (coll.)* short, fat person; *al primer tapón, zurrapas*, unlucky from
the beginning.

taponamiento, *n.m.* tamponage.

taponar, *v.t.* to tampon.

taponazo, *n.m.* knock or blow with a cork or
stopper; pop of the cork.

tapsia, *n.f.* deadly carrot.

tapujarse, *v.r.* to muffle oneself.

tapujo, *n.m.* muffler; *(coll.)* subterfuge, excuse,
false pretext.

taque, *n.m.* noise made by locking a door; rap,
knock at a door.

taquera, *n.f.* stand or rack for billiard-cues.

taquichuela, *n.f. (Par.)* five-stones (children's
play).

taquigrafía, *n.f.* stenography, shorthand.

taquigrafiar, *v.t.* to write in shorthand.

taquigráficamente, *adv.* stenographically, in
shorthand.

taquigráfico, -ca, *a.* stenographic.

taquígrafo, *n.m.* stenographer, shorthand
writer.

taquilla, *n.f.* box, letter-box, slot, letter-file,
locker; box-office; ticket-office, booking-
office; set of pigeon-holes.

taquillero, -ra, *n.m.f.* seller of tickets, person
in charge of a booking office.

taquimetría, *n.f.* tachymetry, tacheometry.

taquímetro, *n.m.* tachymeter, tacheometer.

taquín, *n.m.* knuckle-bone of a sheep.

tara, *n.f. (com.)* tare; tally; *(Ven.)* green grasshopper; *(Col.)* a poisonous snake; *(Chi., Per.)*
a shrub used in dyeing; *menos la tara*, making
allowance for.

tarabilla, *n.f.* clack, clapper; catch, latch, bolt;
fastener or holder; pin or peg holding the
cord of a frame-saw; *(Arg.)* rattle; *(coll.)*
chatterbox.

tarabita, *n.f. (Am.)* main cable of a rope bridge.

taracea, *n.f.* marquetry, chequered work, inlaid work.

taracear, *v.t.* to inlay, make inlaid work.

taragallo, *n.m.* rod attached to a dog's collar.

taraje, *n.m.* tamarisk.

taramba, *n.f.* (*Hond.*) a one-stringed musical instrument.

tarambana, *n.m.f.* (*coll.*) madcap.

tarando, *n.m.* reindeer.

tarángana, *n.f.* kind of salame, like black pudding.

taranta, *n.f.* (*Hond.*) giddiness, dizziness; (*Arg., CR., Ec.*) sudden impulse.

tarantela, *n.f.* (*mus.*) tarantella.

tarantín, *n.m.* (*Cent. Am., Cub.*) useless stuff, rubbish, lumber; (*Ven.*) insignificant shop.

tarántula, *n.f.* tarantula.

tararear, *v.t., v.i.* to hum a tune.

tararira, *n.f.* noisy laughter; (*Arg.*) a fresh-water fish. — *n.m.f.* noisy, laughing person.

tarasa, *n.f.* (*Chi., Per.*) a plant of the Malva-ceous family.

tarasca, *n.f.* serpent's figure borne in the Corpus Christi procession; ugly, lewd wo-man; (*CR., Chi.*) big mouth.

tarascada, *n.f.* bite, wound with the teeth; (*coll.*) pert, rude answer.

tarascar, *v.t.* (conjugated like BUSCAR) to bite (of dogs).

tarascón, -ona, *n.m.f.* (*Arg., Bol., Chi., Ec.*) wound with the teeth, bite; (*coll.*) pert, rude answer.

taray, *n.m.* tamarisk.

tarayal, *n.m.* tamarisk plantation.

tarazana, tarazanal, *n.m.f.* (*naut.*) arsenal, building-yard.

tarazar, *v.t.* (*pret.* **taracé;** *pres. subj.* **tarace**) to bite; to harass, mortify, afflict, molest.

tarazón, *n.m.* large slice.

tarbea, *n.f.* large hall.

tarco, *n.m.* (*Arg.*) a tree of the saxifrage genus.

tardador, -ra, *n.m.f.* delayer, deferrer, tarrier.

tardanaos, *n.m.* (*ichth.*) remora.

tardanza, *n.f.* slowness, delay, lingering, dalliance, detention, tardiness; *en la tar-danza suele estar el peligro,* delays are dan-gerous.

tardar, *v.i., v.r.* to delay, put off; dally, tarry, linger, take a long time; *¿ cuánto tarda ?* how long does it take? *a más tardar,* at the longest, not later than.

tarde, *n.f.* afternoon, evening. — *adv.* late, too late; *buenas tardes,* good afternoon, good evening; *de tarde en tarde,* sometimes, now and then; *hacerse tarde,* to grow late; *tarde o temprano,* sooner or later; *más vale tarde que nunca,* better late than never; *para luego es tarde,* by-and-by is too late (i.e., do it now).

tardecer, *v.i. impers.* (*pres. ind.* **tardece;** *pres. subj.* **tardezca**), to grow late, to become evening.

tardecica, -ita, *n.f.* sundown, toward evening.

tardecillo, -ito, *adv.* (*Am.*) a little late.

tardíamente, *adv.* too late.

tardígrado, -da, *a.* (*zool.*) slow-moving, slow-paced; *n.m.pl.* **tardígrados,** sloths.

tardío, -día, *a.* late, tardy, too late; dilatory, slow.

tardo, -da, *a.* tardy, slow, dull; inactive, lazy, sluggish; laggard, backward.

tardón, -ona, *a.* very tardy, abnormally slow, phlegmatic; heavy, dull.

tarea, *n.f.* task, toil; drudgery; day's work; (*prov.*) measure of olives (about 24 bushels); *tarea de chocolate,* a day's work (of about 46 lb. of chocolate).

tareco, *n.m.* (*Cub., Ec., Ven.*) implement, tool of trade, outfit.

tareche, *n.m.* (*Bol.*) bird of prey, kind of buzzard.

tarida, *n.f.* military transport vessel used in mediæval times in the Mediterranean.

tarifa, *n.f.* tariff, price-list, fare, rate, book of rates, list of charges.

tarima, *n.f.* stand, dais, movable platform; footstool, low bench; bedstead.

tarimilla, *n.f.* small bedstead.

tarimón, *n.m.* large bedstead; large platform.

tarina, *n.f.* (*obs.*) dish for meat.

tarín barín, *adv.* (*coll.*) just about, more or less.

tarja, *n.f.* ancient Spanish coin; tally, check; tally-stick; shield, buckler; *beber sobre tarja,* (*coll.*) to get drink on credit; (*Am.*) visiting card.

tarjador, -ra, *n.m.f.* tally-keeper.

tarjar, *v.t.* to tally.

tarjero, *n.m.* tally-keeper.

tarjeta, *n.f.* small target, small shield; card; (*arch.*) label; tablet with inscription; *tarjeta postal,* postcard; *tarjeta de visita,* visiting card.

tarjeteo, *n.m.* (*coll.*) exchange of cards.

tarjetero, *n.m.* card-case.

tarjetón, *n.m.* large card, show-card.

tarlatana, *n.f.* tarlatan, transparent muslin.

tarma, *n.f.* wood-tick.

taropé, *n.m.* (*Arg., Par.*) a water-lily.

tarquín, *n.m.* mire, mud, slime.

tarquinada, *n.f.* (*coll.*) rape.

tárraga, *n.f.* an ancient Spanish dance.

tarraja, *n.f.* pipe-stock, screw-stock.

tarralí, *n.f.* (*Col.*) a wild climbing plant.

tarraya, *n.f.* (*Col., Ven., PR.*) casting-net.

tarreña, *n.f.* piece of broken china used as castanets.

tarrico, *n.m.* salt-wort.

tarro, *n.m.* jar; glazed earthen pan; milk-pan.

tarsana, *n.f.* (*CR., Ec., Per*) bark of a Sapin-daceæ tree used for washing.

tarso, *n.m.* (*anat.*) tarsus; gambrel, hock.

tarta, *n.f.* tart; cake; baking-pan.

tártago, *n.m.* (*bot.*) spurge; unfortunate inci-dent or event, misfortune; practical joke.

tartajear, *v.i.* to stutter, stammer.

tartajoso, -sa, *a.* stuttering, stammering.

tartalear, *v.i.* to stagger, reel; to be perplexed, dumbfounded.

tartamudear, *v.i.* to stammer, mumble, stut-ter; to fumble; to falter, halt.

tartamudeo, *n.m.;* **tartamudez,** *n.f.* stutter-ing, stammering.

tartamudo, -da, *n.m.f.* stutterer. — *a.* stutter-ing, stammering.

tartán, *n.m.* tartan.

tartana, *n.f.* round-topped two-wheeled car-riage; (*naut.*) tartan.

tartáreo, -rea, *a.* (*poet.*) Tartarean, hellish.

tartarizar, *v.t.* (conjugated like ALZAR) to tartarize.

tártaro, *n.m.* (*poet.*) Tartarus, hell; (*dent.*) tartar; (*chem.*) cream of tartar, argol.

tártaro, -ra, *a.* Tartarian, of Tartary.

tartera, *n.f.* baking-pan, dripping-pan, cake-tin.

tartrato, *n.m.* tartrate.

tártrico, -ca, *a.* tartaric.

taruga, *n.f.* (*Am.*) a kind of vicuña.

tarugo, *n.m.* wooden peg, stopper, plug, bung.

tarumá, *n.m.* (*Arg.*) a tree of the Verbenaceæ family.

tarumba, *n.f. volver a uno tarumba*, to get one confused, rattled.

tas, *n.m.* small anvil used by silversmiths, tinsmiths and plumbers.

tasa, *n.f.* rate, price; assize; appraisement, valuation; rule, measure, standard.

tasación, *n.f.* appraisement, valuation.

tasadamente, *adv.* barely, scantily, scarcely.

tasador, *n.m.* appraiser, valuer.

tasajear, *v.t.* (*Am.*) to jerk; to slash, cut to pieces.

tasajo, *n.m.* jerked beef, hung beef.

tasar, *v.t.* to value, appraise, price; to tax; to regulate, observe rule and order; to give scantily.

tasca, *n.f.* tavern; a low gaming-house; (*Per.*) (*naut.*) cross-currents.

tascador, *n.m.* brake for dressing flax.

tascar, *v.t.* (*pret.* **tasqué**; *pres. subj.* **tasque**) to brake or dress flax; to nibble (grass), crunch, graze, browse; *tascar el freno*, to bite the bridle, resist.

tasco, *n.m.* refuse of flax or hemp; (*naut.*) topping of hemp.

tasconio, *n.m.* a refractory clay.

tasi, *n.m.* (*Arg.*) a wild liana of the Asclepiadaceæ family.

tasquera, *n.f.* dispute, scuffle, wrangle, row.

tasquero, *n.m.* (*Per.*) Indian docker.

tasquil, *n.m.* chip of a stone.

tastana, *n.f.* hard crust on the soil left after a long drought; membrane inside a fruit, as in pomegranates, walnuts, etc.

tástara, *n.f.* coarse bran.

tastaz, *n.m.* polishing powder.

tasto, *n.m.* bad taste of stale food.

tasugo, *n.m.* badger.

tata, *n.m.* (*Am.*) (*coll.*) dad, daddy; nurse-maid; (*prov.*) younger sister.

tatabro, *n.m.* (*Col.*) a species of wild hog.

tatagua, *n.f.* (*Cub.*) a giant nocturnal butterfly.

tataibá, *n.m.* (*Arg., Par.*) mulberry tree.

tatarabuela, *n.f.* great-great-grandmother.

tatarabuelo, *n.m.* great-great-grandfather.

tataradeudo, -da, *n.m.f.* very old and distant relation.

tataranieta, *n.f.* great-great-granddaughter.

tataranieto, *n.m.* great-great-grandson.

tataré, *n.m.* (*Arg., Par.*) a big tree of the genus mimosa, used in cabinet making.

tatas, (**andar a**), *adv.* to begin to toddle; go on all fours.

¡tate! *interj.* beware!, take care!, stay!

tato, *n.m.* (*Chi.*) younger brother; child.

tato, -ta, *n.m.f.*, *a.* stammerer, stutterer.

tatú, *n.m.* (*Arg., Chi.*) variety of giant armadillo.

tatuaje, *n.m.* tattooing, tattooage, tattoo.

tatuar, *v.t.* to tattoo.

taujel, *n.m.* batten.

taumaturgia, *n.f.* thaumaturgy, miracle-working.

taumaturgo, *n.m.* thaumaturge, miracle-worker.

taurino, -na, *a.* taurine, bovine.

tauro, *n.m.* (*astr.*) Taurus, sign of the zodiac.

tauromaquia, *n.f.* art of bull-fighting.

tauromáquico, -ca, *a.* tauromachian.

tautología, *n.f.* tautology.

tautológico, -ca, *a.* tautological.

taxativamente, *adv.* limitedly.

taxativo, -va, *a.* (*law*) restrictive, limited to circumstances.

taxidermia, *n.f.* taxidermy.

taxímetro, *n.m.* taximeter; taxicab, taxi; (*naut.*) instrument resembling the azimuth circle.

taxonomía, *n.f.* taxonomy.

tayuyá, *n.m.* (*Arg.*) a creeping plant of the Cucurbitaceous family.

taz a taz, or **taz por taz**, *adv.* by swapping, in fair exchange.

taza, *n.f.* cup, cupful; basin of a fountain; large wooden bowl; cup guard of a sword.

tazar, *v.t.*, *v.r.* to fray.

tazmía, *n.f.* share of tithes, tithe register.

tazón, *n.m.* large basin, bowl.

te, *n.f.* name of the letter T. — *pron. objective case of* TÚ, thee, to thee.

té, *n.m.* tea; *té de borde* or *té de Méjico*, saltwort.

tea, *n.f.* brand, firebrand, torch; hawser for raising the anchor.

teame, **teamide**, *n.f.* stone said to repel iron.

teatina, *n.f.* (*Chi.*) a gramineous plant used to weave hats.

teatralmente, *adv.* theatrically.

teátrico, -ca; **teatral**, *a.* theatrical.

teatro, *n.m.* stage, theatre, playhouse; drama; theatrical profession; dramatic literature of a country; collection of plays; dramatic art.

teca, *n.f.* teak; teakwood; locket, reliquary.

tecali, *n.m.* (*Mex.*) transparent marble.

tecla, *n.f.* key of a pianoforte, typewriter, etc.; delicate point; *dar en la tecla*, to touch the right chord, hit the mark; *tocar una tecla*, to move cautiously, resort to an expedient.

teclado, *n.m.* key (of a piano, typewriter, etc.), keyboard, manual.

tecle, *n.m.* (*naut.*) single purchase.

teclear, *v.i.* to strike (the keys of a piano, etc.); to drum with the fingers. — *v.t.* to test, try, resort to an expedient.

tecleo, *n.m.* drumming on the keyboard; (*fig.*) scheming, trying.

técnica, *n.f.* technics, technique.

técnicamente, *adv.* technically.

tecnicismo, *n.m.* technics, technicality.

técnico, -ca, *a.* technical.

tecnología, *n.f.* technology.

tecnológico, -ca, *à.* technological.

tecol, *n.m.* (*Mex.*) caterpillar.

tecolote, *n.m.* (*Hond., Mex.*) owl.

tecomate, *n.m.* (*Mex.*) pot made of coarse clay.

techado, *n.m.* roof, roofing, ceiling; shed.

techar, *v.t.* to roof, cover with a roof.

techo, *n.m.* roof, ceiling; cover, shed; habitation, dwelling, shelter, abode; (*aer.*) ceiling.

techumbre, *n.f.* ceiling, upper roof, vaulted roof.

tedero, *n.m.* candlestick, torch-holder.

tediar, *v.t.* to hate, abhor, loathe.

tedio, *n.m.* abhorrence, disgust, loathing, tediousness, ennui.

tedioso, -sa, *a.* tedious, disgusting, loathsome, tiresome.

tefe, *n.m.* (*Col., Ec.*) strip of cloth or leather.

tegue, *n.m.* (*Ven.*) a plant with milky edible tubers.

teguillo, *n.m.* thin board, strip used for ceilings.

tegumento, *n.m.* tegument, covering.

teína, *n.f.* thein.

teinada, *n.f.* cattle shed.

teísmo, *n.m.* theism, deism.

teísta, *n.m.* theist, deist.

teja, *n.f.* roof-tile; linden-tree; steel facings of a sword blade; (*naut.*) hollow cut for scarfing; *a teja vana*, (*fig.*) superficially, carelessly; *de tejas abajo*, in a natural order; *teja de la silla*, (*Mex.*) hind bow of a saddle; *a toca teja*, in cash, cash down.

tejadillo, *n.m.* small roof-tile, coach-roof, shed; card sharper's trick.

tejado, *n.m.* roof, tiled roof; roofed covering, shed.

tejamaní, tejamanil, *n.m.* (*Mex., Cub., PR.*) shingle, wood roof-covering.

tejar, *n.m.* tile-works, tile-kiln. — *v.t.* to tile, cover with tiles.

tejaroz, *n.m.* penthouse, eaves, tiled shed.

tejazo, *n.m.* blow with a tile.

tejedera, *n.f.* weaver (woman); (*ent.*) water-skipper.

tejedor, *n.m.* weaver, cloth-maker; (*ent.*) water-skipper.

tejedora, *n.f.* female weaver.

tejedura, *n.f.* texture, weaving, fabric.

tejeduría, *n.f.* art of weaving; mill, factory.

tejemaneje, *n.m.* (*coll.*) skill, knack; (*Am.*) intrigue, plot, shady business.

tejer, *v.t.* to weave, interweave, wattle, plait; to knit; to make webs (of spiders, silkworms, etc.); to discuss, devise, plot, concoct; to adjust, regulate; (*Chi., Per.*) to intrigue, scheme.

tejera, tejería, *n.f.* tile-kiln.

tejero, *n.m.* tile-maker.

tejido, *n.m.* texture, weaving, tissue, fabric, web.

tejillo, *n.m.* girdle-band, plaited girdle.

tejo, *n.m.* quoit; metal disc or plate; gold bullion; (*bot.*) yew-tree; (*mech.*) bush, pillow-block, socket-plate.

tejocote, *n.m.* (*Mex.*) a sloe-like fruit.

tejoleta, *n.f.* tile, burnt clay; broken tile; brickbat; shuffle-board counter; clapper.

tejolote, *n.m.* (*Mex.*) stone pestle.

tejón, *n.m.* (*zool.*) badger; (*bot.*) yew; round gold ingot.

tejuela, *n.f.* small tile; brickbat; saddle-tree.

tejuelo, *n.m.* book-label; quoit; (*mech.*) bush, pillow-block, socket.

tela, *n.f.* fabric, stuff, cloth; argument, matter, business, thread of a discourse; film; pellicle, membrane; quibble, quirk; cobweb; *tela de araña*, cobweb; *tela encerada*, buckram; *tela de cebolla*, onion-skin; *tela de juicio*, judicial proceeding, mature consideration; *haber tela de que cortar*, to have (*or* be) enough and to spare; *hay tela cortada*, there are a good many difficulties in the matter; *llegarle a uno a las telas del corazón*, to wound (*or* offend) a person deeply; *poner en tela de juicio*, to doubt the success of; *querer más que a las telas de su corazón*, to love more than the apple of one's eye; *ver una cosa por tela de cedazo*, to see a thing confusedly.

telar, *n.m.* loom; frame; (*theat.*) gridiron.

telaraña, *n.f.* cobweb; something flimsy or trifling; *mirar las telarañas*, (*coll.*) to be in a brown study; *tener telarañas en los ojos*, to be blind to one's surroundings; *se cura con una telaraña*, that's easily cured.

telarejo, *n.m.* small loom.

telecomunicación, *n.f.* telecommunication.

telefio, *n.m.* stone-crop.

telefonear, *v.t.* to telephone.

telefonema, *n.m.* telephone message.

telefonía, *n.f.* telephony; *telefonía sin hilos*, wireless telephony.

telefónicamente, *adv.* telephonically.

telefónico, -ca, *a.* telephonic.

telefonista, *n.m.f.* telephonist.

teléfono, *n.m.* telephone.

telegrafía, *n.f.* telegraphy; *telegrafía sin hilos*, wireless telegraphy.

telegrafiar, *v.t.* to telegraph.

telegráficamente, *adv.* telegraphically.

telegráfico, -ca, *a.* telegraphic.

telegrafista, *n.m.f.* telegraph operator.

telégrafo, *n.m.* telegraph; *hacer telégrafos*, to talk by signs; *telégrafo sin hilos*, wireless; *telégrafo marino*, nautical signals; *telégrafo óptico*, semaphore.

telegrama, *n.m.* telegram.

telele, *n.m.* (*Cent. Am., Mex.*) swoon, fainting fit.

telemetría, *n.f.* telemetry.

telemétrico, -ca, *a.* telemetric.

telémetro, *n.m.* telemeter, rangefinder.

telendo, -da, *a.* lively, graceful, gallant.

teleobjetivo, *n.m.* telephotographic object glass.

telepate, *n.m.* (*Hond.*) a troublesome wingless insect.

telepatía, *n.f.* telepathy.

telepático, -ca, *a.* telepathic.

telera, *n.f.* plough pin; cattle pen, corral; (*mech.*) cheek, jaw (of a clamp, press, etc.); (*motor.*) body transom, cross frame; (*artill.*) transom of a gun carriage; (*naut.*) rack block; (*prov.*) heap of copper ore ready for roasting; (*Chi.*) round loaf of brown bread; (*Cub.*) a thin rectangular biscuit.

telescópico, -ca, *a.* telescopic.

telescopio, *n.m.* telescope.

teleta, *n.f.* blotting-paper; sieve in paper-mills.

teletón, *n.m.* strong silken stuff.

televisión, *n.f.* television.

telilla, *n.f.* light woollen stuff; rind of fruit; film on molten silver.

telina, *n.f.* clam, mussel.

telón, *n.m.* (*theat.*) curtain, drop-curtain, drop-scene.

telonio, *n.m.* custom-house, tax-office; *a manera de telonio*, disordered, jumbled up.

telúrico, -ca, *a.* telluric.

telurio, *n.m.* tellurium.

tellina, *n.f.* clam, mussel.

telliz, *n.m.* horse-cloth, saddle-cover.

telliza, *n.f.* bed-cover, bedspread, coverlet.

tema, *n.m.* theme, composition, subject, proposition, text; (*mus.*) theme, motive. — *n.f.* obstinacy; mania, obsession; grudge, animosity; dispute, contention; *tema celeste*, (*astr.*) map of the heavens; *a tema*, obstinately, emulously.

temático, -ca, *a.* thematic, relating to a theme or subject; obstinate.

tembladal, *n.m.* quagmire.

tembladera, *n.f.* tankard; (*ichth.*) cramp-fish, electric ray; (*bot.*) quaking-grass; gem or ornament mounted on a spiral; (*Arg.*) sickness attacking horses.

tembladerilla, *n.f.* (*Chi.*) a plant of the Papilionaceous family.

tembladero, *n.m.* quagmire.

temblador, -ra, *n.m.f.* shaker, trembler, quaker; Quaker. — *a.* quaking, shaking, shivering, trembling.

temblante, *a.* trembling, quavering. — *n.m.* loose bracelet.

temblar, *v.i.* (*pres. indic.* **tiemblo**; *pres. subj.* **tiemble**) to tremble, quake, shiver, thrill, shake with fear, be afraid.

tembleque, *n.m.* diamond ornament for the hair on a spiral.

temblequear, tembletear, *v.i.* to tremble, shake, quiver, quake, thrill.

temblón, -ona, *a.* tremulous, shaking; *hacer la temblona,* to affect timidity.

temblón, *n.m.* aspen-tree.

temblor, *n.m.* trembling; *temblor de tierra,* earthquake.

temblorcillo, *n.m.* slight tremor.

tembloroso, -sa, *a.* tremulous, shivering, shaking.

tembloso, -sa, *a.* tremulous, shivering, shaking.

temedero, -ra, *a.* dread, redoutable.

temedor, -ra, *a.* dreading, fearing. — *n.m.f.* trembler.

temer, *v.t.* to fear, dread, apprehend; to suspect, doubt, misdoubt. — *v.i.* to be afraid, fearful.

temerariamente, *adv.* rashly, temerariously, hastily, inconsiderately.

temerario, -ria, *a.* rash, daring, hasty, overbold; inconsiderate, temerarious, imprudent; baseless, groundless, unfounded.

temeridad, *n.f.* temerity, imprudence, rashness, foolhardiness.

temerón, -ona, *a.* bullying.

temerosamente, *adv.* timorously.

temeroso, -sa, *a.* timid, timorous; fearful, dreadful, awe-inspiring; chicken-hearted.

temible, *a.* dreadful, terrible, awful, frightful.

temor, *n.m.* dread, apprehension, fear, foreboding, suspicion.

temoso, -sa, *a.* stubborn, obstinate.

tempanador, *n.m.* cutter for beehives.

tempanar, *v.t.* to cover the tops of beehives.

témpano, *n.m.* flitch of bacon; kettle-drum, tabour, timbrel; tympan; drum-head, drum-skin; ice-drift, iceberg, ice-floe, ice-field; block, sod, sward; heading of a barrel; cork dome of a beehive; tympan of an arch.

tempate, *n.m.* (*CR., Hond.*) shrub of the Euphorbiaceæ family.

temperación, *n.f.* tempering.

temperadamente, *adv.* temperately.

temperamento, *n.m.* temperament, constitution, temper; climate; compromise, arbitration.

temperancia, *n.f.* temperance, moderation.

temperante, *a.* (*med.*) tempering.

temperar, *v.t.* (*med.*) to temper.

temperatura, *n.f.* temperature, climate, atmospheric conditions.

temperie, *n.f.* climate, temperature, atmospheric conditions.

tempero, *n.m.* seasonableness.

tempestad, *n.f.* tempest, storm. — *pl.* **tempestades,** violent language.

tempestear, *v.i.* to be a tempest; to storm at, abuse.

tempestivamente, *adv.* seasonably, fitly, opportunely.

tempestividad, *n.f.* tempestuousness, seasonableness, opportuneness, fitness.

tempestivo, -va, *a.* seasonable, opportune, timely.

tempestuosamente, *adv.* tempestuously, turbulently.

tempestuoso, -sa, *a.* tempestuous, stormy, turbulent.

tempisque, *n.m.* (*CR., Hond.*) tree of the Sapotaceæ family.

templa, *n.f.* tempera, distemper, size for painting; (*Cub.*) amount of juice of sugar cane contained in an evaporator pan. — *pl.* **templas,** temples (of the head).

templadamente, *adv.* temperately, moderately, abstemiously.

templadera, *n.f.* sluice gate.

templado, -da, *a.* temperate, abstemious, moderate, frugal; hardened, tempered; medium; lukewarm; firm, brave; (*mus.*) tuned; *zona templada,* temperate zone, between the tropics and the polar circle. — *p.p.* [TEMPLAR].

templador, -ra, *n.m.f.* tuner; temperer.

templador, *n.m.* tuning-key; (*Col.*) cashier in a sugar mill; (*Per.*) stockade in bull-rings.

templadura, *n.f.* temperature, tempering, tuning.

templanza, *n.f.* temperance, moderation; abstemiousness, abstinence, sobriety; mildness of climate, temperature or disposition; good disposition of colours.

templar, *v.t.* to temper, moderate, cool, soften, mollify, pacify, calm; to mix; to tune; to allay, quench; to assuage; (*naut.*) to trim the sails; to train (a hawk); to dispose, prepare; to anneal (glass); to blend colours in proportion. — *v.r.* to be moderate, to restrain oneself.

templario, *n.m.* Knight Templar.

temple, *n.m.* temperature; temper (of metals, glass or persons); frame of mind, disposition, temperament, medium; atmospheric conditions; tuning, concord; religion of the Templars; *al temple,* painted with distemper.

templén, *n.m.* temple of a loom.

templete, *n.m.* small temple, temple-shaped ornament; niche; tabernacle, shrine.

templista, *n.m.* painter in distemper.

templo, *n.m.* church, temple, sanctuary, shrine.

témpora, *n.f.* Ember Week, Ember Day.

temporada, *n.f.* space of time, short time, season; *estar de temporada,* to be spending the holiday; *temporada de frío,* cold spell.

temporal, *n.m.* tempest, storm; weather (good or bad); long rainy spell of weather; temporary labourer. — *a.* temporary, temporal, secular, worldly, provisional.

temporalidad, *n.f.* temporality.

temporalizar, *v.t.* (conjugated like ALZAR) to make temporary.

temporalmente, *adv.* temporally, provisionally, transiently; in a worldly manner.

temporáneo, -nea; temporario, -ria, *a.* temporary, unstable, transient, provisional.

temporejar, *v.i.* (*naut.*) to lie to.

temporero, -ra, *a.* seasonal labourer.

temporizador, *n.m.* temporizer.

temporizar, *v.i.* (*pret.* **temporicé**; *pres. subj.* **temporice**) to temporize, conform; while away time.

tempranal, *a.* producing early fruit.

tempranamente, *adv.* prematurely, early.

tempranero, -ra, *a.* early, premature.

tempranilla, *n.f.* early grape.

temprano, -na, *a.* early, premature, soon, previous, anticipated, precocious. — *n.m.* field yielding early crops.

temprano, *adv.* early, soon, prematurely.

temulento, -ta, *a.* intoxicated, inebriated, tipsy, drunk.

ten (*2nd person imp. sing.* of TENER); *ten con ten,* tact, adroitness, wisdom.

tena, *n.f.* shed for cattle, fold, corral.

tenacear, *v.t.* to tear with pincers. — *v.i.* to insist obstinately.

tenacero, *n.m.* maker of pincers or tongs.

tenacidad, *n.f.* tenacity, toughness; adhesiveness; pertinacity, contumacy.

tenacillas, *n.f.pl.* pincers, pliers, nippers, small tongs, curling irons, snuffers; tweezers; sugar tongs; cigarette tongs.

tenáculo, *n.m.* tenaculum.

tenada, *n.f.* fold, cattle shed.

tenallas, *n.f.pl.* pair of tongs or pincers.

tenallón, *n.m.* (*fort.*) tenaillon.

tenante, *n.m.* (*her.*) supporter of a shield.

tenaz, *a.* tenacious, obstinate, firm, stubborn, tough; hard-headed; sticky, adhesive.

tenaza, *n.f.* (*fort.*) tenail; claw. — *pl.* **tenazas,** tongs, pincers, nippers, pliers, forceps; two cards that take the two last tricks; *ser menester tenazas,* to be exceedingly difficult.

tenazada, *n.f.* gripping with tongs or pincers; gripping or biting strongly.

tenazmente, *adv.* tenaciously.

tenazón, *n.m.; a* or *de tenazón,* point-blank, blindly, wildly; unexpectedly.

tenazuelas, *n.f.pl.* tweezers, pliers.

tenca, *n.f.* tench; (*Arg., Chi.*) kind of lark.

tención, *n.f.* holdi: g, retaining.

tendajo, *n.m.* small, tumble-down shop.

tendal, *n.m.* tent, awning, tilt; (*Arg., Chi., Per.*) untidiness, disorder, confusion; (*Cub.*) drying-shed, -room or -floor; (*Ec.*) drying of the cacao nut.

tendalera, *n.f.* (*coll.*) disorder, untidiness, confusion.

tendalero, tendedero, *n.m.* place for drying wool.

tendedor, *n.m.* stretcher, tenter.

tendedura, *n.f.* tension, extending, stretching.

tendejón, *n.m.* sutler's tent; small shop.

tendel, *n.m.* plumb-line; layer of mortar.

tendencia, *n.f.* tendency, inclination, propensity; drift, bent, trend.

ténder, *n.m.* tender of a locomotive.

tender, *v.t.* to stretch, stretch out, unfold, extend, distend, expand; to cast (a net); to lay (pipe, rails, etc.); (*mas.*) to plaster (a wall). — *v.i.* to tend, direct. — *v.r.* to lie down, stretch oneself at full length; to throw all the cards on the table; to run (a horse) at full gallop; to neglect a business.

tenderete, *n.m.* a card game; (*Mex.*) second-hand clothing shop.

tendero, -ra, *n.m.f.* shopkeeper, haberdasher; tentmaker.

tendezuela, *n.f.* small shop.

tendidamente, *adv.* diffusely, diffusively.

tendido *n.m.* row of seats (in circus, bull-ring, etc.); clothes spread out to dry; lace made without lifting from over the pattern; (*gold*

min.) riffle; batch of bread; (*mas.*) coat of plaster; (*arch.*) roof of a house from ridge to eaves.

tendiente, *a.* tending, expanding.

tendinoso, -sa, *a.* tendinous.

tendón, *n.m.* (*anat.*) tendon.

tenducha, tenducho, *n.f.*, *m.* poor insignificant shop.

tenebrario, *n.m.* candlestick; (*astron.*) Hyades.

tenebrosamente, *adv.* tenebrously, gloomily.

tenebrosidad, *n.f.* darkness, obscurity, gloom.

tenebroso, -sa, *a.* dark, gloomy, tenebrous; horrid; obscure in style.

tenedero, *n.m.* anchoring-ground.

tenedor, *n.m.* holder, keeper; (*com.*) holder; guardian, tenant; fork; *tenedor de libros,* book-keeper; *tenedor de póliza,* policy-holder.

teneduría, *n.f.* position of book-keeper; *teneduría de libros,* book-keeping.

tenencia, *n.f.* holding, possession, tenancy, occupancy, tenure, tenement; lieutenancy, lieutenantship.

tener, *v.t.* (*pres. indic.* **tengo;** *pret.* **tuve;** *fut. indic.* **tendré;** *pres. subj.* **tenga**) to have, possess, own, enjoy; to contain, have within, comprehend; to be worth; to fulfil, keep one's word; to take, hold, grip, gripe, hold fast, keep, retain; to support, maintain, sustain; to domineer, subject; to contain; to stop, detain; to be adorned with, gifted with. — *v.i.* to have, possess; to be well off, rich, wealthy. — *v. aux.* to have (*tengo dicho,* I have said); *tener en,* to esteem, value; *tener hambre,* to be hungry; *tener en buenas,* to keep back one's good cards; *tener en menos,* to despise; *tener en contra,* to find difficulties; *tener miedo,* to be afraid; *tener por,* to judge, consider; *tener que,* to have to, be obliged to; *tener gana(s),* to have an inclination, to want; *tener razón,* to be right; *tener consigo,* to have with one; *no tenerlas todas consigo,* to be worried, afraid; *tener buena mano,* to be lucky; *tener sueño,* to be sleepy; *tener buenas tragaderas,* to be very credulous; *tener buenos pies,* to be a good worker; *tener calma,* to be even-tempered; *tener chispa,* to be a sharp fellow; *tener en buen estado,* to keep in good order; *tener lugar,* to take place; *tener la manga ancha,* to be easy-going, lax or broad-minded; *tener mala cabeza,* to be unprincipled; *tener malas pulgas,* to be bad-tempered; *tener malos cascos,* to be scatter-brained; *tener mu..10 pico,* to be a chatterbox; *tener mucha mosca,* to have tons of money; *tener mundo,* to be a man of the world; *tener un pie dentro,* to gain a footing; *tener vista,* to be showy; *dos linajes sólo hay en el mundo, el 'tener' y el 'no tener',* there are only two families in the world, the 'haves' and the 'have-nots.' — *v.r.* to halt, stop; to steady, hold fast; to set on; to adhere; to resist, oppose; *tenerse en pie,* to stand; *tenérselas tiesas* or *tenerse tieso,* to stand firm.

tenería, *n.f.* tannery, tan yard.

tengue, *n.m.* (*Cub.*) a tree of the leguminous family similar to acacia.

tenguerengue, (en) *adv.* (*coll.*) without stability, unstable.

tenia, *n.f.* tape-worm; (*arch.*) fillet.

tenienta, *n.f.* lieutenant's wife.

tenientazgo, *n.m.* lieutenantship, lieutenant's office, office of deputy.

teniente, *n.m.* lieutenant, deputy, substitute.

— *a.* having, owning, possessing; (*coll.*) deaf; miserly, mean; unripe, immature; *teniente de oídos,* hard of hearing.

tenis, *n.m.* tennis.

teníu, *n.m.* (*Chi.*) a tree of the Saxifraga family.

tenor, *n.m.* contents, tenor; literal meaning; drift, purport; current; kind, nature, state, condition; (*mus.*) tenor; tenorist; *a tenor de,* (*com.*) pursuant to, in compliance with; *a este tenor,* on this style, of the same kind.

tenorio, *n.m.* a Don Juan, a lady-killer, male flirt, a rake.

tensión, *n.f.* tension, stretching, extension, tautness, tightness; voltage, potential; being extended; strain, stretch, stress; *alta tensión,* (*elec.*) high tension; *baja tensión,* (*elec.*) low tension.

tenso, -sa, *a.* tense, tight, stiff, taut, stretched, extended.

tensón, *n.f.* (*poet.*) poetical contest on love.

tensor, -ra, *n.m.f., a.* tensile; turnbuckle.

tentación, *n.f.* temptation, enchantment, enticement, allurement.

tentaculado, -da, *a.* tentacled.

tentáculo, *n.m.* tentacle.

tentadero, *n.m.* corral in which young bulls suitable for fighting are tried out and selected.

tentador, *n.m.* the devil.

tentador, -ra, *n.m.f.* tempter, enticer.

tentadura, *n.f.* alloy of silver ore and mercury.

tentalear, *v.t.* to feel, to examine by touch.

tentar, *v.t.* (*pres. indic.* **tiento**; *pres. subj.* **tiente**) to try, attempt, experiment, endeavour; to touch, examine; to tempt, incite, instigate, stimulate; to coax, entice, allure; to grope; to hesitate; (*surg.*) to probe.

tentativa, *n.f.* attempt, trial, essay, test, experiment.

tentativo, -va, *a.* tentative.

tentemozo, *n.m.* prop, support; strap of the noseband; doll weighted in the base.

tentempié, *n.m.* (*coll.*) snack, light luncheon; a child's doll weighted in the base.

tentenelaire, *n.m.f.* a mestizo quadroon.

tentón, *n.m.* (*coll.*) touch; rough handling.

tenue, *a.* thin, tenuous, subtle, delicate, slender; slight, unimportant, worthless, trifling; soft (of a consonant); (*art*) subdued, faint.

tenuemente, *adv.* slightly.

tenuidad, *n.f.* tenuity, thinness, slenderness, weakness; trifle.

tenuta, *n.f.* provisional possession.

tenutario, -ria, *n.m.f., a.* provisional tenant.

teñidura, *n.f.* dyeing, tingeing.

teñir, *v.t.* (*pres. part.* **tiñendo**; *p.p.* **teñido**, **tinto**; *pres. indic.* **tiño**; *pret.* **él tiñó**; *pres. subj.* **tiña**) to dye, tinge, stain; *teñir en rama,* to dye in grain, ingrain.

teobroma, *n.m.* cacao.

teocalí, *n.m.* teocalli, Mexican temple.

teocracia, *n.f.* theocracy.

teocrático, -ca, *a.* theocratic, theocratical.

teodicea, *n.f.* theodicy.

teodolito, *n.m.* theodolite.

teogonía, *n.f.* theogony.

teologal, *a.* theological.

teología, *n.f.* theology, divinity; *no meterse en teologías,* not to meddle with intricate matters.

teológicamente, *adv.* theologically.

teológico, -ca, *a.* theological.

teologizar, *v.i.* (conjugated like ALZAR) to theologize.

teólogo, *n.m.* theologian, divine.

teólogo, -ga, *a.* theological.

teorema, *n.m.* theorem.

teoría, teórica, *n.f.* theory, speculation.

teóricamente, *adv.* theoretically.

teórico, -ca, *a.* theoretical, speculative.

teorizar, *v.i., v.t.* to theorize.

teoso, -sa, *a.* resinous (of wood).

teosofía, *n.f.* theosophy.

teosófico, -ca, *a.* theosophical.

teósofo, -a, *n.m.f.* theosophist.

tepache, *n.m.* (*Mex.*) drink made of pulque, water, pineapple and cloves.

tepalcate, *n.m.* (*Mex.*) potsherd.

tepe, *n.m.* sod, turf.

tepeguage, *n.m.* (*Mex.*) a very hard wood; *a.* (*Mex.*) obstinate, stubborn.

tepeizcuinte, *n.m.* (*CR., Mex.*) paca, a large Central and South American seminocturnal rodent.

tepemechín, *n.m.* (*CR., Hond.*) a fresh-water fish.

tepexilote, *n.m.* (*Mex.*) a palm nut used for beads.

tepozán, *n.m.* (*Mex.*) a plant of the Scrophulariaceous family.

tepú, *n.m.* (*Chi.*) a small tree of the Myrtaceous family.

tequiche, *n.m.* (*Ven.*) meal made of toasted maize, coconut milk and butter.

tequila, *n.f.* (*Mex.*) a drink like gin.

tequio, *n.m.* (*Mex.*) (*obs.*) task, personal service imposed on Indians; bother, damage; ore dug per man-shift.

terapéutica, *n.f.* therapeutics.

terapéutico, -ca, *a.* therapeutic.

tercamente, *adv.* obstinately, stubbornly.

tercena, *n.f.* wholesale tobacco warehouse.

tercenista, *n.m.* wholesale tobacco merchant.

tercer, *a.* (contraction of TERCERO) third.

tercera, *n.f.* piquet (card game) three-of-a-kind; triplets; (*mus.*) third; third string of a guitar; bawd, procuress.

terceramente, *adv.* thirdly.

tercería, *n.f.* arbitration, mediation; arbitration dues; depositary; (*law*) third party.

tercerilla, *n.f.* (*poet.*) triplet.

tercero, -ra, *a.* (before masculine singular adjectives) **tercer,** third.

tercero, *n.m.* third person; procurer, bawd, pimp; umpire, arbitrator, mediator; tithe-collector; middleman; (*eccles.*) tertiary; (*geom.*) sixtieth of a second; *tercero en discordia,* arbitrator.

tercerol, *n.m.* (*naut.*) third in order.

tercerola, *n.f.* short carbine; barrel, cask; tierce.

tercerón, -ona, *n.m.f.* (*Am.*) mulatto.

terceto, *n.m.* tercet, terzet, tierce, triplet, trio.

tercia, *n.f.* third, third part; sequence of three cards; (*eccles.*) tierce; storehouse, barn; (*fenc.*) tierce.

terciado, *n.m.* cutlass, broad sword; ribbon.

terciado, -da, *a.* slanting, tilted, biased, cross-wise; *azúcar terciado,* brown sugar; *pan terciado,* rent of ground paid in grain.

terciana, *n.f.* tertian ague.

tercianario, -ria, *n.m.f.* person with a tertian fever. — *a.* tertian; causing or suffering tertian fever.

tercianela, *n.f.* heavy silk fabric.

terciano, -na, *a.* tertian.

terciar, *v.t.* to place sidewise or diagonally; to divide into three parts; to plough the third time; to carry arms. — *v.i.* to arbitrate, mediate; to join, share, take part; (*Mex., Col.*) to carry goods on one's back. — *v.r.* to be favourable, offer an opportunity.

terciario, *n.m.* rib of a gothic arch.

terciario, -ria, *a.* third; (*geol.*) tertiary.

terciazón, *n.m.* third ploughing.

tercio, *n.m.* third part; (*hist.*) regiment of infantry; part of a mule-load; division of the *Guardia Civil*; third part of the rosary; one of the three stages in fighting a bull; (*Cub.*) bale (of tobacco); *hacer buen* (*mal*) *tercio,* to do a good (*or* bad) turn; *tercio y quinto,* great advantage. — *pl.* **tercios,** strong limbs of a man.

terciopelado, *n.m.* velvet-like stuff.

terciopelado, -da, *a.* velvet-like, velvety.

terciopelero, *n.m.* velvet-weaver.

terciopelo, *n.m.* velvet.

terco, -ca, *a.* obstinate, stubborn, pertinacious; hard, firm.

terebinto, *n.m.* turpentine-tree, terebinth.

terebrante, *a.* piercing (pain).

tereque, *n.m.* (*PR., Ven.*) traps, belongings.

terete, *a.* plump, robust, round.

tergiversación, *n.f.* tergiversation.

tergiversar, *v.t.* to tergiversate, misrepresent, shuffle, shift.

teriaca, *n.f.* theriaca.

teriacal, *a.* theriacal.

teristro, *n.m.* thin shawl or veil.

terliz, *n.m.* tick, ticking; sackcloth, tentcloth.

termal, *a.* thermal.

termas, *n.f.pl.* hot baths; hot springs.

termes, *n.m.* termite.

térmico, -ca, *a.* thermic, thermal.

terminable, *a.* terminable.

terminación, *n.f.* termination, ending, end; conclusion, completion.

terminacho, *n.m.* (*coll.*) rude word; misused word, malapropism, bloomer.

terminador, -ra, *n.m.f.* finisher. — *a.* finishing, completing.

terminajo, *n.m.* (*coll.*) [TERMINACHO].

terminal, *a.* final, ultimate. — *n.m.* (*bot., elec.*) terminal.

terminante, *a.* terminating, ending, closing; decisive, conclusive, clear, definite, precise.

terminantemente, *adv.* peremptorily, positively.

terminar, *v.t., v.i.* to end, finish, terminate, close, complete, consummate. — *v.i., v.r.* to abut, end at; (*med.*) to reach a crisis.

terminativo, -va, *a.* (*phil.*) terminative, respective.

término, *n.m.* end, ending, finish, conclusion, term; landmark, limit, boundary; aim, object, goal; district; diction, conception, expression; (*med.*) crisis of a disease; manner, conduct, behaviour; stipulation, condition; (*arch.*) terminal, stay; word, expression, technical term; (*mus.*) tone, pitch, note; *en buenos términos,* in plain language; *primer término,* (*art*) foreground; *último término,* (*art*) background; *término medio,* (*math.*) average, (*log.*) middle term. — *pl.* **términos,** (*log., astrol.*)

terms; *medios términos,* subterfuge, evasion; *en propios términos,* properly speaking.

terminología, *n.f.* terminology.

terminológico, -ca, *a.* terminological.

terminote, *n.m.* pompous, *recherché* word.

termodinámica, *n.f.* thermodynamics.

termométrico, -ca, *a.* thermometric.

termómetro, *n.m.* thermometer.

termoscopio, *n.m.* thermoscope.

termóstato, *n.m.* thermostat.

termostático, -ca, *a.* thermostatic.

terna, *n.f.* three names submitted for the election of a candidate; ternary number, triad; set of dice.

ternario, *n.m.* three days' devotion.

ternario, -ria, *a.* ternary, ternal, ternate.

terne, *n.m.* bully, hector.

ternecico, -cica; cito-, -cita, *a.* very tender.

ternejal, *a.* bullying.

ternejón, -ona, *a.* easily moved, compassionate.

ternero, -ra, *n.m.f.* calf, veal.

ternerón, -ona, *a.* easily moved, easily weeping, compassionate.

terneruela, *n.f.* sucking calf.

terneza, *n.f.* softness, suavity, delicacy, affection, endearment, fondness, tenderness.

ternilla, *n.f.* gristle, cartilage.

ternilloso, -sa, *a.* gristly, cartilaginous.

terno, *n.m.* ternary number; triad; suit of clothes; vestments for high Mass; curse, oath; tern (in lottery); (*Cub., PR.*) set of jewellery (ear-rings, necklace, and brooch); (*print.*) three printed sheets one within another; *echar ternos,* to swear greatly; *terno seco,* (lottery) unexpected good luck.

ternura, *n.f.* tenderness, delicacy, softness, sensitiveness.

terquedad, terquería, terqueza, *n.f.* stubbornness, obstinacy, inflexibility, contumacy, pertinacity.

terrada, *n.f.* bitumen.

terradillo, *n.m.* small terrace.

terrado, *n.m.* terrace, platform, flat roof of a house.

terraja, *n.f.* screw-plate, die-stock; modelling board.

terraje, *n.m.* rent paid for land.

terrajero, *n.m.* lessee of arable land.

terral, *n.m., a.* land breeze.

Terranova, *n.f.* Newfoundland.

terraplén, terrapleno, *n.m.* (*fort.*) terrace, mound; (*rail.*) embankment, terreplein.

terraplenar, *v.t.* to make a terrace, raise a rampart, embank; fill with earth.

terráqueo, -quea, *a.* terraqueous.

terrateniente, *n.m.* master of property, landowner, land-holder.

terraza, *n.f.* terrace; garden border; two-handled glazed jar.

terrazgo, *n.m.* arable land; land-rent.

terrazguero, *n.m.* lessee of arable land.

terrazo, *n.m.* landscape.

terrear, *v.i.* to be visible (said of the soil showing through crops).

terrecer, *v.t., v.r.* (conjugated like MERECER) to terrify.

terregoso, -sa, *a.* cloddy, full of clods.

terremoto, *n.m.* earthquake.

terrenal, *a.* terrestrial, terrene, mundane, earthly.

terrenidad, *n.f.* quality of the soil.

terreno, -na, *a.* terrene, terrestrial, earthly, worldly, mundane, perishable.

terreno, *n.m.* land, ground, soil, field; quality of the soil; *ganar terreno,* to gain ground; *perder terreno,* to lose ground; *terreno abierto,* (*mil.*) open ground; *medir el terreno,* to examine a matter before engaging in it; *terreno franco,* (*min.*) tract without registered claims.

térreo, -rrea, *a.* earthy.

terrera, *n.f.* declivity, steep ground; (*orn.*) kind of lark.

terrero, *n.m.* terrace, platform, mound, bank of earth, heap of earth; alluvium; (*min.*) dump; mark, target; frail for carrying earth.

terrero, -ra, *a.* earthly; abject, humble; skimming the ground (as birds); (*PR.*) applied to a single-storied house.

terrestre, *a.* terrestrial.

terrezuela, *n.f.* small piece of ground; light, poor soil.

terribilidad, *n.f.* terribleness, awfulness; ferocity, roughness, asperity.

terrible, *a.* terrible, horrible, awful, ferocious, dreadful; unmannerly, rude; (*coll.*) huge, immense.

terriblemente, *adv.* terribly, frightfully.

terrícola, *n.m.f.* inhabitant of the earth.

terrífico, -ca, *a.* terrific, frightful.

terrígeno, -na, *a.* earthborn.

terrino, -na, *a.* terrene, earthy.

territorial, *a.* territorial.

territorialidad, *n.f.* territoriality.

territorio, *n.m.* territory, district, region; land, ground.

terrizo, -za, *a.* earthy, earthen.

terrizo, *n.m.f.* unglazed earthen tub.

terromontero, *n.m.* hill, hillock.

terrón, *n.m.* clod, lump, heap, mound; bagasse of olives; lump of sugar. — *pl.* **terrones,** landed property; *a rapa terrón,* completely, entirely, down to the ground, from the root.

terronazo, *n.m.* blow with a clod.

terroncillo, *n.m.* small lump, small clod.

terror, *n.m.* terror, dread, consternation, fright; the bloodiest period of the French Revolution (April 1793–July 1794).

terrorífico, -ca, *a.* terrorific, terrific, dreadful, bloodcurdling, awful.

terrorismo, *n.m.* terrorism.

terrorista, *n.m.* terrorist.

terrosidad, *n.f.* earthiness, cloddiness.

terroso, -sa, *a.* earthy, cloddy.

terruño, terruzo, *n.m.* piece of ground; territory, native country.

tersar, *v.t.* to smooth, burnish, polish.

tersidad, *n.f.* terseness, polish.

terso, -sa, *a.* smooth, glossy, polished; pure, correct, terse, pithy.

tersura, *n.f.* smoothness, polish; cleanness, purity; terseness.

tertel, *n.m.* (*Chi.*) hard layer of earth under the subsoil.

tertil, *n.m.* ancient silk tax.

tertulia, *n.f.* club, assembly, circle, party, coterie; (*theat.*) gallery, corridor in early Spanish theatres; billiard or card room.

tertuliano, -na, *n.m.f.,* *a.* club member, one of a circle of friends; habitué.

tertulio, -lia, *a.* relating to a meeting of friends.

teruelo, *n.m.* balloting box or urn.

teruteru, *n.m.* (*Am.*) teru-tero, the Cayenne lapwing.

terzón, -ona, *n.m.f.,* *a.* (*prov.*) three years old (heifer).

terzuelo, *n.m.* third part; male falcon.

tesar, *v.t.* (*p.p.* **teso**) (*naut.*) to haul taut, tauten. — *v.i.* to back (of oxen, etc.); *tesar un cabo,* (*naut.*) to haul a rope taut.

tesauro, *n.m.* thesaurus, dictionary, lexicon.

tesela, *n.f.* tessela, mosaic piece.

teselado, -da, *a.* tessellated.

tésera, *n.f.* tessera, countersign, token.

tesis, *n.f.* thesis, dissertation.

teso, *n.m.* bulge, lump, hardiness; brow of a hill.

teso, -sa, *a.* taut, drawn tight. — *p.p. irreg.* [TESAR].

tesón, *n.m.* tenacity, inflexibility, firmness.

tesonería, *n.f.* stubbornness, obstinacy.

tesorera, *n.f.* treasurer's wife; treasuress.

tesorería, *n.f.* treasury, exchequer, treasurer's office, treasurership.

tesorero, *n.m.* treasurer.

tesoro, *n.m.* treasure, wealth, riches; treasury, exchequer; thesaurus, lexicon.

tespíades, *n.f.pl.* (*poet.*) the Muses.

testa, *n.f.* head; forehead, face; front, forepart; (*coll.*) sense, understanding, ability; cleverness; *testa coronada,* monarch, crowned head.

testáceo, -cea, *a.* testaceous.

testación, *n.f.* obliteration, erasure.

testada, *n.f.* stubbornness, obstinacy.

testado, -da, *a.* testate.

testador, *n.m.* testator.

testadora, *n.f.* testatrix.

testadura, *n.f.* obliteration, erasure.

testaférrea, testaferro, *n.m.* man of straw, dummy, figurehead.

testamentaria, *n.f.* testamentary execution; executrix; estate.

testamentario, *n.m.* executor.

testamentario, -ria, *a.* testamentary.

testamento, *n.m.* last will, testament.

testar, *v.t.,* *v.i.* to bequeath, make a last will. — *v.t.* (*obs.*) to scratch out, blot.

testarada, *n.f.* blow with the head; (*fig.*) obstinacy, stubbornness.

testarrón, -ona, *a.* (*coll.*) hard-headed.

testarronería, testarudez, *n.f.* (*coll.*) hard-headedness, stubbornness.

testarudo, -da, *a.* obstinate, inflexible, stubborn, hard-headed.

teste, *n.m.* testis, testicle; (*Arg.*) a coriaceous pimple on the fingers.

testera, *n.f.* front part, fore part; seat facing forward (of a coach); forehead of an animal; head-piece (of a bridle); wall of a furnace.

testerillo, -lla, *a.* (*Arg.*) blaze (of a horse).

testero, *n.m.* ore rock showing vertical and horizontal faces.

testicular, *a.* testicular.

testículo, *n.m.* testicle.

testificación, *n.f.* testification, attestation.

testificante, *a.* attesting, witnessing.

testificar, *v.t.* (*pret.* **testifiqué;** *pres. subj.* **testifique**) to attest, witness, certify, testify.

testificata, *n.f.* affidavit.

testificativo, -va, *a.* that which testifies.

testigo, *n.m.* witness, testifier, voucher; testimony, proof, evidence; *testigo de cargo,* witness for the prosecution; *testigo de descargo,* witness for the defence; *testigo de vista,* eyewitness.

testimonial, *a.* convincing, confirmatory, authentic.

testimoniales, *n.f.pl.* testimonials; certificate of good character.

testimoniar, *v.t.* to testify, attest, bear witness, vouch for, aver.

testimoniero, -ra, *a.* dissembling, hypocritical, bearing false witness.

testimonio, *n.m.* testimony, deposition, profession, attestation, affidavit; *falso testimonio,* false witness.

testón, *n.m.* silver coin bearing a head.

testuz, testuzo, *n.m.* back of the head, poll; nape; in some animals (bulls, goats, etc.) crown of the head.

tesura, *n.f.* stiffness, tautness.

teta, *n.f.* teat, dug, udder, nipple, mammary gland; hummock, hillock; *teta de vaca,* cow's udder; cone-shaped meringue; viper's-grass; *dar la teta,* to nurse, suckle; *mamar una teta,* (*fig.*) to be tied to mother's apronstrings.

tetania, *n.f.* (*med.*) tetanus.

tetánico, -ca, *a.* (*med.*) tetanic.

tétano, tétanos, *n.m.* tetanus, lockjaw.

tetar, *v.t.* to suckle, give suck to.

tetera, *n.f.* tea-pot, tea-kettle; (*Cub., Mex., PR.*) nipple, teat.

tetero, *n.m.* (*Am.*) nursing bottle.

tetica, tetilla, *n.f.* small dug, small teat (of male mammals).

tetigonia, *n.f.* a variety of cicada.

tetón, *n.m.* stub of a pruned branch.

tetona, *a.f.* with large teats.

tetracordio, *n.m.* tetrachord.

tetraedro, *n.m.* tetrahedron.

tetrágono, *n.m.* tetragon.

tetragrama, *n.m.* four-lined stave.

tetralogía, *n.f.* tetralogy.

tetrao, *n.m.* capercailzie.

tetrarca, *n.m.* tetrarch.

tetrarquía, *n.f.* tetrarchate, tetrarchy.

tétricamente, *adv.* gloomily.

tétrico, -ca, *a.* sullen, grave, gloomy, dark.

tetro, -tra, *a.* (*obs.*) black, stained.

tetuda, *a.f.* with large breasts or nipples.

teucali, *n.m.* (*Mex.*) teocalli.

teucrio, *n.m.* germander.

teucro, -cra, *n.m.f., a.* Trojan.

teurgia, *n.f.* black magic.

teutón, *n.m.* Teuton.

teutónico, -ca, *n.m.f., a.* Teutonic, German.

textil, *a.* textile; fibrous.

texto, *n.m.* text, quotation; textbook; (*print.*) great primer type.

textorio, -ria, *a.* textorial.

textual, *a.* textual, textuary.

textualmente, *adv.* textually, according to the text.

textura, *n.f.* texture; weaving; structure, succession, order; tissue.

teyú, *n.m.* (*Arg., Par., Urug.*) iguana.

tez, *n.f.* complexion, skin.

tezado, -da, *a.* very black.

tezontle, *n.m.* (*Mex.*) a kind of porous stone.

ti, *pron.* 2nd *pers. sing.* (genitive, dative, accusative and ablative case of TÚ) thee; *hoy por ti y mañana por mí,* it's your turn today and mine will come tomorrow.

tía, *n.f.* aunt; (*coll.*) good woman; old woman; common, low woman; crone; *cuéntaselo a tu tía,* (*coll.*) tell it to the marines; *no hay tu tía,* it's no use.

tiaca, *n.f.* (*Chi.*) tree of the Saxifragaceous family.

tialina, *n.f.* (*chem.*) pytalin.

tialismo, *n.m.* (*med.*) ptyalism.

tianguis, *n.m.* (*Mex., Philip.*) market; market days.

tiara, *n.f.* tiara; pontificate, dignity of the Pope; royal diadem; Persian head-dress.

tibar, *a.* of very pure gold.

tibe, *n.m.* (*Col.*) corundum; (*Cub.*) whetstone.

tiberio, *n.m.* (*coll.*) turmoil, hubbub, noise.

tibia, *n.f.* shin-bone; flute.

tibiamente, *adv.* tepidly, lukewarmly, carelessly.

tibieza, *n.f.* tepidity, lukewarmness, coolness, frigidity, coldness; carelessness, negligence.

tibio, -bia, *a.* tepid, cold, lukewarm; (*fig.*) lukewarm, unenthusiastic.

tibor, *n.m.* large china jar; (*Cub.*) chamberpot.

tiburón, *n.m.* shark.

tic, *n.m.* jerk, tic, spasmodic movement.

tica, *n.f.* (*Hond.*) children's game with seeds.

tictac, *n.m.* tick-tack.

tichela, *n.f.* (*Bol.*) vessel for collecting rubber.

ticholo, *n.m.* (*Arg.*) snack of guava paste.

tiemblo; tiemble, *pres. indic.; pres. subj.* [TEMBLER].

tiempo, *n.m.* time, term, season, tide; age; occasion, opportunity, leisure; portion; climate, temperature, weather, state, condition; (*gram.*) tense; (*mus.*) tempo, time, measure; *tiempo cargado,* (*naut.*) hazy weather; *tiempo grueso,* heavy weather; *tiempo hecho,* settled weather; *a su tiempo,* (all) in its time; *a tiempo,* timely, in time; *a un tiempo,* at one and the same time; *a tiempo que,* just as; *con tiempo,* in good time, beforehand; *ajustar los tiempos,* to arrange events in their chronological order; *de tiempo en tiempo,* from time to time; *en tiempo,* occasionally; *la carta llegó a su tiempo,* the letter duly arrived; *abre el tiempo,* or, *se alza el tiempo,* the weather is clearing up; *cargarse el tiempo,* to cloud over, become overcast; *dar tiempo al tiempo,* to await an occasion for doing something, make allowances (for a person's behaviour), be considerate; *haga buen o mal tiempo,* rain or shine; *engañar el tiempo,* to kill time; *tomarse tiempo,* to take one's time; *del tiempo de Maricastaña,* a 'chestnut,' an old story; *tiempo ni hora no se ata con soga,* time and tide wait for no man; *en tiempo hábil,* within the appointed time; *tiempo tras tiempo viene,* there are better times coming; *acomodarse al tiempo,* to accommodate oneself to circumstances; *andar con el tiempo,* to swim with the tide; *cual el tiempo, tal el tiento,* accommodate yourself to circumstances; *no son todos los tiempos unos,* all times are not alike; *del tiempo del rey que rabió,* as old as Queen Anne; *dejar al tiempo una cosa,* to let time do its work; *el tiempo cura al enfermo, que no el ungüento,* time is the best healer; *en tiempo de higos no hay amigos,* in prosperity friends are forgotten; *quien en tiempo huye, en tiempo acude,* he who fights and runs away, lives to fight another day; *quien quisiere ser mucho tiempo viejo, comiéncelo presto,* sober habits bring a long life; *tiempo ha,* a long time ago; *tiempo medio,* mean time; *tiempo solar, verdadero* or *de Dios,* solar time; *tiempos heroicos,* heroic age.

tienda, *n.f.* tent; shop, stall; (*naut.*) awning; tilt; *la tienda de los cojos*, the next shop; *abrir* (or *poner*) *tienda*, to open a shop; *alzar tienda*, to shut up shop; *a quien está en su tienda, no le achacan que se halló en la contienda*, crimes are generally imputed to vagabonds rather than to men doing their regular work; *quien tiene tienda, atienda*, be wary about your own interests.

tiendo; tienda, *pres. indic.; pres. subj.* [TENDER].

tienta, *n.f.* (*surg.*) probe; craft, cunning, artfulness; (*bullfight.*) testing the courage of young bulls; *a tientas*, at random, uncertainly, doubtfully; *andar a tientas*, to grope in the dark, to fumble.

tientaguja, *n.f.* boring-rod.

tientaparedes, *n.m.f.* groper (morally or materially).

tiento, *n.m.* touch; halter of a mill horse; (*coll.*) blow, cuff; blind man's stick; tight-rope walker's pole; (*zool.*) tentacle; maulstick; stroke; steadiness of hand; circumspection, prudence; (*mus.*) preliminary flourish, tuning up; *dar un tiento*, to make a trial; *por el tiento*, by the touch; *a tiento*, doubtfully, obscurely; *cual el tiempo, tal el tiento*, accommodate yourself to circumstances.

tiernamente, *adv.* tenderly, compassionately.

tierno, -na, *a.* tender, soft; delicate; fond, affectionate; mild, recent, modern, young.

tierra, *n.f.* earth; land, soil, ground, mould; globe, country, region; native parts, native land; *tierra yerma*, uncultivated ground; *tierra de pan llevar*, wheat-bearing land; *tierra de saca manchas*, fuller's earth; *tierra de año y vez*, land cultivated in alternate years; *tierra a tierra*, (*naut.*) coasting; securely, cautiously; *tierra firme*, continent; *tierra adentro* (*naut.*) inland; *correr hacia la tierra*, (*naut.*) to stand inshore; *tomar tierra*, (*naut.*) to anchor in a port; *besar la tierra*, to fall flat on one's face; *besar uno la tierra que otro pisa*, to worship the very ground one steps on; *coserse con la tierra*, to creep along the ground; *dar con una persona en tierra*, to throw a person down; *echar tierra a una cosa*, to bury a thing in oblivion; *echarse por tierra*, to be humiliated; *poner tierra por medio* (or *en*), to absent oneself, go far away; *por debajo de tierra*, with great secrecy; *saltar en tierra*, (*naut.*) to disembark; *callar y obrar por la tierra y por la mar*, to talk little but use one's utmost exertions; *en cada tierra, su uso, y en cada casa, su costumbre*, do at Rome as the Romans do; *en tierra de ciegos, el tuerto es rey*, a small fish is king among minnows; *no hay tierra mala, si le viene su añada*, there's nothing without its uses; *ser buena tierra para sembrar nabos*, useless fellow.

tiesamente, tieso, *adv.* firmly, strongly, stiffly.

tieso, -sa, *a.* solid, hard, stiff, firm; valiant; strong, robust; stubborn, obstinate, inflexible; taut, rigid, tight; animated; too grave or circumspect; *tieso que tieso*, pertinacity, obstinacy; *tieso de cogote*, (*coll.*) stiff-necked, obstinate, vain; *tenerse tieso* (or *tenérselas tiesas*), (*coll.*) to be firm in one's opinion, opposition, etc.

tiesto, *n.m.* flowerpot; large pot; (*Chi.*) any vessel or receptacle.

tiesura, *n.f.* stiffness, rigidity, severity.

tifo, *n.m.* typhus; *tifo asiático*, Asiatic cholera; *tifo de América*, yellow fever; *tifo de Oriente*, bubonic plague.

tifo, -fa, *a.* (*coll.*) sated, glutted.

tifoideo, -dea, *a.* typhoid.

tifón, *n.m.* typhoon.

tifus, *n.m.* typhus; *tifus icterodes*, yellow fever.

tigra, *n.f.* (*Am.*) female jaguar.

tigre, *n.m.* tiger; (*Am.*) jaguar; (*Ec.*) a bird.

tigrida, tigridia, *n.f.* tiger-flower.

tigrillo, *n.m.* (*Cent. Am., Ec., Ven.*) a small carnivorous mammal.

tigüilote, *n.m.* (*Cent. Am.*) a tree the wood of which is used as a dye.

tija, *n.f.* shaft of a key.

tijera, *n.f.; tijeras*, *n.f.pl.* scissors; any X-shaped tool; carpenter's horse; cooper's mare; sheep-shearer; brace of a coach; small channel; detractor, murmurer; *pl.* side stringers of a truck frame; beams across a stream to catch floating timber; *buena tijera*, great eater *or* great scandalmonger; *hacer tijera*, to twist the mouth (of horses).

tijereta, *n.f.* small scissors; earwig; small tendril of a vine; fork-tail duck.

tijeretada, *n.f.* clip, cut with scissors.

tijeretazo, *n.m.* cut with scissors.

tijeretear, *v.t.* to cut with scissors; (*fig.*) to meddle with other people's business.

tijereteo, *n.m.* act of clipping; snip-snap noise of scissors.

tijerica, -illa, -ita, *n.f.* small scissors.

tijeruela, *n.f.* small tendril of a vine.

tijuil, *n.m.* (*Hond.*) a black bird of the conirostrous order.

tila, *n.f.* linden-tree; linden-flower; infusion of linden-flowers, linden-tea.

tílburi, *n.m.* tilbury.

tildar, *v.t.* to cross out; to mark letters with tilde, as *ñ*; to stigmatize, brand.

tilde, *n.f.* tilde, stroke over a letter (as *ñ*); point, jot, iota, tittle, very small matter.

tildón, *n.m.* long dash or stroke.

tilia, *n.f.* linden-tree.

tiliche, *n.m.* (*Cent. Am., Mex.*) trifle, trinket, knick-knack.

tilichero, *n.m.* (*Am.*) pedlar.

tilín, *n.m.* sound of a bell; *hacer tilín*, to gratify, become a favourite; *en un tilín*, (*Col., Chi., Ven.*) within an ace, almost, pretty near.

tilingo, -ga, *a.* (*Arg., Mex.*) silly, foolish; dull, stupid.

tilma, *n.f.* (*Mex.*) cotton blanket used as cloak.

tilo, *n.m.* linden-tree.

tilla, *n.f.* midship, gangway.

tillado, *n.m.* wooden floor.

tillar, *v.t.* to floor; to plank.

timador, -ra, *n.m.f.* (*coll.*) swindler.

timalo, *n.m.* grayling.

timar, *v.t.* to cheat, swindle; (*coll.*) to gaze into the eyes, gaze lovingly, exchange winks.

timba, *n.f.* (*coll.*) hand in a game; gambling-den; (*Philip.*) bucket; (*Cent. Am., Mex.*) belly, abdomen.

timbal, *n.m.* kettle-drum.

timbaleo, *n.m.* beat of kettle-drum.

timbalero, *n.m.* kettle-drummer.

timbiriche, *n.m.* (*Mex.*) a tree of the Rubiaceous genus with edible fruit.

timbirimba, *n.f.* (*coll.*) game of chance; gaming house.

timbó, *n.m.* (*Arg., Par.*) a tree used for dugout canoes.

timbra, *n.f.* mountain hyssop.

timbrador, *n.m.* stamper; stamping-machine; rubber-stamp.

timbrar, *v.t.* to stamp, seal.

timbre, *n.m.* stamp, postage-stamp; seal; (*her.*) crest; timbre; call bell; tone-colour; quality of the voice; harmonious sound; glorious deed, achievement; stamp duty; *el mejor timbre de su escudo,* the brightest jewel in his crown.

timiama, *n.f.* incense of sweet scents (Hebrew religion).

tímidamente, *adv.* timidly, timorously, fearfully.

timidez, *n.f.* timidity, fear, cowardice.

tímido, -da, *a.* timid, dastardly, cowardly.

timo, *n.m.* grayling; (*coll.*) cheat, swindle; *dar un timo,* to cheat, swindle.

timón, *n.m.* beam of a plough, coach-pole; (*aer.*) rudder; (*fig.*) guiding principle; (*naut.*) helm, rudder; stick of a rocket; *calar el timón,* to hang the rudder; *apear* (or *sacar*) *el timón,* to unship the rudder; *timón de profundidad,* (*aer.*) elevator.

timonear, *v.t.* (*naut.*) to govern (the helm).

timonel, *n.m.* helmsman.

timonera, *n.f.* helmsman's post, pilot-house, wheel-house; (*orn.*) large quill.

timonero, *n.m.* helmsman.

timorato, -ta, *a.* God-fearing; timorous.

timpa, *n.f.* bar of cast-iron in a furnace hearth.

timpánico, -ca, *a.* (*med.*) tympanic.

timpanillo, *n.m.* small kettle-drum; small tympano; (*print.*) inner tympan; (*arch.*) gablet.

tímpano, *n.m.* kettle-drum; (*anat.*) tympanum, eardrum; (*arch., print.*) tympan.

tina, *n.f.* large earthen jar; copper, dyer's vat, bathing-tub, foot-tub.

tinaco, *n.m.* wooden trough, vat, tub.

tinada, *n.f.* woodstack; shed.

tinado, tinador, *n.m.* cattle-shed.

tinaja, *n.f.* large earthen jar; (*Philip.*) liquid measure (about 11 gallons).

tinajería, *n.f.* water-jar-shop.

tinajero, *n.m.* maker or seller of water-jars; (*PR., Ven.*) water-jar-store.

tinajita, -uela, *n.f.* small water-jar.

tinajón, *n.m.* large wide-mouthed jar.

tinapá, *n.m.* (*Philip.*) smoke-dried fish.

tincar, *v.t.* (*Arg., Chi.*) to drive a ball (as in golf).

tincazo, *n.m.* (*Arg., Ec.*) a fillip, flick, usually on the head.

tinción, *n.f.* the action and effect of dyeing or tingeing.

tindalo, *n.m.* (*Philip.*) hardwood-tree.

tinelar, *a.* pertaining to the servants' dining-room.

tinelo, *n.m.* servants' dining-room.

tineta, *n.f.* small tub.

tinge, *n.m.* kind of black owl.

tingladillo, *n.m.* (*naut.*) clinker work.

tinglado, *n.m.* shed roof; temporary platform or stage; trick, intrigue, machination; (*Cub.*) inclined plane for draining sugar-loaves.

tingle, *n.f., a.* glaziers' lead opener.

tinicla, *n.f.* kind of hauberk.

tiniebla, *n.f.* darkness, obscurity. — *pl.* **tinieblas,** darkness; hell; night; gross ignorance; (*eccles.*) tenebræ.

tinillo, *n.m.* tank for collecting must.

tino, *n.m.* skill; prudence, judgment; dexterity, tact, knack; steady aim; wine-press; recipient, vat; tank; *a buen tino,* at a guess; *sacar de tino,* to astonish, exasperate, confound; *salir de tino,* to be out of one's mind.

tinola, *n.f.* (*Philip.*) a soup made of minced chicken, potatoes and pumpkins.

tinta, *n.f.* tint, hue, colour; dyeing process; ink; *tinta de imprenta,* printer's ink; *tinta china,* Indian ink; *tinta simpática,* invisible ink; *correr la tinta,* to be fluid; *saber de buena tinta,* to know on good authority; *recargar las tintas,* to exaggerate the extent or import of something. — *pl.* **tintas,** colours prepared for painting.

tintar, *v.t.* to dye, tinge.

tinte, *n.m.* tint, tincture; paint, colour, tinge, shade, hue; dyeing, staining; dyer's shop; palliation, cloak.

tinterazo, *n.m.* blow with an inkstand.

tinterillada, *n.f.* (*Am.*) trickery, tricky action; lie, fib.

tinterillo, *n.m.* small inkstand; (*Am., coll.*) pettifogger.

tintero, *n.m.* inkstand, inkhorn, inkwell; (*print.*) ink-table; *quedársele a uno en el tintero,* to forget a thing entirely.

tintilla, *n.f.* a red, sweet, astringent wine made in Rota (Cádiz).

tintillo, *n.m.* light-coloured wine.

tintín, *n.m.* clang, clink (of metal).

tintirintín, *n.m.* piercing sound (as of a clarion).

tinto, -ta, *a.* deep-coloured, dyed, tinged; (*CR., Hond.*) dark red; *vino tinto,* red wine. — *p.p. irreg.* [TEÑIR].

tintóreo, -rea, *a.* tinctorial.

tintorería, *n.f.* dyer's shop.

tintorero, -ra, *n.m.f.* dyer; *n.f.* (*ichth.*) female shark.

tintura, *n.f.* dyeing; make-up (ladies); tincture, dye, colour, stain, spot; smattering, superficial knowledge; extract of drugs; *sobre negro no hay tintura,* a bad temperament cannot be mended.

tinturar, *v.t.* to dye, tinge, imbue; to teach superficially.

tiña, *n.f.* scalp ringworm; (*beekeeping*) small spider damaging beehives; (*coll.*) poverty, indigence, want; niggardliness, meanness.

tiñería, *n.f.* (*coll.*) poverty, indigence, misery, meanness.

tiño; él tiñó; tiña, *pres. indic.; 3rd pers. sing. pret.; pres. subj.* [TEÑIR].

tiñoso, -sa, *a.* mangy, afflicted with ringworm; penurious, niggardly, sordid, mean.

tiñuela, *n.f.* ship-worm; (*bot.*) common dodder.

tío, *n.m.* uncle; (*coll.*) good man, old man; *tener un tío en las Indias,* to have a rich friend or relative.

tiorba, *n.f.* theorbo.

tiovivo, *n.m.* merry-go-round.

tipa, *n.f.* (*Am.*) hardwood-tree; (*Arg.*) leather-pouch or bag.

tipiadora, *n.f.* typewriter; typist.

típico, -ca, *a.* typical, characteristic.

tiple, *n.m.* treble, soprano; small guitar; (*naut.*) mast of one piece. — *n.m.f.* soprano singer.

tiplisonante, *a.* (*coll.*) treble-toned.

tipo, *n.m.* type, pattern; figure, model, standard; (*print.*) letter; (*zool.*) class; (*coll.*) fellow, guy.

tipografía, *n.f.* typography, type-setting, printing.

tipográficamente, *adv.* typographically.

tipográfico, -ca, *a.* typographical.

tipógrafo, *n.m.* printer.

tipometría, *n.f.* measuring printing types.

tipómetro, *n.m.* type-gauge, type measure.

tipoy, *n.m.* (*Arg., Par.*) tunic worn by Indian and peasant women.

típula, *n.f.* daddy-long-legs.

tique, *n.m.* (*Chi.*) a tree of the Euphorbiaceous genus.

tiquín, *n.m.* (*Philip.*) bamboo punting-pole.

tiquismiquis, *n.m.* affected or ridiculous scrupulousness or fastidiousness, fussiness.

tiquistiquis, *n.m.* (*Philip.*) bitterwood tree.

tiquízque, *n.m.* (*CR.*) edible plant of the liliaceous order.

tira, *n.f.* stripe, strip, band; (*naut.*) fall. — *pl.* **tiras,** fees in appeal causes.

tirabala, *n.f.* popgun.

tirabeque, *n.m.* tender peas.

tirabotas, *n.m.* boot-hook.

tirabotón, *n.m.* button-hook.

tirabraguero, *n.m.* truss.

tirabuzón, *n.m.* corkscrew.

tiracol, tiracuello, *n.m.* sword-belt.

tirada, *n.f.* throw, cast; distance; stretch; space or lapse of time; (*print.*) edition, circulation (of a book, etc.); (*print.*) off-print; pulling-off, pull; *de* (or *en*) *una tirada*, at one stretch.

tiradera, *n.f.* strap; long Indian arrow; (*sad.*) trace.

tiradero, *n.m.* cover whence a hunter shoots.

tirado, *n.m.* draught, act of drawing; (*print.*) press-work; wire-drawing (gold or silver).

tirado, -da, *a.* long and low (ship); very cheap, thrown away, given away.

tirador, -ra, *n.m.f.* drawer, thrower; sharpshooter; marksman, good shot; (*mech.*) lift, handle, pull, knob, button; bell-pull; fowler; (*print.*) pressman; *tirador de oro*, gold-wire drawer.

tirafondo, *n.m.* metal bolt; (*med.*) kind of alphonsin (forceps).

tiralíneas, *n.m.* ruling-pen, drawing-pen.

tiramiento, *n.m.* tension, stretching, drawing.

tiramira, *n.f.* long narrow ridge of mountains; long line of things or people; long distance.

tiramollar, *v.t.* (*naut.*) to slacken, ease off; to overhaul.

tirana, *n.f.* old Spanish song.

tiranamente, *adv.* tyrannically.

tiranía, *n.f.* tyranny, despotism, despotic government, severity, oppression; ascendency of a passion.

tiránicamente, *adv.* tyrannically.

tiranicida, *n.m., a.* tyrannicide (murderer).

tiranicidio, *n.m.* tyrannicide (murder).

tiránico, -ca, *a.* tyrannical, despotic.

tiranización, *n.f.* tyrannizing.

tiranizadamente, *adv.* tyrannically.

tiranizar, *v.t.* (*pret.* **tiranicé;** *pres. subj.* **tiranice**) to tyrannize, oppress, domineer.

tirano, -na, *a.* tyrannical, arbitrary, despotic. — *n.m.f.* tyrant, despot, oppressor; ruling passion.

tirante, *n.m.* joist; trace, gear, part of harness; (*mech.*) brace, collar-piece; tie-rod, stay-rod; (*arch.*) anchor, truss-rod. — *pl.* **tirantes,** braces; *a tirantes largos*, drawn by a four-horse carriage with two drivers riding postilion. — *a.* taut, drawn, stretched; strained (as relations); extended; drawing, pulling; tightly bound.

tirantez, *n.f.* length, full-length; tightness, tenseness, tension, stretch, strain.

tiranuelo, -le, *n.m.f.* little tyrant, petty tyrant.

tirapié, *n.m.* shoemaker's strap.

tirar, *v.t., v.i.* to throw, cast, dart, fling, throw away, cast off (*or* away), toss, pitch; to resemble; to enlarge, extend; to get along, pull through; to attract, tend; to pull, draw, tug; to last; to bend, incline; to thwart; to lavish; to turn (in any direction); to fire, shoot, discharge (fire-arms); to aim at, aspire to, try to; to acquire, earn; to squander, waste, misspend; (*print.*) to print sheets; to draw metal into threads. — *v.r.* to throw oneself, abandon oneself, give oneself up; *a todo tirar, a más tirar*, to the utmost, at most; *tirarla de*, to set up as; *tirar (por lo) largo*, to spend lavishly; *tirar coces*, to kick, rebel; *tirar un cañonazo*, to fire a gun; *tirar de la espada*, to draw the sword; *tire Vd. a la derecha*, turn to the right; *tira y afloja*, fast and loose; *tirar al blanco*, to shoot at a target; *tirar indirectas*, to throw out hints; *tirar su sueldo*, to draw one's salary.

tirela, *n.f.* striped stuff.

tireta, *n.f.* (*prov.*) lace, latch, thong.

tiricia, *n.f.* (*coll.*) jaundice.

tirilla, *n.f.* strip, frilling, edging; neckband.

tirio, -ria, *n.m.f., a.* Tyrian; *tirios y troyanos*, opposing factions.

tiritaña, *n.f.* thin cloth or silk; flimsy or unsubstantial thing, trifle.

tiritar, *v.i.* to shiver, shake with cold.

tiritón, *n.m.* shivering, chill.

tiritona, *n.f.* shivering (affected).

Tiro, *n.m.* Tyre.

tiro, *n.m.* cast, throw, fling, shot; charge, discharge, mark, aim; firing, report of firing; (*artill.*) piece of ordnance; target practice; shooting-ground, shooting-gallery; team of draught animals; trace (of harness); hoisting rope; flight of stairs; theft; length of a piece of cloth; prank, trick; serious injury; (*min.*) shaft; depth of a shaft; draught of a chimney. — *pl.* **tiros,** sword-belts; *estar a tiro de cañón*, to be within cannon-range; *una pistola de tres tiros*, a three-barrelled pistol; *de tiros largos*, in full dress; *tiro al blanco*, target-shooting; *errar el tiro*, to miss one's shot; *salir el tiro por la culata*, to give the contrary result to that expected.

tirocinio, *n.m.* apprenticeship, novitiate, pupilage.

tiroides, *n.m.* thyroid gland.

tirolés, -esa, *n.m.f., a.* Tyrolese, Tyrolian.

tirolés, *n.m.* pedlar, huckster.

tirón, *n.m.* haul, tug, pull, effort; tyro, beginner, apprentice, raw hand, novice; *de un tirón*, at once, at a stroke; *ni a dos tirones*, not easily obtained.

tirona, *n.f.* fishing-net, seine.

tiroriro, *n.m.* (*coll.*) sound of a wind-instrument. — *pl.* **tiroriros,** (*coll.*) wind-instruments.

tirotear, *v.t.*, *v. recip.* to shoot at random, exchange shots, to skirmish.

tiroteo, *n.m.* shooting at random, sharp-shooting, cross-fire; skirmish.

tirria, *n.f.* (*coll.*) aversion, dislike, antipathy.

tirso, *n.m.* thyrsus, wand.

tirulato, -ta, *a.* stupefied, astounded, aghast.

tirulo, *n.m.* tobacco leaf forming the core of a cigar.

tisana, *n.f.* ptisan; decoction, medicinal drink.

tísico, -ca, *n.m.f.*, *a.* phthisical, consumptive.

tisis, *n.f.* phthisis, consumption.

tiste, *n.m.* (*Cent. Am.*) drink made of toasted flour of maize, cacao, anatta and sugar.

tisú, *n.m.* gold or silver tissue.

titánico, -ca, *a.* titanic, titanesque; colossal, huge, gigantic.

titanio, *n.m.* titanium.

titanio, -nia, *a.* Titanic.

títere, *n.m.* puppet; dwarf, puny little fellow. — *pl.* **títeres**, Punch and Judy show; marionettes; *no dejar*, or *quedar*, *títere con cabeza*, to destroy entirely, to leave nothing.

titeretada, *n.f.* mean trick.

tití, *n.m.* very small monkey.

titilación, *n.f.* titillation, tickling; twinkle.

titilador, -ra; titilante, *a.* titillating, twinkling.

titilar, *v.i.* to titillate, tickle; to sparkle, flash, twinkle.

titímalo, *n.m.* (*bot.*) spurge.

titirimundi, *n.m.* raree-show, a peep-show.

titiritaina, *n.f.* (*coll.*) confused noise of flutes, etc.; noisy mirth.

titiritar, *v.i.* to shiver, tremble (with cold or fear).

titiritero, *n.m.* puppet-player, puppet-show man.

tito, *n.m.* kind of pea or bean.

titubeante, *a.* stammering, hesitating, vacillating, tottering.

titubear, *v.i.* to stammer; to doubt, hesitate, vacillate; to stagger, waver, reel, totter; to toddle.

titubeo, *n.m.* vacillation, hesitation, wavering; totter, toddle, toddling.

titulado, *n.m.* titled person.

titular, *a.* titular, titulary, nominal. — *v.t.* to title, entitle, call, name. — *v.i.* to obtain a title. — *v.r.* to style oneself.

titulillo, *n.m.* petty title; (*print.*) page-heading; *andar en titulillos*, to stick at trifles.

título, *n.m.* title; heading, head-line, caption, label, sign, inscription; right; deed; licence, patent, diploma; title of nobility; titled person; sobriquet, epithet; qualification, merit, desert; foundation (of a right or claim); gilt-edged securities; certificate, bond; professional degree; cause, reason, pretext; *a título*, on pretence; *título al portador*, bearer bond; *título nominativo*, registered bond; *título translativo de dominio*, (*law*) deed conveyance; *título de la deuda*, Government bond.

titundia, *n.f.* (*Cub.*) a popular dance.

tiuque, *n.m.* (*Arg., Chi.*) a bird of prey.

tiza, *n.f.* chalk, whitening, whiting, clay; calcinated stag's horn.

tizna, *n.f.* stain, blackening matter.

tiznado, -da, *a.* (*Cent. Am., Arg., Chi.*) drunk, intoxicated. — *p.p.* [TIZNAR].

tiznadura, *n.f.* smuttiness, smudginess.

tiznajo, *n.m.* (*coll.*) smut, smudge, stain.

tiznar, *v.t.* to stain, smut, tarnish, blot, blacken, smear, begrime; to defame.

tizne, *n.m.* smut, soot, grime.

tiznón, *n.m.* large spot, stain; smear or smudge.

tizo, *n.m.* half-burnt charcoal.

tizón, *n.m.* brand, firebrand; half-burnt wood; stain, spot, wheat crust, blight, mildew; (*fig.*) disgrace; (*arch.*) header.

tizona, *n.f.* (*coll.*) sword.

tizonada, *n.f.*; **tizonazo**, *n.m.* stroke with a firebrand; (*coll.*) hell fire.

tizoncillo, *n.m.* small burning coal.

tizonear, *v.t.* to stir up a fire.

tizonera, *n.f.* heap of half-burnt charcoal.

tizonero, *n.m.* fire poker.

tlaco, *n.m.* (*Am., obs.*) eighth part of a Spanish silver *real*.

tlazol, *n.m.* (*Mex.*) fodder of maize tops.

¡to! *interj.* word used to call a dog.

toa, *n.f.* (*Am.*) rope, hawser.

toalla, *n.f.* towel; pillow-sham.

toalleta, *n.f.* small towel, napkin.

toar, *v.t.* to tow.

toba, *n.f.* calcareous tufa, travertin, calcsinter; (*dent.*) tartar; (*bot.*) cotton-thistle.

toballeta, tobelleta, *n.f.* napkin.

tobillo, *n.m.* ankle.

tobogán, *n.m.* toboggan.

toboba, *n.m.* (*CR.*) a kind of viper.

toca, *n.f.* hood, coif, bonnet, wimple, toque, head-dress; thin stuff; *dos tocas en un hogar, mal se pueden concertar*, no house thrives with two mistresses.

tocado, *n.m.* ornament, head-dress, head-gear, coiffure.

tocado, -da, *a.* touched, felt; infected, tainted, contaminated. — *p.p.* [TOCAR]; *estar tocado de la cabeza*, to be of unsound mind.

tocador, *n.m.* (*mus.*) player, performer; boudoir, dressing-room, toilet-room, toilet-table; kerchief; dressing-case.

tocadorcito, *n.m.* small toilet-table.

tocadura, *n.f.* coiffure, head-gear.

tocamiento, *n.m.* contact, touch, handling; (*fig.*) inspiration.

tocante, *a.* relative, respecting, concerning, relating to, touching.

tocar, *v.t.* (*pret.* **toqué**; *pres. subj.* **toque**) to touch, feel, lay hands on, handle; to play an instrument; to ring, toll a bell; to try (metals), magnetize; (*mil.*) to beat, sound (drum, bugle, etc.); to hit, knock, strike, rap, tap; to prove, test; to inspire, persuade, move; to treat of, discuss; to kiss (of billiard-balls); to infect, communicate; to reap or find out (by experience); (*naut.*) to touch bottom or sandbank; (*art*) to give finishing touches; to comb and dress (the hair). — *v.i.* to belong, appertain; to interest, behove, concern; to fall to one's share; to be one's turn or right; to touch, be contiguous to; to be a duty or obligation; to be related, allied; to rap, knock; to stop in a place or port. — *v.r.* to put on one's hat, be covered; to arrange one's hair; to wimple; *tocar de cerca*, to be nearly related; *tocar a la puerta*, to rap at the door; *tocar en un puerto*, (*naut.*) to touch at a port; *tocar fondo*, to strike aground; *tocar la diana*, (*mil.*) to sound the reveille; *tocar en lo vivo*, to wound to the quick; *tocar a vuelo*, to ring a merry peal (of bells); *a toca teja*, ready money.

tocasalva, *n.f.* rack or tray for glasses.

tocata, *n.f.* toccata; (*coll.*) drubbing, beating.

tocayo, -ya, *a.* namesake.

tocía, *n.f.* tutty.

tocinería, *n.f.* shop or stall where pork is sold.

tocinero, -ra, *n.m.* pork-butcher, pork seller. — *n.f.* table for salting pork.

tocino, *n.m.* bacon, salt pork; lard; in the game of skipping, to jump very rapidly and as long as possible; (*Cub.*) a creeping shrub of the leguminous family; *tocino del cielo,* confection of eggs and syrup; *témpano de tocino,* flitch of bacon.

tocio, -cia, *a.* low, dwarfish (oak-tree).

tocología, *n.f.* tocology, obstetrics.

tocólogo, *n.m.* tocologist, obstetrician.

tocón, *n.m.* tree-stump; stump of an arm or leg.

toconal, *n.m.* olive-yard planted with stumps.

tocoquera, *n.f.* (*Ven.*) noisy party; gaming house of low class.

tocororo, *n.m.* (*orn.*) a Cuban trogon.

tocotoco, *n.m.* (*Ven.*) pelican.

tocte, *n.m.* (*Ec.*, *Per.*) a tree of the Juglandaceous family.

tocuyo, *n.m.* (*S. Am.*) coarse shirtings or sheetings.

toche, *n.m.* (*Col.*, *Ven.*) a bird of the Conirostrum order.

tochedad, *n.f.* rusticity, ignorance, clownishness.

tochimbo, *n.m.* (*Per.*) blast furnace.

tocho, -cha, *a.* clownish, rustic, uncouth; unpolished, homespun. — *n.m.* (*metal.*) bloom, billet; pole, iron bar.

tochura, *n.f.* (*prov.*) ignorance, clownishness.

todabuena, todasana, *n.f.* St. John's-wort.

todavía, *adv.* nevertheless, notwithstanding; still, ever, yet; *todavía no,* not yet.

todito, -ta, *a.* (*coll.*) the whole (emphatic TODO); *todita la noche,* the whole night long.

todo, -da, *a.* all, entire, whole, complete; each, every. — *n.m.* all; whole; everybody; everything. — *pl.* **todos,** everybody, all. — *adv.* entirely, totally; *ante todo,* first of all; *a todo,* at most; *con todo* (*eso*), nevertheless, notwithstanding; *del todo,* entirely, quite; *todo aquel que,* whoever; *todo aquello que,* whatever; *en todo y por todo,* absolutely, wholly; *en un todo,* together, completely, in all its parts; *jugar el todo por el todo,* to risk or stake all; *meterse en todo,* to interfere in everything; *ser el todo,* to be the chief, the principal; *sobre todo,* especially, above all; *me es todo uno,* it's all the same to me; *quien todo lo niega, todo lo confiesa,* he who denies all, confesses all.

todopoderoso, -sa, *a.* all-powerful, almighty; *el Todopoderoso,* Almighty God.

toesa, *n.f.* toise.

tofo, *n.m.* tumour; (*Arg.*, *Chi.*) white refractory clay.

toga, *n.f.* Roman toga; judicial robe or gown.

togado, -da, *a.* togaed, togated.

toisón de oro, *n.m.* Golden Fleece.

tojal, *n.m.* furze clump, gorse or whin.

tojino, *n.m.* (*naut.*) notch, knob; cleat.

tojo, *n.m.* whin, furze; (*Bol.*) lark.

tojosita, *n.f.* (*Cub.*) a variety of pigeon.

tola, *n.f.* (*S. Am.*) name of several shrubs.

tolano, *n.m.* tumour in horse's gums. — *pl.* **tolanos,** short hair on the neck.

toldadura, *n.f.* hangings, awning.

toldar, *v.t.* to cover with an awning or hangings.

toldería, *n.f.* (*Arg.*) Indian camp.

toldero, *n.m.* (*prov.*) salt retailer.

toldilla, *n.f.* (*naut.*) round-house.

toldillo, *n.m.* covered sedan-chair; small awning.

toldo, *n.m.* awning, tilt; pomp, ostentation; (*Arg.*) Indian hut.

tole, tomar el, (*coll.*) to set off very quickly, to flee.

tole, *n.m.* hubbub, clamour, outcry.

toledano, -na, *n.m.f.*, *a.* Toledan; *noche toledana,* sleepless night.

tolerable, *a.* tolerable, sufferable, bearable, endurable; allowable, permissible.

tolerablemente, *adv.* tolerably.

tolerancia, *n.f.* toleration, tolerance, indulgence, permission; allowance, permissible discrepancy or variation.

tolerante, *a.* tolerant; tolerationist.

tolerantismo, *n.m.* toleration, freedom of worship.

tolerar, *v.t.* to tolerate, endure, permit, suffer; to overlook, be indulgent.

tolete, *n.m.* thole, thole-pin; (*Cent. Am.*, *Cub.*, *Ven.*) cudgel, club; (*Col.*) large boat or canoe.

tolmo, *n.m.* a pillar-like rock, tor.

tolondro, tolondrón, *n.m.* contusion after a blow, bump; hare-brained fellow; *a topa tolondro,* rashly, inconsiderately; *a tolondrones,* by fits and starts.

tolteca, *n.*, *a.* relating to the Toltec tribe and language.

tolú, *n.m.* Peruvian balsam.

tolva, *n.f.* mill-hopper, chute.

tolvanera, *n.f.* cloud of dust.

tolla, *n.f.* moss-covered bog; (*Cub.*) trough.

tollo, *n.m.* spotted dog-fish; blind (for hunting); quagmire, bog.

tollón, *n.m.* gorge, narrow passage.

toma, *n.f.* take, taking; receiving, grasp, grip, hold, catch; (*mil.*) capture; dose, portion; water-main; electricity-mains; outlet of a reservoir. — *interj.* well!; there!; why, of course!

tomada, *n.f.* conquest.

tomadero, *n.m.* haft, handle; outlet, opening into a drain.

tomador, -ra, *n.m.f.* taker, receiver; setter, dog that retrieves game; (*naut.*) gasket; (*Arg.*, *Chi.*) drinker, toper; (*com.*) drawee.

tomadura, *n.f.* catch, seizure, gripe, grasp, hold, grip; dose (medicine, drink, etc.).

tomaína, *n.f.* ptomaine.

tomajón, -ona, *a.* (*coll.*) accepting or taking often.

tomar, *v.t.* to take, have, catch, grasp, seize; to receive, accept, get; to overtake, surprise; to purchase, buy; to eat or drink; to select, choose; to pinch (snuff); to occupy, capture, take possession of; to rob, plunder; to overwhelm; to interpret, construe; to understand, apprehend; to assume, undertake; to acquire, contract (habit, vice, etc.); to employ, take into service; to imitate, take off, copy; to cover the female, to take; to take a trick (at cards); (*naut.*) to arrive in port; to take into one's company; to stop play, call a halt (in ball games). — *v.i.* to take; to drink (liquor); to turn to (the right, left), or into;

to take, follow (a road, street, etc.). — *v.r.* to get rusty; *tomar a cuestas*, to carry on one's back; *tomar calor*, to get warm; *tomar frío*, to catch cold; *tomar cuentas*, to examine or audit accounts; *tomar fuerzas*, to gather strength; *tomar sobre sí*, to take upon oneself; *tomar la puerta*, to get away, be off; *tomar el fresco*, to take the air; *tomar el sol*, to take a sun-bath; *tomar lengua(s)*, to inquire, find out; *tomar estado*, to marry or to take holy orders or to take the veil; *tomar por su cuenta*, to take upon one's account; *tomarla* (or *tomarse*) *con alguno*, to pick a quarrel with someone; *tomar el pelo a*, (*coll.*) to chaff, pull one's leg; *tomar a pecho(s)*, to undertake too zealously, to take to heart; *tomar las de Villadiego*, to run off in haste; *tomar razón*, to register, make a note; *tomar la delantera*, to get ahead of, excel; *tomar a uno entre cejas*, to take a dislike to someone; *tomar entre manos*, to take in hand; *tomar por escrito*, to make a note of; *tomar puerto*, (*naut.*) to make port; *tomar rabia*, to become furious; *tomar rizos*, (*naut.*) to reef; *tomar vuelo*, to increase; (*aer.*) to take off; *más vale un 'toma' que dos 'te daré,'* a bird in the hand is worth two in the bush.

Tomás, *n.m.* Thomas.

tomatada, *n.f.* fry of tomatoes.

tomatal, *n.m.* tomato patch or field.

tomatazo, *n.m.* blow with a tomato.

tomate, *n.m.* tomato.

tomatera, *n.f.* tomato-plant.

tomatero, -ra, *n.m.f.* tomato grower or seller.

tomaticán, *n.m.* (*Chi.*) dish or seasoning of tomatoes.

tomatillo, *n.m.* (*Chi.*) a shrub of the Solanaceous genus.

tome, *n.m.* (*Chi.*) a kind of reed mace.

tomeguín, *n.m.* (*Cub.*) a kind of humming-bird.

tomento, *n.m.* coarse tow.

tomillar, *n.m.* thyme-bed.

tomillo, *n.m.* thyme; *tomillo salsero*, sweet marjoram.

tomín, *n.m.* third part of a drachm, Spanish weight; (*Am.*) a silver coin (2½*d.*); ancient tax paid by the Peruvian Indians.

tominejo, -ja, *n.m.f.* humming-bird.

tomismo, *n.m.* Thomism.

tomista, *n., a.* Thomist.

tomiza, *n.f.* bass-rope.

tomo, *n.m.* body, bulk; value, importance, consequence; volume, tome, book; *de tomo y lomo*, of weight and bulk, of importance.

tomón, -ona, *n.m.f., a.* accepting, one given to accepting or taking.

ton, *n.m.* occasion, motive; *sin ton ni son*, without motive or cause, without rime or reason.

tonada, *n.f.* tune, song.

tonadilla, *n.f.* gay, popular song; musical interlude.

tonadillero, *n.m.* writer of tonadillas.

tonalidad, *n.f.* tonality.

tonante, *a.* (*poet.*) thundering (Jupiter).

tonar, *v.i.* (*poet.*) to thunder.

tonca, *n.f.* tonka bean.

tondino, *n.m.* (*arch.*) astragal.

tondo, *n.m.* (*arch.*) round moulding.

tonel, *n.m.* cask, barrel; (*naut.*) ancient measure of displacement (⅝ ton).

tonelada, *n.f.* tun, ton; tonnage duty.

tonelaje, *n.m.* (*naut.*) tonnage, capacity; (*com.*) tonnage dues.

tonelería, *n.f.* cooper's shop, cooper's trade, cooperage, coopering; quantity of barrels, casks, or water-casks.

tonelero, *n.m.* cooper, hooper.

tonelete, *n.m.* little butt, little barrel; kilt, short skirt.

tonga, tongada, *n.f.* layer, stratum; (*Cub.*) lay, tier, row, ledge; (*Arg., Col.*) task.

tongo, *n.m.* (*Arg., Chi.*) 'throwing it', bribe accepted to lose a horse-race or game of pelota.

tónica, *n.f.* key-note, tonic.

tónico, -ca, *n.m.f., a.* tonic, strengthening; (*gram.*) tonic, accented.

tonificador, -ra; tonificante, *a.* tonic, strengthening.

tonificar, *v.t.* (*med.*) to tone up.

tonillo, *n.m.* monotonous tone, sing-song.

tonina, *n.f.* fresh tunny; dolphin.

tono, *n.m.* tone, tune; (*med.*) vigour, strength; (*mus.*) key, pitch; (*art*) degree of luminosity of a colour; general effect of a picture; deportment, manner, social address, conceit; *bajar el tono*, to talk less haughtily; *darse tono*, to give oneself airs or importance; *de buen* (or *mal*) *tono*, cultured (*or* uncultured).

tonsila, *n.f.* (*anat.*) tonsil.

tonsilitis, *n.f.* (*med.*) tonsillitis.

tonsura, *n.f.* tonsure; cutting of hair or wool, shearing, fleecing.

tonsurar, *v.t.* to cut off hair or wool; to give the tonsure; to shear, fleece.

tontada, *n.f.* nonsense, foolishness, silliness.

tontaina, *n.m.f.* (*coll.*) fool, dolt.

tontamente, *adv.* foolishly, stupidly.

tontear, *v.i.* to fool, act foolishly, talk nonsense.

tontedad, tontera, tontería, *n.f.* foolishness, foolery, folly, nonsense.

tontico, *n.m.* little dolt.

tontillo, *n.m.* hoop-skirt; bustle.

tontina, *n.f.* (*com.*) tontine.

tontito, *n.m.* (*Chi.*) goatsucker (*caprimulgus*).

tontivano, -na, *a.* foolishly conceited.

tonto, -ta, *a.* stupid, ignorant, silly, foolish, fatuous. — *n.m.f.* fool, dolt, dunce, nincompoop, noodle, numskull; (*Col., CR., Chi.*) old maid (at cards); (*Chi.*) lariat with balls at one end; *hacer(se) el tonto*, to act the fool; *a tontas y a locas*, without rime or reason; *volver a uno tonto*, to turn a man's brains; *tonto de capirote*, idiot, great fool; *tonto de cuatro suelas*, a perfect simpleton; *no hay tonto para su provecho*, no fool but can serve himself wisely.

tontuelo, -la, *n.m.f.* little fool.

tontuna, *n.f.* foolishness.

toña, *n.f.* tip-cat; bat for this game; (*prov.*) a big loaf of bread; (*prov.*) cake kneaded with oil and honey.

toñina, *n.f.* (*prov.*) fresh tunny-fish.

¡top!, *interj.* (*naut.*) hold, stop.

topa, *n.f.* pulley to hoist the main sails.

topacio, *n.m.* topaz.

topada, *n.f.* butt.

topador, *n.m.* butter (an animal which butts); ready gambler.

topar, *v.t.* to collide, knock, run or strike against; to meet with by chance; to run across, find; (*naut.*) to butt, abut, joint; (*Am.*) to try-out two fighting cocks. — *v.i.* to butt; to accept a bet at cards; to consist in, depend on; to meet with an obstacle; to come out right, succeed; *tope donde tope*, strike where it may.

toparca, *n.m.* toparch, ruler, chief, petty king.

toparquía, *n.f.* toparchy, little state or country.

topatopa, *n.f.* (*Chi., Per.*) a plant of the Scrophularia genus.

tope, *n.m.* top, butt, projecting end; rub; obstacle, hindrance, impediment; summit, apex; quarrel, scuffle; butt, collision, knock, bump; (*mech.*) stop-collar, stop-plate; (*rail.*) buffer; (*naut.*) mast-head, topmast-head; topman; butt-end of a plank; *hasta el tope* (or *los topes*), up to the brim.

topeadura, *n.f.* (*Chi.*) gaucho horse-play.

topera, *n.f.* mole-hole.

topetada, *n.f.* butt by a horned animal; (*coll.*) bump, bumping.

topetar, *v.t.* to butt; to encounter, bump, strike, knock against.

topetazo, topetón, *n.m.* collision, encounter, knock, blow, butt, bump.

topetudo, -da, *a.* accustomed to butt (of animals).

tópico, -ca, *n.m.f., a.* topical.

tópico, *n.m.* (*med.*) topical application; topic, subject.

topil, *n.m.* (*Mex.*) constable, policeman.

topinada, *n.f.* (*coll.*) awkwardness, clumsiness.

topinambur, *n.m.* (*Arg., Bol.*) kind of sweet potato.

topinaria, *n.f.* (*surg.*) talpa, wen.

topinera, *n.f.* mole-hole, mole-hill.

topo, *n.m.* mole; (*coll.*) stumbler, awkward person; dolt, blockhead; (*Am.*) one league and a half; (*Arg., Chi., Per.*) large scarf-pin.

topocho, -cha, *a.* (*Ven.*) plump, fatty.

topografía, *n.f.* topography; surveying.

topográficamente, *adv.* topographically.

topográfico, -ca, *a.* topographical.

topógrafo, *n.m.* topographer; surveyor.

toque, *n.m.* touch; ringing of bells, peal; (*mil.*) call; test, essay, trial, experience, proof (of gold or silver); touchstone; aid, assistance; divine inspiration; purport, gist; (*art*) fine stroke of the brush; (*coll.*) tap on a person; *toque a muerto*, passing bell; *toque de luz*, light in a picture; *dar un toque*, to put one to the test; (*fig., coll.*) to pump, throw out a feeler; *toque de tambor*, beat of a drum; *toque de diana*, reveille; *toque de retreta*, tattoo.

toqueado, *n.m.* rhythmical noise, clapping of hands, stamping of feet, etc.

toquería, *n.f.* collection of women's head-gear; business of toque making.

toquero, *n.m.* head-dress maker, veil-maker.

toqui, *n.m.* (*Chi.*) Araucanian war chief.

toquilla, *n.f.* small veil, small gauze head-covering; small triangular neckerchief; trimming of a hat; woollen knitted shawl; (*Bol., Ec.*) toquilla palm (*Carludovica palmata*).

tora, *n.f.* figure of a bull in fireworks; Jewish family tribute; Pentateuch.

torada, *n.f.* drove of bulls.

toral, *a.* main, principal. — *n.m.* unbleached wax; mould for copper bars; copper bar.

tórax, *n.m.* thorax; chest, breast.

torbellino, *n.m.* whirlwind; avalanche, rush; vortex; (*coll*) boisterous person, lively person.

torca, *n.f.* cavern, a deep hollow place in the earth.

torcal, *n.m.* cavernous region.

torcaz; torcazo, -za, *a.; paloma torcaz,* (*orn.*) ring-dove.

torce, *n.f.* coil or turn of a chain around the neck.

torcecuello, *n.m.* wryneck.

torcedero, *n.m.* twisting-mill.

torcedero, -ra, *a.* twisted.

torcedor, -ra, *n.m.f.* twister, thread frame; twisting mill; (*fig.*) that which causes displeasure; *torcedor de tabaco,* cigar-maker.

torcedura, *n.f.* twisting, sprain; a very low quality wine.

torcer, *v.t.* (*pres. indic.* **tuerzo**; *pres. subj.* **tuerza**) to twist, wind, twine; distort, curve, crook, pervert; to turn, bend, deflect, dissuade; to misinterpret, misconstrue; to induce to change one's mind; to wind (as strands); to sprain (as a foot, arm, etc.). — *v.r.* to turn sour (milk or wine); to roll tobacco leaf; to cheat at gambling; to be dislocated, sprained; *torcer la llave,* to lock, turn the key; *torcer las narices,* to turn up the nose in disgust; *estar torcido con,* to be on bad terms with.

torcida, *n.f.* wick, lamp-wick; (*prov.*) daily meat ration given to the grinder in oil mills.

torcidamente, *adv.* obliquely, crookedly tortuously.

torcidillo, *n.m.* distorted, perverted, sinister interpretation.

torcido, -da, *a.* oblique, crooked, tortuous; twisted, twined, bent.

torcido, *n.m.* twist of sweetmeat; twist, twisted silk; (*prov.*) bad wine.

torcijón, *n.m.* gripes, colic.

torcimiento, *n.m.* turning, twisting, deflection, deviation, twist, sprain; bend, warp; circumlocution, periphrasis.

torculado, -da, *n.m.* screw-shaped.

tórculo, *n.m.* (*print.*) small press; rolling-press.

tordella, *n.f.* large thrush.

tórdiga, *n.f.* neat's leather.

tordillo, -lla, *a.* thrush-coloured, grizzled, greyish.

tordo, *n.m.* thrush, throstle; *tordo loco,* solitary thrush; *tordo de agua,* reed thrush.

tordo, -da, *a.* speckled, dapple (horse).

toreador, *n.m.* bull-fighter.

torear, *v.i.* to fight bulls; to mate a bull to cows. — *v.t.* (*coll.*) to mock, tease, banter.

toreo, *n.m.* bull-fighting.

torería, *n.f.* (*Cub.*) boys' pranks.

torero, *n.m.* bull-fighter.

torero, -ra, *a.* pertaining to bull-fighters.

torete, *n.m.* bullock; current rumour; (*coll.*) puzzle, intricate business; absorbing topic.

torga, *n.f.* yoke for dogs or hogs.

toril, *n.m.* pen for bulls before the fight.

torillo, *n.m.* little bull; dowel; (*zool.*) raphe; a fish of the Acanthopterygian order.

torio, *n.m.* thorium.

toriondez, *n.f.* rut (of cattle).

toriondo, -da, *a.* rutting (as cows).

torito, *n.m.* small bull; bullock; (*Chi.*) a kind of humming-bird; (*Arg., Per.*) rhinoceros beetle; (*Ec.*) variety of orchid; (*Cub.*) a fish of the Plectognath order.

torloroto, *n.m.* shepherd's flute or pipe.

tormagal, *n.m.,* **tormellera,** *n.f.* (*geol.*) place abounding in tors.

tormenta, *n.f.* storm, tempest, hurricane; misfortune, adversity, reverse; heated discussion.

tormentario, *n.m.* gunnery.

tormentario, -ria, *a.* projectile.

tormentila, *n.f.* tormentil, septifoil.

tormentín, *n.m.* (*naut.*) jib-boom.

tormento, *n.m.* torment, torture; anguish, pang, affliction, worry, pain; rack; (*mil.*) battering ordnance; *dar tormento,* to torture, rack; *confesar sin tormento,* (*fig.*) to speak quite frankly without being urged thereto.

tormentoso, -sa, *a.* boisterous, stormy, turbulent; (*naut.*) labouring hard.

tormo, *n.m.* tor, steep rock.

torna, *n.f.* restitution, return; irrigation tap, drain. — *pl.* **tornas,** return, recompense, requital.

tornaboda, *n.f.* day after a wedding, first day of honeymoon; celebrations upon this day.

tornachile, *n.m.* (*Mex.*) thick pepper.

tornada, *n.f.* return from a journey; (*poet.*) envoi, envoy; (*vet.*) tape-worm cyst.

tornadera, *n.f.* winnowing-fork.

tornadizo, -za, *n.m.f., a.* turncoat, deserter.

tornado, *n.m.* hurricane, tornado.

tornadura, *n.f.* return, recompense, requital; a land measure.

tornaguía, *n.f.* landing certificate.

tornalecho, *n.m.* bed canopy.

tornamiento, *n.m.* alteration, turn, change.

tornapunta, *n.f.* (*arch.*) chock, shoe, wedge; (*naut.*) stay, prop, brace.

tornar, *v.t., v.i.* to restore, requite, make restitution, return; to come back again; to do again, repeat; to turn (one's brain); to transform, alter, change. — *v.i.* to return, come back; to repeat, do again. — *v.r.* to change, become, be altered; *tornar por,* to protect, defend; *tornar las espaldas,* to turn a cold shoulder; *tornar a andar las estaciones,* to go back to one's evil ways.

tornasol, *n.m.* (*bot.*) turnsole; shot silk; changeable colour; sunflower; litmus.

tornasolado, -da, *a.* changing colours, shot (of fabrics); iridescent.

tornasolar, *v.t.* to cause changes in colour; to iridesce.

tornátil, *a.* turned (in a lathe); changeable, fickle.

tornatrás, *n.m.f.* half-breed, mestizo.

tornavía, *n.f.* turn-table.

tornaviaje, *n.m.* return voyage.

tornavirón, *n.m.* box, slap.

tornavoz, *n.m.* sounding-board.

torneador, *n.m.* turner; tilter.

torneadura, *n.f.* lathe shavings.

torneante, *n.m., a.* tilter at tournaments; turner.

tornear, *v.t.* to shape by turning. — *v.i.* to turn, wind, go round; to tilt at tournaments; (*fig.*) to meditate, muse.

torneo, *n.m.* tournament, contest; ancient dance; (*vet.*) sturdy.

tornera, *n.f.* door-keeper in a nunnery.

tornería, *n.f.* turning, turnery.

tornero, *n.m.* turner; lathe-maker; (*prov.*) messenger of a nunnery.

tornés, -esa, *a.* ancient coinage struck in Tours.

tornillero, *n.m.* (*coll.*) deserter.

tornillo, *n.m.* screw; clamp, vice; (*mil.*) deser-

cion; *tornillo de aproximación,* tangent screw; *tornillo de banco,* bench vice; *tornillo sin fin,* worm-gear; (*Cent. Am., Ven.*) medicinal plant of the Bombacaceæ family.

torniquete, *n.m.* tourniquet; turnpike, turnstile; swivel; bell-crank.

torniscón, *n.m.* box, slap, cuff.

torno, *n.m.* wheel, axle-tree; winch, windlass; lathe; carriage-brake; spinning-wheel, spindle; whisket; revolving dumbwaiter; bend in a river; circumvolution, gyration; *en torno,* round about; *torno de hilar,* spinning-wheel.

toro, *n.m.* bull; (*arch.*) ogee moulding; (*astr.*) Taurus. — *pl.* **toros,** bull-fight; *ciertos son los toros,* so then it is true; *echarle a uno el toro,* to say off-hand something disagreeable; *hay toros y cañas,* there is bitter controversy; *pelean los toros, y mal para las ramas,* when fathers fall out, children suffer.

toronja, *n.f.* (*bot.*) grape-fruit, shaddock.

toronjil, *n.m.;* **toronjina,** *n.f.* (*bot.*) balm-gentle.

toronjo, *n.m.* shaddock-tree.

toroso, -sa, *a.* strong, robust.

torozón, *n.m.* gripes.

torpe, *a.* dull, slow, heavy; torpid, stupid; rude, indecorous, infamous, disgraceful; lascivious, unchaste, obscene.

torpedear, *v.t.* to torpedo.

torpedeo, *n.m.* torpedoing.

torpedero, *n.m.* torpedo-boat.

torpedo, *n.m.* torpedo; (*ichth.*) electric ray crampfish; streamlined touring-car; *torpedo automóvil,* self-propelling torpedo; *torpedo de botalón,* spar torpedo; *torpedo de fondo, durmiente* or *flotante,* naval mine.

torpemente, *adv.* obscenely, basely; slowly.

torpeza, *n.f.* rudeness, heaviness, dullness; torpidness, torpor; impurity, unchastity, lewdness, obscenity; want of culture; contemptibleness.

torpor, *n.m.* torpor, numbness.

torrado, *n.m.* toasted chick-pea.

torrar, *v.t.* to toast.

torre, *n.f.* tower, turret; belfry, steeple; castle or rook at chess; belvedere; country-house with garden; *torre de costa,* watch-tower; *torre de viento,* castle in the air; *torre de luces,* (*naut.*) lighthouse.

torrear, *v.t.* to fortify with towers.

torrefacción, *n.f.* torrefaction, toasting.

torreja, *n.f.* (*Am.*) [TORRIJA].

torrejón, *n.m.* ill-shaped turret.

torrencial, *a.* torrent-like, torrential, overpowering.

torrentada, *n.f.* sweep of a torrent, impetuous current.

torrente, *n.m.* torrent; avalanche, rush; plenty, abundance.

torrentera, *n.f.* ravine made by a torrent.

torreón, *n.m.* round fortified tower.

torrero, *n.m.* tower-guard; (*prov.*) farmer; *torrero de faro,* lighthouse-keeper.

torreznada, *n.f.* large dish of rashers.

torreznero, *n.m.* (*coll.*) lazy fellow.

torrezno, *n.m.* rasher of bacon.

tórrido, -da, *a.* torrid, parched, hot.

torrija, *n.f.* fritter, bread soaked in milk and eggs or in wine, then fried and sweetened.

torrontera, *n.f.;* **torrontero,** *n.m.* heap of earth left by a freshet.

tórsalo, *n.m.* (*Cent. Am.*) a parasitic worm which burrows under the skin of man or animals.

torsión, *n.f.* torsion, twist, twisting.

torso, *n.m.* trunk or body.

torta, *n.f.* round cake, tart; (*print.*) font; (*print.*) form kept for distribution; (*coll.*) slap in the face with open hand. — *pl.* **tortas** (**bofetadas**), (*Mex.*) cake of ore; *tortas y pan pintado*, trifles; an easy matter, a cinch; *costar la torta un pan*, to pay dearly for one's game.

tortada, *n.f.* large pie of meat or chicken.

tortedad, *n.f.* twistedness.

tortera, *n.f.* baking-pan; deep dish.

tortero, -ra, *n.m.f.* whorl of a spindle.

tortilla, *n.f.* omelet; (*Mex.*) pancake; *hacerse tortilla*, to break into bits; *volverse la tortilla*, to turn the scale, to take an unexpected course.

tortita, *n.f.* small loaf or cake.

tórtola, *n.f.* turtle-dove.

tortolillo, -lla; -ito, -ita, *n.m.f.* small turtle-dove; sweetheart.

tórtolo, *n.m.* cock turtle-dove; beau, lover.

tortor, *n.m.* (*naut.*) twist; (*naut.*) heaver.

tortozón, *a.* a large grape.

tortuga, *n.f.* tortoise; turtle, green turtle; *paso de tortuga*, snail's pace.

tortuosamente, *adv.* tortuously, circuitously.

tortuosidad, *n.f.* tortuosity, tortuousness, sinuosity.

tortuoso, -sa, *a.* tortuous, winding, sinuous.

tortura, *n.f.* torture, rack; flexure, tortuosity, twistedness, torsion; grief, affliction.

torturar, *v.t.* to torment, torture. — *v.r.* to worry, fret.

toruno, *n.m.* (*Chi.*) ox which has been castrated after his third year.

torva, *n.f.* whirl of snow or rain.

torvisca, *n.f.*; **torvisco,** *n.m.* (*bot.*) flax-leaved daphne.

torvo, -va, *a.* stern, severe, grim, fierce.

torzadillo, *n.m.* thin silk twist.

torzal, *n.m.* silk twist, machine twist; cord; (*Arg.*) lasso or fetterlock made of leather.

torzón, *n.m.* (*vet.*) gripes.

torzonado, -da, *a.* contracted, twisted; (*vet.*) suffering from gripes.

tos, *n.f.* cough; *tos ferina*, whooping-cough.

tosca, *n.f.* (*dent.*) tartar, tophus.

toscamente, *adv.* coarsely, rudely, grossly, clownishly.

tosco, -ca, *a.* rough, coarse, unpolished, uncouth, clownish, ill-bred.

tosegoso, -sa, *a.* coughing greatly.

toser, *v.i.* to cough; *toser a*, to defy, challenge.

tosidura, *n.f.* coughing, act of coughing.

tosigar, *v.t.* (*pret.* **tosigué**; *pres. subj.* **tosigue**) to poison.

tósigo, *n.m.* poison; (*fig.*) pain, grief.

tosigoso, -sa, *a.* poisonous, venomous; coughing.

tosquedad, *n.f.* coarseness, roughness, rudeness, clumsiness.

tostada, *n.f.* toast, toasted bread; (*fig.*) disappointment; *dar* (or *pegar*) *una tostada*, (*coll.*) to cheat, disappoint.

tostado, -da, *a.* toasted, tanned; brown; torrid, parched; (*Ec.*) toasted corn.

tostador, -ra, *n.m.f., a.* toaster, toasting; *n.m.* toaster (utensil).

tostadura, *n.f.* toasting.

tostar, *v.t.* to toast, torrefy, roast; to sunburn, tan; (*Chi.*) to spank, flog.(conj. like COSTAR)

tostón, *n.m.* buttered toast; roasted pea; arrow with a burnt, sharpened point; sucking pig; (*Mex.*) silver coin of 50 cents; (*Bol.*) a silver coin of 30 cents.

total, *n.m.* total, whole, totality, sum, complement. — *a.* total, whole, general, universal.

totalidad, *n.f.* totality, aggregate, completeness.

totalitario, -ria, *a.* totalitarian.

totalmente, *adv.* totally, wholly, fully.

totem, *n.m.* totem.

totemismo, *n.m.* totemism.

totí, *n.m.* (*Cub.*) a black bird.

totilimundi, *n.m.* raree-show.

totolate, *n.m.* (*CR.*) chicken louse.

totoloque, *n.m.* (*Mex.*) an ancient Indian game; game of quoits.

totoposte, *n.m.* (*Cent. Am., Mex.*) corn-cake or biscuit.

totora, *n.f.* (*S. Am.*) cat-tail or red mace.

totuma, *n.f.* (*Am.*) cup made from a calabash.

totumo, *n.m.* (*S. Am.*) calabash tree.

toxicar, *v.t.* (conjugated like BUSCAR) to poison.

tóxico, *n.m.* poison.

tóxico, -ca, *a.* toxic, poisonous.

toxicología, *n.f.* toxicology.

toxicológico, -ca, *a.* toxicological.

toxina, *n.f.* (*med.*) toxin.

toza, *n.f.* log, block of wood, stump; piece of bark.

tozal, *n.m.* (*prov.*) summit, peak.

tozalbo, -ba, *a.* white-faced (cattle).

tozar, *v.i.* (*pret.* **tocé**; *pres. subj.* **toce**) to butt with the head; to contend foolishly.

tozo, -za, *a.* low, small, stumpy, dwarfy.

tozolada, *n.f.*; **tozolón,** *n.m.* stroke or blow on the neck.

tozudo, -da, *a.* obstinate, stubborn.

tozuelo, *n.m.* fat part of the neck (of an animal).

traba, *n.f.* ligament, ligature; tie, bond, brace, clasp; impediment, hindrance, obstacle; hobble, clog, fetterlock, fetter, trammel, shackle; lintel, beam.

trabacuenta, *n.f.* mistake, error (in accounts); difference, dispute, controversy.

trabadero, *n.m.* pastern of a horse.

trabado, -da, *a.* joined, connected, braced; thickened, inspissated; strong, robust; (horse) with two white fore-feet. — *p.p.* [TRABAR].

trabadura, *n.f.* bond, junction, union, bracing.

trabajadamente, *adv.* laboriously.

trabajado, -da, *a.* laboured; wrought, machined; tired, weary.

trabajador, -ra, *a.* labouring, painstaking. — *n.m.f.* worker, operative, hand, labourer.

trabajante, *a.* toiling, working.

trabajar, *v.t., v.i.* to work, labour, travail, toil; to manufacture; to till (the soil); to form, shape; to endeavour, contend; to execute, act; to busy oneself; to procure, solicit; to vex, worry, molest, harass; to undergo a strain.

trabajo, *n.m.* work, toil, labour; difficulty, impediment, obstacle, hindrance; fatigue, painfulness, hardship, trouble, trial; occupation, business, task, drudgery; piece of work. — *pl.* **trabajos,** trials; poverty, misery; *trabajo de manos*, manual work, handiwork; *trabajo* *de punto*, knitting; *día de trabajo*, working-day; *trabajos forzados*, hard labour; *cercar a trabajo* (or *de trabajos*) *a uno*, to heap misfortunes on a person; *trabajo le mando*, I warn you it will need some work.

trabajosamente, *adv.* laboriously, difficultly, painfully.

trabajoso, -sa, *a.* laborious, hard, painful; elaborate, overwrought, contrived; sickly, ailing.

trabajuelo, *n.m.* slight work, labour or hardship.

trabal, *a.* clasping.

trabalenguas, *n.m.* tongue-twister, jawbreaker.

trabamiento, *n.m.* joining, uniting, bracing, bond.

trabanco, *n.m.* piece of wood attached to a dog's collar.

trabar, *v.t.* to join, clasp, brace, fasten, bind, connect, unite; to seize, grab, grasp, take hold of; to fetter, shackle; to begin, set about; to thicken, inspissate; to make agree, harmonize; to set the teeth of a saw; *trabar amistad*, to become friends; *trabar batalla*, to combat; *trabar conversación*, to enter upon a long conversation; *trabar conocimiento*, to scrape acquaintance; *trabar ejecución*, (*law*) to distrain; *trabarse la lengua*, to stammer; *trabarse de palabras*, to become angry in a dispute; (*Am.*) to stammer, to be tongue-tied.

trabazón, *n.f.* juncture, connexion, coalescence, union, bracing, bond.

trabe, *n.f.* beam.

trabilla, *n.f.* small clasp or tie; guitar-strap; gaiter-strap; dropped stitch in knitting.

trabón, *n.m.* fetter for horse's foot.

trabuca, *n.f.* fire-cracker.

trabucación, *n.f.* confusion; mistake, blunder.

trabucador, -ra, *n.m.f.* disturber, interrupter, blunderer.

trabucante, *a.* preponderating; blundering, confusing.

trabucar, *v.t.* (*pret.* **trabuqué**; *pres. subj.* **trabuque**) to upset, overturn; to mix up, confound, mistake; to derange, perturbate; to cut the thread of a discourse, interrupt a conversation. — *v.r.* to mistake, equivocate; to become confused.

trabucazo, *n.m.* shot with a blunderbuss; report of a blunderbuss; (*coll.*) sudden shock or fright.

trabuco, *n.m.* blunderbuss, catapult.

trabuquete, *n.m.* catapult; (*naut.*) seine.

traca, *n.f.* (*naut.*) strake.

trácala, *n.f.* (*Mex., PR.*) scheme, trick, artifice.

tracalada, *n.f.* (*Am.*) multitude, large number.

tracalero, -ra, *a.* (*Mex.*) tricky, artful.

tracamundana, *n.f.* (*coll.*) barter of trifles; noisy wrangles, hubbub.

tracción, *n.f.* traction, draught; cartage; tensile stress.

tracería, *n.f.* (*arch.*) tracery.

tracias, *n.m.* north-north-west wind.

tracio, -cia, *a.* Thracian.

tracista, *n.m.* planner, designer; projector; intriguer, schemer.

tracoma, *n.f.* trachoma.

tracto, *n.m.* stretch, lapse, space of time; tract sung at Mass.

tractocarril, *n.m.* car or train that can run on a road or on rails.

tractor, *n.m.* tractor; traction engine; *tractor oruga*, caterpillar tractor.

tradición, *n.f.* tradition; (*law*) formal delivery of property.

tradicional, *a.* traditional.

tradicionalismo, *n.m.* traditionalism.

tradicionalista, *n.m.f.* traditionalist.

tradicionalmente, *adv.* traditionally.

traducción, *n.f.* translation, version, interpretation.

traducible, *a.* translatable.

traducir, *v.t.* (*pres. indic.* **traduzco**; *pres. subj.* **traduzca**; *pret.* **traduje**) to translate, interpret.

traductor, -ra, *n.m.f.* translator.

traedizo, -za, *a.* portable.

traedor, -ra, *n.m.f.* carrier, porter.

traer, *v.t.* (*pres. part.* **trayendo**; *past part.* **traído**; *pres. indic.* **traigo**; *pret.* **traje**; *pres. subj.* **traiga**) to bring, bring over, carry, fetch; to lead, conduct, assign, cause; to attract, draw towards oneself; to contract, manage; to use, wear; to bring about, occasion; to handle; to oblige, compel; to quote (authority); to reduce; to persuade, prevail upon; to bind; to be engaged in, carry on. — *v.r.* to be dressed; to carry oneself; *traer a mal traer*, to vex, disturb, trouble; *traer a cuento*, to turn the conversation round to a point desired; *traer a la mano*, to fetch or carry; *traer entre ojos*, to be suspicious of; *traer en bocas* (or *lenguas*) to censure, speak ill of; *traer perdido a*, to enamour, to be the ruin of; *traer al retortero*, to lead from place to place, *or* to overwork, *or* to lead up the garden path; *traer y llevar cuentos*, to carry tales backwards and forwards.

traeres, *n.m.pl.* ornaments, finery.

trafagador, *n.m.* trafficker, dealer, trader.

trafagante, *a.* trafficking, dealing, trading.

trafagar, *v.i.* (*pret.* **trafagué**; *pres. subj.* **trafague**) to traffic, trade; to travel.

tráfago, *n.m.* traffic, trade, commerce, business; drudgery.

trafagón, -ona, *a.* active, industrious. — *n.m.f.* hustler.

trafalgar, *n.m.* cotton lining.

trafalmeja, -jas, *n.m.f., a.* rowdy, noisy and silly.

traficación, *n.f.* traffic, trade, commerce.

traficante, *n.m.f., a.* merchant, trader.

traficar, *v.i.* (*pret.* **trafiqué**; *pres. subj.* **trafique**) to traffic, trade; to travel, journey.

tráfico, *n.m.* commerce, trade, traffic.

trafulla, *n.f.* (*coll.*) cheating, swindling.

tragacanta, *n.f.* milk-vetch, goat's-thorn.

tragacanto, *n.m.* tragacanth, a whitish or reddish demulcent gum.

tragacete, *n.m.* javelin, dart.

tragaderas, *n.f.pl.* gullet; *tener buenas tragaderas*, to be very credulous.

tragadero, *n.m.* œsophagus, gullet; pit, gulf, vortex; (*naut.*) trough (of the sea).

tragador, -ra, *n.m.f.* glutton, gobbler.

tragahombres, *n.m.* (*coll.*) bully, hector.

tragaldabas, *n.m.* (*coll.*) glutton.

tragaleguas, *n.m.* (*coll.*) great walker, brisk walker.

tragaluz, *n.f.* skylight.

tragamallas, *n.m.* (*coll.*) gormandizer, glutton.

tragantada, *n.f.* large draught of liquor.

tragante, *a.* swallowing. — *n.m.* top opening of a furnace.

tragantón, -ona, *a.* gluttonous, voracious.

tragantona, *n.f.* (*coll.*) plentiful spread, banquet; swallowing or forcing down the throat; (*fig.*) hard pill to swallow.

tragar, *v.t.* (*pret.* **tragué;** *pres. subj.* **trague**) to swallow, devour, glut, engulf. — *v.r.* to swallow; to admit, receive, believe; to dissemble; to pocket an insult; *no poder tragar a uno,* to dislike someone greatly; *tragar el anzuelo,* to swallow the bait, fall for it.

tragasantos, *n.m.f.* (*contempt.*) churchy, sanctimonious.

tragavenado, *n.f.* (*Ven.*) kind of boa (serpent).

tragavirotes, *n.m.* (*coll.*) conceited stiff man, 'stuffed shirt.'

tragazón, *n.f.* voracity, gluttony.

tragedia, *n.f.* tragedy, tragic event, catastrophe, calamity.

trágicamente, *adv.* tragically.

trágico, -ca, *a.* tragic, disastrous, calamitous. — *n.m.f.* tragedian, tragedienne.

tragicomedia, *n.f.* tragi-comedy.

tragicómico, -ca, *a.* tragi-comical.

trago, *n.m.* drink, draught of liquor, swallow, gulp; adversity, calamity, misfortune; (*anat.*) tragus; *a tragos,* slowly, gently, by degrees; *echar un trago,* to take a drink.

tragón, -ona, *n.m.f.* glutton.

tragón, -ona, *a.* gluttonous, voracious, ravenous.

tragonear, *v.t.* (*coll.*) to eat ravenously.

tragonería, *n.f.* gluttony.

tragontina, *n.f.* arum.

traguillo, -ito, *n.m.* short drink.

traición, *n.f.* treason, disloyalty, treachery, faithlessness; *a traición,* treasonably, treacherously; *alta traición,* high treason; *la traición aplace, mas no el que la hace,* even he who profits by treason, hates the traitor.

traicionar, *v.t.* to do treason; to betray.

tracionero, -ra, *a.* treasonous, treacherous.

traída, *n.f.* carriage, conduction.

traído, -da, *a.* brought, fetched, carried; worn, used, threadbare. — *p.p.* [TRAER].

traidor, *n.m.* traitor, betrayer.

traidor, -ra, *a.* treacherous, traitorous, perfidious, false, disloyal, faithless; insidious, deceitful.

traidora, *n.f.* traitress.

traidoramente, *adv.* treacherously, treasonably, traitorously, perfidiously.

traigo; traiga, *pres. indic.; pres. subj.* [TRAER].

trailla, *n.f.* leash, lash; pack-thread; road-scraper, road-leveller; levelling harrow.

traillar, *v.t.* to level (ground).

traína, *n.f.* seine for deep-sea fishing.

trainera, *n.f.* smack for sardine fishing.

traiña, *n.f.* net for sardine fishing.

traite, *n.m.* raising a nap on cloth.

traje, *n.m.* garb, clothes, dress, habit, apparel, suit, costume; mask; *traje de etiqueta,* full dress *or* evening dress; *traje de luces,* bullfighter's garb; *baile de trajes,* fancy-dress ball; *traje de frac,* full evening dress; *traje charro,* (*Mex.*) showy riding costume.

trajear, *v.t.* to clothe.

trajín, *n.m.* carriage; going to and fro.

trajinante, *n.m.* carrier of goods.

trajinar, *v.t.* to cart, transport (goods). — *v.i.* to fidget about; to travel to and fro.

trajinería, *n.f.* carrying trade; express.

trajinero, *n.m.* carrier.

tralla, *n.f.* cord, bass-weed rope; whip-lash.

trama, *n.f.* weft, woof of cloth; twisted silk; fraud, plot, deceit, machination, imposition; (*theat.*) plot, argument of a play or novel.

tramador, -ra, *n.m.f.* weaver; plotter, contriver, deceiver, hatcher.

tramar, *v.t.* to weave; to plot, hatch, contrive. — *v.i.* to blossom (of olive-trees).

tramilla, *n.f.* twine.

tramitación, *n.f.* procedure; transaction, action.

tramitar, *v.t.* to carry through, transact.

trámite, *n.m.* path, transit, passage; (*law*) procedure; business transaction; step.

tramo, *n.m.* morsel, piece; parcel of ground; flight of stairs; panel of a bridge.

tramojo, *n.m.* band for tying the sheaf; trouble, affliction; (*Am.*) tether.

tramontana, *n.f.* north wind; vanity, pride, haughtiness; *perder la tramontana,* to be mad with passion.

tramontano, -na, *a.* transmontane, ultramontane.

tramontar, *v.i.* to pass beyond the mountains; to sink behind the mountains (of the sun). — *v.t.* to fly, flee, escape.

tramoya, *n.f.* machinery in theatres; craft, trick, artifice, wile.

tramoyista, *n.m.* theatre machinist; scene-shifter; stage carpenter, stage hand; swindler, impostor, deceiver.

trampa, *n.f.* trap, snare, pitfall; trap-door; flap or spring door; falling board of a counter; fraud, deceit, trick, chicane, malpractice, stratagem; bad debt; *coger en la trampa,* to surprise in the act (of a crime); *caer en la trampa,* to fall into the trap; *llevarse la trampa,* to fail, miscarry (of an affair, business, etc.).

trampal, *n.m.* quagmire, bog.

trampantojo, *n.m.* (*coll.*) trick, deception.

trampazo, *n.m.* last twist of a cord (in tortures).

trampeador, -ra, *n.m.f., a.* borrower, swindler, sharper, cheat.

trampear, *v.t., v.i.* to swindle, deceive, cheat, impose upon, practise trickery, obtain money by false pretences; to pull through, get along.

trampería, *n.f.* trickery, cheating, chicanery.

trampilla, *n.f.* peep-hole; door of a kitchen-stove; front flap of trousers.

trampista, *n.m.* cheat, swindler, impostor, card-sharper.

trampolín, *n.m.* spring-board.

tramposo, -sa, *n.m.f.* cheat, swindler, trickster. — *a.* deceitful, tricky, swindling.

tranca, *n.f.* bar across a door or window; transverse bar, cross-bar; club, cudgel, truncheon; (*coll.*) drunken condition, drunkenness.

trancada, *n.f.* long stride; blow with a stick; *en dos trancadas,* in a trice.

trancahílo, *n.m.* surgeon's knot.

trancanil, *n.m.* (*naut.*) waterway.

trancar, *v.i.* (*pret.* **tranqué;** *pres. subj.* **tranque**) to take long strides. — *v.t.* to bar (a door, window, etc.).

trancazo, *n.m.* blow with a bar; (*coll.*) influenza, grippe; (*Col., coll.*) fisticuff.

trance, *n.m.* danger, peril; critical moment; last stage of life; (*law*) legal seizure on an execution; *a todo trance*, resolutely, at any price.

trancelín, *n.m.* hatband of gold or silver garnished with precious stones.

tranco, *n.m.* long stride; threshold; *a trancos*, in haste; *en dos trancos*, swiftly, in a moment.

tranchete, *n.m.* (*shoe.*) heel-knife.

trancho, *n.m.* a variety of shad.

tranquera, *n.f.* palisade; (*Am.*) door in a corral palisade.

tranquero, *n.m.* door-jamb, lintel.

tranquil, *n.m.* (*arch.*) plumb line.

tranquilamente, *adv.* quietly, tranquilly, composedly, peacefully.

tranquilar, *v.t.* to check off; to balance (accounts).

tranquilidad, *n.f.* tranquillity, quiet, peace, rest, repose, calmness, reassurance.

tranquilizar, *v.t.* (conjugated like ALZAR) to tranquillize, calm, pacify, appease, quiet, reassure.

tranquilo, -la, *a.* tranquil, quiet, calm, pacific, gentle, placid, easy.

tranquilla, *n.f.* small bar; stop pin or lug; trap, snare, stratagem, artifice, dodge.

tranquillón, *n.m.* maslin, mashlin.

transacción, *n.f.* transaction, adjustment, accommodation, composition, arrangement, dealing.

transalpino, -na, *a.* transalpine.

transandino, -na, *a.* situated beyond the Andes (usually with reference to the Pacific side).

transar, *v.t., v.r.* (*Am.*) to compromise, adjust, settle.

transatlántico, -ca, *a.* transatlantic.

transatlántico, *n.m.* transatlantic steamer.

transbordador, -ra, *a.* transhipping, transferring. — *n.m.* ferry.

transbordar, *v.t.* (*naut.*) to tranship, transport, transfer.

transbordo, *n.m.* transhipment, transportation, transfer.

transcendencia, *n.f.* transcendence.

transcendental, *a.* transcendental.

transcendente, *n.m.* transcendent.

transcender, *v.t., v.i.* to transcend.

transcribir, *v.t.* (conjugated like ESCRIBIR) to transcribe, copy, recopy.

transcripción, *n.f.* transcription; transcript, copy, copying.

transcripto, -ta; transcrito, -ta, *p.p. irreg.* [TRANSCRIBIR].

transcurrir, *v.i.* to pass, elapse; to go off, run.

transcurso, *n.m.* lapse, course of time, process of time.

transeúnte, *a.* transient, transitory. — *n.m.f.* sojourner; passer-by.

transferencia, *n.f.* transference.

transferible, *a.* transferable.

transferidor, -ra, *n.m.f.* transferrer.

transferir, *v.t.* (conjugated like REFERIR) to remove, transport; (*law*) to transfer, convey; to employ a word figuratively.

transfigurable, *a.* changeable, transformable.

transfiguración, *n.f.* transformation, transfiguration.

transfigurar, *v.t.* to transform, transfigure. — *v.r.* to be transfigured.

transfijo, -ja, *a.* transfixed.

transfixión, *n.f.* transfixion.

transflor, *n.m.* enamel painting.

transflorar, transflorear, *v.t.* to paint or decorate in enamel.

transflorar, *v.t.* to trace. — *v.i.* to show through.

transformación, *n.f.* transformation, metamorphosis, change.

transformador, -ra, *n.m.f.* transformer, metamorphoser; *transformador de aceite*, oil-cooled transformer; *transformador de anillo*, ring transformer; *transformador de tensión*, voltage transformer; *transformador de reducción*, step-down transformer.

transformar, *v.t.* to transform, transmute, transfigure. — *v.r.* to assume different manners or sentiments.

transformativo, -va, *a.* transformative.

transformista, *n., a.* transformist; (*theat.*) impersonator playing several characters in rapid mutation.

transfregar, *v.t.* (conjugated like FREGAR) to rub, scrub.

transfretano, -na, *a.* transmarine.

transfretar, *v.t.* to cross an arm of the sea. — *v.i.* to spread, extend.

tránsfuga, tránsfugo, *n.m.* deserter, fugitive, runaway, turncoat.

transfundir, *v.t.* to pour into, transfuse; to communicate, transmit.

transfusión, *n.f.* transfusion; communication, transmission; *transfusión de la sangre*, (*med.*) blood-transfusion.

transfusor, *n., a.* transfuser.

transgredir, *v.t. defect.* to transgress (the only verb-forms used are those having i in their endings).

transgresión, *n.f.* transgression, law-breaking, sin, trespass, offence.

transgresor, -ra, *n.m.f.* transgressor, offender.

transición, *n.f.* transition, removal, change.

transido, -da, *a.* worn out (with grief, etc.), exhausted, famished; avaricious, mean.

transigencia, *n.f.* broad-mindedness, tolerance.

transigente, *a.* accommodating, tolerant, broad-minded.

transigir, *v.t.* (*ind.* **transijo**; *subj.* **transija**) to come to an understanding or a compromise. — *v.i.* to be broad-minded, to compromise.

transitable, *a.* passable, that may be passed through.

transitar, *v.i.* to travel, journey, pass by.

transitivo, -va, *a.* (*gram.*) transitive; (*law*) transferable.

tránsito, *n.m.* passage, transit, transition; removal, change; stopping-place; road; inn; death, passing away of holy persons, especially that of the Virgin Mary; *hacer tránsitos*, to rest at intervals.

transitoriamente, *adv.* transitorily.

transitorio, -ria, *a.* transitory, perishable.

translación, *n.f.* translation, version; move, removal.

translaticiamente, *adv.* metaphorically.

translaticio, -cia, *a.* metaphorical, translatory.

translimitar, *v.t.* to pass beyond the boundary; to go beyond the limits of morality, reason, etc.

translinear, *v.i.* (*law*) to pass from one line of heirs to another.

translucidez, *n.f.* translucence.

translucido, -da, *a.* translucent.

transmarino, -na, *a.* transmarine.

transmigración, *n.f.* transmigration.

transmigrar, *v.i.* to transmigrate.

transminar, *v.t.* to undermine.

transmisibilidad, *n.f.* transmissibility.

transmisible, *a.* transmissible.

transmisión, *n.f.* transmission, transmittal.

transmisor, -ra, *a.* transmitting; *n.m.* (*wire.* and *elec.*) transmitter.

transmitir, *v.t.* to transfer, transmit, make over, convey.

transmudación, transmutación, transmudamiento, *n.m.f.* transmutation, change.

transmudar, *v.t., v.r.* to move to another place; to change, transform, transplant; to convince, persuade.

transmutable, *a.* transmutable, convertible.

transmutación, *n.f.* transmutation.

transmutar, *v.t., v.r.* to transmute.

transmutativo, -va; transmutatorio, -ria, *a.* that which transmutes.

transparencia, *n.f.* transparency, diaphaneity, clearness.

transparentarse, *v.r.* to be transparent, shine through.

transparente, *a.* transparent, limpid, lucid, clear, fine. — *n.m.* altar window; window-shade.

transpirable, *a.* transpirable, perspirable.

transpiración, *n.f.* transpiration, perspiration.

transpirar, *v.i.* to transpire, perspire.

transpirenaico, -ca, *a.* beyond the Pyrenees.

transponer, *v.t.* (conjugated like PONER) to transpose; to transport, transfer; to transplant. — *v.r.* to hide behind (or round the corner); to set below the horizon (the sun, etc.); to be sleepy.

transportación, *n.f.* transportation, carriage, conveyance.

transportador, -ra, *a.* transporting, carrying. — *n.m.* transporter, carrier; (*geom.*) protractor; (*rail.*) ropeway.

transportamiento, *n.m.* transportation, carriage; transport, ecstasy.

transportar, *v.t.* to transport, convey, remove; (*mus.*) to transpose. — *v.r.* to be in a transport, carried away; *estar transportado con,* (*met.*) to be wrapped up in.

transporte, *n.m.* transport, transportation, conveyance; transport ship; fit (of anger, etc.).

transposición, *n.f.* transposition, transposal.

transpuesto, -ta, *p.p. irreg. of* TRANSPONER.

transterminante, *a.* transgressing.

transterminar, *v.t.* to transgress, trespass, go over the border (of a district or country).

transubstanciación, *n.f.* transubstantiation.

transubstancial, *a.* converted into another substance.

transubstanciar, *v.t.* to transubstantiate.

transvasar, *v.t.* to decant.

transverberación, *n.f.* transfixion.

transversal, *a.* transversal.

transversalmente, *adv.* transversally, collaterally.

transverso, -sa, *a.* transverse.

tranvía, *n.m.* tramway.

tranviario, -ria; tranviero, -ra, *n.m.f.* tramway employee. — *a.* relating to tramways.

tranza, *n.f.* (*law*) seizure in an execution.

tranzadera, *n.f.* knot of plaited cords or ribbons.

tranzar, *v.t.* (*pret.* **trancé**; *pres. subj.* **trance**) to cut, truncate; to plait, weave, braid; (*prov.*) to auction, knock down.

tranzón, *n.m.* clearing in a forest.

trapa, *n.f.* (*naut.*) spilling-line; noise made by bawling or stamping with the feet. — *pl.* **trapas,** (*naut.*) relieving-tackle.

trapacear, *v.i.* to deceive artfully.

trapacería, *n.f.* deceit, fraud, counterfeit.

trapacero, -ra, *n.m.f., a.* sharper, swindler, impostor, deceiver; deceiving, fraudulent, false.

trapacete, *n.m.* daybook.

trapacista, *n.m.* cheater, sharper, deceiver.

trapajo, *n.m.* rag, tatter.

trapajoso, -sa, *a.* ragged, tattered.

trápala, *n.f.* stamping with the feet; galloping noise (of a horse); confusion; (*coll.*) deceit. — *n.m.* garrulity, loquacity. — *n.m.f.* (*coll.*) prattler; cheat, humbug.

trapalear, *v.i.* to babble, be loquacious.

trapalón, -ona, *n.m.f., a.* loquacious, deceitful.

trapaza, *n.f.* fraud; trick.

trape, *n.m.* buckram.

trapecio, *n.m.* (*geom.*) trapezium; trapeze.

trapense, *n.m.* Trappist.

trapería, *n.f.* frippery; rag-fair; woollen-drapers' shop or quarter.

trapero, -ra, *n.m.f.* rag-and-bone dealer; rag picker.

trapezoide, *n.m.* (*anat.*) trapezium; (*geom.*) trapezoid.

trapico, *n.m.* little rag.

trapiche, *n.m.* sugar-mill; olive-press; (*Cub.*) small sugar plantation; (*Arg., Chi.*) grinding-machinery.

trapichear, *v.i.* (*coll.*) to retail; to contrive, shift, find a way.

trapicheo, *n.m.* (*coll.*) contriving, shifting.

trapichero, -ra, *n.m.f.* worker in a sugar mill.

trapiento, -ta, *a.* ragged, tattered.

trapillo, *n.m.* little rag; poor or ill-placed lover; small amount of money saved; *estar de trapillo,* to be in deshabille.

trapío, *n.m.* all the sails of a ship, canvas; lively manner; fine appearance and spirit of the fighting-bull.

trapisonda, *n.f.* (*coll.*) bustle, noise, clatter, confusion; snare, deception; (*naut.*) white-caps.

trapisondear, *v.i.* (*coll.*) to foment brawls; to cheat, deceive.

trapito, *n.m.* little rag, tatter; *los trapitos de cristianar,* best Sunday clothes.

trapo, *n.m.* cloth; rag, tatter; sails of a ship; bullfighter's cloak; *con un trapo atrás y otro adelante,* in a miserable condition; *a todo trapo,* with all one's might; efficiently; (*naut.*) with all sails unfurled; *poner como un trapo,* to reprimand severely; *sacar (todos) los trapos a la colada* (or *a relucir*), to make (all) one's faults public property; *soltar el trapo,* to burst out (crying or laughing).

traque, *n.m.* crack of a bursting rocket; fuse of a firework; *a traque barraque,* (*coll.*) all the time, non-stop; whatever the motive.

tráquea, *n.f.* trachea, windpipe.

traqueal, *a.* tracheal.

traquear, *v.i.* to crack, make a loud noise. — *v.t.* to shake, agitate, move to and fro; to handle too much; to frequent.

traqueo, *n.m.* shaking, moving to and fro; noise of artificial fireworks.

traqueotomía, *n.f.* tracheotomy.

traquetear, *v.i., v.t.* to agitate, jolt, move to and fro, handle roughly; to crack (as fireworks or wood).

traqueteo, *n.m.* shaking, jolting, concussion; cracking, creaking.

traquido, *n.m.* report of fire-arms; noise of breaking or splitting wood.

traquita, *n.m.* trachyte.

trarigüe, *n.m.* (*Chi.*) Indian black, red and white belt.

trarilongo, *n.m.* (*Chi.*) Indian head band.

traro, *n.m.* (*Chi.*) a bird of prey.

tras, *prep.* after, behind; beyond; besides. — *n.m.* (*coll.*) behind, backside; knock, rap; *no tener tras que parar*, to be extremely poor.

trasalcoba, *n.f.* alcove behind a recess; dressing-room.

trasalpino, -na, *a.* beyond the Alps.

trasaltar, *n.m.* altar-screen.

trasandino, -na, *a.* transandine, at the other side of the Andes.

trasanteanoche, *adv.* three nights ago.

trasanteayer, *adv.* three days ago.

trasantier, *adv.* (*coll.*) three days ago.

trasañejo, -ja, *a.* three years old.

trasbordo, *n.m.* transhipment; transfer, change (of passengers).

trasca, *n.f.* leather thong.

trascabo, *n.m.* a leg-hold (in wrestling).

trascantón, *n.m.* corner curb-stone; street porter; *dar trascantón*, to hide behind a corner; to shake off; to leave in the lurch.

trascartarse, *v.r.* to remain unplayed (as a trump card).

trascendencia, *n.f.* transcendency; consequence, result.

trascendental, *a.* transcendental; far-reaching; very important.

trascendentalismo, *n.m.* transcendentalism.

trascendente, *a.* transcendent.

trascender, *v.i.* (*pres. indic.* **trasciendo**; *pres. subj.* **trascienda**) to transcend, go beyond, pass beyond, rise above; to extend itself; to emit a strong and pleasant scent; to exhale, be pervasive; (*fig.*) to leak out, transpire. — *v.t.* to penetrate, scrutinize, find out.

trascendido, -da, *a., p.p.* acute.

trascocina, *n.f.* larder; back kitchen.

trascolar, *v.t.* (conjugated like COLAR) to percolate, strain; (*coll.*) to pass over a mountain.

trasconejarse, *v.r.* to squat, to sheer off (of pursued game); to be missing, mislaid.

trascordarse, *v.r.* (conjugated like ACORDAR) to forget.

trascoro, *n.m.* space behind the choir.

trascorral, *n.m.* backyard; (*coll.*) breech, the posteriors.

trascribir, *v.t.* (*p.p.* **trascripto, trascrito**) to transcribe, copy.

trascripción, *n.f.* transcription.

trascuarto, *n.m.* back room; rear apartment.

trascurso, *n.m.* course of time, process of time.

trasdobladura, *n.f.* trebling.

trasdoblar, *v.t.* to treble, triple.

trasdoblo, *n.m.* treble number.

trasdós, *n.m.* (*arch.*) extrados.

trasdosear, *v.t.* to strengthen the back of an arch.

trasechador, *n.m.* waylayer, ensnarer.

trasechar, *v.t.* to ensnare, waylay.

trasegador, *n.m.* one who racks wine.

trasegar, *v.t., v.i.* (conjugated like SEGAR) to overset, turn upside down; to change the place of; to decant, rack (wine).

traseñalador, -ra, *n.m.f.* one who counter-marks.

traseñalar, *v.t.* to mark anew.

trasera, *n.f.* back part, croup.

trasero, -ra, *a.* remaining behind, coming after; hinder, back, rear.

trasero, *n.m.* buttock, rump. — *pl.* **traseros**, (*coll.*) ancestors, predecessors.

trasferidor, *n.m.* transferrer.

trasferir, *v.t.* (*pres. indic.* **trasfiero**; *pres. subj.* **trasfiera**) to transfer [TRANSFERIR].

trasfigurable, *a.*; **trasfiguración**, *n.f.*; **trasfigurar**, *v.t.* [TRANSFIGURABLE].

trasformación, *n.f.* transformation, metamorphosis [TRANSFORMACIÓN].

trasformador, *n.m.* transformer.

trasformamiento, *n.m.* transformation.

trasformar, *v.t.* to transform.

trasfregar, *v.t.* (conjugated like FREGAR) to rub.

trasfretano, -na, *a.* transmarine [TRANSFRETANO].

trásfuga, trásfugo, *n.m.* deserter, fugitive [TRÁNSFUGA].

trasfundición, *n.f.* transfusion.

trasfundir, *v.t.* to transfuse [TRANSFUNDICIÓN].

trasfusión, *n.f.* transfusion [TRANSFUSIÓN].

trasgo, *n.m.* goblin, hobgoblin, sprite.

trasgredir, *v.t.* to transgress [TRANSGREDIR].

trasgresión, *n.f.* transgression, fault, crime.

trasgresor, -ra, *n.m.f.* transgressor, law-breaker.

trasguear, *v.i.* to play the hobgoblin.

trashoguero, *n.m.* back of fireplace; yule-log.

trashoguero, -ra, *a.* idling. — *n.m.f.* idler, loiterer.

trashojar, *v.t.* to turn over the leaves of a book; to glance at a book.

trashumante, *a.* nomadic (of flocks).

trashumar, *v.t.* to move flocks from winter to summer pastures or vice-versa.

trasiego, *n.m.* removal, moving; decanting of liquors.

trasiego; trasiegue, *pres. indic.; pres. subj.* [TRASEGAR].

trasijado, -da, *a.* lank, meagre; of sunken cheeks.

traslación, trasladación, *n.f.* transfer, moving, removal; change of position; adjournment, postponement; version in another language.

trasladador, -ra, *n.m.f.* carrier, mover.

trasladar, *v.t.* to transport, move, remove; to transcribe, translate; to postpone, adjourn.

traslado, *n.m.* copy, imitation; transcript, transcription; likeness, resemblance, counterpart; (*law*) communication, notification.

traslapar, *v.t.* to superpose, overlap.

traslapo, *n.m.* overlapping.

traslaticiamente, *adv.* metaphorically, figuratively.

traslaticio, -cia; traslato, -ta, *a.* metaphorical, figurative.

traslativo, -va, *a.* transferring, conveying.

trasloar, *v.t.* to praise fulsomely.

traslucidez, *n.f.* transparency, clearness.

traslucido, -da, *a.* transparent, pellucid.

trasluciente, *a.* transparent, translucent.

traslucirse, *v.r.* (conjugated like LUCIR) to shine through, be transparent; to conjecture, infer, be inferred.

traslumbramiento, *n.m.* dazzling, dazzlement.

traslumbrar, *v.t.* to dazzle. — *v.r.* to pass swiftly; to vanish; to be dazzled.

trasluz, *n.m.* light passing through a transparent body; reflected or borrowed light; (*art*) transverse light; *al trasluz*, against the light.

trasmallo, *n.m.* trammel net; hammer-handle; iron collar round a hammer head.

trasmano, *n.m.* second player at cards; *a trasmano*, out of the way, off the beaten track.

trasmañana, *n.f.* day after tomorrow.

trasmañanar, *v.t.* to procrastinate.

trasmarino, -na, *a.* transmarine, oversea.

trasmatar, *v.t.* (*coll.*) to assume that oneself will outlive someone else.

trasmigración, *n.f.* transmigration [TRANSMIGRACIÓN].

trasmigrar, *v.i.* to transmigrate.

trasminar, *v.t.* to excavate, undermine; to penetrate, percolate, pierce. — *v.r.* to penetrate, pierce.

trasmisible, *a.* transmissive [TRANSMISIBLE].

trasmisión, *n.f.* transmission.

trasmontar, *v.t.* to pass beyond the mountains.

trasmosto, *n.f.* wine of low quality.

trasmudar, *v.t.* to move, remove, transport [TRANSMUDAR].

trasmutable, *a.* transmutable [TRANSMUTABLE].

trasmutación, *n.f.* transmutation.

trasmutar, *v.t.* to transmute, convert, alter.

trasmutativo, -va; trasmutatorio, -ria, *a.* transmutative.

trasnochada, *n.f.* last night; watch; sleepless night; night attack.

trasnochado, -da, *a.* having watched the whole night; fatigued through watching; care-worn, haggard, worn out, stale; hackneyed, trite.

trasnochador, -ra, *n.m.f.* night-watcher; keeping late hours; (*coll.*) night hawk.

trasnochar, *v.i.* to watch, sit up a whole night, spend the night. — *v.t.* to sleep on a thing, leave it for the next day.

trasnoche, trasnocho, *n.m.* night watch, vigil.

trasnombrar, *v.t.* to change or confuse names.

trasoír, *v.t.* to misunderstand, mistake.

trasojado, -da, *a.* having sunken eyes, worn out, care-worn, emaciated.

trasoñar, *v.i.* (conjugated like SOÑAR) to conceive a visionary idea or supposition as in a dream.

trasovado, -da, *a.* (*bot.*) obovate.

traspalar, *v.t.* to shovel, remove with a shovel; to hoe, weed.

traspaleo, *n.m.* shovelling, hoeing, weeding.

traspapelarse, *v.r.* to be mislaid among other papers.

trasparencia, *n.f.* transparency [TRANSPARENCIA].

trasparentarse, *v.r.* to be transparent.

trasparente, *a.* transparent.

traspasador, -ra, *n.m.f.* trespasser, transgressor.

traspasamiento, *n.m.* transgression, trespass; crossing over (a river); transfixion; transfer; (*fig.*) grief, anguish.

traspasar, *v.t.* to cross, go beyond, pass over; to remove, transfer, transport; to transfix, pierce through; to cross, repass; to return; to convey, transfer; to assign; to trespass, transgress, violate; to exceed proper bounds; to cause great affliction.

traspaso, *n.m.* conveyance, transfer; assignment; transgression, trespass; grief, anguish.

traspatio, *n.m.* (*Per.*) an inner patio.

traspecho, *n.m.* bone ornament on a crossbow.

traspeinar, *v.t.* to comb lightly over.

traspellar, *v.t.* to shut, close.

traspié, *n.m.* leg-hold in wrestling; stumble, slip; *dar traspiés*, to slip up, commit errors.

traspillar, *v.t.* to close, shut. — *v.r.* to grow thin, become emaciated.

traspintar, *v.t.* to show one card and play another. — *v.r.* to show through; (*coll.*) to turn out contrary to one's expectations.

traspirable, *a.* transpirable.

traspiración, *n.f.* transpiration.

traspirar, *v.t.* to transpire, perspire.

trasplantar, *v.t.* to transplant. — *v.r.* (*fig.*) to migrate.

trasplante, *n.m.* transplantation; migration.

trasponedor, -ra, *n.m.f.* transplanter; transposer [TRANSPONEDOR].

trasponer, *v.t.* (conjugated like PONER) to transpose, transport. — *v.r.* to be drowsy, sleepy; to set below the horizon (of planets).

traspongo; trasponga, *pres. indic.; pres. subj.* [TRASPONER].

traspontín, trasportín, traspuntín, *n.m.* small mattresses, usually three in number, placed across the bed under the ordinary mattress; (*motor.*) tip-seat; (*coll.*) buttocks.

trasportación, *n.f.* transportation, conveyance.

trasportamiento, *n.m.* transportation.

trasportar, *v.t.* to transport.

trasporte, *n.m.* transport.

trasposición, *n.f.* transposition.

traspuesta, *n.f.* transport, removal; corner, nook, turning; concealment; disappearance, flight; lurking-place; back court, backyard, back-door; rear outbuilding.

traspuesto, -ta, *p.p. irreg.* [TRASPONER].

traspunte, *n.m.* prompter.

trasquero, *n.m.* leather-cutter.

trasquiladero, *n.m.* sheep-shearing place.

trasquilador, *n.m.* shearer.

trasquiladura, *n.f.* shearing, clipping, cropping.

trasquilar, *v.t.* to shear sheep; to lop, snip, cut the hair irregularly; to curtail, clip; to diminish.

trasquilimocho, -cha, *a.* (*coll.*) close-cropped.

trasquilón, *n.m.* cut of the shears; clipping, shearing; (*coll.*) money lost through trickery; *a trasquilones*, rudely, irregularly.

trastabillar, *v.i.* to reel; to waver; to stammer.

trastada, *n.f.* (*coll.*) inconsiderate act.

trastazo, *n.m.* (*coll.*) blow, thump, hard whack.

traste, *n.m.* (*mus.*) stop, fret, finger-key (of a guitar); (*prov.*) sample-glass, sampling-cup; (*Am.*, *prov.*) rubbish, lumber; *dar al traste*, to ruin; give up for a bad job; *sin trastes*, in a disorderly way.

trasteado, *n.m.* (*mus.*) set of stops or frets (of a guitar, etc.).

trasteador, -ra, *n.m.f.* one who moves furniture; noisy person.

trastear, *v.t.* to put frets upon the handle of a guitar; to play the guitar well; to play the bull with the red cloak; (*coll.*) to manage with tact. — *v.i.* to move furniture around inside a house; to talk in a lively way.

trastejador, *n.m.* roof tiler.

trastejar, *v.t.* to tile; (*fig.*) to inspect, overhaul.

trastejo, *n.m.* tiling; (*fig.*) continuous and disorderly motion.

trasteo, *n.m.* exciting the bull with a red flag; tactful management of a person or business.

trastería, *n.f.* heap of lumber; (*coll.*) rash action.

trastero, -ra, *n.m.f.* garret, lumber-room.

trastesado, -da, *a.* stiff, hardened.

trastesón, *n.m.* superabundance of milk in the udder of a cow.

trastienda, *n.f.* back-room (of a shop); prudence, foresight, precaution.

trasto, *n.m.* furniture; trash, rubbish; (*theat.*) trick-piece; (*theat.*) transformation scene; movables, luggage; useless person. — *pl.* tools of a trade, implements, utensils; bullfighter's weapons.

trastornable, *a.* movable; reckless, fickle; easily upset.

trastornado, -da, *p.p., a.* upset, topsy-turvy; unbalanced, mad.

trastornador, -ra, *n.m.f.* disturber, subverter.

trastornadura, *n.f.;* **trastornamiento,** *n.m.* overturn, overthrow, upsetting.

trastornar, *v.t.* to overturn, upset, overthrow, reverse; to disturb, disarrange, invert; to cause a rising; to confuse, daze, perplex, trouble; to dissuade.

trastorno, *n.m.* overturn, overthrow, upheaval; disturbance, disorder, confusion; reverse, trouble.

trastrabado, -da, *a.* having the far hind-foot and the near fore-foot white (horse).

trastrabarse, *v.r.* to become fuddled.

trastrabillar, *v.i.* to stumble, to reel; to waver, hesitate; to stammer.

trastrás, *n.m.* last but one (in some children's games).

trastrocamiento, *n.m.* transposition, inversion.

trastrocar, *v.t.* (conjugated like TROCAR) to invert, change the order.

trastrueco, trastrueque, *n.m.* inversion, transposition.

trastuelo, *n.m.* useless little person; worthless utensil, trash.

trastulo, *n.m.* pastime, toy.

trastumbar, *v.t.* to drop; to upset, overturn.

trasudadamente, *adv.* with sweat and fatigue.

trasudar, *v.t.* to perspire, sweat.

trasudor, *n.m.* gentle sweat, perspiration.

trasuntar, *v.t.* to copy, transcribe; to abridge.

trasuntivamente, *adv.* compendiously.

trasunto, *n.m.* copy, transcript, likeness, reproduction, image.

trasvenarse, *v.r.* to be forced from the veins; to be spilled (of blood).

trasver, *v.t.* (conjugated like VER) to see through, glimpse; to see erroneously.

trasversal, *a.* transversal [TRANSVERSAL].

trasversalmente, *adv.* transversally.

trasverso, -sa, *a.* transverse.

trasverter, *v.i.* (conjugated like VERTER) to overflow, run over.

trasvinarse, *v.r.* to leak out (of wine); (*coll.*) to be inferred, surmised.

trasvolar, *v.i.* (conjugated like VOLAR) to fly across.

trata, *n.f.* African slave-trade; *trata de blancas,* white slavery.

tratable, *a.* tractable, ductile; kindly, compliant.

tratadico, -illo, -ito, *n.m.* tract, short treatise.

tratadista, *n.m.f.* author of treatises.

tratado, *n.m.* treaty, compact, convention; treatise, tract, tractate.

tratador, -ra, *n.m.f.* mediator, arbitrator, umpire.

tratamiento, *n.m.* treatment, usage; appellation, style of address, courtesy title; (*med.*) treatment.

tratante, *n.m.* provision dealer, trader, merchant. — *a.* treating.

tratar, *v.t.* to treat (a subject, a person, a patient, a substance); discuss; to confer, consult; to trade, traffic, deal, negotiate; to conduct, handle, touch, manage; to use, treat. — *v.i.* to try, endeavour; to discourse; to deal; to have amorous relations. — *v.r.* to maintain intercourse; to be concerned with; to live (well or ill); *tratar con* (or *por*), (*chem.*) to treat with reagents; *tratar de tú,* to call a person 'thee' and 'thou' (the Spanish familiar form of address); *tratar de Vd.,* to address a person ceremoniously.

trato, *n.m.* treatment, conduct, behaviour; use, usage; address, manner; agreement, pact, deal; trade, commerce, traffic; courtesy title, appellation; conversation, intercourse; communication; *mal trato,* bad conduct, ill usage; *tener buen trato,* to be polite, affable.

traumático, -ca, *a.* traumatic.

traumatismo, *n.m.* traumatism.

traumatología, *n.f.* traumatology.

traversa, *n.f.* (*naut.*) back-stay.

través, *n.m.* slant, slope; reverse, calamity, adversity, misfortune; (*arch.*) cross-beam; (*fort.*) traverse, screen; *de través* (or *al través*), across, athwart; *dar al través,* to be stranded; *dar al través con,* to throw away, destroy, misspend; *por el través,* on the beam.

travesaño, *n.m.* cross-beam, transom, traverse, cross-bar, cross-piece; bolster (of a bed).

travesar, *v.t.* (*pres. indic.* **travieso**; *pres. subj.* **traviese**) to cross.

travesear, *v.i.* to jest, joke; to be quick at repartee; to lead a vicious life; to behave improperly; to skip, caper, frisk, romp; to be mischievous.

travesero, *n.m.* bolster; transom.

travesero, -ra, *a.* transverse.

travesía, *n.f.* oblique or transverse position; passage, crossing, sea voyage; side-road, crossing, cross-road; distance; money lost or won at gambling; (*fort.*) traverse works; (*naut.*) side-wind; sailor's pay for a voyage; (*Arg.*) a vast uninhabited waterless region.

travesío, -sía, *a.* traversing; transverse, oblique (wind).

travesío, *n.m.* cross-road, crossing.

travestido, -da, *a.* disguised.

travesura, *n.f.* trick, wile, prank; frolic, caper, antic, gambol; juggle; lively fancy; sprightly talk; mischief.

traviesa, *n.f.* distance across; (*rail.*) sleeper, cross-tie; (*arch.*) rafter; transverse wall; (*min.*) cross level or gallery.

travieso, -sa, *a.* transverse, cross, oblique; restless, uneasy, flighty; turbulent, noisy; shrewd, acute, cunning; lively, frolicsome, prankish, mischievous; dissolute, lewd.

trayecto, *n.m.* voyage, journey; distance, stage, fare-stage.

trayectoria, *n.f.* trajectory.

trayente, *a.* bringing, carrying, conducting.

traza, *n.f.* outline, sketch, draught, plan, project, scheme, device; contrivance; means, manner; plot, artifice; arrangement; looks, appearance, aspect, prospect; *darse trazas,* to find a way.

trazado, *n.m.* sketch, draught, tracing, plan, outline; designing; course, direction, route.

trazado, -da, *a.* traced, outlined; *bien* (or *mal*) *trazado,* of a good (*or* bad) disposition or character.

trazador, -ra, *n.m.f.* planner, sketcher, tracer.

trazar, *v.t.* (*pret.* **tracé**; *pres. subj.* **trace**) to trace, contrive, project, mark out, plan out; scheme, plot; to draw, sketch, outline, design; (*rail.*) to locate.

trazo, *n.m.* sketch, plan, project, design; tracing, moulding; line, stroke of a pen; (*art*) fold of the drapery; *al trazo,* drawn in outline; *trazo magistral,* down-stroke of a letter.

trazumarse, *v.r.* to transude, ooze, leak.

treballa, *n.f.* sauce for goose.

trébedes, *n.f.pl.* trivet, tripod.

trebejo, *n.m.* toy, plaything; jest, joke, fun; chess piece. — *pl.* **trebejos,** implements, tools of an art or trade.

trebejuelo, *n.m.* trifle, toy, gewgaw.

trébol, *n.m.* (*bot.*) trefoil, clover, shamrock.

trece, *n.m.a.* thirteen, thirteenth; *estar en sus trece,* to persist in one's opinion.

trecemesino, -na, *a.* of thirteen months.

trecenario, *n.m.* space of thirteen days.

treceno, -na, *a.* thirteenth.

trecésimo, -ma, *a.* thirtieth.

trecientos, -tas, *a.* three hundred.

trecheador, *n.m.* miner carrying ore by hand.

trechear, *v.t.* to carry ore from hand to hand.

trechel, *a.* spring wheat.

trecheo, *n.m.* handling, carrying from section to section.

trecho, *n.m.* space, distance, stretch; lapse; *a trechos,* by intervals; *de trecho en trecho,* at intervals, from time to time.

tredécimo, -ma, *a.* thirteenth.

trefe, *a.* lean, thin, pliable; spurious, adulterated.

tregua, *n.f.* truce; rest, repose, respite, recess, intermission.

treinta, *a.* thirty, thirtieth.

treintanario, *n.m.* space of thirty days.

trientañal, *a.* containing thirty years.

trientavo, -va, *a.* thirtieth part.

treintena, *n.f.* thirtieth part.

treinteno, -na, *a.* thirtieth.

treja, *n.f.* cushion shot at billiards.

tremebundo, -da, *a.* dreadful, frightful, fearful.

tremedal, *n.m.* marsh, morass, quagmire.

tremendo, -da, *a.* tremendous, dreadful, awful, terrible, fearful; grand, huge, imposing; excessive.

tremente, *a.* trembling.

trementina, *n.f.* turpentine.

tremés, tremesino, -na, *a.* three months old.

tremielga, *n.f.* cramp-fish, electric ray, torpedo.

tremó, tremol, *n.m.* frame of a wall-mirror.

tremolante, *a.* waving in the air.

tremolar, *v.t., v.i.* (*naut.*) to hoist (colours, etc.); to wave.

tremolina, *n.f.* rustling (of the wind); (*coll.*) noise, fuss, bustle, hubbub.

trémolo, *n.m.* tremolo.

tremor, *n.m.* trembling, tremor.

trémulamente, *adv.* tremblingly, tremulously.

tremulante; tremulento, -ta; trémulo, -la, *a.* tremulous, trembling, quivering, shaking.

tren, *n.m.* train; outfit, following, retinue; equipage, suite; pomp, ostentation, show; *tren de casa,* housekeeping; *tren de lavado,* laundry; *tren de recreo,* excursion train; *tren ascendente,* 'up' train (i.e., going towards the capital); *tren descendente,* 'down' train (i.e., going away from the capital); *tren botijo,* excursion train to the coast; *tren carreta,* slow, stopping-train; *tren correo,* mail train; *tren mixto,* passenger and goods train; *tren rápido o expreso,* fast or express train; *tren de aterrizaje,* (*aer.*) landing gear, undercarriage.

trena, *n.f.* sash, scarf; (*slang*) prison, gaol; burnt silver; (*prov.*) twist bread.

trenado, -da, *a.* reticulated, mesh.

trenca, *n.f.* cross-tree in a beehive; main root of a vine.

trencica, -illa, -ita, *n.f.* braid, plait.

trencillar, *v.t.* to ornament with braid.

trencillo, *n.m.* jewelled hat-band of gold or silver.

treno, *n.m.* threnody.

trenque, *n.m.* (*prov.*) wall, fluvial defence.

trenza, *n.f.* plait, braid; braided hair, tresses; plaited silk.

trenzadera, *n.f.* tape; knot of plaited cord.

trenzado, *n.m.* braided hair; (*danc.*) caper; prance of a horse.

trenzar, *v.t.* (*pret.* **trencé**; *pres. subj.* **trence**) to braid or plait the hair. — *v.i.* to prance, cut capers.

treo, *n.m.* cross-jack sail.

trepa, *n.f.* climbing; perforating, boring, drilling; trimming or edging of clothes; grain or flake of polished wood; (*coll.*) flogging, beating; (*coll.*) fraud, artful trick; somersault.

trepadera, *n.f.* (*Cub.*) rope used in climbing coconut palm-trees.

trepado, -da, *a.* strong, robust (animals).

trepado, *n.m.* trimming or edging of clothes; perforation of stamps, cheques, etc.

trepador, -ra, *a.* climber, climbing. — *n.m.* climbing-place. — *n.f.* creeper, climber, ivy. — *pl.* **trepadoras,** climbers.

trepajuncos, *n.m.* kind of reed bird.

trepanar, *v.t.* to trepan, trephine.

trépano, *n.m.* trepan, trephine.

trepante, *a.* climbing; artful, crafty, wily.

trepar, *v.i.* to climb, clamber, mount, creep up. — *v.t.* to trim; to bore, perforate, drill.

trepatroncos, *n.m.* (*orn.*) mason-bird.

trepe, *n.m.* (*coll.*) reprimand, scolding.

trepidar, *v.i.* to shake, quake, quiver, tremble; to vibrate, jar; to be convulsed, tremulous, agitated.

tres, *n.m., a.* three; third; figure 3; third day of a month; at cards, a trey; *como tres y dos son cinco,* as sure as twice two are four, quite clearly. — *n.f.pl.* **las tres,** three o'clock.

tresañal; tresañejo, -ja, *a.* three years old.

tresbolillo, (al), *adv.* (*agric.*) quincunx; (*mech.*) alternating, staggered.

trescientos, -tas, *n., a.* three hundred.

tresdoblar, *v.t.* to triple, treble; to fold three times.

tresdoble, *n.m.* threefold.

tresillista, *n.m.f.* expert in or very fond of ombre (game).

tresillo, *n.m.* ombre, a card game played by three; (*mus.*) triplet; a three-piece suite (furniture); a jewel with three stones (ring, pendant, etc.).

tresmesino, -na, *a.* three months old.

tresnal, *n.m.* (*agric.*) shock, stook.

trestanto, *n.m.* triple amount or number. — *adv.* three times as much.

treta, *n.f.* (*fenc.*) thrust, feint; trick, wile, craft.

trezavo, -va, *a.* thirteenth.

tría, *n.f.* choice, selection.

triaca, *n.f.* theriac; antidote.

triacal, *a.* theriacal.

triache, *n.m.* refuse of coffee-beans.

triangulación, *n.f.* triangulation.

triangulado, -da; triangular, *a.* triangular.

triangularmente, *adv.* triangularly.

triángulo, -la, *a.* triangular.

triángulo, *n.m.* triangle.

triar, *v.t.* to choose, pick out, select. — *v.i.* to go in and out often (of bees); to work (of bees, etc.). — *v.r.* (*prov.*) to curdle (of milk).

tribu, *n.m.f.* tribe, clan.

tribuente, *a.* attributing.

tribulación, *n.f.* tribulation, affliction.

tríbulo, *n.m.* generic name for several plants with prickly stems.

tribuna, *n.f.* tribune; platform; rostrum, pulpit, gallery.

tribunado, *n.m.* tribuneship.

tribunal, *n.m.* tribunal, court of justice, judicature; *tribunal de cuentas,* commissioners of audit; *tribunal tutelar de menores,* juvenile court.

tribunicio, -cia; tribúnico, -ca, *a.* tribunitial.

tribuno, *n.m.* tribune, political orator.

tributación, *n.f.* tribute, contribution; system of taxation; (*prov.*) emphyteusis.

tributante, *n.m.* taxpayer; tribute payer.

tributar, *v.t.* to pay taxes; to pay respect, honour, homage, duties, etc.

tributario, -ria, *a.* tributary. — *n.m.f.* taxpayer.

tributo, *n.m.* tax, contribution, tribute.

tricahue, *n.m.* (*Chi.*) a large parrot of the Andes.

tricenal, *a.* lasting thirty years.

tricentésimo, -ma, *a.* three hundredth, containing three hundred.

tricésimo, -ma, *a.* thirtieth.

triciclo, *n.m.* tricycle.

tricípite, *a.* three-headed.

tricolor, *a.* tri-coloured.

tricorne, *a.* three-horned.

tricornio, *n.m.* three-cornered.

tricotomía, *n.f.* trichotomy.

tridente, *n.m., a.* trident.

triduano, -na, *a.* tertian; lasting three days.

trienal, *a.* triennial.

trienio, *n.m.* triennium, space of three years.

trieñal, trienal, *a.* triennial.

trifásico, -ca, *a.* (*elec.*) three-phase.

trífido, -da, *a.* trifid.

trifinio, *n.m.* meeting-place of three boundaries.

trifolio, *n.m.* trefoil, shamrock.

triforme, *a.* triform.

trifulca, *n.f.* lever for moving the bellows in a foundry; (*coll.*) squabble, quarrel, row.

trifurcado, -da, *a.* trifurcate.

triga, *n.f.* a three-horse cart; three horses in line.

trigal, *n.m.* wheat-field.

trigaza, *n.f.* short straw (of wheat).

trigésimo, -ma, *a.* thirtieth.

trigla, *n.f.* red mullet.

triglifo, *n.m.* triglyph.

trigo, *n.m.* wheat; wheat-field. — *pl.* **trigos,** crops, cornfields; *trigo alonso,* bearded wheat; *trigo candeal,* summer wheat; *trigo chamorro,* winter wheat; *trigo fanfarrón,* Barbary wheat; (*coll.*) *no es lo mismo predicar que dar trigo,* it's easier to preach than to practise.

trígono, *n.m.* (*astron.*) trigon; (*geom.*) triangle.

trigonometría, *n.f.* trigonometry.

trigonométrico, -ca, *a.* trigonometrical.

trigueño, -ña, *a.* brownish, swarthy, brunette.

triguera, *n.f.* Triticum.

triguero, -ra, *a.* wheaten, wheat-growing; growing among wheat.

triguero, *n.m.* sieve for corn; corn-merchant, grain-dealer; (*orn.*) fallow-finch.

trilátero, -ra, *a.* trilateral.

trile, *n.m.* (*Chi.*) blackbird with yellow markings (*Agelæus thilius*).

trilingüe, *a.* trilingual.

trilítero, -ra, *a.* triliteral.

trilogía, *n.f.* trilogy.

trilla, *n.f.* gurnet, red surmullet; (*agric.*) harrow; threshing.

trilladera, *n.f.* separating harrow.

trillado, -da, *a.* threshed, beaten; trite, stale, hackneyed; *camino trillado,* beaten track, common run.

trillador, *n.m.* thresher.

trilladora, *n.f.* threshing machine.

trilladura, *n.f.* threshing.

trillar, *v.t.* to thresh, tread out (corn), beat; to frequent; to repeat.

trillo, *n.m.* threshing harrow, threshing-machine; (*CR., Cub., PR.*) footpath.

trillón, *n.m.* trillion.

trimestral, *a.* trimestral, trimensual, quarterly.

trimestre, *n.m.* term, quarter, space of three months; quarterly payment.

trimielga, *n.f.* (*ichth.*) electric ray, torpedo.

trimotor, *n.m.* three-motor aeroplane.

trinado, *n.m.* trill; tremulous sound, twittering.

trinar, *v.i.* to trill; (*coll.*) to get irritated, angry.

trinca, *n.f.* triad, ternary; (*naut.*) cord; gammoning, seizing; *a la trinca,* (*naut.*) close-hauled.

trincadura, *n.f.* large two-masted barge.

trincafía, *n.f.* splice or patch, made by winding a rope spirally around the object to be tied.

trincar, *v.t.* (*pret.* **trinqué**; *pres. subj.* **trinque**) to break, chop; to skip, leap; to tie, bind, lash; (*naut.*) to fasten, gammon; (*coll.*) to drink liquor. — *v.i.* (*naut.*) to keep close to the wind.

trincha, *n.f.* strap for buckling garments.

trinchante, *n.m.* carver; carving-knife; stone-cutter's hammer. — *a.* carving.

trinchar, *v.t.* to carve.

trinche, *n.m.* (*Col., Chi., Ec., Mex.*) table fork; (*Chi., Ec., Mex.*) sideboard.

trinchera, *n.f.* trench, entrenchment; deep cut, ditch; trench coat; *abrir trincheras,* to begin a siege.

trinchero, *n.m.* trencher; sideboard.

trincherón, *n.m.* large trench or ditch.

trinchete, *n.m.* paring-knife.
trineo, *n.m.* sledge, sled, sleigh.
Trinidad, *n.f.* Trinity.
trinitaria, *n.f.* (*bot.*) heartsease, pansy.
trinitario, -ria, *n.m.f.*, *a.* Trinitarian; (*Mex.*) hired mourner.
trino, -na, *a.* ternary, triadic, trinal, trine.
trino, *n.m.* (*astron.*) trine; (*mus.*) trill.
trinomio, *n.m.* trinomial.
trinquetada, *n.f.* sailing under the foresail.
trinquete, *n.m.* foresail, foremast; main yard of the foremast; (*mech.*) catch, clink, pawl; game of Spanish rackets; *a cada trinquete*, at every step.
trinquetilla, *n.f.* fore staysail.
trinquis, *n.m.* (*coll.*) drink of wine or liquor.
trío, *n.m.* trio.
trióxido, *n.m.* trioxide.
tripa, *n.f.* tripe, gut, intestine, bowel; (*coll.*) belly, large or distended belly, paunch; filling; fillers for cigars; file, docket. — *pl.* **tripas**, intestines, entrails, bowels; core of fruit; inner lining of some feathers; *hacer de tripas corazón*, to pluck up one's courage; *devanar las tripas a*, to annoy or displease greatly; *tener malas tripas*, to be very cruel.
tripartir, *v.t.* to divide into three parts.
tripartito, -ta, *a.* tripartite.
tripe, *n.m.* shag, plush.
tripería, *n.f.* tripe-shop; heap of tripe.
tripero, -ra, *n.m.f.* tripe-seller.
tripero, *n.m.* belly-band; cummerbund.
tripicallero, -ra, *n.m.f.* street tripe-seller.
tripicallos, *n.m.pl.* tripes.
trípili, *n.m.* a Spanish song and dance.
triplano, *n.m.* (*aer.*) triplane.
triple, *a.* triple, treble.
tríplica, *n.m.* (*law, prov.*) rejoinder.
triplicación, *n.f.* multiplication by three.
triplicado, -da, *a.* triplicate.
triplicar, *v.t.* (*pret.* **tripliqué**; *pres. subj.* **triplique**) to triple, treble; (*law*) to rejoin.
tríplice, *a.* treble, triple.
triplicidad, *n.f.* triplicity, trebleness.
triplo, -pla, *a.* triple, treble, triplicate.
trípode, *n.m.* tripod, trivet.
trípol, trípoli, *n.m.* tripoli, rottenstone.
tripolio, *n.m.* sea starwort.
tripón, -ona, *a.* (*coll.*) big-bellied, pot-bellied.
tríptico, *n.m.* triptych; document or book containing three folios.
triptongo, *n.m.* triphthong.
tripudiar, *v.i.* to dance.
tripudio, *n.m.* dance, ball.
tripudo, -da, *a.* big-bellied.
tripulación, *n.f.* (*naut., aer.*) crew.
tripulado, -da, *a.* manned, equipped.
tripulante, *n.m.* member of the crew (ship, airplane).
tripular, *v.t.* to man (ship, plane, airship), fit out, equip.
trique, *n.m.* sharp noise, crack; (*Chi.*) medicinal plant of the Iridaceæ family; (*Chi.*) refreshing drink made of toasted barley.
triquete, *n.m.; a cada triquete*, (*fig.*) at every step.
triquina, *n.f.* trichina.
triquinosis, *n.f.* trichinosis.
triquiñuela, *n.f.* (*coll.*) cheat, fraud, subterfuge.
triquitraque, *n.m.* crack, clack, clashing, clattering; fire-cracker.
trirreme, *n.m.* trireme.

tris, *n.m.* trice, instant, nick of time; noise made by breaking glass; *en un tris*, within an ace; *tris tras*, wearisome repetition.
trisa, *n.f.* shad.
trisca, *n.f.* noise made by stamping the feet on nuts, etc.; fun, uproar, merriment.
triscador, -ra, *n.m.f.* noisy person; saw set, saw wrest, saw swage.
triscar, *v.i.* (*pret.* **trisqué**; *pres. subj.* **trisque**) to stamp the feet; to walk lively; (*fig.*) to frisk, caper, frolic, romp about. — *v.t.* to mingle, mix; to set the teeth of a saw.
trisecar, *v.t.* to trisect.
trisección, *n.f.* trisection.
trisemanal, *a.* thrice a week.
trisílabo, -ba, *a.* trisyllabic.
trismo, *n.m.* lockjaw.
trispasto, *n.m.* three-pulley tackle.
triste, *a.* sad, mournful, sorrowful; morose, sombre, gloomy, dull, heavy; mean, abject, low; dark, murky. — *n.m.* (*Arg., Per.*) a lover's lament (song).
tristemente, *adv.* mournfully, sorrowfully, sadly.
tristeza, *n.f.* grief, sadness, sorrow, affliction, melancholy, gloom.
tristón, -ona, *a.* melancholy, sad.
tristura, *n.f.* [TRISTEZA].
trisulco, -ca, *a.* (*poet.*) three-pronged.
tritíceo, -ea, *a.* wheaten.
tritón, *n.m.* (*myth.*) Triton.
trítono, *n.m.* (*mus.*) minor third.
triturable, *a.* triturable.
trituración, *n.f.* trituration, pulverization.
triturador, -ra, *a.* crusher. — *n.f.* crushing-machine.
triturar, *v.t.* to triturate, crush, mash, grind; to masticate.
triunfador, -ra, *n.m.f.* conqueror, victor.
triunfal, *a.* triumphal.
triunfalmente, *adv.* triumphally.
triunfante, *a.* triumphant, victorious, conquering.
triunfantemente, *adv.* triumphantly.
triunfar, *v.i.* to triumph, exult; to win the day; to conquer; to trump at cards.
triunfo, *n.m.* triumph, victory, conquest, exultation, jubilation; spoils of war; trump card.
triunviral, *a.* triumviral.
triunvirato, *n.m.* triumvirate.
triunviro, *n.m.* triumvir.
trivial, *a.* trivial; vulgar, common, ordinary; frequented, beaten, trodden.
trivialidad, *n.f.* trivialness, triviality; triteness, vulgarity, idleness.
trivialmente, *adv.* trivially.
trivio, *n.m.* cross-road, fork of a road; trivium.
triza, *n.f.* mite, bit, piece, fragment, scrap, shred, particle; (*naut.*) cord, rope; *hacer trizas*, to knock into smithereens.
trocable, *a.* changeable, exchangeable.
trocadamente, *adv.* contrarily, falsely.
trocado, *n.m.* change, small coin.
trocado, -da, *a.* changed, permuted. — *p.p.* [TROCAR]; *a la trocada* (or *a la trocadilla*), in exchange, in the contrary sense.
trocador, -ra, *n.m.f.* one who exchanges or permutes.
trocaico, -ca, *a.* trochaic.
trocamiento, *n.m.* change; distortion; exchange.
trocante, *a.* bartering, exchanging.

trocar, *v.t.* (*pres. indic.* **trueco**; *pret.* **troqué**; *pres. subj.* **trueque**) to exchange, barter; to change; to equivocate; to vomit. — *v.r.* to change; to be changed, reformed; to exchange seats.

trocatinta, *n.f.* (*coll.*) confusing mistake.

trocatinte, *n.m.* mixed, shot or changing colour.

troceo, *n.m.* (*naut.*) parrel, truss.

trocisco, *n.m.* troche, lozenge.

trocla, *n.f.* pulley.

troco, *n.m.* short sun-fish.

trocha, *n.f.* cross-path, short cut; trail; military road; (*Arg.*) gauge.

trochemoche, -a, *adv.* helter-skelter, pell-mell.

trochuela, *n.f.* little path.

trofeo, *n.m.* trophy, emblem of triumph; spoils of war; victory; memorial; military insignia; pageant.

troglodita, *n.f.* troglodyte; voracious eater, glutton; cruel man.

troj, (*Am.*) troja, troje, *n.f.* granary; barn.

trojero, *n.m.* storekeeper, granary-keeper.

trojezado, -da, *a.* shredded, minced.

trola, *n.f.* (*coll.*) fib, hoax, gammon.

trole, *n.m.* (*elec.*) trolley.

trolebús, *n.m.* trolley-bus.

tromba, *n.f.* waterspout.

trombón, *n.m.* trombone; trombone player.

trombosis, *n.f.* thrombosis.

trompa, *n.f.* French horn; horn; elephant's trunk; proboscis; humming top; projecting arch from a wall; (*metal.*) trompe; cradle, vault. — *n.m.* horn-player; *a trompa y talega*, without order or reflection; *trompa de Eustaquio*, Eustachian tube; *trompa de Falopio*, Fallopian tube; *trompa marina*, a one-string musical instrument played with a bow.

trompada, *n.f.*, trompazo, *n.m.* (*coll.*) blow with a top or fist; bump, collision.

trompar, trompear, *v.i.* to whip a top.

trompero, *n.m.* top-maker. — *a.* deceitful.

trompeta, *n.f.* trumpet; trumpet-shell; bugle. — *n.m.* trumpeter, bugler; (*coll.*) noodle, puppet.

trompetada, *n.f.* (*coll.*) foolish remark.

trompetear, *v.i.* (*coll.*) to sound the trumpet.

trompeteo, *n.m.* sounding the bugle or trumpet.

trompetería, *n.f.* brass pipes of an organ.

trompetero, *n.m.* trumpeter, horn-blower.

trompetilla, *n.f.* small trumpet; ear-trumpet; insect's trunk; (*Philip.*) cheroot.

trompicar, *v.t.*, *v.i.* (*pret.* **trompiqué**; *pres. subj.* **trompique**) to trip, to make stumble; (*coll.*) to promote an employee over the head of a senior one. — *v.i.* to stumble frequently; to falter.

trompicón, *n.m.*; trompilladura, *n.f.* stumbling.

trompillo, *n.m.* (*Am.*) bixa-tree.

trompis, *n.m.* (*coll.*) blow with the fist.

trompo, *n.m.* chess-man; top; trochid; *ponerse como un trompo*, to eat and drink one's fill.

trompón, *n.m.* large top; (*bot.*) narcissus; *de trompón*, in a disorderly way, helter-skelter.

tronada, *n.f.* thunderstorm.

tronador, -ra, *n.m.f.* thunderer, thundering; rocket, cracker.

tronante, *a.* thundering.

tronar, *v. impers.* (*pres. indic.* **truena**; *pres. subj.* **truene**) to thunder. — *v.i.* to cause a noise like thunder or the discharge of guns;

to fulminate, denounce violently; to fail in business; *tronar con*, to break off relations with; *por lo que pueda tronar*, for what may happen.

tronca, *n.f.* truncation.

troncal, *a.* relating to the trunk; main, principal.

troncar, *v.t.* (*pret.* **tronqué**; *pres. subj.* **tronque**) to truncate, mutilate.

tronco, *n.m.* trunk of a tree, log, stock; stem, stalk; trunk of an animal; origin of a family; team or pair of horses; unfeeling person; useless, contemptible person; *estar hecho un tronco*, to have no feeling, to be fast asleep.

tronchado, -da, *a.* (*her.*) having a diagonal bar.

tronchar, *v.t.* to cut off, chop off, cut by trunk or root; to break a trunk or stalk; to mutilate.

tronchazo, *n.m.* large stalk; blow with a stalk.

troncho, *n.m.* stalk, stem, sprig.

tronchudo, -da, *a.* stalky, having a long stalk or stem.

tronera, *n.f.* (*naut.*) loophole; port-hole; (*fort.*) embrasure of a battery; dormer, small skylight; opening; harum-scarum fellow; pocket-hole in a billiard-table; squib, cracker.

tronerar, *v.t.* to make embrasures.

tronga, *n.f.* (*vulg.*) concubine, mistress.

tronido, *n.m.* thunder, loud report.

tronitoso, -sa, *a.* (*coll.*) resounding, thundering.

trono, *n.m.* throne, royal dignity; (*eccles.*) shrine. — *pl.* **tronos**, thrones, third choir of angels.

tronquista, *n.m.* coachman driving a pair.

tronzador, *n.m.* two-handed saw.

tronzar, *v.t.* (*pret.* **troncé**; *pres. subj.* **tronce**) to break to pieces, shatter; (*sew.*) to plait.

tronzo, -za, *a.* having one or both ears cut off (horses).

tropa, *n.f.* troops, soldiers; crowd, mass, multitude, crew; (*mil.*) ranks, soldiery; (*S. Am.*) drove of cattle; (*Arg.*) fleet of carts or wagons. — *pl.* **tropas**, army; *en tropa*, in crowds, in disorderly fashion.

tropel, *n.m.* stamping, pattering; rush, tumult, hurry, confusion, bustle; heap; *de* (or *en*) *tropel*, tumultuously, in a throng.

tropelía, *n.f.* rush, precipitation, confusion, hurry; injustice, outrage; vexation.

tropezadero, *n.m.* slippery place; uneven road, stumbling place.

tropezadura, *n.f.* obstructing, stumbling.

tropezar, *v.i.* (*pres. indic.* **tropiezo**; *pret.* **tropecé**; *pres. subj.* **tropiece**) to stumble, slip, to be obstructed; to strike against, hitch; to wrangle, dispute, squabble; to meet accidentally, light upon, stumble upon; to discover a fault. — *v.r.* to stumble; to interfere (of horses).

tropezón, -ona, *a.* stumbling, tripping often.

tropezón, *n.m.* tripping, stumbling; obstacle, difficulty; (*vet.*) interfering; *a tropezones*, (*coll.*) by fits and starts, falling and rising.

tropezoso, -sa, *a.* apt to trip or stumble.

tropical, *a.* tropical.

trópico, *n.m.* tropic.

trópico, -ca, *a.* (*rhet.*) tropical.

tropiezo, *n.m.* stumble, trip, slip; hitch; impediment, obstruction, obstacle; difficulty; fault, error; quarrel, squabble, dispute.

tropo, *n.m.* (*rhet.*) trope.

tropología, *n.f.* tropology.

tropológico, -ca, *a.* tropological.

troque, *n.m.* dyer's knot.

troquel, *n.m.* die (for coins, medals, etc.).

troquelar, *v.t.* to coin, mint.

troqueo, *n.m.* trochee.

trotaconventos, *n.f.* (*coll.*) procuress, bawd.

trotador, -ra, *n.m.f.* trotter.

trotamundos, *n.m.f.* globe-trotter.

trotar, *v.i.* to trot; to hustle.

trote, *n.m.* trot; *al trote,* at a trot, hastily, hurriedly; *para todo trote,* for constant use; *amansar el trote,* to moderate, restrain oneself; *tomar el trote,* (*coll.*) to run away.

trotillo, *n.m.* light trot.

trotón, -ona, *a.* trotting (horse). — *n.m.* horse.

trotona, *n.f.* chaperon.

trotonería, *n.f.* continual trot.

trova, *n.f.* metrical composition; kind of ballad.

trovador, -ra, *n.m.f.* troubadour, minstrel, poet.

trovar, *v.i.* to versify, make poetry. — *v.t.* to invert or pervert the sense of; to misconstrue.

trovero, *n.m.* trouveur, trouvère.

trovista, *n.m.* versifier, ballad-writer, minstrel.

trovo, *n.m.* love-ballad.

Troya, *n.f.* Troy; *aquí fué Troya,* here was Troy, here the trouble begins; *¡ arda Troya !* let happen what will.

troyano, -na, *n.m.f.*, *a.* Trojan.

troza, *n.f.* parrel; tree-trunk or log to be sawn into boards.

trozar, *v.t.* (*pret.* **trocé;** *pres. subj.* **troce**) to break, cut into boards; to shatter; to haul taut the parrel.

trozo, *n.m.* piece, chunk, fragment, bit, extract; mariner's register; boarding-party; (*mil.*) division of a column; selection, passage (from a book, etc.).

trucar, *v.i.* (*pret.* **truqué;** *pres. subj.* **truque**) to play the first card; to pocket a ball at pool.

truculento, -ta, *a.* truculent, fierce.

trucha, *n.f.* trout; crane; *no se toman truchas a bragas enjutas,* you can't catch trout and keep dry; (*Cent. Am.*) small haberdashery shop.

truchero, -ra, *n.m.f.* trout fisherman, trout-seller.

truchimán, -ana, *a.* (*coll.*) fond of business; shrewd or expert buyer.

truchuela, *n.f.* small trout; small dry codfish.

trueco, *n.m.* exchange; *a* (or *en*) *trueco,* in exchange.

trueco, *pres. indic.* [TROCAR].

trueno, *n.m.* thunderclap; report of fire-arms; (*coll.*) harum-scarum, wild youth; big piece of scandal; *dar el trueno gordo,* to do or say something which may do mischief.

trueque, *n.m.* exchange, barter, truck, commutation; *a* (or *en*) *trueque,* in exchange.

trueque, *pres. subj.* [TROCAR].

trufa, *n.f.* fraud, imposition, hoax, lie, deceit; (*bot.*) truffle.

trufador, -ra, *n.m.f.* fabulist, story-teller, liar, fibber, cheat, impostor.

trufar, *v.t.* to stuff with truffles. — *v.i.* to lie, fib, deceive.

truhán, -ana, *n.m.f.* juggler, jester, buffoon; rascal, scoundrel, knave.

truhanada, *n.f.* buffoonery, low jest.

truhanamente, *adv.* jestingly, in a scoundrelly way.

truhanear, *v.i.* to jest, banter; to swindle.

truhanería, *n.f.* buffoonery, low jest; rascality, scoundrelism.

truhanesco, -ca, *a.* rascally, scoundrelly; belonging to a buffoon.

truja, *n.f.* olive-bin in oil mills.

trujal, *n.m.* oil-press, wine-press; oil mill; copper for making soap.

trujamán, triujimán, *n.m.*, *a.* dragoman, interpreter; expert buyer or trader.

trujamanear, *v.i.* to act as an interpreter; to act as broker; to exchange, barter, trade.

trujamanía, *n.f.* brokering, brokerage.

trulla, *n.f.* trowel; bustle, noise, hurly-burly; multitude, crowd.

trullo, *n.m.* teal; vat for the must.

trumao, *n.m.* (*Chi.*) volcanic dust.

trun, *n.m.* (*Chi.*) a variety of bur.

truncadamente, *adv.* in a truncated manner.

truncado, -da, *a.* truncate, truncated. — *p.p.* [TRUNCAR].

truncamiento, *n.m.* truncation, maiming.

truncar, *v.t.* (*pret.* **trunqué;** *pres. subj.* **trunque**) to truncate; maim, mutilate; abridge, cut short.

truque, *n.m.* a game of cards.

truquero, *n.m.* keeper of the pool table.

truquiflor, *n.m.* a game of cards.

trusas, *n.f.pl.* trunk-hose.

tsetsé, *n.f.* tsetse fly.

tú, *pron. pers.* 2nd person, *m.* or *f.* thou; *de tú por tú,* intimately; *tratar de tú,* to address intimately, be on intimate terms.

tu, *pron. poss.; pl.* **tus** (apocope of *tuyo, tuya, tuyos, tuyas,* used only before a noun) thy, thine.

tuatúa, *n.f.* American spurge.

tuáutem, *n.m.* (*coll.*) mover, author, leader, principal person, leading spirit; essential point.

tuba, *n.f.* (*Philip.*) palm wine; (*mus.*) tuba.

tuberculina, *n.f.* (*med.*) tuberculine.

tuberculización, *n.f.* tuberculosis, tuberculization.

tubérculo, *n.m.* tubercle; tuber.

tuberculosis, *n.f.* tuberculosis.

tuberculoso, -sa, *a.* tuberculous.

tubería, *n.f.* tubing, piping; pipe line.

tuberosa, *n.f.* tuberose.

tuberosidad, *n.f.* tuberosity, protuberance, swelling.

tuberoso, -sa, *a.* tuberous.

tubífero, -ra, *a.* provided with tubes.

tubo, *n.m.* tube, pipe, duct; lamp-chimney; *tubo acústico,* speaking tube; *tubo de ensayo,* test tube; *tubo lanzallamas,* flame-thrower; *tubo lanzatorpedos,* torpedo-tube.

tubular, *a.* tubular, tube-shaped.

tucán, *n.m.* toucan.

tucía, *n.f.* tutty.

tuco, *n.m.* (*Cent. Am., Ec., PR.*) stump of a tree, arm or leg; (*Arg.*) glow-worm; (*Per.*) owl.

tuco, -ca, *a.* (*Bol., Ec., PR.*) armless.

tucúquere, *n.m.* (*Chi.*) a large owl.

tucuso, *n.m.* (*Ven.*) humming-bird.

tucutuco, *n.m.* (*Arg.*) kind of mole.

tudel, *n.m.* mouth-piece of a bassoon.

tudesco, -ca, *n.m.f.*, *a.* German, native of Germany.

tudesco, *n.m.* broad cloak.

tueca, tueco, *n.m.f.* stump, stub; hole left by wood-worm in wood.

tuera, *n.f.* (*prov.*) colocynth, bitter apple.

tuerca, *n.f.* nut, female screw.

tuerce, *n.m.* sprain.

tuero, *n.m.* dry wood, fuel, brushwood; spignel.

tuerto, -ta, *a.* one-eyed, squint-eyed. — *p.p. irreg.* [TORCER].

tuerto, *n.m.* injury, wrong. — *pl.* **tuertos,** pains after childbirth; *a tuertas,* on the wrong side, contrariwise; *a tuertas o a derechas* (or *a tuerto o a derecho*), rightly or wrongly, inconsiderately; *con un poco de tuerto, llega el hombre a su derecho,* if you put up with inconveniences for a time, you get your way at last.

tueste, *n.m.* toast, toasting.

tuesto ; tueste, *pres. indic.; pres. subj.* [TOSTAR].

tuétano, *n.m.* marrow; pith of trees; *hasta los tuétanos,* to the marrow.

tufarada, *n.f.* strong scent, strong smell.

tufo, *n.m.* warm exhalation from the earth; vapour, fume, emanation; effluvium, offensive smell; hair falling over the ear; conceit, haughty airs, vanity, snobbishness; (*min.*) tufa.

tugurio, *n.m.* cottage, cabin, shepherd's hut; (*coll.*) miserable little room; 'joint.'

tui, *n.m.* (*Arg.*) small parrot.

tuición, *n.f.* (*law*) tuition, protection, guardianship.

tuina, *n.f.* a long and loose jacket.

tuitivo, -va, *a.* (*law*) defensive, protective.

tul, *n.m.* tulle.

tule, *n.m.* (*Mex.*) rush, reed.

tulipa, *n.f.* small tulip; tulip-shaped lamp-shade.

tulipán, *n.m.* tulip.

tullidez, *n.f.* paralysis (especially of the legs).

tullido, -da, *a.* paralyzed (especially of the legs).

tullidura, *n.f.* dung of birds of prey.

tullimiento, *n.m.* contraction of the tendons.

tullir, *v.i.* to emit dung (of birds). — *v.t.* to injure, wound. — *v.r.* to be crippled.

tumba, *n.f.* tomb, sepulchral monument, catafalque, grave, vault; roof of a coach; driver's seat in state coaches; tumble, somersault; Andalusian dance performed at Christmas.

tumbacuartillos, *n.m.* sot, old toper.

tumbadero, *n.m.* tumbling-place (in gymnasiums).

tumbadillo, *n.m.* (*naut.*) round-house, cuddy.

tumbado, -da, *a.* vaulted, arched.

tumbaga, *n.f.* a very brittle alloy of gold and copper; ring made of this alloy.

tumbar, *v.t.* to tumble, fell, knock down, throw down, heave down; (*fig., coll.*) to inebriate; to overpower, stun. — *v.i.* to tumble, fall down, roll down; (*naut.*) to heel, run aground. — *v.r.* (*coll.*) to lie down to sleep.

tumbilla, *n.f.* horse for airing bed-linen; bed-warmer.

tumbo, *n.m.* tumble, fall, somersault; matter of importance; book containing title-deeds of monasteries, etc.; *tumbo de dado,* imminent peril.

tumbón, *n.m.* coach with rounded roof; trunk with arched lid.

tumbón, -ona, *n.m.f.* (*coll.*) lazy person. — *a.* sly, cunning person.

tumefacción, *n.f.* tumefaction, swelling.

túmido, -da, *a.* swollen, tumid, inflated; elevated; pompous, highflown; (*arch.*) domed.

tumor, *n.m.* tumour.

tumorcico, -illo, -ito, *n.m.* small tumour.

tumulario, -ria, *a.* tumulary.

túmulo, *n.m.* tomb, sepulchre, monument; catafalque; tumulus; funeral pile.

tumulto, *n.m.* tumult, uproar, uprising, commotion, faction, mob.

tumultuante, *a.* fomenting sedition.

tumultuar, *v.i.* to mob, raise a tumult. — *v.r.* to rise in arms.

tumultuariamente, *adv.* tumultuously.

tumultuario, -ria, *a.* tumultuary, tumultuous.

tumultuosamente, *adv.* tumultuously.

tumultuoso, -sa, *a.* tumultuous.

tuna, *n.f.* prickly pear, Indian fig; idle and licentious life, truantship; *andar a la tuna,* (*coll.*) to loiter, play the truant.

tunal, *n.m.* Indian fig-tree.

tunanta, *n., a.* (*coll.*) shrewd, rascally woman.

tunante, *a.* leading a licentious life; truant, crafty, lazy. — *n.m.* truant, idler, rake, rascal, rogue.

tunantear, *v.i.* to act the rogue.

tunantería, *n.f.* vagrancy, truantship.

tunantuelo, -la, *n.m.f.* (*coll.*) little rascal, scamp.

tunar, *v.i.* to loiter about; to loaf, stroll; to lead a loose life.

tunco, *n.m.* (*Hond., Mex.*) hog, swine.

tunda, *n.f.* shearing of cloth; severe chastisement.

tundente, *a.* beating, chastising; producing contusion.

tundición, *n.f.* shearing of cloth.

tundidor, *n.m.* cloth-shearer.

tundidora, *n.f.* cloth-shearing machine.

tundidura, *n.f.* shearing.

tundir, *v.t.* to shear cloth; (*coll.*) to flog, cudgel, whip.

tundizno, *n.m.* shearings from cloth.

tunduque, *n.m.* (*Chi.*) a large brown mouse.

tunear, *v.i.* to act the rogue.

tunecino, -na, *n.m.f., a.* Tunisian.

túnel, *n.m.* tunnel.

Túnez, *n.f.* Tunis.

tungstato, *n.m.* tungstate.

tungsteno, *n.m.* tungsten.

túnica, *n.f.* tunic, chiton; (*anat., bot.*) tunicle, pellicle; integument; long, wide gown, robe; *túnica de Cristo,* (*bot.*) stramonium.

tunicela, *n.f.* tunic; (*eccles.*) tunicle.

túnico, *n.m.* gown, tunic, robe; (*Cub.*) frock, dress; (*Col., CR., Hond., Venez.*) women's tunic; (*Chi.*) woollen monastic dress.

tuno, *n.m.* truant, rake, rascal, rogue; (*Col., Cub.*) prickly pear or Indian fig.

tuno, -na, *a.* truant, loitering, sly, rascally, roguish, cunning.

tuntún, (al buen), *adv.* (*coll.*) at random, heedlessly.

tupa, *n.f.* tight packing; (*coll.*) repletion, satiety; (*Chi.*) a plant of the Lobeliaceous family.

tupaya, *n.f.* (*Philip.*) an insectivorous squirrel.

tupé, *n.m.* toupee, forelock; (*coll.*) self-assurance, cheek.

tupido, -da, *a.* dense, thick; close-woven; blocked, choked.

tupinambo, *n.m.* Jerusalem artichoke.

tupir, *v.t.* to press close, block up, stop up, obstruct. — *v.r.* to stuff oneself, glut, overeat.

turba, *n.f.* crowd, heap, multitude; rabble; peat.

turbación, *n.f.* perturbation; confusion, disorder, light-headedness; embarrassment.

turbadamente, *adv.* confusedly, in a disorderly manner.

turbador, -ra, *n.m.f.* disturber, perturbator.

turbal, *n.m.* peat-bog, peat-bed.

turbamulta, *n.f.* crowd, multitude, rabble.

turbante, *n.m.* turban. — *a.* disturbing.

turbar, *v.t.* to disturb, disquiet, alarm, upset; disarrange, confuse, surprise. — *v.r.* to be discomposed, uneasy.

turbativo, -va, *a.* alarming, troublesome.

turbera, *n.f.* peat-bog, peat-moss.

turbia, *n.f.* muddy water.

turbiamente, *adv.* obscurely, confusedly.

turbidez, *n.f.* turbidity.

túrbido, -da, *a.* turbid, muddy.

turbiedad, turbieza, *n.f.* muddiness, turbidness, turbidity; obscurity of language.

turbina, *n.f.* turbine.

turbino, *n.m.* pulverized turpeth.

turbinto, *n.m.* terebinth.

turbio, -bia, *a.* turbid, troubled, turbulent, disturbed, muddy; dark, obscure, indistinct; unhappy, unfortunate. — *n.m.pl.* **turbios**, dregs.

turbión, *n.m.* squall, heavy rain-shower; hurricane; sweep, rush.

turbit, *n.m.* (*bot.*) turpeth; *turbit mineral*, (*pharm.*) turpeth mineral.

turbonada, *n.f.* tornado, hurricane; waterspout; squall, pelting shower.

turbulencia, *n.f.* turbidness, muddiness; turbulence, disorder, confusion.

turbulentamente, *adv.* turbulently.

turbulento, -ta, *a.* turbid, thick, muddy; turbulent, disorderly, tumultuous.

turca, *n.f.* tipsiness; *coger una turca*, to get tipsy.

turco, -ca, *a.* Turkish. — *n.m.f.* Turk; *el gran turco*, the Sultan of Turkey.

turdido, -da, *a.* (*orn.*) turdine.

túrdiga, *n.f.* strip of hide or new leather.

turdión, *n.m.* ancient Spanish dance.

turgencia, *n.f.* swelling, tumour, turgescence.

turgente, *a.* turgent, turgescent, tumid, turgid, swollen; (*poet.*) prominent.

turibular, *v.t.* (*eccles.*) to cense with a thurible.

turibulario, turiferario, *n.m.* thurifer, censer bearer.

turíbulo, *n.m.* thurible, censer.

turífero, -ra, *a.* thuriferous, incense-bearing.

turismo, *n.m.* tourism, touring.

turista, *n.m.f.* tourist.

turma, *n.f.* testicle; lamb's fry; *turma de tierra*, truffle.

turmalina, *n.f.* (*min.*) tourmaline.

turnar, *v.i.* to alternate, to work by turns.

turnio, -nia, *a.* squint-eyed; torvous.

turno, *n.m.* turn, order, succession; *al turno*, by turns; *por su turno*, in one's turn.

turón, *n.m.* kind of field-mouse.

turquesa, *n.f.* turquoise; bullet-mould.

turquesado, -da, *a.* turquoise.

turquesco, -ca, *a.* Turkish.

turquí, turquino, -na, *a.* deep blue.

Turquía, *n.f.* Turkey.

turrar, *v.t.* to roast, toast, broil.

turrón, *n.m.* sweet similar to nougat or almond paste; (*coll.*) sinecure; *comer del turrón*, to fill a public office.

turronero, *n.m.* maker or seller of *turrón*.

turulato, -ta, *a.* (*coll.*) silly, stupefied.

turumbón, *n.m.* bump on the head.

¡ tus !, *interj.* word used in calling dogs; *sin decir tus ni mus*, (*coll.*) without saying a word.

tusa, *n.f.* (*Bol., Col., Ven.*) corn-cob; (*Cent. Am., Cub.*) 'shucks' or 'husks' of maize; (*Cub.*) cigarette wrapped with a husk of maize; (*Chi.*) 'silks' of ear of corn; (*Chi.*) mane of a horse; (*Col.*) pock-mark; (*Cent. Am., Cub.*) worthless woman.

tusílago, *n.m.* colt's-foot.

¡ tuso !, *interj.* come here or get away (dogs).

tuso, -sa, *a.* (*Col.*) pitted by small-pox; (*PR.*) bobtailed.

tusón, *n.m.* sheep's fleece; (*prov.*) colt under two years old.

tusona, *n.f.* (*prov.*) filly under two years old; (*coll.*) strumpet.

tute, *n.m.* a game of cards.

tutear, *v.t.* to call 'thee' and 'thou'; to address familiarly.

tutela, *n.f.* tutelage, tutorage, guardianship, protection.

tutelar, *a.* tutelar, tutelary.

tuteo, *n.m.* familiar address, calling 'thee' and 'thou.'

tutía, *n.f.* tutty.

tutiplén, (a), *adv.* abundantly, to excess.

tutor, *n.m.* tutor, guardian, instructor; prop for plants.

tutora, *n.f.* tutoress, governess, female guardian.

tutoría, *n.f.* tutelage, guardianship.

tutriz, *n.f.* tutoress, governess.

tuya, *n.f.* thuya.

tuyo, tuya ; tuyos, tuyas, *pron. poss. 2nd pers. m. and f., sing. and pl.* thine; *lo tuyo*, what belongs to thee; *los tuyos*, thy servants (relatives, followers, etc.).

U

U, u, twenty-fourth letter of the Spanish alphabet.

u, *disj. conj.* used in place of *o*, to avoid cacophony, before words beginning with *o* or *ho*, as in *diez u once*, ten or eleven.

u, (en), *adv. hierro en U*, channel iron.

uacari, *n.m.* (*Am.*) a monkey of the cebid family.

ubajay, *n.m.* (*Arg.*) a tree of the Myrtaceæ family.

ube, *n.m.* (*Philip.*) a plant of the Dioscoreaceæ family.

ubérrimo, -ma, *a. superl.* very fruitful, very abundant.

ubí, *n.m.* (*Cub.*) a plant of the Ampelidæ family.

ubicación, *n.f.* ubiquity; situation, position, location.

ubicar, *v.i., v.r.* (conjugated like BUSCAR) to be in a definite place, to lie, be situated.

ubicuidad, *n.f.* ubiquity.

ubicuo, -cua, *a.* ubiquitous, omnipresent.

ubiquitario, *n.m.* (*theol.*) Ubiquitarian.

ubre, *n.f.* udder, teat.

ubrera, *n.f.* (*med.*) thrush.

ucase, *n.m.* ukase.

uchú, *n.m.* (*Per.*) fruit of a shrub of the Capsicum family.

udómetro, *n.m.* udometer, rain-gauge.

uesnorueste, *n.m.* west-north-west.

uessudueste, *n.m.* west-south-west.
ueste, *n.m.* west.
¡ uf !, *interj.* ugh! (denoting weariness or repugnance).
ufanamente, *adv.* ostentatiously, boastfully, proudly, haughtily.
ufanarse, *v.r.* to boast, pride oneself, be haughty.
ufanía, *n.f.* pride, conceit, haughtiness; joy, gaiety, satisfaction, pleasure.
ufano, -na, *a.* proud, haughty, arrogant; cheerful, gay, content; masterly.
ufo, (a), *adv.* parasitically.
ugre, *n.m.* (*CR.*) a tree of the Bixaceæ family.
ujier, *n.m.* usher, doorkeeper. — *ujier de cámara,* usher of the king's privy chamber.
ulala, *n.f.* (*Bol.*) a kind of cactus.
ulano, *n.m.* uhlan.
úlcera, *n.f.* (*med.*) ulcer; (*bot.*) rot.
ulceración, *n.f.* ulceration.
ulcerante, *a.* ulcerating.
ulcerar, *v.t., v.r.* to ulcerate.
ulcerativo, -va, *a.* causing ulcers.
ulceroso, -sa, *a.* ulcerous.
ulcoate, *n.m.* (*Mex.*) a very poisonous snake.
ulmén, *n.m.* (*Chi.*) a rich and influential araucanian.
ulmo, *n.m.* (*Chi.*) a big perennial tree; its bark is used for tanning.
ulpo, *n.m.* (*Chi., Per.*) gruel made of toasted maize.
ulterior, *a.* farther; subsequent.
ulteriormente, *adv.* farther, beyond; subsequently.
últimamente, *adv.* lastly, finally, ultimately; recently, of late.
ultimar, *v.t.* to finish, end, close.
ultimátum, *n.m.* ultimatum.
ultimidad, *n.f.* ultimateness, final stage.
último, -ma, *a.* last, latest, hindmost; remote, extreme, terminal, final; highly finished; most valuable; *a últimos de,* at the end of (a week, month or year); *estar a lo último* (or *a las últimas*), to be well up in; *por último,* lastly, finally.
ultra, *adv.* beyond, besides, moreover; excessively.
ultrajador, -ra, *n.m.f., a.* one who outrages or insults.
ultrajamiento, *n.m.* outrage, affront.
ultrajar, *v.t.* to outrage, offend, abuse; depreciate, despise.
ultraje, *n.m.* outrage, insult; abuse; contempt.
ultrajosamente, *adv.* outrageously.
ultrajoso, -sa, *a.* outrageous, overbearing.
ultramar, *a.* beyond the sea, ultramarine, foreign.
ultramarino, -na, *a.* ultramarine.
ultramarino, *n.m.* ultramarine, finest blue. — *pl.* **ultramarinos,** oversea goods; (*coll.*) grocer's shop.
ultramaro, *n.m.* ultramarine colour.
ultramicroscopio, *n.m.* ultramicroscope.
ultramontanismo, *n.m.* ultramontanism.
ultramontano, -na, *a.* ultramontane.
ultranza, (a), *adv.* to death; at all costs.
ultrapuertos, *n.m.* place beyond the seaports.
ultrarrojo, *a.* infra-red.
ultratumba, *adv.* beyond the tomb.
ultraviolado, -da ; ultravioleta, *a.* ultraviolet.
úlula, *n.f.* scops owl; (*Am.*) screech owl.

ulular, *v.t.* to howl, hoot, shriek, cry aloud.
ululato, *n.m.* screech, howl.
ulva, *n.f.* (*Arg.*) a variety of cactus.
ulluco, *n.m.* (*Bol., Ec., Per.*) the original potato (*ullusus tuberosus*).
umanto, *n.m.* (*Bol.*) a fish common in lake Titicaca.
umareo, *n.m.* (*Per.*) first irrigation of a field recently sown.
umbela, *n.f.* umbel; projection over a balcony or window to carry off the rain-water.
umbelíferas, *n.f.pl.* (*bot.*) umbelliferæ.
umbelífero, -ra, *a.* umbelliferous.
umbilicado, -da, *a.* navel-shaped.
umbilical, *a.* umbilical.
umbral, *n.m.* threshold, lintel; rudiment, beginning, commencement.
umbralar, *v.t.* to lintel, place an architrave.
umbrátil, *a.* umbratile, shady.
umbría, *n.f.* shady place, grove.
umbrío, -bría, *a.* umbrageous, shady.
umbroso, -sa, *a.* shady.
un, *indef. art.* a, an. — *a.* one (apocope of *uno*).
unánime, *a.* unanimous.
unánimemente, *adv.* unanimously.
unanimidad, *n.f.* unanimity.
uncial, *a.* uncial.
unciforme, *a.* unciform.
unción, *n.f.* unction, anointing; (*eccles.*) extreme unction; devotion; storm try-sail. — *pl.* **unciones,** treatment by unctions of mercury.
uncionario, -ria, *a.* being under mercurial treatment.
uncionario, *n.m.* place where mercurial treatment is taken.
uncir, *v.t.* (*pres. indic.* **unzo ;** *pres. subj.* **unza**) to yoke.
undante, *a.* (*poet.*) waving, undulating.
undecágono, *n.m.* undecagon.
undécimo, -ma, *a.* eleventh.
undécuplo, -pla, *a.* eleven times as much.
undísono, -na, *a.* (*poet.*) sounding (of the sea).
undívago, -ga, *a.* (*poet.*) billowy, wavy.
undoso, -sa, *a.* wavy, undulating, undulatory.
undulación, *n.f.* undulation, wave motion.
undular, *v.i.* to rise in waves; to undulate; to wriggle.
undulatorio, -ria, *a.* undulatory.
ungido, *n.m.* anointed priest or king.
ungimiento, *n.m.* unction.
ungir, *v.t.* (*pres. indic.* **unjo ;** *pres. subj.* **unja**) to anoint, consecrate.
ungüentario, -ria, *a.* sweet-scented; unguentary.
ungüentario, *n.m.* perfume-box; anointer, preparer of ointment.
ungüento, *n.m.* unguent, liniment, ointment; perfume, salve, balsam.
unguiculado, -da, *a.* (*zool.*) unguiculate.
ungulado, -da, *a.* ungulate.
unible, *a.* that may be united or joined.
únicamente, *adv.* simply, solely, exclusively, uniquely, only.
único, -ca, *a.* singular, alone, only; single, unique, sole, rare, unparalleled, unmatched.
unicornio, *n.m.* unicorn; rhinoceros; *unicornio de mar,* narwhal.
unidad, *n.f.* unity; union, agreement; unit; singleness, oneness, uniqueness.
unidamente, *adv.* unitedly, jointly, conjunctively, unanimously.
unificación, *n.f.* unification.

unificar, *v.t.* (*pret.* **unifiqué**; *pres. subj.*
  unifique) to unify, unite.
uniformación, *n.f.* standardization, uniformity.
uniformador, -ra, *a.* uniformer; standardizer.
uniformar, *v.t.* to make uniform; to standardize; to put into uniform.
uniforme, *a.* uniform, similar, alike; regular,
  changeless; of even tenour. — *n.m.* uniform;
  regimentals.
uniformemente, *adv.* uniformly.
uniformidad, *n.f.* uniformity, harmony, resemblance.
unigénito, -ta, *a.* only-begotten.
unilateral, *a.* unilateral.
unión, *n.f.* union, conjunction, unity; harmony,
  alliance, confederacy, coalition; resemblance;
  agreement, concord, conformity; contiguity;
  continuity; sameness, similarity; composition, combination; incorporation, coherence;
  wedding, bond of marriage; (*mech.*) attachment, coupling, joint, joining, fastening;
  hoop, ring; linked rings; (*surg.*) closing of the
  lips of a wound; (*com.*) fusion, consolidation;
  (*rail.*) junction; (*Chi.*) lace insertion. — *unión
  hipostática*, (*theol.*) hypostatic union, the
  union of the divine and human natures in
  Christ.
unionista, *a.* unionist.
unípara, *a. fem.* uniparous.
unipersonal, *a.* unipersonal.
unipolar, *a.* (*elec.*) unipolar.
unir, *v.t.* to unite, join, conjoin; to couple,
  attach, connect, fasten, bind, incorporate,
  confederate; to approach, bring together,
  conform, aggregate, coalesce; to harmonize;
  to marry; to consolidate, close the lips of a
  wound. — *v.r.* to join, unite, adhere, associate, be united; to concur; to be contiguous;
  to wed, be married; (*com.*) to merge, consolidate. combine.
unisexual, *a.* unisexual.
unisón, *n.m.* unison.
unisonancia, *n.f.* unisonance; monotony, uniformity of sound.
unísono, -na, *a.* unison, sounding alike; *al
  unísono*, *adv.* in concord, agreement; unanimously.
unitario, -ria, *a.* unitarian; centralizer, supporter of centralization; Unitarian.
unitarismo, *n.m.* Unitarianism.
unitivo, -va, *a.* unitive.
univalvo, -va, *a.* univalve.
universal, *a.* universal, general, œcumenical;
  all-embracing; well-informed, learned.
universalidad, *n.f.* universality.
universalísimo, -ma, *a.* (*log.*) universal.
universalmente, *adv.* universally, generally.
universidad, *n.f.* university, institute for
  higher education; body of persons forming
  an institution; universality; nature as a whole.
universitario, -ria, *a.* university, universi-
  tarian.
universo, -sa, *a.* universal.
universo, *n.m.* universe.
univocación, *n.f.* univocation.
unívocamente, *adv.* univocally, unanimously.
univocarse, *v.r.* (conjugated like BUSCAR) to
  have the same meaning.
unívoco, -ca, *a.* univocal; unanimous.
uno, *n.m.* one, unit, number one.
uno, una, *a.* a, an. one, sole, only. — *pron.* one,

someone, anyone. — *pl.* **unos, unas,** some,
  some people, a few, nearly, about; *unos . . .
  otros*, some . . . others; *cada uno*, each one;
  uno a uno (or *de uno en uno*), one by one, in
  single file; *uno por uno*, first one, then another, etc.; *una cosa*, something (used
  vaguely); *de so uno*, (*obs.*) altogether, all at
  once; *a una*, jointly, together; *uno y otro*, both;
  uno a otro, reciprocally; *es todo uno*, it's all the
  same; *para en uno*, to be agreed *or* together;
  uno que otro, some, a few; *uno tras otro*, successively. — *n.m.* one (number); *uno y no más*,
  never again. — *n.f. la una*, one o'clock.
untador, -ra, *n.m.f.* anointer.
untadura, *n.f.* ointment, liniment; unction,
  anointing.
untamiento, *n.m.* unction, anointing.
untar, *v.t.* to anoint, rub with ointment; to
  smear, oil, grease; (*coll.*) to grease the hand,
  bribe. — *v.r.* to cheat, embezzle; *untar las
  manos*, (*fig.*) to oil the palm, to bribe.
untaza, *n.f.* grease.
unto, *n.m.* grease, fat; ointment, unguent; *unto
  amarillo* (or *unto de rana*), (*coll.*) money given
  as a bribe.
untuosidad, *n.f.* unctuosity, greasiness.
untuoso, -sa, *a.* unctuous, greasy.
untura, *n.f.* ointment, unction, liniment.
uña, *n.f.* nail; hoof, claw, talon; pointed hook;
  crust of sores; thorn; excrescence on the
  lachrymal caruncle; short tree-stump; curved
  beak; stinging tail of the scorpion; (*coll.*)
  light fingers; (*mech.*) gripper, clutch, claw;
  (*mus.*) plectrum; (*naut.*) palm or bill of an anchor; *uña de caballo*, (*bot.*) colt's-foot; *a uña
  de caballo*, at full speed; *uñas de gato y cara
  or hábito de beato*, the face of a saint and the
  deeds of a villain; *hincar la uña*, to overcharge,
  charge exorbitantly; *mostrar la uña*, to discover one's weaknesses; *mostrar las uñas*, (*fig.*)
  to show one's teeth; *sacar las uñas*, to use
  every possible means in a difficulty; *ser uña y
  carne*, to be very close friends; *afilar las
  uñas*, to sharpen one's wits; *caer en las uñas*,
  to fall into the clutches; *cortarse las uñas
  con*, to pick a quarrel with; *largo de uñas*,
  nimble-fingered, thieving; *mirarse las uñas*,
  to be indolent *or* at ease.
uñada, *n.f.* scratch, nip, mark of the nail.
uñarada, *n.f.* scratch with the nail.
uñate, *n.m.* pinch with the nail; chuck-farthing.
uñero, *n.m.* ingrowing nail; (*med.*) felon.
uñeta, *n.f.* little nail; chuck-farthing (boys'
  game); stonecutter's chisel; (*Chi.*) plectrum.
uñi, *n.m.* (*Chi.*) a Myrtaceous shrub.
uñidura, *n.f.* yoking.
uñir, *v.t.* to yoke.
uñoso, -sa, *a.* having long nails.
¡upa!, *interj.* hoop-la! up, up!
upupa, *n.f.* hoopoe.
ura, *n.f.* (*Arg.*) maggot.
uránico, -ca, *a.* uranic.
uranio, *n.m.* uranium.
uranita, *n.f.* uranite.
uranografía, *n.f.* uranography.
uranometría, *n.f.* uranometry.
urao, *n.m.* (*Am.*) hydrous carbonate of
  soda.
urape, *n.m.* (*Ven.*) a leguminous shrub.
uraquear, *v.t.* (*Arg.*) to perforate, bore;
  burrow.
urato, *n.m.* urate.

urbanamente, *adv.* politely, courteously, civilly, complacently.

urbanidad, *n.f.* urbanity, civility, courteousness, politeness.

urbanismo, *n.m.* town-planning.

urbanización, *n.f.* urbanization.

urbanizar, *v.t.* (*pret.* **urbanicé,** *pres. subj.* **urbanice**) to urbanize; to make sociable, polite.

urbano, -na, *a.* urban; urbane, polite, well-bred, courteous; traffic and urban (police).

urbe, *n.f.* large modern city.

urca, *n.f.* hooker, dogger; storeship; (*ichth.*) killer whale.

urce, *n.m.* heath.

urchilla, *n.f.* orchil.

urdidera, *n.f.* warper (woman); warping-frame.

urdidor, -ra, *n.m.f.* warper, warping-frame, warping-mill.

urdidura, *n.f.* warping.

urdiembre, urdimbre, *n.f.* warp, warping-chain.

urdir, *v.t.* to warp; (*fig.*) to contrive, plot, scheme.

urea, *n.f.* (*chem.*) urea.

uremia, *n.f.* (*med.*) uræmia.

urémico, -ca, *a.* (*med.*) uræmic.

urente, *a.* hot, scorching, burning.

uréter, *n.m.* ureter.

urético, -ca, *a.* urethral, belonging to the urethra.

uretra, *n.f.* urethra.

uretritis, *n.f.* urethritis; blennorrhœa.

urgencia, *n.f.* urgency, exigence, obligation.

urgente, *a.* urgent, pressing.

urgentemente, *adv.* urgently.

urgir, *v.i.* (*pres. indic.* **urjo**; *pres. subj.* **urja**) to be urgent, be pressing; to be in force (of laws).

úrico, -ca, *a.* uric.

urinal, urinario, *n.m.* urinal.

urinario, -ria, *a.* urinary.

urna, *n.f.* urn, case, casket, shrine; ballot-box.

urnición, *n.f.* (*prov.*) top-timbers.

uro, *n.m.* aurochs.

urogallo, *n.m.* a large bird of the Gallenæ group.

uromancía, *n.f.* uromancy.

uroscopia, *n.f.* uroscopy.

urpila, *n.f.* (*Arg.*) a small dove.

urque, *n.m.* (*Chi.*) a low-quality potato.

urraca, *n.f.* magpie; *hablar más que una urraca,* to talk excessively.

ursa, *n.f.* (*astr.*) the Bear; *Ursa Mayor,* the Great Bear; *Ursa Menor,* the Little Bear.

ursulina, *n.f.* Ursuline nun.

urticáceo, -cea, *a.* urticaceous.

urticaria, *n.f.* nettle-rash.

urú, *n.m.* (*Arg.*) a kind of partridge.

urubú, *n.m.* (*Am.*) black vulture.

uruguayo, -ya, *n.m.f.,* *a.* Uruguayan; of Uruguay.

urundey, *n.m.* (*Arg.*) a tree of the Terebinthus family.

urutaú, *n.m.* (*Arg.*) a nocturnal bird.

urutí, *n.m.* (*Arg.*) a very small bird with bright feathers.

usadamente, *adv.* according to custom.

usado, -da, *a.* used, employed; threadbare, worn out, second-hand; skilful, experienced; practical; fashionable; frequent.

usagre, *n.m.* (*med.*) infantile eczema; (*vet.*) scald-head.

usaje, *n.m.* usage, custom.

usanza, *n.f.* usage, custom.

usar, *v.t.* to use, make use of, practise, accustom; to wear; to exercise; to enjoy. — *v.i.* to be accustomed to. — *v.r.* to be in fashion or use; to be wont.

usarcé, usarced, *n.m.f.* (*obs.*) (contraction of **vuesa merced**) your honour.

usencia, *n.m.f.* (contraction of **vuesa reverencia**) (*eccles.*) your reverence.

useñoria, *n.m.f.* (contraction of **vuestra señoría**) your lordship (or ladyship).

usgo, *n.m.* loathing.

usía, *n.m.f.* (contraction of **vuestra señoría**) your excellency, your lordship, your ladyship.

usina, *n.f.* (*Arg.*) large industrial establishment; factory.

uso, *n.m.* use, service, employment practice, experience; enjoyment, usufruct; (*com. law*) a uniform and recognized practice; office, exercise; custom, mode, style, fashion; wearing, wear, wear-and-tear; *a uso* (or *al uso*), according to custom; *andar al uso,* to temporize, conform to the times; *en cada tierra su uso,* every country has its own ways.

ustaga, *n.f.* (*naut.*) tie.

usted, *pron. m.f.* (*pl.* **ustedes**), you (polite form), your worship, your honour (written **V.** or **Vd.,** *pl.* **VV.** or **Vds.**).

ustible, *a.* easily combustible.

ustión, *n.f.* ustion.

ustorio, -ria, *a.* ustorious, burning.

usual, *a.* usual, ordinary, customary, current, general; tractable, social.

usualmente, *adv.* usually, ordinarily, generally.

usuario, -ria, *a.* (*law*) having the sole use.

usucapión, *n.f.* (*law*) usucapion.

usucapir, *v.t.* to acquire a right of property by usucapion.

usufructo, *n.m.* usufruct; enjoyment, profit.

usufructuar, *v.t.* to enjoy the usufruct of something. — *v.i.* to be productive, fruitful.

usufructuario, -ria, *n.m.f., a.* usufructuary.

usura, *n.f.* interest, usury; profit, gain.

usurar, *v.i.* [USUREAR].

usurariamente, *adv.* usuriously.

usurario, -ria, *a.* usurious.

usurear, *v.i.* to practise usury; to lend or borrow money on interest; to reap great profit.

usurero, -ra, *n.m.f.* usurer, money-lender.

usurpación, *n.f.* usurpation.

usurpador, -ra, *n.m.f.* usurper.

usurpar, *v.t.* to usurp.

usuta, *n.f.* (*Arg., Bol., Chi.*) sandal worn by Indian women.

uta, *n.f.* (*Per.*) facial ulcers common in the Andes.

utensilio, *n.m.* utensil, implement; device, contrivance. — *pl.* **utensilios,** implements, tools.

uterino, -na, *a.* uterine.

útero, *n.m.* uterus, womb.

uteromanía, *n.f.* hysteria.

uteroscopio, *n.m.* hysteroscope.

útil, *a.* useful, profitable, serviceable, commodious, convenient; (*law*) lawful (applied to time). — *n.m.* utility. — *pl.* **útiles,** utensils, tools.

utilero, -ra, *n.m.f.* (*Am.*) the man or woman in charge of theatrical properties.

utilidad, *n.f.* utility, profit, expediency, usefulness.

utilitario, -ria, *n.m.f.,* *a.* utilitarian.

utilitarismo, *n.m.* utilitarianism.

utilitarista, *n.,* *a.* utilitarian.

utilizable, *a.* usable, utilizable.

utilizar, *v.t.* (*pret.* **utilicé;** *pres. subj.* **utilice**) to make use of, utilize, use. — *v.r.* to profit, be made profitable, take advantage of, profit by.

útilmente, *adv.* usefully, profitably.

utopía, utopia, *n.f.* Utopia.

utópico, -ca, *a.* utopian, dreaming, idealizing.

utopista, *n.m.* utopian schemer, dreamer, idealist.

utrero, -ra, *n.m.f.* bull or heifer from two to three years old.

uva, *n.f.* grape; barberry; tippler; tumour, wart on the eyelid; tumour on the uvula. — *pl.* **uvas,** bunch of grapes; *uva espina* (or *crespa*), gooseberry; *uva pasa,* raisin; *uva de corinto,* currant; *uva de gato,* white stonecrop; *uva marina,* shrubby horsetail; *uva lupina,* wolf's-bane; *uva de raposa,* nightshade; *uva tamínea,* lousewort; *hecho una uva,* very drunk; *conocer las uvas de su majuelo,* to understand one's own business.

uvada, *n.f.* abundance of grapes.

uvaduz, *n.f.* red-berried arbustus.

uval, *a.* resembling, similar to grapes.

uvate, *n.m.* conserve of grapes.

uvayema, *n.f.* kind of wild vine.

uve, *n.f.* name of the letter V.

uverillo, *n.m.* (*Cub., PR.*) a wild tree (*Coccoloba laurifolia*).

uvero, -ra, *a.* belonging or relating to grapes.

uvero, *n.m.* retailer of grapes; (*Am.*) a wild tree of the West Indies and Central America, with edible fruit.

uviar, *v.i.* (*obs.*) to attend, come, arrive.

uvilla, *n.f.* (*Chi.*) a kind of red currant.

uvillo, *n.m.* (*Chi.*) a climbing shrub of the Phytolacca Americana family.

úvula, *n.f.* uvula.

uxoricida, *n.m., a.* wife-murderer, uxoricide.

uxoricidio, *n.m.* wife-murder, uxoricide.

uzas, *n.f.* (*Braz.*) kind of crab.

V

V, v, *n.f.* v, the twenty-fifth letter of the Spanish alphabet; its name is *uve.* **V.** abbreviation of *véase,* see, and of *usted;* **VV.** abbreviation of *ustedes.*

vaca, *n.f.* cow; beef; sole-leather; joint stock of two gambling partners; *vaca de leche,* milch-cow; *vaca de la boda,* one always sought after in distress; laughing-stock; *vaca de San Antón,* ladybird; *más vale vaca en paz, que pollos en agraz,* better little with contentment, than great riches; *si quieres ser rico, calza de vaca y viste de fino,* good clothes are in the long run more economical; *por eso se vende la vaca* or *porque uno come la pierna y otro la falda,* it's fortunate that people have different tastes.

vacación, *n.f.* vacation, intermission, recess. — *pl.* **vacaciones,** holidays.

vacada, *n.f.* drove of cows.

vacancia, *n.f.* vacancy.

vacante, *a.* vacant, disengaged, unoccupied. — *n.f.* vacancy; vacation.

vacar, *v.i.* (*pret.* **vaqué;** *pres. subj.* **vaque**) to be vacant; to give up some work temporarily; to vacate a position; to devote oneself; to lack.

vacarí, *a.* leathern or leather-covered.

vacatura, *n.f.* period of vacancy.

vaciada, *n.f.* (*metall.*) melt.

vaciadero, *n.m.* drain, sink, sewer; dumping-place.

vaciadizo, -za, *a.* mould; cast.

vaciado, *n.m.* form cast (in a mould); act of casting; (*arch.*) excavation; (*arch.*) face of a pedestal below its mouldings.

vaciador, *n.m.* moulder, caster; dumper, emptier, pourer; *vaciador de navajas,* razor grinder.

vaciamiento, *n.m.* casting, moulding; evacuating, emptying, hollowing.

vaciar, *v.t.* to evacuate, empty, exhaust, pour out; to model, form, mould; to grind; (*arch.*) to excavate, hollow; to explain fully; to translate. — *v.i.* to discharge, flow into; to decrease, fall (of waters); to lose colour or lustre. — *v.r.* to overflow, be spilt (of liquors); to divulge; to become empty or vacant.

vaciedad, *n.f.* emptiness, frothiness; silly talk, nonsense.

vaciero, *n.m.* shepherd of barren sheep.

vacilación, *n.f.* vacillation, staggering, reeling; perplexity; hesitation, irresolution.

vacilante, *a.* vacillating, hesitating, unstable, irresolute.

vacilar, *v.i.* to vacillate, fluctuate, waver, hesitate; to stagger, reel.

vacío,-cía, *a.* void, empty, vacuous, disengaged; unoccupied, uninhabited, untenanted; fruitless, idle; concave, hollow; defective; barren (of cattle); unloaded (of carts, horses, etc.); arrogant, presumptuous, vain.

vacío, *n.m.* void, vacuum, empty space; aperture; vacancy; casting-mould; vacuity, cavity, concavity, hollowness; blank, gap, hiatus; flank of animals; Spanish step in dancing; *de vacío,* empty, unemployed; *en vacío,* in vacuo; *freno al vacío,* vacuum-brake; *tacho al vacío,* (*Am.*) vacuum-pan.

vaco, -ca, *a.* vacant. — *n.m.* (*coll.*) ox.

vacuidad, *n.f.* vacuity, emptiness.

vacuna, *n.f.* vaccine; cow-pox.

vacunación, *n.f.* vaccination.

vacunar, *v.t.* to vaccinate.

vacuno, -na, *a.* bovine, belonging to cattle.

vacuo, -cua, *a.* unoccupied, vacant, empty.

vacuo, *n.m.* vacuum.

vacuómetro, *n.m.* vacuum gauge.

vade, *n.m.* case, portfolio, vade-mecum.

vadeable, *a.* fordable; conquerable.

vadear, *v.t.* to wade, ford; to surmount, conquer; to try, sound. — *v.r.* to conduct oneself, behave.

vademécum, *n.m.* vade-mecum; case, portfolio.

vadera, *n.f.* ford, shallow part of a river.

¡vade retro!, *interj.* avaunt! away! get you gone!

vado, *n.m.* ford, shallow part of a river; resource, expedient; *no hallar vado,* to be at a loss how to act; *al vado o a la puente,* one way or the other.

vadoso, -sa, *a.* shallow, shoaly.

vafe, *n.m.* (*prov.*) bold undertaking.

vagabundear, *v.i.* to rove about, loiter about.
vagabundo, -da, *n.m.f.*, *a.* vagabond, vagrant, roamer, rover; tramp, loiterer.
vagamente, *adv.* vaguely.
vagamundear, *v.i.* to loiter about, rove about.
vagamundo, -da, *n.m.f.*, *a.* vagabond, vagrant; roamer, rover; tramp, loiterer.
vagancia, *n.f.* vagrancy.
vagante, *a.* vagrant, wandering.
vagar, *v.i.* (*pret.* **vagué;** *pres. subj.* **vague**) to rove about, loiter about, wander, range; to be idle, at leisure; to revolve in the mind. — *n.m.* idleness, leisure; indolence; slowness; *de vagar*, (*obs.*) slowly.
vagarosamente, *adv.* vagrantly, rovingly.
vagaroso, -sa, *a.* vagrant, errant.
vagido, *n.m.* cry of a new-born child.
vagina, *n.f.* vagina.
vaginal, *a.* vaginal.
vago, -ga, *a.* errant, vagrant; restless, roving; loitering, wandering; undecided, indefinite, unsettled; lax, vague, loose; hesitating, wavering, fluctuating; (*art*) light, airy, vaporous, indistinct, hazy; *n.m.* (*prov.*) uncultivated plot of ground; vagabond, loafer, vagrant; *en vago*, vaguely, unsteadily, unsuccessfully, insecurely.
vagón, *n.m.* wagon; railway coach; goods-van; *vagón cama*, sleeping-car; *vagón restaurante*, dining-car.
vagonada, *n.f.* wagon-load, car-load.
vagoneta, *n.f.* truck, trolley.
vaguada, *n.f.* water-course.
vagueación, *n.f.* restlessness, uneasiness; flight of fancy.
vagueante, *a.* vagrant; wandering, flighty.
vaguear, *v.i.* to loiter, wander, rove, roam.
vaguedad, *n.f.* vagueness, ambiguity, uncertainty; vague statement; levity.
vaguemaestre, *n.m.* (*mil.*) transport master.
vaguido, *n.m.* dizziness, giddiness; peril, risk, danger.
vaguido, -da, *a.* dizzy.
vahaje, *n.m.* gentle breeze.
vahanero, -ra, *a.* (*prov., obs.*) idle, knavish.
vahar, vahear, *v.i.* to exhale, emit (steam, vapour, etc.).
vaharada, *n.f.* vapour, breath, breathing, exhalation.
vaharera, *n.f.* (*med.*) thrush; (*prov.*) unripe melon.
vaharina, *n.f.* (*coll.*) fume, mist, vapour.
vahear, [VAHAR].
vahído, *n.m.* vertigo, giddiness, dizziness.
vaho, *n.m.* steam, vapour; fume, effluvium.
vaina, *n.f.* scabbard, sheath; knife-case, scissors-case; (*bot.*) pod, husk, capsule, cod, legume; (*naut.*) tabling of a flag; (*naut.*) bolt-rope tabling; (*Col., Pan., CR.*) disappointment, annoyance, bother; *so vaina de oro, cuchillo de plomo*, all is not gold that glitters.
vainazas, *n.m.* (*coll.*) lazy, dull person.
vainero, *n.m.* scabbard-maker.
vainica, *n.f.* back-stitch, hem-stitch.
vainilla, *n.f.* vanilla; heliotrope; small husk or pod.
vainiquera, *n.f.* hemstitch worker.
vaivén, *n.m.* fluctuation, vibration, sway, unsteadiness, vacillation, inconstancy; seesaw, swinging movement; giddiness; risk, danger; (*mech.*) reciprocating movement; (*naut.*) line, cord, rope.

vajilla, *n.f.* table-service, dinner-service; (*Mex.*) an ancient tax on jewellery; *vajilla de plata*, silver ware.
val, *n.m.* (contraction of VALLE) vale, valley, dale; (*prov.*) drain, sink, sewer.
valaco, -ca, *n.m.f.*, *a.* Wallachian.
valais, *n.m.* board, a piece of timber about 4 yards long.
valar, *a.* relating to an enclosure.
valdivia, *n.f.* (*Ec.*) a bird of the order of climbers.
valdiviano, *n.m.* (*Chi.*) a dish made of beef, onions and lemon-juice.
vale, *n.m.* farewell, adieu; valediction; bond, promissory note, IOU; bet at cards; token of good marks given to schoolboys, 'star.'
valedero, -ra, *a.* valid, binding, efficacious.
valedor, -ra, *n.m.f.* protector, defender.
valentía, *n.f.* valour, courage, gallantry, manliness, bravery; exploit, feat; boast, brag; great effort; (*art*) dash, fire, imagination; second-hand shoe shop in Madrid; *hambre y valentía*, poverty and pride; *pisar de valentía*, to swagger or strut about.
valentísimo, -ma, *a.* most valiant; most perfect.
valentón, -ona, *a.* blustering, arrogant, haughty, vainglorious.
valentón, *n.m.* hector, bully.
valentonada, *n.f.* brag, boast.
valer, *v.i.* (*pres. indic.* **valgo;** *fut. indic.* **valdré;** *pres. subj.* **valga**) to be worth, worthy, deserving, valuable, marketable; to serve as refuge; to be able, have power, influence, etc.; to prevail; to possess merit; to be current (of money), to be valid; to hold; to amount to, be equivalent to; to be important, useful; to serve as a protection. — *v.t.* to protect, defend, patronize, favour; to yield, produce, bring in; to be worth, valued at. — *v.r.* to employ, make use of; to avail oneself, have recourse. — *n.m.* value; *valer un ojo de la cara*, to be very precious; *más vale* (or *más valiera*) it is (or would be) better; *más vale tarde que nunca*, better late than never; *vale lo que pesa*, he is worth his weight in gold; *valga lo que valiere*, come what may; *no vale la pena*, it's not worth the trouble; *¡válgame Dios!* bless me! good heavens! *¡válgate Dios!* heaven bless you! *lo que mucho vale, mucho cuesta*, nothing good is got without pains; *más vale algo que nada*, half a loaf is better than no bread.
valeriana, *n.f.* valerian.
valerianato, *n.m.* valerianate.
valeriánico, -ca, *a.* valeric.
valerosamente, *adv.* valiantly, courageously.
valerosidad, *n.f.* courage, bravery.
valeroso, -sa, *a.* valiant, courageous, brave, heroic, gallant; powerful, active, strong.
valetudinario, -ria, *a.* valetudinarian, infirm, invalid.
valí, *n.m.* moslem governor.
valía, *n.f.* appraisement, valuation, price; credit, favour, use, worth, influence; party, faction; *a las valías*, at the highest price.
validación, *n.f.* validity; soundness, firmness.
válidamente, *adv.* validly.
validar, *v.t.* to make binding, validate, give validity.
validez, *n.f.* validity, stability, soundness, efficacy.

válido, -da, *a.* valid, prevalent; sound, firm, conclusive, binding, obligatory, weighty.

valido, -da, *a.* relying, confident; esteemed, accepted, favoured, strong, powerful, influential.

valido, *n.m.* favourite; court minion; prime minister.

valiente, *a.* valiant, brave, spirited, gallant, courageous; active, strenuous; efficacious, valid; excessive, very great; strong, robust, vigorous, powerful. — *n.m.* bully, hector, braggart.

valientemente, *adv.* valiantly, strenuously, courageously, manfully; strongly, vigorously; abundantly, excessively; handsomely, elegantly.

valija, *n.f.* valise; mail-bag; post, mail.

valijero, *n.m.* letter-carrier.

valijón, *n.m.* large valise.

valimiento, *n.m.* use, utility; advantage, benefit; value; favouritism, good graces, interest; favour, protection, support.

valioso, -sa, *a.* highly esteemed; very valuable; most influential; wealthy, rich.

valisoletano, -na, *n.m.f.*, *a.* (native or inhabitant) of Valladolid.

valón, -ona, *n.m.f.*, *a.* Walloon; *U valona,* name of the letter W. — *pl.* **valones,** bloomers.

valona, *n.f.* boy's shirt-collar, vandyke collar; (*Col.*, *Ec.*, *Ven.*) the groomed mane of a horse, mule, etc.

valor, *n.m.* value, worth; price; force, validity; equivalency, amount; fortitude, courage, manliness, bravery, gallantry, valour; meaning, importance; power, efficiency, activity; income, revenue; *valor contante,* at cash value; *valor recibido,* for value received. — *pl.* **valores,** securities, stocks, bonds; *valores fiduciarios,* bank-notes.

valorar, valorear, *v.t.* to value, appraise, price; to raise the value.

valoría, *n.f.* price, worth, value.

valquiria, *n.f.* valkyrie.

vals, *n.m.* waltz.

valsar, *v.i.* to waltz.

valuación, *n.f.* valuation, appraisement.

valuador, -ra, *n.m.f.* valuer, appraiser.

valuar, *v.t.* to appraise, value, prize, rate.

valva, *n.f.* (*zool.*) valve.

valvasor, *n.m.* hidalgo, lesser nobleman.

válvula, *n.f.* valve; *válvula de seguridad,* safety valve; *válvula de estrangulación,* throttle valve.

valvular, *a.* valvular.

valvulilla, *n.f.* valve.

valla, *n.f.* barricade, barrier; paling, fence, stockade, hurdle; enclosure; impediment, obstacle; *romper* (or *saltar*) *la valla,* to be foremost in undertaking any matter.

valladar, vallado, *n.m.* enclosure, stockade; obstacle.

valladear, vallar, *v.t.* to hedge, fence, enclose with stakes.

valle, *n.m.* vale, valley, dale, dell, glen; number of cottages or small hamlets in a valley; *valle de lágrimas,* vale of tears.

vallejo, *n.m.* small valley.

vallejuelo, *n.m.* tiny valley, glen, dell.

vallico, *n.m.* rye-grass.

vallisoletano, -na, *n.m.f.*, *a.* (native or inhabitant) of Valladolid.

¡vamos!, *interj.* come now! well! go on! come, come! let's stop!

vampiro, *n.m.* vampire; usurer, skinflint, miser; ghoul.

vanadio, *n.m.* vanadium.

vanagloria, *n.f.* vaingloriousness, ostentation, boastfulness, conceit.

vanagloriarse, *v.r.* to be vainglorious, boast, be proud.

vanagloriosamente, *adv.* vaingloriously.

vanaglorioso, -sa, *a.* vainglorious, ostentatious, conceited.

vanamente, *adv.* vainly, uselessly, unfoundedly, frivolously, idly; arrogantly, proudly, presumptuously; superstitiously.

vandálico, -ca, *a.* Vandalic.

vandalismo, *n.m.* vandalism.

vándalo, -la, *n.m.f.* Vandal.

vanear, *v.i.* to talk nonsense.

vanguardia, *n.f.* van, vanguard.

vanidad, *n.f.* vanity, ostentation, vain show, foppishness, nonsense; meaningless talk; conceit, levity, inanity, shallowness; *hacer vanidad,* to boast.

vanidoso, -sa, *a.* vain, haughty, foppish, showy, conceited.

vanilocuencia, *n.f.* verbosity, pomposity.

vanilocuo, -cua, *a.* vain, useless.

vaniloquio, *n.m.* foolish talk, empty prattler.

vanistorio, *n.m.* (*coll.*) ridiculous or affected vanity; affected fellow.

vano, -na, *a.* vain; empty, inane, shallow, futile, useless, frivolous, fallacious; presumptuous, haughty, arrogant, conceited, foppish; insubstantial; *en vano,* in vain, unnecessarily, uselessly. — *n.m.* opening in a wall.

vánova, *n.f.* coverlet, bedspread.

vapor, *n.m.* vapour, steam, breath; mist, exhalation; faintness, dizziness, vertigo; frenzy; steamer, steamboat. — *pl.* **vapores,** vapours, hysterical fit.

vaporable, *a.* vaporous, exhalable; fumy.

vaporación, vaporización, *n.f.* evaporation, vaporization.

vaporar, vaporear, vaporizar, *v.i.* to evaporate. — *v.t.* to vaporize.

vaporoso, -sa, *a.* vaporous, vapourish; ethereal, cloudy, indistinct.

vapulación, *n.f.; * **vapulamiento,** *n.m.* whipping, flogging.

vapular, vapulear, *v.t.* to whip, flog.

vapuleamiento, vapuleo, *n.m.* whipping, flogging.

vaquear, *v.t.* to cover cows (said of bulls).

vaquería, *n.f.* herd of cattle; dairy.

vaqueriza, *n.f.* winter cattle-shed.

vaquerizo, -za, *a.* relating to cows. — *n.m.f.* herdsman.

vaquero, *n.m.* cowherd, cow-keeper; herdsman; (*bot.*) ulex.

vaquero, -ra, *a.* belonging to cowherds.

vaqueta, *n.f.* cow-hide, sole-leather.

vaquetear, *v.t.* to flog with leather thongs.

vaqueteo, *n.m.* flogging, running the gauntlet.

vaquilla, vaquita, *n.f.* small cow; (*Arg.*, *Chi.*) heifer under two years.

váquira, *n.f.* peccary.

vara, *n.f.* rod, twig; pole, staff; verge, wand; measure of length about 33 in.; emblem of authority; herd of 40 to 50 swine; picador's thrust at a bull; chastisement, discipline;

vara alta, (*fig.*) high hand; *vara de cortina*, curtain-rod; *vara de pescar*, fishing-rod; *vara de Jesé*, tuberose; *vara (de coche de caballos)*, shaft (of a cart); *vara de medir*, yardstick.

varada, *n.f.* (*naut.*) stranding, running aground; (*agric.*) gang of farm hands; job on a farm; (*min.*) three months' work in a mine; (*min.*) quarterly profit and dividend.

varadera, *n.f.* (*naut.*) skid.

varadero, *n.m.* shipyard.

varadura, *n.f.* running aground; grounding of a vessel.

varal, *n.m.* long pole; (*theat.*) side-lights; tall, slender person; (*Arg.*) poles used to dry jerked beef.

varapalo, *n.m.* long pole, blow with a pole; vexation, grief, trouble, damage, reverse.

varar, *v.t.* (*obs.*) to launch; to run aground. — *v.i.* to be stranded, stopped, at a standstill.

varaseto, *n.m.* espalier.

varazo, *n.m.* stroke with a pole or stick.

varbasco, *n.m.* verbascum, mullein.

vardasca, *n.f.* thin twig.

vardascazo, *n.m.* stroke with a twig or switch.

vareador, *n.m.* beater with a pole or staff.

vareaje, *n.m.* retail-trade; selling or measuring by the yard; beating down the fruit of trees.

varear, *v.t.* to beat down fruit; to cudgel; to measure or sell by the yard; to wound with the goad. — *v.r.* to grow thin or lean.

varejón, *n.m.* thick pole or staff.

varenga, *n.f.* (*naut.*) floor-timber.

varengaje, *n.m.* (*naut.*) collection of floor-timbers.

vareo, *n.m.* [VAREAJE].

vareta, *n.f.* small rod or twig; lime-twig; stripe; piquant expression, hint, offensive remark; *irse de vareta*, (*coll.*) to have diarrhœa.

varetazo, *n.m.* stroke with a twig.

varetear, *v.t.* to variegate, make stripes (in fabrics).

varga, *n.f.* steepest part of a hill.

varganal, *n.m.* enclosure, stockade.

várgano, *n.m.* railing or stake of a fence.

varí, *n.m.* (*Chi., Per.*) a bird of prey.

variabilidad, *n.f.* variableness.

variable, *a.* variable, changeable, fickle.

variablemente, *adv.* variably.

variación, *n.f.* variation, varying, change; *variación de la aguja*, variation of the compass.

variado, -da, *a.* variegated, coloured.

variamente, *adv.* variously, differently.

variante, *a.* varying, deviating. — *n.f.* difference, discrepancy; variant reading.

variar, *v.t.* to change, shift, alter; to diversify, variegate. — *v.i.* to vary, turn, change; to differ from, deviate.

várice, varice, *n.f.* (*surg.*) varix.

varicela, *n.f.* chicken-pox.

varicocele, *n.f.* varicocele.

varicoso, -sa, *a.* varicose.

variedad, *n.f.* variety, variation, change, alteration, diversity; (*com.*) assortment.

variedades, *n.f.pl.* miscellaneous, miscellany; *teatro de variedades*, variety theatre.

varilla, *n.f.* small rod; curtain-rod; spindle, pivot; switch; rib or stick of a fan or umbrella; whalebone of corset; (*coll.*) jawbone; (*Chi.*) a shrub of the Papilionaceous family. — *pl.* **varillas,** frame of a sieve.

varillaje, *n.m.* collection of ribs of a fan, umbrella or corset.

varillar, *n.m.* (*Chi.*) place where *varilla* abounds.

vario, -ria, *a.* various, different, divers; variable, inconstant; unsteady, fickle, undecided, vague; variegated. — *pl.* **varios, -as,** various, several.

varioloso, -sa, *a.* variolous, variolar.

varita de San José, *n.f.* (*Hond.*) tuberose.

varón, *n.m.* man, male; man of respectability; (*naut.*) pendant (of rudder); *santo varón*, (*coll.*) worthy but rather dull man; *buen varón*, wise, prudent man.

varona, varonesa, *n.f.* woman; mannish woman.

varonía, male issue.

varonil, *a.* male; manly, masculine, vigorous, spirited.

varonilmente, *adv.* manfully, courageously, valiantly.

Varsovia, *n.f.* Warsaw.

varraco, *n.m.* male hog or boar.

varraquear, *v.i.* (*coll.*) to grunt like a pig; to cry long (of children).

varraquera, *n.f.* (*coll.*) crying spell (of children).

vasallaje, *n.m.* vassalage, servitude, subjection; dependence; liege-money.

vasallo, -lla, *n.m.f.* vassal, subject. — *a.* vassal, subject, tributary, feudatory.

vasar, *n.m.* kitchen-shelf.

vasco, -ca; vascongado, -da, *n.m.f.*, *a.* Basque.

vascuence, *n.m.* Basque language, Biscayan; (*coll.*) jargon, gibberish.

vascular, vasculoso, -sa, *a.* vascular, vasculose.

vase, *v.r.* (*3rd pers. sing. pres. ind. of* IRSE) (*theat.*) exit.

vaselina, *n.f.* Vaseline (*reg. trade mark*).

vasera, *n.f.* glass-rack.

vasico, *n.m.* small glass.

vasija, *n.f.* vessel, receptacle; butt, cask, pipe; *a la vasija nueva dura el resabio de lo que se echó en ella*, habits early formed are never lost.

vasillo, *n.m.* honeycomb cell.

vaso, *n.m.* vessel; vase, jar, tumbler, glass; glassful; (*naut.*) vessel; horse's hoof; artery, vein; receptacle; (*astron.*) Crater, a southern constellation; *vaso de noche*, chamber-pot.

vástago, *n.m.* stem, shoot, bud, tiller, sucker, sapling; scion, descendant, offspring; *vástago del émbolo*, (*mech.*) piston rod; *vástago de válvula*, valve stem.

vastedad, *n.f.* vastness, immensity, extension, extent.

vasto, -ta, *a.* vast, immense, huge.

vate, *n.m.* (*poet.*) bard, poet; diviner, seer.

vaticano, -na, *a.* pertaining to the Vatican.

vaticinador, -ra, *n.m.f.* prophet, diviner.

vaticinante, *a.* foretelling, divining, predicting.

vaticinar, *v.t.* to divine, foretell, predict.

vaticinio, *n.m.* vaticination, divination, prediction.

vatídico, -ca, *a.* (*poet.*) prophetical.

vatio, *n.m.* watt; *vatio-hora*, watt-hour.

vaya, *n.f.* jest, scoff. — *interj.* get along with you! come, come! Gracious! *¡Vaya Vd. con Dios!* farewell; *¡Vaya por Dios!* good heavens *¡vaya una ocurrencia!* what a notion!

¡vaya un lío! here's a pretty state of things!

ve, *n.f.* name of the letter V.

véase, see, vide.

vecera, *n.f.* herd, pack, drove (usually porcine).

vecero, -ra, *n.m.f., a.* alternate performer; (of trees) fruit-bearing in alternate years; customer.

vecinal, *a.* belonging to the neighbourhood; adjacent, neighbouring.

vecinamente, *adv.* near, next, close by, contiguously.

vecindad, *n.f.* population, inhabitants; vicinity, neighbourhood, contiguity, proximity, affinity; *hacer mala vecindad,* to be a troublesome neighbour.

vecindario, *n.m.* population, number of inhabitants in one place; vicinity, neighbourhood.

vecino, -na, *a.* neighbouring, near, adjoining, next; like, resembling; coincident.

vecino, *n.m.* neighbour, inhabitant, housekeeper, freeman, citizen, denizen; *el buen vecino hace tener al hombre mal aliño,* a man is easily spoilt by kindly neighbours.

vectación, *n.f.* riding (in a vehicle).

vector, *n.m.* vector. — *a.* vectorial.

veda, *n.f.* prohibition, interdiction; close season (game). — *n.m.* Veda, each of the four sacred books of the Hindoos.

vedado, *n.m.* enclosure, park, warren.

vedamiento, *n.m.* prohibition.

vedar, *v.t.* to prohibit, forbid; to impede, hinder, obstruct.

vedegambre, *n.m.* hellebore.

vedeja, *n.f.* long lock of hair; forelock; lion's mane.

vedija, *n.f.* tangled lock of wool, tuft of tangled hair.

vedijero, -ra, *n.m.f.* collector of loose locks at shearing.

vedijoso, -sa; vedijudo, -da, *a.* having tangled hair.

vedijuela, *n.f.* small lock of wool.

veduño, *n.m.* quality of vines.

veedor, -ra, *n.m.f.* watcher, spy, prier; busybody; inspector, overseer; provider, caterer; principal equerry to the king.

veeduría, *n.f.* overseer's place or employment; inspector's office; controllership.

vega, *n.f.* plain, meadow, mead, tract of fruitful ground, fertile space; (*Cub.*) tobaccoplantation; (*Chi.*) low and swampy ground.

vegetabilidad, *n.f.* vegetability.

vegetable, *n.m., a.* vegetable.

vegetación, *n.f.* vegetation.

vegetal, *n.m., a.* vegetable, plant.

vegetante, *a.* vegetating, growing, living.

vegetar, *v.i.* to flourish, grow (of plants); (*fig.*) to vegetate.

vegetarianismo, *n.m.* vegetarianism.

vegetariano, -na, *n.m.f., a.* vegetarian.

vegetativo, -va, *a.* vegetative.

vegoso, -sa, *a.* (*Chi.*) damp ground.

veguer, *n.m.* in Aragon, Catalonia and Majorca, magistrate; in Andorra the representative of Spain.

veguería, veguerío, *n.m.f.* jurisdiction and office of a *veguer.*

veguero, *n.m.* (*Cub.*) tobacco-planter; overseer of a *vega;* cigar made of a single leaf.

veguero, -ra, *a.* meadowy.

vehemencia, *n.f.* vehemence, violence, impetuosity; force, fervour, heat.

vehemente, *a.* vehement, impetuous; fiery, fervent; keen, vivid, persuasive.

vehementemente, *adv.* vehemently, fervently, hotly, forcibly.

vehículo, *n.m.* vehicle, carriage; conductor.

veintavo, *n.m.* twentieth part.

veinte, *n.m., a.* twenty, twentieth; *a las veinte,* unseasonably.

veintén, *n.m.* gold dollar.

veintena, *n.f.;* **veintenar,** *n.m.* score, twentieth part.

veintenario, -ria, *a.* containing twenty years.

veinteñal, *a.* lasting twenty years.

veinteocheno, -na; veintiocheno, -na, *a.* twenty-eighth. — *n.m.* cloth with 2,800 threads of warp.

veinteseiseno, -na; veintiseiseno, -na, *a.* twenty-sixth.

veintésimo, -ma, *a.* twentieth.

veinticinco, *a.* twenty-five.

veinticuatreno, -na, *a.* twenty-fourth. — *n.m.* cloth with 2,400 threads of warp.

veinticuatro, *n.m., a.* twenty-four, twentyfourth. — *n.m.* alderman in some Andalusian cities.

veintidós, *n.m., a.* twenty-two.

veintidoseno, -na, *a.* twenty-second.

veintinueve, *n.m., a.* twenty-nine, twentyninth.

veintiocho, *n.m., a.* twenty-eight, twentyeighth.

veintiséis, *n.m., a.* twenty-six, twenty-sixth.

veintiseiseno, -na, *a.* twenty-sixth.

veintisiete, *n.m., a.* twenty-seven, twentyseventh.

veintitrés, *n.m., a.* twenty-three, twenty-third.

veintiún, veintiuno, -na, *n.m., a.* twenty-one.

veintiuna, *n.f.* vingt-et-un.

vejación, *n.f.* ill-treatment, oppression, molestation.

vejamen, *n.m.* taunt; lampoon; ill-treatment.

vejaminista, *n.m.* lampooner.

vejancón, -ona, *n.m.f., a.* decrepit.

vejar, *v.t.* to vex, molest, tease, annoy, harass; to scoff; to censure.

vejarrón, -ona, *n.m.f., a.* (*coll.*) very old.

vejatorio, -ria, *a.* vexatious.

vejazo, -za, *n.m.f., a.* very old; very old person.

vejestorio, *n.m.* peevish or withered old man.

vejeta, *n.f.* crested lark.

vejete, *n.m.* absurd old man.

vejez, *n.f.* old age; decay; peevishness of old age; trite, commonplace story.

vejezuelo, -la, *n.m.f., a.* little old man (or woman).

vejiga, *n.f.* bladder, gall-bladder; blister, pustule; *vejiga de perro,* (*bot.*) common winter cherry.

vejigatorio, *n.m.* blistering plaster, vesicatory.

vejigatorio, -ria, *a.* blistering, raising blisters.

vejigazo, *n.m.* blow with a *vejiga.*

vejigón, *n.m.* large bladder, large blister.

vejigüela, vejiguica, -illa, -ita, *n.f.* small bladder.

vela, *n.f.* watch, watchfulness, vigil, wakefulness, watching, vigilance; wake; watchman, night-guard; pilgrimage; candle; sail; ship; awning; erect ear of an animal; arm of a windmill; vigil before the Eucharist; nuptial mass and veiling; *vela mayor,* mainsail; *vela de trinquete,* foresail; *vela de mesana,* mizen-sail; *a la vela,* equipped, prepared, ready; *hacerse a la vela*, to set sail; *en vela*, vigilantly, without sleeping; *hacer fuerza de vela*, to crowd on sail; *alzar velas*, to raise sail, to leave, quit; *recoger velas*, to be temperate, contain oneself; *tender las velas*, to seize a chance of obtaining one's wishes; *no darle a uno vela en un entierro*, to give one no excuse for meddling.

velación, *n.f.* watch, watching, vigil, wake. — *pl.* **velaciones**, nuptial mass and veiling.

velacho, *n.m.* (*naut.*) fore-topsail.

velada, *n.f.* watch; social evening, soirée.

velado, -da, *n.m.f.* (*coll.*) husband; wife.

velador, -ra, *n.m.f.* watch, watchman, night-guard; observer, spy; keeper, caretaker; large wooden candlestick; small table (usually round) with one leg.

velaje, velamen, *n.m.* canvas, sails, set of sails.

velante, *n.m.f., a.* watching.

velar, *v.i.* to watch, keep watch, keep vigil, wake; to be wakeful, be vigilant, be attentive; (*naut.*) to appear above water (as rocks); to mount guard before the Holy Sacrament. — *v.t.* to watch, guard, keep; (*eccles.*) to marry, veil a bride and bridegroom, give the nuptial benediction; to sit up with a sick person; (*poet.*) to veil, cover, hide. — *v.r.* (*phot.*) to fog (a negative); (*art*) to glaze a picture.

velarte, *n.m.* fine broadcloth.

velatorio, *n.m.* wake, watch by corpse before burial.

veleidad, *n.f.* levity, fickleness, inconstancy; whim; velleity; feeble will.

veleidoso, -sa, *a.* fickle, inconstant, giddy.

velejar, *v.i.* to make use of sails.

velería, *n.f.* tallow-chandler's shop.

velero, *n.m.* tallow-chandler; sail-maker; pilgrim; *buque velero*, sailing-boat.

velero, -ra, *a.* swift-sailing; fond of pilgrimages or vigils.

veleta, *n.f.* vane, weather-cock; pennant, streamer; bob, float or cork of a fishing line; fickle person.

velete, *n.f.* light, thin veil.

velicación, *n.f.* (*med.*) lancing, opening.

velicar, *v.t.* (*med.*) to lance, open, prick.

velico, -illo, -ito, *n.m.* small veil; embroidered gauze.

velicomen, *n.m.* large glass used for toasts.

velilla, -ita, *n.f.* small candle.

velis nolis, *adv.* willy-nilly, willingly or unwillingly.

velívolo, -la, *a.* (*poet.*) sailing-boat with all sails up and full wind.

velmez, *n.m.* tunic worn under the armour.

velo, *n.m.* veil, curtain; (*eccles.*) ceremony of taking the veil; disguise, mask, cover, pretext, pretence; obscurity, confusion, perplexity; *velo del paladar*, (*anat.*) soft palate; *correr el velo*, to pull off the mask, to reveal some secret; *correr* (or *echar*) *un velo sobre*, (*fig.*) to draw a veil over; *tomar el velo*, to take the veil, become a nun.

velocidad, *n.f.* velocity, fleetness, speed; *velocidad angular*, angular velocity; *velocidad periférica*, circumferential velocity; *en gran velocidad*, express, by passenger train (said of goods sent by rail); *en pequeña velocidad*, by goods train (said of goods not sent express).

velocímetro, *n.m.* bicycle speedometer.

velocipédico, -ca, *a.* relating to bicycles.

velocipedismo, *n.m.* cyclism.

velocipedista, *n.m.f.* velocipedist, cyclist.

velocípedo, *n.m.* velocipede, bicycle, tricycle.

velódromo, *n.m.* cycle-track.

velomotor, *n.m.* motor vehicle (especially motor-cycle).

velón, *n.m.* oil-lamp.

velonera, *n.f.* wooden bracket or lamp-stand.

velonero, *n.m.* lamp-maker.

velorio, *n.m.* evening entertainment; ceremony of taking the veil.

veloz, *a.* nimble, swift, fast, fleet, quick.

velozmente, *adv.* swiftly, nimbly, fleetly.

vellera, *n.f.* woman who makes up or removes hair from women's faces.

vello, *n.m.* down, nap, soft hair; gossamer; pubescence; fuzz.

vellocino, *n.m.* fleece; *Vellocino de oro*, the Golden Fleece.

vellón, *n.m.* fleece, lock of wool, wool of one sheep; silver and copper alloy used for coins; a copper coin; *real de vellón*, a small coin.

vellonero, *n.m.* collector or gatherer of fleeces.

vellora, *n.f.* curl in woollen cloth.

vellorí, vellorín, *n.m.* broadcloth of the colour of natural wool.

vellorita, *n.f.* cowslip.

vellosidad, *n.f.* downiness, hirsuteness.

vellosilla, *n.f.* mouse-ear.

velloso, -sa, *a.* hairy, downy.

velludillo, *n.m.* velveteen.

velludo, -da, *a.* shaggy, downy, hairy, woolly.

velludo, *n.m.* velvet, shag.

vellutero, -ra, *n., a.* velvet worker.

vena, *n.f.* vein, blood-vessel; fibre; hollow, cavity; vein in stone or wood; (*min.*) seam, lode; subterranean flow of water; inspiration, poetical vein; *dar en la vena*, to hit upon the right means; *estar de vena*, to be good humoured (or lucky, fortunate); *estar en vena*, to be inspired; *descabezarse una vena*, (*surg.*) to break a blood-vessel.

venablo, *n.m.* javelin, dart; *echar venablos*, to be violently angry.

venadero, *n.m.* place where deer shelter; (*Col., Ec.*) a dog used in deer-hunting.

venado, *n.m.* deer, stag; venison.

venaje, *n.m.* sources of a river.

venal, *a.* venal, of the veins; marketable, salable; mercenary.

venalidad, *n.f.* venality, mercenariness.

venático, -ca, *a.* cranky, erratic, having a vein of madness.

venatorio, -ria, *a.* venatic, venatorial.

vencedor, -ra, *n.m.f.* conqueror, victor, vanquisher.

vencejo, *n.m.* band, string; (*orn.*) swift, martlet, black-martin.

vencer, *v.t.* (*pres. indic.* **venzo**; *pres. subj.* **venza**) to conquer, defeat, vanquish, subdue, prevail upon, overcome, surmount, clear; to surpass, excel, outdo; to gain a lawsuit; to tolerate, suffer, bear; to turn down; to bend, twist. — *v.i.* to conquer, win, succeed, triumph; (*com.*) to mature, fall due. — *v.r.* to govern one's passions.

vencetósigo, *n.m.* swallow-wort, milk-weed.

vencible, *a.* conquerable, superable, vincible.

vencido, -da, *a.* conquered, subdued. — *p.p.* [VÉNCER]; due, payable; *de vencida*, nearly beaten.

vencimiento, *n.m.* victory, conquest; bend, bending, twisting; (*com.*) expiration; *vencimiento de plazo,* maturity of a bill.

venda, *n.f.* band, bandage, fillet, roller; *tener una venda en los ojos,* to be ignorant of the truth.

vendaje, *n.m.* bandage, bandaging, binding with a fillet; (*Col., CR., Ec., Per.*) gratuity, tip.

vendar, *v.t.* to bandage, fillet, tie with a fillet; to hoodwink, blind.

vendaval, *n.m.* violent sea-wind.

vendavalada, *n.f.* southerly storm.

vendedor, -ra, *n.m.f.* seller, vendor, retailer, trader, huckster.

vendehúmos, *n.m. f.* courtier who trades on his or her influence.

vendeja, *n.f.* public sale.

vender, *v.t.* to sell, vend, expose for sale; to betray. — *v.r.* to allow oneself to be bought, give oneself away, give oneself to another's service; to boast; to be sold; to be for sale; *vender por mayor,* to sell in the lump, wholesale; *vender a destajo,* (or *vender al pormenor*), to sell by retail; *venderse caro,* to be difficult to win over; *vender cara la vida,* to fight for one's life; *vender salud,* (*coll.*) to be exuding health; *vender a plazo,* to sell on credit; *vender al contado,* to sell for cash.

vendí, *n.m.* certificate of sale.

vendible, *a.* salable, marketable.

vendido, -da, *a.* sold; (*fig.*) betrayed.

vendiente, *a.* selling.

vendimia, *n.f.* vintage; (*fig.*) large profit or gain.

vendimiador, -ra, *n.m.f.* vintager.

vendimiar, *v.t.* to gather vintage; (*fig.*) to reap benefits unjustly; (*coll.*) to kill, murder.

vendo, *n.m.* selvage of cloth.

venduta, *n.f.* (*Am.*) auction.

vendutero, *n.m.* auctioneer.

Venecia, *p.n.* Venice; *tierra de venecia,* yellow ochre; *sombra de venecia,* shade prepared with lignite.

veneciano, -na, *n.m.f., a.* Venetian.

venencia, *n.f.* tube for sampling sherry.

venenífero, -ra, *a.* (*poet.*) poisonous.

veneno, *n.m.* poison, venom; passion, wrath, fury; pernicious thing.

venenosamente, *adv.* venomously.

venenosidad, *n.f.* poisonousness. venomousness.

venenoso, -sa, *a.* poisonous, venomous.

venera, *n.f.* scallop shell; badge, emblem; spring of water; *empeñar la venera,* to spare no expense.

venerabilísimo, -ma, *a.* most venerable.

venerable, *a.* venerable.

venerablemente, *adv.* venerably.

veneración, *n.f.* veneration, honour, worship.

venerador, -ra, *n.m.f.* worshipper.

venerando, -da, *a.* venerable.

venerante, *a.* worshipping.

venerar, *v.t.* to venerate, worship, respect, reverence, honour.

venéreo, -rea, *a.* venereous, venereal.

venéreo, *n.m.* venereal disease.

venero, *n.m.* (*min.*) vein, lode, bed, seam; radius of sundials; spring of water; origin, source, root.

veneruela, *n.f.* small scallop shell.

veneto, -ta, *n.m.f., a.* Venetian.

venezolanismo, *n.m.* word or phrase peculiar to Venezuela.

venezolano, -na, *n.m.f., a.* Venezuelan.

vengable, *a.* worthy of revenge.

vengador, -ra, *n.m.f.* avenger, revenger.

venganza, *n.f.* revenge, vengeance.

vengar, *v.t.* (pret. **vengué;** *pres. subj.* **vengue**) to revenge, avenge.

vengativamente, *adv.* revengefully.

vengativo, -va, *a.* revengeful, vindictive.

vengo; venga, *pres. indic.; pres. subj.* [VENIR].

venia, *n.f.* forgiveness, pardon; permission, leave; bow with the head; (*law*) licence to a minor to manage his own estate.

venial, *a.* venial, pardonable, excusable.

venialidad, *n.f.* veniality.

venialmente, *adv.* venially.

venida, *n.f.* arrival, return, coming; flood, freshet, overflow of a river; attack in fencing; impetuosity, rashness.

venidero, -ra, *a.* coming, future; *en lo venidero,* henceforth.

venidero, *n.m.* posterity.

venimécum, *n.m.* vade-mecum.

venir, *v.i.* (pres. part. **viniendo;** *pres. indic.* **vengo;** *pres. subj.* **venga;** *pret.* **vine;** *fut. indic.* **vendré**) to come, advance, draw near, arrive; to happen, pass; to arise, follow, succeed; to proceed, originate; to fit, become, suit; to determine, resolve, decide; to deduce, infer; to yield, assent, submit; to approach, be near; to occur, to present itself to the mind; to shoot up, grow; to accompany; to fall; to produce; to effect; to excite; *venir a deshora,* to come at an inopportune moment; *venir a menos,* to decline, decay; *venir a pelo* (or *venir como anillo en dedo* or *venir de perilla*), to come in the nick of time (or to suit perfectly); *venir rodado,* to gain one's end accidentally; *venir a las manos,* to come to blows; *venir angosto,* to fall short of one's expectations; *venir ancho* or *muy ancho,* to get more than one's deserts, do more than satisfy one; *lo que no le va, ni le viene,* what does not concern him; *venga lo que viniere,* come what may; *vengo en ello,* I agree; *si a mano viene,* possibly, perhaps. — *v.r.* to ferment; to attain perfection by fermentation; *venirse a buenas,* to yield; *venirse a casa,* to come home; *venirse al suelo,* to fall to the ground; *venirse durmiendo,* to be falling asleep.

venoso, -sa, *a.* venous, veiny, veined.

venta, *n.f.* sale; market; selling; roadside inn; exposed, inhospitable place; *de venta* (or *en venta*), on sale; *hacer venta,* (*coll.*) to invite to share pot-luck; *ser una venta,* to be a dear place.

ventada, *n.f.* gust, puff, blast of wind.

ventaja, *n.f.* preference, advantage; gain, profit; good; commodity, commodiousness; additional pay; handicap (in sport).

ventajosamente, *adv.* advantageously.

ventajoso, -sa, *a.* advantageous, lucrative, profitable.

ventalla, *n.f.* valve; (*bot.*) pod.

ventalle, *n.m.* fan.

ventana, *n.f.* window; window-shutter; window-frame; *ventana de la nariz,* nostril; *arrojar por la ventana,* (*met.*) to waste, squander; *estar asomado a buena(s) ventana(s),* to be on the point of succeeding to good fortune; *tirar a ventana conocida*, to speak of someone by implication: *tener ventana al cierzo*, to be very conceited.

ventanaje, *n.m.* number or row of windows in a building.

ventanal, *n.m.* large window.

ventanazo, *n.m.* slamming of a window.

ventanear, *v.i.* (*coll.*) to gaze repeatedly from the window.

ventaneo, *n.m.* window-gazing; window-flirting.

ventanera, *n.f.* window-gazer.

ventanero, *n.m.* glazier, window-maker; window-gazer.

ventanico, *n.m.* small window-shutter.

ventanilla, *n.f.* small window (as in a railway carriage); grill (of a booking office).

ventanillo, *n.m.* small window; peep-hole.

ventar, *v.t.*, *v. impers.* to blow (the wind); to smell, scent, sniff; to find, discover; to make known.

ventarrón, *n.m.* violent wind, gust of wind.

venteadura, *n.f.* anemosis or shake (of timber).

ventear, *v. impers.* to blow (wind). — *v.t.* to scent, sniff, smell; to investigate; enquire; to air, expose to the air. — *v.r.* to be filled with air; to have anemosis; to be cracked (of growing timber); (*coll.*) to break wind.

venteo, *n.m.* vent-hole.

venteril, *a.* belonging to a *venta* or small inn.

ventero, -ra, *n.m.f.* keeper of a *venta*; scenting-dog.

ventilación, *n.f.* ventilation; discussion.

ventilador, *n.m.* ventilator.

ventilar, *v.t.* to ventilate, winnow, fan; to discuss, examine. — *v.i.* to circulate (of the air).

ventisca, *n.f.* storm, blizzard.

ventiscar, **ventisquear**, *v. impers.* (conjugated like BUSCAR) to snow hard.

ventisco, *n.m.* snow-storm; snow-drift.

ventiscoso, -sa, *a.* stormy, windy, tempestuous; full of snow-drifts.

ventisquear, *v. impers.* [VENTISCAR].

ventisquero, *n.m.* snow-drift; snow-storm; glacier; snow-capped mountain.

ventola, *n.f.* the force exerted by the wind in striking any object.

ventolera, *n.f.* gust of wind; (*coll.*) vanity, haughtiness, pride; strange idea, whim.

ventolina, *n.f.* light wind.

ventor, -ra, *n.*, *a.* pointer (dog).

ventorrero, *n.m.* exposed, windy place.

ventorrillo, ventorro, *n.m.* small inn or tavern.

ventosa, *n.f.* vent, air-hole; (*med.*) cupping-glass; (*zool.*) sucker; *pegar una ventosa*, to swindle someone out of his money.

ventosear(se), *v.i.*, *v.r.* to break wind.

ventosidad, *n.f.* flatulence.

ventoso, -sa, *a.* windy, flatulent; vain, inflated; tempestuous, stormy.

ventral, *a.* ventral.

ventrecha, *n.f.* the belly of fish.

ventregada, *n.f.* litter, brood; multitude, rush of things.

ventrera, *n.f.* belly-girdle, sash, cummerbund.

ventrezuelo, *n.m.* small belly.

ventrículo, *n.m.* ventricle; stomach.

ventril, *n.m.* counterpoise (in oil-mills).

ventrilocuo, *n.m.* ventriloquist.

ventriloquia, *n.f.* ventriloquism.

ventrón, *n.m.* large belly; (*cook.*) tripe.

ventroso, -sa; **ventrudo, -da**, *a.* big-bellied.

ventura, *n.f.* happiness, felicity; luck, fortune; chance; venture, danger, risk; *a (la) ventura*, at a venture, at hazard; *por ventura*, by chance; *probar ventura*, to try one's luck; *cada uno es artífice de su ventura*, every man is the architect of his own fortune.

venturado, -da, *a* fortunate, lucky.

venturero, -ra, *a.* casual; lucky; vagrant.

venturero, *n.m.* fortune-hunter, adventurer.

venturilla, *n.f.* good luck.

venturina, *n.f.* aventurine, avanturine.

venturo, -ra, *a.* future, coming.

venturosamente, *adv.* luckily, fortunately.

venturoso, -sa, *a.* lucky, fortunate, successful, happy, prosperous; *todo es comenzar a ser venturoso*, it's everything to make a lucky start.

venus, *n.f.* Venus; beautiful woman; sensual pleasure, venery; (*alch.*) copper.

venustidad, *n.f.* beauty, grace.

venusto, -ta, *a.* beautiful, graceful.

ver, *v.t.* (*pres. part.* **viendo**; *p.p.* **visto**; *pres. indic.* **veo**; *pres. subj.* **vea**; *pret.* **vi**) to see, glance; observe, consider, foresee; look at, look into; to call on, visit, examine, inspect, explore; discover, forecast, find out; to imagine, fancy; to acknowledge, realize; (*law*) to try; *¿A ver?* Let us see, What about it? Isn't it so? *al ver*, on seeing, *a mi ver*, in my opinion; *a más ver* (or *hasta más ver*), farewell; *au revoir*; *hacer ver*, to show, make clear; *no tener nada que ver con*, to have nothing to do with; *ver a hurtadillas*, to look over one's shoulders; *ver venir*, to await results; *estar por ver*, to remain to be seen; *ver el cielo abierto*, to see one's great chance; *si te vi, (ya) no me acuerdo*, out of sight, out of mind; *ver las estrellas*, (*coll.*, *fig.*) to see stars; *ver con muchos ojos*, to observe very closely; *ver por vista de ojos*, to see with one's own eyes; *ver mundo*, to see the world, to travel; *ver y creer*, seeing is believing; *lo que veo con los ojos, con el dedo lo señalo*, what I can see with my eyes, I point out with my finger. — *v.r.* to be seen; to be conspicuous *or* obvious; to find oneself (in a state, etc.); to agree, concur; to meet, have an interview; to see oneself in the glass; *verse apurado*, to be in difficulties; *ver(se) en ello*, to consider; *verse con*, to have a talk with; *ya se ve*, it is undeniable, evident; *verse en las astas del toro*, to be in the greatest danger; *verse entre la espada y la pared*, to be in a tight corner. — *n.m.* sight, sense of sight, seeing; view, light, aspect, looks.

vera, *n.f.* edge, border; a South American tree of the Zygophyllaceæ family; *vera efigies*, faithful likeness; *de veras*, really, indeed, in truth.

veracidad, *n.f.* veracity, fidelity, truthfulness.

veranada, *n.f.* summer season (live stock).

veranadero, *n.m.* summer pasture.

veranar, veranear, *v.i.* to spend the summer.

veraneante, *n.m.* summer resident or holiday-maker.

veraneo, *n.m.* summer holiday(s).

veranero, *n.m.* spot where cattle graze in summer.

veraniego, -ga, *a.* relating to summer; weak, light; sickly.

veranillo, *n.m.* late or untimely summer; *veranillo de San Martín*, Indian summer.

verano, *n.m.* summer; dry season.

veras, *n.f.pl.* truth, reality; fervour, earnestness; *de veras,* really, indeed, truthfully; *con muchas veras,* very earnestly.

verascopio, *n.m.* stereoscope.

veratro, *n.m.* hellebore.

veraz, *a.* veracious, truthful.

verba, *n.f.* loquacity, talkativeness.

verbal, *a.* verbal, oral; *(law)* nuncupative.

verbalismo, *n.m.* literalism; system of teaching which emphasizes word memory.

verbalmente, *adv.* verbally, orally.

verbasco, *n.m.* mullein.

verbena, *n.f.* verbena, vervain; night celebration on the vigil of a saint's day; *coger la verbena,* to rise and go out early.

verbenear, *v.i.* to abound, be plentiful; to rush to and fro.

verberación, *n.f.* verberation.

verberar, *v.t.* to verberate, strike, beat.

verbigracia, *adv.* for instance, for example.

verbo, *n.m.* word, expression, term; *(gram.)* verb; *en un verbo,* at once, immediately; *echar verbos,* to curse, swear; *verbo substantivo,* the verb SER, to be; *verbo adjetivo,* any verb, except SER.

verborrea, verbosidad, *n.f.* verbosity, wordiness.

verboso, -sa, *a.* verbose, prolix.

verdacho, *n.m.* *(art)* green earth.

verdad, *n.f.* truth, reality, veracity; axiom, maxim; platitude, truism; *verdad de Perogrullo,* notorious truth; *a mala verdad,* deceitfully, craftily; *a la verdad* (or *de verdad*), in truth, in fact, truly; *en verdad* (or *por verdad*), it is certain; *por cierto y por verdad,* really and truly; *tratar verdad,* to love truth; *decir cuatro verdades,* to speak one's mind very plainly; *la verdad adelgaza y no quiebra,* truth may grow thin but cannot break; *la verdad amarga,* truth is unpleasant.

verdaderamente, *adv.* verily, indeed, truly, in fact.

verdadero, -ra, *a.* true, real, genuine, veritable, sincere, truthful.

verdal, *a.* applied to certain fruits which keep their green colour when ripe, as *ciruela verdal,* greengage.

verdasca, *n.f.* branch, bough, twig.

verde, *n.m.* green, verdure; verdigris; green barley or grass; youth; *darse un verde,* to have a gay time; to do something until one is sick of it; to take time off. — *a.* verdant, green; fresh, immature, undeveloped, unripe; blooming, young; immodest, loose, obscene; *verde limón,* bright green; *verde pardo,* brownish green; *viejo verde,* *(coll.)* old reprobate.

verdea, *n.f.* kind of greenish wine.

verdear, *v.i.* to grow green, look greenish. — *v.t.* *(prov.)* to pick grapes or olives to sell.

verdeceledón, *n.m.* pale sea-green; celadon.

verdecer, *v.i.* *(pres. indic.* verdezco; *pres. subj.* verdezca) to grow green.

verdecico, -ica; -illo, -illa; -ito, -ita, *a.* greenish.

verdecillo, *n.m.* greenfinch.

verdeesmeralda, *a.* emerald green.

verdegal, *n.m.* green field.

verdegay, *n.m., a.* light green.

verdeguear, *v.i.* to grow green.

verdemar, *n.m., a.* sea-green.

verdemontaña, *n.f.* mountain-green.

verderol, *n.m.* kind of green shell-fish.

verderón, *n.m.* *(orn.)* greenfinch.

verdete, *n.m.* verdigris.

verdevejiga, *n.f.* sap-green, deep green.

verdezuelo, *n.m.* greenfinch.

verdín, *n.m.* pond-scums, pond-weed; copper oxide, verdigris; mildew, mould, green snuff; verdure.

verdina, *n.f.* green of unripe fruit and young plants, verdure.

verdinal, *n.m.* green patch in a meadow.

verdinegro, -gra, *a.* deep green, dark green.

verdino, -na, *a.* bright green.

verdiseco, -ca, *a.* pale green; half dry.

verdolaga, *n.f.* purslane; *como verdolaga en huerto,* at one's ease.

verdón, *n.m.* greenfinch.

verdor, *n.m.* verdure, greenness, herbage; strength, freshness, physical vigour. — *pl.* **verdores,** youth, vigorous age.

verdoso, -sa, *a.* greenish, verdant.

verdoyo, *n.m.* green mould; pond-scum.

verdugada, *n.f.* layer of bricks.

verdugado, *n.m.* hoopskirt.

verdugal, *n.m.* young shoots growing after a wood has been burned or cut down.

verdugazo, *n.m.* stroke with a twig.

verdugo, *n.m.* young shoot, tiller, sucker; executioner, headsman, hangman; very cruel person; scourge, lash; hoop, ring; rapier used in a duel; wale, welt, mark of a lash; that which causes pain; *(mas.)* layer of bricks; small ring.

verdugón, *n.m.* long shoot; broad mark of a lash.

verduguillo, *n.m.* small shoot; blight, mildew; rust; small razor; duelling rapier, long narrow sword; *(naut.)* sheer-rail.

verdulera, *n.f.* market woman; *(coll.)* coarse, low woman.

verdulería, *n.f.* greengrocer's shop.

verdulero, *n.m.* greengrocer.

verdura, *n.f.* verdure, verdancy; vigour, luxuriance; *(art)* foliage; obscenity. — *pl.* **verduras,** green vegetables, greens.

verdusco, -ca, *a.* greenish.

verecundo, -da, *a.* bashful, modest, shy.

vereda, *n.f.* path, foot-path; route of travelling preachers; circular order or notice sent to several towns on the same route; *(S. Am.)* pavement; *hacer a uno entrar por vereda,* to keep a person up to his duty.

veredero, *n.m.* messenger sent with dispatches.

veredicto, *n.m.* *(law)* verdict.

verga, *n.f.* penis; cord of crossbow; *(naut.)* yard; *verga seca,* crossjack yard; *vergas en alto,* ready to sail; *vergas en cruz,* with squared yards.

vergajo, *n.m.* pizzle.

vergel, *n.m.* orchard, garden.

vergeta, *n.f.* small twig.

vergeteado, -da, *a.* *(her.)* vergette, paley.

vergonzante, *a.* shamefaced, bashful. — *n.m.f.* honest poor person, shy beggar.

vergonzosamente, *adv.* shamefully; bashfully.

vergonzoso, -sa, *a.* shamefaced, bashful, modest, diffident, shy, contumelious; shameful.

vergonzoso, *n.m.* a kind of armadillo.

verguear, *v.t.* to beat with a rod.

vergüenza, *n.f.* shame; modesty, diffidence, shyness, bashfulness, confusion; affront, disgrace; public punishment; *perder la vergüenza,* to be quite shameless; *ser una mala vergüenza,* to be a nuisance; *más vale vergüenza en cara que mancilla en corazón,* better a blush on the face than a stain on the heart.
verguero, *n.m.* (*prov.*) high constable.
vergueta, *n.f.* small rod or switch.
verguío, -a, *a.* tough and flexible, leathery (of wood).
vericueto, *n.m.* rough and roadless place.
verídico, -ca, *a.* veridical, truth-telling, truthful.
verificación, *n.f.* inquiry, examination, verification, substantiation, confirmation.
verificador, -ra, *n.m.f.* verifier.
verificar, *v.t.* (*pret.* **verifiqué;** *pres. subj.* **verifique**) to verify; examine; prove, confirm, substantiate; to accomplish, carry out, fulfil. — *v.r.* to prove true; be verified, take place.
verificativo, -va, *a.* verifying.
verija, *n.f.* region of the genitals.
veril, *n.m.* edge of a sand-bank.
verilear, *v.i.* to coast around a bank.
verisímil, *a.* probable, likely, credible.
verisimilitud, *n.f.* verisimilitude, probability, likelihood.
verisímilmente, *adv.* probably.
verja, *n.f.* door-grating, window-grating, iron railing.
vermicida, *a.* vermicide.
vermicular, *a.* vermiculous, vermicular, full of worms or grubs.
vermiforme, *a.* vermiform, worm-like.
vermífugo, *n.m.* vermifuge.
verminoso, -sa, *a.* verminous.
vermut, *n.m.* vermouth.
vernáculo, -la, *a.* vernacular, native.
vernal, *a.* vernal, spring, spring-like.
vero, *n.m.* marten (fur); (*her.*) vair.
verónica, *n.f.* speedwell; pass in bull-fighting.
verosímil, *a.* probable, likely.
verosimilitud, *n.f.* verisimilitude, probability, likelihood.
verraco, *n.m.* boar [VERRÓN].
verraquear, *v.i.* (*coll.*) to grunt like a boar; to cry loudly, squawk (of children).
verriondez, *n.f.* rutting-time of boars; withering state of herbs; over-cooking, toughness.
verriondo, -da, *a.* like a boar at rutting-time; withering, flaccid; badly cooked (of greens).
verrón, *n.m.* male hog or boar.
verruga, *n.f.* pimple, wart; (*coll.*) nuisance, bore.
verrugo, *n.m.* (*coll.*) miser, avaricious person.
verrugoso, -sa, *a.* warty.
versado, -da, *a.* versed, conversant, practical, experienced.
versal, *n.f., a.* capital (letter).
versalilla, versalita, *n.f.* small capital letter.
versar, *v.i., v.r.* to go round; to be versed, conversant; with the preposition SOBRE or the adverb ACERCA DE, to treat of, to write upon, to discuss.
versátil, *a.* versatile; changeable, variable, fickle.
versatilidad, *n.f.* versatility, fickleness.
versear, *v.i.* (*coll.*) to versify, to improvise verses.

versecillo, *n.m.* little verse, verselet.
versería, *n.f.* compilation of poems.
versícula, *n.f.* stand for choir-books.
versiculario, *n.m.* chanter of versicles; keeper of the choir books.
versículo, *n.m.* versicle, verse of a chapter.
versificación, *n.f.* versification.
versificador, -ra, *n.m.f.* versifier.
versificar, *v.t., v.i.* (*pret.* **versifiqué;** *pres. subj.* **versifique**) to versify, make verses.
versión, *n.f.* version, translation.
versista, *n.m.* (*coll.*) versifier, poetaster.
verso, *n.m.* verse, stanza; line of poetry; an ancient cannon; *verso blanco* (*libre* or *suelto*), blank verse.
vértebra, *n.f.* vertebra.
vertebrado, -da, *a.* vertebrate.
vertebral, *a.* vertebral.
vertedero, *n.m.* sewer, drain, sink; weir, spillway.
vertedor, -ra, *n.m.f.* conduit, sewer; nightman; weir, spillway; (*naut.*) scoop, bailer.
verter, *v.t.* (*pres. indic.* **vierto;** *pres. subj.* **vierta**) to spill, pour, cast, shed; to empty; to tilt, dump; to translate, construe, interpret; to divulge, reveal, publish; *verter dinero a manos llenas,* to spend money like water. — *v.i.* to run, flow.
vertibilidad, *n.f.* capability of being turned over or changed.
vertible, *a.* moveable, changeable, variable.
vertical, *a.* vertical, upright; (*astron.*) vertical circle.
verticalidad, *n.f.* verticalness.
verticalmente, *adv.* verticality.
vértice, *n.m.* vertex, zenith; apex, top; (*fig.*) crown of the head.
verticidad, *n.f.* rotation.
verticilado, -da, *a.* verticillate.
verticillo, *n.m.* verticil, whorl.
vertiente, *n.m.* watershed, slope. — *a.* flowing, emptying.
vertiginoso, -sa, *a.* giddy, vertiginous.
vértigo, *n.m.* giddiness, dizziness, vertigo; fit of madness.
vertimiento, *n.m.* shedding, effusion.
vesania, *n.f.* madness, insanity.
vesánico, -ca, *a.* insane.
vesícula, *n.f.* vesicle; *vesícula aérea,* air vesicle of the lungs; *vesícula biliar,* gall bladder; *vesícula elemental,* (*biol.*) cell; *vesícula ovárica,* (*zool.*) Graffian follicle; *vesícula seminal,* (*anat.*) sperm sac.
vesicular, *a.* vesicular.
vesiculoso, -sa, *a.* vesiculate.
véspero, *n.m.* vesper, evening star.
vespertillo, *n.m.* bat.
vespertina, *n.f.* evening discourse in universities; evening sermon.
vespertino, -na, *a.* vesperian, of the evening.
vestal, *n.f., a.* vestal virgin.
veste, *n.f.* (*poet.*) clothes, dress.
vestíbulo, *n.m.* vestibule, portal, lobby, hall; (*anat.*) vestibule of the ear.
vestido, *n.m.* dress, garments, clothes, clothing, wearing apparel, vestment, garb; embellishment, ornament; *el vestido del criado dice quién es su señor,* a master is known by his servant.
vestidura, *n.f.* dress, vesture, garb, wearing-apparel. — *pl.* **vestiduras,** vestments.
vestigio, *n.m.* vestige, sign, index, trace, mark;

footstep. — *pl.* **vestigios,** relic, ruins, remains.

vestiglo, *n.m.* a fantastic, formidable creature, monster.

vestimenta, *n.f.;* **vestimento,** *n.m.* clothes, garments. — *pl.* **vestimentas,** ecclesiastical robes.

vestir, *v.t.* (*pres. part.* **vistiendo;** *pres. indic.* **visto;** *pres. subj.* **vista**) to clothe, dress; to don, put on; to wear; adorn; deck, accoutre, embellish; to disguise, cloak; to make clothes for another; to give a semblance or appearance; (*mas.*) to rough-cast. — *v.i.* to dress, be dressed. — *v.r.* to be covered, clothed.

vestuario, *n.m.* vestiary, cloak-room, dressing-room; vesture, clothes, equipment, uniform, apparel; wardrobe, habiliment, outfit; vestry; dress allowance; (*theat.*) green-room, wardrobe, dressing room.

vestugo, *n.m.* olive-stem, olive-bud.

veta, *n.f.* (*min.*) vein, seam, lode; stripe in cloth; vein in wood or marble; grain, flake; *descubrir la veta,* to discover one's feelings or designs.

vetado, -da; veteado, -da, *a.* striped, veined, streaky.

vetear, *v.t.* to variegate; to grain.

veterano, -na, *a.* veteran; experienced, long practised.

veterano, *n.m.* veteran.

veterinaria, *n.f.* veterinary science.

veterinario, *n.m.* veterinary surgeon.

veto, *n.m.* veto; interdict, prohibition.

vetustez, *n.f.* age, oldness, antiquity.

vetusto, -ta, *a.* very ancient, very old.

vez, *n.f.* turn; time, occasion, epoch; herd of swine belonging to the inhabitants of a ward. — *pl.* **veces,** authority or representation given to a substitute; *a la vez,* by turns; *a la vez que,* while, whilst; *a veces,* sometimes, by turns; *a mala vez,* with difficulty, hardly; *cada vez,* each time; *de una vez,* in one stroke, at one and the same time; *de vez en cuando,* from time to time; *dos veces,* twice; *en vez de,* instead of; *más de una vez,* frequently; *hacer las veces de otro,* to supply someone's place; *decir unas veces cesta y otras ballesta,* to speak contradictorily or inconsistently; *tal vez,* perhaps; *tal cual vez,* rarely, once in a way; *tres veces,* thrice, three times; *quien come y condesa, dos veces pone mesa,* economy is prudence; *quien da luego, da dos veces,* he gives twice who gives quickly.

veza, *n.f.* vetch.

vezar, *v.t., v.r.* to accustom, habituate, inure.

vía, *n.f.* way, road; route, via; mode, method, manner, procedure; (*railw.*) grade, line, track; (*zool.*) tube, canal, passage; spiritual life; *vía general,* main line; *vía angosta,* (*rail.*) narrow gauge; *vía ancha,* (*rail.*) broad gauge; *por vía,* in a manner or form; *vía recta,* straight along; *vía reservada,* office of state; *vía crucis* (or *vía sacra*), (*eccles.*) Calvary; *cegar una vía de agua,* (*naut.*) to stop a leak; *a luengas vías, luengas mentiras,* it's easy to make mistakes at a distance; *vía láctea,* Milky Way.

viabilidad, *n.f.* viability; feasibility, practicability.

viable, *a.* viable.

viadera, *n.f.* harness shaft of a loom.

viador, *n.m.* (*theol.*) traveller, passenger (in a mystical sense).

viaducto, *n.m.* viaduct.

viajador, -ra, *n.m.f.* traveller, voyager, journeyer.

viajante, *n.m.f.* traveller, voyager; commercial traveller. — *a.* travelling.

viajar, *v.i.* to travel, journey, voyage.

viajata, *n.f.* short journey, trip, excursion.

viaje, *n.m.* journey, excursion, trip, tour, voyage, travel; passage; road, way; gait; errand; load carried; water main, water supply; (*arch.*) obliquity; *buen viaje,* God-speed, a pleasant journey.

viajero, *n.m.* traveller, passenger; (*Chi.*) messenger of an estancia.

vial, *a.* wayfaring, relating to roads. — *n.m.* garden-path, lane, avenue.

vialidad, *n.f.* highway department; engineering department.

vianda, *n.f.* food, viands, fare, victuals, meat; (*Cub., PR.*) fruit and vegetables of a national dish.

viandante, *n.m.* traveller, passenger; tramp.

viaraza, *n.f.* diarrhœa.

viaticar, *v.t.* to administer the viaticum.

viático, *n.m.* viaticum; provisions for a journey; travelling expenses.

víbora, *n.f.* viper; treacherous person.

viborán, *n.m.* (*Cent. Am.*) a medicinal plant of the Asclepiadaceæ family.

viborezno, *n.m.* young viper, small viper.

viborezno, -na, *a.* viperine, viperous.

vibración, *n.f.* vibration, oscillation; shaking, jar.

vibrador, -ra, *n., a.* (*elec.*) vibrator.

vibrante, *a.* vibrating, shaking.

vibrar, *v.t., v.i.* to vibrate, oscillate; shake; to brandish; to hurl.

vibratorio, -ria, *a.* vibratory.

viburno, *n.m.* viburnum.

vicaría, *n.f.* vicarship, vicarage; curacy.

vicaria, *n.f.* assistant superior in a convent; (*Cub.*) a plant of the Apocynaceæ family.

vicariato, *n.m.* vicarship, vicarage.

vicario, *n.m.* vicar, curate, deputy.

vicario, -ria, *a.* vicarial, vicarious.

vicealmiranta, *n.f.* vessel next in order to the admiral's.

vicealmirantazgo, *n.m.* vice-admiralship.

vicealmirante, *n.m.* vice-admiral.

vicecanciller, *n.m.* vice-chancellor.

viceconsiliario, *n.m.* vice-councillor.

vicecónsul, *n.m.* vice-consul.

viceconsulado, *n.m.* vice-consulate.

vicecristo, vicediós, *n.m.* honorific title of the Pope.

vicegerente, *a.* assistant manager.

vicenal, *a.* of twenty years' duration or occurrence.

vicepresidencia, *n.f.* vice-presidency.

vicepresidente, *n.m.* vice-president.

viceprovincia, *n.f.* (*eccles.*) religious houses enjoying the rank of a province.

viceprovincial, *n.m.* (*eccles.*) the superior of a vice-province.

vicerrector, *n.m.* vice-rector; assistant director.

vicesecretaría, *n.f.* under-secretaryship.

vicesecretario, *n.m.* under-secretary.

vicesimario, -ria, *a.* vicenary.

vicésimo, -ma, *a.* twentieth.

viceversa, *adv.* vice versa, on the contrary. — *n.m.* illogical statement.

vicia, *n.f.* carob bean.

viciado, -da, *p.p., a.* foul, contaminated; vitiated.

viciar, *v.t.* to vitiate, mar, spoil, corrupt; deprave, pervert; to adulterate, counterfeit, forge, falsify; to annul, make void; to misconstrue. — *v.r.* to give oneself up to vice; to contract a (bad) habit.

vicio, *n.m.* vice, viciousness, excess, depravity; artifice, fraud; defect, imperfection, blemish; bad habit, custom; folly, extravagant desire; extravagant or luxuriant growth; waywardness, forwardness (of children); *de vicio*, by habit; *quejarse de vicio*, to complain habitually.

viciosamente, *adv.* viciously, falsely, corruptly.

vicioso, -sa, *a.* vicious, corrupt, defective; abundant, vigorous, luxuriant; overgrown; spoiled, unruly (child).

vicisitud, *n.f.* vicissitude.

vicisitudinario, -ria, *a.* variable, changeable, vicissitudinary.

víctima, *n.f.* victim, sacrifice.

victimario, *n.m.* (*eccles.*) server.

victo, *n.m.* a day's sustenance.

¡víctor!¡vítor!, *interj.* shout, cry of acclamation.

victorear, *v.t.* to acclaim, shout hurrahs.

victoria, *n.f.* victory, triumph, conquest, palm; victoria (carriage); *cantar (la) victoria*, to celebrate a triumph.

victorial, *a.* relating to victory.

victoriosamente, *adv.* victoriously.

victorioso, -sa, *a.* victorious, conquering, triumphant.

vicuña, *n.f.* vicugna, vicunia.

vichoco, -ca, *a.* (*Arg., Chi.*) weak, feeble, disabled.

vid, *n.f.* vine, grape-vine; *de buena vid planta la viña, y de buena madre, la hija*, choose as your wife the daughter of a good mother.

vida, *n.f.* life, living; sustenance, livelihood, food necessary to life; being, existence; living person, human being; conduct, behaviour, deportment; condition, state; liveliness, activity, animation; (*law*) period of ten years; *darse buena vida*, to give oneself up to pleasure; *dar mala vida*, to treat very badly; *hallarse entre la vida y la muerte*, to be hanging between life and death; *tener la vida en un hilo*, to have one's life hanging by a thread; *de por vida*, for one's life, during life; *¡por vida!* by Jove! *hacer vida*, to live together as husband and wife; *mientras dura, vida y dulzura*, enjoy life while you can; *enterrarse en vida*, (*fig.*) to bury oneself alive, retire from the world; *en la vida* (or *en mi vida*), never; *persona de mala vida* (or *de la vida airada*), profligate; *tiene siete vidas*, to bear a charmed life; *el que larga vida vive, mucho mal ha de pasar*, he that lives the longest suffers the most; *date buena vida, temerás más la caída*, he who lives at ease feels misfortunes most.

vidalita, *n.f.* (*Arg.*) a sad love-song.

vidarra, *n.f.* a climbing plant of the Ranunculaceæ family.

vidente, *n.m.* seer. — *a.* seeing.

vidorria, *n.f.* (*Arg., Cub., Ven.*) (*coll.*) sad, miserable life.

vidriado, *n.m.* crockery, glazed earthenware.

vidriar, *v.t.* to varnish, glaze.

vidriera, *n.f.* glass window, show-case, show-window; glass case, glass cover.

vidriería, *n.f.* glass factory, glazier's shop, glassware.

vidriero, *n.m.* glazier, glass-dealer, glass-blower.

vidrio, *n.m.* glass; anything brittle; person easily offended; *ir al vidrio*, to ride in a coach with one's back to the horses, etc.; *pagar los vidrios rotos*, to be punished undeservingly; *vidrios planos*, window-glass; *es de vidrio la mujer*, woman is sensitive and fragile.

vidrioso, -sa, *a.* vitreous, brittle; glassy, slippery; peevish, touchy, irascible; delicate.

vidual, *a.* belonging to widowhood.

vidueño, viduño, *n.m.* variety of vine.

viejarrón, viejazo, *n.m.* very old man.

viejecito, -ta; viejezuelo, -la, *a.* little old man (woman) (endearing).

viejo, -ja, *a.* old, aged; ancient, antiquated; worn-out, stale, old-fashioned; *cuentos de viejas*, old wives' tales; *perro viejo*, (*coll.*) prudent, experienced person; *viejo como la sarna*, as old as the itch; *el viejo que se cura, cien años dura*, with proper care a man may live to be a hundred; *vieja escarmentada, arregazada pasa el agua*, once bitten twice shy.

vienés, -esa, *n.m.f., a.* Viennese.

vientecillo, *n.m.* light wind.

viento, *n.m.* wind, air, gale, breeze; (*artill.*) windage; (*naut.*) wind, course; scent of dogs; nape bone of a dog, between the ears; brace, guy, bracing-rope; something which agitates the mind; vanity, petty pride; *viento escaso*, slack wind; *viento terral*, land breeze; *viento contrario*, foul wind; *vientos generales*, trade winds; *contra viento y marea*, against wind and tide; *cosas de viento*, vain, empty trifles; *moverse a todos vientos*, to be fickle or wavering; *quitar el viento a un bajel*, (*naut.*) to blanket a ship; *con viento limpian el trigo, y los vicios, con castigo*, spare the rod and spoil the child; *quien siembra vientos, recoge tempestades*, he that sows the wind reaps the whirlwind; *sombrero de tres vientos*, three-cornered hat.

vientre, *n.m.* belly, stomach, intestines; fœtus; pregnancy; womb; belly or widest part of vessels; *reses de vientre*, breeding cattle; *servir al vientre*, to live for the belly; *sacar el vientre de mal año*, to sate one's hunger, tuck in well.

vientrecillo, *n.m.* ventricle.

viernes, *n.m.* Friday; fast day; *Viernes Santo*, Good Friday; *cara de viernes*, wan, thin face.

vierteaguas, *n.m.* (*arch.*) flashing.

viga, *n.f.* beam, girder, rafter, joist, baulk; bridge truss; mill beam; quantity of olives produced in one pressing; *viga de aire*, joist; *viga maestra*, continuous girder.

vigencia, *n.f.* (*law*) state of being in force.

vigente, *a.* (*law*) in force, prevailing.

vigesimal, *a.* vigesimal.

vigésimo, -ma, *a.* twentieth.

vigía, *n.f.* watchtower; watch, watching; (*naut.*) shoal, rock. — *n.m.* look-out, watch.

vigiar, *v.t.* to watch, keep a look out.

vigilancia, *n.f.* vigilance, heedfulness, watchfulness.

vigilante, *a.* watchful, vigilant, careful, heedful. — *n.m.* watchman, guard.

vigilantemente, *adv.* vigilantly, heedfully.

vigilar, *v.t., v.i.* to watch, watch over, keep guard; *vigilar de cerca,* to keep a close watch upon.

vigilativo, -va, *a.* causing sleeplessness or wakefulness.

vigilia, *n.f.* watching, watchfulness; nocturnal study; (*eccles.*) vigil, fast; eve; (*mil.*) watch, guard; *comer de vigilia,* to fast, abstain from meat.

vigor, *n.m.* vigour, strength, force, energy.

vigorar, vigorizar, *v.t.* (conjugated like ALZAR) to strengthen, invigorate; to animate, inspirit, encourage.

vigorosamente, *adv.* vigorously, lustily, energetically.

vigorosidad, *n.f.* vigour, strength.

vigoroso, -sa, *a.* vigorous, strong, active.

vigota, *n.f.* (*naut.*) dead-eye; plank of wood 19 ft. × 12 in. × 9 in.

viguería, *n.f.* (*naut.*) timber-work; set of beams or girders.

vigués, -esa, *n.m.f., a.* native of Vigo.

vigueta, *n.f.* small beam; joist; beam.

vihuela, *n.f.* an early guitar, cithern, cittern.

vihuelista, *n.m.f.* cithern-player.

vil, *a.* mean, base, infamous, vile, worthless, despicable, sordid, abject, contemptible, paltry.

vilano, *n.m.* thistledown.

vileza, *n.f.* vileness, meanness, abjectness; depravity; disgraceful or infamous action.

vilipendiar, *v.t.* to contemn, revile.

vilipendio, *n.m.* contempt, disdain.

vilipendioso, -sa, *a.* contemptible.

vilmente, *adv.* vilely, basely, meanly, abjectly, contemptibly, villainously.

vilo, (en), *adv.* insecurely, in the air; in suspense.

vilordo, -da, *a.* slothful, heavy, lazy.

vilorta, *n.f.* willow-ring; game resembling lacrosse; clasp ring of a plough; washer.

vilorto, *n.m.* kind of reed; reed hoop; kind of crosse for playing *vilorta.*

vilos, *n.m.* (*Philip.*) a two-masted coasting-vessel.

vilote, *a.* (*Arg., Chi.*) cowardly, timid, faint-hearted.

viltrotear, *v.i.* (*coll.*) to gad about.

villa, *n.f.* town enjoying certain privileges by charter; country seat, villa; municipal council; town hall; *quien necio es en su villa, necio es en Castilla,* once a fool, always a fool; *quien ruin es en su villa, ruin será en Sevilla,* a scoundrel's habits are never changed.

Villadiego, tomar (or **coger**) **las de,** to run away, to sneak out, 'to beat it.'

villaje, *n.m.* village, hamlet.

villanada, *n.f.* villainous act.

villanaje, *n.m.* villainage, peasantry.

villanamente, *adv.* rudely; villainously.

villancejo, villancete, villancico, *n.m.* Christmas carol.

villanciquero, *n.m.* writer or singer of *villancicos.*

villanchón, -ona, *a.* boorish, rustic, rude.

villanería, *n.f.* meanness, lowness of birth; villainy; vile deed.

villanesca, *n.f.* an ancient Spanish song and dance.

villanesco, -ca, *a.* rustic, boorish, rude.

villanía, *n.f.* meanness, lowness of birth; villainy, villainage, rusticity; vile deed, indecorous word or deed.

villano, -na, *a.* rustic, boorish, low-class; unworthy, worthless; villainous, wicked.

villano, *n.m.* villain, peasant, rustic; an old Spanish melody and dance; *hacer bien a villanos es echar agua en el mar,* to aid boors is to throw water into the sea; *al villano, dale el pie y se tomará la mano,* give a low-bred man an inch he'll take an ell; *el villano en su rincón,* a retiring, unapproachable man.

villanote, *a.* great villain.

villar, *n.m.* village, hamlet.

villazgo, *n.m.* charter of a town; tax laid on towns.

villeta, *n.f.* small town or borough.

villoría, *n.f.* farm-house, farm; settlement, hamlet.

villorín, *n.m.* broadcloth of undyed wool.

villorrio, *n.m.* insignificant, backward village.

vimbre, *n.m.* osier, willow.

vinagrada, *n.f.* cooling drink made with vinegar and sugar.

vinagre, *n.m.* vinegar; sourness, acidity; (*coll.*) peevish person.

vinegrera, *n.f.* vinegar-cruet.

vinagrero, *n.m.* vinegar-seller.

vinagreta, *n.f.* sauce made with onion, oil and vinegar.

vinagrillo, *n.m.* weak vinegar; cosmetic lotion; rose-vinegar; (*Arg., Chi.*) a plant of the Oxalis family.

vinagroso, -sa, *a.* vinegary, sour; (*coll.*) vinegarish, peevish.

vinagrón, *n.m.* wine on the turn.

vinajera, *n.f.* wine vessel for the Mass.

vinariego, *n.m.* vintager.

vinario, -ria, *a.* belonging to wine.

vinatera, *n.f.* (*naut.*) strop, tricing line.

vinatería, *n.f.* vintnery, wine-trade; wine-shop.

vinatero, -ra, *a.* pertaining to wine. — *n.m.* wine-merchant, vintner.

vinaza, *n.f.* wine drawn from the lees.

vinazo, *n.m.* very strong wine.

vincapervinca, *n.f.* periwinkle.

vinculable, *a.* that may be entailed.

vinculación, *n.f.* entail.

vincular, *v.t.* to entail an estate; (*fig.*) to base, found upon; to perpetuate, continue.

vínculo, *n.m.* tie, vinculum, link, chain, bond of union; charge laid upon a foundation; entail.

vincha, *n.f.* (*Arg., Bol., Chi., Per.*) ribbon, handkerchief for the head or hair.

vinchuca, *n.f.* (*Arg., Chi., Per.*) a kind of winged bed-bug.

vindicación, *n.f.* vindication, justification; revenge.

vindicar, *v.t.* (*pret.* **vindiqué;** *pres. subj.* **vindique**) to vindicate, revenge, avenge; to justify, support, defend; to assert; (*law*) to repossess, reclaim, replevy.

vindicativo. -va, *a.* vindictive, revengeful, defensive.

vindicatorio, -ria, *a.* vindicatory.

vindicta, *n.f.* vengeance, revenge; *vindicta*

pública, public punishment; censure of public opinion.

vínico, -ca, *a.* vinic.

vinícola, *n.m.* vintager, vintner.

vinicultor, *n.m.* wine-grower.

vinicultura, *n.f.* viniculture.

viniebla, *n.f.* hound's tongue.

vinificación, *n.f.* wine-making, wine-fermentation.

vinillo, *n.m.* very weak wine.

vino, *n.m.* wine; fermented fruit-juice; *vino de cuerpo,* strong-bodied wine; *vino de lágrima,* virgin-wine; *vino de pasto,* wine for daily use; *vino tinto,* red wine; *vino peleón,* very common wine; *vino de Jerez,* sherry; *vino de Oporto,* port wine; *vino de mi propia cosecha,* wine of my own growing; *vino de coco,* (*Philip.*) coconut milk fermented; *vino de nipa,* (*Philip.*) fermented juice of nipa; *vino generoso,* strong, old wine; *dormir el vino,* to sleep off the effects of one's drink; *el vino, como rey, y el agua, como buey,* wine is a master but water a servant; *ninguno se embriaga del vino de su casa,* home delights are never sweet.

vinolencia, *n.f.* inebriation, excess in drinking.

vinolento, -ta, *a.* fond of drink, given to excess in drinking.

vinosidad, *n.f.* vinosity.

vinoso, -sa, *a.* vinous, vinose.

vinote, *n.m.* remains in the still after distilling wine.

vinta, *n.f.* (*Philip.*) small boat.

vintén, *n.m.* (*Ur.*) small copper coin.

viña, *n.f.* vineyard.

viñadero, *n.m.* vineyard-keeper.

viñador, *n.m.* wine-grower.

viñedo, *n.m.* vineyard, vineyard-country.

viñero, *n.m.* vintager who owns vineyards.

viñeta, *n.f.* vignette.

viñuela, *n.f.* small vineyard.

viola, *n.f.* viola; viol. — *n.m.f.* viola player; (*bot.*) violet.

violáceo, -cea, *a.* violaceous; violet coloured.

violación, *n.f.* violation.

violado, -da, *a.* violated. — *p.p.* [VIOLAR]; violet-coloured, made with violets.

violador, -ra, *n.m.f.* violator, infringer, profaner.

violar, *v.t.* to violate, break, infringe; ravish, rape; to profane, desecrate; to tarnish, spoil.

violencia, *n.f.* violence, impetuousness, force, compulsion; intensity, fury; rape; excess, outrage.

violentamente, *adv.* violently, forcibly.

violentar, *v.t.* to force, violate, constrain; to break into, open by force; to misconstrue. — *v.r.* to be firm with oneself, force oneself to do a thing.

violento, -ta, *a.* violent, furious, impetuous, boisterous; repugnant; unnatural; absurd, erroneous, misconstrued; improper, impolite, unjust.

violero, *n.m.* (*obs.*) viol player.

violeta, *n.f.* violet.

violeto, *n.m.* clingstone peach.

violín, *n.m.* violin, fiddle; violinist, fiddler. — *embolsar el violín,* (*Arg., Ven.*) (*coll.*) to be crest-fallen, dejected; humiliated.

violinista, *n.m.* violinist.

violón, *n.m.* bass-viol, double bass; double bass player; *tocar el violón,* to do something absurd.

violoncelo, violonchelo, *n.m.* violoncello.

violonchelista, *n.m.f.* violoncellist, cellist.

viperino, -na, *a.* viperine, viperous.

vira, *n.f.* kind of light arrow; welt of a shoe.

viracocha, *n.m.f.* (*Chi., Per.*) Spaniard.

virada, *n.f.* (*naut.*) tack, tacking.

virador, *n.m.* top-rope; (*naut.*) viol; (*phot.*) fixative.

virar, *v.t.* (*naut.*) to tack, veer; to wind, twist, heave; (*phot.*) to fix; (*motor.*) to change the direction; *virar de bordo en redondo,* to stand to leeward; *virar para popa,* to heave astern; *virar para proa,* to heave ahead.

viratón, *n.m.* large dart or arrow.

viravira, *n.f.* (*Arg., Chi., Per., Ven.*) a medicinal plant of the Composite order.

virazones, *n.m.pl.* alternate land and sea breezes.

virgen, *n.m.f.* virgin, chaste person. — *n.f.* maiden, maid; the Blessed Virgin; image of the Virgin; standard of the beam in the oil mills; (*astron.*) Virgin, Virgo. — *a.* primitive, untried, new; pure, chaste, undefiled, spotless.

virgiliano, *a.* Virgilian.

virginal; virgíneo, -nea, *a.* virginal, virgin, maiden.

virginia, *n.f.* Virginia tobacco.

virginiano, -na, *n., a.* Virginian.

virginidad, *n.f.* virginity, maidenhood.

virgo, *n.m.* virginity; (*anat.*) hymen; (*astron.*) Virgo.

vírgula, *n.f.* small rod, thin line; cholera germ.

virgulilla, *n.f.* small, or fine stroke; very thin line; comma, apostrophe, diacritical sign.

viril, *a.* virile, manly. — *n.m.* clear glass; (*eccles.*) monstrance.

virilidad, *n.f.* virility, manhood, strength, vigour.

virilmente, *adv.* in a manly way.

virio, *n.m.* loriot, golden oriole.

viripotente, *a.* marriageable, nubile (said of women); vigorous, strong.

virola, *n.f.* collar, hoop; knob of a curtain-rod: check-ring of a goad.

virolento, -ta, *a.* having small-pox; pockmarked.

virón, *n.m.* large dart.

virotazo, *n.m.* wound caused by shaft, dart or arrow.

virote, *n.m.* shaft, dart, arrow; iron rod on a slave's collar; (*coll.*) beau, young blood; (*coll.*) stuffed shirt; (*coll.*) April fool's trick; *cada uno mire por el virote,* let everyone see to his own business.

virotillo, *n.m.* (*arch.*) strut, intertie. — *pl.* **virotillos,** *n.m.pl.* (*arch.*) braces.

virotismo, *n.m.* conceit, pride, airs.

virotón, *n.m.* large arrow or dart.

virreina, *n.f.* vicereine; viceroy's wife.

virreinato, virreino, *n.m.* viceroyship; vice-royalty.

virrey, *n.m.* viceroy.

virtual, *a.* virtual.

virtualidad, *n.f.* virtuality, efficacy.

virtualmente, *adv.* virtually, in effect.

virtud, *n.f.* virtue; power, strength, force, efficacy; integrity, righteousness, rectitude, goodness; virtuous life, habit, disposition; vigour, courage. — *pl.* **virtudes,** fifth choir of the celestial spirits. — *en virtud de,* by or in virtue of.

virtuosamente, *adv.* virtuously.

virtuoso, -sa, *n.m.f.,* *a.* chaste; virtuous, just; virtuoso, a skilled performer in some fine art.

viruela, *n.f.* pock; small-pox, variola. — *viruelas bastardas,* chicken-pox; *viruelas locas,* benign kind of small-pox.

virulencia, *n.f.* virulence, virus; malignance, acrimony.

virulento, -ta, *a.* virulent, malignant; prurient.

virus, *n.m.* virus, poison; contagion.

viruta, *n.f.* wood shaving, cutting, chip.

vis, *n.f.; vis cómica,* (*theat.*) verve.

visaje, *n.m.* grimace, wry face; grin, smirk; *hacer visajes,* to make wry faces.

visajero, -ra, *n.m.f.,* *a.* grimacer, grimacier.

visar, *v.t.* to examine (a document); to visa, mark with a visa; to countersign; (*artill., topog.*) to set the line of sight.

víscera, *n.f.* viscus; viscera.

visceral, *a.* visceral.

visco, *n.m.* bird-lime; (*Arg.*) a tree of the Leguminosæ family.

viscosidad, *n.f.* viscosity, glutinousness.

viscoso, -sa, *a.* viscous, viscid, glutinous.

visera, *n.f.* visor; eye-shade; (*Cub.*) winker.

visibilidad, *n.f.* visibility.

visible, *a.* visible; perceptible, open, apparent, clear, evident, conspicuous.

visiblemente, *adv.* visibly, clearly, evidently.

visigodo, -da, *n.m.f.,* *a.* Visigoth.

visigótico, -ca, *a.* Visigothic.

visillo, *n.m.* short lace curtain.

visión, *n.f.* sight; vision; (*coll.*) ugly or grotesque person, guy; apparition, phantom; dream, fantasy; prophecy, revelation; *ver visiones,* to build castles in the air.

visionario, -ria, *n.m.f.,* *a.* visionary, fanatic, dreamer.

visir, *n.m.* vizier.

visita, *n.f.* visit; visitor, caller, guest, visitant; social call; visitation, inquisition; register, examination, inspection; (*eccles.*) tribunal for the inspection of prisons; hall of that tribunal; *derecho de visita,* right of search; *tener visita,* to have company; *hacer una visita,* to pay a call.

visitación, *n.f.* visitation, visiting, visit.

visitador, -ra, *n.m.f.* visitor, visitant, frequent caller; surveyor, searcher, examiner; *visitador de registro,* tide-waiter.

visitadora, *n.f.* (*Hond., Ven.*) clyster, enema.

visitar, *v.t.* to visit; to pay a visit, call upon; to search, survey, investigate, inquire, examine; (*law*) to search ships; to try weights and measures; to travel, traverse; to appear (of a spirit); to frequent; (*law*) to make an abstract. — *v.r.* to petition prison-inspectors.

visiteo, *n.m.* frequent calling or visiting.

visitero, -ra, *a.* fond of visiting.

visitica, *n.f.* short call.

visivo, -va, *a.* visual.

vislumbrar, *v.t.* to glimpse, catch a glimpse or glimmer; perceive indistinctly; to conjecture; to know imperfectly. — *v.r.* to glimmer.

vislumbre, *n.f.* glimpse, glimmer, glimmering light, faint or imperfect view; surmise, conjecture; confused perception; appearance, semblance.

viso, *n.m.* elevated spot, prospect, outlook; lustre, gleam, sheen, glare, flash; coloured lining or slip worn under a transparent frock; colour, cloak, pretext; appearance, aspect, semblance, apparent likeness; *a dos*

visos, in two ways, from two (*different*) points of view; *al viso,* viewed sideways (of fabrics); *hacer viso,* to attract attention.

visogodo, -da, *n., a.* Visigoth.

visón, *n.m.* (*Am.*) mink.

visor, *n.m.* (*phot.*) view-finder.

visorio, -ria, *a.* visual, optic.

visorio, *n.m.* expert examination.

víspera, *n.f.* eve, day before; (*fig.*) eve, approach, nearness; vesper; forerunner, prelude. — *pl.* **vísperas,** (*eccles.*) vespers; *en vísperas de,* on the eve of.

vista, *n.f.* view, sight, seeing, vision; interview, meeting; eye, eyesight; look, appearance, aspect; landscape, prospect, vista; purpose, intent; apparition; clear perception; opinion, judgment; relation, comparison; (*law*) trial; first stage of a lawsuit; revision of sentence. — *n.m.* customs surveyor; *a vista de,* in view of, in consideration of; *a vista de ojos,* with one's own eyes; *a la vista,* immediately, at sight; *a primera vista,* at first sight; *a vista de pájaro,* from a bird's-eye view; *aguzar la vista,* to sharpen the perception; *apartar la vista,* to withdraw one's gaze or consideration; *comerse con la vista,* to look longingly at; *conocer de vista,* to know by sight; *dar una vista,* to cast a glance; *echar una vista,* to look after, keep an eye on; *echar la vista a,* to select mentally; *en vista de,* in view of, in consequence of; *hacer la vista gorda,* to wink at, turn a blind eye; *¡hasta la vista!* good-bye, au revoir; *pasar la vista por,* to look over, glance over; *perderse de vista,* (*coll.*) to excel; *tener vista,* to be showy, to look well; *volver la vista atrás,* to look back over. — *pl.* **vistas,** meeting, interview, conference; wedding presents from bride and bridegroom to each other; front, collar and cuffs of a shirt; lights of a building.

vistazo, *n.m.* glance; *dar un vistazo,* to cast a glance, to look over.

vistillas, *n.f.pl.* lofty eminence, view-point.

visto, -ta, *a.* clear, obvious, evident; (*law*) whereas. — *p.p. irreg.* [VER]; *está bien* (or *mal*) *visto,* he is (not) respected; *visto es* (or *visto está*), it is evident; *mal visto,* improper; *no visto,* extraordinary; *visto que,* (*law*) considering that (preambulatory clause 'whereas'); *visto bueno* (abbreviation Vᵒ Bᵒ), correct, approved, O.K.

vistosamente, *adv.* beautifully, showily.

vistoso, -sa, *a.* showy, fine, beautiful; glaring, 'loud.'

visual, *a.* visual. — *n.f.* line of sight.

visualidad, *n.f.* visuality.

visura, *n.f.* ocular inspection, expert examination.

vital, *a.* vital, belonging to life; necessary, essential.

vitalicio, -cia, *a.* life-long, lasting for life, during life; *pensión vitalicia,* annuity.

vitalicio, *n.m.* life-insurance policy.

vitalicista, *n.m.f.* person who enjoys a life annuity.

vitalidad, *n.f.* vitality.

vitalismo, *n.m.* vitalism.

vitalista, *n.m.f.* vitalist.

vitando, -da, *a.* that ought to be shunned; execrable, odious.

vitela, *n.f.* calf; vellum, parchment.

vitelina, *a.* vitelline.

vitícola, *a.* viticultural.

viticultura, *n.f.* vine cultivation, viticulture.

vito, *n.m.* Andalusian folksong and dance.

vitola, *n.f.* (*mil.*) ball calibre, standard gauge; standard shape and size for cigars; (*naut.*) templet; (*Am.*) appearance, looks, aspect.

¡vítor!, *interj.* huzza! hurrah! long live! — *n.m.* triumphal pageant; commemorative tablet.

vitorear, *v.t.* to shout, cheer, huzza, acclaim.

vitre, *n.m.* (*naut.*) thin canvas.

vítreo, -rea, *a.* vitreous, glassy.

vitrificable, *a.* vitrificable.

vitrificación, *n.f.* vitrification.

vitrificar, *v.t.* (conjugated like BUSCAR) to vitrify.

vitrina, *n.f.* glasscase, show-case.

vitriólico, -ca, *a.* vitriolic.

vitriolo, *n.m.* vitriol.

vitualla, *n.f.* victuals, provisions, viands, food.

vituallar, *v.t.* to victual.

vítulo marino, *n.m.* sea calf.

vituperable, *a.* vituperable, condemnable, blameworthy.

vituperación, *n.f.* vituperation.

vituperador, -ra, *n.m.f.* blamer, censurer, vituperator.

vituperante, *a.* vituperating, censuring, decrying.

vituperar, *v.t.* to vituperate, censure, reproach, blame, decry, condemn.

vituperio, *n.m.* vituperation, blame, reproach, censure; affront, insult, disgrace, infamy.

vituperiosamente, *adv.* opprobriously, reproachfully.

vituperioso, -sa, *a.* opprobrious, reproachful.

viuda, *n.f.* widow, dowager; (*bot.*) mourning bride; *condesa viuda,* countess dowager; *la viuda llora, y otros cantan en la boda,* proverb illustrating the fickleness of the world.

viudal, *a.* belonging to a widow or widower.

viudedad, *n.f.* widowhood; widow's pension.

viudez, *n.f.* widowhood.

viudita, *n.f.* merry little widow; (*Arg., Chi.*) an insectivorous bird of the genus Psittacus.

viudo, *n.m.* widower; widowed bird.

¡ viva !, *interj.* long live, hurrah. — *n.m.* huzza, shout, cry of acclamation.

vivac, *n.m.* bivouac.

vivacidad, *n.f.* vivacity, liveliness, briskness; brilliancy; energy, vigour.

vivamente, *adv.* vividly; quickly; deeply.

vivandero, *n.m.* sutler.

vivaque, *n.m.* bivouac; night guard.

vivaquear, *v.i.* to bivouac.

vivaqueo, *n.m.* bivouacking.

vivar, *n.m.* warren, burrow; vivarium.

vivaracho, -cha, *a.* (*coll.*) smart, lively, sprightly, frisky.

vivaz, *a.* lively; ingenious; active, vigorous, energetic; bright, witty; perennial, evergreen.

viveral, *n.m.* (*hort.*) nursery.

víveres, *n.m.pl.* provisions, food, eatables; (*mil.*) stores.

vivero, *n.m.* warren; fish-pond, vivarium; (*hort.*) nursery; cloth manufactured in Vivero (Galicia).

viveza, *n.f.* liveliness, vigour; gaiety; activity, sprightliness, briskness, celerity, ardour; acuteness, perspicacity; witticism; lustre,

splendour; marked resemblance; inconsiderate word or deed.

vividero, -ra, *a.* habitable.

vívido, -da, *a.* vivid, bright.

vividor, -ra, *n.m.f.* long liver; economist; sponger.

vivienda, *n.f.* dwelling-house, lodgings, apartments.

viviente, *a.* animated, living.

vivificación, *n.f.* vivification, enlivening.

vivificador, -ra, *n.m.f.* vivifier, life-giver, animator.

vivificante, *a.* vivifying, life-giving.

vivificar, *v.t.* (conjugated like BUSCAR), to vivify, animate, enliven; to refresh, comfort.

vivificativo, -va, *a.* life-giving; animating; comforting.

vivífico, -ca, *a.* vivific.

vivíparo, -ra, *a.* viviparous.

vivir, *v.i.* to live, have life; to enjoy life, fame or happiness; to last, continue, keep; to be, exist; to lodge, dwell, inhabit, reside; to be remembered; to be present (in memory); to temporize; *vivir en grande* (or *a lo grande*), to live luxuriously; *¡ viva Vd. mil años !* long life to you; *¿ quién vive?* (*mil.*) who goes there ? *vive soñando,* he is a dreamer; *vive de invenciones,* he lives on his wits; (*bueno es*) *vivir para ver,* as we live, we learn. — *n.m.* life, living, existence; *mal vivir,* dissipation.

vivisección, *n.f.* vivisection.

vivo, -va, *a.* alive, living; active, quick, vivid, hasty, nimble, smart, lively, efficacious, kindled, live (as fire), intense; acute, ingenious, bright; inconsiderate; diligent; lasting, enduring, constant; excellent; florid; blessed; persuasive, expressive. — *n.m.* raw (flesh); (*vet.*) inflamed swelling on the back; (*arch.*) sharp corner, angle, edge; edging, border; corded seam; *al vivo* (or *a lo vivo*), to the life; *cal viva,* quicklime; *carne viva,* quick flesh (in a wound); *tocar en lo vivo,* to hurt one deeply, wound to the quick; *viva voz,* by word of mouth.

vizcacha, *n.f.* (*Am.*) large kind of hare.

vizcaíno, -na, *n.m.f.* Biscayan.

vizcaitarra, *n.m.f.*, *a.* Biscayan irredentist.

vizcondado, *n.m.* viscountship, viscountcy.

vizconde, *n.m.* viscount.

vizcondesa, *n.f.* viscountess.

vocablo, *n.m.* word, term, diction.

vocabulario, *n.m.* vocabulary, dictionary, lexicon.

vocabulista, *n.m.* lexicographer; student of words.

vocación, *n.f.* vocation, calling; employment, trade.

vocal, *a.* vocal, oral. — *n.f.* vowel. — *n.m.* voter; member of a committee or governing body.

vocalización, *n.f.* (*mus.*) vocalization.

vocalizar, *v.i.* (conjugated like ALZAR) (*mus.*) to vocalize, articulate.

vocalmente, *adv.* vocally, orally.

vocativo, *n.m.* vocative case.

voceador, -ra, *n.m.f.* vociferator; town-crier.

vocear, *v.t.*, *v.i.* to vociferate, clamour, cry out; cry, bawl, scream, howl, hail, halloo; to shout, huzza; to publish, proclaim; (*coll.*) to boast publicly.

vocejón, *n.m.* harsh voice.

vocería, *n.f.* clamour, hallooing, outcry.

vocero, *n.m.* spokesman, mouthpiece, representative.

vociferación, *n.f.* vociferation, outcry, clamour, boast.

vociferador, -ra, *n.m.f.* vociferator, shouter, boaster, bragger.

vociferante, *a.* vociferating.

vociferar, *v.i.* to vociferate; to boast of.

vocinglería, *n.f.* clamour, outcry; loquacity.

vocinglero, -ra, *a.* vociferous, bawling, prattling, chattering. — *n.m.f.* loud babbler.

volada, *n.f.* short flight; (*Mex.*) story, intentional lie.

voladera, *n.f.* float of a water-wheel.

voladero, -ra, *a.* volatile, fleeting, flying.

voladero, *n.m.* precipice, abyss.

voladizo, -za, *a.* projecting, jutting out.

voladizo, *n.m.* corbel.

volado, -da, *a.* (*print.*) superior, set above the line. — *n.m.* sweetmeat of white of egg, sugar and flavour.

volador, -ra, *a.* flying, hanging in he air; blowing up with gunpowder; very swift.

volador, *n.m.* flying-fish; sky-rocket; a hardwood tropical tree of the Laurus family.

voladora, *n.f.* fly-wheel of an engine.

voladura, *n.f.* explosion, blasting, blowing up.

volandas, (en), *adv.* in the air; *en andas y volandas*, in a twinkling, in an instant, rapidly, swiftly.

volandera, *n.f.* runner (in oil-mills); (*coll.*) lie; (*print.*) galley-slice; (*mech.*) washer.

volandero, -ra, *a.* ready to fly, fluttering in the air, suspended in the air; casual, chance, fortuitous; fleeting, unsettled, volatile, variable; *vapor volandero*, (*naut.*) tramp steamer.

volanta, *n.f.* (*West Ind.*) a two-wheeled cab with very long shafts.

volante, *a.* flying, volant, fluttering, unsettled. — *n.m.* light screen; shuttlecock; shuttlecock and battledore; balance beam; flywheel of a machine; head ornament of gauze; flounce of a dress; coiner's stamping-mill; balance wheel of a watch; footman, lackey, flunkey; (*sew.*) flounce; linen coat; flier, note, memorandum; *papel volante*, fly-sheet, pamphlet; (*Cub.*) [VOLANTA].

volantín, *n.m.* fishing-apparatus; (*Arg., Chi., Cub., PR.*) kite.

volantón, *n.m.* fledged bird able to fly.

volapié, *n.m.* manner of killing a bull (bull-fight).

volar, *v.i.* (*pres. indic.* **vuelo**; *pres. subj.* **vuele**) to fly, soar, rise in the air; to flutter, hover; to pass through the air; to run, move swift'y; to vanish, disappear; to make rapid progress, execute very promptly; to jut out, project; to spread rapidly; to burst, explode. — *v.t.* to fly; to blow up, blast, spring (a mine); to exasperate, irritate; to rouse the game; *echar a volar*, to disseminate, publish.

volarse, *v.i.* (*Am.*) to become suddenly irate.

volateo, (al), *adv.* shooting birds on the wing.

volatería, *n.f.* fowling; sporting with hawks; finding by chance; desultory speech; fowls, flock of birds; (*fig.*) wool-gathering, fancy free; *de volatería*, fortuitously, adventitiously.

volátil, *a.* (*chem.*) volatile; flying, wafting; evaporating; changeable, fugitive, inconstant, fickle; fleeting.

volatilidad, *n.f.* (*chem.*) volatility.

volatilización, *n.f.* volatilization.

volatilizar, *v.t.* (conjugated like ALZAR) to volatilize, vaporize.

volatín, volatinero, *n.m.* tight-rope walker, acrobat; acrobatic feat; (*Per.*) acrobatic show.

volatizar, *v.t.* (conjugated like ALZAR) (*chem.*) to volatilize.

volcán, *n.m.* volcano; great ardour, violent passion; excitable or intemperate person; (*Col.*) precipice, steep and broken ground.

volcanejo, *n.m.* little volcano.

volcánico, -ca, *a.* volcanic.

volcar, *v.t.* (*pres. indic.* **vuelco**; *pret.* **volqué**; *pres. subj.* **vuelque**) to make giddy, dizzy; to upset, overturn, turn upside down; to tilt; (*naut.*) to capsize; to make someone change his opinion. — *v.r.* to upset.

volea, *n.f.* swingle-tree; volley (of a ball).

volear, *v.t.* to throw up in the air; to strike in the air (as a ball); (*sowing*) broadcasting by hand.

voleo, *n.m.* blow given to a ball in the air; high step in dancing; a very hard slap in the face; *de un voleo, del primer voleo*, (*coll.*) at one blow, all at once.

volframio, *n.m.* tungsten, wolfram.

volframita, *n.f.* wolframite.

volición, *n.f.* volition.

volitar, *v.i.* to twirl; to flutter.

volitivo, -va, *a.* volitional, volitive.

volquearse, *v.r.* to tumble; to wallow.

volquete, *n.m.* tip-car, tip-cart.

voltaico, -ca, *a.* voltaic.

voltaísmo, *n.m.* (*elect.*) voltaism.

voltaje, *n.m.* voltage.

voltámetro, *n.m.* voltameter.

voltariedad, *n.f.* levity, inconstancy, volatility.

voltario, -ria, *a.* fickle, inconstant, giddy.

volteador, *n.n.* tumbler, vaulter, acrobat.

voltear, *v.t.* to whirl, revolve; to overturn, upset; to change the state or order of things; (*arch.*) to arch, to vault. — *v.i.* to tumble, give a display of tumbling, roll over.

voltejear, *v.t.* to whirl; (*naut.*) to tack.

volteo, *n.m.* act and effect of whirling.

voltereta, volteta, *n.f.* light spring, light tumble, somersault; act of turning up trumps.

volteriano, -na, *n.m.f., a.* Voltairian, cynic, sceptic.

voltímetro, *n.m.* voltameter.

voltio, *n.m.* volt.

voltizo, -za, *a.* twisted; fickle, inconstant.

volubilidad, *n.f.* volubility, inconstancy, fickleness.

voluble, *a.* voluble; easily swayed, inconstant, fickle; (*bot.*) twining.

volublemente, *adv.* volubly.

volumen, *n.m.* volume, bulkiness, size, corpulence; tome, book.

voluminoso, -sa, *a.* voluminous, bulky.

voluntad, *n.f.* will, purpose, volition, free-will; choice, election, determination; benevolence, kindness, goodwill; pleasure, desire; consent, disposition; precept; *a voluntad*, optional, at one's will or pleasure; *de (buena) voluntad*, with pleasure; *mala voluntad*, ill-will, inimical.

voluntariamente, *adv.* spontaneously, voluntarily, fain.

voluntariedad, *n.f.* free-will, voluntariness, spontaneity.

voluntario, -ria, *a.* voluntary, spontaneous.

voluntario, *n.m.* volunteer.

voluntariosamente, *adv.* selfishly, wilfully; spontaneously.

voluntarioso, -sa, *a.* selfish, self-willed, wilful.

voluptuosamente, *adv.* voluptuously, sensuously, licentiously.

voluptuosidad, *n.f.* voluptuousness, licentiousness.

voluptuoso, -sa, *a.* voluptuous, sensuous; licentious, sensual, lustful, lewd.

voluta, *n.f.* (*arch.*) volute.

volvedor, *n.m.* tap-wrench, turn-screw; (*Arg., Col.*) said of a horse that flees back home.

volver (*p.p.* **vuelto;** *pres. indic.* **vuelvo;** *pres. subj.* **vuelva**), *v.t.* to restore, return, repay, give up; to turn, turn over, turn up, turn upside down; to direct, aim; to incline, persuade, convince, convert; to invert; to remit, send back, discharge, turn away; to replace; to translate; to vomit; to recover, regain; to close (a door, etc.); to give back, change; to plough a second time. — *v.i.* to come or go back, return, come again; to deviate; turn to right or left; to resume the thread of a discourse; *volver la puerta,* to shut the door; *volver atrás,* to come or go back; *volver por sí,* to defend oneself; *volver en sí,* to recover one's senses; *volver pies atrás,* to back out of an enterprise; *volver sobre sí,* to examine one's conscience; recoup; regain self-control; *volver a la carga,* to begin a matter over again; *volver a uno loco,* (*fig.*) to drive someone mad; *volver a las andadas,* to drop back into bad ways (of life). — *v.r.* to turn sour; to turn about, turn around; to turn, become; to change, retract an opinion; *volverse blanco,* to become white; *volverse loco,* to become mad, deranged; *volverse la tortilla,* to turn the tables; *volverse patas arriba,* to turn turtle, capsize.

volvible, *a.* revolving, that may be turned.

volvo, vólvulo, *n.m.* (*med.*) volvulus, iliac passion.

vómico, -ca, *a.* vomitive, causing vomiting.

vomipurgante, vomipurgativo, *n., a.* both purgative and emetic.

vomitado, -da, *a.* (*coll.*) palefaced, meagre, thin.

vomitador, -ra, *n.m.f.* one who vomits.

vomitar, *v.t.* to vomit, eject, discharge, throw up, disgorge; to foam; to reveal, discover (a secret), make a clean breast; *vomitar sangre,* (*fig.*) to boast of one's descent; *vomitar veneno,* to utter insults or blasphemies.

vomitel, *n.m.* (*Cub.*) a tree of the Boraginaceæ family.

vomitivo, -va, *n., a.* vomitive, emetic.

vómito, *n.m.* vomiting, vomit; *provocar a vómito,* to nauseate; (*Cub.*) yellow fever.

vomitón, -ona, *a.* puking, vomiting (of sucking child).

vomitona, *n.f.* (*coll.*) violent vomiting.

vomitorio, -ria, *a.* vomitive, vomitory, emetic.

voracidad, *n.f.* voracity, voraciousness, greediness.

vorágine, *n.f.* vortex, whirlpool.

voraginoso, -sa, *a.* voraginous, engulfing, full of whirlpools.

vorahunda, *n.f.* turmoil.

voraz, *a.* voracious, ravenous, greedy; lustful; fierce, destructive.

vorazmente, *adv.* voraciously, gluttonously, greedily.

vormela, *n.f.* kind of spotted weasel.

vórtice, *n.m.* vortex, whirlpool, whirlwind, hurricane, waterspout.

vortiginoso, -sa, *a.* vortical.

vos, *pers .pron. 2nd pers. sing. and pl.*(always with the plural form of the verb), ye, you (obsolete except in poetic, devotional and official styles).

vosotros, -tras, *pers. pron. 2nd pers. pl.*, you (familiar); ye.

votación, *n.f.* voting, balloting; vote.

votador, -ra, *n.m.f.* voter; swearer.

votante, *a.* voter.

votar, *v.i.* to vote; to vow; to give an opinion; to curse, swear. — *v.t.* to dart.

votivo, -va, *a.* votive; offered by a vow.

voto, *n.m.* vow; vote, suffrage; ballot; voter; voice, advice, opinion; wish; supplication to God, prayer; angry or menacing oath; (*eccles.*) votive offering; *voto de calidad* (or *decisivo*), casting vote; *voto de amén,* blind vote; *ser* (or *tener*) *voto,* to have a right to vote; *a pluralidad de votos,* by a majority of votes; *¡voto a Dios! ¡voto al chápiro! ¡voto a tal!* good gracious!

votri, *n.m.* (*Chi.*) a climbing plant.

voz, *n.f.* voice; outcry, clamour; vocable, expression, term, word; vote, suffrage; right to vote; power, authority; rumour, public opinion; pretext, motive; inspiration; (*mus.*) voice, voice-range (tenor, soprano, etc.); (*mus.*) voice, melodic line; (*mil.*) order, mandate, command; (*law*) life; *dar voces,* to cry, call out; *en voz,* verbally; *es voz común,* it is generally rumoured; *a media voz,* in a whisper; *a una voz,* unanimously; *a voces,* in a loud voice; *a voz en cuello* (or *en grito*), in a loud voice; *correr la voz,* to rumour, disclose, reveal; *dar voces al viento,* to shout to no purpose; *echar la voz,* to disclose, divulge; *jugar la voz,* to sing with inflexions; *poner mala voz,* to discredit, speak ill of; *romper la voz,* to shout very loudly; *tomar la voz,* to take up the discussion *or* question; *voz del pueblo, voz del cielo,* the voice of the people is the voice of God (*vox populi vox Dei*).

vozarrón, *n.m.* loud voice, strong voice.

voznar, *v.i.* to cackle like geese, cry like swans.

vuchén, *n.m.* (*Chi.*) legitimate son; potato that grows wild.

vuecelencia, vuecencia, *n.m.f.* (contraction of VUESTRA EXCELENCIA) Your Excellency.

vuelco, *n.m.* overturning, tumble, upset.

vuelillo, *n.m.* lace cuff trimming.

vuelo, *n.m.* flight, flying; wing of a bird; projecting part of a building; fullness of clothes; (*sew.*) wristfall, flounce, ruffle, frill; soaring, loftiness, elevation of thought; leap in pantomimes; (*arch.*) projection, jutting; *a vuelo* (or *al vuelo*), expeditiously, hurryingly; *coger al vuelo,* to do accidentally, achieve quite by chance; *echar a vuelo las campanas,* to ring the bells; *tomar vuelo,* to increase greatly; to progress.

vuelo, *pres. indic.* [VOLAR].

vuelta, *n.f.* turn; twirl, turning, gyration, circuit, circumvolution; deviation from the straight line; turn of an arch; rehearsal, repetition, iteration; change; requital, recompense; back or wrong side, reverse; wards of a key; flogging, lashing, whipping;

(*naut.*) turn, hitch, lashing; return, regress; review of a lesson; going over (a book, a writing, a report, etc.); rotation; bent, inclination; (*sew.*) flounce, ruffle; order of stitches in a hose; (*tail.*) facing, cuff of a sleeve; outing, excursion, trip, short walk or ride, promenade; envelope, roll; surplus money, small change; recollection, reconsideration; unexpected sally, repartee; number of verses repeated; card turned up for a trump; number of times a field has been ploughed; rotation, revolution; potter's wheel; ceiling; vault; *a vuelta* (or *a vueltas*), very near, almost; *a vuelta de*, within, in the course of; *a vuelta de correo*, by return of post; *a la vuelta*, on returning; overleaf; round the corner; (*com.*) on the return, carried forward; *andar a vueltas*, to shuffle; *a vuelta de cabeza*, in the twinkling of an eye; *andar a las vueltas de*, to dog; *dar una vuelta*, to take a walk, take a trip; *dar a vueltas*, to struggle, fight; to endeavour; *dar vueltas*, to walk to and fro, to fuss about; *de vuelta*, on one's return; *¡media vuelta!* (*mil.*) about turn! *¡otra vuelta!* again! *no tener vuelta de hoja*, to be unanswerable; *no hay que darle vuelta*, it's of no use talking; *poner de vuelta y media*, to abuse; *coger las vueltas*, to manage to get rid of something; *tener vueltas*, to be fickle, changeable; *tomar la vuelta de tierra*, (*naut.*) to make for shore.

vuelto, -ta, *a., p.p. irreg.* [VOLVER].

vuelvo; vuelva, *pres. indic.; pres. subj.* [VOLVER].

vuesa, *a.f.* contraction of *vuestra* used before *eminencia, merced*, etc.

vuesamerced, (*obs.*) **vuesarced,** *n.f.* your honour; your worship, your grace.

vueseñoría, *n.f.* contraction of *vuestra señoría*, your lordship, your ladyship.

vuestro, -tra, *a., poss. pron.* your, yours.

vulcanio, -nia, *a.* igneous, vulcanian.

vulcanización, *n.f.* vulcanization.

vulcanizar, *v.t.* (conjugated like ALZAR) to vulcanize.

vulgacho, *n.m.* populace, mob, rabble.

vulgar, *a.* vulgar, ordinary, common, coarse; vernacular.

vulgaridad, *n.f.* vulgarity, vulgarism, coarseness.

vulgarización, *n.f.* vulgarization.

vulgarizar, *v.t.* (*pret.* **vulgaricé;** *pres. subj.* **vulgarice**) to vulgarize, popularize, make vulgar; to translate into the vernacular. — *v.r.* to become vulgar.

vulgarmente, *adv.* vulgarly, commonly.

vulgata, *n.f.* Vulgate.

vulgo, *n.m.* multitude, populace, mob, generality, general public.

vulnerable, *a.* vulnerable.

vulneración, *n.f.* act of wounding.

vulnerar, *v.t.* to injure the reputation.

vulneraria, *n.f.* kidney-vetch, lady's fingers.

vulnerario, -ria, *a.* vulnerary. — *n.m.* (*law*) clergyman guilty of killing or wounding; medicine for the treatment of ulcers or wounds.

vulpécula, vulpeja, *n.f.* bitch-fox.

vulpino, -na, *a.* foxy, vulpine, deceitful, crafty.

vultuoso, -sa, *a.* (*med.*) bloated.

vulvaria, *n.f.* (*Mex.*) a common wild plant.

vulvario, -ria, *a.* vulvar.

W

W, w, letter not belonging to the Spanish alphabet, and found only in foreign words. The Spanish Academy has accepted **wat,** *n.m.* watt, the unit of electric power (the term generally used is **vatio**).

wáter, *n.m.* water-closet, toilet.

X

X, x, twenty-sixth letter of the Spanish alphabet. Many words which in Old Spanish were written with *X* have been changed to *J*: *Don Quixote, Don Quijote; México, Méjico*, etc. — *rayos X*, X-rays, Röntgen rays.

xale, *n.m.* (*Mex.*) residue of meat and fried fat.

xana, *n.f.* nymph of the springs and mountains in Asturia.

xapoípa, *n.f.* kind of pancake.

xaquellas, *n.m.pl.* (*Par.*) an Indian tribe.

xenofobia, *n.f.* xenophobia, hatred of foreigners.

xenófobo, -ba, *n.m.f., a.* hater of foreigners.

xilófono, *n.m.* xylophone.

xilografía, *n.f.* xylography.

xilográfico, -ca, *a.* xylographic.

xilógrafo, *n.m.* xylographer.

xilotila, *n.f.* (*Ec.*) hydrous silicate of magnesia and iron.

xunde, *n.m.* (*Mex.*) straw basket especially used to carry maize.

Y

Y, y, twenty-seventh letter of the Spanish alphabet, called *i griega* or *ye*.

y, *conj.* and.

ya, *adv.* already; presently; finally, now. — *interj.* oh, yes; *ya estamos en ello*, now we understand; *ya caigo en ello*, I quite understand; *ya voy*, I'm just coming (*or* going); *ya esto, ya aquello*, now this, now that; *ya que*, since, seeing that; *¡pues ya!* certainly, of course; *ya se ve*, that's quite clear. — *conj.* whether, or; *ya en la milicia, ya en las letras*, whether (or) in the army or in the arts.

yaacabó, *n.m.* (*Ven.*) an insectivorous bird.

yaba, *n.f.* (*Cub.*) yaba tree and bark.

yabuna, *n.f.* (*Cub.*) a long, creeping grass or weed.

yaca, *n.f.* (*bot.*) yacca-tree.

yacal, *n.m.* (*Philip.*) a tree of the Dipterocarpaceæ family.

yacaré, *n.m.* (*Arg.*) cayman, alligator.

yacedor, *n.m.* boy who leads horses to graze by night.

yacente, *a.* jacent, lying.

yacer, *v.i.* (*pres. indic.* **yazco, yazgo,** or **yago;** *pres. subj.* **yazca, yazga,** or **yaga**) to lie down; to lie (in the grave); to be fixed or situated, to exist; to lie (with), to copulate; to graze by night (horses).

yaciente, *a.* extended, stretched (honeycomb).

yacija, *n.f.* bed; lounge, couch; grave, tomb; *ser de mala yacija*, to be restless at night; to be a vagrant.

yacimiento, *n.m.* bed or deposit of mineral.

yacio, *n.m.* Indian rubber-tree.

yactura, *n.f.* loss, damage.

yagruma (hembra), *n.f.* (*Cub.*) a tree of the Ulmaceæ family.

yagruma (macho), *n.f.* (*Cub.*) a tree of the Araliaceæ family.

yagrumo, *n.m.* (*PR.*, *Ven.*) *yagruma hembra.*

yagua, *n.f.* bark of the royal palm.

yagual, *n.m.* (*CR.*, *Hond.*, *Mex.*) padded ring for carrying weights on the head.

yaguar, *n.m.* jaguar.

yaguasa, *n.f.* (*Cub.*, *Hond.*) a tree duck.

yaguré, *n.m.* (*Am.*) skunk.

yaicuaje, *n.m.* (*Cub.*) a tree of the Sapindaceæ family.

yaichihue, *n.m.* (*Chi.*) a plant of the Bromeliaceæ family.

yaití, *n.m.* (*Cub.*) a hard-wood Euphorbiaceous tree.

yal, *n.m.* (*Chi.*) a small bird.

yamao, *n.m.* (*Cub.*) a tree of the Meliaceæ family.

yámbico, -ca, *a.* iambic.

yambo, *n.m.* iambic foot; (*bot.*) jamboo.

yanacona, *n.,* *a.* (*Am.*) Indian bondsman; (*Bol.*, *Per.*) an Indian partner in husbandry.

yanilla, *n.f.* (*Cub.*) a wild mangrove tree.

yanqui, *n.m.f.* a Yankee.

yantar, *v.t.* (*obs.*) to dine. — *n.m.* viands, food; king's taxes.

yapa, *n.f.* (*Am.*) mercury mixed with silver ore in smelting.

yapar, *v.t.* (*Am.*) to add mercury to silver ore.

yapú, *n.m.* (*Arg.*) a kind of thrush.

yáquil, *n.m.* (*Chi.*) a shrub of the Rhamnaceæ family.

yarará, *n.m.* (*Arg.*, *Bol.*, *Par.*) a poisonous viper.

yaraví, *n.m.* (*Am.*) an Indian type of song.

yarda, *n.f.* English yard.

yare, *n.m.* poisonous juice from bitter yucca; (*Ven.*) bread made from the flour of the sweet yucca.

yarey, *n.m.* (*Cub.*) a palm-tree.

yaro, *n.m.* arum.

yatay, *n.m.* (*Arg.*, *Par.*) a very tall palm-tree.

yate, *n.m.* yacht.

yaya, *n.f.* (*Cub.*) lancewood; (*Per.*) kind of acarus.

yayero, *n.m.* (*Cub.*) intermeddling person, busybody.

ye, name of the letter Y.

yeco, *n.m.* (*Chi.*) sea-crow.

yedra, *n.f.* ivy.

yegua, *n.f.* mare; (*Cent. Am.*) stub of a cigar.

yeguada, yegüería, *n.f.* stud, herd of breeding mares and stallions.

yeguar, *a.* belonging to mares.

yegüero, yegüerizo, *n.m.* keeper of breeding mares.

yeísmo, *n.m.* fault of pronunciation consisting in pronouncing *ll* as *y*: *gayina* for *gallina*, *poyo* for *pollo*.

yelmo, *n.m.* helmet.

yema, *n.f.* bud, button, first shoot; yolk of an egg; heart, centre, middle; best of its kind; *yema del dedo*, fleshy tip of the finger; *yema del invierno*, depth of winter; *dar en la yema*, to hit the nail on the head.

yente, *a.;* *yentes y vinientes*, coming and going, passers-by.

yerba, *n.f.* grass, weed, herb; *yerba cana*, groundsel; *yerba de la princesa*, scented verbena; *yerba doncella*, periwinkle; *yerba mora*, nightshade; *yerba marina* (or *yerba de mar*), seaweed; *yerba mate*, maté, Paraguay tea; *yerba carmín*, Virginian poke; *yerba del ballestero*, white hellebore; *yerba lombriguera*, southernwood; *yerba piojera*, stavesacre; *yerbabuena*, mint; *yerbajo*, wild weed.

yerbatear, *v.i.* (*Am.*) to take maté.

yerbatero, *a.* (*Am.*) person who sells fodder grass.

yergo ; yerga, *pres. indic.; pres. subj.* [ERGUIR].

yermar, *v.t.* to dispeople, desolate, lay waste.

yermo, *n.m.* desert, wilderness, waste country.

yermo, -ma, *a.* waste, uninhabited, desert, treeless, herbless; *tierra yerma*, uncultivated ground.

yerno, *n.m.* son-in-law.

yero, *n.m.* tare, vetch.

yerro, *n.m.* mistake, inadvertency, error, fault. — *pl.* **yerros,** faults, defects, errors; *yerro de cuenta*, miscount, miscalculation; *yerro de imprenta*, printer's error; *deshacer un yerro*, to amend an error.

yerro ; yerre, *pres. indic.; pres. subj.* [ERRAR].

yerto, -ta, *a.* stiff, inflexible, motionless, rigid tight; *quedarse yerto*, to be petrified with amazement.

yervo, *n.m.* tare, bitter vetch.

yesal, yesar, *n.m.* gypsum-pit.

yesca, *n.f.* tinder, punk, spunk, touchwood, fuel; (*fig.*) fuel, stimulus, provocation, temptation; (*fig.*) provocation to drink. — *pl.* **yescas,** tinder-box.

yesera, *n.f.* gypsum-pit; woman-seller of gypsum.

yesería, *n.f.* gypsum-kiln; plasterer's shop; building made of plaster.

yesero, -ra, *a.* belonging to gypsum. — *n.m.f.* plasterer, plaster-burner.

yeso, *n.m.* gypsum, plaster; plaster cast; *yeso mate*, plaster of Paris; *yeso blanco*, whiting, plaster for surface finish; *yeso negro*, grey plaster for base.

yesón, *n.m.* piece of gypsum; plaster rubbish.

yesoso, -sa, *a.* gypseous.

yesquero, *n.m.* tinder-box; tinder-maker, tinder-seller.

yeta, *n.f.* (*Am.*) bad luck; misfortune.

yezgo, *n.m.* dwarf elder.

yista, *n.f.* (*Bol.*) a kind of bread.

yo, *pron.* I, myself. — *n.m.* (*philos.*) ego, I, me.

yocalla, *n.m.* (*Bol.*) ragamuffin.

yodado, -da, *a.* iodic, containing iodine.

yodo, *n.m.* iodine.

yodoformo, *n.m.* iodoform.

yoduración, *n.f.* iodization.

yodurar, *v.t.* to iodize.

yoduro, *n.m.* iodide.

yol, *n.m.* (*Chi.*) leather saddlebag.

yola, *n.f.* (*naut.*) yawl, small boat.

yolero, -ra, *n.m.f.* (*PR.*) person who mans the *yola.*

yolillo, *n.m.* (*C.R.*, *Nic.*) small palm-tree.

yos, *n.m.* (*C.R.*) a plant of the Euphorbia family.

yubarta, *n.f.* finback, rorqual.

yuca, *n.f.* (*bot.*) Adam's needle; yucca.

yucal, *n.m.* yucca field.

yugada, *n.f.* yoke of land.

yugo, *n.m.* yoke; nuptial tie, marriage ceremony; oppressive authority, absolute power; (*naut.*) transom; frame of a church-bell; *sacudir el yugo*, (*fig.*) to free oneself, shake off a yoke; *sujetarse al yugo de otro*, to submit to someone.

yuguero, *n.m.* ploughman, plough-boy.

yugular, *a.* (*anat.*) jugular.

yumbo, -ba, *n., a.* (*Ec.*) Indian (of Quinto).

yunque, *n.m.* anvil; persevering person; *estar al yunque*, to bear up under adverse circumstances.

yunta, *n.f.* pair, couple, yoke of oxen.

yuntería, *n.f.* place where draught-oxen are fed; herd of draught-oxen.

yuntero, *n.m.* plough-boy.

yunto, -ta, *a.* joined, united, close; *arar yunto*, to plough close.

yuraguano, *n.m.* (*Cub.*) fan palm.

yuré, *n.m.* (*CR.*) a kind of small pigeon.

yuruma, *n.f.* (*Ven.*) the pith from certain palms used for making bread.

yusera, *n.f.* stone base in oil mills.

yusión, *n.f.* (*law*) command, precept, mandate.

yute, *n.m.* jute.

yuxtalineal, *a.* in juxtaposition.

yuxtaponer, *v.t.* (conjugated like PONER) to juxtapose, place contiguously.

yuxtaposición, *n.f.* juxtaposition.

yúyere, *n.m.* (*Cub.*) panic.

yuyo, *n.m.* (*Arg., Chi.*) wild weeds; (*Chi.*) hedge mustard; (*Per.*) greens; (*Col., Ec.*) mixed herbs; *yuyo colorado*, (*Arg.*) jujube.

yuyuba, *n.f.* jujube.

Z

Z, z, *n.f.* twenty-eighth letter of the Spanish alphabet, called *zeda* or *zeta*.

¡za!, *interj.* used to scare dogs.

zabarcera, *n.f.* woman greengrocer.

zábida, zábila, *n.f.* (*bot.*) common aloe.

zaborda, *n.f.; * **zabordamiento**, *n.m.* (*naut.*) stranding.

zabordar, *v.i.* (*naut.*) to touch ground; to be stranded.

zabordo, *n.m.* stranding.

zaborro, -rra, *n.m.f.* fat person.

zabra, *n.f.* small two-masted vessel (in the Bay of Biscay).

zabucar, *v.t.* (conjugated like BUSCAR) to agitate, shake.

zabullida, *n.f.* dipping, ducking.

zabullidor, -ra, *n.m.f.* one who dips, or ducks.

zabullidura, *n.f.* ducking, submersion.

zabullimiento, *n.m.* submersion.

zabullir, *v.t.* to plunge, immerse. — *v.r.* to sink.

zaca, *n.f.* leather bucket for bailing in a mine.

zacapela, zacapella, *n.f.* yell, uproar, bustle.

zacate, *n.m.* (*Philip., Mex., Cent. Am.*) hay, fodder.

zacateca, *n.m.* (*Cub.*) undertaker, sexton.

zacatín, *n.m.* place where clothes are sold; (*Col.*) distilling apparatus.

zacatón, *n.m.* (*Mex.*) a tall fodder grass.

zacear, *v.t.* to frighten dogs away by crying *¡za!*

zadorija, *n.f.* yellow poppy.

zafa, *n.f.* (*prov.*) basin, bowl.

zafacoca, *n.f.* (*Am.*) squabble, row, fight.

zafada, *n.f.; * **zafamiento**, *n.m.* flight, escape; (*naut.*) lightening a ship.

zafado, -da, *n., a.* (*Am.*) impudent, insolent.

zafar, *v.t.* to adorn, embellish, deck; (*naut.*) to free, disentangle, lighten a ship. — *v.r.* to

escape, run away; to excuse, decline; to avoid risk; to excuse oneself; to part, break loose, slip off, come off.

zafareche, *n.m.* (*prov.*) tank.

zafarí, *n.m.* variety of pomegranate.

zafariche, *n.m.* (*prov.*) shelf for water jars.

zafarrancho, *n.m.* (*naut.*) clearing for action; (*coll.*) destruction, ravage; scuffle, squabble, wrangle.

zafiamente, *adv.* boorishly, awkwardly, clumsily.

zafiedad, *n.f.* boorishness, rusticity, clumsiness.

zafío, *n.m.* conger eel.

zafio, -fia, *a.* boorish, awkward, uncivil, rude, ignorant.

zafir, zafiro, *n.m.* sapphire.

zafíreo, -rea; zafirino, -na, *a.* sapphire-coloured.

zafo, -fa, *a.* free, disentangled; exempt from danger; (*naut.*) free and clear.

zafones, *n.m.pl.* overalls, chaps.

zafra, *n.f.* drip jar; oil jar; (*min.*) rubbish; leather strap holding the thills of a cart; (*Cub.*) sugar crop; sugar making; season of the sugar harvest.

zafrero, *n.m.* (*min.*) rubbish-clearer.

zaga, *n.f.* load on the back of a carriage; rear part of anything. — *n.m.* last player in a game of cards. — *adv.* behind; *a (la) zaga* or *en zaga*, behind; *no irle en zaga a otro*, (*fig.*) not to be far behind another.

zagal, *n.m.* fine, strong youth; young shepherd; swain; assistant driver of a stage-coach; under-petticoat or skirt.

zagala, *n.f.* young shepherdess; girl, lass.

zagalejo, *n.m.* under-petticoat or skirt. — *n.m.f.* shepherd, shepherdess.

zagalón, -ona, *n.m.f.* overgrown youth or girl.

zagua, *n.f.* saltwort.

zagual, *n.m.* paddle.

zaguán, *n.m.* entrance, porch, hall, vestibule.

zaguanete, *n.m.* small vestibule or entrance; small party of the king's life-guards.

zaguero, -ra, *a.* loitering, laggard, remaining behind; back player at the game of pelota.

zahareño, -ña, *a.* wild, haggard; indocile, intractable; disdainful, unsociable, difficult.

zaharí, *n.f.* (*bot.*) a variety of pomegranate.

zaharrón, *n.m.* clown, motley fool; motley.

zahén, zahena, *n.m.f.* a Moorish coin of very fine gold.

zaheridor, -ra, *n.m.f.* censurer.

zaherimiento, *n.m.* censure, blame.

zaherir, *v.t.* (*pres. part.* **zahiriendo**; *pres. indic.* **zahiero**; *pres. subj.* **zahiera**; *pret.* él **zahirió**) to censure, reproach, blame, upbraid.

zahina, *n.f.* sorghum.

zahinar, *n.m.* land sown with sorghum.

zahinas, *n.f.pl.* (*prov.*) kind of thin porridge.

zahonado, -da, *a.* brownish, dark brown (of animals' legs).

zahondar, *v.t.* to penetrate, dig the ground. — *v.i.* to sink into soft ground (the feet).

zahones, *n.m.pl.* kind of breeches or overalls; chaps.

zahora, *n.f.* gay luncheon party.

zahorar, *v.i.* (*obs.*) to have a second supper; to have a repast with music, etc.

zahorí, *n.m.* soothsayer, diviner; astute, observant person.

zahoriar, *v.t.* to scrutinize, look deeply into.

zahorra, *n.f.* ballast.

zahurda, *n.f.* pig-sty.

zaida, *n.f.* kind of heron.

zaino, -na, *a.* chestnut-coloured (horse); vicious (animal); wicked, treacherous; *mirar de zaino*, to look sidewise or slyly.

zalá, *n.f.* salaam; *hacer la zalá*, (*coll.*) to wheedle.

zalagarda, *n.f.* ambush, ambuscade; snare, trap, gin; skirmish, sham fight; sudden attack, surprise.

zalama, zalamería, *n.f.* flattery, adulation.

zalamear, *v.t.* (*Chi.*) to flatter.

zalamero, -ra, *n.m.f.* wheedler, fawner, flatterer.

zalea, *n.f.* undressed sheepskin.

zalear, *v.t.* to shake, shake out; to frighten dogs away.

zalema, *n.f.* salaam, bow, curtsy.

zaleo, *n.m.* sheepskin damaged by a wolf; shaking to and fro.

zalmedina, *n.m., a.* magistrate in Aragon.

zalona, *n.f.* (*prov.*) large earthen jar.

zallar, *v.t.* to outrig.

zamacuco, *n.m.* (*coll.*) dolt, dunce; intoxication.

zamacuco, -ca, *a.* (*PR.*) cunning, artful.

zamacueca, *n.f.* (*Chi., Per.*) Indian folksong and dance.

zamanca, *n.f.* drubbing, flogging, castigation.

zamarra, *n.f.* sheepskin jacket or coat.

zamarrear, *v.t.* to shake, pull or drag to and fro; to drag about, ill-treat.

zamarreo, *n.m.* dragging, pulling, or shaking about.

zamarrico, *n.m.* portmanteau or bag of sheepskin.

zamarrilla, *n.f.* mountain germander.

zamarro, *n.m.* sheepskin coat; sheepskin, lambskin; (*coll.*) stupid person, dolt, dunce; *pl.* (*Col., Ven.*) chaps.

zamarrón, *n.m.* large sheepskin jacket.

zambaigo, -ga, *n., a.* (*Mex.*) Indian and Chinese half-breed.

zambapalo, *n.m.* ancient dance.

zambarco, *n.m.* broad breast-harness.

zámbigo, -ga, *a.* knock-kneed.

zambo, -ba, *a.* knock-kneed; half-breed (Indian and Negro). — *n.m.* American monkey.

zamboa, *n.f.* kind of quince-tree.

zambomba, *n.f.* sounding-box, kind of drum. — *interj.* gosh!

zambombo, *n.m.* boor, rustic, ill-bred person.

zamborondón, -ona; zamborotudo, -da, *a.* big, boorish and clumsy; ill-shaped.

zambra, *n.f.* Moorish festival; noisy mirth, merrymaking; a Moorish boat.

zambucar, *v.t., v.r.* (conjugated like BUSCAR) to hide, be concealed.

zambuco, *n.m.* squatting, hiding, concealing.

zambullida, *n.f.* submersion, diving, ducking; dipping; (*fenc.*) breast-thrust.

zambullidor, -ra, *n.m.f.* plunger, diver.

zambullir, *v.t., v.r.* to plunge, dive, duck, dip, give a ducking; to hide, conceal oneself; to sink.

zambullo, *n.m.* evacuation stool; (*prov.*) wild olive tree.

Zamora, *n.pr.; No se ganó Zamora en una hora*, Rome wasn't built in a day.

zampabodigos zampabollos, *n.m.* (*coll.*) glutton.

zampalimosnas, *n.m.* (*coll.*) importunate beggar.

zampapalo, zampatortas, *n.m.* glutton; clodhopper.

zampar, *v.t.* to conceal hastily (one thing inside another); to devour eagerly. — *v.r.* to rush in, to thrust oneself in or into.

zampeado, *n.m.* (*arch.*) grillage of timber, steel or masonry.

zampear, *v.t.* to build a foundation of piles.

zampón, -ona, *n., a.* glutton, gormandizer.

zampoña, *n.f.* pan-pipes, rustic flute; (*coll.*) frivolous saying.

zampuzar, *v.t.* (conjugated like ALZAR) to dip plunge, dive; [ZAMPAR].

zampuzo, *n.m.* immersion, submersion, concealment.

zamuro, *n.m.* (*Col., Ven.*) carrion-vulture.

zanahoria, *n.f.* carrot.

zanca, *n.f.* shank; long leg; large pin; (*min.*) shore, prop; string-piece of a staircase; *zancas de araña*, shifts, evasions; *por zancas o por barrancas*, by hook or by crook.

zancada, *n.f.* long stride; *en dos zancadas* expeditiously, quickly.

zancadilla, *n.f.* leg-hold (in wrestling); (*coll.*) deceit, snare, craft, trick.

zancado, -da, *a.* insipid (said of salmon).

zancajear, *v.t.* to walk in a hurry from place to place; to run about or up and down.

zancajera, *n.f.* running-board.

zancajiento, -ta, *a.* bandy-legged.

zancajo, *n.m.* heel-bone; shoe-heel; heel-piece of a stocking; (*coll.*) ill-shaped person; *no llegar a los zancajos*, (*fig.*) not to come up to or near one; *roer los zancajos*, to backbite.

zancajoso, -sa, *a.* bandy-legged; wearing holed and dirty stockings.

zancarrón, *n.m.* large heel-bone; large, fleshless, ugly, withered person; (*coll.*) quack, fraud.

zanco, *n.m.* stilt; stilt-walker, stilt-dancer; (*naut.*) sliding-gunter mast; (*fig.*) *en zancos*, exalted, high up in the world.

zancón, -ona, *a.* long-shanked. — *n.m.* (*Col., Guat., Ven.*) a dress which has become too short.

zancudo, -da, *a.* long-shanked (wading bird). — *n.m.* (*Am.*) mosquito. — *n.f.pl* **zancudas**, genus of wading birds.

zandía, *n.f.* water-melon.

zandunga, *n.f.* elegance, grace; wheedling, cajoling.

zandunguero, -ra, *n.m.f.* (*coll.*) cajoler.

zanfonía, *n.f.* hurdy-gurdy.

zanga, *n.f.* kind of four-hand ombre.

zangala, *n.f.* buckram.

zangamanga, *n.f.* falsehood, trick, deceit.

zanganada, *n.f.* rude, impertinent word or deed.

zangandongo, zangandullo, zangandungo *n.m.* idler, dolt, lazy person.

zanganear, *v.i.* to drone, loaf.

zángano, *n.m.* drone; sluggard, idler, sponger.

zangarilla, *n.f.* (*prov.*) small mill-pond.

zangarilleja, *n.f.* dirty, lazy girl.

zangarrear, *v.i.* (*coll.*) to scrape a guitar.

zangarriana, *n.f.* (*coll.*) melancholy; periodical disease; (*vet.*) ailment of the head, disease of sheep.

zangarrullón, *n.m.* tall, idle lad.
zangolotear, *v.t.* to move violently. — *v.i.* to fidget, move awkwardly. — *v.r.* to rattle (as a window or door).
zangoloteo, *n.m.* waddling; wagging motion; fuss, fidget, bustle.
zangolotino, -na, *n.*, *a.* a babyish adolescent boy (or girl); a mother's darling.
zangón, *n.m.* lazy lad.
zanguanga, *n.f.* (*coll.*) feigned disease; fawning, wheedling.
zanguango, *n.m.* lazy fellow; booby, fool.
zanguango, -ga, *a.* lazy, sluggardly.
zanguayo, *n.m.* (*coll.*) tall idler who acts the simpleton.
zanja, *n.f.* ditch, trench, furrow, drain, conduit, gully; (*Am.*) gap, gully, draw; *abrir las zanjas,* to begin, lay the foundation.
zanjar, *v.t.* to open ditches or drains, excavate; to settle a business amicably; to surmount.
zanjón, *n.m.* deep ditch, large drain.
zanqueador, -ra, *n.m.f.* awkward walker; great walker.
zanqueamiento, *n.m.* waddling.
zanquear, *v.i.* to waddle; trot, run about, walk fast.
zanquilargo, -ga, *a.* long-shanked, long-legged.
zanquilla, zanquita, *n.f.* (*coll.*) disproportionate person; long-legged man.
zanquituerto, -ta, *a.* bandy-legged.
zanquivano, -na, *a.* spindle-shanked.
zapa, *n.f.* spade; (*mil.*) sap, trench; shagreen; rough surface on silver; *caminar a la zapa,* (*mil.*) to advance by trench.
zapador, *n.m.* sapper.
zapallo, *n.m.* (*S. Am.*) calabash-tree; edible calabash; (*Arg.*, *Chi.*) chance, unexpected event, stroke of good luck.
zapapico, *n.m.* pickaxe, mattock.
zapar, *v.i.* to sap, mine.
zaparrada, *n.f.* heavy fall.
zaparrastrar, *v.i.* to trail (of dress).
zaparrastroso, -sa, *a.* dirty, greasy, filthy; ill-made.
zaparrazo, *n.m.* thud, violent fall; sudden calamity.
zapata, *n.f.* leather hinge; shoe of an anchor; false keel; (*Cub.*) socle of a wall; (*mech.*) shoe of a brake; buskin, half-boot; lintel.
zapatazo, *n.m.* large shoe; blow with a shoe; fall, thud, noise of a fall; drumming of foot or hoof; sound of a sail flapping in the wind; *tratar a zapatazos,* to treat badly, despise.
zapateado, *n.m.* Spanish tap dance.
zapateador, -ra, *n.m.f.* tap-dancer.
zapatear, *v.t.* to kick with the shoe; to lead by the nose; (*fenc.*) to strike frequently; to ill-treat. — *v.i.* to flap (sails). — *v.r.* to resist in debate, make a spirited opposition.
zapateo, *n.m.* keeping time by beating the foot.
zapatera, *n.f.* shoemaker's wife; woman who sells shoes.
zapatería, *n.f.* shoemaker's trade, shoemaker's shop; *zapatería de viejo,* cobbler's stall.
zapatero, *n.m.* shoemaker; seller of shoes; (*ichth.*) thread-fish; (*coll.*) card-player who takes no tricks; *zapatero de viejo,* cobbler; *zapatero, a tus zapatos,* mind your own business.
zapatero, -ra, *a.* connected with shoemaking;

hard, badly cooked (of beans); stale (of olives).
zapateta, *n.f.* caper, jump, leap; slap on the sole of a shoe. — *interj.* oh! good gracious!
zapatilla, *n.f.* slipper, little shoe, pump; button of a foil; animal's hoof; leather washer.
zapatillero, *n.m.* slipper-maker.
zapato, *n.m.* shoe; *meter en un zapato,* to cow; *zapatos papales,* overshoes, galoshes; *como tres en un zapato,* like sardines in a tin; *saber donde aprieta el zapato,* to know where the shoe pinches; *ser más necio que su zapato,* to be more stupid than a bat; *andar con zapatos de fieltro,* to go very cunningly (or quietly).
zapatudo, -da, *a.* wearing large shoes; large-hoofed, large-clawed.
¡zape! *interj.* word used to frighten cats away; to denote fright or surprise; used also to refuse to follow on in some card games.
zapear, *v.t.* to frighten cats by crying *zape*.
zapito, *n.m.*; **zapita,** *n.f.* (*prov.*) milk-pail.
zapote, *n.m.* sapota; sapodilla (tree and fruit).
zapotero, *n.m.* sapota-tree.
zapotillo, *n.m.* sapodilla and its fruit.
zapoyol, *n.m.* (*CR.*, *Hond.*) kernel of the sapodilla fruit.
zapoyolito, *n.m.* (*Cent. Am.*) kind of small parakeet.
zapuzar, *v.t.* to duck, dive.
zaque, *n.m.* leather bottle, leather wine-bag; (*coll.*) tippler, drunkard; (*Col.*) chief of a Chibcha tribe.
zaquear, *v.t.* to rack, draw off liquors.
zaquizamí, *n.m.* garret, loft; small, dirty house.
zar, *n.m.* czar, tsar.
zara, *n.f.* maize, Indian corn.
zarabanda, *n.f.* saraband; noise, bustle; (*Mex.*) beating.
zarabandista, *n.m.f.* saraband dancer; merry person.
zaragata, *n.f.* turmoil, quarrel, scuffle.
zaragate, *n.m.* (*Cent. Am.*, *Mex.*, *Per.*, *Ven.*) contemptible, despicable person.
zaragatona, *n.f.* ribgrass, ribwort.
zaragocí, *n.m.* kind of plum.
zaragozano, -na, *n.m.f.*, *a.* native of Saragossa.
zaragüelles, *n.m.pl.* kind of drawers; large and ill-made breeches; overalls; (*bot.*) reed-grass.
zaragutear, *v.t.* (*coll.*) to bungle.
zaragutero, -ra, *n.m.f.* bungler.
zaramagullón, *n.m.* didapper, a small diving-bird.
zarambeque, *n.m.* a merry folksong and dance (of Negroes).
zaramullo, *n.m.* (*Per.*, *Ven.*) busybody.
zaranda, *n.f.* sifter, sieve; (*Ven.*) humming-top.
zarandador, *n.m.* sifter of wheat.
zarandajas, *n.f.pl.* odds and ends, trifles.
zarandar, zarandear, *v.t.* to sift, winnow (corn); to move nimbly; to separate bad from good. — *v.r.* to move to and fro, be in motion; (*Per.*, *PR.*, *Ven.*) to walk affectedly, to swagger.
zarandeo, *n.m.* sifting, winnowing, moving to and fro.

zarandillo, *n.m.* small sieve; (*coll.*) live wire.

zarapatel, *n.m.* kind of salmagundi.

zarapito, *n.m.* curlew.

zaratán, *n.m.* cancer in a woman's breast.

zaraza, *n.f.* chintz. — *pl.* **zarazas**, a poisonous compound for killing rats, etc.

zarazo, -za, *a.* (*S. Am.*) half-ripe fruit.

zarcear, *v.t.* to clean pipes or conduits with briers. — *v.i.* to move to and fro; to pursue game into briers (said of dogs in hunting).

zarceño, -ña, *a.* pertaining to briers.

zarcero, -ra, *n.*, *a.* kind of retriever.

zarceta, *n.f.* widgeon [CERCETA].

zarcillitos, *n.m.pl.* quaking-grass.

zarcillo, *n.m.* vine tendril; drop earring; hoop of a barrel; gardener's hoe.

zarco, -ca, *a.* light-blue (of eyes); wall-eyed.

zargatona, *n.f.* ribgrass, ribwort [ZARAGATONA].

zariano, -na, *a.* belonging to the tsar.

zarigüeya, *n.f.* (*Am.*) opossum.

zarina, *n.f.* tsarina.

zaroche, *n.m.* (*Ec.*) mountain sickness.

zarpa, *n.f.* weighing anchor; dirt or mud on the clothes; claw, paw; footing; *echar la zarpa*, to grip, claw, clutch.

zarpada, *n.f.* blow with a paw.

zarpar, *v.t.* to weigh anchor, to sail.

zarpazo, *n.m.* sound of a falling body; bang, thud; stroke with a paw.

zarpear, *v.t.* (*CR., Hond.*) to bespatter, to bemire.

zarposo, -sa, *a.* bespattered with dirt.

zarracatería, *n.f.* lure, deception.

zarracatín, *n.m.* (*coll.*) haggler, chafferer; miser.

zarramplín, *n.m.* (*coll.*) bungler, botcher.

zarramplinada, *n.f.* work clumsily performed, bungle, muddle.

zarrapastra, *n.f.* dirt or mud on clothes.

zarrapastrón, -ona, *n.m.f.*, *a.* tatterdemalion.

zarrapastrosamente, *adv.* raggedly, dirtily.

zarrapastroso, -sa, *a.* ragged, dirty, slovenly, seedy.

zarria, *n.f.* dirt sticking to clothes; leather thong.

zarriento, -ta, *a.* besmirched, bespattered.

zarza, *n.f.* bramble, blackberry-bush. — *pl.* **zarzas**, thorns; difficulties.

zarzagán, *n.m.* cold north-east wind.

zarzaganete, *n.m.* light north-east wind.

zarzaganillo, *n.m.* violent north-easterly storm.

zarzahán, *n.m.* kind of striped silk.

zarzaidea, *n.f.* raspberry-bush.

zarzal, *n.m.* brier patch; place full of briers or brambles.

zarzamora, *n.f.* blackberry bush; blackberry.

zarzaparrilla, *n.f.* sarsaparilla.

zarzaperruna, zarzarrosa, *n.f.* dog-rose.

zarzo, *n.m.* hurdle, wattle.

zarzoso, -sa, *a.* brambly, briery.

zarzuela, *n.f.* light musical dramatic performance, musical comedy, comic opera.

zarzuelero, -ra, *a.* relating to musical dramas.

zarzuelista, *n.m.f.* writer or composer of musical dramas.

¡zas!, *interj.* tick, rap, expression denoting the sound of repeated blows; *¡zas! ¡zas!* bang!

bang!; *¡y zas! ¡y zas!* and so on, and all the rest of it.

zascandil, *n.m.* (*coll.*) impostor, swindler, upstart, busybody.

zata, zatara, *n.f.* river raft.

zatico, *n.m.* small bit of bread.

zato, *n.m.* piece of bread.

zazoso, -sa, *a.* lisping. — *n.m.f.* lisper.

zeda, *n.f.* name of the letter Z [ZETA].

zedilla, *n.f.* cedilla.

zenit, zenital, *n.m.* zenith [CENIT, CENITAL].

zeta, *n.f.* name of the letter Z.

zigzag, *n.m.* zigzag.

zigzaguear, *v.i.* to zigzag.

zinc, *n.m.* zinc [CINC].

zipizape, *n.m.* (*coll.*) noisy scuffle, rumpus, row.

¡zis, zas!, *interj.* expression denoting the sound of repeated blows.

ziszás, *n.m.* zigzag.

zizaña, *n.f.* darnel.

zoca, *n.f.* square.

zócalo, *n.m.* socle.

zocato, -ta, *a.* over-ripe; left-handed.

zoclo, *n.m.* clog; over-shoe.

zoco, *a.* left-handed. — *n.m.* clog; plinth; (*Morocco*) market; market-place; *andar de zocos en colodros*, to escape Scylla and fall into Charybdis.

zodiacal, *a.* zodiacal.

zodíaco, *n.m.* zodiac.

zofra, *n.f.* Moorish carpet.

zolocho, -cha, *a.* (*coll.*) stupid, silly.

zollipar, *v.i.* (*coll.*) to sob, blub.

zollipo, *n.m.* sob, sobbing.

zoma, *n.f.* coarse flour.

zompo, -pa, *a.* maimed, deformed, crippled.

zona, *n.f.* zone; girdle, band; (*med.*) shingles.

zoncería, *n.f.* insipidity, stupidity, silliness, dullness.

zonchiche, *n.m.* (*CR., Hond.*) a red-headed vulture.

zonote, *n.m.* (*Mex.*) underground lake or deposit of water.

zonzamente, *adv.* sillily, insipidly, stupidly.

zonzo, -za, *a.* insipid, sloppy, stupid, dull, silly. — *n.m.f.* dunce, booby, noodle.

zonzorrión, -ona, *n.m.f.* very dull and stupid person.

zoografía, *n.f.* zoography.

zoolito, *n.m.* zoolite.

zoología, *n.f.* zoology.

zoológico, -ca, *a.* zoological.

zoólogo, *n.m.* zoologist.

zootomía, *n.f.* zootomy.

zootropo, *n.m.* kinematoscope; zoetrope of wheel of life.

zopas, zopitas, *n.m.f.* (*coll.*) one who lisps.

zope, *n.m.* (*CR.*) buzzard.

zopenco, -ca, *a.* doltish, dull. — *n.m.f.* dunce, dolt, blockhead.

zopilote, *n.m.* (*CR., Hond., Mex.*) buzzard.

zopisa, *n.f.* pitch; pitch and wax mixed.

zopo, -pa, *a.* lame, crippled, maimed, deformed. — *n.m.f.* cripple.

zoqueta, *n.f.* a kind of wooden glove used by reapers.

zoquete, *n.m.* chunk, block, short piece of wood; piece of bread; (*coll.*) sluggish, or ugly little person; dunce, dolt; blockhead; belfry; *zoquete de cuchara*, (*naut.*) scoop-handle.

zoquetero, -ra, *a.* beggarly, poor, indigent.

zoquetico, -illo, *n.m.* small morsel of bread.

zoquetudo, -da, *a.* ill-finished, rough.

zorcico, *n.m.* Basque folksong and dance.

zorita, *n.f.* (*orn.*) stock-dove, wood-pigeon.

zorollo, *a.* reaped but not ripe (wheat).

zorongo, *n.m.* folksong and dance (Andalusia); kerchief worn by Aragonese and Navarrese; flat, wide chignon.

zorra, *n.f.* fox; sly person; strumpet, prostitute, harlot; drunkenness, inebriation; truck; *pillar una zorra,* (*coll.*) to get drunk; *a la zorra candilazo,* diamond cut diamond; *la zorra mudará los dientes, mas no las mientes,* the leopard cannot change his spots; *mucho sabe la zorra, pero más quien la toma,* the cleverest man has his master.

zorrastrón, -ona, *n.m.f.* crafty, knavish person, cunning rogue.

zorrazo, *n.m.* great knave, great rogue.

zorrera, *n.f.* fox hole, kennel; room full of smoke; drowsiness, heaviness.

zorrería, *n.f.* artfulness; craft, cunning, knavery.

zorrero, -ra, *a.* slow, tardy, inactive, lagging; cunning, foxy; sailing heavily.

zorrero, *n.m.* terrier, hunting dog; forestkeeper.

zorrilla, zorrita, *n.f.* little bitch fox; (*Arg., Guat., Hond.*) polecat; skunk.

zorro, *n.m.* male fox; knave, cunning fellow. — *pl.* **zorros,** duster made of strips of cloth.

zorrocloco, *n.m.* foxy person, one who appears slothful but is nevertheless shrewd; petting, caress.

zorrón, *n.m.* boozing; cunning foxy person.

zorronglón, -ona, *a.* slow, sulky, muttering.

zorruelo, -la, *n.m.f.* little fox.

zorruno, -na, *a.* vulpine, foxy, fox-like.

zorzal, *n.m.* (*orn.*) thrush; artful, cunning man; (*Chi.*) simpleton; (*ichth.*) a fish of the Acanthopterygii order.

zoster, *n.m.* shingles.

zote, *n.m.* dunce.

zozobra, *n.f.* uneasiness, anguish, anxiety, worry; unlucky throw of the dice; (*naut.*) sinking, foundering, capsizing.

zozobrante, *a.* sinking, in great danger.

zozobrar, *v.i.* (*naut.*) to founder, sink, upset, capsize; to be in great danger; to be afflicted, worry, fret.

zuaca, *n.f.* (*CR.*) practical joke; (*Mex.*) drubbing, flogging, spanking.

zubia, *n.f.* drain, channel for water.

zucarino, -na, *a.* sugary.

zucurco, *n.m.* (*Chi.*) plant of the Umbelliferous family.

zúchil, *n.m.* (*Mex.*) bouquet.

zueco, *n.m.* sabot, wooden shoe, clog; galosh.

zuindá, *n.m.* (*Arg.*) a brown owl.

zuiza, *n.f.* military tournament; quarrel, dispute.

zuizón, *n.m.* spear; (*naut.*) half pike.

zulacar, *v.t.* to cover with bitumen.

zulaque, *n.m.* (*hydraulics*) packing stuff; (*naut.*) oakum.

zulú, *n.m.* (*Cub.*) mourning dress.

zulla, *n.f.* (*coll.*) human excrements; (*bot.*) French honeysuckle.

zullarse, *v.r.* (*coll.*) to go to stool; to break wind.

zullenco, -ca; zullón, -ona, *a.* breaking wind; flatulent.

zullón, *n.m.* flatulence.

zumacal, zumacar, *n.m.* plantation of sumach trees.

zumacar, *v.t.* (conjugated like BUSCAR) to dress hides or pelts with sumach.

zumacaya, *n.f.* a night wading bird.

zumaque, *n.m.* sumach-tree; (*coll.*) wine.

zumaya, *n.f.* owl, barn-owl; goat-sucker; fern-owl.

zumba, *n.f.* the bell of the leading mule or ox of a drove; rattle; jest, joke, raillery; (*Col., Chi., PR.*) sound beating; flogging.

zumbador, -ra, *n.m.f.* one that hums or buzzes; (*elect.*) buzzer; (*PR.*) humming-bird. — *a.* humming, buzzing.

zumbar, *v.i.* to buzz, hum, resound; to be on the point of, on the brink; to ring (the ears). — *v.t., v.r.* to jest, joke; to strike a blow, box one's ears; *hacer zumbar las orejas,* to hurt with a sharp reproof or a blow.

zumbel, *n.m.* frown, angry look; (*coll.*) cord for spinning tops.

zumbido, zumbo, *n.m.* humming, buzzing; ping of a bullet; ringing in the ears; blow, box, cuff.

zumbilín, *n.m.* (*Philip.*) dart, javelin.

zumbón, -ona, *a.* waggish, joking, jocose.

zumbón, *n.m.* jester, joker, wag; (*prov.*) a variety of pigeon.

zumiento, -ta, *a.* succulent, juicy.

zumillo, *n.m.* deadly carrot; dragon's arum; Aaron's beard.

zumo, *n.m.* sap, juice, liquor, moisture; utility, profit; *zumo de cepas* or *parras,* (*coll.*) wine.

zumoso, -sa, *a.* succulent, juicy.

zuna, *n.f.* sunna (Islam); (*prov.*) trickery treachery; viciousness of horses.

zuncuya, *n.f.* (*Hond.*) a bitter-sweet fruit.

zuncho, *n.m.* band, hoop, collar; ferrule.

zunteco, *n.m.* (*Hond.*) a black wasp.

zunzún, *n.m.* (*Cub.*) humming-bird.

zuño, *n.m.* frown, angry mien.

zupay, *n.m.* (*Arg.*) nickname of the devil.

zupia, *n.f.* wine which is turned; refuse, lees, dregs, slop.

zurano, -na, *n.m.f.* stock-dove, wood-pigeon.

zurcidera, *n.f.* darner, sewer; *zurcidera de voluntades,* (*coll.*) pimp, bawd.

zurcido, *n.m.* stitching, darning, fine-drawing.

zurcidor, -ra, *n.m.f.* darner, fine-drawer.

zurcidura, *n.f.* fine-drawing, darning.

zurcir, *v.t.* (*pres. indic.* **zurzo**; *pres. subj.* **zurza**) to darn, to fine-draw; to join, unite, patch; to hatch, concoct(lies).

zurdería, *n.f.* left-handedness.

zurdo, -da, *a.* left-handed; *mano zurda,* left hand; *a zurdas,* the wrong way; *no ser zurdo,* to be very clever, to be not slow.

zurear, *v.i.* to bill and coo (of doves).

zureo, *n.m.* cooing.

zurita, *n.f.* stock-dove.

zuriza, *n.f.* dispute, quarrel.

zuro, -ra, *a.* belonging to a stock-dove.

zuro, *n.m.* corn-cob; stock-dove, wild pigeon.

zurumbático, -ca, *a.* stunned, dumbfounded.

zurumbela, *n.f.* (*Am.*) a singing bird.

zurupa, *n.f.* (*Ven.*) cockroach.

zurupeto, *n.m.* unofficial or intrusive broker.

zurra, *n.f.* currying, tanning of leather; flogging, drubbing; drudgery, toil; quarrel, dispute, scuffle; severe reprimand.

zurrado, -da, *a.* curried, dressed. — *n.m.* (*coll.*) glove.

zurrador, *n.m.* currier, tanner, leather-dresser; one who flogs or drubs.

zurrapa, *n.f.* lees, sediment, grouts, dregs; anything despicable or vile; rubbish, trash; *con zurrapas,* in a dirty manner.

zurrapelo, *n.m.* (*coll.*) severe reprimand.

zurrapiento, -ta; zurraposo, -sa, *a.* turbid, dreggy, roily.

zurrapilla, *n.f.* small lees.

zurrar, *v.t.* to curry, tan, dress (leather); to flog, beat, whip, drub, chastise. — *v.r.* to have an involuntary evacuation of the bowels; to be seized with great fear; *zurrar la badana,* to flog, beat.

zurriaga, *n.f.* whip, thong, long strap; (*orn.*) lark.

zurriagar, *v.t.* (*pret.* **zurriagué;** *pres. subj.* **zurriague**) to flog, chastise, horsewhip.

zurriagazo, *n.m.* whipping; severe stroke or lash; unfortunate calamity; unexpected ill treatment.

zurriago, *n.m.* whip.

zurriar, *v.i.* to hum, buzz; to rattle.

zurribanda, *n.f.* horsewhipping, cowhiding, repeated flogging; noisy quarrel, rumpus, scuffle, fight.

zurriburri, *n.m.* (*coll.*) ragamuffin, scamp; set of rowdies.

zurrido, *n.m.* humming, buzzing, confused noise, rattling noise; blow, stroke with a stick.

zurrir, *v.i.* to hum, buzz; to rattle.

zurrón, *n.m.* shepherd's provision-bag, game-bag; leather-bag; seron or seroon; pith, soft lining of the rind; chaff, husks of grain; (*anat.*) fœtal sac.

zurrona, *n.f.* prostitute.

zurronada, *n.f.* bagful.

zurroncillo, *n.m.* small bag.

zurrusco, *n.m.* (*coll.*) overtoasted slice of bread.

zurullo, *n.m.* (*coll.*) something round and soft; human excrement.

zutano, -na, *a.; zutano y fulano,* such and such a one; so-and-so.

¡zuzo!, *interj.* expression used to call a dog.

zuzón, *n.m.* ragwort, groundsel.

CASSELL'S
ENGLISH-SPANISH DICTIONARY

CASSELL'S

ENGLISH-SPANISH DICTIONARY

A

A, a [ei], primera letra del alfabeto; (*mús.*) la.
a [æ, ə], *art. indef.* un, una; el, la; por; se halla a veces delante del participio activo, para denotar la acción de un verbo; *a-hunting we will go*, iremos a cazar. Puede denotar proporción; *ten shillings a day*, diez chelines por día; se usa tambien en lugar de *in*, *on*, y como prefijo, *abed*, *aboard*, etc.
Aaron's beard, *s.* (*bot.*) especie de hipérico; hiedra de Kenilworth; linaria Cymbalaria; hierba china, especie de saxífraga; saxífraga sarmentosa.
abaca ['æbəkə], (*bot.*) abacá.
aback [ə'bæk], *adv.* detrás, atrás; (*mar.*) en facha; *to lay flat aback*, poner las velas en facha; *to lay the top-sails aback*, poner las gavias en facha. — *s.* superficie plana cuadrada.
abacus, *s.* ábaco; (*arq.*) ábaco; aparador.
abaft [ə'ba:ft], *adv.* (*mar.*) a popa, en popa, hacia la popa, atrás.
abaisance [ə'beisəns], *s.* saludo, reverencia.
abalienation, *s.* enajenación, traspaso.
abandon [ə'bændən], *v.t.* abandonar, dejar, desamparar, desertar; renunciar, desistir; desmantelar; entregar; *to be abandoned*, abandonarse, entregarse. — *s.* abandono, entrega; desamparo; cesión; arrebato.
abandoned, *p.p.* abandonado, desamparado, dejado; entregado a los vicios, vicioso; *an abandoned woman*, una mujer perdida.
abandonee, *s.* (*for.*) cesionario.
abandoner, *s.* abandonador, desamparador, desamparadora; (*for.*) cesionista, *m.f.*
abandoning, *s.* abandono, desamparo; (*for.*) cesión, renuncia.
abandonment, *s.* abandono, desamparo, abandonamiento; (*for.*, *com.*) cesión, dejación de bienes.
abase [ə'beis], *v.t.* bajar, rebajar, disminuir, reducir; humillar, envilecer, abatir, degradar.
abasement, *s.* abatimiento, envilecimiento, humillación, degradación.
abash [ə'bæʃ], *v.t.* avergonzar, sonrojar, consternar; (*fam.*) correr.
abashed, *p.p.* confundido, confuso, avergonzado, corrido.
abashment, *s.* confusión, rubor, vergüenza; consternación.
abasing, *p.p.*, *a.* humillante; vergonzoso. — *s.* humillación.
abatable, *a.* abolible.
abate [ə'beit], *v.t.* bajar, rebajar, disminuir, minorar; debilitar; abolir, hacer cesar; (*for.*) revocar, anular; contristar. — *v.i.* menguar, disminuirse, minorarse, decaer, ceder, ir a menos; derribar, apoderarse de; irse disminuyendo; (*for.*) anularse; (*fig.*) humillar; *the flood begins to abate*, la inundación va a menos.
abatement, *s.* abatimiento, extenuación, cesación, supresión; debilidad, decaimiento;

(*blas.*) brisadas; diminución, rebaja; (*com.*) no *abatement*, precio fijo sin descuento.
abater, *s.* regatero, regatón; demérito.
abating, *s.* abatimiento, apaciguamiento; disminución, rebaja.
abatis, abattis, *s.* (*mil.*) estacada.
abattoir ['æbətwa:ɹ], *s.* matadero.
abb [æb], *s.* urdiembre; *abb-wool*, lana en borra.
abbacy, *s.* abadía; dignidad, rentas, privilegios y jurisdicción de un abad.
abbess, *s.* abadesa.
abbey, *s.* abadía, monasterio, convento; refugio, santuario.
abbot, *s.* abad.
abbotship, *s.* abadía, dignidad y oficio de abad.
abbreviate [ə'bri:vieit], *v.t.* abreviar, reducir, compendiar.
abbreviated, *p.p.*, *a.* abreviado, compendiado; reducido.
abbreviation [əbri:vi'eiʃən], *s.* abreviación, abreviatura; (*mat.*) reducción.
abbreviator, *s.* abreviador, compendiador.
abbreviatory, *a.* abreviatorio.
abbreviature, *s.* abreviatura, signo de abreviación; compendio, epítome.
abdicant ['æbdikənt], *a.* abdicante, renunciante.
abdicate, *v.t.* abdicar, renunciar, dejar, hacer dimisión, desprenderse de. — *v.i.* abdicar un trono, renunciar a un honor o privilegio; (*for.*) desconocer, no reconocer por suyo.
abdication, *s.* abdicación, renuncia; dimisión; (*for.*) denegación de paternidad.
abdomen [æb'doumen], *s.* (*anat.*) abdomen, vientre, barriga.
abdominal [æb'dɔminəl], *a.* abdominal.
abdominous, *a.* panzudo, abultado de vientre.
abduce [æb'dju:s], *v.t.* arrebatar; desviar, separar, apartar; (*anat.*) mover, llevar.
abducent, *a.* (*anat.*) abductor.
abduct, *v.t.* arrebatar; secuestrar; tomar, plagiar.
abduction, *s.* (*anat.*) abducción; (*for.*) rapto, plagio.
abductor, *s.* (*anat.*) abductor; (*for.*) raptor.
abeam [ə'bi:m], *adv.* (*mar.*) por el través.
abear [ə'bɛəɹ], *v.t.* (*prov.*) sufrir, soportar.
abearance, *s.* (*for.*) comportamiento, conducta, porte, proceder.
abed [ə'bed], *adv.* acostado, en cama, en la cama.
aberrance [æ'berəns], **aberrancy,** *s.* error, descamino, extravío, equivocación, desvío.
aberrant, *a.* errado, extraviado, descaminado, equivocado; (*anat.*) anómalo.
aberration, *s.* error, extravío; aberración, desvío.
abet [ə'bet], *v.t.* instigar, animar, excitar, inducir, apoyar, sostener, favorecer, patrocinar.
abetment, abettal, *s.* apoyo, protección, auxilio, favor; instigación, excitación.
abetter, abettor, *s.* promovedor, instigador,

fautor, fomentador, ayudador; (for.) cómplice.

abeyance [ə'beiəns], s. (for.) expectación, expectativa, espera; in abeyance, en suspenso, en reserva, en depósito; lands in abeyance, bienes mostrencos.

abeyant, a. expectante, en expectativa, en reserva; en reposo, durmiente.

abgregation, s. separación de la manada.

abhor [əb'hɔ:ɹ], v.t. aborrecer, detestar, odiar; despreciar, desdeñar; rechazar.

abhorrence, abhorrency, s. aborrecimiento, odio, horror, aversión, detestación, execración.

abhorrent, a. horroroso, horrorizado; detestable, repugnante, aborrecible, antipático, contrario, ajeno, extraño.

abhorrer, s. aborrecedor, enemigo jurado.

abhorring, s. repugnancia, aversión, aborrecimiento; hastío, náusea.

abidance, s. residencia, morada.

abide [ə'baid], v.i. (p.a. **abiding**; pret. **abode**; p.p. **abode**) vivir, habitar, morar, parar, residir; quedar, permanecer; continuar, perseverar. — v.t. sufrir, soportar, aguantar; defender, sostener, atenerse, perseverar; to abide by, atenerse a, mantenerse en, guiarse por, estar con, pasar por, consentir.

abider, s. habitador, habitante, vecino, residente, inquilino.

abiding, s. continuación, perseverancia, estabilidad, permanencia; residencia, morada, espera. — a. permanente; observante.

abigail ['æbigeil], s. doncella, criada.

ability [ə'biliti], s. habilidad, facultad, potencia, poder, capacidad, aptitud, inteligencia, alcance, acierto; haber o bienes, medios; (en el plural) talento, ingenio, v.g.: a man of abilities, hombre de talento; to the best of one's abilities, a más y mejor; (for.) aptitud, poder legal.

abject ['æbdʒekt], a. abyecto, vil, indecente, bajo, despreciable, servil, humillado, abatido; desalmado.

abjectedness, s. abyección, desesperación, humillación, envilecimiento.

abjection, abjectness, s. abyección, vileza, bajeza, abatimiento, servilismo, cobardía.

abjectness [ABJECTION].

abjudicate [æb'dʒu:diceit], v.t. (for.) expropiar, desposeer, despojar.

abjudication, s. (for.) expropiación, abjudicación.

abjuration, s. abjuración.

abjuratory, a. abjuratorio.

abjure [æb'dʒuəɹ], v.t. abjurar, renunciar a; desdecirse; desterrar.

abjurer, s. renunciante, el que abjura o renuncia.

abjuring, s. abjuración, retractación, renuncia.

ablactate [æb'lækteit], v.t. destetar; quitar el pecho a un niño. — s. manera de injertar árboles.

ablactation, s. destete.

ablation [əb'leiʃən], s. (cir.) ablación; quite, acción de quitar; extirpación, separación.

ablative, s., a. lo que quita; (gram.) ablativo.

ablaze [ə'bleiz], a. en fuego, en llamas.

able [eibl], a. capaz, hábil; poderoso, fuerte; experimentado, experto; sano, vigoroso; rico, opulento; to be able, poder, tener poder, estar en el caso.

able-bodied, a. forzudo, robusto, fornido; an able-bodied seaman, (mar.) marinero de primera.

ablegate, v.t. disputar, enviar. — s. ablegado, representante del Papa.

ableness, s. habilidad, capacidad; poder, fuerza, vigor.

ablest ['eiblest], a. superl. [ABLE]; poderosísimo, riquísimo; muy hábil, muy capaz.

ablet, s. (ictiol.) breca.

abloom [ə'blu:m], a., adv. en flor, floreciente.

abluent ['æbluent], a. (med.) detersivo, detergente, diluyente, limpiante.

ablush [ə'bluʃ], a., adv. sonrojante, abochornado.

ablution [æb lu:ʃən], s. ablución, acción de lavar, limpiar.

ably, adv. hábilmente, con habilidad, con maña.

abnegate ['æbnegeit], v.t. negar, rehusar; resignar, renunciar, renegar.

abnegation, s. abnegación, resignación, renuncia, repudiación.

abnegator, s. negador, impugnador.

abnormal [æb'nɔ:məl], a. anormal, irregular, disforme, mal formado.

abnormality, abnormity, s. anomalía, irregularidad, deformidad.

aboard [ə'bɔəɹd], adv. (mar.) a bordo; to go aboard, embarcarse, ir a bordo; to take aboard, embarcar, llevar a bordo.

abode [ə'boud], s. domicilio, habitación, residencia, mansión, morada; to take up one's abode, establecerse. — v.t. (ant.) presagiar. — v.i. ser presagio.

abolish [ə'bɔliʃ], v.t. abolir, anular, revocar; destruir; borrar.

abolishable, a. abolible.

abolisher, s. abolidor, anulador, revocador.

abolishment, s. abolición.

abolition [æbol'iʃən], s. abolición.

abolitionism, s. abolicionismo.

abolitionist, s. abolicionista, m.f., partidario de la abolición de alguna cosa.

abominable [ə'bominəbl], a. abominable, execrable, detestable; impuro, inmundo.

abominableness, s. abominación, horror.

abominably, adv. abominablemente.

abominate, v.t. abominar, detestar, aborrecer.

abomination [əbomin'eiʃən], s. abominación, detestación, odio, polución, corrupción, maldad.

aboriginal [æbə'ridʒinəl], a. originario, primitivo, aborigen.

abortion [ə'bɔ:ɹʃən], s. aborto, malparto; (vet.) abortón; (fig.) proyecto o trabajo abortado, detenido, o malogrado en su desarrollo.

abortionist, s. abortador, abortadora.

abortive, a. abortivo; frustrado, malogrado; infructuoso, inútil, intempestivo. — s. aborto, engendro.

abortiveness, s. aborto, mal éxito.

abound [ə'baund], v.i. abundar; to abound with, abundar en.

abounding, a. y part. abundante (in, with en). — s. abundancia, afluencia.

about [ə'baut], prep. alrededor de, cerca de, hacia, acerca, tocante a, colgante, pendiente; — adv. alrededor, por ahí, aquí y allá; poco más o menos, en contorno, por rodeos; to be about to come, estar para venir; all about, en todas partes; *how much money have you got about you?* ¿ cuánto dinero lleva Vd. encima? *to be about the same*, ir pasando; *to beat about the bush*, andarse por las ramas; *look about you*, tenga Vd. cuidado; *to bring about something*, efectuar una cosa; *what are you about?* ¿ qué va Vd. a hacer? *what's this about?* ¿ qué quiere ser esto? *what are you thinking about?* ¿ en qué piensa Vd.? *there's no mistake about it*, no hay que darle vueltas; *to send one about one's business*, enviar a uno a pasear, despedir a uno; *to turn about*, (mar.) virar, cambiar el rumbo; *about turn*, (mil.) media vuelta a la derecha.

above [ə'bʌv], *prep.* sobre, superior a, encima de, más que, más de. — *adv.* arriba, encima; *above all*, sobre todo; *above-board*, abiertamente, a vista de todos; *above-mentioned*, ya citado, ya mencionado, susodicho, supracitado; *from above*, de arriba, de lo alto, del cielo; *to be above doing something*, ser incapaz de (o superior a) una cosa; *above ground*, vivo, no muerto.

abrade [ə'breid], *v.t.* raer, gastar estragando.

abrasion [ə'breiʒən], *s.* raspadura.

abrasive, *a.* rayante, raspante.

abreast [ə'brest], *adv.* de frente, de costado; (mar.) por el través; *four abreast*, cuatro de frente; *abreast the port*, (mar.) por el tráves del puerto.

abridge [ə'bridʒ], *v.t.* abreviar, compendiar; disminuir, acortar, cercenar; privar, despojar, o quitar; (alg.) reducir.

abridger, *s.* abreviador, compendiador.

abridgment, *s.* compendio, epítome, resumen, recopilación, limitación, contracción; (alg.) reducción.

abroach [ə'broutʃ], *adv.* en estado de difundirse o propagarse; horadando, esparciendo.

abroad [ə'brɔːd], *adv.* fuera de casa; en el extranjero; al extranjero; en todas partes o direcciones; *to go abroad*, pasar al extranjero; *there is a rumour abroad*, corre la voz; *to set abroad*, divulgar, publicar.

abrogate ['æbrogeit], *v.t.* abrogar, anular, revocar.

abrogation ⌊æbro'geiʃən], *s.* abrogación, anulación, revocación, abolición.

abrogative, *a.* abrogable.

abrupt [ə'brʌpt], *a.* quebrado, desigual; pendiente, escarpado; desunido; precipitado, repentino, brusco, bronco, rudo, fogoso. — *s.* abismo, precipicio.

abruption, *s.* rotura; (cir.) fractura.

abruptly, *adv.* precipitadamente, bruscamente, rudamente, ásperamente, ex-abrupto.

abruptness, *s.* aspereza, precipitación, inconsideración; prontitud; sequedad; (fig.) rudeza.

abscess ['æbses], *s.* absceso, apostema.

abscind [æb'sind], *v.t.* cortar, tajar.

abscissa, *s.* (pl. **abscissæ**) (geom.) abscisa.

abscission, *s.* (cir.) abcisión, separación, cortadura.

abscond [æb'skɔnd], *v.i.* esconderse, ocultarse; marcharse, fugarse. — *v.t.* ocultar, tapar; *to abscond with money entrusted to one*, alzarse con el santo y con la limosna.

absconder, *s.* fugitivo; prófugo; (for.) contumaz.

absconding, *s.* huída, fuga.

absence ['æbsəns], *s.* ausencia; distracción;

negligencia, descuido; *leave of absence*, (mil.) permiso, licencia temporal.

absent, *a.* ausente; distraído, abstraído, divertido; enajenado, fuera de sí. — *v.r.* [æb'sent] *to absent oneself*, ausentarse, retirarse.

absent-minded, *a.* absorto, abstraído en meditación, fuera de sí.

absentee, *s.* ausente.

absenteeism, *s.* absentismo.

absenter, *s.* ausente.

absinthe ['æbsinθ], *s.* ajenjo, absintio, absenta.

absinthiated, *a.* mezclado con ajenjo.

absinthium, *s.* ajenjo, artemisia absinthium.

absolute ['æbsəluːt], *a.* absoluto, incondicional, positivo, amplio, completo; perentorio, categórico; irresponsable, libre; arbitrario, autocrático, despótico.

absoluteness, *s.* independencia; amplitud; despotismo, poder absoluto.

absolution, *s.* absolución, perdón.

absolutism, *s.* absolutismo, autocracia, despotismo, la doctrina de la predestinación.

absolutist, *s.* absolutista, autócrata, *m.f.*

absolutory, absolvatory *a.* absolutorio.

absolve [æb'zɔlv], *v.t.* absolver, desligar, exentar, dispensar; justificar; concluir, acabar; resolver; explicar.

absolver, *s.* absolvedor, dispensador.

absolving, *a.* absolutorio.

absonant, absonous, *a.* absurdo; disonante, ridículo, fuera de razón.

absorb [əb'sɔːb], *v.t.* absorber, empapar, embeber, chupar; preocupar, incorporar; *to be absorbed in a book*, estar absorto en un libro.

absorbability, *s.* cualidad o propiedad de ser absorbido.

absorbable, *a.* absorbible, lo que puede ser absorbido.

absorbency, *s.* absorbencia.

absorbent, *s., a.* absorbente; chupador.

absorption, *s.* absorción; (fig.) absorción, ensimismamiento.

absorptive, *a.* absorbente.

abstain [əb'stein], *v.i.* abstenerse, privarse de.

abstainer, *s.* abstinente, sobrio, moderado.

abstaining, *s.* abstinencia. — *a.* abstinente.

abstemious [əb'stiːmiəs], *a.* abstemio, sobrio, moderado, templado, morigerado, continente.

abstemiousness, *s.* sobriedad, moderación, templanza.

abstention [əb'stenʃən], *s.* abstención, abstinencia, privación, detención; el acto de detener o impedir.

absterge [əb'stəːdʒ], *v.t.* absterger, deterger, limpiar, enjugar.

abstergent, *a.* (med.) abstergente, detergente, emoliente.

abstersion, *s.* (med.) abstersión.

abstersive, *s., a.* abstergente; limpiador.

abstinence ['æbstinəns], **abstinency**, *s.* abstinencia, sobriedad, templanza; *day of abstinence*, día de ayuno.

abstinent, *a.* abstinente, sobrio, moderado, mortificado.

abstract [æb'strækt], *v.t.* abstraer, extraer, epitomar, extractar, substraer; considerar separadamente, prescindir. — ['æbstrækt] *a.* abstracto, separado; puro, ideal (opuesto a concreto); substraído; refinado. — *s.* extracto, epítome, resumen, sumario, compendio; abstracción; suma.

abstracted, *a.* abstraído, separado, substraído, robado; puro, sin mezcla; abstruso, metafísico; distraído; ensimismado. — *p.p.* [ABSTRACT].

abstractedness, *s.* abstracción.

abstracter, *s.* extractador, compendiador, abreviador; extractor; ladrón, ratero.

abstraction, *s.* abstracción, distracción, separación, sustracción, robo; recogimiento, retraimiento; noción, idea, concepto; desatención, descuido; ratería, hurto.

abstractive, *a.* abstractivo.

abstractness, *s.* abstracción; separación.

abstruse [æb'struːs], *a.* abstruso, profundo, recóndito, oculto, obscuro, secreto.

abstruseness, abstrusity, *s.* obscuridad, dificultad; misterio, arcano.

absurd [æb'səːɹd], *a.* absurdo, irracional, ridículo, inconsistente, disparatado, prepóstero.

absurdity, *s.* absurdo, absurdidad, despropósito, disparate; *height of absurdity,* colmo de lo absurdo.

absurdness, *s.* absurdo, disparate, irracionalidad.

abundance [ə'bʌndəns], *s.* abundancia, copia, exuberancia, plenitud, afluencia, caudal.

abundant, *a.* abundante, copioso, rico; amplio, lleno, feraz, fecundo, caudaloso.

abusable, *a.* que admite abuso.

abuse [ə'bjuːz], *v.t.* abusar; seducir, engañar; pervertir; profanar; injuriar; violar, ultrajar, maltratar; denostar. — *s.* (ə'bjuːs) abuso; seducción; engaño; contumelia, ofensa, injuria; corruptela, burla, afrenta, ultraje.

abuser, *s.* engañador; seductor, abusador, denostador, embaucador.

abusive, *a.* abusivo, injurioso, ofensivo, insultante, engañoso, grosero.

abusively, *adv.* abusivamente, injuriosamente, impropiamente; *to speak of someone abusively,* poner lengua en uno.

abusiveness, *s.* abuso; insolencia, ofensa, insulto, injuria, vituperio, vituperación.

abut [ə'bʌt], *v.i.* terminar; lindar, confinar; rematar, parar; *abut upon,* salir a, confinar con, terminar en.

abutment, *s.* linde, confín; lindero, mojón; (*arquit.*) pilar, estribo, contrafuerte; botarel; (*carp.*) empalme.

abuttal, *s.* linde, límite.

abutting, *a.* lindante, confinante.—*s.* encrucijada.

abysm, abyss [ə'bizm, ə'bis], *s.* abismo, sima, golfo, báratro, infierno; (*blas.*) el centro del escudo.

abysmal, abyssal, *a.* abismal, insondable (dicho del océano).

acacia [ə'keiʃə], *s.* (*bot.*) acacia, robinia acacia.

academian, academic, *s.* académico, colegial, estudiante de un colegio, cursante en una universidad.

academic [ækə'demik] **academical,** *a.* académico.

academician, academist, *s.* académico.

academism, *s.* platonismo.

academy [ə'kædəmi], *s.* academia; universidad; institución, colegio, escuela.

acajou, *s.* (*Am.*) caoba del Brasil, o falsa caoba.

acanaceous, *a.* (*bot.*) espinoso.

acantha [ə'kænθə], **acanthus,** *s.* (*bot.*) acanto o branca ursina.

acanthine, *a.* de acanto.

acarus, *s.* (*zool.*) ácaro; arador, género de los ácaridos.

acatalectic, *s.* (*poét.*) acataléctico.

acatalepsy [ə'kætəlepsi], *s.* (*med.*) acatalepsis, *f.*

acataleptic, *a.* acataléptico.

acaulescent, acauline, acaulous, *a.* acaule.

accede [æk'siːd], *v.i.* acceder, asentir, consentir; subir, elevarse; lograr, alcanzar, llegar a.

acceding, *s.* elevación (*al trono*).

accelerate [æk'seləreit], *v.t.* acelerar, apresurar. — *v.i.* despacharse, darse prisa, apresurarse.

accelerating, *a.* aceleratriz.

acceleration, *s.* aceleración, apresuramiento, prisa; despacho.

accelerative, *a.* acelerador, impulsivo.

accelerator, *s.* acelerador.

acceleratory, *a.* acelerador.

accent ['æksent], *s.* acento, inflexión de la voz; (*poét. pl.*) palabras, lenguaje. — *v.t.* acentuar, articular.

accentual, *a.* rítmico.

accentuate [æk'sentjueit], *v.t.* acentuar.

accentuation, *s.* acentuación.

accept [æk'sept], *v.t.* aceptar, admitir, recibir, acoger; consentir, aprobar; abrazar; *to be accepted as,* pasar por; *to accept a bill of exchange,* aceptar una letra de cambio.

acceptability, acceptableness, *s.* aceptabilidad; agrado.

acceptable, *a.* admisible, aceptable, agradable, grato, bien recibido.

acceptance, *s.* aceptación, buena acogida, gracia, favor.

acceptation, *s.* aceptación; aprobación, aplauso; recepción, acogida favorable; preferencia; significado, sentido (de una palabra, frase, etc.).

accepter, *s.* aceptador, aceptante.

acception, *s.* acepción.

acceptor, *s.* (*com.*) aceptante, aceptador.

access ['ækses], *s.* acceso, entrada, paso, camino; aumento, acrecentamiento, añadidura; (*med.*) accesión.

accessibility [æksesə'biliti], *s.* facilidad de acercarse.

accessible [æk'sesəbl], *a.* accesible, asequible, conquistable.

accession, *s.* acceso, accesión; aumento; advenimiento; asentimiento, consentimiento; *accession of the king to the throne,* advenimiento del rey al trono; (*for.*) accesión, título o modo de adquirir.

accessory, *a.* accesorio, secundario, contribuyente, concomitante; adicional, adjunto. — *s.* accesorio, cómplice; dependencia.

accidence ['æksidəns], *s.* (*gram.*) libro de rudimentos; accidente; caso fortuito, lance contratiempo.

accident ['æksidənt], *s.* accidente, casualidad; suceso, ocurrencia, evento; lance, azar, golpe; caso, paso, incidente; desgracia; (*mar.*) siniestro; (*gram.*) caso, modo, desinencia; *sad accident,* lance funesto; *by accident,* por casualidad, casualmente, accidentalmente, sin querer.

accidental [æksi'dentəl], *s.* accidente; (*mús.*) accidente, accidental. — *a.* accidental, casual, contingente, fortuito, adventicio.

accidentality, s. accidencia.

accidentalness, s. contingencia, casualidad, caso imprevisto.

accite [ak'sait], v.t. convocar, reunir, citar, llamar.

acclaim, v.t. aclamar, aplaudir. — v.i. victorear.

acclamation [ækləm'eiʃən], **acclaim,** s. aclamación, celebración, aplauso ovación.

acclamatory, a. laudatorio.

acclimate [ə'klaimət], v.t. aclimatar, connaturalizar.

acclimated, a., p.p. aclimatado.

acclimation, s. aclimatación.

acclimatization [ə'klaimətaiz'eiʃən], s. aclimatación.

acclimatize [ə'klaimətaiz], v.t. aclimatar.

acclive, acclivous, a. pendiente, empinado.

acclivity [ə'kliviti], s. cuesta, rampa, subida, ladera; (fig.) dificultad.

accolade [æko'leid], s. acolada; espaldarazo; (mús.) corchete; (arquit.) moldura curva de adorno.

accommodable, a. acomodable.

accommodableness, s. capacidad de acomodarse.

accommodate [ə'kɔmədeit], v.t. acomodar; cuadrar, adecuar, ajustar, arreglar, reglar; proveer, surtir, suministrar; reconciliar; componer; hospedar, alojar; servir, complacer; (com.) prestar dinero. — v.i. conformarse, componerse, convenir. — a. acomodado, apto, útil, conveniente.

accommodateness, s. aptitud, acomodo, conveniencia, utilidad.

accommodating, s. obsequioso, oficioso, servicial, galante, complaciente, acomodadizo.

accommodatingly, adv. cómodamente, aptamente, convenientemente.

accommodation [əkɔməd'eiʃən], s. comodidad, conveniencia, acomodación, acomodamiento, compostura, concierto, arreglo, ajuste, adaptación, reconciliación; dignación; servicio, favor; facilidades, comodidades; habitaciones, alojamiento; préstamo; accommodation note or note, letra de favor; aceptada sin recibir su valor.

accommodator, s. el que maneja, ajusta o acomoda.

accompaniment [ə'kʌmpənimənt], s. acompañamiento.

accompanist, s. (mús.) acompañante, acompañador.

accompany, v.t. acompañar, ir con, asociarse con, (fam.) cohabitar. — v.i. tocar el acompañamiento.

accomplice [ə'kɔmplis], s. cómplice; compañero en delito o crimen.

accomplish [ə'kɔmpliʃ], v.t. cumplir, realizar, efectuar, completar; llevar a cabo, acabar, concluir; desempeñar, lograr; cumplir, verificar; hermosear, adornar.

accomplishable, a. realizable, cumplidero.

accomplished, a. perfecto, cabal, acabado, positivo, completo, consumado, cumplido, distinguido, ejecutado, realizado; elegante; habilidoso; bien educado.

accomplisher, s. perfeccionador, ejecutor.

accomplishing, s. cumplimiento, realización, ejecución, perfeccionamiento.

accomplishment, s. cumplimiento, consumación, complemento, logro, éxito, efectuación;

adquisición, perfección. — pl. **accomplishments,** talentos, prendas, conocimientos.

accord [ə'kɔːd], v.t. acomodar, conciliar, poner de acuerdo; ajustar; acordar, otorgar, conceder; igualar una cosa con otra. — v.i. acordar, concordar, conciliar, convenir, acomodarse, avenirse. — s. acuerdo, convenio, acomodamiento, concierto, armonía, simetría; (for.) transacción, convenio, arreglo; (mús.) acorde; in accord, de acuerdo; of one's own accord, espontáneamente; with one accord, de común acuerdo, unánimamente.

accordable, a. agradable, conciliable, concordable, conforme.

accordance, accordancy, s. conformidad, correspondencia, concordancia, convenio, acuerdo, buena inteligencia.

accordant, a. acorde, conforme, dispuesto, conveniente, propio.

accordantly, adv. acordemente.

according, pres. part., adv. según, conforme; according to, según, conforme a, en cumplimiento de; according as, según que, como.

accordingly, adv. en conformidad, en efecto, en consecuencia, de consiguiente.

accordion [ə'kɔːrdiən], s. (mús.) acordeón.

accost [ə'kɔst], v.t. acercarse, arrimarse; dirigirse a; trabar conversación con.

accostable, a. accesible, tratable, sociable, aseequible.

accosted a. (blas.) acostado; lado a lado.

accouchement [ə'kuːʃmã], s. parto.

accoucheur, s. comadrón, partero; obstetricio.

accoucheuse, s. partera, comadrona.

account [ə'kaunt], s. cuenta, cálculo; período; cómputo; caso; aprecio, estimación; rango, dignidad, consideración, respeto; declaración, nota, relación, cuento, descripción, información, narración, narrativa; modo, motivo; (teneduría) extracto de cuentas; to keep an account, tener cuenta abierta; account-book, libro de cuentas; current account, cuenta corriente; to pay on account, pagar a cuenta; to turn to account, sacar provecho; to take into account, tener en cuenta, tomar en consideración; to settle accounts, ajustar cuentas; persons of no account, personas sin importancia; persons of great account, personas de gran consideración; profit and loss account, cuenta de ganancias y pérdidas; on joint account, de cuenta a mitad; on no account, de ninguna manera; on account of, por motivo de, por cuenta de; on your account, por amor de Vd. (o a cargo de Vd.). — v.t. tener; juzgar, estimar, reputar; numerar, computar, contar; considerar. — v.i. responder, explicar, hacer patente; dar cuenta; to account for, dar razón de, responder de; dar una explicación; there's no accounting for tastes, sobre gustos no hay disputa.

accountability [əkauntə'biliti], **accountableness,** s. contabilidad; responsabilidad; obligación de dar cuentas.

accountable, a. contable; responsable.

accountant, s. tenedor de libros, contador, contable; calculador, aritmético; (for.) reo o demandado en una acción civil.

accounting, s. acto de contar, arreglo de cuentas; contabilidad; accounting-day, día de ajuste de cuentas, día de vencimiento.

accouplement, *s.* ayuntamiento, unión, pareja.

accoutre [ə'ku:təɹ], *v.t.* aviar, ataviar, vestir; *(mil.)* equipar; echar un caparazón; *fully accoutred*, con equipo completo.

accoutrement, *s.* avío, prevención, atavío, apresto, vestido, vestidura, ornamento, equipaje. — *pl. (mil.)* pertrechos, equipo.

accredit [ə'kredit], *v.t.* creer, dar crédito a; dar credenciales a; favorecer, patrocinar, fomentar; *(com.)* acreditar.

accreditation, *s.* crédito, credencial.

accredited, *a.* acreditado, recibido, creído, admitido; (*diplom.*) autorizado. — *p.p.* [ACCREDIT].

accrescence [ə'kri:sens], *s.* acrecencia, aumento, acrecentamiento.

accrescent, *a.* creciente; lo que va en aumento.

accretion, *s.* acrecentamiento, aumento; (*for.*) acrecencia (derecho de).

accretive, *a.* aumentativo, acrecentado, aumentado.

accrue [ə'kru:], *v.i.* crecer, aumentar, acrecentar, tomar incremento; resultar, provenir; *accrued interest*, interés acumulado.

accumbency [ə'kʌmbənsi], *s.* reclinación.

accumbent, *a.* reclinado, apoyado sobre el codo.

accumulate [ə'kjumjuleit], *v.t.* acumular, amontonar; atesorar. — *v.i.* acumularse, amontonarse, aumentarse, crecer. — *a.* amontonado, acumulado.

accumulation, *s.* acumulación, amontonamiento; hacinamiento. — *pl.* ahorros.

accumulative, *a.* acumulativo; acumulador; acumulado, amontonado, añadido.

accumulatively, *adv.* acumulativamente; en montón.

accumulator, *s.* acumulador; amontonador; (*elec.*) acumulador; (*hidr.*) condensador.

accuracy ['ækjurəsi], *s.* cuidado, exactitud, diligencia; precisión, corrección; esmero, primor.

accurate, *a.* exacto, correcto, fiel, puntual; cabal, perfecto; preciso, estricto, primoroso; pulido, acabado.

accurateness, *s.* exactitud, puntualidad, precisión.

accursed [ə'kə:ɹst], *a.* maldito, maldecido; detestable, execrable; perverso, desventurado; infausto, fatal, excomulgado.

accusable [ə'kju:zəbl], *a.* acusable, culpable, delatable.

accusant, *s.* acusador.

accusation [ækju'zeiʃən], *s.* acusación, acriminación, delación, imputación; cargo.

accusative, *s.* acusativo. — *a.* que acusa.

accusatory, *a.* acusatorio.

accuse [ə'kju:z], *v.t.* acusar, delatar, denunciar, imputar, criminar, culpar, tachar, notar, censurar.

accused, *s.* acusado. — *a., p.p.* [ACCUSE].

accuser, *s.* acusador, delator, delatante, denunciador.

accustom [ə'kʌstəm], *v.t.* acostumbrar, habituar, avezar. — *v.i.* soler, tener costumbre.

accustomable *a.* acostumbrado. común, ordinario, habitual.

accustomably, *adv.* acostumbradamente, según costumbre, habitualmente, a menudo, frecuentemente.

accustomance, *s.* costumbre, *f.*, uso, hábito.

accustomarily, *adv.* acostumbradamente, según el uso, comúnmente, ordinariamente.

accustomary, *a.* acostumbrado, usual, ordinario.

accustomed, *a.* usual, acostumbrado, frecuente, habitual; avezado; ducho.

accustomedness, *s.* costumbre, *f.*, hábito, familiaridad.

ace [eis], *s.* as; migaja, partícula, átomo; *within an ace of*, a dos dedos de, a pique de, en un tris.

acentric [ə'sentrik], *a.* sin centro.

acephala [ə'sefələ], **acephales**, *s.pl.* (*zool.*) acéfalos.

acephalous, *a.* acéfalo.

acer ['eisə], *s.* (*bot.*) arce.

acerate, acerated, *a.* puntiagudo.

acerb [ə'sə:ɹb], *a.* agrio, ácido, áspero; acerbo, cruel, riguroso.

acerbate, *v.t.* agriar, exasperar.

acerbity, *s.* acerbidad; amargura, rigor; severidad, agrura, aspereza, crueldad, dureza, desabrimiento.

aceric, acerous, *a.* acerado, espinoso.

acervate ['æsə:veit], *v.t.* amontonar, poner en montón. — *a.* (*hist. nat.*) arracimado.

acervation, *s.* amontonamiento, hacinamiento; montón.

acescency [ə'si:sənsi], *s.* acescencia, agrura, acedía.

acescent, *a.* reputando.

acetabulum, *s.* acetábulo.

acetate ['æsəteit], *s.* (*quím.*) acetato; *acetate of copper*, cardenillo, verdigris.

acetated, *a.* acetoso, agrio.

acetic [ə'si:tik], *a.* acético; *acetic acid* (*quím.*) ácido acético.

acetification, *s.* acetificación.

acetify, *v.t.* acedar, acetificar.

acetimeter [æsi'timətəɹ], *s.* (*quím.*) acetímetro.

acetimetry, *s.* (*quím.*) acetometría.

acetone ['æsitoun], *s.* (*quím.*) acetona.

acetous, acetose, *a.* agrio, acedo, acetoso.

acetylene [ə'setili:n], *s.* acetileno.

Achaean, *a.* aqueo.

ache [eik], *s.* dolor, mal, dolencia; *headache*, dolor de cabeza; *earache*, dolor de oído; *toothache*, dolor de muelas. — *v.i.* doler, padecer dolor; *my head aches*, me duele la cabeza.

achievable [ə'tʃi:vəbl], *a.* ejecutable, hacedero, factible, acabable.

achievance, *s.* hecho notable, hazaña.

achieve, *v.t.* ejecutar, acabar, perfeccionar, ganar, obtener, lograr, alcanzar; llevar a cabo; *to achieve something difficult*, poner una pica en Flandes.

achievement, *s.* ejecución, realización, logro, hecho, obra, hazaña, proeza.

achiever, *s.* ejecutor, hacedor; vencedor.

aching ['eikiŋ], *s.* dolor; desasosiego, incomodidad; pena, pesadumbre, *f.* — *a.* doliente, enfermo, afligido.

achromatic [ækro'mætik], *a.* acromático.

achromatism, *s.* acromatismo.

achromatize, *v.t.* acromatizar.

acicular, *a.* acicular, alesnado.

acid ['æsid], *a.* ácido, agrio, acedo. — *s.* ácido.

acidifiable [əsidi'faiəbl], *a.* acidificable.

acidification [əsidifi'keiʃən], *s.* acidificación.

acidify [ə'sidifai], *v.t.* acedar, acidular, agriar.

acidifying, *a.* acidificante.
acidimeter, *s.* acidímetro, pesa-ácidos.
acidimetry, *s.* acetometría.
acidity, acidness, *s.* agrura, agrio, acedía, acidez.
acidulate, *v.t.* acidular, agriar, avinagrar.
acidule, *s.* acídulo.
acidulous, *a.* agrio, acídulo, acidulado.
acierate, *v.t.* acerar, convertir en acero.
acinose ['æsinouz], **acinous,** granuloso.
acknowledge [æk'nɔlidʒ], *v.t.* reconocer; confesar; agradecer, declarar; *to acknowledge receipt,* acusar recibo.
acknowledgment, *s.* reconocimiento; confesión; gratitud, agradecimiento; concesión, consentimiento; remuneración, recompensa; gratificación; acuse de recibo.
aclinic [ə'klinik], *a.* aclínico.
acme ['ækmi:], *s.* colmo, cumbre, *f.*, cima, pináculo, apogeo.
acolothist, acolyte ['ækolait], *s.* acólito, monacillo.
aconite ['ækonait], *s.* (*bot.*) acónito.
acorn ['eikɔ:rn], *s.* (*bot.*) bellota; (*naut.*) bola de madera.
acorned, *a.* cargado, alimentado o cebado con bellotas.
acotyledon [əkɔti'li:dən], *s.* (*bot.*) acotiledón.
acotyledonous, *a.* acotiledóneo.
acoustic [ə'ku:stik], *a.* acústico.
acoustics, *s.* (*fís.*) acústica.
acquaint [ə'kweint], *v.t.* imponer; instruir, dar a conocer, familiarizar; enterar, informar, dar aviso; advertir, avisar, comunicar; *to acquaint oneself with,* ponerse al corriente de; *to be acquainted with,* conocer.
acquaintance, *s.* conocimiento, trato, familiaridad, relaciones; conocido.
acquaintanceship, *s.* conocimiento, familiaridad, trato.
acquainted, *a.* impuesto, enterado, informado; conocido; relacionado.
acquaintedness, *s.* conocimiento.
acquest [ə'kwest], *s.* (*for.*) adquisición; propiedad no heredada.
acquiesce [ækwi'es], *v.i.* allanarse, asentir, doblegarse; consentir, someterse.
acquiescence, acquiescency, *s.* aquiescencia, asenso, consentimiento, conformidad; resignación, sumisión.
acquiescent, *a.* condescendiente, acomodadizo, deferente, resignado, sumiso, conforme.
acquirability [əkwairə'biliti], *s.* posibilidad de adquirir.
acquirable, *a.* adquirible, que se puede adquirir.
acquire, *v.t.* adquirir, alcanzar, ganar; aprender; obtener; contraer.
acquirement, *s.* adquisición. — *pl.* **acquirements,** conocimientos, talentos, instrucción, saber.
acquirer, *s.* (*for.*) adquirente, adquiridor.
acquisition [ækwi'ziʃən], *s.* adquisición.
acquisitive, *a.* adquisitivo; adquirido, logrado, ganado.
acquisitively, *adv.* por adquisición.
acquisitiveness, *s.* adquisividad.
acquit [ə'kwit], *v.t.* libertar, poner en libertad; descargar, absolver; desempeñar, cumplir; exentar, pagar; relevar, exponer; eximir, exonerar, dispensar; *to acquit oneself well,* desempeñar su obligación o cometido.

acquittal, *s.* absolución, descargo, pago.
acquittance, *s.* descargo; recibo, quita, carta de pago; (*for.*) finiquito.
acquitted, *a.* absuelto. — *p.p.* [ACQUIT].
acre ['eikə], *s.* acre; campo. — *pl.* **acres,** finca, terrenos; *God's acre,* campo santo, cementerio.
acreage, ['eikəridʒ], *s.* área, acres colectivamente.
acred, *a.* hacendado.
acrid ['ækrid], *a.* acre, mordaz, punzante, irritante, picante, corrosivo.
acridity [æ'kriditi:], **acridness,** *s.* acritud, acrimonia.
acrimonious [ækri'mouniəs], *a.* acre, sarcástico, mordaz, picante, corrosivo.
acrimoniously, *adv.* acremente, ásperamente, agriamente.
acrimoniousness, *s.* acritud, amargura, aspereza.
acrimony ['ækriməni], *s.* acrimonia, acritud, aspereza, mordacidad.
acritical [ə'kritikl], *s.* acrítico.
acritude ['ækritju:d], *s.* acritud, amargura, aspereza, causticidad, mordacidad, acrimonia.
acrobat ['ækrəbæt], *s.* acróbata, *m.f.*, volatín, funámbulo.
acrobatic, *a.* acrobático.
acrogen ['ækrodʒen], *s.* (*bot.*) acrógeno.
acromion [ə'kroumi:ən], *s.* (*anat.*) acromio.
acronycal [ə'krɔnikəl], *a.* (*astron.*) acrónico.
acropolis [ə'krɔpolis], *s.* acrópolis, *f.*, ciudadela (especialmente la de Atenas).
across [ə'krɔs], *adv.* de través, al través; al otro lado; de una parte a otra; (*prop.*) por, a través, de medio a medio, por medio de; contra; sobre; *to come across a person,* tropezar con una persona.
acrostic [ə'krɔstik], *s.* poema acróstico. — *a.* acróstico.
acrostically, *adv.* en acrósticos.
act [ækt], *v.i.* hacer, ponerse en movimiento, ponerse en acción, obrar, estar ocupado; conducirse, portarse; marchar, funcionar, ejecutar, operar, actuar; ejercer fuerza mecánica, mental o moral; producir movimiento o efecto. — *v.t.* hacer, cometer, ejecutar; (*teat.*) representar, hacer el papel de; fingir, simular; obrar; mover; ejercer, desempeñar; *to act honestly,* andar a derechas; *to act openly,* andar con la cara descubierta; *to act the fool,* hacer el bufón (o gracioso); *to act the part of,* desempeñar el papel de, ejercer las funciones de; *to act upon,* influir, obrar sobre; *to act with foresight,* tener perspicacia. — *s.* hecho, efecto acción; acto, obra, golpe; *to pass an act,* votar una ley; *to catch in the act,* prender con las manos en la masa; *act of faith,* acto de fe; *act of oblivion,* amnistía.
acting, *s.* acción, representación, obra; ficción, comedia; desempeño. — *a.* en ejercicio, en actividad; interino, suplente; *acting adjutant,* ayudante de servicio; *acting manager,* subgerente, vice-administrador, interventor.
actinic [æk'tinik], **actinical,** *a.* actínico.
actinism, *s.* actinismo.
actinium, *s.* actinio.
actinograph, *s.* actinógrafo.
actinometer, *s.* actinómetro.
actinometric, *a.* actinométrico.

action ['ækʃən], *s.* acto, acción, hecho, obra, operación, ocupación; actividad; movimiento, marcha; batalla; gesticulación; proceso; influencia; (*teat.*) argumento; (*mech.*) golpe, mecanismo; (*for.*) demanda, proceso, litigio; *to bring into action*, poner en movimiento; *to bring an action*, armar un pleito (*o* pedir justicia).

actionable, *a.* punible, criminal, procesable.

actionably, *adv.* de un modo procesario.

active, *a.* activo, ejecutivo, negocioso, diligente; ágil, hábil, listo, pronto, ligero; eficaz; práctico, real; enérgico.

actively, *adv.* activamente, ágilmente, vivamente, eficazmente.

activeness, activity, *s.* actividad, agilidad, vivacidad, vigor; soltura; ejercicio, movimiento, prontitud, eficacia, gallardía.

actless, *a.* inactivo; insípido. flojo, débil; ocioso; sin espíritu.

actor, *s.* (*teat.*) actor, comediante, cómico; (*for.*) demandante.

actress, *s.* actriz, comedianta, cómica.

actual ['æktjuəl], *a.* actual, real, efectivo, práctico.

actuality [æktju'æliti], *s.* actualidad.

actualize ['æktjuəlaiz], *v.t.* (*for.*) actuar; realizar.

actually ['æktjuəli], *adv.* actualmente, al presente, de hecho, en efecto, realmente, efectivamente.

actualness, *s.* actualidad.

actuary ['æktjuəri], *s.* actuario, escribano, secretario, registrador; calculador, matemático.

actuate ['æktjueit], *v.t.* mover, animar, inspirar, impulsar, excitar; poner en acción, guiar.

acuity [ə'kjuːiti], *s.* agudeza, sutileza.

aculeate [ə'kjuːlieit], *a.* (*hist. nat.*) erizado; (*bot.*) espinoso.

aculeiform, *a.* aculeiforme.

aculeous, *a.* (*bot.*) espinoso.

acumen [ə'kjuːmən], *s.* agudeza, penetración; ingenio; vivacidad; perspicacia; sutileza. chispa.

acuminate [ə'kjuːmineit], *v.t.* afilar, aguzar. — *v.i.* terminar en punta. — *a.* agudo; (*biol.*) aguzado, puntiagudo.

acuminated, *a.* agudo, puntiagudo, picudo, punzante, puntoso.

acumination, *s.* punta aguda; penetración, sutileza.

acute [ə'kjuːt], *a.* agudo, delgado, fino, sutil, penetrante; saliente, anguloso; ingenioso, perspicaz; *acute-angled,* (*geom.*) acutángulo.

acutely, *adv.* agudamente, con agudeza.

acuteness, *s.* agudeza, sutileza; perspicacia, penetración, talento; (*med.*) violencia de una enfermedad; período agudo.

adage ['ædidʒ], *s.* adagio, refrán, proverbio.

Adam ['ædəm], *s.* Adán; el género humano; *Adam's ale,* (*fam.*) agua; *Adam's apple,* (*fam.*) nuez de la garganta.

adamant ['ædəmənt], *s.* diamante; (*ant.*) piedra imán; (*fig.*) dureza.

adamantean [ædə'mæntjən], **adamantine,** *a.* diamantino, duro; (*poét.*) impenetrable, adamantino; insensible, indisoluble.

adapt [ə'dæpt], *v.t.* adaptar, acomodar, ajustar, cuadrar, proporcionar; (*teat.*) arreglar, refundir; *to adapt oneself to one's environment,* bailar al son que se toca.

adaptability, *s.* adaptabilidad, elasticidad.

adaptable, adaptive, *a.* adaptable, acomodable, ajustable.

adaptation [ædəp'teiʃən], **adaption,** *s.* adaptación, aplicación.

adaptedness [ə'dæptednes], *s.* adaptación, apropiación.

adapter, *s.* adaptante, el que adapta.

add [æd], *v.t.* añadir, agregar, adicionar, aumentar, acrecentar, juntar, contribuir; *to add up,* sumar.

addendum [ə'dendəm], *s.* (*pl.* **addenda**) apéndice, adición, suplemento.

adder ['ædəɹ], *s.* víbora.

adder's-grass, adder's-wort, escorzonera.

adder's-tongue, (*bot.*) lengua de sierpe, ophioglossum vulgatum.

addible, *a.* añadible, sumable.

addibility, *s.* propiedad de ser añadido.

addict [ə'dikt], *v.t.* dar, dedicar, destinar, aplicar, consagrar.

addicted, *a.,* *p.p.* dado, entregado, afecto a, adicto, apasionado por, partidario; *to be addicted to,* darse a, abandonarse a, entregarse a.

addictedness, *s.* inclinación, propensión; adhesión; gusto.

addiction, *s.* aplicación, disposición, gusto.

addition, *s.* adición, añadidura, aditamento, adjunto, aumento; (*arit.*) suma; *in addition to,* además de.

additional, *a.* adicional.

additionary, *a.* aumentativo.

additive, additory, *a.* aumentativo.

addle [ædl], *a.* podrido, huero, vacío, vano, sin sustancia; infecundo, estéril; *addle-head,* cabeza vacía; *addle-headed,* inepto, chiflado. — *v.t.* podrir, esterilizar. hacer estéril, enhuerar, engorar.

address [ə'dres], *v.t.* preparar, disponer; dirigir; (*com.*) consignar; acercarse a, dirigirse a; arengar; obsequiar; interceder, rogar. — *v.i.* encararse, engestarse. — *s.* petición, memorial; proclama; dedicatoria; destreza, habilidad, maña; señas, dirección; sobrescrito; trato, tratamiento; arenga, alocución, habla, plática, discurso, recurso verbal; garbo, donaire; gracia; galanteo; *to pay one's addresses,* hacer la corte.

addressee, *s.* destinatario (de una carta, mercancías, etc.).

addresser, *s.* suplicante, exponente; comisionado.

adduce [ə'djuːs], *v.t.* alegar, aducir; presentar, producir; traer, llevar.

adducent, *a.* (*anat.*) aductor.

adducible, *a.* aducible.

adduction [ə'dʌkʃən], *s.* (*anat.*) aducción; alegación.

adductive, *a.* aductivo.

adductor, *s.* (*anat.*) aductor.

ademption [ə'dempʃən], *s.* (*for.*) privación, revocación.

adeniform [ə'denifoɹm], *a.* glandiforme.

adenitis [ædə'naitis], *s.* adenitis, *f.*

adenography [ædən'ografi:], *s.* adenografía.

adenoid ['ædənoid], *a.* glandiforme.

adenology, *s.* adenología.

adept [ə'dept], *s.* adepto, perito. — *a.* versado, cursado, consumado, iniciado.

adequacy ['ædəkwəsi], *s.* suficiencia, justa proporción.

adequate, *v.t.* adecuar, asemejar, igualar. — *a.* adecuado, proporcionado, suficiente, competente.

adequateness, adequation, *s.* adecuación, proporción, exacta, igualdad.

adhere [æd'hiəɹ], *v.i.* adherirse, unirse, allegarse, pegarse; aficionarse.

adherence, adherency, *s.* adherencia, anexión, adhesión.

adherent, *a.* adherente, adhesivo, pegajoso; adicto. — *s.* adherente, secuaz, partidario.

adherently, *adv.* parcialmente, con adhesión.

adherer, *s.* adherente, partidario, parcial.

adherescence, *s.* adherencia.

adherescent, *a.* adhesivo, pegajoso.

adhesion [æd'hi:ʒən], *s.* adhesión, adherencia.

adhesive, *a.* adhesivo, adherente, pegajoso, pegadizo, tenaz; *adhesive stamps,* sellos engomados.

adhesively, *adv.* tenazmente, en unión estrecha.

adhesiveness, *s.* adherencia, tenacidad, viscosidad; *(frenol.)* amatividad.

adhibit [əd'hibit], *v.t.* usar, aplicar.

adhibition, *s.* aplicación.

adhortatory [ædhɔɹ'teitəɹi], *a.* exhortativo.

adieu [ə'dju:], *interj.* A Dios, adiós, agur, vale. — *s.* adiós, despedida; *to bid adieu,* despedirse.

adipose ['ædipous], *a.* adiposo, seboso.

adiposity, *s.* adiposidad.

adit ['ædit], *s.* mina, galería de una mina; entrada; *(Mex.)* socavón.

adjacence [ə'dʒeisəns], **adjacency,** *s.* adyacencia, proximidad, vecindad, contigüidad.

adjacent, *a.* adyacente, contiguo, vecino.

adject, *v.t.* añadir, juntar.

adjection, *s.* adición, añadidura.

adjectival [ædʒək'taivəl], *a.* del (o como) adjetivo.

adjective ['ædʒektiv], *s., a.* adjetivo. — *v.t.* adjetivar.

adjoin [ə'dʒɔin], *v.t.* juntar, asociar, unir, lindar. — *v.i.* colindar, estar contiguo, estar cercano.

adjoining, *a.* contiguo, inmediato, adyacente, colindante.

adjourn [ə'dʒə:ɹn], *v.t.* diferir, suspender, retardar, trasladar; alargar; citar; emplazar; remitir; levantar una sesión. — *v.i.* alargarse prorrogarse; retirarse.

adjournment, *s.* aplazamiento; llamamiento, citación; traslación, suspensión; emplazo, emplazamiento; suspensión de una deliberación, hasta un día señalado.

adjudge [ə'dʒʌdʒ], **adjudicate** [ə'dʒu:dikeit], *v.t.* adjudicar; juzgar, decidir, decretar; sentenciar; estimar; pronunciar la sentencia.

adjudger, *s.* adjudicador.

adjudgment, *s.* adjudicación.

adjudicate, *v.t.* [ADJUDGE].

adjudication, *s.* adjudicación.

adjudicative, *a.* adjudicativo.

adjudicator, *s.* adjudicador.

adjunct ['ædʒʌŋkt], *s.* adjunto, accesorio, auxiliar; compañero, colega, *m.,* asociado, socio; *(filos.)* atributo. — *a.* adjunto, junto, contiguo, suplente.

adjunction, *s.* unión, adición; *(for.)* adjunción.

adjunctive, *a.* adjunto, agregado, adjetivado.

adjunctively, *adv.* juntamente, por adición.

adjuration [ædʒu'reiʃən], *s.* adjuración, imprecación, conjuro.

adjure, *v.t.* juramentar, imprecar, adjurar; conjurar, implorar, suplicar, impetrar, tomar juramento a otro.

adjust [ə'dʒʌst], *v.t.* ajustar, asentar, amoldar, concertar, arreglar, acomodar; conciliar; terminar; componer; acordar, formar, conformar, igualar; justificar; proporcionar.

adjustable, *a.* que se puede ajustar.

adjuster, *s.* el que ajusta; ajustador, mediador, tasador.

adjustment, *s.* ajuste, ajustamiento; justificación; acomodamiento; arreglo, transacción; composición, aliño.

adjutancy ['ædʒutənsi], *s.* ayudantía; ayuda, apoyo.

adjutant, *s. (mil.)* ayudante.

adjute, *v.t.* ayudar, dar auxilio.

adjutor, *s.* coadjutor.

adjuvant, *s., a.* adjutor, útil, provechoso, ayudante, auxiliar; *(med.)* pasante.

admeasure [əd'meʒəɹ], *v.t.* medir.

admeasurement, *s.* medición; dimensión, medida; repartimiento.

admeasurer, *s.* medidor.

adminicular, *a.* adminículo.

administer [əd'ministəɹ], *v.t.* administrar, suministrar; dar, surtir, proveer; regir, manejar, contribuir, gobernar; ejercer, desempeñar. — *v.i.* tender, contribuir; *to administer an oath,* tomar juramento.

administerial, *a.* administrativo.

administrable, *a.* que se puede administrar

administrant, *s.* director, administrador, jefe ejecutivo.

administration, *s.* administración; ministerio, gobierno, dirección; distribución; manejo; intendencia, mayordomía.

administrative, *a.* administrativo.

administrator, *s.* administrator; gobernante; testamentario; *(for.)* tenedor de bienes, fideicomisario abintestato.

administratorship, *s.* administración.

administratrix, *s.* administradora, curadora.

admirable ['ædmərəbl], *a.* admirable, admirativo; digno de admiración.

admirableness, admirability, *s.* excelencia.

admiral ['ædmərəl], *s.* almirante; almiranta (nave); *rear-admiral,* contraalmirante; *vice-admiral,* vice-almirante.

admiralship, *s.* almirantía.

admiralty, *s.* almirantazgo; *first lord of the admiralty,* presidente del almirantazgo.

admiration [ædmə'reiʃən], *s.* admiración; sorpresa, pasmo; embobamiento.

admire [əd'maiəɹ], *v.t.* admirar, contemplar. — *v.i.* admirarse.

admirer, *s.* admirador; amante, adorador, apasionado, aficionado; *to be a great admirer of music,* ser muy aficionado a la música.

admiring, *a.* admirativo, de admiración.

admiringly, *adv.* admirativamente, admirablemente, con admiración.

admissibility [ədmisi'biliti], *s.* admisibilidad.

admissible, *a.* admisible, aceptable; lícito, permitido.

admission, *s.* admisión, recepción, acceso; entrada; concesión, asenso; *ticket of admission,* billete de entrada.

admissive, admissory, *a.* que implica admisión.

admit [əd'mit], *v.t.* admitir, recibir; conceder,

asentir; permitir; dar entrada; confesar, reconocer.

admittance, s. admisión, acceso, entrada; precio (o derechos) de entrada, derecho de entrar.

admitter, s. el que admite.

admittible, a. admisible, pertinente.

admix [əd'miks], v.t. mezclar, juntar, unir, incorporar.

admixtion, admixture, s. mixtura, mezcla.

admonish [əd'mɔniʃ], v.t. amonestar, reprender; exhortar; advertir, prevenir, poner en guardia.

admonisher, s. amonestador.

admonishment, s. advertencia, prevención, amonestación, represión.

admonition [ædmo'niʃən], s. admonición, amonestación, aviso, consejo, represión, exhortación.

admonitive [əd'mɔnitiv], a. admonitivo.

admonitively, adv. en forma de amonestación.

admonitor, s. admonitor, censor.

admonitory, a. admonitorio.

adnascent, adnate ['ædneit], a. (bot.) adnato, entenado.

adnoun ['ædnaun], s. (gram.) adjetivo; adjetivo usado como sustantivo.

ado [ə'du:], s. trabajo, dificultad; bullicio, baraúnda, ruido, tumulto; fatiga, pena; much ado about nothing, mucho ruido y pocas nueces; without more ado, sin más ni más; sin más ni menos; sin más acá ni más allá.

adobe, s. adobe, ladrillo cocido al sol.

adolescence [ædo'lesəns], **adolescency,** s. adolescencia.

adolescent, s., a. adolescente.

adonis, s. (ictiol.) adonis (pez).

adopt [ə'dɔpt], v.t. adoptar, prohijar, ahijar; aceptar; tomar, asumir; elegir, escoger.

adopted, a. adoptivo.

adopter, s. adoptador; prohijador, padre adoptivo (o madre adoptiva).

adoption, s. adopción, prohijamiento; elección.

adoptive, a. adoptivo, aparente.

adorability [ədorə'biliti], s. lo adorable.

adorable, a. adorable.

adorableness, s. lo adorable.

adoration [ædo'reiʃən], s. adoración, culto.

adore [ə'doər], v.t. adorar, glorificar, honrar, reverenciar, amar con extremo, idolatrar.

adorer, s. adorante, adorador; (fam.) amante.

adoring, a. adorante, adorador.

adoringly, adv. con adoración· apasionadamente.

adorn, v.t. adornar, ornar, ornamentar, ataviar, embellecer, hermosear, acicalar, engalanar, guarnecer, alhajar; alindar; atildar; honrar, ennoblecer; aderezar.

adorning, s. ornamento, decoración.

adornment, s. adorno, atavío, ornamento, gala, aderezo.

adossed, a. (blas.) adosado.

adown [ə'daun], adv. bajo, abajo, en tierra, en el suelo.

adrenalin, s. adrenalina.

adrift [ə'drift], adv. (mar.) a la deriva; a la ventura; flotando, a merced de las olas; to break adrift, perder las anclas; his mind is all adrift, se le va la cabeza; está delirando.

adrip [ə'drip], adv. goteando.

adroit [ə'drɔit], a. hábil, diestro.

adroitly, adv. hábilmente, diestramente.

adroitness, s. destreza, habilidad, prontitud.

adry [ə'drai], adv. seco, sediento.

adscript ['ædskript], a. escrito después; ligado, subordinado a la tierra; (derecho feudal) siervo, ligio.

adulate ['ædjoleit], v.t. adular, lisonjear.

adulation, s. adulación, lisonja.

adulator, s. adulador, parásito, lisonjero.

adulatory, a. adulador, adulatorio, lisonjero, cumplimentero.

adulatress, s. aduladora, lisonjera.

adult [ə'dʌlt], s., a. adulto.

adulterant s. adulterador, adulterante, falsificador.

adulterate, v.i. adulterar, cometer adulterio. — v.t. adulterar, corromper, impurificar, falsificar, falsear, viciar; sofisticar. — a. adulterino, adulterado, impuro, falso, espurio, corrompido, falsificado; adúltero.

adulterateness, adulteration, s. adulteración, falsificación, contaminación, corrupción, impureza.

adulterer, s. adúltero.

adulteress, s.f. adúltera.

adulterine, s., a. adulterino; espurio.

adulterous, a. adúltero, adulterino, espurio.

adulterously, adv. adúlteramente, adulterinamente.

adultery, s. adulterio; corrupción.

adultness, s. edad adulta.

adumbrant [ə'dʌmbrent], a. bosquejado, trazado, sombreado ligeramente.

adumbrate, v.t. esquiciar, bosquejar, sombrear, delinear, diseñar; prevenir, pronosticar.

adumbration, s. esquicio, trazo, esbozo, bosquejo, diseño; (pint.) adumbración; pronóstico.

aduncity [ə'dʌnsiti], s. corvadura, comba, sinuosidad.

aduncous, a. corvo, encorvado, torcido, ganchoso, sinuoso, adunco.

adust [ə'dʌst], a. adusto, cálido, requemado, consumido; tostado, requemado, abrasado, desecado; moreno, curtido.

adustion, s. adustión, quemadura; inflamación; cauterización.

ad valorem [æd və'lɔːrəm], (com.) por avalúo.

advance [əd'vaːns], v.t. avanzar, adelantar, poner más adelante, pasar adelante; promover; mejorar; ascender; acelerar apresurar; anticipar (dinero), pagar adelantado; sostener; afirmar; encarecer; ofrecer, proponer, insinuar. — v.i. ir adelante, adelantarse; subir (de precio o valor); to advance firmly, echar el pie adelante; to advance in stature, crecer. — s. avance, adelanto, adelantamiento; mejora; progreso, aprovechamiento; suplemento, préstamo; (com.) alza, encarecimiento; (com.) anticipo; insinuación; requerimiento de amores; in advance, de antemano; por adelantado; to get in advance, tomar la delantera; to make the first advances, dar los primeros pasos; advance guard, (mil.) avanzada.

advanced, a. avanzado; precoz.

advancement, s. adelantamiento; progreso, progresión; promoción, ascenso; subida, elevación; prosperidad; (for.) bienes señalados en el contrato matrimonial.

advancer, *s.* promotor; protector; impulsor; adelantador.

advantage [əd'vaːntidʒ], *s.* ventaja, superioridad, preponderancia; pro, provecho, ganancia, aprovechamiento; granjeo, interés, lucro, beneficio; ocasión favorable; valimiento, sobrepaga; prerrogativa; conveniencia, comodidad; *to advantage,* ventajosamente; *to take advantage,* aprovecharse, valerse; engañar; *to have the advantage of,* llevar ventaja a; *advantage-ground,* situación ventajosa, puesto favorable. — *v.t.* aventajar; favorecer, mejorar, proteger, servir; remunerar; promover; adelantar. — *v.i.* medrar, sacar ventaja.

advantageable, advantageous [ædvən'teidʒəs], *a.* provechoso, ventajoso, útil, conveniente, lucrativo, ganancioso.

advantageousness, *s.* ventaja, utilidad, conveniencia.

advent ['ædvənt], *s.* (*igl.*) Adviento; advenimiento, llegada, venida.

adventitious, adventive, *a.* adventicio; accidental, casual; extraño; (*biol.*) advenedizo; (*for.*) adventicio, no hereditario; (*bot.*) formado sin orden, espontáneo.

adventitiously, *adv.* accidentalmente.

adventual, *a.* adventual, casual.

adventure [əd'ventʃəɹ], *s.* aventura, casualidad, contingencia, lance; (*com.*) ancheta, pacotilla. — *v.i.* osar, atreverse, emprender, aventurarse, arriesgarse. — *v.t.* aventurar, arriesgar.

adventurer, *s.* aventurero; (*com.*) pacotillero, anchetero.

adventuresome, *a.* aventurado; aventurero.

adventuresomeness, *s.* audacia, osadía, atrevimiento, temeridad, intrepidez, arrojo.

adventurous, *a.* animoso, valeroso, aventurero, audaz, emprendedor, intrépido, temerario, peligroso, aventurado, osado, arrojado, atrevido, esforzado, arriesgado.

adventurously, *adv.* arriesgadamente, arrojadamente.

adventurousness, *s.* intrepidez, arrojo, osadía, temeridad.

adverb ['ædvəːɹb], *s.* adverbio.

adverbial, *a.* adverbial.

adversary ['ædvəɹsəri], *s.* adversario, contrario, enemigo, antagonista, *m.f.* — *a.* adverso, contrario, opuesto.

adversative [əd'vəːɹsətiv], *a.* adversativo.

adverse ['ædvəːɹs], *a.* adverso, contrario, opuesto; desgraciado; hostil; funesto.

adverseness, *s.* oposición, resistencia, contrariedad.

adversity, *s.* adversidad, desgracia, infortunio, calamidad.

advert [əd'vəːɹt], *v.i.* atender, tener cuidado, hacer reflexión. — *v.t.* cuidar, aconsejar, hacer referencia, advertir, notar, considerar atentamente.

advertence, advertency, *s.* advertencia, prevención, consideración, atención, aviso, observación.

advertent, *a.* atento, vigilante, avisado.

advertise ['ædvəɹtais], *v.t.* advertir, avisar, informar, anunciar, publicar, notificar. — *v.i.* poner un anuncio.

advertised, *a.* advertido, informado, publicado, anunciado. — *p.p.* [ADVERTISE].

advertisement [əd'vəːɹtizmənt], *s.* advertencia, noticia, aviso, anuncio, notificación.

advertiser ['ædvəɹtaizəɹ], *s.* avisador, anunciador, anunciante; diario de avisos.

advertising, *a.* avisador, noticioso; *advertising agent,* agente de publicidad. — *s.* propaganda.

advice [əd'vais], *s.* consejo, dictamen, consultación, deliberación; consulta; conocimiento, reflexión; (*com.*) aviso, informe, noticia; amonestación, advertencia, admonición; opinión, parecer; *to give advice of,* dar aviso de; *letter of advice,* carta de aviso; *advice-boat,* (*mar.*) patache, aviso.

advisability [ədvaizə'biliti], *s.* conveniencia, propiedad.

advisable, *a.* conveniente, aconsejable, prudente, propio.

advisableness, *s.* conveniencia, propiedad, oportunidad, prudencia.

advise [əd'vaiz], *v.t.* aconsejar, dar consejo; guiar, avisar, advertir, apercibir, informar, enterar, notificar, dar noticia; amonestar. — *v.i.* aconsejarse, pedir consejo, tomar consejo; deliberar, considerar, examinar; consultar.

advised, *a.* avisado, aconsejado, advertido, prudente, premeditado, deliberado.

advisedness, *s.* cordura, juicio, prudencia, reflexión, circunspección, deliberación.

advisement, *s.* deliberación, consideración.

adviser, *s.* aconsejador, consejero, advisador, informante, instigador; consultor, monitor, asesor.

advisory, *a.* consultativo.

advocacy ['ædvəkəsi], **advocateship,** *s.* vindicación, defensa, abogacía.

advocate, *v.t.* abogar, defender, sostener, interceder, mediar. — *s.* (*for.*) abogado, letrado; intercesor, favorecedor, medianero, defensor, protector; *devil's advocate,* abogado del diablo.

advocation, *s.* defensa; apología; intercesión; vindicación, apelación.

advowee [ædvou'i], *s.* (*igl.*) patrón, colador.

advowson, *s.* (*igl.*) patronato; colación.

adynamia [ædi'næmiə], *s.* (*med.*) adinamia.

adynamic, *a.* adinámico, débil.

adynamy, *s.* adinamia.

adze [ædz], *s.* azuela. — *v.t.* azolar, desbastar.

ædile ['iːdail], *s.* edil.

ædileship, *s.* edilidad.

ægis ['iːdʒis], *s.* escudo, broquel, égida.

ægyptiacum, *s.* (*vet.*) egipciaco.

æon, *s.* eón.

aerate ['eiəreit], *v.t.* ventilar, airear, dar aire a, renovar el aire de; hacer efervescente; exponer a la acción del aire; impregnar, saturar un líquido de aire o ácido carbónico; arterializar la sangre.

aerated, *a.* gaseoso; *aerated waters,* gaseosa, aguas gaseosas.

aeration, *s.* ventilación; aerificación, aeración.

aerator, *s.* aparato para la aeración.

aerial, *a.* aéreo, de aire; etéreo; atmosférico; (*elec.*) *s.* antena.

aerie, aery, *s.* nido de ave de rapiña; polluelo de estas aves; habitación, refugio colocado a la cima de una roca.

aeriform, *a.* aeriforme.

aerify, *v.t.* (*quím.*) aerificar.

aerodrome, *s.* aeródromo, campo de aterrizaje.

aerodynamics, *s.pl.* aerodinámica.

aerography, *s.* aerografía.

aerolite, aerolith, *s.* aerolito.

aerological, *a.* aerological.
aerologist, *s.* aerólogo.
aerology, *s.* aerología.
aeromancy, *s.* aeromancia.
aerometer, *s.* aerómetro.
aerometric, *a.* aerométrico.
aerometry, *s.* aerometría.
aeronaut, *s.* aeronauta, *m.f.*
aeronautic, *a.* aeronáutico.
aeronautics, *s.* aeronáutica.
aerophoby, *s.* (*med.*) aerofobia.
aerophone, *s.* aerófono.
aeroplane, *s.* aeroplano, avión; *bomber a.*, avión de bombardeo; *fighter a.*, avión de caza, caza, *m.*; *jet a.*, avión de reacción.
aeroscopy, *s.* aeroscopia.
aerostat, *s.* globo aerostático.
aerostatic, *a.* aerostático.
aerostatics, *s.* aerostática.
aerostation, *s.* aerostación.
aeruginous, *a.* herrumbroso, eruginoso, tomado de orín.
aerugo, *s.* orín, moho, óxido del hierro.
æsculapian [eskju:'leipjan], *a.* medicinal.
æsthesia, *s.* estética, teoría de la sensibilidad.
æsthetic [i:s'θetik], *a.* estético.
æsthetics, *s.* estética.
æstival, estival ['estivəl], *a.* estival; estivo, lo que dura todo el estío.
ætiology [i:ti'olədʒi], *s.* etiología.
aetites, *s.* (*min.*) etites.
afar [ə'fa:ɹ], *adv.* lejos, distante, a gran distancia; *from afar*, de lejos, desde lejos; *afar off*, lejos; muy distante, remoto.
afeard [ə'fi:ɹd], *a.* (*ant.*) (*vulg.*) espantado, atemorizado, temeroso, miedoso.
affability [æfə'biliti], *s.* afabilidad, amabilidad, agrado, dulzura, suavidad, cortesanía, urbanidad.
affable, *a.* afable, amable, agradable, atento, cortés.
affableness, *s.* afabilidad, dulzura, cariño.
affair [ə'fɛəɹ], *s.* negocio, asunto; acción, lance; cuestión; (*mil.*) acción, encuentro; *affair of honour*, lance de honor; *it's no affair of his*, no tiene nada que ver con él; *that's his affair*, con su pan se lo coma.
affect [ə'fekt], *v.t.* afectar, impresionar, conmover, enternecer; obrar, causar efecto (en el ánimo); aspirar, anhelar; amar, tener afición; fingir, aparentar; influir, mover; dañar, atacar; perjudicar; frecuentar; habitar; simular; *to affect grief*, llorar con un ojo.
affectation [æfek'teiʃən], *s.* afectación, artificio, afección; dengue.
affected [ə'fektəd], *a.* afectado, denguero; remilgado, relamido; impresionado, emocionado, conmovido, enternecido. — *p.p.* [AFFECT].
affectedness, *s.* afectación, fingimiento.
affecter, *s.* afectador, fingidor.
affecting, *a.* sensible, tierno, interesante, lastimero, lastimoso, patético, conmovedor.
affectingly, *adv.* tiernamente, patéticamente.
affectingness, *s.* facultad de afectar, conmover.
affection, *s.* afección; afecto, amor, afición, cariño, dilección, querencia; impresión; inclinación; benevolencia; (*med.*) dolencia, enfermedad; cualidad, propiedad.
affectionate, *a.* cariñoso, afectuoso, amoroso, aficionado, expresivo, querencioso, benévolo, prendado.

affectionateness, *s.* afecto, cariño, afectuosidad.
affectioned, *a.* (*ant.*) afectado, dispuesto, inclinado, aficionado, vanidoso.
affective, *a.* afectivo, tierno, patético, conmovedor.
afferent ['æfərənt], *a.* (*biol.*) aferente.
affiance [ə'faiəns], *s.* esponsales, palabra de casamiento, contrato matrimonial; confianza, fe, *f.* — *v.t.* firmar los esponsales; *affianced bride*, novia, prometida.
affianced, *s.*, *a.* prometido.
affiant, *s.* (*for.*) deponente, declarante.
affidavit [æfi'deivit], *s.* (*for.*) declaración jurada; atestación, certificación.
affiliable, *a.* afiliable.
affiliate [ə'filieit], *v.t.* prohijar, adoptar; afiliar, ahijar.
affiliated, *a.* prohijado, reconocido, afiliado.
affiliation, *s.* adopción, afiliación; (*for.*) legitimación de un hijo.
affined [ə'faind], *a.* afín.
affinity [ə'finiti], *s.* afinidad, parentesco; conformidad, conexión.
affirm [ə'fə:ɹm], *v.t.* afirmar, asegurar, sostener, aseverar, cerciorar, asentar, certificar, declarar; confirmar, ratificar. — *v.i.* afirmarse; declarar formalmente.
affirmable, *a.* que se puede afirmar.
affirmance, *s.* afirmación, declaración; confirmación, ratificación.
affirmant, *s.* afirmador, firmante; (*for.*) declarante.
affirmation, *s.* afirmación, aserción, aserto, confirmación, ratificación; (*for.*) declaración.
affirmative, *a.* afirmativo. — *s.* aserción, afirmativa; *to reply in the affirmative*, contestar que sí.
affirmatory, *a.* asertorio.
affirmer, *s.* afirmante.
affix [ə'fiks], *v.t.* fijar, hincar, clavar; aplicar, colocar; pegar, unir, ligar; adaptar; añadir. — *s.* (*gram.*) afijo, sufijo; añadidura.
affixer, *s.* pegador.
affixture, *s.* ligatura, adición.
afflation [ə'fleiʃən], *s.* aliento, respiración, inspiración, resuello.
afflatus, *s.* hálito, aliento; (*fig.*) estro, aflato, inspiración, impulso poético.
afflict [ə'flikt], *v.t.* afligir, contristar, acongojar, atribular, angustiar, desconsolar, aquejar, acuitar, desazonar, causar dolor, pena o sentimiento; oprimir, inquietar, atormentar.
afflicter, *s.* atormentador, opresor; azote.
afflicting, *a.* penoso, devorador, atormentador.
affliction, *s.* aflicción, dolor, calamidad, pena, miseria, sentimiento, tribulación, angustia, desconsuelo, pesadumbre; luto, duelo; azote, plaga.
afflictive, *a.* aflictivo, lastimoso, penoso, gravoso, molesto.
affluence ['æfluəns], *s.* afluencia, aflujo, concurrencia; abundancia, copia, opulencia.
affluent, *a.* (*med.*) fluente; afluente, abundante, copioso; rico, opulento. — *s.* afluente.
afflux ['æflʌks], **affluxion,** *s.* fluxión, flujo; afluencia, aflujo; gentío, concurrencia.
afford [ə'foəɹd], *v.t.* dar, proporcionar, producir, conceder; proveer, suplir, abastecer; tener medios (*o* recursos) para; soportar; hacer frente; *to afford an opportunity*, dar

margen; *I cannot afford it*, está fuera del alcance de mis medios.

afforest [əˈfɔrəst], *v.t.* plantar (un bosque).

afforestation, *s.* plantío, plantación, la plantación de un bosque.

affranchise [əˈfræntʃais], *v.t.* manumitir, dar libertad a.

affranchisement, *s.* manumisión.

affray [əˈfrei], *s.* asalto, pendencia, refriega, riña, combate, tumulto. — *v.t.* asustar, espantar.

affreight [əˈfreit], *v.t.* fletar.

affreighter, *s.* fletador.

affreightment, *s.* fletamiento.

affright [əˈfrait], *v.t.* aterrar, espantar, atemorizar, asustar. — *s.* terror, espanto, pánico, susto.

affrighted, *a.* aterrorizado, asustado, atemorizado.

affrightedly, *adv.* temerosamente, con espanto.

affrighter, *s.* asombrador, espantador, el que da miedo o espanta.

affrightment, *s.* terror, espanto.

affront [əˈfrʌnt], *v.t.* afrentar, insultar, denostar, denigrar, provocar, ultrajar; arrostrar, hacer frente. — *s.* afrenta, provocación, ultraje, injuria, insulto, denuesto, agravio, sonrojo.

affronter, *s.* agresor, provocador.

affronting, affrontive, *a.* injurioso, provocativo, afrentoso, ultrajante.

affusion [əˈfjuːʒən], *s.* afusión, aspersión.

Afghan, *s., a.* afgano.

afield [əˈfiːld], *adv.* en el campo; a campo travieso; ausente, a fuera; lejos; fuera del país.

afire [əˈfaiəɹ], *adv.* en fuego, abrasado, ardiendo, encendido, inflamado.

aflame [əˈfleim], *adv.* en llamas.

aflat, *adv.* a nivel del suelo, tendidamente.

afloat [əˈflout], *adv.* (*mar.*) flotante, a flote, a nado, a flor de agua; a bordo; (*fig.*) sin deudas, solvente, sin dificultades; en circulación, corriente.

afoot [əˈfut], *adv.* a pie; en movimiento, en vía de ejecución, en preparación.

afore [əˈfoəɹ], *prep., adv.* (*ant.*) antes, anticipadamente; delante, en frente; (*mar.*) a proa.

aforegoing, *a.* antecedente, precedente.

aforehand, *adv.* de antemano; con preparación.

aforementioned, aforenamed, aforesaid, *a.* susodicho, ya dicho, ya mencionado, sobredicho, antedicho, supracitado, precitado, expresado, consabido.

aforethought, *a.* premeditado; *with malice aforethought*, con premeditación.

aforetime, *adv.* en otro tiempo, en tiempo pasado, antiguamente.

afoul [əˈfaul], *adv.* (*mar.*) en colisión, enredado.

afraid [əˈfreid], *a.* atemorizado, amedrentado, temeroso, tímido, intimidado, espantado.

afresh [əˈfreʃ], *adv.* de nuevo, otra vez.

afront [əˈfrʌnt], *adv.* en frente, al frente, de cara.

aft [aːft], *adv.* (*mar.*) a popa, en popa; *to haul down the mizzen sheet aft*, (*mar.*) cazar del todo la escota de mesana.

after [ˈaːftəɹ], *prep.* después de, tras, detrás de, en seguimiento de; por; según; *the day after to-morrow*, pasado mañana; *day after day*, día por día, cada día; *after the manner*, según,

a la manera de. — *adv.* después, en seguida; *after all*, después de todo; bien pensado todo, considerándolo todo; *soon after*, poco después; *the day after*, el día siguiente; *a long way after*, muy lejos; muy inferior a. — *a.* posterior, ulterior, subsiguiente; *after* se usa en muchas voces compuestas, generalmente en el sentido de después.

after-account, *s.* cuenta nueva.

after-act, *s.* acto subsiguiente.

after-age, *s.* posteridad, tiempo venidero; *after-ages*, tiempos, siglos venideros.

after-attack, *s.* ataque o choque subsiguiente.

after-birth, *s.* secundinas, *f.pl.*; placenta.

after-clap, *s.* golpe inesperado, revés; repetición de un accidente, lance o acción, cuando se creyó terminada la acción principal.

after-comer, *s.* sucesor.

after-crop, *s.* segunda cosecha.

after-damp, *s.* (*min.*) mofeta.

after-dinner, *s.* sobremesa. — *a.* después de comer; *after-dinner sleep*, siesta; *after-dinner speech*, discurso de sobremesa.

after-game, *s.* revancha, desquite, despique.

after-gathering, *s.* espigadura.

after-glow, *s.* resplandor crepuscular.

after-grass, *s.* segunda yerba, segunda cosecha de heno.

after-hope, *s.* esperanza renovada.

after-hours, *s.* deshora, horas extraordinarias.

after-inquiry, *s.* investigación ulterior, examen posterior.

after-law, *s.* ley posterior.

after-life, *s.* en el resto de la vida; vida venidera.

after-math, *s.* segunda siega; (*fig.*) consecuencias.

aftermost, *a.* (*mar.*) último, postrero.

afternoon, *s.* tarde.

after-pains, *s.pl.* (*med.*) entuertos, dolores de sobreparto.

afterpiece, *s.* (*teat.*) sainete, entremés.

after-supper, *a.* después de la cena.

after-taste, *s.* resabio, dejo, gustillo; (*fam.*) sinsabor, pesar, disgusto, mortificación.

after-thought, *s.* reflexión tardía; nueva idea; reparo. — *adv.* con madura reflexión.

after-times, *s.pl.* tiempos venideros, porvenir.

after-touch, *s.* (*pint.*) retoque.

afterward, *a.* (*mar.*) popel.

afterwards, *adv.* después, enseguida, más tarde, en lo venidero; *long afterwards*, mucho tiempo después.

again [əˈgein], *adv.* otra vez, de nuevo, segunda vez, aún, más; además, por otra parte, luego; del mismo modo, recíprocamente; *again and again*, muchas veces, un sinnúmero de veces, repetidas veces, repetidamente; *as much again*, otra vez tanto; otro tanto más; *to do again*, volver a hacer; *come again to-morrow*, vuelva Vd. mañana; *give it to me again*, devuélvamelo.

against [əˈgeinst], *prep.* contra; enfrente; junto, cerca; *over against*, en frente de; *against time*, para ganar tiempo; *to run against*, tropezar con; *against the grain*, a contrapelo.

agamous [əˈgæməs], *a.* (*biol.*) asexual.

agape [əˈgeip], *adv.* de hito en hito, con la boca abierta. — *s.* ágape.

agaric [ˈægərik], *s.* (*bot.*) agárico, garzo.

agate [ˈægeit], *s.* (*min.*) ágata; (*impr.*) caracter de letra de 5½ puntos: se llama *ruby* en Inglaterra.

agate [æ'geit], *adv.* (*prov.*) en camino, en marcha; en movimiento.

agave [ə'geivi], *s.* (*bot.*) agave, pita, maguey.

agaze [ə'geiz], *adv.* en el acto de mirar.

age [eidʒ], *s.* edad; era, evo, siglo; generación; época, tiempo, período; vejez, senectud. — *v.t.*, *v.i.* envejecer; *full age*, mayoría, edad mayor; *golden age*, siglo de oro; *under age*, menor de edad; *tender age*, primera edad; *to come of age*, llegar a la mayoría de edad.

aged ['eidʒəd], *a.* viejo, envejecido, anciano, cargado de años; de la edad de.

agedly, *adv.* como un viejo; a manera de viejo.

agency ['eidʒənsi], *s.* dirección, acción, operación, obra, agencia; intervención, diligencia, gestión, mediación, influencia; medio, fuerza; factoraje; órgano; *free agency*, libre albedrío.

agenda [ə'dʒendə], *s.* agenda.

agent ['eidʒənt], *s.* operativo; agente, comisionista, *m.f.*, comisionado, encargado, factor, delegado, diputado; asistente, apoyo; mediador; (*for.*) mandatario, apoderado. — *a.* operativo.

agentship, *s.* agencia, factoría; el oficio de agente o factor.

agglomerate [ə'gloməreit], *v.t.* aglomerar, amontonar; ovillar. — *v.i.* aglomerarse, amontonarse. — *a.* aglomerado.

agglomeration, *s.* aglomeración, amontonamiento.

agglutinant [ə'gluːtinənt], *a.* conglutinativo, aglutinativo, aglutinante.

agglutinants, *s.pl.* aglutinantes.

agglutinate, *v.t.* conglutinar, aglutinar, pegar, unir.

agglutination, *s.* conglutinación, aglutinación, ligazón, *f.*, trabazón, *f.*

agglutinative, *a.* conglutinativo, aglutinativo, aglutinante, adhesivo.

aggrandize ['ægrəndaiz], *v.t.* agrandar, engrandecer; elevar, exaltar; *to aggrandize oneself*, elevarse. — *v.i.* acrecentarse, aumentarse.

aggrandizement, *s.* engrandecimiento, elevación, exaltación.

aggrandizer, *s.* ensalzador; favorecedor.

aggravate ['ægrəveit], *v.t.* agravar, hacer más enorme, exagerar; hacer menos excusable; amplificar, aumentar; hacer más pesada o dolorosa alguna cosa; irritar, fatigar, molestar, exasperar.

aggravating, *a.* agravante, provocativo, irritante.

aggravation, *s.* agravación, agravamiento, exageración, enormidad; provocación, vejación; inflamación, irritación.

aggregate ['ægrəgeit], *a.* agregado, juntado, unido; colectivo. — *s.* colección, agregado; conjunto, masa, totalidad, total, suma; *in the aggregate*, por junto. — *v.t.* agregar, juntar, unir; ascender a, sumar.

aggregately, *adv.* colectivamente, en junto.

aggregation, *s.* agregación, agregado, colección; conjunto, masa, total.

aggregative, *a.* colectivo, junto.

aggress [ə'gres], *v.i.* lanzar un ataque, empezar una pendencia, ofender. — *v.t.* atacar, acometer, asaltar.

aggression, *s.* agresión, ataque, acometimiento, asalto.

aggressive, *a.* agresivo.

aggressiveness, *s.* carácter agresivo.

aggressor, *s.* agresor, atacador, provocador.

aggrieve [ə'griːv], *v.t.* apenar, afligir, apesadumbrar, vejar, oprimir, gravar, dañar, cometer una injusticia.

aggroup, *v.t.* agrupar.

aghast [ə'gaːst], *a.* espantado, horrorizado, despavorido, estupefacto, fuera de sí, azorado, atolondrado de horror; (*fam.*) con la boca abierta.

agile ['ædʒail], *a.* ágil, ligero, pronto, vivo, expedito.

agileness, agility, *s.* agilidad, soltura, ligereza, prontitud, expedición.

agio ['ædʒiə], *s.* (*com.*) agio, agiotaje.

agistment [ə'dʒistmənt], *s.* pasturaje.

agistor, *s.* (*for.*) guardabosque.

agitable, *a.* agitable, discutible.

agitate, *v.t.* agitar, mover, afectar, conmover; maquinar, imaginar; discutir, disputar, debatir; inquietar, perturbar; alborotar, traquetear.

agitation, *s.* agitación; discusión, ventilación, deliberación; perturbación.

agitator, *s.* agitador, incitador, promotor, instigador, perturbador, revolvedor; (*pol.*) agente provocador.

agleam [ə'gliːm], *a.* (*poét.*) fulguroso, centellante.

aglet ['æglət], **aiglet** ['eiglət], *s.* herrete; lámina u hoja de metal; (*bot.*) antera.

aglow [ə'glou], *a.* encendido en llamas; incandescente; ardiente, brillante.

agnail ['ægneil], *s.* panadizo, uñero.

agnate ['ægneit], *s.* (*for.*) agnado.

agnatic, *a.* agnaticio.

agnation, *s.* agnación, parentesco por la línea masculina.

agnize, *v.t.* reconocer.

agnomination [ægnɔmi'neiʃən], *s.* sobrenombre; agnominación; (*ret.*) aliteración, paronomasia.

agnostic [æg'nɔstik], *s.*, *a.* agnóstico.

agnosticism, *s.* agnosticismo.

ago [ə'gou], *adv.* pasado; hace, ha; largo tiempo, después; *some time ago*, hace algún tiempo; *long ago*, hay mucho tiempo, mucho tiempo ha; *how long ago?* ¿cuánto ha?; *a good while ago*, hace ya algún tiempo.

agog [ə'gɔg], *a.* excitado; ansioso, curioso. — *adv.* ansiosamente, con curiosidad, con deseo, con antojo, con apresuramiento; *to be agog*, estar ansioso; *to set agog*, animar, excitar.

agoing [ə'gouiŋ], *adv.* a punto, dispuesto; en acción, en marcha, en movimiento.

agometer, *s.* (*elec.*) agómetro.

agonic, *a.* agónico, lo que no tiene ángulos.

agonism ['ægɔnism], *s.* agonística; lucha.

agonist, agonistes, *s.* atleta, *m.f.*, combatiente, competidor.

agonistic, agonistical, *a.* atlético, agonal, agonístico.

agonistics, *s.* agonística.

agonize, *v.i.* agonizar, luchar desesperadamente, estar en el tormento. — *v.t.* atormentar, martirizar.

agonizing, *a.* doloroso, agudo, atroz.

agony, *s.* agonía, angustia, zozobra, paroxismo, aflicción extrema; *agony column*, sección de pequeños anuncios personales (en periódico).

agouti [ə'guːti], *s.* (*zool.*) agutí.

agraffe [ə'græf], *s.* broche, grapa.

agrarian [ə'grɛəriən], *a.* agrario; agreste, selvático.

agree [ə'griː], *v.i.* convenir, concordar, concertar, acordar, entenderse, ponerse de acuerdo; ceder; estipular, ajustar; probar; acomodar; acomodarse; sentar bien, asentar; acceder, consentir, avenirse a. — *v.t.* armonizar, reconciliar, acomodar; *to agree together to do something,* quedar en hacer una cosa.

agreeability, *s.* afabilidad, agrado, complacencia.

agreeable, *a.* ameno, dulce, agradable, grato, afable, placentero, deleitoso; conveniente, concorde, proporcionado, conforme; amable.

agreeableness, *s.* conformidad, proporción; afabilidad, agrado; amabilidad; placibilidad, deleite; semejanza.

agreeably, *adv.* agradablemente; conformemente; según, conforme.

agreed, *a.* convenido, determinado, acordado, avenido, establecido, aprobado, ajustado, admitido, aceptado; de acuerdo. — *adv.* perfectamente.

agreement, *s.* acuerdo, concordia, conformidad, unión, correlación, conveniencia; semejanza; convenio, pacto, ajuste; transacción, tratado, contrato, acomodamiento, ajustamiento; estipulación; *by mutual agreement,* de buenas a buenas; *to reach an agreement,* llegar a un acuerdo.

agrestial [ə'grestjəl], **agrestic, agrestical,** *a.* agreste, rústico, tosco, campestre; descortés, grosero.

agricultor ['ægrikʌltər], *s.* agricultor.

agricultural, *a.* agrícola, de la agricultura, de labranza.

agriculturalist, *s.* agricultor; labrador, agrónomo, agrícola.

agriculture, *s.* agricultura.

agriculturism, *s.* geoponía, agricultura.

agriculturist, *s.* agricultor, labrador, agrónomo, agrícola, *m.f.*

agrimony ['ægriməni], *s.* (*bot.*) agrimonia.

agriot, *s.* (*bot.*) guinda.

agronomic [ægrə'nɔmik], *a.* agronómico.

agronomics, agronomy, *s.* agronomía, ciencia agrícola.

agrope [ə'group], *adv.* a tientas.

aground [ə'graund], *adv.* (*mar.*) barado, encallado; (*fig.*) empantanado, embarazado; *to run aground,* (*mar.*) encallar, dar en un bajío; (*fig.*) fracasar, salir mal de un negocio.

ague ['eigjuː], *s.* (*med.*) fiebre intermitente, *f.*; calofrío, escalofrío; *tertian ague,* fiebre terciana; *quartan ague,* fiebre cuartana.

ague-tree, *s.* (*bot.*) sasafrás.

aguish ['eigjuːiʃ], *a.* febricitante, calenturiento; palúdico; febril.

aguishness, *s.* paludismo; calofrío, estado febril.

ah! *interj.* ¡ah! ¡ay!

aha! *interj.* ¡ajá!

ahead [ə'hed], *adv.* más allá, delante, hacia delante; adelante, al frente; (*mar.*) por la proa, avante; *to be ahead,* ir a la cabeza, ir delante; *to get ahead,* adelantarse, ganar la delantera; *go ahead!* ¡adelante!; *to run ahead,* obrar sin reflexión.

aheap [ə'hiːp], *adv.* en montón.

ahem! *interj.* empleada para llamar la atención o ganar tiempo.

ahoy! [ə'hɔi], *interj.* (*mar.*) ¡ahó! ¡ha! ¡ah del barco!

ahull [ə'hʌl], *adv.* (*mar.*) con las velas recogidas, y el timón amarrado al viento.

ahungered [ə'hʌŋgəɹd], **ahungry,** *a.* hambriento, con hambre.

aid [eid], *v.t.* ayudar, auxiliar, socorrer, coadyuvar, apoyar, conllevar, subvenir, sufragar. — *s.* ayuda, asistencia, auxilio, socorro, favor, amparo, subsidio; asistente, ayudante, auxiliante; *first aid,* (*med.*) cura de primera intención; *first-aid post,* casa de socorro.

aide-de-camp, *s.* (*mil.*) ayudante de campo, edecán.

aider, *s.* (*ant.*) ayuda, auxiliare, auxiliador.

aidful, *a.* servicial, compasivo.

aidless, *a.* (*ant.*) desvalido, desamparado, sin ayuda, sin asistencia.

aiglet, *s.* herrete de agujeta o franja.

aigret ['eigret], **aigrette,** *s.* cresta, penacho; (*orn.*) garceta.

ail [eil], *v.t.* afligir, molestar, aquejar, apenar; *what ails you?* ¿Qué le duele a Vd.? ¿qué tiene Vd.? ¿qué hay? — *v.i.* sufrir, estar enfermo, estar indispuesto.

ailing, *a.* doliente, achacoso, enfermizo, malucho.

ailment, *s.* dolencia, indisposición, incomodidad, dolor.

aim [eim], *v.t.* apuntar; tirar, lanzar; asestar, encarar; dirigir. — *v.i.* aspirar, pretender. — *s.* puntería; encaro; blanco, hito; designio, mira; *to take aim at,* encarar, apuntar; *to miss one's aim,* errar el tiro; *to take one's aim well,* tomar bien sus medidas.

aimer, *s.* (*artill.*) puntero.

aimless, *a.* sin objeto, sin designio, a la ventura.

ain't (eint), *contr. vulg.* de *am not, is not,* o *are not.*

air [ɛəɹ], *s.* aire, viento ligero; atmósfera; gas, vapor; aura, zéfiro; exterior, modo; ademán; (*mús.*) tonada; cara, semblante; ademán, porte; *to take the air,* tomar el fresco; *in the open air,* al raso; *to build castles in the air,* hacer castillos en el aire; *open air,* aire libre; *foul air,* aire viciado; *to give oneself airs,* ponerse hueco. — *v.t.* airear, secar, poner el aire, orear, ventilar.

air-balloon, *s.* globo aerostático.

air-bladder, *s.* vejiga llena de aire.

air-born, *a.* (*poét.*) nacido del aire.

air-borne, *a.* llevado por el aire; *to become air-borne,* despegar.

air-brake, *s.* freno neumático.

air-built, *a.* quimérico.

air-cell, *s.* (*bot.*) célula llena de aire.

air-chamber, *s.* cámara de aire.

aircraft, *s.* avión; *aircraft-carrier,* portaaviones, *m. sing.*

air-cushion, *s.* cojín de aire.

air-drill, *s.* taladro de aire comprimido, taladro neumático.

air-field, *s.* campo de aviación.

air force, *s.* fuerza aérea.

air-gun, *s.* escopeta de viento.

air-hole, *s.* respiradero, resolladero, zarcera; registro de hornillo.

airified, *a.* aéreo; ligero, trivial; fútil.

airily, *adv.* ligeramente, vivamente, alegremente.

airiness, *s.* ventilación, oreo; vivacidad, viveza, ligereza, actividad.

airing, s. paseo; ventilación, renovación del aire; caminata, paseata.
air-jacket, s. chaqueta de natación, salvavidas, m.
airless, a. sofocado, falto de ventilación.
air-like, a. ligero como el aire.
air-line, s. línea aérea.
air-mail, s. correo aéreo.
airman, s. aviador.
air-mattress, s. colchón de viento.
air-pipe, s. tubo de ventilación.
air-pocket, s. bache.
air-port, s. aeropuerto.
air-pump, s. bomba de aire, bomba neumática.
air raid, s. bombardeo aéreo.
air-shaft, s. respiradero de mina.
air-ship, s. aeronave, f.
air-stirring, a. que agita el aire.
air-stove, s. aparato de calefacción.
air-tight, a. herméticamente cerrado.
air-trap, s. ventilador, válvula de inodoro.
air-tube, s. portaviento, tubo de ventilación.
air-valve, s. válvula de viento.
air-vessel, s. recipiente de aire.
airy, a. aéreo, ligero, gracioso, esbelto; vano, ilusorio, visionario, quimérico; trivial; fútil; vivaz, alegre; altanero, orgulloso.
aisle [ail], s. (arquit.) ala, nave lateral, costado; pasillo, pasadizo.
aisled, a. que tiene alas, pasillos o naves.
ait [eit], s. isleta en un río.
ajar [ə'dʒaːɹ], a. entreabierto, entornado; en desacuerdo.
akimbo [ə'kimbou], adv. arqueado; en jarras, en asas; to place the arms akimbo, ponerse en jarras.
akin [ə'kin], a. consanguíneo, emparentado; coherente; análogo, homogéneo, semejante, del mismo género.
alabaster ['æləbæstəɹ], s. alabastro. — a. alabastrino.
alack! [ə'læk], **alack-a-day!** (ant.) ¡ay! ¡ay de mí! ¡qué pena! ¡qué lástima!
alacrity [ə'lækriti], s. alegría, buen humor; presteza, alacridad.
alamode [ala'moud], s. humillo, tela fina de seda negra.
alar ['eiləɹ], a. alado, alígero.
alarm [ə'laːɹm], v.t. alarmar, asustar, sorprender; turbar, perturbar, inquietar. — s. alarma, sobresalto, tumulto, alboroto, rebato.
alarm-bell, s. campana de rebato.
alarm-clock, s. despertador.
alarm-gun, s. cañón de rebato.
alarming, a. alarmante; turbativo; sorprendente.
alarmingly, adv. de una manera alarmante, temerosamente, espantosamente.
alarmist, s. alarmista, m.f.
alarm-post, s. atalaya; punto de reunión en caso de rebato.
alarum [ə'lærəm], s. rebato; despertador.
alary ['eilori], a. perteneciente a las alas.
alas! interj. ¡ay!
alate ['eileit], **alated,** a. alado, con alas.
alaternus, (bot.) alaterno, ladierno.
alb ['ælb], s. (igl.) alba, túnica de lienzo blanco.
Albanian, a. albanés, -esa.
albatross ['ælbətrɔs], s. (orn.) albatros.
albeit [ɔːl'biːit], adv., conj. aunque, bien que, no obstante, sin embargo, con todo.
albescent [æl'besənt], a. blanquecino, argentado.

albino [æl'biːnou], s. albino.
albinism, s. albinismo.
album ['ælbəm], s. álbum, librito de memoria.
albumen [æl'bjuːmən], **albumin,** s. (quím.) albúmina, claro de huevo; (bot.) albumen.
albuminoid, a. (med.) albuminoideo. — s.pl. albuminoides.
albuminose, albuminous, a. albuminado, albuminoso.
albuminuric, a. albuminoso.
alburnum [æl'bəːrnəm], a. (bot.) alburno, albura.
alcaic [æl'keiːik], s., a. alcaico.
alcayde, s. alcaide.
alcedo, s. (orn.) martín pescador.
alchemic [æl'kemik], **alchemical,** a. alquímico.
alchemist, s. alquimista, m.f.
alchemistical, a. perteneciente a los alquimistas.
alchemize, v.t. transmutar, convertir.
alchemy, s. alquimia, crisopeya.
alcohol ['ælkəhɔl], s. alcohol.
alcoholate, a. (med.) alcoholato.
alcoholic, a. alcohólico.
alcoholism, s. alcoholismo.
alcoholization, s. alcoholización.
alcoholize, v.t. alcoholar, alcoholizar.
alcoholmeter, alcoholometer, s. alcoholímetro.
Alcoran [ælkɔ'raɪn], s. Alcorán.
alcove ['ælkouv], s. alcoba, retrete; gabinete; glorieta.
aldehyde ['ældiːhaid], s. (quím.) aldehido.
aldehydic, a. aldehídrico.
alder ['ɔːldəɹ], s. (bot.) aliso.
alderman, s. (pl. aldermen) este cargo no existe en la organización municipal española: corresponde casi a Teniente de Alcalde.
aldermanlike, aldermanly, a., adv. magisterial(mente), a manera de regidor, gravemente.
ale [eil], s. cerveza.
aleak [ə'liːk], adv. goteando, derramándose.
ale-bench [eil-bentʃ], s. mostrador de taberna.
ale-brewer, s. cervecero.
ale-conner, s. inspector de cervecerías.
a-lee [əli:], adv. (mar.) a sotavento.
ale-fed, a. alimentado con cerveza.
ale-house, s. cervecería, taberna.
alembic [ə'lembik], s. alambique.
ale-pot, s. jarro de cerveza.
alert [ə'ləːɹt], a. alerta, cuidadoso, vigilante; activo, vivo, dispuesto. — s. (mil.) sorpresa; alarma; on the alert, sobre aviso; en guardia; to be on the alert, abrir el ojo.
alertly, adv. alertamente, vivamente, con actividad.
alertness, s. cuidado, vigilancia; diligencia, actividad; viveza, agilidad.
ale-vat, s. cuba en que fermenta la cerveza.
ale-wife, s. cervecera; pez norteamericano parecido a un sábalo.
alexanders [ælek'sændəɹs], s. (bot.) esmirnio, apio caballar.
Alexandrian, Alexandrine, s., a. alejandrino.
alga ['ælgə], s. (pl. algæ) (bot.) alga.
algal, a. algáceo.
algebra ['ældʒəbrə], s. álgebra.
algebraic [ældʒə'breiik], **algebraical,** a. algebraico.
algebraist, s. algebrista, m.f.

Algerian [æl'dʒiːriən], **Algerine**, s., a. arge- lino.
algid ['ældʒid], a. (med.) álgido.
algidity, s. (med.) algidez, frío, calofrío.
algoid ['ælgɔid], a. parecido al alga.
algorithm, s. algoritmo.
algous ['ælgəs], a. algoso, lleno de algas.
alguazil [ælgwa'zil], s. alguacil, corchete, esbirro.
alias ['eiliæs], adv. de otro modo; por otro nombre. — s. apodo, nombre supuesto, alias.
alibi ['ælibai], s. (for.) coartada; to prove an alibi, probar la coartada.
alible, a. alimenticio, nutritivo.
alien ['eiliən], a. ajeno, extraño; extranjero, forastero; remoto; contrario, discorde. — s. forastero, extranjero.
alienability, s. alienabilidad.
alienable, a. enajenable, traspasable.
alienate, v.t. enajenar, traspasar, transferir, ceder; desviar; malquistar, extrañar, indisponer. — a. ajeno, opuesto.
alienation, s. enajenamiento, extrañamiento; (med.) alienación, descarrío, enajenación; desapropio; alejamiento, desunión, frialdad, desavenencia, desvío; locura.
alienator, s. enajenador.
alienee, s. (for.) persona a quien pasa la propiedad de una cosa.
alienism, s. (med.) frenopatía; estado legal de un extranjero.
alienist, s. (med.) alienista, m.f.
aliferous [ə'lifərəs], a. alígero, alado.
aliform, a. aliforme.
aligerous [ə'lidʒərəs], a. alígero, alado.
alight [ə'lait], v.i. descender, bajar, apearse, posarse, caer, descargar. — a. encendido, iluminado.
align [ə'lain], v.t. alinear, poner en línea.
alignment, s. alineamiento; línea.
alike [ə'laik], a. semejante, igual, parecido, símil, conforme, uniforme. — adv. igualmente, del mismo modo; a la vez, a la par.
aliment ['æliment], s. alimento, sustento.
alimental, a. nutritivo, alimenticio.
alimentariness, s. alimentación, nutrición.
alimentary, a. nutritivo, alimenticio, alimentoso, jugoso; alimentary canal, tubo digestivo.
alimentation, s. alimentación; provisión de víveres.
alimony ['æliməni], s. pensión alimenticia; (for.) alimentos, asistencias.
aline [ə'lain], v.t. alinear. — v.i. ponerse en línea.
alinement, s. alineación.
aliped ['æliped], a. (hist. nat.) alípede, quiróptero. — s. murciélago.
aliquant ['ælikwənt], s., a. (mat.) alicuanta.
aliquot, a. (mat.) alícuota.
alish, a. acervezado.
alisma, s. (bot.) alisma, lirón.
alive [ə'laiv], a. vivo, viviente, no apagado, activo, alegre; sensible, susceptible; úsase mucho para dar énfasis o ponderar: the best man alive, el mejor hombre que existe.
alkalescence [ælkə'lesəns], **alkalescency**, s. (quím.) alcalescencia.
alkalescent, a. alcalescente.
alkali, s. álcali.
alkalify, v.t. alcalizar, alcalificar, convertir en álcali. — v.i. alcalizarse, alcalificarse.

alkaligenous, a. alcalígeno.
alkalimeter, s. alcalímetro.
alkalimetry, s. alcalimetría.
alkaline, a. alcalino.
alkalinity, s. alcalinidad.
alkalization, s. alcalización.
alkalize, v.t. alcalizar.
alkaloid, s., a. alcaloide.
alkanet, s. (bot.) alcama (o alheña) orcaneta; ancusa; onoquiles.
Alkoran [ælkɔ'raːn], s. Alcorán, Corán.
Alkoranic, **Alkoranish**, a. alcoránico, que se refiere al Corán.
all [ɔːl], a. todo, toda, todos, todas; todo el mundo; all aboard, (f.c.) señores viajeros, al tren; all day, todo el día; at all risks, a todo riesgo; on all fours, a cuatro patas; to go on all fours, ir a gatas; all hail, salud; all told, en junto. — s. todo, conjunto, totalidad; all and singular, (for.) todos y cada uno; at all, de ningún modo; before all, ante todo; once for all, de una vez para siempre. — adv. todo, del todo, completamente, enteramente; all along, todo el tiempo, siempre; all but, casi; it is all one, es todo uno; all the better, tanto mejor; all the worse, tanto peor; all at once, all of a sudden, de golpe, de repente; all right! ¡está bien!; all in the wind, (mar.) en facha; for good and all, enteramente, para siempre; not at all, de ningún modo, nada de eso, no por cierto; by all means, absolutamente, sin duda.
all-abandoned, a. abandonado, desamparado por todos.
all-accomplished, a. cumplido, perfecto, cabal.
all-advised, a. aconsejado de todos.
Allah ['ællə], s. Alá.
all-atoning, a. que expía todo.
allay ['əlei], v.t. aliviar, aquietar, calmar, apaciguar, suavizar, reprimir, mitigar, templar, endulzar. — v.i. aliviarse, moderarse, mitigarse, calmarse.
allayer, s. aliviador, apaciguador, calmante, mitigante.
allayment, s. alivio, descanso, desahogo.
all-beauteous, a. bellísimo, hermosísimo.
all-beholding, a. que ve todo.
all-commanding, a. que manda en todas partes.
all-complying, a. muy complaciente.
all-consuming, a. que gasta todo, consume todo.
all-destroying, a. que arruina todo.
all-divining, a. que pronostica sobre todo.
allegation [ælə'geiʃən], s. alegación, alegato; excusa, disculpa; razón.
allegator, s. alegador, afirmante.
allege [ə'ledʒ], v.t. alegar, afirmar, declarar, sostener.
allegeable, a. (for.) alegable.
alleged, a. alegado, afirmado, declarado.
allegement, s. alegación, alegato.
alleger, s. alegador, afirmante, declarante.
allegiance [ə'liːdʒəns], s. lealtad, fidelidad, sumisión, obediencia; homenaje.
allegiant, a. leal. — s. súbdito.
allegoric [ælə'gɔrik], **allegorical**, a. alegórico.
allegorically, adv. alegóricamente.
allegorist, s. alegorista, m.f.
allegorize, v.t. alegorizar, interpretar alegori-

camente. — *v.i.* discurrir alegóricamente, usar alegorías.

allegorizer, *s.* alegorista, *m.f.*; alegorizador.

allegory, *s.* alegoría.

allegretto, *s.* (*mús.*) alegreto.

allegro [ə'leigrou], *s.* (*mús.*) alegro.

all-eloquent, *a.* elocuentísimo, muy elocuente.

alleluia, *s.* aleluya.

allemande, *s.* (danza) alemana, alemanda.

alleviate [ə'li:vieit], *v.t.* aligerar, aliviar, calmar, aplacar, mitigar; (*fig.*) atenuar.

alleviation, *s.* aligeramiento, alivio, paliativo, calmante, mitigación, atenuación.

alleviative, *s.* paliativo.

alley ['æli], *s.* avenida; calle, *f.*, callejuela, callejón, caminillo; pasillo, pasadizo; *blind alley*, callejón sin salida; *bowling-alley*, boliche, boleo; *alley-way*, callejuela, calle estrecha.

All Fools' Day, *s.* día de engaña-bobos, día de Inocentes (primer día de abril).

all-fours, *s.* imperial (juego de naipes); *to go on all-fours*, andar a gatas, a cuatro pies.

all-hail, *interj.* ¡salud!

all-hallows, *s.* día de Todos los Santos.

all-heal, *s.* (*bot.*) panacea.

alliable, *a.* capaz de aliarse.

alliaceous [æli'eiʃəs], *a.* aliáceo.

alliance [ə'laiəns], *s.* alianza, unión, conexión, fusión, liga; parentela, parentesco.

allies ['ælais], *s.pl.* aliados, confederados.

alligate, *v.t.* ligar, atar, afianzar.

alligation, *s.* (*arit.*) aligación, mezcla; unión, *f.*, ligazón, *f.*, atadura.

alligator ['æligeitər], *s.* caimán; (*Méj.*) lagarto.

alligator-apple, *s.* anona.

alligator-pear, *s.* avocado.

alligator-tree, *s.* liquidámbar.

allineation, alinement, *s.* alineación.

all-in wrestling, *s.* lucha libre.

alliteration [əlitə'reiʃən], *s.* aliteración, paronomasia.

alliterative, *a.* aliterado.

all-knowing, *a.* omniscio, que sabe todo.

allocate ['ælokeit], *v.t.* localizar, señalar, asignar, poner aparte; distribuir, asignar una parte.

allocation, *s.* distribución; cupo, cuota.

allocution, *s.* alocución, arenga, discurso.

allodial [ə'loudiəl], *a.* (*for.*) alodial, independiente.

allodium, *s.* alodio, posesión absoluta.

allonge [ə'londʒ], *s.* (*esgr.*) bote, botonazo, estocada.

allopathic [ælo'pæθik], *a.* (*med.*) alopático.

allopathist [ə'lɔpəθist], *s.* alópata, *m.f.*

allopathy, *s.* alopatía.

allot [ə'lɔt], *v.t.* distribuir, dar, conceder, partir, repartir, asignar, destinar, adjudicar.

allotment, *s.* lote, porción, parte, *f.*; asignación, repartimiento; cuota.

allotropic [ælo'trɔpik], *a.* (*quím.*) alotrópico.

allotropism, allotropy, *s.* (*quím.*) alotropía.

allottable, *a.* repartible.

allottee [ælɔt'i:], *s.* adjudicatario.

allotting, *s.* reparto, repartimiento.

allow [ə'lau], *v.t.* admitir, aceptar; dejar, conceder, consentir, permitir, aprobar, confesar; dar, pagar; abonar en cuenta, descontar, deducir, rebajar, señalar, adjudicar.

allowable, *a.* admisible, permisible, tolerable, lícito, legítimo, justo, permitido.

allowableness, *s.* legitimidad, legalidad, propiedad, permiso, exención.

allowance, *s.* permiso, permisión, concesión; ración; indulgencia; gajes, salario, pensión, abono, mesada, alimentos; asignación; licencia, excusa; (*com.*) descuento, rebaja; *to make allowances*, ser indulgente. — *v.t.* poner la ración; (*med.*) poner a dieta, adietar.

alloxanate [ə'lɔksəneit], *s.* (*quím.*) aloxanato.

alloxanic, *a.* aloxánico.

alloxantin, *s.* aloxantina.

alloy [ə'lɔi], *v.t.* ligar, mezclar, alear (los metales); alterar; juntar. — *s.* ley, quilate del oro, ley de la plata; liga, mezcla, aleación, amalgama.

alloyage, *s.* liga, mezcla, aleación.

alloyed, ligado, mezclado; alterado, falsificado. — *p.p.* [ALLOY].

all-penetrating, *a.* que penetra todo.

all-potent, all-powerful, *a.* omnipotente, todopoderoso.

All Saints, *s.* (día de) Todos los Santos.

All Souls, *s.* (día de) los Difuntos.

allspice ['ɔ:lspais], *s.* (*bot.*) baya o fruta del pimiento de Jamaica.

all-sustaining, *a.* sostenedor, mantenedor de todo.

allude [ə'lju:d], *v.t.* aludir, insinuar; (*fam. incorrecto*) referirse.

allure [ə'ljuəɪ], *v.t.* halagar, alucinar, cebar, seducir, atraer, fascinar, tentar.

allured, halagado, atraído, alucinado. — *p.p.* [ALLURE].

allurement, *s.* halago, incentivo, cebo, seducción, atractivo, lisonja, aliciente, añagaza.

allurer, *s.* halagador, seductor, engañador.

alluring, *a.* seductor, engañador, halagüeño, atractivo, atrayente, tentador.

alluringness, *s.* atractivo, aliciente, incentivo, agrado.

allusion [ə'lju:ʒən], *s.* alusión, indirecta sugestión, insinuación.

allusive, *a.* alusivo.

allusiveness, *s.* calidad de ser alusivo.

alluvial [ə'lju:viəl], *a.* aluvial.

alluvion, *s.* aluvión, terrero; inundación; avenida; derrubio.

alluvium, *s.* derrubio, terreno aluvial.

all-wise, *a.* sapientísimo, infinitamente sabio.

ally [ə'lai], *v.t.* hacer alianza; concordar, poner en relación. — *v.r.* aliarse, confederarse. — *s.* ['ælai] aliado, confederado; allegado, pariente.

almagest ['ælmədʒest], *s.* almagesto.

almagra [əl'mægrə], *s.* almagre.

almanac ['ælmənæk], *s.* almanaque, calendario.

almanac-maker, *s.* almanaquero, calendarista.

almandine ['ælməndin], *s.* (*mín.*) almandina.

almightiness, *s.* omnipotencia.

almighty [ɔ:l'maiti], *a.* omnipotente, todopoderoso; *the Almighty*, Dios, el Todopoderoso.

almond ['amənd], *s.* almendra, alloza; almendro, allozo; *sugar almonds*, almendras garapiñadas; *almonds of the throat*, (*anat.*) amígdalas.

almond-oil, *s.* aceite de almendras.

almond-paste, *s.* pasta de almendras.

almond-tree, almendro, allozo.

almond-willow, *s.* (*bot.*) especie de sauce.

almoner ['ælmənəɹ], s. limosnero.
almonry, s. sitio donde se distribuye limosna; habitación de un limosnero.
almost ['ɔːlmoust], adv. casi, cerca de.
alms [aːms], s. limosna, caridad, pitanza; to give alms, hacer limosna, dar limosna; alms-basket, cesto para limosna; alms-box, alms-chest, s. cepillo (o caja) de limosnas.
almsdeed, s. caridad, limosna, obra de caridad.
almsgiver, s. limosnero.
almsgiving, s. caridad.
almshouse, s. hospicio, casa de caridad, asilo de pobres, casa de misericordia.
almsman, s. mendigo, pordiosero, pobre.
almug-tree ['ælmʌg-triː], s. sándalo.
alnage ['ælnidʒ], s. medición por anas.
aloe ['ælou], s. áloe, lináloe; azabara o zábila.
aloes, s., áloe, acíbar; zábida, zábila.
aloetic [ælo'etik], **aloetical**, a. aloético.
aloft [ə'lɔft], adv., prep. arriba, sobre, en alto; to set aloft, subir, elevar.
alone [ə'loun], a. solo, único, solitario, sin compañía. — adv. solamente; let it alone, no lo toque Vd.; let me alone, déjeme Vd. en paz, no me moleste Vd.
along [ə'lɔŋ], adv. a lo largo, por lo largo; adelante, en compañía de, con, junto con; all along, a lo largo; desde el principio al fin; all along the road, todo lo largo del camino; come along with me, venga Vd. conmigo; take me along with you, lléveme Vd. consigo; to get along, medrar.
alongshore, adv. a lo largo de la costa.
alongside, adv., prep. al lado, al costado, costado con costado, junto a, a lo largo de, (mar.) bordo con bordo; to come alongside, (mar.) atracarse al costado.
aloof [ə'luːf], adv. lejos, de lejos, aparte, apartado, a lo largo; to stand aloof, mantenerse apartado.
alopecia [ælə'piːsiə], **alopecy**, s. (med.) alopecia.
aloud [ə'laud], adv. alto, en voz alta.
alow [ə'lou], adv. bajo, abajo; (mar.) lo opuesto a aloft.
alp, s. montaña muy alta; (fig.) formidable obstáculo; pl. los Alpes.
alpaca [æl'pækə], s. alpaca, paco.
alpenstock, s. palo con punta de hierro usado en las ascensiones de los Alpes.
alpha ['ælfə], s. alfa, primera letra del alfabeto griego; sinónimo de principio; alpha and omega, el principio y el fin.
alphabet, s. alfabeto, abecedario, abecé. — v.t. colocar por orden alfabético.
alphabetic, alphabetical, a. alfabético.
alpine ['ælpain], a. alpino, alpestre; elevado, alto.
alpinist, s. alpinista, m.f.
alquifou ['ælkwifuː], s. alquifol.
already [ɔːl'redi], adv. ya, antes de ahora, todavía, a la hora de ésta.
also ['ɔːlsou], adv. también, igualmente, además, aun, del mismo modo.
altar ['ɔːltəɹ], s. altar, ara; high altar, altar mayor.
altarage, s. pie de altar.
altar-cloth, s. mantel del altar.
altar-piece, s. retablo; altar-screen, contra-retablo.
altar-table, s. mesa del altar.
altar-wise, adv. en forma de altar.

alter ['ɔːltəɹ], v.t. mudar, alterar, cambiar, modificar, reformar, enmendar, transformar; to alter course, (mar.) hurtar el rumbo. — v.i. cambiar (se), mudarse, alterarse, demudarse.
alterability, s. alterabilidad.
alterable, a. alterable, mudable.
alterableness, s. alterabilidad.
alterant, a. (med.) alterante, que altera.
alteration, s. alteración, mudanza, innovación, cambio, reforma.
alterative, a. (med.) alterativo. — s. alterante.
altercate, v.i. altercar, disputar, controvertir.
altercation, s. altercación, altercado, disputa, debate, controversia.
alterer, s. alterador.
alternancy, s. alternación, vez, turno, vicisitud.
alternate [ɔːl'tə:ɹnət], a. alterno, recíproco, alternativo; (bot., geom.) alterno. — s. vicisitud. — v.t. ['ɔːltəɹneit] alternar, variar. — v.i. alternar con otro, variarse.
alternately [ɔːl'tə:ɹnətli], adv. alternativamente, alternadamente, reciprocamente, por turno.
alternateness, s. alternación.
alternating ['ɔːltəɹneitiŋ], a. alternante, por turno.
alternation [ɔːltəɹ'neiʃən], s. alternación, turno, vicisitud, vez; (mat.) permutación; (igl.) responsorio, responso.
alternative [ɔːl'tə:ɹnətiv], s. alternativa. — a. alternativo.
alternatively, adv. alternativamente, recíprocamente, por turno.
alternativeness, s. vicisitud, reciprocidad; turno.
alternator, s. (elec.) alternador.
althea ['ælθiə], s. (bot.) malvavisco.
although [ɔːl'ðou], conj. aunque, bien que, si bien, aun cuando, no obstante, sin embargo.
altiloquence [æl'tiləkwens], s. altilocuencia.
altiloquent, a. altilocuente.
altimeter, s. altímetro.
altimetry, s. altimetría.
altisonant [ælti'sounənt], **altisonous**, a. altisonante, altísono, retumbante, pomposo.
altitude ['æltitjuːd], s. altura, altitud; elevación, cima, cumbre, f.
alto ['æltou], s. (mús.) contralto (de la voz); contralto (cantante) m.f.
altogether [ɔːltə'geðəɹ], adv. enteramente, en junto, del todo, por completo, para siempre.
alto-relievo, s. (escul.) alto relieve.
altruism ['æltruːism], s. altruismo, amor al prójimo, benevolencia.
altruist, s., a.; **altruistic**, a. altruista, altruístico.
alum ['æləm], s. alumbre, m. — v.t. (tint.) alumbrar.
alum-stone, s. aluminita.
alum-water, agua de alumbre.
alum-works, alumbrera.
alumed, a. aluminado.
alumina [ə'ljuːminə], **alumine**, s. alumina.
aluming, s. (tint.) aluminaje.
aluminiferous [əljuːmi'nifərəs], a. aluminífero.
aluminiform, a. aluminiforme.
aluminite, s. aluminita.
aluminium, aluminum, s. aluminio.
aluminous, a. aluminoso.

alumish, *a.* aluminado, alumbrado.

alumna(*pl.*-**ae**) *s. f.* graduada.

alumnus (*pl.*-**i**) *s.m.* graduado.

alveary, *s.* colmena; (*anat.*) alveario.

alveolar ['ælvialaɹ], *a.* (*anat.*) alveolar.

alveolate, *a.* alveolado.

alveolus, *s.* alvéolo; cavidad, celdilla.

alveus, *a.* álveo.

alvine ['ælvin], *a.* alvino.

alway ['ɔːlwei], **always,** *adv.* siempre, constantemente, invariablemente.

alyssum ['ælisəm], *s.* (*bot.*) alhelí.

am [æm], 1ª *pers. del indic. del verbo* [BE]. Yo soy o estoy.

amability, *s.* amabilidad, agrado.

amadou, *s.* yesca, hupe, *f.*

amain [ə'mein], *adv.* vigorosamente, violentamente, con precipitación, con fuerza, con vehemencia; (*mar.*) en banda.

amalgam [ə'mælgəm], *s.* amalgama, mezcla.

amalgamate, *v.t.* amalgamar, mezclar, unir, juntar. — *v.i.* amalgamarse, mezclarse, unirse.

amalgamation, *s.* amalgamación; mezcla.

amalgamator, *s.* amalgamador; azoguero.

amanuensis [əmænju'ensis], *s.* amanuense, *m.f.*, escribiente, *m.f.*, secretario.

amaranth ['æmərænθ], *s.* (*bot.*) amaranto, color carmesí.

amaranthine [æmə'rænθin], *a.* encarnado, de amaranto, de color de amaranto, inmarcesible.

amaryllis [æmə'rilis], *s.* (*bot.*) amarilis, *f.*, familia de plantas amarilídeas.

amass [ə'mæs], *v.t.* acumular, amontonar, juntar; *to amass a fortune,* acumular riquezas.

amassment, *s.* cúmulo, montón, agregado, conjunto.

amateur [æmə'təːɹ], *s.* aficionado.

amateurish, *a.* superficial, a manera de aficionado; torpe.

amateurishly, *adv.* desgarbadamente.

amateurship, *s.* carácter de aficionado.

amative ['æmətiv], *a.* amatorio, enamorado, apasionado.

amativeness, *s.* (*frenol.*) amatividad.

amatorial [æmə'toəriəl], **amatorious, amatory** ['æmətəri], *a.* amatorio, erótico; amoroso, de amor.

amaze [ə'meiz], *v.t.* aterrar, espantar, aturdir, confundir, pasmar, dejar perplejo o atónito, sorprender, asombrar, embazar. — *s.* espanto, asombro, pasmo, sorpresa.

amazed, *a.* espantado, maravillado, atónito, pasmado, asombrado. — *p.p.* [AMAZE].

amazedness [ə'meizədnəs], **amazement,** *s.* espanto, asombro, pasmo, confusión, sorpresa, estupefacción, estupor; admiración.

amazing, *a.* pasmoso, asombroso, extraño.

amazingly *adv.* pasmosamente, asombrosamente.

Amazon ['æməzən], *s.* amazona; marimacho.

Amazonian, *a.* amazónico; guerrera.

ambage ['æmbeidʒ], *s.* ambage, camino tortuoso.

ambassade, *s.* embajada.

ambassador [æm'bæsədəɹ], *s.* embajador, legado.

ambassadorial, *a.* propio de un embajador.

ambassadress, *s.* embajadora, embajatriz.

amber ['æmbəɹ], *s.* ámbar; cárabe, electro; *yellow amber,* succino; *amber seed,* ambarina; *black amber,* azabache. — *a.* ambarino.

ambergris ['æmbəɹgriːs], *s.* ámbar gris.

amber-tree, *s.* (*bot.*) escobilla de ámbar.

ambidexter [æmbi'dekstəɹ], *s.* ambidextro; falso, engañoso; prevaricador.

ambidexterity [æmbidek'steriti], *s.* ambidexteridad; doblez, *f.*, simulación.

ambidextrous [æmbi'dekstrəs], *a.* ambidextro; falso, hipócrita.

ambidextrousness, *s.* ambidexteridad.

ambient ['æmbiənt], *a.* ambiente; lo que rodea, lo que anda o está alrededor.

ambigu, *s.* ambigú.

ambiguity [æmbi'gjuːiti], *s.* ambigüedad; doble sentido; incertidumbre, vaguedad.

ambiguous [æm'bigjuːəs], *a.* ambiguo.

ambiguousness, *s.* ambigüedad; doble sentido, incertidumbre, vaguedad.

ambit ['æmbit], *s.* ámbito, circuito, circumferencia, contorno.

ambition [æm'biʃən], *s.* ambición, aspiración. — *v.t.* ambicionar.

ambitionless, *a.* sin ambición.

ambitious, *a.* ambicioso; ávido.

ambitiousness, *s.* ambición, cualidad de ser ambicioso.

amble ['æmbl], *v.i.* amblar, marchar lentamente. — *s.* portante, paso de andadura, paso castellano.

ambler, *s.* caballo que ambla, persona que anda como un caballo amblador.

ambling, *s.* ambladura; amblador.

amblygon, *s.* (*geom.*) ambligonio.

amblyopia [æmbli'oupiə], *s.* (*med.*) ambliopía.

ambrosia [æm'brouziə], *s.* ambrosía; manjar de los dioses, manjar delicado; (*bot.*) ambrosía, género de plantas de la familia de las compuestas.

ambrosial, *a.* ambrosíaco, delicioso, deleitable, celestial, divino.

ambrosian, *a.* ambrosiano.

ambry, aumbry, *s.* armario, alacena, despensa, sausería.

ambs-ace, ames-ace, *s.* ases, ambos ases; el punto más bajo en los dados; mala suerte, infortunio, indignidad.

ambulance ['æmbjuləns], *s.* ambulancia, hospital de sangre, hospital militar ambulante.

ambulant, *a.* ambulante.

ambulate, *v.i.* andar, pasear, ambular.

ambulation, *s.* paseo; locomoción.

ambulative, ambulatory, *a.* ambulante, ambulativo, mudable. — *s.* galería; claustro; sitio para pasearse.

ambury ['æmbəri], *s.* (*vet.*) furúnculo, tumor blando; en un caballo, lo mismo que ANBURY.

ambuscade [æmbəs'keid], *s.* emboscada, celada. — *v.t.* emboscar, atacar desde una emboscada.

ambush ['æmbuʃ], *v.t.* (*mil.*) emboscar; acechar, poner celada. — *v.i.* emboscarse. — *s.* emboscada, celada; sorpresa, acometimiento repentino; *to lay an ambush,* tender una celada; *to lie in ambush,* estar emboscado.

ameer, amir, *s.* amir, emir.

ameliorable, *a.* mejorable.

ameliorate [ə'miːliəreit], *v.t.* mejorar, adelantar, bonificar. — *v.i.* mejorarse.

amelioration, *s.* mejora, mejoramiento; medro; adelanto; perfeccionamiento.

ameliorator, *s.* mejorador, aumentador, perfeccionador.

amen [aːmen], *adv.* amén, así sea; así es.

amenability [əmi:nə'biliti], **amenableness,** s. responsabilidad.

amenable, a. responsable, sujeto a; tratable, dócil.

amend [ə'mend], v.t. enmendar, corregir, reparar, rectificar, reformar, moralizar. — v.i. enmendarse, reformarse, restablecerse.

amendable, a. reparable, reformable, corregible, enmendable.

amendatory, a. correctivo, reformatorio.

amende, s. multa, pena pecuniaria; *amende honorable,* reparación, satisfacción pública.

amender, s. enmendador, corrector.

amendment, s. enmienda, enmendación, rectificación, reformación, reforma, restauración, corrección.

amends, s. indemnización, compensación, recompensa, reparación, satisfacción; *to make amends,* indemnizar, dar satisfacción.

amenity [ə'mi:niti], s. amenidad; afabilidad, bondad de carácter. — *pl.* modales agradables, atractivos, hechiceros.

amenorrhœa, s. (med.) amenorrea.

ament [ə'ment], **amentum,** (bot.) amento, trama, candelilla.

amentaceous [æmen'teiʃəs], a. amentáceo.

amentia [ə'menʃiə], s. demencia, idiotez, f.; fatuidad, imbecilidad.

amerce [ə'mə:ɹs], v.t. multar; imponer pena pecuniaria; cometer una exacción.

amerceable, a. digno de ser multado.

amercement, amerciament, s. multa, exacción.

amercer, s. multador, exactor.

American [ə'merikən], s., a. americano; (E.U.) norteamericano.

Americanism, s. americanismo.

Americanize, v.t. americanizar.

amethyst ['æməθist], s. (min.) amatista; color de amatista.

amethystine, a. de amatista; parecido o semejante a la amatista.

amiability [eimjə'biliti], s. amabilidad.

amiable, a. amable; agradable, cariñoso, afectuoso; atractivo, encantador, amistoso, amigable.

amiableness, s. amabilidad.

amiant ['æmiənt], **amianthus,** (min.) amianto.

amicability [æmikə'biliti], **amicableness,** s. cariño, afecto, amistad, amigabilidad, cordialidad, disposición amistosa, benevolencia.

amicable, a. amigable, amistoso.

amice ['æmis], s. (igl.) amito, muceta, almucia.

amid [ə'mid], **amidst,** prep. entre, en medio de, mezclado con, rodeado por.

amidin ['æmidin], s. (quím.) almidina, parte soluble del almidón.

amidship [ə'midʃip], **amidships,** adv. (mar.) en medio del navío.

amiss [ə'mis], adv. mal; impropiamente, fuera del lugar, fuera del caso; erradamente, culpablemente; *to take amiss,* llevar a mal; *nothing comes amiss to an empty stomach,* a buena hambre no hay pan duro. — a. malo, impropio, culpable, inconveniente, vicioso, impuro.

amity ['æmiti], s. amistad, concordia, bienquerencia.

ammeter ['æmetəɹ], s. (elec.) amperímetro.

ammonia [ə'mouniə], s. (quím.) amoníaco, álcali volátil.

ammoniac, s. amoníaco, sal amoníaca.

ammoniacal, a. amoniacal, amónico.

ammonite ['æmənait], s. (zool.) amonita.

ammonium, s. amonio, radical alcalino hipotético.

ammunition ['æmju'niʃən], s. (mil.) munición; pertrechos, explosivos; *sporting ammunition,* municiones de caza; *ammunition bread,* pan de munición.

amnesia [æm'ni:siə], s. (med.) amnesia.

amnesty ['æmnesti], s. amnistía, indulto.

amnion ['æmniən], s. (zool.) amnios.

amœba [ə'mi:bə], s. amibea (amiba o ameba).

amœboid, a. amebeo.

amomum, s. (bot.) amomo.

among [ə'mʌŋ], **amongst,** prep. entre, mezclado con, en medio de, rodeado de.

amorist ['æmərist], s. amante, galán.

amorous, a. amoroso, apasionado, enamorado, tierno, cariñoso, amatorio, lo que pertenece al amor.

amorousness, s. amor, inclinación amorosa; galantería; terneza.

amorphism [ə'mɔ:ɹfism], s. amorfia; (pol.) anarquismo.

amorphous, a. amorfo, imperfecto, informe; anómalo, heterogéneo.

amort [ə'mɔ:ɹt], a. exánime, abatido, deprimido, amortiguado, taciturno, triste.

amortization [əmɔ:ɹti'zeiʃən], **amortizement,** s. (for.) amortización.

amortize [ə'mɔ:ɹtaiz], v.t. amortizar.

amount [ə'maunt], s. importe; cantidad, suma, monta, cuantía, valor, sustancia, resultado, efecto; *to the amount of,* por la suma de, hasta el completo de. — v.i. importar, llegar, montar, subir, ascender, sumar, venir; *what does it all amount to?* (fig.) ¿ a qué viene eso ?

amour [ə'muɔɹ], s. amores, amoríos, intriga de amor.

amove, v.t. remover, mover, alterar, mudar; (for.) deponer, retirar, quitar a alguno del empeo que tiene.

amperage ['æmpəridʒ], s. (elect.) amperaje.

ampère ['æmpeɔɹ], s. amperio.

ampersand, s. el signo & que significa y (corrupción de *and per se*).

amphibia [æm'fibiə], s.pl. anfibios.

amphibious, a. anfibio; (fig.) híbrido.

amphibiousness, s. naturaleza anfibia, calidad de ser anfibio.

amphibole, s. (min.) anfíbol.

amphibolite, s. anfibolita.

amphibological, a. anfibológico, dudoso, obscuro.

amphibologically, adv. anfibológicamente.

amphibology, s. anfibología, doble sentido.

amphiboly, s. anfibología; ambigüedad.

amphibrach, s. anfíbraco.

amphipoda, n.pl. orden numeroso de crustáceos, con catorce pies.

amphisbæna, s. anfisbena.

amphitheatral, a. anfiteatral.

amphitheatre, s. anfiteatro.

amphitheatric, amphitheatrical, a. anfiteatral.

amphitryon, s. anfitrión.

amphora ['æmfərə], s. ánfora.

amphoric, a. anfóreo.

ample ['æmpl], a. amplio, extendio, extensivo, espacioso, dilatado, extenso, ancho, capaz, abundante, copioso; holgado; dadivoso; magnífico, liberal.

ampleness, s. amplitud, anchura; holgura, profusión, abundancia; magnificencia.

ampliate, v.t. ampliar, extender, dilatar, aumentar, exagerar.

ampliation, s. ampliación; (for.) plazo, término, demora, prorrogación, prórroga, respiro.

ampliative, a. ampliativo, ampliador.

amplificate, v.t. amplificar; agrandar; exagerar.

amplification, s. amplificación; ampliación, extensión.

amplificator, s. amplificador.

amplifier, s. amplificador; aumentador.

amplify, v.t. (ret.) amplificar; ampliar, extender, dilatar, aumentar, agrandar, exagerar. — v.i. extenderse.

amplifying, a. amplificador.

amplitude, s. amplitud, extensión, dilatación; copia, abundancia; capacidad; esplendor.

amply, adv. ampliamente, copiosamente, liberalmente, holgadamente.

ampulla [æm'pulə], s. ampolla.

ampullaceous, a. ampuláceo, ampollar.

amputate ['æmpjuteit], v.t. amputar, desmembrar.

amputation, s. amputación; desmembración.

amuck [ə'mʌk], adv. furiosamente; to run amuck, atacar a ciegas, a troche y moche; correr por las calles, con el propósito de matar a quien se encuentre.

amulet ['æmjulet], s. amuleto, talismán.

amusable, a. entretenido, divertido.

amuse [ə'mju:z], v.t. entretener, divertir, distraer, recrear, solazar; engañar, embobar.

amusement, s. diversión, divertimiento, distracción, recreo, entretenimiento, pasatiempo, juego.

amuser, s. entretenedor, engañador.

amusing, a. divertido, entretenido, festivo, alegre.

amusive, a. divertido, entretenido.

amygdala [æmig'dælə], s. (anat.) amígdala.

amygdalate, a. almendrado. — s. horchata de almendras.

amygdalic, a. amigdalino.

amygdalin, s. (quím.) amigdalina.

amygdaline, a. almendrado.

amygdaloids, s.pl. (min.) amigdalarias.

amyl ['æmil], s. (quím.) amilo, $C_5 H_{11}$.

amylaceous, a. amiláceo.

amylene, a. amilina.

amylic ['æmilik], a. amílico.

amyloid ['æmiloid], a. amiloide.

an [æn], art. un, uno, una; artículo indefinido A al cual se añade la N cuando la voz siguiente empieza por vocal o H muda; an hour, una hora; a horse, un caballo. — conj. si, como si.

ana ['ænə], s. (med.) ana.

anabaptism, s. anabaptismo.

anabaptist, s. anabaptista, m.f.

anabaptistic, anabaptistical, s., a. anabaptístico.

anabolism [ə'næbolism], s. (biol.) el procedimiento de la asimilación de los alimentos.

anacardium [ænə'ka:rdiəm], s. (bot.) anacardo.

anacathartic, s. anacatártico, expectorante.

anachoret, anachorite, s. anacoreta, m.

anachronic, anachronical, a. anacronístico.

anachronism [ə'nækrənism], s. anacronismo.

anachronistic, a. anacronístico.

anaclastics [ænə'klæstiks], s. (opt.) dióptrica.

anaconda [ænə'kɔndə], s. (zool.) anaconda.

anacreontic [ənækri'ɔntik], a. anacreóntico; amoroso. — s. anacréontica; poesía.

anadromous, a. anadromo.

anæmia [ə'ni:miə], s. (med.) anemia.

anæmic, a. anémico.

anæsthesia, s. (med.) anestesia.

anæsthetic [æni:s'θetik], a. anestésico.

anæsthetize [ə'ni:sθətaiz], v.t. anestesiar.

anaglyph ['ænəglif], s. anáglifo.

anagogical [ænə'goudʒikl], a. anagógico, misterioso, místico, espiritual.

anagogics, s. anagogía, sentido místico.

anagram ['ænəgræm], s. anagrama.

anagrammatical, a. anagramático.

anagrammatism, s. anagramatismo.

anagrammatist a. anagramatizador.

anagrammatize, v.i. anagramatizar.

anal ['einəl], a. (anat.) anal.

analecta [ænə'lektə], **analects**, s.pl. analectas.

analectic, a. analéctico.

analemma. s. analema.

analepsis, analepsy, s. (med.) analepsia.

analeptic, s., a. analéptico.

analogical [ænə'lɔdʒikəl], a. analógico.

analogicalness, s. calidad de ser analógico.

analogism, s. analogismo.

analogist, s. analogista, m.f.

analogize, v.t. analogizar, explicar por analogía.

analogous, a. análogo, parecido, semejante, simpático, proporcional.

analogy [ə'nælədʒi], s. analogía, semejanza, correlación, afinidad.

analysis [ə'nælisis], s. análisis, m.f.

analyst ['ænəlist], **analyzer**, s. analizador.

analytic [ænə'litik], **analytical**, a. analítico.

analytics, s. análisis, m.f.; analítica.

analyzable, a. analizable.

analyzableness, s. cualidad de ser analizable.

analyzation, s. análisis, m.f.

analyze ['ænəlaiz], v.t. analizar, hacer análisis.

analyzer, s. analizador.

anamnesis [ænəm'ni:sis], s. doctrina de la reminiscencia de una existencia previa.

anamorphosis [ænəmɔr'fousis], s. anamorfosis, f.

anandrous [ə'nændrəs], a. (bot.) destituto de estambre.

anapæst ['ænəpest], s. anapesto.

anapæstic, anapæstical, a. anapéstico.

anaphora [ə'næfərə], s. (ret.) anáfora.

anaphrodisiac [æn'æfro'diziæk], s. (med.) anafrodisia.

anarchic, anarchical, a. anárquico.

anarchism, anarchy, s. anarquía, confusión, desorden.

anarchist, ['ænərkist], s. anarquista, m.f.

anastatic [ænə'stætik], a. (art.) anastático, en relieve; anastatic printing, impresion anastática; manera de obtener copia en relieve, sobre una plancha de zinc.

anastomose, v.i. unirse por sus extremos las ramificaciones salientes de las arterias y venas.

anastomosis, s. anastomosis, f.

anastomotic [ənəstə'mɔtik], s., a. (med.) anastomótico.

anastrophe [ə'næstrəfi:], s. (gram.) anástrofe, f.

[814]

anathema [ə'næθəmə], *s.* anatema, *m.f.*, excomunión, execración.

anathematism, *s.* excomunión, anatema, *m.f.*

anathematization, *s.* excomunión, acción de excomulgar.

anathematize, *v.t.* anatematizar, excomulgar, maldecir.

anathematizer, *s.* anatematizador, excomulgador.

anatomical [ænə'tɔmikəl], *a.* anatómico.

anatomist [ə'nætəmist], *s.* anatomista, *m.f.*, anatómico.

anatomize, *v.t.* anatomizar; disecar.

anatomy, *s.* anatomía, disección, examen minucioso; disecación; esqueleto; (*fig.*) análisis, *m.f.*

anbury ['ænbəri], *s.* (*vet.*) tumor blando, furúnculo.

ancestors ['ænsəstəɹs], *s.pl.* mayores, antepasados, ascendientes, abuelos; predecesores; (*for.*) ascendientes.

ancestral, *a.* hereditario.

ancestress, *s.* abuela.

ancestry, *s.* linaje, extracción, raza, prosapia, abolengo, alcurnia, serie de antepasados.

anchor ['æŋkəɹ], *s.* ancla, áncora; *sheet anchor,* ancla grande, ancla de esperanza; *anchor back,* galga del ancla; *anchor beam,* serviola; *anchor chocks,* calzos de ancla; *anchor bill,* pico del ancla; *anchor flukes,* orejas del ancla; *anchor stock,* cepo del ancla; *at anchor,* al ancla; *to cast anchor,* echar el ancla; *to ride at anchor,* estar al ancla; *to weigh anchor,* levar el ancla; *to stock the anchor,* encepar el ancla; *to drop* (o *let go*) *anchor,* dar fondo; *best-bower anchor,* ancla de ayuste; *anchor ground,* fondeadero; *kedge anchor,* anclote. — *v.i.* anclar, ancorar, echar las anclas. — *v.t.* ancorar; fijar, asegurar; aferrar.

anchorable, *a.* propio para anclaje.

anchorage, *s.* (*mar.*) anclaje, ancoraje, surgidero; anchadero, agarradero, fondeadero.

anchored, *a.* anclado, surto; en forma de ancla; afirmado, puesto en seguridad. — *p.p.* [ANCHOR].

anchoress, *s.* ermitaña.

anchoret, anchorite, *s.* ermitaño, anacoreta, *m.,* monje.

anchorless, *s.* sin ancla; inseguro; (*mar.*) a la deriva.

anchorsmith, *s.* ancorero.

anchovy [æn'tʃouvi], *s.* (*ict.*) anchoa, anchova; boquerón, haleche.

ancient ['eintʃənt], *a.* antiguo, viejo, fuera de uso.

ancientness, *s.* antigüedad.

anciantry, *s.* antigüedad de linaje.

ancillary [æn'siləri], *a.* subordinado, dependiente, auxiliar, sucursal.

ancipital [æn'sipitəl], **ancipitous,** *a.* de dos caras, de dos cortes.

ancon ['æŋkən], *s.* codo; (*arq.*) ancón.

ancoral ['æŋkərəl], *a.* (*zool.*) en forma de gancho, encorvado.

and [ænd], *conj.* y, e; *conjunción copulativa,* aun, si, que; *by and by,* pronto, luego; *better and better,* cada vez mejor; *now and then,* de vez en cuando; *here and there,* acá y acullá; *two and two,* dos y dos; *ifs and ands,* dimes y diretes; *and yet,* sin embargo.

Andalusian [ændə'lu:ziən], *s., a.* andaluz, andaluza, de Andalucía.

Andean ['ændiən], *a.* andino, de los Andes.

andirons ['ændaiəɹns], *s.pl.* morillos (de hogar).

Andrew ['ændru:], *n.p.* Andrés. — *s.* espada de marca, o de *Andrés Ferrara*; criado, sirviente; *merry-andrew, s.* payaso.

androgynal [æn'drɔdʒinəl], **androgynous,** *a.* andrógino, hermafrodita.

android ['ændrɔid], *s.* autómata (*m.*) en figura de hombre. — *a.* que tiene forma humana.

androphagous [ændrə'feigəs], *a.* antropófago.

anecdote ['ænəkdout], *s.* anécdota.

anecdotic, anecdotical, *a.* anecdótico.

anele, *v.t.* olear, administrar la extremaunción.

anelectric [ænə'lektrik], *a.* (*fis.*) aneléctrico.

anemography [ænəm'ɔgrəfi], *s.* anemografía.

anemology [ænəm'ɔlədʒi], *s.* anemología.

anemometer, *s.* anemómetro.

anemone [ə'neməni], *s.* anémona, anémone.

anemoscope, *s.* anemoscopio.

anent [ə'nent], *prep.* tocante a, por lo concerniente, respecto de, opuesto a, contra; enfrente de.

aneroid ['ænərɔid], *a.* aneroide, aneroideo, sin líquido.

aneuria [ə'nju:riə], *s.* (*med.*) aneuria.

aneurism, *s.* aneurisma, *m.f.*

aneurismal, *a.* aneurismal.

anew [ə'nju:], *adv.* de nuevo, otra vez, aún, nuevamente.

anfractuose [æn'fræktjuous], **anfractuous,** *a.* sinuoso, tortuoso, áspero, desigual.

anfractuosity [ænfræktju'ositi], **anfractuousness,** *s.* sinuosidad, desigualdad, aspereza.

angel ['eindʒəl], *s.* ángel; moneda antigua de oro. — *a.* angélico, angelical; *guardian angel,* ángel de la guarda.

angel-age, *s.* estado de los ángeles.

angel-fish, *s.* (*ict.*) angelote.

angelhood, *s.* condición de ángel.

angelic [æn'dʒelic], **angelical,** *a.* angelical, angélico, seráfico.

angelica, *s.* (*bot.*) angélica.

angelicalness, *s.* perfección, excelencia sobrehumana.

angel-like, *a.* angelical.

angel-shot, *s.* (*mar.*) balas enramadas, palanquetas.

angel-winged, *a.* alado como los ángeles.

angel-worship, *s.* angelolatría, culto de los ángeles.

anger ['æŋgəɹ], *s.* ira, cólera; enojo, disgusto, enfado; coraje, saña, indignación; incomodidad; inflamación de una parte del cuerpo; *to provoke to anger,* encolerizar, causar ira; *a fit of anger,* un acceso de cólera — *v.t.* provocar, enfurecer, irritar, enojar, enfadar, encolerizar, airar, enrabiar.

angered, *a.* encolerizado. — *p.p.* [ANGER].

angerly, *adv.* con ira, airadamente.

angina [æn'dʒainə], *s.* (*med.*) angina; *angina pectoris,* angina de pecho o esternalgia.

angiography [ændʒi'ɔgrəfi], *s.* angiografía.

angiology, *s.* angiología.

angiosperm, *s., a.* angiosperma.

angiotomy, *s.* angiotomía.

angle ['æŋgl], *s.* ángulo; rincón, escuadra, recodo; encuentro; anzuelo, caña de pescar; *visual angle,* ángulo óptico; *angle-bevel,* falsa escuadra; *angle-brace,* cuadral; *angle-rafter,* lima triangular; *angle,* (roofing) caballete. — *v.t.* pescar con caña. — *v.i.* insinuar, insinuarse.

angled, *a.* angular, anguloso, esquinado; *three angled*, triangular; *right-angled*, rectangular; *many-angled*, polígono.

angler, *s.* pescador de caña.

angle-rod, *s.* caña de pescar.

Anglican ['æŋglikən], *s.*, *a.* anglicano.

Anglicanism, *s.* anglicanismo.

Anglicism, *s.* anglicismo.

Anglicize ['æŋglisaiz], *v.t.* traducir o convertir en inglés; dar a la lengua giros y caracteres del idioma inglés.

angling, *s.* arte o práctica de pesca con caña.

Anglo-American ['æŋglou-ə'merikən], *s.*, *a.* anglo-americano.

Anglo-Indian, *s.*, *a.* angloindio.

Anglomania, *s.* anglomanía.

Anglomaniac, *s.* anglómano.

Anglo-Norman, *s.*, *a.* anglo-normando.

anglophobia, *s.* anglofobia.

Anglo-Saxon, *s.*, *a.* anglosajón.

angry, *a.* colérico, irritado, indignado, enfadado, enojado, encolerizado, airado, agitado; (*med.*) inflamado; *to be very angry*, echar chispas, echar sapos y culebras; *to make angry*, encolerizar.

anguiliform [æn'gwilifoəm], *a.* en forma de anguila.

anguish ['æŋgwiʃ], *s.* ansia, pena, congoja, angustia, tormento, aflicción, dolor. — *v.t.* atormentar, torturar, causar angustia.

anguished, *a.* atormentado, angustiado, acongojado, afligido.

angular ['æŋgjuləɪ], *a.* angular, anguloso, esquinado.

angularity, angularness, *s.* angulosidad.

angulate, angulated, *a.* (*bot.*) angular, anguloso.

anhelation [ænhi'leiʃən], *s.* jadeo, anhelación, anhélito.

anhydride [æn'haidraid], *s.* (*quím.*) anhídrido.

anhydrite, *s.* anhidrita.

anhydrous, *a.* anhidro.

anight [ə'nait], **anights,** *adv.* de noche, por la noche, de la noche.

anil ['ænil], *s.* (*bot.*) añil.

anile ['ænail], *a.* vieja, caduca (de una mujer de edad); falta de juicio; que chochea.

aniline ['ænilain], *s.* anilina.

anility [ə'niliti], *s.* vejez de mujer.

animadversion [æniməd'və:ɪʃən], *s.* reflexión, *f.*, animadversión, censura, reparo, reproche, represión.

animadversive, *a.* perceptivo, judicativo.

animadvert, *v.t.* advertir, observar, considerar; censurar, juzgar; reprochar, castigar.

animadverter, *s.* crítico, criticastro, censurador.

animal ['æniməl], *s.* animal, bestia, criatura, ser viviente, bruto; *animal kingdom*, reino animal. — *a.* animal.

animalcular, *a.* animalcular.

animalcule, *s.* animálculo, animalillo.

animalculism, *a.* animalculismo.

animalculist, *s.* animalculista, *m.f.*

animalism, *s.* animalismo, estado animal; sensualidad.

animalist, *s.* pintor o escultor de animales.

animality, *s.* animalidad.

animalization, *s.* animalización.

animalize, *v.t.* animalizar, dar la vida animal.

animate ['ænimeit], *v.t.* dar vida, infundir alma; animar, vivificar, reforzar, infundir ánimo o valor excitar; alentar. — *a.* viviente, animado.

animated, *a.* animado, vigoroso, vivo.

animating, *a.* vivificante, excitante; vivo, alegro; divertido.

animation, *s.* animación, viveza, espíritu, vivacidad.

animative, *a.* vivificante.

animator, *s.* animador, alentador.

anime ['ænimi], *s.* anime, goma del curbaril (árbol de Cayena); goma copal.

animism, *s.* animismo.

animist, *s.* animista, *m.f.*

animosity, *s.* animosidad, encarnizamiento, mala voluntad, odio, rencor, rencilla, encono, aversión, aborrecimiento, ojeriza.

animus, *s.* ánimo, designio, intención.

anise ['ænis], *s.* (*bot.*) anís.

aniseed ['ænisi:d], *s.* simiente de anís.

anisette, *s.* anisete, licor de anís.

anisometric [æniso'metrik], *a.* que no es isómero; de proporciones distintas.

anker ['æŋkəɪ], *s.* medida de líquidos de cerca de 41 litros.

ankle ['æŋkl], *s.* maléolo, tobillo.

ankle-bone, *s.* hueso del tobillo.

anklet, *s.* brazalete para el tobillo.

anna ['ænə], *s.* moneda de la India equivalente a $\frac{1}{16}$ de rupia.

annalist, *s.* analista, cronista, *m.f.*, el que escribe anales.

annals ['ænəls], *s.pl.* anales, crónica; (*igl.*) misas celebradas durante el año; las de aniversario y de cabo de año.

annates ['æneits], *s.* anata.

anneal [ə'ni:l], *v.t.* templar, atemperar, recocer (metales o cristal).

annelid ['ænəlid], *s.*, *a.* anillado.

annex [ə'neks], *v.t.* anexar, agregar, unir, juntar, adjuntar. — *s.* anexo, aditamento, adición; dependencia.

annexary, *s.* adición.

annexation, annexment, *s.* anexión, *f.*, adición, unión, *f.*, conjunción.

annihilable, *a.* aniquilable, destructible.

annihilate [ə'naihəleit], *v.t.* aniquilar, reducir a la nada. — *a.* aniquilado, destruido.

annihilation, *s.* aniquilación, aniquilamiento, anulación, anonadación.

anniversary [æni'və:ɪsəri], *s.* aniversario. — *a.* anual.

annotate ['ænoteit], *v.i* anotar, comentar. — *v.t.* notar, glosar.

annotation, *s.* anotación, apunte, acotación.

annotationist, annotator, *s.* anotador, comentador, ilustrador.

announce [ə'nauns], *v.t.* anunciar, proclamar, publicar, declarar, notificar, comunicar, participar.

announcement, *s.* aviso, anuncio, declaración, advertencia.

announcer, *s.* anunciador, publicador, avisador; (radio) locutor-a.

annoy [ə'nɔi], *v.t.* molestar, fatigar, incomodar, fastidiar, vejar, aburrir, cargar. — *s.* molestia, daño, fastidio.

annoyance, *s.* molestia, pena, incomodidad, daño, disgusto, fastidio, aburrimiento; engorro; chinchorrería.

annoyer, *s.* molestador, chinchorrero.

annoying, *a.* fastidioso, molesto, incómodo, importuno, engorroso, enojoso, molestador.

annual ['ænjuəl], *a.* anual, añal, cadañal. — *s.* aniversario; (*bot.*) planta anual.

annually, *adv.* anualmente, cada año, de año en año.

annuary, *a.* anuario.

annuitant, *s.* rentista, *m f.*, censualista, *m.f.*

annuity [ə'njuiti], *s.* anualidad, renta de un año, renta vitalicia, censual, pensión; *life annuity,* renta vitalicia; *deferred annuity,* renta diferida; *terminable annuity,* renta reembolsable; *to redeem an annuity,* rescatar una renta; *to settle an annuity on,* señalar una renta a.

annul [ə'nʌl], *v.t.* anular, invalidar, revocar, abolir, rescindir, cancelar, derogar, abrogar.

annular ['ænjulər], *a.* anular.

annulate, annulated, *a.* anuloso, anillado.

annulet, *s.* anillejo, sortijilla; (*arq.*) anillo.

annulment [ə'nʌlmənt], *s.* anulación, derogación, rescisión, revocación, cancelación.

annulose ['ænjulous], *a.* anuloso, anillado; rizado.

annunciate [ə'nʌnsieit], *v.t.* anunciar.

annunciation, *s.* anunciación, proclamación, promulgación.

annunciator, *s.* anunciador, avisador, proclamador; indicador.

anode ['ænoud], *s.* (*fís.*) ánodo.

anodyne ['ænədain], *a.* anodino.

anoint [ə'nɔint], *v.t.* untar, ungir, pringar; (*igl.*) olear; administrar la extremaunción; *to anoint the palm,* (*fam.*) untar la mano; (*fam.*) apelear, azotar, zurrar.

anointed, *a.* ungido; (*fam.*) apeleado, azotado.

anointer, *s.* untador el que unta.

anointing, anointment, *s.* untadura, untamiento, unción, consagración.

anomalism [ə'nɔməlism], *s.* anomalía, irregularidad.

anomalistic, *a.* anomalístico.

anomalous, *a.* anómalo, irregular.

anomalousness, anomaly, *s.* anomalía, irregularidad.

anon [ə'nɔn], *adv.* pronto, luego, presto, al instante; en seguida, inmediatamente, luego; *ever and anon,* a menudo.

anonym, *s.* seudónimo.

anonymous [ə'nɔniməs], *a.* anónimo.

anorexy, *s.* anorexia.

anormal [æ'nɔəʌməl], *a.* anormal, irregular.

anosmia [ə'nɔzmiə], *s.* (*med.*) anosmia, anosfresia.

another [ə'nʌðəɹ], *a.* otro, distinto, diferente; *one another,* uno a otro, unos a otros; *one year with another,* un año con otro; buen año, mal año. — *pron.* otro; *love one another,* amáos los unos a los otros.

ansated, *a.* con asas, que tiene asas.

anserine ['ænsərain], *a.* anserino; tonto, necio.

answer ['a:nsəɹ], *v.t.* contestar, responder; satisfacer a, cumplir, obedecer; diputar, refutar; resolver (un problema, etc.); ser suficiente para; convenir a; *this answers my purpose,* esto conviene a mi designio. — *v.i.* responder, dar satisfacción, replicar; ser responsable; corresponder, venir bien, equivaler; (*for.*) comparecer; *to answer for,* responder de, salir fiador de. — *s.* respuesta, contestación, réplica, refutación, solución correcta.

answerable, *a.* contestable; responsable; equivalente, correspondiente, conforme; discutible, refutable; proporcionado.

answerableness, *s.* responsabilidad; relación, proporción, conformidad, correspondencia.

answerer, *s.* fiador, caucionero, respondedor.

answering, *a.* correspondiente, proporcionado, oportuno, conveniente; simpático.

answerless, *a.* sin respuesta.

an't, contracción de *an it,* para *if it;* contracción vulgar de *am not, are not, is not.*

ant [ænt], *s.* hormiga.

anta, *s.* (*zool.*) danta, tapir.

antacid [ænt'æsid], *a.* antiácido, álcali; *s.* remedio para la acidez del estómago.

antagonism [æn'tægənizm], *s.* antagonismo, oposición, hostilidad, rivalidad, contienda.

antagonist, *s.* antagonista, *m.f.,* enemigo, contrario, adversario, rival.

antagonistic, antagonistical, *a.* contrario, opuesto, hostil, en antagonismo.

antagonize, *v.t., v.i.* competir, contender, disputar; ser antagónico.

antalgic, *a.* antálgico, anodino, calmante.

antaphrodisiac [æntəfrə'diziæk], *s., a.* antiafrodisíaco.

antapoplectic ['æntæpə'plektik], *a.* (*med.*) anti-apoplético.

Antarctic [æn'ta:ɹktik], *a.* antártico.

antarthritic [æntar'θritik], *a.* (*med.*) antiartrítico.

antasthmatic [æntæs'mætik], *a.* (*med.*) antiasmático.

ant-bear, *s.* tamandoá.

anteact, *s.* acto anterior.

ant-eater, *s.* hormiguero; tamandoá.

antecede [æntə'si:d], *v.t.* anteceder, preceder.

antecedence, antecedency, *s.* precedencia.

antecedent, *s., a.* antecedente, precedente.

antecedently, *adv.* anteriormente.

antecessor, *s.* antecesor.

antechamber, *s.* antecámara, antesala.

antedate, *v.t.* antedatar; anticipar, retrotraer. — *s.* antedata; anticipación.

antediluvian, *s., a.* antediluviano.

ant-egg, *s.* huevo de hormiga.

antelope, *s.* (*zool.*) antílope; gamuza.

antelucan, *a.* temprano, antes del día.

antemeridian, *a.* antemeridiano, de la mañana, antes de mediodía.

antemetic [æntə'metik], *s., a.* antiemético.

antemundane, *a.* anterior a la creación del mundo.

antenna [æn'tenə], *s.* antena.

antennal, *a.* que pertenece a las antenas.

antenuptial, *a.* antenupcial.

antepaschal, *a.* antepascual.

antepast, *s.* anticipación; gusto anticipado.

antepenult, *s.* antepenúltima.

antepenultimate, *s., a.* antepenúltimo.

antepileptic, *a.* (*med.*) antiepiléptico.

anterior [æn'tiəriəɹ,] *a.* anterior, precedente, delantero.

anteriority, *s.* anterioridad, precedencia, antelación.

ante-room, *s.* antecámara.

anthelmintic [ænθel'mintik], *a.* (*med.*) antielmíntico.

anthem ['ænθəm], *s.* antífona; *national anthem,* himno nacional.

anther ['ænθəɹ], *s.* (*bot.*) antera.

antheral, *a.* anteral, referente a anteras.

antheriferous, a. anterífero.
ant-hill, s. hormiguero.
anthological [ænθə'lɔdʒikəl], a. antológico.
anthology, s. antología, florilegio.
anthophagous, a. antófago.
Anthony's fire, s. (med.) erisipela, Fuego de San Antón.
anthozoa [ænθə'zouə], s. antozoarios, pólipos.
anthracite ['ænθrəsait], s. (min.) antracita.
anthrax ['ænθræks], s. (med.) ántrax; avispero, carbunclo.
anthropography [ænθrə'pɔgrəfi], s. antropografía.
anthropolite, s. antropolito.
anthropological, a. antropológico.
anthropology, s. antropología.
anthropometer, s. antropómetro.
anthropometrical, a. antropométrico.
anthropometry, s. antropometría.
anthropomorphism, s. antropomorfismo.
anthropomorphist, s. antropomorfista, m.f.
anthropomorphous, a. antropomorfo.
anthropophagi, s.pl. antropófagos.
anthropophagous, a. antropófago.
anthroposophy, s. antroposofía.
anthropotomy, s. antropotomía.
anti ['ænti], prefijo. contra, contrario a.
antiarthritic, a. (med.) antiartrítico.
antibilious, a. (med.) antibilioso.
antibrachial, a. anti-braquial.
antic ['æntik], a. extraño, raro, ridículo, grotesco. — s. bufón, truhán, saltimbanqui; figura grotesca; cabriola; travesura. — v.t. poner en ridículo; to cut antics, hacer bufonadas.
anticachectic, a. (med.) anticaquéctico.
anticatarrhal, a. (med.) anticatarral.
Antichrist, s. Anticristo.
antichristian, s., a. anticristiano.
anticipate [æn'tisipeit], v.t. anticipar, prever, prevenir, adelantarse; esperar, prometerse; to anticipate payment, pagar de antemano; to anticipate one's thoughts, beber los pensamientos de alguno. — v.i. anticiparse.
anticipated, a. anticipado, adelantado, prematuro, dado de antemano; prevenido, previsto.
anticipation, s. anticipación, expectación, adelantamiento.
anticipative, a. anticipativo.
anticipator, s., a. anticipador.
anticipatory, a. anticipado, que anticipa.
anticlerical, a. anticlerical.
anticlinal, a. (geol.) anticlinal.
anticness, s. truhanería, bufonada, extravagancia, rareza.
anti-constitutional, a. anticonstitucional.
anti-contagious, a. anticontagioso.
anti-convulsive, a. anticonvulsivo.
anticosmetic, a. anticosmético.
anticyclone, s. anticiclón.
antidotal, a. perteneciente al antídoto.
antidotary, a. antidotario.
antidote ['æntidout], s. antídoto, contraveneno.
antidotical, a. bueno como antídoto.
antiface, s. antifaz.
antifebrile, s., a. (med.) antifebril.
antifriction, s. contra-fricción.
anti-galactic, a. anti-galáctico, antilácteo.
antihysteric, a. antihistérico.
antiliberal, s., a. antiliberal.
antilogy [æn'tilədʒi], s. antilogía.

antiloquist, s. contradictor, opositor.
antimacassar [æntimə'kæsəɹ], s. antimacasar.
anti-ministerial, a.; **anti-ministerialist**, s., a. antiministerial.
antimonarchic, **antimonarchical**, **antimonarchist**, a. antimonárquico.
antimonial, a. antimonial. — s. preparación antimonial.
antimoniate, s., a. (quím.) antimoniato.
antimonic, a. antimónico.
antimonious, a. de antimonio.
antimony ['æntiməni], s. (min.) antimonio.
antimoralist, s. enemigo de la moralidad.
antinomian, s., a. antinomiano.
antinomianism, s. antinomia.
antinomy, s. antinomia, paradoja.
antipapal, **antipapistical**, a. antipapal.
antipathetic, **antipathetical**, a. antipático; contrario, adverso, opuesto.
antipathic, a. antipático.
antipathy, s. antipatía, antagonismo, repugnancia.
antipatriotic, a. antipatriótico.
antiperistaltic, a. (med.) antiperistáltico.
antipestilential, a. antipestilencial.
antiphlogistic, s., a. antiflogístico.
antiphon, s. antífona.
antiphonal, **antiphonical**, a. antifonal.
antiphonary, **antiphoner**, s. antifonal, antifonario.
antiphony, s. antífona.
antiphrasis, s. antífrasis, f.
antipodal, a. antipodal.
antipodes, s.pl. antípodas; (fig.) opuesto, contrario.
antipope, s. antipapa, m.
antipyretic, a. (med.) antipirético, febrífugo.
antiquarian [ænti'kwɛəriən], s. anticuario. — a. relativo a lo antiguo; (impr.) papel de 52½ inches × 30½ inches.
antiquarianism, s. afición a las antigüedades.
antiquary ['æntikwəri], s. anticuario.
antiquate ['æntikweit], v.t. anticuar, anular, abolir el uso de.
antiquated, a. viejo, añejo, anticuado, caído en desuso, fuera de uso, pasado de moda.
antiquatedness, **antiquateness**, s. vetustez, f., vejez, f.
antique [æn'ti:k], a. antiguo. — s. antigüedad, antigualla; after the antique, a la antigua.
antiquely, adv. a la antigua.
antiqueness, s. antigüedad, vetustez, f.
antiquity [æn'tikwiti], s. antigüedad, ancianidad, vetustez, f., vejez, f.
antirepublican, s., a. antirrepublicano.
antirevolutionary, a.; **antirevolutionist**, s. antirrevolucionario.
antirheumatic, a. antirreumático.
antirrhinum, s. (bot.) antirrino.
antiscorbutic, a. antiescorbútico, depurativo.
antisemitic, a. antisemita.
antisemitism, s. antisemitismo.
antisepsis, s. (med.) antisepsia.
antiseptic, a. antiséptico, antipútrido, desinfectante.
antislavery, a. antiesclavista, m.f.; partidario de la manumisión.
antisocial, a. antisocial.
antispasmodic, s., a. antiespasmódico.
antisplenetic, a. (med.) antiesplenético.
antistrophe, s. antistrofa, antistrofe, f.
antisyphilitic, s., a. antisifilítico.

antithesis [æn'tiθəsis], s. (fil.) antítesis, f., contraposición; contraste, oposición.
antithetic, antithetical, a. antitético.
antitoxin, s. (med.) antitoxina.
antitrinitarian, s. antitrinitario.
antitype, s. antitipo, prototipo, tipo modelo, figura, imagen, f.
antitypical, a. antitípico.
antivaccinator, s. contrario a la vacunación.
anti-venereal, s., a. antivenéreo.
anti-vivisection, s. antivivisección.
antler ['æntləɹ], s. cercetas, astas, mogotes del ciervo y venados.
antlered, a. armado de cerecetas o astas.
ant-lion, s. hormigaleón.
antonomasia, s. antonomasia.
antonomastically, adv. antonomásticamente, por antonomasia.
antonym ['æntənim], s. antónimo.
antre, antrum, s. antro, cueva, caverna.
anus ['einəs], s. (anat.) ano.
anvil ['ænvəl], s. yunque, ayunque, bigornia; hand-anvil, bigorneta; the stock of an anvil, cepo de yunque.
anxiety [æŋzaiəti], **anxiousness**, s. ansia, ansiedad, pena, aflicción, abatimiento de ánimo; desvelo, desasosiego, afán, anhelo, inquietud, dificultad, solicitud, cuidado.
anxious ['æŋkʃəs], a. ansioso, inquieto, anheloso, penoso, perturbado, impaciente, deseoso, solícito.
anxiousness, s. [ANXIETY].
any ['eni], pron., adj. cualquier, cualquiera; algún, alguno, alguna; todo, más; en; any, en sentido partitivo no se traduce generalmente: have you any money? tiene Vd. dinero?
anybody ['enibɔdi], **anyone**, pron. alguno, alguien, cualquiera; (con negación) ninguno, nadie; todo el mundo, toda persona.
anyhow ['enihau], adv. de cualquier modo, como quiera que sea, en cualquier caso, sin embargo, con indiferencia, no importa como.
anything, pron. algo, alguna cosa, cualquier cosa; (con negación) nada.
anyway, adv. sin embargo, con todo, salga lo que saliere, de cualquier modo.
anywhere, adv. donde quiera, en todas partes; (con negación) en ninguna parte.
aorist ['eiərist], s. (gram.) aoristo.
aorta [ei'ɔːɹtə], s. (anat.) aorta.
aortal, aortic, a. aórtico.
apace [ə'peis], adv. rápidamente, con presteza o prontitud de prisa.
apagoge, s. (lóg.) apogojía.
apagogical, a. apogógico.
apart [ə'paːɹt], adv. aparte, a un lado, separadamente, a distancia; independientemente; to put apart, poner aparte, separar; apart from, aparte de; to take apart, desmontar, desarmar; to tear apart, deshacer, despedazar.
apartment, s. cuarto, habitación, aposento, piso, vivienda.
apathetic, apathetical, a. apático, indolente, insensible, indiferente, sin pasión por nada.
apathy ['æpəθi], s. apatía, insensibilidad, indolencia, indiferencia, flema.
apatite, s. (min.) apatita, fosfato de cal.
ape [eip], s. mono, simia; (fig.) imitador, remedador. — v.t. imitar, remedar; hacer muecas.

apeak, apeek, adv. verticalmente; (mar.) a pique.
apepsia, apepsy, s. (med.) apepsia.
aper, s. imitador, mimo, ridículo, bufón.
aperient [ə'piəriənt], **aperitive**, a. aperitivo.
aperture ['æpəɹtjəɹ], s. abertura, paso, bujo, portillo, rendija.
apery, s. monería, gesto ridículo.
apetalous, a. (bot.) apétalo, sin pétalos.
apex ['eipeks], s. (pl. apexes o apices) ápice, cima, cúspide, f., punta.
aphaeresis [ə'fiərəsis], s. (gram.) aféresis, f.
aphasia [ə'feziə], s. (med.) afasia.
aphelion [ə'fiːliən], s. (astr.) afelio.
aphesis, s. (gram.) aféresis, f.
aphis ['æfis], s. afido, pulgón.
aphonia [ə'founiə], **aphony**, s. afonía.
aphonic, a. afónico, mundo, sin sonido.
aphorism, s. aforismo.
aphoristic [æfə'ristik], **aphoristical**, a. aforístico, sentencioso.
aphrodisiac, aphrodisiacal, s. afrodisíaco. — a. afrodisíaco; lujurioso, lascivo, sensual.
aphthous, a. (med.) aftoso.
aphyllous, a. (bot.) afilo, sin hojas.
apiary ['eipiəri], s. colmena, colmenar, abejar.
apical, a. cimerə.
apiculture, s. apicultura.
apiece [ə'piːs], adv. por barba, por cabeza, por persona, por pieza, cada uno.
apiology [eipi'ɔlədʒi], s. estudio de las abejas.
apish ['eipiʃ], a. gestero, monesco, remedador, gesticulador; frívolo, fatuo.
apishness, s. monería, monada, imitación burlesca, impertinencia.
apium ['eipiəm], s. (bot.) apio.
apivorous, a. apívoro.
aplanatic [æplə'nætik], a. (opt.) aplanático.
aplomb [ə'plɔ̃], s. aplomo, seguridad, posición recta; postura vertical.
apocalypse [ə'pɔkəlips], s. apocalipsis.
apocalyptic, apocalyptical, a. apocalíptico.
apocopate, v.t. (gram.) apocopar.
apocope, s. apócope, f.
apocrypha [ə'pɔkrifə], s.pl. libros apócrifos (o no canónicos).
apocryphal, a. apócrifo.
apodal, apodous, a. ápodo, sin pies; apedo.
apodictic [æpə'diktik], **apodictical**, a. (didact.) apodíctico, demostrativo, conveniente.
apodictically, adv. con evidencia.
apodosis [ə'pɔdəsis], s. (gram.) apódosis, f.
apodous, a. [APODAL].
apogee ['æpədʒi], s. (astr.) apogeo.
apograph, s. apógrafo.
apolaustic [æpə'laustik], a. entregado a los placeres; abandonado a los vicios.
apologetic [əpɔlə'dʒetik], **apologetical**, a. apologético.
apologetics, s.pl. apologética.
apologist, s. apologista, m.f.
apologize [ə'pɔlədʒaiz], v.t., v.i. apologizar, defender, excusar, disculpar; disculparse, excusarse.
apologizer, s. apologista, m.f., defensor.
apologue ['æpəlɔg], s. apólogo, fábula.
apology, s. apología, defensa, excusa, justificación, satisfacción.
aponeurotic [æponjuː'rɔtik], a. (med.) aponeurótico.

[819]

apoop [ə'puːp], *adv.* (*mar.*) en, hacia, contra, la popa.

apophasis [ə'pofəsis], *s.* (*ret.*) apófasis, *f.*, refutación.

apophisis [ə'pofisis], *s.* (*anat.*) apófisis, *f.*

apophlegmatic, *a.* (*med.*) apoflemático.

apophthegm, *s.* apotegma, *m.*

apoplectic, apoplectical, *a.* apoplético.

apoplexy [æpə'pleksi], *s.* (*med.*) apoplejía.

aport [ə'pɔəɹt], *adv.* (*mar.*) a babor (el timón).

apostasis [ə'postəsis], *s.* (*med.*) apóstasis, *f.*

apostasy, *s.* apostasía.

apostate [ə'posteit], *s.* apóstata, *m.f.*, renegado. — *a.* falso, pérfido, rebelde.

apostatical, *a.* apostático.

apostatize, *v.i.* apostatar, renegar.

apostem, apostema *s.* (*cir.*) absceso, apostema, postema.

apostemate, *v.i.* (*med.*) apostemar.

apostemation, *s.* formación de un apostema o absceso.

apostematous, *a.* apostemoso.

apostle [ə'posl], *s.* apóstol.

apostleship, apostolate, *s.* apostolado.

apostolic, apostolical, *a.* apostólico.

apostrophe [ə'postrəfi], *s.* apóstrofe, *m.f.*; virgulilla.

apostrophic₂ apostrophical, *a.* perteneciente al apóstrofe.

apostrophize, *v.t.* apostrofar.

apothecary [ə'poθəkəri], *s.* boticario, farmacéutico; *apothecary's shop*, botica, farmacia.

apothegm ['æpoθem], *s.* apotegma, *m.*, proloquio.

apothegmatic, apothegmatical, *a.* apotegmático, sentencioso.

apothegmatist, *s.* apotegmatista, *m.f.*

apothegmatize, *v.i.* apotegmatizar.

apotheosis, *s.* apoteosis, *f.*, deificación.

apotheosize, *v.t.* deificar, divinizar.

apozem, *s.* pócima, bebida medicinal.

appal [ə'pɔːl], *v.t.* espantar, aterrar, desanimar.

appalling, *a.* espantoso, aterrador.

appanage ['æpənidʒ], *s.* infantazgo, heredamiento; dependencia.

apparatus [æpə'reitəs], *s.* aparato, instrumento, conjunto de piezas de una máquina; aparejo, apresto; tren; pompa, ostentación; útiles empleados para la obtención de una cosa.

apparel [ə'pærəl], *s.* traje, ropa, vestido, ropaje; adorno, aderezo; (*mar.*) equipo, aparejo. — *v.t.* vestir, trajear; adornar, componer; (*mar.*) equipar, aparejar (un buque).

apparent [ə'pærənt], *a.* claro, patente, obvio, indubitable, evidente, manifesto, cierto; *heir apparent*, presunto heredero.

apparently, *adv.* evidentemente, claramente, manifiestamente, aparentemente, al parecer, a juzgar por las apariencias.

apparition [æpə'riʃən], *s.* aparición, apariencia; visión, fantasma, *m.*, ilusión, espectro.

apparitor [ə'pæritəɹ], *s.* portero, alguacil; ministril, esbirro; bedel de universidad.

appeach [ə'piːtʃ], *v.t.* acusar, denunciar, imputar, (*for.*) tachar, hacer objeción a.

appeal [ə'piːl], *v.i.* apelar, llamar *o* poner por testigo; clamar, recurrir, acudir a, suplicar a; atraer, llamar la atención a. — *s.* apelación, recurso, rogación, petición, súplica, instancia.

appealable, *a.* apelable.

appealer, *s.* apelante, acusador.

appealing, *a.* suplicante; atrayente.

appear [ə'piəɹ], *v.i.* aparecer, aparecerse, manifestarse, estar a la vista; comparecer, presentarse, responder; semejar, parecer; nacer, salir, surgir, brotar, apuntar, rayar; *to make to appear*, demostrar, probar.

appearance, *s.* aparición, presentación, presencia; vista; apariencia, aspecto, semejanza; exterioridad; máscara; aire; porte; verisimilitud, probabilidad; traza, facha, talante; llegada, asomada; (*for.*) comparecencia; el acto de comparecer ante el tribunal o juez; *to keep up appearances*, salvar las apariencias; *to all appearances*, a lo que parece, según parece, probablemente; *first appearance*, (de un artista) estreno; *appearances are deceitful*, (*prov.*) debajo de una mala capa hay un buen bebedor, las apariencias engañan.

appearer, *s.* (*for.*) compareciente.

appearing, *s.* aparición, presentación; llegada; (*for.*) comparecencia. — *a.* aparente.

appeasable, *a.* aplacable, reconciliable.

appeasableness, *s.* aplacabilidad, aplacamiento; cualidad de poder calmar o apaciguar.

appease [ə'piːz], *v.t.* aplacar, apaciguar, reconciliar; pacificar, aquietar, calmar; endulzar; aliviar, mitigar; desenojar, desenfadar, tranquilizar.

appeasement, *s.* apaciguamiento; quietud, paz, *f.*, tranquilidad, pacificación, alivio.

appeaser, *s.* aplacador, apaciguador, pacificador, reconciliador.

appeasable, *a.* apaciguador, tranquilizador.

appellant [ə'pelənt], *s.* apelante, demandante, demandador.

appellate, *a.* de apelación, a que se puede recurrir.

appellation [æpə'leiʃən], *s.* denominación, título, nombre, tratamiento.

appellative [ə'pelətiv], *s.* apelativo; (*fam.*) apellido. — *a.* apelativo, usual, común, opuesto a propio o peculiar.

appellee, *s* (*for.*) demandado; apelado, acusado.

append [ə'pend], *v.t.* colgar, atar; añadir; anexar; poner, fijar, ligar.

appendage, appendance, *s.* dependencia, accesorio, pertenencia; heredamiento, dote; (*bot. & zool.*) apéndice.

appendant, *a.* pendiente, colgante; dependiente, anexo; pegado, unido; accesorio; obligado, indispensable. — *s.* pertenencia, dependencia, accesoria; colgajo.

appendicitis [ə'pendi'saitis], *s.* apendicitis, *f.*

appendicle, *s.* (*bot.*) apendículo.

appendiculate, *a.* (*bot.*) apendiculado.

appendix [ə'pendiks], *s.* (*pl.* **appendixes** o **apendices**) apéndice; suplemento, adición; accesorio; dependencia.

apperception, *s.* (*fil.*) percepción del conocimiento interior.

appertain [æpəɹ'tein], *v.i.* pertenecer, tocar, competer, atañer.

appetence ['æpətəns], **appetency**, *s.* apetencia; anhelo, deseo, ardiente, ganas, avidez, *f.*; inclinación, tendencia natural.

appetent, *a.* ávido, codicioso, muy deseoso, anhelante, apetecedor.

appetibility, *s.* facultad de apetecer.

appetible, *a.* apetecible, deseable.

appetite ['æpətait], *s.* apetito; gana, antojo; hambre, *f.*, gana de comer.

appetitive, *a.* apetitivo, apetitoso, aperitivo.

appetize, *v.t.* excitar, estimular (el apetito).

appetizer, *s.* excitante, estimulante, aperitivo, apetitivo; *to take an appetizer,* (*fam.*) hacer boca, tomar un aperitivo.

appetizing, *a.* apetitivo, apetitoso, aperitivo; excitante, tentador, grato, gustoso.

applaud [ə'plɔːd], *v.t.* aplaudir, dar palmadas, aclamar, alabar; palmotear, palmear; honrar; celebrar. — *v.i.* aplaudir.

applauder, *s.* aplaudidor, alabador, celebrador.

applause, *s.* aplauso, palmoteo; aclamación, alabanza, aprobación; *round of applause,* salva de aplausos.

applausive, *a.* laudatorio.

apple ['æpl], *s.* manzana; *apple of one's eye,* niña del ojo; *apple of discord,* la manzana de la discordia; *Adams's apple,* nuez (*f.*) de la garganta; *bitter-apple,* coloquintida; *cider-apple,* manzana para sidra; *crab-apple,* manzana silvestre; *love-apple,* tomate; *oak-apple,* agalla de roble; *pine-apple,* ananás; *apple-corer,* despepitador de manzanas; *apple-fritter,* fritura de manzanas; *apple-harvest,* cosecha de manzanas; *apple-orchard,* manzanal; *apple-tart,* pastelillo de manzanas; *apple-tree,* manzano; *apple-woman,* vendedora de manzanas; *apple-yard,* huerto; *in apple-pie order,* (*fam.*) en orden perfecto.

appliable, applicable, *a.* aplicable, conforme, pertinente, propio para.

appliance [ə'plaiəns], *s.* aplicación, objeto aplicado; herramienta, accesorio; empleo; aparato, instrumento, recurso, medios; condición; súplica, petición; atención.

applicability, *s.* aplicabilidad.

applicable [ə'plikəbl], *a.* aplicable, pertinente, conforme.

applicableness, *s.* aptitud, disposición, propiedad de ser aplicable.

applicant ['æplikənt], *s.* suplicante; (*for.*) demandante; candidato, pretendiente, aspirante.

application [æpli'keiʃən], *s.* aplicación; empleo, uso; estudio intenso; (*geom.*) superposición; (*art*) adorno; solicitud, memorial, petición, súplica; *to make application to,* dirigirse a, recurrir a; *written application,* solicitud por escrito.

applicatory, *s., a.* aplicativo, aplicable.

apply [ə'plai], *v.t.* aplicar, apropiar, acomodar, adaptar, apropiar; destinar, utilizar, adjudicar; introducir en la práctica; atribuir, imputar; recurrir. — *v.i.* aplicarse, adaptarse, convenir; ocuparse, fijar (la atención); dirigirse, recurrir; *to apply for a position,* solicitar un puesto; *applied science,* ciencia aplicada; *applied for,* pedido; *patent applied for,* se ha solicitado el privilegio; *to apply oneself to,* darse a.

appoint [ə'point], *v.t.* señalar, designar, asignar, determinar, fijar; prescribir, ordenar; decretar; establecer; surtir, equipar; nombrar, elegir. — *v.i.* decidir, ordenar; *well appointed,* bien equipado; *at the appointed time,* a la hora señalada (*o* prescrita).

appointed, *a.* señalado, fijado, determinado, decretado.

appointee, *s.* funcionario nombrado, designado, elegido.

appointer, *s.* ordenador, director, nombrador.

appointment, *s.* estipulación; acuerdo, convenio; establecimiento, decreto; dirección, mandato, orden; equipaje, aparato; adscripción, destino; ordenanza; equipo (de tropas); ración, sueldo, honorarios, gajes; nombramiento, señalamiento; compromiso, cita. — *pl.* equipo, aparejo (de un buque).

apportion [ə'poəriʃən], *v.t.* proporcionar, repartir, prorratear.

apportionateness, *s.* prorrateo, proporción justa.

apportionment, *s.* distribución, división, reparto; rateo, prorrateo, prorrata.

apposite ['æpəzait], *a.* adaptado, apropiado, propio, proporcionado; conveniente, conforme, justo; oportuno, a propósito.

appositeness, *s.* adoptación; propiedad.

apposition [æpə'ziʃən], *s.* añadidura, adición, yuxtaposición; (*gram.*) aposición.

appositive [ə'pozətiv], *a.* (*gram.*) apositivo, aplicable, propio.

appraise [ə'preiz], *v.t.* apreciar, valuar, valorar, aforar, cuantiar, poner precio, tasar; estimar, ponderar.

appraisal, appraisement, *s.* aprecio, aforo, aforamiento, avalúo, tasación, valuación, estimación, justiprecio.

appraiser, *s.* apreciador, avaluador, tasador, aforador, justipreciador.

apprecation [æpriːsi'eiʃən], *s.* deprecación.

apprecatory, *a.* deprecatorio, deprecativo.

appreciable, *a.* apreciable, estimable, notable, sensible, perceptible.

appreciate [ə'priːʃieit], *v.t.* apreciar, estimar, tasar, valuar. — *v.i.* subir de precio, o en valor.

appreciater, *s.* apreciador, estimador, tasador, valuador.

appreciation, *s.* valuación, estimación, aprecio, tasa, avalúo; alza, aumento de precio, sensibilidad, susceptibilidad, percepción, perspicacia.

appreciative, appreciatory, *a.* apreciativo, estimatorio.

apprehend [æpri'hend], *v.t.* comprender, entender, percibir, aprehender, asir, prender, capturar; creer, pensar, suponer, imaginar; temer, recelar, sospechar.

apprehender, *s.* el que aprehende.

apprehensible, *a.* comprensible, aprensivo.

apprehension, *s.* aprehensión; presa, captura, prisión; embargo; aprensión, cuidado, temor, recelo, estimación, idea.

apprehensive, *a.* aprensivo, agudo, penetrante, capaz, perspicaz; sensible, tímido, receloso.

apprehensiveness, *s.* aprehensibilidad, aprensión, temor, timidez, *f.,* recelo.

apprentice [ə'prentis], *s.* aprendiz, mancebo de botica; novicio, tirón, principiante; *to bind* (or *put*) *apprentice,* poner en aprendizaje. — *v.t.* poner a alguno de aprendiz.

apprenticeship, *s.* aprendizaje, noviciado; *to serve one's apprenticeship,* hacer o pasar su aprendizaje.

apprise [ə'praiz], *v.t.* informar, instruir, avisar, comunicar, dar parte.

apprize, *v.t.* valuar, tasar, apreciar.

apprizer, *s.* valuador, tasador.

approach [ə'proutʃ], *v.i.* acercarse, aproximarse (física o moralmente), avecinarse, llegar; parecerse a, semejar, ser parecido. —

v.t. acercar, aproximar; (*hort.*) injertar. — *s.* acceso; proximidad, apropincuación; paso, entrada, camino, avenida. — *pl.* **approaches,** cercanías; (*fort.*) aproches, ataques.

approachable, *a.* accesible, atracable, de fácil acceso, aproximativo, comunicativo.

approacher, *s.* el que se acerca.

approaching, *a.* próximo, cercano, venidero.

approachless, *a.* inaccesible, de difícil acceso.

approbate ['æprəbeit], *v.t.* (*Am.*) aprobar, licenciar, autorizar.

approbation [æprə'beiʃən], *s.* aprobación, aplauso, beneplácito, juicio favourable; consentimiento, autorización.

approbative, approbatory, *a.* aprobativo, aprobatorio.

appropriable [ə'proupriəbl], *a.* apropiable, aplicable.

appropriate [ə'proupriət], *v.t.* apropiar, apropiarse, posesionarse, aplicar, destinar, adaptar, acomodar; enajenar. — *a.* apropiado, propio; peculiar, particular.

appropriateness, *s.* conveniencia, aptitud; propiedad de aplicación.

appropriation, *s.* apropiación; (*for.*) enajenación.

appropriator, *s.* apropiador.

approvable, *a.* digno de aprobación.

approval [ə'pru:vəl], *s.* aprobación; sanción; *on approval,* a prueba.

approve [ə'pru:v], *v.t.* aprobar, consentir; calificar o dar por bueno. — *v.i.* aprobar.

approver, *s.* aprobador, aprobante; (*for.*) denunciador; reo que confiesa su delito y acusa a sus cómplices.

approving, *a.* aprobador.

approvingly, *adv.* con aprobación.

approximate [ə'prɔksimeit], *a.* aproximado, aproximativo, próximo, cercano, inmediato; casi perfecto o completo. — *v.t.* aproximar. — *v.i.* acercarse.

approximately, *adv.* aproximadamente.

approximation, *s.* aproximación, acercamiento.

approximative, *a.* aproximativo.

approximatively, *adv.* aproximadamente, poco más o menos.

appui, *s.* apoyo, sostén; (*mil.*) punto de apoyo.

appulse [ə'pʌls], *s.* contacto, choque, encuentro.

appulsion, *s.* choque, encuentro.

appurtenance [ə'pə:rtənəns], *s.* (*for.*) adjunto, pertenencia, dependencia.

appurtenant, *a.* perteneciente, dependiente, pertinente.

apricot ['eiprikɔt], *s.* (*bot.*) · albaricoque; damasco.

April ['eipril], *s.* abril; *April-fools-day,* el primer día de abril; *April-fool,* el que es burlado el primero de abril.

apron ['eiprən], *s.* delantal, devantal; mandil; (*artill.*) planchada o plomada de cañón; batiente de un dique; plataforma a la entrada de un dique; antepecho; cuero de coche para proteger las piernas; piel grasa que cubre el vientre de un ganso o pato asado; *apron-man,* artesano; *apron strings,* cintas del delantal; *to be tied to the apron strings,* estar dominado por una mujer.

aproned, *a.* vestido con delantal.

apse [æps], *s.* (*arq.*) ábside.

apsis, *s.* (*astr.*) ápside.

apt [æpt], *a.* apto, idóneo, capaz, competente, hábil, propio; inclinado, pertinente, pronto, vivo, dispuesto, fácil; *apt to forgive,* muy indulgente; *apt to break,* frágil; *apt scholar,* estudiante capaz.

aptera ['æptərə], *s.pl.* (*zool.*) ápteros.

apteral, *a.*; **apterous,** *a.* (*ent.*) áptero, sin alas; (*arq.*) sin columnas a los lados.

aptitude ['æptitju:d], *s.* aptitud, capacidad, disposición, tendencia, idoneidad, facilidad.

aptote ['æptout], *s.* (*gram.*) nombre indeclinable.

apyretic, *a.* (*med.*) apirético.

apyrexy ['æpireksi], *s.* (*med.*) apirexia.

apyrous, *a.* (*quím., min.*) no alterado por el calor, como la mica.

aquafortis [ækwə'fɔə.rtis], *s.* agua fuerte.

aquamarine ['ækwəməri:n], *s.* aguamarina.

aquaregia [ækwə'ri:dʒə], *s.* agua regia.

aquarelle, *a.* (*art.*) acuarela.

aquarium [ə'kweəriəm], *s.* acuario, pecera.

Aquarius, *s.* (*astr.*) Acuario.

aquatic, *a.* acuático, acuátil.

aquatint ['ækwətint], *s.* acuatinta.

aqueduct ['ækwədʌkt], *s.* acueducto.

aqueous, aquose, *a.* ácueo, acuoso, aguoso.

aqueousness, aquosity, *s.* acuosidad.

aquiferous, *a.* acuífero.

aquiform, *a.* semejante al agua.

aquiline, *a.* aguileño, encorvado.

Arab, Arabian [ə'reibiən], *s.* árabe, arábico, natural de Arabia; *street arab,* pilluelo, pillete de calle.

arabesque [ærə'besk], *s., a.* arabesco.

Arabian, Arabic, *a.* arábigo, arábico; *Arabic figures,* cifras árabes.

Arabist, *s.* arabista, *m.f.*

arable ['ærəbl], *a.* labrantío, labradero, cultivable.

arachnid, *s.pl.* (*entom.*) arácnidos, aracneidos.

arbalest ['ɑ:.bəlest], **arbalist,** *s.* ballesta.

arbalister, *s.* ballestero.

arbiter ['ɑ:.bitə.r], *s.* arbitrador, árbitro, compromisario; *every man is the arbiter of his fortune,* (*prov.*) cada uno es artífice de su ventura. — *v.t.* arbitrar, juzgar.

arbitrable, *a.* arbitrable.

arbitrage, *s.* (*com.*) arbitrage.

arbitrament, *s.* arbitrio, arbitramento, elección, determinación, compromiso.

arbitrariness, *s.* arbitrariedad, despotismo.

arbitrary, *a.* arbitrario, arbitral, absoluto, despótico.

arbitrate ['ɑ:.bitreit], *v.t.* arbitrar, juzgar, determinar, decidir.

arbitration, *s.* arbitramento; liquidación; arbitración, tercería.

arbitrator, *s.* arbitrador, árbitro; tercero.

arbitratrix, arbitress, *s.f.* arbitradora.

arbitrement, *s.* arbitrio, determinación, elección, compromiso.

arbor, arbour ['ɑ:.bə.r], *s.* árbol; emparrado, bacelar; glorieta, enramada, bosquecillo; (*mec.*) eje, árbol.

arboreal [ɑ:.r'bɔəriəl], **arboreous, arborous,** *a.* arbóreo.

arborescence [ɑ:.rbə'resəns], *a.* (*bot.*) arborescencia; (*min.*) arborización.

arborescent, *a.* arborescente.

arboret, *s.* arbolillo, arbusto, arboleda, soto.

arboretum, *s.* almáciga (o criadero) de árboles.

arboricultural, *a.* relativo a la arboricultura.

arboriculture, s. arboricultura.
arboriculturist, s. arbolista, m.f.
arborization, s. arborización.
arborized, a. (min.) arborizado.
arbour, s. [ARBOR].
arbuscle ['a:ɪbʌsl], s. arbolillo, arbustillo.
arbuscular, a. arbuscular.
arbuscule, s. arbusto, mata.
arbute, s. (bot.) madroño; fresal.
arbutean, a. perteneciente al madroño, al fresal.
arbutus [a:ɪ'bjutəs], s. madroño.
arc [a:ɪk], s. (geom.) arco; arc-lamp (elec.) arco voltaico; arc-light (elec.) arco galvánico.
arcade [a:ɪ'keid], s. arcada; pasaje, galería, cubierta con tiendas en los lados.
Arcadian, a. arcadio. — s. árcade.
arcane [a:ɪ'kein], a. arcano, misterioso.
arcanum, s. (pl. **arcana**) arcano, misterio.
arch [a:ɪtʃ], s. arco; bóveda; curvatura. — v.t. abovedar; arquear, encorvar, enarcar. — v.i. formar bóveda. — a. insigne, grande, de primer orden; picaresco, socarrón, astuto, travieso, malicioso; the arch of heaven, la bóveda celeste; arch of the aorta, (anat.) la corvatura de la aorta; segmental arch, arco abocinado; Gothic arch, pointed arch, arco gótico, arco ojival; semicircular arch, arco de medio punto.
archaic [a:ɪ'keiik], a. arcaico, anticuado, inusitado, desusado.
archaism, s. arcaísmo.
archangel ['a:ɪkeindʒəl], s. arcángel; (bot.) ortiga muerta.
archangelic, a. arcangélico.
archbishop [a:ɪtʃ'biʃəp], s. arzobispo.
archbishopric, s. arzobispado.
archdeacon, s. arcediano.
archdeaconry, archdeaconship, s. arcedianato.
archdiocese, s. arzobispado.
archducal, a. archiducal.
archduchess, a. archiduquesa.
archduchy, s. archiducado.
archduke, s. archiduque.
archdukedom, s. archiducado.
arched, a. arqueado; abovedado, corvo.
archenemy, s. enemigo principal; el demonio.
archeologic, archeological [a:ɪkɪə'lɔdʒikəl], a. arqueológico.
archeologist, s. arqueólogo.
archeology, s. arqueología.
archer ['a:ɪtʃəɪ], s. arquero, ballestero, flechero.
archery, s. tiro de arco, ballestería.
archetypal, a. perteneciente al arquetipo.
archetype ['a:ɪkətaip], s. arquetipo, patrón.
archfoe ['a:ɪtʃfou], s. enemigo principal.
archheresy, s. grande herejía, enorme herejía.
archheretic, s. gran heresiarca.
archhypocrite, s. hipocritón, santurrón.
archidiaconal [a:ɪkidi'ækənəl], a. perteneciente al arcediano.
archiepiscopal, a. arquiepiscopal, arzobispal.
archiepiscopate, s. arzobispado.
archil ['a:ɪkil], s. (bot.) orchilla.
archimandrite, s. archimandrita, m.
Archimedean, a. de Arquímedes.
arching ['a:ɪtʃiŋ], a. arqueado, en forma de arco. — s. arqueo, curvatura.
archipelago [a:ɪkɪ'peləgou], s. archipiélago.

architect ['a:ɪkitekt], s. arquitecto; (fig.) artífice.
architectonic architectonical, a. arquitectónico.
architectonics, s. arquitectura, arte arquitectónico.
architectural, a. arquitectónico.
architecture, s. arquitectura.
architrave, s. arquitrabe.
archival, a. perteneciente al archivo.
archives ['a:ɪkaivz], s.pl. archivos.
archivist, s. archivero, archivista, m.f.
archivolt, s. (arq.) archivolta.
archlike ['a:ɪtʃlaik], a. arqueado, en forma de arco, abovedado.
archly, adv. sutilmente, con malicia, jocosamente.
archness, s. travesura, astucia, sutileza; coquetería.
archon ['a:ɪkən], s. (pl. **archontes**) arconte.
archonship, s. arcontado.
archpriest, s. gran sacerdote; arcipreste.
archstone, s. clave (f.) de bóveda.
archtraitor, s. traidor principal.
archvillain, s. bellaconazo, picarón.
archvillainy, s. gran bellaquería.
archwise, adv. en figura de arco, de bóveda.
archwork, s. construcción de arcos.
arctic ['a:ɪktik], a. ártico, setentrional.
arcuate, a. arqueado.
arcuation, s. arqueo, curvatura, encorvamiento.
ardency ['a:ɪdənsi], **ardentness,** s. ardor, vehemencia, anhelo, calor, ansia.
ardent ['a:ɪdənt], a. ardiente, vehemente, fervoroso, férvido, intensivo, apasionado, fogoso, vivo, ansioso.
ardour ['a:ɪdəɪ], s. ardor, calor, pasión, fervor, vehemencia, acaloramiento.
arduous ['a:ɪdjuəs], a. arduo, alto; escarpado, inaccesible; (fig.) difícil, rudo, penoso.
arduousness, s. arduidad.
are [a:ɪ], v. plural del presente de indicativo del verbo TO BE; we are, you are, they are, somos, sois, son, o estamos, estáis, están.
area ['ɛəriə], s. área, espacio, superficie, f.; patio, corral; zanja; extensión; calvicie, f., alopecia.
areal, a. superficial, del área.
arefaction, s. arefacción, desecación, sequedad.
arefy, v.t. secar, extraer la humedad.
arena [ə'ri:nə], s. arena; liza, campo de combate; arena de un anfiteatro; círculo de acción; (med.) mal de piedra.
arenaceous, arenose, a. arenisco, arenoso, arenáceo.
arenation, s. (med.) arenación.
areometer [ær'ɔmətəɪ], s. areómetro.
areometrical, a. areométrico.
areometry, s. areometría.
argal ['a:ɡəl], **argol,** s. tártaro.
argent ['a:ɪdʒənt], a. (blas.) plata, blanco.
argentation, s. plateadura, baño de plata.
argentiferous, a. (min.) argentífero.
argentine, a. argentino, argénteo, argentoso. — s. metal blanco plateado.
Argentinian, a. argentino.
argil ['a:ɪdʒil], s. arcilla.
argillaceous, argilliferous, a. arcilloso.
argon ['a:ɪɡən], s. (quím.) argo.
argonaut ['a:ɪɡɔnɔ:t], s. (ict., mit.) argonauta, m.

argosy, s. bajel grande mercante, carraca; (*fig.*) buque con rico cargamento; cosa de gran valor y riqueza.

argot [ɑrˈgo], s. jerga, jerigonza, lenguaje propio de ladrones.

argue [ˈɑːɹgjuː], v.i. argüir, impugnar, razonar, debatir, argumentar, disputar, discurrir, controvertir. — v.t. probar, persuadir, hacer ver con razones; argüir, disputar; deducir, inferir, demostrar; *it argues well for him*, habla en su favor.

arguer, s. discutidor, argumentador, arguyente, opinante.

arguing, s. razonamiento, argumento.

argument, s. argumento, tema, m., asunto; (*for.*) alegato; razón, razonamiento, demostración, prueba; controversia, debate.

argumentation [aːɹgjumenˈteiʃən] s. argumentación, raciocinio.

argumentative [aːɹgjuˈmentətiv], a. argumentativo, argumentador, argumentista, demostrativo, razonado.

Argus, s. (*mit.*) Argos; (*fig.*) persona vigilante; (*zool.*) argos, faisán de China.

argute, a. agudo, sutil, perspicaz, astuto; penetrante; (*bot.*) dentado.

arguteness, s. argucia, agudeza, sutileza, perspicacia.

aria [ˈɑːriə], s. (*mús.*) aria.

Arian [ˈɛəriən], s. arriano.

Arianism, s. arrianismo.

arid [ˈærɪd], a. árido, seco, sequizo, enjuto, enjugado.

aridity, aridness, s. aridez; sequedad, esterilidad, enjutez; (*med.*) emaciación.

arietta, s. (*mús.*) arieta, aria corta.

aright [əˈrait], adv. acertadamente, rectamente, sanamente, justamente, puramente, bien.

aril, s. (*bot.*) arila, cubierta o zurrón del grano.

ariolation, s. adivinación.

arise [əˈraiz], v.i. (*pret.* **arose**; *p.p.* **arisen**) subir, elevarse, levantarse, alzarse, surgir, aparecer; ponerse en pie; provenir, proceder; presentarse, ofrecerse; originarse, suscitarse; sublevarse; resucitar.

aristocracy [ærisˈtɔkrəsi], s. aristocracia.

aristocrat [ˈæristəkræt], s. aristócrata, m. f.

aristocratic [ærɪstəˈkrætik], **aristocratical**, a. aristocrático.

aristocraticalness, s. modales aristocráticos.

Aristotelian, a. aristotélico. — s. **Aristotelianism**, aristotelismo, peripato.

arithmancy, s. aritmancia.

arithmetic [əˈriθmətik], s. aritmética.

arithmetical [ærɪθˈmetikəl], a. aritmético.

arithmetically, adv. aritméticamente.

arithmetician, s. aritmético.

arithmometer, s. aritmómetro.

ark [ɑːk], s. arca, cofre grande; (*mar.*) lanchón; *Noah's ark*, arca de Noé; *ark of the Covenant*, el arca de la alianza.

arm [ɑːm], s. brazo, miembro; esfuerzo, poder, fuerza, valor; rama del árbol; (*mar.*) barra del cabrestante; mango del remo; cabo de una verga; brazo de mar; radio; punta de palanca; (*mil.*) arma, instrumento de ataque o defensa; instituto o ramo del servicio militar; *arm's reach*, alcance; *with folded arms*, con los brazos cruzados; *arm in arm*, de bracete; *at arm's length*, a una brazada; (*fig.*) a distancia; *arm-chair*, sillón; *forearm*, antebrazo. — v.t.

armar; fortalecer, reforzar; aprestar, equipar. — v.i. tomar las armas, armarse, levantarse las tropas.

armada, s. armada, flota.

armadillo, s. armadillo, cachicamo.

armament, s. armamento, equipo.

armature, s. (*elec.*) armadura; arma defensiva, armamento, equipo.

arm-chair, s. sillón, silla de brazos; butaca.

armed, a. armado de brazos; armado, provisto de (armas); (*bot.*) espinoso.

Armenian [ɑːrˈmiːniən], s., a. armenio.

armful, s. brazada; lo que se puede abarcar con los brazos.

armhole, s. sobaquera.

armiger [ˈɑːrmɪdʒəɹ], s. armígero; escudero.

armillary, a. armilar, anular.

arming-press, s. prensa de estampar.

Arminian, s., a. arminiano; de la secta de Arminio.

armipotent, a. armipotente.

armistice [ˈɑːrmistis], s. armisticio.

armless, a. desarmado, manco, sin armas; mutilado, sin brazos.

armlet, s. brazal, brazalete.

armorial [ɑːrˈmoəriəl], a. heráldico; *armorial bearings*, escudo de armas.

armoring, s. acorazamiento, blindaje.

armorist, s. heráldico.

armour [ˈɑːrməɹ], s. armadura; *coat-armour*, cota de malla. — v.t. (*mar.*) acorazar, blindar.

armour-bearer, s. escudero.

armoured, a. blindado; *armoured car*, carro blindado.

armourer, s. armero.

armour-plating, s. acorazamiento, blindaje.

armoury, s. armería; heráldica; fábrica de armas.

arm-pit, s. axila, sobaco.

arms, s.pl. armas; instrumentos ofensivos o defensivos; milicia; hostilidad, guerra, como profesión, ciencia o arte; blasones; *to present arms*, presentar armas; *to ground arms*, descansar sobre las armas; *fire-arms*, armas de fuego; *side-arms*, armas blancas; *man at arms*, guerrero, hombre armado; *to lay down arms*, rendir las arms; *to arms!* ¡a las armas!

army, s. ejército; multitud, muchedumbre.

arnatto [əɹˈnætə], s. (*bot.*) bija, achiote.

arnica [ˈɑːrnikə], s. (*bot.*) árnica.

aroint, v. o *interj.* (*ant.*) irse, apartarse; ¡vete! ¡apártate! ¡fuera! ¡afuera!

aroma [əˈroumə], s. aroma; fragancia.

aromatic [ærəˈmætik], **aromatical**, a. aromático, aromoso, odorífero, fragante.

aromatics, s.pl. aromas, especias.

aromatization, s. aromatización.

aromatize, v.t. aromatizar.

aromatizer, s. aromatizador.

arose [əˈrous], v.t. pret. del verbo TO ARISE.

around [əˈraund], prep. en, cerca de, al rededor; — adv. cerca, alrededor; a la redonda, a la vuelta, por todos lados.

arouse [əˈraus], v.t. despertar, excitar, mover, sacudir.

arow, adv. (*poét.*) en fila, en línea.

arpeggio [ɑːrˈpedʒou], s. (*mús.*) arpegio.

arquebus [ˈɑːkwibʌs], s. arcabuz.

arquebusade, s. arcabucería, arcabuzazo.

arquebusier, s. arcabucero.

arrack [ˈærək], s. arak.

arraign [ə'rein], *v.t.* (*for.*) citar, emplazar; acusar, denunciar, hacer cargo de.

arraignment, *s.* (*for.*) emplazo, emplazamiento; denuncia, acusación; proceso; auto; presentación al tribunal.

arrange [ə'reindʒ], *v.t.* colocar, arreglar, poner en orden; acondicionar, coordinar, disponer, preparar, aprestar, ajustar, justificar, formar; (*mús.*) adaptar. — *v.i.* prevenir, convenir, concertar.

arrangement, *s.* colocación, arreglo, orden; medida, distribución, disposición; cálculo; providencia.

arrant ['ærənt], *a.* consumado, notorio, redomado; *an arrant fool*, tonto de siete suelas.

arrantly, *adv.* corruptamente, vergonzosamente, notoriamente, redomadamente.

arras ['ærəs], *s.* tapicería de Arrás.

array [ə'rei], *s.* formación, orden; revista; fila, hilera; (*for.*) formación del jurado; pompa, aparato; (*poét.*) trajes, adorno, compostura, gala, atavío. — *v.t.* colocar, poner en orden; formar; ataviar, vestir, adornar, engalanar.

arrear [ə'riːə], *s.* lo atrasado, lo caído; (*com.*) vencido, debido. — *adv.* hacia atrás; *in arrears*, atrasado.

arrearage, *s.* atrasos, caídos.

arrest [ə'rest], *s.* detención, prisión, arresto; embargo, detención de bienes; parada, cesación de movimiento; interrupción; *under arrest*, preso, en prisión. — *v.t.* detener, parar, impedir el paso; retener, atajar, impedir; fijar (la atención); arrestar, prender; embargar; (*for.*) cesación temporal de un procedimiento.

arrestation, *s.* detención, prisión, arresto.

arrester, *s.* alguacil, corchete, detenedor.

arrhizous, arrhizal, *a.* sin raíces (como ciertas plantas parásitas).

arris ['æris], *s.* (*arq.*) arista; filo; esquina.

arrival, *s.* llegada, entrada, arribo; logro, consecución; *a new arrival*, un recién venido.

arrive [ə'raiv], *v.i.* llegar, arribar; llevar a cabo, alcanzar, conseguir, lograr; acontecer, suceder.

arrogance, arrogancy, arrogantness, *s.* arrogancia, soberbia, orgullo, altivez, presunción, insolencia, altanería.

arrogant ['ærəgənt], *a.* arrogante, insolente, orgulloso, altivo, presuntuoso, soberbio.

arrogate ['ærəgeit], *v.t.* arrogarse, usurpar; alegar algún derecho infundado; atribuirse.

arrogation, *s.* arrogación.

arrow ['ærou], *s.* flecha, saeta; *arrow-grass*, trigloquín; *arrow-head*, punta de flecha; *arrow-root*, arrurruz; *arrow-shaped*, aflechado, sagital.

arrowy, *a.* de flecha, en forma de flecha; rápido.

arse [aːs], *s.* (*vulg.*) culo, trasero, nalgas, posaderas.

arsenal ['aːsənəl], *s.* arsenal, atarazana.

arsenate, arseniate, *s.* (*quím.*) arseniato.

arsenic ['aːsənik], *s.* arsénico; *white arsenic*, ácido arsenioso.

arsenical, *a.* arsenical, de arsénico.

arsenious, *a.* arsenioso.

arsenite, *s.* arsenito.

arsis ['aːsis], *s.* sílaba acentuada.

arson ['aːsən], *s.* incendio premeditado (o de intento).

art [aːt], *s.* arte, ciencia, gremio, oficio;

cautela, maña, destreza, artificio, astucia, habilidad; *fine arts*, bellas artes; *black art*, magia negra; *Arts Faculty*, Facultad de Filosofía; *art gallery*, museo de arte. — *v.t.* segunda pers. indic. del verbo TO BE: tú eres o tú estás.

arterial [aːˈtiəriəl], *a.* arterial.

arterialization [aːˌtiəriəlaiˈzeiʃən], *s.* arterialización.

arterialize, *v.t.* arterializar.

arteriole, *s.* arteriola.

arteriology, *s.* arteriología.

arteriotomy, *s.* arteriotomía.

artery ['aːtəri], *s.* arteria.

artesian [aːˈtiːziən], *s.*, *a.* artesiano; *artesian well*, pozo artesiano.

artful ['aːtful], *a.* artificioso, diestro, ingenioso; industrioso; artificial; astuto, cauteloso; artero, mañero, ladino, socarrón; refinado, redomado, bellaco.

artfulness, *s.* arte, habilidad, industria; artificio, astucia, artería.

arthritic [aːˈθritik], **arthritical**, *a.* (*med.*) artrítico, artético.

arthriticism, *s.* (*med.*) artritismo.

arthritis [aːˈθraitis], *s.* (*med.*) artritis, *f.*, artética.

arthrology, *s.* artrología.

arthrosis, *s.* (*anat.*) artrosis, *f.*, articulación.

artichoke ['aːtitʃouk], *s.* (*bot.*) alcachofa, arcacil; *Jerusalem artichoke*, cotufa.

article ['aːtikl], *s.* artículo; parte de un conjunto; estipulación, término; cosa, objeto; artículo (literario); cláusula, sección; punto de doctrina; *article of merchandise*, mercadería; *small articles*, menudencias; *trifling article*, bagatela; *to be under articles*, estar escriturado; *to sign articles*, escriturarse; *Articles of War*, Regulaciones por las que se rigen la Marina y Ejército de la Gran Bretaña y América del Norte; *Thirty-nine Articles*, Los treinta y nueve artículos de declaración suscritos por los clérigos de la Iglesia Anglicana; *leading article*, artículo de fondo. — *v.i.* capitular, estipular, convenir en. — *v.t.* detallar; (*for.*) acusar, demandar; contratarse, obligarse por contrato; *to article (an apprentice)* poner en aprendizaje.

articled, *a.* capitulado, concertado, puesto por artículos; contratado, obligado por contrato.

articular [aːˈtikjuləl], *a.* articular.

articulate, *a.* articulado, claro, distinto. — *s.* animal articulado. — *v.t.* articular; pronunciar distintamente; formar nudos o articulaciones. — *v.i.* hablar distintamente; estipular.

articulateness, *s.* calidad de ser articulado.

articulation, *s.* articulación, pronunciación; conjuntura; (*bot.*) nudo.

artifice ['aːtifis], *s.* artificio, engaño, estratagema, *m.*, fraude.

artificer, *s.* artífice, artesano.

artificial [aːtiˈfiʃəl], **artificious**, *a.* artificial; artificioso; fingido.

artificiality, *s.* arte, apariencia, carácter artificial.

artificialness, *s.* astucia, arte.

artillerist, *s.* artillero.

artillery [aːˈtiləri], *s.* artillería; *artillery-man*, artillero; *artillery-practice*, ejercicio de cañón.

artisan [aːtiˈzæn], *s.* artesano, artífice.

artist ['aːtist], *s.* artista, *m.f.*, artífice, conocedor.

artistic, artistical, *a.* artístico.
artless ['ɑːɪtles], *a.* natural, cándido, sin arte, sencillo, simple.
artlessly, *adv.* sencillamente, simplemente, naturalmente, cándidamente; (*fam.*) a la buena de Dios.
artlessness, *s.* sencillez, candidez, naturalidad, ingenuidad.
arum ['ɛərəm], *s.* (*bot.*) aro, yaro, sarrillo.
arundinaceous, arundineous, *a.* (*bot.*) arundináceo.
Aryan ['ɛəriən], *s.*, *a.* ario.
as [æz], *conj.* como, así como, así también, del mismo modo que, por lo que; mientras; según, a medida que; tan, igualmente; cuando, a título de, tocante a; *as far, as to,* en cuanto a, por lo que toca a; *as far as,* hasta; *as good as,* tan bueno como; *as it is,* así como así; *as yet,* aún, todavía; *as well as,* tan bien como; *as sure as can be,* sin duda alguna; *as you please,* como Vd. quiera; *as* indica el tiempo, y también el lugar, y entonces se traduce *como,* o *al,* y las mas veces no se expresa; *v.g. as he was at the door,* estando él a la puerta; *as they were walking,* al ir ellos andando; *as I was there,* estando yo allá.
asafœtida [æsə'fetidə], **asafetida,** *s.* asafétida.
asbestic, asbestine, *a.* asbestino, incombustible.
asbestos [æz'bestɔs], *s.* asbesto.
ascend [ə'send], *v.t.,* *v.i.* ascender, subir; adelantar; elevar, encumbrarse.
ascendable, *a.* accesible, de fácil subida.
ascendant, ascendent, *s.* altura, elevación; ascendiente; autoridad, superioridad; poder, influjo; predominio. — *a.* ascendiente, predominante, superior.
ascendancy, ascendency, *s.* ascendiente, poder, influjo.
ascending, *a.* (*astr.*) ascendente.
ascension, *s.* ascensión, subida.
ascensional, *a.* (*astr.*) ascensional.
ascent, *s.* subida, elevación, ascensión; promoción, ascenso; cuesta, pendiente, *f.*
ascertain [æsəɪ'tein], *v.t.* asegurar, fijar, regular, determinar, descubrir, establecer; confirmar, afirmar, indagar, averiguar; descubrir, hallar, cerciorarse.
ascertainable, *a.* asegurable, descubrible, averiguable.
ascertainer, *s.* averiguador, indagador.
ascertainment, *s.* averiguación, comprobación, certitud, conocimiento cierto.
ascetic [ə'setik], *s.* asceta, *m.f.* — *a.* ascético.
asceticism, *s.* asceticismo.
ascites [æ'saitiːz], *s.* (*med.*) ascitis, *f.*
ascitic, ascitical, *a.* ascítico, hidrópico.
ascititious, *a.* adicional.
ascribable, *a.* aplicable, imputable.
ascribe [ə'skraib], *v.t.* adscribir, atribuir, achacar, aplicar, adjudicar.
ascription, *s.* atribución; imputación.
asea [æ'siː], *adv.* sobre el mar, hacia el mar.
asepsis, *s.* (*med.*) asepsia.
aseptic [æ'septik], *a.* aséptico.
asexual [ə'seksjuəl], *a.* (*bot.*) asexual, sin sexo.
ash [æʃ], *s.* fresno; ceniza; *ash-grove,* fresneda; *mountain-ash* o *rowan-tree,* serbal; *ash-tree,* fresno; *ash-colour,* color de ceniza; ceniciento; *ash-fire,* fuego cubierto; *Ash Wednesday,* miércoles de ceniza; *ash-pan,* cenicero, cenizal. — *a.* de fresno.

ashamed [ə'ʃeimd], *a.* avergonzado, vergonzoso, corrido; *to be ashamed,* tener vergüenza.
ashen, *a.* de fresno; ceniciento; pálido.
ashery, *s.* cenicero, depósito de cenizas.
ashes, *s.pl.* ceniza, cenizas, reliquias de un cadáver, restos mortales.
ashlar ['æʃləɪ], **ashler,** *s.* sillar; morrillo.
ashlaring, *s.* ligazones a los cabríos del techo en guardillas.
ashore [ə'ʃoəɪ], *adv.* a tierra, en tierra; *to go ashore,* desembarcar; *to run ashore,* encallar, ir a la costa (un buque).
ashweed [æʃwiːd], *s.* (*bot.*) angélica.
ashy, *a.* cenizoso, ceniciento; *ashy-pale,* lívido, pálido.
Asian, Asiatic, *s.,* *a.* asiático, de Asia.
aside [ə'said], *adv.* al lado, a un lado; oblicuamente, de través; aparte; *adv.,* *s.* (*teat.*) aparte; *to lay aside,* deponer, desechar, abandonar; (*for.*) *to set aside a judgment,* anular una sentencia.
asinine ['æsinain], *a.* asinino, asnal, borriqueño.
ask [aːsk], *v.t.,* *v.i.* preguntar, interrogar; pedir, rogar; convidar, invitar; inquirir, buscar; *to ask a person in,* rogar a uno que pase (o entre); *to ask up, in, down,* rogar que suba, entre, baje; *to ask for* (o *after*) *someone,* preguntar por alguno; *to ask in church,* (*pop.*), publicar las amonestaciones.
askance, askant [ə'skænt], *adv.* al sesgo, de reojo, de soslayo, oblicuamente, con desdén, con recelo.
asker, *s.* inquiridor, suplicante.
askew [ə'skjuː], *adv.* al lado, de lado, al través, de través.
asking, *s.* súplica, ruego, demanda, acción de pedir; publicación (de amonestaciones); *this is the third time of asking,* ésta es la tercera amonestación.
aslant, *adv.,* *prep.* al sesgo, inclinado, oblicuamente.
asleep [ə'sliːp], *adv.* dormido, durmiendo; *to fall asleep,* dormirse, quedarse dormido.
aslope, *adv.* oblicuamente, en declive, en pendiente.
asp, aspic, *s.* (*zool.*) áspid.
aspalathus, *s.* (*bot.*) aspálato.
asparagus [ə'spærəgəs], *s.* (*bot.*) espárrago.
aspect ['æspekt], *s.* aspecto, fase, *f.,* aire, cara, faz, *f.,* semblante; traza, talante, ademan; mirada, ojeada, vista; situación, dirección, disposición; exposición, apariencia, punto de vista; exterior; (*astr.*) aspecto, posición relativa de los planetas.
aspen ['æspən], *s.* (*bot.*) tiemblo; álamo temblón. — *a.* perteneciente al álamo temblón.
asper, *s.* aspro.
asperation, *s.* asperura.
aspergillus, *s.* aspersorio, hisopo.
asperifolious, *a.* (*bot.*) asperfoliado.
asperity, *s.* aspereza, asperura, desigualdad; acerbidad, rudeza, rigidez; severidad, acrimonia.
aspermatous, aspermous, *a.* (*bot.*) aspermo, sin semilla.
asperse [æs'pəːɪs], *v.t.* asperjar, hisopar, rociar; (*fig.*) calumniar, difamar, denigrar.
asperser, *s.* calumniador, infamador.
aspersion, *s.* aspersión; calumnia, difamación; mancha, mácula, tacha; deshonra; rociadura; (*fam.*) rociada, represión; (*igl.*) asperges; *to*

cast aspersion on one, difamar a alguno, calumniarlo.

aspersive, *a.* calumnioso, disfamatorio; escandaloso.

asphalt, asphaltum, *s.* asfalto.

asphalt ['æsfælt], *v.t.* asfaltar.

asphalter, *s.* asfaltador.

asphaltic, *a.* asfáltico.

asphalting, *s.* asfaltado.

asphodel ['æsfədel], *s.* (*bot.*) asfodelo, gamón.

asphyxia [æs'fiksiə], **asphyxiation, asphyxy,** *s.* (*med.*) asfixia, sofocación.

asphyxiate, *v.t.* asfixiar, sofocar.

aspic ['æspik], *s.* áspid; culebrina (pieza de artillería); (*bot.*) espliego; jalea de carne.

aspirant, *s.* aspirante; candidato, pretendiente.

aspirate ['æspəreit], *v.t.* (*gram.*) aspirar, pronunciar con aspiración. — *v.i.* aspirar. — *a.* aspirado. — *s.* letra aspirada.

aspiration, *s.* aspiración, anhelo, deseo vehemente; ambición.

aspirator, *s.* aspirador.

aspiratory, *a.* aspiratorio.

aspire [ə'spaɪəɹ], *v.t., v.i.* aspirar, anhelar, desear con ansia, ambicionar; pretender; (*fig.*) ascender, subir.

aspirin, *s.* aspirina.

aspiring, *a.* ambicioso, aspirante. — *s.* pretensión.

asquint [ə'skwint], *adv.* oblicuamente, al soslayo, de través; *to look asquint,* mirar de soslayo.

ass [æs], *s.* asno, burro, borrico, jumento; (*fig.*) tonto, estúpido, bestia, ignorante; *she-ass,* burra, borrica; *young ass,* pollino; *jack-ass,* garañón; *ass-driver,* burrero.

assagai, assegai ['æsəgai], *s.* azagaya.

assail [ə'seil], *v.t.* acometer, invadir, arremeter, asaltar, atacar, embestir.

assailable, *a.* que puede ser atacado o asaltado.

assailant, assailer, *s.* acometedor, asaltador, agresor, invasor, arremetedor, embestidor.

assailment, *s.* ataque, asalto, agresión, acometida, acometimiento.

assart, *s.* rozamiento; roza. — *v.t.* rozar, desmontar y desbrotar la tierra.

assassin [ə'sæsin], **assassinator,** *s.* asesino.

assassinate, *v.t.* asesinar, matar alevosamente.

assassination, *s.* asesinato.

assault [ə'sɔːlt], *s.* asalto, ataque, salteamiento, agresión, acometimiento; invasión, hostilidad; insulto, ultraje; violación, estupro; *assault-at-arms,* ejercicio de esgrima; *assault and battery,* (*for.*) falta de palabra y obra. — *v.t.* acometer, asaltar, saltear, invadir, atacar, insultar, violar.

assaultable, *a.* (*mil.*) atacable, lo que puede ser asaltado.

assaulter, *a.* agresor, invasor, salteador, asaltador.

assay [ə'sei], *s.* ensayo, ensaye, toque, prueba, experimento; tentativa; estreno; contraste. — *v.t.* ensayar; experimentar; tentar, hacer tentativa; probar, gustar; acrisolar; aquilatar; contrastar.

assayer, *s.* ensayador, fiel contraste.

assaying, *s.* ensayo, ensay (de metales).

assemblage, *s.* colección, grupo, agregado; asamblea, multitud, reunión, *f.,* junta, asociación, concurso; (*mec.*) montaje.

assemblance, *s.* apariencia, representación; reunión, *f.,* congregación, junta.

assemble [ə'sembl], *v.t.* congregar, allegar, juntar, reunir, convocar. — *v.i.* juntarse, reunirse.

assembler, *s.* convocador; instigador.

assembling, *s.* reunión, *f.,* asamblea, junta; acción de convocar, de juntarse.

assembly, *s.* asamblea, junta, concurso, congreso, concilio, congregación, convención, tertulia; (*mil.*) toque de llamada.

assembly-room, *s.* congreso, asamblea, sala de sesiones o de juntas.

assent [ə'sent], *s.* asenso, asentimiento, consentimiento, aprobación; reconocimiento, confesión; beneplácito, aquiescencia. — *v.i.* asentir, aprobar, convenir, obtemperar.

assenter, *s.* consentidor, favorecedor.

assentient, *a.* consentidor.

assentingly, *adv.* con asenso, con aprobación; en signo de aprobación (o asentimiento).

assert [ə'səːt], *v.t.* sostener, mantener, defender, hacer bueno; afirmar, asegurar, aseverar; *to assert one's right,* hacer valer sus derechos; *to assert one's dignity,* sostener su dignidad.

asserter, assertor, *s.* afirmador, defensor, protector, mantenedor; sostén.

assertion, *s.* aserción, aserto, aseveración, afirmación; defensa.

assertive, *a.* afirmativo, asertivo.

assertory, *a.* afirmativo, declaratorio.

assess [ə'ses], *v.t.* amillarar, tasar, fijar; calcular.

assessable, *a.* tasable.

assessment, *s.* amillaramiento, tasación, imposición, tasa de impuestos; valoración, avalúo; (*for.*) fijación de daños y perjuicios.

assessor, *s.* asesor; tasador de impuestos, imponedor de contribuciones.

assessorial, *a.* relativo a la asesoría.

assets ['æsets], *s.pl.* (*com.*) crédito activo, caudal en caja, haber, capital; fondos, valores; *real assets,* bienes raíces; *personal assets,* bienes muebles.

assever [ə'sevəɹ], **asseverate,** *v.t.* aseverar, afirmar, asegurar con solemnidad.

asseveration, *s.* aseveración, afirmación, protesta.

assibilate, *v.t.* pronunciar con sonido sibilante.

assiduity [æsi'djuːiti], *s.* asiduidad, aplicación, diligencia, laboriosidad, constancia.

assiduous [ə'sidjuəs], *a.* asiduo, constante, laborioso, aplicado, continuo, hacendoso, diligente.

assiduousness, *s.* asiduidad, diligencia, constancia.

assign [ə'sain], *v.t.* asignar, especificar, fijar, exponer, destinar, señalar, mostrar, indicar, asignar, diputar, atribuir; (*for.*) consignar, transferir, ceder, traspasar. — *s.* (*for.*) cesionario.

assignable, *a.* asignable; transferible, negociable.

assignat, *s.* asignado.

assignation [æsig'neiʃən], *s.* asignación, consignación, cita; renuncia, cesión, traslación, traspaso.

assignee [æsai'niː], *s.* poderhabiente, apoderado; (derecho común) cesionario; síndico.

assigner, assignor, *s.* asignante, transferidor, transferente, cedente, comitente, cesionista, *m.f.*

assignment, *s.* asignación, señalamiento, cesión; (*for.*) traslación de dominio; escritura de cesión de bienes.

assimilability, *s.* asimilabilidad.
assimilable, *a.* asimilable, semejable.
assimilate [ə'simileit], *v.t.,* *v.i.* asimilar, asemejar, comparar; (*med.*) convertir el alimento en quilo.
assimilation, *s.* asimilación, semejanza.
assimilative, *a.* asimilativo.
assist [ə'sist], *v.t.* ayudar, socorrer, auxiliar, subvenir, sufragar. — *v.i.* asistir, concurrir, hallarse presente.
assistance, *s.* auxilio, sufragio, socorro, apoyo, ayuda, asistencia.
assistant, *s.* auxiliar, asistente, ayudante, adjutor, pasante, dependiente, segundo. — *a.* auxiliar, ayudador; *assistant judge,* juez asesor; *assistant secretary,* subsecretario.
assister, *s.* ayudador, asistente, socorredor.
assistless, *a.* desamparado.
assize [ə'saiz], *s.* tasa; alto tribunal de justicia, que dos veces al año se reúne en cada condado de Inglaterra para ver y fallar causas civiles y criminales; sesión de un tribunal; arancel. — *v.t.* tasar, fijar el precio.
associability, *s.* sociabilidad.
associable, *a.* sociable, asociable.
associate [ə'souʃieit], *v.t.* asociar, acompañar; juntar, unir, combinar, amalgamar. — *v.i.* asociarse, juntarse, mancomunarse; tomar parte; unirse con, ir con. — *a.* asociado, aliado, confederado. — *s.* socio, compañero, consocio, coadjutor, miembro, individuo de una sociedad, cómplice.
association, *s.* asociación, asociamiento, sociedad, unión, *f.*; liga, alianza, confederación; compañía, asamblea.
associative, *a.* asociativo.
associator, *s.* confederado.
assoil [ə'sɔil], *v.t.* resolver, responder; absolver, perdonar.
assonance, *s.* asonancia.
assonant ['æsənənt], *a.* asonante.
assort [ə'sɔːrt], *v.t.* colocar, ordenar, clasificar, poner en orden; proporcionar; surtir, proveer, abastecer. — *v.i.* ajustar, concordarse, convenirse.
assortment, *s.* arreglo, clasificación, colocación; colección; surtido, surtimiento, provisión.
assuage [ə'sweidʒ], *v.t.* mitigar, apaciguar, suavizar, calmar; ablandar, templar, aliviar, atemperar, desalterar. — *v.i.* minorar, disminuir, calmarse.
assuagement, *s.* mitigación, alivio, calma.
assuasive, *a.* dulcificador, lenitivo, mitigativo, calmante.
assuetude ['æsjuːetjuːd], *s.* uso, hábito, costumbre.
assume [ə'sjuːm], *v.t.* asumir, tomar, arrogar, encargarse de; apropiar(se), usurpar, presumir, suponer; *to assume an air,* tomar un aire; *to assume an air of importance,* alzar figura. — *v.i.* arrogarse, atribuirse, apropiarse, presumir de sí mismo.
assumed, *a.* afectado, fingido; falso.
assuming, *a.* arrogante, altivo, presuntuoso. — *s.* presunción.
assumpsit, *s.* (*for.*) pacto, contrato (oral).
assumption [ə'sʌmpʃən], *s.* asunción, toma, apropiación, arrogación, suposición, asunción.
assumptive, *a.* presuntivo, supuesto.
assurance [ə'ʃuərəns], *s.* seguridad, certeza,

confianza, certidumbre, convicción, firmeza, audacia, intrepidez, valor, arrojo; resolución, ánimo; despejo, desenvoltura, desvergüenza, descaro; (*com.*) seguro (v. **insurance**).
assure [ə'ʃuər], *v.t.* asegurar, afirmar, acreditar, protestar, certificar.
assured, *a.* seguro, cierto, indubitable, persuadido; descarado, atrevido, audaz; asegurado.
assuredly [ə'ʃuəredli], *adv.* ciertamente, indubitablemente, sin duda, con toda seguridad, de seguro.
assuredness, *s.* certeza, seguridad.
assurer, *s.* asegurador.
assurgent, *a.* surgente, brotar hacia arriba.
assuring, *a.* asegurado.
Assyrian, *s.,* *a.* asirio.
astatic, *a.* astático.
aster ['æstə], *s.* (*bot.*) áster.
asteriated, *a.* asteriado, estrellado.
asterisk ['æstərisk], *s.* asterisco.
asterism, *s.* (*astr.*) asterismo, constelación; (*impr.*) grupo de asteriscos.
astern [əs'təːrn], *adv.* (*mar.*) por la popa, a popa; *to go astern,* ir hacia atrás.
asteroid ['æstəroid], *s.* asteroide.
asthenia [æs'θiːniə], *s.* (*med.*) astenia.
asthenic, *a.* asténico, débil.
asthma ['æsθmə], *s.* (*med.*) asma.
asthmatic, asthmatical, *s.,* *a.* asmático.
astigmatic [æstig'mætik], *a.* (*opt.*) astigmático.
astigmatism [æ'stigmətizm], *s.* astigmatismo.
astir [ə'stəːr], *adv.* en movimiento, activo.
astonish [ə'stɔniʃ], *v.t.* asombrar, pasmar, sorprender, enajenar, embazar; *to be astonished,* admirarse.
astonishing, *a.* asombroso, pasmoso, sorprendente.
astonishingly, *adv.* pasmosamente, asombrosamente.
astonishingness, *s.* propiedad pasmosa de una cosa, calidad de pasmoso.
astonishment, *s.* pasmo, asombro, espanto, admiración, sorpresa.
astound [ə'staund], *v.t.* asombrar, aterrar, sorprender; aturdir, consternar, pasmar, confundir.
astounding, *a.* asombroso, pasmoso, aterrador, sorprendente, imponente.
astoundment, *s.* aturdimiento, confusión.
astraddle [ə'strædl], *adv.* a horcajadas, a horcajadillas.
astragal, astragalus, *s.* (*arq., bot.*) astrágalo; (*anat.*) astrágalo, chita; (*vulg.*) taba.
astrakhan [æstrə'kæn], *s.* piel de astracán.
astral, *a.* astral, sideral.
astrand [ə'strænd], *adv.* (*mar.*) encallado, varado; echado sobre la costa.
astray [ə'strei], *adv.* desviado, descarriado, errado, fuera del camino; *to go astray,* perderse, extraviarse; *to lead astray,* (*fig.*) descaminar, extraviar.
astrict [ə'strikt], *v.t.* astringir, apretar, astreñir.
astriction, *s.* astricción; (*med.*) astreñimiento.
astride [ə'straid], *adv.* a horcajadas, con una pierna a cada lado.
astringe [ə'strindʒ], *v.t.* (*med.*) astringir, apretar, restringir, comprimir, astreñir; (*fig.*) estrechar, apremiar.
astringency, *s.* astricción, astringencia; (*fig.*) aspereza de carácter.

astringent, *s., a.* astringente, estíptico, constrictivo, austero, áspero, agrio, duro.

astrography [æsˈtrɔgrəfi], *s.* astrografía.

astrolabe [ˈæstrəleib], *s.* astrolabio.

astrologer [æsˈtrolədʒəɹ], **astrologian,** *s.* astrólogo.

astrologic, astrological, *a.* astrológico.

astrology [əˈstrolədʒi], *s.* astrología.

astronomer, [əˈstronəməɹ], *s.* astrónomo, planetario.

astronomic [æstrəˈnɔmik], **astronomical,** *a.* astronómico.

astronomy, *s.* astronomía.

astrophotometry, *s.* (*astr.*) astrofotometría.

astrophysics, *s.* astrofísica.

astrut [əˈstrʌt], *adv.* hinchadamente, pomposamente, pavoneándose.

astute [əˈstjuːt], *a.* astuto, agudo, fino, cauteloso, sagaz.

astuteness, *s.* astucia, penetración, sutileza, sagacidad.

asunder [əˈsʌndəɹ], *adv.* aparte, separadamente, desunidamente, a pedazos; *to cut a thing asunder*, cortar una cosa en dos partes.

aswim [əˈswim], *adv.* a nado, flotante.

asylum [əˈsailəm], *s.* asilo, refugio, retiro, albergue.

asymmetral, asymmetrical, *a.* asimétrico, desproporcionado, irregular.

asymmetry [əˈsimətri], *s.* asimetría, desproporción.

asymptote [ˈæsimptout], *s.* (*geom.*) asíntota.

asymptotic, asymptotical, *a.* asintótico.

asyndeton [əˈsindətən], *s.* (*ret.*) asíndeton.

at [æt], *prep.* a, en, cerca de, sobre; *at all*, en modo alguno; *at all events*, a todo trance, en todo caso; *at your service*, a la disposición de Vd.; *at home*, en casa; en su propio país; (*fig.*) descansadamente; habituado; *at least*, a lo menos; *at first*, al principio; *at last*, por último, por fin, al fin; *at leisure*, despacio; *at most*, a lo más; *at best*, cuando mejor; *at once*, inmediatamente, a la vez, de un golpe; *at no time*, jamás nunca; *at the worst*, a peor andar; *at play*, jugando; *at work*, trabajando; *at sea*, en el mar, (*fig.*) perplejo; *at a pinch*, en un apuro; *at a venture*, a la buena ventura.

atavism [ˈætəvizm], *s.* (*fisiol.*) atavismo.

ataxia, ataxy [əˈtæksi], *s.* (*med.*) ataxia.

ataxic, *a.* atáxico.

ate [et], *v.t.*, *pret.* del verbo TO EAT.

atelier [æˈtelje], *s.* estudio, taller.

Athanasian, *s., a.* atanasiano.

Athaneum, *s.* ateneo.

atheism, *s.* ateísmo.

atheist [ˈeiθiːist], *s.* ateísta, *m.f.*, ateo.

atheistic, atheistical, *a.* ateístico, ateísta, impío.

atheling [ˈæθliŋ], *s.* hidalgo.

athenæum [æθəˈniːəm], *s.* ateneo.

athirst [əˈθəːɹst], *a.* sediento; (*fig.*) que con ansia desea una cosa.

athlete [ˈæθliːt], *s.* atleta, *m.f.*, gimnasta, *m.f.*

athletic, *a.* atlético, musculoso; lacertoso; fuerte, vigoroso, robusto.

athwart [əˈθwɔːɹt], *prep.* al través, a través, de través, por el través, contra; *athwart hawse*, (*mar.*) por el tráves de las barbas; *athwart ship*, (*mar.*) de babor a estribor. — *adv.* contrariamente, a tuertas.

atilt [əˈtilt], *a.* en postura inclinada; en ristre.

Atlantean, *a.* atlántido, atlántico.

Atlantic [ətˈlæntik], *a.* atlántico. — *s.* mar atlántico.

atlas [ˈætləs], *s.* atlas; (*arq.*) atlante, telamón.

atmosphere [ˈætməsfiəɹ], *s.* atmósfera, aire, ambiente.

atmospheric, *a.* atmosférico.

atoll [ˈætɔl], *s.* isla de coral.

atom [ˈætəm], *s.* átomo, corpúsculo, molécula.

atomic [əˈtomik], **atomical,** *a.* atómico; (*quím.*) atomístico; *atomic bomb*, bomba atómica.

atomism, *s.* atomismo.

atomist, *s.* atomista, *m.f.*

atomize, *v.t.* reducir en átomos; pulverizar, rociar.

atomizer, *s.* pulverizador, aromatizador.

atomy, *s.* átomo; (*fig.*) pigmeo, enano.

atomy, *s.* esqueleto, preparación anatómica; (*fig.*) esqueleto.

at one, *adv.* en armonía, a una, en estado de reconciliación, de la misma opinión, juntos.

atone [əˈtoun], *v.t.*, *v.i.* expiar, pagar, purgar; reconciliar, apaciguar, aplacar, propiciar, acordarse; compensar; reparar, dar satisfacción.

atonement, *s.* concordia, asonancia; acuerdo, reconciliación; expiación, propiciación, reparación; sacrificio.

atonic [əˈtonik], *a.* débil; (*gram.*) atónico.

atony, *s.* (*med.*) atonía.

atop [əˈtop], *adv.* encima, en la punta, en la parte superior.

atoxic [æˈtoksik], *a.* atóxico.

atrabilarian, atrabilarious, *a.* (*med.*) atrabiliario, atrabilioso, melancólico, hipocondríaco.

atrabilariousness, *s.* (*med.*) atrabilis, *f.*, melancolía.

atrabiliary, atrabilious, *a.* atrabiliario, atrabilioso, hipocondríaco, melancólico.

atrabilis, *s.* (*med.*) atrabilis, *f.*

atrip [əˈtrip], *adv.* (*mar.*) apeada el ancla; izado en lo más alto de las vergas (velas); vergas en alto.

atrium [ˈeitriəm], *s.* atrio.

atrocious [əˈtrouʃəs], *a.* atroz, enorme, cruel, terrible, perverso.

atrociousness, atrocity, *s.* atrocidad; enormidad; maldad horrible.

atrophic, *a.* atrófico.

atrophy [ˈætrəfi], *s.* (*med.*) atrofía.

atropine [ˈætrəpain], *s.* (*quím.*) atropina.

attach [əˈtætʃ], *v.t.* prender, agarrar, asir, coger; pillar; ligar, atar; pegar; enganchar; juntar, conectar; dar, conceder, asignar; atraer a sí; (*for.*) embargar, secuestrar; ganar, lograr, adquirir; *to be attached to someone*, apegarse a, aficionarse a; *to attach importance to*, dar importancia a; *to attach little importance to*, tener en poco.

attachable, *a.* pegadizo.

attaché [əˈtæʃei], *s.* agregado.

attachment, *s.* enlace, amistad, afecto, adhesión, afición, apego, fidelidad; aprehensión, presa; ligación, unión, *f.*, enlace, adherencia; (*for.*) embargo, secuestro; (*anat.*) ligatura.

attack [əˈtæk], *v.t.* atacar, acometer, embestir; impugnar; combatir, opugnar. — *s.* ataque, acometimiento; (*med.*) acceso.

attacker, *s.* agresor, atacador, acometedor.

attain [əˈtein], *v.t.* ganar, procurar, conseguir,

alcanzar, lograr, obtener, merecer, sacar, reportar. — *v.i.* llegar a.

attainability, attainableness, *s.* accesibilidad.

attainable, *a.* que se puede alcanzar, asequible, accesible, exequible.

attainder, *s.* mancha, tacha, deshonra; imputación de algún delito; (*for.*) proscripción; (*for.*) mu⊖rte civil; *bill of attainder,* decreto de proscripción.

attainment, *s.* logro; adquisición, conseguimiento, consecución, obtención, capacidad de adquirir; conocimientos, instrucción, talento, mérito.

attaint [ə'teint], *v.t.* convencer; viciar, corromper, manchar, deshonrar, infamar; (*for.*) condenar, proscribir. — *a.* convicto de alta traición. — *s.* mancha, baldón, tacha, estigma, *m.*, muerte civil.

attainture, *s.* deshonra, nota de infamia.

attar ['ætəɹ], *s.* esencia, en especial la de rosas.

attemper, *v.t.* atemperar, molificar, mezclar, diluir; conciliar, acomodar, templar.

attempt [ə'tempt], *v.t.* atentar, intentar; arriesgar, aventurar; atacar, embestir; tentar; probar, ensayar, experimentar. — *v.i.* procurar, pretender; *to attempt impossibilities,* intentar lo imposible. — *s.* ataque, atentado; tentativa, intento, prueba, designio, esfuerzo, experimento.

attemptable, *a.* que puede ser atacado, o intentado.

attempter, *s.* emprendedor; promotor; agresor.

attend [ə'tend], *v.t.* atender, acompañar, servir, asistir, cuidar; presentarse, comparecer, concurrir, acudir; esperar; hacerse cargo de, traer tras de sí; cortejar. — *v.i.* atender, oír, prestar atención, poner atención, considerar; esperar; tardar; estar presente.

attendance, *s.* servicio, atención, cuidado; aplicación, asiduidad; asistencia, presencia; corte, *f.*, obsequio; tren, séquito, comitiva, acompañamiento; servidumbre; concurrencia, auditorio, público; (*for.*) comparecencia; *to be in attendance,* estar de servicio; *to dance attendance,* (*fam.*) hacer antesala; estar de plantón; *lady in attendance,* camarera mayor.

attendant, *s.* sirviente, servidor, criado; cortesano; secuaz; acompañante; asistente; galán, cortejo, galanteador, obsequiante; tren, séquito; criado, doméstico. — *a.* concomitante, acompañante.

attent [ə'tent], *a.* atento, solícito, cuidadoso.

attention, *s.* atención, cuidado, aplicación, reflexión, miramiento; *to pay attention to everything,* estar en todo; *attention!* ¡atención!, (*mil.*) ¡firmes! — *pl.* **attentions,** cortejo, galanteo, obsequio.

attentive, *a.* atento, cuidadoso, curioso, solícito; fino, cortés, político; galante, obsequioso.

attentiveness, *s.* circumspección, cuidado, miramiento; cortesía, finura.

attenuant [ə'tenjuənt], *a.* (*med.*) atenuante diluyente, diluente.

attenuate [ə'tenjueit], *v.t.* atenuar, adelgazar, extenuar, minorar, disminuir; hacer menos denso.

attenuated, *a.* atenuado, delgado, diminuto.

attenuation, *s.* atenuación, adelgazamiento, extenuación, flaqueza.

attenuating, *a.* extenuativo.

attest [ə'test], *v.t.* atestiguar, atestar, declarar, afirmar, deponer, certificar, confirmar, autenticar; (*for.*) dar fe.

attest, attestation, *s.* atestación, deposición, testimonio, testificación, confirmación, prueba, certificado.

attester, attestor, *s.* testigo, certificador.

attic ['ætik], *s.* desván, sotabanco, camaranchón, guardilla; *attic storey,* ático, último o más alto piso de la casa.

Attic, *a.* ático, natural de Atenas; clásico, agudo, juicioso, picante.

atticism, *s.* aticismo.

atticize, *v.t.* emplear el dialecto ático. — *v.i.* emplear aticismos.

attire [ə'taiəɹ], *v.t.* ataviar, asear, adornar, engalanar, vestir, componer. — *s.* atavío, adorno, traje, ropa, compostura; (*blas.*) astas de c:ervo.

attirer, *s.* el que adorna o viste a otro.

attitude ['ætitjuːd], *s.* actitud, ademán, posición, postura.

attitudinize, *v.i.* pavonearse, tomar posturas afectadas.

attollent [ə'tɔlent], *s., a.* (*anat.*) elevador.

attorn, *v.t.* asignar, transferir; (*for.*) reconocer a un nuevo dueño. — *v.i.* transferir los bienes o derechos a otro.

attorney [ə'təːɹni], *s.* procurador, agente, apoderado, poderhabiente, delegado, comisionado; *letter of attorney,* poder, procuración.

attorney-general, *s.* fiscal, procurador, síndico general.

attorneyship, *s.* fiscalía, procuraduría, oficio de procurador, agencia, poder.

attract [ə'trækt], *v.t.* atraer; llamar, captar; granjear, interesar.

attractability [ətræktə'biliti], *s.* atractabilidad, cualidad de atraíble.

attractable, *a.* atraíble.

attractile [ə'træktail], *a.* atractivo.

attracting, *a.* atrayente.

attraction, *s.* atracción; atractivo, interés; aliciente; perturbación, desviación de las agujas imantadas; *attraction of cohesion,* atracción molecular.

attractive, *a.* atrayente, atractivo; magnético; interesante.

attractiveness, *s.* fuerza atractiva; gracia.

attractor, *s.* persona o cosa que atrae.

attrahent ['ætrəhent], *s., a.* (*med.*) atrayente, supurativo.

attributable, *a.* imputable.

attribute [ə'tribjut], *v.t.* atribuir, dar, aplicar, achacar, imputar. — ['ætribjuːt], *s.* atributo, calidad, característica; reputación, honra.

attribution, *s.* atribución, atributo.

attributive, *a.* atributivo.

attrist, *v.t.* entristecer.

attrite [ə'trait], *a.* estregado, frotado; (*teol.*) atrito, pesaroso.

attrition [ə'triʃən], *s.* razadura, frotación, trituración, molimiento, desgaste; atrición.

attune [ə'tjuːn], *v.t.* acordar, armonizar, afinar.

atwirl [ə'twəːɹl], *adv.* girando, en rotación, dando vueltas.

atwist [ə'twist], *adv.* torcidamente, al través, sesgado.

aubade, *s.* alborada.

auberge [ou'bɛəɹʒ], *s.* albergue.

aubergine [oubɛəɹˈʒiːn], s. berenjena.
aubin, s. (*equit.*) medio galope.
auburn [ˈɔːbəɹn], a. castaño, moreno rojizo.
auction [ˈɔːkʃən], s. almoneda; subasta; venta pública. — *v.t.* subastar, rematar, vender en almoneda.
auctioneer, s. subastador, pregonero. — *v.t.* vender en subasta.
auction-room, s. martillo, almoneda.
audacious [ɔːˈdeɪʃəs], a. audaz, osado, atrevido, temerario, descarado, denodado, impudente.
audaciousness, audacity, s. audacia, atrevimiento, temeridad, osadía; denuedo, impudencia, descaro; (*fig.*) desuello, desvergüenza.
audibility, s. capacidad de ser oído.
audible [ˈɔːdibl], a. oíble, inteligible, perceptible al oído.
audibleness, s. capacidad de ser oído.
audibly, adv. inteligiblemente; en alta voz.
audience [ˈɔːdiəns], s. audiencia; audición, auditorio, concurso, público; *audience-chamber,* (*for.*) audiencia.
audiphone, s. instrumento que, colocado entre los dientes, transmite el sonido a los nervios auditorios; utilízanlo los sordomudos.
audit [ˈɔːdit], s. glosa, revisión; ajuste o examen de cuentas. — *v.t.* glosar, revisar, examinar, intervenir (una cuenta); (*fig.*) el día del Juicio.
audition [ɔːˈdiʃən], s. audición.
auditive, a. auditivo.
auditor [ˈɔːditəɹ], s. oyente, oidor; (*for.*) auditor; consejero, revisor, interventor; ordenador de pagos.
auditorium [ɔːdiˈtɔːriəm], s. auditorio, sala de teatro, nave de una iglesia, etc.
auditorship, s. auditoría; intervención.
auditory, s. auditorio, concurso, público; audiencia, sala tribunal; *auditory canal* o *nerve,* conducto o nervio auditivo. — *a.* auditivo.
auditress, s. oyente.
Augean, a. perteneciente o referente a Augeas, rey de Elida; (*fig.*) sucísimo.
auger [ˈɔːgəɹ], s. barrena, taladro; *bolting auger,* (*mar.*) barrena de empernar; *auger-shank,* vástago de barrena; *auger-worm,* (*zool.*) broma.
aught [ɔːt], pron. indef. algo, alguna cosa; (*con negación*) nada; *for aught I know,* en cuanto yo sé.
augite [ˈɔːdʒait], s. (*min.*) augita.
augment [ɔːgˈment], v.t. aumentar, acrecentar. — *v.i.* crecer, tomar aumento, tomar incremento. — *s.* añadidura, aumento, acrecentamiento, (*gram.*) afijo.
augmentable, a. aumentable.
augmentation, s. aumentación, aumento, acrecentamiento, añadidura.
augmentative, s., a. aumentativo.
augmenter, s. exagerador, ponderador.
augur [ˈɔːgəɹ], v.t., v.i. augurar, pronosticar, predecir, agorar, ominar, adivinar.
augur, augurer s. augur, agorero, adivino, arúspice.
augural, a. augural.
auguration, s. auguración.
augurial, a. augural.
augurship, s. función de augur.
augury, s. agüero, presagio, pronóstico, auspicio, adivinación, auguración.

august [ɔːˈgʌst], a. augusto, grande, majestuoso, real. — *s.* agosto.
Augustan, a. de Augusto; de Augsburgo.
Augustines, Agustinians, s.pl. agustinos.
augustness, s. majestad, majestuosidad, grandeza.
auk [ɔːk], s. (*orn.*) alca, ave marina del hemisferio boreal.
auld [ɔːld], a. viejo, antiguo; *Auld Reekie,* (vieja humeante) apodo de la ciudad de Edimburgo; *auld lang syne,* (expresión escocesa) se usa para expresar los días pasados, mucho ha, tiempos que fueron.
aulic [ˈɔːlik], a. áulico, palaciego.
aunt [aːnt], **auntie, aunty,** s. tía, la hermana del padre o madre; (*fam.*) tía, comadre, f., mujer vieja.
aura [ˈɔːrə], s. exhalación, vapor; influencia psíquica; magnetismo animal; céfiro, aura; (*patol.*) sensación como un vaho frío que sube a la cabeza, síntoma monitario de la epilepsia y de la histeria.
aural, a. auditivo, auricular.
aurate [ˈɔːrɪət], s. (*quím.*) auratón, aurato, sal de oro.
aurated, a. dorado; (*quím.*) aureado; (*fig.*) brillante, espléndido.
aurelia, s. crisálida, ninfa.
aureole, s. auréola.
auricle [ˈɔːrikl], s. aurícula, pabellón de la oreja.
auricula, s. (*bot.*) oreja de oso.
auricular, a. auricular, oíble, confidencial, secreto; tradicional.
auricularly, adv. secretamente, al oído.
auriculate, auriculated, a. auriculado, que tiene aurículas u orejillas.
auriferous [ɔːˈrifərəs], a. (*poét.*) aurífero, aurígero.
auriform [ˈɔːrifoəɹm], a. en forma de oreja.
auriga [ɔːˈriːgə], s. auriga, m., cochero; (*astr.*) Auriga.
aurigation, s. manejo o práctica de conducir carruajes.
auriscalp, s. (*cir.*) auriscalpo.
auriscope, s. auriscopio.
aurist, s. otólogo.
aurochs [ˈɔːrəks], s. (*zool.*) uro.
aurora [ɔːˈroərə], s. aurora, alborada, alba.
auroral, a. perteneciente a la aurora; matutino; rosáceo.
auscultate [ˈɔːskʌlteit], v.t. (*med.*) auscultar.
auscultation, s. auscultación; atención.
auscultator, s. auscultador.
auscultatory, a. relativo a la auscultación.
auspicate [ˈɔːspikeit], v.t., v.i. pronosticar, predecir, presagiar, inaugurar, pronosticar.
auspice [ˈɔːspis], s. auspicio, presagio; *under the auspices of,* bajo la protección, amparo, favor, apoyo, autoridad.
auspicial, a. perteneciente a los pronósticos, al auspicio.
auspicious, a. próspero, feliz, favorable; benigno, propicio.
auspiciously, adv. prósperamente, felizmente, bajo favorables auspicios.
auspiciousness, s. prosperidad, esperanza de felicidad.
auster [ˈɔːstəɹ], s. austro.
austere [ɔsˈtiːəɹ], a. austero, severo, riguroso, rígido, rudo, adusto; agrio, ácido, acerbo al gusto.

austerely, *adv.* austeramente, severamente.

austereness, austerity, *s.* austeridad, severidad, rigorismo.

Austin ['ɔ:stin], *s.*, *a.* síncope de *Augustin, Augustinian; Austin Friars,* los agustinos.

austral ['ɔ:strəl], *a.* austral.

Australian [ɔ'is'treiliən], *s.*, *a.* australiano, perteneciente a Australia.

Austrian ['ɔ:striən], *s.*, *a.* austríaco, de Austria, natural de Austria.

authentic [ɔ:'θentik], authentical, *a.* auténtico, solemne, cierto, legítimo, original, fehaciente.

authenticalness, authenticity *s.* autenticidad.

authenticate, *v.t.* autenticar, legalizar, autorizar.

authentication, *s.* autenticación.

author ['ɔ:θəɹ], *s.* autor; escritor; causa.

authoress, *s.* autora, escritora.

authoritative ['ɔ:'θɔritətiv], *a.* autorizado, autorizador, autoritativo, imperioso, perentorio, terminante, positivo.

authoritatively, *adv.* autoritativamente, autorizadamente.

authoritativeness, *s.* autoridad sancionada; apariencia autoritativa.

authority [ɔ:'θɔriti], *s.* autoridad, potestad, facultad, poder legal, mando; dominio; crédito; cita, texto; *I have it on the best authority,* lo sé de muy buen original; lo tengo de buena mano; lo sé de buena tinta; *by authority,* (*impr.*) con licencia.

authorizable, *a.* autorizable.

authorization, *s.* autorización, legalización, sanción.

authorize ['ɔ:θəraiz], *v.t.* autorizar, sancionar, facultar, acreditar, legalizar, otorgar.

authorized, *a.* autorizado.

authorless, *a.* sin autor; desautorizado.

authorship, *s.* profesión de escritor, calidad de autor; paternidad literaria; (*fig.*) manantial, origen.

autobiographer, *s.* autobiógrafo.

autobiographic, autobiographical, *a.* autobiográfico.

autobiography [ɔ:təbai'ɔgrəfi], *s.* autobiografía.

auto-boat ['ɔ:təbout], *s.* bote automóvil.

auto-bus, *s.* autobús.

auto-car, *s.* automóvil.

autocracy [ɔ:'tɔkrəsi], *s.* autocracia.

autocrat ['ɔ:təkræt], *s.* autócrata, *m.f.*

autocratic, autocratical, *a.* autocrático.

autocratix, *s.* autócrata.

autocratship, *s.* dignidad de autócrata.

autograph ['ɔ:təgræf], autography, *s.* autógrafo.

autographic, autographical, *a.* autógrafo, autográfico.

autographometer, *s.* autografómetro.

autography, *s.* autografía.

automatic [ɔ:tə'mætik], automatical, *a.* automático.

automaton [ɔ:'tɔmətən], (*pl.* automata) autómata, *m.*

automatous, *a.* automático.

automobile [ɔ:to'mobi:l], *s.* automóvil.

autonomic, *a.* autonómico.

autonomist, *s.* autonomista, *m.f.*

autonomous, *a.* autónomo.

autonomy [ɔ:'tɔnəmi], *s.* autonomía.

autopathic, *a.* autopático.

autopsy ['ɔ:təpsi], *s.* (*med.*) autopsia.

autoscopy, *s.* autoscopia.

autotomy [ɔ:'tɔtəmi], *s.* automía.

autotype, *s.* facsímil, autotipo, copia exacta; retrato impreso de una placa de gelatina.

autumn ['ɔ:təm], *s.* otoño.

autumnal [ɔ:'tʌmnəl], *a.* otoñal, autumnal.

auxiliar, auxiliary [ɔ:g'ziljəri], *a.* auxiliar, auxiliatorio, subsidiario.

avail [ə'veil], *v.t.* aprovechar, hacer uso de; adelantar, promover. — *v.r.* aprovecharse (de), utilizar, servirse (de). — *v.i.* servir, importar, ser útil, ser ventajoso, ayudar; *it avails nothing,* nada importa; a nada conduce. — *s.* provecho, ventaja, utilidad.

available, *a.* útil, ventajoso, aprovechable, provechoso, eficaz; válido, legítimo; disponible; *available assets,* (*com.*) activo disponible.

availableness, *n.m.* eficacia, virtud, actividad, utilidad, ventaja; validez, disponibilidad.

availably *adv.* eficazmente, provechosamente, útilmente.

avalanche ['ævəla:tʃ], *s.* alud, lurte.

avarice ['ævəris], *s.* avaricia, codicia.

avaricious [ævə'riʃəs], *a.* avaro, avariento, miserable.

avariciousness, *s.* avaricia, codicia.

avast [ə'va:st], *adv.* (*mar.*) forte. — *interj.* ¡forte! ¡basta! ¡no más!; *avast heaving!* (*mar.*) forte al virar.

avaunt [ə'vɔ:nt], *interj.* (*ant.*) ¡fuera! ¡fuera de aquí! ¡quítate de delante! ¡quita allá! ¡lejos de aquí!

avenaceous [ævə'neiʃəs], *a.* aveníceo, de o perteneciente a la avena.

avenge [ə'venʒ], *v.t.* vengar, vengarse de, vindicar, castigar.

avengement, *s.* venganza.

avenger, *s.* vengador, castigador.

avengeress, *s.* vengadora.

avenging, *a.* vengador.

avens ['ævənz], *s.* (*bot.*) gariofilea.

aventail ['ævəteil], aventayle, *s.* (*blas.*) ventalla, abertura de la visera de la celada.

aventurine, *s.* venturina.

avenue ['ævənju:], *s.* avenida, alameda, calzada, carrera, vía, entrada, pasadizo.

aver [ə'və:ɹ], *v.t.* asegurar, afirmar, verificar, certificar.

average ['ævəridʒ], *s.* (*for.*) servicio, carga; servidumbre; (*mar.*) avería; parte igual, parte proporcional; término medio; promedio, rateo, prorrateo, tanteo, precio medio; (*mar.*) sombrero o capa del capitán; *rough average,* término medio aproximativo. — *a.* medio, entre uno y otro, uno con otro, típico, ordinario, proporcional. — *v.t., v.i.* comparar y fijar un precio o término medio, ascender por término medio; costar, dar, tomar, tener, ocurrir, etc., como término medio; proporcionar, ratear, tantear.

averment, *s.* afirmación, aseveración, testimonio.

averruncate [ævə'rʌŋkeit], *v.t.* desarraigar, arrancar de raíz, extirpar; podar, escamondar los árboles.

averruncator, *s.* podadera, tijera de podar.

averse [ə'və:ɹs], *a.* adverso, contrario, opuesto, renuente, repugnante, enemigo.

aversely, *adv.* con repugnancia, repugnantemente.

averseness, *s.* aversión, repugnancia, renuencia, mala gana.
aversion, *s.* aversión, disgusto, odio, aborrecimiento.
avert [ə'və:ɹt], *v.t.* desviar, apartar, alejar; separar; impedir, prevenir.
averter, *s.* apartador.
aviary ['eiviəri], *s.* pajarera, averío, avería.
aviate ['eivieit], *v.i.* volar, viajar por los aires en una máquina.
aviation, *s.* aviación.
aviator, *s.* aviador, aviadora.
avicultural [ævi'kʌltjurəl], *a.* relativo a la avicultura.
aviculturist, *s.* avicultor.
avid ['ævid], *a.* ávido, ansioso, codicioso, voraz.
avidity, *s.* avidez, ansia, codicia.
aviso [ə'vi:zou], *s.* consejo, aviso; (*mar.*) patache, buque aviso.
avocado [ævə'ka:dou], *s.* (*bot.*) aguacate, avocado.
avocation [ævo'keiʃən], *s.* avocación, empleo, ocupación; distracción, entretenimiento, pasatiempo, diversión.
avocet, avoset ['ævosət], *s.* (*orn.*) avoceta.
avoid [ə'vɔid], *v.t.* evitar, salvar, escapar, huir, esquivar, eludir; dejar; evacuar, desalojar; (*for.*) anular. — *v.i.* retirarse; escaparse, zafarse.
avoidable, *a.* evitable, eludible; (*for.*) revocable.
avoidance, *s.* evasión, efugio, escapada; evacuación, descargo; vacación; anulación, invalidación.
avoider, *s.* el que evita o evade; conductor; conducente.
avoidless, *a.* (*poét.*) inevitable.
avoirdupois [ævəɹdʒu'pɔiz], *s.* ley de peso inglesa, cuya libra tiene 16 onzas o 7000 granos; sirve para toda clase de géneros excepto drogas, oro, plata y piedras preciosas; (*fig.*) peso, gordura.
avouch [ə'vautʃ], *v.t.*, *v.i.* afirmar, justificar, sostener; alegar; protestar, testimoniar.
avouch, avouchment, *s.* testimonio, declaración.
avouchable, *a.* justificable.
avoucher, *s.* el que justifica (o afirma).
avow [ə'vau], *v.t.* declarar; protestar; confesar; manifestar, profesar.
avowable, *a.* confesable.
avowably, *adv.* francamente, abiertamente.
avowal, *s.* confesión, aprobación, profesión, declaración justificativa.
avowed, *a.* confesado, declarado; manifiesto, evidente, notorio, paladino.
avowee, *s.* patrono de una iglesia o beneficio.
avower, *s.* (*for.*) declarante.
avowry, *s.* (*for.*) justificación de un secuestro o embargo ya ejecutado, o el motivo que se alega para haberlo hecho.
avulsion [ə'vʌlʃən], *s.* arrancamiento, separación; (*cir.*) avulsión.
avuncular [ə'vʌŋkjuləɹ], *a.* de un tío o parecido a un tío; (*vulg.*) perteneciente o referente a un prestamista.
await [ə'weit], *v.t.* esperar, aguardar.
awake [ə'weik], **awaken,** *v.t.* (*pret.* **awoke**; *p.p.* **awaked**) despertar, mover, excitar; hacer volver en sí. — *v.i.* despertar, dejar de dormir, resucitar.

awake, *a.* despierto; *wide-awake,* (*fig.*) alerta.
awakener, *s.* despertador.
awakening, awaking, *s.* despertar, despertamiento.
award [ə'wɔ:ɹd], *v.t.* juzgar, sentenciar, otorgar, conceder, conferir; (*for.*) adjudicar. — *v.i.* decidir, determinar; (*for.*) pronunciar una sentencia. — *s.* determinación, decisión, sentencia, adjudicación.
awardable, *a.* adjudicable.
awarder, *s.* juez árbitro.
aware [ə'wɛəɹ], *a.* cauto, vigilante, orejeado, enterado, sabedor; *to be aware of,* saber.
awash [ə'wɔʃ], *adv.* (*mar.*) a flor de agua, al capricho de las olas.
away [ə'wei], *adv.* lejos, a distancia; fuera, afuera, ausente; continuamente; *away from home,* ausente; *to get away,* huir, escaparse, evadirse; *to go away,* irse, marcharse; *to send away,* despedir; *to make away with,* matar; *to make away with oneself,* suicidarse; *to run away,* huir, escaparse, tomar las de Villadiego; *to work away,* seguir trabajando; *to write, talk away, etc.,* seguir escribiendo, hablando, etc.
away! *interj.* ¡fuera! ¡fuera de aquí! ¡basta! ¡váyase con la música a otra parte! *away with these compliments!* ¡basta de cumplimientos!
awe [ɔ:], *s.* miedo, temor, pavor, espanto; *to strike with awe,* inspirar terror; *to be awe-struck,* quedarse atemorizado; *to stand in awe of,* tener miedo de. — *v.t.* aterrar, despavorir, amedrentar, atemorizar, asombrar, infundir miedo; imponer.
aweary [ə'wi:ri], *a.* (*poét.*) fatigado, cansado.
aweather [ə'weðəɹ], *adv.* (*mar.*) a barlovento.
aweigh [ə'wei], *adv.* (*mar.*) pendiente, a plomo.
awesome ['ɔ:səm], *a.* terrible, temible, aterrador, pavoroso.
awful ['ɔ:fəl], *a.* solemne, imponente; temible, terrible, digno de respeto y reverencia; tremendo, horrible, horrendo, pavoroso, espantoso, terrorífico; enorme; sublime, majestuoso; (*fam.*) muy malo, monstruoso.
awfully, *adv.* respetuosamente; con temor respetuoso; temerosamente; solemnemente; (*fam.*) muy, excesivamente.
awfulness, *s.* solemnidad; veneración; temor reverencial.
awhile [ə'wail], *adv.* un rato; algún tiempo; *not yet awhile,* todavía no, por ahora no.
awkward ['ɔ:kwəɹd], *a.* tosco, zafio, rudo, inculto, torpe, zopenco, agreste; desmañado, desgarbado; indómito; chabacano, indócil; desgraciado; inconveniente; difícil, delicado; embarazoso; peliagudo; (*fig.*) zurdo.
awkwardness, *s.* grosería, torpeza, tosquedad, desmaña.
awl [ɔ:l], *s.* lesna, lezna, alesna, subilla, punzón.
awl-shaped, *a.* alesnado.
awn [ɔ:n], *s.* (*bot.*) arista, la barba de la espiga.
awning, *s.* pabellón; toldo, tendal; (*hort.*) abrigaña; (*mar.*) toldilla; candeleros de los toldos.
awoke [ə'wouk], *pret.* del verbo [AWAKE].
awry [ə'rai], *a.* oblicuo, sesgado, torcido. — *adv.* oblicuamente, torcidamente, de través, al través, erróneamente, impropiamente.
axe [æks], *s.* segur, *f.,* hacha; *pick-axe,* piqueta, zapapico; *cooper's axe,* doladera; *an axe to grind,* (*fam.*) un fin interesado.
axial ['æksiəl], *a.* axil.

axiferous, *a.* axífero.
axil, axilla [æk'zilə], *s.* (*anat.,* *bot.*) axila, sobaco.
axillar, axillary, *a.* axilar.
axinite ['æksineit], *s.* (*min.*) axinita.
axiom ['æksiəm], *s.* axioma, proposición, sentencia o principio sentado, *m.*; verdad evidente.
axiomatic, axiomatical, *a.* axiomático.
axis ['æksis], *s.* (*pl.* **axes**) eje, pivote; (*anat.*) axis.
axle ['æksl], **axle-tree,** *s.* eje; árbol de una máquina; peón de una noria.
axometer [æ'kzomətə], *s.* (*opt.*) axómetro; (*mar.*) axiómetro.
ay, aye [ai], *adv.* sí, seguramente, desde luego.
aye [ai], *adv.* siempre, para siempre jamás.
azalea [ə'zeiliə], *s.* (*bot.*) azalea.
azerole ['æzərɔl], *s.* (*bot.*) acerola.
azimuth ['æziməθ], *s.* (*astr.*) acimut.
azimuthal, *a.* acimutal.
azoic [ə'zouik], *a.* sin vida organica.
azote [ə'zout], *s.* (*quím.*) azoe, nitrógeno.
azotic, *a.* azoico, nítrico.
azotize, *v.t.* azoar, impregnar de azoe.
azure ['æʒəɹ], **azured,** *a.* azul celeste, azulado claro; (*blas.*) azur.
azure, *v.t.* azular.
azurine, *a.* azulado.
azurite, *s.* azurita, malaquita azul.
azurn, *a.* (*poét.*) cerúleo.
azyme ['æzim], *s.* pan ázimo, pan sin levadura.
azymic, azymous, *a.* ázimo, sin levadura.

B

B, b, segunda letra del alfabeto; (*mús.*) si; *not to know A from B,* ser completamente ignorante; *B.A.,* o *A.B.* Bachiller en Artes, Licenciado en Letras; *B.C.* antes de Jesucristo; *LL.B.,* Bachiller en Leyes; *B.Sc.* Bachiller en Ciencias; al final de voces precedida de *m,* o seguida de *t,* es muda, *v.g. dumb, debt.*
baa [ba:], *s.* be, balido. — *v.i.* balar, dar balidos.
babbit metal, babbit's metal, *s.* metal de antifricción; aleación de estaño, zinc, cobre y antimonio.
babble [bæbl], *v.t.,* *v.i.* balbucear; charlar, parlotear; garlar; murmurar, susurrar (un arroyo); decir tonterías. — *s.* charla, garla, parla; charlatanería; susurro, murmullo.
babbler, *s.* hablador, parlador, charlador, garlador, chacharero, charlatán.
babbling, *s.* charla, cháchara, garrulería. — *a.* hablador; murmurador, murmurante.
babe [beib], *s.* criatura; niño, niña; bebé; pequeñuelo; (*fam.*) nene.
babel [beibəl], *s.* babel; confusión, desorden, alboroto, algarabía.
babish [beibiʃ], *a.* infantil, pueril.
baboon [bə'bu:n], *s.* (*zool.*) babuino, cinocéfalo, mandril.
baby [beibi], *s.* nene, criaturita; muñeca. — *v.t.* hacer como niño, tratar como niño. — *a.* infantil.
babyhood, *s.* niñez, primera infancia.
babyish, *a.* niñero, pueril.
babyishness, *s.* puerilidad, niñada.
Babylonian [bæbi'louniən], **Babylonish,** *a.* babilónico, de Babilonia.

Babylonic, Babylonical, *a.* tumultuoso, desordenado.
bac [bæk], *s.* barca de río; cuba de cervecero.
bacca, baccy, *s.* (*vulg.*) abreviación familiar de tabaco.
baccalaureate [bækə'lɔriit], *s.* bachillerato.
baccara, baccarat ['bækərə], *s.* juego de cartas, bacarrat.
baccate ['bækeit], *a.* (*bot.*) que se parece a una baya.
bacchanal bacchanalian, *s.,* *a.* bacante; borracho, alborotador, alborotado, ebrio, báquico.
bacchant, bacchante, *s.* bacante, *f.,* ménade, *f.*
bacchic, bacchical, *a.* báquico.
Bacchus ['bækəs], *s.* (*mit.*) Baco.
bacciferous [bæk'sifərəs], *a.* (*bot.*) bacífero.
bachelor ['bætʃələɹ], *s.* célibe, soltero; bachiller, mancebo; *old bachelor,* solterón; *bachelor of arts,* bachiller en artes.
bachelor's button, *s.* (*bot.*) botón de oro, azulejo.
bachelorship, *s.* celibato, soltería; bachillerato.
bacillar, bacillary, *a.* bacilar, perteneciente a un bacilo.
bacilliform, *a.* (*med.*) baciliforme.
bacillus [bə'siləs], *s.* (*pl.* **bacilli**) bacilo, microbio.
back [bæk], *s.* lomo, cerro; espinazo (de animales); espalda, espaldar (de personas); dorso, metacarpo (de la mano); revés, reverso; fondo, parte posterior; respaldo (de una silla); trasera (de un coche); (*mar.*) galga de ancla; (*mar.*) espalda o quilla de un buque; foro (de un teatro); recazo, lomo, canto, la parte opuesta al filo de un instrumento cortante; *back to back,* espalda con espalda; *behind one's back,* a espaldas de uno; *to cast behind one's back,* perdonar y olvidar, desechar con desdén; *to carry on one's back,* llevar a cuestas; *to have a pain in one's back,* tener dolor de espaldas (o riñones); *to break one's back,* deslomarse; *to see the back of,* librarse de; *to turn one's back,* volver las espaldas, huir; *to turn one's back on,* abandonar, desertar; (*fútbol*) defensa. — *a.* trasero, interior, posterior, de atrás, de detrás, del interior; apartado, separado, lejano, extraviado; atrasado, añejo, viejo; *back number,* entrega atrasada, número atrasado; *back room,* pieza apartada, cuarto interior; *back shop,* trastienda; *back street,* calle apartada; *back stroke,* revés. — *adv.* atrás, detrás; de vuelta, de retorno; otra vez, de nuevo; *to give back,* devolver; *to come back,* volver, regresar; *to stand back,* retroceder; *to bring back,* volver a traer; *to beat back,* rechazar; *to hold back,* retener; *some time back,* hace algún tiempo. — *adv.* después de un verbo tiene por lo general sentido de retrocesión como el prefijo español **re-**. — *interj.* ¡vuélvase Vd.! ¡vuélvanse Vds.! ¡atrás! — *v.t., v.i.* montar, subir a espaldas de; montar a caballo; hacer recular; endosar; sufragar; apostar; apoyar, sostener, justificar, favorecer; *to back out of,* retractar; *to back up,* acular; apoyar.
backbite ['bækbait], *v.t., v.i.* murmurar, difamar, maldecir, desacreditar.
backbiter, *s.* detractor, maldiciente, murmurador.

backbiting, s. detracción, difamación, murmuración, maledicencia, calumnia.

backbitingly, adv. calumniosamente.

back-board ['bækbɔːɹd], s. respaldo, forro, espaldar; (mar.) respaldo o escudo de un bote.

backbone ['bækboun], s. espinazo, espina dorsal, entrecuesto; (fam., fig.) firmeza, decisión, principio moral; to the backbone, hasta los tuétanos, hasta la médula.

backdoor ['bækdɔːɹ], s. puerta trasera; (fig.) pretexto, escapatoria.

backed, a. de respaldo, con respaldo; apoyado, respaldado; (fig.) sostenido, autorizado.

backer, s. sostenedor; apostador.

backfriend ['bækfrend], s. enemigo secreto, falso amigo, traidor.

backgammon [bækgæmən], s. juego de chaquete; backgammon-board, tablas reales.

background ['bækgraund], s. fondo, lontananza, último término.

backhanded, a. dado con el revés de la mano; (fig.) falto de sinceridad; backhanded blow, revés, golpe de revés.

backhouse ['bækhaus], s. trascuarto, el común, la necesaria.

backing, s. apoyo, sostén, garantía, ayuda; el apostar; equitación; retroceso; refuerzo (encuadernación), respaldo, espaldar, forro.

backpiece [bækpiːs], s. espaldar.

backroom [bækruːm], s. pieza trasera.

backset ['bækset], s. contratiempo, contrariedad, revés, infortunio.

backshop [bˈækʃɔp], s. trastienda.

backside ['bæksaid], s. espalda; trasero, posaderas, nalgas, trascorral.

backslide, v.i. apostatar; reincidir; resbalar o caer hacia atrás; torcerse; tergiversar; recaer (moralmente).

backslider, s. apóstata, m.f., renegado.

backsliding, s. apostasía; tergiversación; reincidencia.

backstaff ['bæksta:f], s. (mar.) cuarto de cuadrante.

backstairs ['bækstɛəɹs], s.pl. escalera secreta o excusada; (fig.) vías indirectas; backstairs influence, influencia de cortesanos.

backstays ['bæksteis], s.pl. (mar.) brandales, traversas.

backstitch ['bækstitʃ], s. puntoatrás, pespunte. — v.t., v.i. pespuntar.

backsword ['bæksɔəɹd], s. espada de un solo corte; alfanje.

backward ['bækwəɹd], **backwards**, adv. atrás, atrasadamente, prepósteramente; hacia atrás, de espaldas; al revés, en sentido contrario; to walk backwards, andar de espaldas, caminar hacia atrás; to go backwards and forwards, ir y venir; backward and forward motion, vaivén; to read backwards, leer al revés.

backward, a. atrasado, tardío; lento, pesado, negligente, perezoso, retrógrado, lerdo; retraído, corto, modesto.

backwardation [bækwəɹ'deiʃən], s. (bolsa) importe pagado por el vendedor para poder diferir la entrega de los valores.

backwardly, adv. opuestamente, al revés; de mala gana, con repugnancia.

backwardness, s. atraso, retraso; retardo; lentitud, vacilación; pesadez, torpeza; negligencia, tardanza.

backwater ['bækwɔːtəɹ], s. remanso.

backwoods ['bækwuds], s. región apartada, monte.

back-yard, s. corral.

bacon ['beikən], s. tocino; gammon of bacon, jamón, pernil; to save one's bacon, (fam.) salvar el pellejo.

bacteria [bæk'tiːriə], s.pl. (med.) bacterias.

bacterial, a. bacterial, bactérico.

bacteriologist, s. (med.) bacteriólogo.

bacteriology [bæktiəɹiˈɔlədʒi], s. bacteriología.

bacterium, s. (pl. **bacteria**) bacteria, microbio.

bad [bæd], a. mal, malo; infeliz, desgraciado; perverso, depravado, dañado, dañoso, nocivo; enfermo, indispuesto; podrido. — s. lo malo; gente mala; perdición; from bad to worse, de mal en peor.

bad, bade, pret. [TO BID].

badge [bædʒ], s. divisa; emblema, m., distintivo, símbolo; carácter; sello; insignia, escarapela, condecoración; badges of the stern and quarters, (mar.) escudos de popa. — v.t. señalar, marcar, condecorar.

badgeless, a. sin divisa.

badger, s. (zool.) tejón; vivandero. — v.t. molestar, cansar, atormentar, fatigar, fastidiar.

badger-legged, a. patituerto, estevado; patas de tejón.

badiane ['bædiein], s. (bot.) badiana.

badinage [badin'aːʒ], s. burla, chanza, cháchara, jocosidad.

badly, adv. mal, malamente.

badminton ['bædmintən], s. juego del volante, bádminton.

badness, s. maldad, ruindad; demasía.

baffle ['bæfl], v.t. engañar, burlar, frustrar, impedir, eludir; confundir, contrariar.

baffler, s. engañador, astuto, hábil; impedimento, contrariedad.

baft [ba:ft], s. tejido grosero de algodón; (mar.) atrás, hacia la popa, en popa, a popa.

bag [bæg], s. saco, talega, costal; balón; bolsa; bolsita, vejiguilla; teta, ubre, f.; cigar bag, petaquilla, cigarrera; game bag, morral, zurrón; travelling bag, saco de noche; work bag, saquito de costura; money bag, talega, saco de dinero; to give someone the bag, atrapar, engañar; to pack up bag and baggage, liar el hato, liar el petate, tomar el tole. — v.t. ensacar, entalegar, enzurronar; henchir; llenar; coger, cazar, capturar; hacer billa. — v.i. abotagarse, hincharse; hacer bolsa o pliegue (la ropa); (mar.) desviarse del rumbo.

bagasse [bæˈgæs], s. bagazo, gabazo.

bagatelle [bægəˈtel], s. bagatela, futesa, pamema.

baggage ['bægidʒ], s. (Am.) bagaje; equipaje (de tropa); armatoste, desecho; (fam.) zorra, pelleja, maula.

bagging, s. arpillera.

bagnio ['bænjou], s. casa de baños; baño; lupanar, burdel.

bagpipe ['bægpaip], s. gaita, zampoña, cornamusa.

bagpiper, s. gaitero.

bail [beil], s. caución, fianza, fiador; cogedero; división en un establo; achicador; to go bail, salir fiador. — v.t. caucionar, fiar, dar fianzas, salir fiador; poner en libertad bajo caución o fianza; desaguar, vaciar, achicar (un bote, etc.).

bailable, *a.* (*for.*) caucionable, admisible con caución o fianza.

bail-bond, *s.* (*for.*) fianza, caución.

bailee [beɪˈliː], *s.* (*for.*) depositario.

bailer, bailor, *s.* (*for.*) fiador; comitente.

bailie, *s.* alcalde, baile, magistrado municipal en Escocia.

bailiff [ˈbeilif], *s.* alguacil, corchete; gobernador; baile, ministril; mayordomo.

bailiwick [ˈbeiliwik], *s.* bailía, mayordomía; alguacilazgo.

bailment, *s.* (*for.*) depósito, fianza, prenda, entrega.

bairn [bɛən], *s.* niño, hijo o hija, descendiente (Escocia).

bait [beit], *v.t.* cebar; azuzar; atormentar; (*fig.*) hostigar, acosar, molestar, fatigar; incitar, atraer; poner cebo para atraer. — *v.i.* hacer alto para tomar un refrigerio; dar un pienso a los animales en el camino. — *s.* cebo, carnada, anzuelo; añagaza, señuelo; refrigerio, refresco; pienso; *to take the bait*, tragar el anzuelo; caer en el lazo.

baited, *a.* cebado, atraído; refrigerado.

baiting, *s.* cebo; señuelo, añagaza; refrigerio; *bull-baiting*, lidia de toros con perros.

baize [beiz], *s.* bayeta; *green baize*, tapete verde.

bake [beik], *v.t.* cocer en horno; desecar, calcinar, endurecer. — *v.i.* hornear; *baked meat*, guisado, carne cocida al horno.

bakehouse, *s.* horno, panadería, tahona; fábrica donde se refina el azúcar.

bakemeats, *s.pl.* pastelillos.

baker, *s.* panadero, panadera, hornero; *baker's shop*, panadería, tahona; *baker's dozen*, trece, docena de fraile.

bakery, *s.* panadería, tahona.

baking, *s.* hornada; cochura; cocimiento; *baking pan*, tortera; *baking-powder*, levadura.

bakshish, baksheesh [bækˈʃiːʃ], *s.* propina, gratificación, en los países orientales.

balance [ˈbæləns], *s.* balanza; cotejo, comparación; equilibrio, balance; volante, péndola (de un reloj); (*astr.*) libra; (*com.*) resto, alcance, saldo (de una cuenta); (*arte*) harmonía de dibujo, perfecta proporción; *balance-beam*, balancín, fiel de balanza; *balance-weight*, contrapeso; *balance-sheet*, balance; *balance of trade*, balanza del comercio; *balance-wheel*, volante (de una máquina, reloj, etc.); rueda catalina; *to strike a balance*, hacer (o pasar) balance. — *v.t.* pesar en balanza; balancear, contrapesar; equilibrar; dar finiquito, saldar; pesar, considerar, examinar. — *v.i.* balancear(se); estar en equilibrio; ser iguales en peso (de dos cosas), vacilar, titubear; dudar; agitarse, mecerse.

balancer, *s.* pesador; fiel de balanza; equilibrista, *m.f.*

balancing, *s.* balance, balanceo, equilibrio; *balancing pole*, balancín de los volatineros y funámbulos.

balcony [ˈbælkəni], *s.* balcón; antepecho; galería; (*teat.*) anfiteatro; (*mar.*) galería de popa.

bald [bɔːld], *a.* calvo, pelado, escueto, desnudo, raído, pelón, descubierto; tordillo (caballos); (*fig.*) grosero; soso.

baldachin [ˈbɔːldəkin], *s.* (*arq.*) baldaquín, dosel.

bald-buzzard, *s.* (*zool.*) sangual, halieto.

balderdash [ˈbɔːldədæʃ], *s.* (*vulg.*) galimatías, jerigonza, jerga; disparate; mezcolanza, calabriada. — *v.t.* falsificar, adulterar.

baldhead, *s.*, *a.* calvo.

baldly, *adv.* desnudamente, a descubierto; chabacanamente, groseramente.

baldness, *s.* calvez, calvicie, *f.*, desnudez; alopecia, pelona; grosería, vulgaridad.

bald-pate, *s.*; **bald-pated**, *a.* tonsurado, calvo.

baldric [ˈbɔːldrik], *s.* zona, banda, faja; talabarte, cinturón terciado; tahalí; (*astr.*) zodíaco.

bale [beil], *s.* bala, fardo; miseria, calamidad; *bale goods*, mercancías de pacotilla. — *v.t.* desaguar; embalar, empacar, empaquetar, enfardar; (*mar.*) achicar, sacar el agua del bote.

balefire, *s.* lumbrada; farol; luminaria.

baleful, *a.* calamitoso; pernicioso; siniestro; funesto; triste.

balefully, *adv.* calamitosamente, tristemente, fatalmente, desgraciadamente.

balefulness, *s.* calamidad, desgracia.

baling, *s.* achique.

balister [ˈbælistəɪ], *s.* ballesta.

balize [bæˈliːz], *s.* (*mar.*) boya, valiza.

balk [bɔːk], **baulk**, *s.* viga; madera larga y gruesa; lomo entre surcos; haza de barbecho; (*fig.*) chasco, yerro, fracaso, contratiempo; impedimento, obstáculo. — *v.t.* frustrar, malograr, perder; desbaratar, impedir, poner obstáculo. — *v.i.* rebelarse (un caballo).

ball [bɔːl], *s.* bola; esfera, globo; pelota; bala; ovillo, pelotón; albóndiga, bolita de carne; baile; tripudio; *eyeball*, globo del ojo; *snowball*, bola de nieve; *wash ball*, bola de jabón; *pneumatic ball*, pera de aire comprimido; *dress ball*, sarao; *fancy dress ball*, baile de disfraces; *masked ball*, baile de máscaras; *ball bearings*, cojinete de bolas.

ballad [ˈbæləd], *s.* balada, balata, jácara, romance, trova, canción, copla. — *v.i.* jacarear; coplear.

ballad-maker, ballad-writer, *s.* escritor de baladas, coplista, jacarista, *m.f.*

ballad-monger, *s.* coplero, el que vende baladas.

ballad-singer, *s.* jacarero, cantor.

ballast [ˈbæləst], *s.* (*mar.*) lastre; casquijo, balasto. — *v.t.* (*mar.*) lastrar, echar lastre; contrabalancear.

ballasting, *s.* lastre, materiales para lastrar; lastraje; terraplenaje.

ballet [ˈbælei], *s.* ballet, baile, bailete, bailable, danza.

ballista [bəˈlistə], *s.* ballesta, balista.

ballister [ˈbælistəɪ], *s.* balaustre.

ballistic, *a.* balístico.

ballistics, *s.pl.* balística.

balloon [bəˈluːn], *s.* balón; bomba pirotécnica; (*aeros.*) globo aerostático; (*quím.*) redoma; (*arq.*) bola de columna; *balloon tyre*, neumático balón.

ballooning, *s.* aerostación.

balloonist, *s.* aeronauta, *m.f.*

ballot [ˈbælət], *s.* balota, bolilla o papeleta para votar; votación; escrutinio; *ballot-box*, urna de escrutinio, urna electoral. — *v.t.* balotar, votar con balotas; insacular.

bally [ˈbæli], *a.* (*fam.*) muy, mucho, vasto, enorme, desmedido; úsase también como expletivo sin sentido determinado.

balm [ba:m], *s.* bálsamo, ungüento; (*bot.*) balsamita mayor; toronjil.

balm-gentle, melisa; *balm-mint*, abejera. — *v.t.* embalsamar; (*fig.*) mitigar, suavizar, calmar.

balmy, *a.* balsámico; embalsamado, untuoso, perfumado, fragrante; dulce, suave, calmante; reparador; (*fam.*) idiota, torpe, estúpido.

balneal [bæl′ni:l], **balneatory**, *a.* balneario.

balsam [′bɔ:lsəm], *s.* bálsamo.

balsam-apple, *s.* (*bot.*) balsamina.

balsam-tree, árbol de Judea, bálsamo.

balsamic [bəl′sæmik], **balsamical**, *a.* balsámico; untuoso.

balsamiferous [bəlsə′mifərəs], *a.* balsamífero.

baluster [′bæləstəɹ], *s.* balaustre; barandilla.

balustered, *a.* balaustrado.

balustrade, *s.* balaustrada.

bamboo [bæmbu:], *s.* (*bot.*) bambú, caña.

bamboozle, *v.t.* (*coll.*) engañar; cansar, majar, capotear; burlar, embaucar.

bamboozler, *s.* engañador, trapacero, embaucador.

ban [bæn], *s.* bando, edicto; anuncio, noticia pública; pregón, proclama; excomunión; entredicho; proscripción, destierro; multa, pena pecuniaria. — *v.t.* proscribir, encartar; maldecir, execrar.

banal [′beinəl], *a.* trivial, vulgar; feudal.

banality [bə′næliti], *s.* trivialidad, lugar común; feudo.

banana [bə′na:nə], *s.* plátano, banana; guíneo; cambur; *banana-tree*, banano.

banc, *s.* (*for.*) tribunal; banco de la justicia; *court in banc*, reunión del alto tribunal en pleno.

band [bænd], *s.* faja, venda, tira, cinta, lista, franja, fleje; cadena; ramal; enlace, lazo, unión, conexión, coyunda, gavilla, cuadrilla, partida, *f.*; orquesta, banda, capilla de música; cuello, alzacuello de clérigos, abogados, etc.; (*arq.*) filete, listón; *brass band*, charanga; (*mec.*) correa sin fin; *band-saw*, sierra sin fin; sierra continua. — *v.t.* congregar, juntar; unir; fajar, vendar, ligar, atar, precintar; abanderizar. — *v.i.* asociarse, ligarse, reunirse.

bandage [′bændidʒ], *s.* venda, vendaje, faja. — *v.t.* vendar, ligar, fajar.

bandanna [bæn′dænə], *s.* (*com.*) bandanas; pañuelo de hierbas.

bandbox, *s.* cajita de cartón; cofrecito.

bandelet, *s.* fajita, cintilla; (*arq.*) cordoncillo.

banderole [′bændəroul], *s.* (*mil.*) banderola, corneta.

bandit [′bændit], *s.* (*pl.* **bandits, banditti**) proscrito; bandido, bandolero, salteador de caminos.

bandlet, *s.* (*arq.*) filete, listón.

bandmaster, *s.* músico mayor.

bandog, *s.* mastín; perro grande y fiero.

bandoleer, bandolier, *s.* bandolera.

bandoline [′bændəlin], *s.* bandolina.

bandy [′bændi], *s.* cayado, báculo; juego de pelota. — *v.t.* botar la pelota; pelotear; buscar querella; cambiar, trocar. — *v.i.* pelotear, contender, disputar. — *a.* arqueado, combado, estevado; *to bandy looks*, cambiar una mirada, desafiarse con la vista.

bandy-leg, *s.* zambo, patizambo.

bandy-legged, *a.* estevado.

bane [bein], *s.* veneno, tósigo; (*fig.*) daño, ruina, destrucción, perdición, castigo, muerte, *f.* peste, *f.*; *wolf's bane*, acónito; *rat's bane*, arsénico; *henbane*, beleño. — *v.t.* envenenar, dañar, injuriar.

baneful, *a.* venenoso, pernicioso, dañino, mefítico, destructivo, mortal, ponzoñoso, mortífero, funesto.

banefulness, *s.* calidad venenosa; influencia deletérea.

banewort [beinwəɹt], *s.* (*bot.*) yerba venenosa, especialmente la belladona, la hierbamora y la francesilla.

bang [bæŋ], *v.t.* (*coll.*) cascar, zurrar, sacudir; encasquetar; arrojar, lanzar, disparar, golpear con violencia y ruido; (*Am.*) cortar el cabello de la frente al través. — *v.i.* hacer estrépito, saltar; *to bang the door to*, dar un portazo. — *s.* puñada, golpe del puño, porrazo; detonación; salto, brinco; (*Am.*) el cabello de la frente cortado en línea recta. — *interj.* ¡pan! — *adv.* con estrépito, con un golpe violento.

banging, *s.* (*fam.*) paliza, tunda.

bangle [′bæŋgl], *s.* ajorca.

bangle-eared, *a.* orejudo.

banish [′bæniʃ], *v.t.* desterrar, deportar, despedir, proscribir, extrañar, desnaturalizar, alejar; echar; confinar; relegar, ahuyentar, exterminar.

banisher, *s.* el que destierra.

banishment, *s.* destierro, deportación, expulsión, extrañación.

banister [′bænistəɹ], *s.* baranda, pasamano.

banjo [′bændʒou], *s.* banjo.

bank [bæŋk], *s.* orilla, ribera, márgen; banco; montón; loma, terrero; dique; terraplén, escarpa; (*mar.*) bajo, alfaque, bajío; (*mús.*) teclado; (*com.*) banco, casa de banca; *sandbank*, escollo, banco de arena; *bank-note*, billete de banco; *deposit-bank*, caja de depósitos; *savings-bank*, caja de ahorros. — *v.t.* represar o estancar con dique o reparo; depositar en el banco; contener (agua) con diques; cubrir con cenizas (un fuego). — *v.i.* tener por banquero; (*aer.*) inclinarse al virar.

bankable, *a.* que se puede descontar o depositar.

bankbill, *s.* billete de banco, cédula de banco.

banker, *s.* banquero, cambista, *m.*

banking, *s.* (*com.*) banca, negocios de banquero. — *a.* bancario.

banking-house, *s.* casa de banca.

bankrupt [′bæŋkrʌpt], *a.* insolvente. — *s.* quebrado, fallido. — *v.t.* quebrar, declar(se) insolvente.

bankruptcy [bæŋkrʌpsi], *s.* bancarrota, quiebra.

banner [′bænəɹ], *s.* bandera, estandarte, insignia, pendón, gonfalón.

bannered, *a.* con bandera, provisto de bandera.

banneret, *s.* mesnadero.

bannerol, *s.* bandera pequeña.

bannock [′bænək], *s.* torta, pan de harina de avena.

banns [bæns], *s.* amonestaciones; *to publish the banns*, decir las amonestaciones.

banquet [′bæŋkwet], *s.* banquete, festín. — *v.t.* banquetear, dar banquetes. — *v.i.* asistir, concurrir a banquetes.

banqueter, s. anfitrión, comensal.
banqueting, s. festín; lujo, magnificencia, vida espléndida; el acto de banquetear.
banquette [bã'ket], s. (*fort.*) banqueta; andén; (*E.U. del sur*) acera.
banshee [bænʃiː], s. ser sobrenatural que según la leyenda de los aldeanos irlandeses y escoceses, da gemidos y solloza alrededor de una casa donde la muerte se cierna.
bantam ['bæntəm], s. gallina pequeña de Bantam.
banter ['bæntəɹ], v.t. zumbar, zumbarse; divertirse, burlarse (de); dar matraca, fisgar, chotear, torear. — s. zumba, vaya, burla, chasco, petardo, matraca.
banterer, s. zumbón, burlón, fisgador, embromador, matraquista, m.f.
bantering, s. chifla, burla.
bantling, s. chicuelo, chicuela; muchachuelo.
Bantu [bæn'tuː], a. bantú. — s. miembro de este pueblo; el lenguaje bantú.
banyan, banian, s. (*bot.*) baniano, árbol de la India y de la Persia, higuera india, *ficus indica;* natural de la India oriental de la clase comerciante; (*anglo-ind.*) bata, ropa, talar, prenda de vestir holgada.
baobab, s. baobal, árbol corpulento de Africa central.
baptism ['bæptism], s. bautismo, bautizo; *certificate of baptism,* fe de bautismo; *baptism of blood,* el martirio antes del bautismo; *baptism of fire,* bautismo del Espíritu Santo; entrada de un soldado en fuego por primera vez.
baptismal [bæp'tisməl], a. bautismal.
baptist ['bæptist], s., a. bautista, m.f.
baptistery, baptistry, s. bautisterio, baptisterio, pila bautismal en las iglesias bautistas; (*poét.*) bautismo.
baptistic, baptistical, a. bautismal, del bautismo.
baptise, baptize [bæp'taiz], v.t. bautizar, cristianar, consagrar, purificar, iniciar; dar un nombre o apodo; (*fam.*) echar el agua a. — v.i. administrar el bautismo.
baptiser, baptizer, s. bautizante, el que bautiza.
baptising, baptizing, s. bautismo, bautizo. — a. bautizante.
bar [baːɹ], s. barra; valla, palenque; tranca de puerta o de ventana; (*mar.*) caña del timón; banco de arena o barra a la entrada de un río o de un puerto; lingote; barrote; reja; (*fort.*) barrera; (*fig.*) obstáculo, impedimento; mostrador; estrados, foro, tribunal; (*profesión*) foro; faja, raya, lista; (*mús.*) barra; compás; (*for.*) excepción perentoria a alguna alegación; *in bar of,* (*for.*) como excepción perentoria; *bar gold,* oro en barra(s); *bar iron,* hierro en barra(s); *barlock,* (*mar.*) escálamo; *bar loom,* telar de barras; *barmaid,* moza de taberna; *to be called to the bar,* recibirse de abogado. — v.t. atrancar, barrear, cerrar con barras; impedir, obstar, prohibir, estorbar; excluir, exceptuar; *to bar out,* cerrarle a uno la puerta.
barb [baːɹb], s. barba, arista; púa, lengüeta de saeta; caballo berberisco. — v.t. armar flechas; hacer mordaz, picante, incisivo.
Barbadoes-cherry, s. (*bot.*) guinda de Indias.
Barbadoes tar, s. especie de betún.

barbarian [baːɹ'bɛəriən], s., a. bárbaro, barbárico, salvaje; extranjero; hombre cruel.
barbaric [baːɹ'bærik], a. bárbaro, inculto, exótico, extranjero.
barbarism ['baːɹbəɹizm], s. barbaridad, barbarie, f., barbarismo, salvajismo, crueldad, inhumanidad; ignorancia.
barbarity [baːɹ'bæriti], s. barbaridad, ferocidad, crueldad, inhumanidad, barbarismo.
barbarize ['baːɹbəriz], v.t. barbarizar; cometer barbarismos.
barbarous, a. bárbaro, barbárico, salvaje, troglodita, inculto; ignorante; inhumano, cruel; extranjero.
barbarousness, s. barbarie, f.
barbate, barbated, a. barbado; barbudo, aristado.
barbe [baːɹb], s. (*mil.*) barbeta.
barbecue ['baːɹbəkjuː], v.t. asar (un animal) entero. — s. animal asado entero; parrilla para curar carne; merienda en la que se asan animales enteros; sitio o lugar al aire libre para secar café.
barbed, a. barbado, bardado, armado con lengüetas; *barbed wire,* alambre de púas; espino artificial.
barbel ['baːɹbəl], s. (*ictiol.*) barbo, comiza; (*vet.*) tolano.
barber ['baːɹbəɹ], s. barbero, rapador. — v.t. afeitar, cortar el pelo.
barberry ['baːɹbəri], s. (*bot.*) berberís, bérbero, agracejo, arlo.
barbes, barbles, s.pl. (*vet.*) tolanos.
barbet, s. (*orn.*) barbudo.
barbican ['baːɹbikən], s. (*for.*) barbacana; falsabraga, tronera, aspillera.
barcarole, s. barcarola.
bard [baːɹd], s. (*célt.*) poeta, m., vate; bardo; barda, arnés, jaez; lonja de tocino; (*albar.*) albardilla; (*ictiol.*) mustela de río. — v.t. poner barda a (un caballo); enjaezar; guarnecer con lonjas de tocino.
barded, a. (*blas.*) bardado.
bardic, bardish, a. del bardo o poeta.
bardism, s. bardismo.
bare [bɛəɹ], a. desnudo, descubierto, desprovisto, pelado, raso; raído, usado, gastado; llano, liso; simple, sencillo; desarmado; público; puro, mero, solo; pobre destituto; *to lay bare,* desnudar, descubrir, poner a descubierta; *bare-back,* en pelo; *bare of money,* sin blanca, sin dinero; *bare-fisted,* a brazo partido, a puño cerrado. — v.t. desnudar, despojar, descubrir, privar.
barebacked, a., adv. sin silla, en pelo.
barebone, s. esqueleto; persona muy flaca.
bareboned a. descarnado, acecinado, muy flaco.
barefaced, a. descarado, desvergonzado, insolente, impudente, atrevido, desfachatado.
barefacedly, adv. descaradamente.
barefacedness, s. desvergüenza, descaro, desfachatez.
barefoot, barefooted, a. descalzo.
barehanded, a. sin guantes.
bareheaded, a. descubierto, sin sombrero.
barelegged, a. descalzo; en pernetas.
barely ['bɛəɹli], adv. simplemente, puramente, meramente, solamente; pobremente, escasamente; apenas.
barenecked, a. escotado, con el cuello desnudo.

bareness, s. desnudez, desabrigo; falta de vestidos; miseria, laceria, flaqueza.

bareribbed, a. demacrado, descarnado, muy flaco.

bareworn, a. raído, rapado, usado.

bargain ['baːɹgin], s. contrato, convenio, ajuste, pacto, trato; adquisición; ganga, chiripa, buena compra; compra o venta; *bargain-driver*, regateador; *at a bargain*, baratísimo; *to give into the bargain*, dar encima, dar de más; *to make* (o *strike*) *a bargain*, cerrar un trato (o contrato); *into the bargain*, además, fuera de esto. — v.i. pactar, ajustar, hacer contrato, concertar, contratar, negociar; regatear.

bargainee, s. comprador.

bargainer, s. vendedor.

bargaining, s. regateo, convenio, pacto, trato de venta.

barge [baːɹdʒ], s. bote, falúa o faluca; alijador, lanchón, gabarra, barco de transporte.

bargeman, barger, s. barquero, lanchero.

bargemaster, s. patrón de falúa.

baric [bɛərik], a. barométrico; (*quím.*) de bario.

barilla, s. barrilla; algazul, mazacote.

baritone, s. barítono.

barium [bɛəriəm], s. (*quím.*) bario.

bark [baːɹk], s. corteza; barco, barca; ladrido, latido, aullido; *Peruvian bark*, quina; *angustura bark*, corteza de angostura; *tanner's oak-bark*, casca de roble para curtir. — v.t. descortezar; raer, raspar; cubrir; curtir, teñir. — v.i. ladrar, latir.

barkantine, s. bergantín.

barkbared, a. descortezado.

barked, a. descortezado, despojado de su corteza.

barker, s. descortezador; ladrador, ladrante.

barkery, s. tenería.

barking, s. descortezamiento; ladrido, ladra.

barky, a. cortezudo.

barley ['baːɹli], s. cebada, alcacer; *barley bread*, pan de cebada; *barley-bin*, cebadera; *barley-corn*, grano de cebada; *Scotch barley*, cebada mondada; *pearl barley*, cebada perlada; *barley mow*, montón de cebada; *barley sugar*, alfeñique, caramelo; *barley water*, hordiate.

barm, s. levadura, fermento, jiste.

barmaid, s. moza de bar.

Barmecide, a. (de Barmecida, el príncipe de las Mil y Una Noches) (*fig.*) ilusorio, fantástico.

barmy, a. fermentado, espumoso.

barn [baːɹn], s. granero, hórreo; pajar, henil; troj, f.; *barn-floor*, era; *barn-yard*, patio de granja, era; *barn-owl*, lechuza.

barnabite, s. barnabita.

barnacle ['baːɹnəkl], s. percebe; (*orn.*) barnacla; broma, lapa; acial. — *pl.* **barnacles**, s.pl. (*vet.*) acial; (*vulg.*) gafas, anteojos.

barograph ['baːɹəgræf], s. barógrafo.

barometer [bəˈɹɔmətəɹ], s. barómetro.

barometric, barometrical [bæɹoˈmetɹikl], a. barométrico.

barometrically, adv. barométricamente.

barometrograph, s. barometrógrafo.

baron ['bæɹən], s. barón; (*for. y blas.*) varón, el marido; *a baron of the Exchequer*, un juez de la tesorería; *baron of beef*, solomo.

baronage, s. baronía.

baroness, s.f. baronesa.

baronet, s. título de honor inferior al de barón y superior al de caballero; es el último grado de los hereditarios en Inglaterra.

baronetage, s. dignidad de *baronet*.

baronetcy, s. rango o condición de *baronet*.

baronial [bəˈɹouniəl], a. baronial.

barony, s. baronía.

baroque, s., a. barroco.

baroscope ['baːɹəskoup], s. (*fis.*) baróscopo.

barouche [bəˈɹuːʃ], s. cabriolé; birlocho.

barracan, s. barragán.

barrack ['bæɹək], s. barraca; (*mil.*) cuartel, caserna. — *pl.* **barracks**, cuartel, caserna; *barrack-master*, jefe de cuartel; v.i. (*fam.*), aplaudir irónicamente.

barracoon, s. barracón para negros apresados en la costa africana.

barrage, s. presa de contención; (*mil.*) cortina de fuego.

barrator, s. trapacero, altercador, camorrista, m.f.; (*der. mar.*) patrón de barco culpable de baratería.

barratrous, a. (*der. mar.*) manchado de baratería.

barratry ['bæɹətri], s. (*for.*) embrollo; engaño, trapacería; (*der. mar.*) baratería.

barrel ['bæɹəl], s. barril, barrica, candiota; cañón de escopeta; cañón de pluma; cañón de bomba; caja del tímpano del oído; cuerpo (de animal); huso; caja de tambor; cilindro de un piano de manubrio u organillo; (*mar.*) eje de cabrestante o molinete. — v.t. embarrilar; embanastar; embasar; *barrel-maker*, barrilero; *barrel-organ*, organillo; *barrel-stand*, poíno.

barrelled, a. embarrilado, entonelado; embanastado, encerrado en banasta; cilíndrico, en forma de barril; albardillado, arqueado. — p.p. [BARREL]; *double-barrelled gun*, escopeta de dos cañones.

barren ['bæɹən], a. estéril, árido, infructífero, infructuoso, infecundo, erial.

barrenness s. esterilidad, infecundidad, aridez.

barrenworth, s. (*bot.*) epimedio.

barricade [bæɹiˈkeid], **barricado**, s. barrera, empalizada, valla, barricada; (*mar.*) empalletado.

barricade, v.t. barrear, cerrar con barricadas, obstruir, empalizar, atrancar.

barrier ['bæɹiəɹ], s. barrera, valla, cerca; (*for.*) espaldón, fortaleza; (*fig.*) obstáculo, embarazo, impedimento, término, límite.

barring ['baːɹiŋ], *prep.* salvo, excepto, quitando, además, amén de.

barring-out, s. exclusión.

barrister ['bæɹistəɹ], s. abogado; curial letrado.

bar-room, s. taberna, cantina, sala de refrescos; café (en un teatro, etc.).

barrow ['bæɹou], s. angarillas; cebón, cerdo castrado; (*arq.*) túmulo; escurridor; prenda larga de vestir (sin mangas, hecha de franela, para niños); *hand barrow*, angarillas, parihuela; *wheel barrow*, carretón, carretilla, carretoncillo.

barse, s. (*ictiol.*) pértiga.

barshot, s. (*mar.*) bala enramada; (*arti.*) palanqueta.

barter ['baːɹtəɹ], v.t., v.i. cambiar, trocar, permutar; baratar, traficar; hacer un cambio; trujamanear. — s. cambio, trueque; barata; tráfico.

barterer, *s.* traficante, baratador.
bartery, *s.* trueco, cambio de géneros.
Bartholomew [baːɪˈθɔləmju], *n.p.* Bartolomé; *Bartholomew-day, -tide,* el día de San Bartolomé; temporada o días precedentes a San Bartolomé.
bartizan [baːɪtiˈzæn], *s.* (*fort.*) torrecilla.
barton, *s.* coserío, cortijada.
barwood, *s.* palo campeche.
baryphonia, *s.* (*med.*) barifonía.
baryta [bəˈraitə], **barytes,** *s.* (*quím.*) barita, baritina.
barytic, *s.* barítico.
barytone, *s.* barítono. — *a.* de barítono.
basal, *a.* básico, relativo a la base; fundamental.
basalt [bəˈsɔːlt], *s.* (*geol.*) basalto.
basaltic, *a.* basáltico.
basaltiform, *a.* basaltiforme.
basaltine, *a.* basaltina.
basanite [ˈbæsəneit], *s.* basanita.
base [beis], *a.* bajo, común; humilde; vil, villano, ruin; soez, despreciable; bajo de ley, hablando de oro y plata; bajo, grave, hablando de instrumentos musicales y de voces; ilegítimo, vergonzoso, infame, indigno; poltrón, mandria, cobarde; *base action,* acción baja; *base-born,* bastardo, espurio, hijo natural; *base-court,* patio; *base-minded,* ruin, vil. — *s.* fondo o suelo; base; (*arq.*) basa; pedestal, soporte, basamento, pie, cimiento;(*ant.*) violoncelo; (*ant.mús.*) bajo, grave; juego de baras. — *v.t.* basar, apoyar, fijar sobre; fundar, establecer, fundamentar.
baseless, *a.* desfondado, infundado, temerario, sin apoyo, sin fundamento.
basely, *adv.* bajamente, vilmente.
basement, *s.* (*arq.*) basamento; cuarto bajo, sótano.
baseness, *s.* bajeza, ruindad, vileza, infamia; bastardía, ilegitimidad de nacimiento; avaricia; baja ley (de un metal); mezquinería, tacañería.
bash, [bæʃ], *v.t.* golpear, apuñazar, apalear; hacer añicos.
bashaw, *s.* bajá.
bashful, *a.* vergonzoso, ruboroso, modesto, tímido.
bashfully, *adv.* vergonzosamente, modestamente, tímidamente.
bashfulness, *s.* vergüenza, timidez, modestia, encogimiento, cortedad, apocamiento, esquivez.
bashless, *a.* desvergonzado, descarado, atrevido.
basic [ˈbeisik], *a.* (*quím.*) básico.
basil [ˈbæzil], *s.* (*bot.*) albahaca, alabega; (*carp.*) filo de escoplo o cepillo; (*enc.*) badana. — *v.t.* achaflanar, biselar.
basilic, basilica, *s.* basílica. — *a.* **basilical,** basilicón; perteneciente a una basílica; real, regio.
basilicon [bəˈsilikən], *s.* (*farm.*) basilicón.
basilisk [ˈbæsilisk], *s.* (*zool.*) basilisco.
basin [ˈbeisən], *s.* jofaina, aljofaina, bacía, lebrillo; palangana; alcubilla, cambija, represa, dársena; reserva de un dique; concha de un puerto; arca de agua, depósito de agua; laguna, charca, estanque; hoya, valle; cuenca; fondeadero; tazón de una fuente; platillo de balanza; pilón de fuente o sur-

tidor; represa de un molino; hondonada; (*geol.*) cubeta sinclinal, braquisinclinal; herramienta para la fabricación de lentes convexos; *sugar-basin,* azucarero.
basinet [ˈbæsənet], *s.* bacinete.
basis [ˈbeisis], *s.* (*pl.* **bases**) base, *f.*; basa, estribo, pedestal; cimiento; (*fig.*) fundamento, principio.
bask [baːsk]. *v.i.* calentarse; tomar el sol.
basket, *s.* cesta, canasta; banasta, cesto, cestón; espuerta, cuévano, capazo, capacho; *wicker basket,* cuévano (o cesta) de mimbres.
basket-ball, *s.* juego de balón.
basketful, *s.* cestada, canastada.
basket-maker, *s.* cestero.
basket-making, *s.* cestería.
basket-woman, *s.* cestera.
basket-work, *s.* trabajo de cestería; (*mil.*) cestón, cestonada.
bason [ˈbeisən], *s.* banco o banqueta de sombrerero.
Basque [bæsk], **Basquish** *s., a.* vasco, vascongado; vascuence.
bas-relief, *s.* bajo relieve.
bass [beis], *s.* estera, felpudo; (*ictiol.*) perca, lobina; esparto; atocha. — *s., a.* (*mús.*) bajo; *bass viol,* violoncelo; *double bass,* contrabajo.
basset [ˈbæsət], *s.* baceta; zarcero; *basset-horn,* clarinete tenor; (*min.*) ramos de metales o lechos de piedras que estriban sobre otros en la superficie.
bassinet, *s.* cuna; bacinete.
basso, *s.* (*mús.*) bajo.
bassock [ˈbæsək], *s.* estera, felpudo.
bassoon [bəˈsuːn], *s.* (*mús.*) bajón.
bassoonist, *s.* bajonista, *m.f.*
basswood, *s.* tilo americano.
bast [bæst], *s.* corteza interior del tilo; líber; cuerda, soga, o estera de líber.
bastard [ˈbæstəɪd], *s., a.* bastardo, ilegítimo, espurio; falso, mentido; degenerado.
bastardism, bastardy, *s.* bastardía.
bastardize, *v.t.* bastardear, declarar bastardo.
bastardly, *a.* bastardeado, degenerado, supuesto. — *adv.* como bastardo.
bastardy, *s.* bastardía.
baste [beist], *v.t.* pringar, untar; hilvanar, bastear, embastar; (*fam.*) dar de palos.
bastinade, bastinado, *s.* paliza, bastonada, bastonazo en las plantas de los pies. — *v.t.* apalear, dar una paliza.
basting, *s.* apaleamiento, paliza; basta, embaste, hilván.
bastion [ˈbæstiən], *s.* (*fort.*) bastión, baluarte.
baston, bastoon, *s.* (*arq.*) toro, moldura redonda, bocel.
basyle [ˈbeisail], *s.* (*quím.*) radical, básico.
bat [bæt]. *s.* paleta, maza, cachero, palocorvo; pedazo de ladrillo; esquita; basta; acolchado; (*zool.*) murciélago; *off his own bat,* (*fam.*) de suyo. — *v.t.* golpear con un *bat*; (*Am.*) pestañear; agitarse, moverse.
batable [ˈbeitəbl], *a.* disputable, controvertible.
Batavian, *s., a.* bátavo, de Batavia.
batch [bætʃ], *s.* hornada, cochura; cantidad de pan que se cuece de una vez; número o cantidad de cosas que se reciben o mandan de una vez.
bate [beit], *s.* contienda, debate, disputa, altercación. — *v.t., v.i.* disminuir, minorar, rebajar el precio; minorarse, mermar; re-

mojar, como un cuero o piel; separar y ablandar, como henequén, yute, etc.

bateful, *a.* controvertible, contencioso.

bateless, *a.* indomable.

batement, *s.* diminución, menoscabo, merma.

bath [ba:θ], *s.* baño, cuarto de baño; bañadera; *dry bath*, estufa; *shower bath*, ducha; *hip bath*, baño de asiento; *hot bath*, baño caliente; *foot bath*, pediluvio, baño de pies; *bath house*, casa de baños; *bath room*, sala de baño; *sand bath*, baño de arena; *vapour bath*, baño de vapor; *bath-keeper*, bañero; *Knight of the Bath*, caballero del orden del Baño.

bathe [beið], *v.t.* bañar, lavar, rociar, regar; *to bathe one's face in tears*, estar inundado de lágrimas. — *v.i.* bañarse, estar en el baño.

bather ['beiðəɹ], *s.* bañista, *m.f.*

bathing, *s.* baño, acción de bañar; lavatorio; *bathing-dress*, traje de baño; *bathing-place*, bañadero, balneario, baño, tina; *bathing-season*, estación de baños; *bathing-gown*, peinador para el baño, bata de baño.

bathometer [ba:'θɔmətəɹ], *s.* batómetro.

bathos ['beiθɔs], *s.* (*ret.*) anticlímax.

bating, *prep.* excepto, exceptuando, deduciendo, fuera de, menos; *bating mistakes*, salvo error.

batiste [bə'ti:st], *s.* batista, lienzo fino.

batlet, *s.* batidera.

baton ['bætən], *s.* bastón de mando; (*mús.*) batuta.

baton, batoon, *v.t.* bastonear.

batoon [bə'tu:n], *s.* palo grande, bastón; (*blas.*) bara.

batrachian, *a.* batracio.

batsman, *s.* el que volea la pelota con el *bat*.

battalion [bə'tæliən], *s.* (*mil.*) batallón.

battels, *s.pl.* (Universidad de Oxford) provisiones de la cantina; cuenta de estas provisiones; contabilidad en general de la Universidad.

batten ['bætən], *s.* lata, tabla de chilla, listón de madera; tablilla. — *v.t.* cebar, dar cebo para engordar; (*agr.*) abonar la tierra, estercolar; fertilizar; reparar; *to batten down the hatches*, (*mar.*) cerrar las escotillas, asegurándolas con listones de madera. — *v.i.* engordar, ponerse gordo; revolcarse; saciar un deseo; medrar a expensas de otro.

batter ['bætəɹ], *v.t.* apalear, dar de palos, batir, golpear, cascar; batir en brecha, cañonear; romper, desmenuzar; destruir, demoler, derribar. — *v.i.* hacer barriga o comba (paredes, muros, parapetos, etc.). — *s.* batido; pasta; golpeo, golpeadura; batidor de yeso; (*arq.*) talud.

battered, *a.* batido en brecha; (*tip.*) tipos o planchas rotos o mutilados.

batterer, *s.* destructor, apaleador.

battering, *s.* (*mil.*) cañoneo; *battering-ram*, ariete; *battering-train*, tren de artillería de sitio.

battery, *s.* (*mil.*) batería; (*elec.*) pila, batería; (*for.*) agresión; *assault and battery*, agravios de hecho; *dry battery*, batería de pilas; *storage battery*, acumulador.

batting, *s.* espadillaje, agramaje; (*cer.*) moldeaje; algodón o lana en hojas; *cotton batting*, algodón en rama.

battle ['bætl], *s.* batalla, pelea, combate, lucha, lidia; acción; *pitched battle*, batalla campal; *to fight a battle*, dar un combate; *battle of life*, lucha por la vida; *battle array*, orden de batalla; *battle axe*, hacha de combate. — *v.i.* batallar, combatir, pelear, luchar; *to battle with adversity*, luchar contra la mala fortuna.

battle-array, *s.* [BATTLE].

battled, *a.* almenado.

battledore, *s.* pala, raqueta; *battledore and shuttlecock*, raqueta y volante.

battlement, *s.* almena, tronera; muro almenado.

battlemented, *a.* almenado.

battling, *s.* combate; conflicto.

battology [bə'tɔlədʒi], *s.* batología.

battue [ba'tu:], *s.* batida, montería de caza mayor; (*fig.*) matanza inexcusable.

baubee, bawbee ['bɔ:bi:], *s.* medio penique (en Escocia).

bauble ['bɔ:bl], *s.* [BAWBLE].

bauson ['bɔ:sən], *s.* (*zool.*) tejón.

bauxite ['bouzit], *s.* (*min.*) bauxita.

Bavarian, *s., a.* bávaro.

bavin ['bævin], *s.* (*fort.*) fagina.

bawble, *s.* bijería, chuchería, fruslería, futesa.

bawbling, *a.* mezquino; fruslero, frívolo.

bawcock, *s.* guapo, hombre bien formado.

bawd [bɔ:d], *s.* alcahueta. — *v.i.* alcahuetar. — *v.t.* ensuciar.

bawdiness, *s.* obscenidad, suciedad; alcahuetería.

bawdrick ['bɔ:drik], *s.* cinturón; tahalí; cuerda.

bawdry ['bɔ:dri], *s.* alcahuetería.

bawdy, *a.* obsceno, impuro, indecente, torpe, sucio, impúdico.

bawdy-house, *s.* burdel, mancebía, lupanar.

bawl ['bɔ:l], *v.t., v.i.* vocear, gritar, chillar; ladrar; pregonar.

bawler, *s.* voceador, alborotador, vocinglero, gritador, chillón.

bawling, *a.* gritador, chillador.

bay [bei], *s.* bahía, golfo, rada, puerto abierto, cala, seno, regolfo, ensenada; brazo de mar; (*bot.*) laurel; lauro, premio de la victoria; división de un edificio; parte saliente de una ventana o balcón en forma de mirador; compuerta de un dique; (*ing.*) ojo de puente; pajar, henil; acorralamiento; *at bay*, entre la espada y la pared; *to be at bay*, (*fig.*) hallarse rodeado de enemigos, hallarse en el último trance; *to bring to bay*, reducir a la último extremidad; *bay window*, balcón cerrado, mirador. — *v.i.* ladrar; aullar. — *v.t.* encerrar. — *a.* bayo (caballo).

bayard ['beiəɹd], *s.* caballo bayo; (*fig.*) bobo, simplón, boquiabierto.

bayberry ['beiberi], *s.* (*bot.*) fruto del laurel.

bayed, *a.* a rejas.

baying, *s.* ladrido, aullido.

bayonet ['beiənət], *s.* bayoneta. — *v.t.* atravesar de un bayonetazo; cargar con bayoneta.

bayou ['baiju:], *s.* canalizo, desagüe de un lago, con escasa corriente, casi estancada.

bay-salt, *s.* sal marina.

bay-window, *s.* ventana salediza.

bazaar, bazar, *s.* bazar.

bdellium, *s.* bedelio.

be [bi:], *v.i.* (*indic. sing.* **am, art, is**; *plur.* **are**; *pret.* **was, wast, were**; *p.p.* **been**) ser; estar; tener algún estado, condición o calidad; tener; *there will be*, habrá; *there is, there are*, hay; *there was, there were*, había (o hubo); *I am*, heme aquí; *how are you?* ¿cómo está Vd.? *what is that to me?* ¿qué me hace eso?

I am to go, tengo que ir *o* he de ir; *to be equal to everything,* ser para todo; *my wife to be,* mi futura (esposa); *be that as it may,* sea como (*o* lo que) fuere; *to be* es el verbo auxiliar que sirve para formar la voz pasiva.

beach [bi:tʃ], *s.* costa, ribera, orilla, playa. — *v.t.* encallar (el buque). — *v.i.* desembarcar en una playa.

beached, *a.* playado, expuesto a las olas; encallado.

beachy, *a.* playado, con playas, con riberas.

beacon [ˈbi:kən], *s.* faro, fanal, almenara, ángaro, baliza, boya. — *v.t.* alumbrar, iluminar, encender, poner señales; (*fig.*) guiar.

beaconage, *s.* valizaje; derechos de faros.

beaconed, *a.* avalizado.

bead [bi:d], *s.* bolita; cuerpo globoso; cuenta de rosario; cañutillo, mostacilla, chaquira, burbuja, ampolla, gota; perla; (*arq.*) astrágalo; (*carp.*) filete, nervio; *to thread beads,* enhilar perlas; *to tell one's beads,* rezar. — *pl.* collar de cuentas, abalorios, etc.; rosario. — *v.t.* adornar con abalorios. — *v.i.* ensartar cuentas.

beading, *s.* abalorio; (*arq.*) listón, borde, pestaña.

beadle [ˈbi:dl], *s.* pertiguero, macero; bedel, ministril, alguacil; muñidor.

beadleship, *s.* bedelía.

beadsman, *s.* beato, santurrón.

beadswoman, *s.* beata, devota.

bead-tree, *s.* (*bot.*) coco de Indias.

beagle [bi:gl], *s.* sabueso; alguacil.

beak [bi:k], *s.* pico; hocico; cañón de alambique; (*mar.*) saltillo de proa; espolón; (*fam.*) rostro, boca; (*vulg.*) juez.

beaked, *a.* picudo, encorvado.

beaker, *s.* copa; jícara; (*quím.*) bocal con pico.

beakhead, *s.* (*mar.*) frontón con proa.

beam [bi:m], *s.* astil; (*arq.*) viga maestra, madero, trabe, *f.*; volante, balancín; rayo; cabeza de campana; lanza de coche; rama de venado; enjulio o vara de empaño; brazos de balanza; (*mar.*) bao; rayo de luz, destello; (*fig.*) brillo, esplendor; *on the beam,* por el través; *aftermost beam,* (*mar.*) bao popero; *foremost beam,* (*mar.*) bao proel; *midship beam,* (*mar.*) bao maestro; *abaft the beam,* (*mar.*) por la popa del través. — *v.t., v.i.* lanzar, emitir o arrojar rayos de luz, radiar.

beaming, *a.* radiante, brillante, vivo, alegre.

beamless, *a.* sin rayos, sin brillo, opaco.

beam-tree, *s.* (*bot.*) serbal silvestre.

beamy, *a.* radiante; alegre, vivo; (*mar.*) ancho de baos; enorme, pesado.

bean [bi:n], *s.* haba, habichuela; judía, fréjol, alubia.

bear [bɛəɹ], *v.t., v.i.* (*pret.* **bore**; *p.p.* **borne**) llevar, conducir, cargar, portar; sostener, apoyar; sufrir, soportar; tolerar, aguantar, permitir; tener amor u odio a; mostrar, dar muestras de; producir; dar a luz, parir; tener derecho a, poseer; admitir, permitir; engañar, entretener; empujar, impeler, animar; padecer; criar, tener virtud generativa, llevar fruto; dirigirse a, encaminarse a; tomar el largo; usar alguna insignia de autoridad o distinción; (*com.*) jugar a la baja; *to bear a hand,* (*mar.*) dar una mano, ayudar, socorrer, agarrar; *bear a hand!* ¡manos a la obra!; *to bear away,* vencer, sobrepujar; (*mar.*) arribar todo, amollar

viento en popa; *to bear down,* derribar, arrastrar, ahondar, tropezar; *to bear arms,* portar armas; *to bear back,* retirarse, hacerse atrás; *to bear out,* mantener, sostener, apoyar, corroborar; *to bear upon,* estribar; *to bear company,* acompañar; *to bear fruit,* dar fruto; *to bear a good price,* tener buen precio; *to bear a part,* tener parte, participar; *to bear the charges,* llevar las cargas *o* pagar los gastos; *to bear date,* estar fechado; *to bear in mind,* tener presente, acordarse; *to bear up,* cobrar ánimo; *to bear with,* condonar, conllevar, ser indulgente; *I can't bear with him,* es insoportable; *to bear witness,* atestiguar, testificar, dar testimonio.

bear, *s.* oso, osa; (*com.*) bajista, *m.f.* (Bolsa); *bear's breech,* branca ursina, acanto; *bear's ear,* (*bot.*) oreja de oso; *bear's foot,* (*bot.*) eléboro negro; *bear's skin,* piel de oso; *bear garden,* (*fam.*) merienda de negros; *Great Bear and Little Bear,* (*ast.*) osa mayor y menor; (*ent.*) oruga lanuda del *tiger-moth; The Bear,* Rusia.

bearable, *a.* soportable, sufrible, tolerable.

bearably, *adv.* tolerablemente, pasaderamente.

bearberry, *s.* gayuba, hierba medicinal; la 'cáscara sagrada' de California y el arbusto que la produce; se llama también *bearwood.*

bearbinder, *s.* correhuela.

beard [biəɹd], *s.* barba; barbillas (de peces); (*bot.*) brizna, raspa, arista (de espiga); lengüeta de flecha; barbas de pluma; *grey beard,* barba cana; (*fig.*) anciano. — *v.t.* desbarbar, arrancar la barba, agarrar por la barba; subirse a las barbas.

bearded, *a.* barbado, barbudo; armado con lengüetas.

beardless, *a.* imberbe, joven barbilampiño, desbarbado; (*bot.*) derraspado.

bearer [bɛəɹəɹ], *s.* portador, dador; faquín, mozo de cordel, esportillero, ganapán; sepulturero; árbol fructífero; (*mec.*) chumacera, sostén, apoyo, soporte, gancho; (*impr.*) calzo; *a cross-bearer,* crucífero o crucero, *an ensign-bearer,* porta-estandarte, abanderado.

bearhead, *s.* guarda de osos.

bearing, *s.* colocación, situación; (*arq.*) apoyo, apuntalamiento; (*mec.*) manga de eje, soporte, cojinete; (*mar.*) reconocimiento; maneras, presencia, porte; aire, donaire, gracia; paciencia, aguante; faz, aspecto; relación; fuerza, sentido, valor; producción, fructificación; gestación, conexión, *f.*, preñez; (*blas.*) escudo armorial; extensión; (*mar.*) orientación, marcación, situación, demora; línea de flotación; *beyond all bearing,* insoportable, inaguantable, insufrible; *to take bearings,* abalizarse, marcarse, orientarse; (*top.*) ángulo en el punto de observación entre el meridiano magnético y el objeto.

bearish, *a.* osuno; rudo, áspero, feroz.

bearlike, *a.* semejante al oso.

bear's ear, *s.* (*bot.*) oreja de oso.

bear's foot, *s.* (*bot.*) eléboro negro.

bearskin, *s.* piel (*f.*) de oso; morrión.

beast [bi:st], *s.* bestia, bruto, animal irracional; cuadrúpedo; hombre brutal.

beastlike, *a.* bestial, brutal, abrutado.

beastliness, *s.* bestialidad, brutalidad, suciedad.

beastly, *a.* bestial, brutal. — *adv.* bestialmente, brutalmente.

beat [biːt], *v.t.* (*pret.* **beat**; *p.p.* **beaten**) batir, golpear, pegar, apalear, cascar, sacudir, dar golpes; derrotar, machacar, moler; ganar, vencer, exceder; (*mús.*) tocar (un tambor); dar una batida; pisar; deprimir, abatir; empujar con violencia; (*mil.*) marcar (el compás); (*com.*) rebajar; (*agric.*) trillar; espadillar, majar, agramar. — *v.i.* batir, golpear; palpitar, latir, moverse con pulsación; fluctuar, agitarse; estrellarse, echarse sobre; *to beat to death*, acogotar, herir de muerte; *to beat down* (*the price*), rebajar, regatear; *to beat black and blue*, moler a palos, acardenalar; *to beat a carpet*, sacudir un tapiz; *to beat about the bush*, andarse por las ramas; *to beat hollow*, (*fam.*) dejar tamañito; *to beat a parley*, (*mil.*) pedir parlamento; *to beat one's way*, abrirse camino; *to beat a retreat*, tocar retirada; *to beat back*, reverberar; *to beat in*, hundir; *to beat into*, introducir, hacer entrar; *to beat off*, arrojar, despedir; *to beat out*, lanzar, arrancar; *to beat time*, llevar el compás; *to beat up*, batir (huevos); dar una paliza a; alarmar, sorprender.

beat, *s.* golpe; pulsación, latido, palpitación; oscilación; redoble, toque de tambor; ronda (de policía); quiebro (de la voz); sonido repetido; (*mús.*) compás.

beat (*pret.*), **beaten,** *p.p.* [BEAT]; batido, golpeado, apaleado; arrojado, lanzado (contra); abatido, derribado; vencido, derrotado; trillado, asendereado.

beater, *s.* martillo, pisón, maza; sacudidor, batidor, golpeador, apaleador.

beatific [biːəˈtifik], **beatifical,** *a.* beatífico.

beatification [biːætifikˈeiʃən], *s.* beatificación.

beatify [biːˈætifai], *v.t.* beatificar.

beating [biːtiŋ], *s.* golpeo, batida, batidero; paliza, zurra, tunda, soba, corrección; pulsación, latido; toque de tambor.

beatitude, *s.* beatitud.

beau [bou], *s.* (*pl.* **beaus, beaux**) petimetre, pisaverde; currutaco; galán; pretendiente, chichisbeador.

beau-ideal, *s.* bello ideal.

beauish, *a.* guapo, galán, lucido; fatuo, afectado.

beauteous [ˈbjuːtiəs], (*poét.*) *a.* bello, hermoso, lo perfecto en su línea.

beauteousness, *s.* belleza, hermosura, elegancia, gracia, encantos.

beautification, *s.* embellecimiento.

beautified, *a.* embellecido, hermoseado, adornado. — *p.p.* [BEAUTIFY].

beautifier, *s.* hermoseador.

beautiful [ˈbjuːtifəl], *a.* hermoso, bello, precioso; encantador.

beautifulness, *s.* hermosura, belleza.

beautify, *v.t.* hermosear, adornar, embellecer, componer, acicalar. — *v.i.* embellecer, hermosearse, adquirir belleza.

beautifying, *s.* embellecimiento, adorno; afeite, compostura, adorno, aderezo.

beautiless, *a.* feo, sin belleza.

beauty [ˈbjuːti], *s.* hermosura, belleza, beldad, encanto, gracia, hechizo, preciosidad, perfección; *the beauty of it all*, (*coll.*) lo mejor de todo; *the beauty of the thing*, (*coll.*) lo singular de la cosa.

beauty-spot, *s.* lunar postizo.

beaver [ˈbiːvəɹ], *s.* (*zool.*) castor; piel (*f.*) de castor; guante o sombrero de castor; visera, babera, baberol.

beavered, *a.* que lleva visera o babera.

beaverteen, *s.* (*tej.*) fustán.

becall, *v.t.* dar apodos, (*despectivo*) poner nombres; insultar, ofender de palabra.

becalm, [bəˈkɑːm] *v.t.* calmar, sosegar, serenar; (*mar.*) quedarse en calma.

became [bəˈkeim], *pret.* [BECOME].

because [bəˈkɔːz], *conj.* porque, a causa de; por razón de; por esta razón; *because of*, a causa de.

beccafico [bekəˈfiːkou], *s.* (*orn.*) papafigo.

bechance [bəˈtʃɑːns], *v.t.*, *v.i.* acaecer, suceder, acontecer. — *adv.* accidentalmente, por casualidad.

becharm [bəˈtʃɑːɹm], *v.t.* encantar, captar, cautivar.

bêche-de-mer [beiʃ də mɛəɹ], *s.* cohombro de mar.

bechic, *a.* (*med.*) béquico, pectoral.

beck [bek], *s.* seña, ademán, indicación; riachuelo; (*tint*). cubeta. — *v.t.*, *v.i.* hacer señas, ademanes; reverencia; doblar la rodilla.

becket, *s.* (*mar.*) tojino, cornuza, taco; (*mar.*) vinatera, manzanillo de aparejo.

beckon [ˈbekən], *v.t.* llamar con señas. — *v.i.* hacer señas.

becloud [bəˈklaud], *v.t.* obscurecer, anublar; *beclouded intellect*, (*fig.*) inteligencia obscurecida.

become [bəˈkʌm], *v.t.* (*pret.* **became**; *p.p.* **become**) convenir, sentar, parecer, ir o caer bien, ser propio, estar bien. — *v.i.* hacerse, volverse, convertirse, venir a parar; llegar a ser, ser lo que no era; ponerse a, meterse a; *what will become of me?* ¿ qué será de mí? el verbo inglés *become* con un adjetivo se expresa a veces en español por medio de los prefijos *en* o *a*; *to become cross*, enojarse, enrabiarse, enfadarse, acorarse.

becoming, *a.* conveniente, propio, acomodado, justo; correcto, decente, decoroso; que sienta bien, que va bien.

becomingly, *adv.* decentemente, correctamente, decorosamente; a propósito.

becomingness, *s.* decencia, propiedad, decoro, corrección, compostura, garbo.

becurl [bəˈkəːɹl], *v.t.* rizar; adornar con rizos.

bed [bed], *s.* cama, lecho; tabla, tablar, era de una huerta o jardín; mesa (de billar); (*fig.*) matrimonio; (*geol.*) yacimiento, capa, estrata; álveo, madre, *f.*, cauce; (*mec.*) asiento, banco, fondo; base, *f.*, fundación; macizo de jardín; (*com.*) tonga, camada; afuste de mortero; *double bed*, cama de matrimonio; *feather bed*, colchón de plumas, plumón; *straw bed*, jergón de paja; *death bed*, lecho mortuorio; *folding bed*, cama plegadiza; *bed of state*, cama de respeto; *to go to bed*, acostarse; *to be brought to bed*, parir; *to lie in the bed one has made*, quien mala cama hace, en ella se yace.

bed, *v.t.* acostar, meter en la cama; plantar, sembrar; poner una cosa en tongadas o capas. — *v.i.* acostarse; cohabitar.

bedabble [bəˈdæbl], *v.t.* rociar, salpicar, mojar.

bedarken [bəˈdɑːɹkən], *v.t.* obscurecer, sombrear.

bedash [bəˈdæʃ], **bedaub,** *v.t.* salpicar; ensuciar, embadurnar; vilipendiar.

bedazzle, *v.t.* deslumbrar, desvistar.

bed-bug, s. chinche.

bedchamber [bedtʃeimbəɹ], s. dormitorio, alcoba, cuarto (de dormir).

bedclothes, s.pl. mantas, coberturas de cama, ropa de cama.

bedcover, s. cubrecama, m.

bedded, p.p. acostado, metido en cama.

bedding, s. ropa de cama.

bedeck [bə'dek], v.t. adornar, asear, engalanar, ataviar, acicalar.

bedel [bi:dl], s. bedel.

bedelry, s. bedelía.

bedevil [bə'devəl], v.t. diablear, endemoniar, endiablar; maleficiar; hechizar; enredar, hacer travesuras.

bedew [bə'dju:], v.t. regar, mojar, humedecer, rociar.

bedfellow, s. compañero (o compañera) de cama.

bedhangings, s.pl. cortinas de cama.

bedhead, s. cabecera de cama.

bedight, (poét.) v.t. adornar, hermosear.

bedim, v.t. velar, obscurecer, ofuscar; deslumbrar; desvistar.

bedizen [bə'daizən], v.t. adornar, acicalar, aderezar.

bedlam ['bedləm], s. casa de locos, manicomio; gran bullicio.

bedlamite, s. loco, loca, orate.

bedlamlike, a. que parece loco.

bed-lounge, s. catricofre.

Bedouin ['bedwin], s. beduino; (fig.) vagabundo callejero.

bedpan, s. chata, silleta.

bedplate ['bedpleit], s. (mec.) cama, bancaza.

bedraggle [bə'drægl], v.t. ensuciar, manchar.

bedrench, v.t. empapar, embeber.

bedrid, bedridden ['bedridən], a. postrado en cama.

bedrite [bə'drait], s. derecho conyugal.

bedrock [bedrɔk], s. (min.) lecho de roca.

bedroom [bedru:m], s. alcoba, cuarto (de dormir).

bedrop [bə'drɔp], v.t. salpicar, rociar.

bedside ['bedsaid], s. lado de cama.

bedsore, úlcera de decúbito.

bedspread, s. cubrecama, m., sobrecama, m.

bedstead, s. armazón, armadura de cama.

bedstraw, s. (bot.) gallete, cardo lechero, cuajaleche; paja para jergón.

bedtime, s. hora de acostarse.

beduck [bə'dʌk], v.t. sumergir, zambullir en el agua.

bedung, v.t. engrasar la tierra con estiércol.

bedust, v.t. empolvar, polvorear.

bedward ['bedwəɹd], adv. hacia la cama.

bedwarf [be'dwɔːɹf], v.t. achicar; atontar, entontecer, reducir.

bedye [bə'dai], v.t. teñir.

bee [bi:], s. abeja; (fig.) tertulia, reunión, f.; queen bee, abeja madre, o abeja reina; bumble bee, abejarrón; bee line, la distancia más corta entre dos puntos; línea recta.

bee-bird, s. (orn.) papamoscas, m. sing.

bee-bread, s. panal de miel.

bee-culture, s. apicultura.

bee-eater, s. abejaruco.

bee-garden, s. abejar.

bee-hive, s. colmena.

bee-keeper, s. colmenero.

bee's wax, s. cera.

beech [bi:tʃ], s. (bot.) haya.

beechen, beechy, a. de haya.

beef [bi:f], s. (pl. **beeves**) buey; vaca; carne de vaca; dry beef, cecina; jerked beef, tasajo; salt beef, vaca salada; corned beef, vaca en conserva; roast beef, rosbif, o vaca asada; beef-steak, biftec.

beefeater, s. alabardero.

been [bi:n], p.p. [BE].

beer [biəɹ], s. cerveza; pale beer, cerveza blanca; table beer, or small beer, cerveza floja; stale beer, cerveja agriada.

beer-house, beer-saloon, s. cervecería.

beestings, s. calostro.

bees-wax, s. cera de abejas.

beet, beetrave, beetroot ['bi:tru:t], s. (bot.); remolacha, betarraga.

beetle ['bi:tl], s. (ent.) escarabajo; pisón, maza, aplanadera; martinete; mallo; batón; horn beetle, stag beetle. ciervo volante; Colorado beetle, escarabajo de la patata. — v.i. combar, salir, avanzar; sobresalir; caer sobre; hacer barriga.

beetle-browed, a. cejudo.

beetling, a. prominente, saliente; colgante, pendiente. — s. (tej.) bataneo.

beeves [bi:vs], s.pl. ganado mayor.

befall [bə'fɔ:l], v.i. (pret. befell; p.p. befallen) suceder, acontecer, sobrevenir; whatever befalls, suceda lo que quiera. — v.t. suceder a; ocurrir a.

befit [bə'fit], v.t. convenir, venir bien, acomodarse a, ser propio o digno de.

befitting, a. conveniente, propio, acomodado, digno.

befog [bə'fog], v.t. envolver en niebla; obscurecer, confundir.

befool [bə'fu:l], v.t. infatuar, engañar, entontecer.

before [bə'fɔəɹ], prep., adv. delante (de), ante, en presencia de; en frente (de); más adelante; antes (de), primero, en tiempo pasado, más arriba. — conj. antes que, antes de que; a little before, un poco antes; the night before, la noche anterior.

beforehand, adv. anticipadamente, con anticipación, de antemano; primeramente, ya, previamente; to pay beforehand, dar dinero adelantado.

beforetime, adv. en tiempo pasado, en otro tiempo, tiempo atrás.

befortune, v.i. suceder, acontecer, acaecer.

befoul [bə'faul], v.t. ensuciar, emporcar, embadurnar.

befriend [bə'frend], v.t. favorecer, patrocinar, proteger, amparar.

befringe [bə'frindʒ], v.t. guarnecer con franjas.

beg [beg], v.i. mendigar, pordiosear, vivir de limosna. — v.t. rogar, pedir, suplicar, implorar; to beg the question, (lóg.) dar por admitido el punto que se discute.

began [bə'gæn], pret. [BEGIN].

beget [bə'get], v.t. (pret. beget, begot; p.p. begotten) engendrar, procrear; suscitar, producir, causar.

begetter, s. engendrador, autor, padre.

beggar [begəɹ], s. mendigo; suplicante, pretendiente; miserable; gorrón; beggars can't be choosers, a quien dan, no escoge. — v.t. empobrecer, arruinar, apurar, agotar, reducir a mendicidad o a impotencia; hacer imposible; it beggars description, no hay palabras para describirlo; es imposible dar una idea de ello.

beggarliness, s. miseria, indigencia, pobreza, abyección; mendicidad, mendiguez; pordiosería.

beggarly, a. miserable, pobre. — adv. miserablemente, pobremente, mezquinamente.

begging, s. mendiguez, mendicación, pordioseo. — a. mendicante.

begilded, begilt [bə'gilt], a. dorado.

begin [bə'gin], v.t. (pret. **began, begun;** p.p. **begun**) empezar, comenzar, principiar, iniciar; well begun, half done (prov.) buen principio, la mitad es hecho; obra empezada, medio acabada. — v.i. nacer, principiar a existir.

beginner, s. autor, originador, inventor; principiante, novicio, tirón.

beginning, s. principio, origen, comienzo; génesis, f.

begird [bə'gəːird], v.t. ceñir, rodear; sitiar, poner sitio a.

begirded, begirt, a. ceñido, rodeado, cercado. — p.p. [BEGIRD].

begnaw, v.t. roer.

begone! [bə'gɔn], interj. ¡fuera! ¡vete! ¡quita allá! ¡afuera! ¡apártate de ahí!

begonia [bə'gouniə], s. (bot.) begonia.

begored, a. ensangrentado.

begot [bə'gɔt], **begotten**, pret., p.p. [BEGET].

begrime, v.t. enlodar, embarrar; ennegrecer, embadurnar.

begrimed, a. embadurnado, untado, ennegrecido. — p.p. [BEGRIME].

begrudge [bə'grʌdʒ], v.t. envidiar; repugnar, rehusar; privarse de.

beguile [bə'gail], v.t. engañar, seducir; distraer, hacer olvidar; defraudar; entretener; divertir; to beguile the time, hacer pasar el tiempo.

beguiler, s. engañador, seductor, impostor.

begum ['biːgəm], s. reina, princesa o dama de calidad en India, de religión mahometana.

begun [bə'gʌn], p.p. [BEGIN].

behalf [bə'haːf], s. favor, patrocinio, beneficio, consideración; in behalf, on behalf, a favor, en nombre; on my behalf, por mí.

behave [bə'heiv], v.t., v.i., v.r. contener, gobernar, dominar; proceder, obrar, conducirse, comportarse, portarse.

behaviour [bə'heivjəɹ], s. proceder, conducta, comportamiento, gesto, continente; (mec.) operación, marcha, modal, crianza, maneras, aire.

behead [bə'hed], v.t. decapitar, descabezar.

beheader, s. verdugo; matarife.

beheading, s. decapitación, descabezamiento.

beheld [bə'held], pret., p.p. [BEHOLD].

behest [bə'hest], s. precepto, mandato, requerimiento.

behind [bə'haind], prep., adv. detrás, tras, atrás, hacia atrás; inferior a; en retardo; en zaga; behind one's back, a espaldas, o en ausencia de uno; to remain behind, quedarse atrás.

behindhand, adv. atrasado, retrasado, tardío; con atraso, con retraso.

behold [bə'hould], v.t. (pret. **beheld**) ver, mirar; considerar, contemplar; notar, observar. — interj. ¡he aquí! ¡aquí está! ¡véle aquí! ¡mirad!

beholden, a. deudor, obligado. — p.p. [BEHOLD].

beholder, s. espectador, observador, mirón, testigo.

beholding, a. deudor, obligado; contemplación.

behoof [bə'huːf], s. provecho, utilidad, ventaja.

behoove, behove, v.t. impers. convenir, corresponder, incumbir, importar, tocar, ser útil, ser necesario, ser preciso.

beige [beiʒ], s. tejido de lana sin teñir ni blanquear; sarga; beige, color arena.

being [biːiŋ], ger. [BE]; s. existencia, estado, condición; criatura, ente, ser; esencia; substancia, entidad. — vb. siendo, estando, existiendo; p.a. [BE]. — conj. ya que, puesto que; well being, felicidad, bienandanza, bienestar; for the time being, por el momento; Supreme Being, Dios.

belabour [bə'leibəɹ], v.t. apalear, cascar, pegar; trabajar activamente; elaborar.

belace, v.t. trenzar, entretejer; atar, liar; guarnecer, galonear; (mar.) amarrar.

belaced, a. guarnecido, galoneado, adornado con encaje.

belated [bə'leitəd], a. en retardo, retardado, trasnochado.

belatedness, s. retardo, tardanza.

belaud [bə'laud], v.t. elogiar excesivamente.

belay, [bə'lei], v.t. (mar.) amarrar.

belaying-pins, s. (mar.) cabillas.

belch [beltʃ], v.t. arrojar, echar de sí. — v.i. eructar, regoldar, vomitar, salir. — s. regüeldo, eructación, eructo.

beldam ['beldəm], s. antepasada; bruja, vejezuela, vejestorio.

beleaguer [bə'liːgəɹ], v.t. sitiar, bloquear.

beleaguerer, beleaguering, s., a. sitiador.

belee, v.t. (mar.) sotaventar.

belemnite ['beləmnait], s. (min.) belemnita.

belfry ['belfri], s. campanario.

Belgian ['beldʒiən], a. bélgico, de Bélgica. — s. belga, m.f.

Belgic, a. bélgico.

Belgravia [bel'greiviə], s. barrio aristocrático de Londres.

Belial ['biːliəl], s. Satanás; maldad, perversidad.

belibel, v.t. calumniar, difamar.

belie [bə'lai], v.t. contrahacer, fingir, remedar, desmentir, contradecir, calumniar, engañar, falsear, defraudar.

belied, a. desmentido.

belief [bə'liːf], s. creencia, fe, f., religión; crédito; credo, sentimiento; opinión, f., parecer; convicción; confianza.

believable, a. creíble.

believe [bə'liːv], v.t., v.i. creer, pensar, imaginar; fiarse; opinar; dar crédito; make-believe, pretexto.

believer, s. creyente, cristiano, fiel.

believingly, adv. con fe, con creencia, confiadamente.

belike [bə'laik], adv. probablemente; quizá, tal vez, acaso; aparentemente.

belime [bə'laim], v.t. enligar, enviscar.

belittle [bə'litl], v.t. achicar, deprimir, dar poca importancia.

bell [bel], s. campana; campanilla; cascabel, cencerro, esquila; timbre; chinesco; (bot.) cáliz; passing-bell, doble para los difuntos; to bear (o carry off) the bell, ser el primero, ganar el premio; to ring the bells, tocar las campanas; one bell, (mar.) espacio de media hora; *one to eight bells*, guardia de cuatro horas. — *v.i.* bramar; (*bot.*) crecer en figura de campana.

belladonna [belə'dɔnə], *s.* (*bot.*) belladama, belladona.

bell-buoy, *s.* boya de campana.

bell-crank, *s.* torniquete.

belle [bel], *s.f.* mujer bella, elegante, beldad.

belles-lettres ['bel-letr], *s.* bellas letras, literatura.

bellflower ['belflauəɹ], *s.* (*bot.*) campanilla, campánula.

bell-founder, *s.* campanero; el que funde y vacía campanas.

bell-glass, *s.* campana de cristal.

bell-hanger, *s.* campanillero.

bellicose ['belikous], *a.* belicoso, bélico, guerrero.

bellied ['belid], *a.* panzudo, ventrudo, inflado; prominente; (*arq.*) con barriga, convexo, acombado.

belligerent [bə'lidʒərənt], *s., a.* beligerante, belígero.

bellman ['belmən], *s.* pregonero de campana.

bell-mule, *s.* cebadero.

bellow ['belou], *v.i.* bramar, rugir, mugir, berrear; gritar, vociferar. — *v.t.* emitir un rugido, bramido. — *s.* el mugido de un buey, toro.

bellower, *s.* bramador.

bellowing, *a.* rugiente. — *s.* bramido, bufido, rugido.

bellows, *s.* fuelle.

bellows-fish, (*ict.*) centrisco.

bellows-maker *s.* barquinero.

bell-pull, *s.* botón, tirador (de campanilla).

bellringer ['belriŋəɹ], *s.* tocador de campana, campanero.

bell-rope, *s.* cuerda de campana.

bell-shaped, *a.* acampanado.

bell-tree, *s.* (*mús.*) chinescos.

bell-wether, *s.* manso (carnero).

belly ['beli], *s.* (*pl.* **bellies**) estómago, seno, entrañas, vientre, panza, barriga, bandullo, andorga. — *v.i.* hacer barriga; hartarse; pandear. — *v.t.* llenar, hinchar, inflar, combar.

belly-ache, *s.* dolor de vientre, cólico.

belly-band, *s.* ventrera, cincho, cinto, tripero.

bellyful, *s.* panzada, hartura, hartazgo de comida.

belly-pinched, *a.* hambriento.

belly-worm, *s.* lombriz, *f.*

belong [bə'lɔŋ], *v.i.* pertenecer, concernir, mirar a, tocar a; formar parte de, ser inherente a, residir en, ser natural de.

belonging, *s.* calidad, dote, facultad.

beloved [bə'lʌvd], *s., a.* querido, querida, amado, amada; caro, cara.

below [bə'lou], *prep., adv.* debajo (de), por bajo, abajo, bajo, después (de); inferior en calidad, grado, dignidad, o excelencia; *below par*, (*com.*) a descuento, con pérdida; *below zero*, bajo cero; *here below*, aquí abajo, en este mundo.

belt [belt], *s.* cinto, cinturón, faja, ceñidor; (*cir.*) venda, vendaje; (*arq.*) cornisa; (*geog.*) estrecho; (*mec.*) correa de transmisión; (*ast.*) uno de los anillos de Jupiter; *cross belt*, bandolera; *sword belt*, biricú; *shoulder belt*, tahalí; *belt saw*, sierra de cinta, sierra sin fin. — *v.t.* fajar; cercar, rodear; ceñir a la bandolera.

belvedere, belvidere [belvə'diəɹ], *s.* azotea, mirador.

belvidere, *s.* (*bot.*) escoparia.

bemask [bə'mask], *v.t.* esconder, ocultar, tapar.

bemire [bə'maiəɹ], *v.t.* enlodar, emporcar, encenagar.

bemoan [bə'moun], *v.t.* lamentar, deplorar, plañir.

bemoanable, *a.* lamentable.

bemoaner, *s.* lamentador, plañidor.

bemoaning, *s.* lamentación, lamento.

bemock [bə'mɔk], *v.t.* mofarse de, reírse de.

bemourn [bə'mɔɔɹn], *v.t.* deplorar, sentir, llorar sobre.

bemuddle [bə'mʌdl], *v.t.* embrollar, confundir, dejar estupefacto.

bemuse [bə'mjuːz], *v.t.* confundir, atontar.

bench [bentʃ], *s.* banco, asiento, banca, escabel; luneta; tribunal de justicia; *King's Bench*, tribunal supremo de justicia; *the Bench of Bishops*, el episcopado anglicano colectivamente; jueces, magistrados, tribunal. — *v.t.* construir bancos, mueblar de bancos o asientos.

bencher, *s.* miembro de colegio de abogados; frecuentador de tabernas.

bend [bend], *v.t.* (*pret., p.p.* **bent**) doblar, plegar, encorvar, torcer; combar, empandar; dirigir, inclinar; vencer, sujetar; doblegar; tender; estirar; aplicar, dedicar; hacer bajar, humillar; (*mar.*) amarrar, entalingar, envargar una vela. — *v.i.* doblarse, encorvarse, inclinarse; torcer, hacer un codo; *to bend the head*, inclinarse; *to bend the knee*, doblar la rodilla; *to bend the brow*, fruncir el ceño; *bend one's endeavours*, dirigir sus esfuerzos; *to bend back*, doblarse o inclinarse hacia atrás; *to bend forward*, doblarse o inclinarse hacia delante; *better bend than break*, (*prov.*) más vale doblarse que quebrarse; *to be bent upon*, tener empeño en. — *s.* comba, corva, curvatura, encorvadura; codillo; doblez; inclinación; codo; venda. — *pl.* **bends**, (*mar.*) nudo; ligazón, *f.*, costillas del casco; (*blas.*) bandas, barra.

bendable, *a.* flexible, plegable.

bender, *s.* el que encorva; tirador de arco; (*anat.*) flexor; torcedor, doblador.

bending, *s.* pliegue, doblez, comba, encorvadura; pendiente, *f.*, declive; rodeo, codo, vuelta, inflexión, *f.*, cimbreo.

bendy, *s.* (*blas.*) banda.

beneath [bə'niːθ], *prep., adv.* bajo, debajo, abajo.

benedick, benedict ['benədikt], *s.* benito; hombre casado.

Benedictine, *s., a.* benedictino, benito.

benediction, *s.* bendición, gracia divina, merced.

benefaction [benə'fækʃən], *s.* beneficio, favor, gracia, merced.

benefactor, *s.* bienhechor, benefactor, fundador, patrón.

benefactress, *s.* bienhechora, fundadora, patrona.

benefice ['benifis], *s.* beneficio, prebenda.

beneficed, *a.* beneficiado, prebendado; que goza algún beneficio eclesiástico.

beneficence [bə'nefisəns], *s.* beneficencia, liberalidad; caridad.

beneficent [beni'fisənt], *a.* benéfico, caritativo.

beneficently, adv. benéficamente.
beneficial, a. beneficioso, provechoso, útil, ventajoso.
beneficially, adv. benéficamente, provechosamente, útilmente.
beneficialness, s. beneficiación, provecho, utilidad, ventaja.
beneficiary, s., a. beneficiado, beneficiario; feudatario. — a. beneficial.
benefit ['benəfit], s. beneficio, bondad, gracia, favor, servicio; provecho, utilidad, ventaja; pro, bien, privilegio; (teat.) función de beneficio; for the benefit of, a beneficio de, en provecho de. — v.i. aprovecharse, utilizarse, prevalerse. — v.t. beneficiar, hacer bien.
benevolence [bə'nevələns], s. benevolencia, buena voluntad, amor, afecto, amistad; caridad, humanidad.
benevolent, a. benévolo, caritativo, gracioso, humano.
bengal [beŋ'gɔːl], s. bengala; Bengal light, fuego (o luz) de Bengala.
Bengalee, s., a. bengalí. — a. de Bengala.
Bengalese, s. habitante de Bengala.
benight [bə'nait], v.t. obscurecer, envolver en obscuridad; sumir en ignorancia.
benighted, p.p., a. anochecido; sumido en ignorancia; descarriado, extraviado, errante.
benign [bə'nain], a. benigno, generoso, afable, liberal, favorable, dulce, servicial, obsequioso, saludable.
benignant [bə'nignənt], a. benigno, bienhechor; benéfico, propicio, saludable.
benignity, s. benignidad, benevolencia, bondad, dulzura; salubridad.
benignly, adv. benignamente, con bondad.
benison ['benizn], s. bendición.
bennet ['benət], s. (bot.) gariofilata.
bent [bent], s. encorvadura, curvidad, curvatura, comba; último esfuerzo; disposición, propensión, inclinación, determinación; dirección, tendencia; pendiente, f., declive, cuesta; to follow one's own bent, seguir sus gustos. — a. curvo, combo, corvo. — p.p. encorvado, inclinado, tendido, dirigido, determinado, resuelto.
bent-grass, s. (bot.) agróstida.
benumb [bə'nʌm], v.t. entorpecer; helar; pasmar.
benumbed, a. entumecido, entorpecido; yerto, traspasado de frío.
benumbedness, benumbment, insensibilidad, entumecimiento.
benzamide ['benzəmaid], s. (quím.) benzámida.
benzine ['benziːn], s. (quím.) benzina, bencina.
benzoic, a. (quím.) benzoico.
benzoin, s. benjuí; benzoína.
benzol, benzole, s. benzol.
bepaint, v.t. colorar, teñir.
bepinch, v.t. pellizcar.
bepowder, v.t. empolvar.
bepraise, v.t. lisonjear con exageración.
bepurple, v.t. purpurar, teñir de purpura.
bequeath [bə'kwiːθ], v.t. legar, dejar; transmitir a la posteridad.
bequeather, s. testador, testadora.
bequeathment, s. testamento, acto de testar; legado, manda.
bequest [bə'kwest], s. legado, manda.
berate [bə'reit], v.t. reprender severamente, regañar, reñir, zaherir.

Berber, s., a. bereber.
berberin ['bəːbərin], s. (quím.) berberina.
berberis, berberry, s. (bot.) berberís, agracejo.
bere [biːr], s. (esco.) (bot.) farro.
bereave [bə'riːv], v.t. despojar, arrebatar, robar, quitar, desposeer, acongojar.
bereavement, s. privación, despojo, desamparo; desgracia, aflicción, luto, duelo.
bereaver, s. raptor.
beret, berret, s. boina.
berg [bəːg], s. témpano de hielo.
bergamot ['bəːgəmɔt], s. (bot.) bergamota; bergamoto.
berhyme, v.t. coplear, hacer muchos o malos versos.
Berlin [bəː'lin], a. berlinense, de Berlín. — s. berlina, coche.
berm, s. (fort.) berma, lisera.
berry ['beri], s. baya. — v.i. producir bayas; coger (fresas, etc.).
berry-bearing, a. que produce bayas.
berth [bəːθ], s. (mar.) amarradero, anclaje; camarote; hamaca; empleo, destino; litera (en un coche-cama); to give a wide berth to, apartarse de. — v.t. dar litera, dar empleo.
berthage, s. anclaje.
bertram ['bəːtrəm], s. (bot.) pelitre.
beryl ['beril], s. (min.) berilo, aguamarina.
berylline, a. berilino, de color de berilo.
beryllium [bə'riliəm], a. (quím.) glucinio.
bescrawl [bə'skraul], v.t. garabatear, escarabajear.
beseech [bə'siːtʃ], v.t. suplicar, rogar, pedir, implorar, conjurar, instar.
beseecher, s. rogador, suplicante, implorante.
beseeching, s. ruego, súplica, instancia.
beseechingly, adv. de una manera suplicante.
beseem [bə'siːm], v.t., v.i. cuadrar, convenir, parecer (bien), sentar (bien), aparecerse.
beseeming, s. gracia, decencia, decoro, donaire. — a. conveniente, decoroso.
beseemly, a. decoroso, decente, gracioso.
beset [bə'set], v.t. (pret. y p.p. beset) sitiar, rodear; acosar, perseguir, acechar, importunar; bloquear, obstruir; beset with trials, abrumado de trabajos.
besetting, a. habitual; besetting sin, flaco, vicio.
beshrew [bə'ʃruː], v.t. depravar, corromper (moralmente); maldecir.
beside [bə'said], **besides,** prep., adv. cerca, junto a, al lado (de); excepto; sobre, fuera de, fuera de que; a más de, amén de, además (de), por otra parte; beside oneself, fuera de sí; to be beside oneself with joy, estar loco de contento, estar en la gloria.
besiege [bə'siːdʒ], v.t. sitiar; asediar, acosar.
besieged, a. sitiado, asediado, cercado. — p.p. [BESIEGE].
besieger, s. sitiador; asediador.
beslaver [bə'slavər], v.t. babosear, rociar de babas.
besmear [bə'smiər], v.t. salpicar, ensuciar, emporcar, embadurnar.
besmearer, s. embarrador, embadurnador.
besmirch [bə'sməːtʃ], v.t. ensuciar, amancillar, manchar; embarrar, averiar.
besmoke [bə'smouk], v.t. ahumar.
besmut [bə'smʌt], v.t. tiznar con humo; tiznar con o llenar de hollín.
besnuff [bə'snʌf], v.t. embadurnar de tabaco.

besom ['biːzəm], *s.* escoba, escobón. — *v.t.* barrer, limpiar.

besomer, *s.* barrendero, barrendera.

besort [bə'sɔəɹt], *v.t.* adaptar, ajustar; convenir, ser adaptable, ser propio.

besot [bə'sɔt], *v.t.* infatuar, entontecer, embrutecer, embeleñar.

besottedly, *adv.* tontamente, estúpidamente, fatuamente.

besottedness, *s.* entontecimiento, fatuidad, estupidez, embrutecimiento.

besottingly, *adv.* estúpidamente.

besought [bə'saut], *p.p.* [BESEECH].

bespangle [bə'spæŋgl], *v.t.* matizar, adornar con matices.

bespatter [bə'spætəɹ], *v.t.* enlodar, manchar, salpicar; difamar.

bespeak [bə'spiːk], *v.t.* (*pret.* **bespoke**; *p.p.* **bespoken**) encomendar, mandar, encargar, ordenar, apalabrar; mandar hacer; alquilar; predecir, adivinar; indicar, anunciar; demostrar; prevenir, advertir.

bespeaker, *s.* el que encarga alguna cosa.

bespeckle [bə'spekl], *v.t.* mosquetear, salpicar.

bespice [bə'spais], *v.t.* condimentar.

bespit, *v.t.*, *v.i.* escupir, ensuciar con escupiduras.

bespoke, *pret.*, *p.p.* monidado, prevenido; mandado hacer [BESPEAK]; *bespoke clothing*, ropas hechas a medida.

bespot [bə'spɔt], *v.t.* salpicar, esparcir.

bespread [bə'spred], *v.t.* sembrar, esparcir; cubrir, tender sobre.

besprent [bə'sprent], *a.* (*poét.*) rociado, esparcido.

besprinkle [bə'spriŋkl], *v.t.* rociar, esparcir; regar; cubrir.

besprinkler, *s.* rociador.

besputter, *v.t.* salpicar, ensuciar.

best [best], *a. superl.* [GOOD]; mejor, superior, óptimo, sumamente bueno, más ventajoso. — *adv.* más bien, más oportuno; *best man*, padrino de boda; *second best*, accésit, mejor después del primero; *to like best*, preferir; *to do one's best*, hacer lo mejor posible; *at the best*, a más y mejor; a mayor andar; *to get the best of*, sobrepujar, vencer, llevar ventaja; *to make the best of a bad job*, salir de un mal negocio lo mejor posible.

bestain [bə'stein], *v.t.* manchar; desteñir.

bestead [bə'sted], *v.t.* aprovechar, beneficiar; arreglar, disponer; tratar; servir, hacer favor a; rodear, cercar, acosar.

bestial ['bestiəl], *a.* bestial, brutal, irracional, carnal, abrutado.

bestiality [besti'æliti], *s.* bestialidad, brutalidad, irracionalidad.

bestialize ['bestiəlaiz], *v.t.* enbrutecer.

bestick [bə'stik], *v.t.* traspasar; hincar, clavar.

bestir [bə'stəːɹ], *v.t.* mover, menear, incitar, intrigar.

bestow [bə'stou], *v.t.* dar, conferir, otorgar, agraciar, conceder; dar de limosna; regalar; gastar, emplear; *to bestow compliments*, hacer cumplimientos.

bestowal, *s.* don, dádiva, regalo, presente, gracia.

bestower, *s.* dador, dispensador.

bestraught [bə'strɔːt], *a.* enajenado, fuera de sí; loco, furioso, rabioso.

bestrew [bə'struː], *v.t.* rociar, esparcir, derramar sobre; sembrar, cubrir.

bestride [bə'straid], *v.t.* (*pret.* **bestrode**; *p.p.* **bestrid**, **bestridden**) cabalgar, montar a horcajadas; zanquear; atravesar.

bestud [bə'stʌd], *v.t.* tachonar; sembrar; adornar; cubrir.

bet [bet], *s.* apuesta. — *v.t.* apostar; atravesar; poner; *how much will you bet?* ¿cuánto va? *to bet ten to one*, poner diez a uno.

betake, *v.t.*, *v.r.* (*pret.* **betook**; *p.p.* **betaken**) acudir, recurrir, irse, trasladarse; darse, aplicarse, retirarse.

betel ['biːtəl], *s.* (*bot.*) betel.

bethel ['beθəl], *s.* en Inglaterra, capilla de los disidentes.

bethink [bə'θiŋk], *v.t.* (*pret.* y *p.p.* **bethought**) recordar, recapacitar. — *v.r.*, *v.i.* considerar, pensar, examinar, reflexionar, deliberar.

bethrall, *v.t.* sojuzgar, esclavizar.

bethump, *v.t.* aporrear; dar de puñadas.

betide [bə'taid], *v.t.*, *v.i.* suceder, acontecer, pasar, acaecer, efectuarse, verificarse; indicar, presagiar; *whate'er betide*, suceda lo que quiera; *woe betide thee*, ¡ay de ti!

betime, **betimes**, *adv.* con tiempo, en sazón; pronto, temprano; *to rise betimes*, tomar la mañana.

betoken [bə'toukn], *v.t.* significar, representar; dar muestras de.

betony ['betoni], *s.* (*bot.*) betónica.

betook, *pret.* [BETAKE].

betoss [bə'tɔs], *v.t.* agitar, sacudir, traquear; conmover.

betray [bə'trei], *v.t.* traicionar, vender, hacer traición; decir, descubrir, divulgar, revelar; exponer, arriesgar; mostrar, hacer ver.

betrayal, **betrayment**, *s.* traición, perfidia, alevosía; prevaricación; abuso de confianza; *a betrayal of confidence*, abuso de confianza.

betrayer, *s.* traidor.

betrim [bə'trim], *v.t.* acicalar, pulir, adornar.

betroth [bə'trouð], *v.t.* desposar(se), dar en matrimonio, dar palabra de casamiento, contraer esponsales.

betrothal, *s.* esponsales, noviazgo, desposorio.

betrothed, *a.* desposado, desposada; novio, novia; prometido, prometida; futuro, futura.

betrothment, *s.* esponsales, contrato esponsalicio.

better ['betəɹ], *a. compar.* [GOOD], mejor, superior; *to be better*, valer más, estar mejor; *to make better*, mejorar, enmendar, reformar, corregir; *to grow better*, mejorarse, corregirse. — *s.* superior; superioridad, mejoría, ventaja; apostador, ponedor. — *adv.* mejor, más, más bien; *better off*, en mejor posición, más acomodado; *better and better*, más y mejor, de mejor a mejor; *better so*, más vale así. — *v.t.* mejorar, adelantar, reformar, aumentar; exceder, sobrepujar, aventajar. — *v.i.* mejorarse, ponerse mejor.

bettering, *s.* mejoría, reforma, mejora, adelanto.

betterment, *s.* mejora, mejoramiento, mejoría, adelanto, adelantamiento, medra.

bettermost, *a.* el mejor.

betting ['betiŋ], *s.* apuesta, apostar.

between [bə'twiːn], *prep.* entre; *between you and me*, entre Vd. y yo; *between ourselves*, entre nosotros dos; *between wind and water*, (*mar.*) entre dos aguas; *between decks*, (*mar.*) entrepuentes; *between now and then*, de aquí a allá.

betwixt [bə'twikst], *prep.* entre; *betwixt and between*, entre los dos.
bevel ['bevəl], *s.* cartabón; chaflán; sesgo, bisel. — *a.* sesgado, chaflanado, abiselado, en bisel. — *v.t.* achaflanar, abiselar, sesgar; cortar en angulo, al sesgo. — *v.i.* sesgar, estar al sesgo; *bevel gear*, engranaje cónico.
bevelled, *a.* biselado.
bevelling, *part. pres.* [BEVEL].
beverage, *s.* bebida, brebaje, potación.
bevy ['bevi], *s.* bandada; manada, hato; compañía, junta, grupo, reunión, *f.*; corro, corrillo.
bewail [bə'weil], *v.t.* llorar, lamentar, deplorar, sentir. — *v.i.* llorar, lamentarse, plañir.
bewailable, *a.* lamentable, deplorable.
bewailing, *s.* lamentación, lloro, sentimiento, pena, pesar.
beware [bə'wɛəɹ], *v.i.* guardarse, recelarse, precaverse, recatarse. — *v.t.* cuidar de, mirar por.
beweep [bə'wi:p], *v.t.* llorar, bañar con lágrimas. — *v.i.* plañir.
bewet, *v.t.* mojar, humedecer.
bewhiskered [bə'wiskəɹd], *a.* que tiene patillas.
bewilder [bə'wildəɹ], *v.t.* aturdir, aturrullar, azorar, encandilar, descarriar, descaminar; turbar, desconcertar, embrollar.
bewilderment, *s.* azoramiento, aturdimiento.
bewitch [bə'witʃ], *v.t.* maleficiar, aojar, encantar, hechizar, arrobar, embrujar, fascinar, embelesar.
bewitcher, *s.* encantador, brujo, hechicero; encantador, halagador.
bewitchery, bewitchment, *s.* encantamiento, hechizo, aojo, sortilegio; fascinación.
bewitching, *a.* atractivo, fascinador, encantador, hechicero.
bewitchingly, *adv.* halagüeñamente, de un modo encantador.
bewitchment, *s.* encanto, fascinación, gracia.
bewray [bə'rei], *v.t.* vender, hacer traición; hacer ver, demostrar, descubrir.
bewrayer, *s.* traidor.
bey [bei], *s.* bey.
beyond [bə'jɔnd], *prep., adv.* tras, detrás (de), más allá (de), allende, al otro lado; sobre, fuera (de); ulteriormente; después (de); *beyond doubt*, a no dudarlo; *beyond measure*, desmesuradamente; *beyond dispute*, incontestable. — *adv.* lejos, a lo lejos.
bezan [bə'zæn], *s.* tela de algodón, que se hace en Bengala.
bezant, *s.* moneda bizantina; (*blas.*) bezante.
bezel ['bezl], **bezil**, *s.* bisel, chatón; engaste. — *v.t.* sesgar, chaflanar, abiselar.
bezique [bə'zi:k], *s.* juego de naipes.
bezoar, *s.* bezar, bezoar.
bezoardic, *a.* bezoárico.
bezzle [bezl], *v.t.* disipar, gastar extravagantemente.
biangular [bai'æŋgjuləɹ], *a.* biangular.
bias ['baiəs], *s.* sesgo, través, oblicuidad; carga; propensión, parcialidad, preferencia, disposición, prejuicio, inclinación; tendencia; objeto, motivo. — *a.* sesgado, terciado. — *v.t.* inclinar; preocupar, prevenir. — *adv.* al sesgo.
biassed, parcial, prejuiciado. — *p.p.* [BIAS].
biaxial, *a.* de dos ejes.
bib [bib], *s.* babador, babero, **pechero**; men-

tonera, delantal. — *v.t., v.i.* darse a la bebida, beber a menudo; beborrotear.
bibacious [bi'beiʃəs], *a.* bebedor.
bibasic [bai'beisik], *a.* (*quím.*) bibásico.
bibb [bib], **bibcock**, *s.* grifo, llave, *f.*, espita.
bibber, *s.* bebedor; chispero.
Bible ['baibl], *s.*, biblia.
biblical ['biblikəl], *a.* bíblico.
bibliographer [bibli'ɔgrəfəɹ], *s.* bibliógrafo.
bibliographic [bibliə'græfik], **bibliographical**, *a.* bibliográfico.
bibliographically, *adv.* bibliográficamente.
bibliography [bibli'ɔgrəfi], *s.* bibliografía.
bibliomania [bibliə'meiniə], *s.* bibliomanía.
bibliomaniac, *s.* bibliomaníaco, bibliómano.
bibliophile ['bibliəfail], **bibliophilist**, *s.* bibliófilo.
bibliopolist, *s.* librero.
bibliothecal, *a.* de biblioteca.
biblist, *s.* biblista, *m.f.*
bibulous ['bibjuləs], *a.* esponjoso, poroso; bebedor, avinado, borrachín.
bicapsular [bai'kæpsjuləɹ], *a.* (*bot.*) bicapsular.
bicarbonate [bai'kɑːbənət], *s.* (*quím.*) bicarbonato.
bice, *s.* (*pint.*) azul de Armenia.
bicephalous, *a.* bicéfalo.
biceps ['baiseps], *s.* (*anat.*) bíceps.
bichloride [bai'klɔəraid], *s.* (*quím.*) bicloruro.
bichromate ['baikroumeit], *s.* (*quím.*) bicromato.
bicipital [bai'sipitəl], **bicipitous**, *a.* (*anat.*) bicipital.
bicker ['bikəɹ], *v.t.* golpear, repiquetear. — *v.i.* escaramucear; altercar, disputar, reñir; vacilar; chisporrotear; gorjear, charlar.
bickerer, *s.* escaramuzador; camorrista, *m.f.*
bickering, *s.* escaramuza; riña, pendencia, disputa, contestación.
bickern ['bikəɹn], *s.* bigornia.
bicolour [bai'cʌləɹ], *a.* bicolor.
biconcave [baikən'keiv], *a.* bicóncavo.
biconvex [baikən'veks], *a.* biconvexo.
bicornous [bai'kɔɹnəs], *a.* bicorne.
bicorporal [bai'kɔːɹpərəl], *a.* bicorpóreo.
bicuspid [bai'kʌspid], *a.* bicúspide.
bicycle ['baisikl], *s.* bicicleta, biciclo. — *v.i.* andar en bicicleta.
bicycling, *s.* ciclismo.
bicycler, bicyclist, *s.* biciclista, *m.f.*
bid [bid], *s.* puja, oferta, postura, licitación; — *v.t.* pedir, rogar, convidar; ordenar, mandar; ofrecer, proponer, licitar, dar, pujar; exceder, sobrepujar; pronunciar; proclamar, publicar, anunciar. — *v.i.* hacer una oferta; *to bid adieu*, despedirse; *to bid fair to*, prometer, dar indicios de; *to bid defiance to*, retar, atreverse con, desafiar; *to bid beads*, pasar el rosario; *to bid farewell, welcome*, saludar al partir o llegar.
bidder, *s.* postor, pujador, licitador; *the highest bidder*, el mejor postor.
bidding, *s.* orden, mandato; oferta, puja; invitación; licitación, postura.
biddy ['bidi], *s.* (*fam.*) gallina; pollo, pollito; (*Am.*) corrupción de Brígida; (*fam.*) criada irlandesa.
bide [baid], *v.t.* (*p.p.* **bided, bode**) sufrir, aguantar, esperar; aguardar. — *v.i.* residir, vivir.
bidental [bai'dentəl], *a.* de dos dientes; dentado de dos lados.

bidentate, *a*. (*bot*.) bidente.
bidented, **bidentated**, *a*. bidente.
bidet [ˈbiːdei], *s*. caballito, jaca; bidé.
biding [ˈbaidiŋ], *s*. domicilio, residencia, mansión; espera, estancia.
bield [biːld], (*esco*.) *v.t*. proteger, amparar. — *s*. refugio, protección.
biennial [baiˈeniəl], *a*. bienal, dosañal; (*bot*.) bisanuo. — *s*. planta bienal.
biennially, *adv*. cada dos años.
bier [biəɹ], *s*. carro mortuorio; féretro, ataúd; andas.
bifarious [baiˈfɛəriəs], *a*. duplicado; (*bot*.) bifollado.
biferous [ˈbaifərəs], *a*. (*bot*.) que florece (*o* da cosechas) dos veces al año.
biffin, *s*. manzana, pastel de manzana.
bifid [ˈbaifid], **bifidated**, *a*. (*bot*.) bífido; hendido.
bifold [ˈbaifould], *a*. doble.
biform [ˈbaifɔːɹm], **biformed**, *a*. biforme.
bifronted, *a*. bifronte.
bifurcate [ˈbaifəɹkeit], **bifurcated**, bifurcado, ahorquillado.
bifurcation, *s*. bifurcación.
big [big], *a*. grande, abultado, voluminoso, grueso; hinchado, inflado, lleno, fecundo; espeso; (*fam*.) preñada; (*Am*.) grande, valeroso, noble, magnánimo, generoso; *to look big* o *talk big*, entonarse, darse aires de grandeza, echar bravatas; *big bellied*, ventrudo, barrigón; *big boned*, huesudo; *big bug*, (*Am*., *vulg*.) persona de importancia, especialmente en su propia estimación; *big-end*, (*mec*.) cabeza de biela.
bigamist, *s*. bígamo.
bigamy, *s*. bigamia.
bigger, **biggest**, *a*. compar., superl. [BIG].
biggin, *s*. capillo de niño; cafetera, gorra.
biggish, *a*. grandote.
bight [bait], *s*. caleta, pequeña ensenada; (*mar*.) seno de un cabo, lazo de una cuerda.
bigness, *s*. grandeza, grandor, espesor, grosor, volumen; importancia.
bigot [ˈbigət], *s*.; **bigoted**, *a*. fanático, intolerante; beato, beatón, santurrón.
bigotry, *s*. fanatismo, santurronería, intolerancia.
bike [baik], *s*. (*fam*.) bici, *f*., bicicleta.
bilabiate [baiˈlæbieit], *a*. (*bot*.) bilabiado.
bilamellate [baiˈlæməleit], **bilamellated**, *a*. (*bot*.) bilamelado.
bilander, *s*. (*mar*.) balandra.
bilateral [baiˈlætərəl], *a*. bilateral.
bilberry [ˈbilbəri], *s*. (*bot*.) mírtilo; arándano.
bilbo [ˈbilbou], *s*. (*poét*.) espada, tizona, estoque; toma el nombre de la ciudad de Bilbao.
bilboes, *s.pl*. (*mar*.) cepo con grillos.
bile [bail], *s*. bilis, *f*., cólera, hiel, *f*.; (*fig*.) enojo, ira; mal genio.
bile-duct, *s*. (*méd*.) conducto biliar; hepático.
bile-stone, *s*. cálculo biliar.
bilge [bildʒ], *s*. (*mar*.) pantoque, sentina; *bilge-pumps*, (*mar*.) bombas de carena; *bilge-water*, agua de pantoque. — *v.i*. (*mar*.) averiarse, sufrir una avería; hacer agua (el buque), combar, hacer barriga.
biliary [ˈbiliəri], *a*. biliario.
bilingual [baiˈlingwəl], **bilinguar**, **bilinguous**, *a*. bilingüe.
bilious [ˈbiljəs], *a*. bilioso.
biliousness, *s*. exceso de bilis.

bilk [bilk], *v.t*. engañar, defraudar, chasquear, estafar; no pagar lo que se debe. — *s*. traición, trampa, estafa, engaño; petardo, engañifa.
bill [bil], *s*. pico (de ave); (*agric*.) honcejo, honcino; alabarda, hacha de armas; billete, lista, cédula; cartel, anuncio; factura, cuenta, nota; (*com*.) billete, letra, pagaré; propuesta de ley, estatuto; demanda, petición, queja; *hand bill*, prospecto; *bill-board*, cartelera; *bill broker*, corredor de cambios; *bill of fare*, lista de platos; *bill of exchange*, letra de cambio; *to draw a bill on*, girar una letra sobre (*o* contra); *bill of lading*, conocimiento de carga; *bill of health*, patente de sanidad; *bills payable*, letras pagaderas; *bills receivable*, letras a cobrar; *bill of rights*, una de las leyes fundamentales de Inglaterra (1688).
bill, *v.t*. facturar, cargar en cuenta; publicar por medio de carteles.
billed, *a*. picudo, en forma de pico; *long-billed*, con pico largo; *short-billed*, con pico corto.
billet [ˈbilət], *s*. billete, esquela, billetico; leño para la chimenea; (*mil*.) boleta de alojamiento; *billet-doux*, carta, billetito amoroso. — *v.t*. entregar la boleta de alojamiento; alojar, aposentar. — *v.i*. alojar(se) estar alojado.
billiard [ˈbiljəɹd], *a*. de billar, relativo al juego de billar; *billiard ball*, bola de billar; *billiard cue*, taco; *billiard cloth*, paño de billar; *billiard table*, mesa de billar; *billiard-pocket*, troncra de billar.
billiards, *s*. billar.
billing, *s*. arrullo; caricias.
Billingsgate [ˈbiliŋsgət], *s*. une pescadería de Londres llamada así. — *a*. (*vulg*.) de lenguaje bajo y obsceno, agitanado; lenguaraz (hablando de una mujer).
billion [ˈbiliən], *s*. (*arit*.) billón; mil millones (Francia y America); millón de millones (en Inglaterra y España).
billionth, *s*., *a*. billonésimo.
billow [ˈbilou], *s*. ola grande, oleada, onda. — *v.i*. levantarse, hincharse, crecer como una ola.
billow-beaten, *a*. sacudido o batido par las olas.
billowy, *a*. agitado; hinchado como las olas.
billy [ˈbili], *s*. porra, palitroque.
billy-goat, *s*. macho cabrío.
bilobate [baiˈloubeit], **bilobated**, **bilobed**, *a*. (*bot*.) dicotiledóneo; de dos lóbulos.
bimana [ˈbaimənə], *s.pl*. (*zool*.) bimanos.
bimane, **bimanous**, *a*. bimano.
bimensal [baiˈmensəl], *a*. bimensual.
bimetallic [baiməˈtælik], *a*. bimetálico.
bimetallism, *s*. bimetalismo.
bin [bin], *s*. hucha, arca, arcón para granos, pan, carbón, vino, etc.; *coal-bin*, carbonera. — *v.t*. guardar en hucha o arca.
binary [ˈbainəri], *a*. binario.
bind [baind], *v.t*. atar, apretar, amarrar; trabar, trincar; ceñir, envolver; ribetear, galonear; juntar, unir; encuadernar; escriturar; constipar, restreñir; vendar; obligar, precisar; empeñar; desecar, estreñir; embarazar, impedir; poner a servir; *to bind over*, (*for*.) obligar a comparecer ante el juez. — *v.i*. endurecerse, trabarse, pegarse; ser obligatorio.
binder, *s*. encuadernador; atadero, atador;

(*carp.*) ligazón, *f.*, traviesa, amarra; (*cost.*) ribeteador.

bindery, *s.* oficina o taller de encuadernador.

binding, *s.* venda, tira, cinta, faja; ligadura, ligazón, *f.*, ligamiento; ribete, galón; astringente; encuadernación; *full binding*, pasta entera; *half binding*, media pasta; (*mar.*) *bindings*, herrajes de las vigotas; *Spanish binding*, pasta española, encuadernación con badanas. — *a.* obligatorio; valedero; estíptico; *binding streaks* (*mar.*) esloras.

bindingly, *adv.* obligatoriamente.

bindweed, *s.* (*bot.*) corregüela, correhuela, enredadera, altabaquillo.

bine [bain], *s.* vástago o tallo flexible, especialmente el de lúpulo.

bing, *s.* montón de quijo o ganga; medida de peso de 8 *cwt.* de quijo de plomo (400 kg. apx.).

binnacle ['binəkl], *s.* (*mar.*) bitácora.

binocle, *s.* (*opt.*) binóculo, gemelo.

binocular [bai'nɔkjuləɹ], *a.* binocular. — *s.* anteojo, lente, gemelo.

binoculate, *a.* que tiene dos ojos.

binomial [bai'noumiəl], *s.*, *a.* (*álg.*) binomio.

binoxalate, *s.* (*quím.*) bioxalato.

binoxide [bin'ɔksaid], *s.* bióxido.

biodynamics [baioudai'næmiks], *s.* biodinámica.

biogenesis [baio'dʒenəsis], *s.* biogénesis, *f.*

biographer [bai'ɔgrəfəɹ], *s.* biógrafo.

biographic [baio'græfik], **biographical,** *a.* biográfico.

biography [bai'ɔgrəfi], *s.* biografía.

biological [baiə'lɔdʒikl], *a.* biológico.

biologist [bai'ɔlədʒist], *s.* biólogo.

biology, *s.* biología.

bionomy, *s.* bionomía.

bioplasm ['baiou'plæsm], *s.* (*fisiol.*) bioplasma.

bioplasmic, *a.* bioplásmico.

biparous ['baipərəs], *a.* bíparo.

bipartite [bai'pɑːtait], *a.* (*bot.*) bipartido.

bipartition [baipəɹ'tiʃən], *s.* bipartición.

biped ['baipəd], *s.* bípedo.

bipedal, *a.* bipedal, bípedo.

bipennate [bai'peneit], **bipennated,** *a.* (*zool.*) bipeno.

bipetalous [bai'petələs], *a.* (*bot.*) bipétalo.

biplane ['baiplein], *s.* (*aero.*) biplano. — *a.* ajustable en dos planos diferentes.

biquadrate [baik'wɔdreit], **biquadratic,** *s.* (*álg.*) bicuadrática, bicuadrado.

birch f[bəːtʃ], *s.* (*bot.*) abedul; varillas de abedul.

birchen, *a.* de abedul, abedulino.

bird [bəːɹd], *s.* ave, *f.*, pájaro; *cock-bird*, ave macho; *hen-bird*, ave hembra; *bird of passage*, ave de paso; *bird of prey*, ave de rapiña; *singing-bird*, pájaro cantor; *bird of Paradise*, ave del Paraíso; *jail-bird*, hombre perdido, quincenario; licenciado de presidio; *birds of a feather*, gente de una calaña; *birds of a feather flock together*, Dios los cría, y ellos se juntan; *to kill two birds with one stone*, (*fig.*) matar dos pájaros de una pedrada; *a bird in the hand is worth two in the bush*, más vale pájaro en mano que buitre volando; *bird's-eye-view*, a vista de pájaro; (*fig.*) resumen; *binding-piece*, escopeta de caza.

birdbolt, *s.* saetilla, dardo pequeño.

birdcage, *s.* jaula, alcahaz.

birdcall, *s.* reclamo.

birdcatcher, birder, *s.* pajarero, cazador de pájaros.

bird-eyed, *a.* de ojo de halcón.

bird-fancier, *s.* pajarero, aficionado a pájaros.

bird-like, *a.* semejante a un pájaro.

bird-lime, *s.* liga.

birdman, *s.* pajarero.

bird-organ, *s.* organillo para enseñar a los canarios.

birds-eye, *a.* a vista de pájaro, visto de alto.

bird's-foot, *s.* (*bot.*) pie de pájaro.

bird's-nest, *s.* nido de pájaros.

biretta [bi'retə], *s.* (*igl.*) birreta.

birth [bəːθ], *s.* nacimiento; parto; camada, lechigada; puesto, lugar; causa, principio, origen, linaje, alcurnia, cuna; *to give birth to*, producir, ser origen de, dar lugar a, dar a luz; *new birth*, renacimiento; *untimely birth*, aborto, malparto; *of exalted birth*, de ilustre cuna.

birthday, *s.* cumpleaños, *m. sing.pl.*

birthmark, *s.* marca de nacimiento.

birthplace, *s.* suelo nativo.

birthrate, *s.* natalidad.

birthright, *s.* derechos de nacimiento; primogenitura; mayorazgo; naturalidad.

Biscayan [bis'keiən], *s.*, *a.* vizcaíno.

biscuit ['biskit], *s.* galleta; bizcocho; porcelana cocida antes de ser vidriada.

bisect [bai'sekt], *v.t.* (*geom.*) dividir en dos partes iguales.

bisection, *s.* bisección.

bisexual [bai'seksjuəl], *a.* (*bot.*) bisexual, hermafrodita.

bishop ['biʃəp], *s.* obispo; bebida compuesta de vino, azúcar y zumo de naranjas; tontillo. — *v.t.* (*vulg.*) ahogar a uno; falsificar, arreglar los dientes de un caballo para que no se vea su edad.

bishoplike, *a.* episcopal.

bishopric, *s.* obispado; episcopado; diócesis, *f.*

bisk [bisk], *s.* sopa, caldo; guisado.

bismuth ['bizməθ], *s.* (*quím.*) bismuto.

bison ['baisn], *s.* (*zool.*) bisonte.

bissextile [bi'sekstail], *s.*, *a.* bisiesto.

bister [biːstəɹ], **bistre,** *s.* (*pint.*) bistre.

bistort ['bistɔːɹt], *s.* (*bot.*) dragúnculo, bistorta.

bistoury ['bisturi], *s.* (*cir.*) bisturí.

bisulcous ['baisʌlkəs], *a.* bisulco.

bisulphide [bai'sʌlfaid], *s.* (*quím.*) bisulfuro.

bisulphite, *s.* bisulfito.

bit [bit], *s.* bocado; fragmento, pedazo, trozo, pedacito; brida, bocado del freno; paletón de llave; gusanillo de taladro; *tit-bit*, pedazo delicado, bocado sabroso; *not a bit*, nada, nada de eso; *to take the bit between one's teeth*, desbocarse, rebelarse; *wait a bit*, espere un momentito. — *v.t.* enfrenar, refrenar, echar el freno a. — *prep.* y *p.p.* [BITE].

bitartrate [bai'tɑːɹtreit], *s.* (*quím.*) bitartrato.

bitch [bitʃ], *s.* perra; (*vulg.*) zorra, mujer perdida.

bite [bait], *v.t.* (*pret.* **bit**; *p.p.* **bitten**) morder, roer, mordiscar, corroer, taladrar; picar, mordicar, punzar; murmurar; satirizar; resquemar; defraudar, engañar; (*med.*) agarrar, sujetar; clavar. — *v.i.* morder; picar, asirse; *to bite the dust*, (*fig.*) morder el polvo, caer vencido; *the biter bit*, el engañador engañado; *once bitten, twice shy*, al espontado la sombra le espanta. — *s.* mordedura, mordisco, picada, picadura; resquemo; bocado; (*fig.*) engaño; tarascada, dentellada; (*mec.*) asimiento, cogedura.

biter, *s.* mordedor; engañador, impostor.

biting, *a.* mordaz, acre, corrosivo, cáustico; áspero, picante; mordedor, mordicante, mordiente.

bitt [bit], *s.* (*mar.*) bitas, barraganetes. — *v.t.* (*mar.*) abitar.

bitten, *p.p.* [BITE].

bitter ['bitəɹ], *a.* amargo, cruel, áspero, agudo, severo; miserable, calamitoso; picante, mordaz, satírico, rudo, penoso, desagradable; enconado, encarnizado; crudo. — *s.* amargo, amargura, pena, pesar, disgusto; *bitter salt*, sulfato de magnesia; *bitter-sweet*, dulcamara; *bitter-wort*, genciana.

bitterish, *s.* amargoso.

bitterishness, *s.* amargor, gusto amargo.

bitterly, *adv.* amargamente, agriamente, severamente, con angustia.

bittern ['bitəɹn], *s.* (*orn.*) alcaraván, bitor, ardea.

bitterness, *s.* amargo, amargor, amargura, encono, odio, mala voluntad, rencor; severidad; mordacidad; dolor, pena, angustia.

bitters, *s.* bíter, bebida amarga.

bitts, *s.* (*mar.*) bitas, barraganetes.

bitumed [bi'tju:md], *a.* embetunado.

bitumen [bi'tju:mən], *s.* betún.

bituminate, *v.t.* embetumar.

bituminiferous [bitju:min'ifərəs], *a.* bituminífero.

bituminize, *v.t.* embetunar, impregnar de betún.

bituminous, *a.* bituminoso.

bivalve ['baivælv], **bivalvular**, *a.* bivalvo.

bivaulted [bai'vaultəd], *a.* de doble bóveda.

biventral [bai'ventrəl], *a.* (*anat.*) digástrico.

bivious, *a.* bivial, bifurcado.

bivouac ['bivuæk], *v.i.* (*mil.*) vivaquear. — *s.* vivac, vivaque.

biweekly [bai'wi:kli], *a.* quincenal.

bizarre [bi'zɑ:ɹ], *a.* fantástico, grotesco, raro.

blab [blæb], *v.t.* revelar, divulgar, parlar. — *v.i.* chismear.

blab, blabber, *s.* hablador, lenguaraz; chismoso, parlador.

black [blæk], *v.t.* ennegrecer, oscurecer, dar o teñir de negro; (*fig.*) denigrar, deshonrar. — *v.i.* ennegrecerse. — *s.* negro, color negro; (*blas.*) sable; luto. — *a.* negro, sombrío; ceñudo, tétrico; funesto, calamitoso; horrible, atroz, infame; *to dye black*, teñir de negro; *to wear black*, tomar luto; *black and blue*, lívido, acardenalado, amoratado; *to put a thing in black and white*, poner por escrito una cosa; *black list*, lista de personas sospechosas; *he looks very black*, tiene el aire bien triste; *to look black at*, mirar de través.

blackamoor ['blækəmoeɹ], *s.*(*despec.*) negro; negrillo; moro.

black-art, *s.* nigromancia.

black-ball, *s.* bola negra (para votar); bola de betún. — *v.t.* dar bola negra, votar en contra.

black-beetle, *s.* escarabajo.

blackberry, *s.* (*bot.*) zarza, zarzamora.

blackbird, *s.* (*orn.*) mirlo o merla.

blackboard, *s.* pizarra, encerado.

black-browed, *a.* cejinegro; tenebroso, triste.

black-cap, *s.* (*orn.*) alondra; (*bot.*) frambuesa negra, enea, espadaña común.

black-cattle, *s.* ganado vacuno.

black-cock, *s.* gallo silvestre.

black-currant, *s.* grosella negra; casis, *f.*

blacken, *v.t.* ennegrecer, obscurecer, dar de negro, betunar; tildar, calumniar, difamar, denigrar. — *v.i.* oscurecer, nublarse, ennegrecer.

black-eyed, *a.* ojinegro.

blackguard, *s.* (*fam.*) pillastrón, pelagatos, pillo, tunante. — *a.* grosero, pillo, tosco.

blackguardism, *s.* pillería, tunantada.

blackhaired, *a.* pelinegro.

black-head, *s.* espinilla.

blacking, *s.* betún, lustre de zapatos.

blackish, *a.* negruzco, oscuro, bruno.

black-leg, *s.* petardista, *m.f.*; fullero; (*vet.*) morriña negra; esquirol (*obrerismo*).

blackly, *adv.* atrozmente, infamemente.

blackmail, *s.* chantaje. — *v.t.* arrancar dinero por chantaje.

blackmailer, *s.* chantajista, *m.f.*

blackmouthed, *a.* boquinegro; grosero, vil.

blackness, *s.* negrura, color negro; obscuridad; atrocidad.

black-pudding, *s.* morcilla.

blacksmith, *s.* herrero, chispero, forzador.

blackthorn, *s.* (*bot.*) endrino.

black-vomit, *s.* vómito negro.

blad [blæd], *s.* manotada, golpe con la mano. — *v.t.* herir, dar una bofetada, golpear.

bladder, *s.* (*anat.*) vejiga; ampolla; *bladder-senna*, (*bot.*) espantalobos.

bladderwort ['blædəɹweəɹt], *s.* (*bot.*) utricularia.

bladdery, *a.* vesicular.

blade [bleid], *s.* hoja; brizna; tallo; pala de remo; (*fig.*) jaquetón, valentón, guapo.

blade-bone, *s.* (*anat.*) escápula, espaldilla, omóplato.

bladed, *a.* entallecido; guarnecido de hojas; armado con hojas; (*min.*) laminado.

bladesmith, *s.* espadero.

blain [blein], *s.* vejiga, ampolla, llaga, divieso; (*vet.*) adivas.

blamable ['bleiməbl], *a.* culpable, vituperable, reprensible.

blamableness, *s.* culpabilidad.

blame [bleim], *v.t.* culpar, condenar, inculpar, reprochar, reprender, tachar, censurar, vituperar; *he is to blame*, es culpable, es digno de censura. — *s.* vituperación, censura, reprobación, reproche; delito, culpa, falta.

blameful, *a.* reprensible, culpable, censurable, reo.

blamefulness, *s.* culpabilidad, sinrazón, *f.*, falta, demérito.

blameless, *a.* intachable, inculpable, inocente, puro, irreprensible.

blamelessness, *s.* inocencia, carencia de culpa, inculpabilidad.

blamer, *s.* represor, censurador.

blameworthiness, *s.* culpabilidad, demérito.

blameworthy, *a.* culpable, censurable.

blanch [blɑ:ntʃ], *v.t.* blanquear, emblanquecer; mondar, pelar; hacer palidecer. — *v.i.* blanquear, perder el color, ponerse blanco; palidecer, volver pálido; tomar un sesgo.

blancher, *s.* blanqueador.

blanching, *s.* blanqueo, blanquición, blanquimiento.

blanc-mange, *s.* (*coc.*) manjar blanco.

bland [blænd], *a.* blando, suave, dulce; lisonjero.

blandiloquence [blæn'diləkwəns], s. agasajo, blandura; lisonja, cumplimiento.

blandish ['blændiʃ], v.t. ablandar, suavizar; acariciar, engatusar; halagar, lisonjear.

blandisher, s. halagador, lisonjero, zalamero.

blandishment, s. halago, requiebro, agasajo, caricia, zalamería.

blandness, s. dulzura, suavidad, blandura; amabilidad, atractivo.

blank [blæŋk], a. blanco; (poét.) suelto, libre, sin rima; en blanco, no escrito; sin adorno; sin interés; turbado, confuso, desconcertado; descolorido, pálido; blank cartridge, cartucho sin bala. — s. blanco, hueco, laguna, espacio; suerte o cédula de la lotería que no gana nada; papel en blanco; carta blanca; pedazo de plata u oro destinado a la acuñación. — v.t. perturbar, desconcertar, confundir, hacer palidecer; cancelar, anular.

blanket ['blæŋkət], s. cubierta de lana; manta, frazada; mantilla; colcha, cobertor; (imp.) mantilla, el cordellate que se coloca entre tímpano y timpanillo; to throw (o be) a wet blanket, (fig.) echar un jarro de agua, ser un aguafiestas. — v.t. cubrir con manta; mantear; matraquear, ridiculizar; (mar.) privar de viento a un buque pasando a barlovento.

blankly, adv. en blanco, sin color, sin escrito; desconcertadamente.

blankness, s. espacio, laguna, hueco; confusión, turbación.

blare [blɛəɹ], v.i. sonar como trompeta; bramar, rugir; gritar, vociferar. — s. bramido, rugido; ruido.

blarney ['blɑːɹni], s. adulación, lisonja, zalamería; bola; mentira; fanfarronada.

blaspheme [blæsfiːm], v.t. blasfemar, vilipendiar, injuriar, calumniar. — v.i. decir blasfemias; renegar.

blasphemer, s. blasfemo, blasfemador.

blasphemous ['blæsfəməs], a. blasfemo, blasfematorio; impío.

blasphemy, blaspheming, s. blasfemia.

blast [blɑːst], s. ráfaga, ventarrón, golpe de viento; ventolera, bocanada de aire; soplo; viento terral; rebufo, explosión, voladura; tizón, enfermedad del trigo; son; blast furnace, alto horno; in full blast, en plena marcha. — v.t. marchitar, agostar, secar; (agric.) anieblar, añublar; ahornagar; arruinar, destruir, acabar; castigar; infamar, maldecir; espantar; volar, barrenar, dar barreno. — v.i. secarse, marchitarse.

blaster, s. destructor, calamitoso; detractor.

blasting, s. destrucción, ruina; voladura; vuelo de una mina; marchitamiento, marchitez.

blastment, s. calamidad, plaga repentina.

blatant ['bleitənt], a. ruidoso, vocinglero; agresivo; llamativo, chillón.

blather ['blæðəɹ], v.i. charlar. — s. charla.

blatter ['blætəɹ], v.i. declamar, denigrar; alborotar.

blatterer, s. alabancioso; (fam.) embromador, bromista, m.f.

blaze [bleiz], s. llama, llamarada; fuego, fogata; fogarada, hoguera; incendio; luz brillante, brillo, esplendor; publicación, divulgación; rumor, ruido; estrella o mancha blanca en la frente del caballo; in a blaze, en llamas. — v.i. inflamarse, encenderse; arder; brillar, flamear, resplandecer, lucir. — v.t. inflamar,

encender, hacer llama; publicar, pregonar, divulgar; to blaze about o abroad, publicar, divulgar.

blazer, s. charlador, novelero; brasero, braserillo; chaqueta de franela o seda.

blazing, a. flameante, flamígero, en llamas; resplandeciente, brillante.

blazon ['bleizən], v.t. blasonar; decorar, adornar; celebrar, alabar; proclamar, divulgar, publicar. — s. blasón; divulgación, publicación, celebración.

blazoner, s. heraldo; genealogista, m.f.; blasonador.

blazonry, s. blasón; boato.

bleaberry ['bliːberi], s. (bot.) mírtilo.

bleach [bliːtʃ], v.t. blanquear, emblanquecer, descolorar, palidecer. — v.i. ponerse blanco, palidecer, descolorirse.

bleacher, s. blanqueador.

bleachery, s. blanqueo.

bleaching, s. blanqueadura, blanqueamiento, blanqueo.

bleak [bliːk], a. pálido, descolorido; desabrigado; helado, frío; sombrío; desierto, raso. — s. (ict.) albur, breca.

bleakish, a. frío, glacial.

bleakness, s. frío, frialdad; palidez; destemplanza, intemperie, f.

blear [bliəɹ], a. lagañoso, legañoso; pitarroso, cegajoso; (fig.) engañoso, falaz.

blear-eyed, a. lagañoso; torpe o confuso de entendimiento.

blearedness, s. lagaña, legaña; turbación u ofuscación de la vista.

bleary, a. lagañoso, legañoso.

bleat [bliːt], v.t. balar. — v.i. balar, dar balidos.

bleating, s. balido. — a. balante.

bleb [bleb], s. ampolla, vejiga.

bled, pret. y p.p. [BLEED].

bleed [bliːd], v.i. sangrar, echar o perder sangre; (poét.) verter su sangre; echar savia; chorrear, destilar; morir, fallecer; exudar, llorar (la vid); (fig.) sangrarse; dar dinero de mala voluntad. — v.t. sangrar, sacar sangre; (fam.) sacar dinero; (fam.) pegar un sablazo; to bleed to death, morir desangrado.

bleeder, s. sangrador.

bleeding, s. sangría, sangradura, hemorragia; flujo de sangre; bleeding-heart, (bot.) dicentra, alhelí doble; a bleeding heart, (poét.) corazón traspasado de dolor.

blemish [blemiʃ], v.t. afear, desfigurar; empañar, ensuciar, manchar; denigrar, infamar. — s. defecto, tacha, imperfección, falta; cicatriz, f., lunar; (vulg.) chirlo; (fig.) deshonra, infamia; mancha, mancilla.

blemishless, a. sin tacha, defecto o falta.

blench [blentʃ], v.i. retroceder, recular, cejar; fruncir las cejas; pestañear; estremecerse. — v.t. impedir, hacer abortar. — s. sobresalto; estremecimiento.

blenching, s. retroceso.

blend [blend], v.t. mezclar, fundir, unir, combinar, casar colores (pint.). — v.i. fundirse, confundirse, mezclarse, combinarse, unirse, aliarse, casarse (colores). — s. mixtura, mezcla, combinación; (pint.) degradación.

blende [blend], s. (min.) blenda (sulfuro de cinc).

blennorrhœa [blenoˈriːə], s. (med.) blenorrea.

blent [blent], pret. y p.p. [BLEND].

bless [bles], v.t. bendecir, hacer prosperar,

hacer feliz; santificar, consagrar; persignar, santiguar; alabar; glorificar, exaltar; *bless me,* ¡válgame Dios!

blessed ['blesid], **blest** [blest], *a.* bendito, santo, divino; feliz, dichoso, bienaventurado; beato; escogido; *blessed thistle,* (*bot.*) cardo bendito.

blessedness, *s.* bendición, felicidad, santidad, beatitud, gloria.

blessing, *s.* bendición; benedícite; beneficio, merced, bien, dicha; don; ventaja; gracia, favor divino; culto, adoración.

blest [blest], *p.p.* [BLESS]. — *a.* [BLESSED].

blet [blet], *v.i.* pasarse, echarse a perder, podrirse. — *s.* picadura; podredumbre incipiente.

blethering ['bleðəɹiŋ], *a.* chirlador, chirladora.

blew [bluː], *pret.* [BLOW].

blight [blait], *s.* tizón, pulgón; (*agric.*) enfermedad del trigo, añublo. — *v.t.* atizonar, agostar, esterilizar, añublar, abrasar; (*fig.*) manchar; marchitar, ajar. — *v.i.* atizonarse, añublarse, agostarse.

blind [blaind], *a.* ciego; necio, ignorante, insensato; tenebroso, oscuro; oculto, secreto, escondido; *blind in one eye,* tuerto; *blind alley,* callejón sin salida; *blind pretence,* pretexto falso; *blind man's buff,* gallina ciega; *blind side,* lado flaco. — *v.t.* cegar, deslumbrar, quitar la vista, ofuscar, obcecar; eclipsar; velar, encubrir; (*mil.*) blindar. — *s.* antipara, pantalla, cancel, mampara, venda, velo; escondite; pretexto, engaño, evasiva; máscara. — *pl.* (*fort.*) blinda, blindajes; *Venetian blinds,* celosías; *window-blind,* transparentes, persianas.

blindage, *s.* (*mil.*) blindaje.

blindfold, *a.* vendados (los ojos); (*fig.*) ofuscado; a ciegas. — *v.t.* vendar (los ojos); cubrir, impedir, hacer gorda (la vista); despistar, ofuscar.

blindly, *adv.* a ciegas, ciegamente, sin reflexión, a ojos cerrados.

blindness, *s.* ceguedad, ceguera, obcecación, ofuscación.

blindworm, *s.* (*zool.*) cecilia.

blink [bliŋk], *v.i.* pestañear, parpadear; cerrar los ojos, disimular; evadir, eludir; fulgurar, destellar. — *v.t.* evadir, eludir; colorear, paliar; guiñar; hacer la vista gorda. — *s.* ojeada; vislumbre, pestañeo, guiño, guiñada, destello, reflejo.

blinkard, *s.* cegato, cegajoso.

blinkers, *s.pl.* anteojeras, pantallas.

bliss [blis], *s.* beatitud, bienaventuranza, gloria, felicidad, deleite, arrobamiento.

blissful, *a.* bienaventurado, feliz, dichoso.

blissfully, *adv.* felizmente.

blissfulness, *s.* bienaventuranza, suprema felicidad.

blissless, *a.* infeliz, desgraciado.

blister ['blistəɹ], *s.* vejiga, ampolla, flictena; cantárida, vejigatorio; burbuja. — *v.i.* ampollarse, avejigarse. — *v.t.* ampollar; aplicar un vejigatorio.

blister-fly, *s.* cantárida.

blistery, *a.* cubierto de ampollas.

blite [blæit], *s.* (*bot.*) bledo.

blithe [blaið], **blitheful,** *a.* alegre, contento, gozoso.

blithely, *adv.* alegremente.

blitheness, *s.* alegría, júbilo, contento, gozo, jovialidad.

blithesome, *a.* alegre, vivo, divertido.

blithesomeness, *s.* alegría, animación, júbilo, contento, gozo, jovialidad.

blizzard ['blizəɹd], *s.* ventisca.

bloat [blout], *v.t.* hinchar, henchir; curar, ahumar; entumecer, inflar. — *v.i.* entumecerse, hincharse. — *a.* ahumado; hinchado.

bloated ['bloutid], *a.* hinchado, turgente.

bloatedness, *s.* turgencia, hinchazón.

bloater, *s.* arenque ahumado.

blob [bləb], *s.* gota; burbuja; ampolla; (*mar.*) base de un poste de hierro en un buque.

blobber, *s.* burbuja, ampolla.

blobberlip, *s.* bezo.

blobberlipped, bloblipped, *a.* bezudo.

block [blɔk], *s.* bloque, zoquete, canto, gran pedazo de mármol o granito en bruto; cubo, dado; cepo o tajo de yunque; trozo de madera; manzana de casas; molde; barra de hierro; tajo, tajón; leño; boliche, bolín; (*mar.*) motón; polea, garrucha; cuadernal; (*fig.*) obstáculo, impedimento; *hatter's block,* horma de sombrero; *chopping-block,* tajo de cocina; *stumbling-block,* piedra de escándalo. — *v.t.* bloquear; cerrar, obstruir; tapiar, condenar; (*tip.*) montar (una plancha); (*carp.*) reforzar (un ángulo).

blockade [blɔ'keid], *s.* bloqueo, bloque, obstrucción. — *v.t.* bloquear, poner cerco.

blockader, *s.* bloqueador.

blockhead ['blɔkhed], *s.* (*fig.*) leño, bruto, necio, tonto, naranjo, zoquete, bolonio; pedazo de alcornoque.

blockheaded, *a.* lerdo, estúpido.

block-house, *s.* blocao, fortín.

blockish, *a.* tonto, estúpido, bobo, estólido.

blockishness, *s.* estupidez, estolidez, necedad, tontería.

block-like, *a.* estúpido.

blockmaker, *s.* fabricante de poleas.

bloke [blouk], *s.* (*vulg.*) un fulano, un tío.

blomary, bloomary [bluːməɹi], (*metal.*) horno de refinación.

blond, blonde [blɔnd], *s.* blondo, blonda, rubio, rubia, persona de cabellos rubios; blonda (encaje).

blond-lace, *s.* blonda de seda.

blood [blʌd], *s.* sangre, *f.*; vida, vitalidad; savia; alcurnia, parentesco, linaje; cólera, ira, indignación; pasión, temperamento; hombre animoso; estrago, carnicería, matanza; asesinato; jugo o zumo de alguna cosa; *bad blood,* encono, animosidad; *blood-vessel,* vena de la sangre; *blue blood,* casta pura, sangre azul; *my blood is up,* me hierve la sangre; *to make one's blood run cold,* bajarse la sangre a los talones; *to let blood,* sangrar. — *v.t.* ensangrentar; sangrar, sacar sangre, exasperar. — *a.* sanguino, sanguíneo.

bloodcurdling, *a.* terrorífico.

blooded, *a.* de buena raza, de pura casta.

bloodguiltiness, *s.* homicidio, asesinato.

blood-heat, *s.* calor natural de la sangre es decir, 37,6° centígrados o 98·4° Fahr.

bloodhorse, *s.* caballo de pura raza.

bloodhound, *s.* sabueso.

bloodily, *adv.* cruelmente, cruentamente, encarnizadamente.

bloodiness, *s.* ensangrentamiento, estado sanguinolento; crueldad, carácter sanguinario, sanguinolencia.

bloodless, *a.* exangüe, desangrado, inanimado, muerto; incruento.

blood-let, *v.t.* sangrar.

blood-letter *s.* sangrador, flebotomista, *m.f.*

blood-letting, *s.* flebotomía, sangría.

blood-money, *s.* precio pagado por el derramamiento de sangre, por la comisión de un homicidio o por el descubrimiento del homicida.

blood-poisoning, *s.* septicemia.

blood-red, *a.* encarnado o rojo como la sangre.

blood-relation, *s.* pariente, consanguíneo.

blood-root, *s.* (*bot.*) sanguinaria (*sanguinaria canadensis*).

bloodshed, *s.* efusión de sangre; matanza.

bloodshedder, *s.* homicida, *m.*, asesino.

bloodshedding, *s.* derramamiento de sangre, homicidio, asesinato.

bloodshot, bloodshotten, *a.* ensangrentado; inyectado de sangre (dícese de los ojos).

blood-spavin, *s.* (*vet.*) esparaván.

blood-spitting, *s.* esputo de sangre.

blood-stained, *a.* manchado con sangre; asesino, homicida.

bloodstone, *s.* hematites, albín, alaqueca.

bloodsucker, *s.* sanguijuela; (*fig.*) usurero.

bloodthirstiness, *s.* sed de sangre, *f.*

bloodthirsty, *a.* sanguinario, cruel.

bloodvessel, *s.* vena.

bloodwort, *s.* (*bot.*) sanguinaria.

bloody, *a.* sangriento, cruento, ensangrentado, sanguinolento, sanguinario, bárbaro, cruel, inhumano; *bloody faced*, que tiene cara mala; *bloody-minded*, sanguinario; *bloody red*, sanguíneo. — *v.t.* ensangrentar, manchar con sangre.

bloom [blu:m], *s.* flor, *f.*; florecimiento, florescencia; capullo, corola; belleza, lindeza, frescura, lozanía; (*metal.*) changote; pelusilla que cubre algunos frutos y hojas. — *v.i.* florar, florecer; ser joven; ostentar lozanía.

bloomers, *s.pl.* calzones o pantalones de señoras.

blooming, *a.* floreciente.

bloomingly, *adv.* floridamente, gallardamente.

bloomingness, *s.* florescencia, eflorescencia.

bloomy, *a.* floreciente, florido.

blossom ['blɔsəm]. *s.* flor, *f.*, corola; overo; capullo, botón; floración; niñez, juventud. — *v.i.* florecer, echar flor; prosperar.

blossoming, *s.* florescencia.

blossomy, *a.* lleno de flores, florido, floreciente.

blot [blɔt], *v.t.* borrar, tachar; emborronar; cancelar; ensuciar, empañar, manchar; secar; denigrar. — *v.i.* pasarse, correrse (la tinta); *to blot out*, rayar o borrar lo escrito. — *s.* borrón, mancha de tinta, tacha, raspadura, enmienda; *to make a blot*, echar un borrón.

blotch [blɔtʃ], *s.* pústula, erupción; lunar, mancha, borrón. — *v.t.* cubrir de pústulas; emborronar.

blotchy, *a.* cubierto de pústulas; enlodado, manchado.

blotter, *s.* difamador; borrón, tacha, raspadura; papel secante; borrador.

blotting, *a.* que se mancha; *s.* el acto de manchar.

blotting-paper, *s.* papel secante.

blouse [blauz], *s.* blusa.

blow [blou], *s.* golpe, porrazo, trastazo; choque

moral; revés, desastre, desdicha, desgracia; soplido, resoplido; trompetazo; circunstancia imprevista; ocasión, momento; *blow on the face, blow with the hand*, bofetada; *blow with a chair*, silletazo; *blow with the fist*, puñetazo; *at one blow* o *at a single blow*, de un golpe, de un solo golpe, de una vez; *to come to blows*, venir a las manos; *to strike a blow*, dar un golpe; *to go for a blow*, pasearse para tomar el fresco. — *v.i.* (*pret.* **blew**; *p.p.* **blown**) dar un soplido, soplar; sonar; jadear; florecer, abrirse las flores; pasar. — *v. impers.* hacer viento. — *v.t.* soplar; inflar, henchir de aire; hacer sonar; divulgar algo; tocar un instrumento de aire; cansar, fatigar, hacer perder el aliento; *to blow hot and cold*, estar indeciso, vacilar; *to blow one's nose*, sonarse las narices; *to blow away*, arrojar, arrebatar, disipar; *to blow down*, derribar, echar por tierra; *to blow off*, hacer caer, levantar, arrojar de; dejar salir vapor; *to blow out*, expeler a soplos, apagar a soplos, empujar, arrastrar; *to blow up*, volar; inflar, henchir; encender; *to blow one's brains*, levantarse la tapa de los sesos; *to blow over*, pasar, olvidarse; *to blow one's own trumpet*, alabarse a sí mismo; *how does the wind blow?* (*fig.*) ¿ por dónde va la danza ?

blower, *s.* soplador; tapadera de chimenea; ventilador, aventador, fuelle.

blow-fly, *s.* (*ent.*) moscarda corónida.

blow-gun, *s.* cerbatana, bodoquera.

blowing, *s.* soplo, soplido, sopladura, sopleo; son; ruido del viento. — *a.* tempestuoso; soplante, soplador.

blown, *p.p.* [BLOW].

blow-off, *s.* aparato de expulsión.

blow-out, *s.* reventón; (*pop.*) francachela.

blow-pipe, *s.* soplete; cerbatana.

blowze [blauz], *s.* pandorga (mujer); muchacha carrilluda; especie de gorro.

blowzed, blowzy, *a.* quemado del sol; rubicundo; desaliñado, sucio.

blubber ['blʌbəɹ], *s.* esperma o grasa de ballena; ortiga marina; burbuja, ampolla. — *v.t., v.i.* gimotear, llorar a lágrima viva.

blubbered, *a.* hinchado, inflado, alterado, desfigurado.

bludgeon ['blʌdʒən], *s.* cachiporra; garrote, clava.

blue [blu:], *s.* azul; (*blas.*) azur. — *pl.* **blues**, melancolía. — *a.* azul, azulado, cerúleo; amoratado, lívido (por una contusión); negriazul, sombrío; (*fig.*) triste, melancólico; estricto, severo, puritánico; leal, fiel, genuino; *to look blue*, quedarse confuso; *blue gum*, (*bot.*) eucalipto; *true blue*, leal, fiel; (*mar.*) *Blue Peter*, gallarete que se iza en un buque cuando está dispuesto a hacerse a la mar. — *v.t.* azular, teñir de azul; pavonar.

blue-bell, *s.* (*bot.*) jacinto silvestre.

blue-bird, *s.* (*orn.*) motacila; azulejo.

blue-book, *s.* libro azul de informes oficiales (en Inglaterra).

blue-bottle, *s.* (*bot.*) aciano, liebrecilla; (*ent.*) corónida.

blue-copper, *s.* (*min.*) azurita.

blue-devils, *s.pl.* vapores negros, melancolía; ilusiones del *delirium tremens*.

blue-eyed, *a.* ojizarco, ojiazul.

blueing, *s.* pavonaje.

blue-jacket, *s.* marinero de la Marina Real.

blueness, s. azul.

blue-pill, s. píldora mercurial.

blue-stocking, s. (despectivo) mujer pedante, marisabidilla; literata, bachillera.

blue-stone, s. (min.) sulfato de cobre.

bluey [bluːi], a. azulado.

bluff [blʌf], a. escarpado, enhiesto, a pico; francote; agreste, áspero, rústico; (mar.) obtuso. — s. fanfarronada; baladronada, faramalla. — v.t. fanfarronear; jactarse, baldronar; pretender, simular, mayor fuerza de la que en realidad se tiene.

bluffer, s. fanfarrón, jactancioso.

bluffing, s. la acción de jactarse.

bluffness, s. aspereza, elevación, rudeza.

bluish [bluːiʃ], a. azulado, azulenco, azulino.

bluishness, s. color azulado.

blunder [blʌndəɹ], v.i. disparatar, desatinar, equivocarse, errar. — v.t. embrollar, confundir; to blunder about, hacer las cosas a tientas; to blunder out, divulgar. — s. desatino, disparate, despropósito, error craso, equivocación, atolondramiento.

blunderbuss, s. trabuco, encaro.

blunderer, blunderhead, s. desatinado, aturdido, imprudente, calavera, m.

blunderingly, adv. desatinadamente.

blunt [blʌnt], a. obtuso, embotado, romo, sin punta; bobo; grosero, rudo, bronco, brusco, áspero, descortés; insensible; lerdo, tardo; to grow blunt, o get blunt, entorpecerse; embotarse. — v.t. embotar, enromar; (fig.) enervar; adormecer; calmar, mitigar.

blunting, s. embotadura; restreñimiento.

bluntly, adv. sin filo; sin artificio; llanamente, claramente; bruscamente.

bluntness, s. embotadura, embotamiento; grosería; estupidez; franqueza; viveza de genio con aspereza.

blunt-witted, a. estúpido, lerdo.

blur [bləːɹ], s. borrón, mancha, tacha. — v.t. borrar, tachar, empañar, manchar; cancelar; deshonrar; hacer borroso; embotar, entorpecer. — v.i. ponerse borroso.

blurt [bləːɹt], **blurt out,** v.t. dejar o saltar bruscamente; hablar inconsideradamente, hablar sin ton ni son.

blush [blʌʃ], v.i. abochornarse, ruborizarse, sonrojarse, sonrosearse, ponerse colorado. — v.t. enrojecer, enrojar, sonrojar, abochornar. — s. bochorno, sonrojo, rubor, color rojo; fulgor, vislumbre, apariencia; ojeada, mirada, vistazo.

blush, a. (fig.) encarnado, rojo.

blushful, a. púdico, pudibundo; encarnado, rojo.

blushfully, adv. púdicamente.

blushing, a. brillante, de color vivo; florido; sonrosado; púdico, vergonzoso, sonroseado.

blushingly, adv. ruborosamente.

blushless, a. desvergonzado, descarado, impudente.

bluster [blʌstəɹ], **blustering,** s. ruido, tumulto; violencia, furor; jactancia, fanfarria, fanfarronada; blustery weather, tiempo tumultuoso, tempestad; blustery wind, viento furioso. — v.i. bramar, soplar con furia, hacer ruido tempestuoso; bravear. — v.t. echar a tierra, desgreñar, desarreglar.

blusterer, s. matasiete; alborotador; fanfarrón.

blustering, a. tumultuoso, turbulento, tempestuoso. — s. [BLUSTER]; blustering fellow,

espíritu levantisco; blustering style, estilo hinchado.

blusterous, a. tumultuoso, tempestuoso, ruidoso, fanfarrón.

bo!, boh!, interj. ¡bú!; voz para asustar o causar miedo, especialmente a los niños.

boa [ˈbouə], s. (zool.) boa, serpiente, f.; cuello de piel o pluma para las señoras.

boar [ˈboəɹ], s. verraco; jabalí.

board [boəɹd], s. tabla; tablilla; tablero, banco; mesa; tribunal, consejo, junta; comida, manutención, pensión, pupilaje; alimento; galería principal de una mina; (mar.) bordo; (mar.) bordada entre dos viradas para ganar el barlovento; cartón. — pl. **boards,** tablazón, f.; (teat.) las tablas, escena; to go on board, ir a bordo, embarcarse; free on board (f.o.b.), libre de gastos a bordo; to go by the board, (fig.) abandonarse por completo; board of admiralty, almirantazgo; board of directors (trustees o governors) junta directiva. — v.t. (mar.) abordar; embarcar; acometer, acercarse a; (carp.) entablar, entarimar, enmaderar; dar pupilaje, manutención, tomar de huésped. — v.i. estar a pupilaje.

boardable, a. (mar.) abordable; accesible.

boarder, s. pensionista, m.f., huésped, pupilo; (mar.) abordador.

boarding, s. entabladura, tablazón, f.; pupilaje, pensión; (mar.) abordaje; boarding-pikes, (mar.) chuzos.

boarding-house, s. casa de huéspedes, posada, pensión.

boarding-pupil, s. interno, pensionista, m.f.

boarding-school, s. escuela de internos; pensionado.

boarish [ˈboəɹiʃ], a. jabaluno; cruel, brutal.

boast [boust], v.i. alardear, blasonar; jactarse, vanagloriarse, alabarse. — v.t. ponderar, exaltar, alabar excesivamente. — s. jactancia, vanidad, vanagloria, ostentación, alarde, baladronada.

boaster, s. jaque, fanfarrón, vanaglorioso.

boastful, a. jactancioso, baladrón.

boastfully, adv. ostentosamente, arrogantemente.

boastfulness, boasting, s. alarde, bravata, jactancia, vanagloria, ostentación.

boastingly, adv. ostentosamente, jactanciosamente.

boastless, a. sencillo, simple.

boat [bout], s. buque, barco, bote, barca, lancha, batel, chalupa, vapor; ballast boat, (mar.) bote de lastrar; fishing boat, bote de pescar; life-boat, lancha de socorro, bote salvavidas; packet boat, paquebote; tow-boat, remolcador. — v.t. trasportar en bote; poner a bordo, llevar a bordo. — v.i. navegar, ir en bote.

boatable, a. navegable para botes.

boat-hook, s. bichero, botador.

boat-house, s. cobertizo para meter botes.

boating, s. trasporte por agua, batelaje; paseo en un bote, manejo de un bote.

boatman, boatsman, s. barquero, lanchero, botero.

boatswain [ˈbouzən], s. contramaestre.

bob [bɔb], v.t. mover, agitar; pegar, zurrar; engañar; burlar, chasquear; desmochar, cercenar. — v.i. oscilar, bambolear; colgar; estar pendiente. — s. balanceo, oscilación; balancín; zarcillo, pendiente; borla; pingajo,

colgajo; lenteja de péndulo; volante; balancín de bomba o de máquina de vapor;
repique de campanas; cebo para pescar;
(*poét.*) estrambote; (*mús.*) estribillo; chanza
picante; peluca; (*fam.*) chelín; cortesía,
saludo.

bobbin, *s.* bolillo; broca, canilla; bobina;
fresilla; carrete, carretel, husillo, argadijo.

bobbinet [bɔbi'net], *s.* especie de tul o encaje.

bobby, *s.* (*fam.*) policía, *m.*, guardia de la
paz.

bob-sled, *s.* rastra corta.

bob-stay, *s.* (*mar.*) barbiquejo.

bobtail, *s.* rabo mocho, descolado; ralea,
canalla.

bobtailed, *a.* rabón, mocho.

bobtailiwig, bobwig, *s.* peluca redonda, peluquín.

bocasine ['bɔkəsin], *s.* bocací.

bode [boud], *v.t.* presagiar, pronosticar, presentir. — *v.i.* predecir; prometer.

bodement, *s.* presagio, pronóstico, augurio.

bodice ['bɔdis], *s.* corsé, corpiño, jubón,
cuerpo de vestido.

bodied ['bɔdid], *a.* corpóreo.

bodiless ['bɔdiles], *a.* incorpóreo.

bodiliness, *s.* corporalidad, corporeidad.

bodily, *a.* corpóreo, corporal, material; verdadero, real. — *adv.* corporalmente; enteramente, completamente.

boding ['boudiŋ], *s.* pronóstico, presagio. — *a.*
ominoso, presagioso.

bodkin ['bɔdkin], *s.* punzón de sastre; agujeta,
aguja de jareta; puñal, daga; horquilla para
los cabellos; (*imp.*) punzón para sacar tipos
de una forma.

body ['bɔdi], *s.* cuerpo, tronco; materia; persona; (*igl.*) nave, *f.*; cuerpo, gremio; corporación; división, cuerpo (de ejército); corsé,
jubón, corpiño; espesor, fortaleza; colección;
agregado; solidez, densidad, consistencia;
(*fil.*) materia, substancia, lo que tiene propiedades sensibles; (*geom.*) todo aquello que
posee las tres dimensiones; (*aut.*) carrocería; *dead body*, cadáver; *poor body*, pobre
diablo; *wine of good body*, vino fuerte; *main
body*, grueso. — *v.t.* dar cuerpo, forma o
orden; materializar; representar; *able-bodied*,
robusto, sano; *body-clothes*, manta; *body-
guard*, guardia de corps; seguridad; *busybody*, entrometido; *anybody*, cualquiera;
everybody, cada uno, todos; *nobody*, nadie.

body-snatcher, *s.* el que roba cadáveres.

Boeotian, *s., a.* beocio, -cia; rudo, necio,
grosero.

bog [bɔg], *s.* pantano, ciénaga, armajal, paúl. —
v.t. empantanar; *bog-oak*, lignito de encina;
bog-ore, (*min.*) limonita; *bog-trotter*, habitante
de un país pantanoso.

bogey, bogy [bougi], *s.* espantajo, espectro,
duende, coco.

boggle ['bɔgl], *v.i.* recular, retroceder, cejar;
fluctuar, vacilar, titubear; fingir, disimular.
— *s.* retroceso de un caballo; dificultad;
patochada.

boggled, embrollado, embarazado, alarmado.
— *p.p.* [BOGGLE].

boggler, *s.* hombre irresoluto.

boggy, *a.* pantanoso, palustre.

bogie ['bougi], *s.* espantajo, espectro, loco,
duende; carretilla de cuatro ruedas en la
parte delantera de las locomotoras.

bogus [bougəs], *a.* falso, podrido, espúreo;
bogus affair, negocio sucio.

bogy [BOGEY].

bohea [bo'hi], *s.* nombre antiguo de la mejor
calidad del té de China; hoy se aplica a las
clases inferiores.

Bohemian [bo'hi:miən], *s., a.* bohemio.

boil [bɔil], *v.t., v.i.* cocer, hervir, bullir, pasar
por agua (huevos); salcochar, herventar;
estar extraordinariamente agitado; hervirle
a uno la sangre; *to boil away*, consumir un
líquido a fuerza de cocerlo; *to boil fast*,
hervir a borbotones; *to boil over*, sobrar,
rebosar; *to boil off*, dar una primera cocción
a. — *s.* hervor, ebullición; (*med.*) furúnculo,
tumor, divieso.

boiler, *s.* marmita, olla, caldero, caldera, paila;
boiler iron, hierro en planchas para calderas;
boiler-maker, calderero.

boilery, *s.* distilatorio; casa de calderas.

boiling, *s.* ebullición, hervor, cocción, cochura;
boiling-point, punto de ebullición.

boisterous ['bɔistərəs], *a.* borrascoso, tempestuoso, violento, ruidoso, tumultuoso,
furioso, turbulento, vocinglero, clamoroso,
ruidoso.

boisterousness, *s.* turbulencia, tumulto, vehemencia, impetuosidad, vinglería.

bold [bould], *a.* intrépido, arrojado, ardiente,
valiente; impudente, descarado; temerario,
bravo, denodado audaz; (*mar.*) escarpado,
acantilado; *to make bold to*, tomar la libertad
de, atreverse a.

boldface, *s.* descaro, desvergüenza, impudencia.

boldfaced, *a.* descarado, desvergonzado;
boldfaced type, (*impr.*) letra negra (lo mismo
que *full-face*).

boldly, audazmente, descaradamente, intrépidamente, animosamente.

boldness, *s.* intrepidez, ánimo, resolución, determinación, arrojo, arresto, aliento, valentía,
denuedo, osadía, audacia, atrevimiento,
libertad, descaro, desvergüenza.

bole [boul], *s.* tronco de un árbol; bol, bolo
(tierra usada en pintura y para el bruñido
de oro).

bolide, *s.* (*ast.*) bólido.

boll [boul], *s.* bodoque; cápsula; antigua
medida para granos. — *v.t.* granar.

Bolognese [bɔlə'ni:z], *s., a.* boloñés.

bolster ['boulstər], *s.* travesero, larguero,
almohadón; cojín, cojinete; (*cir.*) cabezal;
(*mar.*) almohada; (*f.c.*) solera de carro; (*mec.*)
travesaño; nabo; caballete; canecillo. — *v.t.*
recostar la cabeza en el travesero; aplicar el
cabezal a una herida; sostener, auxiliar,
mantener, apoyar con una almohada. — *v.i.*
acostarse; pelear con almohadas (los niños).

bolsterer, *s.* apoyo, sostén; (*fig.*) defensor,
sostenedor, mantenedor.

bolt [boult], *s.* dardo, flecha, azagaya; rayo;
cerrojo, pasador; pestillo de cerradura;
borrón, mancha; (*mar.*) perno, clavillas;
(*carp.*) perno, clavija, tolete; salto rápido;
fuga; tamiz muy fino para harina; rollo (de
tela, de unas 30 yds.). — *pl.* **bolts**, grillos,
grilletes. — *v.t.* lanzar, arrojar, soltar, expeler, echar; parlar, hablar sin discreción;
engullir, tragar sin masticar; empernar,
encabillar; cerrar con cerrojo; atrancar (una
puerta); empalmar; (*fig.*) atar, embarazar,

poner estorbos; cerner, examinar, escudriñar.
— *v.i.* saltar de repente; *to bolt in*, entrar de
repente; *to bolt out*, salir de golpe; *to bolt,
bolt off*, tomar las de Villadiego.
bolter, *s.* cedazo, harnero, criba; cordel de
pescar.
bolting, *s.* cerramiento; cernido, cernidura;
discusión; salida o entrada precipitada;
bolting-cloth, tela de cedazo; *bolting-house*,
cernedero; *bolting-mill*, torno.
bolus ['boulǝs], *s. (med.)* bolo; pelotilla, bola.
boma ['boumǝ], *s.* estacada circular.
bomb [bɔm], *s.* bomba; granada; estampido,
estallido, fragor, estruendo; campanada;
bomb shell, bomba, granada, casco de bomba;
bomb proof, a prueba de bomba; *bomb ketch,
bomb vessel*, *(mar.)* bombarda; *atomic bomb*,
bomba atómica; *hydrogen bomb*, bomba de
hidrógeno. — *v.i.* estallar, zumbar. — *v.t.*
bombardear.
bombard [bɔm'bɑːɹd], *s.* bombarda; bombardeo; *(ant.)* barril, tonel. — *v.t.* bombardear, tirar bombas.
bombardier, *s.* bombardero; *bombardier beetle*,
escarabajo bombardero o escopetero.
bombardment, *s.* bombardeo.
bombardon, *s. (mús.)* bombardón.
bombasin, bombasine [bɔmbǝ'ziːn], *s.* bombasí.
bombast ['bɔmbæst], *s.* algodón en rama
engomado; *(fig.)* ampulosidad, hinchazón, *f.*,
estilo hinchado o ampuloso.
bombastic [bɔm'bæstik], *a.* hinchado, pomposo, ampuloso, altisonante.
bombastry, *s.* hinchazón, *f.*, estilo hinchado.
bombax, *s. (bot.)* ceiba de Cuba.
bombazette [bɔmbǝ'zet], *s.* especie de bayeta
ordinaria.
bombazine [bɔmbǝ'ziːn], *s.* bombasín, bombasí; alepín.
bombic, *a.* bómbico.
bombyx [bɔmbiks], *s. (ent.)* bómbice.
bona-fide ['bounǝ'faidi], *(lat.)* de buena fe,
sin engaño.
bon-bon, *s.* confite, dulce.
bond [bɔnd], *s.* lazo, atadura, soga, cinta, vínculo, unión, *f.*, parentesco; empeño, compromiso, obligación, encadenamiento moral;
yugo, esclavitud, prisión; *(com.)* vale, bono,
obligación, pagaré, billete, título de la deuda
de una corporación o nación, almacén,
depósito; *in bond*, en depósito, en almacén. —
a. cautivo, siervo. — *v.t.* gravar con bono;
dar fianza; *(com.)* poner en depósito.
bondage ['bɔndidʒ], *s.* cautiverio, esclavitud,
servidumbre; obligación.
bonded, *a.* afianzado, garantido por escrito;
asegurado, hipotecado; almacenado, deposi-
tado, en depósito.
bonder, *s.* depositario; guarda.
bonding, *s.* depósito; *bonding warehouse*, almacenes de aduana.
bondmaid, *s.* joven esclava o sierva.
bondman, *s.* esclavo, siervo, vasallo.
bondslave, *s.* esclavo.
bondsman, *s.* fiador, seguridad, dita; esclavo.
bondswoman, *s.* esclava; fiadora, dita.
bone [boun], *s.* hueso; raspa o espina del pez;
marfil (de los dientes); barba de ballena,
fragmento de carne. — *pl.* **bones,** *(fig.)*
cenizas, restos mortales, esqueleto; palillos;
especie de castañuelas, dados; *jaw-bone,*

quijada; *whalebone*, ballena; *bone setter*,
algebrista, *m.f.*, curandero; *bone ache*, dolor de
huesos; *bone black*, negro animal; *to pick a
bone*, roer un hueso; *to make no bones of*, no
tener empacho en; *to have a bone to pick with
someone*, tener que habérselas con alguno;
*what's bred in the bone will come out in the
flesh*, genio y figura hasta la sepultura. — *v.t.*
desosar; embollenar, poner ballenas.
boned, *a.* osudo, huesudo, ososo, robusto.
bonelace, *s.* encaje de hilo.
boneless, *s.* pulposo, mollar, sin huesos.
bonfire ['bɔnfaiǝɹ], *s.* hoguera, fogata, fuego de
regocijo.
bonhomie [bɔnhɔmiː], *s.* afabilidad.
bonify ['bounifai], *v.t.* bonificar, abonar, mejorar.
boning ['bouniŋ], *s.* acción de deshuesar;
nivelación de tierras.
bonito, *s.* bonito.
bonnet ['bɔnǝt], *s.* gorro, gorra, capota, toca;
sombrero de mujer; *(fort.)* bonete; *(mec.)*
sombrerete; *(mar.)* bonetas. — *v.t.* cubrir,
apabullar. — *v.i.* descubrirse, hacer cortesía;
encasquetarle el sombrero a uno.
bonniness, *s.* viveza, amabilidad, alegría
natural, hermosura.
bonny, *a.* bonito, lindo, gentil, galán, festivo,
alegre; regordete. — *s. (min.)* filón.
bonny-clabber, *s.* cuajo, leche cuajada *(voz
irlandesa)*.
bonum-magnum ['bounǝm-'mægnǝm], *(bot.)*
especie de ciruela.
bonus ['bounǝs], *s.* adehala; bonificación;
regalo; dividendos ficticios.
bony, *a.* osudo, huesudo.
bonze [bɔnz], *s.* bonzo.
booby ['buːbi], *s.* zote, hombre bobo, necio,
ignorante; *(orn.)* bobo.
boodle ['buːdl], *s. (argot)* dinero, regalo hecho
como soborno, producto de malversación
o hurto.
book [buk], *s.* libro; tomo; libro de asiento. —
v.t. asentar en un libro, inscribir, registrar;
sacar (billetes, entradas)**;** *account book*, libro
de cuentas corrientes; *cash book*, libro de caja;
day book, diario; *invoice book*, libro de facturas; *pocket-book*, cartera; *memorandum-
book*, libro de memoria; *second-hand book*,
libro de ocasión; *school book*, libro de enseñanza; *waste book*, borrador; *book-keeper*,
tenedor de libros; *book-keeping*, teneduría
de libros; *book post*, servicio de impresos;
book-learning, erudición.
bookbinder, *s.* encuadernador de libros.
bookbindery, *s.* taller de encuadernación.
bookbinding, *s.* encuadernación.
book-case, *s.* armario o estante para libros.
book-clasp, *s.* manecilla.
bookful, *s.* contenido de un libro. — *a.* erudito.
booking, *s.* registro, asiento; *booking-clerk*,
vendedor de billetes de pasaje, teatro, etc.;
booking-office, despacho de billetes.
bookish, *a.* estudioso, dado al estudio, versado
en libros, pedante, teórico.
bookishness, *s.* aplicación a los libros; estudiosidad.
bookmaker, *s.* el que compila, imprime o
encuaderna libros; *(por desdoro)* corredor de
apuestas, apostador de profesión.
bookman, *s.* sabio.
bookmark, *s.* señal o marcador de libros.

bookmate, s. condiscípulo.
bookseller, s. librero; *bookseller and publisher,* librero editor.
bookselling, s. librería.
bookshop, s. librería.
bookstall, s. baratillo.
bookstand, s. estante de libros.
bookstore, s. librería.
bookworm, s. polilla, gusano que roe los libros; (*fig.*) bibliófilo; estudiante demasiadamente aplicado.
boom [buːm], (*mar.*) botalón, botavara; cadena para cerrar un puerto; sonido fuerte y profundo como el del cañón, o bramido de las olas; auge, actividad comercial, prosperidad repentina. — *v.t.* favorecer; fomentar, anunciar muchas veces; dar bombo. — *v.i.* (*mar.*) correr a velas desplegadas; bramar; moverse con violencia; hacer un gran ruido y estruendo.
boomerang ['buːməræŋ], s. bumerang; (*fig.*) acto, proceder, o argumento cuyas consecuencias recaen en el autor del mismo.
booming, s. ruido retumbante.
boom-sail, s. (*mar.*) cangreja.
boon [buːn], s. dádiva, presente, regalo; fineza; favor; gracia, merced; bendición, dicha. — *a.* alegre, genial, festivo, jovial; generoso, liberal; próspero, afortunado; *boon companion,* buen compañero.
boor [buəɹ], s. campesino; rústico, patán, aldeano, villano.
boorish, a. rústico, agreste; jíbaro.
boorishly, adv. rústicamente, groseramente, toscamente.
boorishness, s. rusticidad, tosquedad, grosería.
boose [buːz], s. boyeriza.
boost [buːst], v.t. (*fam.*) empujar, alzar.
boot [buːt], v.t., v.i. aprovechar; valer, servir, ser útil, importar; saquear; calzar, calzarse. — s. ganancia, provecho, ventaja, utilidad; bota, botín, borceguí; pesebrón de un coche; *to boot,* además, encima; *boot-black,* limpiabotas; *half-boot,* botín, media bota; *boot-legs,* cortes de botas; *boot-maker,* zapatero, botero; *boot-jack,* sacabotas, m.; *patent-leather boot,* bota de charol; *boot-hook,* tirabotas, m.; *boot-tree,* horma de bota; *the boot is on the other leg,* eso es harina de otro costal; *to put the boot on the wrong leg,* culpar al inocente.
booted, a. calzado (con botas).
booth [buːð], s. cabaña, choza, barraca, puesto, tabladillo.
bootless, a. descalzo; inútil, sin provecho; infructuoso.
bootlessly, adv. inútilmente, infructuosamente, en vano.
bootlessness, s. inutilidad.
boots, s. (en una fonda) limpiabotas, m.
booty ['buːti], s. botín, presa, saqueo; *to play booty,* trampear en el juego.
booze [buːz], v.i. (*fam.*) embriagarse, emborracharse. — s. borrachera; bebida alcohólica.
boozy, a. embriagado, ebrio, borracho, beodo.
bo-peep [bou'piːp], s. escondite.
boracic [bə'ræsik], a. (*quím.*) bórico o borácico
boracite, s. (*min.*) boracita.
borage, s. (*bot.*) borraja.
borate [bɔəreit], s. (*quím.*) borato.
borax ['bɔəræks], s. (*quím.*) bórax, borraz.
bordel ['bɔədəl], s. burdel.
border, s. borde, reborde, orilla, margen;

frontera, límite, confín; orla, banda, franja, guarnición de vestido, ribete, farfalá; borde o lomo de jardín. — *v.i.* confinar, rayar, lindar; acercarse, aproximarse; (*fam.*) rozarse. — *v.t.* guarnecer, ribetear; *to border on,* confinar, tocar; asemejarse.
borderer, s. limítrofe, comarcano, habitante de la frontera.
bordering, a. adyacente, fronterizo, contiguo, cercano, vecino. — s. orladura.
bore [bɔəɹ], v.t. taladrar; barrenar, horadar, perforar, punzar, trepar; explorar, reconocer; penetrar, pasar, atravesar, abrirse (camino); (*fam.*) aburrir, molestar, fastidiar, incomodar; jorobar. — *v.i.* agujerear, hacer agujeros; avanzar, adelantarse; abrirse, dar paso; perforar; explorar. — s. taladro, barreno; calibre de un cañón; (*fam.*) majadero, pelmazo, pesado; ola que forma la marea al subir por un rio.
bore, *pret.* [BEAR].
boreal [bɔəriəl], a. boreal, septentrional.
boreas ['bɔəriæs], s. bóreas, aquilón, cierzo.
borecale [bɔəɹkoul], s. (*bot.*) especie de berza.
boredshaft, s. (*min.*) pozo de indagación.
boree, s. danza popular.
borer, s. barreno, taladro; sonda.
boric ['bɔrik], a. bórico.
boring [bɔəriŋ], a. penetrante, que perfora, taladra o barrena; (*fam.*) molesto, pesado. — s. horadamiento, horadación, trepa, sondeo, taladro.
born [bɔːɹn], a. nacido, destinado. — *p.p.* [BEAR]; *to be born,* nacer; *first-born,* primogénito; *new-born,* recién nacido; *still-born,* nacido muerto; *high-born,* de elevado nacimiento; *low-born,* de humilde nacimiento; *to be born with a silver spoon in one's mouth,* nacer de cabeza, ser afortunado en todo; nacer para ser rico; *to be born lucky,* nacer de pies; *to be born and bred in a place,* nacérsele a uno los dientes en . . .
borne, *p.p.* [BEAR]
borough ['bʌrə], s. burgo, ciudad, villa grande.
borrow ['bɔrou], v.t. tomar fiado o prestado; pedir prestado; apropiarse, hacerse suyo; copiar.
borrowed, a. prestado, dado o tomado en préstamo.
borrower, s. prestamista, m.f.; (*for.*) comodatario.
borrowing, s. préstamo, empréstito.
boscage ['bɔskidʒ], s. soto, floresta; boscaje, espesura.
bosh [bɔʃ], s. bosquijo, borrón, esbozo, trazo; (*fam.*) necedad, tontería, palabrería, galimatías, m. sing.
bosk [bɔsk], s. matorral.
bosky, a. arbolado, frondoso, nemoroso.
Bosnian ['bɔsniən], s., a. bosnio, -nia.
bosom ['buzəm], s. seno, pecho, corazón; centro, fondo, interior; amor, inclinación, afecto, cariño; (*cost.*) pechera; *bosom of the sea,* senos del mar; *bosom friend,* amigo íntimo. — *v.t.* guardar en el seno; encerrar en su pecho; ocultar, tener secreto.
boss [bɔs], s. clavo, tachón; joroba, corcova, giba, protuberancia; abolladura; (*arq.*) pinjante; (*pol.*) cacique, jefe, cabecilla, m.; copa (de freno); lomo (de un libro); patrón, maestro; capataz. — *v.t.* trabajar en relieve; (*fam.*) mandar, dominar.

bossage, s. (*arq.*) almohadilla.
bossed, bossy, a. tachonado; turgente, saliente.
boston ['bɔstən], s. juego de naipes parecido a la malilla; especie de baile.
bot, s. larva de estro.
botanical [bo'tænikl], a. botánico.
botanise, botanize, v.i. herborizar.
botanist ['bɔtənist], s. botánico, botanista, *m.f.*
botany, s. botánica.
botch [bɔtʃ], s. roncha, tumorcillo; remiendo, chapucería; remendón, obra mal hecha; landre, *f.*, úlcera. — v.t. remendar; chafallar, chapuzar; (*fig.*) ensuciar, emporcar, manchar.
botcher, s. sastre o zapatero remendón; (artesano) chapucero.
botchery, s. remiendo; chafallo.
botchy, a. remendado; culcusido.
bot-fly [bɔtflai], s. (*ent.*) estro.
both [bouθ], a., *pron.* ambos, los dos, entrambos; y; tanto . . . como; a la vez; *both* (*of*) *his friends,* sus dos amigos; *both of them,* ellos dos, ambos; *on both sides,* por ambos lados, de uno y otro lado.
bother ['bɔðəi], v.t. incomodar, molestar; (*vulg.*) aturrullar, enojar, confundir, marear. — s. molestia, incomodidad, fastidio, embarazo, tormento.
botheration, s. molestia, disgusto, fastidio.
bothersome, a. molesto, fastidioso, cargante.
Bothnian ['bɔθniən], s., a. botniano.
bots [bɔts], *s.pl.* (*vet.*) lombrices, *f.pl.*; larvas de varias especies de moscas.
bottle ['bɔtl], s. botella, frasco, redoma; gavilla de heno; *sucking bottle, nursing bottle,* biberón, mamadera; *bottle brush,* hisopo, limpiabotellas, *m.*; *to love the bottle,* (*fam.*) ser aficionado a Baco.
bottle-green, s., a. verde botella, verde oscuro.
bottle-holder, s. porta-botellas, *m.*; padrino (en duelo); segundo (en boxeo).
bottler, s. embotellador.
bottling, s. acto de embotellar.
bottom ['bɔtəm], s. fondo, suelo; pie; zanja, cimiento; valle, cañada; ovillo; hondonada; (*mar.*) carena (de un buque); (*mar.*) casco (de nave); cabo; heces, *f.pl.*; base, *f.*, fundamento, motivo; lecho (de un río); posas, nalgas, posaderas, asentaderas; asiento; *at the bottom,* al fondo, en el fondo; *from top to bottom,* de arriba abajo; *to be at the bottom of a thing,* ser el causante de una cosa; *to touch bottom,* tocar fondo. — a. hondo, bajo; fundamental. — v.t. cimentar, fundar, basar, estribar, apoyar; poner asiento, poner fondo. — v.i. fundarse; apoyarse.
bottomed, a. provisto de un fondo; *flat-bottomed,* con fondo llano.
bottoming, s. (*f.c.*) balasto.
bottomless, a. insondable, sin fondo; visionario.
bottomry, s. (*mar.*) casco y quilla; el acto de tomar dinero prestado con hipoteca del barco.
boudoir ['bu'dwɑːr], s. retrete gabinete, tocador de señora.
bough [bau], s. rama de árbol.
bought [bɔːt], s. torcedura, nudo, corvadura; fondo (de la honda). — v. *pret.* y *p.p.* [BUY].
bougie ['buːʒi], s. bujía; (*cir.*) candelilla, tienta, sonda.

boulder ['bouldəi], s. roca, canto, pedrejón, galga, peña.
boulevard ['buːlvɑːɹd], s. paseo, avenida, bulevar.
bounce [bauns], v.i. rebotar, saltar, brincar; estallar; (*fig.*) bravear; lanzarse, echarse; golpear. — v.t. hacer botar, hacer saltar; (*vulg.*) poner en la calle. — s. golpazo, porrazo, golpe fuerte; bote, rebote; salto, brinco; respingo, repullo; fanfarronada, bravata; mentira.
bouncer, s. fanfarrón, guapo; embustero; bola.
bouncing, a. fuerte, vigoroso, bien formado.
bound [baund], s. término, límite, confín, lindero; bote, brinco, salto, corcovo, respingo, rebote, resalto; *to keep within bounds,* no traspasar los límites. — v. *pret.* y *p.p.* [BIND]. — v.t. poner límites; confinar, limitar, deslindar, parcelar; ceñir; botar; hacer saltar. — v.i. saltar, brincar, resaltar, botar; corvetear. — a. atado, ligado; confinado; moral o legalmente obligado, forzado; encuadernado; puesto en aprendizaje, en probación; estreñido; cerrado de vientre; (*fam.*) destinado, predestinado; (*mar.*) destinado (a), cargado (para); *whither bound? ¿adónde va el barco? bound for,* (*mar.*) con destino a; *bound up* (*in*), (*fig.*) absorto, engolfado, enfrascado.
boundary ['baundəri], s. término, coto, límite, linde, frontera, confín.
bounden, a. obligado, precisado, indispensable, obligatorio.
bounder, s. (*fam.*) vanidoso; presuntuoso.
boundless, a. ilimitado, infinito.
boundlessly, adv. sin límites.
boundlessness, s. immensidad, infinidad.
bounteous [bauntjəs], a. liberal, bondadoso, generoso.
bounteousness, s. munificencia, liberalidad, bondad, generosidad.
bountiful, a. generoso, liberal, dadivoso, bienhechor; bueno; fecundo.
bountifully, adv. liberalmente, generosamente.
bountifulness, s. generosidad, liberalidad, largueza.
bounty ['baunti], s. generosidad, liberalidad, munificencia; (*com.*) premio; merced, gracia; concesión, subvención; *bounty money,* enganche.
bouquet ['bukei], s. ramo, ramillete, perfume, aroma del vino.
bourdon [buəɹdən], s. bordón.
bourgeois ['buəɹʒwɑ], s. burgués; común, ordinario; (*impr.*) especie de tipo, entre breviario y entredós; nueve puntos.
bourgeoisie [buəɹʒwɑ'ziː], s. clase media, burguesía.
bourgeon ['bəːɹdʒən], v.i. brotar; retoñar. — s. retoño, yema.
bourn [boəɹn], s. límite, linde; arroyo, riachuelo.
bourse [boəɹs], s. (*com.*) bolsa, lonja.
bout [baut], s. vez; turno; golpe; ataque; (esgrima) asalto; partida; broma, diversión; *at one bout,* de golpe, de una sola vez; *drinking bout,* juerga.
bovine ['bouvain], a. bovino, vacuno.
bow [bau], v.t. encorvar, arquear, doblar; bajar; saludar, hacer reverencia; agobiar, oprimir, agravar. — v.i. doblarse, torcerse; agobiarse; inclinarse; arquearse; saludar;

ceder, someterse. — *s.* reverencia, saludo, cortesía; (*mar.*) proa; *on the bow*, (*mar.*) por la serviola.

bow [bou], *s.* arco, arco iris; ojo de lazo escurridizo; arzón de silla; anillo (de llave, de reloj, etc.); lazo (de corbata, cinta, etc.); *to have two strings to one's bow*, tener muchos medios para conseguir una cosa, ser hombre de recurso. — *v.t.* arquear, encorvar, torcer, doblar.

bowel ['bauəl], *v.t.* destripar, arrancar las entrañas.

bowels, *s. pl.* intestinos, entrañas, tripas; (*fig.*) ternura, compasión; *to move the bowels*, evacuar el vientre.

bower, *s.* glorieta, enramada, lonjeta, cenador; bóveda de verdura; alcoba, retrete; casita de campo; domicilio, morada; *bower-anchor*, (*mar.*) ancla de servidumbre. — *s.* cortijo.

bowery, *a.* frondoso, sombreado, sombrío; cubierto de enramadas.

bowie-knife ['boui'naif], *s.* puñal largo y ancho con dos cortes en la punta; cuchillo de monte.

bowl [boul], *s.* escudilla, cuenco, taza; capa; hueco, concavidad, cóncavo; tazón de fuente; bola, bocha. — *v.t.* voltear; bolear, tirar las bolas; tumbar con una bola; derribar, hacer rodar. — *v.i.* jugar a las bochas.

bowls, *s.pl.* juego de bochas.

bow-legged, *a.* patiestevado, perniabierto.

bowler, *s.* jugador de bolos o bochas; sombrero hongo.

bowline, *s.* (*mar.*) bolina.

bowling, *s.* juego de bolas, boleo.

bowman, *s.* arquero, flechero; (*mar.*) primer remero.

bowse [bauz], *v.t.* (*mar.*) halar a un tiempo.

bow-shot ['boufot], *s.* tiro de flecha; *within bow-shot*, a tiro de ballesta.

bowsprit, *s.* (*mar.*) bauprés.

bowstring, *s.* cuerda de arco.

bow-window, *s.* ventana arqueada, o saliente.

bow-wow [bau-wau], *s.* ladrido de perros.

bowyer ['boujəɹ], *s.* arquero.

box [bɔks], *s.* caja, cajita, cajón; estuche, excusabaraja; arca, cofre, maleta; palco (de teatro); pescante (de coche); bofetada, revés, cachete, cogotazo, manotada; pescante; casilla, casita; (*impr.*) cajetín; (*mar.*) bitácora; (*bot.*) boj; puñetazo; (*mec.*) buje, manguito, émbolo. — *v.t.* encajonar; abofetear, apuñear. — *v.i.* boxear, pelear a puñadas; *hat box*, sombrerera; *alms box*, cepillo de limosna; *band box*, caja de cartón; *country box*, casita de campo; *dice box*, cubilete; *jewel-box*, joyelero, guardajoyas; *letter box*, buzón del correo; *snuff box*, tabaquera; *strong box*, cofre fuerte, caja de caudales; *box in post-office*, apartado de correos; *poor box*, cepillo de limosnas; *hunting box, shooting box*, casita de caza; *box on the ear*, bofetada; *box-office*, (*teat.*) taquilla; *to box the compass*, (*mar.*) cuartear; *Christmas box*, aguinaldo.

Boxer, *s.* bóxer (*chino*).

boxer, *s.* boxeador; embalador; bóxer (*perro*).

box-haul, *v.t.* (*mar.*) dar vuelta la nave cuando no se puede virar por estar demasiado cerca de tierra.

boxing, *s.* boxeo; empaque, envase; madera para encajonar; *Boxing-Day*, el 26 de diciembre, día de los aguinaldos.

boxthorn, *s.* (*bot.*) licio, tamujo.

boxwood, *s.* boj, madera de boj.

boy [bɔi], *s.* niño, chico, muchacho, mozo, chicuelo; lacayo, criado; *cabin-boy*, mozo de cámara; *choir boy*, niño de coro; *yellow boy*, moneda de oro; *school boy*, muchacho de escuela.

boyar [bo'jaːɹ], *s.* boyardo.

boycott ['bɔikɔt], *v.t.* boicotear; excluir; aislar; desacreditar.

boycott, *s.* boicot.

boycotting, *s.* boicoteo.

boyhood ['bɔihud], *s.* infancia, niñez, muchachez, puericia.

boyish, *a.* pueril, amuchachado.

boyishly, *adv.* puerilmente, como niño.

boyishness, *s.* puerilidad, niñada, muchachada.

boyism, *s.* niñada, tontería.

Brabantine ['bræbæntiːn], *a.* brabanzón, de Brabante.

brabble, *v.i.* armar camorra. — *s.* camorra, riña, pendencia; debate.

brabbler ['bræbləɹ], *s.* camorrista, *m.f.*; pendenciero.

braccate ['brækeit], *a.* (*orn.*) paticalzado.

brace [breis], *v.t.* atar, ligar, trabar, atesar, amarrar; estirar; (*carp.*) ensamblar, empatar; cercar, rodear; vigorizar, fortificar; templar (un tambor); (*mar.*) bracear, halar las brazas. — *s.* lazo, atadura; vendaje, cinto; abrazadera, laña, broche, grapón; brazal; (*arq.*) tirante, anclaje, silla, mordaza; sopanda de coche; (*impr.*) corchete; (*carp.*) berbiquí; par (de perdices, etc.); (*cir.*) braguero; *pl.* **braces,** (*mar.*) brazas; tirantes; (*mar.*) *braces of a rudder*, hembras del timón.

bracelet, *s.* brazal, brazalete; ajorca; (*Am.*) pulsera.

bracer, *s.* brazal, abrazadera, laña; cinto, venda; braguero; (*med.*) tónico.

brach [brætʃ], *s.* braca.

brachial ['breikiəl], *a.* braquial.

brachiopods ['brækiəpɔds], **brachiopoda,** *s.* (*zool.*) braquiópodos.

brachium ['breikiəm], *s.* (*pl.* **brachia**) (*zool.*) brazo superior.

bracing ['breisiŋ], *a.* fortificante, tónico. — *s.* amarra, trabazón, *f.*, ligazón, *f.*, refuerzo.

bracken ['brækən], *s.* (*bot.*) helecho, helechal.

bracket ['brækət], *s.* punta, puntal, soporte, listón, listoncillo; can, repisa, rinconera, codillo; (*impr.*) corchete; (*mec.*) bloque, garfio; brazo de lámpara; *cat-head bracket*, (*mar.*) aletas de las serviolas.

brackish ['brækiʃ], *a.* salobre; áspero.

brackishness, *s.* saladura, salmuera, sabor; aspereza.

bract, bractea, *s.* (*bot.*) bráctea.

bracteal, bracteate, *a.* bracteífero.

bracteole, *s.* bractéola.

brad [bræd], *s.* punta, tachuela, hita, espiga, clavo de ala de mosca, o de cabeza perdida.

bradawl ['brædaul], *s.* lesna, punzón, afilado.

brae [brei], *s.* (*esco.*) pendiente, *f.*, ladera.

brag [bræg], *s.* jactancia, bravata, fanfarrón, fanfarronada, andaluzada; farolero; un juego de naipes. — *v.i.* jactarse, fanfarronear, baladronear, alardear, hablar gordo; *to brag of one's riches*, escupir doblones.

braggadocio [brægə'doufiou], *s.* fanfarrón, fanfarría.

braggart ['brægəɹt], s. jactancioso, bravucón.
braggartism, s. jactancia, vana ostentación, fanfarronería.
bragger, s. fanfarrón, matasiete, jaque.
bragget, s. aguamiel, f.
bragging, a. jactancioso. — s. jactancia; embuste, exageración.
Brahma ['brɑːmə], s. Brahma.
Brahmin, s. brahmán, brahmín.
Brahminical [brɑːˈminikəl], a. brahmánico.
Brahminism ['brɑːminizm], s. brahmanismo.
braid [breid], v.t. trenzar, hacer trenzas; acordonar; bordar. — s. trenza, trencilla, lazo, cordoncillo; galón;] fleco, alamar. — a. (Escocia) ancho.
braided, a. acordonado, trenzado, galoneado, bordado de cordoncillo.
brail [breil], v.t. (mar.) cargar (las velas); halar con las candelizas.
brails, s.pl. (mar.) cargaderas, candelizas.
brain [brein], s. cerebro; juicio, entendimiento, talento, cordura. — pl. **brains,** sesos; to blow out one's brains, saltarse la tapa de los sesos. — v.t. descerebrar, volar los sesos a, romper la crisma; hare-brained, sin seso, atolondrado, aturdido; crack-brained, cabeza de chorlito; brain fever, fiebre cerebral.
brainish, a. loco, furioso.
brainless, a. tonto, insensato, sin seso.
brainpan, s. cráneo.
brainsickly, adv. locamente.
brainy, a. listo, talentudo.
braise [breiz], v.t. asar con doble fuego (encima y debajo).
brake [breik], s. freno; (bot.) helecho, helechal; agramadera; (mar.) guimbalete de bomba; retranca; amasadera; bocado de canutillo; maleza, zarzal, matorral; (agr.) grada, palanca, espeque; air-brake, freno atmosférico; automatic brake o self-acting brake, freno automático; brake-man, guardafrenos; brake-van, vagón de cola.
braky ['breiki], a. espinoso, áspero; lleno de malezas.
bramah ['brɑːmə], s. especie de cerradura y su llave.
bramble ['bræmbl], s. (bot.) zarza.
brambling, s. pinzón, especie de pájaro.
brambly, a. zarzoso.
bran [bræn], s. salvado, afrecho.
brancard, s. estiércol.
bran-new, brand-new, a. enteramente nuevo, flamante.
branch [brɑːntʃ], s. rama; ramo, sección, subdivisión, dependencia; ramificación; brazo, ramal, cama del freno; brazo de un candelero; pitón, asta; ramal de ferrocarril; sucursal (de una casa de comercio); cualquier persona con relación a sus progenitores. — v.t. ramificar, dividir en ramas. — v.i. ramificarse, bifurcar; empalmar; echar pitones, ramas o astas; to branch out, echar ramos divergir, extenderse; to branch off, bifurcarse.
branched, a. ramoso, enramado, frondoso.
brancher, s. arbolillo que empieza a echar retoños; halcón ramero.
branchiæ ['bræŋkiə], s.pl. branquias.
branchial, a. branquial.
branchiness, s. frondosidad.
branchless, a. sin ramas, desnudo.

branchlet, s. ramilla, ramita; ramo.
branchy, a. ramoso.
brand [brænd], s. tizón, tea; (poét.) rayo; (poét.) acero, espada; nota de infamia; sello o marca de fábrica; baldón, estigma. — v.t. herrar, marcar con un hierro ardiendo; tiznar, infamar.
brandied, a. encabezado.
brandiron, s. hierro de marcar.
brandish, v.t. blandir, blandear. — s. (esgr.) molinete, floreo.
brand-new, a. [BRAN-NEW].
brandy, brandy-wine, s. coñac.
brangle ['bræŋgl], s. disputa, riña, pendencia. — v.i. reñir, disputar.
brangler, s. pendenciero.
brangling, s. disputa, riña.
branks, s. trigo morisco.
brank-ursine, s. (bot.) brancaursina, acanto.
branlin ['brænlən], s. salmón pequeño.
branny ['bræni], a. casposo, parecido al salvado.
brant [brænt], s. ganso silvestre, también se llama brent.
brasier, brazier ['breiziəɹ], s. brasero; latonero.
brass [brɑːs], s. latón, cobre amarillo; (mús.) metal; (fig.) descaro, desvergüenza; red brass, tumbaga; yellow brass, latón. — v.t. guarnecer de latón.
brassart ['bræsəɹt], s. brazal.
brass-band, s. murga, charanga.
brassfounder, s. fundidor de bronce o latón.
brassiere, s. sostén.
brassiness, s. bronceadura.
brass-money, s. calderilla.
brassish, brassy, a. de latón, de bronce; (fig.) descarado.
brat [bræt], s. rapaz, niño, mocoso.
brattle [brætl], v.i. repiquetear.
bravado [brəˈvɑːdou], s. bravata, baladronada.
brave [breiv], a. bravo, valiente, valeroso, intrépido, bizarro, atrevido, esforzado, airoso; elegante; honrado. — s. fanfarrón, jaque, espadachín. — v.t. desafiar, bravear, acarar, provocar, arrostrar.
bravery, s. valor, valentía, coraje, braveza, heroismo, proeza, ánimo, esfuerzo, esplendor, magnificencia, gallardía, galantería; bravata.
bravo ['brɑːvou], s. asesino asalariado; interj. ¡bravo! ¡bien! ¡bueno!
bravura [brəˈvuərə], s. (mús.) bravura.
brawl [brɔːl], s. alboroto, camorra, pendencia, disputa; quimera. — v.i. alborotar, armar escándalo, armar camorra; v.t. vociferar, vocinglear.
brawler, s. quimerista, m.f.; alborotador, camorrista, m.f.
brawling, s. alboroto, vociglería. — a. ruidoso.
brawn [brɔːn], s. (coc.) embutido; la parte carnosa y muscular del cuerpo; carne de verraco o cerdo; músculo; (fig.) fuerza (o vigor) muscular.
brawner, s. verraco engordado para comer.
brawniness, s. (fig.) fuerza, vigor, fortaleza, musculatura.
brawny, a. carnoso, membrudo, musculoso; fuerte, endurecido.
braxy ['bræksi], s. fiebre carbuncular de los carneros y ovejas; res atacada de esta enfermedad. — a. atacado por la fiebre carbuncular.

bray [brei], *v.t.* majar, triturar, machacar, pulverizar, moler. — *v.i.* rebuznar, roznar. — *s.* rebuzno, roznido, ruido bronco.

brayer, *s.* rebuznador; (*impr.*) moleta, moledor de tinta; (*cir.*) braguero.

braying, *s.* rebuzno, grito.

braze [breiz], *v.t.* trabajar en cobre; soldar con latón; broncear.

brazen, *a.* bronceado, hecho de bronce, hecho de latón; (*fig.*) descarado, desvergonzado. — *v.t.* hacerse descarado, tratar con descaro, tratar con altivez; *to brazen out a thing*, sostener una cosa con impudencia.

brazen-faced, *a.* descarado, desvergonzado.

brazenly, *adv.* descaradamente, impudentemente; *to lie brazenly*, mentir sin suelo.

brazenness, *s.* descaro, desvergüenza.

brazier ['breiziəɹ], *s.* calderero, latonero; brasero, copa.

braziery, *s.* latonería.

Brazil-wood [brə'zil-wud], *s.* madera o palo del Brasil.

Brazilian [brə'ziljən], *s., a.* brasileño.

brazing ['breiziŋ], *s.* soldadura con cobre derretido.

breach [briːtʃ], *s.* brecha, abertura, rotura, fractura, rompimiento, quebrantamiento; infracción, violación, contravención; disensión; ofensa, rompimiento de relaciones; perjuicio, detrimento; *breach of trust*, abuso de confianza (o falta de fidelidad); *breach of promise*, falta de palabra; *breach of confidence*, abuso de confianza; *breach of the peace*, perturbación del orden público; (*mar.*) romper de las olas, salto de la ballena. — *v.t.* (*mil.*) practicar una brecha, batir en brecha.

bread [bred], *s.* pan; alimentos; sustento diario; *to earn one's bread*, ganar (se) la vida; *white bread*, pan blanco; *brown bread*, pan moreno; *household bread*, pan casero; *bread-basket*, cesto para el pan; (*vulg.*) panza; *bread and butter*, pan con mantequilla; (*fam., fig.*) sustento diario; *unleavened bread*, pan ázimo; *home-made bread*, pan casero; *soft bread*, mollete; *rye-bread*, pan de centeno; *to break bread with*, comer con; *he knows on which side his bread is buttered*, sabe donde le aprieta el zapato; *new bread*, pan tierno; *stale bread*, pan duro; *bread-fruit*, árbol del pan; *bread-winner*, ganador de pan, el que mantiene a su familia.

breadless, *a.* pobre, sin pan.

breadstuff, *s.* cereales, granos.

breadth [bredθ], *s.* anchura, ancho; paño; holgura, latitud; liberalidad, catolicidad.

breadthwise, *adv.* a lo ancho.

break [breik], *v.t.* (*pret.* **broke;** *poét.* **brake;** *p.p.* **broken, broke**) romper, quebar, hender; vencer, sobrepujar; quebrantar, fracturar; infringir, violar; abrir (brecha); abatir; dominar, domar; forzar; revelar; imposibilitar, inutilizar; causar quiebra o brancarrota; degradar; estropear, desvencijar, destruir; parar (un golpe), arruinar; interrumpir, impedir, interceptar. — *v.i.* quebrarse, romperse; abrirse, reventarse; exclamar, prorrumpir; hacer bancarrota; estallar; enemistarse; separarse, apartarse con violencia; desmejorarse, decaer; tener la salud quebrantada; florecer, brotar; apuntar; templarse; romper con uno; entrar de repente; mudar, cambiar; echarse a perder (el tiempo);

to break asunder, partir, dividir en dos; *to break a bank*, hacer saltar la banca; *to break cover*, salir de un escondite; *to break a rule*, salir de la regla; *to break down*, abatir derribar, romperse, perder la salud; *to break forth*, brotar, salir, saltar; *to break ground*, empezar la labranza; *to break one's health*, quebrantar la salud; *to break one's heart*, matar a pesadumbres, desgarrar el corazón; *to break the law*, infringir la ley; *to break in*, acostumbrar; domeñar; forzar la entrada; *to break off*, dejar sin concluir; *to break open*, forzar, romper; *to break out*, estallar; *to break silence*, romper el silencio; *to break out into pimples*, cubrirse de granos; *to break up*, demoler, derribar, abatir; *to break up (a meeting)*, levantar la sesión; *to break upon*, estallar, aparecer; *to break with*, romper con; *to break through*, abrirse camino; *to break ground*, comenzar una empresa; *to break a lance with*, oponerse a; *to break wind*, peer, ventosear; *to break a record*, batir un record. — *s.* brecha, abertura; rompimiento; desgarro; roza; punto; rotura, grieta, raja, defecto; freno; principio, comienzo; laguna; alba; blanco; carruaje; (*elec.*) interruptor; vacío; (*gram.*) puntos suspensivos, interrupción, intervalo; pausa, parada; enrayador; (*com.*) baja; *break of day*, aurora, alborada; *to break one's fast*, desayunarse; *to break one's oath*, ser traidor, perjuro.

breakable, *a.* quebradizo, frágil, frangible.

breakage, *s.* fractura, rotura, quebrantamiento; destrozo.

breakdown, *s.* falta de éxito; parada; avería; vuelca, caída, derrumbamiento; crisis, *f.*

breaker, *s.* destructor; infractor; roturador; rompedor, quebrantador; (*mar.*) rompiente, escollo, rompeolas.

breakfast ['brekfəst], *s.* desayuno, almuerzo. — *v.t.* desayunar(se), almorzar.

breakfasting, *s.* almuerzo.

breaking ['breikiŋ], *s.* rompimiento, fractura; quebrantamiento; quiebra; bancarrota; irrupción; interrupción; violación, infracción; (*min.*) arranque; *breaking up*, disolución, cierre.

breakneck, *s.* despeñadero, precipicio. — *a.* precipitado, rápido.

breakshare, *s.* (*vet.*) soltura de vientre.

break-up, *s.* fin, clausura; punto; desorden.

breakwater, *s.* muelle, dique; rompeolas, *m.,* tajamar, escollera.

bream [briːm], *s.* (*ict.*) sargo; *sea-bream*, besugo. — *v.t.* (*mar.*) carenar.

breast [brest], *s.* pecho, seno; mama, teta; pechos, tetas; corazón; interior del hombre; (*fig.*) alma, conciencia; *breast of chicken, etc.*, pechuga; *to make a clean breast of it*, confesarlo todo. — *v.t.* acometer (o atacar) de frente; oponerse a.

breastbone, *s.* (*anat.*) esternón.

breast-collar, *s.* pretal, collera.

breastdeep, breasthigh, *a.* alto hasta el pecho.

breastpin, *s.* prendedor, broche.

breastplate, *s.* peto, coraza, armadura del pecho.

breastpump, *s.* mamadera.

breastrail, *s.* (*mar.*) antepecho.

breastwork, *s.* (*fort.*) terraplén, parapeto; (*mar.*) propao.

breath [breθ], *s.* aliento, hálito, resuello, respiración; soplo (de aire); (*fig.*) existencia, vida; pausa, demora; instante; momento; *to be out of breath*, estar sofocado, estar sin aliento; *to gasp for breath*, jadear; *to be short of breath*, ser corto de resuello; *under one's breath*, en voz baja; *in a breath*, de un tirón, de una vez.

breathable ['briːðəbl], *a.* respirable.

breathe [briːð], *v.t.*, *v.i.* soplar, exhalar; alentar, resollar, respirar; descansar; vivir; aspirar, exhalar; dar aire; revelar; *to breathe one's last*, dar el último suspiro, morir.

breather, *s.* respirador; inspirador, autor; viviente; *to take a breather*, tomar el aire.

breathing ['briːðiŋ], *s.* respiración, resuello; soplo; inspiración; anhelo, deseo, aspiración; descanso, pausa; respiradero; aire suave. — *a.* respiratorio.

breathing-hole, *s.* respiradero.

breathing-place, *s.* pausa, descanso, parada.

breathing-time, *s.* reposo, relajación, descanso; pausa, parada.

breathless ['breθləs], *a.* sofocado, desalentado, muerto, sin aliento.

breathlessness, *s.* desaliento; muerte, *f.*

bred [bred], *pret.* y *p.p.* [BREED].

brede [breid], *s.* trenza, galón, cordón, cordoncillo.

breech [briːtʃ], *s.* trasero; posaderas, nalgas; (*arti.*) recámara. — *v.t.* poner calzones; zurrar; *breech-loader*, fusil que se carga por la recámara. — *pl.* **breeches**, calzones, pantalones; *to wear the breeches*, ponerse los pantalones (de la mujer que gobierna al marido).

breechings, *s.pl.* (*mar.*) bragueros de cañón, grupera del arnés.

breed [briːd], *v.t.* criar, producir, procrear, engendrar, multiplicar; ocasionar, causar; educar, enseñar; padrear; empollar; *well bred*, bien educado. — *v.i.* estar encinta, preñada; nacer, crecer; criar, multiplicarse. — *s.* raza, casta, progenie. *f.*; generación; pollada, camada.

breeder, *s.* criador, autor, padre, productor, progenitor; paridera, hembra fecunda; nodriza; *cattle breeder*, criador de ganados.

breeding, *s.* cría, crianza, enseñanza, educación; urbanidad, modales; (*fisiol.*) gestación; *good breeding*, buena educación, conocimiento del mundo; *cross breeding*, cruzamiento de razas; *bad breeding*, modales groseros.

breeze [briːz], *s.* brisa, airecillo, aura, oreo, viento fresco, viento favorable; (*fig.*) agitación, excitación; murmuración, vago rumor; cenizas calientes, rescoldo; carboncillo, cisco de coque; *stiff breeze*, (*mar.*) viento fuerte. — *v.i.* ventear.

breezeless, *a.* sin aire, inmoble.

breezy, *a.* airoso, oreado, garboso; expuesto a los vientos; refrescado por la brisa.

brent [brent], *a.* liso, sin arrugas; alto, prominente; *brent-goose*, ganso salvaje.

brest [brest], *s.* (*arq.*) toro.

bret [bret], *s.* (*ict.*) rombo.

brethren ['breðrən], *s.pl.* hermanos. — *pl.* [BROTHER].

Breton ['bretən], *s.*, *a.* bretón.

breve [briːv], *s.* (*mús.*) breve.

brevet ['brevət], *s.* título; despacho; (*mil.*) nombramiento, graduación, comisión honoraria. — *v.t.* (*mil.*) graduar.

breviary ['briːviəri], *s.* compendio, epítome, extracto, resumen; breviario.

brevier, *s.* (*impr.*) breviario.

brevipennate, *a.* (*orn.*) brevipennes.

brevipede, *a.* (*orn.*) brevípedo.

brevity ['breviti], *s.* brevedad; concisión.

brew [bruː], *v.t.* batir, trabajar un líquido a fuerza de brazos; hacer *o* fabricar (cerveza, etc.); mezclar; alterar, falsificar; preparar una bebida; (*fig.*) urdir, maquinar, tramar, fraguar. — *v.i.* prepararse, mezclarse, formarse; fermentar, elaborar; *a storm is brewing*, una tempestad se prepara. — *s.* braceaje, trabajo de preparación de la cerveza; mezcla.

brewage, *s.* brebaje.

brewer, *s.* cervecero.

brewery, brewhouse, *s.* cervecería.

brewing, *s.* elaboración de cerveza.

brewis, *s.* caldo, sopa.

bribe [braib], *s.* cohecho, soborno, regalo hecho con objeto de sobornar; cebo; incentivo. — *v.t.* cohechar, sobornar, seducir, corromper, untar las manos de.

briber, *s.* cohechador, corruptor, sobornador.

bribery, *s.* cohecho, soborno.

bric-a-brac [brik-ə-bræk], *s.* bric-a-brac, objetos de arte, artículos curiosos.

brick [brik], *s.* ladrillo; cantidad de ladrillos; (*fam.*) buena persona. — *v.t.* enladrillar.

brickbat, *s.* pedazo de ladrillo, tejoleta, tejuela.

brickdust, *s.* ladrillo molido.

brick-kiln, *s.* horno de cocer ladrillos.

bricklayer, *s.* albañil, enladrillador.

brick-maker, *s.* ladrillero.

brickwork, *s.* enladrillado.

bricky, *a.* ladrilloso.

brickyard, *s.* ladrillal, adobería.

bridal [braidl], *a.* nupcial; *bridal song*, epitalamio. — *s.* boda, fiesta nupcial.

bride, *s.* novia, desposada.

bridecake, *s.* torta, pastel, pan de la boda.

bridechamber, *s.* cámara nupcial.

bridegroom, *s.* novio, desposado.

bridemaid, bridesmaid, *s.* dama de honor.

brideman, bridesman, *s.* padrino de boda.

Bridewell, *s.* nombre de una casa de corrección de Londres.

bridge [bridʒ], *s.* puente; caballete (de la nariz); *Wheatstone-bridge* (*elec.*) balanza de Wheatstone; *drawbridge*, puente levadizo; *suspension bridge*, puente colgante, puente de violín, guitarra, etc.; *bridge* (origen ruso) parecido al tresillo. — *v.t.* levantar *o* construir un puente; (*mil.*) echar un puente volante sobre un río.

bridge-board, *s.* (*arq.*) pie que sostiene una escalera.

bridge-head, *s.* (*fort.*) cabeza de puente.

bridgeward, *s.* custodio de puente.

bridle ['braidl], *s.* brida, freno; (*fisiol.*) frenillo; sujeción. — *v.t.* embridar, enfrenar; reprimir, refrenar, poner el freno a. — *v.i.* levantar, erguir la cabeza, erguirse. — *pl.* (*mar.*) poas.

bridle-curb, *s.* barbada.

bridle-path, *s.* camino de herradura.

bridoon [bri'duːn], *s.* bridón, filete.

brief [briːf], *a.* breve, corto, conciso, sucinto, sumario; pasajero, fugaz, rápido. — *s.* epítome, compendio, sumario, resumen; memorial; (*for.*) escrito, alegato, auto jurídico; (*mús.*) breve; (*igl.*) breve, buleto apostólico.

briefless, *a.* sin causas, sin clientes (*hablando de un abogado*).

briefly, *adv.* brevemente, sucintamente, compendiosamente, en resumen, en pocas palabras, en una palabra.

briefness, *s.* brevedad, concisión.

brier ['braiəɹ], *s.* zarza, espino; rosal silvestre; maleza, escaramujo, agavanzo.

briered, *a.* lleno de espinos.

briery, *a.* zarzoso, lleno de zarzas.

brig, brigantine ['brigənti:n], *s.* (*mar.*) bergantín.

brigade [bri'geid], *s.* brigada. — *v.t.* formar brigadas.

brigadier [brigə'diəɹ], **brigadier-general,** *s.* (*mil.*) brigadier.

brigand ['brigənd], *s.* bandido, bandolero, salteador de caminos, ladrón público.

brigandage, *s.* salteamiento, latrocinio.

brigandine [brigən'di:n], *s.* cota de malla.

bright [brait], *a.* claro, lustroso, brillante, luciente, reluciente, flamante, luminoso, resplandeciente, radiante; límpido; evidente; ilustre, esclarecido; ingenioso, agudo, perspicaz.

bright-eyed, *a.* ojialegre; *to make bright,* pulimentar, poner brillante o reluciente, dar brillo.

brighten, *v.t.* abrillantar, dar luz, dar brillo, dar lustre; avivar, animar; aguzar; despejar; bruñir, pulir; esparcir luz; ilustrar, ennoblecer. — *v.i.* brillar; aclararse, despejarse; pulimentarse; animarse, avivarse, despabilarse.

brightness, *s.* lustre, esplendor, brillo, brillantez, resplandor, claridad; (*fig.*) agudeza, viveza.

Bright's disease, *s.* (*med.*) enfermedad de Bright, glomerulonefritis, *f.*

brill [bril], *s.* (*ict.*) barbosa, mero.

brilliance ['briljəns], **brilliancy,** *s.* brillantez, brillo, lustre, esplendor, resplandor, fulgor.

brilliant, *a.* brillante, radiante, refulgente. — *s.* (*min.*) brillante.

brilliantine, *s.* brillantina.

brilliantness, *s.* brillantez, magnificencia, esplendor.

brills, *s.pl.* pestañas del caballo.

brim [brim], *s.* borde, orilla, extremo, extremidad, labio (de un vaso); ala (de un sombrero). — *v.t.* llenar hasta el borde. — *v.i.* estar de bote en bote.

brimful, *a.* lleno hasta el borde; colmado.

brimfulness, *s.* plenitud, llenura hasta el borde.

brimless, *a.* sin borde, labio, o ala.

brimmer, *s.* copa llena, vaso lleno.

brimming, *a.* rebosando, lleno hasta el borde.

brimstone ['brimstən], *s.* azufre vivo o en canelones.

brimstony, *a.* sulfuroso.

brinded, *a.* moteado, mosqueado, salpicado.

brindle ['brindl], *s.* variedad de colores.

brindled, *a.* abigarrado, mosqueado.

brine [brain], *s.* salmuera; (*poét.*) onda, mar; lágrimas. — *v.t.* salar, poner en salmuera.

bring [briŋ], *v.t.*, *pret.* y *p.p.* [**brought**] llevar, traer, conducir, hacer venir; aportar, causar, producir; atraer; acarrear; inducir, persuadir; recoger; reducir; valer; *to bring about,*

efectuar, poner por obra; *to bring away,* llevarse, quitar, alzar, hacer salir; *to bring back,* retraer, traer de vuelta, devolver; *to bring down,* bajar, traer abajo; (*fig.*) abatir; matar (en la caza); *to bring down the house,* causar grandes aplausos; *to bring forth,* producir; parir; dar a luz; *to bring forward,* impulsar, empujar, dar empuje; (*com.*) trasportar; presentar; *brought forward,* (*com.*) suma anterior, suma y sigue; *to bring in,* reclamar; alegar; producir; reducir; presentar, introducir; declarar; *to bring off,* desempeñar, rescatar, desviar; lograr, conseguir; *to bring on,* transportar; causar, ocasionar; inducir; aguantar; acarrear; *to bring out,* llevar, conducir; publicar; mostrar; descubrir; echar fuera; *to bring over,* persuadir, convertir; *to bring to,* sacar de un desmayo; (*mar.*) ponerse a la capa; *to bring under,* sojuzgar, sujetar, someter; *to bring up,* subir, hacer subir; servir (una comida); presentar; introducir; criar, educar; *to bring to bed,* partear; *to bring to light,* dar a luz; *to bring by the lee,* (*mar.*) tomar por la luna sobre la arribada.

bringer, *s.* portador.

brinish ['brainiʃ], *a.* salobre, salado.

brinishness, *s.* sabor de sal.

brink [briŋk], *s.* orilla, borde, margen, extremo, extremidad; *on the brink of,* (*fig.*) o dos dedos de.

briny [braini], *a.* salobre, salado; *the briny deep,* el mar, el océano.

brisk [brisk], *a.* vivo, activo, alegre; despejado; animado, rápido; fuerte, vigoroso. — *v.t.* animar, atizar, activar, avivar; *to brisk up,* animar(se).

brisket, *s.* pecho (de un animal).

briskness, *s.* viveza, vivacidad, actividad, despejo, alegría, gallardía.

brisky, *a.* cerdoso, hirsuto, erizado; grosero, rudo.

bristle ['brisl], *s.* cerda, porcipelo; seta. — *v.t.*, *v.i.* erizar, erizarse.

Bristol-board [bristl-boəɹd], *s.* cartulina.

Bristol-brick, *s.* piedra para limpiar cuchillos.

Bristol-stone, *s.* diamante de Bristol.

brit [brit], *s.* entomostráceos, alimento de las ballenas; arenque pequeño.

Britannia [bri'tænjə], (*metal.*) *s.* metal inglés, liga de estaño, antimonio, bismuto y cobre.

Britannic, *a.* británico.

British ['britiʃ], *a.* británico.

British gum, *s.* dextrina.

Briton, *s.*, *a.* bretón; británico, inglés.

brittle ['britl], *a.* quebradizo, frágil.

brittleness, *s.* fragilidad, bronquedad.

broach [broutʃ], *s.* asador; lezna, espetón; (*carp.*) broca, mecha; terraja, prendedor, broche, alfiler con gancho; (*arq.*) aguja, chapitel. — *v.t.* ensartar, espetar; barrenar, encentar, decentar; empezar; introducir, hacer público; *to broach to,* (*mar.*) tomar por avante, por la luna.

broacher, *s.* asador; autor.

broad [brɔːd], *a.* ancho, anchuroso, amplio, extenso, vasto; abierto, claro; categórico; basto, grosero; vago, comprensivo, tolerante, liberal; obsceno, pornográfico, indecente, indecoroso, atrevido, descomedido; *in broad daylight,* en medio del día; *as broad as it is long,* igual; *to grow broad,* ensancharse.

broad-axe, s. hacha de carpintero.
broadcast, s. (agr.) siembra al vuelo; emisión (de radio). — v.t. esparcir, diseminar, sembrar al vuelo; radiar.
broadcasting, s. radiodifusión; *broadcasting-station,* emisora.
Broad-Church, s., a. partido liberal de la iglesia.
broad-cloth, s. paño fino.
broaden, v.t. ensanchar, extender a lo ancho.
broadish, a. algo ancho.
broadness, s. ancho, anchura; grosería; atrevimiento, falta de decoro.
broadside, s. (mar.) costado de navío; (mar.) andanada; (imp.) cada lado de un pliego de papel.
broadsword, s. espada larga y ancha; espadón, chafarote.
broadwise, adv. a lo ancho, por lo ancho.
brocade [bro'keid], s. brocado. — v.t. espolinar, decorar con brocado.
brocaded, a. espolinado; de brocado; recamado de oro.
brocage, s. corretaje; comercio de mercancías viejas.
brocatel, brocatello, s. brocatel.
broccoli ['brɔkəli], s. bróculi, brécol.
brochure [brə'ʃuəɹ], s. folleto.
brock [brɔk], s. tejón.
brocket, s. gamo de dos años.
brodekin ['brɔdəkin], s. borceguí.
brogan ['brougən], s. zapato basto.
brogue [broug], s. especie de calzado; abarca; dialecto; jerigonza.
broil [brɔil], s. tumulto, sedición, alboroto; camorra, pendencia, riña; quimera; calor intenso. — v.t. asar, soasar, tostar, turrar. — v.i. asarse; sudar; padecer calor.
broiler, s. parrilla; perturbador, camorrista, m.f.; quimerista, m.f.; pollo a propósito para asar.
brokage, s. corretaje.
broken ['broukən], a. roto, quebrado; (fig.) abatido, quebrantado; accidentado. — p.p. [BREAK]; *broken sleep,* sueño interrumpido; *broken spirit,* espíritu amilanado; *broken language,* lenguaje chapurrado; *to speak broken English,* chapurrar el inglés; *broken voice,* voz cascada.
broken-down, a. arruinado, desahuciado; muy mal de salud, descompuesto, averiado.
broken-hearted, a. desolado, desesperado, angustiado.
brokenly, adv. interrumpidamente, a ratos.
brokenness, s. interrupción; desigualdad.
broken-wind, s. (vet.) huérfago, asma.
brokenwinded, a. (vet.) asmático.
broker ['broukəɹ], s. corredor, cambista, m.f.; chamarilero, almonedero, ropavejero; agente.
brokerage, s. corretaje; correduría.
broma ['broumə], s. harina de cacao.
bromal, s. (quím.) bromal.
bromate, s. (quím.) bromato.
bromine ['broumi:n], s. (quím.) bromo.
bromography [brou'mɔgrəfi], s. bromografía.
bronchia ['brɔŋkiə], **bronchiæ, bronchi,** (anat.) bronquios.
bronchial, bronchic, a. (anat.) bronquial.
bronchitis [brɔŋ'kaitis], s. (med.) bronquitis, f.
bronchocele ['brɔŋkəsi:l], s. (cir.) broncocele.
bronchotomy [brɔŋ'kɔtəmi], s. (cir.) broncotomía.

bronco ['brɔŋkou], s. potro cerril.
brontograph ['brɔntəgræf], s. brontógrafo.
brontometer [brɔn'tɔmətəɹ], s. brontómetro.
bronze [brɔnz], s. bronce; objeto de bronce; color de bronce. — v.t. broncear, pavonar; endurecer; tostar por el sol.
bronzing, s. bronceado.
brooch [broutʃ], s. broche; joya, prendedero, alfiler de pecho.
brood [bru:d], s. progenie, f., generación, producción, raza, casta, ralea; nidada, cría, pollazón, f. — v.i. empollar; cobijar; tramar, preparar en secreto, fraguar; *to brood over,* rumiar.
brooder, s. clueca; incubadora.
brooding, pres. part., a. empollando, calentando.
broodmare, s. yegua.
broody, a. clueca, llueca.
brook [bruk], s. arroyo, cañada. — v.t. digerir, masticar; sufrir, tolerar, aguantar.
brooklet, s. arroyuelo.
brooklime, s. (bot.) becabunga.
brookmint, s. (bot.) menta de agua.
broom [bru:m], s. escoba, barredera; (bot.) hiniesta, retama.
broom-land, s. retamal.
broom-maker, s. escobero.
broomstick, s. palo o mango de escoba.
broomy, a. retamoso.
broth [brɔθ], s. caldo, jigote.
brothel, s. burdel, lupanar.
brother ['brʌðəɹ], s. hermano; colega, m.. cofrade; *brother-in-law,* cuñado; *foster-brother,* hermano de leche; *half-brother,* medio hermano.
brotherhood, s. hermandad; fraternidad, confraternidad, cofradía, congregación.
brotherless, a. sin hermanos.
brotherlike, a. fraternal, de hermano.
brotherly, a. fraternal; afectuoso, cariñoso, bondadoso. — adv. fraternalmente.
brougham [bru:m], s. coche simón.
brought [brɔ:t], pret. y p.p. [BRING].
brow [brau], s. ceja; frente, f., semblante, rostro, sienes, f.pl.; cresta, cima, borde de un precipicio, cumbre de un monte; (fig.) atrevimiento, descaro; *to knit one's brows,* fruncir las cejas, arrugar el entrecejo.
browbeat, v.t. intimidar, imponer; desconcertar.
browbeating, s. ceño, sobrecejo; arrogancia, altivez. — a. ceñudo.
browbound ['braubaund], a. coronado, con sienes ceñidas.
brown [braun], a. moreno, bazo; pardo, castaño; *brown bread,* pan bazo; *brown paper,* papel de estraza; *brown sugar,* azúcar moreno; *brown bear,* oso pardo; *brown owl,* autillo. — s. color moreno, pardo, etc. — v.t. poner moreno, poner tostado; (coc.) tostar.
brownie, s. duende benigno de los campesinos escoceses.
browning, s. bruñido, pulimento.
brownish, a. pardo, con algo de moreno.
brown-linnet, s. (orn.) pardillo.
brownness, s. color moreno o pardo.
browse [brauz], v.t. ramonear, rozar, tascar, herbajar; hojear (un libro).
browser, s. animal que ramonea.
browsing, s. ramoneo.
brucite ['bru:sait], s. (min.) brucita.

bruin ['bruːin], *s.* nombre familiar que se da al oso pardo.

bruise [bruːz], *v.t.* machacar, magullar, majar, golpear, pulverizar. — *s.* magulladura, contusión, golpe, cardenal.

bruiser, *s.* el que magulla; (*fam.*) púgil.

bruising, *s.* presión de uvas; (*vulg.*) leña, paliza; pugilato.

bruit [bruːt], *s.* ruido; rumor; noticia, fama. — *v.t.* echar voz, dar fama; divulgar, publicar.

brumal, *a.* brumal.

brume, *s.* bruma, neblina.

Brummagem ['brʌmədʒəm], *a.* de pacotilla; de poco valor.

brunette [bruːˈnet], *s.* morena, trigueña.

Brunswick black ['brʌnzwik blæk], *s.* charol negro.

brunt [brʌnt], *s.* choque, embate, encuentro violento; golpe; desastre.

brush [brʌʃ], *s.* cepillo, escobilla; brocha, limpiadera, bruza; pincel; choque, combate, pelea, asalto, escaramuza; batida de caza; ramojo, hojarasca; haz de leña menuda; matorral, monte, breñal; *brush-maker*, obrero que hace cepillos; *brushmaking*, fábrica de cepillos. — *v.t.* acepillar, cepillar; bruzar; frotar, restregar, rasar; pintar con brocha. — *v.i.* moverse apresuradamente; pasar ligeramente por encima.

brusher, *s.* cepillador, acepillador.

brushiness, *s.* rudeza, aspereza.

brushing, *s.* frotadura, estregamiento; acepilladura.

brushlike, *a.* semejante a un cepillo.

brushwood, *s.* matorral, breñal, zarzal; broza, ramojo.

brushy, *a.* cerdoso, cerdudo; áspero; velludo; cubierto de matojos.

brusk, brusque [brʌsk], *a.* áspero, rudo, brusco.

Brussels ['brʌslz], *n.p.* Bruselas; *Brussels sprouts*, *s.* bretones.

brutal ['bruːtl], *a.* brutal, bestial, salvaje, inhumano, cruel.

brutalism, brutality, *s.* brutalidad, barbaridad.

brutalize, *v.t.* embrutecer, tratar cruelmente. — *v.i.* embrutecerse.

brute [bruːt], *s.* bruto, persona brutal. — *a.* bruto, grosero, salvaje, feroz, irracional.

brutify, *v.t.* embrutecer. — *v.i.* embrutecerse.

brutish, *a.* brutal, bestial; insensible, abrutado, embrutecido; sensual; fiero, salvaje, feroz.

brutishness, *s.* brutalidad.

brutism, *s.* bruteza, embrutecimiento.

bryony ['braiəni], *s.* (*bot.*) brionia.

bubble ['bʌbl], *s.* burbuja; bola; pompa (de jabón); (*med.*) ampolla, tumor seroso; bagatela; engañifa, apariencia falsa. — *v.i.* burbujear, hacer ampollas, bullir, hervir; murmurar, correr con ruido manso (de un río). — *v.t.* engañar, estafar.

bubbler, *s.* engañador, fullero.

bubbly, *a.* espumoso.

bubby ['bʌbi], *s.* (*vulg.*) pecho de mujer.

bubo ['bjuːbou], *s.* (*med.*) incordio, bubón.

bubonic [bjuːˈbɔnik], *a.* bubónico.

bubonocele, *s.* (*med.*) bubonocele.

buccal ['bʌkl], *a.* bocal.

buccaneers, bucaniers [bʌkəˈniəɹs], *s.pl.* filibusteros.

buccinal ['bʌkinəl], *a.* (*anat.*) bocinal.

buccinator, *s.* (*anat.*) bucinator.

bucentaur, *s.* bucentauro, galera del dux de Venecia.

bucephalus [buˈsefələs], *s.* bucéfalo.

buck [bʌk], *s.* lejía, enjebe, colada; gamo, macho cabrío; petimetre. — *v.t.* colar, enjebar, lavar en la colada. — *v.i.* cubrir el ciervo a la hembra; entrar en celo el venado; reanimarse; caracolear.

buckbasket, *s.* cesto de la colada.

bucket, *s.* cubo, pozal, balde, herrada, acetre; paleta de rueda; válvula de bomba.

bucketful, *s.* cubo lleno.

buckeye ['bʌkai], *s.* (*bot.*) castaña de Indias.

bucking, *s.* legía, colada; lavado, lavadura de la ropa; vábula de bomba.

buckle ['bʌkl], *s.* hebilla; bucle. — *v.t.* hebillar, abrochar con hebilla; embrozar; hacer bucles. — *v.i.* ajustarse, apretar las hebillas; doblarse, encorvarse; *to buckle up*, confinar, limitar; *to buckle to*, aplicarse; *to buckle under*, resignarse.

buckler ['bʌkləɹ], *s.* escudo, rodela, adarga, broquel. — *v.t.* defender.

buckmast ['bʌkmɑst], *s.* hayuco.

buckram ['bʌkrəm], *s.* bocací o bucarán. — *a.* almidonado, engomado, aderezado; tieso, estirado. — *v.t.* engomar, almidonar.

bucksaw, *s.* sierra de bastidor.

buckshorn ['bʌkshoəɹn], *s.* (*bot.*) estrellamar.

buckskin, *s.* piel (*f.*) de ante; coturno.

buckstall, *s.* red tumbadera.

buckthorn ['bʌkθoəɹn], *s.* (*bot.*) ladierno, tamujo.

buckwheat ['bʌkwiːt], *s.* (*bot.*) trigo negro, sarraceno.

bucolic [bjuˈkɔlik], **bucolical**, *a.* bucólico, pastoril. — *s.* bucólica.

bud [bʌd], *s.* pimpollo, brote, cogollo, vástago, botón, yema; capullo; (*fam.*) niño, niña. — *v.i.* brotar, germinar, crecer, florecer; estar en flor. — *v.t.* (*agr.*) injertar de escudete.

Buddha ['bʌdə], *n.pr.* Budha, Buda.

Buddhic, Buddhistic, *a.* búdico.

Buddhism, *s.* budhaísmo, budismo.

budding, *a.* en capullo. — *s.* injerto de escudete; brotadura.

buddle, *s.* (*metal.*) lavadero, artesa. — *v.t.* lavar el mineral.

budge [bʌdʒ], *v.t.* mover. — *v.i.* moverse, menearse, mudarse de posición; hacer lugar. — *a.* pomposo, imponente, formal, grave. — *s.* pellejo curtido de cordero.

budget, *s.* barjuleta, mochila; provisión; presupuesto.

buff [bʌf], *s.* ante, cota de ante, búfalo; color de ante, color amarillo ligero. — *a.* de color de ante, amarillo claro. — *v.t.* linfa cuajada; pulimentar con ante; parar un golpe.

buffalo ['bʌfəlou], *s.* búfalo, piel (*f.*) de búfalo.

buffer, *s.* cojinete; (*esgr. y f.c.*) tope.

buffet ['bʌfət], *s.* puñada, embate, bofetada, sopapo; ajetreo, armario, repostería, alacena; aparador. — *v.i.* abofetear; combatir a puñadas.

buffeter, *s.* abofeteador, púgil.

buffeting, *s.* mano de bofetadas.

buffing-apparatus, *s.* (*f.c.*) aparato de choque.

buffing-block, *s.* (*f.c.*) cojinete, tope.

buffing-spring, *s.* (*f.c.*) resorte de tope o cojinete.

buffoon [bəˈfuːn], *s.* bufón, truhán, juglar.

buffoonery, buffooning, s. bufonada, bufonería, chocarrería.
buffoonish, buffoonlike, a. bufonesco, burlesco, licencioso.
buffoonism, s. maneras de bufón.
bug [bʌg], s. (en inglés se da generalmente este nombre a los insectos hemípteros), chinche; *bed bug*, chinche; *lady-bug*, mariquita; *potato-bug*, doríphora; pretencioso, orgulloso, (vulg.) petimetre.
bugbear, s. espantajo, coco; fantasma, m. — v.t. espantar.
bugger, s. (vulg.) sodomita; bestia, brutal (E.U.); individuo, muchacho.
bugginess, s. infección de chinches.
buggy, a. chinchoso. — s. calesín.
bugle ['bjuːgl], **bugle-horn,** s. clarín, trompeta, corneta de monte, cuerno o trompa de caza; (bot.) búgula, azabache.
bugler, s. trompetero, corneta, m.
bugloss ['bjuːglɔs], s. (bot.) buglosa.
buhl [buːl], s. taracea, marquetería.
build [bild], v.t.; pret. y p.p. [BUILT] edificar, construir, erigir, fabricar, formar, fundar, cimentar, labrar. — v.i. levantar un edificio, fiarse, apoyarse, contar con algo; *to build castles in the air* (in Spain), hacer castillos en el aire; *to build up*, levantar (un edificio), edificar; reconstituir; *to build upon*, contar con, confiar en. — s. estructura, figura, forma.
builder, s. arquitecto, alarife, maestro de obras; autor, creador, constructor.
building, s. construcción, casa, fábrica, edificio, obra; *ship-building*, construcción de navíos.
built [bilt], pret. y p.p. [BUILD].
bulb [bʌlb], s. (bot.) bulbo, cebolla; (elec.) bombilla; cubeta del barómetro; ampolleta del termómetro. — v.i. tomar o crecer en forma de bulbo.
bulbaceous [bəl'beiʃəs], a. bulboso.
bulbed, bulbous, a. bulboso.
bulbiferous [bəl'bifərəs], a. bulbífero.
bulbiform ['bʌlbifɔəɪm], a. bulbiforme.
Bulgarian [bəl'gɛəriən], s., a. búlgaro.
bulge [bʌldʒ], s. pandeo, comba; tripa (de una botella); (mar.) abertura de agua, pantoque. — v.i. combarse, encorvarse; (arq.) hacer barriga; (mar.) abrirse, hacer agua.
bulged, a. encorvado; que hace barriga.
bulginess, s. pandeo, combadura.
bulging, s. combadura, comba. — a. protuberante.
bulimy ['bjuːlimi], **bulimia,** s. (med.) bulimia, hambre canina.
bulk [bʌlk], s. tamaño, bulto, volumen, masa, grandor, magnitud, grosor; corpulencia; balumba; calibre; cabida, capacidad, carga; barriga o comba en algún edificio; banco delante de una tienda exponiendo mercancías; *in bulk*, (com.) al granel.
bulkhead, s. (mar.) propao, mamparo.
bulkiness, s. volumen, bulto, magnitud, masa.
bulky, a. voluminoso, corpulento; repleto, macizo; grueso, abultado, grandote.
bull [bul], s. toro; (ast.) tauro; bula; (fig.) disparate, despropósito; (com.) alcista, m.f.; *John Bull*, apodo dado a la nación inglesa.
bulla, s. (med.) flictena, ampolla.
bullace ['bulɔs], s. (bot.) ciruela silvestre.
bullary, s. bulario.
bullate, a. globuloso.

bull-baiting, s. combate de toros y perros.
bull-calf, s. ternero.
bull-dog, s. alano, perro de presa; revólver de calibre grande.
bullen, s. cañamiza; *bullen-nail*, clavo de tapicero.
bullet ['bulət], s. bala; plomada de pescador.
bulletin ['bulətin], s. boletín.
bull-faced, a. cariancho.
bull-fight, s. corrida de toros.
bull-fighter, s. torero, diestro.
bull-finch, s. (orn.) pinzón real.
bull-head, s. (orn.) chorlito, zote.
bullion ['buljən], s. oro o plata en barras; (com.) metálico; *bullion-office*, oficina de cambios.
bullish, a. disparatado, absurdo.
bullock, s. novillo castrado.
bull's eye ['bulsai], s. claraboya, tragaluz; linterna sorda; centro del blanco; tiro que da en el blanco.
bully ['buli], s. espadachín, camorrista, m.f., matón, rufián, matasiete. — v.t. echar bravatas, insultar; amedrentar, intimidar. — v.i. fanfarronear, bravear. — a. (E.U. fam.) magnífico, excelente; *bully beef*, carne de vaca en conserva.
bullying, s. brutalidad, novatada.
bulrush ['bulrʌʃ], s. junco, enea.
bulrushy, a. juncoso.
bulwark ['bulwəɪk], s. baluarte; (mar.) amurada; fortaleza, plaza fuerte. — v.t. fortificar, fortalecer, poner baluartes.
bum [bʌm], s. (vulg.) asentaderas, nalgas, posaderas; (E.U.) vago, vagabundo. — v.i. (ant.) zumbar, hacer ruido.
bumbailiff [bʌm'beilif], s. corchete; (fig.) alguacil.
bumble-bee, s. abejarrón, moscón.
bumboat, s. (mar.) bote vivandero.
bummer, s. holgazán, ocioso, pillo.
bump [bʌmp], s. hinchazón, f., bulto; joroba, corcova, giba; bollo, chichón; puñetazo, golpe violento; abolladura; barriga, comba; porrazo, trompazo, topetazo. — v.t. golpear, tropezar, dar contra.
bumper, s. copa o vaso lleno; lo que da golpes; (mar.) tope; (f.c. y aut.) parachoques.
bumpkin ['bʌmpkin], s. patán, villano, paleto.
bumptious ['bʌmpʃəs], a. (fam.) presuntuoso, envanecido.
bumptiousness, s. presunción.
bun [bʌn], s. bollo, torta; gazapo; rabo de liebre; moño.
bunch [bʌntʃ], s. bollo, chichón, bullo, protuberancia; corcova, giba; nudo; manojo, atado, hacecillo; comba; racimo, ristra; haz, gavilla; puñado; montón de hierba; bulto, tumor; mechón, copete; penacho. — v.t. agrupar, juntar, reunir, atar, liar, formar haces o manojos, arracimar. — v.i. formar salida o giba; arracimarse.
bunch-backed, a. corcovado, giboso, gibado.
bunchiness, s. espesura, amontonamiento.
bunchy ['bʌntʃi], a. racimoso, arracimado; corcovado, giboso.
bundle ['bʌndl], s. atado, lío, mazo, manojo, haz, fardel, bulto, envoltorio, paquete. — v.t. liar, atar; envolver, empaquetar, enfardelar. — v.i. liar la ropa; disponerse a partir; (E.U.) dormir, sin desnudarse, con persona de diferente sexo.

bung [bʌŋ], s. tapón, tarugo, bitoque; (*vulg.*) tabernero. — *v.t.* atarugar, encorchar.
bungalow ˈbʌŋɡəlou], s. casita de un solo piso.
bunghole [ˈbʌŋboul], s. boca de tonel.
bungle [ˈbʌŋɡl], *v.t.* chapucear, chafallar; echar a perder, estropear. — *v.i.* hacer algo chabacanamente. — *s.* chapucería, chafallo; torpeza.
bungler [ˈbʌŋɡlər], s. chapucero.
bungling, *a.* torpe, inhábil, poco diestro.
bunglingly, *adv.* chapuceramente, chabacanamente, groseramente.
bunion [ˈbʌnjən], s. (*med.*) juanete.
bunk [bʌŋk], s. tarima, litera. — *v.i.* acostarse, dormir en tarima.
bunker, s. arión; carbonera; (*mar.*) pañol del carbón; (*golf*) ʻbunkerʼ, hoya de arena.
bunkum, s. disparate, patrañas, *f.pl.*
bunny [ˈbʌni], s. (*fam.*) conejito, gazapo.
bunt [bʌnt], *v.i.* hincharse, inflar. — *v.t.* topetar, golpear. — *s.* hinchazón *f.* inflación; (*mar.*) fondo (de vela); *bunt of a sail* (*mar.*) batidero de vela; (*agr.*) añublo, tizón; empellón, empujón, topetazo; hongo parásito que ataca al trigo.
bunting, s. (*mar.*) lanilla (para banderas); estameña, colgaduras; (*orn.*) verderón, calandria.
bunting-iron, s. soplete de vidrio.
buntlines, *s.pl.* (*mar.*) brioles.
buoy [bɔi], s. (*mar.*) boya, baliza. — *v.t.* boyar, mantener sobre el agua. — *v.i.* nadar, sobrenadar; *to buoy up*, sostener, apoyar; *life-buoy*, guindola salvavida, boya de naufragio; *sparbuoy*, baliza.
buoyancy [ˈbɔiənsi], s. fluctuación; vivacidad, animación, ligereza; propiedad de mantenerse a nivel; tendencia a remontar, subir (precios, valores, etc.).
buoyant, *a.* boyante, vivaz, ligero, alegre, animado; flexible.
bur, burr [bəːr], s. bardana; carda, cabeza de la cardencha; corteza erizada de la castaña; (*tej.*) nudillo, mota. — *v.t.* (*tej.*) desmotar.
burbot [ˈbəːrbət], s. (*ict.*) mustela.
burden [ˈbəːrdn], s. carga, gravamen, peso; cuidados del ánimo; (*mar.*) cargamento, cargazón, *f.*, porte, tonelaje, capacidad; (*poét.*) estrambote, estribillo; *beast of burden*, bestia de carga, acémila; *life is a burden to me* o *my life has become a burden*, estoy cansado de vivir. — *v.t.* cargar, sobrecargar; agobiar; embarazar; gravar.
burdener, s. cargador, opresor.
burdensome, *a.* gravoso, oneroso, pesado, molesto.
burdensomeness, s. molestia, pesadez.
burdock [ˈbəːrdɔk], s. (*bot.*) bardana.
bureau [bjuəˈrou], s. armario, cómoda; escritorio; oficina, agencia, despacho; bufete; escaparate; papelera.
bureaucracy [bjuəˈrɔkrəsi], s. burocracia.
bureaucrat, s. burócrata, *m.f.*
bureaucratic [bjuərоˈkrætik], *a.* burocrático.
burette [bjuəˈret], s. bureta, probeta.
burg [ˈbʌrə], s. burgo; villa; aldea amurallada.
burgamot, s. bergamota.
burgee [ˈbəːrdʒiː], s. carbón muy menudo a propósito para fraguas; bandera de corneta.
burgess [ˈbəːrdʒes], s. burgués, ciudadano; elector de un burgo.
burgess-ship, s. condición de ciudadano.

burgh [ˈbʌrə], s. burgo, ciudad, villa.
burgher [ˈbəːrɡər], s. habitante, ciudadano; vecino.
burghership, s. ciudadanía.
burghmote, s. tribunal de un burgo.
burglar [ˈbəːrɡlər], s. ladrón, escalador; (*for.*) salteador en poblado; *cat-burglar*, gato.
burglarious [bəːrɡlɛəriəs], *a.* del robo en poblado.
burglary [ˈbəːrɡləri], s. robo de una casa habitada.
burgomaster, s. burgomaestre.
burgrave, s. burgrave.
Burgundy *s.* vino de Borgoña.
burial [ˈberiəl], s. entierro, enterramiento, sepelio; *burial-ground, burial-place*, cementerio; *burial-service*, oficio de difuntos.
burier, s. enterrador, sepulturero.
burin [ˈbjuərin], s. buril, cincel.
burl [bəːrl], *v.t.* batanar, golpear paños; desmotar, desborrar, despinzar. — *s.* borra, mota; nudo, nudillo.
burlap, s. especie de arpillera para sacos.
burler, s. desmotador.
burlesque [bəːrˈlesk], *a.* burlesco, cómico. — *s.* bufón; parodia. — *v.t.* burlar, chasquear, zumbar; poner en ridículo, parodiar.
burletta [bəːrˈletə], s. zarzuela cómica, zarzuelita, entremés con música.
burliness, s. corpulencia, volumen, espesor; (*fig.*) hinchazón, *f.*; fanfarronada.
burly [ˈbəːrli], *a.* voluminoso, corpulento, grueso; túmido; enfático; turbulento.
Burmese *a.* birmano.
burn [bəːrn], *v.t.* (*pret. y p.p.* **burned, burnt**) quemar; requemar; abrasar; incendiar, hacer arder; carbonear; inflamar; cocer; cauterizar; calcinar. — *v.i.* arder, quemarse, consumirse, soflamar. — *s.* quemadura; cocedura (de ladrillos); arroyo, riachuelo; *to burn down*, quemar de arriba abajo; *to burn with impatience*, arder de impaciencia; *to burn out*, reducirse a cenizas; consumirse, apagarse; *to burn up*, consumir completamente en el fuego; *to burn the midnight oil*, (*fig.*) quemarse las cejas.
burnable, *a.* combustible.
burner, s. quemador, abrasador, incendiario; piquera, mechero (de gas o lámpara).
burnet [ˈbəːrnet], s. (*bot.*) sanguisorba, pimpinela.
burning, s. quemadura; inflamación, ardor; abrasamiento, combustión; quema, incendio; (*fig.*) ardor. — *a.* abrasador; ardiente; vehemente; *there is a smell of burning*, huele a quemado; *a burning shame*, una gran vergüenza.
burnish [ˈbəːrniʃ], *v.t.* bruñir, pulir, acicalar, gratar; satinar. — *v.i.* tomar lustre; crecer, aumentarse; extenderse; medrar. — *s.* bruñido, pulimento; brillo, bruñidor, pulidor.
burnoose, burnous [bəːrˈnuːz], s. albornoz.
burnt [bəːrnt], *a.* quemado, abrasado; consumido; cocido. — *p.p.* [BURN]; *a burnt child dreads the fire*, gato escaldado huye del agua fría.
burnt-offering, burnt-sacrifice, s. holocausto.
burr [bəːr], s. arandela en un remache; halo o corona de la luna; raíz de las astas del ciervo; filo o lomo que deja una herramienta al cortar el metal; barbas producidas por el

buril al grabar cobre; cincel triangular; escoria semi-vitrificada; pronunciación gutural de la letra R; piedra de molino; (*carp.*) piedra de agua; (*carp.*) virola, rondana de perno; lóbulo o pulpejo de la oreja. — *v.t., v.i.* pronunciar o hablar con dejo gutural sonando mucho las R.

burrel ['bʌrəl], *s.* manteca de oro, especie de pera.

burrel-fly, *s.* tábano, moscardón.

burrel-shot, *s.* metralla.

burrock ['bʌrək], *s.* pesquera.

burrow ['bʌrou], *s.* madriguera, conejera; (*min.*) cata. — *v.i.* amadrigar; minar como los conejos.

burrow-duck, *s.* (*orn.*) tadorno común.

burr-pump, *s.* bomba de navío.

burr-stone, *s.* piedra de molino.

bursar ['bə:ɪsəɹ], *s.* tesorero de un colegio; estudiante que tiene plaza dotada en algún colegio; colegial de beca.

bursarship, *s.* tesorería.

bursary, *s.* caja, tesorería, economato; beca.

burse [bə:ɪs], *s.* bolsa, saco; (*igl.*) cubierta para cáliz, etc.

burst, *v.i.* (pret. y *p.p.* **burst**) reventar, estallar, volar; saltar; abrirse; descargar, rebosar; brotar; prorrumpir; entrar con impetuosidad. — *v.t.* romper, quebrar. — *s.* reventón, estallido, explosión; supremo esfuerzo; *to burst asunder,* estallar, reventar; *to burst into tears,* deshacerse en lágrimas; *to burst out,* brotar, reventar; surgir; *to burst out laughing,* dar una carcajada, reventar de risa; *to burst out weeping,* deshacerse en lágrimas; *to burst open,* abrir con violencia.

burton ['bə:ɪtən], *s.* (*mar.*) aparejo, palanquín de polea, polispastos.

bury ['beri], *v.t.* enterrar, inhumar, sepultar, soterrar, ocultar, esconder; olvidar, perdonar; *to bury the hatchet,* deponer las armas, hacer la paz; *to bury in oblivion,* echar tierra a.

bury-pear, *s.* pera mantecosa.

burying, *s.* entierro, exequias.

burying-ground, burying-place, *s.* cementerio, campo santo, necrópolis, *f.*; tumba, sepulcro.

bus [bʌs], *s.* (abreviación de omnibus) (*fam.*) ómnibus, autobús.

busby, *s.* chacó de los húsares, artilleros e ingenieros del ejército de la Gran Bretaña.

bush [buʃ], *a.* arbusto, mata; matojo; zarza, espinar; breña, maleza, matorral; ramo; penacho; cola de zorra; guedeja. — *v.t.* arrastrar matas, apoyar con matas; aforrar, con otro metal, la cámara de los cañones; cojinetes de ejes, etc. — *v.i.* espesarse, cerrarse (un monte, etc.); *to beat about the bush,* andarse por las ramas; *good wine needs no bush,* el buen paño en el arca se vende.

bushel, *s.* medida de áridos; fanega, el imperial inglés equivale a 36,35 litros; el americano a 35 litros.

bushiness, *s.* espesor formado por los arbustos y la maleza; estado de lanudo, peludo.

bushing, *s.* (*mec.*) forro de metal; tejo, tejuelo; (*arti.*) grano de un cañón.

bushman *s.* bosquimán.

bushy, *a.* espeso; lleno de arbustos; matoso, peludo.

busily ['bizili], *adv.* diligentemente, solícita-

mente, apresuradamente; atareadamente.

business ['biznis], *s.* empleo, oficio; asunto, negocio; tarea, quehacer, ocupación, tráfico, trabajo; comercio; *line of business,* ramo de negocios; *man of business,* hombre entendido en negocios; *everyone's business is no one's,* asno de muchos, lobos le comen; *What is your business here?* ¿Qué le trae a Vd. por acá?; *it is not my business,* no es cosa mía o no tengo nada que ver con eso; *get about your business,* vaya Vd. a paseo; *to do business for,* trabajar por, negociar por; *business hours,* horas de despacho.

businesslike, *a.* entendido en negocios; práctico, trabajador, sistemático; adaptado a un asunto.

busk [bʌsk], *s.* ballena de corsé.

buskin, *s.* borceguí; coturno; (*fig.*) tragedia.

buskined, *a.* calzado con borceguíes.

buss [bʌs], *s.* beso con estruendo; (*mar.*) bucha pescadora.

bust [bʌst], *s.* busto; pecho de mujer.

bustard, *s.* (*orn.*) avutarda.

bustle, *v.t., v.i.* apresurarse, afanarse, menearse, bullir, hacer ruido. — *s.* bullicio, animación, baraúnda, ruido, bataholas, alboroto; precipitación, prisa; polizón, tontillo.

bustler, *s.* bullebulle.

bustling, *a.* activo, vivo, diligente; afanado; animado, tumultuoso.

busy ['bizi], *a.* ocupado, empleado, activo, diligente, atareado; entremetido; aplicado; bullicioso. — *v.t.* ocupar, emplear; avivar. — *v.i.* ocuparse.

busybody, *s.* entremetido; solícito; oficioso; chismoso; *to be a busybody,* meter la nariz.

but [bʌt], *conj.* pero; sino; sin embargo, no obstante; excepto menos; solamente; más que. — *prep.* sin, excepto. — *adv.* solamente; *I do nothing but work,* no hago más que trabajar; *but little,* poco, un poco; *but few,* muy pocos; *last but one,* penúltimo; *but for,* a no ser por; *but me no buts,* no me pongas peros. — *s.* objeción verbal; antesala, recibidor de una casa.

butcher ['butʃəɹ], *s.* carnicero; hombre sanguinario o cruel; *butcher's meat,* carne para el consumo; *butcher's shop,* carnicería. — *v.t.* matar reses; matar atrozmente; hacer una carnicería, dar muerte cruel.

butcher-bird, *s.* (*orn.*) alcaudón, pegareborda.

butcherliness, *s.* crueldad, inhumanidad.

butcherly, *a.* sanguinario, bárbaro, cruel.

butcher's broom, *s.* (*bot.*) brusco.

butchery, *s.* carnicería; degüello; destrozo, matanza.

butler ['bʌtləɹ], *s.* repostero, sumiller; despensero, mayordomo.

butlerage, *s.* departamento del despensero; antiguo impuesto sobre vinos.

butlery, *s.* despensa.

butment ['bʌtmənt], *s.* contrafuerte; estribo de un arco.

butt [bʌt], *s.* cabo, extremo; empalme plano; terrero; blanco, hito; límite, término, fin; hazmerreír; cabezada, topetada, topetazo; bota; (*arm.*) culata, contrera. — *v.t.* topar, topetar.

butt, butt-end, *s.* pie de árbol; culata de un fusil.

butter ['bʌtəɪ], s. mantequilla; acorneador, topador; *cocoa-butter*, manteca de cacao. — *v.t.* (*fam.*) untar con manteca; adular, lisonjear; doblar las puestas en el juego.

buttercup, s. (*bot.*) ranúnculo, botón de oro.

butter-dish, s. mantequillera.

butterfly, s. mariposa.

butterine, s. manteca artificial.

butteris, s. pujavante.

buttermilk, s. suero de manteca.

butternut, s. nogal blanco.

butterwife, butterwoman, s. mantequera, vendedora de mantequilla.

butterwort, s. (*bot.*) sanícula.

buttery, s. despensa; bodega, botillería. — *a.* mantecoso.

butt-hinge, s. bisagra.

buttock ['bʌtək], **buttocks**, s. trasero, nalgas, posaderas.

button [bʌtn], s. botón, tirador; (*agric.*) capullo; (*arti.*) cascabel; tope de un florete; *I don't care a button*, no (me) importa un bledo. — *v.t.* abotonar. — *v.i.* abotonarse. — *pl.* **buttons**, lacayo, paje.

button-hole, s. ojal, presilla.

button-hole scissors, *s.pl.* tijeras ojaladeras.

button-hook, s. abotonador.

button-maker, s. botonero.

buttress ['bʌtris], s. contrafuerte, estribo, machón, arbotante; (*fig.*) apoyo, sostén. — *v.t.* estribar.

butyric [bju'tirik], *a.* butiroso.

buxom ['bʌksəm], *a.* dócil, amable, obediente; vivo, alegre, jovial, festivo; frescachona juguetona, rolliza, regordeta (mujeres).

buxomly, *adv.* vivamente, jovialmente; obedientemente.

buxomness, s. jovialidad, alegría, buen humor.

buy [bai], *v.t.* (*pret.* y *p.p.* bought) comprar, mercar; adquirir; *to buy in*, comprar por cuenta del dueño; *to buy with ready money*, comprar al contado; *to buy on trust*, comprar al fiado; *to buy up* (*goods*), estancar (géneros), acaparar; *to buy off*, ganar con presentes; *to buy out*, comprar la parte de otro; *to buy a pig in a poke*, comprar un objeto sin conocerlo bien.

buyable, *a.* comprable.

buyer, s. comprador.

buzz [bʌz], s. susurro, soplo, zumbido, murmurio; *buzz saw*, sierra circular. — *v.t.*, *v.i.* zumbar; cuchichear.

buzzard [bʌzəɪd], s. (*orn.*) buharro; modrego, majadero.

buzzer, s. zumbador; murmurador; soplón; chismoso.

by [bai], *prep.* por, a, de, con, en, cerca de, al lado de, junto a, según; *by all means*, cueste lo que cueste; *by bulk*, en grueso, por mayor; *by degrees*, por grados; *by dint of*, a fuerza de; *by day*, de día; *by halves*, a medias; *by hand*, por mensajero; *by post*, por correo; *by land*, por tierra; *by stealth*, a hurtadillas; *by oneself*, solo, a solas; *by water*, por agua; *by no means*, de ningún modo; *by night*, de noche; *by the way*, de paso, entre paréntesis. — *adv.* cerca; *hard by*, aquí cerca, muy cerca; *by and by*, luego, ahora, de aquí a poco; *to put by*, poner aparte, reservar; *to stand by*, sostener, defender, apoyar; (*mar.*) mantenerse cerca de; estar listo, pronto, preparado.

by, bye, s. cosa secundaria; *by the bye*, de paso, entre paréntesis.

by-blow, s. accidente imprevisto.

by-corner, s. esquina retirada.

bygone ['baigɔn], *a.* pasado, transcurrido. — s. lo pasado, lo transcurrido; *let bygones be bygones*, olvidemos lo pasado, o lo pasado pasado.

by-lane, s. sendero, vereda, camino retirado.

by-law, s. reglamento; ley privada o particular.

by-name, s. apodo.

by-path, s. senda descarriada, vereda.

by-place, s. lugar apartado; sitio escusado, retrete.

by-play, s. (*teat.*) juego escénico, escena muda.

by-product, s. producto accesorio o secundario.

byre ['baiəɪ], s. establo, casa de vacas.

by-road, s. camino de travesía.

by-speech, s. digresión.

bystander, s. espectador, asistente. — *pl.* **bystanders**, circunstantes.

by-street, s. callejuela.

by-walk, s. paseo oculto, privado o solitario.

by-way, s. camino desviado.

by-word, s. dicho, adagio, refrán, proverbio; apodo, mote; objeto de burla.

Byzantine [bi'zæntain], *a.* bizantino.

C

C, c [si:], s. tercera letra del alfabeto; (*mús.*) do; esta letra tiene *cinco* sonidos en inglés: como *c* española delante de *a, o, u, l, r, cap, come, cue, clap, crop*; como la *s* castellana, *cessation, cinder*; seguido de *h* suena: (1) como la *ch* española, *chap, chess, chin*; (2) cuando son voces que se derivan del griego o latín, la *ch* suena como *c, k, o que, qui*; *character, christian, chemist*, etc.; (3) en voces derivadas del francés se le da el sonido que tiene en esta lengua, *chaise, machine*, etc.

cab [kæb], s. cabriolé, berlina, cupé; taxi, coche de alquiler; (*f.c.*) casilla del maquinista; *cab-man*, cochero; *cab-stand*, estación de coches; medida hebraica, de capacidad de 1.41 litros.

cabal [kə'bæl], s. cábala, intriga, trama, maquinación. — *v.i.* maquinar, tramar.

cabala, s. cábala de los judíos.

cabalism, s. cabalismo.

cabalist, s. cabalista, *m.*

cabalistic [kəbə'listik], **cabalistical**, *a.* cabalístico.

cabalistically, *adv.* cabalísticamente.

caballer, s. pandillero, maquinador.

caballine, *a.* caballar.

cabaret ['kæbərei], s. cabaret, taberna, restaurant, café con atracciones y baile.

cabbage ['kæbidʒ], s. repollo, col, *f.*, berza; *cabbage-head*, repollo; cogollo de berza; retales etc. que los sastres se apropian; *cabbage-stalk, cabbage-stump*, troncho de col; *savoy cabbage*, berza rizada. — *v.t.* sisar, cercenar, hurtar. — *v.i.* (*agr.*) repollar, acogollarse.

cabby ['kæbi], s. (*fam.*) simón (cochero de punto); taxistea, *m.*

cabin ['kæbin], *s.* cabaña, choza; (*mar.*) cámara, camarote; cuartito; *chief cabin,* cuarto mayor; *fore-cabin,* antecámara; *cabin-boy,* paje de escoba, camarero. — *v.i.* vivir en cabaña o choza, vivir estrechamente. — *v.t.* encerrar en cabaña o choza.

cabinet ['kæbinet], *s.* gabinete, escritorio, bufete; escaparate, vitrina; caja, estuche; (*pol.*) ministerio; *cabinet council,* consejo de ministros; *cabinet maker,* ebanista, *m.*; *cabinet making, cabinet work,* ebanistería. — *a.* ministerial; reservado, secreto.

cable ['keibl], *s.* (*mar.*) cable, maroma, amarra; cable de alambre, cable eléctrico; telégrafo submarino; cablegrama, *m.*; *cable's length,* medida de distancia de 120 brazas. — *v.t.* (*mar.*) proveer de un cable; (*arq.*) hacer junquillos en las estrías de las columnas y pilastras.

cabled, *a.* torcido, hecho cable; (*arq.*) hecho a manera de cable.

cablegram ['keiblgræm], *s.* cablegrama, *m.*

cablet ['keiblət], *s.* (*mar.*) cable pequeño; remolque.

cabling ['keibliŋ], *s.* (*arq.*) junquillos.

cabman ['kæbmən], *s.* calesero, cochero, simón.

caboodle [kə'bu:dl], *s.* (*vulg., E.U.*) muchedumbre, populacho.

caboose [kə'bu:z], *s.* (*mar.*) fogón o cocina a bordo de un barco; (*f.c.*) vagón del conductor.

caboshed [kə'bɔʃt], *a.* (*blas.*) cortado hasta las orejas; sin trazos fisionómicos.

cabotage ['kæbətidʒ], *s.* (*mar.*) cabotaje.

cabriolet [kæbrio'lei], *s.* cabriolé.

caburn ['kæbəɹn], *s.* (*mar.*) cajeta.

ca'canny [kə'kæni], *s.* política de las sociedades obreras de no permitir trabajo excesivo.

cacao, *s.* (*bot.*) cacao.

cachalot ['kæʃəlou], *s.* (*ict.*) cachalote.

cache [kæʃ], *s.* escondite, escondrijo.

cachetic [kə'kektic], **cachetical,** *a.* (*med.*) caquéctico.

cachexy [kə'keksi], *s.* (*med.*) caquexia.

cachinnation [kæki'neiʃən], *s.* carcajada, risotada.

cachou [kæ'ʃu:], *s.* cachú, cato.

cack [kæk](*vulg.*), *v.i.* cagar.

cackle, *v.i.* cacarear, cloquear; (*fig.*) chacharear, picotear; reírse. — *s.* cacareo; cháchara, charla.

cackler, *s.* cacareador; hablador, parlanchín, chismoso.

cackling, *s.* cloqueo; grito del ánade; (*fig.*) cháchara.

cacochymic, cacochymical, *a.* cacoquímico.

cacochymy, *s.* (*med.*) cacoquimia.

cacodemon, *s.* espíritu maligno, pesadilla, persona mala.

cacoethes [kækou'i:θi:z], *s.* costumbre viciosa; malos hábitos; comezón, *f.*, prurito.

cacography [kæ'kɔɡrəfi], *s.* cacografía.

cacoon, *s.* semilla de una planta trepadera de la familia de las leguminosas, y cuyas vainas sirven para la construcción de cajas de rapé, polveras, etc.

cacophonic [kækou'fɔnik], **cacophonical,** *a.* cacofónico.

cacophony [kə'kɔfəni], *s.* cacofonía.

cactus [kæktəs], *s.* (*bot.*) cactus, cacto.

cacumen [kə'kju:mən], *s.* ápice, cumbre.

cacuminate, *v.t.* acabar o terminar en punta o figura piramidal.

cad [kæd], *s.* persona mal educada o gosera; (*ant.*) conductor de ómnibus; mandadero, mozo de cordel; modrego; ayudante, peón.

cadastre [kə'dæstəɹ], *s.* cadastro.

cadaverous [kə'dævərəs], *a.* cadavérico.

cadaverously, *adv.* en estado cadavérico.

cadaverousness, *s.* estado cadavérico.

caddie ['kædi], *s.* muchacho que en el juego de *golf* lleva las mazas; mensajero, recadero.

caddis ['kædis], *s.* jerguilla de lana; trencilla de estambre.

caddish ['kædiʃ], *a.* mal educado, grosero.

caddishness, *s.* grosería.

caddow ['kædou], *s.* (*orn.*) chova.

caddy ['kædi], *s.* lata o cajita para té; [CADDIE].

cade [keid], *s.* animal manso, domesticado; niño mimado, delicado; barril.

cadence ['keidəns], *s.* ritmo, cadencia, compás, modulación. — *v.t.* dar cadencia.

cadency, *s.* cadencia; declinación.

cadent ['keidənt], *a.* (*poét.*) cayente.

cadet [kə'det], *s.* cadete; hermano menor.

cadge [kædʒ], *v.t.* llevar un fardo. — *v.i.* mendigar, dar sablazos, vivir de gorra.

cadger, *s.* placero, revendedor; mendigo, sablista, *m.*, gorrón.

cadi, *s.* cadí.

Cadmean, -ian [kæd'mi:ən], *a.* de Cadmio.

cadmia, *s.* (*quím.*) cadmia.

cadmium ['kædmiːəm], *s.* cadmio.

caduceous, *a.* caduceo.

caducity [kə'dju:siti], *s.* caducidad.

caducous, *a.* caduco, perecedero.

cæcum ['si:kəm], *s.* (*anat.*) intestino ciego.

Cæsarean [si:'zɛəriən], *a.,* cesáreo.

cæsura [si'zjuərə], *s.* (*poét.*) cesura.

cæsural, *a.* que pertence a la cesura.

café ['kæfei], *s.* café, cantina.

caffeic, *a.* sacado del café.

caffein(e) ['kæfiːn], *s.* (*farm.*) cafeína.

caffre, *s.,* *a.* cafre.

caftan ['kæftən], *s.* caftán.

cag [kæg], *s.* (*ant.*) banasta.

cage [keidʒ], *s.* jaula, gayola; cárcel, *f.*, prisión. — *v.t.* enjaular, encerrar en jaula; encarcelar.

cageling ['keidʒliŋ], *s.* pájaro en jaula.

cagmag ['kæɡmæɡ], *s.* carne dura.

caic, caique [ka'i:k], *s.* (*mar.*) caique.

cairn [kɛəɹn], *s.* montón de piedras.

caisson ['keisɔn], *s.* cajón; arcón; (*mil.*) carro de municiones; furgón de artillería; (*mar.*) camello; compuerta de dique; (*arq.*) artesón, casetón.

caitiff ['keitif], *s.* belitre, pícaro despreciable. — *a.* miserable, cobarde, bajo.

caitively ['keitivli], *adv.* cobardemente.

cajole [kə'dʒoul], *v.t.* lisonjear, halagar, adular; engatusar, lagotear, requebrar.

cajoler, *s.* adulador, lisonjeador, zalamero, requebrador.

cajolery, *s.* adulación, lisonja; zalamería, requiebra.

cake [keik], *v.i.* cocer, endurecer; pegarse; coagularse; formar costra. — *v.t.* coagular; hacer una torta, hacer un bollo. — *s.* bollo, pastelillo; pan, pastilla, rollo; tortita.

cake-walk, *s.* (*Am.*) danza de negros.

caking-coal, *s.* (*min.*) hulla grasa.

calabash ['kæləbæʃ], *s.* calabaza curada.

calabash tree, s. calabazo.
Calabrian [kə'læbriən], s., a. calabrés.
caladium [kə'leidiəm], s. (bot.) caladio.
calamiferous [kæləm'ifərəs], a. (bot.) que tiene la forma de caña.
calamine ['kæləmain], s. calamina.
calamint, s. (bot.) calamento.
calamitous [kə'læmitəs], a. calamitoso.
calamitously, adv. calamitosamente.
calamitousness, calamity, s. calamidad.
calamus ['kæləməs], s. (bot.) cálamo, aromático.
calander [kæ'ləndəɹ], s. (ent.) gorgojo.
calandra [kə'lændrə], s. (orn.) calandra.
calapash ['kæləpæʃ], **calapee**, s. carapacho.
calash [kə'læʃ], s. calesa, carretela; capota.
calcar ['kælkəɹ], s. espolón (bot.); horno de reverbero.
calcareous [kæl'kɛəriəs], a. calcáreo, calero, calizo.
calceated ['kælsieitəd], a. calzado.
calceolaria [kælsiə'lɛəriə], s. (bot.) calceolaria.
calcic ['kælsik], a. cálcico.
calciferous [kæl'sifərəs], a. calcáreo, que contiene cal.
calcinable ['kælsinəbl], a. calcinable.
calcinate, v.t. calcinar.
calcination [kælsi'neiʃən], s. calcinación.
calcinatory [kæl'sinətəri], a. calcinatorio.
calcine ['kælsin], v.t. calcinar. — v.i. calcinarse.
calciner, s. hornillo de calcinación.
calcining-furnace, s. horno de calcinación.
calcite, s. (quím.) calcites.
calcium ['kælsi:əm], s. (quím.) calcio.
calcographer [kæl'kɔgrəfəɹ], s. calcógrafo.
calc-spar, s. espato calcáreo.
calculable ['kælkjuləbl], a. calculable.
calculary, a. (med.) calculoso.
calculate, v.t. calcular, contar, computar; adaptar. — v.i. hacer cálculos; fijar por cálculo.
calculated, a. calculado, suputado; dispuesto; preparado, adaptado; premeditado, intencionado. — p.p. [CALCULATE]; well-calculated, muy a propósito.
calculation [kælkju'leiʃən], s. computación, cálculo, cómputo.
calculative, a. que pertenece al cálculo.
calculator, s. calculador.
calculatory, s. calculatorio, que pertenece al cálculo.
calculose, a. (med.) calculoso.
calculous, a. calculoso.
calculus ['kælkjuləs], s. (med.) cálculo; (mat.) cálculo.
caldron ['kɔːldrən], s. caldero, caldera, paila.
Caledonian [kæli'douniən], s., a. caledonio, escocés.
calefacient [kæli'fæsənt], s., a. calefaciente, calentador.
calefaction, s. calefacción, calentamiento.
calefactive, calefactory, a. calefactorio, calentador.
calefactor, s. calefactor, calentador.
calefy ['kælifai], v.t. calentar, caldear.
calendar ['kæləndəɹ], s. calendario, almanaque; lista, tabla; orden del día. — v.t. anotar (un calendario), insertar en el calendario.
calender, s. calandria; derviche. — v.t. dar

calandria; pasar por la calandria; cilindrar, satinar.
calenderer, s. aprensador encargado de pasar las telas por la calandria.
calendering, s. acción de pasar las telas por la calandria.
calends ['kæləndz], s.pl. calendas.
calendula, s. (bot.) caléndula.
calendulin, s. (quím.) calendulina.
calenture, s. calentura, fiebre violenta.
calf [kɑːf], s. (pl. **calves**) becerro, ternero, ternera, cervatillo; piel de becerro; pantorrilla; bobo, mentecato; tonto, imbécil, idiota.
calf-like, a. aternerado, semejante a un ternero.
calfskin, s. becerrillo, becerro o piel de ternero.
caliber, calibre ['kælibəɹ], s. calibre; capacidad, aptitud; especie, f., raza.
calibrate ['kælibreit], v.t. calibrar, graduar.
calibration, s. calibración, graduación.
calice, s. (ant.) cáliz.
calico ['kælikou], s. calicó; zaraza, indiana; percal, cotonía.
calid, a. (ant.) cálido, ardiente.
calidity, s. calor, encendimiento.
caliduct, s. caliducto.
calif, caliph ['keilif], s. califa, m.
califate, caliphate, s. califato, califado.
califship, caliphship, s. califato.
caligation, s. (med.) caligo, perturbación de la vista.
caliginous, a. caliginoso, tenebroso, oscuro.
caliginously, adv. oscuramente, tenebrosamente.
caliginousness, s. oscuridad; estupidez.
calix ['kæliks], s. (bot.) cáliz.
calk [kɔːk], v.t., (mar.) calafatear; (vet.) herrar a ramplón; marcar con tiza, calcar; redondear los bordes de (remache, plancha, etc.) para que ajusten bien. — s. ramplón de herradura.
calker, s. (mar.) calafate.
calkin ['kælkin], s. (vet.) ramplón de herradura.
calking ['kɔːlkiŋ], s. (pint.) calco, calafateo, calafateadura; calking iron, esclopo de calafate.
call [kɔːl], v.t. llamar; apellidar, calificar, nombrar; citar, convocar; apelar, invocar; hacer venir; poner apodos; juntar, congregar; inspirar; proclamar, publicar, pregonar. — v.i. llamar, gritar, dar voces; visitar, ir a ver; pasar; presentarse; to call someone names, poner malos nombres a alguno; to call to mind, hacer memoria, recordar; to call at, detenerse en; to call aloud, gritar, dar voces; to call after, gritar tras; to call again, llamar de nuevo, volver a llamar; to call back, revocar, anular, hacer volver, mandar volver; to call down, hacer bajar; to call for, preguntar por; pedir, reclamar; to call forth, hacer venir, hacer salir; to call in, hacer venir, llamar; volver atrás, introducir; (com.) retirar; to call off, llamar; cancelar, parar, suspender; distraer, apartar, disuadir; to call on, solicitar; reclamar; exhortar, animar; ir a ver; to call out, gritar, vocear; to call someone out, llamar a uno para que salga, hacer salir; to call together, convocar, citar, reunir. — s. llamada; vocación; (fam.) visita; invitación; instancia, llamamiento; pretensión; reclamo, instrumento para llamar a los pájaros; destino, profesión,

empleo; obligación, derecho, autoridad, orden; demanda; inspiración divina; citación, convocatoria; seña, señal, *f.*, aviso; silbo; (*com.*) demanda, pedido de fondos; (*mar.*) pito de contramaestre; *call-bird*, pájaro de reclamar; *call-bell*, campanilla, timbre; *within call*, al alcance de la voz.

caller, *s.* llamador; visita.

calligraphic [kæli'græfik], *a.* caligráfico.

calligraphist [kə'ligrəfist], *s.* calígrafo.

calligraphy, *s.* caligrafía.

calling ['kɔ:liŋ], *s.* profesión, vocación, clase, *f.*, oficio, ejercicio; llamamiento, invitación; votación.

callipers ['kælipəɹz], *s.pl.* compás calibrador.

callisthenic, *a.* gimnástico.

callisthenics, *s.pl.* ejercicios gimnásticos.

callose [kæ'lous], *a.* calloso, endurecido.

callosity [kə'lɔsiti], *s.* callosidad, callo.

callous ['kæləs], *a.* calloso; endurecido, insensible, córneo.

callously, *adv.* insensiblemente, duramente.

callousness, *s.* callosidad, callo; (*fig.*) dureza.

callow ['kælou], *a.* pelado, desplumado; inexperto, joven.

callus ['kæləs], *s.* callo; (*med.*) punto de unión por donde unieron las partes de un hueso roto.

calm [ka:m], *s.* calma, reposo, quietud, sosiego, serenidad, tranquilidad, bonanza. — *a.* quieto, tranquilo, sosegado, sereno; *to grow calm*, calmarse; *dead calm*, (*mar.*) calma chicha. — *v.t.* calmar, tranquilizar, apaciguar, aquietar, aplacar, sosegar. — *v.i.* abonanzarse, calmarse.

calmer, *s.* tranquilizador, apaciguador, sosegador, pacificador; (*med.*) calmante. — *a. compar.* más tranquilo.

calmly, *adv.* sosegadamente, tranquilamente, con calma, con tranquilidad.

calmness, *s.* calma, quietud, reposo, serenidad, tranquilidad, sosiego.

calomel ['kæləmel], *s.* (*med.*) calomelanos.

caloric [kə'lɔrik], *s.* (*fís.*) calórico.

calorifer, *s.* calorífero.

calorific [kælə'rifik], *a.* (*fís.*) calorífico.

calorification [kælərifi'keiʃən], *s.* calorificación.

calorificient [kæləri'fiʃiənt], *a.* calorífico.

calorimeter [kælə'rimətəɹ], *s.* (*fís.*) calorímetro.

calorimetric, *a.* calorimétrico.

calorimetry, *s.* calorimetría.

calorimotor, *s.* (*fís.*) calorimotor.

calory, calorie ['kæləri], *s.* caloría.

calotte [kə'lɔt], *s.* bonete, casquete.

caltha ['kælθə], *s.* (*bot.*) calta, hierba centella.

caltrop ['kæltrəp], *s.* (*bot.*) abrojo; rampojo; (*mil.*) abrojo.

calumba [kə'lʌmbə], *s.* (*bot.*) columbo.

calumet ['kæljumet], *s.* pipa de los indios de América del Norte.

calumniate [kə'lʌmnieit], *v.t., v.i.* calumniar, denigrar.

calumniated, *a.* calumniado.

calumniation [kəlu:mni'eiʃən], *s.* calumnia.

calumniator, *s.* calumniador.

calumniatory, calumnious, *a.* calumnioso, injurioso, difamatorio.

calumniously [kə'lʌmniəsli], *adv.* calumniosamente, injuriosamente.

calumniousness, *s.* calumnia, injuria.

calumny ['kæləmni], *s.* calumnia.

calvary ['kælvəri], *s.* calvario; (*blas.*) cruz montada sobre tres peldaños.

calve [ka:v], *v.i.* parir (la vaca).

Calvinism ['kælvinizm], *s.* calvinismo.

Calvinist, *s.* calvinista, *m.f.*

Calvinistic [kælvi'nistik], **Calvinistical**, *a.* calvinista.

calvish, calfish, *a.* aternerado.

calx [kælks], *s.* (*quím.*) (*pl.* **calxes, calces**) cal, *f.*, yeso.

calycle ['kælikl], **calycul, calyculus**, *s.* (*bot.*) calículo, doble, cáliz.

calyx ['keiliks], (*pl.* **calices, calyxes**), *s.* (*bot.*) cáliz.

cam [kæm], *s.* (*mec.*) álabe, leva, levador.

camber ['kæmbəɹ], *s.* (*mar.*) comba, combadura, alabeo. — *v.t.* combar. — *v.i.* tener comba.

cambered, cambering, *a.* combado, arqueado.

cambial ['kæmbiəl], *a.* que se refiere al giro de letras.

cambist, *s.* (*com.*) banquero; cambista, *m.*

cambistry, *s.* conocimiento del cambio; ciencia de los pesos y medidas.

cambium ['kæmbiəm], *s.* (*bot.*) cambium.

cambrel ['kæmbrəl], *s.* garfio de carnicería.

cambric ['keimbrik], *s.* batista, holán.

came [keim], *p.p.* [COME], listón de plomo usado en los ventanales de iglesias.

camel ['kæməl], *s.* camello; *she-camel*, camella; *camel-driver*, camellero; *camel's hair*, pelo de camello.

camelia [kə'mi:ljə], **camellia**, *s.* (*bot.*) camelia.

camelopard, [kə'meləpa:ɹd], *s.* camello pardal, jirafa.

cameo ['kæmiou], *s.* camafeo.

camera [kæmərə], *s.* cámara obscura; (*anat.*) cavidad; máquina fotográfica.

camisade [kæmi'seid], *s.* (*mil.*) encamisada.

camlet ['kæmlət], *s.* camelote, barragán.

camomile ['kæməmail], *s.* (*bot.*) manzanilla, camomila.

camp [kæmp], *s.* campamento; *camp bedstead*, catre; *camp stool*, catre de tijera; *to pitch a camp*, asentar los reales; *to break up a camp*, levantar el campo, alzar el real. — *v.t.* acampar o alojar un ejército. — *v.i.* acampar.

campaign [kæm'pein], *s.* (*mil.*) campaña. — *v.i.* servir en campaña, salir a campaña.

campaigner, *s.* (*mil.*) veterano.

campaniform [kəm'pænifɔəɹm], *a.* (*bot.*) campaniforme, campanudo.

campanile [kæmpə'ni:li], *s.* linterna, parte superior de una cúpula; campanario de iglesia.

campanology, *s.* campanalogía.

campanula [kəm'pænjulə], *s.* (*bot.*) campánula.

campanulate, *a.* campaniforme.

campeachy [kæm'pi:tʃi], *s.* palo de Campeche.

campestral [kæm'pestəl], **campestrian**, *a.* campesino.

camphine ['kæmfi:n], *s.* espíritu de trementina.

campholic [kæm'fɔlik], *a.* alcanfórico.

camphor ['kæmfəɹ], *s.* alcanfor. — *v.t.* alcanforar.

camphorate, *s.* canforato. — *v.t.* alcanforar. — *a.* alcanforado.

camphor-tree, *s.* alcanforero.

camping ['kæmpiŋ], *a.* campante. — *s.* campamento; (*ant.*) juego del balón.

campion ['kæmpiən], *s.* (*bot.*) colleja.

campshed ['kæmpʃed], *v.t.* reforzar con estacados los bancos de un río para evitar su desgaste.

campus ['kæmpəs], *s.* patio o recinto de colegio.

camwood ['kæmwud], *s.* madera roja del África y Brasil.

can [kæn], *s.* vaso, jarro; lata; portaviandas, *m.*; *oil can,* aceitera; *milk can,* lechero. — *v.t.* conservar en vasos o latas; *canned goods,* conservas alimenticias. — *v.i. def.* (*pret.* **could**) poder, saber. — *v.t.* guardar, conservar, preservar comestibles en latas.

Canaanite ['keinənait], *s.* cananeo.

Canadian [kə'neidiən], *s.*, *a.* canadiense.

canaille ['kænail], *s.* canalla, gentuza.

canal [kə'næl], *s.* canal; acequia; (*arq.*) estría.

canalage, *s.* sistema de canales.

canalization [kænəlai'zeiʃən], *s.* canalización.

canary [kə'nɛəri], *s.* canario; color de canario; vino de Canarias; *canary seed,* alpiste.

canaster [kə'næstər], *s.* clase de tabaco ordinario y basto.

cancel ['kænsəl], *v.t.* cancelar, tachar, borrar; anular, invalidar, limitar, estrechar, poner límites. — *s.* revocar, rescindir; (*impr.*) supresión.

cancellated, *a.* cancelado, borrado; anulado; limitado.

cancellation [kænsə'leiʃən], *s.* canceladura, cancelación, rescisión.

cancer ['kænsər], *s.* (*zool.*) cangrejo; (*med.*) cáncer; (*astr.*) Cáncer.

cancerate, *v.i.* cancerarse, encancerarse.

canceration [kænsə'reiʃən], **cancerousness,** *s.* ulceración cancerosa.

cancerous ['kænsərəs], *a.* canceroso.

cancriform ['kæŋkrifɔ:ɹm], *a.* cancriforme; cancroideo.

cancrine ['kæŋkri:n], *a.* cancriforme.

cancrinite, *s.* cancrinita.

cancrite ['kæŋkrait], *s.* (*zool.*) cancrito.

candelabrum [kændə'leibrəm], *s.* (*pl.* **candelabra**) hachero, blandón; candelabro.

candent ['kændənt], *a.* candente.

Candian ['kændiən], *s.*, *a.* candiota.

candid ['kændid], *a.* cándido, ingenuo, sencillo, íntegro; (*ant.*) blanco; franco.

candidate ['kændideit], *s.* candidato, aspirante, opositor, pretendiente.

candidateship, candidature, *s.* candidatura.

candidly, *adv.* cándidamente, ingenuamente, francamente.

candidness, *s.* candor, candidez.

candied ['kændid], *a.* confitado, garapiñado, almibarado.

candify ['kændifai], *v.t.* cristalizar.

candle ['kændl], *s.* candela, vela, bujía; luz, *f.*

candle-end, *s.* cabo de vela.

candle-holder, *s.* portavela, *m.*

Candlemas, *s.* Candelaria.

candle-snuffers, *s.* despabilador.

candlestick, *s.* candelero, palmatoria.

candle-wick, *s.* pabilo.

candock ['kændɔk], *s.* (*bot.*) lirio de agua.

candor, candour ['kændeɹ], *s.* candor, sinceridad, integridad, sencillez, ingenuidad, franqueza.

candy ['kændi], *v.t.* confitar, almibarar, garapiñar. — *v.i.* confitarse, cristalizarse. — *s.* azúcar candi, cande; (*Am.*) dulce, confite, bonbón.

candytuft, *s.* (*bot.*) carraspique.

cane [kein], *s.* caña o junco de Indias; bastón, báculo; *cane sugar,* azúcar de caña; *sugar cane,* caña de azúcar; *cane (sugar) juice,* zumo de la caña de azúcar. — *v.t.* apalear, dar de palos con un bastón; varear.

canella [kə'nelə], *s.* (*bot.*) canelo, canela.

canescence [kə'nesənt], *s.* blancura.

canescent, *a.* canoso, que blanquea, blanquecino.

canicula [kə'nikjulə], **canicile,** *s.* (*astr.*) canícula, sirio; días caniculares.

canicular, *a.* canicular.

canine ['kænain], *a.* canino, perruno.

caning ['keiniŋ], *s.* paliza, tunda; enrejado de cañas.

canister ['kænistəɹ], *s.* canastillo; lata o caja para té, tabaco, etc.; *canister-shot,* metralla; caja en la que se guardan las hostias antes de ser consagradas.

canker ['kæŋkəɹ], *s.* gangrena, llaga gangrenosa; úlcera; cáncer; corrosión, virulencia. — *v.i.* gangrenarse, corromperse, roerse. — *v.t.* gangrenar, corromper, roer; contaminar.

cankered, *a.* gangrenado, corrompido, virulento.

cankerous, *a.* gangrenoso, canceroso; corrosivo.

cankerworm, *s.* oruga.

cankery, *a.* gangrenado.

cannabis, *s.* cáñamo.

cannel-coal ['kænəl-coul], *s.* hulla grasa.

cannery ['kænəri], *s.* fábrica de conservas.

cannibal ['kænibəl], *s.* caníbal, caribe, antropófago.

cannibalism, *s.* canibalismo.

cannibally, *adv.* cruelmente.

cannikin ['kænikin], *s.* cubo, balde; vaso de metal.

canning ['kæniŋ], *s.* acción de envasar la conserva.

cannon [kænən], *s.* cañón de artillería; cilindro hueco; (en el juego de billar) carambola. — *v.i.* hacer carambolas; chocar violentamente (contra o con).

cannon ball, *s.* bala de cañón.

cannon foundry, *s.* fundición de cañones.

cannon-hole, *s.* (*mar.*) tronera.

cannon-proof, *a.* a prueba de cañón.

cannonade, *s.* cañonazo; cañoneo. — *v.t.* cañonear, acañonear.

cannoneer, cannonier, *s.* cañonero, artillero.

cannoning, *s.* cañonazo.

cannot ['kænət], *contr.* de can y not. [CAN].

cannula ['kænjulə], *s.* (*med.*) cánula, sonda, candelilla.

cannular ['kænjuləɹ], *a.* tubular.

canny ['kæni], *a.* circunspecto, prudente, digno, avisado, cuerdo, sagaz; agradable, garboso.

canoe [kə'nu:], *s.* canoa, piragua.

canon ['kænən], *s.* canon, regla, estatuto, ley, *f.*; canónigo; *canon law,* derecho canónico; (*impr.*) letra gruesa (4 líneas pica).

canoness, *s.f.* canonesa.
canonic [kə'nɔnik], **canonical**, *a.* canónico, canonical.
canonically, *adv.* canónicamente.
canonicalness, *s.* legitimidad canónica.
canonicals, *s.pl.* hábitos eclesiásticos, vestidos clericales.
canonicate, *s.* canonicato.
canonist ['kænənist], *s.* canonista, *m.*, profesor de derecho canónico.
canonistic [kænən'istik], *a.* canónico.
canonization [kænənai'zeiʃən], *s.* canonización.
canonize ['kænənaiz], *v.t.* canonizar.
canonized, *a.* canonizado.
canonry, canonship, *s.* canonjía, canonicato; prebenda.
canopied ['kænəpid], *a.* endoselado.
canopus [kə'noupəs], *s.* (*astr.*) canopea.
canopy ['kænəpi], *s.* dosel, pabellón, palio, baldaquín; bóveda; cielo de cama colgada. — *v.t.* endoselar, cubrir con dosel.
canorous [kə'nɔːrəs], *a.* canoro, claro, armonioso.
cant [kænt], *s.* tono lastimero; afectación de lenguaje; fariseísmo, gazmoñería, hipocresía; jerga, germanía, jerigonza; canto, esquina, chaflán; desplomo, sesgo, inclinación; vaivén. — *a.* fuerte, lozano, vigoroso; ansioso, vehemente; vivo, brioso. — *v.t.* voltear, invertir; ladear, inclinar, poner al sesgo, oblicuar; lanzar, empujar; (*mar.*) volcarse (el buque). — *v.i.* salmodiar; expresarse con afectación, hablar camandulear, con gazmoñería; (*mar.*) virar.
can't [kɑːnt], *contr.* de **can** y **not**. [CAN]
Cantabrian [kə'tæbriən], *s.* cántabro, -bra. — *a.* cantábrico.
Cantabrigian, *s.* estudiante de la Universidad de Cambridge. — *a.* de Cambridge.
cantaloup ['kæntəluːp], *s.* melón de Cantalú.
cantankerous [kæn'tæŋkərəs], *a.* inquieto, revoltoso, pendenciero, quimerista, pronto a hallar faltas.
cantata [kæn'tɑːtə], *s.* (*mús.*) cantata.
canteen [kæn'tiːn], *s.* (*mil.*) cantina; bote de hoja de lata en que los soldados llevan agua o licor.
cantel ['kæntl], **cantle**, *s.* arzón de la silla de montar.
cantel, *s.* [CANTLE].
canter ['kæntəɹ], *s.* medio galope. — *v.i.* andar (el caballo) a paso largo y sentado.
cantharides [kæn'θæridiːz], **cantharis**, *s.* cantáridas.
canthus ['kænθəs], *s.* canto o ángulo del ojo.
canticle ['kæntikl], *s.* cántico.
cantilever ['kæntəliːvəɹ], *s.* (*arq.*) modillón; (*ing.*) puente de contrapeso.
cantillate, *v.t.* canturrear.
cantillation [kænti'leiʃən], *s.* canturreo.
canting ['kæntiŋ], *s.* hipocresía, gazmoñería; lenguaje afectado.
cantingly, *adv.* hipócritamente.
cantle ['kæntl], *v.t.* (*ant.*) cortar en pedazos, desmembrar, dividir. — *s.* (*ant.*) pedazo, trozo, porción, residuo, fragmento; back of borrén, trasero del arzón de silla de montar.
cantlet, *s.* [CANTLE].
canto [kæntou], *s.* canto.
canton ['kæntən], *s.* cantón. — *v.t.* acantonar, acuartelar.

cantonal, *a.* cantonal.
cantonize, *v.t.* acantonar.
cantonment, *s.* acuartelamiento, acontonamiento.
cantor ['kæntəɹ], *s.* chantre.
canula ['kænjulə], *s.* cánula.
canvas ['kænvəs], *s.* cañamazo; (*mar.*) lona, vela, velamen; (*pint.*) telas.
canvass ['kænvəs], *v.t.* examinar, escudriñar; disputar, controvertir. — *v.i.* solicitar votos; ambicionar. — *s.* examen, inspección, investigación, escrutinio, diligencias en las elecciones (para obtener votos).
canvasser, *s.* solicitador; agente electoral.
cany ['keini], *a.* encañado, lleno de cañas, poblado de cañas o juncos.
canyon ['kænjən], **cañon**, *s.* garganta, desfiladero, cañada; barranca, hondanada.
canzonet [kænzə'net], *s.* cantilena, cancioncilla.
caoutchouc ['kautʃuːk], *s.* caucho, gutapercha, goma elástica.
cap [kæp], *s.* gorro, gorra; casquete, birrete, solideo; birreta, capelo; cumbre, *f.*, cima, punto más elevado; (*arq.*) chapitel; (*mar.*) tamboretes; *percussion cap*, (*mil.*) pistón, fulminante, cápsula; *the cap fits*, viene de perilla; *to put on one's thinking cap*, reflexionar; *to set one's cap at*, querer conquistar; *foolscap*, (*papelería*) papel que corresponde al papel de marca o pliego común. — *v.t.* cubrir la cabeza, poner tapa, tocar la cabeza; saludar; dar la última mano, acabar; sobrepujar. — *v.i.* descubrirse, quitarse el gorro.
capability [keipə'biliti], *s.* capacidad, idoneidad, competencia.
capable ['keipəbl], *a.* capaz; idóneo; inteligente, apto, competente, bastante, suficiente.
capableness, *s.* capacidad, idoneidad, competencia.
capacious [kə'peiʃəs], *a.* capaz; amplio, ancho, espacioso, vasto, extenso, grande.
capaciously, *adv.* capazmente, ampliamente; extensivamente.
capaciousness, *s.* capacidad, cabida; extensión, amplitud.
capacitate [kə'pæsəteit], *v.t.* habilitar, hacer capaz; autorizar, dar poder o autoridad.
capacity, *s.* capacidad, cabida; inteligencia, aptitud, suficiencia; poder, facultad; *in the capacity of*, en plan de, en calidad de.
cap-a-pie [kæpə'piː], *adv.* de punta en blanco; de pies a cabeza.
caparison [kə'pærizn], *s.* caparazón, paramento, gualdrapa. — *v.t.* enjaezar, engualdrapar; (*fam.*) vestir soberbiamente.
cape [keip], *s.* cabo, promontorio; capa, esclavina, manteleta; *to double a sail round a cape*, (*mar.*) doblar o montar un cabo.
capelin, *s.* pequeño pez del mar de Newfoundland.
capeline ['kæpəlin], *s.* (*cir.*) capellina.
capella [kə'pelə], *s.* (*astr.*) cabrilla.
capellet, *s.* (*vet.*) esparaván.
caper ['keipəɹ], *s.* cabriola, zapateta, salto, brinco; (*bot.*) alcaparra; travesura. — *v.i.* cabriolar, hacer cabriolas; (*fam.*) saltar, brincar.
caper-bush, *s.* alcaparro.
capercailzie [kæpəɹ'keilji], *s.* becada.
caperer, *s.* danzador, saltador, saltarín.

caper-spurge, s. (bot.) tártago.

capias ['keipiæs], s. (for.) auto ejecutivo, orden de arresto.

capillaceous [kæpi'leiʃəs], a. (bot.) capilaceo, capilar.

capillament [kə'piləmənt], s. (bot.) estambre o hebra de flor; (anat.) fibra.

capillarity [kæpi'læriti], s. (anat.) vaso capilar.

capillary [kə'piləɹi], a. capilar.

capital ['kæpitl], a. capital; fundamental, principal; criminal; magnífico, excelente. — s. capital, metropolí; principal, fondo; (arq.) capitel, chapitel; (gram.) mayúscula; capital punishment, (for.) pena de muerte; capital sentence, (for.) sentencia de muerte.

capitalist, s. capitalista, m.f.

capitalization [kæpitələi'zeiʃən], s. capitalización.

capitalize ['kæpitəlaiz], v.t. capitalizar.

capitally, adv. capitalmente, excelentemente; con pena de muerte.

capitate ['kæpiteit], a. (bot.) capitado.

capitation [kæpi'teiʃən], s. capitación; enca-bezamiento; empadronamiento.

Capitol ['kæpitəl], s. Capitolio.

capitular [kə'pitjuləɹ], s., a. capitular.

capitularly, adv. capitularmente.

capitulary, a. capitular.

capitulate [kə'pitjuleit], v.i. (ant.) dividir en capítulos; (mil.) capitular, rendirse.

capitulation [kəpitju'leiʃən], s. capitulación.

capitulator, s. capitulante.

capon ['keipən], s. capón. — v.t. castrar, capar a un gallo.

caponet ['keipənet], s. caponcillo.

caponiere [keipən'iːəɹ], s. (fort.) caponera.

capot [kə'pou], s. juego de naipes, etc.; capote. — v.t. dar capote.

capote, s. capote; capota.

capped [kæpt], a. cubierto, tocado. — p.p. [CAP].

capper, s. gorrero; soldador de latas de con-serva.

capric ['kæprik], a. (quím.) cáprico.

caprice [kə'priːs], s. capricho, extravagancia, antojo.

capricious [kə'priʃəs], a. caprichoso, extrava-gante, antojadizo.

capriciously, adv. caprichosamente.

capriciousness, s. capricho.

Capricorn ['kæprikɔːɹn], s. (astr.) Capri-cornio.

caprine ['kæprin], **caproic,** a. parecido a una cabra.

capriole ['kæprioul], s. corveta, cabriola, salto de un caballo. — v.i. corvetear, cabriolar.

capsicum ['kæpsikəm], s. (bot.) pimiento, pimienta, pimentero, ají.

capsize ['kæpsaiz], v.t., v.i. (mar.) volcar (el buque); volverse patas arriba.

capstan ['kæpstən], **capstern,** s. cabrestante.

capstone ['kæpstoun], s. (arq.) corona-miento.

capsular ['kæpsjuləɹ], **capsulary,** a. capsular.

capsulate, capsulated, a. contenido en una cápsula.

capsula, capsule, s. (bot.) cápsula.

captain ['kæptən], s. (mil.) capitán; coman-dante, jefe.

captaincy, captainship, s. capitanía; grado y empleo de un capitán.

caption ['kæpʃən], s. (for.) captura, prisión; título, lema, m., rótulo, encabezamiento, epígrafe.

captious, a. capcioso, caviloso, susceptible, quisquilloso.

captiously, adv. capciosamente; falazmente, quisquillosamente.

captiousness, s. cavilosidad, espíritu de con-tradicción.

captivate ['kæptiveit], v.t. cautivar, seducir, fascinar; apresar, hacer prisionero; sub-yugar, someter; (fig.) encantar, seducir.

captivated, a. cautivado, hecho prisionero; (fig.) encantado, seducido.

captivating, a. encantador, seductor, seduc-tivo, atractivo.

captivation, s. captura, encanto, fascinación.

captive [kæptiv], s. cautivo, esclavo; prisio-nero. — a. cautivo. — v.t. cautivar.

captivity [kæp'tiviti], s. cautiverio, cautividad, prisión, esclavitud; fascinación, obsesión.

captor ['kæptəɹ], s. apresador.

capture ['kæptʃəɹ], s. captura; apresamiento; toma, presa, botín; prisión. — v.t. apresar, prender, capturar; (mil.) tomar.

capuchin ['kæpjuʃin], s. capuchino; capucha y capotillo o capuchón; (orn.) paloma co-petuda; (zool.) capuchino, mono de América del Sur.

capucin, s. color anaranjado; (bot.) capuchina.

capulet ['kæpjulet], s. (vet.) espararáu.

car [kaːɹ], s. carro, carreta; vagón; carro triunfal; coche, automóvil; caja de un ascen-sor; dining-car, coche restaurán; sleeping-car, coche camas, coche dormitorio; tramway-car, tranvía, m.; car of a balloon, barquilla.

carabine ['kaːɹəbain], **carbine,** s. carabina.

carabineer [kaːɹəbin'iəɹ], **carabinier,** s. carabinero.

carac ['kæɹək], **carack,** s. (mar.) carraca.

caracal ['kæɹəkl], s. lince de Persia.

caracole ['kæɹəkəl], s. caracol, caracoleo. — v.i. caracolear.

carafe ['kæɹəf], s. garafa.

carambole, s. carambola. — v.i. hacer caram-bolas.

caramel ['kæɹəmel], s. caramelo, azúcar que-mado.

caramelize, v.t. acaramelar.

carapace ['kæɹəpeis], s. concha de la tortuga.

carat ['kæɹət], s. quilate, ley, f., grado, bondad del oro; peso de cuatro granos que sirve para pesar perlas y diamantes.

caravan ['kæɹəvæn], s. caravana; (ant.) caravana, remolque habitación.

caravansary [kæɹə'vænsəɹi], **caravansery,** s. caravanera; posada.

caravel ['kæɹəvel], **carvel,** s. (mar.) carabela.

caraway ['kæɹəwei], s. (bot.) alcaravea; cara-way-seed, carvi.

carbide ['kaːɹbaid], s. (quím.) carburo.

carbine [CARABINE].

carbolic [kaːɹ'bɔlik], s. fenol, fénico.

carbon ['kaːɹbən], s. (quím.) carbono.

carbonaceous [kaːɹbən'eiʃəs], a. carbonoso.

carbonarism, s. carbonarismo.

carbonaro [kaːɹbən'aːɹou], s. carbonario.

carbonate ['kaːɹbəneit], s. (quím.) carbonato. — v.t. carbonatar.

carbonic [kaːɹ'bɔnik], a. carbónico.

carboniferous [kaːɹbən'ifəɹəs], a. carbonífero.

carbonization [kɑːɹbənai'zeiʃən], s. carbonización, carboneo.
carbonize ['kɑːɹbənaiz], v.t. carbonizar.
carbono-hydrous, a. (quím.) hidrocarburado.
carboy ['kɑːɹbɔi], s. damajuana, garrafón, bombona.
carbuncle ['kɑːɹbʌŋkl], s. carbunclo, carbúnculo; (med.) carbunco.
carbuncled, a. engastado con carbunclos; (med.) carbuncoso.
carbuncular [kɑːɹbʌŋkjuləɹ], a. carbuncal.
carburet ['kɑːɹbjuret], s. (quím.) carburo.
carburetted, a. carburado.
carburettor [kɑːɹbə'retəɹ], s. carburador.
carburometer [kɑːɹbə'rɔmətəɹ], s. carburómetro.
carcanet ['kɑːɹkənet], s. (ant.) gargantilla, argolla, collar de perlas o de diamantes.
carcass ['kɑːɹkəs], **carcase**, s. res muerta, o el cuerpo de un animal muerto, caparazón; armazón, f., de una casa; (mar.) armazón o casco de una embarcación; (arti.) carcasa; *carcass butcher*, carnicero por mayor.
carcinoma [kɑːɹsi'noumə], s. (med.) carcinoma, cáncer.
carcinomatous, a. (med.) carcinomatoso, canceroso.
card [kɑːɹd], s. carda; cardencha, almohaza; tarjeta, papeleta; aviso, anuncio; naipe, carta; ficha; cartulina; rosa náutica; *card-case*, tarjetero; *pack of cards*, baraja de naipes; *trump card*, triunfo; *post-card*, tarjeta postal; *visiting-card*, tarjeta de visita; *to speak by the card*, hablar con conocimiento de causa; *card-sharper*, fullero, tramposo. — v.t. cardar, carduzar.
cardamine ['kɑːɹdəmain], s. (bot.) mastuerzo de prado.
cardamom, s. (bot.) cardamomo.
cardass ['kɑːɹdəs], s. carda, cardencha, alanquia.
cardboard ['kɑːɹdbɔəɹd], s. cartón.
carder, s. cardador, carduzador.
cardiac ['kæɹdiæk], a. cardiaco.
cardialgia [kɑːɹdi'ældʒiə], **cardialgy**, s. cardialegia.
cardigan ['kɑːɹdigən], s. chaqueta, camiseta de lana hecha a mano con punto de calceta.
cardinal ['kɑːɹdinəl], s. cardenal; capa de mujer (siglo XVIII). — a. cardinal, fundamental, esencial, principal, primero; purpurado, rojo.
cardinalate, cardinalship, s. cardenalato.
carding ['kɑːɹdiŋ], s. cardadura.
carditis ['kɑːɹ'daitəs], s. (med.) carditis, f.
cardmaker ['kɑːɹdmeikəɹ], s. fabricante de naipes.
cardoon [kɑːɹ'duːn], s. (bot.) cardo silvestre.
care [kɛəɹ], s. cuidado, cautela, vigilancia, atención; solicitud, cuita, inquietud, desasosiego, zozobra, ansiedad; cargo, custodia. — v.i. cuidar, tener cuidado o pena, inquietarse; importar; estimar, hacer caso, apreciar; *to take care of*, guardar, custodiar, tener cuidado de (o con); *care-worn*, devorado de cuidados; *I don't care*, me tiene sin cuidado; *take care of the pence and the pounds will take care of themselves*, cuida tú de los cuartos, que los pesos se cuidan solos.
careen [kə'riːn], v.t. (mar.) carenar; dar de quilla. — v.i. (mar.) dar a la banda, echarse de costado. — s. (mar.) carena.

careenage, s. (mar.) carenaje, carenero.
careening, s. (mar.) carena, carenamiento.
career [kə'riəɹ], s. carrera (armas, letras o ciencias), curso; corrida; profesión. — v.i. correr a todo galope.
careful ['kɛəɹful], a. atento, avisado, solícito, cuidadoso; lleno de cuidados, inquieto, cauteloso, prudente, ansioso; vigilante; diligente; azaroso.
carefully, adv. cuidadosamente, esmeradamente.
carefulness, s. cuidado, cautela, ansiedad; vigilancia, solicitud, diligencia, atención.
careless, a. descuidado, negligente, indiferente, omiso; indolente, perezoso; dejado, flojo; abandonado; desatento, desaplicado; inconsiderado, irreflexivo, alegre, tranquilo, sencillo.
carelessly, adv. descuidadamente, negligentemente, sin esmero.
carelessness, s. descuido, incuria, negligencia, indiferencia, abandono, flojedad, dejadez, desaliño.
caress [kə'res], v.t. acariciar, halagar, mimar. — s. caricia, cariño, halago, mimo.
caressing, a. cariñoso.
caressingly, adv. cariñosamente.
caret ['kærət], s. (impr.) signo de intercalación.
caretaker ['kɛəɹteikəɹ], s. celador, curador, vigilante, guardián, guardiana; portero, portera.
carex ['kɑːreks], s. (bot.) gladio, espadaña, estoque.
cargo ['kɑːɹgou], s. carga, cargamento, cargazón, f., consignación.
carib, caribbee, s. caribe.
caribou ['kæribuː], s. (zool.) caribú, reno norteamericano.
caricature ['kærikətjəɹ], s. caricatura. — v.t. hacer caricaturas, parodiar, ridiculizar.
caricaturist, s. caricaturista, m.f.
caried, a. cariado.
caries ['kɛəriːs], s. (med.) caries, f.
carillon [kə'riljən], s. repique.
carina [kə'riːnə], s. (bot.) carena.
carinate, carinated, a. carenado.
cariosity, cariousness, s. (med.) caries, f.
carious ['kɛəriəs], a. cariado.
cark [kɑːɹk], v.t. (ant.) opresar, causar, molestar, atormentar. — v.i. ser cuidadoso, molestarse.
carl [kɑːɹl], s. patán, rústico, palurdo, grosero.
carline ['kɑːɹlin], **caroline**, s. carlín; (bot.) carlina.
carling ['kɑːɹliŋ], s. (mar.) carlinga.
Carlism ['kɑːɹlizm], s. carlismo.
Carlist ['kɑːɹlist], s. carlista, m.f.
car-load, s. carga de un furgón o de un coche.
Carlovingian, a. carlovingio.
carman ['kɑːɹmən], s. carretero, carretonero.
Carmelite ['kɑːɹməlait], s., a. carmelita, m.f.; tela fina de lana; especie de pera.
carmine ['kɑːɹmin], s. carmín, carmesí.
carnage ['kɑːɹnidʒ], s. carnicería, mortandad, matanza, estrago.
carnal ['kɑːɹnl], s. carnal, sensual, lascivo, lujurioso, brutal.
carnalist, carnalite, s. hombre sensual.
carnality [kɑːɹ'næliti], s. carnalidad, sensualidad, lascivia, lujuria, concupiscencia.

carnalize ['kɑːɹnəlaiz], *v.t.* hacer carnal, corromper, excitar la sensualidad.

carnallite ['kɑːɹnəlait], *s.* (*min.*) hidroclorato de magnesio y potasio, que en forma blanca o rosada se halla en las minas de sal de Prusia y Persia.

carnally, *adv.* carnalmente.

carnation [kɑːɹ'neiʃən], *s.* color de carne; (*pint.*) encarnado, encarnación; (*bot.*) clavel doble.

carneous ['kɑːɹniəs], *a.* carnoso, carnudo.

carnification [kɑːɹnifi'keiʃən], *s.* (*med.*) carnificación.

carnify ['kɑːɹnifai], *v.i.* carnificarse.

carnival ['kɑːɹnivl], *s.* carnaval, carnestolendas.

carnivora [kɑːɹ'nivərə], *s.pl.* (*zool.*) carnívoros.

carnivoracity [kɑːɹnivə'ræsiti], *s.* voracidad carnívora.

carnivorous [kɑːɹ'nivərəs], *a.* carnívoro, carnicero.

carnosity [kɑːɹ'nɔsiti], *s.* carnosidad.

carnous, *a.* carnoso, carnudo.

carob ['kærəb], **carob-bean**, *s.* (*bot.*) algarroba, algarrobo (árbol).

carol ['kærəl], *s.* villancico, canción alegre; gorjeo, trino de las aves. — *v.i.* cantar, celebrar con canciones; gorjear.

Carolinian [kærə'linjən], *s.*, *a.* natural de la Carolina.

carolling, *s.* gorjeo, canto de las aves.

carom ['kærəm], *s.* carambola. — *v.i.* hacer carambola.

carotid [kə'rɔtid], *s.*, *a.* (*anat.*) carótida.

carousal [kə'rauzəl], *s.* festín, orgía; francachela; jarana, gresca.

carouse [kə'rauz], *v.t.*, *v.i.* (*fam.*) jaranear, andar de parranda, correr una juerga; celebrar una orgía; embriagarse. — *s.* jarana, borrachera, francachela.

carouser, *s.* bebedor, jaranero.

carp [kɑːɹp], *s.* (*ict.*) carpa. — *v.i.* interpretar en mala parte; glosar; criticar, censurar, vituperar.

Carpathian [kɑːɹ'peiθjən], *a.* de los Cárpatos.

carpel ['kɑːɹpəl], **carpellum**, *s.* (*bot.*) carpelo.

carpenter ['kɑːɹpəntəɹ], *s.* carpintero, ebanista; (*min.*) ademador.

carpentry, *s.* carpintería; maderaje.

carper, *s.* censurador, criticón, reparón, maldiciente, murmurador.

carpet ['kɑːɹpət], *s.* tapiz, alfombra, tapete; *to be on the carpet*, estar sobre el tapete. — *v.t.* alfombrar, entapizar.

carpet-bag, *s.* talega o saco de viaje, hecho originalmente de alfombra.

carpet-beetle, *s.* antreno.

carpeting, *s.* alfombra, tapete; telas de alfombras.

carpet-layer, *s.* tapicero, alfombrista, *m.f.*

carpet-maker, *s.* alfombrero.

carping ['kɑːɹpiŋ], *a.* capcioso, porfiado, caviloso, reparón. — *s.* efugio, sutileza, censura inmotivada.

carpingly, *adv.* capciosamente; mordazmente.

carpus ['kɑːɹpəs], *s.* (*anat.*) carpo, muñeca.

carrageen [kɑːɹə'giːn], *s.* musgo nutritivo de Irlanda.

carriage ['kæridʒ], *s.* porte, conducción, transporte, acarreo; carruaje, coche, carro; vagón; (*arti.*) cureña de cañón; porte, presencia, continente, aire de una persona; conducta o modo de proceder; carga; cuerpo de una máquina sobre la que funciona el mecanismo (imprenta, torno, taladro, etc.); *carriage free*, franco de porte; *carriage paid*, porte pagado; *carriage and pair*, coche de dos caballos; *carriage builder*, maestro cochero; *to keep one's own carriage*, tener coche particular.

carriageable, *a.* movible; transportable.

carrier ['kæriəɹ], *s.* portador, acarreador, faquín; arriero, carretero; mensajero, mandadero; *carrier pigeon*, paloma mensajera.

carriole ['kɑːɹiol], *s.* carruaje pequeño; (*Canadá*) trineo ornamentado.

carrion ['kæriən], *s.* carroña. — *a.* podrido, mortecino.

carronade [kærə'neid], *s.* (*mil.*) carronada.

carron oil, *s.* mezcla de agua de cal y aceite de linaza para las quemaduras.

carrot ['kærət], *s.* (*bot.*) zanahoria.

carrotiness, *s.* bermejura; color bermejo, pelo color zanahoria.

carroty ['kærəti], *a.* pelirrojo, rubicundo.

carry ['kæri], *v.t.* (*pret.* y *p.p.* **carried**) llevar, conducir, traer; tener consigo; llevar encima; mantener, aguantar, soportar, sostener; conseguir, lograr; importar; incluir, comprender, contener; (*com.*) llevar, transportar, tener surtido de; portear, acarrear, pasar; mover, impulsar, influir, dirigir; tomar, ganar, conquistar; arrebatar o quitar; (*mar.*) arbolar; buscar y traer (como hacen los perros). — *v.i.* alcanzar, llegar, tener alcance; portear (como oficio); *to carry away*, llevarse, quitar, alzar; *to carry arms*, traer armas; cuadrarse; *to carry back*, devolver, restituir; *to carry off*, alzar, robar, llevar, arrastrar; robar; *to carry on*, continuar, ejercer (una profesión); *to carry out*, realizar, llevar a cabo; *to carry over*, transportar, trasladar; *to carry through*, sostener, vencer; *to carry up*, elevar, hacer subir; *to carry all before one*, triunfar, vencer todos los obstáculos; *to carry one's head high*, llevar la cabeza erguida; *to carry into execution*, poner en ejecución; *to carry one's point*, llevar la suya adelante; *to carry forward*, trasportar, pasar a la cuenta; *carried forward* (o *carried over*), pasa al frente o pasa a la vuelta; *to carry the day*, llevarse el día, llevar la victoria, quedar victorioso; *to carry coals to Newcastle*, llevar hierro a Vizcaya.

carrying, *s.* trasporte, transporte.

cart [kɑːɹt], *s.* carro, carromato, carreta, carretón, carruaje; *cartload*, carretada; *cart-rut*, carril; *cart-wheel*, rueda de carro; *to put the cart before the horse*, tomar el rábano por las hojas. — *v.t.* carretear, acarrear. — *v.i.* usar carros.

cartage, *s.* carretaje, conducción, porteo, carreteo, acarreo, acarreamiento.

carte-blanche [kɑːɹt-blɑ̃ʃ], *s.* carta blanca.

cartel ['kɑːɹtəl], *s.* cartel, reglamento; cartel de desafío.

carter ['kɑːɹtəɹ], *s.* carretero, carromatero.

Cartesian [kɑːɹ'tiːsiən], *s.*, *a.* cartesiano.

Cartesianism, *s.* cartesianismo.

cartful ['kɑːɹtful], *s.* carretada.

Carthaginian [kɑːɹθə'dʒiniən], *s.*, *a.* cartaginés.

carthamus [kɑːɹ'θəməs], *s.* (*bot.*) cártamo, azafrán rumí.

Carthusian [kɑːɹˈθjuːzɪən], s., a. cartujo.
cartilage [kɑːɹtilidʒ], s. (anat.) cartílago, ternilla.
cartilaginous [kɑːɹtiˈlædʒinəs], a. cartilaginoso, cartilagíneo.
carting [kɑːɹtiŋ], s. carreteo, acarreo.
cartman, s. carretero.
cartographer [kɑːɹˈtɔgrəfəɹ], s. cartógrafo.
cartographic [kɑːɹtəˈgræfik], **cartographical**, a. cartográfico.
cartographically, adv. con arreglo a la cartografía.
cartography [kɑːɹˈtɔgrəfi], s. cartografía.
cartomancer, s. cartomántico.
cartomancy [kɑːɹtoˈmænsi], s. cartomancia.
carton [kɑːɹtən], s. caja de cartón; tejo blanco en el corazón del blanco de tiro; tiro al blanco.
cartoon, s. cartón, boceto; caricatura.
cartouche [kɑːɹˈtuːʃ], s. cartucho (de balas o metralla); (arq.) cartón.
cartridge [kɑːɹtridʒ], s. cartucho; blank cartridge, cartucho sin bala; cartridge-belt, (o cartridge-box), cartuchera.
cart-rut, s. carril, rodada.
cartulary [kɑːɹtjuləri]. s. cartulario.
cartwright, s. carretero, el que hace carros.
caruncle [kærəŋkl], s. (med.) carúncula.
carve [kɑːɹv], v.t. esculpir; trinchar; cortar, grabar, tallar, entallar, cincelar; hacer plato.
carvel [kɑːɹvəl], s. (mar.) carabela.
carver, s. escultor, grabador, entallador, tallista, m.; cuchillo de trinchar, trinchante, trinchador.
carving, s. escultura, entallado, entalladura, obra de talla; arte de trinchar; acción de trinchar; carving knife, trinchante, cuchillo de trinchar; carving table, trinchero.
caryatid [kæriˈætid], s. cariátide, f.
caryophyllaceous [kæriɔfiˈleiʃəs], a. (bot.) cariofíleo.
cascade [kæsˈkeid], s. cascada, catarata, salto de agua.
case [keis], s. caso, acontecimiento, suceso, asunto, lance, coyuntura; hipótesis, f., suposición; cuestión; estado, condición, situación; (med.) caso; enfermo; contingencia; caja, estuche, vaina, cubierta, funda; (for.) acción, pleito, causa; guardapolvo, caja de reloj; caja de mercancías; (mec.) camisa, chaqueta, forro, manguito; (carp.) bastidor, marco; in case, en (el) caso de que, si acaso; book case, estante de libros; dressing-case, tocador; jewel case, joyelero, cofrecito de joyas; glass case, vitrina, vidriera; needle case, alfiletero; pillow case, funda de almohada; pistol case, pistolera; upper case, (impr.) caja alta (de mayúsculas, versalitas, y signos); lower case, (impr.) caja baja (de minúsculas, números, puntuación y espacios); in any case, de todos modos; to make out one's case, demostrar su tesis; the case in point, el caso en cuestión. — v.t. encajonar, enfundar, cubrir, forrar, encerrar en un estuche; envolver.
caseharden, v.t. acerar, templar el hierro; endurecer.
casehardened, a. acerado, templado; (fig.) endurecido, indiferente.
casein [keiˈsiːn], s. caseína, legúmina, albumina vegetal.

casemate [keismeit], s. (fort.) casamata.
casement [keismənt], s. puerta ventana; (fort.) barbacana; caja, cubierta.
caseous [keisiəs], a. caseoso.
cash [kæʃ], s. dinero contante o de contado, metálico; pago al contado; numerario, efectivo; cajita para guardar el dinero; (com.) caja; petty cash, gastos menores; cash-box, caja, arquilla; cash account, cuenta de caja; cash book, libro de caja; cash down, dinero en mano; a toca teja. — v.t. cambiar, convertir en dinero contante; hacer efectivo (cheque, letra, etc.); descontar.
cashew [kəˈʃuː], s. (bot.) anacardo.
cashier [kəˈʃiəɹ], s. cajero, contador. — v.t. dejar cesante; quitarle a uno de su empleo; (mil.) degradar, desaforar; destituir.
cashiering, s. acción de despedir a un dependiente; destitución; (mil.) degradación.
cashmere [kæʃmiəɹ], s. casimir, cachemira. — a. de cachemira.
cashoo [kəˈʃuː], s. cachunde, f.
casing [keisiŋ], s. carpeta, cubierta; estuche; (anat.) envoltura; (bot.) película de las gramíneas; (arq.) revoque de una pared. — pl. boñiga seca y combustible.
casino [kəˈsiːnou], s. quinta de recreo, casita de campo; casino, círculo.
cask [kɑːsk], s. barril, tonel, pipa; cuba; casco, capacete. — v.t. entonelar, envasar.
casket, s. arquilla, joyelero, cajita para joyas; cofrecito, estuche; (E.U.) ataúd. — v.t. poner en una cajita.
casking, s. acción de meter el vino en los barriles.
Caspian [kæspiən], a. caspio.
casque [kæsk], s. casquete, capacete, almete, casco.
cass [kæs], v.t. (for.) casar, anular.
cassada, cassareep, s. (bot.) cazabe, yuca.
cassation [kəˈseiʃən], s. (for.) casación, anulación.
cassava [kəˈsɑːvə], s. cazabe.
cassia [kæsiə], s. casia.
cassimere [kæsimiəɹ], s. casimir, tela.
cassino, casino [kəˈsiːnou], s. juego de naipes para cuatro jugadores.
cassiterite [kəˈsitərait], s. (min.) casiterita.
cassock [kæsək], s. sotana, balandrán.
cassocked, a. que lleva una sotana.
cassowary [kæsəwəri], s. (orn.) casuario.
cast [kɑːst], v.t. (pret. y p.p. cast) tirar, arrojar, lanzar alguna cosa con la mano; tirar algo por inútil o dañosa; tirar dados, echar suertes; desechar, despedir, soltar; dirigir, volver; vaciar; computar, calcular; (for.) ganar un pleito; modelar; despojar; abortar (hablando de animales); calcular; poner; echar; verter, derramar; negar; adicionar; fundir; empujar; tumbar, derribar, despeñar, dejar caer; mudar (la piel o plumaje); perder (dientes); repartir (papeles de una obra teatral); condenar, imponer una pena. — v.i. idear, maquinar, (agr.) aventar; reflexionar, pensar; amoldarse; hacer un cálculo; combarse, alabearse; perder el color; echar el anzuelo; to cast aside, desechar, dejar de lado, desechar; to cast about, considerar, meditar; to cast anchor, echar (el) ancla; to cast into prison, poner en la cárcel; to cast down, abatir, derribar, echar por

tierra; *to cast lots*, echar a la suerte; *to cast out*, arrojar, echar fuera; *to cast the evil eye*, mirar con malos ojos; *to cast off*, (*mar.*) desamarrar. — *s.* golpe, tiro, echada, lanzamiento, tirada; ojeada; forma, molde; temple; casta; aspecto, formación; fundición; tono, tinte, matiz; distribución de papeles (en los teatros); plancha; *cast-iron*, hierro colado; *cast-off clothes*, ropa vieja; *at one cast*, de un golpe, de una tirada; *to have a cast in one's eye*, bizcar, torcer la vista.

castanea [kəs'teiniə], *s.* (*bot.*) castaño de Indias.

castanets [kæstə'nets], *s.pl.* castañuelas.

castaway ['ka:stəwei], *s.* náufrago; desperdicio, desecho; réprobo, malhechor. — *a.* desechado, abandonado, perdido.

caste [ka:st], *s.* casta, raza.

castellan, *s.* castellano; el alcaide de un castillo.

castellany, castelry, *s.* castellanía.

castellated ['kæstəleited], *a.* encastillado.

caster ['ka:stəɹ], *s.* tirador, echador; calculador; fundidor, vaciador, moldeador; adivino; rodaja, rueda, roldana de mueble; vinagrera; ampolleta.

castigate ['kæstigeit], *v.t.* castigar, corregir.

castigation, *s.* castigo, pena, correción.

castigator, *s.* castigador.

castigatory, *a.* que sirve para castigar.

Castile soap, *s.* jabón de Castilla.

Castilian, *s.*, *a.* castellano.

casting ['ka:stiŋ], *s.* tiro; fundición; moldaje; arreglo, invención, distribución; alabeo; plan, modelo; (*mar.*) echazón, *f.*; *casting vote*, voto decisivo, de calidad.

castle ['ka:sl], *s.* castillo, alcázar, fortaleza; palacio; torre (*f.*) o roque (ajedrez); *to build castles in the air*, ver visiones, o castillos en el aire; *an Englishman's house is his castle*, mientras en mi casa estoy, rey soy. — *v.t.* enrocar (en ajedrez).

castlet, *s.* castillejo.

castling, *s.* (*ant.*) aborto.

castor ['ka:stəɹ], *s.* (*zool.*) castor; sombrero de castor; castóreo; rodaja, roldana.

castoreum, *s.* castóreo.

castorine, *s.* castorine.

castor-oil ['ka:stəɹ-'oil], *s.* aceite de ricino.

castrametation [kæstrəmə'teiʃən], *s.* (*mil.*) castrametación.

castrate ['kæstreit], *v.t.* castrar, capar.

castration [kæs'treiʃən], *s.* castración, capadura.

castrator, *s.* castrador.

castrel ['kæstrəl], *s.* (*orn.*) alfaneque.

casual ['kæsjuəl], *a.* casual, fortuito, accidental.

casually, *adv.* casualmente, fortuitamente.

casualness, *s.* descuido, falta de aplicación, despreocupación.

casualty, *s.* baja, víctima, herido, muerte o desgracia accidental; contingencia, accidente.

casuist ['kæsjuist], *s.* casuista, *m.f.*

casuistic [kæsju'istik], **casuistical**, *a.* casuístico.

casuistically, *adv.* como un casuista.

casuistry [kæsjuistri], *s.* ciencia de los casuistas.

cat [kæt], *s.* gato, gata; (*mar.*) gata; felino; cualquier animal de los que pertenecen a la familia zoológica de que es tipo el gato, como

el león, tigre, leopardo, etc.; *cat's-foot*, (*bot.*) hiedra terrestre; *wild cat*, gato montés; *civet cat*, algalia; *polecat*, veso; *cat's eye*, (*min.*) cimófana; *to make a cat's paw*, echar de manga; *cat o' nine tails*, azote de nueve ramales; *to bell the cat*, poner el cascabel al gato; *to rain cats and dogs*, llover chuzos; *to see which way the cat will jump*, ver qué sesgo toma el asunto; *when the cat's away, the mice will play*, donde no está el dueño, ahí está su duelo.

catacathartic [kætəkə'θa:ɹtik], *s.*, *a.* (*med.*) catártico.

catacausis [kætə'kausis], *s.* (*med.*) catacausis.

catacaustic, *a.* catacáustico.

catacaustics, *s.* catacáustica.

catachresis [kætə'kri:sis], *s.* (*ret.*) catacresis, *f.*

catachrestic, catachrestical, *a.* catacréstico.

cataclysm ['kætəklizm], *s.* cataclismo, inundación, hundimiento, diluvio.

catacombs ['kætəkoums], *s.pl.* catacumbas.

catacoustic [kætə'kaustik], *a.* (*fís.*) catacústico.

catacoustics, *s.* catacústica.

catadioptric [kætədai'ɔptrik], **catadioptrical**, *a.* (*fís.*) catadióptrico.

catafalque ['kætəfælk], *s.* catafalco.

catagmatic, *a.* catagmático.

catalectic [kætə'lektik], *a.* (*ret.*) cataléctico.

catalepsis ['kætəlepsis], **catalepsy**, *s.* (*med.*) catalepsia.

cataleptic, *a.* cataléptico.

catalogue ['kætəlɔg], *s.* catálogo, lista. — *v.t.* poner en catálogo, catalogar.

catalpa [kə'tælpə], *s.* (*bot.*) catalpa.

catalysis [kə'tælisis], *s.* (*quím.*) catálisis, *f.*

catalytic [kætə'litic], *a.* catalítico.

catamenia [kætə'mi:niə], *s.* menstruación, menstruo, regla.

catamount ['kætəmaunt], **catamountain**, *s.* gato montés, gato pardo.

cataphonic [kætə'fɔnik], *a.* catacústico.

cataphonics, *s.* ciencia de los sonidos reflejos.

cataplasm ['kætəplæzm], *s.* cataplasma.

catapult ['kætəpʌlt], *s.* catapulta.

cataract ['kætərækt], *s.* catarata; cascada.

catarrh [kə'ta:ɹ], *s.* catarro, romadizo, resfriado, constipado, fluxión.

catarrhal, catarrhous, *a.* catarral, catarroso.

catastrophe [kə'tæstrɔfi], *s.* catástrofe, *f.*; desenlace.

catbird ['kætbəɹd], *s.* tordo mimo.

cat-boat, *s.* (*mar.*) laúd.

catcall, *s.* silbo, silbido; reclamo.

catch [kætʃ], *v.t.* (*pret.* y *p.p.* **caught**) coger, asir, agarrar, prender, capturar, arrebatar; atrapar; alcanzar, detener, coger al vuelo; sorprender; retener, sujetar, contener; enganchar, engarzar, endentar, engranar; discernir, comprender; tomar, pillar; contagiarse; *to catch at*, tratar de obtener; *to catch cold*, acatarrarse, constiparse, coger un resfriado; *to catch hold of*, agarrarse a, apoderarse de; *to catch up*, coger, alcanzar, empuñar, asir; ponerse al corriente; *to catch it*, (*fam.*) ganarse una reprimenda; *old birds are not caught with chaff*, pájaro viejo no cae en el lazo. — *v.i.* comunicarse, pegarse, propagarse, ser contagioso; enredarse, engancharse; *to be catching*, ser contagioso, pegarse. — *s.* tomadura, cogedura, presa, captura, prisión; embargo, secuestro; (*fam.*) ventaja, provecho; corchete, gancho; pedazo; pesti-

llo; *it's not a great catch,* (*fam.*) no es gran cosa.
catchable, *a.* secuestrable.
catcher, *s.* cogedor, agarrador.
catching, *a.* contagioso, infeccioso. — *s.* captura, presa.
catchpenny, *s.* engañifa.
catchup ['kætʃəp], *s.* salsa picante.
catch-word, *s.* reclamo; (*teat.*) pie; mote, lema, *m.*
catechetic [kætə'ketik], **catechetical,** *a.* catequístico.
catechetics, *s.* catequismo, enseñanza por preguntas y respuestas.
catechetically, *adv.* por preguntas y respuestas.
catechisation [kætəkai'zeiʃən], *s.* catequización.
catechise ['kætəkaiz], *v.t.* catequizar, examinar, preguntar.
catechiser, *s.* catequista, *m.f.*, catequizante.
catechism ['kætəkizm], *s.* catecismo; doctrina.
catechist, *s.* catequista, *m.f.*
catechistic, catechistical, *a.* catequístico.
catechu, *s.* cato, cachunde.
catechumen [kætə'kjuːmən], *s.* catecúmeno.
catechumenical, *a.* catecuménico.
categoric [kætə'gɔrik], **categorical,** *a.* categórico.
categorically, *adv.* categóricamente.
categorise, *v.t.* clasificar, ordenar por categorías.
category, *s.* categoría, clase, *f.*, orden, *m.f.*
catenarian [kætə'nɛəriən], **catenary,** *a.* eslabonado, en forma de cadena.
catenary, *s.* (*geom.*) catenaria.
catenate, *v.t.* eslabonar, encadenar, formar una serie de cadenas.
catenation, *s.* encadenamiento, encadenadura.
cater ['keitər], *s.* cuatro en los naipes, o dados. *v.i.* abastecer, proveer.
caterer, *s.* proveedor, abastecedor, veedor, despensero.
cateress, *s.* proveedora, abastecedora.
caterpillar ['kætəɹpilər], *s.* oruga.
caterwaul ['kætəɹwoːl], *s.* maullido, maullar. — *v.i.* maullar, dar maullidos.
caterwauling, *s.* maullido; batahola.
cates, *s.pl.* golosinas, gollerías.
cat-eyed, *a.* que tiene ojos de gato.
catfish, *s.* (*ict.*) barbo, siluro.
catgut, *s.* cuerda de tripa; merli, tela basta del siglo XVIII.
catharsis [kə'θɑːɹsis], *s.* (*med.*) catarsis, *f.*, purga.
cathartes, *s.* (*orn.*) catarro.
cathartic, cathartical, *s.*, *a.* (*med.*) catártico, purga, purgante, medicina purgante.
cathartically, *adv.* como purgante.
catharticalness, *s.* fuerza catártica, calidad purgante.
cathedra, *s.* cátedra.
cathedral [kə'θiːdrəl], *s.* catedral. — *a.* episcopal.
Catherine wheel ['kæθərin hwiːl], *s.* rueda (de fuegos artificiales); (*arq.*) rosa o ventana circular.
catheter ['kæθətəɹ], *s.* (*cir.*) catéter, algalia, sonda, candelilla.
cathetometer, *s.* catetómetro.
cathetus ['kæθitəs], *s.* (*geom.*) cateto.
cathodal, cathodic, *a.* catódico.
cathode [kæθoud], *s.* cátodo.

cathodegraph, cathodograph, *s.* catodógrafo.
catholic ['kæθəlik], *a.* católico; universal, general; ortodoxo, liberal. — *s.* católico.
catholical [kə'θɔlikl], *a.* católico.
catholicism [kə'θɔlisizm], *s.* catolicismo.
catholicity [kæθə'lisiti], *s.* catolicidad.
catholicize [kə'θɔlisaiz], *v.t.* convertir al catolicismo.
catholicness, *s.* universalidad.
catholicon [kə'θɔlikən], *s.* (*med.*) catolicón, panacea.
cation, *s.* (*elec.*) positivo elemento que se desarrolla en el cátodo en la electrólisis.
catkin ['kætkin], *s.* (*bot.*) candeda, amento.
catlike, *a.* gatesco, gatuno.
catling ['kætliŋ], *s.* (*cir.*) legra, especie de escapelo; cuerdas de tripa; gato pequeño.
catmint, catnip, *s.* (*bot.*) calamento, calaminta.
catopsis, *s.* (*med.*) catopsis.
catoptric, catoptrical, *a.* catóptrico.
catoptrics [kə'tɔptriks], *s.* (*fís.*) catóptrica.
catstail [kætsteil], *s.* (*bot.*) espadaña.
catsup, *s.* salsa picante de setas y tomates.
cattish, *a.* gatuno, gatesco.
cattle ['kætl], *s.* ganado.
cattle-bell, *s.* esquila.
cattle-raising, cattle-ranch, *s.* ganadería.
cattle-rancher, *s.* ganadero.
cattle-shed, *s.* establo.
cattle-show, *s.* exposición de ganados.
cattle-trade, *s.* comercio de ganado.
cattle-truck, *s.* vagón de ganados.
Caucasian [kau'keiziən], *a.* caucásico (raza); caucáseo (cordillera).
caucus ['kɔːkəs], *s.* (*pol.*) junta secreta, conventículo.
caudal ['kɔːdl], *a.* relativo a la cola.
caudate, caudated, *a.* caudato, raboso.
caudicle ['kaudikl], *s.* (*bot.*) apéndice.
caudle ['kɔːdl], *s.* pisto; yema mejida. — *v.t.* componer una bebida confortante.
cauf, *s.* becerro; [CALF].
caught [kɔːt], *pret.* y *p.p.* [CATCH].
caul [kɔːl], *s.* redecilla; fondo de cofia; (*anat.*) membrana.
cauldrife ['kauldrif], *a.* frío, friolento.
cauldron, caldron ['kɔːldrən], *s.* caldero, calderón.
caulescent [kau'lesənt], *a.* (*bot.*) caulescente.
cauliferous [kɔː'lifərəs], *a.* colífero.
cauliflower ['kɔliflauəɹ], *s.* coliflor, *f.*
cauline ['kɔːlain], *a.* caulinario.
caulk [kɔːk], *v.t.* (v. **calk**).
causal ['kɔːzl], *a.* causal. — *s.* conjunción causativa.
causality [kɔː'zæliti], **causation,** *s.* causa, causalidad, principio, origen.
causally ['kɔːzəli], *adv.* de un modo causal.
causative, *a.* causativo, causante.
causatively, *adv.* efectivamente.
cause [kɔːz], *s.* causa, principio, origen; autor; razón, *f.*, pretexto; partido, interés; proceso, litigio; *there's no cause for alarm,* no hay para que asustarse; *without cause,* sin qué ni para qué. — *v.t.* causar, hacer hacer, ocasionar, excitar, producir; mover, compeler, inducir.
causeless, *a.* infundado, injusto, sin razón.
causelessly, *adv.* infundadamente, sin causa.
causelessness, *s.* falta de fundamento, motivo o causa.

causer, *s.* causador, causante, autor.
causeway ['kɔːzwei], **causey**, *s.* arrecife, camino real, terraplén, calzada; acera.
causidical, *a.* causídico.
caustic ['kɔːstik], **caustical**, *a.* cáustico, corrosivo; satírico, picante. — *s.* (*med.*) cáustico; *lunar caustic*, piedra infernal.
caustically, *adv.* mordazmente; de una manera cáustica.
causticity [kaus'tisiti], **causticness**, *s.* causticidad; mordacidad.
cautelous ['kautələs], *a.* cauteloso, cauto; prudente; astuto.
cautelously, *adv.* cautamente, cautelosamente, con cautela.
cauter ['kautəɹ], *s.* cauterio, instrumento para cauterizar.
cauterization [kɔːəriˈzeiʃən], **cauterism**, *s.* cauterización, cauterio.
cauterize ['kɔːtəraiz], *v.t.* cauterizar.
cautery, *s.* cauterio.
caution ['kɔːʃən], *s.* cautela, prevención, precaución, caución, circunspección; prudencia; atención; aviso, amonestación, advertencia. — *v.t.* advertir, prevenir, precaver, avisar, caucionar, amonestar.
cautionary ['kɔːʃənri], *a.* dado en fianzas; admonitor, avisador, preventivo.
cautioner, *s.* fiador, fianza.
cautious ['kɔːʃəs], *a.* cauto, cauteloso, precavido, prudente, avisado, circunspecto, vigilante.
cautiously, *adv.* cautamente, prudentemente.
cautiousness, *s.* cautela, circunspección, vigilancia, previsión, prudencia.
cavalcade [kævəlˈkeid], *s.* cabalgata.
cavalier [kævəˈliəɹ], *s.* caballero; cortejo, galán; jinete. — *a.* caballeresco, marcial; desdeñoso, altivo; desenvuelto, alegre.
cavalierly, *adv.* altivamente; a lo caballero, caballerescamente.
cavalry ['kævəlri], *s.* caballería.
cave [keiv], *s.* cueva, caverna, covacha, guarida, antro, bodega. — *v.i.* hundirse; (*fam.*) ceder, rendirse; *to cave in*, caer en un hoyo.
caveat ['keiviæt], *s.* (*fig.*) aviso, advertencia; (*for.*) intimación al juez para detener un procedimiento; (*E.U.*) aplicación previa para el registro de una patente.
cavern ['kævəɹn], *s.* caverna, antro.
caverned, **cavernous**, *a.* cavernoso.
cavesson, **cavezon**, *s.* cabezón, cabezada; serreta.
caviar, caviare [kæviˈɑːɹ], *s.* cavial, caviar.
cavil ['kævil], *v.i.* cavilar, sutilizar. — *v.t.* contestar; litigar. — *s.* cavilación, evasiva, sofistería, efugio.
caviller, *s.* sofista, *m.f.*, hombre caviloso; enredador, trapacero.
cavilling, *a.* argumentando, cavilando. — *s.* cavilación, cavilosidad, sofistería.
cavillingly, *adv.* cavilosamente.
cavillous, *a.* caviloso, capcioso, puntilloso; disputador.
cavillously, *adv.* deslealmente.
cavillousness, *s.* cavilosidad.
cavity ['kæviti], *s.* cavidad; hondura, hoyo.
caw [kɔː], *v.i.* graznar, grajear.
caw, cawing, *s.* graznido.
cawk [kɔːk], *s.* (*quím.*) sulfato de barita.
cay [kei], *s.* cayo, isleta; escollo.

cayenne pepper [kei'en pepəɹ], *s.* pimentón; pimiento, guindilla.
cayman, *s.* (*zool.*) caimán.
cease [siːs], *v.i.* cesar, dejar de, parar(se); desistir. — *v.t.* parar, suspender, poner fin a.
ceaseless, *a.* incesante, perpetuo, continuo, perenne.
ceaselessly, *adv.* incesantemente, perpetuamente.
ceasing, *s.* cese, cesación, pausa, descanso.
cecity ['sesiti], *s.* ceguedad, ceguera.
cedar ['siːdəɹ], *s.* (*bot.*) cedro.
cedar-like, *a.* semejante al cedro.
cedarn ['siːdəɹn], *a.* cedrino.
cede [siːd], *v.t.* ceder, renunciar, traspasar, transferir.
cedilla [səˈdilə], *s.* cedilla, virgulilla.
cedrate, *s.* (*bot.*) cedro.
cedrine, cedry, *a.* cedrino.
ceil [siːl], *v.t.* cubrir, techar con cielo raso.
ceiling, *s.* techo, cielo raso; (*mar.*) vágara.
celadon ['selədən], *s.* verde claro.
celandine ['seləndain], *s.* (*bot.*) celidonia.
celebrant ['seləbrənt], *s.* celebrante.
celebrate, *v.t.* celebrar, solemnizar; alabar, aplaudir; festejar.
celebrated, *a.* celebrado; célebre, famoso, afamado, renombrado, ilustre.
celebration [seləˈbreiʃən], *s.* celebración, conmemoración, solemnidad; fiesta, festividad, festejo.
celebrator, *s.* celebrador, panegirista, *m.f.*
celebrity [səˈlebriti], *s.* celebridad, fama, renombre.
celeriac [səˈləːɹiæk], *s.* (*bot.*) apio napiforme.
celerity [səˈleriti], *s.* celeridad, ligereza, velocidad, prontitud, rapidez.
celery ['seləri], *s.* (*bot.*) apio.
celestial [səˈlestjəl], *a.* celeste, celestial, célico, divino. — *s.* habitador del cielo; chino; *Celestial Empire*, *s.* China.
celestially, *adv.* celestialmente, divinamente.
celestine, celestite, *s.* (*min.*) celestina.
celiac ['siːliæk], *a.* (*med.*) celíaco.
celibacy, *s.* celibato, soltería.
celibate ['selibeit], *s., a.* celibato, célibe, soltero.
cell [sel], *s.* celda; calabozo; célula, unidad de estructura; nicho, cavidad, alvéolo, celdilla; (*impr.*) cajetín.
cellar, *s.* sótano, cueva, bodega.
cellarage ['seləridʒ], *s.* cueva, sótano; almacenaje *o* gastos de almacenaje en una bodega.
cellarer, cellarist, *s.* cillerero de un monasterio.
cellaret, *s.* frasquera, caja de licores.
cellerer, *s.* despensero.
celliferous [se'lifərəs], *a.* (*bot.*) celulífero.
cello ['tʃelou], *s.* (*mús.*) violoncelo.
cellular ['seljuləɹ], *a.* celular; celulario, celuloso.
cellule, *s.* celdilla, celdita.
celluloid ['seljulɔid], *s.* celuloide.
cellulose ['seljulous], *a.* (*bot.*) celuloso. — *s.* (*quím.*) celulosa.
Celt [kelt], **Kelt**, *s.* celta, *m.f.*; implemento cortante, prehistórico, hecho de piedra o bronce.
Celtiberian, *s.*, *a.* celtibérico, celtíbero.
Celtic, *a.* céltico.
Celticism, *s.* celticismo.

Celtish, *a.* céltico.
cement [sə'ment], *s.* cemento, cimento; mortero, argamasa; (*fig.*) unión, *f.*, enlace, vínculo. — *v.t.* cimentar, pegar, cementar, argamasar, enmasillar, unir con cimento; (*fig.*) asegurar, estrechar, solidar. — *v.i.* unirse, pegarse, hacer liga.
cementation [səmen'teiʃən], *s.* cimentación; ligazón, *f.*, unión, *f.*, pegadura.
cemented, *a.* cimentado.
cementer, *s.* cimentador; vínculo, lazo.
cemetery ['semətri], *s.* cementerio, cimenterio.
cenatory, *a.* de la cena.
Cenobite, *s.* cenobita, *m.f.*
cenobitic, cenobitical, *a.* cenobítico.
cenotaph ['senotæf], *s.* cenotafio.
cense [sens], *v.t.* incensar, perfumar con incenso.
censer, *s.* incensario, brasero, naveta.
censor, *s.* censor, crítico.
censorial [sen'sɔːriəl], **censorian,** *a.* censorio.
censorious, *a.* severo, rígido; crítico, hipercrítico.
censoriously, *adv.* críticamente, severamente.
censoriousness, *s.* inclinación a censurar.
censor-like, *a.* severo, rígido; inclinado a censurar.
censorship ['sensəɹʃip], *s.* censura.
censual, *a.* censual.
censurable ['senʃurəbl], *a.* censurable, digno de censura.
censurableness, *s.* calidad de ser censurable.
censurably, *adv.* censurablemente.
censure ['sensəɹ], *s.* censura, crítica, reprimenda, reprobación, reprensión. — *v.t.* censurar, reprender, culpar, criticar, condenar.
censurer, *s.* censurador, represor, criticador, crítico.
censuring, *a.* censurante.
census ['sensəs], *s.* censo; empadronamiento.
cent [sent], *s.* ciento; (*fam.*) céntimo; (*Am.*) centavo; *per cent,* por ciento.
centage (*ant.*), **percentage,** *s.* tanto por ciento.
centaur ['sentɔːɹ], *s.* centauro.
centaurea, centaury, *s.* (*bot.*) centaura.
centenarian [sentə'nɛəriən], *s.* centenario.
centenary [sen'tenəri], *s.* centenario; centena, centenar; siglo. — *a.* centenario, centenal, secular.
centennial, *a.* centenar, centenario; secular.
centesimal [sen'tesiməl], *a.* (*arit.*) centésimo.
centifolious [senti'fouliəs], *a.* centifolio.
centigrade ['sentigreid], *a.* centígrado.
centigramme, *s.* centigramo.
centilitre, *s.* centilitro.
centime, *s.* céntimo.
centimetre, *s.* centímetro.
centipede, *s.* (*ent.*) ciempiés, escolopendra.
cento, *s.* (*poét.*) centón.
central ['sentrəl], *a.* central, céntrico.
centralism, *s.* centralidad, centralización; centralismo.
centralist, *s.* centralista, *m.f.*
centrality [sen'træliti], *s.* centralidad.
centralization [sentrəlai'zeiʃən], *s.* centralización.
centralize ['sentrəlaiz], *v.t.* centralizar.
centrally, *adv.* centralmente, de una manera central.
centre ['sentəɹ], *s.* centro, medio, foco; origen, núcleo; (*arq.*) cimbra. — *v.t.* centrar, con-

centrar; reunir; centralizar. — *v.i.* colocarse en el centro; terminar; confinar; reunirse.
centric, centrical, *a.* céntrico, central.
centrically, *adv.* centralmente.
centricalness, *s.* situación central.
centricity [sen'trisiti], *s.* estado céntrico.
centrifugal [sen'trifjugəl], *a.* centrífugo.
centripetal [sen'tripətəl], *a.* centrípeto.
centumvir [sen'tʌmvəɹ], *s.* (*pl.* **centumviri**) centunviro.
centumviral, *a.* centunviral.
centumvirate, *s.* centunvirato.
centuple ['sentjupl], *a.* céntuplo, centuplicado.
centuplicate [sen'tuplikət], *v.t.* centuplicar.
centurial [sen'tjuːriəl], *a.* secular, perteneciente a una centuria.
centuriate, *v.t.* dividir por siglos.
centurion [sen'tjuəriən], *s.* centurión.
century ['sentjuri], *s.* siglo, centuria.
cephalalgy [sefə'lældʒi], *s.* (*med.*) cefalalgia.
cephalic, *a.* cefálico. — *s.* medicamento cefálico.
cephalitis [sefə'laitis], *s.* (*med.*) cefalitis, *f.*
cephalomancy, *s.* cefalomancia.
cephalometer, *s.* cefalómetro.
cephalometry, *s.* cefalometría.
Cepheus ['siːfiəs], *s.* (*astr.*) Cefeo.
ceraceous, *a.* ceráceo.
ceramic [sə'ræmik], *a.* cerámico.
ceramics, *s.* cerámica.
cerate ['siːreit], *s.* (*farm.*) cerato.
cerated, *a.* encerado.
ceratrin, *s.* substancia amarga sacada del musgo.
cerbera ['səːɹbərə], *s.* (*bot.*) cerbero.
cere, *v.t.* (*ant.*) encerar, dar con cera.
cereal ['siəriəl], *a.* cereal. — *s.* grano.
cerealia, *s.* cereales.
cerebel, cerebellum [seri'beləm], *s.* cerebelo.
cerebral ['serəbrəl], **cerebrine,** *a.* cerebral.
cerebric, *a.* sacado de la materia cerebral.
cerebrose, *a.* enfermo del cerebro; loco.
cerebrum, *s.* cerebro, celebro; encéfalo.
cerecloth, cerement, *s.* encerado, hule.
ceremonial [seri'mouniəl], *s.*, *pl.* ceremonial; rito externo.
ceremonially, *adv.* con ceremonial.
ceremonious, *a.* ceremonioso, cumplimentero, etiquetero; ceremonial.
ceremoniously, *adv.* ceremoniosamente.
ceremoniousness, *s.* ceremoniosidad; etiqueta.
ceremony ['seriməni], *s.* ceremonia, ceremonial; etiqueta, formalidad; fórmulas exteriores; *without ceremony,* con franqueza, con toda libertad.
cereolite, *s.* (*min.*) mineral ceróideo.
cereous ['siːriəs], *a.* ceroso, de cera.
cerin, *s.* (*quím.*) cerina.
cerite, *s.* (*min.*) cerita.
cerium, *s.* (*min.*) cerio.
ceroon [sə'ruːn], *s.* (*com.*) coracha.
ceroplasty, *s.* ceroplastia.
certain [səːɹtən], *a.* cierto, seguro, evidente, claro, manifiesto, indudable, incontestable; positivo, determinado, fijo; inevitable. — *s.* número o cantidad indefinida; un tal, alguno, cierto.
certainly, *adv.* ciertamente, seguramente, indudablemente, sin duda, sin falla.
certainness, certainty, *s.* certidumbre, certeza; *of a certainty,* a cosa hecha.

certificate [səɹ'tifikət], *s.* certificación, testimonio; certificado; (*com.*) bono, obligación; acta notorial; *birth certificate*, fe (*o* partida) de nacimiento; *baptismal certificate*, fe de bautismo. — *v.t.*, *v.i.* certificar, dar un certificado.

certifier ['səːɹtifaiəɹ], *s.* certificador.

certify, *v.t.* certificar, afirmar, atestiguar.

certitude [sə:ɹtitju:d], *s.* certeza, certidumbre.

cerulean [sə'ruːliən], **ceruleous**, *a.* cerúleo, azul obscuro.

cerumen [sə'ruːmən], *s.* cerumen, cerilla.

cerumineous, *a.* (*med.*) ceruminoso.

ceruse ['siərus], *s.* cerusa, albayalde.

cervical ['sə:ɹvikəl], *a.* (*anat.*) cervical.

cervine ['sə:ɹvain], *a.* cervino, cervuno.

cervus, *s.* (*zool.*) ciervo.

Cesarean [si:'zɛəriən], *a.* (*cir.*) (operación) cesárea, [CÆSAREAN].

cespitose ['si:spitous], *a.* (*bot.*) de césped.

cespitous, *a.* cubierto de césped.

cess [ses], *v.t.* (*ant.*) tasar, amillarar. — *v.i.* (*ant.*) cesar; omitir. — *s.* (*ant.*) tasa, medida, contribución; amillaramiento.

cessation [se'seiʃən], *s.* cesación, discontinuación, cese, paro.

cessibility [sesi'biliti], *s.* facilidad en ceder; inercia.

cessible ['sesibl], *a.* fácil en ceder, inerte; cesible, que se puede ceder.

cession ['seʃən], *s.* cesión, traspaso.

cessionary, *a.* cesionista, cesionario.

cessment ['sesmənt], *s.* trasación, amillaramiento.

cesspool ['sespu:l], *s.* sumidero, foso de letrina.

cestus ['sestəs], *s.* ceñidor de Venus, cinturón, manopla.

cetacea [sə'teisiə], **cetaceans**, *s.* (*hist. nat.*) cetáceos.

cetaceous, *a.* cetáceo.

chad [ʃæd], *s.* (*ict.*) sábalo.

chafe [tʃeif], *v.t.* frotar, estregar; (*ant.*) calentar; enojar, irritar, enfadar. — *v.i.* enfadarse, irritarse, acalorarse, enojarse; estrellarse; raerse; sahornarse; tascar, tascar el freno. — *s.* excoriación; acaloramiento; sahorno.

chafer, *s.* estufilla; escarabajo.

chafery, *s.* fragua, forja.

chaff [tʃɑːf], *s.* ahechadura; zurrón, hollejo; gluma, cascabillo, arista, película; paja menuda; (*vulg.*) befa, burla, zumba, fisga, matraca; *like chaff before the wind*, como las plumas en el viento.

chaffer ['tʃæfəɹ], *v.t.*, *v.i.* regatear, baratear; (*ant.*) comprar, cambiar, traficar. — *s.* regateo; burlador.

chafferer, *s.* regatón, regatero, el que regatea.

chaffering, *s.* regateo.

chaffery, *s.* tráfico.

chaffinch ['tʃæfintʃ], *s.* (*orn.*) pinzón.

chaffless, *a.* mondado; lo que no tiene paja.

chaffy, *a.* pajizo; ligero; sin importancia.

chafing [tʃeifiŋ], *s.* desolladura, escaldadura, fricción; irritación, excoriación, sahorno; agitación, impaciencia.

chagrin [ʃə'grin], *s.* desilusión, mortificación, disgusto, desazón, pena. — *v.t.* mortificar, provocar, enfadar.

chain [tʃein], *s.* cadena, cadenilla; grillete; serie, sucesión; encadenamiento, eslabonamiento; medida de 66 pies o 20·116 metros;

chain-pump, noria; *chain stitch*, punto de cadenilla o cadeneta; *to break one's chains*, sacudir el yugo; *chain-gang*, cadena, o cuerda de presidiarios; *chain plates*, (*mar.*) cadenas de las vigotas; *chain-shot*, (*arti.*) balas enramadas. — *v.t.* encadenar, aherrojar; (*fig.*) esclavizar; unir, juntar, enlazar; *to chain up*, atar con cadenas.

chainless, *a.* desencadenado; suelto, libre de traba.

chainwork, *s.* cadeneta.

chair [tʃeəɹ], *s.* silla; asiento portátil; taburete; cátedra; (*f.c.*) cojinete; sillón; (*fig.*) presidencia; *arm-chair*, silla de brazos, sillón; *bath chair*, silla volante; *easy chair*, silla poltrona; *pivot chair*, silla giratoria; *folding chair*, silla de tijera; *rocking-chair*, mecedora; *sedan chair*, silla de manos; *to take the chair*, presidir; *to be in the chair*, presidir, ocupar la silla presidencial; *to put in the chair*, nombrar presidente.

chairman, *s.* presidente; silletero, sillero.

chairmanship, *s.* función de presidente de una junta, presidencia.

chaise [ʃeiz], *s.* silla volante; calesín; coche de cuatro ruedas; *post chaise*, silla de posta.

chalcedony [kæl'sedəni], *s.* (*min.*) calcedonia.

chalcographer [kæl'kɔgrəfəɹ], *s.* calcógrafo.

chalcography, *s.* calcografía.

Chaldaic [kæl'deiək], *a.* caldaico, caldeo. — *s.* caldeo, lengua caldaica.

Chaldaism, *s.* caldaísmo.

Chaldean [kæl'diːən], *s.*, *a.* caldeo.

chaldron [tʃɔːldrən], *s.* medida para carbón (Newcastle, 53 quintales; E.U. 2,500 libras).

chalet ['ʃælei], *s.* casita de campo, chalet.

chalice ['tʃælis], *s.* cáliz.

chalk [tʃɔːk], *s.* creta, greda, marga; tiza; yeso; clarión; *red chalk*, lápiz rojo; *French chalk*, jaboncillo de sastre, espuma de mar. — *v.t.* engredar, enyesar; marcar, señalar; (*agric.*) margar; *to chalk out*, trazar.

chalkiness, *s.* estado gredoso.

chalky, *a.* gredoso, yesoso.

challenge ['tʃælindʒ], *v.t.* desafiar, retar, provocar; imputar, acusar; recusar; alegar derecho a, exigir, demandar, pretender; (*mil.*) dar el quién vive. — *s.* cartel de desafío; pretensión, demanda; recusación; concurso; (*mil.*) quién vive.

challengeable, *a.* sujeto o expuesto a desafío o acusación; recusable.

challenger, *s.* desafiador, retador, duelista, agresor.

challis ['tʃæləs], *s.* (*com.*) chalí.

chalybeate [kə'libiət], *a.* ferruginoso, calibeado, impregnado con hierro o acero. — *s.* agua ferruginosa.

chalybite ['kælibait], *s.* (*min.*) especie de espato.

chamade [ʃə'mɑːd], *s.* (*mil.*) llamada.

chamber ['tʃeimbəɹ], *s.* cuarto, habitación, cámara; gabinete; sala; (*arti.*) cámara de mina; recámara; *condensing chamber*, condensador; *chamber of commerce*, junta de comercio, cámara de comercio; *chambermaid*, doncella, moza, criada; *chamber-pot*, orinal; *chamber organ*, órgano portátil; *chamber-fellow*, compañero de cuarto; *chamber music*, música de cámara. — *v.t.* encerrar en cámara o aposento.

chambering, *s.* lascivia, libertinaje.

chamberlain, s. chambelán, camarlengo.
chamberlainship, s. oficio de chambelán.
chambrel, s. corvejón (de caballo).
chameleon [kə'miːliən], s. (zool., astr.) camaleón.
chameleonize, v.i. mudar, cambiar de color.
chamfer ['tʃæmfəɹ], v.t. (arq.) achaflanar estriar, acanalar, arrugar. — s. estría, canal; chaflán, bisel, arruga.
chamfrain, s. testera.
chamois ['ʃæmwɑː], s. (zool.) gamuza, ante; piel de ante.
chamomile [kæməmail], s. (bot.) manzanilla, camomila.
champ [tʃæmp], v.t. morder, mascar, mordiscar.
champagne [ʃæm'pein], s. champaña, vino de Champaña.
champaign, s. campiña; (ant.) campo descubierto, campo raso, campo de batalla. — a. abierto, llano.
champer ['tʃæmpəɹ], s. mascador, roedor.
champignon [ʃæm'pinjən], s. (bot.) seta, hongo.
champion [tʃæmpiən], s. campeón, adalid, paladín. — v.t. provocar a duelo (ant.); sostener, defender, proteger.
championess, s. defensora, protectora, campeona; abogada.
championship, s. campeonato.
chance [tʃɑːns], s. fortuna, ventura, suerte, accidente, contingencia, casualidad, azar, suceso, acaso; peligro, riesgo; ocasión, oportunidad, coyuntura; by chance, acaso; por ventura; to take one's chance, aventurarse, correr el riesgo. — pl. (mat.) probabilidades; chance-medley, (for.) homicidio impremeditado en defensa propia. — v.i. acaecer, suceder, acontecer. — a. fortuito, accidental, casual.
chanceful, chancy, a. accidental, fortuito.
chancel ['tʃɑːnsəl], s. santuario; presbiterio, cancel.
chancellor, s. canciller; magistrado; Chancellor of the Exchequer, Ministro de Hacienda.
chancellorship, s. cancillería; función o dignidad de canciller.
chancery ['tʃɑːsəri], s. cancillería, el más alto tribunal de justicia de Inglaterra, después de la Cámara de Lores.
chancre ['ʃænkəɹ], s. (med.) úlcera sifilítica, chancro.
chancrous, a. ulceroso, chancroso.
chandelier [ʃændə'liəɹ], s. araña de luces; candelero, cornucopia.
chandler ['tʃɑːndləɹ], s. cerero, velero; (Am.) pulpería; (Méj.) tienda; corn-chandler, tratante en granos y semillas; ship-chandler, abastecedor de barcos; wax-chandler, cerero; chandler's shop, abacería, lonja, tienda de víveres.
chandlery, s. especería, mercería.
change [tʃeindʒ], v.t. cambiar, alterar, trocar, mudar; transformar, convertir, transmutar. — v.i. variar, mudar; corregirse, transformarse, alterarse; to change hands, cambiar de dueño; to change colour, ruborizarse, palidecer; let us change the subject, doblemos la hoja. — s. cambio, dinero suelto; alteración, variación, variedad, mudanza, transformación, vicisitud; mutación, metamorfosis, f.; substitución, reemplazo, cambiamiento, tro-

camiento, trueque; muda de ropa; (com.) lonja, bolsa; on Change, en la Bolsa; change of the moon, interlunio; change of clothes, muda de ropa; change of life, (med.) la edad crítica.
changeable, a. voluble, variable, inconstante, alterante, mudable, cambiable, cambiante, tornasolado.
changeableness, changeability, s. mutabilidad, instabilidad, alterabilidad, versatilidad, inconstancia, volubilidad.
changeably, adv. inconstantemente, variablemente.
changeful, a. inconstante, variable, variado, veleidoso.
changefully, adv. inconstantemente.
changefulness, s. versatilidad, inconstancia.
changeless, a. inmutable, constante.
changeling ['tʃeindʒliŋ], s. niño sustituido por otro; idiota, m.f., bobo (ant.).
changer, s. cambista, m.f., cambiador; veleta.
changing, a. cambiante, tornasolado. — s. cambio.
channel ['tʃænl], s. canal; acequia; álveo; cauce; (arq.) estría, mediacaña; estuario, estrecho, brazo de mar; conducto, vía; English Channel, canal de la Mancha. — v.t. acanalar, canalizar, establecer canales; surcar; (arq.) estriar; encauzar, conducir.
chant [tʃɑːnt], v.t., v.i. cantar; discantar; celebrar cantando. — s. canto, canto llano; melodía, salmo, sonsonete.
chanter, s. cantor; chantre.
chanticleer ['tʃæntikliəɹ], s. gallo; quiquiriquí; (fam.) despertador.
chantlate [tʃɑːntleit], s. (arq.) alero.
chantress ['tʃɑːntrəs], s.f. cantora, cantatriz, cantante.
chantry, s. capilla.
chaos ['keiəs], s. caos; desorden, confusión.
chaotic [kei'ɔtik], a. caótico.
chap [tʃæp], s. (fam.) mozo, chico, joven, muchacho; grieta, raja, hendidura; mandíbula, quijada; hocico; (coll.) tipo. — v.t. hender, rajar, resquebrajar, agrietar, abrir grietas. — v.i. rajarse, henderse, agrietarse, cuartearse.
chap-book, s. pliego suelto, folleto, novelón vendido por un pacotillero.
chape [tʃeip], s. chapa o charnela de cinturón; contera de espada.
chapel ['tʃæpl], s. capilla, templo, santuario; los cajistas e impresores de una casa comercial, organizados en cuerpo oficial; chapel of ease, capilla sufragánea; chapel master, maestro de capilla; chapel royal, capilla real.
chapeless ['tʃeiples], a. sin chapa o contera.
chapelet ['tʃæplət], s. (equit.) doble estribo; (hidr.) draga de cubos.
chapellany, s. capellanía.
chaperon [ʃæpəroun], s. (ant.) caperuza, capirote; rodrigón; señora que acompaña a una o más señoritas en público. — v.t. acompañar a una señorita.
chapfallen ['tʃæpfɔːlən], a. boquihundido, abatido, desanimado, triste.
chapiter ['tʃæpitəɹ], s. (arq.) capitel.
chaplain ['tʃæplən], s. capellán; limosnero; capellán castrense.
chaplaincy, chaplainship, s. capellanía, cargo de capellán o limosnero.
chaplet ['tʃæplət], s. guirnalda, corona de

flores; rosario; gargantilla, collar; penacho;
(*arquit.*) moldura de cuentas.
chapman, *s.* (*ant.*) comprador; pacotillero,
buhonero.
chappy, *a.* (*fam.*) chico, chiquito, petimetre;
agrietado, rajado.
chaps, *s.pl.* mandíbulas, quijadas del hombre;
hocicos de un animal.
chapter ['tʃæptəɹ], *s.* capítulo, artículo, categoría, lista, serie, *f.*, asunto; (*eccles.*) cabildo;
sucursal de una confraternidad; *chapter-
house*, sala capitular. — *v.t.* corregir en pleno
cabildo; reprender; dividir en capítulos.
chaptrel ['tʃæptrəl], *s.* (*arquit.*) imposta.
char [tʃɑːɹ], *s.* (*ictiol.*) umbra; jornal, trabajo a
jornal; (*fam.*) char, charwoman, criada de
servicio a jornal, mujer de faenas. — *v.t.*
carbonear, carbonizar, reducir a carbón;
(*ant.*) desempeñar una obligación. — *v.i.*
trabajar a jornal, limpiar, fregar (una casa).
charabanc, *s.* carruaje grande u ómnibus con
asientos transversales para excursionistas,
charabán.
character [kærəktəɹ], *s.* carácter, índole, *f.*,
genio, reputación, fama; informe, referencia;
testimonio de conducta; persona, personaje;
calidad; punto de vista; (*teat.*) papel, parte,
f.; marca, señal, representación; descripción,
retrato; *written character*, certificado; *he is
quite a character*, es un verdadero original;
to vindicate one's character, vengar su honor.
— *v.t.* grabar, esculpir; imprimir, señalar;
caracterizar.
characteristic [kærəktə'ristik], *s.* característica, rasgo.
characteristic, characteristical, *a.* característico, típico, propio.
characteristically, *adv.* característicamente.
characteristicalness, *s.* propiedad característica.
characterize ['kærəktəraiz], *v.t.* caracterizar;
esculpir, grabar, señalar.
characterless, *a.* sin carácter.
charade [ʃə'rɑːd], *s.* charada.
charcoal ['tʃɑːkoul], *s.* carbón de leña.
chard [tʃɑːd], *s.* penca del cardo; alcachofa
aporcada.
charge [tʃɑːɹdʒ], *v.t.* cargar, imponer; llenar,
acumular; gravar; comisionar, encargar,
confiar, encomendar, atarear; (*com.*) poner
en cuenta, poner precio, pedir precio; acometer; acusar, denunciar, imputar, censurar;
exhortar, instruir; mandar; conjurar; (*mil.*)
cargar, atacar, acometer. — *v.i.* (*fam.*) pedir
precios altos; atacar; *What do you charge?*
¿Cuánto pide Vd.? *he overcharged me*, me
ha hecho pagar demasiado; *to charge a
battery*, cargar una batería. — *s.* carga, deber,
obligación; precio; gasto, coste, partida,
cláusula; cargo, cuidado; mandato, precepto,
orden; gravamen, imposición, gavela, tributo; comisión; imputación, acusación;
(*mil.*) embestida, ataque, tiro, carga; depósito, encargo, custodia; (*com.*) débito; *to
leave in someone's charge*, dar a uno en
depósito; *to give in charge*, hacer prender;
in charge of, encargado de; *to take charge of*,
encargarse de.
chargeable, *a.* caro, costoso; acusable, imputable; sujeto, obligado.
chargeableness, *s.* coste, gasto.
chargeably, *adv.* costosamente.

charger, *s.* fuente, *f.*, azafate, plato grande;
corcel, caballo de batalla.
charily ['tʃɛərili], *adv.* cautelosamente, con
economía.
chariot ['tʃæriət], *s.* carroza, carro de placer;
carro militar; (siglo XVIII) carruaje ligero,
cupé.
charioteer [tʃæriə'tiəɹ], *s.* cochero, carretero,
auriga, *m.*
charitable ['tʃæritəbl], *a.* caritativo, benéfico,
limosnero, benigno.
charitableness, *s.* caridad.
charitably, *adv.* caritativamente, benéficamente.
charity, *s.* caridad, limosna, beneficencia,
socorro; benevolencia; amor, ternura; una
de las tres virtudes teologales; *charity begins
at home*, la caridad bien ordenada empieza
por uno mismo.
charivari [ʃɑːri'vɑːri], *s.* cencerrada.
charlatan ['ʃɑːɹlətən], *s.* charlatán, curandero,
medicastro.
charlatanic [ʃɑːɹlə'tænik], *a.* empírico, propio
de un charlatán.
charlatanism ['ʃɑːɹlətənizm], *s.* charlatanismo.
charlatanry, *s.* charlatanería, charlatanismo.
Charles's wain, *s.* (*astr.*) osa mayor.
charlock ['tʃɑːɹlək], *s.* (*bot.*) mostaza silvestre.
charlotte, *s.* postre compuesto de fruta, nata
y rebanadas de pan.
charm [tʃɑːɹm], *s.* encanto, embeleso, atractivo, hechizo, gracia; encantamiento, ensalmo, maleficio; amuleto, talismán. — *v.t.*
encantar, hechizar, ensalmar, embelesar,
prendar, arrobar, atraer.
charmer, *s.* encantador, hechicero.
charmful, *a.* lleno de encantos.
charming, *a.* hechicero, delicioso, encantador,
fascinante.
charmingly, *adv.* encantadoramente.
charmingness, *s.* encanto, embeleso, atractivo.
charnel ['tʃɑːɹnəl], *a.* que contiene huesos de
difuntos; *charnel house*, osario, mortuorio.
chart [tʃɑːɹt], *s.* (*mar.*) carta hidrográfica, carta
de navegar, carta de marear, mapa gráfico. —
v.t. poner en la carta, trazar el mapa o el
rumbo.
charter, *s.* cédula, título; carta constitucional;
privilegio exclusivo; escritura auténtica;
(*com.*) fletamento. — *v.t.* estatuir, establecer
por ley; (*mar.*) fletar; (*fam.*) arrendar, alquilar.
chartographer [tʃɑːɹ'tɔgrəfəɹ], *s.* cartógrafo.
chartographic, *a.* cartográfico.
chartography, *s.* cartografía.
charwoman ['tʃɑːɹwumən], *s.* criada provi-
sora.
chary ['tʃɛəri], *a.* cuidadoso, cauteloso; circunspecto; económico, frugal.
chase [tʃeis], *v.t.* cazar; dar caza, perseguir;
cincelar (metales); engastar, montar (piedras
preciosas). — *s.* caza; persecución, seguimiento; cazadero; montería, partida de caza;
(*art.*) calibre de un cañón; (*imp.*) rama;
(*mec.*) ranura, encaje, muesca; *wild goose
chase*, caza infructuosa, caza de ilusiones de
cosas inasequibles.
chaser, *s.* cazador; cincelador; engastador.
chasing, *s.* cinceladura; caza, seguimiento.
chasm [kæzm], *s.* hendidura, rajadura, que-

brada; vacío, hueco; precipicio; ruptura; laguna.

chasseur [ˈʃɑːsəɹ], *s.* (*mil.*) cazador.

chaste [tʃeist], *a.* casto, puro, virtuoso, honesto, castizo, neto.

chastely, *adv.* castamente, púdicamente; correctamente.

chasten, *v.t.* corregir, castigar; reprimir; depurar, limpiar, purificar.

chastener, *s.* castigador, corrector, depurador, limpiador.

chasteness, *s.* castidad, continencia, pureza.

chastening, *s.* castigo, corrección, reprimenda, disciplina.

chaste-tree, *s.* (*bot.*) agnocasto, sauzgatillo.

chastisable [tʃæsˈtaizəbl], *a.* punible, castigable.

chastise [tʃæsˈtaiz], *v.t.* castigar; reprimir, corregir.

chastisement [ˈtʃæstizmənt], *s.* castigo, corrección, punición, pena.

chastiser [tʃæsˈtaizəɹ], *s.* castigador.

chastity [ˈtʃæstiti], *s.* castidad.

chasuble [ˈtʃæzjubl], *s.* casulla.

chat [tʃæt], *v.i.* charlar, parlotear, platicar. — *s.* charla, cháchara, plática, conversación; pájaro de ambos hemisferios, pájaro cantor.

chateau [ˈʃætou], *s.* palacio; hotelito, casa solariega.

chatelaine [ˈʃɑːtələn], *s.* castellana.

chatellany, *s.* castellanía.

chattels [ˈtʃætəls], *s.pl.* bienes muebles, enseres, efectos.

chatter [ˈtʃætəɹ], *v.i.* charlar, parlotear, parlar, cotorrear; rechinar los dientes, dar diente con diente. — *s.* charla, cháchara, parla, garrulería; chirrido.

chatterbox [ˈtʃætəɹbɒks], *s.* charlador, hablador, parlanchín, parlero, cotorra, *f.*; *to be a chatterbox,* tener mucho pico.

chatterer, *s.* charlador, charlante, gárrulo.

chattering, *s.* chirrido de los pájaros; rechino, rechinamiento; locuaz, hablanchín.

chatty, *a.* hablador; (*anglo-ind.*) jarra, olla.

chatwood, *s.* ramojo, leña menuda, astillas de leña.

chauffeur [ˈʃoufəɹ], *s.* chófer.

chaw [tʃɔː], *v.t.* (*fam.*) mascar, masticar. — *s.* (*ant.*) mandíbula; (*fam.*) bocado; *chaw-bacon,* (*fam.*) palurdo, gañán.

cheap [tʃiːp], *a.* barato; de mal gusto, cursi, charro, de pacotilla; (*fig.*) ordinario, vil, barato.

cheapen, *v.t.* regatear; baratear, abaratar, minorar el precio; rebajar o depreciar el valor, posición, o carácter.

cheapener, *s.* regatón.

cheapjack [ˈtʃiːpdʒæk], *s.* vendedor ambulante.

cheaply, *adv.* barato, a precio bajo.

cheapness, *s.* baratura; economía.

cheat [tʃiːt], *v.t.* engañar, defraudar, petardear, entrampar, estafar; trampear, trapacear, enfullar; chasquear. — *s.* trampa, engaño, impostura; timo, petardo; fraude; trampista, petardista, *m.f.*; timador.

cheater, *s.* bribón, tramposo, trampista, *m.f.*, ratero, estafador, timador, petardero, fullero.

cheatery, cheating, *s.* engaño, trampa, fraude, fullería.

check [tʃek], *v.t.* moderar, contener, detener, contrarrestar, parar, refrenar, reprimir, ata-

jar; regañar, reñir; examinar, verificar; dar jaque; sofocar, ahogar; (*com.*) confrontar; (*ferroc.*) facturar. — *v.i.* pararse, detenerse; vacilar; tropezar, chocar; contrariar. — *s.* resistencia, rechazo; restricción, represión, refrenamiento, frenzo; impedimento, obstáculo; contratiempo, derrota, descalabro; (*ferroc.*) billete de equipajes; (*teat.*) billete de salida, contraseña; marca, visto bueno; jaque (en el ajedrez); cuenta (de restaurán); (*com.*) cheque, talón, bono; tela o tejido a cuadros con colores alternando; (*mec.*) retén, freno; reproche; escaque; *to check up,* investigar, examinar, comprobar; *to keep a check on someone,* tener estrechado a uno; vigilar, tener los ojos en uno; *check-book,* libro de cheques, talonario.

checker, *v.t.* taracear, ataracear; diversificar. — *s.* inspector; represor; tablero de ajedrez; *checker-board,* tablero de damas; *checker-work,* obra a cuadros.

checkered, *a.* diversificado, variado; escaqueado, jaquelado; agitado.

checkless, *a.* violento, desenfrenado.

checkmate, *s.* jaque, mate, jaque mate; (*fig.*) derrota. — *v.t.* dar jaque mate; derrotar, deshacer; desconcertar.

checky, *a.* (*blas.*) jaquelado.

cheek [tʃiːk], *s.* mejilla, carrillo, cachete; (*arti.*) gualdera de cureña; (*fam.*) cara dura, descaro, desfachatez, desvergüenza; caja de balanza; (*mec.*) quijada, montante, larguero; banzo, cárcel, *f.*; *to have a lot of cheek,* (*fam.*) tener mucha cara dura, ser informal; *to go cheek by jowl with,* ser camarada de, juntarse con.

cheek-bone, *s.* (*anat.*) juanete, pómulo.

cheeky, *a.* descarado.

cheep [tʃiːp], *v.i.* gorgear, piar, chirriar. — *s.* pío, chirrido.

cheer [tʃiːɹ], *s.* festín, banquete, convite; regocijo, alegría; (*ant.*) aire, ademán, gesto; aplausos, vivas, vítores. — *v.t.* animar, excitar; aplaudir; alegrar. — *v.i.* alegrarse, ponerse alegre; *cheer up!* ¡ánimo!

cheerer, *s.* regocijador, vitoreador.

cheerful, cheery, *a.* alegre, vivo, animado, jovial, placentero.

cheerfully, cheerily, cheerly, *adv.* alegremente, con alegría; con gusto, de buena gana.

cheerfulness, *s.* alegría, jovialidad, buen humor.

cheering, *a.* que alegra, que anima.

cheerless, *a.* triste.

cheese [tʃiːz], *s.* queso, (*ant.*) formaje; *cream cheese,* queso fresco.

cheesecake, *s.* quesadilla.

cheese-curds, *s.* cuajadas.

cheesemonger, *s.* quesero.

cheese-rennet, *s.* cuajaleche.

cheese-vat, *s.* quesera.

cheesy, *a.* caseoso.

cheetah [ˈtʃiːtə], *s.* leopardo indio.

chef [ʃef], *s.* cocinero.

chegoe, *s.* (*entom.*) nigua.

cheirology [kaiˈrɔlədʒi], *s.* quirología.

cheiroptera [kaiˈrɔptərə], *s.* (*zool.*) orden de los mamíferos quirópteros.

chela [ˈkiːlə], *s.* pinza terminal de algunos crustáceos y arácnidos.

cheliform, *a.* queliforme.

chelonian [kiˈlouniən], *a.* quelonio.

chemical ['kemikəl], *a.* químico.
chemically, *adv.* químicamente.
chemicals, *s.pl.* productos químicos.
chemise [ʃə'miːz], *s.* camisa de mujer; (*fort.*) camisa.
chemisette [ʃəmi'set], *s.* camisolín, camiseta de mujer.
chemist ['kemist], *s.* químico; boticario.
chemistry, *s.* química.
chenille [ʃə'niːl], *s.* felpilla.
cheque [tʃek], *s.* (*com.*) cheque, bono, talón.
cherish ['tʃeriʃ], *v.t.* querer, amar; cuidar; apreciar, estimar; favorecer; fomentar, alimentar; acariciar, criar, proteger; abrigar (esperanzas, etc.).
cherisher, *s.* favorecedor, protector.
cherishing, *s.* apoyo, fomento, protección, estima. — *p. pr.* que favorece, que mantiene, que cuida.
cherishingly, *adv.* afectuosamente.
cheroot [ʃə'ruːt], *s.* filipino (cigarro).
cherry [tʃeri], *s.* cereza; madera del cerezo; *cherry tree*, cerezo; *cherry brandy*, cerezas en aguardiente. — *a.* hecho de cereza, hecho de cerezo; de color de cereza.
chert [tʃəːɹt], *s.* (*min.*) horsteno.
cherub ['tʃerəb], *s.* (*pl.* **cherubim**) querubín.
cherubic [tʃə'ruːbik], **cherubical**, *a.* angelical.
chervil [tʃəːɹvil], *s.* (*bot.*) perifollo.
chess [tʃes], *s.* ajedrez.
chess-board, *s.* tablero de ajedrez.
chessel ['tʃesl], *s.* encella.
chessman, *s.* peón, pieza de ajedrez.
chessom, *s.* mantillo.
chest [tʃest], *s.* arca, caja, cofre, cajón; (*anat.*) pecho, tórax; busto; (*com., fig.*) caja, efectivo, capital; *chest of drawers*, cómoda, guardarropa. — *v.t.* guardar, encerrar, meter en una caja.
chested, *a.* de pecho; *narrow-chested*, estrecho de pecho.
chestnut ['tʃestnʌt], *s.* castaña; color de castaña; *chestnut tree*, castaño; *horse chestnut*, castaña de Indias; (*vet.*) callosidad en la cara interior de la pierna de un caballo; (*fam., vulg.*) chiste viejo, pasado de moda. — *a.* castaño; alazán; zaino.
cheval, *s.* apoyo, sostén; caballo, caballete; *cheval-glass*, espejo de vestir.
chevalier [ʃevə'liəɹ], *s.* caballero.
cheverel ['tʃevərəl], *s.* cabritillo; cabritilla (piel). — *a.* de piel de cabrito; suave, flexible.
cheviot, *s.* carnero oriundo de Cheviot (Escocia); paño cheviot.
chevisance, *s.* hazaña.
chevrette, *s.* piel de guante.
chevron ['ʃevrən], *s.* (*blas.*) cheurón, cabrio; (*mil., etc.*) galón, sardineta.
chew [tʃuː], *v.t.* mascar, masticar; (*fig.*) rumiar, meditar, digerir mentalmente. — *s.* pedazo de tabaco o goma para mascar.
chewing, *s.* masticación; meditación.
Chian ['kaiən], *a.* de Quío.
chiaroscuro, *s.* (*pint.*) claroscuro.
chibouk, *s.* chibuca.
chic [ʃiːk], *a.* gentil, elegante, fino, mono. — *s.* chic, elegancia, gentileza, donaire, buen tono.
chic, chica ['tʃiːkə], *s.* especie de color rojo; indio de América del Sur; chica, baile español antecesor del bolero, fandango y cachucha.
chicane [ʃi'kein], *s.* tramoya, trampa, enredo,

cavilación; (*for.*) trampa legal. — *v.t.* embrollar, enredar; criticar sin razón.
chicaner, *s.* sofista, trampista, *m.f.*, enredador.
chicanery, *s.* sofistería, trapacería, embrollo, enredo.
chiches, *s.* (*bot.*) garbanzo.
chick, chicken, *s.* pollo; polluelo, jovencito, niño; *as tender as chicken* (dícese de la cocina), como una leche.
chicken-hearted, *a.* cobarde, medroso.
chicken-pox, *s.* (*med.*) varicela, viruelas locas.
chickling, *a.* pollito, polluelo.
chickpea, *s.* (*bot.*) garbanzo.
chickweed, *s.* (*bot.*) morgelina, pamplina.
chicory, *s.* (*bot.*) achicoria.
chide [tʃaid], *v.t.* (*pret.* **chid**; *p.p.* **chidden**) reprobar, refunfuñar, regañar, increpar. — *v.i.* reñir, regañar, alborotar.
chider, *s.* regañador, regañón.
chiding, *s.* represión, reprimenda, regaño.
chidingly, *adv.* con reprimenda, con reprensión.
chidress, *s.* regañona.
chief [tʃiːf], *s.* jefe, comandante, principal, caudillo, cacique. — *a.* principal, en jefe; primero; grande, superior, mayor; capital; supremo; *chief town*, capital, ciudad principal.
chiefless, *a.* sin jefe.
chiefly, *adv.* principalmente, particularmente, mayormente, sobretodo.
chieftain, *s.* jefe, comandante; capitán, caudillo; cabeza, *m.*
chiffon ['ʃifon], *s.* gasa, soplillo; tejido muy ligero y transparente.
chiffonier, *s.* armario de salón; gabinete, guardarropa; trapero.
chiffre, *s.* (*mús.*) cifra.
chignon, *s.* moño, penca o castaña (aderezo del pelo).
chilblain [tʃilblein], *s.* sabañón.
child [tʃaild], *s.* (*pl.* **children**) niño, niña; hijo, hija; *with child*, encinta, preñada, embarazada.
child-bearing, *s.* parto; *child-bed*, sobreparto.
childe, *s.* doncel, paje.
childhood, *s.* niñez, infancia; niñería, puerilidad.
childish, *a.* infantil, pueril, aniñado, frívolo, trivial; *childish conduct*, niñada, muchachada; *to be childish*, hacer el niño.
childishly, *adv.* puerilmente.
childishness, *s.* puerilidad, niñada.
childless, *a.* sin hijos.
childlike, *a.* pueril, infantil, propio de niño.
children ['tʃildrən], *s.pl.* [CHILD].
chiliad ['kiliəd], *s.* millar, mil años; milenario.
chiliast, *s.* milenario, partidario del milenarismo.
chill [tʃil], *s.* frío; escalofrío, estremecimiento, enfriamiento; resfriado. — *a.* frío, glacial, helado; reservado; desapacible; *to take the chill off*, quitar el frío. — *v.t.* helar, enfriar, resfriar, pasmar; desanimar, desalentar; (*fund.*) templar, endurecer. — *v.i.* escalofriarse.
chilli, *s.* vaina del pimentón secada al sol.
chilliness, *s.* frialdad, sensación del frío; calofrío.
chilling, *a.* resfriador.
chillness, *s.* frío, calofrío.

chilly, *a.* friolento; frío, calofriado. — *adv.* fríamente.

chimæra [kai'miərə], *s.* quimera.

chimb, chime [tʃaim], *s.* jable, gárgol, cabo o remate de barril.

chime, *s.* consonancia de varios instrumentos; juego o repique de campanas, campaneo, repiquete; conformidad, analogía; clave, *f.*; ritmo, armonía. — *v.i.* repicar, repiquetear; sonar con armonía; convenir, concordar. — *v.t.* tañer, tocar con armonía; *to chime in with*, acordarse; *to chime the hour*, dar la hora.

chimer, *s.* campanero; repicador o tañedor de campanas.

chimera, *s.* quimera, monstruo fabuloso; ilusión.

chimere, *s.* sobrepelliz de obispo.

chimerical, *a.* quimérico, imaginario.

chimerically, *adv.* quiméricamente, imaginariamente.

chimney [tʃimni], *s.* chimenea; tubo de lámpara.

chimney-corner, *s.* rincón del fuego.

chimney-piece, *s.* delantero de chimenea.

chimney-pot, *s.* cañón de chimenea.

chimney-sweeper, *s.* deshollinador, limpia-chimeneas.

chimney-top, *s.* tejadillo o sombrerete de chimenea.

chimpanzee [tʃimpæn'zi:], *s.* chimpancé.

chin [tʃin], *s.* barba, barbilla, parte inferior del rostro.

chin-piece, *s.* barbada.

chin-strap, *s.* carrillera, barboquejo.

china ['tʃainə], *s.* china, porcelana, loza.

china-closet, *s.* chinero.

china-man, *s.* mercader de porcelana.

china-ware, *s.* porcelana.

chinchilla [tʃin'tʃilə], *s.* (*zool.*) chinchilla.

chincough ['tʃinkɔf], *s.* (*med.*) coqueluche, tosferina.

chine [tʃain], *s.* espinazo; lomo; solomo. — *v.t.* deslomar.

Chinese [tʃai'ni:z], *a.* chino; chinesco. — *s.* chino; lengua china.

chink [tʃink], *s.* raja, grieta, hendedura, resquebradura, abertura; rajadura; sonido del dinero; (*fam.*) dinero. — *v.i.* henderse, abrirse; sonar, resonar. — *v.t.* hender, rajar; hacer sonar (dinero).

chinky, *a.* hendido, rajado, resquebradizo.

chinned, *a.* barbado.

chinse, *v.t.* (*mar.*) calafatear.

chintz [tʃints], *s.* quimón, zaraza, tela de algodón estampada.

chip [tʃip], *v.t.* desmenuzar, picar; astillar, descantillar. — *v.i.* romperse, quebrarse, abrirse; reventarse, estallar. — *s.* astilla, brizna, viruta; trozo, pedacito; *chip of the old block*, hijo de su padre, de tal palo tal astilla.

chipping, *s.* pedazo, trozo, fragmento; astillón; brizna.

chippy, *a.* abundante en briznas.

chirk [tʃə:k], *s.* petrosílex, horsteno. — *a.* (*E.U., fam.*) jovial, alegre.

chirm, *v.i.* cantar como un pájaro.

chirograph ['kairəgræf], *s.* quirógrafo.

chirographer [kai'rɔgrəfər], *s.* escribano, escribiente.

chirographic [kairə'græfik], **chirographical**, *a.* quirográfico.

chirography [kai'rɔgrəfi], *s.* quirografía.

chirologist [kai'rɔlədʒist], *s.* quirógrafo.

chirology, *s.* quirología.

chiromancer, *s.* quiromántico.

chiromancy, *s.* quiromancia.

chiromanist, chiromantist, *s.* quiromántico.

chiroplast, *s.* quiroplasto.

chiropodist, *s.* pedicuro, callista, *m.f.*

chirosophist, *s.* adivinador.

chirp [tʃə:p], *v.i.* gorjear, chirriar, piar, pipiar. — *s.* chirrido, gorjeo; canto.

chirper, *s.* chirriador, piador, gorjeador, pájaro que gorjea; persona alegre.

chirping, *s.* chirrido, piada.

chirrup ['tʃirəp], *v.t.* animar, excitar; (*fam.*) actuar de claque. — *v.i.* animarse. — *s.* gorjeo, trino.

chisel [tʃizl], *s.* cincel, escoplo, formón; *cold chisel*, escoplo. — *v.t.* escoplear, cincelar, esculpir; (*fam.*) engañar, estafar.

chiselling, *s.* cinceladura; estafa.

chit [tʃit], *s.* chiquillo, chiquilla; tallo, germen, botón, yema; (*ant.*) peca en la cara; hacheta. — *v.i.* brotar. — *v.t.* quitar los brotes.

chit-chat, *s.* charla, cháchara, palique; cuchicheo.

chitterlings ['tʃitəɹliŋz], *s.pl.* (cocina) tripas, asadura, menudos, mondongo; especie de salchicha.

chitty, *a.* pueril, infantil; lleno de retoños; con yemas. — *s.* (*anglo-ind.*) carta o nota, testimonial, referencias de un criado.

chivalric, *a.* caballeresco.

chivalrous ['ʃivəlrəs], *a.* caballeresco, caballeroso.

chivalrously, *adv.* caballerescamente.

chivalry, *s.* caballería, caballerosidad, hidalguía.

chives [tʃaivs], *s.pl.* (*bot.*) cebolleta.

chloral ['klɔərəl], *s.* (*quím.*) cloral.

chlorate ['klɔərət], *s.* clorato.

chloric, *a.* clórico.

chloride, *s.* cloruro.

chloridic, *a.* clorurado.

chlorine ['klɔəri:n], *s.* cloro.

chlorite, *s.* (*min.*) clorita.

chloroform ['klɔrəfɔ:m], *s.* cloroformo. — *v.t.* cloroformizar.

chlorophyll ['klɔəɹəfil], *s.* (*bot.*) clorofila.

chlorosis [klə'rousis], *s.* (*med.*) clorosis, *f.*

chlorotic, *a.* clorótico.

chlorous, *a.* cloroso.

chock [tʃɔk], *s.* calza, cuña, tornapunta; (*mar.*) choque. — *v.i.* cerrar, tapar, llenar (un hueco); *chock full*, colmado, lleno enteramente.

chocolate ['tʃɔkələt], *s.* chocolate.

chocolate-cup, *s.* jícara.

chocolate-pot, *s.* chocolatera.

choice [tʃɔis], *s.* escogimiento, elección, selección, preferencia; cosa elegida; (lo) selecto, más escogido. — *a.* escogido, selecto; exquisito, delicado, excelente; *choice wares*, mercaderías de primera; *Hobson's choice*, o eso o nada, tomarlo o dejarlo.

choiceless, *a.* que no puede escoger; limitado.

choicely, *adv.* escogidamente, primorosamente.

choiceness, *s.* superioridad, excelencia; discernimiento; delicadeza.

choir ['kwaiəɹ], *s.* coro.

choke [tʃouk], *v.t.* ahogar, sofocar, estrangular;

agarrotar; oprimir, suprimir; cerrar, tapar, atascar; embarazar, obstruir. — *v.i.* atragantarse. — *s.* estrangulación; pelusa de alcachofa; *to choke up a pipe*, atascar un tubo; *choke damp*, aire mefítico; *choke full*, colmado, lleno enteramente.

choker, *s.* ahogadero, ahogador, agarrotador; (*fam.*) tapaboca; argumento sin réplica; (*fam.*) corbata, corbatín.

choler ['kɔləɹ], *s.* cólera, bilis, *f.*, . furor, enojo, ira.

cholera ['kɔlərə], *s.* (*med.*) cólera.

choleric, *a.* colérico, bilioso, irascible.

cholericly, *adv.* coléricamente.

cholesterine [kə'lestərin], *s.* colesterina.

choose [tʃuːz], *v.t.* escoger, elegir, optar por; querer, preferir, desear. — *v.i.* tener facultad para elegir; hacer una elección; dar preferencia.

chooser, *s.* escogedor, elector.

choosing, *s.* escogimiento, elección.

chop [tʃɔp], *v.t.* tajar, cortar, separar, picar; desbastar; hender, rajar; trocar, cambiar. — *v.i.* (*ant.*) caer sobre, echarse de repente; dar cortes; interrumpir; (*ant.*) *to chop at*, atrapar con la boca; intentar coger; *to chop off*, tronchar; *to chop about*, virar, girar; *to chop and change*, cambiar con frecuencia, vacilar. — *s.* parte, *f.*, porción; pedazo, trozo; tajada de carne, costilla, chuleta; quijada, mandíbula; grieta, raja; boca; cambio, trueque.

chop-house, *s.* bodegón, figón.

chopper, *s.* hacha, hacheta; cuchilla de carnicero.

chopping, *s.* regateo, tráfico; trueque, cambio; cortadura, tajadura; acción de cortar o tajar; (*mar.*) embate del mar; *chopping-block*, tajadera de cocina; *chopping-knife*, cuchilla tajadera.

choppy, *a.* rajado, hendido, lleno de grietas; picado, agitado (del mar).

chops, *s.pl.* (*fam.*) boca; quijadas.

chopsticks, *s.* palitos chinos (para comer).

choral ['koərəl], *a.* coral.

choralist, *s.* corista, *m.f.*

chorally, *adv.* en coro.

chord [kɔːɹd], *s.* (*mús.*, *geom.*) cuerda; (*mús.*) acorde; (*med.*) cordón. — *v.t.* (*mús.*) encordar. — *v.t.*, *v.i.* templar, armonizar.

chorea [kə'riːə], *s.* (*med.*) corea (baile de San Vito).

choreographic, *a.* coreográfico.

choreography [kɔri'ɔɡrəfi], *s.* coreografía.

choreus [kə'riːəs], **choree,** *s.* coreo.

choriambic [kɔri'æmbik], *s.* coriambo. — *a.* coriámbico.

chorion ['kɔːriən], *s.* (*anat.*) corión.

chorist, chorister, *s.* corista, *m.f.*

chorographer [kɔ'rɔɡrəfəɹ], *s.* corógrafo.

chorographical [kɔrə'ɡræfikəl], *a.* corográfico.

chorography, *s.* corografía.

choroid ['koərɔid], *s.*, *a.* (*anat.*) coroideo.

chorus [koərəs], *s.* coro; grupo, coral; estribillo, estrambote; *to sing in chorus*, contar en coro. — *v.t.*, *v.i.* decir al unísono.

chose [tʃous], *s.* (*for.*) propiedad, bienes, cosa adquirida.

chose, chosen, *pret.*, *p.p.* [CHOOSE].

chough [tʃʌf], *s.* (*ornit.*) chova.

chouse, *v.t.* (*fam.*) engañar, estafar. — *s.* (*vulg.*) tonto, bobalicón; fraude, estafa, engaño; bribón, estafador.

chow [tʃau], *s.* variedad de perro de China.

chowder ['tʃaudəɹ], *s.* (*E.U.*) sopa de pescado; mezcla, potaje.

chrestomathy [kres'tɔməθi], *s.* crestomatía.

chrism [krizm], *s.* crisma, *m.f.*

chrismal, *a.* que se refiere a la crisma.

chrismatory ['krizmətəri], *s.* crismera.

chrisom ['krisəm], *s.* capillo de cristianar; ropaje de bautismo.

Christ [kraist], *s.* Cristo, Jesucristo.

christen, *v.t.* bautizar, cristianar.

Christendom, *s.* cristiandad, cristianismo.

christening, *s.* bautismo, bautizo. — *a.* bautismal.

Christian ['kristjən], *s.*, *a.* cristiano; *Christian name*, nombre de bautismo, nombre de pila.

Christianism, Christianity, *s.* cristianismo.

Christianize, *v.t.* cristianizar, cristianar.

Christianlike, *a.* propio de cristiano.

Christianly, *adv.* cristianamente.

Christless, *a.* impío, herético.

Christmas ['krisməs], *s.* Navidad, Natividad; pascuas de Navidad. — *a.* de Navidad; *Christmas carol*, villancico, cántico de Navidad; *Christmas box*, aguinaldo o regalo de Navidad; *Christmas eve*, Nochebuena, *f.*, víspera de Navidad; *Christmas tree*, árbol de Navidad; *Merry Christmas!* ¡Felices Pascuas!

chromate ['kroumət], *s.* (*quím.*) cromato, sal del ácido crómico.

chromatic [kro'mætik], *s.*, *a.* cromático.

chromatics, *s.* cromática.

chrome [kroum], **chromium,** *s.* cromo; *chromium-plated*, cromado.

chromic, *a.* crómico.

chromocollography ['kroumou-kə'lɔɡrəfi], *s.* procedimiento para imprimir cromolitografías.

chromolithography, *s.* cromolitografía.

chromophotography, *s.* cromofotografía.

chromophotographic, *a.* cromofotográfico.

chromoptometer, *s.* cromoptómetro.

chromoxylography, *s.* cromoxilografía.

chromous, *a.* cromoso.

chrompher, *s.* instrumento para remitir señales de tiempo a distancia por medio de la electricidad.

chronic ['krɔnik], **chronical,** *a.* crónico, inveterado.

chronicle ['krɔnikl], *s.* crónica. — *v.t.* formar (*o* escribir) una crónica.

chronicler, *s.* cronista, *m.f.*, historiador.

chronique, *s.* crónica, anales.

chronogram, *s.* cronograma, *m.*

chronograph ['krɔnəgræf], *s.* cronógrafo.

chronographer, *s.* cronologista, *m.f.*

chronologer [krə'nɔlədʒəɹ], **chronologist,** *s.* cronologista, *m.f.*, cronólogo.

chronologic [krɔnə'lɔdʒik], **chronological,** *a.* cronológico.

chronologically, *adv.* cronológicamente.

chronology [krə'nɔlədʒi], *s.* cronología.

chronometer [krə'nɔmətəɹ], *s.* cronómetro.

chronometric [krɔno'metrik], **chronometrical,** *a.* cronométrico.

chronometry, *s.* cronometría.

chrysalis ['krisəlis], *s.* (*pl.* **chrysalides**) (*hist. nat.*) crisálida.

chrysanthemum [kri'sænθəməm], *s.* (*bot.*) crisantemo.

chrysoberyl [krisou′berəl], *s.* (*min.*) crisoberilo.

chrysolite [′krisəlait], *s.* (*min.*) crisólito.

chrysoprase, *s.* (*min.*) crisoprasa, crisopracio.

chub [tʃʌb], *s.* (*ictiol.*) coto.

chubby, *a.* gordo, regordete, rechoncho; *chubby-faced*, *chubby-cheeked*, cariancho, mofletudo.

chuck [tʃʌk], *v.i.* cloquear, cacarear. — *v.t.* cloquear; (*fam.*) echar, tirar; arrojar; hacer la mamola; dar una sobarbada a. — *s.* cloqueo, golpe seco; mamola; echada; *chuck-farthing*, hoyuelo; (*mec.*) mandril, mangote, plato de torno; cuña, calzo.

chuckle [tʃʌkl], *v.t.*, *v.i.* reír entre dientes; reír o sonreír de satisfacción; cloquear. — *s.* risa ahogada, risita; cloqueo.

chuckle-head, *s.* tonto, cabezota; cabeza de chorlito.

chuckling, *s.* risa ahogada.

chuff [tʃʌf], *s.*, *a.* patán, rústico, áspero, gruñón.

chuffily, *adv.* groseramente.

chuffiness, *s.* grosería, rusticidad.

chuffy, *a.* rechoncho, gordote, grosero, desatento.

chum [tʃʌm], *s.* (*fam.*) compinche, compañero, camarada, condiscípulo, amigo íntimo. — *v.i.* (*fam.*) ser camarada.

chump [tʃʌmp], *s.* tajo, tronco, tarugo, zoquete; lomo de carnero; animalote; majadero, tonto.

chunk, *s.* pedazo grueso de algo; persona o animal rechoncha.

chunky, *a.* corto, grueso, rechoncho.

church [tʃəːrtʃ], *s.* iglesia; templo, edificio consagrado al culto religioso; el clero; *Church of England*, iglesia anglicana; *church-music*, música sagrada; *to go to church*, ir a misa. — *v.t.* purificar, llevar a la iglesia.

churchdom, *s.* autoridad eclesiástica.

churching, *s.* misa de parida, misa de purificación.

churchman, *s.* eclesiástico, sacerdote; miembro de alguna iglesia.

churchwarden, *s.* capiller, fabriquero u obrero de la junta de obras de una iglesia.

churchyard, *s.* cementerio de parroquia.

churl [tʃəːrl], *s.* patán, paleto, palurdo, payo, rústico; avaro.

churlish, *a.* grosero, rudo, rústico, agreste; ruin, escaso.

churlishly, *adv.* rudamente, brutalmente.

churlishness, *s.* rusticidad, rudeza, descortesía.

churly, *a.* arrebatado, brutal.

churn [tʃəːrn], *s.* mantequera; *churn-staff*, batidor. — *v.t.* mazar, batir (manteca o leche); agitar, revolver, menear.

churning, *s.* batido, mazado (de la leche).

churn-owl [′tʃəːrnaul], *s.* (*ornit.*) chotacabras.

churn-staff, *s.* batidera.

chylaceous [kai′leiʃəs], *a.* quilar, quiloso.

chyle [kail], *s.* (*fisiol.*) quilo.

chylifaction [kili′fækʃən], *s.* quilificación.

chylifactive, *a.* quilificativo.

chylous, *s.* quiloso.

chyme [kaim], *s.* (*fisiol.*) quimo.

chymify, *v.t.* quimificar.

chymous, *a.* quimoso.

cibol [′sibəl], *s.* cebolleta; chalota.

ciborium [si′boəɹiəm], *s.* copón; dosel de altar, ciborio.

cicada [si′kɑːdə], *s.* (*entom.*) cigarra, chicharra.

cicatrice, cicatrix, *s.* cicatriz, *f.*

cicatricle, cicatricule, *s.* (*biol.*) germen en la yema del huevo.

cicatrisant, *s.* cicatrizante.

cicatrisive, *a.* cicatrizativo.

cicatrize, *v.t.* cicatrizar. — *v.i.* cicatrizarse.

cicely [′sisəli], *s.* (*bot.*) perifollo, cerafollo.

cicerone [tʃitʃə′rouni], *s.* cicerone, guía, *m.f.*

Ciceronian [sisə′rouniən], *a.* ciceroniano.

cicisbeo, *s.* chichisbeo; amante de una mujer casada.

ciconia, *s.* (*ornit.*) cigüeña.

cicuta [si′kjuːtə], *s.* cicuta.

cider [′saidəɹ], *s.* sidra.

ci-devant, *a.* pasado, anterior.

cierge [səːɹdʒ], *s.* cirio.

cigar [si′gɑːɹ], *s.* cigarro, puro.

cigar-case, *s.* petaca, cigarrera.

cigar-holder, *s.* boquilla.

cigar-shop, *s.* cigarrería, estanco.

cigarette [sigə′ret], *s.* cigarrillo, pitillo.

cigarette-case, *s.* pitillera.

cigarette-paper, *s.* papel de fumar.

ciliary [′siliəri], *a.* ciliar.

ciliate, *a.* (*bot.*) ciliado, pestañoso.

cilicious [si′liʃəs], *a.* cerdoso, hecho de cerdas o crin.

Cimbric, *a.* címbrico.

cimeter [′simətəɹ], *s.* (*ant.*) cimitarra [SCIMITAR].

Cimmerian, *a.* cimerio, cimeriano.

cinch [sintʃ], *v.t.* apretar, forzar. — *s.* cincho, cincha; (*E.U.*, *fam.*), ganga, cosa que se puede hacer a poca costa.

cinchona [sin′kounə], *s.* (*bot.*) cinchona, quina.

cincture [′siŋktʃəɹ], *s.* cinto, ceñidor, cíngulo, cincho; cercado; cerca. — *v.t.* ceñir, cercar, rodear.

cinder [′sindəɹ], *s.* ceniza; cernada. — *pl.* **cinders**, pavesas, cenizas; carbonilla; rescoldo.

Cinderella, *s.* La Cenicienta.

cindery, *a.* mezclado con ceniza.

cinema, *s.* cine.

cinematograph [sinə′mætəgræf], *s.* cinematógrafo.

cineraceous, *a.* ceniciento.

cineraria [sinə′rɛəriə], *s.* (*bot.*) cineraria.

cinerary, *a.* cinerario.

cineration, *s.* incineración.

cinereous, *a.* ceniciento, cinéreo.

cineritious, *a.* cenizoso.

Cingalese [′siŋəliːz], *s.*, *a.* cingalés.

cinnabar [′sinəbɑːɹ], *s.* cinabrio.

cinnamic, *a.* de canela.

cinnamon [′sinəmən], *s.* canela.

cinque [siŋk], *a.* cinco.

cinquefoil, *s.* (*bot.*) quinquefolio, cincoenrama; (*arq.*) pentalóbulo.

cinque-pace, *s.* especie de danza.

Cinque-ports, *s.* los cinco puertos (Hastings, Sandwich, Dover, Romney y Hythe).

cinter, *s.* (*arq.*) cimbra.

cipher [′saifəɹ], *s.* cifra, clave, *f.*; cero; nulidad; (*fig.*) persona insignificante; (*mús.*) sonido prolongado de un cañón de órgano debido a un defecto de válvula. — *v.i.* numerar; calcular. — *v.t.* cifrar, escribir en cifra, calcular.

ciphering, s. cálculo; aritmética.
Circassian [səɹˈkəsjən], a., s. circasiano.
circensial [səɹˈseniəl], **circensian,** a. circense.
circinate, a. (bot.) arrollado hacia adentro.
circinus [ˈsəɹsinəs], s. (astron.) compás.
circle [ˈsəːɹkl], s. círculo, circunferencia; anillo, cerco, ruedo, redondel; corro, corrillo; asamblea, reunión, tertulia; circunlocución; (bot.) verticilo; ciclo, revolución; circunloquio, rodeo. — v.t. mover circularmente; rodear, circundar; cercar. — v.i. circular, dar vueltas.
circlet, s. círculo pequeño, anillo; corona.
circling, a. circulante, redondo.
circuit [ˈsəːɹkit], s. circuito, rotación, rodeo, vuelta, revolución, recinto; (rad.) ámbito; contorno, distrito; visita de los jueces; diadema; anillo; to be on circuit, to go on circuit, viajar para negocios, ir a visitar la parroquia; ir de gira; representarse; short circuit, (elec.) corto circuito. — v.i: dar la vuelta, moverse circularmente. — v.t. andar al rededor.
circuit-breaker, s. (elec.) cortacircuito.
circuitous, a. indirecto, tortuoso.
circuitously, adv. tortuosamente.
circular, a. circular, redondo. — s. circular, aviso, carta circular.
circularly, adv. circularmente.
circulate [ˈsəːɹkjuleit], v.t. divulgar, propalar, esparcir, diseminar; hacer circular, poner en circulación. — v.i. circular, propagarse. — s. (mat.) fracción continua.
circulating, a. circulante; (mat.) (fracción) continua, periódica; circulating medium, moneda corriente.
circulation [səːɹkjuˈleiʃən], s. circulación; tirada (de un periódico); propaganda.
circulative [ˈsəːɹkjulətiv], a. circulatorio.
circulatory, a. circular, circulante; ambulante; (fisiol.) circulatorio.
circumambient [səːɹkəmˈæmbiənt], a. circumambiente; (fisiol.) ambiente.
circumambulate, v.i. circular, andar al rededor, circumambular.
circumcise [ˈsəːɹkəmsaiz], v.t. circuncidar.
circumciser, s. circuncidador.
circumcision [səːɹkəmˈsiʒən], s. circuncisión; purificación espiritual.
circumduct, v.t. circunducir; contradecir, anular; revocar; abrogar.
circumference [səɹˈkʌmfərəns], s. circunferencia, periferia; perímetro, circuito, cerco, círculo.
circumferential, a. circunferencial.
circumflex [ˈsəːɹkəmfleks], s., a. (acento) circunflejo; (impr.) capucha; (anat.) encorvado, arqueado. — v.t. poner el circunflejo.
circumfluence, s. acción de correr las aguas alrededor o en torno de algo.
circumfluent [səɹˈkʌmfluənt], a. circunfluente.
circumfuse [səːɹkəmˈfjuːz], v.t. verter o esparcir en rededor; rodear.
circumfusion, s. difusión, dispersión; acto de esparcir alguna cosa al rededor de otra.
circumjacent [səːɹkəmˈdʒeisənt], a. circunvecino.
circumlocution, s. circunlocución, circunloquio.
circumlocutory [səːɹkəmˈlɔkjutri], a. circunlocutorio, perifrástico.

circummured, a. amurrallado, murado, cercado de murallas.
circumnavigable, a. (mar.) circunnavegable, navegable al rededor.
circumnavigate [səːɹkəmˈnævigeit], v.t. circunnavegar.
circumnavigation, s. circunnavegación.
circumnavigator, s. el que navega al rededor.
circumscribe [ˈsəːɹkəmskraib], v.t. circunscribir, fijar, limitar.
circumscription [səːɹkəmˈskripʃən], s. circunscripción, término, límite.
circumscriptive, a. circunscriptivo.
circumscriptively, adv. circunscritamente.
circumspect [ˈsəːɹkəmspekt], a. circunspecto, prudente, discreto, mirado.
circumspection, s. circunspección, miramiento, cautela, prudencia, reserva, recato, decoro, compostura, pulso.
circumspective, a. circunspecto, mirado.
circumspectively, circumspectly, adv. circunspectamente.
circumspectness, s. cautela, vigilancia, recato.
circumstance [ˈsəːɹkəmstæns], s. circunstancia; accidente; acontecimiento, incidente; detalle, menudencia. — pl. circunstancias; medios, recursos, situación económica; to act according to circumstances, obedecer al tiempo; to be in easy circumstances, estar en buena posición. — v.t. colocar en buen o mal estado, en una posición cualquiera.
circumstantial, a. accidental, casual; secundario, accessorio; circunstanciado, detallado, minucioso, particular; circunstancial, indirecto; circumstantial evidence, prueba de indicios o indiciaria.
circumstantially, adv. circunstanciadamente, incidentalmente; eventualmente.
circumstantiate [səːɹkəmˈstaːnʃieit], v.t. circunstanciar, detallar, relatar circunstanciadamente.
circumvallate, v.t. circunvalar, rodear con fortificaciones.
circumvallation, s. circunvalación.
circumvent [səːɹkəmˈvent], v.t. circunvenir; engañar; entrampar, enredar, embaucar.
circumvention, s. engaño, impostura, fraude, trampa, enredo, estratagema.
circumventive, a. engañoso, delusorio.
circumvest [səːɹkəmˈvest], v.t. circundar, rodear, cercar.
circumvolution, s. circunvolución; (arquit.) voluta; vuelta, rodeo.
circumvolve [səːɹkəmˈvolv], v.t. enrollar, envolver; dar un movimiento circular.
circus [ˈsəːɹkəs], s. circo; arena; hipódromo; plaza circular, redondel.
cirque [ˈsəːɹk], s. espacio circular; (poét.) circo, arena; (geol.) nicho circular entre montes.
cirrhosis [siˈrousis], s. (med.) materia mórbida amarilla que algunos tejidos segregan; enfermedad del hígado.
cirrus [ˈsirəs], s. (meteor.) cirrus; (bot.) cirro, zarcillo; (anat.) apéndice como un hilo que sirve como órgano del tacto.
Cisalpine, a. cisalpino.
Cisatlantic, a. cisatlántico.
cist, s. arquilla, estuche.
Cistercian [sisˈtəːɹʃən], s., a. cisterciense.
cistern [ˈsistəɹn], s. tanque; cisterna, aljibe.
cistus [ˈsistəs], s. (bot.) cisto, cergazo.

cit, *s.* (*ant.*, *fam.*) ciudadano.
citable, *a.* citable.
citadel ['sitədl], *s.* ciudadela.
citation [sai'teiʃən], *s.* citación; cita; mención.
citatory, *a.* citatorio.
cite [sait], *v.t.* citar, citar a juicio; alegar; referirse a.
citer, *s.* citador.
cithara ['siθərə], *s.* (*mús.*) cítara.
citharist, *s.* citarista, *m.f.*
citharistic, *a.* de la cítara.
cithern ['siθəɹn], *s.* (*mús.*) vihuela de péndola.
citizen ['sitizn], *s.* ciudadano; vecino, munícipe; *fellow-citizen*, conciudadano. — *a.* burgués; ciudadano.
citizenship, *s.* ciudadanía.
citrate ['sitreit], *s.* (*quím.*) citrato.
citric, *a.* cítrico.
citrine, *a.* cetrino.
citron ['sitrən], *s.* cidra, toronja; *citron tree*, cidro, acitrón, toronjal; (*min.*) cuarzo transparente de color amarillo.
citrus, *s.* (*bot.*) género de árboles que contiene naranjo, limonero, lima, cidro, etc.
city ['siti], *s.* ciudad; parte antigua de una ciudad. — *a.* municipal, perteneciente a la ciudad.
civet ['sivət], *s.* civeta; algalia; *civet-cat*, gato de algalia.
civic, *a.* cívico, municipal.
civil ['sivəl], *a.* civil, intestino, doméstico; urbano, cortés, afable, decente, decoroso; honesto; *civil list*, presupuesto de la casa real; *Civil Servant*, funcionario; *Civil Service*, servicio público, diplomacia.
civilian [si'viljən], *s.* ciudadano; jurisconsulto, jurisperito; estudiante de leyes. — *a.* civil.
civility, *s.* civilidad, urbanidad, política, cortesía, afabilidad, atención.
civilizable [sivi'laizəbl], *a.* civilizable.
civilization [sivilai'zeiʃən], *s.* civilización.
civilize ['sivilaiz], *v.t.* civilizar, ilustrar.
civilizer, *s.* civilizador.
civilly, *adv.* civilmente; cortésmente.
civism, *s.* civismo, patriotismo; ciudadanía.
clack [klæk], *s.* chasquido, golpeo; charla; tarabilla, cencerra o cítola de molino; clapatela, válvula de bomba; hablador importuno. — *v.i.* cencerrear; restañar, crujir; repiquetear, castañetear; picotear, charlar.
clacker, *s.* cítola de molino; (*fig.*) taravilla, hablador.
clacking, *s.* sonido de armas; charla.
clad [klæd], *a.* vestido, cubierto, aderezado.
claim, *v.t.* reclamar, demandar, pretender, reivindicar, pedir en juico; afirmar, alegar. — *s.* pretensión, título, reclamación, derecho, petición, demanda; llamamiento; *to lay claim to*, pedir en juicio, demandar, exigir; *to admit a claim*, hacer justicia a una reclamación.
claimable, *a.* exigible, de derecho.
claimant, *s.* demandante, actor. — *a.* que implora, que reclama.
claimer, *s.* demandante, el que demanda, el que pide.
claimless, *a.* falto de derecho.
clairvoyant [klɛəɹ'vɔijənt], *s.*, *a.* vidente; lúcido.
clam [klæm], *v.t.* empastar, pegar con liga. — *v.i.* mojarse, humedecerse; pegar; *to clam the bells*, echar las campanas a vuelo, repicar.
— *s.* peine (de molusco); almeja, tellina, telina, chirla.
clamant, *a.* clamante.
clamber ['klæmbəɹ], *v.i.* gatear, trepar, encaramarse.
clamminess, *s.* viscosidad.
clammy ['klæmi], *a.* viscoso, pegajoso, pastoso.
clamorous ['klæmərəs], *a.* clamoroso, ruidoso, tumultuoso, estrepitoso, alborotador, vocinglero.
clamorously, *adv.* clamorosamente, ruidosamente.
clamorousness, *s.* naturaleza inquieta.
clamour, *s.* clamor, clamoreo; algarabía, alboroto, tumulto; gritería, vocería. — *v.i.* clamar, gritar, vociferar. — *v.t.* dar gritos, aturdir con ruido.
clamp [klæmp], *v.t.* empalmar; lañar; encajar, unir, juntar; pisar con ruido y pesadamente. — *s.* empalmadura; abrazadera, mordaza; montón de ladrillos dispuestos para ser cocidos; (*mar.*) durmientes; tenazas, pinzas, tornillo; (*mec.*) grampa, grapa, laña.
clamping, *s.* empalme.
clan [klæn], *s.* clan; pandilla; secta; familia, tribu, *f.*; casta, horda; gente, *f.*, raza.
clandestine [klæn'destin], *a.* clandestino, secreto, furtivo, oculto.
clandestinity, *s.* clandestinidad, secreto.
clang [klæŋ], *s.* rechino; ruido de armas; chirrido; sonido metálico. — *v.i.* rechinar; sonar, resonar. — *v.t.* hacer resonar.
clangorous, *a.* agudo, penetrante, estridente, estruendoso.
clangour, *s.* estruendo, estrépito; graznido, chirrido; ruido estridente.
clank [klæŋk], *v.i.* rechinar, resonar. — *v.t.* hacer resonar, hacer rechinar. — *s.* rechinamiento, ruido estridente; ruido de cadenas; choque de armas. — (*Nota*) denota, usualmente, un sonido más profundo que el *clink*, y menos resonante que el *clang*.
clannish, *a.* del clan, gregario; estrechamente unido.
clanship, *s.* asociación, unión bajo un jefe.
clansman, *s.* miembro de un clan.
clap [klæp], *v.t.* batir, golpear; pegar; apabullar, encajar; aplicar, juntar, estrechar, apretar; empujar; hacer entrar; palmear; *to clap in* (*irons, etc.*) encerrar, sujetar; *to clap spurs to one's horse*, dar de espuelas; *to clap eyes on*, echar la vista a. — *v.i.* (*ant.*) cerrarse ruidosamente; (*ant.*) arrojarse; aplaudir, dar palmadas; *to clap a door to*, cerrar una puerta con violencia. — *s.* estrépito; trueno, rayo; palmoteo, palmada, aplauso; (*vulg.*) gonorrea.
clap-board, *s.* duela de barril o tonel; (*E.U.*) tabla de chilla.
clapper, *s.* palmoteador; badajo de campana; tarabilla de molino, cítola; aldaba; (*mar.*) chapaleta; (*ant.*) madriguera de conejos; tableta, tejoleta.
clapperclaw, *v.t.* (*vulg.*) regañar, maltratar de palabra.
clapping, *s.* aleteo; palmoteo, palmada; aplausos.
clap-trap, *s.* golpe de teatro; artificio para alcanzar popularchería; artificio indigno.
clarabella, *s.* clarabella, registro melodioso del órgano.

clarence ['klærəns], *s.* cupé, carruaje de cuatro ruedas.
Clarendon, *s.* (*impr.*) tipo grueso y compacto.
claret ['klærət], *s.* clarete.
clarification [klærifi'keiʃən], *s.* clarificación.
clarifier, *s.* clarificador.
clarify [klæri'fai], *v.t.* clarificar, aclarar, defecar, purificar, depurar; ilustrar, esclarecer. — *v.i.* clarificarse.
clarinet [klæri'net], *s.* (*mús.*) clarinete.
clarinettist, *s.* clarinete, el que toca el clarinete.
clarion ['klæriən], *s.* (*mús.*) clarín.
clarity ['klæriti], *s.* claridad, resplandor, luz.
clary, *s.* (*bot.*) salvia silvestre.
clash [klæʃ], *v.i.* chocar, tropezar, batir, entrechocarse; contradecir; ser opuesto a otra cosa; oponerse, antagonizar. — *v.t.* batir; golpear. — *s.* choque; crujido, fragor; golpe violento; lucha, refriega; encontrón, colisión; antagonismo, oposición, conflicto; contienda, disputa.
clashing, *s.* choque; ruido; contienda, contradicción, enemistad.
clashingly, *adv.* en conflicto, en oposición.
clasp [klɑːsp], *s.* broche, botoncito, corchete, chapeta, hebilla; abrazo, presilla, gafete, traba, abrazadera; (*mec.*) grapa, cárcel, *f.*—*v.t.* enganchar, abrochar, encorchetar; cercar; incluir; abrazar, ceñir; embrazar.
clasper, *s.* el que, or lo que ase o abraza; (*zool.*) garfios del tarso de los insectos o peces.
class [klɑːs], *s.* clase, *f.,* orden, *m.f.,* categoría; condición, grado, fila, rango; género, especie, *f.*; (*biol.*) subdivisión intermedia entre reino y género; *class books,* libros de clase; *class room,* sala de clases, sala de enseñanza, aula. — *v.t.* clasificar, ordenar, coordinar.
classic ['klæsik], **classical,** *a.* clásico. — *s.* autor clásico.
classically, *adv.* clásicamente.
classicism, *s.* clasicismo.
classicist ['klæsisist], *s.* humanista, *m.f.,* clásico.
classification [klæsifi'keiʃən], *s.* clasificación.
classify [klæsi'fai], *v.t.* clasificar, coordinar.
classmate, *s.* condiscípulo, compañero de clase.
clastic ['klæstik], *a.* (*geol.*) fragmentario compuesto de residuos de varias rocas.
clatter ['klætəɹ], **clat,** *v.i.* resonar, hacer sonido, hacer ruido; charlar, gritar, repiquetear, guachapear. — *v.t.* hacer retumbar. — *s.* ruido, fracaso, estruendo, gresca, bulla, alboroto; charla; repique, martilleo.
clatterer, *s.* alborotador; hablador.
clattering, *s.* estruendo, ruido, fracaso.
clatteringly, *adv.* ruidosamente.
clause [klɔːz], *s.* cláusula, párrafo, período; artículo, estipulación.
claustral, *a.* claustral.
clavate ['kleiveit], **clavated,** *a.* (*bot.*) clavado; que tiene forma de maza o clavo; claveteado.
clavichord ['klævikɔəɹd], *s.* (*mús.*) clavicordio.
clavicle ['klævikl], *s.* (*anat.*) clavícula.
clavicular [klæ'vikjuləɹ], *a.* clavicular.
clavier [klə'viəɹ], *s.* (*mús.*) teclado; pianoforte.
clavy, *s.* (*arquit.*) campana de chimenea.
claw [klɔː], *s.* garra, uña, garfa; gancho, garfio; garabato; (*mar.*) uñas de espeque o pie de cabra; (*bot.*) pecíolo; *claw bar,* espeque con uña; *claw hammer,* martillo de orejas; (*fam.*) frac, casuca. — *v.t.* desgarrar; arañar, rasgar;

arpar, gafar; despedazar; regañar, reñir; (*fig.*) lisonjear; (*mar.*) escapar, tomar el tole.
clay [klei], *s.* arcilla, argilla, argila, greda, barro, tiza; tierra, limo, cieno; (*fig.*) cuerpo humano; restos mortales; *baked clay,* tierra cocida; *clay pit,* barrizal; *potter's clay,* barro de olleros; *pipe clay,* tierra de pipa. — *v.t.* engredar; cubrir con arcilla; abonar (las tierras) con arcillas.
clayey, clayish, *a.* arcilloso.
claymore ['kleimoəɹ], *s.* espada de dos filos de los antiguos escoceses.
cleading ['kliːdiŋ], *s.* (*ferroc.*) funda, forro, cubierta.
clean [kliːn], *a.* limpio; puro, inmaculado, casto, neto, despejado, claro; inocente; entero; desembarazado; diestro; recto, derecho, simétrico; curioso, aseado, afilado; *to make clean,* limpiar; *to make a clean breast of it,* (*fig.*) cantar de plano; confesarlo todo; *to show a clean pair of heels,* huir corriendo; *clean-shaven,* bien afeitado, sin barba, lampiño. — *adv.* (*fam.*) completamente, enteramente, perfectamente. — *v.t.* limpiar, asear; lavar; purificar; desempolvar, desenlodar, desengrasar (las telas); embetunar; lustrar (el calzado); depurar (el oro); mondar.
cleaner, *s.* limpiador.
cleaning, *s.* limpieza, aseo, limpiadura, monda; desengrase, desengrasamiento; desoxidación.
cleanliness ['klenlinəs], *s.* limpieza, aseo, aliño.
cleanly, *a.* limpio, aseado; delicado, puro.
cleanly, cleanlily, *adv.* aseadamente, primorosamente.
cleanness, *s.* aseo, limpieza; delicadeza, inocencia, pureza; salud.
cleansable, *a.* purificable, limpiable.
cleanse [klenz], *v.t.* limpiar, purificar, purgar, lavar, fregar; borrar; expurgar; depurar, absterger.
cleanser, *s.* evacuante, depurativo, purgante, detersivo, purificador, limpiador.
cleansing, *s.* purificación, depuración, detersión, limpiamiento. — *a.* detersorio, mundificativo.
clear [kliəɹ], *a.* claro, transparente, sereno, diáfano; puro, inocente; alegre; neto, líquido; perspicuo, palpable, indisputable, manifiesto, patente, evidente; despejado; imparcial; raso, abierto, franco, libre, explícito, expreso; desempeñado, sin deudas; distinto, sonoro; *clear-sighted,* perspicaz; *clear-headed,* inteligente, sagaz; *the coast is clear,* (*fig.*) no hay peligro. — *adv.* claramente, evidentemente, enteramente, absolutamente. — *v.t.* aclarar, disipar; despejar; desembrollar (un negocio); satisfacer (una hipoteca); desenredar; absolver; liquidar; blanquear, limpiar; desembarazar; purgar; justificar; saltar; satisfacer; franquear, salvar; clarificar, purificar; (*agr.*) tumbar, desmontar, mondar; sacar de la aduana. — *v.i.* aclararse, serenarse; desenredarse, desembarazarse; (*com.*) liquidar cuentas; *to clear for action,* (*mar.*) realizar el zafarrancho de combate; *to clear a lot of money,* ganar mucho dinero; *to clear accounts,* liquidar cuentas; *to clear a path,* (*fig.*) abrir calle, hacer campo; *to clear the table,* levantar la mesa; *to clear the way,*

abrir paso (o camino); *to clear up*, aclarar, sacar en limpio; poner en orden, arreglar; abonanzar, despejarse, serenarse. — *s.* (*arquit.*) claro (espacio no interrumpido).

clearage, *s.* desembarazo, despejo; desmonte.

clearance, *s.* (*com.*) recibo; despacho de aduana; (*mec.*) espacio muerto, tolerancia, juego limpio; *clearance sale*, liquidación de todos los géneros.

clearer, *s.* lo que aclara, ilumina, purifica.

clearing, *s.* justificación, vindicación; aclaramiento, desempeño; arreglo; claro, raso, sitio sin árboles en un bosque, espacio libre.

clearing-house, *s.* banco de liquidación.

clearing-iron, *s.* (*f.c.*) barredera.

clearing-up, arreglo general, limpieza general; ponerse claro (del tiempo).

clearly, *adv.* claramente, evidentemente, libremente; llanamente, abiertamente, sin reserva.

clearness, *s.* claridad, transparencia; esplendor; luz; sinceridad; perspicacia.

cleat [kli:t], *s.* (*mar.*) cornuza, taco, guardainfante, tojino, galápago; estaquitas, tachuelas.

cleavable, *a.* hendible.

cleavage [kli:vidȝ], *s.* hendedura, hendidura; resquebradura; rotura (en minerales); (*min.*) crucero.

cleave, *v.t.* (*pret.* **cleft, clove;** *p.p.* **cleft, cloven**) hender, rajar, partir, dividir; penetrar, abrirse paso. — *v.i.* pegarse; henderse; grietarse, partirse, resquebrar.

cleaver, *s.* hendedor, cortador de leña; hacha, cuchilla, destralero, destral. — *pl.* **cleavers,** (*bot.*) presera, galio, amor de hortelano.

clef [klef], *s.* (*mús.*) clave, *f.*, llave, *f.*; *treble clef*, clave de sol; *bass clef*, clave de fa.

cleft [kleft], *s.* hendedura, rajadura, abertura, cuarteadura, grieta, fisura, resquicio, resquebradura; (*med.*) grietas en el paladar, hendido. — *a.* partido, rajado, hendido. — *pret.* y *p.p.* [CLEAVE].

clematis [klə'mɑ:təs], *s.* (*bot.*) clemátide, *f.*

clemency ['klemənsi], *s.* clemencia, piedad, misericordia, indulgencia.

clement, *a.* clemente, piadoso, misericordioso, indulgente, benigno.

clench [klentʃ], *v.t.* agarrar; asir fuertemente; hacer firme, asegurar; remachar; cerrar convulsivamente (los puños, los dientes).

clepsydra ['klepsidrə], *s.* clepsidra, reloj de agua.

clerestory ['kliəɹstoəri], *s.* (*arq.*) parte más alta de la nave, coro, crucero de una iglesia con pequeñas ventanas.

clergy ['klə:ɹdȝi], *s.* clero; clerecía; *clergy list*, anuario del clero.

clergyman, *s.* clérigo, eclesiástico; secerdote, cura, *m.*

cleric ['klerik], *s.* clérigo. — *a.* clerical.

clerical, *a.* clerical, eclesiástico.

clericalism, *s.* clericalismo.

clerk [klɑ:ɹk], *s.* eclesiástico, clérigo; sacristán; escribiente, oficinista, *m.f.*, amanuense, oficial de secretaría; dependiente; estudiante, escolar; *managing clerk*, primer dependiente; *junior clerk*, (*com.*) meritorio, dependiente menor.

clerkly, *a.* literato.

clerkship, *s.* estado eclesiástico; erudición, instrucción; oficio, empleo de oficinista; escribanía, secretaría.

cleromancy ['klerəmænsi], *s.* cleromancia.

clever ['klevəɹ], *a.* diestro, experto, hábil, avisado, mañoso, listo, capaz, inteligente; (*E.U.*) complaciente.

cleverness, *s.* destreza, habilidad, talento.

clevis ['klevis], *s.* abrazadera, gancho para asegurar los arreos de tiro.

clew [klu:], *s.* hilo ovillado, ovillo de hilo; (*mar.*) puño de vela; guía, pista, norte. — *v.t.* (*mar.*) cargar.

cliché ['kli:ʃei], *s.* (*impr.*, *fot.*) clisé; frase trillada, lugar común.

click [klik], *v.t.* retiñir, palotear; hacer tictac; (*impr.*) compaginar. — *s.* golpe seco, golpeo; picaporte; (*tecn.*) martinete; (*mec.*) trinquete, seguro, fiador, lingüete.

clicker, *s.* pestillo de puerta; (*impr.*) compaginador.

clicket, *s.* llamador, aldaba de puerta; (*ant.*) tarreña.

clicking, *s.* golpeo.

client ['klaiənt], *s.* cliente.

cliented, *a.* acreditado; que tiene clientes.

clientship, *s.* clientela, patrocinio.

cliff [klif], *s.* acantilado; risco, escarpa, cerrajón, escollera.

cliffy, clifty, *a.* acantilado, escarpado.

climacteric [klai'mætərik], *s.* año climatérico.

climacteric, climacterical, *a.* climatérico.

climate ['klaimət], *s.* clima, *m.*, tiempo, temperatura. — *v.i.* habitar, residir en país extranjero.

climatic, climatical, *a.* del clima, relativo al clima.

climatize, *v.t.* aclimatar.

climatology [klaimə'tɔlədȝi], *s.* climatología.

climax ['klaimæks], *s.* (*gram.*) clímax, gradación; colmo, culminación, cenit; desenlace.

climb [klaim], *v.t.* trepar; escalar; subir; montar. — *v.i.* trepar, subir, elevarse, ascender, encaramarse.

climbable, *a.* accesible, que se puede subir.

climber, *s.* trepador, escalador; (*bot.*) enredadera; (*zool.*) trepador (pájaros).

climbing, *s.* subida, ascenso, trepa. — *a.* trepante, trepador.

clime [klaim], *s.* (*poét.*) clima, *m.*; región o porción de tierra.

clinch [klintʃ], *v.t.* agarrar; remachar (un clavo o un argumento); afirmar, fijar, establecer, confirmar; (*man.*) entalingar. — *v.i.* agarrarse; ser remachado. — *s.* pulla, agudeza, equívoco, argumento sin réplica; (*mar.*) entalingadura; (*E.U.*) forcejeo; (*boxeo*) lucha cuerpo a cuerpo, clinch.

clinching, *s.* remache, robladura; (*mar.*) solapadura.

cling [kliŋ], *v.i.* (*pret.* y *p.p.* **clung**) adherirse, pegarse, unirse, agarrarse, arrimarse.

clinging, clingy, *a.* pegajoso, viscoso, adhesivo, colgante.

clinic [klinik], *s.* clínica; (*hist. ecl.*) clínico, el que recibía el bautismo en artículo de muerte.

clinical, *a.* clínico.

clink [kliŋk], *v.i.* retiñir, resonar, retumbar. — *v.t.* tañer, tocar; hacer sonar. — *s.* tañido, retintín.

clinker, *s.* ladrillo refractario; escoria; lava porosa.

clinkstone, *s.* perleta, fonolita.

clinometer [kli'nɔmətəɹ], *s.* clinómetro.

clinometric [klinə'metrik], **clinometrical,** *a.* clinométrico.

clinometry [kli'nɔmətri], s. clinometría.

clinquant ['kliŋkənt], s. oropel. — a. reluciente, brillante.

clip [klip], v.t. cortar con tijeras; esquilar, trasquilar, repelar; cercenar, recortar; tijeretear; podar, mondar; pellizcar, acortar; ceñir, abrazar. — s. tijeretada, tijeretazo, talla; recorte; esquileo, trasquila; cercenadura; abrazo; grapa, pinza, sujetapapeles.

clipper, s. tallador, cercenador, esquilador; cizalla; (mar., aer.) clíper.

clipping, s. cercenadura, recorte, retal; tijereteo.

clique [kli:k], s. pandilla, corrillo.

clitter-clatter, s. charla, parlería, palique.

cloak [klouk], s. capa, manto, albornoz; (fig.) pretexto, excusa, disimulo. — v.t., v.i. encapotar, embozar; (fig.) paliar, ocultar, encubrir.

cloak-room, s. vestuario; tocador; (f.c.) consigna, depósito de equipajes.

clock [klɔk], s. reloj (de pared, de mesa); cuchilla, bordado en la pierna de la media; *alarm* (or *alarum*) *clock*, despertador; *What o'clock is it?* ¿ Qué hora es ?

clock-case, s. caja de reloj.

clock-maker, s. relojero.

clock-work, s. máquina de reloj; máquina de precisión. — a. de movimiento regular.

clod [klɔd], s. terrón, césped; masa; tierra, suelo; pedazo, trozo; idiota, m.f., zoquete; espalda de buey. — v.i. aterronarse; coagularse. — v.t. tirar terrones.

cloddish, a. estúpido, grosero.

cloddy, a. terroso, lleno de terrones; (fig.) terrenal, bajo, grosero.

clodhopper, s. patán.

clodpoll, s. zoquete, rústico.

cloff [klɔf], s. (com.) abono sobre el peso, por la tara, etc.

clog [klɔg], v.t. cargar, embarazar, impedir, empachar; trabar; entorpecer. — v.i. atestarse; embarazarse; agolparse, obstruirse. — s. traba; (fig.) embarazo, impedimento, obstáculo; carga, hipoteca; galocha, zueco, chapín, chanclo, zoclo, chinela.

clog-dance, s. baile de zuecos.

clogginess, s. embarazo, obstáculo, impedimento.

cloggy, a. embarazoso.

cloister ['klɔistəɹ], s. claustro, convento, monasterio. — v.t. enclaustrar, proveer de claustros.

cloisteral, cloistral, a. claustral, retirado, solitario.

cloisterer, s. monje, religioso.

cloistress, s. monja.

cloop [klup], s. onomatopeya con que se representa el ruido producido al descorchar una botella.

close [klouz], v.t. cerrar, unir, juntar, ajustar, entornar, encajar; terminar, acabar, concluir; tupir, incluir, contener. — v.i. cerrarse, juntarse, unirse; terminar, fenecer; agarrarse; atacar; convenirse, estar de acuerdo; darse a partido; acabarse, terminarse; *to close in*, cercar; *to close round*, cercar, rodear; *to close up*, cerrar completamente; *to close with the enemy*, cerrar con el enemigo; luchar mano a mano; *to close with one's friend*, estar de acuerdo con su amigo. — s. conclusión, fin, término; cierre, cierro; caída;

riña, lucha cuerpo a cuerpo; cercado, huerta, prado, atrio (de una catedral). — a. cerrado; sólido, denso, compacto; incomunicado; reservado, callado, íntimo, oculto, secreto; breve, conciso; parejo, igual; reticente, solitario, retirado; sofocante, bochornoso, sin respiradero, opresivo; apretado, ajustado; angosto, estrecho; discreto; compendioso; interesado, avaro, tacaño; escrupuloso; aplicado, atento; obscuro, cubierto, nublado; contiguo, vecino, inmediato; restringido, limitado, escaso; *to bring to a close*, terminar, perorar; llevar a cabo; *close fight*, combate reñido; *close-fisted*, tacaño; *close-fitting*, ajustado, ceñido al cuerpo; *close season*, veda; *close-stool*, sillico; *close study*, aplicación; *close weather*, tiempo bochornoso, pesado, sofocante. — adv. de cerca, estrechamente, apretadamente; *close by*, muy arrimado; muy cerca de, junto a; a mano; *to stick close by a person*, aficionarse a uno, serle fiel.

closely, adv. estrechamente, exactamente, atentamente, cuidadosamente, sólidamente, fuertemente; contiguamente, de cerca; secretamente; *closely packed*, sólidamente empaquetado; *we are closely related*, somos próximos parientes.

closeness, s. encierro; espesura; estrechez; pesantez; discreción, reserva, secreto; densidad; apretamiento; soledad, reclusión; intimidad, amistad; solidez, firmeza; tacañería, avaricia, ruindad; dependencia, conexión, unión; exactitud.

closet [klɔzət], s. gabinete; armario, alacena, retrete, lugar excusado, letrina. — v.t. encerrar en un gabinete; recibir en privado; deliberar o conferenciar en secreto.

closh [klɔʃ], s. (vet.) estrechura de suelos.

closing [klouziŋ], a. final, que termina. — s. cierre, fin, conclusión.

closure, s. clausura; cerradura, cerramiento; conclusión, fin; cierre (de un circuito eléctrico).

clot [klɔt], s. grumo, coágulo, cuajarón; necio, zopenco. — v.i. coagularse, cuajarse; aburujarse, engrumecerse.

cloth [klɔθ], s. lienzo; tejido de algodón; paño, tela; el clero; (teat.) telón de boca; *packing-cloth*, arpillera; *table-cloth*, tapiz de mesa, mantel; *to lay the cloth*, poner el mantel.

clothe [klouð], v.t. vestir, revestir, cubrir, investir, arropar, trajear.

clothes, s.pl. vestido, vestidura, ropaje, vestuario; ropa, ropa de cama; en general, toda clase de ropa; *cast-off clothes* o *old clothes*, ropa usada; *suit of clothes*, traje, vestido completo.

clothes-brush, s. cepillo para ropa.

clothes-hanger, percha.

clothes-horse, s. camilla, enjugador (para secar ropa).

clothes-line, s. tendedera, cuerda de la ropa.

clothes-press, s. armario, guardarropa.

clothier, s. pañero, ropero.

clothing, s. vestidos, ropa; pelaje; revestimiento.

clotty, a. grumoso, coagulado.

cloud [klaud], s. nube, f., nublado, nublo, nubarrón; (fig.) tinieblas, obscuridad; (joy.) mancha; venas en el mármol, piedras preciosas, etc.; acumulación, enjambre, muchedumbre, f., montón; *cloud-burst*, nublada;

under a cloud, en un aprieto; bajo sospecha;
to be in a cloud, vivir en la obscuridad. — *v.t.*
anublar, nublar, obscurecer, cegar, entristecer; abigarrar, motear, jaspear; empañar,
manchar; difamar. — *v.i.* anublarse; obscurecerse.

cloud-capped, *a.* coronado de nubes.

cloud-dispelling, *a.* que disipa las nubes.

cloudily, *adv.* obscuramente, con mucha
niebla.

cloudiness, *s.* nublosidad, densidad, obscuridad.

cloudless, *a.* sin nubes, claro, sereno, despejado.

cloudy, *a.* nublado, nubloso; obscuro; vaporoso; sombrío, tétrico; (*pint.*) nubarrado.

clough [klʌf], *s.* cañada; garganta, desfiladero
de montaña; (*com.*) tara; [CLOFF].

clout [klaut], *s.* rodilla, pedazo de lienzo;
culero, pañal de niño; remiendo; (*mec.*)
cibica, cibicón; (*vulg.*) bofetada; *clout-nails*,
clavos de zapato. — *v.t.* remendar toscamente; chapucear; vendar; (*vulg.*) abofetear.

clove [klouv], *s.* clavillo, clavo de especia;
diente de ajo.

cloven, *a.* hendido, partido, dividido; *cloven
hoof* or *foot*, patihendido, diabólico; *to show
the cloven foot*, (*fig.*) enseñar la oreja.

clover, *s.* (*bot.*) trébol; *to live in clover*, (*fig.*)
vivir lujosamente, pasársela en flores.

clovered, *a.* lleno de trébol.

clown [klaun], *s.* campesino; patán; gracioso
de teatro; bufón; payaso.

clownery, *s.* rusticidad; bufonada, payasada.

clownish, *a.* villano, rudo, rústico, agreste,
grosero; bufón, atontado.

clownishness, *s.* rusticidad, grosería, rustiquez.

cloy [klɔi], *v.t.* (*ant.*) tapar, obstruir; saciar,
hartar; empalagar; (*arti., ant.*) clavar
(cañones).

cloyless, *a.* que no empalaga.

cloyment, *s.* hartura, saciedad; (*med.*) repleción.

cloysome, *a.* empalagoso.

club [klʌb], *s.* clava, porra, cachiporra, garrote;
tranca; basto; club, círculo; tertulia, escote.
— *v.i.* reunirse; cotizarse; contribuir. — *v.t.*
escotar, aporrear, dar garrotazos.

clubber, clubbist, *s.* clubista, *m.f.*

club fist, *s.* puño enorme.

club foot, *s.* patituerto, pateta, pie con torcimiento congénito.

club-footed, *s.* patiabierto.

club-headed, *s.* cabezudo, cabezorro.

club-man, *s.* socio de un club.

cluck [klʌk], *v.i.* cloquear. — *v.t.* llamar
cloqueando.

cluck, clucking, *s.* cloqueo.

clue [klu:], *s.* guía, norte; indicio, pista, rastro.

clump, *s.* trozo, canto, pedazo; grupo; zoquete, tarugo. — *v.i.* patullar.

clumpy, *a.* compuesto de bloques.

clumsily, *adv.* groseramente, zafiamente,
chapuceramente.

clumsiness, *s.* torpeza, desmaña; tosquedad,
grosería.

clumsy [klʌmzi], *a.* torpe, pesado, sin arte,
chabacano, desgarbado; tosco, rudo.

clung [klʌŋ], *pret.* y *p.p.* [CLING].

clupeoid [ˈkluːpiɔid], *a.* semejante al arenque.

cluster [ˈklʌstəɹ], *s.* racimo, ramo, manojo;

enjambre, manada, hato, caterva, pelotón,
multitud, tropel, montón, grupo, agrupación. — *v.i.* arracimarse, agruparse. — *v.t.*
apiñar, amontonar.

clustery, *a.* arracimado, apiñado, agrupado.

clutch [klʌtʃ], *v.t.* agarrar; empuñar, apretar.
— *s.* agarro, embrague, presa; espolón, grapa,
mano, uña, garra; puño; nidada; (*mec.*)
embrague; *to fall into the clutches of*, caer
en las uñas de; *to engage the clutch*, embragar;
to de-clutch, desembragar.

clutter, *s.* baraúnda, batahola; gentío, multitud; confusión, desorden. — *v.t., v.i.* alborotar; hacer estrépito o ruido.

cly [klai], *v.t.* (*germanía*) coger, agarrar, asir,
embargar, secuestrar; (*fig.*) robar, hurtar,
pillar. — *s.* lo robado o hurtado.

clyster, *s.* clístel, enema, jeringazo; ayuda,
lavativa.

clysterize, *v.t.* clisterizar.

co- *pref.* con, junto; mutual; abreviación de
company, compañía (Co.).

coacervate, *v.t.* juntar, amontonar, coacervar.

coach [koutʃ], *s.* coche, carroza, carruaje;
(*f.c.*) vagón; preceptor; entrenador; (*fam.*)
pasante, preparación para un examen, para
una regata o un certamen atlético; (*mar.*)
camarote cerca de la popa de un navío de
guerra; *hackney coach*, coche simón; *stage-
coach*, diligencia; *coach box*, pescante; *coach-
house*, cochera; *coach-maker*, carrocero; *coach-
stand*, punto o estación de carruajes. — *v.t.*
amaestrar, enseñar, instruir, adiestrar; llevar
en coche; (*fam.*) preparar para un examen.
— *v.i.* pasearse en coche; estudiar con un
preceptor.

coachful, *s.* coche lleno de gente.

coaching, *s.* entrenamiento; lecciones particulares.

coachman, *s.* cochero.

coachmanship, *s.* arte de manejar.

coact [kouˈækt], *v.i.* cooperar, obrar de acuerdo; compeler, obligar, forzar.

coaction, *s.* coacción.

coactive, *a.* coactivo, cooperante.

coactively, *adv.* obligatoriamente.

coactivity, *s.* coactividad.

coadjutant [kouˈædʒutənt], *a.* coadyuvante,
auxiliar. — *s.* auxiliar, asistente.

coadjutor, *s.* coadjutor; compañero.

coadjutorship, *s.* cooperación, asistencia; co-
adjutoria.

coadjutrix, *s.f.* coadjutora; abadesa.

coadministrator, *s.* coadministrador.

coadunate, *a.* (*fisiol.*) coadunado.

coagent [kouˈeidʒənt], *s.* coagente, cooperador.

coagulability, *s.* facultad de coagularse.

coagulable, *a.* coagulable.

coagulate [kouˈægjuleit], *v.t.* coagular, cuajar.
— *v.i.* coagularse, cuajarse, espesarse.

coagulation, *s.* coagulación.

coagulator, *s.* coágulo.

coagulatory, *a.* coagulante, coagulatorio.

coagulum, *s.* (*med.*) cuágulo, cuajarón.

coal [koul], *s.* carbón de piedra; (*ant.*) brasa,
tizón; *anthracite coal*, carbón antrácita;
coal-box, caja del carbón; *coal-cellar*,
carbonera; *coal-field*, mina de hulla; *coal-
gas*, gas de alumbrado; *coal-hole*, pañol del
carbón, carbonera; *to call over the coals*,
reprender severamente; *to carry coals to*

Newcastle, llevar hierro a Vizcaya. — *v.t.* proveer de carbón; carbonizar. — *v.i.* proveerse de carbón.

coal-basket, *s.* cesta del carbón.

coal-black, *a.* negro como el carbón.

coalesce [kouə'les], *v.i.* juntarse, unirse, incorporarse, fundirse, coligarse.

coalescence, *s.* fusión, unión, enlace; (*med.*) coalescencia.

coalition [kouə'liʃən], *s.* coalición, confederación, alianza, unión, liga.

coalitionist, *s.* coalicionista, *m.f.*

co-ally, *s.* aliado.

coal-merchant, *s.* mercader de carbón.

coal-mine, *s.* mina de carbón.

coal-miner, *s.* hullero, minero.

coal-pit, *s.* mina de hulla.

coal-tar, *s.* alquitrán.

coal-whipper, *s.* descargador de carbón.

coaly, *a.* carbonífero, carbonoso.

coamings, *s.pl.* (*mar.*) brazola de escotilla, brocal.

coaptation, *s.* coaptación, ajustamiento, arreglo.

coarct [kou'ɑːkt], (*ant.*) **coarctate**, *v.t.* estrechar; restringir; coartar.

coarctate, *a.* comprimido, contraído, estrechado, coartado.

coarctation, *s.* (*med.*) coartación, contracción, estrechamiento, estrechez.

coarse [koəɹs], *a.* basto, ordinario; tosco, grosero, rústico; grueso, burdo; vulgar, descortés, informal, soez.

coarse-grained, *a.* de grano grueso; (*fig.*) tosco, rudo, informal.

coarsely, *adv.* toscamente, groseramente.

coarseness, *s.* tosquedad, vulgaridad, grosería, informalidad.

coast [koust], *s.* costa, ribera, orilla del mar; litoral; *the coast is clear*, no hay peligro, *o* ha pasado el peligro. — *v.i.* (*mar.*) costear, perlongar; (*mec.*) andar en punto muerto. — *v.t.* costear, abordar; *coast-defence ship*, (*mar.*) guardacostas.

coaster, *s.* buque costanero.

coastguard, *s.* guardacosta, *m.*

coasting, *s.* cabotaje.

coastwise, *a. adv.* a lo largo de la costa.

coat [kout], *s.* levita, casaca, frac, chaqueta; traje; hábito; pelo, plumas, lana; capa, mano, *f.* (de pintura, yeso, alquitrán); (*mec.*) cubierta, envoltura, caperuza, funda; túnica del ojo; *frock coat*, redingote, levita; *dress-coat*, frac; *great-coat*, *overcoat*, abrigo, sobretodo; *coat of arms*, escudo de armas; *to turn one's coat*, volver casaca, mudar de partido. — *v.t.* cubrir, vestir, revestir; azogar.

coati [kou'ɑːti], *s.* cuati.

coating, *s.* revestimiento, capa, mano, *f.* (de pintura); barniz; blanqueo, jalbegue; *rough coating*, (*arq.*) enlucido.

coax [kouks], *v.t.* lisonjear, adular, engatusar, halagar, instar.

coaxer, *s.* adulador, mimador, engatusador.

coaxing, *s.* adulación, lisonja, engatusamiento; ruego, caricia.

cob [kob], *s.* cabeza, tusa, mazorca (de maíz); araña; pedrusco, jaco, jaca; bulto montón; cesta o canastillo de mimbres; cisne macho; gaviota; mezcla de arcilla y paja usada en la construcción de paredes. — *v.t.* azotar con una paleta.

cobalt [ko'boːlt], *s.* (*quím.*) cobalto.

cobaltic, *a.* cobáltico.

cobbing, *s.* látigo.

cobble ['kobl], — *v.t.*, *v.i.* chapucear; remendar zapatos.

cobbler, *s.* zapatero, remendón; chapucero.

coble ['koubl], *s.* barca de pescador de fondo chato.

cobnut, *s.* especie de avellana grande.

cobra ['kobrə], *s.* cobra.

cobweb, *s.* telaraña; trama, tramoya; añagaza. — *a.* frágil, débil.

cobwebby, *a.* cubierto de telarañas; transparente, sutil, de gasa.

coca, *s.* coca, hayo.

cocaine [ko'kein], *s.* (*farm.*) cocaína.

coccinella [koksi'nelə], *s.* (*entom.*) cocinela.

coccus ['kokəs], *s.* (*zool.*) coco, cóccido.

coccyx ['koksiks], *s.* (*anat.*) cóccix.

cochineal ['kotʃiniːl], *s.* cochinilla; grana.

cochlearia [kokli'ɛəriə], *s.* (*bot.*) coclearia.

cock [kok], *s.* gallo; macho de una ave; espita, llave, *f.*; grifo, grifón; montoncillo de paja o heno; seguro; estilo o gnomon de reloj de sol; (*fam.*) campeón, caudillo; veleta, giraldilla; pie de gato de escopeta; posición del gatillo de una arma de fuego cuando está montado; armadura del sombrero; aguja de romana; *cocksparrow*, gorrión macho; *cock-spurs*, navajas de gallo; *black cock*, gallo silvestre; *game-cock*, gallo de combate; *turkey cock*, pavo, guanajo; *cock-a-doodle-do*, quiquiriquí; *cock-and-bull-story*, patraña, cuento exagerado; *cock-fight*, riña de gallos; *cock-horse*, caballito; *cock's comb*, cresta de gallo, moñuelo; *old cock* (*vulg.*) forma de saludo entre amigos íntimos. — *v.t.* montar, amartillar, preparar una arma de fuego; hacinar o amontonar (heno); levantar, erguir, enderezar; encandilar (el sombrero). — *v.i.* entonarse, engreírse.

cockade [kə'keid], *s.* cucarda, escarapela.

Cockaigne, *s.* país de quimeras, país de Jauja; Londres.

cockalorum, *s.* hombre diminuto con grandes aires; juego de muchachos llamado 'salta la burra'.

cockatoo [kokə'tuː], *s.* (*orn.*) cacatúa.

cockatrice, *s.* basilisco; (*fig.*) cualquier cosa terrible, mortal.

cockboat, *s.* (*mar.*) barquilla.

cockchafer, *s.* abejorro; melolonta, escarabajo.

cock-crowing, *s.* canto del gallo; aurora.

cocker, *v.t.* acariciar, mimar. — *s.* sabueso pequeño empleado en la caza de la chochaperdiz.

cockerel, *s.* gallipollo, gallito.

cockering, *s.* indulgencia excesiva.

cocket, *s.* sello (de la aduana); certificación de pago (de la aduana).

cock-eyed, *a.* bizco; (*fig.*) torcido, desaliñado.

cock-fight, *s.* riña *o* pelea de gallos.

cockle ['kokl], *s.* caracol de mar, coquina; (*bot.*) vallico, zizaña, barquichuelo. — *v.t.* arrugar; doblar en figura espiral. — *v.i.* plegarse, doblarse; (*mar.*) rizarse (el mar).

cockling, *a.* (*mar.*) erizado de olas blancas. — *s.* enroscamiento.

cock-loft, *s.* desván, zaquizamí.

cockney, *s.* natural de Londres, algunas veces el que carece de educación.

cockpit, s. gallera, reñidero de gallos; casilla del piloto de un avión.

cockroach, s. (*ent.*) corredera, cucaracha.

cockspur, s. espolón de gallo; (*bot.*) especie de níspero.

cocksure, a. (*fam.*) muy seguro, confiado, cierto.

cocktail, s. caballo, generalmente de raza cruzada, y con la cola recortada; por extensión hombre de raza cruzada; bebida espirituosa compuesta de varios licores y helada, coctel.

cocoa ['koukou], s. cacao (árbol, fruto y bebida).

cocoanut, coconut, s. coco (fruto).

cocoon [kə'ku:n], s. capullo del gusano de seda y otros insectos.

cocoonery, s. local donde se crían los gusanos de seda.

coctile ['kɔktail], a. cocido en horno.

coction ['kɔkʃən], s. cocción.

cod [kɔd], s. bacalao, abadejo; (*bot.*) baya, vaina, vainilla; (*anat.*) bolsa; panza; escroto. — *v.t.* envainar, encerrar.

coda, s. (*mús.*) coda.

coddle, *v.t.* dar un hervido, cocer a medias; asar; criar con mimo.

code [koud], s. código, compilación de leyes; cifra, clave, *f.*

codeine ['koudi:n], s. (*quím.*) codeína.

codex ['koudeks], s. códice.

codfish, s. bacalao.

codfisher, s. pescador de bacalao.

codger ['kɔdʒəɹ], s. (*fam.*) hombre tacaño y avariento.

codicil ['kɔdisil], s. codicilo.

codicillary [kɔdi'siləri], a. codicilar.

codification [koudifi'keiʃən], s. codificación (de leyes).

codify [koudi'fai], *v.t.* codificar, compilar (leyes).

codilla, s. la parte más ordinaria del lino o del cáñamo.

codlin, codling, s. bacalao pequeño; manzana para cocer; manzana cocida; *codling-moth,* mariposa tortrícida cuya oruga es el gusano de la manzana: *carpocapsa pomonella.*

codliver-oil, s. aceite de hígado de bacalao.

coeclometer, s. (*astr.*) instrumento para calcular las posiciones de los astros.

co-education, s. coeducación.

co-efficacy, s. coeficacia.

coefficiency, s. coeficiencia, cooperación, concurso.

coefficient [kouə'fiʃənt], s., a. coeficiente.

coefficiently, adv. cooperativamente.

cœlenterate, s. (*zool.*) subdivisión de los metazoides, conteniendo la esponja, la medusa, etc.; (*hist. nat.*) acalefos.

cœliac ['si:liæk], a. (*anat.*) celíaco.

coemption [kou'empʃən], s. acaparamiento, monopolio, logrería.

cœnobite ['si:nəbait], s. cenobita, *m.f.*

coequal [kou'i:kwəl], a. coigual.

coequality, s. igualdad.

coequally, adv. igualmente.

coerce [kou'ə:ɹs], *v.t.* coercer, contener, refrenar, restringir, obligar, forzar.

coercible, a. coercible.

coercibleness, s. coercibilidad.

coercion, s. coerción, sujeción, opresión, fuerza, violencia.

coercive, a. coercitivo, coactivo, obligatorio.

coessential [kouə'senʃəl], a. coesencial, cosustancial.

coetaneous, a. de la misma edad; coetáneo.

coeternal [kouə'tə:ɹnəl], a. (*teo.*) coeterno.

coeternity, s. coeternidad.

coeval [kou'i:vəl], a. coevo, contemporáneo.

coexist [kouəg'zist], *v.i.* coexistir.

coexistence, s. coexistencia.

coexistent, coexisting, a. coexistente.

coextensive [kouəks'tensiv], a. coextensivo.

coffee ['kɔfi], s. café; *black coffee,* café solo; *white coffee,* café con leche.

coffee-bean, coffee-berry, s. grano de café.

coffee-colour, s. color de café.

coffee-cup, s. taza de café.

coffee-house, s. café.

coffee-mill, s. molinillo de café.

coffee-plantation, s. cafetal.

coffee-pot, s. cafetera.

coffee-roaster, s. tostador de café.

coffee-tree, s. café (árbol), cafeto.

coffer ['kɔfəɹ], s. arca, cofre, caja; tesoro; (*arq.*) artesón hondo. — *pl.* **coffers,** fondos, hacienda, tesoro. — *v.t.* atesorar; artesonar; encajonar, meter en un cofre o arca.

coffer-dam, s. represa encofrada, malecón, caja de hierro introducida en el agua para los trabajos de fijar los estribos de un puente, etc.

coffin ['kɔfin], s. ataúd, féretro; cucurucho de papel; parte del casco del caballo que cubre un hueso; (*impr.*) rama. — *v.t.* meter en un ataúd; (*fig.*) encerrar, ocultar, cubrir; *coffin-bone,* hueso que se halla dentro del casco del caballo.

cog [kɔg], *v.t.* puntear una rueda; hacer trampas (con los dados). — *v.i.* trampear, hacer fullerías. — s. punto, diente de rueda; fraude, engaño; botequín; *cog-wheel,* rodezno, rueda dentada.

cogency, s. fuerza lógica o moral; evidencia.

cogent ['koudʒənt], a. fuerte, potente, convincente.

cogently, adv. fuertemente, de una manera irresistible.

cogged, a. dentado, engranado.

cogger ['kɔgəɹ], s. adulador; fullero, tahur.

cogitate ['kɔdʒiteit], *v.i.* meditar, reflexionar, pensar.

cogitation [kɔdʒi'teiʃən], s. reflexión, meditación, pensamiento, deliberación.

cogitative ['kɔdʒitətiv], a. cogitabundo, cogitativo, discursivo, pensativo, reflexivo.

cognac, s. coñac.

cognate ['kɔgneit], a. cognado, consanguíneo; análogo, semejante; pariente, deudo.

cognatic, a. cognático.

cognation, s. cognación, consanguinidad, parentesco; analogía.

cognition [kɔg'niʃən], s. conocimiento, entendimiento.

cognitive, a. cognoscitivo.

cognizable, a. perceptible, conocible.

cognizance, s. conocimiento, comprensión, percepción, observación; divisa, señal, *f.*; (*for.*) competencia, jurisdicción.

cognize, *v.t.* conocer, reconocer.

cognizee, s. (*for.*) censualista que tiene derecho de cobrar una renta.

cognizor, s. (*for.*) censualista que pasa su derecho de cobrar rentas a otra persona.

cognomen [kɔg'noumən], s. sobrenombre, apellido; apodo.
cognominal, a. homónimo, tocayo.
cognominate, v.t. apellidar.
cognomination, s. sobrenombre.
cognoscible [kɔg'nɔsəbl], a. cognoscible, conocible.
cognoscitive, a. cognoscitivo.
cognovit, s. (for.) reconocimiento, por parte del demandado, de la justicia de la demanda y aceptando la decisión del tribunal.
coguardian, [kou'gɑːɹdiən], s. cotutor.
cohabit [kou'hæbit], v.i. cohabitar.
cohabitant, s. cohabitante, convecino.
cohabitation [kouhæbi'teiʃən], s. cohabitación.
coheir [kou'ɛəɹ], s. coheredero.
coheiress, s. coheredera.
cohere [kou'hiəɹ], v.i. adherirse, pegarse, unirse; adaptarse.
coherence, coherency, s. cohesión, coherencia; conexión, unión, enlace; consecuencia, conformidad.
coherent, a. coherente, consiguiente, consecuente; ligado.
cohesibility, s. tendencia a la cohesión.
cohesible, a. susceptible de cohesión.
cohesion [kou'hiːʃən], s. (fís.) cohesión, unión, enlace, conexión.
cohesive [kou'hiːsiv], a. coherente, adherente.
cohesiveness, s. cohesión, adherencia.
cohort ['kouhɔːɹt], s. cohorte.
coif [kɔif], s. cofia, gorra, toca, papalina; birrete. — v.t. cubrir con una cofia.
coiffure ['kwɑfuɹ], s. tocado, peinado.
coign [kɔin], s. esquina, ángulo saliente; coign of vantage, posición ventajosa; (impr.) cuña de impresor.
coil [kɔil], v.t. recoger, doblar en redondo; arrollar; (mar.) adujar (un cable). — v.i. replegarse, encarrujarse, arrollarse. — s. baraúnda; repliegue; (elec.) carrete; lío (de cuerdas); rollo, rosca, espiral; (mar.) adujada, pliegue (de serpiente o culebra).
coin [kɔin], v.t. acuñar, amonedar, batir; inventar, forjar; he is simply coining money, (fig.) está amontonando dinero. — v.i. falsear, falsificar moneda. — s. (ant.) rincón, esquina; (ant.) cuño; moneda, dinero; (com.) efectivo, numerario; to pay someone in his own coin, pagar a uno en la misma moneda; to coin a lie, forjar una mentira.
coinage, s. acuñación; braceaje; sistema monetario; invención.
coincide [kouin'said], v.i. coincidir; concurrir; convenir, convenirse, estar de acuerdo.
coincidence [kou'insidəns], s. casualidad, coincidencia; acuerdo, conformidad.
coincidency, s. coincidencia.
coincident, a. coincidente, concurrente, confirmante; conforme, de acuerdo. — s. coincidencia.
coincidently, adv. por coincidencia.
coindicant, a. concurrente, confirmante.
coiner ['kɔinəɹ], s. acuñador de moneda; monedero falso; fabricador, inventor.
coining, s. acuñación. — a. que acuña moneda; coining press, prensa monetaria.
coir [kɔiəɹ], s. estopa de coco; cuerda de estopa; bonote.
coition [kou'iʃən], s. coito, concúbito, cópula; (astr.) conjunción de los astros.

coke [kouk], s. cok, coque; coke oven, horno de cok. — v.t. convertir en cok.
cola, kola ['koulə], s. cola.
colabourer [kou'leibərəɹ], s. colaborador.
cola-nut, s. nuez de cola.
colander ['kɔləndəɹ], s. coladera, coladero, colador, pasador, cedazo.
colcannon [kɔl'kænən], s. plato irlandés compuesto de patatas y verduras cocidas juntas.
colchicum ['kɔlkikəm], s. (bot.) cólquico.
colcothar ['kɔlkəθɑːɹ], s. (quím.) colcótar.
cold [kould], a. frío, frígido; helado, enfriado; insensible; sin pasiones, indiferente; esquivo, reservado; serio; intratable, seco; insulso, soso, desagradable, sin gracia ni energía; tibio, flojo. — s. frío; resfriado, constipado; to be cold, tener frío; hacer frío; to catch cold, to get cold, to take cold, resfriarse, coger un resfriado, constiparse, estar constipado, acatarrarse; to leave out in the cold, dejar a uno a la luna de Valencia; to give the cold shoulder to, recibir con frialdad; to turn the cold shoulder, obrar con tibieza; to throw cold water on, desanimar.
cold-blooded, a. de sangre fría, frígido; atroz, inhumano, cruel.
cold-chisel, s. cortafrío.
cold cream, s. pomada para suavizar el cutis (ungüento de agua rosada).
cold-hearted, a. insensible.
coldish, a. frío, frescuelo, fresquito.
coldly, adv. fríamente, indiferentemente.
coldness, s. frialdad, frigidez; indiferencia, tibieza, desvío, despego, esquivez.
coleoptera [kɔli'ɔptərə], **coleopterans**, s. coleópteros.
coleopterous, a. coleoptéreo.
co-lessee, s. mediero.
colewort, s. (bot.) col verde, colza, berza.
colic ['kɔlik], s., a. (med.) cólico.
Coliseum [kɔli'siːəm], **Colosseum**, s. Coliseo.
collaborate [kə'læbəreit], v.t. colaborar.
collaboration [kəlæbə'reiʃən], s. colaboración.
collaborator [kə'læbəreitəɹ], s. colaborador.
collapse [kə'læps], s. derrumbamiento, desplome, hundimiento; (med.) colapso, postración; (fig.) fracaso; ruina. — v.i. derrumbarse, desplomarse, hundirse, debilitarse, desfallecer, postrarse; fracasar; desbaratarse; desalentarse.
collar ['kɔləɹ], s. collar, collera; cuello; golilla; pañoleta; cabezada; (mec.) argolla, anillo, cárcel, f.; (mar.) encapilladura; to slip the collar, escaparse. — v.t. poner cuello (o collar) a; (fam.) apercollar; agarrar; (vulg.) coger, hurtar.
collar-bone, s. clavícula, islilla.
collared, a. engolado.
collate [kə'leit], v.t. comparar, compulsar, cotejar, confrontar; colacionar.
collateral [kə'lætərəl], a. colateral; accesorio, indirecto; paralelo; recíproco; subsidiario, subordinado. — s. pariente colateral; (com.) resguardo, garantía; collateral security, (for.) garantía subsidiaria.
collateralness, s. colateralidad, coordinación.
collation [kə'leiʃən], s. colación, comparación, cotejo; refacción; merienda, colación.
collative ['kɔlətiv], a. colativo.
collator [kə'leitəɹ], s. colador de beneficio.
colleague ['kɔliːg], s. colega, m., compañero.

— *v.t.* asociar, agregar. — *v.i.* tener como compañero.

collect [kə'lekt], *v.t.* recoger, juntar, congregar; coleccionar; recaudar, colectar; cobrar; colegir; copilar, compilar; (*agr.*) hacer la cosecha; deducir, inferir; *to collect oneself*, volver en sí, reponerse. — *v.i.* congregar, reunirse; acumularse. — *s.* (*ecl.*) colecta.

collectable, *a.* cobrable.

collected [kə'lektəd], *a.* junto, reunido, congregado; sosegado, calmoso; con sangre fría.

collectedness, *s.* calma, sangre fría.

collectible, *a.* cobrable.

collection [kə'lekʃən], *s.* colección, compilación; cuestación, cuesta; cobro, recaudación; entrada en caja. — *pl.* examen fin de curso en Oxford, Durham, etc.

collective [kə'lektiv], *a.* (*gram.*) colectivo; congregado, agregado.

collectively, *adv.* colectivamente, en masa.

collectiveness, *s.* colectividad, pluralidad, estado colectivo.

collector, *s.* colector, coleccionador, coleccionista, *m.f.*, compilador; cobrador *o* recaudador de contribuciones.

colleen ['kɔli:n], *s.* muchacha del campo de Irlanda.

college ['kɔlidʒ], *s.* colegio; academia; sociedad.

collegial [kɔ'li:dʒiəl], *a.* colegial, del colegio.

collegian, collegiate, *s.* colegial, miembro de un colegio.

collegiate, *a.* colegiado, colegiata.

collet ['kɔlət], *s.* (*mec.*) collar; (*joy.*) engaste; (*bot.*) cerco.

collide [kə'laid], *v.i.* chocar, topar; estar en conflicto; contradecir.

collie ['kɔli], *s.* perro de pastor (Escocia).

collier ['kɔliəɹ], *s.* hullero, minero; (*mar.*) barco carbonero; mercader de carbón.

colliery, *s.* mina de carbón, comercio de carbón.

colligate ['kɔligeit], *v.t.* enlazar, coligar. — *v.i.* coligarse.

colligation [kɔli'geiʃən], *s.* coligación.

collimation, *s.* (*opt.*) colimación.

collineate, *v.t.* poner en línea los ejes de dos lentes; hacer paralelos (rayos de luz); ajustar la visual de un telescopio.

collineator, *s.* colimador.

collineation, *s.* alineación.

colliquable [kə'likwəbl], *a.* colicuable.

colliquament, *s.* materia en fusión; germen de un huevo o embrión.

colliquant, *a.* colicuante, colicuativo.

colliquate ['kɔlikweit], *v.t.* colicuar, derretir. — *v.i.* colicuarse, fundirse, disolverse.

colliquation [kɔli'kweiʃən], *s.* colicuación.

colliquative [kə'likwətiv], *a.* colicuativo.

colliquefaction [kɔlikwə'fækʃən], *s.* colicuefacción.

collision [kə'liʒən], *s.* colisión, choque, topetazo, encuentro; antagonismo, oposición, conflicto.

collocate, *v.t.* colocar, situar. — *a.* colocado, puesto.

collocation [kɔlə'keiʃən], *s.* colocación.

collodion [kə'loudiən], *s.* colodión.

collograph ['kɔləgræf], *s.* fotocolotipia.

colloid ['kɔlɔid], *a.* gelatinoso, no cristalizable; (*min.*) amorfo en parte. — *s.* substancia gelatinosa de difusión diferida como el albumen, etc.

collop ['kɔləp], *s.* tajada; bocado, pedacito.

colloquial [kə'loukwiəl], *a.* familiar, del uso común.

colloquialism, *s.* expresión familiar.

colloquially, *adv.* familiarmente, en estilo familiar.

colloquist, *s.* interlocutor.

colloquy ['kɔləkwi], *s.* coloquio.

collude [kə'lu:d], *v.i.* coludir.

collusion, *s.* colusión.

collusive, *a.* colusorio.

collusiveness, *s.* colusión, convenio fraudulento.

collusory, *a.* colusorio.

collutorium [kə'lu:tɔriəm], *s.* (*med.*) colutorio.

colly ['kɔli], *s.* hollín de carbón, negro de humo, tizne. — *v.t.* manchar, ennegrecer, ensuciar con hollín.

collyrium [kə'liriəm], *s.* (*farm.*) colirio.

colocynth ['kɔləsinθ], *s.* (*bot.*) coloquíntida.

colon ['koulən], *s.* (*gram.*) dos puntos; (*anat.*) colon, parte del intestino ciego.

colonel [kəːɹnəl], *s.* coronel.

colonelcy, colonelship, *s.* coronelía.

colonial [kə'louniəl], *a.* colonial.

colonist ['kɔlənist], *s.* colono.

colonization [kɔlənai'zeiʃən], **colonizing**, *s.* colonización.

colonize, *v.t.* colonizar. — *v.i.* establecerse en colonia.

colonizer, *s.* colonizador.

colonnade [kɔlə'neid], *s.* (*arq.*) columnata, peristilo.

colony ['kɔləni], *s.* colonia.

colophon ['kɔləfən], *s.* colofón.

colophony [kə'lɔfəni], *s.* colofonia.

color, *s.* [COLOUR].

coloration, *s.* coloración; (*farm.*) colorización, colorido.

coloratura [kɔlərə'tju:rə], *s.* (*mús.*) floreos, variaciones, cadencias caprichosas.

colorific, *a.* colorativo.

colorimeter, *s.* (*tecn.*) colorímetro.

colossal [kə'lɔsl], **colossean**, *a.* colosal.

colossus, *s.* coloso.

colostomy [kə'lɔstəmi], *s.* (*cirúg.*) collotomía.

colostrum [kə'lɔstrəm], *s.* calostro.

colour ['kʌləɹ], *s.* color, tinte, matiz; colorido; materia colorante; tez; pintura; (*for.*) *prima facie* derecho. — *pl.* **colours**, estandarte, bandera, pabellón; (*fig.*) pretexto, motivo, excusa, apariencia, semejanza, pretensión; timbre, calidad de tono; carácter en general; genio, disposición del ánimo; calidad emocional; viveza, animación; *dark colour*, color obscuro; *fast colour*, color sólido; *gaudy colour*, color vivo, colorines; *light colour*, color claro; *fresh colour*, tez rosada; *primary colours*, colores primitivos; *water colour*, acuarela; *oil colour*, color al óleo; *colour blindness*, daltonismo; *colour-sergeant*, portaestandarte; *to lose one's colour*, perder el color; *to hoist the colours*, (*mar.*) enarbolar la bandera; *to strike one's colours*, (*mar.*) amainar el pabellón; *under colour of*, so color de, con pretexto de, bajo capa de; *with flying colours*, a banderas desplegadas. — *v.t.* colorar, colorir, pintar, teñir; dar los colores; iluminar; matizar; blanquear (una pared); extenuar, paliar. — *v.i.* colorearse; ponerse colorado; encenderse, enrojecer, ruborizarse.

colourable, *a.* plausible, especioso.

coloured, *a.* colorado, colorido, pintado, teñido, iluminado; plausible, especioso; exagerado; embellecido; persona de color (de raza negra); *high-coloured*, encendido.

colouring, *s.* coloración; estilo, aire, color, pretexto; (*pint.*) colorido; blanqueo.

colourist, *s.* colorista, *m.f.*

colourless, *a.* descolorido, incoloro, sin color.

colporteur ['kɔlpɔːɪtəɪ], *s.* agente, viajante de una sociedad religiosa, que vende o distribuye libros o folletos piadosos.

colt [kɔlt], *s.* potro; mozuelo sin juicio; azote con nudo; *colt's foot*, (*bot.*) tusílago; *to cast one's colt's tooth*, perder el ardor de la juventud.

colter, *s.* reja de arado.

coltish, *a.* juguetón, aturdido, retozón.

coluber ['kɔljubəɪ], *s.* (*zool.*) una de las especies de serpientes inofensivas, *colubriformes*.

columbary, *s.* palomar; (*arqueol.*) columbario.

columbate [kəˈlʌmbeit], *s.* (*quím.*) tantalita.

columbian, *s., a.* colombiano; colombino, relativo a Colón; perteneciente o relativo a los Estados Unidos de Norteamérica.

columbine ['kɔləmbain], *a.* columbino, de la paloma; tornasolado, color cambiante; (*teat.*) Colombina. — *s.* (*bot.*) aguileña.

columella [kɔljuˈmelə], *s.* (*anat.* y *zool.*) varilla, columna o eje central como la de la cóclea; (*bot.*) eje central como el de un musgo.

column ['kɔləm], *s.* (*arq.*) columna, pilar.

columnar, *a.* columnario, en forma de columna.

colza, *s.* colza.

coma ['koumə], *s.* (*med.*) coma, *m.*, letargo; (*astr.*) cabellera; (*bot.*) hebras sedosas que hay en el extremo de algunas semillas.

co-mate, *s.* compañero, camarada, *m.f.* — *a.* cabelludo.

comatoso, comatous, *a.* (*med.*) comatoso, letárgico.

comb [koum], *s.* peine, peineta; rasqueta, almohaza; carda, carducha, rastrillo; cresta de gallo; (*api.*) panal; cresta de ola; cumbre, *f.*, cima; *curry-comb*, almohaza; *large-toothed comb*, escarpidor; *small-toothed comb*, peine lino, lendrera. — *v.t.* peinar; cardar (lana), carduzar; rastrillar (lino). — *v.i.* encresparse y romper (las olas).

combat ['kɔmbæt], *s.* combate, desafío, lucha, pelea, batalla; *single combat*, duelo, combate singular. — *v.i.* pelear, combatir, luchar. — *v.t.* combatir, resistir, impugnar.

combatable [kəˈbætəbl], *a.* combatible.

combatant, *s.* combatiente, campeón. — *a.* combatiente, lidiador, peleador.

combativeness, *s.* combatividad.

combe, *s.* hondonada, valle estrecho entre montes.

combed [koumd], *a.* peinado.

comber, *s.* peinador, cardador (de lana); ola encrestada, cabrilla, rompiente.

combinable [kɔmˈbainəbl], *a.* combinable.

combination [kɔmbiˈneiʃən], *s.* combinación, unión, mezcla; coalición, cábala, complot, liga; concurso (de circunstancias).

combinative, *a.* combinatorio.

combine [kəmˈbain], *v.t.* combinar, mezclar, unir, ajustar, formar. — *v.i.* unirse, juntarse, conspirar, maquinar.

combing [koumiŋ], *s.* peinada, cardadura, rastrillaje; *combing-cloth*, peinador, especie de capa; *combing-machine*, máquina de peinar.

combustibility, *s.* combustibilidad.

combustible [kəmˈbʌstibl], *s., a.* combustible.

combustibleness, *s.* combustibilidad.

combustion, *s.* combustión, quema, incendio; (*fig.*) tumulto, alboroto.

come [kʌm], *v.i.* (*pret.* **came**; *p.p.* **come**) venir, llegar, aproximarse, acercarse; adelantarse, avanzar, aparecer, salir; suceder, acontecer; moverse a la vista, hacerse perceptible; estar presente, existir; llegar a ser, conseguir algo; proceder; (*interj.*) come! come! ¡ea! ¡vámonos! come in! ¡adelante! *come what may*, suceda lo que fuere; *to come about*, acaecer, conseguir, efectuar; *to come across*, (*fig.*) encontrar, tropezar con; *to come after*, seguir, venir después; venir detrás; *to come again*, volver, venir otra vez; *to come apart*, desunirse, deshacerse; *to come at*, alcanzar, conseguir; *to come away*, irse, retirarse; *to come back*, retroceder, volver; *to come before*, anteponerse, llegar antes; *to come between*, interponerse, intervenir; *to come by*, venir por, pasar junto a; obtener, encontrar; *to come down*, descender, bajar; *to come for*, venir a buscar; *to come forth*, adelantarse, salir; *to come forward*, avanzar, adelantar, llegar primero; medrar; *to come home*, volver a casa; *to come in*, entrar, llegar; *to come in for*, exponerse a, estar sometido a; *to come into the world*, venir al mundo, nacer; *to come near*, acercarse; *to come next*, venir después, seguir; *to come of*, venir, proceder de; *to come of age*, llegar a ser mayor de edad; *to come off*, salir bien, tener éxito; realizarse, tener lugar; romperse, soltarse; *to come off a loser*, perder; *to come off without a scratch*, salir limpio de polvo y paja; *to come off well*, salir bien; *to come on*, avanzar, medrar; come on! ¡vamos!; *to come out with*, salir con, dar salida; dejar escapar, aflojar, soltar; *to come over*, pasar por encima; *to come round*, efectuarse, convenir, asentir; restablecerse, volver en sí; *to come short of*, faltar, fracasar, salir mal de; *to come to*, acercarse; llegar a obtener, alcanzar; conseguir; estar reducido a; recobrar los sentidos; *to come to blows*, andar al morro; llegar a las manos; *to come to and fro*, pasar y repasar; *to come to grief*, salir mal parado; *to come to hand*, venir a mano; *to come to nothing*, reducirse a nada, no valer nada; *to come to pass*, acaecer, acontecer, suceder; *to come to terms*, convenirse, aceptar condiciones; *to come together*, juntarse, venir juntos; *to come true*, realizarse; *to come up to*, llegar a, acercarse a, subir a, juntarse con, abordar (un buque); *to come up with*, alcanzar; *to come upon*, embestir, atacar, agarrar, sorprender; encontrarse con, dar con.

comedian [kəˈmiːdiən], *s.* comediante, actor, cómico; escritor de comedias.

comedienne, *s.* cómica, actriz, comedianta.

comedy ['kɔmidi], *s.* comedia.

comeliness ['kʌmlines], *s.* donaire, donosura, hermosura, garbo, modestia, gracia; cortesía.

comely ['kʌmli], *a.* gentil, donoso, apuesto, garboso, hermoso, bien parecido; decente, modesto, honesto. — *adv.* donosamente, decentemente, gentilmente.

come-off, s. peroración, conclusión; salida, pretexto, excusa, escapatoria.

comer, s. viniente; *new-comer*, recién venido.

comestible [kə'mestibl], s., a. comestible.

comet ['kɔmət], s. (*astron.*) cometa, *m.*

cometary, a. cometario.

cometic [kə'metik], a. que se refiere a los cometas.

comet-like, a. semejante a un cometa.

cometography [kɔmə'tɔgrəfi], s. cometografía.

comfit ['kʌmfit], s. confite; *comfit-maker,* confitero.

comfiture, s. confitura.

comfort ['kʌmfəɹt], s. confortación, auxilio, asistencia; comodidad; consuelo, alivio; satisfacción, solaz; bienestar; conveniencia; regalo. — *v.t.* confortar, fortificar; alegrar, divertir; animar, vivificar, alentar; consolar, solazar; (*for.*) ayudar, apoyar.

comfortable, a. cómodo; dulce; consolador, confortativo; *to feel comfortable,* estar bien, sentirse bien; *to be in comfortable circumstances,* pasarlo cómodamente.

comfortableness, s. comodidad; bienestar; consuelo.

comfortably, adv. cómodamente, agradablemente, a pierna suelta.

comforter, s. consolador, confortador; bufanda, tapabocas; (*teo.*) el Espíritu Santo.

comfortless, a. desconsolado, inconsolable, sin consuelo, desesperado; incómodo.

comfrey ['kʌmfri], s. (*bot.*) consuelda.

comic ['kɔmik], **comical,** a. cómico, burlesco, gracioso, bufo. – *s.pl.* comics, (*fam., usu. pl.*) periódico infantil.

comically, adv. cómicamente, burlescamente.

comicalness, s. gracia, jocosidad, chiste, gracejo, carácter cómico.

coming ['kʌmiŋ], a. próximo, venidero, futuro. — s. venida, llegada, advenimiento; *coming-on,* llegada; *coming-out,* salida. — *pl.* renta, ingresos.

comitia [ko'miʃiə], s. comicios.

comitial, a. comicial.

comity ['kɔmiti], s. urbanidad, cortesía, bienquerencia.

comma ['kɔmə], s. (*gram., mús.*) coma; *turned comma,* (*impr.*) virgulilla.

command [kə'mɑːnd], s. mando, poder, dominio, (*mil.*) comando; autoridad, dominación, imperio; mandamiento, mandato, orden, *m., f.;* alcance, perspectiva; recursos, facilidad; cuerpo de tropas bajo el mando de un oficial. — *v.t.* mandar, dictar, comandar, ordenar, regir, dominar, disponer, gobernar, acaudillar, capitanear. — *v.i.* tener poder o autoridad, gobernar, imperar, reinar; *to have at one's command,* tener a su disposición; *to have a good command of a language,* dominar un idioma.

commandable, a. que se puede mandar.

commandant ['kɔməndənt], s. comandante.

commander [kə'mɑːndəɹ], s. comandante, jefe, caudillo, capitán, comendador; *commander-in-chief,* generalísimo.

commandership, s. comandancia, encomienda.

commanding, a. (*mil.*) comandante; dominante; imponente, imperativo.

commandingly, adv. imperativamente; con tono de mando.

commandment, s. mandato, precepto. — *pl.*

the Ten Commandments, mandamientos de la ley de Dios; (*vulg.*) los dedos de las manos.

commando [kə'mɑːndou], s. cuerpo de gente armada llamada para un servicio militar, comando; expedición, incursión de boéres o portugueses en el África del Sur.

commeasurable [kə'meʒurəbl], a. conmensurable.

commemorable [kə'memərəbl], a. memorable.

commemorate, *v.t.* conmemorar.

commemoration [kəmemə'reiʃən], s. conmemoración.

commemorative [kə'memərətiv], a. conmemorativo.

commemoratory [kəmemə'reitəri], a. conmemoratorio.

commence [kə'mens], *v.i.* comenzar, empezar; (Universidad) licenciarse en una facultad. — *v.t.* comenzar, principiar, iniciar, entablar.

commencement, s. principio, comienzo, inauguración.

commend [kə'mend], *v.t.* encomendar, recomendar; ensalzar, alabar; encargar.

commendable, a. recomendable, loable, autorizado.

commendableness, s. mérito.

commendam, s. beneficio tenido en encomienda.

commendation, s. recomendación, cumplimientos, memorias; alabanza, encomio.

commendator, s. comendatario.

commendatory [kɔmen'deitəri], a. comendatario, beneficiado; recomendatorio, encomendero. — s. encomio.

commender [kə'mendəɹ], s. persona que recomienda; panegirista, *m.f.;* alabador.

commensal [kə'mensəl], s. comensal; (*biol.*) asociado (anémona marina; cangrejo hermitaño).

commensalism, commensality, s. comensalía.

commensurability [kəmenʃərə'biliti], s. **commensurableness,** s. conmensurabilidad.

commensurable [kə'menʃərəbl], a. conmensurable, proporcionado.

commensurate, a. conmensurado, proporcionado; conmensurativo. — *v.t.* conmensurar.

commensuration [kəmenʃə'reiʃən], s. conmensuración, proporción.

comment ['kɔment], *v.t.* comentar, anotar. — *v.i.* glosar, escoliar, explicar. — s. comento, glosa, explicación, escolio; observación.

commentary, s. comentario, interpretación, glosa, escolio.

commentate, *v.i.* comentar, anotar, glosar.

commentator, commenter, s. comentador; comentarista, *m.f.*

commentitious [kɔmen'tiʃəs], a. (*ant.*) imaginario, fingido, falso, inventado.

commerce ['kɔməɹs], s. comercio, negocios, contratación, tráfico; amistad, trato familiar, correspondencia; comercio, un juego de naipes; (*fig.*) cópula, coito. — *v.i.* comerciar, traficar, negociar; estar en relaciones, juntarse, asociarse.

commercial [kə'məːɹʃəl], a. comercial, comerciante, mercante, mercantil.

commerge [kə'məːɹdʒ], *v.i.* mezclarse, unirse.

commigrate [kə'maigreit], *v.i.* emigrar con otros.

commination [kɔmi'neiʃən], s. conminación, amenaza.

comminatory, a. conminatorio.

commingle [kə'miŋgl], v.t. mezclar, hacer mezcla de. — v.i. mezclarse, unirse, barajarse.

comminute ['kɔminjut], v.t. moler, desmenuzar, pulverizar; dividir en pedazos menudos.

comminution, s. atenuación; división, pulverización.

commiserable, a. lastimoso, digno de compasión.

commiserate [kə'mizəreit], v.t. apiadarse, compadecerse, tener lástima.

commiseration [kəmizə'reiʃən], s. conmiseración, compasión, piedad.

commiserative [kə'mizərətiv], a. compasivo.

commiserator, s. persona compasiva.

commissarial [kɔmi'sɛəriəl], a. de comisario, concerniente al comisario.

commissariat, s. cuerpo de administración militar; (for., Esco.) comisaría.

commissarist, s. comisaría, comisariato; (mil.) intendencia, administración militar.

commissary ['kɔmisəri], s. comisario; (mil.) intendente militar; delegado.

commissaryship, s. comisariato, comisaría.

commission [kə'miʃən], s. comisión, misión, encargo; cometido, patente; despacho; nombramiento; (com.) mando, comisión; sueldo de comisionista, corretaje; perpetración (de un crimen); to throw up one's commission, dar su dimisión; to put into commission, poner (un buque) en servicio. — v.t. comisionar, autorizar, apoderar, encargar, diputar, facultar; commissioned officer, oficial.

commissional, commissionary, a. comisionado.

commissioner, s. comisionado, factor, apoderado; comisario, comisionista, m.f.; empleado de comercio.

commissure ['kɔmisjuəɹ], s. (anat.) comisura; (arq.) juntura de dos piedras; aplicación de una superficie a otra.

commit [kə'mit], v.t. cometer, perpetrar; encomendar, encargar, confiar; entregar, depositar, encarcelar, encerrar; to commit to memory, aprender de memoria; to commit oneself, comprometerse; to commit to paper, poner por escrito.

commitment, s. auto de prisión o de procesamiento; perpetración; comisión; obligación, compromiso; encierro, encarcelamiento.

committal, s. fianza; consignación; comisión; encierro, encarcelamiento.

committee, s. comisión, diputación, delegación, junta; comité; oficina; (for.) guardián judicial de un demente o imbécil y de sus bienes; joint committee, comisión colectiva; standing committee, comisión permanente.

commix [kə'miks], v.t. mezclar, misturar. — v.i. mezclarse, confundirse, unir.

commixtion, commixture, s. mixtión, mixtura, mezcla, compuesto.

commode [kə'moud], s. cómoda; inodoro; lavabo cubierto; tocado de mujer del siglo XVIII.

commodious [kə'moudiəs], a. cómodo, conveniente, espacioso, útil, holgado.

commodiousness, s. comodidad, conveniencia, holgura.

commodity [kə'mɔditi], s. comodidad; interés, provecho, conveniencia, utilidad, ventaja. — pl. **commodities**, géneros, mercaderías, productos.

commodore ['kɔmədoəɹ], s. (mar.) comodóro, jefe de escuadra; navío capitana.

common ['kɔmən], a. común, usual, corriente, general, público, vulgar, ordinario; bajo, inferior, adocenado; common crier, pregonero; the common man, el hombre medio, el hombre de carne y hueso; common fraction, quebrado; common ground, (fig.) base de acuerdo; common sense, sentido común, sensatez; common sewer, albañal; common soldier, soldado raso; common people, pueblo, masas; populacho; common law, derecho consuetudinario; in common, en común; to be out of the common, no estar en el mapa; it's nothing out of the common, no es cosa del otro jueves. — s. común, comunal, bienes o pastos comunes, terreno comunal. — pl. **commons**, vulgo, pueblo, clase proletaria; Cámara de los Comunes; comida ordinaria; mesa redonda; víveres. — v.i. tener derecho de pastos comunes; vivir juntos.

commonable, a. común, comunal.

commonage, s. derecho de pastar (ganados) en común.

commonalty, s. pueblo, sociedad, comunidad, comunal.

commoner, s. plebeyo, comunero; miembro de la cámara baja; estudiante no interno (en Oxford); partícipe.

commonness, s. frecuencia; comunidad; vulgaridad, ordinariez.

commonplace, a. común, trivial, vulgar. — s. memento, apunte, nota; lugar común; commonplace book, libro de memorias; commonplace topics, lugares comunes.

commonweal, commonwealth, s. estado, nación, cosa pública, república, bienes públicos; comunidad.

commotion [kə'mouʃən], s. conmoción, agitación, perturbación, excitación, tumulto; movimiento de mar.

communal, a. comunal, público.

commune ['kɔmju:n], v.i. conversar, platicar, departir; meditar; comulgar. — s. (pol.) comuna; comunión, intimidad.

communicability [kəmju:nikə'biliti], s. comunicabilidad.

communicable [kə'mju:nikəbl], a. comunicable, comunicativo, contagioso.

communically, adv. con comunicación.

communicant, s. comunicante, comulgante.

communicate [kə'mju:nikeit], v.t. comunicar, dar la comunión; notificar; transmitir; tener correspondencia. — v.i. conmunicarse; comulgar, recibir la sagrada comunión.

communication [kəmju:ni'keiʃən], s. comunicación, acceso, entrada, paso, participación; trato, correspondencia; notificación; carta, mensaje; despacho, oficio; plática, conversación; evil communications corrupt good manners, la manzana podrida pierde a su compañía.

communicative [kə'mju:nikətiv], a. comunicativo: expansivo.

communicativeness, s. comunicabilidad.

communicator, s. comunicador.

communicatory, a. comunicatorio.

communion [kə'mju:njən], s. comunión,

trato familiar, comunicación; confraternidad; congregación; sagrada comunión.

communionist, *s.* miembro de una comunión.

communism, *s.* comunismo.

communist ['kɔmjuːnist], *s.* comunista, *m.f.*

communistic [kɔmjuː'nistik], *a.* perteneciente al comunismo; común.

community [kə'mjuːniti], *s.* comunidad, comun, sociedad, público; corporación; cuerpo político.

commutability [kəmjuːtə'biliti], *s.* conmutabilidad.

commutable [kə'mjuːtəbl], *a.* conmutable, permutable.

commutation [kɔmjuː'teiʃən], *s.* mudanza, alteración; trueque, cambio; (*for.*) conmutación.

commutative [kə'mjuːtətiv], *a.* conmutativo.

commutator, *s.* conmutador.

commute [kə'mjuːt], *v.t.* conmutar, permutar, cambiar, trocar, rescatar; igualarse, abonarse, ajustarse. — *v.i.* conmutar, permutar.

comose ['koumous], *a.* (*bot.*) peludo.

compact ['kɔmpækt], *s.* pacto, concierto, convenio, ajuste, tratado. — *v.t.* consolidar, comprimir, apretar; convenir, pactar, componer, compaginar. — *v.i.* coligarse, unirse con. — *a.* compacto, denso, apretado, cerrado, firme, sólido, macizo; breve, compendioso; compuesto, hecho.

compacted, *a.* consolidado, firme, apretado.

compactly, *adv.* sólidamente, estrechamente; con concisión; de una manera compacta.

compactness, *s.* densidad; estrechez; firmeza, unión, *f.*

compages [kə'pɑːdʒiːs], *s.* trabazón, *f.*, juntura, enlace.

compaginate [kəm'pædʒineit], *v.t.* compaginar, juntar, adaptar, enlazar.

companion [kəm'pænjən], *s.* compañero, socio, camarada, *m.f.*; colega, *m.*, condiscípulo; acompañante; caballero de una orden; (*mar.*) lumbrera; chupeta; *boon companion,* buen compañero; *companion ladder,* escala de toldilla; *companion way,* escalera de la cámara.

companionable, *a.* sociable, agradable.

companionship, *s.* compañía, sociedad; familiaridad entre camaradas; compañerismo.

company ['kʌmpani], *s.* compañía, asociación, sociedad; visitas, tertulia; compañero, acompañante; socio; cuerpo, gremio; (*mar.*) tripulación; *to have company,* tener visitas; *to part company, quit company,* separarse, dar esquinazo; *to keep company,* frecuentar, acompañar; *to keep company with,* cortejar, galantear.

comparable ['kɔmpərəbl], *a.* comparable.

comparative, *a.* comparativo, relativo, respectivo.

compare [kəm'pɛəɹ], *v.t.* comparar, confrontar, cotejar, compulsar, colacionar, comprobar, equiparar, paragonar. — *s.* comparación; cotejo; *beyond compare,* sin comparación, sin igual.

comparing, *s.* comparación.

comparison [kəm'pærisən], *s.* comparación, confrontación, cotejo, comprobación; paralelo, paridad; símil; metáfora.

compartment [kəm'pɑːɹtmənt], *s.* compartimiento; división; departamento; tablero; cajoncito, gaveta; (*her.*) cuartel.

compass ['kʌmpəs], *v.t.* cercar, rodear, circuir; bloquear, sitiar; conseguir, lograr, obtener, alcanzar; acabar, concluir; conspirar; comprender, entender, concebir; trazar, idear, maquinar; *to compass one's designs,* conseguir su objeto. — *s.* círculo, circuito, circunferencia, ámbito; alcance, extensión; (*mús.*) compás; (*fig.*) límites; moderación; poder; espacio; (*mar.*) brújula; aguja de marear; intención, propósito, designio. — *pl.*

compasses, compás.

compassable, *a.* asequible.

compassion [kəm'pæʃən], *s.* compasión; lástima, piedad, conmiseración. — *v.t.* tener lástima.

compassionable, *a.* lastimoso.

compassionate, *a.* compasivo, compasible. — *v.t.* compadecer, tener lástima.

compaternity [kɔmpə'təːniti], *s.* compadrazgo.

compatibility [kəm'pæti'biliti], **compatibleness,** *s.* compatibilidad.

compatible [kəm'pætibl], *a.* compatible.

compatriot, *s.* compatriota, *m.f.*, compatricio, paisano.

compeer [kəm'piəɹ], *s.* compañero, compadre, colega, *m.* — *v.t.* igualar con, ser igual a, rivalizar.

compel [kəm'pel], *v.t.* compeler, constreñir, obligar, precisar, forzar.

compellable, *a.* que puede ser compelido.

compellably, *adv.* a viva fuerza.

compellation [kɔmpə'leiʃən], *s.* tratamiento, denominación, nombre.

compeller [kəm'peləɹ], *s.* compulsor, apremiador.

compend [kəm'pend], *s.* [COMPENDIUM].

compendious [kəm'pendiəs], *a.* compendioso, breve, sucinto, reducido.

compendiousness, *s.* concisión, brevedad.

compendium, compend, *s.* compendio, resumen, epítome, extracto, sinopsis, *f.*

compensable [kəm'pensəbl], *a.* compensable.

compensate ['kɔmpenseit], *v.t.* compensar, indemnizar, reparar, resarcir, remunerar. — *v.i.* compensarse.

compensation [kɔmpen'seiʃən], *s.* compensación, equivalencia; resarcimiento; desagravio; (*for.*) indemnización; *compensation balance, bar* o *pendulum,* volante, balanza, barra o péndulo de compensación de un reloj.

compensative, compensatory, *a.* compensatorio.

compensator, *s.* compensador.

compesce [kəm'pes], *v.t.* (*ant.*) refrenar, contener, restringir, limitar.

compete [kəm'piːt], *v.i.* competir, contender, rivalizar.

competence, competency, *s.* suficiencia, subsistencia; bienestar; lo bastante; aptitud, capacidad; (*for.*) competencia.

competent ['kɔmpetənt], *a.* competente, adecuado, bastante, suficiente, capaz, propio, apto, calificado.

competition [kɔmpə'tiʃən], *s.* competición, competencia; rivalidad, concurrencia; certamen, oposición, concurso.

competitive [kəm'petitiv], *a.* de la competencia, de concurso; *competitive examination,* examen de concurso u oposición.

competitor, *s.* competidor, rival, opositor, antagonista, *m.f.*

competitress, competitrix, *s.* competidora.

compilation [kɔmpi'leiʃən], *s.* compilación, recopilación, colección, recolección.

compile [kəm'pail], *v.t.* compilar, recopilar.

compilement, *s.* compilación, colección.

compiler, *s.* compilador; recopilador.

complacence [kəm'pleisəns], **complacency**, *s.* contento de sí mismo; (*ant.*) complacencia, placer, satisfacción.

complacent, *a.* complaciente, satisfecho.

complacently, *adv.* afablemente; con placer, con satisfacción.

complain [kəm'plein], *v.i.* quejarse, lamentarse, dolerse, querellarse; (*for.*) acusar, demandar.

complainant, *s.* querellante, demandante.

complainer, *s.* lamentador, querellador.

complaining, *s.* lamento, quejido.

complaining, *a.* quejoso.

complaint, *s.* queja, lamento, llanto, quejido; agravio, querella, causa u objeto de un agravio; (*for.*) queja, demanda; mal, enfermedad.

complaisance, *s.* complacencia, condescendencia; afabilidad, cortesía, deseo de agradar.

complaisant, *a.* cortés, atento, complaciente, cumplimentero.

complaisantly, *adv.* cortésmente.

complanate ['kɔmpləneit], *v.t.* (*ant.*) aplanar, allanar. — *a.* llano, aplanado, que está en el mismo plano.

complect [kəm'plekt], *v.t.* entretejer, enlazar.

complement ['kɔmpli:ment], *s.* complemento; colmo; apéndice, accesorio; (*mil.*) contingente, fuerza numérica; (*mar.*) tripulación completa; (*mar.*) complemento de la derrota. — *v.t.* suplir una falta, acabar, hacer cabal o perfecto.

complemental [kɔmpli:'mentl], *s.* completivo.

complementary, *a.* complementario; *complementary colour*, color complementario.

complete [kəm'pli:t], *a.* completo, perfecto, acabado, cumplido, colmado, cabal, consumado, entero, íntegro, lleno, pleno. — *v.t.* completar, acabar, concluir, consumar, terminar.

completely, *adv.* por completo, completamente, perfectamente, enteramente, totalmente, cabalmente.

completement, completeness, *s.* complemento, conclusión, fin; perfección, integridad, entereza; totalidad.

completion, *s.* complemento, terminación, acabamiento; realización, consumación.

completive, *a.* completivo.

completory, *s.* (*ecl.*) completas. — *a.* complementario.

complex ['kɔmpleks], *a.* complejo, complicado, múltiple; compuesto. — *s.* complejo; *inferiority complex*, complejo de inferioridad.

complexion [kəm'plekʃən], *s.* (*ant.*) complexo; tez, cutis; complexión, inclinación, naturaleza, carácter.

complexional, *a.* complexional.

complexity, complexness, *s.* complejidad, complejidad.

compliance [kəm'plaians], *s.* sumisión, docilidad, obediencia; cumplimiento; complacencia, condescendencia, consentimiento.

compliant, *a.* flexible; rendido, sumiso, dócil, obediente, condescendiente, complaciente, acomodaticio, fácil.

complicacy, *s.* complicación, enredo.

complicate ['kɔmplikeit], *v.t.* complicar, confundir, mezclar, embrollar, enredar. — *a.* complicado, complejo, enredado, revesado.

complicateness, complication, *s.* complicación, perplejidad, enredo.

complicity [kəm'plisiti], *s.* complicidad, complicación.

complier [kəm'plaiəɹ], *s.* consentidor, contemporizador, hombre condescendiente.

compliment ['kɔmplimənt], cumplimiento, cumplido; regalo, obsequio; lisonja, galantería; requiebro, piropo; fineza, favor. — *v.t.* cumplimentar. — *v.i.* hacer cumplimientos.

complimental, *a.* cumplido, cortés.

complimentary, *a.* ceremonioso, lisonjero, galante; cumplido, obsequioso; gratuito.

complimenter, *s.* cumplimentero, adulador.

compline ['kɔmplin], *s.* (*ecl.*) completas.

complot ['kɔmplɔt], *s.* trama, conspiración, cábala. — *v.t.* tramar, conspirar, conjurar.

complotter, *s.* conspirador, conjurado.

comply [kəm'plai], *v.i.* cumplir; ceder, condescender, consentir, conformarse, acomodarse, someterse, obedecer; llenar, satisfacer.

component [kəm'pounənt], *a.* componente. — *s.* parte constitutiva.

comport [kəm'poəɹt], *v.t.*, *v.i.* convenir, concordar; tolerar, sufrir, aguantar; comportarse, portarse. — *s.* conducta, porte; comportamiento.

comportable, *a.* conforme, compatible, conveniente.

comportment, *s.* comportamiento, conducta, porte.

compose [kəm'pouz], *v.t.* componer, formar, arreglar, ordenar, colocar; reglar, ajustar; calmar, sosegar, apaciguar; serenar; (*impr.*) preparar; redactar, escribir; crear, inventar, concertar; (*mús.*) componer.

composed, *a.* tranquilo, sosegado, sereno, compuesto.

composedness, *s.* serenidad, tranquilidad, calma, compostura.

composer, *s.* autor, escritor, compositor (de música); (*impr.*) cajista, *m.*; conciliador, componedor.

composing, *s.* (*impr.*) composición; *composing-stick*, (*impr.*) componedor.

compositæ [kəm'pɔsiti], *s.pl.* (*bot.*) compuestas (orden de plantas).

composite ['kɔmpəzait], *a.* compuesto, mixto; (*arit.*) múltiplo; (*arq.*) compuesto, uno de los cinco órdenes de arquitectura. — *s.* compuesto, mezcla, mixtura; (*bot.*) una de las flores o plantas compuestas.

composition [kɔmpə'ziʃən], *s.* composición, compuesto, mezcla, convención, ajuste, acomodamiento, compostura; obra literaria o musical; (*com.*) arreglo, transacción.

compositive [kəm'pɔsitiv], *a.* compuesto, compositivo.

compositor, *s.* arreglador, componedor; (*impr.*) compositor, cajista, *m.*

compossible, *a.* capaz de existir con otra cosa.

compost ['kɔmpɔst], *s.* (*agr.*) abono, estiércol. — *v.t.* abonar, estercolar, engrasar la tierra.

composure [kəm'pouʒəɹ], *s.* compostura; serenidad, tranquilidad, calma, sangre fría; composición.

compotation [kɔmpo'teiʃən], s. el acto de beber en compañía.

compote ['kɔmpɔt], s. compota, dulce.

compound [kɔm'paund], v.t. componer, arreglar, confeccionar, combinar, mezclar, acomodar; transigir. — v.i. componerse; ajustar; ponerse acorde; avenirse, transigir; componer un pleito o desavenencia; hacer un arreglo un deudor con sus acreedores pagando solamente una parte de la deuda. — ['kɔmpaund] a. compuesto, mezclado. — s. mezcla, mixtura; patio exterior de una casa en India o China.

compoundable, a. componible.

compounder, s. compositor; mediador, mezclador.

comprehend [kɔmpri'hend], v.t. comprender; contener, incluir; entender, penetrar; concebir; encerrar.

comprehensible [kɔmpri'hensibl], a. comprensible, inteligible.

comprehensibleness, s. comprensibilidad.

comprehension, s. comprensión, concepción; compendio, sumario; inteligencia.

comprehensive, a. comprensivo; amplio, extenso, vasto.

comprehensively, adv. comprensivamente, con suma extensión.

comprehensiveness, s. comprensión, extensión, alcance, cabida; perspicacia, entendimiento; (frenol.) comprensibilidad. —

compress [kɔm'pres], v.t. comprimir, apretar, estrechar, condensar; reducir, abreviar. — s. compresa; (cir.) cabezal.

compressible [kɔm'presibl], a. compresible, comprimible, apretadizo.

compression, s. compresión; (fig.) concentración; compression ratio, índice de compresión.

compressor, s. compresor.

comprise [kɔm'praiz], v.t. comprender, contener, incluir, encerrar, abrazar, abarcar.

compromise ['kɔmprəmaiz], s. compromiso, obligación; arreglo, transacción, arbitrio, avenencia, componenda, término medio. — v.t. comprometer, conceder, acordar; arbitrar, arreglar, zanjar, transigir; exponer, arriesgar. — v.i. transigir.

compromiser, s. compromisario.

comptograph ['kɔmptəgræf], s. máquina de calcular.

comptroller [kən'troulər], s. contralor, interventor; sobrestante.

compulsatory [kəm'pʌlsətəri], a. (ant.) compulsorio, coactivo.

compulsatively, compulsively, adv. por fuerza, a la fuerza.

compulsion [kəm'pʌlʃən], s. compulsión, coacción, apremio.

compunction [kəm'pʌŋkʃən], s. compunción, remordimiento, contrición.

compunctious, a. compungido, contrito.

compunctive, a. compungivo.

compurgation [kɔmpəɹ'geiʃən], s. compurgación, justificación de veracidad.

computable [kəm'pju:təbl], a. computable, estimable.

computation [kɔmpju:'teiʃən], s. computación, cómputo, cuenta, cálculo.

compute [kəm'pju:t], v.t. computar, contar, calcular, estimar.

computer, s. computista, m.f., calculador; calculadora, f., (máquina).

comrade ['kɔmreid], s. camarada, m.f., compañero, asociado, compinche, amigo.

con, s. contra; the pros and the cons, el pro y el contra; neither pro nor con, ni a favor ni en contra. — v.t. aprender de memoria; saber; (mar.) gobernar un buque.

conatus [kou'nɑ:təs], s. conato, tentativa.

concamerate [kɔnkæmə'reit], v.t. abovedar; dividir en cámaras.

concameration [kɔnkæmə'reiʃən], s. arco, bóveda; pieza abovedada; división en cámaras.

concatenate [kən'kætineit], v.t. concatenar, encadenar. — a. eslabonado.

concatenation [kənkæti'neiʃən], s. concatenación, eslabonamiento, encadenamiento, serie, f., sucesión.

concave ['kɔnkeiv], a. cóncavo, hueco, vacío. — v.t. excavar. — s. hondón, hueco; bóveda.

concaveness, concavity, s. concavidad, hueco, profundidad, vacío.

concavo-concave, s. cóncavo-cóncavo.

concavo-convex, cóncavo-convexo.

conceal [kən'si:l], v.t. callar, tapar, ocultar, esconder, disimular, encubrir, recatar, cubrir con un velo.

concealable, a. disimulable, ocultable, escondible.

concealedness, s. encubrimiento, recato.

concealer, s. ocultador, encubridor.

concealment, s. ocultación, encubrimiento, secreto; misterio; escondrijo, escondite; retiro.

concede [kən'si:d], v.t. conceder, admitir. — v.i. convenir, asentir, acordar.

conceit [kən'si:t], s. concepto, capricho, pensamiento, idea, fantasía, imaginación; amor propio; presunción, arrogancia, engreimiento, vanagloria. — v.t. (ant.) conceptuar, imaginar, concebir; encapricharse, engreírse.

conceited, a. infatuado, afectado, vanidoso, engreído, presumido; vanaglorioso, caprichoso.

conceitedness, s. presunción, vanidad; amor propio; afectación.

conceivable, a. concebible, imaginable, inteligible, creíble.

conceivableness, s. conceptibilidad.

conceivably, adv. de un modo conceptible.

conceive [kən'si:v], v.t. concebir, entender; comprender, imaginar, crear, ingeniar, engendrar, originar; formular, expresar. — v.i. concebir, hacerse preñada (la hembra); imaginar, pensar.

conceiver, s. el que concibe.

concent [kən'sent], s. concento, concentus, s. concento, concierto (de sonidos), consonancia, armonía.

concentrate ['kɔnsəntreit], v.t. concentrar, reconcentrar; enfocar. — a. concentrado.

concentration [kɔnsən'treiʃən], s. concentración, reconcentración.

concentrator, s. concentrador.

concentre [kən'sentəɹ], v.t. concentrar, reconcentrar, enfocar. — v.i. reconcentrarse.

concentric [kən'sentrik], **concentrical**, a. concéntrico.

concentricity [kɔnsən'trisiti], s. concentricidad.

concentus, s. [CONCENT].

concept ['kɔnsept], s. concepto.

conceptibility [kənsepti'biliti], s. conceptibilidad.

conceptible [kən'septibl], a. conceptible.

conception, s. concepción, noción, idea, sentimiento, imagen, f.; conocimiento, comprensión.

conceptious [kən'sepʃəs], a. fecundo, apto para concebir.

conceptive, a. conceptivo, conceptible.

conceptual [kən'septjuəl], a. conceptual.

concern [kən'səːn], v.t. concernir, tocar, importar, pertenecer, interesar, atañer, incumbir; inquietar, desasosegar. — s. negocio, asunto, ocupación; interés, incumbencia; establecimiento, empresa; ansiedad, preocupación, inquietud; cariño, afecto, amor; consecuencia, importancia; casa de comercio; *it's no concern of mine*, no me concierne, no me interesa, ni me va ni me viene.

concerned, a. interesado; inquieto; p.p. [CONCERN].

concernedly, adv. afectuosamente, con cariño, con interés.

concerning, prep. por lo concerniente a, tocante a, respecto a. — s. (ant.) negocio; interés.

concernment, s. interés, negocio; momento, importancia; ansiedad, cuidado, pena.

concert ['kɔnsəːt], s. concierto, convenio, acuerdo, concierto de música; *to act in concert with*, obrar de inteligencia con o de acuerdo con. — v.t. [kən'səːt], concertar, acordar, ajustar. — v.i. ponerse de acuerdo, concertarse.

concertina [kɔnsəɹ'tiːnə], s. (mús.) concertina.

concerto [kən'tʃəːɹtou], s. (mús.) concierto, pieza de concierto.

concession [kən'seʃən], s. cesión, concesión, gracia, licencia, privilegio.

concessionary, s., a. concesionario.

concessive [kən'sesiv], a. concesivo.

concessively, adv. por vía de concesión.

concessory, a. concedente, otorgante.

conch [kɔŋk], s. concha, caracol marino; (arq.) bóveda de concha.

concha, s. (anat.) cavidad del pabellón de la oreja; hueso cornete.

conchiferous [kɔŋ'kifərəs], a. conchífero.

conchiform ['kɔŋkifoəɹm], a. conquiforme.

conchoid ['kɔŋkɔid], a. (geom.) concoideo.

conchoidal, a. concoideo.

conchological [kɔŋkə'lɔdʒikl], a. conquiliológico.

conchologist [kɔŋ'kɔlədʒist], s. conquiliologista, m.f.

conchology, s. conquiliología.

conchylous [kɔŋ'kailəs], a. concoideo.

conciliable [kən'siliəbl], s. conciliábulo. — a. conciliable.

conciliar, a. conciliar.

conciliate, v.t. conciliar, reconciliar, propiciar, granjear.

conciliation [kənsili'eiʃən], s. conciliación, reconciliación.

conciliator, s. conciliador.

conciliatory, a. conciliativo, reconciliatorio.

concinnous [kən'sinəs], a. decente, elegante, armonioso.

concise [kən'sais], a. conciso, corto, breve, compendioso, sucinto, lacónico.

conciseness, s. concisión, brevedad, laconismo.

concision [kən'siʒən], s. corte, cortadura; concisión.

conclamation [kɔnklə'meiʃən], s. clamor, vocería, gritería.

conclave ['kɔnkleiv], s. conclave.

conclavist, s. conclavista, m.

conclude [kən'kluːd], v.t. concluir, acabar, terminar; inferir por raciocinio; determinar, decidir; arreglar; zanjar; (ant.) restringir, coartar. — v.i. finalizar; decidir; argumentar; inferir.

concluding, a. concluyente, último, final.

concludingly, adv. concluyentemente, terminantemente.

conclusion [kən'kluːʒən], s. conclusión, fin; inferencia, deducción; catástrofe, f., desenlace; consecuencia; determinación, decisión; término, terminación.

conclusive, a. conclusivo, decisivo, concluyente, terminante, final.

conclusiveness, s. determinación, resolución.

concoct [kən'kɔkt], v.t. mezclar, confeccionar; (fig.) trazar, urdir, maquinar, tramar; (ant.) descocer, digerir, purificar por el fuego, madurar, hacer madurar.

concoction, s. mixtura, mezcla, cocción, digestión; elaboración; trama, maquinación.

concoctive, a. digestivo; perteneciente a una mezcla.

concolorous [kən'kʌlərəs], a. (hist. nat.) uniforme en el color.

concomitance [kən'kɔmitens], **concomitancy**, s. concomitancia.

concomitant, s. compañero, concomitante. — a. concomitante.

concomitantly, adv. conjuntamente, en compañía.

concord ['kɔnkɔːd], s. concordia; unión, armonía; conformidad; (gram.) concordancia; (mús.) acorde.

concordance, concordancy, s. concordancia, armonía, conformidad.

concordant, a. concordante, conforme, consonante; armonioso.

concordantly, adv. concordemente, de común acuerdo.

concordat [kən'kɔːdət], s. concordato.

concorporate [kən'kɔːɹpəreit], v.t. incorporar, mezclar, unir.

concourse ['kɔŋkoəɹs], s. concurso, multitud; gentío, muchedumbre, f., confluencia; concurrencia; junta.

concreate ['kɔnkrieit], v.t. crear al mismo tiempo.

concrement ['kɔnkrəmənt], s. concremento.

concrescence [kən'kresəns], s. crecimiento, concrescencia.

concrete ['kɔnkriːt], a. concreto; de hormigón. — v.t. concretar, concrecionar, espesar. — v.i. cuajar, condensarse, coagularse. — s. hormigón, mazacote; concreción; término concreto.

concreteness, s. concreción.

concretion [kən'kriːʃən], s. concreción; cálculo.

concretional, a. concrecionado.

concretionary, a. (geol.) concrecionario.

concretive, a. concretado.

concubinage, s. concubinato, contubernio, amancebamiento.

concubinary, a. concubinario.

concubine ['kɔŋkjubain], *s*. concubina, manceba.

concubitus [kən'kju:bitəs], *s*. (*med*.) concúbito.

concupiscence, *s*. concupiscencia.

concupiscent [kən'kju:pisənt], *a*. concupiscente.

concupiscible, *a*. concupiscible.

concur [kən'kə:ɹ], *v.i*. concurrir, estar de acuerdo, convenir, conformarse, juntarse, unirse.

concurrence [kən'kʌrəns], **concurrency**, *s*. concurrencia; coincidencia, casualidad; cooperación, asistencia, ayuda, auxilio; competencia; consentimiento.

concurrent, *a*. concurrente, coincidente, concomitante, coexistente, unánime. — *s*. competidor.

concuss, *v.t*. sacudir, agitar; dañar el cerebro por concusión, o la espina dorsal.

concussion [kən'kʌʃən], *s*. concusión, conmoción, impulso; impacto; rebufo.

concussive, *a*. concusionario.

condemn [kən'dem], *v.t*. condenar, sentenciar; desprobar, censurar, culpar, reprobar; afear, vituperar; confiscar, expropiar, declarar confiscado; condenar por insalubre; expropiar forzosamente; *condemned cell*, celda de los reos de muerte.

condemnable, [kən'deməbl], *a*. condenable, censurable, culpable, vituperable.

condemnation [kɔndəm'neiʃən], *s*. condenación.

condemnatory, *a*. condenatorio.

condemner [kən'demə.ɹ], *s*. condenador.

condensable, *a*. condensable.

condensate, *v.t*. condensar. — *v.i*. condensarse, hacerse más duro. — *a*. condensado, espesado.

condensated, *a*. condensado, comprimido.

condensation [kɔndən'seiʃən], *s*. condensación.

condensative, *a*. condensativo.

condense [kən'dens], *v.t*. condensar, comprimir, hacer más espeso, denso o compacto; reducir, abreviar. — *v.i*. condensarse, espesarse, comprimirse.

condenser, *s*. (*fís*.) condensador.

condensity, *s*. densidad.

condescend [kɔndi'send], *v.i*. (*ant*.) condescender; (*ant*.) someterse; dignarse, obrar con otros de un modo arrogante.

condescendence, condescension, *s*. condescendencia; complacencia, deferencia, afabilidad; arrogancia en el trato con otros.

condescending, *a*. condescendiente, anuente; arrogante.

condign [kən'dain], *a*. condigno; merecido.

condignity, *s*. condignidad, merecimiento, mérito.

condiment ['kɔndimənt], *s*. condimento, aderezo, guisa, salsa, sazón.

condisciple, *s*. condiscípulo.

condition [kən'diʃən], *s*. condición, cualidad; estado, situación, rango; categoría; artículo; cláusula, estipulación; requisito. — *v.t*., *v.i*. condicionar, pactar, estipular.

conditional, *a*. condicional.

conditionality, *s*. restricción, limitación.

conditioned, *a*. condicionado, condicional.

condole [kən'doul], *v.i*. dolerse, condolerse, simpatizar, dar el pésame. — *v.t*. deplorar, lamentar.

condolement, condolence, *s*. condolencia, luto, aflicción, pésame; *to express one's condolence*, dar el pésame.

condone [kən'doun], *v.t*. condonar, perdonar; remitir alguna pena.

condonement, *s*. condonación, indulto, perdón.

condor ['kɔndə.ɹ], *s*. (*orn*.) cóndor.

conduce [kən'dju:s], *v.i*. convenir, ser a propósito, contribuir, conducir, tender.

conducent, *a*. que conviene.

conducible [kən'dju:sibl], *a*. conducente, ventajoso, útil.

conducibleness, conduciveness, *s*., conducencia; ventaja, utilidad.

conducive, *a*. conducente, oportuno, conveniente, útil.

conduct ['kɔndəkt], *s*. conducta, comportamiento, manejo, dirección, gestión, *f*., mando, gobierno, economía; (*mil*.) escolta, conducta. — *v.t*. [kən'dʌkt], conducir, guiar, llevar, dirigir, acompañar; manejar, gestionar; mandar.

conductibility [kəndʌkti'biliti], *s*. (*fís*.) conductibilidad.

conductible [kən'dʌktibl], *a*. conductible.

conduction, *s*. conducción; traída.

conductive, *a*. conductivo, que conduce.

conductivity [kɔndək'tiviti], *s*. conductividad, conductibilidad.

conductor [kən'dʌktə.ɹ], *s*. conductor, guía; director o maestro de orquesta; *lightning conductor*, pararrayo, pararrayos; (*bus*, etc.) cobrador.

conductress, *s*. conductora, directora, ductriz; (*bus*, etc.) cobradora.

conduit ['kɔndɔit], *s*. conducto, encañado, tubo, tubería, arcaduz.

conduplicate [kən'dju:plikeit], *a*. (*bot*.) duplicado, replegado.

conduplication, *s*. duplicación, duplicado.

condyle ['kɔndil], *s*. (*anat*.) cóndilo.

cone [koun], *s*. (*geom*.) cono; (*bot*.) piña; cucurucho; *friction cone*, (*mec*.) cono de fricción.

coney [kouni], *s*. conejo, gazapo.

cone-shaped, *a*. cónico.

cone-wheel, *s*. rueda cónica.

confabulate [kən'fæbjuleit], *v.i*. confabular, platicar, conferir, departir.

confabulation [kənfæbju'leiʃən], *s*. confabulación, conferencia, plática.

confection [kən'fekʃən], *s*. confitura, dulce; confección.

confectionary, *a*. confitado.

confectioner, *s*. confitero; confeccionador.

confectionery, *s*. dulcería, confitería; dulces, confites, confituras.

confederacy [kən'fedərəsi], *s*. confederación, liga, alianza, unión, *f*., cábala.

confederate, *v.t*. confederar, unir. — *v.i*. confederarse, aliarse, unirse. — *s*., *a*. confederado, aliado, ligado; compinche, socio.

confederation [kənfedə'reiʃən], *s*. confederación.

confer [kən'fə:ɹ], *v.i*. conferenciar, consultar. — *v.t*. conferir, dar, otorgar, comparar, confrontar, cotejar; *to confer a favour*, hacer merced.

conference, *s*. conferencia, junta, entrevista; plática, conversación.

conferer, *s*. conferidor, examinador.

conferva, *s*. (*bot*.) género de algas.

confess [kən'fes], *v.t.* confesar; declarar, reconocer; atestiguar. — *v.i.* confesarse, hacer una confesión.

confessed, *a*. evidente, incontestable. — *p.p.* [CONFESS].

confessedly, *adv*. conocidamente, manifiestamente; por confesión propia.

confession [kən'feʃən], *s*. confesión; credo; profesión de fe; confesión sacramental.

confessional, confessionary, *s*. confesionario.

confessor, *s*. confesor, penitente.

confidant ['kɔnfidant], *s*. confidente.

confide ['kənfaid], *v.t.* fiar, confiar, depositar. — *v.i.* confiar, fiarse, contar (con).

confidence ['kɔnfidəns], *s*. confianza, fe, *f*., crédito; ánimo; valor; presunción; confidencia, secreto; *over-confidence*, mucha confianza en sí; presunción.

confident, *a*. seguro, cierto; confiado. — *s*. confidente.

confidential [kɔnfi'denʃəl], *a*. confidencial, íntimo, de confianza, seguro; reservado, secreto.

confidentially, *adv*. confidencialmente, confidentemente.

confidently ['kɔnfidəntli], *adv*. confidencialmente, confiadamente.

confiding [kən'faidiŋ], *a*. confiado; lleno de confianza, que tiene confianza; fiel.

confidingness, *s*. confianza.

configurate [kən'figəreit], *v.i.* (*astr*.) configurar.

configuration [kənfigə'reiʃən], *s*. configuración; (*astr*.) aspecto, posición relativa de los planetas.

configure, *v.t.* configurar, dar forma o figura.

confinable, *a*. limitable.

confine ['kɔnfain], *s*. confín, límite, término, frontera.—*v.i.* [kən'fain], confinar, lindar.—*v.t.* aprisionar, limitar, restringir, reprimir, encerrar, estrechar; *to be confined*, estar de parto; *to be confined to one's bed*, estar enfermo en cama.

confineless, *a*. ilimitado.

confinement, *s*. prisión; (*mil*.) arresto, encierro, clausura, sujeción; destierro, cautiverio; estreñimiento, restricción; parto, sobreparto.

confiner, *s*. vecino, fronterizo, lo que limita, encierra o confina.

confinity [kən'finiti], *s*. cercanía, proximidad.

confirm [kən'fəːrm], *v.t.* confirmar, comprobar, corroborar, ratificar, asegurar, verificar, demostrar, probar, establecer; sancionar; fortalecer.

confirmable, *a*. que puede ser confirmado.

confirmation [kɔnfəɹ'meiʃən], *s*. confirmación, prueba, verificación, revalidación, ratificación.

confirmative [kən'fəːrmətiv], *a*. confirmativo.

confirmatory [kɔnfəɹ'meitəri], *a*. confirmatorio, confirmativo.

confirmedly [kən'fəɹmidli], *adv*. confirmadamente.

confirmedness, *s*. certeza, firmeza.

confirmer, *s*. confirmador, establecedor; (*for*.) confirmante.

confiscable [kən'fiskəbl], *a*. confiscable.

confiscate ['kɔnfiskeit], *v.t.* confiscar, comisar. — *a*. confiscado.

confiscation [kɔnfis'keiʃən], *s*. confiscación, comiso.

confiscator, *s*. confiscador.

confiture [kɔnfi't ʃuər], *s*. confitura, dulce.

confix [kən'fiks], *v.t.* fijar, ligar, atar, enclavar.

conflagrant [kən'fleigrənt], *a*. incendiado.

conflagration [kɔnflə'greiʃən], *s*. conflagración, quema, incendio.

conflation, *s*. combinación de lecciones variantes en una nueva; soplo de varios instrumentos (música) a un tiempo.

conflict [kən'flikt], *v.i.* chocar, luchar, contender, combatir. — *s*. ['kɔnflikt], choque, conflicto, lucha, pugna, contienda, combate, pelea; dolor, pesar; antagonismo.

conflicting, *a*. contrario, opuesto, contradictorio.

confluence ['kɔnfluəns], *s*. confluencia, concurrencia, concurso; conjunto, agregado.

confluent, *a*. confluente. — *s*. río confluyente.

conflux ['kɔnfluks], *s*. confluencia; concurrencia, concurso.

conform [kən'fɔːrm], *v.t.* conformar, ajustar, concordar; *to conform with the times*, andar al uso. — *v.i.* conformarse, someterse.

conformability [kənfɔːrmə'biliti], *s*. conformidad.

conformable [kən'fɔːrməbl], *a*. conforme, concordable, sumiso; proporcionado.

conformableness, *s*. conformidad.

conformably, *adv*. conformemente, en conformidad.

conformation [kɔnfɔːɹ'meiʃən], *s*. conformación, figura.

conformed [kən'fɔːrmd], *a*. conformado.

conformer, *s*. el que se conforma.

conformist, *s*. conformista, *m.f.*, el que está conforme con la religión anglicana.

conformity, *s*. conformidad.

confound [kən'faund], *v.t.* confundir, mezclar, enredar, embrollar; desconcertar, consternar, atolondrar, aturrullar, turbar; avergonzar; destruir; arruinar.

confounded, *a*. (*vulg*.) maldito, abominable, detestable, terrible, enorme.

confoundedly, *adv*. horriblemente, detestablemente.

confoundedness, *s*. confusión, abatimiento.

confounder, *s*. enredador, desolador.

confraternity, *s*. cofradía, confraternidad, hermandad, corporación, sociedad.

confrère ['kɔnfrɛəɹ], *s*. colega, *m*., compañero, consocio.

confrication [kɔnfri'keiʃən], *s*. confricación, frotación.

confront [kən'frʌnt], *v.t.* confrontar, afrontar, arrostrar, acarear; cotejar, comparar, hacer frente a.

confrontation, confrontment, *s*. confrontación, careo.

confronter, *s*. el que confronta.

confuse [kən'fjuːz], *v.t.* confundir, desconcertar, aturrullar, desordenar, turbar; obscurecer; mezclar.

confused, *a*. confuso, azarado; indistinto, turbio.

confusedly, *adv*. confusamente, tumultuosamente, atropelladamente, remotamente, en desorden.

confusedness, *s*. confusión.

confusion [kən'fjuːʒən], *s*. confusión, desorden, caos, ruina, baraúnda, tumulto, embarazo; vergüenza; perturbación, aturdimiento.

confutable [kən'fjutəbl], *a.* refutable.

confutant, *s.* refutador.

confutation [kɔnfju'teiʃən], *s.* refutación, confutación.

confute [kən'fjuːt], *v.t.* confutar, refutar, impugnar.

confuter, *s.* confutador.

congé, congee [kɔ̃ʒei], *s.* licencia, permiso; salutación; despedida; *congé d'élire*, real permiso al deán y cabildo en *sede vacante* para elegir el obispo.

congeal [kən'dʒiːl], *v.t.* congelar, helar, coagular, cuajar. — *v.i.* congelarse, helarse, cuajarse.

congealable, *a.* congelable, helable.

congealedness, congealment, congelation, *s.* congelación.

congee ['kɔndʒi], *v.i.* despedirse, saludar.

congener, congeneric, *a.* congénere.

congenerousness, *s.* homogeneidad.

congenial [kən'dʒiːniəl], *a.* congenial, simpático, cognado, análogo.

congeniality [kəndʒini'æliti], congenialness, *s.* conformidad, afinidad; simpatía; cognación.

congenital [kən'dʒenitəl], *a.* congenital, congénito.

conger ['kɔŋgəɹ], conger-eel, *s.* (*ict.*) congrio.

congeries, *s.* congerie, *f.*

congest [kən'dʒest], *v.i.* acumular, juntar, amontonar; *v.t.* (*med.*) congestionar.

congested, *a.* (*med.*) congestionado, obstruido por humores o sangre; congestionado, aglomerado, atestado; (*bot.*) apretado, apiñado.

congestible, *a.* amontonable, acumulable.

congestion, *s.* congestión, obstrucción.

congestive, *a.* congestivo.

conglobate, *a.* conglobado, amontonado en forma esférica. — *v.t.* conglobar.

conglobe ['kɔngloub], *v.t.* conglobar.

conglobulate [kən'glɔbjuleit], *v.i.* conglobarse.

conglomerate, *v.t.*, *v.i.* conglomerar, aglomerar, congregar, redondear. — *s.*, *a.* conglomerado, redondeado; (*geol.*) roca compuesta de guifarros, llámase también, *pudding-stone.*

conglomeration [kɔnglɔmə'reiʃən], *s.* conglomeración.

conglutinant, *s.*, *a.* aglutinante.

conglutinate [kən'gluːtineit], *v.t.*, *v.i.* conglutinar(se), pegar(se). — *a.* conglutinado.

conglutination [kəngluːti'neiʃən], *s.* conglutinación.

conglutinative [kən'gluːtinətiv], *a.* conglutinativo.

congratulate [kən'grætjuleit], *v.t.* congratular, felicitar; complimentar, dar la enhorabuena a. — *v.i.* felicitarse, congratularse.

congratulation [kəngrætju'leiʃən], *s.* felicitación, enhorabuena, congratulación, pláceme.

congratulator [kən'grætjuleitəɹ], *s.* congratulador, congraciador.

congratulatory, *a.* congratulatorio.

congregate ['kɔŋgrigeit], *v.t.* congregar, reunir, convocar. — *v.i.* juntarse, reunirse, afluir.

congregation [kɔŋgri'geiʃən], *s.* congregación, concurso; masa, colección, agregado, auditorio, asamblea.

congregational, *a.* perteneciente a una congregación, perteneciente al congregacionalismo.

congregationalism, *s.* congregacionalismo.

congregationalist, *s.*, *a.* miembro de la secta congregacionalista.

congress ['kɔngres], *s.* congreso, asamblea, convención, concilio, conferencia junta; (*E.U.*) poder legislativo de los Estados Unidos; cámara de los diputados (España).

congressional [kən'greʃənl], *a.* del congreso.

congressive, *a.* unido, juntado, pegado.

Congressman, *s.* miembro del Congreso de los Estados Unidos.

congrue [kən'gruː], *v.t.* concordar, adecuar, corresponder.

congruence, congruency, congruity, *s.* congruencia, congruidad, conformidad, oportunidad, conveniencia.

congruent, congruous, *a.* congruo, congruente, apto, proporcionado, conforme, conveniente.

conic ['kɔnik], conical, *a.* cónico, coniforme.

conically, *adv.* en forma cónica.

conicalness, *s.* conicidad, forma cónica.

conics, *s.pl.* (*geom.*) sección cónica; parábola, hipérbola, elipse, *f.*; la ciencia de medir conos y sus curvas.

conifer ['kɔnifəɹ], *s.* (*bot.*) conífero.

coniferous [kə'nifərəs], *a.* conífero.

coniform ['kouniforːm], *a.* coniforme, cónico.

conium [kou'naiəm], *s.* (*bot.*) cicuta.

conjecturable, *a.* conjeturable.

conjectural, *a.* conjetural.

conjecturally, *adv.* conjeturalmente, presuntamente, por conjetura.

conjecture [kən'dʒektʃəɹ], *s.* conjetura, suposición, apariencia, sospecha, barrunto. — *v.t.*, *v.i.* conjeturar, sospechar, pronosticar, barruntar.

conjecturer, *s.* conjeturador.

conjoin [kən'dʒɔin], *v.t.* juntar, unir, asociar, conectar, casar. — *v.i.* confederarse, ligarse, unirse.

conjoint ['kɔndʒɔint], *a.* asociado, confederado; aliado, conjunto.

conjointly, *adv.* conjuntamente, unidamente.

conjugal ['kɔndʒugəl], *a.* conjugal, connubial, matrimonial.

conjugally, *adv.* conjugalmente, maritalmente.

conjugate ['kɔndʒugeit], *v.t.* juntar, enlazar; (*gram.*) conjugar; (*biol.*) combinarse, unirse. — *a.* (*bot.*) apareado; (*mat.*, *gram.*) conjugado, recíprocamente coordinado. — *s.* sinónimo.

conjugation [kɔndʒu'geiʃən], *s.* (*gram.*) conjugación; conjunción; (*biol.*) unión, *f.*, fusión.

conjunct [kən'dʒʌŋkt], *a.* conjunto, unido, allegado.

conjunction, *s.* conjunción, unión, *f.*, asociación, liga.

conjunctiva [kɔndʒʌŋk'taivə], *s.* (*anat.*) conjuntiva, membrana mucosa que cubre la superficie posterior de los párpados y la anterior del globo del ojo.

conjunctive, *a.* conjuntivo, conjunto; (*gram.*) subjuntivo.

conjunctiveness, *s.* calidad de juntar o unir.

conjunctly, *adv.* juntamente.

conjuncture, *s.* conjuntura; sazón, *f.*, ocasión; crisis, *f.*; compatibilidad; unión, *f.*, reunión, *f.*

conjuration [kɔndʒu'reiʃən], *s.* conjuración,

conspiración, conjuro; deprecación, súplica, petición.

conjure [kən'dʒuəɹ], *v.t.* conjurar, pedir, rogar con instancia; conjurarse, conspirar; hechizar, encantar; exorcizar. — *v.i.* hacer juegos de manos; usar sortilegios; *to conjure away*, exorcizar; *to conjure up*, evocar.

conjurer ['kʌndʒərə], *s.* conjurador, encontador; prestidigitador, jugador de manos; mago, brujo, nigromante.

conjuring, *s.* hechicería.

conjuror, *s.* [CONJURER].

connascence [kə'næsəns], *s.* nacimiento al mismo tiempo.

connate ['kɔneit], *a.* connato, congénito, innato.

connation, *s.* unión congénita.

connatural [kə'nætjərəl], *a.* connatural, inherente.

connaturalness, *s.* participación de la misma naturaleza.

connect [kə'nekt], *v.t.* juntar, unir; enlazar, atar, trabar; relacionar; (*mec.*) conectar, engargantar; coordinar; aparear. — *v.i.* juntarse, unirse, asociarse; *connecting-link*, corredera, eslabón, enganche; *connecting-rod*, biela, barra de conexión, biela motriz, vástago oscilante de un émbolo.

connected, *a.* conexo, relacionado.

connectedly, *adv.* coordinadamente.

connecting, *a.* coherente. — *s.* conexión, *f.*

connection, connexion, *s.* conexión, *f.*, unión, *f.*, enlace, combinación, encadenación, encadenamiento; atadura, trabazón, *f.*; analogía, relación; secta o comunidad religiosa; familia, parientes, amistad, deudo, afinidad, parentesco; (*f.c.*) empalme; cópula, coito; *to bring into connection with*, poner en relaciones con; *to enter into a connection with*, entrar en relaciones con.

connective [kə'nektiv], *a.* conexivo; *s.* (*gram.*) conjunción; (*bot.*) estambre que une los lóbulos de la antera; *connective tissue*, tejido fibroso que atraviesa el cuerpo entero y sirve para unir y sostener las diversas partes.

connectively, *adv.* conjuntamente, unidamente.

connector, *s.* conector.

conner ['kɔnə], *s.* observador, inspector.

connex [kə'neks], *v.t.* (*ant.*) juntar, unir.

connexion, *s.* [CONNECTION].

connivance [kə'naivens], *s.* connivencia, consentimiento; guiño, guiñada.

connive, *v.i.* disimular, tolerar, consentir, hacer la vista gorda.

conniver, *s.* consentidor, cómplice.

connoisseur [kɔni'sə:ɹ], *s.* conocedor, perito, juez.

connotation [kɔno'teiʃən], *s.* connotación.

connote [kə'nout], *v.t.* (*lóg.*) connotar.

connubial [kə'nju:biəl], *a.* connubial, conyugal.

connumeration [kɔnju:mə'reiʃən], *s.* connumeración.

conoid ['kounɔid], *s.* conoide.

conoidal, conoidic, conoidical, *s.* conoidal.

conquer ['kɔŋkəɹ], *v.t., v.i.* vencer, conquistar, triunfar; sujetar, rendir, domar, superar.

conquerable, *a.* vencible, domable, conquistable.

conquering, *a.* conquistador.

conqueror, *s.* conquistador.

conquest ['kɔŋkwest], *s.* conquista; *the Conquest*, la conquista de Inglaterra por Guillermo de Normandia en el siglo XI.

consanguineous [kɔnsæŋ'gwiniəs], *a.* consanguineo.

consanguinity, *s.* consanguinidad.

conscience ['kɔnʃəns], *s.* conciencia, escrúpulo, dificultad; justicia; veracidad.

conscienceless, *a.* sin conciencia.

conscient ['kɔnʃiənt], *a.* consciente.

conscientious [kɔnʃi'enʃəs], *a.* concienzudo, escrupuloso.

conscientiousness, *s.* rectitud; escrupulosidad.

conscionable ['kɔnʃənəbl], *a.* razonable, justo.

conscionably, *adv.* razonablemente, en conciencia.

conscious ['kɔnʃəs], *a.* consciente; sabedor; *to be conscious of*, tener conocimiento de, darse cuenta de; *to become conscious*, recobrar el sentido, volver en sí.

consciously, *adv.* conscientemente, con conocimiento, a sabiendas.

consciousness, *s.* conocimiento; sentido; *to lose consciousness*, perder el sentido; *to recover* or *regain consciousness*, recobrar el sentido o el conocimiento, volver en sí.

conscript ['kɔnskript], *s.* conscripto, recluta, *m.* — *a.* conscripto, alistado, afiliado.

conscription [kən'skripʃən], *s.* reclutamiento, alistamiento.

consecrate ['kɔnsikreit], *v.t.* consagrar, santificar; ungir; destinar, aplicar; bendecir, beatificar, canonizar; dedicar a Dios. — *a.* consagrado.

consecration [kɔnsi'kreiʃən], *s.* consagración; canonización; dedicación.

consecrator, *s.* consagrante, consagrador.

consecratory, *a.* sacramental.

consectary [kɔn'sektəri], *s.* corolario, deducción obligada.

consecution [kɔnse'kju:ʃən], *s.* serie de consecuencias; sucesión; (*astr.*) consecución.

consecutive [kən'sekjutiv], *a.* consecutivo, consiguiente, sucesivo.

consecutively, *adv.* consecutivamente.

consecutiveness, *s.* carácter consecutivo.

consensual, *a.* consensual.

consensus [kən'sensəs], *s.* consenso; unanimidad, acuerdo; (*met.*) simpatía.

consent [kən'sent], *s.* consentimiento, acuerdo, aquiescencia, venia, asenso, aprobación, permiso; *silence gives consent*, quien calla, otorga; *with one consent*, de común acuerdo. — *v.i.* consentir, condescender, permitir; avenirse.

consentaneous [kɔnsen'teiniəs], *a.* consentáneo, acorde, conforme.

consentaneously, *adv.* consentáneamente, conformemente, acordadamente.

consentaneousness, *s.* consentaneidad, conformidad.

consentient [kən'senʃənt], *a.* consenciente, acorde, uniforme, de opinión unánime.

consequence ['kɔnsikwens], *s.* consecuencia, resultado, efecto; inferencia, deducción; importancia, momento; *of no consequence*, sin importancia; *man of consequence*, hombre de copete.

consequent, *a.* consiguiente, lógico. — *s.* consecuencia; (*filos.*) consiguiente.

consequential [kɔnsi'kwenʃəl], *a.* consiguiente, necesario, lógico; consecutivo; pomposo, altivo; importante.

consequentially, *adv.* consiguientemente, consecuentemente; lógicamente; con aire de importancia.

consequentialness, *s.* engreimiento.

consequently, *adv.* por consiguiente, en consecuencia, consiguientemente.

conservable [kən'səːɪvəbl], *a.* que se puede conservar.

conservancy, *s.* conservación.

conservant, *a.* conservador, conservante.

conservation [kɔnsəɪ'veiʃən], *a.* conservación, preservación, mantenencia, sostenimiento, defensa, protección.

conservatism [kən'səːɪvətizm], *s.* (*pol.*) conservadurismo, moderantismo.

conservative, *a.* conservativo, preservativo; (*pol.*) conservador, moderado.

conservator, *s.* conservador, protector, defensor.

conservatory [kən'səːɪvətəri], *s.* (*mús.*) conservatorio; reservatorio; almacén, depósito; invernáculo; invernadero. — *a.* conservatorio.

conservatrix, *s.* conservadora.

conserve [kən'səːɪv], *v.t.* conservar, cuidar, mantener, guardar; hacer conservas de. — *s.* conserva, compota, dulce.

conserver, *s.* conservador, confitero, conservero.

consider [kən'sidəɪ], *v.t.*, *v.i.* considerar, reflexionar, meditar, deliberar, pensar, opinar, creer; examinar; recompensar; querer, estimar; distinguir.

considerable, *a.* considerable, respetable; importante, cuantioso.

considerableness, *s.* importancia; entidad, valor.

considerably, *adv.* considerablemente, importantemente, grandemente.

considerate, *a.* servicial, solícito; considerado, atento, prudente, moderado, discreto, mirado, circunspecto.

considerateness, *s.* solicitud, amabilidad; moderación, circunspección, prudencia.

consideration [kənsidə'reiʃən], *s.* consideración, reflexión, deliberación, examen; miramiento, respeto; recompensa; valor, importancia; motivo; retorno, retribución, remuneración; (*for.*) motivo, respeto, razón, *f.*, causa; la condición de un contrato sin la cual es nulo.

considering [kən'sidəriŋ], *prep.* en consideración a, en atención a, considerando, en visto de, visto que, a causa de.

consideringly, *adv.* seriamente; amablemente.

consign [kən'sain], *v.t.* consignar; entregar, confiar, enviar, relegar, ceder; depositar; deponer. — *v.i.* someterse; suscribir.

consignatary [kən'signətəri], *s.* consignatario, depositario.

consignation, *s.* consignación; entrega; firma.

consignatory, *s.* el que firma con otros.

consignee [kɔnsai'niː], *s.* consignatario, depositario.

consigner [kən'sainəɪ], *s.* consignador.

consignment, *s.* consignación; remesa, envío; escritura de complot.

consignor, *s.* consignador.

consist [kən'sist], *v.i.* consistir, componerse,

constar, estar compuesto; depender, ser compatible, acordarse.

consistence, consistency, *s.* consistencia, conformidad, correspondencia, consecuencia; conveniencia; permanencia, estabilidad, solidez, densidad; relación.

consistent, *a.* consistente, conveniente, consecuente, conforme; firme, estable, sólido; compatible.

consistently, *adv.* conformemente, en conformidad con; consecuentemente, firmemente.

consistorial [kɔnsis'tɔːriəl], *a.* consistorial.

consistory [kən'sistəri], *s.* consistorio; asamblea, congreso, junta; tribunal de una curia eclesiástica.

consociate [kən'souʃieit], *s.*, *a.* consocio, cómplice, confederado, unido. — *v.t.* asociar, juntar, unir, congregar. — *v.i.* asociarse, juntarse, congregarse.

consociation [kɔnsousi'eiʃən], *s.* unión, *f.*, alianza, liga, asociación, sociedad.

consolable [kən'souləbl], *a.* consolable.

consolation [kɔnsə'leiʃən], *s.* consolación, consuelo, alivio, confortación.

consolator [kɔnsə'leitəɪ], **consoler,** *s.* consolador.

consolatory [kən'sɔlətəri], *a.* consolatorio, consolativo.

console [kən'soul], *v.t.* consolar, confortar. — *s.* consola; (*arq.*) cartela, repisa.

consoler, *s.* consolador.

consolidate [kən'sɔlideit], *v.t.* consolidar; (*mil.*) formar en masa. — *v.i.* consolidarse; endurecerse. — *a.* consolidado.

consolidated, *a.* consolidado.

consolidation [kɔnsɔli'deiʃən], *s.* consolidación.

consolidative, *a.* consolidativo.

consoling [kən'souliŋ], *a.* consolante.

consols ['kɔnsəls], *s.pl.* consolidados; abreviación de *consolidated annuities:* rentas británicas consolidadas.

consommé [kɔn'somei], *s.* consomé.

consonance ['kɔnsənəns], **consonancy,** *s.* consonancia, congruencia, conformidad; relación; armonía; rima.

consonant, *a.* consonante, cónsono, conforme. — *s.* (*gram.*) consonante, *f.*

consonantly, *adv.* conformemente, en conformidad con, consonantemente.

consonantness, *s.* consonancia, conformidad.

consonous ['kɔnsənəs], *a.* (*mús.*) cónsono, acorde, armonioso.

consort ['kɔnsɔːt], *s.* consorte, compañero, socio; cónyuge, esposo, esposa; compañía. — *v.t.* [kən'sɔːt], casar, unir, juntar, asociar; acompañar. — *v.i.* asociarse, acompañarse; frecuentar.

consound [kən'saund], *s.* (*bot.*) consuelda.

conspectus [kən'spektəs], *s.* ojeada, vista general, resumen, compendio, sinopsis, *f.*

conspicuous [kən'spikjuəs], *a.* conspicuo, visible, aparente, claro; ilustre, distinguido, eminente, sobresaliente.

conspicuously, *adv.* claramente, visiblemente, manifiestamente, notablemente.

conspicuousness, *s.* claridad, visibilidad; evidencia; nombradía, fama, celebridad.

conspiracy [kən'spirəsi], *s.* conspiración, conjuración; complot.

conspirant, *a.* conjurado, conspirador, conspirante.

conspiration [kɔnspi'reiʃən], s. conspiración.
conspirator [kən'spirətəɹ], s. conspirado, conspirador.
conspire [kən'spair], v.i. conspirar, maquinar; convenir, concurrir; conjurarse, ligarse.
conspirer, s. conspirador.
conspiring, a. conspirante.
conspiringly, adv. conspirando criminalmente.
constable ['kɔnstəbl], s. agente de policía, policía, m.; condestable; comisario de policía; ministril; alguacil; gobernador.
constableship, s. condestablía.
constabulary [kən'stæbjuləri], s. policía, f.
constancy ['kɔnstənsi], s. constancia, perseverancia; firmeza, estabilidad. fidelidad, permanencia, certeza.
constant, a. constante, firme, continuo, invariable, inmutable; resuelto, perseverante, permanente.
constantly, adv. siempre, constantemente, invariablemente, permanentemente.
constellate ['kɔnstəleit], v.i. lucir como una constelación. — v.t. unir o juntar varios cuerpos resplandecientes en uno.
constellation [kɔnstə'leiʃən], s. (astr.) constelación; (fig.) pléyade, f.
consternation [kɔnstəɹ'neiʃən], s. consternación, espanto, terror.
constipate ['kɔnstipeit], v.t. condensar, espesar; tupir, obstruir; v.i. (med.) constipar.
constipation [kɔnsti'peiʃən],s. estreñimiento; (med.) constipación, estreñimiento de vientre.
constituency, s. constitución; distrito electoral.
constituent [kən'stitjuənt], s. constituyente; elector, votante; delegante, comitente, mandante, mandatario; constituidor; poderdante. — a. elemental, esencial; constituyente.
constitute ['kɔnstitjuːt], v.t. constituir, formar, establecer, organizar; nombrar; componer.
constituter, s. constituidor; comitente.
constitution [kɔnsti'tjuːʃən], s. constitución.
constitutional, a. constitucional, legal. — s. paseo o ejercicio (de salud).
constitutionalism, s. constitucionalismo.
constitutionalist, s. constitucional, constitucionalista, m.f.
constitutionality, s. constitucionalidad.
constitutionally, adv. constitucionalmente.
constitutionary, a. de la constitución.
constitutionist, s. constitucional.
constitutive, a. constitutivo; constituyente; legislativo; esencial.
constrain [kən'strein], v.t. constreñir, obligar, compeler, forzar; impedir, restringir; apretar, comprimir; detener.
constrainable, a. constreñible.
constrainedly, adv. constreñidamente, por fuerza.
constraint, s. constreñimiento, coacción, coartación, apremio; fuerza, violencia; necesidad.
constrict [kən'strikt], v.t. constreñir, apretar; estrechar; atar, ligar, encoger, arrugar.
constriction, s. constricción, contracción, encogimiento.
constrictive, a. (med.) constrictivo.
constrictor, s. (anat.) constrictor; boa constrictor.
constringe [kən'strindʒ], v.t. comprimir, constreñir, estrechar, ligar.

constringent, a. constringente, constrictivo.
construct [kən'strʌkt], v.t. construir, edificar, erigir; idear, imaginar, componer, inventar, fabricar; montar.
constructer, constructor, s. constructor, fabricador, edificador.
construction, s. construcción; edificación, edificio, estructura; obra; explicación, interpretación, sentido.
constructional, a. (gram.) referente a la construcción.
constructive, a. constructivo.
constructiveness, s. aptitud para construir.
constructor, s. [CONSTRUCTER].
constructure [kən'strʌktʃəɹ], s. estructura; fábrica, edificio.
construe [kən'struː], v.t. construir; interpretar, explicar.
constuprate ['kɔnstupreit], v.t. (ant.) constuprar, (ant.) estuprar.
constupration [kɔnstu'preiʃən], s. (ant.) constupración, (ant.) estupro.
consubsist [kɔnsʌb'sist], v.i. existir juntos; coexistir.
consubstantial [kɔnsəb'stænʃəl], a. consubstancial, coesencial.
consubstantiality, s. consubstancialidad.
consubstantiate, v.t. unir en una misma substancia.
consubstantiation [kɔnsəbstænsi'eiʃən], s. consubstanciación.
consuetude ['kɔnswitjuːd], s. consuetud (ant.), uso, costumbre, f.
consuetudinary, a. consuetudinario, habitual.
consul ['kɔnsəl], s. cónsul.
consular, a. consular.
consulate, consulship, s. consulado.
consult [kən'sʌlt], v.t. consultar, considerar, deliberar, discurrir; estudiar; examinar. — v.i. consultarse, aconsejarse. — s. consulta, junta para deliberar.
consultant, s., a. consultante; especialista, m.f.
consultary, a. relativo a la consultación.
consultation [kɔnsel'teiʃən], s. consulta, consultación; deliberación, junta, conferencia.
consultative [kən'sʌltətiv], **consultatory**, a. consultivo.
consulter, s. consultante, consultor.
consumable, a. consumible.
consume [kən'sjuːm], v.t. consumir, acabar, destruir, gastar, disipar. — v.i. consumirse, deshacerse, aniquilarse, acabarse, perecer.
consumer, s. consumidor, destructor, parroquiano, comprador; disipador.
consummate ['kɔnsəmeit], v.t. consumar, completar, acabar. — a. consumado, acabado, cabal, completo, perfecto.
consummation [kɔnsə'meiʃən], a. consumación, acabamiento, fin, extinción.
consumption [kən'sʌmpʃən], s. consumimiento, consunción, disipación, destrucción; desgaste, gasto, uso, consumo; (med.) tisis,f., hectiquez.
consumptive, a. consuntivo,destructivo; (med.) tísico, hético, héctico. — s. tísico, tísica.
consumptiveness, s. predisposición a la tisis, principio de consunción o tisis.
contabescence, s. (med.) tabes, f., marasmo, atrofía; (bot.) esterilidad de los estambres y el polen.
contact ['kɔntækt], s. contacto, tocamiento. — v.t. ponerse en contacto con.

contact-breaker, s. (elec.) ruptor, corta-corriente, interruptor, temblador.

contact-pin, s. (elec.) formón de contacto.

contact-plug, s. (elec.) tarugo de presa corriente.

contagion [kən'teidʒən], s. contagio, peste, f., virus, infección, corrupción, contaminación.

contagious, a. contagioso, infeccioso, pegadizo.

contagiousness, s. carácter contagioso.

contagium [kən'teidʒiəm], s. contagio.

contain [kən'tein], v.t. contener, tener cabida, caber, comprender; incluir, encerrar, abrazar, reprimir, refrenar; abarcar. — v.i. contenerse, abstenerse, vivir en continencia.

containable, a. contenible; que cabe.

container, s. envase, continente.

contaminate [kən'tæmineit], v.t. contaminar, contagiar, inficionar, infestar, corromper, manchar, pervertir, depravar.

contamination, s. contaminación.

contango, s. (bolsa y cambio) comisión pagada por el comprador en consideración del derecho de posponer una liquidación de compra.

contemn [kən'tem], v.t. menospreciar, desestimar, despreciar.

contemner, s. despreciador, menospreciar.

contemperament, s. temperamento.

contemplate ['kɔntəmpleit], v.t., v.i. contemplar, meditar; estudiar; proyectar, tener intención, proponerse.

contemplation [kɔntəm'pleiʃən], s. contemplación; proyecto, intención, expectación.

contemplative [kən'templətiv], a. contemplativo, pensador.

contemplativeness, s. contemplación.

contemplator ['kɔntəmpleitəɹ], s. contemplador.

contemporaneity, s. contemporaneidad.

contemporaneous, a. contemporáneo.

contemporaneousness, s. contemporaneidad.

contemporariness, s. contemporaneidad.

contemporary, a. contemporáneo, coetáneo.

contempt [kən'tempt], s. desprecio, desdén, menosprecio, vilipendio; contempt of court, (for.) contumacia, rebeldía.

contemptibility [kəntempti'biliti], **contemptibleness,** s. bajeza, abyección.

contemptible, a. despreciable, despreciado, vil.

contemptuous [kən'temptʃəs], a. altivo, desdeñoso, insolente, despreciativo, ofensivo.

contemptuousness, s. desdén, desprecio, insolencia, altanería.

contend [kən'tend], v.t. disputar, sostener, afirmar. — v.i. contender, pleitear, porfiar, disputar, lidiar, altercar, competir; pretender, afirmar.

contendent, contender, s. contendedor, competidor, antagonista, m.f.

contending, a. contrario, opuesto.

content [kən'tent], a. contento, satisfecho; en la Cámara de los Pares de Inglaterra, voto afirmativo. — v.t. contentar, satisfacer; complacer; agradar. — s. ['kɔntent], contento, satisfacción, agrado. — pl. **contents,** contenido, capacidad, cabida; tabla de materias.

contented, a. contento, contentado, agradado, resignado, satisfecho, tranquilo.

contentedly, adv. tranquilamente, contentamente.

contentedness, s. contento, calma, satisfacción.

contention [kən'tenʃən], s. contienda, contención, debate, disputa, pugna, pendencia; tema, m.

contentious, a. contencioso, litigioso.

contentiousness, s. espíritu contencioso, espíritu de contradicción.

contentment, s. contento, contentamiento, satisfacción.

conterminal, conterminous, a. contérmino, coextensivo, limítrofe, vecino, confinante.

contest ['kɔntest], v.t. contender, contestar, disputar. — v.i. contender, competir, rivalizar. — s. contienda, disputa, debate, altercación, pugna, lucha, lid, f.; it was a severe contest, fué una acción (o lucha) muy reñida.

contestable [kən'testəbl], a. contestable, disputable.

contestableness, s. carácter disputable.

contestant, s. contendiente, litigante.

contestation [kɔntes'teiʃən], s. altercación, disputa.

contestingly, adv. contenciosamente.

context ['kɔntekst], s. contexto, contenido; contextura, enfoque.

contextual [kən'tekstjuəl], a. relativo al contexto.

contextural, a. relativo a la contextura.

contexture, s. contextura; complexión; entretejido, enlazamiento; constitución.

contiguity [kɔnti'gjuːiti], s. contigüidad, continuidad, inmediación.

contiguous [kɔn'tigjuəs], a. contiguo, junto, adyacente, inmediato.

contiguously, adv. contiguamente, al lado, junto.

contiguousness, s. contigüidad, vecindad.

continence ['kɔntinens], **continency,** s. continencia, castidad, temperancia, templanza.

continent, a. continente, puro, casto; moderado, templado. — s. continente.

continental [kɔnti'nentəl], s., a. continental.

contingence, contingency, s. contingencia, eventualidad, caso imprevisto.

contingent [kɔn'tindʒənt], a. contingente, acaecedero, eventual, accidental, casual. — s. contingencia, casualidad; cuota.

contingentness, s. contingencia, casualidad.

continual [kɔn'tinjuəl], a. continuo, incesante, frecuente.

continually, adv. continuamente, continuadamente.

continualness, s. continuidad, permanencia.

continuance, s. continuación, permanencia; duración; dilación, prolongación; (for.) demora; aplazamiento.

continuate, v.t. (ant.) continuar. — a. (ant.) continuado.

continuation [kɔntinju'eiʃən], s. continuación, prolongación, seguida, serie, f.

continuator, f. continuador.

continue [kɔn'tinjuː], v.t., v.i. continuar, durar, perdurar; perseverar, persistir, prolongar, perpetuar; permanecer, morar.

continued, a. continuo, continuado, prolongado.

continuedly, adv. continuamente, continuadamente.

continuer, s. continuador, perseverador.

continuity [kɔnti'njuːiti], s. continuidad, continuación, coherencia; prolongación.

continuous [kɔn'tinjuəs], *a.* continuo.

continuously, *adv.* continuamente, continuadamente.

cont-line, *s.* (*mar.*) espacio que queda entre barriles estibados.

contorniate [kɔn'tɔːɪnieit], *a.* (*numismática*) rodeado de un profundo surco en el borde interior.

contort [kɔn'tɔːɪt], *v.t.* torcer, retorcer; (*fig.*) falsear, retorcer.

contorted, *a.* (*geol.*) torcido, retorcido (estrata); (*bot.*) arrollado, envuelto.

contortion, *s.* contorción; contorsión, retorcimiento; (*med.*) luxación; (*bot.*) retorcimiento irregular.

contortionist, *s.* acróbata, *m.f.*

contour ['kɔntuəɪ], *s.* contorno; perfil.

contra ['kɔntrə], *prep.* contra. — *s.* haber de una cuenta.

contraband ['kɔntrəbænd], *s.* contrabando. — *a.* prohibido, de contrabando.

contrabandist, *s.* contrabandista, *m.f.*, matutero.

contrabass, *s.* contrabajo.

contraceptive, *s.* (*med.*) preventivo, preservativo, contraceptivo.

contract ['kɔntrækt], *v.t.* contraer, apretar, encoger, estrechar, compendiar, abreviar, reducir; contratar; arrugar; *to contract the brow,* fruncir el ceño; *to contract debts,* contraer deudas. — *v.i.* comprometerse, contratarse; contraerse, encogerse; opilarse, pactar. — *s.* pacto, convenio, contrato; contrata, escritura; esponsales; *to sell by private contract,* vender de buenas a buenas.

contracted, *a.* estrecho, escaso. — *p.p.* [CONTRACT].

contractedness, *s.* contracción; estrechez, apretamiento, opresión; mezquinería, mezquindad.

contractibility [kəntræktə'biliti], **contractibleness,** *s.* contractibilidad.

contractible [kən'træktəbl], (*med.*) *a.* contractible.

contractile [kən'træktail], *a.* contráctil.

contractility, *s.* contractilidad.

contracting, *a.* contratante; contrayente.

contraction, *s.* contracción, abreviación; encogimiento; (*anat.*) crispatura.

contractive, *a.* contractivo.

contractor, *s.* contratante, contratista, *m.f.*; empresario.

contradict [kɔntrə'dikt], *v.t.* contradecir; oponerse, contrariar, negar, desmentir. — *v.i.* negar, replicar.

contradicter, *s.* contradictor.

contradiction, *s.* contradicción; oposición; impugnación; contrariedad, contrasentido, renuncio.

contradictious, *a.* contradictorio.

contradictiousness, *s.* espíritu de contradicción.

contradictive, *a.* contradictorio.

contradictoriness, *s.* espíritu de contradicción.

contradictory, *a.* contradictorio, opuesto, contrario. — *s.* contrariedad; (*lóg.*) contradictoria.

contradistinct [kɔntrədis'tiŋkt], *a.* opuestamente, distinguido.

contradistinction, *s.* contraste; *in contradistinction,* por oposición.

contradistinctive, *a.* que pone en oposición.

contradistinguish, *v.t.* diferenciar, distinguir.

contra-indicate, *v.t.* (*med.*) contraindicar.

contra-indication, *s.* contraindicación.

contralto [kən'træltou], *s.* (*mús.*) contralto, *m.*

contramure ['kɔntrəmjuɪ], *s.* (*fort.*) contramuro.

contraplex ['kɔntrəpleks], *a.* (*tele.*) de or perteneciente a la remisión de mensajes en opuesta dirección por el mismo circuito.

contraposition [kɔntrəpə'ziʃən], *s.* (*blas.*) contraposición.

contrariety [kɔntrə'raiiti], *s.* contrariedad, oposición; discrepancia.

contrariness, *s.* terquedad, contrariedad, oposición.

contrarious, *a.* contrario, opuesto.

contrariwise, *adv.* al contrario, inversamente, al revés.

contrary ['kɔntrəri], *a.* contrario, opuesto, antagónico, adverso, contradictorio, divergente. — *s.* contrario; *on the contrary,* al contrario; *quite the contrary,* todo lo contrario.

contrast ['kɔntrɑst], *s.* contraste. — *v.t.* contrastar, oponer. — *v.i.* contrastar, hacer contraste.

contrate, *a.* (relojería) con dientes o punto en ángulo recto al plano de la rueda.

contravallation [kɔntrəvə'leiʃən], *s.* (*fort.*) contravalación.

contravene [kɔntrə'viːn], *v.t.* contravenir, infringir, violar.

contravener, *s.* contraventor, infractor.

contravention, *s.* contravención, infracción.

contributary [kən'tribjutəri], *a.* contribuyente, contributario.

contribute ['kɔntribjuːt], *v.t.*, *v.i.* contribuir, ayudar, cooperar, concurrir; escribir (un artículo para un periódico, etc.).

contribution [kɔntri'bjuːʃən], *s.* contribución; cooperación; cuota.

contributive [kən'tribjutiv], *a.* contributivo.

contributor, *s.* contribuidor, contribuyente.

contributory, *a.* cooperante.

contrite ['kɔntrait], *a.* arrepentido, penitente, contrito.

contriteness, contrition, *s.* contrición, arrepentimiento, penitencia.

contriturate [kən'tritjureit], *v.t.* triturar.

contrivable [kən'traivəbl], *a.* imaginable.

contrivance, *s.* idea, plan, invención, designio; artificio, ingenio, concepto; aparato, utensilio, mecanismo; maquinación, trama, maña, estratagema.

contrive, *v.t.* idear, inventar, ingeniar, imaginar; maquinar, tramar, urdir, fraguar, darse maña. — *v.i.* buscar un medio o una solución, maquinar, darse maña.

contriver, *s.* inventor, autor, trazador, organizador; arbitrista, *m.f.*

control [kən'troul], *v.t.* inspeccionar, examinar, registrar; gobernar; mandar, regir; controlar(*neologismo*); manejar; dirigir, dominar; reprimir, restringir; intervenir; *controlling interest,* (*com.*) mayoría (acciones u obligaciones votantes). — *s.* dirección, inspección; manejo, control (*neologismo*); dominio, mando, gobierno, poder, autoridad; regulador; sujeción; freno; contrarregistro.

controllable, *a.* sujeto a registro, inspección o dirección.

controller, *s.* contralor, interventor, superintendente, director.

controllership, s. contraloría.

controlment, s. registro, examen, inspección; autoridad; imperio; restricción, sujeción.

controversial [kɔntrə'vəːsiəl], a. contencioso, polémico; debatido, discutible.

controversialist, s. controversista, polemista, m.f.

controversy [kən'trɔvəːsi], s. controversia, polémica, disputa; discusión, debate; pleito.

controvert ['kɔntrəvəːt], v.t. controvertir, disputar, refutar, altercar.

controverter, s. controversista, polemista, m.f.

controvertible, a. controvertible, disputable, discutible.

controvertist, s. controversista, polemista, m.f.

contumacious [kɔntjum'eiʃəs], a. contumaz, rebelde, obstinado, tenaz; (for.) contumaz, rebelde.

contumaciousness, contumacy, s. contumacia, obstinación, rebeldía, terquedad.

contumelious [kɔntju'miːliəs], a. contumelioso, ignominioso, injurioso, ofensivo, sarcástico, afrentoso.

contumeliousness, contumely, s. contumelia, injuria, insulto, ultraje.

contuse [kən'tjuːs], v.t. contundir, magullar.

contusion, s. contusión, magullamiento.

conundrum [kə'nʌndrəm], s. rompecabezas, m., adivinanza, acertijo.

convalesce [kɔnvə'les], v.i. convalecer, reponerse.

convalescence, s. convalecencia, mejoría, restablecimiento de la salud.

convalescent, a. convaleciente; *to be convalescent,* ir mejorando.

convallaria [kɔnvə'lɛəriə], s. (bot.) convalaria, lirio de los valles.

convection [kən'vekʃən], s. acto de llevar o transportar; (fís.) convección.

convene [kən'viːn], v.t. convocar, congregar, juntar, unir; citar; emplazar. — v.i. convenir, juntarse, reunirse.

convener, s. convocador.

convenience, s. conveniencia, comodidad; retrete; *at your earliest convenience,* en cuanto pueda.

convenient, a. conveniente, cómodo, apto, oportuno, útil.

convent ['kɔnvənt], s. convento.

conventicle [kən'ventikl], s. conventículo, conciliábulo.

convention, s. convención; unión, f.; congreso, asamblea, junta.

conventional, a. convencional, estipulado, convenido; emblemático.

conventionalism, s. convencionalismo.

conventual [kən'ventjuəl], a. conventual. — s. conventual, religioso, monje, monja, fraile.

converge [kən'vəːdʒ], v.i. converger.

convergence, s. convergencia.

convergent, converging, a. convergente.

conversable [kən'vəːsəbl], a. conversable, tratable, sociable.

conversableness, s. sociabilidad.

conversant, a. familiar, íntimo, versado, experimentado; conocedor de, versado en.

conversation [kɔnvəː'seiʃən], s. conversación, conferencia, plática, familiaridad, trato familiar; porte, conducta; trato carnal.

conversational, a. dialogal, familiar, corriente; tratable, locuaz, conversable.

conversationalist, s. conversador.

conversative [kən'vəːsətiv], a. conversable.

converse ['kɔnvəːs], v.i. conversar; tratar, tener trato; platicar, departir. — s. conversación, plática, trato, familiaridad, comercio; lo opuesto, lo contrario, proposición opuesta. — a. opuesto, inverso.

conversely, adv. recíprocamente, a la inversa.

conversible, a. convertible.

conversion, s. conversión; mudanza, transformación, transmutación.

conversive, a. conversivo.

convert [kən'vəːt], v.t. convertir, transmutar, cambiar, transformar, mudar; traducir; (metal.) cementar; emplear. — v.i. convertirse, mudarse. — s. ['kɔnvəːt], converso, neófito.

converter, convertor, s. convertidor; (elec.) transformador; (metal.) retorta de cementación o de Bessemer.

convertibility [kənvəːtə'biliti], **convertibleness,** s. convertibilidad.

convertible, a. convertible, trasmutable.

convertibly, adv. recíprocamente, mutuamente.

convex [kɔn'veks], a. convexo. — s. convexidad, cuerpo convexo.

convexity, s. convexidad.

convexness, s. convexidad.

convexo-concave, a. convexo-cóncavo.

convey, v.t. transportar, llevar, enviar, dirigir, conducir, transmitir; (for.) traspasar, transferir; comunicar, participar, expresar.

conveyable, a. conductible, transportable.

conveyance, s. conducción, transporte; vehículo, conducta; cesión, entrega, traspaso; escritura de traspaso.

conveyancing, s. escritura de traspaso.

conveyer, conveyor, s. conductor, mensajero; (mec.) portador, elevador, etc.; cedente.

convict [kən'vikt], v.t. sentenciar, condenar, culpar; convencer; confutar, refutar. — s. ['kɔnvikt] reo, convicto; forzado, presidiario. — a. convencido.

conviction [kən'vikʃən], s. sentencia, condenación; convicción, convencimiento.

convictive, a. convincente.

convince [kən'vins], v.t. convencer, probar, demostrar, persuadir.

convincible, a. convencible, convincente, incontestable.

convincing, a. convincente.

convincingness, s. convicción.

convive [kən'vaiv], v.t. convidar, invitar. — s. convidado a un banquete.

convivial [kən'viviəl], a. convival, jovial, festivo, alegre.

conviviality [kənvivi'æliti], s. buen humor, jovialidad.

convocate ['kɔnvəkeit], v.t. convocar, citar.

convocation [kɔnvə'keiʃən], s. convocación; reunión, f. asamblea.

convoke [kən'vouk], v.t. convocar.

convolute, convoluted, a. enroscado, retorcido, replegado.

convolution [kɔnvə'luːʃən], s. repliegue; enroscadura; desorden; (anat.) circunvolución; (bot.) convolución.

convolve [kən'vɔlv], v.t. arrollar, revolver, enroscar; envolver, retorcer. — v.i. retorcerse, enroscarse.

convolvulaceæ [kənvɔlvju'leisii:], s.pl. (bot.) convolvuláceas.

convolvulus [kən'vɔlvələs], s. convólvulo.

convoy [kɔn'vɔi], v.t. convoyar. — s. ['kɔnvɔi], convoy, conducta, escolta; (mar.) conserva.

convulse [kən'vʌls], v.t. (med.) convulsionar; arrebatar; crispar. — v.i. convulsionarse, irritarse; crisparse; to be convulsed with laughter, morirse (o perderse) de risa.

convulsion, s. convulsión, espasmo; (fig.) conmoción, alboroto, revolución, inquietud, f., agitación violenta; cataclismo.

convulsionary, convulsive, a. convulsivo, espasmódico.

cony ['kouni], s. conejo, gazapo.

coo [ku:], v.i. arrullar; gorjearse (como niños); (fig.) arrullar, decir ternezas.

coo, cooing, s. arrullo; (fig.) halago, caricia, requiebro.

cook [kuk], s. cocinero, cocinera; too many cooks spoil the broth, barco que mandan muchos pilotos pronto va a pique. — v.t., v.i. cocer, cocinar, guisar; (fam.) alterar, falsificar; aderezar.

cooker, s. cocina de gas, horno, fogón.

cookery, s. arte de cocina; cocimiento.

cook-house, s. cocina (milicia, marina, etc.).

cookie, s. (É.U., Esco.) bollo, dulce.

cooking, s. cocina, arte culinerio.

cookshop, s. bodegón.

cool [ku:l], a. frío, fresco; tibio, flojo, indiferente; ligero; as cool as a cucumber, sosegado, gastando flema; como Pedro por su casa. — s. fresco, frescura. — v.t. enfriar, refrescar; entibiar; atemperar, calmar, dulcificar, sosegar, templar. — v.i. refrescar; enfriarse; moderarse, templarse, apaciguarse.

cooler, s. enfriadera; refrigerador; garapiñera, garrafa; (med.) refrigerante; water cooler, alcarraza.

cool-headed, a. calmo, sereno.

coolie, s. culí.

cooling, a. refrescante, atemperante.

coolish, a. fresquito.

coolly, adv. frescamente, fríamente, serenamente.

coolness, s. fresco, frío; tibieza, frialdad, frescura; serenidad, calma.

coom [ku:m], s. hollín (Esco.); pringue; (ant.) grasa de ruedas.

coomb [ku:m], s. medida de áridos (4 fanegas).

coon [ku:n], **racoon** [rə'ku:n], s. mapache, basáride, f.; (despec., E.U.) negro.

coop [ku:p], s. gallinero, caponera; tonel; cuba. — v.t. encerrar, enjaular.

cooper, s. tonelero. — v.t. fabricar barriles.

cooperage, coopering, s. tonelería.

co-operate [kou'ɔpereit], v.i. cooperar; contribuir, coadyuvar.

co-operation [kouɔpə'reiʃən], s. cooperación.

co-operative [kou'ɔpərətiv], a. cooperativo, coadyutorio, cooperante.

co-operator, s. cooperador.

co-ordinate [kou'ɔːɹdineit], v.t. coordinar, clasificar. — a. coordenado.

co-ordinateness, co-ordination, s. coordinación; igualdad.

coot [ku:t], s. (orn.) fúlica, foja.

cop [kɔp], s. (ant.) cumbre, f., cima, punta; copa, copete; moño; penacho; (vulg.) agente de policía. — v.t. (vulg.) arrestar, detener, coger.

copaiba [ko'peibə], **copaiva,** s. copaiba.

copal ['koupəl], s. goma copal.

coparcener [kou'pɑːɹsənəɹ], s. (for.) coheredero.

co-partner, s. consocio, asociado, compañero, copartícipe.

co-partnership, s. asociación, sociedad, compañía; participación.

co-patriot, s. compatriota, m.f.

cope [koup], s. gorro, capucho, caperuza, solideo; bóveda, arco, cúpula; (igl.) capa pluvial. — v.t. cubrir. — v.i. competir, lidiar, venir a las manos; hacer cara a; arrostrar, manejárselas, contender con.

Copernican [kə'pəːɹnikən], a. copernicano.

cope-stone [koup-stoun], **coping-stone,** s. piedra de albardilla.

copier ['kɔpiəɹ], s. copista, copiante; copiador; plagiario.

coping, s. cumbre, f.; albardilla.

coping-stone, s. [COPE-STONE].

copious ['koupiəs], a. copioso, abundante, prolijo.

copiousness, s. copia, difusión, profusión, abundancia; redundancia, prolijidad.

copped [kɔpt], a. copado, copetudo.

copper, s. cobre; vaso de cobre; caldera, calderilla, calderón; vellón; trujal, perol; (vulg.) agente de policía, guindilla, m. — a. cobreño, cobrizo. — v.t. encobrar; forrar de cobre; copper bottomed, encobado, forrado de cobre; copper coloured, cobrizo; copper coin, moneda de cobre (o de vellón).

copperas, s. (quím.) caparrosa.

copperish, coppery, a. cobreño, cobrizo, encobrado.

copper-plate, s. lámina de cobre.

coppersmith, s. calderero.

copperworm, s. polilla; broma, taraza.

coppice ['kɔpis], **copse,** s. soto, maleza, tallar, matorral. — v.t. plantar un tallar.

coproprietor, s. copropietario.

Copt [kɔpt], s. copto.

Coptic, a. cóptico. — s. copto.

copula ['kɔpjulə], s. (lóg.) cópula; (anat.) ligamiento.

copulate ['kɔpjuleit], v.t. (ant.) copular, juntar, unir. — v.i. copularse; unirse, ayuntarse, juntarse. — a. junto, unido.

copulation [kɔpju'leiʃən], s. cópula, coito; (ant.) conjunción, unión, f., ayuntamiento.

copulative ['kɔpjulətiv], a. (gram.) copulativo, conjuntivo.

copulatory [kɔpju'leitəri], a. copulativo, engendrador.

copy ['kɔpi], v.t. copiar, imitar, trasladar un escrito. — s. copia, reproducción, traslado, original, manuscrito; ejemplar; plana, modelo, muestra; imitación; plana (de periódico); fair copy, copia en limpio; rough copy, borrador; to make a fair copy of, poner en limpio.

copy-book, s. cuaderno de escritura.

copygraph, s. hectógrafo.

copyhold, s. (for.) enfiteusis, f.

copyholder, s. enfiteuta, m.f.; arrendador.

copying, s. transcripción, imitación, acción de copiar; copying ink, tinta de copiar; copying press, prensa de copiar.

copyist, s. copista, m.f.

copyright, s. propiedad literaria; derechos de autor; copyright reserved, queda hecho el depósito que marca la ley.

coquet, coquette [ko'ket], v.t., v.i. coquetear,

galantear, hacer coqueterías, requebrar, cortejar.
coquetry, *s.* coqueteo, coquetería.
coquette, *s.* coqueta.
coquettish, *a.* coquetón, de coqueta.
coquettishly, *adv.* con coquetería.
cor [kɔːɹ], *s.*; *cor anglais,* *s.* oboe tenor.
coracite ['kɔrəsait], *s.* (*min.*) coracita.
coracle ['kɔrəkl], *s.* barquilla de pescadores.
coracoid ['kɔrəkɔid], *s., a.* (*anat.*) coracoides, apófisis del omóplato.
coral ['kɔrəl], *s.* coral. — *a.* coralino, de coral; *coral-fisher,* coralero; *coral-fishery,* pesca del coral.
coralline, *a.* coralino. — *s.* coralina.
coralloid, coralloidal, *a.* coralino.
coranto [kə'rɑːntou], *s.* baile ligero ; courante.
corbeil ['kɔːbəl], *s.* (*mil.*) cestón, gavión; (*arq.*) cesta sobre la cabeza de la cariátide.
corbel, corbil ['kɔːbəl], *s.* (*arq.*) ménsula; saledizo; nicho; modillón.
corbie, *s.* (*orn.*) cuervo.
cord [kɔːd], *s.* cuerda, cordel, cabulla, bramante, lazo, cabo, soga; cordón, cordoncillo; pana. — *pl.* medida cúbica para leña de $8' \times 4' \times 4' = 128$ pies cúbicos. — *v.t.* encordelar; atar con cuerdas; *spinal cord,* medula (*o* médula) espinal.
cordage, *s.* (*mar.*) cordaje, cordelería.
cordate, cordated, *a.* (*bot.*) cordiforme.
corded, *a.* encordelado, acordonado, barrado.
corder, *s.* encordonador.
cordial ['kɔːdiəl], *a.* cordial, confortativo; afectuoso, sincero. — *s.* cordial, licor, remedio confortativo.
cordiality [kɔːdi'æliti], **cordialness,** *s.* cordialidad, sinceridad.
cordite ['kɔːdait], *s.* cordita.
cordon ['kɔːdən], *s.* (*mil.*) cordón; parapeto; cíngulo.
cordovan ['kɔːdəvən], *s.* cordobán.
corduroy ['kɔːdjurɔi], *s.* pana; terciopelo de algodón.
cordwain ['kɔːdwein], *s.* cordobán.
cordwainer, *s.* zapatero.
core [kɔəɹ], *s.* corazón, alma, centro; cuesco; núcleo, esencia, substancia; enfermedad del ganado lanar. — *v.t.* quitar el corazón *o* cuesco; *the heart's core,* el fondo del corazón.
co-regency, *s.* corregencia.
co-regent, *s.* corregente.
corer, *s.* despepitador.
co-respondent, *s.* (*for.*) cómplice del demandado en una demanda de divorcio.
corf [kɔːf], *s.* barril *o* canasta de extracción de carbón.
coriaceous [kɔri'eiʃəs], *a.* coriáceo, correoso.
coriander [kɔri'ændəɹ], *s.* (*bot.*) culantro, coriandro.
Corinthian [kə'rinθiən], *a., s.* (*arq.*) corintio.
co-rival, *s.* competidor, rival.
cork [kɔːk], *s.* (*bot.*) alcornoque; corcho; tapón de botella. — *v.t.* tapar con corchos, encorchar; *cork-cutter,* taponero.
corker, *s.* aparato para tapar; (*fam.*) mentira.
corkscrew, *s.* sacacorchos, tirabuzón.
corky, *a.* de corcho; (*fig.*) seco.
cormorant ['kɔːmərənt], *s.* (*orn.*) corvejón; (*fig.*) glotón.
corn [kɔːn], *s.* grano, trigo; cereal; callo; *Indian corn,* maíz; *soft corn,* callosidad, juanete; *to measure another's corn by one's own bushel,*

piensa el ladrón que todos son de su condición.
cornaceous [kɔːɹ'neiʃəs], *a.* relativo al cornejo.
corn-chandler, *s.* revendedor de granos y cereales.
corn-cob, *s.* mazorca de maíz, (*Am.*) tusa.
corn-crake, *s.* (*orn.*) ave zancuda de la familia de los rálidos *Crex pratensis.*
corn-crops, *s.pl.* cereales.
corn-cutter, *s.* pedicuro, callista, *m.f.*
cornea ['kɔːniə], *s.* (*anat.*) córnea.
corned, *a.* salado; *corned beef,* cecina.
cornel ['kɔːnəl], *s.* (*bot.*) cornejo; (*joy.*) cornalina.
cornelian [kɔːɹ'niːliən], *s.* (*min.*) cornerina, cornalina.
corneous ['kɔːniəs], *a.* córneo, hecho de cuerno; calloso.
corner [kɔːnəɹ], *s.* ángulo, esquina, rincón; recodo; escondrijo; (*com.*) monopolio, acaparamiento; apuro, aprieto. — *v.t.* acaparar; arrinconar; (*fam.*) acochinar; (*aut.*) virar, tomar bien las curvas.
cornered, *a.* angulado, esquinado; *three-cornered hat,* sombrero de tres picos; *to be cornered,* (*fam.*) verse entre la espada y la pared.
cornering, *s.* acaparamiento.
corner-stone, *s.* (*arq.*) piedra angular; mocheta; (*fig.*) piedra angular.
corner-wise, *adv.* diagonalmente.
cornet ['kɔːnət], *s.* corneta; portaestandarte; cucurucho; corona del casco; toca de mujer; (*mús.*) cornetín, corneta de llaves.
cornetcy, *s.* grado de portaestandarte.
corneter, cornettist, *s.* cornetín, el que toca el cornetín.
corn-exchange, *s.* lonja, mercado de trigos.
corn-factor, *s.* mercante en trigos.
corn-flag, *s.* (*bot.*) gladiolo, gladio, espadaña.
corn-flour, *s.* harina de maíz.
corn-flower, *s.* (*bot.*) aciano, coronilla, azulejo.
corn-grower, *s.* productor de trigos.
cornice [kɔːnis], *s.* (*arq.*) cornisa.
cornicle, *s.* cuernecico, cuernecillo.
cornific, *a.* que produce cuernos o substancia córnea.
Cornish ['kɔːniʃ], *a.* de Cornualles (*Cornwall*). — *s.* dialecto céltico de Cornualles.
cornist, *s.* corneta, *m.*, el que toca la corneta.
corn-loft, *s.* granero.
corn-meal, *s.* harina de maíz.
corn-mill, *s.* molino.
cornopean [kɔːɹ'noupiən], *s.* corneta de llaves.
corn-plaster, *s.* emplasto para los callos.
corn-poppy, *s.* (*bot.*) ababol, ababa, amapola.
corn-stalk, *s.* paja del trigo.
cornucopia [kɔːnju'koupiə], *s.* cornucopia; cucurucho.
cornuted, *a.* cornudo.
corny, *a.* córneo; (*vulg.*) trillado, manoseado.
corolla [kə'rɔlə], *s.* (*bot.*) corola.
corollary [kə'rɔləri], *s.* corolario; sobrante.
corona [kə'rounə], *s.* (*astr., arq.*) corona.
coronal, *s.* (*anat.*) coronal; corona, guirnalda. — *a.* coronal.
coronary, *a.* (*anat.*) coronario.
coronation [kɔrə'neiʃən], *s.* coronación.
coroner ['kɔrənəɹ], *s.* oficial de la Corona, que indaga las circunstancias de muertes violentas o repentinas.
coronet, *s.* corona; cintillo, guirnalda.

corporal ['kɔːɪpərəl], s. (mil.) cabo, caporal. — a. corporal, corpóreo.
corporality [kɔːɪpɔ'ræliti], s. corporalidad, corporeidad.
corporate ['kɔːɪpərit], a. corporativo.
corporately, adv. en cuerpo, en corporación.
corporation [kɔːɪpə'reiʃən], s. corporación; cabildo, ayuntamiento; cuerpo, sociedad; (fam.) barriga.
corporator, s. individuo de una corporación.
corporeal [kə'pɔːriəl], a. corpóreo, material; tangible; (for.) inmueble.
corporeality [kəpɔəri'æliti], s. corporeidad.
corporeity, s. corporeidad, materialidad.
corporeous [kə'pɔːriəs], a. corpóreo.
corporification [kəpɔːrifi'keiʃən], s. corporificación.
corposant ['kɔːɪpəsənt], s. (mar.) fuego de Santelmo.
corps [kɔːɹ], s. (mil.) cuerpo, corps.
corpse [kɔːɪps], s. cuerpo, cadáver.
corpulence ['kɔːɪpjuləns], **corpulency**, s. corpulencia, grueso, obesidad; densidad.
corpulent, a. corpulento, repleto, grueso, obeso.
corpulently, adv. de mucho cuerpo.
corpus ['kɔːɪpəs], s. cuerpo.
corpuscle ['kɔːɪpəsl], s. corpúsculo, átomo; (biol.) glóbulo. —pl. celdillas de la sangre.
corpuscular, a. corpuscular.
corrade [kə'reid], v.t. (geol.) erosionar, corrasionar.
corral, s. corral.
correct [kə'rekt], v.t. corregir, rectificar, remediar, subsanar, enmendar; deshacer, castigar, reprender, amonestar. — a. correcto, exacto, justo; formal, decoroso, apuesto.
correction, s. corrección, enmienda, enmendación, rectificación; reforma, censura; pena.
correctional, a. correccional, penal.
corrective, a. correctivo, correccional, reformatorial. — s. correctivo, limitación, antídoto.
correctness, s. exactitud, corrección.
corrector, s. corrector, revisor, reformador; (med.) correctivo.
correlate ['kɔrileit], v.i. tener correlación. — v.t. poner en correlación.
correlation [kɔri'leiʃən], s. correlación.
correlative, a., s. correlativo.
correlativeness, s. correlación, correspondencia.
correspond [kɔris'pɔnd], v.i. corresponder; convenir, adaptarse, estar de acuerdo; mantener correspondencia.
correspondence, correspondency, s. correspondencia; relación recíproca, reciprocidad; comunicación, correo.
correspondent, s. corresponsal (de un periódico); correspondiente. — a. correspondiente, conforme, conveniente.
corresponding, a. correspondiente.
correspondive, a. correspondiente, conforme.
corridor ['kɔridɔːɹ], s. (arq.) corredor, pasillo, pasadizo.
corrie, s. (Esco.) hondanada semicircular en la ladera de una montaña.
corrigible ['kɔridʒibl], a. corregible.
corrival [kɔ'raivəl], a. émulo. — s. contrario, rival, competidor.
corroborant, s., a. corroborante.
corroborate [kə'rɔbareit], v.t. corroborar,

confirmar, confortar, fortalecer. — a. corroborado.
corroboration [kərɔbə'reiʃn], s. corroboración, confirmación.
corroborative [kə'rɔbərətiv], a. corroborativo, corroborante. — s. confortativo.
corrode [kə'roud], v.t. corroer, roer, desgastar. — v.i. corroerse, desgastarse.
corrodent, a. corrosivo.
corrodibility [kəroudə'biliti], **corrosibility**, s. calidad de ser corrosible.
corrodible [kə'roudibl], a. corrosible.
corrosion [kə'rouʒən], s. corrosión, roedura.
corrosive, a. corrosivo, corrayente; mordaz; corrosive sublimate, sublimado corrosivo, solimán, bicloruro de mercurio.
corrosiveness, s. calidad de ser corrosivo.
corrugant ['kɔrugənt], a. que hace arrugas; (med.) astringente.
corrugate ['kɔrəgeit], v.t. plegar, arrugar, acanalar, encarrujar. — a. arrugado, encogido, acanalado; corrugated iron, chapa ondulada, lámina de hierro acanalada.
corrugation [kɔrə'geiʃən], s. corrugación, contracción, arruga.
corrugator, s. corrugador; (anat.) músculo contractor.
corrupt [kə'rʌpt], a. corrompido, corrupto, podrido, infecto, putrefacto, pútrido; (fig.) sobornado, viciado, depravado; falsificado, erróneo. — v.t. corromper, malear, seducir, sobornar, pervertir; podrir, infectar; adulterar, viciar. — v.i. corromperse, podrirse.
corrupter, s. corruptor, seductor, sobornador, pervertidor.
corruptibility [kərʌptə'biliti], s. corruptibilidad.
corruptible [kə'rʌptibl], a. corruptible.
corruptibleness, s. corruptibilidad.
corruption [kə'rʌpʃən], s. corrupción, putridez, putrefacción, descomposición, pus, materia purulenta; soborno, cohecho, inmoralidad.
corruptive, a. corruptivo.
corruptless, a. incorruptible, íntegro, recto.
corruptness, s. corrupción, putrefacción, infección.
corruptress, s. corrompedora, corruptora.
corsage [kɔː'sidʒ], s. corpiño.
corsair [kɔː'sɛəɹ], s. corsario, pirata, m.
corse [kɔːɹs], s. (poét.) cadáver, cuerpo muerto.
corselet ['kɔːɹslət], s. corselete; peto (de armadura); (zool.) el pecho de insectos y artrópodos.
corset [kɔːɹsət], s. corsé; cotilla. — v.t. poner un corsé.
corset-maker, s.f. corsetera.
Corsican ['kɔːɹsikən], s., a. corso.
cortège, s. séquito, acompañamiento, comitiva.
cortex ['kɔːɹteks], s. corteza.
cortical ['kɔːɹtikl], a. cortical.
corticate, corticated, a. corticoso, cortezudo.
corundum [kə'rʌndəm], s. (min.) corindón.
coruscant [kə'rʌskənt], a. coruscante, brillante, resplandeciente.
coruscate, v.t. relucir, resplandecer, fulgurar.
coruscation [kɔrəs'keiʃən], s. coruscación, fulgor; brillo, resplandor; relámpago.
corvette [kɔːɹ'vet], s. (mar.) corbeta.
corybantic [kɔri'bæntik], a. coribántico.
corymb ['kɔrim], s. (bot.) corimbo.

corymbiate [kə'rimbiət], **corymbiated**, *a.* (*bot.*) corímbeo.
corypheus [kɔri'fi:əs], *s.* corifeo.
coryza [kə'raizə], *s.* (*med.*), coriza.
cosecant [kou'sekənt], *s.* (*geom.*) cosecante, *f.*
cosentient [kou'senʃənt], *a.* consintiente, concurrente.
cosey, cosy ['kouziʿ], *a.* cómodo, conveniente, agradable.
cosine ['kousain], *s.* (*geom.*) coseno.
cosmetic [kɔz'metik], *s., a.* cosmético.
cosmic ['kɔzmik], **cosmical**, *a.* cósmico; vasto; metódico.
cosmogonal [kɔzmo'gɔnəl], *a.* cosmogónico.
cosmogony, *s.* cosmogonía.
cosmographer, *s.* cosmógrafo.
cosmographic [kɔzmo'græfik], **cosmographical**, *a.* cosmográfico.
cosmography [kɔz'mɔgrəfi], *s.* cosmografía.
cosmological [kɔzmo'lɔdʒikəl], *a.* cosmológico.
cosmologist [kɔz'mɔlədʒist], *s.* cosmólogo.
cosmology, *s.* cosmología.
cosmometry, *s.* cosmometría.
cosmopolitan [kɔzmo'pɔlitən], **cosmopolite**, *s.* cosmopolita, *m.f.*
cosmopolitanism, cosmopolitism, *s.* cosmopolitismo.
cosmorama [kɔzmo'rɑ:mə], *s.* cosmorama, *m.*
cosmos ['kɔzmos], *s.* cosmos, universo.
Cossack ['kɔsæk], *s.* cosaco.
cosset ['kɔsət], *s.* cordero criado sin madre; favorito, niño mimado; animal doméstico. — *v.t.* mimar, acariciar.
cost [kɔst], *s.* coste, costo, costa, precio; gastos, expensas; *at cost*, al costo; *pl.* costos, (*for.*) costas; *to my cost*, a mis expensas; (*fig.*) por mi daño; *cost free*, gratis, libre de gastos; *at all costs*, cueste lo que cueste; *cost of living*, coste de la vida. — *v.i.* costar; *cost what it may*, cueste lo que cueste.
costa ['kɔstə], *s.* (*zool. y fisiol.*) costilla; cualquier cosa que en apariencia o función se asemeja a una costilla.
costal, *a.* costal.
costard, *s.* manzana grande; (*vulg.*) cabeza; persona gorda.
costean [kɔs'ti:n], *v.i.* (*min.*) hundir un pozo minero en busca de un filón.
costermonger, *s.* frutero, buhonero, vendedor ambulante de frutas.
costive ['kɔstiv], *a.* estreñido; (*fig.*) estreñido, mezquino, duro.
costiveness, *s.* constipación, estreñimiento de vientre.
costless ['kɔstləs], *a.* sin coste, sin precio, de balde.
costliness, *s.* alto precio; magnificencia, suntuosidad, lujo.
costly, *a.* costoso; lujoso, magnífico, suntuoso, dispendioso. — *adv.* costosamente.
costmary, *s.* (*bot.*) especie de tanaceto.
costrel ['kɔstrəl], *s.* botella, frasco.
costume ['kɔstju:m], *s.* traje, vestido; disfraz, máscara.
cosy, *a.* [COSEY.]
cot [kɔt], *s.* cabaña, choza; hamaca; catre, cuna, camilla, camita; barquillo.
co-tangent, *s.* (*geom.*) cotangente, *f.*
cote [kout], *s.* corral, redil; *dove-cote*, palomar.
co-tenant, *s.* inquilino que vive en casa con otro.

coterie ['koutəri], *s.* corro, corrillo; tertulia; pandilla literaria.
cothurnus [kə'θə:rnəs], *s.* coturno.
cotillon [kə'ti:jən], *s.* cotillón.
cotquean ['kɔtkwi:n], *s.* (*fam.*) cominero, cazolero.
cotta, *s.* (*igl.*) cota, sobrepelliz, *f.*
cottage ['kɔtidʒ], *s.* choza, casucha, cabaña; casita de campo.
cottager, *s.* rústico, aldeano, el que vive en una choza.
cottar, cotter ['kɔtər], *s.* rústico, aldeano; (*mec.*) chabeta, llave, *f.*
cotton ['kɔtn], *s.* algodón; cotonía. — *v.t.* envolver con algodón. — *v.i.* algodonar; (*fig.*) *to cotton to*, simpatizar, compadecerse, avenirse. — *a.* de algodón.
cotton-gin, *s.* almarrá, *m.*
cotton-plant, *s.* (*bot.*) algodonero.
cotton waste, *s.* desperdicios de algodón.
cotton-wool, *s.* algodón en rama, guata.
cottonwood, *s.* (*E.U.*) álamo.
cottony, *a.* algodonoso, borroso, blando, suave.
cotton-yarn, *s.* hilado de algodón.
cotyle ['kɔtili:], *s.* (*anat.*) cotila.
cotyledon ['kɔti'li:dən], *s.* (*bot.*) cotiledón.
cotyledonous, *a.* (*bot.*) cotiledóneo.
couch [kautʃ], *v.i.* acostarse, reposar, recostarse; agacharse; tenderse, echarse; doblarse, agobiarse. — *v.t.* acostar; (*ant.*) solapar, encubrir, disimular; indicar, implicar; colocar; (*cir.*) operar las cataratas de los ojos; expresar; *to couch in writing*, redactar, poner por escrito; *to couch the lance*, enristrar. — *s.* cama, lecho; silla poltrona; canapé; lecho; yacija.
couchant [kautʃənt], *a.* (*blas.*) acostado, agachado.
coucher, *s.* cartulario; oculista, *m.f.*
couch-grass, *s.* (*bot.*) grama.
couching, *s.* genuflexión, encorvamiento.
cougar ['ku:gər], *s.* (*zool.*) cuguar.
cough [kɔf], *s.* tos, *f.*; *whooping-cough*, tos ferina. — *v.t. to cough up*, esputar. — *v.i.* toser.
cougher, *s.* tosedor.
coughing, *s.* tosidura.
could [kud], *s. pret. indic.* [CAN].
coulisse [ku'li:s], *s.* corredera; (*teat.*) bastidores.
coulter ['koultər], *s.* reja de arado.
council ['kaunsil], *s.* concejo; concilio, junta, sínodo; ayuntamiento.
councillor, *s.* concejal, consejero.
counsel ['kaunsəl], *s.* consejo, aviso, deliberación, determinación, dictamen, parecer; prudencia; sigilo, secreto; abogado; consultor, asesor; *keep your own counsel*, no lo diga usted a nadie. — *v.t.* avisar, aconsejar, dirigir, guiar.
counsellable, *a.* aconsejable.
counsellor, *s.* consejero, confidente; abogado.
counsellorship, *s.* dignidad de consejero.
count [kaunt], *v.t.* contar, numerar, calcular; considerar, reputar; imputar, atribuir. — *v.i.* contar, valer; *to count upon*, contar con, confiar en; *to count one's chickens before they are hatched*, hijo no tener y nombre le poner. — *s.* cuenta, cálculo, cuento; (*for.*) capítulo (de una acusación), cómputo; cláusula, partida; cuantía, valor; cuidado, atención; conde.

countable, *a.* contable, contadero.

countenance ['kauntənəns], *s.* cara, rostro; semblante, talante, aspecto, aire; amparo, apoyo, protección, favor; (*fig.*) patrocinio; *to give countenance* [TO COUNTENANCE]; *to keep one's countenance,* hacer buena cara. — *v.t.* sostener, apoyar, proteger, fomentar, favorecer, defender, mantener.

countenancer, *s.* defensor, protector; fautor.

counter ['kauntəɹ], *s.* calculista, *m.f.*, contador; mostrador; tablero; (*mar.*) bovedilla; antebrazo; tanto, ficha; lo opuesto, lo contrario; pecho del caballo; (*mús.*) contrapaso, contramotivo; porción del zapato que ciñe el talón; *counter-jumper,* (*fam.*) dependiente de una tienda, (*fam.*) hortera, *m.* — *adv.* contra, al contrario, al revés; *to run counter,* oponerse, correr en una dirección opuesta.

counteract [kauntə'rækt], *v.t.* contrariar, impedir; frustrar, neutralizar.

counteraction, *s.* oposición, impedimento, resistencia.

counteractive, *a.* opuesto, contrario. — *s.* opositor.

counter-attraction, *s.* atración opuesta.

counterbalance, *v.t.* contrabalancear, contrapesar, equilibrar, igualar, compensar. — *s.* contrapeso, equilibrio, compensación.

counter-battery, *s.* contrabatería.

counter-buff, *v.t.* rechazar, repeler. — *s.* rechazo.

counterchange, *s.* contracambio. — *v.t.* trocar, cambiar, dar y tomar recíprocamente.

countercharge, *s.* recriminación, acusación del acusado contra el acusador. — *v.t.* (*for.*) reconvenir.

countercharm, *s.* desencanto. — *v.t.* desencantar.

countercheck, *v.t.* contrastar, contrarrestar. — *s.* repulsa, rechazo; oposición.

counter-current, *s.* contracorriente, *f.*

counterdraw, *v.t.* calcar.

counter-evidence, *s.* contra-evidencia, contraprueba.

counterfeit [kauntəɹfi:t], *v.t.* contrahacer, fabricar, falsear, falsificar, forjar, imitar; inventar. — *v.i.* fingir, disimular, disfrazar. — *s.* falseador; falsificación, engaño, impostura; imitación, copia; moneda falsa. — *a.* contrahecho, falso, falsificado, falseado, espurio, fingido.

counterfeiter, *s.* falsificador, falsario, falseador, imitador; engañador.

counterfeiting, *s.* falsificación; imitación.

counterfoil, *s.* talón; matriz, *f.*

counterfort, *s.* contrafuerte; estribo.

counter-guard, *s.* (*fort.*) contraguardia.

counter-irritant, *s.* (*med.*) contrairritante.

countermand, *v.t.* contramandar, revocar; invalidar. — *s.* contramandato, contraorden, *f.*

counter-march, *v.i.* contramarchar; retroceder. — *s.* contramarcha.

countermark, *v.t.* contramarcar, resellar. — *s.* contramarca.

countermine, *v.t.* contraminar; contravenir. — *s.* contramina.

counter-motion, *s.* movimiento contrario; (*fig.*) proposición contraria.

counter-movement, *s.* movimiento contrario.

countermure, *s.* (*fort.*) contramuro, falsabraga. — *v.t.* contramurar.

counter-natural, *a.* contranatural.

counterpace, *s.* contrapaso.

counterpane ['kauntəɹpein], *s.* cobertor; colcha de cama, sobrecama, *m.*, cubrecama, *m.*

counterpart, *s.* contraparte, *f.*; copia, duplicado; (*mús.*) contrapaso, contramotivo.

counter-petition, *s.* petición opuesta. — *v.t.* hacer una petición contraria a otra.

counter-plea, *s.* (*for.*) réplica, reconvención.

counter-plot, *s.* contratreta. — *v.t.* contraminar.

counterpoint, *s.* (*mús.*) contrapunto; (*ant.*) cobertor, colcha.

counterpoise, *s.* contrapeso, equilibrio. — *v.t.* contrapesar, contrabalancear, equilibrar.

counterpoison, *s.* contraveneno; antídoto.

counter-pressure, *s.* contrapresión.

counter-project, *s.* contraproyecto.

counter-proof, *s.* contraprueba.

counter-proposition, *s.* contraproposición.

counter-revolution, *s.* contrarrevolución.

counter-revolutionary, *a.* contrarrevolucionario.

counterscarp, *s.* (*fort.*) contraescarpa.

counter-scuffle, *s.* contestación, lucha.

counter-seal, *v.i.* contrasellar.

counter-security, *s.* subgarantía.

counter-sense, *s.* contrasentido.

countersign, *s.* refrendata; contraseña, consigna; (*mil.*) santo y seña. — *v.t.* refrendar, visar.

counter-signature, *s.* refrendata.

counter-sink, *v.t.* abocardar. — *s.* avellanador.

counter-statute, *s.* estatuto contrario a otro.

counter-stroke, *s.* contragolpe, revés.

counter-tenor, *s.* (*mús.*) contralto, *m.*

counter-tide, *s.* (*mar.*) contramarea.

countervail ['kauntəɹveil], *v.t.* contrapesar, compensar, equivaler.

counter-vallation, *s.* (*fort.*) contravalación.

counter-valuation, *s.* contravaluación.

counterview, *s.* oposición, opinión opuesta.

counter-weight, *s.* contrapeso.

counter-wheel, *v.t.* (*mil.*) evolucionar.

counter-work, *v.t.* contrarrestar; contrariar, resistir, impedir; contraminar.

countess, *s.* condesa.

counting-house, *s.* escritorio, contaduría.

countless, *a.* innumerable, sin número, sin cuento.

countrified, *a.* (*fam.*) campesino, rústico, agreste.

countrify, *v.t.* hacer rústico.

country ['kʌntri], *s.* campo, campiña; región, provincia; país; patria, nación. — *a.* rústico, campesino, rural, agreste, compestre; provincial, de provincia; rudo, grosero; *country box,* casita de campo; *country dance,* contradanza; *country fellow,* rústico, compesino, provincial; *country house,* finca, casa de campo; *country manners,* modales de provincia; *country seat,* casa de campo, quinta; *country squire,* caballero de provincia.

countryman, *s.* (*pl.* **countrymen**) compatriota, *m.f.,* conciudadano; paisano; campesino, aldeano, labrador, patán, paleto; (*Méj.*) payo, (*Cub.*) montero, guajiro.

county ['kaunti], *s.* condado, provincia, distrito territorial. — *a.* del condado, perteneciente al condado; *county town,* capital del condado.

coup [ku:], *s.* golpe maestro.

coupé, coupee, *s.* cupé.

couple ['kʌpl], *s.* par, macho y hembra; pareja; traílla (de perros); *married couple*, matrimonio. — *v.t.* acoplar, parear, aparear; juntar, unir; casar; enchufar, acollarar; ensamblar, enganchar. — *v.i.* tener cópula; casarse; aparearse.

coupler, *s.* aparato de conexión, enganche, acopladura.

couplet, *s.* copla, estrofa; par, pareja.

coupling, *s.* acopladura; ajuste; conexión; lazo; ensambladura, ensamblaje; *coupling-iron*, grapón; *coupling-pin* (*f.c.*) pasador del enganche; *shaft-coupling*, embrague.

coupon ['kupɔn], *s.* cupón, talón.

courage ['kʌridʒ], *s.* coraje, ánimo, valor, valentía, intrepidez, brío, bravura; resolución, firmeza.

courageous [kə'reidʒəs], *a.* valiente, valeroso, brioso, animoso; *courageous man*, hombre de pelo en pecho.

courageousness, *s.* ánimo, valor, intrepidez, aliento.

courier ['kuriəɹ], *s.* correo, estafeta.

course [koəɹs], *s.* curso; corriente, *f.*; camino, vía; carrera, corrida, estadio, campo de carreras; tránsito, paso, paseo; viaje, correría, excursión; marcha; índole, *f.*; (*mar.*) rumbo, derrota, derrotero; ruta; conducta, costumbre, *f.*, porte; regla; plato, cubierto, servicio; corriente de agua, cauce, dirección de un río; (*min.*) filón de mineral; orden, regularidad; ceremonia; (*med.*) regla, menstruación; (*min.*) buzamiento; serie o hilera de piedras o ladrillos en una pared; *pl.* (*mar.*) papahigos, velas mayores. — *v.t.* cazar, dar caza, perseguir, hacer correr. — *v.i.* correr, caminar rápidamente; circular; corretear.

courser, *s.* corcel; corredor, cazador.

coursing, *s.* caza de la liebre.

court [koəɹt], *s.* patio, atrio; comitiva, séquito, cortejo, galanteo; callejón sin salida; palacio, corte; tribunal, estrado; frontón; pista de tenis; *court chaplain*, capellán del rey; *court day*, día de besamanos; (*for.*) día hábil para vistas; *court dress*, traje de corte; *court-martial*, consejo de guerra; *court plaster*, tafetán inglés. — *v.t.* cortejar, solicitar, enamorar, adular, requebrar, festejar; engatusar. — *v.i.* pedir la mano de una mujer; hacer la corte.

courteous ['kə:ɹ- or 'koəɹtiəs], *a.* cortés, fino; político; atento; cumplido; afable, amable.

courteousness, *s.* cortesía; cortesanía, urbanidad, atención.

courtesan [koəɹtə'zæn], *s.* dama cortesana; ramera.

courtesy ['kə:ɹ- or 'koəɹtəsi], *s.* cortesía, reverencia, finura, galantería; gracia, merced, favor; beneplácito, consentimiento. — *v.i.* hacer una reverencia o cortesía.

court-house, *s.* audiencia; palacio de justicia.

courtier, *s.* cortesano, palaciego; (*ant.*) cortejo, cortejante.

court-like, *a.* cortesano, elegante.

courtliness, *s.* cortesía, cortesanía, urbanidad, elegancia.

courtly, *a.* cortesano, cortés, galante, insinuante, elegante.

courtship, *s.* noviazgo; galanteo.

courtyard, *s.* patio.

cousin ['kʌzn], *s.* primo, prima.

cousinhood, *s.* primazgo.

cove [kouv], *s.* cala, caleta, ensenada, ancón, abra; (*arq.*) bóveda, bovedilla. — *v.t.* abovedar, arquear.

covenant ['kʌvənənt], *s.* contrato, pacto, convenio, convención, alianza, liga, ajuste; *the New Covenant*, el Nuevo Testamento. — *v.t.* estipular; empeñar, prometer; contratar. — *v.i.* acordarse, convenir, pactar, estipular.

covenantee, *s.* contratante.

covenanter, *s.* contratante, covenantario.

Coventry ['kɔvəntri], *s.* nombre de una ciudad del condado de Warwickshire; *Coventry blue*, hilo de marcar; *to send one to Coventry*, hacerle el vacío, echarle del mundo, boicotear.

cover ['kʌvəɹ], *v.t.* cubrir, tapar, ocultar; cobijar, abrigar, proteger, defender; empollar; cubrir, fecundar; compensar, resarcir, indemnizar; abrazar, abarcar; dominar; paliar; disimular; recorrer, andar; hacer; ponerse (el sombrero); apuntar; amenazar. — *s.* cubierta, tapa, tapadera, cobertera; capa, sobre, velo, pretexto; (en la mesa) cubierto; abrigo; techado, albergue, cobertizo; forro, funda (de muebles); cobertor, manta de cama; (*caz.*) guarida, maleza, matorral; (*com.*) fondos, efectivo para cubrir letras y pagos.

covering, *s.* vestido, ropa, abrigo; cobija, envoltura; tegumento, pelaje; arropamiento.

coverlet, *s.* colcha, cobertura de cama, cubrecama, *m.*, sobrecama, *m.*, cobertor.

covert ['kʌvəɹt], *s.* cubierto, cubierta; asilo, refugio, guarida, huidero; bandada (en la caza de aves); *femme-couvert* o *feme covert*, (*for.*) exención legal de la mujer casada, por su propio estado. — *a.* cubierto, tapado, oculto, escondido, secreto; (*for.*) bajo protección.

covertness, *s.* obscuridad; secreto.

coverture, *s.* cubierta; defensa, abrigo.

covert-way, *s.* (*fort.*) camino cubierto.

covet ['kʌvət], *v.t.* codiciar, anhelar, ambicionar, apetecer. — *v.i.* desear, aspirar, anhelar.

covetable, *a.* codiciable.

coveter, *s.* codicioso.

covetous, *a.* codicioso, avariento, sórdido, ambicioso.

covetousness, *s.* codicia, avaricia, sordidez, avidez.

covey ['kʌvi], *s.* pollada, nidada; banda, bandada.

covin ['kouvin], *s.* (*for.*) colusión; reunión de brujas.

cow [kau], *s.* vaca; (elefante o cetáceo) hembra. — *v.t.* acobardar, amedrentar, intimidar.

coward ['kauəɹd], *s., a.* cobarde, (*fam.*) collón; tímido, pusilánime.

cowardice, cowardliness, *s.* cobardía.

cowardly, *a.* cobarde, medroso, pusilánime, miedoso, tímido. — *adv.* cobardemente.

cowboy *s.* vaquero, boyero; gaucho, 'cowboy.'

cow-catcher, *s.* (*f.c.*) quitapiedras.

cow-dung, *s.* boñiga.

cower ['kauəɹ], *v.i.* acurrucarse, agacharse, alebrarse, acobardarse.

cow-herd, cow-keeper, *s.* vaquero, boyero.

cowhide, s. piel de vaca; cuero. — v.t. azotar.
cowl [kaul], s. cogulla, capucha, capuz; tejadillo, caballete de chimenea; carenaje, capotaje.
cowlike, a. semejante a la vaca, avacado.
cowman, s. vaquero.
co-worker, s. coadjutor, colaborador.
cowpox, s. (med.) vacuna.
cowry ['kauri], s. cauri.
cowslip, s. (bot.) prímula; vellorita.
coxa, s. (anat. y zool.) coxa.
coxalgic [kɔk'sældʒik], a. (med.) coxálgico.
coxcomb ['kɔkskoum], s. cresta de gallo; mequetrefe, pisaverde, farolero, farolón.
coxcombry, s. presunción, fatuidad, fachenda.
coxswain ['kɔksn], s. (mar.) patrón; nostramo.
coy [kɔi], **coyish**, a. recatado, reservado, modesto, tímido; coquetón.
coy, v.t. halagar; acariciar; lisonjear. — v.i. (ant.) esquivarse, desdeñarse; recatarse.
coyly, adv. timidamente; con coquetería.
coyness, s. timidez, esquivez; modestia, recato; coquetería.
coz, s. contracción de [COUSIN].
cozen ['kʌzn], v.t. defraudar, engañar.
cozenage, s. fraude, engaño, superchería, trampa.
cozener, s. defraudador, engañador, embanador.
cozily, adv.; **cozy**, a. [COSEY].
crab ['kræb], s. cangrejo, cámbaro; manzana silvestre; hombre ridículo; (astr.) cáncer; (mec.) molinete, (mar.) cabrestante. — a. agrio, áspero. — v.t. (cetrería) desgarrar, arañar; (fam.) criticar despiadadamente.
crab-apple s. manzana silvestre.
crabbed, a. impertinente; áspero, avinagrado, escabroso, bronco; enredoso, obscuro, difícil.
crabbedness, s. rigidez; aspereza; desigualdad.
crabby, a. difícil, espinoso.
crabstone, s. ojo de cangrejo.
crack [kræk], s. crujido, estallido; chasquido; estampido; locura, mentecatez, chifladura; hendedura; grieta, rendija, raja; resquicio; muda, mudanza (de la voz); quebraja, rotura; (vulg.) salteador en poblado; fanfarrón. — v.t. hender, rajar; romper, quebrantar, quebrar; destruir; chasquear, restallar; enloquecer, trastornar; destripar. — v.i. reventar, saltar; romperse, henderse, resquebrajarse, abrirse, agrietarse; estallar, crujir; (fam.) arruinarse; jactarse, echar bravatas. — a. famoso, escogido, de primer orden.
cracker, s. fanfarrón, baladrón; petardo; (fam.) patraña; cohete de China, traca; bizcocho delgado y quebradizo: (E.U.) galleta.
cracking, a. que estalla, que quebranta. — s. crujido, hendedura, estallido, chasquido, castañeteo.
crackle, v.i. crujir, chasquear, crepitar, estallar, castañetear. — s. crepitación, crujido, tiroteo.
crackling, s. estallido, crujido, crepitación.
cracknel ['kræknəl], s. hojaldre; galletica.
cracksman, s. (vulg.) salteador en poblado.
cradle ['kreidl], s. cuna, (cir.) caja, tablilla; (fig.) infancia, niñez; origen; (agr.) hoz de rastra; (min.) artesa móvil para lavado del

oro; (mar.) carro salvavidas; basada; (arq.) armazón para la construcción de un arco, alcantarilla, etc. — v.t. mecer, meter en cuna, cunear. — v.i. mecerse en la cuna.
craft [krɑːft], s. arte, m.f.; oficio; artificio, treta, astucia, maña, habilidad; gremio; (mar.) navichuelo, buque, embarcación.
craftily, adv. astutamente, artificiosamente, mañosamente.
craftiness, s. astucia, estratagema, maña, socarronería.
craftsman, s. artífice, artesano.
craftsmaster, s. artífice, maestro.
crafty, a. astuto, artificioso, ladino, taimado.
crag [kræg], s. despeñadero, risco.
craggedness, cragginess, s. escabrosidad, fragosidad, aspereza.
craggy, a. escabroso, escarpado.
cram [kræm], v.t. rellenar, henchir; llenar demasiado; cebar, hartar, atracar, atestar, recalcar, embutir; empujar, meter una cosa en otra con fuerza y violencia. — v.i. atracarse de comida; prepararse en los últimos momentos y algo superficialmente para un examen; sobrecargar la memoria.
crambo ['kræmbou], s. juego que consiste en hallar consonante a una palabra dada.
crammer, s. (fam.) tutor o ayo que prepara para exámenes; mentira.
cramming, s. repaso.
cramp [kræmp], s. (med.) calambre, rampa; (med.) entumecimiento, sujeción, aprieto, estrechez; laña, grapa. — v.t. dar calambre; entumecer; lañar; engrapar; sujetar; apretar, constreñir; enganchar.
crampit, s. contera de espada.
crampon, s. tenazas, garfios.
cran [kræn], s. medida de capacidad que equivale a 45 galones (pescado fresco) o 37,5 galones (pescado salado).
cranage, s. gruaje, derechos o alquiler de grúa en los muelles.
cranberry, s. (bot.) arándano.
crance, s. (mar.) suncho de botalón, especialmente el que forma la cabeza del bauprés.
crane [krein], s. (orn.) grulla, (mec.) grúa; árgana; pescante; sifón; (mar.) abanico; cigüeña de chimenea; wheel-crane, grúa con rueda.
crane-fly, s. (ent.) típula.
crane's bill, s. (bot.) geranio; (cir.) fórceps.
cranial ['kreiniəl], a. del cráneo.
craniognomy [kreini'ɔgnəmi], s. craneología.
craniograph ['kreiniəgræf], s. craneógrafo.
craniological [kreiniə'lɔdʒikl], a. craneológico, referente a la craneología.
craniologist [kreini'ɔlədʒist], s. craneólogo.
craniology, s. craneología.
craniometrical [kreiniə'metrikl], a. craneométrico.
craniometry [kreini'ɔmətri], s. craneometría.
cranioscopy [kreini'ɔskəpi], s. craneoscopia.
cranium ['kreiniəm], s. (anat.) cráneo, casco.
crank [kræŋk], s. hierro de farol; (mec) manivela, manubrio, cigüeña; gancho; biela; sutileza, juego de palabras; (fam.) mentecato, chiflado. — a. vivo, vigoroso, dispuesto, alegre; (mec.) frágil; (mar.) celoso (de una embarcación). — v.r. virar (un motor).
crankiness, s. chifladura; irritabilidad.
crankle ['kræŋkl], v.t., v.i. serpentear, culubrear. — s. recodo, repliegue, vuelta.

cranky, *a.* chiflado, lunático; torcido; inseguro.

crannied ['krænid], *a.* hendido, grietoso.

cranny, *s.* hendedura, grieta, raja; rincón.

crape [kreip], *s.* crespón. — *v.t.* encrespar, rizar; poner crespón.

crapulence ['kræpjuləns], *s.* crápula.

crapulent, crapulous, *a.* crapuloso.

crash [kræʃ], *v.i.* estrellar; romperse; (*aut.*) estrellar, chocar; caerse con estrépito, hundirse; estallar, dar un estallido. — *v.t.* romper, quebrantar, machacar. — *s.* estallido, estampido, fracaso, quiebra, bancarrota; accidente, choque.

crasis ['kreisis], *s.* (*gram.*) sinéresis, *f.*

crass ['kræs], *a.* gordo, grueso, basto, tosco, espeso, denso, craso, torpe.

crassitude, crassness, *s.* crasitud, tosquedad, espesor.

cratch [krætʃ], *s.* rastrillo de pesebre de heno; (*vet.*) grieta.

crate [kreit], *s.* (caja de) embalaje, envase; cesto grande, canasto, cuévano, banasta.

crater, *s.* cráter.

craunch [krɑːntʃ], *v.t.* cascar, romper con los dientes.

cravat [krə'væt], *s.* corbata, corbatín.

crave [kreiv], *v.t., v.i.* suplicar, rogar, implorar, pedir; anhelar, ansiar, apetecer.

craven, *s.* cobarde; gallo sin valor para la riña. — *a.* cobarde, acobardado, pusilánime. — *v.t.* acobardar, intimidar.

craver, *s.* pedigón, pedigüeño, pedidor.

craving, *s.* anhelo, sed, *f.*, deseo ardiente.

craw [krɔː], *s.* buche.

crawfish, crayfish, *s.* cangrejo; langostín, astaco.

crawl [krɔːl], *v.i.* arrastrar(se), serpear; mover(se) con lentitud; avanzar rastreando; andar a gatas. — *s.* arrastramiento; paso de tortuga; (*natación*) 'crawl'; (*mar.*) pozo de barco; corral de pescado.

crawler, *s.* reptil.

crayfish, *s.* [CRAWFISH].

crayon ['kreiən], *s.* lápiz clarión, tiza, dibujo al clarión, pastel, dibujo de lápiz. — *v.t.* dibujar al pastel, bosquejar, esquiciar.

craze [kreiz], *s* manía; locura, delirio, furor, demencia; antojo, capricho; moda. — *v.t.* quebrantar, debilitar, enloquecer, entontecer; romper, pulverizar; cuartear, grietar. — *v.i.* cuartearse; grietarse; perder la razón.

crazed, *a.* grietoso; demente.

crazily, *adv.* insensatamente, locamente.

craziness, *s.* debilidad, locura, inseguridad, desequilibrio.

crazy, *a.* simple, loco, lelo, fatuo, demente; extravagante; desvencijado, dilapidado.

creak [kriːk], *v.i.* crujir, chirriar, rechinar.

creaking, *s.* crujido, rechino, rechinamiento, chirrido.

creaking, creaky, *a.* crujidero, chirriador.

cream [kriːm], *s.* crema, nata; (*fig.*) la flor y nata; *whipped cream,* nata batida; *cream of tartar,* bitartrato de potasa. — *v.t.* desnatar. — *v.i.* criar nata.

creamery, *s.* lechería.

creamy, *a.* lleno de crema o nata; meloso.

crease [kriːs], *s.* pliegue, repliegue, arruga, plegadura, doblez. — *v.t.* plegar, doblar, estriar, acanalar; (*cost.*) repulgar.

creaser, *s.* (*cost.*) repulgador.

create [kri'eit], *v.t.* crear, producir, causar, ocasionar; engendrar, procrear; constituir, nombrar, elegir; *to create a disturbance,* revolver la feria.

creation, *s.* creación, obra; universo; producción; fundación, establecimiento; nombramiento, elección.

creative, *a.* creador, creativo.

creativeness, *s.* genio inventivo, facultad creadora.

creator, *s.* creador; inventor.

creatress, *s.* creadora.

creature ['kriːtjər], *s.* criatura; animal; ser; hechura; semejante; *fellow creature,* semejante.

credence [kriːdəns], *s.* creencia; crédito; asenso, fe, *f.*

credent, *a.* creyente, crédulo, confiado.

credential [kri'denʃəl], *a.* credencial.

credentials, *s.pl.* cartas credenciales.

credibility [kredi'biliti], *s.* credibilidad, probabilidad, verosimilitud.

credible ['kredibl], *a.* creíble, creedero, verosímil.

credibleness, *s.* credibilidad; veracidad.

credibly, *adv.* creíblemente, probablemente.

credit ['kredit], *a.* crédito, creencia, asenso, fe, *f.*; buen nombre; reputación; confianza; autoridad, influjo, valía; *credit balance,* haber; *on credit,* al fiado; *open credit,* letra abierta; *letter of credit,* carta de crédito; *to buy* o *sell on credit,* comprar o vender al fiado, o a plazos. — *v.t.* acreditar, dar fe o crédito; creer; fiar, acreditar, confiar, honrar; dar fama; adatar, abonar, prestar o vender a crédito; dar al fiado.

creditable, *a.* estimable, apreciable, abonado, fidedigno.

creditableness, *s.* reputación.

creditably, *adv.* honorablemente, honrosamente.

credited, *a.* estimado; acreditado, tenido en buena opinión; creído; (*com.*) abonado en cuenta; pasado al haber. — *p.p.* [CREDIT].

creditor, *s.* acreedor; (*com.*) haber.

credo ['kriːdou], *s.* (*igl.*) credo.

credulity [krə'djuːliti], *s.* credulidad.

credulous ['kredjuləs], *a.* crédulo; *to be very credulous,* tener buenas tragaderas.

credulousness, *s.* credulidad.

creed [kriːd], *s.* credo, símbolo; creencia; profesión de fe.

creek [kriːk], *s.* cala, caleta, abra, ensenada; recodo, sinuosidad; riachuelo; cañón.

creeky, *a.* sinuoso, lleno de caletas.

creel [kriːl], *s.* cesta de pescador.

creep [kriːp], *v.i.* (*pret.* y *p.p.* **crept**) arrastrar, arrastrarse, ratear, deslizarse, serpear, andar a gatas, gatear, insinuarse; andar a hurtadillas, a la chitacallando, o de puntillas; sentir hormigueo (sobre la piel, causado por miedo o repugnancia); rebajarse, adular; (*mar.*) rastrear con un garfio o garabato el fondo del mar; *to creep along,* andar arrastrándose; *to creep on,* acercarse poco a poco; *to creep out,* escurrirse, salir sin hacer ruido; *to creep up,* encaramarse; *to creep in* o *into,* insinuarse, deslizarse en.

creeper, *s.* el que se arrastra; reptil; (*orn.*) trepadora; (*bot.*) enredadera; ramplón de zapato; (*mar.*) garfio o garabato.

creephole, s. huronera; agujero que sirve de refugio; (*fig.*) pretexto, escapatoria.

creeping, s. arrastramiento; bajeza.

creepingly, *adv.* a paso de tortuga.

creese [kriːs], s. daga o puñal malayo.

cremate [krə'meit], *v.t.* incinerar.

cremation, s. cremación, incineración.

cremationist, s. partidario de la cremación.

crematorium [kremə'toəriəm], s. horno de cremación.

crematory ['kremətəri], s. crematorio; horno de incineración.

crenated ['kriːneitid], *a.* dentado, festoneado.

crenelate, crenellate ['krenəleit], *v.t.* (*fort.*) almenar; dentar, festonear.

creole ['krioul], s. criollo.

creosote ['kriːəsout], s. creosota.

crepitate ['krepiteit], *v.i.* crepitar, chisporrotear; chirriar.

crepitation [krepi'teiʃən], s. crepitación, chisporroteo.

crept [krept], *pret.* y *p.p.* [CREEP].

crepuscular [kre'pʌskjuləɹ], *a.* crepuscular, crepusculino.

crepuscule ['krepəsl], s. crepúsculo.

crescendo [kreʃendou], s. (*mús.*) crescendo.

crescent ['kresent], *a.* creciente. — s. creciente, *f.*, primer cuarto de la luna; cualquier cosa que tiene figura semicircular; como signo representativo Turquía y Islamismo.

cress [kres], s. (*bot.*) lepidio, mastuerzo; *water-cress*, berro.

cresset, s. fanal, farol, fogaril; antorcha, antorchero.

crest [krest], s. cresta, penacho, copete; cimera; (*blas.*) timbre; cumbre, *f.*, cima; crestón; (*fig.*) orgullo, corage, altanería. — *v.t.* coronar, adornar con una cimera; rayar. — *v.i.* encresparse, encrestarse.

crested ['krestid], *a.* crestado, coronado, encopetado.

crestfallen ['krestfɔːlən], *a.* cabizbajo, acobardado, abatido, con las orejas gachas.

crestless, *a.* sin cimera; sin divisa, sin escudo; de humilde estirpe.

cretaceous [krə'teiʃəs], *a.* cretáceo, gredoso.

Cretan ['kriːtən], *a.* cretense.

cretin ['kriːtin], s. cretino.

cretinism, s. cretinismo.

cretonne ['kretɔn], s. cretona.

crevasse [krə'væs], s. grieta profunda en un ventisquero; (*E.U.*) brecha en el terraplén de un río.

crevice ['krevis], s. hendedura, raja, grieta, abertura, resquebradura.

crew [kruː], s. cuadrilla, hato, banda, tropa; (*mar.*) tripulación.

crewel, s. ovillo (de lana, etc.).

crib [krib], s. pesebre; pesebrera; camita, cuna; casucha, choza; jaula; arcón; cofre, cajón; (*min.*) brocal; estribo flotante; mimbrera para pescar salmón; (*fam.*) plagio; (*fam.*) traducción de un texto clásico (para uso de estudiantes); ratería. — *v.t.* hurtar, quitar; (*fam.*) plagiar.

cribbage, s. juego de naipes.

cribble, s. criba, harnero; aventador. — *v.t.* cerner; agujerear; puntear.

cribriform ['kribrifoəɹm], *a.* (*anat. y bot.*) cribiforme, en forma de criba.

crick [krik], s. chirrido, chirrio; calambre; *crick in the neck*, torticolis.

cricket, s. (*entom.*) grillo; cáncana, taburete; (juego de) crícquet; *to be as cheery as a cricket*, estar como una pascua.

cricketer, s. jugador de crícquet.

cricoid ['kriːkɔid], s., *a.* (*anat.*) cricoides, *f.*

crier ['kraiəɹ], s. pregonero; baladrero; alguacil de cámara.

crikey ['kraiki], *interj.* (*vulg.*) expresión de asombro: ¡diantre! ¡cáscaras! ¡caray!

crime [kraim], s. crimen, ofensa, delito.

Crimean [krai'miːən], *a.* natural de Crimea.

crimeful, *a.* criminal, reo.

crimeless, *a.* inocente.

criminal ['kriminəl], *a.* criminal, criminoso, reo, culpable. — s. criminal, reo, delincuente.

criminality [krimi'næliti], **criminalness**, s. criminalidad, maldad.

criminate, *v.t.* acriminar, acusar.

crimination [krimi'neiʃən], s. criminación, acriminación.

criminative, criminatory, *a.* acriminatorio.

criminator, *a.* acriminator, acusador.

criminology [krimi'nɔlədʒi], s. criminología.

criminous ['kriminəs], *a.* criminal, malvado, inicuo.

crimp [krimp], *a.* quebradizo, desmenuzable. — s. enganchador, reclutador, rizador; traficante en animales de caza. — *v.t.* asir, coger; rizar, encrespar (los cabellos); estampar de relieve.

crimpage, s. rizaje; rizadura; estampado en relieve.

crimping-iron, s. hierros de rizar.

crimple ['krimpl], *v.t.* plegar; fruncir; arrugar; encrespar. — s. pliegue; arruga.

crimson ['krimzən], s., *a.* carmesí. — *v.t.* teñir de carmesí. — *v.i.* enrojecerse, ponerse encendido, ponerse colorado.

crinal ['krainl], *a.* perteneciente o relativo al cabello.

cringe [krindʒ], s. bajeza, adulación. — *v.i.* acobardarse, acarroñarse, rebajarse; hacer la zalá.

cringer, s. adulador servil.

cringing, *a.* bajo, vil, rastrero.

cringle ['kriŋgl], s. (*mar.*) ojo.

crinite ['krainait], *a.* (*bot. y zool.*) crinito, peludo.

crinkle ['kriŋkl], *v.i.* serpentear. — *v.t.* arrugar, rizar. — s. vuelta, recodo, sinuosidad; ondulación.

crinoid, s. crinóideo, género de equinodermos.

crinoline ['krinəlin], s. tela de crin; crinolina, miriñaque, ahuecador.

crinosity [kri'nositi], s. vellosidad.

cripple ['kripl], s., *a.* tullido, paralítico; estropeado, zopo, manco, cojo; (*mar.*) desmantelado, desarbolado. — *v.t.* estropear, mutilar, lisiar, encojar; baldar, tullir; descabalar.

crisis ['kraisis], s. crisis, *f.*

crisp ['krisp], *a.* crespo, rizado; refrescante; frágil, quebradizo; achicharrado, tostado; terso; (*fig.*) vigoroso, decidido, incisivo, mordaz. — *v.t.* crespar, encrespar, rizar; torcer; entrelazar, trenzar; ondular; hacer quebradizo.

crispate, s. (*bot. y zool.*) desigual, sinuoso, arrugado en los bordes.

crispation ['kris'peiʃən], s. encrespadura, crispatura.

crisping-iron, crisping-pin, s. encrespador; tenacillas.
crisply ['krispli], adv. de manera rizada; ondeante; friablemente.
crispness, s. rizaje; crespadura, encrespadura; friabilidad, fragilidad.
crispy, a. rizado, crespo; frágil, desmenuzable; vigorizante, fresco.
criss-cross, a. cruzado, entrelazado.
criterion [krai'tiəriən], s. (pl. **criteria**) criterio.
critic ['kritik], s. crítico, censor. — v.t. (ant.) criticar.
critic, critical, a. crítico, perito; escrupuloso, exacto; peligroso, decisivo.
critically, adv. exactamente, rigurosamente.
criticalness, s. crítica.
criticism ['kritisizm], s. crítica, censura, juicio crítico.
criticize ['kritisaiz], v.t., v.i. criticar; censurar.
criticizer, s. crítico.
critique [kri'ti:k], s. crítica, reseña, juicio crítico.
croak [krouk], v.t., v.i. graznar, crascitar; cantar (la rana); gruñir, croar. — s. graznido; canto de la rana.
croaker, s. gruñidor, regañón, refunfuñador.
croaking, s. graznido, gruñido; canto de la rana.
crochet ['krouʃei], s. corchete; crochet, labor de crochet. — v.t., v.i. hacer crochet.
crock [krɔk], s. escudilla, cazuela, orza; olla de barro; hollín; rocinante; cacharro viejo. — v.t., v.i. tullir(se); manchar(se) con hollín.
crockery, s. vidriado, loza, cacharros.
crocodile ['krɔkədail], s. (zool.) cocodrilo.
crocus ['kroukəs], s. (bot.) azafrán; (metal.) rojo de pulir, croco de marte.
croft [krɔft], s. heredad; huerto, huerta; aledaño.
crofter, s. colono de una granja, hortelano.
cromlech ['krɔmlek], s. crónlech.
crone [kroun], s. (fam.) mujer vieja; (fam.) tía, bruja; oveja vieja.
crony, s. compinche, camarada, m.f.
crook [kruk], s. curva, curvatura, cosa encorvada; gancho; garfio; cayado de pastor; trampa, artificio; (fam.) petardista, m.f., fullero. — v.t. encorvar; torcer; pervertir, contrariar. — v.i. encorvarse, torcerse; corcovarse.
crookback, crookbacked, s., a. giboso, gibado, jorobado, corcovado.
crooked, a. encorvado, corvo, torcido, oblicuo, ladeado; (fig.) avieso, tortuoso, torcido.
crookedly, adv. torcidamente.
crookedness, s. corvadura, corcova; perversidad, tortuosidad.
crooklegged, a. patituerto.
crookneck, s. (E.U.) calabaza.
croon [kru:n], v.t., v.i. canturrear, cantar en tono bajo.
crop [krɔp], s. buche; copa, cima; cosecha, agosto, las mieses; cortadura; recolección; crecimiento de cabello o barba; látigo mocho; buche de ave. — v.t. tajar, cortar, desbrozar; despuntar; trasquilar, segar, cosechar, coger, recoger (frutas, flores). — v.i. producir; crop-eared, desorejado.
cropper, s. cosechador.

cropping, s. corta; pasto; esquileo; talla; cosecha, siega.
croquet ['kroukei], s. juego de croquet.
croquette [kro'ket], s. croqueta.
crosier ['krouziəɹ], s. cruz, f.; báculo pastoral.
cross [krɔs], s. cruz, f.; aspa; (fig.) carga, peso, trabajo; aflicción, desgracia, pena; oposición; reverso de una moneda; cruzamiento de especies; no cross, no crown, no hay atajo sin trabajo. — a. contrario, opuesto, atravesado; enojado, enfadado, caprichoso; cabezudo, regañón; desgraciado, adverso. — adv. al través; en cruz. — v.t. cruzar, atravesar; hacer una cruz; señalar con la señal de la cruz; mezclar las castas de animales; vejar, frustrar. — v.i. cruzar, atravesar; to cross out, tachar, borrar, rayar; to cross over, atravesar; to cross with, estar en desacuerdo; to cross oneself, santiguarse, persignarse.
cross-armed, a. con los brazos cruzados.
cross-arrow, s. flecha de ballesta.
cross-bar, s. tranca, travesaño.
cross-barred, a. atrancado.
cross-bearer, s. crucífero.
cross-bow, s. ballesta.
cross-breed, s. raza cruzada.
cross-breeding, s. cruzamiento de razas.
cross-cut, s. atajo; cortado al través.
cross-examination, s. (for.) repregunta, examen de la parte contraria o del testigo; interrogación, interrogatorio.
cross-examine, v.t. repreguntar.
cross-eyed, a. bizco.
cross-grained, a. veteado; desabrido, intratable, perverso.
crossing, s. contrariedad, contratiempo; travesía, paso; cruce, encrucijada; vado; level crossing, paso a nivel.
cross-legged, a. patizambo; con las piernas cruzadas.
crosslet ['krɔslət], s. crucecita.
crossly, adv. contrariamente, enojadamente.
crossness, s. espíritu de contrariedad; malicia; enfado; mal humor.
cross-piece, s. (carp.) travesaño, cruceta.
cross-road, s. encrucijada, cruce.
cross-row, s. alfabeto.
cross-spur, s. (min.) crucero de cuarzo.
cross-way, s. encrucijada, cruce.
cross-wind, s. viento contrario.
cross-wise, adv. de través; en cruz, en forma de cruz; de parte a parte.
cross-wort, s. (bot.) cruciata.
crotalum ['krɔtələm], s. crótalo.
crotch [krɔtʃ], s. horca, horquilla; bifurcación; (mar.) cabria.
crotched, a. (E.U.) ahorquillado.
crotchet, s. (mús.) corchea, semínima; (impr.) corchete; puntal; (fig.) capricho, rareza, extravagancia, excentricidad.
crotchety ['krɔtʃəti], a. extravagante, excéntrico, caprichoso; raro; (fam.) alunado, chiflado.
crouch [krautʃ], v.i. agacharse, abatirse, bajarse; rebajarse.
croup [kru:p], s. obispillo, rabadilla; anca, grupa; (med.) crup, garrotillo.
croupier, s. ayuda del banquero (en el juego).
crow [krou], s. (orn.) cuervo; corneja; barra, palanca, pie de cabra; canto del gallo; as the crow flies, en línea recta; crow's foot, arruga,

pata de gallo. — *v.i.* cantar (el gallo), cacarear; (*fig.*) gallear, alardear, bravear, jactar, cantar victoria; to *crow over someone*, bravear, afectar superioridad.

crowbar, *s.* pie de cabra.

crowd [kraud], *s.* tropel, gentío, concurso, montón; muchedumbre, *f.*, multitud, turba; populacho, vulgo; tumulto; apretura; agolpamiento. — *v.t.* amontonar, apretar, atestar; to *crowd sail*, (*mar.*) hacer fuerza de vela; to *be crowded*, estar de bote en bote. — *v.i.* apiñarse, estrecharse, remolinarse, agolparse; to *crowd in*, entrar en tumulto.

crowfoot ['kroufut], *s.* (*bot.*) ranúnculo; (*mar.*) araña; (*mil.*) abrojo.

crown [kraun], *s.* corona, diadema; soberanía; premio; láurea, guirnalda de flores; coronilla; tonsura; cima, copa, cumbre, *f.*; moneda de plata de cinco chelines; (*arq.*) clave, *f.* (de bóveda); colmo, complemento. — *v.t.* coronar; premiar, recompensar; completar, dar la última mano.

crowner, *s.* coronador.

crowning, *s.* (*arq.*) coronamiento, remate.

crownless, *a.* sin corona.

crownlet, *s.* corona pequeña.

crown prince, *s.* heredero de la corona.

croze, *s.* ranura en las duelas de barril, para fijar la cabeza; herramienta para hacer esta ranura. — *v.t.* hacer la ranura.

crozier [krouziər], *s.* báculo del obispo.

crucial ['kru:ʃiəl], *a.* (*cir.*) crucial; decisivo, conclusivo, final.

cruciate, *a.* atormentado; (*bot.*) cruciforme.

crucible ['kru:sibl], *s.* crisol.

cruciferous [kru'sifərəs], *a.* crucífero; (*bot.*) crucíferas.

crucifix ['kru:sifiks], *s.* crucifijo.

crucifixion [krusi'fikʃən], *s.* crucifixión.

cruciform ['kru:sifoəɹm], *a.* cruciforme.

crucify ['kru:sifai], *v.t.* crucificar; aspar; (*fig.*) mortificar; atormentar, enojar.

crude [kru:d], *a.* crudo, indigesto; rudo, inculto, grosero, cerril, mal educado; informal, tosco; ordinario; informe, mal elaborado, mal concebido; superficial.

crudeness, crudity, *s.* crudeza, dureza, indigestión; tosquedad.

cruel ['kru:əl], *a.* cruel, feroz, inhumano, sanguinario, bárbaro; atroz, terrible.

cruelness, cruelty, *s.* crueldad, inhumanidad, atrocidad, barbaridad; dureza, tiranía.

cruet ['kru:ət], *s.* ampolleta; vinagrera.

cruise [kru:z], *s.* viaje en buque. — *v.t.* cruzar; navegar; (*aut.*) ir a velocidad de crucero.

cruiser, *s.* (*mar.*) navegante, crucero, guardacostas, *m.*, corsario.

cruller [krʌləɹ], *s.* (*E.U.*) buñuelo.

crumb [krʌm], *s.* miga, migaja, migajón; brizna, pizca. — *v.t.* migar, desmigajar; desmenuzar; empanar.

crumbable, *a.* desmenuzable.

crumble ['krʌmbl], *v.t.* migar, desmigajar; desmenuzar, destrizar. — *v.i.* desmigajarse; desmoronarse; hundirse.

crumby ['krʌmi], *a.* que se desmigaja.

crump [krʌmp], *a.* (*ant.*) corcovado.

crumpet, *s.* bollo blando, mollete.

crumple, *v.t.* arrugar, manosear, apañuscar, chafar, ajar. — *v.i.* contraerse, arrugarse, encogerse; aplastarse; derrumbarse, hun-

dirse, desplomarse; (*fig.*) abatirse, amilanarse, desalentarse.

crumpling, *s.* manzana acorchada.

crunch [krʌntʃ], *v.t.*, *v.i.* crujir; cascar; mascar.

cruor ['kru:əɹ], *s.* cruor.

crupper ['krʌpəɹ], *s.* grupa; grupera, baticola, ataharre.

crural ['kru:ərəl], *a.* crural.

crusade [kru'seid], *s.* cruzada.

crusader, *s.* cruzado.

cruse [kru:z], *s.* frasco, redomita, botellita.

crush [krʌʃ], *v.t.* moler, machacar, aplastar; abrumar, amilanar, arruinar; triturar, estrujar, despachurrar, magullar, apretar, oprimir, comprimir; destruir; sojuzgar. — *v.i.* estar comprimido; condensarse; romperse. — *s.* apretura, apiñamiento; choque, colisión.

crusher, *s.* apretador, opresor; (*min.*) triturador.

crushing, *s.* (*min.*) molienda. — *a.* (*fig.*) aplastante; abrumador, desmoralizador.

crust [krʌst], *s.* costra; (*med.*) escara; pasta; corteza; mendrugo de pan; caparacho, concha. — *v.t.* encostrar, incrustar, cubrir con costra. — *v.i.* encostrarse.

crustacea [krʌs'teiʃiə], *s.pl.* crustáceos.

crustaceous, *a.* crustáceo.

crustation, *s.* incrustación.

crustily ['krʌstili], *adv.* (*fam.*) enojadamente, bruscamente, broncamente.

crustiness, *s.* corteza, dureza de la costra; (*fig., fam.*) mal genio, aspereza.

crusty, *a.* costroso; (*fam.*) rudo, brusco, bronco, áspero.

crutch [krʌtʃ], *s.* muleta, muletilla; horquilla; horcajadura. — *v.t.* apoyar con muletas.

cry [krai], *v.i.* gritar, vocear, exclamar; publicar, pregonar; lamentarse; llorar, aullar; bramar; to *cry down*, menospreciar, culpar; reprimir; to *cry for*, pedir llorando; to *cry for joy*, llorar de alegría; to *cry for mercy*, pedir gracia, pedir perdón; to *cry off*, renunciar; to *cry up*, alabar, aplaudir. — *v.t.* pregonar, publicar. — *s.* (*pl.* **cries**) alarido, grito; lloro, llanto, lamento; aclamación; aplauso; gritería; pregón; publicación, promulgación, llamada o ruego importuno; muta, cuadrilla de perros de caza; *far cry*, camino largo, mucha distancia; *much cry and little wool*, mucho ruido y pocas nueces.

crying, *s.* grito, lloro, plañido, lamento; ruido, clamor; lamento. — *a.* notorio, atroz, injusto, tiránico, lo que pide venganza al cielo.

cryolite ['krɑi'əlait], *s.* (*min.*) criolita.

crypt [kript], *s.* cripta; gruta.

cryptic, cryptical, *a.* escondido, oculto, secreto.

cryptogamia [kriptə'geimiə], *s.pl.* (*bot.*) criptógamas.

cryptogamian, cryptogamic, *a.* criptógamo, acotilodóneo.

cryptogamous, *a.* criptógamo, acotiledóneo.

cryptogamy, *s.* criptogamia.

cryptogram ['kriptəgræm], *s.* cifra.

cryptography [krip'tɔgrəfi], *s.* criptografía.

cryptology, *s.* criptología.

crysoscopy [kri'soskopi], *s.* (*fis.*) crisoscopía.

crystal ['kristl], *s.* cristal.

crystal, crystalline, *a.* cristalino; transparente, claro.

crystallizable [kristə'laizəbl], *a.* cristalizable.

crystallization [kristəlaiˈzeiʃən], s. cristalización.

crystallize [ˈkristəlaiz], v.t. cristalizar. — v.i. cristalizarse.

crystallography [kristəˈlɔgrəfi], s. cristalografía.

crystalloid [ˈkristəlɔid], a. cristaloide.

cub [kʌb], s. cachorro; ballenato; (fig.) zopenco. — v.t. parir (la leona, osa, etc.).

cubature [ˈkjuːbətjuː,ɪ], **cubage**, s. (geom.) cubicación.

cube [kjuːb], s. (geom.) cubo. — v.t. (mat.) cubicar; cube root, raíz cúbica.

cubic, cubical, a. cúbico.

cubicle, s. cubículo.

cubiform, cuboid, a. cúbico.

cubit [ˈkjuːbit], s. (ant.) (anat.) cúbito; codo (medida lineal).

cubital, a. cubital, codal.

cubo-cube, s. (mat.) cubo-cubo.

cuboid [ˈkjuːbɔid], a. cuboide.

cuckold [ˈkʌkəld], s. marido cornudo. — v.t. hacer cornudo, poner los cuernos.

cuckoo [ˈkukuː], s. (orn.) cuclillo, cuco; cucú (el canto).

cucullate [ˈkjuːkəleit], **cucullated**, a. encapillado; con capucha.

cucumber [ˈkjuːkʌmbəɹ], s. (bot.) cohombro, pepino.

cucurbit, s. (bot.) cucúrbita; calabaza.

cucurbitaceæ, s.pl. cucurbitáceas.

cucurbitaceous, a. cucurbitáceo.

cud [kʌd], s. rumia; to chew the cud, rumiar; (fig.) meditar.

cuddle, v.i. abrazarse; agacharse. — v.t. abrazar, acariciar.

cuddy, s. (mar.) camarote de proa; fogón; pañol del cocinero; rústico, patán; asno, burro.

cudgel [ˈkʌdʒəl], s. garrote, palo, tranca, porra. — v.t. apalear, tundir, aporrear; to cudgel one's brains, devanarse los sesos; to take up the cudgels, romper lanzas.

cudgeller, s. apaleador.

cudweed [ˈkʌdwiːd], **cudwort**, s. (ant.) (bot.) gnafalio; algodonera.

cue [kjuː], s. taco de billar; (teat.) apunte; indirecta, sugestión; genio, humor; to give a cue, apuntar.

cuff [kʌf], s. puño (de camisa), bocamanga; puñada, manotada, bofetón, golpe, sopapo, revés; vuelta de vestido. — v.t. dar un sopapo, abofetear. — v.i. reñir o pelear a puñadas, boxear.

cuirass [kwiˈræs], s. coraza.

cuirassier, s. coracero.

cuisine [kwiˈziːn], s. cocina (manera de guisar).

culex [ˈkjuleks], s. (zool.) mosquito.

culinary [ˈkjuːlinəri], a. culinario.

cull [kʌl], v.t. coger; escoger; elegir. — s. (vulg.) necio, bobo; animal de desecho que se ceba para el matadero.

cullender, s. colador, coladera, tamiz.

culler, s. escogedor.

cullet [ˈkʌlət], s. cristal desmenuzado, para refundir.

cullion, s. (ant.) testículo; belitre, tunante, pícaro; bobo.

cullis, s. canalón, muesca.

cully, v.t. (ant.) engañar, engaitar. — s. bobo.

culm [kʌlm], s. cisco; carbón de piedra en polvo o en trozos menudos; (bot.) caña.

culmiferous [kʌlˈmifərəs], a. culmífero.

culminant [ˈkʌlminənt], a. culminante; dominante, predominante.

culminate, v.i. culminar, lograr, alcanzar el punto o grado más alto; (astr.) pasar por el meridiano.

culmination [kʌlmiˈneiʃən], s. culminación; cumbre, f., cima, corona; (fig.) apogeo.

culpability [kʌlpəˈbiliti], s. culpabilidad.

culpable [ˈkʌlpəbl], a. culpable.

culpableness, s. culpabilidad.

culprit [ˈkʌlprit], s. reo, culpable, criminal, delincuente.

cult [kʌlt], s. culto, devoción; respeto, homenaje.

culter, s. reja de arado.

cultivable, a. cultivable.

cultivate [ˈkʌltiveit], v.t. cultivar, beneficiar; estudiar, practicar, ejercer.

cultivation [kʌltiˈveiʃən], s. cultivación; cultura; cultivo; labor, labranza; adelantamiento.

cultivator, s. cultivador, labrador, agricultor; cultivadora, arado de cultivar.

culture [ˈkʌltjəɹ], s. cultura, cultivación; civilización; ilustración. — v.t. cultivar, refinar; criar, educar.

culver [ˈkʌlvəɹ], s. paloma torcaz.

culverin, s. (mil.) culebrina.

culvert [ˈkʌlvəɹt], s. alcantarilla, cloaca.

cumber [ˈkʌmbəɹ], v.t. obstruir, embarazar; oprimir, incomodar, molestar; embrollar, estorbar, impedir.

cumbersome, a. embarazoso, enfadoso, fastidioso, incómodo, pesado, molesto.

cumbersomeness, s. impedimento, embarazo, incomodidad, engorro.

cumbrance [ˈkʌmbrəns], s. carga, peso, impedimento, obstáculo.

cumbrous, a. engorroso, pesado, incómodo, confuso, enfadoso.

cumbrousness, s. embarazo, molestia, incomodidad, impedimento.

cumin [ˈkʌmin], s. (bot.) comino.

cumulate [ˈkjuːmjuleit], v.t. acumular, cumular, amontonar, hacinar.

cumulation [kjuːmjuˈleiʃən], s. acumulación, amontonamiento.

cumulative [ˈkjuːmjulətiv], a. cumulativo.

cumulus [ˈkjuːmjuləs], s. cúmulus, cúmulo.

cuneal [ˈkjuːniəl], **cuneate, cuneiform**, a. cuneiforme.

cunning [ˈkʌniŋ], a. artificioso, mañoso, artero, astuto; marrullero, trapacero, sutil; diestro, hábil, sagaz, experto; disimulado, solapado; (fam., E.U.) divertido, gracioso, mono. — s. astucia, fraude, maña, ardid; sutileza, arte, artificio, artimaña, bellaquería, malicia, marullería, socarronería.

cunningness, s. [CUNNING].

cup [kʌp], s. taza, copa, jícara, pocillo; (bot. e Igles.) cáliz; copa (premio al vencedor de un deporte); (med.) ventosa; (fig.) suerte, f., fortuna; parting cup, espuela; in his cups, ebrio; there's many a slip 'twixt cup and lip, de la mano a la boca se pierde la sopa. — v.t. (med.) aplicar ventosas; ahuecar en forma de taza; (golf) tocar el suelo al golpear la pelota.

cupboard [ˈkʌbəɹd], s. armario, alacena, copera, aparador.

cupel [ˈkjuːpəl], s. copela.

cupellation [kju:pə'leiʃən], s. (quím.) copelación.
cupful ['kʌpful], s. contenido de una taza.
Cupid ['kju:pid], s. Cupido.
cupidity [kju'piditi], s. codicia, avaricia, avidez, deseo o apetito inmoderado.
cupola [kju:pələ], s. (arq.) cúpula, domo; horno de fundición; torre blindada en un buque de guerra.
cupping ['kʌpiŋ], s. (cir.) aplicación de ventosas; cupping-glass, ventosa.
cupreous ['kju:priəs], a. cobrizo, cobreño.
cupriferous [kju'prifərəs], a. cuprífero.
cupule, s. (bot.) cúpula.
cur [kə:ɹ], s. perro de mala casta; (fig.) canalla, m.
curability [kjurə'biliti], s. curabilidad.
curable ['kju:rəbl], a. curable, sanable.
curableness, s. curabilidad.
curaçao [kjuərə'seiou], s. curasao, curazao.
curacy, s. vicariato, vicaría.
curate ['kjuərət], s. vicario, cura, m.
curative, a. curativo.
curator [kjuə'reitəɹ], s. curador; conservador, guardián.
curatrix [kju'reitriks], s. curadora.
curb [kə:ɹb], s. barbada; brocal de pozo; (fig.) freno, restricción, sujeción; (vet.) corvaza, esparaván; bordillo, encintado (de una acera). — v.t. poner la barbada al caballo; (fig.) refrenar, poner freno, moderar.
curd [kə:ɹd], s. cuajada; requesón. — v.t. cuajar, condensar, coagular.
curdle, v.i. cuajarse, coagularse, condensarse, engrumecerse; to curdle (one's blood), (fig.) helarse la sangre. — v.t. coagular, cuajar, espesar, congelar.
curdly, curdy, a. cuajado, coagulado.
cure [kjuəɹ], s. cura, curación, remedio, medicina, medicamento; salazón, f.; cura de almas. — v.t., v.i. curar, sanar, remediar; salar; preservar, ahumar.
cureless, a. incurable.
curer, s. sanador, médico; preparador de salazones.
curfew ['kə:ɹfju:], s. queda, toque de queda, retreta.
curia ['kjuriə], s. curia.
curialistic [kjuriə'listik], a. curial.
curio [kjuəriou], s. objeto curioso.
curiosity [kjuəri'ɔsiti], s. curiosidad; rareza.
curious ['kjuəriəs], a. curioso; singular, extraño, raro; (ant.) cuidadoso, exacto, escrupuloso; delicado; entremetido.
curiousness, s. curiosidad; exactitud; primor, delicadeza.
curl [kə:ɹl], s. rizo, bucle; tortuosidad, sinuosidad; curvatura; ondulación, bocanada de humo; enfermedad de la patata; enfermedad del melocotón; alabeo de la madera. — v.t. rizar, encrespar, enroscar, engrifar, torcer, ensortijar; ondear; jaspear, vetear; fruncir. — v.i. rizarse, ondearse; enroscarse, encarrujarse; to curl up, enroscarse, hacerse un ovillo.
curledness, s. rizo, bucle; sinuosidad; arruga, ondulación.
curlew ['kə:ɹlju:], s. (orn.) chorlito, zarapito.
curliness, s. ensortijamiento; rizo, bucle.
curling [kə:ɹliŋ], s. ensortijamiento; rizado; curling-iron(s), encrespador, rizador, tenacillas.

curly, ensortijado; rizo, rizado, crespo.
curmudgeon [kə:ɹ'mʌdʒən], s. avaro, tacaño, cicatero, mezquino.
currant ['kʌrənt], s. grosella; grosellero; uva o pasa de Corinto; black-currant, grosella negra, grosellero negro.
currency, s. circulación, dinero en circulación; aceptación; moneda o valor corriente; duración; legal currency, valor corriente.
current, a. corriente, popular, general, en boga, común, admitido; presente, del día, de actualidad. — s. corriente, f., progresión, marcha, curso, rebalaje.
currently, adv. corrientemente, generalmente; a la moda.
currentness, s. circulación; corrección; fluidez, pureza; aceptación general.
curricle ['kʌrikl], s. curso, corrida, carriola.
curriculum [kə'rikjuləm], s. curso de estudios en una escuela; programa o plan de las asignaturas.
currier ['kʌriəɹ], s. curtidor, zurrador.
currish ['kʌriʃ], a. perruno; arisco; (fig.) regañón, brutal.
currishness, s. malignidad, morosidad.
curry ['kʌri], v.t. curtir, zurrar, adobar, aderezar; almohazar; lisonjear; to curry favour, insinuarse. — s. especie de condimento de origen indiano.
curry-comb, s. almohaza.
currying, s. zurra; lisonjeo, servilismo.
curse [kə:ɹs], v.t. maldecir, execrar, anatematizar. — v.i. imprecar, blasfemar, renegar, echar maldiciones. — s. maldición, imprecación, juramento, anatema, m.f., blasfemia, reniego; castigo, azote; calamidad.
cursed a. maldecido, execrado, aborrecible, abominable, execrable.
cursedly ['kə:ɹsədli], adv. (fam.) miserablemente, abominablemente.
cursedness, s. abominación; malicia.
curser, s. maldiciente.
cursing, s. maldición, execración.
cursive ['kə:ɹsiv], a. cursivo, corriente.
cursor, s. corredera.
cursorily, adv. precipitadamente, rápidamente, de carrera.
cursoriness, s. precipitación, prisa; descuido.
cursory, a. precipitado; inconsiderado; por encima.
curt [kə:ɹt], a. brusco, áspero, seco; corto.
curtail [kə:ɹ'teil], v.t. cortar, abreviar, cercenar, mutilar; economizar, reducir; desmembrar. — s. (ant.) rabón.
curtailing, s. corte, m.; mutilación; cercenamiento; abreviatura.
curtailment, s. reducción, rebajamiento, abreviación.
curtain ['kə:ɹtən], s. cortina; telón; (fort.) cortina; behind the curtain, en secreto, de escondidas; to draw the curtain, correr la cortina, (fig.) correr un velo, ocultar; to drop the curtain, bajar el telón.
curtain-lecture, s. reconvención conyugal. — v.t. poner cortinas, adornar con cortinas, velar.
curtain-raiser, s. entremés, loa, paso.
curtana [kə:ɹ'tɑ:nə], s. la espada de la misericordia, que es llevada delante de los Reyes de Inglaterra en su coronación.
curtness, s. brevedad, concisión, brusquedad, falta de cortesía.

curtsey, curtsy, *s.* cortesía, reverencia. — *v.i.* hacer una reverencia.

curvated, *a.* corvo, encorvado.

curvation [kəːɹ'veiʃən], *s.* corvadura, encorvadura, curvatura.

curvature ['kəːɹvətʃəɹ], *s.* curvatura, comba, combadura, cimbra.

curve [kəːɹv], *v.t.* encorvar; torcer; (*arq.*) cimbrar. — *v.i.* encorvarse, torcerse, combarse. — *a.* corvo, curvo, encorvado, torcido. — *s.* curva, recodo; (*aut.*) viraje; combadura.

curvedness, *s.* corvatura, comba.

curvet [kəɹ'vet], *s.* capricho, ventolera; corveta; corcovo, salto que da el caballo. — *v.t., v.i.* corcovear; corvetear, cabriolar; saltar de alegría.

curvilinear [kəɹvə'liniəɹ], *a.* curvilíneo.

curving, *s.* curvatura, comba.

curvity, *s.* curvatura, combadura.

cushat ['kuʃət], *s.* paloma torcaz.

cushion ['kuʃən], *s.* cojín, almohadilla, almohadón; (*mec.*) cojinete; banda de sillón; banda de mesa de billar. — *v.t.* adornar con cojines o almohadones; (*billar*) dejar una bola pegada o arrimada a la banda.

cusp [kʌsp], *s.* cúspide, *f.*, punta; cuerno.

cuspated, *a.* puntiagudo, terminado en punta.

cuspid, *s.* colmillo.

cuspidal, *a.* puntiagudo.

cuspidate, cuspidated, *a.* puntiagudo, terminado en punta, cuspidada o apuntillada (dícese de las plantas).

cuspidor, *s.* escupidera.

cuss [kʌs], *s.* (*fam.*) tunante; (*E.U., fam.*) imprecación.

cussedness ['kʌsidnəs], *s.* (*fam.*) malicia; (*fam.*) emperramiento, tozudez.

custard ['kʌstəd], *s.* flan, natillas.

custodian [kəs'toudiən], *s.* custodio, conservador, guardián.

custody [kʌstədi], *s.* custodia, guardia, guarda; prisión, cárcel, *f.*, encierro; cuidado; seguridad, recaudo.

custom [kʌstəm], *s.* costumbre, *f.*, usanza, uso; parroquia, clientela (de una tienda); parroquiano; despacho; salida; venta; (*for.*) consuetud; *custom-duties,* derechos de aduana; *custom-free,* libre de derechos; *custom house,* aduana, oficinas de aduana. — *v.t.* pagar los derechos de aduana. — *v.i.* acostumbrar; aparroquiar.

customable, *a.* frecuente, habitual; adeudable; sujeto al derecho de aduanas.

customarily [kʌstə'mɛərili], *adv.* comúnmente, generalmente, ordinariamente, de costumbre.

customariness, *s.* frecuencia; hábito.

customary ['kʌstəmri], *a.* usual, ordinario, habitual, acostumbrado, usado; (*for.*) consuetudinario, a (o al) fuero.

customer, *s.* parroquiano, cliente, *m.f.*, marchante; (*fam.*) tipo, individuo; *an ugly customer,* bribón, mal pájaro, adversario temible.

cut [kʌt], *v.t.* cortar, recortar, acortar; hender; separar; tronchar, tallar, entallar, esculpir; cincelar, insculpir; mochar, segar; herir, estropear, lastimar, mutilar; destruir; interrumpir; castrar; (*fam.*) negar el saludo, cortar relaciones; dividir, partir; abrirse paso; alzar o cortar los naipes; *to cut across,* tomar un atajo; *to cut asunder,* rasgar,

despedazar, hacer pedazos; *to cut away,* quitar, separar, cercenar; *to cut capers,* cabriolar; *to cut cards,* alzar los naipes; *to cut a dash,* (*fig.*) alzar figura; *to cut down,* derribar, abatir, aserrar; rebajar, reducir; *to cut off,* tajar, separar; amputar, mutilar, destruir, extirpar; cortar completamente; *to cut out,* recortar; (*fam.*) vencer; excluir; abrir; *to cut short,* (*fig.*) acortar, abreviar, interrumpir, echar a otra parte; *to cut up,* cortar, partir, trinchar, disecar; *diamond cut diamond,* de diestro a diestro. — *v.i.* cortarse, herirse; hacer una incisión; cortar bien. — *s.* corte, cortadura; atajo; hendedura; estampa; forma, figura, hechura; tajada, lonja; talla; incisión; cuchillada, herida; corto pasaje; afrenta, desaire; reducción; *cut with a whip,* latigazo; *short cut,* atajo; *to take a short cut,* ir a campo travieso. — *a.* cortado, tajado; interceptado, interrumpido, castrado.

cutaneous [kju'teiniəs], *a.* cutáneo.

cute [kjuːt], *a.* agudo; picante; (*fam.*) mono, lindo.

cuticle [kjuːtikl], *s.* cutícula.

cuticular [kju'tikjuləɹ], *a.* cuticular.

cutlass [kʌtləs], *s.* alfanje, machete; (*mar.*) sable de abordaje.

cutler, *s.* cuchillero.

cutlery, *s.* cuchillería.

cutlet, *s.* chuleta.

cut-off, *s.* (*mec.*) cortavapor; (*elec.*) cortacircuito.

cut-purse, *s.* salteador.

cutter, *s.* cortador; grabador, tallador; (*mar.*) cúter; (*E.U.*) trineo pequeño.

cut-throat, *s.* asesino, sacamantecas, *m.f.*; (*fig.*) bribón, rufián.

cutting ['kʌtiŋ], *s.* cortadura, incisión; corte; talla; recorte; retazo; estaca; cercenadura; alce de naipes; reducción, rebaja. — *a.* cortante; incisivo, mordaz; conmovedor.

cuttle, cuttle-fish, *s.* jibia, sepia.

cuttle-bone, *s.* jibión.

cutwater, *s.* (*mar.*) tajamar.

cutworm, *s.* larva de la mariposa Agrotis.

cuvette [kju'vet], *s.* cubeta.

cyanate ['saiəneit], *s.* (*quím.*) cianato.

cyanic [sai'ænik], *a.* ciánico.

cyanide ['saiənaid], *s.* cianuro.

cyanogen [sai'ænodʒən], *s.* cianógeno.

cyanometer [saiə'nɔmətəɹ], *s.* cianómetro.

cyanotic, *a.* cianótico.

cyanuric, *a.* cianurado.

cyclamen ['sikləmən], *s.* (*bot.*) ciclamino; artanita.

cycle [saikl], *s.* ciclo, período; bicicleta, velocípedo. — *v.i.* ir en bicicleta.

cyclic, cyclical, *a.* cíclico.

cycling, *s.* ciclismo.

cyclist, *s.* ciclista, *m.f.*

cycloid, *s.* (*geom.*) cicloide.

cycloidal [sai'klɔidl], *a.* cicloidal.

cyclometer [sai'klɔmətəɹ], *s.* ciclómetro.

cyclometric [saiklə'metrik], *a.* ciclométrico.

cyclometry [sai'klɔmətri], *s.* ciclometría.

cyclone ['saikloun], *s.* ciclón, huracán.

cyclopean [saiklə'piːən], **cyclopic,** *a.* ciclópico, ciclópeo, gigantesco.

cyclopædic [saiklə'piːdik], *a.* enciclopédico.

cyclopædia, *s.* enciclopedia.

cyclops [saiklɔps], *s.* cíclope.

cyclorama [saiklə'rɑːmə], *s.* ciclorama, *m.f.*

cycloramic, *a*. panorámico.
cyclosis [sai'klousis], *s*. (*biol*.) circulación, como la de la sangre en los animales, o la savia en las plantas.
cyclostyle ['saikləstail], *s*. ciclóstilo. — *v.t*. tirar en el ciclóstilo, ciclostilar (*neologismo*).
cygnet ['signət], *s*. pollo del cisne.
cylinder ['silindəɹ], *s*. cilindro; rollo, rollete; *cylinder head*, (*mec*.) culata.
cylindric, cylindrical, *a*. cilíndrico.
cymbal ['simbəl], *s*. címbalo.
cyme ['saim], *s*. (*bot*.) cima, corimbo.
cymoscope ['saiməskoup], *s*. (*elec*.) cimoscopio.
cymose, cymous ['saimous], *a*. (*bot*.) que tiene cimas.
cynic ['sinik], **cynical**, *a*. cínico.
cynic, *s*. cínico.
cynicalness, cynicism, *s*. cinismo.
cynosure ['sainəzjuəɹ], *s*. (*astr*.) cinosura; osa menor.
cypher ['saifəɹ], *s*. [CIPHER].
cypress ['saipres], *s*. (*bot*.) ciprés.
cyst [sist], **cystis**, *s*. (*anat*.) quiste.
cystic, cystous, *a*. cístico.
cystoscope, *s*. cistoscopio.
cystotomy [sis'tɔtəmi], *s*. cistotomía.
cytisus ['saitəsʌs], *s*. (*bot*.) citiso.
czar [za:ɹ], *s*. zar.
czarevitch ['za:rəvitʃ], **czarowitz**, *s*. zarevitz.
czarina [za'ri:nə], *s*. zarina.
Czech [tʃek], *s*., *a*. checo.

D

D, d [di:], cuarta letra del alfabeto inglés; (*mús*.) re; (*abrev*.) doctor; *D.D*. Doctor en Teología; *LL.D*. Doctor en Leyes; *D.M*. Doctor en Medicina.
dab [dæb], *v.t*. golpear o frotar blandamente; picar; enjugar; estregar suavemente; (*impr*.) clisar. — *s*. golpecito, sopapo; picada, picotazo; manotada; salpicadura; perito, hábil, diestro; (*ict*.) barbada.
dabber, *s*. (*impr*.) bala.
dabble, *v.t*. mojar, humedecer, salpicar, rociar. — *v.i*. chapotear, guachapear; (*fig*.) meterse, entremeterse.
dabbler, *s*. chapuzador; chapucero.
dab-chick, *s*. (*orn*.) somormujo.
dabster, *s*. (*fam*.) diestro, perito, hábil.
dace [deis], *s*. (*ict*.) albur.
dactyl ['dæktil], *s*. dáctilo.
dactylic [dæk'tilik], *a*. dactílico.
dactylograph, *s*. máquina de escribir.
dactylography [dækti'lɔgrəfi], *s*. dactilografía.
dactylology [dækti'lɔlədʒi], *s*. dactilología.
dad [dæd], **daddie, daddy**, *s*. (*fam*.) papá, papaíto, (*Amér., Murcia*) tata, *m*.
daddle ['dædl], *v.i*. andar vacilando.
daddy-long-legs, *s*. arácnido; típula.
dado ['deidou], *s*. (*arq*.) dado, cubo; rodapié.
daff [dæf], *v.t*. desechar, tirar, apartar.
daffodil ['dæfədil], *s*. (*bot*.) narciso, trompón.
daft [dɑ:ft], *a*. necio, tonto, loco, aturdido, bobo, chiflado.
dag [dæg], *s*. pistola de grueso calibre, de los siglos XVI y XVII.
dagger, *s*. daga, puñal; (*impr*.) cruz, *f*., obelisco; *to look daggers at*, mirar airado a uno, comerse a uno con los ojos; *to be at daggers*

drawn, haber moros y cristianos, estar como perro y gato.
daggle, *v.t*. chapuzar; embarrar. — *v.i*. embarrarse, enlodarse.
daggle-tail, *s*. mujer desaliñada.
dago [deigou], *s*. americano descendiente de español, portugués o italiano(*despec*.).
daguerreotype [də'gerotaip], *s*. daguerrotipo.
dahlia ['deiliə], *s*. (*bot*.) dalia.
daily ['deili], *a*. diario, cotidiano; (*astr*.) diurno. — *s*. periódico diario. — *adv*. diariamente, todos los días, cada día, cotidianamente.
daintiness, *s*. delicadeza; pulidez, afectación; elegancia; golosina.
dainty, *a*. delicado, refinado, afectado, exquisito, regalado; elegante; sabroso, gustoso. — *s*. golosina, manjar delicado, chocho, confite.
dairy ['dɛəri], *s*. lechería; quesería, vaquería; *dairy-farm*, casa de vacas; *dairy-maid*, lechera, moza de lechería; *dairy-man*, lechero.
dais ['deiis], *s*. tablado, estrado; grada; dosel.
daisy ['deizi], *s*. margarita, maya; (*E.U., vulg*.) persona o cosa muy admirada.
dale [deil], *s*. valle, cañada.
dalliance ['dæliəns], *s*. diversión, regodeo, retozo, fiesta, dilación, tardanza.
dallier, *s*. bromista, *m.f*.; retozón, juguetón.
dally, *v.i*. bobear, entretenerse; retozar, acariciarse, juguetear; tardar, retardarse, perder tiempo. — *v.t*. dilatar, suspender, gastar, consumir.
Dalmatian [dæl'meiʃən], *s*., *a*. dálmata, *m.f*.
dalmatic [dæl'mætik], *s*. dalmático, dalmática.
dam [dæm], *s*. yegua; (despectivo) madre; mujer; dama (en el juego de damas); azud, *m.f*., dique; límite, linde; presa, represa. — *v.t*. represar, detener, estancar, rebalsar, cerrar, tapar; *to dam up*, contener el agua con diques.
damage ['dæmidʒ], *s*. daño, perjuicio, estropeo, detrimento, deterioro; menoscabo, pérdida; avería. — *pl*. **damages**, (*for*.) daños y perjuicios. — *v.t*. dañar, perjudicar, deteriorar, empecer. — *v.i*. averiarse, dañarse.
damageable, *a*. susceptible de daño.
damask ['dæməsk], *s*. damasco. — *a*. damasquinado, adamascado. — *v.t*. adamascar; matizar; *damask-plum*, ciruela damascena; *damask-rose*, rosa de damasco o encarnada.
dame [deim], *s.f*. dama, señora, dueña, ama; (*fam*.) tía; maestra de niñas.
damn [dæm], *v.t*. condenar, silbar; infernar; maldecir, reprobar, vituperar. — *interj*. (*vulg*.) ¡maldito sea! — *a*. maldito, infernal.
damnable, *a*. detestable, odioso; condenable, infame.
damnably, *adv*. horriblemente, detestablemente.
damnation [dæm'neiʃən], *s*. damnación, condenación, maldición.
damnatory ['dæmnətəri], *a*. condenatorio.
damned, *a*. condenado; aborrecible, detestable; réprobo; maldito.
damnify ['dæmnifai], *v.t*. dañar, perjudicar, injuriar, lastimar.
damp [dæmp], *a*. húmedo, mojado. — *s*. humedad; niebla.
damp, dampen, *v.t*. mojar, humedecer;

enfriar; desanimar, entibiar, desalentar, abatir, amainar.

dampening, damping, s. humectación.

damper, s. apagador; registro de chimenea; regulador de tiro; apagador del piano, sordina.

dampish, a. un poco húmedo.

dampishness, dampness, s. humedad.

damposcope ['dæmpəscoup], s. (min.) damposcopio.

dampy, a. húmedo.

damsel [dæmzəl], s.f. damisela; señorita, muchacha.

damson ['dæmzən], s. (bot.) ciruela damascena; ciruela de Damasco.

dance [dɑːns], v.i. danzar, bailar; brincar, saltar. — v.t. hacer bailar, hacer saltar; to dance attendance, obsequiar. — s. baile, danza; no longer pipe, no longer dance, por dinero baila el perro; to lead one a dance, traer a uno al retortero.

danceable, a. bailable.

dancer, s. danzador, danzante, bailador, bailarín, saltarín.

dancing, a. danzante. — s. baile, danza.

dancing-master, s. maestro de baile.

dancing-room, s. sala de baile.

dandelion ['dændilaiən], s. (bot.) diente de león, amargón.

dander ['dændər], v.i. vagar. — (vulg.) ira, cólera.

dandle ['dændl], v.t. mecer, cunear; acariciar, mimar; hacer saltar sobre las rodillas; tratar a uno como a un niño.

dandler, s. niñero.

dandruff ['dændrəf], s. caspa.

dandy ['dændi], s. petimetre, currutaco, pisaverde, lechuguino, dandi. — a. barbilindo, alindado; (fig., fam.) acertado, estupendo, lindo; dandy-fever, dengue.

dandyish, a. como un petimetre.

dandyism, s. gomosería, dandismo.

Dane [dein], s. danés, dinamarqués.

danewort ['deinwəːt], s. (bot.) yezgo.

danger ['deindʒər], s. peligro; riesgo; contingencia, trance; to be in danger, correr peligro, peligrar.

dangerless, a. seguro, sin peligro.

dangerous, a. peligroso, arriesgado, espinoso, grave.

dangerousness, s. peligro, riesgo, gravedad.

dangle [dæŋgl], v.i. colgar, suspender, pender, estar colgado; columpiar; bambolearse. — v.t. colgar, dejar colgar, columpiar.

dangler, s. pisaverde.

dangling, a. pendiente, fluctuante.

Danish, a. danés, dinamarqués.

dank [dæŋk], a. húmedo, liento. — s. humedad.

dankish, a. algo húmedo.

dankishness, s. humedad.

dap, v.i. pescar con caña en la superficie del agua.

Daphne ['dæfni], s. Dafne, ninfa de Diana; (bot.) Dafne, género de arbustos de la familia de los timéleas.

dapper [dæpər], a. apuesto, gallardo, limpio; vivaz, vivaracho, activo.

dapple, v.t. varetear, abigarrar, salpicar, motear. — a. vareteado, rucio.

dappled, a. rodado, empedrado; abigarrado.

dard [dɑːrd], s. dardo.

dare [dɛəɹ], v.i. atreverse, arriesgarse, aventurarse, osar. — v.t. arrostrar, hacer frente; desafiar, provocar, retar. — s. (fam.) desafío.

dare-devil, s. atrevido, temerario.

darer, s. desafiador.

daring, s. atrevimiento, osadía, bravura, intrepidez. — a. osado, arriesgado, intrépido, atrevido, temerario; emprendedor.

daringness, s. osadía, atrevimiento, intrepidez, bravura.

dark [dɑːrk], a. oscuro, obscuro, sombrío, moreno, opaco; ciego; bruno, negruzco, triste; difícil; enigmático, secreto, ignorante; melancólico, tétrico, tenebroso, fúnebre; (poét.) ciego, ignorante; dark lantern, linterna sorda; dark-room, (fot.) cuarto obscuro. — s. oscuridad, obscuridad; tinieblas, f.pl.; ignorancia; it is growing dark, va a anochecer.

darken, v.t. obscurecer; anublar; ennegrecer; embrollar, confundir; contristar, entristecer; cegar, ofuscar, obcecar; manchar, denigrar. — v.i. obscurecerse.

darkening, s. obscurecimiento; ennegrecimiento.

dark-eyed, a. ojinegro.

darkish, a. algo obscuro.

darkle, v.i. acechar en la obscuridad; permanecer escondido; hacerse obscuro; enojarse, encolerizarse. — v.t. obscurecer.

darkling, a. obscurecido.

darkly, adv. obscuramente, opacamente, secretamente.

dark-minded, a. vengativo.

darkness, s. oscuridad, obscuridad, lobreguez, tinieblas, f.pl., tenebrosidad, opacidad, densidad; obcecación, ofuscación; ignorancia; secreto.

darksome, a. obscuro, sombrío.

darky, s. (despec.) Negro.

darling ['dɑːrliŋ], s. favorito, predilecto. — a. amado, querido, favorito, predilecto. — interj. ¡ amor mío ! ¡ alma mía !

darn [dɑːrn], v.t. zurcir, componer, remendar. — s. zurcido, compostura, remiendo, recosido. — a. (fam.) maldito, infernal.

darnel ['dɑːrnəl], s. (bot.) cizaña, zizaña, rabillo.

darner, s. zurcidor, zurcidora.

darning, s. zurcidura, remiendo, recosido, compostura; darning-needle, aguja de remiendo.

dart [dɑːrt], s. dardo; flecha, saeta; venablo, virote; sarcasmo. — v.t. lanzar, tirar, arrojar, flechar; despedir. — v.i. lanzarse, arrojarse, precipitarse.

darter, s. flechador.

dartre, s. roña o llaga que padecen los corderos, herpes, m.pl.

Darwinism [dɑːrwinizm], s. darvinismo, doctrinas de Darwin.

dash [dæʃ], v.t. arrojar, desechar, lanzar; tirar; golpear, chocar; quebrar, romper; estrellar; rociar, salpicar con agua; borrar, mezclar; confundir, frustrar; precipitar, volcar; reprimir, desanimar; bosquejar, escribir apresuradamente. — v.i. chocar; saltar, estallar, estrellarse, romperse, zabullirse; to dash to pieces, hacer mil pedazos; hacer añicos; to dash off, (a book, etc.) escribir o trazar rápidamente; to dash with, rociar, salpicar, mezclar; to cut a dash, hacer gran papel; to dash one's hopes to the ground, dejar a uno con un palmo de narices. — *s.* colisión, golpe, choque; incursión, embate; ataque, arremetida, arranque; (*fig.*) arrojo, ardor, brío; infusión; (*impr.*) guión; raya, línea; tilde; rasgo, rúbrica; hilo; ostentación; mezcla, sabor, condimento.

dashing, *a.* fogoso; arrojado, precipitado; brillante.

dastard ['dæstəɹd], *s.* collón, cobarde.

dastardize, *v.t.* acobardar, amedrentar.

dastardly, *a.* cobarde, tímido, pusilánime.

data ['deitə], *s.pl.* [DATUM] datos.

datary, *s.* datario.

date [deit], *s.* fecha; data; plazo, duración; (*fam.*) cita, compromiso, vista (frecuentemente de novios); época, tiempo; (*bot.*) dátil. — *v.t.* fechar, datar; citar (solamente de novios). — *v.i.* computar, contar.

dateless, *a.* sin fecha.

dater, *s.* datario.

date-tree, *s.* datilera; palmera.

dative ['deitiv], *s., a.* (*gram.*) dativo; (*for.*) dativo.

datum ['deitəm], *s.* (*pl.* **data**) dato.

datura [də'tjuərə], *s.* plantas de olor fuerte, venenosas, afines a la belladona.

daub [dɔːb], *v.t.* untar; embadurnar; pintorrear, pintarrajar; manchar, ensuciar, embarrar; cubrir, disfrazar. — *s.* embarradura, unto, (*fam.*) pintarrajo.

dauber, *s.* pintamonas, embarrador, pintorreador.

daubing, *s.* mamarracho, afeite; estuco.

dauby, *a.* pegajoso, glutinoso, viscoso.

daughter ['dɔːtəɹ], *s.f.* hija; *god-daughter,* ahijada.

daughter-in-law, *s.f.* nuera.

daughterly, *a.* filial.

daunt [dɔːnt], *v.t.* acobardar, desanimar, espantar, atemorizar, intimidar.

dauntless, *a.* intrépido, impávido.

dauntlessness, *s.* intrepidez, valor.

dauphin [dɔːfin], *s.* delfín.

dauphiness, *s.f.* delfina.

davit ['dævit], *s.* (*mar.*) pescante de ancla, pequeña grúa.

Davy Jones [deivi-dʒounz], *s.* espíritu maligno imaginario, que según la superstición de los marinos tiene gran poder en el mar. **Davy Jones's locker,** nombre que dan al mar como tumba de los náufragos.

Davy lamp, *s.* lámpara de seguridad para minas.

daw [dɔː], *s.* corneja.

dawdle, *v.i.* perder o gastar tiempo; haraganear.

dawdle, dawdler, *s.* bodoque; haragán.

dawn [dɔːn], *v.i.* amanecer, alborear, romper el día; (*fig.*) apuntar, asomar, mostrarse. — *s.* alba, albor; aurora, madrugada; origen, comienzo, principio; fulgor.

dawning, *s.* alba, alborada, el amanecer.

day [dei], *s.* día, *m.*, luz, *f.*; estado del tiempo; jornal, jornada; vida, tiempo, época, período; batalla; *by day,* de día; *to-day,* hoy; *working day,* día laborable, día de trabajo; *day before,* víspera; *next day,* al día siguiente; *day after tomorrow,* pasado mañana; *day before yesterday,* anteayer; *this day week,* de hoy en ocho días; *from day to day,* de día en día; *every other day,* un día sí y otro no; *to this day,* hasta el día de hoy; *dog-days,* canícula; *fast-*

day, día de ayuno; *for ever and a day,* para siempre jamás; *all day long,* todo el día; *good-day!* ¡ buenos días ! *one of these days,* un día de éstos; *lay days,* (*mar.*) días de estadía o demora.

day-book, *s.* diario.

day boy, *s.* alumno externo.

daybreak, *s.* el amanecer, primera luz, alba.

daydream, *s.* ensueño, quimera, ilusión.

daylight, *s.* luz del día.

day-school, *s.* escuela para externos.

dayspring, *s.* albor.

daystar, *s.* lucero del alba.

day-work, *s.* jornal, trabajo del día.

daze [deiz], *v.t.* deslumbrar, ofuscar, aturdir. — *s.* deslumbramiento, ofuscamiento.

dazzle [dæzl], *v.t.* deslumbrar, ofuscar. — *v.i.* delumbrarse, ofuscarse. — *s.* deslumbramiento.

dazzling, *a.* deslumbrante.

dazzlingly, *adv.* de una manera deslumbrante.

deacon ['diːkən], *s.* diácono.

deaconess, *s.* diaconisa.

deaconry, deaconship, *s.* diaconado, diaconía.

dead [ded], *a.* muerto, sin vida; finado, difunto; pesado, entorpecido, frío; vacío; despoblado; inerte, inmóvil; sin fuego, sordo, apagado; triste, desolado; estéril, inútil; monótono; profundo, completo, acabado; seguro, cierto, absoluto; sin eco; sin elasticidad; marchito, sin espíritu; mate, sin brillo; sin variación, monótono; (*igl.*) sumido en el pecado; (*for.*) desprovisto de la vida civil; (*elec.*) que no transmite corriente, interrumpido; (*impr.*) material muerto o para distribuir; *dead calm,* (*mar.*) calma chicha; *dead coal,* carbón apagado; *dead-drunk, a.* borracho perdido, hecho un cuero; *dead head,* gorrero; *dead sound,* ruido sordo; *at dead of night,* en las altas horas de la noche; *Queen Anne's dead!* (*fam.*) es más viejo que (o en) el año de la Nana, ya tiene canas. — *s.* personas muertas; corazón, fondo. — *adv.* enteramente, exactamente, absolutamente.

deaden, *v.t.* amortecer, amortiguar; desvirtuar, adormecer; retardar, parar; apagar; hacer insípido. — *v.i.* perder vitalidad, vigor, vida.

deadish, *a.* sin vida, apagado.

deadliness, *s.* cualidad mortífera.

deadlock, *s.* detención, paro; situación sin salida, sin solución.

deadly, *a.* mortífero, implacable, mortal; (*fam.*) insoportable, terrible. — *adv.* mortalmente, implacablemente.

deadness, *s.* frío, frialdad, insensibilidad, inercia, apatía; amortiguamiento, estagnación.

deadnettle, *s.* (*bot.*) ortiga muerta.

dead-struck, *a.* espantado, aterrado.

deaf [def], *a.* sordo; insensible; *as deaf as a post,* sordo como una tapia; *to turn a deaf ear,* hacerse el sordo, o hacer oídos de mercader; *deaf-mute,* sordomudo.

deafen, *v.t.* ensordecer, asordar.

deafness, *s.* ensordecimiento, sordera.

deal [diːl], *s.* cantidad, porción, parte, *f.*; mano (en el juego de naipes); madera de pino o abeto; tabla; tabla de chilla de 6′ × 7″ × 3″; (*com.*) negociación, trato; *a great deal,* mucho; *a good deal,* bastante. — *v.t.* (*pret.*

y *p.p.* **dealt**) distribuir, repartir; esparcir; desparramar; dar. — *v.i.* traficar, comerciar, negociar, tratar; intervenir, gestionar, mediar; *to deal by,* usar de; *to deal with,* tratar con; *to deal falsely with,* engañar, abusar de; *to deal in,* comerciar en, ocuparse en; *to deal wholesale,* vender por mayor.

dealer, *s.* negociante, tratante, traficante, comerciante, mercader; el que da las cartas; *double dealer,* (*fig.*) hombre de dos caras; *plain dealer,* hombre sincero; *wholesale dealer,* mercader por mayor.

dealing, *s.* proceder, modo de proceder, comportamiento, conducta; tráfico, negocio, comercio; trato, comunicación.

deambulatory [di:ʹæmbjulətəri], *s.* paseo. — *a.* ambulante.

dean [di:n], *s.* deán; decano.

deanery, deanship, *s.* deanato, decanato.

dear [diəɹ], *a.* querido, predilecto, amado; caro, costoso; escaso. — *s.* querido, bien amado; *dear!, dear dear!, oh dear!, dear me!* ¡Dios mío!, ¡Ay!; *my dear,* querido *o* querida.

dearly, *adv.* caramente, costosamente; cariñosamente, tiernamente, amorosamente.

dearness, *s.* cariño, amor, benevolencia, afecto; carestía, precio subido.

dearth [dəːɹθ], *s.* carestía, escasez, esterilidad, hambre, *f.*

death [deθ], *s.* muerte, *f.,* fallecimiento, defunción; estrago; mortandad, mortalidad; condenación; asesinato; *on pain of death,* bajo (o so) pena de muerte; *to be at death's door,* estar a la muerte, estar con la candela en la mano, *o* estar con el credo en la boca; *at death's door,* a las puertas de la muerte.

death-bed, *s.* lecho de muerte.

death-blow, *s.* golpe mortal.

death-chamber, *s.* cámara mortuoria.

deathful, *a.* mortífero, mortal.

deathless, *a.* inmortal.

deathlike, deathly, *a.* mortal, fatal, semejante a la muerte; letárgico; cadavérico.

death-rattle, *s.* sarrillo, estertor.

death's head, *s.* calavera.

death-warrant, *s.* pena mortal.

death-watch, *s.* guardia de un reo de muerte; (*ent.*) anobio.

debacle [diʹbækl], *s.* caída, ruina; fracaso.

debar [dəʹbaːɹ], *v.t.* excluir, no admitir, prohibir.

debark [dəʹbaːɹk], *v.t.* desembarcar.

debarkation [di:baːɹʹkeiʃən], **debarcation,** *s.* desembarco, desembarque.

debase [dəʹbeis], *v.t.* abatir, humillar, rebajar, envilecer, viciar, degradar, deshonrar, adulterar, prostituir, falsificar.

debasement, *s.* abatimiento, degradación, falsificación, adulteración.

debaser, *s.* falsificador; el que abate o envilece.

debatable, *a.* disputable, discutible.

debate [dəʹbeit], *s.* debate, contienda, discusión, disputa, controversia, pendencia, querella. — *v.t.* debatir, contender, disputar, controvertir, considerar. — *v.i.* deliberar, discutir, examinar, reflexionar, pensar.

debatement, *s.* debate, contienda.

debater, *s.* controversista, polemista, *m.f.*

debauch [dəʹbɔːtʃ], *v.t.* corromper, viciar, relajar, sonsacar, sobornar, pervertir; sedu-

cir, violar. — *s.* exceso, desorden, desarreglo; lujuria, glotonería, licencia, libertinaje, vida disoluta, crápula.

debauched, *a.* licencioso, lujurioso.

debauchee, *s.* libertino, calaverón.

debaucher, *s.* sobornador, seductor, constuprador.

debauchery, *s.* libertinaje; intemperancia.

debauchment, *s.* corrupción.

debenture [dəʹbentjəɹ], *s.* (*com.*) obligación, bono, vale, acción; prima de exportación.

debilitate [dəʹbiliteit], *v.t.* debilitar, extenuar, enervar, postrar, depauperar.

debilitation [dəbiliʹteiʃən], *s.* debilitación, extenuación.

debility [dəʹbiliti], *s.* debilidad, extenuación, languidez, atonía.

debit [ʹdebit], *s.* débito, cargo, adeudo; saldo deudor. — *v.t.* cargar, adeudar.

debonair [debəʹnɛəɹ], *a.* cortés, urbano, elegante, complaciente, afable.

debouch [deʹbuːʃ], *v.t., v.i.* (*mil.*) desembocar.

debris [ʹdebri], *s.* escombros, desecho, ruinas, despojos.

debt [det], *s.* deuda, débito, obligación; *bad debt,* crédito irrecuperable; *deeply in debt,* cargado de deudas.

debtee, *s.* acreedor.

debtor, *s.* deudor; cargo.

debut [deiʹbjuː], *s.* (*teat.*) estreno; debut (*galicismo*) o entrada en la sociedad; *to make a debut,* debutar (*galicismo*).

debutant [ʹdebjutənt], *s.m.;* **debutante** [ʹdebjutənt], *s.f.* principiante, el que o la que se presenta en la sociedad, corte, etc. por primera vez, debutante (*galicismo*).

decade [ʹdekəd], *s.* década; decena, decenio.

decadence [ʹdekədəns], **decadency,** *s.* decadencia, ocaso.

decagon [ʹdekəgən], *s.* (*geom.*) decágono.

decagramme [ʹdekəgræm], *s.* decagramo.

decahedral [dekəʹhiːdrəl], *a.;* **decahedron,** *s.* decaedro.

decalitre, *s.* decalitro.

decalogue, *s.* decálogo.

decametre, *s.* decámetro.

decamp [dəʹkæmp], *v.i.* decampar; escaparse, huir.

decampment, *s.* acción de decampar, huida.

decanal [dəʹkeinəl], *a.* lo que pertenece al decanato.

decant [dəʹkænt], *v.t.* decantar, trasegar.

decantation [di:kænʹteiʃən], *s.* decantación, trasiego.

decanter [dəʹkæntəɹ], *s.* garrafa; ampolla.

decapitate [dəʹkæpiteit], *v.t.* decapitar, degollar.

decapitation [dəkæpiʹteiʃən], *s.* decapitación, degüello.

decapod [ʹdekəpɔd], *s.* decápodo.

decarbonization, *s.* descarburación.

decarbonize [di:ʹkaːɹbənaiz], *v.t.* quitar el carbono, descarburar.

decastich, *s.* décima.

decastyle, *s.* (*arq.*) decástilo.

decasyllable, *s.* decasílabo.

decay [dəʹkei], *v.i.* decaer, descaecer; declinar, degenerar, empeorar, desmejorarse, desmedrar, deteriorarse; pudrirse; cariarse; marchitarse, pasarse. — *v.t.* arruinar, destruir, echar a perder. — *s.* descaecimiento, decadencia, desmedro, declinación, menoscabo, mengua, perecimiento; vejez; podredumbre, *f.*, pobreza.

decayed, *a.* decaído, caído, arruinado; degenerado; deteriorado; podrido; cariado.

decease [də'si:s], *s.* muerte, *f.*, fallecimiento, defunción. — *v.i.* morir, fallecer.

deceased, *a.* muerto, fallecido, difunto, finado.

deceit [də'si:t], *s.* engaño, fraude, superchería, impostura, estratagema, disimulo, dolo, artificio, falacia, falsedad.

deceitful, *a.* falso, engañoso, fraudulento, falaz, mentiroso, ilusorio.

deceitfulness, *s.* falsedad, falsía, duplicidad, doblez.

deceivable, *a.* engañadizo, cándido, bobalicón.

deceivably, *adv.* engañosamente.

deceive [də'si:v], *v.t.* engañar, defraudar, embaucar, desengañar, frustrar, burlar.

deceiver, *s.* engañador, impostor, seductor.

December [də'sembəɹ], *s.* diciembre.

decemvir [də'semvəɹ], *s.* (*pl.* **decemvirs**, o **decemviri**) decenviro.

decemviral [də'semvərəl], *a.* decenviral.

decemvirate, *s.* decenvirato.

decency ['di:sənsi], *s.* decencia, decoro, recato, propiedad, compostura, formalidad.

decennary [də'senəri], *s.* decenario.

decennial, *a.* decenal.

decent [di:sənt], *a.* decente, honesto, formal; conveniente, razonable, módico.

decentness, *s.* (*ant.*) decencia, modestia.

decentralization [di:sentrəlai'zeiʃən], *s.* descentralización.

decentralize [də'sentrəlaiz], *v.t.* descentralizar.

deceptible, *a.* engañadizo.

deception [də'sepʃən], *s.* decepción, engaño, superchería, fraude; impostura, dolo, charlatanería.

deceptious, deceptive, *a.* engañoso, ilusorio, falaz.

decern [də'zəɹn], *v.t.* juzgar, estimar; (*for.*) sentenciar.

deciare, *s.* deciárea.

decidable, *a.* decidible.

decide [də'said], *v.t.*, *v.i.* decidir, decidirse, determinar, resolver; sentenciar, juzgar.

decided, *a.* decidido, resuelto, determinado, incontestable, indudable, categórico.

decider, *s.* arbitro.

deciduous [də'sidjuəs], *a.* caedizo, efímero.

decigram ['desigræm], **decigramme**, *s.* decigramo.

decilitre, *s.* decilitro.

decimal, *s.*, *a.* decimal; diezmal.

decimally, *adv.* por decenas; por medio de los decimales.

decimate ['desimeit], *v.t.* diezmar.

decimation [desi'meiʃən], *s.* diezmo; gran destrucción.

decimator, *s.* diezmero; (*fig.*) gran destructor.

decimetre, *s.* decímetro.

decipher [də'saifəɹ], *v.t.* descifrar, interpretar, aclarar.

decipherable, *a.* descifrable.

decipherer, *s.* descifrador.

deciphering, *a.* que descifra. — *s.* desciframiento, interpretación.

decision [də'siʒən], *s.* decisión, determinación, firmeza; resolución, acuerdo.

decisive [də'saisiv], *a.* decisivo, conclusivo, terminante; decidido (*galicismo*).

decisiveness, *s.* autoridad decisiva, firmeza, decisión.

decisory, *a.* decisorio.

deck [dek], *v.t.* vestir, revestir, cubrir; adornar, embellecer, componer, asear, engalanar, ataviar. — *s.* (*mar.*) puente; cubierta; baraja.

decker, *s.* cubridor, ataviador, adornador; *two-decker*, *double-decker*, navío de dos puentes; de dos pisos (autobús, etc.).

deckle, *s.* (en la fabricación de papel) cubierta, bastidor rectangular.

declaim [də'kleim], *v.i.* declamar. — *v.t.* recitar.

declaimant, declaimer, *s.* declamador, perorador.

declaiming, *s.* arenga, oración.

declamation [deklə'meiʃən], *s.* declamación, peroración, arenga.

declamatory [de'klæmətəri], *a.* declamatorio.

declaration [deklə'reiʃən], *s.* declaración, manifiesto, proclamación, aserto, aserción, manifestación, publicación, exposición.

declarative, *a.* declaratorio, declarativo, testificativo.

declaratory, *a.* declaratorio, afirmativo.

declare [də'kleəɹ], *v.t.* declarar, manifestar, proclamar; confesar, asegurar, afirmar. — *v.i.* declarar(se), testificar, deponer.

declared, *a.* declarado, manifestado, abierto. — *p.p.* [DECLARE].

declension [də'klenʃən], *s.* declinación, decadencia, desinencia, disminución, decremento, inclinación, declive.

declinable [də'klainəbl], *a.* declinable.

declination [dekli'neiʃən], *s.* declinación, declive, descenso, decadencia; decremento, deterioro; desviación, desvío; descarrío.

declinator, *s.*; **declinatory**, *s.*, *a.* (*for.*) declinatorio.

decline [də'klain], *v.i.* declinar, inclinar, inclinarse; desviar; renunciar, rehusar, negarse; declinar, menguar, desmejorar. — *v.t.* inclinar; excusar; rechazar; evitar; (*gram.*) declinar. — *s.* declinación, descaecimiento, decadencia; menoscabo; consunción.

decliner, *s.* declinante.

declining, *a.* declinante, inclinante; pendiente.

declivitous, declivous, *a.* inclinado.

declivity [də'klaiviti], *s.* declive, declivio, pendiente, *f.*, escarpa.

decoct [də'kɔkt], *v.t.* (*ant.*) cocer; asimilar, digerir.

decocted, *a.* cocido, hervido, digerido. — *p.p.* [DECOCT].

decoction, *s.* cocción, decocción, cocimiento.

decollate [də'kɔleit], *v.t.* degollar, decapitar.

decollation [dəkɔ'leiʃən], *s.* degollación, degüello.

decolor, *v.t.* [DECOLOUR].

decolorant, *s.* descolorante.

decolorate, *v.t.* descolorar; clarificar, refinar.

decoloration [di:kʌlə'reiʃən], *s.* descoloramiento.

decolour [di:'kʌləɹ], *v.t.* descolorar, blanquear; refinar, clarificar.

decomposable, *a.* descomponible, corruptible.

decompose [di:kɔm'pouz], *v.t.* descomponer, pudrir. — *v.i.* descomponerse, corromperse.

decomposition [di:kɔmpə'ziʃən], s. descomposición, corrupción.

decompound [di:kɔm'paund], a. dos veces compuesto.

decorate ['dekəreit], v.t. decorar, adornar, engalanar, hermosear; condecorar.

decoration [dekə'reiʃən], s. decoración; ornamentación, ornato, adorno, ornamento; condecoración.

decorator ['dekə'reitəɹ], s. decorador, adornista, m.f.

decorous [də'koərəs], a. decoroso; decente, honesto, correcto.

decorousness, s. decoro, corrección, circunspección.

decorticate [di'kɔ:ɹtikeit], v.t. descortezar, descascarar, mondar, pelar.

decorticator, s. descortezador.

decorum [də'kɔ:rəm], s. decoro, decencia, compostura, corrección.

decoy [də'kɔi], v.t. atraer, embaucar; reclamar (a las aves). — s. seducción; señuelo, reclamo, añagaza, cebo; entruchada, entruchón; lazo, trampa.

decrease ['di:kri:s], v.t. disminuir, reducir, minorar. — v.i. decrecer, disminuir, menguar, minorarse. — s. decremento, diminución, descaecimiento, decadencia, reducción, mengua.

decreasingly, adv. en disminución.

decree [də'kri:], s. decreto, ley, f., mandato, edicto, auto. — v.t., v.i. decretar, ordenar, mandar, determinar.

decrement ['dekrəmənt], s. decremento, diminución.

decrepit [də'krepit], a. decrépito.

decrepitate, v.t., v.i. decrepitar.

decrepitation [dəkrepi'teiʃən], s. decrepitación.

decrepitness [də'krepitnəs], **decrepitude**, s. decrepitud.

decrescent [də'kresənt], a. menguante, decreciente.

decretal [də'kri:təl], s. decretal; decretero; rescripto. — a. decretal.

decretion, s. minoración, merma.

decretorily, adv. definitivamente.

decretory, a. decretorio; (ant.) definitivo, decisivo.

decrial [də'kraiəl], s. vituperio; gritería, confusión contra alguno.

decrier, s. vituperador.

decrown [də'kraun], v.t. destronar.

decry [də'krai], v.t. vituperar, desacreditar, rebajar, afear.

decumbent [də'kʌmbənt], a. recostado, reclinado; echado en la cama.

decuple ['dekjupl], s., a. décuplo. — v.t. decuplicar.

decurion, s. decurión.

decussate [də'kʌseit], v.i. cortarse dos líneas en ángulos agudos o en forma de X; cruzarse como las mallas de una red, los nervios en el cuerpo, etc. — a. entrecruzado; (bot.) decusativo.

decussation [di:kə'seiʃən], s. cruzamiento.

dedicate ['dedikeit], v.t. dedicar, aplicar, entregar, consagrar, destinar. — a. dedicado, consagrado.

dedication [dedi'keiʃən], s. dedicación, consagración; dedicatoria.

dedicator ['dedikeitəɹ], s. dedicante.

dedicatory [dedi'keitəri], a. dedicatorio.

deduce [də'dju:s], v.t. deducir, derivar, inferir, concluir, sacar, colegir.

deducement, s. deducción, conclusión, consecuencia.

deducible, a. deducible.

deducive, a. deductivo.

deduct [də'dʌkt], v.t. deducir, sustraer, restar, descontar, rebajar.

deduction, s. deducción; corolario, consecuencia; descuento, rebaja.

deductive, a. deductivo.

deductively, adv. por inferencia, por consecuencia.

deed [di:d], s. hecho, acto, operación, acción; realidad; hazaña, proeza; escritura; (for.) instrumento auténtico; in very deed, en verdad.

deem [di:m], v.t., v.i. juzgar, imaginar, pensar, creer, estimar, suponer, considerar.

deemster, s. (ant.) juez; magistrado en la isla de Man.

deep [di:p], a. hondo, profundo; penetrador, perspicaz; artificioso, grave; abstruso, recóndito; agudo, intenso; cordial; insidioso; obscuro, subido; (ant.) lodoso. — s. piélago; abismo, sima. — adv. profundamente; deep mourning, luto riguroso; deep sea line, plomada, escandallo, sonda.

deepen, v.t. profundizar; obscurecer; entristecer; aumentar. — v.i. profundizarse, hacerse más hondo.

deeply, adv. hondamente, profundamente; intensamente; gravemente, completamente, sumamente.

deepness, s. profundidad, intensidad, gravedad, sagacidad.

deer [diəɹ], s. ciervo, venado; fallow deer, gamo.

deerhound, s. galgo.

deerskin, s. gamuza.

deer-stalker, s. cazador al acecho.

deer-stalking, s. caza al acecho.

deface [də'feis], v.t. desfigurar, mutilar, afear; borrar; destruir; deteriorar.

defacement, s. violación, mutilación; destrucción, rasadura; deterioro, estropeo, afeamiento.

defacer, s. destructor, el que estropea o afea.

defalcate [di'fælkeit], v.i. desfalcar, malversar. — v.t. descabalar, deducir, rebajar.

defalcation [di:fəl'keiʃən], s. desfalco, malversación; (ant.) diminución, deducción; déficit.

defamation [defə'meiʃən], s. difamación, calumnia.

defamatory [də'fæmətəri], a. infamatorio, difamatorio, calumnioso.

defame [di'feim], v.t. difamar, deshonrar, denigrar, desacreditar, calumniar.

defamer, s. difamador, calumniador.

defamingly, adv. de un modo infamatorio.

default [də'fɔ:lt], s. defecto, falta, delito, culpa; omisión; descuido, negligencia; (for.) rebeldía. — v.t. (for.) declarar en rebeldía; ser contumaz. — v.i. violar (un empeño); faltar, delinquir, no cumplir; (for.) caer en rebeldía o contumacia.

defaulter, s. el que falta o no cumple su deber, delincuente, defraudador, desfalcador, malversador, concusionario; (for.) contumaz, rebelde, contribuyente en retardo.

defeasance [dəˈfiːzəns], s. anulación, revocación, abrogación.

defeasible, a. anulable, revocable.

defeat [dəˈfiːt], s. derrota, vencimiento. — v.t. derrotar; frustrar; vencer; (for.) anular, abrogar; desechar; abolir; eludir.

defecate [ˈdefəkeit], v.t. defecar, purgar; depurar; limpiar, clarificar. — v.i. purificarse, clarificarse. — a. depurado, clarificado.

defecation [defəˈkeiʃən], s. defecación, purificación, clarificación.

defect [dəˈfekt], s. defecto, tacha, vicio.

defectible, a. defectible.

defection, s. defección; apostasía; abandono, deserción.

defective, a. defectivo, defectuoso, imperfecto; corto, falto, deficiente.

defectiveness, s. defecto, falta, culpa, imperfección, deficiencia.

defence [dəˈfens], s. defensa, protección.

defenceless, a. sin defensa, a pecho descubierto.

defencelessly, adv. sin defensa.

defencelessness, s. desvalimiento.

defend [dəˈfend], v.t. defender; mantener, preservar, proteger; resguardar, amparar, vindicar, sostener.

defendable, a. defendible.

defendant, s. defensor; (for.) demandado. — a. defensivo.

defender, s. defensor, protector, campeón, abogado, patrono.

defense, s. (E.U.) [DEFENCE].

defensive, a. defensivo, vindicativo. — s. defensiva.

defensively, adv. defensivamente, sobre la defensiva.

defensory, a. defensivo.

defer [dəˈfəːr], v.t. diferir, suspender, aplazar, remitir, posponer. — v.i. demorarse, aguardar; deferir, condescender, consentir, asentir.

deference [deˈfərəns], s. deferencia, sumisión, consideración, condescendencia, respeto.

deferent, a. deferente. — s. vehículo, lo que lleva o conduce; (anat.) canal deferente.

deferential [defəˈrenʃəl], a. deferente, respetuoso.

deferentially, adv. con deferencia, respetuosamente.

deferrer, s. tardador; holgazán.

deferring, s. aplazamiento, dilación.

defiance [dəˈfaiəns], s. desafío, provocación, cartel, reto; insolencia; desobediencia; to set at defiance, hacer mofa; desafiar.

defiant, a. provocador.

defibrinate [dəˈfaibrineit], v.t. desfibrinar.

deficience, deficiency [dəˈfiʃənsi], s. defecto, deficiencia, imperfección, falta; insolvencia.

deficient, a. deficiente, falto, incompleto, defectuoso.

deficiently, adv. defectuosamente.

deficit [ˈdefisit], s. déficit.

defier [dəˈfaiər], s. desafiador, retador.

defiguration [dəfigəˈreiʃən], s. defiguración.

defilade, v.t. (mar. y mil.) desenfilar.

defile [dəˈfail], v.t. manchar, ensuciar, violar, corromper, profanar, viciar. — v.i. desfilar. — s. desfiladero.

defilement, s. contaminación, profanación, violación.

defiler, s. corruptor, violador, contaminador.

definable [dəˈfainəbl], a. definible; determinado.

definably, adv. determinadamente.

define, v.t. definir, describir, explicar, circunscribir, determinar. — v.i. decidir, juzgar.

definer, s. definidor.

definite [ˈdefinit], a. preciso, concreto, definido, terminante, determinado, limitado.

definitely, adv. definitivamente, determinadamente, ciertamente.

definiteness, s. exactitud, precisión, limitación fija de alguna cosa.

definition [defiˈniʃən], s. definición, decisión, determinación; definición, nitidez, claridad (de un lente, etc.).

definitive [dəˈfinitiv], a. definitivo, decisivo, perentorio. — s. lo que define.

definitiveness, s. cualidad de ser definitivo.

deflagrable [ˈdeflagrəbl], a. combustible.

deflagrate, v.t. deflagrar, abrasar, incendiar. v.i. inflamarse, arder con llama repentina y rápidamente.

deflagration [defləˈgreiʃən], s. deflagración, incendio, quema.

deflagrator [ˈdefləgreitər], s. (elec.) deflagrador.

deflate [diˈfleit], v.t. deshinchar, desinflar. — v.i. deshincharse, desinflarse.

deflect [dəˈflekt], v.t. desviar, apartar, ladear. — v.i. desviarse, separarse, apartarse, ladearse.

deflection, deflexion, s. desvío, desviación, declinación de la aguja; (mec.) flexión; (ópt.) deflexión.

deflective, a. que desvía, que produce una deflexión.

deflorate [dəˈfloureit], a. (bot.) desflorado.

defloration [diːfləˈreiʃən], s. desfloración, desfloramiento; escogimiento, selección.

deflower [dəˈflauər], v.t. desflorar, desflorecer; ajar, deslustrar; desflorar, estuprar, desvirgar.

deflowerer, s. estuprador.

deflux [dəˈflʌks], **defluxion**, s. fluxión, destilación, derramamiento.

defoliate [dəˈfoulieit], v.t. deshojar. — a. deshojado.

defoliation [dəfouliˈeiʃən], s. desfoliación; deshoje.

deforce [dəˈfoərs], v.t. (for.) detentar.

deform [dəˈfoːrm], v.t. deformar, desfigurar, degradar, afear.

deformation [defoərˈmeiʃən], s. deformación, alteración, desfiguración.

deformed [dəˈfoːrmd], a. deformado, desfigurado; contrahecho; feo, bajo.

deformity, s. deformidad.

defraud [dəˈfroːd], v.t. defraudar, frustrar, estafar.

defraudation [diːfroːˈdeiʃən], s. defraudación.

defrauder [dəˈfroːdər], s. defraudador, estafador.

defraudment, s. defraudación.

defray [dəˈfrei], v.t. costear, satisfacer, sufragar.

defrayment, s. gasto.

defrock, v.t. exclaustrar.

deft [deft], a. diestro, hábil; apto, mañoso; galán, pulido.

deftly, adv. gallardamente; diestramente.

deftness, s. habilidad, maña; pulidez.

defunct [dəˈfʌŋkt], a. difunto, muerto. — s. difunto.

defy [də'fai], *v.t.* desafiar, retar, provocar a duelo; arrostrar; contravenir; despreciar.

degarnish [də'gɑːɹniʃ], *v.t.* desguarnecer; desmantelar.

degarnishment, *s.* desmueble; desmantelamiento.

degeneracy [də'dʒenərəsi], *s.* degeneración; depravación; degradación.

degenerate, *v.i.* degenerar, decaer, desdecir, descaecer. — *a.* degenerado.

degenerately, *adv.* de un modo degenerado, indignamente, bajamente.

degenerateness, *s.* degeneración, abandono.

degeneration [dədʒenə'reiʃən], *s.* degeneración; envilecimiento, empeoramiento.

deglutinate [də'gluːtineit], *v.t.* despegar; desenligar; extraer, separar el gluten.

deglutition [diːgluˈtiʃən], *s.* deglución.

degradation [degrə'deiʃən], *s.* degradación, deposición, diminución, privación, degeneración.

degrade [də'greid], *v.t.* degradar, envilecer, deshonrar; degradar, minorar, rebajar, reducir.

degradement, *s.* degradación.

degrading, *a.* degradante.

degradingly, *adv.* de una manera degradante.

degree [də'griː], *s.* grado, transición; rango, condición, estado; licencia, grado de licenciado; *to take a degree*, licenciarse, graduarse; *by degrees*, poco a poco.

degust [də'gʌst], *v.t.* catar, gustar.

degustation [diːgʌs'teiʃən], *s.* cata, prueba.

dehisce [də'his], *v.i.* entreabrirse, hendirse.

dehiscent, *a.* dehiscente.

dehortation [diːhɔːɹ'teiʃən], *s.* disuasión.

dehumanize [diːˈhjumənaiz], *v.t.* embrutecer.

dehydrate [diːˈhaidreit], *v.t.* deshidratar.

deification [diːifi'keiʃən], *s.* deificación, apoteosis, *f.*

deiform [diːifoəɹm], *a.* deiforme.

deify, *v.t.* deificar, endiosar, divinizar.

deign [dein], *v.i.* dignarse, condescender, tener la dignación. — *v.t.* conceder, permitir; admitir, considerar digno.

deism ['diːizm], *s.* deísmo.

deist, *s.* deísta, *m. f.*

deistic, deistical, *a.* deístico.

deity, *s.* deidad, divinidad, numen.

deject [də'dʒekt], *v.t.* abatir, afligir, desalentar, desanimar, descorazonar.

deject, dejected, *a.* abatido, afligido, desanimado.

dejectedness, *s.* abatimiento, desaliento.

dejection, *s.* melancolía, tristeza, aflicción; debilidad; deyección, deposición; evacuación.

delaine [də'lein], *s.* muselina de lana, chalí.

delapse [də'læps], *v.i.* (*med.*) descender, bajar.

delate [də'leit], *v.t.* delatar, denunciar.

delation [də'leiʃən], *s.* delación, denuncia.

delator, *s.* delator.

delay [də'lei], *v.t.* dilatar, aplazar, diferir, demorar, suspender; retardar, retrasar, entorpecer, entretener. — *v.i.* detenerse, demorarse, pararse, tardar. — *s.* dilación, tardanza, retardo, retraso, demora, entorpecimiento.

delayer, *s.* temporizador.

deleble, *a.* deleble.

delectable [də'lektəbl], *a.* deleitable, delicioso.

delectableness, delectation, *s.* delicia.

delegate ['deləgət], *v.t.* delegar, diputar, comisionar. — *s.* delegado, diputado, comisionado.

delegation [delə'geiʃən], *s.* delegación, diputación, comisión.

delete [də'liːt], *v.t.* borrar, tachar, testar.

deleterious [delə'tiəriəs], *a.* deletéreo.

deletion [də'liːʃən], *s.* borradura, canceladura.

delf [delf], *s.* mina, cantera; césped.

delft, *s.* loza fina de Delft.

deliberate [də'libəreit], *v.t.* deliberar discurrir, ponderar, considerar. — *v.i.* deliberar, ponderar, aconsejarse, vacilar. — *a.* circunspecto, prudente, cauto, avisado, pensado, reflexionado, premeditado, pausado.

deliberately, *adv.* deliberadamente, premeditadamente, prudentemente.

deliberation [dəlibə'reiʃən], *s.* deliberación, reflexión, premeditación.

deliberative [də'libərətiv], *a.* deliberativo, deliberante.

deliberatively, *adv.* por deliberación.

deliberator, *s.* deliberante.

delible, *a.* deleble, borrable.

delicacy ['delikəsi], *s.* delicadeza, finura; ternura, suavidad; delicadez, debilidad, fragilidad; escrupulosidad, consideración, miramiento; golosina.

delicate, *a.* delicado.

delicately, *adv.* delicadamente, sutilmente.

delicateness, *s.* delicadeza, delicadez.

delicatessen [delikə'tesən], *s.pl.* gollerías.

delicious [de'liʃəs], *a.* delicioso, exquisito, sabroso, delicado, rico.

deliciousness, *s.* delicia, deleite.

delict [də'likt], *s.* delito, delincuencia.

deligation [deli'geiʃən], *s.* (*cir.*) vendaje, ligadura.

delight [de'lait], *s.* deleite, gozo, encanto, placer, delicia. — *v.t.* deleitar, causar placer, encantar, regocijar. — *v.i.* deleitarse, complacerse, recrearse.

delightful, delightsome, *a.* delicioso, deleitoso, agradable, ameno, grato, exquisito.

delightfulness, *s.* delicia, deleite, placer, encanto, amenidad.

delimit [də'limit], *v.t.* deslindar.

delimitation [dəlimi'teiʃən], *s.* deslinde.

delineament [də'liniəmənt], *s.* delineamiento, delineación, bosquejo.

delineate, *v.t.* delinear, trazar, esquiciar.

delineation [dəlini'eiʃən], *s.* delineación, delineamiento, bosquejo, esquicio.

delineator, *s.* delineador, dibujante.

delineatory, *a.* descriptivo.

delinquency [də'liŋkwənsi], *s.* delincuencia, delito.

delinquent, *s., a.* delincuente.

delinquently, *adv.* criminalmente.

deliquate ['delikweit], *v.i.* derretirse, liquidarse.

deliquation [deli'kweiʃən], *s.* delicuescencia, derretimiento, licuación.

deliquesce, *v.i.* liquidarse, hacerse líquido poco a poco por la acción de la humedad.

deliquescence [deli'kwesəns], *s.* delicuescencia, licuación.

deliquiate [de'likwieit], *v.i.* liquidarse.

deliquium [də'likwiəm], *s.* licuación; deliquio, desmayo; (*ant.*) carencia de luz solar, eclipse.

delirious [də'liriəs], *a.* delirante; chocho.

deliriously, *adv.* de una manera delirante.

deliriousness, delirium, s. delirio, desvarío, devaneo.

delitescence, delitescency, s. delitescencia, encubrimiento; (*med.*) delitescencia.

deliver [də'livəɹ], *v.t.* libertar; librar, salvar; tirar, sacar, arrojar, arrancar; dar, rendir, entregar, remitir; resignar, abandonar; comunicar, pronunciar, decir, recitar; (*med.*) partear; *to be delivered of a child,* parir, dar a luz; *to deliver up* (o *over*) entregar.

deliverable, a. (*com.*) disponible.

deliverance, s. rescate; libramiento, liberación; salvación, preservación; (*for.*) absolución; (*ant.*) entrega; (*ant.*) parto.

deliverer, s. libertador, salvador; relator; entregador.

delivery, s. libertad, rescate; libramiento, liberación; cesión, entrega, traspaso, rendición; expedición; descarga; (*com.*) remesa; distribución; parto; dicción; proyección.

dell [del], s. vallejuelo; barranco; cañada.

Delphian ['delfiən], **Delphic,** a. délfico.

delta ['deltə], s. delta.

deltoid ['deltoid], a. deltoide.

delude [də'lju:d], *v.t.* engañar, entrampar, alucinar; chasquear; frustrar; *to delude oneself,* ilusionarse, engañarse.

deluder, s. engañador.

deluge ['delju:dʒ], s. diluvio, inundación; calamidad. — *v.t.* diluviar, inundar.

delusion [də'lju:ʒən], s. dolo, fraude, engaño; decepción, ilusión, error.

delusive, delusory, a. engañoso, falaz, delusorio, delusivo, ilusorio, ilusivo; iluso.

delve [delv], *v.t.* cavar; sondear; ahondar, penetrar; inquirir. — s. hoyo, barranco, hondón, zanja, madriguera.

delver, s. cavador; (*fig.*) trabajador.

demagnetize [di:'mægnətaiz], *v.t.* desmagnetizar, desimantar.

demagogic, demagogical, a. demogógico.

demagogism, s. demogogia.

demagogue ['deməgog], s. demagogo.

demain [də'mein], **demesne,** s. dominio, heredad, tierra solariega, tierras.

demand [də'mɑ:nd], s. demanda, petición, súplica, exigencia; (*com.*) pedido, despacho; (*for.*) petición jurídica, demanda. — *v.t.* demandar, pedir; reclamar; requerir, exigir; preguntar, interrogar.

demandable, a. exigible.

demandant, s. (*for.*) demandador, demandante.

demander, s. demandador; exactor, acreedor.

demarcation, demarkation [di:mɑ:ɹ'keiʃən], s. demarcación, limitación, deslinde.

demean [də'mi:n], *v.t.*, *v.i.* portarse, conducirse; rebajarse, degradarse.

demeanour, s. conducta, porte.

dement [də'ment], *v.t.* enloquecer, volver loco, trastornar el juicio.

demented, a. demente.

dementia, s. demencia, locura.

demerit [di:'merit], s. demérito, desmerecimiento.

demesne, s. [DEMAIN].

demi ['demi], a. medio, semi, casi.

demigod, s. semidiós.

demijohn, s. damajuana.

demise [də'mi:z], s. muerte, f., fallecimiento, defunción (especialmente de un soberano o personaje); trasmisión, traslación, o cesión de dominio. — *v.t.* transferir, ceder; arrendar; legar, dejar en testamento.

demisemiquaver, s. (*mús.*) fusa.

demission [də'miʃən], s. degradación, destitución; dimisión.

demissionary, a. degradante.

demissive, a. humilde.

demit [də'mit], *v.t.* dimitir, resignar, renunciar; deprimir, abatir.

demobilize [di:'moubilaiz], *v.t.* (*mil.*) poner en pie de paz, desmobilizar, desbandar.

democracy [də'mokrəsi], s. democracia.

democrat ['deməkræt], s. demócrata, m.f.

democratic [demə'krætik], **democratical,** a. democrático.

demography [də'mogrəfi], s. demografía.

demolish [də'moliʃ], *v.t.* demoler, derribar, derrocar, arrasar; acabar con, destruir.

demolisher, s. arruinador, destructor, demoledor.

demolishment, demolition, s. destrucción, ruina, demolición, derribo.

demon ['di:mən], s. demonio, diablo.

demonetize, *v.t.* desmonetizar, quitar su valor legal a la moneda o papel moneda.

demoniac, demoniacal, a. demoníaco, endemoniado. — s. energúmeno.

demonology [di:mə'nolədʒi], s. demonología.

demonopathy, s. demonopatía.

demonstrability, s. capacidad de demostración.

demonstrable ['demənstrəbl], a. demostrable.

demonstrableness, s. capacidad de demostración.

demonstrate ['demənstreit], *v.t.* demostrar, probar, hacer patente, hacer ver.

demonstration [demən'streiʃən], s. demostración, evidencia, prueba, manifestación, muestra.

demonstrative [di'monstrətiv], a. demostrativo; expresivo, animado, expansivo.

demonstrator ['demənstreitəɹ], s. demostrador, expositor.

demonstratory [də'monstrətəri], a. que sirve para demostrar.

demoralization [demərəlai'zeiʃən], s. desmoralización.

demoralize [di:'morəlaiz], *v.t.* desmoralizar, desanimar, descorazonar, acobardar.

demotic [di'motik], a. vulgar, popular; demótico.

demulcent [də'mʌlsənt], s., a. demulcente, emoliente.

demur [də'məːɹ], *v.i.* objetar; vacilar, fluctuar. — s. duda, escrúpulo, objeción; vacilación, hesitación; dificultad; pausa.

demure [də'mjuəɹ], a. recatado, púdico; sobrio, serio, formal.

demureness, s. sobriedad, gravedad; recato, gazmoñería.

demurrage [də'mʌridʒ], s. demora, gastos de demora; estadía, detención, vacilación.

demurrer, s. persona irresoluta, persona que pone siempre dificultades; (*for.*) excepción perentoria; alegación que admitiendo los hechos, niega que constituyan causa suficiente.

demy [də'mai], s. marquilla (papelería).

den, s. antro, caverna, guarida; madriguera; escondrijo, rincón. — *v.i.* habitar una caverna.

denary, *a.* decimal; lo que contiene diez.

denationalize, *v.t.* desnacionalizar.

denaturalize, denaturate, *v.t.* desnaturalizar; desfigurar.

dendriform ['dendrifoəɹm], *a.* (*zool.*) dendrítico.

dendrite, *s.* (*min.*) dendrita.

dendrology [den'drɔlədʒi], *s.* dendrografía.

denegation [dine'geiʃən], *s.* denegación.

deniable [də'naiəbl], *a.* negable.

denial [də'naiəl], *s.* negación, negativa; contradicción; repulsa.

denier [də'niːɹ], *s.* negador, contradictor.

denigrate ['diːnigreit], *v.t.* denigrar.

denigration [diːnigreiʃən], *s.* denigración.

denizen ['denizn], *s.* habitante, ciudadano,
residente; (*for.*) extranjero naturalizado.
— *v.t.* naturalizar.

denominate [də'nɔmineit], *v.t.* denominar,
nombrar.

denomination [dənɔmi'neiʃən], *s.* denominación, designación, título; secta.

denominative [də'nɔminətiv], *a.* denominativo.

denominatively, *adv.* denominadamente.

denominator, *s.* denominador.

denotable [diː'noutəbl], *a.* capaz de ser
notado.

denotation [diːno'teiʃən], *s.* denotación.

denotative, *a.* denotativo.

denote [di'nout], *v.t.* denotar, indicar,
anunciar, significar, designar, marcar, señalar.

denotement, *s.* denotación, indicación.

denouement [dei'nuːmã], *s.* desenlace, desenredo.

denounce [də'nauns], *v.t.* denunciar, acusar,
delatar; publicar, promulgar.

denouncement, *s.* denuncia, denunciación,
acusación.

denouncer, *s.* denunciador, delator.

dense [dens], *a.* denso, espeso, cerrado,
apretado, compacto.

density, *s.* densidad, opacidad, espesor.

dent [dent], *v.t.* abollar; mellar. — *s.* abolladura; mella; diente; (*ant.*) indentación.

dental ['dentəl], *s., a.* dental, *f.*; *dental
surgeon*, odontólogo.

dentate, dentated, *a.* dentado; (*blas.*) dentellado, endentado.

dented, *a.* abollado; dentellado.

denticle, *s.* dientecillo, punto saliente.

denticulate [den'tikjulət], **denticulated,** *a.*
dentado, dentellado.

denticulation [dentikju'leiʃən], *s.* endentadura, serie de dientes.

denticule ['dentikjul], *s.* dentículo.

dentifrice, *s.* dentífrico.

dentil, *s.* (*arq.*) dentículo, dentellón.

dentist ['dentist], *s.* dentista, *m.f.*, odontólogo.

dentition [den'tiʃən], *s.* dentición, dentadura.

denudate, *v.t.* desnudar. — *a.* desnudo,
despojado.

denudation [dinju'deiʃən], *s.* despojo de ropa;
denudación.

denude [də'njuːd], *v.t.* desnudar, desvestir,
privar, despojar.

denunciate [də'nʌnsieit], *v.t.* denunciar,
amenazar.

denunciation [dənʌnsi'eiʃən], *s.* acusación,
denuncia, denunciación.

denunciator, *s.* denunciador, delator.

denunciatory [də'nʌnsiətri], *a.* denunciatorio.

deny [də'nai], *v.t.*, *v.i.* negar, contradecir,
desmentir; desdecirse, renegar, abjurar;
rehusar.

deobstruct, *v.t.* (*med.*) desobstruir; desembarazar.

deobstruction, *s.* desobstrucción.

deobstruent, *s., a.* desobstruente.

deodorant, deodorizer, *s., a.* desodorante.

deodorize [diː'oudəraiz], *v.t.* quitar el olor.

deoppilate [diː'ɔpəleit], *v.t.* (*med.*) desopilar.

deoppilation [diːɔpə'leiʃən], *s.* desopilación.

deoxidate [diː'ɔksideit], **deoxidize,** *v.t.* (*quím.*),
desoxigenar, desoxidar.

deoxidation [diɔksə'deiʃən], **deoxidization,**
s. desoxigenación.

depart [də'paːɹt], *v.i.* irse, marcharse, salir,
partir; apartarse, desviarse; desistir; fallecer,
morir. — *v.t.* partir, dividir, separar.

department, *s.* departamento, sección, subdivisión; ramo; despacho; ministerio, negociado; distrito, provincia.

departmental [dipaːɹt'mentl], *a.* departmental.

departure [də'paːɹtjəɹ], *s.* partida, marcha,
salida; desistimiento; desviación, divergencia; (*fig.*) partida, paso, muerte, *f.*; (*mar.*)
diferencia de meridiano.

depasture [dəpaːstjəɹ], *v.i.* pacer.

depauperate [də'paupəreit], *v.t.* empobrecer,
hacer pobre.

depend [də'pend], *v.i.* pender, colgar;
depender; contar con; confiar en; estar
seguro; apoyarse; *to depend upon someone*,
contar con uno.

dependable, *a.* digno de confianza.

dependant, *s.* subalterno, dependiente.

dependence, dependency, *s.* dependencia,
subordinación; sostén, apoyo; accesorio;
colonia; confianza, seguridad.

dependent, *a.* dependiente, sujeto, subordinado, subalterno; contingente, condicional; necesitado; colgante, pendiente.

depending, *a.* pendiente, colgante, dependiente; *depending upon*, según.

deperdition [dipəɹ'diʃən], *s.* perdición, destrucción, ruina.

depict [də'pikt], *v.t.* pintar, retratar, representar; (*fig.*) pintar, describir.

depicture, *v.t.* pintar, retratar; representar;
describir.

depilate ['depileit], *v.t.* quitar el pelo o vello.

depilation [depi'leiʃən], *s.* depilación.

depilatory [di'pilətəri], *s., a.* depilatorio.

deplete [də'pliːt], *v.t.* agotar; disipar; vaciar;
reducir, disminuir.

depletion, *s.* agotamiento, vaciamiento; (*med.*)
depleción.

depletive, depletory, *a.* que agota; que vacía.

deplorable [də'plɔərəbl], *a.* deplorable,
lamentable, lastimoso.

deplorableness, *s.* estado deplorable.

deplore, *v.t.* deplorar, lamentar, dolerse.

deploy [də'plɔi], *v.t., v.i.* (*mil.*) desplegar.

deployment, *s.* (*mil.*) despliegue.

deplumation [diːplu'meiʃən], *s.* muda, desplumadura (de las aves).

deplume [di'pluːm], *v.t.* desplumar.

depolarize [di:poulǝraiz], *v.t.* (*elec.*) despolarizar.

deponent [dǝ'pounǝnt], *s., a.* deponente, declarante.

depopulate [dǝ'pɔpjuleit], *v.t.* despoblar, deshabitar. — *v.i.* despoblarse.

depopulating, *a.* despoblador.

depopulation [dǝpɔpju'leiʃǝn], *s.* despueblo, despoblación.

depopulator, *s.* despoblador, depopulador, asolador.

deport [dǝ'poǝɹt], *v.t.* deportar, desterrar. — *v.i.* conducirse, portarse, gobernarse; *to deport oneself,* portarse, conducirse.

deportation [di:poǝɹ'teiʃǝn], *s.* deportación, destierro.

deportment [di'poǝɹtmǝnt], *s.* porte, conducta, comportamiento, proceder.

deposable [dǝ'pouzǝbl], *a.* que se puede deponer.

deposal, *s.* destitución, deposición, degradación.

depose, *v.t., v.i.* deponer, destituir; atestiguar, testificar, ser testigo.

deposer, *s.* desposeedor; (*for.*) testigo, deponente.

deposit [dǝ'pɔzit], *v.t.* depositar, consignar. — *s.* depósito, sedimento, poso, heces, *f.pl.,* precipitado; adelanto; fianza, prenda. — *v.i.* precipitarse, formar sedimento.

depositary, *s.* depositario, almacén, depósito.

deposition [di:pǝ'ziʃǝn], *s.* deposición, declaración, testimonio; acumulación, depósito; destitución.

depositor [di'pɔzitǝɹ], *s.* deponente; depositador.

depository, *s.* depósito, almacén.

depot ['depou], *s.* depósito, pósito, almacén; despacho; (*E.U.*) estación.

depravation [di:prǝ'veiʃǝn], *s.* depravación, perversión, estragamiento.

deprave [dǝ'preiv], *v.t.* depravar, pervertir, viciar, estragar.

depraved, *a.* depravado, viciado, abandonado. — *p.p.* [DEPRAVE].

depravement, *s.* depravación.

depraver, *s.* depravador.

depravity, *s.* depravación.

deprecate ['deprǝkeit], *v.t., v.i.* deprecar, impetrar; lamentar; desaprobar, criticar.

deprecation [deprǝ'keiʃǝn], *s.* deprecación; desaprobación, crítica.

deprecative, deprecatory, *a.* deprecativo, deprecatorio; reprobador, de desaprobación.

deprecator, *s.* deprecante.

depreciate [dǝ'pri:ʃieit], *v.t.* desestimar, desapreciar, menospreciar; rebajar, abaratar. — *v.i.* bajar de precio; abaratarse.

depreciation [dǝpri:ʃi'eiʃǝn], *s.* depreciación; desestimación, descrédito.

depreciative [dǝ'pri:ʃiǝtiv], *a.* despreciativo, despectivo.

depreciator, *s.* despreciador.

depredate ['deprideit], *v.t.* (*ant.*) depredar, saquear, pillar, robar; desolar, asolar.

depredation [deprǝ'deiʃǝn], *s.* depredación, saqueo, pillaje, devastación.

depredator, *s.* depredador.

depredatory, *a.* depredador.

depress [dǝ'pres], *v.t.* deprimir, rebajar, inclinar, reducir; abatir, desalentar, desanimar; comprimir; (*com.*) entorpecer.

depressed, *a.* desalentado, melancólico, desanimado; deprimido; necesitado.

depressing, *a.* desalentador, depresivo; deprimente; pesimista, *m.f.,* tétrico.

depression, *s.* desaliento, depresión, desánimo, abatimiento; depresión, hueco, concavidad; depresión, compresión.

depressive, *a.* depresivo.

depressor, *s.* depresor, opresor.

deprivable [dǝ'praivǝbl], *a.* revocable, amovible.

deprivation, deprivement, *s.* privación; despojo, pérdida; (*for.*) destitución; carencia.

deprive, *v.t.* privar, quitar, despojar; excluir.

deprivement, *s.* [DEPRIVATION].

depth [depθ], *s.* fondo, profundidad, hondura; abismo; corazón; medio; grueso, espesor; parte interior; viveza (del color); gravedad (del sonido); penetración, sagacidad; *in the depth of winter,* en pleno invierno; *out of one's depth,* (*fig.*) fuera del alcance, en exceso de las fuerzas de uno.

depurate ['depjureit], *v.t.* depurar.

depuration [depju'reiʃǝn], *s.* depuración.

depurative [dǝ'pjuǝrǝtiv], *a.* depurativo.

depuratory, *a.* depuratorio.

deputation [depju'teiʃǝn], *s.* diputación.

depute [dǝ'pju:t], *v.t.* diputar, delegar, nombrar, constituir, enviar.

deputy ['depjuti], *s.* diputado, delegado, comisario, comisionado, enviado, agente, lugarteniente; *deputy governor,* teniente gobernador; *deputy chairman,* vice-presidente.

deracinate [dǝ'ræsineit], *v.t.* desarraigar.

derail [dǝ'reil], *v.t., v.i.* descarrilar.

derailment, *s.* descarrilamiento.

derange [dǝ'reindʒ], *v.t.* desarreglar, desconcertar, desordenar, descomponer; trastornar, hacer perder el juicio.

deranged, *a.* desarreglado, desconcertado; trastornado, enloquecido. — *p.p.* [DERANGE].

derangement, *s.* desarreglo, desorden, descompostura, trastorno, enajenamiento (mental).

Derby ['dɑ:ɹbi], *s.* famosa carrera anual de caballos de tres años, en Epsom; (*E.U.*) sombrero hongo (d-).

derelict ['derǝlikt], *a.* abandonado voluntariamente; negligente, remiso; (*for.*) cualquier cosa abandonada voluntariamente, especialmente un buque en el mar.

dereliction [derǝ'likʃǝn], *s.* desamparo, abandono; dejación.

deride [dǝ'raid], *v.t.* mofar, burlar, escarnecer.

derider, *s.* burlón, zumbón, soflamero.

deridingly, *adv.* irrisoriamente.

derision [dǝ'riʒǝn], *s.* irrisión, escarnio, burla, mofa, ludibrio.

derisive, derisory, *a.* irrisorio.

derivable [dǝ'raivǝbl], *a.* derivable; deducible.

derivably, *adv.* por derivación.

derivate ['deriveit], *s.* derivado.

derivation [deri'veiʃǝn], *s.* derivación, deducción; etimología.

derivative, *a.* derivativo. — *s.* derivado.

derive [dǝ'raiv], *v.t.* derivar; deducir; comunicar. — *v.i.* derivar, derivarse, remontar (a).

derm [dǝ:ɹm], **derma, dermis,** *s.* (*anat.*) dermis, *f.,* cutis, *m.f.*

dermal, dermic, *a.* dérmico, cutáneo.
dermatography, *s.* dermatografía.
dermatoid [ˈdəːɪmətɔid], *a.* dermoide.
dermatologist [dəɪməˈtɔlədʒist], *s.* dermatólogo.
dermatology [dəɪməˈtɔlədʒi], *s.* dermatología.
dermatopathy, *s.* dermatosis, *f.*
derogate [ˈderəgeit], *v.t.,* *v.i.* derogar;
detraer, detractar.
derogation [derəˈgeiʃən], *s.* derogación, detracción.
derogative [deˈrɔgətiv], *a.* derogatorio.
derogatory, *a.* derogatorio.
derrick [ˈderik], *s.* grúa, cabria; cabrestante.
dervis, dervish [ˈdəːɪviʃ], *s.* derviche.
descant [ˈdeskənt], *s.* (*mús.*) discante; discurso,
comentario, disertación. — *v.i.* (*mús.*) discantar; comentar, discurrir.
descanting, *s.* comentario, nota.
descend [dəˈsend], *v.t.,* *v.i.* descender, bajar;
caer; desviarse; rebajarse; invadir.
descendant, *s.* descendiente, *m.f.*
descendent, *a.* descendente.
descension, *s.* descendimiento, descensión,
descenso; caída, declinación; degradación.
descensional, *a.* descensional.
descent, *s.* descenso, descendimiento, descendencia; bajada; pendiente, *f.,* declive;
origen, linaje, posteridad; nacimiento; (*for.*)
herencia; (*mil.*) invasión; rebajamiento,
degradación.
describable, *a.* descriptible.
describe [dəsˈkraib], *v.t.* describir, delinear,
definir, explicar, representar.
description [dəsˈkripʃən], *s.* descripción,
representación; señas; género, clase, *f.,*
calidad, naturaleza.
descriptive, *a.* descriptivo.
descriptively, *adv.* de un modo descriptivo.
descry [dəsˈkrai], *v.t.* avistar, divisar, columbrar, alcanzar a ver.
desecrate [ˈdesəkreit], *v.t.* profanar; secularizar.
desecration [desəˈkreiʃən], *s.* profanación;
secularización.
desert [ˈdezəɪt], *s.* desierto, yermo. — *a.*
desierto, yermo, despoblado, solitario.
desert [dəˈzəːɪt], *v.t.* desamparar, abandonar,
dejar. — *v.t.,* *v.i.* (*mil.*) desertar. — *s.* merecido, mérito o desmérito.
deserter, *s.* desertor, tránsfuga, *m.f.*
desertion, *s.* deserción, abandono, defección.
desertless, *a.* sin mérito, indigno.
deserve [dəˈzəːɪv], *v.t.,* *v.i.* merecer, ser
digno de, tener derecho a.
deservedly, *adv.* merecidamente, condignamente.
deserver, *s.* merecedor.
deserving, *a.* meritorio, merecedor, acreedor,
digno. — *s.* mérito, merecimiento.
deservingly, *adv.* dignamente, merecidamente.
desiccant [ˈdesikənt], *s.,* *a.* (*med.*) desecante.
desiccate [dəˈsikeit], *v.t.* desecar, secar,
enjugar, hacer secar. — *v.i.* secarse, rese-
carse.
desiccation [desiˈkeiʃən], *s.* desecación.
desiccative [dəˈsikətiv], **desiccatory** *a.*
desecativo.
desiderate [dəˈsidərət], *v.t.* desear, querer;
faltar, necesitar.

desideratum [dəsidəˈreitəm], *s.* (*pl.* **desi-**
derata) desiderátum.
design [dəˈzain], *v.t.* idear, inventar, diseñar;
proyectar, intentar, tener intención de;
bosquejar, designar, determinar, dedicar,
maquinar, tramar. — *v.i.* proponerse; hacer
proyectos; hacer diseños. — *s.* dibujo;
designio, diseño, trazo, propósito, proyecto,
empresa, plan, intento, intención.
designable, *a.* que se puede señalar o diseñar.
designate [dezigneit], *v.t.* señalar, designar.
designation [dezigˈneiʃən], *s.* designación,
nombramiento, señalamiento, título.
designative [dəˈzainətiv], *a.* designativo.
designedly [dəˈzainədli], *adv.* de propósito,
intencionalmente.
designer, *s.* dibujante, diseñador, delineador;
intrigante, proyectista, *m.f.,* maquinador.
designing, *a.* insidioso, traidor, astuto,
intrigante. — *s.* dibujo.
designingly, *adv.* insidiosamente.
desinence [ˈdesinəns], *s.* desinencia.
desirable [dəˈzairəbl], *a.* deseable, agradable,
apetecible.
desirableness, *s.* lo deseable, el atractivo.
desire, *s.* deseo, ansia, aspiración, anhelo;
apetito. — *v.t.* desear, querer, ansiar, anhelar, apetecer, tener gana; rogar, suplicar,
pedir.
desirous, *a.* deseoso, ansioso, ganoso; *to be*
desirous, tener gana, estar deseoso.
desirousness, *s.* anhelo, deseo vivo.
desist [dəˈzist], *v.i.* desistir; cesar; detenerse.
desistance, *s.* desistencia, desistimiento,
cesación.
desk [desk], *s.* bufete; pupitre, escritorio.
desolate [ˈdesələt], *a.* desolado, desierto,
despoblado, solitario, abandonado, arruinado. — *v.t.* desolar, devastar, despoblar,
arruinar.
desolately, *adv.* de un modo desolador.
desolateness, *s.* desolación.
desolater, desolator, *s.* desolador, asolador.
desolating, *a.* desolador.
desolation [desəˈleiʃən], *s.* desolación; desierto.
despair [dəsˈpɛəɪ], *v.i.* desesperar, perder
esperanza. — *s.* desesperación.
despairing, *a.* desesperante.
despairingly, *adv.* desesperadamente.
despatch [disˈpætʃ], *v.t.* despachar, remitir,
enviar, expedir; apresurar; concluir, matar,
quitar la vida. — *s.* despacho; prontitud;
expedición; mensaje, telegrama, *m.,* comunicación.
despatcher, *s.* despachador, expedidor.
despatchful, *a.* expedito, diligente.
desperado [despəˈreidou], *s.* desesperado,
malhechor, bandido.
desperate [ˈdespərət], *a.* desesperado, perdido;
arrojado, arriesgado, temerario; violento,
furioso, temible, terrible.
desperately, *adv.* desesperadamente; extremadamente, perdidamente, furiosamente.
desperateness, temeridad, arrojo, furia,
violencia.
desperation [despəˈreiʃən], *s.* desesperación,
encarnizamiento, furor.
despicable [ˈdespikəbl], *a.* despreciable, vil,
ruin.
despicableness, *s.* bajeza, vileza.
despisable [dəˈspaizəbl], *a.* despreciable.

despise, *v.t.* despreciar, menospreciar, desdeñar; detestar, aborrecer.

despisedness, *s.* envilecimiento.

despiser, *s.* despreciador.

despisingly, *adv.* desdeñosamente.

despite [dəs'pait], *s.* despecho, ira; malicia, malquerencia; odio; ultraje. — *prep.* a pesar de, a despecho de, no obstante.

despiteful, *a.* malicioso, rencoroso, vengativo, maligno.

despitefulness, *s.* malignidad, odio, rencor.

despoil [dəs'poil], *v.t.* despojar; robar; privar.

despoiler, *s.* pillador, robador, saqueador.

despoliation [despouli'eiʃən], *s.* despojo.

despond [dəs'pɔnd], *v.i.* desconfiar, desesperar(se), desalentarse, abatirse.—*s.* (*ant.*) desaliento.

despondence, despondency, *a.* desconfianza, desaliento, desesperación.

despondent, *a.* desconfiado, desesperado, desalentado.

despot ['despɔt], *s.* déspota, *m.*, tirano.

despotic, despotical [des'pɔtik], *a.* despótico, tiránico.

despoticalness, despotism, *s.* despotismo.

despumation [despju'meiʃən], *s.* despumación.

desquamate ['deskwəmeit], *v.t.* (*med.*) descamar. — *v.i.* descamarse; exfoliarse.

desquamation, *s.* (*med.*) descamación.

dessert [də'zəːt], *s.* postre.

destinate ['destineit], *v.t.* destinar. — *a.* destinado.

destination [desti'neiʃən], *s.* destinación, destino, paradero.

destine ['destin], *v.t.* destinar; consagrar, dedicar; predestinar.

destiny, *s.* destino, hado.

destitute ['destitjuːt], *a.* destituido, desamparado, abandonado; falto, desprovisto.

destitution [desti'tjuːʃən], *s.* destitución, privación, desamparo, abandono; desnudez; indigencia, miseria.

destroy [dəs'trɔi], *v.t.* destruir, devastar, exterminar, destrozar, asolar, demoler, arrasar, arruinar, dar al traste con; matar, quitar la vida; aniquilar.

destroyable, *a.* destruible.

destroyer, *s.* destruidor, destructor; devastador; (*mar.*) destructor, contratorpedero.

destructibility [dəstrʌti'biliti], *s.* destructibilidad.

destructible [də'strʌktəbl], *a.* destructible, destruible.

destruction, *s.* destrucción, ruina.

destructive, *a.* destructivo, destructor, ruinoso.

destructiveness, *s.* destructibilidad, destructividad.

desuetude ['deswətjuːd], *s.* desuso.

desultoriness ['desəltərinəs], *s.* inconsistencia, inconstancia, frivolidad.

desultory ['desəltəri], *a.* inconstante, variable, inconexo, suelto, no seguido.

detach [də'tatʃ], *v.t.* separar; desprender, despegar; destacar; desatar.

detachable, *a.* separable; despegable.

detachment, *s.* separación; despegadura; (*mil.*) destacamento.

detail ['diːteil], *v.t.* detallar, especificar, particularizar. — *s.* detalle, pormenor.

detain [də'tein], *v.t.* detener; retener, contener, retardar; suspender, impedir; arrestar.

detainer, *s.* (*for.*) detención, orden de arresto; detentador; retenedor.

detainment, *s.* detención.

detect [də'tekt], *v.t.* descubrir, averiguar; percibir, vislumbrar.

detectable, *a.* averiguable, que se puede descubrir.

detecter, detector, *s.* descubridor, averiguador.

detection, *s.* averiguación; revelación, descubrimiento.

detective, *s.*, *a.* detective; policíaco.

detent [də'tent], *s.* retén; fiador, seguro; escape de un reloj.

detention [də'tenʃən], *s.* detención; retención; arresto; encierro, encarcelamiento, cautividad.

deter [də'təːr], *v.t.* acobardar, desanimar, disuadir.

deterge [də'təːrdʒ], *v.t.* deterger, absterger.

detergent [də'təːrdʒent], *a.* detergente, abstergente, detersivo. — *s.* detergente, detersorio.

deteriorate [də'tiəriəreit], *v.t.* deteriorar, desmejorar, empeorar. — *v.i.* deteriorarse, empeorar, ir en decadencia.

deterioration [dətiəriə'reiʃən], *s.* deterioración, deterioro, empeoramiento, desmejoramiento, menoscabo.

determent [də'təːrmənt], *s.* impedimento, obstáculo, disuasión.

determinable [də'təːrminəbl], *a.* determinable, que puede determinarse.

determinant, *a.* determinante, determinativo.

determinate, *a.* determinado, decidido, resuelto, definido, distinto, fijo, determinante; *determinate inflorescence*, (*bot.*) de inflorescencia limitida. — *v.i.* limitar.

determinateness, determination, *s.* determinación, decisión, resolución; (*for.*) auto definitivo; (*log.*) especificación; (*med.*) congestión.

determinative, *a.* determinativo, determinante.

determine [də'təːrmin], *v.t.* determinar, decidir, resolver; fijar, definir, limitar, decretar, establecer. — *v.i.* decidirse, resolverse.

determined, *a.* determinado, decidido, resuelto.

deterrent [də'terənt], *s.*, *a.* disuasión; disuasivo.

detersion [də'təːrʃən], *s.* (*med.*) detersión.

detersive, *a.* detersivo, detersorio, detergente.

detest [də'test], *v.t.* detestar, abominar, execrar, odiar.

detestable, *a.* detestable, aborrecible, abominable.

detestableness, *s.* carácter detestable.

detestation [diːtes'teiʃən], *s.* detestación, abominación, execración, aborrecimiento.

detester [də'testər], *s.* aborrecedor.

dethrone [də'θroun], *v.t.* destronar.

dethronement, *s.* destronamiento.

dethroner, *s.* el que destrona.

detinue ['detinjuː], *s.* (*for.*) detentación.

detonate ['detəneit], *v.i.* detonar, estallar. — *v.t.* hacer estallar, detonar.

detonation [detə'neiʃən], *s.* detonación.

detorsion, detortion, *s.* acto de destorcer.

detort [də'toəɹt], *v.t.* torcer, destorcer.

detour [də'tuːɹ], *s.* rodeo, vuelta, desvío, desviación.

detract [də'trækt], *v.t.* detraer, disminuir, quitar. — *v.i.* detractar, denigrar.

detractingly, *adv.* denigrativamente.

detraction, *s.* detracción, difamación, calumnia, denigración.

detractive, *a.* difamatorio, derogatorio, denigrante.

detractor, *s.* detractor, difamador.

detractory, *a.* derogatorio, infamatorio.

detractress, *s.* detractora.

detrain [də'trein], *v.t., v.i.* bajar o hacer bajar de un tren.

detriment ['detrimənt], *s.* detrimento, perjuicio, daño, pérdida.

detrimental, *a.* perjudicial, desventajoso, dañoso.

detrition [də'triʃən], *s.* desgaste (por frotamiento).

detritus [də'traitəs], *s.* detrito.

detrude [də'truːd], *v.t.* precipitar, hundir.

detruncate [də'trʌŋkeit], *v.t.* truncar, mochar, podar, mutilar, destroncar.

detruncation [diːtrʌŋ'keiʃən], *s.* mutilación, poda, destroncamiento.

detrusion [də'truːʃən], *s.* impulsión, empuje.

deuce [djuːs], *s.* diantre, demonio; el número dos en el juego de cartas o en los dados. *How the deuce? What the deuce?* ¿cómo diablos?

deuced, *a.* (*fam.*) diabólico; excesivo, en extremo.

deuterogamist [djuːtə'rɔgəmist], *s.* deuterógamo, bígamo.

deuterogany, *s.* deuterogamia.

deuteropathy, *s.* deuteropatía.

devastate ['devəsteit], *v.t.* devastar, asolar, arruinar.

devastation [devəs'teiʃən], *s.* devastación, ruina, desolación.

develop [də'veləp], *v.t.* desarrollar, desenvolver, descubrir, desplegar, fomentar, explotar; (*foto.*) revelar. — *v.i.* desarrollarse, evolucionar, desenvolver.

developer, *s.* (*foto.*) revelador.

development, *s.* desarrollo; revelación; progreso, evolución; manifestación, exhibición; crecimiento, fomento; explotación.

devest [də'vest], *v.t.* (*for.*) privar de los bienes, etc.

deviate ['diːvieit], *v.i.* divergir, desviarse; disentir; errar, pecar.

deviation [diːvi'eiʃən], *s.* desviación, divergencia; desvío; extravío; pecado, error; variación, digresión; (*astr.*) deviación.

device [də'vais], *s.* ardid, estratagema; invención, invento, ingenio, artificio; dibujo, proyecto, plan; recurso, expediente; divisa, lema, cifra, mote.

devil [devl], *s.* diablo, demonio; espíritu maligno; (*impr.*) aprendiz; *talk of the devil and his tail appears*, en nombrando al ruin de Roma, luego asoma; *devil fish*, octópodo o pulpo, etc.; *devil's darning-needle*, caballito del diablo, libélula, peine de Venus. — *v.t.* condimentar; emparrillar; cortar (lana).

devilish, *a.* diabólico, satánico, infernal, demoníaco; excesivo.

devilishness, *s.* diablura, naturaleza satánica.

devilkin, *s.* diablillo.

devilment, *s.* bribonada, pillada.

devilry, *s.* diablería, diablura; perversidad.

devious ['diːviəs], *a.* desviado, descarriado, extraviado, perdido, errante, errado, tortuoso.

deviously, *adv.* tortuosamente; a través.

deviousness, *s.* desviación; extravío, descarrío.

devisable [də'vaizəbl], *a.* imaginable; trasmisible.

devisal, *s.* invención; (*for.*) legado, manda.

devise, *v.t.* proyectar, trazar, inventar, idear; legar. — *v.i.* maquinar, formar projectos. — *s.* legado.

devisee [devai'ziː], *s.* legatario.

deviser [də'vaizəɹ], *s.* inventor, autor.

devisor, *s.* testador.

devitalize [di'vaitəlaiz], *v.t.* quitar vitalidad.

devoid [də'vɔid], *a.* vacío, desprovisto, libre, exento.

devoir [də'vwaːɹ], *s.* obsequio, homenaje.

devolution [diːvə'ljuːʃən], *s.* traspaso, transferencia, transmisión; (*for.*) devolución; derecho devoluto; (*biol.*) degeneración de especies.

devolve [də'vɔlv], *v.t.* rodar; trasmitir, entregar, traspasar. — *v.i.* recaer; rodar hacia abajo; incumbir, tocar.

Devonian, *a.* perteneciente al condado de Devon. **Devonian age**, (*geol.*) Edad devoniana o de los peces, subsiguiente a la silúrica.

devote [də'vout], *v.t.* dedicar, consagrar; aplicar, asignar, entregar; condenar; maldecir, execrar.

devoted, *a.* devoto, ferviente; destinado, dedicado, consagrado; afecto, adicto; malhadado, condenado.

devotedness, *s.* devoción, afición, afecto, abnegación; celo.

devotee [devo'tiː], *s.* devoto, beato; aficionado; santurrón, mojigato.

devotion [də'vouʃən], *s.* devoción, piedad, celo, fervor; afecto; lealtad; oración; abnegación.

devotional, *a.* devoto; piadoso, religioso.

devour [də'vauɹ], *v.t.* devorar, consumir, engullir, tragar, destruir.

devourer, *s.* devorador, engullidor, destructor; tragón, comilón.

devouring, *a.* devorante, devorador.

devouringly, *adv.* vorazmente.

devout [də'vaut], *a.* devoto, piadoso, pío, religioso, fervoroso.

devoutness, *s.* piedad, devoción.

dew [djuː], *s.* rocío, sereno, relente. — *v.t.* cubrir, humedecer, rociar, bañar de rocío; refrescar; *dew-bespangled* o *dew-besprent*, cubierto de rocío.

dewberry, *s.* (*bot.*) zarzamora.

dewdrop, *s.* gota de rocío.

dewiness, *s.* estado rociado.

dewlap, *s.* papada de buey.

dew-worm, *s.* lombriz de tierra.

dewy, *a.* rociado.

dexter ['dekstəɹ], *a.* (*blas.*) diestro, derecho; propicio.

dexterity [deks'teriti], *s.* destreza, maña, habilidad.

dexterous ['dekstrəs], *a.* diestro, hábil, ducho, mañoso, experto.

dexterousness, s. destreza, habilidad, maña.
dextral, a. derecho, diestro.
dextrine ['dekstrin], s. (quím.) dextrina.
dextrose, s. dextrosa.
dey [dei], s. dey.
diabetes [daiə'biːtiːs], s. (med.) diabetes, f.
diabetic [daiə'betik], a. diabético.
diabolic [daiə'bɔlik], **diabolical,** a. diabólico.
diabolicalness, s. temperamento diabólico.
diabolism [dai'æbəlizm], s. diablura.
diachylon [dai'ækilən], **diachylum,** s. diaquilón.
diacodium [daiə'koudiəm], s. diacodio.
diaconal [dai'ækənəl], a. diaconal.
diaconate, a. diaconato.
diacoustics [daiə'kaustiks], s. (fís.) diacústica.
diacritical, a. diacrítico.
diadelphia, s. (bot.) diadelfia.
diadem ['daiədem], s. diadema, corona.
diademed, a. coronado.
diæresis, dieresis [dai'iərəsis], s. diéresis, f., crema.
diagnose, diagnosticate, v.t. diagnosticar.
diagnosis [daiəg'nousis], s. diagnosis, f.
diagnostic [daiəg'nɔstik], s., a. diagnóstico.
diagonal [dai'ægənəl], s., a. diagonal.
diagram ['daiəgræm], s. (geom.) diagrama, m.
diagraph, s. diágrafo.
diagraphic [daiə'græfik], **diagraphical,** a. diagráfico.
dial [daiəl], s. reloj de sol, cuadrante; esfera de reloj; brújula; marcador, disco (de teléfono). — v.i., v.t. (tlf.) marcar.
dialect ['daiəlekt], s. dialecto; jerga, algarabía.
dialectic [daiə'lektik], **dialectical,** a. dialéctico, lógico.
dialectician [daiəlek'tiʃən], s. dialéctico, lógico, argumentador.
dialectics [daiə'lektiks], s. dialéctica.
dialist ['daiəlist], s. constructor de relojes de sol.
dialogism [dai'æləgizm], s. dialogismo.
dialogist, s. dialoguista, m.f.
dialogically, dialogistically [daiələ'dʒistikli], adv. en forma de diálogo.
dialogize, v.i. dialogizar.
dialogue ['daiəlɔg], s. diálogo. — v.t., v.i. dialogar, dialogizar.
dialysis [dai'ælisis], s. (quím.) diálisis, f.; (gram.) diéresis, f.; (med.) languidez; (ret.) asíndeton.
dialytic, a. dialítico.
diamagnetic, s., a. diamagnético.
diameter [dai'æmətəɹ], s. diámetro.
diametral [daiə'metrəl], a. diametral.
diametrical, a. diametral.
diamond ['daiəmənd], s. diamante; oros (de los naipes); cortavidrios; (imp.) letra muy pequeña próxima a la letra 'brillante': 4 o 4½ puntos; (geom.) rombo; cut diamond, diamante tallado; rough diamond, diamante en bruto; diamond cutter, diamantista, m.f.; diamond necklace, collar de diamantes. — a. diamantado; rombal.
diandria [dai'ændriə], s. diandria.
diapason [daiə'peizən], s. diapasón.
diaper ['daiəpəɹ], s. servilleta; lienzo adamascado; pañal, culero. — v.t. matizar de diferentes colores; adamascar; labrar.
diaphaneity [daiəfə'niːəti], s. diafanidad, transparencia.

diaphanic [dai'æfənik], **diaphanous,** a. diáfano, transparente, claro.
diaphoresis [daiəfə'riːsis], s. diaforesis, f.
diaphoretic, diaphoretical, a. diaforético.
diaphragm ['daiəfræm], s. diafragma, m.
diaphragmatic [daiəfræg'mætik], a. diafragmático.
diarist ['daiərist], s. diarista, m.f.
diarrhœa [daiə'riːə], s. diarrea.
diarrhœtic, a. purgante.
diarthrosis [daiəɹ'θrousis], s. diartrosis, f.
diary ['daiəri], s. diario, jornal.
diaspore [daiə'spoəɹ], s. diásporo.
diastase, s. diastasia.
diastole [daiə'stoul], s. diástole, f.
diastolic [daiə'stɔlik], a. diastólico.
diatomic, a. diatómico.
diatonic, s., a. diatónico.
diatribe, s. diatriba.
dib, s. (usually pl.) tejo; taba; (pl., vulg.) guita, parné.
dibble ['dibl], s. plantador, almocafre. — v.t. plantar con plantador; escarbar. — v.i. sumergir.
dibstone, s. tejo; taba.
dice [dais], s. (pl. **die**) dados, partida de dados. — v.i. jugar a los dados.
dice-box, s. cubilete de dados.
dicer, s. jugador de dados.
dichotomize, v.t. separar o dividir en dos partes.
dichotomy [dai'kɔtəmi], s. dicotomía.
dichromatic [daikrə'mætik], a. dicromático.
dichromic, a. dicromático.
dickens ['dikinz], s. (vulg.) diantre, dianche.
dicker, v.i. (E.U.) regatear.
dickey, dicky [diki], s. camisola, camisolín; trasera de un coche; delantal.
dicotyledon [daikɔti'liːdən], s. (bot.) dicotiledón. — pl. dicotiledóneas.
dicotyledonous, a. dicotiledóneo.
dictaphone ['diktəfoun], s. dictáfono.
dictate [dik'teit], v.t. dictar; mandar. — s. dictamen; precepto; sugestión; inspiración; dictado.
dictation, s. dictado; precepto.
dictator, s. dictador, el que dicta.
dictatorial [diktə'toəriəl], a. dictatorio, dictatorial; absoluto; arrogante, imperioso.
dictatorship [dik'teitəɹʃip], s. dictadura.
dictatory, a. dominante, arrogante.
dictature, s. dictadura.
diction ['dikʃən], s. dicción, locución, expresión; estilo, lenguaje.
dictionary, s. diccionario, léxico.
dictograph, s. dictógrafo.
dictum, s. (pl. **dicta**) dicho, aforismo; (for.) dictamen de un juez, fallo.
did [did], **didst,** pret. [DO].
didactic [di'dæktik], **didactical,** a. didáctico.
didactics, s. didáctica.
didactylous, didactyle, a. (zool.) didáctilo.
didascalic, a. didascálico.
diddle [didl], v.t. (fam.) entruchar, entrampar. — v.i. vacilar; anadear.
die [dai], v.i. morir, expirar, fallecer, finar, cesar, fenecer; apagarse, extinguirse; agostarse, marchitarse; to die off rapidly, morir como chinches; to die in the flower of one's age, caer en flor. — v.t. estampar con troquel. — s. (pl. **dice**) dado; suerte, f., azar; (pl. **dies**)

troquel, matriz, *f.*, cuño; (*arq.*) cubo; *the die is cast*, es asunto concluido.

diesis [ˈdaiəsis], *s.* diesi, *f.*

diet [ˈdaiət], *s.* comida, manjar; alimento, comida; dieta, régimen. — *v.t.* poner a dieta. — *v.i.* estar a dieta, comer poco.

dietary, *s.* dieta medicinal. — *a.* dietético.

dieter, *s.* el que está a dieta.

dietetic [daiəˈtetik], **dietetical**, *a.* dietético.

dietetics, *s.* dietética.

differ [ˈdifəɹ], *v.i.* diferenciarse; distinguirse; contender, altercar, diferir, disentir, discrepar.

difference, *s.* diferencia, desigualdad, distinción, desemejanza, disparidad, discrepancia, disensión, controversia; tendencia; (*com.*) déficit. — *v.t.* diferenciar, hacer diferencia; distinguir.

different, *a.* diferente, diverso, distinto, desemejante.

differential [difəˈrenʃəl], *a.* diferencial. — *s.* (*mat.*, *aut.*) diferencial, *f.*

differentiate, *v.t.* diferenciar, distinguir. — *v.i.* diferenciarse.

differently, **differingly**, *adv.* diferentemente.

difficult [ˈdifikəlt], *a.* difícil, dificultoso, penoso, arduo, apurado.

difficulty, *s.* dificultad, impedimento, embarazo, oposición, obstáculo, tropiezo, objeción, reparo, inconveniente; *to be in difficulties*, hallarse en un apuro, o verse apurado.

diffidence [ˈdifidəns], *s.* falta de confianza en sí; reserva, modestia, timidez, humildad, recato; huraña.

diffident, *a.* desconfiado, tímido, vergonzoso; corto de genio, apocado.

diffluent, *a.* difluente.

difform [diˈfɔːm], *a.* (*ant.*) disforme, deforme.

difformity, *s.* (*ant.*) deformidad.

diffraction [diˈfrækʃən], *s.* (*fís.*) difracción.

diffuse [diˈfjuiz], *v.t.* difundir, esparramar, derramar, verter, esparcir; propagar, publicar. — *a.* difundido, extendido, esparcido, prolijo, difuso.

diffusedly, *adv.* difusamente.

diffusedness, *s.* difusión, esparcimiento, dispersión.

diffusely, *adv.* difusamente, copiosamente, prolijamente.

diffusible, *a.* difusible.

diffusion, *s.* difusión, esparcimiento; propagación, diseminación, dispersión, prolijidad.

diffusive, *a.* difusivo; difundido, difuso.

diffusively, *adv.* difusamente.

diffusiveness, *s.* difusión, extensión, dispersión.

dig [dig], *v.t.* (*pret.* y *p.p.* **dug**) cavar, excavar, cultivar; sacar, extraer, minar, ahoyar, ahondar; escarbar; penetrar con una punta; (*fig.*) buscar y extraer por medio del trabajo; *to dig up*, desarraigar; *to dig more deeply*, profundizar. — *v.i.* cavar, trabajar con azadón.

digastric [daiˈgæstrik], *a.* digástrico.

digest [diˈdʒest], *s.* digesto, pandectas, *f.pl.*, recopilación. — *v.t.* digerir, asimilar; clasificar, ordenar, codificar; meditar, pensar, rumiar; tolerar, tragar una afrenta. — *v.i.* asimilarse, ser digerible; (*cir.*) supurar;

(*quím.*) cocerse; *to rest and digest*, reposar la comida.

digester, *s.* digeridor, digestor.

digestibility [didʒestəˈbiliti], *s.* digestibilidad.

digestible [diˈdʒestəbl], *a.* digestible, digerible.

digestion [diˈdʒestʃən], *s.* digestión, *f.*; asimilación; descocedura; (*cir.*) supuración.

digestive, *s.*, *a.* digestivo.

digger [ˈdigəɹ], *s.* cavador; (*agr.*) almocafre; *grave-digger*, sepulturero.

dight [dait], *v.t.* adornar, embellecer. — *a.* adornado, embellecido.

digit [ˈdidʒit], *s.* dedo; dígito; cifra.

digital, *a.* digital.

digitalis [didʒiˈteilis], *s.* (*bot.*) digital, *f.*, dedalera.

digitated, *a.* digitado.

diglyph [ˈdaigliʃ], *s.* (*arq.*) diglifo.

dignified [ˈdignifaid], *a.* dignificado, honrado; serio, grave; elevado, majestuoso.

dignify, *v.t.* dignificar; elevar; promover, exaltar, condecorar.

dignitary, *s.* dignatario; dignidad.

dignity, *s.* dignidad, elevación, rango; nobleza; cargo, empleo.

digress [diˈgres], *v.i.* hacer digresión, divagar.

digression [diˈgreʃən], *s.* digresión, divagación.

digressional, *a.* secundario, accesorio.

digressive, *a.* digresivo, discursivo.

dihedral [daiˈhiːdrəl], *a.* (*geom.*) diedro.

dijudication [didʒuːdiˈkeiʃən], *s.* juicio decisivo.

dike [daik], *s.* dique; malecón; (*min.*) vena; canal; (*fig.*) barrera, defensa. — *v.t.* represar, contener por medio de represa.

dilacerate [daiˈlæsəreit], *v.t.* dilacerar; romper.

dilaceration [dailæsəˈreiʃən], *s.* dilaceración.

dilapidate [diˈlæpideit], *v.t.* desmoronar, derribar, destruir; dilapidar, malgastar. — *v.i.* arruinarse.

dilapidation [dilæpiˈdeiʃən], *s.* desmoronamiento, ruina.

dilatability [dileitəˈbiliti], *s.* dilatabilidad.

dilatable [diˈleitibl], *a.* dilatable.

dilatant, *s.*, *a.* dilatador.

dilatation [dileiˈteiʃən], *s.* dilatación.

dilate [diˈleit], *v.t.* dilatar, extender, alargar, amplificar. — *v.i.* dilatarse, extenderse, espaciarse.

dilated, *a.* difuso, prolijo; *p.p.* [DILATE].

dilator, *s.* (*med.*) dilatador.

dilatorily [ˈdilətrəli], *adv.* lentamente, detenidamente, con retardo.

dilatoriness, *s.* tardanza; lentitud; pesadez.

dilatory, *a.* tardo, lento, perezoso; pesado; (*for.*) dilatorio.

dilemma [diˈlemə], *s.* dilema, *m.*; *to be in a dilemma*, estar entre la espada y la pared.

dilettante [diləˈtænti], *s.* aficionado (a las artes y ciencias).

diligence [ˈdilidʒəns], *s.* diligencia, asiduidad, laboriosidad; atención, cuidado; (*coche*) diligencia.

diligent, *a.* diligente, asiduo, activo, solícito, laborioso.

dill [dil], *s.* (*bot.*) eneldo.

dilly-dally [ˈdilidali], *v.i.* malgastar el tiempo; entretenerse en bagatelas.

dilucid [daiˈluːsid], *a.* lúcido, claro.

diluent ['diljuənt], *s.*, *a.* diluente.
dilute [dai'lju:t], *v.t.* diluir, deshacer, disolver; aguar, cortar, templar. — *a.* atenuado, desleído, diluido, disuelto; templado.
diluter, *s.* diluente.
dilution, *s.* dilución.
diluvial, diluvian, *a.* diluviano.
diluvium, *s.* (*geol.*) diluvio.
dim [dim], *a.* tenue, débil; turbio; opaco, sombrío, obscuro; empañado; cegato; indistinto, confuso; misterioso; nublado, turbio de vista; lerdo, boto, necio. — *v.t.* ofuscar, obscurecer; empañar; (*fig.*) turbar, amortiguar (los faros o una luz).
dime [daim], *s.* diezmo; (*E.U.*) 10 centavos.
dimension [di'menʃən], *s.* dimensión, tamaño, medida.
dimidiate [di'midiət], *v.t.* dimidiar.
diminish [di'miniʃ], *v.t.* disminuir, minorar, amenguar, achicar, acortar, reducir, empequeñecer, debilitar, rebajar. — *v.i.* disminuirse, decrecer, debilitarse; degenerar.
diminishing, *a.* menguante, minorativo.
diminution [dimi'nju:ʃən], *s.* disminución, merma, decremento, reducción, rebaja.
diminutive [di'minjutiv], *s.*, *a.* diminuto, diminutivo; mezquino, pequeño, poquito.
diminutiveness, *s.* pequeñez.
dimissory ['dimisəri], *a.* dimisorio.
dimity ['dimiti], *s.* fustán.
dimness, *s.* obscurecimiento, ofuscamiento; torpeza.
dimorphism [dai'mɔ:rfizm], *s.* dimorfismo.
dimorphous, *a.* dimorfo.
dimple ['dimpl], *s.* hoyuelo. — *v.i.* formarse hoyuelos.
dimpled, dimply, *adv.* que tiene hoyuelos.
dim-sighted, *a.* cegato.
din [din], *s.* estruendo, estrépito, barahúnda, batahola. — *v.t.* atolondrar, ensordecer, asordar, aturdir, clamorear.
dine [dain], *v.i.* cenar, comer; *to dine out*, comer fuera de casa. — *v.t.* dar de comer, convidar, dar un convite.
ding [diŋ], *v.t.* arrojar, lanzar violentamente; batir, golpear; urgir, instar repetidamente.
ding-dong, *s.* din-dán, tintín.
dingey, dinghy, *s.* bote, lancha.
dinginess ['dindʒines], *s.* color obscuro; deslustre; suciedad.
dingle ['diŋgl], *s.* cañada.
dingle-dangle, *adv.* (*vulg.*) bamboleando.
dingo ['diŋgou], *s.* perro salvaje de Australia.
dingy ['dindʒi], *a.* empañado, deslucido, deslustrado; manchado; negruzco, sucio.
dining ['dainiŋ], *a.* de la comida; *dining-hall*, refectorio; *dining-room*, comedor; *dining-table*, mesa de comedor.
dinner ['dinəɹ], *s.* cena, comida; banquete; *dinner-jacket*, smoking; *dinner-napkin*, servilleta; *dinner-pail*, portaviandas, *m. sing.*; *dinner-party*, convite; *dinner-service*, servicio de mesa; *dinner-time*, hora de comer.
dint [dint], *s.* (*ant.*) golpe; fuerza; eficacia, abolladura; marca, señal,*f.*; *by dint of*, a fuerza de. — *v.t.* abollar.
dinumeration [dinju:mə'reiʃən], *s.* numeración, enumeración.
diocesan [diɔsəsən], *s.*, *a.* diocesano.
diocese, *s.* diócesis, *f.*
dioptric [dai'ɔptrik], **dioptrical**, *a.* dióptrico.

dioptrics, *s.* dióptrica.
diorama [daiə'rɑ:mə], *s.* diorama, *m.*
dioramic, *a.* diorámico.
dioxide [dai'ɔksaid], *s.* bióxido.
dip [dip], *v.t.* mojar, remojar, bañar, chapuzar, zampuzar, sumergir; (*aut.*) bascular (faros); *to dip the flag*, batir banderas. — *v.i.* sumergirse, chapuzar; meterse en el agua; (*fig.*) penetrar, entrar; inclinarse hacia abajo; (*geol.*) quedarse o hallarse formando ángulo con el horizonte (capas estratas, etc.). — *s.* inmersión; zambullida; inclinación, caída, declivio; depresión; inclinación vertical de la aguja magnética (de una capa estrata; de un eje de carruaje, etc.).
dipetalous [dai'petələs], *a.* dipétalo.
diphtheria [dif'θiəriə], *s.* difteria.
diphtheritic [difθə'retik], *a.* diftérico.
diphtheritis [difθə'raitis], *s.* difteritis, *f.*
diphthong ['difθɔŋ], *s.* diptongo.
diplograph ['diplɔgræf], *s.* diplógrafo.
diploma [di'ploumə], *s.* diploma, *m.*
diplomacy, *s.* diplomática; diplomacia; cuerpo diplomático; tacto, cautela.
diplomat ['diplomæt], *s.* diplomático.
diplomate, *v.t.* (*ant.*) dar un diploma.
diplomatic [diplə'mætik], *a.* diplomático.
diplomatist [di'ploumətist], *s.* diplomático.
dipolar, *a.* (*elec. y ópt.*) que tiene dos polos.
dipper [dipəɹ], *s.* cazo; pinzas para sacar las placas del desarrollador en la fotografía; nombre despectivo aplicado a los Baptistas y Anabaptistas.
dipping, *s.* inmersión; inclinación (de la aguja).
dipping-needle, *s.* aguja magnética.
dipsomania [dipso'meiniə], *s.* dipsomanía.
dipsomaniac, *a.* dipsomaníaco.
dipterous ['diptərəs], *a.* (*ent.*) díptero.
diptych ['diptik], *s.* díptica.
dire [daiəɹ], *a.* horroroso, horrendo, horrible, espantoso, cruel.
direct [di'rekt], *a.* directo, recto, derecho, en línea derecha; inmediato; formal; claro, patente. — *v.t.* dirigir, apuntar, enderezar, encaminar, guiar, conducir; enseñar; gobernar, regir, reglar; disponer, ordenar, mandar.
direction, *s.* dirección, rumbo, sentido, curso; consejo, orden, *m.f.*, mandato, instrucción; sobrescrito, señas; gobierno, administración; manejo; mira, fin; tendencia.
directive, *a.* directivo, directorio.
directly, *adv.* directamente, en línea recta; inmediatamente, al instante, enseguida; precisamente, exactamente; positivamente.
directness, *s.* derechura.
director, *s.* director, administrador; regente; guía, *m.f.*
directorial [direk'tɔəriəl], *a.* directorio, directorial, directivo.
directorship [di'rektəɹʃip], *s.* dirección.
directory, *s.* directorio; guía de forasteros; (*igl.*) añalejo; *telephone directory*, guía de teléfonos.
directress, *s.f.* directora.
directrix, *s.f.*, *a.f.* directriz.
direful [daiəɹful], *a.* horrible, horroroso, horrendo, terrible.
direfulness, direness, *s.* horror, espanto.
dirge [də:ɹdʒ], *s.* canto fúnebre; endecha.
dirigible ['diridʒibl], *s.* dirigible, aeronave, *f.*

diriment, *a.* (*for.*) anulación de matrimonio.

dirk [dəːɹk], *s.* daga, puñal.

dirt [dəːɹt], *s.* lodo, barro, fango, cieno; basura, mugre, *f.*; excremento; porquería; vileza, bajeza; *dirt cheap*, (*fam.*) muy barato.

dirtiness, *s.* suciedad, desaseo; porquería, cochinería, indecencia, bajeza, sordidez, villanía.

dirty, *a.* sucio, puerco, inmundo, mugriento, enlodado, manchado; despreciable, sórdido, bajo, vil; obsceno, indecente. — *v.t.* ensuciar, enlodar, emporcar, manchar.

disability [disə'biliti], *s.* impotencia, incapacidad, inhabilidad; desventaja.

disable [dis'eibl], *v.t.* mutilar, tullir; inhabilitar, inutilizar, incapacitar, imposibilitar; desmantelar, desaparejar.

disabled, *a.* mutilado, tullido, inválido; incapacitado, inhabilitado, inutilizado; arruinado.

disablement, *s.* invalidez, mutilación; inhabilitación.

disabuse [disə'bjuːz], *v.t.* desengañar, hacer conocer el engaño; sacar de error.

disaccommodate [disə'kɔmədeit], *v.t.* incomodar, molestar.

disaccord, *v.i.* desacordar, discordar.

disaccustom [disə'kʌstəm], *v.t.* desacostumbrar.

disadjust, *v.t.* trastornar, desarreglar.

disadvantage [disæd'vɑːnteidʒ], *s.* desventaja, menoscabo; disconveniencia, detrimento. — *v.t.* dañar, menoscabar, perjudicar.

disadvantageous [disædvɑn'teidʒəs], *a.* desventajoso, inconveniente, perjudicial.

disaffect [disə'fekt], *v.t.* indisponer; desaprobar; descontentar, malquistar.

disaffected, *a.* desafecto, desaficionado, disgustado.

disaffectedly, *adv.* con desafecto.

disaffection, *s.* desafecto, desafección, desamor, descontento.

disaffirm [disə'fəːɹm], *v.t.* negar, contradecir, impugnar, invalidar, anular; renunciar, rechazar.

disaffirmance, disaffirmation, *s.* confutación, impugnación; (*for.*) invalidación.

disafforest, *v.t.* (*for.*) abrir un bosque y hacerlo de uso común.

disaggregate [dis'ægrəgeit], *v.t.* desagregar.

disaggregation [disægrə'geiʃən], *s.* desagregación.

disagree [disə'griː], *v.i.* desconvenir, no convenir, disentir, diferir, discordar, discrepar, desavenirse, desarreglar, contender, altercar; sentar mal, probar mal.

disagreeable, *a.* contrario; desagradable, ofensivo, repugnante; displicente, desabrido.

disagreeableness, *s.* contrariedad; carácter desagradable; displicencia.

disagreement, *s.* diferencia, discrepancia, desemejanza; contrariedad, discordia, desacuerdo, descordancia, desavenencia, disenso, disensión.

disallow [disə'lau], *v.t.* negar, denegar, desaprobar; rechazar.

disallowable, *a.* negable; inadmisible; culpable, censurable.

disallowance, *s.* prohibición; desaprobación; denegación, negativa.

disally [disə'lai], *v.t.* anular la alianza; separar.

disanimate [dis'ænimeit], *v.t.* desanimar.

disanimation [disæni'meiʃən], *s.* desaliento.

disannul, *v.t.* anular, invalidar.

disannulment, *s.* anulación.

disappear [disə'piəɹ], *v.i.* desaparecer, perderse de vista, ausentarse.

disappearance, *s.* desaparecimiento, desaparición.

disappoint, *v.t.* frustrar, engañar, contrariar, chasquear; faltar a; (*fam.*) dar camelo; defraudar (una esperanza), desilusionar; *to be disappointed*, llevarse chasco, desilusionarse, estar desilusionado.

disappointment, *s.* contratiempo, revés; disgusto; desilusión; chasco.

disapprobation [disæpro'beiʃən], *s.* desaprobación, reprobación, censura.

disapprobatory, *a.* desaprobador.

disapproval [disə'pruːvəl], *s.* desaprobación, censura.

disapprove, *v.t.* desaprobar, reprobar, censurar, condenar, desechar, rechazar.

disapprovingly, *adv.* con desaprobación.

disarm [dis'ɑːɹm], *v.t.* desarmar; apaciguar, calmar. — *v.i.* deponer las armas, licenciar tropas o fuerzas de mar; poner en pie de paz.

disarmament, *s.* desarmamiento, desarme.

disarmer, *s.* desarmador.

disarming, *s.* desarme, desarmadura.

disarrange [disə'reindʒ], *v.t.* desarreglar, descomponer, desordenar.

disarrangement, *s.* desarreglo, desorden.

disarray [disə'rei], *s.* desarreglo, desorden, confusión; desatavío, trapillo. — *v.t.* desarreglar, desordenar; derrotar; desnudar.

disarticulate [disɑːɹ'tikuleit], *v.t.* desarticular.

disassociate [disə'souʃieit], *v.t.* desunir, separar.

disaster [di'zɑːstəɹ], *s.* desastre, desgracia, desdicha, catástrofe, *f.*

disastrous, *a.* desastroso, calamitoso, desgraciado; funesto, fatal, triste.

disavow [disə'vau], *v.t.* negar, denegar; desaprobar, desconocer, desautorizar.

disavowal, disavowment, *s.* denegación; retractación; repudiación.

disband [dis'bænd], *v.t.* licenciar; despedir, expulsar. — *v.i.* retirarse, despedir; separarse, dispersarse.

disbanding, disbandment, *s.* licenciamiento.

disbar [dis'bɑːɹ], *v.t.* excluir del colegio de abogados; expulsar.

disbark [dis'bɑːɹk], *v.t.* (*mar.*) desembarcar.

disbelief, *s.* incredulidad, escepticismo.

disbelieve [disbə'liːv], *v.t.*, *v.i.* descreer, dudar.

disbeliever, *s.* incrédulo, descreído.

disbench, *v.t.* desbancar.

disbud, *v.t.* desyemar.

disburden, *v.t.*, *v.i.* descargar, aligerar.

disburse [dis'bəːɹs], *v.t.* desembolsar, pagar, gastar.

disbursement, *s.* desembolso; gasto.

disburser, *s.* desembolsador, pagador.

disc [disk], *s.* disco; disc-jockey, jockey de discos.

discard [dis'kɑːɹd], *v.t.* desechar, descartar, excluir; deponer; (naipes) descartarse.

discern [di'zəːɹn], *v.t.* discernir, conocer, descubrir, percibir, distinguir. — *v.i.* discernir, juzgar, percibir.

discerner, *s.* discernidor.

discernible, *a.* perceptible, visible, aparente, sensible.

discerning, *a.* sagaz, perspicaz, despierto, juicioso, discernidor. — *s.* discernimiento.

discernment, *s.* discernimiento, criterio.

discerptible [di'səːɪptibl], *a.* separable.

discharge [dis'tʃɑːɪdʒ], *v.t.* descargar, soltar, tirar, disparar; saldar, pagar; absolver, dar libertad; ejecutar; licenciar; dispensar, eximir; despedir; relevar, exonerar; desembarazar; cumplir, desempeñar; arrojar, vomitar. — *v.i.* descargarse, soltarse. — *s.* descarga; descargo, disparo; desempeño, ejecución; perdón, exoneración, absolución; rescate; dimisión; finiquito, quitanza; desagüe, derrame.

discharger, *s.* descargador; disparador.

disciple [di'saipl], *s.* discípulo, alumno, estudiante, apóstol. — *v.t.* (*ant.*) disciplinar; convertir; hacer discípulos.

discipleship, *s.* discipulado.

disciplinable, *a.* disciplinable.

disciplinal, *a.;* **disciplinarian** [disipli'-neəriən], *s., a.;* **disciplinary,** *a.* disciplinario.

discipline ['disiplin], *a.* disciplina, educación, enseñanza, instrucción; orden, *m.f.,* conducta, regla; rigor, castigo; mortificación; corrección. — *v.t.* disciplinar, instruir, educar, corregir, castigar, reformar; reglar, gobernar, tener en orden.

disclaim [dis'kleim], *v.t.* negar, renunciar, repudiar, desconocer, rechazar; (*for.*) denegar, renunciar; declinar; negar responsabilidad.

disclaimer, *s.* negador, desconocedor; (*for.*) renuncia, abandono.

disclose [dis'klouz], *v.t.* descubrir, destapar; abrir; exponer, publicar, revelar.

disclosure, *s.* descubrimiento, declaración, revelación.

discoidal [dis'kɔidəl], *a.* discoidal.

discoloration [diskʌlə'reiʃən], **discolouration,** *s.* decoloración, descoloramiento.

discolour [dis'kʌləɪ], *v.t.* descolorar, descolorir, desteñir, amortiguar.

discomfit [dis'kʌmfit], *v.t.* derrotar; frustrar, desconcertar.

discomfiture, *s.* derrota; desconcierto.

discomfort [dis'kʌmfəɪt], *s.* molestia, incomodidad. — *v.t.* incomodar; desconsolar, afligir, entristecer.

discommend [diskə'mend], *v.t.* vituperar, censurar.

discommendable, *a.* culpable, censurable.

discommendation [diskəmen'deiʃən], *s.* culpa, censura.

discommode [diskə'moud], *v.t.* incomodar, molestar.

discommodious, *a.* incómodo.

discompose [diskəm'pouz], *v.t.* turbar, perturbar, descomponer, desconcertar, inquietar, desordenar, desarreglar.

discomposure, *s.* descomposición, descompostura, desorden, *m.* (*ant. f.*), confusión, agitación, inquietud, destemple.

disconcert [diskən'səːɪt], *v.t.* desconcertar, turbar, perturbar, confundir.

disconnect [diskə'nekt], *v.t.* desunir, separar, desacoplar, disociar; (*elec.*) desconectar.

disconnection, *s.* desunión, *f.,* separación, desencajamiento.

disconsolate [dis'kɔnsələt], *a.* desconsolado, apesadumbrado, inconsolable, triste, abatido, afligido.

disconsolateness, *s.* desconsuelo, desconsolación.

discontent [diskən'tent], *s.* descontento, desagrado, disgusto. — *a.* descontento, disgustado, quejoso. — *v.t.* descontentar, desagradar, disgustar.

discontented, *a.* descontento, malcontento, disgustado. — *p.p.* [DISCONTENT].

discontentedly, *adv.* de mala gana.

discontentedness, *s.* descontento.

discontinuance [diskən'tinjuens], **discontinuation,** *s.* descontinuación, interrupción, intermisión, cesación, suspensión.

discontinue, *v.t., v.i.* descontinuar, discontinuar, interrumpir; cesar, parar; suspender; desabonarse.

discontinuity [diskɔnti'njuːiti], *s.* descontinuación.

discontinuous [diskən'tinjuəs], *a.* descontinuo, interrumpido.

discord ['diskɔːɪd], *s.* discordia; desacuerdo; desavenencia; disonancia, discordancia, disensión, cisma.

discordance, discordancy, *s.* discordancia, disensión.

discordant, *a.* discordante, discorde, incompatible, incongruo, desavenido.

discordantly, *adv.* incongruentemente, de una manera discordante.

discount ['diskaunt], *s.* descuento, rebaja, menoscuenta, desfalco. — *v.t.* descontar, anticipar, rebajar, desestimar, deducir.

discountable, *a.* descontable.

discountenance [dis'kauntənəns], *s.* desagrado, sequedad. — *v.t.* desconcertar, desfavorecer, confundir, avergonzar; desaprobar, reprobar, poner mala cara.

discounter, *s.* prestamista, *m.f.;* banquero; corredor de cambio.

discourage [dis'kʌridʒ], *v.t.* descorazonar, desanimar, desalentar; disuadir; reprimir, impedir, frustrar.

discouragement, *s.* desaliento, desmayo, desánimo; oposición, reprobación.

discourager, *s.* desalentador, desanimador.

discourse ['diskoəɪs], *s.* disertación, discurso; conversación, plática; razonamiento. — *v.t.* expresar, pronunciar. — *v.i.* conversar, hablar, discursar, disertar, discurrir.

discourser, *s.* orador; escritor.

discoursive, *a.* discursivo.

discourteous [dis'kəːɪtiəs], *a.* descortés, desatento; grosero.

discourtesy, *s.* descortesía, grosería.

discover [dis'kʌvəɪ], *v.t.* descubrir, hallar, encontrar; inventar; manifestar, exponer, exhibir, revelar; *to discover someone's tricks,* conocer el juego.

discoverable, *a.* que se puede descubrir; distinguible; manifiesto, patente.

discoverer, *s.* descubridor, hallador, explorador.

discovery, *s.* descubrimiento; invento, invención; hallazgo; revelación, manifestación.

discredit [dis'kredit], *s.* descrédito, deshonor; desconfianza, oprobio; *to bring into discredit,* desacreditar. — *v.t.* descreer, dudar; desacreditar, difamar; desautorizar.

discreditable, *a.* deshonroso; vergonzoso, ignominioso.

discreet [dis'kri:t], *a.* discreto, circunspecto, juicioso, cuerdo.

discreetness, *s.* discreción, juicio, seso, prudencia.

discrepance, discrepancy [dis'krepənsi], *s.* discrepancia; desacuerdo; contradicción.

discrepant, *a.* discrepante.

discrete, *a.* distinto, separado, desunido; descontinuo; contrario; (*filos.*) no concreto.

discretion [dis'kreʃən], *s.* discreción, prudencia, circunspección, reserva, miramiento; *at* (*one's*) *discretion,* a discreción; *age of discretion,* edad de discreción.

discretional, discretionary, *a.* discrecional.

discretive [dis'kri:tiv], *a.* distinto, separado; disyuntivo.

discriminable, *a.* discernible, distinguible.

discriminate [dis'krimineit], *v.t.,* *v.i.* distinguir; escoger; discernir, diferenciar. — *a.* discernidor, distinguido.

discriminately, *adv.* distintamente, particularmente.

discriminating, *a.* discerniente, característico, distintivo, particular; discernidor, juicioso.

discrimination [diskrimi'neiʃən], *s.* discernimiento, juicio; distinción.

discriminator, *s.* hombre juicioso.

discrown [dis'kraun], *v.t.* destronar, privar de la corona.

disculpate [dis'kʌlpeit], *v.t.* disculpar.

disculpation [diskəl'peiʃən], *s.* disculpa.

discursive [dis'kə:rsiv], *a.* discursivo; digresivo; descosido, vago; errante.

discursiveness, *s.* ilación, calidad de digresivo.

discursory, *a.* racional, lógico.

discus ['diskəs], *s.* disco.

discuss [dis'kʌs], *v.t.* discutir, argüir examinar, tratar, debatir; catar, probar; (*med.*) resolver, disolver.

discussion, *s.* discusión, debate, examen; (*med.*) disolución.

discussive, *a.* (*med.*) discusivo, resolutivo.

discutient [dis'kju:ʃiənt], *a.* (*med.*) resolvente, resolutivo.

disdain [dis'dein], *v.t.* desdeñar, despreciar, menospreciar. — *v.i.* desdeñarse. — *s.* desdén, desprecio, menosprecio.

disdainful, *a.* desdeñoso; arrogante, altanero, altivo.

disdainfulness, *s.* altivez, entono, orgullo.

disease [di'zi:z], *s.* mal, enfermedad, indisposición, achaque, dolencia; malestar, sufrimiento. — *v.t.* enfermar, hacer daño, causar enfermedad, contagiar; afligir, incomodar.

diseased, *a.* enfermado, indispuesto, mórbido, morboso.

diseasedness, *s.* enfermedad, indisposición, morbidez.

disedge, *v.t.* desafilar, embotar, hacer obtuso.

disembark [disem'ba:rk], *v.i.* desembarcar, bajar a tierra. — *v.t.* desembarcar, echar en tierra.

disembarkation [disemba:r'keiʃən], *s.* desembarco, desembarque.

disembarrass [disəm'bærəs], *v.t.* desembarazar, zafar.

disembarrassment, *s.* desembarazo, desencogimiento.

disembitter [disem'bitər], *v.t.* dulcificar.

disembodied [disəm'bɔdid], *a.* incorpóreo, separado del cuerpo; desbandado.

disembody, *v.t.* separar el cuerpo de la carne; desagregar, librar; (*mil.*) licenciar.

disembogue [disəm'boug], *v.t.,* *v.i.* desembocar, descargar, vaciar, desaguar.

disemboguement, *s.* desembogue, desagüe, salida al mar.

disembosom [disəm'buzəm], *v.i.* desahogar, sacar del fondo del corazón.

disembowel [disəm'bauəl], *v.t.* desentrañar, destripar.

disembroil [disəm'brɔil], *v.t.* desembrollar, desenredar.

disembroiling, *s.* desembrollo.

disenable [disə'neibl], *v.t.* debilitar, incapacitar.

disenchant [disən'tʃa:nt], *v.t.* desencantar, deshechizar, desilusionar.

disenchanting, *s.* desencantador.

disenchantment, *s.* desencanto.

disencumber [disən:kʌmbər], *v.t.* desembarazar, descombrar.

disencumbrance, *s.* desembarazo.

disendowment [disən'daumənt], *s.* supresión de un subsidio.

disengage [disən'geidʒ], *v.t.* desenredar, desembarazar; desunir, desacoplar; desasir; desembragar; eximir, librar. — *v.i.* libertarse, librarse, desligarse, soltarse.

disengaged, *a.* desembarazado, suelto, libre; desunido; desocupado, vacante.

disengagement, *s.* desembarazo, desempeño; soltura, ocio; desembrague.

disennoble [disə'noubl], *v.t.* degradar, envilecer.

disentangle [disən'tæŋgl], *v.t.* desenredar, desembrollar, desenmarañar, desligar, desanudar.

disentanglement, *s.* desenredo, desembarazo.

disenthral [disən'θra:l], *v.t.* emancipar.

disenthralment, *s.* emancipación.

disenthrone [disən'θroun], *v.t.* destronar.

disentitle [disən'taitl], *v.t.* privar de un título.

disentomb [disən'tu:m], *v.t.* exhumar, desenterrar.

disestablish [disis'tæbliʃ], *v.t.* quitar a una Iglesia el apoyo del Estado.

disestablishment, *s.* privación a una Iglesia del apoyo del Estado.

disesteem [disəs'ti:m], *v.t.* desestimar, tener en poco, desaprobar. — *s.* desestima, desestimación.

disfavour [dis'feivər], *v.t.* desfavorecer; desairar. — *s.* desfavor, desgracia; desaire; malquerencia.

disfiguration [disfigju'reiʃən], *s.* desfiguración.

disfigure [dis'figər], *v.t.* desfigurar, deformar, afear.

disfigurement, *s.* disfiguración, deformidad.

disforest [dis'fɔrəst], *v.t.* desmontar, talar.

disfranchise [dis'fræntʃais], *v.t.* quitar derechos de ciudadano.

disfranchisement, *s.* privación de derechos.

disfrock [dis'frɔk], *v.t.* exclaustrar [UNFROCK].

disfurnish [dis'fə:rniʃ], *v.t.* despojar, desproveer; desguarnecer; desmueblar.

disgarnish, *v.t.* desguarnecer.

disgorge [dis'gɔ:rdʒ], *v.t.* vomitar; desembuchar; desembocar; arrojar con violencia;

devolver por fuerza, necesidad o temor lo adquirido injustamente, hacer restitución de.

disgorgement, s. vómito; devolución, entrega.

disgrace [dis'greis], s. afrenta, estigma, m., baldón, ignominia, infamia, oprobio, deshonra, vergüenza. — v.t. retirar favor a; causar oprobio, hacer caer en desgracia, disfamar, deshonrar, vilipendiar.

disgraceful, a. vergonzoso, deshonroso, ignominioso.

disgracefully, adv. vergonzosamente, ignominiosamente, en desgracia.

disgracefulness, s. ignominia, vergüenza, oprobio, afrenta, deshonra.

disgregation [disgrə'geiʃən], s. disgregación.

disgruntle [dis'grʌntl], v.t. (fam.) enfadar, disgustar.

disgruntled, a. mohino, disgustado, refunfuñador.

disguise [dis'gaiz], v.t. disfrazar, enmascarar; encubrir; solapar, tapar, ocultar; desfigurar; embriagar. — s. disfraz, máscara, simulación, embozo, velo, rebozo; embriaguez.

disguisement, s. disfraz.

disguising, s. máscara.

disgust [dis'gʌst], s. asco, aversión, repugnancia, tedio, hastío. — v.t. disgustar, repugnar, enfadar, hastiar.

disgustful, a. asqueroso, desagradable.

disgusting, a. desagradable, desabrido, repugnante, ofensivo, asqueroso.

dish [diʃ], s. plato, plato grande, fuente, f.; copera; concavidad; (min.) caja que sirve de medida para el mineral y que contiene 672 inches cúbicas. — v.t., v.i. hacer plato, servir las viandas; (fig.) preparar; hacer cóncavo; (fam.) atrapar, engañar. — pl. **dishes,** vajilla.

dishabille [disə'bil], s. paños menores; ropa de mañana; to be in dishabille, estar de casa.

disharmony, s. discordancia, disonancia.

dish-cloth, dish-clout, s. rodilla, estropajo.

dish-cover, s. cubreplatos, m. sing.

dishearten [dis'haːtən], v.t. descorazonar, desanimar, desalentar.

disherison [dis'herizən], s. desheredación.

dishevel [di'ʃevəl], v.t. desgreñar, desmelenar.

dishevelled, a. desgreñado, desmelenado.

dishful [diʃfəl], s. plato lleno.

dishonest [dis'ɔnist], a. fraudulento, engañoso, falso; malo, ímprobo, pícaro; desleal, infiel.

dishonestly, adv. fraudulentamente, de mala fe.

dishonesty, s. fraudulencia; improbidad, deshonestidad; picardía, dolo, fraude.

dishonour, s. deshonra, ignominia, afrenta, deshonor; (com.) falta de pago. — v.t. deshonrar, infamar, afrentar; desflorar; (com.) negarse a pagar.

dishonourable, a. deshonroso, indecoroso, afrentoso; deshonrado, infamado.

dishonourably, adv. ignominiosamente, deshonrosamente, indignamente.

dishorn [dis'hɔːn], v.t. descornar.

disillusion [disi'ljuːʃən], **disillusionize,** v.t. desilusionar. — s. desilusión.

disinclination [disinkli'neiʃən], s. desafecto, desamor, aversión.

disincline [disin'klain], v.t. desinclinar, malquistar, indisponer.

disincorporate [disin'kɔːpəreit], v.t. desincorporar; disolver una corporación.

disincorporation, s. desincorporación.

disinfect [disin'fekt], v.t. desinficionar, desinfectar.

disinfectant, s., a. desinfectante.

disinfection, s. desinfección.

disingenuous [disin'dʒenjuəs], a. falso, disimulado, insincero; de dos caras; doble.

disingenuously, adv. doblemente, falsamente.

disingenuousness, s. doblez, astucia, mala fe.

disinherit [disin'herit], v.t. desheredar, exheredar.

disinheritance, s. desheredación.

disintegrate [dis'intəgreit], v.t. desagregar, disgregar, despedazar. — v.i. desmoronarse, disgregarse.

disintegration [disintə'greiʃən], s. desagregación, disgregación.

disinter [disin'təː], v.t. desenterriar, exhumar.

disinterest [dis'intərəst], s. desinterés, desprendimiento; desventaja; pérdida.

disinterested, a. desinteresado, imparcial, neutral.

disinterestedness, s. desinterés, abnegación.

disinterment [disin'təːmənt], s. desenterramiento, exhumación.

disinthral [disin'θrɑul], v.t. manumitir; emancipar.

disinvolve [disin'vɔlv], v.t. desenredar, desembrollar, desenvolver.

disjoin [dis'dʒɔin], v.t. desunir; desasir, despegar, apartar, separar. — v.i. desunirse.

disjoint, v.t. desunir, separar, desarreglar, dislocar, desquiciar, desencajar, desarticular, descoyuntar; desmembrar; trinchar. — v.i. desmembrarse. — a. (ant.) dislocado, desarticulado.

disjointed, a. dislocado, desarticulado; inconexo, incoherente, descosido.

disjointedness, s. descoyuntamiento.

disjunct [disd'ʒʌŋkt], a. descoyuntado, dislocado.

disjunction, s. disyunción, dislocación, descoyuntamiento.

disjunctive, a. disyuntivo.

disk [disk], s. disco [DISC].

dislike [dis'laik], v.t. (impersonal) desagradar, no gustar; (personal) detestar, tener aversión a, desaprobar. — s. aversión, antipatía, repugnancia, aborrecimiento.

disliked, malmirado, malquisto. — p.p. [DISLIKE].

disliker, s. desaprobador.

dislimb [dis'lim], v.t. desmembrar.

dislocate ['disləkeit], v.t. dislocar, descoyuntar.

dislocation [dislə'keiʃən], s. dislocación.

dislodge [dis'lɔdʒ], v.t. desalojar; arrojar, echar. — v.i. mudar(se).

dislodgement, s. desalojamiento.

disloyal [dis'lɔiəl], a. desleal; falso, infiel, pérfido, traidor.

disloyalty, s. deslealtad, infidelidad, perfidia, traición.

dismal ['dizməl], a. triste, funesto, lúgubre, deplorable.

dismalness, s. horror, consternación; tristeza; melancolía.

dismantle [dis'mæntl], v.t. desmontar, deshacer; desnudar, desatar; desguarnecer, desmantelar; (mar.) desaparejar.

dismask [dis'maːsk], v.t. desenmascarar.

dismast, *v.t.* desarbolar.
dismay [dis'mei], *v.t.* espantar, aterrar, desanimar, consternar, desmayar. — *s.* congoja, espanto, consternación, desmayo, deliquio.
dismember [dis'membəɹ], *v.t.* desmembrar.
dismembering, *s.* mutilación.
dismemberment, *s.* desmembramiento.
dismiss [dis'mis], *v.t.* despedir, echar, deponer, descartar, desechar, destituir; licenciar; disolver; repudiar; despachar, enviar; (*mil.*) romper filas.
dismissal, dismission, *s.* despedida, despido; dimisión; deposición; destitución; separación; liberación.
dismount [dis'maunt], *v.t.* desmontar, desarmar; (*arti.*) desplantar. — *v.i.* desmontar, apearse; descender, bajar.
disnaturalize, *v.t.* desnaturalizar.
disobedience [diso'biːdiens], *s.* desobediencia, inobediencia, rebeldía, resistencia.
disobedient, *a.* desobediente, refractario.
disobey [diso'bei], *v.t.* desobedecer.
disobligation [disobli'geiʃən], *s.* desaire, acto desagradable.
disoblige [diso'blaidʒ], *v.t.* desobligar, desplacer, disgustar.
disobliged, *a.* desairado, ofendido. — *p.p.* [DISOBLIGE].
disobliging, *a.* desagradable, desatento, ofensivo.
disorder [dis'ɔːɹdəɹ], *s.* desorden, *m.* (*ant. f.*), confusión, desarreglo, desconcierto; indisposición, enfermedad, enajenamiento de la mente; irregularidad, descomposición; motín, alboroto, tumulto. — *v.t.* desordenar, desarreglar, descomponer, desconcertar; perturbar, inquietar, enfadar.
disordered, *a.* desordenado, en desorden; alienado, desvariado, trastornado; enfermo, trastornado.
disorderliness, *s.* desorden, perturbación, confusión.
disorderly, *a.* desordenado, desarreglado; irregular, ilegal; alborotador, turbulento. — *adv.* desordenadamente, turbulentamente, desarregladamente; ilegalmente.
disorganization [disɔːɹgəni'zeiʃən], *s.* desorganización.
disorganize [dis'ɔːɹgənaiz], *v.t.* desorganizar.
disorganizer, *s.* desorganizador.
disorient, disorientate, *v.t.* desorientar; desviar del este; (*fig.*) confundir, ofuscar, extraviar.
disorientation, *s.* desorientación.
disown [dis'oun], *v.t.* negar, renegar; desconocer; renunciar, repudiar.
disparage [dis'pæridʒ], *v.t.* rebajar, desacreditar; disminuir; mofar; desdorar; menospreciar.
disparagement, *s.* censura, detracción, infamia; menosprecio, desprecio; desdoro; (*ant.*) casamiento desigual.
disparagingly, *adv.* desventajosamente; deshonrosamente, desdeñadamente.
disparate, *a.* desigual, diferente, desemejante, discorde. — *s.pl.* cosas tan desemejantes que no admiten comparación entre sí.
disparity [dis'pæriti], *s.* disparidad, desemejanza, desigualdad.
dispark, *v.t.* descercar.

dispart [dis'pɑːɹt], *v.t.* despartir; separar, apartar, dividir. — *v.i.* partirse, dividirse, rajarse. — *s.* vivo de un cañón; *dispartsight*, *s.* (*arti.*) mira de un cañón.
dispassion [dis'pæʃən], *s.* apatía, calma.
dispassionate, *a.* desapasionado; sereno; imparcial.
dispatch, *v.* [DESPATCH].
dispel [dis'pel], *v.t.* dispersar, esparcir; disipar; expeler.
dispensable [dis'pensəbl], *a.* dispensable.
dispensary, *s.* dispensario.
dispensation [dispen'seiʃən], *s.* dispensa, dispensación, exención; distribución, reparto; revelación.
dispensator, *s.* dispensador.
dispensatory, *s.* farmacopea. — *a.* dispensativo, dispensador.
dispense [dis'pens], *v.t.* dispensar, distribuir, repartir, administrar, excusar, eximir. — *s.* (*ant.*) dispensa, dispensación.
dispenser, *s.* dispensador.
dispensing, *a.* dispensativo.
dispeople, *v.t.* despoblar.
dispeopler, *s.* despoblador.
disperge [dis'pəːɹdʒ], *v.t.* (*ant.*) esparcir, rociar.
disperse [dis'pəːɹs], *v.t.* dispersar; desparramar, esparcir; disipar; distribuir. — *v.i.* dispersarse, separarse, disiparse, esparcirse, desaparecer.
dispersedly, *adv.* esparcidamente.
dispersion [dis'pəːɹʃən], *s.* dispersión, esparcimiento, desparrame; desviación, difusión.
dispersive, *a.* dispersivo.
dispirit [dis'pirit], *v.t.* desanimar, desalentar, descorazonar, amilanar.
dispiritedly, *adv.* con desaliento.
dispiritedness, *s.* desaliento, desánimo, amilanamiento.
displace [dis'pleis], *v.t.* dislocar; remover, desalojar, deponer; desplazar; desordenar.
displacement, *s.* destitución; desalojamiento, remoción, mudanza; (*mar.*) desplazamiento; (*geol.*) quiebra, falla; (*quím.*) coladura.
displant [dis'plɑːnt], *v.t.* trasplantar, arrancar; (*fig., ant.*) trasladar, suplantar.
displantation [displɑːn'teiʃən], *s.* trasplantación; (*fig., ant.*) expulsión (de una raza o de un pueblo).
display [dis'plei], *v.t.* desplegar, descoger, abrir, ensanchar, extender; declarar, exponer; mostrar, ostentar, lucir; (*mar.*) enarbolar el pabellón o la bandera. — *s.* despliegue, exhibición; exposición; ostentación, magnificencia, manifestación; parada; espectáculo.
displease [dis'pliːz], *v.t., v.i.* desplacer, desagradar, descontentar, incomodar, ofender, disgustar, enfadar.
displeased, *a.* ofendido, disgustado, incomodado.
displeasing, *a.* desagradable, ofensivo, displicente, antipático.
displeasure [dis'pleʒəɹ], *s.* desplacer, desagrado, descontentamiento, disfavor, desgracia, disgusto.
displode [dis'ploud], *v.t.* (*ant.*) disparar con estallido. — *v.i.* (*ant.*) estallar, hacer explosión.
displosion, *s.* (*ant.*) explosión.

[954]

displume [dis'plu:m], *v.t.* desplumar.

disport [dis'pɔət], *v.t.* juguetear, travesear, lucir, ostentar, gastar. — *v.i.* entretenerse, divertirse, recrearse.

disposable, *a.* disponible.

disposal [dis'pouzəl], *s.* disposición, colocación, arreglo; venta; donación, enajenación; dirección; distribución, repartimiento; *at your disposal*, a su disposición.

dispose [dis'pouz], *v.t.* disponer, arreglar, colocar, adaptar; ordenar, mandar. — *v.i.* disponer; hacer un arreglo; *to dispose of*, vender, traspasar; enajenar, deshacerse de.

disposition [dispə'ziʃən], *s.* disposición, orden, *m.f.*, arreglo, método; inclinación, propensión, aptitud, genio, temple, natural, humor, índole, *f.*, carácter; tendencia.

dispossess [dispə'zes], *v.t.* desposeer, desalojar, (*for.*) desahuciar.

dispossession, *v.t.* desposeimiento, despojo, (*for.*) desahucio.

dispraise [dis'preiz], *v.t.* vituperar, condenar, censurar. — *s.* desprecio, censura, vituperación.

dispraisingly, *adv.* vituperosamente.

dispread [dis'pred], *v.t.* esparcir, dispersar; desplegar. — *v.i.* esparcirse, extenderse, desplegarse.

disproof, *s.* refutación, confutación, impugnación.

disproportion [disprə'poəɹʃən], *s.* desproporción, desigualdad. — *v.t.* desproporcionar.

disproportionable, disproportional, disproportionate, *a.* desproporcionado.

disproportionateness, *s.* desproporción.

disprovable [dis'pru:vəbl], *a.* refutable.

disproval [dis'pru:vəl], *s.* refutación.

disprove [dis'pru:v], *v.t.* confutar, impugnar.

disputable [dis'pju:təbl], *a.* disputable, contestable, problemático, controvertible.

disputant, *s.* disputador, controversista, *m.f.*, contendiente.

disputation [dispju'teiʃən], *s.* disputa, controversia, certamen.

disputatious, disputative, *a.* disputador, caviloso, quisquilloso.

dispute [dis'pju:t], *v.i.* disputar, controvertir, discutir, contender, cuestionar, pleitear. — *v.t.* disputar, pleitear, argüir, refutar, impugnar. — *s.* disputa, controversia; contención, contienda, altercado, riña; debate, discusión; *beyond all dispute*, sin la menor duda; *to be having a dispute*, habérselas con uno; *to be always disputing*, andar en dimes y diretes.

disputer, *s.* disputador; controversista, *m.f.*

disqualification [diskwɔlifi'keiʃən], *s.* inhabilidad, inhabilitación; incapacidad; descalificación.

disqualify [dis'kwɔlifai], *v.t.* inhabilitar; imposibilitar; descalificar.

disquiet [dis'kwaiət], *v.t.* inquietar, atormentar, intranquilizar, desasosegar.

disquiet, disquietude, *s.* inquietud, desasosiego, ansiedad.

disquisition [diskwi'ziʃən], *s.* disquisición; investigación, pesquisa.

disrate [dis'reit], *v.t.* (*mar.*) degradar, rebajar de grado.

disregard [disri'gɑːɹd], *v.t.* no hacer caso de, desatender, descuidar; desdeñar, menos-preciar, desairar. — *s.* desatención, descuido; desprecio, desdén, desaire; omisión, negligencia.

disregardful, *a.* desatento, negligente.

disrelish [dis'reliʃ], *v.t.* (*fig.*) desazonar, disgustar; (*ant.*) causar disgusto, desazonar. — *s.* disgusto, aversión, repugnancia; desabrimiento, desabor; desgana, tedio, hastío, inapetencia.

disrepair, *s.* detioro, estropeo.

disreputable [dis'repjutəbl], *a.* de mala fama, ignominioso, despreciado, desacreditado, vergonzoso.

disreputation, disrepute, *s.* deshonra, descrédito, mala reputación, mala fama, mal nombre.

disrespect [disri'spekt], *s.* irreverencia, desacato, desatención. — *v.t.* despreciar, desatender.

disrespectful, *a.* irrespetuoso, irreverente, descortés, desatento.

disrespectfulness, *s.* irreverencia.

disrobe [dis'roub], *v.t.* desnudar, desvestir, despojar. — *v.i.* desnudarse.

disroot [dis'ru:t], *v.t.* desarraigar; arrancar de los cimientos.

disrupt, *v.t.* trastornar, desorganizar; quebrantar, romper.

disruption [dis'rʌpʃən], *s.* trastorno, desorganización; rotura, fractura, rompimiento, quebrantamiento.

disruptive, *a.* quebrantador.

dissatisfaction [dissætis'fækʃən], *s.* descontento, disgusto.

dissatisfactory, *a.* desplaciente, desagradable.

dissatisfied [dis'sætisfaid], *a.* disgustado, descontento, ofendido. — *p.p.* [DISSATISFY].

dissatisfy, *v.t.* descontentar, desagradar.

dissect [di'sekt], *v.t.* despedazar; disecar, anatomizar; (*fig.*) criticar, analizar.

dissection, *s.* disección, disecación; anatomía, análisis, *m.f.*

dissector, *s.* disector, disecador.

disseisin [dis'si:zən], *s.* despojo, usurpación.

disseisor, *s.* usurpador.

dissemble [di'sembl], *v.t.*, *v.i.* disimular, encubrir, fingir.

dissembler, *s.* disimulador, simulador, fingidor, hipócrita, *m.f.*

dissembling, *s.*, *a.* disimulación; disimulado.

dissemblingly, *adv.* disimuladamente, fingidamente, hipócritamente.

disseminate [di'semineit], *v.t.* diseminar, sembrar; esparcir; (*fig.*) propalar, divulgar.

dissemination [disemi'neiʃən], *s.* diseminación, esparcimiento; divulgación.

disseminator, *s.* propagador, diseminador.

dissension [di'senʃən], *s.* disensión, discordia, contienda, desunión, *f.*, oposición, pendencia, querella.

dissensious, dissentious, *a.* contencioso.

dissent [di'sent], *v.i.* diferir (de opinión), disentir, disidir; rehusar adhesión a una iglesia establecida. — *s.* disensión; disidencia.

dissentaneous [disen'teiniəs], *a.* discorde, contrario.

dissenter [di'sentəɹ], *s.* disidente.

dissentient, *a.* disconforme, opuesto. — *s.* disidente.

dissenting, *s.*, *a.* disidente.

dissentious, *a.* contencioso, pendenciero.

dissert [di'sə:ɪt], *v.i.* disertar, discurrir, disputar.

dissertation [disəɹ'teiʃən], *s.* disertación, tesis, *f.*, memoria.

dissertator, *s.* disertador.

disserve [di'sə:ɪv], *v.t.* dañar, injuriar, perjudicar; deservir.

disservice, *s.* perjuicio; deservicio.

dissever [di'sevəɹ], *v.t.* partir, dividir, desunir, separar.

disseverance, *s.* desunión, *f.*, división, separación.

dissident ['disidənt], *a.* disidente.

dissilient, *a.* (*bot.*) reventado.

dissimilar [di'similəɹ], *a.* desemejante, diferente, disímil, desigual.

dissimilarity [disimi'læriti], **dissimilitude**, *s.* desemejanza, disimilitud, disparidad, diferencia.

dissimulate [di'simjuleit], *v.t., v.i.* disimular, fingir.

dissimulation [disimju'leiʃən], *s.* disimulación, disimulo, hipocresía.

dissipate ['disipeit], *v.t.* disipar, dispersar, esparcir, desparramar; malgastar, desperdiciar. — *v.i.* disiparse, esparcirse, evaporarse, dispersarse, desparramarse; ser pródigo o disoluto.

dissipation, *s.* disipación; vida relajada, disipación, libertinaje; dispersión, evaporación; pérdida; derroche.

dissociable [di'souʃiəbl], *a.* desasociable; separador.

dissociate, *v.t.* desasociar, disociar, desunir, separar, dividir.

dissociation [disousi'eiʃən], *s.* disociación, desunión, *f.*, separación.

dissolubility [disɔlju'biliti], *s.* disolubilidad.

dissoluble [di'sɔljubl], *a.* disoluble.

dissolute ['disəlju:t], *a.* disoluto, licencioso, libertino.

dissoluteness, *s.* disolución, relajación, exceso, enviciamiento.

dissolution [disə'lju:ʃən], *s.* disolución, separación; muerte, *f.*; descomposición; licuación.

dissolvable, *a.* disoluble.

dissolve [di'sɔlv], *v.t.* disolver, deshacer, desatar, desunir, relajar, desleír, derretir; licuar; separar, dispersar; (*for.*) anular, derogar, abrogar. — *v.i.* disolverse, derretirse, liquidarse, evaporarse, descomponerse, deshacerse, aniquilarse, desvanecerse, morir; descaecer, languidecer.

dissolvent, *s., a.* disolutivo, disolvente; (*med.*) resolutivo.

dissolver, *s.* disolvente.

dissonance ['disənəns], *s.* disonancia, desentonación; desconcierto, discordia, contrariedad.

dissonant, *a.* disonante, discordante, contrario, opuesto, discorde.

dissuade [di'sweid], *v.t.* disuadir, desviar, apartar, desaconsejar.

dissuasion, *s.* disuasión, consejo.

dissuasive, *a.* disuasivo. — *s.* disuasión, consejo.

dissuasively, *adv.* de un modo disuasivo.

dissyllabic [disi'læbik], *a.* disílabo.

dissyllable, *s.* disílabo.

distaff ['distɑːf], *s.* rueca; (*fig.*) el sexo femenino.

distain [dis'tein], *v.t.* (*ant.*) manchar, teñir, deslustrar.

distance ['distəns], *s.* distancia; diferencia; alejamiento, lejanía, lontananza; respeto, miramiento; trecho, espacio; (*mús.*) intervalo; esquivez, altivez, frialdad; *at a distance*, a lo lejos, de lejos; *to keep at a distance*, (*fig.*) mantener a distancia; *to keep one's distance*, (*fig.*) mantenerse a distancia. — *v.t.* espaciar; alejar, apartar, desviar; sobrepasar.

distant, *a.* distante, apartado, remoto, lejano; extraño, esquivo; vago; reservado; *to be distant with*, tratar con frialdad.

distantly, *adv.* a distancia, de lejos; reservadamente.

distaste [dis'teist], *s.* aversión, tedio, disgusto, hastío, fastidio; *to cause distaste* (*in*), enfadar, disgustar.

distasteful, *a.* desabrido, chocante, enfadoso, desagradable.

distastefulness, *s.* repugnancia, disgusto, desagrado, aversión.

distemper [dis'tempəɹ], *s.* indisposición, enfermedad, mal; moquillo; desproporción, destemplanza; (*pint.*) temple. — *v.t.* desordenar, irritar, perturbar; (*pint.*) pintar al temple.

distemperature, *s.* intemperie, *f.*; destemplanza, perturbación, desarreglo, desorden, *m.* (*ant. f.*), agitación, confusión; indisposición.

distempering, *s.* pintura al temple.

distend [dis'tend], *v.t.* extender, ensanchar, inflar, hinchar.

distensible, distensive, *a.* dilatable.

distension, distention, *s.* dilatación, inflación, distensión, ensanche.

distent, *a.* inflado, extendido.

distich [distik], *s.* dístico.

distil [dis'til], *v.t.* destilar; disolver; derretir; alambicar, purificar, rectificar. — *v.i.* destilar, gotear, manar poco a poco.

distillation [disti'leiʃən], *s.* destilación.

distillatory, *a.* destilatorio.

distiller [dis'tiləɹ], *s.* destilador, condensador, refinador.

distillery, *s.* destilería; destilatorio.

distinct [dis'tiŋkt], *a.* distinto, diferente, diverso; formal, preciso, claro; expreso.

distinction, *s.* distinción, diferencia; juicio, discernimiento; honor; (examen) sobresaliente.

distinctive, *a.* distintivo, característico.

distinctly, distinctively, *adv.* distintamente.

distinctness, *s.* distinción, claridad.

distinguish [dis'tiŋgwiʃ], *v.t., v.i.* distinguir, discernir, diferenciar, individuar, clasificar; enaltecer, honrar.

distinguishable, *a.* distinguible, perceptible, discernible, notable.

distinguished, *a.* distinguido, notable, eminente, famoso, ilustre; marcado, señalado, de marca mayor. — *p.p.* [DISTINGUISH].

distinguishing, *a.* distintivo.

distinguishment, *s.* distinción.

distort [dis'tɔːɹt], *v.t.* torcer, retorcer; pervertir, falsear; deformar.

distorted, *a.* torcido, retorcido; falseado; deforme. — *p.p.* [DISTORT].

distortion, *s.* deformación; contorción, torcimiento; falseamiento, perversión.

distract [dis'trækt], *v.t.* distraer, interrumpir, separar, apartar; perturbar, enloquecer.

distracted, *a.* distraído; trastornado, loco, demente; aturdido.

distracting, *a.* distrayente, distractivo.

distraction, *s.* distracción; división, separación; confusión, perturbación; locura, frenesí; discordia, desorden; diversión, pasatiempo.

distractive, *a.* perturbador.

distrain [dis'trein], *v.t., v.i.* (*for.*) embargar, secuestrar.

distrainable, *a.* secuestrable.

distrainer, *s.* embargador, secuestrador.

distraint, *s.* embargo, secuestro.

distraught [dis'trɔːt], *a.* atolondrado, turbado, desconcertado; distraído.

distress [dis'tres], *s.* dolor, pena, tristeza, angustia, miseria, apuro; escasez; calamidad; (*for.*) embargo, secuestro; *to put in in distress,* (*mar.*) entrar de arribada forzosa. — *v.t.* afligir, angustiar, congojar; (*for.*) embargar, secuestrar.

distressed, *a.* apurado, afligido.

distressful, *a.* miserable, desdichado, desgraciado.

distressing, *a.* penoso, congojoso, aflictivo.

distributable [dis'tribjutəbl], *a.* repartible.

distributary, *a.* distributivo.

distribute, *v.t.* distribuir, repartir, dividir, disponer, clasificar, arreglar.

distributor (-er), *s.* distribuidor, repartidor, dispensador.

distribution [distri'bjuːʃən], *s.* distribución, división, disposición, clasificación, repartición, repartimiento.

distributive [dis'tribjutiv], *a.* distributivo.

district ['distrikt], *s.* distrito, territorio, comarca, región, barrio; jurisdicción; *district visitor,* señora caritativa (que visita enfermos por encargo de la parroquia).

distrust [dis'trʌst], *v.t.* desconfiar, sospechar, recelar. — *s.* desconfianza, sospecha, recelo.

distrustful, *a.* desconfiado, sospechoso, receloso, modesto, difidente.

distrustfulness, *s.* desconfianza.

distrustless, *a.* (*ant.*) sin sospecha, confiado.

disturb [dis'təːʌb], *v.t.* turbar, perturbar, desordenar; molestar, incomodar; alterar, remover, revolver; distraer, estorbar, interrumpir; desasosegar, inquietar.

disturbance, *s.* disturbio, confusión, desorden, tumulto, alboroto; irresolución, perplejidad.

disturber, *s.* perturbador, inquietador.

disunion [di'sjuːniən], *s.* desunión, *f.,* división, discordancia, desavenencia, separación.

disunionist, *s.* separatista, *m.f.*

disunite [disju'nait], *v.t.* desunir, separar, dividir, desavenir. — *v.i.* desunirse, separarse, desavenirse.

disunity [di'sjuːniti], *s.* desunión, *f.,* separación.

disusage [dis'juːzidʒ], *s.* (*ant.*) desuso, deshabituación.

disuse [dis'juːs], *s.* desuso, deshabituación. — [dis'juːz], *v.t.* desusar, desacostumbrar, deshabituar.

disvalue [dis'vælju], *v.t.* despreciar.

disvouch [dis'vautʃ], *v.t.* desestimar, desacreditar.

disyoke [dis'youk], *v.t.* desuncir.

ditch [ditʃ], *s.* zanja, caz; (*fort.*) foso. — *v.t., v.i.* zanjar, abrir zanjas.

ditcher, *s.* el que abre zanjas.

dither ['diðəɹ], *v.t.* temblar, tiritar; (*fam.*) vacilar.

dithyramb ['diθiræmb], *s.* ditirambo.

dithyrambic, *a.* ditirámbico. — *s.* ditirambo.

ditone ['daitoun], *s.* (*mús.*) dítono.

dittany ['ditəni], *s.* (*bot.*) díctamo, marrubio.

ditto ['ditou], *s., a.* dicho; ídem.

ditty ['diti], *s.* canción, cantinela.

diuresis [daiju'riːsis], *s.* (*med.*) diuresis, *f.*

diuretic, *a.* diurético.

diurnal [dai'əːɹnəl], *a.* cotidiano, diurno, diario. — *s.* diurno, diurnal.

diuturnal [daiə'təːɹnəl], *a.* diuturno.

diuturnity, *s.* diuturnidad.

divagate ['daivəgeit], *v.t.* divagar.

divagation [daivə'geiʃən], *s.* divagación.

divan [di'væn], *s.* diván, otomana.

divaricate [di'værikeit], *v.t., v.i.* bifurcar(se), dividir(se) en dos partes o ramos.

dive [daiv], *v.i.* sumergirse, zabullirse, enfrascarse; sondear; bucear; profundizar. — *s.* zambullidura, buceo; (*E.U.*) timba, taberna ordinaria.

divellent [dai'velənt], *a.* (*quím.*) dividente.

diver ['daivəɹ], *s.* buzo; (*orn.*) somorgujo.

diverge [di'vəːɹdʒ], *v.i.* divergir, diferir, apartarse.

divergence, divergency, *s.* divergencia.

divergent, *a.* divergente.

divergingly, *adv.* divergentemente.

divers ['daivəɹz], *a.pl.* diversos, varios.

diverse [di'vəːɹs], *a.* diverso, distinto, diferente; multiforme.

diversification [divəɹsifi'keiʃən], *s.* diversificación, variación.

diversify [di'vəːɹsifai], *v.t.* diversificar, variar, cambiar.

diversion, *s.* desvío, desviación, diversión; diversión, entretenimiento, pasatiempo.

diversity, *s.* diversidad, variedad, diferencia.

divert, *v.t.* divertir, desviar, distraer, apartar; divertir, recrear, regocijar.

diverting, *a.* divertido.

divertisement, (*ant.*) **divertissement,** *s.* (*ant.*) diversión, recreo; (*teat.*) intermedio.

divest [di'vest], *v.t.* despojar, desnudar; (*for.*) desposeer.

divestiture [di'vestitjuɹ], *s.* despojo; (*for.*) desposeimiento.

dividable [di'vaidəbl], *a.* divisible.

divide, *v.t.* dividir, partir, hendir, distribuir, desunir, separar; repartir, compartir. — *v.i.* dividirse, desunirse, partirse, separarse. — *s.* vertiente, *m.f.*

dividend ['dividənd], *s.* dividendo.

divider [di'vaidəɹ], *s.* partidor; repartidor, distribuidor; (*arit.*) divisor; *dividers,* compás de división.

dividual [di'vidjuəl], *a.* divisible.

divination [divi'neiʃən], *s.* adivinación.

divinatory, *a.* divinatorio.

divine [di'vain], *a.* divino, deífico; sagrado; teológico; (*fig., fam.*) divino, admirable, sublime. — *s.* teólogo, predicador. — *v.t., v.i.* conjeturar, presentir, pronosticar; vaticinar, presagiar, adivinar; *divining-rod,* vara divinatoria.

divineness, *s.* divinidad; perfección.

diviner, *s.* adivino, adivinador.

divineress, *s.f.* adivina, profetisa.

diving ['daiviŋ], *s.* buceo; *diving-bell,* campana de buzo; *diving-dress, diving-suit,* escafandra.

divinity [di'viniti], *s.* divinidad, deidad; teología.

divisibility [divizi'biliti], *s.* divisibilidad.

divisible [di'vizibl], *a.* divisible, divididero, partible.

division [di'viʒən], *s.* división, desunión, *f.*, separación, partición, repartición, distribución, repartimiento, sección, clase, *f.*, parte, *f.*, departamento, compartimiento, discordia; votación de un cuerpo legislativo (como el Parlamento británico); ramal.

divisional, divisionary, *a.* divisorio, divisional.

divisive [di'vaiziv], *a.* divisivo.

divisor, *s.* divisor.

divorce [di'voəɹs], *s.* divorcio; separación, desunión, *f.*; descasamiento. — *v.t.* divorciar, separar, desunir.

divorcee [divoəɹ'si:], *s.* persona divorciada.

divorcement [di'voəɹsmənt], *s.* divorcio.

divorcer, *s.* divorciador.

divulgate [di'vʌlgeit], *v.t.* divulgar, publicar.

divulge [di'vʌldʒ], *v.t.* divulgar, publicar, descubrir, revelar.

divulger, *s.* divulgador, propalador.

divulsion, *s.* desencajamiento, arrancamiento.

divulsive, *a.* desquiciador.

dizen ['daizen], *v.t.* ataviar, endomingar.

dizziness ['dizinəs], *s.* vértigo, vaguido, vahído; desvanecimiento.

dizzy, *a.* desvanecido; vaguido, vertiginoso; aturdido; ligero, voluble. — *v.t.* aturdir; causar vértigos.

do [du:], *v.t., v.i.* (*pret.* **did**; *p.p.* **done**) hacer, ejecutar, obrar, producir; servir; concluir, finalizar, despachar, acabar, terminar; aprovechar; convenir; preparar, arreglar; modificar; cocer, asar, hacer cocer; traducir, verter; hacer el papel de; (*fam.*) engañar, agraviar, injuriar; (*fam.*) matar; (*vulg.*) dar de comer, convidar, festejar; (*fam.*) visitar, ver lo más interesante de una ciudad, etc.; cansar, fatigar, agotar. — *v.i.* conducirse, comportarse, proceder; obrar, trabajar; ser a propósito; salir (bien o mal); estar, hallarse, pasarlo; bastar, ser suficiente para; *to do again,* volver a hacer; *to do away with,* destruir, quitar; *to do for,* despachar; *to do over,* cubrir, untar; *to do up,* arreglar, componer, liar, empaquetar; *to do with,* componérsela; *to do without,* pasar sin; *how do you do?* (al presentarse) mucho gusto; ¿cómo está usted?; *that will do,* eso sirve o eso basta; *to be done for,* (*fig., fam.*) estar hecho polvo; estar perdido, morirse; *well to do,* acomodado, adinerado, hacendado.

do, *s.* (*mús.*) do.

dobbin ['dobin], *s.* caballo de tiro.

dobby ['dobi:], *s.* duende; (*tejidos*) aparato que se coloca en los telares, para tejer pequeñas figuras.

docile ['dousail], *a.* dócil, sumiso, obediente, flexible.

docility [dou'siliti], *s.* docilidad.

docimacy, docimasy ['dɔsiməsi], *s.* docimasia.

dock [dɔk], *s.* dique, dársena, desembarcadero, muelle, astillero; (*for.*) banquillo (de acusados); (*bot.*) bardana; cola cortada; codón. — *v.t.* descolar; rabotear, desrabotear; cortar, cercenar; (*mar.*) poner una

embarcación en el dique; atracar en el muelle o dársena.

dockage, *s.* entrada en dique, derechos de dique, muellaje.

docket, *s.* rótulo; minuta, extracto, sumario; turno, lista; declaración de bancarrota; (*for.*) lista de las causas pendientes. — *v.t.* rotular, poner rótulo a; dar turno a los pleitos pendientes, después de hacer un extracto o sumario.

dockyard, *s.* (*mar.*) arsenal, astillero.

doctor ['dɔktəɹ], *s.* médico, doctor. — *v.t.* doctorar; medicinar, recetar; componer, reparar; (*fam.*) adulterar. — *v.i.* practicar la medicina.

doctoral, *a.* doctoral.

doctorate, *s.* doctorado.

doctoress, *s.f.* doctora.

doctorship, *s.* doctorado.

doctrinal ['dɔktrinəl], *a.* doctrinal; didáctico, instructivo.

doctrinarian [dɔktrin'ɛəriən], *s., a.* doctrinario.

doctrinarianism, *s.* doctrinarismo.

doctrine ['dɔktrin], *s.* doctrina, creencia, dogma, *m.*, enseñanza.

document ['dɔkjumənt], *s.* documento. — *v.t.* documentar.

documental, documentary [dɔkju'mentəl, -'mentəri], *a.* documental, documentario.

dodder ['dɔdəɹ], *v.i.* temblar, tiritar, estremecerse; tambalear.

dodder, *s.* (*bot.*) cuscuta.

doddering, *a.* tambaleante; chocho.

dodecagon, *s.;* **dodecagonal** [doude'kægənəl], *a.* dodecágono.

dodecahedron [doudekə'hi:drən], *s.* dodecaedro.

dodge [dɔdʒ], *s* trampa, astucia, esquinazo, artificio; evasión, evasiva. — *v.t.* eludir, evadir, evitar, esquivar; entrampar, trampear; burlar.

dodger, *s.* trampista, *m.f.*

dodo ['doudou], *s.* (*orn.*) dido.

doe [dou], *s.f.* gama, hembra del conejo, de la liebre, etc.

doer ['du:əɹ], *s.* hacedor; actor; persona activa, agente.

doeskin ['douskin], *s.* ante, piel de gama.

doff [dɔf], *v.t.* quitar, quitarse la ropa o el sombrero en señal de respeto; despojar.

dog [dɔg], *s.* perro, can; morillo; macho de algunos animales; zorro; (*mar.*) pie de cabra; gatillo de una arma de fuego; *house dog,* perro de guardia; *lap dog,* perrito faldero; *dog in the manger,* perro del hortelano; *to go to the dogs,* estar arruinado; *dog cheap,* muy barato; *dog-tired,* muy cansado. — *v.t.* cazar, seguir la pista de.

dog-bane, *s.* matacán.

dog-berry, *s.* cornizola.

dog-cart, *s.* coche de dos ruedas.

dog-days, *s.pl.* canícula.

doge [doudʒ], *s.* dux.

dog-fancier, *s.* perrero.

dog-fish, *s.* lija.

dogged ['dɔgid], *a.* ceñudo, tozudo, terco, intratable; contrario; tenaz.

doggedly, *adv.* brutalmente, ásperamente; tenazmente.

doggedness, *s.* ceño, mohina; aspereza;

maneras brutales; tenacidad, terquedad, pertinacia.

dogger ['dɔgɔɹ], s. (mar.) dogre.

doggerel ['dɔgərəl], a. burlesco. — s. versos burlescos; coplas de ciego, aleluyas.

doggish, a. perruno, regañón, brutal.

dog-grass, s. grama.

dog-hearted, a. cruel.

dog-hole, s. perrera.

dog-kennel, s. perrera.

dog-Latin, s. latín bárbaro, latinajo.

dog-licence, s. permiso para tener perro.

dogma ['dɔgmə], s. dogma, m., axioma, m.

dogmatic, **dogmatical** [dɔg'mætikəl], a. dogmático; arrogante, autoritario.

dogmatics, s. dogmática, dogmatismo.

dogmatism ['dɔgmətizm], s. dogmatismo, arrogancia.

dogmatist, s. dogmatista, m.f., dogmatizador.

dogmatize, v.t. dogmatizar.

dogmatizer, s. dogmatizador.

dog-rose, s. zarza perruna, gavanzo.

dog-show, s. exposición canina.

dog-skin, s. piel de perro.

dog-star, s. Sirio.

dog-tax, s. impuesto sobre los perros.

dog-teeth, s.pl. dientes caninos.

dog-trot, s. trote de perro.

dog-vane, s. (mar.) cataviento.

dog-watch, s. (mar.) guardia de cuartillo.

dogwood [dɔgwud], s. (bot.) cornejo.

doings ['du:iŋz], s.pl. hechos, acciones, acontecimientos, eventos.

doit [dɔit], s. óbolo, moneda holandesa de muy poco valor; (fig.) fruslería, bagatela.

doldrums ['dɔldrəmz], s.pl. desánimo, murria, tristeza; (mar.) calmas ecuatoriales, donde prevalece calma chicha.

dole [doul], s. repartimiento, distribución; porción, parte, f.; limosna; dádiva, don; congoja, angustia. — v.t. repartir, distribuir.

doleful, a. doloroso, lastimoso, lúgubre, triste.

dolefulness, s. tristeza, melancolía, dolor.

dolerite ['dɔlərait], s. dolerita, roca granítica.

dolesome, a. sombrío, melancólico; lastimero, lastimoso, doloroso, triste.

dolichocephalic [dɔlikousə'fælik], **-cephalous**, a. dolicéfalo.

doll [dɔl], s. muñeca; (fig., vulg.) gachí, f., hembra.

dollar, s. dólar; duro, peso; (vulg.) cinco chelines, pieza de una corona.

dolly, s. muñeca; (min.) tabla perforada para lavar quijo o ganga; plataforma alzable; aparato que se usa para clavar pilotes.

dolman ['dɔlmən], s. dolmán.

dolmen, s. dolmen.

dolomite ['dɔləmait], s. (min.) dolomía.

dolorous, a. doloroso, triste, lastimoso.

dolorousness, **dolour**, s. dolor, desolación, aflicción, pena.

dolose [do'lous], a. (for.) doloso, con intento criminal.

dolphin ['dɔlfin], s. delfín; (mar.) poste de amarra.

dolt [dɔlt], s. necio, tonto, bobo, bobalicón.

doltish, a. tonto, estúpido, lerdo, imbécil.

doltishness, s. tontería, estupidez, imbecilidad.

domain [do'mein], s. dominio, imperio, soberanía; heredad, propiedad, finca.

domainal, a. patrimonial.

dome [doum], s. (arq.) cúpula; cimborrio, domo; (poét.) casa, fábrica.

domesday ['du:mzdei], s. [DOOMSDAY].

domestic [do'mestik], **domestical**, a. doméstico, civil, intestino, casero, familiar; manso, domesticado; nativo, nacional. — s. doméstico, criado, sirviente.

domesticate, v.t. domesticar, amansar, naturalizar; civilizar.

domestication [domesti'keiʃən], **domesticity** [domes'tisiti], s. domesticidad; domestiquez; vida casera.

domicile ['dɔmisail], s. domicilio, residencia. — v.t. domiciliar. — v.i. domiciliarse.

domiciliary [dɔmi'siliəri], a. domiciliario.

domiciliate, v.t., v.i. domiciliarse, establecerse.

dominant ['dɔminənt], a., s. dominante; (mús.) dominante, f.

dominate, v.t., v.i. dominar, predominar, mandar.

domination [dɔmi'neiʃən], s. dominación, imperio, tiranía, autoridad, gobierno.

dominative [do'minətiv], a. dominativo, dominante, altivo.

dominator, s. dominador.

domineer [dɔmi'ni:ɹ], v.i., v.t. señorear, dominar con insolencia.

domineering, a. dominante, insolente.

dominical [do'minikəl], a. dominical.

dominie ['dɔmini], s. dómine, maestro de escuela, pedagogo (en Escocia).

dominion [do'miniən], s. dominio, dominación, señorío, imperio, potencia, gobierno, soberanía; distrito, territorio; (for.) posesión, dominio, potestad. — pl. **dominions**, posesiones.

domino ['dɔminou], s. dominó.

don [dɔn], s. catedrático; don, caballero, señor. — v.t. vestirse, ponerse; asumir, presumir.

donate [do'neit], v.t. donar, contribuir.

donation, s. donación, dádiva, don.

donative, a. donativo.

donator, s. donador.

done [dʌn], p.p. [DO]; hecho, ejecutado, acabado, concluido; bien cocido o frito o asado; fatigado, cansado; enfermo grave, herido mortalmente; (fam.) estafado, robado, engatusado; arruinado. — interj. ¡muy bien! ¡de acuerdo! ¡ya está! ¡hecho!

donee [do'ni:], s. (for.) donatario.

donjon ['dʌndʒən], s. torre de vigilia de un castillo, especialmente de uno normando; calabozo.

donkey ['dɔŋki], s. burro, asno, borrico, pollino, jumento.

donor ['dounəɹ], s. donante, donador.

donship, s. caballería, nobleza.

don't [dount], abreviatura [DO NOT].

doodle ['du:dl], s. (vulg.) bobo; haragán; garrapato. — v.i. garabatear, garrapatear.

doom [du:m], v.t. sentenciar, condenar, juzgar, imponer, mandar; destinar a la ruina. — s. juicio, sentencia; suerte, f., sino, hado, destino; determinación; perdición, ruina.

doomsday, s. día del juicio universal.

Doomsday-, **Domesday-book**, s. libro o registro ordenado por Guillermo I el conquistador, que contiene el gran catastro de la propiedad feudal de Inglaterra en 1084-86.

door [doəɹ], *s.* puerta, entrada; portal; zaguán; pasillo; (*fig.*) avenida, acceso; *back door*, puerta trasera; *blind door*, puerta falsa; *folding door*, puerta de dos hojas; *sliding door*, puerta corredera; *street door*, portal, puerta de entrada; *out of doors*, fuera de casa; *to throw open one's doors*, dar hospitalidad.

door-catch, *s.* golpete.

door-chain, *s.* cadena para la puerta.

door-handle, *s.* puño, tirador; aldaba.

door-head, *s.* dintel.

door-keeper, *s.* portero, portera, ujier.

door-knob, *s.* puño, tirador de puerta.

door-latch, *s.* picaporte, pestillo.

door-mat, *s.* felpudo de puerta, esterilla.

door-post, *s.* jamba de puerta.

door-sill, *s.* umbral.

door-way, *s.* entrada, portal.

dope [doup], *s.* (*vulg.*) narcótico, narcóticos; (*vulg.*) información, datos; pasta de opio; grasa para lubricar. — *v.t.* narcotizar.

dor [doːɹ], **dorr**, *s.* (*zool.*) escarabajo estercolero que zumba al volar.

Dorcas [ˈdoːɹkəs], *s.* reunión de señoras caritativas, para hacer prendas de vestir para los pobres.

doree, *s.* (*ictiol.*) gallo, pez de mar.

Dorian [ˈdoəɹiən], **Doric** [ˈdɔrik], *a.* dórico.

dormancy, *s.* reposo, sueño, quietud, descanso.

dormant [ˈdoːɹmənt], *a.* durmiente; latente, oculto, secreto; sin movimiento; inactivo, inusitado.

dormer, *s.* viga maestra; *dormer window*, buharda.

dormitive [ˈdoːɹmətiv], *s.* dormitivo, narcótico, soporífero.

dormitory, *s.* dormitorio (de colegio o monasterio, etc.).

dormouse [ˈdoːɹmaus], *s.* (*zool.*) lirón.

dorsal [doːɹsəl], *a.* dorsal.

dorsum, *s.* dorso.

dory, *s.* (*ictiol.*) ceo.

dosage [ˈdousidʒ], *s.* dosificación.

dose, *s.* dosis, *f.*; (*fig.*) mal trago. — *v.t.* dosificar, medicinar, administrar una dosis.

dosing, *s.* dosificación.

doss [dɔs], *s.* (*fam.*) sueño. — *v.t.* (*fam.*) dormir.

dossal, *s.* retablo; tapices o colgaduras ricas que se colocan detrás del altar.

dossil, *s.* (*cir.*) lechino.

dost [dʌst], 2ª pers. pres. indic. [DO].

dot [dɔt], *s.* tilde, *f.*, punto, virgulita; (*mús.*) puntillo. — *pl.* **dots** (*gram.*) puntos suspensivos. — *v.t.* tildar, puntear. — *v.i.* hacer puntos, poner (los) puntos; *to dot one's i's*, poner los puntos sobre las íes.

dotage [ˈdoutidʒ], *s.* chochez.

dotal, *a.* dotal.

dotard, *s.* chocho, ñoño.

dotation [douˈteiʃən], *s.* dotación.

dote [dout], *v.i.* chochear, caducar; *to dote upon*, amar con exceso, apasionarse de.

doter, *s.* chocho, el que ama con exceso.

dotingly, *adv.* con mucho cariño, apasionadamente, con chochez, con ceguera.

doth [dʌθ], (*ant.*) 3ª pers. pres. indic. [DO].

dotterel [ˈdɔtərəl], *s.* (*orn.*) calandria marina.

dottle, *s.* porción de tabaco dejado en la pipa, sin fumar.

dotty [ˈdɔti], *a.* (*fam.*) alelado, chiflado.

double [ˈdʌbl], *a.* doble, doblado, duplicado; (*fig.*) falso, engañoso; ambiguo. — *s.* doble, duplo; doblez, pliegue, impostura; fantasma, *m.*, aparecido; (*impr.*) duplicado; pliegue, plegadura; (*mús.*) variaciones; (*teat.*) contrafigura. — *v.t.* duplicar, doblar, redoblar, multiplicar por dos; repetir; plegar; (*mar.*) remontar o doblar un cabo. — *v.i.* duplicarse, doblarse; disimular; volver atrás. — *adv.* en doble, dobladamente; dos veces.

double-barrelled, *a.* de dos cañones.

double-bass, *s.* contrabajo.

double-bed, *s.* cama de matrimonio.

double-biting, *a.* de dos filos.

double-bottomed, *a.* de dos fondos.

double-chin, *s.* papada.

double-dealer, *s.* embustero, traidor.

double-dealing, *a.* doblez, trato doble.

double-edged, *a.* de doble filo.

double-entry, *s.* (*com.*) partida doble.

double-faced, *a.* de dos caras; falso, pérfido.

double-minded, *a.* disimulado, insidioso, indeciso.

doubleness, *s.* doblez, dobladura; duplicidad.

doubler, *s.* plegador, doblador.

doublet, *s.* par, pareja; justillo, almilla, casaca.

double-tongued, *a.* lenguaraz, falso, embustero.

doubling, *s.* dobladura, pliegue; vuelta, rodeo.

doubloon [dʌbˈluːn], *s.* doblón.

doubly, *adv.* doblemente, por duplicado.

doubt [daut], *v.t.*, *v.i.* dudar, temer, recelar, desconfiar, vacilar, sospechar. — *s.* duda, sospecha, reparo, incertidumbre, *f.*

doubtable, *a.* dudable.

doubter, *s.* desconfiado, escéptico.

doubtful, *a.* dudoso, incierto, ambiguo, dudable, perplejo, receloso.

doubtfully, *adv.* dudosamente, inciertamente.

doubtfulness, *s.* duda, dificencia, ambigüedad; irresolución, incertidumbre, *f.*

doubtingly, *adv.* dudosamente.

doubtless, doubtlessly, *adv.* indudablemente, indubitablemente, sin duda.

douche [duːʃ], *s.* ducha, regadera. — *v.t.* duchar.

dough [dou], *s.* masa, pasta, amasijo.

dough-nut, *s.* buñuelo, bollito.

doughtiness, *s.* esfuerzo, valentía, denuedo.

doughty [ˈdauti], *a.* bravo, valeroso; fanfarrón.

doughy [ˈdoui], *a.* pastoso, crudo, blando.

douse [daus], *v.t.* zabullir, chapuzar; mojar, remojar; dar, golpear; (*mar.*) recoger, arriar. — *v.i.* zabullirse, chapuzarse.

dove [dʌv], *s.* palomo, paloma; *ring-dove*, paloma torcaz; *turtle-dove*, tórtola.

dove-coloured, *a.* tornasolado.

dove-cot, *s.* palomar.

dovetail, *s.* (*carp.*) cola de milano o de pato. — *v.t.* ensamblar a cola de milano; machihembrar.

dowager [ˈdauədʒəɹ], *s.* viuda que goza el título de su marido; **Queen dowager**, la reina viuda.

dowdy [ˈdaudi], *a.* sucio, desaliñado, zafio.

dowel [ˈdauəl], *s.* botón, macho de madera, espiga de pie derecho.

dower, dowery [ˈdauəri], *s.* dote, viudedad; don, dotación, beneficio; prendas personales.

dowered, *a.* dotado.

dowerless, *a.* sin dote.

down [daun], *s.* plumón, flojel; vello, bozo; loma, collado, terreno en cuesta suave sin árboles usado para el pastoreo en el sur de Inglaterra; duna; penacho; caída, revés de fortuna. — *a.* descendente; pendiente; (*fig.*) alicaído, abatido; *eider down*, edredón. — *prep., adv.* abajo, debajo de, por tierra, en tierra, en la parte inferior, en sujeción; aprecio o paso reducido; al contado; bajo el horizonte; a un volumen menor; *down from*, desde; *down to*, hasta; *down stream*, río abajo; *to take down*, desatar, descolgar; apuntar, anotar; *cash down*, al contado; *up and down*, de arriba abajo; *ups and downs*, vaivenes; *to be down upon*, (*fig.*) tratar con severidad; *upside down*, patas arriba, lo de arriba abajo, revuelto; *down in the mouth*, (*fig.*) alicaído.

downcast, *adj.* inclinado; descendente; abatido, deprimido.

downfall, *s.* caída, ruina, decadencia, degradación, hundimiento.

downfallen, *a.* caído, arruinado.

downhaul, *s.* (*mar.*) cargadera.

downhill, *a.* pendiente, inclinado, en declive, cuesta abajo. — *s.* pendiente, *f.*, cuesta.

downiness, *s.* vellosidad.

downpour, *s.* aguacero, chaparrón.

downright, *adj.* abierto, sincero, franco, manifiesto, claro, categórico, patente; derecho, perpendicular; extremo; (*fam.*) de cuatro suelas. — *adv.* llanamente; perpendicularmente; enteramente.

downstairs, *adv.* abajo, escalera abajo, bajando las escaleras.

downtrodden, *a.* pisado, pisoteado, maltratado, tiranizado.

downward, *a.* pendiente, inclinado. — *adv.* **downward, downwards,** hacia abajo; hasta nuestros días.

downy, *a.* felpudo, velloso, blando, suave; tranquilo, dulce.

dowry ['dauəri], *s.* dote, *m.f.*

doxology [dɔk'sɔlədʒi], *s.* himno de alabanza a Dios; gloria patri.

doze [douz], *v.i.* dormitar, descabezar el sueño. — *s.* sopor, sueño, adormecimiento.

dozen ['dʌzən], *s.* docena; *baker's dozen*, docena de fraile; *to talk nineteen to the dozen*, hablar por los codos.

doziness, *s.* somnolencia, soñolencia, modorra.

dozy ['douzi], *a.* soñoliento, amodorrado.

drab [dræb], *s.* pelleja, prostituta, mujerota, mujerzuela. — *a.* pardusco; triste, monótono.

drabble, *v.t.* enlodar.

drachma ['drækmə], *s.* dracma; gramo.

draco ['dreikou], *s.* (*astr.*) dragón; fuego fatuo.

draconian [drə'kouniən], **draconic** [drə'kɔnik], *a.* draconiano.

draff [dræf], *s.* inmundicia, hez, *f.*, desperdicios.

draffish, draffy, *a.* sucio, inmundo, asqueroso, inútil; despreciable.

draft [drɑ:ft], *s.* (*com.*) libramiento, orden de pago, libranza, póliza; (*mil.*) destacamento; esquicio, dibujo, traza, trazado, plano, plan, diseño, delineación; minuta, borrador, apuntación, esquema, *m.* — *v.t.* dibujar, diseñar, trazar; (*mil.*) destacar.

drag [dræg], *v.t., v.i.* arrastrar, tirar; garrear (el ancla); (*agr.*) rastrillar; rastrear; remolcar; decaer (acción, interés); *to drag the anchor*, (*mar.*) garrear, echarse sobre el ancla. — *s.* carretilla; arpón, garfio; galga, calzadera; trasmallo; (*mar.*) rastra; draga; brancada; (*fig.*) traba, rémora.

drag-boat, *s.* draga.

drag-chain, *s.* cadena para enrayar.

draggle ['drægl], *v.t.* enlodar o ensuciar arrastrando. — *v.i.* enlodarse, emporcarse.

draggle-tailed, *a.* enlodado, sucio.

drag-hook, *s.* enrayador, garfio.

drag-net, *s.* red barredera, brancada.

dragoman ['drægoumən], *s.* (*pl.* **dragomans**) dragomán, trujamán.

dragon ['drægən], *s.* dragón; (*fig.*) hombre o mujer feroz; (*bot.*) dragontea.

dragonet, *s.* dragonete.

dragon-fly, *s.* libélula; (*fam.*) caballito del diablo.

dragonish, *a.* dragontino.

dragon-like, *a.* fiero.

dragonnade, *s.* dragonadas.

dragon-tree, *s.* (*bot.*) drago.

dragoon [drə'gu:n], *s.* (*mil.*) dragón.

drain [drein], *v.t.* filtrar, secar, desecar, desaguar, avenar, agotar, enjugar, colar, escurrir; achicar; sangrar, desangrar; empobrecer, disipar. — *v.i.* filtrarse, destilarse, desaguar. — *s.* desagüe, desecación; desaguadero; reguera, tajea, vertedero, sumidero, fosa, albañal; acequia; zanja de derivación; colador.

drainable, *a.* desaguable.

drainage, *s.* desagüe, avenamiento, desecamiento, destilación, desecación; (*agr.*) drenaje; arroyada.

drainer, *s.* colador, coladero, filtro; secadero.

draining, *s.* desagüe, agotamiento, achique, desecación; drenaje; *draining-board*, escurreplatos, *m.sing.*, escurridor.

drake [dreik], *s.m.* pato, ánade macho.

dram [dræm], *s.* dracma; (*fig.*) grano, gota; (*fam.*) trago de aguardiente; (*fig., fam.*) copita.

drama ['drɑːmə], *s.* drama, *m.*

dramatic, dramatical [drə'mætikəl], *a.* dramático.

dramatis personæ, *s.* personajes.

dramatist ['drɑːmətist], *s.* dramaturgo.

dramatization [drɑːmətai'zeifən], dramatización.

dramatize [drɑːmətaiz], *v.t.* dramatizar.

dramaturgist [drɑmə'təːdʒist], *s.* dramaturgo.

dramaturgy, *s.* dramática.

dram-drinker, *s.* borrachín.

dram-shop, *s.* taberna.

drank [dræŋk], *pret.* [DRINK].

drape [dreip], *v.t.* vestir, colgar, poner colgaduras; entapizar.

draper, *s.* pañero; *linen draper*, lencero.

drapery, *s.* pañería, fábrica de paños; ropaje, cortinas, colgaduras, tapicería.

drastic ['dræstik], *a.* (*med.*) drástico; enérgico, intenso, violento.

drat [dræt], *int.* (*vulg.*) ¡diantre! ¡maldito sea!

draught [drɑːft], *s.* trago, bebida, pócima, brebaje, toma, dosis, *f.*, poción; esquicio, dibujo, traza, trazado, plan, plano, diseño; tracción, tiro, atracción; (*mil.*) destacamento; minuta, borrador, apuntación, esquema, *m.*; corriente de aire, *f.*; (*mar.*) cala o calado de un buque. — **draughts,** *pl.* juego de damas.

draught-board, *s.* tablero de damas.

draught-horse, *s.* caballo de tiro.

draughtsman, *s.* dibujante; delineante; peón del juego de damas.

draughty, *a.* expuesto a corrientes de aire.

draw [droə], *v.t., v.i.* (*pret.* **drew**; *p.p.* **drawn**) tirar, traer, atraer; arrastrar; aspirar; respirar, inspirar; cobrar; tomar, sacar, extraer; atraer, persuadir, inducir; deducir, inferir; arrancar; desenvainar, desnudar (la espada); correr, descorrer (cortinas); mamar, chupar; dibujar, bosquejar, delinear, representar, describir; (*com.*) girar; devengar (interés); redactar, escribir; destripar; secar, desecar; (*mar.*) calar; tirar bien, manar, fluir; proporcionarse, procurarse; moverse, adelantarse; sortear; *to draw along,* arrastrar; *to draw back,* retroceder, recular, volver hacia atrás; *to draw breath,* tomar aliento; *to draw forth,* hacer salir; *to draw from nature,* dibujar al natural; *to draw in,* atraer, seducir, embaucar; *to draw it mild,* (*fam.*) hablar sin exagerar; *to draw near,* acercarse; *to draw off,* extraer, sacar; retirarse; *to draw on,* (*com.*) girar; aproximarse; acercarse (de la noche); *to draw out,* alargar, sacar, dilatar, extender, desarrollar; sondear (una persona); *to draw over,* persuadir; *to draw the veil,* (*fig.*) correr un velo; *to draw together,* juntar; *to draw up,* tirar hacia arriba; redactar; (*mil.*) formar. — *s.* tiro, tirada, arrastre, tracción; retroceso; (*tej.*) pasada, carrera; (*fam.*) exitazo.

drawback, *s.* desventaja, inconveniente; descuento, rebaja.

drawbridge, *s.* puente levadizo.

drawee, *s.* (*com.*) girado, librado.

drawer, *s.* cajón, gaveta, naveta; aguador; mozo de taberna; (*com.*) girador, librador; extractor. — *pl.* **drawers,** calzoncillos, pantalones; *chest of drawers,* cómoda.

drawing, *s.* tiro, tirante, tirada; dibujo; extracción; sorteo.

drawing-board, *s.* tabla de dibujar.

drawing-frame, *s.* estirador.

drawing-master, *s.* profesor de dibujo.

drawing-paper, *s.* papel de dibujar.

drawing-pen, *s.* tiralíneas, *m.sing.*

drawing-room, *s.* salón.

drawing-school, *s.* escuela de dibujo.

drawl [droəl], *v.t., v.i.* arrastrar las palabras.

drawl, drawling, *s.* balbucencia, enunciación lenta.

drawn [droən], *p.p.* [DRAW]. — *a.* macilento, flaco, ojeroso; *long drawn out,* prolijo, pleonástico, latoso, larguísimo.

dray [drei], *s.* carro, carretón, carromato.

drayage, *s.* carretaje, acarreo.

dray-horse, *s.* caballo de carro.

drayman, *s.* carretero, carromatero.

dread [dred], *v.t., v.i.* temer, tener miedo; recelar. — *s.* espanto, terror, pavor. — *a.* espantoso, terrible, tremendo, formidable; respetable, augusto.

dreadful, *a.* terrible, terrorífico, espantoso, horrendo, horrible, tremendo, temible, tremebundo.

dreadfulness, *s.* horror, horridez, terribilidad.

dreadless, *a.* intrépido, sin miedo.

dreadlessness, *s.* intrepidez.

dreadnought ['drednoət], *s.* el que nada teme; tela muy doble; capote y capucha hecho de esta tela; (*mar.*) acorazado de combate construido en 1906 y que revolucionó la construcción naval.

dream [driːm], *s.* sueño, ensueño; ilusión; visión. — *v.t., v.i.* (*pret. y p.p.* **dreamed, dreamt**) soñar, desvariar, imaginar, fantasear, ver en sueños, hacerse ilusiones.

dreamer, *s.* soñador, visionario, iluso, utopista, *m.f.*

dreamily, dreamingly, *adv.* como en sueño, negligentemente.

dreamy, *a.* soñador, soñoliento.

drear [driːər], *s.* (*ant.*) espanto, horror. — *a.* espantoso, lúgubre, sombrío, triste.

drearily, *adv.* espantosamente, funestamente, tristemente.

dreariness, *s.* tristeza; horror, melancolía, lobreguez, soledad.

dreary, *a.* espantoso, lúgubre, sombrío, triste.

dredge [dredʒ], *v.t.* rastrear; enharinar; excavar, limpiar; dragar; polvorear. — *s.* red barredera; caja de harina para espolvorear.

dredger, *s.* pescador; draga; polvorera.

dredging-machine, *s.* draga.

dregginess, *s.* turbiedad, posos, heces, *f.pl.*

dreggish, dreggy, *a.* feculento, turbio.

dregs [dregz], *s.pl.* hez, *f.*, heces, *f.pl.*; sedimento, asiento; escoria, morralla; zupia; desperdicio; *dregs of the people, dregs of the town,* etc., hez del pueblo, populacho, canalla.

drench [drentʃ], *v.t.* empapar, embeber; ensopar, mojar, humedecer; (*vet.*) purgar con violencia. — *s.* tragantada; mojadar (*vet.*) bebida purgante; inundación, diluvio,

dress [dres], *v.t.* alinear, arreglar; allanar, aplanar; adiestrar; engalanar, adornar, acicalar, vestir; almohazar; ajustar, componer; curar (las heridas); preparar, guarnecer, arreglar, cocinar, guisar; aderezar; poner (la mesa); desbastar (madera); adobar, peinar, ataviar; (*mil.*) alinear; amortajar; podar (una viña). — *v.i.* alinearse; vestirse, ataviarse, componerse. — *s.* vestido, túnico, traje; atavío, tocado, compostura; *dress-circle,* (*teat.*) anfiteatro; *dress-coat,* frac; *dress-guard,* (*carr.*) guardafangos; *dress-suit,* traje de etiqueta.

dresser, *s.* aparador, prensador; cocinero; peluquero; moza de cámara; mesa de cocina; zurrador, adobador.

dressing, *s.* traje, vestido; adorno; condimento, salsa, aliño; (*cir.*) cura; (*agr.*) bina, renda; encoladura de paños, acabado en los tejidos; aderezamiento, aderezo; adobo; (*agr.*) abono, estercoladura; corta; *dressing-down,* (*fam.*) felpa, rapapolvo, salmorejo.

dressing-case, *s.* neceser, maleta.

dressing-gown, peinador, bata, batín, quimono.

dressing-room, *s.* cámara, gabinete; (*teat.*) camarín.

dressmaker, *s.* costurera, modista, *m.f.*

dressmaking, *s.* confección de vestidos; arte y oficio de la costurera o modista.

dressy, *a.* (*fam.*) vistoso, elegante, acicalado.

drew [druː], *pret.* [DRAW].

drib [drib], *v.t.* (*ant.*) desfalcar, cortar pedacitos de. — *v.i.* gotear. — *s.* gota.

dribble, *v.t.*, *v.i.* gotear; babear; hacer caer gota a gota; (*fútbol*) regatear.

driblet, *s.* pico, trozo, pedacito, gota.

dried [draid], *a.* desecado, seco. — *p.p.* [DRY].

drier, driest, *a. compar. y superl.* [DRY].

drift [drift], *s.* violencia, impulso, impulsión, móvil, torbellino; chaparrón; tempestad; rumbo, dirección, tendencia, giro; (*mar.*) dirección de una corriente, deriva; ángulo de deriva; cambio a sotavento; (*mec.*) broca, punzón; designio, intento; montón, rimero, hacina; (*fig.*) nube, *f.*, polvareda. — *v.t.* llevar, impeler, apilar, amontonar; (*min.*) abrir (una galería). — *v.i.* devalar, derivar; empujar; amontonarse, apilarse.

driftage, *s.* (*mar.*) deriva; (*arti.*) desviación.

drifting, *s.* empujamiento; amontonamiento.

driftway, *s.* (*mar.*) deriva; (*min.*) galería.

drill [dril], *v.t.* disciplinar, enseñar o hacer el ejercicio; taladrar, barrenar; perforar, trepar, agujerear; (*ant.*) desaguar; (*ant.*) derramar gota a gota. — *v.i.* plantar, sembrar en surcos, en líneas; (*ant.*) gotear; (*mil.*) hacer ejercicios. — *s.* taladro, perforador, broca; arroyuelo; (*joy.*) árbol; (*tej.*) tela cruda, dril; (*mil.*) instrucción; máquina para sembrar; *drill ground,* campo de maniobras; *drill sergeant,* sargento instructor.

drilling, *s.* perforación, trepa; ejercicio militar; siembra con máquina.

drink [driŋk], *v.t.*, *v.i.* (*pret.* **drank**; *p.p.* **drunk**, *ant.* **drunken**) beber, embeber, absorber, chupar; ser bebedor; emborracharse, embriagarse; *to drink down,* tragar; *to drink in,* absorber, embeber; *to drink someone's health,* beber a la salud de, brindar; *to drink like a fish,* beber como una cuba. — *s.* bebida, poción, trago.

drinkable, *a.* potable. — *s.* (*fam.*) bebida.

drinker, *s.* bebedor; borrachín.

drinking, *s.* acción de beber. — *a.* borracho.

drip [drip], *v.t.*, *v.i.* gotear, destilar; chorrear, verter *o* caer gota a gota. — *s.* gota; gotera; reguero; (*arq.*) alero.

dripping, *s.* chorreo, chorreadura; pringue, grasa; *dripping-pan,* pringuera, grasera.

drive [draiv], *v.t.*, *v.i.* (*pret.* **drove**; *p.p.* **driven**) estimular, aguijonear; mover, empujar, impeler, impulsar; inducir; arrojar, echar; llevar, conducir, guiar; reducir; gestionar, forzar, obligar; arrear, esclavizar; meter, clavar; ir en coche, cochear; manejar (caballos), cochear; (*min.*) abrir (una galería); *to drive away, drive off,* echar fuera, desterrar, ahuyentar; *to drive back,* rechazar; *to drive a bargain,* regatear, sacar provecho; *to drive mad,* hacer perder la cabeza; *to drive on,* empujar; seguir la marcha; *to drive out,* arrojar. — *s.* paseo en coche; calzada; avenida; presión, exigencia, urgencia; manada de reses; (*com.*) saldo, liquidación; (*aut.*) conducción; *left* (*right*) *hand drive,* conducción a la izquierda (derecha); (*mec.*) mecanismo de transmisión, transmisión; mando.

drivel [drivəl], *v.i.* babear; chochear, bobear. — *s.* baba; cháchara, ñoñería.

driveller, *s.* baboso, chocho; simple, fatuo.

drivelling, *a.* baboso, chocho. — *s.* baba; (*fig.*) chochez.

driver [draivəɹ], *s.* conductor; chófer; cochero, carretero, carruajero, calesero;

maquinista, *m.f.*; motor, fuerza motriz; (*mar.*) botalón de maricangalla.

driving, *s.* impulso; tendencia; arte de cochear. — *a.* impetuoso, violento, impulsivo; (*mec.*) motor, motriz; *driving-gloves,* guantes para guiar; *driving-shaft,* árbol motor; *driving-wheel,* rueda motriz; *driving-whip,* látigo.

drizzle [drizəl], *v.i.* lloviznar, molliznar, (*Amér.*) garuar. — *v.t.* destilar; rociar, salpicar. — *s.* llovizna, mollina, garúa.

drizzly, *a.* lloviznoso.

droit [drɔit], *s.* (*for.*) derecho, impuesto.

droll [drɔl], *a.* festivo, jocoso, chancero, chistoso, gracioso, raro. — *s.* bufón, chusco; farsa. — *v.i.* chocarrear, bromear.

drollery, *s.* chocarrería, bufonada, bufonería.

drollish, *a.* divertido.

dromedary [drɔmədəri], *s.* dromedario.

drone [droun], *s.* abejón, zangano; (*fig.*) perezoso, holgazán, haragán. — *v.i.* zanganear, holgazanear; zumbar.

droning, *s.* zumbido; (*fig.*) pereza.

dronish, *a.* ocioso.

droop [druːp], *v.i.* inclinar, caer; pender, colgar; descaecer, decaer; desfallecer; consumirse, marchitarse, pasarse; desanimarse, entristecerse. — *v.t.* inclinar, bajar. — *s.* caimiento, desfallecimiento; caída, inclinación.

drooping, *a.* desfalleciente, lánguido, alicaído; caído, inclinado; gacho.

drop [drɔp], *s.* gota, pinta; zarcillo; pendiente, *f.*, declive; pastilla; caimiento, caída; escotillón; *drop by drop,* *o by drops,* gota a gota; *drop curtain,* (*teat.*) telón de boca. — *v.t.* dejar caer, soltar; verter a gotas, derramar, destilar; polvorear, rociar; echar, despedir; dejar, abandonar; desprenderse de, renunciar a, desistir de; parir (los animales); (*fam.*) hacer caer, derribar, matar, (como con arma de fuego). — *v.i.* caer, descender, bajar, gotear, destilar, chorrear; parar, detenerse; caer muerto repentinamente; *to drop a subject,* cambiar de conversación; *to drop a hint,* dar a entender, soltar una indirecta; *to drop a line,* (*fam.*) poner o escribir (una carta); *to drop a curtsy,* hacer una reverencia; *to drop the curtain,* correr el telón; *to drop in,* visitar, entrar al pasar; *to drop off,* decaer, morir; quedar dormido; *to drop out,* desaparecer; separarse, retirarse, quedarse atrás.

droplet, *s.* gotita.

dropping, *s.* destilamiento, goteo; estilicidio; *dropping-bottle,* (*farm.*) cuentagotas, *m.*; *pl.* excrementos de animales, cagada.

droppingly, *adv.* a gotas.

dropsical, dropsied, *a.* hidrópico.

dropsy [drɔpsi], *s.* hidropesía.

dropwort, *s.* (*bot.*) filipéndula.

drosky [drɔʃki], *s.* carruaje ruso.

dross [drɔs], *s.* escoria; espuma; hez, *f.*; sedimento; horrura; basura; borra.

drossiness, *s.* hez, *f.*

drossy, *a.* lleno de escoria, espuma; impuro.

drought [draut], *s.* sequedad, sequía, seca; sed, *f.*; aridez, carestía, escasez.

droughtiness, *s.* sequedad, sequía.

droughty, *a.* seco, árido; sediento.

drove [drouv], *s.* manada, rebaño, recua, vecera, hato; multitud, muchedumbre, *f.*, gentío.

drover, s. ganadero.

drown [draun], v.t. ahogar, sumergir, inundar; sofocar; anegar. — v.i. ahogarse; anegarse.

drowse [drauz], v.t. adormecer. — v.i. adormecerse, amodorrarse, adormitarse.

drowsily, adv. soñolientamente, lentamente.

drowsiness, s. somnolencia, adormecimiento, modorra, soñera.

drowsy, a. soñoliento, adormecido, soporífero, amodorrado.

drub [drʌb], v.t. apalear, sacudir, pegar, tundir. — s. golpe, palo, puñada, paliza, tunda.

drubbing, s. golpes, puñadas, paliza, zurra, felpa.

drudge [drʌdʒ], v.t., v.i. trabajar mucho, afanarse, sudar, remar (en una ocupación desagradable). — s. ganapán; galopín, marmitón.

drudger, s. trabajador, jornalero; ganapán.

drudgery, s. faena ingrata, desagradable y vil.

drudging, s. trabajo penoso.

drudgingly, adv. penosamente, laboriosamente.

drug [drʌg], s. droga; medicamento; (fig.) cosa de poca venta o demanda. — v.t. mezclar con drogas, medicinar, jaropar; adormecer, narcotizar. — v.i. administrar drogas, medicinar.

drugget, s. droguete, buriel.

druggist, s. droguista, m.f., droguero, boticario.

Druid [dru:id], s. druida.

Druidic, a. druídico.

Druidism, s. druidismo.

drum [drʌm], s. tambor, caja; cilindro; barril, cuñete de pescado, de higos, etc.; tímpano del oído; (arq.) campana. — v.t., v.i. tamborilear; tocar el tambor, redoblar, repetir; teclear; zapatear; to drum out, echar a toque de tambor; kettle-drum, timbal; big drum, bombo.

drum-major, s. tambor mayor.

drummer, s. tambor (el que toca), redoblante; (E.U.) viajante.

drumstick, s. baqueta, palillo de tambor.

drunk [drʌŋk], a. borracho, embriagado, ebrio. — p.p. [DRINK]; to get drunk, embriagarse; to make drunk, emborrachar.

drunkard, s. borrachín, pellejo, cuba, f.

drunken, a. ebrio, embriagado, borracho.

drunkenness, s. embriaguez, borrachera, crápula.

drupe [dru:p], s. (bot.) drupa.

druse [dru:z], s. drusa.

dry [drai], a. seco, estéril, árido; sin jugo; desecado; (fig.) frío; enjuto; pobre, adusto; sediento; insulso; mordaz, áspero, guasón, agudo, satírico; crudo, duro; seco (vinos); dry-dock, atarazana, astillero, dique seco; dry nurse, niñera, ama de destete; dry goods, lencería; dry rot, carcoma; to be dry, (fam.) tener sed; dry land, tierra firme. — v.t. secar, desecar, desaguar, enjugar; pasar (fruta o ropa blanca); enjutar, dar sed. — v.i. secarse, desecarse, enjugarse.

dryad [draiəd], s. (mit.) dríada, lirón.

dryer, s. secante; (quím.) desecativo.

drying, a. desecativo.

dryness, s. sequedad, aridez.

drysalter [draisɔəltər], s. traficante en viandas saladas.

dryshod, a. a pie enjuto.

dual [djuːəl], a. dual.

dualism, s. dualidad, dualismo.

dualist, s. dualista, m.f.

duality [djuˈæliti], s. dualidad.

dub [dʌb], v.t. armar caballero; alisar; estregar, aderezar; conferir una dignidad, apellidar, dar título. — v.i. hacer ruido como el de un tambor, hacer tam tam.

dubbing, s. adobo impermeable; (mar.) aparado.

dubious [djuːbiəs], a. dudoso, irresoluto, indeciso, incierto, problemático; equívoco, obscuro, ambiguo; sospechoso.

dubiousness, s. incertidumbre, f., duda.

dubitable [djuːbitəbl], a. dudable.

ducal [djuːkəl], a. ducal.

ducat [dʌkət], s. ducado.

ducatoon [dʌkəˈtuːn], s. ducado de plata de un valor de medio ducado.

duchess [dʌtʃəs], s.f. duquesa.

duchy, s. ducado.

duck [dʌk], s. ánade, pato; hembra del pato en contraposición a drake, o macho; dril, lienzo fuerte no cruzado, para chaquetas, delantales etc.; pl. traje o pantalones hecho de este tejido; cabeceo; reverencia, saludo; zambullida, baño; cabrillas (juego de muchachos); (fam.) mona, querida, pichona; to play at ducks and drakes, hacer saltar una piedra sobre el agua; (fig.) derrochar, desperdiciar, malgastar, perder tiempo. — v.i. zabullirse, chapuzarse; cabecear, bajar la cabeza. — v.t. zabullir, chapuzar, dar chapuz.

ducking, s. zabullida; chapuz, baño de fuerza.

duck-legged, a. corto de piernas.

duckling, s. anadeja, patito.

ducky, s. (vulg., fig.) paloma, pollito, monina.

duct [dʌkt], s. conducto, tubo, canal.

ductile [dʌktail], a. dúctil, maleable; flexible, blando, dócil, tratable.

ductileness, ductility, s. ductilidad; docilidad.

dud, a. (fam.) falso, postizo; inútil, echadizo. — s. moneda falsa.

dude [djuːd], s. petimetre, currutaco.

dudgeon [dʌdʒən], s. la raíz de boj; puño de daga, puñal pequeño; mal humor, enojo, ojeriza; to go off in dudgeon, tomar en mala parte.

duds [dʌdz], s.pl. (vulg.) ropa vieja, trapos, andrajos.

due [djuː], a. debido, vencido, caído, cumplido, devengado; pagadero; apto, conveniente, propio, oportuno; legítimo; aguardado, cuya llegada está prevista o señalada; in due time, oportunamente, a su debido tiempo; due west, (mar.) poniente derecho; adv. debidamente, convenientemente, exactamente. — s. derecho, (lo) debido; to give the devil his due, ser justo hasta con el diablo.

duel [djuːəl], s. duelo, desafío; certamen. — v.t. acometer en duelo. — v.i. batirse, combatir en duelo.

dueller, s. duelista, m.f.

duelling, s. desafío.

duellist, s. duelista, m.f.

duenna [djuˈenə], s.f. dueña.

duet [djuˈet], **duetto,** s. (mús.) duo, dueto.

duff [dʌf], s. (fam.) pudín de harina muy duro, hervido en una bolsa de tejido.

duff, v.t. disimular, estafar, engañar.

duffel, s. (*tejido*) moletón.
dug [dʌg], teta. — v. pret. y p.p. [DIG].
dug-out, s. cueva; trinchera; canoa india, piragua.
duke [dju:k], s. duque.
dukedom, s. ducado.
dulcet ['dʌlsət], a. dulce, suave, agradable, placentero, armonioso.
dulcification [dʌlsifi'keiʃən], s. dulcificación.
dulcify ['dʌlsifai], v.t. dulcificar, (*quím.*) dulzurar, endulzar.
dulcimer, s. (*mús.*) tímpano; dulcémele.
dulcorate ['dʌlkəreit], v.t. (*ant.*) dulcificar.
dulcoration [dulkə'reiʃən], s. (*ant.*) dulcificación.
dull [dʌl], a. pesado; estúpido, torpe, embotado, lerdo, obtuso; soso, insulso, insípido; tosco; lánguido, desvaído, melancólico, pensativo, triste; sordo; opaco, ofuscado, nebuloso, obscuro, cubierto (del cielo), flojo; (*com.*) calmo; modorro, soñoliento; *dull of hearing*, algo sordo o duro de oído. — v.t. embotar, entontecer, entorpecer, obstruir; contristar; apagar, amortiguar; aliviar, suavizar, mitigar; deslumbrar; ofuscar, deslustrar, empañar, deslucir.
dullard ['dʌlɑɪd], s., a. estúpido, tonto.
dull-head, s. zopenco.
dull-sighted, a. cegato.
dull-witted, a. estúpido, lerdo, embotado.
dully, adv. torpemente, estúpidamente.
dulness, dullness, s. torpeza, estupidez, tontería, embotamiento, somnolencia, entorpecimiento; pereza, pesadez; prosaísmo; deslustre.
dulse [dʌls], s. alga marina comestible de Irlanda y Escocia.
duly [dju:li], adv. debidamente, puntualmente, a su debido tiempo.
dumb [dʌm], a. mudo, callado; latente, oculto; (*fam.*) tonto, torpe; *to strike dumb*, dejar sin habla; *dumb show*, pantomima; *dumb waiter*, (*E.U.*) ascensor doméstico; (*Ingl.*) estante giratorio para vajilla, servicio de mesa, etc. — v.t. imponer silencio.
dumbfound, v.t. confundir, hacer callar; dejar sin habla, pasmar.
dumbfounded, a. sin habla, confundido, pasmado.
dumbness, s. mudez.
dummy ['dʌmi], s. mudo; muerto (juego de whist); maniquí para vestidos, pelucas, etc.; contrafigura, títere; chupador (de bebé). — a. fingido, falseado.
dump [dʌmp], v.t. descargar, vaciar de golpe; exportar y vender a bajo precio artículos invendibles en el país de origen. — s.pl. (*fam.*) melancolía, tristeza; vaciamiento; *to dump down*, descargarse de; *to have the dumps*, tener murria.
dumpish, a. melancólico, triste, murrio.
dumpishness, s. tristeza, murria.
dumpling, s. especie de pudín.
dumpy, a. rechoncho, regordete.
dun [dʌn], a. pardo, bruno, castaño (de un caballo). — v.t. importunar (a un deudor). — s. acreedor importuno, apremio.
dunce [dʌns], s. zote, zopenco, tonto.
dunderhead ['dʌndəɹhed], s. zote, tonto, zopenco.
dune [dju:n], s. duna, marisma.
dung [dʌŋ], s. estiércol, fimo; abono; cagada,

cagarruta; *cow-dung*, boñiga; *dog's dung*, canina; *hen-dung*, gallinaza; *horse-dung*, cagajón. — v.t., v.i. estercolar, abonar; emboñigar (telas).
dungeon [dʌndʒən], s. mazmorra, calabozo.
dunghill, s. muladar, estercolero, basurero.
dungy [dʌŋi], a. lleno de estiércol, puerco, sucio.
dunnage ['dʌnidʒ], s. (*mar.*) abarrote.
dunner, s. agente de negocios, cobrador de deudas atrasadas, el que importuna a un deudor.
dunnish, a. moreno claro.
duo ['dju:ou], s. dúo.
duodecimo [dju:ou'desimou], s. libro en dozavo, cuya página es de 4½ pulg. por 7½ pulg.
duodenum [dju:o'di:nəm], s. duodeno.
dupe [dju:p], s. crédulo, incauto, víctima de engaño. — v.t. engañar, embaucar.
duple, v.t. duplicar, doblar.
duple, duplex, a. duplo, doble, dúplice.
duplicate ['dju:plikət], v.t. duplicar, reproducir, copiar, plegar. — s. duplicado, copia. — a. duplicado, doble.
duplication [dju:pli'keiʃən], s. duplicación, doblez, pliegue, plegadura.
duplicator ['dju:plikeitəɹ], s. duplicador, copiador.
duplicature [dju:pli'keitʃəɹ], s. plegadura, pliegue, doblez.
duplicity [dju'plisiti], s. duplicidad, doblez, engaño.
durability [djuərə'biliti], s. duración; estabilidad, permanencia.
durable ['djuərəbl], a. durable, duradero, permanente, estable.
durableness, s. dura, duración.
duramater [djurə'meitəɹ], s. (*anat.*) duramáter, f.; (*zool.*) duramadre, f.
durance ['djuərəns], s. prisión, cautividad, encierro; (en chiste) continuación, duración.
duration [djuə'reiʃən], s. duración, continuación, permanencia, estabilidad.
durbar ['də:ɹbɑɹ], s. corte de un príncipe de la India.
duress [djuə'res], s. encierro, prisión; compulsión, coacción.
during, prep. durante, mientras.
durst, pret. ant. [DARE].
dusk [dʌsk], s. obscuridad; crepúsculo, nochecita. — a. obscuro, obscurecido; *at dusk*, entre dos luces.
duskily, adv. obscuramente.
duskiness, s. obscuridad, principio de la obscuridad.
dusky, a. obscuro; fusco; pardo, moreno.
dust [dʌst], s. polvo; (*fam.*) alboroto, ruido; cenizas, restos mortales; humillación, abyección; basura, barreduras, residuos; (*vulg.*) dinero. — v.t. polvorear, despolvar, despolvorear, quitar el polvo; *saw-dust*, aserraduras; *to raise a dust*, (*fam.*) armar bronquina.
dust-brush, s. plumero.
dust-cap, s. (*aut.*) sombrerete de válvula, tapa guardapolvo.
dust-cart, s. carro de la basura.
duster, s. plumero, guardapolvo; paño para el polvo.
dust-guard, s. guardapolvo.
dust-hole, s. basurero.

dustiness, *s.* polvo, estado polvoriento.
dustman, *s.* basurero, barrendero.
dust-pan, *s.* pala de recoger la basura.
dusty, *a.* polvoroso, polvoriento, lleno de polvo.
Dutch [dʌtʃ], *s.*, *a.* holandés.
duteous [djuːtiəs], *a.* obediente, respetuoso, obsequioso, sumiso.
dutiable, *a.* imponible, sujeto a impuestos.
dutiful, *a.* obediente, sumiso, respetuoso, rendido.
dutifulness, *s.* obediencia, sumisión, respeto.
duty [djuːti], *s.* deber, obligación; sumisión, acatamiento, obediencia; servicio; facción; (*mec.*) trabajo mecánico; derechos, impuesto, adeudo; *duty free*, libre de derechos; *to be on duty*, estar de guardia.
duumvir [djuʌmvəɹ], *s.* (*pl.* **duumviri**) duúnviro.
duumviral, *a.* duunviral.
duumvirate, *s.* duunvirato.
dwale [dweil], *s.* belladona; narcótico; (*blas.*) sable.
dwarf [dwɔːɹf], *s.* enano, enana. — *a.* enano, diminuto. — *v.t.* achicar, empequeñecer; impedir el crecimiento. — *v.i.* achicarse, empequeñecerse.
dwarfish, *a.* enano, pequeño, diminuto, bajo.
dwarfishly, *adv.* como un enano.
dwarfishness, *s.* pequeñez de estatura.
dwell [dwel], *v.i.* habitar, residir, morar, vivir; hallarse; pararse, detenerse; dilatarse.
dweller, *s.* morador, habitante.
dwelling, *s.* domicilio, casa, morada, vivienda.
dwindle [dwindl], *v.t.* disminuir, rebajar. — *v.i.* disminuirse, mermar, menguar; dacaer, degenerar; consumirse.
dyad [ˈdaiəd], *s.* dos unidades tratadas como una; grupo de dos, par, pareja; (*quím.*) elemento diatómico, o radical.
dye [dai], *v.t.*, *v.i.* teñir, tintar, tinturar, colorar. — *s.* tinte, tintura; sello, marca; color, matiz.
dyeing, *s.* tinte, tintura, tintorería.
dyer, *s.* tintorero.
dyer's broom, *s.* (*bot.*) ginesta.
dye-wood, *s.* madera de tinte.
dying [ˈdaiiŋ], *a.* moribundo, mortal, agonizante; mortecino; *dying words*, últimas palabras; *to be dying for*, estar muerto por.
dynam [ˈdainæm], *s.* dinamia.
dynameter [daiˈnæmətəɹ], *s.* dinámetro.
dynametrical, *a.* dinamométrico.
dynamic [daiˈnæmik], **dynamical**, *a.* dinámico, eficaz.
dynamics, *s.pl.* dinámica.
dynamite [ˈdainəmait], *s.* dinamita.
dynamiter, *s.* dinametero.
dynamo [ˈdainəmou], *s.* dinamo, *f.*
dynamometer [dainəˈmɔmətəɹ], *s.* dinamómetro.
dynamometric, **dynamometrical**, *a.* dinamométrico.
dynast, *s.* dinasta, *m.*
dynastic [diˈnæstik], *a.* dinástico.
dynasty [ˈdinəsti], *s.* dinastía.
dyne [dain], *s.* (*fís.*) dina.
dyscrasia [disˈkreisiə], **dyscrasy** [ˈdiskrəsi], *s.* discrasia.
dysenteric [disənˈterik], *a.* disentérico.
dysentery [ˈdisəntri], *s.* disentería.

dyspepsia [disˈpepsiə], **dyspepsy**, *s.* dispepsia.
dyspeptic, *a.* dispéptico; indigesto; quejoso, mórbido.
dysphagia [disˈfeidʒiə], *s.* disfagia.
dysphonia [disˈfouniə], *s.* disfonía.
dyspnœa [dispˈniːə], *s.* disnea.
dysury [diˈsjuəri], *s.* disuria.

E

E, e [iː], quinta letra del alfabeto inglés; (*mús.*) mi.
each [iːtʃ], *pr.*, *a.* cualquier, cualquiera; cada, cada uno, cada una; *each other*, el uno al otro, unos a otros; uno sí y otro no.
eager [iːgəɹ], *a.* deseoso, ansioso, ávido, anhelante, ardiente, fogoso, apasionado, impaciente, vehemente; (*ant.*) agrio, acedo.
eagerness, *s.* ansia, anhelo, ahinco, avidez, vehemencia, violencia.
eagle [iːgl], *s.* (*orn.*) águila; *eagle-eyed*, de vista de lince.
eagless [ˈiːgləs], *s.f.* hembra del águila.
eaglet, *s.* aguilucho.
eagle-winged, *a.* alado como águila.
ear [iəɹ], *s.* oreja, oído; atención; (*bot.*) espiga; asa, asidero; *by ear*, de oído, de oídas; *to prick up one's ears*, aguzar el oído; *to be head over ears in debt*, estar cargado de deudas; *to turn a deaf ear to*, no hacerle a uno el menor caso. — *v.i.* espigar, echar espigas.
earache, *s.* dolor de oídos.
eardrop, *s.* pendiente, zarcillo, (*Cuba*) arete.
ear-drum, *s.* tímpano del oído.
eared, *a.* espigado; *long-eared*, orejudo.
earing, *s.* (*mar.*) empuñidura de una vela; *reef-earings*, (*mar.*) empuñiduras de rizas.
earl [əːɹl], *s.* conde.
earlap, *s.* lóbulo de la oreja.
earldom, *s.* condado.
earless, *a.* desorejado.
earlier, **earliest**, *a. compar.* y *superl.* [EARLY].
earliness, *s.* precocidad; prontitud, presteza; anticipación, antelación.
early, *a.* avanzado, anticipado, precoz; matinal, temprano; primitivo; próximo, cercano a suceder o acontecer; *to rise early*, madrugar; *early riser*, madrugador. — *adv.* temprano; luego; de madrugada; al principio.
earmark, *s.* marca en la oreja; marca, contraseña. — *v.t.* marcar, traseñalar, destinar.
earn [əːɹn], *v.t.* merecer, ganar; devengar.
earnest [ˈəːɹnist], *a.* fervoroso, ardiente; ansioso; serio, sincero, formal; cuidadoso, atento; extremo; activo, diligente, celoso; *earnest entreaties*, vivas instancias. — *s.* seriedad, sinceridad, buena fe; seriedad; primicias; prendas, señal, *f.*; *in earnest*, seriamente, formalmente, de buena fe.
earnestness, *s.* ansia, celo, ardor; seriedad, gravedad, formalidad, diligencia.
earnings, *s.pl.* salario, estipendio, honorarios, paga, jornal; (*com.*) ingresos, ganancias.
earring, *s.* zarcillo, pendiente, arete.
earshot, *s.* alcance del oído.
earth [əːɹθ], *s.* tierra, terreno, suelo; región, país; gente, *f.*, mundo; madriguera; *fuller's earth*, tierra de batán. — *v.i.* retirarse, esconderse, buscar asilo bajo tierra; (*elec.*) (pérdida a) tierra. — *v.t.* cubrir con tierra, enterrar; (*elec.*) poner a tierra.

earth-bank, *s.* terraplén.
earth-board, *s.* orejera del arado.
earth-born, *a.* terrígeno; humano, mortal; de bajo nacimiento.
earthen, *a.* térreo, terroso, de barro.
earthenware, *s.* vajilla (*o* loza) de barro.
earthiness, *s.* terrenidad, materia terrosa; grosería.
earthliness, *s.* terrenidad, mundanalidad.
earthly, *a.* térreo, terrestre, terrero, terreno, terrenal, mundano, temporal, carnal, sensual; *earthly-minded*, mundano.
earth-nut, *s.* trufa, cacahuete, maní.
earthquake, *s.* terremoto, temblor de tierra.
earth-worm, *s.* lombriz de tierra.
earthy, *a.* térreo, terroso; grosero, basto; (*elec.*) puesto a tierra.
eartrumpet, *s.* trompetilla.
earwig ['iəɹwig], *s.* (*entom.*) tijereta; (*fig.*) cuchicheador.
ease [iːz], *s.* quietud, tranquilidad, reposo; holgura, ocio, alivio, comodidad, desahogo, descanso; facilidad, desenvoltura; naturalidad; *at ease*, con desahogo; *with ease*, fácilmente, con facilidad; *to take one's ease*, ponerse a sus anchas. — *v.t.* mitigar, aliviar, suavizar, templar, ablandar; dar alivio; desembarazar, descargar; *to ease off*, (*mar.*) arriar, lascar.
easeful, *a.* quieto, tranquilo.
easel ['iːzl], *s.* caballete.
easeless, *a.* inquieto.
easement ['iːzmənt], *s.* comodidad, descarga, alivio; (*for.*) servidumbre, *f.*
easily, *adv.* fácilmente; tranquilamente.
easiness, *s.* facilidad, suavidad; despejo, soltura, desembarazo; tranquilidad, quietud; gracia; comodidad, bienestar.
east [iːst], *s.* este, oriente, levante. — *a.* oriental, levantino, del este.
Easter ['iːstəɹ], *s.* Pascua de Resurrección, Pascua florida; *Easter Day*, día de Pascua; domingo de resurrección (*o* de gloria); *Easter Eve*, sábado santo, sábado de gloria.
easterly, *a.*, *adv.* oriental, al este, del este, hacia el este.
eastern, *a.* oriental.
eastward, *adv.* hacia el este (*o* oriente).
easy ['iːzi], *a.* fácil; cómodo; holgado, acomodado, accesible, asequible, complaciente; condescendiente; natural, simple; despacio; libre; dulce, suave; afable; cortés, sociable; *easy chair*, butaca, sillón; *to be under easy sail*, (*mar.*) llevar poca vela; *to take it easy*, tomar a su gusto; *by easy stages*, poco a poco; *easy-going*, transigente, acomodadizo, de manga ancha; indolente, tardo, descuidado.
eat [iːt], *v.t.* (*pret.* ate; *p.p.* eaten) comer; cenar, almorzar; masticar; roer; usar, gastar. — *v.t.* mantenerse, sustentarse, alimentarse; comer; morder, roer; *to eat one's words*, (*fig.*) corroer, socavar; desdecirse; *to eat away*, comer con gusto; *to eat up*, comerse, devorar; (*fig.*) devorar, destruir, arruinar.
eatable, *a.* comedero, comestible. — *s.* comestible. — *pl.* **eatables**, comestibles, víveres.
eater, *s.* comedor, camilón, tragón.
eating, *s.* comida.
eating-house, *s.* fonda, hostería, bodegón.
eaves [iːvz], *s.pl.* alero, socarrén, tejaroz.
eavesdrop, *v.i.* espiar, escuchar a las puertas; fisgonear, atisbar.

eavesdropper, *s.* fisgón, escucha, espía, *m.f.*
eavesdropping, *s.* espionaje, fisgoneo.
ebb [eb], *v.i.* retroceder; decaer, disminuir, menguar. — *s.* (*mar.*) menguante, reflujo; (*fig.*) decadencia; *ebb of life*, vejez; *ebb tide*, marea menguante.
ebbing, *s.* reflujo.
ebon ['ebən], *a.* hecho de ébano, negro.
ebonist, *s.* ebanista, *m.f.*
ebonite ['ebənait], *s.* ebonita.
ebonize, *v.t.* ebonizar, dar a la madera el color del ébano.
ebony, *s.* ébano.
ebriety [i'braiəti], *s.* ebriedad, embriaguez.
ebullience [ə'bʌliəns], **ebulliency**, *s.* ebullición; efervescencia.
ebullient, *a.* hirviente.
ebullition [ebu'liʃən], *s.* hervor, ebullición; (*fig.*) viva emoción, transporte; (*quím.*) efervescencia.
eburnean [e'bəːɹniən], *a.* ebúrneo.
ecaudate [e'kɔːdeit], *a.* (*zool.*) sin cola, sin rabo; (*bot.*) sin espiga, sin tallo.
eccentric, eccentrical [ek'sentrikl], *a.* excéntrico; extravagante, disparatado, estrafalario, estrambótico.
eccentric, *s.* excéntrico, persona estrafalaria; (*mec.*) rueda excéntrica; desvío del centro.
eccentricity [eksen'trisiti], *s.* excentricidad.
ecchymosis [eki'mousis], *s.* equimosis, *f.*
ecclesiastic, ecclesiastical [ekliːzi'æstikl], *a.*; **ecclesiastic**, *s.* eclesiástico.
ecclesiology [ekliːzi'ɔlədʒi], *s.* ciencia que trata los asuntos de la Iglesia (especialmente la arquitectura, decoración, etc.).
echelon ['eʃəlɔn], *s.* (*mil.*) escalón.
echinas [ə'kainəs], *s.* (*arq.*) gallón; erizo.
echinate, echinated [ə'kainətid], *a.* (*bot.*) erizado, cubierto de cerdas o púas.
echinoderm [ə'kinədəɹm], *a.* (*zool.*) equinodermo.
echinus, *s.* erizo de mar, equino, estrellamar; (*arq.*) cuarto bocel, miembro de moldura.
echo ['ekou], *s.* eco. — *v.i.* resonar, reverberar, repetir, formar eco. — *v.t.* repercutir, imitar.
echometer [e'kɔmətəɹ], *s.* ecómetro.
echometry, *s.* ecometría.
eclat [ə'klɑ], *s.* esplendor, magnificiencia, lustre; aclamación, aplauso; celebridad, renombre.
eclectic [ə'klektik], *a.* ecléctico; liberal, tolerante.
eclecticism, *s.* eclectismo.
eclipse [ə'klips], *s.* eclipse. — *v.t.* eclipsar, extinguir. — *v.i.* eclipsarse.
ecliptic, *a.* eclíptico. — *s.* eclíptica.
eclogue ['eklɔg], *s.* égloga.
economic, economical [iːkə'nɔmikl], *a.* económico, moderado, frugal; parco.
economics, *s.* economía, política.
economist [ə'kɔnəmist], *s.* economista, *m.f.*, hacendista, *m.f.*
economize, *v.t.*, *v.i.* economizar, ahorrar, administrar con prudencia.
economy, *s.* economía; frugalidad, parsimonia.
ecostate [ə'kɔsteit], *a.* (*bot.*) sin costillas centrales (como algunas hojas).
ecstasy ['ekstəsi], *s.* éxtasis, éxtasi, rapto, arrobamiento, exaltación, transporte. — *v.t.* extasiar.

ecstatic, ecstatical [ek'stætikl], *a.* extático, absorto, arrobado.
ecstatically, *adv.* extáticamente.
ectype ['ektaip], *s.* ectipo, copia.
ecumenic, ecumenical ['i:kju'menikl], *a.* ecuménico.
eczema ['ekzəmə], *s.* (*med.*) eczema, herpe, *m.f.*
edacious [ə'deiʃəs], *a.* voraz, glotón, comedor.
edaciousness, edacity, *s.* voracidad, glotonería.
eddish, *s.* heno tardío.
eddy ['edi], *s.* barra, reflujo de agua; reversa, remanso, regolfo, remolino. — *a.* remolinado. — *v.t., v.i.* arremolinar, remolinar(se), regolfar, remansarse; *eddy wind,* torbellino de viento; *eddy water,* estela, agua muerta.
edema, [ə'di:me], *s.* edema, *m.*
edematous, edematose [ə'di:mətouz], *a.* edematoso.
Eden ['i:dən], *s.* Edén, paraíso.
edentalous [ə'dentələs], *a.* desdentado.
edentate, edentated, *a.* desdentado.
edge [edʒ], *s.* filo, corte; punta, extremidad, agudeza; margen, *m.f.*; borde, canto; orilla, ribete; (*fig.*) acrimonia, amargura, indirecta; *to set one's teeth on edge,* dar dentera; *to be on edge,* (*fig.*) estar en ascuas; *to take the edge off,* embotar. — *v.t., v.i.* aguzar, afilar; ribetear; guarnecer; estimular, excitar, exasperar, aguijonear, incitar; avanzar poco a poco; *to edge away* or *out,* alejarse, salir poquito a poco. — *a.* cortante, afilado.
edged, *a.* agudo, cortante, afilado, acerado; (*fig.*) mordaz.
edgeless, *a.* obtuso, embotado.
edgeways, edgewise, *a.* de filo, de canto, de sesgo, de lado, oblicuamente.
edging, *s.* orla, orilla, ribete; trepado; guarnición.
edible ['edibl], *s., a.* comestible.
edict ['i:dikt], *s.* edicto, decreto, mandato, ordenanza.
edictal, *a.* edictal.
edification [edifi'keiʃən], *s.* edificación, instrucción, ilustración.
edificatory, *a.* edificatorio, instructivo.
edifice ['edifis], *s.* edificio, fábrica.
edificial [edi'fiʃəl], *a.* edificatorio.
edifier ['edifaiəɹ], *s.* edificador, edificante.
edify, *v.t.* edificar, instruir, ilustrar, enseñar.
edifying, *a.* edificante, edificativo. — *s.* edificación.
edile ['i:dail], *s.* edil.
edileship, *s.* edilidad.
edit ['edit], *v.t.* editar; redactar; dirigir, adaptar.
edition [e'diʃən], *s.* edición, publicación, impresión, tirada.
editor ['editəɹ], *s.* editor, director (de un periódico).
editorial [edi'toəriəl], *a.* editorial. — *s.* artículo de fondo.
editorship, *s.* cargo de redactor.
educate ['edjukeit], *v.t.* educar, criar, instruir, enseñar.
educated, *a.* culto.
education [edju'keiʃən], *s.* educación, instrucción, enseñanza, ilustración.
educational, *a.* relativo a la enseñanza.
educator, *s.* educador, instructor, maestro.

educe [ə'dju:s], *v.t.* educir, extraer.
educt [ə'dʌkt], *s.* producto, extracto, resultado.
eduction, *s.* educción.
edulcorate [ə'dʌlkəreit], *v.t.* edulcorar, endulzar, dulzurar.
edulcoration [ədʌlkə'reiʃən], *s.* edulcoración, dulcificación; (*quím.*) purificación de alguna substancia por el lavado.
edulcorative, *a.* dulcificante.
eel [i:l], *s.* anguila; *electric eel,* gimnoto.
e'en, *adv. contr.* [EVEN].
e'er, *adv. contr.* [EVER].
eerie, eery ['iəri], *a.* espantoso, fantástico, espectral, sobrenatural, inexplicable.
eeriness, *n.* ambiente misterioso, espantoso y espectral.
efface [ə'feis], *v.t.* borrar, cancelar, destruir, tachar.
effaceable, *a.* deleble.
effacement, *s.* canceladura; tachón.
effect [ə'fekt], *s.* efecto, resultado, consecuencia, eficacia, eficiencia; realidad, substancia, significado, fin, mira, intento, designio; operación, ejecución; impresión; vigor, fuerza; realización, cumplimiento; *to take effect,* producir su efecto, salir bien; *in effect,* efectivamente. — **effects,** *pl.* efectos, bienes, (muebles o raíces); caudal. — *v.t.* efectuar, producir, ejecutar, poner por obra, llevar a cabo.
effective, *a.* efectivo, eficiente, eficaz, enérgico, operativo.
effectiveness, *s.* eficiencia, eficacia.
effectless, *a.* ineficaz, sin efecto.
effector, *s.* causa eficiente; causador.
effectual [ə'fektjuəl], *a.* eficaz, activo, eficiente.
effectualness, *s.* eficacia.
effectuate, *v.t.* efectuar, ejecutar.
effeminacy [ə'feminəsi], *s.* afeminación, molicie, *f.*
effeminate, *a.* afeminado, voluptuoso. — *s.* hombre afeminado.
effeminateness, *s.* afeminación.
effeminize, *v.t.* afeminar.
efferent ['efərənt], *a.* eferente.
effervesce [efəɹ'ves], *v.i.* hervir, fermentar, estar en efervescencia.
effervescence, *s.* efervescencia.
effervescent, *a.* efervescente.
effervescible, *a.* fermentable.
effervescing, *a.* gaseoso.
effete [ə'fi:t], *a.* usado, gastado, cascado; infructuoso, estéril.
efficacious [efi'keiʃəs], *a.* eficaz, eficiente, activo, vivo, fuerte, poderoso.
efficaciousness, efficacy, *s.* eficacia, eficiencia.
efficience, efficiency [ə'fiʃənsi], *s.* eficiencia, eficacia, actividad, virtud.
efficient, *a.* eficiente, eficaz, activo, competente. — *s.* hacedor, causador; causa eficiente; (*mat.*) factor.
effigy ['efidʒi], *s.* efigie, *f.*, imagen, *f.*, retrato.
efflation [e'fleiʃən], *s.* insuflación, emanación; soplo.
effloresce [eflə'res], *v.i.* (*quím.*) eflorescer(se).
efflorescence, *s.* eflorescencia, florescencia.
efflorescent, *a.* eflorescente, en flor.
effluence ['efluəns], *s.* emanación, efusión, efluxión.
effluent, *a.* efluente.

effluvium [ə'fluːviəm], (*pl.* **effluvia**) efluvio, emanación, exhalación, vaho, tufo.

efflux [e'flʌks], *s.* flujo, derrame; efusión, emanación.

effluxion [e'flʌkʃən], *s.* emanación, exhalación, efluvio.

efforce [e'fəːɹs], *v.t.* forzar, violar, hacer violencia.

effort ['efəɹt], *s.* esfuerzo, empeño, conato; *to make efforts*, esforzarse, hacer esfuerzos.

effortless, *a.* sin esfuerzos.

effrontery [ə'frʌntəri], *s.* desvergüenza, descaro, desfachatez, impudencia.

effulge [ə'fʌldʒ], *v.i.* lucir, resplandecer.

effulgence, *s.* resplandor, esplendor, lustre, fulgor.

effulgent, *a.* resplandeciente, refulgente, esplendoroso.

effuse [ə'fjuːz], *v.t.* derramar, verter, efundir, desparramar. — *v.i.* derramarse; emanar; espaciarse, dilatarse. — *a.* pródigo, disipado; (*bot.*) esparcido, divergente.

effusion, *s.* efusión, derrame, derramamiento, expansión.

effusive, *a.* expansivo, difusivo, demostrativo, comunicativo.

eft [eft], *s.* lagartija, salamandra acuática.

egad! *interj.* (*ant.*) ¡pardiez!

egence ['iːdʒəns], *s.* estado necesitoso.

egg [eg], *s.* huevo; *boiled egg*, huevo pasado por agua; *fried egg*, huevo frito; *new-laid egg*, huevo fresco; *scrambled eggs*, huevos revueltos. — *v.t.* cubrir o mezclar con huevo; *to egg on*, hurgar, incitar, provocar a.

egg-cup, *s.* huevera.

egg-merchant, *s.* huevero.

egg-plant, *s.* berenjena.

egg-shaped, *a.* oviforme.

egg-shell, *s.* cascarón.

egis [iːdʒis], *s.* egida, escudo.

eglantine ['egləntain], *s.* (*bot.*) eglantina; agavanzo.

egoism ['egouizm], *s.* egoísmo.

egoist ['egouist], *s.* egoísta, *m.f.*

egoistic, egoistical [egou'istikl], *a.* egoístico.

egotism ['egoutizm], *s.* egotismo.

egotist, *s.* egoísta, *m.f.*

egotistic, egotistical [egou'tistikl], *a.* egoísta.

egotize ['egoutaiz], *v.i.* alabarse, vanagloriarse, hablar mucho de sí mismo.

egregious [ə'griːdʒəs], *a.* egregio, insigne, notorio.

egregiousness, *s.* eminencia.

egress, egression [i'greʃən], *s.* salida.

egret ['iːgret], *s.* (*orn.*) especie de garza; plumero; (*bot.*) pelusa.

egrette ['iːgret], *s.* plumero, penacho.

egriot ['egriət], *s.* (*bot.*) guinda.

Egyptian [i'dʒipʃən], *s., a.* egipcio, egipciaco.

Egyptologist [iːdʒip'tɔlədʒist], *s.* egiptólogo.

eh [ei], *interj.* ¡eh! ¡he! ¡hola! ¿qué?

eider, eider-duck ['aidəɹdʌk], *s.* (*orn.*) pato de flojel.

eider-down, *s.* edredón, plumazón.

eidograph ['aidəgræf], *s.* eidógrafo.

eight [eit], *a.* ocho.

eighteen, *a.* diez y ocho, dieciocho.

eighteenth, *a.* décimoctavo.

eightfold, *a.* octuplo, óctuple.

eighth [eitθ], *a.* octavo.

eighthly, *a.* en el octavo lugar.

eightieth, *a.* octogésimo.

eight-sided, *a.* octágono.

eighty, *a.* ochenta.

either ['aiðəɹ], *pron., a.* cualquiera, cada uno, cada una, uno de dos, uno u otro, ambos, entrambos. — *conj.* o, sea, ya; también, tampoco.

ejaculate [ə'dʒækjuleit], *v.t.* exclamar, proferir, pronunciar; arrojar, disparar; eyacular.

ejaculation [ədʒækju'leiʃən], *s.* exclamación, jaculatoria; eyaculación, emisión.

ejaculatory, *a.* jaculatorio, súbito, repentino.

eject [ə'dʒekt], *v.t.* arrojar, expeler, echar, expulsar, lanzar, despedir, desalojar, destituir; despojar; (*med.*) evacuar.

ejection, *s.* expulsión, exclusión, echamiento; (*der.*) despojo; (*med.*) evacuación.

ejectment, *s.* expulsión, exclusión; (*der.*) desahucio.

ejector, *s.* eyector, desposeedor, expulsor.

eke [iːk], *v.t.* añadir, aumentar; *to eke out*, economizar, escatimar, componérselas. — *adv.* también, además.

elaborate [ə'læbəreit], *v.t.* elaborar, labrar; amplificar, ampliar. — *a.* elaborado, acabado, trabajado, detallado.

elaborately, *adv.* cuidadosamente, con muchos detalles, primorosamente.

elaborateness, *s.* primor, perfección, corrección; amplificación, enredo.

elaboration [ələbə'reiʃən], *s.* elaboración, obra acabada.

elaborator [ə'læbəreitəɹ], *s.* artífice.

elance [ə'lɑːns], *v.t.* lanzar, arrojar.

eland ['iːlənd], *s.* alce, anta.

elapse [ə'læps], *v.i.* pasar, transcurrir.

elastic [ə'læstik], *a.* elástico. — *s.* elástico, goma.

elasticity [elæs'tisiti], *s.* elasticidad.

elate [ə'leit], *v.t.* exaltar, elevar, endiosar, engreír, ensoberbecer.

elate, elated, *a.* altivo, engreído, exaltado, triunfante; regocijado, jubiloso, animado.

elation [ə'leiʃən], *s.* engreimiento, altivez, elación; regocijo, júbilo, animación.

elbow ['elbou], *s.* codo; recodo, codillo, ángulo; brazo de sillón; *at one's elbow*, (*fig.*) a la mano; *elbow-chair*, silla de brazos, poltrona; *elbow-grease*, juego de codos, trabajo asiduo; *elbow-room*, anchura, libertad, desahogo. — *v.t.* codear, dar codazos, dar de codo a. — *v.i.* formar recodos o esquinas.

elder ['eldəɹ], *a. comp.* mayor, más viejo, más anciano, de más edad. — *s.* anciano, mayor, jefe de familia; (*bot.*) saúco; dignatario, funcionario, eclesiástico. — *pl.* **elders**, ancianos, antepasados.

elder-berry, *s.* baya del saúco.

elderly, *a.* mayor de edad.

eldership, *s.* ancianidad; primogenitura; presbiterato.

eldest, *a. superl.* el más anciano, el mayor, primogénito.

elecampane [elikæm'pein], *s.* (*bot.*) enula campana (*Inula Helenium*).

elect [ə'lekt], *v.t.* elegir, escoger, designar; elegir por mayoría de votos. — *s., a.* elegido, escogido, electo; (*teo.*) predestinado.

election, *s.* elección; (*teo.*) predestinación.

electioneer [əlekʃə'niəɹ], *v.i.* hacer propaganda electoral, solicitar (votos).

electioneering, *s.* maniobras electorales.

elective [ə'lektiv], *a.* electivo.

elector, s. elector.

electoral, a. electoral.

electorate, s. electorado.

electoress, s.f. electriz.

electorial [elek'tɔːriəl], a. electoral.

electorship [ə'lektəɹʃip], s. electorado.

electress, s.f. electriz.

electric, electrical, a. eléctrico; (fig.) vivo, fogoso, magnético.

electrically, adv. eléctricamente.

electrician [elek'triʃən], s. electricista, m.f.

electricity [elek'triciti], s. electricidad.

electrification, s. electrificación.

electrify [ə'lektrifai], v.t. electrizar; (fig.) exaltar, entusiasmar. — v.i. electrizarse.

electrize, v.t. electrizar.

electro, s. electrotipo.

electro-biology [ə'lektrou-bai'ɔlədʒi], s. electro-biología.

electro-chemical, a. electroquímico.

electro-chemistry, s. electroquímica.

electrocute [ə'lektrəkjuːt], v.t. electrocutar.

electrocution [elektrə'kjuːʃən], s. electrocución.

electrode [ə'lektroud], s. electrodo.

electro-dynamic, a. electrodinámico.

electrology [elek'trɔlədʒi], s. electrología.

electrolysis, s. electrólisis, f.

electrolyte [ə'lektrolait], s. electrolito.

electrolytic [əlektrə'litik], a. electrolítico.

electrolyzation [elektrolai'zeiʃən], s. electrolización.

electrolyze [ə'lektrolaiz], v.t. electrolizar.

electro-magnet, s. electroimán.

electro-magnetic, a. electromagnético.

electro-magnetism, s. electromagnetismo.

electro-metallurgy, s. galvanoplástica, galvanoplastia.

electrometer [elek'trɔmətəɹ], s. electrómetro.

electrometrical [elektro'metrikl], a. electrométrico.

electrometry [elek'trɔmətri], s. electrometría.

electro-motion, s. electro-dinamismo.

electro-motive, a. electromotor, electro-motriz, electro-dinámico.

electro-motor, s. electro-motor, motor eléctrico.

electron [ə'lektrən], s. (fís.) electrón.

electro-negative, a. electro-negativo.

electropathy [elek'trɔpəθi], s. electroterapia.

electrophorus, s. electróforo.

electro-plate, v.t. galvanizar, plaquear, platear.

electro-positive, a. electro-positivo.

electroscope [ə'lektrəskoup], s. electroscopio.

electrostatic, a. electrostático.

electrostatics [elektro'stætiks], s. electro-stática.

electrotechnics, s. electrotecnia.

electro-telegraphy, s. telegrafía eléctrica.

electrotype [ə'lektrətaip], s. electrotipia. — v.t. electrotipar.

electuary [ə'lektjuəri], s. electuario.

eleemosynary [elii:'mosinəri], a. caritativo; mendicante. — s. mendigo.

elegance ['eləgəns], s. elegancia, gentileza, galanura, donaire.

elegant, a. elegante, apuesto, galano, gentil.

elegiac [elə'dʒaiək], a. elegíaco.

elegiast, elegist, s. elegíaco, el que escribe elegías.

elegize ['elədʒaiz], v.t., v.i. lamentar, deplorar; hacer una elegía.

elegy, s. elegía.

element ['eləmənt], s. elemento, componente, ingrediente; (biol.) unidad morfológica; (quím.) cuerpo simple; esfera de acción; (elec.) elemento de pila, par. — pl. **elements,** principios, nociones, rudimentos; los elementos; (igl.) pan y vino de la misa.

elemental [elə'mentəl], a. elemental, primordial.

elementary, a. elemental, inicial, rudimental, incipiente.

elephant ['eləfənt], s. elefante.

elephantiasis [eləfən'taiəsis], s. (med.) elefantíasis, f.

elephantine [elə'fæntain], a. elefantino.

elevate ['eləveit], v.t. elevar, levantar, ascender, alzar, exaltar; encaramar, encumbrar; ensoberbecer; inspirar, excitar, animar, alegrar.

elevated, a. alto, elevado, exaltado, excelso. — p.p. [ELEVATE].

elevation [elə'veiʃən], s. elevación, elevamiento, alzamiento, exaltación, encumbramiento; altura, eminencia; (arq.) alzado de un edificio; (astr.) altura de algún cuerpo celeste.

elevator ['eləveitəɹ], s. ascensor (E.U.); escalera móvil (Ingl.); elevador; noria.

elevatory [elə'veitəri], a. que eleva. — s. (cir.) elevatorio.

eleven [ə'levən], a. once.

eleventh, a. onceno, undécimo, once. — s. onzavo, undécima parte; at the eleventh hour, a última hora.

elf [elf], s. (pl. **elves**) duende, peri, trasgo; diablo, demonio, diablillo; enano.

elfin, a. de duendes; fantástico. — s. diablillo, niño travieso.

elfish, a. aduendado, mágico; fantástico, travieso.

elicit [ə'lisit], v.t. descubrir; sacar, educir, sonsacar.

elide [ə'laid], v.t. frustrar, elidir.

eligibility [elidʒi'biliti], s. elegibilidad.

eligible ['elidʒibl], a. elegible, preferible, deseable.

eligibleness, s. elegibilidad.

eliminate [ə'limineit], v.t. eliminar, quitar, descartar, rechazar.

elimination [əlimi'neiʃən], s. eliminación.

eliquation [əlikweiʃən], s. (quím.) licuación.

elision [ə'liʒən], s. elisión.

élite [e'liːt], s. lo mejor, la flor, lo escogido, lo selecto, la flor y nata.

elixate [e'likseit], v.t. extraer por decocción.

elixation [elik'seiʃən], s. decocción, ebullición.

elixir [ə'liksəɹ], s. elixir; tónico, cordial.

Elizabethan [əlizə'biːθən], a. perteneciente a la Reina Isabel I o a su época.

elk [elk], s. anta, alce.

elke, s. cisne salvaje.

ell [el], s. ana (medida de 45 pulgadas en Inglaterra y de 37 en Escocia).

ellipse [e'lips], s. elipse, f., óvalo.

ellipsis, s. (pl. **ellipses**) (gram.) elipsis, f.

ellipsoid, s. elipsoide.

ellipsoidal, a. elipsoidal, elipsidal.

elliptic, elliptical, a. elíptico.

ellipticity [elip'tisiti], s. elipticidad.

elm [elm], s. (bot.) olmo; elm-grove, olmeda.

elmy, *a.* ulmáceo, poblado de olmos.

elocution [elə'kju:ʃən], *s.* elocución; lenguaje, estilo, expresión; declamación, arte de hacer uso de la palabra.

elocutionary, *a.* declamatorio.

elocutionist, *s.* declamador.

eloge [e'loudʒ], *s.* encomio, panegírico; oración fúnebre.

elongate ['i:lɔŋgeit], *v.t.* alargar, extender, prolongar; alejar, apartar. — *v.i.* alejarse, alargarse, prolongarse. — *a.* alargado, estirado.

elongation [i:lɔŋ'geiʃən], *s.* extensión, prolongación; alejamiento, distancia; (*med.*) elongación.

elope [ə'loup], *v.t.* escapar, evadirse, fugarse con un amante.

elopement, *s.* huida, fuga, escapada, evasión, rapto.

eloquence ['eləkwəns], *s.* elocuencia.

eloquent, *a.* elocuente.

else [els], *a.* otro, cualquiera, cualquier. — *adv.* más, además, de otro modo, en otro caso; *or else,* de otro modo; si no; *nothing else,* nada más; *no one else,* ningún otro.

elsewhere, *adv.* en otra parte, de otra parte, a otra parte.

elucidate [e'lju:sideit], *v.t.* elucidar, dilucidar, aclarar.

elucidation [elju:si'deiʃən], *s.* elucidación, dilucidación, aclaración.

elucidative, elucidatory, *a.* explicativo.

elucidator, *s.* expositor, comentador.

elude [e'lju:d], *v.t.* eludir, huir, evadir, esquivar.

eludible, *a.* eludible, evitable.

elusion [e'lju:ʃən], *s.* evasión, escapatoria, subterfugio, fraude.

elusive, *a.* evasivo, ilusivo, artificioso, falaz.

elusoriness, *s.* falacia, engaño, cualidad de ilusorio.

elusory, *a.* engañador, ilusorio, engañoso, falaz.

elute [e'lju:t], *v.t.* (*ant.*) limpiar, lavar.

elution, *s.* levigación.

elutriate [e'lju:trieit], *v.t.* decantar.

elves [elvz], *s.pl.* [ELF].

Elysian [e'liziən], *a.* elíseo.

'em, (*fam.*) elisión de [THEM], caso objetivo del pronombre *they.*

emaciate [e'meiʃieit], *v.t.* debilitar, extenuar, adelgazar. — *v.i.* enflaquecer. — *a.* enflaquecido, flaco; (*med.*) extenuado.

emaciation [emeiʃi'eiʃən], *s.* extenuación, demacración, flaqueza.

emanate ['eməneit], *v.i.* emanar, derivarse, proceder.

emanation [emə'neiʃən], *s.* emanación, exhalación, efluvio.

emanative, *a.* emanante.

emancipate [ə'mænsipeit], *v.t.* emancipar; libertar; manumitir. — *a.* emancipado, manumitido.

emancipation [əmænsi'peiʃən], *s.* emancipación, manumisión.

emarginate [ə'mɑ:rdʒineit], *v.t.* quitar el margen, recortar; (*bot.*) hacer una escotadura en el ápice. — *a.* (*bot.*) escotado, emarginado.

emasculate [ə'mæskjuleit], *v.t.* castrar; capar; afeminar; enervar; mutilar. — *a.* castrado; afeminado, viciado.

embale [em'beil], *v.t.* embalar, enfardar.

embalm [em'bɑ:m], *v.t.* embalsamar, perfumar; conservar.

embalmer, *s.* embalsamador.

embalming, *s.* embalsamamiento.

embank [em'bæŋk], *v.t.* represar; terraplenar.

embankment, *s.* terraplén; dique, malecón, presa; ribera.

embargo [em'bɑ:rgou], *s.* embargo, detención de buques; secuestro de géneros; *to lay an embargo on,* embargar. — *v.t.* embargar, secuestrar, detener.

embark [em'bɑ:rk], *v.t.* (*mar.*) embarcar; (*fig.*) invertir (dinero) en un negocio. — *v.i.* embarcarse; dar principio a alguna ocupación, aventurarse.

embarkation [embɑ:r'keiʃən], *s.* embarque, embarco; embarcación; cargamento, fleto, carga.

embarking, *s.* embarcadero.

embarrass [em'bærəs], *v.t.* turbar, aturdir, desconcertar, avergonzar; enredar; apurar, preocupar.

embarrassing, *a.* desconcertante, vergonzoso; molesto.

embarrassment, *s.* vergüenza, pudor, turbación, perplejidad, perturbación; compromiso, impedimento, dificultad, enredo; penuria.

embassade ['embəseid], *s.* embajada.

embassy, *s.* embajada; (*fam.*) comisión.

embattle [em'bætl], *v.t.* formar en orden de batalla; (*fig.*) fortificar, almenar. — *v.i.* ponerse en orden de batalla.

embattled, *a.* en orden de batalla.

embattlement, *s.* almena, almenaje.

embay [em'bei], *v.t.* (*mar.*) empeñar en una bahía, encerrar; cercar, rodear.

embed [em'bed], *v.t.* encajar, encajonar, encerrar; incrustar, empotrar.

embellish [em'beliʃ], *v.t.* embellecer, ataviar, hermosear, ornar, adornar, aderezar.

embellishment, *s.* adorno, ornato; embellecimiento.

ember ['embər], *s.* ceniza, tizón, ascua, chispa; *ember days,* témporas; *ember-week,* semana de témporas. — *pl.* **embers,** rescoldo; chispas.

embezzle [em'bezl], *v.t.* hurtar; malgastar, disipar, desfalcar.

embezzlement, *s.* hurto, robo, desfalco; malversación; (*for.*) expilación.

embezzler, *s.* malversador; (*for.*) peculador; desfalcador.

embitter [em'bitər], *v.t.* amargar, hacer amargo, agriar, acibarar.

emblaze [em'bleiz], *v.t.* esmaltar; blasonar; adornar con colores brillantes.

emblazon, *v.t.* blasonar; alabar, ensalzar.

emblazoner, *s.* blasonador; heraldo.

emblazonry, *s.* blasón.

emblem ['embləm], *s.* emblema, *m.*, símbolo, signo, cifra, divisa. — *v.t.* representar en emblema.

emblematic, emblematical [emblə'mætikl], *a.* emblemático.

emblematist, *s.* escritor de emblemas.

emblematize, emblemize, *v.t.* simbolizar, representar por medio de emblemas.

emblement ['embləmənt], *s.* (*usu. en pl.*) (*derecho*) derecho de un arrendatario a la cosecha; cosecha, frutos de la tierra sembrada o plantada.

embloom [em'blu:m], *v.t.* (*ant.*) enflorecer.

embodiment [em'bɔdimənt], s. incorporación, personificación.

embody, v.t. incorporar, incluir, englobar; dar cuerpo; personificar; resumir; informar. — v.i. incorporarse, unirse.

embolden [əm'bouldn], v.t. animar, alentar, envalentonar.

embolism ['embəlizm], s. (astr.) embolismo; (med.) embolía.

embolus, s. émbolo.

emborder [em'bɔəɹdəɹ], v.t. guarnecer, orlar, ribetear.

embosom, v.t. poner o encerrar en su seno; (fig.) abrigar, proteger, amar.

emboss [em'bɔs], v.t. relevar, fabricar en relieve, repujar, realzar; adamascar.

embossment, s. abolladura, protuberancia; relieve, realce, resalte.

embottle [em'bɔtl], v.t. embotellar.

embouchure [ã'bu:ʃu:ɹ], s. desembocadura; (mús.) embocadura, boquilla.

embow [em'bau], v.t. (arq.) abovedar.

embowel [em'bauəl], v.t. desentrañar, destripar; enterrar, empotrar.

embower, v.t. emparrar, enramar, abrigar.

embrace [em'breis], v.t. abrazar; abarcar, ceñir, rodear, contener, comprender; asir, admitir, recibir, aceptar, adoptar; seguir; aprovechar. — v.i. abrazarse, dar un abrazo. — s. abrazo.

embracement, s. abrazo; lucha cuerpo a cuerpo; capacidad.

embracer, s. (for.) cohechador.

embracery, s. (for.) cohecho.

embrasure [em'breiʒəɹ], s. (fort.) cañonera, tronera.

embrocate ['embɹəkeit], v.t. (med.) embrocar.

embrocation [embɹə'keiʃən], s. embrocación, embroca.

embroider [em'bɹɔidəɹ], v.t. recamar, bordar; (fig.) bordar de realce, exagerar.

embroiderer, s. bordador; recamador, bordadura.

embroidery, s. bordado, bordadura.

embroil [em'bɹɔil], v.t. embrollar, liar, enredar, confundir.

embroilment, s. alboroto, confusión, intriga, embrollo.

embryo ['embriou], **embryon**, s. embrión, germen. — a. embrionario, en embrión, en germen.

embryologist [embri'ɔlədʒist], s. embriólogo.

embryology, s. embriología.

emend [e'mend], v.t. enmendar, corregir.

emendable, a. corregible.

emendation [i:men'deiʃən], s. enmienda, corrección.

emendator, s. enmendador, corrector.

emendatory, a. enmendador, correccional.

emerald ['eməɹəld], s., a. esmeralda, (de) color de esmeralda; (imp.) tipo intermedio entre la letra miñona y la nomparell: 6½ puntos.

emerge [ə'mə:ɹdʒ], v.i. emerger, brotar, surgir; aparecer, salir, asomarse, mostrarse.

emergence, s. salida, aparición, desarrollo, emergencia; (ant.) aprieto.

emergency, s. aprieto, necesidad, accidente, emergencia; (ant.) salida, aparición.

emergent, a. emergente, repentino, subitáneo, naciente.

emergently, adv. de un modo emergente.

emeritus, a. emérito.

emersion [ə'mə:ɹʃən], s. emergencia, reaparición, emersión.

emery ['eməɹi], s. esmeril.

emery-paper, s. papel de lija, papel esmeril.

emetic [e'metik], s. emético, vomitivo. — a. emético, vomitivo.

emiction [e'mikʃən], s. orina; acción de orinar.

emigrant ['emigrənt], s. emigrante, emigrado.

emigrate, v.i. emigrar, transmigrar.

emigration [emi'greiʃən], s. emigración, expatriación.

émigré ['emigrei], s. emigrante, emigrado.

eminence ['eminəns], **eminency**, s. eminencia, altura, elevación, cuesta; vértice, loma, cima; (fig.) eminencia, distinción, encumbramiento.

eminent, a. eminente, exaltado, conspicuo, distinguido, egregio, supremo.

emir [ə'miəɹ], s. emir, amir.

emissary [emisəri], s. emisario, espía, m.f., agente secreto; desaguadero, canal, orificio; (anat.) conducto excretorio.

emission [e'miʃən], s. emisión, eyaculación, salida.

emissory, a. excretor, que emite.

emit [e'mit], v.t. emitir; arrojar, despedir; (quím.) exhalar.

emmet ['emət], s. hormiga.

emmew, v.t. enjaular.

emollescence [emə'lesens], s. (metal.) ablandamiento, reblandecimiento.

emolliate [e'mɔlieit], v.t. ablandar.

emollient [e'mɔliənt], s., a. emoliente, demulcente, lenitivo.

emolument, s. emolumento, gaje.

emotion [e'mouʃən], s. emoción, perturbación, sensación, sensibilidad.

emotional, a. impresionable, sentimental, sensible; emocionante.

empale [em'peil], v.t. empalar; cercar, rodear con una estacada o cerca.

empalement, s. empalamiento; palizada, empalizada.

empanel [em'pænl], v.t. (for.) citar a los jurados.

emperor ['empərəɹ], s. emperador.

empery, s. imperio, soberanía.

emphasis ['emfəsis], s. énfasis, m.f.

emphasize ['emfəsaiz], v.t. dar énfasis, acentuar, subrayar, recalcar.

emphatic [em'fætik], **emphatical**, a. enfático, categórico, enérgico, fuerte.

emphysema [emfi'si:mə], s. (med.) enfisema, m.

emphyteutic [emfi'tju:tik], a. enfitéutico.

empire ['empair], s. imperio, soberanía.

empiric [em'pirik], s. empírico.

empiric, empirical, a. empírico.

empiricism [em'pirisizm], s. empirismo.

emplacement [em'pleisment], s. emplazamiento.

emplastic [em'plæstik], a. emplástico.

employ [em'plɔi], v.t. emplear, servirse de; ocupar; dar trabajo a. — s. empleo, ocupación, cargo, servicio, puesto.

employable, a. empleable, que puede ser empleado.

employee, s. empleado.

employer, s. amo, dueño, patrón, principal, jefe.

employment, s. empleo, ocupación, trabajo, colocación, acomodo, puesto, destino, cargo; uso, servicio.

empoison [em'pɔizən], v.t. envenenar, atosigar, emponzoñar.
empoisoner, s. envenenador, emponzoñador.
empoisonment, s. envenenamiento.
emporium [em'poəriəm], s. emporio, plaza;
bazar.
empower [em'pauəɹ], v.t. autorizar, comisionar, dar poder, facultar, habilitar.
empress ['emprəs], s.f. emperatriz; (ant.)
emperadora.
emprise [em'praiz], s. (ant.) empresa.
emptier, s. vaciador.
emptiness, s. vacuidad; vacuo, vacío; ayuno;
futilidad.
emption ['empʃən], s. compra, adquisición.
empty ['empti], a. vacío, vacuo, hueco;
desocupado, desalojado; vaco, vacante;
ignorante; superficial, frívolo; vano, inútil;
hambriento. — v.t. vaciar; evacuar; desocupar, agotar, descargar. — v.i. vaciarse;
descargar, desaguar.
emptyings, s.pl. desperdicio, residuo; (E.U.)
heces de cerveza, sidra, etc., usadas como
lavadura.
empurple [em'pə:ɹpl], v.t. purpurar, teñir de
púrpura.
empyreal [em'piriəl], a. empíreo.
empyreal, empyrean, s., a. empíreo.
emu ['i:mju:], s. (orn.) casoar, dromeo.
emulate ['emjuleit], v.t. emular; (ant.)
rivalizar, tener celos.
emulation [emju'leiʃən], s. emulación; (ant.)
envidia, celos.
emulative ['emjulətiv], a. emulativo.
emulator, s. émulo, emulador.
emulgent [e'mʌldʒənt], s., a. (med.) emulgente.
emulous ['emjuləs], a. émulo; (ant.) competidor, celoso.
emulously, adv. a porfía, con emulación, a
competencia.
emulsion [ə'mʌlʃən], s. emulsión.
emulsive, a. emulsivo.
emunctory [ə'mʌŋktəri], s. (med.) emuntorio.
— a. (med.) excretorio.
enable [e'neibl], v.t. facilitar, habilitar, proporcionar, permitir, poner en estado de;
hacer, hacer que.
enact [e'nækt], v.t. efectuar, poner en ejecución, ordenar, mandar, decretar; hacer el
papel de.
enactive, a. sancionado.
enactment, s. decreto, promulgación, estatuto.
enactor, s. ejecutor; legislador.
enallage [e'nælidʒ], s. enálage, f.
enamel [e'næml], v.t. esmaltar; charolar. — s.
esmalte, charol, laca.
enameller, s. esmaltador.
enamelling, s. esmaltadura.
enamour [e'næməɹ], v.t. enamorar; encantar.
enamoured, a. enamorado, prendado. — p.p.
[ENAMOUR].
encage [en'keidʒ], v.t. enjaular; encarcelar.
encamp [en'kæmp], v.i. acamparse. — v.t.
acampar.
encampment, s. campo, campamento.
encase [en'keis], v.t. encajonar, encajar.
encaustic [en'kɔ:stik], s. (pint.) encausto,
(ant.) adustión, f. — a. encáustico.
encave, v.t. embodegar, ocultar, encovar.
enceinte [ɑ̃'sɛ̃:t], s. (fort.) recinto. — a.f.
preñada, encinta.

encephalalgia [ensefə'lældʒiə], s. (med.)
encefalalgia.
encephalic, a. encefálico.
encephalitis [ensefə'laitis], s. encefalitis, f.
encephalon [en'sefələn], s. encéfalo.
enchafe [en'tʃeif], v.t. enfurecer, enojar.
enchain [en'tʃein], v.t. encadenar.
enchainment, s. encadenamiento.
enchant [en'tʃɑ:nt], v.t. encantar, hechizar,
deleitar, embelesar, fascinar.
enchanter, s. encantador, hechicero.
enchanting, a. encantador.
enchantingly, adv. encantadoramente, admirablemente; como por encanto.
enchantress, s. encantadora, seductora; maga,
bruja.
encharge [en'tʃɑ:ɹdʒ], v.t. fiar a, encargar,
comisionar.
enchase [en'tʃeis], v.t. engastar, adornar,
incrustar, embutir, cincelar.
enchasing, s. obra de cinceladura.
encircle [en'sə:ɹkl], v.t. ceñir, cercar, rodear,
circundar, circunvalar.
enclitic, enclitical [en'klitikl], a. (gram.)
enclítico.
encloister [en'klɔistəɹ], v.t. enclaustrar.
enclose [en'klouz], v.t. circundar, rodear,
cercar, circunvalar; adjuntar, incluir.
enclosed, a. adjunto, incluso. — p.p. [EN-
CLOSE].
enclosure, s. cerca, vallado, corral, cercado,
cercamiento; lo incluso, lo contenido, documento anejo.
encloud [en'klaud], v.t. cubrir de una nube.
encomiast [en'koumiæst], s. encomiasta, m.f.
encomiastic, encomiastical, a. encomiástico.
encomium [en'koumiəm], s. encomio, elogio,
panegírico, alabanza.
encompass [en'kʌmpəs], v.t. cercar, circundar.
encompassment, s. cerco, sitio; rodeo,
vuelta; circunlocución.
encore [ɑ̃'kɔ:ɹ], adv. otra vez, de nuevo. —
interj. ¡otra! ¡bis! — v.t. hacer repetir, pedir
la repetición. — s. repetición.
encounter [en'kauntəɹ], s. encuentro; choque;
desafío, duelo; batalla, pelea, combate,
refriega; casualidad. — v.t. encontrar; acometer; dar con, tropezar con. — v.i. oponerse, combatir, pelear; encontrarse por
casualidad.
encourage [en'kʌridʒ], v.t. animar, inspirar
confianza; fomentar, incitar; alentar, infundir ánimo o valor.
encouragement, s. fomento, estímulo, incentivo.
encourager, s. protector, fomentador.
encouraging, a. estimulante, alentador.
encroach [en'kroutʃ], v.i. usurpar, abusar,
pasar los límites, robar, quitar.
encroacher, s. usurpador.
encroachment, s. usurpación, intrusión,
abuso.
encrust [en'krʌst], v.t. incrustar.
encumber [en'kʌmbəɹ], v.t. embarazar, estorbar, gravar, abrumar; sobrecargar, poner
trabas a.
encumberment, encumbrance, s. embarazo,
obstáculo, impedimento, estorbo, traba,
carga, gravamen, pensión.
encyclical [en'siklikl], s. encíclica.

encyclopædia [ensaiklə'piːdiə], encyclopedia, s. enciclopedia.
encyclopedian, encyclopedic, encyclo-
pedical, a. enciclopédico.
encyclopedism, s. enciclopedismo.
encyclopedist, s. enciclopedista, m.f.
encyst [en'sist], v.t. enquistarse.
encysted, a. enquistado.
end [end], s. fin, cabo; extremidad; extremo;
fondo; límite; consumación, cesación, conclusión, terminación, acabamiento, término;
remate, cola; muerte, f.; mira; desenlace;
destino; resolución, determinación; consecuencia; objeto, intento; pieza, fragmento;
end to end, cabeza contra cabeza; from end to
end, de cabo a cabo, de punta a cabo, de un
extremo a otro; in the end, por fin, al fin, en
fin; on end, de cabeza, de pie; (mar.) a plomo,
flechado; two hours on end, dos horas seguidas;
end on, de punta; at the end of the month,
a fines del mes; his hair stands on end,
se le erizan los cabellos; to make an end of,
acabar con; to the end that, a fin de que, para
que; to make both ends meet, (fig.) pasar con
lo que uno tiene. — v.t. acabar, concluir,
terminar, dar fin a. — v.i. terminarse, acabarse; cesar, fenecer.
endamage [en'dæmidʒ], v.t. perjudicar, estropear, dañar.
endamagement, s. perjuicio, daño, estropeo.
endanger [en'deindʒəɹ], v.t. perjudicar, comprometer, arriesgar, poner en peligro.
endear [en'diəɹ], v.t. hacer querer o amar;
(ant.) encarecer, subir el precio.
endearing, a. cariñoso, atractivo.
endearment, s. encarecimiento, encariña-
miento, afición, ternura.
endeavour [en'devəɹ], s. esfuerzo, conato,
empeño. — v.i. esforzarse; hacer un esfuerzo, tentar, ensayar, probar; hacer lo
posible. — v.t. probar, intentar, procurar.
endecagon [en'dekəgən], s. endecágono.
endemial, endemic, endemical [en'demikl],
a. endémico.
endemically, adv. de un modo endémico.
ender ['endəɹ], s. acabador.
endermatic, endermic [en'dəɹmik], a.
endérmico.
enderon ['endəron], s. (fisiol.) dermis, f.
ending ['endiŋ], s. fin, cesación, conclusión;
desenlace; cierre; (geom.) terminación;
(mús.) coda; (gram.) desinencia.
endive ['endiv], s. (bot.) endibia, escarola.
endless ['endles], a. interminable, infinito,
inacabable, continuo, perpetuo.
endlessly, adv. infinitamente, sin fin.
endlessness, s. infinidad, perpetuidad, continuidad.
endlong, adv. a lo largo; en línea recta; continuamente. — a. de pie, en pie, a plomo.
endmost, a. lo más lejano, remoto, extremo.
endocardiac, a. endocardíaco.
endocardium [endou'kɑːɹdiəm], s. endo-
cardio.
endocarp, s. endocarpio.
endometry [en'dɔmətri], s. endometría.
endorse [en'dɔːɹs], v.t. endosar; refrendar,
autorizar, aprobar.
endow [en'dau], v.t. dotar, enriquecer, fundar.
endower, s. dotador.
endowment, s. dotación, dote, fundación;
dotes, dones, prendas, talentos, gracias.

endue [en'djuː], v.t. ponerse (vestidos, etc.),
vestir, cubrir, adornar; dotar, investir.
endurable [en'djuərəbl], a. soportable, tolerable, sufrible, resistible.
endurably, adv. de un modo soportable.
endurance, s. sufrimiento, paciencia, resistencia, continuación, duración; beyond
endurance, insoportable.
endure, v.t. soportar, tolerar, aguantar, sufrir,
sobrellevar, resistir; perdurar, durar, continuar.
endurer, s. paciente, sufridor.
enduring, a. perdurable, permanente, constante; tolerante, paciente, sufrido.
endways, endwise ['endwaiz], adv. de punta,
de pie, derecho.
enema ['enimə], s. enema, m., ayuda, lavativa.
enemy ['enəmi], s. enemigo, adversario; how
goes the enemy? (fam.) ¿qué hora es?
energetic [enəɹ'dʒetik], energetical, a.
enérgico, activo, vigoroso.
energize ['enəɹdʒaiz], v.t. dar energía, dar
vigor. — v.i. obrar con energía.
energy, s. energía, fuerza, vigor.
enervate ['enəɹveit], v.t. enervar, debilitar. —
a. enervado, debilitado.
enervation [enəɹ'veiʃən], s. enervación, debilidad; molicie, f.
enfeeble [en'fiːbl], v.t. debilitar, enervar.
enfeeblement, s. debilidad, desfallecimiento,
flojedad.
enfeebling, a. debilitante.
enfeoff [en'fef], v.t. enfeudar.
enfeoffment, s. enfeudación.
enfilade [enfi'leid], s. fila, hilera; (mil.) fuego
de enfilada, fuego enfilado. — v.t. enfilar,
batir por el costado.
enfold [en'fould], v.t. envolver, abrazar.
enforce [en'fɔːɹs], v.t. fortificar; esforzar, dar
fuerza, obligar; exigir, obtener por fuerza,
violentar, demostrar, inculcar.
enforceable, a. ejecutable.
enforcedly, adv. forzosamente, por fuerza.
enforcement, s. compulsión, coacción; sanción; aprieto.
enforcer, s. forzador.
enfranchise [en'fræntʃaiz], v.t. franquear,
emancipar, conceder franquicia; enfranquecer; manumitir; naturalizar, dar carta de
naturaleza; adoptar.
enfranchisement, s. franquicia; derecho de
ciudadano; emancipación; manumisión.
enfranchiser, s. libertador.
engage [en'geidʒ], v.t. empeñar, apalabrar,
comprometer; ajustar; encomendar, mandar,
ordenar; ocupar, emplear; alistar, alquilar,
tomar en alquiler; distraer, entretener; enganchar; halagar, atraer; contratar, librar
(batalla); (mec.) encajar, engranar; to engage
the clutch, embragar. — v.i. obligarse, contratarse, empeñarse, dar palabra, comprometerse; ocuparse; pelear, dar combate,
venir a las manos.
engaged, a. obligado, empeñado; ocupado;
prometido (para casarse); reservado.
engagement, s. empeño, obligación, contrato;
compromiso, cita; promesa o palabra de casamiento; noviazgo; escritura, ajuste; combate, batalla.
engaging, a. atractivo, agradable, amable, insinuante, simpático.
engender [en'dʒendəɹ], v.t. engendrar, pro-

crear, producir. — *v.i.* engendrarse, producirse.

engild [en'gild], *v.t.* dorar.

engine ['endʒin], *s.* motor; máquina, mecanismo, aparato; locomotora; agente, instrumento; *engine-turning*, torneo a máquina.

engine-driver, *s.* maquinista, *m.*

engineer [endʒin'iːɹ], *s.* ingeniero; mecánico; soldado del cuerpo de los ingenieros; (*E.U.*) maquinista, *m.* — *v.t.* dirigir, como ingeniero, una construcción civil, militar, o mecánica; gestionar, componérselas, arreglar; maquinar (un complot).

engineering, *s.* ingeniería, ciencia del ingeniero; (*fig.*) manejo, dirección.

enginery, *s.* artillería; maquinaria; manejo, invención.

engird [en'gəːɹd], **engirdle**, *v.t.* cercar, ceñir.

English ['eŋgliʃ], *s.*, *a.* inglés. — *v.t.* traducir al inglés.

Englishman, *s.* inglés.

Englishwoman, *s.* inglesa.

engorge [en'gɔːɹdʒ], *v.t.* engullir, devorar, atracar. — *v.i.* atracarse.

engorgement, *s.* voracidad; (*med.*) congestión, *f.*

engraft [en'grɑːft], *v.t.* injertar; imprimir, grabar, fijar ideas en el ánimo.

engrail [en'greil], *v.t.* dentar.

engrain, *v.t.* teñir; (*fig.*) inculcar, imbuir.

engrave [en'greiv], *v.t.* grabar, esculpir, cincelar, burilar.

engraver, *s.* grabador.

engraving, *s.* grabado, lámina, estampa; arte de grabar, grabadura.

engross [en'grous], *v.t.* absorber; copiar, poner en limpio, hacer una transcripción legal; acaparar, monopolizar.

engrosser, *s.* monopolista, *m.f.*, acaparador, calígrafo.

engrossment, *s.* monopolio; transcripción; embelesamiento, embebecimiento.

engulf [en'gʌlf], *v.t.* engolfar, abismar.

engulfed, *a.* engolfado, *p.p.* [ENGULF].

engyscope ['endʒiskoup], *s.* microscopio solar o de reflexión.

enhance [en'hɑːns], *v.t.* elevar, levantar en alto; mejorar, encarecer; aumentar. — *v.i.* elevarse, engrandecerse; encarecer.

enhancement, *s.* encarecimiento, subida de valor, acrecentamiento; mejoría, encarecimiento, realce.

enhancer, *s.* encarecedor.

enharmonic [enhɑə'mɔnik], *s.* enarmónico.

enigma [ə'nigmə], *s.* enigma, *m.*, misterio.

enigmatic, enigmatical [enig'mætikl], *a.* enigmático.

enigmatist [ə'nigmətist], *s.* enigmatista, *m.f.*

enjoin [en'dʒɔin], *v.t.* encargar, ordenar, mandar, imponer; (*for.*) prescribir, prohibir.

enjoinment, *s.* mandato, precepto, orden, *m.f.*

enjoy [en'dʒɔi], *v.t.* gozar de, disfrutar, saborear, gustar de; lograr, tener, poseer.

enjoyable, *a.* gozable, que se puede gozar; agradable, deleitable.

enjoyment, *s.* goce, felicidad, fruición, disfrute, satisfacción, placer, gusto.

enkindle [en'kindl], *v.t.* encender; (*fig.*) inflamar, incitar. — *v.i.* encenderse, inflamarse.

enlace [en'leis], *v.t.* rodear estrechamente, circundar, atar; entrelazar, enredar.

enlarge [en'lɑːɹdʒ], *v.t.* aumentar, agrandar, engrandecer, ensanchar; difundir, extender, dilatar, abultar, engrosar; exagerar; explayar, ampliar, amplificar; (*ant.*) soltar, libertar, sacar de la prisión. — *v.i.* extenderse, difundirse; aumentar, crecer.

enlargement, *s.* aumento, incremento, ensanche, ensanchamiento; agrandamiento, extensión, dilatación, ampliación, amplificación, soltura; (*ant.*) liberación.

enlighten [en'laitən], *v.t.* alumbrar, iluminar; (*fig.*) iluminar, ilustrar, aclarar, esclarecer.

enlightened, *a.* ilustrado; culto, inteligente, civilizado.

enlightener, *s.* alumbrador; instructor.

enlightenment, *s.* ilustración, instrucción; explicación, esclarecimiento.

enlink [en'liŋk], *v.t.* ligar, eslabonar, encadenar.

enlist [en'list], *v.t.* (*mil.*) enganchar, reclutar, alistar; conseguir, atraer, granjear. — *v.i.* alistarse, sentar plaza, engancharse.

enlisting, enlistment, *s.* alistamiento; enganche.

enliven [en'laivən], *v.t.* vivificar, avivar, animar, alentar, alegrar, regocijar.

enlivener, *s.* vivificador, animador.

enlivenment, *s.* animación.

enmesh [en'meʃ], *v.t.* enredar, coger en la red. — *v.t.*, *v.i.* engranar, endentar.

enmity ['enmiti], *s.* enemistad, hostilidad.

ennead [e'niːd], *s.* juego de nueve, especialmente nueve libros o discursos.

ennoble [e'noubl], *v.t.* ennoblecer, ilustrar, engrandecer, esclarecer.

ennoblement, *s.* ennoblecimiento, esclarecimiento.

ennui [ɔn'wiː], *s.* aburrimiento, fastidio, tedio, abulia.

enormity [e'nɔːɹmiti], *s.* enormidad, atrocidad; demasía, exceso.

enormous, *a.* enorme, colosal; desmesurado, descomunal, excesivo; perverso, atroz.

enormousness, *s.* enormidad.

enough [ə'nʌf], *a.* bastante, suficiente, harto, asaz. — *s.* lo bastante, lo suficiente. — *adv.* bastante, suficientemente.

enounce [e'nauns], *v.t.* enunciar, declarar, publicar.

enow [e'nau], *a.*, *adv.* (*ant.*) bastante, suficiente.

enquire [en'kwaiɹ], *v.t.*; **enquirer**, *s.* [INQUIRE].

enrage [en'reidʒ], *v.t.* enfurecer, hacer rabiar, enrabiar, provocar, irritar, exasperar, encolerizar.

enrank, *v.t.* enfilar.

enrapt [en'ræpt], *a.* extasiado, arrebatado.

enrapture, *v.t.* extasiar, arrebatar, arrebar, transportar, enajenar, hacer salir de sí.

enravish, *v.t.* extasiar, arrebatar.

enrich [en'ritʃ], *v.t.* enriquecer; adornar, embellecer; fertilizar, fecundar.

enrichment, *s.* enriquecimiento; embellecimiento, adorno; beneficio, abono.

enring [en'riŋ], *v.t.* rodear, cercar; poner un anillo, adornar con un anillo.

enrobe [en'roub], *v.t.* vestir, adornar con vestidos.

enrol [en'roul], **enroll**, *v.t.* alistar; matricular, inscribir; arrollar, enrollar, envolver.

enroller, s. matriculador; (mil.) reclutador.

enrolment, s. matrícula, inscripción; empadronamiento, reclutamiento, alistamiento.

enroot [en'ruːt], v.t. arraigar, radicar.

ensanguine [en'sæŋgwin], v.t. ensangrentar.

ensate [en'seit], a. (biol.) en forma de espada, ensiforme.

enschedule, v.t. (ant.) inscribir en cédulas.

ensconce [en'skɔns], v.t. colocar, acomodar, establecer; poner a cubierto, resguardar, cubrir; proteger.

ensemble, s. totalidad, conjunto.

enshield, v.t. escudar, defender con escudo.

enshrine [en'ʃrain], v.t. guardar como reliquia.

enshroud [en'ʃraud], v.t. cubrir, abrigar, esconder; amortajar, envolver.

ensiform ['ensifɔːm], a. ensiforme.

ensign ['ensain], s. (mil.) bandera, enseña, pabellón, divisa, insignia; (mil.) alférez, abanderado; (mar.) bandera de popa.

ensilage ['ensilidʒ], s. (agr.) ensilaje. — v.t. ensilar.

enslave [en'sleiv], v.t. esclavizar, avasallar, cautivar, domar.

enslavement, s. esclavitud, servidumbre, f., cautiverio.

enslaver, s. esclavizador, tirano.

ensnare [en'snɛəɹ], v.t. entrampar, engañar, tender un lazo.

ensue [en'sjuː], v.i. seguir, resultar, sobrevenir, suceder.

ensuing, a. resultante; siguiente, próximo.

ensure [en'ʃjuːɹ], v.t. asegurar, afianzar, dar seguridad; dar seguro.

entablature [en'tæblətʃəɹ], **entablement,** s. (arq.) entablamento.

entail [en'teil], s. (for.) vinculación; vínculo; herencia inalienable, mayorazgo; orden de sucesión. — v.t. vincular, asegurar, perpetuar, transmitir; ligar; imponer, ocasionar, acarrear.

entailment, s. (for.) vínculo.

entame [enteim], v.t. domesticar, domar.

entangle [en'tæŋgl], v.t. enredar, embrollar, enmarañar, intrincar. — v.i. enredarse, embrollarse.

entangled, a. embrolloso, intrincado. — p.p. [ENTANGLE]; to be entangled in lawsuits, arderse en pleitos.

entanglement, s. enredo, perplejidad, confusión, complicación, embrollo.

enter ['entəɹ], v.t., v.i. entrar, pasar; penetrar, insertar, ingerir, meter, introducir, introducirse; admitir; registrar; ingresar, matricularse, alistarse, afiliarse, iniciar; (for.) incoar (un proceso o procedimiento), notar, archivar; (com.) declarar, aduanar; to enter upon, empezar, emprender.

enteric [en'terik], a. entérico; enteric fever, fiebre tifoidea.

entering ['entəriŋ], s. entrada, paso.

enteritis [entə'raitəs], s. enteritis, f.

enterprise ['entəɹpraiz], s. empresa, acometimiento, arresto; resolución, iniciativa; espíritu emprendedor, arrojo. — v.t. (ant.) emprender.

enterpriser, s.; **enterprising,** a. emprendedor, arrojado, enérgico, aventurero.

entertain [entəɹ'tein], v.t. festejar, obsequiar, agasajar; mantener; (fig.) concebir; divertir, entretener, distraer, solazar; tomar en consideración, acariciar, abrigar.

entertainer, s. huésped, festejador, anfitrión, dueño, amo; posadero; artista, m.f., cómico, comediante.

entertaining, a. entretenido, divertido, chistoso, alegre.

entertainment, s. festín, festejo, agasajo, convite; hospedaje; acogida, recibimiento, hospitalidad; entretenimiento, pasatiempo, diversión; función teatral espectáculo, diversión.

enthrall, enthral [en'θrɔːl], v.t. esclavizar, sojuzgar; (fig.) captar, encantar.

enthrone [en'θroun], v.t. entronizar.

enthronization, s. entronización.

enthusiasm [en'θjuːziæzm], s. entusiasmo.

enthusiast, s. entusiasta, m.f., aficionado.

enthusiastic [enθjuːzi'æstik], a. entusiasmado, entusiástico.

entice [en'tais], v.t. halagar, acariciar; excitar; seducir, inducir, tentar, atraer.

enticement, s. incitación, incitamiento, instigación, tentación, seducción.

enticer, s. incitador, instigador, tentador, seductor.

enticing, a. atrayente, seductivo, halagüeño.

entire [en'taiəɹ], a. entero, cabal, íntegro, intacto, completo, perfecto; (mat.) integral.

entirely, adv. enteramente, totalmente, absolutamente, completamente, por entero.

entireness, s. totalidad, integridad, entereza.

entirety, s. total, conjunto, totalidad, integridad, entereza.

entitle [en'taitəl], v.t. titular, intitular, calificar, autorizar, dar derecho, privilegio o pretexto.

entity ['entiti], s. entidad, ente, ser, individualidad.

entoil [en'tɔil], v.t. enredar, coger en la trampa.

entomb [en'tuːm], v.t. enterrar, sepultar.

entombment, s. inhumación, sepultura, entierro.

entomological [entəmə'lɔdʒikəl], a. entomológico.

entomologist [entə'mɔlədʒist], s. entomólogo.

entomology, s. entomología.

entourage [ɔn'tuːraːʒ], s. séquito, cortejo.

entr'acte ['ɔntrækt], s. entreacto.

entrails ['entreilz], s.pl. entrañas, vísceras, intestinos, tripas.

entrance ['entrəns], s. entrada; portal; boca, embocadura, embocador, embocadero, ingreso; (mar.) proa de un bugue.

entrance [en'traːns], v.t. arrobar, extasiar, transportar, hechizar, fascinar.

entrance-fee, s. precio de entrada.

entrance-hall, s. vestíbulo, zaguán.

entrant ['entrənt], s. entrante, principiante, novicio.

entrap [en'træp], v.t. entrampar, enredar, engañar, enmarañar, coger con trampa.

entreat [en'triːt], v.t. rogar, suplicar, conjurar, implorar, exorar, impetrar.

entreaty, s. petición, ruego, solicitud, instancia, súplica.

entrée ['ɔntrei], s. privilegio de entrar como visitador; entrada; (coc.) entrada.

entremets ['ɔntrəmeiz], s.pl. entremeses.

entrench [en'trentʃ], v.t. atrincherar. — v.i. infringir.

entrenchment, s. atrincheramiento, trinchera; infracción.

entrepot ['ɔntrəpou], s. almacén, depósito, factoraje.

entresol, s. (arq.) entresuelo.

entrust [en'trʌst], v.t. entregar, confiar, dar en fideicomiso.

entry ['entri], s. entrada, pórtico, zaguán; inscripción, ingreso, asiento, anotación, registro; declaración; ficha, artículo (de catálogos, etc.); (com.) partida; (mar.) registro, declaración de entrada de un barco.

entwine [en'twain], v.t. entrelazar, entretejer.

entwist, v.t. torcer, enroscar, ensortijar.

enucleate [e'nju:klieit], v.t. desanudar, descascarar; (cir.) extirpar, extraer; (fig.) desembrollar.

enucleation [enju:kli'eiʃən], s. (cir.) enucleación.

enumerate [ən'ju:məreit], v.t. enumerar, detallar, contar.

enumeration [enju:mə'reiʃən], s. enumeración, lista, catálogo, recapitulación.

enumerative [e'nju:məɹətiv], a. enumerativo.

enunciate [e'nʌnsieit], v.t. enunciar, declarar, articular, pronunciar. — v.i. hablar.

enunciation [enʌnsi'eiʃən], s. enunciación, declaración pública, articulación, pronunciación.

enunciative, enunciatory [e'nʌnsiətəri], a. enunciativo, declarativo.

envelop [en'veləp], v.t. envolver, aforrar, cubrir.

envelope ['envəloup], s. sobre; envoltura, cubierta.

envelopment [en'veləpmənt], s. envolvimiento, cubierta, funda.

envenom [en'venəm], v.t. envenenar, atosigar, emponzoñar.

enviable ['enviəbl], a. envidiable.

envier, s. envidioso.

envious ['enviəs], a. envidioso, rencoroso.

enviousness, s. envidia.

environ [en'vairən], v.t. rodear, sitiar, cercar, ceñir.

environment, s. ambiente; cercanía.

environs, s.pl. contornos, alrededores, cercanías, inmediaciones, afueras, suburbios.

envisage [en'vizidʒ], v.t. mirar cara a cara, encarar; (fig.) contemplar, encarar, imaginar.

envoy ['envɔi], s. enviado, mensajero, jefe de legación; (poét.) tornada.

envy ['envi], s. envidia, rivalidad, emulación. — v.t., v.i. envidiar, tener envidia, codiciar.

envyingly, adv. envidiosamente.

enwrap [en'ræp], v.t. envolver; (fig.) absorber, captar.

enwrapment, s. envoltura, cubierta.

enwreathe [en'ri:ð], v.t. enguirnaldar.

enzyme ['enzaim], s. enzima, fermento.

Eolian [i:'ouliən], **Eolic**, a. eólico.

epact ['i:pækt], s. epacta.

epaule ['epɔ:l], s. (fort.) espaldón.

epaulement, s. espaldón, parapeto.

epaulette ['epɔ:let], s. (mil.) capona, charretera, hombrera.

epenthesis [e'penθisis], s. (gram.) epéntesis, f.

epenthetic, epenthetical, a. epentético.

epergne [pə:ɹn], s. centro de mesa.

ephelis ['efelis], s. (med.) efélide, f.

ephemera [e'femərə], s. (med.) efémera; (zool.) efímera.

ephemeral, ephemerous, a. efímero.

ephemerides, s.pl. efemérides, f.pl.

ephemeris, s. efemérides, f.pl.

Ephesian [e'fi:ʒən], s., a. efesino.

ephod ['efɔd], s. efod, superhumeral.

epic ['epik], **epical**, a. épico. — s. epopeya, poema épico.

epicardium [epi'ka:ɹdiəm], s. epicardio.

epicarp, s. epicarpo.

epicene ['episi:n], a. epiceno.

epicure ['epikju:ɹ], s.; **Epicurean**, s., a. epicúreo, gastrónomo, sibarita, m.f.

epicurism, s. epicureísmo.

epicycle ['episaikl], s. epiciclo.

epidemic [epi'demik], **epidemical**, a. epidémico, epidemial. — s. epidemia, plaga, peste, f.

epidermic, epidermical, a. epidérmico.

epidermis [epi'də:ɹmis], s. epidermis, f., cutícula.

epigastric [epi'gæstrik], a. epigástrico.

epigastrium, s. epigastrio.

epiglottis [epi'glɔtis], s. epiglotis, f.

epigram ['epigræm], s. epigrama, m.

epigrammatic [epigrə'mætik], **epigrammatical**, a. epigramático.

epigrammatist [epi'græmətist], s. epigramatista, m.f., epigramatario.

epigrammatize, v.t. epigramatizar.

epigraph ['epigræf], s. epígrafe; inscripción.

epilepsy ['epilepsi], s. epilepsia, alferecía.

epileptic, epileptical, a. epiléptico.

epilogistic [epilo'dʒistik], a. epilogal.

epilogize [e'pilodʒaiz], v.t., v.i. epilogar, titular.

epilogue, s. epílogo.

Epiphany [e'pifəni], s. Epifanía, día de los Reyes.

episcopacy [e'piskəpəsi], s. episcopado.

episcopal, episcopalian, a. episcopal, obispal.

episcopate, s. episcopado, obispado. — v.i. (ant.) obrar como obispo.

episode ['episoud], s. episodio; digresión.

episodic, episodical, a. episódico.

episodically, adv. episódicamente, en forma de episodio.

epispastic [epi'spæstik], a. epispástico, vejigatorio.

episperm ['epispə:ɹm], s. episperma.

epistaxis [epis'tæksis], s. epistaxis, f.

epistemology [episte'mɔlədʒi], s. epistemología.

epistle [e'pisl], s. epístola; carta.

epistolary, a. epistolar.

epistolic [epis'tɔlik], **epistolical**, a. epistolar.

epistolography [epistəl'ɔgræfi], s. ciencia epistolar.

epistrophe [e'pistrəfi], s. epístrofe, f.

epistyle ['epistail], s. (arq.), epístolo, arquitrabe.

epitaph ['epitæf], s. epitafio.

epithalamium [epiθə'leimiəm], **epithalamy**, s. epitalamio.

epithelium [epi'θi:liən], s. epitelio.

epithem ['epiθem], s. epítema, epítima.

epithet ['epiθet], s. epíteto. — v.t. titular, intitular.

epithetic, a. calificativo.

epitome [e'pitəmi], s. epítome.

epitomist, s. compendiador.

epitomize, v.t. epitomar, compendiar.

epitomizer, s. epitomador.

epitrope ['epitroup], s. epítrope, f.

epoch ['i:pɔk], s. época, era.

epode ['epoud], s. epodo.

epopee, *s.* poema épico, epopeya.
Epsom salts, *s.pl.* sal de Epsom, sal de Higuera, sulfato de magnesia.
equability [ekwə'biliti], *s.* uniformidad, igualdad; ecuanimidad.
equable ['ekwəbl], *a.* ecuable (*ant.*), uniforme, igual, equivalente; ecuánime.
equal ['i:kwəl], *a.* igual, semejante, exacto, parejo; mismo; adecuado; justo, equitativo, imparcial; indiferente; (*bot.*) simétrico; *to be equal to,* (*fig.*) ponerse al nivel de, servir para, poder con. — *s.* igual; *between equals,* de igual a igual; *without equal,* sin par, sin igual, singular. — *v.t.* igualar, igualarse a, emparejar, compensar.
equality ['i:kwɔliti], *s.* igualdad, uniformidad, paridad.
equalization [i:kwəlai'zeiʃən], **equalisation,** *s.* igualación, igualamiento, iguala.
equalize ['i:kwəlaiz], **equalise,** *v.t., v.i.* igualar.
equally ['i:kwəli], *adv.* igualmente, uniformemente; imparcialmente.
equalness, *s.* igualdad, uniformidad.
equanimity [ekwə'nimiti], *s.* ecuanimidad, serenidad.
equanimous, *s.* ecuánime, constante.
equation [e'kwei3ən], *s.* ecuación.
equator [e'kweitəɪ], *s.* ecuador.
equatorial [ekwə'tɔ:ɹiel], *a.* ecuatorial.
equerry ['ekwəɹi], *s.* caballerizo mayor (o del rey); caballeriza.
equestrian [e'kwestriən], *a.* ecuestre. — *s.* jinete.
equestrianism, *s.* equitación.
equiangular [e:kwi'æŋgju:ləɹ], *a.* equiángulo.
equidistance, *s.* equidistancia.
equidistant, *a.* equidistante.
equidistantly, *adv.* a la misma distancia.
equilateral, *a.* equilátero.
equilibrate, *v.t.* equilibrar.
equilibration, *s.* equilibración, equilibrio.
equilibrious, *a.* equilibre, en equilibrio.
equilibrist, *s.* equilibrista, *m.f.*
equilibrity, *s.* equilibrio.
equilibrium, *s.* equilibrio.
equimultiple, *a.* equimúltiplo.
equine ['i:kwain], *a.* equino, caballar, hípico.
equinoctial [ekwi'nɔkʃəl], *a.* equinoccial. — *s.* línea equinoccial.
equinoctially, *adv.* en dirección equinoccial.
equinox ['ekwinɔks], *s.* equinoccio.
equip [e'kwip], *v.t.* proveer, armar, pertrechar, equipar, aprestar, aparejar, habilitar; (*mar.*) aprestar un navío.
equipage, *s.* bagajes; séquito, tren; (*ant.*) equipaje; (*ant.*) tripulación.
equipment, *s.* equipo, habilitación, aparejo, apresto; armamento; vestuario; pertrechos; material; aparato.
equipoise ['ekwipɔiz], *s.* contrapeso, equilibrio.
equipollence [ekwi'pɔləns], **equipollency,** *s.* equipolencia, equivalencia.
equipollent, *a.* equipolente, equivalente.
equiponderance [ekwi'pɔndəɹəns], *s.* contrapeso, equiponderancia.
equiponderant, *a.* equiponderante.
equitable ['ekwitəbl], *a.* equitativo, imparcial.
equitableness, *s.* equidad, imparcialidad.
equitancy, *s.* equitación.
equitation [ekwi'teiʃən], *s.* equitación.
equity ['ekwiti], *s.* equidad, justicia, rectitud.

equivalence [ek'wivələns], **equivalency,** *s.* equivalencia.
equivalent, *a., s.* equivalente.
equivocacy [e'kwivəkəsi], *s.* ambigüedad, carácter equívoco.
equivocal [e'kwivəkəl], *a.* equívoco, ambiguo. — *s.* equívoco.
equivocally, *adv.* equivocadamente, ambiguamente.
equivocalness, *s.* equívoco, ambigüedad.
equivocate [e'kwivəkeit], *v.i., v.t.* equivocar, tergiversar, usar palabras equívocas.
equivocation [ekwivə'keiʃən], *s.* equívoco, subterfugio, anfibología.
equivocator, *s.* equivoquista, *m.f.*
equivocatory, *a.* equívoco, evasivo.
era ['iəɹə], *s.* era, época, edad.
eradiate [e'reidieit], *v.i.* radiar, irradiar.
eradiation [ereidi'eiʃən], *s.* radiación; brillo.
eradicate [e'rædikeit], *v.t.* desarraigar, destruir, extirpar, erradicar.
eradication [erædi'keiʃən], *s.* erradicación, extirpación, desarraigo.
eradicative [e'rædikətiv], *a.* erradicativo.
erasable [e'reizəbl], *a.* borrable.
erase [e'reiz], *v.t.* borrar, tachar, rayar, cancelar.
erasement, *s.* canceladura; destrucción.
eraser, *s.* raspador.
erasion, erasure, *s.* raspadura, borradura, tachón, extirpación.
ere [ɛəɹ], *adv., conj.* antes, antes (de) que. — *prep.* antes de; *long ere now,* hace ya mucho tiempo.
erect [e'rekt], *v.t.* erigir, elevar, alzar, levantar; edificar, construir; fundar, establecer, instituir; erguir, enderezar. — *a.* derecho, vertical; levantado, erguido, enhiesto.
erectable, *a.* que se puede erigir.
erecter, *s.* constructor, edificador, fundador.
erectile, *a.* eréctil.
erection, *s.* (*med.*) erección; fundación, construcción (de edificios); montaje, instalación; estructura, elevación, edificación, establecimiento.
erectly, *adv.* perpendicularmente.
erectness, *s.* erección, erguimiento; posición recta.
erector, *s.* erector.
erelong [ɛəɹ'lɔŋ], *adv.* dentro de poco tiempo.
eremite ['eremait], *s.* ermitaño.
ereption [e'repʃən], *s.* arrebato, acto de arrebatar.
erethism, *s.* eretismo.
erg, ergon ['ə:ɹgɔn], *s.* ergio.
ergograph ['ə:ɹgougræf], *s.* ergografo.
ergot ['ə:ɹgɔt], *s.* cornezuelo de centeno.
ergotism, *s.* ergotismo.
eristic [e'ristik], *a.* erístico.
ermine ['ə:ɹmin], *s.* (*zool.*) armiño, piel de armiño; (*fig.*) judicatura.
ermined, *a.* armiñado.
erode [e'roud], *v.t.* corroer, roer, comer; (*geol.*) gastar, desnudar.
erodent, *a.* corrosivo, cáustico.
erosion, *s.* erosión, corrosión, desgaste.
erotic [e'rɔtik], *a.* erótico.
erotomania [erɔtə'meiniə], *s.* erotomanía.
erpetology [ə:ɹpet'ɔlədʒi], *s.* erpetología [HERPETOLOGY].
err [ə:ɹ], *v.i.* vagar, desviarse, descarriarse, errar; pecar, apartarse del buen camino.

errable, *a.* falible.

errand ['erənd], *s.* recado, comisión, mensaje, mandado, diligencia.

errant, *a.* errante, errático, vagabundo; *knight errant*, caballero andante.

errantry, *s.* vida errante.

errata [e'reitə], *s.pl.* erratas, fe de erratas.

erratic, *a.* errático, errante, errátil; vagabundo, excéntrico.

erratically, *adv.* erradamente, irregularmente.

erratum, *s.* (*pl.* errata) errata.

erroneous [e'rouniəs], *a.* errado, erróneo, falso, irregular.

erroneousness, *s.* error, falsedad.

error ['erəɹ], *s.* error, yerro, equivocación, descuido, engaño, renuncio, desacierto; pecado.

Erse ['əːɹs], *s.* lenguaje de los montañeses de Escocia.

erst, erstwhile, *adv.*, *a.* primero, antiguo, primeramente, antiguamente, al principio, antes, en otro tiempo.

erubescence [eru'besəns], *s.* erubescencia, rubor.

erubescent, *a.* erubescente, sonrojado, abochornado.

eructate ['erʌkteit], *v.i.* eructar.

eructation [erʌk'teiʃən], *s.* eructación, eructo.

erudite ['erudait], *a.* erudito.

eruditeness, erudition, *s.* erudición.

eruginous [e'rudʒinəs], *a.* eruginoso, ruginoso.

erupt [e'rʌpt], *v.i.* entrar en erupción, estar en erupción; emitir con violencia (como un volcán), salir precipitadamente, prorrumpir.

eruption, *s.* erupción; salpullido.

eruptive, *a.* eruptivo.

erysipelas [eri'sipələs], *s.* (*med.*) erisipela.

erysipelatous, *a.* erisipelatoso.

escalade [eskə'leid], *s.* escalada. — *v.t.* escalar.

escallop, *s.* pechina; endentadura; escalope.

escapade ['eskəpeid], *s.* escapada, aventura, correría, travesura.

escape [es'keip], *v.t.* huir de, evitar, esquivar, escapar, eludir. — *v.i.* huir, escapar, fugarse, salvarse. — *s.* escapada, fuga, huida, escapatoria, evasión, subterfugio; derrame; escape.

escarp [es'kaːɹp], *v.t.* escarpar.

escarp, escarpment, *s.* escarpa.

eschalot ['eʃələt], *s.* chalote.

eschar [es'kaːɹ], *s.* escara, costra.

eschatology [eskə'tolədʒi], *s.* escatología.

escheat [es'tʃiːt], *v.t.* confiscar, caducar en favor del fisco. — *v.i.* adquirir el derecho por *escheat*. — *s.* (*der.*) desherencia; caducación, reversión al fisco por falta de herederos; bienes caducantes o mostrencos.

escheatable, *a.* confiscable.

eschew [es'tʃuː], *v.t.* huir, evitar, evadir.

escort ['eskɔːɹt], *s.* escolta, acompañante, convoy. — *v.t.* escoltar, resguardar, convoyar, acompañar, cortejar.

escritoire ['eskritwaɹː], *s.* escritorio, bufete, escribanía.

Esculapian [eskju'leipiən], *a.* medicinal.

esculent ['eskjuːlənt], *s.*, *a.* comestible, comedero.

escutcheon [es'kʌtʃən], *s.* escudo de armas, blasón.

escutcheoned, *a.* blasonado.

Eskimo ['eskimou], *s.* esquimal, *m.f.*

esophagus [e'sofəgəs], *s.* esófago.

esoteric [esou'terik], *a.* esotérico; reservado, oculto.

espalier [es'pælieɹ], *s.* (*jard.*) espaldar, espaldera. — *v.t.* hacer espalderas.

esparto [es'paːɹtou], *s.* (*bot.*) esparto.

especial [es'peʃəl], *a.* especial, particular, peculiar, notable.

especialness, *s.* especialidad.

esperance, *s.* esperanza.

espial [e'spaiəl], *s.* espionaje.

espionage, *s.* espionaje.

esplanade [esplən'eid], *s.* explanada; plataforma; ribera; paseo.

espousal [e'spauzl], *a.* esponsalicio, nupcial. — *s.* desposorio, esponsales, adhesión. — *s.pl.* esponsales.

espouse, *v.t.*, *v.i.* desposar, desposarse; casarse; (*fig.*) sostener, defender.

espouser, *s.* desposado; protector, mantenedor.

espy [es'pai], *v.t.* espiar; acechar; descubrir, divisar, percibir, columbrar. — *v.i.* vigilar, velar.

esquire [es'kwaiəɹ], *s.* escudero; (*Inglaterra*) título honorífico que se pone detrás del apellido no anteponiéndose *Mr.* y algunas veces corresponde a *Don.*

essay ['esei], *v.t.* ensayar, tentar, intentar; probar, examinar, hacer inspección. — *v.i.* hacer lo posible. — *s.* ensayo, disertación, opúsculo; tentativa; empeño, conato, esfuerzo.

essayist, *s.* ensayista, *m.f.*

essence ['esəns], *s.* esencia, ser; ente; perfume, aceite volátil. — *v.t.* perfumar con esencias.

essential [e'senʃəl], *s.* esencia. — *a.* esencial, substancial, principal, vital, indispensable.

essentiality, essentialness, *s.* esencialidad.

essoin [e'sɔin], *s.* (*der.*) excusa, exención. — *v.t.* excusar, disculpar.

establish [es'tæbliʃ], *v.t.* establecer, instituir, restablecer, fundar, sentar, fijar, erigir; demostrar, verificar, probar; afirmar; sancionar, ratificar.

establisher, *s.* establecedor, fundador.

establishment, *s.* establecimiento; ley, *f.*, ordenanza, estatuto; fundación, institución, domicilio; renta vitalicia.

estate [es'teit], *s.* estado; caudal, hacienda, propiedad; posición, rango; clase, *f.*, condición, sucesión; activo; patrimonio, herencia; finca, fundo; *personal estate*, bienes muebles; *real estate*, bienes inmuebles; *third estate*, estado llano.

esteem [es'tiːm], *v.t.* estimar, considerar, honrar, reputar, apreciar, valuar; tener en precio; juzgar; pensar. — *s.* estima, estimación, aprecio, consideración, crédito.

esteemable, *a.* estimable.

ester, *s.* (*quím.*) éster.

esthetic [es'θetik], *a.* estético.

esthetics, *s.pl.* estética.

estimable ['estiməbl], *a.* estimable, apreciable, precioso; cuantitativo, calculable.

estimableness, *adv.* estimabilidad, aprecio.

estimably, *adv.* de un modo estimable.

estimate ['estimeit], *v.t.* estimar, apreciar, tasar, preciar, computar, calcular, presuponer. — *s.* estimación, tasa, aprecio; cálculo, cómputo; presupuesto; opinión, *f.*

estimation [esti'meiʃən], *s.* estimación, valuación, apreciación, calculación; juicio, opinión; aprecio, estima.

estimative, *a.* estimativo, apreciativo.

estimator, *s.* estimador, apreciador, tasador, computista, *m.f.*

estival ['estivəl], *a.* estival; veraniego.

estivate, *v.i.* veranear.

estivation [esti'veiʃən], *s.* veraneo; (*bot.*) prefloración.

estop [es'tɔp], *v.t.* (*der.*) impedir, excluir o anular o propia demanda.

estoppel, *s.* (*der.*) impedimento, excepción, acción que no puede ser negada legalmente.

estrade [es'treid], *s.* estrado, tarima.

estrange [es'treindʒ], *v.t.* extrañar, alejar, apartar, enajenar, indisponer.

estrangement, *s.* enajenamiento, extrañeza, extrañamiento, alejamiento, desvío.

estray [es'trei], *v.t.* descarriarse; errar. — *s.* animal descarriado.

estreat [es'tri:t], *v.t.* (*der.*) extraer, sacar copia o traslado de un original; compulsar; imponer una multa. — *s.* extracto, compulso.

estuary ['estju:əri], *s.* estuario, estero.

estuate ['estju:eit], *v.t.* borbotar, hervir.

estuation, *s.* ebullición, hervor, agitación.

esurient [e'zju:riənt], *a.* hambriento.

etcetera [et'setərə], **etc.,** (*lat.*) etcétera.

etch [etʃ], *v.t.* grabar al agua fuerte.

etcher, *s.* grabador al agua fuerte.

etching, *s.* aguafuerte, *f.*

etching-needle, *s.* buril de grabador.

eternal ['i:təɹnəl], *a.* eterno, inmortal, perpetuo.

eternity, *s.* eternidad.

eternize, *v.t.* eternizar.

etesian [e'ti:ʒən], *a.* etesio, anualmente periódico (viento).

ether ['i:θəɹ], *s.* éter; cielo; espíritu; (*quím.*) éter.

ethereal [e'θiəriəl], **ethereous,** *a.* etéreo, celeste, vaporoso, aéreo, sutil.

etherealize, *v.t.* (*quím.*) eterificar, espiritualizar.

etherial, *a.* (*quím.*) etérico.

etherification [iθerifi'keiʃən], *s.* eterificación.

etheriform [i'θerifɔ:ɹm], *a.* etéreo.

etherize, *v.t.* eterificar, eterizar.

ethic ['eθik], **ethical,** *a.* ético.

ethics, *s.pl.* ética.

Ethiop ['i:θiəp], *s.* etíope, Negro.

Ethiopian [i:θi'oupiən], *a.* etiópico. — *s.* etíope.

ethnic ['eθnik], **ethnical,** *a.* étnico.

ethnicism ['eθnisizm], *s.* paganismo, gentilismo.

ethnogeny [eθ'nɔdʒəni], *s.* etnogenia.

ethnographer, *s.* etnógrafo.

ethnographic [eθnə'græfik], **ethnographical,** *a.* etnográfico.

ethnography [eθ'nɔgrəfi], *s.* etnografía.

ethnology, *s.* etnología.

ethological [iθə'lɔdʒikəl], *a.* etológico, moral.

ethology [e'θɔlədʒi], *s.* etología.

ethyl ['eθil], *s.,* *a.* (*quím.*) etilo.

etiolate ['i:tioleit], *v.t.,* *v.i.* ahilar(se); blanquear(se).

etiolation, *s.* ahilamiento, descoloración.

etiology [i:ti'ɔlədʒi], *s.* (*med.*) etiología.

etiquette ['etiket], *s.* etiqueta, ceremonial.

etui ['etwi:], *s.* estuche, vaina, caja, bolsa.

etymologer [eti'mɔlədʒəɹ], **etymologist,** *s.* etimologista, *m.f.*

etymological [etimə'lɔdʒikəl], *a.* etimológico.

etymologize [eti'mɔlədʒaiz], *v.t.* etimologizar.

etymology, *s.* etimología.

etymon ['etimɔn], *s.* forma primitiva o radical de una palabra.

eucalyptus [ju:kə'liptəs], *s.* (*bot.*) eucalipto.

eucharist ['ju:kərist], *s.* eucaristía.

eucharistic [ju:kə'ristik], **eucharistical,** *a.* eucarístico.

euchology [ju:'kɔlədʒi], *s.* eucologio.

euchre ['ju:kəɹ], *s.* juego de naipes.

euclorine ['ju:klɔri:n], *s.* gas amarillo y explosivo obtenido de la mezcla del clorato de potasa y el acido clorhídrico.

eudemonism [ju:'di:mənizm], *s.* ramo de la ética que trata de la felicidad.

eudiometer [ju:di'ɔmitəɹ], *s.* (*fís.*) eudiómetro.

eudiometric [ju:dio'metrik], **eudiometrical,** *a.* eudiométrico.

eugenic [ju:'dʒenik], *a.* eugenésico.

eulogic, eulogical [ju:'lɔdʒikəl], *a.* laudatorio.

eulogist ['ju:lədʒist], *s.* elogiador, panegirista, *m.f.*

eulogistic [ju:lə'dʒistik], *a.* laudatorio.

eulogium [ju:'lɔdʒiəm], *s.* elogio.

eulogize ['ju:lədʒaiz], *v.t.* elogiar, encomiar, loar, preconizar, aplaudir.

eulogy, *s.* elogio, encomio, panegírico, alabanza.

eunuch ['ju:nək], *s.* eunuco, capón.

eupatorium [ju:pə'toəriəm], **eupatory** [ju:'peitəri], *s.* (*bot.*) eupatorio, agrimonia.

eupepsy [ju:'pepsi], *s.* (*med.*) eupepsia.

euphemism ['ju:fəmizm], *s.* eufemismo.

euphemistic [ju:fə'mistik], *a.* eufémico.

euphonia [ju:'founiə], *s.* eufonía.

euphonic, euphonical, euphonious, *a.* eufónico.

euphonium [ju:'founiəm], *s.* (*mús.*) eufono.

euphony ['ju:fəni], *s.* eufonía.

euphorbia [ju:'fɔ:ɹbiə], *s.* (*bot.*) euforbio.

euphrasy ['ju:frəsi], *s.* eufrasia.

euphuism ['ju:fju:izm], *s.* (*ret.*) eufuismo.

Eurasian [ju:'reiʒən], *a.* eurasio.

eureka [ju:'ri:kə], *s.* ¡eureka! (¡Lo he hallado!).

eurhythmics, [ju:'riðmiks] **eurhythmy** [ju:'riðmi], *s.* euritmia.

European, *s.,* *a.* europeo.

eurycephalic, eurycephalous [ju:ri'sefələs], *a.* euricéfalo.

Eustachian tube, *n.* (*anat.*) trompa de Eustaquio.

eustyle ['ju:stail], *s.* (*arq.*) éustilo.

euthanasia [ju:θə'neiʃə], *s.* eutanasia, muerte tranquila, sin sufrimiento.

evacuant [e'vækjuənt], *a.* (*med.*) evacuante.

evacuate, *v.t.* evacuar, vaciar, desocupar.

evacuation [evækju:'eiʃən], *s.* evacuación.

evacuative [e'vækju:ətiv], *a.* evacuativo, purgativo.

evade [e'veid], *v.t.,* *v.i.* evadir, escapar, esquivar, huir; eludir.

evanesce [evə'nes], *v.i.* desaparecer, disiparse, desvanecerse.

evanescence, *s.* desvanecimiento, disipación.

evanescent, *a.* efímero, pasajero; inestable.

evangel [e'vændʒəl], *s.* evangelio.

evangelic, evangelical [evæn'dʒelikl], *a.* evangélico.

evangelicism, evangelism, *s.* evangelismo.

evangelist [e'vændʒəlist], *s.* evangelista, *m.*, evangelizador.

evangelization [evændʒəlai'zeiʃən], *s.* acción de evangelizar.

evangelize [e'vændʒəlaiz], *v.t.* evangelizar.

evanish, *v.i.* (*poét.*) desaparecer, desvanecerse.

evaporable [e'væpərəbl], *a.* evaporable.

evaporate, *v.i.* evaporarse; disiparse; (*fam.*) desaparecer, esfumarse. — *v.t.* evaporar, evaporizar, secar, desecar; desvanecer, disipar.

evaporation [evæpə'reiʃən], *s.* evaporación.

evaporative [e'væpərətiv], *a.* evaporativo.

evasion [e'veiʒən], *s.* evasión, evasiva; escapatoria, efugio; excusa, subterfugio.

evasive, *a.* evasivo, ambiguo.

eve, even, *s.* tardecita, vigilia, víspera.

evection [e'vekʃən], *s.* elevación; (*ast.*) evección.

even ['i:vən], *s.* [EVE]. — *a.* llano, plano, igual, uniforme, liso, raso, de nivel, par; constante, firme; suave; justo, imparcial, sereno, invariable; *even with,* al nivel de, en paz con; *to be even with,* (*fig.*) estar saldo con; *to make even,* allanar, compensar, igualar. — *adv.* aún, aun cuando, también, supuesto (que); exactamente, precisamente, enteramente; sin embargo, no obstante; *even as,* como; *even now,* ahora mismo; *not even,* ni siquiera. — *v.t.* igualar, allanar, unir; nivelar, enrasar; desquitar; arreglar, liquidar cuentas. — *v.i.* igualarse, emparejarse, nivelarse.

even-minded, *a.* imperturbable.

even-tempered, *a.* plácido.

evening ['i:vniŋ], *s.* tarde, *f.*, caída de la tarde, vísperas, anochecer; (*fig.*) terminación, final. — *a.* vespertino; *evening function,* velada; *evening star,* véspero, héspero, estrella vespertina; *good evening!* ¡buenas tardes!

evenness, *s.* igualdad, uniformidad; imparcialidad; nivel; lisura, llanura.

evensong, *s.* vísperas.

event [e'vent], *s.* evento, hecho, suceso, caso acontecimiento, acaecimiento; éxito, consecuencia, resultado; desenlace; *at all events,* o *in any event,* sea lo que fuere, o de todos modos; *in the event of,* en caso de (que).

eventerate [e'ventəreit], *v.t.* destripar.

eventful, *a.* fecundo en acontecimientos, memorable, notable, extraordinario, singular.

eventilate, *v.t.* aventar.

eventilation [ventə'leiʃən], *s.* ventilación.

eventual [e'ventjuəl], *a.* eventual; definitivo, fortuito, acaecedero, consiguiente, último, final.

eventuate, *v.i.* acaecer, suceder, acontecer.

ever ['evəɪ], *adv.* siempre, en todo caso, en cualquier tiempo, alguna vez, perpetuamente; en cualquier grado; en todo caso; generalmente; después de una negación o voz limitativa, nunca, jamás; *ever and anon,* de vez en cuando; *hardly ever,* o *scarcely ever,* casi nunca; *for ever and ever,* para siempre o por siempre jamás, o eternamente; *ever since,* desde entonces; *ever so little,* por poco que sea; *as soon as ever you can,* en cuanto pueda.

evergreen, *a.* siempre verde; (*fig.*) siempre joven o tierno. — *s.* (*bot.*) siempreviva.

everlasting, *a.* eterno, sempiterno, perdurable, perpetuo. — *s.* eternidad; ser eterno; sempiterna.

ever-living, *a.* inmortal, perdurable, sempiterno.

evermore, *adv.* eternamente, para siempre jamás.

eversion [e'vəːɪʃən], *s.* eversión, trastorno.

evert [e'vəːɪt], *v.t.* trastornar, volver de dentro afuera.

every ['evəri], *a.* cada uno, cada una; todo, todos; *every day,* cada día; *every-day,* cotidiano; *every other day,* cada dos días o un día si y otro no; *every now and then* o *every so often,* una que otra vez.

everybody, *s.* todo el mundo.

everything, *s.* todo.

everywhere, *adv.* en todas partes.

evict [e'vikt], *v.t.* desposeer; convencer, probar; desalojar, desaposentar; desahuciar; excluir, expulsar.

eviction, *s.* evidencia, prueba; (*der.*) despojo, desahucio.

evidence ['evidens], *s.* evidencia, testimonio, demostración, prueba; testigo; deposición; declaración. — *v.t.* evidenciar, declarar, hacer patente; *to give evidence,* declarar, deponer; *to turn king's evidence,* revelar sus cómplices.

evident, *a.* evidente, patente, claro, manifiesto, notorio.

evidentness, *s.* evidencia.

evil ['i:vəl], *a.* malo, depravado, miserable, perverso, pernicioso, maligno, dañoso; *evil communications corrupt good manners,* quien con lobos anda, a aullar se enseña. — *s.* maldad, depravación, mal, injuria, daño; desgracia, infortunio, calamidad; enfermedad; *king's evil,* escrófula, lamparones; *the Evil One,* el diablo, Satanás. — *adv.* malamente, injuriosamente.

evil-disposed, *a.* malintencionado.

evil-doer, *s.* malvado, malhechor.

evil-favoured, *a.* contrahecho.

evil-minded, *a.* malicioso, mal intencionado.

evilness, *s.* malignidad.

evil-speaker, *s.* mala lengua.

evil-speaking, *a.* maledicencia, calumnia, murmuración.

evince [e'vins], *v.t.* probar, justificar, demostrar, hacer patente. — *v.i.* probar.

evincible, *a.* demostrable.

evincive, *a.* convincente.

evirate ['evireit], *v.t.* castrar, capar.

eviscerate [i'visəreit], *v.t.* destripar, desentrañar.

evitable ['evitəbl], *a.* evitable.

evoke [i'vouk], *v.t.* evocar, llamar; (*for.*) avocar.

evolute ['evəlu:t], *s.* (*geom.*) voluta, evoluta.

evolution, *s.* evolución, desarrollo, desenvolvimiento, despliegue; progreso, marcha, crecimiento; (*mat.*) extracción de una raíz; (*mil. y mar.*) maniobra.

evolutional, evolutionary, *a.* evolucionario; evolutivo.

evolutionism, *s.* evolucionismo.

evolutionist, *s.* táctico, estratégico; evolucionista.

evolve [i'vɔlv], *v.t.* desenvolver, desarrollar,

desplegar; abrir; extraer. — *v.i.* abrirse, extenderse, desplegarse, desenvolverse, desarrollarse.

evolvent, *s.* (*geom.*) evolvente, curva que produce la evoluta.

evulsion [i'vʌlʃən], *s.* (*cir.*) evulsión, arranque.

ewe [juː], *s.f.* oveja.

ewer [juːəɹ], *s.* jarro, aguamanil.

ex [eks], *prefijo* ex; antiguo.

exacerbate [ek'sæsəɹbeit], *v.t.* exacerbar, exasperar, irritar.

exacerbation [eksæsəɹ'beiʃən], *s.* exacerbación, irritación.

exact [ek'zækt], *a.* exacto, cabal; preciso, correcto, estricto, justo, fiel; metódico. — *v.t.* exigir, imponer. — *v.i.* apremiar.

exacter, *s.* exactor.

exacting, *a.* exigente.

exaction, *s.* exacción, extorsión.

exactitude [ek'zæktitjud], *s.* exactitud, puntualidad.

exactness, *s.* exactitud, puntualidad, precisión.

exaggerate [ek'zædʒəreit], *v.t.* exagerar, encarecer, ponderar, abultar.

exaggeration [ekzædʒə'reiʃən], *s.* exageración, ponderación.

exaggeratory [ek'zædʒəreitəri], *a.* exagerativo.

exalt [ek'zɔːlt], *v.t.* exaltar, levantar, elevar, enaltecer, glorificar, honrar; rejocijar, alegrar, sublimar.

exaltation [ekzɔːl'teiʃən], *s.* exaltación, elevación, dignidad; promoción, ensalzamiento; contento, regocijo.

exalted [ek'zɔːltid], *a.* exaltado, eminente, sublime.

examinable [ek'zæminəbl], *a.* investigable, averiguable.

examination [ekzæmi'neiʃən], *s.* examen, investigación, averiguación, verificación; interrogatorio, inspección.

examine [ek'zæmin], *v.t.* examinar, escudriñar, explorar, registrar, reconocer, investigar, inspeccionar, preguntar, tomar declaración, ensayar, inquirir, analizar, aquilatar.

examiner, *s.* examinador, interrogador, escudriñador, inspector.

example [ek'zɑːmpl], *s.* ejemplo, lección; original, ejemplar, muestra, prototipo, paradigma, *m.*; *to set an example,* dar ejemplo; *for example,* por ejemplo.

exampler, *s.* ejemplo; modelo, patrón.

exanimate [ek'zænimeit], *a.* exánime, sin vida, muerto, inanimado, sin ánimo.

exanthema [ek'zænθəmə], *s.* (*med.*) exantema, erupción sarpullido.

exanthematic [ekzænθə'mætic], **exanthematous,** *a.* exantemático, eruptivo.

exarch ['eksɑːɹk], *s.* exarca, *m.*, exarco; legado de un patriarca en la Iglesia griega.

exarchate, *s.* exarcado, distrito, dignidad de un exarca.

exasperate [ek'zæspəreit], *v.t.* exasperar, enojar, irritar, provocar, agravar, amargar. — *a.* exasperado, irritado.

exasperater, *s.* provocador.

exasperation [ekzæspə'reiʃən], *s.* exasperación, provocación, agravación, irritación, enojo.

excandescence [ekzkæn'desens], *s.* (*fís.*) excandecencia.

excavate ['ekskəveit], *v.t.* descarnar; excavar, socavar; cavar, minar; ahondar, vaciar.

excavation [ekskə'veiʃən], *s.* excavación, cavidad, hoyo; escombro.

excavator, *s.* excavador; (máquina) excavadora.

exceed [ek'siːd], *v.t.* exceder, aventajar, descollar, sobrepujar, sobresalir, superar. — *v.i.* excederse, propasarse; aventajarse; preponderar.

exceeding, *a.* excesivo, excedente, superante.

exceedingly, *adv.* excesivamente, sumamente, muy, mucho, en alto grado, eminentemente.

excel [ek'sel], *v.t., v.i.* sobrepujar, sobresalir, aventajar; aventajarse, superar, vencer, ganar, dejar atrás.

excellence, excellency ['ekselənsi], *s.* excelencia; preeminencia, dignidad, rango; bondad.

excellent, *a.* excelente, sobresaliente, primoroso, selecto; *interj.* ¡de perlas!

excelsior [ek'selsiɔɹ], *a.* aun más alto, más elevado, o eminente. — *s.* (*E.U.*) virutas y hebras de madera para empaquetar.

except [ek'sept], *v.t.* exceptuar, excluir, omitir. — *v.i.* excepcionar, declinar, recusar. — *prep.* excepto, si no, a excepción de, con exclusión de, fuera de, menos, a menos que.

excepting, *prep.* a excepción de, fuera de, salvo.

exception, *s.* excepción, exclusión; (*for.*) recusación, objeción, salvedad.

exceptionable, *a.* recusable, tachable.

exceptional, *a.* excepcional, poco común, superior.

exceptious, *a.* impertinente; susceptible; quisquilloso; caviloso.

exceptive, *a.* excepcional, susceptible, quisquilloso.

exceptor, *a.* exceptuador, opositor, censurador.

excern, *v.t.* (*med.*) expeler.

excerpt ['eksəɹpt], *v.t.* escoger, recoger, extractar, citar un texto. — *s.* extracto; selección, cita.

excerption [ek'səːrpʃən], *s.* selección, colección, extracto.

excerptive, *a.* extractador.

excess [ek'ses], *s.* exceso, demasía, sobra, creces, *f.pl.*; inmoderación, destemplanza, transgresión, desorden, desarreglo; (*com.*) sobrante.

excessive, *a.* excesivo, desarreglado, inmoderado.

excessively, *adv.* excesivamente, extremadamente, sobremanera.

excessiveness, *s.* exceso.

exchange [eks'tʃeindʒ], *v.t.* cambiar, trocar, permutar, canjear. — *s.* cambio, trueque, permuta, canje; (*com.*) bolsa, lonja; (*com.*) cambio, giro; *bill of exchange,* letra de cambio.

exchangeable, *a.* cambiable.

exchanger, *s.* cambista, *m.f.*, banquero.

exchequer [eks'tʃekəɹ], *s.* fisco, tesorería; real hacienda; ministerio de hacienda.

excisable [ek'saizəbl], *a.* sujeto al derecho de sisa.

excise ['eksaiz], *s.* impuesto sobre consumos, alcohol y tabaco. — *v.t.* [ek'saiz], aforar; cortar, extirpar.

exciseman, *s.* aforador; aduanero.

excision [ek'siʒən], *s.* (*cir.*) excisión, extirpación.
excitability [eksaitə'biliti], *s.* excitabilidad.
excitable, *a.* excitable.
excitant, *a.* excitante.
excitate, *v.t.* excitar.
excitation [eksai'teiʃən], *s.* excitación, instigación, incitamiento.
excitative [ek'saitətiv], *a.* excitativo, provocativo.
excitator, *s.* (*elec.*) excitador.
excitatory [eksai'teitəri], *a.* excitador.
excite [ek'sait], *v.t.* excitar, provocar, animar, estimular, emocionar.
excitedly, *adv.* acaloradamente, agitadamente, con emoción.
excitement, *s.* estímulo, instigación, incitamiento, excitación; agitación, conmoción, acaloramiento; emoción.
exciter, *s.* motor, incitador, agitador, instigador; (*med.*) excitante.
exciting, *a.* excitante, incitante; conmovedor; emocionante; *exciting cause*, (*med.*) concausa, causa ocasional.
excitive, *a.* excitativo.
exclaim [eks'kleim], *v.i.* clamar, exclamar; *exclaim against*, clamar contra. — *s.* clamor, gritería.
exclaimer, *s.* gritador, declamador.
exclamation [eksklə'meiʃən], *s.* exclamación, clamor, grito; *exclamation mark*, (*gram.*) punto de admiración (!).
exclamative, exclamatory, *a.* exclamativo, exclamatorio.
exclude [eks'klu:d], *v.t.* excluir, exceptuar, rechazar, desechar, echar fuera.
exclusion [eks'klu:ʒən], *s.* exclusión, exclusiva; eliminación, excepción; emisión; expulsión; recusación.
exclusive, *a.* exclusivo, privativo, exceptuado.
exclusively, *adv.* únicamente, exclusivamente.
exclusiveness, *s.* carácter exclusivo.
exclusivism, *s.* sistema de exclusión.
excogitate [eks'kɔdʒiteit], *v.t.* excogitar, pensar, inventar, imaginar.
excogitation [ekskɔdʒi'teiʃən], *s.* meditación, reflexión, invención, pensamiento.
excommunicable [ekskə'mju:nikəbl], *a.* digno de excomunión.
excommunicate, *v.t.* excomulgar, descomulgar, anatematizar. — *s., a.* excomulgado.
excommunication [ekskəmju:ni'keiʃən], *s.* excomunión, descomunión, religioso.
excoriate [eks'kɔərieit], *v.t.* escoriar, desollar, gastar, arrancar, corroer.
excoriation [ekskɔəri'eiʃən], *s.* escoriación, desolladura; (*fig.*) robo, engaño.
excortication [ekskɔəɹti'keiʃən], *s.* descortezamiento, descortezadura.
excrement ['ekskrəmənt], *s.* excremento, estiércol.
excremental [ekskrə'mentəl], *a.* excremental.
excrementitial, excrementitious [ekskrimen'tiʃəs], *a.* excrementicio, excrementoso.
excrescence [eks'kresəns], *s.* excrecencia.
excrescent, *a.* superfluo.
excrete [eks'kri:t], *v.t.* excretar; echar fuera, arrojar. — *s.* excremento.
excretion, *s.* excreción, excremento.
excretive, *a.* excretorio.

excretory, *a.* excretorio. — *s.* órgano excretorio.
excruciate [eks'kru:ʃieit], *v.t.* atormentar, dar tormento a, afligir.
excruciating, *a.* atroz, agudísimo, penosísimo, muy doloroso.
excruciation [ekskru:ʃi'eiʃən], *s.* tortura, suplicio, tormento.
exculpate ['ekskəlpeit], *v.t.* disculpar, excusar, justificar.
exculpation [ekskəl'peiʃən], *s.* disculpa.
exculpatory, *a.* justificativo, disculpador.
excurrent [eks'kʌrənt], *a.* manante, corriente o fluyente hacia fuera (como la sangre del corazón); abriéndose paso hacia el exterior; (*bot.*) saliendo o proyectándose más allá del borde o punto.
excursion [eks'kə:ɹʃən], *s.* paseo, viaje corto, excursión; romería; rodeo; correría; (*mil.*) salida, expedición, digresión; (*mec.*) curso, recorrido; (*astr.*) desviación del curso fijado.
excursionist, *s.* viajero, excursionista, *m.f.*
excursive, *a.* errante, vagante, paseante, viajante; (*fig.*) distraído; errático, pasajero.
excursively, *adv.* caprichosamente.
excursiveness, *s.* extravagancia, calidad de errante.
excusable [eks'kju:zəbl], *a.* excusable, disculpable.
excusableness, *s.* carácter excusable o disculpable.
excusatory [ekskju'zeitəri], *a.* justificativo; apologético.
excuse [eks'kju:z], *v.t.* excusar, disculpar, vindicar; perdonar, remitir, justificar, sincerar; eximir, libertar, exentar, dispensar, disimular, paliar. — *s.* excusa, disculpa, pretexto, defensa, justificación.
excuseless, *a.* inexcusable.
excuser, *s.* excusador, intercesor, apologista, *m.f.*
exeat ['eksiæt], *s.* permiso, (*igl.*) exeat.
execrable [ek'zekrəbl], *a.* execrable, aborrecible, abominable.
execrate ['eksikreit], *v.t.* execrar, abominar, maldecir.
execration [eksi'kreiʃən], *s.* execración.
execratory, *a.* execratorio.
executable ['eksəkjutəbl], *a.* ejecutable.
executant, *s.* ejecutante.
execute ['eksikju:t], *v.t.* ejecutar, cumplir, llevar a cabo, desempeñar; (*for.*) legalizar; ajusticiar.
executer ['eksikju:təɹ], *s.* ejecutor.
execution [eksi'kju:ʃən], *s.* ejecución; embargo, aprehensión; destrucción, mortandad.
executioner, *s.* ejecutor, verdugo.
executive [ek'zekətiv], *a.* ejecutivo. — *s.* poder ejecutivo, el gobierno; la autoridad suprema.
executor, *s.* ejecutor; albacea, testamentario.
executorship, *s.* albaceazgo.
executory, *s.* ejecutorio, ejecutivo, administrativo.
executrix [ek'zekjutriks], *s.* albacea, testamentaria.
exegesis [eksə'dʒi:sis], *s.* exégesis, *f.*, explicación, comentario.
exegete ['eksədʒi:t], *s.* exegeta, *m.f.*
exegetical [eksə'dʒetikl], *a.* exegético.

exemplar [ek'zempləɹ], *s.* ejemplar, original, modelo, dechado.

exemplariness, *s.* ejemplar, modelo; carácter ejemplar.

exemplary, *a.* ejemplar.

exemplification [ekzemplifi'keiʃən], *s.* ejemplificación; (*for.*) copia certificada.

exemplify [ek'zemplifai], *v.t.* ejemplificar, declarar, manifestar; copiar, trasladar.

exempt [ek'zempt], *v.t.* exentar, eximir, libertar, franquear, exceptuar, dispensar. — *a.* exento, libre, franco.

exemptible, *a.* exento, privilegiado, libre.

exemption, *s.* exención, inmunidad, dispensa, franquicia.

exenterate [ek'zentəreit], *v.t.* desentrañar, destripar.

exequatur [eksə'kweitəɹ], *s.* (*igl. dip.*) exequátur.

exequial [ek'zekwiəl], *a.* funerario, funeral.

exequies ['eksəkwis], *s.pl.* exequias, honras fúnebres.

exercisable [eksəɹsaizəbl], *a.* ejercitativo.

exercise ['eksəɹsaiz], *s.* ejercicio, trabajo; tarea; práctica, uso; tema, *m.*; estudio; gimnasia. — *v.t.* ejercitar, ejercer, adiestrar, formar, habituar, atarear; emplear; preocupar; comunicar. — *v.i., v.r.* ejercitarse, adiestrarse; hacer ejercicio; (*mil.*) maniobrar.

exerciser, *s.* ejercitante.

exercitation [eksəɹsai'teiʃən], *s.* ejercitación, ejercicio, práctica.

exergue [ek'zəːɹg], *s.* (*numism.*) exergo.

exert [ek'zəːɹt], *v.t.* arrojar, extender, proyectar; desplegar, demostrar, hacer ver; ejercer; ejecutar; esforzar; emitir; *to exert oneself,* apurarse, hacer un esfuerzo.

exertion, *s.* esfuerzo, conato.

exeunt ['ekziənt], (*teat.*) vanse.

exfoliate [eks'foulieit], *v.t.* (*cir.*) exfoliar. — *v.i.* exfoliarse; (*min.*) quitar láminas, escamas, esquirlas, etc.

exfoliation [eksfouli'eiʃən], *s.* exfoliación.

exhalable [ek'zeiləbl], *a.* exhalable, evaporable.

exhalant, *s., a.* exhalador.

exhalation [eksə'leiʃən], *s.* exhalación.

exhale [eks'heil], *v.t.* exhalar, evaporar, emitir; despedir. — *v.i.* evaporarse; disiparse, desvanecerse.

exhalement, *s.* exhalación.

exhaust [ek'zɔːst], *v.t.* agotar; apurar, extraer, vaciar; cansar; gastar, consumir, disipar; empobrecer, depauperar; enflaquecer, postrar; (*fís.*) aspirar. — *s.* (*mec.*) escape; vapor de escape; *exhaust pipe,* tubo de escape.

exhausted, *a.* agotado, apurado, exhausto.

exhauster, *s.* agotador; (*fís.*) aspirador.

exhaustible, *a.* agotable.

exhausting, *a.* agotador.

exhaustion, *s.* agotamiento, evacuación, vaciamiento; (*fís.*) aspiración; debilitación, enervación, postración.

exhaustive, *a.* minucioso; completo.

exhaustless, *a.* inagotable.

exhaustment, *s.* desecamiento.

exheredation [ekzerə'deiʃən], *s.* (*for.*) desheredamiento.

exhibit [ek'zibit], *v.t.* exhibir, presentar, ofrecer; exponer, mostrar, manifestar; administrar. — *s.* objeto expuesto al público,

o colección de objetos; manifestación; (*for.*) documento fehaciente; prueba.

exhibition [eksi'biʃən], *s.* exhibición, exposición; espectáculo, manifestación, presentación; beca, prebenda, pensión.

exhibitioner, *s.* becario.

exhibitive [ek'zibətiv], *a.* representativo.

exhibitor, *s.* exponente, expositor.

exhibitory, *a.* (*der.*) exhibitorio; que exhibe.

exhilarant [ek'zilərənt], *a.* alegre, divertido, regocijador; estimulante, vigorizante.

exhilarate [ek'ziləreit], *v.t.* alegrar, causar alegría, regocijar, divertir. — *v.i.* recrear; alegrarse.

exhilarating, *a.* estimulador; vigorizador.

exhilaratingly, *adv.* de un modo divertido.

exhilaration [ekzilə'reiʃən], *s.* alegría, alborozo, regocijo.

exhort [ek'zɔːt], *v.t.* exhortar, inducir, excitar.

exhortation [ekzɔːɹ'teiʃən], *s.* exhortación; consejo, aviso.

exhortative [ek'zɔːɹtətiv], *a.* exhortativo.

exhortator, exhorter, *s.* exhortador.

exhortatory, *a.* exhortatorio.

exhumation [ekzju:'meiʃən], *s.* exhumación, desentierro.

exhume [ek'zju:m], *v.t.* exhumar, desenterrar.

exigence, exigency [ek'zidʒənsi], *s.* exigencia, falta, urgencia, necesidad, aprieto, apuro.

exigent, *a.* exigible, exigente. — *s.* urgencia, perplejidad, embarazo.

exiguous [ek'zigjuəs], *a.* exiguo, pequeño.

exile ['ekzail], *s.* destierro; desterrado; expatriación. — *v.t.* desterrar, confinar, deportar.

exilement, *s.* destierro.

exility [ek'ziliti], *s.* exigüidad; tenuidad, pequeñez.

exist [ek'zist], *v.i.* existir, vivir, subsistir.

existence, *s.* existencia, ente, ser, vida.

existent, existing [ek'zistiŋ], *a.* existente.

existentialism [ekzis'tenʃiəlizm], *s.* existencialismo.

exit, *s.* salida; (*teat.*) vase; partida, muerte, *f.*

exode, exodus ['eksədəs], *s.* éxodo, salida, emigración.

exonerate [ek'zɔnəreit], *v.t.* exonerar; disculpar, descargar, aliviar, relevar, vindicar.

exoneration [ekzɔnə'reiʃən], *s.* exoneración, exculpación, descargo, vindicación.

exonerative [ek'zɔnərətiv], *a.* que puede exonerar.

exorable ['eksərəbl], *a.* exorable.

exorbitance [ek'sɔːɹbitəns], *s.* exorbitancia, enormidad, exceso; desorden, extravagancia.

exorbitant, *a.* exorbitante, excesivo, desarreglado, desproporcionado, enorme.

exorcise ['eksɔːɹsaiz], *v.t.* exorcizar, conjurar.

exorciser, exorcist, *s.* exorcista, *m.f.*, conjurador.

exorcism [ekzɔːɹsizm], *s.* exorcismo, conjuro.

exordial [ek'zɔːɹdiəl], *a.* previo, preliminar.

exordium, *s.* exordio, preámbulo.

exosmose ['eksozmouz], *s.* (*fís.*) exósmosis, *f.*

exosmotic [eksos'mɔtik], *a.* exosmótico.

exosseous [ek'sosiəs], *a.*, (*ant.*) desosado.

exoteric, exoterical [eksou'terikl], *a.* exotérico.

exotericism, *s.* trivialidad.

exothermic [eksou'θəːɹmik], *a.* exotérmico.

exotic [ek'zɔtik], *a.* exótico, extranjero, forastero.

expand [eks'pænd], *v.t.* extender, esparcir; tender, alargar, dilatar, ensanchar, desplegar; desarrollar. — *v.i.* desarrollarse, dilatarse, hincharse, ensancharse, desplegarse, abrirse.

expanse, *s.* extensión, espacio.

expansibility [ekspænsi'biliti], *s.* (*fís.*) expansibilidad.

expansible [eks'pænsibl], *a.* expansible, expansivo.

expansibleness, *s.* expansibilidad.

expansion, *s.* expansión; distensión; (*fís.*) dilatación; (*anat.*) prolongación; anchura, largura; desarrollo.

expansive, *a.* expansivo.

expansiveness, *s.* expansibilidad.

ex-parte [eks-pɑ:ɹti], *adv.* (*for.*) de una de las partes.

expatiate [eks'peiʃieit], *v.t.* extender, alargar, amplificar. — *v.i.* espaciarse; extenderse, discurrir; andar errante.

expatiation [ekspeiʃi'eiʃən], *s.* difusión, digresión; irregularidad, prolijidad.

expatiator [eks'peiʃieitəɹ], *s.* amplificador; persona locuaz.

expatiatory, *a.* prolijo, difuso.

expatriate [eks'pætrieit], *v.t.* expatriar, desterrar, desnaturalizar.

expatriation [ekspætri'eiʃən], *s.* expatriación, destierro.

expect [eks'pekt], *v.t.* esperar, aguardar; estar preparado a; fiar, descansar en, contar con. — *v.i.* esperar.

expectable, *a.* esperable, expectable.

expectancy, *s.* expectación, espera, esperanza.

expectant, *a.* expectante; (de una madre) embarazada. — *s.* esperador, el que espera.

expectation [ekspek'teiʃən], *s.* expectación, expectativa, esperanza; *expectation of life*, duración media de la vida.

expectingly [eks'pektiŋli], *adv.* en la expectativa.

expectorant [eks'pektərənt], *s., a.* (*med.*) expectorante.

expectorate, *v.t., v.i.* expectorar.

expectoration [ekspektə'reiʃən], *s.* expectoración, esputo, gargajo.

expectorative [eks'pektərətiv], *a.* expectorativo, expectorante.

expedience, expediency [eks'pi:diənsi], *s.* aptitud, propriedad; utilidad, conveniencia; oportunidad.

expedient, *a.* conveniente, útil, propio, oportuno, expedito, prudente, ventajoso. — *s.* medio, expediente, estratagema, recurso, partido, corte.

expediently, *adv.* convenientemente, aptamente, a propósito.

expedite ['ekspədait], *v.t.* expedir, dar prisa; apresurar, acelerar; facilitar; cursar, dar curso. — *a.* pronto, expeditivo.

expedition [ekspə'diʃən], *s.* prontitud, diligencia; expedición; celeridad, prisa; (*mil.*) expedición.

expeditionary, *a.* expedicionario.

expeditious, *a.* expedito, expeditivo, pronto.

expeditive [eks'pedətiv], *a.* expedito, pronto.

expel [eks'pel], *v.t.* expulsar, arrojar, expeler, echar fuera (por la fuerza, o autoridad), despedir, desterrar, excluir.

expellable, *a.* expulsable, que se puede expeler.

expellant, *a.* expelente.

expeller, *s.* expulsor.

expend [eks'pend], *v.t.* expender, gastar, desembolsar; emplear (tiempo, palabras, dinero, etc.).

expenditure, *s.* gasto, desembolso.

expense [eks'pens], *s.* gasto, costa, costo, coste, expensas, desembolso, (teneduría) egreso; *to go to expense*, meterse en gastos; *at any expense*, a todo coste, a toda costa; *petty expenses*, gastos menudos; *free of expense*, franco de gastos.

expenseless, *a.* sin gastos; poco costoso.

expensive, *a.* pródigo, gastador; costoso; caro; liberal, dispendioso.

expensively, *adv.* costosamente, dispendiosamente.

expensiveness, *s.* prodigalidad; dispendio; precio elevado; carestía.

experience [eks'pi:riens], *s.* experiencia, práctica, incidente, conocimiento, pericia, lance, paso, aventura; *by experience*, por experiencia. — *v.t.* experimentar, probar, sentir, conocer.

experienced, *a.* experimentado, hábil, experto, práctico, versado, perito, amaestrado, aleccionado.

experiment [eks'perimənt], *s.* experimento, ensayo, prueba, probatura, tentativa. — *v.t., v.i.* experimentar.

experimental [eksperi'mentəl], *a.* experimental.

experimentalist, *s.* experimentador.

experimentally, *adv.* experimentalmente, por experiencia.

experimenter, experimentist [eks'periməntist], *s.* experimentador.

expert [ekspə'ɹt], *a.* experto, experimentado, práctico, diestro, hábil. — *s.* experto; juez, *m.*

expertness, *s.* destreza, habilidad, maña, pericia.

expiable ['ekspiəbl], *a.* expiable.

expiate, *v.t.* expiar, purgar, reparar.

expiation [ekspi'eiʃən], *s.* expiación; reparación.

expiator ['ekspiətəɹ], *s.* el que expía.

expiatory, *a.* expiatorio.

expirable [eks'pairəbl], *a.* expirable.

expiration [ekspai'reiʃən], *s.* respiración, exhalación, espiración; expiración; último suspiro, muerte, *f.*; término, terminación, remate; exhalación, vapor.

expire [eks'paiɹ], *v.t.* respirar, exhalar, espirar; espirar; expeler. — *v.i.* morir, expirar; (*for.*) terminar, concluir, cerrar.

expiry, *s.* terminación, fin; (*com.*) vencimiento; *expiry date*, plazo.

explain [eks'plein], *v.t.* explicar, aclarar, dilucidar, interpretar, explanar; desarrollar. — *v.i.* explicarse.

explainable, *a.* explicable.

explainer, *s.* exponente, intérprete, comentador.

explanation [eksplə'neiʃən], *s.* explicación, explanación, interpretación, aclaración, dilucidación.

explanative, explanatory [eksplə'neitəri], *a.* explicativo.

expletive [eks'pli:tiv], *a.* expletivo. — *s.* interjección, partícula, expletiva.

explicable [eks'plikəbl], *a.* explicable.
explicate ['eksplikeit], *v.t.* desplegar, desarrollar; explicar, aclarar, interpretar. — *a.* desplegado, desarrollado.
explication [ekspli'keiʃən], *s.* explicación; desarrollo, manifestación.
explicative, explicatory [eks'plikitəri], *a.* explicativo.
explicator, *s.* expositor, comentador, ilustrador.
explicit [eks'plisit], *a.* explícito, categórico, claro.
explicitness, *s.* claridad, lucidez, franqueza.
explode [eks'ploud], *v.i.* estallar, detonar, reventar, hacer explosión. — *v.t.* volar, hacer saltar; hacer explotar; expeler con violencia; desacreditar, disfamar; condenar, refutar, confundir.
exploit ['eksploit], *s.* hazaña, proeza. — *v.t.* [eks'ploit], explotar, sacar partido de.
exploitation [eksploi'teiʃən], *s.* explotación.
exploiter [eks'ploitər], *s.* explotador.
exploration [eksplə'reiʃən], *s.* exploración; examen, investigación.
explorator, *s.* explorador.
exploratory, *a.* exploratorio.
explore [eks'plo:ɹ], *v.t.* explorar, averiguar, examinar, sondear.
explorer, *s.* explorador.
explosion [eks'plouʒən], *s.* explosión, detonación, voladura.
explosive, *a.* explosivo, fulminante. — *s.* explosivo.
explosively, *adv.* con explosión, por explosión.
exponent [eks'pounənt], *s.* (*mat.*) exponente, expositor, representante.
export [eks'po:ɹt], *v.t.* exportar. — *s.* ['ekspo:ɹt], exportación; *export licence*, permiso de exportación; *export trade*, comercio exterior.
exportable, *a.* exportable.
exportation [ekspo:ɹ'teiʃən], *s.* exportación.
exporter, *s.* exportador.
expose [eks'pouz], *v.t.* exponer; poner en peligro o ridículo; arriesgar; publicar, divulgar; revelar, desenmascarar; comprometer, abandonar.
exposed, *a.* descubierto; expuesto, peligroso.
exposedness, *s.* desamparo, abandono, desvalimiento.
exposer, *s.*, *a.* exponente.
exposition [ekspou'ziʃən], *s.* exposición, exhibición; explicación, explanación, interpretación; desenlace de un drama.
expositive [eks'pouzətiv], *a.* expositivo.
expositor, *s.* expositor, comentador, intérprete; glosario.
expostulate [eks'pɔstjuleit], *v.i.* amonestar reprochar, hacer presente; contender, altercar; debatir.
expostulation [ekspɔstju'leiʃən], *s.* amonestación; protesta; reconvención; disuasión; debate.
expostulator [eks'pɔstjuleitəɹ], *s.* amonestador.
expostulatory, *a.* que contiene una amonestación.
exposure [eks'pouʒəɹ], *s.* manifestación revelación, exposición, orientación; estrépito, escándalo; acción de desenmascarar; (*fot.*) exposición; *exposure meter*, fotómetro.

expound [eks'paund], *v.t.* exponer, declarar, explicar, interpretar, dilucidar, comentar.
expounder, *s.* comentador, expositor.
express [eks'pres], *v.t.* exprimir; decir, expresar, manifestar; explicar, figurar, describir, reproducir, representar, proferir; mandar por expreso. — *s.* expreso, tren expreso. — *a.* expreso, explícito, categórico, claro, especial; pronto, rápido, veloz; exacto, parecido.
expressible, *a.* exprimible, expresable, decible.
expression, *s.* expresión, locución, vocablo, término, gesto.
expressionless, *a.* sin expresión.
expressive, *a.* expresivo, significativo.
expressiveness, *s.* expresión, fuerza de expresión, energía.
expressly, *adv.* expresamente, explícitamente, categóricamente.
expressness, *s.* exactitud, claridad.
expressure, *s.* expresión, prolación.
exprobate ['eksproubeit], *v.t.* vituperar, reconvenir.
exprobation [eksprə'beiʃən], *s.* reprensión, vituperación.
expropriate [eks'prouprieit], *v.t.* expropriar, enajenar.
expropriation [eksproupri'eiʃən], *s.* expropriación, enajenamiento.
expugn ['ekspju:n], *v.t.* expugnar, conquistar, tomar por asalto.
expugnable, *a.* expugnable.
expugnation [ekspju'neiʃən], *s.* expugnación; conquista; toma por asalto.
expugner [eks'pju:nəɹ], *s.* expugnador, vencedor.
expulse [eks'pʌls], *v.t.* expulsar, despedir, echar.
expulsion [eks'pʌlʃən], *s.* expulsión.
expulsive, *a.* expulsivo.
expunction [eks'pʌŋkʃən], *s.* canceladura, borradura, raspadura.
expunge [eks'pʌndʒ], *v.t.* borrar, cancelar, expurgar, rayar, destruir.
expurgate ['ekspəɹgeit], *v.t.* expurgar; corregir.
expurgation [ekspəɹ'geiʃən], *s.* (*med.*) purgante, purga; expurgación, expurgo, purificación.
expurgator [eks'pə:ɹgətəɹ], *s.* purificador, corrector.
expurgatory, *a.* expurgatorio.
expurge [eks'pə:ɹdʒ], *v.t.* expurgar, limpiar.
exquisite ['ekskwisit], *a.* exquisito, excelente, rico, precioso, primoroso, delicado; vivo, agudo (placer o dolor); consumado; intenso, excesivo. — *s.* petimetre, elegante, pisaverde.
exquisiteness, *s.* delicadeza, primor, excelencia, perfección, gusto delicado, gentileza.
exsanguinate [ek'sæŋgwineit], *v.t.* desangrar.
exsanguine, *a.* exangüe.
exscind [ek'sind], *v.t.* cortar, excluir, extirpar.
exsect [ek'sekt], *v.t.* cortar, extirpar, quitar.
exsert [ek'sə:ɹt], *v.t.* proyectar, sobresalir.
ex-serviceman, *s.* excombatiente.
exsiccate ['eksikeit], *v.t.* secar, evaporar, desecar.
exsiccated, *a.* enjugado.
exsiccation [eksi'keiʃən], *s.* desecación.
exsiccative [ek'sikətiv], *a.* disecativo, desecante.

exsuction [ek'sʌkʃən], s. (med.) succión, chupadura.

extant [eks'tænt], a. existente, viviente, actual.

extemporaneous [ekstempə'reiniəs], a. extemporáneo, improviso, repentino.

extemporaneously, adv. extemporáneamente, sin estudio prealable, de improviso.

extemporaneousness, s. improvisación.

extemporary [eks'tempərəri], a. improvisado.

extempore [eks'tempəri], adv. de improviso, de repente; to speak extempore, improvisar. — a. sin previo estudio, improvisado.

extemporiness, s. improvisación.

extemporize, v.i. improvisar.

extemporizer, s. improvisador.

extend [eks'tend], v.t. extender, alargar, amplificar, ensanchar; tender; prolongar; explayar, dilatar; prorrogar, diferir; desarrollar; continuar; proyectar; conceder, ofrecer, dar, facilitar, proporcionar; dar extensión a; dar prórroga. — v.i. extenderse, prolongarse, estirarse.

extendible, a. extensivo.

extensibility [ekstensi'biliti], s. extensibilidad.

extensible [eks'tensibl], a. extensible, extensivo.

extensibleness, s. extensibilidad.

extensile [eks'tensail], a. extensible.

extension [eks'tenʃən], s. extensión, expansión; aumento, ensanche, prolongación; despliegue, adición, anexo; (com.) prórroga.

extensive, a. extensivo, extenso, espacioso, grande, vasto, dilatado.

extensiveness, s. extensión, anchura, extensibilidad, capacidad.

extensor, s. (anat.) extensor.

extent [eks'tent], s. extensión, compás, término, dimensión, tamaño, amplitud, magnitud; alcance; punto, grado; (der.) ejecución; embargo; to a great extent, en sumo grado; to the full extent, en toda su extensión; to a certain extent, hasta cierto punto; to what extent? ¿ hasta qué punto?

extenuate [eks'tenjueit], v.t. disminuir, minorar, atenuar, paliar, mitigar; (ant.) extenuar, desengrosar, adelgazar. — v.i. rarificar.

extenuating, a. atenuante, paliativo.

extenuation [ekstenju'eiʃən], s. extenuación; atenuación, mitigación, paliación.

exterior [eks'tiːriəɹ], a. exterior, externo; manifiesto, visible. — s. exterior, aspecto, exterioridad, porte.

exteriority [eksti:ri'ɔriti], s. exterioridad.

exterminate [eks'təːɹmineit], v.t. exterminar, destruir, desarraigar, eliminar, extirpar.

extermination [ekstəːɹmi'neiʃən], s. exterminación, extirpación, destrucción; eliminación.

exterminator [eks'təːɹmineitəɹ], s. exterminador.

exterminatory, a. exterminador.

extermine, v.t. exterminar.

external [eks'təːɹnəl], a. exterior, externo, extranjero, objetivo. — pl. externals, apariencias; formas exteriores, ceremonias, ritos.

externality [ekstəɹ'næliti], s. exterioridad.

externalize [eks'təːɹnəlaiz], v.t. exteriorizar.

exterrestrial [ekstə'restriəl], a. perteneciente o relativo a las cosas fuera del globo terráqueo.

exterritorial [eksteri'tɔːriəl], a. extraterritorial.

exterritoriality [eksteritoəri'æliti], s. extraterritorialidad.

extinct [eks'tiŋkt], a. extinto; extinguido, apagado, abolido, desaparecido, destruido, suprimido; to become extinct, extinguirse.

extinction, s. extinción, apagamiento, destrucción, supresión, abolición, aniquilación.

extine ['ekstin], s. (bot.) envoltura exterior de un grano de polen.

extinguish [eks'tiŋgwiʃ], v.t. extinguir, apagar, sofocar, suprimir, destruir, perder.

extinguishable, a. extinguible, apagable.

extinguisher, s. apagador, matacandelas, m.; fire extinguisher, extinctor, matafuego.

extinguishment, s. extinción, apagamiento, abolición, aniquilamiento.

extirpate ['ekstəɹpeit], v.t. extirpar, desarraigar, arrancar, destruir; (cir.) escindir.

extirpation [ekstəɹ'peiʃən], s. extirpación, eradicación, exterminio; (cir.) escisión.

extirpator ['ekstəɹpeitəɹ], s. extirpador.

extol [eks'tɔl], v.t. alabar, ensalzar, aplaudir, engrandecer, exaltar, magnificar, glorificar.

extort [eks'tɔːɹt], v.t. arrancar, arrebatar, obtener por fuerza o amenazas. — v.i. cometer extorsión o exacción; to extort money, (fig.) sacar las entrañas.

extorter, s. el que causa extorsión; concusionario.

extortion [eks'tɔːɹʃən], s. extorsión, exacción; lo que se ha obtenido por fuerza o violencia.

extortionary, a. contra derecho o acto ilegal.

extortioner, s. concusionario; opresor.

extra ['ekstrə], a. adicional, suplementario, supernumerario, extraordinario; auxiliar. — s. extra, exceso, gasto extraordinario.

extract [eks'trækt], v.t. extraer, sacar, tirar, arrancar, deducir, (mat.) buscar, hallar una raíz. — s. ['ekstrækt], extracto, pasaje, cita, excerpta; (quím.) tintura.

extraction [eks'trækʃən], s. extracción, origen, descendencia, linaje, alcurnia; (quím.) extracción, separación de una substancia.

extractive, a. extractivo.

extractor, s. extractor, extractador; (cir.) fórceps, sacabalas, m. sing.

extradition [ekstrə'diʃən], s. extradición.

extrados [eks'trædɔs, s. (arq.) trasdós, curva exterior de un arco o bóveda.

extra-judicial, a. extrajudicial.

extra-mundane, a. fuera del mundo, imaginario.

extraneous [eks'treiniəs], a. externo, extranjero, extrínseco.

extraordinariness, s. carácter extraordinario, singularidad, rareza.

extraordinary [ekstrə'ɔːɹdinəri], a. extraordinario, raro, especial, singular.

extravagance [eks'trævəgəns], **extravagancy**, s. extravagancia, disparate; desarreglo, desorden; prodigalidad, profusión, disipación, gastos excesivos.

extravagant, a. extravagante; exorbitante; pródigo, profuso, despilfarrado, gastador; estrafalario, exagerado, singular.

extravagantness. s. extravagancia, exceso, desarreglo.

extravasate [ekstrævə'seit], v.i. extravasarse, derramarse, rebosar fuera de los propios vasos (sangre). — a. extravasado.

extravasation [ekstrævə'seiʃən], s. extravasación.

extreme [eks'triːm], a. extremo, extremado, excesivo, sumo; postrero, último; estricto, severo, riguroso. — s. extremo, extremidad, ápice, punto más elevado; fin, cabo; *to go to extremes*, tomar medidas extremas; *in the extreme*, en sumo grado; *Extreme Unction*, Extremaunción.

extremity [eks'treməti], s. extremidad, rigor, necesidad, apuro.

extricable ['ekstrikəbl], a. fácil de desenredar.

extricate ['ekstrikeit], v.t. desenredar, desembrollar, desembarazar.

extrication [ekstri'keiʃən], s. desenredo, desembarazo.

extrinsic [eks'trinsik], **extrinsical**, a. extrínseco, exterior, externo.

extrorse [eks'trɔːs], a. (bot.) extrorso, que se abre al lado de la flor (se dice de la antera).

extrovert ['ekstrəvəɪt], a. (psic.) extrovertido.

extrude [eks'truːd], v.t. expulsar, expeler, rechazar, empujar, arrojar, desalojar.

extrusion, s. expulsión, rechazo, empuje.

extuberance [eks'tjuːbərəns], s. protuberancia; hinchazón, f.

extuberant, a. prominente, hinchado.

exuberance [ek'zjuːbərəns], s. exuberancia, exceso, superabundancia.

exuberant, a. exuberante, superabundante, frondoso.

exuberate, v.i. sobreabundar.

exudation [ekzju:'deiʃən], s. exudación, transpiración, sudor, lo rezumado.

exude [ek'zjuːd], v.t. sudar, exudar, transpirar. — v.i. rezumar.

exulcerate [ek'zʌlsəreit], v.t. exulcerar; (fig.) irritar, afligir. — v.i. ulcerarse, degenerar en úlcera. — a. ulcerado, agriado, irritado.

exulceration [ekzʌlsə'reiʃən], s. exulceración, corrosión, enconamiento.

exulcerative [ek'zʌlsərətiv], a. exulceratorio.

exult [ek'zʌlt], v.t. triunfar, alegrarse, regocijarse.

exultation [ekzʌl'teiʃən], s. exultación; regocijo; triunfo; transporte, alborozo.

exultingly [ek'zʌltiŋli], adv. con exultación, con triunfo.

exustion [ek'zʌtʃən], s. combustión.

exutory [ek'zjuːtəri], s. (med.) exutorio.

exuviae [ek'zjuːviiː], s.pl. despojos de los animales; (geol.) fósiles en estado fragmentario.

exuviate, v.t., v.i. mudar, cambiar, echar de sí alguna parte (como las plumas las aves, el pelo los cuadrúpedos, los cuernos los cornúpedos, la concha los crustáceos).

eyas ['aiəs], s. halcón niego, halconcillo. — a. implume; (fig.) novicio.

eye [ai], s. ojo; vista, mirada; (cost.) corcheta, agujero; (bot.) yema, botón; ventana redonda; atención, observación, estimación, vigilancia; aspecto, manera, expresión, cara; *blind in one eye*, tuerto; *before one's eyes*, en presencia de alguno; *to have in one's eye* (o *mind's eye*), proponerse; *keep a sharp eye on*, vigilar de cerca; *in a twinkling of the eye*, en un abrir y cerrar de ojos; *to have a cast in the eye*, ser bisojo; *black eye*, ojo negro o amoratado por un golpe; *in the wind's eye*, (mar.) de cara al viento; *eye of the anchor*, (mar.) ojo de la caña del ancla para afianzar el arganeo; *eye of a strap*, (mar.) ojo de gaza; *eye of a stay*, (mar.) ojo del estay. — v.t. ojear, contemplar, observar, mirar, velar.

eyeball, s. globo del ojo.

eye-beam, s. ojeada, vistazo.

eyebright, s. (bot.) eufrasia.

eyebrow, s. ceja.

eyed, a. observado, vigilado; *blear-eyed*, legañoso; *blue-eyed*, ojiazul, que tiene ojos azules.

eye-doctor, s. médico oculista.

eye-drop, s. lágrima.

eye-flap, s. anteojera.

eye-glass, s. anteojo; ocular. — pl. **eye-glasses**, lentes, quevedos.

eye-hole, s. (cost.) ojete.

eye-lash, s. pestaña.

eyeless, a. ciego, sin ojos, privado de la vista.

eyelet, s. resquicio, ojete, abertura; *eyelet-holes of the reefs*, (mar.) ollados de drizos.

eye-lid, s. párpado.

eye-opener, s. sorpresa, revelación.

eye-piece, s. ocular.

eye-pleasing, a. agradable a la vista.

eye-service, s. servicio prestado de mala gana y solo cuando está presente el amo.

eye-shade, s. guardavista, visera.

eyeshot, s. alcance de la mirada.

eyesight, s. vista; observación.

eyesore, s. cosa que hiere la vista; mal de ojos.

eyestring, s. tendón del ojo.

eye-tooth, s. diente canino, colmillo.

eye-water, s. colirio.

eye-witness, s. testigo ocular.

eyot [eit], s. islote, isleta.

eyre [ɛəɪ], s. vuelta, circuito.

eyrie, eyry ['ɛəri], s. nido de ave de rapiña.

F

F, f [ef], sexta letra del alfabeto; esta letra tiene el mismo sonido que en castellano. F en abreviatura representa *Fellow*, socio, o miembro de una sociedad o academia; (mús.) cuarta nota de la escala de *Do Mayor* (corresponde al *Fa* del solfeo).

fa [fɑː], s. (mús.) fa.

faba ['fæbɑ], s. (bot.) haba.

fabaceous [fə'beiʃəs], a. que pertenece a la haba.

fable ['feibl], s. fábula, ficción; apólogo, cuento; mentira. — v.i. componer, escribir una fábula; contar fábulas. — v.t. fingir, inventar, suponer.

fabler, s. fabulista, m.f., cuentero, mentiroso.

fabric ['fæbrik], s. fábrica, obra, edificio; manufactura; textura, tejido, tela, ropa; sistema, m.; género.

fabricate ['fæbrikeit], v.t. fabricar, edificar, labrar, construir; (fig.) forjar; fingir, inventar.

fabrication [fæbri'keiʃən], s. construcción; fabricación; (fig.) ficción, mentira.

fabricator ['fæbrikeitəɪ], s. constructor, fabricador, fabricante; (fig.) falsificador, embustero, inventor.

fabulist, s. fabulista, m.f.

fabulize, fabulise ['fæbju:laiz], v.i. componer o narrar fábulas.

fabulous ['fæbju:ləs], a. fabuloso, ficticio, extraordinario.

fabulousness, s. fabulosidad, invención de cosas fabulosas.

façade [fə'sɑːd], s. fachada, portada, frente, f., frontispicio.

face [feis], *s.* rostro, cara, faz, *f.*, haz, *f.*, lado; cuadrante (de reloj); facha, frontis, fachada; faceta; (*impr.*) ojo (de letra); (*mil.*) frente; semblante, apariencia, aspecto; facie, *f.*, superficie, *f.*, vista; (*fam.*) atrevimiento, descaro, desfachatez; mueca, gesto; *wry face*, mueca; *face value*, (*com.*) valor nominal; *to a person's face*, (*fig.*) a sus barbas; *face to face*, barba a barba *o* cara a cara *o* facha a facha; *to fly in the face of*, (*fig.*) ir contra viento y marea. — *v.t.*, *v.i.* aparentar; encararse, mirar, hacer cara, hacer frente; cubrir, guarnecer, aforar; afrontar, arrostrar; *to face about*, volver la cara; *to face out*, hacer frente, arrostrar, sostener descaradamente; *to face the music*, (*fam.*) hacer frente a las consecuencias.
face-ache, *s.* neuralgia facial.
face-cloth, *s.* sudario.
faced, *a.* carado, encarado, labrado, guarnecido; (*cost.*) forrado; *full faced*, que tiene la cara ancha; *ill faced*, mal encarado; *double faced* o *two faced*, de cara doble.
faceless, *a.* sin cara.
facer, *s.* puñetazo dado en la cara; (*fig.*) revés, percance.
facet ['fæcet], *s.* faceta; (*arq.*) filete. — *v.t.* labrar facetas.
facetious [fə'si:ʃəs], *a.* chistoso, jocoso, salado, gracioso.
facetiousness, *s.* sal, *f.*, chiste, donaire, gracia.
facial ['feiʃəl], *a.* facial.
facile ['fæsail], *a.* fácil, dócil, obediente, afable, vivo, listo, hábil, diestro, accesible.
facileness, *s.* facilidad, docilidad.
facilitate [fə'siliteit], *v.t.* facilitar, minorar el trabajo.
facilitation [fəsili'teiʃən], *s.* facilitación.
facility [fə'siliti], *s.* facilidad, docilidad, afabilidad, conveniencia, habilidad, destreza.
facing ['feisiŋ], *s.* cubierta; paramento. — *pl.* bocamangas, cuello de uniforme.
facsimile [fæk'simili:], *s.* facsímile, copia exacta.
fact [fækt], *s.* hecho, acción; suceso; realidad, verdad; dato, motivo; *in fact*, en verdad, en efecto; *matter of fact*, hecho positivo, hecho cierto; verdad; *matter-of-fact man*, hombre positivo; *as a matter of fact*, el caso es que.
faction ['fækʃən], *s.* facción, bando, pandilla, liga, parcialidad, bandería; tumulto, alboroto.
factional, *a.* faccionario, partidario.
factionist, *s.* faccioso.
factious, *a.* faccioso, revoltoso, sedicioso.
factiousness, *s.* espíritu de partido, espíritu de facción.
factitious [fæk'tiʃəs], *a.* facticio; artificial; fingido.
factitive ['fæktitiv], *a.* hacedor, efectivo, causante.
factor ['fæktər], *s.* factor, agente comisionado; (*mat.*) factor; causa que produce un resultado.
factorage, *s.* (*com.*) comisión; factoraje.
factorship, *s.* agencia, factoría.
factory, *s.* fábrica, taller; manufactura; factoría.
factotum [fæk'toutəm], *s.* factótum.
facultative [fə'kʌltətiv], *a.* facultativo; (*for.*) potestativo.

faculty ['fækəlti], *s.* facultad, aptitud, don, poder, talento; voluntad, raciocinio, sentido; facultad (universitaria).
fad [fæd], *s.* capricho, antojo, novedad, moda, manía, chifladura, comidilla.
faddy, *a.* antojadizo.
fade [feid], *v.t.* marchitar, descolorar, poner pálido; debilitar, desmejorar, enflaquecer. — *v.i.* palidecer, descolorarse; decaer, marchitarse, desvanecerse, desaparecer gradualmente.
faded ['feidid], *a.* marchito, descolorido, desvanecido, desaparecido.
fadeless ['feidles], *a.* que no se descolora.
fading, *s.* descolorimiento; decadencia, flojedad, desaparición. — *a.* decaído, flojo, desaparecido.
fady, *a.* que se descolora, que se marchita.
fæcal ['fi:kl], *a.* fecal.
fæces ['fi:sez], *s.pl.* excrementos.
fæcula ['fækjulə], *s.* (*quím.*) fécula, almidón.
faerie, faery ['fɛəri], *a.* hada, duende, trasgo. — *s.* tierra de las hadas.
fag [fæg], *v.t.* fatigar, cansar; hacer trabajar excesivamente en faenas groseras. — *v.i.* cansarse, desfallecer de cansancio; trabajar como un galopín.
fag-end, *s.* cadillos, pestañas; fin, desperdicio, sobra; (*mar.*) cordón; colilla (de cigarrillo).
faggot, fagot ['fægət], *s.* haz, gavilla o capón de leña; manojo; (*fort.*) fajina; haz de barras de hierro o acero (de 120 libras de peso); bruja, vieja. — *v.t.* liar, hacer líos; recaudar, recoger.
fagotto [fə'gɔtou], *s.* (*mús.*) fagot.
Fahrenheit ['færənait], *a.* referente al termómetro de Fahrenheit.
faience ['feiəns], *s.* loza fina.
fail [feil], *v.t.* faltar a, abandonar, dejar; engañar, frustrar, chasquear, descuidar, no cumplir, omitir, olvidar. — *v.i.* faltar, marrar, fallar, frustrarse, consumirse, fallecer, malograrse, acabar, abortar; desvanecerse, menguar, decaer; (*com.*) quebrar, hacer bancarrota; *do not fail to*, no deje Vd. de; *without fail*, sin falta.
failing, *s.* falta, defecto, desliz; malogro, decadencia.
failure, *s.* fracaso, malogro, fiasco, falla; culpa, falta, omisión, desliz, descuido; (*com.*) quiebra, bancarrota; *failure of issue*, (*for.*) sin dejar prole.
fain [fein], *a.* dispuesto, resignado, conforme; contento; deseoso. — *adv.* de buena gana, gustosamente.
faint [feint], *v.i.* desmayarse, perder el conocimiento; descaecer, desvanecerse; desfallecer; desalentarse, acobardarse, desanimarse. — *a.* lánguido, abatido, pusilánime, tímido; indistinto, delicado tenue, débil, apagado, desmayado, desfallecido; *to feel or get faint*, desmayarse, sentir un desfallecimiento; *to be faint with*, morirse de, estar muerto de.
faint, fainting, *s.* desmayo, deliquio; desfallecimiento; *fainting-fit*, síncope, desmayo; (*med.*) lipotimia.
faint-hearted, *a.* cobarde, pusilánime, medroso, apocado.
faint-heartedness, *s.* miedo, pusilanimidad, cobardía.
faintish, *a.* desfalleciente, flojo; débil.
faintishness, *s.* desfallecimiento.

faintly, *adv.* desmayadamente; débilmente, indistintamente.

faintness, *s.* languidez, lasitud, desaliento, flaqueza, ahilo; timidez; debilidad; lo borroso.

faints, *s.pl.* alcohol obtenido al principio y al final de la destilación del whisky, y que se vende como espíritu de grado inferior.

fair [fɛər], *a.* claro, sereno, despejado; rubio, blanco; inmaculado, limpio, terso; favorable, bonancible, propicio, próspero; imparcial, justo, recto, equitativo; bueno, natural, abierto; perfecto, hermoso, bello; honrado, sincero, franco, razonable, ingenuo; suave, dulce, blando; pasable, ordinario, en buen estado; corriente, mediano, regular; distinto, bien formado; legible, liberal, cortés; *fair to middling*, (*fam.*) bastante bueno; *fair dealing*, honradez; *fair sex*, bello sexo; *fair play*, equidad, proceder leal, juego limpio; *to play fair*, jugar limpio; *fair weather*, buen tiempo; *fair weather friend*, amigo en la prosperidad; *to make a fair copy*, poner en limpio; *fair wind*, viento favorable; *fair name*, nombre honrado, sin tacha; *to be in a fair way to succeed*, estar en buen camino de prosperar; *to give a fair hearing*, oír con imparcialidad; *by fair means*, por medios rectos, honrados; *fair and square*, honrado, a carta cabal; *a fair lady*, una bella mujer. — *adv.* honradamente, imparcialmente, cortésmente, decentemente, felizmente. — *s.* feria; mercado; exposición; (*poét.*) el bello sexo.

fair-complexioned, *a.* de tez blanca.

fair-haired, *a.* de cabellos rubios.

fairing, *s.* ferias, agasajos, dádivas; (*aer.*) fuselado.

fairly, *adv.* imparcialmente, justamente, rectamente; honradamente; medianamente; razonablemente; favorablemente; cabalmente; totalmente; claramente, bellamente, primorosamente.

fairness, *s.* hermosura, belleza; imparcialidad, rectitud, equidad, justicia; candor, honradez; color rubio.

fair-spoken, *a.* cortés, bien hablado.

fairway, *s.* (*mar.*) canalizo; (*dep.*) fairway.

fairy [ˈfɛəri], *s.* hada, duende, trasgo. — *a.* de los duendes.

fairy-land, *s.* tierra de los duendes.

fairylike, *a.* parecido a una hada, aduendado.

fairy-tale, *s.* cuento de hadas.

faith [feiθ], *s.* fe, *f.*, creencia; confianza, crédito; credo, religión, *f.*; buena fe, lealtad, fidelidad, palabra; *to break faith*, faltar a la palabra dada; *in faith*, a la verdad; *in good faith*, de buena fe; *upon my faith*, a fe mía. — *interj.* en verdad.

faithful, *a.* fiel, leal; puntual, exacto; recto, justo; veraz.

faithfully, *adv.* fielmente, firmemente; puntualmente; *yours faithfully*, s.s.s. (su seguro servidor).

faithfulness, *s.* fidelidad, lealtad, honradez, exactitud.

faithless, *a.* infiel, sin fe; desleal, pérfido, fementido, traidor.

faithlessness, *s.* deslealtad, infidelidad, traición.

fake [feik], *s.* (*mar.*) aduja de cable; (*fam.*) noticias inventadas, invención, patraña, trampa, engaño, paparrucha. — *v.t.* adujar,

enroscar; (*fam.*) fingir, inventar falsedades, fantasear; (*fam.*) chalanear; hurtar.

fakir [ˈfeikəɹ], *s.* fakir, alfaquí; (*fam.*) buhonero.

falcate [ˈfælkeit], **falcated**, *a.* falcado, encorvado como una hoz; (*astr.*) aplicado a la luna en su primer creciente y cuarto menguante.

falcation [fælˈkeiʃən], *s.* encorvadura.

falchion [ˈfælʃən], *s.* cimitarra; falce, *f.*

falciform [ˈfælsifɔːɹm], *a.* falciforme, en forma de hoz, de falce.

falcon [ˈfælkən], *s.* (*orn.*) halcón; (*arti.*) falcón.

falconer, *s.* halconero, cetrero.

falconet, *s.* (*arti.*) falconete.

falconry, *s.* halconería, cetrería.

faldstool [ˈfoldstul], *s.* facistol, atril; faldistorio; silla de tijera.

fall [fɔːl], *v.i.* (*pret.* **fell**; *p.p.* **fallen**) caer, caerse; llegar de repente, descender; irse abajo, sumirse, fluir, vaciarse hacia abajo; bajar de nivel; morir repentina o violentamente; perder, declinar, disminuir, minorar, bajar, rebajar (poder, valor, etc.); menguar, decaer; enflaquecer, extenuarse, disiparse; hacer bancarrota o quiebra; degradarse, deshonrarse, apostatar, caer en (pecado, vicio, error); acontecer, acaecer, suceder, pasar; tocar; nacer (dícese de animales); colgar, estar pendiente; inclinarse, doblarse hacia el suelo; *to fall away*, apostatar, enflaquecer, perecer; *to fall down*, dar en, caer al suelo, postrarse; *to fall due*, (*com.*) vencer; *to fall asleep*, dormirse; *to fall back*, retirarse, retroceder; *to fall in*, (*mil.*) alinearse; *to fall in with*, encontrarse con; concurrir, coincidir, acceder; *to fall in love*, enamorarse; *to fall flat*, (*fam.*) tener poco éxito, fracasar; *to fall headlong*, caer de bruces; *to fall ill*, enfermar, caer en cama; *to fall off*, menguar, perecer, enflaquecer; *to fall on*, asaltar, acometer, embestir; *to fall out*, reñir, disputar, regañar; (*impers.*) suceder, acontecer; *to fall short*, faltar, no alcanzar, no llegar; *to fall through*, fracasar; salir mal; *to fall under*, ser del número, estar sujeto a, incurrir; *to fall to*, empezar; *fall to!* ¡manos a la obra! *to fall upon*, atacar, asaltar, embestir; *to fall back upon*, tener en segundo lugar; recurrir; *to fall calm*, (*mar.*) calmar; *to fall into a trap*, tragar el anzuelo; *to fall to pieces*, hacerse pedazos; *to fall to the ground*, venirse al suelo.

fall, *s.* caída; decadencia, declinación; destrucción, desolación, ruina; muerte, *f.*; pérdida; disminución de precio, baja; corte de leña, y la leña cortada; desembocadura; cascada, catarata; salto; (*E.U.*) otoño; (*mar.*) tira de aparejo; (*mús.*) cadencia, bajada de tono; *fall of snow*, nevada.

fallacious [fəˈleiʃəs], *a.* falaz, ilógico, sofístico; ilusorio, delusorio, engañoso, vano.

fallaciousness, *s.* falacia, engaño, sofisma, *m.*, fraude.

fallacy [ˈfæləsi], *s.* falacia, engaño, ilusión, sofistería, error.

fallen [ˈfɔːlən], *a.* caído; derribado, trastornado; arruinado. — *p.p.* [FALL].

faller, *s.* el que cae.

fallibility [fæləˈbiliti], *s.* falibilidad.

fallible [ˈfæləbl], *a.* falible.

falling [ˈfɔːliŋ], *p.a.* cayente; cadente. — *s.*

bajada; caída; declive, inclinación; (*med.*) prolapso; *falling away*, defección, apostasía; *falling down*, postración, derrumbe; *falling in*, derrumbamiento, desmoronamiento; *falling off*, caída, disminución, decadencia; *falling star*, estrella errante (*o* fugaz); *falling sickness*, epilepsia, gota coral, mal caduco.

Fallopian tubes [fə'loupiən], *s.pl.* (*zool.*) trompas de Falopio.

fallow ['fælou], *a.* flavo, leonado; (*agr.*) en descanso, abandonado, descuidado, no sembrado, barbechado; *fallow deer*, corzo; *fallow-finch*, (*orn.*) triguero. — *s.* tierra que descansa; barbecho; *to allow to lie fallow*, dejar en barbecho. — *v.t.* barbechar; desmontar.

fallowing, *s.* (*agr.*) barbechera.

fallowness, *s.* (*agr.*) barbechada.

false [fɔ:ls], *a.* falso, falaz, incorrecto, incierto; fingido, contrahecho, infundado, falseado, postizo; mentido, mendaz, contrario a la verdad; engañoso, pérfido, infiel, desleal, traidor, aleve; irregular, ilegal; falseador, mentiroso; (*mec.*) provisional, simulado, temporáneo, de imitación; (*mús.*) discordante, desafinado; (*biol.*) seudo, cuasi. — *adv.* falsamente; traidoramente.

false-faced, *a.* hipócrita.

false-hearted, *a.* traidor, pérfido, falso, aleve.

false-heartedness, *s.* perfidia, falsedad.

falsehood, *s.* mentira, falsedad, perfidia, engaño, embuste.

falseness, *s.* falsedad, engaño, perfidia, duplicidad.

falsetto [fɔ:l'setou], *a.* (*mús.*) falsete.

falsifiable [fɔ:lsi'faiəbl], *a.* falsificable.

falsification [fɔ:lsifi'keiʃən], *s.* falsificación; confutación; adulteración.

falsifier ['fɔ:lsifaiəɪ], **falsificator**, *s.* falsificador, falsario, embustero.

falsify, *v.t.* falsificar, forjar, falsear, alterar, adulterar, contrahacer; refutar, confutar, desmentir, violar. — *v.i.* mentir, ser falso, decir falsedades.

falsity, *s.* falsedad, mentira.

falter ['fɔ:ltəɪ], *v.t.* balbucear, hablar de una manera balbuciente. — *v.i.* vacilar; tartamudear; titubear.

falter, faltering, *s.* vacilación; temblor; debilidad; tartamudeo.

falteringly, *adv.* de una manera balbuciente.

fame [feim], *s.* fama, renombre, gloria, celebridad, nombradía. — *v.t.* (*ant.*) celebrar; divulgar.

famed, *a.* afamado, famoso, celebrado, renombrado.

fameless, *a.* desconocido, obscuro.

familiar [fə'miljəɪ], *a.* familiar, íntimo, común, ordinario; muy conocido; agradable, amable, afable; fácil, natural; demasiado íntimo; acostumbrado, versado, ducho, instruido, conocedor. — *s.* amigo íntimo; demonio familiar; (*igl.*) familiar, criado de un prelado.

familiarity [fəmili'æriti], *s.* familiaridad, intimidad, confianza, llaneza.

familiarize [fə'miljəraiz], *v.t.* familiarizar, acostumbrar; *v.r.* familiarizarse (con).

family ['fæmili], *s.* familia; raza, cuna, sangre, *f.*, linaje; (*biol.*) familia. — *a.* familiar, de la familia, perteneciente a la familia, casero; *family man*, padre de familia; *in the family*

way, (*fam.*) encinta, embarazada; *family tree*, árbol genealógico.

famine ['fæmin], **famishment**, *s.* hambre, *f.*, carestía.

famish ['fæmiʃ], *v.t.* hambrear; matar de hambre. — *v.i.* morirse de hambre, sufrir con hambre o sed.

famished, *a.* hambriento.

famous [feiməs], *a.* famoso, celebrado, célebre, afamado, eximio, preclaro; señalado, memorable.

fan [fæn], *s.* abanico; ventalle; (*agr.*) aventador, bieldo; (*mec.*) ventilador, volante de molino de viento; (*mar.*) pala del hélice; admirador, aficionado.

fan, *v.t.* abanicar; soplar; ventilar; (*agr.*) aventar, aechar, abalear.

fanatic [fə'nætik], *s.* fanático; beato.

fanatic, fanatical, *a.* fanático; beato; visionario, entusiasta.

fanaticalness, *s.* fervor, ardor, frenesí.

fanaticism, *s.* fanatismo; ardor, fervor, celo.

fan-belt, *s.* correa de transmisión del ventilador.

fan-blast, *s.* tiro de fuelle.

fan-blower, *s.* aventador, soplador.

fancied ['fænsid], *a.* imaginado, imaginario.

fancier, *s.* aficionado a; criador (de animales o aves); soñador, visionario.

fanciful, *a.* antojadizo, imaginativo, fantástico, caprichoso.

fancifulness, *s.* antojo, capricho.

fancy, *s.* fantasía, imaginación, capricho, antojo, ventolera; inclinación, gusto, amor, afecto, afición; idea, imagen, *f.*, concepción; *to take a fancy to*, prendarse de; poner cariño a, antojársele a uno; *fancy dress*, disfraz, traje de capricho; *fancy goods*, objetos o artículos de fantasía; *fancy man*, *fancy woman*, amante, m.f.; *fancy work*, labor. — *a.* caprichoso, ideal, imaginario, extravagante, fantástico; adornador, elegante, bello; (*com.*) de gusto, de capricho. — *v.t.* imaginar, suponer; antojarse, figurarse; querer, gustar, aficionarse a, encapricharse de. — *v.i.* tener un antojo o capricho, aficionarse, apasionarse; fantasear.

fane [fein], *s.* templo, santuario.

fanfare ['fænfɛəɪ], *s.* toque de trompetas; tocata; encuadernación vistosa; procesión o parada ruidosa.

fanfaron, *s.* fanfarrón.

fanfaronade, *s.* fanfarronada. — *v.i.* fanfarronear.

fang [fæŋ], *s.* colmillo (de un animal); raíz de un diente. — *v.t.* (*ant.*) asir, agarrar.

fanged, *a.* que tiene colmillos.

fangless, *a.* descolmillado, sin colmillos.

fanion ['fæniən], *s.* banderola, pequeña bandera.

fanlight, *s.* (*arq.*) tragaluz, *m.*

fanlike, *a.* en forma de abanico, parecido a un abanico.

fannel ['fænl], *s.* manípulo.

fanner, *s.* abanicador, aventador.

fanon ['fænɔn], *s.* (*igl.*) manípulo.

fan-palm, *s.* (*bot.*) miraguano.

fan-shaped, *a.* en forma de abanico.

fantail, *s.* variedad de paloma; pájaro matamoscas de Australia; (*carp.*) cola de milano; *fantail burner*, mechero de abanico (gas).

fantailed, *a.* que tiene la cola en forma de abanico.

fantasia [fæntə'siːə], s. (*mús.*) fantasía.

fantasm ['fæntæzm], s. fantasma, m.

fantastic [fæn'tæstik], **fantastical**, a. fantástico, grotesco; caprichudo, caprichoso; ilusorio, imaginario.

fantastic, s. persona fantástica.

fantasticalness, s. fantasía, capricho, humorada.

fantasy ['fæntəsi], s. fantasía, imagen, f., ensueño; capricho, humorada; (*mús.*) fantasía; idea fantástica; dibujo fantástico.

fantom ['fæntəm], s. fantasma, m., visión, sombra, espectro.

fan-vaulting, s. bóveda de abanico; crucería.

fanwheel, s. rueda aventadora, rueda de paletas.

faquir [fə'kiəɹ], s. [FAKIR].

far [fɑːɹ], adv. lejos, a lo lejos, en lontananza, a distancia, desde lejos; muy, mucho, en gran parte, en alto grado; *far from it*, lejos de eso; ni mucho menos; *by far*, en mucho, con mucho; *far be it from me*, lejos de mí, no permita Dios; *far beyond*, mucho más allá de; *far and wide*, por todas partes; *far away*, *far off*, a lo lejos, a gran distancia; *as far as*, *so far as*, *in so far as*, tanto cuanto, en tanto que; *as far as I can see*, a lo que veo; *how far*, cuán lejos, hasta donde; *thus far*, hasta ahora, hasta aquí; *far too much*, demasiado; *far better*, mucho mejor; *far distant*, muy distante. — a. lejano, remoto, distante; de gran alcance.

farad ['færəd], s. (*elec.*) faradio.

faradic [fə'rædik], a. (*elec.*) farádico.

faradism ['færədizm], s. electricidad por inducción.

faradization [færədai'zeiʃən], s. (*med.*) faradización; aplicación de una corriente farádica.

far-away, a. lejano; distraído.

farce [fɑːɹs], v.t. rellenar, embutir; henchir; (*teat.*) meter morcilla. — s. farsa, sainete, entremés; fiasco; tramoya, enredo; (*coc.*) relleno, albóndiga; ridiculez, cosa vana.

farcical, a. entremesado, burlesco, bufo, ridículo.

farcically, adv. grotescamente, ridículamente.

farcing, s. embutido, relleno.

farcy ['fɑːɹsi], s. (*vet.*) muermo.

fard, v.t. (*ant.*) pintar, colorar. — v.i. pintarse. — s. coloreta.

fardage [fɑːɹdidʒ], s. (*mar.*) fardaje.

fardel [fɑːɹdl], s. fardillo, lío. — v.t. enfardelar.

fare [fɛəɹ], v.i. pasarlo, irle a uno (bien o mal); acontecer, suceder; (*poét.*) ir, andar, viajar; tratarse (en comida); *to fare like a prince*, tratarse a cuerpo de rey. — s. tarifa, precio de pasaje; persona que alquila un coche; pasajero, viajero; comida, vianda; *bill of fare*, lista de platos; *full fare*, billete entero; *half fare*, medio billete.

farewell [fɛəɹ'wel], interj. adiós, ¡vaya Vd. con Dios! — s. despedida. — a. de despedida; *to bid farewell*, despedirse de alguien.

far-famed, a. renombrado.

far-fetched, a. traído de lejos; increíble, improbable.

farina [fə'riːnə], s. (*Am.*) harina de maíz; fécula; (*quím.*) almidón; (*bot.*) polen.

farinaceous [færi'neiʃəs], a. harinoso, farináceo.

farinose ['færinouz], a. farináceo; (*hist. nat.*) cubierto de una substancia blanca, parecida a la harina.

farm [fɑːɹm], s. hacienda, granja, labranza; (*Am.*) estancia, rancho; (*ant.*) arrendamiento; *farm labourer*, labriego, peón. — v.t. cultivar, labrar (la tierra); *to farm out*, arrendar. — v.i. ser granjero.

farmable, a. arrendable; cultivable.

farmer, s. labrador, hacendado, granjero, agricultor, masadero, colono, quitero; rentero; arrendatario; *small farmer*, labriego; labrador; (*Am.*) ranchero, estanciero, sitiero.

farm-hand, s. labriego, labrador.

farm-house, s. alquería, quintería, granja, masada.

farming, s. cultivo, agricultura, labranza, explotación; arrendamiento (de contribuciones o rentas).

farmyard, s. corral de una granja.

farness ['fɑːɹnəs], s. distancia.

faro ['fɛərou], s. faraón (juego de naipes).

farrago [fə'reigou], s. fárrago, broza.

far-reaching, a. de gran alcance.

farrier ['færiəɹ], s. herrador; albéitar, mariscal.

farriery, s. albeitería; taller de herrador.

farrow ['færou], s. lechón; lechigada de puercos. — a. horra; machorra. — v.t. parir (la puerca o marrana).

far-seeing, a. previsor, precavido; que ve a gran distancia.

far-sighted, a. presciente; (*med.*) présbita.

farther ['fɑːɹðəɹ], adv. más lejos, a mayor distancia; ulteriormente, además de, demás de, más adelante. — a. muy lejano, más alejado, ulterior.

farthest, farthermost, a. superl., adv., s. a lo más lejos, muy lejano, muy distante, remotísimo.

farthing ['fɑːɹðiŋ], s. cuarto de penique; blanca, ardite, (*fam.*) ochavo; *I don't care a farthing*, no se me da un pito o un bledo; *to lay one's last farthing*, jugar hasta la camisa.

farthingale, s. verdugado, guardainfante.

fasces ['fæsiːz], s.pl. fasces, f.

fascia ['feiʃə], s. (*anat.*) aponeurosis, f.; (*astr.*) faja alrededor de un planeta; (*arq.*) faja, banda de arquitrabe; cinturón, venda.

fascial, a. (*anat.*) fascial.

fasciate, fasciated, a. fajado, vendado.

fasciation [fæsi'eiʃən], s. vendaje, acto de vendar.

fascicle ['fæsikl], s. racimo, manojo; entrega de un libro u otra publicación; hacecillo, haz pequeño.

fascicled, a. arracimado, fasciculado.

fascicular [fə'sikjuləɹ], a. fascicular.

fascinate ['fæsineit], v.t. fascinar, encantar, alucinar, hechizar, aojar.

fascination [fæsi'neiʃən], s. fascinación, encanto, hechizo, alucinación, aojo.

fascine ['fæsiːn], s. (*fort.*) fajina; haz.

Fascism, s. fascismo.

Fascist, a., s. fascista, m.f.

fash [fæʃ], v.t. (*fam.*) irritar, enojar, enfadar.

fashion ['fæʃən], s. moda, costumbre, uso; estilo, corte; manera, modo; figura, hechura, forma; rango, calidad; esfera; buen tono, elegancia; *people of fashion*, alta sociedad, gente de buen tono; *after the fashion of*, a la manera de; *in fashion*, de moda; *out of* *fashion*, fuera de moda; *fashion plate*, figurín de modas; *fashion pieces*, (*mar*.) aletas, piezas extremas de los yugos. — *v.t.* formar, hacer, amoldar; adaptar, ajustar; hacer a la moda.

fashionable, *a.* de moda, establecido, acostumbrado, hecho o ajustado a la moda; de buen tono, elegante; *fashionable hat*, sombrero a la moda. — *s.* lechuguino, petimetre, currutaco.

fashionableness, *s.* forma, figura, conformidad con la moda predominante.

fashionably, *adv.* a la moda, según la moda.

fashioner, *s.* hacedor.

fast [fɑːst], *v.i.* ayunar, hacer abstinencia. — *s.* ayuno, abstinencia; (*mar*.) amarra, lazo, cable; *to break one's fast*, romper el ayuno. — *a.* firme, fuerte, seguro; veloz, pronto, rápido, ligero, ágil; hecho o ejecutado rápidamente; inmoble, fijo, sólido, estable; fiel, invariable, constante; indeleble, duradero; (*sueño*) profundo; apretado; (*reloj*.) adelantado; gastador, derrochador; disoluto; *fast and loose*, tira y afloja. — *adv.* fuertemente, firmemente; apretadamente, estrechamente; profundamente; de prisa, aprisa; para siempre, duraderamente; no lejos; cerca de; *fast asleep*, profundamente dormido; *to follow fast upon the heels of*, seguir muy de cerca; *to grow fast*, crecer a palmos; *to make fast*, (*mar*.) amarrar.

fast-day, *s.* día de ayuno.

fasten ['fɑːsən], *v.t.* afirmar, atar, asegurar, amarrar; trabar, unir; (*mar*.) trincar, abadernar; cerrar; pegar, fijar; cerrar; abrochar. — *v.i.* fijarse, establecerse; asirse, agarrarse, pegarse; *to fasten upon*, unir, pegar; cargar a alguno con obligaciones; (*fig*.) imputar; *to fasten in*, clavar, hincar, fijar; *to fasten one's eyes upon*, fijar los ojos en.

fastener, *s.* el que asegura o afirma; pasador, asegurador; cerrojo; *paper-fastener*, sujetador de papeles.

fastening, *s.* (*mar*.) encapilladura; atadura, unión, *f.*; ligazón, *f.*, cierre, *m.*

faster ['fɑːstər], *s.* ayunador. — *a.* compar. [FAST].

fastidious [fæs'tidiəs], *a.* fastidioso, descontentadizo, melindroso, despreciador, desdeñoso, esquilimoso, dengoso.

fastidiousness, *s.* melindrería, dengue; enfado, fastidio; sentido crítico.

fasting, *ger.* ayunando, haciendo abstinencia. — *s.* ayuno, abstinencia.

fasting day, *s.* día de ayuno.

fastness, *s.* firmeza, fijeza, solidez, fuerza, seguridad; plaza fuerte, fortaleza; guájaras; velocidad, celeridad, rapidez; disipación, libertinaje, lujuria.

fat [fæt], *a.* gordo, obeso, grueso, corpulento; opulento, rico; manteicoso, graso, enjundioso, pingüe; grosero, tosco, lerdo; lucrativo, ganancioso, provechoso; (*impr*.) abierto, ancho, claro; *to grow fat*, echar carnes.

fat, *s.* gordo, grasa, sebo, manteca, gordura, enjundia; (*fig*.) lo más rico o provechoso de alguna cosa; *to live on the fat of the land*, vivir a cuerpo de rey. — *v.t.*, *v.i.* engordar, nutrir.

fatal ['feitəl], *a.* fatal, mortal, funesto, mortífero; necesario, inevitable.

fatalism, *s.* fatalismo.

fatalist, *s.* fatalista, *m.f.*

fatality [fə'tæliti], *s.* fatalidad, predestinación; infortunio, desgracia; decreto del destino; muerte, *f.*

fatalness ['feitəlnəs], *s.* fatalidad.

fate [feit], *s.* hado, suerte, *f.*, destino, sino, estrella, providencia, predestinación, fortuna; muerte, *f.*, destrucción; *the Fates*, las Parcas.

fated, *a.* fatal, predestinado.

fateful, *a.* fatal, funesto, predestinado.

fat-head, *s.* (*fam*.) bobo.

fat-headed, *a.* lerdo, estúpido.

father ['fɑːðər], *s.* padre; patriarca, *m*.; padre de almas, padre espiritual, confesor; inventor, autor, creador; *father-in-law*, suegro; *father-like*, paternal, como si fuera padre; *like father like son*, de tal pal o tal astilla. — *v.t.* prohijar, declarar por hijo, reconocer o adoptar como hijo; *to father upon*, achacar, imputar, atribuir.

fatherhood, *s.* paternidad.

fatherland, *s.* patria, tierra natal.

fatherless, *a.* huérfano de padre; desautorizado, sin autoridad.

fatherliness, *s.* ternura o amor paternal.

fatherly, *a.* paternal, paterno. — *adv.* paternalmente.

fathom [fæðəm], *s.* (*mar*.) braza; medida de 6 pies; alcance; profundidad, penetración. — *v.t.* sondar, sondear; profundizar, rastrear, tantear, penetrar, examinar a fondo.

fathomable, *a.* sondable, sondeable.

fathomer, *s.* sondeador.

fathomless, *a.* insondable; impenetrable.

fatidical [fə'tidikl], *a.* fatídico, profético.

fatigue [fə'tiːg], *s.* cansancio, fatiga; trabajo; molimiento; ajetreo; *fatigue-dress*, traje de fajina; *fatigue duty*, (*mil*.) faena, fajina; *fatigue-party*, pelotón de castigo. — *v.t.* fatigar, cansar.

fatigued, *a.* cansado, fatigado, molido, rendido. — *p.p.* [FATIGUE].

fatiguing, *a.* cansado, pesado.

fatling ['fætliŋ], *s.* cebón, ceboncillo. — *a.* grueso, gordo, regordete.

fatness, *s.* gordura, grasa, gordo; fecundidad, fertilidad; pingüosidad.

fatten, *v.t.* engordar, alimentar, cebar, nutrir, sainar; (*agr*.) fertilizar, abonar, engrasar, fecundar. — *v.i.* engordar, echar carnes, engrosarse; medrar, prosperar.

fattener, *s.* cebo.

fattiness, *s.* gordura, pringue.

fattish, *a.* gordiflón, regordete; pingüedinoso.

fatty, *a.* untoso, pingüe, craso. — *s.* (*fam*.) topocho, gordiflón; *fatty acid*, ácido graso.

fatuitous, fatuous ['fætjuəs], *a.* fatuo, tonto, insensato, necio, simple; ilusorio, vano.

fatuity [fə'tjuːiti], *s.* fatuidad.

fauces ['fɔːsiz], *s.pl.* fauces, *f.*, garganta, gaznate.

faucet ['fɔːsit], *s.* espita, llave, *f.*, canilla, grifo.

faugh [fɔ], *interj.* (de enfado) ¡puf! ¡bah!

fault [fɔːlt], *s.* falta, desliz, culpa; lunar, defecto, tacha, imperfección; pérdida del rastro, de la pista (en la caza); (*elec*.) avería accidental, defecto o interrupción de la corriente; (*geol*.) falla; *at fault*, culpable; perplejo; *to find fault*, tachar, criticar; poner faltas. — *v.t.* (*geol*.) hallar o producir una falla en. — *v.i.* extraviarse.

fault-finder, criticón, censurador.

faultily, *adv.* defectuosamente, erradamente.

faultiness, *s.* culpa, ofensa, vicio, defecto, falta.

faultless, *a.* perfecto; cabal, acabado, cumplido; sin tacha; sin falta.

faultlessly, *adv.* inculpadamente.

faultlessness, *s.* inculpabilidad; perfección.

faulty, *a.* culpable, deficiente, defectuoso, imperfecto.

faun [fɔːn], *s.* fauno.

fauna, *s.* (*zool.*) fauna.

faunist, *s.* naturalista que estudia una fauna.

favillous ['fæviləs], *a.* ceniciento.

favonian [fə'vouniən], *a.* perteneciente al favonio; favorable, próspero.

favor [FAVOUR].

favour ['feivər], *v.t.,* *v.i.* hacer un favor, prestar un servicio; usar con cuidado, con precaución; favorecer, amparar, fomentar, mirar con favor, patrocinar, proteger, ayudar, socorrer, apoyar; conducir a, contribuir a; suavizar; (*fam.*) parecerse a, asemejarse a. — *s.* favor, cortesía, fineza; merced, gracia; licencia, permiso; beneficio, servicio; favor, agasajo, prenda, obsequio; amparo, protección, patrocinio, socorro, auspicio; preferencia, parcialidad, lenidad, blandura, mitigación, condescendencia; facilitación, acomodación; (*com.*) carta atenta, grata; insignia, colores, *m.pl.*; *to be in favour of,* estar por; ser partidario de; *to hope for favours from,* esperar en; *by your favour,* con permiso de Vd.; *fortune favours the brave,* (*prov.*) a los osados ayuda la fortuna; *to fall out of favour,* caer en desgracia; pasar de moda.

favourable, *a.* favorable, benigno, propicio, benévolo.

favourableness, *s.* benignidad, agrado.

favoured, *a.* favorecido; protegido, amparado; *ill-favoured,* mal carado, feo; *finely favoured, well-favoured,* bien parecido; hermoso.

favourer, *s.* favorecedor.

favourite, *s., a.* favorito, predilecto, privado, preferido, protegido, valido, confidente.

favouritism, *s.* favoritismo.

favourless, *a.* desfavorecido; contrario, adverso.

fawn [fɔːn], *s.* cervato, enodio, cervatillo; color de cervato. — *v.i.* parir (la cierva); halagar, adular, acariciar.

fawner, *s.* adulador, lisonjero, adulón, quitamotas, *m.*, quitapelillos.

fawning, *s.* adulación, lisonja; servilismo, bajeza. — *a.* adulador, servil.

fawningly, *adv.* servilmente, lisonjeramente.

fay [fei], *s.* duende, hada. — *v.t.,* *v.i.* (*ant.*) juntar, unir, empalmar, ajustar; (*mar.*) cuadrar, venir bien una pieza con otra.

fealty ['fiːəlti], *s.* homenaje, lealtad, fidelidad.

fear [fiːr], *s.* miedo, temor, aprensión, recelo, cuidado; veneración, respeto; *for fear of,* por miedo de, por temor de. — *v.i.* temer, tener miedo, horror o aprensión, estar con cuidado, estar inquieto. — *v.t.* temer, recelar, tener miedo, mirar con temor, con reverencia.

fearful, *a.* miedoso, medroso, temeroso, pusilánime, encogido, tímido, respetuoso; terrible, horrendo, espantoso, tremebundo, tremendo; (*fam.*) imponente; *to be fearful,* tener miedo.

fearfully, *adv.* medrosamente, pavorosamente, temerosamente, terriblemente; (*fam.*) enormemente.

fearfulness, *s.* timidez, pusilanimidad, temor, miedo, encogimiento.

fearless, *a.* impertérrito, bravo, intrépido, atrevido, ardiente, arrojado, audaz.

fearlessly, *adv.* intrépidamente, sin temor, sin miedo.

fearlessness, *s.* intrepidez, bravura, valentía, arrojo.

fearsome, *a.* temible, espantoso; asustado, tímido, miedoso.

feasibility [fiːzə'biliti], *s.* posibilidad, capacidad.

feasible ['fiːzəbl], *a.* factible, posible, practicable, hacedero, agible.

feasibleness, *s.* posibilidad, capacidad.

feasibly, *adv.* de un modo factible, practicable.

feast [fiːst], *s.* (*igl.*) fiesta; banquete, comida, cena, festín; convite; regocijo, fiesta, festejo; (*fam.*) comilona; (*fig.*) abundancia. — *v.t.* banquetar, festejar, agasajar; recrear, regalar, deleitar. — *v.i.* deleitarse, entretenerse, gozarse; comer opíparamente.

feaster, *s.* goloso, comilitón; festejador, anfitrión.

feastful, *a.* festivo.

feasting, *s.* banquete, fiesta.

feat [fiːt], *s.* hecho o acción notable; proeza, maravilla, hazaña; juego de manos; valentía.

feather ['feðər], *s.* pluma; plumaje; (*carp.*) lengüeta, barbilla; (*mec.*) cuña, rayo; refuerzo de eje; clase, *f.,* género, especie, *f.,* naturaleza; bagatela, fruslería. — *v.t.* emplumar, cubrir, adornar o enriquecer con plumas; (*carp.*) machihembrar; volver la pala del remo al sacarla del agua, poniéndola casi horizontal. — *v.i.* saltar o cristalizarse un líquido en forma de plumas; cubrirse con plumas; *to cut a feather,* (*mar.*) cortar el agua, navegar con rapidez; estar hecho un brazo de mar; *to pluck a bird's feathers,* desplumar; *to feather one's nest,* enriquecerse a expensas de otro, hacer su agosto; *to show the white feather,* mostrarse cobarde, mostrar cobardía, volverse atrás; *birds of a feather,* pájaros de una misma pluma, lobos de la misma camada; *birds of a feather flock together,* (*prov.*) cada oveja con su pareja; Dios los cría, y ellos se juntan; *feather duster,* plumero; *feather brain,* imbécil, casquivano, tonto; *feather driver,* plumero, batidor de plumas; *feather-bed,* colchón de plumas; plumón; *feather-bone,* imitación de ballena; *feather-seller,* plumajero; *feather-joint,* (*carp.*) encaje de barbilla y farda; *feather-weight,* ligero de peso; de escasa importancia; (boxeo) peso pluma, *m.;* *in high feather,* alegre, vivo; *feather-edged,* achaflanado, biselado.

feathered, *a.* plumado, emplumado; penígero, alado; *feathered tribe,* pájaros.

feathering-wheel, *s.* rueda de paletas movibles.

featherless, *a.* desplumado; implume.

feathery, *a.* plumado, plumoso, cubierto con plumas; ligero como una pluma.

featly ['fiːtli], *adv.* (*ant.*) con destreza.

featness, *s.* (*ant.*) destreza; gentileza.

feature ['fiːtʃəɹ], s. rostro, semblante; facción, forma, figura; rasgo; carácter; facción distintiva; lo más notable. — *pl.* **features,** facciones, fisionomía, rostro, semblante. — *v.t. (fam.)* asemejarse, parecerse; dar importancia, hacer conspicuo, dibujar; presentar (cine).

featured, *a.* formado, cincelado; *(teat.)* anunciado de modo conspicuo; (bien o mal) encarado.

featureless, *a.* sin facciones o rasgos característicos.

febrifacient [febri'feisiənt], *a.* que causa o produce fiebre.

febrific [fə'brifik], *a.* febril, que produce fiebre.

febrifugal [fe'brifjugl], *a.* febrífugo.

febrifuge ['febrifjuːdʒ], s. *(med.)* febrífugo.

febrile ['fiːbrail], *a. (med.)* febril.

February ['februəri], s. febrero.

fecal ['fiːkl], *a.* fecal.

feces ['fiːsiz], *s.pl.* excrementos; heces, *f.pl.*

feckless ['fekləs], *a.* débil; ineficaz.

fecula ['fekjulə], s. almidón.

feculence, feculency, s. feculencia; heces, *f.pl.*, posos, sedimento.

feculent, *a.* feculento, fecal.

fecund ['fekənd], *a.* fecundo, prolífico, fértil.

fecundate, *v.t.* fecundar, fecundizar.

fecundation [fekən'deiʃən], s. fecundación.

fecundize, *v.t.* fecundar, fecundizar.

fecundity [fə'kʌnditi], s. fecundidad, feracidad, abundancia, fertilidad.

fed [fed], *pret.* y *p.p.* [FEED]; *fed-up, (fam.)* harto, hastiado.

federal ['fedərəl], *a.* federal, relativo a una federación, partidario de una federación.

federalism, s. federalismo.

federalist, s. federalista, *m.f.*

federalize, federalise, *v.t.* federalizar, confederar, formar una federación. — *v.i.* confederarse, aliarse.

federate, federated, *a.* aliado, confederado, federal.

federation [fedə'reiʃən], s. confederación, federación, liga.

federative ['fedərətiv], *a.* federativo, unido en una federación.

fee [fiː], s. honorario; propina, retribución, gratificación; derechos; salario, estipendio; *(for.)* feudo; *(for.)* bienes, hacienda de patrimonio; cuota de ingreso. — *v.t.* pagar, gratificar, premiar, retribuir, recompensar, dar propina; sobornar, cohechar; alquilar, tener a sueldo; *fee simple,* dominio absoluto, hacienda libre de condición.

feeable, *a.* recompensable.

feeble ['fiːbl], *a.* débil, lánguido, flaco; flojo, endeble; delicado, tenue; enfermizo; *to grow feeble,* enflaquecerse, debilitarse.

feeble-minded, *a.* ñoño, imbécil; vacilante, irresoluto, falto de inteligencia.

feeble-mindedness, s. idiotez; irresolución.

feebleness, s. debilidad, flaqueza, extenuación; flojedad, endeblez.

feed [fiːd], *v.t.* dar de comer, alimentar, nutrir, pacer, *(mec.)* alimentar; mantener; proveer, suplir lo que falta; deleitar, entretener. — *v.i.* comer, alimentarse; pastar, pacer; cebar, engordar. — s. alimento, comida; pasto, hierba; forraje, pienso; *(mec.)* alimentación; *to feed on* o *upon,* alimentarse de.

feed-bag, s. morral de pienso.

feeder, s. *(mec. y elec.)* alimentador; gorrista, *m.*, criado, parásito, dependiente, paniaguado; comedor, el que come, el que da de comer; afluente de un río; babero (de niño).

feeding, s. forraje, herbaje, pasto, pastura, comida; alimento.

feeding-bottle, s. biberón, mamadera, botellita.

feed-pipe, s. tubo o válvula de alimentación.

feed-pump, s. bomba de alimentación.

feel [fiːl], *v.t.* sentir, percibir por el tacto, tentar, manosear, palpar tocar, experimentar; sondear, examinar; tomar (el pulso). — *v.i.* sentirse, estar, ser (al tacto), tener (frío, hambre, etc.). — s. tacto, palpamiento; tocamiento; percepción, sensación; *I feel cold,* tengo frío; *how do you feel?* ¿cómo está Vd.? ¿cómo se siente Vd.?; *to feel for,* (a person) condolerse de; *to feel mortified,* pasar un bochorno; *to feel for something in the dark,* buscar a tientas.

feeler, s. el que toca o palpa; tentador; tentativa, probatura; *(ent.)* antena, palpo, cuerno, tentáculo.

feeling, s. tacto, sentido del tacto, sensación, percepción; palpamiento, tocamiento; emoción, sentimiento, ternura, sensibilidad, compasión; pasión, calor; *to touch one* o *to touch one's feelings,* tocar en lo vivo; *to touch on the quick,* herir el amor propio. — *a.* tierno, sensible, patético, conmovedor.

feelingly, *adv.* vivamente, con mucha expresión; tiernamente, sensiblemente, de un modo conmovedor.

feet [fiːt], *s.pl.* [FOOT]; pies.

feetless, *a.* sin pies.

feign [fein], *v.t.* fingir, afectar, disimular; pretextar, valerse de un pretexto; idear, imaginar, inventar. — *v.i.* fingir, disimular, referir falsedades; *to feign ignorance,* hacerse el bobo, hacerse chiquito.

feigned, *a.* fingido.

feignedness, s. ficción, disimulo, engaño, fraude.

feigner, s. fingidor.

feigning, s. fingimiento, simulación, disimulo, engaño.

feigningly, *adv.* falsamente, con disimulo, astutamente.

feint [feint], s. ficción, treta, disimulación, artificio; ataque fingido; *(esgr.)* finta; *(mil.)* diversión. — *v.i.* hacer finta.

feldspar ['felzpɑɹ], **felspar, feldspath,** s. *(min.)* feldespato.

feldspathic, s. feldespático, de feldespato.

felicitate [fə'lisiteit], *v.t.* felicitar, cumplimentar, dar el parabién o la enhorabuena, congratular.

felicitation [fəlisi'teiʃən], s. felicitación, congratulación, enhorabuena, parabién.

felicitous [fə'lisitəs], *a.* feliz, dichoso; bienaventurado; oportuno.

felicity [fə'lisiti], s. felicidad, dicha, bienaventuranza, ventura; ocurrencia oportuna.

felid, s. *(zool.)* félido.

feline ['fiːlain], *s., a.* gatuno, gatesco; felino.

fell [fel], s. *(cost.)* sobrecostura, dobladillo, remate del tejido; pelo, vellón; páramo, erial; mineral fino; *(ant.)* cuero, piel, *f.*, pellejo; sierra, peñasco. — *a.* cruel, fiero, bárbaro, feroz, sanguinario, sangriento, inhumano.

fell, v. pret. [FALL].

fell, v.t. derrocar, echar por tierra, derribar, tumbar, tronchar, cortar, talar; desmontar (árboles); acogotar (reses); (cost.) sobrecoser, dobladillar.

fellah, s. (en Oriente) labriego, patán.

feller, s. máquina taladora.

felling, s. corta, corte (de leña), tala.

felloe ['felou], s. pina de la rueda.

fellow ['felou], a. asociado, parejo, parecido, correspondiente. — s. compañero, socio, hermano, camarada, m.; igual, pareja, cosa que hace juego con otra; individuo de algún colegio, sociedad o academia; (fam.) hombre, chico, mozo, tipo, sujeto, persona, individuo; school-fellow, condiscípulo; brave fellow, valiente, buen muchacho o chico; clever young fellow, muchacho listo; worthless fellow, un pícaro; young fellow, joven, muchacho, mozo; to be hail fellow well met (with someone), tratar (a uno) de igual a igual. — v.t. aparear, hacer pareja, igualar, convenir, hermanar.

fellow-being, s. prójimo, semejante.

fellow-boarder, s. compañero de pupilaje.

fellow-citizen, s. conciudadano.

fellow-countryman, s. compatriota, m.f.

fellow-creature, s. prójimo; semejante.

fellow-feeling, s. compasión, simpatía, interés común.

fellow-heir, s. coheredero.

fellow-labourer, s. colaborador; compañero de trabajo.

fellow-member, s. individuo de la misma sociedad.

fellow-partner, s. consocio.

fellow-scholar, s. condiscípulo.

fellowship, s. intimidad, compañerismo, confraternidad; asociación, participación, mancomunidad; reunión, f., sociedad, cuerpo, compañía; colegiatura, plaza pensionada; beca; (arit.) regla de compañía. — v.t., v.i. admitir o aceptar en sociedad; unirse con otros.

fellow-soldier, s. conmilitón.

fellow-student, s. condiscípulo.

felly ['feli], s. pina de la rueda.

felly, adv. cruelmente, ferozmente, bárbaramente.

felo-de-se ['feloudəsi:], s. (for.) suicida, m.f.; suicidio.

felon [fi:lən], s. reo, criminal, felón; panarizo, panadizo, uñero. — a. malvado, criminal; traidor.

felonious [fə'lounias], a. malvado, traidor, villano, perverso, pérfido, felón.

felony ['feləni], s. crimen, delito, felonía.

felsite ['felsait], **felstone,** s. mezcla de cuarzo y feldespato.

felspar ['felspɑː], s. (min.) feldespato.

felt [felt], s. fieltro. — v., p.p. y pret. [FEEL]. — v.t. hacer fieltro; cubrir con fieltro.

felting ['feltiŋ], s. materiales para hacer fieltro; fieltro en cantidad; (carp.) aserrar al hilo.

feluca [fə'lu:kə], s. (mar.) falúa, falucho.

female ['fi:meil], a. femenino, del sexo femenino; (bot.) que tiene pistilo. — s. hembra (mujer, animal o planta); female screw, tuerca, hembra de tornillo.

femalize, v.t. afeminar.

feme covert, s. (for.) mujer casada; feme sole, (for.) soltera, viuda; mujer casada con derechos de propiedad o comercio independiente del marido.

feminality, femineity, s. femineidad; calidad de femenino.

feminine ['feminin], a. femenino, femíneo; femenil, delicado, tierno; afeminado; mujeril, mujeriego; (gram.) del género femenino.

femininity [femi'niniti], s. calidad o estado de femenino; conjunto de las mujeres; el bello sexo.

feminism ['feminizm], s. feminismo.

feminist, s. feminista, m.f.

femoral ['femərəl], a. femoral.

femur ['fi:mər], s. (anat.) fémur.

fen [fen], s. marjal, aguazal, pantano, paúl, fangal; enfermedad mohosa del lúpulo.

fence [fens], s. cerca, barrera, palizada, valla, vallado, seto; cercamiento; esgrima; (mec.) guía; defensa, resguardo, reparo; (vulg.) comprador u ocultador de objetos robados; fence of stakes, empalizada, estacada; wire fence, cerca de alambre; to be on the fence, (Am.) ver venir; to sit on the fence, estar a ver venir. — v.t. cercar, avallar; preservar, custodiar, defender, guardar. — v.i. esgrimir, pelear; luchar, defenderse; (vulg.) negociar en objetos robados.

fenceless, a. abierto, no cercado.

fence-month, s. tiempo de veda (del 9 de junio al 9 de julio).

fencer, s. esgrimidor; tirador de florete; caballo ágil para saltar cercas.

fencible, a. defendible, capaz de defensa. — s. (mil.) soldado destinado a la defensa del país.

fencing, s. esgrima; el acto de construir o erigir fences; materiales para cercas; habilidad en el debate; valladar.

fencing-bout, s. asalto de armas.

fencing-master, s. maestro de esgrima, maestro de armas.

fencing-school, s. escuela de esgrima.

fen-cress, s. (bot.) berro pantanoso.

fen-cricket, s. grillotalpa.

fend [fend], v.t. parar, rechazar, apartar, resguardar; preservar, defender, guardar. — v.i. defenderse, esgrimir, parar; to fend for oneself, ganarse la vida; defenderse.

fender, s. guarda-fuegos. — pl. **fenders,** (mar.) defensas, pallete, andullo; (aut.) guardabarros, m. sing.pl., guardafango, m.

fender-bar, s. batayola.

fender-beam, s. espolón.

fender-board, s. guarda-fangos, m. sing.

fender-pile, s. estacada, empalizada.

fen-duck, s. ánade silvestre.

fenestral [fe'nestrəl], a. perteneciente o parecido a las ventanas.

fenestration [fenes'treiʃən], a. (arq.) ventanaje.

fen-fire, s. fuego fatuo.

Fenian, a. perteneciente o relativo a los fenianos. — s. feniano.

fenks [fenks], s.pl. desperdicios de grasa de ballena que se usa como fertilizante o abono.

fenland, s. tierra pantanosa.

fennec ['fenik], s. animal parecido a la zorra y muy común en Africa (canis zerda).

fennel ['fenəl], s. (bot.) hinojo; giant fennel, (bot.) cañaheja, férula.

fenny, *a.* pantanoso, palustre, lagunoso, paludoso, empantanado.

fent [fent], *s.* abertura; retal.

fenugreek ['fenjuːgriːk], *s.* (*bot.*) fenogreco, alholva.

feod, feodal, feodary, *s.* [FEUD, FEUDAL, FEUDARY].

feoff [fiːf], *v.t.* (*for.*) enfeudar, investir. — *s.* feudo.

feoffee, *s.* feudatario.

feoffer, feoffor, *s.* el que enfeuda.

feoffment, *s.* (*for.*) feudo; investidura; (*for.*) fideicomiso.

feracious [fə'reiʃəs], *a.* feraz, fértil.

feracity [fə'ræsiti], *s.* feracidad, fertilidad.

feral ['ferəl], *a.* feral; feroz, salvaje; silvestre.

ferial, *a.* (*igl.*) ferial.

ferine ['feriːn], *a.* ferino, salvaje, feral, silvestre; en estado natural; maligno. — *s.* fiera, animal feroz.

ferineness, ferity, *s.* fiereza, crueldad, ferocidad, barbaridad.

ferment [fəɹ'ment], *v.t.* hacer fermentar. — *v.i.* fermentar, estar en fermentación; rehervirse; agitarse, estar excitado.

ferment ['fəɹɪmənt], *s.* fermento, fermentación; (*fig.*) agitación, tumulto, movimiento.

fermentability [fəɹmentə'biliti], *s.* calidad de fermentable.

fermentable [fəɹ'mentəbl], *a.* fermentable.

fermentation [fəɹmen'teiʃən], *s.* (*quím.*) fermentación; (*fig.*) agitación, efervescencia.

fermentative [fəɹ'mentətiv], *a.* fermentativo, fermentante.

fermentativeness, *s.* calidad de fermentativo.

fermentescible [fəɹmən'tesibl], *s.* (*quím.*) materia fermentante.

fermentible [fəɹ'mentibl], *a.* fermentable.

fern [fəɹːn], *s.* (*bot.*) helecho, polipodio.

ferny, *a.* abundante en helechos, cubierto de helechos.

ferocious [fə'rouʃəs], *a.* feroz, feral, voraz, rapaz, salvaje, fiero.

ferociousness, ferocity [fə'rɔsiti], *a.* ferocidad, crueldad, fiereza.

ferox [fe'rɔks], *s.* trucha de los Grandes Lagos (*E.U.*).

ferrara [fə'rɑːrə], *s.* espada ferraresa.

ferrate ['fereit], *s.* sal de ácido férrico.

ferreous, ferrean, *a.* férreo, ferrizo.

ferret ['ferət], *s.* (*zool.*) hurón; (*ant.*) listón, hiladillo, bocadillo; filadez. — *v.t.* indagar, rastrear, averiguar; cazar con hurones.

ferreter, *s.* (*fig.*) hurón.

ferriage, ferryage ['feriedʒ], *s.* barcaje, lanchaje, peaje.

ferric ['ferik], *a.* (*quím.*) férrico; perteneciente al hierro.

ferricyanide, *s.* cianuro de hierro, ferricianuro.

ferriferous [fə'rifərəs], *a.* (*min.*) ferrugiento, ferruginoso.

ferrocalcite [ferou'kælsait], *s.* ferrocalcita.

ferrocyanide o ferrocyanate, *s.* ferrocianato, ferrocianuro.

ferroprussiate, *s.* ferroprusiato.

ferrotype ['feroutaip], *s.* ferrotipo.

ferrous ['ferəs], *a.* (*quím.*) ferroso.

ferruginous [fə'ruːdʒinəs], *a.* ferrugineo, ferruginoso; mohoso, enmohecido, aherrumbrado.

ferrule ['ferul], *s.* contera, regatón, casquillo, virola; marco de pizarra; zuncho.

ferry ['feri], *v.t.*, *v.i.* transportar de una a otra orilla; pasar un río en barca; barquear, llevar en barca. — *s.* barca de transporte (a través de un río); embarcadero; pasaje.

ferry-boat, *s.* barca de pasaje, vapor de río.

ferryman, *s.* barquero.

fertile ['fəːɹtail], *a.* fértil, fecundo, feraz, abundante.

fertileness, fertility [fəɹ'tiliti], *s.* fertilidad, abundancia, copia, fecundidad.

fertilization [fəɹtilai'zeiʃən], *s.* (*biol.*) fertilización, fecundación; (*agr.*) abono.

fertilize ['fəːɹtilaiz], *v.t.* fertilizar, hacer fértil, fecundar, abonar.

fertilizer, *s.* (*agr.*) abono.

ferula ['ferulə], *s.* (*bot.*) férula, cañaheja; cetro.

ferule ['ferul], *s.* férula, palmatoria, palmeta. — *v.t.* dar palmetazos, castigar con la férula. — *v.i.* palmetear.

fervency ['fəːɹvənsi], *s.* fervor, calor, ardor; devoción, celo.

fervent, *a.* ferviente, vehemente, vivo, fogoso, ardiente, hirviente, fervoroso.

fervently, *adv.* fervorosamente, ansiosamente.

ferventness, *s.* ardor, celo, fervor.

fervid ['fəːɹvid], *a.* férvido, fogoso, ardiente, vehemente; encendido, incandescente.

fervidity, fervidness, *s.* fervor, calor, ardor; devoción, celo.

fervour, fervor ['fəːɹvəɹ], *s.* fervor, devoción, celo, vehemencia, ardor.

fescennine ['fesənain], *a.* fescenino; obsceno, licencioso; *Fescennine verses*, versos obscenos.

fescue ['feskjuː], *s.* puntero; (*bot.*) festuca; *fescue-grass*, (*bot.*) especie de festuca para pasto.

fesse [fes], *s.* (*blas.*) faja.

festal ['festl], *a.* festivo, solemne, conmemorativo; alegre; juguetón.

fester ['festəɹ], *v.t.* enconar, emponzoñar. — *v.i.* enconarse, ulcerarse; (*fig.*) inflamarse, amargarse. — *s.* úlcera, llaga, tumor purulento.

festival ['festivəl], *a.* festivo. — *s.* fiesta, festividad, día festivo.

festive, *a.* festivo, alegre, gozoso, regocijado.

festivity [fes'tiviti], *s.* regocijo, alegría, alborozo, animación, júbilo; festividad, fiesta.

festoon [fes'tuːn], *s.* festón, guirnalda. — *v.t.* festonear.

festooned, *a.* afestonado.

festucous ['festikəs], *a.* pajizo.

fetal, fœtal ['fiːtl], *a.* fetal.

fetch [fetʃ], *v.t.* ir a buscar, ir a traer, ir por; conducir, traer; lograr, alcanzar, conseguir; hacer, ejecutar; venderse por, producir; sacar, derivar, deducir; (*fam.*) golpear, pegar; (*fam.*) deleitar, agradar; encantar, atraer, captar. — *v.i.* moverse, menearse; (*mar.*) llegar, arribar; *to fetch away*, quitar, llevar; *to fetch a compass*, hacer un rodeo; *to fetch down*, bajar; humillar, abatir; enflaquecer, debilitar; *to fetch in*, hacer entrar, meter dentro; *to fetch off*, sacar, quitar, arrancar; *to fetch out*, sacar a luz, hacer salir; *to fetch up*, subir; *to fetch the pump*, (*mar.*) cebar la bomba. — *s.* acto de ir a buscar o traer; tirada, alcance; treta, estratagema, artificio.

fetch, s. fantasma o doble de una persona viva y que los supersticiosos suponían como precursor de la muerte de dicha persona.

fetcher, s. el que va por algo, el que lleva o trae algo.

fetching, a. atractivo, fascinador.

fête [feit], v.t. festejar, honrar con regocijos. — s. fiesta; *fête-day*, día de fiesta; fiesta onomástica.

fetial ['fi:ʃəl], a. fecial.

fetich ['fetiʃ], s. [FETISH].

fetid ['fetid], a. fétido, hediondo.

fetidness, s. fetidez, hediondez, mal olor, hedor.

fetish ['fetiʃ], s. fetiche, ídolo; (*fig.*) objeto de devoción o adoración.

fetishism, s. fetichismo.

fetlock ['fetlɔk], s. cerneja; trabón.

fetor ['fi:tər], s. fetor, hedor.

fetter ['fetər], v.t. engrillar, encadenar, trabar. — s. grillete, calceta; traba; prisión. — pl. **fetters,** grillos, cadenas, hierros, prisiones.

fetterless, a. desenfrenado, destrabado.

fetter-lock, s. manea, maniota, manija, guadafiones, suelta, traba.

fettle ['fetl], v.t. alisar, poner liso, quitar rebabas; (*fund.*) poner en buen estado. — v.i. emplearse en frioleras. — s. condición, estado.

fettling, s. (*fund.*) brasca.

fetus, fœtus [fi:təs], s. feto.

feu [fju:], s. (*for.*, *Esco.*) feudo; censo.

feud, s. riña, pendencia, disensión, desunión, f., enemistad, contienda; (*for.*) feudo.

feudal, a. feudal.

feudalism, s. feudalismo, sistema feudal, m.

feudality [fju:'dæliti], s. feudalidad.

feudalize ['fju:dəlaiz], v.t. enfeudar.

feudary, a. feudal, feudatario. — s. vasallo; feudatario; procurador.

feudatory [fju:'deitəri], s., a. feudatario.

feudist ['fju:dist], s. feudista, m.

feuilleton ['fəitən], s. folletín.

fever ['fi:vər], s. (*med.*) fiebre, f., calentura; agitación, calor, sobreexcitación; *scarlet fever,* escarlatina; *typhoid fever,* fiebre tifoidea o tabardillo; *typhus fever,* tifo; *spotted fever,* tabardillo pintado; *to set one in a fever,* quemar la sangre. — v.t. causar calentura.

feverfew, s. (*bot.*) matricaria.

feverish, feverous, a. febril, calenturiento, amagado de fiebre, febricitante; caliente, ardoroso, ardiente; (*fig.*) inquieto; *to be feverish,* tener fiebre.

feverishly, adv. de un modo febril.

feverishness, s. estado febril, calentura; desasosiego.

few [fju:], a. pocos, algunos, unos; *a few,* uno que otro, algunos, unos cuantos, algo, en algún grado; *the few,* la minoría.

fewer, a. comp. de *few;* menos; *the fewer the better,* cuantos menos mejor.

fewness, s. escasez, poquedad; pequeño número; corto número; cortedad, brevedad, concisión.

fey [fei], a. (*Esco.*) destinado a morir; moribundo.

fez [fez], s. fez, m., gorro turco.

fiancé [fi'ɑ:nsei], s. novio, desposado, prometido.

fiancée, s. novia, desposada, prometida.

fiasco [fi'æskou], s. fiasco, fracaso, mal éxito; botella, frasco.

fiat ['fi:ət], s. fíat, orden, mandato.

fib [fib], s. embuste, fábula, falsedad, bola, cuento. — v.i. mentir, trufar, embustear, trapacear, contar falsedades.

fibber, s. embustero, trapacero, mentiroso.

fibre [faibər], s. fibra, hebra, filamento; (*fig.*) naturaleza.

fibril [faibril], s. fibrita.

fibrin ['faibrin], **fibrine,** s. fibrina.

fibrinous, a. fibrinoso.

fibroid ['faibrɔid], a. fibroso.

fibroma, s. (*med.*) fibroma, tumor fibroso.

fibrose, fibrous, a. fibroso, ahebrado, hebroso, textil.

fibula ['fibju:lə], s. (*anat.*) peroné; broche, corchete, fíbula.

fibular, a. peroneo.

fichu ['fiʃu:], s. fichú, pañoleta triangular.

fickle ['fikl], a. voluble, inconstante, veleidoso, variable, mudable.

fickleness, s. volubilidad, inconstancia, veleidad, mutabilidad.

fictile ['fiktil], a. capaz de ser amoldado; plástico; figulino.

fiction ['fikʃən], s. ficción, invención; novela, fábula, embuste, mentira; literatura novelesca; (*for.*) ficción de derecho.

fictitious [fik'tiʃəs], a. ficticio, contrahecho; fabuloso; fingido.

fictitiously, adv. fingidamente.

fictitiousness, s. representación fingida.

fictive, a. fingido, imaginario, ficticio.

ficus ['faikəs], s. (*bot.*) higuera.

fid [fid], s. barra que sirve de sostén; (*mar.*) cuña, tarugo grande de madera; pasador; *fid of a topmast,* cuña de mastelero.

fiddle ['fidəl], s. violín; (*vulg.*) engaño, estafa; *fiddle-block,* (*mar.*) motón de poleas diferenciales; *fiddle-bow,* arco de violín; *fiddle-string,* cuerda de violín. — v.i. tocar el violín; jugar, enredar. — v.t. tocar una pieza de música en el violín; (*vulg.*) estafar, engañar, jugar con trampa.

fiddle-de-dee, interj. ¡quiá! ¡tonterías! — s. necedad, disparate.

fiddle-faddle, s. (*fam.*) bagatelas, frioleras; desatino. — a. quisquilloso. — v.t. disparatar.

fiddler, s. violinista, m.f.

fiddlestick, s. arco de violín; bagatela. — pl. **fiddlesticks!** interj. ¡vaya! ¡disparate! ¡tonterías!

fiddley ['fidli], s. (*mar.*) marco o armazón de hierro de las portezuelas de las escotillas-carboneras de un vapor; el espacio debajo de ellas.

fidelity [fai'deliti], s. fidelidad, lealtad, veracidad.

fidget ['fidʒət], v.t. molestar, inquietar. — v.i. ajetrearse, afanarse por nada; atrafagar, mudar de posición con frecuencia. — s. afán, tráfago, agitación.

fidgety, a. (*fam.*) inquieto, agitado, impaciente.

fiducial [fai'dju:ʃəl], a. fiduciario, de confianza; lleno de confianza; (*mat.*) fiducial.

fiducially. adv. confiadamente; confidentemente.

fiduciary [fai′dju:ʃəri], *a.* fiduciario; confiado, resuelto. — *s.* (*for.*) fideicomisario.
fie [fai], *interj.* ¡uf! ¡vaya! ¡Qué asco!
fief [fi:f], *s.* (*for.*) feudo.
field [fi:ld], *s.* campo, campaña, llanura, campiña; (*agr.*) campo, sembrado, terreno cultivado; (*ópt.*) campo; espacio, extensión, esfera de acción; (*mil.*) batalla, campo de batalla, campaña; colectividad de competidores o candidatos; *corn-field,* maizal. — *v.i.* actuar como *fielder* en el juego de cricket; apostar por el *field* contra el favorito. — *v.t.* parar y devolver la pelota en el juego de cricket; *to take the field,* entrar en campaña.
field-artillery, *s.* artillería de campaña.
field-basal, *s.* (*bot.*) albahaca silvestre.
field-book, *s.* manual de agrimensor.
field-day, *s.* día de ejercicios militares; día de excursión científica.
fielded, *a.* acampado; que está en el campo de batalla.
fielder, *s.* en el juego de *cricket,* jugador situado en el *field* para devolver la pelota; perro de caza.
fieldfare, *s.* (*orn.*) zorzal.
field-glass, *s.* anteojos, gemelos.
field-gun, *s.* cañón de campaña.
field-marshal, *s.* capitán general de ejército.
field-mouse, *s.* ratón silvestre.
fiend [fi:nd], *s.* espíritu malo, demonio, diablo; *dope-fiend, drug-fiend,* morfinómano.
fiendish, fiend-like, *a.* diabólico, perverso, endemoniado, malvado.
fiendishness, *s.* maldad, crueldad, perversidad, malicia.
fierce [fiəɹs], *a.* fiero, feroz, cruel, torvo, bárbaro, voraz; furioso, violento, impetuoso, vehemente, apasionado.
fierceness, *s.* fiereza, ferocidad.
fieri-facias [faiəri′feisiəs], *s.* (*for.*) auto ejecutorio.
fieriness, *s.* fuego, calor, fogosidad, ardor, ardimiento, viveza de animo, vehemencia, pasión.
fiery [′faiəri], *a.* ígneo; caliente, ardiente, encendido; vivo, ardoroso, fogoso, vehemente, impaciente, feroz, fiero, furibundo, iracundo, colérico, indómito.
fife [faif], *s.* (*mús.*) pífano. — *v.t., v.i.* tocar el pífano.
fifer, *s.* (tocador de) pífano.
fifteen [fif′ti:n], *s., a.* quince; *to be fifteen,* tener quince años.
fifteenth, *a.* décimoquinto, quindécimo, quinzavo, quinceno; *s.* (*mús.*) quincena.
fifth [fifθ], *a.* quinto. — *s.* quinta (parte); (*mús.*) quinta.
fifthly, *adv.* en quinto lugar, lo quinto.
fiftieth, *a.* quincuagésimo; cincuenta; cincuenteno.
fifty [′fifti], *s., a.* cincuenta.
fig [fig], *s.* (*bot.*) higo; higuera; (*vet.*) verruga en la ranilla de un caballo; (*fam.*) ardite, bledo; (*ant.*) higa; *Indian fig,* (*bot.*) tuna, higo chumbo; *I don't care a fig,* no me importa un bledo; *fig-leaf,* (*fig.*) hoja de parra; *in full fig,* vestido de veinticinco alfileres.
fig-pecker, (*orn.*) becafigo.
fight [fait], *v.t.* (*pret., p.p.* **fought**) pelear, combatir, disputar, reñir, guerrear; luchar, batallar, pugnar, disputar, lidiar, contender; dirigir una batalla; hacer reñir. — *v.i.*

batirse, defenderse, hacer la guerra; *to fight shy of,* evadir (una contienda, una persona); *to fight to a finish,* luchar hasta el fin; *to fight with knives,* andar a puñaladas; *to fight it out,* terminar una disputa peleando; *to fight one's way through,* abrirse paso con las armas. — *s.* batalla, lucha, pelea, combate, lid, *f.,* lidia; *sea-fight,* batalla naval.
fighter, *s.* guerrero, luchador, peleador, combatiente, lidiador, guerreador; duelista, *m.,* espadachín.
fighting, *a.* aguerrido, peleante, combatiente, pugnante. — *s.* combate, riña, querella, disputa, contención.
fig-leaf [′figli:f], *s.* hoja de higuera; (*fig.*) hoja de parra.
figment [′figmənt], *s.* ficción, invención.
figuline [′figju:lain], *s.* objeto figulino.
figurability [figju:rə′biliti], *s.* calidad de figurable.
figurable [′figju:rəbl], *a.* figurable.
figural [′figju:rəl], *a.* que tiene figuras.
figurant [′figju:rənt], *s.* (*teat.*) figurante.
figurante, *s.f.* figuranta.
figurate [′figju:reit], *a.* figurado; (*mus.*) floreado, embellecido.
figuration, *s.* figuración; figura.
figurative [′figju:rətiv], *a.* figurativo, figurado, metafórico; florido; simbólico.
figurativeness, *s.* calidad de figurativo o metafórico.
figure [′figəɹ], *s.* figura, hechura, semejanza, forma; personaje; símbolo, tipo; cuerpo, presencia, talle; dibujo, representación, pintura, imagen, *f.,* estatua; maniquí; viso, papel; distinción; (*com., fam.*) precio, valor; (*arit.*) cifra, número, guarismo; (*gram.*) figura gramatical; (*astrol.*) horóscopo; (*geom.*) figura geométrica; (*ret.*) figura, tropo; (*danz.*) figura. — *v.t., v.i.* figurar, delinear, amoldar, disponer, formar; figurarse, imaginarse; cubrir con figuras, adornar con figuras; simbolizar, representar simbólicamente; (*mus.*) florear; *to figure out,* calcular, computar, hallar por cálculo; *to figure up,* computar, sumar. — *v.i.* hacer papel o figura.
figured, *p.p., a.* adornado, labrado, floreado, estampado; *figured bass,* (*mús.*) bajo cifrado.
figurehead, *s.* (*mar.*) mascarón de proa; figurón, caudillo nominal.
figurine [′figju:ri:n], *s.* figurilla.
figuring, *s.* computación.
figurist, *s.* figurista, *m.f.*
figwort [′figwəɹt], *s.* (*bot.*) escrofularia.
Fijian [fi:′dʒi:ən], **Feejeean,** *a.* de Fijí. — *s.* habitante o lengua aborígine de las Islas Fijí.
filaceous [fi′leijəs], *a.* hebroso, fibroso, estoposo, filamentoso.
filament [′filəmənt], *s.* hebra, fibra, hilo, filamento; (*bot.*) filamento; brizna.
filamentose, filamentous, *a.* filamentoso, hilachoso, fibroso.
filar [′failəɹ], *a.* perteneciente al hilo; semejante a un hilo, que contiene hilos.
filature [′filətʃəɹ], *s.* hilandería; fábrica de hilados.
filbert [′filbəɹt], *s.* (*bot.*) avellana.
filbert, filbert-tree, *s.* avellano.
filch [filtʃ], *v.i.* ratear, sisar, hurtar.
filcher, *s.* garduño, ratero, sisón, ladroncillo.
file [fail], *s.* lima; carpeta, guardapapeles, *m.*

sing., ensartapapeles, *m. sing.*; escofina; colección, legajo, archivo (de papeles, etc.); cola, línea, hilera, fila; catálogo, lista; retahila, ringla; *Indian file, single-file,* fila india; *half-round file,* lima de media caña. — *v.t.* limar, pulir; acumular; enhilar, ensartar; anotar, registrar, presentar, asentar; archivar; clasificar (cartas); manchar, ensuciar. — *v.i.* (*mil.*) marchar en fila; *to file by, file off, file past,* (*mil.*) desfilar.

file-cutter, *s.* picador de limas.

file-fish, *s.* (*ict.*) liga.

filer, *s.* limador, el que lima.

filial ['filiəl], *a.* filial.

filiation [fili'eifən], *s.* filiación; dependencia; prohijamiento, adopción.

filibeg ['filibeg], *s.* falda masculina o zaragüelles a la usanza moderna.

filibuster ['filibʌstəɹ], *v.t., v.i.* ser filibustero, conducirse como filibustero; (*E.U.*) impedir, obstruir la aprobación de leyes, etc. — *s.* filibustero, pirata, *m.*; (*E.U.*) el que obstruye procedimientos parlamentarios.

filibusterism, *s.* filibusterismo.

filiform ['filifɔɹm], *a.* filiforme.

filigrane ['filigrein], **filigree** ['filigriː], *s.* filigrana.

filigreed, *a.* afiligranado.

filings ['failiŋz], *s.pl.* limaduras, limalla.

fill [fil], *v.t.* llenar, rellenar, henchir; hartar; terraplenar; hinchar; macizar; ocupar, desempeñar; contentar, satisfacer; reemplazar, sustituir; (*dent.*) empastar. — *v.i.* dar de beber, echar de beber, llenar el vaso; atracarse, saciarse, hartarse; *to fill in,* terraplenar, llenar un hueco; insertar; *to fill out,* llenar completar; ahuecarse, henchirse; llevar a cabo; *to fill someone's place,* ocupar el puesto de, sustituir; *to fill up,* llenar completamente, colmar; llenar un blanco; *to fill up one's time,* emplear el tiempo; *to fill the bill,* (*fam., E.U.*) llenar los requisitos. — *s.* terraplén; hartazgo, hartura, abundancia, atracón, lo suficiente.

filler, *s.* llenador, henchidor, envasador, embudador; embudo.

fillet ['filət], *s.* prendedero; venda, faja, cinta, tira; filete, solomillo; lista, listón; gusanillo de rosca; carne arrollada y atada con bramante; (*arq.*) filete, listel, tenia. — *v.t.* vendar, fajar, atar o ceñir con venda, faja o cinta; (*arq.*) filetear, adornar con astrágalos.

filling, *s.* henchimiento, suplemento, adición; envase; tripa (tabaco); relleno; (*dent.*) orificación o empastadura.

fillip ['filip], *v.t.* dar un capirotazo; echar, arrojar, tirar o impeler con un capirotazo; estimular, incitar. — *s.* capirotazo; aguijón, estímulo.

fillister ['filistəɹ], *s.* (*carp.*) guillame.

filly ['fili], *s.* potranca; muchacha ligera y retozona.

film [film], *s.* película; telilla, membrana; nube (*f.*) en el ojo; (*foto.*) película; *silent film,* película muda; *talking film,* película sonora; *film-star,* estrella de cine. — *v.t.* cubrir con una película; filmar, fotografiar para el cine. — *v.i.* formarse película.

filminess, *s.* apariencia como de película.

filmy, *a.* membranoso, compuesto de membranas, pelicular.

filose [fai'lous], *a.* (*anat. y bot*) filiforme.

filter ['filtəɹ], *v.t.* filtrar, depurar, colar. — *v.i.*

infiltrarse. — *s.* filtro, filtrador, colador, destiladera.

filth [filθ], *s.* suciedad, porquería, inmundicia; corrupción, impureza, infección; mugre, *f.*, basura, fango.

filthiness, *s.* inmundicia, escualor, asquerosidad, suciedad.

filthy, *a.* sucio, asqueroso, puerco, zarrapastroso; corrompido, inmundo, depravado, obsceno.

filtrate ['filtreit], *v.t.* filtrar. — *s.* líquido filtrado.

filtration, *s.* (*quím.*) filtración, coladura, destilación.

fimbriate ['fimbriət], *v.t.* franjear; ribetear.

fimbriate, fimbriated, fimbricate, fimbricated, *a.* franjeado, laciniado, recortado.

fin [fin], *s.* aleta (de los peces); barba de ballena; (*mec.*) apéndice en forma de aleta; (*vulg.*) la mano.

finable ['fainəbl], *a.* multable, sujeto a una multa.

final ['fainəl], *a.* final, último, perteneciente al fin; terminante, conclusivo, decisivo; terminal; mortal; *a final answer,* respuesta decisiva.

finale [fi'nɑːli], *s.* (*teat.*) final, fin, acto último, escena última; (*mús.*) último movimiento, coda.

finality [fai'næliti], *s.* finalización, finalidad; determinación, decisión; (*filos.*) doctrina finalista.

finally ['fainəli], *adv.* finalmente, en fin, en conclusión, por último, últimamente.

finance [fai'næns, fi'næns], *s.* hacienda pública; ciencia de negocios monetarios, ciencia rentística. — *pl.* **finances,** rentas, utilidades, ingresos, fondos. — *v.t.* financiar, administrar; (*Cuba*) refaccionar, aviar. — *v.i.* administrar rentas; negociar empréstitos; manejar negocios monetarios.

financial [fai'nænʃəl], *a.* financiero, rentístico, monetario, bancario; *financial year,* año económico.

financially, *adv.* rentísticamente, en materia de rentas.

financier [fai'nænsiəɹ], *v.t., v.i.* manejar, administrar o intervenir en negocios monetarios; conducir operaciones rentísticas. — *s.* financiero, banquero, hacendista, *m.f.*, recaudador de rentas públicas.

finback ['finbæk], *s.* (*ict.*) yubarta, especie de ballena.

finch [fintʃ], *s.* (*orn.*) pinzón, picogordo, fringílido; *bull-finch,* pinzón real; *gold-finch,* acanta.

find [faind], *v.t.* (*pret., p.p.* **found**) encontrar, descubrir, hallar, dar con, tropezar con; aprobar, reconocer, conocer por experiencia, admitir; procurar, abastecer, mantener, proveer, surtir, alimentar; saber, resolver, averiguar; adquirir; (*for.*) juzgar, decidir, fallar — *v.i.* descubrir lo que se busca; (*for.*) fallar, pronunciar sentencia; (caza) levantar una zorra; *to find fault* (*with*), poner defectos, poner peros, culpar, reprobar, desaprobar, censurar; *to find out,* resolver, hallar, descubrir; sorprender, imaginar, adivinar; averiguar; *to find it in one's heart,* tener ganas, estar de humor; *to find work for,* dar ocupación o trabajo a; *to find favour with,* caer en gracia de; *seek and ye shall find,* busca y hallarás. — s. encuentro; descubrimiento, hallazgo.

finder, s. hallador; inventor, descubridor; (ópt.) buscador.

finding, s. descubrimiento, invención; (for.) fallo, decisión, sentencia; gasto, mantenimiento. — pl. herramientas y avíos de zapateros y talabarteros.

fine [fain], a. fino, puro, refinado; admirable, excelente; agradable, hermoso, lindo, bello, elegante, galán; escogido, selecto, primoroso, delicado; cortés, bien criado; guapo, gallardo, bien parecido; tenue, delgado, sutil; diestro, sagaz; cortante, agudo; claro, transparente; espléndido, vistoso. — s. multa; (for.) fin, conclusión. — v.t. afinar, refinar, aclarar, clarificar, perfeccionar, dar lustre, lustrar; purificar; multar. — v.i. purificarse; derretirse; adelgazarse; pagar una multa; in fine, por fin, en resumidas cuentas; fine! ¡estupendo!; a fine fellow, un buen mozo.

fine-draw, v.t. zurcir; tirar (alambre).

fine-drawer, s. zurcidor, zurcidora; tiradora de metales.

fine-drawing, s. zurcidura; tirado de un metal.

fineness, s. fineza, excelencia, lustre, esplendor, primor, delicadeza; sutileza, fineza, finura, ingenio; perfección, pureza; ley del metal.

finer, a. comp. de fine; más fino, más hermoso, mejor. — s. refinador de metales.

finery ['fainəri], s. gala, adorno, aderezo, atavío; primor, elegancia, vista; (metal.) fragua en la que el hierro colado se hace maleable; el arte de refinar hierro.

fine-spun, a. alambicado, ingeniosamente delineado.

finesse [fi'nes], v.i. valerse de subterfugios y artificios. — s. artificio, estratagema, sutileza, treta, astucia; tacto, tino, diplomacia, habilidad.

fin-footed, a. palmeado (dícese de aves).

finger ['fiŋgəɹ], s. dedo; cosa parecida a un dedo; dedo (de licor, etc.); mano, f., manecilla (de reloj). — pl. dedos, la mano, el instrumento de alguna obra o arte. — v.t. tocar, manosear; hurtar, sisar; (mús.) tocar, teclear, tañer, pulsar; hacer algo con los dedos. — v.i. tener destreza en los dedos; index finger, dedo índice; middle finger, dedo del corazón; ring finger, dedo anular; little finger, dedo meñique; finger mark, mancha hecha con el dedo; impresión de la yema del pulgar; to have something at one's fingers' ends, saber una cosa al dedillo.

finger-board, s. mástil del violín o guitarra; teclado.

finger-bowl, s. enjuagatorio, enjuague.

finger-breadth, s. anchura del dedo.

fingered, a. que tiene dedos; (bot., zool.) digitado.

fingering, s. acto de tocar ligeramente; manoseo; (mús.) digitación.

finger-nail, s. uña.

finger-post, s. poste indicador.

finger-print, s. impresión dactilar, huella dactilar.

finger-stall, s. dedil.

finial ['finiəl], s. (arq.) florón de pináculo; remate.

finical ['finikəl], **finikin, finicky,** a. delicado, melindroso, afectado, remilgado.

finicality [fini'kæliti], s. remilgo, melindre, mitote, afectación.

finically, adv. afectadamente.

finicalness, s. melindre, afectación.

finish ['finiʃ], v.t. acabar, concluir, terminar, consumar, rematar, poner fin; completar, retocar, dar la última mano, pulir, perfeccionar; (fam.) matar o hacer impotente; vencer. — v.i. fenecer, cesar, finalizar; morir. — s. fin, remate, término, cima, acabamiento, fenecimiento, colmo; pulimento, última mano.

finisher, s. consumador; pulidor, afinador.

finishing, s. acabamiento, consumación; perfección, colmo; pincelada, colmo, última mano. — a. que acaba, concluye o consuma; finishing blow, golpe de gracia; to give the finishing touch, dar la última mano.

finite ['fainait], a. finito; limitado.

finiteness, s. limitación, restricción.

finless ['finles], a. sin aletas, desaletado.

finlike, a. aleteado.

Finn [fin], s. finlandés, -esa.

finned, a. que tiene aletas, aleteado.

Finnic, a. finés. — s. lengua finesa.

Finnish, s., a. finlandés, perteneciente a Finlandia.

finny ['fini], a. armado de aletas; abundante en peces.

fiord ['fiɔːɹd], s. brazo estrecho del mar; ría orillada de altas rocas.

fir [fəɹ], s. (bot.) abeto; pino; fir-tree, abeto; Scotch fir, pino; spruce-fir, pinabete; fir-cone, piña.

fire [faiəɹ], s. fuego, lumbre; materia combustible; quema, incendio, combustión; llama; ardor; pasión, inspiración poetica, viveza; rabia; desgracia, infortunio; tortura, persecución; (Cuba) candela; (mil.) fire! ¡fuego!; fire alarm, alarma de incendios; fire department, servicio de bomberos; fire insurance, seguros contra incendios; under fire, (mil.) expuesto al fuego; to be on fire, (fig.) estar hecho un ascua, estar ardiendo; to miss fire, hacer fogonazo, no disparar; to set fire to o to set on fire, pegar fuego (a), incendiar, quemar; to put out the fire, apagar el fuego; with fire and sword, a sangre y fuego; fire is a good servant, but a bad master, (prov.) sírvete del fuego, mas guárdate de él; he will never set the Thames on fire, (prov.) no inventó la pólvora; out of the frying-pan into the fire, (prov.) huir del fuego y dar en las brasas; St. Anthony's fire, erisipela; St. Elmo's fire, fuego de Santelmo. — v.t. quemar, encender, abrasar, enardecer, inflamar; excitar, animar; avivar el fuego; (fam.) despedir, echar a la calle; (vet.) cauterizar. — v.i. encenderse; enojarse, excitarse, enfadarse; disparar, tirar, hacer fuego, descargar.

fire-arm, s. arma de fuego.

fire-ball, s. (mil.) granada real o de mano.

fire-brand, s. tea, tizón; (fig.) incendiario, cizañero.

fire-brick, s. ladrillo refractario.

fire-dog, s. morillo de hogar.

fire-eater, s. matamoros, m.sing., fierabrás.

fire-engine, s. bomba de incendios.

fire-escape, s. escalera de incendios.

fire-extinguisher, s. extinctor, matafuego.

fire-fly, s. (ent.) luciérnaga.

fire-kiln, s. hornillo.

firelock, s. fusil, escopeta antigua de pedernal.

fireman, s. bombero; fogonero.

fire-new, a. flamante, recién salido de la fragua.

fire-pan, s. brasero.

fireplace, s. hogar.

fire-proof, a. incombustible, a prueba de incendio.

fire-shovel, s. badil, paleta.

firewood ['faɪəɹwud], s. leña.

fireworks, s.pl. fuegos artificiales.

firing, s. leña, carbón.

firk [fəːɹk], v.t. levantar, echar; azotar, dar azotes; impeler.

firkin, s. cuñete, barrilete de 9 galones (40·914 lit.) de capacidad; barril pequeño que se emplea para mantequilla, sebo, etc.

firm [fəːɹm], a. firme, fijo, fuerte, estable, constante, seguro, sólido, duro; tenaz, inflexible. — s. (com.) firma, razón social.

firmament [fəːɹməmənt], s. firmamento.

firmamental [fəːɹməˈmentəl], a. perteneciente al firmamento.

firman ['fəːɹmən], s. firmán.

firmness, s. firmeza, fijeza, consistencia, dureza, solidez, estabilidad; constancia, determinación, resolución, tesón, entereza.

first [fəːɹst], a. primero; pristino, anterior, original, primitivo, delantero; sobresaliente, excelente; temprano. — s. primero; principio. — adv. primero, al principio, antes, en primer lugar; first or last, tarde o temprano; at first, from the first, al principio; first-class, de primera clase o calidad; first cousin, primo hermano, prima hermana.

firstborn, a. primogénito.

first-fruits, s.pl. frutos primerizos; (fig.) primicias.

firstling, s., a. primogénito; primerizo.

firstly, adv. primeramente, en primer lugar.

first-rate, a. preeminente, excelente, de primera clase.

firth [fəːɹθ], s. estuario, brazo del mar.

firwood ['fəːɹwud], s. madera de pino o abeto.

fisc [fisk], s. fisco, erario público, hacienda pública.

fiscal ['fiskəl], s. ministro o secretario de hacienda. — a. fiscal, rentístico, perteneciente al fisco.

fish [fiʃ], s. pez, m.; pescado; (mec.) refuerzo; (mar.) gimelga, gaburón, gemelo; cuenta o ficha usada en varios juegos; flying-fish, pez volador; a fish out of water, una gallina en corral ajeno; fuera de su elemento; he is an odd fish, es un hombre raro; to have other fish to fry, tener otras cosas en qué pensar. — v.t. pescar; buscar, coger, sacar a luz; alcanzar, intentar, reforzar, obtener; empalmar (rieles, etc.), engimelgar.

fish-bone, s. espina de pescado, raspa de pescado.

fish-day, s. día de abstinencia.

fisher, s. pescador; el pekan, marta de América.

fisher-boat, s. barca pescadora.

fisherman ['fiʃəɹmən], s. pescador; barca pescadora.

fishery ['fiʃəɹi], s. pesca, pesquera.

fish-glue, s. colapez, cola de pescado.

fish-hook, s. anzuelo.

fishiness ['fiʃinis], s. forma, sabor o olor de pescado.

fishing, s. pesca, pesquera, pesquería; fishing bait, cebo; fishing rod, caña de pescar; fishing smack, queche, barcolongo; fishing net, red de pescar, almancebe, albéntola, albareque; fishing grounds, pesquera; fishing reel, carretel; fishing fly, mosca artificial; fishing tackle, avíos de pescar; fishing line, cordel de pescar.

fish-market, s. pescadería.

fishmonger, s. pescadero.

fish-plate, s. mordaza; (f.c.) eclisa, placa (o plancha) de unión.

fish-pond, s. vivero, nansa.

fish-spear, s. dardo, arpón.

fish-wife, s.f. pescadera; (fig.) disputadora, marimacho.

fishy ['fiʃi], a. pisciforme; habitado por pescados; que huele o sabe a pescado; abundante en pescado; (fam.) sospechoso; inverosímil.

fissate ['fiseit], a. hendido, grietado.

fissile ['fisil], a. hendible, rajadizo, fisil.

fission ['fiʃən], s. hendimiento; (biol.) fisiparidad; (fís.) fisión.

fissiped ['fisiped], a. fisípedo, bisulco.

fissure ['fiʃəɹ], s. grieta, abertura, hendedura, rajadura, raja, fisura, abra, resquebradura, cuarteo. — v.t. hender. — v.i. agrietarse, cuartearse.

fist [fist], s. puño; (impr.) llamada, manecilla. — v.t. apuñear; apuñar, empuñar, dar puñetazos; with clenched fists, a puño cerrado.

fistic, a. relativo al puño; pugilístico.

fisticuff ['fistikʌf], s. puñada; puñetazo. — pl. pugilato, riña a puñadas.

fistula ['fistjuːlə], s. (cir.) fístula.

fistular, a. fistular, afistolado, fistuloso.

fistulate, a. tubular, hueco como un tubo, afistolado, fistuloso.

fistulous, a. fistuloso.

fit [fit], s. (med.) acceso, paroxismo, parasismo; convulsión, espasmo; accidente; mal, enfermedad; mal de madre; ataque, acometimiento de una enfermedad; pasión, humor, capricho; arranque, arrebato, arrebatimiento; conformidad, conveniencia; encaje, adaptación, ajuste; (sast.) corte, talle o entalladura de un traje; preparación; punto de saponificación; cold fit, escalofrío; fainting-fit, desmayo, síncope; to send one into fits, (fam.) enrabiar, desesperar, volver loco; to go into fits of laughter, (fam.) desternillarse de risa; by fits and starts, espasmódicamente, a tontas y a locas, al tuntún; if the fit takes me, si me da la gana. — a. apto, adecuado, aprestado, pintiparado, dispuesto, cómodo, conveniente, idóneo, a propósito para algo; capaz, hábil; sano; digno, propio, apropiado, compatible, congruo; preparado, listo; decente; (fam.) como si, casi, cuasi; to see o think fit, juzgar conveniente. — v.t. igualar, adaptar, adecuar; ajustar, acomodar, encajar, conformar; equipar, surtir, aprestar, proveer; (cost.) probar un vestido; vestir, calzar. — v.i. convenir, venir bien, corresponder, ser a propósito, compadecerse o compaginarse con; entallarse, ajustarse, sentar, caer (bien o mal); to fit out, proveer, tripular, equipar; armar; to fit into, encajar; concordar con; to fit up, ajustar, componer, acomodar; adornar, alhajar, amueblar.

fitch [fitʃ], **fitchet** ['fitʃit], **fitchew** ['fitʃu], s. (zool.) veso, visón.

fitch-brush ['fitʃbrʌʃ], s. pincel de veso.

fitful ['fitfʌl], a. espasmódico; incierto, vacilante; caprichoso.

fitfully, adv. caprichosamente, espasmódicamente; por intervalos.

fitment ['fitmənt], s. apresto, equipo, provisión; mobiliario, mueblaje.

fitness, s. propiedad, conveniencia, aptitud, oportunidad, tempestividad; vigor, salud, f.

fitter, s. ajustador, unidor, disponedor, acoplador; armador, mecánico; acomodador, proveedor; (cost.) cortador, entallador.

fitting, a. propio, adecuado, digno, conveniente. — s. ajuste, encaje; (cost.) prueba; entalladura, corte. — pl. **fittings**, guarniciones, avíos, maniobras, herrajes, herramientas; fitting-shop, taller de ajuste.

five [faiv], s., a. cinco; five-finger exercises, ejercicios de piano; five-stones, juego de tabas.

five-finger, five-leaf, s. (bot.) cincoenrama.

fivefold, a. quíntuplo.

fiver, s. (fam.) billete de banco de cinco libras; cualquier cosa que cuente cinco.

fives [faivz], s. un juego de pelota; (vet.) adivas.

fives-court, s. frontón.

fix [fiks], v.t. fijar, clavar, asegurar, asentar, sujetar, establecer; decidir, determinar, precisar; señalar (una fecha), ajustar, arreglar, poner en orden, disponer, acondicionar; fijar, parar, detener o concentrar (la atención, etc.); (quím., foto.) fijar; (fam.) reparar, recomponer; (mar.) encapillar; to fix bayonets, calar la bayoneta. — v.i. fijar el domicilio, fijarse, establecerse; decidirse, determinarse; cristalizarse, congelarse, solidificarse; to fix upon, decidir, elegir, escoger; to fix up, (fam.) arreglar, componer; equipar. — s. (fam.) dificultad, apuro, dilema, aprieto; (fund.) brasea; to be in a bad fix, hallarse en un apuro.

fixable, a. fijable.

fixate, v.t. situar; colocar, fijar. — v.i. fijarse.

fixation [fik'seiʃən], s. fijación; fijeza, firmeza, estabilidad; restricción; sujeción; obsesión.

fixative ['fiksətiv], a. que fija, que hace permanente. — s. (tint.) mordente; (foto.) fijador.

fixed, a. fijo, estable, estacionario, permanente; determinado; (com.) a plazo fijo. — p.p. [FIX].

fixedness ['fiksidnis], **fixity** ['fiksiti], s. fijeza, firmeza, inmovilidad, estabilidad; coherencia, fijación.

fixing, s. fijación; acción de fijar. — pl. **fixings**, adornos, decoraciones, efectos, enseres, accesorios.

fixture ['fikstʃər], s. lo que está fijo; instalación; adorno, trasto o mueble fijo; empleado inamovible. — pl. instalación, habilitación de una tienda; gas-fixtures, cañerías y lámparas de gas.

fizgig ['fizgig], s. mujer callejera; peón (de niños); buscapiés, m. sing.; dardo, arpón.

fizz [fiz], v.i. chisporrotear; estar efervescente. — s. chisporroteo; efervescencia; (fam.) gaseosa; champaña.

fizzle [fizl], v.i. chisporrotear; quedar mal, hacer fiasco. — s. champaña o bebida efervescente; (fam.) fiasco; mal éxito.

flabbergast ['flæbəɪgɑːst], v.t. aturdir, dejar sin habla por admiración, asombro o sorpresa.

flabby ['flæbi], a. blando, flojo, lacio.

flabellate ['flæbəleit], **flabelliform**, a. flabeliforme.

flaccid ['flæksid], a. flojo, débil, lacio, flaco, endeble; (med.) fláccido.

flaccidity [flæk'siditi], s. flojedad, debilidad, flaqueza.

flag [flæg], v.t. hacer señales con una bandera; poner una bandera encima; enlosar, embaldosar. — v.i. flaquear, amilanarse; debilitarse, decaer; colgar, pender; vacilar, estar suspenso. — s. bandera, pabellón, estandarte; banderola, banderín; lastra, baldosa, losa, laja, lancha; (bot.) gladiolo espadaña; falso ácoro; flag of truce, o white flag, bandera blanca, bandera de paz; black flag, pabellón (negro) de los piratas; to lower o strike the flag, arriar la bandera; to hoist the flag, izar la bandera.

flagellant ['flædʒelənt], a. flagelante. — s.pl. (igl.) flagelantes.

flagellate, v.i. azotar, flagelar.

flagellation, s. flagelación, disciplina.

flagelliform [flæ'dʒelifɔːɪm], a. flageliforme, en forma de látigo.

flagellum [flə'dʒeləm], s. flagelo, azote; (bot.) renuevo, sarmiento, vástago; (biol.) apéndice parecido a un látigo.

flageolet [flædʒo'let], s. caramillo, dulzaina, octavín; especie de judía verde.

flagginess ['flæginis], s. flojedad.

flagging ['flægiŋ], s. enlosado; conjunto de baldosas o lajas para adoquinar. — a. flojo, lánguido.

flaggy ['flægi], a. parecido a la laja; flojo, endeble, lacio, débil, insípido.

flagitious [flə'dʒiʃəs], a. malvado, facineroso, atroz, abominable, corrompido, vicioso.

flagitiousness, s. maldad, perversidad, atrocidad, villanía.

flag-officer, s. (mar.) almirante, vicealmirante, contraalmirante.

flagon ['flægən], s. frasco, botella.

flagrance ['fleigrəns], **flagrancy**, s. flagrancia, notoriedad, escándalo, impudencia; abrasamiento, ardor, calor, fuego.

flagrant ['fleigrənt], a. notorio, escandaloso, público; ardiente, flagrante, encendido, colorado; grande, insigne.

flag-ship, s. (mar.) capitana.

flagstaff, s. (mar.) asta de bandera, asta de tope.

flagstone, s. losa, baldosa, lastra, laja; (geol.) asperón.

flail [fleil], s. (agr.) mayal; (mil.) mangual. — v.t. desgranar con mayal. — v.i. batir, sacudir.

flair [fleəɪ], s. don especial, instinto.

flake [fleik], s. cascajo, pedacito, copo, vedija, escama, casquito; (mar.) cañizo, hojuela, lámina, laminilla; clavel rayado; flake of fire, chispa, centella; flake of snow o snow-flake, copo de nieve; flake of ice, carámbano. — v.t., v.i. formar hojuelas o escamas; romperse en láminas; descascararse a pedacitos.

flaky, a. lleno de cascajos o casquitos; vedijoso, vedijudo; escamoso o en laminillas; (pastel) hojaldrado; flaky pastry, hojaldre, f.

flam [flæm], s. falsedad, embuste, mentira, chasco; fantasía, capricho. — v.t. mentir, engañar.

flambeau ['flæmbou], *s.* antorcha, hachón; candelabro; caldera para hervir azúcar.
flamboyance, *s.* extravagancia.
flamboyant [flæm'bɔːiənt], *a.* (*arq.*) flamígero; extravagante, llamativo; ampuloso.
flame [fleim], *s.* llama, luz, *f.*, llamarada; flama; fuego; impulso vehemente, pasión, ardor; (*fam.*) amorío; amado. — *v.t.* quemar, chamuscar; encender, inflamar, excitar. — *v.i.* flamear, flagrar, arder, llamear; brillar, resplandecer, fulgurar; encenderse; inflamarse en alguna pasión violenta.
flame-colour, *s.* color de fuego, de llama.
flame-coloured, *a.* de color de llama.
flameless, *a.* sin llama.
flamen ['fleimen], *s.* flamen.
flame-thrower, *s.* lanzallamas, *m.sing.*
flaming ['fleimiŋ], *a.* flamante, llameante; llamativo, faustoso, apasionado, excitante.
flamingo [flə'miŋgou], *s.* (*orn.*) flamenco.
flamy ['fleimi], *a.* inflamado, llameante; de color de llama, de fuego; compuesto de llamas.
flanch [flɑːntʃ], *s.* (*blas.*) figura formada a cada lado del escudo por el segmento de un círculo; usado siempre en pares.
flange [flændʒ], *s.* (*mec.*) reborde, borde, pestaña, realce, oreja, corona, cordón, brida; plancha de cierre. — *v.t.* proveer de brida o reborde. — *v.i.* proyectar, salir.
flange-joint, *s.* junta de bridas.
flange-pipe, *s.* tubo con reborde.
flange-wheel, *s.* rueda con pestaña.
flank [flæŋk], *s.* ijar, ijada; costado, lado; (*mil. y fort.*) ala, flanco. — *a.* por el flanco, lateral; de lado, de costado. — *v.t.* orillar, lindar, confinar; asegurar los flancos de, estar a cada lado de; (*mil.*) flanquear. — *v.i.* lindar con; llegar a.
flanker, *s.* (*fort.*) flanco; flanqueador.
flannel ['flænəl], *s.* franela, flanela.
flap [flæp], *s.* (*sast.*) cartera; faldeta, falda, faldilla; golpe; hoja plegadiza de mesa; cachete, revés; alazo; ala de sombrero; oreja de zapato; mosqueador; labio de una herida. — *v.t.* batir, sacudir, pegar, golpear, rebajar, dejar caer, columpiar, agitar; gualdrapear; mosquear, espantar con el mosqueador; *to flap the wings,* aletear. — *v.i.* batir; colgar; dar gualdrapazos; columpiarse, moverse de arriba abajo, sacudirse, agitarse; *to be in a flap,* (*fam.*) estar agitado.
flap-eared, *a.* orejudo.
flapjack, *s.* torta de sartén.
flap-mouthed, *a.* morrudo, bezudo, hocicudo.
flapper ['flæpəɹ], *s.* golpeador, agitador, batidor; patito; (*fam.*) muchacha joven, polla.
flapping, *s.* batimiento, aletazo, aleteo, acción de sacudirse; (*mar.*) socollada, gualdrapazo.
flare [flɛəɹ], *v.t.* ostentar, ensanchar. — *v.i.* brillar, resplandecer; relampaguear, fulgurar; ensancharse. — *s.* fulgor, brillo; hacha; (*aer.*) cohete de señales; (*cost.*) vuelo; ensanchamiento; *to flare up,* (*fig.*) encolerizarse; *a flare-up,* (*fig.*) arrebato de cólera.
flaring, *a.* fulgurante, resplandeciente; abocinado; chillón.
flash [flæʃ], *s.* relámpago, destello, llamarada, resplandor; fucilazo; instante, momento; ráfaga (de luz); (*ant.*) represa; rasgo de ingenio; *flash-lamp,* linterna; *flash-wheel,* rueda hidráulica; *lightning flash,* relámpago;

shoulder-flash, (*mil.*) emblema, *m.* — *a.* (*fam.*) ladronesco, germanesco; charro; *flash language,* germanía, caló. — *v.t.* hacer brillar; lanzar (una mirada, etc.); encender; transmitir (señales); (*fam.*) lucir (adornos, etc.). — *v.i.* relampaguear, brillar, destellar; pasar como un relámpago.
flashily ['flæʃili], *adv.* con ostentación, con colores chillones; superficialmente.
flashing, *s.* centelleo; soplado del vidrio; golpe de agua.
flashlight ['flæʃlait], *s.* luz de magnesio; linterna eléctrica.
flashy, *a.* llamativo, charro; superficial.
flask [flɑːsk], *s.* frasco, botella, redoma, pomo; (*fund.*) caja de moldear; *vacuum flask,* termos, *m. sing.*
flat [flæt], *s.* llanura, llano, plano, planicie, *f.*; escollo, banco, bajío; (*mús.*) bemol; (*fam.*) mentecato, primo; habitación, cuarto, piso, apartamento; carro de plataforma; palma de la mano; barca chata; plano de una hoja cortante. — *a.* llano, plano, liso, raso, chato; tendido, extendido; aplastado, triste, abatido, sin viveza, sin interés, insípido, sin lustre, mate, flojo, insulso; absoluto, positivo, perentorio, premeditado, categórico; arrasado; (*mús.*) bemol; (*vino, cerveza,* etc.) evaporado. — *v.t.* (*mús.*) bajar de tono, abajar un tono; aplastar, allanar, achatar; evaporar. — *v.i.* (*mús.*) desafinar por lo bajo, bajar el tono; aplastarse, aplanarse; atontarse.
flat-bottomed, *a.* de fondo plano.
flat-footed, *a.* de pies planos; (*fam., E.U.*) resuelto, determinado.
flatlong, *adv.* de plano.
flatly, *adv.* horizontalmente, llanamente; de plano, absolutamente; sin animación ni interés; fríamente; *to deny flatly,* negar de plano (o rotundamente).
flatness, *s.* llanura, lisura, chatedad; insipidez, desabrimiento, insulsez, frialdad; abatimiento, apocamiento.
flat-nosed, *a.* romo, chato.
flatten ['flætən], *v.t.* allanar, achatar, poner chato, aplastar, aplanar, abatir; echar a tierra, derribar; apachurrar; desabrir, desazonar; deprimir; evaporar. — *v.i.* aplanarse, igualarse; perder el espíritu, la viveza, el sabor; atontarse; evaporarse.
flatter ['flætəɹ], *v.t.* adular, lisonjear; agradar, favorecer, causar gusto. — *v.i.* valerse de lisonjas, ser adulador; *to flatter oneself that . . .,* hacerse la ilusión que.
flatterer ['flætərəɹ], *s.* adulador, lisonjero, zalamero.
flattering, *a.* lisonjero, halagüeño.
flattery, *s.* adulación, halago, lisonja, zalamería, requiebro, carantoña.
flattish, *a.* chato, achatado.
flatulence ['flætjuːləns], **flatulency,** *s.* flatulencia; ventosidad; (*fig.*) presunción, hinchazón, *f.*, vanidad.
flatulent ['flætjuːlənt], **flatuous** ['flætjuːʌs], *a.* ventoso, flatulento; (*fig.*) vano, hinchado.
flatus ['fleitʌs], *s.* flato, ventosidad; soplo; hinchazón, *f.*
flatwise ['flætwaiz], *adv.* de llano.
flaunt [flɔːnt], *v.t., v.i.* ondear, lucir; ostentar, lucir; pavonearse. — *s.* alarde, ostentación.
flautist ['flɔːtist], *s.* flautista, *m.f.*

flavescent [flə'vesənt], *a.* amarillento; que se vuelve amarillo.

flavin ['fleivin], *s.* (*quím.*) tinte amarillo obtenido de la corteza del roble negro americano (*quercus tinctoria*).

flavour ['fleivər], *s.* sabor, gusto, gustillo; (*coc.*) salsa, sainete, sazón, *f.* — *v.t.* sazonar, saborear, condimentar; (*fig.*) dar cualidad distintiva a.

flavoured, *a.* gustoso, sabroso. — *p.p.* [FLAVOUR].

flavouring, *s.* sainete, condimento.

flavourless, *a.* sin sabor, insípido, soso.

flavourous, *a.* sabroso, fragante.

flaw [flɔː], *s.* falta, tacha, defecto, imperfección, lunar; grieta, hendidura, resquebradura, paño, pelo, paja; (*mar.*) ráfaga, racha; mancha, falla. — *v.i.* afear, agrietar, hacer imperfecto, estropear.

flawless, *a.* entero, sano, sin tacha, sin imperfecciones, impecable.

flawy, *a.* agrietado, grietoso, lleno de faltas o tachas; sujeto a rachas; (*carp.*) albornado.

flax [flæks], *s.* lino; *to dress flax,* rastrillar lino.

flax-brake, *s.* agramadera.

flax-comb, *s.* rastrillo.

flax-dresser, *s.* rastrillador.

flax-dressing, *s.* rastrilleo del lino.

flaxen ['flæksən], **flaxy,** *a.* de lino, hecho de lino; *flaxen-haired,* blondo, rubio.

flax-seed, *s.* linaza.

flax-weed, *s.* (*bot.*) linaria.

flay [flei], *v.t.* desollar, despellejar, descortezar.

flayer, *s.* desollador, descortezador.

flea [fliː], *s.* pulga; *a flea in one's ear,* amonestación o mala acogida; *he came out with a flea in his ear,* salió con las manos en la cabeza.

fleabane ['fliːbein], *s.* (*bot.*) coniza, pulguera.

flea-bite, *s.* picadura de pulga.

flea-bitten, *a.* picado de pulgas; vil, bajo, menospreciable.

fleam [fliːm], *s.* (*vet.*) fleme, lanceta; arroyo, zanja.

fleawort ['fliːwəːt], *s.* (*bot.*) pulguera, zaragatona.

fleck [flek], *s.* mancha, lunar, copo, vedija; punto de color.

flecker, *v.t.* abigarrar, varetear, señalar con manchas. — *s.* lunar, mancha; copo, vedija; punto de color.

fleckless, *a.* sin mancha, sin lunar; inocente.

flection ['flekʃən], *s.* flexión, inclinación; ojeada, mirada; corvadura; (*gram.*) flexión.

flector ['flektər], *s.* (*anat.*) músculo flexor.

fled [fled], *pret., p.p.* [FLEE].

fledge [fledʒ], *v.t.* emplumar. — *v.i.* emplumarse, emplumecer, pelechar.

fledged, *a.* plumado, alado, plumoso; maduro. — *p.p.* [FLEDGE].

fledgeling ['fledʒliŋ], *s., a.* volantón; (*fig.*) novel, joven, poco conocido.

flee [fliː], *v.t.* (*pret., p.p.* fled) esquivar, huir de, evitar, escapar de. — *v.i.* huir, huirse, escaparse, fugarse; desaparecer.

fleece [fliːs], *s.* vellón, lana. — *v.t.* esquilar, tonsurar; cubrir con lana o nieve; blanquear; (*fig.*) desnudar, robar, despojar; *Order of the Golden Fleece,* orden del Toisón de Oro.

fleeced, *a.* velludo, esquilado.

fleecy, *a.* lanudo; *fleecy clouds,* nubes aborregadas.

fleer [fliər], *v.t.* mofar, burlar. — *v.i.* mofarse, burlarse, hacer muecas. — *s.* burla, mueca; risa falsa.

fleerer, *s.* mofador.

fleet [fliːt], *s.* (*mar.*) armada; flota. — *a.* veloz, rápido, ligero. — *v.t., v.i.* volar, pasar rápidamente, desvanecerse; (*mar.*) despasar, cambiar.

fleet-footed [fliːt'futəd], *a.* alípede, ligero, veloz.

fleeting, *a.* fugaz, transitorio, volandero, pasajero, que pasa rápidamente, momentáneo, efímero.

fleeting-dish, *s.* espumadera.

fleetness, *s.* velocidad, ligereza.

Fleming ['flemiŋ], *s.* flamenco, natural de Flandes.

Flemish ['flemiʃ], *s., a.* flamenco.

flesh [fleʃ], *s.* carne, *f.*; género humano; sensualidad, carnalidad; pasiones groseras; pulpa de las frutas; en teología y bíblica, la naturaleza humana y pecaminosa del hombre; parentela, parientes cercanos. — *v.t.* saciar, hartar; acostumbrar, habituar, endurecer, avezar; descarnar, pelambrar; cebar; *after the flesh,* conforme a la carne; *flesh and blood,* carne y hueso, (*fig.*) hijos, hermanos, parientes; *flesh diet,* dieta de carne; *flesh wound,* herida superficial.

flesh-colour, *s.* color de carne, encarnación.

fleshed, *a.* carnoso, carnudo.

fleshiness, *s.* carnosidad, gordura, corpulencia.

fleshings ['fleʃiŋz], *s.pl.* (*teat.*) mallas, calzones de punto de color de carne; descarnaduras, piltrafas.

fleshless, *a.* descarnado.

fleshliness, *s.* carnalidad.

fleshly, *a.* carnal, animal; corpóreo.

fleshmonger ['fleʃmʌŋgər], *s.* (*ant.*) carnicero; alcahuete.

fleshpot ['fleʃpɔt], *s.* olla, marmita.

fleshy ['fleʃi], *a.* gordo, corpulento, grueso; suculento, pulposo, carnoso, mollar; carnal, animal; corporal.

fletcher ['fletʃər], *s.* flechero.

fleur-de-lis [fləːdə'liː], *s. sing. y pl.* flor de lis, *f.*

fleured [fləːd], *a.* flordelisado.

fleuret ['fləːiet], *s.* florete; ornamento en forma de pequeña flor.

flew [fluː], *pret.* [FLY].

flewed, *a.* boquihendido.

flews [fluːz], *s.pl.* belfos.

flex [fleks], *v.t.* doblar, doblegar, encorvar. — *s.* doblez, encorvadura; (*elec.*) cordón eléctrico.

flexibility [fleksi'biliti], **flexibleness** ['flekziblnis], *s.* flexibilidad, condescendencia, docilidad.

flexible ['flekzibl], *a.* flexible, correoso; dúctil; doblegable, adaptable; conformable, dócil, obediente, plástico.

flexile ['flekzail], *a.* flexible.

flexion ['flekʃən], *s.* flexión; corvadura.

flexor ['fleksər], *s.* (*anat.*) músculo flexor.

flexuose ['fleksjuːous], **flexuous** ['fleksjuːəs], *a.* tortuoso, vario, inconstante; (*bot.*) flexuoso.

flexure ['flekʒuːɹ], *s.* flexión, corvadura, juntura.

flibbertigibbet ['flibəɹtidʒibit], *s.* charlador, -a; una casquivana; un diablo.

flick [flik], *v.t.* tocar ligeramente con un látigo; dar un golpecito a; sacudir. — *v.i.* revolotear. — *s.* golpecito; (*fam.*) película de cine.

flicker ['flikəɹ], *v.i.* vacilar; agitarse; revolotear. — *s.* llama vacilante; aleteo; estremecimiento; (*orn.*, *E.U.*) picamaderos, pájaro carpintero.

flicker-mouse, *s.* murciélago.

flier ['flaiəɹ], *s.* volador; ave volante; aviador; (*mec.*) volante; fugitivo; (*fam.*) cosa veloz; buque rápido, caballo de carrera, tren expreso, etc.; (*impr.*) sacapliegos. — *pl.* peldaños, escalones de una escalera que va en línea recta.

flies [flaiz], *s.pl.* [FLY]; moscas.

flight [flait], *s.* vuelo, volada; bandada de pájaros, etc.; velocidad, rapidez; fuga, huida; exaltación; ímpetu, rebato, arrebato, arranque; elevación de ideas; vuelo de la imaginación; (*for.*) evasión, escape; tramo de escalera; *flight-feather*, remera.

flightiness, *s.* veleidad, capricho; travesura; ligero delirio.

flighty, *a.* volátil, caprichoso, voltario, delirante, inconstante; ligero, travieso; acelerado.

flimflam ['flimflæm], *s.* (*fam.*) soflama, superchería, embuste. — *v.t.* soflamar, engañar con astucia.

flimsily ['flimzili], *adv.* sin consistencia, de un modo endeble.

flimsiness, *s.* endeblez, falta de solidez o consistencia, textura ligera.

flimsy ['flimzi], *a.* débil, endeble; fútil, frívolo, poco sólido, insubstancial, ineficaz.

flinch [flintʃ], *v.i.* titubear, vacilar, faltar a, echar el cuerpo (o el pie) atrás, desviar el cuerpo; retroceder, desistir; acobardarse; (*fam.*) llamarse andana.

flinch, flinching, *s.* vacilación, titubeo, retroceso; *without flinching*, sin titubear, sin vacilar, sin una queja.

flinder ['flindəɹ], *s.* astilla, pedacito, tira, arista, fragmento.

fling [fliŋ], *v.t.* (*pret.*, *p.p.* **flung**) echar, tirar, arrojar, lanzar, esparcir, empujar; vencer, sobrepujar; echar al suelo, derribar. — *v.i.* lanzar un arma arrojadiza; escarnecer, murmurar, mofarse; lanzarse, brincar, saltar, cocear, alborotar(se) (caballos, etc.); *to fling away*, descartar, arrojar, desechar, desperdiciar; *to fling about*, desparramar, esparcir; *to fling open*, abrir de repente; *to fling off*, engañar en la caza; *to fling up*, (*fam.*) abandonar, dejar; echar en cara; *to fling out*, arrojar con fuerza; hablar violentamente, echar chispas; *to fling down*, echar al suelo, demoler, arruinar. — *s.* tiro, echada, echamiento; baile escocés; atrevimiento, bravata; burla, sarcasmo, indirecta, pulla, chufleta; gesto, mueca; brinco, salto; *to have one's fling*, correrla.

flinger ['fliŋəɹ], *s.* arrojador, tirador; escarnecedor, mofador.

flint [flint], *s.* pedernal.

flint-hearted, *a.* cruel, duro, empedernido.

flintiness, *s.* cualidad del pedernal, excesiva dureza.

flint-lock, *s.* llave de chispa.

flinty, *a.* apedernalado, silicoso, de pedernal, pedernalino; (*fig.*) endurecido, empedernido, duro, inflexible, inexorable, cruel.

flip [flip], *v.t.* lanzar, soltar; dar un golpe ligero y rápido; quitar de golpe; chasquear. — *s.* floretada; bebida de vino o cerveza con ron y azúcar.

flip-flap ['flipflæp], *s.* zis-zas; buscapiés; (*vulg.*) salto mortal; especie de tiovivo.

flip-flop ['flipflɔp], *s.* trapa trapa.

flippancy ['flipənsi], *s.* levedad, ligereza, locuacidad, impertinencia.

flippant ['flipənt], *a.* ligero, frívolo; impertinente.

flipper ['flipəɹ], *s.* aleta o pata (de foca, etc.); (*vulg.*) la mano.

flirt [fləːɹt], *v.i.* flirtear, coquetear, cocar; corretear, travesar; hacer cocos o carantoñas; jugar con, divertirse con. — *v.t.* tirar, sacudir, arrojar o menear con ligereza. — *s.* coqueta, cocador o cocadora, coquetón; golpe o meneo rápido; gesto, mofa, burla.

flirtation [fləːɹ'teiʃən], **flirting**, *s.* flirteo, coquetería, coqueteo, galanteo, ligereza.

flit [flit], *v.i.* volar, revolotear; pasar rápidamente, deslizarse; (*fam.*) mudar de domicilio.

flitch [flitʃ], *s.* hoja de tocino; lonja ahumada; (*carp.*) costera, costanera.

flitter ['flitəɹ], *v.i.* aletear; revolotear. — *s.* aleteo; lentejuela.

flittermouse ['flitəɹmaus], *s.* murciélago.

flitting, *s.* fuga, vuelo rápido. — *a.* pasajero, fugitivo, ligero.

flix [fliks], *s.* borra, borrilla, pelusa, pelusilla, especialmente la del castor.

float [flout], *v.i.* flotar, sobrenadar; fluctuar; boyar; nadar; cernerse. — *v.t.* hacer flotar, hacer nadar, poner, mantener o llevar a flote; estropejar, enlucir con talocha; regar; (*com.*) emitir, poner en circulación; intervenir. — *s.* cualquier cosa que flota; (*mar.*) jangada; corcho de una caña de pescar; flotador de nivel de agua; balsa, masa flotante, almadía, boya, maderada; carromato; carroza para procesiones o espectáculos públicos, plataforma con ruedas; salvavidas, *m.*; *to float up*, soldar por dentro; *floatboard*, (*hidr.*) álabe, paleta de rueda; tablero de rodezno de agua.

floatable, *a.* flotable, flotante.

floatage, *s.* flotante.

floater, *s.* flotador, flotante.

floating, *s.* flote, flotación; (*alb.*) revestimiento. — *a.* flotante, boyante; suelto, a flote, no anclado; (*com.*) flotante, en circulación; fluctuante, movible, variable; *floating debt*, deuda flotante; *floating population*, población de tránsito.

floccose ['flɔkous], *a.* (*bot.*) velludo.

flocculence ['flɔkjuːləns], *s.* vellosidad.

flocculent, *a.* velludo, lanudo; (*orn.*) parecido al flojel, al plumón; (*ent.*) cubierto con una substancia viscosa.

flocculose, *a.* que tiene pelusa.

flock [flɔk], *s.* manada, rebaño, bandada, grey, *f.*; conjunto de muchas personas, multitud; congregación; copo o vedija de lana; borra, flojel, tamo, pelusilla; paño deshilado. — *v.i.* congregarse, reunirse, juntarse, atroparse.

flock-bed, *s.* colchón de borra.

flock-paper, *s.* papel aterciopelado.

floe [flou], *s.* de hielo banco.

flog [flɔg], *v.t.* azotar, tundir, zurrar; *never flog* *a willing horse*, caballo que vuela, no quiere espuela.

flogging ['flɔgiŋ], *s.* vapuleo, felpa, tunda, azotaina, zurra, pela, (*Cuba*) monda; (*fam.*) bocabajo.

flood [flʌd], *s.* riada, desbordamiento, avenida, inundación, diluvio, llena; plétora, abundancia; flujo o creciente de la marea; (*poét.*) río, mar; (*min.*) aguada; chorro. — *v.t.* inundar, apantanar, anegar, enaguazar.

flood-gate, *s.* compuerta de esclusa, paradera.

flooding, *s.* inundación; (*med.*) hemorragia uterina.

flood-mark, *s.* nivel de la marea alta.

flood tide, *s.* pleamar, *f.*

floor [flɔ:ɹ], *s.* pavimiento, piso, suelo; piso de una casa; (*mar.*) fondo, plan; (*agr.*) era; (*min.*) fondo de una vena o filón de carbón. — *v.t.* solar, tillar, entarimar; (*fig.*) superar, vencer, derrotar (en un argumento, debate); poner, tender en el suelo; echar al suelo; *ground floor*, piso o cuarto bajo; *main floor*, piso principal; *to have the floor*, tener la palabra.

floor-cloth, *s.* linóleo; trapo de fregar suelos.

floor-heads, *s.pl.* (*mar.*) maniguetes.

flooring, *s.* suelo, pavimiento, piso, tablado.

floor-timbers, *s.pl.* (*mar.*) varengas.

flop [flɔp], *v.t.* batir, aletear, sacudir, hacer golpear. — *v.i.* caer pesadamente, colgar; agitarse; venirse abajo, caerse; hundirse, desplomarse;(*fam.*) fracasar. — *s.* ruido sordo; (*fam.*) fracaso.

flora ['flɔ:ɹə], *s.* flora.

floral ['flɔ:ɹəl], *a.* floral.

Florentine ['flɔrentain], *s.*, *a.* florentino.

florescence [flɔ'resəns], *s.* (*bot.*) florescencia.

florescent, *a.* floreciente.

floret ['flɔ:ret], *s.* (*bot.*) flósculo, florecilla; cadarza; (*ant.*) florete de esgrima.

floriculture [flɔri'kʌltʃəɹ], *s.* floricultura.

floriculturist, *s.* floricultor.

florid ['flɔrid], *a.* florido; rojo, encarnado; vivo, brillante; sobrecargado de adornos; embellecido con flores de retórica.

floridity, floridness, *a.* floridez, estilo florido.

floriferous [flɔ'rifərəs], *a.* florífero, florígero.

florin ['flɔrin], *s.* florín (moneda).

florist ['flɔrist], *s.* florero, florera, florista, *m.f.*

floscule ['flɔskju:l], *s.* (*bot.*) flósculo.

flosculous, *a.* compuesto de flores.

floss [flɔs], *s.* seda floja; borra, penacho del maíz; cadarzo; (*fund.*) escorias que sobrenadan.

floss-silk, *s.* seda floja.

flossy ['flɔsi], *a.* len; lene.

flota ['floutə], *s.* (*mar.*) flota.

flotage ['floutidʒ], *s.* flotante, objetos que flotan; flotación.

flotation [flou'teiʃən], *s.* flotación; teoría de los cuerpos flotantes.

flotilla [flou'tilə], *s.* flotilla.

flotsam ['flɔtsəm], *s.* pecio.

flounce [flauns], *v.t.* (*cost.*) guarnecer, adornar las extremidades de los vestidos. — *v.i.* pernear; brincar de impaciencia, saltar de enojo. — *s.* (*cost.*) volante, cairel, farfalá, fleco, flueco, (*Cuba*) vuelo, (*Mex.*) olán.

flounder ['flaundəɹ], *s.* (*ict.*) lenguado, rodaballo; tumbo, tropiezo. — *v.i.* vacilar, tropezar; revolverse, revolcarse; (*fig.*) confundirse.

flour [flauəɹ], *s.* harina.

flour-bolt, *s.* tamiz, cedazo.

flourish ['flʌriʃ], *v.t.* florear, agitar, vibrar, menear, sacudir; blandir; (*ant.*) embellecer, adornar, exornar. — *v.i.* florecer; prosperar, medrar; rasguear; agitarse en el aire; (*mús.*) florear. — *s.* rasgo, plumada; adorno, floreo; (*esgr.*) molinete; rúbrica; (*mús.*) floreo, preludio; ostentación, fausto.

flourisher, *s.* el que prospera; el que escribe, haciendo rasgos de adorno.

flourishing, *a.* floreciente; que florece; próspero.

floury ['flauəri], *a.* harinoso.

flout [flaut], *v.t.* escarnecer, befar, burlarse de, rechazar con desdén, menospreciar. — *v.i.* burlarse, mofarse, hacer burla o mofa. — *s.* befa, mofa, escarnio, burla.

flouter, *s.* burlador, mofador.

flow [flou], *v.i.* fluir, manar, derramar, correr; proceder, dimanar, provenir; flotar, ondear; abundar; (*mar.*) subir, crecer (la marea); (*med.*) descargar sangre en exceso por el útero. — *v.t.* inundar. — *s.* corriente, *f.*, torrente; flujo, creciente de la marea, *f.*; abundancia, copia, multitud, muchedumbre, desagüe, chorro; (*mil.*) creciente; *to flow away*, deslizarse, pasar; *to flow out* o *from*, correr de; *to flow into*, desaguar.

flower ['flauəɹ], *s.* (*bot.*) flor, *f.*; adorno, belleza; flor y nata, lo mejor y más selecto; planta en flor. — *pl.* **flowers**, (*quím.*) flor; *everlasting flower*, perpetua. — *v.i.* florecer, dar flor, florar; (*ant.*) fermentar, hervir.

flower-bed, *s.* cuadro de jardín, era, macizo.

flower-bud, *s.* capullo, botón de flor.

flowered, *a.* floreado.

floweret, *a.* florecilla, florecita.

flower-garden, *s.* jardín, pensil.

flower-girl, *s.* florera, ramilletera, florista.

floweriness ['flauərines], *s.* abundancia de flores; floreo de palabras.

flowering ['flauəriŋ], *a.* (*bot.*) fanerógamo; floreciente. — *s.* floración, florescencia, eflorescencia.

flower-leaf, *s.* pétalo.

flowerless, *a.* sin flores, que no tiene flores.

flower-piece, *s.* ramillete; (*pint.*) florero.

flower-pot, *s.* tiesto, maceta de flores.

flower-stand, *s.* jardinera.

flower-vase, *s.* jarrón.

flowery, *a.* florido, lleno de flores; poético.

flowing ['flouiŋ], *a.* corriente, fluente, fluctuante, manantial, pendiente, vertiente; colgante, suelto; ondeante, fluctuoso; flúido. — *s.* derrame, flujo, manantial, creciente, *f.*, fluidez.

flowingly, *adv.* abundantemente, copiosamente.

flowingness, *s.* dicción flúida.

flown [floun], huido, escapado; *high-flown*, hinchado. — *p.p.* [FLY].

flu [flu:], (abrev. de *influenza*) *s.* (*fam.*) gripe, *f.*

fluctuant ['flʌktju:ənt], *a.* fluctuoso, fluctuante, vacilante.

fluctuate ['flʌktju:eit], *v.i.* fluctuar, undular, mover, ondear; dudar, vacilar; estar indeciso.

fluctuation [flʌktju:'eiʃən], *s.* fluctuación, balance, duda, agitación, irresolución, incertidumbre, instabilidad, vaivén.

flue [flu:], *s.* cañón o campana de chimenea, humero; cañón de órgano; tamo, pelusa, borra; flus, tubo de caldera; *flue boiler*, caldera tubular.

fluency ['fluːənsi], s. fluidez; labia, afluencia, soltura, facundia, copia, abundancia, volubilidad.

fluent ['fluːənt], a. facundo, afluente; fluente, flúido, líquido, corriente; fácil, suelto; copioso, abundante. — s. agua corriente.

fluently, adv. corrientemente, con facilidad.

fluff [flʌf], s. pelusa, pelillo, vello, borra, lanilla, mota, plumón, tamo; (teat., fam.) papel mal aprendido; a bit of fluff, (vulg.) chica, polla. — v.t. mullir borra, plumón; (fam.) hacer mal.

fluffiness, s. calidad de velloso, plumoso o sedoso.

fluffy, a. cubierto de plumón o vello; plumoso, mullido, blando, sedoso.

fluid ['fluːid], s. flúido, suco, jugo, líquido; gas. — a. flúido.

fluidity [fluˈiditi], **fluidness**, s. fluidez, liquidez.

fluke [fluːk], s. lengüeta de ancla; aleta de la cola de la ballena; uña del arpón; (ict.) acedía, platija; lombriz del ganado lanar; (fam.) chiripa.

flume [fluːm], s. caño, caz, canalizo, canal de esclusa; salto de agua; cañada.

flummery ['flʌməri], s. manjar blanco; (fig.) pelitrique; lisonja grosera, hojarasca.

flung [flʌŋ], pret., p.p. [FLING].

flunk [flʌŋk], v.t. (fam.) faltar, esquivar. — v.i. retroceder, cejar.

flunkey ['flʌŋki], **flunky**, s. lacayo; adulón, lavacaras, hombre servil.

flunkyism, s. servilismo, bajeza.

fluor ['fluːɔːɪ], s. (ant.) fluidez; fluor-spar, (min.) espato flúor.

fluorescence [fluːɪˈesens], s. fluorescencia.

fluorescent, a. fluorescente.

fluorhydric [fluːɔːhaidrik], a. (quím.) fluorhídrico.

fluoric [fluːˈɔrik], a. (quím.) fluórico.

fluorid ['fluːɔrid], **fluoride**, s. (quím.) fluoruro.

fluorin ['fluːɔrin], **fluorine**, s. (quím.) flúor.

fluoroscope [fluːˈɔrəskoup], s. fluoróscopo.

flurry [flʌri], s. perturbación, agitación, conmoción; soplo repentino, racha, ráfaga; barullo; precipitación, prisa; estertor de una ballena herida por el arpón. — v.t. confundir, aturdir, perturbar, atropellar, alarmar, aturrullar.

flush [flʌʃ], v.t. abochornar, sonrojar, poner colorado; igualar, emparejar, nivelar; llenar hasta la superficie; animar; levantar (aves de caza); limpiar con un chorro de agua, inundar con agua. — v.i. salirse, manar, fluir precipitadamente, derramarse repentinamente, llenarse de agua; sonrojarse, ruborizarse, ponerse colorado; echar a volar. — a. igual, parejo, a nivel, nivelado, ras; abundante, copioso; lleno de vigor o vida, fresco, robusto; (fam.) opulento, adinerado, rico; afectado. — s. rubor, color (en las mejillas), bochorno, rubicundez, sonrojo; emoción, agitación, animación; floración; copia, afluencia, abundancia; flujo rápido o copioso; vuelo súbito de un pájaro, bandada de pájaros espantados; flux (juego de naipes); ataque febril; flush-deck, (mar.) puente corrido.

flushing, s. rubor, bochorno, rubicundez; acción de echar agua.

fluster ['flʌstəɪ], v.t. embriagar; aturdir, atropellar, confundir; poner colorado. — s. confusión, aturdimiento; flujo violento.

flustered, a. excitado; aturrullado; (ant.) borracho.

flute [fluːt], s. (mús.) flauta; rizado, pliegue; (arq.) estría. — v.t. estriar, acanalar, encanutar; (Méj.) encarrujar; (cost.) alechugar, plegar, rizar. — v.i. tocar la flauta.

fluter, s. flautista, m.f.

fluting, s. (arq.) estriadura, acanaladura, estría; (cost.) rizado, alechugado, pliegue.

fluting-iron, s. hierro de rizar.

fluting-plane, s. cepillo bocel.

flutist, s. flautista, m.f.

flutter ['flʌtəɪ], v.t. agitar, sacudir, menear; (mar.) flamear; crujir; poner en desorden, desordenar; alterar, aturdir. — v.i. agitarse, menearse, alterarse; revolotear, aletear, alear; pavonearse.

flutter, fluttering, s. agitación, alboroto, tumulto, confusión, baraúnda, vibración, undulación; aleteo; jugada.

fluvial ['fluːviəl], **fluviatic, fluviatile**, a. fluvial, fluviátil.

flux [flʌks], s. flujo; mudanza, alteración, cambio; (med.) fluxión, flujo; (fund.) derretimiento, fusión; (quím.) fundente; confluencia, concurso. — v.t. fundir, derretir, mezclar con un fundente; (med.) purgar.

fluxation [flʌkˈseiʃən], s. flujo, mudanza, cambio.

flexibility [flʌksiˈbiliti], s. fusibilidad, fluxibilidad.

fluxible ['flʌksibl], a. fusible, capaz de fusión.

fluxion ['flʌkʃən], s. flujo; (med.) fluxión, congestión; acto de fluir; fusión, derretimiento; (mat.) cálculo diferencial.

fluxional, fluxionary, a. referente al cálculo diferencial.

fluxionist, s., a. perito en cálculo diferencial.

fly [flai], v.t. (pret. **flew**, p.p. **flown**) hacer volar; enarbolar; (impr.) sacar pliegos; separar con violencia; huir de, evadir, evitar. — v.i. volar; correr, moverse o pasar rápidamente, precipitarse, lanzarse; desaparecer(se); huir, escaparse; estallar, romperse alguna cosa con estallido; saltar, reventar; fluctuar; desplegarse; to fly about, derramarse; (mar.) cambiar el viento con frecuencia; to fly at, lanzarse sobre; echarse encima de; to fly away, volar, escaparse; to fly around, ir de un lado a otro, (fam.) dar prisa; to fly down, bajar volando; to fly off, tomar un vuelo; evaporarse, desaparecer; to fly out, desenfrenarse; to fly open, abrirse de repente; to fly from, escapar, evitar, huir de; to fly into a passion, montarse o encenderse en cólera; to fly in the face of, oponerse atrevidamente a, insultar; with flying colours, con banderas desplegadas; to fly to arms, recurrir a las armas; to let fly, descargar.

fly, s. mosca; mosca artificial (para pescar); calesín; bragueta (de los pantalones); (teat.) telar; she wouldn't hurt a fly, no sabe ni matar una mosca; gad-fly, tábano; Spanish fly, cantárida.

fly-bitten, a. manchado o descolorado por las moscas.

flyblow ['flaiblou], s. cresa, huevo de mosca. — v.t. corromper la carne con cresas.

flyboat, s. (mar.) flibote.

fly-catcher, *s.* (*orn.*) doral, papamoscas, *m. sing.*, moscareta.

flyer ['flaiəɹ], *s.* volador, volante; fugitivo, el que huye; (*impr.*) sacapliegos.

fly-fishing, *s.* pesca con moscas artificialas.

fly-flap, fly-trap, *s.* mosqueador, mosquero, espantamoscas.

flying ['flaiiŋ], *a.* volante; volador; undulante, flotante; veloz, rápido; volátil; desplegado; *flying-boat,* hidroavión; *flying buttress,* (*arq.*) arbotante, botarel; *flying jib,* (*mar.*) petifoque, cuarto foque; *flying fish,* (pez) volador; *flying squad,* escuadra ligera; *to come out with flying colours,* salirle a uno a pedir de boca. — *s.* vuelo; *to shoot flying,* tirar al vuelo.

fly-leaf, *s.* (*impr.*) guarda de un libro.

fly-net, *s.* mosquitero.

fly-wheel, *s.* rueda volante.

foal [foul], *s.* potro; potrillo; buche; borrico. — *v.t., v.i.* parir (una yegua o una burra); dar crías; procrear.

foam [foum], *s.* espuma. — *v.t.* espumar, hacer espuma, arrojar espuma. — *v.i.* espumar, echar espuma o espumarajos; estar colérico, enfadarse.

foamy, *a.* espumajoso, espumoso, con espuma.

fob [fɔb], *s.* faltriquera del reloj. — *v.t.* engañar, defraudar, disimular, pegársela a uno.

focal ['foukəl], *a.* focal, perteneciente al foco, céntrico.

focus ['foukəs], *s.* foco, punto céntrico. — *v.t.* enfocar, afocar; concentrar; *focussing-screen,* (*foto.*) pantalla o visera para poner en foco.

fodder ['fɔdəɹ], *s.* forraje; (*Cuba*) maloja; (*Filip.*) zacate. — *v.t.* dar forraje (a las bestias).

fodderer, *s.* forrajeador.

foe [fou], **foeman** ['foumən], *s.* enemigo, adversario, antagonista, *m.f.*, perseguidor.

foelike ['foulaik], *a.* hostil, como enemigo.

fœtal [fiːtl], *a.* fetal.

fœtid, *a.* [FETID].

fœtus ['fiːtəs], *s.* feto, engendro.

fog [fɔg], *s.* niebla, neblina, bruma, cerrazón, *f.*, calina; (*foto.*) niebla, velo; (*fig.*) perplejidad, confusión. — *v.t.* obscurecer; (*foto.*) velar, cubrir con un velo o una niebla. — *v.i.* ponerse nebuloso, brumoso; (*foto.*) velarse.

fog [fɔg], **fogge** [fɔg], **foggage** ['fɔgidʒ], *s.* segunda cosecha de hierba de una estación; hierba seca que permanece en el campo durante el invierno; (*Esco.*) musgo.

fogginess, *s.* nebulosidad.

foggy, *a.* nebuloso, brumoso, lleno de nieblas; (*foto.*) obscurecido, velado.

fog-horn ['fɔghɔːɹn], *s.* sirena.

fogy ['fougi], **fogey,** *s.* persona de ideas anticuadas; obscurantista, *m.*

fogyism ['fougiizm], *s.* obscurantismo.

foh [fou], *interj.* ¡quita allá! (expresando disgusto o enojo).

foible [fɔibl], *s.* lado flaco, debilidad; parte de la hoja de una espada desde el medio a la punta.

foil [fɔil], *v.t.* anular, frustrar, hacer nulo o vano, contrarrestar, embotar; amortiguar, adormecer. — *s.* hoja delgada de metal; chapa; azogada de un espejo; oropel; pan, u hoja de oro o plata; huella, rastro, pista; (*esgr.*) florete; (*arq.*) hoja, lóbulo; (*fig.*) contraste.

foilable, *a.* vencible.

foiler, *s.* frustrador.

foiling, *s.* (*caz.*) freza; rastro, vestigio.

foist [fɔist], *v.t.* insertar, meter subrepticiamente; imponer, introducir fraudulentamente.

foister, *s.* falsificador, mentiroso.

fold [fould], *s.* doblez, arruga, plegadura, pliegue, repliegue, recogido; envoltorio; abrazo; rebaño, hato; corral, redil, cercado, aprisco; (*fig.*) iglesia, congregación de fieles; (*como sufijo*) vez; *two-fold,* duplo, *four-fold,* cuádruplo. — *v.t.* plegar, doblar; cerrar, envolver, incluir, encerrar; enlazar, abrazar; ajustar; arredillar, meter en redil; *to fold the arms,* cruzar los brazos. — *v.i.* doblarse, plegarse, cerrarse.

folder, *s.* plegador, doblador; plegadera; folleto; carpeta (para papeles).

folderol ['fɔldərɔl], *a.* absurdo, desatinado. — *s.* pampirolada, pampringada, desatino.

folding ['fouldiŋ], *a.* plegadizo, dobladizo, plegable, replegable; plegador, doblador. — *s.* acción de plegar, plegado, plegadura; pliegue, repliegue; *folding bed,* cama plegadiza; *folding chair,* silla plegadiza; *folding door,* puerta de dos hojas, puerta plegadiza; *folding machine,* máquina de plegar, plegadora mecánica; *folding seat,* asiento levadizo.

fold-net, *s.* arañuelo, red para coger pájaros.

foliaceous [fouli'eifəs], *a.* foliáceo; laminado.

foliage ['fouliədʒ], *s.* follaje, frondosidad, verdura, frondura; ramillete de hojas y flores.

foliate ['foulieit], *v.t.* (*metal.*) batir hojas; azogar un espejo. — *a.* frondoso; laminado, batido.

foliated, *a.* (*metal.*) batido, laminado; chapeado; (*arq.*) lobulado; azogado.

foliation [fouli'eifən], **foliature** ['fouliətfjuːəɹ], *s.* (*metal.*) acto de batir hojas de metal; acto de salir o apuntar las hojas; batimiento; laminación; azogamiento; exfoliación; (*bot.*) foliación.

folio ['fouliou], *s.* infolio, página, folio; (*for.*) medida de palabras (72 o 90 en Ingl., 100 en E.U.); cartera para grabados, etc. — *v.t.* foliar.

foliole ['foulioul], *a.* hojuela.

foliose ['foliouz], **folious** ['fouliəs], *a.* frondoso.

folk [fouk], *s.* gente, *f.*; nación, pueblo, raza, género humano. — *pl.* (*fam.*) gente, *f.*, parientes, parentesco.

folk-lore ['foukləːɹ], *s.* folklore, tradiciones y costumbres del vulgo.

folk-song, *s.* canción popular; romance, copla.

folk-speech, *s.* lenguaje vulgar.

follicle ['fɔlikl], *s.* (*bot.*) folículo, hollejo; (*anat.*) folículo; (*ent.*) capullo.

follicular [fɔ'likjuːləɹ], *a.* folicular, foliculoso.

follow ['folou], *v.t.* seguir, ir detrás de; escoltar, ir en compañía de, acompañar; copiar, imitar; resultar; suceder, venir después; acatar, obedecer; perseguir; poner por obra, obrar, conforme a, ejecutar; ejercer (oficio o profesión); cuidar, poner atención, observar; tener en vista; aplicarse a, dedicarse a. — *v.i.* seguirse, originarse, inferirse; seguir, ir o venir detrás; resultar, ser consecuencia de; *it follows,* síguese, resulta; *to follow on,* perseverar, continuar prosiguiendo; *to follow up,* continuar, proseguir; *as follows,* como sigue, del modo siguiente, de esta manera.

follower, *s.* seguidor; asistente, dependiente, acompañante; criado; partidario, allegante, adherente, secuaz, satélite; amante; discípulo; (*mec.*) rueda secundaria; copiador, imitador; tambor de transmisión. — *pl.* séquito, comitiva.

following, *a.* siguiente; resultante; próximo. — *s.* séquito, cortejo, adherentes, comitiva; oficio, profesión, carrera.

folly ['fɔli], *s.* tontería, sandez; bobería, patochada; locura, insensatez, extravagancia, ignorancia; desatino, indiscreción, disparate; debilidad, fragilidad, ligereza; vicio.

foment [fo'ment], *v.t.* fomentar, instigar, incitar, provocar; proteger, patrocinar; (*med.*) fomentar, dar baños calientes, dar calor artificial; *to foment a quarrel*, echar leña al fuego.

fomentation [fomen'teiʃən], *s.* (*med.*) fomentación, fomento; provocación, excitación, instigación.

fomenter, *s.* fomentador, instigador.

fond [fɔnd], *a.* aficionado, apasionado, enamorado; indulgente, amoroso, afectuoso, cariñoso, tierno; acariciado, querido; enloquecido, atontado, vano, loco, extravagante; *to be fond of*, tener cariño a, ser amigo de, ser aficionado a, estar encariñado con.

fondle [fɔndl], *v.t.* mimar, acariciar, hacer halagos.

fondler, *s.* mimador.

fondling, *s.* caricia, mimo; niño mimado; (*ant.*) tonto.

fondness, *s.* afecto, ternura, cariño, pasión, terneza; inclinación, afición, apego.

font [fɔnt], *s.* pila de bautismo; fuente bautismal; (*impr.*) fundición; fuente, *f.*, manantial.

fontanel ['fɔntənel], *s.* (*anat.*) fontanela.

food [fuːd], *s.* alimento, sustento, nutrimento; comida; (*fam.*) manjar; pasto, vituallas, víveres, provisiones; (*fig.*) pábulo, materia.

foodless, *a.* infructuoso, estéril.

fool [fuːl], *s.* tonto, bobo, badulaque, idiota, *m.f.*, necio, mentecato; truhán, bufón, hazmerreír, chocarrero; insensato; *to make a fool of someone*, burlarse de alguno; *to make a fool of oneself*, hacer un papel ridículo; *to play the fool*, hacer el tonto (o el bobo); *one fool makes many*, un tonto hace ciento. — *v.t.* chasquear; engañar, embaucar, defraudar; infatuar, entontecer, embromar; despreciar. — *v.i.* tontear, chancear, divertirse, hacer el mono.

fool, *s.* manjar compuesto de grosellas cocidas con crema, nata, o azúcar.

foolery, *s.* bobería, tontería.

foolhardiness ['fuːlhɑɹdines], *s.* temeridad, locura.

foolhardy, *a.* temerario, arrojado.

foolish ['fuːliʃ], *a.* simple, tonto, bobo, necio, indiscreto, fatuo, loco, sandio; disparatado.

foolishness, *s.* simpleza, necedad, tontería, bobería, mentecatada.

foolscap ['fuːlzkæp], *s.* gorro de bufón; (papel) pliego común.

foot [fut], *s.* (*pl.* **feet** [fiːt]) pie; pata; parte inferior; base, *f.*; pie (12 pulgadas, equivalente a 30·5 cm); (*mil.*) infantería; (*pros.*) pie; *on foot*, de pie, o a pie; (*fig.*) activo, adelantándose; *by foot*, a pie; *from head to foot*, de pies a cabeza; *to put one's foot down*, (*fam.*) expresarse con determinación, tomar una resolución; *to put one's best foot foremost*,

(*fam.*) hacer su posible, o dar prisa; *to put one's foot in it*, (*fam.*) meter la pata; *to trample under foot*, pisotear; *to set on foot*, emprender, poner en pie; *foot by foot*, palmo a palmo. — *v.t.* recorrer, hollar, pisar, pisotear, patear; fijar, establecer; poner pies a; sumar y poner la suma al pie; (*arit., fam.*) pagar una cuenta; costear, pagar las costas, sufragar. — *v.i.* andar, andar a pie, patear, caminar; bailar, saltar, danzar; (*fam.*) sumar guarismos.

football ['futbɔːl], *s.* balón; fútbol, balompié.

footboy, *s.* lacayo.

foot-bridge, *s.* puente para peatones.

footcloth, *s.* gualdrapa.

footed, *a.* que tiene pies o patas; sumado.

footfall ['futfɔːl], *s.* paso, pisada; el sonido de un paso.

foothills ['futhilz], *s.pl.* faldas de la montaña.

foothold ['futhould], *s.* espacio en que cabe el pie; fundamento seguro; posición segura.

footing ['futiŋ], *s.* pie, base, *f.*, fundamento; estado, condición; danza, baile; estribo, zócalo saliente; (*arit.*) suma de una columna; posición firme o segura; *to be on an equal footing*, ser o estar iguales; estar en condiciones iguales; *on a war footing*, bajo pie de guerra; *to gain a footing*, tener un pie dentro.

footless, *a.* sin pies.

footlights ['futlaits], *s.pl.* (*teat.*) candilejas, luces de proscenio.

footling ['fuːtliŋ], *a.* (*fam.*) trivial; disparatado.

footman ['futmən], *s.* lacayo.

footmark, *s.* huella, pisada.

footpace, *s.* descanso de escalera; paso lento o corto.

footpath, *s.* senda, vereda, acera.

footprint, *s.* huella, pisada.

footrule, *s.* regla de doce pulgadas.

foots, *s.pl.* heces, *f.*, sedimentos, poso.

footstalk ['futstɔːk], *s.* (*bot.*) pedúnculo.

footstep ['futstep], *s.* paso; vestigio, señal, *f.*, huella.

footstool, *s.* escabel, escabelo, tarimilla.

footway, *s.* sendero.

fop [fɔp], *s.* petimetre, currutaco, pisaverde; lechuguino; mentecato; presumido.

fopling, *s.* lechuguino, petimetrillo.

foppery ['fɔpəri], *s.* tontería, necedad, bobería; afectación en el vestir; perifollos.

foppish, *a.* vano, ocioso, vanidoso, afectado, presumido.

foppishness, *s.* vanidad, afectación en el vestir.

for [fɔːr], *prep.* por, para, a, de, desde, durante, hacia, por motivo de, en provecho de, en busca de, con destino a, a pesar de, a causa de, en vista de, en consideración a; en cuanto a, con relación a, en vez de, en lugar de, en concepto de; en honor o por el nombre de; mientras. — *conj.* porque, para que, pues; por cuanto, en atención a que; *as for*, en cuanto a, tocante; *for as much*, en cuanto; *for all that*, no obstante, a pesar de eso; *for ever*, para siempre; *for all the world*, ciertamente, verdaderamente; *for good*, de fijo, para no volver; *but for*, si no fuese por, a no ser por; *for all I know*, que sepa yo; *for the future*, en lo venidero.

forage ['fɔridʒ], *v.t.*, *v.i.* forrajear, pasturar, proveer de forraje, buscar forraje; saquear, pillar, hurtar. — *s.* forraje.

forager, *s.* forrajeador.

foramen ['fɔrəmen], s. foramen, agujero, apertura.

foraminous ['fɔ'ræminəs], a. agujereado.

forasmuch [fɔːrəz'mʌtʃ], conj. puesto (que); visto que; en consideración de.

foray ['fɔrei], s. pillaje, saqueo; correría, irrupción. — v.t. pillar, despojar, saquear.

forbade [fəɹ'beid], pret. [FORBID].

forbear [fəɹ'bɛəɹ], v.t., v.i. (pret. **forbore** [fəɹ'bɔːɹ]; p.p. **forborne** [fəɹ'bɔːɹn]), guardarse, abstenerse, reprimirse, contenerse, interrumpirse, cesar, dejar de, pararse, detenerse; I cannot forbear laughing, no puedo menos de reír.

forbearance [fəɹ'bɛərəns], s. clemencia, lenidad, indulgencia; suavidad, dulzura; (for.) morosidad; abstención; interrupción, intermisión.

forbearing, a. paciente, indulgente.

forbid [fəɹ'bid], v.t. (pret. **forbade**; p.p. **forbidden**) prohibir, vedar; estorbar, impedir; God forbid, no quiera (o no permita) Dios. — v.i. prohibir.

forbiddenly, adv. ilícitamente.

forbidding, a. prohibitivo; adusto (de personas); repugnante, repulsivo. — s. oposición, obstáculo.

forbore [fəɹ'bɔːɹ], pret. [FORBEAR].

force [fɔːɹs], s. fuerza, vigor, energía, robustez, fortaleza; (mil.) tropa, fuerzas; precisión, necesidad; violencia, coacción, agravio; importancia, validez, valor, peso; impulso, motivo, causa, móvil; potencia, virtud, poder, eficacia; (fig.) fuego, animación; force pump, bomba impelente; main force, fuerza mayor; in force, vigente, en vigor; tensile force, fuerza de tensión. — v.t. forzar; compeler, impeler, obligar, esforzar, constreñir, precisar; violar; violentar; (agr.) forzar, hacer madurar temprano; (coc.) rellenar, mechar, embutir; apresurar, hacer madurar, avanzar o adelantar; to force from, echar de alguna parte; to force back, rechazar; to force up, hacer subir por fuerza; to force in, clavar, meter o entrar por fuerza; to force out, arrancar o sacar con violencia; to force down, obligar a bajar; (aer.) derribar un avión.

forcedly ['fɔːsedli], adv. forzadamente.

forcedness, s. compulsión, constreñimiento.

forceful, a. fuerte, potente, poderoso; violento.

forceless, a. débil, endeble, sin fuerza.

forcemeat ['fɔːsmiːt], s. (coc.) relleno, salpicón, embutido.

forceps ['fɔːɹseps], s. (cir.) fórceps, pinzas, tenaza; bullet forceps, sacabalas, m. sing.; arterial forceps, pinzas hemostáticas.

forcer ['fɔːɹsəɹ], a. forzador, vencedor; émbolo.

forcible ['fɔːsibl], a. fuerte, potente, poderoso; violento; eficaz; de gran peso; enérgico; concluyente, obligatorio.

forcibleness, s. fuerza, violencia.

forcibly, adv. por fuerza, de fuerza, fuertemente, forzosamente, forzadamente, violentamente.

forcing, a. impelente; madurador; clarificador (de vino). — s. forzamiento.

forcing-bed, s. almajara.

forcing-house, s. invernadero.

forcing-pump, s. bomba impelente.

ford [fɔːd], s. vado. — v.t. vadear, esguazar.

fordable, a. vadeable, esguazable.

fore [fɔːɹ], a. anterior, delantero; (mar.) proel. — adv. anteriormente, antes, delante; (mar.) de proa; fore and aft, de popa a proa.

fore-, prefijo delante, ante, antes.

foreappoint [fɔːrə'pɔint], v.i. preordinar.

forearm ['fɔːrɑːɹm], s. antebrazo.

forearm, s., v.t. armar de antemano; forewarned is forearmed, hombre prevenido vale por dos.

forebode [fɔːɹ'boud], v.t., v.i. pronosticar, saber de antemano, presagiar; antever, presentir; indicar, decir de antemano.

foreboding, s. presentimiento, presagio; (fam.) corazonada.

forecast ['fɔːkɑːst], v.t., v.i. proyectar, trazar; pronosticar, prever, predecir; preparar o arreglar de antemano.

forecast, s. pronóstico, pronosticación; proyecto, plan; previsión.

forecastle ['fouksl], s. (mar.) castillo de proa.

forechosen [fɔːɹ'tʃouzən], a. preelegido.

forecited [fɔːɹ'saitəd], a. precitado, arriba citado.

foreclose [fɔːɹ'klouz], v.t. cerrar, impedir, excluir; (for.) vender por orden judicial.

foreclosure [fɔːɹ'klouʒəɹ], s. (for.) juicio hipotecario; incautación del bien o bienes hipotecados.

foredoom, v.t. predestinar, predeterminar.

fore-end ['fɔːrend], s. delantera.

forefather ['fɔːfɑːðəɹ], s. abuelo, antecesor, ascendiente, progenitor.

forefinger ['fɔːfiŋgəɹ], s. dedo índice.

forefoot, s. mano o pata delantera, pie delantero (de un cuadrúpedo); (mar.) gorja, tajamar.

forefront, s. primer puesto, primera fila; parte más adelantada.

forego [fɔːɹ'gou], v.t. (pret. **forewent**; p.p. **foregone**) ceder, privarse de, renunciar a; adelantarse a, anteceder, ir delante de, preceder; abandonar.

foregoer, s. abuelo, precursor, pregenitor.

foregoing, a. precedente, anterior. — pres. part. [FOREGO].

foregone [fɔːɹ'gɔn], a. predeterminado, decidido de antemano. — p.p. [FOREGO].

foreground ['fɔːgraund], s. (pint.) primer plano, delantera.

forehand, s. cuarto delantero del caballo.

forehanded, a. temprano; (E.U.) acomodado, adinerado.

forehead ['fɔrid], s. frente, f.; descaro.

foreign ['fɔrin], a. extranjero; exterior; exótico; ajeno, distante, remoto; extraño, advenedizo; excluido; foreign-built, (mar.) construido en el extranjero; Foreign Office, (Ingl.) Ministerio de asuntos extranjeros.

foreigner, s. extranjero, forastero.

foreignness, s. inconexión, extranjía, extrañeza.

forejudgment [fɔː'ɹdʒʌdʒmənt], s. prejuicio.

foreknow [fɔːɹ'nou], v.t. prever, saber o conocer de antemano, tener presciencia de alguna cosa.

foreknowledge, s. presciencia.

foreland ['fɔːlənd], s. promontorio, cabo.

forelay, v.t. prevenir.

forelock, s. melena, copete; (mar.) chaveta; forelock bolts, (mar.) pernos de chaveta.

forelook, v.t. mirar de antemano.

foreman ['fɔːmən], s. capataz; sobrestante,

mayoral; oficial mayor, jefe; (*impr.*) regente; (*for.*) presidente del jurado.

foremast ['fɔːɪmǝst], *s.* (*mar.*) palo de trinquete.

forementioned [fɔːɪ'menʃǝnd], *a.* susodicho, antedicho, precitado, ya citado, arriba citado.

foremost ['fɔːɪmoust], *a.* delantero; primero.

forename, *s.* nombre de pila.

forenamed, *a.* susodicho, antedicho, ya citado.

forenoon ['fɔːɪnuːn], *s.* la mañana.

forensic [fɔ'rensik], *a.* forense, perteneciente al foro; causídico.

foreordain [fɔːɪɔːɪ'dein], *v.t.* preordinar, predestinar.

foreordination, *s.* predeterminación.

fore-part, *s.* delantera; primera parte.

forereach ['fɔːɪriːtʃ], *v.t.* (*mar.*) navegar delante de otro buque.

forerun [fɔːɪ'rʌn], *v.t.* (*pret.* **foreran**; *p.p.* **forerun**) preceder; anunciar; adelantarse, ir delante, llegar antes.

forerunner ['fɔːɪrʌnǝɪ], *s.* precursor; predecesor, antecesor; nuncio; pronóstico, presagio, anuncio.

foresaid ['fɔːɪsed], *a.* ya dicho, antedicho, susodicho.

foresail ['fɔːɪsǝl], *s.* (*mar.*) trinquete.

foresee [fɔːɪ'siː], *v.t.* (*pret.* **foresaw**; *p.p.* **foreseen**) prever, tener prisciencia, barruntar, anticipar.

foreseer, *s.* previsor.

foreshadow, *v.t.* prefigurar, simbolizar.

foreship, *s.* (*mar.*) proa.

foreshore ['fɔːɪʃɔːɪ], *s.* playa.

foreshorten [fɔːɪ'ʃɔːɪtǝn], *v.t.* (*pint.*) escorzar.

foreshortening, *s.* (*pint.*) escorzo.

foreshow, *v.t.* pronosticar, predecir; exhibir de antemano.

foresight ['fɔːɪsait], *s.* previsión, prevención, providencia, perspicacia; mira de un fusil; (*tec.*) croquis de nivel.

foresignify, *v.t.* prefigurar, simbolizar; presagiar.

foreskin ['fɔːɪskin], *s.* (*anat.*) prepucio.

foreskirt, *s.* (*cost.*) delantero, parte delantera de una falda o faldón.

foresleeve, *s.* (*cost.*) la parte de la manga entre la muñeca y el codo.

forespeak, *v.t.*, *v.i.* predecir.

forespent [fɔːɪ'spent], *a.* pasado; consumido; fatigado.

forest ['fɔrest], *s.* selva, bosque, monte, floresta. — *v.t.* formar un bosque; arbolar.

forestaff ['fɔːɪstɑːf], *s.* (*mar.*) ballestilla.

forestal ['fɔrestǝl], *a.* forestal.

forestall [fɔːɪstɔːl], *v.t.* anticipar; (*com.*) acopiar, acaparar, monopolizar; prevenir.

forestaller, *s.* monopolista, *m.f.*; acopiador.

forestalling, *s.* anticipación.

forestay, *s.* (*mar.*) estay del trinquete; *forestaytackle*, (*mar.*) candeletón.

forested ['fɔrestǝd], *a.* arbolado.

forester ['fɔrestǝɪ], *s.* guardabosque, guardamonte; habitante de un bosque; montañero, forestero.

forestry, *s.* selvicultura.

foretaste ['fɔːɪteist], *v.t.* gustar o conocer de antemano. — *s.* goce por anticipación; muestra.

foretell [fɔːɪ'tel], *v.t.*, *v.i.* predecir, profetizar, pronosticar, presagiar, prenunciar.

foreteller, *s.* profeta, *m.*

foretelling, *s.* predicción, presagio, profecía, pronóstico.

forethought ['fɔːɪθɔːt], *s.* presciencia, providencia; premeditación; prevención. — *a.* premeditado.

foretoken, *v.t.* prefigurar, simbolizar. — *s.* pronóstico, presagio.

foretop ['fɔːɪtɔp], *s.* (*mar.*) cofa de trinquete.

forever [fɔːɪ'evǝɪ], (*E.U.*) *adv.* siempre; para siempre.

forewarn [fɔːɪ'wɔːɪn], *v.t.* prevenir, avisar, advertir.

forewarning, *s.* advertencia, aviso.

forewind, *s.* viento favorable.

forewoman ['fɔːɪwumǝn], *s.f.* primera oficiala; encargada.

foreword ['fɔːɪwǝːɪd], *s.* prefacio.

foreyard, *s.* (*mar.*) verga del trinquete.

forfeit ['fɔːɪfit], *s.* multa, pena; decomiso; pérdida legal de un derecho; gaje, prenda (en los juegos); *game of forfeits*, juego de prendas. — *a.* multado; perdido, confiscado; sujeto a multa. — *v.t.* perder el título o derecho a una cosa.

forfeitable, *a.* confiscable.

forfeiture ['fɔːɪfitʃǝɪ], *s.* confiscación, decomiso, secuestro, multa, pérdida de bienes.

forfend [fɔːɪ'fend], *v.t.* impedir; desviar; asegurar; *heaven forfend!* ¡líbreme el cielo!

forgather [fɔːɪ'gæðǝɪ], *v.i.* unirse, congregarse, juntarse (con). — *v.t.* ser amigo, o intimar (con).

forgave, *pret.* [FORGIVE].

forge [fɔːɪdʒ], *s.* fragua; herrería; fábrica de metales; forja, hornaza. — *v.t.* forjar, fraguar; inventar; falsear, contrahacer, falsificar; tramar; *to forge off*, o *over*, empeler, empujar. — *v.i.* avanzar; adelantarse; falsificar.

forge-hearth, *s.* atrio, hogar de fábrica.

forger, *s.* forjador, fraguador, falseador, falsificador, falsario.

forgery, *s.* falsificación.

forget [fǝɪ'get], *v.t.* (*pret.* **forgot**; *p.p.* **forgotten**, (*poét.*) **forgot**) olvidar; descuidar, dejar de atender a. — *v.i.* olvidarse, transcordarse, desmemoriarse; *I have forgotten to write*, se me ha quedado en el tintero.

forgetful, *a.* olvidadizo, desmemoriado, descuidado.

forgetfulness, *s.* olvido, negligencia, descuido.

forget-me-not [fǝɪ'getmɪnɔt], *s.* (*bot.*) raspilla, miosota, nomeolvides.

forge-train, *s.* fragua de laminar.

forgetter, *s.* olvidadizo.

forgetting, *s.* descuido, negligencia.

forging ['fɔːɪdʒiŋ], *s.* forja, forjadura.

forgivable [fǝɪ'givǝbl], *s.* perdonable, remisible.

forgive [fǝɪ'giv], *v.t.* perdonar, dispensar, condonar, remitir, indultar.

forgiven, *p.p.* [FORGIVE].

forgiveness, *s.* perdón, indulgencia, condonación, absolución, remisión; misericordia, clemencia.

forgiver, *s.* perdonador.

forgot [fǝɪ'gɔt], *pret.*, **forgotten**, *p.p.* [FORGET].

fork [fɔːɪk], *s.* tenedor; horcadura; (*agr.*) horcón; horca, horquilla; confluencia de un río; bifurcación; (*mús.*) diapasón. — *v.t.*

hacinar o cargar con horca; ahorquillar. — *v.i.* ahorquillarse, bifurcarse.

forked, *a.* horcado, bifurcado, ahorquillado; hendido.

forkedness, *s.* horcadura, horcajadura.

forkhead, *s.* lengüeta de saeta o flecha.

forktail, *s.* (*orn.*) milano, tirano.

forky, *a.* horcado.

forlorn [fəɹˈlɔːɹn], *a.* abandonado, perdido, ruin, desamparado, destituido, olvidado, desesperado; (*fam.*) dejado de la mano de Dios; *forlorn hope*, (*mil.*) pelotón de asalto; (*fig.*) empresa desesperada.

forlornness, *s.* desamparo, soledad, abandono, miseria.

form [fɔːɹm], *s.* forma, figura, patrón, modelo; manera, método, modo; práctica; ritual, ceremonia, formalidad; hechura; arreglo, orden, disposición; molde, manifestación; estado, condición; estilo; elegancia, hermosura; constitución, sistema, *m.*, organización, estructura; matriz, *f.*, horma; manifestación; conducta, porte; clase, *f.* (de escuela); banco, asiento largo; sombra, aparición; cama de liebre; (*impr.*) forma; *in due form*, en debida forma; *in due form of law*, según prescribe la ley; *for form's sake*, por pura fórmula. — *v.t.* formar, modelar, labrar, construir, concebir, idear; componer, ordenar, poner en orden, arreglar; hacer, constituir; colocar, juntar. — *v.i.* formarse, tomar una figura o forma.

formal [ˈfɔːɹməl], *a.* formal, regular, metódico; ceremonioso, etiquetero, formalista, solemne; esencial, constitutivo; exterior.

formaldehyde [fɔːɹˈmældihaid], *s.* (*quím.*) formaldehido.

formalin [ˈfɔːɹməlin], *s.* (*quím.*) formalina.

formalism [ˈfɔːɹməlizm], *s.* formalismo.

formalist [ˈfɔːɹməlist], *s.* formalista, *m.f.*, ceremoniático.

formality [fɔːɹˈmæliti], *s.* formalidad, ceremonia, etiqueta; regla prescrita; esencia.

formally [ˈfɔːɹməli], *adv.* formalmente, con toda solemnidad; en debida forma; realmente.

format [ˈfɔːɹmɑː, ˈfɔːɹmət], *s.* formato.

formate [fɔːɹˈmeit], *s.* (*quím.*) formiato.

formation [fɔːɹˈmeiʃən], *s.* formación; disposición, arreglo; desarrollo; (*geol.*) formación.

formative, *a.* formativo.

forme [fɔːɹm], *s.* (*impr.*) forma, molde.

former [ˈfɔːɹməɹ], *a.* anterior, primero; antecedente, precedente, pasado; *the former*, ése-a, aquél-la, etc. — *s.* formador, plasmador; matriz, *f.*, molde.

formerly, *adv.* antiguamente, en tiempos pasados.

formic [ˈfɔːɹmik], *a.* hormigoso; fórmico.

formicant [ˈfɔːɹmikənt], *a.* (*med.*) formicante.

formication, *s.* hormigueo.

formidable [ˈfɔːɹmidəbl], *a.* formidable, terrible, pavoroso, tremendo.

formidableness, *s.* terror, horror.

formless, *a.* informe, disforme.

formula [ˈfɔːɹmjuːlə], *s.* (*pl.* **formulæ** [ˈfɔːɹmjuːliː], **formulas** [ˈfɔːɹmjuːləz]) fórmula; profesión de fe, credo; (*mat., quím.*) fórmula; (*med.*) receta, récipe.

formulary [ˈfɔːɹmjuːləri], *s.* formulario. — *a.* formal; sujeto a fórmula.

formulate, *v.t.* formular, expresar en una fórmula.

formulize [ˈfɔːɹmjuːlaiz], *v.t.*, *v.i.* formalizar; formular.

fornicate [ˈfɔːɹnikeit], *v.i.* fornicar.

fornicate, fornicated, *a.* (*arq.*) abovedado, arqueado, en forma de bóveda.

fornication, *s.* fornicación, fornicio, cópula carnal; (*arq.*) bóveda.

fornicator, *s.* fornicador, fornicario.

fornicatress, *s.f.* concubina, manceba.

forsake [fəɹˈseik], *v.t.* (*pret.* **forsook** [fəɹˈsuk]; *p.p.* **forsaken** [fəɹˈseikən]) dejar, renunciar a, alejarse de, abandonar, separarse de; desertar, faltar a, desamparar; renegar de; rechazar, desechar.

forsaker, *s.* desertor, apóstata, *m.f.*

forsaking, *s.* abandono.

forsooth [fəɹˈsuːθ], *adv.* (*ant.*) ciertamente. — *interj.* ¡de veras! ¡vaya! (en sentido irónico).

forswear [fɔːɹˈswɛəɹ], *v.t.* (*pret.* **forswore**; *p.p.* **forsworn**) abjurar; renunciar. — *v.i.* perjurar.

forsworn, *p.p.* [FORSWEAR].

fort [fɔːɹt], *s.* fuerte, castillo, fortaleza.

fortalice [ˈfɔːɹtəlis], *s.* fortín.

forte [ˈfɔːɹti], *s.* fuerte, lado fuerte, talento particular.

forte, *s.*, *a.* (*mús.*) forte.

forth [fɔːɹθ], *adv.* delante; fuera, afuera; adelante, en adelante; hacia adelante; públicamente, a la vista; hasta lo último; *and so forth*, y así de lo demás; *from that day forth*, desde aquel día en adelante; *to go* o *come forth*, irse, venir, salir, fuera. — *prep.* fuera de.

forthcoming, *a.* futuro, próximo, que viene; *to be forthcoming*, venir, aparecer.

forthwith [fɔːɹθˈwið], *adv.* inmediatamente, sin dilación, sin tardanza, en el acto.

fortieth [ˈfɔːɹtiəθ], *a.* cuadragésimo; cuarenta. — *s.* cuarentavo.

fortifiable [fɔːɹtiˈfaiəbl], *a.* fortificable.

fortification [fɔːɹtifiˈkeiʃən], *s.* fortificación; fortaleza; plaza fuerte; fortalecimiento. — *pl.* **fortifications,** defensas.

fortifier [ˈfɔːɹtifaiəɹ], *s.* fortificador; fortalecedor; fautor.

fortify [ˈfɔːɹtifai], *v.t.* fortificar; reforzar, fortalecer; fijar, corroborar, confirmar, establecer. — *v.i.* construir defensas.

fortissimo [fɔːɹˈtisimou], *adv.* (*mús.*) fortísimo, muy fuerte.

fortitude [ˈfɔːɹtitjuːd], *s.* fortaleza, firmeza, entereza, resolución, nobleza de ánima; fuerza, vigor.

fortlet [ˈfɔːɹtlet], *s.* fortín.

fortnight [ˈfɔːɹtnait], *s.* quincena, quince días, dos semanas.

fortnightly, *a.* quincenal, una vez cada quince días. — *adv.* quincenalmente.

fortress [ˈfɔːɹtres], *s.* fortaleza, castillo, ciudadela, fuerte, alcázar.

fortuitous [fɔːɹˈtjuːitəs], *a.* fortuito, accidental, eventual, casual, impensado.

fortuitousness, *s.* casualidad, eventualidad, acontecimiento impensado.

fortuity [fɔːɹˈtjuːiti], *s.* caso fortuito; accidente.

fortunate, *a.* fortunado, afortunado, dichoso, feliz, venturoso.

fortune [ˈfɔːɹtjuːn], *s.* fortuna, ventura, suerte, *f.*; hacienda, dinero, dote, caudal, bienes; sino, destino; buenaventura; *fortune-hunter*, buscador de dotes; aventurero; *to enjoy good fortune,* campar con su estrella.

fortuneless, *a.* sin fortuna, sin bienes.

fortune-teller, *s.* sortílego, adivino, adivinadora.

fortune-telling, *s.* sortilegio.

forty ['fɔːti], *s., a.* cuarenta; cuarentena; *to be forty,* tener cuarenta años.

forum ['fɔːrəm], *s.* plaza, foro; juzgado, tribunal.

forward ['fɔːwəd], *adv.* adelante, más allá, hacia adelante; *from that time forward,* desde entonces; *from this time forward,* o *henceforward,* de aquí en adelante; en lo venidero; *to go forward,* adelantar, ir hacia adelante. — *a.* delantero, que va delante; anterior; activo, pronto; precoz, adelantado; desenvuelto; osado, audaz, atrevido, emprendedor; vivo, apresurado, listo. — *s.* (*dep.*) delantero. — *v.t.* enviar, despachar, remitir, expedir, mandar, transmitir, encaminar; apresurar, impeler, activar, promover, patrocinar; adelantar; hacer crecer; *forwarder* o *forwarding merchant,* comisionista expedidor.

forwardly, *adv.* anteriormente, con descaro, descaradamente; en lugar delantero.

forwardness, *s.* adelantamiento, progreso; precocidad; ansia; ligereza, apresuramiento, prontitud; audacia, ahinco, descaro, atrevimiento, confianza excesiva.

forwards, *adv.* adelante, más allá, hacia adelante.

foss [fɔs], **fosse,** *s.* (*fort.*) foso.

fossa ['fɔsə], *s.* (*anat.*) fosa.

fossil ['fɔsil], *s., a.* fósil; (*fam.*) vejestorio.

fossiliferous [fɔsil'ifərʌs], *a.* fosilífero.

fossilist ['fɔsilist], *s.* paleontólogo.

fossilization [fɔsilai'zeiʃən], *s.* fosilización.

fossilize, *v.t.* fosilizar; convertir en fósil; petrificar; (*fig.*) hacer anticuado. — *v.i.* fosilizarse, petrificarse.

fossilology [fɔsi'lɔlədʒi], *s.* paleontología.

fossorial [fɔ'sɔːriəl], *a.* cavador, que cava, a propósito para cavar; *fossorial wasp,* (*zool.*) avispa cavadora.

foster ['fɔstər], *v.t.* criar, nutrir, alentar; consolar; dar alas, mimar.

fosterage, *s.* el estado de ser hijo de leche.

foster-brother, *s.* hermano de leche.

foster-child, *s.* hijo o hija de leche.

foster-father, *s.m.* padre adoptivo.

fostering, *s.* nutrimento, alimento.

fosterling, *s.* hijo o hija de leche.

foster-mother, *s.f.* madre adoptiva.

foster-nurse, *s.f.* nodriza, ama de leche.

foster-sister, *s.f.* hermana de leche.

fother ['fɔðər], *v.t.* (*mar.*) cerrar una apertura o avería en el barco por medio de una vela o estopa.

fother, *s.* galápago de plomo para lastre; masa de plomo de 992·5 kg.

fought [fɔːt], *pret., p.p.* [FIGHT].

foul [faul], *a.* sucio, asqueroso, puerco; obsceno, indecente; inmundo, impuro, fétido, hediondo, mefítico, pestífero, pestilente, viciado (aire); injurioso; desagradable, contrario; que hace daño; atascado, enredado, obstruido; injusto, sin derecho; detestable, malvado, vil, bajo, horrible; (*fam.*) malo, atroz; (*impr.*) lleno de erratas; *foul copy,* borrador; *foulmouthed,* mal hablado, obsceno; *foul weather,* mal tiempo; *foul means,* medios indignos; *by*

fair means or foul, a buenas o a malas; *to fall foul of,* abordar (un buque). — *s.* acción de ensuciar o enredarse una cosa en otra; juego sucio; (en base-ball) caída de la pelota fuera de las líneas cuadro. — *v.t.* ensuciar, emporcar; abordar, chocar con; violar las reglas. — *v.i.* ensuciarse; (*mar.*) chocar; (en base-ball) caer la pelota fuera de las líneas.

foulard ['fuːlɑːrd], *s.* fular, tela de seda fina; pañuelo de fular.

foulness ['faulnis], *s.* asquerosidad, impureza, porquería.

found [faund], *pret., p.p.* [FIND].

found, *v.t.* cimentar; dar principio a, fundar, instituir, apoyar, establecer; edificar; fijar, asentar; (*fund.*) fundir, derretir.

foundation [faun'deiʃən], *s.* fundación, principio, origen, establecimiento, erección; (*cost.*) forro, refuerzo; (*ing.*) firme; dotación; fundamento, apoyo, base, *f.,* entibo; (*arq.*) cimiento; (*mec.*) asiento, pie, lecho; *foundation school,* escuela dotada; *foundation scholar,* pensionado (en un colegio); *to lay the foundations,* abrir las zanjas.

foundationless, *a.* sin fundamento.

founder, *s.* fundador; (*fund.*) fundidor; (*vet.*) despeadura. — *v.t.* (*mar.*) hacer zozobrar; despear los pies del caballo. — *v.i.* (*mar.*) irse a pique; salir mal, fracasar, desplomarse.

founderous, *a.* que hace zozobrar; lleno de baches (de caminos).

founding, *s.* fundición; establecimiento, fundación.

foundling ['faundliŋ], *s.* niño expósito, cunero; *foundling hospital,* casa de expósitos, inclusa; (*Mex.*) la cuna.

foundry ['faundri], *s.* fundición; fábrica en que se funde, fundería, ferrería.

fount [faunt], **fountain** ['fauntin], *s.* fuente, *f.;* origen, principio, fontana, fundamento; manantial, nacimiento de un río.

fountain-pen, *s.* (pluma) estilográfica.

four [fɔːr], *s., a.* cuatro; *four in hand, coach and four,* carruaje tirado por cuatro caballos; *four-o-clock,* (*bot.*) dondiego de noche; *to go upon all-fours,* gatear, andar a gatas.

four-cornered, *a.* cuadrangular.

fourfold, *a.* cuadruplo.

four-footed, *a.* cuadrúpedo.

four-in-hand [fɔːrin'hænd], *s.* carruaje tirado por cuatro caballos; (*ant.*) especie de corbata.

fourpence ['fɔːrpəns], *s.* cuatro peniques.

fourscore ['fɔːrskɔːr], *s.* ochenta; octogenario.

fourteen [fɔːr'tiːn], *s., a.* catorce.

fourteenth, *a.* catorceno, décimocuarto, catorce.

fourth [fɔːrθ], *a.* cuarto; cuarta parte; cuatro.

fourthly, *adv.* en cuarto lugar.

fovilla [fə'vilə], *s.* fovila.

fowl [faul], *s.* gallo, gallina; pollo; ave, *f.,* aves en general. — *pl.* **fowls,** volatera, aves de corral. — *v.i.* cazar aves, ir de caza.

fowler, *s.* cazador (de aves).

fowling, *s.* volatería, caza (de aves).

fowling-net, *s.* red (para cazar pájaros).

fowling-piece, *s.* escopeta.

fox [fɔks], *s.* zorra, raposa, zorro; (*fig.*) zorro, bellaco; (*mar.*) rebenque; *fox-case,* piel de zorra. — *v.i.* cazar zorras; agriarse, acedarse (vino, etc.); disimular; ponerse rojizo, descolorarse (páginas, etc.). — *v.t.* acedar; (*fam.*) confundir; emborrachar.

foxed, *p.p.*, *a.* descolorido.

foxglove, *s.* (*bot.*) digital, dedalera.

fox-hound, *s.* perro zorrero o raposero.

fox-hunter, *s.* cazador de zorras.

foxiness, *s.* astucia; acedía; descolorimiento.

foxish, fox-like, *a.* astuto, bellaco, engañoso, taimado.

foxship ['fɔksʃip], *s.* zorrería.

foxtail, *s.* (*bot.*) cola de zorra, carricera.

foxwood, *s.* madera descolorida o podrida.

foxy ['fɔksi], *a.* raposuno, zorruno; rojizo; tomado, agriado; astuto, taimado; manchado, descolorido.

foyer ['fɔijei], *s.* (*teat.*) salón de descanso; (*fund.*) cubilote.

fracas ['fræka:], *s.* contienda ruidosa, pelea, riña, tumulto, batahola.

fraction ['frækʃən], *s.* fragmento, trozo, porción; (*arit.*) fracción, número quebrado; rotura, rompimiento.

fractional, *a.* fraccionario.

fractious ['frækʃəs], *a.* reacio, rebelón, repropio, regañón, enojadizo.

fracture ['fræktʃə], *s.* rotura, rompimiento, quebrantamiento; (*cir.*) fractura; *compound fracture,* fractura conminuta. — *v.t.* quebrar, fracturar, romper.

fragile ['frædʒail], *a.* frágil, rompedero, quebradizo, deleznable; débil, delicado, caduco, perecedero.

fragility [frə'dʒiliti], **fragileness,** *s.* fragilidad; flaqueza, debilidad; friabilidad, instabilidad.

fragment ['frægmənt], *s.* fragmento; trozo; *to break into fragments,* hacer añicos.

fragmentary, *a.* fragmentario.

fragor ['freigɔː], *s.* estallido.

fragrance ['freigrəns], **fragrancy,** *s.* fragancia, perfume, aroma, *m.*, buen olor.

fragrant, *a.* fragante, oloroso, aromático, aromoso.

fragrantly, *adv.* con fragancia.

frail [freil], *a.* frágil, deleznable, quebradizo; endeble, débil, delicado. — *s.* capacho, canasta, sera, serón, espuerta.

frailness, frailty, *s.* fragilidad, friabilidad, debilidad, flaqueza, inconstancia, instabilidad, caducidad.

framable ['freiməbl], *a.* componible, que se puede construir.

frambœsia [fræm'biːziə], *s.* (*med.*) erupción cutánea y contagiosa de los trópicos peculiar de los negros.

frame [freim], *v.t.* fabricar, construir, formar; armar; ajustar, componer; inventar, forjar, trazar, idear; dirigir, arreglar; colocar o encerrar en un marco; servir de marco o cerco. — *s.* composición, figura, forma, hechura, estructura, constitución, construcción, forjadura, arreglo; armadura, armazón, *f.*, bastidor, entramado, esqueleto; marco, cerco; molde para barras de jabón; (*cost.*) bastidor para bordar; (*tej.*) telar; (*mar.*) cuaderna, costillaje; (*hort.*) estructura o caja de vidrio para proteger las plantas de las heladas; (*impr.*) chibalete; (*fig.*) talante, disposición.

framer, *s.* constructor, armador; inventor, autor, forjador; fabricante de marcos.

frame-saw, *s.* sierra montada o de bastidor.

framework, *s.* armadura, armazón, *f.*, esqueleto, entramado, sostén.

framing, *s.* acto de construir; armadura, armazón, *f.*

franc [fræŋk], *s.* franco (moneda).

franchise ['fræntʃaiz], *s.* derecho político, jurisdicción; exención, privilegio, franquicia, inmunidad; derecho de sufragio; asilo, santuario; encartación. — *v.t.* exentar, franquear, conceder franquicias.

franchisement ['fræntʃizmənt], *s.* liberación, libertad, exención, franqueza, soltura.

Franciscan [fræn'siskən], *s.*, *a.* franciscano.

frangible ['frændʒibl], *a.* frangible, frágil, quebradizo, perecedero.

frangipani [frændʒi'pæni], *s.* perfume que se obtiene del jazmín rojo.

frank [fræŋk], *a.* franco, sincero, abierto, ingenuo, natural; campechano, francote; exento, libre, privilegiado. — *s.* carta franca. — *v.t.* franquear (una carta).

frankincense ['fræŋkinsens], *s.* incienso.

Frankish, *s.*, *a.* franco.

frankness, *a.* ingenuidad, sinceridad; candor, franqueza, lisura.

Franks, *s.pl.* francos.

frantic ['fræntik], *a.* frenético, enfurecido, furioso.

franticness, *s.* frenesí, furor.

frap [fræp], *v.t.* (*mar.*) atortorar un buque.

frass [fræs], *s.* excremento de la larva.

fraternal [frə'təːnəl], *a.* fraternal.

fraternity [frə'təːniti], *s.* fraternidad, hermandad, hermanazgo; confraternidad, sociedad, congregación, compañía, gremio, junta.

fraternization [frætənai'zeiʃən], *s.* fraternidad, hermandad.

fraternize, *v.i.* fraternizar, hermanarse, hermanar.

fratricidal [frætri'saidəl], *a.* relativo al fratricidio.

fratricide ['frætrisaid], *s.* fratricidio; fratricida, *m.*

fratry, fratery ['frætri], *s.* refectorio en un convento o monasterio.

fraud [frɔːd], *s.* fraude, superchería, engaño, artificio; timo, petardo; trapalón, timador.

fraudful, *a.* pérfido, engañoso, engañador, traidor, de mala fe, fraudulento, astuto, artificioso.

fraudless, *a.* sin fraude, libre de fraude.

fraudulence ['frɔːdjuːləns], **fraudulency,** *s.* fraude, engaño, fraudulencia.

fraudulent, *a.* fraudulento, engañoso.

fraught [frɔːt], *a.* cargado, lleno, atestado.

fraxinella [fræksi'nelə], *s.* (*bot.*) fraxinela, fresnillo, díctamo blanco.

fray [frei], *s.* riña, querella, contienda, disputa, combate, refriega; rozamiento, raedura, raboseadura, desgaste, refregadura, deshiladura. — *v.t.* ludir, raer, rozar, tazar, rabosear. — *v.i.* deshilacharse, deshilarse, destejerse, tazarse, gastarse.

fraying, *s.* rozamiento, raedura, desgaste, deshiladura.

freak [friːk], *s.* capricho, fantasía, antojo; monstruosidad, rareza, extravagancia, fenómeno; *freak of nature,* aborto de la naturaleza. — *v.t.* varetear; gayar, abigarrar.

freakish, *a.* caprichoso, antojadizo, raro, extravagante, fantástico.

freakishness, *s.* calidad de caprichoso, fantástico, o monstruoso; extravagancia; monstruosidad.

freckle [frekl], s. peca. — v.t. motear. — v.i. tener pecas, ponerse pecoso.

freckled, freckly, a. pecoso; moteado.

freckledness, s. estado de pecoso.

freckle-faced, a. pecoso, con cara pecosa.

free [fri:], a. libre, emancipado, independiente, manumiso, horro; autónomo; libertado; deshonesto, torpe, disoluto, licencioso, atrevido, desenfrenado, insubordinado; despejado, accesible, desembarazado, franco; vacante, desocupado; privilegiado, exento; inmune, dispensado; abierto, generoso, liberal; voluntario, permitido, discrecional; ingenuo; gratuito, de gracia, de balde; (mar.) flojo, zafo, suelto, vacante; desatado; activo, vivo, gallardo; airoso, cortés; escotero; *free and easy*, despreocupado, desenvuelto; *free of charge*, libre de gastos; *free on board*, (com.) libre de gastos a bordo; *free trade*, (pol.) libre cambio; *free trader*, librecambista, m.f.; *free will*, libre albedrío; *to make free with*, usar con mucha libertad; *post free*, franco. — v.t. libertar, poner en libertad; rescatar, librar; sacar o preservar de riesgo; exentar, eximir; desvedar; manumitir, zafar, desembarazar; abrirse camino.

freebooter ['fri:bu:tǝɹ], s. pirata, m., filibustero.

freebooting, s. saqueo, pillaje, piratería.

free-born, a. nacido libre; (for.) ingenuo.

freedman ['fri:dmǝn], s. esclavo manumitido, liberto.

freedom ['fri:dǝm], s. libertad, independencia; inmunidad, exención; licencia, franqueza, familiaridad atrevida; soltura, facilidad; comodidad; *freedom of the press*, libertad de la prensa; *freedom of worship*, libertad de culto; *freedom of speech*, libertad de la palabra.

free-hearted, a. generoso, liberal, cordial.

freehold, s. (for.) feudo franco, dominio absoluto.

freeholder ['fri:houldǝɹ], s. feudo franco, dueño, propietario absoluto de una finca.

freelance ['fri:lɑ:ns], s., a. (mil.) aventurero, mercenario; (fig.) independiente.

freeman ['fri:mǝn], s. hombre independiente, hombre libre; ciudadano de honor.

freemartin ['fri:mɑ:ɹtin], s. ternera nacida al mismo tiempo que un ternero.

Freemason ['fri:meisǝn], s. francmasón.

Freemasonry, s. masonería, francmasonería.

free-minded, a. desembarazado, libre de cuidados.

freeness, s. libertad, franqueza; liberalidad; sinceridad.

freer ['fri:ǝɹ], s. libertador. — a. compar. [FREE]; más libre.

free-spoken, a. franco, dicho sin reserva.

freestone, s. piedra franca, piedra blanda y arenosa; (bot.) abridero, durazno.

free-thinker, s. librepensador.

free-thinking, s. libertad de pensar; libertinaje.

freeze [fri:z], (pret. **froze**; p.p. **frozen**), v.t. congelar, helar, matar de frío; *to freeze out*, (fam., E.U.) excluir o alejar, tratando con frialdad. — v.i. helarse, helar, escarchar, paralizarse de miedo.

freezer, s. refrigerador, congelador; sorbetera.

freezing, a. glacial, frigorífico.

freezing-point, s. punto de congelación; congelamiento, hielo.

freight [freit], v.t. fletar; dar o tomar un buque a flete; cargar. — s. carga, cargazón, f.; flete; *freight-car*, (f.c.) vagón de mercancías.

freightage ['freitidʒ], s. carga, cargamento, transportación, flete.

freighter, s. fletador, cargador; buque de carga.

French [frentʃ], s., a. francés; idioma francés; *French bean*, judía, habichuela, frisol, frijol; *French chalk*, blanco de Meudón; *French roof*, (arq.) mansarda; *to take French leave*, escurrir la bola, tomar el pendingue; *in the French fashion*, a la francesa.

Frenchify, v.t. afrancesar.

Frenchlike, a. afrancesado.

Frenchman ['frentʃmǝn], s.m. francés.

Frenchwoman, s.f. francesa.

frenetic [fre'netik], a. frenético, furioso.

frenzied ['frenzid], a. frenético.

frenzy ['frenzi], s. frenesí, furor, locura, manía, extravío, devaneo, enajenamiento del juicio.

frequency ['fri:kwǝnci], s. frecuencia; *high frequency*, alta frecuencia.

frequent ['fri:kwǝnt], a. frecuente; habitual, corriente, usado, usual, ordinario, regular, común.

frequent [fri'kwent], v.t. frecuentar, visitar muchas veces; *to frequent the streets*, desempedrar las calles.

frequentation, s. frecuentación.

frequentative [fri'kwentǝtiv], a. frecuentativo.

frequenter [fri'kwentǝɹ], s. frecuentador.

fresco ['freskou], pl. **frescoes**, s. fresco, pintura al fresco. — v.t. pintar al fresco.

fresh [freʃ], s. fresco, nuevo; que reanima o devuelve las fuerzas; refrescante, refrigerante; entremetido, presumido, oficioso, descocado; vivo, fuerte, robusto, sano; novicio, inexperto; lozano (flor, planta, etc.); puro (aire); reciente; recién llegado; sobrio; *fresh water*, agua dulce; *a fresh-blown flower*, una flor recién abierta; *fresh bread*, pan tierno; *fresh from*, acabado de; *fresh hand*, novicio. — s. avenida, riada, desbordamiento, inundación; mezcla de agua dulce y salada en los ríos y bahías; manantial.

freshen, v.t. refrescar, refrigerar, desalar. — v.i. refrescarse, avivarse.

freshet ['freʃit], s. avenida, crecida, inundación, riada.

freshman ['freʃmǝn], s. estudiante de primer año; novato.

freshness, s. frescura, frescor; viveza, lozanía, delicadeza, hermosura, verdor, renovación del vigor.

fret [fret], v.t. rozar, gastar, raer, rabosear; corroer, desgastar; irritar, agitar, enfadar, enojar; bordar en realce, recamar, varetear, adornar con calados. — v.i. rozarse, gastarse, tazarse, consumirse, impacientarse, incomodarse, apurarse, angustiarse, enojarse, enfadarse, inquietarse, agitarse; lamentarse, afligirse, entristecerse. — s. roce, rozamiento; raedura, raspadura, rozadura; enfado, enojo, apuro, irritación; desgaste; (med., ant.) empeine; hervor; realce, relieve, cinceladura; calado; (arq.) greca; (mús.) traste de guitarra.

fretful, a. displicente, mohino, enojadizo, colérico, molesto, incómodo.

fretfully, *adv.* con mal humor; de mala gana.

fretfulness, *s.* mal humor, mal genio.

fretted, *a.* calado, estriado. — *p.p.* [FRET].

fretsaw, *s.* sierra de calados.

fretwork, *s.* greca, adorno; (*carp.*) calado.

friability [fraiǝ'biliti], *s.* friabilidad.

friable ['fraiǝbl], *a.* friable, desmenuzable.

friar ['fraiǝɹ], *s.* fraile; *black friar,* fraile dominicano; *white friar,* carmelita, *m.*; *grey friar,* franciscano; *friar's lantern,* fuego fatuo.

friar-like, *a.* frailero, frailesco.

friary ['fraiǝri], *s.* convento de frailes. — *a.* frailero, frailesco.

fribble [fribl], *v.i.* bobear, tontear, vacilar. — *a.* vano, inútil, frívolo. — *s.* persona frívola; persona despreciable; pisaverde; fruslería.

fricandeau ['frikǝndou], *s.* fricandó.

fricassee [frikǝ'siː], *s.* (*coc.*) fricasé. — *v.t.* hacer fricasé.

fricative ['frikǝtiv], *s., a.* (*gram.*) fricativo.

friction ['frikʃǝn], *s.* fricción, frote, frotación, frotadura, roce, frotamiento; friega, refregón; *friction clutch,* manguito de fricción; *friction gearing,* engranaje de fricción.

Friday ['fraidi], *s.* viernes; *Good Friday,* viernes santo.

fried [fraid], *a.* frito. — *p.p.* [FRY].

friend [frend], *s.* amigo, amiga, compañero, aliado, persona favorable, favorecedor; cuáquero; partidario, adherente; *to be friends again,* reconciliarse, hacer las paces; *bosom friend,* amigo de corazón, amigo íntimo; *friend at court,* amigo influyente; *short reckonings make long friends,* (*prov.*) las cuentas claras hacen los buenos amigos; *a friend in need is a friend indeed,* (*prov.*) en la necesidad se conoce al buen amigo.

friendless, *a.* desamparado, desvalido, sin amigos, sin protección.

friendly, *a.* amigable, amistoso; benévolo, favorable, servicial, propicio.

friendliness, *s.* amistad.

friendship, *s.* amistad, intimidad, afecto, favor.

frieze [friːz], *s.* (*tej.*) frisa; (*arq.*) friso, arrocabe.

frieze-like, *a.* semejante a una frisa.

frigate ['frigǝt], *s.* (*mar.*) fragata; *frigate bird,* fragata, rabihorcado.

fright, *s.* susto, espanto, terror, pavor; (persona) esperpento, espantajo; *to take fright,* asustarse.

frighten, *v.t.* espantar, amedrentar, asustar, causar horror o espanto, amilanar, aterrorizar; *to frighten away,* ahuyentar.

frightful, *a.* espantoso, horrible, horroroso, horrendo, pavoroso, terrible, tremebundo, temible; feísimo.

frightfulness, *s.* horror, espanto.

frigid ['fridʒid], *a.* frío, helado, frígido; gélido, indiferente.

frigidity [fri'dʒiditi], *s.* frialdad, frío, frigidez; tibieza, negligencia, indiferencia.

frigidly, *adv.* fríamente, con frialdad.

frigorific [frigǝ'rifik], *a.* frigorífico, helado, frío.

frill [fril], *s.* (*cost.*) escarola, lechuga; chorrera, pechera, faralá. — *pl.* **frills,** (*fam.*, *E.U.*) aires, arrequives. — *v.t.* (*cost.*) alechugar, escarolar, guarnecer con pecheras. — *v.i.* escarolarse.

fringe [frindʒ], *s.* (*cost.*) fleco; borde, orla;

franja; margen, orilla; guarnición. — *v.t.* guarnecer con fleco, orlar, ribetear, orillar, franjear.

fringeless, *a.* sin fleco, sin ribete, sin franjas.

fringe-maker, *s.* fabricante de franjas.

fringy ['frindʒi], *a.* floqueado, adornado con franjas.

fripperer ['fripǝɹǝɹ], *s.* ropavejero, baratillero, prendero.

frippery ['fripǝri], *s.* prendería; trapería; vestidos viejos, ropa vieja; ropavejería, fruslería, bobería; baratillo. — *a.* despreciable, frívolo.

friseur ['friːzǝːɹ], *s.* peluquero.

frisk [frisk], *v.i.* saltar, cabriolar, brincar; travesear, retozar. — *s.* retozo; salto, brinco, gambeta.

frisket ['friskit], *s.* (*impr.*) frasqueta.

friskiness ['friskinis], *s.* retozo, viveza, vivacidad.

frisky, *a.* juguetón, gallardo, desparpajado, alegre, retozón, vivo, vivaracho.

frit [frit], *s.* frita. — *v.t.* derretir.

frith [friθ], **firth** [fǝːɹθ], *s.* estrecho o brazo de mar.

fritillary [fri'tilǝri], *s.* (*bot.*) fritilaria.

fritter ['fritǝɹ], *s.* buñuelo, fritura, fruta de sartén, frisuelo; torrezno, tajada. — *v.t.* desmenuzar, desperdiciar.

frivolity [fri'vɔliti], *s.* frivolidad, trivialidad.

frivolous ['frivǝlǝs], *a.* frívolo, superficial, trivial, fruslero.

frivolousness, *s.* frivolidad.

frizz [friz], **frizzle,** *v.t.* frisar, encrespar, rizar. — *s.* bucle, rizo.

frizzler, *s.* frisador, rizador.

fro [frou], *adv.* atrás, hacia atrás; *to and fro,* de un lado a otro; *to go to and fro,* ir y venir.

frock [frɔk], *s.* (*cost.*) vestido (de mujer o de niño); sotana (de cura); *smock frock,* sayo.

frock-coat, *s.* levita.

frog [frɔg], *s.* rana; (*sast.*) alamar, recamo; (*f.c.*) corazón, rana; (*vet.*) ranilla del caballo; *a frog in the throat,* carraspera.

frog-lettuce, *s.* (*bot.*) espiga de agua.

frolic ['frɔlik], *s.* juego, traversura; retozo, fantasía, capricho, extravagancia. — *a.* alegre, vivo, travieso, caprichoso, juguetón. — *v.i.* loquear, retozar, jaranear, juguetear, triscar.

frolicsome ['frɔliksǝm], *a.* juguetón, retozón, travieso, alegre.

from [frɔm], *prep.* de, después, desde; a fuerza de; por, de parte de, debido a, a causa de; con; conforme, según; *from behind,* desde atrás; *from beyond,* de más allá; *from afar,* de lejos, desde lejos; *from amidst,* de entre, del centro de; *from the midst de;* *from above,* desde arriba, de lo alto; *from beneath,* de abajo, de lo hondo; *from among,* de entre; *from memory,* de memoria; *from off,* fuera de; desde lejos de; *from without,* de fuera; *from out,* de, desde, del fondo de; *from on high,* desde lo alto; *from nature,* del natural; *from under,* de debajo; *from time to time,* de cuando en cuando; *from that time* (*onwards*), desde aquel tiempo, desde entonces; *from top to toe,* de pies a cabeza; *from hence,* de aquí, desde aquí; *from long ago,* desde hace mucho tiempo.

frond [frɔnd], *s.* fronda; hoja.

frondage, *s.* frondosidad.

frondescence [frɔn'desǝns], *s.* frondescencia.

frondescent, *a.* (*bot.*) frondescente.
frondiferous, *a.* frondífero.
frondose ['frɔndouz], *a.* frondoso.
front [frʌnt], *s.* frente, *f.*, cara, faz, *f.*; (*arq.*) frontispicio, fachada; (*mil.*) frente, *m.*; (*teat.*) sala, auditorio; (*zap.*) caña de una bota; (*igl.*) frontal, portal; (*cost.*) pechera, camisolín, delantera; (*carr.*) testera. — *a.* delantero, anterior, frontero, frontal; *front to front*, cara a cara; *front door*, puerta de entrada; *front room*, cuarto que da a la calle; *front view*, vista al frente. — *v.t.* hacer frente a, oponerse a; estar en frente de, mirar, poner frente o fachada; arrostrar. — *v.i.* estar al frente o de frente; dar a, caer a.
frontage ['frʌntidʒ], *s.* extensión lineal de frente.
frontal ['frʌntəl], *s.* (*anat.*) hueso frontal; frontero (venda); (*arq.*) frontón; (*igl.*) frontal. — *a.* frontero, anterior; frental, frontal, relativo a la frente.
fronted, *a.* que tiene fachada.
frontier ['frɔntiəɹ], *s.* frontera. — *a.* frontero, fronterizo.
frontispiece ['frʌntispiːs], *s.* (*impr.*) portada; (*arq.*) fachada, frontis, frontispicio.
frontless, *s.* sin frente; (*ant.*) desvergonzado, descarado.
frontlet, *s.* venda para la frente; (*arq.*) frontón de mira; (*orn.*) margen de la cabeza detrás del pico de las aves.
frost [frɔːst], *s.* helada, hielo; *frost-bitten*, helado; *white frost*, *hoar frost*, escarcha; *frost-nail*, tacón de herradura. — *v.t.* congelar; escarchar; dañar (el frío); deslustrar, despulir. — *v.i.* helar, congelarse.
frosted, *a.* escarchado; mate; (vidrio) despulido, deslustrado; garapiñado. — *p.p.* [FROST].
frostiness, *s.* escarcha; helamiento.
frosting, *s.* capa de clara de huevo batida con azúcar; deslustre o imitación de escarcha en los metales, etc.
frostwork, *s.* garapiña, garapiñado, ramajes de la escarcha.
frosty, *a.* que tiene o parece escarcha; helado, muy frío; cano, canoso; indiferente, insensible.
froth [frɔːθ], *s.* espuma; (*fig.*) frivolidad, bambolla, paja. — *v.i.* espumar, criar espuma. — *v.t.* hacer espuma.
frothily, *adv.* con espuma; sin substancia, frívolamente, superficialmente.
frothiness, *s.* espumosidad; frivolidad, vaciedad.
frothy, *a.* espumoso, espumajoso, cubierto de espuma; vano, frívolo, superficial.
frouzy ['frauzi], *a.* desaliñado, sucio, desaseado; mal peinado.
froward ['frouəɹd], *a.* indócil, incorregible, protervo, díscolo; impertinente, insolente.
frowardness, *s.* indocilidad, insolencia, mal genio, mal humor, petulancia.
frown [fraun], *v.t.* poner mala cara, mirar con ceño. — *v.i.* fruncir el entrecejo, ponerse ceñudo, poner mal gesto, enfurruñarse; *to frown upon*, mirar a uno de mal ojo; *to frown anyone down*, avergonzar, hacer bajar la cara, sonrojar. — *s.* ceño, sobrecejo, entrecejo; desagrado, enfado, enojo; esguince; *frowns of fortune*, reveses de fortuna.
frowning, *a.* torvo, fosco, ceñudo.

frowningly, *adv.* con ceño, de mal ojo, enojadamente.
frowst [fraust], *s.* mala ventilación, mal olor (en una habitación).
frowzy ['frauzi], *a.* desaseado, desaliñado, sucio; mal peinado.
froze, *pret.* [FREEZE].
frozen ['frouzən], helado, congelado; (*fam.*) muy frío. — *p.p.* [FREEZE].
fructescence [frʌk'tesəns], *s.* fructificación.
fructiferous [frʌk'tifərəs], *a.* fructífero.
fructification [frʌktifi'keiʃən], *s.* (*bot.*) fructificación, fecundación.
fructify ['frʌktifai], *v.t.* fertilizar, fecundar. — *v.i.* fructificar, dar fruto.
frugal ['fruːgəl], *a.* económico, frugal; sobrio, templado.
frugality [fruː'gæliti], *s.* economía; parsimonia, frugalidad, parcidad, templanza, moderación, sobriedad.
frugiferous [fruː'dʒifərəs], *a.* fructífero.
frugivorous [fruː'dʒivərəs], *a.* frugívoro.
fruit [fruːt], *s.* fruta; fruto; (*fig.*) producto; postres; resultado, efecto; provecho, utilidad; *stone fruit*, fruta de hueso. — *v.i.* producir fruta, dar fruto.
fruitage, *s.* fruta; fruto, efecto, producto.
fruit-bearing, *a.* frutal.
fruit-drier, *s.* secadero de frutas.
fruiter, *s.* arbol frutero; (*mar.*) buque frutero.
fruiterer, *s.* frutero.
fruitery ['fruːtəri], *s.* fruta; frutería.
fruitful ['fruːtful], *a.* fructífero, fértil, feraz; útil, provechoso, ventajoso, fructoso, ópimo; prolífico, fecundo, copioso, abundante.
fruitfulness, *s.* fertilidad, fecundidad.
fruition [fruː'iʃən], *s.* fruición; gusto, goce, complacencia.
fruitless, *a.* estéril, infructuoso; vano, ocioso, inútil.
fruitlessness, *s.* esterilidad; infructuosidad.
fruit-parer, *s.* mondafruta, *m.*
fruit-piece, *s.* (*pint.*) frutaje.
fruit-tree, *s.* frutal, árbol frutal.
fruity, *a.* de olor o de sabor de fruta.
frumentaceous [fruːmen'teiʃəs], *a.* frumenticio.
frumenty ['fruːmenti], *s.* manjar hecho de trigo y leche.
frump [frʌmp], *s.* vieja vestida a la antigua; vieja regañona.
frustrate [frʌs'treit], *v.t.* frustrar, defraudar, privar, burlar; anular, hacer nulo. — *a.* burlado, frustrado, fallido, inútil, desventajoso, vano, nulo.
frustration [frʌs'treiʃən], *s.* frustración; defraudación; contratiempo; privación.
frustrative, frustratory, *a.* frustratorio, engañoso, falaz.
frustum ['frʌstəm], *s.* (*geom.*) tronco; trozo (de columna).
frutescence [fruː'tesəns], *s.* fructescencia.
frutescent, *a.* fruticoso.
fruticose ['fruːtikouz], *a.* fruticoso.
fry [frai], *s.* (*pl.* fries) (*coc.*) fritada; cría (de animales, peces, etc.); *small fry*, (*fam.*) cosa o gente sin importancia. — *v.t.* freír. — *v.i.* freírse; achicharrarse; *I have other fish to fry*, tengo otras cosas en que pensar.
frying-pan, *s.* sartén, *f.*; *out of the frying-pan*

into the fire, huir del fuego (*o* saltar de la sartén) y dar en las brasas.

fuchsia [fjuːʃə], *s.* fucsia.

fucoid [ˈfjuːkɔid], *a.* fucáceo, fucóideo. — *s.* alga parecida al fuco.

fucus [ˈfjukəs], *s.* fuco, ova.

fuddle [fʌdl], *v.t.* emborrachar. — *v.i.* emborracharse.

fuddled, *a.* peneque, calamocano.

fudge [fʌdʒ], *s.* embuste, cuento; dulce de chocolate; *interj.* ¡quita allá! ¡vaya! — *v.t.* arreglar torpemente; contrahacer; (*impr.*) insertar noticias de última hora.

fuel [ˈfjuːəl], *s.* combustible; aliciente, pábulo; *to add fuel to the flames*, echar leña al fuego. — *v.t.* proveer con leña u otro combustible.

fueller, *s.* el que provee con leña.

fugacious [fjuːˈgeiʃəs], *a.* fugaz, volátil, instable; efímero, transitorio.

fugaciousness, fugacity, *s.* fugacidad, volatalidad, instabilidad.

fugh [fjuː], *interj.* ¡fo! (asco o enfado).

fugitive [ˈfjuːdʒitiv], *a.* fugitivo, prófugo; pasajero, perecedero; fugaz, huidizo, vagabundo, volátil; expulsado, desterrado. — *s.* fugitivo, desertor, apóstata, *m.f.*, tránsfuga, *m.f.*, contumaz, refugiado.

fugitiveness, *s.* fugacidad, instabilidad.

fugleman [ˈfjuːgəlmən], *s.* (*mil.*) jefe de fila.

fugue [fjuːg], *s* (*mús.*) fuga.

-ful [-fəl], *sufijo,* lleno de, abundante en; que contiene.

fulcrum [ˈfʌlkrəm], *s.* (*mec.*) fulcro, alzaprima; (*bot.*) apéndice, accesoria.

fulfil [fulˈfil], *v.t.* colmar, llenar; realizar; cumplir.

fulfiller, *s.* el que cumple.

fulfilment, *s.* cumplimiento, ejecución completa, desempeño, colmo.

fulgency [ˈfʌldʒənsi], **fulgor,** *s.* fulgor, esplendor, resplandor.

fulgent [ˈfʌldʒənt], *a.* fulgente, fúlgido, brillante.

fulgurate [ˈfʌlgjuːreit], *v.i.* fulgurar.

fuliginous [fəˈlidʒinəs], *a.* fuliginoso, tiznado, denegrido.

fuliginously, *adv.* de un modo fuliginoso.

full [ful], *v.t.* dar amplitud a; (*tej.*) batanar, abatanar; hacer más espeso, compacto o más grueso. — *v.i.* hacerse lleno, hacerse espeso, llenarse, espesarse; plegarse, fruncirse; llegar la luna a su plenilunio. — *a.* lleno, repleto, gordo; completo, atestado; cumplido, pleno, amplio; abundante, copioso, preñado; ahito, harto, saciado; plenario; beodo, ebrio; fuerte, perfecto, maduro; abrumado; amigo, aficionado; *full dress, a.* de gala; *s.* traje de etiqueta; *full stop,* punto final; *full moon,* plenilunio; *full sea,* mar bravío; *full length,* de cuerpo entero; *full speed,* toda velocidad; *full weight,* peso cabal; *full cock,* amartillado; *to keep the sails full,* (*mar.*) andar a buena vela. — *s.* lleno, complemento; saciedad; colmo; plenilunio; total, totalidad, todo. — *adv.* enteramente, de lleno, del todo; en pleno, totalmente; derechamente; *full well,* muy bien; *full three years,* tres años cumplidos.

fullage [ˈfulidʒ], *s.* lo que se paga por abatanar el paño.

full-blooded, *a.* pletórico; de sangre pura; (*fig.*) viril; apasionado.

full-blown, *a.* abierto; hinchado por el viento; maduro, en plena flor.

full-charged, *a.* sobrecargado.

fuller [ˈfulər], *s.* batanero; *fuller's-earth,* (*tej.*) galactita, tierra de sacamanchas, tierra de batán; *fuller's thistle,* capota, cardencha, cardo de bataneros.

fullery, *s.* batán.

full-faced, *a.* carilleno.

full-grown, *a.* maduro; *a full-grown man,* hombre hecho.

fulling-mill, *s.* batán.

fully [ˈfuli], *adv.* enteramente, completamente, plenamente.

fulminant [ˈfʌlminənt], *a.* fulminante.

fulminate [ˈfʌlmineit], *v.t., v.i.* volar, estallar, hacer explosión; fulminar; detonar, tronar, dar un estallido; censurar, condenar; excomulgar. — *s.* (*quím.*) fulminato.

fulminating, *a.* fulminante.

fulmination, *s.* fulminación, detonación, trueno.

fulminatory, *a.* fulminante, fulmíneo, fulminoso.

fulmine [ˈfʌlmin], *v.t.* fulminar, lanzar con explosión. — *v.i.* tronar.

fulminic, *a.* (*quím.*) fulmínico.

fulness [ˈfulnis], **fullness,** *s.* plenitud, llenura, copia, abundancia; complemento; saciedad, hartura.

fulsome [ˈfulsəm], *a.* insincero, hipócrita; (*ant.*) asqueroso, repugnante.

fulsomeness, *s.* insinceridad, hipocresía.

fulvid [ˈfʌlvid], **fulvous,** *a.* color leonado, amarillo rojizo.

fumage [ˈfjuːmədʒ], *s.* humazga.

fumarole [ˈfjuːməroul], *s.* fumarola.

fumble [fʌmbl], *v.t., v.i.* chapucear; manosear; parar una pelota desmañadamente; andar a tientas.

fumbler, *s.* chapucero.

fumbling, *a.* incierto, vacilante; chapucero.

fume [fjuːm], *s.* vaho, humo, vapor, gas, emanación, tufo; cólera, acaloramiento; presunción, vanidad. — *v.t.* ahumar; sahumar; avahar; fumigar; exhalar; exponer a ciertos vapores; *to fume away,* evaporarse. — *v.i.* humear; echar humo; exhalar vapores; enojarse, encolerizarse, arder en cólera.

fumigate [ˈfjuːmigeit], *v.t.* fumigar, ahumar; desinfectar; perfumar, sahumar.

fumigation, *s.* sahumerio, sahumo; (*med.*) fumigación.

fumigator, *s.* fumigador; máquina fumigatoria.

fumigatory, *s., a.* fumigatorio.

fuming, *s.* sahumerio; acto de humear o ahumar; enojo. — *a.* humeante, fumante; encolerizado, furioso.

fumingly, *adv.* con humo.

fumish [ˈfjuːmiʃ], *a.* de color de humo.

fumitory [ˈfjuːmitəri], *s.* (*bot.*) fumaria.

fumy, *a.* humoso, fumoso.

fun, *s.* broma, chunga, guasa, chanza, chiste, entretenimiento, diversión, chacota, chirigota, burla, chuscada; *to make fun of,* burlarse de, mofar; *to say in fun,* decir en broma; *for fun,* o *in fun,* en broma; *to poke fun at,* burlarse de.

funambulatory, *a.* relativo o que imita volatines.

funambulist [fjuː'næmbjuːlist], *s.* funámbulo, volatín.

function ['fʌŋkʃən], *s.* función, desempeño; ejercicio, oficio, ocupación; ceremonia, acto; potencia, facultad; (*mat.*, *fisiol.*) función. — *v.i.* funcionar.

functional, *a.* funcional.

functionary ['fʌŋkʃənəri], *s.* funcionario, empleado.

functionate, *v.i.* ejercer una función.

fund [fʌnd], *s.* fondo, capital, caudal; reserva, acopio. — *pl.* **funds**, fondos públicos; (*fam.*) dinero contante, capital convertible, dinero; *sinking fund*, fondo de amortización. — *v.t.* consolidar una deuda; acumular, tener en reserva.

fundable, *a.* consolidable.

fundament ['fʌndəmənt], *s.* fundamento, cimiento, principio; ano.

fundamental [fʌndə'mentəl], *a.* fundamental, esencial, cardinal. — *s.* fundamento, radical.

funded, *a.* consolidado; convertido en préstamo permanente.

fund-holder, *s.* rentista, *m.f.*

fundus ['fʌndəs], *s.* fondo, base, *f.*, fundamento, parte fundamental.

funeral ['fjuːnərəl], *a.* funeral, fúnebre, funerario. — *s.* funeral, funerales, exequias; entierro, duelo, cortejo; *funeral furnisher*, director de pompas fúnebres; *funeral service*, misa de difuntos.

funereal [fjuː'niəriəl], *a.* fúnebre, funéreo, funesto, triste.

fungible ['fʌndʒibl], *a.* (*for.*) que puede ser reemplazado por otra cosa de la misma clase. — *s.pl.* mercancías movibles que pueden ser valuadas por peso o medida.

fungiform ['fʌndʒifoːɹm], *a.* fungóideo.

fungoid ['fʌŋgɔid], *a.* fungoso, fungóideo.

fungosity [fʌŋ'gɔsiti], *s.* fungosidad.

fungous, *a.* fungoso, esponjoso, poroso.

fungus ['fuŋgəs], *s.* (*pl.* **fungi**) (*bot.*) hongo; tizón, moho; (*med.*) carnosidad, excrecencia.

funicle ['fjuːnikl], *s.* (*med.*) cuerdecilla, funículo, ligamento pequeño.

funicular [fjuː'nikjuːləɹ], *a.* funicular.

funk [fʌŋk], *s.* temor, miedo; cobarde; *to be in a blue funk*, tener mucho miedo. — *v.i.* espantarse, atemorizarse. — *v.t.* asustar; despedir humo o malos olores, apestar.

funnel ['fʌnəl], *s.* embudo; cañón, humero; (*fund.*) boca de carga; (*mar.*) chimenea de un vapor.

funnel-shaped, *a.* en forma de embudo; (*bot.*) infundibuliforme.

funny ['fʌni], *a.* cómico, burlesco, alegre, divertido, chistoso, bufón, chusco, gracioso; (*fam.*) curioso, raro, extraño; *funny-bone*, hueso de la risa.

fur [fəːɹ], *s.* piel, *f.*, forro de pieles; pelo; peletería; sarro, borra, roya; saburra (de la lengua). — *v.t.* cubrir, forrar o adornar con pieles finas; amaestrar con tabletas; depositar sarro; quitar incrustaciones a las calderas; *to fur a ship*, aforrar un buque. — *v.i.* formarse incrustaciones.

furacious [fjuː'reiʃəs], *a.* rapaz.

furacity [fjuː'ræsiti], *s.* rapacidad.

furbelow ['fəːɹbelou], *s.* farfalá, vuelo, volante. — *v.t.* adornar con volantes.

furbish ['fəːɹbiʃ], *v.t.* acicalar, pulir, limpiar.

furbishable, *a.* capaz de ser pulido.

furcate ['fəːɹkeit], *a.* ahorquillado, hendido.

furcation, *s.* bifurcación, horcajadura.

furcular ['fəːɹkjuːləɹ], *a.* horcado.

furfur, *s.* (*med.*) caspa, escamitas.

furfuraceous [fəːɹfjuː'reiʃəs], *a.* furfuráceo, parecido al salvado o a la caspa.

furfurol ['fəːɹfjuːrəl], *s.* (*quím.*) aceite obtenido de la destilación seca del azúcar, o de la destilación del salvado con una mezcla de ácido sulfúrico diluido.

furious ['fjuːriəs], *a.* furioso, furibundo, sañudo, frenético, iracundo, airado, violento.

furiousness, *s.* frenesí, furia.

furl [fəːɹl], *v.t.* plegar, recoger; encoger, contraer; (*mar.*) aferrar; *furling lines*, aferravelas.

furlong ['fəːɹlɔŋ], *s.* estadio, octava parte de una milla, equivalente a 201 m. aprox.

furlough ['fəːɹlou], *s.* (*mil.*) licencia, permiso. — *v.t.* dar licencia.

furnace ['fəːɹnis], *s.* horno, hornillo; fornalla, hogar de caldera, de máquina; calorífero; fundición, fundería; *furnace bar*, (*fund.*) botador; *furnace charger*, cebadera; *furnace hoist*, grúa o cabria de horno.

furnish ['fəːɹniʃ], *v.t.* surtir, proveer, suplir; equipar, aparejar; procurar, suministrar, proporcionar; decorar, alhajar; amoblar, adornar, amueblar.

furnisher, *s.* equipador, guarnecedor, decorador; proveedor, aparejador.

furnishing, *s.* habilitación, equipo, suministro. — *pl.* **furnishings**, accesorios, mueblaje, mobiliario; avíos.

furnishment, *s.* surtimiento, surtido.

furniture ['fəːɹnitʃəɹ], *s.* ajuar, moblaje o mueblaje; equipo, guarnición, aderezo; decoraciones, adornos; (*impr.*) fornitura; (*mar.*) aparejo; *a piece of furniture*, mueble; *furniture van*, camión de mudanza.

furor ['fjuːrɔːɹ], **furore** [fjuː'rɔːri], *s.* furor, furia, rabia; frenesí; aplauso, entusiasmo, gran éxito.

furred [fəːɹd], *a.* forrado, cubierto de piel; cargado, cubierto con sarro.

furrier ['fʌriəɹ], *s.* peletero.

furriery, *s.* peletería.

furring, *s.* forro o guarnición de pieles; tabletas para enlucidos; incrustaciones de una caldera; operación de limpiar una caldera; sarro; (*carp.*) contrapar de armadura falsa.

furrow ['fʌrou], *s.* (*agr.*) surco; canaliza, tajea, zanja, reguera; (*fig.*) arruga, señal, *f.*, marca; (*carp.*) muesca, encaje, gargol; (*arq.*) estría, mediacaña. — *v.t.* surcar, hacer surcos; estriar; *furrow-faced*, (con la) cara arrugada.

furry ['fəːri], *a.* hecho de pieles, adornado con pieles; peludo; sarroso.

further ['fəːɹðəɹ], *a. compar.* [FAR] ulterior, más lejos, más separado, más distante; adicional, nuevo; más amplio; *till further orders*, hasta nueva orden; *on the further side of*, más allá de. — *adv.* más lejos, más allá; aun, además, además de eso, cuanto más. — *v.t.* adelantar, promover, apoyar, ayudar, asistir.

furtherance ['fəːɹðərəns], *s.* adelantamiento, progreso, socorro, ayuda, promoción, apoyo, asistencia.

furtherer, *s.* promotor, patrón, protector, fautor.

furthermore [fəːɹðəɹ'mɔːɹ], *adv.* además, cuanto más, a más de esto; (*for.*) otrosí.

furthermost ['fəːɹðəɹmoust], *a.* más lejano, más remoto.

furthest ['fəːðest], *a., adv.* más lejos, más remoto; extremo, último; muy distante.

furtive ['fəːɹtiv], *a.* furtivo, oculto, secreto, hecho a escondidas.

furuncle ['fʌrʌŋkl], *s.* furúnculo, divieso, grano.

furuncular, *a.* furunculoso.

fury ['fjuːri], *s.* furia, ira, furor, cólera, rabia, entusiasmo, frenesí, arrebatamiento; (*fig.*) fiera, mujer furiosa o colérica.

furze [fəːɹz], *s.* (*bot.*) aulaga, tojo, hiniesta espinosa.

furzy, *a.* retamero, lleno de aulagas.

fuscous ['fʌskəs], *a.* fusco.

fuse [fjuːz], *v.t.* fundir, derretir. — *v.i.* derretirse, fundirse. — *s.* espoleta, cebo, pebete, mecha; (*elec.*) fusible; *fuse box,* caja de fusibles; *to blow a fuse,* fundir un fusible.

fusee [fjuː'ziː], *s.* fósforo; caracol o husillo de reloj; (*arti.*) espoleta, espiga, pipa.

fuse-extractor, *s.* sacaespoletas, *m.*

fusel-oil ['fjuːzələil], *s.* (*quím.*) compuesto aceitoso y alcohólico obtenido de la destilación del aguardiente.

fuse-setter, *s.* recalcador de espoletas.

fusibility [fjuːzi'biliti], *s.* fusibilidad.

fusible, *a.* fusil, fusible, conflátil, fundible.

fusiform ['fjuːzifɔːɹm], *a.* fusiforme.

fusil ['fjuːzəl], *s.* fusil de chispa, escopeta de pistón. — *a.* fundible.

fusileer, fusilier [fjuːzi'liəɹ], *s.* (*mil.*) fusilero.

fusillade [fjuːzileid], *s.* (*arti.*) descarga cerrada, tiroteo.

fusing ['fjuːziŋ], *a.* fundente, de fusión; *fusing point,* punto de fusión.

fusion, *s.* fusión, licuación, fundición, derretimiento; conflación; unión, *f.*

fuss [fʌs], *s.* ajetreo, bulla, alboroto, ruido, desasosiego, bullicio, tremolina. — *v.t.* molestar, preocupar, turbar. — *v.i.* zangolotear, agitarse, ajetrearse, inquietarse, preocuparse.

fussy, *a.* remilgado, inquieto, molesto; exigente, minucioso.

fust [fʌst], *s.* fuste.

fustian ['fʌstʃən], *s.* (*tej.*) fustán; (*fig.*) énfasis. — *a.* hecho de fustán; altisonante, enfático.

fustic ['fʌstik], *s.* fustoc, fustete.

fustigate ['fʌstigeit], *v.t.* fustigar, apalear.

fustigation, *s.* castigo o pena de azotes o latigazos.

fustiness ['fʌstinis], *s.* enmohecimiento; rancidez; hediondez, hedor.

fusty ['fʌsti], *a.* mohoso, rancio.

futile ['fjuːtail], *a.* fútil, frívolo, vano, inútil.

futility [fjuː'tiliti], *s.* futilidad; superficialidad.

futtock ['fʌtək], *s.* (*mar.*) genol, singlón, barraganete, arraigada; *futtock-shrouds,* pernadas de las arraigadas.

future ['fjuːtʃəɹ], *a.* futuro, venidero, venturo. — *s.* porvenir, futuro.

futurism, *s.* futurismo.

futurist ['fjuːtərist], *s.* futurista, *m.f.*

futurity [fjuː'tjuːriti], *s.* futuro, porvenir.

fuzz [fʌz], *v.i.* soltar pelusa; deshilarse, deshilacharse, desflecarse. — *s.* pelusa, tamo, borra, lanilla, hilacha menuda.

fuzz-ball, *s.* (*bot.*) bejín.

fuzziness, *s.* vellosidad.

fuzzy ['fʌzi], *a.* velloso, parecido a lanilla, cubierto de pelusa.

fy [fai], *interj.* ¡qué verguenza! ¡uf! ¡vaya!

fyke [faik], *s.* nasa, red para pescar de forma cónica y con boca ancha.

G

G, g [dʒi], séptima letra del alfabeto inglés; tiene dos sonidos: uno igual a la g castellana ante *a, o, u;* el otro igual a la ll de América; (*mús.*) sol; *G clef,* clave de sol, *f.*

gab [gæb], *v.t., v.i.* (*fam.*) parlotear, charlar, picotear. — *s.* (*fam.*) locuacidad, cháchara; garabato, gancho; *to have the gift of the gab,* tener la lengua muy suelta.

gabardine ['gæbəɹdiːn], **gaberdine**, *s.* gabacha, gabardina.

gabble [gæbl], *v.t., v.i.* charlar, parlotear, picotear, cotorrear, cacarear, hablar de hilván. — *s.* algarabía; cotorreo, charla; graznido.

gabbler, *s.* charlador, hablador, parlador, chacharero, picotero, charlante.

gabbro ['gæbrou], *s.* (*geol.*) roca compuesta de feldespato y diálaga.

gabion ['geibiən], *s.* (*fort.*) gavión, cestón.

gable ['geibəl], *s.* (*arq.*) faldón; gablete.

gable-end, *s.* socarrén, alero.

gad [gæd], *v.i.* andorrear, callejear, corretear, pindonguear; *on the gad,* (*fam.*) correteando, callejeando. — *s.* (*min.*) cuña, aguja, taladro, punzón; aguijón, chuzo; clavo grande.

gadabout ['gædəbaut], *s.* placero. — *a.* callejero, cantonero.

gadder, *s.* callejero, andorrero, correntón; mujer cantonera.

gadding, *s.* vagancia, briba, peregrinación.

gaddingly, *adv.* haraganamente.

gadfly ['gædflai], *s.* tábano.

gadhelic [gə'delik], *a.* gaélico.

gadroon [gə'druːn], *s.* (*arq.*) godron.

gadwall ['gædwəl], *s.* ánade silvestre grande (*Anas strepera*).

Gael [geil], *s.* escocés; celta, *m.f.*

Gaelic ['geilik], **Galic** ['gælik], *s., a.* gaélico, céltico.

gaff [gæf], *s.* arpón o garfio; espolón de gallo; (*mar.*) botavara, berlinga.

gaff-boom, *s.* (*mar.*) verga de cangreja.

gaffer ['gæfəɹ], *s.* viejo, vejete (tiene casi el significado de tío, maese, compadre).

gaffle ['gæfəl], *s.* espolón, navaja de gallo.

gaff-sail, *s.* (*mar.*) vela de cangreja.

gag [gæg], *v.t.* amordazar; hacer callar; (*teat.*) meter morcilla; provocar bascas, náuseas. — *v.i.* nausear, tener náuseas. — *s.* mordaza; (*vet.*) acial; asco, lo que produce bascas; (*teat.*) morcilla; chiste.

gage [geidʒ], **gauge**, *s.* regla de medir, medida; indicador; norma, calibrador; (*mar.*) barlovento, calado. — *v.t.* aforar, medir, calibrar, graduar, escantillar; apreciar, comprometer, estimar, avaluar; (*mar.*) arquear.

gage, *s.* prenda, caución; guante, reto, gaje; variedad de ciruela; *greengage,* ciruela verdal, claudia. — *v.t.* empeñar, dar en prenda; apostar.

gager, gauger, *s.* aforador, arqueador, graduador.

gagger ['gægəɪ], s. el que amordaza.
gaggle ['gægəl], v.i. graznar.
gaiety ['geiiti], s. jovialidad, alborozo, alegría; broma, algazara; viveza, ufanía, ostentación, fausto, pompa.
gaily ['geili], adv. alegremente.
gain [gein], s. ganancia, beneficio, ventaja, lucro, interés, provecho, granjería; logro; usura; (carp.) gárgol, ranura. — v.t. ganar, llevar, sacar, adquirir, llegar a, reportar, granjear, conseguir, alcanzar, lograr; conquistar, vencer, llevar la palma; devengar; apaciguar, propiciar; conciliar; (carp.) hacer gárgoles; to gain the day, vencer, triunfar; to gain the wind, (mar.) ganar el barlovento. — v.i. ganar, medrar, mejorar, crecer, lograr, alcanzar, obtener una ventaja, sacar provecho, aumentar; aproximarse, acercarse, avanzar, adelantar; enriquecerse; prevalecer; to gain upon, alcanzar.
gainable, a. ganable, asequible, capaz de ser adquirido.
gainer, s. ganador.
gainful, a. ganancioso, lucrativo, ventajoso, provechoso.
gainfulness, s. provecho, ganancia.
gainless, a. desventajoso, infructuoso.
gainlessness, s. inutilidad, infructuosidad.
gainsay [gein'sei], v.t. (pret., p.p. gainsaid) negar; contradecir; contrariar.
gainsayer, s. contradictor, adversario.
gainsaying, s. oposición, contradicción.
gait [geit], s. marcha, andadura, paso, modo de andar; continente; porte; (Esco.) viaje, camino.
gaiter ['geitəɪ], s. botín, botina; polaina.
gala ['geilə, 'gɑːlə], s. gala, fiesta; gala-day, festividad.
galactic [gə'læktik], a. galáctico, relativo a la galaxia.
galactometer [gələæk'tomətəɪ], s. galactómetro, lactómetro.
galangal [gə'læŋgəl], s. (bot.) galanga.
galantine ['gælənti:n], s. plato de carne servido en forma de gelatina.
galaxy ['gæləksi], s. (astr.) galaxía, vía láctea; grupo brillante.
galbanum ['gælbənəm], s. gálbano.
gale [geil], s. viento fuerte, ventarrón; (mar.) temporal; (fig.) algazara; pago periódico del alquiler.
galea, s. yelmo, casco, galea.
galeate ['gælieit], galeated, a. cubierto con yelmo.
galena [gæ'li:nə], s. (min.) galena; sulfuro de plomo nativo.
galenic, galenical, a. galénico; que contiene galena; que se refiere a Galeno.
Galenismo, s. galenismo.
Galenist ['gælənist], s. galenista, m.f.
Galilean [gæli'li:ən], s. galileo.
galiot ['gæliət], s. (mar.) galeota.
galipot ['gælipɔt], s. galipote, resina.
galium ['gæliəm], s. (bot.) cuajaleche.
gall [gɔːl], s. hiel, f., bilis, f.; odio, hiel, f., rencor; aversión; aspereza, amargura, malignidad, malicia; desfachatez, tupe, (fam.) descaro; (vet.) rozadura, matadura, gall; gall-apple, gall-nut, (bot.) agalla; gall-stones, cálculos hepáticos; gall-fly, cinipo. — v.t., v.i. ludir, gastar, raspar, rozar; desollar; dañar,

fatigar, irritar, ahelear, hostigar; desollarse, rozar.
gallant ['gælənt], a. galante, cortés; cortejador, galanteador. — v.t. galantear, requebrar, cortejar. — s. galán, galanteador; cortejo; chichisbeo.
gallant, a. valeroso, animoso, intrépido, valiente, bizarro; caballeroso.
gallantness, s. bizarría, elegancia.
gallantry ['gæləntri], s. bizarría, gallardía, valentía, heroísmo, valor; caballerosidad; cortejo, galantería, galanteo; amores, amistad, trato.
gallate ['gæleit], s. (quím.) galato; agallato.
galleass ['gæliəs], s. galeaza.
galleon ['gæljən], s. (mar.) galeón.
gallery ['gæləri], s. galería, tribuna; pasadizo, corredor; corrido, balcón; (teat.) paraíso, gallinero, cazuela; (b.a.) colección, galería; (min.) socavón, pozo, galería; (fort.) galería; (mar.) crujía, galería; art gallery, museo de arte.
galley ['gæli], s. (mar.) galera; cocina; fogón; (Ingl.) falúa; (impr.) galera.
galley-proof, s. galerada.
galley-slave, s. galeote.
galley-tiles, s.pl. azulejos.
galliard ['gæljəɪd], a. (ant.) vivo, alegre. — s. gallarda.
Gallic ['gælik], **Gallican**, a. galo, galicano; gallic acid, (quím.) ácido agálico.
Gallicism ['gælisizm], s. galicismo.
Gallicize ['gælisaiz], v.t. afrancesar, hablar o escribir usando galicismos.
galligaskins [gæli'gæskinz], s.pl. calzacalzones, medias grandes.
gallimaufry [gæli'mɔːfri], s. jigote, picadillo, ropa vieja, etc.; (fig.) mezcla ridícula de cosas contrarias; mezcolanza.
gallinaceous [gæli'neiʃəs], a. gallináceo.
gallinule ['gælinjuːl], s. gallineta, fúlica.
galliot ['gæliət], s. (mar.) galeota.
gallipot ['gælipɔt], s. orza, bote, pote, vasija de barro vidriada.
gallium ['gæliəm], s. (quím.) galio.
gallivant [gæli'vænt], v.i. (fam.) callejear.
gall-less, a. sin hiel; dulce, apacible.
gallon ['gælən], s. galón.
galloon [gə'luːn], s. (tej.) galón; trencilla; ribecillo.
gallop ['gæləp], s. galope; at full gallop, a rienda suelta, a galope tendido. — v.t. hacer galopar (un caballo). — v.i. galopar; ir aprisa.
gallopade [gælə'peid], s. caracoleo; (mús.) galop.
galloper, s. hombre o caballo que galopa.
Galloway ['gæləwei], s. jaca escocesa.
gallows ['gælouz], s. horca, patíbulo; montante, armazón, f.; gallows-bird, criminal digno de la horca, carne de patíbulo. — pl. (fam., E.U.) tirantes del pantalón.
gally ['gæli], a. amargo; que contiene hiel.
galop ['gæləp], s. (baile) galop.
galore [gə'lɔːɪ], s., adv. en abundancia; muchísimos.
galosh [gə'lɔʃ], **galoshe**, s. galocha, choclo, zueco, chanclo, zapatón; polaina, botín.
galvanic [gæl'vænik], a. galvánico.
galvanism ['gælvənizm], s. galvanismo.
galvanization, s. galvanización.

galvanize ['gælvənaiz], *v.t.* galvanizar; comunicar energía.

galvanometer [gælvə'nɔmətəɹ], *s.* galvanómetro.

galvanometric, *a.* galvanométrico.

galvanometry, *s.* galvanometría.

gam [gæm], *s.* (*mar.*) manada de ballenas; compañía de pescadores de ballenas.

gamb [gæmb], *s.* (*blas.*) dibujo o figura de pierna de animal en un escudo de armas.

gamba ['gæmbə], *s.* (*anat.*) el metacarpo o el metatarso.

gambade [gæm'beid], **gambado**, *s.* polaina. — *pl.* guardaestribos o cubiertas de cuero.

gambet ['gæmbet], *s.* (*orn.*) especie de maubecha.

gambier ['gæmbiəɹ], *s.* extracto de las hojas de la *Uncaria gambir*, usado en medicina como astringente y en la tintorería y tenería.

gambit ['gæmbit], *s.* (*ajedrez*) gambito; (*fig.*) táctica.

gamble ['gæmbəl], *v.i.* jugar por dinero; especular financialmente; jugar con trampas; frecuentar garitos; *to gamble for large stakes*, jugar grueso; *gambling-den*, o *gambling hell*, garito, timba, casa de juego. — *s.* (*fam.*) jugada.

gambler, *s.* jugador, garitero, tahur, fullero.

gambling, *s.* juego.

gamboge ['gæmboudʒ], *s.* gomaguta, gutagamba.

gambol ['gæmbəl], *v.i.* brincar, saltar, caracolear; travesear, juguetear. — *s.* brinco, cabriola, caracoleo, travesura, zapateta.

gambrel ['gæmbrəl], *s.* corvejón, jarrete; gancho, garabato; *gambrel roof*, (*arq.*) techo a la holandesa, de ángulo obtuso.

game [geim], *s.* juego, entretenimiento, pasatiempo; chanza, mofa, burla; partida o partido de juego; caza; *game leg*, (*fam.*) pierna estropeada; *the game is up*, se ha levantado la caza; (*fam.*) ¡se acabó!; la cosa ha fracasado. — *a.* valeroso, animoso, esforzado; (*coc.*) manido, salvajino; (*fam.*) peleón, indómito, bravo, que quiere jugar o pelear. — *v.t., v.i.* jugar; jugar fuerte; entretenerse con algun juego o diversión.

game-bag, *s.* zurrón, morral.

game-cock, *s.* gallo inglés o de pelea.

game-keeper, *s.* guardabosque, guarda de coto, *m.*

gamesome, *a.* juguetón, retozón.

gamesomeness, *s.* festividad, alegría, juguete.

gamester ['geimstəɹ], *s.* tahur, jugador; garitero; fullero; bufón chocarrero.

gamic ['gæmik], *a.* (*biol.*) sexual.

gaming ['geimiŋ], *s.* juego; *gaming house*, casa de juego, garito; *gaming table*, mesa de juego, tablero.

gammer ['gæməɹ], *s.f.* vieja, tía, comadre, abuela, abuelita.

gammon ['gæmən], *s.* jamón; (*fam.*) añagaza, chasco, trola; lance del juego de chaquete; (*fam.*) bobería, necedad. — *v.t.* engañar, chasquear; curar jamón; ganar doble partida de chaquete; (*mar.*) trincar.

gammoning, *s.* trinca.

gammoning-hole, *s.* groera de trinca.

gamopetalous ['gæmou'petələs], *a.* (*bot.*) gamopétalo, monopétalo.

gamosepalous, *a.* (*bot.*) gamosépalo, monosépalo.

gamut ['gamʌt], *s.* (*mús.*) gama, escala.

ganch [gæntʃ], *v.t.* empalar.

gander ['gændəɹ], *s.* (*orn.*) ánsar, ganso.

gang [gæŋ], *s.* cuadrilla, pelotón, pandilla, banda; juego de herramientas; revezo; (*min.*) gangar; *press-gang*, ronda de matrícula.

gang-board, *s.* (*mar.*) plancha, andamio.

ganglion ['gæŋgliən], *s.* (*anat.*) ganglio.

ganglionic, *a.* ganglionar.

gang-plank, *s.* pasamano, plancha.

gang-plough, *s.* arado de reja múltiple.

gangrenate ['gæŋgreneit], **gangrene**, *v.t.* gangrenar. — *v.i.* gangrenarse.

gangrene ['gæŋgriːn], *s.* gangrena.

gangrenous, *a.* gangrenoso.

gang-saw, *s.* sierra múltiple.

gangster ['gæŋstəɹ], *s.* gángster, pistolero.

gangue [gæŋ], *s.* (*min.*) ganga.

gangway ['gæŋwei], *s.* (*mar.*) pasamano, portalón, tilla.

gannet ['gænit], *s.* (*orn.*) bubia.

ganoid ['gænɔid], *a.* (*ict.*) ganoideo.

gantry ['gæntri], *s.* grúa corrediza.

gaol [dʒeil], *s.* cárcel, *f.*, prisión; *gaol-bird*, presidiario. — *v.t.* encarcelar.

gaoler, *s.* carcelero, alcaide, guardia, *m.f.*

gap [gæp], *s.* buco, portillo, boquete, raja, brecha, resquicio, abertura, hueco; vacío, espacio, claro, laguna; hondonada; barranca; quebrada. — *v.i.* abrir una brecha.

gape [geip], *v.i.* bostezar; boquear; abrirse, estar abierta, hendirse, abrirse en grietas; estar con la boca abierta; anhelar, ansiar, papar moscas, embobarse. — *s.* bostezo; brecha, hendedura, abertura; boqueado.

gaper, *s.* bostezador; papamoscas, *m.*, bobalicón.

gar [gɑːɹ], *s.* (*ict.*) sollo, belona.

garage [gɑːɹ], *s.* garaje. — *v.t.* poner en un garaje.

garancin ['gærənsin], *s.* (*quím.*) materia colorante obtenida por la acción del ácido sulfúrico sobre la rubia.

garb [gɑːɹb], *s.* vestido, vestidura, traje; (*blas.*) espiga.

garbage ['gɑːɹbidʒ], *s.* basura, desperdicios, desechos.

garbel ['gɑːɹbəl], *s.* (*mar.*) aparadura.

garble ['gɑːɹbəl], *v.t.* alterar, pervertir, mutilar, falsificar, garbillar; escoger, entresacar. — *s.pl.* (*com.*) desecho de especias.

garbler, *s.* garbillador; falsificador, alterador.

garboard, *s.* (*mar.*) aparadura, tablón de aparadura.

garden ['gɑːɹdən], *s.* jardín; huerta, huerto. — *a.* de jardín; *garden city*, ciudad jardín; *garden party*, fiesta de jardín. — *v.t., v.i.* hacer plantar o cultivar jardines o huertos.

gardener, *s.* jardinero, hortelano.

gardenia [gɑːɹ'diːniə], *s.* (*bot.*) gardenia.

gardening ['gɑːɹdəniŋ], *s.* horticultura, jardinería.

garden-mould, *s.* tierra vegetal.

garfish ['gɑːɹfiʃ], *s.* (*ict.*) belona.

gargantuan [gɑːɹ'gæntjuən], *a.* inmenso, enorme, increíble, colosal.

gargarism ['gɑːɹgərizm], *s.* gargarismo.

gargarize, *v.t.* gargarizar, hacer gárgaras.

garget ['gɑːɹdʒet], *s.* (*vet.*) inflamación de la cabeza o la garganta del ganado; enfermedad de las ubres.

gargle ['gɑːɹgəl], *v.i., v.t.* gargarizar, hacer gárgaras. — *s.* gárgara, gargarismo; colutorio, enjuague.

gargoyle ['gɑːɹgɔil], s. (arq.) gárgola.
garish ['gɛəriʃ], a. deslumbrante, deslumbrador; charro; llamativo; pomposo, ostentoso; extravagante.
garishness, s. relumbrón, oropel; ostentación, pompa.
garland ['gɑːɹlənd], s. guirnalda, corona, florón; crestomatía; (mar.) roñada; (arq.) festón. — v.t. enguirnaldar.
garlic ['gɑːɹlik], s. ajo.
garlicky, a. que huele o sabe a ajo.
garment ['gɑːɹmənt], s. vestido, prenda de vestir. — pl. **garments**, ropa.
garner ['gɑːɹnəɹ], v.t. entrojar, almacenar el grano. — s. granero, acopio, horreo.
garnet ['gɑːɹnet], s. granate; (mar.) aparejo de carga, candeletón.
garnish ['gɑːɹniʃ], v.t. (coc.) aderezar, componer, adornar, ornar, guarnecer, ataviar; (for.) prevenir, notificar; aprestar. — s. (coc.) aderezo; adorno, guarnición.
garnisher, s. aderezador; guarnecedor, el que pone guarniciones.
garnishment, s. ornamento, adorno; (for.) entredicho.
garniture, s. guarnición, gayadura, adorno.
garpike ['gɑːɹpaik], s. (ict.) belona.
garret ['gærət], s. buharda, guardilla, desván, zaquizamí.
garrison ['gærisən], s. (mil.) guarnición. — v.t guarnecer; guarnicionar.
garrote [gəˈrɔt], v.t. dar garrote; agarrotar; agarrar por la garganta.
garrulity [gəˈruːliti], s. garrulidad, charla, locuacidad, cháchara.
garrulous ['gærjuːləs], a. gárrulo, locuaz, lenguaz, parlero.
garter ['gɑːɹtəɹ], s. liga, atadero, cenojil, jarretera; Order of the Garter, Orden de la Jarretera. — v.t. atar con cenojil; investir con la Orden de la Jarretera.
garter-fish, s. (ict.) lepidopo.
garth [gɑːɹθ], s. corral, patio, jardín; hierba.
gas [gæs], s. gas; mechero de gas, luz de gas; (fig.) palabrería; gasolina; gas-burner, mechero, quemador, boquilla; gas-fitting, instalación de gas; gas-light, luz de gas, mechero de gas; gas-holder, gas-tank, gasómetro; gas-main, cañería principal de gas; gas-meter, contador; gas-works, fábrica de gas; poison gas, gas asfixiante. — v.t. asfixiar con gas; (mil.) atacar con gas.
gasconade [gæskəˈneid], s. gasconada, fanfarronada. — v.i. jactarse, fanfarronear.
gaselier [gæsəˈliəɹ], s. candelabro (para gas).
gaseous ['geisiəs], a. gaseoso, gaseiforme; insubstancial.
gash [gæʃ], v.t. acuchillar, dar una cuchillada, hacer un chirlo. — s. cuchillada, herida; incisión.
gashful, a. lleno de cuchilladas; (fig.) terrible, espantoso.
gasification [gæsifiˈkeiʃən], s. gasificación.
gasify, v.t. gasificar, convertir en gas, aerificar.
gasket ['gæskit], s. (mec.) aro de empaquetadura. — pl. **gaskets**, (mar.) tomadores, cajetas.
gaskins ['gæskinz], s.pl. empaquetadura de cáñamo o estopa; (ant.) especie de medias anchas.
gasogen ['gæsədʒin], **gasogene**, s. gasógeno.

gasolene ['gæsoliːn], s. gasoleno, gasolina.
gasolier [gæsəˈliəɹ], s. candelabro colgante (para gas).
gasometer [gəˈsɔmetəɹ], s. gasómetro.
gasometry, s. gasometría.
gasoscope ['gæsoskoup], s. instrumento usado para descubrir la presencia de hidrógeno carburado, en minas, edificios, etc.
gasp [gɑːsp], v.t., v.i. emitir sonidos entrecortados; boquear, respirar con dificultad; suspirar, anhelar. — s. boqueada; acción de respirar entrecortadamente; to be at one's last gasp, estar dando la última boqueada; (fig.) haber hecho los últimos esfuerzos.
gasteropod [gæsˈterəpɔd], **gastropod**, s., a. gasterópodo.
gastralgia [gæsˈtrældʒə], s. gastralgia.
gastralgie, a. gastrálgico.
gastric ['gæstrik], a. gástrico.
gastriloquous, a. ventrílocuo.
gastritis [gæsˈtraitis], s. gastritis, f.
gastronomer [gæsˈtrɔnəməɹ], **gastronomist**, s. gastrónomo.
gastronomic, gastronomical, a. gastronómico.
gastronomy [gæsˈtrɔnəmi], s. gastronomía.
gastropod, s. [GASTEROPOD].
gate [geit], s. puerta, portillo, entrada; rastrillo, poterna; barrera, talanquera; compuertas de esclusa; (dep.) concurrencia. — v.t. prohibir de salir de la Universidad; flood-gate, paradera.
gated, a. que tiene puertas.
gate-keeper, gateward, s. portero; (f.c.) guardabarrera, m.
gateway ['geitwei], s. paso, entrada, portillo.
gather ['gæðəɹ], v.t. reunir, coger, recoger, rebuscar, cosechar, amontonar; acumular, acopiar; ganar; plegar, arrugar; juntar, unir, alzar, congregar, recolectar; (impr.) ordenar las páginas; (cost.) fruncir; deducir, inferir, colegir; to gather dust, cubrirse de polvo; to gather breath, tomar aliento; to gather crops, levantar las cosechas, hacer el verano; to gather grapes, vendimiar; to gather strength, recuperarse, tomar fuerzas; to gather flesh, criar carnes. — v.i. unirse, aumentarse, congregarse, juntarse; amontonarse, acumularse; contraerse, concentrarse, condensarse; formarse pus; cerrarse (el cielo). — s. (cost.) frunce, pliegue, plegado; deslustre (del paño).
gatherable, a. deducible; que puede juntarse o cosecharse.
gatherer, s. colector; vendimiador, segador; (cost.) fruncidor.
gathering, s. asamblea, muchedumbre, hacinamiento, acción de amontonar, amontonamiento, acumulación; contracción, fruncimiento; colecta, cuesta, demanda; (med.) acumulación de pus, absceso; (cost.) fruncido.
gauche [gouʃ], a. torpe, zurdo.
gaucherie ['gouʃəri], s. torpeza.
gaud [gɔːd], s. objeto charro.
gaudery, s. lujo ostentoso; (vulg.) charrada.
gaudiness ['gɔːdinis], s. oropel; pompa, ostentación, fausto; charrada.
gaudish, gaudy ['gɔːdi], a. ostentoso, llamativo, chillón, charro.
gauge [geidʒ], s. regla de medir; indicador; (mar.) calado; calibre (de fusil); (f.c.) entre-

vía; medida; *broad (narrow) gauge railway*, ferrocarril de vía ancha (estrecha); *pressure gauge*, manómetro. — *v.t.* medir; calibrar; calcular; (*mar.*) arquear.
gauger, *s.* arqueador, aforador, graduador.
gauging, *s.* acto de medir o aforar, aforo, aforamiento; medición; (*mar.*) arqueaje.
Gaul [gɔːl], *s.* Galia; galo.
Gaulish, *a.* galicano.
gaultheria [gɔːlˈθiəriə], *s.* gualteria.
gaunt, *a.* flaco, flojo, delgado, desvaído.
gauntlet [ˈgɔːntlet], *s.* manopla; guantelete; (*mil.*) baquetas; *to throw (o fling) down the gauntlet*, echar el guante, retar; *to run the gauntlet*, correr las baquetas.
gauze [gɔːz], *s.* gasa, cendal; *wire-gauze*, tela metálica; *silk gauze*, gasa de seda; *linen gauze*, clarín.
gauziness, *s.* diafanidad.
gauzy, *a.* delgado, diáfano; de gasa.
gave, *pret.* [GIVE].
gavel [ˈgævəl], *s.* mazo de albañil; mazo empleado por el presidente en una reunión; gavilla; gabela.
gavelock [ˈgævlɔk], *s.* palanca de hierro.
gavial, *s.* cocodrilo del Ganges.
gavot [gəˈvɔt], **gavotte**, *s.* gavota.
gawk [gɔːk], *s.* pápano, bobo; (*fam.*) cuclillo. — *v.i.* cometer torpezas; mirar boquiabierto.
gawky [gɔːki], *s.* papanatas, zote. — *a.* bobo, tonto, torpe, rudo, desgarbado.
gay [gei], *a.* alegre, festivo, de buen humor, jovial; ligero, calavera, correntón; ufano, llamativo, gayo, vistoso.
gayness, *s.* alegría, jovialidad.
gaysome, *a.* alegre, jovial, de buen humor.
gaze [geiz], *v.i.* mirar, contemplar, considerar. — *s.* contemplación, mirada.
gazebo [gəˈziːbou], *s.* torreón, miranda.
gazelle [gəˈzel], *s.* gacela.
gazer, *s.* mirón, el que mira por mera curiosidad.
gazette [gəˈzet], *s.* gaceta; periódico; anuncio o nombramiento oficial. — *v.i.* publicar o anunciar en la Gaceta (o periódico oficial); nombrar oficialmente.
gazetteer [gæzəˈtiəɹ], *s.* gacetero; nomenclador o diccionario geográfico.
gazing-stock, *s.* hazmerreír.
gazogene [ˈgæzədʒiːn], *s.* aparato para la fabricación de bebidas gaseosas.
gear [giəɹ], *s.* (*mec.*) engranaje; juego; (*mar.*) aparejo; atavíos, guarniciones; herramientas; utensilios; *pl.* **gears**, (*mar.*) drizas; *in gear*, engranado, en juego; *out of gear*, desengranado; *gear-block*, cuadernal; *first gear*, primera velocidad; *neutral gear*, punto muerto; *gear-box*, caja de velocidades; *gear-lever*, palanca de cambio de velocidades; *to put in gear*, engranar; poner en marcha. — *v.t.* aparejar, preparar, enjaezar; armar, montar; (*mec.*) engranar, conectar, encajar, endentar, embragar. — *v.i.* venir o estar en juego.
gearing, *s.* (*mec.*) encaje, engranaje; (*mar.*) drizas, sogas y aparejos.
geat [dʒiːt], *s.* (*fund.*) boca del molde.
gecko [ˈgekou], *s.* lagarto de Malaya.
gee [dʒiː], *v.t.* arrear hacia la derecha. — *v.i.* torcer hacia la derecha. — *interj.* ¡arre! — *s.* nombre de la letra *g*; *gee-gee*, voz infantil para designar un caballo.

geese [giːs], *s.pl.* [GOOSE].
geezer [ˈgiːzəɹ], *s.*   (*vulg.*) viejo, vieja, (*teat.*) característica.
Gehenna [geˈhenə], *s.* Gehena, infierno.
gelatine [ˈdʒelətiːn], *s.* gelatina.
gelatinate [dʒelˈætineit], **gelatinize**, *v.t.*, *v.i.* convertir o convertirse en substancia gelatinosa.
gelatinous [dʒelˈætinəs], *a.* gelatinoso.
gelation [dʒeˈleiʃən], *s.* helamiento.
geld [geld], *v.t.* (*vet.*) castrar, capar; castrar las colmenas. — *s.* multa, tributo antiguo.
gelder, *s.* castrador, capador.
gelding [ˈgeldiŋ], *s.* capón, caballo capado.
gelid [ˈdʒelid], *a.* (*poét.*) helado, gélido.
gelidity, gelidness, *s.* frío extremo.
gelignite [ˈdʒelignait], *s.* gelignita.
gem [dʒem], *s.* gema; joyel, joya, presea, alhaja; preciosidad. — *v.t.* adornar con piedras preciosas. — *v.i.* abotonar, arrojar el botón una planta.
gemel [ˈdʒemel], *s.*, *a.* gemelo, mellizo; *gemel ring*, sortija de alianza; formada por dos o mas anillos.
geminate [ˈdʒemineit], *s.* (*bot.*) gemino, gemelo. — *v.t.* duplicar.
gemination, *s.* duplicación, repetición.
Gemini [ˈdʒemini], *s.* (*astr.*) Géminis.
gemma [dʒemə], *s.* (*bot.*) botón, yema.
gemmate [ˈdʒemeit], *a.* que tiene yemas o botones.
gemmation, *s.* (*zool.*, *bot.*) gemación; vernación.
gemmeous [ˈdʒeməs], *a.* que se asemeja a una piedra preciosa.
gemmule [ˈdʒemjuːl], *s.* (*bot.*) botoncillo, botón pequeño.
gemsbok [ˈgemzbɔk], *s.* antílope grande del Africa del Sur.
gender [ˈdʒendəɹ], *s.* (*gram.*) género; sexo. — *v.t.* engendrar; producir, causar.
genealogical [dʒiːniəˈlɔdʒikəl], *a.* genealógico.
genealogist [dʒiːniˈælədʒist], *s.* genealogista, *m.f.*
genealogy [dʒiːniˈælədʒi], *s.* genealogía.
generable, *a.* generable.
general [ˈdʒenərəl], *a.* general, indeterminado, extensivo; corriente, usual, común; público, universal. — *s.* (*mil.*) general; generala, toque de tambor; generalidad, mayor parte; *in general*, en general, por lo común.
generalissimo [dʒenərəˈlisimou], *s.* generalísimo.
generality [dʒenəˈræliti], **generalty,** *s.* generalidad.
generalization [dʒenərəlaiˈzeiʃən], *s.* generalización.
generalize, *v.t.* generalizar.
generalness, *s.* extensión, frecuencia.
generalship [ˈdʒenərəlʃip], *s.* generalato; dirección, jefatura.
generant [ˈdʒenərənt], *a.* generativo. — *s.* generante, principio generativo.
generate [ˈdʒenəreit], *v.t.* engendrar, procrear, propagar; causar, ocasionar, producir; (*mat.*, *mec.*) generar.
generation [dʒenəˈreiʃən], *s.* generación, procreación, reproducción, engendramiento; familia, linaje, progenie, *f.*, prole, *f.*; siglo, edad; (*mat.*, *fís.*) generación.
generative, *a.* generativo, prolífico, fecundo.

generator, s. padre, engendrador, procreador; (*elec.*) generador; dínamo.

generatrix, s. madre, *f.*; (*mat.*) generatriz, *f.*; (*elec.*) dínamo.

generic [dʒeʹnerik], **generical,** a. genérico.

generosity [dʒenəʹrositi], s. generosidad, liberalidad, largueza, bizarría.

generous, a. generoso, liberal, desprendido, dadivoso; amplio, holgado; noble, franco, abierto, magnánimo; estimulante, vigoroso.

generousness [ʹdʒenərəsnes], s. generosidad, nobleza, magnanimidad, bizarría.

genesis [ʹdʒenesis], s. génesis, origen, creación, principio; Génesis.

genet [ʹdʒenet], s. jineta; jaca.

genetic, a. genesiaco, genésico.

genetics [dʒeʹnetiks], s. genética.

geneva [dʒəʹniːvə], s. ginebra (bebida).

Genevan, s., a. ginebrino, ginebrés; calvinista, *m.f.*

genial [ʹdʒiːniəl], a. genial, cordial, afable, bondadoso; nupcial, generativo; confortante.

geniality [dʒiːniʹæliti], s. afabilidad, cordialidad.

geniculate [dʒeʹnikjuːleit], **geniculated,** a. articulado, doblado; (*bot.*) arrodillado, nudoso.

geniculation, s. genuflexión; (*bot.*) articulación, nudosidad.

genii [ʹdʒiːniai], s.pl. genios.

genista [dʒeʹnistə], s. retama.

genital [ʹdʒenitəl], a. genital. — s.pl. genitales.

genitive [ʹdʒenitiv], s., a. (*gram.*) genitivo.

genitor [ʹdʒenitəɹ], s. padre.

genius [ʹdʒiːniəs], s. (*pl.* **genii**) genio (fuerza); (*pl.* **geniuses**), genio (persona), talento, ingenio.

Genoese [dʒenouʹiːz], s., a. genovés.

genteel [dʒenʹtiːl], a. urbano, cortés, señoril, caballeroso, bien criado; apuesto, gentil, elegante, lindo; formal.

genteelness, s. gentileza, urbanidad, dulzura; formalidad.

gentian [ʹdʒenʃən], s. genciana.

gentianella, s. especie de azul.

Gentile [ʹdʒentail], s., a. gentil, gentílico, pagano; (*gram.*) gentilicio.

gentilism [ʹdʒentilizm], s. gentilismo, gentilidad.

gentilitious, a. gentilicio.

gentility [dʒenʹtiliti], s. gentilidad, gentilismo, nobleza, buen nacimiento, gentileza, donosura, garbo, donaire, gracia.

gentle [dʒentl], a. halcón adiestrado; gusano usado como ceho para pescar. — a. suave, blando, apacible, manso, dócil, dulce, benévolo, moderado, benigno, tranquilo; bien nacido.

gentlefolk, s. gente bien nacida.

gentleman [ʹdʒentlmən], s.m. caballero, señor; *gentleman-like,* señoril, caballeroso; *gentleman farmer,* hacendado agricultor; *independent gentleman,* hacendado, rentista, *m.*

gentlemanliness, gentlemanship, s. caballerosidad, porte de caballero, hidalguía.

gentlemanly, a. caballeroso, señoril, galante, urbano, civil; hidalgo.

gentleness, s. dulzura, suavidad, docilidad, blandura, urbanidad, mansedumbre, caballerosidad, nobleza; delicadeza.

gentlewoman, s.f. señora, dama; dama de honor.

Gentoo [dʒenʹtuː], s. indio oriental.

gentry [ʹdʒentri], s. clase media; gente, *f.* (*en sentido irónico*); *light-fingered gentry,* rateros, carteristas, *m.pl.*, descuideros.

genuflection [dʒenjuːʹflekʃən], s. genuflexión.

genuine [ʹdʒenjuːin], a. genuino, verdadero, sin falsedad, real, legítimo, auténtico, propio, sincero, no afectado, puro; (*zool.*) típico.

genuineness, s. pureza, autenticidad, legitimidad.

genus [ʹdʒiːnəs, ʹdʒenəs], s. género.

geocentric [dʒiːouʹsentrik], a. geocéntrico.

geode [ʹdʒiːoud], s. geoda, drusa.

geodesic, geodesical, a. geodésico.

geodesy [dʒiːʹɔdesi], s. geodesia, topografía.

geodetic, geodetical, a. geodésico.

geogenic [dʒiːouʹdʒenik], a. geogénico, geogónico.

geognosy, s. geognosia.

geographer [dʒiːʹɔgrəfəɹ], s. geógrafo.

geographic [dʒiːouʹgræfik], **geographical,** a. geográfico.

geography [dʒiːʹɔgrəfi], s. geografía.

geologic [dʒiːouʹlɔdʒik], **geological,** a. geológico.

geologist [dʒiːʹɔlədʒist], s. geólogo.

geologize [dʒiːʹɔlədʒaiz], v.i. estudiar la geología.

geology [dʒiːʹɔlɔdʒi], s. geología.

geomancy [ʹdʒiːoumænsi], s. geomancia.

geometer [dʒiːʹɔmetəɹ], s. geómetra, *m.*

geometric [dʒiːouʹmetrik], **geometrical,** a. geométrico, geometral.

geometrician [dʒiːɔmeʹtriʃən], s. geómetra, *m.f.*

geometridae, s.pl. geometrinos.

geometrize, v.i. geometrizar.

geometry [dʒiːʹɔmetri], s. geometría.

geomorphy, s. geomorfía.

geonomic, a. geonómico.

geonomy [dʒiːʹɔnəmi], s. geonomía.

geophagous, a. geófago.

geophysics [dʒiːouʹfiziks], s. geofísica.

geoponic, geoponical, a. geopónico.

geoponics, s. geopónica, agricultura; economía rural.

georama, s. georama, *m.*, globo geográfico.

george [dʒɔːɹdʒ], s. placa de la orden de la Jarretera; (*sast.*) cuello; (*mar.*) garganta de polea; antigua peluca; figura que representa a San Jorge.

Georgian [ʹdʒɔːɹdʒən], s., a. georgiano.

georgic, georgical, a. geórgico.

geoscopy [dʒiːʹɔskəpi], s. geoscopia.

geranium [dʒeʹreiniəm], s. geranio.

gerent [ʹdʒerənt], s. director, gerente.

gerfalcon [ʹdʒɔːɹfælkən], s. (*orn.*) gerifalte.

germ [dʒəːɹm], s. germen; (*bot.*) brote, yema, simiente, *f.*, botón, ovario, embrión; (*biol.*) embrión; origen, principio, rudimento; microbio.

german, a. pariente; *cousin german,* primo hermano, primo carnal.

German [ʹdʒəːɹmən], s., a. alemán; germánico, tudesco; (idioma) alemán; *German silver,* alpaca, metal blanco, plata alemana; *German tinder,* yesca; *German measles,* rubéola.

germander [dʒəːɹʹmændəɹ], s. pinillo, maro.

germane [dʒəːɹʹmein], a. relativo, aliado, pariente.

Germanic [dʒəːɹʹmænik], a. germánico, alemanisco.

Germanism, s. germanismo.
germanity, s. hermandad.
germanium [dʒəːˈmeiniəm], s. germanio.
germicidal [dʒəːˈmiˈsaidəl], a.; **germicide,** s. germicida, m.
germiculture, s. cultivo de bacteria.
germinal [ˈdʒəːˌminəl], **germinative,** a. seminal, semental.
germinate [ˈdʒəːˌmineit], v.i. brotar, germinar; desarrollarse. — v.t. producir.
germination, s. germinación.
germon [ˈdʒəːˌmon], s. atún de larga aleta.
gerontic [dʒeˈrɔntik], a. senil, perteneciente a la vejez.
gerrymander [dʒeriˈmændəɹ], v.t. (fam.) manipular el censo electoral, hacer pucheros electorales.
gerund [ˈdʒerʌnd], s. (gram.) gerundio.
gerundive, s. (gram.) gerundio adjetivado.
gesso [ˈdʒesou], s. yeso mate.
gest [dʒest], **geste,** s. (ant.) acto, hecho; narración de aventuras, romance.
gestation [dʒesˈteiʃən], s. gestación, preñez, preñado; embarazo.
gestatory, a. gestatorio.
gesticulate [dʒesˈtikjuːleit], v.i. gesticular, accionar, hacer gestos, hacer ademanes. — v.t. imitar, remedar.
gesticulation, s. gesticulación.
gesticulator, s. gestero, el que acciona o hace gestos.
gesticulatory, a. gesticular.
gesture [ˈdʒestʃəɹ], s. gesto, acción, signo, ademán, seña, mohín. — v.i. accionar; gesticular; hacer gestos.
get [get], v.t. (pret. **got**; p.p. **got, gotten**) recibir, ganar, granjear, adquirir, conseguir, alcanzar, obtener, reportar, llevar (premio, ventaja, etc.), traer; hacer ser, hacer que, mandar, disponer; procrear, engendrar; aprender de memoria; inducir, persuadir, animar, influir, incitar, lograr, procurar; ir a buscar; (fam.) poseer, tener, estar obligado, haber de ser; to have got to, tener que; to have got, (fam.) tener, poseer; get you gone! ¡váyase Vd.! — v.i. alcanzar o ganar poco a poco; ponerse, volverse, hallarse, estar; llegar; meterse, introducirse; to get better, mejorar de salud; to get home, llegar a casa o a la meta; to get about, divulgarse, hacerse público; levantarse (un convaleciente); to get at, ir a, llegar; descubrir, averiguar; atacar; to get warm, hacer más calor o tener más calor; to get along, hacer andar, adelantar(se), seguir; to get a husband (or wife), casarse; to get away, sacar, quitar, escaparse, huirse; you can't get away from that, (fam.) no hay que darle vueltas; no hay escape; to get back, recobrar, volver, regresar; to get behind, penetrar, quedarse atrás, perder terreno; to get clear, salir bien (de un apuro, etc.); to get dark, ponerse oscuro; to get down, bajar, apearse; to get forward, o on, adelantarse; to get in, entrar, alcanzar, hacer entrar, introducir(se); to get off, deshacerse de, despachar, escapar, salir; (vulg.) casarse; to get on, seguir, suceder, meter, acertar, montar a caballo, estar bien, medrar; to get out, v.t. quitar. — v.i. salir, bajar, apearse; to get out of the way, apartase a un lado; to get out of order, descomponerse; to get over, vencer, sobrepujar; to get over an illness, convalecer, reponerse; to get ready, preparar, aparejarse; to get rid of, deshacerse de; to get a start, empezar, adelantar; to get through, pasar por, atravesar; to get up, subir, levantarse, preparar; (fam.) aprender de memoria; to get well again, restablecerse; to get a woman with child, poner encinta a una mujer; to get wind of, (fam.) recibir (un informe) por casualidad; get out of it! ¡anda a pasear! ¡quítate de ahí! get at it! o get to work at it! ¡manos a la obra!

get, s. engendramiento, engendro, acto de engendrar; casta, progenie, f.; producto.
getter, s. engendrador, procreador; el que procura, adquiere o consigue algo.
getting, s. adquisición, ganancia; engendramiento.
geum [ˈdʒiːəm], s. género de plantas rosáceas que comprende la Gariofilea.
gewgaw [ˈgjuːgɔ:], s. chuchería, brinquillo, juguete de niños, miriñaque, friolera.
geyser [ˈgeizəɹ, ˈgiːzəɹ], s. geiser, ojo de agua.
ghastliness [ˈgɑːstlinis], s. palidez.
ghastly [ˈgɑːstli], a. lívido, cadavérico; horrible, espantoso; lúgubre.
ghee [giː], s. aceite de manteca clarificada.
gherkin [ˈgəːˌkin], s. pepinillo, cohombrillo; encurtido.
Ghibelline [ˈgibeˈliːn], s. gibelino.
ghost [goust], s. aparecido, sombra, espectro, duende, fantasma, m.; alma, espíritu; ánima en pena; (foto., ópt.) imagen falsa o secundaria; mancha; imagen, f., traza leve; the Holy Ghost, el Espíritu Santo; to give up the ghost, entregar el alma a Dios, fallecer; to have not the ghost of a suspicion, no tener la menor sospecha; there's not the ghost of a doubt, no cabe la menor duda.
ghost-like, a. cadavérico, seco; parecido a un espectro.
ghostliness, s. espiritualidad.
ghostly [ˈgoustli], a. espiritual; bueno, santo; espectral; misterioso.
ghoul [guːl], s. vampiro; demonio.
ghurry [ˈgʌri], s. clepsidra; reloj de agua; hora india.
giant [ˈdʒaiənt], s. gigante; coloso; giant powder, especie de dinamita. — a. gigantesco, colosal.
giantess, s.f. giganta.
giant-like, a. giganteo, gigantesco.
giaour [dʒauɹ], s. infiel; nombre que los musulmanes dan a los cristianos.
gib, jib [dʒib], s. chaleta, chaveta, cuña, contraclavija; aguilón, brazo de grúa. — v.t. acunar, asegurar con chaveta. — v.i. rebelarse el caballo, destrizar.
gib, v.t. destripar; castrar. — s. gato, particularmente el gato castrado; cárcel, f., prisión.
gibber [ˈdʒibəɹ], v.i. farfullar, hablar en jerga.
gibberish, s. jerigonza, jerga, habladuría incoherente, farfulla. — a. falto de sentido.
gibbet [ˈdʒibit], s. horca, patíbulo; muerte en el patíbulo. — v.t. ahorcar, colgar en la horca, exponer en la horca.
gibbon [ˈgibən], s. (zool.) gibón.
gibbosity, s. giba, jiba, corcova.
gibbous [ˈgibəs], a. convexo, giboso, jiboso, jibado, corcovado, encorvado, jorobado.
gibbousness, s. convexidad, corvadura.
gib-cat [ˈgibkæt], s. gato castrado.
gibe [dʒaib], v.t. escarnecer, burlar, mofar,

burlarse de, mofarse de, ridiculizar. — *v.i.* burlarse, chunguearse, hacer mofa, hacer burla. — *s.* escarnio, burla, mofa; chufleta.
giber, *s.* escarnecedor, mofador.
gibingly, *adv.* con burla, de burlas, con desprecio, con desdén.
giblets ['dʒiblits], *s.pl.* menudillos de ave; (*fig.*) andrajos, guiñapos.
gibus ['dʒaibəs], *s.* clac (sombrero).
giddiness ['gidinis], *s.* vértigo, vahido, vaivén, desvanecimiento; devaneo, desvarío; veleidad, instabilidad, inconstancia, atolondramiento, aturdimiento.
giddy ['gidi], *a.* vertiginoso; voluble, voltario, inconstante, casquivano, ligero, aturdido, necio, bobo, pelele, atolondrado, veleidoso.
giddy-head, giddy-pate, *s.* persona frívola.
giddy-headed, *a.* ligero de cascos, frívolo, inconstante, voluble; imprudente.
gift ['gift], *s.* donación; dádiva, donativo; regalo, gracia, merced, presente, favor, obsequio, oblación, estrena, ofrenda; prenda, don, dote; talento natural; *deed of gift,* instrumento (o contrato) de donación; *Christmas* (o *New Year's*) *gift,* aguinaldo; *to have the gift of the gab,* (*fam.*) tener mucha lengua; *never look a gift horse in the mouth,* (*prov.*) a caballo regalado no hay que mirarle el diente. — *v.t.* dotar, agraciar, adornar con dotes.
gifted, *a.* dotado, talentoso, agraciado, hábil.
giftedness, *s.* estado de poseer grandes talentos.
gig [gig], *s.* birlocho, calesa, calesín, quitrín; (*mar.*) esquife, bote, falúa, lancha; percha, máquina para tundir paño; trompo, peonza, perinola; arpón; calaverada; chacota.
gigantic, *a.* giganteo, gigantesco, enorme, colosal.
giggle ['gigəl], *v.i.* reírse sin motivo; reírse por nada, reírse convulsivamente. — *s.* risa ahogada, risa falsa, convulsiva; risa sin motivo.
giggler, *s.* persona reidora, persona que ríe sin motivo.
giglet, *s.* (*ant.*) muchacha retozona o juguetona.
gig-mill, *s.* máquina de perchar, percha.
gigolo ['dʒigolou], *s.* bailarín profesional en una sala de baile.
gigot, *s.* pierna de carnero; (*mar.*) áurica (vela).
Gilbertian [gil'bəːtiən], *a.* absurdo, al revés, de abajo arriba; paradójico.
gild [gild], *v.t.* (*pret. y p.p.* **gilded** o **gilt**), dorar, cubrir de oro; iluminar; dar brillo o lustre, dar un barniz superficial y aparente.
gilder, *s.* dorador; charolista, *m.*
gilding, *s.* doradura; dorado.
gilia ['dʒiliə], *s.* (*bot.*) gilia; planta americana de la familia de las polemoniáceas.
gill [dʒil], *s.* medida de líquidos (¼ pinta); (*ant.*) *gill-flirt,* pelandusca, moza lasciva; (*bot.*) hiedra terrestre.
gill [gil], *s.* (*ict.*) agalla, branquia; barranco; rambla; (*fam.*) papada.
gillaroo [gila'ruː], *s.* variedad irlandesa de la trucha común.
gillie ['gili], *s.* (en las montañas de Escocia) criado, mozo, sirviente.
gilliflower ['dʒiliflauɹ], **gillyflower,** *s.* (*bot.*) alhelí.
gilt [gilt], *a.* dorado, áureo. — *pret. y p.p.* [GILD]. — *s.* dorado; oro en hojuelas; falso brillo; oropel.

gilthead, *s.* (*ict.*) dorada; salema; espátula.
gimbals ['dʒimbəlz], *s.pl.* (*mar.*) balancines de la brújula.
gimcrack ['dʒimkræk], *a.* baratillo, de poco valor. — *s.* chuchería.
gimlet ['gimlət], *s.* barrena pequeña.
gimmal ['dʒiməl], *s.pl.* par o serie de eslabones.
gimp [gimp], *v.* **jimp.**
gin [dʒin], *s.* almarrá; desmotadora de algodón; cabria, cabrestante portátil; molinete, husillo; bomba movida por un molino de viento; armadijo, trampa; martinete; ginebra; *gin-palace,* taberna vistosa; *gin-shop,* (*fam.*) taberna; *gin fizz,* (*fam.*) bebida compuesta de ginebra y gaseosa. — *v.t.* entrampar, coger con una trampa; alijar, desmotar el algodón.
ginger ['dʒindʒəɹ], *s.* (*bot.*) jengibre; *ginger-ale,* o *ginger beer,* cerveza de jengibre.
ginger-bread, *s.* pan o galletita de jengibre.
gingerly, *a.* cauteloso, escrupuloso, quisquilloso. — *adv.* cuidadosamente, cautelosamente.
gingerness, *s.* escrupulosidad.
ginger-snap, *s.* galletita de jengibre.
gingham ['giŋəm], *s.* carranclán, guinga.
gingili ['dʒindʒili], *s.* sésamo.
gingival ['dʒindʒivəl], *a.* perteneciente a las encías.
ginseng [dʒin'seŋ], *s.* ginseng.
gip [dʒip], *v.t.* destripar los pescados.
gipsy ['dʒipsi], *s.* gitano. — (*ant.*) muchacha engañadora; *gipsy-winch,* grúa de soporte lateral. — *a.* gitanesco, picarón; (*ant.*) egipcio.
gipsyism, *s.* gitanismo, gitanería, vida gitanesca.
giraffe [dʒi'rɑːf], *s.* jirafa; (*astr.*) constelación Camelopardalis.
girandole ['dʒirəndoul], *s.* candelabro; girándula; (*joy.*) pendiente.
girasol ['dʒirəsol], *s.* especie de ópalo.
gird [gəːd], *v.t.* (*pret. y p.p.* **girded** o **girt**) ceñir; cercar, rodear; vestir; investir. — *v.i.* mofarse, burlarse, hacer burla o mofa; *to gird a sword,* ceñir espada. — *s.* escarnio, mofa, burla.
girder, *s.* (*arq.*) viga, jácena, durmiente; persona satírica.
girding, *s.* ceñidor, ceñidura.
girdle ['gəːdəl], *s.* cinto, cinturón, ceñidor, pretina, cincho; faja; cíngulo; cerco, círculo, circunferencia, zona; zodíaco; *pelvic girdle,* cinturón pélvico; *pectoral girdle,* cinturón escapular. — *v.t.* ceñir, cercar, circundar, rodear, atar con cinto; hacer una incisión circular en el tronco de un árbol.
girdle-belt, *s.* ceñidor.
girl [gəːl], *s.f.* muchacha, niña, doncellita; (*fam.*) doncella, criada, moza; (*fam.*) novia, amiga; *best girl,* (*fam.*) la amada.
girlhood, *s.* doncellez; soltería.
girlish, *a.* juvenil, de niña; de muchacha; *girlish prank,* niñada.
girlishly, *adv.* como una niña o muchacha.
Girondist [dʒi'rondist], *s., a.* girondino.
girt [gəːt], *a.* (*mar.*) amarrado de modo a contrarrestar el viento o marea; (*ent.*) braceado. — *pret.* [GIRD].
girth [gəːθ], *s.* cincha; faja, cinto; periferia. — *v.t.* ceñir, cinchar.
girth-straps, *s.pl.* correas de cincha.

girt-line, s. (*mar.*) andarivel.

gist [dʒist], s. substancia; el grano de un asunto, clave, f., punto capital.

give [giv], v.t. (*pret.* **gave;** p.p. **given**) dar, donar; dejar, ceder, traspasar; confiar, aplicar, remitir, entregar; dar permiso o licencia; conceder, otorgar, ofrecer, presentar como producto o resultado; conferir; recompensar, premiar, pagar; causar, ser el autor u ocasión de, ocasionar; dedicar, consagrar; renunciar, sacrificar, desprenderse de; empeñar (la palabra); divulgar; presumir, suponer; pronunciar; mostrar, demostrar, exhibir, explicar, enseñar; autorizar, rendirse (con *up*). — v.i. dar libremente, ser dadivoso; aflojarse, ablandarse; cejar, ceder, recular; dar de sí; dar, mirar hacia una parte, tener vistas (con *on* o *upon*); *to give away,* dar libremente, deshacerse de, regalar, transferir, enajenar; (*vulg.*) divulgar por descuido o tontería; (*fam.*) traicionar; dar en matrimonio; *to give back,* restituir; *to give in,* ceder, recular, retirarse; *to give it to some-one,* (*fam.*) dar de palos, reprender severamente; *to give off,* emitir; *to give over,* entregar, (*fam.*) cesar, dejar de hacer algo, parar, descontinuar, abandonar; detenerse, desistir; darse o entregarse a vicio, pasión o voluntad ajena; *to give out,* emitir, proclamar, divulgar; darse por vencido, estar agotado; *to give up,* entregar, renunciar, abandonar, desanimarse; *to give up for lost,* dar por perdido; *give it up,* he abandonado la esperanza *o* me doy por vencido; *to give a guess,* (*fam.*) adivinar; *to give ground,* retroceder, retirarse; *to give heed,* reparar, advertir; *to give birth to,* dar a luz; *to give credit,* dar crédito, dar fe; *to give ear,* escuchar; *to give a portion,* dotar, entregar una cuota; *to give leave,* dar permiso o licencia; *to give the lie,* desmentir; *to give oneself to,* o *give one's mind to,* aplicarse a; *to give place,* hacer lugar; *to give the slip,* sustraerse, huirse; *to give trouble,* incomodar; *to give warning,* advertir; *to give way,* ceder, flaquear, hundirse (la tierra); (*mar.*) empezar a remar, remar con ritmo creciente; *to give one's greetings* (o *respects*) *to,* saludar; *to give no quarter,* no dejar soldado con vida; no dar cuartel; *silence gives consent,* quien calla, otorga.

given, a. dado; inclinado, adicto; citado, expresado; (*mat.*) dado, conocido, concedido. — p.p. [GIVE].

giver, s. donador, donante, dador, distribuyente.

gizzard [ˈgizəd], s. molleja de ave; *to fret one's gizzard,* romperse los cascos, devanarse los sesos.

glabrous [ˈglæbrəs], a. liso, calvo, llano, sin pelo.

glacial [ˈgleiʃəl], a. glacial, helado.

glaciate [ˈgleisieit], v.t. (*geol.*) cubrir con hielo glacial; (*artes y oficios*) producir un efecto parecido al de hielo. — v.i. helarse.

glaciation, s. helamiento, congelación.

glacier [ˈglæsiə], s. ventisquero, glaciar.

glacis [ˈglæsiː], s. (*fort.*) glacis.

glad [glæd], a. alegre, gozoso, contento; agradecido; agradable; *to be glad,* celebrar, alegrarse.

glad, gladden, (*poét.*) v.t. alegrar, regocijar.

gladder, s. regocijador.

glade [gleid], s. claro, raso, parte de un bosque sin árboles.

gladiator [ˈglædieitə], s. gladiador, gladiator.

gladiatorial, gladiatory, a. gladiatorio.

gladiole [ˈglædioul], **gladiolus,** s. gladio.

gladiolus, s. espadaña, gladiolo.

gladly [ˈglædli], adv. alegremente; de buena gana, con mucho gusto, con placer.

gladness, s. alegría, gozo, placer, buen humor, regocijo.

gladsome, a. alegre, contento.

gladsomeness, s. alegría, buen humor, regocijo; gracia, donaire.

Gladstone [ˈglædstən], s. maleta o portamantas ligero.

glair [glɛə], s. clara de huevo empleada en la encuadernación y dorado; cualquier substancia viscosa o resbaladiza. — v.t. untar con clara de huevo.

glairy, a. viscoso, pegajoso.

glamour [ˈglæmə], s. encanto, hechizo; embeleso, artificialidad, fascinación; brujería.

glance [glɑːns], s. mirada, vista, vistazo, ojeada; pensamiento repentino y pasajero; intuito, relámpago, fulgor; vislumbre; desviación (por choque); (*min.*) mineral lustroso; *at the first glance,* a la simple vista, a primera vista; *copper glance,* cobre sulfurado vidrioso; *glance coal,* antracita. — v.t. mirar de soslayo; despedir o disparar oblicuamente. — v.i. ojear, mirar de prisa; lanzar miradas; dar un vistazo, dar una ojeada; tocar o herir oblicuamente; rebotar, divergir, desviar; centellear, brillar, fulgurar; *to glance over a book,* hojear un libro; *to glance off,* desviarse (al chocar).

glancing [ˈglɑːnsiŋ], a. indirecto, oblicuo, de paso.

gland [glænd], s. (*anat., bot.*) glándula; bellota; (*mec.*) collarín, cuello.

glandered, glanderous, a. muermoso.

glanders, s. (*vet.*) muermo.

glandiferous [glænˈdifərəs], a. glandífero.

glandiform, a. glandiforme, abellotado.

glandular [ˈglændjulə], **glandulous,** a. glanduloso, glandular, relativo a las glándulas.

glandule [ˈglændjuːl], s. glandulilla.

glandulosity, s. calidad de glanduloso; conjunto de glándulas.

glans, s. (*pl.* **glandes**) bellota; (*anat.*) balano.

glare [glɛə], v.i. relumbrar, brillar, ser muy brillante; echar fuego por los ojos; echar miradas de indignación; tener colores chillones. — v.t. deslumbrar. — s. deslumbramiento, viso, brillo; mirada feroz y penetrante; superficie lisa y vidriosa. — a. liso y resbaladizo.

glaring, a. brillante, deslumbrante, deslumbrador; evidente, notorio; de mirada penetrante. — p.a. [GLARE].

glaringly, adv. evidentemente, notoriamente.

glass [glɑːs], s. vidrio; cualquier objeto hecho de vidrio; vaso, copa; cristal de ventana; espejo; lente; termómetro o barómetro; reloj de arena; contenido de un vaso o copa. — pl. **glasses,** anteojos; (*mar.*) ampolletas; espejuelos; gafas, lentes, quevedos; *ground glass,* vidrio deslustrado o esmerilado; *cut glass,* cristal tallado; *burning glass,* espejo ustorio; *magnifying glass,* vidrio de aumento; *looking glass,* espejo; *spy-glass,* catalejo; *cupping glass,* ventosa.

glass-blower, s. vidriero.

glassful, s. vaso; contenido de un vaso.

glass-house, s. vidriería; invernadero.

glassiness, s. calidad de vidrioso; lisura.

glasslike, a. liso; transparente como el vidrio.

glass-maker, glassman, s. vidriero.

glass-shop, s. vidriería.

glassware, s. cristalería, vajilla de cristal.

glasswork, s. fábrica de vidrio o cristales; vidriería, cristalería.

glasswort, s. sosa, barrilla, matojo, almarjo.

glassy, a. vítreo, vidrioso, cristalino.

glaucoma [glɔ:'koumə], s. glaucoma.

glaucous ['glɔ:kəs], a. verdemar; (bot.) cubierto de una pelusa azulada, como las uvas.

glaucus, s. (zool.) glauco.

glave [gleiv], **glaive,** s. arma parecida a la alabarda; espada ancha.

glaze [gleiz], v.t. vidriar; poner vidrios a una ventana; dar una apariencia vidriosa; satinar, glasear; barnizar, embarnizar; apomazar. — s. superficie lisa y lustrosa, substancia que da lustre; barniz, lustre.

glazed, a. vidriado; glaseado; satinado. — p.p. [GLAZE].

glazier ['gleiʒəɹ], s. vidriero.

glazing, s. vidriado; satinado; barnizado; superficie lustrosa; lustre, barniz; cristalería, vidriería, oficio del vidriero.

gleam [gli:m], s. relámpago, destello, resplandor, rayo, fulgor, viso, brillo, centelleo. — v.i. relampaguear, centellear, brillar, lucir, fulgurar.

gleaming, a. reluciente, resplandeciente.

glean [gli:n], v.t. espigar, respigar, coger las espigas; juntar, recoger, rebuscar, arrebañar. — s. moraga; rebusco, rebusca.

gleaner, s. espigador, espigadera; rebuscador, respigador, recogedor, arrebanador.

gleaning, s. rebusco, rebusca; moraga, arrebanadura.

glebe [gli:b], s. gleba, terrón, césped; (min.) extensión de tierra que contiene mineral; (Ingl.) tierras beneficiales de un cura.

glebous, a. gleboso.

glede [gli:d], s. (orn.) milano.

glee [gli:], s. alegría, júbilo, gozo; (mús.) canción para voces solas.

gleeful, gleesome, a. alegre, gozoso, jubiloso, jovial.

gleeman, s. (ant.) cantor ambulante.

gleet [gli:t], s. blenorragia.

gleety, a. blenorrágico.

glen [glen], s. cañada, hoyada, hocino.

glene ['gli:ni:], s. (anat.) globo del ojo; fosa.

glengarry [glen'gæri], s. gorro escocés de lana.

glenoid, a. glenoideo.

gliadin ['glaiədin], **gliadine,** s. gluten.

glib [glib], a. voluble, suelto de lengua, corriente.

glibness, s. volubilidad, desate, facundia.

glide [glaid], v.t. resbalar, deslizarse, moverse o correr suavemente, escurrirse; (aer.) planear. — s. deslizamiento, escurrimiento.; (aer.) planeo.

glider ['glaidəɹ], s. (aer.) planeador.

gliding, s. vuelo a vela.

gliff, s. ojeada rápida; susto, espanto.

glim [glim], s. (fam.) pequeña luz, candela.

glimmer ['gliməɹ], s. vislumbre, resplandor tenue; (min.) mica; viso, luz débil. — v.i. vislumbrarse, rielar, brillar débilmente, alborear, alumbrar.

glimmering, a. vacilante, luciente, naciente. — s. vislumbre, viso, luz incierta, débil resplandor.

glimpse [glimps], s. ojeada, vistazo; vislumbre; reflejo; apariencia ligera. — v.t. ver con una ojeada, mirar rápidamente. — v.i. ojear, mirar rápidamente, dar un vistazo; lucir o brillar por un momento.

glint [glint], v.t. reflejar, relucir. — v.i. lucir o brillar a intervalos; destellar; saltar de rechazo.

glissade [gli'sɑ:d, gli'seid], s. (alpinismo) resbalada.

glisten ['glisən], v.i. relucir, brillar, relumbrar, rielar, resplandecer (comúnmente por reflexión).

glister ['glistəɹ], v.i. lucir, relucir, brillar, resplandecer, centellear, chispear.

glistering, a. brillante, lustroso.

glitter ['glitəɹ], v.i. relucir, resplandecer; centellear, rutilar, lucir, chispear, brillar.

glitter, glittering, s. lustre, esplendor, brillo, resplandor; oropel; all is not gold that glitters, (prov.) no es oro todo lo que reluce o todo lo blanco no es harina.

glittering, a. lustroso, reluciente, brillante, resplandeciente.

gloam [gloum], v.t., v.i. obscurecer, obscurecerse, anochecer.

gloaming, s. crepúsculo vespertino, anochecida, el anochecer.

gloat [glout], v.i. deleitarse (en el daño ajeno), mirar con satisfacción maliciosa, manifestar satisfacción maligna.

globate ['gloubeit], **globated,** a. esférico, globular, en forma de globo.

globe [gloub], s. esfera, bola, globo; mundo, pecera globular; bombilla de una lámpara.

globe-fish, s. orbe.

globigerina [gloubidʒə'rainə], s. genio de foraminíferos protozoarios.

globose ['globouz], a. globoso, redondo, esférico.

globosity, s. esfericidad, redondez.

globular ['globju:ləɹ], a. esférico, globular.

globule, s. glóbulo, globulillo.

globulose, globulous, a. globuloso.

glomerate ['glɔmərət], v.t. aglomerar, conglomerar, ovillar, formar una bola. — a. aglomerado, conglomerado.

glomeration, s. conglobación.

glomerule ['glɔməru:l], s. glomérula.

gloom [glu:m], s. obscuridad, tenebrosidad, tinieblas, lobreguez; tristeza, melancolía. — v.i. encapotarse, obscurecerse; entristecerse; lucir confusa o tenuemente. — v.t. encapotar, obscurecer, llenar de obscuridad.

gloominess, s. obscuridad, lobreguez, tenebrosidad; melancolía, tristeza, abatimiento; nublado; adustez.

gloomy, a. tenebroso, lóbrego, obscuro, lúgubre, sombrío; triste, melancólico, tétrico; desalentado, abatido, nublado.

glorification [glɔ:rifi'keiʃən], s. glorificación, apoteosis, f.; (fam.) celebración, fiesta.

glorify ['glɔ:rifai], v.t. glorificar, alabar, celebrar, honrar, exaltar.

gloriole ['glɔ:rioul], s. aureola.

glorious ['glɔ:riəs], a. glorioso, magnífico, ilustre.

gloriousness, s. gloria, esplendor.

glory ['glɔ:ri], s. gloria, alabanza, celebridad,

renombre, honra, fama; magnificencia, esplendor; cielo, paraíso, gloria; lustre, brillantez, resplandor; exaltación, adoración; aureola; lauro; *to be at the height of one's glory,* estar uno en sus glorias. — *v.i.* gloriarse, preciarse, jactarse, llenarse de orgullo.

gloss [glɔs], *s.* lustre, brillo, viso; disculpa, paliativo; apariencia superficial; oropel; barniz; comentario, glosa, escolio. — *v.t.* pulir, pulimentar, barnizar, glasear, satinar, lustrar; paliar, colorear. — *v.t., v.i.* glosar, postillar, comentar, notar, interpretar, escoliar.

glossa ['glɔsə], *s.* (*anat.*) lengua.

glossarial [glɔs'ɛəriəl], *a.* de glosa.

glossarist, *s.* glosador, comentador.

glossary ['glɔsəri], *s.* glosario, nomenclador, vocabulario.

glossiness, *s.* pulimento, lustre, apariencia superficil.

glossist, *s.* glosador, comentador, pulidor.

glossographer, *s.* glosador, glosógrafo, comentador.

glossography, *s.* arte de glosar *o* de hacer glosarios; (*anat.*) descripción de la lengua.

glossy ['glɔsi], *a.* lustroso, glaseado, brillante, satinado; especioso, superficial.

glottis ['glɔtis], *s.* glotis.

glove [glʌv], *s.* guante. — *pl.* **gloves**, guantes para el pugilato; *to fit like a glove,* venirle a uno de molde; *to be hand in glove,* ser inseparables, ser uña y carne; *to handle without gloves,* tratar severamente. — *v.t.* enguantar, cubrir como con guante. — *v.i.* enguantarse.

glove-fight, *s.* boxeo.

glove-money, *s.* (*Ingl.*) gratificación a los criados; propina.

glover, *s.* guantero.

glove-stretcher, *s.* abridor de guantes.

glow [glou], *v.t.* calentar, encender. — *v.i.* dar luz o calor sin llama; inflamarse, encenderse, arder, abrasarse (hablando de pasiones del ánimo); relucir, brillar, lucir, resplandecer; tener colores vivos. — *s.* calor vivo, encendimiento; vehemencia de una pasión; viveza de color; soflama.

glower, *v.i.* mirar con ceño, poner mala cara, tratar con severidad.

glowing, *a.* resplandeciente, ardiente; encendido, colorado; estuoso; *to speak in glowing terms of,* elogiar.

glowingly, *adv.* de un modo resplandeciente; *to speak glowingly of,* elogiar.

glow-worm, *s.* luciérnaga, cocuyo.

gloxinia [glɔk'ziniə], *s.* flor de la familia de las escrofulariáceas, muy hermosa.

gloze [glouz], *v.i.* paliar, colorear, excusarse. — *s.* lisonja, adulación.

glozing, *s.* paliativo; adulación.

glucin ['glu:sin], **glucina**, *s.* (*quím.*) glucina.

glucinum, *s.* (*quím.*) glucinio.

glucose ['glu:kous], *s.* glucosa.

glue [glu:], *s.* cola, ajicola; liga, visco; gluten; *fish-glue,* colapez. — *v.t.* encolar, pegar, aglutinar, ligar, unir.

glue-pot, *s.* cazo de cola.

gluer, *s.* el que encola.

gluey ['glu:i], **gluish**, *a.* viscoso, pegajoso, glutinoso.

glueyness, *s.* viscosidad, glutinosidad.

gluing ['glu:iŋ], *a.* que encola.

glum [glʌm], *a.* malhumorado, displicente, moroso, triste, abatido.

glumaceous, *a.* glumáceo.

glume [glu:m], *s.* (*bot.*) gluma.

glut [glʌt], *v.t.* hartar, saturar, saciar, atracar; colmar; atarugar, atascar; sobrellenar; *to glut the market,* (*com.*) inundar el mercado. — *v.i.* tragar, devorar, ahitarse, engullir(se). — *s.* hartura, plétora, hartazgo, llenura, superabundancia; (*alb.*) ripio de ladrillo; cuña de madera.

gluteal ['glu:tiəl], *a.* glúteo, nalgar.

gluten ['glu:tən], *s.* gluten.

gluteous ['glu:tiəs], *s.* músculo glúteo.

glutinosity, glutinousness, *s.* glutinosidad, viscosidad.

glutinous ['glu:tinəs], *a.* glutinoso, pegajoso, viscoso, gelatinoso.

glutted ['glʌtəd], *a.* harto, repleto, ahito. — *p.p.* [GLUT].

glutton ['glʌtən], *s.* glotón, tragaldabas, *m.,* tragón, empachado; (*zool.*) carcajú.

gluttonize, *v.i.* glotonear.

gluttonous, *a.* glotón; goloso.

gluttony, *s.* glotonería, gula.

glyceric, *a.* de glicerina.

glycerin ['glisəri:n], **glycerine**, *s.* glicerina.

glycogen ['glaikodʒən], *s.* glicógeno.

glycol ['glaikɔl], *s.* glicol.

glyph [glif], *s.* (*arq.*) glifo; estría.

glyptic ['gliptik], *s.* glíptica.

glyptography, *s.* gliptografía.

gnarl [nɑːl], *v.t.* torcer. — *v.i.* (*ant.*) gruñir. — *s.* nudo (en el árbol o la madera).

gnarled, gnarly, *a.* nudoso, retorcido.

gnash [næʃ], *v.t.* rechinar, crujir (los dientes).

gnat [næt], *s.* mosquito, cínife.

gnathic ['næθik], *a.* perteneciente o relativo a la mandíbula humana.

gnathism, *s.* clasificación de la raza humana según las medidas de la mandíbula.

gnaw [nɔː], *v.t.* roer, comer poco a poco; morder, mordicar; ratonar; corroer; carcomer.

gnawer, *s.* roedor; el que roe o muerde.

gneiss [nais], *s.* gneis.

gnetaceous, *a.* gnetáceo.

gnome [noum], *s.* máxima, aforismo; gnomo, trasgo, enano; (*orn.*) especie de colibrí.

gnomic ['nɔmik], **gnomical**, *a.* sentencioso, gnómico, críptico, oculto.

gnomon ['nomɔn], *s.* gnomon.

gnomonic, gnomonical, *a.* sentencioso, gnómico.

gnomonics, *s.* gnomónica.

gnostic ['nɔstik], *s.* gnóstico.

gnosticism ['nɔstisizm], *s.* gnosticismo.

gnu [nju:], *s.* bucéfalo.

go [gou], *v.t.* (*pret.* **went**; *p.p.* **gone**; *3rd pers. indic. sing.* **goes**) ir, apostar en el juego; interesar, tener participación en, contribuir con, responder por; asentir a, tolerar; *to go halves,* ir a medias; *to go bail,* salir fiador. — *v.i.* ir, irse; estar, ser; marchar(se), partir, moverse, pasar de un sitio a otro; pasear, caminar, andar; salir, escapar, huir; funcionar, trabajar, andar; seguir, proseguir; acudir, dirigirse a, recurrir; venir, convenir, ir, sentar, o caer bien; morirse, estarse muriendo; tender, contribuir, concurrir; valer, ser valido, aceptarse como bueno; venderse, tener venta; (*impers.*) pasar, acaecer, acabarse una cosa; cambiar, mudar de situación, opinión, etc.;

pasar (por); estar preñada, en cinta; debilitarse, decaer; influir; ir en busca de; ser aplicable; tocar a; ser desembolsado, ser gastado; andar (máquina o reloj); (como verbo auxiliar) ir a hacer, intentar, proponer, tener designio de; *how goes it?* (*fam.*) ¿qué tal? *to go about*, dar vueltas, rodear, desviarse, procurar, intentar, andar; (*mar.*) virar de bordo; *to go about one's business*, irse, o meterse en lo que le importa; *to go abroad*, marchar, marcharse, partir, salir de su país, divulgarse una cosa; *to go after*, seguir a alguno; *to go against*, ir en contra de, oponerse a; *to go along*, seguir, continuar, proseguir; *to go along with*, acompañar; *to go astray*, descaminarse, descarriarse, perder el camino; *to go away*, irse, marcharse; *to go away with*, acompañar (a una persona), llevarse (una cosa); *to go back*, retroceder, regresar, retirarse, volverse atrás, desistir, ceder; *to go back on one's word*, faltar a su palabra, desdecirse, retractarse; *to go before*, preceder, adelantarse; ir delante; *to go behind*, seguir, ir detrás de; (*fig.*) engañar; *to go between*, mediar, terciar, interponerse; *to go beyond*, pasar más allá de, exceder, sobrepujar; *to go by*, pasar, dirigirse por, tomar como regla; pasar por alto, pretermitir; escurrirse, escabullirse, pasar sin ser visto; pasar cerca; *to go down*, descender, bajar, ponerse (el sol), tragar(se); hundirse un buque; persuadirse, creer algo; *to go down stream*, ir con la corriente; *to go far*, ir muy lejos; (*fig.*) tener mucha influencia, valer mucho; *to go as far as*, ir hasta, llegar a; *to go for*, ir en busca de, ser reputado por; (*fam.*) declararse partidario de; *to go forth*, salir, aparecer; *to go forward*, proseguir, adelantar; *to go from*, separarse, partirse; *to go hard with*, pasarlo mal; *to go in*, entrar, penetrar; *to go in for*, practicar, favorecer, empezar; *to go into*, entrar, penetrar, participar en, discutir, investigar; *to go it*, (*fam.*) seguir, esforzarse; *to go near*, acercarse a; *to go off*, irse, marcharse, dispararse, pasar, salir (bien o mal); (*fam.*) morirse; *to go on*, pasar, continuar, seguir, adelantarse, atacar, progresar; *to go over*, pasar, atravesar, pasarse a, desertar; *to go out*, salir; apagarse, morirse, extinguirse; *to go out of the way*, desorientarse, apartarse del camino; *to go through*, salir con, llevar a cabo, recorrer completamente, enhilar, ensertar, hender; *go to!* ¡vaya!; *to go under*, llamarse por (tal o cual nombre), pasar por (tal persona); quebrar, quedar vencido; *to go up*, subir; *to go upon*, fundarse en, emprender; *to go with*, acompañar; *to go without*, pasarse sin, estar sin, arreglarse sin; *to go the whole length* o *to go the whole hog*, hacerlo todo, arriesgarlo todo; *to let go one's hold*, soltar la presa; *to be all the go*, (*fam.*) hacer furor, estar en boga. — *s.* (*pl.* goes) energía, empuje; espíritu, vida; giro, marcha de los asuntos; mano (en el juego); (*fam.*) moda, furor, auge; el acto de ir; *it's all the go*, es la moda; *it's my go*, me toca a mí; *to have a go*, probar suerte.

goad [goud], *s.* aguijada, aijada, aguijón, pincho, focino. — *v.t.* aguijar, picar, pinchar, agarrochear, aguijonear; incitar, estimular.

goadsman, *s.* agarrochador, boyero.

goad-stick, *s.* garrocha, rejo; goadspur, acicate.

go-ahead ['gouəhed], *a.* (*fam.*) emprendedor, enérgico, activo; *interj.* ¡adelante!

goal [goul], *s.* meta, término; objeto, fin, motivo.

goat [gout], *s.* cabra, cabrón, chivo, chiva; *he-goat*, o *goat-buck*, cabrón, macho cabrío; *wild-goat*, cabra montés.

goat-beard, *s.* (*bot.*) barba cabruna.

goatee [gou'tiː], *s.* perilla.

goatherd ['gouthəːɹd], *s.* cabrero.

goatish, *a.* cabrerizo; cabruno, chotuno; lascivo.

goatskin, *s.* piel de cabra.

goat's-rue, *s.* (*bot.*) gálega, ruda cabruña.

goat's-thorn, *s.* (*bot.*) tragacanto, alquitira.

goatsucker ['goutsʌkəɹ], *s.* (*orn.*) caprimulga, chotacabras, *f.*

gob [gɔb], *s.* pedazo, trozo; bocado; escombros, escombrera.

gobbet ['gɔbit], *s.* canto de piedra; bocado; pedacito.

gobble ['gɔbəl], *v.t.* engullir, tragar; tragar vorazmente, devorar. — *v.i.* hacer ruido en la garganta como los pavos. — *s.* voz del pavo.

gobbler, *s.* engullidor, glotón, tragón, tragador; (*fam.*) pavo, (*Méx.*) guajolote; (*Cuba*) guanajo.

go-between ['goubətwiːn], *s.* mediador, medianero; alcahuete; entremetido; tercero.

goblet ['gɔblit], *s.* copa.

goblin ['gɔblin], *s.* trasgo, duende, espíritu errante.

go-by ['goubai], *s.* desaire; menosprecio, repulsa; esquinazo.

go-cart, *s.* carretilla, castillejo, andaderas.

God [gɔd], *s.* Dios; deidad; *God-forsaken*, dejado de la mano de Dios; *God forbid*, no quiera Dios; *thank God*, gracias a Dios.

godchild, *s.* ahijado, ahijada.

goddaughter [gɔ'dɔːtəɹ], *s.* ahijada.

goddess, *s.* diosa, deidad, diva.

godfather, *s.* padrino.

God-fearing, *a.* reverente, temeroso de Dios.

Godhead, *s.* deidad, divinidad.

godless, *a.* infiel, impío, ateo.

godlessness, *s.* impiedad, ateísmo.

godlike, *a.* divino, deiforme.

godliness, *s.* piedad, santidad, devoción.

godly, *a.* piadoso, religioso, devoto, justificado.

godmother, *s.* madrina.

godsend, *s.* divina merced; (*fam.*) buena suerte; bendición.

godship, *s.* divinidad.

godson, *s.m.* ahijado.

Godspeed, *s.* bienandanza.

God speed! *interj.* ¡buena suerte! ¡buen viaje!

Godward, *adv.* hacia Dios.

godwit ['gɔdwit], *s.* (*orn.*) francolín.

goer ['gouəɹ], *s.* andadoɹ, paseante, ambulante, vagabundo.

goffer ['gɔfəɹ], *v.t.* rizar, encrespar; estampar cuero. — *s.* rizado.

goggle ['gɔgəl], *v.t.*, *v.i.* torcer o abrir los ojos de una manera afectada. — *s.* torcimiento de los ojos. — *pl.* goggles, anteojos de camino; anteojeras.

goggle-eyed, *a.* de ojos saltones.

goggle-eyes, *s.* ojos saltones.

going ['gouiŋ], *a.*, *ger.* [GO]. — *s.* paso, andar, andadura; ida, marcha, partida; estado del camino; preñado, preñez; *goings and comings*, idas y venidas.

goings-on [gouiŋz'ɔn], *s.pl.* hechos, ocurrencias, sucesos; andanzas.

goitre, goiter ['gɔitəɹ], *s.* papera.

goitred, goitrous, *a.* que tiene papera.

gold [gould], *s.* oro; riqueza, dinero; color de oro; *all is not gold that glitters,* (*prov.*) no es oro todo lo que reluce; *gold foil,* oro batido o en hojas; *gold lace,* galón o encaje de oro.

gold-bearing, *a.* aurífero.

gold-beater, *s.* batihoja, *m.,* batidor de oro.

gold-dust, *s.* polvo de oro; (*bot.*) alisón.

golden, *a.* áureo, de oro; precioso, excelente; de gran valor; lustroso, brillante; de color de oro, rubio, amarillento; feliz; *golden wedding,* bodas de oro; *golden number,* (*astr.*) número áureo; *golden mean,* justo medio.

golden-thistle, *s.* (*bot.*) cardillo.

goldfinch ['gouldfintʃ], *s.* jilguero, cardelina, pintacilgo.

goldfish, *s.* carpa dorada.

gold-size, *s.* barniz de color de oro.

goldsmith, *s.* orífice, orfebre.

goldstone, *s.* venturina.

gold-thread, *s.* hilo de oro.

goldy-locks, *s.* (*bot.*) crisocomo.

golf [gɔlf], *s.* golf.

golf-club, *s.* palo de golf; club de golf.

golliwog ['gɔliwɔg], *s.* muñeca negra de trapo.

gondola ['gɔndoulə], *s.* góndola.

gondolier [gɔndo'liəɹ], *s.* gondolero.

gone [gɔn], *a.* ido, pasado; arruinado, perdido; muerto, fallecido, apagado. — *p.p.* [GO].

gonfalon ['gɔnfələn], **gonfanon,** *s.* confalón, pendón.

gonfalonier, *s.* confalonero.

gong [gɔŋ], *s.* gong, batintín.

goniometer [gɔni'ɔmətəɹ], *s.* goniómetro.

goniometric, geometrical, *a.* goniométrico.

goniometry, *s.* goniometría.

gonococco [gɔno'kɔkou], *s.* gonococo.

gonorrhœa [gɔno'riə], *s.* (*med.*) gonorrea, blenorragia; (*vulg.*) purgación.

gonorrhœal, *a.* gonorréico.

good [gud], *a.* bueno; excelente; útil, apto, saludable, ventajoso, conveniente; perfecto, completo, virtuoso, justo, religioso; verdadero, genuino, legítimo, válido; bondadoso, benévolo, misericordioso, clemente; dócil, obediente, cariñoso, de buena índole; amplio, considerable, grande; hábil, experto, sobresaliente; digno. — *adv.* bien, rectamente. — *interj.* ¡bueno! ¡bien! — *s.* bien, provecho, adelantamiento, prosperidad, ventaja. — *pl.* **goods,** mercancías; *for good and all,* de seguro; *as good as,* tanto como; casi; *good-bye,* adiós; *as good as done,* cosa hecha; *to be as good as one's word,* cumplir lo prometido; *good day,* buenos días; *a good deal,* mucho, bastante; *in good earnest,* seriamente, de veras, de fijo; *Good Friday,* Viernes Santo; *he is good for nothing,* no vale tres pepinos, no vale nada; *good morning* o *good morrow,* buenos días; *good night,* buenas noches; *in good time,* a tiempo; *good turn,* gracia, favor; *a good while,* un buen rato; *to be a good walker,* tener buenos pies; *what is the good of it?* ¿para qué sirve? *for good* (o *for good and all*), para siempre, de cierto, definitivamente;

to go for good, ir (o marcharse) para no volver; *to hold good,* continuar en toda su fuerza, ser valedero; *to return good for evil,* pagar los azotes al verdugo; volver bien por mal; *to make good,* justificar, probar, suplir lo que falta, indemnizar, lograr, acetar; *to think good,* juzgar a propósito; *much good may it do you,* buen provecho le haga.

good-fortune, *s.* dicha, felicidad, buena suerte.

good-humour, *s.* jovialidad, buen humor.

good-humoured, *a.* alegre, bienhumorado.

goodish, *a.* algo bueno, bastante bueno, regular; holgado; amplio, algo grande, considerable.

goodliness, *s.* belleza, hermosura, elegancia, gracia.

good-looking, *a.* hermoso, bonito, guapo.

goodly, *a.* hermoso, guapo, bien parecido; excelente, atractivo, agradable; vistoso; considerable, abultado, bastante grande, algo numeroso; *a goodly prospect,* hermosa perspectiva, o buenas esperanzas.

goodman ['gudmən], *s.* (*ant.*) señor, dueño; amo; marido.

good-natured, *a.* bondadoso, benévolo, afable.

good-naturedly, *adv.* afablemente, amistosamente.

goodness, *s.* bondad, benevolencia; virtud; fineza, favor. — *interj.* ¡por Dios! ¡caramba!

goods [gudz], *s.pl.* géneros, mercancías, mercaderías, efectos, bienes; muebles; *goods train,* tren de mercancías; *goods shed,* almacén, depósito, cobertizo; *goods wagon, goods van,* vagón de mercancías, furgón; *green goods,* (*E.U.*) billetes falsificados.

good-wife, *s.* (*ant.*) señora, ama de la casa; esposa.

goodwill, *s.* clientela, parroquia, buen crédito (de una casa comercial).

good-will, *s.* sinceridad, benevolencia.

goody, *s., a.* bonachón, pazguato, Juan Lanas, mojigato; (*fam.*) comadre, *f.; pl.* (*fam.*) confitura, dulce; *goody-goody,* santurrón, beato.

goosander [gu:'sændəɹ], *s.* (*orn.*) mergánsar, mergo, cuervo marino.

goose [gu:s], *s.* (*pl.* **geese**) ganso o gansa, ánsar; oca; juego de la oca; bobo, tonto, necio, persona muy simple o inocente; (*pl.* **gooses**) plancha de sastre.

gooseberry ['guzbəri], *s.* (*bot.*) uva espina; variedad de grosella.

goose-cap, *s.* bobo, tonto, pazguato, ganso.

goose-flesh, *s.* (*fig.*) carne de gallina, *f.*

goose-foot, *s.* (*bot.*) chual.

goose-herd, *s.* ansarero.

goose-neck, *s.* (*mar.*) gancho de botalones; arbotante; pescante de bote; cuello de cisne.

goose-quill, *s.* pluma de ave, pluma de ganso, cañón.

goose-wings, *s.* (*mar.*) calzones.

gopher ['goufəɹ], *s.* geomís.

gopher-wood, *s.* (*bot.*) árbol de madera amarilla; madera con que se construyó el arca de Noé.

gordian ['gɔ:diən], *a.* gordiano; *gordian knot,* nudo gordiano.

gore [gɔ:ɹ], *a.* sangre, *f.,* sangre cuajada, cruor, cuajarón; (*cost.*) cuchillo, nesga; pedazo de terreno triangular; ensanche triangular del vestido; (*mar.*) tabla triangular. — *v.t.* herir con puñal o con los cuernos, acornear; hacer o poner nesga o cuchillo.

gorge [gɔːɹdʒ], *s.* gorja, gola, garganta, gaznate; acción de engullir, trago, bocado; barranco, cañada, desfiladero, abra; cuello de un vestido; apretujón. — *v.t.* engullir, tragar; saciar, hartar; comer, demasiado; atiborrar. — *v.t.* hartarse, atracarse, saciarse, apiarse.

gorged, *a.* que tiene garganta; que ha comido demasiado, hartado.

gorgeous ['gɔːɹdʒəs], *a.* brillante, vistoso, grandioso, esplendoroso, magnífico, suntuoso, primoroso.

gorgeousness, *s.* esplendor, magnificencia, suntuosidad.

gorget ['gɔːɹdʒet], *s.* (*mil.*) gola, golilla, gorguera, gorjal; (*cost.*) gorguera; (*orn.*) collar, mancha de color en la garganta de ciertas aves; (*cir.*) cuchilla para fístulas.

gorgon ['gɔːɹgən], *s.* gorgona; cualquier cosa fea y horrible.

gorilla [gə'rilə], *s.* gorila.

gormand ['gɔːɹmənd], **gourmand**, *s.* glotón, gomia, goloso.

gormandize ['gɔːɹməndaiz], *v.i.* glotonear, comer con gula.

gormandizer, *s.* glotonazo, golosazo, golmajo, tragamallas, *m.f.*

gorse [gɔːɹs], *s.* árgoma, hiniesta espinosa.

gory ['gɔːri], *a.* sangriento, ensangrentado, cubierto de sangre.

goshawk ['gɔshɔːk], *s.* (*orn.*) azor.

gosling ['gɔzliŋ], *s.* (*orn.*) ansarino, gansarón; *gosling-green*, color verdoso amarillento.

gospel ['gɔspəl], *s.* evangelio; (*fam.*) verdad, cosa cierta, cosa indudable. — *v.t.* evangelizar; instruir en los preceptos del Evangelio; cristianizar.

gospeller, *s.* evangelista, *m.f.*; evangelistero; misionero.

gospellize, *v.t.* evangelizar, cristianizar.

gossamer ['gɔsəməɹ], *s.* hilo finísimo; telaraña; capa de tela impermeable; (*tej.*) gloria, gasa sutilísima.

gossamer, gossamery, *a.* sutil, delgado.

gossip ['gɔsip], *s.* charla, chisme, chismería, charladuría, parladuría, picotería, hablilla, murmuración; padrino, madrina, compadre, comadre, *f.*; chismoso, murmurador, cuentista, *m.f.*, charlantín. — *v.i.* charlar, picotear, parlotear, chismear.

gossiping, *s.* charla, murmuración, chismografía.

got [gɔt], *pret.* y *p.p.* [GET].

Goth [gɔθ], *s.* godo.

Gothic, *a.* gótico, relativo a los godos. — *s.* godo, lengua godo; (*fig.*) bárbaro, rudo, grosero, ignorante.

Gothicism ['gɔθisizm], *s.* idioma godo; estilo gótico; rudeza, barbarie, *f.*

gotten, *p.p.* [GET].

gouge [gaudʒ], *s.* (*carp.*) gubia, mediacaña; ranura, canal. — *v.t.* excavar, escoplear con una gubia; sacar, arrancar, vaciar; llevar ventaja, regatear, sacar un ojo con el dedo pulgar.

gouge-channel, *s.* (*mar.*) gubiadura.

gourd ['guəɹd], *s.* calabaza, calabacino, calabacera, melón; *bottle-gourd*, calabaza vinatera.

gourmand, *s.* [GORMAND].

gourmandize, *v.i.* [GORMANDIZE].

gourmet ['guəɹmei], *s.* gastrónomo.

gout [gaut], *s.* (*med.*) gota, artritis, *f.*; podagra.

gout, *s.* gusto; inclinación.

goutiness, *s.* afección gotosa.

goutwort, *s.* (*bot.*) angélica.

gouty ['gauti], *a.* gotoso.

govern ['gʌvəɹn], *v.t.*, *v.i.* governar, guiar, regir, dirigir, administrar, regentar, tener dominio, comandar, dominar; moderar, domar, enfrenar, embridar, manejar; (*gram.*) regir; (*mar.*) gobernar.

governable, *a.* dócil, sumiso, obediente, sujeto; manejable.

governance, *s.* gobierno, autoridad, poder, ejercicio del poder.

governess, *s.* aya, institutriz, *f.*, maestra, gobernadora.

government ['gʌvəɹnmənt], *s.* gobierno, ministerio, gobernación, administración pública; autoridad, dominio; manejo, dirección, porte, conducta; (*gram.*) régimen.

governmental [gʌvəɹn'mentəl], *a.* gubernamental, gubernativo, relativo al ministerio o a la administración pública.

governor ['gʌvəɹnəɹ], *s.* gobernador; administrador; (*fam.*) padre; (*ant.*) ayo, tutor; piloto, capitán; (*mec.*) regulador; moderador; *fan* o *fly-governor*, (*mec.*) volante regulador.

gowan ['gauən], *s.* margarita.

gown ['gaun], *s.* vestido talar, traje de mujer, vestidura talar, túnica, toga, bata; *dressing-gown*, bata.

gowned, *a.* vestido, vestido de toga; *well-gowned*, bien vestido, bien vestida.

gownman ['gaunmən], **gownsman**, *s.* togado; paisano, civil; clérigo; ciudadano.

grab [græb], *v.t.* coger, asir, copar, agarrar, apresar, arrebatar; prender; posesionarse violentamente o fraudulentamente. — *s.* (*fam.*) agarro, asimiento, apresamiento, toma; arrebatina; presa; copo; (*fam.*) sisa, robo; (*mec.*) gancho, garfio, aparato para asir. — *v.t.* tentar, palpar, reconocer por medio del tacto.

grabble ['græbəl], *v.i.* ir a tientas; postrarse; tenderse de cuatro patas.

grace [greis], *s.* gracia, garbo, donaire, gracejo; donosura, hermosura, elegancia, despejo; beneficio, don, merced, favor, indulgencia, remisión, perdón; afabilidad; concesión, privilegio; disposición, gana, talante, título de honor que se da a los duques y arzobispos, Alteza, Excelencia, Ilustrísima; bendición de la mesa; *to say grace*, dar gracias, bendecir la mesa; *days of grace*, (*com.*) días de gracia. — *pl.* **graces**, juego con aros y palillos; *good graces*, favor, amistad, patrocinio, amparo. — *v.t.* favorecer; agraciar; adornar, hermosear; conceder una gracia.

graceful, *a.* gracioso, agraciado, donairoso, primoroso, gallardo, garrido, garboso, donoso, elegante, cortés, decoroso; natural, fácil.

gracefully ['greisfəli], *adv.* con gracia, graciosamente, airosamente, donosamente, elegantemente.

gracefulness, *s.* gracia, donaire, donosura, gallardía, gentileza, elegancia, garbo, sal, *f.*

graceless, *a.* réprobo, malvado; abandonado, desesperado, dejado de la mano de Dios.

gracelessly, *adv.* sin gracia, depravadamente, sin elegancia.

gracelessness, *s.* depravación.

Graces ['greisiz], *s.pl.* las tres Gracias.

gracile ['græsil], *a.* grácil, sutil, delgado.

gracious ['greiʃəs], *a.* benigno, bueno, bondadoso, virtuoso, benévolo; cortés, grato, afable, gracioso, agradable, favorable, primoroso; *gracious me,* o *goodness gracious! (interj.)* ¡válgame Dios!

graciousness, *s.* gracia, dulzura, afabilidad, bondad, benignidad.

grackle ['grækəl], *s.* especie de grajo o estornino; *(E.U.)* mirlo americano.

gradate [grə'deit], *v.t.* graduar; *(pint.)* degradar.

gradation [grə'deiʃən], *s.* graduación; grado, rango; paso gradual; *(pint.)* degradación; serie, *f.*; *(mús.)* gradación.

gradatory [grə'deitəri], *a.* graduado, gradual; dispuesto o a propósito para andar. — *s.* *(arq.)* gradas, escalones.

grade [greid], *s.* grado, rango, graduación; *(zool.)* casta u orden de animales producido por el cruzamiento con los de una casta superior; *(ing.)* pendiente, *f.*, inclinación, declive; *on the down grade,* cuesta abajo; *on the up grade,* cuesta arriba. — *v.t.* graduar, clasificar, colocar por grados; *(ing.)* nivelar, igualar, explanar; *to grade up,* cruzar, mejorar (castas de animales).

grader, *s.* *(ing.)* nivelador.

gradient ['greidiənt], *a.* ambulante, pendiente; moviente, que baja o se levanta por grados. — *s.* *(ing.)* desnivel, rampa, declive, pendiente, *f.*, inclinación; *(meteor.)* grado del aumento o disminución (de temperatura, presión, etc.).

gradienter, *s.* nivel de agrimensor.

gradin ['greidin], **gradine,** *s.* grada, escalón; gradino de escultor.

grading, *s.* *(ing.)* nivelación.

gradual ['grædjuːəl], *s.* *(igl.)* gradual. — *a.* gradual; graduado; que baja o se levanta por grados.

gradualness, *s.* calidad de gradual.

graduate ['grædjuːeit], *v.t.* graduar, conferir un grado universitario; adelantar, subir, o aumentar por grados; modificar, aumentar o disminuir gradualmente; graduar, dividir y señalar por grados. — *v.i.* graduarse, recibirse, pasarse, tomar la borla; cambiar gradualmente, pasar por grados. — *s.* licenciado universitario; *(quím.)* graduador, probeta. — *a.* graduado, recibido.

graduation, *s.* graduación, acto de obtener o conferir grados universitarios; acción y efecto de modificar o dividir un espacio en partes iguales.

graduator, *s.* graduador.

graduction [grə'dʌkʃən], *s.* *(astr.)* la división de arcos circulares en grados, minutos y segundos.

Graecism ['griːsizm], *s.* grecismo.

graffito [grə'fiːtou], *s.* *(arq.)* esgrafiado; inscripción; dibujo.

graft [graːft], *s.* *(agr.)* injerto, púa, acodo, aguja; *(cir.)* injerto de piel; *(E.U., vulg.)* estafa; soborno. — *v.t.* injertar, ingerir, incorporar, unir, insertar; *(cir.)* transferir. — *v.i.* hacer injertos.

grafter, *s.* injertador.

grafting, *s.* injertación, injerto, ingeridura; *grafting twig,* estaca; *grafting knife,* abridor; *groove-grafting,* injerto de canutillo; *cleft-grafting,* injerto en púa; *crown-grafting,* injerto de coronilla; *tongue-grafting, whip-grafting,* injerto de lengüeta.

grail [greil], *s.* grial; *the Holy Grail,* el Santo Grial.

grain [grein], *s.* grano; cereal; fruto y semilla de las mieses; porción o parte menuda, fruta, semilla, pipa o petita de fruta; fibra, veta, o trepa de cuerpos fibrosos; pizca; peso equivalente a 0·0648 gramos; flor del cuero; granilla del paño; *(tint.)* grana, cochinilla, color rojo; genio, índole, *f.*, disposición; *cross-grain,* a contrahilo; *to dye in (the) grain,* teñir la lana en rama; *against the grain,* a repelo, contra pelo, con repugnancia, de mala gana. — *v.t.* granular, agranelar, vetear, granear, imitar la trepa de madera, etc.

grain-cleaner, *s.* aventador.

grain-fork, *s.* bieldo.

graining, *s.* graneladura, graneo.

grain-moth, grain-weevil, *s.* gorgojo.

grainy, *a.* granado, graneado, granoso.

gram [græm], **gramme,** *s.* gramo.

grama-grass, *s.* *(ant.)* grama.

gramercy [grə'məːɹsi], *interj.* *(ant.)* ¡gracias! ¡muchas gracias!

graminaceous [græmi'neiʃəs], **gramineous,** *a.* gramíneo.

graminivorous [græmi'nivərəs], *a.* graminívoro.

grammar ['græməɹ], *s.* gramática; buen decir, lenguaje correcto; tratado elemental de una ciencia, elementos, principios; *grammar-school,* escuela de gramática; *(Ingl.)* colegio de segunda enseñanza; *(E.U.)* escuela pública, escuela de primera enseñanza.

grammarian [grə'məriən], *s.* gramático, maestro de gramática; dómine; humanista, *m.*

grammatical [grə'mætikəl], *a.* gramático, gramatical.

grammatically, *adv.* gramaticalmente.

grammaticalness, *s.* corrección gramatical.

grammatist ['græmətist], *s.* gramático.

grampus ['græmpəs], *s.* orco; delfín.

granary ['grænəri], *s.* granero, troj, hórreo, alhóndiga, alfolí.

grand [grænd], *a.* gran, grande, grandioso; noble, augusto, ilustre, comprensivo; sublime, elevado, majestuoso, solemne, magnífico, espléndido.

grandam ['grændəm], *s.f.* *(ant.)* abuela; vieja, anciana.

grand-aunt, *s.f.* tía abuela.

grandchild ['græntʃaild], *s.* nieto, nieta.

grand-daughter, *s.f.* nieta.

grand-duke [grænd'djuːk], *s.* granduque; archiduque; *(orn.)* duque, buho; buho maximus.

grandee [græn'diː], *s.* grande de un reino, prócer.

grandeur ['grændjəɹ], *s.* grandeza, esplendor, pompa, fausto, magnificencia.

grandfather, *s.m.* abuelo; *great-grandfather,* bisabuelo; *great-great-grandfather,* tatarabuelo; *grandfather-clock,* reloj de péndulo.

grandiloquence [græn'dilokwəns], *s.* grandilocuencia, altilocuencia.

grandiloquent, grandiloquose, *a.* grandílocuo.

grandiose ['grændiouz], *a.* grandioso, imponente; pomposo, hinchado, bombástico.

grandmother, *s.f.* abuela; *great-grandmother,* bisabuela; *great-great-grandmother,* tatarabuela.

grandnephew ['grændnevju:], *s.m.* sobrino (nieto de un hermano o de una hermana).

grandness, *s.* grandor, grandeza, grandiosidad, esplendor, pompa.

grandniece, *s.f.* sobrina (nieta de un hermano o de una hermana).

grand-sire ['grændsaiɹ], *s.m.* abuelo.

grandson, *s.m.* nieto.

grand-uncle, *s.m.* tío del padre o de la madre, hermano del abuelo o de la abuela.

grange [greindʒ], *s.* granja, cortijo, hacienda, alquería; casa de labranza, casa de campo; *(ant.)* granero.

granger, *s.* labriego, patán; *(E.U.)* miembro de la sociedad llamada *Patrons of Husbandry* (patronos de la agricultura).

graniferous [grə'nifərəs], *a.* granífero, granoso, lleno de granos, que tiene granos.

granite ['grænit], *s.* granito.

granitic, granitical, *a.* granítico.

granivorous [grə'nivərəs], *a.* granívoro.

grannom ['grænəm], *s.* mosca de cuatro alas, que sirve como cebo para pescar.

granny ['græni], *s. f. (fam.)* abuela, vieja, comadre.

grant [grɑ:nt], *v.t.* conceder, dar, permitir, dispensar, hacer gracia, hacer merced, otorgar; convenir en, asentir, dar de barato; conferir, ceder, transferir, transmitir el título de una propiedad, etc.; *to take for granted,* dar por supuesto, presuponer. — *s.* cesión, don, dádiva, concesión, donación, merced; gracia, permiso, subvención, privilegio; documento que confiere un privilegio o concesión; asentimiento, asenso; *(for.)* carta de gracia.

grantable, *a.* dable, permisible, capaz de ser otorgado, que se puede otorgar o conceder.

grantee [grɑ:n'ti:], *s.* cesionario, concesionario, donatario, adjudicatario.

grantor, *s.* cesionista, *m.f.,* cesionario, otorgador.

granular ['grænju:ləɹ], **granulary,** *a.* granular, granoso, granuloso, granujoso.

granulate ['grænju:leit], *v.t.* granular; granear, granar (pólvora); *(fund.)* granallar. — *v.i.* granularse.

granulated, *a.* graneado, granulado; moteado; en grano o en polvo. — *p.p.* [GRANULATE].

granulation, *s.* granulación; superficie granulada; *(med.)* granazón, *f.,* encarnación.

granule ['grænju:l], *s.* gránulo, granito, granillo.

granulous, *a.* granuloso, granujoso, granilloso.

grape [greip], *s.* uva; *pl. (vet.)* grapa, sarna que las caballerías padecen en las patas; *bear's grape,* madroño.

grape-fruit, *s.* toronja.

grape-hyacinth, *s.* almizclena.

grapeless, *a.* sin uva.

grapery ['greipəri], *s.* invernadero o criadero de uvas.

grape-shot, *(arti.)* balas encadenadas o enramadas, metralla.

grape-skin, *s.* hollejo.

grape-stone, *s.* granuja, simiente de uva.

grape-sugar, *s.* glucosa.

grape-vine, *s.* vid, *f.,* parra.

graphic ['græfik], **graphical,** *a.* gráfico, perteneciente al grabado.

graphically, *adv.* gráficamente, de un modo gráfico o pintoresco.

graphite ['græfait], *s. (min.)* grafito, plombagina; lápiz.

graphitic [grə'fitik], *a.* grafítico.

grapholite ['græfolait], *s.* pizarra.

graphometer, *s.* grafómetro, instrumento para levantar o transportar planos.

graphophone ['græfofoun], *s.* especie de fonógrafo.

grapline ['græplain], **grapling** ['græpliŋ], **grapnel** ['græpnəl], *s. (mar.)* anclote, rezón; arpeo, gancho, garabato, cloque, rastra, rebanadera.

grapple ['græpəl], *v.t.* agarrar, garrafinar, agarrafar, asir; amarrar. — *v.i.* agarrarse, engarrafarse; *(mar.)* atracarse, abordarse. — *s.* riña, lucha, pelea; rastra, gafa, cloque, garabato, arpeo.

grappling, *s. (mar.)* rezón; aferramiento.

grappling-iron, *s.* cloque, arpeo de abordaje.

grapy ['greipi], *a.* lleno o hecho de uvas.

grasp [grɑ:sp], *v.t.* empuñar, coger, asir, agarrar; usurpar, tomar, apoderarse de; *(fig.)* abarcar, comprender, alcanzar, saber. — *v.i.* usurpar, envidiar; *grasp all, lose all, (prov.)* quien todo lo quiere, todo lo pierde; quien mucho abarca, poco aprieta. — *s.* acción de agarrar; asimiento, agarro; garras; puño, puñado; usurpación; comprensión; poder, posesión.

grasper, *s.* agarrador.

grasping, *a.* codicioso, avaro.

grass [grɑ:s], *s.* hierba, yerba, pasto, herbaje, césped. — *v.t.* cubrir de hierba; apacentar; blanquear lino. — *v.i.* criar hierba. *-grass-widow,* mujer separada(temporalmente) de su marido; *grass-widower,* marido separado (temporalmente) de su mujer; *to let the grass grow under one's feet,* perder el tiempo.

grass-green, *a.* verde como la hierba.

grass-grown, *s.* cubierto de hierba.

grasshopper ['grɑ:shɔpəɹ], *s.* langosta, langostón, cigarra, saltamontes, saltón; palanca de cada tecla del pianoforte.

grassiness, *s.* abundancia de hierba.

grassless, *a.* sin hierba.

grass-mower, *s.* dallador.

grassy, *a.* herboso, lleno de hierba; herbáceo.

grate [greit], *s.* reja; parrilla de hogar; rejilla, verja, rejado. — *v.t.* raspar; rallar; enrejar; frotar, hacer rechinar; emparrillar; *(fig.)* molestar, irritar, fastidiar. — *v.i.* ludir, rozar, rozarse, estregarse; chirriar, rechinar; raer.

grateful ['greitfəl], *a.* agradecido, reconocido; gustoso, grato, agradable; *be grateful for small mercies,* de lo ajeno, lo que quisiere su dueño.

gratefulness, *s.* gratitud, reconocimiento, agradecimiento; gusto, agrado.

grater ['greitəɹ], *s.* rallo, rallador, raspador.

graticulate [grə'tikju:leit], *v.t.* cuadricular.

gratification [grætifi'keiʃən], *s.* satisfacción, fruición, placer, gusto, complacencia, deleite; recompensa, gratificación, propina.

gratify ['grætifai], *v.t.* satisfacer, complacer, cumplir con, dar gusto a, agradar, contentar; premiar, gratificar, recompensar.

grating ['greitiŋ], *a.* rechinante, discordante,

chirriante, irritante, mal sonante; ofensivo, áspero; penoso, rudo, duro. — *s.* reja, verja, rejado, enrejado; chirrido, rechinamiento; emparrillado; escurridero; (*ópt.*) retícula de microscopio. — *pl.* **gratings**, (*mar.*) ajedrez, *m.*, jareta, enjaretado; enrejado.

gratitude ['grætitjuːd], *s.* gratitud, reconocimiento, agradecimiento.

gratuitous [grə'tjuːitəs], *a.* gratuito, gratis, gratisdato, voluntario, sin pago, sin prueba; de gracia, gracioso; injustificado, sin necesidad.

gratuity [grə'tjuːiti], *s.* gratificación, remuneración, propina, recompensa.

gratulate, *v.t.* (*ant.*) felicitar, congratular.

gratulatory [grætju'leitəri], *a.* congratulatorio; *gratulatory letters*, cartas de enhorabuena.

gravamen [grə'veimen], *s.* (*for.*) gravamen; agravio; causa substancial de una acción.

grave [greiv], *v.t.*, *v.i.* (*pret.* **graved**; *p.p.* **graved** o **graven**) grabar; cincelar, esculpir; (*mar.*) despalmar.

grave, *s.* sepultura, hoya, fosa, cárcava; sepulcro, tumba; muerte, *f.*; (*gram.*) acento grave. — *a.* grave, serio, severo, circunspecto, honesto, importante, difícil, arduo; solemne, formal; (*gram.*) grave; (*mús.*) grave, bajo, profundo.

grave-clothes, *s.pl.* mortaja.

grave-digger, *s.* sepulturero.

gravel ['grævəl], *s.* cascajo, casquijo, guijo, sablón, arena gruesa, sábulo; (*med.*) litiasis, *f.*, arenilla, mal de piedra; *gravel pit*, arenaria; *gravel walk*, paseo enarenado. — *v.t.* arenar, enarenar, cubrir con cascajo; embarazar, confundir, inquietar, enmarañar.

graveless, *a.* insepulto.

gravelly ['grævəli], *a.* arenisco, guijoso, cascajoso, guijarreño.

graven ['greivən], *a.* grabado, esculpido. — *p.p.* [GRAVE].

graveness, *s.* gravedad, seriedad, compostura, circunspección.

graver, *s.* buril, chaple; gradino; cincel; punzón; cincelador, grabador.

Graves' disease, *s.* bocio exoftálmico.

gravestone ['greivstoun], *s.* monumento fúnebre, lápida sepulcral.

graveyard ['greivjɑːd], *s.* cementerio.

gravid ['grævid], *a.* preñada, embarazada, encinta.

gravimeter ['grævimiːtəɹ], *s.* gravímetro.

graving ['greiviŋ], *s.* grabado; (*mar.*) carena; *graving-dock*, dique seco.

gravitate ['græviteit], *v.i.* gravitar, gravear.

gravitation, *s.* gravitación; inclinación, tendencia, atracción universal; gravedad.

gravity ['græviti], *s.* gravedad, pesantez, majestad, seriedad; importancia; *centre of gravity*, centro de gravedad; *law of gravity*, ley de la gravedad; *specific gravity*, peso específico.

gravure [grə'vjuːɹ], *s.* grabado, fotograbado.

gravy ['greivi], *s.* salsa, jugo, pringue, unto, caldillo.

gray, **grey** [grei], *a.* gris; cano, encanecido. — *s.* color gris; animal gris; *dark gray*, gris obscuro; *gray horse*, caballo tordo; *gray-headed*, canoso, encanecido, envejecido. — *v.t.*, *v.i.* poner o volverse gris o cano; encanecer.

gray-beard, *s.* barbicano, hombre ya entrado en años.

gray-bearded, *a.* barbicano.

gray fly, *s.* trompetilla, mosca gris.

grayish ['greiiʃ], *a.* agrisado, griseo; tordillo; entrecano.

grayling ['greiliŋ], *s.* (*ict.*) umbla.

grayness, *s.* calidad de ser gris.

graze [greiz], *v.i.* pacer, apacentarse, pastar, herbajar; rasar, rozar, tocar ligeramente. — *v.t.* pastorear, apacentar, llevar al campo: dar pienso, hierba, forraje; rasar, raspar, pasar rozando o volando. — *s.* acción de rozar, rozamiento, raspadura, roce; pasto, apacentamiento.

grazer, *s.* animal que pace o se apacienta.

grazier ['greizəɹ], *s.* ganadero.

grease [griːs], *s.* grasa, saín, manteca, gordura, unto o sebo de un animal; (*vet.*) aguajas.

grease-box, (*mec.*) caja de sebo. — *v.t.* engrasar, ensebar, untar, pringar; manchar con grasa, lubricar; corromper, sobornar con dinero.

greaser ['griːzəɹ], *s.* engrasador; lubricante; lubricador; (*E.U.*, **despec.**) hispanoamericano o mejicano.

greasily ['griːzili], *adv.* crasamente.

greasiness ['griːzinis], *s.* pringue, mugre, *f.*, gordura.

greasy ['griːzi], *a.* grasiento, mugriento, craso, lardoso, aceitoso, pringado, pringoso, churriento; (*fam.*) servil, lisonjero; (*vet.*) atacado de la enfermedad de las aguajas.

great [greit], *a.* gran, grande, grueso, magno, enorme, vasto, desmedido; mucho, numeroso, muchísimo; largo, prolongado, dilatado; importante, considerable, principal; henchido, lleno, preñado, gordo; familiar, íntimo; ilustre, poderoso, eminente, noble, magnánimo; admirable, adorable, sublime, maravilloso; grandioso, magnífico, solemne, imponente, orgulloso, valiente; indica la tercera o cuarta generación (*great-grandson*, biznieto; *great-granddaughter*, biznieta; *great-grandfather*, bisabuelo; *great-great-grandfather*, tercer abuelo, etc.).

great-bellied, *a.* barrigudo; preñada.

great-coat, *s.* sobretodo, abrigo, levitón.

greaten ['greitən], *v.t.* (*ant.*) agrandar, engrandecer. — *v.i.* crecer, aumentarse.

greater ['greitəɹ], *a. comp.* [GREAT]; mayor, más grande; *Greater Britain*, el imperio colonial de la Gran Bretaña.

greatest, *a. sup.* [GREAT]; máximo, sumo.

great-hearted, *a.* magnánimo, animado, valiente, de alma grande.

greatly, *adv.* muy, mucho; grandemente; magnánimamente, ilustremente, noblemente.

greatness, *s.* grandeza; amplitud, grandor, magnitud, extensión; grandiosidad; fausto, nobleza, majestad, poder, dignidad; magnanimidad, grandeza de alma.

greaves [griːvz], *s.pl.* (*mil.*) grebas, espinilleras, canilleras; (*coc.*) chicharrones.

grebe [griːb], *s.* colimbo.

Grecian ['griːʃən], *s.* griego; helenista, *m.f.* — *a.* griego, greco.

Grecianize, **Grecize**, *v.t.*, *v.i.* grecizar, greguizar.

Grecism ['griːsizm], *s.* grecismo, helenismo.

Greco-Latin [griːkou'lætin], *a.* greco-latino.

Greco-Roman, *a.* grecorromano.

greed [gri:d], **greediness**, *s.* voracidad, gula; codicia, avaricia; ansia, anhelo.

greedy [gri:di], *a.* voraz, goloso, insaciable; avaro, codicioso; anhelante, ansioso, apasionado, deseoso.

Greek, *s.* griego; lengua griega; helenista, *m.f.*; (*fam.*) gringo, jerga, lenguaje ininteligible. — *a.* griego; helénico.

Greekish [gri:kiʃ], *a.* griego.

green [gri:n], *a.* verde; verdoso; no maduro; novicio, inexperto, novato; fresco, nuevo, reciente, tierno, joven, acabado de hacer; crudo; floreciente, lozano, gallardo; pálido, descolorido. — *s.* color verde, verdura, verdor; prado, pradera, lugar cubierto de hierba. — *pl.* **greens**, (*coc.*) verduras, hortaliza; *sea-green*, verde mar; *bottle-green*, verde botella; *green corn*, (*Ingl.*) trigo nuevo; (*Am.*) maíz tierno; (*Mex.*) elote; *green ware*, loza cruda; *green vitriol*, caparrosa, sulfato de hierro; *green-eyed*, de ojos verdes; *green hand*, novicio, tirón, principiante; *green-laver* o *green-sloke*, alga marina comestible. — *v.t.* teñir o pintar de verde, dar color verde a. — *v.i.* verdear.

greenback, *s.* (*E.U.*) papel moneda, billete del gobierno.

greenfinch, *s.* verdecillo, verderón, verderol, cloris.

greengrocer [gri:ngrousəɪ], *s.* verdulero.

greenhorn [gri:nhɔ:n], *s.* (*fam.*) tirón, aprendiz, principiante, persona sin experiencia, paleto, palurdo; (*Cuba*) bozal.

greenhouse, *s.* conservatorio; invernáculo.

greening, *s.* acto de verdear, o de volverse verde; variedad de manzana verdosa.

greenish, *a.* verdoso, verdusco.

greenly, *adv.* nuevamente, recientemente; sin madurez.

greenness [gri:nnis], *s.* verdura, verdor, verdín; frescura, vigor; falta de experiencia; novedad.

greenroom, *s.* (*teat.*) sala de espera de los actores; almacén destinado a contener loza cruda, o tela acabada de tejer.

greensand, *s.* arenisca verde.

greensickness, *s.* (*med.*) clorosis, *f.*

greenstall, *s.* puesto para vender frutas y verduras.

greensward, *s.* césped, alfombra de hierba.

greenwood, *s.* bosque verde, selva frondosa.

greet [gri:t], *v.t.* saludar, llamar, dar la bienvenida a; hablar cortésmente. — *v.i.* encontrarse y saludarse; (*Escocia*) llorar, lamentarse.

greeting, *s.* salutación, saludo; en los instrumentos públicos, ¡salud!

gregarious [gre'gɛəriəs], *a.* gregario, rebañego, gregal.

gregariously, *adv.* gregariamente, a manadas.

gregariousness, *s.* tendencia a andar en manadas o rebaños.

Gregorian [gre'gɔ:riən], *a.* gregoriano.

gremial [gri:miəl], *a.* lo que pertenece o refiere al regazo; perteneciente a gremios; gremial.

grenade [gre'neid], *s.* granada, granada real, bomba.

grenadier [grenə'diəɪ], *s.* granadero.

grenadine [grenədi:n], *s.* (*tej.*) granadina.

grew [gru:], *pret.* [GROW].

grey [grei], *a.* gris [GRAY].

greyhound, *s.* galgo, galga; lebrel; vapor muy veloz.

grice [grais], *s.* gorrino, lechón; osezno, cachorro.

grid [grid], *s.* parrilla, reja; criba de alambre; (*elec.*) red.

griddle [gridəl], *s.* (*coc.*) tartera; tapadera de fogón; *griddle cake*, (*Am.*) pastelillo, fritura de harina.

gridiron [gridai.ɪn], *s.* parrillas; (*teat.*) telar; (*mar.*) andamiada, basada de esqueleto.

grief [gri:f], *s.* pesar, pesadumbre, pena, aflicción, tristeza, dolor, duelo, luto, sentimiento, congoja.

griefless, *a.* exento de pena, sin agravio.

grievance [gri:vəns], *s.* pesar, agravio, injusticia, entuerto, perjuicio, pesadumbre.

grieve [gri:v], *v.t.* agraviar, lastimar, afligir, oprimir; apesadumbrar. — *v.i.* sentir, dolerse, afligirse, apesadumbrarse, lamentarse, entristecerse, ponerse triste; *to grieve to death*, morirse de pena.

grievingly, *adv.* apesaradamente.

grievous [gri:vəs], *a.* gravoso, aflictivo, doloroso, lastimoso, penoso; fiero, cruel, atroz; oneroso, enorme, grave; provocativo, ofensivo.

grievousness, *s.* dolor, aflicción, pena; enormidad, atrocidad, calamidad.

griffin [grifin], *s.* grifo; (*fam.*) (dueña) carabina.

griffon [grifən], *s.* buitre, *Gyps fulvus*; perro zorrero.

grig [grig], *s.* (*ent.*) cigarra, grillo; (*ict.*) anguila pequeña; *as merry as a grig*, alegre como un grillo.

grill [gril], *v.t.* asar en parrillas; molestar, tormentar, atormentar. — *s.* parrillas; manjar asado en parrillas.

grillade, *s.* carbonada, manjar asado en parrillas.

grillage [grilidʒ], *s.* emparrillado.

grille [gril], *s.* verja, reja, enrejado, calado de adorno.

grilse [grils], *s.* salmón joven cuando regresa por primera vez del mar.

grim [grim], · *a.* torvo, severo, disforme, feo, ceñudo, regañón, horrendo; formidable; inflexible; *grim-faced* o *grim-visaged*, malcarado.

grimace [gri'meis], *s.* visaje, gesto, mueca.

grimalkin [griməlkin], *s.* gatazo, gata vieja; (*fig.*) vieja de mal genio, bruja, arpía.

grime [graim], *s.* tizne, porquería, mugre, *f.* — *v.t.* ensuciar, tiznar, llenar de mugre.

grimness [grimnis], *s.* grima, horror, espanto.

grimy [graimi], *a.* tiznado, sucio, mugriento, manchado.

grin [grin], *v.i.* sonreír mostrando los dientes. — *s.* mueca, visaje; sonrisa burlona o maliciosa.

grind [graind], *v.t.* (*pret.* y *p.p.* **ground**) moler, triturar; frotar, rallar, refregar, estregar; vaciar, pulverizar, amolar, afilar; gravar, acosar, agobiar, molestar, oprimir; mascar; pulir, bruñir; (*fam.*) estudiar con ahinco; dar matraca; dar vueltas a un manubrio; (*Cuba*) chotear. — *v.i.* hacer andar (la rueda de un molino); ludir, rozar, frotar; pulirse, deslustrarse (el vidrio), afilarse.

grinder, *s.* molinero, molendero; afilador; muela, piedra de molino o de amolar;

moledor; amolador; molino, molinillo; diente, muela, molar, quijal.

grindery, s. tienda de amolador; herramientas para curtidor.

grinding, s. pulverización, molimiento, molienda, moledura; bruñido, pulimento; amoladura; moliente.

grinding-mill, s. trapiche.

grinding-roll, s. maza de trapiche.

grindstone ['graindstən], s. amoladera, muela, volandera, piedra de afilar.

grinner, s. el que se sonríe y enseña los dientes.

grip [grip], s. apretón de mano; modo especial de darse la mano (los masones, etc.); empuñamiento, agarro; (E.U.) saco de mano; agarradero, mango, puño, asidero; (f.c.) garra, afiador, retén; capacidad de agarrar y retener o alcanzar, comprender. — pl. combate mano a mano, cuerpo a cuerpo. — v.t. agarrar, asir, cerrar, empuñar. — v.i. agarrarse con fuerza, tener firmemente.

gripe [graip], v.t. agarrar, asir, cerrar, empuñar; (mec.) morder; pellizcar, dar pellizcos; dar cólico; afligir, acongojar. — v.i. agarrar fuertemente; padecer cólico; (fam.) quejarse mucho; sacar dinero por exacción; (mar.) navegar de bolina contra timón; ceñir demasiado el viento. — s. toma, asimiento, agarro; sujeción; (mec.) zarpa, uña, abrazadera, grapa, freno de malacate; (fig.) esclavitud; garra; (mar.) pie del tajamar; mango, puño, empuñadura, manija, agarradero; opresión, apuro, aprieto. — pl. **gripes,** dolor cólico, apretón, torozón, retortijón; (mar.) obenque, bozas de lancha; trincas; tenedor de ancla.

griper ['graipər], s. userero.

griping, s. dolor, aflicción, retortijón.

gripingly, adv. con dolor del estómago.

grippe [grip], s. (med.) influenza, gripe, f.; (vulg.) trancazo, dengue.

gripper, s. (impr.) uña; (elec.) soporte del carbón de una lámpara de arco.

grisly ['grizli], a. espantoso, terrible, horroroso.

grist [grist], s. molienda; abasto, provisión, suministro.

gristle ['grisəl], s. cartílago, ternilla.

gristly ['gristli], a. cartilaginoso.

grit [grit], s. arena, cascajo; partículas ásperas y duras; (geol.) arenisca silicosa; (fam.) entereza, firmeza de carácter, ánimo, valor; (agr.) moyuelo. — pl. **grits,** sémola, farro.

grittiness, s. arenosidad, contextura arenosa; fortitud, ánimo, valor, entereza.

gritty, a. arenoso, arenisco, sabuloso; valeroso, animoso, esforzado.

grizzle ['grizəl], s. color gris, mezclilla.

grizzled, a. tordillo; (pelo) gris.

grizzly ['grizli], a. pardo, gríseo, pardusco. — s. (min.) criba para separar las piedras; grizzly bear, oso pardo.

groan [groun], v.i. gemir, suspirar, lanzar quejidos, dar gemidos. — s. gemido, quejido, mugido, suspiro.

groaning, s. lamento, lamentación, quejido, gemido.

groat [grout], s. (ant.) moneda inglesa del valor de cuatro peniques. — pl. **groats,** sémola, avena o trigo mondado y medio molido.

groatsworth ['groutswəːrθ], s. valor de un groat.

grocer ['grousər], s. especiero, abacero, lonjista, m.; tienda de ultramarinos; (Am.) pulpero, (Cuba) bodeguero, (Mex.) tendero; greengrocer, bercero; grocer's shop, abacería, especiería, (Am.) pulpería, (Cuba) bodega, (Mex.) tienda de abarrotes.

grocery ['grousəri], s. (E.U.) abacería, lonja. — pl. **groceries,** especierías, víveres, comestibles, ultramarinos; (Am.) abarrotes.

grog [grɔg], s. mezcla de ron y agua; grog-shop, taberna.

groggy ['grɔgi], a. medio borracho, calamocano; vacilante, inseguro; medio atontado.

grogram ['grɔgrəm], s. (tej.) gorgorán, cordellate.

groin [grɔin], s. ingle, f., empeine; (arq.) arista de encuentro, esquina viva, espiga; hocico de cerdo. — v.t. (arq.) formar aristas. — v.i. gemir, suspirar, lamentarse.

grommet ['grɔmit], s. anillo de cuerda; (mar.) roñada o grillete de las velas de estay.

gromwell ['grɔmwəl], s. (bot.) género de hierba rastrera de la familia de las borrajas.

groom [grum], s. mozo de mulas o de caballos; palafrenero; establero; lacayo; novio, hombre recién casado; groomsman, padrino de boda; groom in waiting, camarero de semana de palacio; groom of the bedchamber, ayuda de cámara del rey; groom of the chamber, caballerizo de cámara. — v.t. cuidar, almohazar los caballos; (fam.) peinar y vestir.

groove [gruːv], s. muesca, encaje, rebajo, encastre, estría, acanaladura, gárgol, ranura; surco; (mil.) rayadura; (fig.) rutina, hábito fijo. — v.t. acanalar; hacer estrías, muescas o ranuras; runar.

grope [group], v.t., v.i. tentar, andar a tientas; buscar tentando, buscar a ciegas.

groper, s. el que tienta o busca a obscuras.

gros, grosgrain, s. (tej.) gro.

grosbeak ['grousbiːk], s. (orn.) cardenal, loxia; picogordo.

gross [grous], a. craso; espeso, denso; gordo, grueso, corpulento; basto, tosco, grosero; obsceno, chocante, vergonzoso, indecoroso; lerdo, estúpido; descortés; (com.) bruto; gross weight, peso bruto; gross amount, importe total. — s. (pl. **gross**) gruesa (doce docenas); totalidad, conjunto; mayor parte, grueso; in gross, o in the gross, en grueso, por junto, en conjunto; by the gross, por mayor; por gruesas; small gross, diez docenas; great gross, doce gruesas.

gross-headed, a. lerdo, estúpido.

grossly ['grousli], adv. en bruto; groseramente, crasamente, toscamente.

grossness, s. grosería, tosquedad, rusticidad, ordinariez, rudeza, incivilidad, desvergüenza; grosura; espesor, densidad.

grossular ['grɔsjuːlər], s. (min.) grosularia.

grot [grɔt], s. (poét.) gruta.

grotesque [grou'tesk], a. grotesco, grutesco, desproporcionado, incongruo, fantástico.

grotto ['grɔtou], s. gruta, antro, covacha, caverna.

ground [graund], s. tierra, suelo, terreno, piso, pavimento; solar, heredad, posesión; país, territorio, región, f.; base, f., fundamento, principio; (pint.) fondo, campo, baño, capa; motivo, causa, razón, f., pie; (elec.) tierra; (mil.) campo de batalla; (mar.) tenedero. — pl. **grounds,** sedimento, poso, heces, f.pl., terrenos, parque, jardín; *to be on one's own ground*, (*fig.*) ocuparse uno en una cosa que conoce bien; *to break new ground*, (*fig.*) empezar una empresa nueva; *to fall to the ground*, (*fig.*) fracasar, no salir bien; *to gain ground*, (*fig.*) ganar terreno, hacer progresos; *to give ground* o *lose ground*, (*fig.*) perder terreno; *to hold* o *stand one's ground*, mantenerse firme. — *v.t.* fundar, apoyar, cimentar, zanjar, establecer, poner a tierra, sacar a tierra. — *v.i.* (*mar.*) tocar, varar.

ground, *a.* molido; *p.p.* [GRIND].

groundage ['graundidʒ], *s.* (*mar.*) derecho de puerto, derecho de anclaje.

groundedly, *adv.* firmemente.

ground-floor, *s.* piso bajo.

grounding, *s.* (*mar.*) encalladura; acto de varar.

ground-ivy, *s.* hiedra terrestre.

groundless, *a.* infundado.

groundlessly, *adv.* infundadamente, sin motivo, sin razón.

groundlessness, *s.* falta de razón o fundamento; futilidad, poca fuerza (de un argumento).

groundling, *s.* animal terrestre; (*ict.*) loche, loja; villano, persona vil.

ground-pine, *s.* camepitios, pinillo.

ground-plan, *s.* plano horizontal; delineación del piso bajo de un edificio; bosquejo general.

ground-plot, *s.* solar, sitio, terreno en el que se levanta un edificio.

ground-rent, *s.* alquiler por el terreno en que se levanta un edificio.

groundsel o **groundsil** ['graundsəl], *s.* umbral de puerta; (*bot.*) zuzón, hierba cana.

ground-tackle, *s.* (*mar.*) amarrazón de ancla.

ground-work, *s.* plan, plano de alguna cosa; base, *f.*, fundamento, cimiento; principio, razón fundamental, *f.*

group [gruːp], *s.* grupo, agrupación, corrillo; orden, serie, *f.*, clase, *f.*; combinación, conjunto. — *v.t.* agrupar, poner en un grupo.

grouse [graus], *s.* (*orn.*) ortega; queja. — *v.i.* rezongar, quejarse.

grout [graut], *s.* (*alb.*) mezcla para llenar juntas; mortero muy claro y cascajo; enlucido; sémola, farro; harina basta. — *pl.* **grouts,** heces, *f.pl.*, sedimento, zurrapas. — *v.t.* hurgar.

grouty, *a.* turbio, fangoso; intratable, áspero, arisco, regañón.

grove [grouv], *s.* arboleda, alameda, soto, enramada, boscaje, bosquecillo; *pine grove*, pinar; *oak grove*, robledal, robledo.

grovel ['grɔvəl], *v.i.* serpear, arrastrarse; (*fig.*) envilecerse, bajarse.

groveller, *s.* hombre servil y rastrero, hombre de poco valor, cobarde.

grovelling, *a.* servil, rastrero.

grow [grou], *v.t.* (*pret.* **grew**; *p.p.* **grown**) cultivar, hacer crecer o nacer algún vegetal. — *v.i.* nacer, crecer, vegetar; adelantar, medrar, proceder; tomar aumento, aumentarse, desarrollarse, provenir, progresar, formarse; extenderse, dilatarse; ponerse, volverse; pegarse, unirse; echar raíces, fijarse; *to grow dark*, obscurecer, anochecer, cerrar el día; *to grow old*, entrar en edad, envejecer; *to grow hot*, acalorarse; *to grow well*, restablecerse; *to grow better*, ponerse mejor; enmendarse, corregirse; *to grow worse*, empeorar; *to*

grow into fashion, hacerse de moda, hacerse (la) moda; *to grow out of fashion*, pasar de moda; *to grow up*, brotar, arrogar, apuntar, crecer, desarrollarse; *to grow less*, disminuir; *to grow near*, o *on*, acercarse; *to grow big*, engordar, crecer, aumentarse; *to grow cold*, enfriarse; *to grow dear*, encarecerse; *to grow late*, hacerse tarde; *to grow fat*, engordar, engruesar; *to grow rich*, enriquecerse; *to grow poor*, empobrecerse; *to grow out of esteem*, perder el crédito; *to grow out of use*, caer en desuso; *to grow strong*, ponerse fuerte, reponerse, restablecerse; *to grow tame*, domesticarse; *to grow tired* o *weary*, cansarse.

grower, *s.* labrador, productor, cultivador, arrendador; el que crece.

growl [graul], *v.i.* regañar, gruñir, rezongar, refunfuñar. — *v.t.* decir gruñendo. — *s.* regañamiento, refunfuño, gruñido.

growler, *s.* perro gruñidor; refunfuñador, regañón; (*vulg.*) coche.

grown [groun], *a.* crecido, hecho, espigado, desarrollado; cubierto, lleno (de hierbas, maleza, etc.); dominante, prevalente; *grown up*, adulto, crecido, (hombre) hecho.

growth [grouθ], *s.* crecimiento, desarrollo; vegetación; producción, producto; aumento, acrecentamiento, acrecencia, extensión, ampliación, adelantamiento, mejora, medro, progreso, aprovechamiento; altura, estatura completa; cosecha (vino); (*med.*) tumor.

grub [grʌb], *v.t.*, *v.i.* rozar, desarraigar, desyerbar; cavar, azadonar; emplearse en oficios bajos; (*vulg.*) comer. — *s.* gorgojo, larva; (*vulg.*) alimento, comestibles, manducatoria; persona desaliñada; (*E.U.*) raíz arrancada; *grub-ax*, legón, picaza; *grubbing-hoe*, escarda.

grubber, *s.* desyerbador; arrancador de raíces.

grubby, *a.* gusarapiento; (*fam.*) sucio.

Grub Street, *s.* nombre antiguo de una calle de Londres en la que vivían escritores de poco mérito y muy pobres; por extensión, escritorzuelos, escritores mercenarios.

grudge [grʌdʒ], *v.t.* envidiar, apetecer, codiciar; dar de mala gana, escatimar. — *v.i.* murmurar; repugnar. — *s.* enemistad antigua, rencor, rencilla, enemiga, ojeriza, tirria, resentimiento, mal grado.

grudging ['grʌdʒiŋ], *a.* envidioso; mezquino; de mala gana.

grudgingly, *adv.* con repugnancia, de mala gana.

gruel ['gruːəl], *s.* gachas, *f.pl.*; (*Méj.*) atole.

gruesome ['gruːsəm], *a.* horrible, horrendo, espantoso, fantástico.

gruff [grʌf], *a.* ceñudo, áspero, malhumorado, grosero, arisco, tosco, mal engestado.

gruffness, *s.* aspereza, ceño, sequedad, mal humor.

grum [grʌm], *a.* áspero, severo; gutural.

grumble ['grʌmbəl], *v.i.* refunfuñar, gruñir, rezongar, regañar, murmurar, quejarse. — *s.* regaño, refunfuñadura, quejumbre, gruñido.

grumbler, *s.* refunfuñador, regañón, gruñidor, regañador, rezongador, malcontento.

grumbling, *s.* refunfuñadura, murmuración, descontento, queja.

grumblingly, *adv.* refunfuñando; con descontento.

grume [gruːm], *s.* grumo, cuajarón, masa viscosa.

grummet ['grʌmet], *s.* (*mar.*) bozas rabizadas;

(*arti.*) taco hecho de cuerda y atacado entre la carga y el proyectil.

grumous [ˈgruːməs], *a.* grumoso, coagulado, espeso; (*bot.*) amacollado.

grumpy [ˈgrʌmpi], *a.* gruñón, quejoso, áspero, rudo, malhumorado.

grunt [grʌnt], *v.i.* gruñir; murmurar, refunfuñar, quejarse; arruar.

grunt, grunting, *s.* gruñido; (*ict.*) hemulón (pez americano).

grunter, *s.* gruñidor; (*fam.*) cerdo.

gruntingly, *adv.* regañando, refunfuñando.

gruntling, *s.* lechón, cochinillo.

guaco [ˈgwɑːkou], *s.* (*bot.*) guaco.

guaiac [ˈgwaiək], **guaiacum** [ˈgwaikəm], *s.* (*bot.*) guayaco o guayacán, lodoñero; resina del guayaco; palo santo.

guana [ˈgwɑːnə], *s.* iguana.

guanaco [gwəˈnɑːkou], *s.* guanaco, llama.

guano [ˈgwɑːnou], *s.* guano, huano. — *v.t.* abonar con guano.

guarantee [gærənˈtiː], *v.t.* garantizar, asegurar, responder por, respaldar, salir fiador, salir responsable, afianzar; dar fianza o caución. — *s.* (*for.*) persona por quien otra responde o sale fiadora; garantía, fianza.

guarantor [gærənˈtɔːr], *s.* garante, fiador.

guaranty [ˈgærənti], *s.* (*for.*) garantía, fianza, caución.

guard [gɑːrd], *v.t.*, *v.i.* guardar, custodiar, defender, conservar, preservar, proteger; vigilar; prevenirse, estar sobre sí, estar prevenido; guardarse.—*s.* guarda, *m.f.*, guardia, *m.f.*; vigilancia; centinela, *m.f.*, vigilante; defensa, protección, custodia, resguardo; estado de defensa; prevención, precaución, cautela; guarnición de una espada o vestido; cadena de un reloj; medio de protección; (*f.c.*) conductor de tren; *to be on one's guard,* estar sobre sí o sobre aviso; *to be off one's guard,* estar desprevenido; *to come off guard,* (*mil.*) salir de guardia; *to mount guard,* (*mil.*) montar la guardia; *on guard,* alerta; *rearguard,* retaguardia; *vanguard,* vanguardia.

guardable, *a.* capaz de ser guardado.

guarded, *a.* cauteloso.

guardedness, *s.* cautela, circunspección, precaución.

guardian [ˈgɑːrdiən], *s.* guardián, custodio, guarda, *m.f.*; (*for.*) tutor, curador. — *a.* que guarda, que ampara, tutelar; *guardian angel,* ángel custodio, ángel de la guarda.

guardianship, *s.* tutela, patronato; protección, amparo, custodia, guardianía; (*for.*) tutoría, curaduría.

guardless, *a.* sin amparo, sin defensa.

guard-rail, *s.* (*f.c.*) contracarril.

guard-room, *s.* (*mil.*) cuarto de guardia, calabozo.

guard-ship, *s.* navío de guardia.

guava [ˈgwɑːvə], *s.* guayabo; guayaba.

gubernatorial [gʌbərnəˈtɔːriəl], *a.;* (*E.U.*) gubernativo, relativo a un gobernador.

gudgeon [ˈgʌdʒən], *s.* (*ict.*) gobio; (*fig.*) chiripa, ganga; (*fig.*) zote, ganso, mentecato, bobo; (*mar.*) hembra (del timón); (*mec.*) gorrón; pernete; cojinete de un eje, perno, luchadero o cuello de eje; pezón metálico de un eje de madera.

guelder-rose [ˈgeldərrouz], *s.* viburno.

Guelf [gwelf], **Guelph,** *s.* güelfo.

guerdon [ˈgəːrdən], *s.* galardón, premio, recompensa.

guérite [ˈgeiriːt], *s.* (*mil.*) garita.

guernsey [ˈgəːrnzi], *s.* jersey (originalmente de Guernsey); *Guernsey cow,* res vacuna de la isla de Guernsey.

guerrilla [geˈrilə], *s.* (*mil.*) guerrillero; partida, guerrilla; (*Am.*) montonero, montonera.

guess [ges], *v.t.*, *v.i.* conjeturar, barruntar, sospechar, suponer; atinar, adivinar, acertar; (*fam., E.U.*) pensar, imaginar, imaginarse, creer, juzgar; *to guess rightly,* caer en el chiste; *you may guess the rest,* puede Vd. imaginarse lo demás. — *s.* barrunto, conjetura, suposición, adivinación, sospecha.

guesser, *s.* conjeturador, adivinador.

guess-rope, *s.* (*mar.*) guía de falsa amarra.

guesswork, *s.* conjetura, casualidad, obra hecha por conjetura o al acaso.

guest [gest], *s.* huésped, convidado; pensionista, *m.f.*, inquilino; visita, forastero; animal o vegetal parásito; *guest-chamber,* cuarto de respeto, habitación destinada a los huéspedes de una casa.

guffaw [gʌˈfɔː], *s.* carcajada, risotada.

guidable [ˈgaidəbl], *a.* dócil, manejable.

guidance [ˈgaidəns], *s.* guía, dirección, gobierno, conducta.

guide [gaid], *v.t.* guiar, encaminar, dirigir, encauzar, ajustar, gobernar, arreglar, poner en orden, influir. — *s.* guía, *m.f.*, conductor, director, mentor; modelo; guía (libro); (*impr.*) modante; pauta, patrón; corredera.

guide-board, *s.* hito.

guide-book, *s.* guía (de turistas).

guideless, *a.* sin guía ni director; sin gobierno.

guide-lines, *s.pl.* pauta, falsilla.

guide-post, *s.* hito, poste indicador.

guidon [ˈgaidən], *s.* (*mil.*) guión; portaguión.

guild [gild], *s.* gremio, comunidad, cuerpo, corporación, hermandad.

guilder, *s.* florín holandés.

guildhall [gildˈhɔːl], *s.* casa de ayuntamiento, casa consistorial.

guile [gail], **guilefulness** [ˈgailfəlnis], *s.* astucia, engaño, superchería; traición, perfidia; artificio, estratagema, chasco.

guileful, *a.* astuto, aleve, traidor, engañoso.

guilefulness, *s.* [GUILE].

guileless [ˈgailles], *a.* sencillo, cándido, franco, sincero, sin engaño, sin artificio.

guilelessness, *s.* inocencia, sencillez, franqueza, sinceridad.

guillemot [ˈgilimɔt], *s.* alca, uria.

guillotine [ˈgilotiːn], *s.* guillotina. — *v.t.* degollar, guillotinar.

guilt [gilt], *s.* culpabilidad, delito, culpa, falta, crimen, pecado.

guiltiness, *s.* criminalidad, maldad, culpabilidad.

guiltless, *a.* inocente, libre de culpa; virgen; puro, sin tacha; ignorante.

guiltlessness, *s.* inocencia, inculpabilidad.

guilty [ˈgilti], *a.* reo, delincuente, culpable; malvado, perverso, vicioso; convicto, sujeto a una pena; *guilty of death,* reo de muerte; *to plead guilty,* confesarse culpable; *to be found guilty,* ser declarado culpable.

guimpe [gimp], *s.* (*cost.*) camisolín.

guinea [ˈgini], *s.* guinea (21 chelines).

guinea-fowl, *s.* gallina de Guinea.

guinea-pepper, s. pimiento de Guinea.

guinea-pig, s. conejillo de Indias; cobayo; (*Cuba*) curiel.

guise [gaiz], s. modo, forma, manera; máscara, color, pretexto, capa; apariencia, continente; costumbre, práctica; *under the guise of*, socolor, bajo capa de; *in this guise*, de este modo, de esta forma.

guitar [gi'tɑːɹ], s. guitarra.

gulch [gʌltʃ], s. quebrada, rambla, valle estrecho.

gules [gjuːlz], s. (*blas.*) gules.

gulf [gʌlf], s. golfo, seno; abismo, sima, vorágine, f.; (*fig.*) gran dificultad u obstáculo; *Gulf Stream*, corriente del Golfo de Méjico.

gulf-weed, s. sargazo, gran alga marina.

gull [gʌl], v.t. engañar, petardear, defraudar, estafar, sisar, timar. — s. (*orn.*) gaviota; bodoque, bobo, primo; fraude, engaño, petardo, estafa, timo.

gull-catcher, s. engañador, impostor, petardista, *m.f.*

gullery, s. engaño, fraude, petardo, impostura.

gullet ['gʌlit], s. gaznate, gola, tragadero; (*anat.*) esófago; trinchera profunda, zanja.

gullibility [gʌli'biliti], s. tragadero, tragaderas, credulidad.

gullible [gʌlibəl], a. bobo, simple, crédulo.

gully ['gʌli], v.t. formar canal, acanalar. — s. carcava, barranca, hondonada; zanja honda.

gully-hole, s. albañal, sumidero.

gulosity [gjuː'lɔsiti], s. flotonería, voracidad; (*fig.*) ansia, codicia.

gulp [gʌlp], v.t. engullir, tragar; *to gulp down*, tragar; *to gulp up*, vomitar, vaciar. — s. trago.

gum [gʌm], s. goma; (*anat.*) encía. — v.t. engomar, pegar.

gum-arabic, s. guacia, goma arábiga.

gumbo ['gʌmbou], s. (*bot.*) quingombó, quimbombó; sopa de quimbombó; dialecto criollo (en Luisiana).

gum-boil, s. flemón.

gum-elastic, s. goma elástica, caucho.

gum-lac, s. goma laca.

gummiferous [gʌm'ifərəs], a. gomífero.

gumminess ['gʌminis], s. gomosidad.

gummous, gummy, a. gomoso, engomado, pegajoso, cubierto de goma.

gump [gʌmp], s. (*fam.*) páparo, payo, simplón.

gumption ['gʌmʃən], s. (*fam.*) perspicacia, habilidad; sentido común; (*pint.*) arte de preparar colores.

gum-tree, s. eucalipto; *to be up a gum-tree*, (*fam.*) estar en un apuro.

gum-water, s. aguagoma.

gun [gʌn], s. arma de fuego; fusil, cañón, carabina; pistola, revólver; escopeta de caza; disparo de arma de fuego, cañonazo; *air-gun*, escopeta de viento; *double-barrelled gun*, escopeta de dos cañones; *field-gun*, pieza de campaña; *to spike a gun*, clavar un cañón.

gun-barrel, s. cañón de fusil.

gunboat, s. (*mar.*) cañonero.

gun-carriage, s. afuste.

gunflint, s. piedra de chispa, piedra de lumbre, pedernal.

gunnage ['gʌnidʒ], s. número y peso de los cañones de un buque.

gunnel ['gʌnəl], s. (*mar.*) regala, borda.

gunner, s. (*mar.*) condestable; escopetero; artillero.

gunnery, s. artillería.

gunning, s. caza.

gunports, s.pl. (*mar.*) portas.

gunpowder, s. pólvora.

gunshot, s. tiro de fusil; alcance; escopetazo; *within gunshot*, al alcance de fusil, a tiro de escopeta.

gunsmith, s. armero, arcabucero.

gunwale ['gʌnəl], s. borda, regala.

gurgitation [gəːɹdʒi'teiʃən], s. vorágine, f., remolino, borbotón, borbollón.

gurgle ['gəːɹgəl], v.i. gorgotear. — s. gorgoteo, murmullo, salida de un líquido con ruido.

gurglet ['gəːɹglet], s. alcarraza.

gurnard ['gəːɹnəd], **gurnet,** s. trigla, alcotana, golondrina.

gush [gʌʃ], v.t. derramar, verter. — v.i. brotar, manar, fluir, chorrear; ser extremoso. — s. chorro, borbotón; extremos, efusión.

gushing, a. extremoso.

gusset ['gʌset], s. (*cost.*) escudete, contrete; codo de hierro, hierro angular.

gust [gʌst], s. ráfaga, ventolera, racha; soplo fuerte, bocanada de aire; (*mar.*) sobreviento, fugada; parasismo, arrebato; acceso, transporte; deleite, inclinación, afición; discernimiento, elección; gusto, sentido del paladar.

gustation, s. gustadura, gustación.

gustatory, gustative, a. gustable, gustoso.

gusto ['gʌstou], s. sabor, afición, placer, gusto.

gusty, a. borrascoso, chubascoso, tempestuoso.

gut [gʌt], s. intestino, tripa; cuerda de tripa; paso estrecho; (*mar.*) estrecho. — pl. **guts,** (*vulg.*) estómago; gula; valor, ánimo. — v.t. desventrar, destripar, desentrañar.

gutta ['gʌtə], s. (*farm.*) gota; **gutta serena;** (*med.*) gota serena.

gutta-percha [gʌtə'pəːɹtʃə], s. gutapercha.

gutter ['gʌtəɹ], s.canalón, gotera; alcantarilla; caneta; cloaca para el desagüe; arbollón, zanja, albañal, acequia; arroyo de calle; estría, canal de ebanistería. — v.t. acanalar, estriar; construir albañales, etc.; poner canalones. — v.i. caer en gotas, acanalarse; correrse.

guttural ['gʌtərəl], s., a. gutural.

gutturality, gutturalness, s. calidad de gutural.

guy [gai], s. tirante, guía, viento; persona fantástica o mal vestida; ente ridículo, mamarracho; (*fam., E.U.*) individuo; (*mar.*) retenida, patarráez, m. — v.t. (*mar.*) sujetar con vientos o retenida; (*fam.*) hacer burla o mofa de.

guzzle ['gʌzəl], v.t. beber mucho; engullir, tragar. — v.i. emborracharse; engullir.

guzzler, s. bebedor, borracho, borrachín; pellejo de vino.

gymnasium [dʒim'neiʒəm], s. gimnasio; liceo, colegio, escuela superior.

gymnast ['dʒimnæst], s. gimnasta, *m.f.*, atleta, *m.f.*

gymnastic [dʒim'næstik], **gymnastical,** a. gimnástico, gímnico.

gymnastics, s.pl. gimnástica.

gymnosophist [dʒim'nɔsofist], s. gimnosofista, *m.f.*

gymnosperm ['dʒimnospəːɹm], s. (*bot.*) planta gimnosperma.

gymnospermous, a. (*bot.*) gimnospermo.

gynæceum [gaini'si:əm], s. gineceo.
gynæcologist [gaini'kɔlodʒist], s. ginecólogo.
gynæcology, s. ginecología.
gynarchy ['dʒainɑːki], **gynæocracy**, s. ginecocracia.
gyp [dʒip], s. en las universidades de Cambridge y Durham, criado, sirviente.
gypseous, gypsine, a. gipsoso, yesoso.
gypsum ['dʒipsəm], s. yeso, aljez, m., aljezón; *crude gypsum*, aljez; *gypsum-pit*, yesal.
gypsy ['dʒipsi], s. [GIPSY].
gyral ['dʒairəl], a. giratorio; (*anat.*) referente a las circunvoluciones del cerebro.
gyrate [dʒai'reit], v.i. girar, rodar, revolver, dar vueltas.
gyration, s. giro, vuelta, revolución, rotación.
gyratory, s. giratorio.
gyre [dʒaiɹ], s. giro, girada, vuelta.
gyrfalcon ['dʒɔːɹfɔlkən], s. gerifalte.
gyromancy ['dʒairo'mænsi], s. giromancia.
gyroscope ['dʒairoskoup], s. giroscopio.
gyrostatics, s. girostática.
gyve [dʒaiv], v.t. encadenar; apiolar.
gyves [dzaivz], s.pl. grillos; esposas, manillas.

H

H, h [eitʃ], octava letra del alfabeto inglés; esta letra tiene un sonido algo más suave que la J española; en algunas palabras como *hour*, *heir*, *honest*, etc., es muda; al final de palabra como en *bough*, *plough*, es muda; en algunas voces, como *enough*, *cough*, da a la *g* el sonido de *f*.
ha [hɑː], *interj.* ah! ¡ja, ja, ja!
haberdasher ['hæbərdæʃəɹ], s. camisero, mercero, tendero que vende artículos para caballeros.
haberdashery [hæbəɹ'dæʃəri], s. camisería, mercería, pasamanería.
habergeon ['hæbəɹdʒən], s. coraza, cota de malla.
habiliment [hə'bilimənt], s. prenda de vestir. — *pl.* **habiliments**, vestuario, ropa, traje, vestidos.
habilitate [ha'biliteit], v.t. pertrechar, aviar, habilitar.
habilitation, s. habilitación; aptitud.
habit ['hæbit], s. hábito, costumbre, uso, rutina; vestido, hábito; condición, estado, complexión, constitución; *riding-habit*, (*equit.*) traje de amazona, traje de montar; *to get in the habit*, tomar la costumbre, tomar el tema. — *v.t.* ataviar, vestir, adornar.
habitable ['hæbitəbl], a. habitable.
habitableness, s. habitabilidad.
habitant, s. habitante, morador.
habitat ['hæbitæt], s. medio; habitación.
habitation [hæbi'teiʃən], s. habitación, morada, domicilio.
habited, a. vestido, ataviado. — *p.p.* [HABIT].
habitual [hə'bitjuːəl], a. habitual, acostumbrado, usual, inveterado.
habituate [hə'bitjuːeit], v.t., v.i. habituar, habituarse; acostumbrarse.
habitude ['hæbitjuːd], s. hábito, habituación, costumbre; familiaridad; relaciones, amistad, trato.

habitué [hæbi'tjuːei], s. tertuliano, parroquiano, cliente, concurrente.
hachure [hɑːˈʃuːɹ], s. rayado. — v.t. sombrear con líneas, rayar.
hack [hæk], s. caballo de alquiler, alquilón, cuartago, rocín; peón, trabajador; (*E.U.*) simón, coche de alquiler; muesca, tajo, corte, cuchillada; azuela, hacha, cuchilla; pico; (*fam.*) tos seca; *hack-saw*, sierra para metal; *hack writer*, escritor mercenario. — v.t. acuchillar, machetear; cortar, picar, tajar; mellar, hacer muescas; allanar o picar piedras; alquilar (coche o caballo). — v.i. tajar, cortar; alquilarse, prostituirse, venderse; toser con tos seca; escribir artículos etc. mal pagados.
hackle ['hækəl], v.t. rastrillar, hacer pedazos, romper en pedazos. — s. rastrillo; mosca para pescar; fibra no hilada.
hackman ['hækmən], s. cochero de alquiler, simón.
hackmatack ['hækmətæk], s. alerce o lárice americano.
hackney ['hækni], s. caballo pequeño, caballo de alquiler, rocín, cuartago; alquilón. — a. alquilado; común; gastado, cansado; *hackney coach*, coche de alquiler o simón; *hackney coachman*, cochero de alquiler. — v.t. gastar, repetir, vulgarizar; llevar en coche de alquiler.
hackneyed, a. trillado, gastado, manoseado. — *p.p.* [HACKNEY].
had [hæd], *pret.* y *p.p.* [HAVE].
haddock ['hædək], s. róbalo.
hade [heid], s. (*min.*) buzamiento, descenso escarpado.
Hades ['heidiːz], s. el infierno; Hades.
hæ-, v. **he-**.
haft [hɑːft], s. mango, agarradera, asa, manija, puño, cabo, guarnición.
hag [hæg], s. bruja, hechicera; vejarrona fea. — v.t. aterrar, atormentar, acosar, infundir terror.
hag-born, a. nacido de bruja.
haggard ['hægəɹd], a. trasnochado, ojeroso, macilento; consumido, desfigurado; zahareño, intratable, montaraz. — s. halcón; sujeto indómito, fiera.
haggis ['hægis], s. plato escocés (picadillo hervido).
haggish ['hægiʃ], a. de bruja, feo, horroroso.
haggle ['hægəl], v.t. tajar, machetear, destrozar. — v.i. regatear; cavilar; porfiar, hacer demandas y respuestas.
haggler, s. tajador; el que regatea, regatero, regatón.
hagiographal, a. hagiógrafo.
hagiographer [hægi'ɔgrəfəɹ], s. hagiógrafo.
hagiography [hægi'ɔgrəfi], s. hagiografía.
hagiolatry, s. hagiolatría.
hagiology [hægi'ɔlodʒi], s. hagiología.
hag-ridden, a. embrujado.
hah [hɑː], *interj.* ¡ah! ¡ja, ja, ja!
ha-ha ['hɑːhɑː], s. foso con escarpa, cerca hundida.
haik [heik], s. jaique árabe.
hail [heil], s. granizo, pedrisco, piedra; grito, llamada; saludo. — *interj.* ¡salve! ¡salud! ¡Dios te guarde! — v.t., v.i. granizar; aclamar, saludar; llamar, vocear; recibir o saludar con aclamaciones; *within hail*, al habla; *hailstorm*, granizada, pedrisquero; *to hail from*, venir o proceder de; *hail-fellow*, com-

pañero, camarada; *to hail a ship*, (*mar.*) ponerse al habla.

hailshot, *s.* perdigones, munición menuda.

hailstone, *s.* piedra de granizo.

haily ['heili], *a.* lleno de granizo, granujado.

hair [hɛəɹ], *s.* pelo, cabello, cabellera, vello; pelillo, fibra, hebra, hilo, filamento; *hairbrush*, cepillo para la cabeza; *head of hair*, cabellera; *false hair*, pelo postizo; *against the hair*, a contrapelo; *to a hair*, exactamente; perfectamente; *horse-hair*, crin; *hair shirt*, cilicio; *hair spring*, pelo o muelle (de reloj) muy fino; *to dress the hair*, peinarse.

hairbreadth, *s.* ancho de un pelo; casi nada; *to have a hairbreadth escape*, librarse de buena, salir de un apuro, escapar por un pelo.

hair-cloth, *s.* cilicio; esterilla para sillas, tela de crin.

hair-dresser, *s.* peluquero; peinador, peinadora.

hair-dressing, *s.* peinado.

haired, *a.* peludo, cabelludo; *curly-haired*, de pelo rizado o encrespado; *red-haired*, pelirrojo; *grey-haired*, canoso; *black-haired*, pelinegro.

hairiness, *s.* pelaje, calidad de peludo.

hairless, *a.* pelón, pelado, calvo.

hairpin, *s.* horquilla; gancho.

hair-sieve ['hɛəɹsiv], *s.* tamiz de cerda.

hair-splitting ['hɛəɹsplitiŋ], *s.* quisquilla, distinción sin importancia. — *a.* quisquilloso.

hairy, *a.* peludo, cubierto de pelo, velloso, velludo, peloso, cabelludo, hirsuto; crinito, caudato.

Haitian ['heitiən], *a.* haitiano.

hake [heik], *s.* merlango, merluza.

halation [həˈleiʃən], *s.* (*fot.*) aparición de un halo, de una aureola.

halberd ['hælbəɹd], *s.* alabarda.

halberdier [hælbəɹˈdiəɹ], *s.* alabardero.

halcyon ['hælsiən], *a.* quieto, tranquilo, apacible, pacífico, sereno; *halcyon days*, días tranquilos; veranillo de San Martín. — *s.* (*orn.*) alcedón, alción, (*m.*), martín pescador.

hale [heil], *a.* sano, fuerte, robusto, vigoroso; entero, ileso. — *v.t.* tirar, halar, arrastrar, llevar con violencia.

half [hɑːf], *s.* (*pl.* **halves**) mitad; parte media de un todo. — *a.* medio; casi, semi-; *half and half*, mitad de uno y mitad de otro; *half seas over*, medio borracho; *half a loaf is better than no bread*, (*prov.*) del agua vertida, alguna cogida.

half-blood, *s.* medio hermano, media hermana.

half-breed, half-caste, *s.*, *a.* mestizo.

half-cock, *a.* en seguro.

half-crown [hɑːfˈkraun], *s.* moneda inglesa del valor de dos chelines y medio.

halfer, *s.* gamo castrado.

half-mast, *s.* (a) media asta. — *v.t.* poner a media asta.

half-moon, *s.* semilunio.

halfpenny ['heipni], *s.* moneda de cobre inglesa del valor de medio penique.

half-wit, *s.* tonto, bobo.

halibut ['hælibət], *s.* hipogloso.

halieutic [hæliˈjuːtik], *a.* perteneciente o referente a la pesca. —*s.pl.* el arte de la pesca; tratado de pesca.

hall [hɔːl], *s.* vestíbulo, antecámara, zaguán; gran salón; corredor, pasadizo; sala de un tribunal; sala de sesiones; edificio público;

casa de ayuntamiento; *hall-mark*, marca de ley; *music-hall*, teatro de variedades; *City Hall*, casa de la ciudad o del Ayuntamiento.

hallelujah [hæliˈluːjə], *s.* (*igl.*) aleluya.

halliard ['hæljɑːd], *s.* (*mar.*) driza.

hallo [həˈlou], **halloa** ['hælou], *interj.* ¡hola! ¡oiga! ¡oye! ¡eh!

halloo [həˈluː], *s.* grita, vocería. — *interj.* ¡busca! ¡sus! — *v.t.*, *v.i.* gritar, dar grita, vocear, llamar o azuzar a gritos, insultar con clamores.

hallooing [həˈluːiŋ], *s.* grito alto, grita, vocería.

hallow ['hælou], *v.t.* consagrar, santificar; reverenciar; *All-Hallows*, día de Todos los Santos.

Hallowe'en, Hallow-eve, *s.* víspera de Todos los Santos.

Hallowmass, *s.* fiesta de Todos los Santos.

hallucinate [həˈluːsineit], *v.i.* alucinarse, confundirse, equivocarse.

hallucination, *s.* alucinación, equivocación, error; disparate.

halo ['heilou], *s.* halo, halón, cerco, corona, nimbo, aureola.

halogen ['hælodʒen], *s.* halógeno.

halography [həˈlɔɡrəfi], *s.* halografía.

haloid ['hælɔːid], *a.* haloideo. — *s.* sal haloidea.

halt [hɔlt], *v.i.* cojear, renquear, andar cojo; tartamudear; dudar, vacilar; pararse, detenerse; estar alto; estar imperfecto. — *v.t.* detener, parar. — *a.* cojo, encojado; lisiado, estropeado. — *s.* cojera; parada, alto; detención.

halter ['hɔltəɹ], *s.* cabestro, cabezada, ronzal; jáquima, ramal; dogal; cuerda, soga; cojo. — *v.t.* poner el cabestro o dogal; cabestrar, echar el ronzal; encordar.

halting, *a.* cojo; incierto, vacilante.

halve [hɑːv], *v.t.* dividir en dos mitades, demediar; machihembrar; ser o formar la mitad de.

halves [hɑːvz], *s.pl.* de *half*; *to go halves*, ir a medias, tener partes iguales; *halves!* a la parte me llamo.

halyard ['hæljəd], *s.* (*mar.*) driza; *peak-halyard*, driza del pico; *throat halyards*, drizas del foque mayor.

ham [hæm], *s.* pernil, jamón; (*anat.*) corva.

hamadryad, *s.* amadríada.

hamartiology [hæmɑːtiˈɔlədʒi], *s.* doctrina del pecado; tratado del pecado.

hamate ['heimət], *a.* enredado, encorvado, ganchoso.

hame [heim], *s.* horcate.

hamlet ['hæmlət], *s.* aldea, aldehuela, lugar, pueblo, villorrio, caserío, lugarillo.

hammer ['hæməɹ], *s.* martillo; rastrillo o percutor de arma de fuego; pilón o maza de martinete; macillo del piano; *tack-hammer*, martillo para puntillas; *claw-hammer*, martillo de orejas; *drop-hammer*, martinete; *sledge-hammer*, mazo o macho de herrero; *paving-hammer*, pisón de empedrador; *clench-hammer*, martillo de presa. — *v.t.* martillar, dar golpes con el martillo; machacar, golpear, cutir, batir; forjar; clavar; lucubrar; idear, trabajar con el entendimiento; *to hammer one's brains*, devanarse los sesos. — *v.i.* martillar, dar golpes; repiquetear; trabajar asiduamente.

hammercloth, s. paño del pescante de un coche.
hammerer, s. martillador.
hammerhead, s. (ict.) cornudilla, pez martillo.
hammering, s. martilleo; ruido de martillazos; repujado.
hammerman, s. martillador.
hammock ['hæmək], s. hamaca.
hamper ['hæmpəɹ], s. cuévano, canasta, banasto, cesto grande; traba, impedimento; (mar.) aparejo. — v.t. enmarañar, embarazar, enredar, estorbar; encanastar, encestar.
hamstring ['hæmstriŋ], s. tendón de la corva. — v.t. desjarretar, cortar las piernas por el jarrete.
hanaper ['hænəpəɹ], s. cesta para documentos u objetos de valor; erario, tesorería.
hand [hænd], s. mano, f.; (fig.) ejecución, mano de obra; maña, habilidad, destreza; operario, obrero; lado (derecho o izquierdo); horario o secundario, manecilla o aguja de reloj; peón, brazo, jornalero; operario u operaria; persona, gente, f.; carácter de letra; mano, medida de 4 pulgadas; firma, rúbrica; trabajo, acción, agencia; poder, posesión, dominación; mano, f., cartas (en el juego); prenda de esponsales o matrimonio; influencia, disciplina; at hand, a la mano, cerca, junto; clean hands, (fig.) honradez; light hand, suavidad, dulzura, economía; heavy hand, dureza, tiranía, gasto inútil; in hand, de contado, por de pronto; near at hand, junto, a la mano; to change hands, cambiar de dueño; to be in good hands, estar muy bien; to come to hand, llegar a su debido tiempo o hallarse a la mano; to bring up by hand, dar de mamar artificialmente; to get one's hand in, adquirir habilidad por medio de la práctica; to get the upper hand, o to get the whip hand, llevar la ventaja; to lay hands on, echar mano a; to lend a hand, ayudar, dar una mano; to be short of hands, carecer de operarios; to live from hand to mouth, ir arrastrando; to shake hands, estrechar o apretar la mano a; to take in hand, tomar entre manos; to turn one's hand to, meter mano en, emprender; to wash one's hands of, lavarse las manos, declinar responsabilidad; to be someone's right hand, ser la mano derecha de uno; all hands below! (mar.) ¡abajo todo el mundo!; all hands on deck! ¡todo el mundo arriba!; to have well in hand, estar sobre; given under my hand, firmado de mi puño y letra; hand in hand, (fig.) de acuerdo; hands off!, ¡manos quedas!, ¡no me toques!, ¡no tocar!; off-hand, despreocupado, inconsideradamente, sin consideración; on hand, en poder, en posesión, a la mano, puntual; out of hand, inmediatamente, rebelde, rebelón, difícil; second-hand, de segunda mano; second-hand bookseller, librero de viejo; second-hand clothes shop, ropavejería. — v.t. dar, alargar, proporcionar; conducir, guiar; manejar, mover con la mano. — v.i. cooperar, concertarse, ir de acuerdo; to hand down, bajar, pasar de arriba a abajo, transmitir; to hand in(to), ayudar a entrar; to hand round, hacer circular.
handball, s. pelota; juego de pelota; bola hueca.
handbarrow, s. angarillas, parihuela.
handbell, s. campanilla, esquila.
handbill, s. cartel.

handbook, s. manual, guía.
handbow, s. arco de mano.
handbreadth, s. palmo menor.
handcuff, s. manilla, esposas. — v.t. maniatar.
handed, a. que tiene mano; de mano. — p.p. [HAND]; empty-handed, con las manos vacías; high-handed, imperioso; arbitrario; left-handed, zurdo; dado con la mano izquierda; right-handed, que usa la mano derecha; dado con la mano derecha; hard-handed, de mano pesada; one-handed, manco; four-handed, a cuatro manos; open-handed, generoso, liberal; single-handed, con una mano; por sí solo, sin ayuda.
hander, s. el que entrega o transmite.
handful ['hændful], s. puñado, manojo, mano llena, manípulo; by handfuls, a manos llenas; double handful, almuerza.
hand-glass, s. espejo de mano.
handicap ['hændikæp], v.t. poner obstáculos; (fig.) perjudicar; impedir. — s. obstáculo; desventaja; (dep.) handicap.
handicraft ['hændikrɑːft], s. mano de obra; oficio, arte mecánico; (ant.) mecánico, menestral.
handicraftsman ['hændikrɑːftsmən], s. artesano, artífice, mecánico.
handily ['hændili], adv. mañosamente, con destreza.
handiness, s. maña, destreza, habilidad.
handiwork, handywork, s. obra mecánica, obraje, maniobra, artefacto.
handkerchief ['hæŋkətʃif], s. pañuelo.
handle ['hændəl], v.t. palpar, manosear, tocar; dirigir; tratar; hacer tratable; manejar, manipular; poner mango a; comerciar en; practicar. — v.i. manejarse; hacer uso de las manos, trabajar con las manos; handle with care, con cuidado, frágil. — s. mango, manija, manubrio, varilla, puño, asidero, asa, cabo, tirador; (vulg.) apodo; (fam.) título, tratamiento.
handless ['hændles], a. manco, sin manos.
handling ['hændliŋ], s. acto de manejar, manejo, tocamiento, manoseo; toque; manipulación, maniobra; ardid, astucia.
handmaid ['hændmeid], **handmaiden,** s.f. criada, doncella, asistenta.
hand-mill, s. molinillo.
handsel, hansel ['hænsəl], s. estrena, prenda, garantía de un contrato. — v.t. estrenar, dar prenda en garantía.
handsome ['hænsəm], a. hermoso, gentil, lindo, guapo, garrido; elegante, distinguido, fino, correcto; honrado, excelente, primoroso; noble, dadivoso, generoso, liberal, amplio, noble.
handsomeness, s. hermosura, elegancia, gracia; generosidad.
handspike, s. (mar.) espeque.
handstaff, s. jabalina.
handwork, s. obra hecha a mano.
handwriting ['hændraitiŋ], s. letra, caligrafía; quirografía; escritura.
handy [hændi], a. manual; próximo, a la mano; de fácil acceso, cerca, fácil de manejar; mañoso, hábil, diestro, socorrido.
handywork, s. [HANDIWORK]
hang [hæŋ], v.t. (pret., p.p. hung, hanged) colgar, suspender; ahorcar (en este sentido el participio pasado es hanged); endoselar; levantar en alto; inclinar; entapizar; poner

colgaduras; empapelar la pared; (*mar.*) montar, calar (el timón). — *v.i.* colgar(se), caer, pender; pegarse, ir al retortero, agregarse a uno; vacilar, fluctuar; amenazar, ser inminente; sufrir la pena de horca, ser ahorcado; vigilar, aguardar; dilatar, tardar; estar en duda; depender, estar pendiente de; formar pendiente; colgarse o abrazarse al cuello de uno; seguir en el mismo estado; *to hang back*, rehusar ir adelante, vacilar en vez de ir adelante; *to hang down*, bajar, colgar; *to hang out*, enarbolar, desplegar; *to hang over*, inclinarse, cabecear; *to hang up*, levantar, suspender; *to hang together*, acordarse; *to hang upon*, atender a, mirar con gran afecto; *to hang round*, (*fam.*) tardar, (*fam.*) pegarse; *to hang fire*, (*mil.*) suspender el fuego, (*fam.*) no hacerse una cosa al debido tiempo, no tener gran éxito; *hang it!* ¡diablos! — *s.* manera como cuelga una cosa; (*fam.*) maña, destreza; (*fam.*) uso, idea general; *I don't care a hang!* ¡Ruede la bola!

hangdog [ˈhæŋdɔg], *s.* camastrón, mataperros. — *a.* bajo, tacaño, de apariencia vil.

hanger [ˈhæŋəɹ], *s.* colgadero, soporte colgante; (*impr.*) espito; alfanje; campanillero; *paper-hanger*, empapelador; *bell-hanger*, campanillero.

hanger-on [hæŋəɹˈɔn], *s.* dependiente; haragán; mogollón, ladilla, moscón, pegote; paseante de corte; familiar.

hanging, *s.* ahorcadura, muerte en la horca. — *a.* colgante, pendiente, suspendido. — *pl.* **hangings**, tapices, colgaduras, cortinajes; *to deserve hanging*, oler a soga.

hangman, *s.* verdugo.

hangnail, *s.* padrastro, respigón.

hangnest, *s.* oropéndola.

hank [hæŋk], *s.* madeja, ovillo; rollo de cuerda, adujada; (*fam.*) inclinación, influencia. — *v.i.* hacer madejas u ovillos; ovillar, adujar.

hanker [ˈhæŋkəɹ], *v.i.* ansiar, apetecer.

hankering, *s.* gana, ansia, anhelo, apetencia, deseo, antojo, inclinación, afición.

hanse [hæns], *s.* ansa; unión mercantil, *f.*, lonja, bolsa.

Hanseatic [hænsiˈætik], *a.* anseático.

hansom [ˈhænsəm] (**cab**), *s.* cabriolé con el pescante en la zaga.

hap [hæp], *s.* caso, acaso, lance; accidente, casualidad, azar, fortuna, suerte, *f.* — *v.i.* acontecer, suceder, acaecer.

ha'penny [ˈheipni], *s.* contracción de HALF-PENNY, medio penique.

haphazard [hæpˈhæzəd], *s.* suerte, *f.*, lance, accidente. — *a.* fortuito, casual.

hapless [ˈhæples], *a.* desgraciado, desamparado, desventurado, miserable.

haply [ˈhæpli], *adv.* quizá, quizás; por casualidad, casualmente.

ha'p'orth [ˈheipəθ], *s.* contracción de HALF-PENNY-WORTH, lo que se vende por medio penique.

happen [ˈhæpən], *v.i.* acontecer, acaecer, pasar, ocurrir, sobrevenir, suceder por casualidad; hallarse accidentalmente en; parar en; *to happen on*, tropezar con, encontrar casualmente; *whatever happens*, suceda lo que suceda *o* venga lo que viniere *o* salga lo que saliere; *to happen in*, (*fam.*) entrar (*o* hacer una visita) al pasar.

happening, *s.* acontecimiento, suceso, sucedido.

happiness [ˈhæpines], *s.* felicidad, dicha, prosperidad, ventura.

happy [ˈhæpi], *a.* feliz, dichoso, bienhadado, afortunado, bienaventurado, fausto; bienhallado, oportuno; desembarazado, expedito.

harangue [hæˈræŋ], *s.* arenga, perorata, oración, alocución. — *v.t.* arengar. — *v.i.* pronunciar un discurso.

haranguer, *s.* orador.

harass [ˈhærəs], *v.t.* cansar, fatigar, hostigar, incomodar, acosar, vejar, atormentar; (*mil.*) perseguir, hostigar, hostilizar.

harassment, *s.* hostigamiento, fatiga, cansancio.

harbinger [ˈhɑːɹbindʒəɹ], *s.* el que va delante, precursor, heraldo, nuncio; presagio. — *v.t.* anunciar, presagiar.

harbour [ˈhɑːɹbəɹ], *s.* puerto; seguro; albergue, asilo, abrigo; *harbour master*, capitán de puerto; *harbour dues*, derechos de puerto. — *v.t.* abrigar, defender, amparar, resguardar; guardar, conservar, acariciar, profesar; hospedar, acoger, albergar; concebir, imaginar. — *v.i.* refugiarse, ampararse, recibir amparo, hospedarse.

harbourage, *s.* puerto; amparo, refugio, asilo.

harbourer, *s.* amparador, acogedor, albergador; encubridor.

harbourless, *s.* desamparado, destituido de asilo.

hard [hɑːɹd], *a.* duro, firme, sólido, endurecido; insensible, cruel; trabajoso, difícil, dificultoso, penoso, arduo; opresivo, injusto, ofensivo; rígido, severo, riguroso; tieso, inflexible, fuerte, vigoroso, sufrido; tosco, áspero, grosero, bronco; miserable, mezquino; (*fam.*) malvado, perverso; cruda, gorda (agua); *hard earned*, ganado con dificultad; *hard of hearing*, duro de oído, medio sordo; *hard words*, palabras injuriosas; *hard cash*, (*com.*) moneda sonante, efectivo; *hard drinking*, borrachera. — *s.* piso de camino duro. — *adv.* cerca, a la mano, diligentemente, con ahinco; con impaciencia, con inquietud, aprisa, ligeramente; tempestuosamente; con dureza, reciamente, con fuerza; difícilmente, con dificultad; (*mar.*) todo, enteramente, al límite extremo; *hard-a-port*, a babor todo; *hard by*, muy cerca, inmediato; *it rains hard*, llueve a cántaros; *hard and fast*, de cal y canto, a macha martillo; *to be hard up*, hallarse en apuros, estar a la cuarta pregunta; *to grow hard*, endurecerse; *to be hard put to it*, estar en apuros, encontrar gran dificultad.

hard-bitten, *a.* de carácter duro.

hard-bound, *a.* estreñido.

harden [ˈhɑːɹdn], *v.t.* endurecer, poner duro; curtir, encallecer; solidar; templar; robustecer; hacer obstinado, insensible, indiferente, firme o constante. — *v.i.* endurecerse, empedernirse.

hardener, *s.* el que o lo que endurece.

hard-favoured, *a.* feo, de semblante desagradable.

hard-favouredness, *s.* fealdad.

hard-handed, *a.* trabajador; despótico, severo.

hard-headed, *a.* terco.

hard-hearted, *a.* empedernido, cruel, inhumano.

hard-heartedness, s. insensibilidad, crueldad, inhumanidad.

hardihood ['hɑːɹdihud], s. atrevimiento, valor, temeridad, impudencia, descaro.

hardiness ['hɑːɹdinis], s. ánimo, valor, osadía, intrepidez; vigor, robustez.

hardly ['hɑːɹdli], adv. apenas, difícilmente, con dificultad; de mala gana; no del todo; escasamente; duramente, ásperamente, severamente.

hard-mouthed ['hɑːɹdmauðd], a. boquiduro, de boca dura (caballos).

hardness ['hɑːɹdnis], s. dureza, solidez, firmeza; crueldad, obscuridad, severidad, inhumanidad, obduración; trabajo, pena; penuria, escasez; aspereza, rigor; fiereza, ferocidad.

hards [hɑːɹdz], s.pl. desperdicios de lino o lana.

hardship ['hɑːɹdʃip], s. privación; trabajo, pena, fatiga; opresión, injuria, injusticia, gravamen.

hardtack, s. galleta de munición.

hardware ['hɑːɹdwɛəɾ], s. quincalla, quincallería, quinquillería, ferretería.

hardwareman, s. quincallero, ferretero.

hardwood, s. madera dura.

hard-worked, a. que trabaja mucho.

hardy ['hɑːɹdi], a. fuerte, endurecido, robusto; intrépido, bravo; osado, atrevido; (bot.) resistente, que aguanta bien el frío, que sobrevive el invierno.

hare [hɛəɹ], s. liebre, f.; (astr.) constelación Lepus; hare and hounds, juego campestre en que se imita la caza de las liebres; young hare, lebratillo; hare-hunting, caza de liebres; mad as a March hare, loco de atar, extravagante, insensato.

harebell, s. (bot.) campánula.

hare-brained, a. cabeza de chorlito, ligero de cascos, tolondro; precipitado, inconstante.

harefoot, s. pie de liebre; (poét.) corredor ágil.

hare-hearted, a. temeroso, cobarde.

harehound ['hɛəɹhaund], s. lebrel, galgo.

harelip [hɛəɹ'lip], s. labio leporino.

harelipped, a. labihendido, boquiconejuno.

harem ['hɛəɹəm], s. harén, harem, serrallo.

haremint ['hɛəɹmint], s. (bot.) yaro, manto de Santa María.

hare's-ear ['hɛəɹziəɹ], s. (bot.) oreja de liebre, hierba de Europa.

hare's-foot, s. (bot.) pie de liebre, variedad de trébol.

hare's lettuce, s. (bot.) ajonjera.

haricot ['hærikou], s. guisado con habichuelas; fréjol, judía, habichuela.

hark [hɑːɹk], **harken** ['hɑːɹkən] o **hearken,** v.t., v.i. oír con atención, escuchar, atender; interj. ¡oye! ¡oiga! ¡mira!

harl [hɑːɹl], s. hebras de lino; filamento.

harlequin ['hɑːɹlikwin], s. arlequín, gracioso, botarga, bufón. — v.t., v.i. bufonear, chasquear, decir gracias.

harlequinade [hɑːɹlikwi'neid], s. arlequinada, pantomima.

harlot ['hɑːɹlət], s.f. ramera, prostituta, meretriz. — a. meretricio, ruin, vil. — v.i. prostituirse.

harlotry, s. prostitución.

harm [hɑːɹm], s. detrimento, perjuicio, daño, agravio, peligro, ofensa, mal, injuria, maldad, desgracia. — v.t. dañar, agraviar, ofender, herir, perjudicar.

harmala ['hɑːɹmələ], s. (bot.) ruda silvestre.

harmaline, s. (quím.) alcaloide cristalino blanco, obtenido de la semilla de la ruda.

harmful ['hɑːɹmfəl], a. dañoso, nocivo, pernicioso, perjudicial, peligroso.

harmfulness, s. maldad, daño, calidad de nocivo.

harmless, a. innocuo, inocente; sano y salvo; libre de daño, ileso; to hold harmless, librar de responsabilidad.

harmlessness, s. inocencia, sencillez, calidad de no ser nocivo.

harmonic [hɑːɹ'mɔnik], s. armónico. — pl. armonía.

harmonic, harmonical, a. armónico.

harmonica, s. (mús.) armónica.

harmonicon, s. (mús.) armónica, organillo.

harmonious [hɑːɹ'mouniəs], a. armónico, consono, armonioso, musical; proporcionado, simétrico.

harmoniousness, s. armonía, sonoridad.

harmonist ['hɑːɹmənist], s. armonista, m.f. músico.

harmonium [hɑːɹ'mouniəm], s. (mús.) armonio.

harmonize ['hɑːɹmənaiz], **harmonise,** v.t. armonizar, hermanar, ajustar, poner de acuerdo, concertar. — v.i. armonizarse, congeniar, concordar; convenir, consonar, corresponder.

harmonizer, s. conciliador; (mús.) armonista, m.f.

harmony ['hɑːɹməni], s. armonía; concordancia, uniformidad, concordia, consonancia.

harness ['hɑːɹnes], s. atalaje, arreos y paramentos, jaeces, guarniciones; (fig.) servicio activo; (mil.) arnés; (mec.) aparejo; equipo. — v.t. atalajar, enjaezar, acollarar, enganchar; armar con arnés.

harness-maker, s. guarnicionero.

harp [hɑːɹp], s. (mús., astr.) arpa. — v.t., v.t. tocar o tañer el arpa; to harp on o upon, repetir, porfiar, machacar.

harper, harpist, s. arpista, m.f.

harping, s. tañido del arpa; repetición enfadosa. — pl. **harpings,** (mar.) cucharros; jaretas; redondos de la proa; bagaras o maestras.

harpist, s. arpista, m.f.

harpoon [hɑːɹ'puːn], s. arpón, cloque. — v.t. arponear.

harpooneer [hɑːɹpu'niəɹ], **harpooner,** s. arponero.

harpsichord ['hɑːɹpsikɔːɹd], s. arpicordio.

harpy ['hɑːɹpi], s. arpía; (orn.) arpella.

harquebuss ['hɑːɹkwibʌs], s. arcabuz.

harquebussier, s. arcabucero.

harridan ['hæridən], s. vieja rencorosa; bruja.

harrier ['hæriəɹ], s. lebrel; asolador, pillador, molestador; ave de rapiña, parecida al milano.

harrow ['hærou], s. (agr.) grada, trilla, rastro; escarificador. — v.t. (agr.) gradar, escarificar; (fig.) atormentar, inquietar, perturbar.

harrower, s. el que desmenuza la tierra.

harrowing ['hærouiŋ], a. conmovedor, angustioso.

harry ['hæri], v.t. pillar, saquear, asolar; molestar, cansar, inquietar, acosar.

harsh [hɑːɹʃ], a. áspero, acerbo, agrio, rígido, duro, bronco, austero, riguroso, desagradable; desapacible, tosco, malcondicionado.

harshness, s. aspereza, austeridad, rudeza,

acerbidad; rigor, severidad, mal humor; bronquedad.

hart [haːɪt], *s.* ciervo de cinco años; (*mar.*) motón de vigota.

hartshorn [ˈhaːɪtshɔːɪn], *s.* amoníaco; (*bot.*) variedad de llantén; cuerno de ciervo.

hartstongue [ˈhaːɪtstʌŋ], *s.* (*bot.*) escolopendra.

harum-scarum [hɛərəmˈskɛərəm], *a.* precipitado, atolondrado; al tuntún, a troche y moche, patas arriba; *to be a harum-scarum*, tener malos cascos.

haruspex [həˈrʌspeks], **haruspice**, *s.* arúspice.

harvest [ˈhaːɪvest], *s.* cosecha, esquilmo, siega, mies, *f.*, agosto; producto, fruto; *harvest moon*, luna de la cosecha; *harvest-home*, (*Ingl.*) fiesta o coro de segadores. — *v.t.* cosechar, esquilmar, segar, recoger las mieses, el fruto, hacer su agosto.

harvest-bug, *s.* mita, arador.

harvester, *s.* segador; (máquina) segadora.

harvester, harvest-man, *s.* agostero, cosechero.

harvest-fly, *s.* cigarra, chicharra, cicada.

has [hæz], 3ª. *pers. pres. ind.* [HAVE].

hash [hæʃ], *v.t.* picar, hacer pedazos, hacer picadillo. — *s.* picadillo; jigote, salpicón.

hashish [ˈhæʃiːʃ], **hasheesh**, *s.* haxix, hachich.

haslet [ˈhæzlet], *s.* asadura de puerco.

hasp [haːsp], *s.* aldaba de candado; broche. — *v.t.* abrochar; cerrar con aldaba.

hassock [ˈhæsək], *s.* banqueta, escabel; ruedo de estera; cojín.

hastate [ˈhæsteit], *a.* (*bot.*) alabardado; de punta aguda.

haste [heist], *s.* prisa, diligencia, presteza, acucia, premura; expedición, festinación, precipitación, velocidad; urgencia; *to be in haste*, estar de prisa, tener prisa; *to make haste*, darse prisa, despacharse, apresurarse; *more haste, less speed*, quien más corre, menos vuela.

haste, hasten, *v.t.* acelerar, precipitar, apresurar, activar, acuciar, avivar. — *v.i.* darse prisa, apresurarse, moverse rápidamente, ser pronto.

hastener, *s.* avivador.

hastiness [ˈheistinis], *s.* prisa, prontitud, presteza, precipitación, diligencia; impaciencia.

hasting [ˈheistiŋ], *a.* precipitado; sin la debida reflexión; madurando antes de su tiempo normal. — *s.pl.* guisantes tempranos.

hasty [ˈheisti], *a.* pronto, ligero, apresurado, vivo; arrojado, precipitado; temprano; *hasty-pudding*, (*coc.*) especie de papilla, gachas.

hat [hæt], *s.* sombrero; capelo; (*fig.*) dignidad de cardenal; *Panama hat*, sombrero de jipijapa; sombrero panamá; *silk hat, tall hat, high hat* (*vulg.* *chimney-pot hat, stove-pipe hat*), sombrero de copa (alta); *cocked hat*, tricornio, sombrero de tres picos; *to pass round the hat*, pasar el cepillo, hacer una colecta; *to put on one's hat*, ponerse el sombrero; *to take off one's hat*, quitarse el sombrero.

hat-band, *s.* cinta, cintillo de sombrero.

hat-box, hat-case, *s.* sombrerera.

hatch [hætʃ], *v.t.* criar pollos, empollar, incubar; maquinar, tramar, idear, fraguar; sombrear (un grabado). — *v.i.* empollarse, salir del cascarón; madurarse; *to count one's chickens before they are hatched*, echar la

cuenta sin la huéspeda. — *s.* cría, nidada, pollada, pollazón, *f.*; portezuela, trampa; salida del cascarón; media puerta; (*hidr.*) paradera, compuerta; exclusa en un canal o río para coger peces; (*mar.*) cuartel; portezuelas para cerrar las escotillas; *to be under hatches*, andar a sombra de tejado; (*fig.*) estar en miseria, en la cárcel, etc.

hatch-bar, (*mar.*) barra de escotilla.

hatchel [ˈhætʃəl], *s.* rastrillo. — *v.t.* rastrillar; (*fig.*) contrariar, fastidiar, impacientar.

hatcheller, *s.* rastrillador.

hatcher, *s.* tramador, trazador.

hatchet [ˈhætʃet], *s.* destral, hacha pequeña, machado; *to bury the hatchet*, hacer la paz, olvidar lo pasado; *to dig up* (o *take up*) *the hatchet*, hacer la guerra.

hatchet-face, *s.* cara delgada, enjuta.

hatchet-faced, *a.* de facciones enjutas.

hatching [ˈhætʃiŋ], *s.* incubación; (*b.a.*) acto de sombrear, rayado.

hatchment, *s.* (*blas.*) escudo de armas.

hatchway [ˈhætʃwei], *s.* (*mar.*) escotilla; *magazine-hatchway*, escotilla de popa; *main-hatchway*, escotilla mayor; *fore-hatchway*, escotilla de proa.

hate [heit], *v.t.* detestar, odiar, aborrecer, abominar. — *s.* odio, detestación, aborrecimiento, aversión.

hateful, *a.* aborrecible, detestable, odioso; rencoroso, maligno, malévolo.

hatefulness, *s.* odiosidad.

hater, *s.* aborrecedor; *woman-hater*, misógino, enemigo o aborrecedor de las mujeres.

hath [hæθ], 3ª. *pers. pres. ind. sing.* [HAVE].

hating [ˈheitiŋ], *s.* aversión, aborrecimiento, acto de odiar o abominar.

hat-maker, *s.* sombrerero.

hat-pin, *s.* alfiler o pasador de sombrero.

hatred [ˈheitred], *s.* odio, mala voluntad, aversión, aborrecimiento, enemistad, malignidad.

hatted [ˈhætid], *a.* que lleva sombrero.

hatter, *s.* sombrerero; *as mad as a hatter*, loco de remate.

hauberk [ˈhoubəːɪk], *s.* (*mil.*) coraza, plaquín, camisote.

haughtiness [ˈhoːtinis], *s.* altanería, soberbia, arrogancia, orgullo, altivez, presunción, humos.

haughty [ˈhoːti], *a.* soberbio, altivo, altanero, orgulloso, presuntuoso, arrogante, vanidoso, entonado, vano.

haul [hoːl], *v.t.* tirar, arrastrar; (*mar.*) ronzar, halar, aballestar, cazar; *to haul the wind*, abarloar, ceñir el viento; *to haul down the colours*, arriar la bandera; *haul home*, caza y atraca; *to haul aft the sheets*, cazar las escotas. — *s.* tirón o estirón, hala; redada; arrastre.

hauling, *s.* estirón, hala, acción de halar.

hauling-line, *s.* guía.

haulm [hoːm], **haum**, *s.* paja, rastrojo.

haunch [hoːntʃ], *s.* anca, culata, grupa; (*arq.*) riñón de la bóveda; *haunch of venison*, pierna (de venado).

haunt [hoːnt], *v.t.* frecuentar, acudir muchas veces a; visitar frecuentemente; causar obsesión; rondar, perseguir, molestar. — *s.* guarida; hábito, querencia, costumbre; lugar que uno frecuenta.

haunted, *a.* encantado, frecuentado. — *p.p.* [HAUNT]; *to be haunted*, tener duendes.

hausen ['hauzən], *s.* el gran esturión blanco; ballena blanca del mar ártico.

haustellum [hɔː'steləm], *s.* trompa (de las mariposas, moscas, etc.).

hautboy ['houbɔi], *s.* (*mús.*) oboe; (*bot.*) especie de fresa.

have [hæv], *v.t.* (*pret. y p.p.* had; *ger.* having) tener, haber; traer, llevar, tomar; recibir, obtener; contener, incluir, comprender; poseer; padecer, sufrir; sentir, experimentar, gozar; procurar, mandar, hacer; profesar, concebir; poner por obra, efectuar; parir, dar a luz; haber de, tener que, deber; mirar, apreciar, estimar; estar a punto de; saber; parir, engendrar; vencer, tener a uno a su merced; tener en la mento; entrampar, enredar, engañar; *to have at a person*, desafiar a uno, provocarle a combate; *to have about* (o *on*) *one*, llevar o tener consigo; *to have as lief*, serle a uno igual; querer de buena gana; *to have down*, bajar; *to have from*, saber por; *to have in*, hacer entrar; *to have it out*, concluir un negocio, hablar francamente, poner las cosas claras; *to have by heart*, saber de memoria; *to have a mind*, tener gana, deseo, pensamiento de hacer algo; *to have nothing to do with*, no tener nada que ver con; *to have on*, llevar (un vestido); (*vulg.*) tomar el pelo, engañar; *to have rather*, preferir; *to have up*, hacer subir; *as luck would have it*, por fortuna.

havelock ['hævlɒk], *s.* (*mil.*) forro, cogotera.

haven ['heivən], *s.* puerto, abra, fondeadero; abrigo, asilo.

haver ['heivər], *s.* poseedor, tenedor; disparate. — *v.i.* (*Esco.*) decir tonterías. — *s.pl.* charla inconsiderada, necedad.

haversack ['hævərsæk], *s.* mochila, barjuleta.

having ['hæviŋ], *s.* bienes, haber, hacienda.

havoc ['hævək], *s.* estrago, destrucción, tala, asolamiento, ruina, desolación. — *v.t.* asolar, talar, destruir, estragar.

haw [hɔː], *s.* (*bot.*) acerola; cañada, cercado; baya y simiente del espino blanco. — *v.t.*, *v.i.* volver o hacer volver a la izquierda (caballerías o bueyes; lo opuesto a *gee*); *to haw and gee*, vacilar, ir de un lado a otro, estar irresoluto. — *v.i.* tartamudear; tartalear.

Hawaiian [hɑ:'weijən], *a.* de Hawaii.

hawk [hɔːk], *s.* halcón; *hawk-moth*, esfinge, *f.*, cabeza de muerto (mariposa). — *v.t.* cazar con halcón; espectorar, gargajear, arrancar flema; pregonar mercancía por las calles.

hawker, *s.* buhonero, mercachifle, revendedor, pregonero; falconero.

hawk-eyed ['hɔːkaid], *a.* de ojos de lince.

hawking, *s.* cetrería; buhonería.

hawk-nosed, *a.* aguileño, de nariz aguileña.

hawk-owl, *s.* úlula, autillo.

hawk's-bell, *s.* cascabel.

hawkweed, *s.* (*bot.*) hieracio, hierba del gavilán.

hawse [hɔːz], *s.* (*mar.*) proa del buque, en que están los escobenes; distancia o longitud de un cable.

hawse-hole, *s.* escobén.

hawse-plugs, *s.pl.* tacos de los escobenes.

hawser ['hɔːzər], *s.* (*mar.*) cable, estacha, guindaleza.

hawthorn ['hɔːθɔːrn], *s.* espino blanco, espina blanca, oxiacanto, acerolo.

hay [hei], *s.* heno, paja de heno, forraje; seto, vallado, cercado; (*Am.*) zacate; (*esgr.*) estocada; danza en círculo; *hay rake*, rastrillo para heno; *hay spreader* o *hay tedder*, esparcidora de heno; *make hay while the sun shines*, al buen día meterle en casa.

haycock, *s.* almiar, montón o niara de heno.

hay-fever, *s.* romadizo.

hay-field, *s.* henar.

hayfork, *s.* bieldo, horca.

hay-loft, *s.* henil.

hayrick, *s.* almiar, montón de heno.

hayseed, *s.* patán, paleto; simiente de heno, *f.*

haystack, *s.* niara, almiar o montón de heno.

hazard ['hæzəd], *s.* azar, suerte, *f.*, acaso, casualidad, ventura, peligro, accidente, albur, riesgo; tronera (juego de billar), juego de azar a los dados; *at all hazards*, a toda costa, o cueste lo que cueste. — *v.t.* arriesgar, exponer, aventurar, poner en riesgo. — *v.i.* arriesgarse, correr un albur, probar la suerte, aventurarse; correr riesgo.

hazardable ['hæzədəbl], *a.* que se puede aventurar; peligroso, osado, arriesgado.

hazarder, *s.* jugador; el que arriesga.

hazardous ['hæzədəs], *a.* arriesgado, peligroso.

hazardousness, *s.* riesgo, peligro.

haze [heiz], *s.* tufo, niebla, calina, bruma; ofuscamiento mental. — *v.i.* abrumarse la atmósfera, estar nebuloso el tiempo, hacer tufo. — *v.t.* dar culebra (en los colegios); hacer a uno víctima de chanzas; (*mar.*) cansar, fatigar con trabajos pesados.

hazel ['heizəl], *s.* avellano.

hazel-grouse, *s.* (*orn.*) ortega.

hazel-nut, *s.* avellana. — *a.* castaño, del color de avellana.

haziness ['heizinis], *s.* tufo, fosca, obscuridad.

hazing, *s.* culebra, culebrazo, novatada.

hazy ['heizi], *a.* anieblado, nublado, nebuloso, cargado de humo, brumoso, caliginoso; vago, confuso.

he [hiː], *pron. pers. masc.*, 3ª *pers. sing.* él; *pron. indef.* el, aquel; alguien; algunas veces se emplea para determinar el genero masculino de un animal: *he-goat*, macho cabrío; *he-cat*, gato macho.

head [hed], *s.* cabeza; testa; primer puesto; cima; posición de jefe; extremo, punta; parte principal o superior; cara de una moneda; título, encabezamiento; caudillo, cabecilla, jefe; res, cabeza de ganado; avance, adelantamiento, prosperidad, progreso; talento, juicio, capacidad, crisis, *f.*; astas de ciervo o venado; (*mar.*) proa; nacimiento, fuente, *f.*, manantial; cofia; soltura del freno; *arrow-head*, punta de un dardo; *head of a cabbage*, repollo de col; *head of a bed*, cabecera; *head of a cask*, fondo de un barril; *head of a sail*, gratil; *from head to foot*, de pies a cabeza; *to give a horse his head*, dar rienda suelta a un caballo; *a head and shoulders superior*, (*fig.*) mucho mejor, por fuerza; a las buenas o a las malas; *on* (o *under*) *this head*, sobre este punto; asunto o particular; *head over ears*, (*fig.*) completamente; *head to sea*, (*mar.*) con la proa a la mar; *to make head against*, hacer frente a; *two heads are better than one*, (*prov.*) más valen (o ven) cuatro ojos que dos; *to be head over ears in debt*, estar comido de deudas; *to hit the nail on the head*, dar en el clavo; *I can make neither head nor tail of it*, no puedo comprenderlo o descifrarlo en absoluto; no tiene pies ni cabeza; *to make head against*, hacer frente a. — *v.t.* poner cabeza; dirigir, gobernar, mandar; podar; degollar; adelantar, cortar la retirada. — *v.i.* adelantarse; acogollarse, repollar; anudar; provenir, tomar su origen.

headache ['hedeik], *s.* dolor de cabeza.

headboard, *s.* cabecera de cama.

head-dress, *s.* cofia, tocado.

headed, *a.* que tiene cabeza; titulado; *clear-headed* o *long-headed*, perspicaz; *thick-headed*, duro de mollera, de pocos alcances, mentecato.

header, *s.* el que pone fondos a las cubas, cabezas a los clavos; cabezada, golpe en la cabeza; caída, zambullida de cabeza; descabezador de las mieses; (*alb.*) primer acabecero; cabecilla; *to take a header*, irse de cabeza.

head-gear ['hedgiəɹ], *s.* cofia, tocado.

headily ['hedili], *adv.* desatinadamente, obstinadamente.

headiness, *s.* terquedad, obstinación; desatino; sacudida; encabezamiento del vino.

heading, *s.* título, epígrafe, encabezamiento; membrete; témpano, tapa; frente, *f.*; (*min.*) galería, socavón.

headland ['hedlənd], *s.* cabo, punta, promontorio, castro.

headledge, *s.* (*mar.*) contrabrazola.

headless, *a.* descabezado, degollado; acéfalo; ignorante, obstinado, inconsiderado.

headlight, *s.* linterna de locomotora; (*mar.*) farol de tope; faros (de automóvil, etc.).

headlong, *a.* temerario, arrojado, precipitado; imprudente; inconsiderado, despeñadero. — *adv.* de cabeza, de prisa, de sopetón, precipitadamente; temerariamente, inconsideradamente, sin pensarlo; de hoz y de coz, al tuntún.

headman, *s.* jefe.

headmaster [hed'mɑːstəɹ], *s.* director (de un colegio).

headmistress [hed'mistris], *s.* directora.

headphone ['hedfoun], *s.* auricular.

headquarters [hed'kwɔːtəɹz], *s.* (*mil.*) cuartel general; oficina principal.

head-sail, *s.* vela delantera.

headship, *s.* jefatura, cargo de jefe; gobierno, autoridad.

headsman ['hedzmən], *s.* verdugo, degollador; (*min.*) minero que acarrea el carbón desde la cara del filón a la vagoneta; (*mar.*) marinero que patronea la embarcación al arponear una ballena.

headstone ['hedstoun], *s.* lápida sepulcral; piedra fundamental de un edificio.

headstrong ['hedstrɔŋ], *a.* terco, cabezudo, testarudo, obstinado, aferrado, reacio, encalabrinado, indócil.

headstrongness, *s.* terquedad, pertinacia, obstinación, encaprichamiento, aferramiento.

headtire, *s.* escofieta.

headway ['hedwei], *s.* adelantamiento, progreso, ímpetu, avance; (*mar.*) marcha de un buque; (*f.c.*) intervalo o distancia entre dos trenes consecutivos.

headwind [hed'wind], *s.* viento en contra.

head-work ['hedwəːɹk], *s.* trabajo mental.

heady ['hedi], *a.* temerario, arrojado; violento, impetuoso; fuerte, encabezado (vino).

heal [hiːl], *v.t.* sanar, curar; remediar; ajustar; componer, reconciliar; purificar. — *v.i.* recobrar la salud, sanar; *to heal up*, cicatrizarse.

healable, *a.* curable, sanable; lo que puede curarse.

heald, *s.* (*tej.*) lizo de un telar.

healer, *s.* sanador, curador, medicinante, médico.

healing, *a.* sanativo, curativo, medicinal, saludable, emoliente; pacífico, conciliador. — *s.* curar, curación.

health [helθ], *s.* salud, *f.*, sanidad; pureza; brindis; *health officer*, oficial de sanidad, de cuarentena; *bill of health*, patente de sanidad; *Your health!* ¡A su salud!

healthful, *a.* sano, saludable, salubre, salutífero.

healthfulness, *s.* salud, salubridad, sanidad, bondad.

health-giving, *a.* saludable, salubre.

healthiness, *s.* estado sano, sanidad, goce de buena salud.

healthless, *s.* enfermo, enfermizo, débil.

healthy ['helθi], *a.* sano, fuerte, bueno; saludable, sanativo.

heap [hiːp], *s.* montón, pila, cúmulo, rimero, acervo; (*fam.*) muchedumbre, multitud, gentío, turba; *in heaps*, a montones. — *v.t.* amontonar, acumular, apilar, colmar, juntar.

heaper, *s.* amontonador.

hear [hiəɹ], *v.t.* (*pret.*, *p.p.* **heard**) oír, entender, escuchar, hacer caso; dar audiencia; obedecer; conceder, otorgar. — *v.i.* oír, escuchar; saber, tener noticia, oír decir, estar informado, tener entendido; *to hear a person out*, oír a uno hasta el fin.

heard [həːɹd], *pret.* y *p.p.* [HEAR].

hearer ['hiəɹəɹ], *s.* oidor, oyente.

hearing, *s.* oído; alcance del oído; audición; (*for.*) examen de testigos; acción de oír; *within hearing*, al alcance del oído; *hard of hearing*, algo sordo, duro de oído; *to refuse a hearing*, negar los oídos.

hearken ['hɑːɹkən], *v.i.* oír o seguir con atención, escuchar, atender, tomar en consideración.

hearsay ['hiəɹsei], *s.* rumor, fama, voz común; *by hearsay*, de oídas.

hearse [həːɹs], *s.* coche fúnebre; féretro, ataúd. — *v.t.* encerrar o colocar en un ataúd.

hearse-cloth, *s.* palio, paño mortuorio.

hearse-like, *a.* lúgubre, fúnebre.

heart [hɑːɹt], *s.* corazón; (*fig.*) centro de los afectos; interior, centro, fondo; valor, esfuerzo, ánimo; amor, benevolencia, voluntad, caridad, generosidad; copas (en los naipes); *heart disease*, enfermedad del corazón; *a heart to heart talk*, una conversación íntima; *at heart*, en el fondo; *by heart*, de memoria; *to find it in one's heart*, desear; *to take to heart*, desconsolarse, afligirse por; *to take the heart out of*, desanimar; *to have one's heart in one's mouth*, tener el alma entre los dientes; estar con el alma en un hilo; *to die of a broken heart*, morir de pena, pesadumbre o tristeza; *to wear one's heart on one's sleeve*, llevar el corazón en la mano; *heart and soul*, con toda el alma.

heartache ['hɑːɹteik], *s.* angustia, aflicción, pesar, inquietud, congoja, pena.

heart-blood, s. sangre del corazón, f.; (fig.) esencia, vida.

heart-break, s. angustia, congoja, pena.

heart-breaking, a. congojoso, desolador.

heart-broken, a. penetrado de dolor, de congoja.

heartburn, s. acedía, cardialgia.

heartburning, s. acedía, cardialgia; animosidad, rencilla, odio. — a. intenso, sentido, profundo.

hearted, a. que tiene su asiento u origen en el corazón; kind-hearted, bondadoso; faint-hearted, tímido, pusilánime.

hearten ['hɑːɹtən], v.t. animar, fortificar, alentar; (agr.) abonar, estercolar, engrasar.

heartener, s. animador.

heartfelt ['hɑːɹtfelt], a. sincero, cordial, sentido, de corazón.

hearth [hɑːɹθ], s. hogar, fogón; chimenea, hogar doméstico; (fig.) casa.

hearth-money, s. fogaje.

heartily ['hɑːɹtili], adv. sinceramente, cordialmente; de corazón; to laugh heartily, reírse a más no poder.

heartiness, s. cordialidad, sinceridad, ánimo, fuerza, vigor.

heartless ['hɑːɹtles], s. sin cariño, sin corazón; cruel, inhumano, sin piedad; pusilánime, tímido, cobarde, amilanado.

heartlessly, adv. cruelmente, inhumanamente, sin piedad; tímidamente, pusilánimemente.

heartlessness, s. falta de corazón; falta de ánimo, simpatía o piedad.

heart-rending ['hɑːɹtrendiŋ], a. penetrante, agudo, que destroza el corazón.

heart's-ease ['hɑːɹtziːz], s. (bot.) pensamiento, trinitaria.

heart-shaped, a. acorazonado.

heart-sick, a. afligido, dolorido, desconsolado.

heart-sore, a. apesadumbrado, afligido.

heart-strings, s.pl. fibras del corazón.

heart-whole, a. desamorado; sincero; intrépido, valiente.

hearty ['hɑːɹti], a. cordial, sincero, sentido; voraz; sano, robusto, vigoroso; gustoso, grato; alegre.

heat [hiːt], s. calor, fogosidad, vehemencia; ardor, acaloramiento; viveza demasiada, odio, cólera, animosidad; (fund.) carga de un horno; fermentación; celo de los animales; carrera o corrida de caballos; red heat, calor llevado al rojo; white heat, candencia, incandescencia; heat-stroke, insolación; heat unit, caloría; in heat, en celo, salida (hembra de ciertos animales). — v.t. calentar, encender; acalorar; caldear; causar ardor, acalorar; excitar. — v.i. hervir, fermentar, arder, acalorarse, calentarse, encolerizarse, estar poseído de una pasión.

heater, s. calentador, calorífero, estufa; aparato de calefacción.

heath [hiːθ], s. (bot.) brezo; páramo, brezal, matorral.

heath-cock, s. (orn.) gallo silvestre.

heathen ['hiːðən], s. gentil, pagano, idólatra, m.f.; ateísta, m.f., ateo.

heathen, heathenish, a. gentílico, bárbaro, feroz, salvaje, idólatra.

heathenism, s. gentilismo, gentilidad, idolatría, paganismo.

heathenize, v.t. hacer a uno pagano o idólatra.

heather ['heðəɹ], s. brezo, brezal, matorral, bermejuela.

heathery, heathy, a. lleno o cubierto de brezos, matoso.

heating ['hiːtiŋ], s. calefacción. — a. caluroso; calefaciente; que da o produce calor.

heatless, a. frío, sin calor.

heave [hiːv], v.t. (pret., p.p. **heaved, hove**) alzar, elevar, levantar; lanzar, echar fuera, largar, arrojar; (mar.) izar; virar; exhalar, prorrumpir; inflar, hinchar; (geol.) fracturar; to heave a sigh, exhalar un suspiro; to heave the lead, escandallar, echar el escandallo. — v.i. palpitar, respirar con dificultad, palpitar el corazón; levantarse y bajarse alternativamente; jadear; suspirar hondo; tener náuseas; trabajar penosamente; (mar.) virar; heave ho! (mar.) ¡vira!; to heave to, ponerse al pairo o en facha; to heave down, descubrir la quilla; to heave overboard, echar a la mar; to heave the log, (mar.) echar la corredera. — s. elevación; levantamiento, alzadura; esfuerzo; estertor, hinchazón del pecho, f.; náusea; henchidura de una ola; (geol.) falla; heave-offering, un sacrificio de los judíos.

heaven ['hevən], s. cielo; región etérea, f., firmamento; felicidad; poder supremo; Dios, Providencia.

heaven-born, a. celeste, angelical, divino.

heaven-built, a. construido por los dioses.

heaven-gifted, a. dotado por el cielo.

heavenliness ['hevənlines], s. felicidad o excelencia suprema.

heaven-loved, a. favorecido de Dios.

heavenly ['hevənli], a. celeste, celestial, divino.

heavenward ['hevənwəd], a., adv. hacia el cielo.

heaver ['hiːvəɹ], s. (mar.) alzaprima; cargador; coal-heaver, cargador de carbón.

heaves [hiːvz], s.pl. (vet.) huérfago.

heaviness ['hevines], s. pesadez, peso, pesantez, gravedad; languidez, sueño, modorra; tardanza, pereza; abatimiento, tristeza, aflicción, angustia, carga, opresión.

heaving ['hiːviŋ], s. palpitación; (mar.) oleada, hinchazón de las olas, f.

heaving-line, s. estacha, calabrote.

heavy ['hevi], a. pesado, ponderoso; poderoso, macizo, fuerte, grueso, doble; denso, amazacotado, espeso; enfadoso, penoso, molesto, duro, violento, opresivo; grave, gravoso, oneroso; difícil; frío; recargado, cargado; triste, pesaroso, melancólico; lento, tardo, lerdo, estúpido, soñoliento; considerable, importante; arcilloso; indigesto.

hebdomad ['hebdomæd], s. hebdómada.

hebdomadal [heb'domədəl], **hebdomadary,** a. hebdomadario, semanal.

hebetation [hebe'teiʃən], **hebetude,** s. estupidez, entorpecimiento, embotamiento.

Hebraic [hiː'breiik], a. hebreo, hebraico.

Hebraism ['hiːbreiizm], s. hebraísmo.

Hebraist, s. hebraista, m.f., hebraizante.

Hebraize ['hiːbreiaiz], v.t. hebraizar, hacer hebreo, verter al hebreo. — v.i. volverse hebreo, adoptar costumbres hebreas.

Hebrew ['hiːbruː], s. hebreo, judío, lengua hebrea. — a. hebraico, hebreo.

hecatomb ['hekətəm], s. hecatombe, f.; matanza, carnicería.

heck [hek], s. enrejado, verja, trampa para

coger peces; recipiente para forraje; volante de una máquina de hilar.

heckle ['hekəl], s. rastrillo. — v.t. rastrillar; contrariar; interrumpir, importunar con preguntas.

hectare ['hektɛəɹ], s. hectárea.

hectic ['hektik], a. hético, héctico; febril. — s. tisis, f., consunción, fiebre hética, f.

hectogram ['hektəgræm], s. hectogramo.

hectograph ['hektəgræf], s. hectógrafo.

hectolitre, s. hectólitre.

hectometre, s. hectómetro.

hector, s. matón, matasiete, fanfarrón, fierabrás, perdonavidas, m. — v.i. breavear, baladronear, echar fieros o bravatas. — v.t. amenazar, intimidar con fieros o bravatas.

heddle ['hedəl], s. malla, lizos de un telar.

hedera ['hedərə], s. hiedra.

hedge [hedʒ], s. seto, vallado de zarzas; como prefijo significa vil, despreciable; *quickset hedge*, seto vivo; *stake hedge*, cerca; *hedge-school*, escuela baja y que antiguamente en Irlanda se conducía al aire libre. — v.t. cercar con seto, vallar; rodear; circundar; proteger, defender; impedir, obstruir, tapar. — v.i. esconderse, agacharse; cubrirse; ponerse al abrigo; compensar o igualar una apuesta con otra en sentido contrario; evitar una contestación o resolución categórica, no comprometerse.

hedge-born, a. de linaje bajo.

hedge-creeper, s. vagamundo.

hedgehog ['hedʒhog], s. erizo; (*fig.*) persona irritable o intratable.

hedge-mustard, s. jaramago, erísimo.

hedge-nettle, s. galiopsis.

hedgepig, s. erizo joven.

hedge-priest, s. clérigo iliterato, clerizonte.

hedger, s. el que hace setos o cercados; el que compensa o iguala sus apuestas.

hedgerow ['hedʒrou], s. seto vivo.

hedge-sparrow, s. curruca.

hedging-bill, s. podadera de setos.

hedonism ['hedonizm], s. hedonismo.

hedonist, s. hedonista, m.f.

heed [hiːd], v.t. atender, observar, escuchar, considerar, notar, prestar atención a, hacer caso de. — v.i. prestar atención, hacer caso, considerar. — s. cuidado, cautela, aprecio, atención, precaución, seriedad, sobriedad, observación, reparo, gravedad, regularidad; *to take no heed of*, no hacer caso de; *to give no heed to*, echar en saco roto (un consejo).

heedful ['hiːdful], a. vigilante, cauteloso, atento, cauto, exacto, cuidadoso, prudente, circunspecto.

heedfulness, s. vigilancia, atención, cautela, cuidado, circunspección.

heedless ['hiːdles], a. desatento, negligente, omiso, distraído, descuidado, incauto, atolondrado.

heedlessness, s. descuido, negligencia, omisión, imprudencia, inadvertencia, distracción.

heel [hiːl], s. (*anat.*) talón, calcañal; (*mar.*) coz o pie de palo; tacón; parte inferior; talón de una media; mano de vaca; *down at heel*, de aspecto descuidado; *from head to heels*, de pies a cabeza; *head over heels*, patas arriba; *to be at someone's heels*, perseguir a uno; *to cool one's heels*, esperar mucho tiempo; *to kick one's heels*, (*fig.*) tascar el freno; *to lay by the heels*, poner grillos; *to show a clean pair of*

heels, huir, poner pies en polvorosa. — v.t. poner talón; agarrar por los talones; poner espolones al gallo. — v.i. (*mar.*) ladearse, inclinarse, tumbarse a un lado.

heeler, s. taconero; gallo que usa bien los espolones; (*vulg., E.U.*) politicastro, teniente de un cacique político.

heel-maker, s. taconero.

heel-piece ['hiːlpiːs], s. talón, tapa. — v.t. poner tapas a los zapatos.

heft [heft], s. mango, asa, cabo; (*fam., E.U.*) bulto, mayor parte; peso, pesadez. — v.t. levantar, alzar en peso, probar el peso; sompesar. — v.i. (*fam.*) pesar, tener cierto peso.

hefty ['hefti], a. fuerte, grueso, membrudo.

Hegelian [he'dʒiːliən], a. hegeliano.

Hegelianism, s. hegelianismo.

hegemonic [he'gemonik], a. predominante, dominante.

hegemony [he'gemoni], s. hegemonía, supremacía, preeminencia.

hegira ['hedʒirə], s. hégira, égira.

heifer, s. vaquilla, vaca que no ha parido, novilla, churra; *heifer calf*, ternera.

heigh-ho ['hei'hou], *interj.* ¡ay!

height [hait], s. altura, elevación, alto; collado, loma, montaña, colina, cerro; estatura, talla, alzada; sumidad, ápice, extremidad, extremo, eminencia, cima, cumbre; sublimidad, excelencia, colmo; *the height of folly*, el colmo de la locura; *at its height*, en su apogeo; en su punto culminante.

heighten ['haitən], v.t. realzar, elevar, levantar; avivar; ascender, adelantar; exaltar, sublimar; ilustrar, adornar, mejorar, perfeccionar, agravar, abultar, exagerar; recalcar, acentuar. — v.i. levantarse, aumentarse, acrecentarse.

heightening, s. adorno; realce.

heinous ['heinəs], a. atroz, malvado, nefando, horrible, grave.

heinousness, a. atrocidad, perversidad, enormidad.

heir [ɛəɹ], s. heredero; *heir presumptive*, heredero presunto; *heir at law*, heredero legal; *joint heir*, coheredero.

heir-apparent [ɛəɹə'pærənt], s. heredero forzoso.

heirdom ['ɛəɹdəm], **heirship**, s. herencia, derecho de heredar; bienes heredados.

heiress ['ɛəres], s. heredera.

heirless, a. sin heredero.

heirloom ['ɛəɹluːm], s. (*for.*) bienes muebles vinculados; herencia; atavismo.

helcoid ['helkoid], a. parecido a una úlcera.

helcology [hel'kolədʒi], s. parte de la patología que trata de las úlceras.

heliac ['hiːliək], **heliacal**, a. helíaco.

helianthemum [heli'ænθeməm], s. jaguarzo.

helical ['helikəl], a. espiral; *helical line*, hélice, f., espira.

helicoid ['helikoid], a. helicoidal. — s. (*geom.*) helicoide.

Helicon ['helikən], s. Helicón, Parnaso.

heliocentric [hiːliou'sentrik], **heliocentrical**, a. heliocéntrico.

heliochrome ['hiːliokroum], s. (*foto.*) heliocromo.

heliograph ['hiːliogræf], s. heliógrafo; helióstato; heliotropo. — v.i. hacer señales con el heliógrafo o el helióstato.

heliographic, a. heliográfico.
heliography [hi:li'ɔgrəfi], s. transmisión de señales por medio del heliógrafo; descripción de la superficie del sol; heliografía, fotografía (del sol).
heliolatry [hi:li'ɔlətri], s. culto del sol.
heliometer [hi:li'ɔmetəɹ], s. heliómetro.
helioscope ['hi:lioskoup], s. helioscopio.
heliospherical [hi:lio'sferikəl], a. esférico como el sol.
heliostat ['hi:liostæt], s. helióstato.
heliotrope ['hi:liotroup], s. (bot.) heliotropo, vainilla; olor o color de esta flor; (min.) heliotropo, heliotropio; (fís.) heliotropo.
heliotype ['hi:liotaip], s. heliotipo, fotograbado. — v.t. reproducir por medio del heliotipo. — v.i. imprimir un heliotipo.
heliotypy, s. procedimiento del fotograbado o heliotipo.
helispheric, helispherical, a. espiral.
helium ['hi:liəm], s. helio.
helix ['hi:liks], s. hélice, f., espira, voluta; (anat.) hélice, f., reborde del pabellón de la oreja; caracol de tierra de la familia de los helícidos.
hell [hel], s. infierno; desván; garito; (impr.) caja de letras inservibles; cajón de sastre; hell fire, fuego o tormento del infierno; hell gate, umbral del infierno.
hell-born, a. nacido en el infierno, infernal.
hell-cat, s. bruja; mujer fiera.
hellebore ['helibo:ɹ], s. eléboro, verdegambre, veratro.
Hellenic [he'li:nik], a. helénico, heleno, greciano; gentílico.
Hellenism ['helinizm], s. helenismo, grecismo.
Hellenist, s. helenista, m.f.; judío greguizante.
Hellenistic, a. helénico.
Hellenize, v.i. grecizar.
hell-hag, s. bruja del infierno.
hell-hound ['helhaund], s. perro del infierno, el Cancerbero; agente infernal; persona feroz e inhumana.
hellish ['heliʃ], a. infernal, malvado, diabólico.
hellishness, s. diablura, malicia infernal.
hello [he'lou], interj. ¡hola!
hellward, adv. y a. hacia el infierno.
helm [helm], s. (mar.) timón, el conjunto de timón, su caña y rueda; gobernalle; yelmo, capacete; dirección, gobierno, puesto de autoridad; to hang the helm, calar el timón; to shift the helm, cambiar el timón. — v.t. gobernar el timón, timonear, guiar; cubrir con yelmo.
helmed, a. que lleva yelmo o casco. — p.p. [HELM].
helmet ['helmet], s. yelmo, celada, capacete, almete, casco, morrión; helmet-flower, acónito, matalobos.
helmeted, a. que lleva yelmo o casco.
helminth ['helminθ], s. lombriz, f., helminto.
helminthic [hel'minθik], a. helmíntico; vermífugo.
helminthology [helmin'θɔlədʒi], s. helmintología.
helmless ['helmles], a. sin timón.
helmport, s. (mar.) limera del timón.
helmsman ['helmzmən], s. timonero, timonel.
helot ['helət], s. ilota, m.f.
helotism, s. ilotismo.
help [help], v.t., v.i. ayudar, asistir, socorrer, auxiliar, amparar, patrocinar, favorecer,

sostener; librar, aliviar, reparar, remediar; servir (a la mesa); abstenerse, evitar, dejar de hacer. — v.i. ayudar, concurrir, contribuir; to help back, ayudar a regresar; to help forward, adelantar, promover, activar, ayudar a delantarse; to help down, ayudar a bajar; to help on, servir, ofrecer; contribuir; proporcionar; ayudar, coadyuvar; to help out, ayudar a salir; sacar de un peligro o mal paso; I cannot help it, no puedo dejar de hacerlo; no puedo remediarlo; to help one another, favorecerse mutuamente; I cannot help going, no puedo menos de ir; Heaven helps those that help themselves, (prov.) a quien madruga, Dios la ayuda; a Dios rogando y con la maza dando. — s. ayuda, auxilio, socorro, asistencia, apoyo, remedio, protección, arrimo, favor, amparo; medio, recurso; descanso; (E.U.) criada, sirvienta, jornalera; by the help of, con auxilio de; to cry out for help, pedir socorro; there is no help for it, no hay más remedio, no tiene remedio (o quite); with God's help, Dios mediante.
helper, s. auxiliador, socorredor, asistente, fautor, ayuda.
helpful, a. útil, provechoso; saludable; sano.
helpfulness, s. asistencia, utilidad.
helping ['helpiŋ], s. ración, porción de comida.
helpless, a. desvalido, imposibilitado; irremediable; destituído, desamparado, abandonado; desmañado; inerte.
helplessness, s. desamparo; impotencia, debilidad, falta de energía y fuerzas.
helpmate ['helpmeit], s. compañero, asistente; auxiliar.
helter-skelter ['heltəɹskeltəɹ], adv. atropelladamente, sin orden ni concierto, confusamente, a trochemoche, a trompa y talega, al tuntún.
helve [helv], s. mango, astil de hacha o destral. — v.t. poner mango o cabo a; to throw the helve after the hatchet, echar la soga tras el caldero.
Helvetian [hel'vi:ʃən], **Helvetic,** a. helvético, helvecio, de Suiza, suizo.
hem [hem], s. (cost.) dobladillo, bastilla, repulgo, orilla, borde; ribete. — interj. ¡eh! — v.t. (cost.) dobladillar, bastillar, repulgar, ribetear, orillar; rodear, cercar, encerrar. — v.i. fingir tos, toser de fingido, espirar con violencia.
hemal ['hi:məl], **hæmal,** a. perteneciente a la sangre.
hematin ['hemətin], s. hematina.
hematite ['hemətait], s. hematita.
hematosis [hemə'tousis], s. hematosis, f.
hematoxylin [hemə'tɔksilin], s. hematoxilina.
hemicrania [hemi'kreiniə], **hemicrany,** s. hemicránea, jaqueca.
hemicycle ['hemisaikəl], s. hemiciclo, semicírculo.
hemiplegia [hemi'pli:dʒiə], **hemiplegy,** s. hemiplejía.
hemiplegic, a. hemipléjico.
hemipterous [he'miptərəs], a. hemíptero.
hemisphere ['hemisfiəɹ], s. hemisferio.
hemispheric [hemi'sferik], **hemispherical,** a. hemisférico, semiesférico.
hemistich ['hemistik], **hemestic,** s. (poét.) hemistiquio.
hemlock ['hemlɔk], s. cicuta.

hemoglobin [hemo'gləbin], **hæmoglobin,** s. hemoglobina.
hemorrhage ['heməridʒ], s. hemorragia.
hemorrhoidal, a. hemorroidal.
hemorrhoids ['hemərɔidz], s.pl. hemorroides, f.
hemp [hemp], s. cáñamo; *Indian hemp,* canabina; *raw hemp,* cáñamo sin peinar; *bastard-hemp,* cañamón; *hemp agrimony,* eupatorio vulgar.
hemp-beater, s. espadillador, espadador de cáñamo.
hemp-brake, s. maza, espadilla.
hemp-breaker, s. agramador.
hemp-close, s. cañamar.
hemp-comb, s. peine para pasar el cáñamo despues de rastrillado.
hemp-dresser, s. batidor.
hempen, a. cañameño.
hemp-seed, s. cañamón.
hempy, a. semejante al cáñamo.
hem-stitch ['hemstitʃ], v.t. (cost.) hacer una vainica.
hen [hen], s.f. gallina; hembra de cualquier ave. — pl. **hens,** pollos, gallinas, aves domésticas; *guinea-hen,* gallina de Guinea o de Indias, pintada; *moor-hen,* zarceta; *turkey-hen,* pava; *brood hen,* gallina clueca.
henbane ['henbein], s. (bot.) beleño.
hence [hens], adv. de aquí, desde aquí, fuera de aquí; por lo tanto, en consecuencia de esto; por esto; *far hence,* lejos de aquí; *ten years hence,* de aquí a diez años; *get thee hence!* (ant.) ¡largo de aquí!
henceforth [hens'fɔːrθ], adv. de aquí en adelante; en lo futuro, en adelante.
henceforward [hens'fɔːrwəd], adv. desde ahora, de aquí en adelante; en lo venidero; para siempre.
henchman ['hentʃmən], s. agente; criado; escudero; secuaz servil.
hen-coop ['henkuːp], s. gallinero.
hendecagon [hen'dekəgən], s. endecágono.
hendecasyllable [hendekə'siləbəl], s. verso endecasílabo.
hen-house ['henhaus], s. gallinero.
henna ['henə], s. alheña.
hennery ['henəri], s. gallinero.
henpeck ['henpek], v.t. dominar, fastidiar, importunar (la mujer al marido); (fam.) llevar los calzones.
henpecked, a. dominado por su mujer.
hen-roost ['henruːst], s. gallinero.
henry ['henri], s. (elec.) henrio.
hepatic [he'pætik], **hepatical,** s. hepático; de color de hígado.
hepatica [he'pætikə], s. hepática.
hepatite ['hepətait], s. hepatita.
heptachord ['heptəkɔːrd], s. heptacordio.
heptad ['heptæd], s. setena.
heptagon ['heptəgən], s. heptágono.
heptagonal [hep'tægənəl], a. heptagonal.
heptarchy ['heptɑːrki], s. heptarquía.
Heptateuch ['heptə'tjuːk], s. Heptateuco.
her [həːr], pron. (caso acusativo o dativo de **she**) la, le, ella, a ella; (caso posesivo de **she**) su, de ella.
herald ['herəld], s. heraldo, rey de armas; publicador; precursor.
heraldic [he'rældik], a. heráldico, genealógico.
heraldry ['herəldri], s. heráldica, blasón.
heraldship, s. oficio de heraldo.

herb [həːrb], s. hierba; *pot-herbs,* hortalizas; *salad-herbs,* hierbas para ensalada; *sweet herbs,* hierbas odoríferas.
herbaceous [həːr'beiʃəs], a. herbáceo.
herbage ['həːrbidʒ], s. herbaje, pasto, hierba; (for.) derecho de pasto en bosque o tierras agenas.
herbaged, a. cubierto de hierba.
herbal [həːrbəl], a. herbario.
herbalism [həːrbəl'izm], s. conocimiento de las hierbas.
herbalist, herbarist, herbist, s. herbolario, herbario, botánico.
herbarious [həːr'bɛəriəs], a. herbario.
herbarium [həːr'bɛəriəm], s. herbario seco.
herbarize, v.i. herborizar.
herbescent [həːr'besənt], a. herbáceo.
herbivorous [həːr'bivərəs], a. herbívoro.
herbless ['həːrbles], a. sin hierbas, yermo.
herborization, s. herborización.
herborize ['həːrbəraiz], v.i. herborizar.
herborizer, s. herborizante, herborizador.
herbose ['həːrbouz], **herbous, herby,** a. herboso, herbáceo.
herbwoman, s. herbolaria; verdulera.
Herculean [həːr'kjuːliən], a. hercúleo.
herd [həːrd], s. hato, rebaño, grey, f., manada, piara, ganado; manadero, vaquerizo; tropel, junta, asamblea, reunión, f., multitud; chusma, gentuza, vulgo; guarda de ganado; *shepherd,* pastor de ovejas; *goatherd,* cabrero; *swineherd,* porquero; *cowherd,* vaquero, boyero; *herd's grass,* alfalfa; *common herd,* vulgo, gentuza. — v.t. reunir en hatos. — v.i. ir en manadas, ir en compañía con otros.
herdic, s. carruaje americano de dos o cuatro ruedas para el transporte de viajeros.
herdsman [həːr'dzmən], s. guarda de ganado, m., zagal, pastor, manadero, vaquerizo.
herdwick ['həːrdwik], s. raza de carneros que se crían en las montañas de Cumberland y Westmorland.
here [hiər], adv. aquí; acá; ahí; por aquí; en este momento, ahora, en este punto; en esta época, en este mundo, en esta vida; *here and there,* aquí y allá, acá y acullá; *here below,* en esta vida, en la tierra; *here it is,* aquí está; *here goes,* (fam.) ahí va; *here's a go o here's a mess,* (fam.) ahora sí que la hemos hecho; *here's (a health) to you,* a la salud de Vd.; *here I am,* heme aquí; *here he is, here she is, here they are,* hele aquí, hela aquí, helos aquí.
hereabouts ['hiərəbauts], adv. aquí alrededor, en estas cercanías, en estas inmediaciones, por aquí cerca.
hereafter [hiər'ɑːftər], adv. en el tiempo venidero, en lo futuro. — s. estado futuro.
hereat [hiər'æt], adv. a esto, en esto, por eso.
hereby [hiər'bai], adv. por esto, por la presente, por este medio, por estas.
hereditable [heri'ditəbəl], a. heredable, que puede ser heredado.
hereditament [heri'ditəmənt], s. (for.) todo lo que puede heredarse.
hereditary [he'reditəri], a. hereditario.
herefrom [hiər'frɔm], adv. de aquí, desde aquí; a causa de esto.
herein [hiər'in], **hereinto,** adv. aquí dentro; incluso.
hereinafter [hiərin'ɑːftər], adv. después, más abajo, más adelante.

hereof [hiəɹˈɔv], *adv.* de esto, de eso, acerca de esto, de aquí.

hereon [hiəɹˈɔn], *adv.* sobre esto, sobre este punto.

heresiarch [heˈriːziɑːɹk], *s.* heresiarca, *m.f.*

heresiarchy, *s.* gran herejía.

heresy [ˈheresi], *s.* herejía.

heretic [ˈheretik], *s.* hereje.

heretical [heˈretikəl], *a.* herético, heretical.

heretically, *adv.* heréticamente.

hereto [hiəɹˈtuː], *adv.* a esto, a este fin.

heretofore [hiəɹtoˈfoːɹ], *adv.* en otro tiempo, antes, en tiempos pasados, antiguamente; hasta ahora, hasta aquí, hasta el día. — *s.* tiempo pasado, antaño.

hereunder [hiəɹˈʌndəɹ], *adv.* bajo esto, en virtud de esto.

hereunto [hiəɹˈʌntuː], *adv.* a esto, a eso.

hereupon [hiəɹəˈpɔn], *adv.* sobre esto, a esto.

herewith [hiəɹˈwið], *adv.* adjunto, con esto, junto con esto.

heritable [ˈheritəbəl], *a.* que se puede heredar.

heritage [ˈheritidʒ], *s.* herencia; interés, porción; estado heredado.

hermaphrodite [həːɹˈmæfrodait], *a.* (*zool.*, *bot.*) hermafrodita. — *s.* hermafrodito, hermafrodita, andrógino; (*mar.*) bergantín goleta.

hermaphroditic [həːɹmæfroˈditik], **hermaphroditical**, *a.* hermafrodita.

hermaphroditism, **hermaphrodism**, *s.* hermafroditismo.

hermeneutic [həːɹmeˈnjuːtik], **hermeneutical**, *a.* hermenéutico.

hermeneutics, *a.* hermenéutica.

hermetic [həːɹˈmetik], **hermetical** [həːɹˈmetikəl], *a.* hermético.

hermit [ˈhəːɹmit], *s.* ermitaño, eremita, *m.*, asceta, *m.*, anacoreta, *m.*, solitario.

hermitage [ˈhəːɹmitidʒ], *s.* ermita; clase de vino francés.

hermitary, *s.* celda de ermitaño aneja a un monasterio.

hermitess, *s.* ermitaña.

hermitical [həːɹˈmitikəl], *a.* eremítico.

hern [həːɹn], **heron** [ˈherən], *s.* garza, ardeola, airón.

hernia [ˈhəːɹniə], *s.* hernia, quebradura, relajación.

hernial, *a.* herniario, herniado.

hernshaw [ˈhəːɹnʃoː], *s.* garza.

hero [ˈhiəɹou], *s.* héroe, campeón, persona principal o eminente; protagonista (de un drama, etc.), *m.*; personaje ilustre, semidiós; *hero-worship*, culto extremado a un héroe.

heroic [heˈrouik], **heroical** [heˈrouikəl], *a.* heroico, épico; sublime, grande, noble, valeroso, magnánimo, ilustre.

heroicalness, *s.* heroicidad.

heroin [ˈheroin], *s.* (*quím.*) heroína.

heroine [ˈheroin], *s.* heroína.

heroism [ˈheroizm], *s.* heroísmo, heroicidad, grandeza, proeza, hazaña.

heron [ˈherən], *s.* garza, ardeola; airón.

heronry [ˈherənri], **herony**, *s.* lugar en que se crían las garzas.

heron's-bill, (*bot.*) pico de garza.

herpes [ˈhəːɹpiːz], *s.* herpes, *m.f.pl.*

herpetic [həːɹˈpetik], *a.* herpético.

herpetism [ˈhəːɹpetizm], *s.* herpetismo.

herpetology [həːɹpeˈtɔlədʒi], *s.* herpetología.

herring [ˈheriŋ], *s.* arenque; *red herring*, arenque ahumado; (*fig.*) distracción.

hers [həːɹz], *pron. pos. f.* suyo, suya, de ella; el suyo, la suya, los suyos, las suyas.

herschelite [ˈhəːɹʃəlait], *s.* (*min.*) cristal ortorrombal, silicato sin color o semitransparente de aluminio, calcio y sodio.

herse [həːɹs], *s.* (*fort.*) rastrillo; enrejado; caballo de frisia.

herself [həɹˈself], *pron.* ella misma, sí misma.

hersilion [həɹˈsiliən], *s.* (*mil.*) caballo de frisa.

hesitancy [ˈhezitənsi], *s.* duda, hesitación, irresolución, incertidumbre, indeterminación, indecisión.

hesitant [ˈhezitənt], *a.* vacilante, titubeante, irresoluto, indeciso.

hesitate [ˈheziteit], *v.i.* dudar, tardar, pausar, vacilar; balbucear, titubear, tartamudear.

hesitation [heziˈteiʃən], *s.* hesitación, irresolución, duda, titubeo, indecisión, vacilación, perplejidad; balbucencia.

Hesper [ˈhespəɹ], *s.* Héspero, Venus, estrella vespertina.

Hesperian [hesˈpiəriən], *a.* hespérido; occidental. — *s.* habitante de un país occidental.

Hessian [ˈheʃən], *a.* pertenenciente al ducado de Hesse; *Hessian fly*, cecidomio. — *s.* harpillera.

hest [hest], *s.* (*ant.*) mandato, precepto, orden.

heteroclite [ˈhetəroklait], *s.*, *a.* heteróclito, irregular.

heterodox [ˈhetəroˈdɔks], *a.* heterodoxo.

heterodoxy [hetəroˈdɔksi], *s.* heterodoxia.

heterogamous [hetəˈrɔgəməs], *a.* (*bot.*) heterógamo.

heterogeneity [hetəroˈdʒiːniti], **heterogenousness**, *s.* heterogeneidad.

heterogeneous [hetəroˈdʒiːniəs], *a.* heterogéneo.

hew [hjuː], *v.t.* (*pret.* **hewed**; *p.p.* **hewn**, **hewed**) tajar, picar, cortar; labrar, trabajar (una cosa); hachear, dolar, desbastar, descortezar. — *v.i.* golpear, acuchillar; *to hew in pieces*, destrozar; *to hew out*, modelar en bruto; abrir paso.

hewer [hjuːəɹ], *s.* cortador de madera, cantero; desbastador; picapedrero.

hexachord [ˈheksəkoːɹd], *s.* hexacordo.

hexagon [ˈheksəgɔn], *s.* hexágono, seisavo.

hexagonal [hekˈzægənəl], *a.* hexagonal, sexagonal, seisavado.

hexahedron [heksəˈhiːdrɔn], *s.* hexaedro.

hexameter [hekˈsæmetəɹ], *s.* hexámetro.

hexametric [heksəˈmetrik], **hexametrical**, *a.* hexámetro, que se compone de hexámetros.

hexangular [heksˈæŋgjuːləɹ], *a.* hexángulo, hexágono.

hexapod [ˈheksəpɔd], *s.*, *a.* hexápodo.

hexastyle [ˈheksəstail], *s.* hexástilo.

hey [hei], *interj.* ¡he! ¡eh!

heyday [ˈheidei], *s.* colmo, apogeo. — *interj.* ¡hola!

hiatus [haiˈeitəs], *s.* blanco, laguna, espacio, vacío, salto (en un manuscrito); grieta, raja, hendedura, abertura; hiato.

hibernal [haiˈbəːɹnəl], *a.* hibernal, hiemal, invernizo, invernal.

hibernate [ˈhaibəɹneit], *v.i.* invernar; estar retirado e inactivo, vegetar.

hibernation [haibəɹˈneiʃən], *s.* invernada.

Hibernian [haiˈbəːɹniən], *s.* irlandés, hibernés, de Hibernia.

Hibernianism, Hibernicism, *s.* idiotismo irlandés.

hibiscus [hi'biskəs], *s.* hibisco.

hiccough, hiccup, hickup ['hikʌp], *s.* hipo. — *v.i.* hipar, tener hipo.

hickory ['hikəri], *s.* nogal americano.

hid [hid], *pret., p.p. (ant.)* [HIDE].

hidden ['hidən], *a.* oculto, secretamente, recóndito, escondido, latente. — *p.p.* [HIDE].

hide [haid], *s.* cuero, pellejo, piel, *f.*; *to dress hides,* adobar y curtir cueros; *raw hide,* cuero sin curtir; *I'll tan his hide for him,* *(fam.)* yo le calentaré el pellejo. — *pl.* corambre.

hide [haid], *v.t. (pret.* hid; *p.p.* hidden *o* hid) esconder, ocultar, retirar de la vista, tapar, encubrir, disimular; dar latigazos castigar a uno con vergajo; *to hide the face from,* volverse de espaldas, ocultar el rostro de. — *v.i.* esconderse, ocultarse; *hide and seek,* juego del escondite.

hidebound ['haidbaund], *a.* obstinado, conservador, reaccionario; *(med.)* que tiene la piel endurecida.

hideous ['hidiəs], *a.* horrible, horrendo, feo, espantoso, repugnante, deforme, monstruoso.

hideousness, *s.* horror, espanto; deformidad, fealdad.

hiding ['haidiŋ], *s.* ocultación, encumbrimiento; retrete, retiro; *(fam.)* zurra, paliza.

hiding-place, *s.* escondite.

hidrotic [hi'drɔtik], *a. (med.)* hidrótico, que causa o produce sudor.

hie [hai], *v.t.* activar, apresurar; pasar con rapidez, correr. — *v.i.* darse prisa, apresurarse; *hie thee home,* apresúrate a volver a casa; *hie thee,* date prisa.

hierarch ['haiərɑːk], *s.* jerarca, *m.,* pontífice, prelado.

hierarchal, hierarchical [haiə'rɑːkikəl], *a.* jerárquico.

hierarchism, *s.* jerarquía, principios del gobierno eclesiástico.

hierarchy ['haiərɑːki], *s.* jerarquía, gobierno eclesiástico.

hieratic [haiə'rætik], **hieratical,** *a.* jerárquico, hierático, sacerdotal; consagrado.

hieroglyph ['haiəroglif], **hieroglyphic,** *s.* jeroglífico.

hieroglyphic [haiəro'glifik], *a.* jeroglífico, hieroglífico.

hierography [haiə'rɔgrəfi], *s.* escritura sagrada

hierolatry [haiə'rɔlətri], *s.* hierolatría.

hierologic, *a.* hierológico.

hierology [haiə'rɔlədʒi], *s.* hierología.

hieromancy ['hairomænsi], *s.* hieromancia.

hierophant ['hairofænt], *s.* hierofante.

hifalutin [haifə'luːtin], *a. (fam.)* hinchado, pomposo, retumbante.

higgle [higəl], *v.i.* regatear, altercar, porfiar sobre un precio.

higgledy-piggledy ['higəldi'pigəldi], *adv. (fam.)* confusamente.

higgler ['higləɪ], *s.* zarracatin; el que regatea.

high [hai], *a.* alto, grande, enorme, elevado, levantado, enhiesto, empinado; eminente, pingorotudo, copetudo; encumbrado; altivɔ, solemne, altanerc, despótico, arrogante, jactancioso, orgulloso; poderoso, vivo, fuerte; dificultoso, arduo, difícil; severo, opresivo, tiránico; ilustre, noble, sublime; fogoso, ardiente, borrascoso; violento, turbulento, tempestuoso; cumplido, lleno, caro,

de precio subido; de color vivo o subido; *(mús.)* alto, agudo; fuerte, picante, corrompido, mal oliente, pasado, podrido; impetuoso, vehemente; indómito; *(vulg.)* borracho; *high life,* mundo elegante; *high mass,* misa mayor; *high road,* carretera, camino real; *high handed,* despótico, altanero; *high and dry,* completamente seco, fuera del agua; *high and mighty,* arrogante, orgulloso; *high day,* día solemne, fiesta; *high days and holidays,* días de fiesta; *it was high time to do it,* ya era hora de hacerlo; *to bear one's head high,* llevar la cabeza erguida; *high terms,* términos lisonjeros *o* precio subido; *on high,* arriba; *the Most High,* el Altísimo; *to run high (the sea),* estar muy crecida. — *adv.* arriba, sobre; alto; sumamente, profundamente, grandemente; a un precio alto o subido; a voces, a gritos, en alto tono.

high-born, *a.* noble, ilustre de nacimiento.

high-coloured, *a.* de color subido.

highest, *superl.* [HIGH,]; el más alto; supremo sumo, superbo.

highfalutin [haifə'luːtin], *a. (fam., E.U.)* hinchado, retumbante, pomposo.

high-handed, *a.* despótico, altanero, tiránico.

high-hearted, *a.* de pelo en pecho, bravo, animoso, valiente.

high-heeled, *a.* de tacones altos.

high-keyed, *a. (mús.)* agudo; impresionable.

highland ['hailənd], *s.* país montañoso.

highlander, *s.* montañés, serrano, gaelo, montañés de Escocia.

highlandish ['hailəndiʃ], *a.* montañés.

highly ['haili], *adv.* altamente; sumamente, en sumo grado, en gran manera, infinitamente; levantadamente, elevadamente; arrogantemente, altivamente, ambiciosamente, encarecidamente; con aprecio, estimación o concepto; *to think highly of oneself* tener gran concepto de sí mismo.

high-minded, *a.* magnánimo; altanero; ambicioso.

highness, *a.* altura, elevación; celsitud; Alteza (título de).

high-priest, *s.* jerarca, *m.*

high-reaching, *a.* ambicioso; lo que alcanza gran altura.

high-seasoned, *a.* picante.

high-spirited, *a.* atrevido, osado.

hight [haɪt], *a. (ant.)* llamado, nombrado.

high-toned, *a.* de tono alto, honrado, honroso; *(fam., E.U.)* de buen gusto.

highty-tighty [haiti'taiti], *a. interj.* ¡hola! ¡tate!

highway ['haiwei], *s.* camino real; carretera, calzada, carrera.

highwayman ['haiweimən], *s.* bandido, forajido, ladrón, salteador de caminos.

high-wrought ['hairɔːt], *a.* primorosamente trabajado; muy agitado.

hilarious [hi'lɛəriəs], *a.* alegre, bullicioso.

hilarity [hi'læriti], *a.* hilaridad, júbilo, alegría, regocijo.

Hilary Term ['hiləri'təːm], *s. (for.)* uno de los cuatro períodos del año en que está abierto el Alto Tribunal de Justicia.

hill [hil], *s.* collado, colina, eminencia, monte, loma, cuesta, otero, cerro, altozano; montoncillo; *down-hill,* cuesta abajo; *up-hill,* cuesta arriba; *ant-hill,* hormiguero; *up hill* *and down dale*, por montes y valles. — *v.t.* aporcar. — *v.i.* amontonarse.

hilliness ['hilinis], *s.* montuosidad.

hillman ['hilmən], *s.* (*Am.*) arribeño.

hillock ['hilək], *s.* colina, altillo, montecillo, loma, morón, otero, cerrejón, mogote.

hillside, *s.* lado de una colina, ladera.

hilltop, *s.* cima, cumbre.

hilly ['hili], *a.* montañoso, montuoso.

hilt [hilt], *s.* (*arm.*) puño, empuñadura; (*fig.*) *up to the hilt*, hasta lo sumo, hasta lo último.

hilted, *a.* que tiene puño o guarnición.

hilum ['hailəm], *s.* (*bot.*) ombligo de una semilla; yema de un haba; ojo de un frejol; núcleo de un grano de almidón; (*anat.*) hilo.

him [him], *pron. pers. m.* (caso acusativo de **he**) a él, le, lo, se; *to him*, a él; *of him*, de él; *give it to him*, déselo Vd.

himself [him'self], *pron. pers.* reflexivo, él, él mismo, se, sí, sí mismo; *he will go himself*, irá en persona; *he will go by himself*, irá solo.

hind [haind], *a.* trasero, posterior, zaguero. — *s.* cierva; (*ant.*) criado; patán, rústico; *hind foremost*, lo de atrás delante.

hinder ['haindəɹ], *a.* posterior, trasero.

hinder ['hindəɹ], *v.t.* impedir, embarazar, poner obstáculos, estorbar, detener, obstruir, demorar. — *v.i.* poner obstáculos o trabas; oponerse.

hinderer, *s.* obstructor, estorbador.

hindermost ['haindəɹməst], **hindmost** ['haindməst], *a.* postrero, último, postrimero.

Hindi ['hindi], **Hindoo, Hindu** ['hindu:], *s.* indostano, indostánico.

hindrance ['hindrəns], *s.* impedimento, obstáculo, estorbo, embarazo.

Hindustani [hindu'stɑ:ni], *a.* indostanés. — *s.* (idioma) indostani.

hinge [hindʒ], *s.* gozne, bisagra, charnela, alguaza, resorte, eje principal; *blank-hinge*, bisagra de doble acción; *butt-hinge*, quicio; *dove-tail hinge*, (*mar.*) bisagras a cola de pato; *hinge-post*, quicial; *hinge-joint*, (*anat.*) coyuntura; *to come off its hinges*, salirse de sus casillas. — *v.t.* poner goznes a, engoznar; enquiciar; encorvar; fijar. — *v.i.* girar sobre un gozne; dar vueltas; depender.

hinny ['hini], *v.i.* relinchar. — *s.* macho, mulo (producto de caballo y burra).

hint [hint], *v.t.* apuntar, insinuar, tocar ligeramente, intimar, indicar, sugerir indirectamente. — *v.i.* echar una indirecta, sugerir, dar a entender; *to hint at*, aludir a, hacer una alusión, hacer entrever, dar a entender. — *s.* indirecta, alusión, sugestión, insinuación, idea, aviso, pulla; *to throw out hints*, tirar indirectas.

hinterland ['hintəɹlənd], *s.* región situada más allá de la costa; tierra adentro.

hintingly ['hintiŋli], *adv.* por insinuación, a medias palabras.

hip [hip], *s.* (*anat.*) cadera; (*arq.*) caballete; (*bot.*) fruto del escaramujo, agavanzo; *hip bath*, baño de asiento, semicupio; *hip shot*, renco; *hip roof*, (*arq.*) techo a cuatro vertientes; *to catch on the hip*, llevar ventaja sobre; *to smite hip and thigh*, derrotar completamente. — *v.t.* descaderar, echar sobre la cadera, fracturar la cadera; (*arq.*) construir un techo con cubierta a cuatro aguas.

hip, hipped, hippish, *s.* hipocondríaco.

hip-bone, *s.* cía.

hip-gout, *s.* ciática.

hippocampus [hipo'kæmpəs], *s.* hipocampo, caballo marino; (*anat.*) nombre de dos eminencias del cerebro.

hippocras ['hipokræs], *s.* hipocrás.

Hippocratism [hi'pokrətizm], *s.* doctrina médica de Hipócrates.

hippodrome ['hipodroum], *s.* hipódromo, circo.

hippogriff ['hipogrif], *s.* hipogrifo, caballo con alas.

hippophagy [hi'pofəgi], *s.* hipofagia.

hippopotamus [hipo'potəməs], *s.* hipopótamo.

hippuric [hi'pju:rik], *a.* hipúrico.

hipshot ['hipʃot], *a.* descaderado.

hipwort ['hipwə:ɹt], *s.* escaramujo.

hircine ['hə:ɹsain], *a.* cabrío, cabruno.

hire [haiɹ], *v.t.* alquilar, dar o tomar en arriendo; asoldar, ajornalar, asalariar; arrendar; sobornar, cohechar; *to hire out*, alquilar, alquilarse, dar en alquiler; ponerse a servir. — *s.* alquiler, arriendo; soborno; jornal, salario, estipendio.

hireling ['haiɹliŋ], *s.* alquilón, jornalero, persona asalariada; hombre mercenario. — *a.* mercenario, venal.

hirer ['hairəɹ], *s.* alquilador, arrendador.

hirsute ['hə:ɹsju:t], *a.* hirsuto, velludo, peludo; grosero, áspero.

hirsuteness, *s.* vellosidad.

his [hiz], *pron.* (posesivo o genitivo de **he**) *m.* el suyo, la suya, los suyos, las suyas (de él). — *a. posesivo*, su, sus (de él); suyo, suya, suyos, suyas.

hispid ['hispid], *a.* híspido, cerdoso.

hiss [his], *v.t.* silbar, sisear, burlarse de. — *v.i.* silbar, producir un silbido, chiflar; hacer burla, burlarse. — *s.* silbido, siseo, burla, escarnio.

hissing, *s.* silbido, silba, siseo, chifla.

hissingly, *adv.* a silbidos, por medio de silbidos.

hist [hist], *interj.* ¡chito! ¡chitón! ¡silencio!

histologic [histo'lodʒik], **histological**, *a.* histológico.

histologist [his'tolodʒist], *s.* histólogo.

histology [his'tolodʒi], *s.* histología.

historian [his'to:riən], *s.* historiador.

historic [his'torik], **historical**, *a.* histórico, historial.

historiographer [histori'ogrəfəɹ], *s.* historiógrafo.

historiography, *s.* historiografía.

history ['histəri], *s.* historia.

histrionic [histri'onik], **histrionical**, *a.* histriónico, teatral.

hit [hit], *v.t.* (*pret., p.p.* **hit**) dar, golpear, pegar, cutir; acertar, atinar, encontrar, dar con, dar en; lograr, conseguir; *to hit the nail on the head*, acertar; dar en el hito, dar en el clavo, acertar; *to hit the mark*, dar en el blanco. — *v.i.* ludir, rozar, tocar, chocar; acontecer o acaecer felizmente, salir bien; acertar, tener buen éxito; encontrar por casualidad, tropezar; *to hit off*, describir o expresar acertadamente o exactamente; *to hit against*, dar contra, chocar con; *to hit upon*, hallar, encontrar. — *s.* golpe, choque, coscorrón; suerte feliz, *f.*, golpe de fortuna; rasgo de ingenio; chanza, chiste; (*teat.*) éxito; *lucky hit*, éxito, golpe de fortuna, occurrencia feliz; *hit or miss*, (*fam.*) sea como fuere; a todo riesgo.

hitch [hitʃ], *v.t.* atar, acoplar, ligar, sujetar, enganchar; (*mar.*) amarrar; mover a tirones o saltos. — *v.i.* saltar, moverse a saltos; enredarse; rozarse con los pies; caer dentro; (*fam.*) llevarse bien con otro, estar de acuerdo, ser compatible con otro. — *s.* alto, parada; obstáculo, impedimento, tropiezo, dificultad; acción de coger o tirar; (*mar.*) vuelta de cabo; tirón.

hitchel ['hitʃəl], *v.t.* rastrillar.

hither ['hiðəɹ], *adv.* acá, hacia acá; a este fin; *hither* o *come hither*, ven acá. — *a.* citerior; *on the hither side of*, aquende, de este lado, más joven de.

hithermost ['hiðəɹməst], *a.* más cercano, próximo.

hitherto [hiðəɹ'tuː], *adv.* hasta aquí, hasta ahora.

hive [haiv], *s.* colmena; emporio; enjambre de abejas. — *pl.* **hives**, (*med.*) ronchas, urticaria. — *v.t.* enjambrar, encorchar, encerrar en las colmenas. — *v.i.* vivir juntos como en colmena, encerrarse muchas personas juntas.

hiver, *s.* colmenero.

ho [hou], **hoa!** *interj.* ¡eh! ¡basta! ¡so! ¡cho! ¡jo!

hoar [hoːɹ], *a.* blanco, cano; nevado; mohoso. — *s.* canicie, *f.*

hoard [hoːɹd], *v.t.*, *v.i.* atesorar, amontonar, guardar, recoger, acumular, hacinar, almacenar, recolectar, acaudalar, hacer repuesto. — *s.* provisión, montón, repuesto, repuesto oculto, acumulamiento; tesoro escondido.

hoarder, *s.* atesorador, el que oculta repuestos.

hoarding, *s.* amontonamiento; tablilla de avisos; cerca provisional.

hoarfrost ['hoːɹfroːst], *s.* escarcha blanca.

hoarhound, horehound ['hoːɹhaund], *s.* (*bot.*) marrubio.

hoariness ['hoːrinis], *s.* blancura; moho; canicie, *f.*, canas de viejo, vejez.

hoarse [hoːɹs], *a.* ronco, rauco, enronquecido, bronco.

hoarsely ['hoːɹsli], *adv.* roncamente; *to speak hoarsely*, hablar ronco.

hoarseness, *s.* ronquera, enronquecimiento, carraspera.

hoary ['hoːri], *a.* blanco, blanquecino; cano, canoso; escarchado; mohoso; venerable.

hoax [houks], *s.* engaño, burla, bola, paparrucha, petardo, broma, filfa, mentira. — *v.t.* engañar, dar un petardo, burlar.

hob [hob], *s.* antehogar, repisa interior del hogar; mandril para hacer roscas de tornillo; cubo de rueda; punzón de embutir; tángano; plancha de taladro; (*ant.*) patán; *to play hob with*, trastornar, poner en confusión.

hobble ['hobəl], *v.t.* poner trabas, maniatar; apear; embarazar, enredar. — *v.i.* cojear; hacer versos desiguales o irregulares. — *s.* cojera; manea, traba, maniota; berengenal, atolladero, dificultad.

hobbledehoy ['hobəldihoi], *s.* zagal (*esp.* torpe y desmañado).

hobby ['hobi], *s.* recreación, pasatiempo; manía; jaca; caballico (juguete); (*orn.*) sacre; zoquete; *everyone has his hobby*, (*prov.*) cada loco con su tema.

hobby-horse, *s.* caballito o caballico (juguete); (*fig.*) manía, tema o empeño predilecto.

hobgoblin ['hobgoblin], *s.* duende, espectro, trasgo, cachidiablo, espíritu.

hobnail ['hobneil], *s.* tachuela.

hob-nailed, *a.* clavado con tachuelas.

hob-nob ['hobnob], *v.i.* beber juntos, tener intimidad.

hobo ['houbou], *s.* (*E.U.*) vagabundo, holgazán.

hock [hok], *s.* vino del Rin; corva, tarso, jarrete, corvejón, pernil. — *v.t.* desjarretar, cortar los jarretes.

hockey ['hoki], *s.* juego de pelota con palo encorvado.

hockle ['hokəl], *v.t.* desjarretar.

hocus ['houkəs], *v.t.* engañar, chasquear; atontar con drogas.

hocus-pocus ['houkəs'poukəs], *s.* treta, titiritero, birbirloque, pasapasa.

hod [hod], *s.* artesa; cuezo.

hod-carrier, *s.* peón de albañil.

hodge-podge ['hodʒpodʒ], *s.* almodrote, bodrio; baturrillo.

hodiernal [houdi'əːnəl], *a.* de hoy, de hoy día.

hodman ['hodmən], *s.* peón de albañil, manobre.

hoe [hou], *s.* azada, azadón; (*Mex.*) coa. — *v.t.* cavar, azadonar, sachar.

hoeing ['houiŋ], *s.* sachadura.

hog [hog], *s.* puerco, cochino, cerdo, marrano, gorrino; (*mar.*) escobón; (*fam.*) persona sucia, o egoísta; *to go the whole hog*, (*fam.*) llegar hasta el último límite, ir al extremo. — *v.t.* (*mar.*) limpiar el casco de un buque debajo del agua; afretar, rapar el pelo; partir (una embarcación) por el medio; (*fam., E.U.*) tomar demasiado. — *v.i.* arquearse, torcerse, combarse.

hog-fennel, *s.* servato, ervato.

hog-herd, *s.* porquero, porquerizo.

hoggish ['hogiʃ], *a.* porcino, porcuno.

hoggishly, *adv.* puercamente, cochinamente; vorazmente, vilmente.

hoggishness, *s.* porquería, cochinada; voracidad, glotonería.

hog-pen, hog-sty, *s.* porqueriza, zahurda, pocilga.

hogshead ['hogzhed], *s.* pipa, bocoy, tonel.

hoiden ['hoiden], *s.* muchacha traviesa, tunantuela. — *a.* atrevida, desenvuelta, grosera, rústica. — *v.i.* retozar o saltar de un modo indecoroso o grosero.

hoist [hoist], *v.t.* alzar, elevar, suspender, guindar, levantar; (*mar.*) izar, enarbolar, drizar. — *s.* cabría, pescante, malacate, grúa, montacargas, *m.*, ascensor, elevador; medida vertical de una bandera; ascensión, levantamiento, enarboladura.

hoisting-rope, *s.* braga.

hoity-toity ['hoiti'toiti], *a.* (*fam.*) fachendero, engreído, descuidado, juguetón. — *interj.* ¡tate! ¡ola!

hold [hould], *v.t.* (*pret.*, **held**; *p.p.* **held**, (*ant.*) **holden**) tener, coger asir, agarrar, aguantar, retener, reservar; limitar, estrechar, restringir; detener, contener; sostener, mantener; caber, tener cabida o capacidad, contener en sí, poseer, ocupar, reputar, estar en posesión de; juzgar, entender; gozar, disfrutar; continuar, proseguir; llevar a cabo, celebrar; obligar; guardar; apostar, hacer una apuesta; observar; conservar. — *v.i.* estar en vigor, valer, ser válido; seguir, proseguir;

mantenerse firme, sostenerse, aguantar; durar, continuar; tener fuerza; abstenerse, refrenarse; estar en posesión; depender, estar dependiente de; deducir; *to hold back*, resistir, retener, guardar; *to hold forth*, mostrar, revelar; (*fam.*) arengar, predicar, hablar en público; *to hold in*, refrenar, refrenarse, contenerse; *to hold off*, alejar, apartar, alejarse, separarse; *to hold on*, seguir, proseguir, prolongar, continuar; *to hold out*, proponer, ofrecer, extender, sostener, durar, alargar, proferir; *to hold up*, alzar, levantar, sostener, proteger, sostenerse, mantenerse, cesar, terminar; parar (un tren, etc.) con motivo de robarlo, atracar; *to hold one's tongue*, callar; *to hold oneself in*, contener la risa (o cólera); *to hold with*, ser de la opinión de, estar de acuerdo con. — *s.* acción de prender asir, o agarrar; presa; asidero, agarradero, mango, asa, etc.; cárcel, *f.*, prisión, custodia; (*mar.*) bodega; *afterhold*, (*mar.*) bodega de popa; *forehold*, (*mar.*) bodega de proa; *to trim the hold*, (*mar.*) abarrotar; *depth of the hold*, (*mar.*) puntal de la bodega; apresamiento; escondite, paraje oculto; fortaleza, fuerte; influencia, poder; *to lay hold of*, apoderarse de. — *interj.* ¡tente! ¡para! ¡quieto!

holdback, *s.* restricción, freno; (*carr.*) cejadero.

holder, *s.* tenedor, poseedor, posesor, teniente; (*for.*) tenedor; arrendatario, arrendador, propietario; mantenedor; inquilino; agarrador, asidero, agarradero, cabo, mango, asa, puño; apoyo; (*mar.*) marinero de la bodega; *bond-holder*, (*com.*) obligacionista, *m.f.*; *pen-holder*, portaplumas, *m.*; *stockholder, shareholder*, accionista, *m.f.*; *plate-holder*, (*foto.*) porta-placas, *m.*; *holder of shares*, accionista, *m.f.*

holdfast ['houldfɑːst], *s.* (*mec.*) barrilete, grapón, laña, grapa; apoyo, sostén; mordaza, prensa; (*fam.*) hombre muy avaro.

holding, *s.* tenencia, posesión, pertenencia; inquilinato, arrendamiento, influencia, poder; *holding-ground*, (*mar.*) buen fondo.

hole [houl], *s.* agujero, horado, orificio, cavidad, hueco, boquete, hoyo; cueva, choza, cabaña; vivienda vil y mala; perforación; seno; (*fam.*) atolladero, aprieto; gran aprieto; (*fig.*) excusa; mancha, defecto en el carácter. — *v.t.* agujerear, perforar, cavar, taladrar; meter en la tronera (juego de billar). — *v.i.* meterse, entrar; deslizarse; invernar.

holiday ['hɔlidei], *s.* día festivo, festividad, fiesta, día feriado; aniversario; (*mar.*) mancha, punto que se ha dejado sin pintar o alquitranar. — *pl.* **holidays**, vacaciones. — *a.* alegre, festivo.

holiness ['houlinis], *s.* santidad, beatitud; perfección, integridad; *His Holiness*, Su Santidad.

holing ['houliŋ], *s.* perforación; taladro para introducir un clavo, perno, etc.

holland ['hɔlənd], *s.* (*tej.*) holanda; *brown holland*, holanda cruda. — *pl.* **hollands**, ginebra.

hollo [hə'lou], **holl(o)a** ['hɔlə], *interj.* ¡eh! ¡hola! — *s.* grito, grita.

hollow ['hɔlou], *a.* hueco, vacío, cóncavo; profundo, cavernoso, grave, sepulcral; hundido; insincero, falso, disimulado, traidor, doble; *hollow-hearted*, solapado. — *s.* cueva, caverna, cavidad; concavidad, hueco; paso, ranura, canal; valle, cañada; hoyo. — *v.t.*

excavar, ahuecar, ahondar, vaciar; acopar, escotar.

hollowness, *s.* cavidad, vacío, hueco; falsía, doblez, falacia, simulación.

hollow-root, *s.* moscatelina, palomilla.

holly ['hɔli], *s.* acebo; agrifolio.

hollyhock ['hɔlihɔk], *s.* malva hortense.

holm [houm], *s.* isleta de río; rambla; (*bot.*) acebo.

holm-oak, *s.* encina.

holocaust ['hɔlokɔːst], *s.* holocausto; matanza, hecatombe, *f.*; sacrificio.

holograph ['hɔlogræf], *s.* hológrafo.

holographic, *a.* hológrafo, ológrafo.

holster ['houlstəɹ], *s.* pistolera, funda de pistola.

holster-cap, *s.* tapafunda.

holt [hoult], *s.* bosque, monte.

holy ['houli], *a.* santo, pío; sacro, sagrado, santificado, consagrado; almo, puro, inmaculado; *Holy Ghost, Holy Spirit*, Espíritu Santo; *Holy Office*, Santo Oficio; *holy day*, día de fiesta, disanto; *holy water*, agua bendita; *holy oil*, crisma, óleo; *Holy Week*, Semana Santa; *holy-water sprinkler*, hisopo; *holy writ*, la Sagrada Escritura; *holy wars*, cruzadas; *Holy Thursday*, jueves santo; día de la Ascensión.

holystone ['houlistoun], *s.* (*mar.*) piedra bendita, trozo de arenisca. — *v.t.* (*mar.*) limpiar la cubierta con piedra bendita.

homage ['hɔmidʒ], *s.* homenaje, respeto, reverencia; *to do* (o *pay*) *homage*, rendir homenaje. — *v.t.* reverenciar, acatar, honrar.

homageable, *a.* sujeto a homenaje.

home [houm], *s.* hogar, casa propia, morada, habitación, mansión; patria, suelo patrio; vivienda, domicilio, residencia; asilo, hospicio, casa de huérfanos; posada, albergue, refugio, hospedería; (*dep.*) meta, límite, término. — *a.* doméstico, de casa; regional, nacional, del país; indígena, nativo, natal; eficaz, certero, que da en el blanco, que hiere en lo vivo. — *adv.* a casa; en casa; en el sitio en que debe estar; al país, en la tierra de uno; al propósito; estrechamente, íntimamente, eficazmente; *at home*, en casa, en su patria, libre, como en su propia casa; *to come home*, volver a su país; *to be away from home*, estar fuera de casa; *to go to one's long home*, morir, fallecer; *to strike home*, dar en el blanco; *to take home*, llevar a casa; *there's no place like home*, mi casa y mi hogar cien doblas val. — *v.i.* volar al palomar (palomas); (*fig.*) ir a casa, sentir nostalgia por la casa. — *v.t.* enviar, soltar (palomas) al palomar; proveer, proporcionar un hogar.

home-born, *a.* doméstico, indígena, natural.

home-bred, *a.* natural, nativo, casero; agreste, inculto, rudo.

home-keeping, *a.* de gustos caseros.

homeless, *a.* destituído; sin casa ni hogar; mostrenco.

homelike, *a.* semejante al hogar doméstico; cómodo, agradable.

homeliness ['houmlinis], *s.* simpleza, sencillez; grosería, rudeza; fealdad.

homely ['houmli], *a.* casero, sencillo, doméstico, llano, liso; rústico, inculto; (*E.U.*) feo, de facciones ordinarias; vulgar, grosero. — *adv.* llanamente, simplemente; como de casa; groseramente.

home-made, *a.* fabricado en el país, hecho en casa.

homeopathic [houmio'pæθik], **homœopathic**, *a.* homeopático.

homeopathy [houmi'opəθi], **homœopathy**, *s.* homeopatía.

Homeric [ho'merik], *a.* homérico.

homesick ['houmsik], *a.* nostálgico.

homesickness, *s.* nostalgia, añoranza.

homespun ['houmspʌn], *a.* casero, hecho o hilado en casa; tocho, basto; vulgar, común. — *s.* tela tejida en casa.

homestead ['houmsted], *s.* casa solariega, casa propia; granja, estancia; (*E.U.*) tierra cedida por el gobierno para el establecimiento de una familia según la ley del año 1862.

homeward ['houmwəd], *adv.* hacia casa, hacia su país; de vuelta; *homeward bound*, de regreso, de vuelta.

homicidal [həmi'saidəl], *a.* sanguinario, matador, homicida.

homicide ['homisaid], *s.* homicidio; homicida, *m.f.*

homiletic [homi'letik], **homiletical**, *a.* homilético.

homiletics, *s.* homilética, oratoria sagrada.

homilist ['homilist], *s.* predicador de homilías.

homily ['homili], *s.* homilía; sermón.

homing ['houmiŋ], *a.* que regresa a casa (paloma).

hominy ['homini], *s.* maíz molido, maíz machacado.

homœ-, *v.* **home-**.

homogen ['homodʒen], *s.* estructora o parte homogénea.

homogeneal [homo'dʒi:niəl], **homogeneous** [homo'dʒi:niəs], *a.* homogéneo; parecido.

homogeneity [homodʒen'i:iti], **homogeneousness**, *a.* homogeneidad, semejanza, uniformidad.

homograph ['homogræf], *s.* vocablo homógrafo.

homographic, *a.* homógrafo.

homologation [homələ'geiʃən], *s.* (*for.*) homologación.

homologous [homələ'gəs], *a.* homólogo.

homologue ['homolog], *s.* parte de una cosa homóloga a otra.

homonym ['homonim], *s.* homónimo.

homonymous [ho'moniməs], *a.* homónimo, equívoco, ambiguo.

homonymy [ho'monimi], *s.* homonimia; equivocación; ambigüedad.

homophone ['homofoun], *s.* palabra o letra homófona.

homophonous, *a.* homófono.

homophony [hom'ofəni], *s.* identidad de sonido de dos palabras de distinta significación.

homosexual [homo'sekzju:əl], *a., s.* homosexual.

homotonous [hom'otənəs], *a.* que tiene el mismo tono; parecido, uniforme.

homunculus [ho'mʌŋkju:ləs], *s.* homúnculo; hombrecito, enano.

hone [houn], *s.* piedra de afilar. — *v.t.* afilar, vaciar, asentar (navajas, etc.).

honest ['onest], *a.* honrado, recto, probo, delicado, justo, íntegro, sincero; leal, equitativo; fiel; (hablando de mujeres) honesta, recatada, casta; *honest dealing*, proceder leal,

buena fe; *honest people*, gente honrada, gente de bien; *honest fellow*, hombre de bien.

honesty ['onesti], *s.* honradez, equidad, probidad, integridad, justicia; decencia, honestidad, decoro; (*bot.*) lunaria.

honey ['hʌni], *s.* miel, *f.*; dulzura. — *v.t.* enmelar, cubrir con miel. — *v.i.* hablar cariñosamente.

honey-ant, *s.* especie de hormiga.

honey-bee, *s.* abeja de miel.

honeycomb, *s.* panal (de abejas); (*arti.*) escarabajos, fallas en la fundición de cañones.

honeycombed, *a.* lleno de celdillas.

honeyed ['hʌnid], *a.* dulce, meloso, melifluo, enmelado, cubierto de miel.

honeyedness, *s.* dulzura, halago.

honey-flower, *s.* ceriflor, *f.*

honeyless, *a.* sin miel.

honeymoon ['hʌnimu:n], *s.* luna de miel.

honey-mouthed, *a.* melifluo, adulador.

honeysuckle ['hʌnisʌkəl], *s.* madreselva.

honey-sweet, *a.* dulce como la miel.

honorarium ['onɛəriəm], *s.* honorarios, emolumentos.

honorary ['onərəri], *s.* honorario, honorífico, honroso. — *s.* honorarios.

honour ['onəɹ], **honor**, *s.* honra; rectitud, probidad, honradez, fidelidad, integridad; veneración, reverencia; obsequio público; reputación, gloria, fama; dignidad, señorío, honor, lauro, empleo, cargo, blasón; decoración, ornamento; civildad, cortesía; pudor, recato, castidad, vergüenza; magnanimidad; las cuatro figuras (as, rey, caballo y sota) del palo de triunfo (naipes); *court of honour*, tribunal de honor; *Your Honour*, título que se da a los jueces; *word of honour*, palabra de honor; *honour bright*, (*fam.*) a fe de honor, bajo mi palabra de honor; *point of honour*, pundonor; *on my honour*, por mi fe, o por mi honor; *act of honour*, (*com.*) protesta de intervención; *last honours*, honras fúnebres. — *v.t.* honrar, respetar, reverenciar, venerar, estimar; enaltecer; glorificar; laurear, condecorar; dar un empleo; (*com.*) pagar, aceptar, honrar.

honourable ['onərəbl], *a.* honorable, noble, ilustre, esclarecido; grande, honrado, honroso, honorífico, magnánimo, equitativo, justo.

honourableness, *s.* honradez, honestidad, eminencia.

honourer, *s.* honrador.

hood [hud], *s.* capucha, capirote, capilla, caperuza; (*Univ.*) muceta de graduados; fuelle de carruaje; carroza de la escalera; (*mar.*) caperuza de palo; (*mar.*) sombrero de la escalera; sombrerete de chimenea; campana del hogar; tapa de la bomba. — *v.t.* cubrir con capirote, caperuza, o capucha; ocultar, cegar, tapar.

-hood [-həd], sufijo que denota estado, condición o totalidad; equivale al sufijo castellano -dad o -ez.

hoodlum ['hu:dləm], *s.* (*fam., E.U.*) gamberro; rufián, malhechor, pistolero.

hoodoo ['hu:du:], *v.t.* (*fam., E.U.*) aojar. — *s.* mal de ojo; aojador.

hoodwink ['hudwiŋk], *v.t.* vendar los ojos; tapar, ocultar, encubrir; engañar.

hoof [hu:f], *s.* (*pl.* **hoofs, hooves**) casco de las bestias; animal ungulado; pesuña o pezuña;

(*geom.*) cono truncado; *hoof-paring*, despalmador, pujavante. — *v.i.* andar, moverse despacio; ir a pie; (*vulg.*) cocear.

hoof-bound, *a.* estrecho o corto de cascos.

hoofed, *a.* que tiene cascos, ungulado.

hook [huk], *s.* gancho, garfio, garabato; garra; grapón, arpón, arponcillo; anzuelo; corchete, prendedero; hoz, *f.*; aliciente, atractivo; (*mús.*) rabo de una corchea o nota más corta; *hook-bill*, pico encorvado; *hook-nose*, nariz aguileña; *hooks and eyes*, (*cost.*) corchetes y corchetas, broches; *off the hooks*, agitado, distraído; *to be off the hooks*, (*fam.*) no tenerlas todas consigo; *on one's own hook*, (*fam.*) por cuenta propia, sin depender de otro; *by hook or by crook*, a tuertas o a derechas; a buenas o a malas. — *v.t.* enganchar, coger con gancho, garfear, engafar, encorchetar, garabatear, prender; encornar, dar una cornada; embestir con los cuernos; atrapar, atraer, engatusar, engañar; (*fam.*) ratear, hurtar.

hookah ['huːkə], *s.* narguile.

hooked ['hukd], *a.* enganchado; ganchudo, ganchoso, encorvado.

hookedness, *s.* encorvadura.

hooker, *s.* cosa que engancha.

hooky, *a.* ganchudo, lleno de ganchos; *to play hooky*, (*vulg., escuelas*) hacer novillos.

hooligan ['huːligən], *s.* gamberro.

hooliganism, *s.* gamberrismo.

hoop [huːp], *s.* aro, cerco, arco, fleje, zuncho; anilla, argolla, vilorta; (*mec.*) collar, collarín; virola; grito; (*joy.*) sortija, ajorca, arete, zarcillo; *hoop-la!* ¡arriba, upa! *hoop-skirt*, tontillo, ahuecador. — *v.t.* poner arcos o cercos a; rodear, cercar, cenir. — *v.i.* gritar, vociferar; ojear.

hooper, *s.* tonelero.

hooping-cough ['huːpiŋkɔf], *s.* tos ferina.

hoopoe, hoopoo ['huːpou], *s.* abubilla, puput, upupa.

hoot [huːt], *v.t.* ojear, espantar. — *v.i.* gritar, huchear, ulular; dar gritos. — *s.* grito, grita, clamor, ruido; *hoot-owl*, buho que ulula.

hooter, *s.* el que grita; silbato, sirena de vapor; bocina de automóvil.

hooting ['huːtiŋ], *s.* grito, grita, acto de gritar; silbido (de sirena).

hoove [huːv], **hove** [houv], **hooven,** *s.* (*vet.*) enfermedad del ganado (distensión del abdomen por gases).

hop [hɔp], *v.t.* saltar, brinchar; mezclar el lúpulo en la cerveza. — *v.i.* saltar, dar saltos, andar a la pata coja, cojear; recoger lúpulo. — *s.* brinco, salto; (*bot.*) lúpulo, hombrecillo; (*fam.*) baile, sarao.

hop-bine, *s.* vástago de lúpulo.

hope [houp], *s.* esperanza, confianza; apoyo, sostén; expectativa; cosa esperada o ansiada; valle; bahía. — *v.t., v.i.* esperar, desear, confiar, tener esperanza.

hopeful, *a.* lleno de esperanzas, de grandes esperanzas; que da esperanza o promete.

hopefully, *adv.* con esperanza.

hopefulness, *s.* buena disposición, apariencia de buenos resultados.

hopeless, *a.* desesperado, desesperanzado, desahuciado; incurable, irremediable.

hopelessly, *adv.* sin esperanza, desesperadamente; *he is hopelessly behindhand*, tarda un siglo.

hopingly, *adv.* con esperanza.

hoplite ['hɔplait], *s.* hoplita, *m.*

hopper ['hɔpəɹ], *s.* el que salta a la pata coja; (*agr.*) sementero; (*min.*) tolva.

hop-picker ['hɔppikəɹ], *s.* sementero; el que trabaja en la recolección del lúpulo.

hopple ['hɔpəl], *v.t.* trabar o atar un caballo. — *s.* traba, maniota, manea, atadura.

hopscotch ['hɔpskɔtʃ], *s.* coxcojilla, infernáculo, 'a la pata ciega'; (*Am.*) rayuela.

horal ['hɔːrəl], **horary** ['hɔːrəri], *a.* horario; por horas.

Horatian [hoˈreiʃən], *a.* horaciano.

horde [hɔːd], *s.* horda; aduar, ranchería. — *v.i.* formar hordas; vivir en hordas.

hordeolum [hɔːˈdiˈouləm], *s.* orzuelo.

horehound, *s.* marrubio.

horizon [hoˈraizən], *s.* horizonte.

horizontal [hɔriˈzɔntəl], *a.* horizontal.

horizontality, *s.* horizontalidad.

hormone [hɔːˈmoun], *s.* hormona.

horn [hɔːn], *s.* cuerno, asta; (*zool.*) tentáculo; cuerna; (*Am.*) cacho; palpo, antena; (*mús.*) trompa; trompa de caza, cuerno de caza, corneta de monte; bocina; callosidad o dureza en la piel; (*Cuba*) fortuto; objeto de cuerno; cuerno de la luna; (*fig.*) honor, poder; brazo de mar, lago o río en forma de cuerno; *shoe-horn*, calzador de zapatos; *ink-horn*, tintero. — *v.t.* poner cuernos; dar una cornada, hacer cornudo; dar una cencerrada.

hornbeam ['hɔːnbiːm], *s.* carpe, ojaranzo, carpinus.

hornbill, *s.* cálao.

hornblende ['hɔːnblend], *s.* hornblenda.

horn-blower, *s.* trompetero, bocinero.

hornbook ['hɔːnbuk], *s.* cartilla, cuaderno de gramática elemental.

horned, *a.* cornudo; (*poét.*) cornígero; enastado; encornado; de cuerno, formado como cuerno; *horned owl*, buho norteamericano con cuernos; *horned cattle*, ganado vacuno.

hornet ['hɔːnet], *s.* avispa, avispón, crabrón; *to stir up a hornet's nest*, meterse en un avispero; excitar la hostilidad de mucha gente.

hornet-fly, *s.* avispón.

hornfish, *s.* (*ict.*) aguja.

hornify ['hɔːnifai], *v.t.* hacer semejante al cuerno.

horning, *s.* media luna.

hornish, *a.* duro; córneo.

hornless, *a.* que no tiene cuernos.

hornpipe ['hɔːnpaip], *s.* baile predilecto de los marineros que ejecuta una sola persona; chirimía.

hornsilver, *s.* (*min.*) plata córnea; cloruro de plata.

hornwork, *s.* (*fort.*) hornabeque.

horny ['hɔːni], *a.* hecho de cuerno; parecido al cuerno, córneo; calloso.

horography [hoˈrɔgrafi], *s.* gnomónica.

horologe [horoˈloudʒ], *s.* reloj.

horologic [horoˈlɔdʒik], **horological,** *a.* que se refiere a la gnomónica.

horometry [hoˈrɔmetri], *s.* horometría.

horoscope ['hɔroskoup], *s.* horóscopo.

horrent ['hɔrənt], *s.* (*poét.*) erizado; horrendo, horrible, espantoso.

horrible ['hɔribəl], *a.* horrible, terrible, espantoso, horrendo; enorme.

horribleness, *s.* horribilidad.

horrid ['hɔrid], *a.* horrible, hórrido, espantoso; dañoso, ofensivo; áspero; tenebroso, obscuro.

horridness, *s.* horridez, horror, enormidad.

horrific [hɔ'rifik], *a.* horrífico.

horrify ['hɔrifai], *v.t.* horrorizar, horripilar.

horrifying ['hɔrifaiiŋ], *a.* horripilante.

horrisonous, *a.* horrisono.

horror ['hɔrəɹ], *s.* horror, terror, espanto, consternación; desastre, catástrofe, *f.*, calamidad; detestación, aborrecimiento, odio; *the horrors,* (*fam.*) melancolía, delirium tremens.

horse [hɔːs], *s.* caballo; (*mil.*) caballería; caballete, bastidor, burro, borrico; potro en que se castiga a los soldados; tendedor; (*fam.*) traducción, apuntes, clave, *f.*; mania; *carriage-horse,* caballo de tiro; *cart-horse,* caballo de carro; *pack-horse,* caballo de carga; *runaway horse,* caballo desbocado; *saddle-horse,* caballo de silla; *iron horse,* locomotora; *dark horse,* caballo que no inspira confianza, candidato desconocido; *to ride a horse at full gallop,* poner un caballo a rienda suelta; *to ride the high horse,* mostrarse orgulloso.

horse-ant, *s.* hormiga roja.

horseback ['hɔːsbæk], *s.* lomo de caballo o asiento de jinete; *to ride horseback,* montar a caballo.

horse-bean, *s.* haba panosa o caballuna.

horse-car, *s.* carro de tranvía.

horse-chestnut [hɔːs'tʃesnʌt], *s.* castaño de Indias; la castaña que produce.

horse-colt, *s.* potro.

horse-comb, *s.* almohaza.

horse-doctor, *s.* veterinario, albéitar.

horse-dung, *s.* estiércol de caballos.

horse-flesh, *s.* carne de caballo, *f.*; conjunto de caballos; variedad de caoba de las Bahamas.

horse-fly, *s.* tábano; moscarda, garrapata.

horse-guards ['hɔːsgɑːdz], *s.pl.* guardias de a caballo; cuartel general del ejército en Gran Bretaña.

horsehair ['hɔːshɛəɹ], *s.* crin de caballo.

horse-leech, *s.* sanguijuela; albéitar; persona pordiosera, molesta, garrona.

horseman ['hɔːsmən], *s.* jinete, caballero, cabalgador, caballista, *m.*; (*mil.*) soldado de caballería.

horsemanship ['hɔːsmənʃip], *s.* manejo, equitación.

horse-mill, *s.* molino de sangre.

horsemint, *s.* mastranzo.

horse-play, *s.* payasada, chanza pesada, broma de mal gusto.

horse-power, *s.* caballo de fuerza.

horse-radish, *s.* rábano picante o rústico.

horseshoe ['hɔːsʃuː], *s.* herradura; lo que tiene forma de herradura; (*Am.*) casquillo; (*zool.*) límulo, cangrejo.

horsetail, *s.* (*bot.*) cola de caballo.

horsewhip ['hɔːswip], *s.* látigo; (*Méx.*) cuarta, azote; (*Cuba*) chucho. — *v.t.* azotar, zurriagar, cruzar con látigo.

horsewoman ['hɔːswumən], *s.* amazona.

horsiness, *a.* afición a los caballos.

horsing ['hɔːsiŋ], *s.* asiento del amolador de cuchillos; tunda que se da a un muchacho llevado a cuestas por otro.

horsy, horsey ['hɔːsi], *a.* caballar, hípico, caballuno; chalán.

hortation [hɔːr'teiʃən], *s.* exhortación.

hortative [hɔːrtə'tiv], **hortatory,** *a.* exhortatorio.

hortensial [hɔːr'tenʃəl], *a.* hortense, hortelano, apto para jardín.

horticultural [hɔːti'kʌltjuːrəl], *a.* hortícola.

horticulture ['hɔːrtikʌltʃəɹ], *s.* horticultura, jardinería.

horticulturist [hɔːti'kʌltʃuːrist], *s.* horticultor, hortelano.

hosanna [hou'zænə], *s.* hosana.

hose [houz], *s.* calceta; calzas, calcetines, medias; manguera; *hose-pipes,* tubos de manguera; *half-hose,* calcetines; *great hose,* zaragüelles; *hoseman,* manguero; *lawn hose,* mangueras de regar prados; *hose-reel,* carretel de manguera.

hosier ['houʒəɹ], *s.* mediero, calcetero.

hosiery ['houʒəri], *s.* calcetería; calcetines, medias.

hospice ['hɔspis], *s.* hospicio, hospedería.

hospitable ['hɔspitəbəl], *a.* hospitalario, caritativo, benigno con los huéspedes.

hospitableness, *s.* hospitalidad.

hospital ['hɔspitəl], *s.* hospital; hospicio; (*ant.*) colegio; (*ant.*) fonda; *maternity hospital,* casa de maternidad; *hospital ship,* barco (o buque) hospital; *hospital wagon,* carro de ambulancia; *lock hospital,* (*Ingl.*) hospital de enfermedades venéreas.

hospitality [hɔspi'tæliti], *s.* hospitalidad.

hospitaller, hospitaler ['hɔspitələɹ], *s.* hospitalario; hospitalero, hospiciano.

hospitium [hɔs'piʃəm], *s.* hospicio.

host [houst], *s.* patrón, hostalero, hospedero, posadero, mesonero; hueste, *f.*, multitud, ejército; huésped, anfitrión; gran número, sinnúmero; (*igl.*) hostia; *to reckon without one's host,* hacer la cuenta sin la huéspeda.

hostage ['hɔstidʒ], *s.* rehén, prenda, gaje.

hostel ['hɔstəl], *s.* posada, hostería, hostal; casa de huéspedes para estudiantes.

hostelry ['hɔstəlri], **hostlery,** *s.* posada, hostería, mesón, hospedería, hostal, parador.

hostess ['houstes], *s.* posadera, patrona, mesonera, ama, huéspeda.

hostile ['hɔstail], *a.* hostil, enemigo.

hostility [hɔs'tiliti], *s.* hostilidad, guerra.

hostilize, *v.t.* hostilizar.

hostler ['ɔstləɹ], *s.* establero, palafrenero, mozo de paja y cebada.

hot [hɔt], *a.* caliente, cálido; ardiente; caluroso; urente; tórrido; fogoso, fervoroso, ardiente, impaciente; furioso, violento, colérico; acre, picante; (*fam.*) intolerable; *to make hot,* calentar; *to grow hot,* calentarse, encenderse; *to be burning hot,* quemarse, hacer mucho calor; *hot blast,* tiro o corriente de aire caliente; *hot mustard,* mostaza muy picante; *piping hot,* caliente hasta bullir, hirviendo; *hot and heavy,* (*fam.*) furioso; *hot-blooded,* de sangre ardiente; *hot-headed,* vehemente, exaltado, fogoso; *to be in hot water,* estar en ascuas.

hotbed, *s.* era, almajara; (*fig.*) foco, plantel.

hot-brained, *a.* furioso, violento.

hotchpot ['hɔtʃpɔt], *s.* (*for.*) reunión o amalgamación de los bienes de un intestado a fin de hacer partes iguales para los coherederos.

hotel [hou'tel], *s.* hotel, fonda, posada; palacio.

hot-headed [hɔt'hedid], *a.* vehemente, colérico, fogoso, violento.

hothouse ['hɔthaus], s. invernadero, invernáculo; estufa.

hotly ['hɔtli], adv. con calor, calurosamente; lascivamente; vehementemente.

hot-potch, hotch-potch, s. almodrote, gatuperio.

hotspur ['hɔtspə:ɹ], s., a. temerario; atolondrado; violento, fogoso.

Hottentot ['hɔtəntɔt], s. hotentote.

hough [hɔk], v.t. desjarretar, descuadrillar. — s. jarrete, corvejón de las bestias.

hound [haund], s. perro, sabueso, podenco; hombre vil, collón; (mar.) cacholas; bloodhound, sabueso ventor; greyhound, galgo, lebrel. — v.t. cazar, seguir la pista; soltar los perros; to hound out, echar, despedir.

hound-tree, s. cornejo.

hound's tongue, s. (bot.) cinoglosa, viniebla, lengua de perro.

hour ['auəɹ], s. hora; estación, momento, trance. — pl. hours, (igl.) horas (rezos); jornada, horas de trabajo; to keep bad hours, volver a deshora; to keep good hours, volver a casa (o retirarse) temprano; small hours, altas horas de la noche; to strike the hour, dar la hora.

hour-glass, s. ampolleta, reloj de arena.

hour-hand, s. horario, saetilla, aguja, mano.

hour-plate, s. esfera de reloj.

houri ['hu:ri], s. hurí, f.

hourly ['auəli], adv. a cada hora; frecuentemente, por horas. — a. por horas, frecuente.

house ['haus], s. casa; casalicio; edificio, domicilio, hogar, residencia; comunidad, monasterio, convento; linaje, familia, descendencia; (com.) casa de comercio, establecimiento mercantil; razón social, f.; cámara de un cuerpo legislativo; casilla del tablero de ajedrez; (teat.) sala, público; ale-house, cervecería, venta; coffee-house, café; pigeon-house, palomar; summer-house, glorieta; to bring down the house, provocar aplauso general; workhouse, hospicio, asilo. — v.t. tener en casa, dar casa a, albergar; poner a cubierto; ocultar; (mar.) afianzar o cubrir cuando hay borrasca. — v.i. residir.

housebreaker ['hausbreikəɹ], s. ladrón de casas.

house-breaking, s. robo de casa.

house-dog, s. perro de guarda, mastín.

household ['haushould], s. casa, familia; household furniture, menaje de una casa; king's household, casa real; household bread, pan casero, pan bazo.

householder, s. amo de casa, padre de familia.

housekeeper ['hauski:pəɹ], s. ama de llaves, ama de gobierno; mujer de su casa.

housekeeping, s. manejo o cuidado de la casa. — a. doméstico, casero.

houseleek, s. siempreviva, hierba puntera.

houseless, a. sin casa, sin habitación.

housemaid, s. criada, sirvienta.

house-rent, s. alquiler de casa.

housetop, s. techo, azotea, tejado; to shout from the housetops, pregonar a los cuatro vientos.

housewarming, s. tertulia con que se celebra el estreno de una casa.

housewife ['hauswaif], s. ama de una casa; ama de gobierno, ama de llaves; mujer casera, madre de familia; estuche o cajita de costura; agujetero.

housewifely, adv. con economía doméstica. — a. económica y cuidadosa.

housewifery, s. gobierno de una casa; economía doméstica.

housing ['hauziŋ], s. alojamiento; construcción de vivienda; albergue, abrigo; (mec.) muesca, encaje, rebajo; almacenaje; (arq.) nicho; chumacera; (mar.) piola; mantilla, gualdrapa; habitación.

hove [houv], pret. [HEAVE]. — s. enfermedad del ganado.

hovel ['hovəl], s. cobertizo, cabaña, choza. — v.t. abrigar en cabaña.

hover ['hovəɹ], v.t. cubrir con las alas. — v.i. cernerse; revolotear, aletear; estar suspenso en el aire; rondar; dudar; colgar.

hovering, s. revoloteo; el cernerse (de aves de rapiña).

how [hau], adv. como, de qué modo; a qué precio; cuán, cuanto; en que extensión; hasta qué punto; por qué; how long? ¿cuánto tiempo? how far? ¿a qué distancia? ¿cuánto dista? how do you do? ¿cómo le va a Vd.? ¿cómo está Vd.? how few! ¡qué pocos! ¡cuán pocos! how is it? ¿cómo es? ¿cómo sucede? how so? ¿por qué? ¿cómo? how much? ¿cuánto? how many? ¿cuántos? ¿cuántas? how little! ¡qué pocos! ¡cuán pocos! to know how to, saber. — s. modo, manera.

howbeit [hau'bi:it], adv. sea como fuere, así como así, no obstante, sin embargo que, de cualquier modo que.

howdah ['haudɑ:], s. castillo.

howel ['hawəl], s. (carp.) doladera.

however [hau'evəɹ], adv. como quiera que sea, de cualquier modo, en todo caso, a lo menos. — conj. empero, con todo, no obstante, sin embargo.

howitzer ['hauitzəɹ], s. (arti.) obús.

howl [haul], v.i. aullar; gritar; quejarse, gemir; dar alaridos; bramar, rugir. — v.t. gritar, chillar. — s. aullido, latido; alarido; ululato; gemido; bramido; rugido.

howler, s. aullador; gritador; gemidor; mono chillón; (fam.) plancha.

howlet, s. lechuza.

howling, s. aullido; grito; lamento.

howsoever [hausou'evəɹ], adv. como quiera; sin embargo; aunque.

hoy [hɔi], s. (mar.) caraba; interj. (mar.) ¡hola!

hoyden ['hɔidən], s. muchacha traviesa, tunantuela, paya, moza agreste.

hub [hʌb], s. (carr.) cubo de la rueda; chito; clavo, perno, eje, centro; manguito de doble bocina para juntas o empalmes; punzón para hacer troqueles; hub cap, tapa de cubo.

hubbub ['hʌbʌb], s. grito, ruido, tumulto, bulla, alboroto, batahola, enredo.

huckaback ['hʌkəbæk], s. (tej.) alemanisco.

huckleberry ['hʌkəlberi], s. arándano.

hucklebone ['hʌkəlboun], s. cía, hueso de la cadera.

huckster ['hʌkstəɹ], s. regatón, mercachifle, buhonero, revendedor, chalán, pícaro, perillán. — v.i. regatonear, revender.

hucksterage, s. regatonería; tráfico en géneros de poco valor.

hucksteress, s. regatona, revendedora.

huddle ['hʌdəl], v.t. amontonar, tapujar, confundir, arrebujar, mezclar; atrabancar. — v.i. arracimarse, agruparse, amontonarse, venir confusamente. — s. tropel, baraúnda, confusión, desorden, alboroto.

huddler, s. chapucero.
hue [hju:], s. color, tinte, matiz; gritería, grita, clamor; *hue and cry,* alarma, somatén.
huff [hʌf], s. enfado, enojo; gruñido, bufido. — *v.t.* hinchar, inflar; ofender, maltratar de palabra; injuriar; bravear, bufar; soplar una dama en el juego. — *v.i.* hincharse, engreírse; bufar; enfadarse; patear.
huffish, a. irascible, petulante, arrogante, insolente, impertinente.
huffishly, adv. con petulancia, insolentemente; con enfado.
huffishness, s. petulancia, insolencia, arrogancia, impertinencia.
huffy, a. arrogante, irascible, petulante, malhumorado; engreído, hinchado.
hug [hʌg], v.t. abrazar, halagar, acariciar; abrazarse fuertemente a; (*mar.*) navegar muy cerca de (la costa); *to hug the wind,* ceñir el viento; *to hug oneself.* congratularse. — s. abrazo apretado; abracijo; zancadilla.
huge [hju:dʒ], a. vasto, grande, inmenso, gigante, enorme, tremendo; garrafal.
hugeness, s. magnitud, grandeza enorme, enormidad, inmensidad.
hugger-mugger [ˈhʌgəɹmʌgəɹ], s. (*ant.*) reserva, secreto; desorden, confusión. — a. (*ant.*) secreto, reservado; descuidado, confuso.
Huguenot [ˈhju:gənɔt], s. hugonote.
hulk [hʌlk], s. (*mar.*) casco arrumbado, carraca; mamotreto; armatoste; masa, cuerpo abultado.
hulking, hulky, a. tosco, pesado, grueso.
hull [hʌl], s. cáscara, corteza; (*mar.*) casco de un buque; vaina de legumbre; *a-hull,* (*mar.*) a palo seco. — v.t. mondar, pelar, descascarar, descortezar; agujerear el casco de un buque a cañonazos. — v.i. (*mar.*) (*ant.*) navegar a palo seco.
hullabaloo [ˈhʌləbəˈlu:], s. alboroto, bulla, batahola, gritería, tumulto.
hullo [hʌˈlou], interj., s. [HALLO].
hully [ˈhʌli], a. cascarudo.
hum [hʌm], v.t. canturrear, tararear. — v.i. zumbar; canturrear; hablar entre dientes; heder; *to make things hum,* (*fam.*) desplegar actividad, ser muy activo. — s. susurro, baraúnda, zumbido; voz inarticulada; filfa, engaño, chasco, burla; interj. ¡ya! ¡hum!
human [ˈhju:mən], a. humano. — s. mortal, ser humano.
humane [hju:mein], a. humano, filantrópico, humanitario, apacible, afable, compasivo; benigno; cortés.
humanism [ˈhju:mənizm], s. humanismo.
humanist, s. humanista, m.f.
humanitarian [hju:mæniˈtɛəriən], a. humanitario. — s. filántropo; humanitario.
humanitarianism, s. humanitarismo.
humanity [hju:ˈmæniti], s. humanidad, benignidad, benevolencia; género humano. — pl. **the humanities,** humanidades, letras humanas.
humanize [ˈhju:mənaiz], v.t. humanar, civilizar, humanizar, suavizar. — v.i. humanizar.
humankind [hju:mənˈkaind], s. humanidad, género humano, especie humana.
humation [hju:ˈmeiʃən], s. entierro.
humble [hʌmbəl], a. humilde, sumiso, modesto, bajo. — v.t. humillar, postrar,

achicar, deprimir, hollar, desensoberbecer, domar, abatir; confundir.
humble-bee [ˈhʌmbəlbi:], s. abejorro.
humble-mouthed, a. blando, manso, dulce.
humbleness, s. humildad.
humble-pie [hʌmbəlˈpai], s. empanada de *humbles*; *to eat humble-pie,* retractarse, desdecirse, humillarse.
humbler, s. humillador.
humbles, s.pl. despojos o entrañas de venado.
humbling, s. humillación, rendimiento, abatimiento.
humbug [ˈhʌmbʌg], s. embeleco, bambolla, trampantojo, patraña, engaño, engañifa, trampa, decepción, fraude, embuste; charlatán; vaya, cantaleta, zumba; farsante, embaucador, embustero. — v.t. embaucar, engañar, chasquear.
humdrum [ˈhʌmdrʌm], a. torpe, pesado, monótono, cansado. — s. fastidio, aburrimiento, fatiga, enojo; posma, persona cargante, zorrocloco; charla o cantilena fastidiosa. — v.i. pasar el tiempo monótonamente.
humeral [ˈhju:mərəl], a. humeral.
humerus [ˈhju:mərəs], s. (*anat.*) húmero.
humic [ˈhju:mik], a. perteneciente al suelo o tierra; *humic acid,* ácido húmico.
humid [ˈhju:mid], a. húmedo.
humidity [hju:ˈmiditi], s. humedad.
humiliate [hju:ˈmilieit], v.t. humillar, degradar, mortificar, confundir; (*fam.*) poner de vuelta y media.
humiliation [hju:miliˈeiʃən], s. humillación, degradación, mortificación.
humility [hju:ˈmiliti], s. humildad, modestia, encogimiento, sumisión.
hummer [ˈhʌməɹ], s. zumbón.
humming, s. zumbido, susurro. — a. zumbador.
humming-bird [ˈhʌmiŋbə:ɹd], s. colibrí, picaflor, pájaro mosca, chupamiel, tucuso, tominejo; (*Am. Cent.*) guainambí.
hummock [ˈhʌmək], s. montecillo, montecito, colina, morón, mogote.
humoral [ˈhju:mərəl], a. (*med.*) humoral.
humoralism, humorism, s. (*med.*) humorismo; ingenio, gracejo.
humoresque [ˈhju:moresk], s. (*mús.*) humoresca; (*lit.*) humorada.
humorist, s. humorista, m.f.
humorous [ˈhju:mərəs], **humourous,** a. humorístico, chistoso, festivo.
humorousness, s. jocosidad, donaire, gracejo; humorada.
humorsome [ˈhju:məɹˈsəm], a. caprichudo, caprichoso, antojadizo; chistoso, gracioso; enojoso.
humour [ˈhju:məɹ], **humor,** s. humor; carácter, índole, f., genio, ingenio, talante, natural; sal, f., chiste, agudeza, chanza; humorada, capricho, fantasía; aguadija; (*fam.*) erupción cutánea; *dry humour,* chiste socarrón; *broad humour,* payasada; farsa; *to be in humour* (o *in good humour*), estar de buen humor (o talante); *to be out of humour* (o *in ill humour*), estar de mal humor o no estar para fiestas; *to take someone in the humour,* llegarse a alguno en un momento favorable. — v.t. complacer, agradar, satisfacer, acceder, dar gusto; mimar; acomodar a, adaptarse a; consentir en; desempeñar bien; cumplir; dar alma a.
hump [hʌmp], s. giba, corcova, joroba. — v.t.

encorvarse, doblar la espalda. — *v.r.* (*fam.*) hacer un esfuerzo.

humpback ['hʌmpbæk], *s.* giba, corcova, joroba; jorobado; *humpbacked*, jorobado, giboso, corcovado.

humped, *a.* jorobado, corcovado. — *p.p.* [HUMP].

humpty-dumpty ['hʌmti'dʌmti], *s.* persona baja y gruesa, rechoncha; cualquier cosa que una vez caída no puede componerse.

humpy, *a.* giboso.

Hun [hʌn], *s.* huno; (*fam.*) alemán.

hunch [hʌntʃ], *v.t.* empujar, doblar la espalda, dar de puñadas; dar empellones; dar codazos. — *s.* giba, corcova; empellón, empujón, codazo, puñada, golpe.

hunchback ['hʌntʃbæk], **hunchbacked,** *a.* jorobado, giboso, corcovado.

hundred ['hʌndred], *a.* ciento. — *s.* centena, centenar; ciento; división de los condados en Inglaterra en ciertos distritos; *hundredweight*, ciento doce libras (equivale a 50·8 kg.); *by hundreds*, a centenares; *hundred-legs*, ciempiés; *hundredfold*, centuplo, cien veces; *to increase a hundredfold*, centuplicar.

hundredth ['hʌndredθ], *a.* centésimo, ciento.

hung [hʌŋ], *pret.*, *p.p.* [HANG].

hung-beef, *s.* tasajo, cecina de vaca.

Hungarian [hʌŋ'gɛəriən], *a.* húngaro, de Hungría.

hunger ['hʌŋgər], *s.* hambre, *f.*; apetito, gana, apetencia; anhelo, deseo grande o vehemente; *hunger is the best sauce*, a buena hambre no hay pan duro, ni falta salsa a ninguno. — *v.i.* hambrear; desear con ansia.

hunger-bitten, *a.* atormentado por el hambre.

hungry ['hʌŋgri], *a.* hambriento, famélico; deseoso, ganoso; pobre (dícese de las tierras); *to be hungry,* o *to feel hungry,* tener hambre.

hunk [hʌŋk], *s.* (*fam.*) buen pedazo; rebanada gruesa.

hunks [hʌŋks], *s.* hombre avaro.

hunt [hʌnt], *v.t.* montear, cazar; recorrer, registrar, buscar; seguir, perseguir. — *v.i.* cazar; hacer un registro minucioso, buscar una cosa; ir de caza, seguir la pista, ir en busca; *to hunt up and down,* buscar por todos lados; *to hunt after,* buscar, correr tras, desear con ansia; *to hunt counter,* ir contra la pista; *to hunt out,* buscar con empeño, buscar con éxito, descubrir. — *s.* caza, cacería, montería; acosamiento, perseguimiento; asociación de cazadores; jauría, cuadrilla de perros para cazar; *hunt's up,* toque matinal para despertar a los monteros.

hunter, *s.* montero, cazador; caballo de caza; podenco; *hunter's cap,* montera, gorra de caza.

hunting, *s.* montería, cacería, caza; *happy hunting-ground,* terreno favorable, lugar predilecto.

hunting-box, *s.* pabellón de caza.

hunting-horn, *s.* cuerno de caza.

hunting-lodge, *s.* pabellón de caza.

hunting-match, *s.* partida de caza.

hunting-watch, *s.* saboneta.

huntress ['hʌntres], *s.* cazadora.

huntsman ['hʌntsmən], *s.* montero, cazador, cazador de monte.

hurdle ['hə:rdəl], *s.* zarzo, valla, cañizo; adral; valla portátil en las carreras de caballos; fábrica de cosas hechas con varas o mimbres;

(*mil.*) fagina, cestón, gabión; *hurdle-race,* carrera de obstáculos. — *v.t.* hacer o colocar cañizos; hacer cercas de palos y mimbres; defender con faginas.

hurds [hə:rdz], *s.* estopas, desechos de cáñamo o lino. — *v.i.* saltar vallas.

hurdy-gurdy ['hə:rdigə:rdi], *s.* (*mús.*) organillo.

hurl, *v.t.* tirar, arrojar, lanzar, precipitar con violencia, pegar (un grito). — *v.i.* lanzarse, arrojarse; dar alaridos; *to hurl oneself into ruin,* arruinarse. — *s.* tiro, lanzamiento.

hurlbat ['hə:rlbæt], *s.* especie de garrote o cachiporra.

hurler, *s.* el que arroja.

hurling, *s.* antiguo juego de pelota parecido al football.

hurlyburly ['hə:rlibə:rli], *s.* batahola, gritería, trulla, baraúnda, tumulto, alboroto, confusión.

hurrah [hu'rɑ:], **hurray,** *interj.* ¡viva! ¡hurra! — *v.t.*, *v.i.* aclamar, aplaudir, vitorear.

hurricane ['hʌrikən], *s.* huracán; tormenta, tempestad; *hurricane lamp,* lámpara sorda.

hurried ['hʌrid], *s.* apresurado, precipitado, hecho de prisa. — *p.p.* [HURRY]; *hurried note,* billete escrito a escape; *hurried away,* arrastrado; llevado por la fuerza, arrebatado.

hurrier ['hʌriər], *s.* apresurador, acelerador.

hurry ['hʌri], *v.t.* acelerar, apresurar, dar prisa; atropellar; apurar, activar, apremiar, acuciar, no dar respiro; precipitar; (*min.*) arrastrar un vagón de hulla. — *v.i.* apresurarse, atropellarse, darse prisa; precipitarse; *to hurry after,* correr detrás de, en pos de; *to hurry back,* volver de prisa; *to hurry in,* entrar (o hacer entrar) de prisa; *to hurry into,* (*fig.*) empezar sin consideración; *to hurry off,* salir de prisa; *to hurry on,* precipitar, apresurar, empujar, apresurarse; *to hurry over,* pasar (o hacer pasar) rápidamente; *to hurry over a thing,* despachar una cosa, hacer una cosa con prisa; *to hurry up,* (*fam.*) dar(se) prisa; *there's no hurry,* no corre prisa. — *s.* precipitación; confusión, desorden.

hurry-scurry ['hʌriskʌri], *adv.* confusamente, en tropel, en tumulto.

hurst [hə:rst], *s.* bosquecillo, colina poblada de árboles.

hurt [hə:rt], *v.t.* (*pret.*, *p.p.* **hurt**) dañar, lastimar, hacer mal o daño, lisiar, herir, estropear; ofender, injuriar; damnificar, perjudicar. — *v.i.* doler; (*impers.*) *to hurt the feelings of someone,* lastimar, ofender a uno. — *s.* golpe, herida, lesión, magulladura, contusión, lastimadura; daño, mal, perjuicio, detrimento. — *a.* lastimado, lisiado, herido; perjudicado. — *p.p.* [HURT].

hurter, *s.* dañador.

hurtful, *a.* perjudicial, dañoso, pernicioso, nocivo, dañino.

hurtfulness ['hə:rtfəlnis], *s.* nocividad; naturaleza dañina, perniciosa.

hurtle ['hə:rtəl], *v.t.* arrojar, estrellar, chocar contra. — *v.i.* arrojarse, tirarse, embestir con gran fuerza y ruido, caer. — *s.* choque.

hurtleberry ['hə:rtəlberi], *s.* arándano.

hurtless, *a.* inocente; intacto, ileso.

husband ['huzbənd], *s.* marido, esposo. — *v.t.* procurar marido a; gobernar con economía; ahorrar, economizar; ser o pasar por marido de, hacer el papel de marido.

husbandless, *a.* soltera, viudad, sin marido.

husbandman ['hʌzbəndmən], s. agricultor, viñador, labrador, granjero.

husbandry ['hʌzbəndri], s. labranza, agricultura; frugalidad, economía, ahorro, parsimonia; producción agrícola; economía doméstica.

hush [hʌʃ], v.t. apaciguar, sosegar, aquietar, callar, acallar; calmar, mitigar; *to hush up*, ocultar, mantener secreto, echar tierra a. — v.i. estar quieto, enmudecer, callar, estar callado. — s. silencio, quietud; *hush-money*, chantaje; *interj.* ¡chitón! ¡silencio!

husk [hʌsk], s. cáscara, vaina, pellejo, vainilla, hollejo, cascabillo; desperdicio; bagazo. — v.t. descascarar, pelar, desvainar, mondar, despellejar, deshollejar.

husked, a. que tiene cáscara, vaina o pellejo.

husker, s. descascarador, desgranador; abridor.

huskiness ['hʌskinis], s. ronquera; calidad de cascarudo o cortezudo; estado de tener cáscara, vaina o pellejo.

husking ['hʌskiŋ], s. acto de descascarar y desgranar maíz.

husking-bee ['hʌskiŋ'biː], s. (*Am.*) reunión de vecinos para desgranar maíz.

husky ['hʌski], s. cascarudo, cortezudo; ronco, rauco; (*fam.*) robusto, fuerte. — s. perro esquimal.

hussar [hu'zɑːr], s. (*mil.*) húsar.

hussy ['hʌzi], s. buena pieza, pícara, picarona, tunanta; buena alhaja; estuche o bolsa de costura.

husting ['hʌstiŋ], s. asamblea, junta; consejo o tribunal en la ciudad de Londres. — *pl.* **hustings**, tribuna pública para discursos electorales.

hustle ['hʌsəl], v.t. mezclar, confundir, escaramuzar; atropellar, sacudir, empujar. — v.i. andar a empellones; moverse con dificultad; apiñarse; (*fam.*) patear, pernear, triscar, patullar.

hustler ['hʌslər], s. (*fam.*) hombre de gran energía, trafagón, bullebulle, afanador, buscavidas, m.

huswife ['hʌzif], s.f. [HOUSEWIFE].

hut [hʌt], s. choza, barraca, cabaña, huta. — v.t. alojar en una choza. — v.i. vivir en una choza.

hutch [hʌtʃ], s. arca, cofre, cesto; artesa; ratonera; hucha; conejera; amasadera; trampa; (*min.*) cuba. — v.t. guardar en cofre, atesorar; recoger.

hut-urn, s. urna cineraria.

huzza [hʌ'zɑː], v.t. recibir con vivas. — v.i. aclamar, aplaudir, vitorear; *interj.* ¡viva! ¡hurra!

hyacinth ['haiəsinθ], s. jacinto.

hyacinthine [haiə'sinθain], s. jacintino.

hyæna, hyena [hai'iːnə], s. hiena, ana.

hyaline ['haiəlin], a. (*fis.*) hialino; cristalino, transparente, vidrioso.

hybrid ['haibrid], **hybridous**, a. mestizo, híbrido.

hybridism ['haibridizm], **hybridity**, s. hibridismo.

hybridize ['haibridaiz], v.t. producir o generar híbridos. — v.t., v.i. ser capaz de cruzamiento.

hydatid ['haidətid], s. (*med.*) hidátide, f.

hydra ['haidrə], s. (*zool.*, *astr.*) hidra.

hydracid [hai'dræsid], s. hidrácido.

hydragogue ['haidrə'gɔg], s. hidragogo.

hydrangea [hai'dreindʒə], s. hortensia.

hydrant ['haidrənt], s. boca de riego.

hydratation [haidrə'teiʃən], **hydration** [hai'dreiʃən], s. hidratación.

hydrate ['haidreit], s. hidrato. — v.t. hidratar.

hydraulic [hai'drɔːlik], **hydraulical**, a. hidráulico. — *pl.* **hydraulics**, hidráulica.

hydric ['haidrik], a. hídrico.

hydriodic, a. iodo-hídrico.

hydrocarbon [haidro'kɑːɪbən], s. hidrocarburo.

hydrocele ['haidrosiːl], s. hidrocele, f.

hydrocephalus [haidro'sefələs], s. hidrocéfalo.

hydrochlorate [haidro'klɔːreit], s. hidroclorato, clorhidrato.

hydrochloric [haidro'klɔrik], a. hidroclórico, clorhídrico.

hydrocyanic [haidrosai'ænik], a. hidrociánico.

hydrodynamic [haidrodai'næmik], a. hidrodinámico.

hydrodynamics, s. hidrodinámica.

hydrofluoric [haidrofluːˈɔrik], a. fluorhídrico.

hydrogen ['haidrodʒən], s. hidrógeno; *hydrogen bomb*, bomba de hidrógeno.

hydrogenate [hai'drɔdʒeneit], **hydrogenize** [hai'drɔdʒənaiz], v.t. hidrogenar.

hydrogenous [hai'drɔdʒənəs], a. hidrogenado.

hydrographer [hai'drɔgrəfəɪ], s. hidrógrafo.

hydrographic, hydrographical, a. hidrográfico.

hydrography [hai'drɔgrəfi], s. hidrografía.

hydrokinetic [haidrokai'netik], a. hidromecánico.

hydrologic [haidro'lɔdʒik], **hydrological**, a. hidrológico.

hydrology [hai'drɔlodʒi], s. hidrología.

hydrolysis [hai'drɔlisis], s. hidrólisis, f.

hydromancy ['haidromænsi], s. hidromancia.

hydromel ['haidromel], s. hidromel, aguamiel, f.

hydrometallurgy [haidrome'tæləːɪdʒi], s. hidrometalurgia.

hydrometeor [haidro'miːtiəɪ], s. hidrometeoro.

hydrometer [hai'drɔmetəɪ], s. hidrómetro; pesalicores; fluviómetro.

hydrometric [haidro'metrik], a. hidrométrico; *hydrometric pendulum*, péndulo hidrométrico.

hydrometry, s. hidrometría.

hydropathic [haidro'pæθik], a. hidropático.

hydropathy [hai'drɔpəθi], s. hidropatía.

hydrophobia [haidro'foubiə], **hydrophoby**, s. hidrofobia, rabia, mal de rabia.

hydropic [hai'drɔpik], **hydropical**, a. hidrópico.

hydropsy ['haidrɔpsi], s. hidropesía.

hydroscope ['haidroskoup], s. hidroscopio.

hydrostat ['haidrostæt], s. hidróstato.

hydrostatic [haidro'stætik], **hydrostatical**, a. hidrostático.

hydrostatics, s. hidrostática.

hydrosulphide [haidro'sʌlfaid], s. hidrosulfuro, sulfhidrato.

hydrotherapeutic [haidroθerə'pjuːtik], s., a. hidroterápico.

hydrotherapeutics, hydrotherapy, s. hidroterapia, hidropatía.

hydrothermal [haidro'θəːɪməl], a. hidrotermal.

hydrothorax [haidro'θɔːɪæks], s. hidrotórax.

hydrous ['haidrəs], a. acuoso, aguado.

hydrus ['haidrəs], s. serpiente de agua, f.
hyena [HYÆNA].
hyetal [hai'i: təl], a. pluvial, lluvioso, perteneciente a la lluvia.
hyetometer, s. pluvímetro.
hygiene ['haidʒi:n], **hygienics**, s. higiene, f., profiláctica.
hygienic [haidʒ'enik], a. higiénico.
hygienist [hai'dʒiənist], s. higienista, m.f.
hygrometer [hai'grɔmetəɹ], s. higrómetro.
hygrometric, **hygrometrical**, a. higrométrico.
hygrometry, s. higrometría.
hygroscope ['haigroskoup], s. higroscopio.
hygroscopic, **hygroscopical**, a. higroscópico.
hyla ['hailə], s. rubeta, rana del género Hyla.
hylicism ['hailisizm], **hylism**, s. materialismo.
hylotheism, s. panteísmo.
hymen ['haimən], s. himeneo; (anat.) himen, virgo.
hymeneal [hai'meniəl], **hymenean**, s. (poét.) epitalamio. — a. nupcial, relativo a las bodas.
Hymenoptera [haimen'ɔp tərə], s.pl. himenópteros.
hymn [him], s. himno. — v.t. alabar con himnos. — v.i. cantar himnos.
hymnal ['himnəl], s. libro de himnos.
hymnic, a. perteneciente a los himnos.
hymnology [him'nɔlədʒi], s. estudio, tratado o colección de himnos.
hyoid ['haiɔid], s. hioides, m.sing.
hyper ['haipəɹ], pref. sobre; excesivo.
hyperæmia [haipe'ri:miə], **hyperemia**, s. hiperemia.
hyperbola [hai'pə:ɹbolə], s. hipérbola.
hyperbole [hai'pə:ɹboli:], s. hipérbole, f.
hyperbolic [haipəɹ'bolik], **hyperbolical**, a. hiperbólico, ponderativo.
hyperbolist, s. exagerador.
hyperbolize, v.i. usar de hipérboles. — v.t. exagerar, expresar en lenguaje hiperbólico.
hyperborean [haipəɹ'bo:ɹiən], s., a. hiperbóreo.
hypercritic [haipəɹ'kritik], s., a. hipercrítico. — s. crítico inflexible.
hypercritical, a. severo en la crítica.
hyperdulia [haipəɹ'dju:liə], **hyperduly**, s. hiperdulía.
hypericon [hai'perikɔn], **hypericum**, s. hipérico, hipericón.
hypermeter [hai'pə:ɹmetəɹ], s. hipermetría.
hyperphysical [haipəɹ'fizikəl], a. sobrenatural.
hypertrophic [haipəɹ'trɔfik], a. hipertrófico.
hypertrophied [hai'pə:ɹtrofid], a. hipertrofiado.
hypertrophy [hai'pə:ɹtrofi], s. hipertrofia; (fig.) aumento excesivo. — v.t., v.i. hipertroficarse.
hyphen ['haifən], s. división, guión.
hyphenate ['haifəneit], v.t. separar con guión.
hyphenation, s. separación de sílabas con guiones.
hypnosis [hip'nousis], s. hipnosis, f.
hypnotic [hip'nɔtik], a. hipnótico, medicamento que produce el sueño.
hypnotism ['hipnotizm], s. hipnotismo, hipnalismo, mesmerismo.
hypnotize ['hipnotaiz], v.t. hipnotizar, causar sueño hipnótico, magnetizar.
hypnotizer, s. hipnotizador, magnetizador.

hypocaust ['haipokɔ:st], s. hipocausto.
hypochondria [haipəɹ'kondriə], s. hipocondría.
hypochondriac [haipər'kɔndriæk], s. hipocondríaco.
hypochondriac, **hypochondriacal**, a. hipocondríaco, hipocóndrico, melancólico.
hypochondriacism, s. hipocondría.
hypochondriasis [haipəɹkon'draiəsis], s. hipocondría.
hypocondrium, s. hipocondrio.
hypocrisy [hi'pokrəsi], s. hipocresía, disimulo, mojigatería, camandulería.
hypocrite ['hipokrit], s. hipócrita, m.f., mojigato, beatón.
hypocritical [hipo'kritikəl], a. hipócrita, falso, disimulado.
hypocycloid [haipo'saiklɔid], s. hipocicloide.
hypoderm [haipodə:ɹm], s. hipodermis.
hypodermatic, **hypodermic** [haipo'də:mik], a. subcutáneo, hipodérmico.
hypogæal, **hypogeal** [haipo'dʒi:əl], a. subterráneo; hipogénico, oculto en la tierra, colocado debajo de la tierra.
hypogastric [haipo'gæstrik], a. hipogástrico.
hypogastrium, s. hipogastro, bajovientre.
hypogeum [haipo'dʒi:əm], s. hipogeo.
hypophosphite [haipo'fosfait], s. hipofosfito.
hypostasis [hai'postəsis], s. base, f., fundamento; (teol.) hipóstasis, f.; (med.) sedimento de la orina.
hypostatic [haipo'stætik], **hypostatical**, a. hipostático; personal; constitutivo.
hyposulphate [haipo'sʌlfeit], s. hiposulfato.
hyposulphite [haipo'sʌlfait], s. hiposulfito.
hypotenuse [hai'potənju:z], **hypothenuse**, s. hipotenusa.
hypothecate [hai'poθikeit], v.t. hipotecar, pignorar, empeñar.
hypothecation, s. pignoración.
hypothecator, s. el que pignora o da en hipoteca.
hypothesis [hai'poθesis], s. hipótesis, f.
hypothetic [haipo'θetik], **hypothetical**, a. hipotético.
hypsometer [hip'sometəɹ], s. hipsómetro.
hypsometric, **hypsometrical**, a. hipsométrico.
hypsometry, s. hipsometría.
hyrse [hə:ɹs], s. mijo.
hyson ['haisən], s. cha, especie de te verde.
hyssop ['hisəp], s. hisopo.
hysteria [his'tiəɹiə], s. histerismo.
hysteric [his'terik], **hysterical**, a. histérico.
hysterics, s. histerismo.
hysterotomy [histə'rotomi], s. histerotomia.
hythe [haið], s. puerto pequeño.

I

I, i [ai], novena letra del alfabeto inglés. Esta letra tiene, en inglés, varios sonidos; larga y semejante al diptongo español ai pronunciado como un solo sonido como en bind, find, mild; breve como la i castellana en pin, bin, fin; otro sonido parecido al grupo alemán oe o al francés eu e intermedio entre la e y la o castellana en dirk, sir, bird.
I [ai], pron. pers. yo.
iambic [ai'æmbik], a. yámbico. — s. yambo; verso yámbico.

iambus [ai'æmbəs], *s.* yambo.
Iberian [ai'biəriən], *a.* ibérico.
ibex ['aibeks], *s.* íbice, cabra montés.
ibis ['aibis], *s.* íbis.
Icarian [ai'kɛəriən], *a.* icario; arriesgado.
ice [ais], *s.* hielo; garapiña, sorbete, granizado.
— *v.t.* helar, cubrir de hielo; garapiñar, cuajar de azúcar.
iceberg ['aisbəːɹg], *s.* iceberg.
ice-bound ['aisbaund], *a.* rodeado de hielos; aprisionado por los hielos.
ice-box, *s.* nevera, refrigerador.
ice-breaker ['aisbreikəɹ], *s.* barco rompehielos.
ice-built ['aisbilt], *a.* formado de hielo.
ice-cream, *s.* helado, mantecado.
ice-field, *s.* campo de hielo.
ice-floe ['aisflou], *s.* témpano de hielo flotante.
ice-house, *s.* nevería.
iceman, *s.* nevero; vendedor de hielo.
Icelandic [ais'lændik], *a.* islandés.
Iceland moss, *s.* liquen o musgo de Islandia.
ichneumon [ik'njuːmən], *s.* icneumon, especie de garduña; *ichneumon fly,* especie de insecto himenóptero.
ichnographical, *a.* icnográfico.
ichonography [ik'nɔgrəfi], *s.* icnografía.
ichor [ai'kɔːɹ], *s.* icor.
ichorous, *a.* icoroso.
ichthyocolla [ikθiou'kɔlə], *s.* colapez, cola de pescado.
ichthyologic [ikθiou'lɔdʒik], *a.* ictiológico.
ichthyologist [ikθi'ɔlodʒist], *s.* ictiólogo.
ichthyology [ikθi'ɔlodʒi], *s.* ictiología.
ichthyophagous [ikθi'ɔfəgəs], *a.* ictiófago.
ichthyophagy, *s.* ictiofagía.
ichthyosaurus [ikθio'sɔːɹəs], *s.* ictiosauro.
icicle ['aisikəl], *s.* cerrión, carámbano.
icily ['aisili], *adv.* fríamente, frígidamente, con frialdad.
iciness, icyness, *s.* frigidez.
icing ['aisiŋ], *s.* capa de azúcar garapiñado.
icon ['aikɔn], *s.* icono; imagen, representación; grabado, ilustración.
iconoclast [ai'kɔnoklæst], *s.* iconoclasta, *m.f.*
iconoclastic, *a.* iconoclasta, conoclástico.
iconography [aikə'nɔgrəfi], *s.* iconografía.
icosahedron [aikosə'hiːdrɔn], *s.* icosaedro.
icteric [ik'terik], **icterical,** *s.*, *a.* ictérico.
ictus ['iktʌs], *s.* (*med.*) pulsación; latido; golpecito; (*prosodia*) acento tónico.
icy ['aisi], *a.* helado, frío, álgido.
I'd [aid], *contr.* [I HAD o I WOULD].
idea [ai'diə], *s.* idea, pensamiento, concepto, imagen mental; plan, proyecto, propósito.
ideal [ai'diːəl], *a.* ideal, mental, intelectual; utópico; perfecto. — *s.* ideal, sumo de perfección, modelo, prototipo.
idealism [ai'diːəlizm], *s.* idealismo.
idealist [ai'diːəlist], *s.* idealista, *m.f.*
idealistic [aidiːə'listik], *a.* idealista.
ideality [aidi'æliti], **idealness,** *s.* idealidad.
idealization [aidiəlai'zeiʃən], *s.* idealización.
idealize [aidiə'laiz], *v.t.*, *v.i.* idealizar, dar carácter ideal, hacer ideal; espiritualizar, exaltar.
identical [ai'dentikəl], *a.* idéntico, mismo, igual.
identicalness, *s.* identidad.
identification [aidentifi'keiʃən], *s.* identificación.
identify [ai'dentifai], *v.t.* identificar, identificarse con; probar ser lo mismo; asemejar.

identity [ai'dentiti], *s.* identidad; *identity card,* carnet de identidad.
ideograph ['idiogræf], *s.* ideograma, *m.*; pintura, jeroglífico, símbolo.
ideographic, *s.* ideográfico.
ideography [idi'ɔgrəfi], *s.* ideografía.
ideologist [idi'ɔlodʒist], *s.* ideólogo.
ideology, *s.* ideología.
ides [aidz], *s.pl.* idus.
idiocy ['idiəsi], *s.* idiotez, idiotismo, necedad.
idiom ['idiəm], *s.* idiotismo; modismo, locución; genio o índole de una lengua; jerga, habla, lenguaje.
idiomatic [idio'mætik], **idiomatical,** *a.* idiomático.
idiopathic [idio'pæθik], **idiopathical,** *a.* idiopático.
idiopathy [idi'ɔpəθi], *s.* idiopatía.
idiosyncrasy [idio'siŋkrəsi], *s.* idiosincrasia.
idiosyncratic [idiosin'krætik], *a.* idiosincrásico.
idiot ['idiət], *s.* idiota, *m f.*, imbécil; tonto, necio, bobo.
idiotic [idi'ɔtik], *a.* idiota, tonto, imbécil, necio, bobo, simple.
idiotism ['idiotizm], *s.* idiotismo, modismo; barbarismo; ignorancia, necedad.
idiotize, *v.i.* embrutecerse, volverse tonto.
idle ['aidəl], *a.* ocioso, desocupado; inútil, vano; haragán, perezoso, holgazán; frívolo, baldío, fútil; parado; *idle story,* cuento de viejas; *idle thing,* bagatela; *idle fellow,* haragán, callejero. — *v.t.* gastar ociosamente, malgastar. — *v.i.* haraganear, holgazanear; estar ocioso; (*mec.*) girar en marcha lenta.
idle-headed, *a.* desrazonable; infatuado.
idleness ['aidəlnəs], *s.* ociosidad, ocio; inutilidad, negligencia, trivialidad, frivolidad; haraganería, pereza, holgazanería, futilidad; paro.
idle-pated, *a.* tonto, estúpido, majadero.
idler ['aidləɹ], *s.* haragán, poltrón, holgazán, azotacalles, *m.*, novillero.
idling ['aidliŋ], *s.* pereza, vaguedad; (*mec.*) marcha lenta.
idol ['aidəl], *s.* ídolo, imagen, *f.*
idolater [ai'dɔlətəɹ], *s.* idólatra, *m.f.*; admirador, amante.
idolatress, *s.* mujer idólatra.
idolatrous [ai'dɔlətrəs], *a.* idólatra, idolátrico.
idolatrously, *adv.* idolatradamente.
idolatry [ai'dɔlətri], *s.* idolatría.
idolize ['aidəlaiz], *v.t.* idolatrar; adorar; amar con exceso.
idyl ['aidil], **idyll,** *s.* idilio.
idyllic [ai'dilik], *a.* idílico; pastoril.
if [if], *conj.* si; aunque, en caso que, supuesto que, dado que, aun cuando; *if so be,* supuesto que, con tal que; *without ifs or buts* (o *ifs and ands*), sin si ni pero, o sin ambajes ni rodajes.
i'faith [i'feiθ], *adv.* (*ant.*) a fe mía.
igad [i'gæd], *interj.* (*ant.*) por Dios.
igloo ['i:gluː], *s.* choza de hielo (de los esquimales).
igneous ['igniəs], *a.* ígneo.
igniferous [ig'nifərəs], *a.* ignífero.
ignis fatuus [ignis'fætjuːəs], *s.* fuego fatuo.
ignitable [ig'naitəbəl], *a.* inflamable.
ignite [ig'nait], *v.t.* encender, pegar fuego a; hacer luminoso. — *v.i.* encenderse, inflamarse, enrojecerse.
ignitible [ig'naitəbəl], *a.* inflamable.

ignition [ig'niʃən], s. ignición; inflamación; (*mec.*) encendido.

ignobility [igno'biliti], s. villanía, bajeza.

ignoble [ig'noubəl], a. innoble, villano, plebeyo; bajo, indigno, humilde, vil, cobarde, de casta inferior.

ignobleness, s. bajeza, vileza, falta de nobleza.

ignominious [igno'miniəs], a. ignominioso.

ignominy ['ignomini], s. ignominia, deshonra, infamia.

ignoramus [igno'reiməs], s. ignorante, simple, tonto.

ignorance ['ignorəns], s. ignorancia, desconocimiento, inadvertencia.

ignorant ['ignorənt], a. ignorante; ajeno; lego, desconocedor; indocto.

ignore ['igno:ɹ], v.t. desconocer, no hacer caso de, pasar por alto; (*for.*) sobreseer; rechazar; (*ant.*) ignorar.

iguana [ig'wɑ:nə], s. iguana.

ileac ['iliək], a. ilíaco.

ileum ['iliəm], s. íleon (intestino).

ileus ['iliəs], s. ileo.

ilex, s. encina; coscoja.

iliac, a. ilíaco.

ilium, s. ílion (hueso).

ilk [ilk], a. (*Esco.*) mismo; úsase impropiamente como substantivo; *of that ilk*, de este género, de esta especie.

I'll [ail], contr. [I SHALL o I WILL].

ill [il], a. malo, enfermo, doliente; desgraciado, funesto; perverso; insaluble, malsano, dañino; ordinario, grosero; de calidad inferior; poco diestro, inhábil; *to put an ill construction on*, tomar a mal, interpretar en mal sentido; *to take ill*, llevar a mal; *to be ill spoken of*, tener mala reputación; *to bear ill will to someone*, guardar rencor a alguno; *ill weeds grow apace*, la mala hierba crece a la vista. — s. maldad, mal, infortunio, desgracia. — adv. malamente, mal; *to take a thing ill*, llevar a mal.

ill-advised, a. imprudente.

ill-affected, a. mal intencionado.

illapse [il'æps], s. acceso; (*teol.*) descenso, inspiración.

illation [i'leiʃən], s. ilación, inferencia, consecuencia.

illative ['ilətiv], a. ilativo, conclusivo. — s. conjunción ilativa; lo que indica ilación.

illatively, adv. por ilación, por inferencia.

ill-contrived, a. mal arreglado, mal dispuesto.

ill-disposed, a. mal intencionado.

illegal [i'li:gəl], a. ilegal.

illegality [ile'gæliti], **illegalness**, s. ilegalidad.

illegalize, v.t. hacer ilegal.

illegibility [iledʒi'biliti], s. calidad de ilegible.

illegible [i'ledʒibəl], a. ilegible.

illegitimacy [ile'dʒitiməsi], s. ilegitimidad.

illegitimate [ile'dʒitimit], a. ilegítimo, bastardo; erróneo, ilógico; falso, espurio; desautorizado. — v.t. ilegitimar.

illegitimation [ilegiti'meiʃən], s. ilegitimidad, bastardía, falsedad, impostura.

ill-fated, a. malaventurado, desdichado, desgraciado.

ill-favoured, a. feo, disforme.

ill-gotten, a. mal adquirido.

ill-grounded, a. mal fundado.

illiberal [i'libərəl], a. iliberal, tacaño, ruin, miserable, mezquino; corto de alcances, estrecho de inteligencia, estrecho de miras;

indigno de una persona bien educada, innoble.

illiberality [ilibe'ræliti], s. tacañería, ruindad, miseria; intolerancia.

illicit [i'lisit], a. ilícito; ilegal.

illicitness, s. calidad de ilícito, de carácter ilícito, ilegalidad.

illimitable [i'limitəbəl], a. ilimitado; indeterminado; infinito.

illision [i'liʒən], s. choque, colisión, golpe.

illiteracy [i'litərəsi], s. analfabetismo.

illiterate [i'litərit], a. analfabeto, iliterato.

illiterateness, illiterature, s. analfabetismo.

ill-liking, ill-looking, a. mal carado.

ill-luck, s. desdicha, desgracia.

ill-nature, s. malevolencia, mal genio.

ill-natured, a. malévolo, nocivo, duro, áspero, malicioso; (*fam.*) de cáscara amarga.

illness ['ilnes], s. mal, enfermedad; depravación.

illogical [i'lodʒikəl], a. ilógico, absurdo, irracional.

illogicality [ilodʒi'kæliti], **illogicalness**, s. falta de lógica, sin razón.

ill-pleased, a. malcontento, enojado.

ill-shaped, a. disforme, irregular, mal hecho.

ill-starred, a. desgraciado, desdichado.

ill-temper, s. morosidad, irritabilidad.

ill-treated, a. maltratado, injuriado.

illude [i'lu:d], v.t. engañar, defraudar, estafar; mofar, escarnecer.

illume [i'lju:m], v.t. (*poét.*) iluminar, aclarar; dorar.

illuminant [i'lju:minənt], a. iluminador, iluminante. — s. substancia iluminativa.

illuminate [i'lju:mineit], v.t. iluminar, alumbrar; esclarecer, aclarar; inspirar; (*b.a.*) iluminar. — v.i. hacer luminarias.

illuminate [i'lju:minit], **illuminated**, a. iluminado; bien instruido. — p.p. [ILLUMINATE].

illuminati [ilju:mi'nɑ:ti:], s.pl. secta de los iluminados o alumbrados.

illumination [ilju:mi'neiʃən], s. iluminación, alumbramiento, alumbrado; brillo, esplendor; luminarias; inspiración; (*b.a.*) iluminación.

illuminative, a. iluminativo.

illuminator [ilju:mi'neitəɹ], s. el que ilumina; iluminador, reflector (lámpara, lente, etc.).

illumine [i'lju:min], v.t. iluminar, alumbrar.

ill-usage, s. mal trato.

illusion [i'lju:ʒən], v.t. ilusión, espejismo, ensueño; falsa apariencia, engaño, embaimiento; *Illusions, farewell!* ¡el gozo en el pozo!

illusive [i'lju:ziv], a. ilusivo, falso, ilusorio, engañoso.

illusiveness, s. ilusión, embaimiento, engaño, apariencia falsa.

illusory [i'lju:zəri], a. ilusorio; engañoso, prestigioso, artificioso, fantástico.

illustrate ['iləstreit], v.t. ilustrar; aclarar, elucidar; esclarecer; (*ant.*) engrandecer, ennoblecer; (*b.a.*) ilustrar.

illustration [iləs'treiʃən], s. ilustración, elucidación; ejemplo; (*b.a.*) ilustración, lámina, dibujo, cuadro, grabado.

illustrative [i'lʌstrətiv], a. illustrativo, explicativo.

illustrator ['iləstreitəɹ], s. ilustrador.

illustrious [i'lʌstriəs], a. ilustre, ínclito, preclaro, conspicuo, esclarecido; célebre, insigne.

illustriousness, *s.* eminencia, nobleza, grandeza.

ill-will, *s.* mala voluntad, aversión, tedio.

I'm [aim], *contr.* [I AM]; soy, estoy.

image ['imid3], *s.* imagen, *f.*, estatua, efigie, *f.*; pintura, retrato; representación, figura; simulacro; (*ópt.*) imagen, *f.*; semejanza, parecido; idea. — *v.t.* figurar, reflejar, reproducir, representar; imaginar; parecerse a; *image-worship*, culto de las imágenes.

imagery ['imid3əri], *s.* (*b.a.*) imaginería; (estilo) metáforas, *f.pl.*; (*ant.*) imaginación.

imaginable [i'mæd3inəbəl], *a.* imaginable, figurable.

imaginary [i'mæd3inəri], *a.* imaginario, fantástico.

imagination [imæd3i'neiʃən], **imagining,** *s.* imaginación, magín, fantasía; inventiva, imaginativa; concepción, visión, aprehensión, imagen, *f.*, idea, pensamiento.

imaginative [i'mæd3inətiv], *a.* imaginativo; imaginario.

imagine [i'mæd3in], *v.t.* imaginar, concebir, premeditar, idear, inventar, discurrir, imaginarse; (*fam.*) conjeturar, figurarse, suponer. — *v.i.* crear, fantasear, imaginarse, figurarse.

imaginer, *s.* el que imagina o inventa.

imam [im'ɑ:m], *s.* imán.

imbalm, imbank, etc. Véase em-, etc.

imbecile ['imbesi:l], *s., a.* imbécil, tonto, necio, débil.

imbecility [imbe'siliti], *s.* imbecilidad; necedad.

imbed [im'bed], *v.t.* encajar, enclavar, encastrar, empotrar.

imbibe [im'baib], *v.t.* beber, embeber, chupar, absorber; empapar(se), saturarse, calarse; esponjarse; (*fig.*) empaparse (de una idea). — *v.i.* (*fam.*) beber (vino).

imbiber, *s.* embebedor.

imbibition, *s.* imbibición.

imbricate ['imbrikeit], **imbricated,** *a.* imbricado, sobrepuesto, encaballado.

imbrication, *s.* imbricación, superposición.

imbroglio [im'brouliou], *s.* embrollo, enredo, complicación, lío, engaño.

imbrue [im'bru:], *v.t.* mojar, remojar, empapar, embeber, calar.

imbrute [im'bru:t], *v.t.* embrutecer. — *v.i.* embrutecerse, reducirse al estado de bruto.

imbue [im'bju:], *v.t.* calar, infiltrar, empapar, penetrar, imbuir, infundir; teñir, tinturar.

imide ['imaid], *s.* compuesto derivado de amoniaco.

imitability, *s.* calidad de imitable.

imitable ['imitəbl], *a.* imitable.

imitate ['imiteit], *v.t.* imitar, contrahacer, remedar; copiar, tomar por modelo, seguir el ejemplo de.

imitation [imi'teiʃən], *s.* imitación, copia, modelo.

imitational, *a.* imitador.

imitative ['imitətiv], *a.* imitativo; imitatorio.

imitator ['imiteitəɹ], *s.* imitador.

immaculacy [i'mækjuləsi], **immaculateness,** *s.* pureza, inocencia.

immaculate [i'mækju:lət], *a.* inmaculado, sin mancha, puro, limpio.

immaculateness, *s.* pureza, inocencia.

immalleable [i'mæliəbəl], *a.* que no es maleable.

immanence ['imənəns], **immanency,** *s.* inmanencia; inherencia.

immanent ['imənənt], *a.* inmanente, intrínseco, inherente, interno.

Immanuel [i'mænju:el], *n.pr.* Emanuel.

immaterial [imə'tiəriəl], *a.* inmaterial, incorpóreo; sin importancia, fútil, frívolo; *to be immaterial*, no hacer al caso.

immaterialism, *s.* inmaterialismo, espiritismo, idealismo.

immaterialist, *s.* inmaterialista, *m.f.*, espiritista, *m.f.*, idealista, *m.f.*

immateriality, *s.* inmaterialidad, incorporeidad, espiritualidad.

immaterialized, *a.* incorpóreo, espiritual.

immaterialness, *s.* inmaterialidad.

immature ['imətʃju:əɹ], *a.* inmaturo, verde, crudo; imperfecto, prematuro, adelantado, precoz, temprano.

immatureness, immaturity, *s.* calidad de inmaturo, falta de sazón.

immeasurability, immeasureableness, *s.* inmensidad, inmensurabilidad, inconmensurabilidad.

immeasurable [i'meʒərəbəl], *a.* inmensurable, inconmensurable, inmenso, desmesurado.

immediacy [i'mi:diəsi], *s.* inmediación, contigüidad, proximidad.

immediate [i'mi:d3it], *a.* inmediato, contiguo, seguido, cercano; próximo, perentorio, urgente, instantáneo; intuitivo; directo.

immediately [i'mi:d3itli], *adv.* inmediatamente, al instante, al momento, en seguida; próximamente; directamente.

immediateness, *s.* inmediación, calidad de inmediato, presencia inmediata.

immedicable [i'medikəbəl], *a.* incurable, irremediable.

immemorial [ime'mɔ:riəl], *a.* inmemorial, inmemorable.

immemorially, *adv.* inmemorialmente, inmemorablemente, desde tiempo inmemorial.

immense [i'mens], *a.* inmenso, ilimitado, infinito; desmedido; vasto.

immenseness, immensity, *s.* inmensidad, infinidad, vastedad, grandeza sin límites.

immensurability [imenʃurə'biliti], *s.* inconmensurabilidad, inmensurabilidad.

immensurable, immensurate, *a.* inmensurable.

immerge [i'mə:ɹd3], *v.t.* sumergir, zambullir. — *v.i.* sumergirse; ocultarse.

immerse [i'mə:ɹs], *v.t.* sumergir, anegar, zambullir; bautizar por la inmersión; hundir, sumir.

immersed, *a.* sumergido, hundido. — *p.p.* [IMMERSE].

immersion [i'mə:ɹʃən], *s.* inmersión, sumersión, hundimiento, zampuzo.

immersionist, *s., a.* inmersionista, *m.f.*

immethodical, *a.* sin método, falto de orden.

immigrant ['imigrənt], *s.* inmigrante.

immigrate [imigreit], *v.i.* inmigrar; establecerse en un país nuevo.

immigration [imi'greiʃən], *s.* inmigración.

imminence ['iminəns], *s.* inminencia; proximidad.

imminent ['iminənt], *a.* inminente.

immiscibility, *s.* inmiscibilidad.

immiscible [i'misibəl], *a.* inmiscible.

immission [i'miʃən], *s.* introducción, inyección.

immit, *v.t.* introducir, inyectar.

immitigable [i'mitigəbəl], *a.* inmitigable.

immobile [ı'moubail], *a.* inmóvil, inmovible, inmoble; impasible.

immobility [imou'biliti], *s.* inmovilidad, estabilidad, falta de movimiento.

immoderate [i'mɔdərit], *a.* inmoderado, excesivo; desarreglado, intemperante, irrazonable.

immoderateness [i'mɔdəritnes], **immoderation** [imɔdər'eiʃən], *s.* inmoderación, desarreglo, exceso.

immodest [i'mɔdest], *a.* inmodesto, impúdico, impuro, deshonesto, indecente, indecoroso; atrevido, insolente, impudente.

immodesty [i'mɔdesti], *s.* inmodestia, indecoro, impudicia, indecencia.

immolate ['imoleit], *v.t.* inmolar; sacrificar.

immolation [imo'leiʃən], *s.* inmolación; sacrificio.

immolator, *s.* inmolador; sacrificador.

immoral [i'mɔrəl], *a.* inmoral, licencioso, depravado, corrompido, vicioso.

immorality [imɔ'ræliti], *s.* inmoralidad, corrupción.

immortal [i'mɔːɹtəl], *s., a.* inmortal, eterno, perpetuo.

immortality [imɔːɹ'tæliti], *s.* inmortalidad.

immortalization, *s.* perpetuación, acto de inmortalizar.

immortalize [i'mɔːɹtəlaiz], *v.t.* inmortalizar, perpetuar, eternizar.

immortelle ['imɔːɹtel], *s.* perpetua, siempreviva.

immovability [imuːvə'biliti], *s.* inmovilidad, inmutabilidad, inamovilidad; inalterabilidad; insensibilidad.

immovable [i'muːvəbəl], *a.* inmóvil, inamovible, inmovible, inmoto, fijo; impasible, apático, insensible; inalterable, firme, fijo, inflexible, inmoble, inmutable; (*for.*) inmueble. — *pl.* **immovables,** bienes raíces.

immune [i'mjuːn], *s., a.* inmune, exento.

immunity [i'mjuːniti], *s.* inmunidad, privilegio, libertad, exención, franquicia.

immunize, *v.t.* inmunizar.

immure [i'mjuːɹ], *v.t.* emparedar, cercar con muros.

immutability [imjuːtə'biliti], **immutableness** [i'mjuːtəblnis], *s.* inmutabilidad, constancia, firmeza.

immutable [i'mjuːtəbəl], *a.* inmutable, inalterable.

imp [imp], *s.* diablillo, trasgo, duende; (*fam.*) tunantuelo, picaruelo, muchacho o niño travieso.

impact [im'pækt], *v.t.* empaquetar; unir varias cosas entre sí fuertemente.

impact ['impækt], *s.* impacto, golpe, impacción, colisión, choque.

impaction, *s.* atasco, infarto; presión.

impair [im'pɛəɹ], *v.t.* empeorar, perjudicar, dañar, debilitar, deteriorar, menoscabar, echar a perder. — *v.i.* empeorar, ir de mal en peor, echarse a perder. — *a.* impar. — *s.* número impar.

impairer, *s.* el que (*o* lo que) disminuye o empeora.

impairment, *s.* empeoramiento, menoscabo, deterioro, deterioración.

impale [im'peil], *v.t.* empalar; cercar.

impalpability [impælpə'biliti], *s.* impalpabilidad, calidad de impalpable.

impalpable [im'pælpəbəl], *a.* impalpable, intangible, finísimo; incomprensible, ininteligible; sin realidad.

impanation [impə'neiʃən], *s.* empanación, transubstanciación.

impanel [im'pænəl], *v.t.* formar la lista de los jurados; inscribir en esta lista.

imparity [im'pæriti], *s.* desigualdad, diferencia, disparidad; desproporción; indivisibilidad.

impart [im'pɑːɹt], *v.t.* dar participación; dar parte, comunicar, hacer saber; conceder, dar, conferir.

impartial [im'pɑːɹʃəl], *a.* imparcial.

impartiality [impɑːɹʃi'æliti], *s.* imparcialidad, equidad; desinterés.

impartible [im'pɑːɹtibəl], *a.* impartible, indivisible; concedible; comunicable.

impassability [impæsə'biliti], *s.* calidad de intransitable.

impassable [im'pɑːsəbəl], *a.* intransitable, impracticable.

impasse ['impɑːs], *s.* callejón sin salida; (*fig.*) obstáculo invencible.

impassibility [impæsi'biliti], **impassibleness,** *s.* impasibilidad; inmutabilidad.

impassible [im'pæsibəl], *a.* impasible, insensible, impávido, apático, sin emoción.

impassion [im'pæʃən], *v.t.* (*poét.*) conmover, excitar, mover las pasiones. — *v.i.* apasionarse.

impassionable, *a.* conmovible.

impassionate, *v.t.* apasionar; afectar, conmover.

impassioned [im'pæʃənd], *a.* apasionado, extremoso, vehemente.

impassive [im'pæsiv], *a.* impassible.

impassiveness, *s.* impasibilidad.

impaste [im'peist], *v.t.* hacer pasta; poner en forma de pasta; (*pint.*) empastar.

impatible [im'pætibl], *a.* intolerable.

impatience [im'peiʃəns], *s.* impaciencia, desasosiego, apresuramiento, irritabilidad, intolerancia, petulancia.

impatient [im'peiʃənt], *a.* impaciente, intolerante, inquieto, apresurado.

impawn [im'pɔːn], *v.t.* empeñar, dar o dejar en prenda.

impeach [im'piːtʃ], *v.t.* acusar, denunciar, acriminar, delatar, encausar, poner en tela de juicio; imputar; poner tachas a, hacer objeción a, residenciar.

impeachable, *a.* delatable, censurable.

impeacher, *s.* acusador, delator, denunciador.

impeachment, *s.* acusación, delación, imputación, tacha, desdoro, reconvención.

impeccability [impekə'biliti], *s.* impecabilidad.

impeccable [im'pekəbəl], *a.* impecable, incapaz de pecar.

impeccancy, *s.* impecabilidad, incapacidad de pecar.

impeccant, *a.* exento de pecar.

impecuniosity [impekjuːni'ɔsiti], *s.* inopia, falta de dinero.

impecunious [impe'kjuːniəs], *a.* pobre, sin recursos, sin dinero.

impede [im'piːd], *v.t.* impedir, retardar, dificultar, estorbar, obstruir.

impediment [im'pedimənt], *s.* impedimento,

estorbo, tropiezo, embarazo, obstáculo; traba, obstrucción, cortapisa.

impedimenta [impedi'mentə], *s.pl.* (*mil.*) impedimenta; (*fam.*) equipaje, efectos.

impedimental, *a.* que impide o sirve de obstáculo.

impeditive [im'peditiv], *a.* impeditivo.

impel [im'pel], *v.t.* impeler, hacer avanzar, empujar, impulsar, excitar, mover, incitar, apretar, apurar.

impellent [im'pelənt], *a.* impelente; impulsor. — *s.* empuje, móvil, motor, autor, inspirador.

impeller, *s.* impulsor, motor, el que impele.

impend [im'pend], *v.t., v.i.* pender; (*fig.*) amagar, amenazar, ser inminente.

impendence, impendency, *s.* inminencia, amenaza, amago.

impendent [im'pendənt], **impending,** *a.* inminente, amenazante, pendiente.

impenetrability [impenetrə'biliti], *s.* impenetrabilidad.

impenetrable [im'penetrəbəl], *a.* impenetrable, intransitable, denso, abstruso, espeso; difícil de comprender.

impenetrableness, *s.* impenetrabilidad.

impenitence [im'penitəns], **impenitency,** *s.* impenitencia, obstinación.

impenitent [im'penitənt], *s., a.* impenitente, obstinado.

impenitently, *adv.* sin contrición, sin penitencia.

impennate [im'penət], *a.* impennado, que tiene alas cortas.

imperative [im'perətiv], *a.* imperativo, perentorio, imperioso. — *s.* mandato perentorio; (*gram.*) modo imperativo.

imperceptibility [impəɹsepti'biliti], **imperceptibleness,** *s.* imperceptibilidad.

imperceptible [impəɹ'septəbəl], *a.* imperceptible, incognoscible.

imperception [impəɹ'sepʃən], *s.* impercepción.

imperceptive, impercipient, *a.* incapaz de percibir.

imperfect [im'pəːɹfekt], *a.* imperfecto, defectuoso, descabal, incompleto. — *s., a.* (*gram.*) imperfecto.

imperfection [impəɹ'fekʃən], *s.* imperfección, falta; lunar, tacha, defecto.

imperfectness, *s.* imperfección, falta, defecto.

imperforable, *a.* imperforable.

imperforate [im'pəːɹfəreit], **imperforated,** *a.* imperforado.

imperforation, *s.* imperforación, obstrucción, cerramiento.

imperial [im'piəriəl], *a.* imperial; principal, soberano, predominante. — *s.* pera, perilla; (*arq.*) cúpula morisca.

imperialism, *s.* imperialismo, carácter imperial.

imperialist, *s.* imperialista, *m.f.*

imperil [im'peril], *v.t.* poner en peligro, poner en riesgo, arriesgar.

imperious [im'piəriəs], *a.* imperioso, absoluto, orgulloso, dominante, despótico, arrogante; perentorio, urgente, irresistible.

imperiousness, *s.* autoridad, mando; altivez, arrogancia.

imperishable [im'periʃəbəl], *a.* imperecedero, indestructible; eterno, immortal.

impermanence [im'pəːɹmənəns], **impermanency,** *s.* inestabilidad.

impermanent [im'pəːɹmənənt], *a.* que no es permanente.

impermeability, *s.* impermeabilidad.

impermeable [im'pəːɹmiəbəl], *a.* impermeable, impenetrable.

impersonal [im'pəːɹsonəl], *a.* impersonal.

impersonate [im'pəːɹsoneit], *v.t.* personificar; (*teat.*) representar.

impersonation [impəːɹso'neiʃən], *s.* personificatión; (*teat.*) representación, papel.

impersonator, *s.* personificador; (*teat.*) el que hace el papel de.

impertinence [im'pəːɹtinəns], **impertinency,** *s.* impertinencia, insolencia; absurdo; extravagancia; importunidad; cosa de poca importancia.

impertinent [im'pəːɹtinənt], *a.* impertinente; desvergonzado, atrevido, importuno, cansado, descortés, insolente, inoportuno, incómodo.

imperturbability, *s.* imperturbabilidad, calma, serenidad, frialdad.

imperturbable [impəɹ'təːɹbəbel], *a.* imperturbable, sereno, calmo, tranquilo.

imperturbation, *s.* tranquilidad, serenidad, calma, frialdad.

imperturbed [impəɹ'təːbɹd], *a.* tranquilo, sereno, quieto, sosegado.

impervious [im'pəːɹviəs], *a.* impenetrable, impermeable.

imperviousness, *s.* impenetrabilidad.

impetigo [impe'taigou], *s.* impétigo.

impetuosity [impetju'ɔsiti], *s.* ímpetu, impetuosidad, vehemencia, violencia.

impetuous [im'petju:əs], *a.* impetuoso, arrebatado, violento, vehemente.

impetuousness, *s.* impetuosidad, arranque, violencia, viveza.

impetus ['impetəs], *s.* ímpetu, momento, impulsión; (*fig.*) impulso, incentivo, inspiración.

imphee ['imfi:], *s.* caña africana de azúcar.

impiety [im'paiiti], *s.* impiedad, irreligiosidad, irreligión.

impinge [im'pindʒ], *v.i.* tocar, tropezar, golpear, chocar.

impious ['impiəs], *a.* impío, malvado, sacrílego, irreligioso, perverso, profano.

impiousness, *s.* impiedad, irreverencia.

impish ['impiʃ], *a.* travieso, endiablado, malicioso.

implacability [implækə'biliti], **implacableness** [im'plækəbəlnis], *s.* implacabilidad, rencor.

implacable [im'plækəbəl], *a.* implacable, irreconciliable, inexorable.

implacental [implə'sentəl], *a.* que no tiene placenta. — *s.* mamífero que no tiene placenta.

implant [im'plɑːnt], *v.t.* plantar, ingerir, fijar, acodar; (*fig.*) inculcar, sembrar.

implantation, *s.* injertación, plantación; (*fig.*) inculcación.

implausible [im'plɔːzibəl], *a.* que no es plausible.

implead [im'pli:d], *v.t.* (*for.*) acusar, demandar; proceder contra, poner pleito.

implement ['implimənt], *s.* herramienta, instrumento. — *pl.* utensilios, aperos, útiles, trebejos, enseres.

implete [im'pli:t], *v.t.* llenar, colmar.

impletion, *s.* acto de llenar; llenura, colmo, plenitud.

implicate ['implikeit], *v.t.* implicar, envolver, complicar; enredar, embrollar.

implication [impli'keiʃən], *s.* implicación, ilación, inferencia, deducción; complicidad; complicación.

implicative [im'plikətiv], *a.* implicativo, implicante, deductivo, que se infiere.

implicatively, *adv.* por implicación, por deducción, por inferencia.

implicit [im'plisit], *a.* implícito, sobretendido; completo, sin reserva, absoluto; *implicit faith* (o *trust*), fe ciega.

implicitly, *adv.* implícitamente, tácitamente; sin reserva, sin preguntas.

implicitness, *s.* calidad de implícito.

implied [im'plaid], *a.* implícito, contenido, incluido, sobreentendido. — *p.p.* [IMPLY]; *to be implied,* sobreentenderse.

implore [im'plo:ɹ], *v.t.* implorar, rogar, suplicar, conjurar, pedir con instancia.

implorer, *s.* solicitador.

imploringly, *adv.* de un modo suplicante o implorante.

imply [im'plai], *v.t.* querer decir, dar a entender, denotar, significar; implicar; envolver.

impolite [im'polait], *a.* descortés, impolítico, grosero.

impoliteness, *s.* desatención, descortesía, impolítica.

impolitic [im'politik], *a.* imprudente, indiscreto; impolítico.

imponderability [impondərə'biliti], *s.* imponderabilidad.

imponderable [im'pondərəbəl], *a.* imponderable.

imporosity [impo:'rositi], *s.* densidad, falta de poros.

imporous [im'po:rəs], *a.* sin poros, sólido, macizo.

import [im'po:ɹt], *v.t.* (*com.*) importar; introducir; significar, denotar; interesar, ser de importancia, implicar. — *v.i.* convenir, tener importancia, importar, ser de entidad.

import ['impo:ɹt], *s.* tendencia, significación, sentido; importancia, peso, valor, consecuencia, entidad, momento. — *pl.* (*com.*) **imports,** importaciones; *import duty,* derechos de entrada, derechos de aduana; *import licence,* permiso de importación.

importable, *a.* importable.

importance [im'po:ɹtəns], *s.* importancia, peso, consideración, autoridad, crédito; valor, cuenta; presunción, vanidad, importunidad; fachenda; consecuencia.

important [im'po:ɹtənt], *a.* importante, considerable, esencial, valioso; fachendero, presuntuoso; afectado; pomposo.

importation [impo:ɹ'teiʃən], *s.* (*com.*) importación, entrada.

importer, *s.* importador.

importunacy [im'po:ɹtjuːnəsi], **importunateness,** *s.* importunidad.

importunate [im'po:ɹtjuːnit], *a.* importuno, insistente, pesado; machacón; apremiante, urgente.

importune ['impo:ɹtjuːn], *v.t., v.i.* importunar, porfiar, instar, machacar, pedir con instancia.

importuner, *s.* importunador; (*fam.*) mazacote.

importunity [impo:ɹ'tjuːniti], *s.* importunación, importunidad, porfía.

imposable, *a.* imponible, pechero, sujeto a impuestos.

impose [im'pouz], *v.t.* imponer, cargar; prescribir, infligir; hacer pasar como bueno; hacer recibir, obligar a aceptar; (*impr.*) imponer; (*igl.*) imponer (las manos); colocar por influencia. — *v.i.* imponerse, engañar, embaucar; *to impose on* (o *upon*), engañar, embaucar; *to be imposed upon,* ser engañado; *to impose a fine upon,* castigar en la bolsa, multar.

imposer, *s.* imponedor, el que impone.

imposing, *a.* imponente, impresivo, tremendo; *imposing-stone* (o *table*), (*impr.*) piedra (o mesa) de imponer.

imposition [impo'ziʃən], *s.* imposición; violencia, impresión, impostura, fraude, ficción, engaño; impuesto, tributo, carga, gabela; tarea extraordinaria; (*impr.*) imposición.

impossibility [imposi'biliti], *s.* imposibilidad, imposible.

impossible [im'posibəl], *a.* imposible; (*for.*) impracticable; (*mat.*) imaginario.

impost ['impost], *s.* impuesto, gabela, tributo, contribución; (*arq.*) imposta.

impostor, *s.* impostor, embustero, trapacista, *m.f.,* embaucador.

imposture [im'postʃəɹ], *s.* impostura, engaño, fraude, falsedad.

impotence ['impotəns], **impotency** ['impotənsi], *s.* impotencia, incapacidad, debilidad.

impotent ['impotent], *a.* impotente, sin potencia, impedido; tullido, baldado, débil, incapaz.

impound [im'paund], *v.t.* encerrar, aprisionar, acorralar, apoderarse de, restringir; (*for.*) depositar, poner en custodia.

impoverish [im'povəriʃ], *v.t.* empobrecer, depauperar; deteriorar, menguar.

impoverishment, *s.* empobrecimiento.

impracticability [impræktikə'biliti], **impracticableness,** *s.* impracticabilidad, imposibilidad; obstinación, terquedad.

impracticable [im'præktikəbəl], *a.* impracticable, imposible, infactible; irrazonable, intratable, terco; inútil, de ningún servicio.

imprecate ['imprekeit], *v.t.* imprecar, maldecir.

imprecation, *s.* imprecación, reniego, maldición.

imprecatory, *a.* imprecatorio.

impregnable [im'pregnəbəl], *a.* inexpugnable, inconquistable; impregnable.

impregnate ['impregneit], *v.t.* empreñar, fecundar, hacer concebir, fecundizar, embarazar; saturar, impregnar; imbuir, penetrar con un principio activo. — *a.* impregnado; embarazada, empreñada.

impregnation, *s.* fecundación; infusión; fertilización; impregnación.

impresario [impres'ɑːrio], *s.* empresario.

imprescriptible [impre'skriptəbəl], *a.* imprescriptible.

impress [im'pres], *v.t.* imprimir, estampar, grabar; fijar; marcar; inculcar; impresionar; influir; (*mil.*) reclutar, enganchar; expropiar.

impress ['impres], *s.* impresión, marca, señal, *f.,*

huella; (*mil.*) leva, enganche, recluta, forzosa;
expropiación; mote, divisa, lema, empresa.
impressibility, *s.* facilidad de impresionarse,
capacidad de recibir impresiones.
impressible [im′presibəl], *a.* impresionable,
que recibe fácilmente impresiones; que se
puede estampar, imprimir o marcar.
impression [im′preʃən], *s.* impresión, acción y
efecto de imprimir; sigilación, señal, *f.*, huella,
marca, sello, estampado; idea vaga, recuerdo
confuso o vago; (*impr.*) impresión, edición.
impressionable, *a.* impresionable, susceptible.
impressional, *a.* referente a la impresión.
impressionism, *s.* impresionismo.
impressionist, *s.* impresionista, *m.f.*
impressionistic, *a.* impresionista.
impressive [im′presiv], *a.* impresionante;
grandioso, solemne, notable.
impressiveness, *s.* calidad impresionante;
grandiosidad.
impressment [im′presmənt], *s.* expropiación;
requisición, requisa; (*mil.*) leva, enganche.
imprest [′imprest], *v.t.* hacer un anticipo. —
s. anticipo, pago adelantado.
imprimis [im′praimis], *adv.* en primer lugar.
imprint [im′print], *v.t.* imprimir, estampar,
marcar por medio de presión; grabar en al
ánimo.
imprint [′imprint], *s.* impresión, señal, *f.*,
marca, huella; (*impr.*) pie de imprenta.
imprison [im′prizən], *v.t.* encerrar, encarcelar,
aprisionar, poner preso.
imprisonment, *s.* prisión, reclusión, encierro,
encarcelación; *false imprisonment*, prisión
ilegal.
improbability [improbə′biliti], *s.* improbabilidad, inverosimilitud.
improbable [im′probəbəl], *a.* improbable, inverosímil.
improbation, *s.* reprobación, desaprobación.
improbity [im′proubiti], *s.* improbidad.
impromptu [im′promtju:], *a.* impremeditado.
— *adv.* de repente, en el acto. — *s.* repente,
ímpetu; improvisación, obra improvisada.
improper [im′propəɹ], *a.* impropio, inconveniente, inepto; indecoroso, grosero, indecente; irregular, impolítico; incorrecto.
impropriate [im′prouprieit], *v.t.* apropiarse;
expropiar o secularizar bienes eclesiásticos.
— *a.* secularizado.
impropriation, *s.* secularización de bienes
eclesiásticos.
impropriator, *s.* el que se apropia un beneficio.
impropriety [impro′praiəti], *s.* impropiedad,
inconveniencia, incongruencia, indecoro,
descortesía.
improvability, improvableness, *s.* perfectibilidad, capacidad de perfeccionarse.
improvable [im′pru:vəbəl], *a.* mejorable, perfectible; cultivable, laborable; útil, aprovechable.
improve [im′pru:v], *v.t.*, *v.i.* mejorar, bonificar, adelantar, avanzar, aumentar, perfeccionar; embellecer, hermosear; (*agr.*) beneficiar, cultivar, abonar, labrar; enmendar,
corregir, rectificar; formentar; urbanizar,
construir; (*min.*) explotar, trabajar; utilizar,
aprovechar, sacar partido de. — *v.i.* mejorarse, medrar, progresar, hacer progresos,
adelantar; (*com.*) subir, encarecer, aumentar
de valor, estar en alza.

improvement [im′pru:vmənt], *s.* mejora,
mejoría, perfeccionamiento, mejoramiento,
adelanto; provecho, aplicación, buen empleo,
ventaja, utilidad; progreso, medra, adelantamiento; cultivo, labranza; laboreo; fomento;
reforma; instrucción, edificación, construcción, urbanización; alivio, mejoría en la
salud.
improver, *s.* adelantador, beneficiador, enmendador, mejorador; aprendiza de costurera.
improvidence [im′providəns], *s.* improvidencia, imprevisión, falta de previsión,
descuido, desprevención.
improvident [im′providənt], *a.* impróvido,
desprevenido, descuidado, inconsiderado,
imprudente.
improvisate [im′provizeit], *a.* improvisado,
impensado, no premeditado.
improvisation, *s.* improvisación; obra improvisada.
improvisator, improviser, *s.* improvisador,
repentista, *m.f.*
improvisatorial, improvisatory, *a.* improvisado.
improvise [′improvaiz], *v.t.*, *v.i.* improvisar,
repentizar.
improviser, *s.* improvisador.
imprudence [im′pru:dəns], *s.* imprudencia,
irreflexión, indiscreción, inconsideración.
imprudent, *a.* imprudente, irreflexivo, indiscreto, inconsiderado.
impuberal [im′pju:bərəl], *a.* impúber, impúbero.
impudence [′impju:dəns], *s.* impudencia,
desfachatez, insolencia, atrevimiento, desvergüenza, descaro, avilantez, inmodestia,
procacidad.
impudent [′impju:dənt], *a.* impudente, desfachatado, descarado, audaz, deslenguado,
insolente; inmodesto, impúdico, desvergonzado.
impudicity [impju:′disiti], *s.* impudicicia,
deshonestidad, inmodestia.
impugn [im′pju:n], *v.t.* impugnar, poner en
tela de juicio, contrariar, contradecir.
impugnable [im′pju:nəbəl], *a.* impugnable.
impugner, *s.* impugnador.
impugnment [im′pju:nmənt], *s.* impugnación.
impuissant [im′pwisənt], *a.* sin poder, impotente.
impulse [′impʌls], *s.* impulso, ímpetu, impulsión; instigación, estímulo, motivo; corazonada, hombrada, arranque.
impulsion [im′pʌlʃən], *s.* impulsión, ímpetu,
impulso, empuje.
impulsive [im′pʌlsiv], *s.*, *a.* impulsivo, impelente.
impunity [im′pju:niti], *s.* impunidad; *with
impunity*, impunemente.
impure [im′pju:əɹ], *a.* impuro, sucio; impúdico, inmundo, deshonesto; sórdido;
adulterado; profano; incorrecto (lenguaje).
impureness, impurity, *s.* impureza; impurificación; adulteración; torpeza, liviandad,
deshonestidad.
impurple [im′pɔ:ɹpəl], *v.t.* teñir de púrpura,
purpurar.
imputable [im′pju:təbəl], *a.* imputable.
imputableness, *s.* imputabilidad.
imputation [impju:′teiʃən], *s.* imputación,
reproche, nota, acusación, censura, reconvención.

imputative, *a.* imputable.
impute [im'pju:t], *v.t.* imputar, achacar, atribuir, incusar.
imputer, *s.* imputador.
in [in], *prep.* en, por, de, durante, con, dentro, de, mientras, de aquí, bajo, a fin de; *in time*, con tiempo; *in writing*, por escrito; *in the night*, de noche o durante la noche; *in the reign of*, en (o bajo) el reinado de; *in order to*, a fin de; *in so far as* o *in as much as*, en cuanto, en vista de que; *in that*, porque, a causa de; *in the meantime*, entre tanto; *to be in great hopes*, abrigar grandes esperanzas; *to be in the right*, tener razón. — *adv.* dentro, adentro; aquí, ahí, allí; en casa; adelante; *Is Mr. X in?* ¿ Está el Sr. X? *to drive in a nail*, clavar un clavo en su lugar; *Come in!* o *Walk in!* ¡ Pase Vd.! *to be in for it*, (*fam.*) no poder evitar (un castigo, etc.); *to be in with someone*, (*fam.*) ser íntimo con alguien.
in-, prefijo con el que se forman muchos vocablos y denota en unos casos interioridad y en otros negación o privación.
inability [inə'biliti], *s.* inhabilidad, ineptitud, insuficiencia, incapacidad; impotencia, falta de fuerzas, falta de medios.
inaccessibility [inæksesi'biliti], *s.* inaccesibilidad.
inaccessible [inæk'sesəbəl], *a.* inaccesible.
inaccuracy [in'ækju:rəsi], *s.* inexactitud, incorrección, impropiedad, defecto, error, falta.
inaccurate [in'ækju:rit], *a.* inexacto, erróneo, incorrecto, impropio.
inaction [in'ækʃən], *s.* inacción, holgazanería, descanso.
inactive [in'æktiv], *a.* inactivo, parado, ocioso, perezoso, indolente, inerte, negligente, flojo.
inactivity [inæk'tiviti], *s.* inactividad, desidia, ociosidad, flojedad, inercia.
inadaptable [inə'dæptəbəl], *a.* inadaptable.
inadequacy [in'ædikwəsi], *s.* insuficiencia; desproporción; imperfección.
inadequate [in'ædikwit], *a.* inadecuado, incompleto, insuficiente.
inadequateness, *s.* insuficiencia; imperfección; defecto de proporción.
inadmissible [inəd'misəbəl], *s.* inadmisible.
inadvertence [inəd'və:rtəns], **inadvertency**, *s.* inadvertencia.
inadvertent [inəd'və:rtənt], *a.* inadvertido, accidental, descuidado, negligente, atolondrado.
inadvisable [inəd'vaizəbəl], *a.* inconveniente, impropio, no aconsejable.
inalienable [in'eiliənəbəl], *a.* inalienable, inajenable.
inalterability, *a.* inalterabilidad.
inalterable [in'ɔltərəbəl], *a.* inalterable.
inamorato [inæmo'rɑːtou], *s.* (*fem.* **-ata**) enamorado, enamorada.
inane [in'ein], *a.* vano, sandio, soso, mentecato, atontado, inane, insubstancial. — *s.* vacío, infinito, espacio desocupado.
inanimate [in'ænimit], **inanimated**, *a.* inanimado, exánime, sin alma, sin vida.
inanimateness, **inanimation**, *s.* falta de animación, de vida, de espíritu.
inanition [inə'niʃən], *s.* inanición; vaciedad, debilidad.
inanity [in'æniti], *s.* inanición; sandez, vacuidad, vanidad, insubstancialidad, inutilidad, nulidad.

inappeasable [inə'piːzəbəl], *a.* implacable.
inappellable [inə'peləbəl], *a.* inapelable, final, absoluto.
inappetence [in'æpetəns], **inappetency**, *s.* inapetencia.
inapplicability, *s.* ineptitud.
inapplicable [in'æplikəbəl], *a.* inaplicable.
inapplication, *s.* inaplicación, desaplicación, desidia, indolencia.
inapposite [in'æpozit], *a.* inconveniente, no pertinente, fuera de propósito.
inappreciable [inə'priːʃəbəl], *a.* inapreciable, inestimable.
inapprehensible, *a.* incomprensible, ininteligible.
inapprehensive [inæpri'hensiv], *a.* descuidado, negligente, indolente.
inapproachable [inə'proutʃəbəl], *a.* inaccesible, inasequible, de difícil acceso.
inappropriate [inə'proupriət], *a.* inadecuado, impropio, poco apropiado; inoportuno.
inappropriateness, *s.* impropiedad, incorrección, inconveniencia, inoportunidad.
inapt [in'æpt], *a.* no apto, impropio; inepto.
inaptitude [in'æptitjuːd], *s.* ineptitud, insuficiencia.
inarable [in'ærəbəl], *a.* no arable, incultivable.
inarch [in'ɑːtʃ], *v.t.* injertar por aproximación.
inarticulate [inɑːɹ'tikjulit], *a.* inarticulado, incapaz de hablar; (*zool.*) inarticulado.
inarticulately, *adv.* de un modo inarticulado.
inarticulateness, *s.* inarticulación; tartamudez.
inartificial [inɑːɹti'fiʃəl], *a.* natural, simple, sin artificio, sencillo; contrario a las reglas del arte.
inartistic [inɑːɹ'tistik], *a.* falto de arte; inartístico.
inartistically, *adv.* sin gusto, sin arte.
inasmuch [inaz'mʌtʃ], *adv.* considerando, puesto que, visto que, ya que, en vista que; en cuanto.
inattention, *s.* desatención, inadvertencia, distracción, descuido.
inattentive [inə'tentiv], *a.* desatento, distraído, descuidado.
inaudibility, **inaudibleness**, *s.* dificultad o incapacidad de ser oído.
inaudible [in'ɔːdibəl], *a.* inaudible, que no puede oírse.
inaugural [in'ɔːgjurəl], *a.* inaugural.
inaugurate [in'ɔːgjureit], *v.t.* inaugurar, dedicar, consagrar; comenzar, abrir, originar, principiar, iniciar; instalar, investir.
inauguration, *s.* inauguración, estreno, instalación.
inauguratory, *a.* inauguratorio.
inauspicious [inɔːs'piʃəs], *a.* poco propicio, infeliz, desfavorable.
inauspiciously, *adv.* desgraciadamente, bajo malos auspicios.
inauspiciousness, *s.* malos auspicios, infelicidad.
inbeing ['inbiːiŋ], *s.* inherencia, inseparabilidad.
inboard ['inbɔːɹd], *a., adv.* (*mar.*) interior, dentro del casco; (*mec.*) hacia dentro, hacia el interior.
inborn [in'bɔːɹn], *a.* ingénito, innato, de nacimiento, connatural.
inbreathe [in'briːð], *v.t.* inspirar, infundir.
inbred [in'bred], *a.* innato, ingénito, natural.

inbreed ['inbri:d], *v.i.* producir, crear; reproducir con padre de la misma familia.
inbreeding, *s.* endogamia.
inca [iŋkə], *s.* inca, *m.f.* — *a.* incaico.
incage [in'keidʒ], *v.t.* enjaular, encerrar.
incalculable [in'kælkju:ləbəl], *a.* incalculable.
incalescence, incalescency, *s.* calor incipiente.
incalescent [inkə'lesent], *a.* cuyo calor va aumentando.
incandesce, *v.t.* encandecer.
incandescence, incandescency, *s.* incandescencia, encendimiento, candencia.
incandescent [inkən'desənt], *a.* incandescente, candente, hecho ascua.
incantation [inkæn'teiʃən], *s.* encantación, encantamiento, encanto, conjuro.
incantator, *s.* conjuro, mago, brujo.
incantatory, *a.* mágico.
incapability [inkeipə'biliti], **incapableness,** *s.* inhabilidad, incapacidad, falta de capacidad, ineptitud.
incapable [in'keipəbəl], *a.* incapaz, inepto, inhábil, incompetente, falto de talento.
incapacious [inkə'peiʃəs], *a.* poco capaz, angosto, estrecho.
incapaciousness, *s.* angostura, estrechez.
incapacitate [inkə'pæsiteit], *v.t.* incapacitar, imposibilitar, inhabilitar, debilitar.
incapacitation, *s.* inhabilitación.
incapacity [inkə'pæsiti], *s.* incapacidad, insuficiencia, inhabilidad.
incarcerate [in'ka:ɹsəreit], *v.t.* encarcelar, aprisionar, poner en la cárcel. — *a.* encarcelado.
incarceration, *s.* encarcelación, prisión, encarcelamiento; (*cir.*) estrangulación (de una hernia).
incarnadine [in'ka:ɹnədain], *v.t.* encarnar, dar color de carne. — *a.* encarnadino, color de carne.
incarnate, *v.t.* [in'ka:ɹneit] encarnar, tomar carne. — *a.* [in'ka:ɹnit], encarnado, de color de carne.
incarnation, *s.* encarnación, encarnadura; (*cir.*) encarnación.
incarnative, *s.* encarnativo.
incase [in'keis], *v.t.* encajar, encerrar, incluir, encajonar.
incasement, *s.* encerramiento; encaje.
incastellate [in'kæsteleit], *v.t.* encerrar dentro de un castillo.
incautious [in'kɔ:ʃəs], *a.* incauto, descuidado, imprudente, negligente.
incautiousness, *s.* falta de cautela, descuido, negligencia.
incavation [inkə'veiʃən], *a.* ahuecamiento; excavación.
incendiarism [in'sendiərizm], *s.* incendiarismo.
incendiary, *a.* incendiario. — *s.* petrolero, incendiario; (*fig.*) cizañero, sedicioso, revoltoso, inflamatorio.
incense ['insens], *s.* incienso; olíbano; perfume agradable; (*fig.*) lisonja, alabanza.
incense [in'sens], *v.t.* exasperar, irritar, encolerizar, sulfurar; (*igl.*) incensar, perfumar con incienso.
incensement, *s.* rabia, furia, ira, arrebato, cólera.
incension, *s.* encendimiento.

incensive, *a.* provocativo, incitativo.
incensor, *s.* incitador, el que inflama las pasiones.
incensory, *s.* incensario.
incentive [in'sentiv], *s.* incentivo, impulso, estímulo, motivo, móvil. — *a.* incitativo.
incept [in'sept], *v.t.* emprender; (*biol.*) recibir, tomar, asimilar, absorber.
inception [in'sepʃən], *s.* principio, comienzo, estreno.
inceptive, *a.* incipiente, incoativo.
inceration [insə'reiʃən], *s.* enceramiento.
incerative, *a.* que se pega como cera.
incertitude [in'sə:ɹtitju:d], *s.* incertidumbre, duda, obscuridad.
incessable [in'sesəbəl], *a.* incesable, incesante, continuo, constante.
incessant [in'sesənt], *a.* incesante, constante, incesable.
incest ['insest], *s.* incesto.
incestuous [in'sestju:əs], *a.* incestuoso.
inch [intʃ], *s.* pulgada; pizca; *inch by inch,* o *by inches,* a pulgadas, palmo a palmo; (*fig.*) pedacitos; *a man every inch of him,* hombre hecho y derecho; *within an inch,* poco más o menos; *within an inch of,* a dos dedos de; *give him an inch and he'll take an ell,* (*prov.*) dale el pie y se tomará la mano. — *v.t.* mover poco a poco. — *v.i.* avanzar o retirarse poco a poco.
inched, *a.* marcado o dividido en pulgadas; de tantas pulgadas.
inchmeal ['intʃmi:l], *adv.* por pulgadas; poco a poco.
inchoate ['inkouit], *a.* principiado, incoado, comenzado, imperfecto. — *v.t.* ['inkoueit] incoar, principiar.
inchoately, *adv.* en el primer grado.
inchoation, *s.* principio.
inchoative, *a.* incipiente, incoativo.
incidence ['insidəns], *s.* incidencia; carga, gravamen, gabela.
incident ['insidənt], *a.* incidente; casual, fortuito; acontecedero, probable; dependiente de, concomitante. — *s.* casualidad, incidente, acaecimiento, acontecimiento, lance, ocurrencia; digresión, episodio.
incidental [insi'dentəl], *a.* incidental, contingente, incidente; concomitante; casual.
incinerate [in'sinəreit], *v.t.* incinerar, consumir, reducir a cenizas.
incineration, *s.* incineración.
incipience, incipiency, *s.* principio.
incipient [in'sipiənt], *a.* incipiente.
incircumspection [insə:ɹkəm'spekʃən], *s.* falta de circunspección, inadvertencia.
incise [in'saiz], *v.t.* tallar, grabar, tajar, esculpir, hacer obras de talla; hacer incisión, cortar.
incised, *a.* inciso, cortado.
incision [in'siʒən], **incisure,** *s.* cisión, abscisión, cisura, incisión; corte, cortadura, recorte.
incisive [in'saiziv], *a.* incisivo, incisorio; mordaz; agudo.
incisor [in'saizəɹ], *a.* incisivo, propio para cortar. — *s.* diente incisivo.
incisorial, incisory, *a.* incisorio.
incitant [in'saitənt], *a.* provocativo, incitativo, incitante. — *s.* estímulo, aguijatorio, incentivo.
incitation, *s.* incitación, instigación.

incite [in'sait], *v.t.* incitar, instigar, mover, aguijonear, estimular, acuciar.

incitement, *s.* incitación, incitamento, instigación; aguijón, estímulo, aliciente, incentivo.

inciter, *s.* incitador, concitador, instigador.

incitingly, *adv.* incitantemente, de un modo estimulante, incitante, o alentador.

incivility [insi'viliti], *s.* incivilidad, descortesía, desatención, inurbanidad.

inclavated, *a.* fijo, enclavado.

inclemency, *s.* inclemencia, intemperie, *f.*; crueldad, rigor, severidad; aprieto, apuro, aflicción; revés, desgracia.

inclement [in'klemənt], *a.* inclemente, severo, duro; adverso, malandante, contrario; tempestuoso, riguroso, borrascoso.

inclinable [in'klainəbəl], *a.* favorable, inclinado.

inclination [inkli'neiʃən], *s.* inclinación, declivio, declive, descenso; afición, afecto, amor; tendencia, propensión; reverencia, acatamiento; predilección; (*farm.*) decantación.

inclinatory, *a.* inclinativo, ladeado.

incline [in'klain], *v.t.* inclinar, enderezar, torcer, ladear; doblegar, doblar. — *v.i.* inclinarse, ladearse, hacer pendiente, bajar; propender, tirar a (un color), tender a; hacer reverencia o acatamiento; sentir inclinación o predilección. — *s.* declivio, (*f.c.*) declive.

inclined, *a.* inclinado, oblicuo, propenso, prono, proclive. — *p.p.* [INCLINE].

incloister [in'klɔistəɪ], *v.t.* enclaustrar.

include [in'klu:d], *v.t.* incluir, encerrar; englobar, abrazar, comprender, contener.

including, *pa.* incluso, inclusive.

inclusion [in'klu:ʒən], *s.* inclusión, restricción, limitación; contenido.

inclusive [in'klu:ziv], *a.* inclusivo.

inclusively, *adv.* inclusivamente, inclusive.

incogitable [in'kɔdʒitəbəl], *a.* inconcebible.

incogitancy, *s.* irreflexión.

incogitant, *a.* irreflexivo; inconsiderado.

incognito [in'kɔgnitou], *a., adv., s.* incógnito, de incógnito, de oculto.

incognizable, *a.* no cognoscible.

incoherence, incoherency, *s.* incoherencia, inconsistencia, inconsecuencia, inconexión.

incoherent [inko'hiərənt], *a.* incoherente, inconexo, suelto, inconsecuente.

incoherently, *adv.* con incoherencia, sin conexión.

incombustibility, incombustibleness, *s.* incombustibilidad.

incombustible [inkəm'bʌstibəl], *a.* incombustible.

income ['inkəm], *s.* renta, ingreso, entrada, censo; (*com.*) rédito; *income tax,* impuesto de utilidades.

incomer, *s.* el que entra; recién llegado.

incoming, *a.* entrante, que está por llegar. — *s.* llegada, entrada, arribo; renta.

incommensurability, *s.* inconmensurabilidad.

incommensurable [inkə'menʃju:rəbəl], *a.* inconmensurable.

incommensurate [inkə'menʃju:rit], *a.* desproporcionado, insuficiente.

incommode [inkə'moud], *v.t.* incomodar, molestar, desacomodar, fastidiar.

incommodious [inkə'moudiəs], *a.* incómodo, molesto, inconveniente, estrecho.

incommodiousness, incommodity, *s.* incomodidad, molestia, inconveniencia.

incommunicability, incommunicableness, *s.* incomunicabilidad.

incommunicable [inkə'mju:nikəbəl], *a.* incomunicable; indecible.

incommunicative [inkə'mju:nikətiv], *a.* inconversable, insociable, intratable, poco comunicativo.

incommunicativeness, *s.* carácter intratable.

incommutability, *s.* inconmutabilidad.

incommutable [inkə'mju:təbəl], *a.* inconmutable.

incomparable [in'kɔmpərəbəl], *a.* incomparable, sin igual, sin parelelo.

incomparableness [in'kɔmpərəbəlnis], *s.* excelencia incomparable.

incompassionate [inkəm'pæʃənit], *a.* incompasivo, desapiadado.

incompatibility, *s.* incompatibilidad, contrariedad.

incompatible [inkəm'pætibəl], *a.* incompatible.

incompetence, incompetency, *s.* incompetencia, insuficiencia, inhabilidad, ineptitud.

incompetent [in'kɔmpetənt], *a.* incompetente, inepto; (*for.*) inadmisible, que no puede invocarse en derecho.

incomplete [inkəm'pli:t], *a.* incompleto, imperfecto, falto, descabal.

incompleteness, *s.* estado incompleto; imperfección, falta.

incomplex [in'kɔmpleks], *s., a.* incomplejo.

incompliance [inkəm'plaiəns], *s.* indocilidad, desobediencia.

incomprehensibility, incomprehensibleness, *s.* incomprensibilidad.

incomprehensible [inkɔmpri'hensibəl], *a.* incomprensible, impenetrable.

incomprehension, *s.* falta de comprensión.

incomprehensive, *a.* limitado, que no abarca, que no tiene la extensión deseada.

incomprehensiveness, *s.* incomprensibilidad.

incompressibility, *s.* resistencia a la compresión.

incompressible [inkəm'presibəl], *a.* incomprimible.

inconcealable [inkən'si:ləbəl], *a.* que no se puede ocultar.

inconceivability, inconceivableness, *s.* incomprensibilidad; implicación.

inconceivable [inkən'si:vəbəl], *a.* inconcebible, inimaginable, incomprensible; (*lóg.*) implicatorio, contradictorio.

inconclusive [inkən'klu:siv], *a.* inconcluyente, indeciso, que no convence.

inconclusively, *adv.* sin conclusión, de un modo que no convence.

inconclusiveness, *s.* falta de conclusión.

incondite [in'kɔndit], *a.* irregular, no acabado, mal construido.

incongruence, incongruity, *s.* incongruencia, inconexión, desproporción, falta de relación.

incongruent [in'kɔngru:ənt], *a.* incongruente.

incongruous [in'kɔŋgru:əs], *a.* incongruo, incongruente, desproporcionado, inconexo.

incongruousness, *s.* incongruencia.

inconsequence [in'kɔnsikwəns], *s.* inconsecuencia.

inconsequent, *a.* inconsecuente, ilógico, inconsistente, informal, inconsiguiente.

inconsequential, *a.* inconsecuente, inconexo.

inconsiderable [inkən'sidərəbəl], *a.* insignificante, inconsiderable, inapreciable.

inconsiderableness, *s.* insignificancia, falta de importancia.

inconsiderate [inkən'sidərit], *a.* inconsiderado, inadvertido; irreflexivo, desconsiderado, malmirado.

inconsiderateness, inconsideration, *s.* inconsideración, inadvertencia.

inconsistence, inconsistency, *s.* incompatibilidad, incongruencia, inconsistencia, contradicción, mutabilidad, inconsecuencia.

inconsistent [inkən'sistənt], *a.* inconsistente, contradictorio, variable, mudable, incompatible, implicatorio, inconsecuente, inconstante, veleidoso.

inconsolable [inkən'souləbəl], *a.* inconsolable.

inconsonance [in'kɔnsonəns], **inconsonancy,** *s.* falta de consonancia, de armonía.

inconspicuous [inkən'spikju:əs], *a.* no conspicuo, insignificante, sin importancia.

inconstancy, *s.* inconstancia, instabilidad, diversidad, mudanza.

inconstant [in'kɔnstənt], *a.* inconstante, voluble, mudable, variable.

inconsumable [inkən'sju:məbəl], *a.* que no se puede consumir.

incontestable [inkən'testəbəl], *a.* incontestable, irrecusable, indisputable, irrefragable.

incontiguous [inkən'tigju:əs], *a.* no contiguo, separado.

incontinence, incontinency, *s.* incontinencia; lascivia; (*med.*) incontinencia.

incontinent [in'kɔntinənt], *a.* incontinente, desenfrenado; incesante. — *adv.* (*ant.*) inmediatamente.

incontinently, *adv.* incontinentemente; al instante, inmediatamente.

incontrollable [inkən'trouləbəl], *a.* ingobernable, indomable.

incontrovertible [inkɔntro'və:rtibəl], *a.* incontrovertible, irrefragable, incontrastable, indisputable.

inconvenience, inconveniency, *s.* inconveniencia, incomodidad, dificultad, desventaja, inconveniente, estorbo, molestia, embarazo. — *v.t.* incomodar, molestar, estorbar, embarazar, causar inconvenientes.

inconvenient [inkən'vi:niənt], *a.* incómodo, molesto, impropio, embarazoso, fastidioso, inconveniente; inoportuno.

inconversable, *a.* inconversable, intratable, insociable.

inconversant [inkən'və:rsənt], *a.* que no conoce o entiende (de).

inconvertible [inkən'və:rtibəl], *a.* inconvertible.

inconvincible, *a.* inconvencible, incontrastable.

inco-ordinate [inkou'ɔ:rdinit], *a.* no coordinado, incoordinado.

incorporate [in'kɔ:rpəreit], *v.t.* dar cuerpo o forma material; formar corporación, gremio, etc.; incorporar, agregar; asociar. — *v.i.* incorporarse, unirse, agregarse, asociarse. — *a.* incorporado, unido, asociado; conmisto, mezclado; incorporal, incorpóreo, inmaterial.

incorporation, *s.* incorporación, asociación, organización, formación de una corporación, etc.

incorporeal [inkɔ:r'pɔ:riəl], *a.* incorporal, incorpóreo, inmaterial.

incorporeity, *s.* incorporeidad.

incorrect [inkə'rekt], *a.* incorrecto, inexacto, falso, erróneo; inmoral.

incorrectness, *s.* inexactitud, impropiedad; incorrección, inconveniencia, descuido.

incorrigible [in'kɔridʒibəl], *a.* incorregible, empecatado, indócil, terco, obstinado.

incorrigibility, incorrigibleness, *s.* incorregibilidad, indocilidad, terquedad, obstinación.

incorrodible [inkə'roudibəl], *a.* lo que no puede corroerse.

incorrupt [inkə'rʌpt], *a.* incorrupto; probo, íntegro, recto.

incorruptibility, *s.* incorruptibilidad.

incorruptible, *a.* incorruptible, incorrupto, probo.

incorruption, *s.* incorrupción.

incorruptive, *s.* incorrupto.

incorruptness, *s.* incorrupción.

incrassate ['inkræseit], *v.t.* espesar, encrasar, condensar, engrosar. — *v.i.* condensarse, espesarse, engrosarse. — *a.* encrasado.

incrassation, *s.* engrasación, espesura, condensación; hinchazón, *f.*

incrassative, *a.* incrasante, espesativo.

increasable, *a.* aumentable.

increase [in'kri:s], *v.t.* acrecentar, aumentar; agrandar, abultar, alargar. — *v.i.* crecer, acrecentarse, tomar vuelo, tomar cuerpo, multiplicarse; arreciar, engrandecer.

increase ['inkri:s], *s.* aumento. acrecentamiento, acrecencia, crecimiento, adelantamiento, incremento, engrandecimiento, desarrollo; provecho, interés, ganancia; cosecha, producto; progenie, *f.*, generación; creciente (de las aguas); creciente, (de la luna), *f.*

increaser, *s.* aumentador, acrecentador, productor.

increasingly, *adv.* en aumento, con creces; en creciente.

increate, *a.* (*poét.*) increado.

incredibility, incredibleness, *s.* incredibilidad.

incredible [in'kredibəl], *a.* increíble.

incredulity, incredulousness, *s.* incredulidad.

incredulous [in'kredju:ləs], *a.* incrédulo, escéptico.

incremate ['inkremeit], *v.t.* incinerar.

increment ['inkrimənt], *s.* incremento, aumento, crecimiento; adición, agregación, añadidura; (*mat.*) incremento; (*ret.*) gradación, clímax.

increpate ['inkrepeit], *v.t.* increpar.

increscent [in'kresənt], *a.* creciente (dícese de la luna).

incriminate [in'krimineit], *v.t.* criminar, acriminar, incriminar, acusar.

incrimination, *s.* criminación, acriminación, incriminación.

incrust [in'krʌst], **incrustate,** *v.t.* encostrar; incrustar, adornar con incrustaciones.

incrustation, *s.* incrustación, encostradura, embutido.

incubate ['iŋkju:beit], *v.t., v.i.* empollar, incubar; (*fig.*) pensar, madurar.

incubation, *s.* incubación, empolladura; (*med.*) incubación.

incubator, *s.* empollador; incubadora.

incubus ['iŋkju:bəs], *s.* íncubo; pesadilla; (*fig.*) carga.

inculcate ['inkʌlkeit], v.t. inculcar.
inculcation, s. inculcación.
inculcator, s. inculcador.
inculpable [in'kʌlpəbəl], s. inculpable, irreprensible; inocente, exento de culpa.
inculpableness, s. inculpabilidad.
inculpate ['inkʌlpeit], v.t. culpar, inculpar, imputar.
inculpation, s. culpación, inculpación.
inculpatory, a. inculpador, imputador, que inculpa.
incumbency, s. posesión o duración de un beneficio eclesiástico; incumbencia, obligación, cargo.
incumbent [in'kʌmbənt], a. obligatorio, preciso, exigido, demandado, apoyado, colocado, sostenido. — s. (igl.) beneficiado; empleado con posesión de su cargo.
incumber, v.t. embarazar, sobrecargar, abrumar, gravar, estorbar.
incumbrance, s. embarazo, estorbo, obstáculo, impedimento; pensión, gravamen, imposición, carga.
incur [in'kə:ɹ], v.t. contraer, incurrir; atraerse, causarse.
incurability, incurableness, s. calidad de incurable.
incurable [in'kju:rəbəl], a. incurable, irremediable, irreparable, insanable. — s. incurable.
incuriosity, s. falta de curiosidad, indiferencia.
incurious [in'kju:riəs], a. indiferente; incurioso, omiso, descuidado, negligente.
incuriously, adv. sin curiosidad; descuidadamente, negligentemente.
incuriousness, s. falta de curiosidad, incuria, descuido, omisión, negligencia.
incursion [in'kə:ɹʃən], s. incursión, correría.
incurvate ['inkə:ɹveit], incurve, v.t. encorvar, torcer, doblar. — a. encorvado, torcido, doblado.
incurvation, s. encorvadura, encorvamiento, curvatura; genuflexión, reverencia.
incurvity, s. corvadura, inflexión.
incus ['inkəs], s. (anat.) yunque.
incuse [in'kju:z], v.t. estampar, acuñar.
incussion [in'kʌʃən], s. sacudimiento violento.
indebted [in'detid], a. adeudado, endeudado, empeñado; reconocido, obligado.
indebtedness, s. estado de deudor, adeudo; deuda pasiva; importe o suma de las deudas, obligación.
indebtment, s. adeudo.
indecency [in'di:sənsi], s. indecencia, deshonestidad, inmodestia, indecoro, vulgaridad, grosería.
indecent [in'di:sənt], a. indecente, obsceno, torpe, grosero, indecoroso, pornográfico; impropio.
indecipherable [indi'saifərəbəl], a. indescifrable.
indecision [indi'siʒən], s. indecisión, irresolución.
indecisive [indi'saiziv], a. indeciso, irresoluto, dudoso, indeterminado.
indecisiveness, s. estado o calidad de indecisión o irresolución.
indeclinable [indi'klainəbəl], a. indeclinable. — s. nombre que no se declina.
indeclinably, adv. sin declinación, sin variación, invariablemente.
indecorous [in'dekərəs], a. indecoroso, irrespetuoso, indecente, vil, indigno.

indecorousness, indecorum, s. indecoro, indecencia, ignominia.
indeed [in'di:d], adv. verdaderamente, seguramente, realmente, de veras, a la verdad, claro está, ya, sí; por cierto; indeed? ¿de veras? ¿es posible? ¿le parece?
indefatigability, indefatigableness, s. calidad de infatigable o incansable.
indefatigable [indi'fætigəbəl], a. infatigable, incansable.
indefeasibility, s. irrevocabilidad.
indefeasible [indi'fi:zəbəl], a. (for.) irrevocable, inabrogable, inquebrantable.
indefectibility, s. indefectibilidad.
indefectible [indi'fektəbəl], a. indefectible.
indefensible, a. indefendible, insostenible.
indefensive [indi'fenziv], a. indefenso.
indefinable [indi'fainəbəl], a. indefinible.
indefinite [in'definit], a. indefinidio, incierto, indeterminado; vago, imperceptible, sutil.
indefiniteness, s. calidad de indefinido.
indehiscence, s. indehiscencia.
indehiscent [inde'hisənt], a. indehiscente.
indeliberate [inde'libərət], a. indeliberado, impremeditado.
indelibility, s. calidad de indeleble.
indelible [in'delibəl], a. indeleble; irrevocable.
indelicacy, s. inmodestia, indecoro, grosería, inurbanidad.
indelicate [in'delikit], a. indecoroso, inmodesto; grosero, inurbano.
indemnification [indemnifi'keiʃən], s. indemnización, resarcimiento.
indemnify [in'demnifai], v.t. indemnizar, compensar, resarcir, reparar.
indemnity [in'demniti], s. indemnización, demnidad, reparación, resarcimiento, contrafianza, garantía; indemnity bond, contrafianza.
indemonstrable [inde'monstrəbəl], a. indemostrable.
indent [in'dent], v.t. dentar, mellar, endentar; requisar; (impr.) sangrar. — v.i. ponerse dentado, mellarse. — s. mella, diente, cortadura dentada.
indentation, s. mella, diente, muesca, piquete, corte, cortadura dentada.
indented, a. dentado; (bot.) dentellado. — p.p. [INDENT].
indention, s. abolladura, desigualdad, mella; (impr.) sangría.
indenture ['indentʃəɹ], s. (for.) escritura, contrato, instrumento, carta partida, documento. — v.t. obligar, ligar por contrato, escriturar.
independence [indi'pendəns], independency, s. independencia, autonomía, libertad; posición holgada, bienestar.
independent [indi'pendənt], a. independiente, separado, desunido; acomodado, adinerado; fácil, libre, cómodo; intrépido; que vive de sus rentas.
indescribable [inde'skraibəbəl], a. indescriptible.
indestructibility, s. indestructibilidad.
indestructible [inde'strʌktəbəl], a. indestructible.
indeterminable [inde'tə:ɹminəbəl], a. indeterminable.
indeterminate [inde'tə:ɹminit], a. indeterminado, indefinido, inexacto.
indeterminateness, indetermination, s. indeterminación, irresolución, duda.

indetermined, *a.* indeterminado, irresuelto, irresoluto, vacilante.

index ['indeks], *s.* (*pl.* **indexes, indices**) índice, tabla de materias; dedo índice; manecilla (de reloj, etc.); indicio, señal, *f.*, indicación; *index card*, ficha; *card index*, fichero; *index gauge*, compás de graduación; *index-plate*, plataforma; *expurgatorial index*, índice expurgatorio. — *v.t.* poner índice a; poner en el índice.

indexterity [indeks'teriti], *s.* desmaña, falta de destreza.

India ['india], *s.* India; *India ink*, tinta china; *India-proof*, prueba en papel de China; *India-paper*, papel de China.

Indiaman ['indiamən], *s.* buque que hace el comercio con la India.

Indian ['indiən], *a.* indio; indo, índico; (*E.U.*) de maíz, hecho de maíz. — *s.* indio, indiano; *Indian corn*, maíz; *Indian millet*, alcandía; *Indian summer*, veranillo de San Martín; *Indian pink*, clavelón de Indias; *Indian cress*, capuchina; *Indian meal*, harina de maíz; *Indian red*, almagre; *Red Indian*, piel roja, *m.f.*

india-rubber [india'rʌbər], *s.* caucho, cauchuco, goma elástica; (*Méx.*) hule.

indicant ['indikənt], *a.* indicante.

indicate ['indikeit], *v.t.* indicar, designar, señalar, anunciar, intimar.

indication, *s.* indicación, indicio; signo; señal, *f.*; muestra, manifestación.

indicative, *a.* indicativo.

indicator, *s.* indicador, apuntador, señalador; manómetro.

indicatory, *a.* demostrativo, indicatorio.

indices ['indisi:z], *s.pl.* [INDEX].

indict [in'dait], *v.t.* acusar ante el juez; (*for.*) procesar, encausar, demandar.

indictable [in'dəitəbəl], *a.* procesable, denunciable, sujeto a denuncia.

indictee, *s.* acusado, procesado.

indicter, *s.* denunciante, acusador, fiscal.

indiction, *s.* indicción.

indictment [in'dəitmənt], *s.* sumaria; acusación, denuncia; proceso.

Indies ['indiz], *s.pl.* Indias; *West Indies*, las Antillas.

indifference, indifferency, *s.* indiferencia, desapego, desinterés; desvío, apatía, tibieza; frialdad, neutralidad, imparcialidad.

indifferent [in'difərənt], *a.* indiferente, apático, desapegado; pasadero, mediano, ordinario, pasable, tal cual; desapasionado, neutral, imparcial.

indigence, indigency, *s.* indigencia, necesidad, pobreza, inopia, penuria.

indigenous [in'didʒənəs], *a.* índigena, natural, nativo; innato.

indigent ['indidʒənt], *a.* indigente, necesitado, pobre; falto.

indigested, *a.* indigesto, mal digerido, crudo.

indigestible [indi'dʒestibəl], *a.* indigestible, indigesto.

indigestion [indi'dʒestʃən], *s.* indigestión, apepsia; empacho.

indignant [in'dignənt], *a.* indignado; *to make indignant*, dar rabia a, indignar.

indignantly, *adv.* con indignación.

indignation, *s.* indignación, cólera, desprecio, despecho.

indignity [in'digniti], *s.* indignidad, afrenta, ultraje; oprobio.

indigo ['indigou], *s.* añil, índigo; *indigo-plant, indigo-tree*, índigo, jiquilete.

indirect [in'direkt], *a.* indirecto, torcido, oblicuo; inicuo, deshonesto.

indirection, indirectness, *s.* oblicuidad, tortuosidad; rodeo; efugio; conducta torcida; vía indirecta; doblez.

indiretin [indi'ri:tin], *s.* compuesto resinoso obtenido por la descomposición de la glucosa del añil.

indiscernible [indi'sə:ɹnəbəl], *a.* indiscernible, imperceptible.

indisciplinable, *a.* indisciplinable.

indiscoverable [indi'skʌvərəbəl], *a.* indescubrible.

indiscreet [indi'skri:t], *a.* indiscreto, irreflexivo, imprudente, impolítico, incauto, inconsiderado.

indiscrete, *a.* que no está separado o desunido.

indiscretion [indi'skreʃən], *s.* indiscreción, irreflexión, inconsideración, imprudencia.

indiscriminate [indi'skriminit], *a.* promiscuo, indistinto, confuso, general.

indiscriminating, *a.* indiscriminado, que no hace distinción alguna.

indiscrimination, *s.* falta de distinción.

indispensability, indispensableness, *s.* indispensabilidad, necesidad, calidad de indispensable.

indispensable [indi'spensəbəl], *a.* indispensable, imprescindible; preciso.

indispose [indi'spouz], *v.t.* indisponer; malquistar, enemistar; *to be indisposed*, estar indispuesto.

indisposedness, *s.* indisposición, repugnancia, desavenencia, desazón.

indisposition [indis'poziʃən], *s.* indisposición, falta de salud, desazón, *f.*, achaque, destemplanza; falta de inclinación; desavenencia, desafecto.

indisputable [indi'spju:təbəl], *a.* indisputable, irrebatible, incontestable.

indisputableness, *s.* certeza.

indissolubility, indissolubleness, *s.* indisolubilidad.

indissoluble [indi'sɔlju:bəl], **indissolvable,** *a.* indisoluble, insoluble; obligatorio, permanente, estable, firme.

indistinct [indi'stiŋt], *a.* indistinto, confuso; vago, obscuro.

indistinction, *s.* indistinción, obscuridad, confusión, falta de claridad; igualdad de rango.

indistinctness, *s.* confusión, incertidumbre, obscuridad.

indistinguishable [indi'stiŋgwiʃəbəl], *a.* indistinguible.

indite [in'dait], *v.t.* redactar, escribir, componer, poner por escrito; dictar.

inditement, *s.* redacción, composición, escritura.

inditer, *s.* redactor, escritor, autor.

indium ['indiəm], *s.* indio (metal).

individual [indi'vidju:əl], *a.* solo, único, particular, individual, singular, individuo. — *s.* individuo, sujeto, particular, persona particular.

individualism, *s.* individualismo.

individualist, *s.* individualista, *m.f.*

individualistic, *a.* individualista.

individuality [individju:'æliti], *s.* individualidad.

individualize, *v.t.* individualizar, individuar, particularizar.

individuate, *v.t.* individualizar, individuar, particularizar. — *a.* individual, numérico.

individuation, *s.* acción de individuar; producción de individuos.

indivisibility, indivisibleness, *s.* indivisibilidad.

indivisible [indi'vizəbəl], *a.* indivisible, incapaz de división, individuo, impartible.

indocile [in'dousail], *a.* indócil, cerril.

indocility, *s.* indocilidad, aspereza, dureza, obstinación, pertinacia.

indoctrinate [in'dɔktrineit], *v.t.* doctrinar, disciplinar, enseñar, instruir.

indoctrination, *s.* instrucción, enseñanza.

Indo-European [indouju:ro'pi:ən], **Indo-Germanic,** *a.* indoeuropeo, indogermánico.

indolence, *s.* indolencia, desidia, pereza; (*med.*) ausencia de dolor.

indolent ['indolənt], *a.* indolente, holgazán, perezoso; (*med.*) insensible, sin dolor.

indomitable [in'dɔmitəbəl], *a.* indomable, indómito.

indoor [in'dɔ:ɪ], *a.* interior, interno; de puertas adentro.

indoors [in'dɔ:ɪz], *adv.* dentro, adentro, en casa.

indorsable, *a.* endosable, endorsable, confirmable.

indorse [in'dɔ:ɪs], *v.t.* (*com.*) endosar, endorsar; respaldar; abonar, garantizar; sancionar, confirmar, apoyar, aprobar.

indorsee, *s.* (*com.*) endosado, portador.

indorsement, *s.* (*com.*) endoso, endorso, contenta; sobrescrito, respaldo, rótulo; garantía, aval; sanción, confirmación, ratificación, aprobación.

indorser, indorsor, *s.* (*com.*) endosante, endosador.

indraft, indraught ['indrɑ:ft], *s.* absorción, aspiración, succión, entrada, acto de atraer.

indrawn ['indrɔ:n], *a.* sorbido, inspirado, atraído; con voz ahogada; abstraído, distraído.

indubitable [in'dju:bitəbəl], *a.* indudable, positivo, indubitable, seguro, cierto.

indubitableness, *s.* certeza, estado de indudable.

induce [in'dju:s], *v.t.* inducir, mover, inclinar, instigar, inspirar, influir, incitar, producir, ocasionar, causar; inferir; (*elec.*) inducir.

inducement, *s.* inducimiento, móvil, incitamento, aliciente; persuasión.

inducer, *s.* inducidor, inspirador, persuadidor.

inducible, *a.* deducible; que se puede causar o producir.

induct [in'dʌkt], *v.t.* instalar, dar posesión a; obtener o sacar por inducción; iniciar.

induction, *s.* inducción, ilación; prólogo, introducción, preámbulo; instalación; (*mec.*) introducción, entrada, ingreso; (*elec.*) inducción; *induction coil,* carrete de inducción.

inductive, *a.* inductivo, ilativo; (*elec.*) inductivo, inductor, inductriz; introductor.

inductively, *adv.* por inducción, inductivamente, por inferencia.

inductivity, *s.* inductividad.

inductometer, *s.* inductómetro.

inductophone [indʌkto'foun], *s.* inductófono.

inductor, *s.* instalador, el que instala; (*elec.*) inductor.

indue [in'dju:], *v.t.* vestir; investir; cubrir con vestido; dotar.

indulge [in'dʌldʒ], *v.t.* consentir, malcriar, mimar; animar, dar gusto, condescender, gratificar, favorecer, tolerar; satisfacer, contentar; dar gratuitamente, proporcionar, conceder, dar permiso. — *v.i. to indulge in,* entregarse a, satisfacer completamente, permitirse, gozar.

indulgence, indulgency, *s.* abandonamiento, abandono; afecto, halago, cariño; inclinación a perdonar o a sufrir; mimo, disimulo, indulgencia, facilidad, placer, lenidad; exceso; (*com.*) prórroga; favor, complacencia, gracia; (*igl.*) indulgencia; dispensa.

indulgent, *a.* indulgente, complaciente, condescendiente, fácil, lenitivo, tierno, favorable, clemente.

indulgential, *a.* (*igl.*) indulgente.

indulger, *s.* indulgente.

indult [in'dʌlt], *s.* (*igl.*) indulto; dispensa, gracia, privilegio, exención.

indurate ['indju:reit], *v.t.* endurecer, hacer duro. — *v.i.* endurecerse, empedernirse. — *a.* duro, endurecido, obstinado, impenitente.

induration, *s.* acción de endurecer, endurecimiento; dureza de corazón; (*med.*) dureza, induración.

industrial [in'dʌstriəl], *a.* industrial. — *s.* artesano, industrial; *pl.* (*com.*) acción o obligación de una sociedad industrial, anónima.

industrialism, *s.* industrialismo; industria, trabajo.

industrialist [in'dʌstriəlist], *s.* industrial.

industrious [in'dʌstriəs], *a.* industrioso, laborioso, diligente, aplicado, hecho con industria.

industry ['indʌstri], *s.* industria, laboriosidad, diligencia, actividad; esmero, destreza, fabricación; (*com.*) industria.

indwell [in'dwel], *v.t., v.i.* residir, morar, habitar.

indweller, *s.* habitante.

indwelling, *a.* morador, residente. — *s.* presencia, existencia interior.

inebriant, *a.* embriagador, que embriaga. — *s.* lo que embriaga.

inebriate [in'i:brieit], *v.t.* embriagar, emborrachar; cegar, infatuar, desvanecer. — *v.i.* embriagarse, emborracharse. — *a.* ebrio, borracho. — *s.* borracho, beodo.

inebriation, *s.* embriaguez, borrachera.

inedible [in'edibəl], *a.* no comestible, incomible.

inedited [in'editid], *a.* inédito, no publicado, no redactado.

ineffable [in'efəbəl], *a.* inefable, indecible.

ineffableness, *s.* inefabilidad.

ineffaceable [ine'feisəbəl], *a.* imborrable, indeleble.

ineffective [ine'fektiv], *a.* ineficaz, impotente, inútil, vano.

ineffectual [ine'fektjuːəl], *a.* ineficaz, incapaz de obrar, sin efecto.

ineffectualness, *s.* ineficacia.

inefficacious [inefi'keiʃəs], *a.* ineficaz.

inefficaciousness, inefficacy, inefficiency, *s.* ineficacia.

inefficient [ine'fiʃənt], *a.* ineficaz.

inelastic [ine'læstik], *a.* falto de elasticidad.

inelasticity [inelæs'tisiti], *s.* carencia de elasticidad.

inelegant [in'eligənt], *a.* inelegante, sin elegancia.

inelegantly, *adv.* sin elegancia.

ineligibility, *s.* inelegibilidad.

ineligible [in'elidʒəbəl], *a.* inelegible.

ineloquent [in'elokwənt], *a.* infacundo.

ineluctable [ine'lʌktəbəl], *a.* ineluctable, inevitable, irresistible.

inept [in'ept], *a.* inepto; absurdo, tonto, necio.

ineptitude [in'eptitjuːd], **ineptness,** *s.* ineptitud, incapacidad.

inequal [in'iːkwəl], *a.* desigual.

inequality [ini'kwɔliti], *s.* disigualidad, disparidad, falta de proporción, diferencia, desemejanza; escabrosidad, aspereza; insuficiencia; injusticia.

inequitable [in'ekwitəbəl], *a.* injusto.

ineradicable [ini'rædikəbəl], *a.* que no se puede desarraigar; indeleble.

inerrable [in'erəbəl], **inerrant,** *a.* inerrable, libre o exento de error, infalible.

inert [in'əːrt], *a.* inerte, flojo, pesado; inanimado, sin vida.

inertia [in'əːrʃə], *s.* flojedad, desidia, inacción; (*fís.*) inercia.

inertness, *s.* flojedad, inacción.

inescapable [ines'keipəbəl], *a.* inevitable, ineludible.

inescutcheon [ines'kʌtʃən], *s.* escudo de armas pequeño dentro de otro mayor.

inestimable [in'estiməbəl], *a.* inestimable, inapreciable.

inevitable [in'evitəbəl], *a.* inevitable, ineludible.

inevitability, inevitableness, *s.* calidad de inevitable.

inexact [inek'zækt], *a.* inexacto; incorrecto.

inexcusable [inek'skjuːzəbəl], *a.* inexcusable, imperdonable, indisculpable, injustificable.

inexcusableness, *s.* lo que no admite disculpa.

inexecutable [ineksi'kjuːtəbəl], *a.* incapaz de ser ejecutado, o efectuado.

inexhaustible [inek'zɔːstəbəl], **inexhaustive,** *a.* inexhausto, inagotable.

inexhaustibleness, *s.* estado o calidad de inagotable.

inexistence, *s.* inexistencia.

inexistent [inek'zistənt], *a.* inexistente, que no existe; que existe dentro, o con.

inexorability, inexorableness, *s.* inflexibilidad.

inexorable [in'ekzərəbəl], *a.* inexorable, inflexible, duro.

inexpansible [inek'spænsəbəl], *a.* incapaz de expansión.

inexpedience, inexpediency, *s.* inoportunidad, inconveniencia, impropiedad.

inexpedient [inek'spiːdiənt], *a.* impropio, inconveniente, inoportuno.

inexpensive [inek'spensiv], *a.* barato.

inexperience [inek'spiəriəns], *s.* inexperiencia, impericia.

inexperienced, inexpert, *a.* inexperto, novel, inexperimentado, inhábil.

inexpiable [in'ekspiəbəl], *a.* inexpiable; lo que no puede ser satisfecho o perdonado.

inexpiableness, *s.* calidad de inexpiable.

inexplicability, inexplicableness, *s.* calidad o estado de inexplicable.

inexplicable [inek'splikəbəl], *a.* inexplicable, inenarrable.

inexplicit [inek'splisit], *a.* no explícito.

inexplorable [inek'splɔːrəbəl], *a.* que no se puede explorar.

inexpressible [inek'spresəbəl], *a.* indecible, inefable.

inexpressive, *a.* falto de expresión; (*poét.*) indecible.

inextinguishability, *s.* calidad de inextinguible.

inextinguishable [inek'stiŋgwiʃəbəl], *s.* inextinguible, inapagable.

inextricable [in'ekstrikəbəl], *a.* inextricable, enmarañado, intrincado, confuso.

inextricableness, *s.* estado de inextricable.

infall ['infɔːl], *s.* ataque, incursión; sitio por donde entra el agua en un estanque.

infallibility, infallibleness, *s.* infalibilidad, incapacidad de engañar(se).

infallible [in'fælibəl], *a.* infalible, seguro, indefectible, cierto.

infamous ['infəməs], *a.* infame, vil, vergonzoso, desacreditado, ignominioso; infamatorio, infamante; odioso, aborrecible.

infamousness, infamy, *s.* infamia, deshonra, descrédito, oprobio, vituperio, baldón.

infancy ['infənsi], *s.* infancia, niñez; (*for.*) minoridad, menor edad.

infant ['infənt], *s.* niño, niña, criatura; (*for.*) menor. — *a.* infantil; menor de edad; naciente, joven; *infant school*, escuela de párvulos.

infanticidal, *a.* que se refiere al infanticidio.

infanticide [in'fæntisaid], *s.* infanticidio; infanticida, *m.f.*

infantile ['infəntail], **infantine** ['infəntain], *a.* infantil, pueril, propio de niño.

infantry ['infəntri], *s.* infantería; peones.

infantryman, *s.* infante, peón.

infatuate [in'fætjuːeit], *v.t.* infatuar, embobar, atontar, cegar, preocupar.

infatuate, infatuated, *a.* infatuado, locamente enamorado.

infatuation, *s.* infatuación, encaprichamiento, apasionamiento.

infeasibility, infeasibleness, *s.* impracticabilidad.

infeasible [in'fiːzəbəl], *a.* impracticable.

infect [in'fekt], *v.t.* infectar, inficionar, apestar, contagiar; (*fig.*) corromper.

infection, *s.* acción de infectar, infección, infestación, contagio; miasma; corrupción de costumbres; (*for.*) tacha de ilegalidad.

infectious [in'fekʃəs], *a.* infecto, pestilencial, inficionado; infeccioso, infectivo; corruptor; pestilente.

infectiously, *adv.* por infección.

infectiousness, *s.* calidad o propiedad de inficionar.

infective [in'fektiv], *a.* infeccioso, infectivo, pestilente.

infecund [in'fekʌnd], *a.* infecundo, estéril.

infecundity, *s.* infecundidad, esterilidad.

infelicitous [infe'lisitəs], *a.* inepto, poco conveniente; desatinado; desdichado, desgraciado, infeliz.

infelicity [infe'lisiti], *s.* infelicidad, desdicha, desgracia, infortunio; impropiedad; ineptitud; falta de tino.

infer [in'fəːr], *v.t.* inferir, deducir, colegir,

concluir, probar, implicar, mostrar. — *v.i.* sacar una consecuencia.

inferable, *a.* deducible.

inference ['infərəns], *s.* inferencia, ilación, deducción, corolario, consecuencia.

inferential [infə'renʃəl], *a.* ilativo.

inferentially, *adv.* por inferencia.

inferior ['infiəriə], *a.* inferior, subordinado, subalterno; debajo, más bajo; inferior en calidad; (*mús.*) de tono más bajo; (*impr.*) inferior, más bajo del nivel de la línea, como los números en H_2SO_4; *to be inferior*, quedarse atrás. — *s.* inferior, subalterno.

inferiority [infiəri'ɔriti], *s.* inferioridad; *inferiority complex*, complejo de inferioridad.

infernal [in'fə:nəl], *a.* infernal.

infernalness, *s.* estado de infernal.

infertile [in'fə:tail], *a.* infecundo, estéril, infértil.

infertility, *s.* infecundidad, esterilidad.

infest [in'fest], *v.t.* infestar, plagar, incomodar, apestar, inficionar.

infestation, *s.* infestación; disturbio, molestia.

infestive, *s.* triste, melancólico.

infeudation [infju:dei'ʃən], *s.* enfeudación.

infidel ['infidəl], *s.* infiel, pagano, gentil. — *a.* descreído, infiel; fementido, desleal, pérfido.

infidelity [infi'deliti], *s.* infidelidad; falta de fe; perfidia, alevosía, deslealtad.

infighting ['infaitiŋ], *s.* lucha cuerpo a cuerpo (en el boxeo).

infiltrate ['infiltreit], *v.t.* infiltrar, calar. — *v.i.* infiltrarse, penetrar, recalar.

infiltration, *s.* infiltración, acto de infiltrar; (*med.*) infarto blando.

infinite ['infinit], *a.* infinito, ilimitado, inmenso; sin fin, sin término; innumerable.

infiniteness, *s.* infinidad, estado de infinito.

infinitesimal [infini'tesiməl], *a.* infinitesimal. — *s.* cantidad infinitésima.

infinitive [in'finitiv], *a.* infinitivo. — *s.* (*gram.*) infinitivo.

infinitude [in'finitju:d], *s.* infinidad; muchedumbre innumerable.

infinity [in'finiti], *s.* infinidad, inmensidad, espacio sin límites; infinito.

infirm [in'fə:m], *a.* enfermo, enfermizo, doliente, inválido; (*fam.*) enclenque, achacoso, canijo, entecado, valetudinario, débil, frágil; inestable, poco firme; (*for.*) anulable, que se puede invalidar.

infirmary, *s.* enfermería, hospital.

infirmity, *s.* enfermedad, mal, achaque, dolencia, indisposición; fragilidad, flaquedad, flaqueza; desliz, falta, traspié.

infirmness, *s.* debilidad, flaqueza, extenuación.

infix [in'fiks], *v.t.* clavar, encajar, inculcar, imprimir, grabar en el alma. — *s.* (*gram.*) partícula que se interpone en una palabra para modificar su significación.

inflame [in'fleim], *v.t.* inflamar, hacer arder, encender; acalorar, encandilar, provocar, irritar, azuzar, enardecer, avivar; agravar, exagerar. — *v.i.* arder, encenderse; (*med.*) hincharse, inflamarse.

inflamed, *a.* encendido, acalorado, ardiendo; irritado, inflamado, enardecido. — *p.p.* [INFLAME].

inflamer, *s.* inflamador, enardecedor.

inflaming, *s.* enardecimiento, inflamación.

inflammability, inflammableness, *s.* calidad de inflamable.

inflammable [in'flæməbəl], *a.* inflamable.

inflammation [inflə'meiʃən], *s.* (*med.*) inflamación, enardecimiento, encendimiento.

inflammatory [in'flæmətəri], *a.* inflamatorio, incendiario; (*med.*) inflamatorio.

inflate [in'fleit], *v.t.* soplar, hinchar, inflar, ahuecar, entumecer, envanecer, engreír.

inflated, *a.* hinchado, inflado, tumido, engreído, entumecido; afectado, pomposo.

inflation, *s.* inflación, ahuecamiento, entumecimiento, hinchazón, *f.*; (*com.*) inflación; pompa, engreimiento, envanecimiento.

inflationist, *s.* inflacionista, *m.f.*

inflect [in'flekt], *v.t.* torcer, doblar, encorvar; acentuar; variar, mudar, modular; (*gram.*) declinar, conjugar.

inflection, inflexion, *s.* inflexión, dobladura; modulación de la voz, acento; (*gram.*) inflexión, desinencia, terminación.

inflectional, *a.* que tiene desinencias.

inflective, *a.* capaz de doblar o torcer.

inflexibility, inflexibleness, *s.* inflexibilidad, obstinación, pertinacia, dureza.

inflexible [in'fleksibəl], *a.* inflexible, inexorable, inalterable, obstinado.

inflexion, *s.* [INFLECTION].

inflict [in'flikt], *v.t.* infligir, descargar, imponer; *to inflict (disgrace, etc.) upon*, cubrir de (oprobio, etc.).

infliction [in'flikʃən], *s.* imposición, aplicación, pena, castigo.

inflictive, *a.* que se impone o inflige.

inflorescence [inflo'resəns], *s.* inflorescencia, florescencia.

inflow ['inflou], *s.* flujo, afluencia.

influence ['influəns], *s.* influencia, influjo, valimiento; (*elec.*) inducción. — *v.t.* influir, intervenir, comunicar, modificar, alterar, cambiar.

influencing, *s.* influencia, influjo.

influent ['influ:ənt], *a.* que fluye hacia dentro.

influential [influ'enʃəl], *a.* influente, influyente, que tiene influencia.

influentially, *adv.* por medio de influencia o influjo.

influenza [influ:'enzə], *s.* gripe, *f.*, trancazo.

influx ['inflʌks], *s.* flujo, influjo, instilación, intromisión; afluencia; entrada, desembocadura.

influxion, *s.* infusión.

infold [in'fould], *v.t.* envolver, arrollar, abrazar, apretar, estrechar, incluir.

inform [in'fɔ:m], *v.t.* informar, comunicar, participar, avisar, enterar, notificar, noticiar, dar noticias a, hacer saber a, enseñar, instruir; informar, infundir vida a, dar forma a, animar, modelar. — *v.i.* denunciar; dar parte, delatar.

informal, *a.* informal, irregular; sin ceremonia, de confianza, casero.

informality [infɔ:'mæliti], *s.* informalidad, irregularidad; hecho informal, acto sencillo, falta de ceremonia.

informant [in'fɔ:mənt], *s.* informante, informador; denunciador.

information [infə'meiʃən], *s.* informe, instrucción, información, noticia, aviso; delación, acusación, denunciación; saber, conocimientos.

informative [in'fɔ:mətiv], *a.* informativo.

informed, *a.* informe, inteligente, instruido. — *p.p.* [INFORM].

informer, *s.* delator, denunciador, delatante; informador, informante; soplón, espía, *m.f.*; el que forma, anima o amolda; *to turn informer,* delatar, hacerse delator.

infracted [in'fræktid], *s.* roto, quebrantado.

infraction, *s.* quebrantamiento, rompimiento; transgresión, infracción, violación, desafuero, contravención.

infractor, *s.* infractor, contraventor, transgresor.

inframammary [infrə'mæməri], *a.* situado debajo de los pechos.

inframaxillary [infrəmæk'ziləri], *s.* quijada inferior. — *a.* perteneciente a la quijada inferior.

infrangible [in'frændʒibəl], *a.* infrangible, inquebrantable.

infrangibleness, *s.* calidad o estado de infrangible.

infraorbital [infrə'ɔːrbitəl], *a.* situado debajo de la órbita del ojo.

infra-red [infrɑ:'red], *a.* infrarrojo.

infrequence, infrequency, *s.* infrecuencia, rareza, raridad.

infrequent [in'fri:kwənt], *a.* raro, infrecuente, poco común.

infringe [in'frindʒ], *v.t.* infringir, violar, quebrantar, contravenir a. — *v.i.* violar (derechos, privilegios, etc.).

infringement, *s.* infracción, transgresión, violación, contravención, quebrantamiento.

infringer, *s.* violador, quebrantador, contraventor, infractor.

infumed [in'fju:md], *a.* desecado al humo.

infundibular [infʌn'dibju:lər], *a.* infundibuliforme.

infuriate [in'fju:rieit], *v.t.* enfurecer, irritar, enojar, hacer rabioso, volver loco.

infuriate, infuriated, *a.* enfurecido, furioso, rabioso.

infuscation [infʌs'keiʃən], *s.* obscurecimiento.

infuse [in'fju:z], *v.t.* infundir, inculcar, imbuir, instilar; comunicar a, introducir en, inspirar; poner en infusión; infiltrar.

infused, *a.* infundido, infuso. — *p.p.* [INFUSE].

infuser, *s.* el que infunde o anima.

infusibility, infusibleness, *s.* infusibilidad.

infusible, *a.* infusible, infundible, que no sufre fusión.

infusion [in'fju:ʒən], *s.* infusión, instilación, inspiración; (*farm.*) maceración.

infusive, *a.* capaz de infundir.

infusoria [infju:'zɔ:riə], *s.pl.* infusorios.

infusorial, *a.* infusorio; *infusorial earth,* tierra de infusorios.

infusorian, infusory, *s., a.* infusorio.

ingate ['ingeit], *s.* (*fund.*) bebedero; (*min.*) boca de una galería.

ingathering ['ingæðəriŋ], *s.* cosecha, acto de recoger los frutos.

ingeminate [in'dʒemineit], *a.* doble, duplicado, reduplicado, repetido. — *v.t.* duplicar, reduplicar, repetir.

ingemination, *s.* duplicación, reduplicación.

ingenerable, *a.* ingenerable.

ingenerate [in'dʒenəreit], *a.* innato; ingénito. — *v.t.* engendrar, procrear, producir.

ingenious, *a.* ingenioso, talentoso, mañoso; apto, hábil, sutil.

ingeniousness [in'dʒi:niəsnis], *s.* ingeniosidad, sutileza, destreza, industria.

ingenuity [indʒen'ju:iti], *s.* ingeniosidad, facultad inventiva; maña, destreza, habilidad; ingeniatura.

ingenuous [in'dʒenju:əs], *a.* ingenuo, franco, sincero, natural, claro, real.

ingenuousness, *s.* ingenuidad, candidez, sinceridad.

ingest [in'dʒest], *v.t.* ingerir.

ingesta, *s.pl.* alimento tomado; (*fig.*) cosas ingeridas o incorporadas.

ingestion, *s.* ingestión.

ingle ['ingəl], *s.* fuego, llama.

inglenook ['ingəlnuk], *s.* rincón del hogar.

inglorious [in'glɔ:riəs], *a.* afrentoso, vergonzoso, ignominioso; obscuro, bajo, deshonroso.

ingloriousness, *s.* ignominia, deshonra, vileza, obscuridad.

ingoing [in'gouiŋ], *a.* entrante, que entra. — *s.* entrada, ingreso.

ingot ['ingət], *s.* lingote; *ingot of copper,* galápago de cobre; *ingot of gold,* tejo de oro; riel, barra o padazo de metal.

ingraft [in'grɑ:ft], *v.t.* (*agr.*) injertar; (*fig.*) grabar, inculcar, inspirar, imprimir.

ingrafting, *s.* injertación, enjertación, acto de injertar.

ingraftment, *s.* injerto, enjerto.

ingrain [in'grein], *a.* teñido en rama; inculcado, impreso; *ingrain carpet,* alfombra teñida en rama.

ingrain, *v.t.* teñir en rama; teñir con grana o cochinilla; fijar, impregnar.

ingrained, *a.* (*fig.*) innato, congénito.

ingrate ['ingreit], *s., a.* ingrato, desagradecido, desapacible. — *s.* persona ingrata.

ingratiate [in'greiʃieit], *v.t.* insinuarse, captarse, granjearse o ganar la voluntad o el favor, congraciarse.

ingratiating, *a.* obsequioso.

ingratitude [in'grætitju:d], *s.* ingratitud, desagradecimiento.

ingredient [in'gri:diənt], *s.* ingrediente.

ingress ['ingres], *s.* ingreso, entrada; acceso, facultad de entrar.

ingression, *s.* ingreso, entrada, incorporación.

ingrowing [in'grouiŋ], *a.* que crece hacia dentro; *ingrowing nail,* uñero.

inguinal [in'gwainəl], *a.* inguinal.

ingulf [in'gʌlf], *v.t.* sumir, engolfar, embocar, hacer arrebatarse, precipitar con violencia.

ingurgitate [in'gə:rdʒiteit], *v.i.* tragar, beber copiosamente; hartarse. — *s.* voracidad, ingurgitación, glotonería.

inhabit [in'hæbit], *v.t.* habitar, ocupar. — *v.i.* (*ant.*) habitar, residir, vivir.

inhabitability, *s.* habitabilidad.

inhabitable [in'hæbitəbəl], *a.* habitable; (*ant.*) inhabitable, no habitable.

inhabitance, *s.* habitación, morada, residencia.

inhabitant, *s.* habitante, habitador, morador, vecino, lugareño.

inhabitation, *s.* habitación, domicilio, morada.

inhabited, *a.* poblado, habitado. — *p.p.* [INHABIT].

inhabiter, *s.* (*fem.* **inhabiter, inhabitress**) habitador, morador, habitante, vecino.

inhalation [inhə'leiʃən], *s.* inspiración, acto de inspirar; (*med.*) inhalación.

inhale [in'heil], *v.t.* inspirar, aspirar, inhalar.

inharmonic [inhɑ:'mɔnik], **inharmonical,** *a.* dísono, disonante, inarmónico.

inharmonious, *a.* discordante; inarmónico, poco armonioso, disonante.

inhaul ['inhɔːl], s. (mar.) cabo que sirve para halar una berlinga, como por ejemplo el botalón de foque.

inhere [in'hiər], v.i. inherir, ser inherente, tener unión íntima.

inherence, inherency, s. inherencia.

inherent, a. inherente, inmanente; intrínseco, innato, esencial.

inherit [in'herit], v.t. heredar. — v.i. suceder como heredero.

inheritable, a. heredable, hereditable.

inheritance, s. herencia, patrimonio, abolengo.

inheritor, s. heredero.

inheritress, inheritrix, s. heredera.

inhesion [in'hiːʒən], s. inherencia, unión, f., adhesión.

inhibit [in'hibit], v.t. inhibir, detener, contener, impedir; vedar, prohibir; (igl.) prohibir.

inhibition [inhi'biʃən], s. inhibición, impedimento, prohibición; (for.) inhibición.

inhibitory [in'hibitəri], **inhibitive** [in'hibitiv], a. inhibitorio.

inhive [in'haiv], v.t. enjambrar.

inhospitable [in'hɔspitəbəl], a. inhospitalario, inhospedable, inhospitable.

inhospitality [inhɔspi'tæliti], s. inhospitalidad.

inhuman [in'hjuːmən], a. inhumano, cruel, desalmado, riguroso, desapiadado.

inhumanity [inhju:'mæniti], s. inhumanidad, desalmamiento, crueldad, barbarie, f.

inhumation [inhju:'meiʃən], s. entierro, sepultura.

inhume [in'hjuːm], **inhumate** ['inhjuːmeit], v.t. inhumar, sepultar, enterrar.

inimical [in'imikəl], a. enemigo, hostil, contrario, opuesto.

inimitability, s. imposibilidad de ser imitado.

inimitable [in'imitəbəl], a. inimitable.

inimitableness, s. estado o calidad de inimitable.

iniquitous [in'ikwitəs], a. inicuo, injusto, malvado, facineroso.

iniquity [in'ikwiti], s. iniquidad, injusticia, perfidia, pravedad, maldad, picardía.

initial [in'iʃəl], a. inicial, incipiente. — s. (letra) inicial, f.

initiate [in'iʃieit], v.t. iniciar, promover, empezar, comenzar, poner en pie, entablar, admitir, introducir. — v.i. tomar la iniciativa.

initiate, initiated, a. adepto, iniciado, instruido.

initiating, a. iniciativo.

initiation [iniʃi'eiʃən], s. iniciación, estreno, principio, comienzo, primer uso.

initiative [in'iʃiətiv], a. iniciativo. — s. primer paso, iniciativa.

initiator, s. iniciador.

initiatory, a. iniciativo.

inject [in'dʒekt], v.t. inyectar; introducir.

injection, s. inyección.

injector, s. inyector.

injoin [in'dʒɔin], v.t. encargar, ordenar.

injudicial [indʒuː'diʃəl], a. informal, ilegal.

injudicious [indʒuː'diʃəs], a. indiscreto, sin discreción, poco juicioso, imprudente.

injudiciousness, s. indiscreción, imprudencia.

injunction [in'dʒʌŋkʃən], s. mandato, mandamiento, precepto, requerimiento; (for.) embargo, entredicho.

injure ['indʒəɪ], v.t. injuriar, ofender, agraviar; menoscabar, molestar, dañar, lastimar, perjudicar, lisiar.

injurer, s. injuriador, agraviador, injuriante, ofensor.

injurious [in'dʒuːriəs], a. dañoso, pernicioso, perjudicial, dañino, nocivo, ofensivo, contumelioso.

injuriousness, s. injuria, daño, perjuicio, menoscabo, nocividad.

injury ['indʒəri], s. injuria, agravio, daño, perjuicio, sinrazón, f., mal, lesión, menoscabo, detrimento; afrenta, ofensa, baldón, insulto.

injustice [in'dʒʌstis], s. injusticia, agravio, sinrazón, f., entuerto.

ink [iŋk], s. tinta; *indelible* o *marking-ink*, tinta indeleble, tinta de marcar; *copying-ink*, tinta de copiar; *India-ink*, tinta china; *invisible ink*, tinta simpática; *ink duct*, (impr.) tintero de prensa; *ink-roller*, (impr.) rulo, rodillo. — v.t. entintar, dar tinta a, teñir o tiznar con tinta, untar de tinta.

ink-ball, s. bala de entintar.

ink-bottle, s. tintero, botella de tinta.

ink-eraser, s. raedor.

inkhorn ['iŋkhɔːn], s. tintero de bolsillo. — a. pomposo, pedantesco.

inkiness, s. entintamiento.

inkle ['iŋkəl], s. cinta.

inkling ['iŋkliŋ], s. sospecha, noción; (ant.) insinuación.

inkmaker, s. fabricante de tinta.

inknot [in'nɔt], v.t. atar, añudar.

inkstand, inkwell, s. tintero.

inky ['iŋki], a. parecido a la tinta; manchado de tinta, cubierto de tinta.

inlace [in'leis], v.t. adornar con cordones.

inlaid [in'leid], pret., p.p. [INLAY]; *inlaid work*, embutido, incrustación, taracea.

inland ['inlənd], a. interior; nacional, del país, regional. — s. interior de un país. — adv. tierra adentro.

inlander, s. el que habita tierra adentro; tierradentreño.

inlay ['inlei], v.t. (pret., p.p. **inlaid**) embutir; taracear, ataracear, incrustar, hacer ataujía o mosaico.

inlay, s. taracea, embutido.

inlayer, s. incrustador, obrero que hace taracea, operario en taracea.

inlaying, s. arte de ataracear, embutir o incrustar.

inlet ['inlet], s. entrada, abra, cala, caleta, ensenada; estero, estuario; boca de entrada.

inlock [in'lɔk], s. encerrar, encajar.

inly ['inli], adv. interiormente.

inmate ['inmeit], s. inquilino, interno, huésped, habitador.

inmost ['inməst], **innermost** ['inəɹməst], a. íntimo, profundo, recóndito, secreto, oculto.

inn [in], s. posada, mesón, fonda, parador, venta, hospedería, hostal; *Inns of Court*, colegios de abogados en Londres.

innate [i'neit], a. innato, propio, natural, connatural, ingénito.

innately, adv. por modo ingénito; naturalmente.

innateness, s. calidad o estado de innato o ingénito.

innavigable [i'nævigəbəl], a. innavegable.

inner ['inəɹ], a. interior; *inner tube*, cámara de aire.

innermost, a. [INMOST].

innervate ['inəɹveit], *v.t.* proveer de nervios; causar inervación o estímulo nervioso.

innervation, *s.* inervación.

innerve [i'nəːɹv], *v.t.* dar vigor, dar fuerza, vigorizar.

innings ['iniŋz], *s.* (en cricket, base-ball, etc.) turno del batsman; (*fig.*) turno en el mando o gobierno.

innkeeper ['inki:rəɹ], *s.* posadero, fondista, *m.f.*, mesonero, hospedero, hostelero, tabernero.

innocence ['inosəns], **innocency** ['inosənsi], *s.* inocencia, pureza; simplicidad, sencillez.

innocent ['inosənt], *a.* inocente, puro; simple, cándido; innocuo, inofensivo; tonto. — *s.* inocente, párvulo; tonto, inocentón.

innocuous [i'nɔkjuːəs], *a.* innocuo, inocente, inofensivo; sencillo.

innocuousness, *s.* innocuidad.

innominate [i'nɔminit], *a.* (*anat.*) innominado; anónimo.

innovate ['inoveit], *v.t.* innovar, hacer innovaciones.

innovation, *s.* innovación, innovamiento, novedad.

innovator, *s.* innovador.

innoxious [i'nɔkʃəs], *a.* innocuo, innocivo; inocente.

innoxiousness, *s.* innocuidad.

innuendo [inju:'endou], *s.* indirecta, pulla, insinuación.

innumerability, *s.* innumerabilidad.

innumerable [i'njuːmərəbəl], *a.* innumerable, incontable.

innumerableness, *s.* innumerabilidad.

innumerous [i'njuːmərəs], *a.* innumerable.

innutrition [inju:'triʃən], *s.* falta de nutrición.

inobservable [inɔb'zəːɹvəbəl], *a.* inobservable.

inobservance, *s.* inobservancia.

inoculate [i'nɔkjuːleit], *v.t.*, *v.i.* (*med.*) inocular; (*fig.*) imbuir, infundir; inficionar, infectar; (*agr.*) injertar en escudo.

inoculation [inɔkju:leiʃən], *s.* (*med.*) inoculación; infección, contaminación; (*agr.*) injertación en escudo.

inoculator, *s.* inoculador.

inodorous [in'oudərəs], *a.* inodoro, sin olor.

inoffensive [ino'fensiv], *a.* inofensivo.

inoffensiveness, *s.* inocencia, calidad de inofensivo.

inofficial [ino'fiʃəl], *a.* no oficial.

inoperative [in'ɔpərətiv], *a.* ineficaz.

inopportune [in'ɔpəɹtjuːn], *a.* inoportuno, inconveniente.

inopportuneness, *s.* inoportunidad.

inordinacy, *s.* desarreglo, desorden; exceso.

inordinate [in'ɔːɹdinit], *a.* inordenado, desordenado, desarreglado, irregular, excesivo.

inordinateness, *s.* desorden, demasía, exceso.

inorganic [inɔːɹ'gænik], *a.* inorgánico.

inosculate [in'ɔskjuːleit], *v.t.* unir por anastomosis. — *v.i.* anastomarse.

inosculation [inɔskjuːleiʃən], *s.* anastomosis, *f.*

inquest ['iŋkwest], *s.* (*for.*) indagación, examen, averiguación, información o pesquisa judicial; jurado que hace una pesquisa; juicio de indemnización.

inquiet [in'kwaiət], *v.t.* inquietar, destorbar.

inquietude, *s.* inquietud, descontento, desasosiego.

inquirable [in'kwairəbəl], *a.* investigable.

inquire [in'kwaiəɹ], *v.t.*, *v.i.* inquirir, averi-

guar, examinar, preguntar, informarse; *to inquire into*, hacer preguntas sobre; investigar, examinar; *to inquire about* (o *after* o *for*), preguntar por; *to inquire of*, preguntar, investigar.

inquirer, *s.* inquiridor, examinador, investigador, escrutador, pesquisidor, averiguador, preguntón.

inquiry [in'kwairi], *s.* interrogación, indagación, examinación, pesquisa, escudriñamiento, pregunta, información, investigación.

inquisition [inkwi'ziʃən], *s.* inquisición; escudriñamiento, investigación; *the Inquisition*, el Santo Oficio, Inquisición.

inquisitional, *a.* inquisitorial.

inquisitive [in'kwizətiv], *a.* inquisitivo, curioso, preguntón, investigador.

inquisitiveness, *s.* curiosidad, deseo de saber.

inquisitor, *s.* inquisidor; inquiridor, investigador.

inquisitorial [inkwizi'tɔːriəl], *a.* inquisitorial.

inracinate [in'ræsineit], *v.t.* arraigar, implantar.

inroad ['inroud], *s.* incursión, irrupción, invasión, correría.

inrush ['inrʌʃ], *s.* empuje, invasión.

insalivate [in'sæliveit], *v.t.* insalivar, mezclar con saliva.

insalivation, *s.* insalivación.

insalubrious [insə'ljuːbriəs], *a.* insalubre, malsano.

insalubrity, *s.* insalubridad.

insane [in'sein], *a.* loco, insano, demente, insensato; de locos o para locos; *home for the insane* (o *asylum*), casa de locos, manicomio.

insanitary [in'sænitəri], *a.* antihigiénico, malsano.

insanity [in'sæniti], *s.* locura, insania, manía, demencia, enajenación mental.

insatiable [in'seiʃəbəl], *a.* insaciable.

insatiableness, insatiateness, *s.* insaciabilidad.

insatiate [in'seiʃət], *a.* insaciable.

inscribe [in'skraib], *v.t.* inscribir, grabar; dedicar; apuntar.

inscriber, *s.* el que inscribe.

inscription [in'skripʃən], *s.* inscripción; registro; rótulo, letrero; dedicatoria.

inscriptive, *a.* inscrito, inscripto.

inscrutability, *s.* inescrutabilidad.

inscrutable [in'skruːtəbəl], *a.* inescrutable, insondable, inescudriñable.

inseam ['insiːm], *s.* costura interior.

insect ['insekt], *s.* insecto; *insect-powder*, polvos insecticidas.

insectean, insectile, *a.* insectil.

insecticide [in'sektisaid], *s.* insecticida, *m.*

insection [in'sekʃən], *s.* incisión.

insectivorous [insek'tivərəs], *a.* insectívoro.

insecure [insi'kjuːəɹ], *a.* inseguro, poco firme, poco sólido; precario.

insecurity [insi'kjuːriti], *s.* inseguridad, incertidumbre; riesgo, peligro.

inseminate [in'semineit], *v.t.* fecundar; (*fig.*) implantar; (*ant.*) sembrar.

insensate [in'sensit], *a.* insensato.

insensibility [insensi'biliti], *s.* insensibilidad; insensatez, estupidez; torpeza.

insensible [in'sensibəl], *a.* insensible; duro de corazón, impasible, indiferente; imperceptible.

insensibleness, *s.* insensibilidad.

insentient [in'senʃənt], *a.* insensible.

inseparability, inseparableness, *s.* inseparabilidad.

inseparable [in'sepərəbəl], *a.* inseparable, indivisible.

inseparate [in'sepərit], *a.* no separado, unido.

insert [in'sə:.t], *v.t.* insertar, introducir, ingerir, encajar, meter, intercalar, inserir, hacer insertar.

insertion [in'sə:.ɪʃən], *s.* inserción; metimiento; (*cost.*) entredós, tira labrada.

inserviceable [in'sə:.ɪvisəbəl], *a.* inservible.

inset ['inset], *s.* intercalación, adición; flujo o marea montante. — *v.t.* fijar, meter, plantar.

inshell [in'ʃel], *v.t.* encascarar.

inshore ['inʃɔ:.ɹ], *a.* cercano a la orilla. — *adv.* hacia la orilla, cerca de la orilla.

inshrine [in'ʃrain], *v.t.* guardar como reliquia.

insiccation [insi'keiʃən], *s.* desecación.

inside [in'said], *a.* interior, interno, que está dentro o adentro. — *s.* interior, la parte de adentro; forro; contenido; viajero del interior; (*fam.*) entrañas, estómago. — *adv.* dentro, adentro, en el interior; *inside out,* de dentro afuera; al revés.

insidious [in'sidiəs], *a.* insidioso, engañoso, solapado.

insidiousness, *s.* insidia; traición.

insight ['insait], *s.* discernimiento, perspicacia; percepción clara; conocimiento profundo.

insignia [in'signiə], *s.pl.* insignias, estandartes.

insignificance, insignificancy, *s.* insignificancia, poca importancia, friolera, nulidad.

insignificant [insig'nifikənt], *a.* insignificante, insignificativo, frívolo, despreciable, nulo.

insincere [insin'siə.ɹ], *a.* insincero, doble, hipócrita; turbado, agitado; corrompido.

insincerity [insin'seriti], *s.* insinceridad, hipocresía, falsedad.

insinuate [in'sinju:eit], *v.t.* insinuar, apuntar, sugerir, indicar, dar a entender. — *v.r.* insinuarse, introducirse, intimar. — *v.i.* insinuarse; echar indirectas.

insinuating, *a.* insinuativo.

insinuation, *s.* insinuación; sugestión, pulla, indirecta.

insinuative, *a.* insinuante, insinuativo.

insinuator, *s.* insinuante, insinuador.

insipid [in'sipid], *a.* insípido, desaborido, desabrido, soso, insulso.

insipidity [insi'piditi], **insipidness,** *s.* insipidez, desabrimiento, desabor, sosería, insulsez.

insist [in'sist], *v.i.* insistir, instar, porfiar, persistir; *to insist on,* insistir en; pedir enfáticamente; aseverar positivamente.

insistence, insistency, *s.* insistencia, porfía.

insistent [in'sistənt], *a.* insistente, porfiado, persistente; conspicuo.

insition [in'siʃən], *s.* injertación.

insnare [in'snɛə.ɹ], *v.t.* tender un lazo, entrampar, engañar.

insobriety [inso'braiiti], *s.* embriaguez, borrachera, falta de sobriedad.

insolate ['insoleit], *v.t.* insolar, secar al sol.

insolation, *s.* acto de secar al sol; blanqueo; (*med.*) insolación.

insole ['insoul], *s.* plantilla.

insolence, insolency, *s.* insolencia, demasía, procacidad, atrevimiento, descaro, altanería, orgullo.

insolent ['insolənt], *a.* insolente, descomedido, procaz, altanero, atrevido, arrogante.

insolubility, insolubleness, *s.* indisolubilidad, insolubilidad.

insoluble [in'sɔlju:bəl], *a.* insoluble, indisoluble.

insolvable [in'sɔlvəbəl], *a.* insoluble; inexplicable; (*ant.*) que no se puede saldar o pagar.

insolvency [in'sɔlvensi], *s.* insolvencia.

insolvent [in'sɔlvənt], *a.* insolvente.

insomnia [in'sɔmniə], *s.* insomnio, desvelo.

insomnious, *a.* insomne, desvelado.

insomnolence [in'sɔmnoləns], *s.* falta de sueño.

insomuch [insou'mʌtʃ], *adv.* de manera que, de suerte que, de modo que, de tal modo que, hasta el punto que.

inspect [in'spekt], *v.t.* reconocer, examinar, registrar, investigar, inspeccionar.

inspection, *s.* inspección, visita, reconocimiento, registro, examen.

inspector, *s.* inspector, interventor, superintendente, sobrestante, veedor, registrador, contralor; jefe de policía.

inspectorate [in'spektərət], *s.* distrito, cargo o empleo de un inspector.

insphere [in'sfeir], *v.t.* colocar en una esfera.

inspirable, *a.* inspirable.

inspiration [inspi'reiʃən], *s.* inspiración.

inspirationist, *s.* defensor de la doctrina de la inspiración.

inspiratory, *a.* inspirador, inspirativo, inspiratorio.

inspire [in'spaiə.ɹ], *v.t.* inspirar, aspirar, inhalar; instilar, imbuir, comunicar; estimular, iluminar, animar; sugerir. — *v.i.* inspirar el aire; soplar suavemente.

inspirer, *s.* inspirador.

inspirit [in'spirit], *v.t.* alentar, vigorizar, animar, estimular, infundir espíritu.

inspissate [in'spiseit], *v.t.* espesar, trabar, condensar, incrasar. — *a.* espeso.

inspissation, *s.* condensación, acto de espesar.

instability [instə'biliti], *s.* instabilidad, mutabilidad, inconstancia.

instable [in'steibəl], *a.* inconstante, variable, voltario, vario, mudable.

install [in'stɔ:l], *v.t.* instalar; dar posesión; colocar.

installation, *s.* instalación; montaje, emplazamiento.

instalment [in'stɔ:lmənt], *s.* (*com.*) plazo; entrega; instalación.

instance ['instəns], *s.* caso; ejemplo; ruego, instancia, solicitación; prueba; (*for.*) instancia, expediente; *in the first instance,* en primer lugar; *for instance,* por ejemplo; *at the instance of,* a ruego de, a instancia de. — *v.t.* poner por caso, citar como ejemplo o prueba.

instancy, *s.* insistencia, urgencia, instancia; solicitación porfiada.

instant ['instənt], *a.* inminente, perentorio, importuno, inmediato, pronto, actual, presente, corriente, al instante. — *s.* instante, punto, momento, tiempo señalado, santiamén, periquete; mes corriente o presente.

instantaneous [instən'teiniəs], *a.* instantáneo, hecho en un instante.

instanter [in'stæntə.ɹ], **instantly** ['instəntli], *adv.* al instante, instantáneamente, inmediatamente, en un momento.

instate [in'steit], *v.t.* instalar, colocar.
instead [in'sted], *adv.* en lugar (de), en vez (de).
instep ['instep], *s.* empeine o garganta del pie; parte anterior de la pata trasera de una caballería.
instigate ['instigeit], *v.t.* instigar, incitar, excitar, mover, espolear, fomentar.
instigation, *s.* instigación, provocación, sugestión.
instigator, *s.* instigador, concitador, incitador.
instil [in'stil], *v.t.* instilar; (*fig.*) insinuar, inculcar, inspirar, infundir, introducir.
instillation [insti'leiʃən], **instil(l)ment**, *s.* instilación; insinuación.
instiller, *s.* el que instila o insinúa.
instinct ['instiŋt], *s.* instinto.
instinct [in'stiŋt], *a.* animado, movido, impulsado.
instinctive [in'stiŋtiv], *a.* instintivo, espontáneo, impulsado.
institor, *s.* (*for.*) institor, factor.
institute ['institjuːt], *v.t.* instituir, establecer, crear, fundar; poner por obra, poner en operación; empezar, entablar, incoar, iniciar; (*igl.*) conferir un beneficio. — *s.* instituto, establecimiento; principio, regla, máxima. — *pl.* **institutes**, instituta, instituciones.
institution [insti'tjuːʃən], *s.* institución; instituto; fundación, establecimiento; comienzo, acto incoativo; derecho positivo; educación, enseñanza; (*for.*) nombramiento de heredero; (*igl.*) institución canónica.
institutional, institutionary, *a.* institucional; prescrito; rudimentario, elemental.
institutive, *a.* instituente, instituidor, instituyente; instituido, establecido.
institutor, *s.* instituidor, fundador, institutor.
institutress, *s.* fundadora.
instruct [in'strʌkt], *v.t.* instruir, enseñar, educar, amaestrar, doctrinar, aleccionar, enterar, imponer, dar órdenes a, dar instrucciones a, mandar.
instructer, *s.* [INSTRUCTOR].
instructible, *a.* instruible.
instruction [in'strʌkʃən], *s.* instrucción, enseñanza, educación, enseñamiento; conocimiento o saber adquirido.
instructive, *a.* instructivo.
instructiveness, *s.* calidad de instructivo; poder de instruir.
instructor, *s.* instructor, educador, maestro, pedagogo.
instructress, *s.f.* instructora, institutriz, maestra.
instrument ['instruːmənt], *s.* instrumento; máquina, herramienta, utensilio; (*for.*) escritura, acta, instrumento, documento; medio, agente; *wind instrument*, instrumento de viento; *stringed instrument*, instrumento de cuerda. — *v.t.* (*mús.*) instrumentar.
instrumental [instruː'mentəl], *a.* instrumental.
instrumentalist, instrumentist, *s.* (*mús.*) instrumentista, *m.f.*
instrumentality [instruːmen'tæliti], *s.* agencia, mediación.
instrumentation, *s.* (*mús.*) instrumentación; ejecución instrumental; agencia.
insubjection [insəb'dʒekʃən], *s.* insumisión, inobediencia.
insubordinate [insə'bɔːdinit], *a.* insubordinado, refractario.
insubordination, *s.* insubordinación, indisciplina.

insubstantial [insəb'stænʃəl], *a.* insubstancial; irreal.
insufferable [in'sʌfərəbl], *a.* insufrible, detestable, insoportable, pesado, intolerable.
insufficience, insufficiency, *s.* insuficiencia, incapacidad.
insufficient [insə'fiʃənt], *a.* insuficiente; incapaz, inepto, inhábil, impotente.
insufficiently, *adv.* insuficientemente; por carta de menos.
insufflate ['insəfleit], *v.t.* insuflar, soplar en o sobre; respirar sobre.
insufflation, *s.* soplo; (*med.*) insuflación.
insufflator, *s.* insuflador.
insular ['insjuːlər], *a.* insular, isleño; estrecho de miras, escaso, iliberal, mezquino; aislado.
insularity [insjuː'læriti], *s.* estado o cualidad insular o isleña; iliberalidad, estrechez de miras.
insulate ['insjuːleit], *v.t.* aislar.
insulated, *a.* aislado, apartado; exento, solitario, escueto; (*astr.*) remoto; (*elec.*) aislado.
insulation, *s.* aislamiento.
insulator, *s.* aislador.
insult ['insʌlt], *s.* insulto, denuesto, ultraje, afrenta, injuria; *to add insult to injury*, sobre cuernos, penitencia.
insult [in'sʌlt], *v.t.* insultar, ultrajar, denigrar, pisar, ajar, injuriar, afrentar, despreciar.
insulter, *s.* insultador, denostador.
insulting, *a.* insultante, injurioso, ultrajante, insolente.
insuperability, insuperableness, *s.* calidad de insuperable.
insuperable [in'sjuːpərəbl], *a.* insuperable, invencible.
insupportable [insə'pɔːtəbl], *a.* insoportable, insufrible, inaguantable, intolerable.
insupportableness, *s.* calidad de insoportable.
insuppressible [insə'presəbl], *a.* que no se puede suprimir.
insurable [in'ʃuərəbl], *a.* asegurable, capaz de ser asegurado.
insurance [in'ʃuərəns], *s.* (*com.*) seguro, aseguramiento, aseguración; prima o premio del seguro; sistema de seguros; garantía, seguridad; cantidad total del seguro; *fire insurance*, seguro contra incendio; *life insurance*, seguro de vida; *endowment insurance*, seguro dotal; *accident insurance*, seguro contra accidentes; *insurance agent*, agente de seguros; *insurance company*, compañía de seguros; *insurance policy*, póliza de seguros.
insure [in'ʃuər], *v.t.* (*com.*) asegurar; afianzar, garantizar. — *v.i.* asegurarse.
insurer, *s.* asegurador.
insurgent [in'səːrdʒənt], *s.*, *a.* insurrecto, insurgente, sublevado, rebelde.
insurmountable [insəːr'mauntəbl], *a.* insuperable, incontrastable, insalvable.
insurrection [insə'rekʃən], *s.* insurrección, rebelión, levantamiento, conjuración, sublevación, sedición, tumulto.
insurrectional, insurrectionary, *a.* insurreccional, revolucionario, tumultuoso, rebelde.
insurrectionist, *s.* insurrecto.
insusceptible [insə'septəbl], *a.* no susceptible, insensible.
intact [in'tækt], *a.* intacto, íntegro.
intactness, *s.* integridad.
intagliated, *a.* entallado, estampado, grabado.

intaglio [in'tæljou], *s.* obra de talla, obra de entalladura; (*joy.*) entalle.

intake ['inteik], *s.* toma; (*tej.*) menguado; orificio de entrada; (*mec.*) válvula de admisión; admisión.

intangibility, intangibleness, *s.* cualidad de intangible.

intangible [in'tænjibəl], *a.* intangible; incomprensible; impalpable.

integer ['inted3əɹ], *s.* entero, número entero, total.

integral ['intigrəl], **integrant** ['integrənt], *a.* íntegro, integrante, integral; total, entero, completo, perfecto, sano; intrínseco. — *s.* (*mat.*) integral; *integral calculus,* cálculo integral.

integralism, integrality, *s.* integridad.

integrate ['integreit], *v.t.* integrar, formar un todo; indicar la suma; (*mat.*) integrar. — *v.i.* integrarse, completarse.

integration, *s.* integración, reintegro.

integrity [in'tegriti], *s.* integridad, honradez, probidad, entereza.

integument [in'tegju:mənt], *s.* tegumento, integumento, cubierta natural, túnica.

integumental, integumentary, *a.* integumentario.

intellect ['intelekt], *s.* intelecto, entendimiento, intelectiva, inteligencia; gente de talento.

intellection, *s.* intelección.

intellective, *a.* intelectivo.

intellectual [inte'lektjuəl], *a.* intelectual, ideal, mental. — *s.* intelectual.

intellectuality [intelektju:'æliti], *s.* entendimiento, intelectualidad, facultad intelectual.

intelligence [in'telid3əns], *s.* inteligencia; entendimiento, mente, *f.*, intelectiva, talento; informe; penetración; correspondencia mutua, harmonía, acuerdo; noticia, aviso; conocimiento, comprensión; ser inteligente; *intelligence bureau,* oficina de información; *to give intelligence,* dar aviso; *latest intelligence,* últimas noticias; *Intelligence Service,* Inteligencia.

intelligencer, *s.* mensajero, noticiero, espía, *m.f.*

intelligent [in'telid3ənt], *a.* inteligente, ilustrado, talentoso; sensato, sabio, instruido, perito.

intelligibility, intelligibleness, *s.* comprensibilidad, claridad, perspicuidad.

intelligible [in'telid3əbəl], *a.* inteligible, distinto, claro, perspicuo.

intemperance [in'tempərəns], *s.* intemperancia, exceso, destemplanza, desarreglo.

intemperate [in'tempərit], *a.* destemplado, intemperante, desenfrenado, inmoderado, desarreglado, desmandado, desmedido, excesivo.

intemperateness, *s.* inmoderación, intemperancia; demasía, exceso; intemperie, *f.*

intend [in'tend], *v.t.* intentar, proponerse, proyectar, aplicar, destinar, señalar, determinar; querer decir, significar.

intendancy, *s.* intendencia.

intendant, *s.* intendente.

intended, *s.* (*fam.*) desposado, desposada, prometido, prometida, novio, novia.

intendedly, *adv.* adredo, exprofeso, con intención.

intendment, *s.* (*for.*) intento o espíritu de una ley; (*ant.*) intención, designio.

intense [in'tens], *a.* intenso, fuerte, ardiente, fogoso, intensivo, estirado, excesivo, vivo, violento, vehemente; sumo, extremado; (*foto.*) duro (negativo); esforzado.

intenseness, *s.* intensidad, vehemencia, vigor, fuerza; fogosidad, ardor.

intensifier [in'tensifaiəɹ], *s.* el que o lo que hace más intenso; (*foto.*) baño para reforzar un negativo.

intensify [in'tensifai], *v.t.* hacer más intenso; (*foto.*) reforzar un negativo. — *v.i.* volverse intenso.

intension [in'tenʃən], *s.* intensión; intensidad; tensión; (*lóg.*) contenido.

intensity, *s.* intensidad, fuerza, exceso, vehemencia, vigor; tensión; (*fís.*) intensidad, energía; (*foto.*) fuerza de un negativo.

intensive [in'tensiv], *a.* intensivo; completo; entero; (*lóg.*) relativo al contenido; (*gram.*) enfático.

intent [in'tent], *a.* atento, dedicado, asiduo; resuelto a, decidido; absorto; *to be intent upon,* pensar sólo en. — *s.* intento; designio, intención, deseo, ánimo, propósito; *to all intents and purposes,* en todos sentidos, prácticamente; (*for.*) para todos los casos y efectos que haya lugar.

intention [in'tenʃən], *s.* intención, determinación, designio, ánimo, fin, mira; (*cir.*) curso o procedimiento natural; (*for.*) propósito deliberado, consciente; *healing by first intention,* (*cir.*) cura de primera intención, sin supuración; *healing by second intention,* cura por cicatrización, después de la supuración.

intentional, *a.* intencional.

intentness, *s.* aplicación asidua, afición, atención.

inter [in'təːɹ], *v.t.* enterrar, soterrar, sepultar, inhumar.

inter- ['intəɹ], *prefijo,* entre, en medio, mutuamente.

interact [intəɹ'ækt], *v.t.* obrar entre sí, recíprocamente; afectar el uno al otro.

interact ['intəɹækt], *s.* (*teat.*) entreacto; intermedio.

interaction, *s.* acción recíproca; acción intermedia; influencia recíproca.

interarticular [intəɹɑːɹ'tikju:ləɹ], *a.* interarticular.

interbreed [intəɹ'briːd], *v.t., v.i.* cruzar, producir híbridos.

intercalary [intəɹ'kæləri], *a.* intercalar.

intercalate, *v.t.* intercalar, interpolar, interponer.

intercalation, *s.* intercalación, interpolación.

intercede [intəɹ'siːd], *v.i.* interceder, abogar, mediar, interponerse, hablar (por).

interceder, *s.* intercesor.

interceding, *s.* intercesión, mediación.

intercept [intəɹ'sept], *v.t.* interceptar; sorprender, coger, atajar, detener, obstruir, cerrar el paso.

interception, *s.* interceptación, atajo.

interceptor, *s.* avión de caza.

intercession, *s.* intercesión, mediación, oración.

intercessor [intəɹ'sesəɹ], *s.* intercesor, mediador; administrador durante un interregno; (*igl.*) obispo que administra una sede vacante.

intercessory, *s.* intercesorio.

interchain [intəɹ'tʃein], *v.t.* encadenar, entrelazar.

interchange [intəɹ'tʃeindʒ], *v.t.* alternar, permutar, trocar, variar, cambiar. — *v.i.* alternarse, trocarse, suceder con alternación.

interchange, interchangement, *s.* intercambio, correspondencia; tráfico, negociación, comercio; permutación, permuta, vicisitud, sucesión mutua.

interchangeability, interchangeableness, *s.* permutabilidad, cualidad de permutable.

interchangeable [intəɹ'tʃeindʒəbəl], *a.* permutable; intercambiable; recíproco, mutuo; sucesivo.

interchangeably, *adv.* alternativamente, recíprocamente, mutuamente.

intercipient [intəɹ'sipiənt], *s., a.* interceptador, atajador; (cosa) que intercepta.

interclude [intəɹ'klu:d], *v.t.* obstruir, interceptar; tapar, ocultar.

interclusion, *s.* interceptación, obstrucción.

intercolumnar [intəɹkə'lʌmnəɹ], *a.* (anat., arq.) intercolumnar.

intercolumniation, *s.* intercolumnio.

intercommunicate [intəɹko'mju:nikeit], *v.i.* comunicarse con otro, mantener comunicación.

intercommunication, *s.* comunicación mutua.

intercostal [intəɹ'kɔstəl], *a.* intercostal.

intercourse ['intəɹko:ɹs], *s.* comercio, tráfico; comunicación, correspondencia, roce, trato; (*com.*) intercambio, giro; *sexual intercourse,* coito, cópula.

intercross [intəɹ'krɔs], *v.t.* entrecruzar; hibridar, cruzar castas. — *v.i.* entrecruzarse.

intercrossing, *s.* cruzamiento.

intercurrence [intəɹ'kʌɹəns], *s.* ocurrencia, intervención.

intercurrent, *a.* intercurrente.

intercutaneous [intəɹkju:'teiniəs], *a.* intercutáneo.

interdependence, *s.* dependencia mutua.

interdependent [intəɹde'pendənt], *a.* dependiente uno de otro.

interdict [intəɹ'dikt], *v.t.* interdecir, vedar, prohibir, poner entredicho, entredecir.

interdict ['intəɹdikt], **interdiction** [intəɹ'dikʃən], *s.* veto, prohibición; interdicto, censura eclesiastica, interdicción, entredicho.

interdictive, interdictory, *a.* que interdice, veda o prohibe.

interdigital [intəɹ'didʒitəl], *a.* interdigital.

interest ['intəɹest], *v.t.* interesar, empeñar. — *v.i.* interesarse, tomar parte. — *s.* interés, provecho, utilidad, lucro, beneficio; curiosidad, atención; simpatía; (*com.*) rédito, interés; influencia, influjo, empeño; participación; *compound interest,* interés compuesto; *to put out on interest,* dar a interés.

interesting, *s.* interesante, atractivo.

interfere [intəɹ'fiəɹ], *v.i.* meterse, imponerse, interponerse, intervenir, mezclarse, entremeterse; embarazar, impedir, oponerse, poner obstáculos; chocar; (*vet.*) tropezar, rozarse un pie con el otro (los caballos).

interference, *s.* intervención, interposición, mediación; impedimento, obstáculo; (ópt.) interferencia; (rad.) parásitos.

interfering, *s.* oposición, intervención, interposición, contrariedad; (*vet.*) alcance, rozadura, tropezón, *f.* — *a.* entremetido.

interfluent [intəɹ'flu:ənt], **interfluous,** *a.* que fluye por medio de otras cosas.

interfuse [intəɹ'fju:z], *v.t.* hacer pasar a través de, hacer fluir juntamente, mezclar. — *v.i.* fluir uno en otro; mezclarse.

interfusion, *s.* mezcla, combinación.

interim ['intəɹim], *s.* intermedio, ínterin; *in the interim,* entre tanto, en el ínterin. — *a.* interino, provisional.

interior [in'tiəɹiəɹ], *a.* interior, interno. — *s.* interior, parte de adentro.

interjacent [intəɹ'dʒeisənt], *a.* interyacente, interpuesto.

interject [intəɹ'dʒekt], *v.t.* interponer, poner en medio, insertar. — *v.i.* interponerse, intervenir.

interjection, *s.* (gram.) interjección; intervención, interposición; exclamación.

interjoin [intəɹ'dʒɔin], *v.t.* unir mutuamente.

interlace [intəɹ'leis], *v.t.* entrelazar, entremezclar.

interlard [intəɹ'lɑ:ɹd], *v.t.* (coc.) mechar; interpolar, entreponer, insertar, entretejer, entremezclar.

interleave [intəɹ'li:v], *v.t.* interfoliar, interpaginar, interpolar.

interline [intəɹ'lain], *v.t.* interlinear, entrerrenglonar, escribir entre renglones.

interlinear [intəɹ'liniəɹ], **interlineary,** *a.* interlineal.

interlineation, interlining, *s.* interlineación, entrerrenglonadura, corrección interlineal.

interlining, *s.* (cost.) entretela.

interlink [intəɹ'liŋk], *v.t.* eslabonar, encadenar.

interlock [intəɹ'lɔk], *v.t., v.i.* trabar, engargantar, engranar; entrelazarse, unirse.

interlocution, *s.* interlocución, diálogo, plática.

interlocutor, *s.* interlocutor.

interlocutory [intəɹlo'kju:təɹi], *a.* dialogístico; interlocutorio.

interlope [inter'loup], *v.i.* entremeterse sin derecho; traficar sin licencia; mezclarse en bandos.

interloper, *s.* entremetido, intruso; (com.) intérlope.

interlude ['intəɹlu:d], *s.* intermedio, entremés; sainete, farsa o baile representado entre los actos de una comedia; (mús.) interludio.

interlunar [intəɹ'lu:nəɹ], **interlunary,** *a.* perteneciente al interlunio.

intermarriage [intəɹ'mæridʒ], *s.* matrimonio o casamiento de personas de distintas razas, matrimonio entre parientes.

intermarry [intəɹ'mæri], *v.i.* casarse (parientes o personas de distintas razas).

intermeddle [intəɹ'medəl], *v.t.* mezclar, entremezclar. — *v.i.* entremeterse, inmiscuirse, ingerirse, mezclarse, meterse.

intermeddler, *s.* entremetido, refitolero.

intermedial [intəɹ'mi:diəl], **intermediate** [intəɹ'mi:dʒit], *a.* intermedio, medio, medianero.

intermediary, *s., a.* intermediario, intermedio, medio, intermediado.

intermediate [intəɹ'mi:dieit], *v.i.* intervenir.

intermediately, *adv.* por intervención.

intermediation, *s.* intervención, mediación.

intermedium [intəɹ'mi:diəm], *s.* intermediario, intermedio; agente intermedio.

interment [in'tə:ɹmənt], *s.* entierro, funeral, sepultura, inhumación.

interminable [in'tə:ɪminəbəl], *a.* interminable, ilimitado, inacabable, infinito.

interminate, *a.* interminable, ilimitado, ínfinito.

intermingle [intəɪ'miŋgəl], *v.t.* entremezclar, entreverar. — *v.i.* mezclarse.

intermission [intəɪ'miʃən], *s.* intermisión, interrupción, tregua; pausa, intermitencia; intermedio; tiempo intermedio.

intermissive, *a.* intermitente.

intermit [intəɪ'mit], *v.t.* intermitir, interpolar. — *v.i.* descontinuar, cesar, interrumpirse, suspender, parar.

intermittent, *a.* intermitente, cuartanal.

intermittingly, *adv.* con intermisión, a intervalos.

intermix [intəɪ'miks], *v.t.* entremezclar, entretejer, entreverar, interpolar. — *v.i.* entremezclarse, mezclarse, compenetrarse.

intermixture, *s.* entremezcladura, mezcla; masa de ingredientes mezclados.

intermural [intəɪ'mju:rəl], *a.* entremural, emparedado.

intern [in'tə:ɪn], *v.t.* encerrar, poner a buen recaudo. — *s.* (*med.*) interno.

internal, *a.* interno, doméstico, interior, íntimo, intestino; inherente, real, intrínseco; *internal combustion engine*, motor de combustión interna.

international [intəɪ'næʃənɔl], *a.* internacional; *international law*, derecho internacional *o* derecho de gentes; *Third International*, la Tercera Internacional.

internationalist, *s.* internacionalista, *m.f.*

internationalize, *v.t.* hacer internacional.

internecine [intəɪ'ni:sain], *a.* sanguinario, sin cuartel, a muerte; de exterminación mutua.

internodal [intəɪ'noudəl], **internodial** [intəɪ'noudiəl], *a.* colocado entre dos nudos o articulaciones; relativo a un internodio.

internode, **internodium**, *s.* internodio, entrenudo.

internuncio [intəɪ'nʌnsiou], *s.* internuncio.

interosseous [intəɪ'ɔsiəs], *a.* interóseo.

interpellate [in'tə:ɪpeleit], *v.t.* interpelar.

interpellation, *s.* interpelación, interrupción, ruego ardiente.

interpenetrate [intəɪ'penetreit], *v.t.*, *v.i.* compenetrar, compenetrarse, penetrar(se) mutuamente, penetrar completamente.

interplead [intəɪ'pli:d], *v.i.* (*for.*) litigar entre sí varios demandantes.

interpledge [intəɪ'pledʒ], *v.t.* dar y tomar recíprocamente una cosa como prenda.

interpolate [in'tə:ɪpoleit], *v.t.* interpolar, interponer, insertar.

interpolation, *s.* interpolación, entrerrenglonadura, añadidura.

interpolator, *s.* interpolador.

interposal, *s.* interposición, intervención, asistencia, mediación.

interpose [intəɪ'pouz], *v.t.* interponer, entreponer, interpolar. — *v.i.* interponerse, intervenir, mediar, intermediar; interrumpir, hacer objeción.

interposer, *s.* mediador, el que interviene o interpone.

interposition [intəɪpo'ziʃən], *s.* interposición, mediación, intervención.

interpret [in'tə:ɪprit], *v.t.* interpretar, explanar, explicar, descifrar, traducir; ilustrar, representar.

interpretable, *a.* interpretable, capaz de explicación.

interpretation [intəɪpre'teiʃən], *s.* interpretación, explicación, traducción, exposición.

interpretative, *a.* interpretativo.

interpreter [in'tə:ɪpretəɪ], *s.* intérprete, traductor, interpretador, trujamán.

interregnum [intəɪ'regnʌm], *s.* interregno, período de transición o espera, intervalo.

interrogate [in'terogeit], *v.t.* interrogar, examinar, preguntar. — *v.i.* hacer preguntas, hacer un interrogatorio.

interrogation, *s.* interrogación, pesquisa, pregunta; *point of interrogation*, (*impr.*) interrogación, signo (*o* punto) de interrogación.

interrogative [intə'rɔgətiv], *a.* interrogativo. — *s.* palabra interrogativa.

interrogator, *s.* interrogante, preguntador.

interrogatory [intə'rɔgətəri], *s.* interrogatorio, examen, serie de preguntas. — *a.* interrogativo.

interrupt [intə'rʌpt], *v.t.* interrumpir, perturbar, estorbar; dividir, separar, entrecortar, entorpecer, intermitir, cortar el hilo (de una conversación).

interruptedly, *adv.* interrumpidamente.

interrupter, *s.* interruptor; (*elec.*) interruptor.

interruption, *s.* interrupción, interposición, obstáculo, embarazo, suspensión, intermisión, paréntesis, *f.*

interscapular [intəɪ'skæpju:ləɪ], *a.* interescapular.

intersecant [intəɪ'si:kənt], *a.* cortante, separante.

intersect [intəɪ'sekt], *v.t.*, *v.i.* entrecortar, cruzarse, entrecortarse, intersecarse.

intersection, *s.* intersección; arista.

interspace [intəɪ'speis], *s.* intervalo, espacio medio, intersticio.

intersperse [intəɪ'spə:ɪs], *v.t.* esparcir, entremezclar; diseminar.

interspersion, *s.* esparcimiento de una cosa entre otras.

interspinal [intəɪ'spainəl], *a.* interespinal, interespinoso.

interstate [intəɪ'steit], *a.* relativo a las relaciones entre diferentes estados; *interstate commerce*, comercio interior.

interstellar ·[intəɪ'steləɪ], *a.* interestelar, intersideral.

interstice [in'tə:ɪstis], *s.* intersticio, hendedura, resquicio; intervalo, intermedio.

interstitial [intəɪ'stiʃəl], *a.* que tiene intersticios.

intertexture [intəɪ'tekstjəɪ], *s.* entretejido, entretejimiento, entretejedura, contexto.

intertie [intəɪ'tai], *s.* travesaño.

intertropical [intəɪ'trɔpikəl], *a.* intertropical.

intertwine [intəɪ'twain], **intertwist** [intəɪ'twist], *v.t.* entretejer, entrelazar; (*mar.*) acolchar.

interval ['intəɪvəl], *s.* intervalo, claro, espacio, blanco, intersticio, intermedio, espera, remisión, intermisión; (*mús.*) intervalo; *at infrequent intervals*, de tarde en tarde.

interveined [intəɪ'veind], *a.* interpolado, cortado como las venas.

intervene [intəɪ'vi:n], *v.i.* intervenir, interrumpir, mediar; interponerse, ponerse por medio, atravesarse; ocurrir, sobrevenir, impedir, embarazar.

intervenient [intəɹˈviːniənt], *a.* interpuesto, ocurrido, que interrumpe.

intervening, *a.* intermedio, interpuesto, intercurrente.

intervention [intəɹˈvenʃən], *s.* intervención, mediación, interposición; concurrencia, asistencia.

intervertebral [intəɹˈvəːɹtəbrəl], *a.* intervertebral.

interview [ˈintəɹvjuː], *s.* interview, entrevista, vistas, conferencia. — *v.t.* avistarse, entrevistarse (con).

interviewer, *s.* reportero, periodista, *m.f.*; interrogador.

intervolve [intəɹˈvolv], *v.t.* envolver una cosa dentro de otra.

interweave [intəɹˈwiːv], *v.t.* entretejer, entrelazar, enlazar, entremeter.

interweaving, *s.* entretejimiento, entretejedura.

interwreathe [intəɹˈriːð], *v.t.* tejer en forma de guirnalda.

intestable, *a.* legalmente incapacitado para hacer testamento.

intestacy [inˈtestəsi], *s.* falta de testamento.

intestate [inˈtestit], *a.* intestado, abintestato.

intestinal [inˈtestinəl], *a.* intestinal, relativo a los intestinos, intestino, interior.

intestine [inˈtestin], *a.* interior, doméstico, intestino, interno.

intestine, intestines, *s.* intestino(s); tripa(s); *large intestine,* intestino grueso; *small intestine,* intestino delgado.

intimacy [ˈintiməsi], *s.* intimidad, confianza, familiaridad.

intimate [ˈintimeit], *a.* íntimo, interior; familiar, cordial, estrecho; interno; apegado. — *s.* amigo íntimo, confidente. — *v.t.* insinuar, intimar, indicar, dar a entender indirectamente.

intimation, *s.* insinuación, indirecta, intimación, prevención, pulla, indicio, aviso indirecto.

intimidate [inˈtimideit], *v.t.* intimidar, infundir miedo, aterrar, amedrentar, acobardar, espantar, acoquinar.

intimidation, *s.* intimidación, acoquinamiento.

intimidatory, *a.* intimidador.

into [ˈintuː], *prep.* en, dentro, adentro, hacia el interior, por ademàs de; *into the bargain,* por añadidura, por demás.

intolerability, intolerableness, *s.* intolerabilidad.

intolerable [inˈtolərəbəl], *a.* intolerable, insoportable, insufrible, inaguantable.

intolerance, intolerancy, *s.* intolerancia.

intolerant, *s., a.* intolerante, falto de tolerancia.

intolerantly, *adv.* con intolerancia.

intoleration [intoləɹˈreiʃən], *s.* intolerantismo.

intomb [intuːm], *v.t.* enterrar, sepultar.

intonate [ˈintɔneit], *v.i.* entonar, cantar, solfear.

intonation, *s.* entonación, entonamiento, acción de entonar; modulación de la voz.

intone [inˈtoun], *v.t., v.i.* entonar; cantar o recitar en un tono; salmear, salmodiar.

intorsion, intortion, *s.* intorsión, torcedura.

intort [inˈtɔːɹt], *v.t.* torcer.

intoxicant [inˈtɔksikənt], *s.* bebida alcohólica; lo que embriaga los sentidos.

intoxicate [inˈtɔksikeit], *v.t.* embriagar, emborrachar; (*med.*) envenenar, intoxicar, atosigar, emponzoñar; excitar hasta el frenesí. —

a. ebrio, borracho, embriagado, emborrachado.

intoxication, *s.* embriaguez, beodez, borrachez, borrachera, crápula; (*med.*) intoxicación, envenenamiento; (*fig.*) arrebatamiento, entusiasmo, transportamiento.

intra [intrə], *prefijo,* dentro.

intractability, intractableness, *s.* estado de intratable; obstinación, dureza, terquedad, porfía.

intractable [inˈtræktəbəl], *a.* intratable, zahareño, recreído, áspero, terco, duro, obstinado.

intrados [ˈintrədos], *s.* intradós.

intramural [intrəˈmjuːrəl], *a.* intramuros.

intranquillity [intrænˈkwiliti], *s.* desasosiego; intranquilidad.

intransient [inˈtrænʒənt], *a.* inmutable, permanente.

intransigence [inˈtrænzidʒəns], *s.* intransigencia.

intransigent, *a.* intransigentes.

intransitive [inˈtrænzitiv], *a.* intransitivo.

intransmutability, *s.* intransmutabilidad.

intransmutable [intrænsˈmjuːtəbəl], *a.* intransmutable.

intrench [inˈtrentʃ], *v.t.* atrincherar, llenar de hoyos. — *v.i.* invadir, usurpar.

intrenchment, *s.* atrincheramiento.

intrepid [inˈtrepid], *a.* intrépido, arrojado, impertérrito, denodado, osado.

intrepidity [intreˈpiditi], *s.* intrepidez, osadía, arrojo, denuedo.

intricacy [ˈintrikəsi], **intricateness** [ˈintrikitnis], *s.* intrincación, embrollo, confusión, intrincamiento, enredo, embarazo, dificultad, obscuridad, perplejidad.

intricate [ˈintrikit], *a.* intrincado, enredado, revuelto, confuso, complicado. — *v.t.* intrincar, enredar.

intrigue [inˈtriːg], *s.* intriga, trama, manejo, confusión, embrollo; amaño, arte; enredo (de una comedia); galanteo, intriga amorosa, lío. — *v.i.* intrigar, tramar; tener intrigas amorosas.

intriguer, *s.* intrigante, embudista, *m.f.*, tracista, *m.f.*, embrollador, entremetido, zaramullo; amante.

intriguing, *a.* enredador, intrigante; (*fam.*) atrayente, fascinador.

intrinsic [inˈtrinsik], **intrinsical,** *a.* intrínseco, verdadero, inherente, esencial, interno, interior.

intrinsicalness, *s.* realidad; valor o mérito intrínseco.

introduce [introˈdjuːs], *v.t.* introducir, insertar, ingerir, meter; empezar, establecer; dar entrada; proponer, presentar; facilitar; poner en uso, hacer adoptar; dar motivo, causar, ocasionar; dar a conocer.

introducer, *s.* introductor.

introduction [introˈdʌkʃən], *s.* introducción, proemio, prólogo; iniciación, presentación, metimiento, inserción; *letter of introduction,* carta de presentación.

introductive, *a.* introductivo.

introductor, *s.* introductor.

introductory [introˈdʌktəri], *a.* preliminar, introductivo, proemial.

introgression [introˈgreʃən], *s.* entrada.

introit [ˈintroit], *s.* introito.

intromission [introˈmiʃən], *s.* introducción, admisión, iniciación.

intromit [intro'mit], *v.t.* introducir, insertar; admitir, dar entrada a. — *v.i.* entremeterse, ingerirse, mezclarse, tomar posesión.

intromittent, *a.* que introduce, que echa dentro.

introspect ['introspekt], *v.t.* mirar lo interior de alguna cosa, mirar adentro. — *v.i.* hacer examen de conciencia, o de sus motivos, mirar dentro de sí.

introspection [intro'spekʃən], *s.* examen de conciencia, introspección.

introspective, *a.* introspectivo.

introsusception [introsʌ'sepʃən], *s.* acto de recibir dentro.

introvert ['introvəːɹt], *v.t.* volver hacia dentro. — *s., a.* introverso.

intrude [in'truːd], *v.i.* intrusarse, entremeterse, introducirse sin permiso, inmiscuirse, ingerirse. — *v.t.* meter, forzar, presentar o introducir sin permiso.

intruder, *s.* intruso, entremetido.

intrusion [in'truːʒən], *s.* intrusión, impertinencia, entremetimiento; (*geol.*) intromisión.

intrusional, *a.* intruso.

intrusive, *a.* intruso, impertinente, manifacero, fastidioso, importuno.

intrusiveness, *s.* intrusión, importunidad, tendencia a intrusarse.

intrust [in'trʌst], *v.t.* fiar, dar, confiar, entregar; poner en depósito.

intuition [intju'iʃən], *s.* intuición.

intuitive [in'tjuːitiv], *a.* intuitivo.

intumesce [intju'mes], *v.i.* hincharse, entumecerse.

intumescence, intumescency, *s.* entumecimiento, intumescencia, levantamiento, hinchazón, *f.*, tumor.

intumescent, *a.* intumescente; hinchado.

intwine [in'twain], *v.t.* entrelazar, enlazar.

inula ['injuːlə], *s.* énula campana.

inulin ['injuːlin], *s.* inulina.

inumbrate ['inʌmbreit], *v.t.* echar sombra sobre.

inunction [in'ʌŋkʃən], *s.* untura, untadura, friega.

inundate ['inʌndeit], *v.t.* inundar, apantanar, anegar; abrumar.

inundation, *s.* inundación, desbordamiento, anegación, diluvio.

inurbane [in'əːːbein], *a.* inurbano, rudo, descortés.

inurbaneness, inurbanity, *s.* inurbanidad.

inure [in'juːəɹ], *v.t.* avezar, habituar, acostumbrar, endurecer por el uso. — *v.i.* tener efecto; quedar para, pasar a.

inured, *a.* avezado, baqueteado, hecho a, endurecido. — *p.p.* [INURE].

inurement, *s.* práctica, uso, hábito, costumbre.

inurn [in'əːɹn], *v.t.* poner en una urna cineraria.

inutility [inju'tiliti], *s.* inutilidad.

invade [in'veid], *v.t.* invadir, usurpar, acometer, embestir, asaltar, violar; *to invade one's rights*, violar los derechos de alguno.

invader, *s.* invasor, usurpador, asaltador, acometedor, agresor, violador.

invaginate [in'vædʒineit], *v.t.* envainar, enchufar, meter en una vaina. — *a.* envainado, enchufado.

invagination, *s.* enchufamiento, intususcepción, invaginación.

invalid [in'vælid], *a.* inválido, írrito, nulo.

invalid ['invəliːd], *s.* inválido, enfermo.

invalid, *v.t.* matricular en el registro de inválidos; invalidar, lisiar, estropear; *to invalid out of the army*, licenciar por invalidez.

invalidate [in'vælideit], *v.t.* invalidar, anular; (*for.*) privar de valor legal.

invalidation, *s.* invalidación.

invalidism ['invəliːdizm], *s.* baldadura crónica.

invalidity [invə'liditi], **invalidness** [in'vælidnis], *s.* invalidación; (*for.*) nulidad; debilidad.

invaluable [in'væljuːəbəl], *a.* inestimable, inapreciable, invaluable.

invariability, invariableness, *s.* invariabilidad.

invariable [in'vɛəriəbəl], *a.* invariable.

invasion [in'veiʃən], *s.* invasión, irrupción, infracción, agresión; arremetida; usurpación.

invasive, *a.* hostil, invasor, agresivo.

invective [in'vektiv], *s.* invectiva, vituperio; filípica. — *a.* ultrajante, ofensivo, injurioso, abusivo.

inveigh [in'vei], *v.i.* prorrumpir en invectivas, desencadenarse contra alguno.

inveigher, *s.* declamador, ultrajador.

inveigle [in'veigəl], *v.t.* seducir, embaír, engañar, engatusar.

inveiglement, *s.* engañifa, embaimiento, seducción.

inveigler, *s.* seductor.

inveil [in'veil], *v.t.* cubrir con un velo.

invent [in'vent], *v.t.* inventar, descubrir, hallar; idear, discurrir, componer, tramar, fraguar, fingir, forjar, sacar de su cabeza.

invention, *s.* invención, descubrimiento, hallazgo, invento; maña, inventiva, ingenio; mentira, ficción, falsedad, embuste.

inventive, *a.* inventivo, ingenioso, fecundo en expedientes.

inventor, *s.* inventor, descubridor, autor; invencionero, trazador.

inventorial [invən'toːriəl], *a.* perteneciente al inventario.

inventorially, *adv.* con inventario, por inventario.

inventory ['invəntəri], *s.* inventario, recuento, catálogo. — *v.t.* inventariar, hacer un inventario.

inventress, *s.* inventora.

Inverness [invəɹ'nes], *a.* especie de gabán sin mangas y con una esclavina sobre los hombros.

inverse [in'vəːɹs], *a.* inverso, trastrocado, invertido, trastornado.

inversion, *s.* inversión, trastrocamiento, transmutación.

invert [in'vəːɹt], *v.t.* invertir, trastornar, trastrocar, poner o volver al revés, transponer, mudar, cambiar.

invertebral [in'vəːɹtibrəl], **invertebrate** [in'vəːɹtibrit], *s., a.* invertebrado.

inverted, *a.* invertido, inverso; *inverted commas*, comillas.

invest [in'vest], *v.t.* (*com.*) invertir; investir, dar, conferir, vestir, adornar, cubrir, poner; (*mil.*) sitiar, cercar, rodear.

investigable, *a.* investigable, averiguable, escudriñable.

investigate [in'vestigeit], *v.t.* investigar, buscar, indagar, examinar, averiguar, inquirir, explorar.

investigation, *s.* investigación, averiguación, pesquisa, indagación, escrutinio.

investigative, *a.* investigador.

investigator, s. investigador, averiguador, indagador.

investiture [in'vestitʃəɪ], s. investidura, instalación.

investment [in'vestmənt], s. (com.) inversión; investidura, instalación; (mil.) sitio, cerco; (biol.) envoltura; cubierta. — pl. (com.) fondos, acciones.

inveteracy, inveterateness, s. hábito o costumbre inveterada.

inveterate [in'vetərit], a. inveterado, habitual, arraigado.

invidious [in'vidiəs], a. envidioso; aborrecible, injusto, detestable, odioso.

invidiousness, s. calidad de envidioso.

invigilate [in'vidʒileit], v.i. vigilar, velar, cuidar que se cumplan las ordenanzas durante un examen.

invigorate [in'vigəreit], v.t. vigorizar, fortificar, dar vigor; (fig.) vigorar, confortar.

invigoration, s. acto y efecto de vigorizar.

invincibility, invincibleness, s. calidad de invencible.

invincible [in'vinsibəl], a. invencible, invicto.

inviolability, inviolableness, s. inviolabilidad.

inviolable [in'vaiɒləbəl], a. inviolable, infrangible, inquebrantable.

inviolate [in'vaiɒleit], **inviolated,** a. inviolado, inviolable, íntegro, incorrupto.

inviscate ['inviskeit], v.t hacer viscoso.

invisibility, invisibleness, s. invisibilidad.

invisible [in'vizibəl], a. invisible; invisible ink, tinta simpática.

invitation [invi'teiʃən], s. invitación, convite, instancia, llamamiento.

invitatory, a. invitador. — s. invitatorio.

invite [in'vait], v.t. convidar, brindar, invitar, atraer, mover, tentar, incitar, llamar, estimular, instar, animar. — s. (fam.) invitación, convite.

inviter, s. convidador, invitador.

inviting, a. atractivo, seductor, seductivo, halagador, incitante.

invitingness, s. atractivo, aliciente.

invocation [invo'keiʃən], s. invocación; (for.) suplicatorio, mandamiento, exhorto.

invoice ['invɔis], s. (com.) factura. — v.t. facturar.

invoke, v.t. invocar, implorar, llamar, rogar, suplicar; (for.) expedir suplicatorio o mandamiento.

involucral [in'vɒljuːkrəl], a. involucral.

involucrate, involucred, a. involucrado, provisto de un involucro.

involucre [invo'ljuːkəɪ], **involucrum** [invo-'ljuːkrəm], s. (bot.) involucro; (anat.) envoltura membranosa.

involuntariness, s. involuntariedad.

involuntary [in'vɒləntəri], a. involuntario.

involute [in'vɒljuːt], a. intrincado; enrollado en espiral; vuelto o encorvado hacia dentro. — s. evolvente, involuta.

involution, s. envolvimiento, envolvedero; complicación; enredo, embrollo.

involve, v.t. envolver, enrollar; torcer, retorcer, intrincar, enredar, complicar, enmarañar; comprometer, implicar, revolver, involucrar; (mat.) multiplicar, elevar (a una potencia). — v.r. meterse.

involvedness, s. envolvimiento, intrincación, complicación.

invulnerability, invulnerableness, s. invulnerabilidad.

invulnerable [in'vʌlnərəbəl], a. invulnerable.

inward ['inwəd], **inwards** ['inwədz], adv. interiormente, hacia lo interior, hacia dentro, adentro.

inward, a. interior, interno; oculto, secreto; doméstico. — s. interior; lo de dentro. — pl. inwards, (fam.) entrañas.

inwardness ['inwədnis], s. calidad, naturaleza o estado interior, estado de ser interior; intimidad.

inweave [in'wiːv], v.t. entretejer, enlazar.

inwrap, v.t. envolver.

inwrought [in'rɔːt], a. labrado, incrustado, embutido.

iodic [ai'ɒdik], a. yodado.

iodide ['aiodaid], s. yoduro.

iodine ['aiodain], s. yodo.

iodism ['aiodizm], s. yodismo.

iodize, v.t. echar yodo a, someter a la influencia del yodo; (foto.) exponer a los vapores del yodo.

iodoform [ai'odofɔːm], s. yodoformo.

ion ['aiən], s. ion.

Ionic [ai'ɒnik], a. jónico.

iota [ai'outə], s. jota, tilde, ápice, punto.

IOU ['ai'ou'juː], (abreviatura fonética de I owe you, yo le debo). — s. abonaré, pagaré.

ipecac ['ipikæk], **ipecacuanha** [ipikækjuː-'ɑːnə], s. ipecacuana, bejuquillo.

ipomœa [ipo'miːə], s. ipomea.

Iranian [ai'reniən], a. iranio.

irascibility, irascibleness, s. iracundia.

irascible [i'ræsibəl], a. irascible, colérico.

irate [ai'reit], a. encolerizado, airado, enfurecido.

ire [aiəɪ], s. ira, iracundia, cólera, enfado, enojo.

ireful, a. iracundo, colérico.

irenic [ai'riːnik], **irenical,** a. conciliador, pacífico.

iridaceous [iri'deiʃəs], a. irideo.

iridesce [iri'des], v.i. irisar.

iridescence, s. iradación, cambiante, tornasol.

iridescent, a. iridiscente, irisado, tornasolado.

iridium [i'ridiəm], s. iridio.

iris ['airis], s. (anat., opt.) iris; arco iris; (bot.) flor de lis, f.

Irish ['airiʃ], s., a. irlandés, natural de Irlanda, lengua de Irlanda.

Irishism, s. locución irlandesa, rasgo irlandés.

Irishman ['airiʃmən], s.m. irlandés.

Irishwoman, s.f. irlandesa.

iritis [ai'raitis], s. iritis, f.

irk [əːk], v.t., v.i. fastidiar, cansar, aburrir.

irksome ['əːksəm], a. tedioso, enfadoso, fastidioso, cansado, cargante.

irksomeness, s. tedio, molestia, fastidio, cansancio.

iron ['aiəɹn], s. hierro, fierro; cualquier herramienta, utensilio o arma de hierro. — pl. irons, cadenas, hierros, grilletes, prisiones; bar iron, hierro en barras; cast iron, hierro colado; sheet iron, hierro en planchas; smoothing iron, plancha; to put (o throw) into irons, echar grillos, aprisionar; to have too many irons in the fire, tener demasiados asuntos entre manos. — a. férreo; impenetrable, duro, áspero, severo, obstinado, indomable. — v.t. aplanchar, alisar con una plancha, planchar; aprisionar.

iron-bound, *a.* rodeado de arcos de hierro; (*fig.*) inflexible.

ironclad ['aiəɹnklæd], *s.* acorazado, buque de guerra blindado.

iron-clad, *a.* blindado; (*fig.*) riguroso, leonino; fuerte.

ironed, *a.* planchado, aplanchado; armado; engrillado, aherrojado. — *p.p.* [IRON].

ironer, *s.* planchadora.

iron-founder, *s.* fundidor de hierro.

iron-hearted, *a.* severo, duro, inflexible.

ironic [ai'rɔnik], **ironical** [ai'rɔnikəl], *a.* irónico.

ironing, *s.* planchado; *ironing board,* tabla de planchar.

ironmonger ['aiəɹnmʌŋgəɹ], *s.* quinquillero, ferretero; *ironmonger's shop,* ferretería.

ironmongery, *s.* ferretería, cerrajería.

iron-mould, *s.* mancha de orín de hierro.

ironside, ironsides, *s., a.* enérgico, fuerte, terrible en la guerra; soldado del ejército de Cromwell.

ironsided, *a.* lo que tiene un lado o lados de hierro.

ironware, *s.* artículos de ferretería.

ironwood, *s.* madera de hierro; (*Am.*) palo hacha.

ironwork, *s.* herraje.

ironwort, *s.* sideritis.

irony ['airəni], *s.* ironía. — *a.* férreo, ferrugiento.

Iroquois ['irɔkwɑ:], *s.* iroqués.

irradiance [i'reidiəns], **irradiancy,** *s.* irradiación, lustre, esplendor.

irradiate [i'reidieit], *v.t.* irradiar; iluminar; inspirar; esparcir. — *v.i.* lucir, brillar. — *a.* (*poét.*) resplandeciente, iluminado, brillante, claro.

irradiation, *s.* irradiación; esplendor, brillo; iluminación.

irradiative, *a.* radiante, refulgente.

irradicate [i'rædikeit], *v.t.* arraigar.

irrational [i'ræʃənəl], *a.* irracional, desrazonable, ilógico, absurdo.

irrationality, *s.* irracionalidad.

irreclaimable [iri'kleiməbəl], *a.* irredimible, incorregible, obstinado, indomable, indómito.

irreconcilable [irekon'sailəbəl], *a.* irreconciliable, intransigente, inconciliable, incompatible, incomponible, implacable.

irreconcilableness, *s.* imposibilidad de reconciliarse.

irreconcilement, irreconciliation, *s.* falta de reconciliación, discordia, estado de guerra.

irrecoverable [ire'kʌvərəbəl], *a.* irreparable, irrecuperable; irremediable, incobrable.

irrecoverableness, *s.* calidad de irrecuperable.

irrecuperable [ire'kju:pərəbəl], *a.* irrecuperable, irremediable.

irredeemable [ire'di:məbəl], *a.* irredimible, irremisible.

irreducible [ire'dju:səbəl], *a.* irreducible.

irrefragability, *s.* fuerza incontestable de un argumento.

irrefragable [ire'frægəbəl], *a.* irrefragable, indisputable, incontestable.

irrefutable [i'refju:təbəl], *a.* irrefutable, irrefragable, indisputable, incontestable, indubitable, cierto.

irregular [i'regju:ləɹ], *a.* irregular; anómalo, anormal; extraño, raro, estrambótico; desa-

rreglado, desordenado. — *s.* soldado de tropas irregulares; charlatán.

irregularity [iregju:'læriti], *s.* irregularidad, anomalía; desorden, desarreglo, demasía, exceso.

irrelative [i'relətiv], *a.* inconexo, sin regla, sin orden.

irrelevance [i'relevəns], *s.* inoportunidad, inconexión; despropósito; impertinencia.

irrelevant, *a.* inaplicable, fuera de propósito; inoportuno; desatinado.

irrelevantly, *adv.* fuera de propósito, desatinadamente.

irrelievable [ire'li:vəbəl], *a.* irremediable, irreparable.

irreligious [ire'lidʒəs], *a.* irreligioso, impío, indevoto, profano.

irremediable [ire'mi:diəbəl], *a.* irremediable, irreparable; incorregible; incurable, insanable.

irremediableness, *s.* estado o calidad de irremediable.

irremissible [ire'misəbəl], *a.* irremisible, imperdonable, incapaz de perdón.

irremissibleness, *s.* calidad de irremisible.

irremovable [ire'mɔ:vəbəl], *a.* inamovible; inmutable.

irreparability, *s.* estado de irreparable.

irreparable [ire'pærəbəl], *a.* irreparable.

irrepealable [ire'pi:ləbəl], *a.* inabrogable, irrevocable.

irreplaceable [ire'pleisəbəl], *a.* irreemplazable.

irreprehensible [irepre'hensəbəl], *a.* irreprensible.

irrepressible [ire'presəbəl], *a.* incorregible, indomable.

irreproachable [ire'proutʃəbəl], *a.* intachable, irreprensible, incensurable, irreprochable.

irreprovable [ire'pru:vəbəl], *a.* irreprensible, irreprochable.

irresistance, *s.* pasividad, paciencia.

irresistibility, irresistibleness, *s.* fuerza o poder irresistible.

irresistible [ire'zistəbəl], *a.* irresistible.

irresoluble [ire'sɔlju:bəl], *a.* irresoluble.

irresolubleness, *s.* calidad de irresoluble.

irresolute [i'rezolju:t], *a.* irresoluto, vacilante, irresuelto, indeciso.

irresoluteness, *s.* irresolución.

irresolution, *s.* irresolución, vacilación, indecisión, duda.

irresolvable [ire'sɔlvəbəl], *a.* inseparable; insoluble.

irrespective [ire'spektiv], *a.* inconsiderado, sin consideración; independiente, aparte, que no hace el caso.

irresponsibility, *s.* irresponsabilidad.

irresponsible [ire'spɔnsəbəl], *a.* irresponsable.

irresponsive [ire'spɔnziv], *a.* que no responde.

irretentive [ire'tentiv], *a.* que no retiene.

irretraceable [ire'treisəbəl], *a.* que no se puede desandar.

irretrievable [ire'tri:vəbəl], *a.* irrecuperable, irreparable, incobrable.

irreverence, *s.* irreverencia, falta de reverencia.

irreverent [i'revərənt], *a.* irreverente, falto de reverencia, profano, irrespetuoso, desatento.

irreversibility, irreversibleness, *s.* estado de irrevocable, imposibilidad de volverse del revés; irrevocabilidad.

irreversible [ire'və:ɹsəbəl], *a.* que no se

puede volver al revés; irrevocable, inquebrantable.
irreversibly, *adv.* sin poderse revocar o invertir.
irrevocability, irrevocableness, *s.* irrevocabilidad.
irrevocable [i'revokəbəl], *a.* irrevocable, inquebrantable.
irrigable ['irigəbəl], *a.* regadizo.
irrigate ['irigeit], *v.t.* regar; mojar, bañar, humedecer; (*med.*) irrigar.
irrigation, *s.* riego; regadura, regamiento; (*med.*) irrigación; *irrigation channel*, acequia, canal de riego.
irrigator, *s.* carro de riego; (*med.*) irrigador.
irrision [i'riʒən], *s.* irrisión, mofa, burla, desprecio.
irritability, *s.* irritabilidad, propensión a irritarse.
irritable ['iritəbəl], *a.* irritable, enfadadizo, irascible.
irritableness, *s.* iracundia, irritabilidad.
irritant ['iritənt], *s.*, *a.* irritante, (lo) que irrita; (*for.*) írrito.
irritate, *v.t.* irritar, amostazar, exasperar; enconar; estimular, provocar.
irritation [iri'teiʃən], *s.* irritación, irritamiento, provocación.
irritative, irritatory, *a.* irritador, provocativo, irritante.
irruption [i'rʌpʃən], *s.* irrupción, invasión.
irruptive, *a.* invasor.
is [iz], *3ª pers. sing. pres. ind.* [BE].
isagogical [aizə'gɔgikəl], *a.* isagógico.
isagon ['aisəgɔn], *s.* iságono.
ischiatic [iski'ætik], *a.* isquiático.
ischium ['iskiəm], *s.* isquion.
isenergic [aise'nə:rdʒik], *a.* (*fís.*) de igual energía.
iserine ['aisərin], *s.* iserina.
Ishmaelite ['iʃməlait], *s.* ismaelita, *m.f.*
isinglass ['aiziŋglɑːs], *s.* colapez, cola de pescado.
Islam [iz'lɑːm], **Islamism** ['izləmizm], *s.* islam, islamismo.
Islamic, *a.* islámico.
island ['ailənd], *s.* isla, ínsula.
islander, *s.* isleño.
isle [ail], *s.* isla, ínsula.
islet ['ailet], *s.* isleta, cayo.
ism [izm], *s.* teoría, doctrina (usualmente despectivo).
isobaric [aiso'bærik], *a.* isobárico.
isochromatic [aisokro'mætik], *a.* isocromático.
isochronal [ai'sɔkrənəl], **isochronous,** *a.* isócrono.
isolate ['aisoleit], *v.t.* aislar, apartar, separar.
isolated, *a.* aislado, solitario, retirado; esporádico; incomunicado. — *p.p.* [ISOLATE].
isolation, *s.* aislamiento, soledad, separación.
isolator, *s.* aislador.
isomeric [aiso'merik], *a.* isomérico.
isomerism, *s.* isomerismo, isomorfia.
isometric [aiso'metrik], **isometrical,** *a.* isométrico.
isomorphism [aiso'mɔːrfizm], *s.* isomorfismo, isomorfia.
isomorphous, *a.* isomorfo.
isonomy [ai'sɔnəmi], *s.* igualdad ante la ley.
isopathy [ai'sɔpəθi], *s.* teoría de que una dolencia puede ser curada por un producto de la misma.

isosceles [ai'sɔseliːz], *a.* isósceles.
isotherm ['aisoθə:ɪm], *s.* línea isoterma.
isothermal, *a.* isotermo.
isotope ['aisotoup], *s.* isotope, isotopo.
Israelite ['izrəlait], *s.* israelita, *m.f.*, hebreo, judío.
Israelitish, Israelitic, *a.* israelítico, judío.
issuable ['iʃjuːəbəl], *a.* emisible.
issue ['iʃjuː], *s.* (*impr.*) edición, impresión, tirada; (*com. y bolsa*) emisión de valores; rentas, réditos, beneficio, producto; prole, *f.*, hijos, progenie, *f.*, sucesión; egreso, salida; evento, resultado, consecuencia, término, fin, éxito, conclusión; fuente, *f.*, nacimiento, principio; decisión; (*med.*) fontículo, exutorio, cauterio; *cause at issue*, causa que está para verse o sentenciarse; *point at issue*, punto que se discute, punto en cuestión; *without issue*, sin sucesión; *at issue*, en disputa; *issue of blood*, pérdida de sangre; *to join issue*, tener pareceres contrarios, llevar la contraria; contradecirse mutuamente; *to join issues*, zurcir voluntades. — *v.t.* echar, arrojar, brotar; despachar, expedir; (*impr.*) dar a luz, publicar; (*com.*) librar, emitir, poner en circulación. — *v.i.* salir, surgir, nacer, brotar, prorrumpir, manar, fluir; provenir, venir, proceder; terminarse, acabarse, resolverse, resultar.
issued, expedido; emitido; descendido. — *p.p.* [ISSUE].
issueless, *a.* sin sucesión.
issuing, *s.* salida.
Isthmian ['istmiən], *a.* ístmico.
isthmus ['istməs], *s.* istmo.
it [it], *pron. neut.* (*pl.* they) se aplica a cosas inanimadas, y a niños y animales cuyo sexo no puede determinarse, él, ella, ello, lo, la, le; *it*, en las frases impersonales, se usa como sujeto gramatical y no se traduce, como: *it is warm*, hace calor; úsase asimismo como objeto indefinido de los verbos transitivos o intransitivos.
Italian [i'tæljən], *s.*, *a.* italiano.
Italianize, *v.t.* italianizar, hacer italiano.
italic [i'tælik], *a.* itálico; (*impr.*) bastardillo. — *s.* bastardilla, letra bastardilla, letra itálica.
italicize [i'tælisaiz], *v.t.* poner letras bastardillas; subrayar, dar énfasis.
itch [itʃ], *s.* sarna, picor, picazón, *f.*, comezón, *f.*, prurito, flujo. — *v.i.* picar, sentir comezón o picazón, sentir prurito, antojarse, padecer deseo vehemente.
itching, *s.* escozor, picazón, *f.*, picor, hormigueo, comezón, *f.*, prurito.
itch-insect, itch-mite, *s.* ácaro, arador.
itchy, *a.* sarnoso; picante, hormigoso.
item ['aitem], *adv.* ítem; otrosí, además. — *s.* partida, párrafo, artículo.
itemize ['aitəmaiz], *v.t.* detallar, razonar, especificar, apuntar.
iterable, *a.* iterable, capaz de repetirse.
iterant ['itərənt], *a.* iterativo.
iterate, *v.t.* iterar, reiterar, repetir; inculcar.
iteration [itər'eiʃən], *s.* iteración, vuelta, repetición.
iterative, *a.* iterativo; (*gram.*) frecuentativo.
itinerant [ai'tinərənt], *a.* itinerante, viandante; errante, ambulante.
itinerary [ai'tinərəri], *s.* itinerario, ruta, derrotero; guía de viajeros; relación de un viaje.

— *a.* itinerario, hecho en viaje, relativo a un viaje.

itinerate, *v.i.* viajar, seguir un itinerario.

its [its], su (de él, de ella, de ello).

it's [its], *abrev. de* **it is**; es, está.

itself [it'self], *pron. neut.* el mismo, la misma, lo mismo.

I've [aiv], *abrev. de* **I have**; yo he, yo tengo.

ivied ['aivid], *a.* cubierto de hiedra.

ivory ['aivəri], *s.* marfil. — *pl.* **ivories**, (*vulg.*) cosas hechas de marfil; bolas de billar; (*fam.*) dientes. — *a.* ebúrneo, de marfil; *ivory palm*, tagua.

ivy [aivi], *s.* hiedra, yedra; *ground ivy*, hiedra terrestre; *poison ivy*, especie de zumaque, arbusto trepador.

J

J, j [dʒei], décima letra del alfabeto inglés.

jab [dʒæb], *v.t.* (*fam.*) pinchar con violencia; golpear. — *s.* hurgonazo, pinchazo, punzado, golpe violento.

jabber [dʒæbəɹ], *v.i.* charlar, hablar mucho y sin substancia; mascar, farfullar; (*fam.*) disparatar; hablar en jerigonza, marmotear. — *s.* jerga, guirigay, jerigonza, farfulla, algarabía, charla.

jabberer, *s.* farfullador, parlanchín.

jaborandi [dʒæbo'rændi], *s.* jaborandi, pilocarpo.

jacaranda [dʒækə'rændə], *s.* jacarandá, abey.

jacent ['dʒeisənt], *a.* yacente.

jacinth ['dʒæsinθ], *s.* (*bot.*) jacinto; (*min.*) circón.

Jack [dʒæk], *s.* dim. de John; Juanito, Juanillo; hombre; marinero; mozo; macho de varios animales; barrilete; prensa; cárcel, *f.*; burro; armazón, *f.*; borriquete; sacabotas; (*mec.*) gato; torno de asador; martinete, palillo del piano; cota de malla; carda; (*mar.*) bandera de proa; bola pequeña, boliche; sota (de la baraja); (*ict.*) lucio, luso; *Jack by the hedge*, (*bot.*) erísimo; *Jack o'lantern*, fuego fatuo; *Jack sauce*, hombre descarado; *Jack pudding*, bufón, arlequín; *jack towel*, toalla colgada de un rodillo giratorio; *Jack Ketch*, verdugo; *Jack of all trades and master of none*, (*prov.*) aprendiz de todo y oficial de nada; *he is a regular Jack of all trades*, de todo sabe un poco.

jackal ['dʒækɔ:l], *s.* chacal.

jackanapes ['dʒækəneips], *s.* mequetrefe, pisaverde; tonto, bobo.

jackass ['dʒækæs], *s.* garañón, borrico, asno; (*fig.*) necio, tonto, imbécil, asno.

jack-boot ['dʒækbu:t], *s.* bota de montar.

jackdaw ['dʒækdɔ:], *s.* (*orn.*) grajo, chova.

jacket ['dʒæket], *s.* chaqueta, jaqueta, jubón; (*mec.*) camisa, chaqueta, cubierta del cilindro; (*fam.*) piel de la patata. — *v.t.* enchaquetar; *to dust a person's jacket*, (*fig.*) darle a uno una tunda.

jack-knife, *s.* navaja sevillana.

jackscrew, *s.* gato cornaquí.

jackstaff, *s.* asta de bandera.

jackstone, *s.* taba, pito.

jackstraw, *s.* efigie de paja, *f.*; espantapájaros; hombre insignificante; paja, pajita. — *pl.* juego con pajitas.

jack-tree, *s.* artocarpo.

Jacobin ['dʒækobin], *s.* (*pol.*) jacobino; (*igl.*) dominico; pichón capuchino; antimonárquico, demagogo; irreligioso.

Jacobinic, Jacobinical, *s.* jacobínico.

Jacobinism, *s.* jacobinismo.

Jacobinize, *v.t.* infundir los principios de los jacobinos.

Jacobite ['dʒækobait], *s., a.* jacobita, *m.f.*

Jacob's-ladder [dʒeikəbz'lædəɹ], *s.* (*bot.*) polemonio azul; (*mar.*) escala de jarcias; *Jacob's staff*, bordón de peregrino; báculo de Jacob; astrolabio.

jaconet ['dʒækonet], *s.* chaconá, chaconada.

jactation [dʒæk'teiʃən], **jactitation** [dʒækti-'teiʃən], *s.* agitación, ajetreo.

jaculate ['dʒækju:leit], *v.t.* lanzar, arrojar.

jaculatory, *s.* lanzamiento. — *a.* disparado; jaculatorio.

jade [dʒeid], *s.* rocín, jamelgo, jaco; (despectivo) mujercilla, picarona, bruja, mala pécora; (*min.*) nefrita, piedra nefrítica; lemanita, jade. — *v.t.* cansar, acosar, sujetar, tiranizar, maltratar. — *v.i.* jadear, desalentarse, desanimarse.

jadish ['dʒeidiʃ], *a.* viciosa (yegua); incontinente, impúdica (mujer).

jag [dʒæg], *v.t.* dentar, mellar, formar dientes en. — *s.* diente, mella, muesca, melladura; (*fam.*) pitima, turca, chispa; carga para un caballo.

jagged ['dʒægid], **jaggy** ['dʒægi], *a.* mellado, dentado, recortado de una manera desigual.

jaggedness, *s.* melladura, estado de dentellado.

jaggy, *a.* dentado, dentellado.

jaguar ['dʒægju:ə], *s.* jaguar.

jail [dʒeil], *s.* cárcel, *f.*, prisión, gayola, calabozo; *jail fever*, tifo, fiebre de las cárceles.

jailbird, *s.* el que ha estado encarcelado; malhechor, presidiario, criminal.

jailer, *s.* carcelero, alcaide, calabocero.

jalap ['dʒæləp], *s.* jalapa.

jalousie ['ʒælu:zi:], *s.* celosía.

jam [dʒæm], *s.* compota, conserva, mermelada; agolpamiento, aprieto, apretura, apiñadura; bata de niño; (*fam.*) aprieto, apuro. — *v.t.* apiñar; estrechar, apretar, acuñar, estrujar, apachurrar; (*mec.*) atascar; (*rad.*) causar interferencia; hacer confitura de. — *v.i.* atorarse, agolparse, quedarse apretado e inmóvil.

Jamaica [dʒə'meikə], *s.* Jamaica; *Jamaica pepper*, (*bot.*) pimienta; *Jamaica wood*, brasilete; palo campeche; caoba fina; *Jamaica rum*, ron de Jamaica.

Jamaican, *a.* jamaicano.

jamb [dʒæm], *s.* jamba, quicial, montante.

jambe, *s.* canillera, greba.

jamboree ['dʒæmbori:], *s.* lance del juego de euchre; fiesta popular; (*fam.*) francachela.

jangle ['dʒæŋgəl], *v.t.* hacer sonar discordemente. — *v.i.* sonar discordemente; (*ant.*) reñir, altercar; charlar, decir tonterías. — *s.* sonido discordante; disputa, altercado, querella, riña.

jangler, *s.* parlanchín, disputador.

jangling ['dʒæŋgliŋ], *s.* sonido discordante; charla; riña, pendencia.

janissary ['dʒænisəri], *s.* genízaro.

janitor ['dʒænitəɹ], *s.* conserje, portero, bedel.

jannock ['dʒænək], *s.* pan de avena.

Jansenism ['dʒænsənizm], *s.* jansenismo.

January ['dʒænju:əri], *s.* enero.

Japan [dʒə'pæn], s. Japón; charol, laca, barniz; *Japan earth*, tierra japónica. — *v.t.* charolar, charolear, embarnizar.

Japanese [dʒæpə'niːz], s. japonés, natural del Japón, idioma japonés. — *a.* japonés, relativo al Japón.

Japhetic, *a.* jafético.

japonica [dʒə'pɔnikə], s. camelia japonesa.

jar [dʒɑːɹ], *v.t.* sacudir, hacer vibrar o trepidar, agitar; hacer discordar. — *v.i.* chirriar, hacer un ruido desagradable; reñir, desavenirse, disputar, contender, trepidar, vibrar; chocar, ludir; (*mús.*) discordar, desentonar. — *s.* jarro, jarra; botija, tarro, cántaro, tinaja, orza; trepidación, vibración; choque, sacudida, pendencia, riña, disensión; ruido, chirrido, ruido desagradable; *on a jar*, o *on the jar*, entreabierto.

jardinière [ʒɑːɹdini'ɛɹ], s. jardinera, florero.

jargon ['dʒɑːɹɡən], s. jerga, guirigay, jerigonza, monserga; lenguaje técnico; (*min.*) jacinto.

jarl [dʒɑːɹl], s. antiguo jefe escandinavo.

jarring [dʒɑːriŋ], s. disonancia, ruido discorde; contienda. — *a.* discorde, disonante, en conflicto.

jasmine ['dʒæsmin], **jessamine** ['dʒesəmin], s. jazmín.

jasper ['dʒæspəɹ], s. jaspe.

jaundice ['dʒɔːndis], s. (*med.*) ictericia; (*fig.*) envidia. — *v.t.* causar ictericia; (*fig.*) causar envidia; desilusionar.

jaundiced, *a.* ictérico, ictericiado; cetrino; (*fig.*) envidioso; desilusionado. — *p.p.* [JAUNDICE].

jaunt [dʒɔːnt], *v.i.* corretear, ir y venir. — *s.* excursión, paseata, caminata; llanta, pina.

jauntiness, s. viveza, gentileza, ligereza, garbo.

jaunty, *a.* vistoso, airoso, garboso, delicado, gentil, galán, ostentoso.

Javanese [dʒɑːvə'niːz], s., *a.* javanés, javo.

javelin ['dʒævlin], s. jabalina, venablo.

jaw [dʒɔː], s. quijada, mandíbula; (*mec.*) boca, quijada, telera; hueso maxilar; (*fig.*) abismo, garas; (*vulg.*) charla, palabrería, vituperio; *jaws of hell*, boca del infierno. — *v.t.* (*fam.*) reñir. — *v.i.* (*fam.*) charlar, hablar demasiado; refunfuñar.

jaw-bone, s. quijada, mandíbula.

jaw-breaker, s. (*fam.*) palabra difícil, trabalenguas, *m.*

jaw-teeth, *s.pl.* muelas.

jay [dʒei], s. arrendajo.

jealous ['dʒeləs], *a.* celoso, receloso, desconfiado, suspicaz, envidioso.

jealousy, jealousness, s. celos; inquietud, sospecha, recelo, vigilancia, desconfianza, suspicacia.

jean [dʒiːn], s. (*tej.*) coquillo.

jeer [dʒiəɹ], *v.t.*, *v.i.* befar, escarnecer, tratar con escarnio, mofar, burlarse. — *s.* befa, mofa, burla, escarnio; (*mar.*) guindaste con sus drizas.

jeerer, s. escarnecedor, burlador, mofador.

jeering, s. escarnio, burla.

jeeringly, *adv.* con escarnio.

Jehovah [dʒe'houvə], s. Jehová.

jehu ['dʒiːhjuː], s. cochero, auriga, *m.*, especialmente el que guía veloz o furiosamente; *to drive like a Jehu*, ir desempedrando las calles.

jejune [dʒe'dʒuːn], *a.* insípido, estéril, seco; pobre, tibio; insubstancial.

jejuneness, jejunity, s. carestía, esterilidad,

sequedad; pobreza; tibieza; insubstancialidad; insulsez.

jejunum, s. (*anat.*) yeyuno.

jellied ['dʒelid], *a.* gelatinoso, dulce como una jalea.

jelly ['dʒeli], s. jalea, gelatina, jaletina.

jelly-fish, s. medusa, aguamar.

jemmy ['dʒemi], s. palanqueta, pie de cabra.

jennet ['dʒenit], s. jaca, caballo chico; jaca española.

jenny ['dʒeni], s. torno, máquina para hilar; jumenta, burra, asna, borrica; *jenny-wren*, reyezuelo.

jeopard ['dʒepəd], **jeopardize** ['dʒepədaiz], *v.t.* arriesgar, comprometer, exponer a daño.

jeopardy ['dʒepədi], s. exposición, peligro, riesgo a daño.

jerboa [dʒəɹ'bouə], s. gerbo.

jeremiad [dʒeri'maiəd], s. jeremiada, lamentación.

jerfalcon ['dʒəːɹfɔlkən], s. gerifalte.

jerk [dʒəːɹk], s. tirón, sacudida, sobarbada, vibración, sacudimiento; brinco, salto, respingo; (*equit.*) sobarbada; (*mar.*) socollada, gualdrapazo. — *v.t.* arrojar, dar un tirón, mover a tirones; sacudir, traquetear, echar convulsivamente; tasajear carne; *jerked beef*, tasajo. — *v.i.* vibrar; sacudir; moverse a tirones.

jerker, s. tirador, sacudidor.

jerkin ['dʒəːɹkin], s. justillo; chaquetón; coleto de ante sin mangas; (*orn.*) especie de halcón.

jerky, *a.* espasmódico.

jerry-builder ['dʒeribildəɹ], s. mal constructor.

jerry-built, *a.* mal construido.

Jersey ['dʒəːɹzi], s. estambre fino; toro o vaca de la isla de Jersey; jersey.

Jerusalem [dʒe'ruːsələm], s. Jerusalén; *Jerusalem artichoke*, cotufa, pataca, aguaturma.

jess [dʒes], s. pihuela.

jessamine ['dʒesəmin], s. jazmín, jasmín.

jesse, s. árbol geneológico de Jesucristo, en forma de candelabro.

jest [dʒest], *v.i.* bufonearse, bromear, burlarse, zumbar, jaranear, chancearse, chunguearse, chulear. — *s.* chanza, broma, burla, guasa, hazmerreír, chiste, zumba, chunga, chacota, chirigota, matraca.

jester, s. bufón, burlón, fisgón, chancero, mofador.

jesting, s. mofadura, bufonería.

jestingly, *adv.* de burlas.

Jesuit ['dʒezjuːit], s. jesuita, *m.*; (*fig.*) intrigante.

Jesuitic, jesuitical, *a.* jesuítico; ajesuitado.

Jesuitism, s. jesuitismo.

jet [dʒet], s. (*min.*) azabache; chorro, fuente, *f.*, surtidor, chorretada; caño o tubo de salida; *gas-jet*, mechero o quemador de gas; *jet-engine*, motor de reacción; *jet-aeroplane*, avión de reacción. — *v.t.* echar, lanzar, arrojar. — *v.i.* salir en chorro, chorrear; sobresalir.

jet-black, *a.* negro como el azabache.

jetsam ['dʒetsəm], **jetson**, s. (*mar.*) echazón, *f.*; (*for.*) pecio.

jettee, s. [JETTY].

jettison ['dʒetizən], *v.t.* (*mar.*) echar, arrojar mercancías al mar (para aligerar un buque). — *s.* (*mar.*) echazón, *f.*; (*for.*) pecio.

jetty ['dʒeti], **jettee**, *a.* azabachado, de azabache, negro. — *s.* malecón, dique, muelle, rompeolas, *m.*, espolón; (*arq.*) salidizo, proyección.

Jew [dʒuː], *s.* judío, israelita, *m.f.*

jewel [ˈdʒuːəl], *s.* joya, alhaja, prenda, piedra preciosa, presea, venera. — *pl.* **jewels**, pedrería. — *v.t.* adornar con piedras preciosas.

jewel-box, jewel-case, *s.* joyero, joyelero, escriño.

jeweller [ˈdʒuːələr], *s.* joyero, platero, diamantista, *m.f.*, enjoyelador.

jewellery [ˈdʒuːəlri], *s.* joyas, pedrería, joyería, prendería; aderezo.

jewel-like, *a.* brillante como una joya.

Jewess [ˈdʒuːes], *s.f.* judía.

jewfish, *s.* guasa.

Jewish, *a.* judaico, judío, israelítico.

Jewry [ˈdʒuːri], *s.* Judea, Judería.

Jews'-harp, *s.* birimbao.

Jew's-mallow, *s.* (*bot.*) corchoro, planta tiliácea.

Jezebel [ˈdʒezəbəl], *s.* mujer cruel y viciosa.

jib [dʒib], *s.* aguilón, pescante (de una grúa); (*mar.*) foque, maraguto; *jib-boom*, botalón de foque; *flying-jib*, cuarto, foque; *middle-jib*, segundo foque; *standing-jib*, contrafoque; (*fam.*) cara. — *v.i.* rehusar; negarse a; *to jib at*, asustarse ante, no tener ánimo para.

jibe [dʒaib], *v.t.* (*mar.*) mudar un botavante.

jiffy [ˈdʒifi], *s.* (*fam.*) instante, momento, periquete.

jig [dʒig], *s.* jiga; bromazo, chasco, petardo; trampa; (*mec.*) conductor o guía para fabricar piezas idénticas; anzuelo, emplomado; (*min.*) criba. — *v.t.* (*mús.*) cantar o tocar una jiga; separar con criba; sacudir; (*mec.*) formar o adaptar por medio de guías; dar un bromazo. — *v.i.* bailar una jiga; bailotear; pescar con anzuelo emplomado.

jigger [ˈdʒigər], *s.* bailador, bailador de jiga; criba; (*ing.*) aparejo hidráulico; (*min.*) enganche; aparato con movimiento de vaivén; (*ent.*) nigua, pulga; (*mar.*) aparejuelo; (*mar.*) cangreja de mesana.

jig-jog [ˈdʒigdʒog], *s.* (*fam.*) sacudimiento.

jig-saw, *s.* sierra de vaivén; *jig-saw puzzle*, rompecabezas, *m.sing.*

jill [dʒil], *s.* moza; querida; taza, jícara; hurón hembra.

jilt [dʒilt], *s.* coquetona. — *v.t.* (*fam.*) plantar, dejar colgado; (*fam.*) dar calabazas (a).

Jim Crow [dʒimˈkrou], *s.* (*mec.*) herramienta para curvar o enderezar raíles; (*min.*) pie de cabra con uña; (*E.U. despec.*) un negro.

jimmy [ˈdʒimi], *s.* [JEMMY].

jimp [dʒimp], *a.* (*Esco.*) delgado, delicado, fino.

jingle [ˈdʒiŋgəl], *v.t.*, *v.i.* retiñir, sonar, tintinar; rimar. — *s.* retintín, sonido metálico; rima pueril, aleluya; cascabel.

jinglet [ˈdʒiŋglet], *s.* escrupulillo de cascabel.

jingo [ˈdʒiŋgou], *s.* (*fam.*) partidario de una política agresiva.

jinn [dʒin], *s.* genio, en la mitología árabe; espíritu bueno o malo.

jippo [ˈdʒipou], *s.* jubón, jaqueta.

job [dʒob], *s.* tarea; remiendo; destajo; granjería, agiotaje; socaliña, engañifa; ganga, cucaña; (*fam.*) empleo, ocupación, negocio, trabajo; circunstancia, suceso; *bad job*, lástima o mal negocio; *odd job*, trabajo de poca importancia; *job lot*, colección miscelánea; (*com.*) lote, saldo de mercancías.

v.t. comprar en grueso y revender; regatear; trabajar al destajo; herir, dar una mojada; pinchar; subarrendar. — *v.i.* cambalachear, chalanear.

jobber [ˈdʒobər], *s.* agiotador, agiotista, *m.f.*; remendero, remendón; destajero, destajista, *m.f.*; (*com.*) traficante medianero, corredor; el que se emplea en negocios bajos y no muy honorables.

jobbery, *s.* engañifa; agiotaje.

jobbing, *s.* cambalache.

jockey [ˈdʒoki], *s.* jockey; engañabobos, petardista, *m.f.*; chalán. — *v.t.* trampear, petardear, engañar; cruzar, ponerse delante de otro en una carrera.

jocose [dʒoˈkous], *a.* jocoso, festivo, burlesco, chancero, jovial, guasón.

jocoseness [dʒoˈkousnis], **jocosity** [dʒoˈkositi], *s.* jocosidad, alegría, chanza.

jocular [ˈdʒokjuːlər], **joculatory** [dʒokjuːˈleitəri], *a.* jocoso, guasón, chancero, divertido, gracioso, chistoso, burlesco.

jocularity, *s.* jocosidad, festividad.

jocund [ˈdʒoukʌnd, ˈdʒokʌnd], *a.* alegre, festivo, jovial, agradable.

jocundity [dʒoˈkʌnditi], **jocundness** [dʒoˈkʌndnis], *s.* alegría, jovialidad.

jog [dʒog], *v.t.* empujar; (*fig.*) excitar suavemente, estimular; dar (con el codo, etc.). — *v.i.* traquearse, bombolearse; *to jog along*, seguir adelante; (*fig.*) irse defendiendo; *to jog the memory*, refrescar la memoria. — *s.* empujoncito, empellón, sacudimiento, golpecito; zangoloteo, traqueo, bazuqueo, trote lento; estímulo; (*mec.*) muesca cuadrada.

jogging, *s.* traqueo, sacudimiento.

joggle [ˈdʒogəl], *v.t.*, *v.i.* agitar(se) o mover(se) con sacudidas suaves; vacilar; unir por medio de muescas.

John [dʒon], *s.m.* Juan; muchacho, tipo nacional; *John Bull*, tipo del pueblo inglés.

john-apple, *s.* especie de manzana tardía.

john-dory, *s.* fabro, dorado.

johnny-cake, *s.* (*E.U.*) torta de maíz.

join [dʒoin], *v.t.* juntar, unir, ensamblar, acoplar; casar; añadir, trabar, enlazar; anexar; (*com.*) asociar; chocar, aunarse, embestir; agregarse, juntarse, incorporarse o unirse a; *to join battle*, librar batalla. — *v.i.* unirse, reunirse, juntarse; asociarse, aliarse, agregarse, confederarse; estar junto.

joinder [ˈdʒoindər], *s.* (*for.*) junta, asociación, unión.

joiner, *s.* ebanista, *m.f.*, carpintero de obra prima, ensamblador.

joinery [ˈdʒoinəri], *s.* ensambladura, juntura, ebanistería.

joining, *s.* unión, *f.*, juntura, coyuntura, bisagra; *joining press*, (*carp.*) cepo.

joint [dʒoint], *s.* juntura, unión, *f.*, junta, ensambladura, empalme; nudillo; conexión, enganche; (*anat.*) articulación, coyuntura; gozne, charnela, bisagra; (*bot.*) nudo; (*alb.*) degolladura; cuarto de un animal; encuentro de un ave; (*E.U., vulg.*) lugar de reunión, sitio; *out of joint*, dislocado; desunido, despegado, desconcertado, descoyuntado; desordenado, confuso. — *a.* unido, combinado, agrupado, solidario, indiviso, colectivo; asociado, participante, copartícipe; dividido, repartido, distribuído; *joint heir*, coheredero; *joint bolt*, perno; *joint consent*, común acuerdo; *joint stock*, capital social; fondos en común; *joint-stock company*, compañía por acciones, sociedad anónima; *joint pipe*, manguito, golilla. — *v.t.* juntar, agregar, unir; descuartizar; formar nudos, articulaciones o coyunturas; hacer alianza o confederación. — *v.i.* unirse por medio de articulaciones.

jointed, *a.* nudoso, lleno de junturas, articulado; de movimiento.

jointer, *s.* (*carp.*) juntera.

jointly ['dʒɔintli], *adv.* juntamente, colectivamente, conjuntamente, mancomunadamente, unidamente; *jointly and severally*, todos y cada uno de por sí.

jointress, *s.* mujer que posee alguna cosa por derecho de viudedad.

joint-stool, *s.* asiento plegadizo.

jointure ['dʒɔintʃəɹ], *s.* (*for.*) viudedad.

joist [dʒɔist], *s.* viga, vigueta de bovedilla o suelo.

joke [dʒouk], *s.* chanza, chuscada, chiste; burla, guasa, chunga, chocarrería, camelo; *bad joke*, broma pesada; *in joke*, en chanza, de broma, de burlas; *to crack a joke*, decir un chiste; *practical joke*, bromazo, petardo, chasco. — *v.i.* chancear, chancearse.

joker, *s.* burlón, bromista, *m.f.*, guasón, chancero; comodín (naipe).

joking, *s.* chiste, burla, broma.

jokingly, *adv.* de burlas, en chanza.

jolliness ['dʒɔlinis], **jollity** ['dʒɔliti], *s.* jovialidad, alegría, viveza, broma, regocijo.

jolly ['dʒɔli], *a.* alegre, jovial, festivo, jaranero, airoso, gallardo, agradable, divertido, placentero; achispado. — *v.t.* (*fam.*) candonguear.

jolly-boat, *s.* botequín, serení.

Jolly Roger [dʒɔli'rɔdʒəɹ], *s.* bandera negra de los piratas con un cráneo y dos huesos cruzados.

jolt [dʒoult], *v.t.* traquear, traquetear, sacudir, dar sacudidas. — *v.i.* traquearse, bambolearse.

jolt, jolting, *s.* sacudimiento, traqueteo, salto, sacudida.

jolter, *s.* lo que traquea, lo que sacude.

jongleur ['ʒɔŋɡləːɹ], *s.* juglar.

jonquil ['dʒɔŋkwil], *s.* junquillo.

joss [dʒɔs], *s.* ídolo o dios chino; *joss-house*, templo para ídolos chinos; *joss-stick*, pebete.

jostle ['dʒɔsəl], *v.t.* rempujar, codear, empellar, apretar. — *v.i.* empujarse. — *s.* empellón, empujón.

jot [dʒɔt], *s.* pizca, jota, tilde, punto, ápice; *every jot*, todo; *not a jot*, ni agua. — *v.t. to jot down*, apuntar, tomar notas.

jotting, *s.* apunte, nota.

joule [dʒuːl], *s.* julio.

jounce [dʒauns], *v.t.*, *v.i.* (*fam.*) sacudir, sacudirse, traquear, traquetear. — *s.* sacudimiento, traqueteo.

journal ['dʒəːɹnəl], *s.* diario; periódico; revista; jornal (*mec.*) luchadero, manga de eje; (*com.*) jornal.

journal-bearing, *s.* cojinete.

journal-box, *s.* (*f.c.*) caja de sebo.

journalism ['dʒəːɹnəlizm], *s.* periodismo.

journalist, *s.* periodista, *m.f.*; diarista, *m.f.*

journalistic, *a.* periodístico.

journalize ['dʒəːɹnəlaiz], *v.t.* (*com.*) pasar al jornal. — *v.i.* apuntar en un diario.

journey ['dʒəːɹni], *s.* viaje; tránsito; pasaje;

jornada; *journey work*, jornal. — *v.i.* viajar, ir de viaje; recorrer un trayecto.

journeyman ['dʒəːɹnimən], *s.* jornalero; *journeyman tailor*, oficial de sastre.

joust [dʒaust], *s.* justa, torneo. — *v.i.* justar.

jovial ['dʒouviəl], *a.* jovial, alegre, festivo.

joviality [dʒouvi'æliti], **jovialness**, *s.* jovialidad, buen humor, festividad, regocijo.

jowl [dʒaul], *s.* carrillo, quijada; cabeza de pescado aderezada.

jowler, *s.* especie de perro.

joy [dʒɔi], *s.* alegría, alborozo, júbilo, regocijo, albricias; ufanía, deleite, gozo, gusto, placer, complacencia; *to wish someone joy*, desear felicidad a uno, dar la enhorabuena. — *v.i.* (*poét.*) regocijarse, alegrarse.

joy-bells, *s.* campanas de regocijo.

joyful, *a.* alegre, gozoso, regocijado, contento, festivo, jubiloso, placentero.

joyfulness, *s.* gozo, júbilo, alegría.

joyless, *a.* triste, sin gozo, sin alegría, lúgubre.

joylessness, *s.* tristeza, melancolía, oscuridad.

joyous, *a.* alegre, gozoso, festivo.

joyousness, *s.* gozo, dicha.

jubilant ['dʒuːbilənt], *a.* alborozado, regocijado, jubiloso.

jubilate, *v.i.* alegrarse, regocijarse, jubilar.

jubilation [dʒuːbi'leiʃən], *s.* júbilo, alegría, regocijo.

jubilee ['dʒuːbiliː], *s.* jubileo.

Judaic [dʒuː'deik], **Judaical** [dʒuː'deiikəl], *a.* judío, judaico, hebreo.

Judaism ['dʒuːdeiizm], *s.* judaísmo.

Judaize, *v.i.* judaizar.

Judaizer, *s.* judaizante.

Judas-tree ['dʒuːdəstriː], *s.* árbol del amor, árbol de Judas, algarrobo loco.

judge [dʒʌdʒ], *s.* juez, *m.*, magistrado; conocedor, perito; *to be no judge of*, no entender de, no ser juez en. — *v.t.* juzgar, estimar, considerar, conceptuar; (*for.*) sentenciar, criticar, censurar. — *v.i.* juzgar, opinar; (*for.*) fallar como juez, sentenciar, hacer o formar juicio; distinguir, discernir.

judgement ['dʒʌdʒmənt], **judgment**, *s.* juicio, criterio, discreción, caletre, discernimiento; sentir, dictamen, opinión, *f.*, voto; fallo, decisión, sentencia del juez; ejecutoria; *the last judgment*, juicio final; *in my judgment*, según creo; *to the best of my judgment*, según mi leal saber y entender.

judger, *s.* el que juzga, juez.

judgeship, *s.* judicatura, magistratura.

judgment-seat, *s.* tribunal.

judicable ['dʒuːdikəbəl], *a.* que puede ser juzgado.

judicative, *s.* judicativo.

judicatory ['dʒuːdi'keitəɹi], *s.* tribunal de justicia, justicia, judicatura. — *a.* judicial; jurídico.

judicature ['dʒuːdikətʃuːɹ], *s.* judicatura, magistratura, juzgado.

judicial [dʒuː'diʃəl], *a.* judicial, penal.

judiciary [dʒuː'diʃəɹi], *a.* judiciario; judicial. — *s.* administración de justicia; magistratura.

judicious [dʒuː'diʃəs], *a.* juicioso, prudente, cuerdo, sensato, mirado, circunspecto.

judiciousness, *s.* cordura, buen juicio, sensatez.

jug [dʒʌɡ], *s.* jarro; cántaro; pote; (*vulg.*) cárcel, *f.* — *v.t.* (*coc.*) estofar; (*vulg.*) encarcelar. — *v.i.* trinar (dicho del ruiseñor).

juggle ['dʒʌɡəl], *v.i.* hacer juegos malabares;

engañar, fingir, hacer trampas; (*ant.*) escamotear. — *s.* juegos malabares; (*ant.*) escamoteo; engaño, impostura, truhanería.

juggler, *s.* malabarista, *m.f.*; (*ant.*) prestidigitador; (*ant.*) juglar; engañador, estafador.

jugglery, juggling, *s.* juegos malabares; impostura, engaño, truhanería, trampa.

jugular ['dʒʌgjuːləɹ], *a.* yugular. — *s.* vena yugular.

jugulate ['dʒʌgjuːleit], *v.t.* degollar.

jugulation, *s.* degüello, degollación.

juice [dʒuːs], *s.* zumo, jugo, suco; (*Cuba*) guarapo; (*fam.*) electricidad; (*fam.*) gasolina; *digestive juices*, jugos digestivos.

juiceless, *a.* seco, sin jugo, sin zumo, sin sucos.

juiciness, *s.* jugosidad, suculencia.

juicy, *a.* jugoso, sucoso, zumiento, zumoso, suculento.

jujube ['dʒuːdʒuːb], *s.* azufaifa, yuyuba, guinja, jinjol; *jujube-tree*, guinjo, azufaifo.

julep ['dʒuːlep], *s.* julepe.

julienne [ʒuːliˈen], *s.* sopa juliene, caldo claro con legumbres.

July ['dʒuːlai], *s.* julio.

jumble ['dʒʌmbəl], *v.t.* mezclar, emburujar, arrebujar, revolver confusamente, confundir. — *v.i.* mezclarse, confundirse, revolverse. — *s.* mezcla, bazuqueo, enredo, revoltillo, embrollo, enredo, confusión; bollito delgado y dulce.

jumbler, *s.* mezclador, embrollón.

jump [dʒʌmp], *v.t.* saltar por encima de, saltar al otro lado de; saltarse, pasar por, omitir; arriesgar; en el juego de damas, comer un peón; (*fam.*) usurpar, tomar por fuerza o engaño. — *v.i.* saltar; cabriolar, brincar, dar saltos, sacudirse, traquearse, convenir, concordar; *to jump at*, apresurarse a aceptar; *to jump over*, saltar por encima; *to jump on one*, (*fam.*) poner a uno de oro y azul; *to jump one's bail*, fugarse el que esta bajo fianza; *to jump to a conclusion*, deducir o juzgar sin reflexión. — *s.* salto, cabriola, brinco; distancia o extensión de un salto; (*min.*) falla de una vena; *on the jump*, de un salto, al vuelo; inquieto.

jumper, *s.* saltador, brincador; blusa (de marinero, etc.); jersey, sweater; rastra; (*mec.*) barreta de mina, taladro de mano.

junction ['dʒʌŋkʃən], *s.* junta, unión, *f.*, adición, agregación; acopladura, trabadura; (*f.c.*) empalme, estación de empalme.

juncture ['dʒʌŋktʃəɹ], *s.* junta, juntura; articulación, coyuntura; sazón, *f.*, ocasión, momento crítico, oportunidad; trance.

June [dʒuːn], *s.* junio.

June-bug, *s.* insecto que en los E.U. aparece en junio.

jungle ['dʒʌŋgəl], *s.* selva, jungla; (*fig.*) maraña, zarzal; *jungle-fever*, fiebre palúdica.

junior ['dʒuːniəɹ], *a., s.* más joven, hijo, el menor; (*igl.*) junior; *junior partner*, socio menos antiguo; *John Smith Junior*, John Smith, hijo.

juniorate, *s.* jovenado.

juniority [dʒuːniˈɔriti], *s.* condición de más joven.

juniper ['dʒuːnipəɹ], *s.* enebro, junípero; *juniper-berry*, nebrina.

junk [dʒʌŋk], *s.* (*mar.*) junco, champán; chicote, trozada; trastos viejos; hierro viejo;

(*mar.*) trozos de cable, de cuerda, etc.; cecina.

junket ['dʒʌŋket], *v.t., v.i.* dar o tener un convite, obsequiar, festejar.

junket, junketing, *s.* festín, tiberio, francachela.

junto, *s.* cábala, cabildeo, facción.

jupe [dʒuːp], *s.* falda de mujer.

jural, *a.* forénsico.

Jurassic [dʒuˈræsik], *a.* jurásico.

jurat ['dʒuːrət], *s.* jurado, magistrado.

juratory [dʒuːˈreitəri], *a.* juratorio.

juridic [dʒuːˈridik], **juridical**, *a.* jurídico, judicial.

jurisconsult [dʒuːriskonˈsʌlt], *s.* jurisconsulto, abogado.

jurisdiction [dʒuːrisˈdikʃən], *s.* jurisdicción; fuero, potestad, poderío.

jurisdictional, *a.* jurisdiccional.

jurisdictive, *a.* que tiene jurisdicción.

jurisprudence [dʒuːrisˈpruːdəns], *s.* jurisprudencia.

jurisprudent, *s., a.* jurisperito, abogado, jurisprudente.

jurist ['dʒuːrist], *s.* jurista, *m.f.*, legista, *m.f.*, jurisperito, jurisconsulto.

juror ['dʒuːrəɹ], *s.* (*for.*) jurado (miembro de un jurado); *grand-juror*, individuo del gran jurado.

jury ['dʒuːri], *s.* (*for.*) jurado (cuerpo e institución); *grand jury*, gran jurado de acusación; *petty jury*, jurado de juicio.

jury-box, *s.* tribuna del jurado.

juryman ['dʒuːrimən], *s.* jurado (individuo).

jurymast ['dʒuːrimɑːst], *s.* (*mar.*) bandola.

jussive ['dʒʌsiv], *a.* (*gram.*) expresando orden, mando o dominio.

just [dʒʌst], *a.* justo, imparcial, equitativo, verdadero; íntegro, recto, virtuoso, honrado, inocente, puro; cabal, completo, entero; exacto; lícito; proporcionado, ordenado, arreglado. — *adv.* apuradamente, tasadamente; precisamente, justamente, exactamente, cabalmente; apenas, casi, no más que; recién, nuevo, nuevamente; poco ha (o hace), dentro de un momento; sólo, solamente; en el mismo instante; nuevamente, de nuevo; *just as*, al momento que, al tiempo que; no bien; cuando; *just as (like)*, lo mismo que, semejante a; *just as if*, lo mismo como si; *just by*, aquí cerca; *just beyond*, un poco más allá; *just now*, ahora mismo, en este mismo instante, poco hace; *just as you please*, como Vd. guste; *to have only just time*, tener justamente el tiempo preciso; *just so*, según y como; *that's just like him*, son cosas suyas (o cosas de él).

just, joust, *s.* justa, torneo. — *v.i.* justar, lidiar.

justice ['dʒʌstis], *s.* justicia, equidad; rectitud, razón, *f.*, derecho, imparcialidad; (*for.*) juez; *justice of the peace*, juez municipal.

justiceship, *s.* justiciazgo, judicatura.

justiciary [dʒʌsˈtiʃəri], *a.* judicial. — *s.* juez, magistrado.

justifiable [dʒʌstiˈfaiəbəl], *a.* justificable.

justifiableness, *s.* posibilidad de ser justificado.

justifiably, *adv.* justificadamente.

justification [dʒʌstifiˈkeiʃən], *s.* justificación; descargo, defensa.

justificative, justificatory, *a.* justificativo, defensivo.

justificator, *s.* justificador, defensor.

justifier, *s.* justificador, ajustador; justificante; calibrador.

justify ['dʒʌstifai], *v.t.* justificar, probar en justicia, defender, vindicar, sincerar; absolver; (*teol.*) absolver, perdonar, reinstalar en gracia; (*impr.*) justificar, ajustar.

justle ['dʒʌsəl], *v.t.* codear, rempujar.

justness ['dʒʌstnis], *s.* justicia, precisión, equidad; propiedad, exactitud, regularidad.

jut [dʒʌt], *v.i.* sobresalir, proyectar, extenderse más allá, combarse. — *s.* salidizo, proyección, vuelo, retallo, **resalto;** *jut window,* ventana saliente.

jute [dʒuːt], *s.* yute, cáñamo chino.

juvenescence [dʒuːvəˈnesəns], *s.* renovación de la juventud.

juvenescent, *a.* rejuveneciente, que se remoza.

juvenile ['dʒuːvənail], *a.* juvenil, joven. — *s.* mocito, joven galancete.

juvenility [dʒuːvəˈniliti], *s.* mocedad, juventud, ardor, viveza, ligereza.

juxtaposition [dʒʌkstəpoˈziʃən], *s.* yuxtaposición, contigüidad.

K

K, k [kei], undécima letra del alfabeto inglés. Esta letra tiene en inglés, el mismo sonido que la *c* española delante de *a, o, u;* antes de la *n* no se pronuncia.

Kabyle [kəˈbail], *s.* cabila.

Kafir ['kæfəɪ], **Kaffir,** *s.* cafre, idioma de los cafres; infiel (entre los mahometanos).

kail [keil], **kale,** *s.* (*bot.*) bretón, col rizada.

Kaiser ['kaizəɪ], *s.* Káiser, emperador de Alemania.

kaleidoscope [kəˈlaidoskoup], *s.* caleidoscopio.

kaleidoscopic, *a.* caleidoscópico; variado, pintoresco.

kalendar ['kælendəɪ], *s.* calendario, almanaque.

kali ['kæli, kɑːli], *s.* barrilla, hierba.

kalif [kəˈliːf], *s.* califa, *m.*

kalifate, *s.* califato.

kalmia ['kælmiə], *s.* kalmia.

Kalmuck ['kælmʌk], *s.* calmuco.

Kanaka [kəˈnækə], *s.* natural de las islas de Hawai.

kangaroo [kæŋgəˈruː], *s.* canguro.

Kantian ['kæntiən], *s.* kantiano.

Kantianism, *s.* kantismo.

kaolin ['keioulin], *s.* caolín.

kapok ['keipɔk], *s.* miraguano.

karat ['kærət], *s.* quilate.

katabolism [kəˈtæbolizm], *s.* catabolismo.

katydid ['keitidid], *s.* (*E.U.*) insecto ortóptero.

kauri ['kauri], **kawrie,** *s.* pino de la Nueva Zelandia; resina de este pino.

kayak [kai'æk], *s.* canoa esquimal.

kazoo [kəˈzuː], *s.* chicharra (instrumento).

keck [kek], *v.i.* arquear, querer vomitar. — *s.* tallo hueco, tallo de cicuta.

keckle ['kekəl], *v.t.* (*mar.*) aforrar un cable. — *v.i.* [CACKLE].

keckson ['keksən], **kecksy** ['keksi], *s.* cicuta.

kedge [kedʒ], *s.* anclote.

keel [kiːl], *s.* (*bot.*) quilla; (*mar.*) quilla; *false keel,* zapata de quilla. — *v.t.* poner la quilla; surcar el mar; dar carena; refrescar, enfriar.

keelage ['kiːlidʒ], *s.* (*mar.*) derechos de quilla.

keelfat, *s.* garapiñera.

keelhaul ['kiːlhɔːl], *v.t.* (*mar.*) pasar por debajo de la quilla (castigo).

keeling, *s.* especie de merluza.

keelson ['kiːlsən], *s.* sobrequilla.

keen, *a.* afilado; agudo, sutil, vivo, penetrante; aguzado; ladino, astuto; vehemente, ansioso; perspicaz; mordaz, picante, acre, incisivo, desabrido, satírico.

keenness ['kiːnnes], *s.* agudeza; viveza, perspicacia, sutileza; aspereza, rigor (del frío, etc.); anhelo, ansia, gana; entusiasmo, aplicación; acrimonia.

keep [kiːp], *v.t.* (*pret., p.p.* **kept**) tener, mantener, retener, conservar, guardar, librar, custodiar, proteger, preservar, cuidar, defender; reservar, ocultar; impedir, detener, entretener; dirigir, atender a (una tienda); llevar (los libros de comercio); sostener, proveer, mantener; proseguir, continuar, seguir; celebrar, solemnizar; guardar, cumplir, observar; poner por escrito. — *v.i.* mantenerse, sostenerse; soler, acostumbrar; continuar, perseverar, permanecer, quedar; residir, vivir; tener cuidado de alguna cosa; *to keep aloof,* apartarse, alejarse, mantenerse (o quedarse) aparte; no entremeterse; *to keep at it,* (*fam.*) persistir, perseverar; *to keep away,* tener a uno alejado o apartado; *to keep back,* retener, guardar, ocultar, impedir, restringir; *to keep books,* (*com.*) llevar los libros; *to keep company with,* acompañar, estar con; *to keep down,* sujetar; tener en un lugar subordinado; tener humillado; *to keep from,* defender, guardar; impedir; *to keep in,* refrenar, reprimir, contener, tener en sujeción; esconder, ocultar, quedarse en casa; *to keep in awe,* hacerse temer; *to keep something in mind,* tener presente una cosa, o conservar la memoria de una cosa; *to keep late hours,* trasnochar; *to keep off,* impedir, tener alejado, mantener(se) separado; *to keep on,* seguir, proseguir, adelantar; *to keep out,* impedir a uno que entre, no permitir entrar, no entrar, mantenerse alejado; *to keep one's eye on someone,* no perder de vista a uno; *to keep under,* sujetar, tener en sujeción; *to keep up,* conservar, mantener, continuar, no ceder; *to keep (to) one's bed,* guardar cama; *to keep one's temper,* contenerse, ser dueño de sí mismo o tener calma; *to keep strict silence,* no decir malo ni bueno o no decir esta boca es mía; *to keep strictly to the text,* atenerse a la letra; *to keep the land aboard,* (*mar.*) mantenerse inmediato a la tierra; *to keep the sea,* (*mar.*) mantenerse mar afuera; *to keep off,* (*mar.*) mantenerse distante, no arrimarse. — *s.* mantenimiento, medios; cuidado, custodia; guarda, guardia; torreón, alcázar, castillo; *give for keeps,* (*fam.*) dar para siempre o para retener.

keeper, *s.* guarda, *m.f.,* guardador, guardián, custodio, defendedor, defensor; carcelero; tenedor; guardabosque; *keeper of the great seal,* guardasellos del Rey, Gran Canciller; *book-keeper,* tenedor de libros.

keepership, *s.* guardería, alcaidía.

keeping, *s.* cargo, mantenimiento, custodia; cuidado, defensa, preservación; guarda; concordancia; congruencia; *book-keeping,* teneduría de libros; *not in keeping,* no congruente, mal avenido.

keepsake ['kipseik], s. dádiva, regalo, recuerdo, presente.
keeve [ki:v], s. cuba, tina, vasija en que fermenta la cerveza.
keever, s. enfriadera de cerveza.
keg [keg], s. cuñete, barrilito.
kelp [kelp], s. algas marinas y sus cenizas de las que se obtiene el yodo.
kelpie ['kelpi], s. (*Esco.*) duende del agua.
Kelt [kelt], s. celta.
Keltic, a. céltico.
kelter, s. buen orden.
kemp [kemp], s. la parte más basta de la lana.
ken [ken], v.t. saber, conocer; divisar, espiar, reconocer. — s. alcance de la vista.
Kendal green ['kendəl'gri:n], s. especie de paño verde (originario de *Kendal*).
kennel ['kenəl], s. perrera; traílla; jauría; (*fig.*) canalizo, arroyo; zorrera. — v.t., v.i. tener en perrera, estar en perrera.
keno, s. especie de lotería.
kent [kent], s. asta, palo largo, garrocha, venablo.
kentledge ['kentledʒ], s. (*mar.*) enjunque.
kepi ['kepi], s. quepis.
kept [kept], pret., p.p. [KEEP].
keramic [ke'ræmik], a. cerámico.
keratitis [kerə'taitis], s. queratitis, f.
kerb [kə:ɹb], s. bordillo de acera.
kerb-stone, s. brocal de pozo; bordillo (de acera).
kerchief ['kə:ɹtʃif], s. pañuelo, tocado de mujer, cofia.
kerchiefed, a. adornado con pañuelo.
kerf [kə:ɹf], s. abertura hecha por una sierra, hacha, etc.
kerite ['kerait], s. cauchú artificial usado como aislante en la electricidad.
kermes ['kə:ɹmi:z], s. quermes, grana; *Kermes Oak*, coscoja.
kermis ['kə:ɹmis], s. quermese, f.
kern [kə:ɹn], s. última gavilla de la cosecha; fiesta con que se celebra la gavilla; (*impr.*) hombre de una letra; patán; soldado irlandés. — v.i. (*agr.*) granar, formarse en granos.
kernel ['kə:ɹnəl], s. almendra, semilla; grano de maíz; pepita de manzana; (*fig.*) meollo, médula, núcleo. — v.i. formarse almendra.
kernelled, a. que tiene almendra, pepita o hueso.
kernelly, a. almendrado, lleno de almendras.
kernelwort, s. escrofularia.
kerosene ['kerosi:n], s. nafta, parafina líquida.
kersey ['kə:ɹzi], s. buriel.
kerseymere ['kə:ɹzimiəɹ], s. casimiro o casimira.
kestrel ['kestrəl], s. cernícalo.
ketch [ketʃ], s. queche.
ketchup ['ketʃəp], s. salsa picante.
ketone ['ki:toun], s. ketona.
kettle ['ketəl], s. caldero; cafetera; calderilla; calderico, caldereta; *tea-kettle*, tetera; *here's a kettle of fish!* ¡vaya un lío!
kettledrum ['ketəldɹʌm], s. timbal, atabal.
kettledrummer, s. timbalero, atabalero.
kettlepins, s. juego de bolos.
kevel ['kevəl], s. (*mar.*) manigueta, maniguetón; (*zool.*) gacela.
kevel-head, s. escalamote, abitón.
kex [keks], s. (*bot.*) cicuta; tallo hueco y seco.
key [ki:], s. llave, f.; buscapié; clave, f., destor-

nillador; cuña; chaveta, chabeta; (*arq.*) clave, f., dovela; (*arti.*) sotrozo; (*enc.*) clavija; (*elec.*) llave, f., conmutador; tecla (de piano, etc.); tono; llave de los instrumentos de viento; (*mar.*) cayo, isleta; muelle; *pass key* o *skeleton key*, llave maestra; *key action*, (*mús.*) teclado; *in a high key*, en tono alto; *in key*, en harmonía, de acuerdo; *to be under lock and key*, estar bajo siete llaves, o estar bien guardado.
keyboard ['ki:bɔ:ɹd], s. teclado.
keyed [ki:d], a. que tiene llaves o teclas; templado, afinado; estirado.
keyhole ['ki:houl], s. ojo de la llave, agujero.
keystone, s. (*arq.*) piedra clave.
khaki ['kɑ:ki], s. caqui.
khan [kæn, kɑ:n], s. kan, khan; caravanera.
khedive [ke'di:v], s. jedive, kedive.
kibble ['kibəl], s. (*min.*) cubo de hierro para extraer el mineral.
kibe [kaib], s. grieta en la piel; sabañón ulcerado.
kibed, kiby, a. lleno de sabañones.
kick [kik], v.t. acocear, cocear, tirar coces. — v.i. patear, dar patadas, dar puntapiés, dar coces, pernear; (*fam.*) respingar, oponerse; quejarse; *to kick against the pricks*, dar coces contra el aguijón; *to kick one out*, echar a alguno a puntapiés (o a patadas); *to kick up a shindy*, (*fam.*) armar un escándalo (o una bronca); *to kick the bucket*, morir. — s. patada, puntapié, puntillazo; coz, f.; (*fam.*) respingo, oposición, queja, protesta; depresión en el fondo de una botella de vidrio.
kicker, s. acoceador, pateador, coceador; (*fam.*) reparón, quejumbroso.
kicking, s. acoceamiento, coceadura, acción de cocear, pateadura, pataleo.
kickshaw ['kikʃɔ:], s. patarata, monada, bagatela, fruslería; ridiculez; pisto, almodrote.
kid [kid], s. cabrito, chivato; cabritilla; carne de cabrito; (*mar.*) gamella; (*fam.*) chico, chica, niño, niña; muchachito, muchachita; haz de brezos. — pl. kids, (*fam.*) guantes o zapatos de cabritilla. — v.i. parir cabritos; (*vulg.*) engañar.
kiddle ['kidəl], s. presa o represa en un río con redes o trampas para pescar.
kidling, s. choto, cabritillo.
kidnap ['kidnæp], v.t. secuestrar; (*Am.*) plagiar.
kidnapper, s. ladrón de niños, secuestrador.
kidnapping, s. secuestro; (*Am.*) plagio.
kidney ['kidni], s. riñón; (*ant.*) pasiones, afectos; temperamento, índole, f.; *of the same kidney*, del mismo palo.
kidney-bean, s. judía, frijol, frejol, habichuela.
kidney-shaped, a. reniforme.
kidney-vetch, s. vulneraria.
kidney-wort, s. (*bot.*) ombligo.
kilderkin ['kildəɹkin], s. medio barril (de 18 galones).
kill [kil], v.t. matar; amortiguar, destruir, privar de vigor, quitar la vida; descartar; neutralizar; cancelar, suprimir, anular; hacer una carnicería; *to kill oneself with work*, fatigarse, cansarse con demasiado trabajo; *to kill two birds with one stone*, matar dos pájaros de un tiro. — s. riachuelo, caleta, arroyo.
killdee [kil'di], **killdeer** ['kildiəɹ], s. (*orn.*) egialites, frailecillo norteamericano.
killer, s. matador; asesino.

killick, s. (*mar.*) piedra, trozo de hierro, o anclote para anclar un bote de pesca.

killing, a. matador; irresistible; destructivo; (*fam.*) ridículo, risible, divertido. — s. occisión, matanza.

kill-joy, s. aguafiestas, *m. f. sing. pl.*

killow ['kilou], s. tierra negruzca, tierra gallinera.

kiln [kiln], s. horno, estufa; *brick-kiln*, ladrillera, ladrillal; *lime-kiln*, calera.

kilndry ['kilndrai], *v.t.* secar en horno.

kilo ['ki:lou, 'kilou], *pref. y abrev.* [KILOGRAM].

kilogram, kilogramme ['kilogræm], s. kilo(gramo).

kilogrammeter, s. kilográmetro.

kilojoule ['kilodʒu:l], s. kilojulio.

kilolitre ['kiloli:tə.ɪ], s. kilolitro.

kilometre ['kilomi:tə.ɪ], s. kilómetro.

kilometric, s. kilométrico.

kilowatt ['kilowɔt], s. kilovatio.

kilt [kilt], s. falda escocesa.

kimono [ki'mounou], s. quimono.

kin [kin], s. parentesco, vínculo; parentela, parientes, linaje; especie, *f.*, clase, *f.*; *all of a kin*, (*fig.*) lobos de una camada; *next of kin*, pariente próximo. — a. pariente, familiar; allegado, congenial, de la misma naturaleza.

kind [kaind], a. benigno, benévolo, bondadoso, benéfico, afable, cariñoso; favorable; manso. — s. género, clase, *f.*, especie, *f.*; naturaleza, modo, manera; calaña, calidad; linaje; *in a kind*, en cierto modo, de cierta manera; *in kind*, del mismo modo, con algo parecido; (*com.*) con mercancías (en vez de dinero); *human kind*, género humano; *kind of*, (*fam.*) algo, como si.

kindergarten ['kində.ɪgɑː.ɪtən], s. jardín de la infancia.

kind-hearted [kaind'hɑː.ɪtid], a. bondadoso.

kind-heartedness, s. bondad, benevolencia.

kindle ['kindəl], *v.t.* encender, quemar, pegar fuego; enardecer, inflamar; iluminar; *kindling-wood*, leña. — *v.i.* prender, arder, quemarse, iluminarse; inflamarse, avivarse; (*ant.*) parir (liebres u otros animales).

kindliness ['kaindlinis], s. bondad, benevolencia; buena índole.

kindly ['kaindli], a. benigno, amable, cariñoso; blando, suave, tratable; provechoso, beneficioso; (*ant.*) natural, idóneo, propio.

kindness ['kaindnis], s. bondad, benevolencia, buena voluntad, cariño, afecto, humanidad, benignidad; gracia, atención, favor, fineza, caridad, beneficio.

kindred ['kindred], s. parentesco, cognación, consanguinidad, sangre, *f.*; casta, parentela, tribu, *f.* — a. emparentado, consanguíneo, deudo, hermano, parejo.

kine [kain], *s.pl.* vacas (antiguo plural de *cow*).

kinematics [kine'mætiks], s. (*fís.*) cinemática.

kinetic [kai'netik], a. dinámico.

kinetics, s. dinámica.

kinetoscope [kai'netoskoup], s. cinematógrafo.

king [kiŋ], s. rey, soberano, monarca, *m.f.*; (juego de damas); dama) (naipes o ajedrez) rey; *king's evil*, lamparón, escrófula; (*fig.*) el que o lo que es preeminente en cualquier esfera; *king's yellow*, color amarillo hecho de oropimente, o arsénico amarillo. — *v.t.* elevar a la dignidad de rey; (juego de damas) coronar un peón.

king-bird, s. tirano, muscícapa.

king-bolt, s. perno pinzote, perno real.

king-crab, s. límulo.

kingcraft, s. arte de reinar, arte de gobernar.

king-cup, s. (*bot.*) botón de oro.

kingdom ['kiŋdəm], s. reino, monarquía; región, *f.*, extensión de tierra.

kingfisher ['kiŋfiʃə.ɪ], s. guardarrío, martín pescador, alción, *m.*

kinghood, s. soberanía, dignidad de rey.

kinglet, s. reyezuelo; (*orn.*) abadejo, régulo.

kinglike ['kiŋlaik], **kingly,** a. real, regio, soberano, majestuoso, augusto, pomposo.

king-pin, s. perno real; (*E.U.*) persona de gran importancia.

king-post, s. (*arq.*) pendolón, colgante.

kingship ['kiŋʃip], s. majestad, dignidad real; trono, corona, cetro; monarquía.

kingspear, s. gamón.

kink [kiŋk], s. retorcimiento, ensortijamiento, retortijón; (*mar.*) coca, ojal; (*fam.*) capricho, chifladura. — *v.t.*, *v.i.* formar cocas, ensortijarse, torcerse, retorcerse, encarrujarse, enredarse.

kinky, a. que tiene cocas; pasudo; ensortijado, grifo, encarrujado; (*fam.*) chiflado.

kino [ki:nou], s. quino.

kinsfolk ['kinzfouk], s. parentela, parientes.

kinship, s. parentesco.

kinsman ['kinzmən], s. pariente, deudo.

kinswoman, s. parienta.

kiosk ['ki:ɔsk], s. quiosco.

kip [kip], s. (*ten.*) piel de res pequeña; (*vulg.*) casa de huéspedes mala; cama; *kip-leather*, *kip-skin*, becerro.

kipe [kaip], s. nasa, butrón, buitrón.

kipper [kipə.ɪ], s. salmón macho durante la época de la freza; arenque ahumado. — *v.t.* curar pescado al humo.

kirk [kə:.ɪk], s. (*Esco.*) iglesia.

kirtle ['kə:.ɪtəl], s. capa, manto; chupa larga.

kirtled, a. vestido con manto o capa.

kismet ['kizmet], s. hado, destino.

kiss [kis], *v.t.* besar, acariciar, hacer caricias; rozar, tocar suavemente; (*billar*) tocar; *to kiss the rod*, aceptar un castigo; *to kiss the dust*, morder el polvo. — s. beso, ósculo; (en el billar) pelo; dulce, merengue.

kiss-curl, s. aladar.

kisser, s. besador, besucador; (*vulg.*) boca.

kist [kist], s. (*Esco.*) arca, cofre; ataúd de piedra prehistórico.

kit [kit], s. gatito; colodra, tineta; (*mil.*) equipo; avíos, juego o caja de herramientas, apresto, aparejo; cubo; tiple (guitarría); violín de tres cuerdas; (*foto.*) marquito, interior del porta-placas.

kit-bag, s. mochila.

kit-cat, s. tertulia política; (*pint.*) lienzo o retrato de medio cuerpo.

kitchen ['kitʃin], s. cocina; *kitchen maid*, *kitchen wench*, fregona, fregatriz; *kitchen-range*, cocina económica, fogón a la inglesa; *kitchen-garden*, huerta; *kitchen-boy*, *kitchen-knave*, pinche, galopillo; marmitón; *kitchen utensils*, batería de cocina.

kite [kait], s. cometa, pandorga, barrilete, (*Cuba*) papalote; (*orn.*) milano; (*fig.*) fullero, petardista, *m.f.*; (*mar.*) sobrejuanete, foque volante; *kite-flying*, acción de remontar una cometa; (*fam.*) negociación de pagarés sin valor.

kith [kiθ], *s.* conocidos, amistades; *kith and kin,* parientes y amigos.

kitten ['kitən], **kitling,** *s.* gatito, gatico, michito. — *v.i.* parir la gata.

kittenish, *a.* de gatito; juguetón.

kittiwake ['kitiweik], *s.* (*orn.*) risa, especie de gaviota.

kitty ['kiti], *s.* gatito, minino.

kleptomania [klepto'meiniə], *s.* cleptomanía.

kleptomaniac, *s., a.* cleptómano.

knack [næk], *s.* maña, don, tino, destreza, acierto, prontitud, habilidad, arte, gracia; chuchería; treta. — *v.i.* estallar, crujir, rechinar; hablar afectadamente.

knacker, *s.* soguero, cordelero; matarife de caballos; tratante en artículos de segunda mano (casas, buques, etc.).

knag [næg], *s.* nudo duro en la madera.

knaggy, *a.* nudoso; áspero.

knap [næp], *v.t.* romper, golpear. — *v.i.* crujir, estallar, rechinar.

knapsack ['næpsæk], *s.* mochila, alforja, barjuleta, fardel.

knapweed, *s.* cabezuela; varias especies de centáurea.

knave [neiv], *s.* bribón, pícaro, bellaco, truhán; sota de naipes; (*ant.*) muchacho, criado.

knavery ['neivəri], **knavishness** ['neiviʃnis], *s.* picardía, travesura, bribonada, bellaquería, charranería.

knavish, *a.* travieso, fraudulento, malicioso.

knead [ni:d], *v.t.* amasar, heñir, sobar.

kneader, *s.* amasador, panadero.

kneading, *s.* amasadura, acción de amasar, soba; *kneading trough,* amasadera, artesa, masera.

knee [ni:], *s.* rodilla; (*mar.*) curva; (*mec.*) codo, codillo, ángulo, escuadra; *knee breeches,* calzón corto; *knee deep,* metido hasta las rodillas; *knee high,* hasta la rodilla; *knee timber,* madera para curvas; *knee tribute,* genuflexión. — *v.t.* suplicar de rodillas. — *v.i.* arrodillarse para pedir.

knee-cap, *s.* rodillera, rótula.

knee-crooking, *s.* obsequioso.

knee-joint, *s.* articulación de la rodilla.

knee-jointed, *a.* encorvado, angular.

kneed, *a.* articulado, acodillado; nudoso.

kneeholly, kneeholm, *s.* (*bot.*) brusco.

kneel [ni:l], *v.i.* arrodillarse, hincar (o doblar) la rodilla, ponerse de hinojos.

kneeler, *s.* el que se arrodilla; escabel.

knee-pan, *s.* (*anat.*) rótula, choquezuela.

knell [nel], *s.* doble, tañido fúnebre, toque de difuntos; (*fig.*) mal agüero. — *v.t., v.i.* (*poét.*) doblar, tocar las campanas a muerto; dar un sonido lúgubre o de aviso.

knew [nju:], *pret.* [KNOW].

knickerbockers ['nikəɹbɔkəɹz], *s.* calzón corto, bragas.

knick-knack ['niknæk], *s.* (*fam.*) chuchería, bujería, juguete.

knife [naif], *s.* (*pl.* **knives** [naivz]) cuchillo, navaja, cuchilla; (*ant.*) espada, puñal; *carving-knife,* cuchillo de trinchar, trinchante; *pen-knife,* cortaplumas, *m.*; *pocket-knife,* navaja; *pruning-knife,* podadera; *war to the knife,* guerra a muerte. — *v.t.* (*fam.*) acuchillar, matar con un cuchillo; (*E.U.*) vencer, arruinar por medio de intrigas.

knight [nait], *s.* caballero; campeón; caballo del ajedrez; *knight of the shears,* (*fam.*) sastre;

knight of St. Crispin, (*fam.*) zapatero; *Knight of the Order of the Garter,* caballero de la Orden de la Jarretera. — *v.t.* armar, hacer o crear caballero, condecorar, encomendar.

knight-errant [nait'erənt], *s.* caballero andante.

knight-errantry, *s.* caballería andante.

knighthead ['naithed], *s.* (*mar.*) tragante exterior del bauprés; *knighthead of the windlass,* cepos (o bitas) del molinete; *knightheads of the gears,* guindastes.

knighthood ['naithud], *s.* caballería, dignidad de caballero, encomienda.

knightliness ['naitlinis], *s.* cualidades o deberes de caballero.

knightly, *a.* caballeresco.

knit [nit], *v.t., v.i.* (*pret., p.p.* **knit** o **knitted**) hacer punto; (*fig.*) juntar, anudar, atar, unir, enlazar, entretejer; contraer; tejer; (*fig.*) unirse, trabarse; *to knit the eyebrows,* fruncir las cejas; *knitted stockings,* medias de punto. — *s.* tejido.

knittable, *a.* capaz de ser tejido o unido.

knitter, *s.* calcetero, mediero.

knitting, *s.* trabajo de punto; acción de hacer calceta; unión, *f.*; *knitting machine,* máquina para hacer punto; *knitting needle,* aguja de hacer punto; *knitting work,* trabajo de punto.

knittle ['nitəl], *s.* (*mar.*) sardineta, cordoncillo de bolsa.

knob [nɔb], *s.* prominencia, eminencia, protuberancia, bulto; nudo en la madera; (*arq.*) abollón; borlita o bolita, perilla, gorrón, botón; puño (de bastón); (*mar.*) tojino; *door-knob,* tirador de puerta.

knobbed, knobby, *a.* lleno de bultos o nudos; que tiene eminencias, montañoso; terco, obstinado, difícil.

knobbiness, *a.* calidad de lo que tiene bultos.

knock [nɔk], *v.t., v.i.* chocar, topar, encontrarse; tocar; llamar (a una puerta), golpear, pegar, dar golpes, aporrear, macear; cutir; *to knock down,* echar por tierra de un golpe, derribar; (*com.*) abatir, desarmar; *to knock down to the highest bidder,* rematar al mejor postor; *to knock in,* martillar, amartillar; hacer entrar por medio de golpes; *to knock on the head,* romper la cabeza, dar en la cabeza; (*fig.*) frustrar, destruir el efecto de; *to knock off,* hacer saltar por medio de golpes; descontinuar, cesar, suspender; (*fam.*) hacer o ejecutar prontamente; descontar, rebajar; *to knock out,* sacar, quitar; dejar fuera de combate, 'noquear'; atontar; *to knock together,* construir toscamente o de prisa; *to knock under,* someterse, rendirse; *to knock up,* despertar; cansar, poner enfermo a. — *s.* choque, porrazo, golpe, topetazo, llamada, toque, aldabonazo.

knock-about, *a.* violento (dicho de farsas); de uso constante; *knock-about suit,* traje de batalla.

knock-down, *a.* derribador; *knock-down price,* reserva, precio mínimo.

knocker, *s.* golpeador; aldaba, llamador, aldabilla, aldabón; (*folklore*) gnomo que indica la presencia de un metal precioso, golpeando.

knocking, *s.* aldabazo, aldabonazo, llamada a la puerta, acto de llamar a la puerta.

knock-kneed, *a.* zambo, patizambo.

knoll [nɔl], *v.t., v.i.* doblar, tocar las campanas a muerto, sonar (como campana). — *s.*

colina, loma, otero; cumbre o cima de una loma; doblar o doble de las campanas.

knop [nɔp], *s.* prominencia, protuberancia, bulto; (*arq.*) florón.

knosp [nɔsp], *s.* (*bot.*) botón, capullo; (*arq.*) florón.

knot [nɔt], *s.* nudo, ligadura, atadura; nudo de madera, nudo de plantas; vínculo; lazo; maraña, enredo de un drama; grupo, corrillo; asociación, colección, confederación, reunión, *f.*; embrollo, dificultad, confusión, intriga; (*mar.*) nudo, milla náutica; punto arduo o dificultoso; (*orn.*) canuto, tríngido; *loose knot*, nudo flojo; *hard knot*, nudo apretado; *running knot*, o *slip-knot*, nudo corredizo; *knots of the log line*, (*mar.*) señales de la corredera. — *v.t.* anudar, añudar, atar con nudos, enredar, juntar, unir, intrincar. — *v.i.* echar nudos (las plantas); formar nudos, hacer nudos.

knotgrass, *s.* centinodia; grama.

knotless, *a.* sin nudos.

knotted, *a.* nudoso, anudado, lleno de lazos.

knottiness [ˈnɔtinis], *s.* abundancia de nudos; dificultad; desigualdad; bulto.

knotty [ˈnɔti], *a.* nudoso; áspero, duro; difícil, intrincado.

knot-wood, *s.* madera nudosa.

knout [naut], *s.* knut, azote antiguo ruso.

know [nou], (*pret.* **knew,** *p.p.* **known**) *v.t.* saber, conocer; distinguir, discernir; comprender, entender, estar al corriente de; reconocer, hacerse cargo, caer en algo; *to know perfectly*, saber al dedillo, saber de memoria. — *v.i.* saber, conocer, comprender, estar informado, tener noticia o conocimiento, obtener experiencia; informarse, enterarse; *to know how many beans make five*, saber cuántas son cinco.

knowable [ˈnouəbəl], *a.* conocible.

knower, *s.* sabio, conocedor.

know-how, *s.* pericia, conocimiento técnico.

knowing [ˈnouiŋ], *a.* instruido, inteligente, entendido, hábil, diestro. — *s.* conocimiento, inteligencia; *worth knowing*, digno de conocerse (o de saberse).

knowingly, *adv.* conocidamente, hábilmente; con conocimiento de causa, a ciencia cierta; a sabiendas; con cierta malicia.

knowledge [ˈnɔledʒ], *s.* conocimiento, erudición, ciencia, instrucción, saber, noticia, experiencia práctica, apariencia, inteligencia, pericia; *to the best of my knowledge*, según mi leal saber y entender; *not to my knowledge*, no que yo sepa; *without my knowledge*, sin saberlo yo.

known [noun], conocido, noto, reconocido, sabido, comprendido. — *p.p.* [KNOW]; *to make known*, hacer saber, participar, declarar, publicar; *as is well known*, como es bien sabido, como ya se sabe.

knub [nʌb], *s.* terrón, bulto, protuberancia, borlita. — *pl.* desperdicio de la seda al hilarla del capullo.

knuckle [ˈnʌkəl], *s.* nudillo, artejo, juntura de los dedos; (*mec.*) charnela; jarrete de ternero; (*mar.*) codillo de una curva. — *v.i.* someterse, rendirse, abandonar la partida.

knuckled, *a.* nudoso.

knur [nəː], **knurl** [nəːl], *s.* nudo, protuberancia, substancia dura.

knurled, knurry, *a.* lleno de nudos, nudoso.

kobold [kɔˈbəld], *s.* gnomo.

koniscope [ˈkɔniscoup], *s.* instrumento para medir la cantidad de polvo en la atmósfera.

kopeck [ˈkoupek], *s.* copec.

kopje [ˈkɔpi], *s.* colina, montecillo.

Koran [koˈræn, koˈrɑːn], *s.* Alcorán o Corán.

kosher [ˈkouʃəɹ], *a.* permitido por la ley judía.

koumiss [kuˈmis], **koomiss,** o **kumiss,** *s.* kumis, caracosmos, leche fermentada de yegua.

kow-tow [kauˈtau], *s.* reverencia. — *v.i.* saludar humildemente; (*fig.*) humillarse.

kraal [krɑːl], *s.* población de hotentotes; corral, redil, reunión de barracas.

kyanise, kyanize [ˈkaiənaiz], *v.t.* dar a la madera un baño de sublimado corrosivo.

kymograph [ˈkaimogræf], *s.* instrumento para medir las ondas de oscilación, como las pulsaciones de la sangre.

L

L, l [el], duodécima letra del alfabeto inglés. Esta letra tiene la misma pronunciación que en español excepto que seguida de *f, k* o *m* es muda; en varias palabras es semilíquida como en *cattle, trouble.*

L, *s.* abrev. de libra esterlina; (*E.U. local*) ferrocarril elevado; *LL.B.* o *LL.D.* Bachiller o Doctor en ambos derechos.

la [lɑː], *s.* (*mús.*) la, *m.* — *interj.* ¡vamos! ¡por Dios!

labarum [ˈlæbəɹəm], *s.* lábaro; norma.

labdanum [ˈlæbdənəm], *s.* ládano.

labefaction [læbiˈfækʃən], *s.* decadencia, decaimiento, declinación; enflaquecimiento.

label [ˈleibəl], *s.* marbete, rótula, rotulata, membrete, letrero, etiqueta. — *v.t.* rotular, marcar; señalar con un rótulo, poner etiqueta; clasificar, designar.

labellum [ləˈbeləm], *s.* (*bot.*) pétalo inferior de una orquídea; (*ent.*) parte de la trompa de un insecto díptero.

labial [ˈleibiəl], *a.* labial; que tiene labios o bordes. — *s.* letra labial.

labiate [ˈleibiət], **labiated,** *s., a.* (*bot.*) labiado, dividido a modo de labios.

labiodental [leibioˈdentəl], *a.* labiodental. — *s.* labiodental, *f.*

labionasal [leibioˈneizəl], *a.* labionasal. — *s.* labionasal, *f.*

labium [ˈleibiəm], *s.* (*pl.* **labia**) labio.

laboratory [ˈlæborətəri], *s.* laboratorio; (*mil.*) taller de arsenal.

labour [ˈleibəɹ], *s.* trabajo, pena, labor, *f.*, fatiga; obra, faena, ejercicio, quehacer, tarea; dolores de parto; la clase obrera; aprieto, apuro; tráfago; (*mar.*) violento balanceo o cabeceo de un buque; *hard labour*, trabajo arduo, rudo; trabajo forzado en una prision; *to be in labour*, estar de parto; *to labour without result* (o *in vain*) o *to have one's labour for one's pains*, trabajar en balde, o machacar en hierro frío, o azotar el aire; *labour-saving*, que ahorra trabajo. — *v.i.* trabajar, forcejar, afanarse, esforzarse; sufrir; estar de parto; hacer una cosa con dificultad; (*mar.*) cabecear, balancear(se), trabajar contra viento y marea. — *v.t.* elaborar, fabricar, labrar, pulir, perfeccionar; hacer trabajar, activar, formar con trabajo; arar, cultivar.

labourer, s. peón, gañán, bracero, labrador, jornalero.

labouring, s. trabajo, esfuerzo; *labouring beast,* bestia de carga.

laborious [lə'bɔːrɪəs], a. laborioso, trabajoso, penoso, afanoso; diligente, industrioso, trabajador; difícil, ímprobo, arduo.

laboriousness, s. laboriosidad, trabajo, dificultad, afán, aplicación, diligencia.

laborsome, laboursome, a. trabajoso, ímprobo, penoso, arduo.

labradorite [læbrədo'rait], s. labradorita.

labrum ['læbrəm], s. labro.

laburnum [lə'bəːnəm], s. laburno.

labyrinth ['læbirinθ], s. laberinto, dédalo.

labyrinthian, labyrinthic, a. laberíntico, intrincado, enmarañado, confuso.

lac [lak], s. laca.

lac [lak], **lakh,** s. suma de cien mil (generalmente de rupias).

lace [leis], s. encaje, puntas, puntilla, blonda, pasamano, randa, galón de oro o plata; cuerda, cinta, cordón; (*ant.*) lazo, trampa; *thread lace,* encaje de hilo, puntas de hilo; *lace pillow,* almohadilla para hacer encajes; *point lace,* punta, encaje hecho con aguja. — *v.t.* atar, abrochar, ajustar (zapatos, vestidos, etc.) con lazos o cordones; galonear, guarnecer con encajes, galones o cordones; enlazar, encordonar, acordonar; entrelazar; (*fam.*) azotar; rayar con líneas muy finas.

Lacedæmonian [læsidi'mouniən], a. lacedemón, lacedemonio.

lace-frame, s. telar para encajes.

lace-man, s. pasamanero.

lacerable ['læsərəbəl], a. que se puede lacerar.

lacerate ['læsəreit], *v.t.* lacerar, despedazar, rasgar, hacer pedazos, lastimar.

laceration, a. laceración, despedazamiento, desgarradura, desgarrón, rasgón.

lacertian, s. (*zool.*) lacertídeo. — s. lacerto, lagarto.

lacewing, s. crisopo.

lace-woman, *s.f.* pasamanera, vendedora de encajes.

laches ['lætʃez], s. (*for.*) negligencia culpable; negligencia, dejadez.

lachrymal ['lækriməl], a. lacrimal. — s. hueso lacrimal.

lachrymary, a. que contiene lágrimas.

lachrymation [lækri'meiʃən], s. derramamiento o efusión de lágrimas.

lachrymose ['lækrimouz], a. lloroso, llorón.

lacing ['leisiŋ], s. acto de enlazar o enlace, enlazamiento; atar; pieza de espaldar; cuerda, cordón, cordoncillo; (*fam.*) zurra, tunda; uso de corsés; *tight lacing,* hábito de apretarse el corsé.

lacinia [lə'siniə], s. lacinia.

laciniate [lə'siniət], **laciniated** [lə'sinieitid], a. laciniado, dentado, serrado, adornado con randas.

lack [læk], *v.t., v.i.* carecer, faltar, necesitar, estar necesitado. — s. falta, carencia, menester, necesidad, escasez.

lackadaisical [lækə'deisikəl], a. sentimental, lánguido, negligente, perezoso.

lack-a-day [lækə'dei], *interj.* (*ant.*) ¡mal día! ¡día aciago!

lacker, s. el que hace falta. — *v.t.* barnizar.

lackey ['læki], s. lacayo. — *v.t., v.i.* servir como lacayo; ser criado de alguno.

lacking, a. falto, defectivo.

lacklove, s. desamorado.

lacklustre ['læklʌstəɹ], a. deslustrado, falto de brillo.

laconic [lə'kɔnik], **laconical,** a. lacónico, conciso, breve, corto, compendioso.

laconism [lækə'nizm], s. laconismo, estilo lacónico.

lacquer ['lækəɹ], *v.t.* barnizar; dar una capa de laca a. — s. laca; *lacquer work,* objetos de laca.

lacquering, s. acción de barnizar con laca, adorno o capa de laca.

lacrimal ['lækriməl], a. lacrimal, lagrimal. — s. (*anat.*) hueso lagrimal.

lacrimary ['lækriməri], a. lacrimal, que contiene lágrimas.

lacrimation, s. llanto, lloro, derramamiento de lágrimas.

lacrimatory [lækri'meitəri], a. lacrimatorio.

lacrimose ['lækrimouz], a. lacrimoso, lloroso, llorón, plañidero.

lacrosse [lɑ'krɔːs], s. lacrosse, juego de pelota.

lactary ['læktəɹi], a. lácteo, lactario. — s. lechería.

lactate ['lækteit], s. lactato.

lactation, s. lactancia, lactación, crianza.

lacteal ['læktiəl], a. lácteo, quilífero.

lacteous, a. lácteo, lactario.

lactescence [læk'tesəns], s. lactescencia.

lactescent, a. lácteo, lactario.

lactic ['læktik], s. láctico.

lactiferous, a. lactífero, lechal.

lactifuge ['læktifjuːdʒ], s. lactífugo.

lactine ['læktin], **lactose** ['læktouz], s. lactina, lactosa, azúcar de leche.

lactometer [læk'tɔmetəɹ], s. lactómetro, galactómetro.

lactone, s. lactona.

lactucarium, s. lactucario.

lactumen ['læktjuːmən], s. lactumen.

lacuna [lə'khuːnə], s. laguna, claro, blanco, falta, abertura, espacio; hoyo, hueco.

lacunal [lə'kjuːnəl], **lacunar** [lə'kjuːnəɹ], **lacunose** [lə'kjuːnouz], a. que tiene lagunas, claros u hoyos.

lacunar, s. lagunar, lacunario, artesonado.

lacustral [lə'kʌstrəl], **lacustrine** [lə'kʌstrin], a. lacustre.

lad [læd], s. mozo, muchacho, joven, garzón, mozalbete.

ladanum ['lædənəm], a. ládano.

ladder [lædəɹ], s. escala portátil, escalera de mano; subidero, escalón; *extension ladder,* escalera doble, escalera de extensión; *step-ladder,* escalera de mano; *ladder ropes,* brandales; *rope ladder,* escala de cuerda; *accommodation ladder,* (*mar.*) escala real; *quarter-deck ladder,* escala del alcázar; *quarter o poop ladder,* (*mar.*) escala de popa o de toldilla.

lade [leid], s. desaguadero, canal de desagüe; embocadero, desembocadero. — *v.t.* (*p.p.* **laded** o **laden**) cargar, poner carga; sacar agua; echar en, verter. — *v.i.* (*mar.*) hacer agua, abrir agua.

lading ['leidiŋ], s. carga, cargamento, cargazón, *f.,* flete; *bill of lading,* conocimiento (o póliza) de embarque.

ladle ['leidəl], s. cucharón, cuchara grande, cazo, cacillo; vertidor; (*arti.*) cuchara; (*hidr.*) álabe, paleta del rodezno de un molino. — *v.t.* achicar, sacar, vaciar (líquido con un cucharón).

ladleful, *s.* cucharada.

lady ['leidi], *s.* señora, señorita, dama; ama; mujer bien educada; (*Ingl.*) tratamiento que se da a la esposa o hija de un par o caballero que tenga título del reino; *Lady Day*, día de la Anunciación de Nuestra Señora; *lady killer*, galanteador, Don Juan; *lady love*, amada, querida; *lady in waiting*, dama de una reina o princesa.

lady-bird, lady-bug, lady-fly, *s.* (*ent.*) mariquita, coquito (*o* vaca) de San Antón.

lady-fern, *s.* aspidio.

ladyship ['leidiʃip], *s.f.* señoría; *Your Ladyship*, Su Señoría.

lady's mantle, *s.* (*bot.*) alquímila, pie de león.

lady's-slipper, (*bot.*) zueco.

ladysmock, *s.* (*bot.*) cardamina.

lag [læg], *a.* rezagado, último, trasero, postrero, posterior. — *s.* (*mec.*) retardación de movimiento, listón de madera. — *v.i.* remolonear, rezagarse, roncear; tardar, quedarse atrás. — *v.t.* proteger cañería (con fieltro, etc.).

lagan ['lægən], *s.* (*for.*) despojos de un naufragio o mercancías, en el fondo del mar y generalmente marcados con una boya.

lager ['lɑ:gəɹ], *s.* especie de cerveza, ligera y clara.

laggard ['lægəɹd], **lagger,** *s.*, *a.* moroso, rezagado, perezoso, tardío, holgazán, haragán.

lagging, *s.* movimiento retardado; protección de cañería.

lagoon [lə'gu:n], *s.* laguna, lagunajo, charca, concavidad.

laic ['leiik], **laical** ['leiikəl], *a.* laical, lego, laico, secular, seglar.

laic ['leiik], *s.* lego seglar.

laid [leid], *pret. y p.p.* [LAY].

lain [lein], *p.p.* [LIE].

lair [leəɹ], *s.* cubil, cueva de fieras, guarida.

laird [leəɹd], *s.* (*Esco.*) lord; hacendado.

laity ['leiiti], *s.* estado seglar o laico.

lake [leik], *s.* lago, laguna, charco, pantano, estanque; (*pint.*) laca.

lakelet, *s.* laguna, laguito, lago pequeño.

lakh [læk], *s.* cien mil.

lallation [lə'leiʃən], *s.* vicio de pronunciación que consiste en dar a la *r* el sonido de *l*.

lama ['lɑ:mə], *s.* lama, *m.* (del Tibet).

lamaism ['lɑ:mɑ:izm], *s.* lamaísmo.

lamb [læm], *s.* cordero, borrego, borrega, borro, borra; persona apacible o inocente. — *v.i.* parir corderos.

lambative ['læmbətiv], *a.* que se lame. — *s.* (*fam.*) lamedor; medicina que se lame.

lambent ['læmbənt], *a.* ligero, undulante; radiante.

lamb-fry, *s.* turma, criadilla.

lambkin ['læmkin], *s.* corderito.

lamb-like, *a.* manso, inocente.

lambrekin ['læmbrikin], **lambrequin,** *s.* guardamalleta, sobrepuerta.

lambskin ['læmzkin], *s.* corderina.

lamb's lettuce, *s.* valerianilla, macha.

lamb's-wool, *s.* lana de cordero, cerveza.

lame [leim], *a.* cojo, zopo, renco, lisiado, estropeado, derrengado; imperfecto, defectuoso; *lame comparison*, comparación defectuosa; *to go lame*, cojear, andar cojeando;

lame excuse, disculpa frívola. — *v.t.* lisiar. estropear, derrengar, encojar.

lamella [lə'melə], *s.* (*pl.* **lamellæ**) laminilla, hoja delgada, hojuela.

lamellar [lə'meləɹ], *a.* laminar, compuesto de láminas.

lamellate, lamellated, *a.* laminado, hecho de láminas, hojaldrado.

lamelliform, *a.* lameliforme, en forma de láminas.

lamely ['leimli], *adv.* con cojera; débilmente, imperfectamente, defectuosamente.

lameness ['leimnis], *s.* cojera, derrengadura; defecto, imperfección, falta, estado de lisiado.

lament [lə'ment], *v.t.*, *v.i.* lamentar, lamentarse, afligir, afligirse, llorar, deplorar, dolerse, plañir. — *s.* lamento, queja.

lamentable [lə'mentəbəl], *a.* lamentable, deplorable, lamentoso, lastimoso, sensible, lastimero, flébil.

lamentation [læmen'teiʃən], *s.* lamentación, duelo, lamento, plañido, gemido.

lamenting, *s.* lamentación.

lamina ['læminə], *s.* (*pl.* **laminæ**) lámina, hoja, planchita, capa, chapa.

laminable, *a.* laminable.

laminar ['læminəɹ], *a.* laminar, compuesto de hojas.

laminate, laminated, *a.* laminado. — *v.t.* batir o laminar en hojas o láminas delgadas.

Lammas ['læməs], *s.* (*igl.*) fiesta del día primero de agosto.

lammergeyer ['læməɹ'gaiəɹ], *s.* quebrantahuesos.

lamp [læmp], *s.* lámpara, lustro, farol, candil, velón.

lampas ['læmpəs], **lampers** ['læmpəɹz], *s.* (*vet.*) inflamación en la parte superior de la boca de los caballos.

lampblack ['læmpblæk], *s.* humo de pez, hollín de resina, negro de humo; (*Méx.*) humo de ocote.

lamp-burner, *s.* mechero, piquera.

lamp-chimney, *s.* tubo de lámpara, (*Cuba*) bombillo.

lamp-holder, *s.* porta-lámparas, *m.*

lamplight ['læmplait], *s.* luz de una lámpara; luz artificial.

lamplighter, *s.* farolero, lamparero; cerillero, encendedor de lámparas.

lampoon [læm'pu:n], *s.* pasquín, libelo. — *v.t.* satirizar, pasquinar.

lampooner, *s.* escritor de pasquines.

lamp-post, *s.* pie de farol (de la calle).

lamprey ['læmprei], *s.* lamprea.

lamp-shade, *s.* pantalla de lámpara.

lanary ['lænəri], *s.* almacén para lana.

lanate ['læneit], **lanated** [lə'neitid], *a.* lanoso; (*bot.*) lanudo.

lance [lɑ:ns], *s.* lanza, asta, pica; lanzada, lancetada, lancetazo; bisturí, lanceta; lancero, el que usa de una lanza. — *v.t.* lancear, dar una lanzada; cortar, penetrar; (*cir.*) abrir una apostema con lanceta.

lance-bucket, *s.* cuja.

lanceolate ['lɑ:nsioleit], *a.* lanceolado.

lancer ['lɑ:nsəɹ], *s.* alanceador, el que lancea; (*mil.*) lancero. — *pl.* **lancers,** lanceros (danza).

lancet, *s.* (*cir.*) lanceta, sangradera; (*arq.*) arco puntiagudo; (*ent.*) trompetilla.

lancewood, *s.* palo de lanza; (*bot.*) anona, yaya.

lancinate [lɑːnsiˈneit], *v.t.* lacerar, despedazar.

lancination, *s.* laceración; dolor lancinante.

land [lænd], *s.* tierra; terreno; suelo, terruño; bienes raíces, posesiones, hacienda; reino, región, *f.*, país, territorio, provincia; continente, tierra firme; nación; *to make the land,* (*mar.*) acercar la nave a la costa, descubrir tierra; *to know how the land lies,* estar al corriente de un asunto; saber a que atenerse; *to see how the land lies,* sondar el terreno; *land surveyor,* agrimensor; *land surveying,* geodesia, agrimensura. — *v.t., v.i.* desembarcar, poner en tierra, saltar en tierra; (*aer.*) aterrizar.

land-agent, *s.* corredor de fincas rurales.

landau [ˈlændou], *s.* landó.

landed, *a.* hacendado, que tiene hacienda; desembarcado; *landed property,* bienes raíces. — *p.p.* [LAND].

landfall [ˈlændfɔːl], *s.* herencia de tierras; desprendimiento de tierras; (*mar.*) recalada.

landgrave [ˈlændgreiv], *s.* langrave.

landgraviate, *s.* langraviado, langraviato.

landholder, *s.* terrateniente, hacendado.

landing, *s.* desembarco, desembarque, desembarcadero; apeadero; pasillo, rellano, descanso de escalera; (*aer.*) aterrizaje; *landing-place,* desembarcadero; *landing-strip,* pista de aterrizaje.

land-jobber, *s.* corredor de bienes raíces.

landlady, *s.* ama, casera, mesonera, huéspeda, patrona, posadera.

landless, *a.* pobre, sin tierras, sin bienes, sin fortuna.

landlocked, *a.* cercado de tierra, abrigado de los vientos por la tierra.

landloper, *s.* venturero, vagamundo.

landlord, *s.* propietario o dueño de tierras o casas; amo, posadero; arrendador; patrón, casero.

landlordism, *s.* autoridad del propietario; conjunto de hacendados o proprietarios.

land-lubber, *s.* marinero bisoño.

landman, landsman, *s.* el que vive en tierra.

landmark, *s.* mojón, coto, marca, linde. — *pl.* **landmarks** (*mar.*) marcas.

land-measure, *s.* uvada.

landowner, *s.* terrateniente, hacendado.

land-poor, *a.* que posee muchas tierras de poco valor.

landscape [ˈlændskeip], *s.* paisaje, país, campiña, vista, boscaje.

landslide, landslip, *s.* derrumbe, derrumbamiento, desprendimiento de tierra, revenimiento; tierra que se ha derrumbado; (*Méx.*) desliz.

landsman [ˈlændzmən], *s.* [LANDMAN].

land-tax, *s.* impuesto sobre tierras.

landward [ˈlændwəd], *adv.* hacia la tierra.

lane [lein], *s.* senda, vereda, callejuela, calle; (*mar.*) ruta o derrotero fijo.

language [ˈlæŋgwidʒ], *s.* idioma, *m.*, lenguaje, habla, lengua; expresión; vocabulario.

languedoc [læŋgwiˈdok], *s.* lengua de oc, lemosín.

languet [ˈlæŋgwet], *s.* lengüeta, orejeta.

languid [ˈlæŋgwid], *a.* lánguido, débil, flojo, flaco; mustio, lacio, decaído; sin animación o interés.

languidness, *s.* languidez, caimiento, desmadejamiento, falta de fuerza.

languish [ˈlæŋgwiʃ], *v.i.* languidecer, enflaquecer, debilitar, adolecer, decaer, extenuar(se), consumir(se), padecer lentamente; agostarse; ponerse mustio; entibiarse, encalmarse, aflojar; mirar con ternura.

languishing, *s.* languidez, flaqueza. — *a.* lánguido, afligido, decaído; derretido, enamorado, amartelado.

languishment, *s.* languidez, desmadejamiento; debilidad, angustia, consumimiento.

languor [ˈlæŋgəɹ], *s.* desfallecimiento, dejamiento, languidez, flojedad, postración, descaecimiento, diminución de ánimo.

languorous, *a.* lánguido, débil, flojo.

laniard [ˈlænjəd], *s.* [LANYARD].

laniary [ˈlænjəɹi], *a.* propio para lacerar o rasgar. — *s.* colmillo, diente canino.

laniferous [lænˈifərəs], **lanigerous** [lænˈidʒərəs], **lanuginous** [lænˈjuːdʒinəs], *a.* lanudo, lanoso, lanífero, lanuginoso, velludo.

lank [læŋk], *a.* flaco, enteco, flojo, seco, descarnado, delgado, desfallecido; *lank hair,* cabellos largos y lacios.

lankness, *s.* flaqueza, flojedad.

lanky, *a.* (*fam.*) larguirucho, langaruto, delgaducho.

lanner [ˈlænəɹ], *s.* alcotán; *lanneret,* alcotanillo.

lanolin [ˈlænolin], *s.* lanolina.

lansquenet [ˈlɑːnskənet], *s.* sacanete; cascarela; piquero de a pie.

lantern [ˈlæntəɹn], *s.* linterna, farol, fanal; (*mar.*) faro, fanal; (*arq.*) linterna; *lantern-jawed,* carienjuto; *lantern jaws,* carilargo; *magic lantern,* linterna mágica; *lantern-jack,* fuego fatuo; *dark lantern,* linterna sorda.

lantern-maker, *s.* linternero.

lanyard [ˈlænjəd], *s.* (*mar.*) acollador; (*arti.*) correa tirafrictor.

Laodicean [leiodiˈsiːən], *a.* laodicense; (*fig.*) indiferente, tibio, irreligioso.

lap [læp], *s.* falda, faldón, faldones, enfaldo, regazo, rodillas; longitud o extensión determinada; presilla ; pliegue, doblez; solapa de una ensambladura; salidizo, parte saliente, parte sobrepuesta de una cosa sobre otra; vuelta completa de una pista; (*mec.*) rueda de labrar metales joyas y bruñir; (*fig.*) refugio, santuario; *lap-dog,* perrillo faldero; *lapstone,* (*zap.*) piedra de batir el cuero; *lap-joint,* junta o ensambladura solapada; *lap-seam,* (*cost.*) costura rebatida; *lap-hemmer,* rebatidor; *lap-board* o *table,* tabla faldera que usan los sastres. — *v.t.* sobreponer, superponer, encaballar, solapar; arrollar, envolver; doblar sobre sí, replegarse sobre; caer, recaer; alcanzar, adelantarse a, pasar delante de; reposar, reclinar; plegar, hacer pliegues; tocar, bañar, besar (el agua); lamer; pulir, labrar (joyas o metales); cruzar; exceder, hacer salidizo; *to lap up,* beber a lengüetadas, beber vorazmente. — *v.i.* estar sobrepuesto o replegado; lamer; susurrar, hacer un sonido suave (del agua); traslaparse.

laparotomy [læpəˈrɒtəmi], *s.* laparotomía.

lapel [ˈlæpəl], *s.* solapa.

lapful [ˈlæpful], *s.* lo que puede caber en el regazo.

lapidary [ˈlæpidəɹi], *s.* lapidario. — *a.* lapidario; inscripto sobre piedra; lapídeo.

lapidate [ˈlæpideit], *v.t.* labrar las piedras preciosas; apedrear.

lapidation, *s.* lapidación, apedreamiento.

lapidescence [læpi'desəns], s. lapidificación, concreción de piedra.
lapidescent, a. que petrifica.
lapidific [læpi'difik], a. lapidífico.
lapidification, s. lapidificación.
lapidist, s. lapidario.
lapis lazuli ['læpis 'læzju:li], s. lapislázuli, lazulita.
Lapland, s. Laponia.
Laplander ['læpləndəɹ], s. lapón.
lapper ['læpəɹ], s. el que lame.
lappet ['læpet], s. caídas de toca o escofiesta; moco de pavo.
lapsable, a. (for.) prescriptible; susceptible de caer.
lapse [læps], s. lapso, caída, transcurso, curso, intervalo de tiempo; desliz, traspié, error, yerro, falta, equivocación; (for.) prescripción, translación de derecho o dominio; after the lapse of time, andando el tiempo o con el transcurso del tiempo. — v.t. dejar caer. — v.i. pasar, transcurrir; deslizarse, decaer; escurrir; caer en algún defecto, desliz o error; (for.) caducar, prescribir.
lapsed, a. caído, caducado, deslizado, cumplido, prescrito, omitido. — p.p. [LAPSE].
lapwing ['læpwiŋ], s. frailecillo, avefría.
lapwork, s. obra entrelazada o entretejida.
larboard ['lɑ:bəɹd], s. (ant.) babor.
larcener ['lɑ:ɹsenəɹ], **larcenist** ['lɑ:ɹsenist], s. ladrón, ratero.
larceny ['lɑ:ɹsəni], s. (for.) ratería, latrocinio, hurto de poco valor; petty larceny, (ant.) robo (de menos de 12 peniques); grand larceny, (ant.) robo (de más de 12 peniques).
larch [lɑ:ɹtʃ], s. lárice, alerce.
lard [lɑ:ɹd], s. manteca de cerdo, tocino gordo, cochevira. — v.t. (coc.) lardar, lardear; mechar, engordar, guarnecer, entreverar; larding pin, mechera.
lardaceous [lɑ:ɹ'deiʃəs], a. lardoso, grasiento; (med.) craso, gordo.
larder ['lɑ:ɹdəɹ], s. despensa, reposte.
larderer, s. despensero.
lardy, s. lardoso, graso, mantecoso.
large ['lɑ:ɹdʒ], a. grande, grueso, abultado; amplio, vasto, espacioso, ancho, capaz, extenso, holgado, cumplido; lato; dilatado, difuso, copioso; (ant.) largo, liberal, franco, espléndido; considerable, cuantioso; at large, extensamente; en general; a lo largo; en libertad; sin limitación; to talk large, (fam.) darse tono. — adv. (mar.) con viento a la cuadra; (fam.) con jactancia.
large-handed, a. de manos grandes; liberal, dadivoso; codicioso, rapaz.
large-hearted, a. magnánimo, desprendido, generoso.
large-heartedness, s. liberalidad, generosidad, largueza.
largeness ['lɑ:ɹdʒnis], s. grandor, extensión, amplitud, anchura, grandeza de ánimo, liberalidad, generosidad.
larger ['lɑ:ɹdʒəɹ], **largest** ['lɑ:ɹdʒest], comp. y superl. [LARGE]; (el) más grande, mayor; máximo.
largess ['lɑ:ɹdʒes], s. (ant.) largueza; don, dádiva, regalo, presente.
lariat ['læriət], s. reata; lazo, mangana.
lark [lɑ:ɹk], s. (orn.) alondra, terrera, calandria; (fam.) calaverada, parranda, francachela,

holgorio; to have a lark, estar de juerga, bromear, hacer de las suyas; meadow-lark, titlark, alondra de los prados. — v.i. bromear.
larkspur ['lɑ:ɹkspə:ɹ], s. (bot.) delfinio, espuela de caballero.
larrup ['lærəp], v.t. (fam.) zurrar, zurriagar, tundir.
larva ['lɑ:ɹvə], s. larva.
larval ['lɑ:ɹvəl], a. larval.
larvate ['lɑ:ɹveit], **larvated** [lɑ:ɹ'veitid], a. larvado, larval.
laryngeal [lə'rindʒiəl], a. laríngeo.
laryngitis [lærin'dʒaitis], s. laringitis, f.
laryngoscope [læ'riŋgoskoup], s. laringoscopio.
laryngoscopy, s. laringoscopia.
laryngotomy, s. laringotomía.
larynx ['læriŋks], s. laringe, f.
Lascar ['læskɑ:ɹ], s. láscar.
lascivious [lə'siviəs], a. lascivo, lúbrico, lujurioso, incontinente, salaz.
lasciviousness, s. lascivia, lujuria, incontinencia.
lash [læʃ], s. látigo, verdugo, fusta, fuete, rebenque; invectiva, sarcasmo, injuria, azote, latigazo, fuetazo, ramalazo; chasquido; embate de las olas; pestaña; drooping lashes, pestañas caídas. — v.i. dar latigazos; azotar; romper contra un objeto (como las olas); mover con violencia; satirizar, zaherir, reprochar, censurar; (mar.) amarrar, ligar, trincar. — v.i. latiguear, chasquear el látigo; to lash out, desenfrenarse, desordenarse.
lasher, s. azotador.
lashing, s. ligadura, atadura; cabo de cuerda, lazo; (mar.) amarra, amarradura; castigo de azotes; acción de lanzar invectivas; lashing rings, (mar.) argollas de amura; lashing rope, braga.
lasket ['læskit], s. (mar.) badaza de boneta.
lass [læs], s. doncella, moza, zagala, muchacha, chavala, aldeana.
lassie ['læsi], s. muchachita, niña, mozuela.
lassitude ['læsitju:d], s. lasitud, cansancio, fatiga, languidez, dejadez, flojedad.
lasso [læ'su:], v.t. lazar, manganear, coger con un lazo. — s. lazo, guasco, mangana.
lassoer [læ'su:əɹ], s. lazador.
last [lɑ:st], a. último, postrero, postrimero, pasado, final, extremo; last night, anoche; last week, la semana pasada; at last, últimamente, al cabo, al fin, finalmente; al fin y al cabo, al cabo y a la postre; to the last, hasta el fin, hasta lo último; last but one, penúltimo; last but two, antepenúltimo; to be on one's last legs, estar a la muerte; (fig.) estar a la quinta pregunta. — adv. la última vez, al fin, finalmente. — s. (zap.) horma; (mar.) lastre de una embarcación; término, fin, conclusión; el último, lo último — v.i. durar, perdurar, permanecer, continuar, seguir; sostenerse; guardarse, conservarse, subsistir, vivir.
lastage, s. (mar.) espacio para el cargamento; (ant.) lastre.
laster, s. (zap.) ahormador.
lasting, s. duradero, perpetuo, durable, permanente, perdurable, constante. — s. (tej.) sempiternas.
lastingly, adv. perpetuamente, para siempre.
lastingness, s. duración, continuación, perpetuidad.

lastly, *adv.* últimamente, en conclusión, finalmente, por último, por fin.

last-maker, *s.* hormero.

latch [lætʃ], *s.* aldaba, aldabilla, picaporte, cerrojo; *the latch string is always out,* venga Vd. cuando guste. — *v.t.* cerrar con aldaba; unir, ajustar.

latchet ['lætʃit], *s.* agujeta o cordón de zapato.

latch-key, *s.* llavín.

latch-string, *s.* cordón de aldaba.

late [leit], *a.* tardío; tardo, lento; remoto, lejano; postrero, último; reciente, moderno; difunto; *to be late,* llegar tarde; *to keep late hours,* retirarse tarde, acostarse a deshora; *late in years,* de edad provecta. — *adv.* tarde; poco ha, antes, últimamente; fuera de tiempo; *to make one late,* retardar; *late in the year,* al fin del año; *of late,* de poco tiempo acá, de poco tiempo a esta parte; *too late,* demasiado tarde; *better late than never,* (*prov.*) más vale tarde que nunca.

lateen [lə'ti:n], *a.* latino; *lateen-sail,* (*mar.*) vela latina, vela de burro.

lateener, *s.* falucho.

lately ['leitli], *adv.* poco ha, no ha mucho, poco tiempo hace, recientemente, modernamente, últimamente.

latency ['leitənsi], *s.* estado latente, obscuridad.

lateness ['leitnis], *s.* retraso; hora (etc.) avanzada.

latent ['leitənt], *a.* latente, oculto, escondido.

later ['leitər], *a.*, *adv.* (*comp.* **late**) más tarde; luego, después; posterior, subsecuente, más reciente; *sooner or later,* tarde o temprano; *a little later,* a los pocos días (momentos, etc.).

lateral ['lætərəl], *a.* lateral, ladero.

Lateran ['lætərən], *a.* lateranense.

laterite ['lætərait], *a.* arcilla roja y ferruginosa.

latescent [lə'tesənt], *a.* que se va obscureciendo u ocultando.

latest ['leitist], *a.*, *adv.* (*superl.* **late**) el último; últimamente, reciente, novísimo, fresco.

latex ['leiteks], *s.* látex.

lath [lɑ:θ]. *s.* (*alb.*) lata, listón. — *v.t.* poner latas en. — *v.i.* (*alb.*) listonar, hacer un enlatado.

lathe [leið], *s.* (*mec.*) torno; (*tej.*) marco o cama de telar.

lathe-bed, *s.* banco del torno.

lathe-dog, *s.* trinquete de mandril.

lathe-drill, *s.* torno de taladrar.

lather [lɑ:ðər], *v.t.* enjabonar para afeitar. — *v.i.* espumar, hacer espuma. — *s.* jabonadura(s), espuma de jabón.

lathing ['leiðiŋ], *s.* (*alb.*) enlatado, enlistonado.

lathy, *a.* largo y delgado como lata.

Latin ['lætin], *a.* latino. — *s.* latín, lengua latina.

Latinism, *s.* latinismo.

Latinist, *s.* latinista, *m.f.*

Latinity, *s.* latinidad, estilo latino.

Latinize, *v.t.* latinizar. — *v.i.* emplear latinismos.

latirostrous [læti'rɔstrəs], *a.* latirrostra.

latish ['leitiʃ], *a.* (*fam.*) algo tardío, algo retrasado. — *adv.* algo tarde.

latitude ['lætitju:d], *s.* latitud; difusión, anchura, extensión; amplitud, laxitud; libertad. — *pl.* climas, *m.*, regiones, *f.*

latitudinal [læti'tju:dinəl], *a.* latitudinal.

latitudinarian [lætitju:di'nɛəriən], *s.*, *a.* latitudinario, amplio, libre, sin freno.

latitudinarianism, *s.* latitud en materias religiosas.

latria ['lætriə], *s.* latría.

latrine [lə'tri:n], *s.* letrina.

latten ['lætən], *s.* latón, azófar.

latter ['lætər], *a.* posterior, moderno, más reciente; éste o esto, el último de dos cosas de las que se habla; *latter-day,* de nuestros días; *Latter-day Saints,* el pueblo mormón.

lattice ['lætis], *s.* celosía, rastel, enrejado de listoncillos. — *v.t.* enrejar, poner celosías, hacer un enrejado.

laud [lɔ:d], *s.* elogio, alabanza. — *pl.* **lauds,** (*igl.*) laudes, *f.pl.* — *v.t.* alabar, celebrar, elogiar, loar; *to laud to the skies,* poner sobre las estrellas.

laudability, laudableness, *s.* calidad de laudable, mérito.

laudable ['lɔ:dəbəl], *a.* laudable, loable, recomendable, digno de alabanza, que merece alabanza.

laudanum ['lɔdnəm], *s.* láudano.

laudative ['lɔ:dətiv], **laudatory** ['lɔ:dətəri], *a.* laudatorio. — *s.* panegírico.

lauder, *s.* loador.

laugh [lɑ:f], *v.i.* reír; estar contento o alegre; sonreír. — *v.t.*, *v.i.* escarnecer, burlar, mofar; *to laugh at,* reírse de, ridiculizar, mofarse; *to laugh at one to his face,* reírsele a uno en las barbas; *to laugh out,* reírse a carcajadas; echarse a reír; *to laugh down,* ridiculizar; hacer callar a un orador a carcajadas; *to laugh in one's sleeve,* reírse interiormente. — *s.* risa, risada; *horse-laugh,* risotada, carcajada; *to turn off with a laugh,* hacer burla de una cosa, tomarla a broma.

laughable ['lɑ:fəbəl], *a.* risible, ridículo, reidero, divertido.

laugher, *s.* reidor.

laughing, *a.* riente, risueño, alegre, reidor. — *s.* risa, alegría; *laughing-gas,* gas exhilarante, protóxido de ázoe; *laughing stock,* hazmerreír, fábula del mundo; *laughing eyes,* ojos alegres.

laughingly, *adv.* alegremente, irrisoriamente.

laughter ['lɑ:ftər], *s.* risa, risada, hilaridad, carcajada.

launch [lɔ:ntʃ], *v.t.* botar o echar al agua; empezar, principiar; llevar adelante, acometer, dar principio a, lanzar, arrojar. — *v.i.* arrojarse, echarse, lanzarse, salir. — *s.* (*mar.*) botadura de un buque; lanzamiento; (*mar.*) lancha, chalupa.

launder ['lɔ:ndər], *v.t.* lavar (la ropa).

launderer, *s.* lavandero.

laundress ['lɔ:ndres], *s.* lavandera.

laundry ['lɔ:ndri], *s.* lavadero; tren de lavado, (*fam.*) ropa lavada. — *v.t.* (*fam.*) lavar y planchar la ropa.

laureate ['lɔ:rieit], *a.* laureado, coronado con laurel. — *s.* poeta laureado.

laureateship, *s.* dignidad de poeta laureado.

laureation, *s.* acto de recibir algún grado académico.

laurel ['lɔrəl], *s.* laurel, lauro, lauréola; corona de laurel, distinción, honor; *to crown with laurel,* laurear.

laurelled, *a.* laureado, coronado con laurel.

Laurentian [lɔ'renʃən], *a.* lorenziano.

laurestine ['lɔ:restain], **laurestinus** [lɔ:res'tainəs], *s.* durillo, viburno.

lava ['lɑ:və], *s.* lava.

lavation [lə'veiʃən], **lavement** ['leivmənt], s. lavadura, lavatorio, lavado.

lavatory, s. lavatorio, lavadero; loción; retrete, wáter.

lave, v.t., v.i. lavar, bañar; bañarse, lavarse; sacar (agua).

lavement, s. lavado, acción de lavar; lavativa, enema.

lavender ['lævəndəɹ], s. espliego, alhucema, lavándula; *lavender-water*, agua de lavanda; *lavender cotton*, santolina.

laver ['leivəɹ], s. aguamanil, vasija, jofaina, lavadero; ova, alga comestible.

lavish ['læviʃ], a. pródigo, gastador, manirroto, descabellado, despilfarrado, profuso. — v.t. desparramar, malbaratar, disipar, malgastar, prodigar, malrotar, sacrificar, despreciar (su vida, su sangre, etc.).

lavisher, s. pródigo, malgastador.

lavishment, lavishness, s. despilfarro, profusión, prodigalidad, disipación.

law [lɔ:], s. ley, f., estatuto; código de leyes; principio, regla, norma de conducta; litigio judicial, jurisprudencia, derecho, leyes en general; ley de la naturaleza; (*bíb.*) tora, libro de la ley judía; *to follow the law*, estudiar leyes; *to go to law with*, poner pleito a; *to take the law into one's own hands*, hacerse justicia por sí mismo; *in point of law*, (*for.*) desde el punto de vista legal; *law of nations*, (*for.*) derecho internacional.

law, lawk, lawks, interj. (*vulg.*) ¡Oh!, ¡caramba! ¡demonio!

law-breaker, s. transgresor, el que viola la ley.

law-day, s. día en que están abiertos los tribunales.

lawful, a. legal, jurídico, según derecho, conforme a la ley; permitido, justo, legítimo, lícito, válido; *lawful goods*, géneros permitidos o lícitos.

lawfulness, s. legalidad, legitimidad.

lawgiver ['lɔ:givəɹ], s. legislador.

lawgiving, a. legislativo.

lawless, a. ilegal; desordenado, desaforado, desarreglado.

lawlessness, s. desorden, desobediencia.

lawmaker, s. legislador.

lawn [lɔ:n], s. prado, césped; (*tej.*) linón, tela fina; *long lawn*, estopilla; (*fig.*) la dignidad de obispo. — a. hecho de linón.

lawn-mower ['lɔ:nmouəɹ], s. segadora o cortadora de césped.

lawny, a. parecido a un prado verde, que tiene campos de césped; hecho o vestido de linón.

lawsuit ['lɔ:sju:t], s. pleito, litigio, litigación, acción, proceso, causa, lite, f.

lawyer ['lɔ:jəɹ], s. abogado, jurisperito, jurista, m.f., letrado, jurisconsulto.

lawyerlike, lawyerly, adv. a manera de un abogado, judicial.

lax [læks], a. laxo, suelto, laso, desatado, flojo, poroso; (*fig.*) vago, indeterminado, descuidado, omiso; indisciplinado; corriente de vientre.

laxation [læk'seiʃən], s. laxación.

laxative ['læksətiv], a. laxativo, laxante. — s. laxante, purgante.

laxativeness, s. virtud o propiedad laxante.

laxity ['læksiti], **laxness** ['læksnis], s. laxitud, flojedad, soltura, aflojamiento; anchura, desahogo, relajación, relajamiento; diarrea, despeño.

lay [lei], pret. [LIE].

lay [lei], v.t. (*pret., p.p.* **laid**) poner, fijar, tender, extender, colocar; echar, abatir, derrocar, tumbar, derribar; ordenar, mandar; instalar; matar (el polvo); poner (un huevo, la mesa, etc.); imponer (cargas, tributos, etc.); enterrar; aquietar, calmar, sosegar, apaciguar; propagar (las plantas); (*impr.*) poner, calzar; apostar; pintar, trazar, proyectar, discurrir; presentar, exhibir, exponer, poner de manifiesto; achacar, imputar, atribuir; juntar, añadir; depositar; (*mil.*) apuntar (un cañón). — v.i. poner, aovar (las gallinas, etc.); situarse, colocarse; apostar; tramar, formar (planes); (*mar.*) venir o ir como mandado; *to lay about one*, dar golpes con energía; *to lay aft*, (*mar.*) ir a popa; *to lay apart*, poner a parte; *to lay aside* (o *away*), echar o poner a un lado; *to lay before*, desplegar, exponer a la vista; mostrar, manifestar, exponer (agravios, quejas, etc.); *to lay by*, conservar, guardar; *to lay claim to*, reclamar; *to lay down*, sostener o sentar una opinión, pagar, devolver, rendir las armas; restituir; *to lay hold of*, agarrar, coger, asir; *to lay in*, comprar, atesorar; *to lay on*, aplicar, extender; *to lay open*, descubrir, demostrar, hacer ver; *to lay out*, desplegar, disponer, desembolsar; *to lay to*, acometer, acusar; *to lay waste*, asolar, pasar a sangre y fuego; *to lay to heart*, tomar a pechos; *to lay under*, someter, sojuzgar; *to lay up*, guardar, atesorar, acumular, juntar, amontonar, apretar, cerrar. — v.i. guardar cama; *to lay upon*, cargar, imponer; *to lay hands on someone*, pegar a uno; *to lay the blame on someone*, echar la culpa a uno. — s. caída, contorno, dirección relativa; negocio; cantidad de hilo; ganancia; cama, lecho; balada, romance, canción. — a. lego, seglar, secular, no eclesiástico, no profesional; *lay clerk*, (*igl.*) sochantre; *lay figure*, maniquí.

layer ['leiəɹ], s. lecho, capa, cama, tonga, tongada; (*alb.*) hilada; (*geol.*) estrato; (*agr.*) pimpollo, vástago; jerpa, acodo, renuevo de alguna planta; gallina ponedora. — v.t. (*agr.*) acodar.

layering ['leiəriŋ], s. (*agr.*) acodadura.

layette [lei'et], s. canastilla.

laying ['leiiŋ], s. acto de colocar, colocación; postura (del huevo); (*alb.*) primera capa de un enlucido. — a. situado, colocado; (*mar.*) anclado; *laying-press*, (*enc.*) prensa de cepillo; *laying-hook*, manubrio del cordelero; *laying-in*, (*pint.*) esbozo; *laying-walk*, cordelería; *laying-on of hands*, imposición de manos.

layman ['leimən], s. lego, seglar.

layout ['leiaut], s. plan; disposición.

laystall, s. establo.

lazar ['læzəɹ], s. lázaro, leproso, lazarino.

lazaret ['læzəret], **lazaretto** [læzə'retou], **lazar-house** ['læzəɹhaus], s. lazareto.

lazar-like, lazarly, a. lazarino.

lazarwort, s. laserpicio.

laze [leiz], v.i. holgazanear, ser vago, perezoso; estar a sus anchas. — v.t. malgastar (tiempo o dinero) por pereza. — s. pereza, holgazanería.

laziness ['leizinis], s. pereza, gandulería, indolencia, galbana, holgazanería, desidia, haraganería, ociosidad.

lazuli ['læzju:lai], s. lapislázuli.

lazy ['leizi], *a.* perezoso, flojo, ocioso, desidioso, holgazán, haragán, tardo, gandul; *lazy-bones*, vago, gandul.

lea [li:], *s.* prado, pradera; llanura; medida (variable) de hilado.

leach [li:tʃ], *v.t.* lixiviar; colar la ropa; extraer el líquido de algún material. — *s.* cenizas de lejía; colada; lixiviación; *leach tub*, cubo, tina o colador de ropa.

leachy, *a.* penetrable, permeable, poroso.

lead [led], *s.* (*min.*) plomo; (*impr.*) interlínea, regleta; (*mar.*) sondalesa, escandallo; *lead-line* o *hand-lead*, sondalesa; *deep-sea-lead*, escandallo mayor; *black lead*, lápiz-plomo, plombagina, grafito; *white lead*, albayalde; *red lead*, almagra, almagre; *yellow lead*, albayalde calcinado; *sugar of lead*, azúcar de plomo, acetato de plomo; *lead pencil*, lápiz; *to heave the lead*, (*mar.*) echar la sonda. — *v.t.* (*pret.*, *p.p.* **leaded**) emplomar, forrar o guarnecer con plomo; (*impr.*) interlinear, espaciar, regletear.

lead [li:d], *s.* primer lugar, primacía, (en el juego) mano; delantera; salida (palo que juega el que es mano); *to take the lead*, tomar la delantera. — *v.t.* (*pret.*, *p.p.* **led**) llevar de la mano, conducir, dirigir, guiar; ir delante, ir a la cabeza; regir, mandar, gobernar; (*mús.*) llevar la batuta; encausar; derivar, adestrar, amaestrar, enseñar; atraer, halagar, inducir, motivar, mover; gastar o emplear (el tiempo). — *v.i.* guiar, conducir, enseñar el camino; dominar, mandar en jefe; ser mano (en el juego); *to lead along*, conducir, acompañar; *to lead in* (o *into*), introducir; *to lead* (*a horse*) *to water*, llevar a abrevar (un caballo); *to lead astray*, descarriar, extraviar, desviar, seducir; *to lead the way*, mostrar el camino, llevar la delantera; *to lead off*, principiar; *to lead a good life*, vivir bien; *to lead out of the way*, descarriar; *to lead a new life*, enmendarse.

leaded ['ledid], *p.p.*, *a.* (*impr.*) interlineado; plomado, emplomado.

leaden ['ledən], *a.* hecho de plomo, plomizo, plomoso, aplomado; (*fig.*) pesado; lento, tardo, estúpido.

leaden-footed, *a.* lento, tardo.

leaden-hearted, *a.* insensible.

leader ['li:dəɹ], *s.* guía, *m.f.*, guiador, conductor; jefe, general, comandante, capitán; guión, bastonero; (*alb.*) condutal, canalera; caudillo, principal, corifeo, cabecilla, *m.* cabeza, *m.*; caballo delantero; (*mús.*) director (de coro o de orquesta); primer violín; (*impr.*) puntos suspensivos; artículo de fondo; (*min.*) nervadura, vena, filón; (*mec.*) rueda motriz.

leadership, *s.* dirección; jefatura; mando.

leading ['li:diŋ], *a.* principal, primero, capital; *leading strings*, andadores; (*fig.*) refrenamiento, disciplina; *leading man*, jefe de partido; *leading wheels*, ruedas delanteras; *to have the leading hands at cards*, ser mano en el juego. — *s.* guía, conducción; dirección de orquesta; *to be out of leading-strings*, haber salido de mantillas.

leading ['lediŋ], *s.* emplomadura; (*impr.*) interlineación.

leadsman ['ledzmən], *s.* (*mar.*) sondeador.

leadwort ['ledwəːɹt], *s.* velesa.

leady ['ledi], *a.* aplomado, plomizo, parecido al plomo.

leaf [li:f], *s.* (*pl.* **leaves**) (*bot.*) hoja; hoja o plancha de metal; hoja (de un libro, de una mesa, puerta, etc.); *leaf brass*, oropel; *fly-leaf*, (*impr.*) guarda; *to turn down a leaf*, hacer un pliegue a la hoja; *overleaf*, o *over the leaf*, a la vuelta; *to turn over a new leaf*, doblar la hoja, enmendar uno su conducta; *leaf lard*, manteca en rama. — *v.i.* echar hojas; hacerse frondoso.

leafage ['li:fidʒ], *s.* follaje, frondaje.

leafed, leafy, *a.* frondoso, hojoso.

leafiness, *s.* follaje, frondaje, abundancia de hojas.

leafless, *a.* áfilo, deshojado, sin follaje.

leaflet ['li:flet], *s.* hojilla, hojuela.

leaf-stalk, *s.* (*bot.*) pezón.

league [li:g], *s.* liga, alianza, confederación; pandilla; asociación, unión, *f.*; legua. — *v.i.* confederarse, ligarse, unirse, aliarse, acomunarse.

leagued, *a.* confederado, aliado, ligado, coligado, conjurado.

leaguer ['li:gəɹ], *s.* miembro de una liga; conjurado, coligado.

leak [li:k], *s.* rendija, grieta, raja; gotera; fuga o escape de gas o vapor; (*mar.*) vía de agua; goteo, filtración; *to spring a leak*, (*mar.*) hacer agua, abrir agua (un barco); *to fother a leak*, (*mar.*) atajar, cegar una vía de agua. — *v.i.* gotear, hacer agua, salirse; derramarse, trazumarse, rezumarse.

leakage ['li:kidʒ], *s.* goteo, filtración; (*com.*) avería, pérdida, merma, derrame.

leaky ['li:ki], *a.* llovedizo; haciendo agua, que hace agua, que se rezuma; resquebrajado; roto; (*fam.*) locuaz, indiscreto.

leal [li:əl], *a.* (*Esco.*) leal, sincero, fiel; *the land of the leal*, la morada de los bienaventurados, la Gloria.

lean [li:n], *v.i.* apoyarse, recostarse, reclinarse, repantigarse; ladearse, torcerse, inclinarse, encorvarse; tener propensión a. — *v.t.* apoyar, reclinar; torcer, inclinar, encorvar; *to lean over*, adelantarse hacia alguna parte; *to lean upon*, acodarse; *to lean against*, apoyarse en, arrimarse a. — *a.* flaco, magro; enjuto, delgado; (*fig.*) mezquino, chupado; necesitado. — *s.* carne mollar, *f.*, carne magra.

lean, leaning, *s.* inclinación, disposición, propensión.

leanly, *adv.* pobremente; sin gordura.

leanness ['li:nnes], *s.* flaqueza, flacura, magrura, magrez, delgadez; pobreza.

lean-to ['li:ntu:], *s.* (*arq.*) colgadizo.

lean-witted, *a.* tonto, necio.

leap [li:p], *v.i.* saltar, brincar, correr rápidamente, brotar, salir con ímpetu; corvetear; batir o palpitar el corazón. — *v.t.* saltar, brincar; cubrir (el macho a la hembra); *to leap for joy*, saltar de gozo. — *s.* salto, brinco, paso repentino; asalto; coito de los animales; cestón para pescado.

leaper, *s.* saltador, brincador.

leap-frog ['li:pfrɔg], *s.* salto.

leapingly ['li:piŋli], *adv.* a brincos, a saltos.

leap-year ['li:pjəːɹ], *s.* año bisiesto.

learn [ləɹn], *v.t.*, *v.i.* (*pret.*, *p.p.* **learned** o **learnt**) aprender, recibir (o tener) noticia de, saber, adquirir conocimientos de, enterarse de, fijar en la mente, instruirse; *live and learn*, vivir para ver.

learnable, *a.* que puede aprenderse.

learned ['ləːɹned], *a.* docto, erudito, hábil,

diestro, ilustrado, sabio, inteligente; versado, perito, entendido, experto, de buenas letras; *the learned*, los doctos, los literatos, los sabios; *my learned brother*. (*for.*) mi ilustrado colega; *the learned world*, el mundo de las letras.

learner ['lə:ɹnəɹ], *s.* tirón, bisoño, principiante, aprendiz; escolar, estudiante, discípulo.

learning, *s.* letras, literatura; ciencia, saber, sabiduría, erudición, estudio, ilustración.

leasable ['liːsəbl], *a.* arrendable.

lease [liːs], *s.* (*for.*) arriendo, escritura de arrendamiento; (*tej.*) paso, cruce; locación, inquilinato. — *v.t.* arrendar, dar en arriendo.

leasehold ['liːshould], *s.* censo. — *a.* censatario.

leaser, *s.* concesionario; arrendatario; (*ant.*) espigador.

leash [liːʃ], *s.* pihuela, traílla, correa; tres, par y medio; (*tej.*) lizo. — *v.t.* atraillar, atar con correa o cuerda.

least [liːst], *a.* (*superl.* **little**) el menor, el mínimo, el más pequeño; mínimo, menos importante. — *adv.* (lo) menos; *not in the least*, de ningún modo, de ninguna manera, bajo ningún concepto; *at least, at the least* o *at leastwise*, al menos, a lo menos, o por lo menos.

leat [liːt], *s.* cauce, caz.

leather ['leðəɹ], *s.* cuero, cordobán, pellejo, piel curtida; (*vulg.*) el balón del fútbol, o la pelota del cricket; los guantes de boxeo; *patent leather*, charol; *alum leather, rawed leather*, cuero blanco; *sheep's leather*, badana; *wash leather*, gamuza. — *a.* de cuero; *leather belt*, correa; *leather dresser*, curtidor, pellejero; *leather cutter*, vendedor de cuero curtido por menor; *leather belting*, correaje. — *v.t.* guarnecer con cuero; hacer cuero; pegar, golpear, zurrar, dar una tunda.

leatherette [leðə'ret], *s.* cartón cuero.

leatherhead ['leðəɹhed], *s.* (*orn.*) frailecico, tropidorinco; (*fig.*) tonto, estúpido, bodoque.

leathern ['leðəɹn], *a.* de cuero, de cordobán; correoso, coriáceo.

leathery ['leðəri], *a.* coriáceo, correoso; de cuero; curtido (piel, etc.).

leave [liːv], *s.* licencia, venia, permiso; despedida; *to take leave*, despedirse; *leave-taking*, despedida; *by your leave*, con permiso de Vd.; *leave of absence*, licencia; *to take French leave*, despedirse a la francesa; *without so much as a 'by your leave,'* sin decir oxte ni moxte. — *v.t., v.i.* (*pret., p.p.* **left**) dejar, dejar estar; desamparar, abandonar; legar; dar, ceder o renunciar una cosa a favor de otro; despojarse; marcharse, partir, irse, salir de un lugar; entregar, confiar en depósito; cesar, desistir; *to leave out*, omitir, excluir, olvidar, desatender, descuidar; *to leave off*, quitarse, cesar, descontinuar, parar; *to leave issue*, dejar hijos o sucesión; *to leave behind*, dejar atrás; dejar en pos; *'to be left till called for,'* (de las cartas) lista de correos. — *v.i.* (*pret., p.p.* **leaved**) echar hojas.

leaved, *a.* hojoso; de hojas.

leaveless, *a.* sin licencia.

leaven ['levən], *s.* levadura, fermento. — *v.t.* fermentar, leudar; penetrar, imbuir; (*ant.*) corromper; *leavened bread*, pan de levadura.

leavening ['levəniŋ], *s.* fermento.

leavenous, *a.* que contiene fermento.

leaves [liːvz], *s.pl.* [LEAF] hojas; cortes; *gilt leaves*, (de libros) cortes dorados; *marbled leaves*, cortes jaspeados.

leaving ['liːviŋ], *s.* partida, marcha, acción de partir, de marcharse. — *pl.* **leavings,** sobras, relieves; desperdicios; desechos; residuo, sobra.

lecher ['letʃəɹ], *s.* hombre disoluto, libertino, putañero.

lecherous, *a.* lujurioso, lascivo, impúdico.

lecherousness, lechery, *s.* lujuria, lascivia, salacidad.

lecithin ['lesiθin], *s.* lecitina.

lectern ['lektəɹn], **lecturn,** *s.* atril, facistol de iglesia.

lection ['lekʃən], *s.* lección, lectura; letra, texto.

lectionary, *s.* leccionario.

lector ['lektəɹ], *s.* lector, lectorado.

lecture ['lektʃəɹ], *s.* conferencia, discurso, disertación; corrección, fraterna; lección, clase, *f.*; homilía, plática, razonamiento, represión; *curtain lecture*, reconvención privada (entre esposos); *lecture-room*, sala de conferencias, sala de clases, aula. — *v.t.* disertar, discursar; dar una conferencia; reprender, leer la cartilla a; sermonear; hablar excátedra, instruir, enseñar. — *v.i.* dar conferencias.

lecturer, *s.* lector, instructor, profesor, catedrático, disertante, discursante, conferenciante.

lectureship, *s.* lectoría, lectorado.

lecturn, *s.* [LECTERN].

led [led], *pret., p.p.* [LEAD]; *led horse*, caballo de mano.

ledge [ledʒ], *s.* anaquel; capa, tonga, borde, tongada; arrecife. — *pl.* **ledges,** (*mar.*) barrotes, latas de los baos.

ledger ['ledʒəɹ], *s.* (*com.*) libro mayor; traviesa de andamio, solera de emparrillado.

lee [liː], *s.* (*mar.*) sotavento; socaire. — *a.* (*mar.*) sotaventado; *lee side*, banda de sotavento; *lee shore*, (*mar.*) costa de sotavento; *lee tide*, marea de donde viene el viento; *under the lee*, a sotavento; *to have lee room*, tener buen sotavento; *on the lee beam*, a la banda de sotavento.

leech [liːtʃ], *s.* sanguijuela; (*fig.*) gorrón; (*mar.*) caídas; (*ant.*) médico; *leech lines*, apagapenoles; *leech-rope*, relinga de las caídas; *artificial leech*, ventosa; *horse-leech*, albéitar. — (*ant.*) *v.t.* curar, sanar.

leek [liːk], *s.* puerro.

leer [liəɹ], *s.* mirada maliciosa, mirada lasciva, mirada de soslayo o de reojo; (*tec.*) templador. — *v.i.* mirar de soslayo o de reojo; mirar con malicia o con lascivia.

leeringly, *adv.* con risa muy fea; con mirada de soslayo.

lees [liːz], *s.pl.* heces, *f.*, poso, sedimento, zurrapa, borras, feculencia, madre, *f.*

leeward ['luːəɹd], *a.* (*mar.*) sotavento, sotaventeador, roncero; *to leeward*, a sotavento; *leeward-tide*, marea en la dirección del viento; *to stand to leeward*, virar de bordo en redondo.

leeway ['liːwei], *s.* (*mar.*) deriva, abatimiento; desviación; tardanza.

left [left], *pret., p.p.* [LEAVE]. — *a.* siniestro, izquierdo; *left-luggage office*, consigna; *left-overs*, sobras, desperdicios.

left-hand ['lefthænd], *a.* zurdo; izquierdo; que rueda, da vueltas, o se mueve hacia la mano izquierda.

left-handed, *a.* zurdo; vueltas o gira hacia la izquierda; (*fig.*) desmañado; torpe; malicioso, torcido; morganático.

left-off, *a.* puesto a un lado, desechado.

leg [leg], *s.* pierna; pata de los animales; pie o pata de un mueble; caña de media o de bota; pierna de pantalón; (*mar.*) bordada; etapa; (*geom.*) lado de un triángulo; pernil (de carne de cerdo); *on one's last legs,* a la muerte, agonizante; sin recursos; *to be on one's legs again,* recobrar la salud; *to have not a leg to stand on,* no poder disculparse; *to leave someone not a leg to stand on,* poner a uno entre la espada y la pared; *to get on one's hind legs,* (*fam.*) levantarse para hablar; *upon its legs,* en pie, firmemente establecido; *to take leg-bail,* tomar las de Villadiego; *to pull one's leg,* (*fam.*) tomar el pelo a uno.

legacy ['legəsi], *s.* legado, manda; herencia; *legacy hunter,* el que anda a caza de herencias; *legacy duty,* derechos de herencia.

legal ['li:gəl], *a.* legal, jurídico, legítimo, lícito; permitido o provisto por la ley.

legality [li'gæliti], *s.* legalidad, legitimidad.

legalization [li:gəlai'zeiʃən], *s.* legalización; refrendación, refrendo.

legalize, *v.t.* legalizar, autorizar, legitimar; interpretar a la letra, refrendar.

legate ['legət], *s.* (*igl.*) legado; diputado, enviado.

legatee [legə'ti:], *s.* legatario.

legateship, *s.* legacía.

legatine ['legətain], *a.* hecho por un legado o que pertenece a él.

legation [le'geiʃən], *s.* legación, misión.

legato [le'gɑ:tou], *adv.* (*mús.*) ligado.

legator [le'geitəɹ], *s.* testador, el que haciendo testamento deja legados.

legend ['ledʒənd], *s.* leyenda; legenda; fábula; saga; letrero, inscripción, divisa, empresa; relación, narración.

legendary, *a.* legendario. — *s.* legendario.

leger ['ledʒəɹ], *a.* (*ant.*) ligero y delicado; *leger-lines,* (*mús.*) líneas adicionales al pentagrama; *leger space,* espacio comprendido por estas líneas.

legerdemain [ledʒəɹdə'mein], *s.* juego de manos, ligereza de manos, pasapasa, prestidigitación.

legged [legd, 'legid], *a.* de piernas, que tiene piernas empernado; *three-legged stool,* banquillo de tres pies.

legging ['legin], *s.* polaina, botín, guardapierna, sobrecalza.

Leghorn [le'goːɹn], *s.* sombrero de paja de Italia; raza de gallinas.

legibility [ledʒi'biliti], *s.* legibilidad.

legible ['ledʒibəl], *a.* legible, leíble.

legion ['li:dʒən], *s.* legión, *f.*; gran número; tropa, multitud.

legionary ['li:dʒənəri], *s., a.* legionario.

legislate ['ledʒisleit], *v.i.* legislar, dar o hacer leyes.

legislation, *s.* legislación.

legislative ['ledʒislətiv], *a.* legislativo.

legislator, *s.* legislador.

legislatorial [ledʒislə'tɔːriəl], *a.* perteneciente o relativo a la legislación o a una legislatura.

legislatorship, *s.* oficio o dignidad de legislador; facultad de hacer leyes.

legislatress, *s.* legisladora.

legislature ['ledʒislətʃəɹ], *s.* legislatura, cuerpo legislativo.

legist ['li:dʒist], *s.* legista, *m.f.*, jurisconsulto.

legitimacy [le'dʒitiməsi], *s.* legitimidad, legalidad; nacimiento legítimo; pureza.

legitimate [le'dʒitimit], *a.* legítimo; lícito, justo, legal; genuino, auténtico. — *v.t.* legitimar.

legitimateness, *s.* legitimidad, legalidad.

legitimation, *s.* legitimación.

legitimist [le'dʒitimist], *s.* legitimista, *m.f.*

legitimize, *v.t.* legitimar.

legume ['legju:m], **legumen** ['legjumən], *s.* legumbre, vaina.

leguminous [le'gju:minəs], *a.* leguminoso.

leisure ['leʒəɹ], *s.* ocio, vagancia, ociosidad, desocupación, holganza, comodidad; oportunidad, conveniencia; *at leisure,* despacio, con sosiego, cómodamente; *to be at leisure,* estar desocupado; *leisure hours,* horas libres, desocupadas, horas de ocio.

leisurely, *a.* pausado, deliberado. — *adv.* despacio, con cachaza, desocupadamente, deliberadamente.

leman ['lemən], *s.(ant.)* galán, *m.*, amante, *m.f.*

lemma ['lemə], *s.* (*log., mat.*) lema.

lemma, *s.* (*bot.*) lemnáceo, lentícula.

lemon ['lemən], *s.* limón; *lemon tree,* limonero; *lemon grove,* limonar; *lemon drop,* pastilla de limón; *candied lemon,* acitrón; *lemon coloured,* cetrino. — *a.* hecho o sazonado con limón; de color de limón, cetrino.

lemonade [lemo'neid], *s.* limonada.

lemur ['li:məɹ], *s.* lémur.

lend [lend], *v.t.* prestar; *to lend a hand,* dar una mano, ayudar; *to lend one's aid,* dar ayuda; prestar auxilio; *to lend an ear,* prestar atención, prestar oído.

lendable, *a.* prestable, prestadizo.

lender, *s.* prestador, prestamista, *m.f.*; logrero, mutuante.

lending, *s.* préstamo, empréstito; *lending library,* biblioteca circulante.

lene [li:n], *a.* suave, no aspirado. — *s.* consonante no aspirada.

length [lenθ], *s.* longitud, largo, largura, largor, largueza; extensión, distancia, dilatación; duración, o espacio de tiempo; alcance (de un tiro, etc.); echada; *at length,* al fin, finalmente; extensamente; *full length,* (*b.a.*) de cuerpo entero; *at full length,* a lo largo, de todo el largo; *to write at great length,* dejar correr la pluma.

lengthen ['lenθən], *v.t.* alargar, extender, estirar, dilatar, prolongar. — *v.i.* aumentarse, prolongarse, alargarse, dilatarse.

lengthening, *s.* alargamiento, prolongación, continuación.

lengthwise ['lenθwaiz], *adv.* longitudinalmente; a lo largo.

lengthy, *a.* bastante largo, demasiado largo; difuso, prolijo.

leniency ['li:niənsi], *a.* suavidad, lenidad.

lenient ['li:niənt], *a.* benigno, indulgente, clemente, lenitivo, misericordioso; leniente, laxativo.

lenify ['lenifai], *v.t.* lenificar, suavizar, ablandar.

lenitive ['lenitiv], *a.* lenitivo, molificativo,

mitigativo. — *s.* lenitivo, remedio que ablanda o suaviza; laxante.

lenity ['leniti], *s.* lenidad, suavidad, blandura.

lens [lenz], *s.* (*pl.* **lenses**) (*ópt.*) lente; (*anat.*) cristalino.

lent [lent], *pret.*, *p.p.* [LEND]; prestado. — *s.* Cuaresma.

lenten ['lentən], *a.* cuadragesimal, cuaresmal; pobre, escaso.

lenticel ['lentisel], *s.* (*bot.*) lentezuela.

lenticula, *s.* lente pequeño.

lenticular [len'tikju:lər], **lentiform** ['lenti-fɔ:ɹm], *a.* lenticular.

lentiginous [len'tidʒinəs], *a.* (*bot.*, *zool.*) pecoso; casposo.

lentil ['lentəl], *s.* lenteja.

lentiscus [len'tiskəs], **lentisk** ['lentisk], *s.* lentisco.

Leo ['li:ou], *s.* (*astr.*) León.

leonine ['li:ounain], *a.* leonino.

leopard ['lepəɹd], *s.* leopardo, pardal.

leopard's-bane, *s.* dorónico.

lepadide ['lepədaid], *s.* lápade, *f.*, percebe.

leper ['lepəɹ], *s.* leproso, lazarino.

leperous ['lepərəs, 'lepɹəs], *a.* leproso.

lepidoptera [lepi'dɔptərə], *s.* lepidópteros.

lepidopterous, *a.* lepidóptero.

leporine ['lepɔrin], *a.* lebruno.

leprose ['leprouz], *a.* (*bot.*) casposo, escamoso.

leprosity, *s.* calidad de escamoso o casposo.

leprosy ['lepɹəsi], *s.* lepra; elefancía.

leprous ['lepɹəs], *a.* leproso, lazarino.

leprousness, *s.* leprosidad.

Lepus ['li:pəs], *s.* (*astr.*) Liebre, *f.*

lese-majesty ['li:z'mædʒesti], *s.* lesa majestad.

lesion ['li:ʒən], *s.* lesión.

less [les], *a.* (*comp.* **little**) menor, menos, inferior. — *adv.* menos, en grado más bajo, en grado más pequeño; *to grow less*, disminuir(se), achicarse; *more or less*, más o menos; *so much the less*, tanto menos cuanto; *less and less*, de menos en menos; *to make less*, aminorar, mermar, escatimar, disminuir. — *s.* menos.

-less ['lis, -les], *sufijo*, terminación negativa o privativa; sin; *childless*, sin hijos; *hopeless*, sin esperanza; *penniless*, sin un céntimo, etc.

lessee [le'si:], *s.* arrendatario, censero, rentero, inquilino, el que toma en arrendamiento.

lessen ['lesən], *v.t.* minorar, aminorar, disminuir, achicar, mermar, acortar, menoscabar, reducir; degradar, rebajar, privar. — *v.i.* bajarse, degradarse; disminuirse, mermar.

lesser, *a.* (*comp.* **little**) menor, más pequeño.

lesson ['lesən], *s.* lección, lectura; fraterna, corrección, reprensión; enseñanza, precepto, instrucción; conocimiento, saber; (*igl.*) lección. — *v.t.* enseñar; reprender.

lessor ['lesər], *s.* arrendante, arrendador.

lest [lest], *conj.* para que no, por miedo de, de miedo que, a fin de que no.

let [let], *v.t.* (*pret.*, *p.p.* **let**) dejar, no impedir, permitir, conceder; alquilar; arrendar; (*ant.*) estorbar, impedir. — *v.i.* ser arrendado, ser alquilado; como verbo auxiliar, equivale al subjunctivo: *let him come*, que venga; *a house to let*, una casa por alquilar; *to let be*, dejar en su estado actual, no entremeterse; *to let down*, dejar caer, dejar bajar; (*fig.*) engañar; *to let in*, admitir, recibir; *to let loose*, soltar, desatar, desencadenar; *to let off*, perdonar, excusar; disparar, descargar; *to let out*, dejar salir, poner en libertad; arrendar, alquilar;

to let blood, sangrar, hacerse sangrar; *to let fly*, disparar; *to let go*, soltar; *to let know*, advertir, hacer saber; *let us go*, vámonos. — *s.* obstáculo, estorbo, impedimento; *without let or hindrance*, sin estorbo ni obstáculo.

lethal ['li:θəl], *a.* letal, mortal.

lethargic [le'θɑ:ɹdʒik], **lethargical** [le'θɑ:ɹdʒikəl], *a.* letárgico, aletargado.

lethargied, *a.* aletargado.

lethargize, *v.t.* aletargar.

lethargy ['leθəɹdʒi], *s.* letargo, aletargamiento; inacción, apatía; estupor, entorpecimiento, enajenamiento, torpeza.

Lethe ['li:θi], *s.* Leteo.

Lethean, *a.* léteo.

lethiferous [le'θifərəs], *a.* somnífero.

Lett [let], *s.* letón.

letten ['letən], *p.p.* (*for.*) alquilado, arrendado.

letter ['letəɹ], *s.* letra; carta, carta misiva; epístola, comunicación; (*impr.*) letra, carácter, tipo; sentido o interpretación literal. — *pl.* **letters**, literatura, erudición, letras; *letter of exchange*, letra de cambio; *letter of licence*, moratoria; *letter rogatory*, (*for.*) suplicatoria; *letters of safe-conduct*, salvoconducto. — *v.t.* estampar con letras; rotular.

letter-book, *s.* libro copiador.

letter-box, *s.* buzón.

letter-carrier, *s.* cartero.

letter-case, *s.* cartera.

lettered ['letəɹd], *a.* letrado, instruido, literato, docto, erudito.

letter-file, *s.* guardacartas, *m.*, archivo.

letter-foundry, *s.* fundición.

lettering, *s.* letrero, rótulo, inscripción; estampilla.

letterpress, *s.* impresión, obra impresa; texto. — *a.* impreso.

lettuce ['letis], *s.* lechuga.

leucin ['lju:sin], **leucine**, *s.* leucina.

leucocyte ['lju:kosait], *s.* leucocito.

leucoma [lju:'koumə], *s.* albugo.

leucorrhœa [lju:ko'riə], *s.* leucorrea, flores blancas.

Levant [le'vænt], *s.* levante, oriente. — *a.* oriental.

Levanter [le'væntəɹ], *s.* viento de levante.

levantine [le'væntain], *a.* levantino.

levantines, *s.pl.* (*tej.*) levantín.

levator [le'veitəɹ], *s.* músculo elevador; (*cir.*) levantador.

levee ['levi], *s.* corte, *f.*, besamanos, recepción; dique, ribero, malecón.

level ['levəl], *a.* plano, llano, igual; liso, raso; a nivel, nivelado, allanado; derecho, recto; (*fig.*) parejo, uniforme, igual a otra cosa; honrado, probo; (*fam.*) de buen juicio, juicioso, discreto, equilibrado; *level crossing*, (*f.c.*) paso a nivel; *to make level*, allanar, nivelar; (*alb.*) enrasar; *to do one's level best*, (*fam.*) hacer su posible; *to be level*, estar al nivel. — *s.* llano, llanura; nivel o altura media; plano, ras, nivel; igualdad; (*min.*) galería horizontal, piso; *dead level*, monotonía, uniformidad, planicie inmensa. — *adv.* a nivel, ras; en derechura; igualmente; con puntería; lisa y llanamente. — *v.t.* nivelar, igualar, allanar, aplanar; arrasar, derribar; encaminar, dirigir, apuntar, asestar; adaptar, ajustar, proporcionar; emparejar; (*alb.*) enrasar. — *v.i.* apuntar (una arma); hacer nivelaciones los agrimensores.

level-headed, *a*. sagaz, juicioso.
leveller ['levələɹ], *s*. allanador, igualador, aplanador; nivelador; aplanadera.
levelling, *s*. nivelación; aplanamiento, allanamiento, arrasamiento; igualación; (*alb*.) enrasado.
levelness, *s*. igualdad, nivel, allanamiento.
lever ['liːvəɹ], *s*. palanca, alzaprima, barra, leva, espeque, mangueta; escape de reloj; manubrio; torniquete.
leverage ['liːvəˈridʒ], *s*. sistema de palancas, *m*.; punto de apoyo; (*fig*.) influencia, poder.
leveret ['levəret], *s*. lebrato, lebratillo.
leviable ['leviəbəl], *a*. exigible.
leviathan [le'vaiəθən], *s*. leviatán.
levigate ['levigeit], *v.t.* levigar; pulverizar, reducir a polvo. — *a*. aligerado, alisado, reducido a polvo.
levigation, *s*. levigación; pulverización.
levitate ['leviteit], *v.t.* aligerar.
levitation, *s*. aligeramiento.
Levite ['liːvait], *s*. levita, *m.f.*
Levitic [le'vitik], **Levitical** [le'vitikəl], *a*. levítico.
levity ['leviti], *s*. levedad, ligereza; liviandad, veleidad, frivolidad, inconstancia; vanidad.
levulose ['levjuːlouz], *s*. levulosa.
levy, *v.t.* hacer leva, reclutar, enganchar; exigir tributos; (*for*.) embargar, ejecutar. — *s*. leva, enganche, recluta; (*for*.) embargo, ejecución; exacción de tributos, colectación, recaudación.
lewd [ljuːd], *a*. lujurioso, sensual, lascivo, impúdico, salaz, deshonesto, libidinoso, obsceno, disoluto, libertino, depravado, perverso.
lewdness, *s*. lascivia, lubricidad, sensualidad, lujuria, incontinencia, impudicicia, licencia, libertinaje, relajación, desenfreno.
lewis ['luːis], **lewisson** ['luːisən], *s*. clavija para alzar piedras, castañuela de cantera; retén, grapa.
lexical ['leksikəl], *a*. lexicográfico, relativo al léxico.
lexicographer [leksiˈkɔgrəfəɹ], *s*. lexicógrafo.
lexicographic, *a*. lexicográfico.
lexicography, *s*. lexicografía.
lexicological, *a*. lexicológico.
lexicologist, *s*. lexicólogo.
lexicology [leksiˈkɔlodʒi], *s*. lexicología.
lexicon ['leksikən], *s*. léxico, lexicón, vocabulario, diccionario.
liability [laiəˈbiliti], *s*. riesgo, exposición; propensión, inclinación; responsabilidad, obligación, pasivo, deuda pasiva; *limited (liability) company*, (*com*.) sociedad anónima. — *pl*. **liabilities**, (*com*.) pasivo, deudas pasivas.
liable [laiəbəl], *a*. sujeto, obligado, expuesto, deudor, responsable; propenso, inclinado.
liaison [liːˈeizən], *s*. lío; coordinación; amorío; *liaison officer*, oficial de enlace.
liana [liˈɑːnə], **liane** [liːˈɑːn], *s*. jagüey.
liar ['laiəɹ], *s*. mentiroso, embustero.
lias ['laiəs], *s*. lías.
libation [laiˈbeiʃən], *s*. libación.
libel ['laibəl], *s*. libelo; calumnia, difamación. — *v.t., v.i.* satirizar; calumniar, difamar.
libellant, *s*. (*for*.) actor o demandante ante el tribunal del Almirantazgo.
libeller, *s*. libelista, *m.f.*, infamador, difamador, calumniador.

libelling, *s*. difamación.
libellous, *a*. infamatorio, difamatorio.
libellula [liˈbeljuːlə], *s*. libélula, caballito del diablo.
liberal ['libərəl], *a*., *s*. liberal, dadivoso, generoso, bizarro, pródigo, munífico; abundante, espléndido; franco; (*pol*.) liberal; honorífico, caballeroso; *liberal arts*, artes liberales, *f.pl*.; *liberal-minded*, tolerante; *liberal profession*, carrera liberal.
liberalism ['libərəlizm], *s*. liberalismo.
liberality [libəˈræliti], *s*. liberalidad, dadivosidad, generosidad, munificencia, largueza, bizarría.
liberalize, *v.t.* liberalizar, hacer liberal, etc.
liberate ['libəreit], *v.t.* libertar, librar, redimir; manumitir.
liberation, *s*. liberación, relevación, redención.
liberator, *s*. librador, libertador.
libertarian [libəˈtɛəriən], *a*. libertario.
libertinage [libəɹˈtiːnidʒ], **libertinism** ['libəɹtinizm], *s*. libertinaje; licencia, desenfreno; estado de libertino.
libertine ['libəɹtin], *a*., *s*. libertino, disoluto. — *s*. (*hist*.) libertino, hijo de liberto.
liberty ['libəɹti], *s*. libertad; libre albedrío; prerrogativa, inmunidad, privilegio, exención, franquicia; osada familiaridad; franqueza; liberación, soltura de presos o cautivos; permiso, licencia.
libidinous [liˈbidinəs], *a*. libidinoso, liviano, lascivo, deshonesto, lujurioso, impúdico, disoluto, salaz.
libidinousness, *s*. lascivia, desenfreno, lujuria, impudicia.
Libra ['laibrə], *s*. Libra.
librarian [laiˈbrɛəriən], *s*. bibliotecario.
librarianship, *s*. empleo u oficio de bibliotecario.
library ['laibrəri], *s*. biblioteca; estudio, escritorio, despacho; librería.
librate [laiˈbreit], *v.t.* balancear, equilibrar, poner en equilibrio.
libration [laiˈbreiʃən], *s*. libración, balance, equilibrio.
libratory, *a*. oscilatorio; que balancea.
librettist [liˈbretist], *s*. autor de libretos.
libretto [liˈbretou], *s*. libro, libreto.
Libyan ['libiən], *s*., *a*. libio.
lice [lais], *s.pl*. [LOUSE]; piojos.
licebane, *s*. albarraz, hierba piojera.
licence ['laisəns], *s*. licencia; permiso, autorización, facultad; despacho, título, cédula; pase; desorden, libertad inmoderada, desarreglo, libertinaje, desenfreno; diploma, certificado que contiene un permiso.
licensable [laiˈsensəbəl], *a*. permisible, permitiero.
license, *v.t.* licenciar, dar licencia o permiso; facultar, autorizar, permitir; dar cédula, despacho o privilegio; soltar, dar soltura.
licensee [laisənˈsiː], *s*. concesionario.
licenser, *s*. persona que da licencia.
licentiate [laiˈsenʃit], *s*. licenciado.
licentious [laiˈsenʃəs], *a*. licencioso, libertino, desenfrenado, desordenado, disoluto.
licentiousness, *s*. licencia, disipación, disolución, desarreglo, desenfrenamiento, libertinaje.
lichen ['laikən], *s*. liquen.

lich-gate ['litʃgeit], s. sotechado a la entrada de un cementerio.

lich-owl, s. lechuza.

licit ['lisit], a. lícito, permitido.

licitness, s. licitud.

lick [lik], v.t. lamer; (vulg.) cascar, golpear, aporrear, dar una tunda; (mec.) absorber; sobrepujar, vencer; to lick the dust, morder el polvo. — s. lamedura, lametada, lengüetada; (E.U.) salagar, lamedero; (fam.) mojicón, bofetón, cachete.

licker, s. lamedor; (mec.) lubricador automático.

lickerish ['likəriʃ], a. sabroso, apetitoso; salaz, libidinoso.

lickerishness, s. delicadeza de paladar, regalo.

lickspittle ['likspitəl], s. quitapelillos, parásito, hombre servil.

licorice, liquorice ['likəris], s. regaliz, alcazuz, orozuz.

lictor ['liktəɹ], s. lictor.

lid [lid], s. tapa, tapador; párpado (del ojo); tapadera; (bot.) opérculo; guardapolvo de reloj.

lie [lai], s. mentira, ficción, embuste, vanidad, falsedad, error; mentís, desmentida; postura, positura, posición, caída, situación, yacimiento; cubil; (f.c.) desviadero; white lie, mentirilla; to give the lie, dar un mentís.

lie [lai], v.i. (pret., p.p. **lied**; part. pres. **lying**) mentir, embustear, decir mentiras, faltar a la verdad.

lie [lai], v.i. (pret. **lay**; p.p. **lain**) echarse, tenderse, tumbarse; reposar, estar acostado, acostarse; descansar recostado, apoyarse; estar tendido o echado, yacer; pernoctar, habitar, morar, residir; apretarse, estrecharse; consistir; ubicar, estar situado; estar una persona o cosa en un lugar o paraje; estar en la mano, tocar o corresponder a uno; estar pendiente; depender; (for.) ser sostenible, defendible (una acción, objeción, etc.); to lie at anchor, (mar.) estar sobre las áncoras; to lie along, (mar.) dar a la banda; to lie at heart, tomar a pechos una cosa o tenerla clavada en el corazón; to lie at, importunar, molestar; to lie at stake, estar muy interesado en algo; to lie at the point of death, estar a punto de morir, estar expirando; to lie about, estar esparcido; to lie by, reposar, estar tranquilo o quieto; to lie down, acostarse, reposar; to lie in, estar de parto; (fam.) quedarse en la cama; to lie in wait, espiar, acechar; to lie in the way, ser obstáculo, impedimento, embarazo; to lie upon, ser obligatorio, pesar sobre; to lie over, aplazarse; (com.) posponerse; to lie under, estar sujeto a; estar expuesto a, acusado; to lie with, vivir o dormir con; to lie up, descansar; to lie sick, guardar cama; to lie to, (mar.) estar a la capa; to lie on, (mar.) estar en carga.

lief [li:f], a. (ant.) agradable, querido; I had as lief, preferiría. — adv. de buena gana, de buena voluntad, de buen grado, bien dispuesto.

liege [li:dʒ], a. ligio; feudatorio. — s. vasallo, súbdito, soberano, señor de vasallos.

liegeman ['li:dʒmən], s. vasallo.

lien ['li:ən], s. (for.) derecho de retención, embargo preventivo para el cobro de una deuda; gravamen, obligación.

lienteric [li:ən'terik], s. lientérico.

lientery, s. lientería.

lieu [lju:], s. (fr.) lugar, sitio; in lieu of, en lugar de, en vez de.

lieutenancy, s. tenencia, lugartenencia, tenientazgo.

lieutenant [lef'tenənt], s. teniente, lugarteniente; (mil.) teniente.

lieutenantship, s. tenencia, tenientazgo, oficio de lugarteniente.

life [laif], s. vida; existencia; conducta; viveza, prontitud, fuego, ardor, vivacidad, animación, movimiento, espíritu; mundo; semejanza o forma exacta; idea vivificante o central. — a. vitalicio, de por vida; life preserver, salvavidas, m.; to depart this life, fallecer; I would stake my life upon its being so, pondría mi cabeza a que es así; from life, del natural; high life, alta sociedad; to the life, al vivo.

life-annuity, s. fondo vitalicio.

life-belt, s. (cinturón) salvavidas, m. sing.

life-blood, s. sangre vital, f.; (fig.) alma, vida.

lifeboat, s. lancha salvavidas.

life-buoy ['laifbɔi], s. boya salvavidas.

life-giving, a. vivificante.

lifeguard, s. guardia de corps.

life-insurance, s. seguro de vida.

lifeless, a. muerto, inanimado, exánime, flojo, falto de fuerza; inhabitado; amortiguado.

lifelessly, adv. sin espíritu, sin vigor.

lifelike, a. que parece vivo, natural.

life-line, s. cable de salvamento.

lifelong, a. de toda la vida.

lifesized, a. de tamaño natural.

lifetime, s. curso de la vida.

lift [lift], v.t. alzar, levantar, elevar; exaltar, ensalzar; quitar la presión; enriscar; envanecer, ensoberbecer, engreír; soliviar; sopesar; (fam.) hurtar; quitar, llevarse. — v.i. hacer fuerza para levantar alguna cosa; disiparse (una niebla); to lift one's hat, quitarse el sombrero; to lift up, levantar, alzar; to lift up the heel against, tratar con insolencia y desprecio; to lift up the hand, levantar la mano, pegar; (fig.) jurar, prestar juramento levantando la mano; to lift the horn, tratar con insolencia y con desdén; establecer en autoridad; to lift up the voice, levantar la voz; gritar. — s. esfuerzo para levantar un peso; solivio, soliviadura; elevación, alzamiento; máquina o utensilio para alzar; asa, tirador; elevador, ascensor; alza, calzo; at one lift, de un golpe; to give one a lift, ayudar a uno a levantarse; llevar en coche. — pl. **lifts**, (mar.) amantillos; topping-lifts, (mar.) amantillos de la botaborra; handing-lifts, (mar.) mostachos.

lifter, s. alzador, elevador; calzo; ratero, ladrón.

lifting, s. acto de levantar; levantamiento.

lifting-jack, s. gato, cric.

ligament ['ligəmənt], s. (anat.) ligamento; ligazón, f., ligadura, traba.

ligamental [ligə'mentəl], **ligamentous** [ligə'mentəs], a. ligamentoso.

ligate [li'geit], v.t. (cir.) atar con ligadura.

ligation [li'geiʃən], s. ligación.

ligature ['ligətʃəɹ], s. (cir., mec. y mús.) ligadura; (impr.) letras ligadas.

light [lait], s. luz, f., emisión de luz; claro, claridad, resplandor; luz, f., vela, bujía, lámpara, farol; vidrio de ventana; claraboya, ventana, tragaluz; candela, lumbre; noticia, aviso, publicidad; ilustración, conocimiento;

punto de vista, aspecto; (*pint.*) luz, *f.*; vista, visión; día, *m.*; alba, amanecer; inteligencia; percepción. — *a.* leve, ligero; fácil; frívolo, liviano, mutable, inconstante, fútil, superficial; llevadero; desembarazado, ágil; alegre, vivo; incontinente; resplandeciente, reluciente, claro, brillante; rubio, blondo; *light supper*, colación; *to make light of*, burlarse de, tomar en broma; *light o'love*, mujer liviana. — *v.t.* encender; alumbrar, iluminar, dar luz a; (*mar.*) aligerar, hacer más ligero. — *v.i.* hallar, encontrar, tropezar; desmontarse, apearse, desembarcar; descansar; parar.

light-armed, *a.* armado levemente.

light-borne, *a.* llevado o traído por la luz.

lightbrain, *s.* casquivano, hombre frívolo.

lighten, *v.t.* iluminar, alumbrar, dar luz; descargar, aligerar, quitar peso; exonerar; (*mar.*) alijar; aclarar, hacer más claro; aliviar; alegrar, regocijar, infundir gozo o alegría. — *v.i.* ponerse ligero, disminuir de peso; relampaguear, brillar; hablar con violencia; caer, descender.

lightening ['laitəniŋ], *s.* alba, alborada; aligeramiento.

lighter, *a.* (*comp.* **light**); más ligero; más claro. — *s.* (*mar.*) lanchón, barcaza, alijador, chalana, gabarra; alumbrador, encendedor; *cigarette lighter*, encendedor, mechero.

lighterage ['laitəridʒ], *s.* alijo, arrimaje, gabarraje.

lighterman, *s.* lanchonero, gabarrero.

light-fingered, *a.* ligero de dedos, ratero, ladrón.

light-footed, *a.* ligero de pies.

light-headed, *a.* casquivano; delirante; aturdido.

light-hearted, *a.* festivo, alegre.

light-horse, *s.* (*mil.*) caballería ligera.

lighthouse ['laithaus], *s.* faro.

lighting, *s.* iluminación, alumbrado.

light-keeper, *s.* farolero; torrero.

lightless, *a.* obscuro, sin luz, falto de luz.

lightly, *adv.* ligeramente, levemente, a la ligera; prontamente; fácilmente; sin razón, sin motivo; con alegría, alegremente, airosamente; livianamente, deshonestamente; *lightly come, lightly go*, (*prov.*) como se viene, se va, *o* los dineros del sacristán, cantando se vienen y cantando se van.

light-minded, *a.* variable, inconstante, voluble.

light-money, *s.* (*mar.*) derechos de faro o de fuego.

lightness, *s.* levedad, ligereza; velocidad, agilidad; inconstancia; frivolidad; liviandad, deshonestidad.

lightning ['laitniŋ], *s.* relámpago, rayo, relampagueo; *sheet-lightning*, fucilazos; *lightning conductor*, pararrayos; *lightning-proof*, a prueba de rayos; *as quick as lightning*, (*fam.*) como una pólvora.

light railway, *s.* ferrocarril de vía estrecha.

light-room, *s.* (*mar.*) caja de faroles del pañol de pólvora o lampión.

lights ['laits], *s.pl.* bofes.

light-ship, *s.* buque faro.

lightsome ['laitsəm], *a.* alegre, festivo, juguetón; (*poét.*) luminoso.

lightsomeness, *s.* claridad; alegría.

light-weight, *s.* peso ligero (boxeo). — *a.* de peso ligero.

light-year, *s.* año de luz.

ligneous ['ligniəs], **lignous,** *a.* leñoso.

ligniferous, *a.* leñífero.

lignify ['lignifai], *v.t.*, *v.i.* convertir(se) en madera.

lignite ['lignait], *s.* lignito.

lignum-vitæ [lignəm'vaiti:], *s.* guayaco, guayacán, palo santo.

ligulate ['ligju:lit], *a.* (flor) acintillada, semiflosculosa o ligulada.

ligure ['ligju:əɹ], *s.* ligurio.

like [laik], *a.* parecido, igual, semejante; creíble, probable, verosímil, verisímil; lo mismo que, equivalente; ganoso, deseoso. — *s.* semejanza, semejante, igual. — *adv.* como, como si, del mismo modo que, igual que; probablemente, verisímilmente; *in like manner*, del mismo modo; *to give like for like*, pagar en la misma moneda; *like father, like son*, (*prov.*) el hijo de la gata, ratones mata; *like master, like man*, (*prov.*) de tal palo, tal astilla *o* tal para cual; *he has not his like*, no tiene igual; *to look like*, parecerse a; *to be as like as two peas*, parecerse como dos gotas de agua. — *v.t.*, *v.i.* gustar de, hallar agrado en, tener gusto en, contentarse con; querer, amar; estar contento de, hallar (bien o mal); *as you like (it)*, como Vd. quiera, *o* como Vd. guste; *I like it*, me gusta.

likelihood ['laiklihud], **likeliness** ['laiklinis], *s.* probabilidad, posibilidad, verisimilitud.

likely ['laikli], *a.* probable, verosímil; bien parecido; creíble, plausible; loable; placentero; apto, idóneo, a propósito. — *adv.* probablemente, según todas las apariencias; *it is likely enough*, no sería extraño.

liken ['laikən], *v.t.* comparar, asemejar.

likeness ['laiknis], *s.* semejanza, parecido; igualdad, conformidad; forma, viso, aire, apariencia; retrato; semeja, semejante; *a speaking likeness*, un retrato fiel, un retrato que habla.

likewise, *adv.* también, asimismo, igualmente, además.

liking, *s.* inclinación, gusto, afición, deseo, agrado; preferencia, aprobación.

lilac ['lailək], *s.* lila, lilas. — *a.* de color de lila.

liliaceous [lili'eiʃəs], *a.* liliáceo.

lilied ['lilid], *a.* adornado con lirios.

Lilliputian [lili'pju:ʃən], *s.*, *a.* liliputiense.

lilt [lilt], *v.t.*, *v.i.* bailar o cantar alegremente. — *s.* canción; ritmo.

lily ['lili], *s.* azucena; lirio; flor de lis, *f.*; *water lily*, ninfea, nenúfar; *lily of the valley*, muguete; lirio de los valles; *day lily*, hemerocálide.

lilywort ['liliwəːt], *s.* liliácea.

Lima [li:mə, laimə], *Lima wood*, brasilete; *lima beans*, habas de Lima.

limaceous [li'meiʃəs], *a.* limáceo.

Limax ['laimæks], *s.* babosa, babaza.

limb [lim], *s.* miembro (del cuerpo); (*fig.*) miembro, socio, individuo; rama de árbol; borde, orilla, remate, extremo; (*astr.*) limbo; corona graduada del sextante; (*fam.*) joven travieso o malévolo. — *v.t.* poner miembros; desmembrar, despedazar.

limbed, *a.* membrudo, ramoso, fornido.

limber ['limbəɹ], *a.* flojo, blando, flexible. — *s.* (*arti.*) avantrén de cureña, armón; (*mar.*) groera del canal del agua; *limber-holes*, (*mar.*) imbornales de las varengas; *limber boards*, (*mar.*) panas imbornales de las varengas;

limber rope, cabo imbornalero. — *v.t.* poner flexible, manejable o blando; *to limber up*, poner o colocar el armón; poner el avantrén a una cureña; (*fam.*) entrenar(se).

limberness ['limbəɹnis], *s.* flexibilidad.

limbless ['limles], *a.* desmembrado.

limbo ['limbou], *s.* limbo.

lime [laim], *s.* cal, *f.*; liga; (*bot.*) lima; *limelight*, luz de calcio; (*fig.*) la luz de publicidad; *lime water*, agua de cal; *lime kiln*, calera; *lime juice*, zumo de lima; *lime twig*, vareta; *lime tree*, (*bot.*) limero; tilia, tilo. — *v.t.* encalar, enmarañar; untar o coger con liga; (*agr.*) abonar con cal; (*alb.*) unir con betún, mortero, argamasa, o mezcla.

lime-burner, *s.* calero.

limehound, *s.* sabueso; perro grande de caza.

limerick ['limərik], *s.* cierta copla de cinco versos.

limestone ['laimstoun], *s.* piedra de cal, piedra caliza.

limit ['limit], *s.* límite, término, fin; aledaño, meta; linde, lindero; frontera, raya, confín, comarca; freno, obstáculo, limitación, impedimento. — *v.t.* limitar, fijar, determinar; restringir; coartar.

limitable, *a.* restringible.

limitary, *a.* limitáneo, fronterizo, limítrofe, confinante.

limitation [limi'teiʃən], *s.* limitación, acotamiento, restricción, modificación.

limited ['limitid], *a.* limitado, restricto, poco, escaso; finito. — *p.p.* [LIMIT]; *limited train*, (*f.c.*) tren compuesto sólo de coches de primera clase; *limited partnership*, sociedad en comandita; *limited company*, sociedad anónima.

limiter, *s.* limitador.

limitless, *a.* ilimitado.

limn [lim], *v.t.* pintar, iluminar; retratar; dibujar.

limner ['limnəɹ], *s.* pintor; dibujador; retratista, *m.f.*

limning, *s.* pintura, acción de pintar.

limous [laiməs], *a.* cenagoso, fangoso.

limp [limp], *s.* cojera. — *a.* débil, flojo, flexible, blando, débil de carácter. — *v.i.* cojear; (*mec.*) cojear, agotar irregularmente.

limper, *s.* cojo.

limpet ['limpet], *s.* lapa, lápade, *f.*

limpid ['limpid], *a.* límpido, cristalino, puro.

limpidity [lim'piditi], **limpidness** ['limpidnis], *s.* limpidez.

limping, *s.* cojera.

limpingly, *adv.* con cojera.

limy ['laimi], *a.* calizo; viscoso, glutinoso, pegajoso.

Linaceae [li'neisiə], *s.pl.* lináceas.

linaceous [li'neiʃəs], *a.* lináceo.

linch-pin ['lintʃpin], *s.* sotrozo, estornija, perno, pasador; (*arti.*) pezonera.

linden ['lindən], **linden-tree**, *s.* tilo, tila, teja, patagua.

line [lain], *s.* línea, renglón; cordel, cuerda; rasgo, perfil, trazo, contorno; carta muy breve, esquela; raya, arruga; (*f.c.*) vía, trayecto; línea de vapores; línea telegráfica, raya, fila, hilera, ringlera, andana; frontera, linde, línea divisoria, confín, término, límite; serie, *f.*, sucesión, descendencia; contorno, trazo, croquis, esquicio; sedal; (*com.*) renglón, clase, *f.*, surtido, cantidad de

géneros de una clase; línea de conducta, curse de acción; hilo de un discurso; ramo de negocios; (*mar.*) cuerda, cabo, vaivén; (*mil.*) línea (de defensa, de batalla, etc.); (*geog.*) ecuador, línea equinoccial; (*impr.*) línea, renglón; (*mat.*) línea; verso. — *pl.* **lines**, versos; *branch line*, (*f.c.*) ramal, vía lateral; *junction line*, línea de empalme; *line-keeper*, (*f.c.*) guardavía, *m.*; *lead line*, (*mar.*) sondalesa; *leech-lines*, (*mar.*) apagapenoles; *log-line*, (*mar.*) corredera; *tape-line*, lienza; *towing-line*, estacha, remolque; *line-reel*, carretel de la caña de pescar; *hard lines*, (*fam.*) lástima, apuro, situación difícil; *line engraving*, grabado de líneas; *to write a few lines*, enviar cuatro líneas (o renglones). — *v.t.* linear, rayar, trazar líneas, hacer líneas sobre; alinear; delinear; colocar, poner o disponer en fila, en hileras; aleccionar; enseñar; (*mec.*) ajustar; leer en alta voz, línea por línea; forrar, aforrar; revestir, guarnecer; hacer concebir (hablando de animales). — *v.i.* estar en línea; colocarse en fila, o en posición (para fútbol, etc.); *to have one's purse* (o *pocket*) *well lined*, tener el riñón bien cubierto.

lineage ['liniedʒ], *s.* línea, linaje, genealogía, prosapia, abolengo, descendencia.

lineal ['liniəl], *a.* lineal; descendiente, hereditario, emparentado.

lineally, *adv.* en línea recta.

lineament ['liniəmənt], *s.* lineamento, facción del rostro.

linear, *a.* lineal; longitudinal; (*zool., bot.*) linear; *linear measure*, medida de longitud.

lineate ['linieit], **lineated** ['linieitid], *a.* señalado con líneas.

lineation, *s.* delineación, dibujo de líneas.

lined [laind], *a.* rayado; forrado; arrugado. — *p.p.* [LINE].

lineman ['lainmən], *s.* tendedor de alambres telegráficos.

linen ['linin], *s.* lienzo, lino; género de lino, tela hecha de lino, ropa blanca; *bed-linen*, sábanas, ropa de cama; *bleached linen*, lienzo blanqueado; *linen cambric*, olán batista, cambray; *table linen*, mantelería; *linen damask*, damasco de hilo, alemanisco; *baby-linen*, pañales; *linen draper*, lencero; *change of linen*, muda de ropa; *linen goods*, o *linen trade*, lencería; *linen prover*, cuentahilos.

liner ['lainəɹ], *s.* (*mar.*) buque de vapor; transatlántico; rayador; delineador; forrador; forro.

ling [liŋ], *s.* (*bot.*) brezo; (*ict.*) abadejo.

-ling, sufijo dim., v.g. stripling, mozuelo.

ling-aloe, *s.* (*bot.*) lináloe.

linger ['liŋgəɹ], *v.i.* demorarse, tardar, dilatarse, consumirse, tardar mucho, ir pasando, ir despacio; padecer lentamente.

lingerer ['liŋgərəɹ], *s.* el que tarda o dilata.

lingerie ['lɑːngəri:], *s.* (*fr.*) ropa blanca.

lingering ['liŋgəriŋ], *a.* lento, tardo, prolongado, lánguido, pesado, moroso. — *s.* tardanza, dilación.

lingo ['liŋgou], *s.* (*fam.*) jerga, algarabía, greguería, dialecto.

lingot, *s.* molde de lingote, riel.

linguadental [liŋgwi'dentəl], *a.* linguodental.

lingual ['liŋgwəl], *a.* lingual, relativo a la lengua. — *s.* sonido lingual.

linguist ['liŋgwist], *s.* lingüista, *m.f.*

linguistic [liŋ'gwistik], *a.* lingüístico. — *pl.* **linguistics**, lingüística.

liniment ['linimənt], s. linimento, untura.

lining ['lainiŋ], s. forro, aforro; (mar.) embono, encofrado.

link [liŋk], s. eslabón, anillo de cadena; (mec.) varilla de conexión; hacha de viento; enlace, enganche; medida de unos 201 mm.; *link motion*, (mec.) cuadrante de la corredera. — *v.t.* enlazar, ligar, unir, reunir, trabar, juntar, eslabonar, engarzar, encadenar. — *v.i.* tener conexión; unirse en matrimonio. — *pl.* **links**, campo de golf.

linkboy, linkman, s. paje de hacha.

linnet ['linit], s. pardillo.

linoleum [li'nouliəm], s. linóleo.

linotype ['lainotaip], s. linotipo; linotipia (máquina).

linseed ['linsi:d], s. linaza.

linsey-woolsey ['linzi'wulzi], s., a. de lana y lino mezclados; basto, grosero.

linstock ['linstɔk], **lintstock**, s. disparador, botafuego.

lint [lint], s. hila, hilaza; (cir.) hilas.

lintel ['lintəl], s. (arq.) lintel, dintel, tranquero.

lion ['laiən], s. león; (fig.) celebridad; (astr.) León; *lion's share*, parte del león, mayor parte, f.

lioness ['laiənes], s.f. leona.

lion-like, a. aleonado.

lion's foot, s. (bot.) alquemila, pie de león.

lion's tail, s. (bot.) leonuro.

lip [lip], s. labio; labio de una herida; boca, habla; borde, extremidad, pico de jarro; (vulg.) descaro, desvergüenza; *to make a lip*, hacer muecas, befar, hacer gestos; *to smack one's lips*, (fig.) chuparse los dedos.

lip-glue, s. cola de boca.

lip-labour, s. jarabe de pico, palabras vanas.

lipothymy [li'pɔθimi], s. lipotimia, desmayo, desfallecimiento, síncope.

lipped [lipd], a. que tiene labios; *blubber-lipped*, belfo, hocicudo, morrudo.

lipper, s. (mar.) mar picada.

lippitude ['lipitju:d], s. legaña.

lip-reading, s. interpretación del movimiento de los labios.

lip-salve, s. ungüento para los labios.

lip-service, s. servicio de boca, devoción de boca.

liquable ['likwəbəl], a. licuable, liquidable.

liquate ['likweit], v.t. liquidar, derretir. — v.i. derretirse, licuarse, fundirse, liquidarse.

liquation, liquefaction, s. licuación, licuefacción, liquidación, fusión, propiedad de disolverse.

liquefiable, a. liquidable, licuable.

liquefy ['likwifai], v.t. licuar, derretir, liquidar, descuajar, descoagular, disolver, deshacer. — v.i. liquidarse, derretirse.

liquescence [li'kwesəns], **liquescency** [li-'kwesənsi], s. licuescencia.

liquescent, a. licuescente.

liqueur [li'kju:əɹ], s. licor.

liquid ['likwid], a. líquido, fluído; límpido, claro; acuoso; *liquid securities*, valores realizables. — s. líquido, fluído; agua, licor; sonido líquido.

liquidambar [likwi'dæmbɑːɹ], s. liquidámbar; *liquidambar-tree*, ocozol, estoraque.

liquidate ['likwideit], v.t. líquidar, saldar cuentas, ajustar las cuentas.

liquidation, s. liquidación.

liquidator, s. depositario, síndico.

liquidity [li'kwiditi], **liquidness** ['likwidnis], s. liquidez, fluidez; sutileza.

liquor ['likəɹ], s. licor, aguardiente, espíritu; (E.U.) bebida alcohólica; baño, licor, solución, fluído; *malt liquor*, cerveza; *tan liquor*, baño de casca; *liquor-case*, cantina, frasquera.

liquorice ['likəris], s. orozuz, regaliz.

lisle thread ['lailθred], s. hilo de escocia.

lisp [lisp], v.t., v.i. cecear; balbucir. — s. ceceo; balbucencia.

lisper, s. el que cecea, el que balbucea.

lisping, a. ceceoso; balbuciente.

lissom ['lisəm], **lissome**, a. flexible.

list [list], s. lista, catálogo, cédula, nómina, matrícula; rol; (tej.) orilla, borde del paño, lista, cenefa, tira; (carp.) tabloncillo; (arq.) filete, listel, listelo, listón, orla, barandal; (poét.) borde, cabo, límite; (ant.) deseo, gana, voluntad; (mar.) falsa banda, bandeo; liza (para torneos). — v.t. registrar, matricular, poner en una lista, inscribir; (mil.) alistar; (com.) cotizar, facturar; cercar una liza para torneos; guarnecer con cenefas o listones; (poét.) escuchar; prestar atención; (mar.) dar carena al buque. — v.i. (mar.) dar a la banda, inclinarse a la banda, escorar; (ant.) querer.

listed, a. listado, listeado; (com.) cotizado.

listel ['listəl], s. listel, filete.

listen ['lisən], v.t., v.i. escuchar, oír, atender; conformarse, obedecer; *to stop listening to one who is speaking*, dejar a uno con la palabra en la boca.

listener, s. escuchante, escuchador; (rad.) oyente, radiooyente; escucha, espía, m.f.; *listeners hear no good of themselves*, (prov.) quien escucha, su mal oye.

Listerine ['listərin], s. (trade mark) listerina.

Listerism ['listərizm], s. listerismo (procedimiento antiséptico practicado por primera vez por Lord Lister).

listing, s. orilla de paño, cenefa, tira.

listless ['listles], a. lánguido, apático, desatento, indiferente.

listlessness, s. languidez, apatía, indiferencia.

lit [lit], pret., p.p. [LIGHT].

litany ['litəni], s. letanía.

liter ['litəɹ], s. litro.

literal ['litərəl], a. literal, exacto, recto; positivista, m.f.

literalism, s. exactitud, sentido literal; positivismo; (b.a.) naturalismo.

literalist, a. escrupulosamente exacto. — s. el que se adhiere a la letra; positivista, m.f.

literally ['litərəli], adv. literalmente, según la letra, al pie de la letra.

literalness, s. exactitud literal; materialidad, positivismo.

literary ['litərəri], a. literario.

literate ['litərit], s., a. literato; (igl. angl.) el candidato a órdenes sagradas que no posee un grado académico.

literati [litə'rɑːtiː], s.pl. literatos, sabios, eruditos, doctos.

literatim [litə'reitim], adv. letra por letra, a la letra; según la letra, literalmente.

literature ['litərətʃəɹ], s. literatura; obras literarias; bellas letras; trabajo literario; erudición, conocimiento de las letras; *light literature*, literatura amena.

litharge ['liθɑːɹdʒ], *s.* litarge, litargirio, almártaga.

lithate ['liθeit], *s.* urato.

lithe [laið], *a.* flexible, manejable, delgado, blando.

litheness, *s.* flexibilidad, flojedad; blandura; agilidad; delgadez.

litherly ['liðəɹli], *a.* (ant.) artificioso; travieso, malicioso, depravado, disoluto. — *adv.* (ant.) tardamente, perezosamente.

lithesome, *a.* flexible, ligero, ágil.

lithia ['liθiə], *s.* litina.

lithiasis [li'θiəsis], *s.* litiasis, *f.*, mal de piedra.

lithic ['liθik], *a.* lítico.

lithium ['liθiəm], *s.* litio.

lithogenesy [liθo'dʒenesi], *s.* litogenesia.

lithograph ['liθogræf], *v.t., v.i.* litografiar. — *s.* litografía (impresión).

lithographer [li'θogrəfəɹ], *s.* litógrafo.

lithographic, *a.* litográfico.

lithography [li'θogrəfi], *s.* litografía (arte).

lithoid ['liθoid], **lithoidal** [li'θoidəl], *a.* litoideo, de aspecto pétreo.

lithologic, lithological, *a.* litológico.

lithologist [li'θolodʒist], *s.* litólogo.

lithology [li'θolodʒi], *s.* litología; (med.) tratado sobre los cálculos.

lithophyte ['liθofait], *s.* litófito, especie de zoófito.

lithotomist, *s.* litotomista, *m.f.*

lithotomy [li'θɔtomi], *s.* litotomía, talla.

lithotrite ['liθotrait], *s.* litotrictor.

lithotrity, *s.* litotricia.

Lithuanian [liθjuːeiniən], *a.* lituano. — *s.* habitante de la Lituania.

litigant ['litigənt], *s., a.* litigante, contendiente, pleiteante.

litigate ['litigeit], *v.t., v.i.* litigar, pleitear, contender, tener pleito pendiente.

litigation, *s.* litigio, litigación, pleito.

litigator, *s.* pleiteador.

litigious ['litidʒəs], *a.* litigioso.

litigiously, *adv.* de un modo litigioso.

litigiousness, *s.* inclinación a tener pleitos.

litmus ['litməs], *s.* tornasol en pasta.

litotes [lai'toutiːz], *s.* lítote, *f.*

litre ['liːtəɹ], *s.* litro.

litter ['litəɹ], *s.* litera, cama portátil, camilla, parihuela, andas; lechigada, camada, cachillada, ventregada; cama de paja para las caballerías; (fig.) desechos, cachos, objetos en desorden, estado de desorden, fragmentos esparcidos; desorden, desarreglo. — *v.t.* parir (los animales); hacer un lecho de paja para el ganado, cubrir con paja; esparcir, poner en desorden, desordenar. — *v.i.* tenderse sobre la paja; parir (los animales).

littérateur ['litərətəːɹ], *s.* literato.

little [litəl], *a.* (comp. **less, lesser**, *fam.* **littler**; *super.* **least**, *fam.* **littlest**) poco, escaso, limitado; pequeño, parvo, chico, menudo, mezquino, diminutivo; corto, escatimado; breve; de poca importancia, insignificante; ligero, mediano; despreciable, ruin; *little by little*, poco a poco; *a little one*, un chiquillo, un bebe; *be it never so little*, por poco que sea. — *s.* poco, parte o porción pequeña. — *adv.* poco, escasamente.

littleness, *s.* pequeñez, poquedad, parvedad, cortedad, menudencia; ruindad, bajeza, mezquindad, falta de dignidad.

littoral ['litərəl], *s.* litoral, costa, playa. — *a.* litoral, costanero.

liturgic [li'təːɹdʒik], **liturgical**, *a.* litúrgico.

liturgy ['litəɹdʒi], *s.* liturgia.

live [liv], *v.t.* pasar, llevar (una vida); habituarse a, hacerse a, conformarse a. — *v.i.* vivir, tener vida, existir; subsistir, mantenerse; morar, residir, habitar, parar; vegetar; (mar.) estar o quedar a flote, salvarse; *to live and learn*, vivir para ver, escarmentar; *to live up to*, vivir en conformidad con, vivir dentro de; *to live from hand to mouth*, vivir al día; *to live down*, sobrevivir a; refutar (una calumnia), borrar (una falta); *to live up to one's promise*, cumplir lo prometido; *to live up to one's income*, comerse todas las rentas; *to live in a dream*, vivir soñando.

live [laiv], *a.* vivo, en vida; ardiente, abrasador, brillante; activo, enérgico; efectivo, eficaz, listo; (impr.) útil; (elec.) con corriente; cargado (proyectiles); *live-box*, porta-animálculos (para el microscopio); *live coal*, brasa, carbón ardiente; *live stock*, ganadería.

liveable, *a.* digno de vida.

livelihood ['laivlihud], *s.* vida, mantenimiento, subsistencia.

livelily ['laivlili], *adv.* de un modo vivo o enérgico.

liveliness ['laivlinis], *s.* vida, viveza, vivacidad, agilidad, prontitud, actividad, despejo.

livelong ['livloŋ, 'laivloŋ], *a.* todo, entero, largo; *all the livelong day*, todo el santo día.

lively ['laivli], *a.* vivo, vivaz, vivaracho; rápido, apresurado; gallardo, galán, airoso; vigoroso, brioso, enérgico; animado, bullicioso; eficaz, intensivo. — *adv.* vigorosamente, enérgicamente; vivamente, a lo vivo; aprisa.

live-oak ['laivouk], *s.* variedad de la encina americana (Quercus virens).

liver ['livəɹ], *s.* vividor, viviente; hígado; higadilla; pájaro fabuloso que se supone dió el nombre a Liverpool; *liver complaint*, mal de hígado.

livered ['livəɹd], *a.* de hígado, que tiene hígado; *white-livered* o *lily-livered*, cobarde.

liveried, *a.* que lleva librea.

liverwort, *s.* hepática.

livery ['livəɹi], *s.* librea; uniforme; cochería de alquiler; (for.) entrega, acto de dar o tomar posesión de tierras; ración; *livery coach*, carruaje de alquiler; *livery stable*, pensión de caballos; cochería de alquiler; *livery horse*, caballo de alquiler.

liveryman ['livəɹimən], *s.* dueño de cochería de alquiler; ciudadano de honor de Londres. — *pl.* **liverymen**, criados de librea.

lives [laivz], *s.pl.* [LIFE].

livid ['livid], *a.* lívido, cárdeno, amoratado, acardenalado; *to be livid*, (fam.) estar negro.

lividity [li'viditi], **lividness** ['lividnis], *s.* lividez; cardenal.

living ['liviŋ], *s.* modo de vivir o de ganar la vida, mantenimiento, o subsistencia; beneficio eclesiástico; vida, potencia vital. — *pl.* **the living**, los vivientes, los vivos. — *a.* vivo, vigoroso animado, viviente; *living-room*, sala de estar.

lixivial [lik'ziviəl], **lixiviate** [lik'ziviət], *a.* lixiviado, lejival.

lixiviate [lik'zivieit], *v.t.* lixiviar; hacer lejía. — *a.* convertido en lejía.

lixiviation, *s.* lixiviación.
lixivium, *s.* lejía.
lizard ['lizəd], *s.* (*zool.*) saurio, lagarto, lagartija.
llama ['lɑ:mə], *s.* (*zool.*) llama (del Perú).
Lloyd's ['lɔidz], *s.* corporación de corredores de seguros marítimos; clasificación y registro de los buques de todas las naciones, etc.
lo [lou], *interj.* he aquí, ved aquí, mirad.
loach [loutʃ], *s.* (*ict.*) locha, loja, lobo, espirenque.
load [loud], *s.* carga, peso, gravamen; presión; (*mec.*) resistencia; opresión, agobio; fardo; *boat-load,* barcada; *cart-load,* carretada; *ship-load,* cargamento de un buque; *load-line, load-water line,* línea de un buque, línea de flotación. — *v.t.* cargar, echar o poner algún peso; embarazar, impedir; llenar, colmar, agobiar; *to load the dice,* cargar los dados. — *v.i.* cargar, tomar carga.
loader, *s.* cargador, embarcador.
loadstar, *s.* estrella polar, cinosura; (*fig.*) norte, [LODESTAR].
loadstone, *s.* imán [LODESTONE].
loaf [louf], *s.* hogaza de pan; panecillo, bollo; *loaf of sugar,* pan (o pilón o terrón) de azúcar; *loaf sugar,* azúcar de pilón; *loaves and fishes,* (*fig.*) ganancias. — *v.t., v.i.* haraganear, holgazanear, bribonear, gandulear.
loafer, *s.* haragán, holgazán, gandul, tunante, arrimón, cantonero, corrillero, pelafustán.
loam [loum], *s.* marga; arcilla plástica; (*fund.*) tierra de moldeo. — *v.t.* untar con marga; cubrir con arcilla.
loamy, *a.* margoso, gredoso, gredal.
loan [loun], *s.* préstamo; prestación, presti-monio; (*com.*) empréstito; (*for.*) mutuo, comodato; *loan-office,* casa de empeños. — *v.i.* prestar.
loath [louθ], *a.* poco dispuesto, desinclinado, disgustado.
loathe [louð], *v.t.* detestar, abominar, tener hastío, estar harto de. — *v.i.* (*ant.*) tener hastío, sentir fastidio, disgusto o aborrecimiento.
loather, *s.* el que siente disgusto, tedio o aborrecimiento.
loathful, *a.* lleno de tedio o aversión.
loathing, *s.* repugnancia, asco, hastío.
loathingly, *adv.* de mala gana, con repugnancia, con asco.
loathsome, *a.* nauseabundo, asqueroso.
loathsomeness, *s.* calidad de repugnante o asqueroso, asquerosidad.
loaves [louvz], *pl.* [LOAF].
lob [lɔb], *s.* masa, mezcla blanda y espesa; patán, pelmazo; (en lawn-tennis), voleo alto y tendido de la pelota; (en cricket) voleo bajo. — *v.t.* hacer un *lob* con la pelota; *lob-worm,* lombriz para cebo.
lobar ['loubər], *a.* lobular.
lobate ['loubeit], **lobated,** *a.* lobulado.
lobby ['lɔbi], *s.* paso, pasillo, corredor; ante-cámara, vestíbulo, tribuna, galería; (*pol.*) camarilla de cabilderos. — *v.t., v.i.* (*pol.*) cabildear.
lobbying ['lɔbiiŋ], *s.* (*pol.*) cabildeo.
lobbyist ['lɔbiist], *s.* (*pol.*) cabildero.
lobe [loub], *s.* lóbulo, lobo.
lobed, *a.* lobado, lobulado.
lobelia [lo'bi:liə], *s.* lobelia.
loblolly [lɔb'lɔli], *s.* polenta; patán, pelmazo;

loblolly man o *boy,* criado del cirujano de un buque.
lobster ['lɔbstər], *s.* langosta de mar, cangrejo de mar.
lobulate ['lɔbju:lit], *a.* lobulado.
lobule, *s. dim.* lobulillo.
local ['loukəl], *a.* local, de la región; *local remedies,* remedios externos, tópicos. — *s.* (*vulg.*) taberna; (*E.U.*) noticias de interés local; (*elec.*) batería o circuito local; (*f.c.*) suburbano.
locale, *s.* ambiente.
localism ['loukəlizm], *s.* costumbre, idiotismo o locución local; provincialismo.
locality [lo'kæliti], *s.* localidad, posición, situación.
localization, *s.* localización.
localize ['loukəlaiz], *v.t.* localizar, orientar.
locally ['loukəli], *adv.* localmente.
locate [lo'keit], *v.t.* colocar; situar; (*f.c.*) trazar la línea.
located, *a.* sito, situado. — *p.p.* [LOCATE].
location, *s.* colocación, ubicación; sitio, localidad; situación, posición; (*f.c.*) trazado de la línea.
loch [lɔx, lɔk], *s.* (*Esco.*) lago; ensenada.
lochia ['lɔkiə], *s.pl.* loquios.
lock [lɔk], *s.* cerradura, cerraja; esclusa, represa, compuerta; llave, *f.* (de las armas de fuego); cercado, vallado, cerca; bucle, rizo, trenza, guedeja; trabas, maniotas; borla; vedija de lana; *spring-lock,* cerradura de muelle; *under lock and key,* debajo de llave, debajo de siete llaves. — *v.t.* cerrar con llave o candado, tener debajo de llave, acerrojar, candar; hacer pasar por una esclusa; poner cerradura; juntar, atar, trabar; (*impr.*) acuñar, cerrar la forma; abrazar, coger en los brazos. — *v.i.* cerrarse con llave; unirse (o entrelazarse) una cosa con otra; *to lock in,* encerrar, poner bajo llave; *to lock one out,* cerrar la puerta a uno para que no entre; *to lock up,* encerrar; *to lock the stable when the steed is gone,* (*prov.*) después de ido el conejo, tomamos el consejo.
lockage ['lɔkidʒ], *s.* materiales de una esclusa; diferencia de nivel en un canal de esclusas; portazgo o derechos de esclusa.
locker, *s.* cajón, gaveta, alacena, armario, ropero; cerrador; *shot-locker,* (*mar.*) chillera. — *pl.* **lockers,** cajonada.
locket ['lɔkit], *s.* guardapelo, medallón, broche, relicario.
lock-jaw, *s.* (*med.*) trismo, tétano; (*Cuba*) pasmo.
lock-nut, *s.* contratuerca, tuerca de seguridad.
lock-out, *s.* (*econ. polít.*) cierre (de fábrica) por los dueños (correlativo de huelga).
lockram, *s.* lienzo basto, estopa.
locksmith, *s.* cerrajero.
lockup, *s.* calabozo; (*fam.*) cárcel, *f.*
locomobile [louko'moubil], *s.f., a.* locomóvil, locomovible.
locomotion [louko'mouʃən], *s.* locomoción, potencia locomotriz.
locomotive [louko'moutiv], *a.* locomotor, locomotriz, locomóvil. — *s.* (*f.c.*) locomotora, *f.*
locomotor [louko'moutər], *a.* locomotor, locomotriz; *locomotor ataxia,* ataxia locomotriz.
locular ['lɔkjulər], *a.* locular, loculado.

locum-tenens [loukəm'ti:nenz], _s._ (_pl._ **tenentes**), interino.

locust ['loukəst], _s._ langosta, saltamontes; (_E.U._) cicada, cigarra; _locust_ o _locust-tree_, (_bot._) robinia; algarrobo.

locution [lo'kju:ʃən], _s._ locución, frase, _f._; (_ant._) modo de hablar.

lode [loud], _s._ (_min._) filón, veta, vena; (_hidr._) reguera, acequia.

lodestar ['loudsta:ɹ], _s._ cinosura, estrella polar; (_fig._) norte, estrella de guía.

lodestone, _s._ piedra imán, calamita.

lodge [lɔdʒ], _v.t._ alojar, aposentar, hospedar, poner en alojamiento, albergar, dar hospedaje; plantar, introducir, fijar, colocar; cubrir, abrigar; dar a guardar, poner a recaudo, fijar en la memoria. — _v.i._ residir, habitar, vivir, parar, morar, alojarse, hospedarse; tenderse, echarse; _lodging-knees_, (_mar._) curvas valonas; _to lodge a complaint against_, dar una queja contra. — _s._ casa de guarda; pabellón; casita pequeña o accesoria a otra mayor; logia; guarida, antro; _porter's lodge_, portería, covacha o cuarto del portero.

lodger, _s._ huésped, inquilino, morador.

lodging, _s._ posada, habitación, vivienda, hospedería; albergue, aposentamiento; hospedaje; (_mil._) alojamiento; morada, residencia. — _pl._ **lodgings**, pensión, habitaciones, cuartos alquilados; _lodging house_, pensión o casa de huéspedes; _board and lodging_, pensión completa.

lodgment ['lɔdʒmənt], _s._ colocación; amontonamiento, acumulación; alojamiento; (_mil._) atrincheramiento.

loft [lɔft], _s._ desván, buharda, sobrado; henil, pajar; _hayloft_, henil.

loftily ['lɔftili], _adv._ en alto, muy alto, elevadamente, levantadamente; hinchadamente, altivamente, pomposamente.

loftiness, _s._ altura, elevación; excelsitud, sublimidad; altivez, altanería, orgullo, soberbia; majestad.

lofty ['lɔfti], _s._ altísimo, elevado, levantado; sublime, excelso, eminente; encrestado, encumbrado, pingorotudo; altivo, orgulloso, soberbio.

log [lɔg], _s._ leño, palo, toza, tronco; (_mar._) barquilla de la corredera; _log-board_, (_mar._) tableta de bitácora; _log-line_, (_mar._) corredera; _log-book_, cuaderno de bitácora; diario de navegación; _log-cabin_, o _log-hut_, cabaña rústica hecha con troncos de árboles; _log-reel_, carretel, devanadera.

loganberry ['lougənberi], _s._ mora; _loganberry bush_, moral.

logarithm ['lɔgəriðm], _s._ logaritmo.

logarithmic, logarithmical, _a._ logarítmico.

loggerhead ['lɔgəɹhed], _s._ zote, necio; cierta tortuga marina de gran tamaño; (_orn._) pega reborda de los E.U.; _at loggerheads_, riñendo, a la greña; _to fall_, o _come_ o _get to loggerheads_, venir a las manos, andar al pelo, andar en cuentos, estar de cuerno.

loggerheaded, _a._ tonto, necio, zote.

logic ['lɔdʒik], _s._ lógica.

logical ['lɔdʒikəl], _a._ lógico, exacto, preciso, escrupuloso, rígido.

logician [lo'dʒiʃən], _s._ lógico, profesor de lógica, dialéctico.

logistics [lo'dʒistiks], _s.pl._ logística.

logman ['lɔgmən], _s._ leñero.

logogram [lɔgo'græm], _s._ abreviatura o signo que indica una palabra; logogrifo.

logograph, _s._ palabra escrita.

logogriph, _s._ logogrifo, enigma en verso.

logomachy [lo'gɔməki], _s._ logomaquia; juego de formar anagramas.

logroll ['lɔgroul], _v.t._ hacer rodar tozas.

log-rolling, _s._ tarea de rodar tozas; (_pol._) cabildeo de politicastros.

logwood, _s._ palo de Campeche, palo de tinte.

loin [lɔin], _s._ ijada, ijar; _loin-cloth_, taparrabo. — _pl._ **loins**, lomos.

loiter ['lɔitəɹ], _v.i._ holgazanear, haraganear, vagar; perder o malgastar el tiempo; andar muy despacio; tardar.

loiterer, _s._ vagabundo, haragán, holgazán, negligente, perezoso.

loitering, _a._ vago, haragán, holgazán, perezoso, negligente. — _s._ vagancia.

lolium ['louliəm], _s._ (_bot._) joyo, cizaña.

loll [lɔl], _v.i._ apoyarse, recostarse, tenderse; colgar, estar colgando, colgar hacia fuera (la lengua). — _v.t._ sacar la lengua.

Lollard ['lɔla:ɹd], _s._ lolardo (nombre de una secta de reformadores de los siglos XIV y XV).

lollypop ['lɔlipɔp], _s._ variedad de melcocha o arropía; (_fam._) dulce, confitura.

loment ['loumənt], _s._ (_bot._) lomento.

London ['lʌndən], _n.pr._ Londres. _London pride_, saxifraga irlandesa (saxifraga umbrosa); _London tuft_, clavel de poeta.

Londoner, _s._ londinense, natural o habitante de Londres.

lone [loun], _a._ solitario, solo, aislado, inhabitado; soltera, viuda.

loneliness, _s._ soledad; sentimiento de melancolía en el que está solo.

lonely, _a._ solitario, abandonado, solo; amante de la soledad.

loneness, _s._ soledad.

lonesome, _a._ solitario, desierto.

lonesomeness, _s._ soledad, abandono; sentimiento de melancolía en el que está solo.

long [lɔŋ], _a._ largo, extenso, prolongado, luengo; de largo, de longitud; continuo; enfadoso, aburrido; tardo, lento, dilatorio; (_com._) que guarda acciones en espera de alza; _long measure_, medida de longitud; _two metres long_, dos metros de largo (o de longitud); _in the long run_, a la larga. — _adv._ a una gran distancia; mucho; durante, en toda la extensión, continuamente; _long ago_, o _long since_, mucho tiempo ha; _long after_, mucho después; _long drawn out_, prolongado, tedio; _long headed_, sagaz, astuto; _long primer_, (_impr._) entredós, letra de diez puntos; _long sighted_, que ve a gran distancia, présbita, présbite; (_fig._) sagaz, previsor, precavido; _ere long_, antes de mucho; _as long as_, o _so long as_, mientras (que), en tanto que, con tal que; _how long is it since?_ ¿cuánto tiempo hace? _all my life long_, toda mi vida; _not long before_, poco tiempo antes; _no longer_, no más. — _s._ longitud, largo; sílaba larga; (_mús._) longa. — _pl._ (_com._) los que guardan acciones en espera de alza; _the long and the short of it_, la substancia, el resumen; _the long and the short of it is_ o _to make a long story short_, en resumidas cuentas, sin ambages ni rodeos, total. — _v.i._ desear con vehemencia, ansiar, anhelar, tener ganas, antojarse.

longanimity [lɔŋgə'nimiti], s. longanimidad.
long-boat, s. lancha, falúa.
longe [lɔndʒ], s. estocada, golpe; pista.
longer ['lɔŋgəɹ], **longest**, a. compar. y superl. [LONG].
longeval [lɔn'dʒiːvəl], **longevous**, a. longevo.
longevity [lɔn'dʒeviti], s. longevidad, ancianidad.
longhand ['lɔŋhænd], s. escritura ordinaria sin abreviaciones, contrario de [SHORTHAND].
longicorn ['lɔndʒikɔːɹn], s., a. longicornio.
longimanous [lɔndʒi'meinəs], a. longimano, manos-largas.
longing ['lɔŋiŋ], s. deseo vehemente, anhelo, golondro, ansia, gana.
longingly, adv. impacientemente, vehementemente.
longish, a. algo largo, un poco largo.
longitude ['lɔndʒtjuːd], s. longitud.
longitudinal, a. longitudinal.
longitudinally, adv. longitudinalmente, a lo largo.
long-legged, a. zanquilargo.
long-lived ['lɔŋlivd], a. de vida larga, longevo.
longly ['lɔŋli], adv. por mucho tiempo, prolijamente; extensamente.
longness, s. largura.
longshoreman ['lɔŋʃɔːɹmən], s. estibador, trabajador de muelle; pescador, coquinero.
longspun, a. dilatado, prolijo.
long-sufferance, long-suffering, s. paciencia, sufrimiento (de las injurias); clemencia.
long-suffering, a. paciente.
longways ['lɔŋweiz], adv. longitudinalmente.
loo [luː], **lu**, s. juego de naipes, parecido al euchre.—v.t. (en el juego de loo) dar capote; dar bola.
loof [luːf], s. (mar.) lof; la palma de la mano.
look [luk], v.t., v.i. mirar, ojear, dar una mirada; considerar, contemplar, pensar; poner cuidado, tener cuidado; esperar; estar frente a, dar o caer a; parecer, tener traza de; tener (buen o mal) aspecto; parecerse a; lucir (bien o mal); buscar; to look about, mirar alrededor; observar; to look at, mirar a; considerar; atender; to look about one, estar alerta, vigilar; to look after, cuidar; tener cuidado de; atender; prestar atención a, buscar, inquirir, investigar; to look back upon, reflexionar sobre; to look black, tener mala cara, tener ceño; to look big, entonarse; to look for, buscar; esperar; to look down upon, mirar con desprecio, despreciar; to look into, examinar, considerar, inspeccionar, investigar; to look like, parecerse a, semejarse a; to look on, considerar, estimar, juzgar; mirar, ver; dar o caer a; ser espectador; to look out, estar alerta, tener cuidado; estar o andar a la mira; look out! ¡cuidado!; to look out of, asomarse a; to look over, dar una mirada a, examinar someramente; hojear (un libro); to look out for, buscar; esperar, aguardar; tener cuidado con, guardarse de; to look through, examinar, inspeccionar, hacer un registro; to look sharp, tener ojo avisor, estar muy alerta, tener mucho cuidado; apresurarse, dar prisa; to look to, cuidar de, velar por; atender a; hacer responsable; observar, considerar, esperar de; to look to it, estar con cuidado; estar sobre sí; to look up, (fig.) ir mejorando; buscar con cuidado hasta encontrar; to look

up to, respetar, reverenciar; to look daggers, echar chispas (por los ojos); to look well, tener buena cara; to look after oneself, cuidar del número uno; look before you leap, antes que te cases, mira lo que haces; to look through rose-coloured spectacles, bañarse en agua rosada. — s. mirada, ojeada, vistazo; semblante, aspecto, cara, aire, ademán; facha, catadura; apariencia, cariz; look! ¡mira! ¡cuidado!
looker, looker-on, s. mirador, mirón, espectador.
looking, s. mirada; expectación; good (o fine) looking, guapo, bien parecido.
looking-glass, s. espejo.
look-out, s. vigía, vigilancia, observación; mirador, miradero, garita, atalaya, vigía, m.f.; to be on the look-out, estar a la mira; that's his look-out, allá él; to keep a sharp look-out, despabilar los ojos.
loom [luːm], s. telar; presencia, aparición; (mar.) guión del remo; loom-shuttle, lanzadera mecánica. — v.i. asomar, aparecer; descollar; lucir, relucir.
looming, s. (ópt.) espejismo.
loon [luːn], s. bobo, necio, estúpido; (orn.) somorgujo.
loop [luːp], s. gaza, lazo, nudo; ojal, presilla, alamar; anillo; recodo, comba, curva, vuelta; (fort.) aspillera; (mec.) abrazadera, anilla; (aer.) rizo. — v.t. enlazar; asegurar con una presilla; hacer gazas, formar festones o curvas. — v.i. andar haciendo curvas; (aer.) to loop the loop, hacer, o rizar, el rizo.
looped [luːpd], a. ojalado, lleno de ojales. — p.p. [LOOP].
looper, s. engazador.
loophole ['luːphoul], s. abertura, mirador; (fort.) aspillera, tronera; escapatoria, efugio, excusa.
loopholed, a. que tiene troneras o aspilleras.
loop-maker, s. ojaladero, presillero.
loose [luːs], v.t. desatar, desenlazar, desprender, desliar; dar alivio, aliviar; aflojar, desapretar; soltar, libertar, librar, sacar de algún mal paso, desenredar; desocupar; to loose one's hold of (o on), soltar, abandonar. — a. suelto, desatado, desenredado, desprendido, movible, flojo, holgado; suelto de vientre; vago, indeterminado, indefinido; libre, relajado, descuidado, negligente, remiso, licencioso, disoluto; suelto, en libertad; holgado, flotante (vestido); loose bodied, suelto, ancho, holgado (vestido); to grow loose, desbandarse, desprenderse; to break (o get) loose, escaparse de la prisión, soltarse, zafarse, desencadenarse, recobrar la libertad, ponerse en libertad; to hang loose, colgar, pender, flotar; to let loose, soltar; poner en libertad. — s. libertad; soltura; to give loose to, dar rienda suelta a.
loosely, adv. sueltamente, flojamente, con desenvoltura, negligentemente, holgadamente, sin cohesión.
loosen ['luːsən], v.t. aflojar, laxar, soltar, desunir, desliar, desceñir, desligar, desatar; relajar, solver, librar, libertar, ablandar; soltar el vientre; to loosen the sails (mar.) largar, descargar las velas. — v.i. desunirse, desatarse, separarse, desasirse.
looseness ['luːsnis], s. aflojamiento, flojedad, holgura; libertad, relajación, licencia, des-

garro; flujo de vientre, diarrea, cursos, correncia, soltura.

loosening [ˈluːsəniŋ], a. laxante. — s. laxación, desatadura, aflojadura.

loosestrife [ˈluːstraif], s. (bot.) lasimaquia, planta del género Lythrum.

loot [luːt], v.t. saquear, pillar; llevarse como botín. — s. botín, pillaje.

lop [lɔp], v.t. desmochar, descabezar, chapodar; podar (viñas); maestrear; cortar y doblar hacia abajo. — v.i. colgar; (mar.) romper (el mar) en olas cortas y gruesas. — s. rama podada; oreja gacha; pulga.

lope [loup], v.t., v.i. andar a saltos, o a zancadas; saltar. — s. galope tendido.

lopper [ˈlɔpəɪ], s. podador de árboles.

lopping, s. poda, desmoche; rama cortada.

lopsided [lɔpˈsaidid], a. al sesgo, al bies, a tuertas; más pesado de un lado que de otro, desequilibrado; (fig.) desequilibrado, maniático.

loquacious [loˈkweiʃəs], a. locuaz, lenguaz, charlador, palabrero, hablador.

loquaciousness [loˈkweiʃəsnis], **loquacity** [loˈkwæsiti], s. locuacidad, habladuría, charla, parla, parladuría, picotería.

lord [lɔːɪd], s. señor, monarca, m.; Dios, el Señor; marido, amo, dueño, patrón; lord, barón (títulos); castellano; House of Lords, Cámara de los Lores; Lord Chamberlain, Camarero Mayor; Lord High Steward, Mayordomo Mayor; Lord Chief Justice, Presidente del tribunal supremo (de Inglaterra); Lord Mayor, alcalde o corregidor; Lord's Day, el día del Señor; Lord's Prayer, padrenuestro; Lord's Supper, la Ultima Cena; Sacramento de la Eucaristía; Lord's table, altar de la sagrada eucaristía; comunión, Eucaristía. — v.t. investir con la dignidad de par de Inglaterra; dar el título de lord; gobernar, mandar. — v.i. señorear, dominar, mandar despóticamente; to lord it over, señorear, mandar imperiosamente a.

lording, lordling, s. (despec.) hidalguillo, señorito, pequeño lord, hidalgo de gatera; señor de poco más o menos.

lordliness, s. dignidad, señorío; altivez, orgullo.

lordly, a. perteneciente a un lord; señoril; altivo, orgulloso, imperioso. — adv. señorilmente, altivamente, imperiosamente.

lordship, s. señorío, dominio, poder; señoría, excelencia; your lordship, Usía, Vuecencia, Excelencia.

lore [lɔːɹ], s. erudición, ciencia, conocimientos, saber; doctrina, instrucción, enseñanza; (hist. nat.) parte semejante a una tira o correa.

lorgnette [lɔːˈnjet], s. impertinentes; gemelos con mango.

lorica [ˈlɔrikəɪ], s. peto, loriga; (zool.) cubierta protectora; brasca o luten para los crisoles.

loricate [lɔriˈkeit], v.t. enchapar, planchear, cubrir con planchas protectoras. — a. plancheado, enchapado.

lorication, s. enchapado.

loriot [ˈlɔriət], s. (orn.) oropéndola de Europa.

loris [ˈlɔris], s. (zool.) loris, especie de lemur.

lorn [lɔːɪn], a. dejado, abandonado, sin parientes ni amigos.

lorry [ˈlɔri], s. camión; (min.) camioneta.

lory [ˈlɔːri], s. (orn.) especie de loro de color escarlata.

losable, loseable [ˈluːzəbl], a. fácil de perder.

lose [luːz], (pret. y p.p. lost), v.t. perder; malograr; malbaratar, desperdiciar, malgastar, disipar; hacer perder; exponer a la pérdida, la ignominia o la ruina; to lose ground, perder terreno; to lose one's senses, perder el seso; to lose one's temper, perder los estribos; to lose one's way, perderse, andar perdido, extraviarse. — v.r. perderse, extraviarse. — v.i. perder, tener una pérdida; declinar, decaer; atrasar (un reloj).

loser, s. perdedor, el que pierde algo, el que no consigue lo que desea.

losing, s. pérdida, diminución.

loss [lɔs], s. pérdida, daño, desventaja, detrimento, merma, menoscabo; perecimiento; perdición, destrucción, privación; mal éxito; fracaso; desperdicio, disipación; quiebra; at a loss, con pérdida, con quebranto; en duda, perplejo, sin saber qué hacer; to be at a loss, no atinar, desatinar, no poder dar en la tecla.

lost [lɔst], pret., p.p. [LOSE]. — a. perdido; frustrado; malgastado, desperdiciado; malogrado; descarriado, extraviado, desorientado, perplejo, confuso; arruinado; condenado, insensible; to lose one's heart to, enamorarse de; the remark was not lost upon him, no dejó de advertir esta observación; lost in thought, absorto, ensimismado.

lot [lɔt], s. lote; suerte, f., fortuna, sino, hado, estrella, destino; solar, extensión de terreno para la venta o para edificar; cuota, parte, f., partija, porción; (fam.) gran cantidad, mucho; it fell to his lot, le cupo la suerte; lots of (fam.) mucho, muchos, la mar de; a lot of money, gran cantidad de dinero; to cast (o draw) lots, echar suertes. — v.t. asignar, repartir, dividir, distribuir, destinar.

lote [lout], s. (bot.) loto.

loth [louθ], a. poco dispuesto, desinclinado, disgustado.

lothario [loˈθɛəriou], s. libertino, tunante.

lotion [ˈlouʃən], s. loción, ablución.

lotos, lotus [ˈloutəs], s. (bot.) loto, ninfea, nenúfar, almez, azufaifo; lotus-eater, lotófago, lujurioso; lotus-tree, loto, almez.

lottery [ˈlɔtəri], s. lotería, rifa; lottery office, lotería, expendeduría de billetes de lotería.

lotto [ˈlɔtou], s. lotería (juego casero).

loud [laud], a. ruidoso, alto, recio, fuerte, clamoroso, estrepitoso, estentoreo, turbulento, escandaloso; (fam.) charro, chillón, llamativo; (fam.) vulgar, de mal gusto; (vulg.) de olor muy fuerte; to speak loud, hablar alto. — adv. ruidosamente, con ruido, en alta voz.

loudly, adv. ruidosamente, alborotadamente, con mucho ruido.

loudness, s. ruido, sonoridad, alboroto, turbulencia; (fam.) vulgaridad, mal gusto.

loudspeaker, s. (rad.) altavoz.

lough [lɔx, lɔk], s. lago, laguna.

louis [ˈluːi], s. luis de oro.

lounge [laundʒ], v.i. haraganear, holgazanear, corretear, gandulear, callejear; tenderse, repantigarse; ponerse uno a sus anchas; to lounge about the streets, azotar las calles. — s. haraganería, holgazanería; sala de estar, salón; lugar donde se sestea; sofá, canapé.

lounger, s. haragán, holgazán, ocioso, gandul, azotacalles.

lour [lauəɹ], *v.i.* encapotarse (el cielo); mirar con ceño, poner mala cara.

louse [laus], *s.* (*pl.* **lice**) piojo, cáncano; *crab-louse*, ladilla; *dog-louse*, garrapata; *plant-louse*, áfido; pulgón. — *v.t.* despiojar.

lousewort, *s.* (*bot.*) albarraz; hierba piojera.

lousily ['lauzili], *adv.* con piojería; (*vulg.*) mezquinamente, de un modo vil, bajo.

lousiness, *s.* piojería.

lousy ['lauzi], *a.* pésimo, piojento, piojoso; pedicular; (*vulg.*) infame, astroso, miserable, vil; soez; (*Méj.*) cicatero.

lout [laut], *s.* patán, zafio, rústico; zamacuco. — *v.i.* demorarse, perder el tiempo, tardar, callejear; doblarse, someterse.

loutish, *a.* rústico, tosco, rudo, grosero.

louver ['lu:vəɹ], *s.* (*arq.*) lumbrera, lucerna.

louver-boards, *s.pl.* tejadillos.

lovability [lʌvə'biliti], **lovableness** ['lʌvəbəlnis], *s.* amabilidad, atractivo.

lovable, *a.* amable, simpático.

lovage ['lʌvidʒ], *s.* (*bot.*) ligústico.

love [lʌv], *v.t.* querer, amar, tener cariño; adorar; tener inclinación o afición a, gustar de. — *v.i.* estar enamorado; deleitarse, tener gusto en. — *s.* amor, cariño, inclinación, afecto; (persona amada) amor, cariño; pasión sexual; galanteo; el dios amor, Cupido; (en lawn-tennis y otros juegos), cero, nada; *to fall in love with*, enamorarse de; *to be out of love with*, tener repugnancia por; *to be madly in love with*, estar loco por; *to be in love with*, estar enamorado de; *to make love*, hacer el amor, galantear, cortejar; *love-affair*, intriga amorosa; *self-love*, amor propio; *love-fit*, transporte, o arrebato de amor; *love-letter*, esquela, billete o carta amorosa; *love-lass*, cortejo, amada; *love-knot*, nudo o lazo de amor; *love-lock*, rizo largo con lazo; *love-making*, amorío, galanteo, corte; *love-secret*, secreto entre amantes; *love-suit*, trato amoroso, cortejo, galanteo; *love-shaft*, flecha de Cupido; *love-song*, canción amorosa; *love-tricks*, tretas de amantes o enamorados; *love-token*, estrena, prenda de amor; regalo en señal de amor; *love-tale*, requiebros, amoricones; *love is blind*, quien feo ama, hermoso le parece; *love-potion*, filtro; *love-thought*, pensamiento amoroso.

love-apple (ant.), *s.* (*bot.*) tomate.

love-bird, *s.* (*orn.*) perico, periquito.

love-feast, *s.* ágape.

love-in-a-mist [lʌvinə'mist], *s.* (*bot.*) neguilla; pasionaria.

lovelace ['lʌvleis], *s.* seductor, libertino.

loveless, *a.* falto de amor, sin amor, desamorado; insensible, hurón.

love-lies-bleeding [lʌvlaiz'bli:diŋ], *s.* (*bot.*) especie de amaranto.

loveliness ['lʌvlinis], *s.* amabilidad, agrado, encanto; belleza, hermosura.

love-lorn ['lʌvlɔːɹn], *a.* abandonado por un amante, sin amante.

lovely ['lʌvli], *a.* amable, cariñoso; hermoso, agradable, atractivo; deleitoso, ameno.

lovely, lovelily, *adv.* amablemente, con cariño; con alegría; hermosamente.

lover, *s.* amante, amador, galanteador, galán, cortejo; querido.

lovesick, *a.* enamoricado, enamorado, herido por Cupido.

lovesome, *a.* amable.

loving, *a.* amante, amoroso, afectuoso, cariñoso, benigno, apacible, aficionado; *loving-cup*, copa que pasa de mano en mano entre amigos.

lovingkindness [lʌviŋ'kaindnis], *s.* cariño, misericordia.

lovingness, *s.* afección, cariño, terneza, afecto, afabilidad.

low [lou], *a.* (*comp.* **lower**, *superl.* **lowest**), bajo, poco elevado, pequeño; económico, barato, módico; profundo, hondo; débil, gravemente enfermo; abatido, amilanado, desanimado; pobre, sumiso, reverente, humilde; respetuoso; deshonrado, deshonroso, vulgar, vil, ruin, menospreciable; (*igl. ang.*) inclinado a la doctrina evangélica, con ritual muy sencillo; *low brow*, (*fam.*) poco culto; *Low Countries*, Países Bajos; *low-born*, de humilde cuna, bajo; *low latitude*, latitud cercana al ecuador; *low day*, día de trabajo; *in low spirits* o *low-spirited*, abatido, amilanado, desanimado, descorazonado, acobardado; *in a low voice*, en voz baja; *low fever*, calentura lenta; *low trick*, mala pasada (o partida); *low neck*, escote; *low-necked*, escotado; *Low Mass*, misa privada, o rezada; *low-pitched*, grave (de tono); *Low Sunday*, domingo de cuasimodo; *low tide*, *low water*, menguante, *f.*, aguas de menguante, reflujo, bajamar (del mar), *f.*, estiaje (del río). — *adv.* bajo, abajo, cerca del suelo, en la parte inferior; bajamente; barato, a precio bajo; sumisamente; vilmente; en voz baja; en tono bajo (o profundo). — *v.i.* mugir, dar mugidos, berrear. — *s.* mugido, berrido; (en los naipes) triunfo más bajo; (*prov.*) fuego, llama.

lowbell ['loubel], *s.* cencerro; campanilla para coger pájaros por la noche. — *v.t.* cazar pájaros con campanilla y luz.

low-church ['loutʃəːɹtʃ], *a.* evangélico, opuesto al ritualismo; *low churchman*, partidario del evangelismo, antagonista del ritualismo.

lower ['louəɹ], *v.t.* bajar, poner más bajo o en lugar inferior, descender; abajar, agachar, humillar, abatir; rebajar, disminuir, minorar; *to lower the sails*, (*mar.*) arriar las velas. — *v.i.* bajar, disminuirse, minorarse, menguar; encapotarse, encubrirse (el cielo); mirar con ceño; *to lower away*, (*mar.*) arriar. — *a. comp.* [LOW]; más bajo; *lower-case*, (*impr.*) caja baja; letras minúsculas.

lowering, *a.* sombrío, encapotado, nebuloso; amenazador.

loweringly, *adv.* nubladamente; con ceño, con sobreceño.

lowermost, lowest, *a.* el más bajo, bajísimo, ínfimo.

lowing, *s.* mugido, bramido.

lowland ['loulənd], *s.* tierra baja. — *pl.* **Lowlands**, tierras bajas (sur y oeste de Escocia).

lowlander, *s.* abajeño.

lowlily, *adv.* bajamente; vilmente.

lowliness, *s.* humildad.

lowly, *a.* humilde, sumiso; vil, ruin, despreciable; bajo, rastrero. — *adv.* humildemente, modestamente; vilmente.

low-minded [lou'maindid], *a.* ruin, vil.

lowness ['lounis], *s.* pequeñez, bajeza, vileza, ruindad; abatimiento, postración; sumisión, reverencia, humildad; disminución de precio, baratura; suavidad o debilidad del sonido; gravedad o profundidad del sonido o tono.

loxodrome ['lɔkzo'droum], s. loxodromia, línea loxodrómica.

loxodromic, a. loxodrómico; *loxodromic line*, línea loxodrómica.

loyal ['lɔiəl], a. leal, fiel, constante.

loyalist, s. (*pol.*) partidario del rey, realista, *m.f.*

loyalty ['lɔiəlti], s. lealtad, fidelidad.

lozenge ['lɔzəndʒ], s. (*farm.*) pastilla; (*geom.*) rombo; (*blas.*) losanje, lisonja.

lozenged, a. rombal, que tiene forma de rombo o losanje.

lozengy, a. (*blas.*) lisonjado.

lu [lu:], s. (*ant.*) juego de naipes.

lubber [lʌbəɹ], s. gordiflón, bobalicón, tomajón, harazán, perezoso; marinero de agua dulce; joven sin experiencia; *lubber's hole*, (*mar.*) boca de lobo.

lubberly, a. poltrón, haragán, perezoso, holgazán. — *adv.* toscamente, zafiamente.

lubricant ['lju:brikənt], s. lubricante. — a. lubricativo, lubricante.

lubricate ['lju:brikeit], v.t. engrasar, lubricar, lubrificar, hacer lúbrico; untar; *lubricating oil*, aceite lubricante.

lubrication, lubrifaction, lubrification, s. engrase, engrasación, lubricación, lubrificación.

lubricator , s. engrasador, lubricador.

lubricity [lju:'brisiti], s. lubricidad, lisura; lujuria, incontinencia, lascivia; instabilidad, inconstancia, ligereza.

lubricous ['lju:bri:kəs], a. lúbrico, deslizadero, inconstante; lúbrico, lascivo.

luce [lu:s, lju:s], s. (*ict.*) lucio.

lucent ['lju:sənt], a. luciente, reluciente.

lucern [lu:'səɹn], s. (*bot.*) mielga, alfalfa; *lucern-field*, alfalfal.

lucid ['lju:sid], a. luciente, diáfano, brillante, luminoso; (*fig.*) lúcido, transparente, claro.

lucidity, lucidness, s. (*fig.*) perspicuidad, lucidez, claridad; esplendor, lucimiento.

Lucifer ['lu:sifəɹ], s. lucero, estrella del alba; Lucifer, Luzbel; *lucifer* o *lucifer-match*, fósforo de fricción.

Luciferian [lu:si'fiərən], a. luciferino, diabólico, endiablado.

luciferous, a. lucífero, luminoso, resplandeciente.

luck [lʌk], s. suerte, *f.*, azar, acaso, ventura, casualidad; *good luck*, (buena) suerte, fortuna, dicha, feliz casualidad; *bad luck*, mala suerte; *for luck*, para traer fortuna (o suerte); *to be in luck*, estar de suerte; *to try one's luck*, probar fortuna; *to take pot luck*, (*fam.*) comer lo que haya, sin ceremonia, (*fig.*) probar fortuna; *no such luck!* ¡ni mucho menos! ¡ni por pienso! *better luck tomorrow!* mañana será otro día.

luckily, adv. por fortuna, afortunadamente, felizmente, por dicha, dichosamente.

luckiness, s. dicha, buena fortuna, (buena) suerte, felicidad.

luckless, a. malaventurado, infeliz, desdichado, desgraciado, desventurado.

lucky, a. afortunado, feliz, venturoso, dichoso, propicio, bienhadado, favorable, de buena sombra; *to be born under a lucky star*, nacer en buena hora.

lucrative ['lju:krətiv], a. lucrativo, ganancioso, provechoso.

lucre ['lu:kəɹ], s. lucro, ganancia, usura.

lucubrate ['lju:kju:breit], v.t. lucubrar.

lucubration, s. lucubración, acto de lucubrar.

lucubratory, a. que se lucubra.

luculent ['lju:kju:lənt], a. luciente, claro; cierto, evidente, indubitable.

ludicrous ['lju:dikrəs], a. burlesco, absurdo, ridículo, risible, alegre.

ludicrousness, s. ridiculez, extravagancia.

luff [lʌf], s. (*mar.*) gratil, cachete de proa; orzada; *luff-tackle*, (*mar.*) aparejo de bolinear. — v.t. (*mar.*) ceñir el viento, orzar, bolinear; *to luff up*, tomar por avante; *to keep one's luff*, orzar; *to spring the luff*, partir el puño; *to luff round*, (*mar.*) meter todo a lof.

lug [lʌg], s. (*fam.*) tirón, estirón; cosa lenta y pesada; acto de tirar, cosa tirada; oreja, cosa parecida a una oreja, lóbulo de la oreja; asa, agarradera; correa de las varas de un carruaje; jamba de chimenea; pértiga; medida de tierra usualmente de 5·0292 m; *lug sail*, (*mar.*) vela al tercio. — v.t. tirar (de); (*mar.*) halar; *to lug away* (o *off*), arrastrar, llevarse arrastrando; *to lug in* (o *into*), arrastrar hacia dentro; *to lug out*, (*ant.*) sacar la espada.

luggage ['lʌgidʒ], s. equipaje, trastos efectos; petate; (*Amér.*) tarecos; (*ant.*) fardería, cosa pesada y embarazosa; *luggage-train*, (*f.c.*) tren de mercancías.

lugger ['lʌgəɹ], s. (*mar.*) lugre.

lugubrious [lju:'gju:briəs], a. lúgubre, funesto, fúnebre, lóbrego.

lugworm ['lʌgwə:ɹm], s. lombriz que sirve de cebo para pescar, arenícola.

lukewarm ['lju:kwɔ:ɹm], a. tibio, templado; (*fig.*) tibio, indiferente.

lukewarmness, s. tibieza, calor moderado; (*fig.*) tibieza, indiferencia.

lull [lʌl], v.t. arrullar, adormecer, aquietar, calmar, sosegar, mitigar. — s. momento de calma o de silencio, tregua(s).

lullaby ['lʌləbai], s. canción de cuna, arrullo.

lum [lʌm], s. (*Esco. y prov.*) chimenea de cabaña.

lumbago [lʌm'beigou], s. lumbago.

lumbar ['lʌmbɑ:ɹ], a. lumbar.

lumber ['lʌmbəɹ], s. tablones, tablas, tablazón, madera, maderas, maderaje; armatoste; balumba; trastos, muebles viejos; *lumber-room*, leonera, camaranchón; *lumber-yard*, almacén de madera para construcción, maderería. — v.t. amontonar trastos, o cosas inútiles. — v.i. andar pesadamente; (*ant.*) producir un ruido sordo.

lumbering, a. pesado (en el andar), torpe, desmañado, lerdo.

lumberman, s. hachero.

luminary ['lju:minəri], s. lumbrera, luminar, astro.

luminescence [lju:mi'nesəns], s. fosforescencia.

luminescent, a. fosforescente.

luminiferous [lju:mi'nifərəs], luminoso.

luminous ['lju:minəs], a. luminoso, luciente, brillante, resplandeciente, iluminado; lúcido, perspicuo, evidente.

luminousness, luminosity, s. brillo, brillantez, resplandor, claridad, lucidez, intensidad de luz, calidad de luminoso.

lump [lʌmp], s. pedazo, bollo, masa, montón; terrón (de azúcar); bulto, burujón, hinchazón, f., protuberancia; by (o in) the lump, (com.) por mayor, a bulto, por grueso, por junto; to have a lump in one's throat, atravesarle un nudo en la garganta. — v.t. comprar (o tomar) por mayor, por junto, por grueso; amontonar. — v.i. aterronarse, aborujarse, apelotonarse.

lumper, s. descargador; (vulg.) contratista pequeño.

lumping, a. (fam.) grueso, pesado, grande, abundante.

lumpish, a. grueso, pesado; tosco, torpe, lerdo.

lumpishness, s. pesadez; tosquedad, torpeza; tardanza.

lumpy, a. aterronado, apelmazado, lleno de terrones.

lunacy ['lu:nəsi], s. locura, demencia.

lunar ['lu:nəɹ], **lunary** ['lu:nəɹi], a. lunar, luniforme, lunario, lunático, lunado; (bot.) lunaria anual, hierba de la plata.

lunarian, s. habitante de la luna. — a. lunar.

lunate, lunated, a. lunado, luniforme, lunar.

lunatic ['lu:nətik], s., a. lunático, loco, alunado, avenado.

lunation [lu:'neiʃən], s. lunación.

lunch [lʌntʃ], **luncheon** ['lʌntʃən], s. almuerzo, merienda; luncheon basket, fiambrero; luncheon room, merendero. — v.i. almorzar, merendar.

lune [lu:n], s. luna, media luna, lúnula. — pl. caprichos, arranques.

lunette [lu:'net], s. (arch., fort.) luneta, media luna.

lung [lʌŋ], s. pulmón. — pl. livianos, bofes (de animales).

lunge [lʌndʒ], s. estocada; arremetida, embestida; cuerda larga o rienda usada en domesticar un caballo. — v.i. (esgr.) dar una estocada, dar un bote; abalanzarse.

lungwort ['lʌŋwə:ɹt], s. (bot.) pulmonaria oficinal.

luniform ['lu:nifɔ:ɹm], a. luniforme, lunado.

lunisolar [lu:ni'souləɹ], a. lunisolar.

lunt [lʌnt], s. mecha de cañón; bocanada de humo; llamarada.

lunular ['lu:nju:ləɹ], **lunulate** ['lu:nju:leit], a. lunado.

lunulated, a. (bot.) lunado.

lunule, s. lúnula.

lupin, lupine ['lu:pin], s. (bot.) lupino, altramuz. — a. lupino, de lobo.

lupuline, s. lupulino.

lurch [lə:ɹtʃ], s. brusco movimiento; vaivén, sacudida; (mar.) guiñada; to leave in the lurch, dejar en las astas del toro, dejar en el atolladero, dejar plantado, dejar abandonar. — v.i. (ant.) trampear, obrar con doblez; hacer bruscos movimientos, tambalearse; (mar.) guiñar, cabecear; ganar una partida doble.

lurcher, s. acechador; estafador, embaucador, trampeador; perro de caza.

lure [lju:əɹ], s. señuelo, añagaza, armadijo, engaño, reclamo. — v.t. inducir, persuadir, atraer; tentar; entruchar, engañar.

lurid ['lju:rid], a. (fig.) ominoso, terrible, violento; cárdeno; funesto, triste; ojeroso, pálido.

lurk [lə:ɹk], v.i. espiar, acechar, ocultarse, esconderse, emboscarse.

lurker, s. acechador, el que se oculta, espía.

lurking, a. escondido, secreto, en acecho; que se oculta; lurking-place, emboscada, escondrijo, escondite, guarida.

lurry [lʌri], s. (min.) carretón, carretilla, vagoneta.

luscious ['lʌʃəs], a. meloso, almibarado; delicioso, grato, sabroso; empalagoso.

lusciousness, s. melosidad, dulzura.

lush [lʌʃ], a. jugoso, suculento, lozano. — s. (vulg.) bebida alcohólica. — v.i. beber. — v.t. emborrachar.

lust [lʌst], **lustfulness** ['lʌstfəlnis], s. lascivia, lujuria, sensualidad, concupiscencia, incontinencia, salacidad. — v.i. lujuriar, desear vehementemente, codiciar.

lustful, a. lujurioso, voluptuoso, incontinente, sensual, impúdico, lascivo, libidinoso.

lustfulness, s. [LUST].

lustily ['lʌstili], adv. fuertemente, vigorosamente, robustamente, con fuerza.

lustiness, s. vigor, lozanía, robustez.

lusting, s. concupiscencia, lujuria, codicia.

lustral ['lʌstrəl], a. lustral, lústrico.

lustration, s. lustración, purificación.

lustre ['lʌstəɹ], s. lustre, brillantez, brillo; araña de cristal; lucimiento, esplendor; lustro.

lustreless, a. deslustrado, sin brillo.

lustring ['lʌstriŋ], s. lustrina.

lustrous ['lʌstrəs], a. lustroso, brillante.

lustrum ['lʌstrəm], s. lustro, quinquenio; lustración.

lustwort, (bot.) rocío del sol.

lusty, a. robusto, forzudo, vigoroso, fornido, lozano.

lute [lju:t], s. (mús.) laúd; vihuela; raspador de ladrillares; lutén o lodo y cemento para junturas. — v.t. enlodar, tapar con lodo; enrasar un ladrillar.

luteolin, s. luteína.

luter, lutist, s. tañedor de laúd.

lutestring ['lju:tstriŋ], s. cuerda de laúd.

Lutheran ['lu:θərən], s., a. luterano.

Lutheranism, s. luteranismo.

lutose ['lu:touz], a. lodoso, cenagoso.

luxate ['lʌkseit], v.t. luxar.

luxation, s. luxación.

luxuriance [lʌk'ʒju:riəns], s. lozanía, frondosidad, exuberancia; demasía, superabundancia.

luxuriant, a. lozano, frondoso, lujuriante, exuberante, superabundante; superfluo.

luxuriantly, adv. lozanamente, abundantemente, con profusión.

luxuriate [lʌk'ʒju:rieit], v.i. crecer con exuberancia, lozanear; (fig.) deleitarse, regodearse; (fig.) vivir con lujo, lozanear.

luxurious, a. lujoso, suntuoso; (ant.) lujurioso, voluptuoso.

luxuriousness, s. suntuosidad, lujo.

luxury ['lʌkʒəri], s. lujo; (ant.) lujuria, lascivia.

lycanthropy [lai'kænθropi], s. licantropía.

lyceum [lai'siəm], s. liceo.

lycopodium [laiko'poudiəm], s. licopodio.

lyddite ['lidait], s. lidita, explosivo a base de ácido pícrico.

Lydian ['lidiən], s., a. lidio.

lye [lai], s. lejía; (f.c.) desviadero.

lying ['laiiŋ], s. mentira, embuste, falsedad. —

a. mentiroso, falso; recostado, tumbado; yacente, situado, sito, echado.

lying-in [laiiŋ'in], *s.* parto.

lying-in-hospital, *s.* casa de maternidad.

lyingly, *adv.* mentirosamente.

lying-to, *s.* (*mar.*) al pairo, en facha.

lymph [limf], *s.* (*anat., poét.*) linfa; vacuna.

lymphate ['limfeit], **lymphated** [lim'feited], *a.* linfático.

lymphatic [lim'fætik], *s.* vaso linfático. — *a.* linfático.

lynch [lintʃ], *v.t.* linchar, ahorcar.

lynx [links], *s.* lince; *lynx-eyed*, *a.* de ojos linces; con ojos de lince.

lyrate ['laireit], *a.* (*mús.*) de la forma de lira. — *s.* lira.

lyre ['laiəɹ], *s.* (*mús.*) lira.

lyre-bird, *s.* (*orn.*) pájaro lira.

lyric ['lirik], **lyrical** ['lirikəl], *a.* lírico.

lyric, *s.* poema lírico, poesía lírica.

lyricism ['lirisizm], *s.* lirismo.

lyrist, *s.* tocador de lira; poeta lírico.

lysis ['laisis], *s.* lisis, *f.*

M

M, m [em], *s.* decimatercia letra del alfabeto inglés; como abreviatura: mil, maestro, miembro; *MS.*, manuscrito; *M.A.*, Maestro en Artes; *M.B.*, Bachiller en Medicina; *M.C.*, Miembro del Congreso (*E.U.*); *M.P.*, Miembro del Parlamento (*Ingl.*). — *pl. MSS.*, manuscritos.

ma [mɑː], *s.f.* (*vulg.*) contr. de *mama* o *mamma*, mamá.

ma'am [mæm, mɑːm], *s.f.* contr. de *madam*, señora.

Mac [mæk], **Mc** [mək], **M'**, prefijo que significa 'hijo de' (de origen escocés o irlandés). — **mac**, *s.* (*vulg.*) [MACKINTOSH].

macabre [mə'kɑːbəɹ], *a.* macabro.

macadam [mə'kædəm], *s.* macadán, macadam, pavimiento de macadam.

macadamize, *v.t.* macadamizar, afirmar con macadam.

macaque [mə'keik], *s.* (*zool.*) macaco.

macaroni [mækə'rouni], *s.* macarrones; pisaverde.

macaronic [mækə'rɔnik], *s., a.* macarronea, macarrónico.

macaronics, *s.pl.* poesía macarrónica.

macaroon [mækə'ruːn], *s.* macarrón, almendrado.

macassar [mə'kæsəɹ], *s.* aceite macasar.

macaw [mə'kɔː], *s.* (*orn.*) macagua, guacamayo.

Maccabean [mækə'biən], *a.* macabeo.

mace [meis], *s.* maza; macis, *f.*, macia.

mace-bearer, macer, *s.* macero.

macerate ['mæsəreit], *v.t.* macerar; enflaquecer.

maceration, *s.* maceración, enflaquecimiento.

Machiavellian, *s.* maquiavelista, *m.f.* — *a.* maquiavélico.

Machiavellism, *s.* maquiavelismo.

machicolation [mə'tʃikoleiʃən], *s.* (*arq.*) ladronera, matacán.

machinate ['mækineit], *v.t., v.i.* maquinar, fraguar, tramar.

machination, *s.* maquinación, conjura, trama.

machinator, *s.* maquinador, maquinante.

machine [mə'ʃiːn], *s.* máquina, aparato; (*pol.*) camarilla; *machine-made*, hecho a máquina; (*sewing-*)*machine*, máquina de coser. — *v.t.* labrar a máquina; coser a máquina.

machine-gun, *s.* ametralladora, cañón automático.

machinery [mə'ʃiːnəri], *s.* mecánica, mecanismo, maquinaria; (*fig.*) mecanismo, sistema, *m.*

machinist, *s.* maquinista, *m.f.*, mecánico.

mackerel ['mækərəl], *s.* escombro, caballa. — *a.* aborregado.

mackintosh ['mækintɔʃ], *s.* impermeable.

mackle ['mækəl], *s.* maculatura. — *v.t.* macular, repintar.

macrobian [mə'kroubiən], *s.* macrobiano.

macrocephalous [mækro'sefələs], *a.* macrocéfalo.

macrocosm ['mækroukɔzm], *s.* macrocosmo.

macula ['mækjuːlə], *s.* mácula.

maculate, *v.t.* macular. — *a.* maculado.

maculation, *s.* mácula, mancilla.

maculature, *s.* maculatura.

mad [mæd], *a.* (*comp.* **madder**, *sup.* **maddest**), loco, rabioso, demente, maníaco, desesperado, distraído, insensato, furioso, lunático, furibundo, enajenado; (*fam.*) enfadado; *to be or go mad*, enloquecer, volverse loco, perder el seso, estar loco, estar fuera de sí.

madam ['mædəm], *s.f.* señora, madama.

mad-apple, *s.* berengena.

madbrain, madcap, *s., a.* calavera, *m.f.*, botarate, loco.

madden ['mædən], *v.t.* enloquecer; exasperar, enfurecer. — *v.i.* enloquecerse, perder el juicio, volverse loco.

maddening, *a.* exasperante.

madder ['mædəɹ], *s.* (*bot.*) rubia. — *v.t.* teñir con rubia.

made [meid], *a.* hecho, creado, fabricado, producido, confeccionado; próspero. — *p.p.* [MAKE].

made-up [meid'ʌp], *a.* acabado, completo; artificial; confeccionado, hecho; compuesto, pintado (del rostro).

madefaction [mædi'fækʃən], *s.* majada, mojadura.

Madeira [mə'diərə], *s.* vino de Madera.

madhouse ['mædhaus], *s.* manicomio, casa de locos.

madly, *adv.* locamente, insensatamente, furiosamente.

madman ['mædmən], *s.* loco, insensato, demente, maniático.

madness, *s.* locura, demencia, manía, furor, rabia.

madonna [mə'dɔnə], *s.f.* Madona, Señora; representación de la Virgén.

madrepore ['mædripɔːɹ], *s.* madrépora.

madrigal ['mædrigəl], *s.* madrigal.

Madrilenian [mædrilliːniən], *s., a.* madrileño, matritense.

madwort ['mædwɔːɹt], *s.* aliso, marrubio.

maelstrom ['meilstrɔm], *s.* remolino.

mænad ['miːnæd], (*pl.* **mænads**) *s.* ménade, sacerdotisa de Baco.

magazine, *s.* almacén; depósito; recámara de un fusil; revista, periódico; (*mar.*) polvorína pañol de pólvora, Santabárbara.

magdalen ['mægdələn], *s.* prostituta arrepentida, reformada; asilo u hospicio para tales mujeres.

mage [meidʒ], *s.* mago.

magenta [mə'dʒentə], *s.* color magenta.

maggot ['mægət], *s.* cresa, larva, gusano; (*fig.*) antojo, fantasía, capricho.

maggoty, *a.* gusaniento; (*fig.*) caprichoso, fantástico.

magi ['meidʒai], *s.pl.* magos, los Reyes Magos.

magian ['meidʒən], *a.* mago, de los magos.

magic ['mædʒik], *s.* magia, mágica; (*fig.*) encanto; *as if by magic*, por ensalmo. — *a.* mágico, encantador; *magic lantern*, linterna mágica.

magical, *a.* mágico, encantado.

magically, *adv.* mágicamente, maravillosamente, por encantamiento.

magician [mə'dʒiʃən], *s.* mago, nigromante.

magisterial [mædʒi'stiəriəl], *a.* magisterial, magistral; imperioso.

magisterialness, *s.* magisterio, autoridad magistral.

magistery, *s.* magisterio; decreto magisterial.

magistracy ['mædʒistrəsi], *s.* magistratura.

magistrate ['mædʒistreit], *s.* magistrado; juez de paz, justicia.

Magna Charta [mægnə'kɑːɹtə], *s.* la Carta Magna sellada por el Rey John (1215) en la que están compendiadas las libertades del pueblo inglés.

magnanimity [mægnə'nimiti], *s.* magnanimidad, generosidad.

magnanimous [mæg'næniməs], *a.* magnánimo, generoso.

magnate ['mægneit], *s.* magnate.

magnesia [mæg'niːʒə], *s.* magnesia.

magnesian, magnesic, *a.* magnésico, magnesiano.

magnesium, *s.* magnesio.

magnet ['mægnət], *s.* imán, calamita.

magnetic [mæg'netik], **magnetical** [mæg'netikəl], *a.* magnético.

magnetically, *adv.* magnéticamente, atractivamente.

magneticalness, *s.* calidad de magnético.

magnetics, *s.* magnetismo.

magnetism ['mægnetizm], *s.* magnetismo; atractivo personal.

magnetizable [mægne'taizəbəl], *a.* magnetizable.

magnetization, *s.* magnetización.

magnetize ['mægnetaiz], *v.t.* magnetizar, imantar. — *v.i.* imanarse, imantarse.

magnetizer, *s.* magnetizador.

magnifiable [mægni'faiəbəl], *a.* capaz de ser magnificado.

magnific, magnifical, *a.* magnífico.

magnification [mægnifi'keiʃən], *s.* magnificación, enaltecimiento; (*ópt.*) amplificación.

magnificence, *s.* magnificencia, esplendor, grandiosidad.

magnificent [mæg'nifisənt], *a.* magnífico, suntuoso, grandioso.

magnifier ['mægnifaiəɹ], *s.* panegirista, *m.f.*; lente, microscopio, amplificador, vidrio de aumento.

magnify ['mægnifai], *v.t.* (*fig.*) magnificar, engrandecer; aumentar, amplificar.

magnifying ['mægnifaiiŋ], *a.* amplificante, que amplifica, que magnifica, que engrandece; *magnifying glass*, lente de aumento.

magniloquence, *s.* altilocuencia.

magniloquent [mæg'nilokwənt], *a.* grandílocuo.

magnitude, *s.* magnitud.

magnolia [mæg'nouliə], *s.* magnolia.

magnum ['mægnəm], *s.* gran botella (conteniendo 2 cuartos o sea 2·273 litros).

magpie ['mægpai], *s.* marica, picaza, urraca.

Magyar ['mɔdjɑːr], *s., a.* magiar.

maharaja [mɑːhə'rɑːdʒe], *s.* maharajá, *m.*

mahlstick ['mɑːlstik], *s.* tiento de pintor.

mahogany [mə'hɔgəni], *s.* caoba.

Mahometan [mə'hɔmetən], *s., a.* mahometano.

Mahometanism, *s.* Mahometismo.

maid [meid], *s.f.* doncella, sirvienta, fámula, criada; doncella, moza, virgen; soltera; (*ict.*) lija; *maid of honour*, dama de honor; *nursery maid*, niñera; *old maid*, solterona, (*fam.*) jamona.

maiden ['meidən], *s.f.* doncella; virgen; soltera; zagala. — *a.* de virgen, de joven, virgíneo, virginal; nuevo, fresco, pristino, primero; puro; *maiden name*, apellido de soltera; *maiden speech*, primer discurso.

maidenhair, *s.* (*bot.*) culantrillo, (*ant.*) brenca.

maidenhead, maidenhood, maidhood, *s.* virginidad, doncellez.

maidenlike, *a.* virginal, virgíneo, pudoroso, candoroso. — *adv.* púdicamente, pudorosamente, candorosamente.

maidenliness, *s.* pudor, dulzura.

maidenly, *a.* virginal, virgíneo, pudoroso. — *adv.* púdicamente, pudorosamente.

mail [meil], *s.* cota de malla, jacerina; correo, correspondencia, mala, valija. — *v.t.* revestir (*o armar*) con cota de malla; echar al correo, enviar por correo; *royal mail*, mala real.

mail-bag, *s.* valija, mala, portacartas, *m.sing.*

mail-coach, *s.* correo.

mail-order, *s.* pedido postal.

mail-steamer, *s.* vapor correo.

mail-train, *s.* correo, tren correo.

maim [meim], *v.t.* mutilar, estropear, lisiar, mancar, tullir. — *s.* pérdida del uso de un miembro; mutilación, manquera, daño.

maimed, *a.* estropeado, manco, mutilado, mútilo, zopo, tullido.

maimedness, *s.* mutilación, mancamiento.

main [mein], *a.* grande, mayor, principal, más importante, fuerte, esencial; *main road*, carretera, camino real; *main-sheet*, (*mar.*) escota mayor; *main-brace*, (*mar.*) brazo mayor; *main-yard*, (*mar.*) verga mayor; *mainmast*, (*mar.*) palo mayor; *main-topmast*, (*mar.*) mastelero mayor; *main-topyard*, (*mar.*) verga de gavia; *main-topsail*, (*mar.*) vela de gavia; *main wall*, pared maestra. — *s.* vigor, robustez, fuerza; esfuerzo violento; océano, alta mar; continente, la parte principal de la tierra como opuesto a isla; cloaca colectora, cañería maestra, cable eléctrico, de alimentación, etc.; *Spanish main*, la costa N.E. de la América del Sur y la parte adyacente del mar de las Antillas; *in the main*, principalmente; *with might and main*, con toda fuerza, con todas sus fuerzas.

mainland ['meinlənd], *s.* continente, tierra firme.

mainly, *adv.* sobre todo, principalmente, primeramente.

mainprize ['meinpraiz], *v.t.* (*for., ant.*)

libertar bajo caución. — s. (for.) libertad bajo caución, auto de la sala de justicia, ordenando la aceptación de fianza.

mainsail ['meinsəl], s. (mar.) vela mayor.

maintain [mein'tein, mən'tein], v.t. tener, mantener, sustentar, sostener, guardar, defender; proveer; alimentar.

maintainable, a. sostenible, defendible.

maintainer, s. mantenedor, protector, defensor, patrón.

maintenance ['meintənəns], s. mantenimiento, alimentación; protección, defensa; apoyo, sostén, sostenimiento; manutención, conservación, duración.

maize [meiz], s. maíz.

majestic [mə'dʒestik], a. majestuoso, grande, sublime, magnífico, pomposo.

majestically [mə'dʒestikəli], adv. majestuosamente.

majesty ['mædʒesti], s. majestad, majestuosidad, soberanía.

majolica [mə'jɔlikə], s. mayólica.

major ['meidʒəɹ], a. mayor, más grande, principal; (mús.) mayor. — s. (mil.) mayor, comandante; major general, general de división; (for.) mayor de edad; proposición mayor.

majoration, s. aumento.

major-domo [meidʒəɹ'doumou], s. mayordomo.

majority [mə'dʒɔriti], s. mayoría, mayor número; mayor de edad.

majuscule ['mædʒəskjuːl], s. mayúscula, letra mayúscula.

make [meik], v.t. (pret. y p.p. **made**) hacer, producir, formar, crear; ocasionar, constituir, causar, practicar, ejecutar, efectuar; confeccionar, fabricar, componer; adquirir, ganar (dinero); procurar, obtener; calcular; alcanzar; elaborar; aderezar; disponer; proporcionar; granjear; trabajar; pronunciar, referir, relatar, hablar; forzar, obligar, constreñir, compeler; cruzar, atravesar; sacar; terminar, acabar, poner fin a, completar; (mar.) avistar, descubrir, llegar a; convenir en; deducir, inferir; hacer fortuna. — v.i. hacerse; dirigirse, ir, encaminarse, volverse; corresponder; tener efecto, contribuir, servir, concordar; levantarse, fluir (de las mareas); to make after, seguir, perseguir; to make again, hacer de nuevo, rehacer; to make amends, indemnizar, compensar; to make angry, enfadar, enojar; to make as if, fingir, hacer como; to make away, huirse; to make away with, hurtar, llevarse; malgastar, disipar, malbaratar; matar, destruir; to make believe, fingir; to make fast, amarrar, asegurar; to make free, libertar; to make good, mantener, mejorar, garantizar; responder de; probar, justificar, completar, suplir, indemnizar, reparar; acertar, salir bien, tener éxito; to make haste, darse prisa, apresurarse; to make known, publicar, dar a saber; to make oneself known, darse a conocer; to make light of, menospreciar, no preocuparse, ostentar desprecio ocupación; to make love, cortejar, galantear, hacer el amor; to make merry, divertirse; to make a mistake, equivocarse; to make much of, estimar, apreciar; to make off, escaparse; to make off with, alzarse con; to make out, descifrar, comprender, explicar; to make

sure, asegurar(se), estar seguro; to make up, indemnizar, recompensar; formar, reunir, componer; acabar, completar; ajustar, reconciliar, hacer las paces, conciliar, apaciguar; pintarse; contar mentiras, fábulas, etc.; (impr.) compaginar; to make up to, (fam.) obsequiar; to make no matter, no importar; to make up one's mind, resolverse, hacer ánimo; to make water, orinar, hacer aguas; to make way, abrir paso; to make one's way in the world, progresar, avanzar; to make a pass, tirar una estocada; (fig., fam.) camelar, hacer guiños, hacer la rueda; to make more sail, (mar.) largar las velas; to make sense, tener sentido; to make shift, sacar partido; to make speed, ir rápidamente; to make use of, hacer uso de; money makes money, dinero llama dinero. — s. forma, figura; estructura; hechura; marca, construcción, fábrica, producción, manufactura, producto.

makebelieve ['meikbeliːv], a. falso, fingido. — s. artificio, pretexto, mentira, ficción.

makepeace ['meikpiːs], s. pacificador, mediador.

maker [meikəɹ], s. hacedor, creador, autor; artífice, fabricante; el Creador Supremo.

makeshift ['meikʃift], s. expediente, substituto, suplente; (ant.) cribón, ladronzuelo. — a. provisional, temporero.

make-up ['meikʌp], s. maquillaje; afeites; carácter, modo de ser; conjunto; modo de vestirse; disfraz; (impr.) imposición de tipos; novela, historia, ficción.

makeweight ['meikweit], s. complemento de peso, suplente, contrapeso, equilibrio, compensación.

making ['meikiŋ], s. forma, estructura, composición, hechura, trabajo. — pl. ganancias, provechos.

malachite ['mæləkait], s. malaquita.

malacology [mælə'kɔlodʒi], s. malacología.

maladdress ['mælədres], s. descortesía; falta de gracia; grosería.

maladjustment [mælə'dʒʌstmənt], s. ajuste defectuoso; inadaptación (psicológica).

maladministration [mælədmini'streiʃən], s. mala administración, desconcierto, despilfarro.

maladroit [mælə'drɔit], a. desmañado, torpe.

malady ['mælədi], s. enfermedad, dolencia, mal.

malaga ['mæləgə], s. vino de Málaga.

malaise [mə'leiz], s. malestar, indisposición.

malapert ['mæləpəːɹt], a. descarado, desvergonzado, descomedido.

malapertness, s. impertinencia, insolencia.

malapropos [mælæpro'pou], a. impropio, mal a propósito, fuera de propósito, disparatado. — adv. impropiamente.

malapropism, s. impertinencia, barbarismo, disparate.

malaria [mə'lɛəriə], s. aire malsano de las regiones pantanosas; (med.) paludismo.

malarial, malarious, a. palúdico, malsano.

malcontent ['mælkɔntent], a. malcontento, malcontentadizo. — s. malcontento.

malcontentedness, s. descontento, disgusto.

male [meil], s. (animal) macho; varón, hombre. — a. macho, masculino, varón, varonil; (bot.) estaminado; male screw, macho, tornillo; female screw, hembra, tuerca.

malediction [mæli'dikʃən], s. maldición.
malefactor ['mælifæktəɹ], s. malhechor.
malefic, a. maléfico.
malefice, s. maleficio.
maleficent, a. maléfico, maligno.
malevolencè, s. malevolencia, mala voluntad, encono.
malevolent [mə'levolənt], a. malévolo, maligno.
malfeasance [mæl'fi:zəns], s. conducta reprochable, ilegal, especialmente por parte de una persona con cargo oficial.
malformation [mælfɔːɹ'meiʃən], s. conformación defectuosa o viciosa, deformidad.
malformed, a. mal formado, contrahecho, mal hecho, deformado.
malic ['meilik], a. (quím.) málico.
malice ['mælis], s. malicia, malignidad, ruindad, mala intención; (ant.) maldad.
malicious [mə'liʃəs], a. malicioso, maléfico, maligno, ruin.
maliciousness, s. malignidad, malicia, mala intención.
malign [mə'lain], a. maligno, malicioso, pernicioso, dañino. — v.t. calumniar, perjudicar, envidiar. — v.i. tener rancor, ser malicioso.
malignancy, s. malignidad, malevolencia, malicia.
malignant [mə'lignənt], a. maligno, malicioso, malévolo; (med.) virulento, maligno.
malignity [mə'ligniti], s. malignidad, virulencia.
malinger [mə'liŋgəɹ], v.i. fingirse enfermo para no tener que trabajar.
malingerer, s. maula, m.f. (fam.), el que se finge enfermo.
malingering, s. enfermedad fingida. — a. malucho, que se finge enfermo.
malison ['mælizən], s. (poét.) maldición.
malkin ['mɔlkin], s. (ant.) gato; escoba para lavar, escobillón, aljofifa; deshollinador de horno; fregona mala, criada sucia; marrana, mujer sucia y desaliñada.
mall [mɔːl], s. mallo, mazo; calle, f., paseo público.
mallard ['mæləɹd], s. lavanco, ánade silvestre.
malleability, s. maleabilidad.
malleable ['mæliəbəl], a. maleable.
malleableness, s. maleabilidad.
malleate ['mælieit], v.t. martillar, trabajar a martillo.
malleation, s. maleación.
malleolar [mæli'ouləɹ], a. maleolar.
malleolus, s. maléolo.
mallet ['mælit], s. mallo, martillo, mazo, maceta.
mallow ['mælou], s. (bot.) malva; marsh mallow, malvavisco.
malm [mɑːm], s. roca cretácea friable, la que con arcilla y arena se usa para la fabricación de ladrillos.
malmsey ['mɑːmzi], s. malvasía.
malodorous [mæl'oudorəs], a. hediondo, que huele mal.
malpractice [mæl'præktis], s. ilegalidad, abuso; inmoralidad, tratamiento erróneo, impropio o perjudicial (de un médico).
malt [mɔːlt], s. malta. — v.t. hacer germinar la cebada.
Maltese [mɔl'tiːz], s., a. Maltés.
malt-floor, s. suelo para germinar cebada.

Malthusian [mæl'θjuːzən], s., a. maltusiano.
malting ['mɔːltiŋ], s. maltaje.
malt-liquor, s. cerveza.
malt-man, maltster, s. cervecero, preparador de malta.
maltreat [mæl'triːt], v.t. maltratar.
maltreatment, s. maltratamiento.
malvaceous [mæl'veiʃəs], a. malváceo.
malversation [mælvəːɹ'seiʃən], s. malversación.
mama, mamma [mə'mɑː], s.f. mamá; (ant.) mama, teta.
mamaluke, mameluke ['mæmiluːk], s. mameluco.
mammal ['mæməl], s. mamífero.
mammalia [mə'meiliə], s.pl. mamíferos.
mammalian, a. mamífero.
mammary ['mæməri], a. mamario.
mammee [mə'miː], s. mamey.
mammifer ['mæmifəɹ], s. mamífero.
mammiferous, a. mamífero.
mammiform, a. mamiforme; atetado.
mammilla [mə'milə], s. mamila, mamella.
mammillary, a. mamilar.
mammillated, a. mamellado, apezonado.
mammock ['mæmək], v.t. hacer pedazos, despedazar. — s. pedazo, fragmento.
mammon ['mæmən], s. becerro de oro.
mammoth ['mæmɔθ], s. mamut. — a. gigantesco, enorme.
man [mæn], s. (pl., men) hombre; el género humano; varón; persona; servidor, criado; peón, pieza (juego de damas); (mar.) barco, buque, navío; alguien, cualquiera; good man, hombre de bien; head man, jefe; per man, por barba o por cabeza; to a man, como un solo hombre o unánimemente; man of war, buque de guerra; man of the world, hombre de mundo; Man overboard! ¡Hombre al agua!; man about town, (fam.) señorito; hombre de mundo; man-eater, man-eating, s., a. caníbal, antropófago; man-hole, hoyo, pozo; man-in-the-moon, mujer de la luna; man-in-the-street, hombre de la calle, hombre de carne y hueso. — v.t. guarnecer con tropas; armar, dotar; (mar.) tripular, equipar, amarinar; (mil.) fortificar, guarnecer, poner guarnición.
manacle ['mænəkəl], s. manilla. — pl. **manacles,** esposas. — v.t. maniatar, encadenar, poner las esposas.
manage ['mænidʒ], v.t. manejar, conducir, hacer andar, llevar, dirigir, usar, manipular, guiar, regir, administrar, gobernar; tratar con prudencia; gestionar, procurar; domar, amansar. — v.i. arreglarse, obrar, acertar, hallar modo; ingeniarse, componérselas.
manageable ['mænidʒəbəl], a. manejable, tratable, dócil, flexible.
manageableness, s. flexibilidad; docilidad, suavidad, mansedumbre.
management ['mænidʒmənt], s. manejo; conducta, proceder, dirección, gobierno, negociación, gestión, f., administración; (com.) gerencia, dirección; empleo, uso; destreza, prudencia; empresa, intendencia.
manager, s. administrador, empresario, director, superintendente, regente; gestor, gerente; intrigante.
managerial [mænə'dʒiəriəl], a. directivo, administrativo.
managing, a. que conduce o dirige; intrigante.

manatee [mænə'tiː], s. manatí, vaca marina.
mancipation [mænsi'peiʃən], s. (for.) mancipación.
manciple ['mænsipəl], s. administrador, mayordomo, intendente.
mandarin ['mændərin], s. mandarín; (naranja) mandarina; lengua mandarina; amarillo de mandarín.
mandate ['mændeit], s. mandato, mandamiento.
mandatory ['mændətəri], s. mandatorio; agente.
mandible [mændibəl], s. mandíbula, quijada.
mandibular [mæn'dibjuːləɹ], a. mandibular.
mandibulate, a. mandibulado.
mandolin, mandoline ['mændolin], s. (mús.) mandolina.
mandragora [mæn'drægərə], **mandrake** ['mændreik], mandrágora.
mandrel ['mændrəl], s. mandril; taladro; (prov.) pico de minero.
manducate ['mændjuːkeit], v.t. manducar.
manducation, s. manducación.
mane [mein], s. crin, f., clin, f. (de caballo), crines; melena (de león, etc.).
man-eater, s. antropófago.
maned, a. crinado.
manege ['meiniːz], s. picadero, escuela de equitación; manejo, equitación. — v.t. adiestrar (un caballo).
manes, s. manes.
manful ['mænful], a. bravo, esforzado, viril; noble.
manfully, adv. varonilmente, bravamente; noblemente; estoicamente.
manfulness, s. virilidad, aliento, bravura, esfuerzo; nobleza; estoicismo.
manganate ['mæŋgənit], s. manganato.
manganese [mæŋgə'niːz], s. manganeso.
manganic [mɑŋ'gænik], a. mangánico.
manganous, a. manganoso.
mange [meindʒ], s. (vet.) sarna perruna, roña.
manger ['meindʒəɹ], s. pesebre.
manginess, s. estado sarnoso, sarnazo, roña.
mangle ['mæŋgəl], s. calandria, 'mangle'; máquina de aplanchar. — v.t. pasar por la calandria; lacerar, desgarrar, mutilar, destrozar, despedazar, estropear; satinar, alisar.
mangler, s. destrozador, despedazador; lustrador.
mangling, s. despedazamiento, laceración, mutilación; acción de pasar por la calandria.
mango ['mæŋgou], s. mango, manguey, manga.
mangrove ['mæŋgrouv], s. manglar.
mangy ['meindʒi], a. sarnoso.
man-hater ['mænheitəɹ], s. misántropo; mujer que aborrece a los hombres.
manhole ['mænhoul], s. registro, pozo de visita, agujero de hombre.
manhood, s. virilidad; masculinidad, hombradía, hombría de bien; naturaleza humana.
mania ['meiniə], s. manía, frenesí; (fig.) manía, obsesión, capricho obsesionado.
maniac ['meiniæk], s., a. maníaco, maniático.
maniacal [mə'nəiəkəl], a. maníaco, maniático.
maniacally, adv. maniáticamente.
Manichæism, s. maniqueísmo.
Manichæan [mæni'kiən], a. maniqueo.
manichord ['mænikɔːɹd], s. manicordio.
manicure ['mænikjuːəɹ], s. tratamiento de las

manos y de las uñas, manicura. — v.t. cuidar y curar las manos y uñas.
manicurist, s. manicuro, -a.
manifest ['mænifest], a. manifiesto. — v.t. manifestar, expresar, declarar, hacer ver, hacer patente, revelar, demostrar. — s. (mar.) manifiesto, conocimiento, hoja de ruta.
manifestable, a. demostrable.
manifestation, s. manifestación, revelación, demostración, declaración.
manifestness, s. evidencia palpable.
manifesto [mæni'festou], s. manifiesto, proclama, declaración.
manifold ['mænifould], a. multíplice, múltiple, numeroso, diverso, vario. — v.t. sacar muchas copias al mismo tiempo.
manikin ['mænikin], s. maniquí, hombrecillo, muñeco.
manila, manilla [mə'nilə], s. cigarro filipino, abacá, cáñamo de Manila.
manioc ['mæniɔk], s. (bot.) cazabe, harinaza hecha con la raíz de la yuca.
maniple, manipule ['mænipəl], s. manípulo.
manipular, a. manipular, manuable.
manipulate [mə'nipjuːleit], v.t. manipular, manejar.
manipulation, s. manipulación, manejo.
manipulative, a. manipulante.
manipulator, s. manipulador.
man-killer ['mænkiləɹ], s. homicida, m.f.
mankind [mæn'kaind], s. humanidad, el género humano, los hombres en general.
manlike, a. varonil, viril, bravo, animoso, esforzado, de hombre, hombruno.
manliness ['mænlines], s. hombradía, valentía, bravura.
manly, a. varonil, viril; noble; estoico. — adv. varonilmente, virilmente.
manna ['mænə], s. maná; (bot.) ládano, mangla.
mannequin ['mænikin], s. modelo, maniquí.
manner ['mænəɹ], s. manera, método, género, modo, especie, f., forma, traza, ademán, aire; hábito, costumbre, práctica, maña. — pl. **manners**, modales, conducta, crianza, educación, urbanidad, comportamiento; in this manner, o in such a manner, de este modo, de esta forma, así; in a manner, hasta cierto punto; by all manner of means, seguramente, o de todos modos; by no manner of means, de ningún modo; manners maketh man, se puede juzgar a un hombre por sus modales; mannered, amanerado; ill-mannered, mal educado, mal criado; well-mannered, bien educado, bien criado.
mannerism ['mænəɹizm], s. amaneramiento.
mannerist, s. manerista, m.f., amanerado.
mannerliness ['mænəɹlinis], s. buena educación, cortesanía, urbanidad, política.
mannerly ['mænəɹli], a. político, cortés, urbano, bien criado. — adv. políticamente, urbanamente.
mannikin, s. [MANIKIN].
mannish ['mæniʃ], a. masculino, varonil; hombruno, ahombrado.
manœuvre [mə'nuːvəɹ], s. (mil.) maniobra, evolución; artificio. — v.i. maniobrar (tropas o flota), ejecutar maniobras. — v.t. hacer maniobrar; tramar, intrigar, manipular, negociar artificiosamente.

manœuvrer [mə'nuːvrəɹ], *s.* maniobrista, *m.f.*
manœuvring, *a.* que maniobra, que ejecuta evoluciones, que intriga. — *s.* maniobras.
manometer [mə'nɔmetəɹ], *s.* manómetro.
manometrical, *a.* manométrico.
manor ['mænəɹ], **manor-house** ['mænəɹhaus], *s.* señorío o jurisdicción territorial, feudo; hacienda, finca solariega, casa señorial, palacio, hotel, hotelito.
manorial [mə'nɔːriəl], *s.* señorial.
manpower, *s.* mano de obra, *f.*
mansard roof ['mænsɑːɹd ruːf], *s.* techo de boardilla, aboardillado.
manse [mæns], *s.* rectoría; quinta, hacienda, granja; residencia.
manservant ['mænsəɹvənt], *s.* criado.
mansion ['mænʃən], *s.* casa solariega, finca, hotel, hotelito; mansión, residencia, morada; *Mansion House,* palacio del *Lord Mayor* o alcalde de Londres. — *pl.* edificio grande con pisos de alquiler.
manslaughter ['mænslɔːtəɹ], *s.* homicidio fortuito o intencionado.
mantel ['mæntəl], *s.* manto de una chimenea; *mantelpiece,* repisa de chimenea.
mantelet, mantlet, *s.* manteleta, capotillo; *(mil.)* mantelete.
mantic ['mæntik], *a.* relativo a la profecía o divinación.
mantilla [mæn'tiljə], *s.* mantilla.
mantis ['mæntis], *s.* *(entom.)* cortón, mantis, rezadora.
mantissa [mæn'tisə], *s.* mantisa.
mantle ['mæntəl], *s.* capa, manta, manto, manteo, manteleta; manguito incandescente, camisa (de luz de gas); *(fig.)* máscara. — *v.t.* velar, cubrir con una capa, tapar. — *v.i.* extenderse, divertirse; extender las alas.
mantled, *a.* cubierto con una capa.
manual ['mænjuəl], *a.* manual, manuable. — *s.* manual; *(mús.)* teclado de órgano.
manubrium [mə'njuːbriəm], *s.* manubrio.
manufactory [mænju'fæktəri], *s.* fábrica, manufactura, taller.
manufacture [mænju'fæktʃəɹ], *s.* manufactura, fábrica, artefacto, fabricación; obra, producto. — *v.t.* hacer, manufacturar, fabricar, labrar, obrar. — *v.i.* ser fabricante.
manufacturer, *s.* fabricante, manufacturero.
manufacturing, *a.* fabril, manufacturero, industrial. — *s.* fabricación, industria.
manumission [mænju'miʃən], *s.* manumisión, liberación.
manumit [mænju'mit], *v.t.* manumitir, emancipar.
manumotor [mænju'moutəɹ], *s.* cochecito de inválido movido a mano.
manurable, *a.* cultivable.
manure [mə'njuəɹ], *s.* abono, fiemo, estiércol. — *v.t.* abonar, estercolar, engrasar.
manuscript ['mænjuːskript], *s.*, *a.* manuscrito; original de imprenta.
Manx [mæŋks], *s.*, *a.* habitante o lenguaje de la isla de Man.
many ['meni], *a.* muchos, diversos, varios; *a great many,* muchísimos; *how many,* cuantos; *so many,* tantos; *as many as,* tantos como; *too many,* demasiado(s); *one too many,* uno de sobra; *many a many a one,* muchos; *many a time,* muchas veces; *twice as many o as many more,* otros tantos. — *s.* gran número; *the many,* la mayoría, la multitud, las masas.

many-coloured, *a.* multicolor, policromo, abigarrado.
many-flowered, *a.* de muchas flores, multifloro.
many-headed, *a.* de muchas cabezas.
many-hued, *a.* matizado.
many-peopled, *a.* populoso, numeroso.
manyplies ['meniplaiz], *s.* omaso, el tercer estómago de los rumiantes.
many-sided, *a.* multilátero; *(fig.)* versátil.
map [mæp], *s.* mapa, *m.*, mapamundi, carta geográfica, plano (topográfico). — *v.t.* trazar o delinear mapas; *to map out,* trazar, planear; *(fig.)* proyectar, planear, trazar.
maple, *s.* *(bot.)* arce, ácer, plátano falso, meple; *maple sugar,* azúcar de meple; *maple syrup,* guarapo de meple; *maple wood,* meple.
mapping, map-making, *s.* cartografía.
mar [mɑːɹ], *v.t.* dañar, echar a perder, corromper, dañar, desfigurar, estropear, frustrar, viciar, malear. — *s.* *(ant.)* borrón, mancha; desventaja, estorbo.
marabout ['mærəbuːt], *s.* morabito.
marasmus [mə'ræzməs], *s.* marasmo.
maraud [mə'rɔːd], *v.t.*, *v.i.* merodear, pillar.
marauder, *s.* merodeador, merodista, *m.f.*
marauding, *s.* merodeo, pillaje. — *a.* merodeante.
maravedi [mæri'vedi], *s.* maravedí.
marble ['mɑːɹbəl], *s.* mármol; canica (bolita de juego); *(impr.)* piedra de imponer; *Elgin marbles,* la crónica de Atenas contenida en mármol (Museo Británico). — *pl.* **marbles,** juego de canicas. — *a.* de mármol, marmóreo; *(fig.)* empedernido, duro, insensible. — *v.t.* jaspear.
marbled, *a.* marmóreo; marmoleño; jaspeado.
marble-polisher, *s.* marmolista, *m.f.*
marble-works, *s.pl.* marmolería.
marbling, *s.* marmoración; jaspeadura.
marbly, *a.* marmóreo.
marc [mɑːɹk], *s.* hollejo.
marcasite ['mɑːɹkəzait], *s.* marcasita, marquesita, pirita blanca.
march [mɑːɹtʃ], *v.i.* marchar (en fila, o en orden, o con resolución), desfilar; estar contiguo, lindar; *to march on,* seguir caminando; *to march out,* irse, salir; *to march past,* desfilar; *to march up,* adelantar, avanzar. — *v.t.* hacer marchar, poner en marcha; *to march out,* hacer salir. — *s.* marcha, movimiento; progreso, adelanto; frontera (el de marzo); *quick march,* paso doble; *to steal a march on,* ganar por la mano; *march-past,* desfile. — *pl.* **marches,** fronteras.
marching, *a.* de marcha, en marcha. — *s.* marcha.
marchioness ['mɑːɹʃənes], *s.f.* marquesa.
marchpane ['mɑːɹtʃpein], *s.* mazapán.
marcid ['mɑːɹsid], *a.* *(ant.)* macilento, flaco, magro.
marconigram [mɑːɹ'kounigræm], *s.* marconigrama, *m.*
mare [mɛəɹ], *s.f.* yegua; *mare's nest,* *(fig.)* cuento falso; *mare's tail,* *(bot.)* cola de caballo.
margaric [mɑːɹ'gærik], *a.* margárico.
margarine ['mɑːɹdʒəriːn, 'mɑːɹgəriːn], *s.* margarina, manteca.
margarite ['mɑːɹgərait], *s.* *(min.)* margarita, perla mica.

marge ['mɑːɹdʒ], **margin** ['mɑːɹdʒin], s. margen, orilla, lado, borde; provisión, reserva; (tip.) blanco; (com.) reserva, sobrante, depósito en mano; (vulg.) [MARGARINE]. — v.t. margenar, marginar, escribir en margen, poner margen a. — v.i. depositar fondos en manos de un agente, como reserva.

marginal, a. marginal; *marginal note* o *marginal reading*, acotación.

marginally, adv. al margen.

marginate, a. marginado.

margrave ['mɑːɹgɹəv], s. margrave.

margraviate, s. margraviato.

margravine ['mɑːɹgɹəviːn], s.f. mujer de un margrave.

marguerite ['mɑːɹgəriːt], s. (bot.) margarita.

Marian ['mɛəriən], a. mariano, de María.

marigold ['mærigould], s. (bot.) caléndula, flamenquilla, clavelón.

marinade [mæri'neid], s. escabeche.

marine [mə'riːn], a. marino, naval, oceánico, náutico; de mar. — s. marino, soldado de marina; marina, fuerza naval; buques en general; *tell that to the marines*, a otro perro con ese hueso.

mariner ['mærinəɹ], s. marino, marinero.

Mariolatry [mɛəri'ɔlətri], s. culto excesivo de la virgen María.

marionette [mæriɔ'net], s. títere, marioneta.

marital ['mæritəl], a. marital.

maritime ['mæritaim], s. marítimo.

marjoram ['mɑːɹdʒərəm], s. mejorana, amáraco, orégano.

mark [mɑːɹk], s. marca, señal, f., seña; observación, nota, impresión, vestigio, indicación, indicio, traza, rastro, huella; nota (de examen); prueba; marco; símbolo, signo, blanco; distinción, rango, eminencia; regla, norma; (mar.) piratería; *book-mark*, registro; *trade-mark*, marca de fábrica; *high water mark*, nivel de marea alta; *low water mark*, nivel de marea baja; *to hit the mark*, dar en el blanco (o golpe); *save the mark!* ¡salva sea la parte! *to make one's mark*, firmar con una cruz; (fig.) distinguirse; *a man of mark*, hombre de categoría. — v.t., v.i. marcar, caracterizar, señalar; advertir, observar, notar, acotar; *to mark down*, anotar, observar precisamente; (com.) marcar a precio más bajo; *to mark out*, señalar, mostrar; elegir, destinar.

markedly ['mɑːɹkedli], adv. marcadamente.

marker, s. marcador; ficha, marca; *book-marker*, registro.

market ['mɑːɹket], s. mercado; tráfico, venta; feria, bazar, emporio; precio, curso, plaza, plazuela; *fish-market*, pescadería; *market-day*, día de mercado; *market-price*, precio corriente; *ready market*, fácil salida. — v.t., v.i. vender (o comprar) en el mercado.

marketable, a. comerciable, vendible, de venta de buena calidad, corriente.

market-garden, s. huerto, huerta.

market-gardener, s. hortelano.

marketing, s. mercado, tráfico, compra o venta.

market-place, s. mercado; plaza.

marking ['mɑːɹkiŋ], s. marcación; *marking ink*, tinta de marcar.

marksman ['mɑːɹksmən], s. tirador, tiro, el que tira con acierto.

marksmanship, s. buena puntería.

marl [mɑːɹl], s. marga, greda. — v.t. margar, abonar con marga; (mar.) empalomar, trincafiar.

marlaceous [mɑːɹ'leiʃəs], a. margoso.

marline ['mɑːɹlin], s. (mar.) merlín. — v.t. (mar.) coser con merlín.

marline-spike ['mɑːɹlinspaik], s. (mar.) pasador.

marling ['mɑːɹliŋ], s. acción de margar.

marl-pit, s. margal, marguera, gredal.

marly, a. margoso, gredoso.

marmalade ['mɑːɹməleid], s. mermelada de naranjas.

marmoration [mɑːɹmo'reiʃən], s. marmoración.

marmoreal [mɑːɹ'moːriəl], **marmorean** ['mɑːɹ'moːriən], a. marmóreo.

marmose ['mɑːɹmouz], s. marmoso.

marmot ['mɑːɹmɔt], s. marmota, monote.

maroon [mə'ruːn], s. cimarrón, color castaño; persona abandonada en una isla desolada; (pirotécnica) morterete. — a. castaño. — v.t. abandonar en una costa desierta. — v.i. (E.U.) merendar al aire libre.

marplot ['mɑːɹplɔt], s. enredador, aguafiestas.

marquee [mɑːɹ'kiː], s. marquesina; gran tienda.

marquess ['mɑːɹkwis], s. marqués.

marquetry ['mɑːɹketri], s. marquetería, ataracea.

marquis ['mɑːɹkwis], s. marqués.

marquisate ['mɑːɹkwizeit], s. marquesado.

marquise [mɑːɹ'kiːz], s. marquesa.

marriage ['mæridʒ], s. matrimonio, maridaje, casamiento, boda, himeneo, nupcias, enlace. — a. matrimonial, conyugal.

marriageable, a. núbil, casadero.

marriage-bell, s. campana de bodas.

marriage-contract, s. contrato de matrimonio.

marriage-licence, s. dispensa de amonestación.

marriage-portion, s. dote.

married, a. casado; conyugal, matrimonial, connubial; *married couple*, cónyuges, matrimonio.

marrow ['mærou], s. médula (o medula), tuétano; meollo; esencia, esencial; *vegetable marrow*, variedad de la calabaza, cucúrbita ovífera.

marrow-bone, s. caña o hueso medular. — pl. (fam.) rodillas; puños.

marrowish, a. meduloso.

marrowless, s. sin medula.

marrowy, a. meduloso, medular.

marry ['mæri], v.t. casar, unir (o juntar) en matrimonio; dar en matrimonio; casarse con, tomar por marido (o por mujer). — v.i. casarse, contraer matrimonio; interj. (ant.) ¡de veras! ¡por mi fe!

Mars [mɑːɹz], s. Marte.

marsh [mɑːɹʃ], s. pantano, tremedal, ciénaga, marisma, laguna, marjal, fangal; *marsh land*, lugar pantanoso; *salt marsh*, saladar.

marshal ['mɑːɹʃəl], s. mariscal; maestro de ceremonias; alguacil; bastonero; mariscal de logis; (mil.) mariscal de campo; (E.U.) jefe de policía; oficial del tribunal de justicia. — v.t. ordenar, dirigir, adiestrar, arreglar, poner en orden, guiar. — v.i. juntarse, ordenarse, tomar posiciones.

marshaller, s. ordenador, arreglador.

marshalship, s. mariscalía, mariscalato.
marsh-mallow [mɑ:ɪʃ'mælou], s. (bot.) malvavisco.
marsh-marigold, s. (bot.) calta, centella.
marshy, a. pantanoso, lagunoso, cenagoso, palustre.
marsupial [mɑ:ɪ'sju:piəl], **marsupiate** [mɑ:ɪ'sju:pieit], s., a. marsupial.
mart [mɑ:ɪt], s. emporio, mercado público, feria, sala de ventas. — v.t., v.i. (ant.) traficar, vender y comprar.
martel [mɑ:ɪtəl], s. (blas.) martillo.
martello tower [mɑ:ɪ'telou 'tauəɪ], s. atalaya, torre de guarda en las costas.
marten ['mɑ:ɪtən], s. (zool.) marta, fuina, garduña; piel de marta.
martial ['mɑ:ɪʃəl], a. marcial, guerrero, de guerra, de batalla; belicoso, bélico; court martial, consejo de guerra; martial law, estado de sitio.
martialist, s. guerreador.
martially, adv. de una manera marcial.
Martian ['mɑ:ɪʃən], a. de Marte. — s. habitante de Marte.
martin ['mɑ:ɪtin], s. (orn.) avión, vencejo.
martinet [mɑ:ɪti'net], s. oficial severo, rigorista, m.f.
martingal ['mɑ:ɪtiŋgəl], **martingale**, s. martingala, gamarra; (mar.) moco del bauprés.
Martinmas ['mɑ:ɪtinməs], s. fiesta de San Martín (el 11 de Noviembre).
martyr ['mɑ:ɪtəɪ], s. mártir. — v.t. martirizar.
martyrdom ['mɑ:ɪtəɪdəm], s. martirio.
martyrize, v.t. martirizar, ofrecer como mártir.
martyrologist, s. martirologista, m.f.
martyrology [mɑ:ɪti'rolodʒi], s. martirologio.
marvel ['mɑ:ɪvəl], s. maravilla, prodigio. — v.i. maravillar(se), estar admirado, admirarse, asombrarse.
marvellous ['mɑ:ɪvələs], a. maravilloso, admirable, estupendo.
marvellousness, s. carácter maravilloso, lo maravilloso, maravilla, singularidad, extrañeza.
mascot ['mæskɔt], s. mascota, talismán.
masculine ['mæskju:lin], a. masculino, macho, machuno, varonil, viril; (mat.) impar; (ret.) agudo; masculine woman, marimacho, f., mujer hombruna.
masculinity [mæskju:'liniti], s. masculinidad.
mash [mæʃ], s. mezcla de ingredientes, masa; puré; amasijo; malta; fárrago, baturrillo. — v.t. mezclar, amasar, magullar, triturar, estrujar, revolver, majar; (vulg.) cortejar, hacer cocos.
masher, s. (vulg.) petimetre, joven ridículo.
mashing, s. acción de mezclar, mezclamiento.
mashy, a. mezclado, amasado, revuelto, magullado.
mask [mɑ:sk], s. máscara, disfraz, careta, carátula, carantoña, antifaz; mascarilla; persona disfrazada; mascarada, mojiganga; capa, pretexto, velo; disimulo, color, apariencia; (arq.) mascarón, parapeto; (mil.) cubierta natural o artificial para cubrir fuerzas o baterías; to take off the mask, quitarse la máscara. — v.t. poner máscara, enmascarar, disfrazar, disimular, ocultar. — v.i. enmascararse, disfrazarse, andar enmascarado.

masker, s. máscara, mascarón.
maslin ['mæslin], s. mezcla de granos especialmente de trigo y centeno.
mason ['meisən], s. albañil; masón, franc-masón.
mason-bird, s. trepatroncos.
masonic [mə'sɔnik], a. masónico; masonic lodge, logia de franc-masones.
masonry ['meisənri], a. albañilería; franc-masonería.
masque ['mɑ:sk], s. mascarada, mojiganga.
masquerade [mɑ:skə'reid], s. mascarada, baile de máscaras; máscara, disfraz. — v.i. enmascararse, disfrazarse, ir disfrazado.
masquerader, s. máscara, mascarón, m.f.
mass [mæs], s. masa, montón, multitud, gran número; cuerpo informe, volumen, bulto, mole, f., cuerpo compacto; misa; High Mass, misa mayor; Low Mass, misa rezada; in the mass, en conjunto; the masses, las masas, el vulgo, la plebe; mass-production, fabricación en serie. — v.t. reunir en masa, amasar, juntar. — v.i. juntarse, formar masas.
massacre ['mæsəkəɪ], s. carnicería, matanza, mortandad. — v.t. destrozar, degollar, hacer una carnicería.
massage ['mæsɑ:ʒ], s. masaje, soba; fricción. — v.t. sobar.
masseur ['mæsə:ɪ], s.m. **masseuse** ['mæsə:ɪz], s.f. masajista, m.f.
massiness ['mæsinis], (ant.), **massiveness** ['mæsivnis], s. solidez, peso, pesadez, bulto.
massive ['massiv], **massy** ['mæsi], (ant.), a. macizo, abultado, sólido, ponderoso, grueso.
mast [mɑ:st], s. (mar.) mastelero, mástil, palo; (bot.) bellota; fabuco (del haya, etc.); fore mast, (mar.) palo de trinquete; main mast, (mar.) palo mayor; mizen mast, (mar.) palo de mesana; top masts, (mar.) masteleros; standing masts, palos principales. — pl. masts, (mar.) arboladura. — v.t. (mar.) arbolar.
master ['mɑ:stəɪ], s. maestro, maestre, señor, amo, director, dueño, propietario; preceptor, maestro, profesor (de escuela); jefe; oficial; señorito; (mar.) patrón, capitán, maestre; experto, diestro, perito; to be master of the situation, ser dueño del baile; to be master of (a language), dominar, conocer a fondo; like master, like man, como canta el abad, responde el sacristán; Master of the Horse, caballerizo mayor; Master of the Ordnance, director general de artillería; Master of the Rolls, archivero general; past master, hombre experto; master key, llave maestra; master mind, inteligencia superior, ingenio; master stroke, golpe maestro; master builder, maestro de obras. — v.t. dominar, sujetar, conocer (o saber) a fondo; conquistar, maestrear, someter, domar, reprimir, gobernar; ser superior en; sobreponerse a. — v.i. ser superior en. — a. magistral, principal, superior.
masterdom, s. mando, dominio, maestría.
masterful, a. dominante, imperioso, arbitrario, tiránico; hábil, diestro, capaz.
masterless, a. libre, independiente; rebelde; indómito.
masterliness, s. maestría.
masterly, a. dominante, magistral, maestro, imperioso. — adv. de mano maestra, con maestría.

masterpiece, *s.* obra maestra, obra magistral.

mastership, *s.* maestría, magisterio, preeminencia, superioridad.

masterwort, *s.* imperatoria.

mastery ['mɑːstəri], *s.* maestría, dominio, poder, gobierno, habilidad, destreza, ventaja, preeminencia, superioridad.

masthead ['mɑːsthed], *s.* cabeza del mástil, vigía, tope. — *v.t.* alzar el tope del mástil; mandar un marinero al tope como castigo.

mastic ['mæstik], *s.* mástique, almáciga, almástica; *mastic-tree,* lentisco.

masticate ['mæstikeit], *v.i.* masticar, mascar.

mastication, *s.* masticación.

masticator, *s.* masticador, mascador.

masticatory, *s., a.* masticatorio.

mastiff ['mæstif], *s.* mastín.

mastless ['mɑːstles], *a.* desarbolado.

mastodon ['mæstodɔn], *s.* mastodonte.

mastoid ['mæstɔid], *a.* mastoide. — *s.* mastoides.

masturbate ['mæstəbeit], *v.i.* masturbarse.

masturbation, *s.* masturbación.

mat [mæt], *s.* estera, esterilla, felpudo, petate; (*mar.*) pallete, empalletado; mate, superficie mate. — *v.t.* esterar; tejer; desgreñar; enredar; producir una superficie mate. — *v.i.* enredarse.

matador ['mætədɔː], *s.* matador, espada, *m.*, primer espada, diestro; (en los juegos de tresillo, cascarela, etc.) los tres naipes de estuche; un juego al dominó.

match [mætʃ], *s.* fósforo, cerilla, pajuela; (*arti.*) mecha, cuerdamecha, cuerdacalada; partido, juego; alianza, boda, casamiento; certamen, contienda, combate, lucha, concurso; apuesta, semejante, igual; pareja, compañero; competidor, contrincante; *fencing match,* asalto de armas; *even match,* partida igual; *to meet one's match,* dar con (o encontrar) la horma de su zapato; *to be no match for,* no poder con. — *v.t.* igualar a; proporcionar; hermanar, emparejar, aparear; casar. — *v.i.* concordarse; casarse; aparearse; hermanarse, convenir; hacer juego con.

matchable, *a.* igual, proporcionado, comparable, adaptable.

match-box, *s.* fosforera, cajita de cerillas.

matchet ['mætʃət], *s.* machete.

matchless ['mætʃles], *a.* incomparable, sin igual, sin rival, sin par.

matchlessly, *adv.* incomparablemente.

matchlessness, *s.* incomparabilidad, estado de incomparable.

matchlock, *s.* mosquete, llave de mosquete.

matchmaker, *s.* fabricante de cerillas; casamentero.

mate [meit], *s.* (*fam.*) camarada, *m.f.*, compañero *o* compañera; cónyuge, consorte, *m.f.*; pareja; comensal; hermano, socio, condiscípulo; mate (en el juego de ajedrez); (*mar.*) contramaestre. — *v.t.* casar, desposar; igualar, aparear; resistir, hacer frente; competir; ajustar, asombrar, aplastar; dar jaque mate.

mateless, *a.* sin compañero, soltero, falto de consorte.

mater ['meitə], *s.f.* (*anat.*) máter; (*fam.*) madre, mamá.

material [mə'tiəriəl], *a.* material, físico, corpóreo, sustancial, esencial, principal, importante, potente, grave, serio. — *s.*

materia, asunto, material, ingrediente; género; *raw material,* materia prima.

materialism, *s.* materialismo.

materialist, *s.* materialista, *m.f.*

materialistic, *a.* materialista.

materiality [mætiəri'æliti], *s.* materialidad, corporeidad.

materialization, *s.* encarnación.

materialize [mə'tiəriəlaiz], *v.t.* materializar, exteriorizar, dar cuerpo. — *v.i.* hacerse corpóreo, tomar cuerpo.

materially [mə'tiəriəli], *adv.* materialmente, esencialmente.

materialness, *s.* materialidad, importancia.

maternal [mə'təːnəl], *a.* maternal, materno.

maternally, *adv.* maternalmente.

maternity [mə'təːniti], *s.* maternidad.

math [mɑθ], *s.* cosecha del heno; *aftermath,* retoño del heno, segunda siega; resultados, consecuencias, repercusiones.

mathematic [mæθə'mætik], **mathematical** [mæθə'mætikəl], *a.* matemático.

mathematically, *adv.* matemáticamente.

mathematician [mæθəmə'tiʃən], *s.* matemático.

mathematics [mæθə'mætiks], *s.pl.* matemática(s).

matin ['mætin], *s.* (*ant.*) mañana. — *a.* matutino.

matinal ['mætinəl], *a.* matinal, matutino.

matinée ['mætinei], *s.* (*teat.*) función de tarde.

matins ['mætinz], *s.* maitines.

matrice ['mætris], **matrix** ['mætriks], *s.* matriz, *f.*; (*anat.*) útero; (*impr.*) matriz, *f.*, molde; (*biol.*) substancia intercelular; (*geol.*) quijo.

matricidal, *a.* relativo al matricidio.

matricide ['mætrisaid], *s.* matricidio; matricida, *m.f.*

matricula [mə'trikjuːlə], *s.* matrícula.

matriculate, *v.t., v.i.* matricular(se). — *s., a.* matriculado.

matriculation [mətrikjuː'leiʃən], *s.* matrícula, matriculación; empadronamiento.

matrimonial [mætri'mouniəl], *a.* matrimonial, marital, conyugal.

matrimonially, *adv.* matrimonialmente.

matrimony ['mætriməni], *s.* matrimonio, casamiento; juego de naipes entre cinco o más personas.

matrix, *s.* [MATRICE].

matron ['meitrən], *s.f.* matrona, directora de un hospital o instituto; madre de familia; ama de llaves.

matronize, *v.t.* aparecer o dar la apariencia de matrona; acompañar a una soltera a bailes, reuniones, etc.

matt [mæt], *s., a.* mate.

matte [mæt], *a.* mate de cobre.

matter ['mætə], *s.* materia; cuerpo, substancia, cosa; quehacer; causa, razón, sujeto, objeto, ocasión; motivo; cuestión, proposición, negocio, asunto; hecho; suma, cantidad; entidad, consecuencia, importancia; (*med.*) pus; (*impr.*) tipo compuesto; *What is the matter?* ¿De qué se trata? ¿Qué pasa? *What is the matter with you?* ¿Qué tiene Vd.? ¿Qué le pasa a Vd.? *no matter,* no importa; *What matter?* ¿Qué importa? *a light (o small) matter,* poca cosa; *matter of course,* cosa natural; *matter of fact,* hecho, cosa hecha, cosa positiva, realidad;

as a matter of fact, en realidad. — *v.i.* importar, convenir, ser de consecuencia, hacer al caso; (*med.*) supurar, formarse pus.

matterless, *a.* sin importancia, fútil.

matting, *s.* estera, esterado; (*mar.*) empalletado.

mattock ['mætɔk], *s.* azadón de peto; piqueta, zapapico.

mattress ['mætres], *s.* colchón; *spring mattress*, colchón de muelles.

maturant, *s., a.* (*agr.*) madurativo, madurante.

maturate ['mætjuːreit], *v.t.* madurar; (*med.*) hacer madurar, hacer supurar. — *v.i.* madurar; (*med.*) supurar francamente.

maturation, *s.* maduración; (*med.*) supuración.

maturative, *a.* madurativo.

mature [mə'tjuːəɹ], *a.* maduro, sazonado; (*fig.*) maduro, juicioso, completo, acabado; (*com.*) pagadero, vencido. — *v.t.* hacer madurar, madurar, sazonar. — *v.i.* madurar(se); (*com.*) vencer, cumplirse (un plazo).

matureness [mə'tjuːəɹnes], **maturity** [mə'tjuːriti], *s.* madurez, maduración, edad madura; (*com.*) vencimiento.

matutinal [mə'tjuːtinəl], *a.* matutino.

mat-weed, *s.* esparto.

maudlin ['mɔːdlin], *a.* calamocano, algo ebrio; sensiblero, chocho, lelo, calamocano.

maugre ['mɔːgəɹ], *adv.* (*ant.*) a pesar de, no obstante.

maul [mɔːl], *s.* mazo, maza, porra, machota; (*mar.*) mandarria. — *v.t.* apalear, aporrear, macear, maltratar.

maulstick ['mɔːlstik, 'mɑːlstik], *s.* (*pint.*) bastoncillo, tiento.

maund [mɔːnd], *s.* cesto, canastillo.

maunder, *v.t.* murmurar, gruñir, refunfuñar, quejarse; mendigar.

maunderer, *s.* murmurador, regañón.

Maundy ['mɔːndi], *s.* (*igl.*) mandato, lavatorio; *Maundy Thursday*, jueves santo.

mausoleum [mɔːso'liəm], *s.* mausoleo, panteón.

mauve [mouv], *s.* malva; color de malva. — *a.* de color de malva, púrpura o lila.

mavis ['meivis], *s.* malvis, zorzal.

maw [mɔː], *s.* cuajar; molleja, buche; (*despec.*) el estómago humano; (*vulg.*) la boca.

mawkish ['mɔːkiʃ], *a.* sensiblero, ñoño, lelo; (*ant.*) insípido, nauseabundo.

mawkishness, *s.* sensiblería, ñoñez; (*ant.*) insipidez, náusea.

maw-seed, *s.* simiente de adormideras.

maw-worm, *s.* lombriz, *f.*

maxilla [mək'zilə], *s.* hueso maxilar.

maxillar, maxillary, *a.* maxilar.

maxim ['mæksim], *s.* máxima, apotegma, aforismo.

maximum ['mæksiməm], *s.* máximum, máximo. — *a.* máximo, mayor.

may [mei], *v. auxil.* (*pret.* **might**) poder(se); ser posible, tener permiso; tener licencia, libertad, facultad; ser lícito, legal, permitido; tener el poder moral; contingencia, incertidumbre; *it may be*, puede ser o se puede. — *s.* (mes de) mayo; (*fig.*) juventud, primavera de la vida. — *v.t.* coger flores de mayo.

may-apple, *s.* mandrágora.

maybe [mei'biː], **mayhap** [mei'hæp], *adv.* acaso, quizá(s), tal vez.

may-beetle, *s.* saltón.

may-blossom, *s.* espina blanca, maya.

May-day ['meidei], *s.* día primero de mayo.

may-flower, *s.* maya, flor de mayo.

may-fly, *s.* mosca de mayo.

may-lily, *s.* lirio de los valles.

mayonnaise [meiə'neiz], *s.* salsa mayonesa.

mayor [meəɹ], *s.* alcalde.

mayoralty ['meərəlti], *s.* alcaldía, funciones de alcalde.

mayoress ['meəres], *s.f.* alcaldesa, corregidora; mujer o hija del alcalde.

maypole, *s.* cucaña, árbol de mayo.

may-weed, *s.* manzanilla loca.

mazard ['mæzɑːd], *s.* (*bot.*) guinda.

mazarine ['mæzərin], *s., a.* color azul subido.

maze [meiz], *s.* laberinto; (*fig.*) enredo, embolismo, confusión, duda, perplejidad. — *v.t.* descarriar, extraviar; confundir, asombrar. — *v.i.* vacilar.

mazurka [mə'zɑːkə], *s.* mazurca.

mazy ['meizi], *a.* confuso, perplejo, embrollado, embarazado.

me [miː], *pron. pers.* me, a mí; *with me*, conmigo.

mead [miːd], *s.* aguamiel, hidromel, meloja.

mead [miːd] (*poét.*), **meadow** ['medou], *s.* prado, pradera, vega; *meadow land*, pastos.

meadow-saffron, *s.* villorita, quitameriendas, cólquico.

meadow-sweet, *s.* (*bot.*) ulmaria, barba de cabra.

meadowy, *a.* de pradera; lleno de prados.

meagre ['miːgəɹ], *a.* magro, flaco, pobre, cuaresmal, enjuto, escaso, exiguo.

meagreness, *s.* flacura, flaqueza, pobreza, escasez.

meal [miːl], *s.* harina; comida, sustento; (*prov.*) la leche producida por una vaca en un ordeño. — *v.i.* tomar una comida.

mealiness, *s.* melosidad; calidad harinosa.

meal-man, *s.m.* harinero.

meal-tub, *s.* arcón para harina.

meal-worm, *s.* gusanillo de harina.

mealy, *a.* harinoso, farináceo; meloso; *mealy-mouthed*, hipócrita, doble, falso, mojigato.

mean [miːn], *a.* bajo, inferior, ruin, sórdido, abyecto, vil; basto, humilde, pobre, abatido; despreciable, insignificante, indigno, mezquino, mediano, tacaño, servil, vulgar; medio, del medio, mediano; intermedio, intermediario. — *s.* medio, medianía, mediocridad. — *pl.* **means**, medio, modo, forma, expediente; diligencia; instrumento, arbitrio; medios, dinero, renta, fondos, recursos, caudal; *by all means*, sin falta, no faltaba más; sin duda; *by fair means*, por la suavidad, o por medios lícitos; *by foul means*, por la fuerza o por malos medios; *by no means*, de ningún modo, ni por sombra; *by means of*, por medio de; *by this* (o *that*) *means*, de este modo, por este medio; *by some means or other*, de una manera u otra; *to be a man of means*, tener cuartos; *to be a man de medios*.

mean, *v.t., v.i.* (*pret. y p.p.* **meant**) significar, querer decir, decir en serio, dar a entender; implicar; intentar; pretender, proponerse; *to mean well*, tener buenas intenciones; *well-meaning*, bien intencionado.

meander [mi'ændəɹ], *s.* laberinto, meandro. — *v.i.* serpentear, serpear, errar, vagar; divagar.

meandering, *a.* serpentino.

meaning ['mi:niŋ], *s.* significado, acepción, significación, sentido; fin, intención, designio; *double meaning*, sentido doble, equívoco, ambigüedad.

meaningless, *a.* insignificante, sin sentido, insensato.

meanness ['mi:nnis], *s.* mediocridad, mezquindad, roñería, inferioridad, humildad; villanía, vileza, bajeza; tacañería; bastardía, infamia.

meant [ment], *pret. y p.p.* [MEAN].

meantime [mi:n'taim], **meanwhile** [mi:n-'wail], *adv.* en el intervalo, mientras tanto, entretanto. — *s.* ínterin.

measled, *a.* roñoso; (cerdos y bueyes) enfermo de sarampión.

measles ['mi:zəlz], *s.* sarampión, rubéola; roña (en cerdos, etc., causada por la lombriz solitaria).

measly ['mi:zli], *a.* roñoso; (*fam.*) pobre, despreciable, insignificante.

measurable ['meʒərəbəl], *a.* mensurable; moderado.

measurableness, *s.* mensurabilidad.

measurably, *adv.* moderadamente; mesuradamente.

measure ['meʒəɹ], *s.* medida, dimensión, volumen, capacidad, cantidad, tamaño, extensión; (*ret.*) cantidad de las sílabas en los versos; metro, cadencia; compás; modo, grado, graduación, moderación, tasa; disposición; proporción, regla; modelo, tipo; medios, recursos; proyecto de ley; *in some measure*, de algún modo; *beyond measure*, excesivamente; *in (a) great measure*, en gran manera, en alto grado; *long measure*, medida de longitud; *square measure*, medida de superficie; *common measure*, (*mús.*) compás ordinario (de cuatro por cuatro); *to take measures*, tomar las medidas necesarias. — *v.t.* medir, mensurar, proporcionar, ajustar, distribuir, señalar, graduar, juzgar, estimar, valuar; *to measure one's length*, medir el suelo. — *v.i.* medir, tomar una medida.

measured, *a.* medido, calculado, uniforme; limitado, restringido; proporcionado, rítmico, pausado, contado.

measureless, *a.* sin medida, inmensurable, inmenso.

measurement, *s.* medición, mensuración, dimensión, medida.

measurer, *s.* medidor, agrimensor.

measuring, *s.* medida, medición; agrimensura.

meat [mi:t], *s.* carne, *f.*, vianda; *chopped* o *minced meat*, picadillo; *cold meat*, fiambre; *stewed meat*, estofado, cocido; *butcher's meat*, carne de carnicería; *roast meat*, asado; *meat-saw*, serrucho; *meat-ball*, albóndiga; *meat-market*, carnicería; *meat-pie*, empanada; *meat-hook*, escarpia; *one man's meat is another man's poison*, lo que a uno cura a otro mata.

meatus [mi:'eitəs], *s.* meato.

meaty [mi:ti], *a.* carnoso.

mechanic [me'kænik], **mechanical** [me-'kænikəl], *a.* mecánico; maquinal; materialista. — *s.* mecánico.

mechanician [mekə'niʃən], *s.* mecánico, maquinista, *m.f.*

mechanics [me'kæniks], *s.* mecánica, maquinaria.

mechanism ['mekənizm], *s.* mecanismo, maquinaria.

mechanist, *s.* mecánico, maquinista, *m.f.*

mechanize ['mekənaiz], *v.t.* motorizar; construir mecánicamente.

meconate ['mekəneit], *s.* meconato.

meconic, *a.* mecónico.

meconium [me'kouniəm], *s.* meconio, alhorre.

medal ['medəl], *s.* medalla.

medallion [me'dæljən], *s.* medallón.

medallist ['medəlist], *s.* medallista, *m.f.*, colector de medallas, grabador de medallas.

meddle ['medəl], *v.i.* meterse, entremeterse, entrometerse, ingerirse, ocuparse; tocar, manosear (sin permiso o derecho); *don't meddle in what doesn't concern you*, lo que no has de comer, déjalo cocer.

meddler, *s.* intrigante, entremetido.

meddlesome, *a.* intrigante; curioso, entremetido; oficioso, intruso.

meddlesomeness, *s.* entremetimiento.

meddling, *a.* entremetido, oficioso, intrigante. — *s.* oficiosidad, intervención.

media ['mi:diə], *s.pl.* [MEDIUM]; (*anat.*) la túnica media de un vaso.

mediæval, **medieval** [medi'i:vəl], *a.* medieval.

medial ['mi:diəl], *a.* medio, del medio, del centro.

median ['mi:diən]; *a.* mediano; del medio.

mediant ['mi:diənt], *s.* (*mús.*) tercera.

mediate ['mi:dieit], *v.t.* mediar, interponerse; procurar, facilitar, diligenciar. — *v.i.* mediar, arbitrar, intervenir. — *a.* mediato, intermedio, interpuesto.

mediation [mi:di'eiʃən], *s.* mediación, intervención, interposición, intercesión, tercería.

mediatization [mi:diətai'zeiʃən], *s.* mediatización.

mediatize, *v.t.* mediatizar.

mediator ['mi:dieitəɹ], *s.* mediador, medianero, corredor, árbitro, tercero, avenidor, intercesor.

mediatorial, *a.* de mediador, medianero.

mediatorship, *s.* oficio o papel de mediador.

mediatrix [mi:di'eitriks], *s.f.* medianera.

medicable ['medikəbəl], *a.* medicable.

medical, *a.* médico, medicinal, medical, de medicina, curativo.

medically ['medikəlli], *adv.* medicalmente, en calidad de médico.

medicament [me'dikəmənt], *s.* medicamento, remedio.

medicamental, *a.* medicamentoso, curativo, sanador.

medicaster ['medikæstəɹ], *s.* medicastro, curandero, empírico, charlatán.

medicate ['medikeit], *v.t.* medicinar, hacer medicinal.

medication, *s.* medicación.

medicative, *a.* medicinal.

medicinal [me'disinəl], *a.* medicinal, médico, de médico, medicamentoso, curativo.

medicine ['medisin, 'medsin], *s.* medicina, medicamento, pócima; *medicine chest*, farmacia portátil, botiquín. — *v.t.* obrar, operar, curar.

medieval, *a.* [MEDIÆVAL].

mediocre ['mi:dioukəɹ], *a.* mediocre, mediano, ordinario, trivial.

mediocrity [mi:di'ɔkriti], *s.* mediocridad, medianía.

meditate ['mediteit], *v.t., v.i.* meditar, premeditar, idear, ponderar, reflexionar; proyectar, contemplar, tramar, considerar.

meditation, *s.* meditación, reflexión.

meditative ['mediteitiv], *a.* meditativo, contemplativo.

meditatively, *adv.* con meditación.

Mediterranean [meditə'reiniən], *a.* mediterráneo. — *s.* el mar Mediterráneo.

medium ['mi:diəm], *s.* (*pl.* **mediums, media**) medio, expediente; intermedio, intermediario; (*espiritismo*) médium, *m.f.*; (*fís.*) éter, atmósfera; (*lóg.*) término; (*mat.*) mediana; (*pint.*) medio, vehículo. — *a.* mediano, mediocre, intermedio; *medium-sized,* de tamaño (*o* grandor) mediano.

medlar ['medləɹ], *s.* níspero, níspera.

medley ['medli], *s.* mezcla, mixtura, miscelánea, mescolanza; revoltijo, fárrago. — *a.* mezclado, mixto.

medulla [me'dʌlə], *s.* tuétano, médula.

medullar, medullary, *a.* medular.

medusa [me'dju:zə], *s.* medusa, aguamar.

meed [mi:d], *s.* recompensa, premio, galardón, mérito.

meek [mi:k], *a.* suave, modesto, manso, humilde, sumiso, dócil, apacible, amable.

meeken, *v.t.* sauvizar.

meekness, *s.* suavidad, mansedumbre, modestia, humildad, docilidad.

meerschaum ['miəɹʃəm], *s.* espuma de mar; pipa de espuma de mar.

meet [mi:t], *s.* reunión *o* concurso de cazadores, lugar donde se reúnen los cazadores. — *a.* conveniente, a propósito, útil, idóneo, apto, propio. — *v.t.* (*pret.* y *p.p.* met) hacer frente a, encontrar; tocar una cosa a otra; tropezar con, hallar; citar, convocar; obtener, recibir; prevenir; pagar, honrar, saldar, sufragar; refutar; combatir con. — *v.i.* encontrarse; juntarse, reunirse, congregarse, verse; pelear, rozar, chocar; estar expuesto a; carearse, abocarse; descubrir; venir a las manos; responder; verse, empezar a conocer, entrar en tratos; *to go to meet,* ir al encuentro de; *to meet one's death,* hallar la muerte; *to meet one's expenses,* hacer frente a sus gastos; *pleased to meet you,* mucho gusto en conocerle; *to meet someone half way,* partir la diferencia; *till we meet (again),* hasta luego, hasta la vista.

meeting, *s.* encuentro, entrevista, cita, consultación, conferencia; desafío, duelo; sesión, reunión, *f.*, concurso, congreso, asamblea, junta, mitin; confluencia (de ríos).

meetly, *adv.* convenientemente, a propósito.

meetness, *s.* conveniencia, propiedad, aptitud.

megalith ['megəliθ], *s.* menhir.

megalithic, *a.* megalítico.

megalomania [megəlo'meiniə], *s.* megalomanía.

megalomaniac, *s.*, *a.* megalómano.

megaphone ['megəfoun], *s.* megáfono, portavoz, *m.*

megrim ['mi:grim], *s.* jaqueca, hemicránea.

meiosis [mai'ousis], *s.* (*ret.*) lítote, *f.*; (*pat.*) mejoramiento, reducción o atenuación en los síntomas.

melancholia [melən'kouliə], *s.* melancolía, enajenación mental.

melancholic [melən'kɔlik], **melancholy** ['melənkəli], *a.* melancólico, hipocondríaco, lúgubre, cetrino, tristón.

melancholy, *s.* melancolía, hipocondría, tristeza.

melange ['melɑ:nʒ], *s.* mezcla.

melanosis [melə'nousis], *s.* (*med.*) melanosis, *f.*, cáncer negro.

melic ['melik], *a.* mélico, lírico.

melilot ['melilot], *s.* mililoto, trébol dulce.

melinite ['melinait], *s.* melinita.

meliorate ['mi:liəreit], *v.t.* mejorar, adelantar, bonificar. — *v.i.* mejorarse.

melioration, *s.* mejora, mejoramiento, adelanto, medra.

melissa [me'lisə], *s.* melisa.

melliferous [me'lifərəs], *a.* melífero.

mellifluence, *s.* melifluidad, suavidad, dulzura.

mellifluent [me'lifluːənt], **mellifluous,** *a.* melífluo, melificado:

mellow ['melou], *a.* dulce, suave, tierno, blando; mantecoso, pastoso; meloso; sazonado, maduro; dulce, suave, melodioso; mórbido; (*fam.*) calamocano, medio borracho. — *v.t.* ablandar, suavizar, madurar; sazonar. — *v.i.* madurar(se).

mellowness, *s.* suavidad, melosidad; blandura; sazón, *f.*, madurez; pastosidad.

mellowy, *a.* dulce, blando, suave.

melodic [me'lɔdik], *a.* melódico.

melodious [me'loudiəs], *a.* melodioso. — *adv.* melodiosamente.

melodiousness, *s.* melodía.

melodist ['melodist], *s.* melodista, *m.f.*

melodize, *v.t.* hacer melodioso. — *v.i.* hacer melodía.

melodrama ['melodrɑ:mə], *s.* melodrama, *m.*

melodramatic [melodrə'mætik], *a.* melodramático.

melodramatist [melo'dræmətist], *s.* autor de melodramas.

melody ['melodi], *s.* melodía.

melon ['melən], *s.* melón; sandía.

melt [melt], *v.t.* (*p.p.* **melted, molten**) fundir, derretir, evaporar, disolver, licuar, liquidar; reducir; (*fig.*) enternecer, ablandar, aplacar; consumir, gastar, disolver, evaporar; *to melt a heart of stone,* ablandar las piedras. — *v.i.* fundirse, derretirse, liquidarse, desvanecerse, disiparse; (*fig.*) enternecerse, amilanarse, confundirse; *to melt into tears,* deshacerse en lágrimas, llorar a lágrima viva, (*fam.*) llorar a moco tendido.

melter, *s.* fundidor; crisol.

melting, *a.* fusorio, lo que funde, fundente. — *s.* fusión, derretimiento.

meltingly, *adv.* tiernamente.

melting-pan, *s.* cazo.

melting-pot, *s.* crisol.

melton ['meltən], *s.* chaqueta de caza, cazadora; tejido con pelusa usado para abrigos.

member ['membəɹ], *s.* miembro; individuo, socio.

membered, *a.* membrudo, fornido; (*blas.*) membrado.

membership ['membəɹʃip], *s.* sociedad, comunidad; número de socios, matrícula; calidad de socio.

membrane ['membrein], *s.* (*anat.*) membrana; trozo de pergamino.

membranaceous, membraneous, membranous, membraniform, *a.* membranoso, membranáceo, membraniforme.

memento [me'mentou], *s.* memento, memoria, recuerdo.

memoir ['memwɑːɹ], *s.* memoria, relación, informe.

memorable ['memərəbəl], *a.* memorable.

memorably, *adv.* memorablemente.

memorandum [memo'rændəm], *pl.* **memoranda**, *s.* memoria, nota, apunte, memorándum.

memorial [me'mɔːriəl], *s.* memorial, recuerdo, nota; monumento (conmemorativo); memorial, petición, súplica, instancia; (*for.*) memorial. — *a.* conmemorativo.

memorialist, *s.* memorialista, *m.f.*, suplicante, solicitante.

memorialize, *v.t.* hacer (*o* presentar) una petición.

memorize ['memoraiz], *v.t.* conservar memoria de, recordar, memorar, aprender de memoria.

memory ['meməri], *s.* memoria, reminiscencia, recuerdo; retentiva; recordación, conmemoración, fama.

men [men], *s.pl.* [MAN].

menace ['menəs], *v.t.*, *v.i.* amenazar. — *s.* amenaza.

menacer, *s.* amenazador.

menacing ['menəsiŋ], *a.* amenazante, amenazador.

menacingly, *adv.* de una manera amenazadora.

ménage ['menɑːʒ], *s.* familia; manejo de una casa, economía doméstica.

menagerie [men'ɑːdʒəri, men'ædʒəri], *s.* colección o casa de fieras.

mend [mend], *v.t.* enmendar, reformar, rehacer, retocar, mejorar; apedazar, componer, recomponer, remendar, reparar; zurcir; corregir, subsanar, enmendar, remediar. — *v.i.* enmendarse, corregirse, reformarse; curarse, restablecerse, reponerse. — *s.* reforma, mejoría; remiendo; zurcido.

mendable, *a.* corregible, reparable, componible, reformable.

mendacious [men'deiʃəs], *a.* mentiroso, mendaz, engañoso, embustero, falso.

mendaciousness, mendacity, *s.* engaño, embuste; falsedad, mentira.

mender, *s.* componedor, reparador, reformador.

mendicancy, *s.* mendicidad, mendiguez.

mendicant ['mendikənt], *s.*, *a.* mendigo, mendicante.

mendicity [men'disiti], *s.* mendicidad, mendiguez.

menhir ['menhiəɹ], *s.* menhir.

menial ['miːniəl], *a.* doméstico, servil, bajo. — *s.* doméstico, criado o criada, lacayo.

meninges [men'indʒiːz], *s.pl.* [MENINX].

meningitis [menin'dʒaitis], *s.* meningitis, *f.*

meninx ['meniŋks], *s.* meninge, *f.*

meniscus [me'niskəs], *s.* (*ópt.* y *fís.*) menisco; (*geom.*) lúnula.

menology [me'nɔlodʒi], *s.* menologio.

menopause ['menoupɔːz], *s.* menopausia.

menorrhagia [meno'reidʒə], *s.* menorragia.

mensal ['mensəl], *a.* lo que pertenece a la mesa; mensual, cada mes.

menses ['mensiːz], *s.* menstruo.

menstrual ['menstruːəl], *a.* menstrual, mensual.

menstruate, *v.i.* menstruar.

menstruation, *s.* menstruación.

menstruous ['menstruːəs], *a.* menstruo, menstruoso, mensual.

menstruum ['menstruːəm], *s.* (*quím.*) menstruo, disolvente, excipiente líquido.

mensurability, *s.* mensurabilidad.

mensurable ['menʃuːrəbəl], *a.* mensurable.

mensural ['menʃuːrəl], *a.* mensural.

mensuration, *s.* mensura, medición, medida; mensura (ramo de las matemáticas).

mental ['mentəl], *a.* mental, intelectual, ideal, moral; *mental home* o *hospital*, manicomio.

mentha ['menθə], *s.* menta.

menthol ['menθəl], *s.* mentol.

mention ['menʃən], *s.* mención, alusión, recuerdo. — *v.t.* mencionar, mentar, hacer mención de, hablar de.

mentionable, *a.* mencionable.

mentor ['mentəɹ], *s.* mentor.

menu ['menjuː], *s.* lista de platos, carta, menú.

mephitic [me'fitik], **mephitical**, *a.* mefítico.

mephitis [me'faitis], *s.* mefitis, *f.*

mercantile ['məːɹkəntail], *a.* mercantil, mercante, comercial.

mercantilism, *s.* mercantilismo.

mercenarily, *adv.* mercenariamente.

mercenariness, *s.* venalidad.

mercenary ['məːɹsenəri], *a.* mercenario, interesado, venal. — *s.* mercenario.

mercer ['məːɹsəɹ], *s.* mercero, sedero.

mercerize ['məːɹsəraiz], *v.t.* mercerizar.

mercership, *s.* mercería, sedería.

mercery, *s.* mercería, sedería.

merchandise ['məːɹtʃəndaiz], *s.* mercadería, mercancía. — *v.i.*, *v.t.* traficar, comerciar, negociar.

merchant, ى. mercader, mercantil, mercante, negociante, comerciante, traficante. — *a.* mercantil, mercante, mercader, comercial; *merchant iron*, hierro en barras; *merchant-like*, mercantil; *merchant ship* o *merchantman*, buque mercante; *merchant service* o *navy*, marina mercante.

merchantable, *a.* vendible, comerciable, de buena calidad, de recibo, corriente.

merciful ['məːɹsiful], *a.* clemente, misericordioso, benigno, piadoso, compasivo.

mercifulness, *s.* misericordia, piedad, compasión, clemencia, indulgencia.

merciless, *a.* sin misericordia, sin piedad, inhumano, desapiadado, desalmado.

mercilessly, *adv.* sin misericordia, sin piedad, cruelmente.

mercilessness, ى. falta de misericordia, inhumanidad, crueldad.

mercurial [məɹ'kjuːriəl], *a.* mercurial, mercúrico, de mercurio; (*fig.*) activo, vivo, jovial, volátil, versátil. — *s.* (*med.*) preparación mercurial.

mercurialize, *v.t.* someter a un tratamiento mercurial.

mercury ['məːɹkjuːri], *s.* mercurio, azogue; (*bot.*) mercurial; (*fig.*) mensajero, gacetero; (*fig.*) ardor, vivacidad, desparpajo, desembarazo; gaceta o papel periódico; (*astr.*, *mit.*) Mercurio.

mercy ['məːɹsi], *s.* misericordia, clemencia, gracia, perdón, compasión, piedad, merced; *to be at the mercy of*, estar a la merced de; *to cry (for) mercy*, pedir gracia; *to show mercy*, usar de misericordia.

mercy-seat, *s.* propiciatorio.
mere [miəɹ], *a.* mero, solo, simple, franco, puro, sin mezcla, nada más que. — *s.* estanque, lago, laguna; límite, lindero.
merely, *adv.* simplemente, meramente, puramente, sólo, solamente, nada más que.
meretricious [meri'triʃəs], *a.* de mal gusto, charro, de oropel, chillón; (*ant.*) meretricio.
meretriciousness, *s.* mal gusto; (*ant.*) putería, puñatería.
merganser [məɹ'gænsəɹ], *s.* mergo, mergánsar.
merge [məːɹdʒ], *v.t.* fundir, combinar, unir, sumergir; fusionar; apagar, absorber. — *v.i.* hundirse, estar hundido; fundirse, mezclarse, absorberse; fusionarse.
meridian [me'ridiən], *s.* (*astr., geog.*) meridiano; mediodía; auge, apogeo, cenit. — *a.* meridiano, de mediodía.
meridional, *a.* meridional.
meridionally, *adv.* hacia el mediodía, al mediodía, al sur.
meringue [me'ræŋ], *s.* merengue.
merino [me'riːnou], *a.* merino, hecho de merino. — *s.* paño merino, carnero merino.
merit ['merit], *s.* mérito, merecimiento. — *v.t.* merecer, ser digno de.
meritorious [meri'toːriəs], *a.* meritorio, benemérito.
meritoriously, *adv.* meritoriamente, merecidamente.
meritoriousness, *adv.* merecimiento, mérito.
merle [məːɹl], *s.* (*poét.*) mirlo, merla.
merlin ['məːɹlin], *s.* (*orn.*) merlín, esmerejón.
merlon, *s.* merlón, almena.
merluce ['məːɹluːs], *s.* merluza.
mermaid ['məːɹmeid], *s.f.* sirena.
merman ['məːɹmən], *s.* tritón.
Merovingian [mero'viŋgiən], *a.* merovingio.
merrily ['merili], *adv., s.* regocijadamente, jovialmente.
merriment, merriness, *s.* júbilo, regocijo, diversión; fiesta, zambra.
merry ['meri], *a.* divertido, jovial, festivo, regocijado, gozoso, placentero, risueño; *to be merry,* estar de fiesta, estar de bulla; *to make merry,* regodearse, regocijarse, divertirse.
merry-andrew, *s.* bufón, chocarrero.
merry-go-round ['merigouraund], *s.* caballitos, tiovivo.
merry-hearted, *a.* de humor jovial.
merry-make, *v.i.* regodearse, regocijarse.
merry-making, *s.* regodeo, holgorio, gaudeamus, (*fam.*) juerga, júbilo; fiesta, festividades.
merry-thought ['meriθɔːt], *s.* hueso de la pechuga (de una ave).
mersion ['məːɹʃən], *s.* inmersión.
meseems [me'siːmz], *v. impers.* (*poét., ant.*) tengo para mí, paréceme.
mesenteric [mesən'terik], *a.* mesentérico.
mesentery ['mesəntəri], *s.* mesenterio.
mesh [meʃ], *s.* malla de red, obra de malla; lazo, trampa; (*mec.*) engranaje. — *pl.* **meshes,** red, randa. — *v.t.* coger en la red, enredar. — *v.i.* enredarse.
meshy, *a.* hecho de malla; reticular.
mesial ['miːziəl], *a.* mediano.
meslin, *s.* tranquillón, comuña, mixtura.
mesmeric [mez'merik], *a.* mesmérico, relativo al mesmerismo.

mesmerism ['mezmərizm], *s.* mesmerismo, hipnotismo.
mesmerist, mesmerizer, *s.* magnetizador.
mesmerization, *s.* mesmerización.
mesmerize, *v.t.* hipnotizar, magnetizar; fascinar, hechizar.
mesmerizer, *s.* persona que hipnotiza.
mesocarp ['miːzokɑːɹp], *s.* mesocarpio.
mesocolon [meso'koulən], *s.* mesocolon.
mess [mes], *s.* manjar, plato, porción, ración, cantidad; desorden, revoltijo, confusión; suciedad; rancho; embarazo; (*mil.*) mesa, comida; *to make a mess,* hacer embrollos. — *v.t.* dar de comer, dar rancho; desordenar, desarreglar; *to mess up,* desordenar; echar a perder. — *v.i.* comer en rancho, hacer rancho, arrancharse; desordenar, hacer un revoltijo.
message ['mesidʒ], *s.* mensaje, comunicación, recado, encargo, comisión, aviso, parte, *m.*
messenger ['mesendʒəɹ], *s.* mensajero, recadero, mandadero, portero, nuncio, heraldo; mozo de esquina; precursor; (*mar.*) aparejo para levar el ancla.
messieurs, messrs. ['mesəɹz], *s.pl.* señores.
messmate ['mesmeit], *s.* compañero de rancho, comensal.
messuage ['mesjuːidʒ], *s.* (*for.*) casa de vivienda y dependencias; menaje, ajuar de casa.
met [met], *pret., p.p.* [MEET].
metabolism [me'tæbolizm], *s.* metabolismo.
metacarpal [metə'kɑːɹpəl], *a.* metacarpiano, del metacarpo.
metacarpus, *s.* metacarpo.
metacentre [metə'sentəɹ], *s.* metacentro.
metachromatism [metə'krɔmətizm], *s.* cambio de color.
metachronism, *s.* metacronismo.
metage ['miːtidʒ], *s.* medición de carbón.
metal ['metəl], *s.* metal; aleación, liga; grava (de caminos); (*f.c.*) balasto; vidrio en fusión; (*fig.*) bravura, valor, esencia, cualidad esencial, temple; *metal work,* metalistería; *metal worker,* metalario.
metalepsis [metə'lepsis], *s.* metalepsis, *f.*
metaleptic [metə'leptik], *a.* metaléptico.
metaleptically, *adv.* por metalepsis, por transposición.
metalled, (*f.c.*) terraplenado; cubierto de grava.
metallic [me'tælik], *a.* metálico.
metalliferous [metə'lifərəs], *a.* metalífero.
metalline ['metəlain], *a.* metálico.
metallist ['metəlist], *s.* metalario.
metallization, *s.* metalización.
metallize, *v.t.* metalizar.
metallographer [metə'lɔgrəfəɹ], *s.* metalógrafo.
metallography, *s.* metalografía.
metalloid ['metəlɔid], *s., a.* metaloide.
metalloidal, *a.* metaloide.
metallurgic [metə'ləːɹdʒik], **metallurgical,** *a.* metalúrgico.
metallurgist [metə'ləːɹdʒist], *s.* metalúrgico, metalario, metalista, *m.f.*
metallurgy ['metələːɹdʒi], *s.* metalurgia, metálica.
metameric [metə'merik], *a.* metamérico.
metamorphic, *a.* metamórfico.
metamorphism [metə'mɔːɹfizm], *s.* metamorfismo.
metamorphize [metə'mɔːɹfaiz], **metamor-**

phose [metəmɔːɹˈfouz], v.t. metamorfosear.
metamorphose [metəmɔːɹˈfouz], **metamorphosis** [metəˈmɔːɹfosis], s. metamorfosis, f., metamorfosi, f.
metaphor [ˈmetəfəɹ], s. metáfora.
metaphoric [metəˈfɔrik], **metaphorical**, a. metafórico.
metaphorist, s. metaforista, m.f.
metaphrase [ˈmetəfreiz], s. metafrasis, m.f., traducción literal.
metaphrast [ˈmetəfræst], s. metafrasta, m.f., traductor literal.
metaphrastic, a. metafrástico, literal.
metaphysic [metəˈfizik], **metaphysical** [metəˈfizikəl], a. metafísico.
metaphysically, adv. metafísicamente.
metaphysician [metəfiˈziʃən], s. metafísico.
metaphysics [metəˈfiziks], s. metafísica.
metaplasm [ˈmetəplæzm], s. metaplasmo.
metastasis [metəˈstæsis], s. metástasis, f.
metathesis [metəˈθiːsis], s. metátesis, f.
mete [miːt], v.t. medir, distribuir, repartir; prorratear; ser conforme a medida. — s. medida, límite.
metempsychosis [metemsaiˈkousis], s. metempsicosis (o metempsícosis), f.
meteograph [ˈmiːtiogræf], s. meteorógrafo.
meteor [ˈmiːtiɔɹ], s. meteoro (o metéoro), estrella fugaz.
meteoric [miːtiˈɔrik], a. meteórico, meteorológico.
meteorism, s. meteorismo.
meteorite [ˈmiːtioˈrait], s. meteorito, aerolito.
meteoritic, a. meteórico.
meteorolite, s. meteorolito, meteorito.
meteorologic, meteorological, a. meteorológico.
meteorologist, s. meteorólogo, meteorologista, m.f.
meteorology [miːtioˈrɔlodʒi], s. meteorología.
meteoroscope, s. meteoroscopio.
meteorous, a. meteórico.
meter [ˈmiːtəɹ], s. medidor, mensurador, contador; gas-meter, gasómetro; contador de gas (etc.).
methane [ˈmeθein], s. metano.
metheglin [meˈθeglin], s. aguamiel, hidromel.
methinks [miˈθiŋks], v. impers. (ant.) tengo para mí, paréceme.
method [ˈmeθəd], s. método, orden, m.f., procedimiento, sistema, m., manera, regla, forma, medio; regularidad.
methodic [meˈθɔdik], **methodical** [meˈθɔdikəl], a. metódico, ordenado, sistemático.
methodism [ˈmeθodizm], s. metodismo, método.
methodist [ˈmeθodist], s. metodista, m.f.
methodistic [meθoˈdistik], a. metodístico, de metodista.
methodize, v.t. metodizar, clasificar, ordenar, arreglar metódicamente, regularizar.
methomania [meθoˈmeiniə], s. metomanía.
methought [miˈθɔːt], pret. del v. impers. methinks.
methyl [ˈmeθil], s. metilo.
methylene [ˈmeθiliːn], s. metileno.
methylic [meˈθilik], a. metílico.
metonymical, a. metonímico.
metonymy [meˈtɔnimi], s. metonimia.
metope [ˈmetoup], s. (arq.) métopa; (zool.) frente, f., faz, f.
metoposcopy [metəˈpɔskopi], s. metoposcopia.

metre [ˈmiːtəɹ], s. metro.
metric [ˈmetrik], **metrical** [ˈmetrikəl], a. métrico.
metrically, adv. métricamente.
metrician, metrist, s. metrista, m.f., versificador.
metrological, a. metrológico.
metrology [meˈtrɔlodʒi], s. metrología.
metronome [ˈmetronoum], s. metrónomo.
metropolis [meˈtrɔpolis], s. metrópoli, f.
metropolitan [metroˈpɔlitən], s., a. metropolitano.
metrorrhagia [metroˈreidʒiə], s. metrorragia.
mettle [metəl], s. valor, bravura, bizarría, coraje; vivacidad, brío, temple, fuego.
mettlesome, adv. vivo, vivaz, ardiente, fogoso, brioso.
mettlesomeness, s. vivacidad, brío; fuego, ardor.
mew [mjuː], s. (orn.) gaviota (de la familia de láridos); maullido, maúllo (del gato); jaula para halcones cuando mudan; encierro, prisión; establo, caballeriza. — pl. las caballerizas reales de Londres; casa de vecindad. — v.t. enjaular, mudar sus plumas las aves; (fig.) encerrar, encarcelar. — v.i. maullar o miar el gato; estar de muda los animales.
mewing [mjuːiŋ], s. maullido, maído; muda.
mewl [mjuːl], v.i. llorar como niño, chillar; maullar (el gato). — s. lloro de niño.
mewling, s. lloro de niño; maullido.
Mexican [ˈmeksikən], s., a. mejicano.
mezzanine [ˈmezəniːn, ˈmezənin], s. entresuelo.
mezzotint [ˈmedzotint], s. media tinta; estampa de humo.
mi [miː], s. (mús.) mi, la nota E.
miaow [miˈau], s. miau, onomatopeya del maúllo del gato. — v.t. maullar (el gato).
miasma [maiˈæzmə], s. (pl. **miasmata**) miasma, m.
miasmal, miasmatic, a. miasmático, abundante en miasma.
mica [ˈmaikə], s. mica.
micaceous [maiˈkeiʃəs], a. micáceo.
mice [mais], s.pl. [MOUSE].
Michaelmas [ˈmikəlməs], s. día de San Miguel, sanmiguelada.
miche [mitʃ], v.i. esconderse.
mickle [ˈmikəl], a. (prov.) mucho; grande.
microbe [ˈmaikroub], s. microbio.
microbial, microbic, a. microbiano.
microbicide, s. microbicida.
microbiology [maikrobaiˈɔlodʒi], s. microbiología.
microcephalia [maikroseˈfeiliə], **microcephaly** [maikroˈsefali], s. microcefalia.
microcephalic, microcephalous, a. microcéfalo.
micrococcal [maikroˈkɔkəl], a. microcócal.
micrococcus, s. micrococo.
microcosm [ˈmaikrokɔzm], s. microcosmo.
microcosmical, a. microcósmico.
micrograph [ˈmaikrogræf], s. micrógrafo.
micrographer, micrographist, s. micrógrafo.
micrography [maiˈkrɔgrəfi], s. micrografía.
micrometer [maiˈkrɔmetəɹ], s. micrómetro.
micrometric, micrometrical, a. micrométrico.
micrometry, s. micrometría.
microphone [ˈmaikrofoun], s. micrófono.

microphyte ['maikrofait], *s.* micrófito.
microscope ['maikroskoup], *s.* microscopio.
microscopic [maikro'skɔpik], **microscopical** [maikro'skɔpikəl], *a.* microscópico.
microscopist, *s.* microscopista, *m.f.*
microscopy [mai'krɔskəpi], *s.* microscopia.
micturition, *s.* micción.
micturate ['miktjuːreit], *v.i.* orinar.
mid [mid], *a. (superl.* **midmost)** medio, de medio. — *prep. (poét.)* entre, en medio de; a mediados de. — *s.* medio, centro; *mid-course*, medio camino, o media carrera; *mid-Lent*, media cuaresma; *mid-seas*, mar abierto; *mid-way*, medio camino; *mid-week*, en medio de la semana; *in mid-winter*, en pleno invierno.
midday ['middei], *s.* mediodía, *m.* — *a.* del mediodía, meridional.
midden ['midən], *s.* muladar, albañal, basurero.
middle ['midəl], *a.* medio, del medio, central, del centro; intermediar, intermedio; *Middle Ages*, edad media; *middle finger*, dedo del corazón. — *s.* medio, mitad, mediados, centro, corazón, promedio, cintura; *in the middle of May*, a mediados de Mayo.
middle-aged, *a.* de mediana edad, de edad madura.
middleman ['midəlmæn], *s.* agente de negocios; corredor.
middlemost ['midəlmoust], *a.* lo más céntrico, colocado en el centro.
middle-sized, *a.* de mediano tamaño, de mediana estatura.
middling ['midliŋ], *a.* mediano, regular, mediocre, moderado, ordinario, pasadero.
middy ['midi], *s.m.* cadete de marina.
midge [midʒ], *s.* mosquito, mosca de agua; *(fig.)* enano.
midget ['midʒit], *s.* mosquita; chiquillo; enanito.
midland ['midlənd], *a.* del centro, del interior de un país. — *pl.* **Midlands**, los condados del centro de Inglaterra.
midnight ['midnait], *s.* media noche. — *a.* de medianoche, nocturno.
midrib ['midrib], *s.* nervadura mediana.
midriff ['midrif], *s.* diafragma, *m.*
midship ['midʃip], *s.* medio de un buque. — *a.* en medio del buque.
midshipman ['midʃipmən], *s.* aspirante de marina; guardiamarina, *m.*
midships ['midʃips], *s.pl.* cuaderna maestra. — *adv.* al través.
midst [midst], *s.* centro, medio; *in the midst of*, en medio de. — *prep. (poét.)* entre.
midsummer ['midsʌmər], *s.* medio del verano, pleno verano, solsticio estival, fiesta de San Juan.
midway, *a., adv.* en medio del camino, a medio camino.
midwife ['midwif], *s.f. (pl.* **midwives)** partera, comadre, *f.*, comadrona. — *v.t.* partear. — *v.i.* ejercer la profesión de comadrona o partera.
midwifery ['midwifri], *s.* obstetricia, partería.
midwinter ['midwintər], *s.* pleno invierno.
mien [miːn], *s.* aire, semblante; porte, facha.
miff [mif], *v.t.* desagradar, ofender, enojar, enfadar. — *s.* bochorno; disgusto.
might [mait], *v. pret. cond.* [MAY]. — *s.* fuerza, vigor, poder; *with all his might* o *with might*

and main, con todas sus fuerzas, a puño cerrado, a más no poder.
mightily, *adv.* fuertemente, poderosamente, enérgicamente.
mightiness, *s.* potencia, grandeza, fuerza, poder, poderío.
mighty, *a.* fuerte, poderoso, potente, grande, vigoroso, eficaz; enorme; valiente; importante; *(fam.)* mucho, muy, extremamente.
mignonette [minjo'net], *s. (bot.)* reseda.
migrate ['maigreit], *v.i.* emigrar.
migrating, *a.* migratorio.
migration, *s.* migración, emigración.
migratory ['maigrətəri], *a.* migratorio, nómada, peregrino; *migratory bird*, pájaro de paso.
Milanese [milə'niːz], *s., a.* milanés.
milch [miltʃ], *a.* lechero, lactífero, que da leche.
mild [maild], *a.* dulce, blando, suave, benigno, indulgente, moderado, apacible, dócil, manso; ligero, leve.
mildew ['mildjuː], *s.* mildeu, mildiu, moho, añublo, borra, tizón, voya, pelusilla; mancha de humedad. — *v.t., v.i.* atizonarse (el trigo), añublar(se), enmohecer(se).
mildness, *s.* dulzura, suavidad, afabilidad, lenidad, apacibilidad, mansedumbre, indulgencia.
mile [mail], *s.* milla (1·609 m); *geographical* o *nautical mile* (1·852 m).
mileage ['mailidʒ], *s.* distancia en millas, kilometraje.
milepost, milestone, *s.* piedra millera (o miliar), mojón.
milesian [mai'liːʒən], *s., a.* irlandés, hibernés, hibernico.
milfoil ['milfɔil], *s.* cientoenrama, milenrama, milhojas.
miliaria [mili'ɛəriə], *s.* fiebre miliar.
miliary, *a.* miliar.
militancy, *s.* estado de militante, belicosidad.
militant ['militənt], *a.* militante, combatiente, guerrero, belicoso.
militarily, *adv.* militarmente.
militarism ['militərizm], *s.* militarismo.
military ['militəri], *a.* militar, marcial, guerrero, bélico, de guerra. — *s.* soldados, soldadesca, milicia, tropas.
militate ['militeit], *v.i.* militar, combatir, pelear, oponerse.
militia [mi'liʃə], *s.* milicia, guardia nacional.
militiaman [mi'liʃəmən], *s.* miliciano.
milk [milk], *s.* leche, *f.*; jugo de ciertas plantas; *buttermilk*, suero de leche; *milk of almonds*, almendrada; *milk-and-water*, *(fam.)* de carácter débil, vacilante. — *v.t.* ordeñar; extraer de; *(fig.)* apurar. — *v.i.* dar leche.
milk-can, *s.* lechera, lecherón.
milker, *s.* ordeñador.
milk-fever, *s.* fiebre láctea.
milkiness, *s.* lactescencia, propiedad láctea; suavidad, dulzura.
milkmaid, *s.f.* lechera.
milkman, *s.m.* lechero.
milk-pail, *s.* ordeñadero, colodra.
milkpan, *s.* lechera, ordeñadero.
milksop, *s.* sopa de leche; *(fig.)* marica, *m.*
milk-thistle, *s.* titimalo.
milk-vetch, *s.* astrágalo, regaliz silvestre.
milkwoman, *s.f.* lechera.
milkwort, *s.* enforbio, polígala.

milky, *a.* lechoso, de leche, lactífero, lacticíneo, lácteo; *Milky Way,* vía láctea.

mill [mil], *s.* molino; fábrica; taller; tejeduría, hilandería, fábrica de hilados o tejidos; (*E.U.*) milésimo de dólar; rueda de lapidario; (*fam.*) pugilato; *coffee-mill,* molinillo de café; *horse-mill,* tahona; *rolling-mill,* laminador; *saw-mill,* molino de aserrar; *water-mill,* molino de agua; *wind-mill,* molino de viento; *fulling-mill,* batán; *mill-race,* canal o cañal de molino; *to go through the mill,* saber, o conocer, o aprender una cosa a fondo. — *v.t.* moler, majar, desmenuzar, pulverizar; acordonar o labrar el canto de las monedas; (*fam.*) dar puñetazos; *to put a person through the mill,* hacer sufrir a uno.

mill-board, *s.* cartón doble, cartón de encuadernar.

mill-dam, *s.* esclusa, represa, dique.

mill-dust, *s.* harija.

millenarian [mile'nɛəriən], **millenary,** *s., a.* milenario.

millennial [mil'eniəl], *a.* milenario.

millennium [mi'leniəm], *s.* milenario, mileno.

milleped ['miliped], *s.* cientopiés, ciempiés, miriápodo, escolopendra.

millepore ['milipɔːɹ], *s.* miléporo.

miller ['miləɹ], *s.* molinero, molendero, tahonero; mariposa nocturna con las alas blanquecinas y empolvadas; *miller's thumb,* (*ictiol.*) gobio.

millesimal [mi'leziməl], *a.* milésimo.

millet ['milit], *s.* mijo.

mill-hand, *s.* obrero (de molino).

mill-hopper, *s.* tolva de molino.

milliard ['miljəd], *s.* mil millones.

milliary ['miljəri], *a.* miliario. — *s.* piedra miliar.

milligram, milligramme ['miligræm], *s.* miligramo.

millilitre ['milili:tər], *s.* mililitro.

millimetre ['milimi:tər], *s.* milímetro.

milliner ['milinəɹ], *s.* sombrero. — *a.* modista, *m.f.*

millinery ['milinəri], *s.* modas, ocupación de una modista; cintas o flores para los sombreros de señora.

milling, *s.* molienda, acción de moler; (*monedas*) acordonamiento, cordón, cordoncillo, acuñación; (*fam.*) paliza, puñetazos.

million ['miljən], *s.* millón.

millionaire [miljə'nɛəɹ], *s.* millonario.

millionary, *a.* millonario.

millioned, *a.* amillonado.

millionth ['miljənθ], *a.* millonésimo.

mill-pond, *s.* charca, alberca.

millstone, *s.* muela de molino, piedra molar; *to have a millstone about one's neck,* tener la cuerda al cuello.

mill-wheel, *s.* rueda de molino.

millwright, *s.* constructor de molinos.

milt [milt], *s.* bazo, lechecillas. — *v.t.* (*ictiol.*) fecundar, aovar, impregnar.

milter, *s.* pez macho.

mime [maim], *s.* mimo, mímica, pantomima; bufón, truhán, farsante. — *v.t.* mimear. — *v.i.* remedar, representar una pantomima.

mimeograph ['mimiogræf], *s.* mimeógrafo.

mimer ['maiməɹ], *s.* mimo, bufón.

mimesis [mai'mi:sis], *s.* mimesis, *f.*

mimetic [mi'metik], *a.* mimico, imitativo.

mimic ['mimik], **mimical,** *a.* mímico, burlesco, imitativo.

mimic, *s.* imitador, mimo, pantomimo, remedador, bufón. — *v.t.* imitar, remedar, contrahacer.

mimically, *adv.* mímicamente, burlescamente.

mimicry ['mimikri], *s.* bufonada, bufonería, imitación burlesca; monería, remedo, pantomima, farsa.

mimosa, *s.* mimosa.

mimosis [mi'mousis], *s.* (*med.*) semejanza.

mimulus ['mimju:ləs], *s.* mímulo.

minacious [mi'neiʃəs], *a.* amenazador.

minaret ['minəret], *s.* minarete.

minatory ['minətəri], *a.* amenazador, amenazante.

mince [mins], *v.t.* desmenuzar; picar (carne), hacer picadillo; medir (palabras); atenuar, paliar; afectar, hablar con afectación; *he does not mince matters,* no anda en cumplimientos. — *v.i.* andar con pasos menuditos; ser afectado; hablar con melindre.

mincemeat ['minsmi:t], *s.* carne picada.

mincepie ['minspai], *s.* pastel de pasas y especias.

mincing ['minsiŋ], *a.* afectado, remilgado.

mincingly, *adv.* con afectación; a pedacitos; superficialmente.

mind [maind], *s.* mente, *f.,* alma, espíritu, inteligencia, entendimiento, ingenio; gana, gusto, ánimo, afición, voluntad, afecto, deseo, inclinación; pensamiento, razón, *f.,* sentimiento, parecer, dictamen, opinión; recuerdo, memoria; intención, propósito, resolución; *of one mind,* unánimes; *to give one's mind,* aplicarse; *of sound mind,* en su cabal juicio; *to have a mind to,* tener ganas de; *to make up one's mind,* decidirse, resolverse, estar resuelto, tomar un partido; *to change one's mind,* cambiar de propósito; *to have gone out of one's mind,* haber perdido el juicio; *to call to mind,* traer a la memoria; *to bear* (o *have*) *in mind,* tener presente, tener en consideración; *to have a mind to,* estar dispuesto a, . (*fam.*) pedírselo el cuerpo; *to put in mind,* recordar; *to speak one's mind,* decir su parecer; *many men, many minds,* tantas cabezas, tantas sentencias; *time out of mind,* tiempo inmemorial; *never mind,* no haga Vd. caso. — *v.t.* observar, notar, reparar; mirar, considerar, prestar atención; vigilar, cuidar; proponerse; ponerse en guardia; recordar; obcecder. — *v.i.* prestar atención, atender; tener ganas; ser obediente; acordarse; *mind him,* tenga Vd. cuidado con él; *to mind one's own business,* andar las estaciones; *mind your own business,* métase Vd. en lo que le concierne; *to mind one's p's and q's,* poner los puntos sobre las íes.

minded, *a.* inclinado, propenso, dispuesto; *high-minded,* de pensamientos nobles y elevados; *right-minded,* de espíritu justo; *evil-minded,* mal intencionado; *weak-minded,* débil, pusilánime.

mindedness, *s.* inclinación, disposición.

mindful, *a.* atento, diligente; cuidadoso, vigilante.

mindfulness, *s.* cuidado, atención, circunspección, prudencia.

mindless, *a.* descuidado, negligente, olvidadizo; insensato, necio.

mine [main], *pron.*, *adj.* posesivo mío, míos, mía, mías; el mío, lo mío, etc.; *a friend of mine*, un amigo mío.

mine, *s.* mina. — *v.t.* minar, contraminar, zapar, consumir, destruir, extraer (minerales), explotar (minas). — *v.i.* hacer una mina, explotar una mina, minar, zapar; dedicarse a la minería.

miner ['mainəɹ], *s.* minero, (*Méj.*) barretero; zapador, minador.

mineral ['minərəl], *s.*, *a.* mineral; *mineral oil*, petróleo; *mineral water*, gaseosa, agua mineral.

mineralization, *s.* mineralización.

mineralize ['minərəlaiz], *v.t.* mineralizar.

mineralizer, *s.* mineralizador.

mineralogic, **mineralogical**, *a.* mineralógico.

mineralogist [minə'rælodʒist], *s.* mineralogista, *m.f.*

mineralogy [minə'rælodʒi], *s.* mineralogía.

minever ['minivəɹ], *s.* (*zool.*) marta.

mingle ['miŋgəl], *v.t.* mezclar, mixturar, confundir, incorporar, unir. — *v.i.* mezclarse, confundirse, juntarse.

mingler ['miŋgləɹ], *s.* mezclador.

mingling ['miŋgliŋ], *s.* mezcla.

miniate ['minieit], *v.t.* pintar o teñir con bermellón. — *a.* bermellón, rojo.

miniature ['miniətʃəɹ], *s.* miniatura. — *a.* en miniatura, en corta escala.

miniaturist, *s.* miniaturista, *m.f.*

minify ['minifai], *v.t.* empequeñecer, disminuir, depreciar.

minikin ['minikin], *a.* pequeñín, menudo; remilgada (*usu. f.*). — *s.* cosa baladí, pequeñín; alfilerito; favorito.

minim ['minim], *s.* pigmeo, enano; pescadillo; (*farm.*) mínimo (0·0616 mililitro de agua); (*mús.*) mínima, blanca; (*igl.*) religioso de la orden de San Francisco de Paula.

minimal ['miniməl], *a.* mínimo.

minimize ['minimaiz], *v.t.* reducir al grado mínimo, mitigar, disminuir; achicar; menospreciar, tener en menos.

minimum ['miniməm], *s.* mínimo, mínimum.

minimus, *s.* más pequeño. — *a.* (*escuela*) el menor de los estudiantes de un mismo apellido.

mining ['mainiŋ], *a.* minero, de mina; de minero. — *s,* minería, mineraje, explotación de minas.

minion ['minjən], *s.* favorito, valido, predilecto, privado; (*impr.*) miñona; paniaguado. — *a.* lindo, delicado, cuco.

minister ['ministəɹ], *s.* ministro, agente; ejecutor, delegado, sustituto; embajador; cura, *m.*, pastor, sacerdote, eclesiástico; oficiante; *Prime Minister*, primer ministro. — *v.t.* ministrar, suministrar, administrar, socorrer, dar, proveer. — *v.i.* servir, ministrar; atender, asistir; contribuir, tender, administrar; (*igl.*) oficiar, decir misa, celebrar los oficios divinos; cuidar; llenar.

ministerial [minis'tiəriəl], *a.* ministerial, eclesiástico, sacerdotal; del gobierno, del ministro.

ministerialism, *s.* ministerialismo.

ministering ['ministəriŋ], *s.* socorro, asistencia, ayuda, servicio.

ministrant ['ministrənt], *s.*, *a.* ministrante, sirviente, oficiante.

ministration [minis'treiʃən], *s.* servicio, agencia; (*igl.*) ministerio, oficio eclesiástico.

ministry ['ministri], *s.* ministerio, incumbencia, servicio, intervención, ayuda, oficio, cargo; gabinete, consejo de ministros; clero; profesión de pastor protestante; *Ministry of Education*, ministerio de Educación Nacional, ministerio de Instrucción Pública y Bellas Artes; *Ministry of Health*, ministerio de Sanidad; *Ministry of War*, ministerio de la Guerra; *Ministry of Work*, ministerio del Trabajo; *Ministry of State*, ministerio de la Gobernación, ministerio de lo Interior; *Ministry of Works*, ministerio de Obras Públicas, ministerio de Industria y Comercio.

minium ['miniəm], *s.* minio, azarcón.

miniver ['minivəɹ], *s.* [MINEVER].

mink [miŋk], *s.* visón, piel de visón.

minnow ['minou], *s.* pez pequeño de río (*phoxinus aphya*).

minor ['mainəɹ], *a.* menor, más pequeño menor de edad, inferior; secundario, de menos importancia. — *s.* menor; (*mús.*) tono menor; (*lóg.*) proposición segunda de un silogismo; fraile Franciscano; *minor key*, (*mús.*) tono menor.

minorite ['mainərait], *a.* franciscano. — *s.* minorita, *m.*

minority [mi'nɔːriti, mai'nɔːriti], *s.* minoridad, menor edad; minoría.

minotaur ['minotɔːɹ], *s.* minotauro.

minster ['minstəɹ], *s.* monasterio; catedral, *f.*, basílica.

minstrel ['minstrel], *s.* juglar, trovador, ministril, bardo; músico, cantor.

minstrelsy ['minstrelsi], *s.* música, canto, coro; arte del trovador; gaya ciencia.

mint [mint], *s.* casa de moneda; (*fig.*) tesoro, mina; (*bot.*) menta, hierbabuena, matapulgas, *f.*; *to have a mint of money*, (*fam.*) tener un dineral. — *v.t.* acuñar; forjar, fraguar; inventar.

mintage, *s.* moneda acuñada; braceaje; derecho de cuño.

minter, *s.* acuñador; forjador, inventor.

minuend ['minjuːend], *s.* minuendo.

minuet ['minjuːet], *s.* minuete, minué.

minus ['mainəs], *a.*, *prep.* menos; sin, falto de, desprovisto de. — *s.* (signo) menos; cantidad negativa.

minuscule [mi'nʌskjuːl], *s.* minúscula.

minute ['minit], *s.* minuto, momento, instante; nota, acta, minuta; módulo. — *v.t.* minutar, apuntar, anotar; *minute-book*, minutario, libro de minutas; *minute-hand*, minutero.

minute [mai'njuːt], *a.* menudo, diminuto, minucioso.

minutely [mai'njuːtli], *adv.* exactamente, circunstanciadamente, por menor, minuciosamente; detalladamente.

minutely ['minitli], *a.*, *adv.* a cada minuto, por minutos, a intervalos de un minuto.

minuteness [mai'njuːtnis], *s.* menudencia, minucia, minuciosidad, cortedad, parvedad, exigüidad, pequeñez.

minutia ['minjuːʃə], *pl.* **minutiæ**, *s.* minucia, menudencia.

minx [miŋks], *s.* (*zool.*) marta; (*fig.*) coqueta, bribona; moza descarada.

miracle ['mirəkəl], *s.* milagro, maravilla, prodigio; *miracle play*, pieza parecida al auto alegórico, 'milagro'; *miracle worker* o *miracle monger*, milagrero, impostor, embustero.

miraculous [mi'rækjuːləs], *a.* milagroso, maravilloso.

miraculously, *adv.* milagrosamente, por milagro.

miraculousness, *s.* estado de milagroso, lo maravilloso, lo extraordinario.

mirage [mi'rɑːʒ], *s.* espejismo.

mire [maiəɹ], *s.* cieno, limo, fango; lodazal, cenagal. — *v.t.* enlodar, encenegar. — *v.i.* atascarse, caer en el fango, enlodarse.

miriness ['mairines], *s.* suciedad.

mirk [məːɹk], **mirky** ['məːɹki], *a.* tenebroso, lóbrego, oscuro.

mirror ['mirəɹ], *s.* espejo; (*fig.*) modelo, ejemplar. — *v.t.* reflejar, espejear.

mirth [məːɹθ], **mirthfulness** ['məːɹθfəlnes], *s.* alegría, regocijo, júbilo, jovialidad, contento.

mirthful, *a.* alegre, jovial, gozoso, regocijado, contento.

mirthless, *a.* melancólico, abatido, sin alegría.

miry ['mairi], *a.* cenagoso, fangoso.

misadventure [misəd'ventʃəɹ], *s.* desgracia, infortunio, desventura, revés; accidente.

misadventured, *a.* desgraciado.

misadvised [misəd'vaizd], *a.* mal aconsejado.

misalliance [misə'laiəns], *s.* mal casamiento, matrimonio con persona de estado social inferior; asociación, union o alianza impropias.

misallied [misə'laid], *a.* mal casado.

misanthrope ['misənθroup], **misanthropist** [mi'sænθrəpist], *s.* misántropo.

misanthropic [misən'θrɔpik], **misanthropical,** *a.* misantrópico.

misanthropy [mi'sænθrəpi], *s.* misantropía.

misapplication, *s.* aplicación mala o falsa.

misapply, *v.t.* aplicar mal, hacer mal uso de.

misapprehend [misæpri'hend], *v.t.* entender mal.

misapprehension, *s.* equivocación, error, engaño, yerro, falso concepto.

misappropriate [misə'prouprieit], *v.t.* malversar.

misappropriation, *s.* apropiación errónea.

misbecome [misbe'kʌm], *v.i.* desconvenir, caer o sentar mal, no convenir, no cuadrar.

misbecoming, *a.* desproporcionado, impropio, indecoroso.

misbecomingness, *s.* desproporción, indecencia, impropiedad.

misbegot [misbe'gɔt], **misbegotten** [misbe'gɔtən], *a.* bastardo, ilegítimo; (*fig.*) espantoso, feo, despreciable.

misbehave [misbe'heiv], *v.i.* conducirse mal, portarse mal, proceder mal.

misbehaved, *a.* mal educado, mal criado.

misbehaviour [misbe'heivjəɹ], *s.* mala conducta, grosería, mal comportamiento, mala acción.

misbelief [misbe'liːf], *s.* falsa creencia, error; (*ant.*) incredulidad.

misbelieve, *v.i.* equivocarse, estar en error; profesar una falsa creencia.

misbeliever, *s.* incrédulo, infiel.

misbelieving, *a.* infiel, heterodoxo.

miscalculate [mis'kælkjuːleit], *v.t.* calcular mal.

miscalculation, *s.* mal cálculo, error, cuenta errada.

miscall [mis'kɔːl], *v.t.* nombrar equivocadamente; (*prov.*) ultrajar, insultar.

miscarriage [mis'kæridʒ], *s.* malogro, fracaso; aborto, malparto; *miscarriage of justice*, error judicial, injusticia cometida por un tribunal.

miscarry, *v.i.* salir mal, frustrarse, malograrse; abortar, malparir.

miscast [mis'kɑːst], *v.t.* calcular mal, contar mal; (*teat.*) repartir mal, dar mal papel.

miscegenation [misidʒe'neiʃən], *s.* mezcla de razas, especialmente de las razas negra y blanca.

miscellanea [mise'leiniə], *s.* miscelánea.

miscellaneous [mise'leiniəs], *a.* misceláneo, mezclado, diverso, mixto.

miscellaneously, *adv.* de una manera mixta.

miscellany [mi'seləni], *s.* miscelánea.

mischance [mis'tʃɑns], *s.* mala fortuna, desdicha, desgracia, desventura, infortunio, desastre, fatalidad.

mischarge [mis'tʃɑːɹdʒ], *s.* error de precio. — *v.t.* alegar erróneamente, cargar equivocadamente en cuenta.

mischief ['mistʃif], *s.* daño, mal, perjuicio, desgracia, malicia, agravio, pérdida, injuria; diablura, travesura; (*fam.*) diablillo; *to make mischief*, sembrar zizaña; *from* (o *out of*) *pure mischief*, por pura maldad.

mischief-maker, *s.* dañador; enredador; tea de la discordia.

mischief-making, *a.* perjudicial, dañino.

mischievous ['mistʃivəs], *a.* malvado, malo, dañoso, dañino, malicioso, perverso, perjudicial, malévolo; chismoso, enredador, travieso, revoltoso; juguetón.

mischievousness, *s.* malicia, malignidad, maldad; picardía, travesura.

miscibility [misi'biliti], *s.* cualidad miscible, lo miscible.

miscible, *a.* miscible, mezclable.

miscitation [mi'sai'teiʃən], *s.* cita falsa o equivocada.

miscite [mis'sait], *v.t.* citar falsamente o equivocadamente.

misclaim [mis'kleim], *s.* pretensión mal fundada.

miscompute [miskəm'pjuːt], *v.t.* contar mal.

misconceive [miskən'siːv], *v.t.*, *v.i.* juzgar mal, formar concepto falso.

misconception [miskən'sepʃən], *s.* idea *o* concepción falsa; equivocación, concepto equivocado.

misconduct [mis'kɔndəkt], *s.* mala conducta, mal porte (especialmente adulterio). — *v.t.* desacertar, conducir mal, dirigir mal. — *v.i.* conducirse mal.

misconjecture [miskən'dʒektʃəɹ], *s.* conjetura falsa o equivocada. — *v.t.* hacer conjeturas falsas.

misconstruction, *s.* interpretación falsa o errónea.

misconstrue [miskən'struː], *v.t.* interpretar equivocadamente, torcer el sentido de.

miscount [mis'kaunt], *v.t.*, *v.i.* contar mal, calcular mal, descontarse, equivocarse en la cuenta.

miscreance ['miskriəns], *s.* (*ant.*) falsa creencia.

miscreant ['miskriənt], *s.*, *a.* malandrín, perverso, malvado; bribón; (*ant.*) descreído, infiel.

misdate [mis'deit], *s.* fecha falsa. — *v.t.* fechar falsamente.

misdeal [mis'di:l], *v.t.* (en el juego) dar mal las cartas.

misdeed, *s.* malhecho, delito, fechoría.

misdeem [mis'di:m], *v.t.* juzgar mal, formar juicios equivocados.

misdemean [misdi'mi:n] (**oneself**), *v.t.* conducirse mal, portarse mal, tener mala conducta.

misdemeanour [misdi'mi:nəɹ], *s.* mala conducta; delito, crimen, (*for.*) fechoría.

misdirect [misdai'rekt], *v.t.* dirigir mal.

misdirection, *s.* mala dirección; informe falso; (*for.*) error cometido por un juez al hacer el resumen de una causa ante el jurado.

misdoer, *s.* el que comete una falta, malhechor.

misdoing [mis'du:iŋ], *s.* delito, mala acción, falta, crimen, yerro, ofensa.

misdoubt [mis'daut], *s.* (*ant.*) sospecha, recelo, irresolución. — *v.t.* dudar de, sospechar.

misdoubtful, *a.* (*ant.*) que duda o sospecha, que inspira la duda.

misemploy [misem'plɔi], *v.t.* hacer mal uso de, emplear mal, abusar.

mise en scène [mi:zɒŋ'sein], *s.* (*teat.*) aparato escénico, escenario; (*fig.*) escenario, circunstancias.

misentry ['misəntri], *s.* entrada errada, anotación incorrecta.

miser ['maizəɹ], *s.* avaro, avariento, tacaño; barrena grande para abrir pozos.

miserable ['mizərəbəl], *a.* desgraciado, lastimoso, desdichado, infeliz, angustiado, cuitado; miserable, sin valor, sin importancia, despreciable.

miserableness, *s.* tristeza, melancolía, desesperación; miseria, pobreza.

miserably, *adv.* miserablemente, pobremente, mezquinamente.

miserere [mizə'rɛəri], *s.* (*igl.*) miserere.

miserly ['maizəɹli], *a.* avariento, mezquino, tacaño.

misery ['mizəri], *s.* sufrimiento, pena, suplicio, desesperación, melancolía; miseria, pobreza, desgracia.

misestimate [mis'estimeit], *v.t.* apreciar de una manera errónea.

misfaith [mis'feiθ], *s.* fe equivocada.

misfashion [mis'fæʃən], *v.t.* formar mal, hacer una cosa al revés.

misfeasance [mis'fi:zəns], *s.* (*for.*) ejecución de un hecho legal de una manera ilegal, especialmente con negligencia; infidencia.

misfire [mis'faiəɹ], *s.* falla de un tiro, carga explosiva, etc. — *v.i.* fallar una arma de fuego, etc.

misfit [mis'fit], *v.t.*, *v.i.* sentar mal, no ajustar bien, no ser a propósito o propio. — *s.* lo que no sienta o cae o ajusta bien.

misform [mis'fɔ:m], *v.t.* formar mal.

misfortune [mis'fɔ:tʃu:n], *s.* desgracia, infortunio, desventura, calamidad, contratiempo, desdicha, adversidad, desastre; *misfortunes never come singly*, bien vengas mal, si vienes solo.

misgive [mis'giv], *v.t. impers.* llenar de recelos, llenar de dudas, hacer temer, hacer dudar. — *v.i.* ser receloso.

misgiving, *s.* desconfianza, recelo, presentimiento.

misgotten [mis'gɔtən], *a.* mal adquirido, mal ganado.

misgovern [mis'gʌvəɹn], *v.t.* desgobernar, gobernar mal.

misgoverned, *a.* mal gobernado.

misgovernment, *s.* desgobierno, mala conducta, mala administración, desorden.

misguidance [mis'gaidəns], *s.* dirección falsa o errada, extravío.

misguide, *v.t.* descaminar, extraviar, descarriar.

mishap [mis'hæp], *s.* desventura, desgracia, trastorno, contratiempo, accidente.

mishmash ['miʃmæʃ], *s.* mezcolanza.

misinform [misin'fɔ:m], *v.t.* informar mal, dar informes erróneos.

misinformation, *s.* información falsa, aviso erróneo.

misinformer, *s.* el que da informes falsos.

misinstruct [misin'strʌkt], *v.t.* informar mal, instruir mal.

misintelligence [misin'telidʒəns], *s.* informes erróneos, aviso falso; desacuerdo.

misinterpret [misin'tə:ɹpret], *v.t.* interpretar mal, entender mal.

misinterpretation, *s.* mala interpretación; tergiversación.

misjoin [mis'dʒɔin], *v.t.* unir, ajustar, acomodar o adecuar mal.

misjudge [mis'dʒʌdʒ], *v.t.* juzgar mal, formar conceptos erróneos. — *v.i.* engañarse, equivocarse, errar.

misjudgment, *s.* juicio falso, erróneo o injusto; idea falsa.

mislay [mis'lei], *v.t.* extraviar, transpapelar, perder.

mislead [mis'li:d], *v.t.* extraviar, descaminar, descarriar, despistar; engañar, alucinar, pervertir, seducir.

misleader, *s.* engañador, seductor, corruptor.

misleading, *a.* falso, engañoso.

mislike [mis'laik], *v.t.* no querer, desaprobar.

mismanage [mis'mænidʒ], *v.t.* administrar mal, dirigir mal.

mismanagement, *s.* desgobierno, desbarajuste, mala administración, mala dirección; desarreglo, desconcierto.

mismanager, *s.* mal administrador, mal gerente.

misname [mis'neim], *v.t.* trasnombrar, dar un nombre falso.

misnomer [mis'nouməɹ], *s.* error de nombre, nombre falso o equivocado.

misogamist [mis'ɔgəmist], *s.* misógamo.

misogamy [mi'sɔgəmi], *s.* misogamia.

misogynist, *s.* misógino.

misogyny [mi'sɔdʒəni], *s.* misoginia.

misplace [mis'pleis], *v.t.* colocar mal, poner alguna cosa fuera de su lugar; extraviar.

mispoint [mis'pɔint], *v.t.* puntuar mal.

misprint [mis'print], *v.t.* imprimir mal, cometer erratas en la impresión. — *s.* error de imprenta, errata.

misprision [mis'priʒən], *s.* (*for.*) ocultación de un crimen.

misprize, *v.t.* despreciar, hacer poco caso de.

mispronounce [mispro'nauns], *v.i.* pronunciar mal o incorrectamente.

mispronunciation, *s.* pronunciación incorrecta.

misproportion [mispro'pɔ:ɹʃən], *v.t.* desproporcionar.

misquotation, s. cita falsa o equivocada.

misquote [mis'kwout], v.t. citar inexactamente.

misrate [mis'reit], v.t. valuar mal.

misread [mis'ri:d], v.t. leer mal.

misreckon [mis'rekən], v.t. calcular mal.

misreckoning, s. cálculo erróneo, cuenta falsa.

misrelate [misre'leit], v.t. referir o relatar falsamente.

misreport [misre'pɔ:it], v.t. relatar falsamente, tergiversar, falsificar; citar inexactamente; (ant.) propagar chismes. — s. relación falsa, tergiversación; relación inexacta; informe inexacto.

misrepresent [misrepre'zent], v.t. falsificar, pervertir, desfigurar, tergiversar.

misrepresentation, s. relación o representación falsa, tergiversación; relación o representación inexacta.

misrule [mis'ru:l], v.t. desgobernar. — s. desorden, confusión, tumulto.

miss [mis], v.t. errar, equivocar, no acertar, omitir, engañarse de, perder, no hallar; tener necesidad de, echar de menos a; pasar sin, carecer, abstenerse de; pasar por alto. — v.i. faltar, frustrarse, desgraciarse, malograrse, fallar, errar, salir mal; errar el tiro, el golpe, etc., no dar en el blanco. — s. señorita, muchacha; (ant.) manceba; fracaso, malogro, errada, error, pérdida, falta; culpa involuntaria; desprecio.

missal ['misəl], s. misal.

missel-thrush ['misəlθrʌʃ], s. tordo grande de Europa (*Turdus viscivorus*).

misshape [mis'ʃeip], v.t. deformar, desfigurar, dar mala forma a.

misshaped, misshapen, a. deforme, disforme, desfigurado.

missile ['misail], s. proyectil. — a. arrojadizo.

missing ['misiŋ], a. perdido, extraviado, ausente; *to be missing,* faltar, estar extraviado.

mission ['miʃən], s. misión; comisión; envío; destino; embajada; legación.

missionary ['miʃənəri], s. misionero, misionario. — a. misionero.

missis, missus ['misiz], s.f. (vulg.) señora, esposa; (vulg.) señora, ama.

missive ['misiv], a. misivo, arrojado, lanzado, enviadizo. — s. misiva, comunicación escrita.

misspeak [mis'spi:k], v.t. pronunciar mal. — v.i. hablar mal.

misspell [mis'spel], v.t. deletrear mal, escribir con mala ortografía.

misspelling, s. ortografía incorrecta, error de ortografía.

misspend [mis'spend], v.t. disipar, gastar mal, malbaratar, desperdiciar, prodigar.

misstate [mis'steit], v.t. exponer mal, relatar mal, desnaturalizar, desfigurar.

misstatement, s. relación inexacta.

misstep [mis'step], v.i. tropezar, dar un paso equivocado. — s. desliz, tropiezo.

missy ['misi], s. (festivo) señorita.

mist [mist], s. neblina, calina, bruma, llovizna; vaho, vapor; calígine, f., obscuridad. — v.t. cubrir de neblina, anieblar, anublar, obscurecer, empañar. — v.i. lloviznar.

mistakable, mistakeable [mis'teikəbəl], a. susceptible de error.

mistake [mis'teik], v.t. (pret. **mistook**; p.p. **mistaken**) comprender mal, trabucar,

trasoír, entender mal; confundir, equivocar. — v.i. equivocarse, engañarse, errar. — s. error, equivocación, engaño, trabucación, renuncio; (And) no mistake! (fam.) Sin duda alguna, ¡ Ya lo creo !

mistaken, p.p. incorrecto, erróneo, equivocado, desacertado.

mistakenly, adv. equivocadamente.

misteach [mis'ti:tʃ], v.t. (pret. y p.p. **mistaught**) instruir mal, enseñar mal.

mister ['mistəɪ], s. (abrev. MR), señor, don.

misterm [mis'tə:ɪmɪ], v.t. dar un nombre equivocado.

mistily ['mistili], adv. oscuramente, vagamente.

mistime, v.t., v.i. dejar pasar la hora oportuna, hacer o decir fuera de tiempo.

mistimed, p.p., a. fuera de tiempo, inoportuno, intempestivo.

mistiness, s. nebulosidad, calígine, f.

mistle ['misəl], v.i. (ant.) lloviznar.

mistletoe ['misəltou], s. muérdago, liga, visco.

mistook [mis'tuk], prep., p.p. [MISTAKE].

mistranslate [mistræns'leit], v.t. traducir inexactamente, traducir mal.

mistranslation, s. traducción inexacta o infiel.

mistress ['mistris], s. (abrev. MRS), señora, ama, dueña; reina, soberana; amiga, querida, concubina; maestra, mujer diestra en un arte; mujer cortejada, amada; *Mistress of the Robes,* camarera mayor de una reina; *to be mistress of a language,* dominar una lengua; *to be one's own mistress,* ser dueña de sus acciones.

mistrial [mis'traiəl], s. (for.) causa o pleito viciado de nulidad, por error, empate o desacuerdo del jurado.

mistrust [mis'trʌst], v.t. dudar de, recelar de, desconfiar de. — s. recelo, falta de confianza, desconfianza.

mistrustful, a. desconfiado, receloso, suspicaz.

mistrustfully, mistrustingly, adv. desconfiadamente, con desconfianza.

mistrustfulness, s. desconfianza, suspicacia, recelo.

mistrustless, a. confiado.

mistune [mis'tju:n], v.t. desentonar, desacordar.

mistutor [mis'tju:təɪ], v.t. instruir mal.

misty ['misti], a. nebuloso, brumoso, nublado, calinoso, anublado; empañado.

misunderstand [misʌndəɪ'stænd], v.t. entender mal, comprender mal, equivocarse, trasoír; tomar en sentido erróneo.

misunderstanding, s. concepto falso, interpretación errónea, equivocación; mala inteligencia; disensión, desavenencia.

misusage [mis'ju:zidʒ], s. abuso, mal trato.

misuse [mis'ju:z], v.t. tratar mal, maltratar, abusar.

mite [mait], s. ácaro, insecto aracnoide; óbolo, blanca, ardite; (fig.) gorgojo, mota, pizca; cosa muy pequeña, especialmente un infante.

mitigable, a. capaz de ser mitigado.

mitigant ['mitigənt], a. mitigativo, mitigante, lenitivo, sedativo, calmante.

mitigate ['mitigeit], v.t. mitigar, aliviar, calmar, suavizar.

mitigation, s. mitigación, alivio.

mitigatory, a. mitigador, mitigativo; (med.) sedativo, lenitivo, calmante.

mitral ['maitrəl], *a.* mitral.
mitre ['maitəɹ], *s.* mitra; dignidad de obispo; caperuza de chimenea; (*carp.*) inglete. — *v.t.* adornar con mitra, conferir una mitra; (*carp.*) cortar, o unir con ingletes, ingletear.
mitred ['maitəɹd], *a.* mitrado; (*carp.*) ingleteado.
mitt [mit], **mitten** ['mitən], *s.* mitón; especie de guante; (*fig.*) *to give the mitten*, dar calabazas a un pretendiente; despedir de un empleo, etc.; *a cat in mittens is no mouser*, gato enguantado no caza ratones.
mittimus ['mitiməs], *s.* (*for.*) auto de prisión, orden de arresto.
mix [miks], *v.t.* mezclar, mixturar; incorporar, unir, asociar, juntar; aderezar; amasar. — *v.i.* mezclarse, confundirse, barajarse; llevarse bien, congeniar.
mixable, *a.* que puede mezclarse.
mixen ['mikzən], *s.* estercolero, muladar.
mixer, *s.* mezclador.
mixture ['mikstʃəɹ] *s.* mezcla; ligación, mescolanza, mixtura; poción.
mizen, mizzen ['mizən], *s.* (*mar.*) mesana; *mizen-mast*, palo de mesana; *mizen-shrouds*, jarcia de mesana; *to balance the mizen*, tomar rizos en la mesana.
mizmaze ['mizmeiz], *s.* dédalo, laberinto.
mizzle ['mizəl], *v.i.* (*prov.*) lloviznar, molliznar. — *s.* (*prov.*) llovizna.
mnemonic [ne'mɔnik], **mnemonical** [ne-'mɔnikəl], *a.* mnemotécnico.
mnemonics [ne'mɔniks], *s.* mnemónica, mnemotecnia.
moan [moun], *v.t.* lamentar, llorar, deplorar, sentir. — *v.i.* quejarse, lamentarse, afligirse, gemir. — *s.* queja, quejido, lamento, plañido, gemido.
moanful, *a.* lamentable, lúgubre, quejumbroso.
moanfully, *adv.* lamentablemente, con muchos gemidos.
moat [mout], *s.* mota, foso. — *v.t.* rodear con un foso.
mob [mɔb], *s.* tropel, tumulto; populacho, gentuza, canalla, plebe, *f.*; gorra de mujer. — *v.i.* tumultuar, atropellar, incitar al desorden; (*vulg.*) aclamar, festejar tumultuosamente.
mobbish, *a.* tumultuoso.
mobile ['moubail], *a.* movible, móvil, ambulante; movedizo, variable, inconstante. — *s.* cosa movible.
mobility [mo'biliti], *s.* movilidad; instabilidad, volubilidad.
mobilization, *s.* movilización.
mobilize ['moubilaiz], *v.t.* movilizar. — *v.i.* movilizarse.
moccasin ['mɔkəsin], *s.* mocasín.
mocha ['mɔtʃə], *s.* moca; variedad de calcedonia dendrítica.
mock [mɔk], *v.t.* mofar, escarnecer, befar, burlar, burlarse de, ridiculizar; remedar, copiar, imitar; engañar, burlar. — *v.i.* reírse, burlarse. — *s.* mofa, burla, befa, escarnio; risada; ironía, mímica. — *a.* falso, contrahecho, ficticio; burlesco, irónico, satírico; *mock-orange,* (*bot.*) jeringuilla.
mockable, *a.* ridículo.
mocker, *s.* mofador, escarnecedor, burlador, burlón.
mockery, *s.* mofa, befa, burla, ridículo, irrisión; remedo.

mocking, *s.* mofa, burla, escarnio.
mocking-bird, *s.* cerción; (*Amér.*) sinsonte, bababuí.
mockingly, *adv.* con mofa, con burla, irónicamente.
mocking-thrush, *s.* mirlo burlón (*Harporhynchus rufus*).
modal ['moudəl], *a.* modal.
modality [mo'dæliti], *s.* modalidad.
mode [moud], *s.* modo, manera, forma; usanza, moda; accidente; grado, graduación; (*gram.*) modo; (*fil.*) modo; (*mús.*) tono, modo.
model ['mɔdəl], *s.* modelo, patrón; horma, molde; ejemplar, ejemplo, muestra, tipo; pauta; imagen; (*mar.*) gálibo; figurín, bosquejo, diseño; modelo vivo. — *v.t., v.i.* modelar, moldear, formar. — *a.* modelo, ejemplar, perfecto, ideal.
modeller ['mɔdələɹ], *s.* modelador, dibujador, diseñador, trazador.
modelling, *s.* modelado; modelo. — *a.* modelador.
moderate ['mɔdəɹit, 'mɔdəɹeit], *a.* moderado, mesurado, templado, modesto, sencillo, parco, pacato, razonable, sobrio; arreglado, módico; mediano, mediocre; quieto, tranquilo; bonancible, apacible, suave; pasadero. — *v.t.* moderar, templar, modificar, limitar, reprimir, restringir. — *v.i.* moderarse, apaciguarse; presidir en una reunión.
moderation [mɔdəɹ'eiʃən], *s.* moderación, templanza; economía, sobriedad; (*Univ. de Oxford*) primer examen público para un grado.
moderator ['mɔdəɹeitəɹ], *s.* moderador, árbitro; (*mec.*) regulador; presidente; (*Univ. de Oxford y Camb.*) examinador universitario.
moderatorship, *s.* funciones de moderador.
moderatrix, *s.f.* moderadora.
modern ['mɔdəɹn], *s., a.* moderno, reciente, nuevo.
modernism, *s.* modernismo; uso moderno, creencias modernas.
modernist, *s.* modernista, *m.f.*
modernize, *v.t.* modernizar; (*arq.*) restaurar.
modernness, *s.* novedad.
modest ['mɔdest], *a.* modesto, moderado; recatado, púdico, pudoroso, decente, humilde.
modesty ['mɔdesti], *s.* modestia; decencia, pudor, recato, reserva, humildad.
modicum ['mɔdikəm], *s.* pitanza, poco, cantidad pequeña.
modifiable, *a.* modificable.
modification [mɔdifi'keiʃən], *s.* modificación.
modifier, *s.* modificador.
modify ['mɔdifai], *v.t.* modificar, moderar.
modillion, modillon [mo'diljən], *s.* modillón, cartela.
modish ['moudiʃ], *a.* a la moda, conforme a la moda, hecho según la moda, en boga; elegante.
modishly, *adv.* a la moda, según la moda.
modishness, *s.* afición a la moda; elegancia.
modular, *a.* modular.
modulate ['mɔdju:leit], *v.t.* modular.
modulation, *s.* (*mús.*) modulación; (*arq.*) módulo.
module ['mɔdju:l], *s.* modelo, imagen, *f.*; (*arq.*) módulo.

modulus, *s.* (*mat.*) módulo.
modus ['moudəs], *s.* modo, método, manera.
mofette [mo'fet], *s.* mofeta.
mogul [mo'gʌl], *s.* mogol.
mohair ['mouheəɹ], *s.* pelo de cabra de angora.
Mohammedan [mo'hæmidən], *a.* mahometano.
Mohammedanism, *s.* mahometismo.
Mohawk ['mouhɔːk], *s.* mohock, tribu de indios de los E.U.
moidore ['mɔidɔːɹ], *s.* moidoro.
moiety ['mɔiiti], *s.* mitad.
moil [mɔil], *v.t.*, *v.i.* fatigar(se), inquietar(se), afanarse. — *s.* mancha, suciedad.
moire [mwɑːɹ], *s.* moaré, muaré.
moist [mɔist], *a.* húmedo; suculento, jugoso.
moisten ['mɔisən], *v.t.* humedecer, mojar ligeramente, humectar.
moistener, *s.* humedecedor.
moistness, moisture, *s.* humedad; jugosidad, sudor.
moke [mouk], *s.* asno; (*Austral.*) caballejo de mala muerte.
molar ['mouləɹ], *a.* molar. — *s.* diente molar, muela.
molasses [mo'læsis], *s.* melote, melaza.
Moldavian [mɔl'deiviən], *s.* moldavo.
mole [moul], *s.* (*zool.*) topo; (*med.*) grano de belleza; mancha, lunar; (*mar.*) muelle, dique, espolón, malecón, mole.
mole-cast, *s.* montoncillo de tierra.
mole-cricket, *s.* topogrillo, grillotalpa.
molecular [mo'lekju:ləɹ], *a.* molecular.
molecule ['mɔlikju:l], *s.* molécula.
mole-eyed, *a.* (*fam.*) ciego, cegato.
mole-hill, *s.* topinera.
moleskin ['moulskin], *s.* ratina, molesquina, piel de topo.
molest [mo'lest], *v.t.* molestar, vejar, incomodar, hostigar; molestar, fastidiar, manosear.
molestation, *s.* molestia, incomodidad, inconveniente, persecución, importunidad, vejación.
mollient ['mɔliənt], *a.* emoliente, molitivo.
mollifiable [mɔli'faiəbəl], *a.* molificable.
mollification [mɔlifi'keiʃən], *s.* molificación, ablandamiento.
mollifier, *s.* emoliente; ablandador, mitigador; (*fig.*) pacificador.
mollify ['mɔlifai], *v.t.* molificar, ablandar, mitigar, suavizar.
mollusc ['mɔlʌsk], molluscan, mollusk, *s.* molusco, marisco. — *a.* perteneciente a los moluscos.
mollusca [mo'lʌskə], *s.pl.* moluscos.
mollycoddle ['mɔlikɔdəl], *s.* (*fam.*) (hombre) alfeñique, niño mimado. — *v.t.* mimar.
molossus, *s.* moloso.
molten, *a.* fundido. — *p.p.* [MELT].
molybdate, *s.* molibdato.
molybdenum [mo'libdənəm], *s.* molibdeno.
moment ['moumənt], *s.* momento, instante, minuto; (*mec.*) impulso, fuerza; causa, origen; importancia, consecuencia, peso; *at this moment*, en este momento; *in a moment*, en un momento.
momentarily, *adv.* momentáneamente.
momentary ['moumməntəri], *a.* momentáneo.
momentous [mo'mentəs], *a.* importantísimo, trascendental, grave.
momentously, *adv.* con importancia, con gravedad.

momentousness, *s.* gravedad, importancia.
momentum [mo'mentəm], *s.* momento; ímpetu, impulsión, fuerza.
monachal ['mɔnəkəl], *a.* monacal, monástico.
monachism, *s.* monaquismo.
monad ['mɔnəd], *s.* mónada.
monadic, monadical, *a.* de mónada.
monarch ['mɔnɑːɹk], *s.* monarca, *m.*
monarchal, monarchic, monarchical, *a.* monárquico.
monarchically, *adv.* monárquicamente.
monarchism, *s.* monarquismo.
monarchiste, *s.* monárquico.
monarchize, *v.i.* reinar (el monarca); hacer monárquico.
monarchy ['mɔnɑːɹki], *s.* monarquía.
monastery ['mɔnəstəri], *s.* monasterio.
monastic [mo'næstik], monastical [mo'næstikəl], *a.* monástico, monasterial, monacal.
monastically, *adv.* monásticamente.
monasticism [mo'næstisizm], *s.* monasticidad.
Monday ['mʌndi], *s.* lunes.
monetary ['mʌnitəri], *a.* monetario, pecuniario.
monetization, *s.* monetización.
monetize ['mʌnitaiz], *v.t.* monetizar.
money ['mʌni], *s.* moneda, dinero, divisas; fondos, caudal, efectivo, riqueza; *bad money*, moneda falsa; *even money*, cuenta redonda; *paper money*, papel moneda; *old money*, cuenta obscura; *ready money*, dinero contante; *to make money*, ganar dinero; *to put out money*, poner dinero a interés; *money-bill*, ley de hacienda; *moneylender*, prestamista, *m.f.*; *moneywort*, (*bot.*) lisimaquia, mimularia.
money-bag, *s.* bolso, talega.
money-box, *s.* hucha, caja.
money-broker, *s.* corredor de cambios.
money-changer, *s.* cambista, *m.f.*
money-changing, *s.* cambio de monedas.
moneyed ['mʌnid], *a.* adinerado, acomodado, de fondos; *moneyed man*, capitalista, *m.*
moneyer, *s.* monedero.
money-market, *s.* lonja, bolsa.
money-order, *s.* giro postal, libranza postal.
monger ['mʌŋgəɹ], *s.* traficante, tratante, vendedor; . *fishmonger*, pescadero; *ironmonger*, quincallero, ferretero; *whoremonger*, alcahuete.
mongoose ['mʌŋ'guːs], *s.* mangosta.
mongrel ['mʌŋgrəl], *s.*, *a.* mestizo, atravesado, cruzado, perro mestizo.
monism ['mɔnizm], *s.* (*biol.*) unidad de origen.
monition [mo'niʃən], *s.* amonestación, prevención, aviso, advertencia.
monitive ['mɔnitiv], *a.* monitorio.
monitor ['mɔnitəɹ], *s.* monitor, amonestador, admonitor.
monitorial, *a.* monitorio.
monitory ['mɔnitəri], *a.* monitorio, instructivo. — *s.* amonestación, prevención, aviso, advertencia.
monitress, *s.f.* admonitora.
monk [mʌŋk], *s.* monje, fraile.
monkery, *s.* monasterio; vida monástica.
monkey ['mʌŋki], *s.* mono; maza; (*fam.*) diablillo, picaruelo; (*mec.*) trinquete, grapa; fiador de martinete; pequeño crisol para fundir vidrio; (*vulg.*) la suma de £500 o de $500; mezcla de ácido clorhídrico y zinc para soldar; *she-monkey*, mona; *to monkey about*,

(*fam.*) hacer monadas; *monkey-tricks*, (*fam.*) monerías.

monkish ['mʌŋkiʃ], *a.* monástico.

monk's-hood, *s.* (*bot.*) acónito; acónito napelo, napelo.

monochord ['mɔnokɔːɹd], *s.* monocordio.

monochromatic, *a.* monocromático.

monochrome ['mɔnokroum], *s.*, *a.* monocromo.

monocle ['mɔnəkəl], *s.* monóculo.

monocotyledon [mɔnoukɔti'liːdən], *s.* monocotiledón.

monocotyledonous, *a.* monocotiledóneo.

monocular [mɔ'nɔkjuːləɹ], **monoculous** [mɔ'nɔkjuːləs], *a.* monóculo.

monocycle ['mɔnosaikəl], *s.* bicicleta con una rueda.

monody ['mɔnodi], *s.* monodia.

monogamist [mɔ'nɔgəmist], *s.* monógamo.

monogamous, *a.* monógamo.

monogamy [mɔ'nɔgəmi], *s.* monogamia.

monogram ['mɔnogræm], *s.* monograma, *m.*

monograph ['mɔnogræf], *s.* monografía.

monographic, monographical, *a.* monográfico.

monography [mɔ'nɔgrəfi], *s.* monografía; dibujo sin colores.

monolith ['mɔnoliθ], *s.* monolito.

monolithic [mɔno'liθik], *a.* monolítico.

monologist, *s.* monologista, *m.f.*

monologue ['mɔnolɔg], *s.* monólogo.

monomane, *s.* monómano.

monomania [mɔno'meiniə], *s.* monomanía.

monomaniac, *s.* monómano. — *a.* monomaníaco, monomaniático.

monometallism [mɔno'metəlizm], *s.* monometalismo.

monopetalous [mɔno'petələs], *a.* monopétalo.

monoplane ['mɔnoplein], *s.* monoplano.

monopolist [mɔ'nɔpolist], **monopolizer** [mɔnɔpo'laizəɹ], *s.* monopolista, *m.f.*, acaparador.

monopolization, *s.* monopolización.

monopolize [mɔ'nɔpolaiz], *v.t.* monopolizar, acaparar.

monopoly [mɔ'nɔpoli], *s.* monopolio; estanco.

monosepalous [mɔno'sepələs], *a.* monosépalo.

monospermous [mɔno'spəːɹməs], *a.* monospermo.

monosyllabic [mɔnosi'læbik], *a.* monosilábico.

monosyllable ['mɔnosiləbəl], *s.* monosílabo.

monotheism ['mɔnoθiizm], *s.* monoteísmo.

monotheist, *s.* monoteísta, *m.f.*

monotheistic, *a.* monoteístico, monoteísta.

monotone ['mɔnotoun], *s.* monotonía.

monotonous [mɔ'nɔtənəs], *a.* monótono.

monotonously, *adv.* de un modo monótono.

monotony [mɔ'nɔtəni], *s.* monotonía.

monoxide [mɔn'ɔksaid], *s.* monóxido.

monsoon [mɔn'suːn], *s.* monzón, *m.f.*

monster ['mɔnstəɹ], *s.* monstruo. — *a.* monstruoso, prodigioso, magno, enorme, extraordinario.

monstrance ['mɔnstrəns], *s.* (*igl.*) custodia, viril.

monstrosity [mɔn'strɔsiti], *s.* monstruosidád.

monstrous ['mɔnstrəs], *a.* monstruoso; descomunal, prodigioso; horrible. — *adv.* (*fam.*) enormemente, excesivamente.

monstrously, *adv.* monstruosamente, prodigiosamente, enormemente.

monstrousness, *s.* monstruosidad, enormidad.

month [mʌnθ], *s.* mes; *in a month of Sundays*, (*fam.*) en mucho tiempo.

monthly, *a.* mensual. — *s.* publicación mensual. — *adv.* mensualmente.

monticle ['mɔntikəl], *s.* montecillo.

monument ['mɔnjuːmənt], *s.* monumento.

monumental [mɔnjuː'mentəl], *a.* monumental, conmemorativo; monumental, notable.

moo [muː], *v.i.* berrear, mugir, hacer mu.

mood [muːd], *s.* talante, capricho, humor, genio, cólera; (*gram.*) *to be in the mood*, estar de vena.

moodily, *adv.* caprichosamente; con mal humor.

moodiness, *s.* irritación, melancolía, mal humor; cólera; extravagancia, capricho.

moody, *a.* de mal humor, irritable, taciturno, melancólico; caprichoso, mudadizo.

moon [muːn], *s.* luna; (*poét.*) mes. — *v.i.* brillar (como la luna); (*fam.*) andar de vagar, estar abatido, mirar a las musarañas; cazar de noche. — *v.t.* exponer a los rayos de la luna.

moonbeam, *s.* rayo lunar.

moon-blind, *a.* cegato.

moon-calf, *s.* bobo, tonto; (*ant.*) mola, monstruo.

moon-daisy, *s.* margarita mayor, crisantemo, floriblanco.

moon-eyed, *a.* de ojos lunáticos, bizco, bisojo, ciego.

moon-fern, *s.* botriquio, helecho común (*Botrichium lunaria*).

moonflower, *s.* especie de ipomea nocturna (*Ipomœa bona nox*).

moonish, *a.* lunático, simple, tonto.

moonless, *a.* sin luna, sin claridad de luna.

moonlight ['muːnlait], *s.* claro de luna, luz de la luna. — *a.* **moonlit** ['muːnlit], iluminado por la luna, de luna; *moonlight flitting*, cambiar los trastos durante la noche para no pagar al casero o a la patrona.

moonseed, *s.* cualquier planta del género Menispermo.

moonshine, *s.* claridad de la luna; (*fig.*) ensueño, fábula, sueños dorados, ilusión.

moonstruck ['muːnstrʌk], *a.* lunático.

moonwort, *s.* lunaria.

moony, *a.* (*fig.*) lunático, simple, tonto; lunado. — *s.* bobo.

Moor [muəɹ], *s.* moro.

moor [muəɹ], *s.* páramo, pantano, ciénaga, marjal. — *v.t.* (*mar.*) amarrar, atar, afirmar. — *v.i.* anclar, estar anclado, estar amarrado.

moor-buzzard, *s.* (*orn.*) circo, especie de halcón.

moorcock, *s.m.* macho de la cerceta, lagópedo de Escocia (*Lagopus scoticus*).

moorhen, *s.f.* cerceta.

mooring, *s.* (*mar.*) amarra; reguera; *mooring-ground*, anclaje.

moorish, moory, *a.* pantanoso, cenagoso, charcoso.

Moorish, *a.* moro, morisco, moruno.

moorland, *s.* pantano, marjal, brezal.

moose [muːs], *s.* alce, mosa, anta.

moot [muːt], *v.t.* suscitar, promover o tratar de (un asunto); (*ant.*) disputar, discutir, argüir, cuestionar. — *v.i.* defender una causa ficticia. — *s.* (*ant.*) tesis, *f.*, debate, discusión; junta, conceja; *moot case* o *point*, pleito fingido; cuestión discutible.

mooting, *s.* ejercicio de discusión jurídica.

mop [mɔp], *s.* escoba, estropajo, aljofifa, fregajo; mueca; mechón, copete, puñado de cabellos; cabos de algodón, cerdas, etc.; (*mar.*) lampazo. — *v.t.* aljofifar, fregar, lavar o limpiar con una escoba; (*mar.*) lampacear.

mope [moup], *v.i.* estar abatido, aburrirse, fastidiarse, entontecerse, ser bobo. — *v.t.* atontar; abatir, desanimar, fastidiar. — *s.* hombre atontado o abatido.

mopingly, *adv.* de una manera abatida o estúpida.

mopish ['moupiʃ], *a.* atontado, abatido, adormecido.

mopishness, *s.* abatimiento.

moppet ['mɔpit], *s.* gachona, querida, cariño, amor; (*fam.*) mocita, gachí; (*ant.*) muñeca de trapo.

moquette [mɔ'ket], *s.* moqueta.

moraine [mo'rein], *s.* (*geol.*) morena.

moral ['mɔrəl], *a.* moral, ético; virtuoso, púdico, casto, honesto, recto, honrado. — *s.* moraleja. — *pl.* moralidad; ética, moral, *f.*; costumbres, *f.pl.*; integridad.

morale [mo'rɑ:l], *s.* moral, *f.*, confianza, aliento.

moralist, *s.* moralista, *m.f.*

morality [mɔ'ræliti], *s.* moralidad, moral, *f.*, ética, rectitud, honestidad, formalidad.

moralization, *s.* moralización.

moralize ['mɔrəlaiz], *v.t.* moralizar. — *v.i.* moralizar.

moralizer, *s.* moralizador.

moralizing, *s.* moralización. — *a.* moralizador.

morally ['mɔrəli], *adv.* moralmente, honradamente, virtuosamente; prácticamente, casi, poco menos de.

morass [mo'ræs], *s.* pantano, ciénaga, cenegal, marisma.

moratorium [mɔrə'tɔ:riəm], *s.* moratoria.

Moravian [mo'reiviən], *s.*, *a.* moravo.

morbid ['mɔ:ibid], *a.* mórbido, morboso, insano.

morbidity, *s.* estado mórbido.

morbidly, *adv.* de una manera mórbida.

morbidness, *s.* estado mórbido, disposición mórbida.

morbific, morbifical, *a.* morbífico, mórbido, malsano.

mordacious [mɔ:ɪ'deiʃəs], *a.* mordaz, satírico.

mordacity [mɔ:ɪ'dæsiti], *s.* mordacidad.

mordant ['mɔ:ɪdənt], *s.*, *a.* mordente, mordiente; mordaz.

mordent ['mɔ:ɪdənt], *s.* (*mús.*) mordente.

mordicant ['mɔ:ɪdikənt], *a.* corrosivo.

more [mɔ:ɪ], *a.* (*superl.* **most**) más, adicional, más numeroso; mayor; en mayor número; *more haste, less space,* cuanto más se corre, menos se anda. — *adv.* más; *more and more,* cada vez más; *once more,* otra vez, una vez más; *so much the more,* tanto más; *the more the merrier,* cuantos más locos hay, más se ríe; *to be no more,* haber fallecido, haber dejado de existir; *the more one has, the more one wants,* cuanto más tiene, más quiere.

moreen [mo'ri:n], *s.* filipichín, tela de lana.

morel [mo'rel], *s.* crespilla, colmenilla múrgura; hierba mora, especie de solano. — *a.* moreno.

moreover [mɔ:r'ouvəɪ], *adv.* además, por

otra parte, a más, además de eso; también, ítem, otrosí.

moresque [mo'resk], *s.*, *a.* morisco, arabesco.

morganatic [mɔ:ɪgə'nætik], *a.* morganático.

moribund ['mɔribʌnd], *a.* moribundo.

morion ['mɔriən], *s.* morrión, casco.

morisco [mo'riskou], **morisk** [mo'risk], *s.* morisco; danza morisca; arabesco. — *a.* morisco.

morling ['mɔ:ɪliŋ], *s.* lana muerta.

Mormon ['mɔ:ɪmən], *s.* mormón. — *a.* mormónico.

mormonism, *s.* mormonismo.

morn [mɔ:ɪn], *s.* (*poét.*) mañana, aurora, alborada.

morning ['mɔ:ɪniŋ], *s.* mañana, aurora, alborada; madrugada; *good morning,* buenos días; *early in the morning,* de madrugada, muy de mañana; *to-morrow morning,* mañana por la mañana. — *a.* de mañana, matutino, matinal; *morning gown,* bata; *morning star,* (*astr.*) lucero del alba.

Moroccan, *s.*, *a.* marroquí, marrueco.

Morocco, *s.* Marruecos.

morocco [mo'rɔkou], *s.* (*cuero*) marroquí, tafilete.

morose [mo'rous], *a.* abatido, malhumorado, saturnino, bronco, áspero; moroso, tardo.

morosely, *adv.* morosamente, ásperamente, broncamente.

moroseness, morosity, *s.* acrimonia, aspereza, mal humor; morosidad, dilación.

morphia ['mɔ:ɪfiə], **morphine** ['mɔ:ɪfi:n], *s.* morfina.

morphinism, *s.* morfinismo.

morphinomania [mɔ:ɪfino'meiniə], **morphiomania** [mɔ:ɪfio'meiniə], *s.* abuso excesivo de morfina.

morphological [mɔ:ɪfo'lɔdʒikəl], *a.* morfológico.

morphology [mɔ:ɪ'fɔlɔdʒi], *s.* morfología.

morphosis, *s.* morfosis, *f.*

morrice, morris ['mɔris], *s.* danza morisca, mojiganga.

morrow ['mɔrou], *s.* mañana, día siguiente; *to-morrow,* mañana; *day after to-morrow,* pasado mañana.

morse [mɔ:ɪs], *s.* (*zool.*) morsa; (*teleg.*) Morse; *Morse code,* clave telegráfica de Morse.

morsel ['mɔ:ɪsəl], *s.* pedazo, bocado, manjar.

mort, *s.* muerte, *f.*; hurra, victoria; (*ict.*) salmón de tres años.

mortal ['mɔ:ɪtəl], *a.* mortal, mortífero; grave, fatal, letal; humano; (*fam.*) extremo, violento; prolijo, fastidioso. — *s.* mortal, ser humano.

mortality ['mɔ:ɪ'tæliti], *s.* mortalidad, mortandad; mortalidad, naturaleza mortal.

mortally ['mɔ:ɪtəli], *adv.* mortalmente, a muerte; (*fam.*) extremamente.

mortar ['mɔ:ɪtəɪ], *s.* mortero, argamasa, almirez.

mortgage ['mɔ:ɪgidʒ], *s.* hipoteca. — *v.t.* hipotecar.

mortgageable, *a.* hipotecable.

mortgagee [mɔ:ɪgə'dʒi:], *s.* acreedor hipotecario.

mortgager, *s.* deudor hipotecario.

mortiferous [mɔ:ɪ'tifərəs], *a.* mortífero, mortal.

mortification [mɔ:ɪtifi'keiʃən], *s.* mortificación, descomposición; (*med.*) gangrena; humillación, bochorno.

mortify ['mɔːtifai], *v.t.* mortificar, hacer gangrenar; (*fig.*) humillar, abochornar; herir el amor propio; subyugar, castigar, domar. — *v.i.* mortificarse, gangrenarse, descomponerse, corromperse.

mortifying, *a.* mortificante, humillante.

mortise ['mɔːtis], *v.t.* hacer una mortaja. — *s.* mortaja, cotana, muesca, entalladura.

mortmain ['mɔːtmein], *s.* (*der.*) manos muertas.

mortuary ['mɔːtjuːəri], *s.* mortuorio, cementerio, depósito de cadáveres. — *a.* mortuorio.

mosaic [moˈzeiik], *s.* mosaico, obra en mosaico.

mosaic [moˈzeiik], **mosaical** [moˈzeiikəl], *a.* mosaico.

mosaically, *adv.* en mosaico.

moschatel [mɔskəˈtel], *s.* moscatelina, hierba almizcle.

Moslem ['mɔzlem], *s.* musulmán. — *a.* musulmán, muslímico, mahometano.

moslings ['mɔzliŋz], *s.pl.* tiras delgadas de cuero producidas al descarnar los cueros para curtir.

mosque [mɔsk], *s.* mezquita.

mosquito [mɔsˈkiːtou], *s.* mosquito, cínife; *mosquito net*, mosquitero.

moss [mɔs], *s.* musgo, musco, moho; pantano, ciénaga, tremedal.

moss-grown, *a.* musgoso, mohoso.

mossiness, *s.* abundancia de musgo; estado mohoso.

moss-rose, *s.* rosa musgosa.

moss-trooper, *s.* bandido, bandolero.

mossy, *a.* musgoso, mohoso.

most [moust], *a.* la mayor parte de, lo(s) más de, la mayoría de. — *adv.* lo más, sumamente, en extremo, muy, en sumo grado. — *s.* principal, mayor número, mayor parte, más; *at the most*, a todo tirar, a lo más; *to make the most of*, sacar el mejor partido posible de; *most of all*, sobretodo; *for the most part*, en su mayor parte.

mostly, *adv.* ordinariamente, principalmente, par lo común, mayormente, en su mayor parte.

mote [mout], *s.* mota, partícula; (*ant.*) átomo; (*ant.*) detalle, cosa baladí; mota, cerro; mota, mancha.

motet [moˈtet], *s.* motete.

moth [mɔθ], *s.* polilla, alevilla, falena.

moth-eaten, *a.* apolillado.

mother ['mʌðər], *s.f.* madre; matrona; madre (religiosa), abadesa, priora; (*fam.*) tía, mujer muy vieja; enmohecimiento; origen, causa; zurrapa, madre del vino; incubadora; *mother-in-law*, suegra; *step-mother*, madrastra; *grand-mother*, abuela. — *a.* materno, natal, de madre; vernáculo; metropolitano, nacional; *mother country*, patria; *mother church*, iglesia metropolitana; *mother tongue*, lengua madre; *mother-of-pearl*, madreperla, nácar; *mother wit*, ingenio; *mother of thyme*, (*bot.*) serpol. — *v.t.* servir de madre a; ahijar; mimar. — *v.i.* criar madre (el vino, los licores, etc.).

motherhood ['mʌðəhud], *s.* maternidad.

motherless, *a.* sin madre.

motherliness, *s.* cariño maternal, maternidad.

motherly, *a.* maternal, materno; mimoso. — *adv.* maternalmente.

motherwort, *s.* agripalma.

mothy ['mɔθi], *a.* apolillado.

motif [mouˈtiːf], *s.* motivo, tema, *m.*

motile ['mouˈtail], *a.* movible.

motion ['mouʃən], *s.* movimiento, moción, mudanza; cambio de postura; meneo, aire, ademán, ímpetu, impulso; señal, *f.*, signo, seña; propuesta, proposición; (*mec.*) juego, operación; (*med.*) evacuación; (*for.*) pedimento; *to carry a motion*, hacer adoptar una moción; *to make a motion*, proponer, hacer una proposición; *to put in motion*, poner en movimiento o marcha. — *v.i.* hacer una señal, hacer señas.

motionless, *a.* inmóvil, inmovible, yerto, sin movimiento.

motive ['moutiv], *s.* motivo, razón, *f.*, causa, móvil, estímulo, impulso; tema, *m.*, asunto. — *a.* motor, motriz, moviente; *motive power*, fuerza motriz.

motley ['mɔtli], *a.* abigarrado, pintorreado, vestido de colorines, variado, mezclado. — *s.* traje abigarrado; mezcla de colores; payaso, gracioso con traje pintarrajado.

motor ['moutər], *a.* motor, motriz; *motor-boat*, bote automóvil; *motor-car*, coche automóvil; *motor-cycle*, motocicleta. — *s.* motor; máquina, motriz, *f.*; (*fam.*) automóvil, coche.

motoring, *s.* automovilismo.

motorist ['moutərist], *s.* automovilista, *m.f.*, motorista, *m.f.*

motorman ['moutəmæn], *s.* conductor de tren (o tranvía) eléctrico.

motory ['moutəri], *a.* motor.

mottle ['mɔtəl], *v.t.* jaspear, motear, abigarrar. — *s.* mancha.

mottled, *a.* jaspeado, moteado, esquizado, mosqueado; abigarrado, pintarrajado, pintojo; tordo. — *p.p.* [MOTTLE]; *mottled soap*, jabón de Marsella.

motto ['mɔtou], *s.* mote, divisa, lema, *m.*, leyenda.

moufflon ['muːflɔn], *s.* musmón.

mould [mould], *s.* moho, tierra vegetal; modelo, patrón; matriz, molde; (*mar.*) grúa de tablas; (*arq.*) moldura; verdín, orín, mancha de orín. — *v.t.* enmohecer, cubrir con tierra; moldar, amoldar, moldear; formar, amasar, vaciar; (*mar.*) galivar. — *v.i.* enmohecerse.

mouldable, *a.* capaz de ser amoldado.

moulder ['mouldər], *s.* moldeador. — *v.t.* convertir en polvo, destruir, consumir, degastar. — *v.i.* reducirse a polvo, desgastarse, consumirse, desmoronarse.

mouldering ['moulddəriŋ], *a.* que (se) reduce a polvo; que (se) consume. — *s.* desmoronamiento, desgaste.

mouldiness, *s.* moho.

moulding, *s.* (*arq.*) moldura, lengüeta; amoldamiento; vaciamiento; (*fig.*) formación.

mouldy, *a.* mohoso, enmohecido.

moulinet [muːliˈnet], *s.* molinete.

moult [moult], *v.i.* mudar (la pluma), emplumar, desplumar. — *s.* muda.

moulting, *s.* muda (de pluma).

mound [maund], *s.* atrincheramiento, dique; baluarte, terraplén, montón de tierra, montículo, terrero, morón; (*blas.*) mundo, esfera, atributo de un monarca. — *v.t.*

atrincherar, fortalecer con un dique; amontonar.

mount [maunt], *v.i.* subir(se), elevarse, ascender, montar; ascender, aumentar. — *v.t.* levantar, alzar, subir, montar; cabalgar; poner a caballo; enaltecer; engastar (una joya); (*teat.*) poner en escena; (*arti.*) portar, armar, artillar; *to mount guard,* (*mil.*) entrar la guardia; *to mount the throne,* subir al trono; *to mount a trooper,* poner un jinete a caballo. — *s.* monte, montaña, cabalgadura, montadura; terraplén, baluarte; apeadero; borde (de un cuadro); (*mil.*) monta (toque de clarín).

mountable, *a.* que se puede subir o montar.

mountain ['mauntin], *s.* montaña, sierra, monte; masa enorme, montón; *mountain-railway,* ferrocarril funicular; *mountain-side,* falda, pendiente (de montaña), *f.*; *mountains high,* (*mar., fig.*) olas como montañas; *to make mountains out of molehills,* hacer de una mosca (o pulga) un elefante. — *a.* montés, montañés; *mountain chain,* cordillera, sierra; *mountain ash,* mostajo, mostellar, serbal de los cazadores.

mountaineer [maunti'niəɹ], *s.* montañés, montaraz; alpinista, *m.f.* — *v.i.* dedicarse o estar aficionado al alpinismo.

mountaineering, *s.* alpinismo.

mountainous, *a.* montañoso, montuoso, montaraz, peñascoso; (*fig.*) enorme.

mountainousness, *s.* montuosidad.

mountebank ['mauntibæŋk], *s.* saltimbanqui, saltabanco; charlatán, truhán, juglar. — *v.t.* engañar por medio de charlatanerías.

mounting, *s.* ascensión, elevación, subida; montaje, montura, armadura, armamento, equipo; engaste.

mourn [mɔːɹn], *v.i.* llorar, quejarse, afligirse, dolerse, lamentarse, gemir, plañir, apesadumbrarse; vestirse de luto, llevar luto, estar de luto, enlutarse. — *v.t.* llorar, deplorar, lamentar, sentir; llevar luto por.

mourner, *s.* afligido, enlutado, el que llora, doliente, dolorido; plañidera; *chief mourner,* el que guía el duelo y recibe los pésames.

mournful, *a.* melancólico, lastimero, deplorable, funesto, fúnebre, lúgubre, (*poét.*) fúnereo.

mournfulness, *s.* aflicción, pesar, desconsuelo, duelo, melancolía.

mourning, *a.* deplorable, afligido, luctuoso, lamentoso, fúnebre, fúnereo, de luto. — *s.* llanto, lamento, duelo, luto, aflicción, dolor, desconsuelo, gemido, plañido; luto, vestido o prendas de luto; *to go into mourning,* tomar el luto; *to be in mourning,* estar de luto; *to come out of mourning,* dejar el luto; *half mourning,* medio luto; *deep mourning,* luto riguroso; *mourning-bride, mourning-widow,* (*bot.*) escabiosa; *mourning-dove,* paloma de la Carolina.

mouse [maus], *s.* (*pl.* **mice**) ratón; (*mar.*) barrilete; *field-mouse,* turcón. — *v.t., v.i.* cazar ratones, coger ratones; desgarrar; (*mar.*) amarrar (un gancho), abarbetar.

mouse-coloured, *a.* pardusco.

mouse-ear, *s.* miosota, vellosillo, pelosilla oficinal.

mouse-hole, *s.* agujero de ratón.

mouser ['mausəɹ], *s.* cazador de ratones.

mouse-tail, *s.* (*bot.*) miosuro.

mouse-trap, *s.* ratonera. — *a.* ratonero.

mousing, *s.* caza de ratones.

moustache [məs'tɑːʃ], *s.* bigote, mostacho.

mouth [mauθ], *s.* boca; orificio; embocadura, desembocadura, embocadero; (*fig.*) entrada; (instrumento musical) boquilla; gesto, mueca; *to make one's mouth water,* hacer venir el agua a la boca, *o* hacerse agua la boca; *to stop someone's mouth,* (*fig.*) imponer silencio a uno; *to make mouths,* hacer una mueca; *down in the mouth,* cabizbajo, alicaído. — *v.t.* pronunciar; vocear, declamar, hablar alto; reprochar, insultar; comer, mascar. — *v.i.* vociferar, hablar a gritos.

mouthed [mauðd], *a.* que tiene boca, provisto de una boca; *foul-mouthed,* que tiene mala lengua, mal hablado; *hard-mouthed,* boquiduro; *mealy-mouthed,* hipócrita, doble, mojigato, almibarado; *wide-mouthed,* bocudo.

mouther, *s.* declamador.

mouthful ['mauθful], *s.* bocado, bocadito; pizca.

mouthing ['mauðiŋ], *s.* pronunciación afectada.

mouthless, *a.* desbocado.

mouth-organ ['mauθɔːɹgən], *s.* organillo de boca.

mouth-piece, *s.* embocadura, boquilla, bocal, estrangul; (*fig.*) intérprete, portavoz.

movable ['muːvəbəl], *a.* movedizo, móvil, movible; mobiliario. — *pl.* **movables,** muebles, bienes muebles, mobiliario, efectos.

movableness, *s.* movilidad.

movably, *adv.* de un modo movible.

move [muːv], *v.t.* mover, mudar; trasladar, mudar; incitar, excitar, impeler, impulsar; conmover, alterar, remover; enternecer; sacudir, menear; *to move to laughter,* hacer reír o causar risa; *to be moved,* enternecerse, conmoverse. — *v.i.* moverse, ponerse en movimiento; menearse; pasearse; sacudir; mudar de sitio; mudar de casa; vacilar; ir, caminar, andar, ponerse en marcha, marchar; adelantar, progresar, avanzar; trasladarse; entrar en acción, empezar a obrar; exonerarse el vientre; *to move about o around,* ir y venir; pasearse; remover; *to move along,* circular, pasearse; *to move away,* marcharse, irse; alejarse, retirarse; *to move down,* bajar; *to move forward,* avanzar, adelantarse; *to move in,* entrar, tomar posesión de (una casa); *to move out,* salir, mudar de casa, abandonar una casa; *to move round,* dar vueltas; girar; *to move to laughter,* hacer reír; *to move to tears,* hacer llorar; *to move up,* subir, ascender; mejorar. — *s.* movimiento, paso, suerte, *f.,* turno, jugada, mano, *f.* (en el juego); *to make a good move,* dar un paso acertado; *it's your move,* le toca a Vd. (jugar); *to miss one's move,* errar una jugada; *on the move,* de viaje.

movement, *s.* moción, movimiento, marcha; (*mil.*) evolución, maniobra, acto, paso, meneo, rodeo, vuelta; incidente, acción, agitación, actividad, excitación; disposición; evacuación, cámara; (*com.*) circulación; (*mús.*) movimiento, tiempo, compás; (*mús.*) movimiento, tiempo, parte, *f.*; (*literatura*) movimiento, tendencia.

mover, s. motor, motriz, f., móvil, movedor, autor de una moción.

moving, a. motor, motriz; conmovedor, emocionante, excitante, tierno, patético; *moving staircase,* escalera giratoria. — s. movimiento, moción, impulso; partida, salida, marcha; traslado, mudanza, cambio de domicilio.

mow [mou], s. hórreo, granero, henil, troj, f., cámara, haz, f., hacina, pila. — v.t. (p.p. **mowed, mown)** poner en haces, entrojar. — v.t., v.i. segar, guadañar. — v.i. hacer muecas.

mower [mouəɹ], s. segador, guadañero; segadora mecánica.

mowing, s. siega; mies, f.; terreno segado; mueca, gesta; *mowing machine,* segadora mecánica.

much [mʌtʃ], a. mucho, grande, largo, abundante, copioso. — adv. mucho, muy, tanto, excesivamente, grandemente, en gran manera, con mucho; *as* (o *so*) *much as,* tanto como; *so much,* tanto; *so much the better,* tanto mejor; *how much?,* ¿cuánto?; *too much* o *over much,* demasiado; excesivo; *much the same,* casi lo mismo, poco más o menos; *as much more,* otro tanto más; *much ado about nothing,* mucho ruido y pocas nueces, nada entre dos platos, poco mal y bien quejado; *however much,* por mucho que; *I thought as much,* (fam.) ya me lo figuraba; *not much,* (vulg.) ni por asomo, ni por pienso, ciertamente no. — s. abundancia, copia, plenitud, gran cantidad, muchedumbre, multitud; *much never cost little,* nunca mucho costó poco; *to make much of,* dar importancia a; atender a, tener en mucho a; mimar; *not to think much of,* tener en poco a.

muchness [mʌtʃnis], s. demasía, cantidad; (fam.) *much of a muchness,* lo mismo poco más o menos, otro que tal.

mucid [mjuːsid], a. mohoso, viscoso, glutinoso.

mucilage [mjuːsilidʒ], s. mucílago.

mucilaginous, muciparous, a. viscoso, mucilaginoso.

muck [mʌk], s. fiemo, estiércol, abono, basura; (fig.) porquería, suciedad; cosa de poco valor. — v.t. estercolar, abonar; *to muck up,* (vulg.) estropear, chapucear, ensuciar.

muck-heap, muck-hill, s. estercolero, muladar.

muckiness, s. inmundicia, basura, suciedad, porquería.

muckle [mʌkəl], a. (prov.) mucho; grande.

muckworm, s. gusano de estercolero; (fig.) avariento, ruin, mezquino, miserable.

mucky [mʌki], a. (fam.) asqueroso; despreciable, vil.

mucoid [mjuːkɔid], a. mucoso.

mucor, s. moco, moho, mucosidad.

mucosity, s. mucosidad.

mucous [mjuːkəs], a. mucoso, mocoso, flemoso, viscoso, glutinoso, pegajoso.

mucousness, s. mucosidad, viscosidad, moco.

mucus [mjuːkəs], s. moco, mucosidad; (bot.) mucílago vegetal.

mud [mʌd], s. barro, lodo, fango, cieno, limo; *mud-lighter,* gañil, lancha de draga; *mud-bath,* baño de cieno; *mud-wall,* tapia. — v.t.

encenagar, empantanar, enfangar, enlodar, ensuciar, enturbiar.

mudɑily, adv. suciamente, turbiamente.

muddiness, s. suciedad; turbieza, turbulencia.

muddle [mʌdəl], v.t. embriagar; entontecer, atontar, embotar; aturdir, dejar peplejo, enredar, turbar; enturbiar, ensuciar. — v.i. estar atontado; *to muddle along,* (fam.) hacerse un lío; no acertar; *to make a muddle,* armar un lío. — s. confusión, embrollo.

muddled, muddle-headed, a. atontado; achispado; torpe; desordenado.

muddy, a. sucio, fangoso, lodoso, cenagoso, barroso; turbio, enturbiado; tonto, confuso. — v.t. manchar, enturbiar, ensuciar, encenagar, empantanar; entontecer; turbar, obscurecer.

mudlark, s. galopín, pocero.

mudwort, s. limosela.

muezzin [muːˈezin], s. muecín, almuecín.

muff [mʌf], s. manguito; (orn.) curruca; maleta, m., desmañado; cubierta (para radiador de coche). — v.t. no acertar, hacer sin destreza.

muffin [mʌfin], s. mollete, bɔdigo, especie de panecillo.

muffle [mʌfəl], v.t. embozar, arrebozar, encapotar, tapar, ocultar; apagar, ensordecer; enfundar, enlutar (un tambor); cubrir con un crespón. — v.i. refunfuñar. — s. mufla; hocico, morro; funda; horno de arcilla.

muffled, a. sordo. — p.p. [MUFFLE].

muffler, s. embozo, bufanda, tapaboca, m., velo; guante de púgil; sordina de piano.

mufti [mʌfti], s. muftí; traje paisano.

mug [mʌg], s. pichel, cubilete; (vulg.) hocico, jeta, facha; (vulg.) ganso, primo, torpe, maleta, m.

muggish [mʌgiʃ], **muggy** [mʌgi], a. bochornoso, caluroso y húmedo.

mug-house, s. (vulg.) cervecería, taberna.

mugil, s. mugo, sargo.

mugweed, s. cuajaleche cruzado.

mugwort, s. artemisa, vulgar.

mugwump [mʌgwʌmp], s. (polit., E.U.) miembro del partido Republicano que se reserva el derecho de votar con absoluta independencia.

mulatress, s.f. mulata.

mulatto [mjuːˈlætou], s. mulato.

mulberry [mʌlbəri], s. (bot.) mora.

mulberry-tree, s. morera.

mulch [mʌltʃ], s. paja, estiércol, etc. que se echa alrededor del tronco de un árbol para conservar la humedad y abrigar las raíces.

mulct [mʌlkt], s. multa. — v.t. multar.

mule [mjuːl], s. mulo, mula, macho; máquina de hilar y retorcer; (bot.) planta híbrida; *pack mule,* acémila.

mule-chair, s. jamuga.

mule-driver [mjuːldraivəɹ], **muleteer** [mjuːleˈtiəɹ], s. muletero, mulero, acemilero, arriero.

mule-jenny, s. hilandera.

muliebrity [mjuːliˈiːbriti], s. naturaleza o costumbres de la mujer; nubilidad; afeminación, delicadeza.

mulish [mjuːliʃ], a. mular; híbrido; terco.

mulishness, s. terquedad.

mull [mʌl], v.t. calentar vino, cerveza, etc. con

especias. — *v.i.* ponderar, meditar. — *s.* promontorio, cabo; (*fam.*) confusión, desacierto, fracaso; muselina fina.

mullein ['mʌlin], *s.* verbasco, gordolobo.

mullet ['mʌlet], *s.* mújol, mújil, salmonete, barbo de mar; (*blas.*) estrellita, espuela; espolín.

mulligatawny [mʌligə'tɔːni], *s.* especie de sopa muy condimentada de origen indio.

mulligrubs ['mʌligrʌbz], *s.* mal humor; retortijón de tripas, cólico.

mullion ['mʌljən], *s.* crucero de ventana.

multangular [mʌl'tæŋgjuːləɹ], *a.* multangular.

multicapsular [mʌlti'kæpsjuːləɹ], *a.* multicapsular.

multidentate, *a.* multidentado.

multifarious [mʌlti'fɛəriəs], *a.* multifario, diverso, vario.

multifariousness, *s.* variedad, diversidad, desemejanza.

multifidous [mʌl'tifidəs], *a.* multífido.

multiflorous [mʌl'tiflorəs], *a.* multifloro.

multiform ['mʌltifɔːɹm], *a.* multiforme, de diversas formas, variado.

multiformity, *s.* multiformidad.

multilateral [mʌlti'lætərəl], *a.* multilátero.

multiloquent [mʌl'tilokwənt], **multiloquous** [mʌl'tilokwəs], *a.* moltilocuo, parlero, parlanchín.

multimillionaire [mʌltimiljo'nɛəɹ], *s.* multimillonario.

multiparous [mʌl'tipərəs], *a.f.* multípara.

multipartite, *a.* multipartido.

multiped ['mʌltiped], *s.* ciempiés, cientopiés, escolopendra. — *a.* multípedo.

multiple, *a.* multíplice, múltiple. — *s.* múltiplo, multíplice.

multiplex ['mʌltipleks], *a.* multíplice.

multipliable [mʌlti'plaiəbəl], **multiplicable**, *a.* multiplicable.

multiplicand [mʌltipli'kænd], *s.* multiplicando.

multiplicate [mʌl'tiplikit], *a.* multiplicado.

multiplication, *s.* multiplicación.

multiplicative, *a.* multiplicador, multiplicativo.

multiplicator, *s.* multiplicador.

multiplicity [mʌlti'plisiti], *s.* multiplicidad.

multiplier, *s.* multiplicador.

multiply ['mʌltiplai], *v.t.* multiplicar. — *v.i.* multiplicar(se).

multipolar [mʌlti'pouləɹ], *a.* multipolar.

multitude ['mʌltitjuːd], *s.* multitud, muchedumbre, sinnúmero; vulgo, masas; gentío, populacho.

multitudinary, multitudinous, *a.* numeroso.

multitudinousness, *s.* gran número, multitud, muchedumbre, sinnúmero.

multivalve ['mʌltivælv], *s., a.* multivalvo.

multure ['mʌltʃəɹ], *s.* maquila.

mum [mʌm], *a.* (*fam.*) silencioso, callado. — *s.* (*fam.*) mamá; (*ant.*) cerveza fuerte. — *interj.* ¡chito! ¡chitón! — *v.t., v.i.* enmascararse; guardar silencio.

mumble ['mʌmbəl], *v.t., v.i.* refunfuñar, murmullar; gruñir; mascar; barbotar; barbullar, hablar entre dientes.

mumbler, *s.* gruñidor, farfulla, farfullador.

mumblingly, *adv.* entre dientes; de manera refunfuñona.

mummer ['mʌməɹ], *s.* máscara, *m.f.*, momero.

mummery, *s.* mascarada; momería, mojiganga.

mummification [mʌmifi'keiʃən], *s.* momificación.

mummiform, *a.* en forma de momia.

mummify ['mʌmifai], *v.t.* momificar.

mumming ['mʌmiŋ], *s.* mascarada, mojiganga, momería. — *a.* relativo a una mascarada.

mummy ['mʌmi], *s.* momia; (*fam.*) mamá, mamaíta.

mump [mʌmp], *v.t.* morder, mascar, mordiscar; farfullar; (*vulg.*) mendigar.

mumper, *s.* (*vulg.*) mendigo.

mumping, *s.* (*vulg.*) mendicidad; astucia de mendigo.

mumpish, *a.* malhumorado, moroso, intratable, de mal humor.

mumpishness, *s.* morosidad.

mumps [mʌmps], *s.* (*med.*) parótidas, paperas; (*fig.*) murria.

munch [mʌntʃ], *v.t.* mascar, mascujar, mascullar, masticar.

muncher, *s.* tragón, comilón.

mundane [mʌn'dein], *a.* mundano.

municipal [mju:'nisipəl], *a.* municipal; *municipal government*, gobierno municipal, ayuntamiento.

municipality [mju:nisi'pæliti], *s.* municipalidad, municipio.

munificence, *s.* munificencia.

munificent [mju:'nifisənt], *a.* munífico.

muniment ['mju:nimənt], *s.* título, escritura, papel, documento de importancia guardado como defensa legal y prueba; (*ant.*) fortaleza; apoyo, defensa.

munitions [mju:'niʃəns], *s.pl.* municiones; *munitions dump*, depósito de municiones.

mural ['mju:rəl], *a.* mural; vertical, escarpado. — *s.* pintura mural; mapa mural.

murder ['məːɹdəɹ], *s.* asesinato. — *v.t.* asesinar; exterminar, destruir; degollar; (*fig.*) estropear, desfigurar, mutilar.

murderer, *s.* asesino, homicida, *m.*

murderess, *s.f.* asesina.

murderous, *a.* sanguinario, bárbaro, homicida, asesino.

mure [mju:əɹ], *v.t.* cercar con murallas.

murex, *s.* (*zool.*) múrice.

muriate ['mju:riət], *s.* muriato, clorhidrato.

muriatic, *a.* muriático, clorhídrico.

murk [məːɹk], *s.* oscuridad, lobreguez, tinieblas.

murk, murky, *a.* oscuro, lóbrego, tenebroso; tenebroso, accidentado, borrascoso.

murkily, *adv.* oscuramente.

murkiness, *s.* lobreguez, tinieblas; lo borrascoso.

murmur ['məːɹməɹ], *s.* murmullo, murmurio; queja; susurro, rumor. — *v.i.* murmurar, refunfuñar, gruñir, regañar; murmurar, susurrar, hablar en voz baja.

murmurer, *s.* murmurador, gruñidor.

murmuring, *s.* murmuración, murmullo. — *a.* murmurante, susurrante; quejumbroso.

murphy ['məːɹfi], *s.* (*vulg.*) patata.

murrain ['mʌrən], *s.* morriña.

murrey ['mʌri], *a.* morado, mezcla de rojo y negro.

muscadel [mʌskə'del], **muscadine** ['mʌskədin], **muscat** ['mʌskət], **muscatel** [mʌskə'tel], *s.* moscatel.

muscardine ['mʌskaːɹdin], *s.* muscardina, enfermedad fatal del gusano de seda.

muscle ['mʌsəl], s. (anat.) músculo; (zool.) almeja.

muscoid ['mʌskɔid], a. musgoso.

Muscovite ['mʌskovait], s., a. moscovita, m.f.

muscular ['mʌskju:lɔɹ], a. muscular; musculoso, membrudo, fornido.

muscularity, s. fuerzas musculares, muscolosidad.

musculous, a. musculoso.

muse [mju:z], s. musa, numen, estro; ingenio poético, inspiración. — v.t. meditar, pensar, considerar. — v.i. meditar, distraerse, rumiar, mirar a las musarañas.

museful, a. meditabundo, cogitabundo, pensativo.

muser, s. el que medita.

museum [mju:'ziəm], s. museo.

mush [mʌʃ], s. cualquier cosa blanda y mollar; potaje de harina de maíz y leche; (vulg.) paraguas, m.sing.; (vulg.) compadre, chico.

mushroom ['mʌʃrum], s. seta, hongo; (fig.) hombre advenedizo, nuevorico. — a. hecho con setas; (fig.) advenedizo, efímero, rápido.

mushy, a. (fam.) pulposo, mollar.

music ['mju:zik], s. música; composición musical; music-hall, (teatro de) variedades, café concierto; music-master, profesor de música; music-stand, atril, pupitre; music-stool, banqueta o taburete de piano;

musical ['mju:zikəl], a. musical, músico, armonioso, armónico; aficionado a la música; musical box, caja de música; musical comedy, zarzuela, tonadilla, comedia musical.

musically, adv. musicalmente, armoniosamente.

musician [mju:'ziʃən], s. músico.

music-mad, a. melómano.

musing ['mju:ziŋ], s. meditación, contemplación, ensueño. — a. meditabundo, pensativo.

musingly, adv. de un modo contemplativo.

musk [mʌsk], s. almizcle, musco; (bot.) almizcleña.

musk-apple, s. manzana camuesa.

musk-beetle, s. calicromo.

musk-cat, s. (zool.) desmán.

musk-cherry, s. cereza almizcleña.

musk-deer, s. almizclero.

musked, a. almizclado.

musket ['mʌsket], s. mosquete; (ant.) gavilán macho (ave).

musketeer [mʌskə'tiəɹ], s. mosquetero.

musketoon [mʌskə'tu:n], s. trabuco.

musketry ['mʌsketri], s. mosquetería, fusilería.

musket-shot, s. fusilazo.

musk-grape, s. moscatel.

muskiness ['mʌskinis], s. olor de almizcle.

musk-melon, s. melón almizclero o de Castilla.

musk-ox, s. buey almizclero.

musk-pear, s. mosqueruela, pera almizcleña.

musk-rat, s. rata almizclera.

musk-rose, s. rosa almizcleña.

musky, a. almizclado, almizclero, almizcleño.

Muslim ['mʌzlim], s., a. musulmán, mahometano.

muslin, s. muselina; bengala; cambric muslin, batista. — a. de muselina, hecho de muselina.

musquash ['mʌskwɔʃ], s. almizclera.

muss [mʌs], s. (E.U.) estado de confusión o desorden; (vulg.) sarracina, riña. — v.t. desarreglar, poner en confusión y desorden [MESS].

mussel ['mʌsəl], s. almeja.

Mussulman ['mʌsəlmən], s. musulmán.

must [mʌst], v. auxil. deber, tener que, haber de, ser necesario (o preciso), estar precisado, estar obligado, ser menester; convenir; deber de; I must go, tengo que ir, es preciso que vaya. — s. moho; mosto, zumo. — v.t. enmohecer. — v.i. enmohecerse.

mustache, s. [MOUSTACHE].

mustang ['mʌstæŋ], s. potro mesteño.

mustard ['mʌstəɹd], s. mostaza; mustard-pot, mostacera; mustard-gas, gas mostaza; mustard-paper, mustard-poultice, sinapismo.

musteline ['mʌstəlain], a. mustelino.

muster ['mʌstəɹ], v.t., v.i. pasar lista, pasar muestra, pasar revista; reunir(se), juntar(se); exhibir, mostrar, revelar; to muster one's courage, cobrar (o recobrar) ánimo. — s. concurso, reunión, f.; muestra, alarde, llamada, reseña, revista; lista (de tropas), (mar.) rol; to pass muster, pasar muestra, ser aceptable; muster-roll, matrícula de revista; (mar.) rol de la tripulación; muster-book, libro de revistas; muster-master, comisario de revistas.

mustily ['mʌstili], adv. con moho.

mustiness, s. moho, husmo.

musty, a. enmohecido, mohoso, añejo; rancio, mustio; pasado, pasado de moda; triste.

mutability [mju:tə'biliti], s. mutabilidad.

mutable ['mju:təbəl], a. mudable, instable.

mutableness, s. mutabilidad.

mutation [mju:'teiʃən], s. mutación, mudanza, variación, alteración.

mute [mju:t], a. mudo; callado, silencioso, tranquilo. — s. mudo; (mús.) sordina; tullidura, fiemo de pájaros; (gram.) muda; deaf-mute, sordomudo; to stand mute, (for.) negarse a responder ante la justicia. — v.i. tullir, arrojar tullidura.

mutely, adv. mudamente, sin hablar palabra, en silencio, calladamente.

muteness, s. mudez, silencio.

mutilate ['mju:tileit], v.t. mutilar, tronchar, estropear, cercenar.

mutilation, s. mutilación.

mutilator, s. mutilador.

mutineer [mju:ti'niəɹ], s. amotinador, amotinado, sedicioso.

mutinous ['mju:tinəs], a. amotinado, sedicioso, faccioso.

mutinousness, s. amotinamiento, sedición.

mutiny ['mju:tini], s. amotinamiento, motín, sublevación, insubordinación. — v.t., v.i. amotinarse, rebelarse, sublevarse.

mutism ['mju:tizm], s. mutismo, mudez.

mutter ['mʌtəɹ], v.i. murmurar, refunfuñar, musitar; decir entre dientes, mascullar. — s. murmuración, murmurio; rumor.

mutterer, s. gruñón, rezongador.

muttering, s. refunfuño; murmurio.

mutteringly, adv. inarticuladamente, en voz baja.

mutton ['mʌtən], s. carnero, carne de carnero; mutton-chop, chuleta (o costilla) de carnero; mutton-fist, (vulg.) manaza grande y colorada; mutton-ham, pierna de carnero salada y curada.

mutual ['mju:tju:əl], a. mutual, mutuo, recíproco.

mutuality [mju:tju:'æliti], s. mutualidad, reciprocidad, reciprocación.

mutually, adv. mutuamente, recíprocamente.

mutuary [ˈmjuːtjuːəri], s. mutuatario.
muzzle [ˈmʌzəl], s. hocico, morro, jeta; bozal, frenillo, risuelo (para hurones), mordaza; abertura; boca de arma de fuego; *muzzle energy*, energía original; *muzzle-velocity*, velocidad inicial. — *v.t.* embozar, abozalar; imponer silencio, hacer callar.
muzzle-loader, s. arma que se carga por la boca.
muzzy [ˈmʌzi], a. (*vulg.*) borracho, emborrachado; olvidadizo, distraído.
my [mai], a. mi, mis; mío, mía, míos, mías. — *interj.* (oh) my! (*vulg.*) ¡hombre!
mycology [maiˈkɔlodʒi], s. micología, micetología.
myocardium [maioˈkɑːɹdiəm], s. miocardio.
myography [maiˈɔɡrəfi], s. miografía.
myope [ˈmaioup], **myops** [ˈmaiɔps], s. miope, *m.f.*
myopia [maiˈoupiə], **myopy**, s. miopia.
myopic, a. miope.
myosis [maiˈousis], s. miosis, *f.*
myosotis [maioˈsoutis], s. miosota.
myriad [ˈmiriəd], s. miríada, gran número.
myriagram [ˈmiriəɡræm], s. miriagramo.
myrialiter [ˈmiriəliːtəɹ], s. mirialitro.
myriameter, s. miriámetro.
myriapod [ˈmiriəpɔd], s. miriápodo.
myrmidon [ˈməːɹmidən], s. rufián, esbirro, hombre grosero.
myrrh [məːɹ], s. mirra.
myrrhic, a. mirrado, mirrino.
myrtiform, a. mirtiforme, mirtino.
myrtle [ˈməːɹtəl], s. mirto, arrayán.
myself [maiˈself], *pron. pers.* yo mismo, yo; me, a mí, a mí mismo.
mysterious [miˈstiəriəs], a. misterioso.
mysteriously, *adv.* misteriosamente.
mysteriousness, s. misterio, naturaleza misteriosa, obscuridad; embarazo.
mystery [ˈmistəri], s. misterio, arcano; (*ant.*) profesión, oficio; (*teat.*) comedia parecida al auto sacramental, misterio.
mystic, s. místico.
mystic [ˈmistik], **mystical** [ˈmistikəl], a. místico; misterioso, oscuro, simbólico, emblemático.
mysticalness, s. misticidad, mística.
mysticism [ˈmistisizm], s. misticismo, mística.
mystification, s. mistificación, ofuscación, superchería.
mystify [ˈmistifai], *v.t.* mistificar, desconcertar, confundir, ofuscar, anieblar.
myth [miθ], s. mito, fábula, ficción.
mythic [ˈmiθik], **mythical** [ˈmiθikəl], a. mítico, imaginario, fabuloso.
mythologic, mythological, a. mitológico.
mythologist [miˈθɔlodʒist], s. mitologista, *m.f.*, mitólogo.
mythologize, s. convertir en mito, interpretar mitológicamente.
mythology [miˈθɔlodʒi], s. mitología.

N

N, n [en], décimacuarta letra del alfabeto inglés; (*impr.*) n. o en, unidad de medida; (*mat.*) número indefinido.
nab [næb], *v.t.* (*vulg.*) coger, atrapar, prender.
nabob [ˈneibɔb], s. nabab; ricacho, hombre rico.
nacarat [ˈnækəræt], s. color nacarado.

nacelle [nəˈsel], s. barquilla de un globo; góndola de un dirigible.
nacre [ˈneikəɹ], s. nácar, madreperla. — a. nacarado, nacarino.
nadir [ˈnædəɹ], s. nadir.
nag [næɡ], s. jaco, jaca, haca. — *v.t., v.i.* regañar, machacar, encocorar, jeringar constantemente.
naiad [ˈnaiəd], s. náyade, *f.*
naïf [ˈnɑːiːf], a. sencillo, cándido.
nail [neil], s. uña; pezuña; garra; clavo; punta; tachón, roblón; medida (de 2¼ pulgadas); *on the nail*, al instante, en el acto; *to bite one's nails*, comerse las uñas; *to drive a nail home*, dar en el clavo; *to hit the nail on the head*, dar en el hito, acertar; *to nail a lie to the counter* (o *platform*), demostrar que una cosa es mentira. — *v.t.* clavar, enclavar, clavetear, empernar; adornar con clavos; *to nail down*, cerrar con clavos; *to nail up*, sujetar con clavos.
nail-cleaner, s. limpiauñas, *m.sing.*
nailer, s. chapucero, fabricante de clavos.
nailery, s. fábrica de clavos.
nail-maker, s. clavero.
nainsook [ˈneinsuk], s. nansú.
naissant [ˈneisənt], s. (*blas.*) naciente.
naïve [nɑːiːv], a. ingenuo, sencillo, simple, cándido, candoroso, natural.
naïveté [nɑːiːvitei], s. ingenuidad, simplicidad, candor, candidez.
naked [ˈneikid], a. desnudo, nudo; sencillo, simple, puro, mero; sin adorno; descamisado; desarmado, sin defensa; claro, patente; pobre, indigente; *stark naked*, en cueros, desnudo como la palma de la mano; *the naked truth*, verdad pura, sin quitar ni poner; *naked sword*, espada desnuda, desenvainada; *with the naked eye*, a (la) simple vista.
nakedly, *adv.* desnudamente, nudamente, en cueros; claramente.
nakedness, s. desnudez; desabrigo; falta de defensa; (*fig.*) miseria, pobreza; falta de adorno.
namby-pamby [ˈnæmbipæmbi], a. soso, (*fam.*) ñoño, insípido, melindroso. — s. melindre, pamplina, ñoñería, ñoñez; persona ñoña o sosa o melindrosa.
name [neim], s. nombre; título; mote, apodo; (*fig.*) fama, nombradía, reputación, opinión, crédito; poder, autoridad, representación; *in the name of*, en nombre de, de parte de; *in God's name*, por el amor de Dios; *by the name of*, bajo el nombre de; *in name*, de nombre; *to call names*, poner motes (a), decir injurias; *what is his name?* ¿cómo se llama?; *Christian name*, nombre de pila. — *v.t.* nombrar, apellidar, llamar, poner nombre, nominar, mentar; nombrar, elegir; mencionar; señalar, fijar, especificar, designar; citar; proferir; *to be named*, llamarse.
named [neimd], a. nombrado, elegido, designado, mencionado, citado. — *p.p.* [NAME]; *above named*, arriba citado.
name-day, s. fiesta onomástica, día del santo, santo.
nameless, a. anónimo, innominado; desconocido; indecible.
namely [ˈneimli], *adv.* a saber; particularmente, señaladamente.
namesake [ˈneimseik], s. homónimo; tocayo; (*ant.*) colombroño.

nankeen [næn'ki:n], *s.* nanquín.
nanny-goat ['nænigout], *s.* (*vulg.*) cabra.
nap [næp], *s.* siesta, sueño ligero o corto, (*fam.*) duermevela, *m.*, (*fam.*) canóniga; pelusa, lanilla, borra, vello; juego de naipes; *to take a nap*, echar, o dormir la siesta, dormitar, descabezar el sueño; quedarse hecho, quedarse frío, estar descuidado. — *v.t.* cardar (paño), carmenar, sacar pelo. — *v.i.* echar, o dormir la siesta, dormitar, descabezar el sueño; *to be caught napping*, quedarse hecho, quedarse frío, ser sorprendido, estar desprevenido.
nape [neip], *s.* nuca, cogote.
napery ['neipəri], *s.* ropa blanca, artículo de lienzo, mantelería.
naphtha ['næfθə], *s.* nafta.
naphthalene ['næfθəli:n], **naphthaline** [næfθəlin], *s.* naftalina.
naphthol ['næfθɔl], *s.* naftol.
napkin ['næpkin], *s.* servilleta; toalla pequeña; (*prov.*) pañuelo de bolsillo; *napkin-ring*, servilletero.
napless, *a.* sin pelusa, raído.
napoleon [nə'pouliən], *s.* antigua moneda francesa; juego de naipes.
napper ['næpəɹ], *s.* (*vulg.*) cabeza.
nappiness, *s.* vellosidad; gana de dormir.
nappy ['næpi], *a.* velloso, peludo; fuerte (de la cerveza).
narcissus [naː'sisəs], *s.* narciso.
narcolepsy [naːˈkoˈlepsi], *s.* narcolepsia.
narcosis [naːɹ'kousis], *s.* narcosis, *f.*, narcotismo.
narcotic [naːɹ'kɔtik], *a.* narcótico, opiado; narcotizador. — *s.* narcótico, opiato.
narcotical, *a.* narcótico.
narcotine ['naːɹkotain], *s.* narcotina.
narcotism ['naːɹkətizm], *s.* narcotismo.
narcotization, *s.* narcotismo.
narcotize, *v.t.* narcotizar.
nard [naːɹd], *s.* nardo.
nardine ['naːɹdain], *s.* nardino.
narrate [nə'reit], *v.t.* narrar, relacionar, relatar, referir.
narration, *s.* narración, relato, relación, cuento, reseña.
narrative ['nærətiv], *a.* narrativo. — *s.* narrativa, relación, relato.
narrator, *s.* narrador, relator, relatador.
narratory, *a.* narratorio.
narrow ['nærou], *a.* estrecho, angosto; encogido, apretado; limitado, reducido; breve, escaso, corto; apocado; próximo, cercano; minucioso; mezquino, ruin, tacaño, avariento; escrupuloso; atento; mojigato, santurrón; iliberal, intransigente; *narrow escape*, escapada difícil; *to have a narrow escape*, salvarse en una tabla; *narrow-minded*, corto de miras; santurrón, mojigato; *narrow-gauge*, (*f.c.*) ferrocarril económico o de vía estrecha (de menos de 1·435 m); *narrow circumstances*, pobreza, estrechez. — *pl.* (*mar.*) estrecho, paso; desfiladero entre montañas. — *v.t.* estrechar, reducir, encoger, angostar; limitar, disminuir. — *v.i.* estrecharse, encogerse, reducirse; andar los caballos con las patas muy juntas.
narrowing, *s.* estrechamiento; reducción, mengua, limitación.
narrowly, *adv.* estrechamente, angostamente,

reducidamente, mezquinamente; escasamente, exactamente.
narrowness, *s.* angostura, apretura, estrechez; miseria, pobreza; mojigatería.
narwhal ['naːɹwəl], *s.* narval.
nasal ['neizəl], *a.* nasal. — *s.* (*anat.*) hueso de la nariz; (*gram.*) letra nasal, sonido nasal.
nasality [nə'zæliti], *s.* sonido nasal, calidad nasal.
nasally, *adv.* nasalmente, con sonido nasal.
nasard ['næzəɹd], *s.* nasardo.
nascent ['neisənt], *a.* naciente, creciente.
naseberry ['neizberi], *s.* níspero.
nastily ['naːstili], *adv.* mal, suciamente, asquerosamente, puercamente.
nastiness, *s.* suciedad, obscenidad, bascosidad, porquería.
nasturtium [nə'stəːɹʃəm], *s.* (*bot.*) capuchina, nasturcia.
nasty ['naːsti], *a.* sucio, impuro, puerco, asqueroso, obsceno, sórdido, indecente, deshonesto, pornográfico; odioso, vicioso, nauseabundo; rencoroso; intratable.
natal ['neitəl], *a.* natal, nativo.
natality [nə'tæliti], *s.* natalidad.
natant, *a.* (*poét.*) nadante; (*bot.*) flotando; (*blas.*) pez representado como nadando en un escudo de armas.
natatorial [nætə'tɔːriəl], *a.* nadador, natatorio.
natatory [nə'teitəri], *a.* natatorio.
natch [nætʃ], *s.* anca, nalga, solomo de vaca.
nation ['neiʃən], *s.* nación, país; pueblo; estado; muchedumbre.
national ['næʃənəl], *a.* nacional; público, general; patriótico; *national debt*, deuda pública. — *s.* nacional, *m.f.*
nationalism, *s.* nacionalismo, amor a la patria; rasgo característico nacional.
nationality [næʃə'næliti], *s.* nacionalidad, ciudadanía; patriotismo.
nationalize ['næʃənə'laiz], *v.t.* nacionalizar.
nationally, *adv.* nacionalmente.
native ['neitiv], *a.* nativo, natal, original, originario, natural, nacional, oriundo, patrio; virgen; *native land*, patria, tierra; *native soil*, terruño, tierra natal; *native place*, lugar (o suelo) natal; *native tongue* o *native language*, lengua maternal. — *s.* nacional, natural, indígena; producto nacional.
nativeness, *s.* estado natural, cualidad de nativo.
nativity [nə'tiviti], *s.* natividad, navidad; nacimiento.
natron ['neitrən, 'nætrən], *s.* natrón.
natterjack ['nætəɹdʒæk], *s.* sapo europeo (*Bufo calamita*).
nattily ['nætili], *adv.* garbosamente, lindamente.
nattiness, *s.* garbo, (*fam.*) majeza, elegancia.
natty, *a.* garboso, (*fam.*) majo, fino, elegante.
natural ['nætʃjuːɹəl], *a.* natural, sencillo, genuino, llano; nativo; natural, corriente; ilegítimo, bastardo; (*mús.*) natural. — *s.* (*mús.*) becuadro.
naturalism, *s.* naturalismo.
naturalist, *s.* naturalista, *m.f.*
naturalization, *s.* naturalización; aclimatación.
naturalize ['nætʃjuːɹəlaiz], *v.t.* naturalizar, aclimatar, habituar.
naturalness, *s.* naturalidad, sencillez, ingenuidad.

M N

nature ['neitʃəɹ], s. naturaleza, natura; constitución, complexión, índole, f.; natural, genio, idiosincrasia, carácter; calidad, especie, f., clase, f., género; espontaneidad, naturalidad; benignidad, mansedumbre; *from nature*, del natural, al natural; *good nature*, benignidad, benevolencia, bondad; *ill nature*, maldad, mal ánimo, (*fam.*) mala leche.

natured, *a.*, *good-natured*, bondadoso, generoso, liberal; *ill-natured*, de mal ánimo, (*fam.*) de mala leche.

naught [nɔːt], s. nada, cero; *to set at naught*, tener en menos, despreciar. — *a.* sin valor; (*ant.*) malo, perverso, indigno, perdido, arruinado.

naughtily ['nɔːtili], *adv.* traviesamente, con picardía, juguetonamente; malvadamente, inicuamente, perversamente.

naughtiness, *s.* travesura, picardía, chiquillada; desobediencia, mala conducta; perversidad, iniquidad, malignidad, maldad.

naughty ['nɔːti], *a.* travieso, díscolo, pícaro; juguetón, picaruelo; desobediente; malo, perverso, malvado, desobediente.

nausea ['nɔːʃə], s. náusea, asco.

nauseant, *a.* (*med.*) nauseabundo.

nauseate ['nɔːsieit, 'nɔːʃieit], *v.t.*, *v.i.* nausear, apestar; tener asco; dar asco, causar aversión.

nauseative ['nɔːsiətiv], **nauseous** ['nɔːʃəs], *a.* nauseoso, nauseativo, nauseabundo, apestoso, asqueroso.

nauseously, *adv.* de un modo nauseabundo, asquerosamente.

nauseousness, *s.* asco, asquerosidad, náusea.

nautic ['nɔːtik], **nautical** ['nɔːtikəl], *a.* náutico.

nautically, *adv.* náuticamente.

naval ['neivəl], *a.* naval, marítimo, de marina.

nave [neiv], s. (*arq.*) nave; cubo, maza, el centro de una rueda de carruaje.

navel ['neivəl], s. (*anat.*) ombligo; (*fig.*) centro, medio; *navel cord*, cordón umbilical.

navel-gall, s. matadura.

navel-shaped, *a.* umbilicado.

navelwort, s. (*bot.*) oreja de monje.

navew ['neivjuː], s. nabiza, colinabo.

navigable ['nævigəbəl], *a.* navegable.

navigableness, navigability, s. navegabilidad, cualidad de navegable.

navigably, *adv.* de un modo navegable.

navigate ['nævigeit], *v.t.*, *v.i.* navegar; marear, dirigir un buque.

navigation, s. navegación, náutica; mareaje.

navigator, s. navegador, navegante, mareante, marino, piloto.

navvy ['nævi], s. peón, bracero, jornalero.

navy ['neivi], s. marina (de guerra); armada.

nawab [nə'wɔːb], s. nababo, nabab.

nay [nei], *adv.* (*ant.*) no, de ningún modo; aun; no sólo eso; más que eso; no sólo; sino; *nay more*, es más o hay más. — s. negación, denegación; voto negativo; repulsa.

Nazarene [næzə'riːn], s. nazareno; (*fig.*) cristiano.

naze [neiz], s. cabo, promontorio.

neap [niːp], s. (*mar.*) bajo. — *a.* (*mar.*) bajo, ínfimo.

Neapolitan [niːə'pɔlitən], s., *a.* napolitano.

near [niəɹ], *prep.* cerca de, junto a, inmediato a, próximo a, hacia, por; *to sail near the wind*, (*mar.*) navegar ciñendo el viento. — *adv.* cerca; casi; cuasi; próximamente; *quite near*, cerquita, muy cerca; *near at hand*, a mano; *to draw near*, acercarse. — *a.* próximo, cercano, inmediato, vecino, contiguo, propincuo; mezquino, tacaño, avaro; inminente; allegado, estrecho, íntimo; corto; cordial; literal, exacto; *near side*, lado izquierdo (*Ing.*), lado derecho (*E.U.*); *near-by*, cercano, vecino; cerquita. — *v.t.*, *v.i.* acercarse (a).

nearly ['niəɹli], *adv.* casi, por poco, poco más o menos, aproximadamente; cerca, de cerca, cercanamente, a poca distancia; mezquinamente, miserablemente; íntimamente, estrechamente; próximamente.

nearness, *s.* proximidad, cercanía, propincuidad; amistad, estrecha; consanguinidad; inminencia; mezquindad; ruindad, tacañería.

near-sighted, *a.* miope, corto de vista.

near-sightedness, *s.* miopía.

neat [niːt], *a.* aseado, esmerado, nítido, limpio; primoroso, pulcro, pulido, mondo, neto; gallardo; de frase elegante y concisa; bien proporcionado, bien hecho; puro, casto, sin mezcla, natural. — s. vaca o buey, ganado vacuno.

'neath [niːθ], *prep.* (*poét.*) bajo, so, debajo de.

neatherd ['niːthəɹd], s. vaquero.

neatness ['niːtnis], *s.* aseo, esmero, nitidez, limpieza; elegancia, hermosura, pulcritud, delicadeza.

neb [neb], s. (*prov.*) pico; nariz, f., hocico; cabo, punta; boca.

nebular ['nebjuːləɹ], **nebulous** ['nebjuːləs], *a.* nebuloso, nublado.

nebulizer, *s.* pulverizador; rociador.

nebulosity, nebulousness, *s.* nebulosidad.

necessarily ['nesisəɹili], *adv.* necesariamente, precisamente, esencialmente.

necessariness, *s.* necesidad.

necessary ['nesisəɹi], *a.* necesario, inevitable, forzoso, preciso, esencial; conclusivo, decisivo; intuitivo. — s. lo necesario, el requisito; (*ant.*) letrina; *to be necessary*, ser necesario o preciso; hacer falta; faltar.

necessitate [ne'sesiteit], *v.t.* necesitar, exigir, obligar, requerir.

necessitous [ne'sesitəs], *a.* necesitado, pobre, indigente.

necessitously, *adv.* con necesidad.

necessitousness, *s.* necesidad, indigencia, pobreza.

necessity [ne'sesiti], *s.* necesidad, presición, exigencia; necesidad, indigencia; *necessity knows no law*, la necesidad carece de ley.

neck [nek], s. cuello; pescuezo; gollete; garganta; mango; clavijero (de violín, guitarra, etc.); lengua de tierra; (*arq.*) collarino; (*geog.*) istmo, península; desfiladero, estrecho; (*vulg.*) descaro, desfachatez; (*cost.*) escote, degolladura; *stiff neck*, tortícolis, f.; *to stiffen one's neck*, obstinarse; *to break one's neck*, desnucarse; *neck and crop*, inmediatamente, a tontas y a locas; *neck or nothing*, todo o nada; a toda costa; o perdiz, o no comerla; *low neck*, (*cost.*) escote; *to wring the neck (of)*, torcer el pescuezo (a).

necked, *a.* con cuello; *long-necked*, cuellilargo; *stiff-necked*, cuellierguido.

neckerchief ['nekəɹtʃif], s. corbata, corbatín, pañuelo de cuello, bobillo.

necking, (*vulg.*, *E.U.*) sobo, magreo, arrumacos, halagos, amoricones.
necklace ['neklǝs], *s.* collar.
neck-line, *s.* escotadura, escote.
necktie ['nektai], *s.* corbata.
necrological [nekro'lɔdʒikǝl], *a.* necrológico.
necrologist [ne'krɔlodʒist], *s.* necrologista, *m.f.*
necrology [ne'krɔlodʒi], *s.* necrología.
necromancer ['nekromænsǝɹ], *s.* nigromante, brujo.
necromancy ['nekromænsi], *s.* nigromancia, brujería.
necromantic, *a.* nigromántico.
necropolis [ne'krɔpolis], *s.* necrópolis, *f.*
necrosis [ne'krousis], *s.* necrosis, *f.*
necrotomy [ne'krɔtǝmi], *s.* necrotomía.
nectar ['nektɑːɹ], *s.* néctar.
nectarean, nectareous, nectarial, *a.* nectáreo.
nectarine ['nektǝrin], *s.* variedad del melocotón. — *a.* dulce como néctar, nectáreo, nectarino.
nectary ['nektǝri], *s.* nectario.
need [niːd], *s.* necesidad; cosa necesaria; necesidad, miseria, indigencia; falta, urgencia, carencia; *to stand in need of,* necesitar; *if need be,* si hay necesidad, si fuera necesario; *if need were,* si hubiera necesidad; *in case of need,* en caso de necesidad. — *v.i.* ser menester; haber menester; tener necesidad o precisión; carecer; hacer falta; faltar. — *v.t.* necesitar, pedir, requerir, tener necesidad de; *good wine needs no bush,* el buen paño en arca se vende.
needer, *s.* necesitado.
needful, *a.* necesario, preciso, indispensable.
needfulness, *s.* necesidad, urgencia.
needily, *adv.* pobremente.
neediness, *s.* necesidad, estrechez, miseria.
needle ['niːdǝl], *s.* aguja; palillo para hacer media; estilo; (*mar.*) brújula; (*arq.*) chapitel; roca acicular; obelisco; *darning-needle,* aguja de zurcir; *dipping-needle,* aguja de inclinación; *knitting-needle,* aguja de malla; *magnetic needle,* aguja de marear. — *v.i.* cristalizar en forma de aguja. — *v.t.* hacer o coser con aguja; trabajar o elaborar con la aguja; penetrar, ir a través; (*vulg.*) fastidiar, enojar.
needle-case, *s.* alfiletero.
needle-fish, *s.* (*ictiol.*) aguja.
needleful, *s.* hebra de hilo.
needle-holder, *s.* portaagujas, *m.sing.*
needler, *s.* el que hace agujas.
needle-shaped, *a.* acicular.
needless ['nidlis], *a.* superfluo, innecesario, inútil.
needlessly, *adv.* inútilmente, en vano.
needlessness, *s.* superfluidad, inutilidad.
needlewoman, *s.f.* costurera.
needlework, *s.* costura, bordado de agua, obra de punto.
needs [niːdz], *adv.* necesariamente, esencialmente, indispensablemente; *I must needs go,* tengo que ir; *it must needs be,* es absolutamente necesario.
needy ['niːdi], *a.* necesitado, apurado, menesteroso.
ne'er [nɛǝɹ], *adv. contr.* (*poét.*) [NEVER].
nef [nef], *s.* (*arq.*) nave, *f.*
nefarious [ne'fɛǝriǝs], *a.* nefario, nefando.

nefariousness, *s.* atrocidad, maldad.
negation [ne'geiʃǝn], *s.* negación, negativa; carencia, falta.
negative ['negǝtiv], *a.* negativo. — *s.* negativa, denegación; veto; clisé; (*foto.*) negativo. — *v.t.* denegar, negar, desaprobar, desechar; oponerse a, poner veto a, votar en contra de.
negativeness, *s.* cualidad de negativo.
neglect [ne'glekt], *v.t.* descuidar, desatender, faltar a, menospreciar, omitir, no hacer caso de, olvidar, abandonar, arrinconar. — *s.* descuido, olvido, abandono, desuso, omisión, negligencia; dejadez, indiferencia; desprecio, menosprecio, desdén; *to fall into,* or *suffer neglect,* caer en desuso.
neglectful [ne'glektful], *a.* negligente, descuidado.
neglectfulness, *s.* [NEGLIGENCE].
negligee ['negliʒei], *s.* bata, batín (de mujeres).
negligence ['neglidʒǝns], **neglectfulness** [ne'glekfǝlnis], *s.* negligencia, descuido, incuria, dejadez, pereza; omisión; tibieza; abandono; desaliño.
negligent ['neglidʒǝnt], *a.* negligente, descuidado, dejado, perezoso, flojo.
negligible ['neglidʒibǝl], *a.* desatendible, omisible, sin importancia, sin valor.
negotiability, *s.* negociabilidad.
negotiable [ne'gouʃiǝbǝl], *a.* negociable.
negotiate [ne'gouʃieit], *v.t.*, *v.i.* negociar, tratar, agenciar, gestionar; ajustar.
negotiation, *s.* negociación, negocio, transacción, gestión.
negotiator, *s.* negociador, manipulante, gestor.
Negress ['niːgres], *s.f.* (*despec.*) negra.
Negro ['niːgrou], *s.* (*pl.* **Negroes**) negro, negra.
Negroid ['niːgrɔid], *s.*, *a.* negroide, parecido a un negro.
Negro-land, *s.* tierra de los negros.
Negrophile ['negrofil], *s.* antiesclavista, *m.f.*
Negrophobia [negro'foubiǝ], *s.* odio contra los negros.
negus ['niːgǝs], *s.* nego; carraspada, sangría (bebida).
neigh [nei], *v.i.* relinchar. — *s.* relincho, relinchido.
neighbour ['neibǝɹ], *s.* vecino; prójimo. — *v.t.* ser vecino de; estar contiguo a, estar cerca de; confinar. — *a.* vecino.
neighbourhood, *s.* vecindad, vecindario; proximidad, cercanía, inmediación, inmediaciones, alrededores, redonda.
neighbourliness, *s.* cortesía de vecindad, urbanidad.
neighbourly, *a.* atento, urbano, amigable. — *adv.* atentamente, civilmente.
neighing ['neiiŋ], *s.* relincho, relinchido.
neither ['naiðǝɹ], *conj.* ni, ni siquiera, tampoco. — *adv.* tampoco. — *pron.* ni (el) uno ni (el) otro, ni (la) una ni (la) otra, ninguno, ninguna. — *a.* ninguno, ninguna.
nemesis ['nemisis], *s.* némesis, *f.*; justicia.
nenuphar ['nenjuːfɑːɹ], *s.* nenúfar.
neo ['niːou], *pref.* reciente, nuevo.
neologic, neological, *a.* neológico.
neologism [niː'ɔlodʒizm], *s.* neologismo.
neologist, *s.* neólogo.
neology [niːɔlodʒi], *s.* neología.
neomenia [niːo'miːniǝ], *s.* neomenia.
neon ['niːɔn], *s.* (*quím.*) neón.
neophobia [niːo'foubiǝ], *s.* neofobia.
neophyte ['niːofait], *s.* neófito; novicio.

neoplasm ['niːoplæzm], s. neoplasma, m.
neoplatonism [niːo'pleitənizm], s. neoplatonismo.
neoteric [niːo'terik], **neoterical** [niːo'terikəl], a. neotérico.
nepenthe [ne'penθi], s. nepente.
nephew ['nevjuː], s.m. sobrino.
nephrite, s. piedra nefrítica.
nephritic [ne'fritik], **nephritical**, a. nefrítico.
nephritic, s. remedio nefrítico.
nephritis [ne'fraitis], s. nefritis, f.
nepotism, s. nepotismo.
Neptune ['neptʃjuːn], s. Neptuno.
Neptunian [nep'tjuːniən], a. neptuniano.
nereid ['niːreiid], s. nereida.
neroli ['niːroliː], s. esencia de flor de naranja amarga.
nerve [nəːɹv], s. nervio; (bot.) nervadura; (poét.) músculo; (fig.) nervio, fuerza, vigor, fortaleza; valor, ánimo; (fam.) descaro, desfachatez. — v.t. vigorizar, dar fuerza, dar vigor, animar, alentar.
nerved, a. nervudo.
nerveless, a. sin nervio, enervado.
nervine ['nəːɹvain], a. nervino.
nerviness ['nəːɹvinis], s. nervosidad.
nervous ['nəːɹvəs], a. nervioso, tímido, nervoso; nervudo, vigoroso, fuerte.
nervousness, s. nervosidad, nerviosidad, timidez; fuerza, vigor.
nervure ['nəːɹvjuːɹ], s. nervadura.
nervy ['nəːɹvi], a. nervioso, débil.
nescience ['neʃəns], s. nesciencia, ignorancia.
ness [nes], s. cabo, promontorio.
nest [nest], s. nido, nidada; papelera; conjunto o juego de nichos, cajones, gavetas; estante; madriguera, guarida; casa, habitación, morada; nest egg, nidal; (fig.) economías, ahorros; dote; to make a nest, anidar; to look for a mare's nest, buscar tres pies al gato; nest of thieves, cueva (o guarida) de ladrones. — v.t., v.i. hacerse nidos, anidar, nidificar; buscar nidos.
nestle ['nesəl], v.i. apretarse, arranarse, arrimarse; anidarse, enjaular, enjaularse; to nestle up to, arrimarse a, apretarse contra.
nestling ['nestliŋ], s. ave recién salido del nido, pollo.
net [net], s. red, f.; malla; trampa, artificio. — a. neto; puro, limpio; reticular; cogido con red. — v.t. producir o recibir (un beneficio) neto, sacar el producto neto de una cosa; enredar, prender, coger, pescar o cazar con red. — v.i. hacer redes.
nether ['neðəɹ], a. más bajo, inferior.
nethermost ['neðəɹməst], a. lo más bajo, lo inferior.
net-maker, s. redero.
netting ['netiŋ], a. obra de malla, randa; pesca; (mar.) enjaretados, redes para defenderse de abordajes o de torpedos.
nettle ['netəl], s. (bot.) ortiga; dead nettle, lamio blanco, ortiga muerta; great nettle, ortiga dioica; Roman nettle, ortiga pilulífera; small nettle, ortiga picante; red dead nettle, lamio purpúreo. — v.t. picar, provocar, irritar.
nettle-rash, s. urticaria.
nettle-tree, s. almez, almezo.
network, s. red, f.; malla; randa; (fig.) red, f.
neuralgia [njuː'rældʒə], s. neuralgia.
neuralgic, a. neurálgico.

neurasthenia [njuːrəs'θiːniə], s. neurastenia.
neurasthenic, a. neurasténico.
neurology [njuː'rɔlodʒi], s. neurología.
neuropter ['njuːrɔptəɹ], s. neuróptero.
neurosis [njuː'rousis], s. neurosis, f.
neurotic [njuː'rɔtik], s., a. neurótico, nervioso.
neurotomy, s. neurotomía.
neuter ['njuːtəɹ], a. neutro, neutral, indiferente.
neutral ['njuːtrəl], a. neutral, neutro, indiferente, ni bueno ni malo. — s. neutral; neutral gear, marcha neutra.
neutrality [njuː'træliti], s. neutralidad.
neutralization, s. neutralización.
neutralize ['njuːtrəlaiz], v.t. neutralizar.
never ['nevəɹ], adv. nunca, jamás; de ningún modo, en ningún tiempo; por más que; never again, nunca jamás, nunca más; never a word, ni una palabra; never a one, ni uno; never a whit, ni (una) pizca; never mind, no importa; be it never so little, por poco (o pequeño) que sea; be it never so great, por mucho (o grande) que sea.
never-ceasing [nevəɹ'siːsiŋ], **never-ending** [nevəɹ'endiŋ], a. perpetuo, continuo, sin fin, de nunca acabar.
never-failing, a. infalible, inagotable.
nevermore [nevəɹ'mɔːɹ], adv. nunca jamás.
nevertheless [nevəɹðə'les], adv. sin embargo, no obstante, con todo, a pesar de todo.
new [njuː], a. nuevo, fresco, moderno, reciente; tierno, blando (del pan); no acostumbrado; renovado; brand new, o bran new, nuevo del todo, enteramente nuevo, flamante. — adv. recientemente, modernamente, nuevamente, de nuevo; new-laid egg, huevo fresco; the New Year, el año nuevo; new bread, pan fresco, pan tierno; the New World, el Nuevo Mundo; new moon, luna nueva, novilunio; new rich, ricacho, nuevo rico, advenedizo; New Testament, Nuevo Testamento.
new-born, a. recién nacido.
new-comer, s. recién llegado.
newel ['njuːəl], s. columna o pilar central de una escalera de caracol; poste en la parte superior e inferior de una escalera, que sostiene el pasamanos.
new-fangled [njuː'fæŋgəld], a. nuevo, inventado por novedad.
Newfoundland [njuː'faundlənd], s. Terranova; perro de Terranova.
Newgate ['njuːgit], s. antigua cárcel de Londres derribada en 1902; Newgate Calendar, lista de los prisioneros en Newgate.
newish ['njuːiʃ], a. bastante nuevo, casi nuevo, reciente.
new-laid ['njuːleid], a. recién puesto.
newly, adv. nuevamente, recientemente.
newness, s. novedad; inexperiencia; innovación; cualidad de moderno; principio.
news [njuːz], s. noticias, nuevas, novedades, aviso; gacetilla; actualidades; news agency, agencia de anuncios; newsagent, vendedor de periódicos; agente de la prensa, noticiero; news-bulletin, (boletín de) noticias; news-items, noticias, actualidades; news-reel, actualidades (cinematográficas); news-stand, quiosco de periódicos; what is the news? ¿qué hay de nuevo? ¿qué noticias hay? this was news to me, me cogió de nuevo; no news is good news, falta de noticias, buena señal.

newsboy, *s.m.* repartidor de periódicos, vendedor de periódicos.

newsmonger, *s.* amigo de noticias, persona que trae noticias; correveidile.

newspaper, *s.* periódico, diario, gaceta.

newsroom, *s.* gabinete de lectura.

newsvendor, *s.* vendedor de periódicos.

newswriter, *s.* gacetero, gacetillero, redactor, noticiero.

newt [nju:t], *s.* tritón, salamandra acuática.

next [nekst], *a.* próximo, primero, más cercano, siguiente, sucesivo, contiguo, vecino, inmediato, del lado; *on the next page*, a la vuelta; *on the next day*, al día siguiente; *the next day*, el día siguiente; *the next of kin*, los familiares, los suyos, etc., los parientes cercanos; *the next heir*, el presunto heredero; *next week*, a la semana que viene; *next year*, el año que viene; *the next word*, la palabra que sigue; *next to impossible*, casi imposible, que raya en lo imposible; *what next?* y luego ¿qué? — *adv.* luego, inmediatamente después; cerca. — *prep.* lo más cerca a.

nexus ['neksəs], *s.* nexo, vínculo, lazo.

nib [nib], *s.* pico; punta, extremo; punto de una pluma. — *v.t.* poner una pluma en un mango; hacer punta, aguzar, afilar el punto (de una pluma de ave).

nibbed [nibd], *a.* picudo, que tiene pico.

nibble ['nibəl], *v.t.* roer, mascullar; picar, picotear; morder, mordiscar; tomar una corta porción; pacer; criticar, denigrar, satirizar, despreciar. — *v.i.* mordiscar, morder, criticar, satirizar.

nibbler, *s.* el que pica, persona que come poco a la vez; animal que mordisca; pez que muerde el anzuelo; persona que critica, criticastro.

nice [nais], *a.* simpático, amable; fino, refinado, delicado, exquisito; tierno; gustoso, lindo, delicioso, agradable; bonito, gracioso, hermoso, elegante, primoroso, esmerado; fastidioso, difícil de contentar; fácil de resentirse; sutil; exacto; solícito, diligente; cauto, prudente, circunspecto, escrupuloso; mirado; bueno, gentil, amable; *to be nice*, hacer el delicado; *nice distinction*, sutileza; *nice point*, punto delicado; *he's a nice person*, (*iron.*) ¡buen apunte es!; *nice-looking*, guapo, mona (de muchachas); formal, elegante.

nicely, *adv.* bien, delicadamente, con delicadeza, primorosamente, con esmero, exactamente, sutilmente, con formalidad.

niceness, *s.* amabilidad, refinamiento, formalidad; delicadeza, exactitud, esmero.

nicety ['naisiti], *s.* delicadeza, sutileza, exactitud, esmero, circunspección, discreción, argucia, refinamiento; *to a nicety*, con la mayor precisión.

niche [nitʃ], *s.* nicho.

nick [nik], *s.* escote; tarja; muesca; ocasión oportuna; punto crítico, momento preciso; (*impr.*) cran; *in the nick of time*, de perilla, a pelo, muy a propósito, oportunamente; al momento preciso; *Old Nick*, (*fam.*) patillas, el diablo. — *v.t.* tarjar; cortar en muescas; acertar, dar en el hito; llegar a tiempo.

nickel ['nikəl], *a.* níquel, niquelio; (*E.U.*) moneda de cinco centavos.

nickel-plated, *a.* niquelado.

nickel-plater, *s.* niquelador.

nickel-silver, *s.* metal blanco.

nicker, *s.* (*vulg.*) ladrón.

nicker, *s.*; nicking, *s.*; nick-nack, *s.* [NICK].

nickering, *s.* acción de robar, acción de engañar.

nick-nack ['niknæk], *s.* friolera, fruslería, chuchería, baratija.

nickname [nikneim], *s.* opodo, mote. — *v.t.* poner un apodo a, motejar.

nicotine ['nikoti:n], *s.* nicotina.

nictate ['nikteit], *v.i.* parpadear, pestañear; guiñar el ojo, ojear.

nictation, *s.* nictación, pestañeo, guiñadura.

nidification [nidifi'keiʃən], *s.* nidificación, acto de hacer nidos.

nidorosity [nido'rɔsiti], *s.* eructación, eructo.

nidulate ['nidju:leit], *v.t.*, *v.i.* nidificar, anidar, hacer nidos.

nidulation, *s.* incubación, tiempo de quedar en el nido.

niece [ni:s], *s.f.* sobrina.

niggard ['nigəɪd], *s.* hombre avaro, tacaño. — *a.* avaro, avariento, tacaño, miserable, escaso, económico. — *v.t.* (*ant.*) escasear, dar poco.

niggardish, niggardly, *a.* avariento, sórdido, mezquino, tacaño, ruin.

niggardliness ['nigəɪdlinis], niggardness, *s.* tacañería, ruindad, miseria.

niggardly, *a.* tacaño, ruin, mezquino.

nigger ['nigəɪ], *s.* (*fam.*, *despec.*) negro, negra.

niggle ['nigəl], *v.i.* pormenorizar; tardar mucho, irse muriendo; retozar, travesear.

niggling ['nigliŋ], *a.* nimio, mezquino, insignificante.

nigh [nai], *a.* cercano, próximo, vecino. — *adv.* cerca, próximamente, inmediato, junto a, cuasi o casi. — *prep.* cerca de, no lejos de; *to draw nigh*, acercarse; *nigh at hand*, a la mano.

nighly, *adv.* cercanamente.

nighness, *s.* proximidad, cercanía.

night [nait] *s.* noche, *f.*; oscuridad, tinieblas; (*fig.*) melancolía, dolor, tristeza; *at o by night*, de noche; *last night*, anoche; *to-night*, esta noche; *Good night*, Buenas noches; *to spend the night*, pasar la noche, pernoctar.

nightbird, *s.* pájaro nocturno; (*fig.*, *fam.*) trasnochador.

nightcap, *s.* gorro de dormir; (*fig.*) la última copa antes de acostarse.

nightdress, nightgown, *s.* camisa de dormir; bata.

nightfall, *s.* anochecer, crepúsculo, atardecer, boca de noche.

nightfire, *s.* fuego de Santelmo; fuego fatuo.

nightingale ['naitiŋgeil], *s.* ruiseñor.

nightless, *a.* que no tiene noches.

night-light, *s.* lamparilla de noche.

nightly ['naitli], *a.* nocturno. — *adv.* de noche, por la(s) noche(s).

nightmare, *s.* pesadilla.

nightshade, *s.* (*bot.*) hierbamora, belladona, beleño.

night-stool, *s.* sillico.

night-walk, *s.* paseo de noche.

night-walker, *s.* somnámbulo; noctívago.

night-walking, *s.* somnambulismo.

night-watch, *s.* ronda de noche.

night-watchman, *s.* sereno; vigilante.

nigrescent [ni'gresənt], *a.* negruzco, ennegrecido.
nigrification [nigrifi'keiʃən], *s.* ennegrecimiento.
nihilism ['naiilizm], *s.* nihilismo.
nihilist, *s.* nihilista, *m.f.*
nihility [nai'hiliti], *s.* nulidad, nada.
nil [nil], nada; (*com.*) nulo.
nill [nil], *v.t.* (*ant.*) no querer, negarse,
rehusar. — *s.* chispa de bronce fundido;
will he, nill he o *willy-nilly*, que quiera que
no quiera, de buena o mala gana.
nimble ['nimbəl], *a.* ligero, activo, listo, vivo,
ágil.
nimble-footed, *a.* ligero de pies.
nimbleness, *s.* ligereza, agilidad, celeridad,
actividad, expedición, destreza.
nimble-witted, *a.* listo, despierto, vivo.
nimbly ['nimbli], *adv.* vivamente, ágilmente,
con ligereza.
nimbosity [nim'bɔsiti], *s.* tormenta.
nimbus ['nimbəs], *s.* nimbo, auréola, círculo
de luz.
nimiety [ni'maiiti], *s.* nimiedad.
nimious ['nimiəs], *a.* nimio.
nincompoop ['ninkəmpu:p], *s.* badulaque,
simplón.
nine [nain], *s., a.* nueve; *up to the nines*, (*fam.*)
de veinticinco alfileres; *the Nine* (*poét.*) las
nueve musas.
ninefold, *a., adv.* nueve veces.
nine-holes, *s.* boliche.
ninepence ['nainpəns], *s.* nueve peniques.
ninepins ['nainpinz], *s.* bolos, juego de bolos.
nineteen [nain'ti:n], *s., a.* diez y nueve,
diecinueve.
nineteenth [nain'ti:nθ], *a.* décimonono, diez y
nueve.
ninetieth ['naintiəθ], *a.* nonagésimo, noventa.
ninety ['nainti], *s., a.* noventa.
ninny ['nini], *s.* imbécil, mentecato, simple,
simplón, bobo, zote.
ninth [nainθ], *a.* noveno, nono, nueve. — *s.*
novena parte.
ninthly, *adv.* en nono lugar.
niobium [nai'oubiəm], *s.* niobio.
nip [nip], *v.t.* pellizcar; morder, cortar;
esquilar; penetrar; quemar, marchitar;
destruir; arañar, rasguñar; picar, zaherir,
satirizar; helar, secar los frutos antes de
madurar; *to nip in the bud*, destruir en germen, cortar en flor. — *s.* pellizco, dentellada,
uñada; cortadura pequeña y ligera; escarcha,
helada; sarcasmo, sátira, dicho mordaz;
sorbo, sorbito.
nipper, *s.* satírico; pinza; pala; (*vulg.*) muchacho, chacho, crío, chiquillo.
nippers, *s.pl.* tenazas, alicates; (*mar.*) mojelas,
badernas.
nipping, *s.* rasguño, araño, mordedura. — *a.*
picante, mordaz.
nipple ['nipəl], *s.* pezón; chimenea (de fusil);
nipple shield, pezonera.
nipplewort, *s.* lapsana común.
nit [nit], *s.* liendre, *f.*
nitid ['nitid], *a.* nítido, claro, resplandeciente.
nitrate ['naitreit], *s.* nitrato.
nitre ['naitəɹ], *s.* nitro.
nitric ['naitrik], *a.* nítrico, azoico.
nitrogen ['naitrodʒən], *s.* nitrógeno.
nitro-glycerine [naitro'glisərin], *s.* nitroglicerina.

nitrous ['naitrəs], **nitry** ['naitri], *a.* nitroso,
que contiene nitro.
nitty ['niti], *a.* lendroso, lleno de liendres.
nival ['naivəl], **niveous** ['niviəs], *a.* nevoso,
blanco como la nieve.
no [nou], *adv.* no, de ningún modo. — *a.*
ninguno, ningún; *no man*, o *no one*, nadie;
by no means, de ningún modo; *no matter*,
no importa; *to no purpose*, inútilmente, en
vano; *no where*, en ninguna parte; *no more
of this*, no más de eso.
nob [nob], *s.* (*vulg.*) petimetre; jefe.
nobiliary [no'biliəri], *s.* nobiliario.
nobilitate, *v.t.* ennoblecer, hacer noble.
nobilitation, *s.* ennoblecimiento.
nobility [no'biliti], *s.* nobleza; grandeza,
sublimidad, dignidad.
noble ['noubəl], *a.* noble; principal; generoso,
magnánimo. — *s.* noble, hidalgo.
nobleman ['noubəlmən], *s.* noble, hidalgo.
nobleness ['noubəlnes], **noblesse** [nou'bles],
s. nobleza, magnificencia, grandeza, lustre.
noblewoman, *s.f.* mujer noble.
nobly ['noubli], *adv.* noblemente, con nobleza,
generosamente.
nobody ['noubədi], *s.* nadie, ninguno; *to be a
nobody*, no ser nada.
nocent ['nousənt], *a.* nocivo; culpable,
delincuente, criminal.
nock [nɔk], *s.* muesca, abertura; (*mar.*) puno
de la boca (vela).
noctambulism, *s.* noctambulismo.
noctambulist [nɔk'tæmbju:list], *s.* noctámbulo.
nocturn ['nɔktə:n], *s.* nocturno.
nocturn, nocturnal, nocturnous, *ı.* nocturno, nocturnal.
nocturnally, *adv.* de noche.
nocuity [nɔ'kju:iti], *s.* nocuidad.
nocuous ['nɔkju:əs], *a.* nocivo.
nod [nɔd], *v.i.* cabecear, hacer una señal con la
cabeza, inclinar la cabeza, inclinarse, dar
cabezadas; amodorrarse, adormecerse. —
v.t. mover (la cabeza), sacudir; significar
(con un movimiento de la cabeza); *to nod
approbation*, hacer un signo de aprobación.
— *s.* cabeceo, cabezada, señal hecha con la
cabeza; reverencia, mocha, inclinación de la
cabeza; *Land of Nod*, sueño, mu, *f.*
nodal ['noudəl], *a.* nodal.
nodated ['noudeitid], *a.* nudoso.
nodation, *s.* acto de hacer nudos.
nodder ['nɔdəɹ], *a.* el que inclina la cabeza,
el que da cabezadas.
noddle ['nɔdəl], *s.* (*vulg.*) mollera; calamorra,
coca, cachola.
noddy ['nɔdi], *s.* tonto, imbécil, simple, simplón;
calesa; ave de la especie de pájaros bobos.
node [noud], *s.* nudo.
nodose ['nɔdouz], *a.* nudoso.
nodosity [nɔ'dɔsiti], *s.* nudosidad, abundancia
de nudos.
nodous, *a.* nudoso, lleno de nudos.
nodular ['nɔdju:ləɹ], *a.* parecido a un nudo.
nodule ['nɔdju:l], *s.* nudillo.
noetic [nou'etik], **noetical**, *a.* mental,
intuitivo.
nog [nɔg], *s.* bote; (*mar.*) cabilla para escotas;
clavija; perno; una cerveza fuerte.
noggin ['nɔgin], *s.* vaso pequeño, medida de
líquidos de 1.42 decil.
nogging, *s.* tabique.

noise [nɔiz], s. ruido, estruendo, sonido, zumbido; bulla, gritería, clamor; fama, nombre, novedad. — v.t. esparcir, divulgar; to noise abroad, divulgar. — v.i. hacer un ruido desapacible.

noiseful, a. ruidoso.

noiseless, a. sin ruido, callado, tranquilo, quedo.

noiselessly, adv. silenciosamente, tranquilamente, sin ruido.

noiselessness, s. tranquilidad, calma.

noisette [nwɑ:'zet], s. variedad de rosa, cruce de China con almizclera. — pl. pedacitos de carnero, ternera, etc. cocidos de una manera especial.

noisily ['nɔizili], adv. ruidosamente, bulliciosamente.

noisiness, s. tumulto, ruido, estrépito, alboroto.

noisome ['nɔisəm], a. nocivo, ofensivo, malsano, asqueroso, fétido, dañoso, repugnante, desagradable.

noisomely, adv. con olor fétido.

noisomeness, s. náusea, asco, fastidio, asquerosidad, infección.

noisy ['nɔizi], a. ruidoso, turbulento, bullicioso, clamoroso, estrepitoso.

noli-me-tangere [noulaimi:'tændʒəri], s. (bot.) nometoca, o impaciente nometoca; (med.) nolimetángere, nometoques.

nolition [no'liʃən], s. nolición.

nomad ['noumæd], s. nómada, m.f.; errante, sin asiento fijo.

nomad, nomadic, a. nómada.

nome [noum], s. nomo; distrito, región, provincia (especialmente de Grecia o Egipto).

nomenclator, s. nomenclator.

nomenclature [no'menklətʃəɹ], s. nomenclatura, nombre.

nominal ['nɔminəl], a. nominal, en el nombre.

nominalism, s. nominalismo.

nominalist, s. nominalista, m.f.

nominally, adv. nominalmente, por nombre.

nominate ['nɔmineit], v.t. nombrar, elegir, señalar.

nominately, adv. nominativamente, particularmente.

nomination, s. nominación, nombramiento, presentación.

nominative ['nɔminətiv], a. nominativo. — s. nominativo.

nominator, s. nominador, presentador.

nominee [nɔmi'ni:], s. candidato nombrado, persona nombrada.

nominor, s. nominador.

non [nɔn], pref. des-, in-, no, poco, falta de.

non-acceptance, s. falta de aceptación.

nonage ['nounidʒ, 'nɔnidʒ], s. minoridad, menor edad.

nonagenarian [nɔnədʒe'nɛəriən], s. nonagenario.

nonagesimal [nɔnə'dʒeziməl], a. nonagésimo.

nonagon ['nɔnəgən], s. nonágono.

non-appearance, s. ausencia, falta de comparición; (for.) contumacia, rebeldía.

non-attendance, s. falta de asistencia.

nonce [nɔns], s. tiempo o ocasión presente, actualidad; for the nonce, al presente, actualmente, hoy en día; (ant.) adrede.

nonchalant ['nɔnʃələnt], a. descuidado, negligente, frío.

non-combatant, a. no combatiente.

non-commissioned officer, s. (mil.) cabo, sargento o suboficial.

non-condensing, a. sin condensador.

non-conductor, s. (fís.) mal conductor.

nonconformist [nɔnkon'fɔ:ɹmist], s. nonconformista, m.f., disidente.

nonconformity [nɔnkon'fɔ:ɹmiti], s. disidencia, desconformidad.

non-delivery, s. falta de envío o de entrega.

nondescript ['nɔndiskript], a. indefinible, casual, mediocre; que no está descrito. — s. persona o cosa indefinible.

none [nʌn], pron. indef. nadie, ninguno, ninguna; nada; none of that, nada de eso; to be none the worse, no hallarse peor; he has none, no tiene. — a. no, ninguno. — adv. de ninguna manera; nada de; fuera.

nonentity [nɔn'entiti], s. nada, falta de existencia; ficción, algo imaginario; persona de ninguna importancia.

nones [nounz], s.pl. nonas; (igl.) nona.

nonesuch ['nʌnsʌtʃ], s. persona o cosa sin igual, sin par.

non-execution, s. falta de ejecución.

nonpareil [nɔnpə'rel], s. cosa excelente, sin igual; (impr.) nonparel, letra de seis puntos. — a. excelente, precioso, magnífico, sin rival, sin igual.

non-payment, s. falta de pago.

nonplus ['nɔnplʌs], s. perplejidad, embarazo; (fam.) apuro. — v.t. confundir, embarazar, arrinconar, poner en apuros, estrechar (en una disputa).

non-resident, a. no residente, ausente.

nonsense ['nɔnsəns], s. desatino, disparate, absurdidad, necedad, impertinencia, tontería, jerigonza, jerga; to talk nonsense, echar coplas de repente.

nonsensical [nɔn'sensikəl], a. desatinado, absurdo, impertinente.

nonsensicalness, s. disparate, absurdidad.

nonsolvency, s. insolvencia.

nonsolvent [nɔn'sɔlvənt], a. insolvente.

nonsuit ['nɔnsju:t], s. (der.) desistimiento. — v.t. absolver de la instancia.

non-voter, abstencionista, m.f.

noodle [nu:dəl], s. (fam.) simplón, tonto, mentecato; tallarín, pasta.

nook [nuk], s. sitio retirado y apacible, rincón, ángulo; escondrijo.

noon [nu:n], **noonday** ['nu:ndei], **noontide** ['nu:ntaid], s. mediodía, m.; punto culminante, apogeo.

nooning, s. siesta. — a. de mediodía.

noose [nu:s], s. lazo, lazo corredizo; (fig.) trampa, red, f. — v.t. apretar con lazo; enlazar; entrampar.

nopal ['noupəl], s. nopal.

nor [nɔ:ɹ], conj. ni, no; tampoco; nor was this all, y esto no era todo.

norm [nɔ:ɹm], s. norma, modelo, regla; (biol.) unidad típica de conformación.

normal ['nɔ:ɹməl], a. normal; (geom.) perpendicular.

Norman ['nɔ:ɹmən], s., a. normando; (mar.) burel del molinete.

Norse [nɔ:ɹs], a. escandinavo, noruego.

north [nɔ:ɹθ], s. norte, septentrión. — a. del norte, septentrional; north-east, nordeste; north-west, noroeste.

northerly ['nɔ:ɹðəɹli], a. del norte, septentrional, setentrional.

northern ['nɔːɪðəɪn], *a.* al norte, hacia el norte.
northernmost, *a.* situado más el norte.
northward ['nɔːɪθwəɪd], *a.*, *adv.*; **northwards**, *adv.* hacia el norte.
Norwegian [nɔːɪ'wiːdʒən], *s.*, *a.* noruego.
nose [nouz], *s.* nariz, *f.*; hocico (de ciertos animales); olfato; (*fig.*) sagacidad; tobera, cañuto, proa, pitón (de cántaro, etc.), pico, punto; *pug nose*, nariz remachada; *Roman nose*, nariz aguileña; *snub nose*, nariz chata (o roma o aplastada); *turn-up nose*, nariz arremangada; *to blow one's nose*, sonarse las narices (o los mocos); *to lead by the nose*, llevar por la punta de los narices (o agarrado por las narices); *to follow one's nose*, seguir en línea recta; *to poke one's nose into*, entremeterse en; *to turn up one's nose at*, mirar con desprecio; desdeñar; *to have one's nose out of joint*, no estar en el candelero; *to put one's nose out of joint*, suplantar, desquiciar a uno; *to speak through the nose*, ganguear; *under one's very nose*, a las barbas de uno. — *v.t.*, *v.i.* oler, olfatear; hacer frente, encararse, oponerse.
nose-bag, *s.* cebadera, morral.
nose-band, *s.* muserola.
nosebleed, *s.* hemorragia nasal, epistaxis, *f.*; (*bot.*) milenrama.
nosed, *a.* con nariz; *long-nosed*, narigudo.
nosegay, *s.* ramillete.
noseless, *a.* desnarigado.
nosography [no'sɔgrəfi], *s.* nosografía.
nosology [no'sɔlodʒi], *s.* nosología.
nostalgia [nɔs'tældʒiə], *s.* nostalgia, querencia.
nostril ['nɔstrəl], *s.* ventana de la nariz, *f.* — *pl.* narices, *f.pl.*
nostrum ['nɔstrəm], *s.* remedio secreto, panacea; (*fig.*) proyecto, panacea, arbitrio (de policastro o charlatán).
not [nɔt], *adv.* no, de ningún modo; *not at all*, de ningún modo; *not but*, no es que; *why not?* ¿cómo no? o ¿porqué no? *not to say*, por no decir; *he had not so much as heard*, ni siquiera había oído; *I think not*, creo que no, no lo creo.
notability [noutə'biliti], *s.* notabilidad, importancia, singularidad.
notable ['noutəbəl], *a.* notable, señalado; considerable. — *s.* notable, persona eminente.
notableness ['noutəbəlnis], *s.* notabilidad; economía; cuidado.
notary ['noutəri], *s.* notario, escribano.
notation [no'teiʃən], *s.* notación, anotación; (*mús.*) notación; (*mat.*) numeración.
notch [nɔtʃ], *s.* mella, muesca, abertura, ranura, mortaja, tajadura, hendidura; (*anat.*) escotadura. — *v.t.* mellar, hacer muescas, escotar.
notchboard, *s.* pie de una escalera.
note [nout], *s.* nota; señal, *f.*, marca; aprecio, caso, apunte, apuntación; censura, reparo; importancia, consecuencia, distinción, carácter; reputación; billete, esquela; vale, pagaré; noticia, aviso; indirecta; (*mús.*) nota, tecla; sonido, tono, voz, *f.*, acento; (*gram.*) punto; *note of exclamation*, (*gram.*) punto de exclamación; *note of hand o promissory note*, pagaré; *to take note of*, tomar nota de, hacer cargo de; *bank-note*, billete de banco. — *v.t.* reparar, fijarse en, observar, advertir, notar, marcar, distinguir; (*com.*) apuntar; censurar, imputar culpa; (*mús.*) componer.

note-book, *s.* libro de apuntes; cuaderno.
noted, *a.* conocido, famoso, célebre, afamado, renombrado, eminente, insigne.
notedly, *adv.* perfectamente, notablemente, atentamente.
notedness, *s.* fama, celebridad, reputación.
noteless, *a.* sin reputación, sin fama, oscuro.
noteworthy ['noutwəːɪði], *a.* notable, digno de ser anotado, digno de atención.
nothing ['nʌθiŋ], *s.* nada, ninguna cosa; bagatela; (*mat.*) cero; *for nothing*, gratuitamente, de balde; *to be nothing to* (one), no importar a; *to be good for nothing*, no servir para nada, ser inútil; *to come to nothing*, fracasar, reducirse a nada, aniquilarse; *to have nothing to do with*, no tener nada que ver con; no ser (o no tener) arte ni parte en; *to make nothing of*, no sacar nada de, no comprender, no reparar en. — *adv.* en nada, de ninguna manera, de ningún grado; *nothing daunted*, sin temor; *nothing to speak of*, no vale cosa, poca cosa.
nothingness, *s.* nada, nadería, cosa de ninguna importancia.
notice ['noutis], *s.* aviso, informe; observación, nota, reparo; cuidado, atención; conocimiento; cartel, anuncio; plazo; *to give notice*, avisar, hacer saber; *to give notice to*, despedir; *to be under notice*, estar despedido, llevar dimisorias; *to give notice of*, notificar, hacer saber; *to give short notice*, dar corto plazo, conceder un breve plazo; *to take notice of*, observar, notar, advertir; hacer caso de; *to attract notice*, atraer la atención; *at short notice*, a corto plazo; *until further notice*, hasta nuevo aviso; *worthy of notice*, digno de atención; *notice-board*, tablón (o tablero) de aviso; poste indicador. — *v.t.* advertir, reparar en, fijarse en, notar, mirar, observar; cuidar de; atender a; mencionar; hacer observar.
noticeable ['noutisəbəl], *a.* digno de atención.
notification [noutifi'keiʃən], *s.* notificación, acto de notificar, aviso.
notify ['noutifai], *v.t.* notificar, declarar, avisar, dar aviso, hacer saber, informar, significar.
noting ['noutiŋ], *s.* acto de tomar notas.
notion ['nouʃən], *s.* noción, concepto, voto, parecer, dictamen, opinión, pensamiento, idea; (*fam.*) intención, inclinación, designio.
notional, *a.* imaginario, fantástico, ideal.
notionally, *adv.* idealmente, imaginariamente.
notoriety [noutə'raiiti], *s.* mala notoriedad, escándalo; notoriedad.
notorious [no'tɔːɪiəs], *a.* notoriamente malo; notario.
notoriousness, *s.* mala notoriedad, escándalo.
notwithstanding [nɔtwið'stændiŋ], *adv.*, *prep.*, *conj.* no obstante, a pesar de (que), bien que, con todo, sin embargo; por más que.
nought [nɔːt], *s.* nada; *to set at nought*, despreciar, no hacer caso de, desafiar.
noun [naun], *s.* substantivo, nombre.
nourish ['nʌriʃ], *v.t.* nutrir, alimentar, sustentar, mantener; (*fig.*) fomentar, alentar; educar, criar. — *v.i.* tomar carnes.
nourishable, *a.* nutritivo, nutricio, susceptible de nutrimento, que sirve para nutrir.
nourisher, *s.* nutridor, alimentador, persona que nutre.
nourishing, *a.* alimenticio, nutritivo.

nourishment, *s.* alimento, nutrimento, sustento, nutrición.

nousle ['nausəl], *v.t.* alimentar; entrampar.

novaculite [no'vækju:lait], *s.* (*geol.*) piedra de sentar navajas.

novation [no'veiʃən], *s.* novación, renovación de una obligación.

novel ['nɔvəl], *s.* novela; (*for.*) novela; decreto o constitución, nueva y suplementaria. — *a.* nuevo, moderno, novel.

novelism, *s.* innovación.

novelist, *s.* novelista, *m.f.*, novelador.

novelty ['nɔvəlti], *s.* novedad, innovación.

November [no'vembəɹ], *s.* noviembre.

novenary [no'vi:nəri], *a.* novenario.

novennial [no'veniəl], *a.* que dura u ocurre cada nueve años.

novercal [no'vəːɹkəl], *a.* propio o perteneciente a madrastra.

novice ['nɔvis], *s.* principiante, *m.f.*; (*igl.*) novicio.

novitiate [no'viʃit], *s.* noviciado, aprendizaje.

now [nau], *adv.* actualmente, ahora, en este instante, después de esto, de aquí a poco, poco ha; entonces; ya; ahora bien; *just now,* ahora mismo; *how now?* ¿cómo? ¿qué tal? ¿qué es esto? *till now,* o *until now,* hasta aquí, hasta ahora, hasta el presente; *now . . . now . . . ,* ora . . . ora, ya . . . ya; *now and again* (o *now and then*), de vez en cuando, de cuando en cuando. — *conj.* mas, pues, luego que, supuesto que. — *interj.* ¡vamos! — *s.* momento actual, momento presente, actualidad.

nowadays ['nauədeiz], *adv.* hoy día, hoy por hoy, en nuestros días, en nuestros tiempos.

nowhere ['nouwɛəɹ], *adv.* en ninguna parte.

nowise ['nouwaiz], *adv.* de ningún modo, de modo alguno, de ninguna manera.

noxious ['nɔkʃəs], *a.* pernicioso, nocivo, dañoso.

noxiousness, *s.* dañabilidad.

nozzle ['nɔzəl], *s.* nariz, *f.*, hocico; extremidad, pico, canuto, boquerel (de manguera), boquilla, tobera.

Nubian ['nju:biən], *s.*, *a.* nubio.

nubiferous [nju:'bifərəs], *a.* nubiloso, nubloso.

nubilate ['nju:bileit], *v.t.* anublar.

nubile ['nju:bil], *a.* núbil.

nucleus ['nju:kliəs], *s.* núcleo.

nude [nju:d], *a.* en cueros, en cueros vivos, en carnes, nudo, desnudo; (*for.*) hecho sin consideración, y por lo tanto nulo.

nudge [nʌdʒ], *v.t.* dar un codazo, tocar ligeramente para advertir o para llamar la atención. — *s.* codazo.

nudity ['nju:diti], *s.* desnudez.

nugacity [nju:'gæsiti], *s.* fruslería.

nugatory ['nju:gətəri], *a.* nugatorio, fútil, frívolo, frustráneo.

nugget ['nʌgit], *s.* pepita de metal virgen, en especial la de oro.

nuggety, *a.* abundante en pepitas.

nuisance ['nju:səns], *s.* molestia, incomodidad, fastidio, plaga, suplicio; indecencia, vergüenza; *to make a nuisance of oneself,* meterse en todo, estar de más; *What a nuisance!* ¡Qué lata! ¡Qué fastidio!; *commit no nuisance,* se prohibe hacer aguas, se prohibe depositar inmundicias.

null [nʌl], *a.* nulo, ineficaz, inútil, inválido,

sin valor, sin fuerza; *null and void,* de ningún valor y efecto. — *v.t.* anular.

nullify ['nʌlifai], *v.t.* anular, invalidar.

nullity ['nʌliti], *s.* nulidad, falta de existencia.

numb [nʌm], *a.* entorpecido, entumecido, adormecido; atontado, aturdido. — *v.t.* entumecer, entorpecer, causar torpor.

number ['nʌmbəɹ], *v.t.* contar, calcular, numerar; dar, o poner, número a; foliar; ascender a. — *s.* número, multitud, cantidad; versos, poesía, armonía, cadencia; entrega, ejemplar; (*gram.*) número (nombres y verbos); *back number,* número atrasado; (*fam.*) persona anticuada; *round numbers,* números redondos, pares; *number one,* (*fam.*) uno mismo, sí mismo; *to look after number one,* cuidar de sí mismo.

numberer, *s.* calculador, contador, numerador, el que numera.

numbering, *s.* numeración, enumeración.

numberless, *a.* innumerable, sin número.

numb-fish ['nʌmfiʃ], *s.* torpedo.

numbles ['nʌmbəlz], *s.pl.* entrañas de venado.

numbness ['nʌmnis], *s.* entorpecimiento, torpor, adormecimiento.

numerable ['nju:mərəbəl], *a.* numerable.

numeral ['nju:mərəl], *a.* numeral.

numerally, *adv.* numéricamente, individualmente.

numerary ['nju:mərəri], *a.* numerario.

numerate ['nju:məreit], *v.t.* numerar, contar.

numeration, *s.* numeración.

numerator, *s.* contador; (*arit.*) numerador.

numeric [nju:'merik], **numerical** [nju:'merikəl], *a.* numérico.

numerically, *adv.* numéricamente, individualmente.

numerist, *s.* contador.

numerous ['nju:mərəs], *a.* numeroso, en gran número, muchos.

numerousness, *s.* numerosidad, muchedumbre; cadencia.

Numidian [nju:'midiən], *s.*, *a.* Númida, *m.f.*

numismatic, *a.* numismático.

numismatics [nju:mis'mætiks], *s.pl.* numismática.

numismatographer, *s.* numismatógrafo.

numismatography [nju:mismə'tɔgrəfi], *s.* numismatografía.

numismatologist, *s.* numismático.

numismatology [nju:mismə'tɔlodʒi], *s.* numismática.

numskull ['nʌmskʌl], *s.* bobo, simplón, zote.

numskulled, *a.* lerdo, tonto, necio.

nun [nʌn], *s.f.* monja; (*orn.*) paro; *nun-buoy,* (*mar.*) boya de barrilete.

nuncio ['nʌnsiou], *s.* nuncio, enviado papal.

nuncupative ['nʌnkju:pətiv], **nuncupatory** ['nʌnkju:pətəri], *a.* nuncupativo.

nunnery ['nʌnəri], *s.* convento de monjas.

nuphar ['nju:fɑːɹ], *s.* nenúfar amarillo.

nuptial ['nʌpʃəl], *a.* nupcial; *nuptial ode,* epitalamio.

nuptials, *s.pl.* nupcias, bodas.

nurse [nəːɹs], *s.* nodriza, niñera, ama de cría; enfermero, enfermera; *wet nurse,* ama de leche, nodriza; (*Méj.*) chichigua; (*Cuba*) criandera; (*selvicultura*) árbol para proteger a otros; especie de tiburón; *nurse-bee,* abeja neutra que cuida de la cría; *to put to nurse,* poner en ama. — *v.t.* criar, alimentar, mantener; dar alas; cuidar enfermos; dar de mamar, amamantar; fomentar, animar. — *v.i.* cuidar enfermos; dar de mamar; mamar, chupar la leche.

nursemaid, nursery maid, *s.f.* niñera.

nurser, *s.* criador, promotor.

nursery ['nəːɹsri], *s.* plantel, semillero, almáciga; invernadero; crianza; cuarto o habitación de los niños pequeños; *nursery governess,* aya; *nursery rhymes,* cuentos de niños.

nursing, *s.* amamantamiento; acto de criar.

nursling ['nəːɹsliŋ], *s.* criatura, niño, niño criado, niño mimado, favorito.

nurture ['nəːɹtʃəɹ], *s.* nutrimento, educación. — *v.t.* criar, enseñar, educar.

nut [nʌt], *s.* nuez, *f.*; tuerca (de tornillo); (*vulg.*) calamorra, coca, cachola; (*vulg.*) pisaverde, petimetre; (*mar.*) oreja (de ancla); *cashew nut,* anacardo; *hazel nut,* avellana; *to crack nuts,* romper nueces; *he's a hard nut to crack,* es duro de pelar; *to give someone a hard nut to crack,* dar a uno que roer. — *v.t.* coger nueces.

nutation [njuːˈteiʃən], *s.* nutación.

nut-brown, *a.* avellanado (color).

nut-cracker, *s.* cascanueces, *m.*

nut-gall, *s.* agalla de monte.

nut-hatch, nutpecker, *s.* picamadero.

nutmeg ['nʌtmeg], *s.* nuez moscada.

nut-oil, *s.* aceite de nueces.

nutria ['njuːtriə], *s.* (*zool.*) nutria; (*Arg., Chi.*) coipo, coipu.

nutrication, *s.* modo de nutrirse.

nutrient ['njuːtriənt], *a.* nutritivo. — *s.* alimento.

nutriment ['njuːtrimənt], *s.* nutrimento, alimento.

nutrimental, *a.* nutrimental.

nutrition [njuːˈtriʃən], *s.* nutrición, nutrimento.

nutritious, *a.* nutricio, nutritivo, alimentoso.

nutritive ['njuːtritiv], *a.* nutritivo.

nurture, *s.* nutrición, nutrimento.

nutshell, *s.* cáscara de nuez; *in a nutshell,* (*fig.*) en una palabra, en resumidas cuentas.

nutting ['nʌtiŋ], *s.* acción de coger avellanas.

nut-tree, *s.* avellano.

nux-vomica [nʌksˈvɔmikə], *s.* nuez vómica.

nuzzle ['nʌzəl], *v.t., v.i.* fomentar, criar; anidar(se), esconder(se); andar con el hocico hacia abajo; cavar con el hocico.

nye [nai], *s.* (*prov.*) bandada de faisanes.

nymph [nimf], *s.f.* ninfa; aldeana; palomilla.

nympha ['nimfə], *s.* (*zool.*) ninfa, palomilla, crisálida; (*anat.*) ninfas.

nymphæa [nimˈfiːə], *s.* (*bot.*) ninfea, nenúfar.

nymphlike, *a.* como una ninfa.

nymphomania [nimfoˈmeiniə], *s.* ninfomanía, furor uterino.

nymphomaniac, *s.* ninfómana.

nymphosis [nimˈfousis], *s.* transformación en ninfas.

O

O, o [ou], décimaquinta letra del alfabeto inglés. — *interj.* ¡o! ¡oh! ¡ojalá! — *s.* cero.

oaf [ouf], *s.* niño cambiado por las brujas; zoquete, bobalicón, persona de poca inteligencia.

oafish [oufiʃ], *a.* lerdo, torpe.

oafishness, *s.* torpeza, estupidez.

oak [ouk], *s.* roble; encina; *cork oak,* alcornoque, roble de corcho; *scarlet oak,* coscoja; *oak-apple,* agalla; *oak bark,* corteza de roble; *oak gall,* bugalla; *oak grove,* robledo, robledal.

oaken ['oukən], *a.* roblizo, de roble.

oakling, *s.* roble tierno.

oakum ['oukəm], *s.* (*mar.*) estopa (para calafatear).

oaky, *a.* de roble, fuerte, duro.

oar ['ɔːɹ], *s.* remo; remero; *to bend to the oars,* hacer fuerza de remos; *to lie on the oars,* cesar de remar. — *v.i.* remar. — *v.t.* hacer ir remando.

oared, *a.* provisto de remos.

oar-maker, *s.* remero.

oarsman ['ɔːɹzmən], *s.* (*pl.* **oarsmen**) remador, remero.

oasis [ouˈeisis], *s.* (*pl.* **oases**) oasis.

oast [oust], *s.* horno para lúpulo.

oat [out], *s.* (*bot.*) avena; *to sow one's wild oats,* (*fig.*) arrojar el fuego de la juventud, pasar las mocedades, andarse a la flor del berro.

oaten, *a.* de avena, aveníceo.

oat-field, *s.* avenal.

oath [ouθ], *s.* juramento, jura; reniego; blasfemia; *to take the oath,* prestar juramento; *upon one's oath,* bajo juramento; *to put someone upon oath,* hacer prestar juramento.

oatmeal ['outmiːl], *s.* harina de avena, gachas, puches.

obbligato [ɔbliˈgɑːtou], *s.* (*mús.*) obligado.

obduracy ['ɔbdjuːrəsi], *s.* obstinación, endurecimiento, obcecación, terquedad.

obdurate ['ɔbdjuːrit], *a.* obstinado, endurecido, inexorable, inflexible, insensible, terco.

obdurateness, *s.* obstinación, terquedad, endurecimiento de corazón.

obedience, *s.* obediencia, obedecimiento, sumisión.

obedient [oˈbiːdiənt], *a.* obediente, respetuoso, dócil, sumiso.

obeisance [oˈbeisəns], *s.* reverencia, saludo, cortesía, homenaje, acatamiento.

obelisk ['ɔbelisk], *s.* obelisco; (*impr.*) obelo, cruz, *f.*

obese [oˈbiːs], *a.* obeso, gordo, grueso.

obeseness, obesity, *s.* obesidad.

obey [oˈbei], *v.t.* obedecer, cumplir, estar sujeto a.

obfuscate [ɔbˈfʌskit], *v.t.* ofuscar, obcecar.

obfuscation, *s.* ofuscación, obcecación, ceguera.

obit ['ɔbit, 'oubit], *s.* (*ant.*) óbito, fallecimiento, defunción; exequias, funeral.

obitual, *a.* obituario.

obituary [oˈbitjuːəri], *a.* obituario, mortuorio. — *s.* necrología.

object ['ɔbdʒekt], *s.* objeto, artículo, cosa, efecto, sujeto; materia, causa; fin; (*mil.*) objetivo; (*gram.*) complemento, régimen directo; *object lens,* (*opt.*) objetivo; *object-lesson,* lección práctica.

object [ɔbˈdʒekt], *v.t.* objetar, oponer, imputar, aducir. — *v.i.* objetar, oponerse, poner objeción, poner reparos, protestar; *if you don't object,* si no tiene inconveniente, si no le importa.

objectify [ɔbˈdʒektifai], **objectivize** [ɔbˈdʒektivaiz], *v.t.* objetivar.

objection [ɔb'dʒekʃən], s. reproche, objeción, tacha; oposición, reparo, dificultad, inconveniente; *to take objection*, poner objeción; *to have* (o *take*) *no objection*, no oponerse, no tener inconveniente, no importarle; no ofenderse, no disgustarse.

objectionable [ɔb'dʒekʃənəbəl], *a.* inadmisible, reprensible, censurable.

objective [ɔb'dʒektiv], s., *a.* objetivo; (*gram.*) directo acusativo, o complemento de un verbo transitivo o de una preposición; (*mil.*) objetivo.

objectivity [ɔbdʒek'tiviti], s. objetividad.

objectless, *a.* sin objeto.

objector, s. objetante, el que pone objeciones.

objurgate ['ɔbdʒəɹgeit], *v.t.* reprender, reconvenir, regañar, reñir.

objurgation, s. represión, reconvención, regaño, reprimenda.

objurgatory, *a.* reprobatorio, relativo a una represión.

oblate ['ɔbleit], s. (*igl.*) oblata, hostia, beato. — *a.* consagrado al culto; aplastado en los polos.

oblateness, s. aplastamiento.

oblation [ɔb'leiʃən], s. oblación, ofrenda, sacrificio.

obligate ['ɔbligeit], *v.t.* (*fam.*) obligar, empeñar, comprometer, constreñir, precisar.

obligation, s. obligación, empeño, vínculo, precisión, compromiso, incumbencia, deber; *of obligation*, (*igl.*) de precepto.

obligatory [ɔbli'geitəri], *a.* obligatorio.

oblige [ɔ'blaidʒ], *v.t.* obligar, compeler, precisar, constreñir; agradar, complacer, hacer un favor a, servir, favorecer; *I am much obliged*, estoy muy agradecido o reconocido.

obligee [ɔblai'dʒi:], s. (*der.*) acreedor.

obliging, *a.* complaciente, servicial, servidor, obsequioso, oficioso.

obligingly, *adv.* complacientemente, atentamente, cortésmente.

obligor ['ɔbligɔɹ], s. (*der.*) deudor, obligado.

oblique [ɔ'bli:k], *a.* oblicuo, diagonal, sesgado, torcido, inclinado; travesío; indirecto, evasivo, siniestro; (*gram.*) oblicuo; cualquiera de los casos excepto el nominativo y el vocativo; colateral (de parientes).

obliquely, *adv.* oblicuamente, diagonalmente, al sesgo; indirectamente.

obliqueness [ɔ'bli:knis], **obliquity** [ɔ'blikwiti], s. oblicuidad, sesgo, irregularidad, desviación.

obliterate [ɔ'blitəreit], *v.t.* borrar, anular, testar, tachar, apagar; destruir, arrasar, consumir; olvidar; (*med.*) obliterar.

obliteration, s. extinción, canceladura, cancelación; testadura, testación; (*med.*) obliteración.

oblivion [ɔ'bliviən], s. olvido; *act of oblivion*, amnistía general.

oblivious [ɔ'bliviəs], *a.* olvidadizo, desmemoriado; absorto, abstraído.

obliviousness, s. olvido.

oblong ['ɔblɔŋ], *a.* oblongo. — s. figura oblonga, cuadrilongo.

obloquy ['ɔblokwi], s. infamia, baldón, vilipendio.

obmutescence [ɔbmju:'tesəns], s. pérdida de la palabra; silencio.

obnoxious [ɔb'nɔkʃəs], *a.* aborrecible, detestable, censurable, culpable, reprensible; ofensivo, dañoso, perjudicial.

obnoxiousness, s. odiosidad, carácter odioso; sujeción.

oboe ['oubou], s. oboe.

oboist ['oubouist], **oboe player**, s. oboe, el que toca el aboe.

obole ['ɔbɔl], **obolus** ['ɔbɔləs], s. óbolo.

obovate [ɔb'ouvət], *a.* (*bot.*) trasovado.

obreption [ɔb'repʃən], s. obrepción.

obreptitious [ɔbrep'tiʃəs], *a.* obrepticio.

obscene [ɔb'si:n], *a.* obsceno, impúdico, indecente, pornográfico, sucio, torpe.

obsceneness [ɔb'si:nnes], **obscenity** [ɔb'seniti], s. obscenidad, suciedad, impureza, indecencia.

obscurantism [ɔbskju:'ræntizm], s. obscurantismo.

obscurantist, s. obscurantista, *m.f.*

obscuration [ɔbskju:'reiʃən], s. obscurecimiento.

obscure [ɔb'skju:əɹ], *a.* obscuro, tenebroso, lóbrego; oculto, abstruso, enigmático, enrevesado; humilde, desconocido; confuso, indistinto. — *v.t.* obscurecer, eclipsar, entenebrecer, esconder.

obscurely, *adv.* obscuramente, ocultamente, confusamente, opacamente.

obscureness [ɔb'skju:əɹnis], **obscurity** [ɔb'skju:riti], s. obscuridad, lobreguez, densidad, tenebrosidad, vaguedad, confusión.

obsecrate ['ɔbsekreit], *v.t.* implorar, suplicar.

obsecration, s. obsecración; uno de los rezos de la letanía que en inglés empieza con *by* y en latín con *per*.

obsequies ['ɔbsekwiz], *s.pl.* exequias, ritos fúnebres.

obsequious [ɔb'si:kwiəs], *a.* servil, zalamero.

obsequiousness, s. obsequiosidad, sumisión, servilismo.

observable [ɔb'zə:ɹvəbəl], *a.* observable, notable.

observance [ɔb'zə:ɹvəns], s. observancia, uso, deber, cumplimiento, acatamiento, práctica; rito, ceremonia religiosa; respeto, cuidado exacto.

observant, *a.* observador, observante, atento, vigilante, obediente.

observation [ɔbzəɹ'veiʃən], s. observación; escrutinio; experiencia; comento, advertencia, opinión; *to place under observation*, poner en observancia; *observation post*, puesto de observancia.

observatory [ɔb'zə:ɹvətəri], s. observatorio, mirador, atalaya.

observe [ɔb'zə:ɹv], *v.t.*, *v.i.* observar, hacer observar; expresar, decir, advertir; reparar, atisbar, mirar, ver; vigilar, velar; cumplir (con).

observer, s. observador, atisbador, acechador.

observing, *a.* observador, atento, observante, cuidadoso.

obsess [ɔb'ses], *v.t.* sitiar, acosar, perseguir, causar obsesión.

obsession [ɔb'seʃən], s. obsesión.

obsidional [ɔb'sidiənəl], *a.* obsidional.

obsolescence [ɔbso'lesəns], s. tendencia a caer en desuso, acto de caer en desuso; estado de haber caído en desuso.

obsolescent, *a.* que cae en desuso, que envejece.

obsolete ['ɔbsoli:t], *a.* fuera de uso, anticuado, desusado, (*ant.*) obsoleto; (*biol.*) atrofiado.

obsoleteness, s. desuso.

obstacle ['ɔbstəkəl], s. obstáculo, impedimento, traba, cortapisa, inconveniente, embarazo, contrariedad.

obstetric [ɔb'stetrik], **obstetrical** [ɔb'stetrikəl], a. obstétrico.

obstetrician [ɔbste'triʃən], s. comadrón, partero.

obstetrics [ɔb'stetriks], s. obstetricia, partería.

obstinacy ['ɔbstinəsi], s. obstinación, terquedad, pertinacia, emperramiento, contumacia; persistencia, porfía.

obstinate ['ɔbstinit], a. obstinado, terco. testarudo, contumaz, rebelde, tozudo, cabezón; porfiado, pertinaz.

obstinately, adv. obstinadamente, tercamente, tenazmente, erre que erre; porfiadamente, a porfía, pertinazmente.

obstinateness, s. obstinación, terquedad, ccntumacia; persistencia, porfía.

obstipation [ɔbsti'peiʃən], s. (med.) estreñimiento.

obstreperous [ɔb'strepərəs], a. estrepitoso, ruidoso, turbulento, estridente.

obstreperousness, s. estrépito, bulla, baraúnda, clamor.

obstriction [ɔb'strikʃən], s. obligación, constreñimiento.

obstruct [ɔb'strʌkt], v.t. estorbar, obstruir, impedir, atorar, cerrar, tupir, dificultar, retardar, interrumpir, detener.

obstruction [ɔb'strʌkʃən], s. estorbo, obstrucción, impedimento, obstáculo, entorpecimiento, atasco, inconveniente, dificultad.

obstructionism, s. obstruccionismo.

obstructionist, s. obstruccionista, m.f.

obstructive, obstruent [ɔb'struːənt], a., s. obstructivo; obstáculo, traba.

obstruent, a. (med.) opilativo, obstructivo.

obtain [ɔb'tein], v.t. obtener, adquirir, alcanzar, conseguir, lograr, recibir, tener. — v.i. establecerse, prevalecer, existir, regir, ser costumbre, ser uso, ser moda.

obtainable, a. asequible.

obtainer, s. el que obtiene.

obtainment, s. obtención, conseguimiento, consecución, logro.

obtest [ɔb'test], v.t. suplicar, rogar, solicitar, conjurar, adjurar. — v.i. protestar.

obtestation, s. súplica, encarecimiento.

obtrude [ɔb'truːd], v.t. imponer, entrometer, entremeter. — v.i. ser importuno, intrusarse, entrometerse, entremeterse.

obtruder, s. intruso, entremetido, entrometido.

obtruncate [ɔb'trʌŋkeit], v.t. desmochar, podar, decapitar.

obtruncation, s. desmoche.

obtrusion [ɔb'truːʒən], s. intrusión, entremetimiento, entrometimiento.

obtrusive [ɔb'truːziv], a. entremetido, entrometido, intruso, importuno, indiscreto, majadero.

obtund [ɔb'tʌnd], v.t. amortiguar, embotar; adormecer.

obturate ['ɔbtjuːreit], v.t. obturar.

obturation, s. obturación.

obturator, s. obturador.

obtuse [ɔb'tjuːs], a. obtuso, embotado, lerdo, torpe, estúpido; sin punta, romo; sordo, apagado (ruidos o sonidos); *obtuse-angled*, a. obtusángulo.

obtusely, adv. obtusamente, estúpidamente, sordamente, lerdamente, torpemente.

obtuseness, s. estado de obtuso, embotamiento, embotadura, falta de inteligencia.

obtusion [ɔb'tjuːʒən], s. embotamiento, estado de obtuso.

obverse ['ɔbvəːs], s. anverso. — a. del anverso.

obversely, adv. a manera de anverso.

obvert [ɔb'vəːt], v.t. (ant.) volver hacia, volver de frente a.

obviate ['ɔbvieit], v.t. obviar, evitar, apartar, quitar, precaver.

obvious ['ɔbviəs], a. obvio, manifiesto, evidente, claro, patente; poco sutil, abierto, conspicuo.

obviously, adv. claramente, evidentemente, manifiestamente, patentemente.

obviousness, s. evidencia, claridad; (fig.) trasparencia.

ocarina [ɔkə'riːnə], s. ocarina.

occasion [ɔ'keiʃən], s. ocasión, acontecimiento, ocurrencia, acaecimiento, caso, lance, casualidad, oportunidad, coyuntura, sazón, f.; causa, motivo, razón, f.; proporción; *to have occasion to*, haber de, tener que; *on occasion*, en caso de necesidad, cuando se ofrece la oportunidad, a su debido tiempo; *on the first occasion*, a la primera ocasión; *to take this occasion*, aprovechar la oportunidad; *as occasion requires* (o *dictates*), en caso necesario. — v.t. dar motivo, ocasionar, causar, producir, excitar, mover, traer.

occasionable, a. que puede ser ocasionado.

occasional, a. poco frecuente, infrecuente, de vez en cuando, ocasional; (ant.) ocasional, accidental, fortuito, casual, contingente; de ocasión.

occasionally [ɔ'keiʃənəli], adv. de vez en cuando, ocasionalmente; (ant.) por contingencia, ocasionalmente.

occasioner, s. ocasionador, causador, autor; causa, motivo.

occident ['ɔksidənt], s. occidente, ocaso, poniente.

occidental [ɔksi'dentəl], a. occidental, occiduo.

occiduous [ɔk'sidjuːəs], a. occidental.

occipital [ɔk'sipitəl], a. occipital.

occiput ['ɔksipət], s. occipucio, colodrillo.

occlude [ɔk'luːd], v.t. cerrar, tapar; (med.) ocluir.

occlusion [ɔ'kluːʒən], s. (med.) oclusión.

occult [ɔ'kʌlt], a. oculto, misterioso, invisible; mágico; desconocido, ignoto, ignorado.

occultation [ɔkʌl'teiʃən], s. (astr.) ocultación, desaparición.

occultism ['ɔkəltizm], s. ocultismo.

occultist, s. ocultista, m.f.

occultly, adv. ocultamente.

occultness, s. carácter oculto, ocultación.

occupancy ['ɔkjuːpənsi], s. ocupación, tenencia, posesión.

occupant, a. ocupador, dueño, poseedor, el que ocupa o posee, inquilino.

occupation [ɔkjuː'peiʃən], s. ocupación, posesión, toma de posesión; tenencia, inquilinato; ocupación, oficio, profesión, empleo; trabajo, labor, tarea.

occupier ['ɔkjuːpaiə], s. ocupante, ocupador, inquilino.

occupy ['ɔkjuːpai], v.t. ocupar, emplear; hacer uso de; ocupar, habitar; ocuparse de, ocuparse en; estar instalado en.

occur [ɔ'kəːr], v.i. ocurrir, acontecer, acaecer,

suceder, pasar; encontrarse; aparecer; ocurrirse, venir a la imaginación o memoria.

occurrence [ɔ'kʌrəns], *s.* acontecimiento, caso, suceso, acaecimiento, lance, ocurrencia; *to be of frequent occurrence*, suceder a menudo.

occurrent, *a.* que ocurre, incidental.

ocean ['ouʃən], *s.* océano, piélago; (*fig.*) mar, *f.*, abundancia.

oceanic [ouʃi'ænik], *a.* oceánico, del océano, inmenso.

ocellate ['ɔseleit], **ocellated,** *a.* ojoso.

ocelot ['ouselɔt], *s.* (*zool.*) ocelote.

ochre ['oukəɹ], *s.* ocre, sil.

ochreous ['oukriəs], *a.* ocroso.

o'clock [o'klɔk], locución, contracción de *of the clock*, significando la hora; *What o'clock is it?* ¿Qué hora es?; *It is four o'clock*, Son las cuatro.

octagon ['ɔktəgən], *s.* octágono.

octagonal [ɔk'tægɔnəl], *a.* octágono, octagonal.

octahedral, *a.* octaédrico.

octahedron [ɔktə'hi:drən], *s.* octaedro.

octandria [ɔk'tændriə], *s.* octandria.

octandrian, octandrous, *a.* octándrico.

octangular [ɔk'tæŋgju:ləɹ], *a.* octangular.

octant ['ɔktənt], *s., a.* octante.

octave ['ɔkteiv], *s.* octava; medida para líquidos (61·371 lit.). — *a.* octavo, ochavo.

octavo [ɔk'teivou], *s.* en-octavo, en-8vo.

octennial [ɔk'teniəl], *a.* de ocho años.

octet [ɔk'tet], *s.* octeto.

octillion [ɔk'tiljən], *s.* octillón.

October [ɔk'toubəɹ], *s.* octubre; cerveza o sidra hecha en octubre.

octogenarian, *s., a.; octogenary, a.* octogenario.

octopetalous [ɔkto'petələs], *a.* (*bot.*) octopétalo.

octopus ['ɔktɔpəs], *s.* pulpo, pólipo, jibia octópoda.

octosyllabic, *a.* octosílabo.

octosyllable [ɔkto'siləbəl], *s.* octosílabo.

octroi ['ɔktrwɑ:], *s.* (*fr.*) fielato, derechos de puerta.

octuple ['ɔktju:pəl], *s., a.* óctuplo.

ocular ['ɔkju:ləɹ], *a.* ocular, visual.

ocularly, *adv.* ocularmente, visiblemente.

oculist ['ɔkju:list], *s.* oculista, *m.f.*

odalisk, odalisque ['ɔdəlisk], *s.* odalisca.

odd [ɔd], *a.* impar; sobrante, de más, de pico, pico, tanto, excedente; raro, extraño, singular, curioso, irregular, accidental, casual, extraordinario, original, excéntrico, descarrillado; desemparejado, sin pareja; único, solo, suelto; *odd or even*, pares o nones; *fifty odd pounds*, cincuenta libras y pico, o cincuenta y tantas libras; *at odd times*, de vez en cuando; en momentos imprevistos.

oddity ['ɔditi], *s.* particularidad, singularidad, rareza; despropósito; persona o cosa singular.

oddly, *adv.* raramente, curiosamente, extraordinariamente, extrañamente, singularmente, desigualmente.

oddment ['ɔdmənt], *s.* retazo, retal, baratija.

oddness, *s.* singularidad, disparidad, desigualdad, extravagancia, rareza.

odds [ɔdz], *s.pl.* desigualdad, disparidad, diferencia; apuesta desigual; superioridad,

ventaja; suerte, *f.*, destino; disputa, riña, pendencia; *to be at odds*, estar de punta, estar siempre riñendo; *odds and ends*, piezas, retazos; *to be made up of odds and ends*, estar hecho de piezas; *to give odds*, dar puntos (o dar ventaja en una apuesta); *to fight against odds*, luchar contra una fuerza superior; *to set at odds*, poner en desorden, desunir, malquistar; *what odds does it make?* ¿qué importa?

ode [oud], *s.* oda.

odious ['oudiəs], *a.* odioso, aborrecible, aborrecido, detestable, abominable, asqueroso.

odiousness ['oudiəsnis], **odium** ['oudiəm], *s.* odiosidad, odio.

odograph ['oudogræf], **odometer** [o'dɔmitəɹ], *s.* odómetro.

odometrical, *a.* odométrico.

odontalgia [oudɔn'tældʒə], **odontalgy** [oudɔn'tældʒi], *s.* odontalgia.

odontalgic, *a.* odontálgico.

odontograph [ou'dɔntogræf], *s.* odontógrafo.

odontoid [ou'dɔntoid], *a.* odontoide, odontóideo.

odontology [oudɔn'tɔlodʒi], *s.* odontología.

odorant ['oudəɹənt], *a.* odorífero.

odoriferous [oudo'riferəs], *a.* odorífero.

odoriferousness, *s.* perfume, fragancia.

odorous ['oudorəs], *a.* odorífero, oloroso, perfumado, fragante.

odorousness, *s.* olor, perfume, fragancia, aroma, *m.*

odour ['oudəɹ], *s.* olor, perfume, aroma, *m.*, fragancia; reputación, estimación.

odourless, *a.* inodoro.

odyssey ['ɔdisi], *s.* odisea.

œcumenical [i:kju:'menikəl], *a.* [ECUMENICAL].

œdema [i:'di:mə], *s.* [EDEMA].

œdematous [i:'di:mətəs], *a.* [EDEMATOUS].

œsophagus [i:'sɔfəgəs], *s.* [ESOPHAGUS].

œstrum ['i:strʌm], *s.* brama; (*poét.*) estro.

œstrus, *s.* tábano.

of [ɔv], *prep.* de, en, para, por, sobre, según, tocante a; desde, fuera de, proveniente de, entre; *of course*, por supuesto, desde luego, naturalmente, como es natural, claro está, bien entendido; *of late*, últimamente, recientemente; *of old*, antiguamente; en otro tiempo, antes; *of all things*, ante todo, sobre todo; *a friend of mine*, un amigo mío, uno de mis amigos.

off [ɔ:f], *adv.* lejos, fuera de aquí, a distancia; por arriba; enteramente, completamente, del todo; *off and on*, ya bien, ya mal, de vez en cuando, por intervalos, de una manera intermitente; *far off* o *a long way off*, muy lejos, a una gran distancia; *to be off*, irse, marcharse; *the wedding is off*, se ha deshecho la boda; *is there anything off?* (*com.*) ¿hay descuento? *to put off*, aplazar, diferir; *hands off!* ¡manos quietas! *hats off!* ¡abajo los sombreros! ¡quítense los sombreros!; *to stand off*, mantenerse apartado; *to tell off*, contar; (*fam.*) regañar; *to have one's shoes off*, estar descalzo; *to be well off*, tener un buen pasar, estar holgado, ser rico, (*vulg.*) tener el riñón bien cubierto; *to ward off*, parar; *I will see you off*, iré a despedirle; *to turn off* (*gas, etc.*) cerrar la llave (del gas, etc.); *to send off*, expedir, mandar, despachar. — *interj.* ¡fuera! ¡vaya! ¡anda! ¡vete de aquí! ¡fuera de aquí!

¡anda a paseo! *off with his head!* ¡que le corten la cabeza! — *prep.* lejos de, fuera de, desde, de; (*mar.*) a la altura de, frente a; *off colour*, desteñido; falta de color (joyas, piedras, etc.); (*fig.*) malucho, triste, enfermo; (*fam.*) verde; *it is a street off Piccadilly*, es una calle que arranca de Piccadilly. — *a.* derecho (de un animal, o la pata de un animal); libre, de fiesta, de asueto; errado, equivocado; más distante, a mayor distancia, más lejano; *off side*, (*aut.*) lado derecho (*Ing.*), lado izquierdo (*E.U.*); *off season*, estación muerta.

offal ['ɔfəl], *s.* relieves, sobras, asadura; menudillos; desecho, desperdicio.

offence, offense [ɔ'fens], *s.* ofensa, agravio, injuria, afrenta, ultraje, contravención, delito, pecado, falta, culpa, crimen, agresión; *to take offence*, ofenderse, darse por sentido; *there's no offence taken*, no importa, no hay daño; *there's no offence meant*, sin ofender a Vd.

offenceless, *a.* inofensivo.

offend [ɔ'fend], *v.t.* ofender, irritar, agraviar, provocar, enfadar, escandalizar, desagradar, ultrajar, contravenir, transgresar. — *v.i.* ofender, pecar, faltar, delinquir, disgustar, desagradar.

offender, *s.* ofensor, criminal, delincuente, culpable, pecador, transgresor, agraviador.

offensive [ɔ'fensiv], *a.* ofensivo, injurioso, perjudicial, desagradable, ultrajante, agresivo. — *s.* ofensiva, ataque.

offensiveness, *s.* ofensa, injuria, afrenta, desazón, *f.*

offer ['ɔfəɹ], *v.t.* ofrecer, presentar, deparar, proponer, prometer, brindar; sacrificar, inmolar. — *v.i.* ofrecerse, presentarse; estar a la mano; sobrevenir, ocurrir; intentar. — *s.* oferta, ofrecimiento; demanda; promesa, palabra; intento, esfuerzo; envite; declaración de amor; propuesta, proposición; donativo, don.

offerable, *a.* presentable, ofrecible.

offerer, *s.* ofrecedor, sacrificador, oferente.

offering, *s.* ofrenda, sacrificio, oblación, tributo; oferta, ofrecimiento; *burnt offering*, holocausto; *votive offering*, exvoto.

offertory ['ɔfəɹtəri], *s.* oferta, ofrenda, ofrecimiento; (*igl.*) ofertorio; *offertory box*, cepo, cepillo del Santísimo.

off-hand [ɔ:f'hænd], *a.* brusco, descomedido; improvisado, sin preparación, sin ceremonia, de repente, de sopetón.

office ['ɔfis], *s.* oficio, ejercicio, cargo, empleo, ocupación, colocación, destino, puesto, ministerio, función; servicio divino; despacho, oficina, dependencia, bufete, estudio, escritorio; departamento, negociado, agencia; (*igl.*) oficios, rezo; empleados de oficina (colectivamente); letrina; *Jack in office*, pequeño empleado; *ticket office*, despacho de billetes; *post office*, administración de correos, casa de correos, estafeta; estanco; *to be in office*, estar colocado, estar en el poder; *to do the office of*, servir de, hacer el oficio de. — *pl.* **offices**, servicio, ayuda, favor; oficinas, departamentos; (*igl.*) oficios, rezos.

officer ['ɔfisəɹ], oficial, funcionario; agente de policía; empleado, dependiente; ujier; *customs officer*, aduanero; *staff officer*, oficial de estado mayor; *commissioned officer*,

(*mil.*) oficial, subalterno; *non-commissioned officer*, (*mil.*) sargento, cabo, suboficial. — *v.t.* proveer de oficiales; mandar como oficial.

official [ɔ'fiʃəl], *a.* oficial, público, de oficio, autorizado. — *s.* encargado, autorizado, oficial, funcionario, juez.

officialdom [ɔ'fiʃəldəm], **officialism** [ɔ'fiʃəlizm], *s.* funcionarismo, formalismo, burocracia.

officiality, *s.* oficialidad.

officially [ɔ'fiʃəli], *adv.* oficialmente, de oficio.

officiate [ɔ'fiʃieit], *v.i.* oficiar, ejercer, ejercer funciones, funcionar, desempeñar un cargo; *to officiate for*, reemplazar, sustituir.

officiating, *a.* oficiante, reemplazante, suplente.

officinal [ɔ'fisinəl], *s.* oficinal. — *s.* droga oficinal.

officious [ɔ'fiʃəs], *a.* entremetido, oficioso; (*ant.*) obsequioso, servicial, oficioso.

officiousness, *s.* entrometimiento, oficiosidad; (*ant.*) obsequiosidad, oficiosidad.

offing ['ɔfiŋ], *s.* (*mar.*) alta mar, mar afuera, mar ancha.

offish, *a.* reservado, intratable, adusto.

off-print, *s.* tirada aparte, separata.

offscouring [ɔ:f'skauəriŋ], *s.* desecho, hez, *f.*, lavaduras, basura.

offset ['ɔ:fset], *s.* compensación, equivalencia, balance, equivalente; botón, pimpollo, vástago, tallo nuevo; (*geog.*) estribo, estribación, terraplén. — *v.t.* compensar, balancear, equivalar, equiparar, contrapesar; terraplenar.

offshoot ['ɔ:fʃu:t], *s.* vástago, tallo, ramal.

off-side, *s.* (*aut., etc.*) lado derecho (*Ing.*), lado izquierdo (*E.U.*); (*deportes*) 'ofside', fuera de juego.

offspring ['ɔ:fspriŋ], *s.* descendiente, vástago, niños, hijos, descendientes, descendencia, prole, *f.*, posteridad; casta, linaje.

offward ['ɔ:fwəɹd], *adv.* (*mar.*) hacia el largo de la costa.

often, oftentimes, (*ant.*) oft, (*ant.*) **ofttimes**, *adv.* frecuentemente, muchas veces, con frecuencia, a menudo o amenudo; *how often?* ¿cuántas veces? *so often*, tantas veces; *as often as*, siempre que, tantas veces como; *too often*, demasiado a menudo.

ogee [ou'dʒi:], *s.* cimacio, gola.

ogival [ou'dʒaivəl], *a.* ogival, en ogiva, aristado.

ogive ['oudʒaiv], *s.* ojiva. — *a.* ogival, en ogiva, aristado.

ogle ['ougəl], *v.t.*, *v.i.* guiñar, ojear, comerse con los ojos a, echar miradas amorosas. — *s.* guiñada, ojeada, mirada al soslayo.

ogler, *s.* guiñador.

ogling, *s.* guiño, ojeada, acción de mirar al soslayo.

ogre ['ougəɹ], *s.* ogro, monstruo, gigante.

ogress, *s.f.* ogresa, ogro hembra.

oh [ou], *interj.* ¡oh! ¡ay!

ohm [oum], *s.* ohmio.

ohmic, *a.* óhmico.

oho [ou'hou], *interj.* ¡ajá!

oil [ɔil], *s.* aceite, óleo; *salad oil*, aceite para ensaladas, mayonesa; *palm oil*, aceite del Senegal; *to burn the midnight oil*, quemarse las cejas; *to strike oil*, encontrar buena suerte de súbito. — *v.t.* aceitar, engrasar, lubrificar, untar, ungir, olear; hacer suave y agradable.

oil-beetle, *s.* carraleja.
oil-cake, *s.* torta de linaza, torta de borujo.
oil-can, *s.* aceitera, alcuza.
oilcloth, *s.* hule, encerado.
oiler, *s.* engrasador, aceitero, aceitador; buque aceitero.
oiliness, *s.* naturaleza aceitosa, oleaginosidad, oleosidad, untuosidad.
oilman, *s.m.* mercader de aceites.
oil-painting, *s.* pintura al óleo.
oil-press, *s.* almazara, trujal.
oil-shop, *s.* aceitería.
oilskin, *s.* hule, encerado, impermeable.
oil-stove, *s.* estufa de aceite.
oil-tank, *s.* almijara.
oily, *a.* oleaginoso, aceitoso; untuoso, grasiento; (*fig.*) zalamero; sin escrúpulos.
ointment ['ɔintmənt], *s.* ungüento, unto, untura.
O.K. ['ou'kei], *a.*, *interj.* (*vulg.*) muy bien; perfectamente; entendido. — *v.t.* aprobar.
old [ould], *a.* viejo, anciano, antiguo, añejo, añoso; de edad (de); anticuado, usado, acabado, gastado; inveterado, avejentado; familiar, de costumbre; *Old Style*, (*impr.*) estilo antiguo; *to grow old*, envejecer; *to be old enough*, tener bastante edad; *to be twenty years old*, tener veinte años; *of old*, antiguamente; *old clothes*, ropa vieja; *old wine*, vino añejo; *how old are you?* ¿cuántos años tiene Vd.? *old maid*, solterona; mona (juego de naipes); *old bachelor*, solterón; *old-fashioned*, fuera de moda; del tiempo de maricastaña; *old fogy*, vejarrón, vejazo. vejete; *old boy*, *chap*, o *fellow*, (*fam.*) amigo, amigo mío, compadre.
olden ['ouldən], *a.* (*poét.*) antiguo, viejo, pasado. — *v.i.* hacerse viejo, envejecer.
oldish, *a.* antiguo, avejentado, poco viejo.
oldness, *s.* vejez; antigüedad, ancianidad, envejecimiento.
oleaceous [ouli'eiʃəs], *a.* oleáceo.
oleaginous [ouli'ædʒinəs], *a.* oleaginoso, aceitoso.
oleander [ouli'ændər], *s.* adelfa, baladre.
oleaster [ouli'æstər], *s.* oleastro, olivo silvestre, acebuche.
oleate ['oulieit], *s.* oleato.
oleic [ou'li:ik], *a.* oleico.
olein [ou'li:in], *s.* oleína.
oleometer [ouli'ɔmetər], *s.* oleómetro.
oleose ['ouliouz], **oleous** ['ouliəs], *a.* oleoso.
oleracious [ɔlə'reiʃəs], *a.* oleráceo.
olfactive [ɔl'fæktiv], **olfactory** [ɔl'fæktəri], *a.* olfactorio.
oliban ['ɔlibæn], **olibanum** [ɔ'libənəm], *s.* olíbano.
oligarch ['ɔligɑ:rk], *s.* oligarca, *m.*
oligarchic, oligarchical, *a.* oligárquico.
oligarchy, *s.* oligarquía.
olio ['ouliou], *s.* olla podrida; mezcla, miscelánea.
olivaceous [ɔli'veiʃəs], *a.* oliváceo, aceitunado.
olivary ['ɔlivəri], *a.* oliviforme, olivario.
olive [ɔliv], *s.* olivo; oliva, aceituna; *wild olive*, acebuchina; *wild olive tree*, acebuche. — *a.* aceitunado, aceitunil.
olive-bearing, *a.* olivífero.
olive-coloured, *a.* aceitunado.
oliver ['ɔlivər], *s.* martillo mecánico accionado con el pie, usado en la fabricación de clavos, etc.

olivet ['ɔlivet], *s.* botón en forma de aceituna; perla falsa usada en el comercio con salvajes.
olive-tree, *s.* olivo, aceituno.
olivine ['ɔlivain], *s.* variedad de crisólito.
Olympiad [o'limpiæd], *s.* olimpíada.
Olympian [o'limpiən], **Olympic** [o'limpik], *a.* olímpico.
Olympus [o'limpəs], *s.* olimpo.
ombre ['ɔmbər], *s.* tresillo (juego de naipes).
omega ['oumegə], *s.* omega, fin.
omelet ['ɔmlet], *s.* tortilla de huevos.
omen ['oumen], *s.* agüero, presagio, pronóstico.
omened, *a.* de buen o mal agüero, fatídico; *ill-omened*, de mal agüero, mal hadado.
omentum [o'mentəm], *s.* omento, redaño.
ominous ['ɔminəs], *a.* ominoso, siniestro, azaroso, nefasto, fatal, pronosticador, presagioso.
ominously, *adv.* ominosamente, de mal agüero, fatalmente.
ominousness, *s.* fatalidad.
omissible [o'misəbəl], *a.* que se puede omitir.
omission [o'miʃən], *s.* omisión, exclusión, supresión, preterición, descuido, olvido.
omissive, *a.* que omite, que olvida.
omit [o'mit], *v.t.* omitir, saltar, descuidar, excluir, desechar, suprimir, pretermitir, prescindir de, pasar por alto, dejar de mencionar.
omittance, *s.* omisión.
omnibus ['ɔmnibəs], *s.* autobús, ómnibus. — *a.* que comprende varias cosas de obras coleccionadas.
omnifarious [ɔmni'fɛəriəs], *a.* omnímodo, de todos los géneros.
omniparous [ɔm'nipərəs], *a.* omníparo.
omnipotence, omnipotency, *s.* omnipotencia.
omnipotent [ɔm'nipotənt], *a.* omnipotente, todopoderoso.
omnipresence, *s.* omnipresencia, ubicuidad.
omnipresent [ɔmni'prezənt], *a.* omnipresente, ubicuo.
omniscience, omnisciency, *s.* omnisciencia.
omniscient [ɔm'niʃənt], *a.* omnisciente, omniscio, omnisapiente.
omnium ['ɔmniəm], *s.* (*bolsa*) el agregado valor de las diferentes acciones, obligaciones o valores en que un empréstito está fundado; (*fam.*) mezcla, confusión, barullo.
omnivorous [ɔm'nivorəs], *a.* omnívoro, codicioso, glotón.
omoplate ['oumopleit], *s.* omóplato, espaldilla.
omphalic ['ɔmfəlik], *a.* umbilical.
on [ɔn], *prep.* sobre, encima, en; hacia, con dirección a; después de, inmediatamente después, tras; acerca, tocante a, concerniente a, respecto a; *to live on*, vivir de; *on arriving*, al llegar; *on his arrival* (o *arriving*), a su llegada; *on account of*, a causa de; *on no account* para nada en el mundo; *on condition that*, con tal que; *on an average*, por término medio; *on every side*, por todos lados; *on board*, a bordo de; *on the contrary*, al contrario; *on foot*, a pie; *on horseback*, a caballo; *on the right*, a la (mano) derecha; *on the left*, a la (mano) izquierda; *on the wing*, volando; *on the point of*, a punto de; *on purpose*, de propósito, ex profeso, expresamente; *on my part*, por parte mía; *on a sudden*, de golpe, de repente; *on second thoughts*, después de

maduro examen; *to be on one's guard*, estar en guardia. — *interj.* ¡adelante! ¡vamos! — *adv.* encima; adelante, sobre; encendida (la luz), funcionando, puesto en marcha; sin cesar, progresivamente; a lo largo; *on and off*, por intervalos, de vez en cuando; *on and on*, siempre, sin cesar; *and so on*, y así sucesivamente, etcétera; *come on!* ¡ven acá! ¡vamos! *go on!* ¡siga Vd.! *move on!*, ¡adelante Vd.!; *to have on*, llevar puesto; *to have one's shoes on*, estar calzado; *on the tenth of July*, el 10 de julio.

onager [ˈɔnəgəɹ], *s.* onagro.

onanism [ˈounənizm], *s.* onanismo.

once [wʌns], *adv.* una vez, antiguamente, en otro tiempo; *at once*, sin parar, de una vez, de repente, al mismo tiempo; enseguida, inmediatamente, al momento; *once more*, otra vez, una vez más; *once for all*, una vez para siempre; *once in a way*, o *for once*, una vez siquiera; *once upon a time*, érase una vez, había una vez, mucho tiempo ha, en otros tiempos; *once bit, twice shy*, gato escaldado del agua fría huye.

one, *a.* un, uno, una; único, solo; un tal, cierto; común. — *pron.* uno; se; alguno, alguien, cualquiera; el uno, la una; uno solo; *any one*, cualquiera, quienquiera, todo el mundo; *each one*, *every one*, cada uno; *one by one*, uno a uno; *one and all*, todos sin excepción; *no one*, nadie; *some one*, alguno; *such a one*, fulano, fulana; *one o'clock*, la una; *it's all one to me*, lo mismo me da, me es igual.

one-eyed [wʌnˈaid], *a.* tuerto.

one-handed, *a.* manco.

one-horse, *a.* de un caballo; (*fam.*) pobre, sin importancia.

oneness [ˈwʌnnis], *s.* unidad; singularidad.

onerous [ˈounəɹəs], *a.* oneroso, pesado, gravoso, opresivo.

one's [wʌnz], *pron. pos.* [ONE], su, sus, de uno.

oneself [wʌnˈself], *pron. refl.* se, sí, sí mismo; *to come to oneself*, volver en sí.

one-sided, *a.* parcial, injusto.

onion [ˈʌnjən], *s.* cebolla.

onion-bed, *s.* cebollera, cebollar.

only [ˈounli], *adj.* solo, único, raro, singular. — *adv.* sólo, solamente, tan sólo, no... sino, no más que, únicamente. — *conj.* sólo que, pero, si no fuera que.

onomatopœia [ɔnɔmætoˈpiːə], *s.* onamatopeya.

onrush [ˈɔnrʌʃ], *s.* arremetida, embestida.

onset [ˈɔnset], **onslaught** [ˈɔnslɔːt], *s.* asalto, ataque furioso, primer choque, acceso, arremetida, arranque.

ontologic [ɔntoˈlɔdʒik], **ontological** [ɔntoˈlɔdʒikəl], *a.* ontológico.

ontologist, *s.* ontólogo.

ontology, *s.* ontología.

onus [ˈounəs], *s.* cargo, obligación, responsabilidad.

onward [ˈɔnwəd], **onwards** [ˈɔnwədz], *adv.* adelante, en adelante, progresivamente, en lo venidero.

onward, *adj.* adelantado, progresivo, avanzado.

onyx [ˈɔniks, ˈouniks], *s.* ónix, ónice.

oolite [ˈouolait], *s.* oolito.

oolitic, *a.* oolítico.

oological, *a.* oológico.

oology [ouˈolodʒi], *s.* oología.

ooze [uːz], *v.i.* filtrar, manar, fluir, exudar,

rezumarse. — *v.t.* sudar. — *s.* legamo, fango, limo, cieno; chorro suave; adobo.

oozing, *s.* rezumo.

oozy, *a.* fangoso, cenagoso, lamoso.

opacity [oˈpæsiti], *s.* opacidad, obscuridad.

opal [ˈoupəl], *s.* ópalo.

opalesce [oupəˈles], *v.i.* irisar.

opalescence, *s.* opalescencia, cualidad de opalino.

opalescent [oupəˈlesənt], *a.* opalino, iridiscente.

opaline [ˈoupəlain], *a.* opalino.

opaque [ouˈpeik], *a.* opaco; sombrío, obscuro, incomprensible; mate, sin brillo.

opaqueness, *s.* opacidad.

ope [oup], *poét.*) *v.t.*, *v.i.* abrir. — *a.* abierto.

open [ˈoupən], *v.t.* abrir; empezar, dar principio, inaugurar, encentar; deshacer, romper; desplegar, destapar; descubrir, explicar, revelar, desenvolver; abrir paso, abrir camino, franquear, hacer accesible; establecer, cortar, rajar, hender; aumentar, ensanchar; (*for.*) dar principio, exponer la causa antes de presentar el testimonio o prueba. — *v.i.* abrirse; entreabrirse, dividirse; desplegarse, destaparse, descubrirse; asomarse, aparecer; empezar, comenzar, estrenarse; *to open on* o *on to*, dar a, mirar a; *to open up*, abrir; (*fig.*) hacer accesible. — *a.* abierto, descubierto, desplegado, destapado, desembarazado, descampado, descercado; llano, ingenuo, franco, honesto, honrado; libre; visible, desnudo; raso; extendido; sin atar, sin sellar, desempaquetado; dispuesto, receptivo, aparejado, preparado, listo, pronto; manifiesto, evidente, patente, claro; directo; templado, suave; (*com.*) pendiente; *slightly open*, entreabierto, in the open air, al aire libre, al raso, a la intemperie; *in the open street*, en medio de la calle, en plena calle; *open country*, país abierto; *open fields*, campo raso; *an open question*, una cuestión pendiente; *open shame*, vergüenza pública; *in open court*, en pleno tribunal; *an open secret*, un secreto a voces; *to lay open*, descubrir; *to lie open*, exponerse; *to draw open*, abrir de par en par; *to keep the bowels open*, tener el vientre libre.

opener, *s.* abridor.

open-eyed, *a.* vigilante, alerta.

open-handed, *a.* generoso, liberal, dadivoso.

open-hearted, *a.* cándido, llano, franco, ingenuo, abierto.

opening, *s.* abertura; ranura; entrada; tronera; portillo, buco, brecha; inauguración, apertura, principio, comienzo; estreno; coyuntura, oportunidad, ocasión; (*com.*) salida; campo abierto, raso; vacante, *f.*, oportunidad; claro; (*min.*) cala, galería.

openly, *adv.* abiertamente, francamente; públicamente, al descubierto.

openness, *s.* ausencia de obstáculos; franqueza, llaneza, ingenuidad, claridad, publicidad.

openwork, *s.* (*cost.*) calado, deshilado.

opera [ˈɔpəɹə], *s.* ópera; *opera-glass(es)*, gemelos de teatro; *opera-hat*, clac; *opera-singer*, cantante de ópera, operista, *m.f.*; *opera-goer*, (*fam.*) aficionado a la ópera; *comic* o *light opera*, zarzuela.

operameter [ɔpərˈæmitəɹ], *s.* operámetro.

operate [ˈɔpəreit], *v.t.*, *v.i.* operar, obrar,

producir efecto, hacer funcionar, manejar, dirigir, gobernar; efectuar, llevar a cabo; (*com.*) especular; (*cir.*) operar.

operatic [ɔpə'rætik], *a.* de ópera, operístico.
operating, *a.* de operación, operante.
operation [ɔpə'reiʃən], *s.* operación, acción, función, efecto, oficio, manipulación, movimiento, procedimiento; (*cir.*) operación.
operative, *a.* activo, eficaz, operativo. — *s.* artesano, operario, obrero, trabajador, maquinista, *m.f.*
operator, *s.* operario, agente; maquinista, *m.f.*; (*telephone*) *operator*, telefonista, *m.f.*, telegrafista, *m.f.*; (*cir.*) operador.
opercular [o'pəːɹkjuːləɹ], *s.* opérculo.
operculate, *a.* operculado.
operculum [o'pəːɹkjuːləm], *s.* opérculo.
operetta [ɔpə'retə], *s.* opereta, zarzuela.
operose ['ɔpərouz], *a.* laborioso, penoso, trabajoso.
ophidian [o'fidiən], *s.*, *a.* ofidiano, ofidio.
ophioglossum [ɔfio'glɔsəm], *s.* ofiglosa.
ophite ['ɔfait], *s.* ofita.
ophthalmia [ɔf'θælmiə], *s.* oftalmía.
ophthalmic, *a.* oftálmico.
ophthalmologist, *s.* oftalmólogo.
ophthalmology [ɔfθæl'mɔlodʒi], *s.* oftalmología.
ophthalmoscope, *s.* oftalmoscopio.
ophthalmy [ɔf'θælmi], *s.* oftalmía.
opiate ['oupiət], *s.* opiato, opiata, narcótico. — *a.* opiado, narcótico, soporífero. — *v.t.* administrar opio.
opinable [o'painəbəl], *a.* opinable.
opine [o'pain], *v.t.*, *v.i.* opinar.
opiniated [o'pinieitid], *a.* obstinado, terco.
opiniative [o'pinjətiv], *a.* obstinado, terco; hipotético.
opiniativeness, *s.* obstinación, terquedad.
opinion [o'pinjən], *s.* opinión, *f.*, juicio, parecer, dictamen, idea, concepto, pensamiento, sentir, acuerdo; estimación, reputación, fama; *in my opinion*, a mi modo de ver; *to be of opinion*, ser de opinión, opinar; *to be of the same opinion*, quedar de acuerdo, concurrir; *What is your opinion?* ¿Qué opinión tiene Usted? ¿Qué le parece a Usted?
opinionated [o'pinjəneitid], *a.* obstinado, terco, opinativo, testarudo, pertinaz, presuntuoso.
opinionately, opinionatedly, *adv.* obstinadamente, pertinazmente.
opinionativeness, *s.* obstinación, terquedad.
opium ['oupiəm], *s.* opio; *opium-addict*, opiómano, opiófago.
opobalsam [ɔpo'bɔːlsəm], *s.* opobálsamo.
opodeldoc [ɔpo'deldɔk], *s.* (*farm.*) linimento de jabón disuelto en alcohol y alcanfor.
opopanax [o'pɔpənæks], *s.* opopónaco.
opossum [o'pɔsəm], *s.* zorra mochilera, (*Amér.*) zarigüeya.
oppilation [ɔpi'leiʃən], *s.* opilación.
opponent [ɔ'pouɹənt], *a.* opuesto, contrario, antagónico, en frente. — *s.* antagonista, *m.f.*, adversario, rival, contrario, opositor, competidor, contrincante.
opportune ['ɔpəːɹtjuːn], *a.* oportuno, conveniente, tempestivo.
opportunely, *adv.* oportunamente, a tiempo, a propósito.
opportuneness, *s.* oportunidad.

opportunism ['ɔpɔːɹtjuːnizm], *s.* oportunismo.
opportunist, *s.* oportunista, *m.f.*
opportunity [ɔpɔːɹtjuːniti], *s.* oportunidad, ocasión, sazón, *f.*, covuntura; *opportunity makes the thief*, la ocasión hace el ladrón, puerta abierta al santo tienta.
opposable [ɔ'pouzəbəl], *a.* oponible.
oppose [ɔ'pouz], *v.t.* oponer, poner un impedimento, contraponer, resistir, combatir, luchar contra, oponerse a, hacer frente a. — *v.i.* oponerse, estar frente a frente, obstar, argüir, resistirse.
opposed, *a.* contrario, opuesto, antagónico, desafecto. — *p.p.* [OPPOSE].
opposer, *s.* antagonista, *m.f.*, adversario, opugnador, rival.
opposite ['ɔpozit], *a.* contrario, opuesto, antagónico, adverso; de enfrente, frente a; frontero, fronterizo; otro, diferente. — *s.* antagonista, *m.f.*, adversario; (lo) contrario, (lo) opuesto.
oppositely, *adv.* opuestamente, en frente.
oppositeness *s.* contraste; situación opuesta; contrariedad.
opposition [ɔpo'ziʃən], *s.* oposición; contrariedad; contraste; contradicción; objeción, aversión; resistencia, opugnación; obstáculo, impedimento.
oppositional, *a.* (*pol.*) de la oposición.
oppositionist, *s.* (*pol.*) miembro de la oposición, oposicionista, *m.f.*
oppress [ɔ'pres], *s.* oprimir, tiranizar, gravar, abrumar, aquejar, afligir; agobiar; supeditar, aprensar; (*ant.*) apretar, comprimir.
oppression [ɔ'preʃən], *s.* opresión, tiranía, vejación; descorazonamiento; miseria; calamidad, pesadez; opresión de pecho, ahogo, sofocación.
oppressive [ɔ'presiv], *a.* opresivo, sofocante; molesto, pesado, gravoso; duro, tiránico, inhumano; bochornoso, opresivo; agobiante, abrumador.
oppressively, *adv.* opresivamente, duramente.
oppressiveness, *s.* opresión, carácter opresivo.
oppressor, *s.* opresor, tirano.
opprobrious [ɔ'proubriəs], *a.* oprobioso, vituperioso, infamante, ultrajante; injurioso.
opprobriousness, *s.* oprobio, vituperio; ignominia.
opprobrium [ɔ'proubriəm], *s.* oprobio, afrenta, injuria, deshonra.
oppugn [ɔ'pjuːn], *v.t.* opugnar, combatir.
oppugnancy, oppugnation, *s.* opugnación.
oppugner [ɔ'pjuːnəɹ], *s.* opugnador.
optative ['ɔptətiv], *s.*, *a.* optativo; (*gram.*) modo optativo.
optatively, *adv.* optativamente.
optic ['ɔptik], **optical**, *a.* óptico, visorio, de la vista.
optic, *s.* (*fam.*) ojo.
optician [ɔp'tiʃən], *s.* óptico.
optics ['ɔptiks], *s.* óptica.
optimism ['ɔptimizm], *s.* optimismo.
optimist, *s.* optimista, *m.f.*
optimistic, *a.* optimista.
option ['ɔpʃən], *s.* opción.
optional ['ɔpʃənəl], *a.* discrecional, facultativo, libre.
optionally, *adv.* facultativamente.
optometer [ɔp'tɔmetəɹ], *s.* optómetro.
opulence ['ɔpjuːləns], **opulency** ['ɔpjuːlənsi], *s.* opulencia, copia, lozanía.

opulent ['ɔpjuːlənt], *a.* opulento, acaudalado.

opulently, *adv.* opulentamente, caudalosamente.

opuntia [oˈpʌnʃə], *s.* nopal, higuera de tuna.

opus ['oupəs], *s.* (*pl.* **opera**) obra literaria o musical.

opuscule [oˈpʌskjuːl], *s.* opúsculo.

or [ɔːɹ], *conj.* o, u, alias, o sea; *either . . . or,* o . . . o, *sea . . . sea.* — *s.* (*blas.*) oro.

oracle ['ɔrəkəl], *s.* oráculo. — *v.i.* revelar oráculos.

oracular [oˈrækjuːlər], **oraculous** [oˈrækjuːləs], *a.* fatídico; dogmático, positivo; ambiguo, obscuro, oculto.

oral ['ɔːrəl], *a.* oral, verbal, hablado.

orally, *adv.* oralmente, verbalmente, de palabra.

orange ['ɔrəndʒ], *s.* (*bot.*) naranja; color de naranja; *orange blossom,* azahar; *orange-coloured,* anaranjado; *orange-tree,* naranjo; *orange-woman,* naranjera. — *a.* anaranjado, de naranja; *Orangeman,* Orangista, miembro del partido protestante extremista de Irlanda.

orangeade [ɔrəndʒˈeid], *s.* naranjada (bebida), gaseosa.

orangery [ɔrəndʒəri], *s.* naranjal, naranjería.

orang-outang [oˈræŋuˈtæŋ], *s.* orangután.

oration [oˈreiʃən], *s.* oración, arenga, disertación, discurso, razonamiento, locución.

orator ['ɔrətər], *s.* orador, predicador; suplicante, o querellante ante el tribunal.

oratorial [ɔrəˈtɔːriəl], **oratorical** [ɔrəˈtɔrikəl], *a.* oratorio, retórico.

oratorially, oratorically, *adv.* de una manera retórica u oratoria.

oratorio [ɔrəˈtɔːriou], *s.* (*mús.*) oratorio.

oratory ['ɔrətəri], *s.* oratoria, elocuencia; oratorio, capilla; (*igl.*) congregación.

orb [ɔːb], *s.* orbe, globo, esfera, astro, (*poét.*) ojo. — *v.t.* formar (en) círculo; rodear, redondear, cercar, englobar.

orbed [ɔːbd], *a.* circular, esférico, redondo, redondeado; que tiene ojos.

orbic ['ɔːbik], **orbical** ['ɔːbikəl], *a.* orbicular, esférico.

orbicular [ɔːrˈbikjuːlər], *a.* orbicular, esférico.

orbicularness, *s.* esfericidad, forma orbicular.

orbiculate, orbiculated, *a.* orbicular.

orbit ['ɔːbit], *s.* órbita.

orbital, orbitual, *a.* orbital, orbitario.

orca ['ɔːkə], *s.* orca, orco (cetácea).

orcanet ['ɔːkənet], *s.* orcaneta.

orchal ['ɔːkəl], *s.* acedera.

orchard ['ɔːtʃbrəd], *s.* vergel, huerto, huerta, pomar, cigarral.

orcharding, *s.* horticultura, cultura de los verjeles.

orchardist, *s.* horticultor, arboricultor.

orchestra ['ɔːkestrə], *s.* orquesta.

orchestral, *a.* de orquesta.

orchestrate, *v.t.* instrumentar.

orchestration, *s.* instrumentación.

orchid ['ɔːkid], **orchis** ['ɔːkis], *s.* orquidácea, orquídea.

orchidaceous [ɔːkiˈdeiʃəs], *a.* orquídeo, orquidáceo.

orchil ['ɔːkil], **orchilla** [ɔːrˈkilə], *s.* colorante obtenido de la Archilla (*Roccella tinctoria*).

ordain [ɔːdein], *v.t.* ordenar, prescribir, decretar, mandar; constituir, instituir, esta-

blecer; (*igl.*) ordenar, conferir órdenes sagradas.

ordainable, *a.* que se puede ordenar.

ordainer, *s.* ordenador.

ordeal [ɔːˈdiːl], *s.* ordalías, prueba rigurosa, experiencia penosa; aprieto.

order ['ɔːdər], *s.* orden, *m.f.*; reglamento, regla; estado, clase, *f.*, serie, *f.*; regularidad, arreglo; medio, medida, forma, método; orden, *f.*, disposición, mandamiento, precepto, ordenanza, mandato; (*com.*) endoso, pedido, encargo, comisión; sistema, *m.*, usanza; asociación, sociedad, círculo; condecoración honorífica. — *pl.* **orders,** (*igl.*) órdenes sagradas; *in order to,* para, con motivo de, a fin de; *to keep in order,* tener en buen estado; *to put* (o *set*) *in order,* ordenar, arreglar; *made to order,* hecho de encargo; *to be in order,* estar en regla; *by order and on account of,* (*com.*) por orden y por cuenta de; *till further orders,* hasta nueva orden; *order-book,* (*com.*) libro de pedidos. — *v.t.* mandar, ordenar; disponer, arreglar, poner en orden; (*com.*) pedir, encargar; metodizar, regularizar; (*igl.*) ordenar, conferir las órdenes sagradas; *to order in,* mandar entrar, mandar traer; *to order away* (o *off*), despedir, mandar salir; *to order out,* mandar salir; *to order up,* mandar subir; *to take* (*holy*) *orders,* ordenarse; *order arms!* (*mil.*) ¡descansen!; *out of order,* averiado, estropeado; fuera del orden del día.

orderer, *s.* ordenador.

ordering, *s.* orden, *m.*, disposición, manejo.

orderless, *a.* sin orden, desordenado, irregular.

orderliness, *s.* aseo, método, orden.

orderly, *a.* ordenado, metódico, aseado; bien arreglado, en regla, en orden; tranquilo, quieto, apacible; (*mil.*) de ordenanza(s); *orderly officer,* (*mil.*) oficial del día. — *adv.* en buen orden, bien dispuesto, regularmente, metódicamente, ordenadamente. — *s.* (*mil.*) ordenanza, *m.*, asistente, practicante.

ordinal ['ɔːdinəl], *a.* ordinal. — *s.* número ordinal; (*igl.*) ritual.

ordinance ['ɔːdinəns], *s.* ordenanza, estatuto, reglamento; ceremonia, rito.

ordinary ['ɔːdinəri], *a.* corriente, ordinario, común; metódico, ordenado, normal; ordinario, vulgar, bajo, mediano. — *s.* ordinario; capellán; juez ordinario; mesa redonda; vulgo, masa; (*igl.*) ordinario.

ordinate ['ɔːdineit], *a.* regular, ordenado, metódico. — *s.* (*geom.*) ordenada.

ordinately, *adv.* de una manera regular.

ordination [ɔːdiˈneiʃən], *s.* (*igl.*) ordenación; disposición, buen orden, arreglo.

ordnance ['ɔːdnəns], *s.* artillería; municiones, pertrechos de guerra; *ordnance map,* mapa del estado mayor.

ordure ['ɔːdjuːr], *s.* basura, porquería, inmundicia, excremento.

ore [ɔːr], *s.* mena, ganga, quijo.

oread ['ɔːriæd], *s.* oréade, *f.*, orea.

orgal ['ɔːgəl], *s.* tártaro, heces secas.

organ ['ɔːgən], *s.* órgano; organillo; periódico, diario; *barrel-organ, street-organ,* organillo portátil; *piano-organ,* piano de manubrio; *organ-grinder,* tocador de organillo; *organ-loft,* tribuna de órgano; *organ-pipe,* tubo de órgano.

organ-blower, *s.* entonador.

organ-builder, s. organero.
organdi, organdy [ˈɔːɹgəndi], s. organdí; muselina ligera.
organic [ɔːɹˈgænik], a. orgánico, organizado, sistematizado.
organism [ˈɔːɹgənizm], s. organismo, estructura orgánica.
organist, s. organista, m.f.
organization [ɔːɹgənaiˈzeiʃən], s. organización, organismo, sociedad.
organize, v.t. organizar, disponer, constituir, arreglar. — v.i. organizarse, unirse, juntarse.
organographic(al), a. organográfico.
organography [ɔːɹgəˈnɔgrəfi], s. organografía.
organology [ɔːɹgəˈnɔlodʒi], s. organología.
orgasm [ˈɔːɹgæzm], s. orgasmo; excitación.
orgeat [ˈɔːɹdʒiət, ˈɔːɹʒɑː], s. horchata.
orgiastic, a. orgiástico.
orgy [ˈɔːɹdʒi], s. orgía.
oriel [ˈɔːriəl], s. mirador, ventana circular, alcoba.
orient [ˈɔːriənt], a. oriental, naciente; resplandeciente, brillante. — s. oriente, este. — v.t. orientar.
oriental [ɔːriˈentəl], a. oriental, del oriente. — s. oriental.
orientalism, s. orientalismo.
orientalist, s. orientalista, m.f.
orientalize, v.t. orientalizar.
orientate [ˈɔːriənteit], v.t. orientar. — v.i. caer hacia el este.
orientation, s. orientación.
orifice [ˈɔrifis], s. orificio, ranura, abertura, boca.
oriflamme [ˈɔriflæm], s. oriflama.
origan [ˈɔrigən], **origanum** [oˈrigənəm], s. orégano.
origin [ˈɔridʒin], s. origen, fuente, f., manantial, germen, procedencia, fundamento; familia, ascendencia.
original [ɔˈridʒinəl], a. original, primitivo, primero, prístino, radical; novel, nuevo. — s. original, origen, prototipo, primer escrito; persona de temperamento original.
originality [ɔridʒiˈnæliti], s. originalidad.
originally [ɔˈridʒinəli], adv. originalmente, originariamente.
originalness, s. originalidad.
originate, v.t. crear, originar, engendrar, hacer nacer. — v.i. originarse, traer su origen, emanar, dimanar.
origination, s. origen, creación.
originator, s. autor, móvil, causa primera.
oriole [ˈɔːrioul], s. (orn.) oriol, oropéndola.
orison [ˈɔrizən], s. (ant.) oración, plegaria.
orle [ɔːrl], s. orla; (arq.) filete, listón, orla.
orlet [ˈɔːrlet], **orlo** [ˈɔːrlou], s. (arq.) orla.
orlop [ˈɔːrlop], s. (mar.) sollado, entrepuente.
ormolu [ˈɔːrməluː], s. bronce dorado.
ornament [ˈɔːrnəmənt], s. ornamento, ornato, adorno, atavío, paramento, compostura; condecoración, insignia. — v.t. adornar, decorar, exornar, ornamentar.
ornamental [ɔːrnəˈmentəl], a. ornamental, decorativo.
ornamentally, adv. ornadamente.
ornamentation, s. ornamentación, decorado.
ornamentist, s. adornista, m.f.
ornate [ɔːrˈneit], a. ataviado, churrigueresco, vistoso, barroco; embellecido, ornamentado.
ornateness, s. vistosidad, magnificencia, atavío; adorno, embellecimiento.

ornithological [ɔːrniθoˈlodʒikəl], a. ornitológico.
ornithologist [ɔːrniˈθolodʒist], s. ornitólogo.
ornithology [ɔːrniˈθolodʒi], s. ornitología.
ornithomancy [ɔːrˈnaiθomænsi], s. ornitomancia.
orographic [ɔrouˈgræfik], a. orográfico.
orography [ɔˈrogrəfi], s. orografía.
oroide [ˈɔrɔid], s. bronce dorado.
orological [ɔroˈlodʒikəl], a. orológico.
orology [ɔˈrolodʒi], s. orología.
orotund [ˈɔrotʌnd], a. rotundo.
orphan [ˈɔːrfən], s. huérfano, huérfana. — a. huérfano. — v.t. reducir al estado de orfandad, dejar huérfano a.
orphanage [ˈɔːrfənidʒ], s. inclusa, orfanato, hospicio; orfandad.
orphaned, a. huérfano.
orphanhood, s. orfandad.
Orphean [ɔːrˈfiːən], **Orphic** [ˈɔːrfik], a. órfico.
orpiment [ˈɔːrpimənt], **orpin** [ˈɔːrpin], s. oropimente.
orpine [ˈɔːrpin], s. piñuela, telefio.
orrery [ˈɔrəri], s. planetario.
orris [ˈɔris], s. galón, trencilla; (bot.) lirio; orris-root, raíz de iris florentina.
ort [ɔːrt], s. fragmento, resto, sobra.
orthochromatic [ɔːrθoukrouˈmætik], a. ortocromático.
orthodox [ˈɔːrθodoks], a. ortodoxo; formal, convencional, correcto.
orthodoxy, s. ortodoxia.
orthoepical, a. ortológico.
orthoepist, s. ortólogo.
orthoepy [ɔːrˈθoˈiːpi], s. ortología.
orthogon [ˈɔːrθogon], s. ortogonio.
orthogonal, a. ortogonal.
orthographer, s. ortógrafo.
orthographic [ɔːrθoˈgræfik], a. ortográfico.
orthographist, s. ortógrafo.
orthography [ɔːrˈθogrəfi], s. ortografía.
orthometry [ɔːrˈθometri], s. ortometría.
orthopædic [ɔːrθoˈpiːdik], a. ortopédico.
orthopædy, s. ortopedia.
orthoptera [ɔːrˈθoptərə], s.pl. ortópteros.
ortive [ˈɔːrtiv], a. ortivo.
ortolan [ˈɔːrtolən], s. (orn.) hortelano; verderol.
oryx [ˈɔriks], s. (zool.) orix.
oscillancy, oscillation, s. oscilación, balanceo, vibración.
oscillate [ˈɔsileit], v.t. hacer oscilar, balancear. — v.i. oscilar, balancearse, fluctuar, vibrar.
oscillating, a. oscilante.
oscillator, s. oscilador.
oscillatory, a. oscilatorio, oscilante.
oscitancy, s. bostezo; descuido; indolencia.
oscitant [ˈɔsitənt], a. bostezante, indolente, soñoliento.
oscitation, s. bostezo.
osculate [ˈɔskjuːleit], v.i. besar.
osculation, s. ósculo.
osculatory, a. osculatorio.
osier [ˈouʒər], s. (bot.) mimbrera, sarga, sauce. — a. mimbreño, de mimbre; osier ground, mimbreral; golden osier, sauce vitelino, mimbrera ama.
osmic [ˈozmik], a. ósmico.
osmium [ˈozmiəm], s. osmio.
osmose, osmosis, s. osmosis, f.
osmotic [ozˈmotik], a. osmótico.
osprey [ˈosprei], s. águila osífraga, atahorma.
ossarium [ɔˈsɛəriəm], s. osario.

osselet ['ɔselet], *s.* huesecillo.
osseous ['ɔsiəs], *a.* huesoso, ososo, óseo.
ossicle ['ɔsikəl], *s.* huesecillo.
ossific [ɔs'ifik], *a.* osífico.
ossification, *s.* osificación.
ossify ['ɔsifai], *v.t.* osificar. — *v.i.* osificarse.
ossifrage ['ɔsifridʒ], *s.* ositraga, quebrantahuesos.
ossivorous [ɔs'ivərəs], *a.* osívoro.
ossuary ['ɔsjuːəri], *s.* osario, osar.
osteitis [ɔsti'aitis], *s.* osteítis, *f.*
ostensibility, *s.* cualidad de ostensible.
ostensible [ɔs'tensibəl], *a.* ostensible, plausible, aparente.
ostensive, *a.* ostensivo, evidente, aparente.
ostent [ɔs'tent], *s.* apariencia, señal, *f.*, manifestación, prodigio.
ostentation [ɔsten'teiʃən], *s.* fausto, boato, pompa, alarde, aparato, jactancia, ostentación; (*ant.*) manifestación, ostentación.
ostentatious, *a.* pomposo, faustoso, jactancioso, ufano, vanaglorioso, ostentativo.
ostentatiousness, *s.* fausto, boato, vanagloria, jactancia, vanidad, ostentación.
osteocolia [ɔsteo'kouliə], *s.* osteocola.
osteogeny [ɔsti'ɔdʒəni], *s.* osteogenía.
osteography, *s.* osteografía.
osteolite ['ɔstiolait], *s.* osteolito.
osteologer, osteologist, *s.* osteólogo, osteógrafo.
osteology [ɔsti'ɔlodʒi], *s.* osteología.
osteoma [ɔsti'oumə], *s.* osteoma, *m.*
osteotomy [ɔsti'ɔtomi], *s.* osteotomía.
ostiary ['ɔstiəri], *s.* ostiario; ostial.
ostler [ɔslə], *s.* establero, mozo de cuadra.
ostlery, *s.* hostería.
ostosis [ɔs'tousis], *s.* osificación.
ostracean [ɔs'treiʃən], *a.* ostráceo, ostrero.
ostracism, *s.* ostracismo.
ostracize ['ɔstrəsaiz], *v.t.* desterrar, expulsar, excomulgar.
ostreiculture, *s.* ostricultura.
ostrich ['ɔstritʃ], *s.* avestruz.
Ostrogoth ['ɔstrougɔθ], *s.* ostrogodo.
otacoustic [ɔtə'kaustik], *a.* otacústico.
otalgia [ou'tældʒə], *s.* otalgia.
other ['ʌðəɹ], *a.* otro, diferente, distinto, nuevo; *the other day*, hace poco (tiempo); *every other day*, un día sí (y) otro no. — *pron.* otro, el otro, otra cosa; *to have other fish to fry*, tener otras cosas que hacer. — *adv.* (con **than**) más (que), otra cosa (que), además de.
otherwise ['ʌðəɹwaiz], *adv.* de otra manera, otramente, de otro modo; por otra parte; si no.
otic ['outik], *a.* ótico, de la oreja, auricular.
otiose ['ouʃiouz], *a.* ocioso, holgazán; ocioso, infructuoso.
otitis [ou'taitis], *s.* otitis, *f.*
otolith ['outoliθ], *s.* otolito.
otologist, *s.* otólogo.
otology [ou'tolodʒi], *s.* otología.
otorrhagia [outo'reidʒə], *s.* otorragía.
otoscope ['outoskoup], *s.* otoscopio.
otoscopy, *s.* otoscopia.
ototomy [ou'tɔtomi], *s.* ototomía.
ottar ['ɔtəɹ], **otto**, *s.* esencia, aceite esencial, aroma, *f.* [ATTAR].
otter ['ɔtəɹ], *s.* nutria, nutra; piel de nutria, *f.*; *sea otter*, nutria de mar.
otter-coloured, *a.* alutrado.

ottoman ['ɔtomən], *a.* otomano, turco. — *s.* otomano, turco; otomana.
ouch [autʃ], *s.* collar, adorno de oro, engaste, montura.
ought [ɔːt], *v. aux.* deber, deber de, ser necesario, ser menester, tener la obligación de; convenir, ser conveniente. — *s.* nada (corrup. vulg. de *naught*). — *s. adv.* [AUGHT].
ounce [auns], *s.* onza; *ounce avoirdupois*, 28·350 grs., *ounce troy*, 31·103 grs.; (*zool.*) onza; onza de oro.
our [auəɹ], *a.* nuestro, nuestra, nuestros, nuestras; *the Our Father*, el Padrenuestro.
ours [auəɹz], *pron.* el nuestro, la nuestra, los nuestros, las nuestras.
ourself [auəɹ'self], *pron.* (*pl.* **ourselves**) [auəɹ'selvz]) nosotros (mismos), nosotras (mismas); *between ourselves*, entre bastidores.
ourang [o'ræŋ], *s.* [ORANG-OUTAN].
ousel ['uːzəl], *s.* (*orn.*) mirlo, mirla [OUZEL].
oust [aust], *v.t.* expulsar, echar fuera, desalojar, desposeer, desaposentar; sacar, quitar; (*mil.*) desemboscar.
ouster, *s.* (*for.*) evicción, desahucio, despojo.
out [aut], *adv.* fuera, defuera, afuera; fuera de casa, ausente; salido; exteriormente; descubierto; aparecido, publicado; destituido; apagado, extinguido; acabado, agotado; francamente, sinceramente, abiertamente; enteramente, completamente; conocido, existente; equivocado, desacertado, en error; de huelga; fuera de juego; *to be out*, no estar en casa; no estar de moda; quedar cesante; estar extinguido, apagado; salir a luz; estar fuera de juego; *all sails out*, con velas desplegadas; *just out*, (de un libro) acaba de publicarse; *the supply is out*, no hay más, agotado; *out and out*, completamente; *out at elbow*, agujereado, roto por los codos; *out at heels*, con zapatos rotos; *way out*, salida; *to speak out*, hablar distintamente, sin rodeos; *to be out with someone*, estar reñido con uno; *the best thing out*, (*fam.*) la mejor cosa que existe; *to set out*, ponerse en camino, marcharse, partir. — **out of**, *prep.* fuera de; más allá de; además de, sobre; en; de; por; sin; *to be out of patience*, perder la paciencia; *I am out of paper*, se me acabó el papel, ya no me queda papel; *to be out of a place* (o *job*), estar sin colocación; *to fall out with*, reñir con; *out of time*, discordante; *out of kindness*, por amistad; *out of humour*, de mal humor; *out of idleness*, por pereza; *out of sight*, fuera del alcance de la vista; *out of breath*, sin aliento; *out of character*, inconveniente, impropio, fuera de propósito; *out of measure*, desmesurado; *out of order*, descompuesto, averiado; desordenado; *out of print*, agotado; *it is out of the question*, no puede ser; *out of sorts*, indispuesto; *out of tune*, desentonado; *out of the way*, lejano, inaccesible, desviado; *time out of mind*, tiempo inmemorial; *out of one's mind*, fuera de sí. — *out*, *interj.* ¡fuera!, ¡fuera de aquí!; *out with it!* ¡hable Vd. sin rodeos! — **out**, *s.* exterior, parte de afuera; exterioridad; lugar exterior; (*impr.*) omisión. — *v.t.* expulsar, expeler, despojar, desposeer. — *a.* externo; distante, remoto, lejano.
outact [aut'ækt], *v.t.* superar, exceder.
outargue, *v.t.* hacer callar, reducir al silencio (en argumentación).

---

outbalance, *v.t.* exceder en, preponderar en.

outbid, *v.t.* pujar, sobrepujar, mejorar.

outbidder, *s.* pujador, ponedor.

outbidding, *s.* puja, encarecimiento.

outbound, *a.* destinado a un país extranjero; de travesía.

outbrave, *v.t.* arrostrar los peligros, sobrepujar en audacia, magnificencia o garbo.

outbrazen, *v.t.* exceder en descaro.

outbreak, *v.t.* erupción, irrupción, explosión; ataque; disturbio, tumulto; pasión; *outbreak of war,* declaración de guerra.

outbreathe, *v.t.* dejar sin aliento; jadear, exhalar.

outbuild, *v.t.* construir mejor que.

outbuilding ['autbildiŋ], *s.* accesoria, construcción exterior, dependencia, anexo.

outburn, *v.t.* quemar más que.

outburst, *s.* (*fig.*) explosión, erupción, acceso, arranque.

outcast ['autkɑːst], *a.* repudiado, rechazado, desechado, expulso, desterrado, perdido, arrojado, inútil. — *s.* proscrito, desterrado, paria, *m.f.*

outclass, *v.t.* sobrepujar, exceder, ser superior a.

outcome ['autkʌm], *s.* resultado, consecuencia, éxito.

outcry ['autkrai], *s.* clamor, clamoreo, alboroto, alarido, vocería, gritería.

outdare, *v.t.* osar, atreverse más que otro; desafiar, arrostrar.

outdate, *v.t.* anticuar; *outdated,* anticuado, fuera de moda.

outdistance, *v.t.* dejar atrás.

outdo, *v.t.* sobrepujar, superar, exceder, descollar, vencer.

outdoor, *a.* fuera de la casa, al aire libre, en campo abierto, al raso; externo.

outdrink, *v.t.* beber más que otro.

outdwell, *v.t.* quedarse más tiempo que otro.

outer ['autəɹ], *a.* exterior, externo. — *s.* (*tiro*) círculo exterior de un blanco.

outerly, *adv.* hacia fuera, hacia afuera; exteriormente.

outermost, *a.* extremo, más exterior.

outface, *v.t.* retar, desafiar, arrostrar, humillar.

outfall, *s.* canal, desembocadero, despeñadero.

outfield, *s.* campo abierto.

outfit, *s.* armamento; equipo, apresto, tren, ajuar, juego; traje; pertrechos. — *v.t.* aviar, habilitar, equipar.

outfitter, *s.* abastecedor, proveedor, confeccionador; armador.

outfitting, *s.* equipo, abastecimiento.

outflank, *v.t.* (*mil.*) flanquear.

outflow, *v.t.* deslizarse hacia afuera. — *s.* salida, efusión, flujo, derrame.

outfly, *v.t.* exceder en vuelo; escapar.

outgeneral, *v.t.* (*mil.*) vencer en táctica.

outgive, *v.t.* exceder en generosidad.

outgo, *v.t.* exceder, vencer, aventajar; pasar. — *v.i.* tomar la delantera, adelantarse. — *s.* gasto, lo gastado; expendido, costas.

outgoing, *s.* salida, partida, ida. — *a.* saliente, cesante.

outgoings, *s.pl.* gastos, costas, desembolso, expendio.

outgrow, *v.t.* sobrecrecer, crecer más que; ser ya viejo para.

outgrowth, *s.* excrecencia, consecuencia, resultado.

outguard, *s.* guardia avanzada.

out-Herod, *v.t.; to out-Herod Herod,* exceder en violencia, crueldad o disparates.

outhouse, *s.* accesoria, sotechado, tejadillo, dependencia.

outing ['autiŋ], *s.* paseo, salida, vuelta, caminata, excursión.

outlandish, *a.* extraño, raro, ridículo, disparatado; rústico, grosero; (*ant.*) remoto, extranjero.

outlast, *v.t.* sobrevivir a, tirar más que.

outlaw ['autlɔː], *s.* proscripto, desterrado; bandido, bandolero, forajido. — *v.t.* proscribir.

outlawed, *a.* proscripto.

outlawry, *s.* proscripción, rebeldía.

outlay, *s.* gasto, gastos, desembolso, expendición, expendio.

outleap, *v.t.* pasar saltando.

outlet ['autlet], *s.* salida, orificio; desaguadero, desagüe.

outlie, *v.t.* mentir más que otro.

outline ['autlain], *v.t.* delinear, bosquejar, perfilar, recortar, trazar, esquiciar; (*fig.*) bosquejar, esbozar. — *s.* bosquejo, contorno, traza, trazado, perfil, croquis, recorte; (*fig.*) esbozo, esquema, *m.; to be outlined against,* destacarse contra.

outlive, *v.t.* sobrevivir a, durar más tiempo que.

outliver, *s.* sobreviviente.

outlook, *v.t.* turbar con la mirada, hacer bajar los ojos. — *s.* perspectiva; viso, aspecto, vista; atalaya, vigía, guardia, centinela.

outlying, *a.* distante, extranjero, exterior, extrínseco.

outmarch, *v.t.* dejar atrás a.

outmeasure, *v.t.* exceder en medida a.

outmost, *a.* más exterior.

outnumber, *v.t.* exceder en número.

outpace, *v.t.* dejar atrás a, preceder.

outpass, *v.t.* adelantar, pasar más allá de, dejar atrás a.

outpost ['autpoust], *s.* puesto avanzado, avanzada.

outpour, *v.t.* (*poét.*) verter, chorrear.

outpour, outpouring, *s.* derramamiento, chorreo, chorro; (*fig.*) efusión.

output ['autput], *s.* producción total; capacidad.

outrage ['autreidʒ], *v.t.* ultrajar, injuriar, violentar, maltratar; desflorar, violar. — *s.* ultraje, injuria, atropello, violencia, afrenta, atrocidad; violación, rapto.

outrageous [aut'reidʒəs], *a.* ultrajante, injurioso, violento, turbulento, ultrajoso, afrentoso, ofensivo, tumultuoso; atroz, enorme, tremendo; desenfrenado.

outrageousness, *s.* furor, violencia, turbulencia; escándalo, violencia, enormidad.

outreach, *v.t.* pasar más adelante de, alcanzar; pasar más allá de lo que se debe.

outreason, *v.t.* vencer en argumento.

outride, *v.t.* ganar la delantera a caballo. — *v.i.* andar a caballo junto al estribo de un carruaje.

outrider, *s.* ujier, batidor.

outrigger, *s.* (*mar.*) esquife, pescante de banda para carenar; horqueta, cuerno, tangón, puntal de tope.

outright, *a.* franco, abierto, sincero, llano; franco, rotundo, completo. — *adv.* abiertamente, sin reserva; completamente, entera-mente, inmediatamente; sin violencia; *to laugh outright*, reír a carcajadas.

outroot, *v.t.* extirpar, desarraigar.

outrun, *v.t.* correr más que, vencer en una carrera.

outsail, *v.i.* ser más velero que, navegar más y mejor.

outsell, *v.t.* vender más caro (*o* más aprisa) que otro.

outset ['autset], *s.* principio, comienzo, inauguración.

outshine, *v.t.* exceder en brillantez, dejar deslucido. — *v.i.* brillar, resplandecer, lucir.

outside [aut'said], *s.* exterior, extremo, ex-tremidad; sobrefaz, *f.*, apariencia superficial; (*fam.*) imperial, *f.* (de autobús o tranvía); *at the outside*, a lo más, a más tirar, a lo sumo. — *a.* exterior, externo, aparente, extrínseco, superficial; extremo; neutral.

outsider, *s.* forastero, extraño; (*fam.*) intruso; (carreras de caballos, etc.) caballo *o* com-petidor no incluido entre los favoritos, 'outsider'.

outskirt, *s.* linde, borde, orilla. — *pl.* **out-skirts**, confines, arrabales, inmediaciones, suburbios.

outspeak, *v.t.* hablar más que otro; exceder en locuacidad; explicarse clara y francamente.

outspoken, *a.* franco, abierto, sincero.

outspread, *v.t.* extender, desplegar; esparcir, difundir, propagar.

outstand, *v.t.* resistir a, arrostrar.

outstanding, *a.* sobresaliente, destacado, excelente; sobresaliente, saledizo, salidizo, prominente; (*com.*) corriente, pendiente, no pagado.

outstare, *v.t.* mirar de hito en hito.

outstep, *v.t.* ir más allá que; adelantar.

outstretch, *v.t.* extender, desplegar, alargar.

outstrip, *v.t.* sobrepujar, avanzar más, aventa-jar; ganar, pasar, dejar atrás.

outtalk, *v.t.* hablar más que otro; reducir al silencio.

outvalue, *v.t.* valer más que.

outvie, *v.t.* sobresalir, exceder, sobrepujar.

outvote, *v.t.* ganar más votos que otro.

outwalk, *v.t.* andar más que, dejar atrás a.

outward ['autwəɹd], *a.* exterior, externo, extrínseco, superficial, aparente, visible, extraño, extranjero, remoto; (*teol.*) corpóreo, carnal. — *adv.* fuera, afuera, exteriormente, superficialmente; (*mar.*) de ida; *outward bound*, con rumbo a un puerto extranjero; *outward journey*, ida. — *s.* exterior.

outwardly, *adv.* exteriormente, superficial-mente, aparentemente, en apariencia, ex-trínsecamente.

outwardness, *s.* exterioridad.

outwards, *adv.* al exterior.

outwear [aut'wɛəɹ], *v.t.* durar más tiempo que; consumir, gastar; usar hasta el fin.

outweigh, *v.t.* exceder en peso, preponderar; (*fig.*) preponderar, sobrepujar.

outwit, *v.t.* sobresalir en astucia, ser más listo que, engañar.

outwork, *s.* (*fort.*) obra exterior, obra avan-zada.

outworn, *a.* gastado, usado.

outwrite, *v.t.* escribir más que otro.

ouzel ['uːzəl], *s.* mirlo, mirla, merla; *water-ouzel*, mirlo de agua.

oval ['ouvəl], *s.* óvalo. — *a.* oval, ovalado.

ovarian [ou'vɛəriən], *a.* ovárico.

ovarious, *a.* de huevos.

ovaritis [ouvə'raitis], *s.* ovaritis, *f.*

ovary ['ouvəri], *s.* (*anat.*) ovario; (*orn.*) overa, huevera.

ovate, ovated, *a.* ovado.

ovation [ou'veiʃən], *s.* ovación.

oven ['ʌvən], *s.* horno, hornillo.

over ['ouvəɹ], *prep.* sobre, en, encima de, por encima de; por, al través; allende de, al otro lado de; más de. — *adv.* encima, por encima; de un lado a otro; al otro lado; demasiado; además; de ancho, a lo ancho; de arriba abajo; al revés, patas arriba; sobre; otra vez; desde el principio al fin; al fin; mientras, durante; *over again*, de nuevo, otra vez; *over and over again*, repetidas veces; *to cross over*, atravesar, pasar al otro lado (de); *to run over*, atropellar; revisar, pasar por en-cima de; *to be over twenty*, tener más de veinte años; *over and above all that*, además de todo eso; *over the way*, al otro lado de la calle; *head over ears o over head and ears*, por encima de las orejas; *to be all over mud*, estar cubierto de lodo; *all over*, por todas partes; *all the world over*, por todo el mundo; *it's all over*, se acabó; *it's all over with him*, es hombre perdido; *please turn over*, (*P.T.O.*) a la vuelta.

overact, *v.t.*, *v.i.* exagerar (un papel).

overalls ['ouvərɔːlz], *s.pl.* zafones, zahones, mono.

over-anxious, *a.* demasiado inquieto o ansioso.

overarch, *v.t.* abovedar.

overawe, *v.t.* intimidar, imponer respeto.

overbalance, *v.t.* hacer perder el equilibrio; exceder en peso, preponderar; llevar ventaja. — *v.i.* perder el equilibrio, caerse. — *s.* exceso de peso, preponderancia.

overbear, *v.t.* (*pret.* **overbore**; *p.p.* **over-borne**) vencer, domar, sujetar, reprimir, subyugar, sojuzgar, oprimir, abrumar, ago-biar. — *v.i.* llevar demasiado fruto.

overbearing, *a.* despótico, imperioso, domi-nante, altivo.

overbearingly, *adv.* imperiosamente, des-póticamente.

overbid, *v.t.* ofrecer más que. — *v.i.* ofrecer demasiado.

overbig, *a.* demasiado grande.

overblow, *v.t.* disipar soplando; (*mar.*) soplar con excesiva violencia (del viento).

overboard ['ouvəɹbɔːɹd], *adv.* (*mar.*) al mar, al agua; *to throw overboard*, (*fig.*) desechar, arrinconar, descartar, echar *o* tirar por la borda.

overboil, *v.t.*, *v.i.* hervir demasiado.

overbold, *a.* descarado, temerario, pre-suntuoso.

overburden, *v.t.* sobrecargar, agobiar.

over-busy, *a.* demasiado ocupado.

overbuy, *v.t.* comprar muy caro, comprar demasiado.

overcareful, *a.* demasiado cuidadoso.

overcast ['ouvəɹkɑːst], *v.t.* anublar; cubrir, obscurecer; entristecer; (*cost.*) sobrehilar; (*cir.*) cicatrizar. — *v.i.* anublarse, cubrirse. — *a.* nublado, anublado; oscurecido, cu-bierto, sombrío, cerrado.

overcautious, *a.* demasiado circunspecto.

overcharge, *v.t.* recargar, encarecer, cobrar

más de lo justo; sobrecargar; exagerar, oprimir. — *s.* recargo de precio, precio excesivo; cargo excesivo, exceso de carga.

overcloud, *v.t.* cubrir de nubes, anublar; entristecer.

overcoat ['ouvəɹkout], *s.* abrigo, sobretodo, gabán, levitón, paletó.

overcome [ouvəɹ'kʌm], *v.t.* subyugar, sojuzgar, domar, conquistar, superar, vencer, rendir, sujetar, sorprender. — *v.i.* sobreponerse, ganar la superioridad, hacerse superior; *to be overcome*, estar rendido, aturdido, turbado, o confuso.

overconfidence, *s.* demasiada confianza de sí, presunción.

overcrowd, *v.t.* amontonar demasiado, atestar, apiñar.

overcrowded, *a.* atestado. — *p.p.* [OVERCROWD].

overcrowding, *s.* amontamiento excesivo.

overdate, *v.t.* posfechar.

overdo [ouvəɹ'duː], *v.i.* (*pret.* **overdid**; *p.p.* **overdone**) hacer más de lo necesario. — *v.t.* exagerar; extralimitar; fatigar demasiado; llevar al exceso; cocer demasiado; abrumar, agobiar de trabajo; *to overdo it*, (*fam.*) cansarse excesivamente, trabajar demasiado.

overdone, *p.p.* demasiado cocido o asado, pasado; rendido, cansado; exagerado.

overdose, *s.* dosis excesiva o tóxica.

overdraft, *s.* (*com.*) giro en descubierto, crédito abierto.

overdraw, *v.t.* (*pret.* **overdrew**; *p.p.* **overdrawn**) (*com.*) girar en descubierto, exceder su crédito; exagerar.

overdress, *v.t.* adornar demasiado. — *v.i.* adornarse con exceso, vestirse de un modo cursi.

overdrink, *v.i.* beber con exceso.

overdrive, *v.t.* fatigar, hacer trabajar demasiado.

overdue, *a.* retrasado, en retardo; prescripto; (*com.*) vencido y no pagado.

overeat, *v.i.* comer demasiado, hartarse, tupirse.

over-eating, *s.* atracón, panzada, hartazgo.

overestimate, *v.t.* estimar demasiado, dar un valor excesivo a, presuponer. — *s.* presupuesto o avalúo excesivo.

overexcite, *v.t.* sobrexcitar, sobreexcitar.

overexcitement, *s.* sobrexcitación, sobreexcitación.

overexpose, *v.t.* (*foto.*) dar exceso de (*o* demasiada) exposición.

overexposure, *s.* (*foto.*) sobreexposición.

overfeed, *v.t.* sobrealimentar, hartar, saciar. — *v.i.* atracarse, empaparse, tupirse.

overfeeding, *s.* sobrealimentación; atracón, panzada, hartazgo.

overflow [ouvəɹ'flou], *v.i.* salir de madre, derramarse, desbordarse, rebosar, rebasar. — *v.t.* sobrellenar; inundar.

overflow ['ouvəɹflou], *s.* inundación, diluvio, avenida; (*mec.*) vertedero, descarga; desbordamiento, derrame, anegación.

overflowing, *a.* (*fig.*) rebosante, superabundante.

overfly, *v.i.* pasar volando, atravesar volando.

over-forward, *a.* demasiado apresurado; descarado.

overfree, *a.* demasiado libre; pródigo.

overfreight, *v.t.* sobrecargar.

overfull, *a.* demasiado lleno.

overgo, *v.t.* sobresalir, sobrepujar.

overgrow, *v.t.* (*pret.* **overgrew**; *p.p.* **overgrown**) revestir; entapizar; cubrir con plantas, crecer más que. — *v.i.* crecer (*o* desarrollarse) demasiado.

overgrown, *a.* entapizado, lleno, revestido, cubierto; demasiado, grande, enorme, inmenso.

overgrowth, *s.* exuberancia, vegetación exuberante, frondosidad.

overhang, *v.t.* estar pendiente; sobresalir por encima, suspender, colgar; dar a, mirar a; amenazar. — *v.i.* inclinar, desplomarse, estar pendiente, colgar. — *s.* (*arq.*) alero.

overhanging, *a.* suspendido, colgado sobre.

overhaste, **overhastiness**, *s.* precipitación.

overhasty, *a.* precipitado, demasiado apresurado.

overhaul, *v.t.* revisar, reexaminar, recorrer; hacer reparaciones generales, reparar, componer; alcanzar, ir ganando; (*mar.*) recorrer, tiramollar. — *s.* (*mec.*) recorrido, reparación y examen completo.

overhead, *adv.* sobre la cabeza, en lo alto, encima, arriba. — *a.* colgante, elevado, aéreo (*f.* ., etc.).

overhear, *v.t.* sorprender (una conversación), oír por casualidad; alcanzar a oír.

overheat, *v.t.* calentar demasiado, recalentar, acalorar.

over-issue, *s.* emisión exagerada.

overjoyed, *a.* arrebatado de alegría, encantado, encantadísimo.

overkind, *a.* excesivamente cariñoso.

overkindness, *a.* bondad excesiva.

overlade, *v.t.* sobrecargar.

overland, *a.* que pasa por tierra, trascontinental. — *adv.* por tierra.

overlap, *v.t.* recubrir, solapar, extenderse sobre, montarse sobre. — *v.i.* recubrirse. — *s.* recubrimiento, solape.

overlay, *v.t.* cubrir (con), dar una capa a, colocar (sobre); platear, dorar; ahogar; anublar, obscurecer; (*impr.*) calzar.

overlie, *v.t.* estar tendido sobre.

overload, *v.t.* sobrecargar, recargar.

overlook, *v.t.* mirar desde lo alto, tener vista a, caer a, dar a, dominar; mirar por encima, revisar, repasar; vigilar, inspeccionar, examinar, cuidar de; no hacer caso de, no notar, no fijarse en; pasar por alto, tolerar, perdonar, disimular, hacer la vista gorda.

overlooker, *s.* inspector, celador, veedor, sobrestante, vigilante; contramaestre.

overmaster, *v.t.* dominar, señorear.

overmatch, *v.t.* vencer, superar, sobrepujar, agobiar, abrumar. — *s.* fuerza superior, persona con fuerza o destreza superior.

overmeasure, *s.* medida excesiva, porción excesiva, colmo. — *v.t.* dar demasiada estimación, importancia o valor.

over-modest, *a.* demasiado modesto; remilgado.

overmuch, *a.*, *adv.* demasiado, excesivo, con exceso, superfluo, en demasía.

over-nice, *a.* demasiado escrupuloso, remilgado.

overnight, *s.* velada, noche pasada. — *adv.* durante la noche, de noche; *to stay overnight*, pasar la noche, pernoctar.

overpass, *v.t.* atravesar, salvar; pasar por alto,

omitir, olvidar; descuidar; exceder, sobrepujar; menospreciar, mirar con indiferencia.

overpay, *v.t.* pagar demasiado.

overpayment, *s.* pago excesivo.

overpeople, *v.t.* poblar demasiado.

overplus, *s.* sobrante, excedente, sobra, residuo, remanente.

overpower, *v.t.* subyugar, dominar, domar, predominar; colmar; abrumar, oprimir, supeditar.

overpowering, *a.* abrumador, dominante, superior.

overpoweringly, *adv.* con fuerza superior.

overpress, *v.t.* oprimir, abrumar, apretar demasiado, aplastar; importunar; (*mar.*) cargar las velas.

overprize, *v.t.* estimar o valuar con exceso.

over-production, *s.* exceso de producción.

overprompt, *a.* demasiado pronto.

overpromptness, *s.* prontitud excesiva.

overrate [ouvəɹˈreit], *v.t.* encarecer, valuar o apreciar con exceso.

overreach, *v.t., v.i.* extenderse más allá, ser más listo, exceder, pasar; extender o alargar demasiado (una extremidad o el cuerpo); estafar, trampear; elevarse; sorprender; tirar alto; alcanzar; fraguar; (*vet.*) rozar; (*mar.*) dar una virada o una bordada más allá de lo necesario; *to overreach oneself,* extralimitarse, excederse, pasarse.

override [ouvəɹˈraid], *v.t.* pasar por encima de; fatigar (un caballo); supeditar, vencer; dar de mano a, poner a un lado, rechazar; cubrir enteramente, montarse sobre.

overripe, *a.* demasiado maduro, papandujo.

overroast, *v.t.* asar demasiado.

overrule [ouvəɹˈruːl], *v.t., v.i.* denegar, desechar; dominar, predominar; ser superior (a); dirigir, regir, governar; inspeccionar, registrar; (*for.*) desechar, denegar.

overruler, *s.* gobernador, director.

overruling, *a.* que gobierna, que dirige.

overrun [ouvəɹˈrʌn], *v.t.* recorrer, hacer correrías; invadir, devastar, desolar, plagar, infestar, pisar; desbordar, pasar (una seña o límite); (*impr.*) reportar, retocar; fatigar (una máquina). — *v.i.* excederse, adelantarse; desbordarse, inundar, rebosar, estar muy abundante. — *s.* (*impr.*) reporte; (*auto.*) arrastrado del motor.

overrunner, *s.* invasor.

overrunning, *a.* invasor. — *s.* invasión.

overscrupulous, *a.* demasiado escrupuloso, remilgado

oversea [ˈouvəɹsiː], *a.* ultramarino; extranjero. — *adv.* ultramar.

oversee, *v.t.* (*pret.* oversaw; *p.p.* overseen) examinar, inspeccionar, registrar; revistar, celar, vigilar.

overseer, *s.* capataz, mayoral, veedor, superintendente, sobrestante, celador; limosnero de una parroquia.

oversell, *v.t.* vender demasiado caro, vender demasiado (más de lo que se tiene).

overset, *v.t.* volcar, hacer volcar, derribar, voltear, tumbar, trastornar, arruinar. — *v.i.* volcarse, caerse.

overshade, overshadow, *v.t., v.i.* hacer sombra, dar sombra, sombrear, asombrar, cubrir; (*fig.*) poner al abrigo, obscurecer, eclipsar.

overshoe, *s.* (*E.U.*) golocha, chanclo.

overshoot, *v.t.* (*pret.* y *p.p.* **overshot**) ir más allá de, tirar más allá del blanco; exceder, pasar rápidamente. — *v.i.* pasar de lo justo, pasar de raya; *overshot wheel,* rueda hidráulica de artesas.

oversight [ˈouvəɹsait], *s.* olvido, omisión, descuido, equivocación, inadvertencia; examen, inspección, vigilancia, superintendencia.

overskip, *v.t.* pasar saltando; saltar, omitir, evitar.

overskirt, *s.* sobrefalda.

oversleep, *v.t., v.i.* dormir demasiado, pegarse las sábanas.

oversleeves, *s.pl.* mangotes.

overspent, *a.* apurado, agotado, extenuado.

overspread, *v.t.* cubrir; desparramar, esparcir, tender, regar.

overstate, *v.i.* exagerar.

overstep, *v.t.* traspasar, pasar de los límites, propasar. — *v.i.* excederse, extralimitarse, ir más allá.

overstock, *v.t.* colmar, atestar; abarrotar. — *s.* colmo, superabundancia, surtido excesivo.

overstore, *v.t.* aprovisionar con exceso.

overstrain, *v.t.* apretar demasiado. — *v.i.* esforzarse demasiado, hacer esfuerzos muy grandes. — *s.* tensión excesiva.

overstretch, *v.t.* estirar demasiado.

overstrew, *v.t.* derramar, esparcir, desparramar.

overstrung, *a.* demasiado excitable, muy sensible, altamente nervioso; *overstrung piano,* piano cruzado.

oversway, *v.t.* dominar, mandar u ordenar con tiranía; predominar.

overswell, *v.t.* rebosar.

overt [ˈouvəɹt], *a.* abierto, público, evidente, patente.

overtake, *v.t.* alcanzar, pasar, dejar atrás a; coger, atrapar, atajar, sorprender en el acto.

overtask, *v.t.* atarear demasiado.

overtax, *v.t.* agobiar con impuestos; (*fig.*) agobiar, oprimir; *to overtax oneself,* esforzarse demasiado, cansarse.

overthrow, *v.t.* echar abajo, trastornar, deponer, derribar, demoler, destruir, volcar, tumbar, vencer, destronar. — *s.* derribo, vuelco, derrocamiento, destronamiento, trastorno, trastornamiento, derrota, destrucción; (*dep.*) voleo demasiado fuerte.

overthrower, *s.* trastornador, derrotador.

overthwart, *prep.* (*ant.*) a través, de lado a lado. — *a.* (*ant.*) opuesto, contrario, adverso.

overtime [ˈouvəɹtaim], *s.* horas suplementarias o extraordinarias de trabajo.

overtire, *v.t.* cansar completamente, fatigar demasiado.

overtop, *v.t.* elevarse sobre, sobresalir; (*fig.*) exceder, sobrepujar, elevarse sobre, descollar sobre.

overture [ˈouvəɹtʃəɹ], *s.* (*mús.*) obertura; declaración, insinuación, proposición, propuesta.

overturn, *v.t.* volcar, trastornar, trastrocar, derrocar, trastumbar, voltear, subvertir, trabucar.

overvalue, *v.t.* encarecer, estimar demasiado, ponderar.

overwatch, *v.t.* cansar con vigilias.

overweary, *v.t.* exceder en trabajo.

overween, *v.i.* presumir

overweening, s. presunción. — a. presuntuoso, altanero, arrogante.

overweigh, v.t. pesar más, prevalecer, preponderar.

overweight, s. peso excesivo, sobrepeso; preponderancia, superioridad.

overwhelm, v.t. abrumar, hundir, sumir, abatir, soterrar, sumergir, engolfar, oprimir, confundir.

overwhelming, a. abrumador, opresor, opresivo, preponderante, dominante, irresistible.

overwise, a. demasiado prudente, sabihondo.

overwork, v.i. trabajar demasiado. — v.t. fatigar, hacer trabajar con exceso, imponer demasiado trabajo, esclavizar. — s. trabajo excesivo.

overworn, a. usado, raído; abrumado de fatiga.

overwrought, a. sobreexcitado, excitadísimo, nervioso; rendido por exceso de trabajo.

ovicular [ou'vikju:lə.ɪ], a. ovicular.

oviduct ['ouvidʌkt], s. oviducto.

oviferous [ou'vifərəs], a. ovífero.

oviform ['ouvifɔ:ɪm], a. oviforme, ovoide, aovado.

ovine ['ouvain], a. ovino, ovejuno, lanar.

oviparous [ou'vipərəs], a. ovíparo.

oviposit [ouvi'pozit], v.t. (ent.) poner huevos; depositar huevos con el ovipositor.

ovoid ['ouvɔid], **ovoidal** [ou'vɔidəl], a. ovoide, aovado.

ovolo ['ouvolou], s. óvolo, equino, cuarto bocel.

ovoviviparous [ouvovi'vipərəs], a. ovovivíparo.

ovule ['ouvju:l], s. óvulo.

ovum ['ouvəm], s. (pl. **ova**) (biol.) huevo.

owe [ou], v.t. deber, ser deudor de, adeudar, estar obligado a. — v.i. estar endeudado, tener deudas.

owing ['ouiŋ], a. debido; to be owing to, ser debido a, ser atribuible a; owing to, a o por causa de.

owl [aul], s. lechuza, mochuelo, buho, miloca; barn owl, mochuelo, alucón; screech owl, úlula; owl light, crepúsculo.

owlet ['aulet], s. buho pequeño.

owlish, owl-like, a. de lechuza, de buho, semejante a la lechuza.

own [oun], a. propio, suyo, particular, individual, peculiar, verdadero, mismo, real; own cousin, primo hermano; of one's own accord, espontáneamente, por propio acuerdo; with one's own hand, de su puño y letra o de su propio puño; it's his own fault, es culpa suya. — v.t. poseer, tener, ser dueño de; confesar; reconocer, aseverar.

owner, s. proprietario, dueño, poseedor.

ownerless, a. sin dueño; mostrenco.

ownership, s. propiedad, posesión, dominio, pertenencia.

ox [ɔks], s. (pl. **oxen**) buey.

oxalate ['ɔkzəleit], s. oxalato.

oxalic [ɔk'zælik], a. oxálico.

ox-driver, s. boyero.

oxen ['ɔkzən], s.pl. [ox].

ox-eye, s. (bot., mar.) ojo de buey; (orn.) pajarito; ox-eye daisy, (bot.) manzanilla loca.

ox-fly, s. estro, tábano.

ox-goad, s. aguijada.

ox-herd, s. boyero.

ox-house, ox-stall, s. boyera, boyeriza.

oxidant, s. oxidante.

oxidate ['ɔkzideit], v.t. oxidar.

oxidation, s. oxidación.

oxide ['ɔksaid], s. óxido.

oxidize ['ɔksidaiz], v.t. oxidar, oxigenar.

oxidizement, s. oxidación.

oxlip ['ɔkslip], s. prímula.

Oxonian [ɔk'zouniən], s., a. estudiante o licenciado de la Universidad de Oxford.

ox-tongue, s. lengua de buey; (bot.) buglosa.

oxygen ['ɔksidʒən], s. oxígeno.

oxygenate ['ɔksidʒənait], v.t. oxigenar, oxidar.

oxygenation, s. oxigenación, oxidación.

oxygenic [ɔksi'dʒenik], a. oxigenado.

oxygenizable, a. oxigenable.

oxygenize, v.t. oxigenar.

oxygenous [ɔk'sidʒənəs], a. de oxígeno.

oxygon ['ɔksigɔn], s. triángulo oxigonio.

oxygonal, oxygonial, a. oxigonio.

oxyhydrogen [ɔksi'haidrodʒən], s. gas oxhídrico.

oxysalt, s. oxisal, f.

oxytone ['ɔksitoun], s. (gram.) sonido agudo, palabra aguda. — a. agudo.

oyer ['ɔiə.ɪ], s. (for.) audición, vista, audiencia.

oyez ['oujes], interj. ¡oíd!

oyster ['ɔistə.ɪ], s. ostra, ostión, ostrón; oyster-culture, ostricultura; oyster-bed, oyster-farm, ostrero, banco de ostras; oyster-dredger, pescador de ostras; oyster-house, ostrería; oyster-wench o oyster-woman, vendedora de ostras.

ozæna, ozena [ou'zi:nə], s. ocena.

ozone ['ouzoun], s. ozono, ozona.

ozonic, ozonous, a. que contiene ozono.

ozonify, ozonize, v.t. ozonizar, ozonificar, combinar con ozono.

ozonometer [ouzo'nɔmitə.ɪ], s. ozonómetro.

P

P, p [pi:], décimasexta letra del alfabeto inglés. Tiene un sonido algo más fuerte que la española. Al principio de palabra cuando va seguida de s, t, o n es muda, como en psora, ptomaine, pneumonia. Si va seguida de h pierde su sonido pronunciándose las dos como f. Como abreviatura significa página o piano; to mind one's p's and q's, (fam.) ir con pie o pies de plomo, medir las palabras; poner los puntos sobre las íes.

pa [pɑ:], s. (fam.) papá.

pabular ['pæbju:lə.ɪ], a. alimentoso, nutritivo.

pabulum ['pæbju:ləm], s. pábulo, alimento, sustento, pasto.

paca ['pækə], s. (zool.) paca.

pace [peis], s. paso; marcha, modo de andar, andadura, portante; aire; medida de unas 30 pulgadas; (arq.) tablado, estrado; to keep pace with, seguir a un paso igual a, andar con una persona al mismo paso que él. — v.t. medir a pasos, andar a pasos medidos, marchar el paso. — v.i. pasear, andar, marchar, ir a pasos lentos; ambular.

paced, a. paso; slow-paced, de paso lento.

pacer, s. andador; caballo que va a paso de andadura.

pacha ['pæfɑ:], s. bajá.

pachyderm ['pækidə.ɪm], s. paquidermo.

pachydermatous, a. paquidermo.

pacific [pə'sifik], *a.* pacífico, sosegado, tranquilo, quieto.

pacificate, *v.t.* pacificar, apaciguar, sosegar.

pacification [pæsifi'keiʃən], *s.* pacificación, apaciguamiento.

pacificator, pacifier, *s.* pacificador, apaciguador.

pacificatory, *a.* pacificador.

pacifier, *s.* pacificador.

pacifism, *s.* pacifismo.

pacifist ['pæsifist], *s.* pacifista, *m.f.*

pacify ['pæsifai], *v.t.* pacificar, apaciguar, sosegar, calmar, tranquilizar, conciliar, templar, aplacar, aquietar.

pack [pæk], *v.t., v.i.* embalar, envasar, empaquetar, empacar, enfardar, enfardelar; embarillar, encajonar, embaular; hacer el baúl; apretar, atestar; enviar, despachar; consolidarse, formar una masa; *to pack off,* (*fam.*) despedir. — *s.* fardo, peso, carga, bala; paca; lío, paquete; baraja de naipes; perrada, muta, jauría, vuelo de perdices, manada, hato, hatajo; cuadrilla; *pack of thieves,* cuadrilla de malhechores; *to pack on all sail,* (*mar.*) desplegar las velas, a todo trapo.

package ['pækidʒ], *s.* paquete, embalaje, envase, embalo; fardo, bulto, burujo; (*mar.*) abarrote; (*com.*) gastos de embalar o empaquetar las mercancías.

pack-cloth, *s.* arpillera.

packer, *s.* embalador.

packet, *s.* paquete; (*mar.*) paquebote; correo, mala; valija; dineral; *to make one's packet,* (*fam.*) hacer su pacotilla.

pack-horse, *s.* caballo de carga.

packing, *s.* embalaje, envase, enfardeladura; *packing-case,* cajón de embalaje.

packman, *s.* buhonero.

pack-saddle, *s.* albarda, basto.

pack-thread, *s.* bramante.

pack-train, *s.* reata.

pact [pækt], *s.* pacto, convenio, convención, ajuste.

pad [pæd], *s.* almohadilla, cojinete; tapón, tarugo; pechera; postizo; rodete; (*vulg.*) senda, camino; (*vulg.*) salteamiento de camino; haca, jaca; silla de montar blanda; puño (de látigo); colchoncillo; *blotting-pad,* secante; *inking-pad,* almohadilla para entintar; *writing-pad,* bloc. — *v.t.* acolchar; rellenar de borra, emborrar, forrar; meter paja (en un libro, etc.). — *v.i.* andar poco a poco; (*ant.*) saltear; llevar postizos; escribir prolijamente, emplear frases demasiado largas.

padding, *s.* borra, algodón; almohadilla, relleno; (*fig.*) ripio, paja.

paddle ['pædəl], *v.i.* chapotear, guachapear; remar; dar palmaditas; impeler con canalete. — *s.* canalete, zagual, remo grande, pagay; trampa, escotillón.

paddle-board, *s.* paleta (de rueda hidráulica).

paddle-box, *s.* tambor.

paddle-door, *s.* paradera.

paddler, *s.* remero.

paddle-steamer, *s.* vapor de paletas.

paddle-wheel, *s.* paleta (de vapor).

paddock ['pædək], *s.* prado, parque, dehesa; picadero (junto a un hipódromo); (*Esco.*) sapo, escuerzo; (*min.*) tanque.

Paddy ['pædi], *s.* (*fam.*) irlandés.

padlock ['pædlɔk], *s.* candado. — *v.t.* cerrar con candado, echar el candado.

padre ['pɑːdrei], *s.* (*mil., mar.*) cura castrense.

pæan ['piːən], *s.* himno de triunfo.

pagan ['peigən], *s.* pagano. — *a.* pagano, gentílico.

paganish, *a.* pagano.

paganism, *s.* paganismo.

paganize, *v.t., v.i.* hacer pagano, hacerse pagano.

page [peidʒ], *s.* paje, escudero, asistente, criado; página, hoja, plana; (*fig.*) hoja, episodio. — *v.t.* paginar, foliar.

pageant ['pædʒənt], *s.* espectáculo público, procesión, pompa; exterioridad, apariencia. — *a.* ostentoso, pomposo, faustoso.

pageantry, *s.* fausto, pompa, fasto, exterioridad, aparato.

paginate ['pædʒineit], *v.t.* paginar, foliar.

pagination, paging, *s.* paginación, foliación.

pagoda [pə'goudə], *s.* pagoda; moneda de oro de la India.

paid [peid], *pret. y p.p.* [PAY].

pail [peil], *s.* cubo, cubeta, pozal, herrada, coldra; (*mar.*) balda.

pailful, *s.* cubada, lo que cabe en un cubo.

pain [pein], *s.* dolor; pena, tormento, sufrimiento, inquietud; *on pain of death,* so pena de muerte. — *pl.* pains, esmero; ansiedad, inquietud, solicitud; dolores de parto; *to take pains,* afanarse, empeñarse, esmerarse; *to be in pain,* dolerse, sufrir, padecer; *to be at pains to,* tomarse el trabajo de. — *v.t.* doler, afligir, apenar, hacer padecer; inquietar, atormentar, acongojar, angustiar.

painful, *a.* dolorido; desconsolado, aflictivo, afligido, atormentado; doloroso; industrioso, penoso, arduo, trabajoso, laborioso, ímprobo.

painfulness, *s.* dolor, aflicción, trabajo, pena, fatiga.

painless, *a.* sin dolor, sin pena.

painlessness, *s.* ausencia de dolor.

painstaker, *s.* trabajador, afanador.

painstaking ['peinzteikiŋ], *a.* esmerado, afanoso, laborioso.

paint [peint], *v.t.* pintar; (*fig.*) pintar, representar, describir. — *v.i.* pintar, pintarse, dedicarse a la pintura; afeitarse, arrebolarse. — *s.* pintura, color, colorete, afeite, arrebol; *coat of paint,* capa de pintura.

paint-box, *s.* caja de colores.

paint-brush, *s.* pincel, brocha.

painter, *s.* pintor; (*mar.*) amarra (de un bote).

painting, *s.* pintura, arte pictórico; cuadro, pintura; coloración.

paintress, *s.f.* pintora.

pair [pɛəɹ], *s.* pareja; par; macho y hembra, marido y mujer; tramo (de escalera); yunta (de bueyes); *pair of scissors, of spectacles,* par de tijeras, de anteojos; (*pol.*) dos miembros de partidos opuestos que se abstienen de votar, anulando así mutuamente su voto. — *v.t.* parear, aparear, igualar, hermanar, casar. — *v.i.* hacer pareja; parearse, aparearse, igualarse, hermanarse, juntarse; ajustarse.

pairing, *s.* pareamiento, pareo.

pajama, *s.* (*E.U.*) [PYJAMA].

pal [pæl], *s.* (*vulg.*) camarada, *m.f.*, compinche, *m.f.*, compadre.

palace ['pælis, 'pæləs], *s.* palacio.

paladin ['pælədin], *s.* paladín.

palæ-, [PALE-].

palanquin   pan

palanquin [pælən'kiːn], s. palanquín.

palatable ['pælətəbəl], a. sabroso, apetitoso; aceptable, agradable.

palatal ['pælətəl], s., a. paladial.

palate ['pælət], s. paladar; paladeo, gusto. — v.t. gustar.

palatial [pə'leiʃəl], a. palacial, palaciego, palatino, de un palacio; del paladar.

palatinate [pə'lætinit], s. palatinado.

palatine ['pælətain], s., a. palatino, paladial; *county palatine*, palatinado.

palaver [pə'laːvəɹ], s. palabrería, palabras ridículas; zalamería, lisonja; discusión, conferencia o plática larga, palique. — v.t., v.i. adular, lisonjear, engatusar; charlar, estar de palique.

palaverer, s. adulador.

pale [peil], a. pálido, descolorido, claro; apagado; *to grow pale*, palidecer. — s. estaca; límite, mojón, recinto, cerca; estacada, palizada, empalizada; (*fig.*) seno, gremio, sociedad, esfera; distrito, territorio, región; (*blas.*) palo (de escudo). — v.t., v.i. empalizar, rodear, cercar; palidecer, poner pálido, hacer palidecer, (hacer) perder el color; (*fig.*) desmedrar, perder.

pale-face, s. cara pálida, m.f.

pale-faced, a. de rostro pálido.

paleness, s. palidez.

paleographer, s. paleógrafo.

paleographic, paleographical, a. paleográfico.

paleography [pæli'ɔgrəfi], s. paleografía.

paleologist, s. paleólogo.

paleology [pæli'ɔlodʒi], s. paleología.

paleontological, a. paleontológico.

paleontologist, s. paleontólogo.

paleontology [pælion'tɔlodʒi], s. paleontología.

palestra [pæ'lestrə], s. palestra, gimnasio.

palette ['pælet], s. (*pint.*) paleta; *palette-knife*, espátula.

palfrey [pɔːlfri], s. palafrén.

palification [pælifi'keiʃən], s. empalización.

palimpsest ['pælimpsest], s. palimpsesto.

palindrome ['pælindroum], s. palindromia.

paling ['peiliŋ], s. palizada, estacada, valla, palenque.

palinode ['pælinoud], s. palinodia.

palisade [pæli'seid], s. palizada, empalizada, estacada, palenque, frisa. — v.t. empalizar.

palish ['peiliʃ], a. paliducho, algo pálido.

pall [pɔːl], s. (*igl.*) palio, palia; manto, manto de ceremonia; paño mortuorio; velo; (*fig.*) tristeza, aflicción; *pall bearers*, dolientes. — v.i. perder el sabor, hacerse insípido; (*ant.*) evaporarse; (*ant.*) desvanecerse; desmedrar, perder. — v.t. (*ant.*) fatigar, desalentar, debilitar; empalagar, desvirtuar, quitar el sabor.

palladium [pə'leidiəm], s. (*fig.*) paladión, salvaguardia; garantía; (*min.*) paladio.

pallet ['pælet], s. lecho miserable; camilla, jergón; jergón de pintor, paleta de reloj, fiador de rueda, linguete, retén; herramienta de albañilería y de alfarero; válvula de cañón de órgano; *pallet-knife*, espátula de pintor.

palliate ['pælieit], v.t. paliar, mitigar; disimular, excusar, disculpar, encubrir.

palliation, s. paliación, alivio, mitigación.

palliative ['pæliətiv], s., a. paliativo.

pallid ['pælid], a. pálido, descolorido.

pallidity, pallidness, s. palidez.

pallor ['pæləɹ], s. palidez.

palm [pɑːm], s. palma; palmera, palmo; palma de la mano; (*fig.*) palma, victoria; (*mar.*) rempujo; *palm tree*, palmera; *Palm Sunday*, domingo de Ramos; *palm bird*, (*orn.*) tejedor; *to carry off the palm*, alcanzar (o llevar) la palma, llevar la victoria. — v.t. manosear, manejar, manipular; escamotar, engañar, defraudar; cubrir con palmas; *to palm something off upon*, pegar la o una tostada, embaucar.

Palma-Christi [pælmə'kristai], s. (*bot.*) palma-cristi, higuera infernal.

palmar ['pælmɑːɹ], a. palmar.

palmary ['pɑːməri], a. palmario, palmar, principal.

palmate, palmated, a. palmar, palmeado, palmípedo.

palmer ['pɑːməɹ], s. palmero, peregrino, romero; palmeta; tahur.

palmetto [pæl'metou], s. (*bot.*) areca, palma, palmito.

palmiferous, a. palmífero.

palmiped ['pælmiped], a. palmípedo, palmeado.

palmistry ['pɑːmistri], s. quiromancia; escamoteo.

palmy ['pɑːmi], a. palmeado; palmar; glorioso, espléndido, floreciente, próspero, triunfal.

palp [pælp], **palpus** [pælpəs], s. palpo.

palpability, s. palpabilidad.

palpable ['pælpəbəl], a. palpable.

palpation [pæl'peiʃən], s. palpación, palpamiento, palpadura.

palpitate ['pælpiteit], v.i. palpitar, latir.

palpitation, s. palpitación, latido.

palsied ['pɔːlzid], a. paralizado, paralítico, perlático. — p.p. [PALSY].

palsy ['pɔːlzi], s. parálisis, f., perlesía; apatía, ineficacia. — v.t. paralizar.

palter ['pɔːltəɹ], v.i. usar de rodeos; estafar, petardear; regatear.

palterer, s. petardista, m.f.

paltriness ['pɔːltrinis], s. mezquindad, vileza, bajeza.

paltry ['pɔːltri], a. mezquino, miserable, despreciable, vil.

paludal [pæ'ljuːdəl], a. palúdico, palustre.

paly ['peili], a. (*poét.*) pálido; marchito; (*blas.*) barrado, palado.

pampas ['pæmpəs], s.pl. pampas.

pamper ['pæmpəɹ], v.t. mimar, acariciar; (*ant.*) atracar, hartar.

pampered, a. mimado; muy bien alimentado o servido.

pamperer, s. acariciador, persona que mima o que atraca.

pamphlet ['pæmflet], s. folleto, libelo, impreso.

pamphleteer [pæmfletiəɹ], s. folletista, m.f., foliculario.

pan [pæn], s. cazo, cazuela, cacerola, cuenco, caldero, barreño, lebrillo; (*carp.*) quicio; (*min.*) gamella; cazoleta de una arma de fuego; (*mec.*) rangua, tejuelo; *Pan* (*mit.*) el dios Pan; *brain-pan*, sesera, cráneo; *dripping-pan*, grasera; *baking-pan*, tartera; *frying-pan*, sartén, f.; *sauce-pan*, cacerola; *warming-pan*, calentador; *to flash in the pan*, dar higa un

fusil; *knee-pan*, rótula, choquezuela. — *v.t.*
(*min.*) separar el oro en una gamella; (*fam.*)
lograr, alcanzar; servir en una cazuela. —
v.i. to *pan out well*, dar buen resultado.

panacea [pænə'siəɹ], *s.* panacea.

panache [pə'nɑːʃ], *s.* penacho.

pancake ['pænkeik], *s.* hojuela, **tortita**, fruta
de sartén.

pancratic [pæn'krætik], *a.* pancrático, gimnástico, atlético.

pancreas ['pænkriəs], *s.* páncreas.

pancreatic [pænkri'ætik], *a.* pancreático.

pandect ['pændekt], *s.* tratado, digesto,
recopilación. — *pl.* **pandects**, pandectas.

pandemonium [pændə'mouniəm], *s.* pandemonio, baraúnda, batahola, infierno.

pander ['pændəɹ], *v.t.*, *v.i.* ser el tercero,
hacerse el medianero, alcahuetear; to *pander
to*, mimar, complacer. — *s.* tercero, medianero, alcahuete.

panderess, *s.f.* alcahueta.

pane [pein], *s.* vidrio (de una vidriera); hoja
de vidrio; (*ant.*) cuadro, cuadrado, tablero;
cara, faz, *f.*, faceta, lado.

paned, *a.* hecho a cuadros.

panegyric [pæni'dʒirik], *s.* panegírico.

panegyric, panegyrical, *a.* panegírico.

panegyrist, *s.*, *a.* panegirista, *m.f.*

panegyrize, *v.t.*, *v.i.* panegirizar, hacer el
panegírico.

panel ['pænəl], *s.* entrepaño, cuarterón,
artesón, tablero, tabica, anaquel; lista, registro; (*for.*) lista de los jurados; jurado; el
prisionero o los prisioneros en el banquillo.
— *v.t.* formar tableros, hacer en forma de
cuarterones.

paneless ['peinlis], *a.* sin vidrios, sin cristales.

pang [pæŋ], *s.* punzada (de dolor); dolor
agudo; angustia, remordimiento, congoja,
pena; *birth-pangs*, dolores de parto.

panic ['pænik], *s.* terror, miedo, pánico, consternación. — *a.* pánico.

panic-grass, *s.* panizo, zahina, mijo.

panicle ['pænikəl], *s.* panícula, panoja,
panocha.

paniculated [pə'nikju:leitid], *a.* apanojado.

panification [pænifi'keiʃən], *s.* panificación.

pannage ['pænidʒ], *s.* bellotera; derecho de
bellotera; el pago de este derecho.

pannier ['pænjəɹ], *s.* canasto de mimbre;
cesto, cuévano; canasta, canastón; (*arq.*)
cestón; tontillo (vestido de mujer).

pannikin ['pænikin], *s.* cazo, cacillo.

panoply ['pænopli], *s.* panoplia.

panorama [pænə'rɑːmə], *s.* panorama, *m.*

panoramic, *a.* panorámico.

pansy ['pænzi], *s.* (*bot.*) pensamiento, trinitaria.

pant [pænt], *v.i.* jadear, resollar, acezar; hipar
(del perro); palpitar; suspirar, anhelar; to
pant after, anhelar, suspirar por; perseguir
jadeando. — *s.* jadeo; palpitación, latido. — *pl.*
pants, (*fam.*) [PANTALOONS].

pantaloon [pæntə'luːn], *s.* pantalón; arlequín,
gracioso, bufón. — *pl.* **pantaloons**, pantalones, calzones.

panter, *s.* anheloso, jadeante.

pantheism ['pænθiizm], *s.* panteísmo.

pantheist, *s.* panteísta, *m.f.*

pantheistic, pantheistical, *a.* panteístico.

pantheologist, *s.* panteólogo.

pantheology [pænθi'ɔlodʒi], *s.* panteología.

pantheon ['pænθiən], *s.* panteón.

panther ['pænθəɹ], *s.* pantera.

pantile ['pæntail], *s.* canalón, teja.

panting ['pæntiŋ], *s.* jadeo, resuello; palpitación. — *a.* jadeante; anheloso.

pantingly, *adv.* con palpitación, con anhelo,
anhelantemente, con resuello.

pantograph ['pæntogræf], *s.* pantógrafo.

pantographic, *a.* pantográfico.

pantography [pæn'tɔgrəfi], *s.* pantografía.

pantomime ['pæntomaɪm], *s.* pantomima;
variedades, revista (de teatro); mímica.

pantomimic [pænto'mimik], *a.* pantomímico.

pantomimist, *s.* pantomimo.

pantophobia [pænto'foubiə], *s.* pantofobia.

pantry ['pæntri], *s.* despensa.

pap [pæp], *s.* teta, ᴘezón; papa, papilla,
puches; carne de la fruta; mogote. — *v.t.*
alimentar con papilla.

papa [pə'pɑː], *s.* ᴘapá.

papacy ['peipəsi], *s.* papado, pontificado.

papal ['peipəl], *a.* papal, pontifical.

papaverous [pə'pævərəs], *a.* papaveráceo,
amapolado.

papaw [pə'pɔː], *s.* papayo, papaya.

paper ['peipəɹ], *s.* papel, hoja de papel;
periódico; disertación, ensayo; (*com.*) letra,
pagaré, valor; documento; paquete; *on
paper*, escrito, impreso; *blotting-paper*,
secante, papel secante; *brown paper*, papel
alquitranado; *cream-laid paper*, papel acanillado; *drawing-paper*, papel de dibujo; *laid
paper*, papel acantillado; *letter-paper* o *note-
paper*, papel de cartas; *litmus-paper*, papel de
tornasol; *tissue-paper*, papel de seda; *vellum-
paper*, papel vitela; *wall-paper*, papel de
empapelar; *waste paper*, papel de desecho;
weekly paper, periódico semanal; *wrapping-
paper*, papel de envolver; *monthly paper*,
periódico mensual; *quarterly paper*, periódico
trimestral; *quire of paper*, mano de papel, *f.*;
ream of paper, resma de papel; *outside
quires*, costeras, papel quebrado; *large paper*,
papel marquilla; *emery paper*, papel esmeril;
sand paper, papel de lija. — *a.* de papel,
hecho de papel. — *v.t.* envolver con papel;
empapelar, entapizar con papel.

paper-clip, *s.* sujetapapeles, abrazadera.

paper-cutter, *s.* cortapapeles.

paper-folder, *s.* plegadera.

paper-hanger, *s.* empapelador.

paper-hanging, *m.* empapelado.

paper-knife, *s.* cortapapel.

paper-weight, *s.* pisapapel, prensapapeles.

papescent [pə'pesent], *a.* pulposo, carnoso.

papier-máché ['pæpjəɹ-'mæʃei], *s.* cartón
piedra.

papilionaceous [pəpiljɔn'eiʃəs], *a.* papilio-
náceo, amariposado.

papillary [pə'piləri], **papillous** [pə'piləs], *a.*
papilar.

papist ['peipist], *s.* papista, *m.f.*

papistic, papistical, *a.* papístico, papal.

papistry, *s.* papismo.

pappose ['pæpous], **pappous** ['pæpəs], *a.*
velloso, velludo.

pappus, *s.* (*bot.*) vilano.

pappy ['pæpi], *a.* pulposo, blando, jugoso,
mollar.

papula ['pæpju:lə], **papule** ['pæpju:l], *s.*
pápula.

papular, papulous, *a.* lleno de pápulas.

papyrography [pæpi'rɔgrəfi], *s*. papirografía.
papyrus [pə'pairəs], *s*. papiro.
par [paːɹ], *s*. (*com*.) par, paridad, nivel, equivalencia; *at par*, a la par; *par value*, valor nominal; *below par*, a descuento; *above par*, a premio; *to be on a par with*, (*fig*.) estar al nivel de, ser igual a, correr parejas con.
parable ['pærəbəl], *s*. parábola.
parabola [pə'ræbolə], *s*. (*geom*.) parábola.
parabole [pə'ræboli], *s*. (*ret*.) comparación.
parabolic [pærə'bɔlik], **parabolical** [pærə-'bɔlikəl], *a*. parabólico.
paraboliform, *a*. paraboliforme.
paraboloid [pə'ræbolɔid], *s*. paraboloide.
parachronism [pə'rækronizm], *s*. paracronismo.
parachute [pærə'ʃjuːt], *s*. paracaídas, *m*.
parachutist, *m*. paracaidista, *m.f.*
paraclete ['pærəkliːt], *s*. paráclito, paracleto.
parade [pə'reid], *s*. cabalgata, procesión, paseo público; (*mil*.) parada, revista de tropas; gala, alarde, pompa, ostentación; (*esg*.) quite, parada, repulsa; *parade ground*, plaza de armas. — *v.t.*, *v.i.* marchar en orden militar, pasar revista a, formar en parada; cabalgar, pasear; fachandear, alardear, hacer gala.
paradigm ['pærədaim], *s*. paradigma, *m*.
paradigmatic [pærədig'mætik], *a*. ejemplar.
paradise ['pærədais], *s*. paraíso.
paradisiacal, paradisaic, *a*. paradisiaco, paradisíaco.
paradox ['pærədɔks], *s*. paradoja, contrasentido.
paradoxical, *a*. paradojo, paradójico.
paraffin ['pærəfiːn, 'pærəfin], *s*. parafina.
paragoge [pærə'gɔdʒi], *s*. (*gram*.) paragoge.
paragogic, paragogical, *a*. paragógico.
paragon ['pærəgon], *s*. ejemplar, dechado; (*ant*.) parangón, comparación; (*impr*.) parangona. — *v.t.* (*poét*.) comparar.
paragram ['pærəgræm], *s*. equivoquillo.
paragraph ['pærəgraːf], *s*. párrafo, suelto. — *v.t.* dividir en párrafos.
paragraphic, paragraphical, *a*. escrito en párrafos sueltos.
paralipsis [pærə'lipsis], *s*. (*ret*.) paralipse, *f*.
parallactic, parallactical, *a*. paraláctico.
parallax ['pærəlæks], *s*. paralaje, *f*., paralasis, *f*., paralaxi, *f*.
parallel ['pærəlel], *a*. paralelo, semejante, igual. — *s*. paralelo, línea paralela; conformidad, semejanza; comparación, cotejo; copia; par, igual; (*mil*.) paralela; *without parallel*, sin ejemplo. — *v.t.* hacer paralelas, paralelizar; igualar, parangonar.
parallelable, *a*. que puede tener paralelo.
parallelism, *s*. paralelismo.
parallelogram [pærə'lelogræm], *s*. paralelogramo.
paralogism [pə'rælodʒizm], *s*. paralogismo.
paralogize, *v.i.* paralogizar.
paralyse ['pærəlaiz], *v.t.* paralizar.
paralysis [pə'rælisis], *s*. parálisis, *f*., perlesía; (*fig*.) paralización, estancamiento.
paralytic [pærə'litik], *s*. paralítico.
paralytic, paralytical, *a*. paralítico, perlático.
paralyzation, *s*. paralización.
paralyze, *v.t.* paralizar.
parameter [pə'ræmitəɹ], *s*. parámetro.
paramorphism [pærə'mɔːɹfizm], *s*. paramorfismo, paramorfosis, *f*.

paramount ['pærəmaunt], *a*. supremo, soberano, eminente, principalísimo, sumo. — *s*. (*ant*.) jefe supremo, soberano.
paramour ['pærəmuɹ], *s*. cortejo, amante, querido, querida.
paranymph ['pærənimf], *s*. paraninfo; defensor, portavoz; apoyo, ayuda.
parapet ['pærəpet], *s*. parapeto, antepecho, baranda, talanquera, mampuesto.
paraphernalia [pærəfəɹ'neiliə], *s.pl.* atavíos, adornos, arreos; (*for*.) bienes parafernales.
paraphrase ['pærəfreiz], *s*. paráfrasis, *f*. — *v.t.* parafrasear.
paraphraser, *s*. parafraseador, parafraste.
paraphrast ['pærəfræst], *s*. parafraste.
paraphrastic, paraphrastical, *a*. parafrástico.
parasite ['pærəsait], *s*. parásito, parasito; (*fig*.) parásito, gorrero, gorrón, sicofante.
parasitic [pærə'sitik], **parasitical** [pærə-'sitikəl], *a*. parásito, parasítico.
parasitically, *adv*. parasitamente, a modo de parásito.
parasitism ['pærəsitizm], *s*. parasitismo.
parasol [pærə'sɔl, 'pærəsɔl], *s*. parasol, sombrilla, quitasol.
parboil ['paːɹbɔil], *v.t.* medio cocer, salcochar.
parbuckle ['paːɹbʌkəl], *s*. tiravira. — *v.t.* levantar o bajar por medio de un tiravira.
parcel ['paːɹsəl], *s*. paquete, bulto, lío, burujo; atado, manojo; cantidad, porción; pandilla, corrillos, hato; partecilla; partida, cuadrilla; *part and parcel*, carne y hueso; *parcel post*, servicio de paquetes postales; *parcel of ground*, solar, lote, parcela de terreno. — *v.t.* dividir, partir; repartir, distribuir; empaquetar; *to parcel out*, repartir, hacer particiones; *to parcel the seams*, (*mar*.) aforrar las costuras; *parcelling*, (*mar*.) capa.
parcener ['paːɹəsənəɹ], *s*. coheredero.
parch [paːɹtʃ], *v.t.* tostar, secar, asolanar, agostar. — *v.i.* quemarse, tostarse, abrasarse.
parched, *a*. secado, agostado; muerto de sed.
parchedness, *s*. aridez, sequedad.
parching, *a*. abrasador, ardiente, secante.
parchment ['paːɹtʃmənt], *s*. pergamino, vitela.
pard [paːɹd], *s*. (*zool*.) leopardo; (*vulg*.) compinche, asociado.
pardon ['paːɹdən], *v.t.* perdonar, dispensar, absolver; conceder gracia, indultar, condonar, excusar, relevar. — *s*. perdón, remisión, absolución, indulto, gracia.
pardonable, *a*. perdonable, excusable, disculpable, venial.
pardonableness, *s*. disculpabilidad, venialidad.
pardoner, *s*. perdonador.
pardoning, *s*. remisión.
pare [pɛəɹ], *v.t.* cortar, recortar; pelar, cercenar, mondar; desbastar, descantillar; raspar, rallar; (*fig*.) escatimar.
paregoric [pæri'gɔrik], *a*. paregórico, anodino, calmante. — *s*. elixir paregórico, tintura alcanforada de opio.
parent ['pɛərənt], *s*. padre o madre; antecesor; autor; origen, fuente, *f*., causa. — *pl*. **parents**, padres. — *a*. principal, materna, madre, matriz.
parentage ['pɛərəntidʒ], *s*. extracción, origen, nacimiento, parentela, linaje, familia, alcurnia, cepa.

parental [pə'rentəl], *a.* paternal, maternal.
parentalism, *s.* paternalismo.
parenthesis [pə'renθesis], *s.* paréntesis.
parenthetic [pæren'θetik], **parenthetical,** *a.* por paréntesis, entre paréntesis.
parenthetically, *adv.* entre paréntesis.
parenthood ['pɛərənthud], *s.* paternidad o maternidad.
parenticide [pə'rentisaid], *s.* parricida, *m.f.*; parricidio.
parentless ['pɛərəntles], *a.* sin padres, huérfano.
parer ['pɛərəɹ], *s.* desbarbador, mondador, pelador.
paresis ['pæresis], *s.* paresia.
parget ['pɑːɹdʒet], *s.* yeso; enlucido. — *v.t.* blanquear (las paredes), enyesar, enlucir.
pargeter, *s.* blanqueador.
pargeting, *s.* blanqueo, argamasa, enlucido, estuco.
parhelion [pɑːɹ'hiːliən], *s.* parhelia, parhelio.
pariah ['pæriə], *s.* paria, *m.f.*
Parian ['pɛəriən], *a.* de Paros, pario.
parietal [pə'raietəl], *a.* (*anat.*) parietal; (*E.U.*) interno, pensionado; paredaño, mural.
parietary, *s.* parietaria.
paring ['pɛəriŋ], *s.* raedura, peladura, raspadura, mondadura; corteza, pellejo, cáscara, cortadura; desecho, desperdicio.
paring-knife, *s.* tranchete, trinchete, cuchilleja.
Parisian [pə'risiən], *s.* parisiense; *plaster of Paris,* yeso, escayola.
parish ['pæriʃ], *s.* parroquia, curato, feligresía; pueblo. — *a.* parroquial; *parish church,* parroquia, iglesia parroquial; *parish clerk,* sacristán.
parishioner [pə'riʃənəɹ], *s.* parroquiano, feligrés.
parisyllabic [pærisi'læbik], *a.* parisilábico.
paritor ['pæritəɹ], *s.* (*ant.*) bedel, alguacil.
parity ['pæriti], *s.* paridad.
park [pɑːɹk], *s.* parque, vedado, jardín público; campo abierto; *artillery-park,* parque de artillería. — *v.t.* estacionar (un vehículo); cercar, cerrar (un coto).
parking, *s.* estacionamiento; *parking place* o *station,* parque de estacionamiento; *No Parking,* Prohibido estacionarse.
parlance ['pɑːɹləns], *s.* habla, lenguaje, idioma, *m.*
parley ['pɑːɹli], *s.* (*mil.*) parlamento; plática, conferencia; (*ant.*) habla, lenguaje; *to come to a parley,* parlamentar. — *v.i.* (*mil.*) parlamentar; conferenciar.
parliament ['pɑːɹləmənt], *s.* parlamento, cortes, *f.pl.*
parliamentarian [pɑːɹləmen'tɛəriən], *s., a.* parlamentario.
parliamentarism [pɑːɹlə'mentərizm], *s.* parlamentarismo.
parliamentary [pɑːɹlə'mentəri], *a.* parlamentario.
parlour ['pɑːɹləɹ], *s.* parlatorio, locutorio; sala de recibo, sala de confianza.
Parmesan ['pɑːɹmezən], *s.* parmesano; *Parmesan cheese,* queso de Parma.
Parnassus [pɑːɹ'næsəs], *s.* Parnaso.
parochial [pə'roukiəl], *a.* parroquial, parroquiano; (*fig.*) provincial, estrecho, despreciable.
parochiality, *s.* parroquialidad.

parochially, *adv.* por parroquias.
parodic [pə'rɔdik], *a.* paródico.
parodist ['pærodist], *s.* parodista, *m.f.*
parody ['pærodi], *s.* parodia. — *v.t.* parodiar.
parole [pə'roul], *s.* palabra, promesa verbal, promesa de honor; (*mil.*) santo y seña. — *v.t.* poner en libertad bajo palabra.
paronomasia [pərɔnɔ'meiʒiə], *s.* paronomasia.
paronym ['pæronim], *s.* voz parónima.
paronymous, *a.* paronímico, parónimo.
paronymy [pə'rɔnimi], *s.* paronimia.
parotid [pə'rɔtid], *s.* parótida. — *a.* parotídeo.
paroxysm ['pærɔksizm], *s.* paroxismo, acceso, arrebato.
paroxysmal, *a.* paroxismal.
parquet [pɑːɹket], **parquetry** [pɑːɹketri], *s.* mosaico de madera; (*E.U.*) en los teatros, lugar destinado a las butacas o lunetas.
parr [pɑːɹ], *s.* murgón, esguín.
parrakeet ['pærəkiːt], *s.* periquito, cotorra.
parricidal [pæri'saidəl], *a.* parricida.
parricide ['pærisaid], *s.* parricida, *m.f.*, parricidio.
parrot ['pærət], *s.* papagayo, loro; *parrot-fish,* escaro.
parry ['pæri], *v.t., v.i.* parar, rechazar, quitar, reparar; esgrimir.
parry, parrying, *s.* parada, reparo, quite.
parse [pɑːɹz], *v.t.* (*gram.*) analizar.
Parsee [pɑːɹ'siː], *s., a.* parsi.
parsimonious [pɑːɹsi'mouniəs], *a.* parsimonioso, parco, mezquino.
parsimoniously, *adv.* con parsimonia, parcamente, mezquinamente.
parsimoniousness, parsimony, *s.* parsimonia, parquedad, mezquindad.
parsing ['pɑːɹziŋ], *s.* (*gram.*) análisis, *m.f.*
parsley ['pɑːɹsli], *s.* (*bot.*) perejil.
parsnip ['pɑːɹsnip], *s.* chirivía, berraza.
parson ['pɑːɹsən], *s.* cura, *m.,* clérigo, párroco, rector, sacerdote.
parsonage ['pɑːɹsənidʒ], *s.* curato, rectoría, casa del cura.
part [pɑːɹt], *s.* parte, *f.,* porción, trozo, pedazo, fragmento, pieza; entrega (de una publicación); miembro, socio, paraje, región, *f.,* sitio, lugar; papel (de actor o actriz); obligación, deber; (*mús.*) voz, *f.,* melodía. — *pl.* **parts,** talento, prendas, dotes; *for my part,* por mi parte, por lo que a mí toca; *man of parts,* hombre de buenas prendas; *foreign parts,* países extranjeros, el extranjero; *private parts,* partes pudendas, vergüenzas; *in part,* en parte; *in parts,* por entregas; *part and parcel,* carne y hueso *o* uña y carne; *part owner,* condueño; *to take part in,* tomar parte en, participar de; *to take in good part,* tomar a buena parte; *to play a part,* hacer, representar *o* desempeñar un papel. — *v.t.* partir, repartir, dividir, separar. — *v.i.* separarse, desunirse, partirse, desprenderse; despedirse, marcharse, irse; (*mar.*) apartarse del ancla; *to part the hair,* hacerse la raya; *to part from,* despedirse de; *to part with,* deshacerse de.
partake [pɑːɹ'teik], *v.t., v.i.* (*pret.* **partook;** *p.p.* **partaken**) tener *o* tomar parte, participar; partir, repartir.
partaker, *s.* partícipe, participante, *m.f.*; cómplice, *m.f.*
partaking, *s.* participación, complicidad.
parterre [pɑːɹ'tɛəɹ], *s.* cuadro de jardín,

macizo de flores; (*E.U.*) patio de un teatro debajo de las galerías.

parthenogenesis [pɑːɹθenou'dʒenesis], *s.* partenogénesis, *f.*

partial ['pɑːɹʃəl], *a.* parcial; *to be partial to,* tener afición a.

partiality [pɑːɹʃi'æliti], *s.* parcialidad, preferencia, prejuicio.

partially ['pɑːɹʃəli], *adv.* parcialmente, con parcialidad, en parte.

partibility, *s.* divisibilidad.

partible ['pɑːɹtəbəl], *a.* partible, divisible.

participable, *a.* participable.

participant [pɑːɹ'tisipənt], *a.* partícipe, participante.

participate [pɑːɹ'tisipeit], *v.t., v.i.* participar (de), tomar parte (en).

participation, *s.* participación, distribución, repartimiento.

participator, *s.* participante.

participial [pɑːɹti'sipiəl], *a.* participial.

participially, *adv.* participialmente.

participle ['pɑːɹ'tisipəl], *s.* (*gram.*) participio.

particle ['pɑːɹtikəl], *s.* partícula; átomo, pizca; (*gram.*) partícula.

parti-coloured ['pɑːɹtikʌlərd], *a.* abigarrado.

particular [pə'tikjuːləɹ], *a.* particular, especial, peculiar, singular; exacto, preciso; escrupuloso, minucioso, exigente; privado, individual, propio; íntimo, delicado; extraordinario, notable, distinguido; predilecto; descontentadizo, quisquilloso; extraño, raro, extravagante. — *s.* particular, particularidad, pormenor, detalle, circunstancia particular; caso individual, punto de importancia, punto esencial; artículo; *in particular,* en particular, particularmente, especialmente; *to go into particulars,* detallar, entrar en detalles, concretar.

particularity [pətikjuːlæriti], *s.* particularidad.

particularize, *v.t.* particularizar, singularizar, especificar, detallar. — *v.i.* entrar en detalles.

particularly, *adv.* en particular, particularmente, especialmente.

parting ['pɑːɹtiŋ], *s.* despedida, marcha, partida, adiós; rompimiento, rotura; raya, línea divisoria, bifurcación; separación; reparto.

partisan ['pɑːɹtizæn], *s.* partidario; guerrillero. — *a.* partidario, parcial, de partido.

partition [pɑːɹ'tiʃən], *s.* repartimiento; partición, división, separación; pared, *f.*; tabique; (*carp.*) mampara; (*mús., ant.*) partitura. — *v.t.* partir, separar, dividir; repartir, distribuir.

partitive ['pɑːɹtitiv], *a.* (*gram.*) partitivo.

partly ['pɑːɹtli], *adv.* en cierto modo, en parte.

partner ['pɑːɹtnəɹ], *s.* socio, partícipe, *m.f.*; asociado, interesado; compañero, compañera, camarada, *m.f.*; consorte, cónyuge; pareja; parcionero, aparcero; *sleeping partner,* socio comanditario.

partnership, *s.* asociación, sociedad, consorcio, interés social.

partook, *pret.* [PARTAKE].

partridge ['pɑːɹtridʒ], *s.* perdiz, *f.*; perdigón.

parturient [pɑːɹ'tjuːriənt], *a.* parturiente.

parturition [pɑːɹtjuːriʃən], *s.* parto, alumbramiento.

party ['pɑːɹti], *s.* partido; grupo, facción; individuo, sujeto, (*for.*) parte, *f.,* cómplice,

m.f., interesado; partida, bando, banda; fiesta en casa, reunión, *f.,* festejo, convite, tertulia, velada; *party man,* hombre de partido, partidario; *to be a party to,* ser cómplice en; aprobar.

parvenu ['pɑːɹvenjuː], *s., a.* advenedizo, medrado.

parvis ['pɑːɹvis], *s.* (*arq.*) atrio; espacio alrededor del tabernáculo en una sinagoga.

Paschal ['pæskəl], *a.* Pascual.

pasha ['pæʃɑː], *s.* bajá, *m.*

pashalic ['pæʃɑːlik], *s.* bajalato.

pasigraphy [pə'sigrəfi], *s.* sistema universal de escritura por medio de signos representando ideas en vez de palabras.

pasque-flower ['pæskflauəɹ], *s.* anémone pulsatila.

pasquinade [pæskwin'eid], *s.* pasquín, pasquinada.

pass [pɑːs], *v.t.* (*p.p.* **passed, past**) pasar, traspasar, atravesar, cruzar; pasar, alcanzar, dejar atrás; hacer pasar; portear, trasponer; superar, exceder, aventajar; tolerar, consentir, aprobar; filtrar, colar, cerner; trasladar, transferir; pasar, dar, alargar; aprobar (en un examen); *to pass compliments,* lisonjear; *to pass remarks,* hacer observaciones; *to pass sentence,* pronunciar sentencia, fallar; *to pass one's word,* empeñar su palabra. — *v.i.* pasar; transitar, caminar, andar; morir, fallecer; excederse, propasarse; dejar de hacer, omitir; correr, deslizarse (tiempo); acontecer, ocurrir, suceder; desvanecerse, disiparse, acabarse, cesar; (*esg.*) dar una estocada, hacer un pase; *to pass along,* pasar a lo largo (de); *to pass away,* desvanecer, consumir; fallecer, morir; *to pass by,* pasar (cerca de); (*fig.*) pasar por, olvidar, perdonar, dispensar, pasar por alto; *to pass for,* pasar por, hacerse pasar por; *to pass off,* pasar, suceder, (*fig.*) salir; *to pass oneself off as,* hacerse pasar por; *to pass on,* pasar, seguir andando, circular; fallecer, finar; *to pass over,* cruzar, atravesar, pasar por; excusar, pasar por alto; *to pass out,* salir; (*fam.*) desmayarse, caerse redondo; *to pass up,* subir; *let it pass!* ¡no haga Vd. caso!

pass, *s.* paso, pasillo; camino; puerto; pasaporte, salvoconducto, pase, permiso, licencia; pasaje, estrecho, garganta, desembocadero, desfiladero; aprieto, crisis, *f.,* situación; estado, condición, crisis, *f.;* aprobado (de exámenes); (*teat.*) billete de favor; (*esg.*) estocada; *pass-key,* llave maestra, ganzúa; *pass-book,* libreta de banco; *free pass,* pase, billete de favor.

passable ['pɑːsəbəl], *a.* transitable, pasadero; tolerable, regular.

passably, *adv.* tolerablemente, medianamente, pasaderamente.

passado [pə'sɑːdou], *s.* estocada.

passage ['pæsidʒ], *s.* pasaje; travesía; pasada, tránsito; camino; travesía, navegación, viaje; entrada, acceso; corredor, pasillo, pasadizo; acontecimiento, episodio, incidente, ocurrencia; pasaje, trozo (de un libro, etc.); desafío, lance, encuentro; migración (de las aves); deposición; aprobación (de una ley).

passant ['pæsənt], *s.* pasante.

passenger ['pæsəndʒəɹ], *s.* pasajero, viajero, viandante.

passer [pɑːsəɹ], **passer-by** [pɑːsəɹˈbai], *s.* transeúnte, pasante, paseante, peatón, viandante.

passibility [pæsiˈbiliti], *s.* pasibilidad.

passible [ˈpæsibəl], *a.* pasible.

passing [ˈpɑːsiŋ], *s.* pasaje, paso, pasada; tránsito, muerte, *f.*, fallecimiento. — *a.* pasajero, fugaz, transitorio, momentáneo; *in passing*, de paso, a propósito. — *adv.* (*poét.*) eminentemente, extraordinariamente; *passing bell*, toque de difuntos.

passion [ˈpæʃən], *s.* pasión; saña cólera, ira; ardor; *passion-flower*, (*bot.*) pasionaria, (en el Perú) ñorbo; *to fly into a passion*, encolerizarse, montor en cólera.

passionate, *a.* apasionado, arrebatado; colérico, irascible; ardiente, vivo, intenso, impetuoso.

passionateness, *s.* vehemencia, impetuosidad, arrebatamiento.

passionless, *a.* indiferente, frío, insensible, pasivo.

passive [ˈpæsiv], *a.* pasivo, inactivo, quieto, inerte. — *s.* (*gram.*) voz pasiva.

passiveness, passivity, *s.* pasibilidad, paciencia, tranquilidad, calma.

Passover [ˈpɑːsouvəɹ], *s.* pascua de los hebreos.

passport [ˈpɑːspɔːɹt], *s.* pasaporte.

password [ˈpɑːswəːɹd], *s.* palabra de pase, contraseña, santo y seña.

past [pɑːst], *a.* pasado, transcurrido, terminado, consumado, concluido, último; *times past*, o *days past*, antaño. — *s.* pasado, antecedentes, historia; (*gram.*) pretérito; *to have a past*, (*fam.*) tener malos antecedentes. — *prep.* después de, más de, fuera de, sin, ex-, que fué; *it is past mending*, ya no tiene remedio; *past all doubt*, sin ninguna duda; *past belief*, increíble; *past bearing*, insoportable; *past recovery*, incurable; *past hope*, sin esperanza; *past dispute*, incontestable.

paste [peist], *s.* pasta; *paste diamonds*, diamantes imitados. — *v.t.* empastar, engrudar, pegar.

pasteboard, *s.* cartón; tablilla de madera para hacer pasteles. — *a.* acartonado, de cartón.

pastel [ˈpæstəl], *s.* (*art.*) pastel; (*bot.*) hierba pastel o glasto.

pastern [ˈpæstəɹn], *s.* ranilla, trabadera, cuartilla del caballo.

pastil, pastille [ˈpæstiːl], *s.* pastilla, tableta.

pastime [ˈpɑːstaim], *s.* pasatiempo, entretenimiento, recreación, diversión.

pastor [ˈpɑːstəɹ], *s.* pastor, clérigo; (*orn.*) estornino.

pastoral, *a.* pastoral, pastoricio, pastoril. — *s.* (*igl.*) pastoral, *f.*; bucólica, pastorela; carta pastoral.

pastorate, pastorship, *s.* estado o funciones de pastor espiritual, cura de almas.

pastry [ˈpeistri], *s.* pasta; torta, tartaleta; pasteles, pastelería; *pastry-cook*, pastelero.

pasturage [ˈpɑːstʃjuːridʒ], *s.* pasto, pastura, pasturaje, hierbas; ganadería; apacentamiento.

pasture [ˈpɑːstʃəɹ], *s.* pasto, pastura, hierba, dehesa, pacedura. — *v.t.* pastar, apacentar, pastorear. — *v.i.* pastar, herbajar, pacer.

pasty [ˈpeisti], *s.* pastel. — *a.* pastoso; pálido, macilento, (*fam.*) de cara de viernes.

pat [pæt], *s.* golpecillo, golpecito, pasagonzalo; pastilla; caricia, mamola; ruido de pasos. —

v.t. dar golpecitos, palmaditas; acariciar con la mano, hacer la mamola. — *a.* (*fam.*) a propósito; propio, justo, en punto, exacto, oportuno. — *adv.* justamente, convenientemente, a propósito, aptamente.

patch [pætʃ], *s.* pieza; lunar (de tafetán), mancha, pedazo de tierra; parche, remiendo, apaño; *cross-patch*, (*fam.*) malhumorado. — *v.t.* componer, aderezar, remendar, apedazar, apañar; (*fam.*) chafallar, chapuzar; emplastar, paliar; *to patch up*, (*fig.*) hacer las paces; remendar, reparar; *not to be a patch on*, (*fam.*) no servir para descalzar a, no llegar al zancajo o a los zancajos a.

patcher, *s.* remendón, chafallón.

patchouli [ˈpætʃuːli], *s.* planta o perfume pachulí.

patchwork [ˈpætʃwəːɹk], *s.* remiendo; chapucería; labor de retacitos; (*fig.*) entapizada; (*fig.*) mezcolanza.

patchy [ˈpætʃi], *a.* cubierto de parches (*fig.*); desigual, manchado.

pate [peit], *s.* (*fam.*) bola, testa, cabeza.

pated, *a.* que tiene cabeza.

patella [pəˈtelə], *s.* (*anat.*) rótula, choquezuela de la rodilla; (*zool.*) género de moluscos que contiene las lepas o lepadas.

paten [ˈpætən], *s.* plato, placa; (*igl.*) patena.

patent [ˈpætənt, ˈpeitənt], *a.* patente, patentado; patente, evidente; *patent leather*, cuero barnizado, charol. — *s.* patente, privilegio de invención, privilegio exclusivo; título, diploma, *m.*; franquicia, cédula oficial, carta patente. — *v.t.* obtener o conceder un privilegio exclusivo.

patentee [pætənˈtiː, peitənˈtiː], *s.* el que obtiene privilegio exclusivo; privilegiado.

patentor, *s.* el que concede un privilegio exclusivo.

pater [ˈpeitəɹ], *s.* padrenuestro o paternóster; (*vulg.*) padre, papá.

paternal [pəˈtəːɹnəl], *a.* paternal, paterno.

paternally, *adv.* paternalmente.

paternity [pəˈtəːɹniti], *s.* paternidad, origen, linaje.

paternoster [ˈpætəɹˈnɔstəɹ], *s.* paternóster, padrenuestro, rosario; (*arq.*) contera.

path [pɑːθ], *s.* senda, sendero, vía, camino, paso, huella, vereda, acera; curso; *bridle path*, camino de herradura. — *v.i.* andar.

pathetic [pəˈθetik], *a.* patético.

patheticalness, *s.* carácter patético, lo patético.

pathless [ˈpɑːθles], *a.* sin camino, sin senda.

pathologic [pæθoˈlɔdʒik], **pathological** [pæθoˈlɔdúikəl], *a.* patológico.

pathologist [pəˈθɔlɔdʒist], *s.* patólogo.

pathology [pəˈθɔlɔdʒi], *s.* patología.

pathos [ˈpeiθɔs], *s.* patetismo, lo patético.

pathway [ˈpɑːθwei], *s.* senda, sendero, vereda.

patibulary [pəˈtibjuːləri], *a.* patibulario.

patience [ˈpeiʃəns], *s.* paciencia; (*bot.*) romaza; solitario (juego de naipes); *to try one's patience*, probar la paciencia a, tentar de o la paciencia a; *to lose patience*, perder la paciencia, impacientarse; montar en cólera.

patient [ˈpeiʃənt], *a.* paciente, pacienzudo, sufrido, tolerante. — *s.* paciente, enfermo, doliente; sujeto pasivo.

patly [ˈpætli], *adv.* a propósito, en punto, cómodamente, convenientemente.

patness, *s.* aptitud, oportunidad, conveniencia.

patois [ˈpætwɑː], *s.* dialecto, jerga.

patriarch ['peitriɑːık], s. patriarca, m.
patriarchal, patriarchic, a. patriarcal.
patriarchate, patriarchship, s. patriarcado.
patrician [pə'triʃən], s., a. patricio.
patricide ['pætrisəid], s. parricida, m.f.; parricidio.
patrimonial [pætri'mouniəl], a. patrimonial.
patrimony ['pætriməni], s. patrimonio.
patriot ['pætriət], s. patriota, m.f. — a. patriota, patriótico.
patriotic [pætri'ɔtik], a. patriótico.
patriotism ['pætriotizm], s. patriotismo, amor a la patria.
patristic [pə'tristik], a. patrístico.
patristics, s. patrística, patrología.
patrol [pə'troul], s. patrulla, ronda; *patrol-man,* rondador. — v.t. patrullar, rondar, hacer la ronda. — v.i. patrullar.
patron ['peitrən, 'pætrən], s. mecenas, protector, patrono, patrocinador, patrón, apadrinador, amparador.
patronage ['pætrənidʒ], s. patronazgo, patronato, patrocinio, amparo, clientela.
patronal [pə'trounəl], a. perteneciente al patrón, tutelar.
patroness ['pætrones], s.f., protectora, patrocinadora, patrona, madrina.
patronize ['pætronaiz], v.t. patrocinar, apadrinar, proteger, apoyar, fomentar; dignarse, tratar con arrogancia; (*fam.*) ser parroquiano de.
patronizer, s. patrocinador, patrón, protector.
patronizing, a. que patrocina, que protege; altivo, arrogante.
patronless, a. sin protector, sin patrón, desamparado.
patronymic [pætro'nimik], s., a. patronímico.
patten ['pætən], s. galocha, chanclo, chinela, zueco; (*arq.*) cimiento, fundamento de una pared, etc.; base de una columna.
patter ['pætəɹ], v.t., v.i. patear, patalear, hacer ruido de pasos; murmurar padrenuestros.
patter, pattering, s. pataleo; ruido de pasos; ruido de gotas de agua; parladuría, habladuría.
pattern ['pætəɹn], s. modelo, ejemplo, muestra, patrón, ejemplar; diseño, molde, dechado, escantillón; norma, regla, pauta; *pattern card,* (*com.*) mostruario. — v.t. copiar, imitar; servir de ejemplo.
patty ['pæti], s. pastelillo, fajardo, empanada.
patty-pan, s. tartera, molde para pastelillos.
patulous ['pætjuːləs], a. extendido, abierto.
paucity ['pɔːsiti], s. poco, poquedad, escasez, f., parquedad, número pequeño.
Pauline ['pɔːlain], a. Paulista, de San Pablo.
paunch [pɔːntʃ], s. panza, barriga; rumen de los rumiantes; (*mar.*) gimelga, pallete. — v.t. desbarrigar.
pauper ['pɔːpəɹ], s. pobre, indigente.
pauperism, s. pauperismo.
pauperize, v.t. depauperar, empobrecer, reducir a la pobreza.
pause [pɔːz], s. pausa; reposo; cesación, suspensión, parada; irresolución, hesitación, vacilación; (*mús.*) pausa. — v.i. pausar, cesar, parar, hacer una pausa, detenerse, interrumpirse.
pausingly, adv. por pausas.
pave [peiv], v.t. empedrar, solar, embaldosar, pavimentar, adoquinar, enlosar, enladrillar;

to pave the way for, (*fig.*) facilitar el camino para, preparar para.
pavement ['peivmənt], s. pavimento, empedrado, solado, adoquinado; acera.
paver, pavier, s. empedrador, solador.
pavilion [pə'viljən], s. pabellón, tienda; quiosco; glorieta, cenador (de jardín), dosel; bandera; pabellón (de la oreja); (*arq.*) ala. — v.t. surtir con pabellones; cobijar bajo un pabellón.
paving ['peiviŋ], s. empedrado, adoquinado, pavimento, soladura; *paving-stone,* adoquín.
paw [pɔː], s. pata, garra, zarpa; (*vulg.*) la mano. — v.i. patear, piafar. — v.t. dar golpes con las garras; arañar; manosear, sobar, acariciar.
pawl [pɔːl], s. (*mar.*) linguete, trinquete; (*mec.*) retén, seguro; diente de encaje; paleta de reloj; *supporter of the pawl,* (*mar.*) descanso del linguete; *hanging pawls,* (*mar.*) linguete de por alto.
pawn [pɔːn], s. garantía, empeño; (*fig.*) prenda; peón (ajedrez); *in pawn,* en prenda, empeñado; *pawn ticket,* papeleta de empeño. — v.t. empeñar, dar en prenda, pignorar, dejar en prenda; *he has pawned his boots,* (*fig.*) está empeñado hasta los ojos.
pawnbroker, s. prestamista, m.f., prendero; (*for.*) comodatario.
pawnee [pɔː'niː], s. prestamista, m.f., prestador.
pawner, s. prendador, el que toma prestado.
pawnshop, s. monte de piedad, casa de préstamos, casa de empeños.
pay [pei], v.t. (*pret., p.p.* paid) pagar, saldar, recompensar; costear, abonar; cumplir, satisfacer, desempeñar, devolver; desembolsar, gastar; presentar, ofrecer; corresponder; sufrir (un castigo); ser provechoso; *to pay attention,* prestar o dar atención; *to pay attentions to,* galantear, cortejar; *to pay back,* restituir, devolver, reembolsar; (*fig.*) pagar en la misma moneda, pagar con las setenas; *to pay down,* pagar al contado (o en dinero contante); *to pay by instalments,* pagar a plazos; *to pay in full,* saldar; *to pay with interest,* (*fig.*) pagar con creces, pagar con las setenas; *to pay a call,* hacer una visita; *to pay off,* pagar y despedir, saldar; *to pay out a cable,* (*mar.*) arriar un cable; *to pay the piper,* (*fig.*) pagar los vidrios rotos. — v.i. pagar, recompensar, hacer aprovechar, dar provecho, ser provechoso; sufrir un castigo; *to pay through the nose,* ser un desuello, costar un ojo de la cara; *to pay for it,* (*fig.*) estar escarmentado, pagarla, pagarlas. — s. pago, paga, sueldo, salario, honorarios, estipendio, quitación, gaje, recompensa, compensación; (*mil.*) prest, pre, soldada; *half-pay,* medio sueldo; *half-pay officer,* oficial retirado; *pay-day,* día de pago; *pay-roll,* nómina; *pay-dirt,* tierra o arenilla con cantidad provechosa de oro.
payable, a. pagadero, reembolsable; acera.
payee [pei'iː], s. (*com.*) portador.
payer, s. pagador.
paymaster, s. pagador, contador; (*mil.*) habilitado; *Paymaster-General,* ordenador de pagos.
payment ['peimənt], s. pago, pagamento, paga; (*fig.*) paga, recompensa, premio; *to suspend payment,* suspender sus pagos; *cash*

payment, pago en especie, al contado; *full payment*, saldo; *on payment of*, mediante, mediante el pago de.

pay-office, *s.* pagaduría.

pea [pi:], *s.* (*pl.* **peas, pease**) guisante, chícharo; *chick-pea*, garbanzo.

peace [pi:s], *s.* paz, *f.*, quietud, sosiego; paz pública; *to hold one's peace*, callarse, guardar silencio; *to make peace*, hacer las paces; *peace establishment*, (*mil.*) pie de paz. — *interj.* ¡paz! ¡chito! ¡silencio! ¡calle!

peaceable ['pi:səbəl], *a.* tranquilo, pacífico, apacible, sosegado.

peaceableness, *s.* tranquilidad, quietud, sosiego.

peaceably, *adv.* pacíficamente.

peaceful ['pi:sfəl], *a.* tranquilo, pacífico, apacible.

peacefully, *adv.* pacíficamente, tranquilamente.

peacefulness, *s.* tranquilidad, quietud, calma, *m.*

peaceless, *a.* sin paz, sin tranquilidad.

peace-loving, *a.* pacífico.

peace-maker, *s.* conciliador, pacificador.

peace-offering, *s.* sacrificio propiciatorio.

peace-officer, *s.* alguacil, agente de paz.

peach [pi:tʃ], *s.* melocotón, pérsico, durazno, albérchigo; (*fam.*, *fig.*) (cosa) de mieles, de oro, buena pieza. — *v.t.* (*vulg.*) acusar, delatar a un cómplice.

peachick ['pi:tʃik], *s.* pavito real.

peacock ['pi:kɔk], *s.* pavón, pavo real.

pea-gun, *s.* cerbatana.

peahen [pi:hen], *s.f.* pava real.

peajacket, *s.* chaquetón de piloto, marsellés.

peak [pi:k], *s.* pico, picacho, cumbre, *f.*, cúspide, *f.*; (*fig.*) cumbre, *f.*, cima, *m.*, auge, apogeo; punta; visera (de gorra, etc.); (*mar.*) pena, penol, pico, espiga de vela; *peak-halliards*, (*mar.*) drizas de la pena. — *v.i.* adolecer, enflaquecer, consumirse, tener apariencia de enfermo y macilento. — *v.t. to peak up*, (*mar.*) amantillar el pico, levantar una verga contra el mástil.

peaked, *a.* puntiagudo; (*fam.*) indispuesto, enfermizo.

peaking, *a.* enfermizo.

peakish, peaky, *a.* picudo, picoteado.

peal [pi:l], *s.* repique, juego de campanas; estrépito, estruendo; *in a peal*, a vuelo; *peal of laughter*, risotada, carcajada. — *v.i.* tronar, retronar, repicar. — *v.t.* agitar, aturdir, celebrar.

pea-nut ['pi:nʌt], *s.* cacahuete, cacahué, cacahuey, (*Cuba*) maní.

pear [pɛəɹ], *s.* pera.

pearl [pə:ɹl], *s.* perla, aljófar; (*med.*) nube, *f.*, catarata; (*impr.*) perla, tipo de cinco puntos; *mother of pearl*, madreperla, nácar; *pearl white*, blanco de perla; *to cast one's pearls before swine*, echar margaritas a puercos. — *v.t.* perlar; adornar con perlas. — *v.i.* parecer a una perla; pescar perlas.

pearl-ash, *s.* potasa purificada.

pearl-barley, *s.* cebada perlada, cebada sin cáscara.

pearled, *a.* aljofarado, perlado.

pearl-fishery, *s.* pesca de perlas.

pearly, *a.* perlino, de perla.

peart [piəɹt], *a.* (*ant.*) alegre, jovial [PERT].

pear-tree, *s.* peral.

peasant ['pezənt], *s.*, *a.* aldeano, rústico, labrador, labriego, campesino.

peasantry ['pezəntri], *s.* paisanaje, gente del campo, aldeanos, lugareños.

peascod ['pi:zkɔd], *s.* vaina de guisantes.

pease [pi:z], *s.pl.* [PEA].

pea-shooter, *s.* cerbatana.

peat [pi:t], *s.* turba; *peat-bog*, turbera, turbal, pantano turboso; *peat-moss*, musgo de pantano.

peaty, *a.* turboso.

pea-weevil, *s.* (*entom.*) gorgojo.

pebble ['pebəl], *s.* guijarrò, guija, china, matacán; ágata. — *v.t.*, *v.i.* granular, abollonar.

pebbly, *a.* guijarroso, guijoso.

peccability [pekə'biliti], *s.* fragilidad, disposición al pecado.

peccable ['pekəbəl], *a.* pecable.

peccadillo [pekə'dilou], *s.* pecadillo.

peccancy ['pekənsi], *s.* defecto, vicio, disposición al pecado.

peccant ['pekənt], *a.* pecador, pecante; ofensivo, corrompido, vicioso, defectuoso; mórbido.

peck [pek], *s.* medida de áridos (9·09 litros); celemín; picotada, picotazo; (*fam.*) montón, gran cantidad. — *v.t.* picotear, picar, recoger con el pico; picar, punzar, herir; rozar con los labios; *to peck at*, picar, picotear; (*fig.*) comiscar, picar. — *v.i.* picotear.

pecker, *s.* pájaro que pica, picoteador; (*orn.*) picoverde.

pecten ['pektən], *s.* membrana en forma de peine que algunas aves y reptiles tienen sobre los ojos; festón de una concha.

pectin ['pektin], *s.* pectina.

pectinal, *a.* pectíneo. — *s.* (*ictiol.*) pectinal.

pectinate, pectinated, *a.* pectiniforme.

pectoral ['pektərəl], *a.* pectoral. — *s.* (*mil.*) peto; (*igl.*) pectoral.

peculate ['pekju:leit], *v.t.*, *v.i.* desfalcar, malversar.

peculation, *s.* peculado, desfalco, malversación.

peculator, *s.* peculador, malversador, desfalcador.

peculiar [pe'kju:liəɹ], *a.* peculiar, particular, propio, privativo; raro, extraordinario.

peculiarity [pekju:li'æriti], *s.* particularidad, peculiaridad.

peculiarize, *v.t.* particularizar, individualizar, apropiar.

peculiarly [pe'kju:liəɹli], *adv.* peculiarmente, particularmente; en particular; de modo extraño.

pecuniary [pe'kju:niəri], *a.* pecuniario.

pecunious [pe'kju:niəs], *a.* adinerado.

pedagogic [pedə'gɔgik], *a.* pedagógico.

pedagogics, *s.* pedagogía.

pedagogism, *s.* pedantismo.

pedagogue ['pedəgɔg], *s.* pedagogo; pedante.

pedagogy ['pedəgɔgi], *s.* pedagogía, pedantismo.

pedal ['pedəl], *a.* de pie, del pie, perteneciente al pie. — *s.* pedal; (*mús.*) bajo continuo. — *v.i.* pedalear.

pedant ['pedənt], *s.* pedante.

pedantic [pe'dæntik], *a.* pedante, pedantesco.

pedantry ['pedəntri], *s.* pedantería, pedantismo.

peddle ['pedəl], *v.i.* ser buhonero, vender cosas de buhonería. — *v.t.* vender (cosas de buhonería); vender por las calles o de casa en casa; revender, vender por menor.

peddler ['pedləɹ], *s.* buhonero, baratillero, revendedor.

peddlery, *s.* buhonería; artículos de buhonería.

peddling, *s.* buhonería. — *a.* fútil, mezquino.

pedestal ['pedestəl], *s.* pedestal, peana.

pedestrian [pe'destriən], *s.* peón, peatón, andador, andarín. — *a.* caminante, pedestre, a pie; (*fig.*) trillado, ordinario, vulgar.

pedicle ['pedikəl], *s.* (*bot.*) pedúnculo; pedicelo; (*med.*) pedículo.

pedicular [pe'dikju:ləɹ], **pediculous** [pe-'dikju:ləs], *a.* pedicular.

pedigree ['pediɡri:], *s.* genealogía, árbol genealógico, linaje. — *a.* de casta, de raza.

pediment ['pedimənt], *s.* (*arq.*) frontón, frontis, tímpano, témpano.

pedlar ['pedləɹ], *s.* buhonero, baratillero, revendedor.

pedometer [pe'dɔmitəɹ], *s.* pedómetro.

peduncle, *s.* pedúnculo.

peduncular [pe'dʌŋkju:ləɹ], *a.* peduncular.

pedunculate, pedunculated, *a.* pedunculado.

peek [pi:k], *v.t.* (*fam.*) atisbar, mirar por hendiduras, espiar, fisgonear.

peel [pi:l], *v.t.* pelar, descortezar, mondar, desollar, deshollejar, descascarar. — *v.i.* mondarse, pelarse, descascararse. — *s.* corteza, cáscara, hollejo, pellejo; pala de horno; (*mar.*) pala del remo; (*impr.*) colgador, espito.

peeler, *s.* mondador, pelador, descortezador; *vulg.* polizonte, guindilla, *m.*

peen [pi:n], *s.* la punta del martillo opuesta a la cara; *peen-hammer*, martillo de punta.

peep [pi:p], *v.i.* atisbar, mirar a hurtadillas; aparecer, asomar; mostrarse; despuntar (alba); pipiar, piar. — *s.* atisbo; asomo, ojeada, mirada; primera aparición; pío, piada; *peep of day*, despunte del día; *Peeping Tom*, mirón.

peeper, *s.* el que mira a hurtadillas, atisbador; polluelo, pollito; (*fam.*) ojo.

peep-hole, *s.* atisbadero.

peer [piəɹ], *s.* par, igual, semejante; par del reino, grande, noble de Inglaterra; camarada, *m.f.*, campañero. — *v.i.* escudriñar, husmear; apuntar, asomar, aparecer, salir.

peerage ['piəridʒ], *s.* dignidad de par.

peeress ['piəres], *s.f.* paresa.

peerless, *a.* sin par, incomparable, sin igual.

peerlessly, *adv.* incomparablemente, sin igual, sin par.

peerlessness, *s.* superioridad incomparable.

peevish ['pi:viʃ], *a.* enojadizo, rencilloso, enfadadizo, enfadoso, regañón, displicente, pueril; bobo.

peevishly, *adv.* de mal humor, impertinentemente, displicentemente, con displicencia.

peevishness, *s.* mal humor, mal genio, displicencia.

peewit ['pi:wit], *s.* avefría.

peg [peg], *s.* clavija, estaca, estaquilla, espita, espiga, sobina, taco; (*fig.*) grado, punto; (*fig.*) excusa, pretexto; *to come down a peg*, bajar un punto; *to take down a peg*, bajar los humos a, cortar las alas a. — *v.t.* enclavi-

jar, clavar, estaquillar, encabillar, atarugar, empernar; *to peg away*, (*fam.*) batirse el cobre, machacar; *to peg out*, (*vulg.*) diñarla, estirar la pierna.

pegging ['pegiŋ], *s.* pernería.

peg-ladder, *s.* escala de cotorra.

pegmatite ['pegmətait], *s.* pegmatita.

peg-top, *s.* peonza.

pejoration, *s.* deterioro, decadencia.

pejorative ['pi:dʒoreitiv, pe'dʒɔrətiv], *a.* despectivo, peyorativo.

pekan ['pekən], *s.* mustela de la América del Norte.

pekoe ['pekou], *s.* té negro superior.

pelagic [pe'leidʒik], *a.* pelágico, oceánico.

pelargonium [pelɑːɹ'gouniəm], *s.* pelargonio.

pelerine ['pelərin, 'peləri:n], *s.* pelerina, esclavina.

pelf [pelf], *s.* (*despectivo*) bienes, judiada.

pelican ['pelikən], *s.* pelícano, pelicano.

pelisse [pe'li:s], *s.* pelliza; ropón.

pell [pel], *s.* (*ant.*) piel, *f.*, pellejo, cuero; pergamino.

pellet ['pelet], *s.* pella, pelotilla; píldora; bola, bolita, bodoque.

pellicle ['pelikəl], *s.* película, cutícula, túnica, hollejo; lapa, telilla.

pellitory ['pelitəri], *s.* (*bot.*) cañarroya; *pellitory of Spain*, pelitre, manzanilla pelitre.

pell-mell [pel'mel], *adv.* a trochemoche, confusamente, atropelladamente, al tuntún.

pellucid [pe'lju:sid], *a.* translúcido, diáfano, cristalino.

pellucidity, pellucidness, *s.* diafanidad; (*fis.*) pelucidad.

pelt [pelt], *s.* piel, *f.*, pellejo, cuero, zalea; corambre; golpe, golpazo. — *v.t.* arrojar, apedrear, llover. — *v.i.* azotar, seguir apedreando, caer con fuerza (como la lluvia).

pelting, *s.* golpeo, lapidación. — *a.* furioso; *pelting rain*, lluvia copiosa.

pelt-monger, *s.* pellejero.

peltry ['peltri], *s.* peletería, corambre, pieles, pellejos.

pelvic ['pelvik], *a.* pelviano.

pelvimeter, *s.* pelvímetro.

pelvis ['pelvis], *s.* pelvis, *f.*

pemmican ['pemikən], *s.* carne preparada para viajes.

pen [pen], *s.* pluma; escritura; corral, parque; alcahaz, caponera; pocilga; *fountain-pen*, estilográfica, estilo, *f.*; *slip of the pen*, error de pluma; *pen-drawing*, o *pen-sketch*, dibujo a la pluma. — *v.t.* escribir; componer; acorralar, encerrar.

penal ['pi:nəl], *a.* penal, sujeto a castigo; *penal servitude*, presidio, pena de trabajos forzados.

penalty ['penəlti], *s.* pena, castigo, multa.

penance ['penəns], *s.* penitencia.

penates [pe'neiti:z], *s.* penates, *m.pl.*

pence [pens], *s.pl.* [PENNY].

penchant ['penʃənt, 'pɔŋʃɔŋ], *s.* tendencia, afición, inclinación.

pencil ['pensəl], *s.* lapiz, pincel; (*ópt.*) hacecillo (de luz). — *v.t.* dibujar, lapizar.

pencil-case, *s.* lapicero.

pendant ['pendənt], *s.* pendiente, pinjante, medallón, péndola, arete; araña de lámpara; (*mar.*) amante, gallardete; apéndice; (*arq.*) adorno que cuelga.

pendency, *s.* suspensión, dilación, demora.

pendent ['pendənt], *a.* pendiente, colgante, suspendido, pinjante, péndulo, salidizo.
pendentive, *s.* (*arq.*) pechina.
pending, *a.* pendiente, colgante, indeciso, suspenso. — *prep.* durante, mientras, en el intervalo.
pendulosity, pendulousness, *s.* suspensión.
pendulous ['pendju:ləs], *a.* pendiente, colgante, suspenso, suspendido.
pendulum ['pendju:ləm], *s.* péndulo, péndola.
penetrability, *s.* penetrabilidad.
penetrable ['penetrəbəl], *a.* penetrable.
penetrableness, *s.* penetrabilidad.
penetrant ['penetrənt], *a.* penetrante.
penetrate ['penetreit], *v.t.*, *v.i.* penetrar, taladrar, entrar, horadar; atravesar, pasar a través; profundizar; conmover; (*fig.*) penetrar, comprender.
penetrating, *a.* penetrante, penetrador; (*fig.*) penetrante, agudo, astuto.
penetration, *s.* penetración.
penetrative, *a.* penetrante, penetrativo.
penguin ['pengwin], *s.* pingüino, pájaro bobo.
penholder, *s.* portaplumas, *m.*
penicillin, *s.* penicilina.
peninsula [pe'ninsju:lə], *s.* península.
peninsular [pe'ninsju:lɑːɹ], *a.* peninsular.
peninsulate, *v.t.* formar una península.
penis ['pi:nis], *s.* pene.
penitence ['penitəns], **penitency** ['penitənsi], *s.* penitencia, contrición, arrepentimiento.
penitent ['penitənt], *a.* penitente, contrito, arrepentido. — *s.* penitente.
penitential [peni'tenʃəl], *a.* penitencial; penal.
penitentially, *adv.* de una manera penitencial.
penitentiary [peni'tenʃəri], *a.* penitenciario, de penitencia. — *s.* casa de corrección; casa penitenciaria, presidio, cárcel modelo; (*igl.*) penitenciario, confesor.
penitently, *adv.* con penitencia.
penknife ['pennaif], *s.* cortaplumas, *m.*
penman ['penmən], (*pl.* **penmen**) calígrafo; autor, escritor; pendolista, *m.*
penmanship, *s.* caligrafía.
penna ['penə], *s.* (*orn.*) pena.
pen-name, *s.* seudónimo.
pennant ['penənt], *s.* flámula, gallardete, banderola, insignia; (*mar.*) amante.
pennate ['penit], **pennated** ['penɔtid], *a.* peniforme, alado.
penniless ['peniles], *a.* sin dinero, sin blanca, muy pobre.
pennilessness, *s.* pobreza extrema.
pennon ['penɔn], *s.* pendón, flámula, banderola.
penny ['peni], *s.* (*pl.* **pennies, pence**) penique (duodécima parte de un chelín); (*fam.*) dinero; *to be without a penny,* estar a la cuarta pregunta; *to turn an honest penny,* ganar la vida honradamente; *in for a penny, in for a pound,* preso por uno, preso por ciento, o perdido por uno, perdido por todo; *penny-a-liner,* gacetillero; *penny dreadful,* (despectivo) folletín; *penny wise,* que hace pequeños ahorros a costa de sumas importantes; *penny-in-the-slot machine,* tragaperras, *m.*
pennyroyal, *s.* (*bot.*) poleo.
pennyweight, *s.* (*joy.*) escrúpulo.
pennyworth, *s.* valor de un penique.
penology [pe'nɔlodʒi], *s.* penología.
pensile ['pensail], *a.* pensil, suspendido, colgado.

pension ['penʃən], *s.* pensión, renta, beca, cesantía, retiro; pensión de familia, casa de huéspedes; pensión, hospedaje. — *v.t.* pensionar; *to pension off,* jubilar.
pensionary ['penʃənəri], *a.* pensionado. — *s.* pensionista, *m.f.,* pensionado.
pensioner ['penʃənəɹ], *s.* pensionista, *m.f.,* pensionado; beca; (*mil. y mar.*) inválido.
pensive ['pensiv], *a.* pensativo, meditabundo; sombrío, triste, cabizbajo.
pensiveness, *s.* meditación profunda; melancolía, tristeza.
penstock, *s.* paradera; portaplumas, *m.*
pent [pent], *a.* encerrado. — *p.p.* [PEN]. — *s.* clausura.
pentachord ['pentəkɔːɹd], *s.* pentacordio.
pentad ['pentæd], *s.* grupo de cinco cosas.
pentagon ['pentəgən], *s.* pentágono.
pentagonal, *a.* pentágono, pentagonal.
pentameter [pen'tæmetəɹ], *s.* pentámetro. — *a.* pentamétrico.
pentarchy ['pentɑːɹki], *s.* pentarquía.
Pentateuch ['pentətjuːk], *s.* pentateuco.
Pentecost, *s.* pentecostés, pascua.
pent-house ['penthaus], *s.* sobradillo, tejadillo, tejaroz.
pent-up, *a.* encerrado, enjaulado; (*fig.*) reprimido, ahogado.
penult [pe'nʌlt], *s.* penúltima (sílaba).
penultimate [pen'ʌltimit], *a.* penúltimo.
penumbra [pe'nʌmbrə], *s.* penumbra.
penurious [pe'njuːriəs], *a.* indigente, muy pobre; escaso; tacaño, ruin.
penuriously, *adv.* indigentemente, pobremente, miserablemente, estrechamente, escasamente.
penuriousness, *s.* indigencia, escasez, miseria; tacañería, ruindad.
penury ['penjuːri], *s.* penuria, pobreza extrema, indigencia, miseria, estrechez, inopia.
penwiper, *s.* enjugaplumas, limpiaplumas, *m.*
peon ['piːən], *s.* peón; criado, soldado de a pie en la India.
peony, *s.* (*bot.*) peonía.
people ['piːpəl], *s.* pueblo, nación; población, gente, *f.,* personas, habitantes; vulgo, populacho; *common people,* gentuza, gentualla; *people say,* se dice. — *v.t.* poblar.
pepper ['pepəɹ], *s.* pimienta; pimiento, pimentero. — *v.t.* sazonar con pimienta; golpear, acribillar.
peppercorn ['pepəɹkɔːɹn], *s.* semilla o grano de pimienta; (*fig.*) chuchería, niñería.
peppergrass, pepperwort, *s.* lepidio.
peppermint ['pepəɹmint], *s.* (*bot.*) menta, piperita, hierbabuena, yerbabuena; pastilla de menta.
peppery, *a.* picante; irascible, colérico.
pepsine ['pepsin], *s.* pepsina.
peptone ['peptoun], *s.* peptona.
peptonic, *a.* peptónico.
peptonize, *v.t.* peptonizar.
per [pəːɹ], *prep.* por; *per annum,* al año; *per cent,* por ciento; *per diem,* diario, al día; *per se,* por sí mismo.
peradventure [pəɹəd'ventʃəɹ], *adv.* por casualidad, por ventura, acaso.
perambulate [pə'ræmbjuːleit], *v.t.*, *v.i.* ambular, recorrer, transitar.
perambulation, *s.* ambulación, paseo.
perambulator, *s.* coche o cochecito o cochecillo de niño.

percale [pəɹˈkeil], *s.* percal.
perceivable, *a.* perceptible, sensible.
perceive [pəɹˈsiːv], *v.t.* darse cuenta de, entender, comprender, conocer; percibir, sentir, observar, advertir.
perceiver, *s.* el que percibe.
percentage [pəɹˈsentidʒ], *s.* porcentaje, tanto por ciento.
perceptibility, *s.* perceptibilidad.
perceptible [pəɹˈseptibəl], *a.* perceptible, sensible, palpable.
perception [pəɹˈsepʃən], *s.* percepción, observación; penetración, agudeza, sensibilidad; (*for.*) percibo (de rentas, etc.).
perceptivity [pəɹsepˈtiviti], *s.* percepción, perceptibilidad.
perch [pəːɹtʃ], *s.* (*ictiol.*) perca; pértica (medida agraria de longitud equivalente a 5·229 m); percha, alcándara. — *v.i.* posar, posarse, ponerse en percha. — *v.t.* emperchar, empingorotar.
perchance [pəɹˈtʃɑːns], *adv.* tal vez, acaso, por ventura.
perchloride [pəɹˈklɔːraid], *s.* percloruro.
percipient [pəɹˈsipiənt], *a.* dotado de percepción, agudo, penetrante.
percolate [ˈpəːɹkoleit], *v.t.* colar, pasar, filtrar, infiltrar, rezumar. — *v.i.* colarse, filtrarse.
percolation, *s.* coladura, filtración, infiltración.
percolator, *s.* colador, filtro.
percuss [pəɹˈkʌs], *v.t.* percutir, golpear, herir.
percussion [pəɹˈkʌʃən], *s.* percusión, choque; resonación; *percussion-cap*, cápsula, pistón, fulminante.
percussive, percutient, *a.* percuciente.
perdition [pəɹˈdiʃən], *s.* perdición, ruina.
perdurable [pəɹˈdjuːɹəbəl], *a.* perdurable.
peregrinate [ˈperigrineit], *v.t.* peregrinar.
peregrination, *s.* peregrinación.
peregrine [ˈperigrin], *a.* peregrino, pasajero, migratorio.
peremptoriness, *s.* carácter perentorio.
peremptory [pəˈremptəri], *a.* perentorio, definitivo; imperioso, dictatorial, intolerante.
perennial [pəˈreniəl], *a.* perenne, perennal, perpetuo. — *s.* planta vivaz.
perfect [ˈpəːɹfekt], *a.* perfecto, cabal, acabado. — *s.* (*gram.*) tiempo perfecto. — *v.t.* perfeccionar, hacer perfecto, redondear, completar.
perfecter, *s.* perfeccionador.
perfectibility, *s.* perfectibilidad.
perfectible, *a.* perfectible.
perfection [pəɹˈfekʃən], *s.* perfección; *to perfection*, a la perfección.
perfectionist, *s.* perfeccionista, *m.f.*
perfective, *a.* perfectivo, que hace perfecto.
perfectly [ˈpəːɹfektli], *adv.* perfectamente, cabalmente; completamente, enteramente, del todo.
perfectness, *s.* perfección, excelencia.
perfervid [pəɹˈfəːɹvid], *a.* muy férvido, ardiente, celoso.
perfidious [pəɹˈfidiəs], *a.* pérfido, fementido.
perfidiousness, perfidy, *s.* perfidia, alevosía.
perfoliate [pəɹˈfoulieit], *a.* (*bot.*) perfoliado.
perforate [ˈpəːɹforeit], *v.t.* perforar, taladrar, horadar, agujerear, punzar.
perforation, *s.* perforación, horadación; agujero.

perforator, *s.* perforador, horadador, taladro, barrena.
perforce [pəɹˈfɔːɹs], *adv.* por fuerza, a la fuerza, forzosamente.
perform [pəɹˈfɔːɹm], *v.t.* ejecutar, poner por obra, efectuar, llevar a cabo, realizar, hacer; desempeñar, llenar, cumplir, representar. — *v.i.* representar, desempeñar un papel; cantar, tocar, realizar (una obra musical).
performable, *a.* ejecutable, factible, practicable.
performance [pəɹˈfɔːɹməns], *s.* ejecución, cumplimiento; composición, obra, acción, hazaña; función, representación, desempeño.
performer, *s.* ejecutor, ejecutante; cómico, actor, actriz, *f.*, artista, *m.f.*, representante.
perfume [ˈpəːɹfjuːm], *s.* perfume, aroma, *m.*, fragancia, olor fragante; (*Perú*) agua rica. — *v.t.* perfumar, aromatizar, embalsamar, sahumar, incensar.
perfumer, *s.* perfumador, perfumista, *m.f.*, perfumero, sahumador.
perfumery [pəɹˈfjuːməri], *s.* perfumería.
perfuming, *a.* que perfuma. — *s.* acción de perfumar.
perfunctorily [pəɹˈfʌŋktərili], *adv.* perfunctoriamente, descuidadamente, superficialmente, muy por encima, sin interés.
perfunctoriness, *s.* descuido, negligencia.
perfunctory, *a.* perfunctorio, superficial, ligero, indolente, negligente.
perfuse [pəɹˈfjuːz], *v.t.* difundir, extender sobre, rociar, esparcir.
pergola [ˈpəːɹgolə], *s.* glorieta, emparrado, cenador.
perhaps [pəɹˈhæps], *adv.* quizá, quizás, tal vez, acaso, puede ser.
peri [ˈpiəri], *s.* peri, *f.*, hada.
perianth [ˈperiænθ], **perianthum**, *s.* periantio.
pericardial [periˈkɑːɹdiəl], *a.* pericardino.
pericardium, *s.* pericardio.
pericarp [ˈperikɑːɹp], *s.* pericarpo.
pericranium [periˈkreiniəm], *s.* pericráneo.
perigee [ˈperidʒiː], *s.* perigeo.
perigonium [periˈgouniəm], *s.* perigonio.
perihelion [periˈhiːliən], *s.* perihelio.
peril [ˈperil], *s.* peligro, riesgo, trance. — *v.i.* estar en peligro, peligrar. — *v.t.* exponer al peligro, poner en peligro.
perilous, *a.* peligroso, arriesgado, aventurado, expuesto.
perilousness, *s.* peligro, situación peligrosa.
perimeter [peˈrimitəɹ], *s.* perímetro.
period [ˈpiəriəd], *s.* período, edad, *f.*, tiempo, época; serie, *f.*, ciclo, revolución; cláusula; punto final; conclusión, término; (*med.*) regla, menstruación.
periodic [piəriˈɔdik], **periodical** [piəriˈɔdikəl], *a.* periódico.
periodical, *s.* publicación periódica, revista, periódico.
periodically, *adv.* periódicamente.
periodicalness, periodicity, *s.* periodicidad.
periosteum [periˈɔstiəm], *s.* periostio.
periostitis, *s.* periostitis, *f.*
peripatetic [peripəˈtetik], *s.*, *a.* peripatético.
peripateticism, *s.* peripatetismo.
peripheral [peˈrifərəl], *a.* periférico.
peripheric, peripherical, *a.* periférico.
periphery [peˈrifəri], *s.* periferia.
periphrase [ˈperifreiz], **periphrasis**, *s.* perífrasis, *f.*, perífrasi, *f.*

periphrase, *v.t.*, *v.i.* perifrasear.
periphrastic, periphrastical, *a.* perifrástico, perifraseado.
periplus ['periplʌs], *s.* periplo.
periptery, *s.* períptero.
perique [pe'ri:k], *s.* (*E.U.*) tabaco de Luisiana.
periscope ['periskoup], *s.* periscopio.
periscopic, *a.* periscópico.
perish ['periʃ], *v.i.* perecer; marchitarse; acabar, fenecer.
perishability, *s.* naturaleza perecedera.
perishable ['periʃəbəl], *a.* perecedero.
perishableness, *s.* carácter perecedero.
perishably, *adv.* de una manera perecedera.
perisperm ['perispəɹm], *s.* perispermo.
peristaltic [peri'stæltik], *a.* peristáltico.
peristyle ['peristail], *s.* peristilo.
peritoneum [peri'touniəm], *s.* peritoneo.
peritonitis [perito'naitis], *s.* peritonitis, *f.*
periwig ['periwig], *s.* peluca; peluquín.
periwinkle ['periwiŋkəl], *s.* litorina, caracol marino; (*bot.*) pervencha, pervinca.
perjure ['pə:ɹdʒəɹ], *v.t.*, *v.i.* perjurar, jurar en falso; *to perjure oneself*, perjurarse. — *s.* perjuro.
perjurer, *s.* perjurador, perjuro.
perjury ['pə:ɹdʒəri], *s.* perjurio; *to commit perjury*, jurar en falso.
perk [pə:ɹk], *a.* descarado, descocado; vivaracho, gallardo, desparpajado. — *v.i.* levantarse, erguirse; *to perk up*, (*fam.*) cobrar ánimo, animarse, reponerse, despejarse. — *v.t.* adornar, vestir, decorar; erguir, levantar la cabeza.
perky, *a.* (*fam.*) descarado, desenvuelto; vivaracho, gallardo, alegre.
permanence ['pə:ɹmənəns], **permanency** ['pə:ɹmənənsi], *s.* permanencia, estabilidad, fijeza.
permanent ['pə:ɹmənənt], *a.* permanente, duradero, estable, fijo.
permanganate [pəɹ'mæŋɡənit], *s.* permanganato.
permeability, *s.* permeabilidad.
permeable ['pə:ɹmiəbəl], *a.* permeable.
permeate ['pə:ɹmieit], *v.t.* penetrar, atravesar, calar, pasar.
permeation, *s.* penetración, impregnación, infiltración.
permeative, *a.* permeativo, penetrativo.
permissible [pəɹ'misəbəl], *a.* permisible, admisible, permitidero, tolerable.
permission [pəɹ'miʃən], *s.* permiso, licencia, permisión, venia.
permissive [pəɹ'misiv], *a.* permisivo, permitido, tolerado, consentido.
permissory, *a.* permisible.
permit [pəɹ'mit], *v.t.* permitir, consentir, tolerar.
permit ['pə:ɹmit], *s.* permiso, licencia, guía, pasavante, pase.
permittance, *s.* permisión.
permutable, *a.* permutable.
permutableness, *s.* permutabilidad.
permutably, *adv.* por cambio.
permutation [pəɹmju:'teiʃən], *s.* permutación, permuta, trueque.
permute [pəɹ'mju:t], *v.t.* permutar, trocar.
pern [pə:ɹn], *s.* buaro, buharro.
pernicious [pəɹ'niʃəs], *a.* pernicioso, perjudicial.

perniciousness, *s.* carácter pernicioso, malignidad, malicia.
pernickety [pəɹ'nikiti], *a.* (*fam.*) melindroso, descontentadizo; remilgado, exigente.
perorate ['peroreit], *v.i.* perorar.
peroration, *s.* peroración.
peroxide [pe'rɔksaid], *s.* peróxido.
peroxidize, *v.t.*, *v.i.* peroxidar.
perpend [pəɹ'pend], *v.t.* ponderar, parar mientes (en).
perpender, *s.* (*arq.*) perpiaño.
perpendicular [pəɹpen'dikju:ləɹ], *s.*, *a.* perpendicular.
perpendicularity, *s.* perpendicularidad.
perpetrate ['pə:ɹpetreit], *v.t.* perpetrar, cometer, consumar.
perpetration, *s.* perpetración, comisión.
perpetrator, *s.* perpetrador.
perpetual [pəɹ'petju:əl], *a.* perpetuo, continuo, incesante; eterno, vitalicio.
perpetuate, *v.t.* perpetuar, eternizar, inmortalizar.
perpetuation [pəɹpetju:'eiʃən], *s.* perpetuación.
perpetuity [pəɹpe'tju:iti], *s.* perpetuidad.
perplex [pəɹ'pleks], *v.t.* confundir, perturbar, embrollar, aturrullar, aturdir, enmarañar, enredar, atormentar.
perplexed, *a.* perplejo, intrincado, enredado, confuso, irresoluto, dudoso.
perplexing, *a.* inquietante; confuso, intrincado.
perplexity, perplexedness, *s.* perplejidad, confusión, irresolución, vacilación, inquietud, duda, enredo.
perquisite ['pə:ɹkwizit], *s.* percance, gajes, buscas, emolumentos, regalía, propina, adehala.
perquisition, *s.* pesquisa, investigación.
perron ['perɔn], *s.* (*arq.*) escalinata (en la parte exterior de un edificio), grada.
perroquet ['peroukei], *s.* cotorra.
perry ['peri], *s.* sidra de peras.
persecute ['pə:ɹsikju:t], *v.t.* molestar, hostigar, acosar, vejar, importunar, perseguir.
persecution, *s.* persecución, acosamiento, vejación.
persecutive, *a.* perseguidor, que persigue.
persecutor, *s.* perseguidor, acosador.
perseverance [pəɹse'viərəns], *s.* perseverancia, persistencia, constancia, empeño.
persevere [pəɹse'viəɹ], *v.t.* perseverar, persistir, empeñarse.
persevering, *a.* perseverante, persistente, constante, porfiado, (*Amér.*, *Andalucía*) empeñoso.
Persian ['pə:ɹʃən], *a.* persa, de Persia, pérsico, persiano. — *s.* persa, *m.f.*; persiano; lengua persa; (*tej.*) persiana; *Persian blinds*, celosías; *Persian wheel*, azuda, azud; noria.
Persic ['pə:ɹsik], *a.* pérsico, persa.
persicot ['pə:ɹsikou], *s.* bebida cordial hecha de melocotón, macerado con alcohol.
persimmon [pəɹ'simən], *s.* fruto del dióspiro.
persist [pəɹ'sist], *v.i.* persistir, porfiar, empeñarse, insistir, perseverar; mantener; permanecer, quedarse.
persistence, persistency, *s.* persistencia, insistencia, porfía; constancia; obstinación, permanencia, duración, continuación.
persistent, persisting, *a.* persistente, perseverante, resuelto, firme, invariable; permanente, continuo.

persistently, persistingly, *adv.* con persistencia.

persistive, *a.* perseverante.

person ['pəːɪsən], *s.* persona, *f.*, personaje, individuo, carácter, personalidad; ente, (*fam.*) quídam, (*fam.*) tipo; papel (de un actor); *in person*, personalmente, en persona. — *pl.* **persons,** gente.

personable, *a.* de buena presencia, bien parecido.

personage, *s.* personaje.

personal, *a.* personal, en persona, privado, particular; (*for.*) mobiliario, mueble; *personal estate*, bienes muebles.

personalism, *s.* personalidad.

personality [pərsoˈnæliti], *s.* personalidad, individualidad, personaje.

personalize, *v.t.* personalizar; (*ret.*) personificar.

personally, *adv.* personalmente.

personalty ['pəːɪsonəlti], *s.* bienes muebles.

personate ['pəːɪsoneit], *v.t.* representar, hacer el papel de; hacerse pasar por, fingir; contrahacer, remedar.

personation, *s.* disfraz; personificación; usurpación del nombre de otro.

personator, *s.* el que hace el papel de otro *o* se hace pasar por otro.

personification [pərsɔnifiˈkeiʃən], *s.* personificación; (*ret.*) personificación, prosopeya.

personify, *v.t.* personificar.

personnel [pəːɪsoˈnel], *s.* personal.

perspective [pərˈspektiv], *s.* perspectiva; vista; *in perspective*, en perspectiva. — *a.* perspectivo, en perspectiva.

perspectively, *adv.* según las reglas de la perspectiva.

perspicacious [pərspiˈkeiʃəs], *a.* perspicaz, penetrante.

perspicaciousness, perspicacity [pərspiˈkæsiti], *s.* perspicacia, agudeza, penetración.

perspicuity [pərspiˈkjuːiti], *s.* perspicuidad, lucidez; (*fig.*) penetración, agudeza.

perspicuous [pərˈspikjuːəs], *a.* perspicuo, lúcido.

perspicuousness, *s.* perspicuidad, claridad.

perspiration [pərspəˈreiʃən], *s.* transpiración, sudor; *to be bathed in perspiration*, estar hecho un pollo de agua.

perspirative, perspiratory, *a.* sudorífico.

perspire [pərˈspaiəɪ], *v.i.* transpirar, sudar, resudar, trasudar.

persuadable, *a.* persuasible.

persuade [pərˈsweid], *v.t.* persuadir, inducir, mover, influir.

persuader, *s.* persuador, persuadidor, persuasor.

persuasibility, *s.* calidad de persuasible.

persuasible, *a.* persuasible.

persuasion [pərˈsweiʒən], *s.* persuasión, instigación; denominación, secta; persuasiva.

persuasive [pərˈsweiziv], *a.* persuasivo. — *s.* aliciente, incentivo, anzuelo.

persuasiveness, *s.* persuasiva.

persuasory [pərˈsweizəri], *a.* persuasivo.

persulphate [pərˈsʌlfeit], *v.t.* persulfato.

pert [pəːɪt], *a.* listo, vivo, vivaracho, gallardo; descarado, descocado, desenvuelto, fresco.

pertain [pərˈtein], *v.i.* pertenecer, concernir, tocar, referirse a, atañer.

pertinacious [pərtiˈneiʃəs], *a.* pertinaz, porfiado, tenaz; incesante, continuo, constante.

pertinacity [pərtiˈnæsiti], *s.* tenacidad, porfía, pertinacia, perseverancia, constancia.

pertinence ['pəːɪtinəns], **pertinency** ['pəːɪtinənsi], *s.* pertenencia, conexión, conveniencia.

pertinent, *a.* pertinente, atinado, a propósito.

pertinentness, *s.* pertinencia, conveniencia, oportunidad.

pertness, *s.* viveza, gallardía; descaro, descoco, desenvoltura, desfachatez, frescura, desembarazo.

perturb [pərˈtəːɪb], *v.t.* perturbar, conturbar, inquietar, agitar.

perturbable [pərˈtəːɪbəbəl], *a.* perturbable.

perturbation, *s.* perturbación, agitación, desorden, confusión, alborotamiento.

perturbator, perturber, *s.* perturbador, agitador.

peruke [peˈruːk], *s.* peluca, peluquín; *peruke-maker,* peluquero.

perusal [peˈruːzəl], *s.* lectura cuidadosa; (*ant.*) escudriño.

peruse, *v.t.* repasar, leer con cuidado; (*ant.*) examinar, escudriñar.

Peruvian [peˈruːviən], *s., a.* peruano, perulero, peruviano; *Peruvian bark,* cascarilla, quina.

pervade [pərˈveid], *v.t.* esparcirse, compenetrarse, penetrar, atravesar; ocupar, llenar.

pervasion [pərˈveiʒən], *s.* penetración; esparcimiento.

perverse [pərˈvəːɪs], *a.* perverso, depravado; intratable, refractario, contrario, petulante, contumaz.

perversely, *adv.* perversamente, con perversidad.

perverseness, *s.* perversidad, contumacia, terquedad; maldad, malicia.

perversion, *s.* perversión, pervertimiento; contumacia.

perversity, *s.* perversidad; contumacia, obstinación.

perversive, *a.* perversivo.

pervert [pərˈvəːɪt], *v.t.* pervertir, corromper, desnaturalizar; tergiversar, falsear, falsificar, viciar, malear, alterar. — *v.i.* apartarse del camino recto; apostatar, renegar. — *s.* renegado, apóstata, *m.f.*, pervertido.

perverter, *s.* pervertidor.

pervertible, *a.* pervertible.

pervious ['pəːɪviəs], *a.* penetrable, permeable; *pervious to light,* diáfano.

perviousness, *s.* penetrabilidad, permeabilidad.

pesky ['peski], *a.* (*fam., E.U.*) molesto, incómodo; cargante.

pessary ['pesəri], *s.* pesario.

pessimism ['pesimizm], *s.* pesimismo.

pessimist, *a.* **pessimistic,** *a.* pesimista, *m.f.*

pest [pest], *s.* peste, *f.*, plaga, pestilencia; insecto nocivo; (*fig.*) plaga, pestilencia; *pest-house,* lazareto.

pester, *v.t.* molestar, importunar, incomodar, vejar, cansar, cargar, amolar.

pesterer, *s.* importuno, (*vulg.*) majadero, moscón, pejiguera.

pestiferous [pesˈtifərəs], *a.* pestífero, pestilente, pestilencial.

pestilence ['pestiləns], *s.* pestilencia, peste, *f.*

pestilent, *a.* pestilente, pestífero.

pestilential [pestiˈlenʃəl], *a.* pestilencial.

pestle ['pestəl], *s.* pistadero, majadero de mortero, mano de almirez, *f.* — *v.t.* majar, moler en un mortero.

pet [pet], *s.* animal doméstico; favorito; niño mimado; (*fam.*) querida, amor mío; berrinche, despecho, mal humor. — *a.* domesticado; favorito; mimado; *pet name*, apodo, mote; *to fly into a pet*, emberrincharse. — *v.t.* mimar; acariciar.

petal ['petəl], *s.* pétalo.

petaled, petalous, *a.* petaláceo.

petaliferous, *a.* que tiene pétalos.

petalism, *s.* petalismo.

petard [pe'tɑːɹd], *s.* petardo.

petarder, *s.* petardero.

petasus ['petəsəs], *s.* petaso.

peter ['piːtəɹ], *v.i.*; *to peter out*, agotarse, disminuir, desaparecer poco a poco.

Peter; *to rob Peter to pay Paul*, desnudar un santo para vestir a otro; ganar el cielo con rosario ajeno; *Peter's penny*, dinero de San Pedro; *Peter's fish*, merluza.

petiolate ['petioleit], **petioled** ['petiould], *a.* peciolado.

petiole ['petioul], *s.* peciolo.

petition [pe'tiʃən], *s.* petición, memorial, súplica, demanda, representación, instancia. — *v.t.* suplicar, pedir, rogar, orar, dirigir un memorial.

petitionary, *a.* petitorio, demandante, suplicante.

petitioner, *s.* peticionario, memorialista, *m.f.*, suplicante, representante.

petrel ['petrel], *s.* (*orn.*) petrel.

petrescence [pe'tresəns], *s.* petrificación.

petrescent, *a.* que se petrifica.

petrifaction [petri'fækʃən], **petrification** [petrifi'keiʃən], *s.* petrificación.

petrifactive, *a.* petrificante.

petrifiable [petri'faiəbəl], *a.* que puede petrificarse.

petrific [pe'trifik], *a.* petrificante.

petrify ['petrifai], *v.t.* petrificar; (*fig.*) petrificar (de asombro). — *v.i.* petrificarse.

petrifying, *a.* petrificante, petrífico; (*fig.*) petrificante, asombrante.

petrography [pe'trɔgrəfi], *s.* petrografía, tratado de las piedras.

petrol ['petrəl], *s.* gasolina, gas, petróleo; (*auto.*) *petrol-pump*, bomba de gasolina, surtidor de (*o* bomba para distribuir) gasolina.

petroleum [pe'trouliəm], *s.* petróleo bruto, crudos.

petroliferous [petro'lifərəs], *a.* petrolífero.

petrology [pe'trɔlodʒi], *s.* petrología.

petrous ['petrəs], *a.* pétreo, petroso.

petticoat ['petikout], *s.* enaguas, justillo, combinación, zagalejo, basquiña, fustán, guardapiés, faldas; (*elec.*) aislador de campana (de hilos telegráficos); *petticoat-pipe*, tubo de escape de la caja de humos, eyector para activar el tiro (de locomotora). — *a.* propio de las mujeres.

pettifogger ['petifɔgəɹ], *s.* picapleitos, leguleyo, sofista, *m.f.*

pettifoggery [peti'fɔgəri], *s.* trapacería, abogacía, sofismo.

pettifogging, *s.* sofista, charlatán, embaidor, quisquilloso.

pettiness ['petinis], *s.* pequeñez, mezquindad, insignificancia.

pettish, *a.* enojadizo, quisquilloso, áspero, bronco, regañón, displicente.

pettishness, *s.* berrinche, mal humor, displicencia, capricho, enojo.

petty ['peti], *a.* despreciable, mezquino, insignificante; inferior, subalterno; (*ant.*) pequeño; *petty king*, reyezuelo; *petty larceny*, hurto menor; *petty cash*, gastos menores.

petulance ['petjuːləns], **petulancy** ['petjuːlənsi], *s.* berrinche, displicencia, mal humor, mal genio; (*ant.*) petulancia, descaro.

petulant, *a.* displicente, enojadizo, malhumorado; (*ant.*) petulante, descarado.

petunia [pe'tjuːniə], *s.* petunia.

pew [pjuː], *s.* banco de iglesia.

pewit ['piːwit], *s.* (*orn.*) avefría, frailecillo [PEEWIT].

pewter ['pjuːtəɹ], *s.* peltre. — *a.* de peltre.

pewterer, *s.* peltrero, estañador.

phaeton ['feitən], *s.* faetón; (*ent.*) meliteo.

phalanx ['fælæŋks], *s.* (*pl.* **phalanges, phalanxes**) falange, *f.*

phallic ['fælik], *a.* fálico.

phantasm ['fæntæzm], **phantasma** [fæn'tæzmə], *s.* fantasma, *m.*

phantasmagoria [fæntæsmə'gɔːriə], *s.* fantasmagoría.

phantasmagoric, *a.* fantasmagórico.

phantom ['fæntəm], *s.* fantasma, *m.*, espectro, estantigua, visión, sombra.

pharisaic [færi'seik], **pharisaical** [færi'seikəl], *a.* farisaico.

pharisaically, *adv.* de modo farisaico.

pharisaicalness, pharisaism, *s.* farisaísmo.

Pharisee ['færisiː], *s.* fariseo.

pharmaceutic [fɑːɹmə'sjuːtic], **pharmaceutical** [fɑːɹmə'sjuːtikəl], *a.* farmacéutico.

pharmaceutics, *s.pl.* farmacéutica.

pharmacologist, *s.* farmacéutica, farmacopola, *m.f.*

pharmacology [fɑːɹmə'kɔlodʒi], *s.* farmacología.

pharmacopœia [fɑːɹməko'piə], *s.* farmacopea.

pharmacy ['fɑːɹməsi], *s.* farmacia.

pharos ['feərɔs], **phare** [feəɹ], *s.* faro.

pharyngoscope [fæ'riŋgoskoup], *s.* faringoscopio.

pharynx ['færiŋks], *s.* faringe, *f.*

phase [feiz], *s.* fase, *f.*, aspecto.

pheasant ['fezənt], *s.* faisán.

phenacetin [fe'næsətin], *s.* fenacetina.

phenazone ['fenəzoun], *s.* antipirina.

phenic ['fenik], *a.* fénico.

phenix ['feniks], *m.* fénix. (*ant. f.*).

phenol ['fenɔl], *s.* fenol, ácido fénico.

phenomenal [fe'nɔminəl], *a.* fenomenal.

phenomenon [fe'nɔminən], *s.* (*pl.* **phenomena**) fenómeno.

phenyl ['fenil], *s.* (*quím.*) fenilo.

phew [fjuː], *interj.* ¡uf! ¡caramba! ¡de buena!

phial [faiəl], *s.* redoma, redomilla, fraseo.

Philadelphian [filə'delfiən], *a.* de Filadelfia; de Ptolomeo Filadelfo.

philander [fi'lændəɹ], *v.i.* hacer cocos, galantear. — *s.* (*ant.*) pretendiente, amante.

philanderer, *s.* tenorio, galanteador.

philanthropic [filən'θrɔpik], **philanthropical** [filən'θrɔpikəl], *a.* filantrópico.

philanthropy [fi'lænθropi], *s.* filantropía, humanidad.

philanthropist, *s.* filántropo.

philatelic [filə'telik], *a.* filatélico.

philatelist, *s.* filatelista, *m.f.*

philately [fi'lætəli], *s.* filatelia.

philharmonic [filhɑːɹ'mɔnik] *a.* filarmónico.

philhellene ['filheli:n], **philhellenist** [filhe-'li:nist], s. filoheleno.
philippic [fi'lipik], s. filípica.
Philistine ['filistain], s., a. filisteo; inculto, iletrado.
philologist, s. filólogo.
philologic, philological, a. filológico.
philology [fi'lɔlodʒi], s. filología.
philomel ['filomel], s. (poét.) filomela.
philopena [filo'pi:nə], s. juego casero de prendas.
philosopher [fi'lɔsofəɹ], s. filósofo, sabio; natural philosopher, físico; philosopher's stone, piedra filosofal.
philosophic [filo'sɔfik], **philosophical** [filo-'sɔfikəl], a. filósofo, filosófico.
philosophism, s. filosofismo.
philosophist, s. filosofista, m.f.
philosophize, v.i. filosofar.
philosophy [fi'lɔsofi], s. filosofía, metafísica; fortaleza de ánimo; natural philosophy, física.
philotechnic [failo'teknik], a. filotécnico.
philter, philtre ['filtəɹ], s. filtro. — v.t. hechizar con filtro.
phimosis [fai'mousis], s. fimosis, f.
phiz [fiz], s. (vulg.) facha, cara, fisionomía.
phlebitis [fle'baitis], s. flebitis, f.
phlebotomist, s. flebótomo, flebotomiano.
phlebotomize, v.t. sangrar.
phlebotomy [fle'bɔtomi], s. flebotomía.
phlegm [flem], s. flema, gargajo; (fig.) flema, apatía, lentitud, cachaza.
phlegmasia, s. flegmasia.
phlegmatic [fleg'mætik], a. flemático.
phlegmatically, adv. flemáticamente.
phlegmon, s. flemón.
phlegmonous, a. flegmóneo, flemonoso.
phlogistic [flo'dʒistik], a. (quím.) flogístico; (med.) inflamatorio.
phlogiston [flo'dʒistɔn], s. flogisto.
phlox [flɔks], s. flox, f.
phobia ['foubiə], s. fobia, aversión mórbida.
phoca ['foukə], s. foca.
phoebe bird ['fi:bi bə:ɹd], s. febe (Sayornis phoebe).
Phœnician [fe'ni:ʃən], s., a. fenicio.
phœnix ['fi:niks], s. fénix, m. (ant. f.).
phonetic, phonetical, a. fonético.
phonetics [fo'netiks], s. fonética.
phonic ['founik, 'fɔnik], a. fónico.
phonograph ['founogræf], s. fonógrafo.
phonographer, s. taquígrafo fonético.
phonographic, phonographical, a. fonográfico.
phonography [fo'nɔgrəfi], s. fonografía.
phonology [fo'nɔlodʒi], s. fonología.
phonometer, s. fonómetro.
phonometric, a. fonométrico.
phonometry [fo'nɔmetri], s. fonometría.
phonotypic, a. fonotípico.
phonotypy ['founotaipi], s. fonotipia.
phosphate ['fɔsfeit], s. fosfato.
phosphatic, a. fosfático.
phosphor ['fɔsfɔɹ], s. (quím.) fósforo; Phosphor, fósforo, la estrella matutina.
phosphorate, v.t. impregnar de fósforo.
phosphoresce, v.i. fosforescer, ser fosforescente.
phosphorescence [fɔsfo'resəns], s. fosforescencia.
phosphorescent, a. fosforescente.

phosphoric [fɔs'fɔrik], a. fosfórico.
phosphorite, s. fosforita.
phosphorization, s. fosforización.
phosphorize ['fɔsforaiz], v.t. fosforescer.
phosphorous, a. fosforoso.
phosphorus, s. fósforo.
phosphuret, s. fosfuro.
photogenic [fouto'dʒenik], a. fotogénico.
photograph ['foutogræf], s. fotografía; photo, foto, f. — v.t. fotografiar, retratar, sacar un retrato.
photographer [fo'tɔgrəfəɹ], s. fotógrafo.
photographic [fouto'græfik], a. fotográfico.
photography [fo'tɔgrəfi], s. fotografía.
photogravure [foutogrə'vju:əɹ], s. fotograbado.
photolithograph, v.t. fotolitografiar.
photolithographic, a. fotolitográfico.
photolithography [foutoli'θɔgrəfi], s. fotolitografía.
photometer [fo'tɔmetəɹ], s. fotómetro.
photometric, a. fotométrico.
photometry [fo'tɔmetri], s. fotometría.
photophone ['foutofoun], s. fotófono.
photosphere ['foutosfiəɹ], s. fotosfera.
phototypography, s. fototipografía.
phototypy ['foutotaipi], s. fototipia.
phrase [freiz], s. frase, f., locución, modismo, período, estilo; (mús.) frase, f., cláusula; phrase-book, manual de conversación. — v.t. frasear, expresar, redactar.
phraseologist, s. fraseologista, m.f.
phraseology [freizi'ɔlodʒi], s. fraseología, estilo, construcción.
phrenetic [fre'netik], a. frenético. — s. frenético.
phrenetically, adv. frenéticamente.
phrenitis [fre naitis], s. frenitis, f., fiebre cerebral, frenesí.
phrenologic, phrenological, a. frenológico.
phrenologist, s. frenólogo.
phrenology [fre'nɔlodʒi], s. frenología.
phrenopathy [fre'nɔpəθi], s. frenopatía.
Phrygian ['fridʒən], a. frigio.
phthisical ['tizikəl], a. tísico.
phthisis ['taisis], s. tisis, f.
phylactery [fi'læktəri], s. filacteria.
phyllite ['filait], s. filita.
phyllome ['filoum], s. (bot.) hoja.
phyllotaxis [filo'tæksis], s. filotaxia.
phylloxera [fi'lɔkzərə], s. filoxera.
phylogeny [fi'lɔdʒeni], s. filogenia.
physic ['fizik], s. medicina; purga, purgante; remedio. — v.t. purgar, medicamentar, medicinar.
physical, a. físico; médico, medicinal; físico, material.
physician [fi'ziʃən], s. médico; (ant.) físico.
physicist ['fizisist], s. físico.
physicky, a. purgante.
physics, s. física.
physiognomic, physiognomical, a. fisionómico.
physiognomist [fizi'ɔnomist], s. fisónomo, fisonomista, m.f.
physiognomy [fizi'ɔnomi], s. fisonomía, estudio de la fisionomía; fisionomía.
physiologic [fizio'lɔdʒik], **physiological** [fizio'lɔdʒikəl], a. fisiológico.
physiologist [fizi'ɔlodʒist], s. fisiólogo.
physiology [fizi'ɔlodʒi], s. fisiología.
physique [fi'zi:k], s. físico, presencia, figura.

phytologist, *s*. fitólogo.

phytology [fai'tɔlodʒi], *s*. fitología.

pia mater ['paiə'meitəɪ], *s*. (*anat*.) piamáter, *f*.; (*fig*.) los sesos.

pianissimo [pi:ə'nisimou], *a*., *adv*. (*mús*.) pianísimo.

pianist ['pi:ənist], *s*. pianista, *m.f*.

piano [pi'ænou, pi:'ɑ:nou], *s*. (*mús*.) pianoforte, piano. — *a*., *adv*. piano, dulcemente; *grand piano*, piano de cola; *baby grand piano*, piano de media cola; *upright piano*, piano vertical; *piano tuner*, afinador de pianos; *to play the piano*, tocar el piano.

pianoforte [pi:ænou'fɔ:ɪti], *s*. (*mús*.) pianoforte, piano.

piastre [pi'æstəɪ], *s*. escudo, duro, peso; moneda turca.

piazza [pi'ætsəɪ], *s*. plaza; pórtico, colunata, galería.

pibroch ['pi:brɔk], *s*. música marcial tocada con la gaita; (*poét*.) gaita.

pica ['paikə], *s*. (*med*.) pica; (*orn*.) urraca; (*impr*.) cícero.

picamar ['pikəmɑ:ɪ], *s*. compuesto oleoso obtenido de la destilación del alquitrán de madera.

picaroon [pikə'ru:n], *s*. pirata, *m*.; ladrón, picarón.

piccaninny, pickaninny ['pikənini], *s*. (*despec*.) muchacho negro, muchacha negra.

piceous ['pisiəs], *a*. negro de azabache, negro marrón o rojizo; inflamable.

pick [pik], *v.t*. elegir, escoger, recoger, tomar, coger; picar, agujerear, romper con pico, picotear; limpiar, mondar; robar, hurtar, ratear; descañonar (una ave); abrir (una cerradura) con ganzúa; *to pick a bone*, roer un hueso; ajustar cuentas, dar para peras; *to pick and choose*, melindrear; titubear, vacilar; *to pick to pieces*, (*fig*.) criticar, critiquizar, fiscalizar; *to pick a quarrel*, buscar camorra; *to pick someone's pocket*, limpiar la faltriquera a; *to pick off*, arrancar; fusilar; *to pick out*, recoger, coger, elegir; *to pick up*, recoger, coger; encontrar; *to pick up a bargain*, dar con una ganga; *to have a bone to pick with someone*, tener que ajustar cuentas con uno, habérselas con; *pick-me-up*, bebida o medicina para restablecerse; trinquis (*fam*.). — *v.i*. comer poco, comer bocaditos; comiscar, picar. — *s*. escogimiento; pico, martillo; mondadientes; ganzúa, punzón; suciedad, porquería; cosecha.

pickaback ['pikəbæk], *adv*. sobre los hombros.

pickaninny, *s*. [PICCANINNY].

pickaxe ['pikæks], *s*. pico, piqueta, espiocha, zapapico.

picked, *a*. selecto, escogido, precioso; espinoso; puntiagudo; mondado, limpio. — *p.p*. [PICK].

picker, *s*. escogedor, escardador; (*tej*.) recibidor.

pickerel ['pikərəl], *s*. sollo pequeño.

picket ['pikit], *s*. estaca, piquete; (*mil*.) piquete. — *v.t*. atar a la estaca; cercar con estacas; (*mil*.) colocar de guardia, poner piquetes.

picking, *s*. cosecha, recolección; roedura, acción de roer un hueso; monda, limpia; arrancamiento; escogimiento, elección; robo,

hurto; picadura. — *pl*. **pickings**, residuos, desperdicios, desechos; hurtos, raterías.

pickle ['pikəl], *s*. escabeche, salmuera, adobo; encurtido; condición, estado; (*fam*.) enredo, apuro, lío; (*fam*.) diablillo, picaruelo, niño travieso; *to have a rod in pickle for*, tenérsela guardada a; *mixed pickles*, mescolanza, mixtifori. — *v.t*. escabechar, adobar, encurtir, conservar en adobo; regañar, reñir.

picklock, *s*. ganzúa; llave falsa; ladrón nocturno.

pickpocket, pickpurse, *s*. ratero, cortabolsas, carterista, *m*.

pickthank, *s*. (*ant*.) complaciente, oficioso, zalamero; entrometido.

Pickwickian [pik'wikiən], *a*. relativo o referente a Mr. Pickwick; (*fig*.) hipotético; optimista; no literal.

picnic ['piknik], *s*. excursión al campo, partida de campo, romería, jira. — *v.i*. ir de excursión o de romería o de jira al campo.

pictotee [piko'ti:], *s*. clavel moteado.

picrate ['pikrit], *s*. picrato.

picric ['pikrik], *a*. pícrico.

Pict [pikt], *s*. picto, individuo de una antigua raza que habitaba la Caledonia.

pictograph ['piktogræf], *s*. pictografía.

pictorial [pik'tɔ:riəl], *a*. pictórico, gráfico.

pictorially, *adv*. de una manera pictórica.

picture ['piktʃəɪ], *s*. cuadro, pintura; retrato; diseño; ilustración; lámina; semejanza, imagen, *f*., estampa, grabado; fotografía; *picture book*, libro de estampas, libro con láminas; *to be the picture of someone*, ser el retrato de uno; *to be the picture of grief*, ser una imagen del dolor. — *v.t*. pintar, dibujar, hacer un cuadro, hacer el retrato de; imaginar, figurarse; (*fig*.) pintar, describir.

picturesque [piktʃəɪ'esk], *a*. pintoresco.

picturesqueness, *s*. pintoresco.

piddle ['pidəl], *v.i*. (*vulg*.) mear, orinar; comiscar, picar la comida; escatimar, emplearse en bagatelas.

piddler, *s*. hombre mezquino, escatimoso y despreciable.

piddling, *a*. mezquino y despreciable.

pidgin-English [pidʒin'iŋgliʃ], *s*. inglés chapurrado; mezcla de chino, portugués y malayo usado en el Oriente; *it's not my pidgin*, (*fam*.) *v*. **pigeon**.

pie [pai], *s*. pastel, tarta, empanada; (*orn*.) marica, urraca; (*impr*.) masa mezclada de tipos de imprenta; *to have a finger in the pie*, meter cuchara, tener metida la mano en la masa.

piebald ['paibɔ:ld], *s*., *a*. pío, manchado, abigarrado; (*fig*.) mestizo.

piece [pi:s], *s*. pedazo, fragmento, pieza, trozo; porción; remiendo, retazo, cacho; división, parte, *f*., sección; obra, composición, escrito; hecho, cosa; rasgo; acto, acción; cuadro; casco (de botella); (*arti*.) pieza (cañón, fusil, escopeta); *piece of advice*, consejo; *piece of furniture*, mueble; *piece of ground*, solar; *piece of money*, pieza; *piece of news*, noticia, informe; *piece work*, obra o trabajo a destajo; *piece of wit*, agudeza, chiste; *all of a piece*, de una sola pieza; *to pull to pieces*, despedazar, desgarrar; *to come to pieces*, deshacerse, desarmarse, desbaratarse; *to break in pieces*, hacer añicos; *to cut an army to pieces*, destrozar un ejército; *to give* *someone a piece of one's mind*, decirle a uno las verdades del barquero. — *v.t.* unir, juntar, remendar, apedazar, echar pedazos; *to piece out*, prolongar, alargar; *to piece up*, reparar, remendar, apedazar.

pieceless, *a.* todo de una pieza.

piecemeal ['piːsmiːl], *adv.* en pedazos, en fragmentos, a bocados, a bocaditos, a pedacitos; por partes.

piecer, *s.* remendón.

pied [paid], *a.* manchado, variegado, abigarrado, pío, de varios colores, abigarrado.

piedness, *s.* variedad de colores.

pier [piəɹ], *s.* embarcadero; desembarcadero; muelle, malecón; espolón, escollera; pila, pilar, pilón, estribo de puente; (*arq.*) entrepaño; *pier-glass*, tremó, espejo de cuerpo entero; *pier-table*, consola.

pierage ['piəridʒ], *s.* muellaje.

pierce [piəɹs], *v.t.* penetrar, taladrar, agujerear, horadar, clavar, pinchar, acribillar, traspasar, atravesar; abrir paso o camino a la fuerza; *pierced with sorrow*, traspasado de dolor. — *v.i.* penetrar, internarse.

piercer, *s.* aguijón, taladro.

piercing, *a.* penetrante; cortante; agudo. — *s.* abertura, penetración.

piercingness, *s.* penetración, agudeza.

pierrot ['piərou], *s.* payaso, bufón, cómico.

pietism ['paiitizm], *s.* pietismo.

pietist, *s.* pietista, *m.f.*

piety ['paiiti], *s.* piedad, devoción, santidad.

piffle ['pifəl], *v.i.* disparatar, hablar en camelo. — *s.* disparates, boberías, patochadas, patrañas.

piffling, *a.* disparatado, fútil, ñoño.

pig [pig], *s.* puerco, cerdo, cochino, marrano, cochinillo, lechón; (*fund.*) barra, lingote, tejo, pigote; *guinea pig*, conejo de India; *sucking pig*, lechoncillo; *to buy a pig in a poke*, comprar o hacer a ciegas, salga pez o salga rana, al buen tuntún. — *v.i.* parir (la puerca); vivir como cochinos, vivir mal; *to pig it*, (*vulg.*) vivir cochinamente.

pigeon ['pidʒin], *s.* palomo, paloma, pichón; (*fig.*) bobalicón; *carrier-pigeon*, paloma mensajera; *wild pigeon*, paloma torcaz; *pigeon-dung*, palomina; *pigeon-breast*, deformidad causada por la raquitis; *that's his pigeon*, (*fam.*), allá él, con su pan se lo coma.

pigeon-foot, *s.* (*bot.*) pie de milano.

pigeon-hearted, *a.* cobarde, tímido.

pigeon-house, *s.* palomar.

pigeonry, *s.* palomar.

piggery ['pigəri], *s.* pocilga, chiquero, zahurda.

piggin ['pigin], *s.* cubo pequeño generalmente de madera.

piggish, *a.* de cochino; sucio, puerco, voraz.

pig-headed, *a.* cabezudo, estúpido, terco.

pig-iron, *s.* hierro en barras.

pigmean ['pigmiən], *a.* de pigmeo.

pigment ['pigmənt], *s.* pigmento, pintura, color.

pigmy ['pigmi], *s.* pigmeo, enano. — *a.* muy pequeño.

pignut ['pignʌt], *s.* (*E.U.*) nuez del nogal (*Carya porcina*).

pigsty ['pigstai], *s.* pocilga.

pigtail ['pigteil], *s.* coleta.

pike [paik], *s.* (*ict.*) sollo, lucio; pica, guincho, chuzo; (*agr.*) horca, horquilla; camino de

barrera; barrera de portazgo; (*E.U.*) carretera, ruta nacional.

piked, *a.* puntiagudo.

pikeman, *s.* piquero, chucero.

pikestaff, *s.* asta de pica; *as plain as a pikestaff*, a bola vista, de clavo pasado, está visto.

pilar ['pailɑːɹ], *a.* perteneciente o relativo al cabello.

pilaster [pi'læstəɹ], *s.* pilastra.

pilch, *s.* envoltorio de franela para infantes.

pilchard ['piltʃəɹd], *s.* sardina, arenque.

pile [pail], *s.* pila, montón, hacina, rimero, cúmulo; pilote, estaca; pira, hoguera; pelo; fibra, pelo, pelillo; edificio grande y macizo; cruz de una moneda; (*elec.*) pila galvánica; *atomic pile*, pila atómica; *funeral pile*, pira; *to make one's pile*, (*fig., fam.*) hacer su pacotilla. — *pl.* **piles**, almorranas, hemorroides, *f.* — *v.t.* apilar, amontonar, acumular; clavar estacas; formar pabellones con los fusiles; *to pile up*, amontonarse; (*fam.*) estrellarse, encallar.

pileate ['pailieit], **pileated** ['pailieitid], *a.* en forma de sombrero.

pileous ['pailiəs], *s.* píleo.

pilework ['pailwəːɹk], *s.* pilotaje, estructura de pilotes.

pilfer ['pilfəɹ], *v.t.* hurtar, ratear, birlar, sisar.

pilferer, *s.* ratero, sisón.

pilfering, *s.* ratería, sisa.

pilgrim ['pilgrim], *s.* peregrino, romero. — *v.i.* peregrinar, ir de romería.

pilgrimage, *s.* peregrinación, romería.

pill [pil], *s.* píldora; sinsabor, desazón, *f.*; (*vulg.*) machaca, posma, *m.f.* — *pl.* (*vulg.*) bolas de billar. — *v.t.* medicinar con píldoras.

pillage ['pilidʒ], *v.t.* pillar, robar, hurtar, saquear. — *s.* pillaje, saqueo, rapiña, depredación, botín.

pillager, *s.* pillador, saqueador, hurtador.

pillar ['piləɹ], *s.* pilar, columna, puntal; (*fig.*) soporte, sostén; *to go from pillar to post*, ir de Ceca en Meca.

pillared, *a.* sostenido con columnas.

pillion ['piljən], *s.* sillón, albarda, grupera, grupa.

pillory ['pilori], *s.* cepo, picota. — *v.t.* empicotar.

pillow ['pilou], *s.* almohada, cabezal; (*mec.*) cojín, cojinete; *pillow of the bowsprit*, (*mar.*) tragante del bauprés; *pillow-case*, funda de almohada. — *v.t.* poner sobre la almohada.

pilose, **pilous** ['pailəs], *a.* piloso, peludo, velloso.

pilosity, *s.* vellosidad.

pilot ['pailət], *s.* piloto, práctico, guía; carta de marear; consejero; (*f.c.*) trompa, quitapiedras (de la locomotora); *pilot-balloon*, globo de ensayo. — *v.t.* dirigir, aconsejar, guiar, gobernar; pilotar, pilotear (buque, avión, etc.).

pilotage, **piloting**, *s.* pilotaje, practicaje.

pilot-bird, *s.* (*orn.*) pájaro-piloto.

pilot-fish, *s.* (*ict.*) piloto.

pimp [pimp], *s.* alcahuete. — *v.i.* alcahuetear, echacorvear.

pimpernel ['pimpəɹnel], *s.* pimpinela, pamplina.

pimping, *a.* (*fam.*) muy pequeño, miserable, fútil, mezquino; enfermizo, enclenque.

pimple ['pimpəl], *s.* grano, pupa, barro.

pimpled, *a.* engranujado, granujiento.

pimply, *a.* barroso, granujiento.

pin [pin], *s.* alfiler, espiga, pasador, clavija, perno, clavo, clavillo; prendedor, broche; pequeño barril de 4½ galones. — *pl.* (*vulg.*) las piernas; *drawing-pin*, chinche; *firing-pin*, aguja de percusión; *hair-pin*, horquilla para el cabello; *linch-pin*, pezonera; *rolling-pin*, hataca, rodillo; *pin-case*, alfiletero; *pin-head*, cabeza de alfiler; cosa muy pequeña; *pin-point*, punta de alfiler; *pin money*, (dinero para) alfileres; *I don't care a pin*, no se me da un bledo. — *v.t.* prender o asegurar con alfileres; remangar con alfileres; *to pin up*, recoger y asegurar con alfileres o horquillas; *to pin one's faith to*, confiar absolutamente en.

pinafore ['pinəfɔ:ɹ], *s.* delantal de niño.

pince-nez ['pɑ:nsnei], *s.* quevedos.

pincers ['pinsəɹz], *s.pl.* tenazas, tenazuelas, tenacillas, pinzas, entenallas; (*zool.*) pinza.

pinch [pintʃ], *v.t.* pellizcar, repizcar; apretar, aplastar; apretar con pinzas; oprimir, perseguir; adelgazar, contraer; quitar, arrancar; agarrar, morder (animales); sufrir, experimentar (hambre, frío, etc.); (*fam.*) hurtar, birlar; coger, meter a la sombra, prender; (*mar.*) ceñir el viento (un buque). — *v.i.* pellizcar, acosar, apretar; escatimar; limitar gastos, ahorrar, economizar; padecer, sufrir; picar; *to know where the shoe pinches*, saber dónde aprieta el zapato. — *s.* pellizco, pizco; opresión, apuro, aprieto; tormento, dolor; extrema necesidad; pulgarada, polvo; *at a pinch*, en caso de apuro.

pinchbeck ['pintʃbek], *s.* similor; (*fig.*) falso, oropel.

pinchers, *s.pl.* tenazas.

pinchfist, *s.* avaro.

pinching, *a.* que aprieta, que pellizca; urgente. — *s.* apretón, pellizco.

pincushion ['pinkuʃən], *s.* acerico.

Pindaric [pin'dærik], *a.* Pindárico.

pine [pain], *s.* pino, madera de pino; *pitch-pine*, pino de tea; *Scots-pine*, pino de Escocia; *pine-marten*, marta cibelina; *pine-tree State*, (*E.U.*) el estado de Maine. — *v.i.* descaecer, languidecer estar lánguido, desfallecer, consumirse, anelar; *to pine away*, languidecer, morirse de pena. — *v.t.* hacer descaecer; *to pine after* (o *for*), desear con vehemencia, suspirar por.

pineapple ['painæpəl], *s.* ananás, ananá, *m.*, piña (de América).

pine-cone, *s.* piña.

pine-house, pinery, *s.* invernadero de ananás.

pinene ['paini:n], *s.* pineno.

pinfold ['pinfould], *s.* redil.

ping [piŋ], *s.* silbido de una bala; zas, pum, tris.

ping-pong ['piŋpɔŋ], *s.* ping-pong, pin-pon, tenis de mesa.

pinguid ['piŋgwid], *a.* craso, gordo, pingüe.

pining ['painiŋ], *a.* lánguido, abatido. — *s.* deseo vehemente, anhelo, languidez.

pinion ['pinjən], *s.* piñón, ala de ave, alón; (*mec.*) piñón. — *v.t.* atar las alas; poner esposas, maniatar; encadenar, agarrotar.

pinioned, *a.* alado; maniatado.

pink [piŋk], *a.* rojizo. — *s.* (*bot.*) clavel, dianto, clavelito; color de rosa; casaquín de caza; espejo; modelo; (*mar.*) *pink-sterned*,

de proa puntiaguda; (*cost.*) picadura; *he is the pink of politeness*, es muy cortés; *in the pink of health*, en sana salud. — *a.* rosado. — *v.t.* ojetear, calar, picar. — *v.i.* guiñar; (*auto.*) picar.

pinker, *s.* recortador, picador.

pinkeye, *s.* catarro epidémico de los caballos, acompañado de oftalmía; oftalmía purulenta contagiosa.

pinking, *s.* recortadura; picadura.

pinkish, pinky, *a.* rosado.

pinna ['pinə], *s.* (*zool.*) ala, aleta; (*anat.*) pabellón externo del oído.

pinnace ['pinəs], *s.* pinaza.

pinnacle ['pinəkəl], *s.* (*arq.*) pináculo; cumbre, *f.*, cima, remate, fastigio.

pinnate ['pineit], **pinnated,** *a.* (*bot.*) pinado, alado.

pinnatafid [pi'nætəfid], *a.* pinatífido.

pinner ['pinəɹ], *s.* (*ant.*) especie de toca de mujer; (*prov.*) delantal.

pinnigrade ['pinigreid], *a.* (*zool.*) que se mueve por medio de aletas (v.g. la foca).

pinnock ['pinək], *s.* (*orn.*) paro.

pinnule ['pinju:l], *s.* (*bot.*) pínula, hojuela; (*zool.*) aleta pequeña.

pint [paint], *s.* pinta (47 centilitros, octava parte de galón).

pintle ['pintəl], *s.* clavija; macho de timón.

pinwheel, *s.* molinete de juegos artificiales; rueda de engranaje con clavijas.

pinworm, *s.* gusano pequeño.

piolet [pi'oulei], *s.* pico de trepador de hielo.

pioneer [paio'niəɹ], *s.* explorador, iniciador, descubridor; (*mil.*) zapador, gastador, palero. — *v.t.*, *v.i.* explorar, ir delante, abrir un camino, guiar, introducir, promover.

pious ['paiəs], *a.* piadoso, pío, devoto, religioso.

pip [pip], *s.* pepita; moquillo; punto (en el juego). — *v.i.* piar. — *v.t.* romper el cascarón (el polluelo, etc.).

pipe [paip], *s.* cañón, tubo, caño, conducto; pipa; (*mús.*) caramillo, churumbela; (*mar.*) chiflo; silbo, silbido; tonel (usual de 105 galones); casco; *branch pipe*, tubo de empalme; *discharging-pipe*, tubo de descarga; *main pipe*, tubo principal; *waste pipe*, tubo de relleno; *water pipe*, conducto de agua, cañería; *pipe clay*, blanquizal, tierra de pipas; *to pipe-clay*, blanquear con tierra de pipas. — *pl.* la gaita. — *v.t.* tocar la flauta; silbar. — *v.i.* gritar, pipar; tocar la gaita; *to pipe one's eye*, (*fam.*) soltar el trapo, hacer pucheros, llorar a lágrima viva.

pipe-laying, *s.* instalación de cañerías.

piper, *s.* flautista, *m.f.*, gaitero, flautero.

pipe-stock, *s.* terraja.

pipe-tree, *s.* lila.

pipette [pi'pet], *s.* pipeta.

piping, *s.* cordoncillo; gemido; tubería, cañería; (*mar.*) raya de cuerda; (*cost.*) cordoncillo, vivo; *piping hot*, muy caliente, hirviente.

pipit, *s.* especie de alondra del género *Anthus*.

pipkin ['pipkin], *s.* pucherito, ollita.

pippin ['pipin], *s.* (*bot.*) esperiega, camuesa.

piquancy ['pi:kənsi], *s.* acrimonia, picante.

piquant ['pi:kənt], *a.* picante, sazonado; (*fig.*) sabroso, gustoso, incitante, estimulante; (*ant.*) picante, mordaz.

pique [pi:k], *s.* pique, resentimiento, rencilla,

desabrimiento, desazón, *f.*; pundonor; piqué, tela de algodón. — *v.t.* picar, provocar, enojar, ofender, irritar, hendir; *to pique oneself on,* jactarse, picarse de.

piquet [pi'ket, 'piket], *s.* séptimo, juego de los cientos.

piracy ['pairəsi], *s.* piratería.

pirate [paiərət], *s.* pirata, *m.,* corsario; (*fig.*) plagiario. — *v.t.* falsificar. — *v.i.* piratear, plagiar, hurtar, robar.

pirated, *a.* falsificado.

piratical [pai'rætikəl], *a.* pirático.

pirn [pəːn], *s.* carrete, huso, lanzadera, bobina.

pirogue [pi'roug], *a.* piragua.

pirouette [piro'et], *s.* pirueta, girada. — *v.i.* hacer piruetas.

piscatorial [piskə'tɔːriəl], **piscatory** ['piskətəri], *a.* piscatorio.

pisciculture ['pisikʌltʃəɹ], *s.* piscicultura.

pisciculturist, *s.* piscicultor.

piscina [pi'siːnə], *s.* piscina.

piscinal, *a.* relativo a la piscina.

piscine, *a.* de pescado.

piscivorous [pi'sivərəs], *a.* piscívoro, ictiófago.

pish [piʃ], *interj.* ¡quita allá! — *v.i.* expresar desprecio.

pismire ['pismaiəɹ], *s.* (*entom.*) hormiga.

pisolite ['pisolait], *s.* variedad de calcita.

piss [pis], *v.i.* (*vulg.*) orinar, mear. — *s.* orina.

pissasphalt ['pisəsfælt], *s.* pisasfalto.

pistachio [pis'tɑːʃou], *s.* (*bot.*) pistacho, alfóncigo.

pistil ['pistil], *s.* pistilo.

pistol ['pistəl], *s.* pistola, revólver. — *v.t.* tirar con pistola, matar de un pistolazo.

pistole [pis'toul], *s.* doblón de oro.

piston ['pistən], *s.* macho, émbolo, pistón; (*mús.*) llave, *f.,* pistón; *piston boss,* cubo de émbolo; *piston pin,* (*mec.*) pasador del pistón, muñón de pie de biela; *piston ring,* aro del pistón; *piston rod,* biela, vástago del émbolo; *piston stroke,* carrera del embolo.

pit [pit], *s.* hoyo, hoya, carcavuezo, cárcava, mina; abismo, precipicio, foso; (*teat.*) platea, patio de teatro; boca (del estómago); *armpit,* sobaco; *coal pit,* mina de carbón; *pit-head,* pozo de mina. — *v.t.* marcar con hoyos, carcañar, cavar, excavar; picar.

pitapat ['pitəpæt], *s.* palpitación, tictac. — *adv.* de una manera palpitante.

pitch [pitʃ], *s.* pez, *f.,* betún, alquitrán, brea, resina; echada, echamiento; grado, pendiente, *f.,* declive, bajada; tiro, alcance; (*mús.*) diapasón, tono; (*mar.*) cabezada; extremo, término, punto, fin; *as dark as pitch,* o *pitch-black,* obscuro como boca de lobo, negro como el azabache; *pitch-brush,* escopero; *highest pitch,* (*fig.*) apogeo, cumbre, *f.,* *to carry to too high a pitch,* ir demasiado allá; *concert pitch,* diapasón normal; *to a proper pitch,* hasta un grado razonable; *pitch and toss,* cara o cruz; *pitch-blende,* pech blenda, variedad de uraninita. — *v.t.* plantar, fijar, arreglar; formar, colocar hundir, ordenar; echar, arrojar, tirar; embrear; betunar; arrojar con una horquilla; *pitched battle,* batalla campal. — *v.i.* caerse, caer de cabeza, caerse hacia abajo; empedrar; escoger; balancear; (*mar.*) cabacear un buque; (*mús.*) entonar; establecerse,

fijarse, instalarse; arrojarse; *to pitch into,* echarse en, acometer; *to pitch tents,* (*mil.*) acampar; (*fam.*) reñir con, buscar camorra con.

pitcher, *s.* cántaro, bocal, pichel, jarro; botador, arrojador; en el *baseball,* el que tira la pelota; (*bot.*) ascidia; *little pitchers have long ears,* las paredes oyen.

pitch-farthing, *s.* (juego de) hoyuelo.

pitch-fork, *s.* horca, horquilla; (*mús.*) diapasón normal.

pitchiness, *s.* obscuridad, negrura.

pitching, *s.* balanceo, cuneo; cabeceo, cabeceamiento, cabezada (de un buque). — *a.* inclinado.

pitch-pipe, *s.* diapasón.

pitchy ['pitʃi], *a.* embreado, piceo, peceño, obscuro, negro.

piteous ['pitiəs], *a.* miserable, lastimoso, lastimero; tierno, compasivo.

piteousness, *s.* compasión, ternura; estado miserable y lastimoso.

pitfall ['pitfɔːl], *s.* lazo, trampa, hoya cubierta; (*fig.*) defecto, (*fam.*) pero, peligro latente.

pith [piθ], *s.* meollo de planta; médula; médula espinal; (*fig.*) médula, robustez, energía, vigor, fuerza; substancia, jugo; quinta esencia. — *v.t.* quitar el meollo (o la médula) a.

pithily ['piθili], *adv.* fuertemente, enérgicamente.

pithiness, *s.* fuerza, vigor, energía, eficacia, importancia.

pithless, *a.* falto de meollo; débil.

pithy ['piθi], *a.* meduloso; eficaz, enérgico; sentencioso, expresivo.

pitiable ['pitiəbəl], *a.* sensible, lastimoso, enternecedor, digno de compasión; detestable, despreciable.

pitiableness, *s.* estado lastimoso.

pitiful ['pitiful], *a.* compasivo, lastimoso, sensible, enternecedor; miserable, despreciable.

pitifulness, *s.* compasión, piedad, misericordia, ternura; ruindad, mezquindad, estado lastimoso.

pitiless, *a.* inhumano, cruel, desapiadado, duro de corazón.

pitilessness, *s.* dureza de corazón, inhumanidad.

pitman ['pitmən], *s.* (*pl.* **pitmen**) minero, aserrador de foso.

piton ['piːtɔŋ], *s.* barra, estaca para fijar una cuerda en precipicios.

pittance ['pitəns], *s.* pitanza, ración, porción.

pitted ['pitid], *a.* picado, cacarañado.

pituita, *s.* pituita, moco.

pituitous [pi'tjuːitəs], *a.* pituitoso.

pity ['piti], *s.* piedad, misericordia, conmiseración, compasión, lástima; *for pity's sake,* por piedad. — *v.t.* compadecer, tener lástima. — *v.i.* apiadarse, perdonar, enternecer, tener piedad.

pivot ['pivət], *s.* quicio, pivote, espiga, espigón, gorrón; (*fig.*) eje, polo, punto de partida. — *v.t.* colocar sobre un eje; proveer de pivote. — *v.i.* girar sobre un eje.

pix [piks], *s.* [PYX].

pixy, pixey, pixie ['piksi, piksi], (*pl.* **pixies**) *s.* duende, *f.,* hada.

pizzle ['pizəl], *s.* vergajo de buey.

placability [plækə'biliti], s. placabilidad, dulzura, clemencia.

placable ['plækəbəl], a. placable, aplacable.

placard ['plækɑːɹd], s. cartel, letrero, anuncio, placarte. — v.t. poner carteles (en); publicar por medio de carteles.

placate [plə'keit], v.t. apaciguar, aplacar, conciliar.

placation, s. aplacamiento.

place [pleis], s. sitio, lugar, parte, f., local, paraje; dignidad, empleo, puesto; calle corta y estrecha, callejón; residencia; punto, grado; rango, posición; acomodo; mansión; espacio, asiento, cabida; (mil.) fortaleza, plaza, puesto militar; lugar, texto, pasaje; (com.) asilo; place of refuge, asilo; trading-place, plaza de comercio; watering-place, playa, estación balnearia; abrevedero; in the first place, en primer lugar; in the next place, luego; in place of, en lujar de, en vez de; in no place, en ninguna parte; in the next place, luego, después; out of place, fuera de lugar, mal a propósito; to give place, ceder el paso; to take place, ocurrir, suceder, verificarse, celebrarse; to take the place of, sustituir. — v.t. poner, colocar, situar, fijar, plantar, instalar, establecer, destinar; prestar a interés; señalar, asignar, destinar a un deber.

placenta [plə'sentə], s. placenta.

placer, s. colocador, el que coloca; placer, lavadero de oro o metal precioso.

placet ['pleiset], s. permiso.

placid ['plæsid], a. plácido, tranquilo, apacible, sosegado, benigno.

placidity [plə'siditi], s. apacibilidad, afabilidad, placidez, serenidad.

plagal ['pleigəl], a. (mús.) plagal.

plagiarism ['pleidʒiərizm], s. plagio.

plagiarist, s. plagiario.

plagiarize ['pleidʒəraiz], v.i. plagiar. — v.t. cometer plagios.

plagiary ['pleidʒəri], s. plagio. — a. plagiario.

plagium ['pleidʒəm], s. (for.) secuestro de una persona.

plague [pleig], s. plaga, azote, peste, f., pestilencia; (fig.) plaga, pestilencia, calamidad, miseria; a plague on, llévese el diablo. — v.t. plagar, molestar, atormentar; apestar, infestar, importunar, vejar.

plaguily, adv. (fam.) molestamente.

plaguy ['pleigi], a. (fam.) molesto, enfadoso, apestado.

plaice [pleis], s. (ict.) platija.

plaid [plæd], s. manta escosesa; tartán; diseño en forma de cuadros. — a. variejado.

plain [plein], a. raso, igual, llano, plano, liso; llano, sencillo, sin adorno; claro, distinto, evidente, manifiesto; fácil, simple, sencillo; sincero, ingenuo, natural, puro, bueno, recto, verdadero; humilde, de humilde cuna; ordinario; tupido; feo; plain cooking, cocina casera; plain figures, números visibles; in plain terms, en términos claros; plain chant o plainsong, canto llano; plain dealing, buena fe; a plain man, un hombre sincero; the plain truth, la pura verdad. — adv. claro, claramente, llanamente, sinceramente, distintamente. — s. llano, llanura, llanada, planada, planicie, f.; (geom.) plano. — v.t. (ant.) lamentar. — v.i. (ant.) quejarse, lamentarse, llorar.

plain-dealing, a. sincero, franco. — s. sinceridad, buena fe.

plainly, adv. llanamente, sencillamente, francamente, claramente, evidentemente, de veras.

plainness, s. igualdad, llanura; sencillez, claridad, sinceridad, franqueza; ordinariez, fealdad.

plainsong, s. (igl.) canto llano.

plain-spoken, a. abierto, franco.

plaint [pleint], s. acusación, cargo; (poét.) queja, quejido, lamento.

plaintiff ['pleintif], s. (for.) demandador, demandante.

plaintive ['pleintiv], a. lamentoso, lastimoso, quejumbroso, dolorido.

plaintiveness, s. tono lastimoso, calidad de lastimoso.

plait [plæt], s. (cost.) pliegue, doblez, plegado, alforza; trenza (de cabellos). — v.t. trenzar, alechugar, tejer, encarrujar, encañonar.

plaiter, s. tejedor.

plaiting, s. trenza, trenzado.

plan [plæn], s. plan, proyecto; plano, mapa, m.; planta, diseño, traza, trazado; to draw a plan, levantar un plano. — v.t. proyectar, trazar (un plan), planear; (planta de edificio, etc.) planear, trazar.

planch [plɑːntʃ], s. plancha de metal o refractaria usada por los esmaltadores.

planchet ['plɑːntʃət], s. tejuelo, disco metálico para acuñar.

planchette [plɑːn'ʃet], s. plancheta, tabla de escritura mesmérica.

plane [plein], s. (geom.) plano, superficie plana; (carp.) cepillo; (bot.) plátano; nivel; (fam.) avión. — a. llano, plano. — v.t. acepillar, allanar, desbastar; alisar.

plane-tree, s. plátano (árbol).

planer, s. acepillador; (impr.) tamborilete.

planet ['plænit], s. planeta, m.

planetary ['plænitəri], a. planetario.

planimeter [plæ'nimitəɹ], s. planímetro.

planimetric, planimetrical, a. planimétrico.

planimetry [plæ'nimitri], s. planimetría.

planing ['pleiniŋ], s. acepilladura.

planish ['plæniʃ], v.t. allanar, aplanar, alisar, pulir.

planisher, v.t. planador, aplanador, alisador.

planisphere ['plænisfiəɹ], s. planisferio.

plank [plæŋk], s. tabla gruesa, tablón. — pl. tablado, entablado, entarimado. — v.t. entarimar, entablar, enmaderar; (min.) encofrar.

planking, s. entablado, tablado; tablazón.

plankton, s. plancton.

planner ['plænəɹ], s. proyectista, m.f., calculista, m.f.; trazador, tracista, m.f.

planometry [plə'nɔmetri], s. planometría.

plant [plɑːnt], s. (bot.) planta, hierba, mata; material; (mec.) instalación, equipo. — v.t. plantar, sembrar, colocar, instalar, poner, fundar, establecer.

plantain ['plæntən], s. (bot.) llantén; plátano (musa paradisiaca).

plantation [plɑːn'teiʃən], s. plantación, plantel, plantío, colonia; siembra, ingenio, hacienda; ostrera, ostral.

planter ['plɑːntəɹ], s. plantador, cultivador, colono, hacendado.

plantigrade ['plæntigreid], a. plantígrado. — s. animal plantígrado.

planting ['plɑːntiŋ], s. plantación; arboricultura.

plant-louse ['plɑːntlaus], s. brugo.

plaque [plɑːk], s. placa, plancha; medalla; disco; (*pat.*, *zool.*, *etc.*) disco, marca circular en la superficie del cuerpo.

plash [plæʃ], s. charco, charquillo, aguazal, lagunajo, chapoteo, chapaleteo. — *v.t.*, *v.i.* chapotear, chapalear; salpicar; (*pint.*) manchar.

plashy, a. pantanoso; manchado.

plasm [plæzm], s. molde, matriz, *f.*; (*biol.*) plasma, *m.*

plasma ['plæzmə], s. plasma, *m.*

plasmic, a. plasmático.

plaster ['plɑːstəɪ], s. yeso; argamasa, mortero; enlucido; estuco; esparadrapo (medicamento); *court plaster*, tafetán inglés; *mustard plaster*, sinapismo; *plaster of Paris*, escayola; *plaster work*, enyesado, enlucido. — *v.t.* enyesar, enlucir; emplastar, poner emplastos; revocar; (*fig.*) embadurnar, untar, embarrar.

plasterer, s. yesero; enjalbegador, estuquista, *m.f.*, revocador; plasmante.

plastering, a. que enyesa. — s. acción de enyesar; enyesado, obra de yeso, enlucido; emplastadura; embarradura.

plastic ['plæstik], a. plástico; *plastic art*, plástica; *plastic surgery*, cirugía plástica. — s. plástico; *plastics*, plástica.

plasticine, s. plasticina.

plasticity [plæs'tisiti], s. plasticidad.

plastron ['plæstrɒn], s. plastrón, pechera, peto; (*zool.*) concha inferior de las tortugas; parte semejante de los anfibios.

plat [plæt], s. trenza, cintilla; pedazo de tierra, parcela, solar; mapa de un terreno acotado; (*mar.*) baderna. — a. (*prov.*) llano, liso. — *v.t.* entretejer, trenzar; parcelar un terreno.

platane, platan, s. plátano oriental.

platband ['plætbænd], s. acirate, arriate de un jardín; faja de la cornisa.

plate [pleit], s. plancha, planchuela, lámina, hoja, chapa; plato; contenido de un plato; vajilla en general (de oro, plata, etc.); (*impr.*) clisé, estereotipo, electrotipo; grabado, ilustración; (*foto.*) placa; dentadura postiza; (*elec.*) elemento de una pila; *dinner plate*, plato de comer; *gold plate*, vajilla de oro; *silver plate*, vajilla de plata; *soup plate*, sopero; *plate-armour*, blindaje; *plate-basket*, cesto para platos; *plate-rack*, escurreplatos, espetera, colador; *plate-holder*, (*foto.*) portaplaca, *m.*; *plate-room*, repostería. — *v.t.* planchear; platear, dorar, niquelar, azogar, estañar; blindar.

plateau ['plætou], s. mesa, meseta, altillanura, altiplanicie, *f.*; bandeja.

plateful, s. plato, plato lleno, platada.

platform ['plætfɔːm], s. plataforma; tablado, tribuna, andamio; cadalso; terraplén; (*f.c.*) andén; plataforma (de un tranvía); (*E.U.*) programa, declaración formal de principios.

plating ['pleitiŋ], s. plateadura, niquelado, estañadura, galvanización; blindaje.

platinode ['plætinoud], s. cátodo o polo negativo de un elemento voltaico.

platinum ['plætinəm], s. platino, platina; *platinum black*, polvo negro de platino.

platitude ['plætitjuːd], s. perogrullada, trivialidad.

platonic [plə'tɒnik], a. platónico.

Platonism ['pleitonizm], s. platonismo.

Platonist, Platonizer, s. platónico.

platoon [plə'tuːn], s. (*mil.*) pelotón.

platter ['plætəɪ], s. plato grande, fuente, *f.*, platel; (*E.U.*) plato.

platting, s. trenza; acción de trenzar.

plaudit ['plɔːdit], s. aclamación, aplauso.

plausibility, s. plausibilidad.

plausible ['plɔːzibəl], a. plausible.

plausibleness, s. plausibilidad.

plausive ['plɔːziv], a. (*ant.*) plausible; laudatorio.

play [plei], *v.i.* jugar; (*mús.*) tañer, tocar; representar, dar, poner en escena una comedia; burlarse, bromear, chancearse; divertirse, entretenerse, recrearse; enredar, retozar, travesear, juguetear; correr (aguas); (*mec.*) funcionar, moverse; conducirse, portarse; ondear, ondular, flotar. — *v.t.* poner en movimiento, hacer andar; interpretar, ejecutar, tocar; hacer o desempeñar el papel de representar; remedar; manejar, manipular, menear; hacer uso de, valerse de; *to play away* (*money*), perder jugando; *to play fair*, jugar limpio; *to play false*, engañar; *to play the fool*, hacer(se) el tonto; *to play high*, jugar fuerte; *to play out* (*the game*), jugar hasta el fin; *to play upon one*, burlarse de uno, explotar; *to play a trick upon*, hacer una mala jugada a, engañar; *to play truant*, hacer novillos; *to play words*, hacer equívoco de vocablos; *to play off*, hacer alarde; contraponer, oponer; *to play into someone's hands*, hacer a uno el caldo gordo; *to play second fiddle*, hacer un papel secundario. — s. juego, recreo, divertimiento, diversión; broma, jugada; espectáculo, representación, función, comedia, drama, *m.*, pieza; movimiento, acción, funcionamiento, operación; libertad de acción, remonte, vuelo; (*mec.*) huelgo, holgura, anchura; *foul play*, perfidia, alevosía, vileza, mala pasada; *full of play*, chancero; *child's play*, (*fig.*) niñerías, poca cosa, cosa facilísima; *free play*, rienda suelta; *fair play*, juego limpio; *in play*, en chanza; *play upon words*, equívoco, retruécano; *it is as good as a play*, es una verdadera comedia; *to bring into play*, poner en movimiento.

playbill, s. cartel de teatro.

player, s. jugador; actor, comediante, cómico; músico, tocador, instrumentista, *m.f.*

playfellow, playmate, s. compañero de juego.

playful, s. travieso, juguetón, retozón.

playfully, adv. por chanza, festivamente, alegremente, por modo de juego.

playgoer, s. aficionado al teatro.

playground, s. patio de recreo (especialmente de una escuela).

playhouse, s. teatro, coliseo.

playing-card, s. naipe.

plaything, s. juguete.

play-time, s. horas de recreo.

playwright ['pleirait], **playwriter** ['pleiraitəɪ], s. autor dramático, dramaturgo.

plea [pliː], s. apología, excusa, defensa, disculpa; pretexto, excepción; argumentación, argumento; súplica, ruego, instancia; (*for.*) alegato, defensa; respuesta o declaración del acusado; acción, litigio, proceso.

plead [pli:d], *v.t.* abogar, pleitear; defender; alegar, argüir, raciocinar; disculpar, interceder, excusar. — *v.i.* sostener, opener, interceder, disculpar, rogar, suplicar; declararse, declarar o responder el acusado si es culpable o no.

pleadable, *a.* defendible; alegable.

pleader, *s.* defensor, abogado.

pleading, *s.* defensa, alegación.

pleasant ['plezənt], *a.* grato, agradable, divertido, delicioso, gustoso, placentero, apacible, ameno, tratable, simpático.

pleasantness, *s.* delicia, recreo, agrado, placer, satisfacción.

pleasantry ['plezəntri], *s.* chanza, agudeza, chocarrería, broma, humorada.

please [pli:z], *v.t.* gustar, agradar, satisfacer, deleitar, dar gusto, complacer, contentar. — *v.i.* agradar, querer, gozar, servirse, gustar de, gustar, tener gusto en, tener a bien, placer; *please God*, ¡plegue a Dios! ¡quiera Dios! *if you please*, si usted no tiene inconveniente, con su permiso, si usted gusta; *please go in*, tenga Vd. la bondad de entrar, haga Vd. el favor de entrar, entre Vd. por favor, sírvase Vd. entrar; *to be hard to please*, ser muy exigente; *whatever you please*, lo que le dé la gana, lo que le parezca bien.

pleased, *a.* contento, satisfecho, feliz. — *p.p.* [PLEASE].

pleasing, *a.* agradable, gustoso, grato, placentero, jovial.

pleasingly, *adv.* agradablemente, donosamente.

pleasingness, *s.* gracia, atractivo, calidad de agradable.

pleasurable [pleʒə·əbəl], *a.* divertido, deleitante, festivo, grato, agradable.

pleasurableness, *s.* deleite, agrado, atractivo.

pleasurably ['pleʒərəbli], *adv.* con deleite, con gusto, placenteramente.

pleasure ['pleʒɹ], *s.* deleite, gusto, placer, complacencia, agrado, satisfacción, gozo; arbitrio, deseo; *to take pleasure in*, tener el honor de; disfrutar de; complacerse en; *at pleasure*, a voluntad; *what is your pleasure?* ¿qué desea Vd.? *pleasure-boat*, bote de recreo; *pleasure-ground*, parque o jardín de recreo; *pleasure-trip*, partida de placer, excursión turística. — *v.t.* complacer, dar gusto a, hacer favor a. — *v.i.* complacerse (en); disfrutar (de).

pleat [pli:t], *v.t.* (*fam.*) plegar, hacer dobleces o pliegues. — *s.* (*cost.*) pliegue, doblez, plegadura en la ropa; [PLAIT].

plebe ['pli:bi], *s.* (*E.U.*, *fam.*) estudiante de primer año (Academia Militar o Naval).

plebeian [ple'biən], *s.*, *a.* plebeyo, vulgar.

plebeianism, *s.* estado o calidad de plebeyo.

plebiscite ['plebisit], *s.* plebiscito.

plebs, *s.* (*vulg.*) populacho, plebe, *f.*, vulgo.

plectrum ['plektrəm], (*pl.* **plectra**), *s.* plectro, púa.

pledge [pledʒ], *s.* prenda, fianza, empeño, rehén; voto, brindis; *to put in pledge*, empeñar. — *v.t.* empeñar, garantizar, dar en prenda, dar fianza; brindar por; comprometerse a; *to pledge one's word*, dar su palabra.

pledger, *s.* prendador, depositador, depositante; garante, *m.f.*

pledget, *s.* planchuela de hilas; taruguito.

pleiads ['plaiədz], **pleiades** ['plaiədi:z], *s.pl.* (*astr.*) pléyades, *f.pl.*

plenary ['pli:nəri], *a.* completo, entero, lleno; (*teol.*, *for.*) plenario.

plenipotence, *s.* plenipotencia.

plenipotent ['plenipotent], *a.* todopoderoso, con poder pleno.

plenipotentiary [plenipo'tenfəri], *s.*, *a.* plenipotenciario.

plenish ['plenif], *v.t.* llenar, rellenar, reequipar.

plenitude ['plenitju:d], *s.* plenitud, abundancia, copia.

plenteous ['plentiəs], *a.* abundante, copioso, fértil, fructífero.

plenteousness, *s.* abundancia, fertilidad.

plentiful ['plentifəl], *a.* abundante, copioso, fértil, feraz, profuso.

plentifully, *adv.* abundantemente, copiosamente, a puñados.

plenty ['plenti], *s.* abundancia, copia, fertilidad, profusión, (*fam.*) la mar de; demasía, de sobra.

plenum ['pli:nəm], *s.* plenitud, pleno, plétora.

pleonasm ['pli:onæzm], *s.* pleonasmo.

pleonastic, pleonastical, *a.* pleonástico.

plethora ['pleθərə], *s.* (*med.*) plétora; (*fig.*) plétora, hartura.

plethoric [ple'θɔ:rik], *a.* pletórico.

pleura ['plu:rə], *s.* pleura.

pleural, *a.* pleurítico.

pleurisy ['plu:risi], *s.* pleuresía, pleuritis, *f.*

pleuritic, pleuritical, *a.* pleurítico.

plexiform ['pleksifɔ:m], *a.* reticular, complicado.

plexus ['pleksəs], *s.* (*anat.*) plexo; trabazón, *f.*, entrelazamiento, red, *f.*

pliability [plaiə'biliti], *s.* blandura, docilidad, flexibilidad, elasticidad.

pliable ['plaiəbəl], *a.* dócil, blando, flexible, doblegable.

pliableness, *s.* docilidad, blandura, flexibilidad, elasticidad.

pliably, *adv.* flexiblemente, con blandura.

pliancy ['plaiənsi], *s.* flexibilidad, docilidad, blandura, elasticidad.

pliant ['plaiənt], *a.* flexible, doblegable; blando; dócil, manejable; cimbreño.

pliantness, *s.* flexibilidad, blandura, docilidad.

plicate ['plaikət], **plicated** ['plaikətid], *a.* plegado sobre sí mismo, como un abanico.

pliers ['plaiəɹz], *s.pl.* alicates, tenacillas, tenallas; *flat-pointed pliers*, alicates de boca; *sharp-pointed pliers*, alicates de punta.

plight [plait], *s.* embarazo, apuro, aprieto, trance. — *v.t.* empeñar, prometer en matrimonio, dar palabra; contraer esponsales; *a sorry* (o *woeful*) *plight*, un estado lastimoso.

plim [plim], *v.i.* engordar, rellenarse. — *v.t.* causar hinchazón.

Plimsoll's mark ['plimsəlz'mɑ:1k], *s.* marca Plimsoll.

plinth [plinθ], *s.* plinto, orlo.

pliocene ['plaiosi:n], *s.* plioceno.

plod [plɔd], *v.i.* andar penosamente y despacio; (*fig.*) afanarse, atrafagar, trabajar con perseverancia, estudiar con aplicación; *to plod on*, seguir trabajando.

plodding, *s.* trafagón, hombre trabajador.

plodding, *a.* tráfago, laborioso, afanoso.

plot [plɔt], *s.* plantación; solar, parcela, terreno pequeño; trama, conspiración, in-

triga, enredo, conjura, estratagema, *m.*;
traza, idea, proyecto; argumento, trama (de
drama, etc.); *to lay a plot*, tramar. — *v.t.*
delinear; idear, trazar, urdir, tramar. — *v.i.*
conspirar, tramar, urdir, intrigar, maquinar.
plotter, *s.* conjurado, conspirador, maquinador, tramador.
plotting, *s.* maquinación, trama, conspiración;
delineación.
plough [plau], *s.* arado; lengüeta; agricultura;
snow-plough, quitanieves; *gang-plough*, arado
de reja múltiple; *plough-plane*, guillame,
cepillo acanalado; *Plough Monday*, el
primer lunes después de la Epifanía. — *v.t.*
arar, labrar; surcar (las ondas); hender (el
aire); arrejacar.
ploughboy ['plaubɔi], *s.* yuguero, mozo de
arado, gañán.
plougher, *s.* arador, surcador.
ploughing, *s.* aradura, labranza.
ploughman ['plaumən], *s.* arador, labrador,
yuguero, patán, rústico.
ploughshare, *s.* reja de arado.
ploughtail, *s.* mancera.
plover ['plʌvəɪ], *s.* avefría; *bastard plover*,
frailecillo.
plow, *s.*, *v.t.* (*E.U.*) [PLOUGH].
pluck [plʌk], *v.t.* arrancar, coger, desarraigar;
pelar, desplumar; (*mús.*) puntear; tirar. —
v.i. dar un tirón; *to pluck up courage*, hacer
de tripas corazón. — *s.* tirón, estirón;
asadura; (*fam.*) ánimo, valor, resolución,
denuedo; (*fam.*) suspenso en exámenes,
calabazas.
plucker, *s.* persona que coge, que arranca.
plucky, *a.* (*fam.*) valeroso, valiente, animoso,
denodado, resuelto, esforzado.
plug [plʌg], *s.* tapón, tarugo, zoquete, nudillo,
taco; llave (de fuente), *f.*; (*elec.*) enchufe;
empastadura (de dientes); rollo de tabaco;
émbolo; caña; espita; (*fam.*) rocín; (*E.U.*,
vulg.) sombrero de copa, chistera. — *v.t.*
atarugar, tapar (con tapón), obturar; empastar, orificar; (*elec.*) *to plug in*, enchufar.
plum [plʌm], *s.* (*bot.*) ciruela, ciruelo, pasa;
(*fig.*) turrón, golosina; (*fam.*) fortuna, riquezas; *plum cake*, pastel con pasas; *plum tree*,
ciruelo.
plumage ['pluːmidʒ], *s.* plumaje, plumazón;
atavío, adorno.
plumagery, *s.* plumajería.
plumb [plʌm], *s.* plomada. — *a.* perpendículo,
aplomo; recto; *out of plumb*, desviado;
plumb-line, (*arq.*) tranquil, plomada. — *adv.*
a plomo, verticalmente, perpendicularmente.
— *v.t.* aplomar, sondar, sondear.
plumbago [plʌmˈbeigou], *s.* mina de plomo;
plombagina, grafito; (*bot.*) plombagíneas.
plumbean ['plʌmbiən], **plumbeous** ['plʌm-
bəs], *a.* plomado, plomizo, plúmbeo,
plúmbico.
plumber ['plʌməɪ], *s.* plomero, emplomador;
cañero, instalador de cañerías.
plumbiferous [plʌmˈbifərəs], *a.* plombífero.
plumbing ['plʌmiŋ], *s.* oficio del plomero;
emplomadura, tubería; instalación de cañerías.
plume [pluːm], *s.* pluma, plumaje, penacho de
pluma; altivez, orgullo; laurel, plomo. — *v.t.*
desplumar, pelar; ajustar, componer (plumas); adornar con plumas, emplumar; *to
plume oneself*, jactarse, vanagloriarse.

plumeless, *a.* implume.
plumiferous [pluːˈmifərəs], **plumigerous**
[pluːˈmidʒərəs], *a.* plumífero.
plumiped ['pluːmiped], *s.* ave calzada. — *a.*
plumípedo, calzado.
plummet ['plʌmit], *s.* plomada; sonda,
sondaleza.
plumose, **plumous** ['pluːməs], *a.* plúmeo,
plumoso.
plump [plʌmp], *a.* rollizo, regordete, gordiflón,
gordinflón; (*ant.*) brusco; *plump-faced*, carilleno. — *adv.* de repente, de golpe. — *s.*
bandada de aves; espesura de árboles. — *v.t.*
soltar, dejar caer, arrojar, tirar; hinchar, engordar, dilatar; (*fig.*, *fam.*) *to plump for*,
abogar por, votar por. — *v.i.* hincharse,
ponerse gordo, llenarse; caer a plomo.
plumper, *s.* cosa que abulta o hincha, abulta-
miento; caída a plomo; (*vulg.*) mentirón.
plumply, *adv.* redondamente, llenamente.
plumpness, *s.* corpulencia, gordura.
plumula ['pluːmjuːlə], **plumule** ['pluːmjuːl],
s. (*orn.*) plúmula; (*bot.*) plúmula.
plumy ['pluːmi], *a.* plumado, plumoso, empenachado.
plunder ['plʌndəɪ], *v.t.* saquear, pillar, despojar. — *s.* pillaje, saqueo, despojo, botín,
pecorea; (*vulg.*) provecho, ganancia.
plunderer, *s.* ladrón, pillador, saqueador, rapiñador.
plunge [plʌndʒ], *v.t.* chapuzar, hundir,
sumergir, zampuzar, zambullir; precipitar,
arrojar. — *v.i.* sumergirse, precipitarse, zambullirse; arrojarse, lanzarse; saltar; encabritarse (el caballo, avión o buque, etc.);
jugarse el todo. — *s.* sumersión, zambullida,
zampuzo; (*ant.*) apuro, aprieto; abismo;
arrojo, salto, embestida.
plungeon ['plʌndʒən], *s.* (*orn.*) somorgujo,
mergo.
plunger, *s.* buzo; (*mec.*) chupón, émbolo;
(*fam.*) jugador o bolsista desenfrenado.
pluperfect [pluːˈpəːɪfekt], *a.* pluscuamperfecto.
plural ['pluːrəl], *s.*, *a.* plural.
pluralism, *s.* pluralidad; (*filos.*) pluralismo.
plurality, *s.* pluralidad, mayoría, multitud.
pluralize, *v.t.* pluralizar.
plurally, *adv.* en plural.
plus [plʌs], *a.*, *adv.* más; (*mat.*, *eléc.*) positivo.
plus fours, *s.* pantalones de golf.
plush [plʌʃ], *s.* tripe, felpa. — *a.* afelpado.
plutarchy ['pluːtɑːɪki], *s.* oligarquía.
plutocracy [pluːˈtɔkrəsi], *s.* plutocracia.
plutocrat ['pluːtokræt], *s.* plutócrata, *m.f.*
plutocratic, *a.* plutocrático.
pluvial ['pluːviəl], *s.* (*igl.*) capa pluvial.
pluvial, **pluvious**, *a.* pluvial, lluvioso.
pluviograph ['pluːviogræf], *s.* pluviógrafo.
pluviometer [pluːviˈɔmetər], *s.* pluviómetro.
ply [plai], *v.t.* aplicar, aplicarse a, dedicarse a;
ocupar, emplear; practicar, ejercer; trabajar
con ahinco (aguja, herramienta, etc.);
manejar, usar; atacar; *to ply with questions*,
matar con preguntas, importunar. — *v.i.*
doblegarse, ceder, trabajar con asiduidad;
mantenerse; ir y venir; ir de prisa; (*mar.*)
barloventear; hacer el servicio. — *s.* pliegue,
doblez; inclinación, propensión (capa de
tela, etc.); *three-ply*, de tres hojas o capas;
three-ply wood, madera contraplacada o contrachapada, tablero.

plyings ['plaiiŋz], *s.pl.* servicio (de buques, etc.); solicitud, instancia; (*mar.*) esfuerzo de vela contra el viento.

Plymouth Brethren ['pliməθ 'breðren], *s.pl.* secta evangélica establecida en Plymouth cerca de 1830, sin clero ni credo regular.

pneumatic [nju:'mætik], *a.* neumático.

pneumatics, *s.pl.* neumática.

pneumatology [nju:mə'tɔlodʒi], *s.* neumatología.

pneumonia [nju:'mouniə], *s.* (*med.*) pulmonía, neumonía.

pneumonic, *a.* neumónico, pulmoníaco, pulmonar.

poa ['pouə], *s.* (*bot.*) poa.

poach [poutʃ], *v.t.* escalfar (huevos); cazar o pescar furtivamente (en terreno vedado); (*fig.*) invadir, hurtar. — *v.i.* cazar o pescar furtivamente; meterse en los negocios de otros; encenagarse un terreno.

poacher, *s.* el que caza o pesca en vedado; sartén para escalfar huevos.

poachiness, *s.* humedad.

poaching, *s.* caza furtiva, hurto de caza en vedado.

poachy, *a.* húmedo, pantanoso.

pock [pɔk], *s.* viruela, postilla, pústula; *pock-marked*, picado de viruelas.

pocket ['pɔkət], *s.* bolsillo, faltriquera; bolsa, saco; receptáculo, cavidad; (*fig.*) dinero, recursos, interés; (*min.*) bolsa; *air-pocket*, (*aer.*) bache; *pocket-argument*, razón de interés; *pocket-book*, cartera, portamonedas, *m.*; *pocket-handkerchief*, pañuelo de bolsillo; *pocket-knife*, navaja, cortaplumas, *m.*; *pocket-money*, alfileres, dinerillo; *in pocket*, con ganancia; *to be in pocket*, ganar; *out of pocket*, con pérdida; *to pick a pocket*, vaciar un bolsillo. — *v.t.* embolsar, embolsillar, meter en el bolsillo; apropiarse, tomar; *to pocket one's pride*, tragarse una injuria, tragarse el orgullo, reprimirse; *to pocket an insult*, tragarse una injuria.

pocky, *a.* picado de viruelas; cacarañoso; sifilítico.

pod [pɔd], *s.* (*bot.*) vaina; cápsula de una flor; manada; pericarpo. — *v.i.* criar vainas; hincharse, llenarse.

podagra ['pɔdægrə], *s.* podagra.

podge [pɔdʒ], *s.* (*vulg.*) persona gordinflona.

podocarp ['pɔdoka:rp], *s.* (*bot.*) sostén, v. gr. un pecíolo.

poe-bird ['poubə:rd], *s.* pájaro de Nueva Zelandia (*Prosthemadera Novæ-Zeelandiæ*).

poem ['pouem], *s.* poema, *m.*, poesía.

poesy ['pouezi], *s.* poesía, arte poética.

poet ['pouet], *s.* poeta, *m.*, vate.

poetaster [poue'tæstər], *s.* poetastro.

poetess ['pouetes], *s.*, *f.* poetisa.

poetic [pou'etik], **poetical**, *a.* poético.

poetics [pou'etiks], *s.* poética, arte poética.

poetize, *v.i.* poetizar, versificar.

poetry ['pouetri], *s.* poesía, poética, versos.

pogrom [po'grɔm], *s.* 'pogrom,' degüello y saqueo organizado contra una clase de la población especialmente contra los judíos en Rusia.

poignancy, *s.* fuerza conmovedora, patetismo; acrimonia, acerbidad; angustia, congoja.

poignant ['pɔinənt], *a.* conmovedor, emocionante, patético; acerbo, punzante, mordaz; penetrante, agudo.

point [pɔint], *s.* punta; punto; (*geog.*) cabo, promontorio, punta de tierra; aguja, agujeta; (*f.c.*) aguja; puntillo, pundonor; cola, rabo; sal, *f.*; intención; chiste, agudeza; punto de vista; cuestión; pormenor, detalle; objeto, punto, fin; ocasión, momento, instante; puntería; grado (de una escala); peculiaridad, rasgo característico, característica; (*mar.*) rumbo (la división del plano en la rosa náutica); (*com.*) entero (en la fluctuación de los valores); (*gram.*) signo de puntuación, punto final; (*impr.*) punto tipográfico; puntura; *to gain one's point*, conseguir sus fines; *to be on the point of*, estar a punto de; *to come to the point*, llegar al caso, venir al caso; *to score a point*, ganar un tanto; *to speak to the point*, ir al grano; *in point*, a propósito, al caso; *in point of*, tocante a, en cuanto a; *at the point of death*, en artículo de muerte; *on all points*, de todos lados. — *pl.* **points**, (*f.c.*) cambiavía, *m.*, agujas; *on the points* (*baile*), de puntillas. — *v.t.* apuntar; aguzar, afilar, adelgazar; dirigir, encarar, asestar; (*gram.*) puntuar; *to point out*, mostrar, indicar, señalar, apuntar; (*alb.*) unir con mortero, rellenar (juntas), llenar. — *v.i.* señalar; parar, mostrar la caza; *to point at*, señalar con el dedo; *to point to*, señalar, indicar; volverse hacia.

point-blank [pɔint'blæŋk], *adv.*, *a.* de punto en blanco; a bocajarro, a quema ropa. — *s.* tiro a quema ropa, tiro asestado.

pointed, *a.* puntiagudo, agudo, aguzado, afilado, puntuado; picante; (*arq.*) ojival; (*fig.*) directo, satírico, epigramático, áspero, directo, acentuado; intencionado.

pointedly, *adv.* sutilmente; explícitamente, categóricamente; intencionadamente.

pointedness, *s.* aspereza, picantez, acrimonia, agudeza, intención.

pointer, *s.* indicador, índice; apuntador, puntero; aguja; buril, punta; perro perdiguero; manecilla de reloj; (*f.c.*) palanca de aguja; (*astr.*) las dos estrellas de la Osa Mayor, en cuya dirección se halla la estrella polar.

pointing, *s.* puntuación; indicación, señalamiento; puntería; aguzadura, afiladura; (*mar.*) rabo de rata; (*com.*) marca; (*alb.*) mamposteado, relleno de juntas.

point-lace, *s.* puntas, encaje en general.

pointless, *a.* sin punta, obtuso; insubstancial; impertinente, fútil.

pointsman, *s.* (*f.c.*) guardaagujas, guardabarreras, *m.*

poise [pɔiz], *s.* contrapeso, equilibrio, balanza; reposo, elegancia, garbo, donosura, compostura; aplomo, serenidad; porte. — *v.t.* equilibrar, balancear, equiparar, contrapesar; examinar, pesar; (*ant.*) oprimir, abrumar. — *v.i.* estar suspendido, posarse; dudar.

poison ['pɔizən], *s.* veneno, ponzoña, tósigo. — *v.t.* envenenar, emponzoñar, atosigar; (*fig.*) inficionar, corromper.

poison-elder, *s.* zumaque.

poisoner, *s.* envenenador; (*fig.*) seductor, corruptor.

poison-ivy, *s.* especie de zumaque.

poison-nut, *s.* nuez vómica.

poisonous, *a.* venenoso, ponzoñoso, tóxico, emponzoñado; (*fig.*) ponzoñoso, pernicioso.

poisonousness, *s.* venenosidad, naturaleza venenosa.

poke [pouk], *s.* bolsa, barjuleta, saquito, saquillo; empuje, emrᵘjón; hurgonada, hurgonazo; (*ict.*) vejiga de aire. — *v.t.*, *v.i.* hurgar, atizar; golpear, empujar; sacar, asomar; andar a tientas; *to poke about*, andar *o* buscar a tientas; *to go poking one's nose into everything*, meter su cucharada en todo; *to buy a pig in a poke*, comprar *o* hacer a ciegas, salga pez o salga rana, al buen tuntún; *to poke fun at*, burlarse de, mofarse de.

poker [ˈpoukəɹ], *s.* tizonero, atizador, atizadero, hurgón, espetón; 'póker,' juego de naipes.

pokeweed [ˈpoukwiːd], *s.* fitolaca, hierba carmín.

poky [ˈpouki], *a.* (*fam.*) pequeño, miserable, apretado, encogido; tacaño, mezquino.

polacre [poˈleikəɹ], *s.* polacra.

Polar [ˈpoulɑːɹ], *a.* polar; *Polar bear*, oso blanco.

polariscope [poˈlæriskoup], *s.* polariscopio.

polarity [poˈlæriti], *s.* polaridad.

polarization, *s.* polarización.

polarize [ˈpouləraiz], *v.t.* polarizar.

polary, *a.* polar.

pole [poul], *s.* (*geog., elec.*) polo; pértiga; palo, asta, estaca, paral, mira, piquete; zanca; balancín; lanza (de un coche); muestra (de barbero); (*mar.*) mástil; medida de longitud (5½ yds.). — *v.t.* armar, llevar o sostener con palos; empujar con palos; clavar estacas.

poleaxe [ˈpoulæks], *s.* hachuela de mano.

polecat, *s.* mofeta, veso.

polemic [poˈlemik], **polemical** [poˈlemikəl], *a.* polémico.

polemic, *s.* polemista, *m.f.*; polémica.

polemics, *s.pl.* polémica.

police [poˈliːs], *s.* policía; *police constable* *o* *police officer*, agente de policía; *police station*, comisaría de policía. — *v.t.* poner o apostar polizontes.

policed [poˈliːst], *a.* bien gobernado, administrado, o vigilado.

policeman [poˈliːsmən], *s.* policía, *m.*, guardia, *m.*, polizonte.

policewoman, *s.* agente femenino de policía.

policy [ˈpolisi], *s.* política, programa político; prudencia, sagacidad; curso de acción; póliza de seguro.

poliomyelitis [poulioumaieˈlaitis], *s.* poliomielitis, *f.*

polish [ˈpoliʃ], *s.* pulimento, lustre, bruñido, barniz; tersura; urbanidad, cortesía. — *v.t.* pulir, pulimentar, bruñir, dar brillo, alisar, satinar; (*fig.*) adiestrar; educar, civilizar; (*fam.*) desasnar; *to polish off*, (*fam.*) terminar, acabar con; matar; comerse, engullir. — *v.i.* pulirse, alisarse; recibir lustre.

Polish [ˈpouliʃ], *a.* polaco, polonés.

polishable [ˈpoliʃəbəl], *a.* susceptible de adquirir brillo.

polished, *a.* pulido, bruñido; culto, refinado, ilustrado, cortés, desentorpecido, civilizado. — *p.p.* [POLISH].

polishedness, *s.* bruñidura, tersura; urbanidad, cortesanía.

polisher, *s.* pulidor, pulidero, bruñidor, alisador.

polishing, *s.* bruñidura, brillo.

polite [poˈlait], *a.* cortés, urbano, atento, fino, bien educado.

politely, *adv.* cortésmente, urbanamente, atentamente.

politeness, *s.* cortesía, urbanidad, buena crianza.

politic [ˈpolitik], *a.* político, civil; circunspecto, prudente, sagaz.

political [poˈlitikəl], *a.* político.

politically, *adv.* políticamente.

politician [poliˈtiʃən], *s.* político.

politicly [poˈlitikli], *adv.* prudentemente, astutamente.

politics [ˈpolitiks], *s.pl.* política.

polity [ˈpoliti], *s.* constitución política; comunidad.

polka [ˈpolkə], *s.* polca.

poll [poul], *s.* lista electoral, escrutinio, elección; padrón, empadronamiento, nómina; cabeza, persona; matrícula; votación; colegio electoral, urnas electorales; cotillo de destral *o* martillo; *to come out head of the poll*, tener mayoría. — *v.t.* descabezar (árboles); registrar, escrutar; encabezar; dar voto; recoger (votos); empadronar, matricular. — *v.i.* votar en las elecciones.

poll, polly, *s.* (*fam.*) loro, papagayo.

pollack [ˈpolək], *s.* abadejo, pescadilla.

pollard [ˈpolɑːd], *s.* árbol desmochado; (*ict.*) esperinque, coto, salvado; res descornada; res *o* árbol mocho. — *v.t.* desmochar.

pollen [ˈpolən], *s.* (*bot.*) polen; salvado fino.

poller [ˈpoulər], *s.* desmochador; votante; (*ant.*) barbero; (*ant.*) despojador.

polling [ˈpoulin], *s.* votación, escrutinio, verificación de los votos; *polling-booth*, colegio electoral.

polliwog [ˈpoliwog], *s.* renacuajo.

poll-tax [ˈpoultæks], *s.* capitación.

pollute [poˈluːt], *v.t.* ensuciar, manchar; mancillar, impurificar; profanar.

pollutedness, *s.* contaminación; profanación; corrupción; polución, efusión del semen.

polluter, *s.* contaminador; profanador; corruptor.

pollution [poˈluːʃən], *s.* contaminación; profanación; corrupción; polución, efusión del semen.

polo [ˈpoulou], *s.* polo (juego).

polonaise [poloˈneiz], *s.* (*mús.*) polonesa; (*sast.*) polaca.

polony [poˈlouni], *s.* salchicha de cerdo a medio cocer.

poltroon [polˈtruːn], *s.* cobarde, pusilánime, mandria; (*ant.*) poltrón, haragán.

poltroonery, *s.* cobardía.

poltroonish, *a.* pusilánime.

poly [ˈpouli], *s.* zamarrilla.

polyandria [poliˈændriə], **polyandry** [poliˈændri], *s.* poliandria; (*bot.*) poliandria.

polyanthus [poliˈænθəs], *s.* (*bot.*) primavera.

polyarchy [ˈpoliɑːrki], *s.* poliarquía.

polychromatic, *a.* policromático.

polychrome [ˈpolikroum], *s.* policromo.

polygamist [poˈligəmist], *s.* polígamo.

polygamous, *a.* polígamo.

polygamy [poˈligəmi], *s.* poligamia.

polygastric [poliˈgæstrik], *a.* poligástrico.

polygenesis [poliˈdʒenesis], *s.* poligénesis, *f.*

polyglot [ˈpoliglot], *s.*, *a.* polígloto, poligloto.

polygon [ˈpoligən], *s.* polígono.

polygonal [poˈligənəl], *a.* poligonal, polígono.

polygraphy [pɔ'ligrəfi], s. poligrafía.
polygraphic, polygraphical, a. poligráfico.
polyhedral [pɔli'hi:drəl], a. poliédrico.
polyhedron, s. poliedro.
Polynesian [pɔli'ni:ʒən], a. polinesio.
polynome ['pɔlinoum], s. polinomio.
polyp ['pɔlip], s. (zool.) pólipo; zoófito.
polypetalous [pɔli'petələs], a. polipétalo.
polypod ['pɔlipɔd], **polypody** ['pɔlipɔdi], s. polipodio.
polypus ['pɔlipəs], s. (med.) pólipo.
polyscope ['pɔli'skoup], s. poliscopio.
polysepalous [pɔli'sepələs], a. polisépalo.
polysyllabic [pɔlisi'læbik], a. polisílabo, polisilábico.
polysyllable [pɔli'siləbəl], s. polisílabo.
polytechnic [pɔli'teknik], a. politécnico.
polytheism ['pɔliθi:izm], s. politeísmo.
polytheist, s. politeísta, m.f.
polytheistic, polytheistical, a. politeísta.
polythene, s., a. politeno; politénico.
pomace ['pʌməs], s. el desecho de manzanas después de la obtención de la sidra.
pomaceous [po'meiʃəs], a. pomáceo.
pomade [po'mɑːd], **pomatum** [po'meitəm], s. pomada. — v.t. untar con pomada.
pomander ['poumændər], s. bola o poma olorosa que se acostumbraba a llevar encima de uno para evitar una infección.
pome [poum], s. pomo.
pomegranate ['pɔmgrænət], s. granada; pomegranate tree, granado.
pommel ['pʌməl], s. pomo (de un arzón, de una espada o de un cañón); (arq.) perilla. — v.t. pegar, apalear, aporrear, cascar.
pommelling, s. puñetazo, puñada.
pomp [pɔmp], s. pompa, fausto, magnificencia, ceremonia.
pom-pom ['pɔmpɔm], s. cañón automático antiaéreo y de tiro rápido; pompón.
pomposity [pɔm'pɔsiti], s. alarde, jactancia, vanidad, pomposidad; (estilo) pomposidad, hinchazón, f.
pompous ['pɔmpəs], a. jactancioso, vano, pomposo; (estilo) pomposo, hinchado.
pompousness, s. alarde, jactancia, vanidad, pomposidad; pompa, ceremonia; (estilo) pomposidad, hinchazón, f.
pond [pɔnd], s. estanque, alberca, charca, vivero. — v.i. hacer un estanque; fish-pond, vivero; horse-pond, abrevadero.
ponder, v.t. ponderar, considerar, examinar, pesar, estudiar. — v.i. meditar, considerar, reflexionar.
ponderability, ponderableness, s. ponderabilidad.
ponderable ['pɔndərəbəl], a. ponderable.
ponderer, s. ponderador.
ponderosity [pɔndə'rɔsiti], s. balumbo; pesadez, languidez; ponderosidad, gravedad.
ponderous ['pɔndərəs], a. abultado, rebultado; pesadísimo; (ant.) ponderoso, grave.
ponderousness, s. balumbo, bulto; pesadez; hinchazón, f.; (ant.) ponderosidad, gravedad.
poniard ['pɔnjɑːd], s. puñal, almarada. — v.t. herir con puñal, dar de puñaladas.
pontage ['pɔntidʒ], s. pontaje, pontazgo.
pontiff ['pɔntif], s. pontífice.
pontifical, a. pontifical, pontificio.
pontificals [pɔn'tifikəlz], s.pl. adornos, pontificales.

pontificate [pɔn'tifikit], s. pontificado, papazgo, papado. — v.i. pontificar.
pontil ['pɔntil], s. barra de hierro usada en la fabricación del cristal.
pontlevis ['pɔnlevi:], s. puente levadizo; (equit.) el constante encabritarse del caballo.
pontoon [pɔn'tuːn], s. pontón; (mar.) barcaza chata.
pony ['pouni], s. (pl. ponies) haca, jaca, caballito.
poodle ['puːdəl], s. perro de lanas.
pooh [puː], interj. ¡bah!
pooh-pooh, v.t. tratar con desprecio, con desdén, hacer mofa.
pool [puːl], s. estanque, charco, balsa, laguna, rebalsa, alberca, hoya, hoyo (en un río); polla (en el juego); truco, piña (en el billar); conjunto, fusión, combinación; football pools, apuestas de fútbol, quinas. — v.t. formar una polla; pagar a escote; mancomunar intereses.
poop [puːp], s. popa, toldilla. — v.t. empopar, abordar por la popa.
poor [puːə], a. pobre; desgraciado, infeliz, pobre de; malo, flojo; the poor, los pobres; as poor as a church mouse, pobre como ratón de iglesia; in poor health, falto de salud, enclenque.
poor-box, s. cepillo de pobres.
poor-house, s. casa de caridad.
poorly, adv. pobremente, escasamente. — a. indispuesto; enfermizo, enclenque, deficiencia.
poorness, s. pobreza.
poor-rate, s. contribución que se pagaba para socorrer a los necesitados.
poor-spirited, a. abatido, bajo, ruin, apocado.
pop [pɔp], v.t. meter de repente; soltar, tirar, disparar; hacer; ¡pum! con. — v.i. salir o saltar (como un cohete); entrar o salir de sopetón; dar un chasquido; to pop in, (fam.) bajar de repente; to pop in, (fam.) visitar, ir a ver; entrar de repente; to pop out, (fam.) salir de casa; salir de repente; to pop off, (fam.) marcharse, salir; (vulg.) estirar la pata; to pop the question, (fam.) hacer una declaración de amor (u ofrecimiento de casamiento). — interj. ¡pum! ¡paf! — s. chasquido, ruido seco, detonación; taponazo, pistoletazo; (fam.) concierto popular; (fam.) gaseosa, champaña; (E.U., fam.) papá.
pope [poup], s. papa, m., pontífice.
popedom, s. papado, papazgo.
popery ['poupəri], s. (despec.) papismo.
pope's head, s. escobillón para limpiar techos.
pop-eye, s. ojo saltón.
pop-eyed ['pɔpaid], a. de ojos saltones.
pop-gun, s. escopeta de viento, tirabala, m.
popinjay ['pɔpindʒei], s. (orn.) papagayo, loro; picamaderos; (fig.) doncel, pisaverde.
popish ['poupiʃ], a. papista; (ant.) papal.
poplar ['pɔplər], s. (bot.) álamo, chopo temblón.
poplin ['pɔplin], s. papelina, popelina.
poppy ['pɔpi], s. adormidera, amapola, ababa.
poppycock, s. (vulg.) tontería presumida, majadería, patrañas.
poppy-head, s. cabeza de adormidera.
populace ['pɔpjuːlis], s. pueblo; populacho, gentuza, chusma.
popular ['pɔpjuːlər], a. popular, comunero.

popularity [pɔpju:'læriti], *s.* popularidad.
popularize ['pɔpju:ləraiz], *v.t.* popularizar, divulgar, vulgarizar.
populate ['pɔpju:leit], *v.t.* poblar. — *v.i.* propagarse, multiplicarse.
population, *s.* población, populación.
populin ['pɔpju:lin], *s.* substancia cristalizada obtenida del álamo temblón.
populous ['pɔpju:ləs], *a.* populoso, pobladísimo.
populously, *adv.* pobladamente.
populousness, *s.* populosidad, población.
porbeagle ['pɔ:ɹbi:gəl], *s.* tiburón de la familia Lamna.
porcate ['pɔ:ɹkit], **-cated,** *a.* surcado.
porcelain ['pɔ:ɹselein, 'pɔ:ɹslin], *s.* porcelana. — *a.* de porcelana.
porch [pɔ:ɹtʃ], (*arq.*) atrio, pórtico, porche; vestíbulo, entrada.
porcine ['pɔ:ɹsain], *a.* porcino, porcuno, de puerco.
porcupine ['pɔ:ɹkju:pain], *s.* puerco espín.
pore [pɔ:ɹ], *s.* poro. — *v.i. to pore over a book,* leer un libro con mucha atención.
porer, *s.* persona estudiosa.
porgy ['pɔ:ɹdʒi], *s.* pargo, pagro.
porifera [pɔ'rifərə], *s.pl.* (*zool.*) las esponjas.
pork [pɔ:ɹk], *s.* carne de puerco, cerdo, tocino; *salt pork,* saladillo; *pork-butcher,* salchichero; *pork chop,* chuleta de cerdo.
porker, porket, *s.* lechoncillo, cochino, gorrino, marrano.
pornographic [pɔ:ɹno'græfik], *a.* pornográfico.
pornography [pɔ:ɹ'nɔgrəfi], *s.* pornografía.
porosity [pɔ:'rɔsiti], *s.* porosidad.
porous ['pɔ:rəs], *a.* poroso.
porously, *adv.* con porosidad.
porousness, *s.* porosidad.
porphyritic [pɔ:ɹfi'ritik], *a.* porfídico.
porphyry ['pɔ:ɹfiri], *s.* pórfido.
porpoise ['pɔ:ɹpəs], *s.* marsopa, puerco marino.
porridge ['pɔridʒ], *s.* potaje; gachas, puches.
porrigo [pɔ'raigou], *s.* enfermedad de la piel que afecta al cuero cabelludo.
porringer ['pɔrindʒəɹ], *s.* escudilla.
port [pɔ:ɹt], *s.* puerto; porta, portañola, tronera; (*mar.*) babor; garbo, airɛ, presencia, continente, porte; *Port wine,* vino de Oporto; *bonded port,* puerto para depósito; *free port,* puerto franco, puerto libre de derechos; *sea port,* ciudad marítima; *port admiral,* comandante de un puerto; *port bar,* barra para cerrar las troneras; barra de arena a la entrada de un puerto; barra de babor; *port dues,* derechos de puerto; *port-hole,* tronera, porta, portañola. — *v.t.* cargar, llevar; (*mar.*) poner a babor; (*mil.*) terciar, llevar el fusil terciado. — *v.i.* (*mar.*) andar a babor.
portability, *s.* cualidad portátil.
portable ['pɔ:ɹtəbəl], *a.* portátil.
portage ['pɔ:ɹtidʒ], *s.* porte, portaje, portazgo; transporte, conducción.
portal ['pɔ:ɹtəl], *s.* (*arq.*) portada; portal, vestíbulo; (*anat.*) *portal vein,* vena porta.
port-crayon [pɔ:ɹt'kreijɔn], *s.* lapicero.
portcullis [pɔ:ɹt'kʌlis], *s.* rastrillo.
portend [pɔ:ɹ'tend], *v.t.* pronosticar, presagiar.
portent ['pɔ:ɹtənt], *s.* portento, mal agüero, augurio, presagio.
portentous [pɔ:ɹ'tentəs], *a.* portentoso, prodigioso, ominoso, monstruoso, de mal agüero.

porter ['pɔ:ɹtəɹ], *s.* portero, conserje, portera; mozo de estación, mozo de cordel; portador, porteador, faquín, comisionista, *m.f.*; cerveza.
porterage ['pɔ:ɹtəridʒ], *s.* porte, portaje; transporte.
portfire, *s.* lanzafuegos, botafuego.
portfolio [pɔ:ɹt'fouliou], *s.* cartera, carpeta; (*pol.*) cartera, ministerio.
portico ['pɔ:ɹtikou], *s.* pórtico, portal; soportal, atrio, porche.
portion ['pɔ:ɹʃən], *s.* porción, parte, *f.,* pedazo, cuota, dote, *m.f.* — *v.t.* dividir, partir, repartir, distribuir, dotar.
portioner, *s.* repartidor.
portionless, *a.* indotado, sin dote.
portliness ['pɔ:ɹtlinis], *s.* porte majestuoso; corpulencia.
portly ['pɔ:ɹtli], *a.* corpulento, grueso, rollizo; majestuoso.
portmanteau [pɔ:ɹt'mæntou], *s.* maleta.
portrait ['pɔ:ɹtrit], *s.* retrato; *portrait-painter,* retratista, *m.f.*
portraiture ['pɔ:ɹtrətʃəɹ], *s.* retrato, representación; bosquejo, pintura.
portray [pɔ:ɹ'trei], *v.t.* retratar, describir, pintar.
portrayal, *s.* representación gráfica.
portrayer, *s.* pintor.
portress ['pɔ:ɹtres], *s.f.* portera.
Portuguese [pɔ:ɹtju:'gi:z], *s., a.* portugués.
pory ['pɔ:ri], *a.* poroso.
pose [pouz], *v.t.* plantear, afirmar, proponer; colocar en cierta actitud; confundir, refutar. — *v.i.* colocarse en cierta postura; adoptar actitudes *o* posturas falsas; *to pose as,* hacerse pasar por, dársela de, fingir ser. — *s.* actitud, postura; postura vana, aire de afectación, empaque, prosopopeya.
poser, *s.* escudriñador; examinador; (*fam.*) problema, pregunta difícil, pega.
posit ['pɔzit], *v.t.* (*lóg.*) afirmar, proponer.
position [pɔ'ziʃən], *s.* posición, situación, colocación; categoría, condición, estado; postura, actitud; colocación, empleo; (*lóg.*) proposición, aserto; *in a position to,* en estado de.
positive ['pɔzitiv], *a.* positivo, indudable, concreto, preciso; dogmático, categórico, enfático; porfiado, obstinado, terco. — *s.* (*gram.*) positivo; (*foto.*) (prueba) positiva; (*filos.*) positivista.
positiveness, *s.* carácter positivo; realidad, seguridad, certeza; terquedad, obstinación, porfía.
positivism, *s.* positivismo.
positivist, *s.* positivista, *m.f.*
posology [pɔ'zɔlodʒi], *s.* (*med.*) posología; (*mat.*) doctrina o ciencia de la cantidad.
posse ['pɔsi], *s.* posibilidad; pelotón.
possess [pɔ'zes], *v.t.* poseer, tener, tener en su poder, ser dueño de; apoderarse de, gozar, dominar, señorear; *to be possessed of,* poseer; *one possessed,* energúmeno.
possession [pɔ'zeʃən], *s.* posesión, poder, pertenencia, dominio. — *pl.* riquezas, bienes; *to take possession of,* entrar en posesión de.
possessive, *a.* posesivo, posesional.
possessor, *s.* poseedor, posesor; (*com.*) portador.
possessory, *a.* posesorio.

posset ['pɔset], s. bebida de leche cuajada con cerveza, vino, etc.

possibility [pɔsi'biliti], s. posibilidad, contingencia.

possible ['pɔsibəl], a. posible; *as soon as possible*, cuanto antes; *it is possible that*, puede ser que.

possibly ['pɔsibli], adv. posiblemente, quizá, quizás, acaso, tal vez.

possum ['pɔsəm], s. (*fam.*) zarigüeya [OPOSSUM]; *to play possum*, desatenderse, no hacer caso; hacerse el tonto.

post [poust], s. poste, pilar; estafeta, correo, mala, posta; empleo, colocación, vacante, f., puesto; paraje; (*mil.*) guarnición, plaza, puesto avanzada; *Last Post*, Retreta; *finger post*, poste indicador; *as deaf as a post*, sordo como una tapia; *by return of post*, a vuelta de correo; *post free*, franco de porte; *from pillar to post*, de Herodes a Pilatos, de Ceca en Meca. — *v.t.* echar o llevar al correo; cartelear, poner carteles; colocar, situar, apostar; tener al corriente; (*com.*) pasar los asientos de un libro a otro; registrar. — *v.i.* viajar en posta, correr la posta; ir de prisa, apresurarse.

postage ['poustidʒ], s. porte, franqueo; viaje en posta; *postage stamp*, sello de correo.

postal ['poustəl], a. postal; *postal note*, (*E.U.*) vale postal de menos de $5; *postal order*, orden postal de pago, giro postal.

post-bag, s. saco de los despachos; saco de correspondencia.

post-card, s. tarjeta, tarjeta postal.

post-chaise, s. coche de posta.

post-date, v.t. posfechar.

posted, a. puesto, colocado. — *p.p.* [POST]; *posted up*, al corriente.

poster ['poustəɹ], s. cartel; cartelero, cartelón; papelón; correro; caballo de posta; (*com.*) tenedor de libros; *bill-poster*, fijador de carteles.

posterior [pɔs'tiəriəɹ], s. trasero, asentaderas. — a. posterior.

posteriority, s. posterioridad.

posteriorly, adv. posteriormente.

posteriors [pɔs'tiəriəɹz], s.pl. nalgas, posaderas, asentaderas.

posterity [pɔs'teriti], s. posteridad.

postern ['pɔstən], s. puerta trasera; (*fort.*) poterna, postigo.

postfix [poust'fiks], s. (*gram.*) sufijo. — v.t. añadir (un sufijo).

postgraduate [poust'grædju:it], s. estudiante licenciado o que desarrolla investigaciones superiores en una universidad. — a. de investigaciones superiores, de estudiantes licenciados.

post-haste [poust'heist], a. urgente, apresurado. — s. diligencia, presteza. — adv. a toda prisa, a raja tabla.

posthumous ['pɔstjuːməs], a. póstumo.

posthumously, adv. después del fallecimiento.

postil ['pɔstil], v.t. (*ant.*) postilar, apostillar. — s. postila, apostilla.

postilion, s. postillón.

postillate ['pɔstileit], v.t. (*ant.*) postilar, apostillar.

postliminy [pɔst'limini], s. postliminio.

postman ['poustmən], s. cartero.

postmark, s. matasellos.

postmaster, s. administrador de correos.

post-meridian ['poust me'ridiən], a. postmeridiano, de la tarde; abreviación: *p.m.*

post-mortem [poust'mɔːɪtem], adv. (*Lat.*) después de la muerte. — s. necropsia, autopsia.

post-obit [poust'ɔbit], a. (*for.*) teniendo efecto, valor, o fuerza después de la muerte.

post-office ['poustɔfis], s. casa de correos, estafeta.

post-paid, a. franco de porte.

postpone [poust'poun], v.t. diferir, aplazar, posponer, postergar.

postponement, s. aplazamiento, postergación.

postscript ['poustskript], s. posdata.

postulant ['pɔstjuːlənt], s. postulante; (*igl.*) postulador, novicio.

postulate ['pɔstjuːlit], v.t. postular, arrogarse, atribuirse. — s. postulado.

postulation, s. postulación, póstula; petición.

postulatory, a. postulatorio, supuesto.

posture ['pɔstʃəɹ], s. postura, actitud; situación, estado, disposición. — v.t., v.i. poner(se) en alguna postura.

post-war, s. postguerra. — a. de la postguerra.

posy ['pouzi], s. ramillete de flores; mote, cifra.

pot [pɔt], s. olla, marmita, puchero; piñata, caldereta, cacharro; orinal; *flower-pot*, tiesto, florero; *melting-pot*, crisol; *milk-pot*, jarro para leche; *pot-belly*, barriga; *pot-bellied*, barrigón, barrigudo, panzudo; *pot-boiler*, obra hecha de prisa para ganarse la vida; *to go to pot*, (*fam.*) echarse a perder, estar arruinado; *to keep the pot boiling*, ganar bastante para vivir; *to have pots of money*, (*fam.*) tener mucha mosca; *it is like the pot calling the kettle black*, dijo la sartén a la caldera, ¡ quítate allá culinegra ! — v.t. preservar, conservar; (*coc.*) estofar; plantar en tiestos. — v.i. disparar, tirar; (*ant.*) achisparse.

potable ['poutəbəl], a. potable.

potage ['poutɑːʒ], s. potaje.

potash ['pɔtæʃ], s. potasa.

potassium [po'tæsiəm], s. potasio.

potation, s. trago; potación, bebida.

potato [po'teitou], s. (*bot.*) patata; (*Amér.*) papa; *potato starch*, almidón; *sweet potato*, batata, patata dulce de Málaga; (*Cuba*) boniato; (*Méj.*) camote; *small potatoes*, (*vulg.*) cosas de chicha y nabo.

pot-cheese, s. requesón.

poteen [po'tiːn], s. whisky irlandés.

potency ['poutənsi], s. potencia, fuerza, poder, autoridad, influjo, vigor.

potent ['poutənt], a. potente, fuerte, poderoso, influyente, eficaz.

potentate ['poutənteit], s. potentado.

potential [po'tenʃəl], a. potencial; virtual; (*ant.*) potente, poderoso; eficaz, efectivo; (*fis.*, *gram.*) potencial; (*mat.*) función potencial.

potentiality, s. potencialidad.

Potentilla [poten'tilə], s. (*bot.*) cincoeurama.

potentiometer [potenʃi'ɔmetəɹ], s. potenciómetro.

potentness, s. poder, potencia.

pother ['pɔðəɹ], s. alboroto, tumulto, baraúnda, bullicio. — v.t., v.i. aturdir, atormentar, alborotar sin necesidad.

pot-herb ['pɔthəːɹb], s. hortaliza.

pot-hole, s. bache.

pothook ['pɔthuk], s. garabato; llar, gramallera.

pot-house, s. tabernucho.
potion ['pouʃən], s. poción, pócima, brebaje.
pot-lead, s. grafito.
pot-luck, s. fortuna del puchero; *to take pot-luck,* (*fam.*) hacer penitencia, hacer algo al buen tuntún.
potman ['pɔtmən], s. mozo de taberna.
pot-pourri [poupu'ri:], s. (*mús.*) popurrí; baturrillo.
potsherd ['pɔtʃəːɹd], s. casco, tiesto.
pottage ['pɔtidʒ], s. potaje, acemita, menestra.
pottager, s. escudilla.
potter ['pɔtəɹ], s. alfarero, alcarracero, ollero. — *v.i.* divertirse con tonterías, andar de vagar; *potter's field,* cementerio de los pobres, hoyanca (*fam.*); *potter's wheel,* rueda de alfarero.
pottery, s. alfarería, ollería, cocharros.
pottle ['pɔtəl], s. medida líquida de cuatro pintas, azumbre, *f.*; cesto, cesta; vaso, jarro.
pouch [pautʃ], s. faltriquera, saquito, bolsa, bolsón; tabaquera; buche; barrigón; (*zool.*) bolsa; vejiga; (*bot.*) silícula. — *v.t.* embolsar; engullir, tragar. — *v.i.* (*E.U.*) hacer pucheritos.
poudrette [pu:'dret], s. abono compuesto de letrina, yeso y carbón de leña.
pouf [puf], s. cojín o almohadilla; peinado femenino del siglo 18.
poulpe [pu:lp], s. (*ict.*) pulpo.
poulterer ['poultərəɹ], s. gallinero, pollero.
poultice ['poultis], s. bizma, emplasto, apósito, cataplasma. — *v.t.* bizmar.
poultry ['poultri], s. aves caseras, aves de corral, volatería.
pounce [pauns], s. calada, zarpada, embestida; zarpa, garra; sandáraca, grasa, grasilla, muñequilla de carbón. — *v.t.* agarrar, embestir, abalanzarse, caer sobre; (*ant.*) horadar, agujerear; dar una zarpada; polvorear con sandáraca. — *v.i.* caer a plomo, cálarse, embestir.
pouncet-box, s. caja para perfumes; cajita agujereada para polvos de goma sandáraca.
pound [paund], s. libra; libra esterlina; depósito; corral de concejo; *pound foolish,* derrochador, gastador. — *v.t.* golpear, majar, moler, machacar, pulverizar; encerrar.
poundage, s. comisión, deducción; derecho de entrada.
pounder, s. golpeador, moledor, majador; cañón; triturador; mano de mortero, *f.*
pour [pɔːɹ], *v.t.* echar, verter; emitir, arrojar; vaciar; derramar, desparramar. — *v.i.* fluir; salir a borbotones, salir atropelladamente; arremeter, acometer; *to pour with rain,* diluviar, llover chuzos, llover a cántaros; *pouring rain,* lluvia fuerte; *it never rains but it pours,* bien vengas mal si vienes solo.
pourer, s. trasegador, vaciador.
pout [paut], s. hocico, pucherito; (*orn.*) francolín; berrinche; (*ict.*) mustela de río, abadejo, faneca. — *v.i.* hacer pucheritos, estar de hocico, poner mal gesto; amohinarse, enfurruñarse; hinchar el pecho (las aves como el palomo, etc.).
pouter, s. (*orn.*) pichón de cuello grueso, paloma buchona; persona ceñuda.
pouting, s. pucheritos, berrinche.
poverty ['pɔvəɹti], s. pobreza, estrechez, miseria.
powder ['paudəɹ], s. pólvora; polvo, polvillo;

polvos de tocador; *powder magazine,* (*mar. y arti.*) santabárbara, almacén de pólvora. — *v.t.* pulverizar, empolvar, reducir a polvos; espolvorear, polvorear. — *v.i.* caer en polvo; pulverizarse; ponerse polvos.
powder-box, s. polvorera.
powder-flask, powder-horn, s. frasco de pólvora, frasco para pólvora.
powdering, s. pulverización; acción de empolvar; salazón.
powder-puff, s. penacho o borla de empolvar.
powdery, a. polvoriento, empolvado, desmenuzado.
power ['pauəɹ], s. poder, potestad; poderío; pujanza, fuerza; propiedad, facultad; potencia, dominación, dominio, imperio, autoridad, mando; influjo, ascendiente; energía, fuerza motriz; (*vulg.*) gran número, cantidad; *power of attorney,* (*for.*) procuración, poder; *the Western Powers,* las potencias occidentales; *power-station o power-house,* central de energía eléctrica, *f.*
powerful, a. poderoso, potente; fuerte; intenso, eficaz; imperioso.
powerfulness, s. poderío, fuerza, eficacia, energía.
powerless, a. sin poder, impotente, ineficaz.
powerlessness, s. impotencia.
power-loom, s. telar mecánico.
pow-wow, powwow ['pauwau], s. junta india; exorcismo; (*fam.*) deliberación, discusión, conversación.
pox [pɔks], s. viruelas; (*fam.*) sífilis, *f.*
practicability, s. posibilidad de hacerse.
practicable ['præktikəbəl], a. practicable, factible, hacedero; accesible.
practicably, adv. prácticamente, posiblemente.
practical ['præktikəl], a. práctico, experto, versado.
practically, adv. en práctica, prácticamente; moralmente, virtualmente, casi.
practicalness, s. carácter práctico.
practice ['præktis], s. práctica, uso, costumbre, *f.*; experiencia; método, profesión, regla; clientela, parroquia; ejercicio; tiro; artificios, estratagemas; *to make it one's practice to,* soler, acostumbrarse a; *to put into practice,* poner en obra.
practician [præk'tiʃən], s. práctico.
practise ['præktis], *v.t.* poner en práctica, practicar; ejercitar, ensayar; ejercitarse en. — *v.i.* practicar, ejercer (una profesión), ejercitar, ensayar, estudiar; *to practise at a target,* (*mil.*) tirar al blanco.
practised, a. práctico; experimentado, hábil. — *p.p.* [PRACTISE].
practiser, s. practicante, el que practica, el que ejerce una profesión.
practising, a. en ejercicio, que ejerce una profesión. — s. repetición; ensayo, repaso; ejercicio, práctica; acción de practicar.
practitioner [præk'tiʃənəɹ], s. practicante, práctico; médico que ejerce; *general practitioner,* médico de familia.
prætorium [pri'tɔ:riəm], s. pretorio.
pragmatic [præg'mætik], **pragmatical** [præg'mætikəl], a. pragmático, activo, práctico.
prairie ['preəri], s. pradera, pradería, llanura, sabana, pampa; *prairie chicken,* (*orn.*) chocha; *prairie dog,* (*zool.*) aranata.

praise [preiz], s. elogio, alabanza, encomio, loor; fama, celebridad, reputación, renombre; glorificación, lisonja. — v.t. alabar, loar, aplaudir, exaltar, hacer elogios de, preconizar, glorificar, encomiar, ensalzar, celebrar; bendecir.

praiseless, a. sin alabanza.

praiser, s. loador, aprobador, ensalzador, celebrador, panegirista, m.f.

praiseworthily, adv. loablemente, laudablemente.

praiseworthiness, s. mérito, carácter loable.

praiseworthy ['preizwəːɹði], a. loable, laudable, digno de alabanza.

praline ['prɑːliːn], s. almendra tostada.

pram ¡præm], s. (mar.) barco chato; (fam.) [PERAMBULATOR].

prance [prɑːns], v.i. cabriolar, cabriolear, encabritarse; trenzar. — s. cabriola; trenzado.

prancer, s. caballo pisador.

prancing, s. cabriolas; trenzado; aire altanero.

prank ¡præŋk], s. travesura, locura, extravagancia, picardihuela; to play one's pranks, hacer de las suyas. — v.t. adornar, hermosear. — v.i. to prank up, to be pranked up, ataviarse, adornarse con exceso.

prankish, a. malicioso, travieso, retozón.

prate [preit], v.i. charlar, parlotear, chacharear. — s. charla, cháchara.

prater, s. hablador, charlador, charlatán.

prating, s. charla, cháchara. — a. charlador.

pratingly, adv. charlando, con cháchara.

pratique ['prætik, prə'tiːk], s. (mar.) libre plática.

prattle [prætəl], v.t. balbucear. — v.i. charlar, parlotear, chacharear. — s. charla, parlería, charlatanería, garrulería, parloteo, cháchara; (fig.) parloteo, murmullo, rumor.

prattler, s. charlador, parlanchín, hablador; chismoso.

pravity [præviti], s. depravación, pravidad, perversidad, iniquidad.

prawn [prɔːn], s. (ict.) camarón, gamba.

praxis ['præksis], s. práctica, modelos, ejercicios, (ant.) praxis, f.

pray [prei], v.t., v.i. rezar, orar; rogar, suplicar, implorar.

prayer [prɛəɹ], s. oración, rezo; plegaria, súplica; Lord's Prayer, padrenuestro, oración dominical; prayer book, libro de rezo, devocionario.

prayerfulness ['prɛəɹfəlnis], s. devoción, piedad; inclinación a rezar.

praying ['preiiŋ], s. rezos; suplicación.

preach [priːtʃ], v.t., v.i. predicar, sermonear; to preach to no effect, dar voces al lobo, predicar en desierto.

preacher, s. predicador.

preaching, s. predicación; sermón.

preachment, s. (despec.) prédica, sermoneo.

pre-acquaint [priːə'kweint], v.t. comunicar o advertir de antemano.

pre-admonish [priːəd'mɔniʃ], v.t. advertir de antemano.

pre-admonition [priːædmɔ'niʃən], s. advertencia prealable.

preamble [priː'æmbəl], s. preámbulo, exordio.

pre-arrange [priːə'reindʒ], v.t. arreglar de antemano, predisponer (las cosas).

prebend ['prebənd], s. prebenda; prebendado.

prebendary ['prebəndəri], s. prebendado, racionero.

precarious [pre'kɛəriəs], a. precario, azaroso, incierto, inseguro, arriesgado, peligroso.

precariousness, s. estado precario, condición incierta, incertidumbre, f.

precatory [pre'keitəri], a. mendicante.

precaution [pre'kɔːʃən], s. precaución, cautela, reserva.

precautionary, a. preventivo.

precede [pre'siːd], v.t. preceder, anteceder; anteponer; sobresalir. — v.i. tener la primacia, ir delante.

precedence ['presidəns], **precedency** [pre'siːdənsi], s. prioridad, anterioridad, superioridad, precedencia, primacía.

precedent [pre'siːdənt], a. precedente, antecedente, prior, anterior, ejemplar.

precedent ['presidənt], s. precedente, antecedente, ejemplo.

precedented, a. que tiene precedente.

preceding [pre'siːdiŋ], a. precedente.

precentor [pre'sentəɹ], s. chantre, capiscol.

precept ['priːsept], s. precepto; (for.) mandato.

preceptive, a. preceptivo.

preceptor, s. preceptor.

preceptorial [priːsep'tɔːriəl], a. preceptoral.

preceptory [pre'septəri], a. preceptoral. — s. preceptoria.

preceptress, s.f. preceptora.

precession [pre'seʃən], s. precesión, precedencia; (astr.) precesión de los equinoccios.

precinct ['priːsiŋkt], s. recinto; linde, lindero; distrito electoral, barrio. — pl. recinto; alrededores, afueras.

precious ['preʃəs], a. precioso, costoso, de gran valor, preciado; caro, querido, amado; (iron., fam.) famoso; culterano, hinchado, ampuloso; remilgado, cursi (fam.). — (adv.) considerablemente, bastante; to be very precious, costar un ojo de la cara.

preciousness, s. preciosidad, gran precio, gran valor; culteranismo, culterano, hinchazón, f., ampulosidad; remilgo, hinchazón, f.

precipice ['presipis], s. precipicio, despeñadero, derrumbadero.

precipitance [pre'sipitəns], **precipitancy** [pre'sipitənsi], s. precipitación, gran prisa.

precipitant, a. precipitado, que se precipita, arrojado, arrebatado. — s. (quím.) precipitante.

precipitantly, adv. precipitadamente.

precipitate [pre'sipiteit], v.t. precipitar, acelerar, apresurar; despeñar, arrojar, derrumbar; (quím.) precipitar. — v.i. precipitarse, arrojarse, despeñarse. — a. precipitado, que se precipita. — s. (quím.) precipitado.

precipitately, adv. precipitadamente, apresuradamente, de corrida.

precipitation [presipi'teiʃən], s. precipitación, imprudencia; precipitación, apresuramiento; derrumbamiento; (quím.) precipitado.

precipitous [pre'sipitəs], a. precipitoso, acantilado, escarpado.

precipitously, adv. precipitadamente, en precipicio.

precipitousness, s. carácter escarpado, acantilado o precipitoso.

précis ['preisiː], s. resumen, sumario.

precise [pre'sais], a. preciso, puntual, exacto; formal, escrupuloso, estricto, justo; terminante, perentorio; (*fam.*) singular, particular; propio, idéntico; pedante, ceremonioso.

precisely, *adv.* precisamente, exactamente; escrupulosamente; cabalmente, justamente; ceremoniosamente, formalmente.

preciseness, *s.* precisión, exactitud, puntualidad; escrúpulo, escrupulosidad.

precisian [pre'siʒən], *s.* rigorista, formulista, *m.f.*, ceremonioso.

precision [pre'siʒən], *s.* precisión, exactitud; escrupulosidad.

preclude [pre'klu:d], *v.t.* evitar, impedir; excluir; *to preclude the possibility of*, hacer imposible.

preclusion, *s.* exclusión.

preclusive, *a.* que excluye.

preclusively, *adv.* con exclusión.

precocious [pre'kouʃəs], *a.* precoz.

precociously, *adv.* con precocidad.

precociousness, precocity, *s.* precocidad.

precogitation [pri:kɔdʒi'teiʃən], *s.* premeditación.

precognition [pri:kɔg'niʃən], *s.* precognición.

precompose [pri:kəm'pouz], *v.t.* componer de antemano.

preconceit [pri:kən'si:t], *s.* concepto anticipado, preocupación.

preconceive [pri:kənsi:v], *v.t.* preconcebir.

preconceived, *a.* preconcebido.

preconception [pri:kən'sepʃən], *s.* opinión *o* concepto preconcebido; prejuicio.

preconcert [pri:kənsə:ɪt], *s.* concertar, acordar de antemano, predisponer.

pre-Conquest [pri:'kɔŋkwest], *s.* anterior a la conquista de Inglaterra por los normandos (1066).

preconscious [pri:'kɔnʃəs], *a.* referente *o* relativo al estado anterior al de recobrar el sentido.

precurrent [pri:'kʌrənt], *a.* ocurriendo de antemano; precursorio.

precursive [pri:'kə:ɪsiv], **precursory** [pri:'kə:ɪsəri], *a.* precursor.

precursor, *s.* precursor.

predatory ['predətəri], *a.* rapaz, voraz, de rapiña, que vive de sus presas, de presa, hurto *o* rapiña.

predecease [pri:de'si:s], *v.t.* morir antes que (otro), (*for.*) premorir.

predecessor [pri:de'sesəɪ], *s.* predecesor, antecesor; antepasado.

predestinarian [pri:desti'nɛəriən], *s., a.* partidario de la doctrina de la predestinación.

predestinarianism, *s.* doctrina de la predestinación.

predestinate [pri:'destineit], *v.t.* predestinar.

predestination, *s.* predestinación.

predestinator, *s.* predestinante.

predestine [pri:'destin], *v.t.* predestinar.

predeterminate [pri:de'tə:ɪminit], *a.* predeterminado.

predetermination, *s.* predeterminación.

predetermine [pri:de'tə:ɪmin], *v.t.* predeterminar, predestinar.

predial ['pri:diəl], *a.* predial.

predicable ['predikəbəl], *s., a.* predicable; (*lóg.*) predicable, categorema.

predicament [pre'dikəmənt], *s.* apuro, trance; (*filos.*) predicamento, categoría; *in a regular predicament*, (*fam.*) en las astas del toro.

predicamental, *a.* predicamental.

predicate ['predikeit], *v.t.* (*lóg.*) predicar,

afirmar un predicado. — *v.i.* predicarse, afirmarse. — *s.* (*gram., lóg.*) predicado, absoluto.

predication, *s.* (*lóg.*) predicación, aseveración; (*ant.*) predicación, sermón.

predict [pre'dikt], *v.t.* predecir, profetizar, pronosticar, adivinar.

prediction, *s.* predicción, pronóstico, profecía, vaticinio.

predictive, *a.* que predice.

predictor, *s.* pronosticador, adivino.

predigestion [pri:di'dʒestʃən], *s.* peptonización del alimento, digestión artificial.

predilection [predi'lekʃən], *s.* predilección.

predisponent, *a.* predisponente.

predispose [pri:dis'pouz], *v.t.* predisponer.

predisposition [pri:dispə'ziʃən], *s.* predisposición, propensión.

predominance [pre'dɔminəns], **predominancy** [pre'dɔminənsi], *s.* predominio, predominación.

predominant, *a.* predominante.

predominate [pre'dɔmineit], *v.t.* predominar, prevalecer.

pre-elect [pri:e'lekt], *v.t.* nombrar *o* elegir de antemano.

pre-election, *s.* elección anterior.

pre-eminence, *s.* preeminencia, supremacía, primacía.

pre-eminent [pri:'eminənt], *a.* preeminente, superlativo, supremo, extremo, extraordinario.

preen [pri:n], *v.t.* limpiar y concertar sus plumas (las aves); *to preen oneself*, darse tono, jactarse; componerse, afeitarse.

pre-engage [pri:en'geidʒ], *v.t.* apalabrar, obligar o empeñar de antemano.

pre-engagement, *s.* obligación o empeño anterior, compromiso.

pre-establish [pri:es'tæbliʃ], *v.t.* preestablecer, establecer de antemano.

pre-exist [pri:ek'zist], *v.i.* preexistir.

pre-existence, *s.* preexistencia.

pre-existent, *a.* preexistente.

preface ['prefəs, 'prefis], *s.* prólogo, proemio; (*igl.*) prefacio. — *v.t.* poner un prólogo a; (*fig.*) dar comienzo a. — *v.i.* hacer un exordio, empezar.

prefatory ['prefətəri], *a.* preliminar.

prefect ['pri:fekt], *s.* prefecto; decurión, estudiante con encargos especiales.

prefecture ['pri:fektju:əɪ], *s.* prefectura.

prefer [pre'fə:ɪ], *v.t.* preferir, dar preferencia a; anteponer; elevar, ascender, exaltar, adelantar; elegir, escoger; presentar, ofrecer en público, ofrecer solemnemente.

preferable ['prefərəbəl], *a.* preferible, preferente.

preferableness, *s.* estado de preferible.

preferably, *adv.* preferiblemente, preferentemente.

preference, *s.* preferencia, predilección; prelación.

preferential [prefə'renʃəl], *a.* de preferencia; que tiene preferencia.

preferment [pre'fə:ɪmənt], *s.* promoción, ascenso, elevación, adelantamiento; preferencia, puesto eminente.

preferrer, *s.* persona que prefiere.

prefiguration [pri:figju:'reiʃən], **prefigurement** [pri:'figəɪmənt], *s.* prefiguración.

prefigurative, *a.* que prefigura.

prefigure [pri:'figəɹ], v.t. prefigurar.
prefix [pre'fiks], s. prefijo, afijo. — v.t. prefijar, anteponer; fijar, determinar o establecer de antemano.
preform [pri:'fɔ:ɹm], v.t. formar de antemano.
preformation, s. formación previa.
prefulgence [pre'fʌldʒəns], s. resplandor.
pregnancy, s. embarazo, preñez, preñado; (fig.) fertilidad, fecundidad; (fig.) gravedad, profundidad.
pregnant ['pregnənt], a. embarazada, encinta, preñada; (fig.) fértil, fecundo; (fig.) grave, profundo.
prehensile [pri:'hensail], a. prensil.
prehension [pre'henʃən], s. prensión.
prehistoric [pri:his'tɔrik], **prehistorical** [pri:his'tɔrikəl], a. prehistórico.
prejudge [pri:'dʒʌdʒ], v.t. prejuzgar.
prejudgment, s. juicio sin examen, prejuicio.
prejudicate [pre'dʒu:dikeit], v.t. (ant.) prejuzgar. — v.i. (ant.) tener prejuicios.
prejudication, s. prejuicio, acto de juzgar de antemano.
prejudice ['predʒu:dis], s. prejuicio; (for.) perjuicio; daño, desventaja. — v.t. perjudicar, dañar, hacer daño; sugestionar, influir, predisponer.
prejudiced, a. parcial, de prejuicios. — p.p. [PREJUDICE].
prejudicial [predʒu:'diʃəl], a. perjudicial, dañoso, nocivo, pernicioso, funesto.
prelacy ['preləsi], s. prelacía, episcopado.
prelate ['prelət], s. prelado.
prelateship, s. prelatura, prelacía.
prelatic [pre'lætik], **prelatical** [pre'lætikəl], a. de prelado.
prelect [pre'lekt], v.i. pronunciar un discurso, conferenciar.
prelection, s. conferencia universitaria o pública; lectura de antemano.
prelector, s. catedrático.
preliminary [pre'liminəri], a. preliminar, preparativo, antecedente, introductorio.
prelude [pre'lju:d], s. preludio, prelusión; presagio. — v.t., v.i. preludiar.
preluder, s. el que hace preludios.
preludial, prelusive, prelusory, a. preparatorio, preliminar, proemial, introductorio, previo.
premature [pri:mə'tʃju:əɹ], a. prematuro, intempestivo.
prematureness, s. precocidad, madurez antes del tiempo, lo intempestivo.
premeditate [pri:'mediteit], v.t. premeditar. — v.i. pensar de antemano.
premeditated, a. premeditado.
premeditation, s. premeditación.
premier ['premiəɹ], a. primero, principal, jefe. — s. primer ministro, presidente del consejo.
première, s. estreno (de un drama).
premiership ['premiəɹʃip], s. presidencia del consejo, oficio de primer ministro.
premise [pre'maiz], v.t. exponer anticipada-mente. — v.i. sentar o establecer premisas. — s. (lóg.) premisa.
premises ['premisis], s.pl. (lóg.) premisas; (for.) asertos, aserciones; recinto, local, establecimiento, tierras.
premium ['pri:miəm], s. premio, remuneración, galardón; (com., mar.) prima, premio; at a premium, a beneficio, a prima.
premonish [pre'mɔniʃ], v.t. prevenir, advertir.

premonition [premɔn'iʃən], s. presentimiento; presagio, advertencia.
premonitory [pri'mɔnitəri], a. preventivo.
premotion [pri:'mouʃən], s. premoción.
prenominate [pri:'nɔmineit], v.t. nombrar primero.
prenomination, s. acción de nombrar primero.
prentice ['prentis], s. aprendiz.
preobtain [pri:ɔb'tein], v.t. obtener de ante-mano.
preoccupancy, s. preocupación; ocupación previa; derecho de ocupación.
preoccupation [pri:ɔkju:'peiʃən], s. preocupación, prejuicio; obsesión, preocupación; ocupación previa.
preoccupied [pri:'ɔkju:paid], a. absorto, pre-ocupado; obseso, preocupado; preocupado, perturbado.
preoccupy, v.t. obsesionar, preocupar; ab-sorber, atraer, preocupar; preocupar, per-turbar; ocupar antes que otro.
preordain [pri:ɔ:ɹ'dein], v.t. preordenar; (teo.) predestinar, preordinar.
preordinance [pri:'ɔ:ɹdinəns], **preordination** [pri:ɔ:ɹdi'neiʃən], s. preordinación.
prepaid [pri:'peid], a. franqueado; pagado de antemano.
preparation [prepə'reiʃən], s. preparación, preparativo, apresto, disposición, adapta-ción; preparado (de medicamentos); aparato; manipulación, fabricación.
preparative [pre'pærətiv], a. preparativo, preparatorio, previo. — s. preparativo, apresto.
preparatively, adv. previamente, anticipada-mente.
preparatory [pre'pærətəri], a. preparatorio, previo, preliminar.
prepare [pre'pɛəɹ], v.t. preparar, aparejar, aviar, aprestar, equipar, disponer, prevenir; aderezar, adobar, confeccionar, proveer de; establecer, fundar. — v.i. hacer preparativos, prepararse, disponerse, alistarse.
prepared, a. preparado, dispuesto; alerto. — p.p. [PREPARE].
preparedly, adv. preventivamente.
preparedness, s. estado de preparación, prevención.
preparer, s. preparador.
prepay [pri:'pei], v.t. (pret., p.p. **prepaid**) pagar adelantado, franquear.
prepayment, s. pago adelantado, franqueo.
prepense [pre'pens], a. premeditado. — v.t. (ant.) premeditar.
preperception [pri:pəɹ'sepʃən], s. percepción previa.
preponderance [pre'pɔndərəns], **prepon-derancy** [pre'pɔndərənsi], s. preponde-rancia, predominación.
preponderant, a. preponderante, predomi-nante.
preponderate [pre'pɔndəreit], v.t., v.i. pre-ponderar, prevalecer, predominar.
preponderating, a. preponderante.
preponderation, s. preponderancia.
preposition [prepo'ziʃən], s. preposición.
prepositional, prepositive, a. preposicional, prepositivo.
prepositive [pre'pɔzitiv], s. partícula, pre-positiva. — a. prefijo, antepuesto.
prepositor, s. (en algunas escuelas) decurión.

prepossess [pri:po'zes], *v.t.* predisponer, sugestionar, influir; llenar de preocupaciones, preocupar; ocupar antes que otro.

prepossessing, *a.* simpático, amable, atractivo.

prepossession, *s.* predisposición, parcialidad; preferencia, predilección; prejuicio; ocupación o posesión previa.

preposterous [pre'pɔstərəs], *a.* absurdo, ridículo, disparatado; prepóstero, invertido.

preposterousness, *s.* ridiculez, lo disparatado; preposteración.

prepotent [pre'poutənt], *a.* prepotente, predominante; muy poderoso; con fuerza o influencia superior.

pre-prandial [pri:'prændiəl], *a.* sucedido o realizado antes de comer.

prepuce ['pri:pju:s], *s.* prepucio.

pre-Raphaelite [pri:'ræfəlait], *s.*, *a.* pre-rrafaelista, *m.f.*

prerequisite [pri:'rekwizit], *s.*, *a.* requisito (previo).

preresolve [pri:rezɔlv], *v.t.* resolver anticipadamente.

prerogative [pre'rɔgətiv], *s.* prerrogativa, privilegio. — *a.* privilegiado.

presage ['presidʒ], *s.* presagio, pronóstico. — *v.t.* presagiar, predecir, pronosticar, vaticinar.

presageful, *a.* lleno de presagios.

presbyopia [prezbi'oupiə], *s.* presbicia.

presbyter ['prezbitəɹ], *s.* presbítero.

presbyterial [prezbi'tiəriəl], **presbyterian** [prezbi'tiəriən], *a.* presbiteral, presbiteriano. — *s.* presbiteriano.

presbyterianism, *s.* presbiterianismo.

presbytery ['prezbitəri], *s.* presbiterio.

prescience ['preʃəns], *s.* presciencia.

prescient ['preʃənt], *a.* presciente.

prescind [pre'sind], *v.t.*, *v.i.* separar, abstraer; prescindir.

prescribe [pre'skraib], *v.t.* prescribir; (*med.*) recetar. — *v.i.* prescribir; (*med.*) hacer una receta, prescribir un remedio; (*for.*) prescribir, dar leyes o reglas.

prescript ['pri:skript], *s.* regla, ordenanza, norma; (*filos.*) prescrito.

prescriptibility, *s.* calidad de prescriptible.

prescriptible, *a.* prescriptible; (*for.*) adquirible por prescripción.

prescription [pre'skripʃən], *s.* prescripción, disposición, precepto; (*med.*) receta.

prescriptive [pre'skriptiv], *a.* de prescripción, autorizado por la costumbre; (*for.*) adquirido por prescripción.

presence ['prezəns], *s.* presencia, asistencia; porte, aspecto, aire, presencia; personalidad impresionante; asamblea; aparición; *presence-chamber*, salón de recepción; *presence of mind*, serenidad, presencia de ánimo; *to lose one's presence of mind*, perder la cabeza; *Real Presencia*, Presencia de Dios.

present ['prezənt], *a.* actual, presente; (*com.*) corriente; *to be present at*, asistir a; presenciar. — *s.* presente, actualidad; (*gram.*) tiempo presente; regalo. — *pl.* **presents**, (*for.*) escrituras presentes; *to make a present of*, regalar; *at present*, actualmente, ahora, al presente; *by these presents*, (*for.*) por las presentes.

present [pre'zent], *v.t.* presentar, regalar, dar, entregar, proporcionar, ofrecer; hacer un obsequio de; sugerir, indicar; repre-

sentar, mostrar, exponer, manifestar; (*for.*) denunciar, acusar; *to present arms*, (*mil.*) presentar armas.

presentability, *s.* calidad de presentable.

presentable [pre'zentəbəl], *a.* presentable.

presentation [prezen'teiʃən], *s.* presentación; agasajo, homenaje, obsequio; exposición, presentación; *presentation copy*, ejemplar de regalo; *on presentation of*, (*com.*) a presentación de.

presentative, *a.* que tiene derecho de presentación.

presentee [prezen'ti:], *s.* (*igl.*) presentado (a un beneficio).

presenter, *s.* presentador; obsequiador; el que presenta a un beneficio.

presential, *a.* presencial.

presentiment [pre'zentimənt], *s.* presentimiento; corazonada.

presently ['prezəntli], *adv.* pronto, luego, ya, dentro de poco, de aquí a poco tiempo; (*ant.*) al presente.

presentment [pre'zentmənt], *s.* presentación, introducción; retrato, representación, semejanza; (*for.*) denuncia, acusación.

preservable [pre'zə:ɹvəbəl], *a.* preservable, que se puede preservar.

preservation [prezə:ɹ'veiʃən], *s.* preservación, resguardo, conservación.

preservative [pre'zə:ɹvətiv], *a.* preservativo, conservativo. — *s.* salvaguardia, *m.*, defensa, preservativo; conservador.

preserve [pre'zə:ɹv], *v.t.* preservar, conservar; proteger, resguardar; reservar, retener, guardar; asegurar, garantizar; (*coc.*) hacer conservas de, confitar, almibarar. — *s.pl.* **preserves**, conserva; compota, confitura; vedado, coto.

preserver, *s.* preservador, conservador; persona o cosa que conserva; *life-preserver*, salvavidas, *m.*; cintura de salvamento.

preside [pre'zaid], *v.i.* presidir, dirigir, gobernar; *to preside over*, presidir.

presidency, *s.* presidencia.

president ['prezidənt], *s.* presidente, presidenta, *f.*

presidential [prezi'denʃəl], *a.* presidencial.

presidentship, *s.* presidencia.

presider, *s.* persona que preside, presidente.

presidial [pre'zidiəl], **presidiary**, *a.* perteneciente o relativo a la guarnición de un fuerte, una plaza, etc.

presiding [pre'zaidiŋ], *a.* que preside, presidente; tutelar.

pre-signify [pri:'signifai], *v.t.* significar, hacer saber de antemano.

press [pres], *v.t.* apretar, comprimir, estrujar, prensar, aprensar; exprimir; afligir, angustiar, abrumar, oprimir; compeler, forzar, impeler, importunar, obligar; dar prisa, apremiar, apresurar; hacer adelantar; (*mil.*) enganchar, hacer levas; acosar, hostigar, perseguir; ajustar, recalcar; planchar, alisar, satinar; dar un apretón; *I am pressed for time*, me falta tiempo; *to hot-press*, satinar, prensar con planchas calientes. — *v.i.* acudir, apresurarse; adelantarse; urgir; pesar, ejercer presión; ser importuno; influir en el ánimo; perseguir; agolparse, apiñarse; *to press against*, arrimarse a, pegarse a; *to press forward*, *press on*, empujar, avanzar, embestir; seguir la marcha, apretar el paso; *to* *press upon one's mind*, ocuparle a uno el espíritu; *to press for*, exigir, apoyar, reclamar, meter en prensa. — *s.* urgencia, prisa; prensa; empujón, apretón; presión; armario, escaparate; muchedumbre, *f.*, turba, apiñamiento; leva forzada; estampa, imprenta, casa editorial; (*mar.*) fuerza de velas; (*mil.*) enganche, leva; *in the press*, en o bajo prensa; *to send to press*, poner bajo prensa; *press-money*, (*mil.*) prima de enganche; *press-proof*, (*impr.*) prueba de prensa; *freedom of the press*, libertad de imprenta.

press-agent, *s.* agente de relaciones públicas.

presser, *s.* prensador; planchador, satinador, lustrador.

press-gang, *s.* ronda de matrícula.

pressing, *a.* urgente, importuno, apremiante. — *s.* presión, prensadura, prensado, apretura; expresión (de zumo, etc.); planchado; satinación de papel; recalcadura; *pressing-iron*, plancha.

pressingly, *adv.* urgentemente.

pression ['preʃən], *s.* presión.

pressman ['presmən], *s.* prensador, tirador; periodista, *m.f.*, reportero; impresor; (*mil.*) reclutador.

press-room, *s.* taller de imprenta; sala o cuarto de máquinas de una imprenta.

press-stud ['presstʌd], *s.* botón (o corchete) automático.

pressure ['preʃər], *s.* presión; opresión; impulso; peso; apremio, prisa, premura, urgencia; impulso, ímpetu; apretón; (*elec.*) carga, tensión, potencial; (*fís.*) gravitación; prensadura (de la uva); *pressure-cooker*, autoclave, *f.*; *pressure-gauge*, manómetro.

press-work, *s.* (*impr.*) impresión, tiro, tirada.

prestation [pres'teiʃən], *s.* censo.

prestidigitation [prestididʒi'teiʃən], *s.* prestidigitación.

prestige [pres'ti:ʒ], *s.* prestigio.

presumable [pre'zju:məbəl], *a.* presumible.

presumably, *adv.* presumiblemente.

presume [pre'zju:m], *v.t.* presumir, conjeturar, suponer, sospechar. — *v.i.* jactarse, vanagloriarse, presumir.

presumer, *s.* el que presume, presumido, hombre presuntuoso o arrogante.

presuming, *a.* presumido, presuntuoso.

presumption [pre'zʌmʃən], *s.* probabilidad, conjetura, sospecha, suposición; (*for.*) presunción; presunción, vanagloria.

presumptive [pre'zʌmtiv], *a.* presunto, presuntivo; (*ant.*) presuntuoso.

presumptuous [pre'zʌmtju:əs], *a.* presuntuoso, presumido; (*ant.*) presuntivo.

presumptuousness, *s.* presunción, presuntuosidad, engreimiento.

presuppose [pri:sə'pouz], *v.t.* presuponer, dar por cierto, suponer de antemano.

pretence [pre'tens], *s.* pretexto, fingimiento, apariencia, afectación, simulación; pretensión, intención; *on o under pretence of*, so pretexto de; *to make a pretence of*, fingir, simular.

pretenceless, *a.* sin pretensiones; sin pretexto.

pretend [pre'tend], *v.t.* pretextar, fingir, simular, aparentar, afectar, alegar falsamente; pretender, intentar.

pretended, *a.* falso, hipócrita; putativo.

pretender, *s.* pretendiente, pretensor; persona que finge, hipócrita, *m.f.*

pretension, *s.* simulación, pretexto, excusa; pretensión vana, afirmación gratuita, afectación; pretensión.

pretentious [pre'tenʃəs], *a.* presuntuoso, presumido, cursi (*fam.*), hinchado, ampuloso.

pretentiousness, *s.* presunción, presuntuosidad, cursilería, lo cursi, hinchazón, *f.*, ampulosidad.

preterite ['pretərit], *s.* pretérito. — *a.* pasado, pretérito.

preterition [pretə'riʃən], *s.* pretérición.

pretermission [pri:tər'miʃən], *s.* pretermisión.

pretermit [pri:tər'mit], *v.t.* pretermitir, omitir.

preternatural [pri:tər'nætʃju:rəl], *a.* preternatural, contranatural.

preterperfect [pri:tər'pə:rfekt], *a.* pretérito perfecto.

preterpluperfect [pri:tərplu:'pə:rfekt], *a.* pluscuamperfecto.

pretext ['pri:tekst], *s.* pretexto, socapa, socolor.

pretor ['pri:tər], *s.* pretor.

pretorial [pre'tɔ:riəl], **pretorian** [pre'tɔ:riən], *a.* pretoriano, pretorial.

prettiness ['pritinis], *s.* lo bonito, lindeza, gracia.

pretty ['priti], *a.* bonito, lindo, (*fam.*) guapo, (*fam.*) mono; *a pretty mess you made of it*, valiente lío se ha armado Vd. — *adv.* bastante, suficiente, algo, un poco, regular; *pretty well*, regular, tal cual; *pretty nearly*, poco más o menos, a corta diferencia.

pre-typify [pri:'tipifai], *v.t.* simbolizar, figurar de antemano.

prevail [pre'veil], *v.i.* prevalecer, predominar, preponderar; triunfar, vencer; *to prevail over*, aventajar, vencer; *to prevail upon*, inducir, persuadir, ganar; *to prevail with*, persuadir, convencer.

prevailing, *a.* predominante, reinante; general, común, extendido; *prevailing winds*, vientos alisios o de dirección dominante.

prevalence ['prevələns], **prevalency** ['prevələnsi], *s.* predominio, preponderancia, superioridad.

prevalent ['prevələnt], *a.* prevaleciente, predominante, reinante; general, común.

prevaricate [pre'værikeit], *v.i.* (*for.*) prevaricar; tergiversar.

prevarication, *s.* (*for.*) prevaricación, prevaricato; tergiversación.

prevaricator, *s.* prevaricador; tergiversador.

prevenance ['prevənəns], **prevenancy**, *s.* anticipación a las necesidades o deseos de otros; cortesía, obsequio.

prevenient [pre'vi:niənt], *a.* preveniente, preventivo.

prevent [pre'vent], *v.t.* prevenir, impedir, estorbar, frustrar, evitar, desbaratar, atajar, precaver; (*ant.*) preceder, guiar, ir delante; llegar más temprano.

preventable, *a.* evitable.

preventative, *s.* [PREVENTIVE].

preventer, *s.* estorbador, persona que impide, persona que previene; (*mar.*) berlinga, soga, perno auxiliar.

prevention, *s.* prevención, cautela, caución; obstáculo, estorbo, embarazo.

preventive, preventative, *a.* preventivo, impeditivo; preservativo, profiláctico. — *s.* preservativo; (*mar.*) guardacosta.

preview [pri:'vju:], *s.* previa representación (de un cine); vista de antemano.

previous ['pri:viəs], *a.* previo, antecedente, anterior, precedente, anticipado, de antemano.

previously, *adv.* previamente, anteriormente, anticipadamente, de antemano.

previousness, *s.* prioridad, anterioridad.

previse [pre'vaiz], *v.t.* prever; conocer de antemano, prevenir o avisar.

prevision [pri:'viʒən], *s.* previsión.

prewarn [pri:'wɔ:ɪn], *v.t.* advertir de antemano.

prey [prei], *s.* presa; víctima, *f.*; botín, pillaje, robo, despojo, rapiña, depredación; *bird of prey,* ave de rapiña; *to be a prey to,* estar en presa de, ser presa de. — *v.i.* devorar (presas); pillar, hurtar, rapiñar, robar, hacer presa; consumir, oprimir.

preyer, *s.* pillador; devorador; robador, ladrón.

pribble ['pribəl], *s.* conversación ociosa, sin ton ni son.

price [prais], *s.* precio, valor, valía, coste, costo, monta; premio, recompensa, galardón; *price list,* tarifa, lista de precios; *cost price,* precio de coste; *opening price,* (*com.*) primer curso (en la Bolsa); *the lowest price,* el último precio; *closing price,* último curso (en la Bolsa); *market price,* precio corriente; *under price,* por menos del precio; *at any price,* cueste lo que cueste; *not at any price,* (*fam.*) por nada del mundo; *to set a price upon someone's head,* poner a precio la cabeza de alguno. — *v.t.* valuar, valorar, estimar, tasar, apreciar, fijar un precio.

priced, *a.* valuado. — *p.p.* [PRICE].

priceless, *a.* sin precio; inapreciable, precioso, que no tiene precio; (*fig., fam.*) salado, divertidísimo.

prick [prik], *v.t.* picar, punzar, clavar(se), hincar, pinchar, apuntar; (*fig.*) aguijar, aguijonear, aguzar, avivar (*equit.*) aguijar, aguijonear; (*mar.*) cartear; (*ant.*) poner en música; *to prick up one's ears,* aguzar las orejas, prestar atención. — *v.i.* picarse; pinchar; galopar, arrimar las espuelas; (*prov.*) componerse, afeitarse. — *s.* aguijón, punzón, picadura, puntura, hincadura; alfilerazo, agujazo, pinchazo; remordimiento, escrúpulo; rastro, pista; momento, punto; blanco; *to kick against the pricks,* tirar coces contra el aguijón.

pricker, *s.* punzón, aguijón, lezna, lesna; jinete.

pricket, *s.* cervato o gamo de un año; punta sobre que se pude clavar una vela.

pricking, *s.* punzada, picadura; picazón, *f.*, picor, escozor.

prickle ['prikəl], *s.* espin.., púa, pincha; picazón, *f.*, picor, escozor.

prickleback, *s.* espinocha.

prickleness, *s.* calidad de espinoso.

prickly, *a.* espinoso, lleno de púas; *prickly pear,* nopal, higo chumbo.

prickwood, *s.* bonetero.

pride [praid], *s.* soberbia, engreimiento, altivez, jactancia; orgullo, dignidad; aparato, esplendor, majestuosidad, pompa. — *v.t.,*

v.r. enorgullecerse, ensoberbecerse, vanagloriarse; *to take pride in,* enorgullecerse de, estar orgulloso de; *to pride oneself upon,* jactarse de, preciarse de.

prideful, *a.* soberbio, altanero.

prier ['praiəɪ], *s.* escudriñador, atisbador, persona curiosa.

priest [pri:st], *s.* sacerdote, cura, *m.*

priestcraft, *s.* intriga eclesiástica.

priestess, *s.f.* sacerdotisa.

priesthood ['pri:sthud], *s.* sacerdocio; clero, clerecía.

priestlike, *a.* de cura.

priestly ['pri:stli], *a.* sacerdotal.

priest-ridden, *a* (*despec.*) dominado por el clero.

prig [prig], *s.* empingorotado, fatuo, cursi (*fam.*); pisaverde; mojigato, hipócrita, *m.f.*; (*vulg.*) ladronzuelo, caco. — *v.t.* (*vulg.*) hurtar, robar.

priggery, *s.* fatuidad, hinchazón, *f.*, cursilería; mojigatería, gazmoñería.

priggish ['prigiʃ], *a.* empingorotado, fatuo, cursi (*fam.*); mojigato, gazmoño; (*ant., vulg.*) ratero, sisón.

prim [prim], *a.* perıpuesto, etiquetero, estirado, repulido, almidonado, remilgado. — *v.t.* ataviar, hacer carantoñas. — *v.i.* ponerse de veinticinco alfileres.

primacy ['praiməsi], *s.* primacía.

primage ['praimidʒ], *s.* (*mar.*) capa.

primal ['praiməl], *a.* primero, originario, prístino.

primarily, *adv.* primitivamente, en el principio, en primer lugar; principalmente.

primariness, *s.* primacía.

primary ['praiməri], *s.* lo primero; que ocupa el primer lugar en orden, graduación o importancia; (*astro.*) planeta primario; (*E.U.*) mitin de electores para nombrar candidatos; (*elec.*) circuito primario; (*orn.*) pluma grande de la ala de un ave.

primary, *a.* primario; (*elec., geol.*) primario.

primate ['praimıt], *s.* primado.

primateship, *s.* (*igl.*) primacía.

primatial [prai'meiʃəl], *a.* primacial.

prime [praim], *s.* alba, aurora, amanecer, madrugada, albor; principio, origen; (*fig.*) flor, *f.*, crema, nata; (*igl.*) (hora) prima; (*mat.*) número primo. — *a.* primero; primitivo, prístino, original; de primera clase, excelente, primoroso; principal; temprano, precoz. — *v.t.* cebar (las armas); preparar, aprestar, aparejar, alistar; (*pint.*) imprimar; (*fam.*) dar instrucciones, informar, prevenir. — *v.i.* estar cebado; estar listo, estar preparado.

primely, *adv.* principalmente, en primer lugar; primorosamente, excelentemente, en alto grado.

primeness, *s.* primor, excelencia, buena calidad.

primer ['praiməɪ], *s.* abecedario, cartilla para los niños; libro escolar, libro de texto elemental; (*arti.*) pistón, fulminante, cebador; devocionario; (*impr.*) *long primer,* letra de diez puntos; *great primer,* letra de dieciocho puntos. — *a.* primero, primario.

primero [pri'mɛəɪou], *s.* juego de naipes que estuvo de moda en los siglos 16 y 17, el original juego de póker.

primeval [praim'i:vəl], *a.* primitivo, prístino.

priming ['praimiŋ], s. cebo (de armas); preparación; (*pint*.) imprimación, encolado; *priming-horn*, cebador; *priming-tube*, estopín.

primiparous [prai'mipərəs], a. (*obst*.) primeriza.

primitive ['primitiv], s., a. primitivo, primordial, prístino; (*biol*.) rudimentario; (*despec*.) anticuado, rudimentario.

primitiveness, s. estado primitivo, estado original.

primly ['primli], adv. con afectación, escrupulosamente, afectadamente, remilgadamente; gravemente.

primness, s. gravedad afectada, dengue, remilgo, exceso de formalidad, escrupulosidad.

primogenital [praimou'dʒenitəl], a. primogénito.

primogenitor, s. progenitor.

primogeniture [praimou'dʒenitʃər], s. primogenitura.

primordial [praim'ɔːrdiəl], a. primordial. — s. primer principio, origen.

primrose ['primrouz], s. (*bot*.) primavera, prímula. — a. de color amarillo verdoso claro; *Primrose Day*, aniversario de la muerte de lord Beaconsfield (Disraeli), el 19 de abril.

prince [prins], s. príncipe, infante; *Prince (of darkness)*, Príncipe de las tinieblas; *Prince of Peace*, Príncipe de la Paz, Jesucristo.

princedom, s. principado.

princelet, princeling, s. principillo.

princelike, a. de príncipe.

princeliness, s. magnificencia, munificencia.

princely ['prinsli], a. principesco; magnífico; digno de un príncipe.

princess, s.f. princesa.

principal ['prinsipəl], a. principal. — s. principal, presidente, gobernador, director, rector; (*arq*.) jamba de fuerza; (*for*.) causante, comitente, principal acusado.

principality [prinsi'æliti], s. principado.

principally ['prinsipəli], adv. principalmente, mayormente, máxime.

principalness, s. principalidad.

principle ['prinsipəl], s. principio, axioma, m.; principio, regla; *in principle*, en principio. — v.t. infundir o establecer principios.

prink [priŋk], v.t., v.i. (*vulg*.) ataviar(se), componerse, afeitar(se); limpiarse (un pájaro).

print [print], v.t. imprimir, estampar, tirar, dar a la estampa, dar a luz; (*fig*.) grabar en la memoria; (*foto*.) tirar una prueba. — v.i. publicar un libro, hacer una tirada; ser impresor; imprimirse. — s. impresión, estampa; folleto, volante, impreso; grabado; plancha, lámina; (*foto*.) prueba positiva; molde; señal, f., marca, huella; tela impresa, indiana; muestra; *in print*, en letra de molde, impreso; *out of print*, agotado; *print shop*, estampería.

printed, a. impreso; *printed fabric*, (tejido) estampado; *printed matter*, impresos.

printer, s. impresor, tipógrafo, cajista, m.f.

printing, s. imprenta, tipografía, impresión, impreso; estampa; estampación.

printing-house, printing office, s. imprenta.

printing-press, s. prensa tipográfica.

printless, a. que no deja señal.

print-seller, s. estampero.

prior ['praiər], s. prior. — a. precedente, anterior, antecedente, prior, previo.

priorate, s. priorato.

prioress, s.f. priora.

priority [prai'ɔriti], s. prioridad, antelación, prelación, precedencia.

priorship, s. priorato, priorazgo.

priory ['praiəri], s. priorato.

prise [praiz], v.t. abrir como o con una palanca, alzaprimar [PRIZE].

prism [prizm], s. prisma, m.

prismatic [priz'mætik], **prismatical** [priz'mætikəl], a. prismático.

prismoid, a. prismoide, en forma de prisma.

prison ['prizən], s. cárcel, f., prisión. — v.t. encarcelar, aprisionar.

prisoner, s. prisionero, preso; reo, acusado; *to take prisoner*, hacer prisionero, prender; *prisoner's base*, rescate (juego de muchachos).

prison-house, s. cárcel, f.; (*fig*.) encierro.

prison-keeper, s. conserje de una cárcel, carcelero.

pristine ['pristain], a. prístino.

prithee ['priði], interj. (ant., contr. de *I pray thee*) te ruego.

prittle-prattle ['pritəlprætəl], s. cháchara; balbuceo.

privacy ['praivəsi, 'privəsi], **privateness** ['praivətnis], s. soledad, retiro, aislamiento, retraimiento, recogimiento, apartamiento; reserva, secreto.

private ['praivit], a. particular, personal, privado, secreto; apartado, reservado, privado, retirado; clandestino, oculto; solo, solitario; reticente, callado; confidencial; excusado; *private hearing*, (*for*.) audiencia a puertas cerradas; *in private*, confidencialmente, entre Usted y yo; en secreto, a puerta cerrada; *to be private*, estar solo; *strictly private*, muy reservado; *private parts*, partes pudendas, vergüenzas. — s. soldado raso.

privateer [praivə'tiər], s. corsario. — v.i. corsear, armar en corso.

privateering, s. corso.

privately ['praivitli], adv. secretamente, reservadamente, a puertas cerradas, a escondidas.

privateness, s. [PRIVACY].

privation [prai'veiʃən], s. privación, carencia.

privative ['praivətiv], a. privativo; (*gram*.) negativo. — s. carácter privativo; (*gram*.) prefijo negativo.

privet [privit], s. (*bot*.) alheña, ligustro.

privilege ['privilidʒ], s. privilegio, prerrogativa, exención, indulto. — v.t. privilegiar.

privily ['privili], adv. secretamente, reservadamente, a escondidas.

privity ['priviti], s. confianza, secreto, informe reservado.

privy ['privi], a. privado; excusado, clandestino, cómplice; enterado. — s. privada, letrina, retrete, lugar excusado; (*for*.) copartícipe.

prize [praiz], s. premio, recompensa, galardón; presa, captura, botín; suerte, f., buena suerte; ganancia, adquisición, ventaja; (*fam*.) chiripa; *to be a lawful prize*, ser de buena presa; *to draw a prize*, sacar un premio; *first prize*, premio mayor, premio gordo (de lotería). — v.t. estimar, apreciar; (ant.) valorar, valuar, tasar; alzaprimar; *to prize open*, abrir con una palanca, alzaprimar.

prize-fight, *s.* pugilato, contienda de boxeo.
prize-fighter, *s.* púgil, boxeador.
prize-fighting, *s.* pugilato, boxeo.
prizeman ['praizmən], *s.* laureado.
prizer, *s.* (*ant.*) apreciador, valorador, tasador.
pro, *prep.* pro. — *s.* voto afirmativo; (*vulg.*) futbolista, jugador de cricket, etc. profesional; (*vulg.*) puta, mujer pública; *pro and con,* el pro y el contra.
probabilism ['prɔbəbilizm], *s.* probabilismo.
probabilist, *s.* probabilista, *m.f.*
probability [prɔbə'biliti], *s.* probabilidad; verisimilitud.
probable ['prɔbəbəl], *a.* probable; verosímil.
probang ['proubæŋ], *s.* (*cir.*) sonda esofágica.
probate ['proubeit], *s.* prueba, verificación (de los testamentos), copia auténtica de un testamento. — *a.* (*for.*) testamentario.
probation, *s.* probación, noviciado; (*for.*) libertad vigilada; (*ant.*) prueba.
probational, probationary, *a.* probatorio.
probationer [pro'beiʃənər], *s.* novicio, aprendiz, principiante.
probationership, *s.* noviciado.
probative, probatory, *a.* probatorio.
probe [proub], *v.t.* reconocer con la tienta; (*fig.*) sondar, explorar; tentar, registrar, escudriñar. — *s.* tienta, cánula, sonda; (*fig., fam.*) investigación.
probity ['proubiti], *s.* probidad.
problem ['prɔbləm], *s.* problema, *m.*
problematic [prɔble'mætik], **problematical** [prɔble'mætikəl], *a.* problemático.
proboscis [pro'bɔsis], *s.* probóscide; (*irónico*) nariz, *f.,* narigón.
procacious [pro'keiʃəs], *a.* procaz, petulante, impudente.
procedure [pro'si:dʒər], *s.* procedimiento; proceder; operación; (*for.*) tramitación, actuación.
proceed [pro'si:d], *v.i.* proceder, dimanar, originarse, provenir; avanzar, adelantar; continuar, proseguir; empezar, poner manos a la obra, echar mano, obrar; instituir, tramitar; *to proceed against,* armar un pleito contra; *to proceed warily,* emplear precauciones; *to proceed to blows,* llegar a las manos.
proceeding, *s.* proceder, procedimiento; porte, conducta; transacción; proceso; continuación; (*for.*) trámite, procedimiento. — *pl.* **proceedings,** autos, actas, actuaciones; expediente; procedimiento.
proceeds ['prousi:dz], *s.pl.* producto, reditos, rentas.
process ['prouses], *s.* proceso, procedimiento; adelantamiento, continuación, progreso; método, sistema, *m.*; tratamiento, manipulación, operación, sucesión, serie, *f.,* curso; (*for.*) causa, proceso; expediente, autos; (*zool.*) excrecencia, protuberancia; (*bot.*) apéndice; *in process of time,* andando el tiempo. — *v.t.* encausar, procesar; esterilizar bajo presión; fotograbar.
procession, *s.* procesión, desfile, cabalgata, cortejo.
processional, *a.* procesional. — *s.* (libro) procesionario.
processionary, *a.* procesional.
proclaim [pro'kleim], *v.t.* proclamar, publicar, promulgar, declarar, pregonar, vocear; proscribir, poner fuera de la ley.

proclaimer, *s.* proclamador, el que proclama, el que promulga.
proclamation [prɔklə'meiʃən], *s.* proclamación, publicación, proclama, pregón; edicto, decreto.
proclitic [pro'klitik], *a.* proclítico.
proclivity [pro'kliviti], *s.* proclividad.
proconsul [prou'kɔnsəl], *s.* procónsul.
proconsular, *a.* proconsular.
proconsulate, proconsulship, *s.* proconsulado.
procrastinate [pro'kræstineit], *v.t., v.i.* perecear (*fam.*), dar largas, dilatar, diferir, retardar.
procrastination, *s.* dilatorias, largas, pereza, vacilación, dilación, demora, tardanza.
procrastinator, *s.* moroso, perezoso, pelmazo.
procreant ['proukriənt], *a.* procreante.
procreate ['proukrieit], *v.t.* procrear, criar, engendrar.
procreative, *a.* procreador, generativo.
procreativeness, *s.* facultad de procrear, fertilidad.
procreator, *s.* procreador.
proctor ['prɔktər], *s.* (*for.*) procurador, apoderado; abogado, censor (de una universidad). — *v.t.* dirigir, conducir.
proctorage, *s.* procuración.
proctorship, *s.* procura, procuraduría, procuración; oficio de procurador.
procumbent [prou'kʌmbənt], *a.* postrado, inclinado, tendido, yacente.
procurable [pro'kju:rəbəl], *a.* asequible, proporcionable.
procuration, *s.* (*for.*) procuración, gestión, manejo; poder; alcahuetería.
procurator ['prɔkju:reitər], *s.* procurador, apoderado.
procuratorship, *s.* cargo de procurador.
procure [pro'kju:ər], *v.t.* lograr, conseguir, alcanzar, obtener; alcahuetear. — *v.i.* alcahuetear, andar en tercerías.
procurement, *s.* alcahuetería; obtención, logro; procuración, manejo.
procurer, *s.* tercero, alcahuete, (*fam.*) gancho; (*ant.*) procurador; el que consigue.
procuress, *s.f.* alcahueta, tercera.
prod [prɔd], *v.t.* picar, punzar, aguijonear. — *s.* pincho, pinchazo, aguijón.
prodigal ['prɔdigəl], *s., a.* pródigo, derrochador, manirroto.
prodigality [prɔdi'gæliti], *s.* prodigalidad, despilfarro; (*fig.*) prodigalidad, profusión.
prodigious [pro'didʒəs], *a.* prodigioso, vasto, enorme, inmenso, excesivo, extraordinario.
prodigiousness, *s.* prodigiosidad, enormidad.
prodigy ['prɔdidʒi], *s.* prodigio, maravilla, pasmo.
prodomic [pro'dɔmik], *a.* prodómico.
produce [pro'dju:s], *v.t.* producir, generar; engendrar; causar, motivar, ocasionar; criar; manifestar, mostrar, presentar; (*geom.*) extender, alargar, prolongar; (*com.*) manufacturar, fabricar; (*teat.*) dirigir, realizar, poner en escena; (*com.*) rendir. — *v.i.* producir, dar producto.
produce ['prɔdju:s], *s.* producto, producción; provisiones, mercancías, géneros.
producer [pro'dju:sər], *s.* (*teat.*) director de escena; produciente, productor.
producible, *a.* producible.
producibleness, *s.* producibilidad.

producing, *a.* productivo.
product ['prodʌkt], *s.* producto, producción; resultado, efecto; (*com.*) rendición, renta.
productible, *a.* productible.
productile [pro'dʌktail], *a.* dúctil.
production [pro'dʌkʃən], *s.* producción, producto; (*teat.*) dirección (escénica), realización; (*fig.*) obra, fruto.
productive [pro'dʌktiv], *a.* productivo, fértil, fecundo, prolífico, feraz.
productiveness, productivity, *s.* potencia productiva, producibilidad, fecundidad, fertilidad.
proem ['prouem], *s.* proemio, prefacio, exordio.
proemial [pro'i:miəl], *a.* proemial, preliminar.
profanation [profə'neiʃən], *s.* profanación, desacato, prostitución.
profane [pro'fein], *a.* profano, secular, irreverente; blasfemo, profano. — *v.t.* profanar, prostituir, desprestigiar.
profaneness, profanity, *s.* profanidad, desacato; lenguaje profano, blasfemia.
profaner, *s.* profanador.
profess [pro'fes], *v.t.* profesar; declarar, afirmar, confesar. — *v.i.* hacer profesión; actuar como profesor o catedrático; ejercer una profesión; ordenarse.
professed, *a.* manifiesto, declarado; profeso; de profesión. — *p.p.* [PROFESS].
profession [pro'feʃən], *s.* profesión, carrera; profesión, manifestación, declaración.
professional, *a.* profesional, de profesión, de la profesión, dedicado a una carrera. — *s.* (*deportes*) profesional.
professionally, *adv.* de profesión, en su profesión; ex profeso; públicamente.
professor [pro'fesər], *s.* catedrático principal y jefe de un departamento; (*ant.* o *irónico*) profesor, maestro; declarador, profesan te.
professorial [profe'so:riəl], *a.* de un catedrático o de catedráticos (jefes de departamentos); profesorial, pedagógico.
professorship, *s.* cátedra principal; profesorado.
proffer ['profər], *v.t.* ofrendar, brindar, ofrecer, proponer. — *s.* propuesta, oferta, ofrecimiento.
profferer, *s.* ofrecedor.
proficience [pro'fiʃəns], (*ant.*), **proficiency** [pro'fiʃənsi], *s.* habilidad, pericia; (*ant.*) adelantos, progresos.
proficient, *a.* hábil, perito, experto; (*ant.*) proficiente. — *s.* perito; (*ant.*) proficiente.
profile ['proufi:l, 'proufail], *s.* perfil; recorte, contorno; *in profile*, de perfil. — *v.t.* perfilar.
profit ['profit], *s.* provecho, utilidad, beneficio, ganancia, ventaja, lucro, rendimiento, rendición; *gross profit*, ganancia total, o en bruto; *net profit*, beneficio neto, ganancia neta. — *v.t.* ser útil a, ser ventajoso para, aprovechar. — *v.i.* aprovechar, ganar, lucrar, sacar provecho, sacar utilidad.
profitable ['profitəbəl], *a.* provechoso, lucrativo, gananacioso, fructuoso, ventajoso, útil.
profitableness, *s.* ganancia, provecho, ventaja, lucro.
profiteer [profi'tiər], *v.i.* usurear, explotar una necesidad general o calamidad nacional. — *s.* estraperlista, *m.f.*, usurero, explotador.

profitless, *a.* infructuoso.
profitlessly, *adv.* sin ventaja, sin provecho.
profligacy ['profligəsi], *s.* libertinaje, desenfreno, estrago; perversidad, maldad.
profligate ['profligit], *a.* libertino, disipado, abandonado, perdido, relajado. — *s.* hombre libertino, hombre abandonado, calavera, *m.*, disoluto.
profligately, *adv.* licenciosamente, disolutamente.
profound [pro'faund], *a.* profundo, hondo.
profundity [pro'fʌnditi], *s.* profundidad, hondura.
profuse [pro'fju:s], *a.* profuso, pródigo, lozano.
profuseness, profusion, *s.* profusión, prodigalidad, superabundancia, exceso.
prog [prog], *v.i.* (*prov.*) mendigar; escarbar, buscar que comer; hurtar. — *s.pl.* (*vulg.*) víveres, provisiones.
progenitor [pro'dʒenitər], *s.* progenitor, antepasado.
progeniture, *s.* progenitura.
progeny ['prodʒəni], *s.* progenie, *f.*, prole, *f.*, progenitura.
prognathism, *s.* prognatismo.
prognathous [prog'neiθəs], *a.* prognato.
prognosis [prog'nousis], *s.* (*med.*) pronóstico; pronóstico, vaticinio; (*meteorologia*) prognosis, *f.*
prognostic [prog'nostik], *s.* pronóstico, presagio.
prognosticable, *a.* pronosticable.
prognosticate, *v.t.* pronosticar, presagiar.
prognostication, *s.* pronosticación, pronóstico, presagio, signo.
prognosticator, *s.* pronosticador, vaticinador.
programme ['prougræm], *s.* programa, *m.*; prospecto, plan; cartel, anuncio.
progress ['prougres], *s.* progreso, adelanto, adelantamiento, aprovechamiento; mejora, mejoramiento; desarrollo; jornada, curso; pasaje, paso, corriente; *to make progress*, adelantar, hacer progresos, mejorar.
progress [pro'gres], *v.i.* llevar adelante. — *v.i.* progresar, hacer progresos; avanzar, marchar, adelantar.
progression [pro'greʃən], *s.* progresión, progreso; curso, adelantamiento; carrera, marcha; (*mat.*) progresión.
progressional, progressive, *a.* progresivo.
progressiveness, *s.* progresión, marcha progresiva.
prohibit [pro'hibit], *v.t.* prohibir, impedir, vedar, interdecir, impedir, privar.
prohibiter, *s.* el que prohibe.
prohibition, *s.* prohibición, veda; veto; prohibicionismo (de bebidas alcohólicas).
prohibitionist, *s.* (*E.U.*) prohibicionista (de bebidas alcohólicas), *m.f.*
prohibitive [pro'hibitiv], **prohibitory** [pro'hibitəri], *a.* prohibitivo, prohibitorio.
project [pro'dʒekt], *v.t.* proyectar, echar, arrojar, despedir; trazar, proyectar, delinear; proyectar, idear. — *v.i.* salir fuera, resalir, sobresalir, resaltar, destacar.
project ['prodʒekt], *s.* proyecto, plan; proyecto, traza, diseño.
projectile [pro'dʒektail], *s.* proyectil. — *a.* proyectante; arrojadizo.
projecting, *a.* saledizo, voladizo, saliente, saltón (ojos, dientes, etc.).

projection [proˈdʒekʃən], s. proyección, resalte; lanzamiento, echamiento; (arq.) saledizo, proyectura, vuelo, delineación; (geom.) proyección.

projector, s. proyectista, m.f., autor de un proyecto; aparato de proyección.

projecture [proˈdʒektʃəɹ], s. (arq.) proyectura, saledizo, vuelo.

prolapse [proˈlæps], s. prolapso. — v.i. caerse hacia adelante.

prolate [ˈprouleit], a. (geom.) prolongado hacia los polos.

prolegomenon [proleˈgomenɔn], s. prolegómeno.

prolepsis [proˈlepsis], s. prolepsis, f.

proleptic, proleptical, a. antecedente, previo.

proletarian [prouleˈtɛəriən], a. proletario; jornalero, peón, vulgar, plebeyo.

proletariate [prouleˈtɛəriət], s. proletariado, vulgo.

prolific [proˈlifik], a. prolífico, fecundo, fértil.

prolificness, s. fertilidad, fecundidad.

prolix [ˈprouliks], a. prolijo, difuso, verboso, dilatado; ampuloso, pesado, enfadoso.

prolixity, prolixness, s. prolijidad; ampulosidad, pesadez.

prolocutor [proˈlɔkjuːtəɹ], s. presidente de una asamblea, junta del clero; intercesor, portavoz, m.

prolocutorship, s. presidencia.

prologue [ˈprouloɡ], s. prólogo, introito, exordio, proemio. — v.t. prologar.

prolong [proˈlɔŋ], v.t. prolongar, dilatar, alargar, diferir.

prolongation [prolɔŋˈgeiʃən], s. prolongación, dilatación.

prolonger [proˈlɔŋəɹ], s. prolongador.

prolusion [proˈljuːʒən], s. prolusión, prelusión.

promenade [ˈprɔmenɑːd], s. paseo, bulevar; paseo, paseata; (E.U.) baile (en un colegio); promenade-deck, (mar.) cubierta de paseo. — v.i. pasearse.

promenader, s. paseante.

prominence [ˈprɔminəns], s. prominencia, protuberancia; eminencia; distinción; (arq.) saledizo, resalto.

prominent [ˈprɔminənt], a. prominente, saliente, protuberante; sobresaliente, eminente, conspicuo, distinguido; (arq.) saledizo, proyectante.

prominently, adv. de un modo prominente; eminentemente, marcadamente, de un modo importante; (arq.) en saledizo.

promiscuous [proˈmiskjuːəs], a. promiscuo; (vulg.) negligente, desidioso, licencioso, libertino, disipado.

promiscuousness, s. promiscuidad; (vulg.) negligencia, desidia, libertinaje.

promise [ˈprɔmis], s. promesa, palabra dada; esperanza, promisión, oferta, ofrecimiento; to break one's promise, faltar a su palabra; to keep one's promise, cumplir su palabra o promesa; under promise of, bajo (su) palabra de; promises are like pie crust, palabras y plumas el viento las lleva. — v.t., v.i. prometer.

promiser, s. prometedor.

promising, a. prometedor, que promete, prometiente, que da esperanzas.

promissory [proˈmisəri], a. promisorio, que

contiene una promesa; promissory note, pagaré, abonaré, vale.

promontory [ˈprɔməntəri], s. promontorio, punta, cabo.

promote [proˈmout], v.t. promover, fomentar, secundar, favorecer; suscitar, provocar; animar, alentar, estimular; desarrollar, extender, acrecentar; mejorar, adelantar, ascender; (com.) agenciar, gestionar; organizar una empresa.

promoter, s. promotor, promovedor, gestor, protector; el que secunda; empresario.

promotion, s. promoción, adelantamiento, ascenso; fomento; desarrollo, engrandecimiento; protección.

promotive, a. promovedor, que protege.

prompt [prɔmpt], a. pronto, vivo, expedito, listo, veloz; exacto, puntual; resoluto, resuelto; diligente, activo; en punto (de la hora); prompt payment, dinero contante, pago al contado; prompt-book, (teat.) libro del traspunte o apuntador. — v.t. impeler, impulsar, incitar, alentar, animar, mover, inspirar, dictar, sugerir, insinuar, soplar, susurrar en voz baja (en clase); (teat.) apuntar.

prompt-book, s. (teat.) libro del apuntador o traspunte.

prompt-box, s. concha del apuntador.

prompter, s. persona que anima o que impele, incitador, instigador; (teat.) apuntador, traspunte, consueta, m.

promptitude [ˈprɔmptiˈtjuːd], **promptness** [ˈprɔmptnis], s. prontitud, puntualidad, rapidez, presteza, diligencia; buena voluntad.

promptly [ˈprɔmptli], adv. prontamente, prestamente, puntualmente.

promulgate [ˈprɔmʌlgeit], v.t. promulgar; proclamar, publicar.

promulgation, s. promulgación; publicación, declaración oficial.

promulgator, s. promulgador, publicador.

prone [proun], a. prono, acostado boca abajo; prono, dispuesto, propenso.

proneness, s. postración; propensión, inclinación.

prong [prɔŋ], s. horca, horquilla; diente, punta (de tenedor, horquilla, etc.), púa; pitón de asta, punta de colmillo. — v.t. atravesar, traspasar, pinchar, herir con un prong.

prongbuck, pronghorn, s. antílope norteamericano (Antilocapra Americana).

pronged, a. dentado, dentellado, provisto de púas.

pronominal [proˈnominəl], a. pronominal.

pronoun [ˈprounaun], s. pronombre.

pronounce [proˈnauns], v.t. pronunciar, declarar, proferir; articular; recitar; (for.) pronunciar, fallar, dar (sentencia). — v.i. pronunciarse, declararse.

pronounceable, a. pronunciable.

pronounced, a. pronunciado, marcado, fuerte. — p.p. [PRONOUNCE].

pronouncement, s. proclama, manifiesto, declaración; (for.) pronunciamiento.

pronouncer, s. pronunciador.

pronouncing, a. de pronunciación.

pronunciation [pronʌnsiˈeiʃən], s. pronunciación, articulación, fonación.

proof [pruːf], s. prueba, comprobación, evidencia, experiencia, demostración; ensayo, experimento; graduación normal de

licores alcohólicos; impenetrabilidad; (*impr.*)
prueba; *bomb-proof*, a prueba de bomba;
fireproof, incombustible; *waterproof*, impermeable, a prueba de agua; *written proof*,
prueba por escrito; *to put to the proof*,
meter a prueba. — *a.* a prueba, de prueba;
impenetrable.

proofless, *a.* falto de prueba, no probado.

proof-reader, *s.* corrector de pruebas.

proof-reading, *s.* corrección de pruebas.

proof-sheet, *s.* (*impr.*) prueba limpia, prueba.

prop [prɔp], *s.* apoyo, sostén, apeo, paral,
puntal; (*agr.*) rodrigón, tentemozo; (*mar.*)
puntal; (*min.*) entibo, adema; (*arq.*) contrafuerte. — *v.t.* apoyar, sostener; acodalar,
ahorquillar, escorar; apuntalar, entibar.

propagable ['prɔpəgəbəl], *a.* propagable, que
puede propagarse.

propaganda [prɔpə'gændə], *s.* propaganda,
propaganda política.

propagandism, *s.* propagandismo.

propagandist, *s.* propagandista, *m.f.*

propagate ['prɔpəgeit], *v.t.* propagar. — *v.i.*
propagarse.

propagation, *s.* propagación.

propagative, *a.* propagativo.

propagator, *s.* propagador.

propel [pro'pel], *v.t.* propulsar, impeler;
lanzar (un proyectil); poner en movimiento.

propellent, *a.* propulsor, impelente.

propeller, *s.* propulsor, impulsor; (*mec.*)
hélice, *f.* (de un buque, avión, etc.).

propend [pro'pend], *v.t.* inclinarse.

propense [pro'pens], *a.* inclinado hacia;
dispuesto.

propension, *s.* propensión, inclinación, tendencia.

propensity [pro'pensiti], *s.* propensión, inclinación, tendencia.

proper ['prɔpəɹ], *a.* propio, idóneo, particular,
peculiar; conveniente, apropiado, a propósito, apto, adecuado, natural; formal,
decoroso, decente; (*despec.*) ceremonioso,
almidonado; exacto, justo, correcto; (*gram.*)
propio (nombre); *proper fraction*, (*mat.*)
quebrado propio.

properness, *s.* propiedad, aptitud, conveniencia; formalidad, decoro; (*despec.*) ceremoniosidad, pulcritud excesiva.

property ['prɔpəɹti], *s.* propiedad, cualidad,
peculiaridad; bienes, bienes raíces, hacienda,
heredad, posesión, pertenencia; *real property*,
bienes inmuebles; *personal property*, bienes
muebles. — *pl.* bienes; bienes raíces; (*teat.*)
decorados, guardarropía, aderezo, accesorios.

prophecy ['prɔfesi], *s.* profecía, vaticinio.

prophesier, *s.* profeta, *m.*, profetizador.

prophesy ['prɔfesai], *v.t.*, *v.i.* profetizar,
vaticinar.

prophesying, *s.* profecía, vaticinio.

prophet ['prɔfet], *s.* profeta, *m.*

prophetess, *s.f.* profetisa.

prophetic [pro'fetik], **prophetical** [pro'fetikəl],
a. profético.

prophylactic [profi'læktik], *s.*, *a.* (*med.*) profiláctico, preventivo.

prophylaxis ['prɔfilæksi], *s.* profilaxis, *f.*

propinquity [pro'piŋkwiti], *s.* parentesco,
proximidad (de tiempo), propincuidad,
cercanía (de lugar).

propitiable [pro'piʃiəbəl], *a.* que se puede
propiciar.

propitiate [pro'piʃieit], *v.t.* propiciar, aplacar,
apaciguar, ablandar. — *v.i.* hacer expiación.

propitiation, *s.* propiciación, expiación.

propitiator, *s.* propiciador.

propitiatorily, *adv.* por propiciación.

propitiatory [pro'piʃieitəri], *s.*, *a.* propiciatorio.

propitious [pro'piʃəs], *a.* propicio, benéfico,
benigno, feliz, favorable.

propitiousness, *s.* calidad de propicio,
benevolencia, bondad.

proponent [pro'pounənt], *s.* proponedor,
proponente.

proportion [pro'pɔːɹʃən], *s.* proporción, correlación, correspondencia; porción, parte,
f.; (*mɪt.*) razón, *f.*, relación; ajuste, simetría,
medida; *in proportion as*, en proporción, a
medida que, conforme; *out of proportion*,
desproporcionado. — *v.t.* proporcionar, tantear, ajustar; repartir.

proportionable, *a.* proporcionable, proporcionado.

proportionableness, *s.* proporcionalidad.

proportionably, *adv.* proporcionadamente,
proporcionablemente.

proportional, *a.* proporcional, en proporción.
— *s.* (*mat.*) proporcional.

proportionally, *adv.* proporcionalmente, en
proporción.

proportionate, *v.t.* proporcionar, ajustar. — *a.*
proporcionado, ajustado, correspondiente.

proportionless, *a.* desproporcionado, sin proporción.

proposal [pro'pouzəl], *s.* proposición, ofrecimiento, propuesta, oferta; propósito, proyecto; *proposal of marriage*, declaración de
amor.

propose [pro'pouz], *v.t.* proponer; brindar.
— *v.i.* proponerse, declararse.

proposer, *s.* proponedor, proponente.

proposition [prɔpo'ziʃən], *s.* proposición,
propuesta, oferta; propósito, proyecto.

propound [pro'paund], *v.t.* proponer, ofrecer,
exponer, presentar.

propounder, *s.* proponedor, proponente.

propped, *pret.*, *p.p.* [PROP].

propping ['prɔpiŋ], *s.* sostén; puntal, apuntalamiento; (*agr.*) estaca.

proprietary [pro'praiətəri], *s.* propietario,
dueño; pertenencia, propiedad. — *a.* de
propietario.

proprietor [pro'praiətəɹ], *s.* propietario, dueño,
amo.

proprietorship, *s.* estado de ser propietario.

proprietress, *s.f.* propietaria, dueña.

propriety [pro'praiiti], *s.* propiedad; formalidad, corrección; urbanidad, decencia; conveniencia, decoro.

props [prɔps], *s.pl.* (*vulg.*, *teat.*) guardarropía,
aderezos.

propugnator, *s.* defensor.

propulsion [pro'pʌlʃən], *s.* reacción, retroacción, impulso, impulsión; (*ant.*) propulsión, propulsa; *jet-propulsion*, propulsión a
chorro, propulsión de reacción, de retroacción.

propulsive, propulsory, *a.* propulsor, impelente.

pro rata [prou'reitə], *a.* prorrata.

prorogate ['prɔrogeit], *v.t.* prorrogar.

prorogation, *s.* prorrogación, prórroga.

prorogue [prou'roug], *v.t.* prorrogar; (*pol.*)
suspender las sesiones del Parlamento.

prosaic [pro'zeiik], *a*. prosaico.
prosaically, *adv*. prosaicamente.
prosaism, *s*. prosaísmo.
proscenium [pro'si:niəm], *s*. proscenio.
proscribe [pro'skraib], *v.t.* proscribir, desterrar; reprobar, condenar; proscribir, vedar.
proscriber, *s*. proscriptor.
proscript, *s*. proscrito, desterrado.
proscription [pro'skripʃən], *s*. proscripción, encartamiento.
proscriptive, *a*. proscriptivo.
prose [prouz], *s*. prosa. — *a*. de prosa, en prosa, prosaico. — *v.t.* escribir en prosa; *prose-writer*, prosista, *m.f.*, prosador.
prosecute ['prosikju:t], *v.t.* proseguir, continuar, llevar adelante; (*for.*) procesar, acusar. — *v.i.* seguir un pleito, pedir en juicio, proponer.
prosecution, *s*. prosecución, cumplimiento, desarrollo; (*for.*) acusación; (*for.*) parte actora, actor, demandante, fiscal.
prosecutor, *s*. (*for.*) demandante, actor, acusador, fiscal; el que prosigue.
prosecutrix, *s.f.* (*for.*) acusadora, demandante.
proselyte ['prosəlait], *s*. prosélito. — *v.t.* convertir, hacer prosélitos.
proselytism ['prosəlaitizm], *s*. (*despec.*) proselitismo.
proselytize, *v.t.*, *v.i.* hacer prosélitos, apostolizar; (*despec.*) apostolizar.
proser ['prouzər], *s*. prosador, prosista, *m.f.*; escritor de estilo hinchado, hablador, (*fam.*) prosador.
prosily ['prouzili], *adv*. prosaicamente.
prosody ['prouzədi], *s*. prosodia.
prosopopœia [prosopo'piər], *s*. (*ret.*) prosopopeya.
prospect ['prospekt], *s*. perspectiva, vista, panorama, *m*., paisaje; perspectivas, expectativa, esperanza; aspecto, traza; probabilidad, previsión; exposición; punto de vista; orientación, situación; *man of* (o *with*) *good prospects*, hombre de porvenir.
prospect [pro'spekt], *v.t.* (*min.*) catear, explorar, tratar de descubrir minerales; prometer, dar buenas esperanzas; (*com.*) comprador o parroquiano probable.
prospection, *s*. previsión.
prospective, *a*. previsor, prevenido, anticipado, venidero, en perspectiva. — *s*. perspectiva.
prospectively, *adv*. en perspectiva.
prospectiveness, *s*. perspectiva.
prospector, *s*. (*min.*) explorador, operador.
prospectus [pro'spektəs], *s*. prospecto, programa, *m*.
prosper ['prospər], *v.t.* prosperar, favorecer, hacer medrar. — *v.i.* prosperar, florecer, medrar.
prosperity [pros'periti], *s*. prosperidad, medro, bienandanza, bonanza.
prosperous ['prospərəs], *a*. próspero, floreciente; que medra, adinerado, acomodado, opulento.
prosperousness, *s*. prosperidad.
prostate ['prosteit], *s*. próstata.
prostatic, *a*. prostático.
prosthesis ['prosθesis], *s*. prótesis, *f*.
prostitute ['prostitju:t], *s*. prostituta, ramera; mercenario. — *a*. prostituto, prostituido, mercenario. — *v.t.* prostituir.

prostitution, *s*. prostitución; (*fig.*) prostitución.
prostitutor, *s*. persona que prostituye.
prostrate ['prostreit], *a*. prosternado, postrado, humillado; (*biol.*) procumbente, tendido. — *v.t.* postrar; tender; demoler, derribar, arruinar; rendir; trastornar. — *v.i.* prosternarse, postrarse.
prostration, *s*. prostración; abatimiento; (*med.*) agotamiento, adinamia.
prosy ['prouzi], *a*. prosaico, prolijo, hinchado, ampuloso.
protasis ['protəsis], *s*. prótasis, *f*.
protatic, *a*. protático.
protean ['proutiən], *a*. proteico.
protect [pro'tekt], *v.t.* proteger, amparar, favorecer, patrocinar, resguardar, guarecer.
protection [pro'tekʃən], *s*. protección, amparo, patrocinio; garantía, defensa, salvaguardia, *f*., salvoconducto; (*pol.*) proteccionismo.
protectionism, *s*. proteccionismo.
protectionist, *s*. proteccionista, *m.f.*
protective [pro'tektiv], *a*. protector; proteccionista. — *s*. amparo, resguardo, abrigo, reparo; (*cir.*) cubierta aséptica.
protector, *s*. protector, amparador, patrono.
protectoral, protectorial, *a*. de protector.
protectorate [pro'tektərit], *s*. protectorado, protectoría.
protectorship, *s*. protectorado.
protectress, protectrix, *s.f.* protectriz, protectora.
protein ['prouti:n], *s*. proteína.
protend [pro'tend], *v.t.* tender, alargar.
protest [pro'test], *v.t.* protestar, declarar; (*com.*) protestar una letra de cambio. — *v.i.* protestar (de o contra), quejar(se).
protest ['proutest], *s*. protesta, queja, protestación; (*com.*) protesto.
protestant ['protestənt], *s*., *a*. protestante.
Protestantism, *s*. protestantismo.
protestation [protes'teiʃən], *s*. protesta, protestación, declaración.
protester, *s*. persona que protesta.
protocol ['proutoukol], *s*. protocolo. — *v.t.* protocolizar, protocolar. — *v.i.* formular un protocolo.
protomartyr [proutou'ma:tər], *s*. protomártir.
protoplasm ['proutouplæzm], *s*. protoplasma, *m*.
prototype ['proutoutaip], *s*. prototipo, arquetipo, ejemplar.
prototypical, *a*. prototípico.
protoxide [pro'toksaid], *s*. protóxido.
protoxidize, *v.t.* protoxidar.
protract [pro'trækt], *v.t.* prolongar, dilatar, diferir, retardar; alargar; (*ingen.*) levantar un plano; trazar un mapa por medio del pitipié o del semicírculo.
protracted, *a*. prolongado; (*fig.*) prolongado, dilatado, demorado. — *p.p.* [PROLONGAR].
protracter, *s*. prolongador, persona que prolonga.
protraction, *s*. prolongación; (*fig.*) prolongación, dilatación, retardo, demora.
protractor, *s*. prolongador; (*mat.*) transportador; (*anat.*) músculo extensor.
protrude [pro'tru:d], *v.t.* hacer salir, hacer destacar, sacar fuera; interponer, entrometer. — *v.i.* salir fuera, destacar, sobresalir, abultar.

protrusion [pro'truːʒən], *s.* bulto, prominencia; interposición, entrometimiento.
protrusive, *a.* que hace salir, que empuja hacia adelante.
protuberance [pro'tjuːbərəns], *s.* protuberancia, prominencia, bulto.
protuberant, *a.* prominente, saliente, abultado.
protuberate, *v.i.* sobresalir, abultar.
proud [praud], *a.* orgulloso, noble; soberbio, ufano, orgulloso, engreído, arrogante, envanecido, altivo, altanero; espléndido, magnífico, noble, bello, grande; (*med.*) fungoso; *to be proud of*, estar orgulloso de, estar contento *o* satisfecho de; preciarse de, ufanarse de, pagarse de; *proud flesh*, carnosidad, bezo.
proudish, *a.* algo orgulloso.
provable, *a.* comprobable.
prove [pruːv], *v.t.* probar, evidenciar, comprobar, demostrar; (*ant.*) experimentar, poner a prueba; (*for.*) hacer público (un testamento); (*impr.*) sacar una prueba. — *v.i.* resultar, hallarse, salir.
proveditor [pro'veditəɹ], *s.* proveedor, abastecedor.
proven ['prouvən], *a.* probado, comprobado, demostrado. — *p.p. irreg.* [PROVE].
provenance ['provenəns], *s.* procedencia, origen, fuente, *f.*
provender ['provendəɹ], *s.* forraje, provisión de heno.
prover [pruːvəɹ], *s.* persona que prueba.
proverb ['provəɹb], *s.* refrán, adagio, proverbio. — *v.t.*, *v.i.* proverbiar; mencionar en un proverbio.
proverbial, *a.* proverbial; (*fig.*) proverbial, notorio.
proviant ['proviənt], *s.* provisiones, abastecimientos, especialmente para un ejército.
provide [pro'vaid], *v.t.* proveer, proporcionar, prevenir; contratar, estipular, convenir; abastecer, suministrar, suplir, surtir, habilitar; sufragar los gastos. — *v.i.* abastecer, proveer o proporcionar lo necesario; precaverse, tener cuidado, tomar sus precauciones; prepararse; *provided that*, con tal que, a condición que, siempre que, dado que; *he is well provided*, tiene todo lo que necesita, está proveído; *to provide against*, prevenir, precaver; *the Lord will provide*, Dios dará.
provided, *a.*, *p.p.* [PROVIDE]. — *conj.* con tal que, a condición que, siempre que, dado que.
providence ['providəns], *s.* providencia, prevención; frugalidad, economía, cautela; *Providence of God*, Providencia de Dios.
provident ['providənt], *a.* providente, próvido, prevenido; cauto, cuidadoso, económico.
providential [provi'denʃəl], *a.* providencial.
providently, *adv.* próvidamente; prudentemente.
provider [pro'vaidəɹ], *s.* proveedor, provisor, abastecedor, suministrador.
province ['provins], *s.* provincia, región; (*fig.*) esfera, materia; incumbencia, obligación, competencia.
provincial [pro'vinʃəl], *a.* provincial; provinciano, grosero, campesino. — *s.* provinciano; (*igl.*) provincial.
provincialism, *s.* provincialismo.
provine ['prouvain], *v.t.* amugronar.
provision [pro'viʒən], *s.* provisión, abasteci-

miento, aprovisionamiento; bastimentos, víveres; (*for.*) estipulación, cláusula; medida, convenio, ajuste, requisito; *to make provision for*, proveer(se); encargarse de; asegurar el porvenir, hacer provisión de; *provisions* (*shop*), (tienda de) ultramarinos.
provisional, *a.* provisional, provisorio, interino.
provisionally, *adv.* provisionalmente, interinamente.
proviso [pro'vaizou], *s.* condición, estipulación, requisito, caución.
provisor [pro'vaizəɹ], *s.* proveedor.
provisorily, *adv.* condicionalmente.
provisory, *a.* provisorio, provisional, condicional.
provocation [provo'keiʃən], *s.* provocación.
provocative [pro'vokətiv], *a.* provocativo, provocador.
provoke [pro'vouk], *v.t.* provocar, amostazar, encolerizar; provocar, promover, inducir. — *v.i.* excitar la cólera, causar enojo.
provoker, *s.* provocador.
provoking, *a.* provocante, provocativo.
provokingly, *adv.* de un modo provocativo.
provost ['provəst], *s.* preboste; provisor; (*Esco.*) alcalde; (*Ingl.*) director de colegio; *Provost Marshal*, (*mil.*) capitán preboste.
provostship, *s.* prebostazgo.
prow [prau], *s.* proa, tajamar.
prowess ['praues], *s.* proeza, valentía, hazaña.
prowl [praul], *v.i.* rondar, acechar, andar de caza; rondar, vagabundear, callejear; rondar (con intentos de robar); merodear. — *s.* ronda, acecho; vagabundeo, callejeo, ronda; merodeo.
prowler, *s.* acechador, robador; vagamundo, andorrero, rondador; merodeador.
proximate ['proksimit], *a.* inmediato, próximo.
proximately, *adv.* inmediatamente, próximamente.
proximity [prok'zimiti], *s.* proximidad, inmediación, cercanía, vecindad.
proxy ['proksi], *s.* poder, procuración; poderhabiente, delegado, apoderado; *to be married by proxy*, casarse por poderes.
prude [pruːd], *s.f.* mojigata, gazmoña, remilgada, hazañera, beata.
prudence, *s.* prudencia, discreción, cordura, cautela.
prudent ['pruːdənt], *a.* prudente, discreto, cuerdo, cauto.
prudential [pru'denʃəl], *a.* prudencial, prudente.
prudery ['pruːdəri], *s.* melindre, remilgo; mojigatería, gazmoñería, beatería.
prudish ['pruːdiʃ], *a.* mojigato, gazmoño, remilgado, hazañero, beato.
pruinose ['pruːinouz], *a.* (*hist. nat.*) cubierto con polvillo o pelusa; parecido a la escarcha.
prune [pruːn], *v.t.*, *v.i.* podar, cortar, expurgar, escamondar; adornar(se), componerse, ataviar(se). — *s.* ciruela pasa; (*bot.*) ciruela.
prunella [pru'nelə], *s.* (*tej.*) carro de oro, sempiterna; (*med.*) angina.
prunello [pru'nelou], *s.* (*bot.*) bruñola.
pruner, *s.* podador.
pruniferous [pru'nifərəs], *a.* que produce ciruelas.
pruning ['pruːniŋ], *s.* poda, monda, escamonda, remonda.

pruning-hook, pruning-knife, s. podadera, podón, márcola.

pruning-shears, s.pl. podaderas.

prunt [prʌnt], s. adorno de cristal, etc., soldado o impreso en otro cristal, vaso, etc.; herramienta para este fin.

prurience ['pruːriəns], **pruriency** ['pruːriənsi], s. lujuria, lascivia; prurito, picazón, f., comezón, f.

prurient, a. lascivo, salaz, lujurioso; curioso, picante, desasosegado; que pica.

prurigo [pruː'raigou], s. (med.) prurigo.

Prussian ['prʌʃən], s., a. prusiano; Prussian blue, azul de Prusia.

prussiate ['prʌsiət], s. prusiato.

prussic ['prʌsik], a. prúsico; prussic acid, ácido prúsico.

pry [prai], v.i. espiar, atisbar, acechar, fisgonear, escudriñar; (mec.) alzaprimar, mover o levantar con palanca; Paul pry, persona muy curiosa, mirón; to pry into other people's business, meterse en asuntos ajenos. — v.t. (E.U.) alzaprimar [PRIZE]; to pry out a secret, arrancar un secreto. — s. fisgoneo; mirón; (E.U.) alzaprima.

prying, s. fisgoneo, curiosidad, comezón, m. — a. fisgón, curioso, fisgador, mirón.

pryingly, adv. con fisgoneo, comezón o curiosidad.

psalm [sɑːm], s. salmo, himno.

psalmist, s. salmista, m.

psalmody, s. salmodia.

psalter ['sɔltəɹ], s. salterio, salmodia.

psaltery, s. (mús.) salterio.

pseudo ['sjuːdou], a. seudo, falso, pretendido.

pseudomorphous [sjuːdou'mɔːɹfəs], a. seudomorfo.

pseudonym ['sjuːdonim], s.; **pseudonymous,** a. seudónimo.

pseudoscope ['sjuːdoskoup], s. seudoscopio.

pshaw [pʃɔː], interj. ¡fo! ¡fu! ¡bah! ¡fuera! — v.t., v.i. desdeñar.

psora ['sɔːrə], s. sora, sarna.

psoriasis [so'raiəsis], s. (med.) soriasis, f.

psychiatrist [sai'kaiətrist], s. psiquíatra, psiquiatra, m.f.

psychiatry [sai'kaiətri], s. psiquiatría.

psycho-analyse, v.t. psicoanalizar.

psycho-analysis [saikou'ænælisis], s. psicoanálisis, m.f.

psycho-analyst, s. psicoanalista, m.f.

psychologic [saiko'lɔdʒik], **psychological** [saiko'lɔdʒikəl], a. psicológico.

psychologist [sai'kɔlodʒist], s. psicólogo.

psychology [sai'kɔlodʒi], s. psicología.

psychopathic [saiko'pæθik], a. psicopático.

psychosis [sai'kousis], s. psicosis, f.

psychrometer [sai'krɔmetəɹ], s. psicómetro.

ptarmigan ['tɑːɹmigən], s. lagópedo, chocha de nieve.

ptisan ['tizən], s. tisana.

ptomaine ['toumein], s. ptomaína.

ptyalin ['taiəlin], s. ptialina.

ptyalism, s. tialismo.

pub [pʌb], s. (fam.) taberna.

puberty ['pjuːbəɹti], s. pubertad, pubescencia.

pubes ['pjuːbiːz], s. pubis, pubes.

pubescence [pjuː'besəns], s. pubescencia, pubertad.

pubescent, a. pubescente, púbero, púber.

pubic ['pjuːbik], a. pubiano.

public ['pʌblik], a. público. — s. público;

in public, públicamente, en público; public house, taberna, posada, venta; public school, escuela de alumnos internos de tipo tradicional (v. gr. Eton, Harrow); public spirited, patriótico.

publican ['pʌblikən], s. publicano; tabernero, posadero, mesonero.

publication [pʌbli'keiʃən], s. publicación, promulgación.

publicist ['pʌblisist], s. publicista, m.f.

publicity [pʌb'lisiti], s. publicidad.

publicness, s. publicidad.

publish ['pʌbliʃ], v.t. publicar, promulgar, divulgar, difundir; dar a luz, sacar a luz, dar a la imprenta, publicar; editar; propalar.

publisher, s. editor, librero; promulgador, publicador.

puccoon [pə'kuːn], s. (bot.) orcaneta, onoquiles, f.

puce [pjuːs], **puce-coloured,** a. color de pulga.

puck [pʌk], s. duende; picaruelo, trasgo.

pucker, v.t. arrugar, recoger, plegar, hacer pliegues; fruncir. — s. arruga, pliegue; fruncido; (vulg.) agitación, embrollo.

puckish, a. de duende; picaruelo, travieso.

puddening ['pudəniŋ], s. (mar.) rollo de cuerda usados como parachoques contra muelles, etc.

pudding ['pudiŋ], s. pudín, budín; black pudding, morcilla.

pudding-headed, a. necio, tonto.

puddle ['pʌdəl], s. charco; (ant.) charca, poza, lodazal, cenagal; (fig., prov.) embrollo, lío. — v.t. enlodar, enfangar, cimentar; (fund.) pudelar, purificar la fundición. — v.i. (fam.) patullar.

puddler, s. (fund.) pudelador.

puddling, s. (fund.) pudelación, pudelaje, purificación de la fundición; amasijo; (hidr.) cimentación.

puddly, a. lleno de charcos; cenagoso, lodoso.

pudency ['pjuːdənsi], s. pudor, recato.

pudge [pʌdʒ], a. gordiflón, gordinflón, regordete.

pudgy, a. gordiflón, gordinflón, regordete.

pudicity [pjuː'disiti], s. pudor, pudicicia.

puerile ['pjuːərail], a. pueril, infantil, fútil.

puerility [pjuːə'riliti], s. puerilidad, niñería, niñada.

puerperal [pjuː'əːɹpərəl], a. puerperal; puerperal fever, fiebre puerperal, f.

puet ['pjuːit], s. gallineta.

puff [pʌf], s. bufido, soplo, resoplido; fumarada, bocanada de humo, ventada; rizado; borla para empolvar; elogio exagerado, reclamo; jactancia, charlatanería; (coc.) bollo esponjado, macarrón, bamba; puff pastry, pastel relleno; puff of wind, ventarrón, ráfaga, racha; puff-adder, víbora. — v.t. inflar, hinchar; soplar; engreír, envanecer, ensoberbecer; ensalzar, alabar, dar bombo, elogiar demasiado; (cost.) abollonar; to puff away, dar soplidos o resoplidos, disipar a soplos; to puff out, apagar a soplos; to puff up, henchir(se), hinchar(se), ahuecar(se). — v.i. hinchar(se), inflarse; envanecerse, engreírse; bufar, dar bufidos, resoplar; abotagarse; to puff and blow, jadear.

puff-ball, s. (bot.) bejín.

puffer, s. soplador; (fam. de niños) tren; chalán.

puffily, *adv.* hinchadamente.
puffin ['pʌfin], *s.* mergo, alca.
puffiness, *s.* hinchazón, *f.*; (*med.*) intumescencia.
puffingly, *adv.* hinchadamente.
puffy ['pʌfi], *a.* inflado, hinchado, entumecido; jadeante; (*fig.*) pomposo, campanudo.
pug [pʌg], *s.* perro dogo pequeño; (*alb.*) torta; (*Ang.-Ind.*) huella de un animal. — *v.t.* (*alb.*) embarrar, cimentar.
pug-dog, *s.* perro dogo pequeño.
pug-faced, *a.* de hocico de mono.
pugging, *s.* amasijo.
pugil ['pju:dʒil], *s.* pulgarada, lo que cabe entre el pulgar y los dos primeros dedos.
pugilism ['pju:dʒilizm], *s.* pugilato.
pugilist, *s.* púgil.
pugilistic, *a.* pugnante, pugnaz.
pugnacious [pʌg'neiʃəs], *a.* pugnaz, pendenciero, batallador.
pugnaciously, *adv.* de un modo pugnaz.
pugnacity [pʌg'næsiti], *s.* pugnacidad.
pug-nosed, *a.* (de nariz) respingona o roma.
puisne ['pju:ni], *a.* inferior en grado, más joven; (*for.*) reciente, nuevo, juez pedáneo.
puissance ['pju:isənt], *s.* pujanza, potencia, poder.
puissant, *a.* pujante, poderoso, fuerte.
puke [pju:k], *v.t.*, *v.i.* vomitar, nausear, basquear.
puke, puker, *s.* vomitivo; vomitador.
pulchritude ['pʌlkritju:d], *s.* pulcritud.
pule [pju:l], *v.i.* pipiar, piar como un pollo; lloriquear, gemir.
puling ['pju:liŋ], *s.* piada, pío, grito del pollo; lloriqueo. — *a.* llorón, que lloriquea.
pull [pul], *s.* estirón, tirón, arrancada, sacudimiento, sacudida; tirador (de puerta); campanillazo; (*fam.*) enchufe, influencia, tarea; ventaja; ejercicio de remos; (*impr.*) impresión hecha con la prensa de mano; (*dep.*) una jugada de golf; (*carreras*) el acto de retardar la velocidad del caballo con objeto de perder; *to take a pull*, (*impr.*) sacar una prueba. — *v.t.* tirar, arrastrar, halar, estirar, sacar, arrancar, remar, bogar; coger, recoger; desgarrar, rasgar; chupar; (*impr.*) sacar (una prueba). — *v.i.* tirar con violencia; (*mar.*) remar; *to pull a long face*, (*fam.*) poner la cara larga; *to pull through*, salir de un trance; salir de apuros; reponerse, sanar; *to pull away*, arrancar (un vehículo), remar; quitar con violencia; *to pull about*, arrastrar por acá y acullá; *to pull ahead*, (*mar.*) halar avante; *to pull back*, retirar hacia atrás, hacer recular; *to pull down*, derribar, demoler; deponer, abatir, humillar; *to pull in*, traer o tirar hacia adentro; enfrenar, frenar; entrar, parar; *to pull one's leg*, (*fam.*) tomar el pelo a uno; *to pull off*, quitar(se) (vestidos), arrancar, deshacer; (*fam.*) conseguir, lograr, salirse con; *to pull out*, sacar; *to pull to pieces*, hacer pedazos; *to pull round*, (*fam.*) sanar, reponerse; *to pull up*, (*v.t.*) desarraigar, extirpar, levantar; (*v.i.*) hacer alto, frenar, enfrenar.
puller, *s.* el que tira, el que arranca.
puller-down, *s.* demoledor.
pullet ['pulit], *s.* polla, pollita.
pulley ['puli], *s.* polea; (*mar.*) garrucha, cuadernal.

pullicat ['pulikət], *s.* especie de pañuelo a cuadros originario de Pulicat (Madras).
pullman ['pulmən], *s.*; *Pullman car*, coche de lujo, cochecama, *m.*, coche restaurante.
pullulate ['pulju:leit], *v.i.* pulular.
pullulation, *s.* germinación; progenie, *f.*
pulmonary ['pʌlmonəri], *a.* pulmonar. — *s.* (*bot.*) pulmonaria.
pulmonic [pʌl'monik], *a.* pulmonar, pulmoníaco. — *s.* pectoral; tísico.
pulp [pʌlp], *s.* pulpa; (*bot.*) carne (de fruta), arilo; pasta (para hacer papel); (*min.*) mineral pulverizado y mezclado con agua. — *v.t.* descortezar; reducir a pulpa; *to beat to a pulp*, (*fig., fam.*) poner como un pulpo.
pulpiness, pulpousness, *s.* estado pulposo.
pulpous, *a.* pulposo, mollar.
pulpit ['pulpit], *s.* púlpito; tribuna (de orador).
pulpwood ['pʌlpwud], *s.* pulpa de madera para fabricar papel.
pulsate [pʌl'seit], *v.i.* pulsar, latir, tener latidos, tener palpitaciones, batir.
pulsatile ['pʌlsətail], *a.* pulsátil, pulsativo, latiente; de percusión.
pulsation [pʌl'seiʃən], *s.* pulsación, latido.
pulsative, *a.* pulsativo.
pulsator, *s.* pulsímetro.
pulsatory, *a.* pulsátil, pulsativo, latiente.
pulse [pʌls], *s.* pulso; pulsación, vibración, latido; (*fig.*) ritmo, vibración, latido; legumbres, *f.pl.*; *to feel one's pulse*, tomar el pulso a uno; (*fig.*) tantear. — *v.i.* pulsar, batir, latir.
pulseless, *a.* sin pulso.
pulsimeter [pʌl'simitə], *s.* pulsímetro, esfigmómetro.
pulsion ['pʌlʃən], *s.* impulso, tracción.
pulverizable, *a.* pulverizable, triturable.
pulverization, *s.* pulverización, trituración.
pulverize ['pʌlvəraiz], *v.t.* pulverizar, moler, triturar, desmenuzar, machacar.
pulverizer, *s.* pulverizador.
pulverulence [pʌl'verju:ləns], *s.* polvareda, abundancia de polvo.
pulverulent, *a.* polvoriento, pulverulento.
puma ['pju:mə], *s.* puma.
pumice ['pʌmis], *s.* piedra pómez. — *v.t.* apomazar.
pump [pʌmp], *s.* bomba; (*fam.*) zapatilla, escarpín; *to man the pump*, (*mar.*) armar la bomba; *air-pump*, maquina-neumática; *force-pump*, bomba impelente; *lifting-pump*, bomba elevadora; *petrol-pump*, bomba de gasolina (de un motor); surtidor de gasolina (en un garaje); *suction-pump*, bomba aspirante. — *v.t.* bombear, dar a la bomba; (*fig.*) tantear, sondear, sonsacar; *to pump up*, hinchar, inflar. — *v.i.* dar a la bomba.
pump-box, *s.* (*mar.*) mortero de bomba.
pump-brake, *s.* (*mar.*) guimbalete; freno o amortiguador hidráulico.
pumper, *s.* bombero; (*fam.*) sonsacador.
pumpkin ['pʌmpkin], *s.* calabaza; calabacera.
pun [pʌn], *s.* equívoco, retruécano, juego de vocablos. — *v.i.* decir equívocos, jugar con el vocablo. — *v.t.* triturar, machacar, moler [POUND].
punch [pʌntʃ], *s.* puñetazo, puñada, puñete, moquete, cachete, mojicón (*fam.*); punzón; sacabocados; ponche (bebida); revés; arlequín o bufón de los volatines. — *v.i.*, *v.t.* punzar, pungir, horadar con punzón;

empujar, hurgar; dar puñetazos, pegar un puñetazo, acachetear, apuñear (*fam.*).

punch-bowl, s. ponchera.

puncheon ['pʌntʃən], s. punzón, cuño, contrapunzón, estampador; (*carp.*) montante, pie derecho; tonel que contiene de 72 a 120 galones.

puncher, s. punzador, punzón; (E.U.) vaquero.

punchinello [pʌntʃi'nelou], s. polichinela, títere.

punchy, a. rechoncho.

punctate ['pʌŋteit], **punctated** [pʌŋk'teitid], a. puntiagudo, formado en punta.

punctilio [pʌŋk'tiliou], s. puntillo; formalidad, escrupulosidad, exactitud minuciosa.

punctilious [pʌŋk'tiliəs], a. puntilloso, puntoso, escrupuloso, delicado.

punctiliously, adv. con exactitud minuciosa, con puntillo.

punctiliousness, s. puntualidad, delicadez, miramiento, pundonor, puntillo.

punctual ['pʌŋktjuəl], a. puntual, exacto, fiel, justo, preciso.

punctuality [pʌŋktju:'æliti], s. puntualidad, formalidad, exactitud.

punctually ['pʌŋktjuəli], adv. puntualmente, exactamente, formalmente.

punctuate ['pʌŋktju:eit], v.t. puntuar; (*fig.*) interponer, intercalar; (*fig.*) subrayar.

punctuation, s. puntuación.

puncture ['pʌŋktʃər], s. pinchazo; perforación; puntura, picada, picadura, punzada, punzadura. — v.t. pinchar; perforar; punzar, picar, agujerear.

pundit ['pʌndit], s. bracmán sabio; experto; (*despec.*) sabihondo.

pungency ['pʌndʒənsi], s. naturaleza picante; mordacidad, acerbidad, acrimonia; punta, sabor.

pungent ['pʌndʒənt], a. picante, pungente; mordicante, mordaz; áspero, acre; (*hist. nat.*) punzante, puntiagudo.

pungently, adv. de un modo picante.

Punic ['pju:nik], a. púnico; (*fig.*) falso, pérfido.

puniceous [pju:'nifəs], a. rojo vivo; purpúreo.

puniness ['pju:ninis], s. mezquindad, delicadeza, encanijamiento.

punish ['pʌniʃ], v.t. castigar, corregir, mortificar; pegar, penar.

punishable ['pʌniʃəbəl], a. punible, penable.

punishability, punishableness, s. carácter punible, penalidad.

punisher, s. castigador.

punishment, s. castigo, punición, penitencia, pena.

punitive ['pju:nitiv], **punitory** ['pju:nitəri], a. punitivo, penal.

punk [pʌŋk], s. pebete, yesca, hupe, f.; prostituta, ramera.

punner, s. herramienta para apisonar tierra.

punnet ['pʌnit], s. cesto pequeño para exponer flores, frutas, etc.

punster ['pʌnstər], s. equivoquista, m.f.

punt [pʌnt], s. barquichuelo plano, batea; (*mar.*) plancha de agua; (*dep.*) puntapié dado a un balón. — v.t., v.i. impeler una batea; ir en batea; despedir un balón con un puntapié.

punter, s. el que va en una balea; pelete (en juegos de azar), punto.

punty, s. pontil; marca redonda en un objeto de cristal.

puny ['pju:ni], a. mezquino; encanijado, enfermizo, delicado.

pup [pʌp], s. cachorro, cachorrito. — v.i. parir (de una perra).

pupa ['pju:pə], s. crisálida, ninfa.

pupil ['pju:pəl], s. pupila, niña del ojo; (*for.*) pupilo; discípulo, alumno.

pupilage, s. pupilaje; (*for.*) minoridad.

pupilary ['pju:piləri], a. pupilar.

puppet ['pʌpit], s. títere, muñeca, muñeco, monigote; (*fig.*) maniquí, monigote, muñeco, paniaguado.

puppet-play, puppet-show, s. representación de títeres, retablo.

puppy ['pʌpi], s. perrillo, perrezno, cachorro; (*fig.*) pisaverde, trompeta, m.

puppyish, a. parecido a un cachorro; tontivano, fatuo.

puppyism, s. hinchazón, f., virotismo, fatuidad.

Purbeck ['pə:ɪbek], s. piedra de la península de Purbeck en Dorset, usada como mármol fino.

purblind ['pə:ɪblaind], a. miope, cegato; ciego; torpe.

purchasable, a. comprable.

purchase ['pə:ɪtʃis], v.t. comprar, obtener; feriar, mercar; (*mec.*) izar, levantar; (*mar.*) levantar el ancla. — s. compra; (*for.*) obtención, adquisición; botín; (*mar.*) aparato, aparejo; palanca; *purchase-money*, precio de compra; *to get a purchase*, tener por donde agarrar.

purchaser, s. comprador, adquiridor, adquirente.

pure ['pjuər], a. puro.

purée ['pju:rei], s. (*coc.*) puré.

purely ['pju:əli], adv. puramente, meramente, sencillamente, simplemente.

pureness, s. pureza.

purfle [pə:ɪfəl], v.t. bordar, orlar, recamar, adornar con bordados. — s. orla, perfil, borde adornado.

purgation [pə:ɪ'geiʃən], s. purgación, purgamiento; (*for.*) purgación.

purgative ['pə:ɪgətiv], a. purgativo, purgante, purgador. — s. purgante, purga.

purgatorial [pə:ɪgə'to:riəl], a. purgativo, del purgatorio.

purgatory ['pə:ɪgətəri], s. purgatorio.

purge [pə:ɪdʒ], v.t. purgar, depurar, expurgar, acrisolar. — v.i. purgarse. — s. purga, purgante, catártico; purgación, purgamiento, depuración.

purger, s. purgante, purga, purificador; purgador.

purging, s. purgación, purificación; expiación; depuración; purga. — a. purgativo.

purification [pju:rifi'keiʃən], s. purificación, depuración, expiación.

purificator, purifier, s. purificador.

puriform ['pju:rifo:ɪm], a. puriforme.

purify ['pju:rifai], v.t. purificar, purgar, depurar, expurgar, expiar. — v.i. purificarse, clarificarse.

purifying, s. purificación, purgación.

purin ['pju:rin], s. purina.

purism ['pju:ərizm], s. purismo.

purist, s. purista, m.f.

Puritan ['pju:ritən], s., a. puritano.

puritanic [pju:ri'tænik], **puritanical** [pju:ri-

'tænikəl], *a.* puritano; (*despec.*) nimiamente escrupuloso.

puritanically, *adv.* como puritano.

Puritanism ['pjuːritənizm], *s.* puritanismo.

purity ['pjuːriti], *s.* pureza.

purl [pəːl], *v.t.* (*cost.*) perfilar, guarnecer con bordado o fleco; orlar; arremolinar, envolver. — *v.i.* murmurar, susurrar (de las aguas); ondular; arremolinarse. — *s.* perfil, pliegue de vestido; cerveza de ajenjos; ondulación; (*cost.*) orla; espiral de hilo de oro o plata; variedad de punto en la calceta; murmullo, susurro (de las aguas).

purlieu ['pəːljuː], *s.* confín, confines, linde, lindero, mojoneras; (*ant.*) alrededores.

purlin ['pəːlin], *s.* (*arq.*) ejión, fabalcón; viga que sostiene los cabrios.

purling ['pəːling], *s.* murmullo, susurro (de agua). — *a.* murmurante, que murmura.

purloin [pəːˈlɔin], *v.t.* robar, hurtar, sustraer.

purloiner, *s.* ladrón, plagiario, ratero.

purloining, *s.* robo, plagio.

purple ['pəːpəl], *s.* púrpura, color morado; múrice; trábea; dignidad real, dignidad de reyes, dignidad de cardenales. — *pl.* tabardillo pintado. — *a.* purpúreo; purpurino, morado; regio, imperial; (*poét.*) purpurino; sangriento. — *v.t.* purpurar, teñir de púrpura, purpurear. — *v.i.* purpurear; ruborizarse.

purplish, purply, *a.* purpurino, morado.

purport ['pəːpɔːt], *s.* sentido, significado, significación; intención, designio, objeto; tenor, substancia.

purport [pəːˈpɔːt], *v.t.*, *v.i.* tender a mostrar; implicar, querer decir, significar; pretender, intentar, proponerse.

purpose ['pəːpəs], *s.* proyecto, plan, propósito, motivo, intención, utilidad, designio, mira; resolución, determinación, voluntad; objeto, fin, efecto, resultado; cuestión, proposición; negocio, hecho; *to what purpose*, para qué, con qué motivo, con qué fin; *to no purpose*, inútilmente, sin efecto; por demás; *to the purpose*, al propósito, al caso, al grano; *on purpose*, expresamente, de propósito, adrede. — *v.t.*, *v.i.* tener la intención, intentar, proyectar, proponer, proponerse.

purposeless, *a.* vago, sin objeto, sin propósito.

purposely, *adv.* de intento, adrede, expresamente, de propósito.

purpura ['pəːpjuːrə], *s.* púrpura; (*med.*) escorbuto.

purpurate ['pəːpjuːreit], *s.* purpurato.

purpurine ['pəːpjuːrin], *s.* purpurina.

purr, purring, *s.* ronroneo.

purr [pəː], *v.i.* ronronear. — *v.t.* decir murmurando.

purse [pəːs], *s.* bolsa, portamonedas, *m.*; premio; riqueza, hacienda; derrama, colecta; (*zool.*) buche; *purse-strings*, cordones de la bolsa, cerradero; *well-lined purse*, (*fig.*) bolsa llena; *you cannot make a silk purse out of a sow's ear*, de ruin paño nunca buen sayo. — *v.t.* embolsar, embolsillar; apretar (los labios); fruncir.

purseful, *s.* cantidad que contiene una bolsa.

purse-proud, *a.* envanecido por la riqueza, orgulloso de sus riquezas.

purser, *s.* (*mar.*) contador; maestre de raciones, sobrecargo.

pursiness, *s.* disnea.

purslain, purslane ['pəːslin], *s.* (*bot.*) verdolaga.

pursuable [pəːˈsjuːəbəl], *a.* proseguible.

pursuance, *s.* prosecución, seguimiento, cumplimiento; *in pursuance of*, en virtud de.

pursuant [pəːˈsjuːənt], *a.* conforme, consiguiente, en virtud (de), en fuerza (de).

pursue [pəːˈsjuː], *v.t.*, *v.i.* seguir (una carrera, oficio, etc.); continuar; perseguir, acosar, dar caza; ejercer, dedicarse a; (*for.*) demandar, poner pleito, procesar.

pursuer, *s.* perseguidor; (*for.*) demandante.

pursuit [pəːˈsjuːt], *s.* perseguimiento, acosamiento; persecución, caza; busca, búsqueda; seguimiento, continuación, prosecución; pretensión; empeño, conato; ocupación. — *pl.* **pursuits**, ocupaciones, estudios.

pursuivant ['pəːswivənt], *s.* (*mil.*, *her.*) persevante.

pursy ['pəːsi], *a.* asmático; hinchado, obeso; arrugado; acaudalado; envanecido por su riqueza.

purtenance ['pəːtenəns], *s.* asadura de un animal.

purulence, purulency, *s.* purulencia.

purulent ['pjuːrulənt], *a.* purulento.

purvey [pəːˈvei], *v.t.*, *v.i.* proveer, suministrar, surtir, abastecer.

purveyance, *s.* abastecimiento, suministro, abasto.

purveyor, *s.* abastecedor, proveedor, suministrador.

purview ['pəːvjuː], *s.* estipulación, condición; esfera, extensión; (*for.*) alcance, límite de una disposición legal.

pus [pʌs], *s.* pus.

push [puʃ], *v.t.* empujar, impeler, rempujar; obligar, apretar, apremiar, estrechar; proseguir, molestar, importunar; activar, promover, apurar; *to push forward* o *on*, echar adelante; *to push back*, echar atrás, hacer retroceder, rechazar; *to push off*, apartar con la mano; desatracar (un bote); *to push away*, alejar, rechazar; *to push down*, derribar, abatir; *to push further*, seguir adelante. — *v.i.* empujar, dar un empujón, dar una estocada, dar empellones, estoquear; hacer un esfuerzo, acometer; apresurarse, darse prisa; *to push forward, to push on*, apresurarse, adelantarse; *to push back*, retroceder; *to be pushed*, (*fam.*) estar atareado, faltarle tiempo; estar en un aprieto; *to push off*, (*vulg.*) coger la calle, largarse, tomar el trote; *to push in*, entrometerse; introducirse a codazos. — *s.* empujón, empuje, empellón, rempujón; picada, punzada; impulsión, impulso; embestida, arremetida, asalto, conato; (*fam.*) esfuerzo, iniciativa, energía; (*fam.*) aprieto, apuro, momento crítico; pulsador, botón (eléctrico); *at a push*, (*fig.*, *fam.*) en un apuro, en caso de necesidad.

pushing, *a.* vigoroso, enérgico, agresivo, eficaz, diligente, activo, emprendedor.

pushpin, *s.* juego de alfileres, juego de pajitas.

pusillanimity [pjuːziˈlænimiti], *s.* pusilanimidad.

pusillanimous [pjuːziˈlæniməs], *a.* pusilánime, apocado.

pusillanimously, *adv.* pusilánimemente.

puss [pus], **pussy** ['pusi], *s.* minino, micho, gatito, gatita; chica, guapa; liebre, *f.*; *Puss! Puss!* ¡Miz, miz!

pussy-cat, *s.* gato, gata; (*bot.*) el amento del sauce.
pussy-willow, *s.* sauce pequeño americano (*Salix discolor*).
pustular [ˈpʌstjuːləɪ], *a.* (*bot.*) pustulado, pustuloso.
pustulate, *v.t.* cubrir de vejigas. — *v.i.* formarse pústulas.
pustule [ˈpʌstjuːl], *s.* pústula, postilla, buba, grano.
pustulous, *a.* pustuloso, postilloso, puposo.
put [put], *v.t.* poner, meter, colocar; proponer; exponer; disponer; entregar; confiar; situar; expresar, declarar, interpretar; prevenir; lanzar, arrojar; presentar para ser discutido; hacer o dirigir (una pregunta); obligar a una persona a hacer algo contra su voluntad, imponer, obligar; traducir; *to put into practice*, poner en uso; *to put about*, divulgar, hacer correr; enojar; (*mar.*) cambiar de rumbo; *to put aside*, poner a un lado, descartar, desechar; *to put away*, apartar, echar fuera, repudiar, divorciar, despedir; guardarse, dejar; poner en salvo; ahorrar; (*fam.*) embuchar, comerse; *to put back*, apartar, retirar hacia atrás, atrasar, retardar; reponer, devolver; *to put by*, poner de lado, arrimar, arrinconar, desviar, apartar; ahorrar; poner en salvo; *to put down*, deponer, bajar, descender; abatir, degradar, humillar, deprimir, reprimir, sofocar; anotar, apuntar, poner; *to put forth*, adelantar, extender; publicar, exponer, dar a luz; brotar, producir; germinar; *to put forward*, exponer, adelantar, adelantarse, llevar adelante; *to put in*, meter dentro de, introducir, presentar, insertar, ingerir; (*mar.*) entrar en un puerto, arribar; *to put in an appearance*, comparecer, presentarse, llegar; *to put in for*, solicitar (una vacante, etc.), presentarse para; *to put in writing*, poner por escrito; *to put in mind*, recordar; *to put off*, dilatar, diferir, aplazar, suspender; apartar, desechar, posponer; quitarse, despojarse; desilusionar; *to put off one's clothes*, desnudarse; *to put on*, ponerse; atribuir, echar, imputar; poner encima de; disimular, fingir; imponer; *to put on land* (o *shore*), desembarcar, echar a tierra; *to put out*, sacar; echar, expeler, echar fuera, arrojar, despachar, despedir; germinar, brotar; dislocar; apagar, matar (la luz, etc.); tachar, borrar; distraer; cortar; poner a interés, dar a logro; dar a luz, publicar; mostrar; irritar, enfadar, enojar, molestar; *to put oneself out for another*, dar su brazo a torcer, sacrificarse, incomodarse, molestarse; *to put out to nurse*, dar a criar; *to put out to sea*, hacer(se) a la mar, zarpar; *to put over*, sobreponer; diferir, dilatar; (*fig.*) conseguir, salir bien; exponer; realizar; *to put an end to*, acabar; *to put a question*, hacer una pregunta, preguntar; *to put a stop to*, poner coto a; *to put to*, añadir, agregar; exponer; usar, ejercitar; abandonar, dejar; enganchar; *to put to bed*, acostar, poner en cama; *to put to death*, dar la muerte, quitar la vida; *to put to flight*, hacer huir, poner en fuga; *to put to the sword*, pasar a cuchillo; *to put to the vote*, poner a votación; *to put together*, juntar, acumular, amontonar, reunir; *to put up*, poner encima, poner en venta; aumentar; poner en su lugar, construir, edificar; presentar, proponer,

ofrecer; poner en escena; poner dinero (en una apuesta); presentarse como candidato; alojar y convidar; publicar las amonestaciones; poner en lugar seguro; *to put up one's umbrella*, abrir su paraguas; *to put up one's sword*, envainar la espada; *to put up for sale*, poner en venta; *to put up with*, resignarse a, aguantar, tolerar; *to put upon*, poner en, poner encima de; persuadir, incitar; oprimir, hacer padecer; acusar; imprimir. — *v.i.* ir, moverse; (*mar.*) seguir rumbo, dirigirse; germinar, brotar.
put [pʌt], *s.* tiro, golpe; (*vulg.*) palurdo, bobo; extremidad, necesidad; juego de naipes; (*com.*) privilegio, opción.
putative [ˈpjuːtətiv], *a.* supuesto, reputado; putativo.
puteal [ˈpjuːtiəl], *s.* brocal de pozo.
putid [ˈpjuːtid], *a.* sucio, puerco, impuro, inmundo; bajo, vil, ruin, de ningún valor.
putlog [ˈputlɔg], *s.* (*arq.*) almojaya.
put-off [ˈputɔf], *s.* dilatorias, retraso; excusa, escapatoria.
putrefaction [pjuːtriˈfækʃən], *s.* putrefacción, podredura.
putrefactive, *a.* putrefactivo, putrido.
putrefiable [pjuːtriˈfaiəbəl], *a.* capaz de pudrirse.
putrefy [ˈpjuːtrifai], *v.t.* pudrir, podrir, podrecer.
putrescence [pjuːˈtresəns], *s.* putrefacción, pudrición, pudrimiento.
putrescent, *a.* podrido, pútrido, que se pudre.
putrid [ˈpjuːtrid], *a.* podrido, pútrido, putrefacto, carroño.
putridity [pjuːˈtriditi], *s.* pudredumbre, *f.*, podredumbre, *f.*, putridez.
putt [pʌt], *v.t.* (*golf*) dar un golpe a la pelota con el ponedor (palo de golf) para que ésta caiga en el hoyo. — *s.* el golpe.
puttee [ˈpʌti], *s.* especie de venda de lana que se usaba, especialmente en el ejército inglés, como polaina.
putter [ˈpʌtəɪ], *s.* ponedor, uno de los palos del juego de golf.
putter [ˈputəɪ], *s.* ponedor, persona que pone.
putter-on, *s.* instigador, incitador; fingidor.
putting [ˈputiŋ], *s.* acción de poner.
putting-green [ˈpʌtiŋgriːn], espacio en el campo de golf donde se halla el hoyo.
puttock [ˈpʌtɔk], *s.* milano.
putty [ˈpʌti], *s.* masilla; potea. — *v.t.* poner masilla, revocar con cemento.
put-up [ˈputʌp], *a.* (*vulg.*) tramado, urdido; confabulado.
puzzle [ˈpʌzəl], *v.t.* traer perplejo o desconcertado, desconcertar, inquietar, intrigar, confundir, aturrullar; embrollar, enredar, embarazar; (*fig.*) alambicar. — *v.i.* preguntarse, estar perplejo; embrollarse, enredarse. — *s.* enigma, *m.*, rompecabezas, *m.*, problema arduo, acertijo, adivinaja; perplejidad, inquietud; embrollo, enredo.
puzzler, *s.* persona o cosa que embaraza.
puzzling, *a.* extraño, de difícil resolución, intrigante; enredador, embarazador.
pycnite [ˈpiknait], *s.* variedad de topacio.
pye [pai], *s.* mezcla confusa de tipos de imprenta.
pygmean [pigˈmiːən], **pygmy**, *a.* de pigmeo. — *s.* pigmeo, enano.
pyjamas [piˈdʒɑːməs], *s.pl.* pijama, *m.*

pylon ['pailɔn], s. (arq. egipcia) pilón, portada monumental; (aer.) torre, f., poste de señal; torre de lanzamiento de un dirigible; (elec.) poste telegráfico o de conducción de fuerza en alta tensión, pilono.

pyloric [pai'lɔːrik], a. pilórico.

pylorous [pai'lɔːrəs], s. píloro.

pyracanth ['pairəkænθ], s. piracanto.

pyramid ['pirəmid], s. pirámide, f.

pyramidal [pi'ræmidəl], a. piramidal.

pyramidically, adv. en forma de pirámide, piramidalmente.

pyre ['paiəɹ], s. pira, hoguera.

Pyrenean [pirə'niːən], a. pirenaico, de los Pirineos.

Pyrenees, s. Pirineos.

pyretic [pai'retik], a. pirético.

pyretology, s. piretología.

pyrexia [pai'reksiə], s. pirexia.

pyrites [pai'raitiːz], s. pirita.

pyritic [pai'ritik], a. piritoso.

pyrogallic [pairo'gælik], a. pirogálico.

pyrogenous [pai'rɔdʒənəs], a. pirógeno, ígneo.

pyrography, s. pirografía.

pyroligneous, pyrolignous, a. pirolignoso, piroleñoso.

pyrology [pai'rɔlodʒi], s. pirología.

pyrometer [pai'rɔmetəɹ], s. pirómetro.

pyrometry, s. pirometría.

pyrophorous [pai'rɔfərəs], a. piroforoso.

pyrophorus, s. piróforo.

pyrophotometer [pairo'foutomiːtəɹ], s. pirofotómetro.

pyroscope ['pairoskoup], s. piroscopio.

pyrotechnic [pairo'teknik], **pyrotechnical**, a. pirotécnico.

pyrotechnics, pyrotechny, s. pirotecnia.

pyroxene [pai'rɔkziːn], s. piroxena.

pyrrhic ['pirik], s., a. pírrico (danza griega); (poét.) pirriquio; Pyrrhic victory, victoria costosa por demás.

Pythagorean [paiθəgo'riːən], **pythagoric** [paiθə'gɔːrik], **pythagorical**, a. pitagórico.

Pythagorism [pai'θægorizm], s. pitagorismo.

python ['paiθɔn], s. pitón.

pythoness ['paiθənes], s. pitonisa.

pythonic [pai'θɔnik], a. pitónico.

pyx [piks], s. copón, píxide, f.; caja de la brújula.

Q

Q, q [kjuː], decimaséptima letra del alfabeto inglés. Se pronuncia como que, qui, del castellano; como c fuerte y como cue, cui: etiquette, etiquet; antique, antic; banquet, bancuet; quiver, cuiver.

quack [kwæk], v.i. parpar, graznar (un pato); jactarse; charlar, chacharear, charlatanear. — s. graznido (del pato); medicastro, matasanos, curandero, ensalmador; charlatán, saltimbanco; quack-doctor; medicastro, curandero, matasanos, ensalmador.

quackery, s. charlatanería, charlatanismo, empirismo; curandería, curanderismo, ensalmos.

quackish, a. de charlatán; curanderil.

quacksalver ['kwæksælvəɹ], s. medicastro, curandero, medicucho.

quad [kwɔd], s. cuadrángulo o patio como el

de un colegio, etc.; (impr.) cuadrado, cuadratín; (fam.) uno de hijos cuádruplos.

quadragenarian [kwɔdrədʒe'neəriən], s. cuadragenario.

quadragesima [kwɔdrə'dʒezimə], s. cuadragésima, cuaresma.

quadragesimal, a. cuadragesimal.

quadrangle ['kwɔdræŋgəl], s. (geom.) cuadrángulo; (arq.) patio.

quadrangular, a. cuadrangular.

quadrant ['kwɔdrənt], s. (geom.) cuadrante; cuarto de círculo, cuarto; (mar.) octante; (mec.) sector oscilante.

quadrantal, a. cuadrantal.

quadrat ['kwɔdrət], s. (impr.) cuadrado, cuadratín.

quadrate ['kwɔdrit], a. cuadrado. — s. (anat.) hueso cuadrado; (astr.) cuadrado aspecto; (mús.) becuadro. — v.t., v.i. (fig.) cuadrar, corresponder, convenir; (mat., etc.) cuadrar.

quadratic, a. cuadrado; (mat.) ecuación de segundo grado; (cristal.) cuadrático. — s. cuadrática, ecuación de segundo grado.

quadrature ['kwɔdrətʃəɹ], s. cuadratura, cuadrado; (mec.) escuadreo.

quadrels ['kwɔdrəlz], s.pl. (arq.) piedras cuadradas.

quadrennial [kwɔd'reniəl], a. cuadrenial.

quadrennially, adv. cada cuatro años.

quadricycle ['kwɔdrisaikəl], s. cuadriciclo.

quadriga [kwɔd'raigə], s. cuadriga.

quadrilateral [kwɔdri'lætərəl], s., a. cuadrilátero.

quadrille [kwɔ'dril], s. contradanza; cuatrillo (juego de naipes); cuadrilla.

quadrillion [kwɔd'riljən], s. cuatrillón.

quadrinomial [kwɔdri'noumiəl], a. cuadrínomo. — s. cuadrinomio.

quadripartite [kwɔdri'pɑːɹtait], s. cuadripartido.

quadrisyllable [kwɔdri'siləbəl], s. cuadrisílabo.

quadrivium [kwɔd'riviəm], s. cuadrivio.

quadroon [kwɔd'ruːn], s. cuarterón.

quadrumane ['kwɔdru:mein], s. cuadrumano.

quadrumanous, a. cuadrumano.

quadruped ['kwɔdru:ped], s., a. cuadrúpedo.

quadrupedal, a. cuadrupedal.

quadruple [kwɔd'ru:pəl], s., a. cuádruplo, cuádruple. — v.t., v.i. cuadruplicar, cuatrodoblar.

quadruplet, s. cuádruple; uno de hijos cuádruplos, gemelo.

quadruplex, a. cuádruple.

quadruplicate, v.t. cuadruplicar. — a. cuadruplicado.

quadruplication, s. cuadruplicación.

quadruply, adv. al cuádruplo, cuatro veces tanto.

quaff [kwɔf], v.t., v.i. beber a grandes tragos, beber copiosamente, tragar, potar. — s. trago.

quaffer, s. bebedor, potador.

quagga ['kwægə], s. cuaga.

quaggy ['kwægi], a. pantanoso, fangoso, blando.

quagmire ['kwægmaiəɹ], s. cenagal, tremedal, tembladal.

quail [kweil], v.i. desanimarse, descorazonarse, acobardarse, languidecer, perder el valor, cejar. — v.t. domar, subyugar; desanimar, desalentar, amilanar. — s. (orn.) codorniz, parpayuela.

quailing, *s.* doma, subyugación; descaecimiento, desaliento, amilanamiento. — *a.* descorazonado, acobardado, desalentado.

quaint [kweint], *a.* singular, original, fantástico, curioso, raro, original, extraño; pintoresco, bonito; fino, afectado, pretencioso; excéntrico, extravagante.

quaintly, *adv.* de una manera fantástica, original; de manera arcaica pero agradable.

quaintness, *s.* curiosidad, rareza, singularidad; carácter pintoresco o bonito, preciosidad; esmero, afectación.

quake [kweik], *v.i.* estremecerse, tremer; (*personas*) estar agitado, estremecerse, trepidar. — *s.* estremecimiento, temblor; agitación, estremecimiento, trepidación; *earthquake,* terremoto.

Quaker ['kweikəɹ], *s.* cuáquero, cuákero.

Quakerish, *a.* de cuáquero.

Quakerism, *s.* cuaquerismo.

quakerly, *a.* de cuáquero.

quaking ['kweikiŋ], *a.* movedizo, temblador, temblante, que tiembla; temblón, tembloroso. — *s.* estremecimiento; agitación, trepidación, temblor; *quaking-grass,* cualquiera planta del género Briza.

qualifiable [kwɔli'faiəbəl], *a.* calificable, susceptible.

qualification [kwɔlifi'keiʃən], *s.* calificación, calidad, requisito, cualidad; condición, estado; capacidad, idoneidad; título; mitigación, modificación, disminución, atenuación.

qualificator, *s.* (*igl.*) calificador.

qualified ['kwɔlifaid], *a.* capaz, propio, idóneo, competente, apto; autorizado, dotado, calificado, (*for.*) habilitado; modificado, (*for.*) restringido, limitado. — *p.p.* [QUALIFY].

qualifier, *s.* (*gram.*) calificativo.

qualify ['kwɔlifai], *v.t., v.i.* hacer(se) apto, hacer(se) capaz o idóneo; poner(se) en estado (de), preparar; hallarse en disposición (para), ser competente para; autorizar, determinar, calificar, fijar; modificar, moderar, limitar, restringir, suavizar, templar; (*for.*) habilitar; limitar, restringir; (*E.U.*) prestar juramento antes de entrar en funciones.

qualifying, *a.* calificativo; preparativo.

qualitative ['kwɔlitətiv], *a.* cualitativo.

quality ['kwɔliti], *s.* cualidad, propiedad; disposición, inclinación, naturaleza, virtud; poder, condición; calidad, clase, *f.*; título, prendas; categoría, alta posición social.

qualm [kwɔːm, kwɑːm], *s.* escrúpulo, remordimiento; basca, náusea; desfallecimiento.

qualmish, *a.* basco, con náusea; escrupuloso.

qualmishness, *s.* náusea, ganas de vomitar; escrupulosidad.

quandary, *s.* incertidumbre, *f.*, perplejidad, duda, apuro.

quant [kwɔnt], *s.* vara para empujar la batea.

quantify ['kwɔntifai], *v.t.* determinar la cantidad, contar, medir; expresar la cantidad.

quantitative ['kwɔntitətiv], **quantitive** ['kwɔntitiv], *a.* cuantitativo.

quantitatively, *adv.* de una manera cuantitativa.

quantity ['kwɔntiti], *s.* cantidad, número, agregado, suma; masa, volumen; gran cantidad, gran número; (*elec.*) intensidad de una corriente.

quantum, *s.* (*fís.*) cuanto; unidad cuántica; cantidad. — *a.* cuántico.

quarantine ['kwɔrəntiːn], *s.* cuarentena, cuarenta días; lazareto; *to be in quarantine,* hacer cuarentena. — *v.t.* poner en cuarentena.

quarrel ['kwɔrel], *s.* riña, reyerta, querella, pendencia, disputa, contienda, camorra, pelotera, bronca, oposición, altercación, porfía, quimera, desavenencia; especie de flecha usada en tiempos antiguos; vidrio o loseta romboidal; *to pick a quarrel,* armar pendencia. — *v.i.* reñir, contender, disputar(se), altercar, pelear, romper (con), desavenirse.

quarreller, *s.* pendenciero, quimerista, *m.f.*, reñidor.

quarrelling, *s.* pendencia, riña, disputa, lucha, desacuerdo.

quarrelsome, *a.* reñidor, pendenciero, quimerista, peleón.

quarrelsomely, *adv.* alborotadamente.

quarrelsomeness, *s.* temperamento pendenciero, pugnacidad, petulancia.

quarrier ['kwɔriəɹ], *s.* cantero, picapedrero.

quarry ['kwɔri], *s.* cantera, pedrera; presa, ralea, caza muerta; cuadro, rombo (de vidrio). — *v.t.* extraer, sacar de una cantera; devorar, hacer su presa de.

quarrying, *s.* extracción; cantería.

quarryman ['kwɔrimən], *s.* cantero, cavador de cantera; picapedrero.

quart [kwɔːɹt], *s.* cuarto de galón (aprx. 1·13 litros); cuarta.

quartan ['kwɔːɹtən], *s.* (*med.*) cuartana. — *a.* cuartanal.

quartation, *s.* incuartación, encartación.

quarter ['kwɔːɹtəɹ], *s.* cuarto, cuarta parte; cuarto de quintal, arroba; cuarto de hora; barrio, vecindad; región, comarca, parte, *f.*; trimestre; procedencia, origen, lado; (*astr.*) cuarto de luna; (*E.U.*) cuarto del dólar; (*mar.*) cuarta, cuadra de popa; (*carp.*) cuarterón, entrepaño; cuartel, merced, indulgencia, clemencia, gracia; *to give no quarter,* no dar cuartel. — *pl.* **quarters,** habitaciones, vivienda, domicilio, alojamiento, (*mil.*) cuartel; *the four quarters of the globe,* las cuatro partes del mundo; *from all quarters,* de todos lados; *to take up quarters in,* alojarse en; *to get to close quarters,* llegar a las manos. — *a.* cuarto. — *v.t.* dividir, partir, cuartear, hacer cuartos, descuartizar; dividir en cuarteles; (*mil.*) acantonar, acuartelar; hospedar, alojar; romper en pedazos; (*blas.*) cuartelar. — *v.i.* alojarse, tomar sus cuarteles.

quarterage, *s.* sueldo trimestral; cuartel, alojamiento.

quarter-day, *s.* día en que se pagan los alquileres.

quarter-deck, *s.* (*mar.*) alcázar.

quartering, *s.* acción de alojar, acuartelamiento; descuartizamiento.

quarterly, *a.* trimestral. — *s.* revista o publicación trimestral. — *adv.* trimestralmente; por cuartos.

quartermaster ['kwɔːɹtəɹmɑːstəɹ], *s.* (*mil.*) intendente, comisario de guerra, comisario ordenador; (*mar.*) cabo de brigadas; sotomaestro.

quartern ['kwɔːɹtəɹn], *a.* de cuatro. — *s.*

cuarto de pinta; cuarta; *quartern loaf*, pan de cuatro libras.

quartet, quartette [kwɔ:'tet], *s.* (*mús.*, *poét.*) cuarteto, cuartete, cuarteta.

quartile ['kwɔ:til], *s.* (*astr.*) cuadrado.

quarto ['kwɔ:tou], *s.* (*impr.*, *enc.*) papel en cuarto, libro en cuarto. — *a.* en cuarto.

quartz [kwɔ:tz], *s.* (*min.*) cuarzo.

quartzite ['kwɔ:tzait], *s.* (*geol.*) cuarcita.

quartzose, quartzy, *a.* cuarzoso.

quash [kwɔʃ], *v.t.* anular, invalidar, derogar, abrogar; subyugar, domar, aplastar, reprimir.

quasi ['kweizai], *a.*, *adv.* casi, cuasi-.

quasimodo [kwæsi'moudou], *s.* domingo de Quasimodo.

quassation [kwæs'eiʃən], *s.* agitación, sacudida.

quassia ['kwɔʃə, 'kwæʃə], *s.* (*bot.*) cuasia.

quater-centenary [kwætəɹsen'ti:nəri], *s.* cuarto centenario.

quaternary [kwɔ'tə:nəri], *a.* cuaternario, cuarto en orden; cuadrángulo. — *s.* cuaterno.

quaternion [kwɔ'tə:niən], *s.* cuaternidad, banda, serie o fila de cuatro.

quatrain ['kwɔtrein], *s.* cuarteto, cuarteta, redondilla.

quatrefoil ['kætɹfɔil], *s.* hoja o flor compuesta de cuatro divisiones o lóbulos.

quaver ['kweivəɹ], *s.* trino, gorjeo, vibración, trémolo; (*mús.*) corchea; *semiquaver*, (*mús.*) semicorchea. — *v.i.* gorjear, trinar, gorgoritear, gargantear, vibrar; temblar. — *v.t.* cantar o decir con gorjeos, quiebros o acentos temblorosos.

quavering, *s.* trino, gorjeo, gorgorito. — *a.* temblante, temblón, tembloroso; vacilante.

quay [ki:], *s.* muelle, desembarcadero. — *v.t.* proveer de muelles.

quayage ['ki:idʒ], *s.* derecho de muelle.

queachy ['kwi:tʃi], *a.* movedizo.

quean [kwi:n], *s.f.* mujer de mala vida, dama cortesana, mujercilla; moza, buena moza.

queasiness ['kwi:zinis], *s.* náusea, hastío, propensión a la náusea, ganas de vomitar; escrúpulos, escrupulosidad; malestar.

queasy ['kwi:zi], *a.* propenso a la nausea; mareado; nauseabundo, nauseoso, bascoso; escrupuloso, severo; inquieto.

queen [kwi:n], *s.f.* reina, soberana; mujer preeminente; dama (en el juego de damas); figura que equivale al caballo (en el juego de naipes); *queen bee*, enjambrera, abeja reina; *queen consort*, esposa del rey; *queen dowager*, reina viuda; *queen mother*, reina madre; *queen of the meadows*, (*bot.*) ulmaria, espírea. — *v.t.* hacer reina; *to queen it*, hacerse la reina, darse tono.

queen-like, *a.* de reina.

queenliness, *s.* majestad de una reina, dignidad de reina.

queenly, *a.* de reina, como reina; regio, real.

queer [kwiəɹ], *a.* raro, extraño, singular, curioso, original, excéntrico, estrafalario, estrambótico, misterioso; sospechoso; chiflado, chalado; malucho, un poco enfermo, vaguido, desmayado; (*vulg.*) invertido, (*vulg.*) maricón; *there's something queer about this*, aquí hay gato encerrado; *in queer street*, (*fam.*) apurado, en mala situación. — *v.t.* poner en mal estado, comprometer; *to queer the pitch*, meter letra, complicar, poner chinitas.

queerish, *a.* bastante extraño.

queerness, *s.* rareza, singularidad, particularidad, extrañeza; extravagancia.

quell [kwel], *v.t.* reprimir, ahogar, sofocar; calmar, aquietar, apaciguar; hacer cesar; domar, sojuzgar, subyugar. — *v.i.* apagarse, apaciguarse, morir.

queller, *s.* domador, sojuzgador, opresor.

quench [kwentʃ], *v.t.* apagar, matar (luz o fuego), extinguir; sosegar, apaciguar, calmar; (*fig.*) satisfacer, apagar, sosegar; templar, enfriar (hierro); apagar la sed. — *v.i.* enfriarse.

quenchable, *a.* extinguible, destruible, apagable.

quencher, *s.* apagador, sosegador.

quenchless, *a.* inextinguible, implacable.

quercitron ['kwə:ɹsitrən], *s.* roble negro norte-americano y su cáscara.

querimonious [kweri'mouniəs], *a.* lastimero, quejicoso.

querimoniousness, *s.* disposición a quejarse, gimoteo.

querist ['kwiərist], *s.* preguntador, inquiridor.

quern [kwə:ɹn], *s.* molino de mano.

querulous ['kweru:ləs], *a.* querelloso, quejicoso, lastimero.

querulousness, *s.* disposición de quejarse, quejumbre, *f.*, querella; gimoteo, mal genio, mal humor.

query ['kwiəri], *s.* pregunta, cuestión, duda; signo de interrogación. — *v.t.* informarse acerca de, inquirir; pesquisar, indagar; examinar; dudar; marcar con un interrogante. — *v.i.* preguntar, interrogar, hacer preguntas, expresar una duda.

quest [kwest], *s.* búsqueda, busca; examen, investigación, pesquisa, indagación, averiguación, informe. — *v.t.*, *v.i.* averiguar, buscar, investigar; *in quest of*, en busca de.

question ['kwestʃən], *s.* pregunta; interrogación; cuestión, problema, *m.*; interrogatorio; duda; asunto, materia, tema, *m.*; (*for.*) proceso, pleito, juicio; cuestión de tormento; examinación jurídica; (*pol.*) interpelación; *beyond question*, indudablemente, fuera de duda; *to ask a question*, hacer una pregunta; *to be in question*, tratarse (de algo); *to beg the question*, hacer una petición de principio; *to call in question*, poner en duda, poner en cuestión; *the question is*, el caso es; *there is no question about it*, no cabe duda acerca de ello; *out of the question*, fuera de la cuestión, imposible; *that is the question*, he ahí la cuestión, he ahí de lo que se trata. — *v.t.* preguntar, interrogar, examinar; cuestionar; poner en duda, dudar; objetar, oponerse a, recusar; desconfiar de. — *v.i.* preguntar, averiguar, informarse, inquirir, escudriñar, poner en duda, dudar.

questionable, *a.* cuestionable; opinable, dudoso, controvertible; sospechoso.

questionableness, *s.* naturaleza sospechosa, naturaleza dudosa.

questionably, *adv.* problemáticamente.

questionary, *a.* en forma de cuestión, cuestionario.

questioner, *s.* preguntador, inquiridor.

questioning, *s.* interrogatorio; dudas, preguntas; averiguación.

questionless, *s.* ciertamente, sin duda; que no hace preguntas.

question-mark, *s.* signo de interrogación.
questor ['kwestəɪ], *s.* cuestor.
questorship, *s.* cuestura.
queue [kju:], *s.* cola, hilera (personas); coleta (cabello). — *v.i.* hacer cola; *to queue up*, hacer cola.
quey [kwei], *s.* vaca joven que no ha parido, novilla.
quibble ['kwibəl], *s.* subterfugio, juego de palabras; sutileza, argucia, equívoco. — *v.i.* argüir, ergotizar, buscar escapatorias, sutilizar, hacer uso de sofismas.
quibbler, *s.* sofista, *m.f.*, ergotista, *m.f.*, pleitista, *m.f.*, equivoquista, *m.f.*
quick [kwik], *a.* rápido, presto, acelerado, veloz; ágil, activo, ligero; listo, vivo, penetrante, agudo, ardiente, diligente; petulante, irritable, precipitado; disponible, efectivo; *(ant.)* preñada, encinta, embarazada; *the quick and the dead,* los vivos y los muertos; *quick-eyed,* con vista penetrante; *quick-fire,* *(arti.)* de tiro rápido; *quick-march* o *quick-time,* *(mús.)* paso doble; *quick-sighted,* de vista penetrante; *quick-tempered,* irritable, colérico; *quick-witted,* listo, agudo, salado; *to be quick,* darse prisa; *to be quick at one's work,* trabajar de prisa; ser perito; hábil en el trabajo; *to be quick of hearing,* tener buen oído. — *adv.* rápidamente, con rapidez, velozmente, con presteza; en seguida; pronto; prontamente, vivamente. — *s.* sensibilidad; lo vivo; carne viva; lo más hondo (del alma, de la sensibilidad); *to cut to the quick,* herir en lo vivo; *to sting to the quick,* picar hasta lo vivo.
quick-beam, *s.* fresno silvestre.
quicken ['kwikən], *v.t.* vivificar, resucitar, dar vida, animar, avivar, devolver la vida a; acelerar, urgir, apresurar; excitar, aguzar; *to quicken one's appetite,* aguzar el apetito; *to quicken one's step,* alargar o avivar el paso. — *v.i.* avivarse, estar vivo, tener vida, vivificarse, animarse, revivir.
quickener, *s.* vivificador, acelerador, avivador.
quickening, *a.* vivificante. — *s.* vivificación, avivamiento.
quickfiring [kwik'faiəriŋ], *a.* de tiro rápido (de un cañón).
quicklime ['kwiklaim], *s.* cal viva.
quickly ['kwikli], *adv.* rápidamente, con rapidez, velozmente, con presteza; pronto; vivamente, de prisa, aprisa.
quickness, *s.* rapidez, prontitud, velocidad, celeridad, presteza; viveza, vivacidad; agudeza, penetración, sagacidad.
quicksand, *s.* arena movediza.
quickset, *s.* planta viva. — *v.t.* rodear de un seto vivo; *quickset hedge,* seto vivo.
quicksilver ['kwiksilvəɪ], *s.* azogue, mercurio. — *v.t.* azogar.
quicksilvered, *a.* cubierto de azogue.
quickstep, *s.* *(mús.)* paso doble, paso redoblado, pasacalle, *m.*
quid [kwid], *s.* mascada, rollo de tabaco; *(vulg.)* libra esterlina; el quid.
quiddle ['kwidəl], *v.i.* *(E.U.)* gastar o pasar el tiempo en pequeñeces, andar de vagar.
quidnunc ['kwidnʌŋk], *s.* preguntón; chismoso.
quiesce, *v.i.* aquietarse, callarse; *(fonética)* hacerse mudo un sonido.

quiescence, quiescency, *s.* quietud, descanso, reposo.
quiescent [kwai'esənt], *a.* tranquilo, en reposo, inactivo; quieto; *(fonética)* mudo.
quiet ['kwaiət], *a.* callado, tranquilo, silencioso; sosegado, sereno, manso, suave, apacible; sencillo, modesto, reposado, sereno; quieto, inmóvil, quedo, tranquilo; (color) bajo, poco vivo, suave; *to be quiet,* callarse; estar callado, estar silencioso; *Be quiet!* ¡Cállate!; *to let one be quiet,* dejar en paz. — *s.* tranquilidad, sosiego, descanso, reposo, quietud, calma, paz, *f.* — *v.t.* tranquilizar, apaciguar, calmar, sedar, aquietar, sosegar.
quieting, *a.* calmante.
quietism, *s.* quietismo.
quietist, *s.* quietista, *m.f.*
quietness, *s.* tranquilidad, quietud, calma, reposo, sosiego, paz, *f.*
quietude ['kwaiitju:d], *s.* quietud, tranquilidad, reposo, sosiego.
quietus [kwai'i:təs], *s.* quitanza, finiquito, carta de pago; fallecimiento, muerte, *f.*; quietud, sueño de la muerte.
quill [kwil], *s.* pluma de ganso, pluma de ave; cañón de pluma; púa de puerco espín; pluma para escribir; devanador; estría; *men of the quill,* escritores, la profesión de las letras. — *v.t.* rizar, plegar, encañonar, desplumar, arrancar plumas; *(cost.)* rizar, hacer un encarrujado.
quillon ['ki:jɔŋ], *s.* gavilón de espada.
quilt [kwilt], *s.* colcha, manta acolchada, cobertor acolchado. — *v.t.* colchar, acolchar, estofar, acojinar.
quilter, *s.* colchero, acolchador.
quilting, *s.* acción de acolchar, colchadura; *(mar.)* cajera; *(tej.)* piqué.
quina ['kwinə], *s.* quina.
quinary, *a.* quinario.
quince [kwins], *s.* membrillo; *quince tree,* membrillero, membrillo; *quince jelly,* carne de membrillo, codoñate.
quincentenary [kwinsen'ti:nəri], *s.* quinto centenario.
quincuncial [kwin'kʌnʃəl], *a.* que tiene figura de quincuence.
quincunx ['kwinkʌŋks], *s.* quincuence, tresbolillo.
quindecagon [kwin'dekəgən], *s.* *(geom.)* quindecágono.
quinia ['kwiniə], *s.* quinina.
quiniary, *a.* quinario.
quinine [kwi'ni:n], *s.* quinina.
quinol ['kwinəl], *s.* hidroquinona.
quinquagenarian [kwinkwidʒe'nɛəriən], *s.* quincuagenario; cincuentón.
quinquagesima [kwinkwə'dʒezimə], *s.* quincuagésima.
quinquennial [kwin'kweniəl], *a.* quinquenal.
quinquina [kin'ki:nə, kwin'kwainə], *s.* *(bot.)* quina, cinchona.
quinsy ['kwinzi], *s.* angina.
quint [kwint], *s.* quinta; conjunto de cinco; *(mús.)* quinta.
quintain ['kwintən], *s.* juego de langa a caballo.
quintal ['kwintəl], *s.* quintal.
quintessence [kwin'tesəns], *s.* quintaesencia.
quintessential [kwinte'senʃəl], *a.* de la quinta esencia, depuradísimo.
quintette [kwin'tet], *s.* quinteto.
quintile ['kwintil], *s.* quintil.

quintillion [kwin'tiljən], s. quintillón (E.U. y Fr.) la tercera potencia de un millón; (Ing. y Esp.) quinta potencia de un millón.

quintuple ['kwintju:pəl], a. quíntuplo. — v.t. quintuplicar.

quinze [kwinz, kɑːŋz], s. juego de naipes semejante al veintiuno pero con quince puntos.

quip [kwip], v.t., v.i. bromear; zaherir, burlarse, echar pullas. — s. chiste; chufleta, pulla, sarcasmo.

quire [kwaiəɪ], s. mano de papel, f.; (igl.) (ant.) coro. — v.t., v.i. cantar en coro, hacer coro, cantar en concierto; formar manos de papel.

quirk [kwəːɪk], s. sutileza, argucia; refugio, desviación; capricho; giro, recodo, rodeo, escapatoria; pulla, arranque; (arq.) copada, caveto, muesca entre las molduras.

quirkish, a. sutil, equivoquista; evasivo, embrollón, enredador; caprichoso; gracioso, salado.

quirt [kwəːɪt], s. látigo con mango corto y correa de cuero retorcido; (Méj.) cuarta.

quit [kwit], v.t. abandonar, dejar, renunciar; ceder, resignar; satisfacer, desempeñar; soltar; desocupar, evacuar; ejecutar; (fam.) desistir de, dejar de; irse de, marcharse de. — v.i. desistir, cesar; to give notice to quit, dar aviso para que se marche, desahuciar, dar aviso de desahucio; quit that nonsense, (fam.) déjate de tonterías. — a. libre, descargado, absuelto; to be quit of, estar libre de, zafarse de; to be quits, estar desquitado, pata es la traviesa.

quitch-grass ['kwitʃgrɑːs], s. (bot.) grama.

quitclaim ['kwitkleim], s. (for.) renuncia, cesión definitiva; (com.) finiquito.

quite [kwait], adv. completamente, absolutamente, en extremo, totalmente, perfectamente, enteramente; (fam.) muy, mucho; bastante.

quit-rent ['kwitrent], s. (ant.) censo pagable para librarse del servicio feudal.

quits [kwitz], adv., interj. (fam.) en paz, desquitado, empatado.

quittance ['kwitəns], s. quitanza, desempeño, descargo, finiquito; remuneración, recompensa; liberación.

quitter, s. el que deja, el que desiste; (E.U.) desertor, cobarde; dejado.

quiver ['kwivəɪ], s. carcaj, aljaba; temblor. — v.i. estremecerse, temblar, palpitar, vibrar, agitarse.

quivering, s. temblor, tremor, estremecimiento, vibración.

quixotic [kwik'zɔtik], a. quijotesco.

quixotism ['kwiksotizm], s. quijotismo, quijotería.

quiz [kwiz], s. enigma, m., acertijo; broma, chanza, guasa, burla, engaño, burlón; patraña, chacota; persona estrafalaria o estrambótica; (E.U., fam.) interrogatorio, exámenes. — v.t. engañar, burlar, chulear, candonguear; mistificar, intrigar; mirar con un anteojo, mirar de hito en hito; (E.U., fam.) interrogar.

quizzer, s. mistificador, burlón; (E.U., fam.) interrogante, examinador.

quizzical, a. burlón, bufón, zumbón, bromista, guasón, gracioso; estrafalario, caprichoso.

quizzing, s. burla, chasco; mistificación; quizzing-glass, monóculo.

quod [kwɔd], s. (vulg.) cárcel, f.

quodlibet ['kwɔdlibet], s. equívoco, sutileza; (mús.) miscelánea.

quoin [kwɔin], s. rincón, ángulo, esquina; (imp., mec.) cuña; (arq.) diente, adaraja, clave (f.) de arco, piedra angular.

quoit [kwɔit], s. herrón, tejo. — pl. quoits, juego de tejos.

quondam, a. antiguo, que fué, de otro tiempo.

quorum ['kwɔːrəm], s. quórum.

quota ['kwoutə], s. cupo, cuota, contingente, escota, prorrata.

quotable, a. citable.

quotation [kwou'teiʃən], s. cita, citación; (com.) cotización; quotation marks, (impr.) comillas.

quote [kwout], v.t. citar; (com.) cotizar. — s. cita. — pl. (impr.) comillas [QUOTATION MARKS].

quoter, s. citador, cotizador.

quoth [kwouθ], v. def. pret. (ant.); quoth I, dije yo; quoth he, dijo él.

quotha, interj. (ant.) ¡de veras!

quotidian [kwo'tidiən], a. cotidiano, diario. — s. cosa diaria; (med.) calentura cotidiana.

quotient ['kwouʃənt], s. cociente, cuociente.

R

R, r [ɑːɪ], décimaoctava letra del alfabeto inglés; the three Rs, (fam.) lectura, escritura, y aritmética (reading, 'riting, 'rithmetic).

rabat [rɑ'bɑː], s. cuello eclesiástico usado por los sacerdotes franceses.

rabbet ['ræbet], s. ranura; (mar.) alefriz; (carp.) ensambladura, encaje, rebajo. — v.t. practicar una ranura; ensamblar, encajar.

rabbi ['ræbai], **rabbin** ['ræbin], s. rabí, rabino.

rabbinic, rabbinical, a. rabínico.

rabbinic [rə'binik], s. lengua rabínica.

rabbinism ['ræbinizm], s. rabinismo.

rabbinist, s. rabinista, m.f.

rabbit ['ræbit], s. conejo; doe rabbit, coneja; young rabbit, gazapo, gazapillo; rabbit-hole, rabbit-warren, conejera. — v.i. cazar conejos; apiñarse.

rabble ['ræbəl], s. gentuza, gentualla, populacho, gentío, plebe, f., canalla, morralla, chusma; (fund.) barra de pudelar.

rabid ['ræbid], a. rabioso; canino, devorador.

rabidness, s. rabia.

rabies ['reibiiːz], s. rabia, hidrofobia.

raccoon [rə'kuːn], s. [RACOON].

race [reis], s. raza, casta, estirpe, f., descendencia, prole, f., casa, familia, tribu, f., pueblo, linaje, hijos, posteridad, progenitura, generación; fragancia, nariz, f., sabor (del vino); curso, carrera, regata, corrida, marcha; lucha, contienda, competencia; apuesta; corriente de agua, canal, estrecho, caz, saetín; pista de caballo en la noria; (tej.) paso; boat race, regata; race course, estadio, hipódromo; race ground, campo de carreras; human race, género humano. — v.i. correr, ir de prisa; luchar en las carreras; (mec.) desbocarse, dispararse. — v.t. hacer ir de prisa, correr en competencia con.

race, s. raíz, f.; race-ginger, raíz de gengibre sin moler.

raceme [rə'siːm], s. (bot.) racimo, pedúnculo común.

racemose ['ræsiməs], **racemous**, a. racimoso.

racer, s. caballo de carrera, coche de carrera (etc.); carrerista, m.f., corredor.

raceway, s. (elec.) canal para conductores eléctricos; (mec.) muesca por la que corre una lanzadera, etc.; (E.U.) canal de molino, caz, saetín.

rachis ['rækis], s. (pl. **rachides**) (bot.) raquis, raspa; cañón de pluma; espinazo.

rachitic [rə'kitik], a. (med.) raquítico.

rachitis [rə'kaitis], s. (med.) raquitis, f.

racial ['reiʃəl], a. racial, de la casta o nación.

racily ['reisili], adv. de un modo vivo, picante, enérgico.

raciness, s. aroma del vino; carácter, energía, picante.

racing, s. carrera. — a. de carrera.

rack [ræk], s. rueda, caballete; rambla, bastidor; rueca; enrejado de madera; potro de tormento; (fig.) suplicio; entrepaso, portante; (mec.) armero, astillero; percha, espetera; nube tenue, f.; comedero, pesebre; (mec.) cremallera; escaleta; (coc.) morillos de asador; *rack-railway*, ferrocarril de cremallera; *bottle-rack*, botellero; *rack rent*, arriendo exorbitante; *to go to rack and ruin*, arruinarse completamente. — v.t. atormentar, dar tormento, torturar; apretar; llegar al último grado; exigir; despedazar, rasgar; oprimir, agobiar, vejar; (mar.) amarrar; trasegar, trasvasar. — v.i. cometer exacciones; disiparse, elevarse en vapor; andar a trote cochinero.

rackabones, s. (E.U., fam.) persona o animal muy flaco.

rackarock, s. pólvora de mina, explosivo compuesto de clorato de potasio y nitrobenzol.

racket ['rækit], s. estrépito, barullo, barahunda, zurriburri; raqueta (de tenis); francachela; zapato de nieve; (fam.) trampa, estafa. — v.t., v.i. hacer ruido, meter bulla; dar con una raqueta, pelotear.

racketer, s. alborotador; camorrista, m.f.

racketing, s. alegría ruidosa.

rackety ['rækiti], a. bullicioso, ruidoso.

racking, s. tortura, suplicio.

racoon [rə'kuːn], s. mapache, basáride, f.

racy ['reisi], a. fragante, que tiene aroma; enérgico, vigoroso; chispeante, picante.

radar ['reidɑːɹ], s. radar.

raddle ['rædəl], s. soto; percha. — v.t. trenzar, entrelazar; pintar de almagre, pintar mal.

raddock ['rædɔk], s. petirrojo.

radial ['reidiəl], a. radial, radiado.

radian ['reidiən], s. (geom.) radián.

radiance, radiancy, s. resplandor, esplendor, brillo.

radiant ['reidiənt], a. radiante, brillante, radioso, resplandeciente, espléndido; (bot.) radiado. — s. (geom.) línea radial.

radiate ['reidieit], v.i. brillar, resplandecer, echar rayos, centellear. — v.t. alumbrar, iluminar, irradiar. — a. (bot.) radiado.

radiated, a. radiante, radioso; radiado.

radiation, s. radiación (topográfica o calorífica); irradiación (radioactiva).

radiator, s. radiador; aparato de calefacción.

radical ['rædikəl], a. radical, fundamental, esencial, original; extremo, importantísimo,

completo; (gram.) primitivo; (bot.) radicoso, radical, raigal. — s. radical.

radicalism, s. radicalismo.

radicalness, s. naturaleza radical.

radication [rædi'keiʃən], s. radicación, arraigo.

radicle ['rædikəl], s. raicilla, radícula.

radio, s. radio, f.; radiocomunicación; *radio announcer*, locutor; *radio broadcast*, emisión; *radio listener*, radiooyente, radioyente, m.f.; *radio receiver*, radiorreceptor; aparato de radio; *radio transmitter*, (radio)emisora.

radioactive [reidiou'æktiv], a. radioactivo.

radioactivity, s. radioactividad.

radioamplifier, s. radioamplificador.

radiobroadcast, v.t. y v.i. radiodifundir.

radiobroadcasting, s. radiodifusión. — a. perifónico, difusor.

radiodetector, s. detector de ondas eléctricas.

radiogram, s. radiograma, m.; radiogramola.

radiograph, s. radiografía. — v.t. radiografiar.

radiographer [reidi'ɔgrəfəɹ], s. radiografista, m.f.

radiography [reidi'ɔgrəfi], s. radiografía.

radiologist [reidi'ɔlodʒist], s. radiólogo.

radiology [reidi'ɔlodʒi], s. radiología.

radiometer [reidi'ɔmetəɹ], s. radiómetro.

radiophare, s. estación baliza, radio faro.

radiotelegraphy, s. radiotelegrafía.

radiotherapeutics [reidiouθerə'pjuːtiks], s. radioterapia.

radish ['rædiʃ], s. rábano, rabanillo.

radium ['reidiəm], s. radio.

radius ['reidiəs], s. (pl. **radii**) radio; rayo; flor ligulada.

radix ['reidiks], s. (pl. **radices**) raíz, f.; (mat.) base, f.; (gram.) radical.

raff [ræf], s. montón; almodrote; fárrago; populacho, gentío.

raffia ['ræfiə], s. rafia.

raffish, a. disoluto, degenerado.

raffle ['ræfəl], s. rifa, sorteo, lotería. — v.t. rifar, sortear.

raffler, s. persona que rifa.

raft [rɑːft], s. balsa, jangada, almadía, maderada. — v.t. llevar sobre una balsa, transportar en balsa.

rafter, s. viga, cabrio, traviesa, costanera. — v.t. construir con vigas.

raftsman, s. almadiero.

rag [ræg], s. trapo, harapo, andrajo, jirón, guiñapo, pingajo, arambel; (fam.) papelucho; jolgorio (de estudiantes), novatada; *in rags*, harapiento; *rag, tag and bobtail*, canalla, gentuza; *rag dealer*, mercader de trapos; *rag picker*, trapero; *rag bolt*, (mar.) perno harponado. — v.t. marear, irritar, hacer bromas pesadas o de mal género.

ragamuffin ['rægəmʌfin], s. galopín, pelagatos.

rage [reidʒ], s. rabia, furor, enojo, cólera, ira, violencia, furia, manía, pasión, ardor, intensidad, avidez, anhelo, entusiasmo, vehemencia, encarnizamiento; *all the rage*, (fam.) muy en boga. — v.i. enfurecerse, encolerizarse, enojarse, bramar, rabiar.

rageful, a. rabioso, furioso, violento.

ragged ['rægid], a. rasgado, roto, andrajoso, harapiento, trapajoso, haraposo; escabroso, desmochado, áspero, desigual.

raggedness, s. calidad de haraposo; estado andrajoso; escabrosidad, aspereza, desigualdad de terreno.

raging [′reidʒiŋ], *a.* rabioso, furioso, violento, bramador. — *s.* rabia, violencia, furor, impetuosidad.

raglan [′ræglən], *s.* raglán.

ragman, *s.* trapero.

ragoût [rə′guː], *s.* estofado.

ragpicker, *s.* trapero.

ragstone, *s.* piedra de amolar.

ragtag [′rægtæg], *s.* chusma.

ragtime, *s.* (*mús.*) tiempo sincopado.

ragwort, *s.* hierba de Santiago.

raid [reid], *s.* incursión, correría, irrupción; ataque; bombardeo. — *v.t.* invadir; atacar; bombardear.

rail [reil], *s.* barra, barrera, cerca, barandilla, antepecho, baranda, balustrada; pasamano; (*arq.*) traviesa; (*mar.*) batayola, cairel; brazal, galón; carril, riel, raíl, ferrocarril; (*orn.*) ave zancuda; *to go off the rails,* descarrilar. — *v.t.* enfilar; cercar con balustradas, con barras, etc.; colocar rieles; *to rail in,* cerrar un enrejado; *to rail off,* separar. — *v.i.* injuriar, burlarse de, mofarse de; *to rail at,* vituperar; injuriar de palabra (a); protestar contra.

railer, *s.* maldiciente, murmurador, el que injuria.

railhead, *s.* término de la vía; (*mil.*) estación de ferrocarril para víveres y municiones.

railing, *a.* ultrajante, injurioso. — *s.* lenguaje injurioso; estacada; enrejado; balustrada, baranda, barandilla, pasamano, antepecho.

railingly, *adv.* injuriosamente.

raillery [′reiləri], *s.* burla, bufonada, chocarrería, escarnio.

railroad [′reilroud], **railway** [′reilwei], *s.* ferrocarril, camino de hierro, vía férrea, ferrovía; *narrow-gauge railway,* ferrocarril de vía estrecha; *railway-carriage,* vagón; *railway-compartment,* departamento; *railway-engine,* locomotora; *railway-guard,* jefe del tren; *railway-platform,* andén; *railway-porter,* mozo (de estación); *railway-station,* estación.

railwayman, *s.* ferroviario.

raiment [′reimənt], *s.* ropa, vestido, traje.

rain [rein], *s.* lluvia; *to pour with rain,* llover a cántaros; *rain or shine,* llueva o no; *pouring rain,* aguacero. — *v.i.* llover; *to rain cats and dogs,* o *to rain pitchforks,* llover a cántaros; llover chuzos. — *v.t.* (*fig.*) derramar copiosamente, llover.

rainbow, *s.* arco iris; *rainbow-hued,* iridiscente.

raincoat, *s.* impermeable.

raindrop, *s.* gota de lluvia.

rainfall, *s.* aguacero; cantidad de lluvia.

rain-gauge, *s.* pluviómetro.

raininess [′reininis], *s.* tendencia a la lluvia; estado lluvioso del tiempo.

rainstorm, *s.* aguacero, temporal, chubasco, tempestad de agua.

rain-tight, *a.* impermeable.

rain-water, *s.* agua de lluvia.

rainy, *a.* lluvioso, de lluvia, pluvioso.

raise [reiz], *v.t.* levantar, alzar, elevar, enarbolar, poner en pie; promover; fundar, erigir, fabricar, construir, erguir, edificar; brotar, resucitar; exigir; cultivar, criar; suscitar; aumentar, subir, ascender, encarecer, ensalzar, engrandecer, exaltar; incitar, animar, inspirar, armar, sublevar, excitar; evocar, llamar; causar, producir;

ocasionar; hacer concebir; hacer surgir; acumular; procurar (dinero); reunir, allegar, recoger; (*mar.*) guindar; avistar tierra, etc.; *to raise recruits,* hacer leva de reclutas; *to raise expectations,* infundir esperanzas; *to raise Cain,* (*fam.*) armar una marimorena; *to raise money on,* empeñar; *to raise an outcry,* armar un alboroto; *to raise a point,* hacer una observación. — *s.* alzamiento, levantamiento; (*fam.*) aumento, ascenso.

raiser, *s.* fundador, cultivador, productor, educador; *cattle raiser,* ganadero.

raising, *s.* acción de levantar, acción de elevar; elevación, fundación, producción, cría; aumento, engrandecimiento, ensalzamiento, levantamiento, recaudación; evocación (de los espíritus).

raisin [′reizən], *s.* pasa, uva seca.

raj, *s.* [rɑːʒ], *s.* soberanía, señorío.

raja, rajah [′rɑːdʒə], *s.* rajá.

rake [reik], *s.* (*agr.*) rastro; rastrillo, mielga; libertino, tuno, calavera, *m.*; (*mar.*) lanzamiento. — *v.t.* rastrillar, rascar, barrer, raspar; recoger, reunir; hurgar, atizar; cubrir con tierra; buscar, rebuscar, escudriñar; remover; (*mil.*) enfilar; *to rake out,* desembarazar; *to rake together,* recoger; *to rake up,* rebuscar, recoger. — *v.i.* pasar el rastro; pasar con violencia; rascar, ahorrar; buscar minuciosamente, rebuscar; escudriñar; registrar; (*mar.*) inclinarse.

rakehell, *s.* disoluto, libertino, perdido.

raker, *s.* rastrilladora, raedera.

raki [′rɑːki], *s.* coñac turco.

raking [′reikiŋ], *s.* rastrilleo, rastrillada, roza; terreno arrastrado; libertinaje. — *a.* oblicuo.

rakish, *a.* corrompido, libertino, perdido, licencioso; (*mar.*) de mástiles muy inclinados; elegante.

rakishness, *s.* libertinaje, disolución; (*mar.*) caída, inclinación de los palos; elegancia.

rale [reil], *s.* (*med.*) estertor.

rally [′ræli], *v.t.* (*mil.*) reunir, rehacer, replegar, recoger; reanimar; ridiculizar, burlarse de, dar zumba. — *v.i.* (*mil.*) reunirse, rehacerse, replegarse, reanimarse, recobrar las fuerzas; zumbarse, chancearse. — *s.* reunión de tropas dispersas; recuperación; mofa, burla.

ram [ræm], *s.* morueco, carnero; (*astr.*) Aries; (*mec.*) martinete, pisón; ariete hidráulico; (*mar.*) espolón, buque con espolón; *battering ram,* ariete. — *v.t.* atacar, apisonar, pisonear, empujar con violencia, apretar; hundir, atracar; henchir, atestar, amontonar.

ramble [′ræmbəl], *v.i.* vagar, callejear, corretear; serpentear, dar vueltas; holgazanear; (*fig.*) divagar. — *s.* carrera, correría; excursión, paseo.

rambler [′ræmblər], *s.* callejero, vagabundo, divagador, paseador, holgazán; excursionista, *m.f.*

rambling, *a.* errante, (*fam.*) holgazán; incoherente. — *s.* divagación.

ramblingly, *adv.* a la aventura; de una manera vaga.

ramé [ra′mei], *a.* (*blas.*) adornado.

ramekin [′ræmikin], *s.* (*coc.*) plato compuesto de queso, huevos, y migas de pan, etc.

rameous [′reiməs], *a.* de rama.

ramification [ræmifi′keiʃən], *s.* ramificación, ramal.

ramify ['ræmifai], *v.t.* dividir en ramas o ramales. — *v.i.* ramificarse.

rammer ['ræməɹ], *s.* maza; atacador; baqueta de fusil; (*mar.*) espolón.

ramose ['ræmous], *a.* ramoso.

ramp [ræmp], *v.t., v.i.* saltar, brincar; trepar. — *s.* salto, brinco; declive, rampa; estafa.

rampage [ræm'peidʒ], *s.* alboroto, agitación. — *v.i.* rabiar, gritar, alborotar.

rampancy, *s.* exuberancia, extravagancia, superabundancia; imperio.

rampant ['ræmpənt], *a.* exuberante, dominante; desenfrenado, excesivo; lozano, ufano; (*blas.*) rampante; (*arq.*) con estribo o contrafuerte más alto que otro.

rampart ['ræmpaːt], *v.t.* guarnecer con murallas. — *s.* (*fort.*) terraplén, plataforma; muralla, muro; baluarte.

rampion ['ræmpiən], *s.* rapónchigo.

ramrod ['ræmrɔd], *s.* baqueta de fusil, roquete, atacador, cargador.

ramshackle ['ræmʃækəl], *a.* descalabrado, desvencijado, destartalado, ruinoso.

ramulose ['ræmjuːləs], **-lous**, *a.* ramoso.

ran, *pret.* [RUN].

ranch [rɑːntʃ, ræntʃ], *s.* rancho, hacienda (de ganado).

rancher, ranchman, *s.* hacendado, ganadero; boyero; (*Méj.*) ranchero.

rancid ['rænsid], *a.* rancio, acedo, rancioso; *to get rancid*, arranciarse.

rancidity [ræn'siditi], *s.* rancidez.

rancorous ['ræŋkərəs], *a.* rencoroso.

rancour ['ræŋkəɹ], *s.* rencor, odio profundo, encono, enemiga.

rand [rænd], *s.* calzo del zapato; (*Africa del Sur*) tierra alta que bordea la cuenca de un río.

randan ['rændæn], *s.* bote propulsado por tres remeros, el del centro bogando con dos remos.

random ['rændəm], *s.* casualidad, azar, aventura, acaso; desacierto, desatino; *at random*, al azar, a la ventura, a la aventura, a troche y moche; *to speak at random*, hablar a tontas y a locas. — *a.* fortuito, casual, impensado; *random shot*, tiro al aire, tiro sin puntería.

randy, *a.* cachondo.

ranee ['rɑːniː], *s.* esposa de rajá.

rang, *pret.* [RING].

range [reindʒ], *v.t.* colocar, ordenar, colocar metódicamente, poner en fila, alinear, arreglar, clasificar; distribuir; vagar, recorrer, batir (el monte); saltar por; (*mar.*) costear, navegar cerca de, ir a lo largo de. — *v.i.* vagar; ir de una parte a otra; fluctuar, variar; estar en línea; adherirse, ponerse al lado; extenderse; (*arti.*) tener alcance. — *s.* serie, *f.*, clase, *f.*, orden, rango; línea, ringlera, hilera, fila; duración, transcurso; sierra, cordillera, cadena (de montañas); excursión, expedición, paseo, vuelta; carrera, campo; extensión, círculo; vasta extensión de terrenos de pasto; espacio, esfera, distancia; (*arti.*) alcance, alza; campo (o polígono) de tiro; hornillo, reja de cocina; cocina económica; (*mar.*) aduja.

range-finder, *s.* telémetro.

ranger, *s.* guardamayor de bosque; batidor; perro ventor; vagamundo, andorrero. — *pl.* cuerpo de tropas montadas.

rangership, *s.* cargo de guardamayor de bosque.

ranging, *s.* orden, colocamiento, acción de colocar en línea; excursión, paseo, expedición; (*tip.*) alineación.

rank [ræŋk], *s.* rango, grado, graduación, distinción, orden, clase, *f.*, posición, esfera; (*mil.*) fila, hilera; línea, ringlera; *to break the ranks*, (*mil.*) romper las filas. — *pl.* **ranks**, tropas, soldados rasos. — *v.t.* arreglar, colocar, comparar; ordenar, clasificar; poner en fila. — *v.i.* estar colocado, colocarse, ponerse en orden, ocupar un puesto, ocupar un rango; tener tal o cual grado de clasificación; *to rank high*, ocupar un puesto elevado. — *a.* fuerte, vigoroso, violento; insigne, rematado, acabado, famoso; notorio; exuberante, lozano, fértil; rico; enorme, grosero; rancio; espeso, cerrado; fétido.

rankle ['ræŋkəl], *v.i.* irritarse, enconarse; inflamarse; envenenarse, ulcerarse. — *v.t.* agriar, irritar, inflamar, envenenar, ulcerar.

rankling ['ræŋkliŋ], *s.* inflamación, irritación, furor, violencia. — *a.* envenenado, violento, que irrita, que inflama.

rankness, *s.* vigor, fuerza; fertilidad, exuberancia; exceso, exageración; fetidez, rancidez.

ransack ['rænsæk], *v.t.* saquear, pillar, robar; escudriñar, rebuscar, explorar, registrar.

ransom ['rænsəm], *v.t.* rescatar, redimir, recobrar. — *s.* rescate, redención.

ransomless, *a.* irredimible, irrescatable.

rant [rænt], *v.i.* declamar, desvariar, gritar, delirar, disparatar, exagerar. — *s.* declamación, lenguaje exagerado, desvarío.

ranter, *s.* declamador, vociferador, energúmeno.

ranting, *a.* declamatorio, exagerado.

ranula ['rænjuːlə], *s.* ránula.

ranunculus [rə'nʌŋkjuːləs], *s.* ranúnculo.

rap [ræp], *v.t., v.i.* golpear vivamente; tocar, llamar, dar un golpe seco. — *v.t.* arrebatar, transportar; quitar; tomar ávidamente; tropezar; *to rap out*, proferir vivamente. — *s.* golpe seco, golpecito; coz, *f.*; ardite, bledo.

rapacious [rə'peiʃəs], *a.* rapaz, rapiego.

rapaciously, *adv.* con rapacidad.

rapaciousness, rapacity, *s.* rapacidad.

rape [reip], *s.* estupro, violación; rapto; robo, rapiña; (*bot.*) colza; nabo silvestre; granuja. — *v.t.* forzar, violar, desflorar.

rap-full, *a.* (*mar.*) con las velas henchidas cuando el buque ciñe el viento.

rapid ['ræpid], *a.* rápido, veloz, vivo, arrebatado. — *s.pl.* **rapids**, rápido, rabión (de río).

rapidity [rə'piditi], **rapidness** ['ræpidnis], *s.* rapidez, celeridad, velocidad.

rapier ['reipiəɹ], *s.* espetón, espadín, estoque; *rapier-fish*, pez espada.

rapine ['ræpin], *s.* rapiña, robo; violencia, fuerza.

rapparee ['ræpəriː], *s.* irlandés ladrón.

rappee [rə'piː], *s.* rapé.

rapper ['ræpəɹ], *s.* golpeador, llamador; aldaba, aldabón; juramento.

rapscallion [ræp'skæljːən], *s.* vagabundo.

rapt [ræpt], *a.* transportado, arrebatado o extasiado.

rapture ['ræptʃəɹ], *s.* rapto, éxtasis, transporte, pasmo, enajenamiento, arrebatamiento, arrobamiento, embelesamiento, embeleso.

raptured, rapturous, *a.* arrebatado, arrobado, con éxtasis.

rapturously, *adv.* con éxtasis.

rare [rɛəɹ], *a.* sutil, raro, extraordinario, fino, delicado, sorprendente, sobresaliente, excelente; precioso; ralo, claro (de la atmósfera); esparcido; (*coc.*) poco asado, medio crudo.

raree-show ['rɛəri:ʃou], *s.* tutilimundi, mundinovi.

rarefaction [rɛəri'fækʃən], *s.* rarefacción, enrarecimiento.

rarefiable [rɛəri'faiəbəl], *a.* capaz de rarefacción.

rarefy ['rɛərifai], *v.t.* rarificar, enrarecer. — *v.i.* rarificarse, enrarecerse, dilatarse, extenderse.

rareness ['rɛənis], **rarity** ['rɛəriti], *s.* raridad, rareza, estado raro, curiosidad, singularidad, superioridad, excelencia, preciosidad; rarefacción; tenuidad.

rareripe, *a.* precoz, anticipado, temprano. — *s.* fruto precoz.

rascal ['raːskəl], *s.* bribón, pícaro, bellaco, belitre, tuno, tunante, truhán.

rascality [raːsˈkæliti], *s.* bribonería; bellaquería, truhanería, tunantada; canalla.

rascallion [raːsˈkæljən], *s.* vagabundo, villano, bergante, canalla, *m.*

rascally ['raːskəli], *a.* bajo, vil, indigno, ruin, mezquino, truhanesco.

rase [reiz], *v.t.* rascar, pasar rozando; demoler, destruir, arrasar; borrar.

rash [ræʃ], *a.* imprudente, temerario, arrojado, precipitado, arrebatado, irreflexivo, inconsiderado, atolondrado. — *s.* erupción; sarpullido.

rasher, *a. compar.* más temerario, más irreflexivo. — *s.* magra, lonja de tocino.

rashness, *s.* temeridad, audacia, arrojo, irreflexión, precipitación; atolondramiento.

rasp [raːsp], *s.* raspador, raspa, escofina, escarpelo, limatón, rallo; sonido estridente. — *v.t.* raspar, rallar, escofinar; raer, rallar.

raspatory ['raːspətəri], *a.* raspador; (*cir.*) legra.

raspberry ['raːzbəri], *s.* frambuesa, sangüesa; frambueso; *raspberry bush*, frambueso.

rasper, *s.* raspador, rallo; (*vulg.*) persona o cosa extraordinaria; individuo desagradable.

rasping, *s.* raspadura, raedura. — *a.* raspante, raedor; áspero, ronco; irritable.

rasure ['reiʒəɹ], *s.* acción de raspar, acción de borrar.

rat [ræt], *s.* rata; (*fig.*) traidor, renegado; canalla, *m.f.*; esquirol; desertor; *to smell a rat*, (*fig.*) oler el poste, sospechar. — *v.t., v.i.* cazar ratas; (*fam.*) hacerse esquirol; *to rat on*, traicionar (a), delatar (a).

ratable ['reitəbəl], *a.* imponible, sujeto a contribución; valuable.

ratafia [rætəˈfiːə], *s.* ratafia.

ratch [rætʃ], *s.* cremallera, rueda dentada con trinquete.

ratchet, *s.* (*mec.*) trinquete; rueda dentada; diente del caracol.

rate [reit], *s.* razón, *f.*, proporción; tarifa, valor, precio; rango, grado; manera, modo; ración; (*com.*) curso, valuación, tasa; velocidad; contribución (municipal), derecho; tipo (de interés, etc.); clasificación; (*mar.*) clase; *at the rate of*, a razón de; *at that rate*, de ese modo; *at any rate*, no obstante, por lo menos, de todos modos, de cualquier modo; *first rate*, muy bien, de primera clase, de primera; *second rate*, de segunda clase; *third rate*, de tercera

clase, muy pobre, muy mal. — *s.pl.* **rates**, contribuciones, inquilinato. — *v.t., v.i.* tasar, valuar, evaluar, imponer un derecho, una contribución o tasa; apreciar, hacer una apreciación; reñir; regañar; estimar, contar, justipreciar; *to rate someone unmercifully*, poner a uno de vuelta y media.

rateable, *a.* [RATABLE].

rather ['raːðəɹ], *adv.* más bien, antes, más, bastante, un poco, algo; mejor, antes bien, de preferencia; tal vez, puede ser, quizá; al contrario; *I had rather*, o *I would rather*, me gustaría más, preferiría; *the rather as* (o *because*), tanto más cuanto que.

ratification [rætifiˈkeiʃən], *s.* ratificación, confirmación, sanción, aprobación.

ratifier ['rætifaiəɹ], *s.* ratificador, confirmador.

ratify ['rætifai], *v.t.* ratificar, aprobar, confirmar, sancionar.

rating ['reitiŋ], *s.* clasificación, valuación, evaluación; (*mar.*) marinero de guerra; (*mec.*) capacidad o potencia normal.

ratio ['reiʃou], *s.* razón, *f.*, causa, relación, proporción.

ratiocinant, *a.* raciocinador, razonador.

ratiocination [ræʃiosinˈeiʃən], *s.* raciocinación, razonamiento, argumento.

ration ['ræʃən], *s.* ración; *ration-book*, cartilla de abastecimiento.

rational ['ræʃənəl], *a.* razonable, razonado, racional, inteligente, juicioso, motivado; (*mat.*) racional.

rational, *s.* (*igl., ant.*) racional.

rationale [ræʃənˈeili], *s.* exposición, análisis, *m.f.*; razón fundamental, *f.*

rationalism ['ræʃənəlizm], *s.* racionalismo.

rationalist, *s., a.* racionalista, *m.f.*

rationality, rationalness, *s.* racionalidad.

rationalization, *s.* (*mat.*) supresión de radicales.

ratite ['rætait], *s.* (*orn.*) corredora (ave).

ratline ['rætlin], **rattling** ['rætliŋ], *s.* (*mar.*) rebenque, flechaste, frenillo.

ratoon [rəˈtuːn], *s.* vástago, renuevo, soca de caña de azúcar.

rat-tail, *s.* (*carp.*) lima de cola de rata.

rattan [rəˈtæn], *s.* roten o rota; junquillo, bejuco.

ratteen [rəˈtiːn], *s.* ratina.

ratter ['rætəɹ], *s.* gato o perro ratonero.

ratting, *s.* deserción, apostasía; actuar de esquirol; caza de ratas.

rattle ['rætəl], *v.i.* zurrar, zurriar, hacer ruido, matraquear, resonar, rechinar, sonar, repiquetear; dar el estertor; parlotear, charlatanear; *to rattle away*, (*fam.*) parlotear, hablar muy de prisa. — *v.t.* hacer resonar, hacer sonar; batir con ruido; zurrir, zumbar; aturdir, atolondrar, aturrullar; regañar, reñir; gritar; (*mar.*) atar con rebenques. — *s.* ruido; rechinamiento, rechinido, rechino; vocería; matraca; carraca; sonajero (de niño); estertor; charla, parla; zumbido, zurrido; cascabel (de serpiente); *death rattle*, agonía, estertor.

rattle-brained, rattle-headed, *a.* atolondrado, casquivano, ligero de cascos.

rattler, *s.* (*fam.*) parlanchín; serpiente de cascabel.

rattle-snake, *s.* serpiente de cascabel, crótalo.

rattlesnake-root, *s.* lechera.

rattling, *s.* estertor; ruido; parla, cháchara. —

a. ruidoso, impetuoso. — *a., adv.* (*fam.*) soberbio, magnífico, sorprendente, excelente.

rat-trap, *s.* ratonera.

raucity ['rɔːsiti], *s.* ronquera, ronquedad.

raucous ['rɔːkəs], *a.* rauco, ronco.

ravage ['rævidʒ], *s.* asolamiento, estrago, destrucción, ruina, destrozo, saqueo. — *v.t.* saquear, pillar, asolar, destruir; arruinar; ajar (la tez).

ravager, *s.* asolador, saqueador, pillador.

rave [reiv], *v.i.* delirar, devanear, decir disparates, desvariar, encolerizarse, enfurecerse, bramar; *to rave about a person,* (*fam.*) estar loco por. — *s.* adral de un carro.

ravel ['rævəl], *v.t.* deshilar, destorcer, deshilachar, destejer, deshebrar, deshacer; (*ant.*) enredar, embrollar, enmarañar; desenredar, desenmarañar. — *v.i.* (*ant.*) enredarse, confundirse; deshilarse, deshacerse.

ravelin ['rævəlin], *s.* (*fort.*) rebellín.

ravelling, *s.*; **ravellings,** *s.pl.* hilacha, hila, deshiladura.

raven ['reivən], *s.* cuervo. — *a.* parecido a un cuervo, negro.

raven, ravin ['rævən], *v.t.* devorar, hacer presa de, prender, apresar. — *v.i.* entregarse al saqueo; echarse sobre la presa.

ravener ['rævənəɹ], *s.* saqueador; pájaro de rapiña.

ravening ['rævəniŋ], *s.* rapiña, rapacidad, voracidad.

ravening, ravenous, *a.* voraz, codicioso, hambriento, famélico, rapaz.

ravin ['rævin], *s.* rapiña, presa; *beast of ravin,* animal de presa.

ravine [rə'viːn], *s.* quebrada, barranca, hondonada, garganta.

raving ['reiviŋ], *a.* furioso, delirante, desvariado, en delirio; loco, frenético; extravagante; *raving mad,* loco de atar. — *s.* delirio, desvarío.

ravingly, *adv.* locamente, desvariadamente, con frenesí.

ravish ['ræviʃ], *v.t.* violar, forzar, estuprar; arrebatar, atraer, encantar.

ravisher, *s.* estuprador, violador, forzador.

ravishing, *a.* arrebatador, encantador, embriagador.

ravishingly, *adv.* de una manera encantadora.

ravishment, *s.* rapto, violación, estupro, desfloramiento; éxtasis, transporte, arrobamiento.

raw [rɔː], *a.* crudo, pelado, poco maduro, verde; ignorante; descarnado, vivo, desollado; doloroso; matado, llagado; nuevo, fresco; indigesto; crudo, desapacible, frío y húmedo (del tiempo); bisoño, novato; vulgar; tosco, brutal; (*com.*) en bruto; *raw flesh,* carne viva; *raw meat,* carne cruda; *raw material,* materia primera (o prima), materia bruta; *raw hand,* novicio, tirón; *raw cotton,* algodón en rama; *raw spirits,* alcohol puro; *raw silk,* seda en rama devanada; *raw sugar,* azúcar bruto; *raw hide,* cuero crudo.

raw-boned, *a.* descarnado, huesudo.

rawhead, *s.* espantajo, espectro, fantasma, *m.*

rawish, *a.* algo crudo; un poco frío y húmedo (del tiempo).

rawness, *s.* frío húmedo; crudeza; ignorancia, falta de experiencia.

ray [rei], *s.* rayo, brillo; raya; (*geom.*) radio; hilera; (*ict.*) raya; (*bot.*) lígula. — *v.t.* rayar; dardear, lanzar (rayos). — *v.i.* emitir rayos.

ray-grass, *s.* vallico.

rayon ['reijon], *s.* radio; (*tej.*) rayón.

raze [reiz], *v.t.* arrasar, subvertir, extirpar, demoler, destruir; (*fam.*) afeitar.

razee [rə'ziː], *s.* (*mar.*) buque rebajado.

razor ['reizəɹ], *s.* navaja de afeitar; colmillo del jabalí; *safety razor,* máquina de afeitar; *razor case,* navajero; *razor shell,* navaja (marisco); *razor blade,* hoja de afeitar. — *pl.* **razors,** colmillos de jabalí.

razor-bill, *s.* (*orn.*) alca.

re [riː], *s.* (*mús.*) re. — *prep.* (*for.*) causa, litigio, acción; (*com.*) acerca de, concerniente a.

reabsorb [riəb'sɔːɹb], *v.t.* reabsorber, resorber.

reabsorption, *s.* reabsorción, resorción.

reaccess [ri'ækses], *s.* (*med.*) recidiva.

reach [riːtʃ], *v.t.* tender, extender, alargar; alcanzar, conseguir, obtener, penetrar, lograr, ir hasta, llegar a las manos de; reportar; estirar; asir llegar a o hasta. — *v.i.* extenderse, llegar, penetrar, alcanzar; (*mar.*) ceñir el viento, navegar de bolina; esforzarse; vomitar; *to reach after,* hacer esfuerzos para alcanzar; *to reach one's heart,* tocar al corazón. — *s.* alcance, poder; distancia, extensión; facultad; capacidad; penetración, vista; designio, proyecto, plan; medio; artificio, estratagema; (*mar.*) bordada; *within reach of,* al alcance de; *out of reach,* fuera de alcance.

reaching, *s.* esfuerzo para alcanzar; esfuerzo para vomitar, vómito.

react [ri'ækt], *v.i.* reaccionar; resistir.

reacting, reactive, *a.* reactivo.

reaction, *s.* reacción; resistencia.

reactionary, reactionist, *s.* reaccionario, retrógrado.

reactivity, *s.* tendencia reactiva; nueva actividad.

read [riːd], *v.t.* (*pret.* y *p.p.* **read**) leer; estudiar, aprender; aconsejar, descifrar, interpretar, enseñar, avisar, amonestar; (*mús.*) leer. — *v.i.* decir, querer decir, significar; rezar; *to read aloud,* leer en alta voz; *to read to oneself,* leer para sí; *to read about,* enterarse de; *to read offhand,* leer de corrida; *to read over,* recorrer; *to read between the lines,* leer entre líneas; *to read proofs,* (*impr.*) corregir pruebas; *to read on,* seguir (o continuar) leyendo; *to read right through,* leer de cabo a rabo.

read [red], *a.* instruido, enseñado. — *p.p.* [READ]; *well-read,* instruido, erudito.

readable ['riːdəbəl], *a.* legible, leíble; interesante, entretenido, ameno.

readableness, *s.* calidad de legible.

reader ['riːdəɹ], *s.* lector, leyente; libro de lectura; (*impr.*) corrector; (*igl.*) lector; catedrático; *to be a great reader,* leer mucho.

readership, *s.* lectoría, lectorado, cátedra.

readily ['redili], *adv.* prontamente, luego; de buena gana, con gusto; fácilmente.

readiness ['redinis], *s.* disposición; prontitud, aptitud, facilidad, expedición, desembarazo; viveza, vivacidad; *to be in readiness,* estar preparada.

reading, *s.* lectura; disertación; estudio; glosa, variante, *f.*, lección; interpretación; conferencia; solución; (*teat.*) desempeño (de un papel); *reading-book,* libro de lectura; *reading-*

desk, atril, facistol; *reading-room*, gabinete de lectura, sala de lectura.

re-adjourn, *v.t.* diferir otra vez.

re-adjust, *v.t.* reajustar; (*impr.*) recorrer.

re-adjustment, *s.* reajuste.

re-admission, *s.* readmisión.

re-admit, *v.t.* readmitir, volver a admitir.

re-admittance, *s.* readmisión.

ready ['redi], *a.* pronto, listo; ágil, ligero, presto, vivo; efectivo, contante; útil, disponible; prevenido, aprestado, preparado, aparejado, fácil, natural; gustoso, propenso, inclinado, dispuesto; al alcance, a la mano; *to make ready*, preparar; *to be ready for anything*, estar a todo; *ready money*, dinero contante, dinero en mano. — *adv.* presto, prontamente; *ready made clothes*, vestidos ya hechos.

re-affirm, *v.t.*, *v.i.* afirmar de nuevo, reiterar.

re-afforest, *v.t.* repoblar de árboles.

re-afforestation, *s.* repoblación de montes.

reagent [ri:'eidʒənt], *s.* reactivo.

re-aggravation, *s.* (*der.*) tercera y última monición.

real ['ri:əl], *a.* real, verdadero, positivo, genuino, sincero, efectivo; (*der.*) inmoble, inmueble; *real property*, bienes raíces.

realgar [ri:'ælgɑ:ɹ], *s.* rejalgar.

realism [ri:ə'lizm], *s.* realismo.

realist, *s.* realista, *m.f.*

realistic, *a.* realista; natural.

reality [ri:'æliti], *s.* realidad, carácter real; verdad; entidad.

realizable [ri:ə'laizəbəl], *a.* realizable, factible.

realization, *s.* realización.

realize ['ri:əlaiz], *v.t.* realizar; darse cuenta de; sentir en toda su fuerza; creer en; tener por cierto; efectuar, verificar; convertir en dinero contante; vender bienes raíces; llevar a cabo, cumplir; ganar.

really ['riəli], *adv.* en realidad, realmente, en efecto, efectivamente, verdaderamente.

realm [relm], *s.* reino, dominio; región; (*fig.*) esfera.

realtor, *s.* (*E.U.*) agente de fincas, agente de casas.

realty ['ri:əlti], *s.* (*der.*) bienes raíces; naturaleza inmobiliaria.

ream [ri:m], *s.* resma (de papel). — *v.t.* escariar; (*mar.*) ensanchar gradualmente una costura de los tallones para calafatear.

reamer, *s.* escariador.

re-animate, *v.t.* reanimar, resucitar.

re-animation, *s.* acción de reanimar.

re-annex, *v.t.* reunir, volver a unir.

reap [ri:p], *v.t.*, *v.i.* segar, cosechar, hacer la siega, hacer la cosecha, hacer el agosto; sacar fruto, sacar provecho, recibir la recompensa de su trabajo.

reaper, *s.* segador; segadora mecánica.

reaping, *s.* siega, cosecha; *reaping-machine*, segadora.

re-appear, *v.i.* reaparecer.

re-appearance, *s.* reaparición.

re-apply, *v.t.*, *v.i.* aplicar de nuevo; presentarse de nuevo.

re-appoint, *v.t.* nombrar de nuevo; fijar de nuevo; designar.

re-appointment, *s.* designación nueva; segundo nombramiento.

rear [riəɹ], *a.* inferior, postrero, último, trasero, posterior; *rear-admiral*, contraalmirante; *rear rank*, última fila; *rearguard*,

retaguardia. — *s.* fondo; retaguardia; última clase; espalda, cola, parte posterior; *to be in the rear*, estar a la cola; *to bring up the rear*, cerrar la marcha. — *v.t.* levantar, elevar, alzar, construir; criar, alimentar, cultivar, educar, instruir. — *v.i.* empinarse, encabritarse (el caballo).

rearmost ['riəɹmost], *a.* último, postrero.

rearmouse ['riəɹmaus], *s.* murciélago.

rearward ['riəɹwəd], *adv.* hacia atrás. — *a.* último, postrero. — *s.* retaguardia.

re-ascend, *v.i.* volver a subir, subir de nuevo.

re-ascension, *s.* ascensión nueva.

re-ascent, *s.* subida.

reason [ri:zən], *s.* razón, *f.*, argumento, motivo, causa; fundamento; prueba; justicia, derecho; entendimiento, conocimiento, intuición, sensatez; moderación; (*lóg.*) antecedente, principio; premisa, particularmente la premisa menor; *it stands to reason*, así lo pide la razón, es lógico; *by reason of*, a causa de; *there's no reason for it*, no hay para qué. — *v.t.*, *v.i.* razonar, raciocinar, discutir, argüir, discurrir, probar.

reasonable, *a.* razonable, racional; módico, arreglado, moderado, acomodado; excogitable; equitativo, justo.

reasonableness, *s.* razón, *f.*, racionalidad, naturaleza razonable, moderación, equidad, justicia.

reasoner, *s.* razonador, dialéctico.

reasoning, *s.* raciocinio, razonamiento, argumento, discurso.

reasonless, *a.* desrazonable, sin razón.

re-assemble, *v.t.* reunir, juntar de nuevo. — *v.i.* reunirse.

re-assert, *v.t.* asegurar de nuevo, afirmar de nuevo.

re-assume, *v.t.* reasumir.

re-assumption, *a.* reasunción.

re-assurance, *s.* afirmación nueva (o repetida); (*com.*) segundo seguro; confianza restablecida.

re-assure [ri:ə'ʃjuəɹ], *v.t.* asegurar de nuevo; tranquilizar.

re-attempt, *v.t.* ensayar de nuevo.

reave [ri:v] (*pret. y part. p.* **reaved**, *poét.* **reft**), *v.t.* pillar, hurtar.

re-baptism, *s.* rebautismo.

re-baptize, *v.t.* rebautizar.

rebate ['ri:beit], *v.t.* rebajar, deducir, descontar, disminuir; (*blas.*) embotar; humillear, abajar; practicar una ranura. — *s.* (*carp.*) encaje, ranura, cepillo; majadero; asperón.

rebate, rebatement, *s.* diminución; deducción, reducción; (*com.*) descuento, rebaja.

rebec ['ri:bek], *s.* rabel.

rebel ['rebel], *s.*, *a.* rebelde, insurgente, insurrecto, faccioso.

rebel [re'bel], *v.i.* rebelarse, levantarse, alzarse, sublevarse, insurreccionarse.

rebellion [re'beljən], *s.* rebelión, *f.*, insurrección, levantamiento, sublevación.

rebellious, *a.* rebelde, amotinado, insubordinado, sublevado, refractario.

rebelliousness, *s.* insubordinación, rebeldía.

reblossom, *v.i.* florecer de nuevo.

rebore [ri:'bɔ:ɹ], *v.a.* (*aut.*) descarbonizar.

rebound [ri'baund], *v.i.* rebotar, resaltar, repercutir, resurtir; recular (un arma de fuego, etc.). — *v.t.* hacer botar, hacer saltar; rechazar. — *s.* resalto, rebote, repercusión, resurtida, rechazo.

rebuff [ri'bʌf], v.t. rebatir, rechazar. — s. repercusión; repulsa, rechazo; denegación.

rebuild [ri:'bild], v.t. (pret. y p.p. **rebuilt**) reedificar, reconstruir.

rebukable, a. vituperable.

rebuke [ri'bju:k], v.t. regañar, reñir; reprender, increpar, reprochar, censurar; castigar. — s. repulsa, reprimenda, reprensión; censura; reproche; castigo, bofetada, revés.

rebuker, s. reprensor, censor.

rebus ['ri:bəs], s. jeroglífico (diversión).

rebut [ri'bʌt], v.t. rechazar, rehusar, refutar, contradecir. — v.i. retirarse, replicar.

rebuttal [ri'bʌtəl], s. refutación.

rebutter, s. respuesta, contrarréplica; el que la hace.

recalcitrant [ri'kælsitrənt], s., a. recalcitrante, obstinado, rehacio.

recalesce, v.i. recalentarse (esp. hierro y acero).

recalescence [ri:kə'lesəns], s. recalescencia.

recall [ri'kɔ:l], v.t. revocar, retractar, llamar, hacer volver, anular; recordar; despedir, deponer, destituir (de un oficio). — s. revocación, retractación; recordación; llamada; (mil.) toque de llamada.

recant [ri'kænt], v.t. retractar. — v.i. retractarse, desdecirse, cantar la palinodia.

recantation, s. recantación, retractación, palinodia.

recanter, s. persona que se retracta, retrayente.

recapitulate [ri:kə'pitju:leit], v.t. recapitular; resumir.

recapitulation, s. recapitulación, resumen, sumario.

recapitulatory, a. recapitulatorio, que recapitula.

recaption [ri:kæpʃən], s. (der.) nuevo embargo; recobro de bienes, etc.

recapture [ri:'kæptʃəɹ], s. represa. — v.t. represar, volver a tomar.

recast [ri:'kæst], v.t. (pret. y p.p. **recast**) (fund.) refundir, fundir de nuevo; reformar; volver a calcular.

recede [re'si:d], v.i. retroceder, recular, alejarse, apartarse, retirarse; retractarse, desdecirse, desistir, volverse atrás; desviarse, inclinarse. — v.t. ceder de nuevo; devolver a su anterior poseedor.

receipt [re:'si:t], s. recibimiento, recepción; carta de pago, descargo, cobranza; recibo; receta, fórmula; receipt-book, libro de ingresos; on receipt of, al recibir, o al recibo de; receipts and outgoings, entrada y salida. — v.t., v.i. dar un recibo (de), extender recibo; formar recibo; poner el recibí.

receipted, a. pagado, satisfecho, que lleva el recibí.

receipts, s.pl. entradas, ingresos.

receivable, a. recibidero, admisible, a recibir.

receive [re:si:v], v.t. recibir, tomar, aceptar, admitir; aprobar; agasajar; cobrar, percibir; contener, receptar; hospedar, acoger; received payment, recibí; to receive the sacrament, comulgar.

receivedness, s. aceptación, aprobación.

receiver, s. recibidor, receptador, receptor; depositario, consignatario; recipiente, montera, campana; (rad.) receptor; (tele.) auricular; (der.) síndico (de quiebra); receptador (de objetos robados).

receivership, s. receptoría; sindicatura.

receiving, s. recepción; encubrimiento.

recense [ri:sens], v.t. revisar, reseñar, verificar; hacer un censo.

recension [ri'senʃən], s. revisión, revista, texto revisado, enumeración, verificación, censo, reseña.

recent ['ri:sənt], a. reciente, moderno, nuevo, flamante, fresco, tierno.

recently, adv. recientemente, nuevamente, hace poco.

recentness, s. origen reciente, novedad.

receptacle [re'septəkəl], s. receptáculo.

receptibility, s. receptividad, capacidad para recibir.

reception [re'sepʃən], s. recepción, recibimiento, acogida; readmisión, vuelta; facultad de recibir; recibo; besamanos; audiencia.

receptive [re'septiv], a. receptivo, capaz de recibir, que quiere recibir.

recess [re'ses], s. alejamiento, partida; suspensión, vacación, tregua; reclusión, retiro; (arq.) fondo; entrada; escondrijo, alcoba, nicho, lugar apartado; vacaciones.

recession [re'seʃən], s. receso, retroceso, desistimiento, retirada; renuncia, concesión; restitución.

rechange, v.t. volver a cambiar.

recharge [ri:'tʃɑ:ɹdʒ], v.t. volver a cargar, recargar; acusar de nuevo.

recheat, s. toque de trompa para llamar los perros.

recherché [ri'ʃɛəɹʃei], a. rebuscado; raro, selecto.

recidivism, s. reincidencia.

recidivist [re'sidivist], s. reincidente.

recipe ['resipi], s. receta, récipe.

recipient [re'sipiənt], s. recibidor, recipiente, receptor, persona que recibe.

reciprocal [re'siprokəl], a. recíproco, mutuo, alternativo, alterno, permutable. — s. recíproca.

reciprocality, reciprocalness, s. reciprocidad.

reciprocate [re'siprouket], v.t., v.i. reciprocar, ser recíproco, reciprocarse, permutar, corresponder, cambiar, hacer cambio de; oscilar; alternar; tener movimiento alternativo; estar a la recíproca.

reciprocating, a. que reciproca; que cambia de vaivén; alternativo.

reciprocation, s. reciprocación.

reciprocity [resi'prɔsiti], s. reciprocidad.

recision [re'siʒən], s. resección.

recital [re'saitəl], s. recitación, relación, declamación, narración, repetición, descripción, enumeración; (mús.) recital.

recitation [resi'teiʃən], s. recitación, repetición, declamación.

recitative [re'sitətiv], s. (mús.) recitado.

recite [re'sait], v.t. recitar, relatar, referir, narrar, contar, citar. — v.i. recitar, declamar.

reciter, s. recitador, declamador.

reck [rek], v.t. (poét.) tener cuidado de, inquietarse de. — v.i. cuidar, inquietarse.

reckless, a. descuidado, indiferente; temerario, atrevido, precipitado, atolondrado; derrochador.

recklessness, s. descuido, indiferencia, imprudencia, negligencia, atrevimiento, temeridad.

reckon ['rekən], v.t., v.i. contar, calcular, computar, tantear, numerar, enumerar;

apreciar, considerar, estimar; (*E.U.*) creer, suponer; *to reckon up*, adicionar; *to reckon upon* o *reckon with*, contar con; *to reckon without one's host*, hacer la cuenta sin la huéspeda.

reckoner, *s.* contador, calculador; *ready reckoner*, libro de cuentas ya hechas.

reckoning, *s.* cálculo, cómputo, cuenta, tanteo; ajuste de cuentas; escote; factura, memoria; (*mar.*) *dead reckoning*, estima; *day of reckoning*, el día del juicio final.

reclaim [ri:'kleim], *v.t.* reclamar, vindicar, revindicar; reducir; reformar, corregir; oponerse; domesticar, amansar, domeñar, desecar (un pantano).

reclaimable, *a.* reclamable, que puede ser reclamado, que puede ser corregido.

reclamation [reklə'meiʃən], *s.* reclamación, corrección, reforma; restauración; cultivo, mejoramiento.

réclame [rei'klɑ:m], *s.* reclamo; (*fam.*) bombo.

reclination, *s.* reclinación.

recline [re'klain], *v.t.* reclinar, inclinar, recostar. — *v.i.* reposar, descansar, reclinarse, recostarse.

reclining, *a.* inclinado, recostado.

reclose [ri:'klouz], *v.t.* volver a cerrar.

recluse [re'klu:z], *a.* recluso, encerrado, solitario. — *s.* persona retirada del mundo; eremita, *m.*, monje.

recluseness, reclusion, *s.* retiro, reclusión, recogimiento, soledad; aislamiento.

reclusive, *a.* recluso, solitario, aislado.

recognition [rekog'niʃən], *s.* reconocimiento, agradecimiento; saludo.

recognizable, *a.* que puede ser conocido o reconocido.

recognizance [re'kognizəns, re'konizəns], *s.* reconocimiento; confesión; (*der.*) obligación.

recognize ['rekəgnaiz], *v.t.* reconocer, conocer; admitir, confesar, conceder. — *v.i.* (*der.*) subscribir una obligación.

recoil [re'koil], *v.i.* retroceder, cejar, recular, retirarse, volver atrás; desdecirse, rebelarse; rebufar. — *s.* rechazo, reculada; retroceso, coz, rebufo; horror, repugnancia, terror; culatazo (de un fusil).

recoiling, *s.* reculada; aversión, horror, repugnancia.

recoilingly, *adv.* reculando.

recoin [ri:'koin], *v.t.* resellar; acuñar de nuevo.

recoinage, *s.* resello; acuñación nueva; nueva moneda.

recollect [rekə'lekt], *v.t.* recordar, acordarse de; reconocer; recobrar, reunir, juntar de nuevo. — *s.* (*igl.*) recoleto.

recollection, *s.* recuerdo, memoria, reminiscencia, recordación.

recollective, *a.* recordativo.

recombine, *v.t.* combinar de nuevo.

recommence [ri:kə'mens], *v.t.* volver a comenzar, comenzar de nuevo.

recommencement, *s.* acción de volver a comenzar.

recommend [rekə'mend], *v.t.* recomendar; encomendar, acreditar; encarecer, alabar.

recommendable, *a.* recomendable, digno de ser alabado.

recommendation, *s.* recomendación, encarecimiento; apostilla.

recommendatory, *a.* recomendatario.

recommender, *s.* persona que recomienda.

recommit [ri:ko'mit], *v.t.* confiar de nuevo; trasladar de nuevo; volver a prender, encarcelar; cometer de nuevo.

recommitment, recommittal, *s.* acto de volver a confiar, trasladar o encarcelar.

recompense ['rekompens], *s.* recompensa, reparación, indemnidad, compensación; remuneración, retribución. — *v.t.* recompensar, compensar, indemnizar, retribuir, remunerar, reintegrar, reparar.

recompose [ri:kompouz], *v.t.* volver a calmar, tranquilizar; recomponer, volver a componer; volver a ajustar; rehacer.

recomposition, *s.* recomposición.

reconcilable, *a.* reconciliable, conciliable, componible.

reconcile ['rekonsail], *v.t.* reconciliar; conciliar; concordar, componer, acomodar. — *v.t.*, *v.r.* resignarse, avenirse, arreglarse, conformarse, compadecerse.

reconcilement, *s.* reconciliación.

reconciler, *s.* reconciliador, conciliador.

reconciliation [rekonsili'eiʃən], *s.* conciliación, reconciliación; ajuste, conformidad.

reconciliatory [rekon'siliətəri], *a.* reconciliador, propio para reconciliar.

recondense, *v.t.* volver a condensar.

recondite ['rekondait], *a.* recóndito, secreto, oculto; abstruso, profundo, difícil.

recondition [ri:kon'diʃən], *v.t.* (*mec.*) reacondicionar; rectificar.

reconduct, *v.t.* volver a conducir.

reconfirm, *v.t.* reconfirmar.

reconnaissance [re'konisəns], *s.* (*mil.*) reconocimiento; exploración.

reconnoitre ['rekonoitər], *v.t.* (*mil.*) reconocer; examinar; explorar, inspeccionar. — *v.i.* practicar un reconocimiento.

reconquer [ri:'konkər], *v.t.* reconquistar.

reconquest, *s.* reconquista.

reconsecrate, *v.t.* volver a consagrar.

reconsecration, *s.* nueva consagración.

reconsider [ri:kon'sidər], *v.t.* volver a considerar, volver a discutir.

reconsideration, *s.* nueva consideración, nueva reflexión.

reconstruct [ri:kon'strʌkt], *v.t.* reconstruir, restablecer, reedificar.

reconstruction, *s.* reconstrucción, reedificación, restablecimiento.

reconvene, *v.t.* reunir de nuevo, convocar de nuevo.

reconvention, *s.* reconvención.

reconversion, *s.* reconversión.

reconvert, *v.t.* volver a convertir.

reconvey, *v.t.* volver a llevar; reponer, restituir.

record [re'ko:rd], *v.t.* registrar, inscribir; protocolar; archivar; marcar, indicar, apuntar, grabar (discos).

record ['reko:rd], *s.* registro, protocolo, partida, inscripción; copia auténtica; datos; testimonio, recuerdo; anales, archivo, documento, acta; relación, crónica, historia; hoja de servicios; antecedentes de una persona; disco (de gramófono); (*der.*) memorial, proceso verbal; informe, expediente; (*dep.*) 'record'; *record office*, archivo; *to break* (o *beat*) *the record*, batir el 'record'; *to hold the record*, conservar el 'record' obtenido.

recorder [re'ko:rdər], *s.* registrador, archivero;

recopilador; (*mús.*) caramillo; (*mec.*) indicador, contador; grabador (de un disco); (*der.*) juez municipal.

recording, *a.* registrador. — *s.* registro; registro acústico, grabación (de discos).

recount [riːˈkaunt], *v.t.* recontar, referir, relatar, detallar, recitar. — *s.* recuento.

recountment, *s.* relato, relación.

recoup [reˈkoup], *v.t.* retener para indemnizarse; desquitar, reintegrar. — *s.* indemnización, descuento, reintegro, desquite.

recourse [reˈkoːɹs], *s.* recurso, remedio, acceso, auxilio, refugio; *to have recourse to*, recurrir a.

recover [reˈkʌvəɹ], *v.t.* restablecer, reparar, recobrar, recuperar, desempeñar, rescatar, volver a tomar, volver a ganar; remediar, reparar; (*for.*) reivindicar; *to recover oneself*, volver en sí. — *v.i.* restablecerse, reponerse, rehacerse, recobrar la salud; reintegrarse o resarcirse; (*for.*) ganar un pleito.

re-cover [riːˈkʌvəɹ], *v.t.* volver a cubrir o tapar.

recoverable [reˈkʌvərəbəl], *a.* recuperable, curable.

recovery [reˈkʌvəri], *s.* recobro, recuperación, restablecimiento, mejoría, convalecencia; cobranza; rescate, redención; (*for.*) reivindicación; *past all recovery*, sin remedio, desahuciado.

recreant [ˈrekriənt], *a.* pusilánime, cobarde; apóstata, falso, desleal. — *s.* cobarde, poltrón; traidor, apóstata, *m.f.*; desertor.

recreate [ˈrekrieit], *v.t.* recrear; divertir, deleitar. — *v.i.* recrearse, distraerse, divertirse.

recreation [rekriˈeiʃən], *s.* recreación, recreo, entretenimiento, pasatiempo, diversión.

recreative, *a.* recreativo, agradable, divertido, entretenido.

recrement [ˈrekrimənt], *s.* (*ant.*) recremento; (*med.*) hez, escoria.

recremental, recrementitious, *a.* recrementicio; (*med.*) recrementoso.

recriminate [reˈkrimineit], *v.t.*, *v.i.* recriminar.

recrimination, *s.* recriminación, reconvención.

recross [riːˈkrɔːs], *v.t.* volver a atravesar, volver a pasar, volver a cruzar.

recrudesce, *v.i.* recrudecer(se).

recrudescence [rekruˈdesəns], *s.* recrudescencia, recrudecimiento.

recruit [reˈkruːt], *v.t.* (*mil.*) reclutar, alistar; restablecer, rehacer, reparar, reponer. — *v.i.* reclutarse; reanimarse, reponerse, restablecerse. — *s.* (*mil.*) recluta, *m.*; novicio; suministro.

recruiter, *s.* reclutador.

recruiting, recruitment, *s.* reclutamiento.

rectal [ˈrektəl], *a.* del recto.

rectangle [ˈrektæŋgəl], *s.* rectángulo.

rectangular [rekˈtæŋgjuːləɹ], *a.* rectangular.

rectifiable [rektiˈfaiəbəl], *a.* rectificable.

rectification [rektifiˈkeiʃən], *s.* rectificación, enmendación, corrección; (*quím.*, *geom.*, *elec.*) rectificación.

rectifier, *s.* rectificador; (*elec.*) enderezador, rectificador.

rectify [ˈrektifai], *v.t.* rectificar, corregir, enmendar; (*quím.*) rectificar; (*elec.*) enderezar.

rectigrade [ˈrektigreid], *a.* rectígrado.

rectilineal [rektiˈliniəl], **rectilinear** [rektiˈliniəɹ], *a.* rectilíneo.

rectitude [ˈrektitjuːd], *s.* rectitud, derechura, equidad, corrección, formalidad.

recto [ˈrektou], *s.* recto.

rector [ˈrektəɹ], *s.* rector.

rectoral, rectorial, *a.* rectoral.

rectorate, rectorship, *s.* rectorado, rectoría.

rectory, *s.* rectoría, presbiterio.

rectrix [ˈrektriks], *s.* pluma timonera.

rectum [ˈrektəm], *s.* (*anat.*) recto.

recumbence, recumbency, *s.* reclinación, postura acostada; reposo.

recumbent [reˈkʌmbənt], *a.* reclinado, recostado, yacente.

recuperate [reˈkjuːpəreit], *v.t.* recobrar, recuperar. — *v.i.* restablecerse, reponerse, rehacerse.

recuperation, *s.* recuperación, recobro.

recuperative, *a.* recuperativo.

recur [reˈkəːɹ], *v.i.* repetirse, volver, recurrir, ofrecerse a la memoria.

recurrence [reˈkʌrəns], **recurrency** [reˈkʌrənsi], *s.* recurso, retorno, vuelta; repetición, reaparición.

recurrent [reˈkʌrənt], *a.* que vuelve, que recurre, periódico; (*anat.*) recurrente.

recurvate, *v.t.* encorvar, torcer. — *a.* encorvado.

recurvation, *s.* encorvadura; flexión hacia atrás.

recurve, *v.t.* encorvar, torcer.

recurved, recurvous, *a.* (*bot.*) encorvado; (*zool.*) encorvado hacia arriba (el pico).

recusancy, *s.* recusación, falta de conformidad.

recusant [ˈrekjuːzənt], *s.*, *a.* recusante (en religión).

recusation, *s.* (*der.*) recusación.

red [red], *a.* rojo, encarnado, colorado, enrojecido, encendido, sanguíneo; rojo, comunista, revolucionario; *red letter day*, día de fiesta, día notable, día señalado; *red tape*, balduque; (*fig.*) burocratismo; *to turn red*, ponerse colorado, ruborizarse. — *s.* rojez, encarnado, color rojo, color de sangre.

redaction [reˈdækʃən], *s.* redacción.

redactor, *s.* redactor.

redan [reˈdæn], *s.* (*fort.*) estrella.

redbird [ˈredbəːɹd], *s.* (*orn.*) cardenal.

redbreast, *s.* pechirrojo, petirrojo.

redbud, *s.* ciclamor.

redbug, *s.* nigua.

red-cap, *s.* cardelina, jilguero; (*vulg.*) policía militar.

redcoat, *s.* (*hist.*, *fam.*) soldado.

redden [ˈredən], *v.t.* teñir de color rojo. — *v.i.* sonrojarse.

reddish [ˈrediʃ], *a.* rojizo.

reddle [ˈredəl], *s.* almagre, almazarrón.

redeem [reˈdiːm], *v.t.* redimir, rescatar, desempeñar, libertar; recompensar, reintegrar, reparar; amortizar; resarcir, compensar; cumplir (una promesa); volver a tomar; (*teol.*) redimir.

redeemable, *a.* redimible, rescatable, amortizable.

redeemableness, *s.* calidad de redimible.

redeemer, *s.* redentor, rescatador; *The Redeemer*, el Redentor.

redeeming, *a.* que redime, que rescata; *redeeming feature*, (*for.*) circunstancia atenuante.

redeliberate, *v.i.* redeliberar, volver a discutir.

redeliver, *v.t.* restituir, devolver, entregar de nuevo.

redeliverance, redelivery, *s.* restitución.

redemand, *v.t.* volver a pedir, volver a preguntar.

redemise, *v.t.* (*for.*) restituir, devolver.

redemption [re'demʃən], *s.* redención, rescate, desempeño, liberación; amortización.

redemptive, *a.* de rescate.

redemptorist [re'demptərist], *s.* redentorista, *m.f.*

redescend [ri:de'send], *v.t.*, *v.i.* volver a bajar.

red-haired [red'hɛəɹd], *a.* pelirrojo.

red-handed, *a.* (*fig.*) en flagrante.

redhead, *s.* pelirrojo, pelirroja.

redhibition [redhi'biʃən], *s.* (*der.*) redhibición.

red-hot, *a.* enrojecido al fuego, candente.

redingote ['rediŋgout], *s.* redingote.

redintegrate, *v.t.* reintegrar, restablecer. — *a.* reintegrado, restablecido, renovado.

redintegration [redinti'greiʃən], *s.* reintegración, reintegro; restablecimiento, renovación, restauración.

redirect [ri:dai'rekt], *v.t.* reexpedir.

redissolve, *v.t.* volver a disolver.

redistribute, *v.t.* volver a distribuir.

redistribution, *s.* repartición nueva.

redness ['rednis], *s.* rojez, color rojo.

redolence, redolency, *s.* perfume, fragancia.

redolent ['redolənt], *a.* de fuerte y penetrante olor; fragante, oloroso; (*fig.*) reminiscente.

redouble [ri:'dʌbəl], *v.t.* redoblar, reduplicar; aumentar; repetir. — *v.i.* redoblarse.

redoubt [re'daut], *s.* reducto.

redoubtable [re'dautəbəl], *a.* formidable, terrible, tremendo.

redound [re'daund], *v.i.* redundar (en).

redpole, redpoll, *s.* pardilla.

redraft [ri:'drɑ:ft], *v.t.* tirar de nuevo, trazar de nuevo, dibujar de nuevo. — *s.* copia; nuevo dibujo, nuevo borrador; (*com.*) resaca.

redraw [ri:'drɔ:], *v.t.* tirar de nuevo, hacer un nuevo borrador. — *v.i.* (*com.*) resacar.

redress [re'dres], *v.t.* enderezar; remediar, compensar, resarcir, reformar, reparar, rectificar, corregir; hacer justicia; *to redress a wrong*, deshacer un agravio. — *s.* corrección, enmienda, satisfacción, reparación, desagravio; consuelo, alivio; enderezamiento; remedio; compensación.

re-dress [ri:'dres], *v.t.*, *v.i.* vestir de nuevo, vestirse de nuevo.

redresser, *s.* reformador, reparador, remediador.

redressive, *a.* correctivo, consolatorio.

redshank, *s.* (*orn.*) especie de maubecha del género *Totanus*.

redshirt, *s.* revolucionario (apl. esp. a los comunistas).

redskin, *s.* piel roja, *m.*

redstreak, *s.* manzana de rosa.

redtop, *s.* alfalfa.

reduce [re'dju:s], *v.t.* reducir, disminuir, minorar, rebajar, acortar, mermar, reformar, convertir; sojuzgar, subyugar, someter; (*mil.*) degradar; contraer, abreviar, ceñir, compendiar; (*mat., quím., cir.*) reducir.

reducer, *s.* reductor, achicador.

reducible, *a.* reductible, reducible.

reducibleness, *s.* reducibilidad, calidad de reducible.

reduction [re'dʌkʃən], *s.* reducción, disminución, reducimiento, rebaja; conquista, toma, sujeción; (*arit. y foto.*) reducción.

reductive, *a.* reductivo.

redundance, redundancy, *s.* redundancia, pleonasmo, abundancia, superabundancia, exceso.

redundant [re'dʌndənt], *a.* redundante, excesivo, superfluo, pleonástico.

reduplicate [ri:'dju:plikeit], *v.t.* reduplicar, redoblar, multiplicar, repetir. — *a.* reduplicado.

reduplication, *s.* reduplicación, repetición, aumento.

redwing, *s.* tordo rojo del antiguo continente; mirlo americano.

redwood, *s.* pino gigantesco de California.

re-dye, *v.t.* teñir de nuevo; volver a teñir.

reebok ['ri:bɔk], *s.* antílope pequeño de África.

re-echo [ri:'ekou], *v.t.*, *v.i.* resonar, repercutir, responder, repetir(se). — *s.* eco repetido.

reed [ri:d], *s.* (*bot.*) caña, cañuela, junquillo; (*poét.*) saeta, flecha; (*mús.*) lengüeta; dulzaina, caramillo; cualquier instrumento de boquilla; peine de tejedor; (*arq.*) baqueta; (*fig.*) poesía pastoril; (*min.*) tubo para cebar un barreno; *reed organ*, armonio.

reed-bunting, *s.* (*orn.*) verderón.

reeded, *a.* cubierto de cañas.

reeden, *a.* de caña.

re-edify [ri:'edifai], *v.t.* reedificar.

reedy, *a.* cañado, cañoso, lleno de cañas; (*mús.*) de tono agudo y delgado.

reef [ri:f], *s.* (*mar.*) rizo; arrecife, escollo, bajío, cayo; (*min.*) filón. — *v.t.* (*mar.*) tomar rizos, arrizar.

reefer, *s.* (*mar.*) rizador; especie de chaquetón; (*mar., fam.*) guardiamarina; (*vulg.*) cigarrillo de haxix.

reefy, *a.* lleno de arrecifes.

reek [ri:k], *v.i.* ahumar. — *v.i.* echar humo, humear, vahar, vahear, exhalar un vapor; oler. — *s.* vapor, humo, exhalación; olor.

reeky, *a.* humeante, ahumado.

reel [ri:əl], *s.* aspa, aspador, aspadera, argadijo, devanadera; carrete, carretel; (*Esco.*) contradanza. — *v.i.* hacer eses; vacilar, titubear, tambalear, bambolear. — *v.i.* devanar, aspar; *my head reels*, se me va la cabeza.

re-elect [ri:e'lekt], *v.t.* reelegir.

re-election, *s.* reelección.

re-eligibility, *s.* estado reeligible.

re-eligible, *a.* reeligible.

re-embark [ri:em'bɑ:k], *v.t.*, *v.i.* (*mar.*) reembarcar, embarcarse por segunda vez.

re-embarkation, re-embarcation, *s.* reembarco.

re-embody, *v.t.* reincorporar.

re-enact [ri:en'ækt], *v.t.* establecer de nuevo; revalidar una ley.

re-enactment, *s.* restablecimiento (de una ley).

re-enforce [ri:en'fɔ:s], *v.t.* reforzar, volver a fortificar; establecer de nuevo.

re-enforcement, *s.* refuerzo.

re-engage [ri:en'geidʒ], *v.t.* volver a empeñar; reescriturar; reenganchar. — *v.i.* empeñarse por segunda vez.

re-engagement, *s.* nuevo ataque; nuevo empeño; reenganchamiento.

re-enlist, *v.t.* alistar de nuevo, enganchar de nuevo.

re-enlistment, *s.* reenganche.

re-enter [riːˈenter], *v.t.*, *v.i.* volver a entrar, reingresar.

re-entering, *a.* reentrante.

re-entrance, re-entry, *s.* nueva entrada.

re-establish [riːesˈtæbliʃ], *v.t.* restablecer, restaurar, volver a poner.

re-established, *a.* restablecido.

re-establishment, *s.* restablecimiento, restauración.

reeve [riːv], *s.* (*ant.*) mayordomo; (*ant.*) magistrado; (Canadá) alcalde. — *v.t.* (*mar.*) laborear.

re-examination, *s.* reexaminación, nuevo examen, revista, repaso.

re-examine, *v.t.* reexaminar, repasar.

re-exchange, *s.* recambio.

re-export, *s.* reexportación. — *v.t.* reexportar, volver a exportar, exportar lo importado.

re-exportation, *s.* reexportación.

refection [reˈfekʃən], *s.* refección, colación.

refective, *a.* que refresca.

refectory [reˈfektəri], *s.* refectorio.

refer [reˈfəː], *v.t.* referir, dirigir, remitir, enviar, trasladar, encaminar, atribuir, asignar, someter. — *v.i.* referirse; tener relación, aludir, importar; recurrir, dirigirse.

referable [ˈrefərəbəl], *a.* referible, asignable, atribuible.

referee [refəˈriː], *s.* árbitro; garante; (*for.*) juez arbitrador, ponente.

reference [ˈrefərəns], *s.* referencia; alusión; nota, mención; recomendación, informes; señal, *f.*, marca; (*impr.*) llamada; remisión; fiador; (*der.*) arbitramento, arbitramiento; *to have* (o *bear*) *no reference to*, no atenerse a; *with reference to*, en cuanto a, respecto a (o de), con referencia a.

referendary, *a.* referendario.

referendum [refəˈrendəm], *s.* (*dipl.*) referéndum; (*pol.*) plebiscito.

referential, *a.* referente.

refill [riːˈfil], *v.t.* rellenar, rehenchir; reenvasar, llenar de nuevo.

refine [reˈfain], *v.t.* refinar, clarificar, purificar, afinar; acrisolar; pulir; mejorar, perfeccionar. — *v.i.* refinarse, purificarse, pulirse.

refined, *a.* refinado, purificado, clarificado, afinado, pulido; fino, cortés.

refinedness, refinement, *s.* refinamiento, refinación, refinadura; sutileza, astucia refinada; afectación; cortesía, elegancia, urbanidad, gentileza, cultura, pureza; quintaesencia.

refiner, *s.* refinador.

refinery, *s.* refinería.

refining, *s.* refinadura, refinación.

refit [riːˈfit], *v.t.* reparar, rehabilitar, componer; (*mar.*) recorrer. — *s.* recorrido.

refix [riːˈfiks], *v.t.* fijar de nuevo.

reflect [reˈflekt], *v.t.*, *v.i.* reflejar, reflectar, reverberar, repercutir, reflexionar, considerar; repensar, discurrir; *to reflect on*, reprobar, reprochar; desdorar, deslustrar, deslucir, perjudicar.

reflectingly, *adv.* con reflexión.

reflection, reflexion [reˈflekʃən], *s.* (*fís.* y *psic.*) reflexión; reflejo; reverberación, repercusión; consideración, meditación; reproche, censura, tacha, baldón; (*anat.*) repliegue; acción refleja.

reflective, *a.* reflector; reflexivo, meditabundo, meditativo.

reflector, *s.* (*ópt.*) reflector, reverbero.

reflex [ˈriːfleks], *a.* reflejo, por reflexión. — *s.* reflexión, reflejo; (*anat.*) acción refleja. — *v.t.* reflejar, dirigir inclinar o volver hacia atrás.

reflexibility, *s.* reflexibilidad.

reflexible [reˈfleksəbəl], *a.* reflexible.

reflexive, *a.* reflexivo; (*fís.*) reflector.

refloat [riːˈflout], *v.t.*, *v.i.* reflotar, poner otra vez a flote, desvarar.

reflorescence [riːfloːˈresəns], *s.* acción de reflorecer.

reflourish, *v.i.* reflorecer.

reflow, *v.i.* refluir.

refluence, refluency, *s.* reflujo.

refluent, *a.* refluente.

reflux [ˈriːflʌks], *s.* reflujo.

refoot, *v.t.* cabecear (un calcetín).

reform [reˈfoːm], *s.* reforma. — *v.t.* reformar, formar de nuevo, rehacer, reconstruir; corregir, mejorar, convertir, enmendar. — *v.i.* reformarse, corregirse, enmendarse.

reformation [refoːˈmeiʃən], *s.* reformación, reforma; nueva formación; *the Reformation*, la Reforma.

reformative [reˈfoːmətiv], *a.* reformador, reformatorio.

reformatory, *a.* reformador, reformatorio. — *s.* casa de corrección.

reformer, *s.* reformador, reformista, *m.f.*

reforming, *a.* reformador.

reformist, *s.* reformista, *m.f.*

refound [riːˈfaund], *v.t.* refundir.

refract [reˈfrækt], *v.t.* refractar, refringir.

refracting, *a.* refringente.

refraction, *s.* refracción.

refractive, *a.* refractor, refringente.

refractometer, *s.* refractómetro.

refractor, *s.* refractor; telescopio de refracción.

refractoriness, *s.* obstinación, rebeldía, terquedad, porfía, contumacia, desobediencia.

refractory [reˈfræktəri], *a.* refractario, contumaz, terco (*equit.*) repropio. — *s.* refractario.

refragable [reˈfrægəbəl], *a.* impugnable, refutable.

refrain [reˈfrein], *s.* estribillo, estrambote. — *v.t.* detener, refrenar, contener, moderar, reprimir. — *v.i.* refrenarse, contenerse, abstenerse; *to refrain from weeping*, contener las lágrimas.

reframe [riːˈfreim], *v.t.* rehacer, reconstruir, volver a poner en cuadro.

refrangibility, *s.* refrangibilidad.

refrangible [reˈfrændʒibəl], *a.* refrangible, capaz de refracción.

refresh [reˈfreʃ], *v.t.* refrescar, vivificar, renovar; descansar, suavizar; enfriar, templar el calor, refrigerar. — *v.i.* tomar un refresco.

refresher, *s.* refrescador, refrigerador, bebida que refresca; cursillo de vacaciones; (*for.*) estipendio adicional (de abogado).

refreshing, *a.* refrigerante, refrescante.

refreshment, *s.* refresco, alivio, reposo, descanso; refrigerio.

refrigerant, *a.*, *s.* refrigerante, refrigerativo.

refrigerate [reˈfridʒəreit], *v.t.* refrigerar, enfriar, resfriar, refrescar.

refrigerating, *a.* refrigerante, resfriador; *refrigerating plant* o *machine*, máquina de hacer hielo.

refrigeration, *s.* enfriamiento.

refrigerative, *a.* refrigerante, refrigerativo.

refrigerator [re'fridʒəreitəɹ], *s.* nevera, heladera, máquina frigorífica, refrigerador.

refuge ['refju:dʒ], *s.* refugio, asilo, abrigo, albergue, guarida; protección, amparo; subterfugio, escapatoria; *to take refuge*, refugarse; *house of refuge*, asilo. — *v.t.* dar asilo a.

refugee [refju:'dʒi:], *s.* refugiado; asilado; desterrado.

refulgence, refulgency, *s.* refulgencia, resplandor, esplendor, brillo, brillantez.

refulgent [re'fʌldʒənt], *a.* refulgente, brillante, resplandeciente, radiante.

refund [re'fʌnd], *v.t.* restituir, devolver, reintegrar, reembolsar; (*com.*) consolidar, amortizar.

refundable, *a.* restituible.

refunding, *s.* reembolso.

refurbish [ri:'fə:ɹbiʃ], *v.t.* adornar de nuevo; restaurar.

refusal [re'fju:zəl], *s.* repulsa, negativa; denegación; elección, opción, exclusiva; preferencia.

refuse [re'fju:z], *v.t., v.i.* rehusar, renunciar, repulsar, negar, denegar, oponerse, negarse; rechazar, desechar; resistirse a.

refuse ['refju:s], *s.* desecho, barredura, basura, residuo, sobra, desperdicio. — *a.* desechado, de desecho.

re-fuse [ri:'fju:z], *v.t.* refundir.

refuser, *s.* rehusador.

refutable ['refju:təbəl], *a.* refutable, rebatible, impugnable.

refutation [refju:'teiʃən], *s.* refutación, impugnación.

refutatory, *a.* refutatorio.

refute [re'fju:t], *v.t.* refutar, impugnar, rebatir, contradecir.

regain [ri:'gein], *v.t.* recobrar, recuperar, volver a tomar, volver a ganar lo perdido.

regal ['ri:gəl], *a.* real, regio. — *s.* organillo portátil.

regale [re'geil], *v.t.* regalar, festejar, agasajar, recrear, deleitar. — *v.i., v.r.* regalarse.

regalement, *s.* regalo, regalamiento, festejo.

regalia [re'geiliə], *s.pl.* insignias, regalias; cigarro puro habano de calidad superior.

regality [ri:'gæliti], *s.* soberanía, realeza.

regard [re'gɑːɹd], *v.t.* mirar, observar, reparar, atender, poner atención; considerar, juzgar, reputar, estimar, apreciar; tener cuidado; venerar, respetar; concernir, tocar; relacionarse con, referir a. — *s.* mirada, miramiento; atención, consideración, deferencia, veneración, acatamiento, respeto; referencia, relación; motivo, razón, *f.*; *with regard to*, o *as regards*, respecto a, tocante a; *without regard to*, sin respeto alguno a; *out of regard to*, por respeto a; *to pay regard to*, tener miramientos con; *regard being had to*, o *regard being paid to the fact that*, en vista de que; *kindest regards to*, muchos recuerdos a, mil afectos a.

regardful, *a.* mirado, atento, cuidadoso, circunspecto.

regarding, *prep.* tocante a, con respecto a, en cuanto a.

regardless, *a.* descuidado, negligente, indiferente; poco atento; *regardless of consequences*, sin reparar en barras.

regardlessness, *s.* descuido, negligencia, indiferencia.

regatta [re'gætə], *s.* regata.

regency ['ri:dʒənsi], *s.* regencia, gobierno; *the Regency*, (*hist. de Ingl.*) período de 1810–20.

regeneracy [re'dʒenərəsi], *s.* regeneración.

regenerate [re'dʒenəreit], *v.t.* regenerar, reproducir, reengendrar. — *a.* regenerado, reengendrado.

regenerateness, *s.* regeneración, estado de regenerado.

regenerating, regenerative, regeneratory, *a.* regenerador.

regeneration [ri:dʒene'reiʃən], *s.* regeneración, renacimiento.

regenerative, *a.* regenerativo, regenerador.

regent ['ri:dʒənt], *a.* regente, reinante. — *s.* regente; gobernador, gobernante.

regentship, *s.* regencia.

regerminate [ri:'dʒə:ɹmineit], *v.i.* retoñar.

regicide ['redʒisaid], *s.* regicida, *m.f.*; regicidio.

régime [re'dʒi:m], *s.* régimen; gobierno.

regimen ['redʒimən], *s.* (*med., gram.*) régimen.

regiment ['redʒimənt], *s.* (*mil.*) regimiento. — *v.t.* regimentar.

regimental, *a.* regimentario, que pertenece a un regimiento.

regimentals [redʒi'mentəlz], *s.pl.* uniforme militar.

region ['ri:dʒən], *s.* región, *f.*, distrito, país, tierra, territorio, comarca, espacio.

regional, *a.* regional.

regionalism, *s.* regionalismo.

register ['redʒistəɹ], *s.* registro; archivo, protocolo; matrícula, registrador; inscripción; lista, rol; contador, indicador; regulador de calorífero; cédula, albalá; *church register*, libro de parroquia. — *v.t.* registrar, inscribir en un registro, protocolar, matricular, encartar; marcar, indicar; certificar (una carta); (*mar.*) abanderar, matricular. — *v.i.* inscribirse, matricularse; (*impr.*) estar en registro.

registrar ['redʒistrɑːɹ], *s.* registrador, guardaregistros; archivero, secretario.

registrarship, *s.* funciones de archivero.

registration [redʒis'treiʃən], *s.* asiento, registro; inscripción, encabezamiento, empadronamiento.

registry ['redʒistri], *s.* archivo; registro, protocolo; matrícula; *registry office*, oficina del registro civil; agencia doméstica (para criados).

regius ['ri:dʒiəs], *a.* real; nombrado por el rey (aplicado a ciertas cátedras).

reglet ['reglet], *s.* (*arq.*) filete; (*impr.*) regleta, corondel.

regma ['regmə], *s.* (*pl.* **regmata**) (*bot.*) fruta compuesta de varias celdas, dehiscente (que se abre espontáneamente) al madurar.

regnancy, *s.* reino.

regnant ['regnənt], *a.* reinante, predominante.

regorge [ri:'gɔːɹdʒ], *v.t.* vomitar; engullir, tragar; rebosar.

regraft [ri:'grɑːft], *v.t.* volver a injertar.

regrate [re'greit], *v.t.* (*ant.*) revender, regatear.

regress [re'gres], *s.* regreso, vuelta, retorno. — *v.i.* regresar, retornar, volver.

regression [re'greʃən], *s.* regresión.

regressive, *a.* regresivo, retrógrado.

regret [re'gret], *s.* disgusto, pena, pesar, pesadumbre, sentimiento, remordimiento, compunción; excusa; *to send one's regrets,* mandar sus excusas. — *v.i.* sentir, deplorar, lamentar, condolerse, arrepentirse.

regretful, *a.* triste, pesaroso, sentido.

regrettable, *a.* sensible, lamentable.

regular ['regju:lə.ɪ], *a.* regular, regulado, exacto, ordenado, metódico, arreglado; verdadero, franco, famoso; normal, corriente, natural; uniforme; autorizado; formal; (*com.*) mediano; (*geom.*) regular. — *s.* parroquiano permanente; soldado de línea; (*igl.*) regular.

regularity [regju:'læriti], *s.* regularidad, simetría, orden, método; *for the sake of regularity*, para mayor regularidad.

regulate ['regju:leit], *v.t.* regular, arreglar, disponer, ordenar; disciplinar; regularizar.

regulation, *s.* regulación, reglamento, arreglo, regla, método, régimen. — *a.* corriente, ordinario, de ordenanza. — *pl.* **regulations**, reglamento; (*mil.*) ordenanzas militares.

regulative, *a.* reglamentario, ordenativo.

regulator, *s.* regulador; guía, registro; (*mec.*) regulador; registro (de reloj).

regurgitate [ri:'gə:ɪdʒiteit], *v.t.*, *v.i.* regurgitar, redundar.

regurgitation, *s.* regurgitación.

rehabilitate [ri:hə'biliteit], *v.t.* rehabilitar, reintegrar, restablecer.

rehabilitation, *s.* rehabilitación.

rehash [ri:'hæʃ], *s.* (*fam.*) refundición. — *v.t.* refundir; (*fam.*) recomponer sin cuidado.

re-hearing, *s.* (*der.*) nuevo examen, nueva vista.

rehearsal [re'hə:ɪsəl], *s.* repetición; recitación, relación minuciosa; repaso; (*teat.*) ensayo.

rehearse [re'hə:ɪs], *v.t.* repetir, recitar, narrar, referir; repasar; (*teat.*) ensayar.

rehearser, *s.* recitador, narrador, contador.

reheat [ri:'hi:t], *v.t.* recalentar.

reign [rein], *v.i.* reinar, imperar, prevalecer, predominar, estar en boga. — *s.* reinado, reino, imperio, soberanía, dominio; *in the reign of*, bajo el reinado de.

reigning, *a.* reinante, dominante, predominante; *reigning fashion*, moda actual.

reimburse [ri:'imbə:ɪs], *v.t.* reembolsar, reintegrar, indemnizar.

reimbursement, *s.* reembolso, reintegración, indemnización.

reimburser, *s.* persona que reembolsa.

reimpress, *v.t.* reimprimir.

reimpression, *s.* reimpresión.

reimprison, *v.t.* volver a encarcelar.

reimprisonment, *s.* nuevo encarcelamiento.

rein [rein], *s.* rienda; (*fig.*) licencia; (*fig.*) dirección, gobierno, poder, autoridad; *to give rein to*, dar licencia a, abrir la mano a. — *pl.* **reins**, (*ant.*) riñones. — *v.t.* gobernar, dirigir; refrenar, contener. — *v.i.* obedecer a las riendas.

reincarnation [ri:inkɑ:ɪ'neiʃən], *s.* reencarnación.

reincorporate, *v.t.* reincorporar.

reindeer ['reindiə.ɪ], *s.* reno.

reinforce [ri:'info:ɪs], *v.t.* reforzar; *reinforced concrete*, hormigón armado.

reinforcement, *s.* refuerzo; (*ing.*) armadura (del hormigón armado).

reinless ['reinlis], *a.* sin riendas, desenfrenado.

reinsert, *v.t.* insertar de nuevo.

reinsertion, *s.* reinserción.

reinstall, *v.t.* reinstalar, rehabilitar, restablecer.

reinstalment, *s.* reinstalación, restablecimiento, rehabilitación.

reinstate [ri:'insteit], *v.t.* reinstalar, reintegrar, restablecer, rehabilitar.

reinstatement, *s.* reintegración, restablecimiento.

reinsurance, *s.* reseguro.

reinsure, *v.t.* volver a asegurar.

reintroduce, *v.t.* volver a introducir.

reintroduction, *s.* reintroducción.

reinvest, *v.t.* reinvertir; investir de nuevo.

reinvestment, *s.* reinversión; nuevo investimiento.

reinvestigate, *v.t.* investigar de nuevo.

reinvestigation, *s.* nueva investigación.

reinvigorate, *v.t.* volver a dar vigor a; vigorizar.

reissue, *v.t.* emitir de nuevo, volver a emitir. — *v.i.* volver a salir. — *s.* nueva emisión, reedición.

reiterate [ri:'itəreit], *v.t.* reiterar, repetir.

reiteratedly, *adv.* repetidas veces.

reiteration, *s.* reiteración, repetición.

reject [re'dʒekt], *v.t.*, *v.i.* rechazar, recusar, renunciar, rehusar, repeler, rehuir; negar, denegar; excluir, desechar, repudiar, despreciar, expeler, arrojar; arrinconar, descartar.

rejectable, *a.* recusable, inadmisible.

rejection, *s.* rechazamiento, repulsa, repudiación, desecho, exclusión.

rejoice [re'dʒɔis], *v.i.* regocijarse, gozarse, alegrarse. — *v.t.* alegrar, regocijar.

rejoicing, *s.* alegría, regocijo, fiesta, júbilo, festividad.

rejoin [ri:'dʒɔin], *v.t.* volver a juntar, reunirse con. — *v.i.* (*for.*) responder, replicar.

rejoinder [re'dʒɔində.ɪ], *s.* réplica, contra-rréplica, respuesta.

rejoint, *v.t.* reunir; (*alb.*) llenar con mortero.

re-judge, *v.t.* juzgar de nuevo.

rejuvenate [ri:'dʒu:veneit], *v.t.* rejuvenecer, remozar.

rejuvenation, rejuvenescence, *s.* rejuvenecimiento, remozamiento.

rekindle, *v.t.* volver a encender.

relais [re'lei], *s.* (*fort.*) estrecho espacio entre el terraplén y el foso de un fuerte.

re-land, *v.t.*, *v.i.* desembarcar de nuevo; (*aer.*) aterrizar de nuevo.

relapse [re'læps], *v.i.* recaer, reincidir, renegar. — *s.* recaída, reincidencia; (*med.*) recidiva.

relate [re'leit], *v.t.* relatar, referir, recitar, narrar, contar; relacionar; emparentar. — *v.i.* relacionarse (con); pertenecer, tocar (a).

related, *a.* afín, conexo, emparentado; allegado. — *p.p.* [RELATE].

relater, *s.* narrador, contador, relator.

relating, *a.* que concierne, que se refiere.

relation [re'leiʃən], *s.* relación, relato, narración; referencia, respecto, correspondencia, conexión, interdependencia; parentesco, pariente, deudo; *with* (o *in*) *relation to*, respecto a, con relación a. — *pl.* **relations**, parentela.

relationship [re'leiʃənʃip], *s.* parentesco, afinidad, cognación.

relative ['relətiv], *a.* relativo, pertinente. — *s.* pariente; (*gram.*) pronombre relativo.

relativeness, *s.* relación, respecto.

relativism ['relətivizm], *s.* relativismo.

relativity [relə'tiviti], *s.* relatividad.

relax [re′læks], *v.t.* relajar, aflojar, soltar, laxar, remitir, dar reposo a, ablandar, mitigar; ceder; aliviar el estreñimiento; causar languidez. — *v.i.* aflojar; ceder, consentir; descansar, distraerse; sucumbir; enfriarse; mitigarse.

relaxation, *s.* aflojamiento, flojedad, aflojadura, disminución, relajación, relajamiento (de nervios, músculos, etc.); descanso, reposo, solaz, distracción, recreo, asueto; lenidad, mitigación.

relaxative, *a.* laxativo.

relaxing, *a.* laxante.

relay [re′lei], *s.* muda, remuda, revezo, parada, posta; relevo; (*elec.*) relé; (*rad.*) retransmisión; *relay-race*, carrera de relevos. — *v.t.* reemplazar, volver a poner; mandar por posta; (*elec.*) reemitir; (*rad.*) retransmitir.

release [re′li:s], *v.t.* soltar, desprender, desagarrar, eximir, realquilar, libertar; aflojar, relajar; aliviar; dar al público. — *s.* soltura, libertad; absolución, exoneración, remisión, descargo; quita, finiquito, recibo; cesión (de un derecho); publicación; representación; alivio.

relegate [′relegeit], *v.t.* desterrar, relegar.

relent [re′lent], *v.i.* ceder, ablandar, suavizarse, desenojarse, templarse; enternecerse, aplacarse.

relenting, *s.* enternecimiento, suavizamiento; relajación.

relentless, *a.* inflexible, inexorable, implacable, empedernido.

re-let [ri:′let], *v.t.* volver a alquilar.

relevance, relevancy, *s.* pertinencia, relación.

relevant [′relevənt], *a.* pertinente, aplicable, a propósito; apropiado.

reliable [re′laiəbəl], *a.* confiable, seguro, digno de confianza.

reliance, *s.* confianza, seguridad.

reliant [re′laiənt], *a.* confiado.

relic [′relik], *s.* resto, reliquia, residuo, vestigio.

relict [′relikt], *s.* viuda; reliquia.

relief [re′li:f], *s.* alivio, consuelo, socorro, asistencia, ayuda; aligeramiento, relevación; (*b.a.*) relieve; reparación, desagravio; indemnización; (*mil.*) relevo de centinela; *out-door relief*, socorros a domicilio.

relieve [re′li:v], *v.t.* relevar, remediar, aliviar, socorrer, consolar; exonerar, descargar; mitigar, suavizar, ablandar; relevar (centinelas); (*pint.*) dar relieve, poner en relieve, hacer resaltar; (*for.*) reparar, desagraviar, hacer justicia.

relieving, *a.* que alivia; *relieving arch,* (*arq.*) sobrearco.

re-light [ri:′lait], *v.t.* volver a encender.

religion [re′lidʒən], *s.* religión.

religionary, *a.* religioso.

religionist, *s.* religionario.

religiosity [relidʒi′ɔsiti], *s.* religiosidad.

religious [re′lidʒəs], *a.* religioso, piadoso, devoto, pío, concienzudo, fiel. — *s.* religioso, monje, monja.

religiousness, *s.* religiosidad, piedad.

relinquish [re′liŋkwiʃ], *v.t.* abandonar, renunciar, dejar, desertar; abstenerse, cesar; desistir de, ceder.

relinquishment, *s.* renuncia, abandono, dejación.

reliquary [′relikwəri], *s.* relicario.

relish [′reliʃ], *v.t.* gustar, dar gusto a, gustar de, hacer con fruición; aprobar; saborear, paladear; condimentar, sazonar, dar sabor a. — *v.i.* tener un gusto agradable, saber bien. — *s.* sabor, gusto, apetencia; dejo, sazón, *f.*, condimento; perfume; encanto, goce, fruición; (*carp.*) hombro de espiga.

relishable, *a.* gustoso, sabroso, apetitoso, de un gusto agradable.

relishing, *a.* apetitoso.

re-live [ri:′liv], *v.i.* revivir.

reload [ri:′loud], *v.t.* recargar, cargar de nuevo.

relucent [re′lu:sənt], *a.* reluciente.

reluctance, *s.* repugnancia, aversión, disgusto; desgana.

reluctant [re′lʌktənt], *a.* renuente, mal dispuesto, repugnante, recalcitrante.

reluctantly, *adv.* a contrapelo, de mala gana.

relume [re′lju:m], **relumine** [re′lju:min], *v.t.* encender de nuevo, alumbrar de nuevo.

rely [re′lai], *v.i.* tener confianza, confiar, fiar, fiarse, dar fe; contar; descansar.

remain [re′mein], *v.i.* quedar, quedarse, quedar en pie, permanecer, continuar, persistir; restar, faltar; *it remains to be done*, está (o queda) por hacer; *it remains to be seen*, allá veremos.

remainder, *s.* residuo, resto, remanente, alcance; (*der.*) reversibilidad; (*arit.*) residuo. — *a.* restante.

remains [re′meinz], *s.pl.* restos; desechos, ruinas, despojos, reliquias, sobras; obras póstumas.

re-make [ri:′meik], *v.t.* rehacer, hacer de nuevo.

remand [re′mɑ:nd], *v.t.* hacer venir, llamar, volver a llamar; (*for.*) reencarcelar. — *s.* reencarcelamiento.

remark [re′mɑ:ɹk], *v.t.* observar, notar, hacer notar, hacer observar. — *s.* observación, advertencia, reparo, nota.

remarkable, *a.* notable, singular, extraordinario, maravilloso, famoso, interesante, insigne.

remarkableness, *s.* singularidad.

remarker, *s.* anotador, observador.

re-marriage [ri:′mæridʒ], *s.* segundas nupcias.

re-marry, *v.t.* casar de nuevo; (*mar.*) fornecer con nuevos mástiles. — *v.i.* casarse de nuevo.

remediable [re′mi:diəbəl], *a.* remediable, reparable, curable.

remedial [re′mi:diəl], *a.* remediador; curativo, terapéutico.

remediless [′remediles], *a.* sin remedio, irremediable, incurable.

remedilessness, *s.* estado irremediable.

remedy [′remedi], *s.* remedio, medicamento; recurso; *it is past remedy*, no tiene remedio; *there's a remedy for all things*, también hay bulas para difuntos. — *v.t.* curar, remediar, poner remedio a, sanar, reparar.

re-melt [ri:′melt], *v.t.* refundir.

remember [re′membəɹ], *v.t.* recordar, acordarse de, caer en, hacer acordar, hacer mención de, tener presente, hacer presente; *remember me to him*, preséntele Vd. mis recuerdos.

remembrance [re′membrəns], *s.* recuerdo, memoria, retentiva, nota, recordación, conmemoración.

remembrancer, *s.* recuerdo, memento; recordador, recordatorio; memorial.

remigration [riːmaiˈgreiʃən], s. emigración nueva; vuelta.

remind [reˈmaind], v.t. recordar, acordar, avisar, dar a conocer, hacer presente.

reminder, s. recuerdo, recordativo, recordatorio, advertencia.

reminiscence, s. reminiscencia.

reminiscent [remiˈnisənt], a. recordativo, rememorativo.

remise [reˈmiːz], s. (for.) restitución, cesión. — v.t. restituir, ceder, devolver.

remiss [reˈmis], a. descuidado, remiso, negligente, inexacto, perezoso, lento, flojo, tibio.

remissible, a. remisible, perdonable.

remission [reˈmiʃən], s. remisión, absolución, perdón, debilitación, abandono; diminución, rebaja, minoración, reducción (de una multa, pena, etc.); asueto, descanso; (med.) remisión; (com.) remesa.

remissive, a. que remite, que relaja.

remissness, s. descuido, negligencia, flojedad, remisión.

remissory [reˈmisəri], a. remisorio.

remit [reˈmit], v.t. remitir, perdonar, condonar, aflojar, relajar; referir, debilitar; eximir, exonerar; trasladar, enviar, mandar, transmitir; disminuir; (com.) hacer remesas, remesar; (for.) referir, someter, trasladar a un tribunal inferior. — v.i. debilitar(se), calmarse, suavizarse; hacer remesas.

remitment, s. remisión, exoneración, gracia; remesa.

remittal [reˈmitəl], s. renuncia, abandono, cesión; remesa.

remittance, s. (com.) remesa, giro, letra de cambio.

remittent, a. (med.) remitente (fiebre o calentura).

remitter, s. (com.) remitente; (for.) restitución (derecho, título, etc.).

remnant [ˈremnənt], s. residuo, resto, remanente; retazo, retal. — pl. **remnants**, relieves, restos, desechos.

remodel [riːˈmɔdəl], v.t. volver a modelar; reconstruir, rehacer.

remonstrance [reˈmɔnstrəns], s. advertencia, protesta, represión, amonestación, reconvención, censura; memorial, representación.

remonstrant, s. peticionario, exponente. — a. en son de protesta, queja o reconvención.

remonstrate [reˈmɔnstreit], v.t. objetar, protestar, reconvenir.

remora [ˈremərə], s. obstáculo, impedimento; (ict.) rémora.

remorse [reˈmɔːrs], s. remordimiento, compunción.

remorseful, a. lleno de remordimientos; compasivo, arrepentido.

remorseless, a. inexorable, implacable, cruel.

remorselessness, s. inhumanidad, crueldad.

remote [reˈmout], a. remoto, lejano, apartado, retirado, distante; ajeno, extraño; ligero; *remote control*, mando a distancia.

remotely, adv. lejos, a lo lejos, remotamente.

remoteness, s. lejanía, distancia, alejamiento.

remould [riːˈmould], v.t. remodelar, dar nueva forma.

remount [riːˈmaunt], v.t., v.i. remontar, volver a subir; (mil.) remontar, remontarse. — s. (mil.) remonta.

removability, s. removilidad, movilidad.

removable [reˈmuːvəbəl], a. removible, trasportable.

removal [reˈmuːvəl], s. removimiento, remoción, traslación; traslado, mudanza; alejamiento, apartamiento; cambio de casa, cambio de domicilio; cambio de sitio; ausencia; extirpación, eliminación, salida; *removal van*, camión de mudanzas.

remove [reˈmuːv], v.t. remover, quitar, sacar, arrancar, extirpar; mudar (casa); suprimir; trasladar, alejar, cambiar, hacer cambiar, desviar, separar; apartar, desarrimar; despedir, destituir, obviar, deponer, derogar, transportar, transferir; *cousin once removed*, primo hermano. — v.i. mudarse, apartarse, alejarse, retirarse, irse, trasladarse, cambiar de sitio, cambiar de casa. — s. traslado, cambio de sitio; cambio de domicilio, mudanza; mudada, alejamiento; partida, escalón, grado, paso, intervalo; jugada (ajedrez); grado de parentesco.

remover, s. quitador, mudador; mozo de mudanza.

remunerable, a. remunerable, digno de remuneración.

remunerate [reˈmjuːnəreit], v.t. remunerar, pagar, recompensar, premiar, retribuir.

remuneration, s. remuneración, retribución, recompensa.

remunerative, a. remunatorio, lucrativo, provechoso.

remunerator, s. remunerador.

remurmur, v.t. volver a decir en voz baja, repetir en voz baja. — v.i. volver a murmurar.

renaissance [reˈneisɔns], s. renacimiento.

renal [ˈriːnəl], a. renal.

renard [ˈrenɑːrd], s. (ant.) zorro, zorra.

renascence, renascency, s. renacimiento.

renascent [reˈnæsənt], a. renaciente.

rencounter [renˈkauntəɹ], s. choque; combate; encuentro; duelo; pendencia. — v.t. y v.i. encontrar(se); embestir(se).

rend [rend], v.t. desgarrar, rasgar, arrancar, rajar, hender, hacer pedazos, lacerar; desunir, separar; *to rend asunder*, hender. — s. (mar.) costura de los tablones.

render, v.t. devolver, restituir; volverse, volver, poner, dar, hacer; pagar, verter, traducir; prestar, rendir, suministrar; expresar; (mús.) interpretar, ejecutar; (alb.) enlucir; derretir, clarificar, hervir; *to render thanks*, dar gracias; *to render a service*, prestar un servicio; *to render into*, traducir, verter al; *to render accounts*, dar cuenta.

renderer, s. el que devuelve, el que traduce, el que interpreta.

rendering, s. devolución; traducción, versión; (alb.) enlucimiento.

rendezvous [ˈrɔndeivuː], s. cita, lugar de cita; reunión, f. — v.t. dar cita. — v.i. acudir a una cita; reunirse, juntarse.

rendition [renˈdiʃən], s. rendición; (E.U.) versión, traducción; (mús., teat.) interpretación, ejecución; (com.) rendimiento, producción.

renegade [ˈrenegeid], **renegado**, s. renegado, apóstata, m.f.

renegue [reˈniːg], v.i. (naipes) no seguir el palo jugado.

renew [reˈnjuː], v.t. renovar, rehacer, reanudar, reengendrar; (com.) extender, prorrogar. — v.i. renovarse, empezar de nuevo, rejuvenecerse.

renewable, *a.* renovable.
renewal [re′njuːəl], *s.* renovación, renuevo, reanudación; (*com.*) prórroga.
renewedness, *s.* renovación, renovamiento.
renewing, *s.* renovamiento.
reniform [′renifɔːɹm], *a.* reniforme.
renitence, renitency, *s.* renitencia.
renitent [′renitənt], *a.* renitente.
rennet [′renet], *s.* cuajo; (*bot.*) cuajaleche.
renominate [riː′nɔmineit], *v.t.* nombrar de nuevo.
renounce [re′nauns], *v.t.* renunciar, rehusar, rechazar, renegar, abnegar, abandonar, abjurar, abdicar; (naipes) renunciar.
renouncement, *s.* renuncia.
renouncer, *s.* renunciador.
renouncing, *s.* renuncia.
renovate [′renoveit], *v.t.* rehacer, renovar, hacer renacer; purificar, limpiar.
renovating, *a.* renovador.
renovation, *s.* renovación, renuevo, rehacimiento, regeneración, limpiadura; compostura; (*teol.*) regeneración.
renovator, *s.* renovador.
renown [re′naun], *s.* renombre, fama, nombradía, celebridad, reputación.
renowned, *a.* renombrado, célebre, famoso, afamado.
rent [rent], *s.* alquiler; renta; arriendo, arrendamiento; crédito; rotura; rasgo, rasgón, rasgadura; desgarro, desgarrón; grieta, raja, hendedura; cisma; *rent-free*, sin pagar alquiler. — *v.t.* alquilar, arrendar, dar en arrendamiento, tomar en arrendamiento. — *v.i.* alquilarse.
rentable, *a.* arrendable.
rental [rentəl], *s.* arriendo, renta, arrendamiento, alquiler.
renter, *s.* rentero, arrendante, arrendador, alquilador, propietario, dueño; inquilino.
rentier, *s.* rentista, *m.f.*
renuent [re′njuːənt], *a.* renuente.
renule [′renjuːl], *s.* lobulillo renal o pequeño riñón (en algunos animales).
renunciation [renʌnsi′eiʃən], *s.* renunciación, renuncia.
renverse [ren′vəːɹs], *v.t.* volver atrás; (*mec.*) invertir; trabucar, trastornar.
reobtain, *v.t.* obtener de nuevo.
reoccupy, *v.t.* reocupar.
reopen, *v.t.* volver a abrir.
reordain, *v.t.* volver a mandar, volver a ordenar.
reordinance, *s.* repetición de una orden.
reordination, *s.* nueva ordenación.
reorganization, *s.* reorganización.
reorganize, *v.t.* reorganizar.
rep [rep], *s.* (*tej.*) reps.
repack [riː′pæk], *v.t.* reempacar; reenvasar; volver a hacer (una maleta).
repair [re′pɛəɹ], *v.t.* reparar, restaurar, remendar, aderezar, componer, recomponer; renovar; remediar, enmendar, subsanar, restablecer; resarcir o indemnizar; recorrer; (*mar.*) carenar; (*zap.*) remontar. — *v.i.* ir a alguna parte, irse, encaminarse, refugiarse. — *s.* reparación, remiendo, reparo, compostura, composición, arreglo, restauración; (*mar.*) recorrido; (*zap.*) remonta; *to keep in repair*, conservar en buen estado; *out of repair*, descompuesto, en mal estado.
repairable [re′pɛərəbəl], *a.* reparable, remediable.

repairer, *s.* reparador, restaurador.
repairing, *s.* reparación, restauración; (*zap.*) remonta.
reparable [′repərəbəl], *a.* reparable.
reparation [repə′reiʃən], *s.* reparación, renovación; compensación, indemnización, satisfacción, resarcimiento.
reparative, *a.* reparatorio, reparativo.
repartee [repɑːɹ′tiː], *s.* réplica, respuesta picante; agudeza. — *v.i.* dar respuestas picantes.
repartition [repɑːɹ′tiʃən], *s.* repartición, repartimiento.
repass [riː′pɑːs], *v.t.*, *v.i.* repasar, volver a pasar.
repast, *s.* comida, colación, alimento. — *v.t.* alimentar, nutrir.
repasture, *s.* alimento, sustento.
repatriate [riː′pætrieit], *v.t.* repatriar.
repay [riː′pei], (*pret. y p.p.* **repaid**), *v.t.* volver a pagar, recompensar; repagar, restituir, retornar, reintegrar, reembolsar; pagar en la misma moneda. — *v.i.* hacer un pago.
repayable, *a.* reembolsable.
repayment, *s.* reembolso, pago, devolución.
repeal [re′piːl], *v.t.* abrogar, revocar, derogar, abolir, anular. — *s.* revocación, anulación, abrogación, derogación.
repealable, *a.* revocable, anulable, abrogable.
repealer, *s.* revocador, anulador.
repeat [re′piːt], *v.t.* repetir, reiterar; recitar de memoria; volver a decir; duplicar; repasar; ensayar. — *s.* (*mús.*) repetición.
repeatedly, *adv.* repetidamente, repetidas veces, reiteradamente.
repeater, *s.* repetidor, repetidora; recitador; reloj de repetición; arma de repetición; (*elec.*) repetidor; (*E.U. pol.*) el que trata de votar dos o más veces en una elección.
repeating, *s.* acción de repetir. — *a.* de repetición.
repel [re′pel], *v.t.* rechazar, repeler, repulsar, resistir, ahuyentar. — *v.i.* ser repulsivo.
repellency, *s.* repulsión, fuerza repulsiva.
repellent [re′pelənt], *a.* repelente, repulsivo, repercusivo; impermeable; (*med.*) remedio repercusivo.
repent [re′pent], *v.t.*, *v.i.* arrepentirse. — *a.* (*bot., zool., etc.*) rastrero, que se arrastra.
repentance, *s.* arrepentimiento, contrición.
repentant, *a.* arrepentido, penitente, contrito.
repentantly, repentingly, *adv.* con arrepentimiento.
repeople [riː′piːpəl], *v.t.* repoblar.
repercuss, *v.t.* repercutir, reverberar, rechazar.
repercussion [riːpəɹ′kʌʃən], *s.* repercusión, reverberación, rechazo.
repercussive, *a.* repercusivo.
repertoire [′repəɹtwɑːɹ], *s.* repertorio.
repertory [′repəɹtəri], *s.* repertorio; colección, depósito; lista, índice, inventario; *repertory theatre*, o *company*, teatro de repertorio. — *a.* de repertorio.
repetition [repi′tiʃən], *s.* repetición, reiteración, repaso.
repine [re′pain], *v.i.* quejarse, apurarse; gemir, afligirse; tener nostalgia.
repining, *s.* queja, dolor, pesar, descontento, nostalgia. — *a.* dispuesto a murmurar, dispuesto a afligirse, descontento.

replace [ri:pleis], *v.t.* reponer, colocar de nuevo; substituir, reemplazar; reembolsar, restituir, devolver.

replaceable, *a.* reemplazable, renovable.

replacement, *s.* colocación en su lugar, reemplazo, substitución; restitución.

replacing-switch, *s.* (*f.c.*) aparato colocado en los rieles para volver a ellos vagones descarrilados.

replait, *v.t.* plegar repetidas veces.

replant, *v.t.* replantar.

replenish [re'pleniʃ], *v.t.* rellenar, rehenchir; aprovisionar, proveer, llenar. — *v.i.* llenarse.

replenishment, *s.* acción de llenar, acción de proveer, aprovisionamiento.

replete [re'pli:t], *a.* lleno, completamente lleno, repleto.

repleteness, repletion, *s.* repleción, plenitud.

replevin [re'plevin], *s.* (*der.*) desembargo, auto de desembargo.

replevy [re'plevi], *v.t.* (*der.*) recobrar mercancías embargadas dando una garantía de someterse a un tribunal de justicia.

replica ['replikə], *s.* réplica, duplicado.

replicant, *s.* replicante, replicador.

replicate ['replikeit], *a.* (*bot.*) replegado. — *s.* (*mús.*) tono una o más octavas más alto o más bajo que el original.

replication, *s.* réplica, respuesta; repetición; repliegue; (*for.*) réplica.

replier [re'plaiər], *s.* replicante.

reply [re'plai], *s.* réplica, respuesta, contestación. — *v.t.*, *v.i.* responder, contestar, reponer, replicar.

repolish [ri:'poliʃ], *v.t.* repulir.

report [re'po:t], *v.t.* referir, contar, relatar, hacer relación, informar, dar noticia, dar parte, enterar, manifestar; redactar un informe o dictamen; reportar; divulgar, propalar; denunciar; estenografiar. — *v.i.* presentar informes; ser reportero; comparecer, personarse; *it is reported*, se dice, corre la voz, corre la fama. — *s.* voz, *f.*, opinión, *f.*, rumor, manifiesto, memoria, noticia, anuncia, dicho, relato, informe, dictamen, relación; parte, *f.*; detonación, estallido, estampido; sumaria; reputación, fama; hablilla; crónica, reportaje (de periódico); actas; *current report*, rumor que corre.

reporter, *s.* (*for.*) relator; reportero, periodista, *m.f.*; *Reporters' gallery*, tribuna de periodistas.

reporting, *s.* relato.

reposal [re'pouzəl], **repose**, *s.* reposo, descanso, calma, tranquilidad, quietud, sueño.

repose [re'pouz], *v.t.* confiar, poner o tener (confianza). — *v.i.* reposar, descansar, dormir; tenderse, reclinarse, recostarse.

reposit [re'pozit], *v.t.* depositar, colocar, poner.

reposition, *s.* reposición; restablecimiento; (*cir.*) reducción.

repository [re'pozitəri], *s.* repositorio, depósito, dispensa, almacén, tienda.

repossess [ri:po'zes], *v.t.* recobrar, recuperar.

repossession, *s.* recuperación, reintegro.

repoussé [re'pu:sei], *a.* repujado.

reprehend [repri'hend], *v.t.* reprender, censurar, tachar, regañar, reñir; imputar, acusar.

reprehender, *s.* represor, censor, crítico.

reprehensible [repri'hensəbəl], *a.* reprensible, reprobable, censurable.

reprehensibleness, *s.* culpabilidad, calidad de reprensible.

reprehension, *s.* reprensión, regaño, censura, amonestación.

reprehensive, reprehensory, *a.* represor, digno de represión.

represent [repre'zent], *v.t.* representar, manifestar, simbolizar, exponer, describir.

representable, *a.* representable.

representation [reprezen'teiʃən], *s.* representación.

representative [repre'zentətiv], *a.* representativo, representante, típico. — *s.* representante, delegado, apoderado; símbolo.

representativeness, *s.* carácter representativo.

representer, *s.* representante.

repress [re'pres], *v.t.* reprimir, dominar, sofocar, sojuzgar, sujetar, contener.

repression, *s.* represión.

repressive, *a.* represivo.

reprieve [re'pri:v], *v.t.* (*for.*) suspender la ejecución; perdonar; aliviar, librar temporalmente. — *s.* suspensión; perdón.

reprimand [repri'ma:nd], *v.t.* reprender, censurar, corregir, reñir, reconvenir. — *s.* reprimenda, reprensión, corrección.

reprint [ri:'print], *v.t.* reimprimir. — *s.* reimpresión, nueva tirada.

reprisal [re'praizəl], *s.* represalia.

reprise, *s.* represa; (*mús.*) repetición; estribillo.

reproach [re'proutʃ], *v.t.* reprochar, acusar, reconvenir, vituperar, increpar, culpar, censurar; echar en las barbas, echar en cara. — *s.* reproche, vituperación, increpación, tacha, improperio, contumelia, vituperio, reconvención, censura, baldón.

reproachable, *a.* reprochable, censurable, reprensible.

reproachful, *a.* vergonzoso, ignominioso, infame; lleno de reproches; severo.

reprobate ['reprobeit], *s.*, *a.* réprobo, falso, malvado, perverso, malo. — *v.t.* reprobar, desaprobar, condenar.

reprobation [repro'beiʃən], *s.* reprobación, desaprobación, condenación.

reprobative, reprobatory, *a.* reprobatorio, reprobador.

reproduce [ri:pro'dju:s], *v.t.* reproducir; copiar.

reproducer, *s.* reproductor.

reproducible, *a.* reproducible.

reproduction [ri:pro'dʌkʃən], *s.* reproducción; copia; trasunto.

reproductive, reproductory, *a.* reproductor, reproductivo.

reproof [re'pru:f], *s.* reprensión, reprobación, reconvención, reproche, censura.

reprovable, *a.* reprensible, censurable, culpable.

reprove [re'pru:v], *v.t.* reprobar, censurar, culpar, reprender, condenar, acusar.

reprover, *s.* represor, censor, reprobador.

reprovingly, *adv.* reprobadamente, con reprobación.

reprovision [ri:pro'viʒən], *v.t.* aprovisionar de nuevo (buque, ejército, etc.).

reptant ['reptənt], *a.* (*hist. nat.*) reptante; rastrero, que se arrastra.

reptile ['reptail], *s.*, *a.* reptil.

reptilian [rep'tiliən], *s. y a.* reptil.

republic [re'pʌblik], *s.* república.

republican, *s.*, *a.* republicano.

republicanism, *s.* republicanismo.
republicanize, *v.t.* republicanizar.
republication [ri:pʌbli'keiʃən], *s.* reimpresión; nueva publicación; (*for.*) renovación de un testamento.
republish [ri:'pʌbliʃ], *v.t.* publicar por segunda vez; renovar, reimprimir.
repudiable, *a.* repudiable.
repudiate [re'pju:dieit], *v.t.* repudiar, renunciar, repeler, desechar; divorciarse (de la esposa).
repudiation, *s.* repudiación, repudio; divorcio.
repugnance, *s.* repugnancia, aversión, desgana, contrariedad, resistencia.
repugnant [re'pʌgnənt], *a.* repugnante; opuesto; incompatible; antipático, repulsivo; *to be repugnant to,* repugnar a.
repugnantly, *adv.* con repugnancia, de mala gana.
repullulate [re'pʌlju:leit], *v.i.* pulular de nuevo; (*med.*) reaparecer (una enfermedad).
repulse [re'pʌls], *s.* repulsa, rehuso, rechazo. — *v.t.* repulsar; rechazar, desechar, repeler.
repulsion, *s.* aversión, repugnancia, rechazamiento; (*fís.*) repulsión.
repulsive, *a.* repulsivo, repelente, repugnante, chocante.
repulsiveness, *s.* fuerza repulsiva; carácter repugnante o repulsivo.
repurchase [ri:'pə:tʃis], *v.t.* recomprar. — *s.* cosa comprada de nuevo.
reputable ['repju:təbəl], *a.* respetable, estimable, honroso, honrado, intachable, lícito.
reputableness, *s.* cualidad de ser respetable, estimable, honroso.
reputation [repju:'teiʃən], **repute** [re'pju:t], *s.* reputación, crédito, nombre, renombre, fama, estimación, nombradía.
repute [re'pju:t], *v.t.* reputar, tener por, estimar, juzgar. — *s.* reputación, estimación, crédito, fama; *of repute,* renombrado, famoso.
reputed, *a.* reputado; putativo: *to be reputed,* tener fama de.
reputeless, *a.* desacreditado, ınfame.
request [re'kwest], *s.* ruego, petición, pedimento, encargo, súplica, solicitud, instancia; (*com.*) pedido, demanda; *at the request of,* a petición de, a solicitud de; *in great request,* muy concurrido, en gran honor, en boga; *in request,* en boga, en demanda. — *v.t.* rogar, suplicar, pedir, encargar, solicitar.
requester, *s.* solicitador, suplicante.
re-quicken [ri:'kwikən], *v.t.* reanimar; hacer revivir.
requiem ['ri:kwiem, 'rekwiəm], *s.* réquiem; *Requiem Mass,* misa de difuntos.
requirable, *a.* que se puede requerir.
require [re'kwaiɹ], *v.t.* requerir, solicitar, demandar, exigir, pedir, necesitar. — *v.i.* ser necesario.
requirement, *s.* demanda, requisito, necesidad, requerimiento, exigencia; estipulación.
requirer, *s.* requeridor.
requisite ['rekwizit], *a.* necesario, esencial, preciso, forzoso, indispensable. — *s.* requisito.
requisiteness, *s.* necesidad, precisión.
requisition [rekwi'ziʃən], *s.* requisición, demanda, requisito, pedimento, súplica, petición; necesidad; (*der.*) requisitoria; (*com.*) demanda, solicitud.
requisitory, *a.* requisitorio.

requital [re'kwaitəl], *s.* retorno, torna, paga, satisfacción, compensación, acción recíproca; represalia, desquite.
requite [re'kwait], *v.t.* tornar, retornar, devolver, desquitar; reconocer; recompensar, pagar, corresponder; pagar en la misma moneda.
rerail [ri:'reil], *v.t.* volver a encarrilar.
reredos ['riərədɔs], *s.* retablo.
resail [ri:'seil], *v.i.* reembarcarse.
resale, *s.* reventa.
resalute, *v.t.* volver a saludar.
rescind [re'sind], *v.t.* rescindir, abrogar, anular.
rescindable, *a.* anulable.
rescission [re'siʒən], *s.* rescisión, revocación, anulación, abolición; incisión.
rescissory, *a.* rescisorio.
rescript ['ri:skript], *s.* rescripto, edicto.
rescue ['reskju:], *v.t.* rescatar, salvar, redimir, libertar, librar; preservar. — *s.* recobro, libramiento, rescate; socorro, salvamento.
rescuer, *s.* libertador, salvador, rescatador.
research [re'sə:ɹtʃ], *s.* investigación, investigaciones, indagación. — *v.t.*, *v.i.* investigar, hacer investigaciones.
re-seat [ri:'si:t], *v.t.* sentar de nuevo, asentar de nuevo; restablecer; poner un fondo a asiento nuevo.
resect [re'sekt], *v.t.* (*cir.*) resecar.
resection [re'sekʃən], *s.* resección.
reseda [re'si:də], *s.* (*bot.*) reseda; color grisverde muy pálido.
re-seize, *v.t.* volver a coger.
re-sell, *v.t.* revender, volver a vender.
resemblance [re'zembləns], *s.* semejanza, parecido, imagen, *f.*; analogía, conformidad, similitud.
resemble [re'zembəl], *v.t.* asemejar, asemejarse a, parecerse a, tener semejanza con.
resent [re'zent], *v.t.* resentirse de; agraviarse por, sentir (por), ofenderse (por).
resentful, *a.* resentido; agraviado, ofendido; vengativo.
resentfulness, *s.* resentimiento.
resentive, *a.* suceptible, irritable.
resentment, *s.* resentimiento, enfado, queja.
reservation [rezəɹ'veiʃən], *s.* reservación, reserva; restricción, segunda intención, doble sentido, salvedad; (*E.U.*) territorio reservado para los indios.
reserve [re'zə:ɹv], *v.t.* reservar, retirar, conservar, guardar, retener; excluir, exceptuar. — *s.* reservación, reserva, reticencia; circunspección; custodia, guarda; silencio, sigilo, cautela; (*mil.*) reserva, retén; *without reserve,* completamente, enteramente, sin reserva.
reserved, *a.* reservado, guardado, circunspecto, discreto, modesto, callado, taciturno.
reservedness, *s.* reserva, cautela, circunspección.
reservist, *s.* reservista, *m.f.*
reservoir, *s.* depósito; estanque, alberca; cubeta; presada; (*com.*) surtido de reserva.
reset [ri:'set], *v.t.* volver a poner; volver a montar; (*impr.*) recomponer.
resetting, *s.* (*impr.*) recomposición.
resettle [ri:'setəl], *v.t.* restablecer; tranquilizar de nuevo.
resettlement, *s.* restablecimiento, reinstalación.
reshape [ri:'ʃeip], *v.t.* reformar.

reship [riːˈʃip], *v.t.* reembarcar.

reshipment, *s.* reembarco, reembarque.

reside [reˈzaid], *v.i.* residir, morar, vivir, parar.

residence [ˈrezidəns], *s.* residencia, domicilio, morada, habitación; permanencia, estada.

Residency, *s.* Residencia oficial de un ministro residente.

resident, *a.* residente, habitante, vecino, morador, habitador. — *s.* residente; permanente; inherente; (*dipl.*) ministro residente.

residential [reziˈdenʃəl], *a.* residencial.

residual [reˈzidjuːəl], **residuary** [reˈzidjuːəri], *a.* residuo, restante, que queda; *residuary legatee,* heredero universal; *residual magnetism,* (*elec.*) magnetismo remanente.

residue [ˈrezidjuː], *s.* residuo, sobrante, remanente, resto, resta.

residuum [reˈzidjuːəm], *s.* residuo, resta.

resign [reˈzain], *v.t.,* *v.i.* resignar, ceder, renunciar, abandonar, dejar, hacer dejación, dimitir. — *v.t.* firmar otra vez. — *v.r.* resignarse, rendirse, someterse.

resignation [rezigˈneiʃən], *s.* resignación, renuncia, dejación, dimisión; conformidad.

resigned [reˈzaind], *a.* resignado, submisivo, conforme.

resignee [rezaiˈniː], *s.* resignatario.

resigner, *s.* resignante, dimisionario.

resilience, resiliency, *s.* resalto; elasticidad.

resilient [reˈziliənt], *a.* resaltante; elástico.

resin [ˈrezin], *s.* resina; colofonia (para arcos de violín, etc.).

resinaceous, *a.* resinoso.

resiniferous, *a.* resinífero.

resinoid [ˈrezinɔid], *a.* parecido a la resina.

resinous [ˈrezinəs], *a.* resinoso.

resinousness, *s.* calidad de resinoso.

resipiscence [reˈsipisəns], *s.* reconocimiento de un error; arrepentimiento.

resist [reˈzist], *v.t.,* *v.i.* resistir, repeler, negarse (a), rechazar; impedir, oponerse (a); contrariar, detener.

resistance, *s.* resistencia, oposición; defensa; (*der.*) rebelión, *f.*; (*elec.*) resistencia; *resistance box,* (*elec.*) caja de resistencias; *resistance coil,* bobina de resistencia; *resistance frame,* reostato de cuadro.

resistant, resistent, *a.* resistente.

resister, *s.* oponente.

resistibility, resistibleness, *s.* resistibilidad.

resistible, *a.* resistible.

resisting, *a.* resistente.

resistless, *a.* irresistible.

resistlessness, *s.* calidad de irresistible.

resole [riːˈsoul], *v.t.* (*zap.*) sobresolar, remontar.

resolute [ˈrezoluːt, ˈrezoljuːt], *a.* resuelto, determinado, firme.

resoluteness, *s.* resolución, determinación, denuedo, firmeza.

resolution [rezoˈluːʃən], *s.* resolución, decisión, denuedo, brío, ánimo, determinación, firmeza; solución, resolución; análisis; proposición, propósito; resolución, acuerdo (de una junta o asamblea); (*mec.*) descomposición; análisis (químico, mecánico o mental); (*med.*) resolución de un tumor, etc. sin supurar; *to act with resolution,* echar el pecho al agua.

resolvable, *a.* resoluble, soluble.

resolve [reˈzɔlv], *v.t.* resolver, determinar, decidir; declarar, explicar, informar; tratar de, estar dispuesto a; reducir, descomponer, analizar; dar solución a, desatar, aclarar. — *v.i.* decidirse, resolverse; acordar, tomar un acuerdo; disolverse, fundirse, transformarse. — *s.* resolución, determinación; acuerdo; propósito.

resolvedly, *adv.* resueltamente, decididamente.

resolvedness, *s.* resolución.

resolvent [reˈzɔlvənt], *s.* disolvente, solutivo. — *a.* disolvente, resolvente.

resolver, *s.* el que resuelve.

resolving, *s.* resolución.

resonance, *s.* resonancia, resonación, retumbo.

resonant [ˈrezonənt], *a.* resonante, retumbante, reverberante, sonoro.

resonator, *s.* resonador.

resorb [reˈsɔːrb], *v.t.* reabsorber.

resorcin [reˈzɔːrsin], *s.* resorcina.

resorption [reˈsɔːrbʃən], *s.* reabsorción, resorción.

resort [reˈzɔːrt], *v.i.* ir, acudir, concurrir, frecuentar, recurrir; echar mano de, hacer uso de; pasar a. — *s.* concurrencia, concurso, asamblea, frecuentación; recurso, refugio; medio, junta, visita; punto de reunión, cita; sitio frecuentado; *last resort,* último recurso; *summer resort,* lugar de veraneo; *health resort,* balneario, lugar de curación.

resound [reˈzaund], *v.t.* repetir (el sonido); repercutir, rechazar el sonido; celebrar, cantar. — *v.i.* resonar, tener resonancia, retumbar, rimbombar, formar eco, transcender, tener fama.

re-sound [riːˈsaund], *v.t.* volver a sonar.

resounding [reˈzaundiŋ], *a.* resonante.

resource [reˈsɔːrs], *s.* recurso, arbitrio, medio, resorte, expediente. — *pl.* recursos, medios pecuniarios; riqueza.

resourceful, *a.* fértil en recursos.

resourceless, *a.* sin recurso; desprovisto de medios.

re-sow [riːˈsou], *v.t.* volver a sembrar.

respect [reˈspekt], *v.t.* respetar, estimar; honrar; acatar, hacer acepción de; corresponder, tocar, referir, concernir; guardar, conservar. — *s.* respeto, estimación, consideración; miramiento; cumplimiento, observancia, acatamiento, homenaje; motivo, consideración; respecto; *with respect to,* (con) respecto a, en cuanto a, tocante a; *in all respects, in every respect,* por todos conceptos; *in other respects,* por lo demás, por otra parte; *in some respect(s),* de algún modo; *out of respect to,* (o *for*), por consideración a; *respect of persons,* acepción de personas; *to pay one's respects,* cumplimentar, dar los cumplimientos.

respectability [respektəˈbiliti], **respectableness** [reˈspektəbəlnis], *s.* respetabilidad, honorabilidad; crédito.

respectable [reˈspektəbəl], *a.* respetable, estimable, honroso, acreditado, autorizado; (*fam.*) regular, pasable, mediano, tal cual, bastante bueno, considerable.

respecter, *s.* respetador, persona que respeta.

respectful, *a.* respetuoso.

respectfulness, *s.* conducta respetuosa.

respecting, *prep.* con respecto a, tocante a, en cuanto a, relativamente a.

respective, *a.* respectivo; relativo; particular, individual, sendo.

respirability, respirableness, *s.* respirabilidad.

respirable ['respirəbəl], *a.* respirable.
respiration [respi'reiʃən], *s.* respiración, respiro; descanso, desahogo.
respirator ['respireitəɹ], *s.* respirador.
respiratory, *a.* respiratorio.
respire [re'spaiəɹ], *v.i.* respirar; resollar, ẹxhalar, espirar; descansar, tomar aliento.
respite ['respait], *s.* respiro, tregua, pausa, espera, suspensión; plazo, prórroga. — *v.t.* suspender, diferir, prorrogar, aplazar, dar treguas a, conceder plazo a.
resplendence, resplendency, *s.* resplandor, lustre, fulgor, brillo, esplendor.
resplendent [re'splendent], *a.* resplandeciente, esplendente, brillante.
respond [re'spɔnd], *v.i.* responder, contestar; corresponder; mostrar simpatía; obedecer; (*E.U.*) satisfacer una deuda.
response [re'spɔns], *s.* respuesta, réplica, contestación; (*fig.*, *mec.*) réplica, reacción.
responsibility [responsi'biliti], *s.* responsabilidad.
responsible [res'pɔnsibəl], *a.* responsable.
responsive [res'pɔnsiv], *a.* respondiente, respondedor; simpático; sensible; conforme, correspondiente; (*der.*) responsivo.
responsiveness, *s.* simpatía; conformidad, correspondencia.
responsory [res'pɔnsəri], *s.* responsorio. — *a.* (*ant.*) respondiente.
rest [rest], *s.* descanso, reposo; quietud, tranquilidad, paz, *f.*; sueño; asueto, holganza, tregua, inacción; apoyo, sustentáculo, base, *f.*, soporte, estribo, arrimo; posada, descansadero; detención, parada; restante, sobra, resto, residuo; ristre, cuja; excedente, sobrante; saldo semanal (del Banco de Inglaterra); (*mús.*) pausa, silencio; (*poét.*) cesura; *the rest,* (*sing.*) lo demás; (*pl.*) los demás; *to get a good night's rest,* pasar una buena noche. — *v.t.* descansar, calmar; proporcionar descanso a; apoyar, poner, colocar, asentar. — *v.i.* descansar, reposar, holgar, estar en paz; dormir; apoyar, apoyarse en, cargar sobre; contar (con), depender (de); yacer; parar, cesar; morir; permanecer, quedar; atenerse a; (*for.*) acabar (un informe); *to rest assured,* estar cierto; *to rest with,* tocar a.
restaurant ['restorənt], *s.* restaurante, restaurán.
restful ['restful], *a.* quieto, tranquilo, reposado, sosegado.
rest-harrow [rest'hærou] *s.* (*bot.*) gatuña, detienebuey.
resting, *s.* reposo, descanso; *resting-place,* descansadero; (*fig.*) la tumba.
restitution [resti'tju:ʃən], *s.* restitución, restablecimiento; torna, devolución, reintegración, indemnización, reparación, recuperación, recobro.
restive ['restiv], *a.* inquieto, impaciente, ingobernable; (*equit.*) repropio.
restiveness, *s.* obstinación, terquedad, inquietud, impaciencia.
restless ['restles], *a.* desasosegado, intranquilo, impaciente, inquieto; desvelado, insomne; inconstante; travieso, agitado; bullicioso, alborotadizo, revoltoso.
restlessness, *s.* desasosiego, inquietud, impaciencia; agitación continua; insomnio, desvelo.

restock [ri:'stɔk], *v.t.* volver a surtir, llenar de nuevo o abastecer; (*agr.*) renovar, restablecer, replantar (un bosque, etc.).
restorable [re'stɔ:əbəl], *a.* restituible.
restoration [resto'reiʃən], *s.* restauración, restitución, renovación, reparación, rehabilitación, reintegración, restablecimiento.
restorative [res'tɔ:rətiv], *a.* restaurativo, restaurante. — *s.* restaurativo.
restore [re'stɔ:ɹ], *v.t.* restaurar, rehacer, restituir, devolver, retornar, reparar, reedificar, reconstruir, restablecer, recuperar; reintegrar; compensar, resarcir; *to restore to life,* devolver la vida a.
restorer, *s.* restaurador, restituidor, reparador.
restrain [re'strein], *v.t.* restriñir, restringir, apretar, contener, reprimir, detener, refrenar, enfrenar, constreñir, limitar, impedir, coartar, coercer; (*der.*) vedar, prohibir.
restrainable, *a.* restringible.
restraint, *s.* refrenamiento, constreñimiento, freno, sujeción, limitación, cohibición, prohibición, coerción, restricción.
restrict [re'strikt], *v.t.* restringir, limitar, coartar.
restriction [re'strikʃən], *s.* restricción, coartación, limitación.
restrictive, *a.* restrictivo.
restringency, *s.* restringencia.
restringent [re'strindʒənt], *a.* restringente, restriñente.
result [re'zʌlt], *v.i.* resultar, inferirse, seguirse; *to result in,* acabar por, terminar en, venir a parar en. — *s.* resultado, resulta, consecuencia, efecto, conclusión, fin.
resultance, *s.* resultancia, resultado.
resultant, *s.* consecuencia, resultado; (*mec.*) resultante. — *a.* resultante.
resultant, resulting, *a.* resultante; *resulting use,* (*for.*) usufructo resultante.
resumable [re'zju:məbəl], *a.* que se puede reasumir.
resume [re'zju:m], *v.t.* reasumir, empezar de nuevo, reanudar; recobrar, recuperar, reocupar; *to resume one's seat,* volver a ocupar su asiento. — *v.i.* seguir, continuar, tomar el hilo.
résumé ['rezju:mei], *s.* resumen, sumario, recapitulación.
resumption [re'zʌmʃən], *s.* reasunción.
resumptive, *a.* reasuntivo.
resupinate [ri'sju:pineit], *a.* (*bot.*) boca arriba, supino.
resupination, *s.* posición supina.
resurge [re'sə:ɹdʒ], *v.i.* resurgir, volver a alzarse.
resurgence, *s.* resurrección.
resurgent [re'sə:ɹdʒənt], *a.* resurrecto.
resurrect [rezə'rekt], *v.t.* resucitar; (*fam.*) exhumar, desenterrar.
resurrection [rezə'rekʃən], *s.* resurrección.
resurrectionist, *s.* resurreccionista, *m.f.*, desenterrador de cadáveres.
re-survey [ri:sə:ɹ'vei], *s.* revisión. — *v.t.* volver a ver, rever.
resuscitate [re'sʌsiteit], *v.t.* resucitar.
resuscitation, *s.* resurrección, renovación, renacimiento.
resuscitator, *s.* resucitador.
ret [ret], *v.t.* embalsar; enriar (cáñamo o lino).
retable [re'teibəl], *s.* retablo.

retail ['ri:teil], *v.t.* vender por menor, vender al menudeo, revender, regatonear; contar; repetir. — *s.* venta por menor, reventa, menudeo; *by retail*, a la menuda. — *a.* por menor.

retailer, *s.* vendedor al por menor; narrador.

retailment, *s.* venta por menor.

retain [re'tein], *v.t.* retener, guardar, quedarse con; conservar; ajornalar, contratar; (*der.*) ajustar (a un abogado).

retainable, *a.* que se puede retener.

retainer, *s.* partidario, adherente; criado, dependiente, asistente; retenedor; miembro de una comitiva; honorario.

retaining, *a.* que retiene, que conserva; *retaining fee,* honorario; *retaining wall,* pared de sostén, muro de apoyo.

re-take, *v.t.* volver a tomar.

re-taking, *s.* acto de volver a tomar.

retaliate [re'tælieit], *v.t.*, *v.i.* talionar, desquitarse, vengarse, pagar en la misma moneda; usar de represalias.

retaliation, *s.* desquite, despique, desagravio, represalias, satisfacción.

retaliative [re'tæliətiv], **retaliatory** [retæli-'eitəri], *a.* vengativo, que se venga, que usa de represalias.

retard [re'ta:ɹd], *v.t.* retardar, detener, diferir, atrasar, retrasar, aplazar, demorar, dilatar.

retard, retardation, retardment, *s.* retardo, retardación, atraso, retraso.

retardative, retardatory, *a.* retardador.

retarder, *s.* retardador.

retch [ri:tʃ, retʃ], *v.i.* arquear, tener bascas, esforzarse para vomitar.

re-tell [ri:'tel], *v.t.* repetir, volver a narrar.

retention [re'tenʃən], *s.* retención, conservación, retentiva, memoria; (*med.*) retención (de orina, etc.).

retentive, *a.* retentivo.

retentiveness, *s.* retentiva, tenacidad.

reticence, *s.* reticencia, reserva.

reticent ['retisənt], *a.* reticente, reservado, discreto.

reticle ['retikəl], *s.* retículo.

reticular [re'tikju:ləɹ], *a.* reticular.

reticulate, *v.t.*, *v.i.* formar a modo de red.

reticulated, *a.* reticular, trenado.

reticulation, *s.* disposición reticular.

reticule ['retikju:l], *s.* retículo, redecilla; bolsa.

reticulum [re'tikju:ləm], *s.* retículo; (*zool.*) redecilla.

retiform ['retifɔ:ɹm], *a.* retiforme, reticular.

retina ['retinə], *s.* retina.

retinalite ['retinəlait], *s.* retinalita.

retinoscopy [reti'nɔskopi], *s.* examen de la retina con el oftalmoscopio.

retinue ['retinju:], *s.* comitiva, tren, acompañamiento, séquito.

retiral [re'taiərəl], *s.* (*com.*) recogida.

retire [re'taiəɹ], *v.i.* retirarse, irse a acostar; dejar un empleo; volver atrás, retroceder; refugiarse, recogerse, separarse, apartarse; retraerse; jubilarse; *to retire from business,* retirarse de los negocios. — *v.t.* (*com.*) recoger, retirar de la circulación; separar, apartar; jubilar. — *s.* (*ant.*) retiro.

retired, *a.* retirado; aislado, apartado; retraído; (*com.*) recogido; jubilado, retirado. — *p.p.* [RETIRE]; *retired life,* vida retirada o solitaria; *to put on the retired list,* dar el retiro a, jubilar.

retiredness, *s.* retiro, soledad, recogimiento.

retirement, *s.* retiramiento, retiro; lugar apartado, lugar retirado; retraimiento; jubilación.

retiring, *a.* retraído, reservado, recatado, austero; prudente, discreto, modesto; referente a la jubilación.

retorsion [re'tɔ:ɹʃən], *s.* represalia.

retort [re'tɔ:ɹt], *v.i.* replicar. — *v.t.* retorcer; devolver (una acusación, etc.), rechazar. — *s.* redargüición; réplica mordaz; (*quím.*) retorta, destilador.

retorter, *s.* el que replica, rechaza, etc.

retortion, *s.* retorcedura, retorcimiento, retorsión; represalia.

retouch [ri:'tʌtʃ], *v.t.* volver a tocar, retocar, limar, modificar, pulir; (*foto.*) retocar. — *s.* retoque, última mano; *retouching frame,* bastidor de retocar.

retoucher, *s.* (*foto.*) retocador.

retrace [ri:'treis], *v.t.* desandar, volver atrás, volver a seguir las huellas, seguir las huellas retrocediendo; repasar un trazado; buscar el origen; relatar, narrar; representar a la memoria una cosa pasada; *to retrace one's steps,* volver sobre sus pasos.

retract [re'trækt], *v.t.* retractar, retirar, encoger, retraer. — *v.i.* retractarse, desdecirse, cantar la palinodia; encogerse.

retractable, retractible, *a.* retractable; retráctil.

retractation [retræk'teiʃən], **retraction** [re-'trækʃən], *s.* retracción; retractación; contracción.

retractile [re'træktail], *a.* retráctil.

retractive, *a.* que tiende a retractar.

retractor, *s.* el que o lo que retracta; (*anat.*) músculo contractor; (*cir.*) retractor; (*armas de fuego*) expulsor.

retreat [re'tri:t], *s.* retiro, soledad, retraimiento; asilo, refugio; (*mil.*) retirada; retreta; receso; (*igl.*) retiro. — *v.i.* (*mil.*) retirarse, batirse en retirada; cejar; retroceder; escaparse, refugiarse; retraerse; (*esgr.*) dar un paso atrás; apartarse.

retrench [re'trentʃ], *v.t.* cercenar, acortar, cortar, abreviar, disminuir; podar, mondar; (*mil.*) atrincherar. — *v.i.* reducirse, economizar, vivir con economía, ahorrar, cercenar los gastos.

retrenchment, *s.* cercenadura, cercenamiento; rebaja, diminución; economía; (*mil.*) trinchera, atrincheramiento.

retrial [ri:'traiəl], *s.* (*for.*) nuevo proceso; revisión.

retribute [re'tribju:t], *v.t.* retribuir, recompensar, dar en pago.

retribution [retri'bju:ʃən], *s.* retribución, pago, recompensa; pena incurrida, justo castigo; (*teol.*) la distribución de premios y castigos en la vida futura.

retributive, retributory, *a.* retribuyente.

retrievability, retrievableness, *s.* posibilidad de recuperación, estado de los que pueden repararse.

retrievable [re'tri:vəbəl], *a.* recuperable; reparable.

retrieval [re'tri:vəl], *s.* cobranza, recobro, recuperación; reintegración.

retrieve [re'tri:v], *v.t.* recuperar, resarcirse, recobrar, volver a ganar, desquitarse; remediar, reparar, componer, restaurar, restablecer; cobrar (la caza); revocar; *to* *retrieve one's fortunes,* levantar la cabeza. — *v.i.* cobrar la caza.

retriever, *s.* perro cobrador; sabueso, perdiguero.

retroact [retro'ækt], *v.i.* tener fuerza retroactiva.

retroaction, *s.* (*for.*) retroactividad.

retroactive, *a.* retroactivo.

retrocede [retro'si:d], *v.t.* (*for.*) hacer retrocesión, devolver. — *v.i.* retroceder, recular.

retrocession [retro'seʃən], *s.* (*for.*) retrocesión; retroceso.

retroflex ['retrofleks], *a.* doblado hacia atrás.

retroflexion, *s.* repliegue, inflexión hacia atrás.

retrogradation, *s.* retrogradación.

retrograde ['retrogreid], *a.* retrógrado; opuesto, contrario. — *v.i.* retrogradar, desandar, retroceder.

retrogression [retro'greʃən], *s.* retrogradación; (*med.*) retroceso; regresión; (*astr.*) retrogradación.

retrogressive, *a.* retrógrado.

retrospect ['retrospekt], *s.* mirada retrospectiva, reflexión sobre el pasado; *in retrospect,* retrospectivamente.

retrospection [retro'spekʃən], *s.* retrospección.

retrospective, *a.* retrospectivo.

retroussé [re'tru:sei], *a.* respingado.

retroversion, *s.* inclinación hacia atrás.

retrovert [retro'və:t], *v.t.* desviar (un órgano) hacia atrás.

retry [ri:'trai], *v.t.* (*for.*) rever, repasar.

return [re'tə:n], *v.t.* volver, devolver, remitir, transmitir, volver a enviar, restituir; dar en cambio, recompensar; agradecer, reconocer (un favor, etc.); pagar, corresponder (a), retribuir, retornar; dar, rendir; producir (utilidad); (*pol.*) elegir, anunciar como elegido; *to return a kindness,* corresponder a un beneficio; *to return answer,* contestar, dar respuesta; *to return thanks,* dar las gracias; *to return good for evil,* devolver bien por mal; *to return a verdict,* dar o pronunciar un fallo. — *v.i.* volver, retornar, regresar, recurrir; repetir, reiterar; reaparecer, presentarse de nuevo; redargüir, reponer, responder, replicar; (*for.*) revertir; volver al estado anterior; volver de nuevo, dar otra vuelta. — *s.* vuelta, retorno, regreso; torna, pago, paga, recompensa, satisfacción, retribución, correspondencia (a un favor, etc.); respuesta, redargüición, réplica; restablecimiento, restitución, devolución, reinstalación; ganancia, provecho, utilidad, rédito; reaparición; repetición; estado; relación, informe oficial; retorno, cambio, trueque, intercambio, revolución; recaída; curva, vuelta, desviación; (*arq.*) ala; vuelta de moldura, marco, etc.; (*for.*) diligencia; (*pol.*) elección; lista, padrón, censo. — *pl.* tablas estadísticas; resultados (electorales); *in return,* en cambio, en recíproca correspondencia; *election return,* resultado del escrutinio; *return ticket,* billete de ida y vuelta; *by return of post,* a vuelta de correo; *return day,* (*for.*) día en el que el demandado debe comparecer en el juzgado.

returnable, *a.* devolutivo; que se puede devolver; restituible, reintegrable; (*for.*) devolutorio, restitutorio; devolutivo.

returner, *s.* el que devuelve.

returning-officer, *s.* oficial que preside en una elección.

retuse [re'tju:s], *a.* achatado.

reunion [ri:'ju:niən], *s.* reunión, *f.*; reconciliación; junta; tertulia.

reunite [ri:ju:'nait], *v.t.* reunir, juntar; reconciliar. — *v.i.* reunirse, reconciliarse, juntarse.

revamp, *v.t.* (*zap.*) remontar.

reveal [re'vi:l], *v.t.* revelar, descubrir, manifestar, mostrar, enseñar, divulgar, publicar.

revealer, *s.* revelador.

reveille [re'væli], *s.* (*mil.*) diana.

revel ['revəl], *v.i.* jaranear, ir de parranda, andar en borracheras; gozarse, divertirse con gran algazara. — *s.* algazara, jarana, francachela, borrachera; *to hold high revel,* retozar con el verde.

revelation [reve'leiʃən], *s.* revelación; Apocalipsis.

reveller ['revelər], *s.* calavera, *m.*, borrasquero; trasnochador; juerguista, *m.f.*

revelry ['revəlri], *s.* jarana, francachela, borrachera, algazara, juerga.

revenant ['revenənt], *s.* fantasma, *m.*; uno que vuelve.

revendication [ri:vendi'keiʃən], *s.* reivindicación.

revenge [re'vendʒ], *v.t., v.i.* vengar, vindicar, vengarse (de); tomar satisfacción (de). — *s.* venganza; despique, desquite, desagravio.

revengeful, *a.* vengativo, vindicativo.

revengefulness, *s.* venganza, ansia de vengarse, encono; carácter vengativo.

revengeless, *a.* sin venganza, no vengado.

revenger, *s.* vengador.

revengingly, *adv.* con venganza.

revenue ['revenju:], *s.* rentas públicas; (*com.*) rédito; entrada, ingreso, provento; rédito; beneficio, recompensa; *revenue officer,* aduanero, empleado de aduana; *revenue cutter,* (*mar.*) guardacostas, *m.,* escampavía, *f.;* *Inland Revenue,* delegación de contribuciones.

reverberant [re'və:rbərənt], *a.* repercusivo; resonante, retumbante.

reverberate [re'və:rbəreit], *v.t., v.i.* resonar, repercutir, rechazar, retumbar; reflejar, reverberar.

reverberation, *s.* retumbo, eco; reflexión, reverberación.

reverberator, *s.* reverberador, reverbero.

reverberatory, *a.* de reverbero, que reverbera o refleja. — *s.* horno de reverbero.

revere [re'viər], *v.t.* reverenciar, respetar, venerar, honrar, acatar.

reverence ['reverəns], *s.* reverencia, respeto; veneración; acatamiento; (*igl.*) Reverencia (título y tratamiento); reverencia (inclinación del cuerpo); *saving your reverence,* con perdón de Vd.; *to do* (o *pay*) *reverence,* rendir homenaje; *saving your reverence,* (*fam.*) salvo vuestro respeto. — *v.t.* reverenciar, venerar, honrar, respetar.

reverencer, *s.* reverenciador.

reverend ['reverənd], *a.* reverendo, venerable; (*igl.*) Reverendo (título y tratamiento); *most reverend, right reverend,* Ilustrísimo, Reverendísimo.

reverent ['reverənt], *a.* reverente; humilde, sumiso, respetuoso.

reverential [reve'renʃəl], *a.* reverencial, respetuoso.

reverer [re'viərər], *s.* venerador.

reverie ['reveri], *s.* ensueño; arrobamiento, embelesamiento; (*mús.*) fantasía.

revers [re'viɔɹ], *s.* vueltas, solapas (de una chaqueta, etc.).

reversal [re'vɔːɹsəl], *s.* reversión, trastrocamiento, inversión; (*ópt.*) cambio de una línea obscura en una brillante y viceversa; (*for.*) revocación.

reverse, *v.t.* trastrocar, preposterar, invertir, volver al revés, volver lo de arriba abajo; trastornar, voltear, volcar; (*mec.*) poner en marcha atrás; dar contravapor; (*for.*) revocar, abolir, anular. — *v.i.* cambiarse en lo contrario o volver a un estado anterior. — *a.* inverso, reverso, invertido; contrario, opuesto; (*mec.*) de marcha atrás. — *s.* lo contrario, lo opuesto; reversión, inversión; dorso, respaldo, revés, reverso; descalabro, contratiempo, mudanza, vicisitud; marcha atrás; *quite the reverse,* muy al contrario; *reverse-gear,* marcha atrás; *reverse-operation,* (*mat.*) operación inversa; *reverse-turn,* (*mec.*) cambio de dirección.

reversedly [re'vɔːɹsedli], **reversely** [re'vɔːɹsli], *adv.* al revés, con lo de arriba abajo.

reverseless, *a.* que no se puede trastrocar o invertir.

reversible [re'vɔːɹsəbəl], *a.* volvible, reversible; versátil; de dos caras; de vaivén; (*mec.*) reversible; (*for.*) revocable. — *s.* (*tej.*) género de dos caras.

reversing, *a.*, *s.*; *reversing gear,* aparato de cambio de marcha; *reversing key,* (*elec.*) inversor.

reversion [re'vɔːɹʃən], *s.* reversión; futura, derecho de sucesión (de un cargo).

reversionary, *a.* (*for.*) reversible.

reversioner, *s.* el que tiene derecho de reversión.

revert [re'vɔːɹt], *v.i.* retroceder, volverse atrás, resurtir, volver, recudir; (*for.*) revertir; (*biol.*) saltar atrás.

revertible, *a.* reversible.

revest [ri:'vest], *v.t.* revestir, volver a vestir; restablecer.

revestiary [re'vestiəri], *s.* guardarropa; (*igl.*) sacristía.

revet [re'vet], *v.t.* (*alb.*) revestir.

revetment, *s.* revestimiento.

revictual [ri:'vitəl], *v.t.* volver a proveer de víveres.

review [re'vju:], *v.t.* rever, ver de nuevo, remirar; criticar, examinar, analizar, revisar, repasar; escribir una reseña de (un libro); (*mil.*) pasar revista, revistar. — *v.i.* escribir una revista. — *s.* revista, repaso, examen, escrutinio, segunda vista, análisis, *m.f.*; revista (publicación periódica); reseña, juicio crítico; repaso; (*mil.*) revista, parada; (*for.*) revisión.

reviewer, *s.* crítico, revistero; examinador, inspector; revisor.

revigorate [ri:'vigoreit], *v.t.* vigorizar de nuevo.

revile [re'vail], *v.t.* vituperar, ultrajar, injuriar, denigrar, despreciar, disfamar, denostar, vilipendiar.

revilement, *s.* contumelia, ultraje, oprobio, denuesto, vilipendio.

reviler, *s.* vilipendiador, injuriador, denostador.

revilingly, *adv.* injuriosamente, con oprobio, afrentosamente.

revindicate [ri:'vindikeit], *v.t.* reivindicar.

revisal [re'vaizəl], *s.* revisión, revista.

revise [re'vaiz], *v.t.* repasar, rever, volver a examinar, releer; limar, revisar, corregir.

revise, *s.* revista, revisión; (*impr.*) segunda prueba; *second revise,* tercera prueba.

revised, *a.* revisado, corregido. — *p.p.* [REVISE]; *Revised Version,* traducción (corregida) de la Biblia del año 1870–84.

reviser, revisor, *s.* revisor, superintendente, examinador; (*impr.*) corrector de pruebas.

revision [re'viʒən], *s.* repaso, revisión; (*impr.*) corrección de pruebas.

revisit [ri:'vizit], *v.t.* volver a visitar, visitar de nuevo.

revisory [re'vaizəri], *a.* revisor.

revitalize [ri:'vaitəlaiz], *v.t.* revivificar, vivificar de nuevo.

revival [re'vaivəl], *s.* renacimiento, restablecimiento, restauración; despertamiento religioso; (*teat.*) representación de obras antiguas.

revivalist, *s.* predicador protestante que recorre un país para despertar la fe.

revive [re'vaiv], *v.t.* dar nueva vida a, hacer revivir, restablecer, revivificar, restaurar, renovar; animar, excitar; dar nuevo vigor a, despertar, avigorar; hacer recordar; despertar la memoria. — *v.i.* revivir; reanimarse, renovarse, resucitar, restablecerse; volver a vivir, volver en sí, recobrar los sentidos; florecer de nuevo, renacer.

reviver, *s.* vivificador.

revivification [ri:vivifi'keiʃən], *s.* vivificación, revivificación.

revivify [ri:'vivifai], *v.t.* revivificar, hacer revivir. — *v.i.* restablecer, revivir.

revocable ['revokəbəl], *a.* revocable.

revocableness, *s.* calidad de revocable.

revocation [revo'keiʃən], *s.* revocación; derogación.

revoke [re'vouk], *v.t.* revocar, abolir, anular, derogar, cancelar. — *v.i.* (en los juegos de naipes) hacer un renuncio.

revolt [re'voult], *v.i.* levantarse, rebelarse, amotinarse, sublevarse; desertar, volver casaca; sentir repugnación o repulsión. — *v.t.* rebelar, sublevar, revolucionar; chocar, repugnar, irritar, indignar. — *s.* revuelta, levantamiento, sublevación, deserción, rebelión, *f.*

revolter, *s.* rebelde, amotinado, sublevado, desertor.

revolting, *a.* odioso, repugnante, irritante, chocante.

revolute ['revolju:t], *a.* (*bot.*) enrollado hacia atrás.

revolution [revo'lu:ʃən], *s.* revolución; ciclo; rotación, mudanza violenta, alteración, vuelta, giro; (*mec.*) revolución, vuelta.

revolutionary, revolutionist, *s., a.* revolucionario.

revolutionize, *v.t.* revolucionar, sublevar.

revolvable, *a.* giratorio.

revolve [re'vɔlv], *v.i.* revolverse, moverse circularmente, rodar; girar, dar vueltas; suceder periódicamente. — *v.t.* voltear, hacer girar o rodar, arrollar, revolver; dar vueltas sobre un eje; discurrir, meditar, ponderar.

revolver [re'vɔlvəɹ], *s.* revólver.

revolving, *a.* giratorio.

revulsion [re'vʌlʃən], s. revulsión, cambio repentino, reacción; reculada; apartamiento, removimiento, retroceso; (*med.*) revulsión, reacción.

revulsive [re'vʌlsiv], a. (*med.*) revulsivo, revulsorio.

reward [re'wɔːɹd], v.t. premiar, galardonar, retribuir, recompensar, remunerar, gratificar. — s. premio, galardón, recompensa; pago, gratificación, retribución, remuneración; castigo merecido.

rewardable, a. remunerable, digno de premio.

rewarder, s. gratificador, premiador, remunerador.

reweigh [riː'wei], v.t. repesar.

reword [riː'wəːɹd], v.t. expresar de otra manera.

reynard ['reinɑːɹd], s. zorro.

rhapontic [ra'pɔntik], s. rapóntico.

rhapsodist, s. autor de rapsodias; rapsodista, m.f.

rhapsodize ['ræpsodaiz], v.t., v.i. cantar o recitar rapsodias.

rhapsody ['ræpsodi], s. rapsodia.

rhea ['riːə], s. avestruz de la América del Sur.

Rhenish ['reniʃ], a. del Rin. — s. vino del Rin.

rheometer [riː'ɔmetəɹ], s. reómetro.

rheophore ['riːofoːɹ], s. reóforo.

rheostat ['riostæt], s. reóstato.

rhesus ['riːsəs], s. uno de los macacos, mono de la India.

rhetoric ['retorik], s. retórica.

rhetorical [re'tɔrikəl], a. retórico.

rhetorician, s. retórico.

rheum [ruːm], s. (*ant.*) reuma, fluxión, destilación, corrimiento; (*bot.*) género de plantas que comprende el ruibarbo.

rheumatic [ruː'mætik], a. reumático.

rheumatism [ruːmə'tizm], s. reumatismo.

rheumy ['ruːmi], a. catarroso; legañoso (los ojos); (*fig.*) húmedo.

rhinitis [rai'naitis], s. rinitis, f., romadizo, catarro nasal.

rhinoceri(c)al [raino'serikəl], **rhinocerotic** [rainose'rɔtik], a. rinoceróntico.

rhinoceros [rai'nɔsərəs], s. rinoceronte; *female rhinoceros*, abada.

rhinoplastic [raino'plæstik], a. rinoplástico.

rhinoplasty, s. rinoplastia.

rhizome ['raizoum], **rhizoma** [rai'zoumə], s. rizoma.

rhizopod ['raizopɔd], s. animal rizópodo.

rhodium ['roudiəm], s. rodio.

rhododendron [roudo'dendrɔn], s. rododendro.

rhomb [rɔmb], **rhombus** ['rɔmbəs], s. rombo; (*blas.*) losange.

rhombic, a. rombal, que tiene figura de rombo.

rhombohedron [rombo'hiːdrən], s. romboedro.

rhomboid ['rɔmbɔid], s. romboide.

rhomboidal, a. romboidal.

rhubarb ['ruːbɑːɹb], s. ruibarbo.

rhumb [rʌmb], s. (*mar.*) rumbo.

rhyme [raim], s. rima, consonancia, consonante; verso, poesía; *without rhyme or reason*, sin ton ni son, a tontas y a locas, sin qué ni por qué, sin pies ni cabeza. — v.t., v.i. hacer versos, componer versos, versificar; rimar, metrificar, armonizarse.

rhymer, rhymester, versificador, rimador, poetastro, versista, m.f.

rhythm [riðm], s. ritmo, cadencia, medida; (*med.*) periodicidad; armonía.

rhythmic ['riðmik], **rhythmical** ['riðmikəl], a. rítmico, con ritmo, cadencioso, armónico.

rib [rib], s. costilla; (*mec.*) pestaña, reborde; (*bot.*) nervadura de las hojas; (*mar.*) cuaderna; (*mar.*) ligazón, f.; (*arq.*) faja, listón, nervadura, nervio; viga de tejado, cabrio; varilla (de paraguas); tirante, varenga de hierro; (*pl.*) *ribs of a ship*, (*mar.*) costillaje. — v.t. encarrujar; afianzar con rebordes a pestañas; marcar con rayas, listones o filetes; (*cost.*) hacer un vivo.

ribald ['ribald], a. obsceno, ribaldo, lascivo, lujurioso. — s. persona impúdica.

ribaldry ['ribaldri], s. ribaldería, escabrosidad, indecencia.

riband ['ribənd], s. cinta, listón. — v.t. encintar, adornar con cintas.

rib-bands, ribbands, s.pl. (*mar.*) bagaras.

ribbed [ribd], s. encarrujado, guarnecido de costillas.

ribbon ['ribən], s. cinta, listón, colonia; galón; faja, tira, banda. — pl. (*fam.*) riendas; perifollos; *baby ribbon*, cintilla angosta; *ribbon grass*, (*bot.*) alpiste. — v.t. encintar. — a. hecho de cinta; de forma de cinta.

ribwort ['ribwəːɹt], s. llantén, arta, plantaina.

rice [rais], s. arroz; *rice bird*, (*orn.*) pajarito americano que se cría en los arrozales; *rice field*, arrozal; *rice paper*, papel de paja de arroz; papel de China; *rice-pudding*, arroz con leche.

rich [ritʃ], a. rico, opulento, adinerado, pudiente, acaudalado; abundante, copioso, caudaloso, caro, costoso, precioso, valioso, suntuoso, de valor; fértil, opimo, feraz, pingüe; empalagoso; rico, sabroso, muy sazonado, suculento; excelente, exquisito; (*fam.*) jocoso, gracioso, divertido o ridículo; *rich hues*, matices vivos; *rich wine*, vino generoso.

riches ['ritʃiz], s.pl. riqueza, caudales, opulencia, abundancia de bienes; magnificencia, pompa.

richness, s. riqueza, opulencia; fertilidad; primor, magnificencia, suntuosidad; abundancia, copia; riqueza, suculencia; pinguosidad, crasitud.

rick [rik], s. niara, almiar, hacina. — v.t. hacer niaras o hacinas.

rickets ['rikits], s. raquitis, f., raquitismo.

rickety ['rikiti], a. desvencijado, destartalado; tambaleante; (*med.*) raquítico.

rickshaw ['rikʃɔː], s. riksha, carruaje ligero.

ricochet ['rikoʃei], v.t. hacer fuego de rebote. — v.i. rebotar. — s. rebote.

rictus ['riktəs], s. abertura, anchura de la boca abierta en un hombre o animal; (*bot.*) la apertura de una corola de doble labio.

rid [rid], v.t. (*pret.* **ridded, rid**; *p.p.* **rid**) desembarazar, desocupar, quitar de encima, librar, zafar; (*ant.*) libertar, redimir; *to be rid of*, estar libre o exento de, deshacerse de; *to rid oneself of, to get rid of*, desembarazarse de, librarse de, deshacerse de, zafarse de.

riddance ['ridəns], s. libramiento; zafada.

ridden, p.p. [RIDE].

riddle ['ridəl], s. acertijo, adivinanza, enigma, m.; misterio; quisicosa; garbillo, harnero,

criba, cribo. — *v.t.* resolver o desatar enigmas, garbillar, cribar, adivinar acertijos; acribillar. — *v.i.* hablar enigmáticamente.
riddler, *s.* garbillador.
riddling, *s.* cribadura. — *a.* enigmático, obscuro.
ride [raid], *v.t.* (*pret.* **rode;** *p.p.* **ridden**) cabalgar, correr, dirigir o manejar (un caballo, etc.); ir montado en o sobre; hender o surcar las olas; (*fig.*) oprimir, tiranizar, dominar (a). — *v.i.* montar a caballo, cabalgar, dar un paseo (a caballo o en carruaje), andar o ir en coche; (*mar.*) estar fondeado; flotar; (*mec.*) rodar, tener juego, funcionar; *to ride out,* (*mar.*) luchar felizmente contra una tempestad; *to ride at anchor,* (*mar.*) estar fondeado; *to ride on shanks' mare,* (*fam.*) andar a pie; *to ride easy,* mantenerse bien al ancla; *to ride down,* atropellar, pisotear, pasar por encima; *to ride roughshod* (*over*), pisotear; mandar a puntapiés (a). — *s.* paseo (a caballo o en coche); camino de herradura.
rider, *s.* caballero, jinete, cabalgador; picador; biciclista, *m.f.*; ruante; hojuela pegada a un documento; cosa que va montada sobre otra; (*mar.*) sobreplán, *f.*, cochinata; añadidura; corolario.
riders, *s.pl.* (*mar.*) sobreplanes, *f.pl.*
ridge [ridʒ], *s.* espinazo, lomo; cerro, colina, loma, serranía, cadena de colinas, serrijón; (*agr.*) caballón, camellón, lomo; costurón, arruga; (*arq.*) caballete del tejado; arrecife, escollo. — *v.t.* (*agr.*) alomar; acanalar, arrugar, encaballar; formar lomas o camellones, o surcos; *ridge pole,* (*arq.*) parhilera; madero horizontal de una tienda de campaña; *ridge piece, ridge plate,* (*arq.*) cima, cumbre, *f.*
ridgel [ʹridʒəl], *s.* ciclán.
ridgy, *a.* surcado, acanalado, hecho a surcos; desigual.
ridicule [ʹridikjuːl], *s.* ridículo, burla, irrisión; extravagancia, ridiculez. — *v.t.* ridiculizar, befar, escarnecer, poner en ridículo, tornar en ridículo; hacer mofa de alguien.
ridiculous [riʹdikjuːləs], *a.* ridículo, grotesco, extravagante, risible, estrambótico.
ridiculousness, *s.* calidad o estado de ridículo.
riding [ʹraidiŋ], *s.* acción de andar a caballo o en coche, paseo, excursión (a caballo o en coche); camino de herradura; cabalgata; manejo, equitación; movimiento, marcha (de un vehículo); comarca. — *a.* que se emplea para caminar a caballo o en coche; (*mar.*) fondeado, al ancla; *riding-habit,* traje de amazona, vestido de montar; *riding-cloak, riding-coat,* redingote; *riding-school,* escuela de equitación; *riding-hood,* capirote o capucho, gabán; *riding-whip,* látigo de montar; *riding-boots,* botas de montar.
ridotto [riʹdɔtou], *s.* (*ant.*) sarao, baile (esp. de máscaras).
rife [raif], *a.* abundante, corriente, numeroso, común; que domina, que reina.
rifeness, *s.* abundancia.
riffle [ʹrifəl], *s.* (*min.*) ranura en el fondo de una gamella.
riffler, *s.* escofina encorvada.
riff-raff [ʹrifræf], *s.* gentuza, canalla; desperdicio, desecho.
rifle [ʹraifəl], *s.* carabina, rifle; especie de piedra de afilar guadañas. — *pl.* tropas

armadas con rifles; *rifle-pits,* pozos para rifleros; *rifle-shot,* fusilazo; tiro de fusil. — *v.t.* robar, pillar; rayar (una arma).
rifleman [ʹraifəlmən], *s.* carabinero, riflero, fusilero.
rifler, *s.* saqueador, salteador, pillador, robador.
rift [rift], *s.* hendedura, grieta, rendija, reventón; desemboque, cuarteadura, vado; ola que lame la playa. — *v.t.* hender, dividir. — *v.i.* reventar, partirse, regoldar.
rig [rig], *v.t.* (con *out*) ataviar, asear, adornar, guarnir; (*mar.*) enjarciar; (con *out* o *up*) aparejar, equipar; *to rig the market,* manipular el mercado para hacer subir o bajar los precios a capricho. — *s.* (*fam.*) traje; tren de carruaje o caballos; burla, mala partida; (*mar.*) apresto, equipo; aparato de pesca; (*mar.*) aparejo; mujercilla.
rigadoon [rigəʹduːn], *s.* rigodón.
rigescent [riʹdʒesənt], *a.* volviéndose rígido, tieso o entumecido.
rigger [ʹrigə], *s.* (*mar.*) aparejador.
rigging [ʹrigiŋ], *s.* (*mar.*) aparejo, jarcia, cordaje, maniobra, maniobras, enjarciadura, cordelería; *rigging-loft,* (*teat.*) telar.
riggish, *a.* lascivo.
right [rait], *a.* recto; correcto; razonable; cierto, real, verdadero; legal; moral; genuino; propio, conveniente; apropiado; derecho, directo, en línea recta; sano, en buen estado; ordenado, ajustado; derecho (contrario de izquierdo); cuerdo; bien dispuesto, bien arreglado; derecho (contrario de revés, en las telas); *to be right,* tener razón; *right hand* o *right hand man,* brazo derecho; *to be in one's right mind,* estar en su juicio. — *adv.* rectamente, perfectamente, cabalmente; justamente, exactamente, correctamente; debidamente; precisamente, derechamente; muy; al instante, ahora mismo, inmediatamente; *right honourable,* excelentísimo, muy respetable, muy honorable; *right reverend,* reverendísimo; *right or wrong,* a tuertas o a derechas; *to put right,* poner en orden, poner en el camino derecho. — *s.* derecho, ley moral, *f.*, rectitud, equidad, justicia; razón, *f.*; título, dominio, propiedad; autoridad, poder; prerrogativa, privilegio; la derecha (opuesto a la izquierda); *by right(s),* en derecho; *to the right,* a la derecha; *to rights,* derecho, derechamente; *to put* (o *set*) *to rights,* poner en orden, componer. — *v.t.* hacer justicia a; poner en el camino derecho; enderezar.
righteous [ʹraitʃəs], *a.* justo, equitativo; recto; moral, honrado, virtuoso.
righteousness, *s.* rectitud, equidad, justicia, virtud, honradez.
righter [ʹraitə], *s.* enderezador de tuertos o agravios; persona que hace justicia.
rightful, *a.* legítimo, recto, justo, equitativo.
rightfulness, *s.* derechura; equidad, rectitud, justicia.
right-handed [raitʹhænded], *a.* que se sirve de la mano derecha; *right-handed screw,* tornillo de rosca a la derecha.
right-minded, *a.* honrado, recto; prudente.
rightness, *s.* rectitud, justicia; derechura.
rigid [ʹridʒid], *a.* inflexible, rígido, tieso; exacto, preciso, estricto; austero, rigoroso, severo; yerto.
rigidity [riʹdʒiditi], **rigidness** [ʹridʒidnes], *s.*

rigidez, tesura, inflexibilidad; rigor, austeridad; tosquedad, terquedad, falta de gracia.

rigmarole ['rigmǝroul], *s.* jerigonza, galimatías, *m.*; monserga.

rigor, rigour ['rigǝɹ], *s.* rigor, inflexibilidad, tesura; dureza, inclemencia, austeridad, severidad; rigor, escrupulosidad, exactitud; terquedad, tesón; (*med.*) escalofrío.

rigorism ['rigorizm], *s.* rigorismo.

rigorist, *s.* rigorista, *m.f.*

rigorous ['rigorǝs], *a.* riguroso, estricto, duro, inclemente, severo, inflexible.

rigorousness, *s.* severidad, rigurosidad, rigor.

rile [rail], *v.t.* (*fam.*) sulfurar, irritar, encolerizar.

rill [ril], *s.* riachuelo, arroyuelo.

rillet ['rilet], *s.* arroyuelo, reguero.

rim [rim], *s.* canto, margen, borde, orilla; cerco, reborde, arco; llanta, aro; (*mar.*) la superficie del mar.

rime [raim], *s.* [RHYME]; *rime* es la forma menos usada, aunque correcta.

rime, *s.* escarcha. — *v.t.* cubrir con escarcha.

rimose, rimous ['raimǝs], *a.* hendido, agrietado, rajado.

rimple ['rimpǝl], *v.t.* arrugar, hacer pliegues. — *s.* arruga, pliegue.

rimy ['raimi], *a.* escarchado, blanco con escarcha.

rind [raind], *s.* corteza, pellejo o piel de ciertas frutas, hollejo; piel, *f.* — *v.t.* mondar, descortezar, deshollejar, quitar el hollejo, pelar.

rinderpest ['rindǝɹpest], *s.* morriña.

ring [riŋ], *s.* anillo; círculo, faja circular, circunferencia, aro, cerco, anilla, argolla, virola; circo, arena, escena de un espectáculo; redondel, liza; (*joy.*) sortija; cintillo, ojera; camarilla; corro o corrillo de gente; juego de campanas, repique o tañido de campanas, campaneo, campanilleo, toque de campanilla; susurro, rumor, estruendo, ruido, clamor; sonido metálico; (*mar.*) arganeo, virola con chaveta; *wedding ring,* anillo (o sortija) de matrimonio; *ear ring,* zarcillo; *ring dove,* paloma torcaz, zurita o zorita; *seal ring,* sortija que sirve de sello; *ring finger,* dedo anular; *ring bone,* (*vet.*) sobrehueso de caballo. — *v.t.* (*p.p.* y *pret.* **ringed**) rodear, circundar, cercar; formar un corro alrededor de, anillar, ensortijar; poner un anillo; adornar con anillos; (*agr.*) quitar una tira circular de corteza. — *v.i.* moverse en círculo, formar círculo. — *v.t.* (*pret.* **rang, rung**; *p.p.* **rung**); sonar, tocar, repicar, tañer (campanas); anunciar, celebrar, proclamar (con repique de campanas); llamar o convocar, por medio de una campana; tocar (un timbre o una campanilla); reiterar, repetir; *to ring up,* o *give a ring,* (*fam.*) llamar, hablar por teléfono. — *v.i.* sonar, retiñir, tañer; zumbar los oídos; resonar, retumbar; estar lleno de la fama de una cosa.

ringent ['rindʒǝnt], *a.* (*bot.*) bostezante (de una flor).

ringer ['riŋǝɹ], *s.* tocador de campanas, campanero.

ringing ['riŋiŋ], *a.* que repica, que toca las campanas; resonante, retumbante. — *s.* campaneo, retintín, repique de campana.

ringleader ['riŋli:dǝɹ], *s.* cabecilla, *m.*

ringlet ['riŋlet], *s.* anillejo, círculo; rizo, bucle.

ring-shaped, *a.* circular, en forma de sortija, bucle.

ringtail ['riŋteil], *s.* (*orn.*) especie de milano; (*mar.*) vela adicional colocada más a popa de la maricangalla.

ringworm ['riŋwǝːɹm], *s.* tiña, empeine, culebrilla.

rink [riŋk], *s.* pista; *skating-rink,* sala de patinar; pista de patinar.

rinse [rins], *v.t.* lavar; enjuagar, deslavar, aclarar. — *s.* enjuague; aclarado (de ropa).

rinsing, *s.* enjuagadura, deslavadura, escurridura.

riot ['raiǝt], *s.* tumulto, alboroto, sedición, asonada, motín, bullanga; exceso, desorden, desenfreno; borrachera. — *v.i.* armar motines, causar tumultos; andar en borracheras, vivir desenfrenadamente.

rioter, *s.* alborotador, abanderizador, amotinador; (*fam.*) bullanguero, libertino, disoluto, jaranero.

riotous, *a.* amotinado, sedicioso; desarreglado, disoluto, libertino; desenfrenado; bullicioso.

riotousness, *s.* disolución, desorden, desenfreno, estado de tumulto.

rip [rip], *v.t.* (con *up, open* o *off*) hender, lacerar, rasgar, romper, rajar, partir; (*cost.*) descoser, (con *out* o *away*) cortar, destripar, arrancar, destrozar; descoser, soltar; (*carp.*) aserrar en la dirección de la veta, linear, hilar; (con *up*) sondear o estudiar a fondo, penetrar al fondo de, descubrir; *to rip out an oath,* jurar con violencia. — *v.i.* henderse, rasgarse, romperse. — *s.* laceración, rasgón, rasgadura; *rip saw,* sierra de hender; *young rip,* (*fam.*) bribón, pícaro.

riparian [rai'pɛǝriǝn], *a.* ribereño.

riparious [rai'pɛǝriǝs], *a.* ribereño.

ripe [raip], *a.* maduro; acabado, consumado, hecho; en sazón; preparado, pronto, a propósito; colorado, rosado.

ripen ['raipǝn], *v.t., v.i.* madurar, llegar a madurez, poner en estado de madurar; sazonar.

ripeness ['raipnes], *s.* madurez; sazón, *f.*

ripper ['ripǝɹ], *s.* rasgador, el que rasga, el que descose; (*fam.*) tipo estupendo, cosa estupenda.

ripping, *s.* rasgadura; descosedura, deshiladura; laceración; descubrimiento; *ripping-iron,* (*mar.*) descalcador; *ripping-line,* (*aer.*) cabo de desgarre (con que se maneja la faja de desgarre); *ripping-panel,* (*aer.*) faja de desgarre. — *a.* (*fam.*) estupendo.

ripple ['ripǝl], *v.t.* rizar, ondear; sacudir o desgargolar el cáñamo. — *v.i.* agitarse, rizarse (la superficie del agua); murmurar, susurrar. — *s.* ondulación, escarceo, oleadita, onda, rizo (del agua); carda o peine para desgargolar; murmullo de las aguas.

rippling, *a.* que se riza, murmura, etc. — *s.* escarceo, ondulación.

riprap ['ripræp], *v.t.* (*E.U.*) (*alb.*) reforzar con broma. — *s.* (*alb.*) cascajo, broma, ripio; cimiento hecho de cascajo.

rip-saw, *s.* (*carp.*) sierra de hender tablas.

rise [raiz], *v.i.* (*pret.* **rose**; *p.p.* **risen**) subir, ascender, remontarse, elevarse; suspender una sesión; ponerse en pie, salir de la cama, levantarse; nacer, asomar por el horizonte, salir (el sol); levantarse, rebelarse, sublevarse; nacer, salir, brotar (las plantas, los manantiales); surgir, aparecer, presentarse; provenir; armarse, sobrevenir, suscitarse (una disputa, etc.); ascender (en empleo); hincharse, aumentar de volumen; mejorar de posición, medrar, encumbrarse; resucitar; elevarse en estilo; encarecerse, subir el precio; *to rise to one's feet*, ponerse en pie, levantarse. — *s.* levantamiento, elevación, ascensión; crecimiento o desarrollo; nacimiento (de un manantial); subida, cuesta; encarecimiento, subida de precios, alza en los valores; altura, eminencia; inclinación, pendiente, *f.*, salida (de un astro, del sol); fuente, *f.*, origen, principio, causa, manantial; crecida, creciente (de un río, etc.); medro, adelantamiento, ascenso en grado, etc.; (*arq.*) flecha (de un arco); elevación de la voz; (*carp.*) altura de una contrahuella; *rise and fall (of stocks)*, alza y baja (en los fondos); *rise (of a hill)*, pendiente (de una colina), *f.*; *to give rise to*, dar origen a, causar, motivar.

risen ['rizən], *p.p.* [RISE].

riser ['raizər], *s.* el que se levanta; (*carp.*) contrahuella; (*elec.*, *etc.*) conductor o tubo ascendente; *early riser*, madrugador.

risibility, *s.* risibilidad, facultad de reír.

risible ['raizəbəl], *a.* reidor; irrisorio, risible, ridículo.

rising ['raiziŋ], *a.* naciente; creciente; próspero; subiente; saliente, ascendente. — *s.* subimiento, subida, ascenso; levantamiento, insurrección; renacimiento, resurrección; levadura, fermento; (*astr.*) orto, salida; protuberancia, prominencia; acto de cerrar una sesión.

risk [risk], *s.* riesgo, contingencia, peligro, exposición; (en el juego), albur. — *v.t.* arriesgar, poner en riesgo, exponer, aventurar, correr un albur.

risker, *s.* persona que arriesga.

risky ['riski], *a.* peligroso, expuesto, arriesgado; temerario, imprudente; indelicado, verde.

rissole ['risoul], *s.* albóndiga.

rite [rait], *s.* rito, ceremonia; *funeral rites*, exequias, ritos fúnebres.

ritual ['ritjuːəl], *s.*, *a.* ritual, ceremonial. — *s.* rito, ceremonia.

ritualism, *s.* ritualidad, ritualismo.

ritualist, *s.*, *a.* ritualista, *m.f.*, rubriquista, *m.f.*

ritualistic, *a.* ritualista.

ritually, *adv.* según el ritual, conforme al ritual o a los ritos, de rúbrica.

rival ['raivəl], *a.* rival, competidor. — *s.* rival, competidor. — *v.t.* competir, ser el igual de pugnar, emular, entrar en competencia con, rivalizar con. — *v.i.* rivalizar.

rivalry ['raivəlri], *s.* rivalidad, emulación, competencia, competición, esfuerzo.

rive [raiv], *v.t* (*pret.* **rived**; *p.p.* **rived**, **riven**) rajar, hender. — *v.i.* henderse.

river ['rivər], *s.* río; (*fig.*) copia, corriente, *f.*, flujo copioso; *river basin*, cuenca de río; *river bed*, lecho, álveo, madre de un río; *up the river*, río arriba; *down the river*, río abajo; *river dragon*, cocodrilo, caimán; *river horse*, hipopótamo; *river god*, dios tutelar de un río.

riverside ['rivərsaid], *s.*, *a.* orilla o margen de un río; ribera.

rivet ['rivit], *s.* remache, redoblón, roblón;

rivet knob, embutidera. — *v.t.* remachar; roblar, redoblar; (*fig.*) asegurar, afianzar; clavar (los ojos, etc.).

riveting, *s.* robladura, remache.

rivose ['raivous], *a.* (*ent.*) surcado, lleno de surcos.

rivulet ['rivjuːlet], *s.* riachuelo, río pequeño, arroyo, cañada.

roach [routʃ], *s.* (*ict.*) escarcho; (*ent.*) cucaracha; (*mar.*) combadura de la parte inferior de una vela; (*E.U.*) crin de un caballo dejado muy corto.

road [roud], *s.* camino, carretera, camino real, vía; carrera, viaje, paso, curso; (*mar.*) rada, bahía; *cross-road*, encrucijada; *turnpike road*, camino con portazgo; *by-road*, *side road*, atajo, sendero, trocha; *road runner*, (*orn.*) cuclillo de tierra; *high road*, *main road*, camino real, carretera.

roadstead, *s.* rada, fondeadero, ensenada.

roadster, *s.* automóvil de turismo; bicicleta de carreras; caballo de aguante; (*mar.*) barco capaz de aprovecharse de una rada.

roadway, *s.* carretera, calzada.

roam [roum], *v.t.*, *v.i.* vagar, andar vagando, ir errante, vaguear, andar sin dirección fija.

roamer, *s.* vagabundo, vagamundo, hombre errante.

roan [roun], *a.* roano, ruano, sabino, rosillo. — *s.* caballo ruano; badana de color ruano; color ruano.

roar [rɔːr], *v.i.* rugir, mugir, bramar; estallar. — *s.* rugido (el león), mugido (el toro), bramido, bufido; vocerío, grito, gritería; estruendo, ruido grande; estallido.

roarer, *s.* bramador.

roaring, *a.* bramante, rugiente; (*fig.*) tremendo, enorme. — *s.* ronquido.

roast [roust], *v.t.* (*coc.*) asar; calcinar; tostar; (*fam.*) mofarse, burlarse, rechiflar, ridiculizar; *to roast coffee*, tostar café. — *a.* asado; tostado; *roast beef*, carne de vaca asado o carne asada, rosbif; *roast meat*, asado o carne asada. — *s.* carne asada, o buena para asar; asado.

roaster, *s.* asador, tostador; cocinero que asa; pollo o lechón propio para ser asado.

roasting, *s.* acción de asar; tostadura; (*metal.*) torrefacción, calcinación; (*fam.*) censura, rechifla, burla, pesada, zurra.

rob [rɔb], *v.t.*, *v.i.* robar, burlar, hurtar, pillar, saltear, saquear, privar, quitar.

robber, *s.* ladrón; *highway robber*, salteador, bandolero.

robbery ['rɔbəri], *s.* robo, hurto, latrocinio, pillaje, saqueo, salteamiento; *to commit highway robbery*, saltear.

robe [roub], *s.* túnico, túnica, manto, ropaje; traje talar, toga; ropón; manta de coche; corte de vestido; *counsellor's robe*, garnacha; *master of the robes*, jefe de la guardarropa. — *v.t.* vestir, ataviar, vestir de gala o de ceremonia. — *v.i.* vestirse, ponerse trajes; cubrirse; *robing-room*, guardarropa; vestuario.

robin ['rɔbin], *s.* (*orn.*) pechicolorado, petirrojo.

roborant ['roubərənt], *a.* roborante, roborativo.

robust [ro'bʌst], *a.* robusto, fuerte, vigoroso, fornido, trabado, membrudo.

robustness, *s.* robustez, vigor, fuerza.

roc, ruc, rukh [rɔk], *s.* rocho, ruc.

rochet ['rɔtʃet], *s.* (*igl.*) roquete; (*ict.*) trigla roja.

rock [rɔk], s. roca, peña, peñasco; (*fig.*) amparo, protección, defensa, solidez; escollo, arrecife, laja; (*fig.*) fundamento sólido; *rock alum*, alumbre de roca; jebe; *rock bass*, (*ict.*) papagayo; *rock candy*, azúcar candi; *rock crystal*, cristal de roca, cuarzo; *rock crusher*, triturador; *rock salt*, sal de piedra, *f.*, sal gema; *rock rose*, estepa, cisto; *rock water*, agua que mana de las rocas, agua cristalina; *the Rock*, Gibraltar, el Peñón. — *v.t.* mecer, balancear; calmar, sosegar; arrullar. — *v.i.* bambolear, oscilar.

rock-bound, *a*. rodeado de penascos.

rocker, *s*. cunera; balancín, mecedor; mecedora, silla mecedora; columpio (*Cuba*).

rocket [ˈrɔket], *s*. cohete, volador; (*bot.*) oruga, jaramago, hespéride, *f.*; (*fam.*) reprimenda; *sky rocket*, cohete.

rockiness [ˈrɔkinis], *s*. abundancia de rocas; fragosidad.

rocking, *a*. mecedor; oscilatorio, vacilante; *rocking-horse*, caballo mecedor, caballito; *rocking-chair*, mecedora. — *s*. balance, balanceo.

rock-oil, *s*. petróleo.

rockwork [ˈrɔkwəːk], *s*. gruta artificial, roca artificial.

rocky, *a*. formado de rocas, peñascoso, roqueño, roquero, pedregoso, endurecido, duro; *Rocky Mountains*, Montañas Roqueñas.

rococo [roˈkoukou], *a.*, *s*. rococó.

rod [rɔd], *s*. caña, vara, varilla; cetro; bastón de mando; vara de alcalde o de alguacil; (*fig.*) corrección, disciplina, severidad, castigo; dominación, poder, varilla de virtudes; caña de pescar; vara de medir; varilla o barra de cortina; pértica (medida); jalón; (*mec.*) vástago; (*fig.*) tribu, *f.*, raza; *to give the rod*, dar azotes, azotar; *to rule with a rod of iron*, gobernar con mano de hierro; *connecting-rod*, (*mec.*) biela; *angling-rod*, caña de pescar.

rode [roud], *pret.* [RIDE].

rodent [ˈroudənt], *s.*, *a*. roedor.

rodomontade [rɔdomɔnˈteid], *s*. bravata, fanfarronada, baladronada. — *v.i.* baladronear, bravear, fanfarronear.

roe [rou], *s*. corzo; hueva, huevecillos, ovas de pescado; *roe-stone*, (*min.*) oolita.

roebuck [ˈroubʌk], **roe-deer** [ˈroudiəɹ], *s*. corzo.

rogation [roˈgeiʃən], *s*. (*igl.*) rogativa; ruego, súplica. — *pl.* **Rogations**, (*igl.*) rogaciones, letanías cantadas en las procesiones de las cuatro témporas.

rogatory [roˈgeitəri], *a*. rogatorio.

rogue [roug], *s*. bribón, tunante, pícaro, pillo, bellaco, villano, ruin, pillastre, persona traviesa; vagamundo; (*fam.*) tunantuelo; (*for.*, *Ingl.*) pordiosero, vagabundo, vago; elefante feroz y peligroso; *rogue's gallery*, retratos de malhechores que colecciona la policía para su identificación; *rogue's yarn*, (*mar.*) hilo de ladrones.

roguery [ˈrougəri], *s*. picardía, bellaquería, ruindad; (*fam.*) retozo, travesura.

rogueship, *s*. propiedades de un bribón.

roguish [ˈrougiʃ], *a*. pícaro, picaresco, tuno, belitre; (*fam.*) travieso, chistoso, juguetón, burlón, decidor.

roguishly, *adv*. pícaramente, picarescamente, bellacamente.

roguishness, *s*. picardía, lo pícaro, lo travieso; tunantada, bellaquería, bribonada, ladronera, mala partida.

roil [rɔil], *v.t.* enturbiar, enlodar; irritar, vejar.

roily, *a*. turbio; agitado.

roister [ˈrɔistəɹ], *s*. fanfarrón, baladrón. — *v.i.* bravear, fanfarronear, echar bravatas.

rôle [roul], *s*. papel; *to play a rôle*, hacer un papel.

roll [roul], *v.t.* rodar, hacer rodar; voltear, girar, volver; (*fund.*) laminar, alisar, cilindrar, allanar con rodillo; abarquillar, arrollar, enrollar; redoblar (el tambor); fajar, envolver; mover, poner en blanco (los ojos); vibrar la lengua (para pronunciar la *rr*); vibrar la voz (para hacer un trino). — *v.i.* rodar, dar vueltas, revolver, revolverse, girar, volver; ondear, fluctuar, ondular, flotar; agitarse (las olas); caer dando vueltas; resonar, retumbar, retemblar; arrollarse, encarrujarse, abarquillarse; bambolearse, balancearse; dar un redoble de tambores; vivir con gran lujo, tener abundancia de algo; *to roll up*, enrollar, arrollar; abarquillar; *to roll about*, rodar, andar de acá para allá, divagar; *to roll in money, to be rolling in money* (o *wealth*), nadar en dinero, en la abundancia; *to roll down*, bajar rodando; *a rolling stone gathers no moss*, (*prov.*) piedra movediza nunca moho cobija. — *s*. rollo; registro, catálogo, matrícula, nómina, lista, rol; rodillo, cilindro; bollo, mollete, panecillo; redoble (de tambores); balanceo, bamboleo; retumbo del trueno; oleaje; (*arq.*) roleo, voluta; (*cir.*) mecha. — *pl.* archivos; *roll call*, acto de pasar lista; *French roll*, panecillo francés; *roll-top desk*, escritorio de tapa rodadera.

roller, *s*. rodillo, cilindro, tambor; alisador; allanador, arrollador, aplanadera; (*cir.*) venda, faja; (*impr.*) rulo, rodillo; ola larga; (*mar.*) roldana, polines, rolletes; *roller skate*, patín de ruedas; *roller bearing*, cojinete de rodillos.

rollick [ˈrɔlik], *v.i.* travesear, moverse con ademán retozón, retozar.

rollicking, *a*. jovial; retozón, juguetón, travieso.

rolling [ˈrouliŋ], *a*. rodadero; rodadizo, rodador, rodante, rotante; ondulado, quebrado (terreno). — *s*. acto de rodar, rodadura; balanceo, cuneo; revuelco; fajamiento; enrollamiento; (*aer.*) escora lateral; *rolling-pin*, rodillo de pastelero; *rolling-mill*, (*metal.*) taller para hacer láminas, taller para laminar; laminador; *rolling stone*, (*geol.*) galga, canto rodado; (*fig.*) persona que no se queda en un empleo; persona inconstante; *rolling-stock*, (*f.c.*) material móvil; *rolling tackle*, (*mar.*) aparejo de rolin.

roly-poly [ˈroulipouli], *a*. rechoncho, gordiflón. — *s*. pudín en forma de rollo; (*fam.*) persona gordiflona.

Romaic [roˈmeiik], *a*. romaico.

Roman [ˈroumən], *a*. romano; romanesco; papal, católico romano; austero, severo; valeroso, noble; *Roman letter*, *Roman type*, (*impr.*) letra romana, tipo romano; *Roman candle*, candela romana.

Romance [roˈmæns], **Romanic** [roˈmænik], *a*. romance; neolatino.

romance [roˈmæns], *s*. romance; cuento,

ficción, novela, fábula; aventura, drama, *m.*;
romanticismo; amorío; (*mús.*) romanza. —
v.i. fingir fábulas; mentir.

romancer, romancist, *s.* romancero, escritor
de romances, novelista, *m.f.*; visionario,
chismoso, chismeador; mentiroso, embustero.

Romanesque [romən'esk], *a.* romanesco;
romance; (*arq.*) románico.

Romanism [roumən'izm], *s.* dogmas de la
Iglesia católica romana.

Romanist, *s.*, *a.* católico romano.

Romanize ['roumənaiz], *v.t.* convertir al
catolicismo; usar los modismos de los cató-
licos romanos; propender a sus opiniones.

romantic [ro'mæntik], *a.* romántico; novelesco; sentimental.

romantically, *adv.* de un modo romántico.

romanticism [ro'mæntisizm], *s.* romanticismo.

romanticist, *s.* escritor romántico.

Romany ['romәni], *s.*, *a.* gitano; caló.

Rome [roum], *s.*, Roma; *when in Rome do as
Rome does,* (*refrán*) por donde fueres, haz
como vieres.

Romish ['roumiʃ], *a.* católico romano.

romp [romp], *s.* muchacha retozona; retozo.
— *v.i.* retozar, juguetear, brincar, travesear,
triscar.

rompish, *a.* retozón.

rondeau [rondou], **rondel** [rondel], *s.* (*poét.*)
rondel, redondilla; (*mús.*) rondó.

rondelle ['rondel], *s.* pieza circular o disco de
metal, vidrio, etc.; (*fund.*) costra o escama
formada sobre metal fundido al enfriarse.

rondo ['rondou], *s.* (*mús.*) rondó.

rood [ru:d], *s.* cruz, *f.*, crucifijo; pértica (5½
yardas); cuarto de acre cuadrado; *rood
screen,* mampara del presbiterio.

roof [ro:f], *s.* tejado, azotea, techado; cubierta;
imperial de una diligencia; (*fig.*) casa, hogar,
habitación; paladar (de la boca); *flat roof,*
azotea, ajarafe, terrado; *tile roof,* tejado;
roof of the mouth, paladar. — *v.t.* techar,
cubrir con techo; alojar, abrigar.

roofage ['ru:fidʒ], *s.* materiales para techo.

roofed, *a.* techado.

roofer, *s.* constructor de tejados.

roofing, *s.* (*arq.*) techado, cubierta; albergue;
material para techos; *roofing-slate,* pizarra de
techar.

roof-tile, *s.* teja, cobija.

roof-tree, *s.* cumbrera.

rook [ruk], *s.* (*orn.*) corneja, corvato; roque,
torre (del juego de ajedrez); (*fam.*) trampista, *m.f.* — *v.t.* (*vulg.*) robar, estafar.

rookery ['rukəri], *s.* manada de cornejas;
colonia de aves marinas o de focas; casa
destartalada y ruinosa.

rooky, *a.* habitado por cornejas.

room [rum], *s.* lugar, sitio, paraje, puesto,
espacio, plaza; tiempo, oportunidad, ocasión;
cuarto, aposento, cámara, pieza, habitación;
motivo, causa; *state room,* (*mar.*) camarote,
pañol; *back room,* cuarto o pieza de detrás;
cuarto interior; *front room,* aposento o
cuarto de delante; *dining-room,* comedor;
drawing-room, salón; *retiring-room,* tocador,
retrete; *bath room,* cuarto de baño; *sitting-
room,* habitación, sala, salón; *lecture room,*
aula, sala de clase; *to make room,* abrir paso,
hacer lugar; *to give room,* hacer lugar; dar
puesto, retirarse; *room mate,* compañero de

cuarto; *there is no room for him here,* no cabe
aquí; *there is no room for doubt,* no cabe duda,
no hay duda posible. — *v.i.* (*fam.*) habitar,
tener una habitación o aposento, alojarse.

roomful, *s.* cuanto cabe en un aposento.

roominess, *s.* espaciosidad, amplitud, holgura.

roomy ['rumi], *a.* espacioso, capaz, dilatado,
holgado, amplio.

roost [ru:st], *s.* pértiga o percha de gallinero;
sueño, reposo, descanso (de las aves domésticas); (*fam.*) lugar de descanso; (*E.U.*) per-
chada; *to rule the roost,* dominar, mandar,
tener vara alta. — *v.i.* dormir, descansar (las
aves) en una percha; (*fam.*) alojarse, acostarse; *chickens come home to roost,* no hay
deuda que no se pague.

rooster ['ru:stər], *s.* gallo.

root [ru:t], *s.* raíz, *f.*; parte inferior, *f.*; pie;
principio, origen; tronco, estirpe *f.*; (*mús.*)
base, *f.*, nota fundamental; *to take root* (o
strike root), echar raíces, arraigarse; *cube root,*
(*mat.*) raíz cúbica. — *v.t.*, *v.i.* arraigar,
hozar; levantar con el hocico, hocicar;
afianzarse, arraigarse, echar o criar raíces;
grabar profundamente; estar establecido,
estar fijo; *to root up* (o *out*), arrancar de raíz,
desarraigar; extirpar, extinguir; desterrar.

rooted, *a.* radical; arraigado.

rooter, *s.* el que arranca de raíz; jabalí, puerco.

rootlet, *s. dim.* raicilla, radícula.

rootstock, *s.* (*bot.*) rizoma; (*fig.*) origen.

rooty, *a.* lleno de raíces; radicoso, parecido a
raíces.

rope [roup], *s.* soga, cordel, cuerda; maroma;
sirga, cabo; driza, toa; cobra, reata; sarta,
trenza, ristra; fila, hilera; *ropes of a ship,*
(*mar.*) jarcia, cordaje; *bolt rope,* relinga; *buoy
rope,* orinque; *entering rope,* guardamancebo
del portalón; *rope yard,* cordelería; *rope yarn,*
filástica; *rope dancer,* volatín, bailarín de
cuerda; *rope trick,* truco de las cuerdas;
rope work, trabajo hecho de cuerdas; *rope
ladder,* escala de cuerdas; *to be at the end of
one's rope,* estar sin recursos; quedarse en la
calle; *to know the ropes,* (*fig.*) saber cuantas
son cinco, conocer a fondo; *to give someone
the rope's end,* castigar a uno golpeándole con
un cabo de cuerda; *ropemaker,* cordelero. —
v.t. atar, amarrar con una cuerda; rodear con
soga; (*fam.*) engatusar, embaucar; (*E.U.*)
coger con lazo. — *v.i.* hacer hebras o madeja;
to rope in, (*fam.*) atraer a una empresa;
(*fam., E.U.*) engañar, embaucar; *roper-in,*
gaucho, donillero.

rope-bands, *s.pl.* (*mar.*) envergues.

ropery ['roupəri], *s.* cordelería; (*fam.*)
tunantería.

ropewalk, *s.* cordelería.

rope-walker, *s.* volatinero, maromero.

ropiness ['roupinis], *s.* viscosidad; tenacidad.

ropish, ropy, *a.* viscoso, pegajoso, glutinoso.

roquet ['roukei], *v.t.* en el juego de croquet,
dar la bola del que juega contra otra. — *s.*
choque de dichas bolas, acción de chocar una
bola contra otra.

rorqual ['ro:kwəl], *s.* (*ict.*) rorcual, balenóp-
tero.

rosaceous [ro'zeiʃəs], *a.* (*bot.*) róseo, rosáceo.

rosaniline [ros'ænilain], *s.* rosanilina.

rosary ['rouzəri], *s.* (*igl.*) rosario; guirnalda o
corona de rosas; macizo o jardín de rosales;
(*fig.*) crestomatía.

rose [rouz], *pret.* [RISE].

rose, *s.* rosa; rosal; color de rosa; roseta; (*arq.*) rosetón; remate perforado de una regadera; *dog rose,* agavanzo, rosal silvestre, escaramujo; *honey of roses,* miel rosada; *tea-rose,* rosa de té; *Bengal* (o *monthly*) *rose,* rosa de China; rosa de todo el año; *under the rose,* (*fig.*) bajo cuerda, secretamente; *rose-beetle, rose-bug, rose-chafer,* insectos coleópteros dañinos a los rosales; *rose-window,* (*arq.*) rosetón, ventana con rosetón; *no rose without its thorn,* (*prov.*) no hay rosa sin espina; a cada gusto su susto; quien coma la carne, que roa el hueso.

rose-apple, *s.* pomarrosa.

roseate ['rouzieit], *a.* rosado; róseo.

rose-bay, *s.* adelfa, baladre.

rose-bud, *s.* pimpollo o capullo de rosa; (una) joven, niña adolescente.

rose-bush, *s.* rosal.

rosegall, *s.* zarzarrosa.

rosemary ['rouzməri], *s.* romero, rosmarino.

roseola [ro'ziːolə], *s.* roseola, sarpullido.

rose-tree, *s.* rosal.

rosette [ro'zet], *s.* rosa, roseta; mona, escarapela; (*arq.*) rosetón, florón.

rosewater, *s.* agua rosada, agua de rosas.

rosewood, *s.* palisandro, palo de rosa.

Rosicrucian [rouzi'kruːʃən], *s., a.* rosacruz.

rosied ['rouzid], *a.* rosado, róseo.

rosin ['rɔzin], *s.* trementina, abetinote, resina. — *v.t.* dar con resina.

rosiny ['rɔzini], *a.* resinoso.

Rosmarinus [rɔzmə'riːnəs], *s.* rosmarino, romero.

rosolio, *s.* rosoli (licor).

roster ['rɔstər], *s.* (*mil.*) rol, lista; registro, matrícula, nómina, lista de deberes de los oficiales, orden del día.

rostral ['rɔstrəl], *a.* rostral, que tiene rostro.

rostrate ['rɔstrit], *a.* (*zool.*) rostrado.

rostrum ['rɔstrəm], *s.* tribuna; (*mar.*) rostro, espolón; (*zool.*) rostro, hocico, pico; cañón de alambique.

rosy ['rouzi], *a.* róseo, rosado, roso, de color de rosa; sonrojado; (*fig.*) lisonjero, agradable, optimista, glorioso; *rosy-fingered,* (*poét.*) con dedos de rosa; *rosy-hued,* rosado, de color de rosa, con tez rosada.

rot [rɔt], *v.i.* pudrirse, podrirse; malearse, echarse a perder, corromperse; estar estancado; padecer de morriña (las ovejas); ir a menos; irse consumiendo poco a poco; corromperse moralmente. — *v.t.* pudrir; enriar, resolver en podre. — *s.* putrefacción, podredumbre, podre, *f.*; (*vet.*) morriña; (*fam.*) borricada, tontada, sandez, disparate; (*bot.*) enfermedad de las plantas, causada por los hongos.

rota ['routə], *s.* rol, lista, nómina; orden del día, rutina, orden de los deberes (de oficiales, etc.).

rotary ['routəri], *a.* giratorio, rotatorio, rotante, rotativo; *rotary press,* (*impr.*) prensa rotativa.

rotate [ro'teit], *v.t., v.i.* girar, dar vueltas, rodar o hacer rodar sobre un eje; turnar, alternar, cambiar, revezar; desamelgar un terreno. — *a.* en forma de rueda, rotante, que forma círculo alrededor de una parte; (*bot.*) de venas radiales; (*ent.*) que forma círculo.

rotation, *s.* rotación, turno, giro, vicisitud, ruedo, vuelta, alternativa; *in rotation* (o *by rotation*), por turno, alternativamente; *rotation of crops,* rotación de cultivos.

rotative, rotatory, *a.* rotante, rotatorio, en rotación, giratorio.

rotator, *s.* lo que hace rodar, lo que causa rotación; (*anat.*) músculo rotador; hélice (de la corredera); (*elec.*) rotor.

rote [rout], *s.* lo que se aprende de memoria; *to learn by rote,* aprender de memoria o de coro.

rother ['rɔðəɹ], *s.* buey.

rotifera [ro'tifərə], *s.pl.* rotíferos, infusorios rodadores.

rotiform ['routifɔːɹm], *a.* rotiforme, en forma de rueda o estrella.

rotor ['routəɹ], *s.* pieza giratoria; (*hidr.*) rotor, rueda móvil de una turbina; (*elec.*) pequeño motor; (*aut.*) rotor.

rotten ['rɔtən], *a.* podrido, carroño, putrefacto; cariado; corrompido; endeble; (*fam.*) malísimo, pésimo, en mal estado; *rotten egg,* huevo empollado; *rotten trick,* (*fam.*) mala partida.

rottenness ['rɔtənnis], *s.* podredumbre, putridez, putrefacción, pudrición.

rottenstone ['rɔtənstoun], *s.* trípol o trípoli.

rotter ['rɔtəɹ], *s.* (*vulg.*) persona indeseable; calavera, *m.*, perdido.

rotund [ro'tʌnd], *a.* rotundo, redondo, circular, esférico; orbicular.

rotunda [ro'tʌndə], *s.* rotonda, rotunda.

rotundifolious [rotʌndi'foulios], *a.* que tiene las hojas redondas.

rotundity [ro'tʌnditi], *s.* rotundidad, redondez, esfericidad; protuberancia redonda.

rouble ['ruːbəl], *s.* rublo.

roué ['ruːei], *s.* libertino.

rouge [ruːʒ], *s.* arrebol, afeite, colorete; (*joy.*) azafrán de Marte, color encarnado, colorado, rojizo. — *a.* encarnado. — *v.t., v.r.* arrebolarse, pintarse, afeitarse, darse colorete; pulir con rojo de joyero.

rough [rʌf], *a.* áspero, tosco; erizado; quebrado, escabroso, fragoso; duro, severo, cruel, rígido, desapacible; peludo, encrespado; áspero al tacto; bruto, cerril, inculto, rudo, ordinario, brusco, grosero, arrogante, insolente; chapucero, mal acabado; áspero, agrio al gusto; bronco, ingrato al oído; borrascoso, tempestuoso; general, aproximado, aproximativo; mal peinado, desgreñado; *rough diamond,* diamante en bruto; (*fig.*) persona ineducada pero de buen fondo; *rough sea,* mar alborotado; *rough wind,* viento borrascoso; *rough sketch* (o *draft*), boceto, bosquejo; *rough rider,* jinete arrojado; domador de caballos; *rough setter,* (*alb.*) mampostero; *rough guess,* valuación aproximada; *at a rough guess,* a ojo de buen cubero; *to make a rough draft* (o *rough-draft*), hacer un boceto o borrador, bosquejar, trazar rudamente; *to ride rough-shod,* ir en derechura al grano, imponerse con arrogancia; *to rough-hew,* desbastar; *rough shod,* herrado con clavos que impiden resbalar en el hielo; *to rough-dry,* secar sin planchar; *rough and tumble,* desordenado, sin restricción ni regla. — *s.* estado tosco; rufián, matón, belitre; vista general; *in the rough,* en bruto, sin pulimento. — *v.t.* hacer áspero, poner áspero, escabroso, tosco; labrar toscamente; (*fam.*) molestar, irritar; *to rough it*, vivir sin comodidades, o en duras condiciones.

roughcast ['rʌfkɑːst], *s.* modelo en bruto; (*alb.*) mortero grueso; obra sin acabar. — *v.t.* bosquejar, hacer toscamente.

roughen ['rʌfən], *v.t.*, *v.i.* poner(se) áspero o tosco, volver(se) rudo; *to roughen a horse*, domar un caballo.

roughness, *s.* aspereza, tosquedad, rudeza, escabrosidad; dureza, severidad; bronquedad, bruteza, grosería; tormenta, tempestad; chapucería.

rouleau ['ruːlou], *s.* cartucho de dinero; cucurucho, rollo, alcartaz.

roulette [ru'let], *s.* ruleta; roleta de grabador.

round [raund], *a.* redondo, orbicular, circular, esférico, cilíndrico; rotundo, lleno; semi-circular; cabal; sonoro; cuantioso, grande; franco, sincero, claro, liso, ingenuo, llano; amplio, generoso, liberal; vivo, rápido, acelerado, veloz; honrado, justo; terminante, categórico; *round fee*, o *round figure*, honorarios amplios; *round robin*, petición en que las firmas están dispuestas en círculo; *round sum*, cifra redonda; *round shouldered*, cargado de espaldas; *to make round*, redondear, dar figura redonda; *to bring up with a round turn*, obligar a hacer una parada repentina; *not to have enough to go round*, haber más días que longanizas. — *s.* orbe, círculo, esfera; peldaño (de escala), escalón, paso; vuelta, giro, rodeo, revolución, rotación; redondez; rodaja de carne; listón o travesaño (de silla); (*mil.*) ronda; salva, andanada, disparo, descarga, tiro; (*arq.*) mediacana; (*mil.*) cartucho con bala; rutina, serie, *f.*, curso; ruta, circuito, camino; (*dep.*) vuelta, turno; (*boxeo*) asalto; (*mús.*) rondó; danza, baile; *to go the rounds*, ir de ronda. — *adv.* alrededor, en derredor, circularmente; redondamente, por todos lados, por todas partes; *round about*, por el lado opuesto; por todos lados, a la redonda; *all-round man*, persona experta en todos los detalles de su profesión; *to go round*, andar alrededor, dar vueltas; *my head goes round*, se me va la cabeza; *all the year round*, todo el año. — *prep.* alrededor de. — *v.t.* redondear, arredondar; cercar, moverse alrededor, ceñir, rodear, dar vuelta a; perfeccionar, acabar; *to round in*, (*mar.*) halar en redondo. — *v.i.* hacerse redondo, redondearse; desarrollarse, perfeccionarse; rondar; dar vueltas; hablar al oído, susurrar; *to round on*, volverse contra; *to round off*, redondear; *to round to*, (*mar.*) orzar; *to round up*, colmar; (*mar.*) halar.

roundabout ['raundəbaut], *a.* indirecto, vago; desviado. — *s.* chaleco, chaqueta; tío vivo; glorieta de circulación, redondel (de tráfico).

roundel ['raundəl], **roundelay** ['raundilei], *s.* (*mús.*) melodía; baile en círculo; rondo.

round-faced, *a.* carirredondo.

roundhand, *s.* letra redonda.

Roundhead ['raundhed], *s.* (*Ingl.*) 'cabeza redonda,' apodo despectivo que se daba a los puritanos durante las guerras civiles del siglo diecisiete.

roundheaded, *a.* repolludo.

roundhouse, *s.* (*mar.*) toldilla, chupeta, tumbadillo; (*E.U.*, *f.c.*) rotunda, casa de máquinas.

rounding, *s.* curvatura; (*mar.*) forro de cable.

roundish, *a.* casi redondo, medio redondo.

roundly, *adv.* redondamente, absolutamente, francamente, claramente, abiertamente, sin rodeos, sin cumplimentos; aproximadamente.

roundness, *s.* redondez, sinceridad, claridad, buena fe.

roundsman ['raundzmən], *s.* (*E.U.*) rondador de policía.

round-up, *v.t.* rodear, recoger el ganado para marcarlo, etc. — *s.* rodeo del ganado.

roup [ruːp], *s.* angina, crup de las aves domésticas.

roupy, *a.* enronquecido, ronco.

rouse [rauz], *v.t.* despertar, despabilar, desadormecer, animar, avispar, atizar, excitar, provocar; levantar la caza; (*mar.*) halar, arronzar. — *v.i.* despertar, despertarse, animarse, despabilarse, moverse. — *s.* tragazo de licor.

rouser, *s.* despertador, excitador; (*vulg.*) mentira, bola, embuste.

roust [raust], *v.t.* (*fam.*) despertar, sacudir, hacer huir. — *v.i.* moverse con energía, ser activo.

roustabout ['raustəbaut], *s.* (*E.U.*) peón, trabajador en los vapores de río; gañán.

rout [raut], *s.* rota, huida, derrota, destrozo; chusma, jabardillo, garulla, reunión de gente baja; (*for.*) alboroto, tumulto, asonada. — *v.t.* derrotar, desbaratar, arrollar, destruir, hacer huir, poner en fuga, destrozar; (con *out*) arrancar hozando; (*carp.*) rebajar.

route [ruːt], *s.* ruta, vía, rumbo, camino, carrera; trazado, línea, delineación, curso, marcha.

router ['rautər], *s.* (*carp.*) cepillo de machihembrar, moldear, etc. — *v.t.* hacer molduras, embutar.

routinary, routine, *a.* rutinario.

routine ['ruːtiːn], *s.* rutina, hábito, costumbre, práctica.

rove [rouv], *v.t.* (*tej.*) torcer el hilo antes de encanillarlo; pasar por un agujero, enhebrar, ensartar. — *v.i.* corretear, vaguear, vagar, correr acá y acullá; *to rove the seas*, piratear. — *s.* correría, acto de correr, paseo; arandela de remache; hilado, madeja de lana tirada.

rover, *s.* errante, vagamundo, andorrero, tunante; pirata, *m.*

roving, *s.* primera torsión. — *a.* errante, vagabundo.

row [rou], *s.* hilera, línea, fila; remadura; paseo (en lancha o bote). — *v.i.* (*mar.*) remar, bogar, trabajar con el remo. — *v.t.* conducir remando, pasear por agua.

row [rau], *v.i.* pelearse, armar un escándalo, armar un zipizape. — *s.* camorra, zipizape, riña, trifulca, pendencia, zambra, alboroto.

rowan ['rouən, 'rauən], *s.* fresno alpestre; fruto del fresno alpestre.

rowboat ['roubout], *s.* (*mar.*) bote, barca de remos, lancha.

rowdy ['raudi], *a.* alborotador, ruidoso. — *s.* gamberro, quimerista, *m.*, zaragatero, alborotador, rufián, pelafustán.

rowdyism, *s.* gamberrismo, pillería, bellaquería, tunantería, alboroto.

rowel ['rauəl], *s.* rodaja de espuela; (*vet.*) sedal. — *v.t.* poner sedal.

rower ['rouər], *s.* remero, bogador.

rowlock ['rʌlək], *s.* chumacera, escalamera.
royal ['rɔiəl], *a.* real, majestuoso, regio, noble, magnífico, ilustre, magnánimo; excelente, exquisito, superior; *to have a right royal time*, divertirse en grande. — *s.* tamaño de papel (de 19 × 24 pulgadas para escribir y de 20 × 25 para imprenta); (*mar.*) juanete, sobrejuanete; punta superior del asta del ciervo; mogote.
royalism, *s.* realismo, adhesión a la monarquía.
royalist, *s.* realista, *m.f.*, monárquico, partidario de la monarquía.
royalty ['rɔiəlti], *s.* realeza, majestad real, soberanía; derecho de privilegio o de autor; prerrogativas reales; regalía.
rub [rʌb], *v.t.* estregar, restregar, fregar, regregar, frotar, limpiar; ludir, tocar; testar, raer, raspar; fastidiar, incomodar, inquietar, molestar. — *v.i.* rozar, pasar raspando o frotando; ir a contrapelo, ser desagradable o molesto; desenredarse; librarse de un peligro; *to rub away*, quitar frotando; seguir frotando; *to rub down* (*a horse*), limpiar (un caballo); *to rub along* (u *on*), (*fam.*) ir tirando; *to rub in*, hacer penetrar por los poros frotando; (*fam.*) machacar, insistir, reiterar; *to rub out*, borrar; *to rub off*, borrar, quitar; limpiar frotando; *to rub up*, aguijonear, excitar; repasar, pulir, retocar; *to rub* (*up*) *the wrong way*, frotar a contrapelo; irritar, incomodar. — *s.* ludimiento, frotamiento, roce, estregamiento; sarcasmo, denuesto; embarazo, tropiezo, obstáculo, dificultad; *there's the rub*, (*fam.*) ése es el cuento, ahí está la cosa.
rub-a-dub, *s.* rataplán.
rubber ['rʌbəɪ], *s.* caucho, goma elástica, goma de borrar; fregador, frotador; rodilla, estropajo, estregadera, aljofifa; jugada final que decide un empate; partida de juego; escofina. — *pl.* **rubbers,** zapatos (*o* chanclos) de goma. — *a.* hecho de caucho o goma elástica.
rubberize ['rʌbəraiz], *v.t.* engomar, impregnar, cubrir de goma o caucho.
rubbing, *s.* fricción, roce, frotación, estregamiento, rozamiento; soba.
rubbish ['rʌbiʃ], *s.* basura; escombro, ruinas, ripio, cascajo, broza, rudera, desecho, morralla, zupia, desperdicio; trasto; andrajos; porquería; *rubbish!* ¡qué tontería!
rubble ['rʌbəl], *s.* ripios, morrillo, cascote, mampuesto; *rubble-work*, mampostería, enripiado.
rubefacient [ru:be'feiʃənt], *s., a.* rubefaciente.
rubescence, rubicundity, *s.* rubicundez.
rubescent [ru:'besənt], **rubicund** ['ru:bikənd], *a.* rubicundo, sonrosado.
rubiaceous [ru:bi'eiʃəs], *a.* rubiáceo.
rubied ['ru:bid], *a.* adornado con rubíes; de color de rubí.
rubific [ru:'bifik], *a.* que rubifica.
rubify, *v.t.* rubificar.
rubiginous [ru:'bidʒinəs], *a.* añublado.
rubigo [ru:'baigou], *s.* añublo, tizón.
rubric ['ru:brik], *a.* rubro, rojo, rojizo. — *s.* rúbrica; rasgo de la firma; título, encabezamiento; división, sección.
rubrical, *a.* de rúbrica.
rubricate ['ru:brikeit], *a.* rubicundo, rubio, iluminado, escrito o impreso de color rojo. — *v.t.* marcar o iluminar con encarnado.
ruby ['ru:bi], *s.* rubí; color encarnado vivo, carmín; (*Ingl.*, *impr.*) tipo de 5½ puntos. — *a.* rubeo, rubicundo, rojo, rojo vivo; *ruby-throat*, (*orn.*) colibrí norteamericano. — *v.t.* rubificar, enrojecer.
ruche [ru:ʃ], *s.* (*cost.*) golilla, lechuguilla.
ruck [rʌk], *s.* montón, multitud, muchedumbre, especialmente la masa de caballos rezagados en una carrera; arruga; enojo, enfado. — *v.t.* arrugar, ajar.
rucksack ['ruksæk], *s.* mochila.
rudder ['rʌdəɪ], *s.* (*mar.*) timón, gobernalle; (*fig.*) gobierno, dirección; *rudder-chain*, (*mar.*) varón del timón; *rudder-pintles*, (*mar.*) machos del timón; *rudder-hole*, limera del timón; *rudder-post*, (*mar.*) codaste; (*aer.*) eje del timón; *rudder-stock*, cabeza del timón.
ruddiness ['rʌdinis], *s.* rojez, rubicundez, color de rubí.
ruddy ['rʌdi], *a.* rojo, rojizo, colorado, encendido, frescote; (*fam.*) maldito, puñetero; *ruddy complexion*, tez sanguínea.
rude [ru:d], *a.* rudo, ordinario, brusco, rústico, sin crianza, ignorante, grosero, descortés, impolítico; tosco, chabacano, basto, chapucero, mal hecho, informe, imperfecto; violento, fiero, turbulento; desigual, escabroso; severo, inflexible.
rudeness, *s.* grosería, patanería, ordinariez, descortesía; tosquedad, rusticidad, ignorancia, crudeza, insolencia, brutalidad; rudeza, aspereza, dureza.
rudiment ['ru:dimənt], *s.* rudimento, elemento, principio; germen, embrión.
rudimental, *a.* rudimental, relativo a los rudimentos.
rudimentarily, *adv.* de un modo rudimentario.
rudimentary [ru:di'mentəri], *a.* rudimental, elemental, rudimentario; germinal, abortivo, embrionario.
rue [ru:], *v.t.*, *v.i.* llorar, sentir, lamentar, pesarle a uno, arrepentirse. — *s.* (*bot.*) ruda; infusión o cocimiento de ruda; trago amargo; arrepentimiento, pesar.
rueful, *a.* lamentable, triste, lastimoso, deplorable; terrible.
ruefulness, *s.* tristeza, pesar, pena, aflicción.
ruff [rʌf], *s.* (*cost.*) lechuguilla, golilla, gorguera, escarola; paloma moñuda; collarín natural de plumas o de pelo que tienen algunos animales; (*ict.*) navo marino.
ruffian ['rʌfien], *s.* rufián, malhechor, ladrón; bruto; asesino; bandolero, bergante. — *a.* brutal, inhumano, belitre; semejante a un bandolero o salteador.
ruffianish, *a.* propio de un malvado.
ruffianism, *s.* bellaquería.
ruffianly, ruffian-like, *a.* forajido, arrufianado.
ruffle ['rʌfəl], *v.t.* (*cost.*) rizar, fruncir un volante, adornar con puños o manguitos; desazonar, incomodar, enfadar, fastidiar, irritar; arrugar, ajar, desaliñar, confundir, descomponer, desordenar, desaderezar; vejar; redoblar (el tambor) con un sonido apagado. — *v.i.* rizarse, arrugarse, desarreglarse; tremolar; incomodarse, enojarse, fastidiarse, aburrirse, argumentar, pelear. — *s.* (*cost.*) volante fruncido; vuelta o puño de camisola; redoble apagado de tambor en la milicia; desazón, *f.*, irritación, enojo; escarceo del agua; conmoción, disputa.

ruffler ['rʌfləɹ], s. matón, matasiete; accesorio para máquina de coser para fruncir o rizar.

rufous ['ru:fəs], a. rufo, leonado, bermejo, rojizo, color de orín.

rug [rʌg], s. paño burdo; alfombrilla, felpudo, tapete, ruedo; manta peluda, manta de viaje; perro de lanas.

rugate ['ru:git], a. rugoso, rizado, arrugado.

Rugby ['rʌgbi], s. rugby.

rugged ['rʌgid], a. áspero, abrupto, escabroso, desigual, escarpado; basto, tosco; desapacible; inculto; descomedido, severo, desvergonzado; bronco; regañón, ceñudo, arrugado; severo; borrascoso, tempestuoso; (*E.U.*) robusto, vigoroso.

ruggedness, s. rudeza, escabrosidad, aspereza.

rugose, rugous ['ru:gəs], a. rizado, arrugado, lleno de arrugas, rugoso.

rugosity [ru:'gɔsiti], s. rugosidad.

ruin ['ru:in], s. ruina, arruinamiento; decadencia, caída; destrucción, destrozo, tala, devastación; bancarrota; perdición, corrupción, vicio, degradación, pérdida de reputación; *to bring one to ruin,* perder a uno. — *pl.* **ruins,** escombros, ruinas; vestigios, residuos. — *v.t.* derribar, arruinar, derruir, demoler, derrumbar, destruir, devastar; echar a perder; seducir (a una mujer); estropear, desbaratar; empobrecer, hundir. — *v.i.* decaer; arruinarse, caer en ruinas; causar o producir ruina.

ruination [ru:in'eiʃən], s. arruinamiento, ruina, perdición.

ruinous ['ru:inəs], a. ruinoso, desmantelado; fatal, funesto, pernicioso, desastroso.

ruinousness, s. arruinamiento, acción de arruinar.

rulable ['ru:ləbəl], a. gobernable, manejable, dirigible, sujeto a reglas; permisible, permitido, lícito.

rule [ru:l], s. mando, dominación, poder, autoridad, señorío, dominio; regla, precepto, estatuto, canon; regimen, gobierno; (*arq.*) ságoma, escantillón; tasa, modelo, medida, método, pauta, guía, norma; principio; (*for.*) auto, fallo de un tribunal; regla (para medir); (*impr.*) filete, raya; arreglo, buen orden, regularidad; línea; *to be the rule,* ser de regla; *rules and regulations,* reglamento; *to make it a rule,* hacerse (o imponerse) la regla (o costumbre) de; *to bear rule,* mandar. — *v.t.* gobernar, dominar, regir, mandar, subyugar, reprimir, moderar, contener; (*for.*) decidir, disciplinar, determinar, disponer; dirigir, guiar; establecer una regla, una ley; rayar, trazar rayas, marcar con rayas o líneas (papel); reglar; arreglar, ordenar; *to rule out,* (*for.*) no admitir, no recibir, desechar. — *v.i.* mandar, tener mando o autoridad; dominar, señorear, regir, gobernar, reinar, imperar; prevalecer, privar, estar en boga; formular una decisión, establecer (o poner) una regla; (*com.*) mantenerse, permanecer en determinado estado o nivel; *to rule over,* mandar, dominar, gobernar.

ruler, s. gobernador, gobernante; regla para trazar líneas.

ruling, s. (*for.*) decisión, fallo, orden reglamentaria, disposición; rayado; rayadura; *ruling price,* (*com.*) precio predominante; *ruling-pen,* tiralíneas, *m.sing.*; *ruling-machine,* máquina para rayar.

rullion ['rʌljən], s. zapato de cuero sin adobar.

rum [rʌm], s. ron; (*Méx.*) chinguirito. — *a.* (*fam., Ingl.*) extraño, singular; raro.

rumble ['rʌmbəl], *v.t., v.i.* retumbar, rugir; producir un sonido sordo y continuo; alborotar; avanzar con estruendo; (*fam.*) descubrir. — *s.* rumor, ruido sordo y prolongado; estruendo; asiento elevado o pescante situado detrás de un coche.

rumbler, s. lo que hace un ruido sordo y continuo.

rumbustious [rʌm'bʌstʃəs], a. ruidoso, tumultuoso.

rumen ['ru:men], s. (*zool.*) omaso, panza.

rumgumption [rʌm'gʌmʃən], s. (*Esco.*) sentido común.

ruminant ['ru:minənt], s., a. rumiador, rumiante; (*fig.*) meditativo.

ruminate ['ru:mineit], *v.t., v.i.* rumiar, masticar; (*fig.*) reflexionar, considerar, pensar con reflexión, con madurez.

rumination, s. rumia, rumiadura; (*fig.*) meditación.

ruminative ['ru:minətiv], a. reflexivo, que reflexiona; dado a la meditación.

rummage ['rʌmidʒ], *v.t., v.i.* (*mar.*) estibar, arrumar; revolver, explorar, escudriñar; agitar (un líquido); (con *out* o *up*) hallar, desenterrar. — *v.i.* revolver todo en busca de una cosa, ir trastornándolo todo. — *s.* revuelta, desorden, trastorno.

rummager, s. saqueador, explorador.

rumour ['ru:məɹ], s. rumor, runrún. — *v.t.* divulgar, propalar, esparcir; *it is rumoured,* se dice comúnmente.

rump [rʌmp], s. rabadilla u obispillo de ave; anca; solomo de vaca; (*despec.*) trasero, nalga.

rumple ['rʌmpəl], *v.t.* arrugar, hacer pliegues, apañuscar, ajar, chafar. — *s.* arruga, doblez, pliegue irregular, ajamiento, estrujadura.

rumpus ['rʌmpəs], s. batahola.

rumpy ['rʌmpi], s. gato sin cola originario de la isla de Man.

run ['rʌn], *v.t.* (*pret.* **ran**; *p.p.* **run**) correr, recorrer, hacer correr; cazar, perseguir; echar, empujar, impeler; tirar (una línea); pasar (la vista); picar, clavar, herir de punta; meter, hacer entrar, introducir; (*cost.*) bastear, coser en una línea contínua; atravesar, cruzar; verter, derramar, manar; fundir, derretir, moldear; manejar, dirigir (una máquina, institución, empresa); hacer o efectuar corriendo; verter, echar, manar, descargar; hacer derretirse, arriesgar, aventurar. — *v.i.* correr, ir corriendo, seguir corriendo, pasar rápidamente, hender el aire, volar, deslizarse, resbalarse; andar, marchar; competir, lidiar, huir, apresurarse; cambiarse rápidamente; derretirse, derramarse, manar, gotear, fluir, rezumarse, chorrear; (*teat.*) representarse consecutivamente; (*med.*) supurar; suceder, ocurrir; decir, leer; estar admitido; estar en fuerza, en boga, en operación, en actividad, desarrollarse por medio de acrecimiento; continuar, seguir, proseguir, proceder; correr a porfía; ser fácil (del estilo); inclinarse, tender, tener predisposición; hacer contrabando; *to run across,* atravesar corriendo, tropezar con, encontrarse con, encontrar por casualidad; *to run about,* andar de una parte a otra; *to run* *against*, chocar, topar, dar contra; *to run after*, ir tras de, seguir; perseguir; aspirar a, anhelar por; *to run ahead*, correr delante; *to run aground*, (*mar.*) encallar; zozobrar; *to run away*, huir, escapar, tomar soleta, zafarse; *to run away with*, arrebatar, precipitar, fugarse con; *to run along*, correr a lo largo; correr por todo un espacio; *to run back*, volver atrás, retroceder; *to run behind*, correr detrás; quedarse atrás; *to run by*, ser conocido por; pasar por; *to run counter*, oponerse; ir en contra; *to run down*, dar caza; (*mar.*) echar a pique; envilecer, difamar, vilipendiar; oprimir, agobiar; gastar la salud; pararse (un reloj); acabarse (la cuerda); quebrantar, postrar; gotear, chorrear, destilar; *to run foul of*, (*mar.*) chocar, abordar; *to run in*, entrar; coincidir, convenir; (*impr.*) recorrer; encerrar; *to run in the blood* (o *in the family*), venir de familia, estar en la sangre; *to run in for the land*, (*mar.*) andar con lo proa a tierra; *to run into*, meterse de cabeza en, chocar o topar con; *to run off*, desviar; vaciar, desecar; pasar rápidamente de una cosa a otra; repetir, decir de coro; *to run off with*, huirse con; *to run on*, continuar; *to run out*, salir (o salirse) corriendo, gastarse, acabarse, concluirse; dilatarse, extenderse; esparcirse, derramarse, escurrirse; *the deed runs thus*, la escritura dice o reza así; *to run out a warp*, (*mar.*) tender una espía; *to run over*, repasar, revisar de prisa; darramarse, rebosar, salir de madre; pasar por encima, atropellar; pasar al otro lado; *to run to*, acudir; correr a o hacia; propender, tender; correr al socorro de uno; *to run through*, atravesar, pasar de parte a parte; traspasar; derrochar, malbaratar; leer por encima, hojear; *to run up*, (*cost.*) remendar, repasar; sumar, hacer una suma; incurrir, hacer subir una cuenta; montar o edificar de prisa; contraerse, encogerse; crecerse, aumentarse; levantar, dar más altura a, izar; *to run on* (o *upon*), mencionar de paso; versar sobre, referirse a; correr por encima de; acometer; *to run up and down*, correr de una parte a otra; subir y bajar corriendo; *to run to seed*, granar; *to run the hazard* (o *the risk*), correr peligro; *to run the gauntlet*, pasar por baquetas; *as they run*, (*com.*) al barrer, sin escoger; *to have a run to run*, (*com.*) vencer dentro de ocho días. — *a.* extraído; derretido; vaciado. — *p.p.* [RUN]. — *s.* corrida, curso, carrera, marcha; (*mil.*) marcha forzada; paseo, vuelta, excursión, viajecito, jornada; batida de caza; carrera, hilera; sitio frecuentado; (*mar.*) singladura; recorrido; (*teat.*) serie de representaciones consecutivas de una pieza; curso, período de operación, continuación, serie, *f.*; (*mec.*) marcha, movimiento, operación; duración, vida de alguna cosa; aceptación, aprobación; libre uso, discreción o libertad en el uso de una cosa, gusto, voluntad; hilo del discurso; asedio de un banco por los imponedores; ribazón, *f.*; terreno de pasto, migración; (*min.*) caída (de la caja de un elevador); inclinación, dirección, buzamiento; galería inclinada; (*mar.*) racel; (*mús.*) escala; *a day's run*, (*mar.*) singladura; *good* (o *bad*) *run at play*, buena (o mala) suerte en el juego; *in the long run*, al fin y al cabo; tarde o temprano; a la corta o a la larga, a la postre;

run of mine, (*min.*) producto (mineral, carbón, etc.).

runabout [ˈrʌnəbaut], *s.* vagabundo; (*carr.*) birlocho; (*aut.*) coche ligero.

runagate [ˈrʌnəgeit], *s.* (*ant.*) renegado, apóstata, *m.f.*; vagamundo.

runaway [ˈrʌnəwei], *s.*, *a.* tránsfuga, *m.f.*, desertor, fugitivo; fuga; caballo desbocado; *runaway match*, casamiento que sigue a una fuga.

runcinate [ˈrʌnsineit], *a.* (*bot.*) dentado hacia atrás.

rundlet [ˈrʌndlet], *s.* barrilejo.

rune [ruːn], *s.* runa.

rung [rʌŋ], *pret.*, *p.p.* [RING]. — *s.* peldaño de escala, travesaño de silla; barrote, listón; (*mar.*) varengas, planes.

rung-heads, *s.pl.* (*mar.*) escoas, puntas de escoa.

runic [ˈruːnik], *a.* rúnico, runo. — *s.* (*impr.*) tipo llamado rúnico.

runlet [ˈrʌnlet], **runnel** [ˈrʌnəl], *s.* arroyuelo.

runner [ˈrʌnəɹ], *s.* corredor; mensajero; contrabandista, *m.f.*; peatón, andarín; vástago; agente, factor; maquinista, *m.*; fugitivo; (*mol.*) corredera, muela, volandera; alguacil, corchete; anillo movible; (*bot.*) serpa, jerpa; (*hidr.*) rueda móvil (de turbina); pasador corredizo; *runner of a crowfoot*, (*mar.*) perigallo de araña; *runner of a tackle*, (*mar.*) amante de aparejo.

running, *s.* carrera, corrida, curso; celo de ciertos animales; contrabando, matute; (*med.*) corrimiento; laboreo. — *a.* corredor; corriente; (*med.*) supurante; rápido, por encima; repetido; *twice running*, dos veces seguidas; *running hand*, letra corrida; *running headline* (o *title*), (*impr.*) título de página; *running rigging*, (*mar.*) cabos de labor; *running water*, agua viva, agua corriente, agua de pie. — *adv.* en sucesión.

runnion [ˈrʌnjən], ’*s.* pelafustán, pandorgo.

runround [ˈrʌnraund], *s.* panadizo.

runt [rʌnt], *s.* redrojo; paloma; enano.

runway [ˈrʌnwei], *s.* (*E.U.*) lecho, cauce, madre, *f.*; senda; (*f.c.*) vía; (*aer.*) pista de aterrizaje.

rupee [ruːˈpiː], *s.* rupía.

rupture [ˈrʌptʃəɹ], *s.* rompimiento, rotura, quebrantamiento, destrozo; reventazón, *f.*; (*med.*) potra, quebradura, hernia; ruptura, riña, hostilidad, desavenencia. — *v.t.* romper, fracturar, quebrar; hacer pedazos, reventar. — *v.i.* abrirse, romperse, henderse, reventar, rejarse.

rupturewort, *s.* milengrana, herniaria.

rural [ˈruːrəl], *a.* rural, campestre, campesino, rústico, guajiro.

rurality [ruːˈræliti], **ruralness** [ˈruːrəlnis], *s.* calidad de rural.

ruralize [ˈruːrəlaiz], *v.t.* dar forma campestre a.

ruse [ruːz], *s.* ardid, artimaña, astucia, estafa, engaño.

rush [rʌʃ], *s.* ímpetu, acometida, embestida; torrente, tropel, cúmulo, apretura, agolpamiento; prisa, furia, presión; carrera precipitada, precipitación; asedio; procedimiento enérgico; (*bot.*) junco, enea, junquillo; (*E.U.*) lucha violenta; bagatela, friolera, chuchería; concurso, gentío; *rush rope*, aderra; *it is not worth a rush*, no vale un bledo (*o* un ardite). — *v.t.* empujar (*o* arrojar) con violencia; despachar con prontitud, activar, precipitar, acelerar; (en fútbol) llevar el balón a través del campo enemigo. — *v.i.* arrojarse, precipitarse, abalanzarse; agolparse; embestir, acometer; *to rush in*, entrar de rondón; *to rush forward*, arrojarse con ímpetu; *to rush in upon*, entrar sin avisar, sorprender; *to rush through*, ejecutar de prisa; *to rush out*, exponerse atrevidamente; *to rush out*, salir precipitadamente.

rush-bottomed ['rʌʃbɔtəmd], *a.* con asiento de enea (*o* de junco).

rusher, *s.* embestidor; (en fútbol) el que cruza el campo enemigo con el balón.

rushlight ['rʌʃlait], *s.* especie de vela con pábilo de junco.

rushy, *a.* juncoso, juncino, cubierto de juncos.

rusk [rʌsk], *s.* galleta, rosca, sequillo.

russet ['rʌset], *a.* bermejo, bermejizo; rojizo; tosco, burdo, grosero; *russet leather*, cuero bermejo. — *s.* color bermejo; cuero bermejo; paño burdo; (*bot.*) manzana asperiega.

russety, *s.* bermejizo.

Russia, *s.* Rusia.

russia ['rʌʃə], **russia leather** [rʌʃə'leðəɹ], *s.* cuero o piel de Rusia; vaqueta de Moscovia.

Russian ['rʌʃən], *a.* ruso, de Rusia. — *s.* ruso (natural e idioma).

rust [rʌst], *s.* orín, herrín, herrumbre, robín, roya, moho (óxido rojizo de hierro); (*bot.*) añublo, tizón, hongo que produce esa enfermedad; defecto, mancha. — *v.i.* enmohecerse, aherrumbrarse, ponerse mohoso; embotarse, entorpecerse. — *v.t.* enmohecer, poner mohoso; aherrumbrar; embotar o entorpecer (el entendimiento).

rustic ['rʌstik], *a.* rústico, agrario, rural, agreste; campesino, aldeano, villano; sin artificio, sencillo; palurdo, morral, grosero, inculto, tocho. — *s.* patán, rústico, villano, paleto, labriego; (*Cuba*) guajiro.

rusticate ['rʌstikeit], *v.i.* rusticar, veranear, vivir en el campo, retirarse del mundo. — *v.t.* enviar al campo; expulsar temporalmente de una universidad; (*arq.*) biselar las juntas.

rustication, *s.* rusticación, acción de rusticar, estado de vivir en el campo.

rusticity [rʌs'tisiti], *s.* rusticidad, rustiquez; rudeza, grosería; simpleza.

rustily ['rʌstili], *adv.* con herrumbre; enmohecimiento, falta de uso.

rustiness, *s.* enmohecimiento, herrumbre; falta de uso; torpeza.

rustle ['rʌsəl], *v.t.*, *v.i.* susurrar, crujir (la seda o las hojas secas), producir un sonido de rozamiento; (*fam.*, *E.U.*) pernear, patear, moverse con actividad; robar ganado. — *s.* susurro, crujido, rozamiento.

rustler ['rʌsləɹ], *s.* persona o cosa que susurra; (*fam.*, *E.U.*) hombre activo o emprendedor; ladrón de ganado.

rusty ['rʌsti], *a.* oriniento, mohoso, ruginoso, herrumbroso; entorpecido, torpe por falta de práctica; rojizo, amarillento; rancio; rudo, ronco, bronco.

rut [rʌt], *s.* rodera, rodada, carril, releje, surco; rutina, hábito arraigado; costumbre; brama, toriondez, celo (de los animales); brama, bramido, mugido; sendero trillado; batahola, ruido, alboroto; *rutting time*, estación de

celo. — *v.t.* hacer rodadas o surcos. — *v.i.* bramar, estar en celo (los animales).

rutabaga [ruːtə'beigə], *s.* naba de Suecia.

rutaceous [ruː'teiʃəs], *a.* rutáceo.

ruth [ruːθ], *s.* (*ant.*) compasión, conmiseración, desgracia.

ruthenium [ruː'θiːniəm], *s.* rutenio.

ruthless ['ruːθlis], *a.* cruel, insensible, endurecido, despiadado, falto de piedad.

ruthlessness, *s.* crueldad, falta de piedad.

rutile [ruːtail], *s.* rutilio (bióxido rojo de titanio).

ruttish ['rʌtiʃ], *a.* toriondo, lascivo, libidinoso, salido.

rutty ['rʌti], *a.* lleno de surcos.

rye [rai], *s.* centeno; (*fam.*, *E.U.*) whisky destilado de centeno; *rye straw*, paja centenaza; *rye grass*, ballico, grama de centeno.

ryot ['raiət], *s.* (en la India) labrador, labriego, villano.

S

S, s [es], *s.* s; décimanona letra del alfabeto inglés. Tiene dos sonidos principales: como la *s* castellana en *casa*, y como la *s* castellana en *mismo*. La forma *'s* es signo posesivo o genitivo; *'s* es contracción de *is*, es.

sabal ['sæbəl], *s.* sabal.

Sabbatarian [sæbə'tɛəriən], *s.*, *a.* sabatario; persona que observa con mucho rigor el domingo.

Sabbatarianism, Sabbatism, *s.* observancia rígida del sábado.

Sabbath ['sæbəθ], *s.* sábado (judío); domingo (cristiano).

sabbatic [sə'bætik], **sabbatical** [sə'bætikəl], *a.* sabático, sabatino.

Sabian ['seibiən], *s.*, *a.* sabeo, (persona) que adora el sol.

Sabianism, *s.* sabeísmo.

sabine [sæb'ain], *s.* (*bot.*) sabina.

Sabine, *a.* sabino.

sable ['seibəl], *s.* (*zool.*) cebellina, marta cebellina; su piel. — *a.* (*blas.*) sable, negro; (*poét.*) negro.

sabot ['sæbou], *s.* zueco, almadreña; (*arti.*) salero de granada.

sabotage [sæbou'taːʒ], *s.* sabotaje. — *v.t.* sabotear.

saboteur ['sæbotəːɹ], *s.* saboteador.

sabre ['seibəɹ], *s.* sable. — *v.t.* acuchillar, herir a sablazos.

sabulosity [sæbju'lɔsiti], *s.* calidad de sabuloso, arenoso.

sac [sæk], *s.* (*biol.*) saco, cavidad, receptáculo, bolsa.

saccate ['sækeit], *a.* en forma de bolsa o saco.

sacchariferous [sækə'rifərəs], *a.* sacarífero.

saccharimeter [sækə'rimitəɹ], **saccharometer** [sækə'rɔmitəɹ], *s.* sacarímetro, sacarómetro.

saccharin(e) ['sækərin], *s.* sacarina.

saccharine, saccharous, *a.* sacarino, azucarado.

saccharoid ['sækərɔid], *a.* sacaroideo.

saccharose ['sækərous], *s.* sacarosa.

sacerdotal [sæsəɹ'doutəl], *a.* sacerdotal.

sacerdotalism, *s.* carácter y métodos sacerdotales; clericalismo.

sachem ['sɑːtʃem, 'sætʃem], s. (*E.U.*) cacique indio.

sachet ['sæʃei], s. sachet, perfumador.

sack [sæk], s. saco, costal, saca, talega; medida de tres fanegas; (*mil.*) saqueo de una plaza, saco, botín; vino blanco generoso (de España y Canarias); (*sast.*) saco; bata americana; chaqueta del siglo 17 y 18; *to give the sack*, (*fam.*) echar, despedir; *to get the sack*, (*fam.*) ser despedido; *sack race*, carrera de hombres metidos en sacos. — *v.t.* ensacar, meter en un saco; (*mil.*) saquear; (*fam.*) des pedir; *to sack up*, ensacar.

sackbut ['sækbət], s. sacabuche.

sackcloth, s. harpillera.

sacker ['sækəɹ], s. saqueador, persona que saquea.

sackful ['sækful], s. costal o saco lleno.

sacque [sæk], s. (*cost.*) saco, chaqueta.

sacrament ['sækrəmənt], s. sacramento; eucaristía; *to receive the sacrament*, comulgar.

sacramental [sækrə'mentəl], a. sacramental.

sacramentarian [sækrəmen'tɛəriən], a. sacramental. — s. (*igl.*) sacramentario.

sacramentary, a. sacramental. — s. (*igl.*) sacramentario (libro).

sacrarium [sə'krɛəriəm], s. (*igl.*) sagrario; (*arq.*) capillita.

sacred ['seikred], a. sagrado, consagrado, sacro, santo; digno de reverencia; inviolable, particular.

sacredness, s. santidad, carácter sagrado; inviolabilidad.

sacrifice ['sækrifais], v.t. sacrificar, inmolar; matar, destruir; abandonar, renunciar. — v.i. sacrificar, ofrecer sacrificios. — s. inmolación, sacrificio; víctima; (*fig.*) sacrificio.

sacrificer, s. sacrificador.

sacrificial [sækri'fiʃəl], a. sacrificador; de la naturaleza de un sacrificio; empleado en los sacrificios.

sacrilege ['sækrilednʒ], s. sacrilegio.

sacrilegious [sækri'lednʒəs], a. sacrílego.

sacring ['sækriŋ], s. consagración.

sacrist ['sækrist], **sacristan** ['sækristən], s. sacristán.

sacristy, s. sacristía.

sacrosanct ['sækrosæŋkt], a. sacrosanto.

sacrum ['seikrəm], s. sacro.

sad [sæd], a. triste, pensativo, pesaroso, cariacontecido, melancólico; perverso, cruel, malo; lastimoso, lastimero; lóbrego, fúnebre, lúgubre, funéreo; aciago, funesto, nefasto, infausto, calamitoso; (*ant.*) obscuro, sombrío; (*fig.*) travieso, malicioso, pícaro; *to make sad*, entristecer, afligir; *to grow sad*, entristecerse; *sad dog*, (*fig.*) pícaro, diablillo.

sadden ['sædən], v.t. entristecer, contristar, poner triste, causar o dar tristeza a; (*tint.*) rebajar un color. — v.i. entristecerse, ponerse triste.

saddle ['sædəl], s. silla de montar (a caballo o en bicicleta); enjalma; (*mec.*) silla, cojinete; lo que tiene la forma de una silla; soporte, caballete de asiento (de una caldera); silla de los cilindros (de una locomotora); depresión, paso, garganta (de una montaña); cuarto trasero de una res; *hunting saddle*, galápago; *saddle of mutton*, lomo de carnero; *pack-saddle*, basto, albarda, aceruelo; *saddle cloth*, mantilla de silla; *saddle cover*, acitara; telliz; *saddle maker*, sillero; *saddle horse*,

caballo de silla; *saddle tree*, fuste de silla; arzón, tejuelo. — *v.t.* ensillar, poner la silla a, enalbardar; cargar, poner a cuestas; *to saddle oneself with*, echarse al hombro.

saddlebacked, a. ensillado, encorvado, ancho de espaldas.

saddle-bag, s. alforja, (*Méx.*) cojinillo.

saddle-bow, s. arzón.

saddle-galled, a. lastimado por la silla.

saddler ['sædləɹ], s. sillero, talabartero.

saddlerock ['sædəlrɔk], s. (*E.U.*) variedad de ostra grande.

saddlery ['sædləri], s. talabartería, herraje de sillero.

saddle-tree, s. fuste de silla.

Sadducee ['sædjuːsiː], s. saduceo.

Sadduceeism, s. saduceísmo.

sad-iron ['sædəiən], s. plancha para la ropa.

sadism ['seidizm], s. sadismo.

sadist, s. sadista, *m.f.*

sadistic, a. sadista.

sadly ['sædli], adv. tristemente; *to be sadly*, (*fam.*) estar indispuesto.

sadness ['sædnis], s. tristeza, melancolía, pesadumbre, entristecimiento.

safe [seif], a. seguro, salvo; intacto, incolume, ileso, sin lesión; cierto; leal, digno de confianza; *safe keeping*, guarda, custodia, depósito; *safe and sound*, sano y salvo; *to be safe from the rain*, estar al abrigo de la lluvia; *it is safe to say*, es indudable que. — s. caja de caudales; alacena, despensa.

safe-conduct, s. salvoconducto.

safeguard ['seifgɑːɹd], s. salvaguardia, defensa; protección; precaución; salvoconducto; escolta. — *v.t.* proteger, guardar.

safely ['seifli], adv. seguramente, sin peligro, a salvo, felizmente.

safeness, s. estado o condición de seguridad.

safety ['seifti], s. seguridad, resguardo; incolumidad; *safety-pin*, imperdible; *safety-belt*, cinto de seguridad, salvavidas, *m.*; *safety-catch*, fiador; *safety-curtain*, telón de seguridad; *safety-lamp*, (*min.*) lámpara de seguridad; *safety-valve*, válvula de seguridad.

saffian ['sæfiən], s. cuero de cabra o carnero curtido con zumaque y teñido de amarillo o rojo.

safflower ['sæflauəɹ], s. alazor, cártamo, azafrán bastardo.

saffron ['sæfrən], s. azafrán. — a. azafranado, de color de azafrán.

sag [sæg], v.t. combar, hacer doblegar. — v.i. combarse, ceder, doblegarse; hundirse; rezagarse; aflojar, flaquear; (*mar.*) irse a la ronza. — s. hundimiento, comba.

saga ['sɑːgə], s. saga; epopeya.

sagacious [sə'geiʃəs], a. sagaz, avisado, perspicaz; penetrante, sutil, listo, vivo, ladino.

sagaciousness [sə'geiʃəsnis], **sagacity** [sə'gæsiti], s. sagacidad, astucia, perspicacia; sutileza, penetración.

sagamore ['sægəmɔːɹ], s. (*E.U.*) cacique indio.

sagapenum [sægə'piːnəm], s. sagapeno.

sage [seidʒ], s. (*bot.*) salvia; filósofo, sabio; *sage brush*, artemisa. — a. sabio; sagaz, grave; prudente; cuerdo.

sageness, s. sabiduría, prudencia, cordura, gravedad.

saggar ['sægɑːɹ], s. caja refractaria para cocer porcelana fina.

sagittal ['sædʒitəl], a. sagital.
Sagittaria [sædʒi'tɛəriə], s. sagitaria, saetilla.
Sagittarius, s. Sagitario.
sago ['seigou], s, sagú.
saguaro [sægu:'ɑːrou], s. pitahaya.
sahib ['sɑːib], s. señor (tratamiento indio).
said [sed], a. citado, antedicho, ya nombrado. — p.p. [SAY].
sail [seil], s. (mar.) vela; excursión o paseo en barco; velero; aspa (de molino); (mec.) ala; main-sail, (mar.) vela mayor; main-top-sail, gavia; fore-sail, trinquete; main-top-gallant-royal, sobrejuanete mayor; main-top-gallant-sail, juanete mayor; fore-top-sail, velacho; fore-top-gallant-sail, juanete de proa; mizzen-sail, mesana; mizzen-top-sail, sobremesana; mizzen-top-gallant-sail, juanete de mesana; studding-sail, rastrera, ala; fore-stay-sail, trinquetilla; sprit-sail, cebadera; stay-sail, vela de estay; to set sail, hacerse a la vela; to strike sail, arriar una vela; fleet of seventeen sail of the line, escuadra de diecisiete navíos de línea. — v.i. darse a la vela, hacerse a la vela, navegar; zarpar; ir o viajar por río, lago o mar; ir embarcado; dar un paseo en barco; flotar, ir por el aire, mecerse en el aire; deslizarse; moverse majestuosamente. — v.t. guiar, gobernar (una embarcación); surcar, navegar por, viajar en; to sail close hauled o to sail close with the wind, ceñir el viento, bolinear; to sail along the coast, costear; to sail back, tomar puerto; to sail before the wind, navegar viento en popa, navegar a dos puños; to sail with the wind on the beam, navegar con el viento a través; to make sail, partir, desplegar las velas, zarpar.
sailable, a. navegable a la vela.
sailcloth, s. lona.
sailer ['seiləɹ], s. buque de vela, embarcación, navío; good sailer, fine sailer, navío velero.
sailing ['seiliŋ], s. acto de darse a la vela, de zarpar; zarpa; náutica, navegación; sailing-boat, barco de vela, barco velero, barca; sailing-orders, orden de salida dada a un buque; sailing-directions, noticias marítimas; plain sailing, fácil avance o progreso; (fig.) coser y cantar; plane sailing, navegación sobre la carta de marear; great-circle sailing, navegación circular; sailing master, piloto.
sail-loft, s. tinglado, almacén de velas.
sail-maker, s. fabricante de velas.
sailor ['seiləɹ], s. marinero, marino, hombre de mar.
sailyard, s. verga.
sainfoin ['seinfɔin], s. mielga, pipirigallo.
saint [seint], s. santo, santa; (fig.) ángel. — a. santo; como título (generalmente abreviado St.) San, Santo, Santa; St. Vitus' dance, (med.) corea, baile de San Vito; St. Bernard, perro de San Bernardo; St. John's bread, (bot.) algarrobo; St. John's wort, hipérico, corazoncillo, hierba de San Juan. — v.t. canonizar. — v.i. obrar como un santo; fingir santidad.
sainted, a. santo; consagrado, sagrado, bendito; piadoso, devoto, virtuoso.
saintlike, saintly, a. propio de un santo, que obra como un santo.
saintliness, s. santidad, santificación.
saintship ['seintʃip], **sainthood** ['seinthud], s. santidad, carácter de santo.
saith [seθ], (ant.) 3a. pers. pres. indic. [SAY];

dice; how saith it? o what saith it? ¿qué dice?
sake [seik], s. causa, fin, motivo, razón, f., objeto; respeto, amor, consideración; for politeness' sake, por política; for goodness' sake, o for God's sake, por Dios; por amor de Dios; for your sake, por Vd., en obsequio a Vd., por respeto a Vd.; for brevity's sake, en obsequio de la brevedad; do it for my sake, hágalo Vd. por mí.
saker ['seikəɹ], s. (orn., arti.) sacre.
sal [sæl], s. (quím., farm.) sal, f.; sal soda, sosa, carbonato de sodio; sal ammoniac, sal amoniaco.
salaam [sə'læm], **salam** [sə'lɑːm], v.t., v.i. hacer zalamas. — s. zalema.
salability [seilə'biliti], **salableness** ['seiləbəlnis], s. facilidad de ser vendida una cosa.
salable ['seiləbəl], a. vendible, que puede ser vendido, de fácil venta, realizable, venal.
salacious [sə'leiʃəs], a. salaz, lascivo, lujurioso.
salaciousness [sə'leiʃəsnis], **salacity** [sə'læsiti], s. salacidad, lascivia, lujuria.
salad ['sæləd], s. ensalada; salad-oil, aceite para ensaladas; salad-dressing, mayonesa; salad bowl, salad dish, ensaladera.
salal ['sæləl], s. arbusto perenne de California (Gaultheria shallon).
salamander ['sæləmændəɹ], s. salamandra, salamanquesa; salamander's hair o wool, (min.) asbesto, amianto.
salamandrine, a. semejante a la salamandra.
salaried ['sælərid], a. asalariado.
salary ['sæləri], s. salario; honorarios; paga, sueldo.
sale [seil], s. venta; almoneda, subasta; voga, demanda, mercado; oportunidad de vender; for sale, u on sale, de venta; sale by auction, subasta, almoneda; on sale or return, (com.) contrato de retroventa.
saleable, saleableness, etc. [SALABLE, SALABLENESS, etc.].
salep ['sæləp], s. salep.
saleratus [sælə'reitəs], s. (coc.) bicarbonato de sosa o potasa para usos culinarios.
salesman ['seilzmən], s.m. vendedor; dependiente de tienda.
saleswoman, s.f. vendedora; dependiente de tienda.
Salian ['seiliən], a. y s. salio.
Salic ['seilik], a. sálico; Salic law, ley sálica.
salicaceous [sæli'keiʃəs], a. salicíneo.
salicetum [sæli'siːtəm], s. salceda.
salicin, salicine ['sælisin], s. salicina.
salicylate, s. salicilato.
salicylic [sæli'silik], a. salicílico.
salience, s. proyección, salidizo.
salient ['seiliənt], a. surgente, saliente, saltante; conspicuo, notable. — s. saliente, resalto, esquina, ángulo; (fort. y mil.) saliente.
saliferous [sə'lifərəs], a. salífero.
salifiable [sæli'faiəbəl], a. salificable.
salify ['sælifai], v.t. salificar.
saline ['seilain], **salinous** [sə'lainəs], a. salino, que contiene sal.
salineness, s. calidad de salino.
salinometer [sæli'nɔmetəɹ], s. pesasales, m.sing.
saliva [sə'laivə], s. saliva, esputo.
salival [sə'laivəl], **salivary** [sə'laivəri], a. salival; salivoso.
salivant, s. sialismo. — a. salival.

salivate ['sæliveit], *v.t.* desalivar.
salivation, *s.* babeo, desalivación, salivación.
sallet ['sælet], *s.* (*ant.*) celada.
sallow ['sælou], *a.* cetrino, lívido, pálido, descolorido, amarillo. — *s.* (*bot.*) sarga.
sallowness, *s.* palidez, lividez, amarillez.
sally ['sæli], *s.* (*mil.*) salida, surtida; ímpetu, arranque, arrancada; paseo, excursión; salida de pie de banco, humorada; (*arq.*) saledizo, vuelo, saliente; *sallies of wit*, agudezas, rasgos de ingenio, ocurrencias chistosas o saladas. — *v.i.* salir, hacer una salida, avanzar con denuedo, tener un arranque.
sallyport, *s.* (*fort.*) surtida.
salmagundi [sælmə'gʌndi], *s.* salpicón; (*fig.*) baturrillo, mescolanza.
salmiac ['sælmiək], *s.* sal amoniaco natural.
salmon ['sæmən], *s.* salmón; color de salmón; *salmon trout*, trucha salmonada.
salol ['seilɔl], *s.* salol.
Salomonic [sælo'mɔnik], *a.* salomónico.
salon ['sælɔŋ], *s.* salón.
saloon [sə'luːn], *s.* salón, sala de visitas, gran sala; (*f.c.*) coche salón; cámara (de un vapor); (*E.U.*) taberna, cantina; *saloon keeper*, tabernero.
salpiglossis [sælpi'glɔsis], *s.* planta herbácea de América del Sur.
salsify ['sælsifai], *s.* salsifí.
salt [sɔːlt], *s.* sal, *f.*, sabor, gusto; (*quím.*) sal, *f.*; ingenio chispeante, gracia, viveza, agudeza; incredulidad; *old salt*, (*mar.*) lobo de mar. — *pl.* **salts**, sales medicinales, *f.*; (*fam.*) sal de higuera. — *a.* salado; curado o conservado con sal; impregnado de sales; salobre, salino; *salt box*, salero de cocina; *salt cellar*, salero de mesa; *salt junk*, (*mar.*) carne de buey dura, tasajo de rancho; *rock salt*, sal gema; *salt lick*, salegar, lamedero; *salt mines*, minas de sal; *salt marsh*, saladar o marisma; *salt pan*, caldera en que se hace la sal, saladar; *salt pit*, saladar, lagunajo; *salt meat*, carne salada, cecina; *salt spring*, fuente de agua salada; *salt tub*, saladero; *he's not worth his salt*, no vale el pan que come. — *v.t.* salar, salpresar, curar con sal, sazonar con sal, arencar; salpimentar; (*fig.*) sazonar, purificar; (*fam.*) poner mineral subrepticiamente en una mina para darle valor.
saltant ['sæltənt], *a.* saltante.
saltation [sæl'teiʃən], *s.* saltación, salto; palpitación.
saltatorial [sæltə'tɔːriəl], **saltatory** [sæl-'teitəri], *a.* saltón.
salter ['sɔːltəɹ], *s.* salador; salinero.
saltern, *s.* salina.
saltigrade ['sæltigreid], *a.* saltígrado.
salting ['sɔːltiŋ], *s.* acción de salar, salazón, *f.*; *salting-tub*, saladero.
saltire ['sæltaiəɹ], *s.* (*blas.*) sotuer; cruz de San Andrés.
saltish ['sɔːltiʃ], *a.* algo salado, salobre, sabroso.
saltless, *a.* soso, desabrido, insulso, insípido.
salt-maker, *s.* salinero.
saltmarsh, *s.* saladar, marisma.
saltness, *s.* sabor de sal.
saltpeter, **saltpetre** [sɔːlt'piːtəɹ], *s.* nitro, salitre; *saltpetre-maker*, salitrero; *saltpetre house o works*, nitrería; salitrería.
saltworks, *s.* salina.

saltwort, *s.* barrilla, sosa.
salty ['sɔːlti], *a.* salado; salobre, salobreño.
salubrious [sə'ljuːbriəs], *a.* salubre, saludable, salutífero.
salubriousness, **salubrity**, *s.* salubridad.
salutariness, *s.* salubridad.
salutary ['sæljuːtəri], *a.* saludable, salubre, salutífero, sano.
salutation [sæljuː'teiʃən], *s.* salutación, saludo; enhorabuena, bienvenida, parabién.
salutatory, *a.* saludador. — *s.* discurso de bienvenida.
salute [sə'ljuːt, sæ'luːt], *v.t.*, *v.i.* saludar, ofrecer un saludo, mostrar respeto (a); (*mil.*) cuadrarse; (*ant.*) besar. — *s.* salutación; saludo; salva, honras militares o navales; (*ant.*) abrazo, beso.
salvability, **salvableness**, *s.* posibilidad de ser redimido o de salvarse.
salvable ['sælvəbəl], *a.* que puede salvarse.
salvage ['sælvidʒ], *s.* salvamento; *salvage money*, derecho de salvamento.
salvarsan [sæl'vɑːɹsən], *s.* salvarsán.
salvation [sæl'veiʃən], *s.* salvación; *Salvation Army*, Ejército de la Salvación.
salve [sælv], *s.* emplasto, pomada, ungüento; remedio, socorro, auxilio. — *v.t.* curar una herida con ungüentos o emplastos; remediar, socorrer, auxiliar, salvar.
salver, *s.* salvilla, bandeja.
salvia ['sælviə], *s.* salvia.
salvo ['sælvou], *s.* salvedad, excepción, reservación, restricción mental, subterfugio, escapatoria; salva de artillería.
salvor ['sælvəɹ], *s.* persona o buque efectuando un salvamento.
sam [sæm], **sammy** ['sæmi], *v.t.* humedecer o secar parcialmente un cuero en el proceso de manufactura.
samara ['sæmərə], *s.* sámara.
Samaritan [sə'mæritən], *s.*, *a.* samaritano, samarita *m.f.*
Sambo ['sæmbou], *s.* negro, mulato.
same [seim], *a.* mismo, idéntico; igual; *the same*, el mismo, lo mismo, la misma, los mismos, las mismas; todo uno; otro tanto; *much the same as*, casi como; *it is all the same (to me)*, lo mismo (me) da, (para mí) es todo uno; *if it is the same to you*, si a Vd. le es igual.
sameness ['seimnes], *s.* igualdad, identidad; parecido exacto.
samiel ['seimiəl], *s.* el simún.
samite ['sæmait], *s.* rica tela de seda de la Edad Media con urdimbre de seis hilos.
samlet ['sæmlet], *s.* salmón joven.
samovar ['sæmovɑːɹ], *s.* samovar.
samp [sæmp], *s.* (*E.U.*) maíz descortezado y molido para hacer gachas; potaje de samp.
samphire ['sæmfaiəɹ], *s.* hinojo marino.
sample ['sɑːmple], *s.* muestra; prueba, ejemplo; patrón, dechado; cata; *sample room*, cuarto de muestras; (*vulg.*) taberna. — *v.t.* sacar una muestra; probar, catar.
sampler ['sɑːmpləɹ], *s.* probador, catador; (*cost.*) dechado; *bottom samplers*, catadores de fondo; *soil sampler*, (*ing.*) cuchara de sondeo.
sanative ['sænətiv], *a.* curativo, sanativo, que sana.
sanativeness, *s.* calidad de sanativo.

sanatorium [sænə'tɔːriəm], s. sanatorio, estación balnearia, casa de salud.

sanatory ['sænətəri], a. sanador, sanitario.

sanctification [sæntifi'keiʃən], s. santificación; consagración.

sanctifier ['sæŋktifaiəɹ], s. santificador.

sanctify ['sæŋktifai], v.t. santificar.

sanctimonious [sæŋkti'mouniəs], a. beato, santucho, mojigato.

sanctimoniously, adv. con mojigatería, con santimonia, con apariencia de santidad.

sanctimoniousness, s. santurronería, santimonia, mojigatería, apariencia de santidad.

sanctimony ['sæŋktiməni], s. santimonia, santurronería, beatería, apariencia de santidad.

sanction ['sæŋkʃən], s. sanción; confirmación, justificación, ratificación; decreto, mandato. — v.t. sancionar, ratificar, autorizar, confirmar, validar, dar fuerza de ley.

sanctity ['sæŋktiti], s. santidad, estado de santo o sagrado, calidad o estado de obligatorio; inviolabilidad.

sanctuary ['sæŋktjuəri], s. santuario, templo; lugar santo, refugio sagrado, asilo; to take sanctuary, acogerse a sagrado.

sanctum ['sæŋktəm], s. paraje sagrado; (fam.) despacho u oficina particular, retrete.

sand [sænd], s. arena; (E.U., fam.) fuerza de carácter, sufrimiento; dinero contante, caudales; valor. — pl. **sands,** arenal, playa de arena; horas de la vida; small sand, arenilla; (Méj.) marmajita o margajita; sand bank, banco de arena; sand-blasting, chorro de arena; sand bar, barra de arena; sand-blind, muy corto de vista; sand dune, duna; sand glass, reloj de arena; sand wasp, avispa de arena; sand fly, (ent.) jijene; sand box, salvadera, arenillero; (f.c.) depósito de arena en una locomotora, caja de enarenar. — v.t. arenar, cubrir de arena, mezclar de arena, enarenar.

sandal ['sændəl], s. sandalia; abarca; hempen sandal, alpargata.

sandalwood ['sændəlwud], s. sándalo.

sandarac, sandarach ['sændəræk], s. sandáraca, grasilla; sandarach-tree, tuya; enebro.

sandbox-tree, s. hura.

sanded ['sændəd], a. arenoso, lleno de arena, cubierto de arena, arenisco; del color de arena; pecoso.

sanderling ['sændəɹliŋ], s. pequeño pájaro acuático (Calidris arenaria).

sanders ['sændəɹz], s. sándalo.

sandiness ['sændinis], s. naturaleza arenosa; rubio bermejizo.

sandiver ['sændivəɹ], s. anatrón.

sandpaper ['sændpeipəɹ], s. papel de lija. — v.t. lijar.

sandpiper ['sændpaipəɹ], s. gallineta, tringa.

sandpit, s. arenal.

sandstone, s. arenisca.

sandwich ['sændwitʃ], s. sándwich, emparedado; bocadillo; combinación de cosas diferentes alternadas; sandwich-man, hombre sándwich. — v.t. colocar entre dos capas; insertar, intercalar.

sandy, a. arenoso, arenisco; sabuloso; rufo; (E.U., vulg.) bravo, valiente, animoso.

sane [sein], a. sano, cuerdo; prudente, sagaz.

saneness, s. cordura, sanidad de ánimo; prudencia.

sang [sæŋ], pret. [SING].

sangaree [sæŋgə'riː], s. sangría (bebida).

Sangrail ['sæŋgreil], s. grial.

sanguiferous [sæŋ'gwifərəs], a. sanguífero, sanguificativo.

sanguification, s. sanguificación.

sanguifier ['sæŋgwifaiəɹ], s. cosa que puede convertirse en sangre.

sanguify, v.i. sanguificar, criar sangre.

sanguinariness, s. calidad de sanguinario.

sanguinary ['sæŋgwinəri], a. sanguinario, sangriento; cruel, inhumano, bárbaro.

sanguine ['sæŋgwin], a. confiado, lleno de esperanza, entusiasta; temerario, atrevido, vehemente, ardiente, violento, impetuoso; sanguinoso, sanguíneo, sanguino, pletórico. — s. color de sangre.

sanguineness, s. plenitud de sangre, de esperanza, confianza, ardor o entusiasmo; plétora.

sanguineous [sæŋ'gwiniəs], a. sanguino, sanguíneo, sanguinoso; de color de sangre, encarnado.

Sanhedrin, Sanhedrim ['sænedrin], s. sanedrín, sanhedrín o sinedrio; (fig.) asamblea.

sanicle ['sænikəl], s. sanícula.

sanies ['seiniːz], s. sanies, f., icor, pus icoroso.

sanious ['seiniəs], a. sanioso, icoroso, purulento.

sanitarian [sæni'tɛəriən], s., a. sanitario, perteneciente a la salud pública.

sanitarium [sæni'tɛəriəm], s. sanatorio.

sanitary ['sænitəri], a. sanitario.

sanitation [sæni'teiʃən], s. higiene, f.; sanidad pública; instalación sanitaria.

sanity ['sæniti], s. cordura, juicio sano; sentido común; sanidad.

Sanskrit ['sænskrit], **Sanscrit,** s., a. sánscrito.

Santa Claus [sæntə'klɔːz], s. Papá Noel.

santal ['sæntəl], s. sándalo.

santon ['sæntən], s. santón, fraile turco.

santonica [sæn'tɔnikə], s. santónico.

santonin, santonine ['sæntonin], s. santonina.

sap [sæp], s. savia; (fig.) vida, fuerza, vitalidad; (fort.) zapa; (fam.) necio, panoli; sap wood, alburno; (carp.) sámago. — v.t. zapar, minar, abrir camino debajo de la tierra; chupar la savia; (fig.) agotar, debilitar. — v.i. hacer trabajos de zapa; obrar por bajo mano; caminar debajo de tierra.

sapajou ['sæpədʒuː], s. sapajú, zamba.

sapan-wood ['sæpənwud], s. sapán.

sapful ['sæpful], a. lleno de savia.

saphenous [sə'fiːnəs], a. (anat.) superficial, manifiesto.

sapid ['sæpid], a. sápido, sabroso, gustoso.

sapidity, sapidness, s. sapidez, sabor, gusto.

sapience, s. sabiduría; sapiencia.

sapient ['seipiənt], a. sabio; sagaz.

sapiential, a. sapiencial.

sapless ['sæples], a. seco, sin jugo.

sapling ['sæpliŋ], s. renuevo, vástago, serpollo; árbol joven; persona joven; cachorro de lebrel.

sapodilla [sæpo'dilə], s. zapotillo, chicozapote.

saponaceous [sæpo'neiʃəs], a. jabonoso, saponáceo.

saponifiable, a. saponificable.

saponification [səpɔnifi'keiʃən], s. saponificación.

saponify [sə'pɔnifai], v.t. saponificar, convertir en jabón.

saporific [sæpo'rifik], *a.* saporífero.
sapota [sə'poutə], *s.* zapote.
sapper ['sæpəɹ], *s.* (*mil.*) zapador, gastador.
Sapphic ['sæfik], *a.* sáfico. — *s.* verso sáfico.
sapphire ['sæfaiəɹ], *s.* zafiro, zafir, zafira; color de zafiro, cerúleo.
sapphirine, *a.* zafíreo, zafirino. — *s.* (*min.*) zafirina.
sappiness ['sæpinis], *s.* abundancia de savia, jugosidad; necedad.
sappy ['sæpi], *a.* lleno de savia; jugoso; inmaturo, pueril, necio.
saraband ['særəbænd], *s.* zarabanda.
Saracen ['særəsən], *s.* sarraceno, moro.
Saracenic [særə'senik], *a.* sarracénico, moro.
sarbacand ['sɑːɹbəkænd], *s.* cerbatana.
sarcasm ['sɑːɹkæzm], *s.* sarcasmo.
sarcastic [sɑːɹ'kæstik], **sarcastical** [sɑːɹ'kæstikəl], *a.* sarcástico, irónico.
sarcel ['sɑːɹsəl], *s.* pluma del alón del halcón.
sarcenet ['sɑːɹsənet], *s.* tafetán de Florencia.
sarcine ['sɑːɹsain], *s.* compuesto nitrogenado contenido en la carne.
sarcocarp ['sɑːɹkokɑːɹp], *s.* sarcocarpio.
sarcocele ['sɑːɹkosiːl], *s.* sarcocele.
sarcocolla [sɑːɹko'kɔlə], *s.* sarcócola.
sarcode ['sɑːɹkoud], *s.* sarcoda, protoplasma animal.
sarcologic, sarcological, *a.* sarcológico.
sarcology [sɑːɹ'kɔlodʒi], *s.* sarcología.
sarcoma [sɑːɹ'koumə], *s.* sarcoma.
sarcomatous, *a.* sarcomatoso.
sarcophagous, *a.* carnívoro.
sarcophagus [sɑːɹ'kɔfəgəs], *s.* sarcófago, ataúd de piedra.
sarcotic [sɑːɹ'kɔtik], *s.*, *a.* sarcótico.
sard [sɑːɹd], *s.* sardio.
sardel ['sɑːɹdəl], **sardine** [sɑːɹ'diːn], *s.* (*ict.*) sardina; (*joy.*) sardio.
Sardinian [sɑːɹ'diniən], *a.* sardo.
sardius ['sɑːɹdiəs], *s.* sardio.
sardonic [sɑːɹ'dɔnik], *s.*, *a.* sardónico, burlador, burlón, (persona) sin sinceridad, no natural.
sardonyx ['sɑːɹdoniks], *s.* sardónice, *f.*
sargasso [sɑːɹ'gæsou], *s.* sargazo (alga).
sark [sɑːɹk], *s.* (*Esco.*) camisa.
sarkinite ['sɑːɹkinait], *s.* arsenito rojo de manganeso.
sarment ['sɑːɹmənt], **sarmentum** [sɑːɹ'mentəm], *s.* sarmiento, vástago rastrero.
sarmentose [sɑːɹmen'touz], *a.* sarmentoso.
sarsaparilla [sɑːɹsəpə'rilə], **sarsa** ['sɑːɹsə], *s.* zarzaparrilla.
sarsenet ['sɑːɹsenet], **sarsnet** ['sɑːɹsnet], *s.* tafetán de Florencia.
sartage ['sɑːɹtidʒ], *s.* tala (de una arboleda).
sartorial [sɑːɹ'toːriəl], *a.* sartorio.
sash [sæʃ], *s.* faja; cinto, cinturón; marco (de ventana); *sash-window*, ventana de guillotina.
sassafras ['sæsəfræs], *s.* sasafrás.
sat [sæt], *pret. y p.p.* [SIT].
Satan ['seitən], *s.* Satanás, el diablo.
satanic [sə'tænik], **satanical** [sə'tænikəl], *a.* satánico, infernal, diabólico.
satchel ['sætʃəl], *s.* vademécum, cartapacio (de escolar), burjaca, bolsa, saquito de mano; mochila; cartera.
sate [seit], *v.t.* hartar, saciar; hastiar.
sateen [sə'tiːn], *s.* satén, rasete.
satellite ['sætelait], *s.* satélite.
satiable ['seiʃəbəl], *a.* saciable.

satiate ['seiʃieit], *v.t.* saciar, satisfacer completamente, hartar, ahitar, llenar, saturar, colmar, sobrellenar, apestar, sobrecargar. — *v.i.* hartarse, saciarse. — *a.* harto, sacio, saciado, ahito, satisfecho; saturado, sobrellenado, sobrecargado.
satiation [seiʃi'eiʃən], *s.* hartazgo, hartura, saciedad, acto de hartarse, efecto de hartarse.
satiety [sə'taiiti], *s.* saciedad, plenitud, hartura, colmo, repleción.
satin ['sætin], *s.* (*tej.*) raso; *satin damask*, raso adamascado; *satin bird*, pájaro de Australia (*Ptilenorhyncus violaceus*); *satin flower*, lunaria.
satinet, *s.* satinete; rasete.
satin-wood, *s.* palo águila, palo áloe, doradillo.
satiny, *a.* arrasado.
satire ['sætaiəɹ], *s.* sátira; dicho agudo o mordaz.
satiric [sə'tirik], **satirical** [sə'tirikəl], *a.* satírico.
satirist ['sætərist], *s.* escritor satírico.
satirize, *v.t.* satirizar.
satisfaction [sætis'fækʃən], *s.* satisfacción; contentamiento, contento; gozo, fruición; desquite; recompensa, reparación; finiquito, pago final, pago de una deuda; desagravio.
satisfactoriness, *s.* carácter satisfactorio.
satisfactory [sætis'fæktəri], *a.* satisfactorio; expiatorio; suficiente.
satisfied, *a.* satisfecho, contento; pagado. — *p.p.* [SATISFY]; *to be easily satisfied*, pasarse con poco.
satisfy ['sætisfai], *v.t.* satisfacer, dar solución a; contentar; colmar, saciar; convencer; pagar, resarcir, recompensar. — *v.i.* satisfacer, dar o causar satisfacción.
satrap ['sætrəp], *s.* sátrapa, *m.*
satrapy, *s.* satrapía.
saturable ['sætjuːrəbəl], *a.* saturable.
saturant, *a.* saturador. — *s.* substancia que neutraliza la acidez o la alcalinidad de otra.
saturate ['sætjuːreit], *v.t.* saturar; mojar, embeber, empapar, impregnar; (*quím.*) saturar; imbuir, inculcar; colmar, llenar al extremo.
saturation, *s.* saturación.
Saturday ['sætəɹdi], *s.* sábado.
Saturn ['sætəɹn], *s.* Saturno.
Saturnalia [sætəɹ'neiliə], *s.* saturnales, *f.pl.*
Saturnalian, *a.* de las saturnales; saturnal, licencioso.
Saturnian [sə'təːɹniən], *a.* saturnal; feliz, dichoso.
saturnine [sə'təːɹnain], *a.* saturnino; silencioso, triste, melancólico; (*ant., quím.*) plomizo; *saturnine poisoning*, saturnismo.
saturnite, *s.* saturnita.
satyr ['sætəɹ], *s.* sátiro.
satyriasis [sæti'raiəsis], *s.* satiriasis, *f.*
satyric [sə'tirik], *a.* satírico.
sauce [sɔːs], *s.* salsa, moje, aderezo; (*E.U.*) ensalada; compota; (*fam.*) desfachatez; *apple-sauce*, compota de manzana. — *v.t.* condimentar, sazonar; (*fam.*) ser respondón, impertinente, decir insolencias o desvergüenzas, desvergonzarse.
sauce-boat, sauce-dish, *s.* salsera.
saucebox, *s.* muchacho descarado y atrevido.
saucepan, *s.* cacerola.
saucer ['sɔːsəɹ], *s.* platillo; salsera, salsereta.
sauciness ['sɔːsines], *s.* descaro, descoco,

insolencia, desfachatez, desmandamiento, desvergüenza.

saucisse [sou'siːs], s. (*arti*.) salchicha.

saucy ['sɔːsi], a. respondón, descarado, desvergonzado, atrevido, desfachatado, impudente, insolente.

sauerkraut ['sauəɹkraut], s. choucroute, f.

saunter ['sɔːntəɹ], v.i. vagar, pasearse; haraganear. — s. paseo, vuelta.

sauntering, s. vagancia, paseo.

Sauria ['sɔːriə], s.pl. saurios.

saurian, a. saurio.

sausage ['sɔsidʒ], s. salchicha; embutido; chorizo, longaniza; *large sausage*, salchichón; *sausage stuffer*, jeringa choricera.

savable, a. conservable; que se puede salvar.

savage ['sævidʒ], a. salvaje; silvestre; inculto; bárbaro; brutal, bravío, feroz, enfurecido, cruel. — s. salvaje, hombre inculto y bárbaro.

savageness ['sævidʒnis], **savagery** ['sævədʒəri], s. salvajez, barbarie, f., salvajismo, ferocidad, crueldad.

savanna [sæ'vænə], s. sabana, pradera.

savant ['sævɔŋ], s. sabio.

save [seiv], v.t. salvar, librar; ahorrar, economizar; reservar, conservar, guardar; evitar; aprovecharse de; eximir, proteger; dispensar; *God save the king!* ¡Viva el rey! — *prep.* salvo, excepto. — *conj.* sino, a menos que, a no ser que, si no es más que.

save-all ['seivɔːl], s. baloncita, apuracabos, m.sing.; (*mar.*) vela rastrera.

saveloy ['sævelɔi], s. embutido de puerco salado y muy sazonado.

saver ['seivəɹ], s. libertador; auxiliador; economizador, ahorrador.

savin ['sævin], s. sabina, junípero; cedro rojo.

saving ['seiviŋ], a. ahorrativo, económico, frugal; salvador; calificativo; *saving clause*, cláusula que contiene una salvedad (o reserva). — s. economía, ahorro; salvedad. — *pl.* **savings**, ahorros; *savings bank*, banco o caja de ahorros. — *prep.* con excepción de, fuera de, excepto, salvo.

savingness, s. ahorro, economía; frugalidad.

saviour ['seivjəɹ], s. salvador; *the Saviour*, el Salvador, el Redentor.

savory ['seivəri], s. (*bot.*) ajedrea.

savour ['seivəɹ], s. sabor, gustillo, gusto, dejo; sainete; olor, perfume. — v.t. saborear, sazonar, dar sabor, dar gusto. — v.i. (con *of*) saber (a), oler (a), tener sabor, gusto u olor de.

savouriness, s. sabor, buen gusto; fragancia.

savoury ['seivəri], a. sabroso, agradable, delicado, apetitoso, aperitivo, fragante. — s. (*bot*.) ajedrea; entremés salado.

savoy [sə'vɔi], s. (*bot*.) variedad de col o berza con hojas arrugadas.

Savoyard [sə'vɔijɑːɹd], s., a. saboyano, de Saboya.

saw [sɔː], s. (*carp*.) sierra; refrán, dicho, sentencia, proverbio; *cross-cut saw*, sierra de trozar; *hand-saw*, sierra o serrucho de mano; *pit-saw*, sierra abrazadera; *jig-saw*, sierra vaivén; *rompecabezas*, m.; *fret-saw*, sierra de calar o de punto. — v.t. (p.p. sawed y sawn) serrar, aserrar. — v.i. ser serrado; usar una sierra.

saw, pret. [SEE].

saw-bill, s. pájaro de la América tropical aliado del martín pescador.

saw-bones, s. (*vulg*.) un médico cirujano.

sawbuck, s. cabrilla de aserrar.

saw-doctor, s. máquina para cortar dientes en una sierra.

sawdust, s. aserraduras, serrín.

saw-fish, s. (*ict*.) priste, pez sierra.

saw-fly, s. mosca de sierra, (*Tenthredinidæ*).

sawhorse, s. caballete, cabrilla.

sawmill, s. aserradero, molino de aserrar.

sawn [sɔːn], p.p. *irreg*. [SAW]; aserrado.

sawpit, s. aserradero.

sawwort ['sɔːwəɹt], s. serrátula.

saw-wrest, s. triscador.

sawyer ['sɔːjəɹ], s. aserrador, serrador, chiquichaque; (*E.U*.) árbol caído en un río.

sax [sæks], s. hachuela (o martillo) de pizarrero.

saxatile ['sæksətail], **saxicolous**, a. saxátil.

saxe [sæks], s. (*foto*.) papel de Sajonia, papel albuminado.

saxe-blue, s. azul de Sajonia.

saxhorn ['sækshɔːɹn], s. bombardino; bombardón.

saxifrage ['sæksifridʒ], s. saxífraga.

Saxon ['sæksən], a. sajón, de Sajonia. — s. sajón; anglosajón; lengua sajona.

saxophone ['sæksofoun], s. saxófono.

say [sei], v.t. (pret. y p.p. said) decir, hablar; alegar, afirmar; repetir, recitar; presumir, suponer; *it is said*, o *they say*, se dice, dicen; *to say over again*, volver a decir, repetir; *I have something to say to you*, tengo que hablar con Vd.; *you don't say so!* ¡calle Vd.! o ¿de veras? *say what you like* (o *will*), diga Vd. lo que diga; *no sooner said than done*, dicho y hecho, o lo dicho, hecho. — v.i. decir, hacer una aserción; *to say on*, continuar hablando; *that is to say*, es decir, quiere decir; *to say on*, continuar hablando; *I say!* ¡hola! ¡escucha, oye! — s. uso de la palabra, afirmación, discurso; (*fam*.) turno de hablar; (*tej*.) sarga fina y delgada; especie de seda o raso.

saying ['seiiŋ], s. dicho, lo que se dice; aserto, relato; refrán, dicho, adagio, sentencia, proverbio; *as the saying is*, como se dice.

scab [skæb], s. (*cir*.) costra, escara; (*vet*.) roña, escabro; (*despec*.) hombre ruin o roñoso; esquirol. — v.i. criar costra sobre una llaga.

scabbard ['skæbɑːɹd], s. vaina de espada, cuchillera, funda.

scabbed ['skæbd], **scabby** ['skæbi], a. cubierto de costras, costroso, postilloso; roñoso; tiñoso; vil, ruin, miserable, despreciable.

scabbiness, s. calidad de costroso, roñoso o tiñoso.

scabies ['skeibiːz], s. sarna.

scabious ['skeibiəs], a. sarnoso. — s. escabiosa.

scabrous ['skæbrəs], a. escabroso, áspero, desigual.

scabrousness, s. escabrosidad; aspereza.

scabwort ['skæbwəɹt], s. énula campana.

scad [skæd], s. (*ict*.) escombro; sábalo, alosa.

scaffold ['skæfold], s. andamio, tablado; patíbulo, cadalso. — v.t. construir o instalar tablados o andamios; tender cadáveres sobre andamio.

scaffolding, s. construcción de andamios; castillaje, andamiada; bastidor de apoyo, armazón, f., paral, arrimadero, sostén.

scaglia ['skɑːljə], s. piedra caliza italiana.

scagliola [skɑː'ljoulə], s. estuco.

scalar ['skeilɑːɹ], *a.* (*mat.*) numérico, no vectorial. — *s.* cantidad puramente numérica.

scalariform, *a.* escaleriforme; (*biol.*) células o vasos que presentan la apariencia de escalera.

scalawag, scallawag, scalliwag ['skæliwæg], *s.* (*fam.*, *E.U.*) bribón, pícaro; persona o animal sin valor.

scald [skɔːld], *v.t.* escaldar, quemar con un líquido muy caliente; limpiar con agua muy caliente; (*coc.*) escalfar. — *s.* quema, quemadura, escaldadura; escalda, bardo escandinavo. — *a.* tiñoso; ruin, miserable, sin valor.

scald-head, *s.* tiña; acores, usagre.

scale [skeil], *s.* platillo de balanza; balanza, báscula; (*astr.*) Libra; costra, costrita; escama (de peces y reptiles); (*mat.*) escala; graduación regular, división en grados; (*bot.*) escama, hoja rudimentaria; plancha, lámina pequeña, laminita, hojuela; chispa; incrustación en las calderas; (*mús.*) escala, gama; escalón; escalada; *scales of iron*, chispas de fragua; *pair of scales*, peso de cruz; *on a large scale*, en gran escala, en grande; *on a small scale*, en pequeña escala, en pequeño. — *v.t.* escamar, cubrir con escamas; desescamar, quitar las escamas; pelar, descascarar o raspar; descortezar; incrustar; escatinar, cercenar; medir por escala, hacer un dibujo por escala; escalar, encaramarse, subir; balancear, averiguar el peso por medio de balanzas; tener (tanto) peso; pesar; comparar; igualar; graduar; *to scale down*, reducir o rebajar según una escala. — *v.i.* descostrarse; formarse incrustaciones o escamas; desconcharse, pelarse; formar a modo de escalera, servir como escalera.

scaled, *a.* escamado, escamudo, con escamas, escamoso; escalado, subido.

scalene [skei'liːn], *a.* (*geom.*) escaleno; (*anat.*) escaleno (músculo). — *s.* (*geom.*) triángulo escaleno.

scalepan, *s.* platillo de balanza.

scaler, *s.* escalador; rascador.

scaliness, *s.* escamosidad.

scaling, *s.* acción de escamar, escamadura; acción de escalar, escalada; (*mil.*) escalamiento; *scaling-ladders*, escalas de sitio, escalas de asalto.

scall [skɔːl], *s.* tiña.

scalled, *a.* tiñoso, costroso.

scallion ['skæljən], *s.* chalote, ascalonia, cebolleta.

scallop ['skæləp, 'skɔləp], *s.* (*ict.*) venera, pechina; (*cost.*) festón, recortadura, recorte, onda; concha de un romero; platito en forma de concha para ostras. — *v.t.* festonear, ondear; (*coc.*) asar ostras empanadas.

scalp [skælp], *s.* pericráneo; cuero cabelludo; frente, *f.*, cabeza. — *v.t.* quitar el pericráneo con la cabellera; (*fam.*, *E.U.*) comprar y revender.

scalpel ['skælpəl], *s.* escalpelo; bisturí.

scalper, *s.* (*fam.*, *E.U.*) revendedor de billetes de ferrocarril a precios reducidos; (*cir.*) escalpelo.

scalping ['skælpiŋ], *s.* acción de arrancar la piel del cráneo (como hacen los salvajes); *scalping-knife*, cuchillo que usan los salvajes para esta operación.

scaly ['skeili], *a.* escamudo, escamoso, con-

chado; incrustado (caldera); herrumbroso; (*fam.*) vil, deshonrado, ruin.

scammony ['skæməni], *s.* escamonea.

scamp [skæmp], *s.* bribón, pícaro, tuno. — *v.t.* frangollar.

scamper, *v.i.* escaparse, huir, escabullirse, andar muy de prisa. — *s.* fuga, huída precipitada.

scan [skæn], *v.t.* escudriñar, examinar con mucho cuidado, registrar; escandir, medir (versos).

scandal ['skændəl], *s.* escándalo; difamación, maledicencia; censura, reproche; oprobio, baldón, caída, ignominia, infamia, mancha; *scandal bearer*, detractor; *scandal-monger*, murmurador.

scandalize, *v.t.* causar escándalo a, escandalizar; difamar; acusar falsamente.

scandalous, *a.* escandaloso; chocante; infame, vergonzoso; ofensivo, difamatorio, calumnioso.

scandalousness, *s.* carácter escandaloso.

scandent ['skændənt], *a.* trepador.

Scandinavian [skændi'neiviən], *s.* escandinavo; idioma escandinavo. — *a.* escandinavo.

scansion ['skænʃən], *s.* escansión.

scansorial [skæn'sɔːriəl], **scansorious** [skæn'sɔːriəs], *a.* trepador, apto para trepar, que trepa.

scant [skænt], *v.t.* escatimar, cercenar, escasear, estrechar, limitar la provisión de una cosa. — *v.i.* (*mar.*) virar, cambiar, caer, disminuir(se) (el viento). — *a.* escaso, corto, parco, limitado; estrecho, angosto; apenas suficiente, insuficiente.

scantiness, scantness, *s.* estrechez, angostura; exigüidad, rareza, insuficiencia, escasez, miseria.

scantling, *s.* cuartón, madero, barrote; escantillón; colección de cuartones; *the scantlings,* (*mar.*) grúas de tablas.

scanty ['skænti], *a.* escaso, escatimado, parco, estrecho, limitado, corto, pequeño; económico, que ahorra, parsimonioso.

scape [skeip], *s.* (*bot.*) escapo, bohordo; (*ent.*) cuerno, antena; (*orn.*) cañón de una pluma; (*arq.*) fuste de una columna. — *v.t.*, *v.i.* (*ant.*) escapar, huir.

scapegoat ['skeipgout], *s.* cabeza de turco, víctima propiciatoria; *to be a scapegoat for,* pagar el pato por.

scapegrace ['skeipgreis], *s.* travieso, pícaro.

scapement, *s.* escape (de reloj).

scaphander [skə'fændəɹ], *s.* escafandra.

scaphoid ['skæfɔid], *a.* navicular, en forma de nave; escafoideo. — *s.* (*anat.*) escafoides.

scapinade [skæpi'neid], *s.* treta vil, acción de pilluelo (de Scapin de Molière).

scapple ['skæpəl], *v.t.* reducir una piedra a cierto nivel con el cortafrío.

scapula ['skæpjuːlə], *s.* escápula, omóplato, espaldilla, hueso de la espaldilla.

scapular, scapulary, *a.* escapular. — *s.* (*igl.*) escapulario; (*cir.*) vendaje para el omóplato.

scar [skɑːɹ], *s.* cicatriz, *f.*; chirlo, costurón; (*ict.*) escaro; peñasco, farallón, roca pelada. — *v.t.* marcar con una cicatriz.

scarab ['skærəb], *s.* ateuco, escarabajo sagrado (de los egipcios).

scaramouch ['skærəmuːʃ], *s.* bufón, botarga.

scarce [skɛəɹs], *a.* raro, contado, escaso, que escasea.

scarcely, *adv.* escasamente, apenas, con dificultad; no bien, poco.

scarceness ['skɛəɹsnis], **scarcity** ['skɛəɹsiti], *s.* carestía, penuria, escasez; raridad, rareza; esterilidad.

scare [skɛəɹ], *v.t.* asustar, espantar, causar espanto o miedo a, intimidar, amedrentar; *to scare away*, espantar, ahuyentar. — *s.* susto, sobresalto, alarma.

scarecrow, *s.* espantajo; (*fig.*) esperpento, adefesio; persona o cosa que da miedo.

scaremonger ['skɛəɹmʌŋgəɹ], *s.* propalador de rumores de calamidades.

scarf [skɑːɹf], *s.* (*pl.* **scarfs, scarves**) bufanda; corbata; chalina; faja; (*carp.*) escarpe, ensambladura, empalme. — *v.t.* (*carp.*) ensamblar, empotrar, empalmar, charpar; encabezar; adornar con una banda, poner en banda; terciar.

scarfing, *s.* empalme, acopladura, encabezadura, ensambladura; biselado.

scarf-joint, *s.* (*carp.*) junta a diente de sierra.

scarfpin, *s.* alfiler de corbata.

scarfskin, *s.* cutícula, epidermis, *f.*

scarification [skærifi'keiʃən], *s.* escarificación, sajadura.

scarificator, *s.* escarificador.

scarifier ['skærifaiəɹ], *s.* sajador, escarificador; (*agr.*) escarificador.

scarify, *v.t.* (*cir.*) escarificar, sajar, hacer incisiones con el escarificador; (*agr.*) escarificar; (*fig.*) criticar severamente, satirizar.

scarious ['skɛəɹiəs], **scariose** ['skɛəɹiouz], *a.* (*bot.*) escarioso; delgado, seco.

scarlatina [skɑːɹlə'tiːnə], *s.* escarlatina.

scarlet ['skɑːɹlet], *s.* escarlata, grana, color encarnado vivo; *scarlet fever*, escarlatina, escarlata; *scarlet oak*, coscoja. — *a.* de color escarlata.

scarp [skɑːɹp], *v.t.* hacer escarpa, cortar en declive. — *s.* (*fort.*) escarpa; pendiente, *f.*, declive.

scarry ['skɑːɹi], *a.* que tiene cicatrices.

scart, *v.t.* rascar, raer; grabar. — *s.* rasguño, marca; (*fig.*) persona miserable.

scary, *a.* (*fam.*) medroso, asustadizo, pusilánime.

scat [skæt], *interj.* ¡zape!

scath, scathe [skeið], *v.t.* desbaratar, dañar severamente.

scathe, *s.* acto de desbaratar, desbarate, daño, perjuicio.

scatheless ['skeiðles], *a.* libre de daño, sano y salvo.

scathing ['skeiðiŋ], *a.* mordaz, cáustico.

scatology [skə'tolodʒi], *s.* (*pat.*) escatología.

scatological [skæto'lodʒikəl], *a.* (*pat.*) escatológico.

scatter ['skætəɹ], *v.t.* esparcir, derramar, desparramar, desperdigar; derrotar, dispersar; disipar, malgastar. — *v.i.* dispersarse, esparcirse; disiparse.

scatter-brain, *s.* casquivano, cabeza de chorlito.

scatter-brained, *a.* atolondrado, inconstante.

scattered, *a.* disipado, disperso, desparramado, esparcido; (*bot.*) apartado, irregular. — *p.p.* [SCATTER].

scatteringly, *adv.* esparcidamente.

scaup [skɔːp], *s.* (*orn.*) pato marino.

scavenge ['skævendʒ], *v.t.* recoger o retirar la basura.

scavenger ['skævendʒəɹ], *s.* basurero; animal que se alimenta de carroña; empleado que recoge algodón suelto en las hilaturas; *scavenger beetle*, escarabajo clavicornio.

scenario [se'nɑːriou], *s.* guión; argumento.

scend [send], *v.i.* (*mar.*) arfar, cabecear (un buque). — *s.* arfada.

scene [siːn], *s.* escena, vista, perspectiva, paisaje; (*teat.*) escena, escenario; escena o episodio de un drama; decoración; cuadro que divide un acto; lugar de un acontecimiento; lance, arrebato, incidente, escándalo, impulso apasionado; *behind the scenes*, entre bastidores; *to appear on the scene*, presentarse; *to bring on the scene*, poner en escena.

sceneful, *a.* abundante en escenas o imagenes.

scene-painter, *s.* pintor escenógrafo.

scenery ['siːnəri], *s.* perspectiva, vista, paisaje; (*teat.*) escenario, decoraciones.

scene-shifter, *s.* tramoyista, *m.f.*

scenic ['senik], *a.* escénico, artístico; pintoresco.

scenographer, *s.* escenógrafo.

scenographical, *a.* escenográfico.

scenography [se'nɔgrəfi], *s.* escenografía.

scent [sent], *s.* olfato; olor, fragancia, perfume; rastro, pista; mal olor. — *v.t.*, *v.i.* oler, husmear, olfatear, ventear; perfumar; sospechar, concebir una sospecha.

scentless, *a.* sin olfato; inodoro, sin olor, que no tiene olor.

sceptic ['skeptik], *s.* escéptico.

sceptical, *a.* escéptico.

scepticism ['skeptisizm], *s.* escepticismo.

sceptre, scepter ['septəɹ], *s.* cetro.

sceptred, *a.* que tiene o lleva cetro; real, regio, imperial.

schedule ['ʃedjuːl], *v.t.* inventariar, catalogar; incluir en una lista, catálogo o inventario. — *s.* cédula; lista, nota, inventario, catálogo, descripción; anexo, documento, escrito suplementario a otro; horario (de f.c., etc.); plan, programa, *m.*

schema ['skiːmə], *s.* sumario, cuadro, sinopsis, *f.*; diagrama, *m.*; esquema, *m.*

schematic [ske'mætik], *a.* esquemático.

scheme [skiːm], *s.* plan, proyecto, designio; diseño, bosquejo, diagrama, *m.*, traza; modelo, esquema, *m.*, planta; sistema, *m.*, disposición, arreglo; ardid, treta, artificio. — *v.t.*, *v.i.* formar un plan, formar planes o proyectos, idear, proyectar, trazar, urdir, tramar, intrigar.

scheme-arch, *s.* (*arq.*) arco de forma circular, pero de menor extensión que un semicírculo.

schemer, *s.* invencionero, proyectista, *m.f.*, tracista, *m.f.*; intrigante, maquinador.

schiller ['ʃiləɹ], *s.* (*min.*) el brillo bronceado peculiar de ciertos minerales.

schism [sizm], *s.* (*igl.*) cisma, *m.f.*; separación, división, escisión, desavenencia.

schismatic [siz'mætik], *s.* cismático, disidente, fundador de un cisma.

schismatic, schismatical, *a.* cismático, disidente.

schismatize ['sizmətaiz], *v.i.* tomar parte en un cisma.

schist [ʃist], *s.* esquisto.

schistose, schistous, schistic, *a.* esquistoso.

schnaps [ʃnæps], *s.* licor parecido a la ginebra de Holanda.

scholar ['skɔlǝɹ], *s.* escolar, alumno, estudiante, colegial; literato, letrado, hombre erudito, o docto; discípulo; becario; *fellow scholar,* condiscípulo, compañero de colegio; *day scholar,* alumno externo; *classical scholar,* humanista, *m.f.,* helenista, *m.f.,* latinista, *m.f.;* *to be no scholar,* haber recibido poca instrucción; carecer de talento.

scholarly, scholar-like, *a.* de estudiante, de escolar, de literato. — *adv.* como sabio, como literato.

scholarship, *s.* saber, erudición, ciencia; beca.

scholastic [skɔ'læstik], **scholastical** [skɔ-'læstikǝl], *a.* escolástico, escolar, estudiantil, estudiantino; pedantesco; (*filos.*) escolástico.

scholasticism, *s.* escolasticismo.

scholiast ['skouliæst], *s.* escoliador.

scholium ['skouliǝm], *s.* escolio, glosa.

school [sku:l], *s.* escuela, colegio; facultad; departamento (de universidad); banco (de peces); sistema, *m.;* método de vida; *boarding school,* colegio de internos, pupilaje; *charity school,* escuela gratuita; *school book,* libro de clase, libro de texto; *school teacher,* maestro (o maestra) de escuela; *grammar school,* instituto de segunda enseñanza; *private school,* colegio particular; *in school,* en clase; *to go to school,* ir a la escuela, entrar en clase. — *v.t.* instruir, enseñar; reprender, disciplinar; adiestrar, amaestrar. — *v.i.* ir (o moverse) juntos, como los peces; moverse en masa.

schoolboy, *s.m.* muchacho de escuela, colegial.

schooled, *a.* enseñado, amaestrado. — *p.p.* [SCHOOL].

schoolfellow, *s.* compañero de colegio, condiscípulo.

schoolgirl, *s.f.* colegiala.

schoolhouse, *s.* escuela (el edificio).

schooling, *s.* instrucción elemental; enseñanza, educación; precio de la escuela, remuneración u honorarios del maestro; experiencia.

schoolman, *s.* (*filos.*) escolástico; escritor sobre teología escolástica.

schoolmaster, *s.* maestro de escuela; maestro.

schoolmate, *s.* compañero de colegio, condiscípulo.

schoolmistress, *s.f.* maestra; preceptora.

schooner ['sku:nǝɹ], *s.* (*mar.*) goleta; (*E.U.*) galera con toldo que usan los emigrantes; (*fam.*) vaso alto para cerveza.

schorl [ʃɔ:l], *s.* (*min.*) chorlo; turmalina.

sciagraph ['saiǝgræf], *s.* (*arq.*) sección vertical.

sciagraphical, *a.* esciagráfico.

sciagraphy, *s.* (*arq., astr.*) esciagrafía.

sciatica [sai'ætikǝ], *s.* ciática.

sciatic(al), *a.* ciático, isquiático.

science ['saiǝns], *s.* ciencia; sabiduría; conocimiento, pericia, destreza.

scientific [saiǝn'tifik], **scientifical** [saiǝn-'tifikǝl], *a.* científico; sistemático, exacto; sabio; perito, muy hábil.

scientist ['saiǝntist], *s.* hombre de ciencia, científico.

scimitar ['simitɑ:ɹ], *s.* cimitarra.

scintilla [sin'tilǝ], *s.* centella, chispa; traza, partícula, tilde.

scintillant, *a.* que echa chispas, centelleante.

scintillate ['sintileit], *v.i.* chispear, centellear, destellar.

scintillation, *s.* chispazo, centelleo, destello; titilación.

sciolist ['saiolist], *s.* semisabio, erudito a la violeta.

scion ['saion], (*agr.*) púa, acodo, esqueje, plantón; hijo (o hija), descendiente; vástago, verduguillo, renuevo.

scioptic [sai'ɔptik], *a.* escióptico.

scirrhosity, *s.* calidad de escirroso.

scirrhous ['sirǝs], *a.* (*med.*) cirroso, escirroso, endurecido.

scirrhus ['sirǝs], *s.* (*med.*) cirro, escirro; tumor endurecido.

scissel ['sisǝl], *s.* desperdicios, desechos o recortes de metal; escoria.

scission ['siʒǝn], *s.* corte, división, partición, separación.

scissor ['sizǝɹ], *v.t., v.i.* cortar(se), con tijeras.

scissors ['sizǝɹz], *s.pl.* tijeras.

scissure ['sisjǝɹ], *s.* cisura, cortadura, hendedura; cisma, escisión.

Sclav ['slɑ:v], **Sclavic** ['slævik], *s., a.* eslavo.

scleroma [skle'roumǝ], *s.* escleroma.

sclerosis [skle'rousis], *s.* esclerosis, *f.*

sclerotic [skle'rɔtik], *a.* escleroso, que padece esclerosis; opaco, endurecido.

sclerotica, *s.* esclerótica.

sclerotitis [sklero'taitis], *s.* esclerotitis, *f.*

scobs [skɔbz], *s.* aserraduras, limaduras, rasuras; escobina; escoria.

scoff [skɔf], *v.i.* mofarse (de), burlarse (de). — *s.* mofa, burla, escarnio, befa; hazmerreír; (*fam.*) zampar (comida).

scoffer, *s.* burlón, mofador.

scoffingly, *adv.* con mofa y escarnio.

scold [skould], *v.t., v.i.* regañar, reñir, increpar, reprender, refunfuñar, rezongar; *to scold one up and down,* o *to scold one's head off,* poner a uno como un trapo. — *s.f.* mujer regañona.

scolding, *s.* regaño, trepe, reprensión; *scolding match,* pelotera.

scoliosis [skouli'ousis], *s.* escoliosis, *f.*

scollop ['skɔlǝp], *s.* [*v.* SCALLOP].

scolopendra [skolo'pendrǝ], *s.* escolopendra, ciempiés.

scomber ['skɔmbǝɹ], *s.* (*ict.*) escombro, caballa.

sconce [skɔns], *s.* cobertizo, salidizo; (*fam.*) cabeza; (*fort.*) defensa, baluarte, fortín; yelmo; sentido, juicio, seso; (*univ.*) multa por ligera travesura; anaquel fijo; farolillo, linterna con panal exterior, linterna sorda; cornucopia, candelabro de pared. — *v.t.* fortificar con baluarte; multar.

scoop [sku:p], *s.* pala de mano; paleta; cuchara, cucharón de draga; paletada, cucharada; achique; cavidad, hueco; (*fam.*) ganancia; (*fam.*) reportaje sensacional que publica un periódico antes que los demás; (*mar.*) vertedor, achicador; acto de cavar, de ahuecar; *scoop net,* red barredera. — *v.t.* sacar con pala o cuchara; vaciar, achicar; cavar, ahuecar, excavar, socavar; ganar, obtener.

scooper, *s.* achicador, vaciador; cavador.

scoot [sku:t], *v.i.* (*fam., E.U.*) tomar las de Villadiego; pasar, volar.

scooter, *s.* patinete (de niño); patineta; scúter.

scope [skoup], *s.* alcance, campo, extensión; lugar, espacio o esfera de acción; plan, propósito, fin, intento, objeto, designio, intención; (*mar.*) bitadura; *to give free scope* (o *full scope*), dar carta blanca, dar rienda suelta.

scorbutic [skɔːɹˈbjuːtik], **scorbutical** [skɔːrˈbjuːtikəl], *a.* escorbútico o con propensión a escorbuto.

scorch [skɔːɹtʃ], *v.t.* chamuscar, sollamar, socarrar, aburar, tostar, rescaldar; abrasar, agostar (el sol). — *v.i.* quemarse, secarse; agostarse, abrasarse (las plantas); *to scorch along*, (*fam.*) ir como un relámpago.

scorcher, *s.* (*fam.*) día muy caluroso; jinete o biciclista que va con excesiva velocidad; reproche o censura cáustica.

scorching, *a.* ardiente, abrasador, caliente; (*fig.*) mordaz.

scordium [ˈskɔːɹdiəm], *s.* escordio.

score [skɔːəɹ], *s.* muesca, incisión, canalita; (*mar.*) entalladura; tantos, tanteo, escote (en el juego); marca, señal, *f.*, línea, raya; (*dep.*) tanteo, marca; cuenta; razón, *f.*, motivo, consideración; (*mús.*) partitura; *on the score of*, en consideración a, con motivo de; *to pay one's score*, pagar sus deudas, su escote; *to put to someone's score*, poner en cuenta de uno; *upon what score?* ¿con qué motivo?; *to pay off old scores*, saldar cuentas viejas (vengarse). — *v.t.* rayar, marcar con líneas cortaduras, etc.; azotar; marcar con latigazos; escoplear; borrar, testar, tachar; censurar severamente; apuntar, poner en cuenta; sentar; (*mús.*) orquestar; (*dep.*) ganar (puntos), marcar (un gol); llevar ventaja (en un juego); hacer muescas, rayas o señales.

score, *s.* veintena, veinte; *three score*, sesenta.

scorer, *s.* marcador, (*dep.*) ganador (o marcador) de tantos; martillo; coime.

scoria [ˈskɔːɹiə], *s.* escoria, horrura, cagafierro. — *pl.* **scoriæ**, escorias volcánicas.

scoriaceous [skɔriˈeiʃəs], *a.* escoriáceo.

scorification [skɔrifiˈkeiʃən], *s.* escorificación.

scoriform, *a.* escoriforme.

scorify [ˈskɔrifai], *v.t.* escorificar.

scoring [ˈskɔːriŋ], *s.* rayado, borradura; orquestración; guión sonoro (cine).

scorn [skɔːɹn], *v.t.*, *v.i.* despreciar, desdeñar; rechazar desdeñosamente, escarnecer; burlarse de, poner en ridículo. — *s.* desdén, menosprecio, desprecio, ludibrio, escarnio, irrisión, mofa.

scorner, *s.* despreciador, escarnecedor, desdeñador.

scornful, *a.* desdeñoso, insolente, despreciativo.

scornfulness, *s.* desprecio, desdén, calidad de desdeñoso.

scorodite [skɔroˈdait], *s.* arseniato de hierro natural.

scorper [ˈskɔːɹpəɹ], *s.* gubia, (herramienta) para trabajar madera, metal o en la joyería.

Scorpio [ˈskɔːɹpiou], *s.* Escorpión.

scorpion [ˈskɔːɹpiən], *s.* escorpión, alacrán; (*bib.*) látigo, azote; (*astr.*) Escorpión; *scorpion wort*, alacranera, hierba del alacrán; *scorpion fly*, panorpo, escorpión mosca; *scorpion grass*, especie de miosotis.

scot [skɔt], *s.* escote; tasa, contribución; multa; *scot free*, libre de tasa; impune, impunemente.

Scot, *s.* escocés, natural de Escocia.

scotch, *v.t.* (*ant.*) escoplear; (*fig.*) extirpar;

matar; frustrar; calzar (una rueda). — *s.* cortadura, corte, incisión; rasguño; trazo para jugar al *hopscotch* (infernáculo); calzo, calza, cuña, galga amarra de un carruaje; *butterscotch*, melcocha amasada con mantequilla.

Scotch [skɔtʃ], **Scottish** [ˈskɔtiʃ], *a.* escocés; *Scotch fiddle*, (*vulg.*) sarna; *Scotch thistle*, cardo borriquero, emblema nacional de Escocia. — *s.* pueblo escocés; la lengua escocesa.

scotcher, *s.* travesaño.

Scotchman, Scotsman, *s.* escocés.

scoter [ˈskoutəɹ], *s.* (*orn.*) foja; ánade negro marino.

scotia [ˈskouʃə], *s.* (*arq.*) escocia, nacela.

Scotism [ˈskɔtizm], *s.* escotismo, doctrina de Escoto.

Scotist [ˈskoutist], *s.* escotista, *m.f.*

scotoma [skoˈtoumə], *s.* (*med.*) escotoma.

scotomy, *s.* (*med.*) escotomía.

scoundrel [ˈskaundrel], *s.* canalla, *m.f.*, truhán, belitre, pillo, bergante, bribón.

scoundrelism, *s.* truhanería, canallada, pillería, picardía, bajeza.

scoundrelly, *a.* canallesco, vil.

scour [skauəɹ], *v.t.*, *v.i.* fregar, limpiar, estregar, lavar; componer, recorrer; escurar, desengrasar; blanquear; purgar; registrar, explorar, pasar rápidamente cerca de, batir (el monte), expeler, ahuyentar; formar cauce; correr de una parte a otra, corretear. — *s.* chorro; corriente rápida; diarrea del ganado.

scourer, *s.* limpiador, sacamanchas, *m.*, desengrasador; azotacalles, *m.*; purgante eficaz.

scourge [skɔːɹdʒ], *s.* azote, látigo, flagelo, correa, disciplina; calamidad; castigo severo, plaga. — *v.t.* azotar, flagelar, dar con un látigo; hostigar, castigar, mortificar, acosar.

scourger, *s.* azotador, castigador.

scouring, *s.* acción de fregar, escurar, etc.; fregado, fregadura, estregadura; purga; desengrase; diarrea.

scout [skaut], *s.* (*mil.*) explorador, descubridor, escucha, batidor; *boy scout*, explorador. — *v.i.* (*mil.*) explorar, reconocer. — *v.t.* rechazar con desdén; reírse, burlarse, escarnecer.

scow [skau], *s.* (*E.U.*) lanchón, alijador.

scowl [skaul], *v.i.* mirar con ceño, enfurruñarse, poner mal gesto o mala cara; ponerse ceñudo, tener mal cariz. — *v.t.* repeler, rechazar. — *s.* ceño, semblante ceñudo, sobrecejo, mal cariz.

scowling, *s.* ceño.

scowlingly, *adv.* con ceño.

scrabble [ˈskræbəl], *v.t.* trazar caracteres irregulares, escarabajear, garabatear; recoger, amontonar de prisa. — *v.i.* emborronar papel, hacer garabatos, escarbar; buscar a cuatro patas. — *s.* escarabajeo; escarbo.

scrag [skræg], *s.* cualquier cosa flaca y basta o áspera; pedazo de carne magra, cuello; retal.

scragged [ˈskrægid], *a.* áspero, escabroso, desigual; descarnado, flaco.

scraggedness, scragginess, *s.* flaqueza, extenuación, desigualdad, escabrosidad, aspereza.

scraggy [ˈskrægi], *a.* áspero; descarnado, flaco, macilento.

scramble [ˈskræmbəl], *v.t.* arrebatar; (*coc.*)

revolver. — *v.i.* trepar, subir gateando; (*bot.*) trepar; andar a la rebatiña; hacer esfuerzos para alcanzar; *scrambled eggs*, huevos revueltos; *to scramble up*, trepar; *to scramble over*, pasar gateando. — *s.* trepa; arrebatiña, contienda; esfuerzo, lucha.

scrambler, *s.* trepador; persona que anda a la rebatiña.

scrannel ['skrænəl], *a.* (*ant.*) flaco, macilento; discorde.

scrap [skræp], *s.* migaja, mendrugo; sobras; pedacito, trozo, fragmento; chatarra; (*fam.*) riña, pendencia, camorra. — *v.i.* (*vulg.*) reñir, armar pendencia. — *v.t.* echar a la basura, descartar.

scrap-book, *s.* álbum de recortes.

scrape [skreip], *v.t.*, *v.i.* raer, rascar, raspar, arañar; recoger; arrebañar; amontonar poco a poco; restregar los pies; tocar mal (un instrumento); (*mar.*) dar un raspadillo a; *to scrape up* (o *together*), amontonar poco a poco, a fuerza de ahorro; *to scrape off*, *out* o *from*, quitar o barrar raspando; *to scrape up acquaintance*, trabar conocimiento (o amistad); *to scrape through*, aprobar (un examen) por milagro. — *s.* acción o efecto de raspar, raspadura, rasguño, raedura, arañazo; ruido de raspar; enredo, maraña, lío, restregadura de pies contra el suelo; apuro, empeño, aprieto, lance apretado, dificultad, embarazo, berenjenal.

scraper, *s.* rascador, estregadera, garatura, raspador, raedera; (*mar.*) rasquetas; arañador, escarbador; mal violinista, *m.f.*, rascatripas, *m.f.*; (tenería) descarnador.

scraping ['skreipiŋ], *s.* acción de raer o raspar, raedura, raspadura, raimento; escarbo. — *pl.* **scrapings**, ahorros; raspaduras.

scrap-iron, *s.* hierro viejo, chatarra.

scratch [skrætʃ], *v.t.*, *v.i.* rascar, raspar; hacer un rasguño, rasguñar, carpir; arañar, raer; rayar (el vidrio); cavar, escarbar; garrapatear, escribir mal; *to scratch out*, borrar, cancelar, testar; *to scratch out someone's eyes*, sacar a uno los ojos con las uñas. — *s.* rasguño, arañazo, araño, rascadura; borradura, tachón, tildón; línea o raya ligera, marca en una superficie; (*dep.*) línea de partida en una carrera; peluquín; peluca para una parte de la cabeza; (*E.U.*, en el billar) chiripa, bambarria. — *pl.* **scratches**, (*vet.*) galápago, espundia.

scratcher, *s.* arañador, escarbador.

scratchingly, *adv.* rascando, arañando.

scratchwork ['skrætʃwəːk], *s.* (*alb.*) enfoscado; (*b.a.*) pintura el fresco, esgrafiado.

scrawl [skrɔːl], *v.t.* garrapatear, borrajear, escribir mal, garabatear. — *s.* garabatos, garrapatos.

scrawler, *s.* garabateador, persona que escribe garabatos.

scrawniness, *s.* flaqueza, flacura.

scrawny ['skrɔːni], *a.* huesoso y flaco, esquelético.

screak [skriːk], *v.i.* chirriar, rechinar, chillar. — *s.* chirrido, rechinamiento.

scream [skriːm], *v.t.*, *v.i.* chillar, gritar, vocear, vociferar, dar alaridos, dar gritos. — *s.* grito, alarido, chillido.

screamer, *s.* chillón; (*orn.*) ave gritadora.

screaming, *s.* gritería, vocería, alarida.

scree [skriː], *s.* (*geol.*) deyecciones; escombros.

screech [skriːtʃ], *v.i.* chillar, dar chillidos, dar alaridos. — *s.* chillido, alarido, grito.

screech-owl ['skriːtʃaul], *s.* úlula, autillo, zumaya.

screechy, *a.* chillante, chillón, agudo.

screed [skriːd], *s.* invectiva, tirada, arenga; (*alb.*) maestra, referencia; tira larga, jirón, retazo; gálibo, plantilla.

screen [skriːn], *s.* biombo; mampara; (*igl.*) cancel; (*elec.*) pantalla; pantalla (de cine); (*mil.*) cortina; reja, tabique, defensa, abrigo, reparo; albitana, cerca; criba, zaranda, harnero; pantalla de chimenea. — *v.t.* abrigar, esconder, ocultar, encubrir; cribar, cerner; defender, proteger, resguardar; sustraer (a un castigo). — *pl.* **screenings**, desperdicios.

screw [skruː], *s.* tornillo, vuelta de tornillo; rosca, tuerca; hélice (de barco, avión), *f.*; concha de hélice; vapor de hélice; (*vulg.*) tacaño, cicatero; presión, fuerza; (*vulg.*) paga, salario, jornal; *screw tap*, matriz o molde para hacer tornillos; *round-head screw*, tornillo de cabeza redonda; *right-handed screw*, tornillo de filete a la derecha; *left-handed screw*, tornillo zurdo (o reverso); *female screw*, tuerca; *screw nails*, clavos de rosca; *screw thread*, espira del tornillo; *cork screw*, tirabuzón, sacacorchos; *set screw*, tornillo montado. — *v.t.* atornillar; forzar, comprimir, estrechar, oprimir; deformar, torcer, retorcer, afear retorciendo; torcer (o fijar) con tornillos; hacer visajes; apremiar, apretar. — *v.i.* retorcerse o dar vueltas una cosa en forma de rosca o espiral; ejercer extorsión u opresión; *to screw in*, atornillar; meter por fuerza; *to screw down*, atornillar, fijar con tornillo; *to screw out*, hacer salir a viva fuerza; sonsacar con astucia; *to screw one's wits*, calentarse los sesos; *to screw up*, *to screw up to the pitch*, (*fig.*) excitar, aguijonear; *to screw up one's courage*, tomar coraje.

screwdriver, *s.* destornillador.

screw-eyes, *s.pl.* armellas.

screw-jack, *s.* gato, cric.

screw-plate, **screw-stock**, *s.* terraja.

screw-wrench ['skruːrentʃ], *s.* llave inglesa.

scribble ['skribəl], *v.t.* escribir de prisa; garrapatear, borrajear, escarabajear. — *s.* escrito mal formado; garabato; escrito de poco mérito.

scribbler, *s.* mal escritor, escritor de poca fama.

scribe [skraib], *s.* calígrafo; notario público; escribiente, amanuense, escriba, *m.*; escritor. — *v.t.* rayar, marcar, puntear; (*carp.*) juntar, ajustar, ensamblar, corrocar, esgarabotar.

scrim [skrim], *s.* tejido muy fuerte de algodón o lino usado en la tapicería de muebles.

scrimmage ['skrimidʒ], *s.* arrebatina, contienda, escaramuza, jaleo, lucha cuerpo a cuerpo; (rugby) mêlée, *f.*

scrimp [skrimp], *v.t.*, *v.i.* escatinar, acortar, estrechar, reducir. — *a.* escaso, corto, reducido, estrecho. — *s.* avaro.

scrimping, *a.* mezquino, parsimonioso.

scrimpy, *a.* (*fam.*) muy pequeño, muy estrecho.

scrimshaw ['skrimʃɔː], *v.t.* y *v.i.* decorar (marfil, conchas, etc.) con tallados, dibujos de color, etc.

scrip [skrip], *s.* cédula; (*com.*) póliza, acción o

certificado con carácter de vale; bolsa, taleguilla, zurrón, morral; *scrip holder*, tenedor de vales o certificados provisionales.

script [skript], *s.* letra, mano, letra cursiva; (*impr.*) plumilla inglesa; (*for.*) escritura original; texto (original, mecanografiado); manuscrito; guión, plató (de cine).

scriptural ['skriptʃjuːrəl], *a.* bíblico; autorizado por la Sagrada Escritura.

scripturally, *adv.* de una manera bíblica; conforme a la Sagrada Escritura.

Scripture ['skriptʃjuːəɹ], *s.* Sagrada Escritura.

scrivener ['skrivənəɹ], *s.* (*ant.*) plumista, *m.*; tagarote, escribano, notario público.

scrofula ['skrɔfjuːlə], *s.* escrófula.

scrofulism, *s.* escrofulismo.

scrofulous, *a.* escrofuloso.

scroll [skroul], *s.* rollo de papel o pergamino; (*arq.*) voluta; rasgo, rúbrica.

scroll-saw, *s.* sierra de contornear.

scrotal ['skroutəl], *a.* escrotal.

scrotocele [skrouto'siːl], *s.* escrotocele, *f.*

scrotum ['skroutəm], *s.* escroto.

scrub [skrʌb], *v.t.* fregar, estregar; restregar; limpiar. — *a.* achaparrado, desmirriado; mezquino, inferior. — *s.* fregado; limpieza; fricción; matorral, maleza.

scrubbed, scrubby, *a.* achaparrado; (terreno) cubierto de maleza; insignificante, pobre, mezquino.

scrubber, *s.* restregador; cepillo de fregar; purificador de gas (por medio del agua); limpiasuelos; (*quím. y met.*) depurador.

scrubbing, *s.* fregadura, restregón, fregado; *scrubbing-brush*, cepillo para el suelo.

scruff [skrʌf], *s.* nuca.

scrum [skrʌm], **scrummage** ['skrʌmidʒ], *s.* (*rugby*) mêlée, *f.*

scrumptious ['skrʌmpʃəs], *a.* (*fam.*) exquisito, delicioso.

scruple ['skruːpəl], *s.* escrúpulo, duda, aprensión; (*farm.*) escrúpulo, peso de 20 granos; cantidad muy pequeña, ínfima. — *v.t.*, *v.i.* escrupulizar, tener escrúpulos, tener dudas, vacilar por razones de conciencia.

scrupulous ['skruːpjuːləs], *a.* escrupuloso, concienzudo, delicado; temeroso, dudoso; cauto, cuidadoso; preciso, exacto, riguroso, estricto, exigente.

scrupulousness, scrupulosity, *s.* escrupulosidad; meticulosidad.

scrutator [skruː'teitəɹ], *s.* escudriñador.

scrutineer [skruːti'niəɹ], *s.* escrutador, escudriñador.

scrutinize ['skruːtinaiz], *v.t.* escudriñar, escrutar, averiguar, inquirir, sondear, examinar a fondo.

scrutinous ['skruːtinəs], *a.* curioso.

scrutiny ['skruːtini], *s.* escrutinio, escudriñamiento, examen, averiguación.

scrutoire ['skruːtwɑːɹ], *s.* escritorio, pupitre, papelera.

scud [skʌd], *v.i.* correr, volar, moverse o deslizarse rápidamente; atravesar de prisa; *to scud before the wind*, (*mar.*) correr viento en popa; *to scud under bare poles*, (*mar.*) correr a palo seco. — *s.* carrera rápida, precipitada; celaje, nubes (ligeras, impulsadas por el viento); espuma del mar; chubasco ligero y pasajero.

scuff [skʌf], *v.t.*, *v.i.* (*fam.*) ponerse áspera una superficie; arrastrar los pies.

scuffle ['skʌfəl], *s.* pelea, riña, refriega, arrebatiña, altercación, sarracina, pendencia, contienda, reyerta. — *v.i.* pelear, venir a las manos, forcejear, reñir, altercar.

scull [skʌl], *s.* remo de espadilla, remo largo; botecito, botequín. — *v.t.*, *v.i.* cinglar, bogar con espadilla.

scullboat, *s.* barquillo, botecito; (*mar.*) sereni.

sculler, *s.* bote de espadilla; remero de bote; cinglador.

scullery ['skʌləri], *s.* fregadero, espetera.

scullion ['skʌljən], *s.* marmitón, galopín de cocina, pinche; sollastre, persona despreciable; *scullion wench*, fregona.

sculper ['skʌlpəɹ], *s.* buril, cincel.

sculpin ['skʌlpin], *s.* (*ict.*) coto espinoso.

sculptor ['skʌlptəɹ], *s.* escultor, estatuario, entallador.

sculptress ['skʌlptres], *s.f.* escultora, mujer que esculpe.

sculptural ['skʌlptʃjuːrəl], *a.* escultural.

sculpture ['skʌlptʃəɹ], *s.* escultura. — *v.t.* esculpir, entallar, cincelar, labrar en madera, piedra, etc.

sculpturesque [skʌlptjuː'resk], *a.* escultural; majestuoso, bello y frío.

scum [skʌm], *s.* espuma, hez, *f.*, nata, escoria; (*fig.*) desecho, canalla, hez del pueblo. — *v.t.* espumar, quitar la espuma.

scumble ['skʌmbəl], *v.t.* (*pint.*) dar glacis. — *s.* unión de colores, glacis.

scummy ['skʌmi], *a.* espumoso; cubierto de escoria.

scupper ['skʌpəɹ], *s.* (*mar.*) imbornal, embornal; *scupper-hole*, imbornal, embornal; *scupper-nails*, estoperoles. — *v.t.* hundir (un barco).

scurf [skəːf], *s.* caspa; costra; tiña de los árboles.

scurfiness, *s.* estado casposo o costroso.

scurfy, *a.* casposo, costroso.

scurrility [skʌ'riliti], *s.* grosería, indecencia, procacidad, insolencia, desvergüenza, improperio, baldón, lenguaje grosero; bufonada, bufonería.

scurrilous ['skʌriləs], *a.* grosero, indecente, procaz, vil, bajo, insolente, difamatorio, chocante, oprobioso.

scurrilousness, *s.* cualidad de procaz o insolente; improperio; grosería; lenguaje vulgar.

scurry ['skʌri], *v.t.* poner en fuga, barrer, hacer mover de prisa. — *v.i.* echar a correr, apretar a correr, escabullirse, escaparse. — *s.* fuga precipitada; remolino, vuelta, ventolera.

scurvied, *a.* escorbútico.

scurvily ['skəːvili], *adv.* vilmente, ignominiosamente, groseramente, mezquinamente.

scurviness, *s.* ruindad, torpeza, vileza, indignidad, malignidad, descortesía, desatención.

scurvy ['skəːvi], *s.* escorbuto. — *a.* vil, despreciable, ruin.

scurvy-grass, *s.* coclearia.

scutate, *a.* (*zool.*) escutiforme; (*bot.*) escuteliforme.

scutch [skʌtʃ], *v.t.* agramar, tascar, espadar, espadillar (lino, etc.). — *s.* estopa.

scutch-blade, *s.* agramadera.

scutcheon ['skʌtʃən], *s.* escudo de armas; planchuela; batidera, escudete de metal.

scutellate ['skjuːtileit], *a*. escuteliforme.

scutiform ['skjuːtifɔːm], *a*. escutiforme.

scuttle ['skʌtəl], *s*. escotillón; trampa; carrera corta; agujero, barreño; cubo, balde; paso acelerado; *coal scuttle*, cubo (para carbón); *cabin scuttles*, (*mar*.) luces (*o* lumbreras) de camarote; *scuttles of the mast*, (*mar*.) fogonaduras. — *v.i.* apretar a correr. — *v.t.* (*mar*.) echar a pique; hacer aberturas en el fondo de, dar barreno a, barrenar.

scye [sai], *s*. (*sast*.) apertura donde se inserta la manga.

scythe [saið], *s*. guadaña, dalle. — *v.t.* guadañar.

scythed, *a*. armado de guadaña.

Scythian ['siðiən], *s.*, *a*. escita, *m.f.*

'sdeath [s'deθ], *interj*. ¡vive Dios!

sea [siː], *s*. mar, océano; ola grande, curso de las ondas, olaje, oleaje, oleada; marejada; abundancia (grande o excesiva); *sea anemone*, anémone de mar; *sea gate*, punto de salida al mar, oleada larga; compuerta de marea; *sea level*, nivel del mar; *sea room*, espacio suficiente para maniobrar una embarcación; *sea water*, agua salada; *at sea*, en el mar; *to be* (*quite*) *at sea*, (*fig*.) estar perplejo, no saber qué hacer; *beyond* (*the*) *sea*, allende el mar; *half seas over*, medio borracho; *heavy sea*, ola fuerte, mar de leva; *high sea*, mar gruesa; *high sea o main sea*, mar ancha, alta mar; (*for*.) más allá de la marca de la bajamar; *high-swelling sea*, mar de leva; *narrow sea*, estrecho de mar; *to have* (*o get*) *one's sea legs*, poder andar por la cubierta de un buque sin cansarse, andar con pies de mar; *to put to sea*, hacerse a la vela, salir a la mar; *the sea runs high*, la mar está muy crecida.

sea-bank, *s*. orilla del mar, muralla de mar.

sea-bass, *s*. serrano.

sea-biscuit, *s*. galleta de marinero.

seaboard ['siːbɔːd], *s*. costa, playa, litoral. — *a*. costanero, litoral, vecino al mar.

sea-bream, *s*. besugo.

sea-breeze, *s*. viento de mar.

sea-brief, *s*. carta marítima.

sea-cabbage, *s*. berza marina.

sea-calf, *s*. foca o becerro marino.

sea-cap, *s*. gorra de marinero.

sea-cob, *s*. gaviota.

sea-cow, *s*. vaca marina, manatí.

sea-dragon, *s*. araña o dragón marino.

sea-eagle, *s*. halieto, águila pescadora.

seafarer ['siːfɛərər], *s*. marino, navegante, marinero.

seafaring, *a*. marino, marinero, navegante. — *s*. vida del marinero.

sea-fennel, *s*. (*bot*.) hinojo marino.

seafood, *s*. (*E.U.*) pescado, mariscos.

sea-girt, *a*. rodeado o cercado por el mar.

seagoing ['siːgouiŋ], *a*. marinero de altura; navegante.

sea-green, *a*. verdemar, color verde oscuro.

sea-gull, *s*. gaviota.

sea-hog, *s*. puerco marino, marsopla.

sea-holly, *s*. (*bot*.) cardo corredor.

sea-horse, *s*. caballo marino, hipocampo.

seakale ['siːkeil], *s*. berza marina.

seal [siːl], *s*. sello; sigilo, signáculo; timbre; acto de sellar, acto de poner fin a una cosa; selladura, sigilación; marca o señal característica; precinto; firma; autenticación; fianza; sacramento; (*hidr*.) obturación;

líquido obturador; sello del *Privy Council*; *Custom-house seal*, marchamo; *privy seal*, sello privado; *great seal*, gran sello; *to affix one's seal*, poner su sello; *keeper of the seals*, guardasellos; *under the hand and seal of*, firmado y sellado por; *seal ring*, sortija con sello. — *v.t.* sellar, sigilar, poner el sello sobre; precintar; concluir, poner fin; estampar; confirmar, afirmar, afianzar; marchamar; cerrar (cartas, paquetes, etc., con lacre o goma); (*igl*.) santiguar; confirmar, bautizar; guardar secreto; (*mec*.) tapar con chapaleta; (*alb*.) empotrar, encastrar; *to seal up*, cerrar (con lacre, etc.).

seal, *s*. (*zool*.) foca, becerro marino. — *v.i.* cazar focas.

sealer, *s*. sellador; cazador de focas.

sealing-wax ['siːliŋwæks], *s*. lacre.

sealskin ['siːlskin], *s*. piel de foca.

seam [siːm], *s*. (*cost*.) costura; reborde; (*mec*.) junta, juntura; (*cir*.) sutura; grieta, hendedura, raja, rendija; arruga; cicatriz, *f.*, costurón; (*geol., min*.) filón, vena, hilo, capa delgada, veta, yacimiento; (*mar*.) costura de los tablones; (*fund*.) rebaba; *to pay the seams*, (*mar*.) embrear las costuras. — *v.t.* hacer costuras, coser, juntar; señalar con cicatrices. — *v.i.* henderse, rajarse.

sea-maid, sea-maiden, *s.f.* sirena.

seaman ['siːmən], *s*. marinero, nauta, marino; *seamanlike*, marineramente.

seamanly, *a*. marino, marinesco.

seamanship, *s*. náutica, marina, marinaje, marinería, habilidad en la navegación.

seamew ['siːmjuː], *s*. gaviota.

seamless, *a*. inconsútil, sin costura; *seamless stockings*, medias sin costura.

seamstress ['semstres], *s.f.* costurera.

seamy ['siːmi], *a*. con costuras; *the seamy side*, (*fig*.) el lado peor.

sean [sein], *s*. jabega, red barredera; [*v*. SEINE].

séance ['seiɔns], *s*. sesión; en especial reunión de espiritistas.

sea-nettle, *s*. ortiga de mar.

sea-ooze, *s*. cieno de mar.

sea-otter, *s*. nutria marina.

seapiece ['siːpiːs], *s*. (*pint*.) cuadro marina.

seaplane ['siːplein], *s*. hidroavión.

sea-pool, *s*. laguna de agua salada, marisma.

sea-port, *s*. puerto de mar.

sear [siər], *a*. seco, ajado, agostado, marchito (hojas, flores, plantas). — *s*. (*arm*.) fiador que mantiene el gatillo en seguro; *sear spring*, muelle real. — *v.t.* agostar, marchitar, secar, disecar, quemar la superficie de, tostar, chamuscar; endurecer, hacer insensible o calloso; cauterizar.

sea-raven, *s*. cormorán.

search [səːtʃ], *v.t.*, *v.i.* buscar, explorar, examinar con cuidado, registrar; escudriñar; investigar, enterarse de, informarse de, indagar, inquirir; (*cir*.) tentar, reconocer con la tienta (una herida); probar, poner a prueba; *to search into*, examinar, investigar; *to search after*, preguntar por; inquirir, indagar; *to search for*, buscar; procurar, solicitar; *to search out*, descubrir o encontrar buscando. — *s*. registro, acto de registrar, visita, reconocimiento; averiguación, pesquisa, examen, investigación, indagación; busca, buscada; *search warrant*, (*for*.) auto de registro; *right of search*, (*mar*.) derecho de visita.

searchable, *a.* que puede buscarse o explorarse; investigable.

searcher, *s.* buscador, explorador, pesquisidor, escudriñador, indagador, registrador, inquiridor, escrutador; (*arti.*) gato de registro; vista, inspector; (*cir.*) explorador, sonda, tienta; (*ópt.*) buscador.

searching, *a.* penetrante, escrutador; completo, cabal.

searchlight [ˈsəːʌtʃlait], *s.* reflector, proyector eléctrico.

sea-risk, *s.* riesgo o peligro de mar.

sea-rocket, *s.* (*bot.*) alga marina.

sea-rover, *s.* corsario, pirata, *m.*

sea-serpent, *s.* serpiente de mar, *f.*

sea-shark, *s.* tiburón.

sea-shell, *s.* concha marina.

sea-shore, seaside, *s.* playa, ribera, costa u orilla del mar.

seasick [ˈsiːsik], *a.* mareado; *to be seasick,* estar mareado, (*fam.*) cambiar la peseta.

seasickness, *s.* mareo, mareamiento.

season [ˈsiːzən], *s.* estación (del año); sazón, *f.*, tiempo; época, momento; temporada; *in season,* en sazón, en tiempo oportuno, a su tiempo; *out of season,* fuera de sazón; *dull season,* (*com.*) estación muerta; *to be in season,* ser de la estación; *in due season,* en tiempo oportuno, a su debido tiempo; *hunting* (o *open*) *season,* tiempo de caza; *close season,* veda. — *v.t.* sazonar; aliñar, aderezar, condimentar; infundir, imbuir, persuadir; aclimatar, acostumbrar, habituar, moderar, templar, hacer más agradable. — *v.i.* secarse, endurecerse: madurarse, sazonarse, habituarse, aclimatarse.

seasonable [ˈsiːzənəbəl], *a.* oportuno, conveniente, tempestivo, favorable, a propósito; de estación.

seasonableness, *s.* sazón, *f.*, oportunidad de tiempo.

seasonably, *adv.* en sazón, oportunamente.

seasoning [ˈsiːzəniŋ], *s.* (*coc.*) sazón, *f.*, aliño, condimento; punto (o madurez) de algunas cosas; sainete, chiste, salsa (o sal) de un cuento; aclimatación.

seat [siːt], *s.* asiento; banco, silla; escaño; posaderas, nalgas; fondillos de los calzones; sitio, paraje, posición, lugar, puesto, situación; domicilio; residencia, morada; finca, mansión, quinta; privilegio; *country seat,* casa solar; *seat of war,* teatro de la guerra; *seat-back,* respaldo, espaldar; *to hold a seat in Parliament,* ser diputado a Cortes. — *v.t.* sentar, asentar; tener asientos para; colocar en asientos; poner asiento a (una silla); fijar, arraigar, afianzar; echar fondillos (a un pantalón); sentar (una válvula, etc.). — *v.i.* asentar.

seating, *s.* acción de sentar (o de sentarse); asientos; (*mec.*) lecho, asiento, base, *f.*; material para entapizar muebles; *seating capacity,* cabida (de personas sentadas).

sea-tossed, *a.* batido por el mar.

sea-unicorn, *s.* narval, unicornio de mar.

sea-urchin, *s.* erizo de mar.

sea-wall, *s.* muralla de mar, dique, banco de arena.

sea-ward, *s.* [SEAWARD].

seaward [ˈsiːwəd], *adv.* hacia el mar. — *a.* dirigido hacia el mar.

seaway, *s.* (*mar.*) mar gruesa, mar alborotada.

seaweed, *s.* alga marina, planta de mar, ajomate, ova.

sea-wolf, *s.* lobo marino.

seaworthiness, *s.* buen estado de una embarcación.

seaworthy [ˈsiːwəːʌði], *a.* marinero, en buen estado para hacerse a la mar.

sebaceous [seˈbeiʃəs], *a.* sebáceo, seboso.

sebacic [seˈbæsik], *a.* sebácico; *sebacic acid,* ácido sebácico.

sebate [ˈsiːbeit], *s.* sebato.

secant [ˈsiːkənt, ˈsekənt], *s.* (*geom.*) secante. — *a.* cortante.

secede [seˈsiːd], *v.i.* separarse, apartarse.

seceder, *s.* separatista, *m.f.*

secession [seˈseʃən], *s.* secesión, separación, apartamiento.

secessionism, *s.* separatismo.

secessionist, *s.* separatista, *m.f.*, secesionista, *m.f.*

seclude [seˈkluːd], *v.t.* apartar, encerrar, recluir, excluir, alejar, confinar, aislar, alejarse de otros.

secluded, *a.* alejado, desviado, aislado, apartado, retirado, solitario. — *p.p.* [SECLUDE].

seclusion [seˈkluːʒən], *s.* reclusión, apartamiento, exclusión, retraimiento, aislamiento, soledad, retiro.

second [ˈsekənd], *a.* segundo; inferior; secundario, subordinado; igual, otro, idéntico; *second-class,* de segunda clase, de grado inferior; *second cabin,* (*mar.*) segunda clase; *second rate,* de segunda clase o categoría; *second hand,* secundario (del reloj); *second lieutenant,* alférez, *m.*; *second sight,* doble vista, conocimiento de lo futuro; *second son,* segundón; *to be second to none,* no ser inferior a nadie; *on second thoughts,* después de pensarlo bien; *to be second nature,* ser otra naturaleza; *to play second fiddle,* hacer un papel secundario. — *s.* segundo, brazo derecho; auxilio, apoyo; ayudante, ayuda, auxiliar; sostenedor, defensor; segundo (boxeo); padrino (en un desafío); (*mús.*) segunda; segundo (de tiempo), momento, instante; *second best,* segundo; *to come off second best,* llevar lo peor. — *pl.* mercancías de segunda o de calidad inferior. — *v.t.* apoyar, apadrinar, sostener, ayudar, favorecer, auxiliar; secundar o apoyar una proposición; ser segundo, asegundar, segundar; prestar.

secondariness [ˈsekəndərines], *s.* propiedad de ser secundario.

secondary [ˈsekəndəri], *a.* secundario; subalterno, subordinado; resultante; accesorio; subsecuente; (*elec., fís., etc.*) secundario; *secondary battery,* (*elec.*) acumulador. — *s.* lugarteniente, diputado, delegado, subalterno; (*astr.*) círculo secundario; (*orn.*) pluma grande de la segunda articulación; planeta secundario, satélite; (*ent.*) ala posterior.

seconder [ˈsekəndəʌ], *s.* el que apoya o secunda una proposición.

second-hand [sekəndˈhænd], *s.* segunda mano; *at second-hand,* de segunda mano; por imitación; de oídas. — *a.* de lance, de segunda mano.

secondly, *adv.* en segundo lugar.

secrecy [ˈsiːkrisi], *s.* secreto, reserva, sigilo; misterio; clandestinidad; retiro, soledad.

secret [ˈsiːkret], *a.* secreto, misterioso, oculto;

recóndito, retirado, esotérico, escondido; clandestino; silencioso, callado, privado, reservado; *secret service*, servicio de espionaje. — *s.* secreto; llave, *f.*, clave, *f.*; misterio, arcano; razón oculta; *in secret*, secretamente, en secreto. — *pl.* **secrets**, partes pudendas o genitales.

secretariat [sekre´tɛəriət], *s.* secretaría; secretariado.

secretary [´sekretəri], *s.* secretario; amanuense, *m.f.*; escritorio, pupitre, papelera; ministro del gobierno, presidente de un ministerio; *assistant secretary*, subsecretario, secretario auxiliar; *corresponding secretary*, secretario correspondiente; *Secretary of State*, Ministro de Estado; (*E.U.*) Secretario de Relaciones Exteriores; *Secretary to the Treasury*, Ministro de Hacienda; *Secretary of State for War*, Ministro de la Guerra; *Secretary of the Interior*, (*E.U.*) Ministro de Gobernación.

secretary-bird, *s.* serpentario.

secretaryship [´sekretəriʃip], *s.* secretaría, cargo de secretario.

secrete [se´kri:t], *v.t.* esconder, ocultar, desviar, recatar, encubrir; (*med.*) secretar, separar.

secretion [se´kri:ʃən], *s.* (*med.*) secreción, acto de secretar; escondimiento, ocultación.

secretitious, *a.* segregado, separado.

secretive [se´kri:tiv], *a.* callado, reservado; (*med.*) secretorio.

secretiveness, *s.* inclinación a esconder o ocultar.

secretness [´si:kretnes], *s.* secreto, sigilo.

secretory [se´kri:təri], *a.* secretorio.

sect, *s.* secta, denominación; pandilla, partido, orden, *m.f.*

sectant [´sektənt], *s.* (*mat.*) sectante.

sectarian [sek´tɛəriən], *s.*, *a.* sectario.

sectarianism, *s.* sectarismo; adhesión excesiva a una secta.

sectary [´sektəri], *s.* sectario; secuaz; discípulo.

sectile [´sektail], *a.* sectil.

section [´sekʃən], *s.* sección, división; cortadura, tajadura; parte, *f.*, porción; negociado, subdivisión, departamento; compartimento; sección o corte transversal (de un edificio, de una máquina, etc.); (*impr.*) párrafo, signo; (*mil.*) media compañía; (*E.U.*) división de terreno de 1 milla en cuadro; *section-cutter*, instrumento para cortar secciones para el microscopio.

sectional, *a.* seccionario; hecho de secciones o compartimentos; regional, local.

sectionalism, *s.* regionalismo; espíritu de partido.

sector [´sektɔɹ], *s.* (*geom.*) sector; compás de proporción.

secular [´sekju:lǝɹ], *a.* secular; seglar, profano, temporal, mundano; efectuado en el curso de siglos. — *s.* seglar, lego.

secularity [sekju:´læriti], *s.* mundanalidad, afición o apego a las cosas mundanas.

secularization, *s.* secularización, exclaustración.

secularize [´sekju:ləraiz], *v.t.* secularizar, hacer secular, exclaustrar. — *v.i.* aseglararse.

secundine [´sekəndin], *s.* (*zool.*) secundinas.

secure [se´kju:ɔɹ], *a.* seguro, libre de peligro; indudable, cierto; firme, inexpugnable, fuerte; (*ant.*) confiado, despreocupado. —

v.t. asegurar, resguardar; poner en salvo, proteger, salvar; dar garantías, garantizar; afirmar, refirmar, afianzar; coger, prender, encerrar, aprisionar; lograr, procurarse, adquirir, obtener, hacerse dueño de.

secureness, *s.* seguridad, calidad de seguro; falta de cuidado.

security [se´kju:riti], *s.* seguridad, aseguramiento, afianzamiento, protección, defensa; firmeza; confianza, tranquilidad; fianza, garantía, prenda, caución, salvaguardia, resguardo; falta de cautela, exceso de confianza, descuido; fiador. — *pl.* **securities,** (*com.*) vales, valores, títulos, obligaciones, garantías de pago; *to stand security for,* salir fiador por.

sedan [se´dæn], *s.* silla de manos.

sedate [se´deit], *a.* sentado, formal, sosegado, apacible, sereno, serio, juicioso.

sedateness, *s.* compostura, serenidad, tranquilidad, quietud, calma.

sedative [´sedətiv], *s.*, *a.* sedativo, calmante.

sedentariness, *s.* vida sedentaria, falta de actividad, pereza.

sedentary [´sedentəri], *a.* sedentario; de poca acción, inactivo; perezoso, flojo; (*zool.*) sedentario.

sedge [sedʒ], *s.* juncia, enea, junco.

sedge-warbler, *s.* (*orn.*) curruca.

sedgy [´sedʒi], *a.* abundante en juncias.

sediment [´sedimənt], *s.* sedimento, hez, *f.*; poso, asiento, zurrapas; borras; (*geol.*) tierras de aluvión.

sedimental, sedimentary, *a.* sedimentario, sedimental.

sedimentation [sedimən´teiʃən], *s.* sedimentación.

sedition [se´diʃən], *s.* sedición, tumulto, sublevación, revuelta, motín, bullicio, levantamiento popular.

seditious [se´diʃəs], *a.* sedicioso, tumultuoso, revoltoso, faccioso, amotinado.

seditiousness, *s.* calidad de sedicioso.

seduce [se´dju:s], *v.t.* seducir; pervertir, descaminar, desviar, corromper; deshonrar.

seducement, *s.* seducción, acción de seducir.

seducer, *s.* seductor, persona que seduce.

seducible, *a.* capaz de ser seducido.

seduction [se´dʌkʃən], *s.* seducción.

seductive [se´dʌktiv], *a.* seductivo, atractivo, halagüeño; persuasivo.

seductress, *s.f.* seductora.

sedulity [se´dju:liti], *s.* diligencia, aplicación, asiduidad, ahinco, cuidado celoso.

sedulous [´sedju:ləs], *a.* asiduo, aplicado, diligente, cuidadoso.

sedulousness, *s.* celo, ahinco, asiduidad, aplicación, diligencia, cuidado celoso.

sedum [´si:dəm], *s.* género de las crasuláceas.

see [si:], *v.t.*, *v.i.* (*pret.* **saw**; *p.p.* **seen;** *ger.* **seeing**) ver; mirar, observar, discernir; avistar, divisar; percibir; comprender; presenciar; visitar, hacer una visita; recibir visitas; acompañar, servir de escolta (a una persona hasta su casa); (*póker*) aceptar un envite. — *imp.* **see** (en citas) vide, véase; *let me see,* deje que lo piense, deme tiempo de reflexionar; *to be well* (o *ill*) *seen in,* estar versado en, ser perito (o ignorar); *to see about,* hacerse cargo, tomarlo a. sí; *I'll see to it,* déjelo a mi cargo; *to see daylight,* (*fam.*, *E.U.*) empezar a comprender; *to see* *life*, ver el mundo, experimentar la vida; *to see into*, examinar a fondo, penetrar en; *to see afar off*, ver de lejos, contemplar el porvenir; *to see the point*, caer en la cuenta; *let us see*, vamos a ver.

see, *s.* sede, *f.*; *Holy See*, Santa Sede.

seed [si:d], *s.* semilla, simiente, *f.*; origen, causa primitiva, semen, esperma, germen, principio generador; generación, casta, progenie, *f.*; *seed of a fruit*, pepita, hueso, cuesco; *animal seed*, esperma, semen; *seed drill*, sembradora; *seed corn*, trigo o maíz para sembrar; *seed time*, siembra, sementera; *seed pearl*, aljófar, rostrillo; *seed cake*, torta de semillas aromáticas; *to run to seed*, granar, convertirse todo en semillas, agotarse; *seedlac*, laca seca; *seed-vessel*, pericarpio. — *v.t.* sembrar; despepitar; adornar con figuras parecidas a semillas. — *v.i.* hacer la siembra, sembrar semillas; granar, desgargolar.

seed-basket, *s.* sembradera.

seed-bud, *s.* germen, botón.

seeder, *s.* sembradora, máquina de sembrar.

seediness, *s.* calidad de granado o de andrajoso.

seedling, *s.* planta de semillero.

seedlip, seedlop, *s.* sementero.

seedplot, *s.* semillero, plantel.

seedsman ['si:dzmən], *s.* sembrador; persona que siembra granos; tratante en semillas o simientes.

seedy ['si:di], *a.* granado, lleno de granos; abundante en semillas; (*fam.*) andrajoso, descamisado, desharrapado; indispuesto, malucho.

seeing ['si:iŋ], *s.* vista, visión, acto de ver; *seeing is believing*, (*prov.*) ver y creer. — *conj. seeing* o *seeing that*, visto que, siendo así que, puesto que.

seek [si:k], *v.t.*, *v.i.* (*pret.*, *p.p.* **sought**) buscar, procurar hallar, ir en busca de, inquirir; pretender, aspirar, solicitar, ambicionar; preguntar, suplicar, rogar, pedir, interrogar; procurar, intentar; dirigirse a, recurrir, acudir; *to seek after*, buscar, inquirir; pretender, solicitar; pesquisar; perseguir; *to seek for*, andar buscando, inquiriendo o preguntando por; procurar conseguir; *to seek out*, buscar por todos lados, hacer esfuerzos para conseguir; *to seek one's life*, querer matar a uno.

seeker, *s.* buscador, investigador, inquiridor.

seel [si:l], *v.t.* tapar o coser los ojos, cerrar los ojos, cegar (un halcón o gavilán); (*fig.*) engañar. — *v.i.* (*mar.*) tumbarse (sobre una banda).

seem [si:m], *v.i.* parecer, parecerle (a uno una cosa); darse un aire (a alguno); *it seems*, parece, se dice, según parece.

seemer, *s.* persona que parece.

seeming, *s.* apariencia, parecer, exterior; apariencia falsa. — *a.* aparente, parecido, especioso.

seemingly, *adv.* al parecer, aparentemente.

seemingness, *s.* exterioridad, apariencia; plausibilidad.

seemliness, *s.* decoro, gracia, gallardía, decencia; bien parecer; propiedad.

seemly ['si:mli], *a.* decente, propio, correcto, decoroso.

seen, *p.p.* [SEE].

seep [si:p], *v.t.* (*E.U.*) colar, pasar. — *v.i.* colarse, rezumarse, escurrirse.

seepage, *s.* coladura, escape.

seer [siəɹ], *s.* profeta, *m.*, adivinador, vidente; veedor, persona que ve.

seersucker ['siəɹsʌkəɹ], *s.* sirsaca, carranclán fino de la India.

see-saw ['si:sɔ:], *s.* vaivén, balance; columpio (de niños); persona que vacila. — *a.* de vaivén, de balance, que vacila. — *v.i.* balancear, columpiarse, dar o hacer balances.

seethe [si:ð], *v.t.* (*p.p.* **seethed**, (*ant.*) **sodden** o **sod**) hacer hervir, hacer cocer; (*farm.*) elijar. — *v.i.* hervir, bullir; (*fig.*) bullir, estar negro.

seether, *s.* caldera, marmita.

segment ['segmənt], *s.* segmento, parte dividida o cortada, sección; (*geom.*) segmento de un círculo.

segmental [seg'mentəl], **segmentary** ['segməntəri], *a.* segmentario.

segmentation [segmən'teiʃən], *s.* acción o efecto de dividir en segmentos.

segregate ['segregeit], *v.t.*, *v.i.* segregar, desagregar, separar; segregarse. — *a.* segregado, separado, apartado; selecto.

segregation, *s.* segregación, desagregación, separación, apartamiento.

Seidlitz powders ['sedlitz'paudəɹz], *s.* polvos de Seidlitz.

seignior, seigneur ['seinjəɹ], *s.* (*der.*) señor.

seigniory, seigneury, *s.* señoría, señorío.

seignorage, *s.* señoreaje; derecho de braceaje.

seignorial [sein'jɔ:riəl], *a.* señoril, independiente.

seine [sein], *v.t.*, *v.i.* pescar con jábega o red barredera. — *s.* jábega, red barredera, buitrago.

seismic ['saizmik], **seismical**, *a.* sísmico.

seismograph ['saizmogræf], **seismometer** [saiz'mɔmetəɹ], *s.* sismógrafo, sismómetro.

seismology [saiz'mɔlodʒi], *s.* sismología.

seizable ['si:zəbəl], *a.* expuesto a ser asido o embargado.

seize [si:z], *v.t.*, *v.i.* asir, tomar, agarrar, coger, empuñar; (*der.*) secuestrar, embargar, decomisar, tomar bajo la custodia de la ley; poner en posesión; (*mar.*) amarrar, dar una ligadura, aferrar; prender, apiolar, apresar; sobrecoger, apoderarse de; (*fig.*) comprender; darse cuenta de; *to be seized with fear*, estar sobrecogido o embargado por el terror; *to seize on* (o *upon*), asir, apoderarse de, agarrar, coger; embargar; *to seize up*, (*mec.*) agarrotarse, atascarse.

seizer, *s.* agarrador; secuestrador; persona que ase o embarga.

seizin, seisin ['si:zin], *s.* (*for.*) posesión, acto de poseer; cosa poseída; toma de posesión.

seizing, *s.* toma de posesión; (*mar.*) trinca, traba; aferramiento, ligadura.

seizure ['si:ʒəɹ], *s.* acto de asir, asimiento; prendimiento, aprehensión, prisión; presa, captura; cosa asida; (*med.*) ataque; (*mec.*) agarrotamiento; (*for.*) secuestro, embargo, comiso.

sejant, sejeant ['si:dʒənt], *a.* (*blas.*) sentado.

selachian [se'leikiən], *s.*, *a.* selacio.

seldom ['seldəm], *adv.* raramente, rara vez.

select [se'lekt], *v.t.* escoger, triar, elegir, optar por entresacar. — *a.* preferido, selecto, escogido, florido, granado, exclusivo.

selection [se'lekʃən], *s.* selección, escogimiento, elección, tría.

selective [se'lektiv], *a.* selectivo; *selective tuning*, sintonización selectiva.

selectness, *s.* calidad de selecto o escogido.
selector [se'lektəɹ], *s.* escogedor, persona que escoge, que elige; (*elec.*) selector.
selenite ['selənait], *s.* (*min.*, *quím.*) espejuelo, selenita.
selenium [se'li:niəm], *s.* selenio.
selenography [selen'ɔgrəfi], *s.* selenografía.
self [self], *a.* mismo, idéntico; propio; puro, no mezclado (colores). — *s.* (*pl.* **selves**) persona, personalidad, individuo; se, sí mismo; yo mismo. Unido a pronombres personales, a algunos adjetivos posesivos y al pronombre *one* forma pronombres reflexivos, o bien da más fuerza a la expresión: *myself*, yo mismo, me; *himself*, *herself*, *itself*, se; *ourselves*, *yourselves*, *themselves*, nos, os, se.
self, *a.* en ciertos casos *self* se separa del adjetivo posesivo y entonces se traduce por el pronombre respectivo como *my other self*, mi otro yo; *my wife and self*, mi esposa y yo.
self-abased, *a.* humillado por la conciencia de su falta.
self-acting, *a.* automático.
self-binder, *s.* máquina de segar con atador automático.
self-centred, *a.* egocéntrico.
self-command, *s.* dominio de sí mismo.
self-complacency, *s.* complacencia en sí mismo.
self-conceit, *s.* arrogancia, vanidad, presunción.
self-conceited, *a.* presuntuoso, arrogante, presumido.
self-confidence, *s.* confianza en sí mismo.
self-conscious, *a.* confuso, tímido.
self-consciousness, *s.* confusión, timidez.
self-control, *s.* dominio de sí mismo.
self-convicted, *a.* convicto por confesión propia.
self-defeating, *a.* contraproducente.
self-defence, *s.* defensa propia; (*for.*) legítima defensa.
self-delusion, *s.* engaño de sí mismo.
self-denial, *s.* abnegación de sí mismo.
self-denying, *a.* abnegado.
self-esteem, *s.* buena opinión de sí mismo.
self-evident, *a.* patente, evidente por sí mismo; *self-evident proposition*, verdad de perogrullo.
self-excitation, *s.* (*elec.*) autoexcitación.
self-excite, *v.* autoexcitar.
self-existent, *a.* existente por sí mismo, eterno.
self-feeder, *s.* (*mec.*) de alimentación automática.
self-government, *s.* dominio sobre sí mismo; autonomía.
self-heal, *s.* (*bot.*) sanícula, planta.
self-importance, *s.* altivez, orgullo, concepto exagerado de la importancia propia.
self-induction, *s.* (*elec.*) autoinducción.
self-interest, *s.* propio interés.
selfish ['selfiʃ], *a.* interesado, egoísta.
selfishness, *s.* amor propio, egoísmo.
selfless ['selfles], *a.* desinteresado.
self-love, *s.* amor propio.
self-made, *a.* levantado por sus propios medios y esfuerzos, autodidacto.
self-moving, *a.* automotor.
self-murder, *s.* suicidio.
self-murderer, *s.* suicida, *m.f.*
self-reliant, *a.* confiado en sí mismo.

self-respect, *s.* pundonor; decoro; respeto de sí mismo; dignidad.
self-righteous, *a.* justo en la propia estimación.
self-sacrifice, *s.* sacrificio de sí mismo, abnegación.
selfsame ['selfseim], *a.* mismo, idéntico.
self-service, *s.* propio servicio, sin camareros o dependientes (de ciertos restaurantes, etc.).
self-starter, *s.* (*auto.*) arranque automático.
self-styled, *a.* que se llama a sí mismo, llamado.
self-will, *s.* obstinación, terquedad, porfía, tozudez.
self-winding, *a.* de cuerda automática (de ciertos relojes).
sell [sel], *v.t.* (*pret.*, *p.p.* **sold**) vender, traspasar o entregar por dinero; hacer traición; (*vulg.*) faltar a la palabra, engañar, estafar, entrampar. — *v.i.* vender, traficar, hacer el comercio; tener despacho, tener buena venta; hallar compradores; venderse; *to sell at auction*, almonedear, vender en pública subasta; *to sell on credit*, vender al fiado (*o* a plazos); *to sell for ready money*, vender al contado; *to sell underhand*, vender bajo mano; *to sell long stock*, (*com.*) vender acciones que uno posee en abundancia; *to sell off*, vender una gran cantidad de cosas juntas; *to sell at retail*, vender a destajo (*o* al por menor); *to sell wholesale*, vender al por mayor.
seller, *s.* vendedor.
seltzer ['seltzəɹ], *s.* agua de Seltz, agua carbónica.
selvage ['selvidʒ], *s.* (*tej.*) hirma, orillo de paño; orilla, borde, orla, lista; (*min.*) salbanda. — *pl.* **selvages**, (*mar.*) estrobos.
selves [selvz], *pr. pl.* [SELF].
semantics [se'mæntiks], *s.* semántica.
semaphore ['seməfɔ:ɹ], *s.* semáforo; (*f.c.*) disco, telégrafo de señales.
semaphoric [semə'fɔrik], **semaphorical,** *a.* semafórico.
semasiology [semeizi'ɔlodʒi], *s.* semasiología, semántica.
semblance ['sembləns], *s.* semejanza exterior, apariencia; máscara, ademán, ficción, velo; forma visible, imagen, *f.*
semeiology [si:mai'ɔlodʒi], *s.* semiología.
semen ['si:men], *s.* semen; (*bot.*) simiente, *f.*, semilla.
semester [se'mestəɹ], *s.* semestre escolar (5 meses).
semi- ['semi], *prefijo,* semi, medio.
semiannual [semi'ænju:əl], *a.* semianual, semestral.
semiannular, *a.* semianular.
semibreve ['semibri:v], **semibrief,** *s.* (*mús.*) semibreve, *f.*, redonda; *semibreve rest*, aspiración de semibreve.
semicircle ['semisə:ɹkəl], *s.* semicírculo, medio círculo, hemiciclo.
semicircular [semi'sə:ɹkju:ləɹ], **semicircled,** *a.* semicircular.
semicircumference, *s.* semicircunferencia.
semicolon ['semikoulən], *s.* punto y coma (;).
semidiameter, *s.* semidiámetro.
semidiaphanous, *a.* semidiáfano.
semidouble, *a.* (*bot.*), *s.* (*igl.*) semidoble.
semifloret [semi'flɔ:ret], *s.* semiflósculo.
semifloscular, semifloscuous, *a.* semifloscular.

semifluid, *a.* semiflúido.
semiglobular, *a.* semiesférico.
semilunar [semi'lu:nəɹ], *a.* semilunar.
semimetal, *s.* semimetal.
semimonthly, *a.* quincenal. — *s.* publicacion quincenal.
seminal ['seminəl], *a.* seminal, espermático; elemental, embrionario; (*bot.*) seminal, sementino.
seminar ['seminɑ:ɹ], *s.* seminario.
seminarist ['seminərist], *s.* seminarista, *m.f.*
seminary ['seminəri], *s.* seminario; colegio. — *a.* seminal; perteneciente a un seminario.
semination [semi'neiʃən], *s.* (*ant.*) acción de sembrar, sembradura, sementera; propagación, diseminación.
seminific, seminifical, *a.* seminal, seminífero; sementino.
semi-official [semiɔ'fiʃəl], *a.* oficioso, semioficial.
semiordinate, *s.* semiordenada.
semi-precious, *a.* (*joy.*) semiprecioso.
semiquadrate, semiquartile, *s.* semicuadrado.
semiquaver ['semikweivəɹ], *s.* semicorchea.
semiquintile, *s.* semiquintil.
semisextile, *s.* semisexti:.
semispherical, *a.* semiesférico, hemisférico.
Semite ['semait], *a.* semítico. — *s.* semita, *m.f.*
Semitic [se'mitik], *a.* semítico. — *s.* lengua semítica.
semitone ['semitoun], *s.* semitono.
semivocal [semi'voukəl], *a.* semivocal.
semivowel, *s.* semivocal, *f.*
semiweekly, *a.* bisemanal. — *s.* publicación bisemanal.
semolina [semo'li:nə], *s.* sémola.
sempiternal [sempi'tə:ɹnəl], *a.* sempiterno.
sempiternity, *s.* perpetuidad.
sempstress ['sempstres], *s.f.* costurera.
senary ['si:nəri], *a.* senario, que contiene seis unidades.
senate ['senət], *s.* senado; *senate house*, senado.
senator ['senətəɹ], *s.* senador, consejero.
senatorial [senə'tɔːriəl], *a.* senatorio.
senatorship, *s.* senaduría.
send [send], *v.t.* (*pret.*, *p.p.* **sent**) enviar, mandar, despachar, remitir, expedir, remesar; producir, emitir, dirigir, arrojar, lanzar, echar, tirar; conceder, dar; difundir, extender, propagar; infligir; volver (loco, etc.); permitir; hacer sobrevenir o acontecer. — *v.i.* enviar; (*mar.*) arfar, cabecear; *to send back*, devolver, mandar volver, enviar de vuelta, enviar otra vez; *to send away*, despedir, poner en la calle, enviar lejos, a otra parte; *to send for*, enviar a buscar, enviar a llamar, enviar por; *to send down*, hacer bajar, (*fam.*) suspender (a un estudiante); *to send forth* (o *out*), enviar adelante, hacer marchar, echar, emitir, arrojar, exhalar, despedir, producir, dar a luz; *to send word*, mandar o pasar aviso, enviar un recado; *to send in*, hacer entrar; anunciar, introducir; *to send forward*, enviar hacia adelante; *to send off*, hacer partir, expedir; *to send up*, enviar arriba, mandar subir; (*fam.*, *E.U.*) enviar a la cárcel; *to send someone about his business*, echar a pasear.
sender, *s.* remitente; (*elec.*) transmisor.
send-off, *s.* (*fam.*) despedida afectuosa.
senescence, *s.* vejez, senectud.

senescent [se'nesənt], *a.* que envejece; característico de la vejez.
seneschal ['seneskəl], *s.* senescal.
senile ['si:nail], *a.* senil, caduco, perteneciente a la vejez.
senility [se'niliti], *s.* senectud.
senior ['si:niəɹ], *a.* mayor, de mayor edad; superior en grado, más anciano, más antiguo, decano. — *s.* señor mayor, anciano; socio más antiguo; decano; (*E.U.*) escolar del último curso en un colegio.
seniority [si:ni'ɔriti], *s.* antigüedad; ancianidad.
senna ['senə], *s.* sen, sena.
sennight ['senait], *s.* (*abrev.* de *seven night*), (*ant.*) semana.
sennit ['senit], *s.* (*mar.*) cajeta.
sensation [sen'seiʃən], *s.* sensación; excitación.
sensational, *a.* sensacional.
sensationalism, *s.* (*filos.*) sensualismo; efectismo.
sense [sens], *s.* sentido; juicio, entendimiento, prudencia, inteligencia, mente, *f.*, razón, *f.*; sentido, significación, interpretación, significado; sensación; sentimiento; (*geom.*) dirección; *to be out of one's senses*, haber perdido el juicio; *common sense*, sentido común; *sense perception*, percepción sensitiva.
senseless, *a.* insensible, inerte, sin conocimiento, privado de sentido; sin sentido, disparatado, absurdo; necio, insensato.
senselessness, *s.* tontería, necedad, insensatez, absurdo.
sensibility [sensi'biliti], *s.* sensibilidad; finura, precisión (de instrumentos).
sensible ['sensibəl], *a.* sensible; consciente (de); cuerdo, razonable, juicioso, sesudo; sensato; perceptible; sensitivo; *to be sensible of*, estar consciente de, estar persuadido de, darse cuenta de. — *s.* (*mús.*) sensible.
sensibleness, *s.* sensación, sensibilidad; cordura, sensatez.
sensitive ['sensitiv], *a.* sensitivo; sensible, impresionable; sentido, tierno, delicado; (*foto.*) sensibilizado; *sensitive plant*, sensitiva, mimosa.
sensitiveness, *s.* calidad de sensible o sensitivo, sensibilidad; delicadeza, precisión.
sensitize ['sensitaiz], *v.t.* hacer sensible; (*foto.*) sensibilizar.
sensorial [sen'sɔːriəl], **sensory** ['sensəri], *a.*; **sensorium**, **sensory**, *s.* sensorio.
sensual ['senʃjuəl], *a.* sensual; lujurioso, lascivo, voluptuoso.
sensualism, *s.* sensualismo, sensualidad.
sensualist ['senʃjuəlist], *s.* persona sensual, sibarita, *m.f.*; (*filos.*) sensualista, *m.f.*
sensuality [senʃju'æliti], *s.* sensualidad, voluptuosidad.
sensualize ['senʃjuəlaiz], *v.t.* hacer sensual, lascivo, o voluptuoso.
sensuous ['sensjuːəs], *a.* sensorio, sensitivo; sensible, tierno, apasionado, afectivo, patético.
sensuousness, *s.* sensualidad; sensibilidad.
sent [sent], *pret.*, *p.p.* [SEND].
sentence ['sentəns], *s.* (*gram.*) frase, *f.*; (*for.*) sentencia, condena; fallo; dictamen, parecer, opinión, *f.*, determinación; máxima, dicho, sentencia; (*mús.*) frase, *f.* — *v.t.* sentenciar, condenar.

sentential [sen'tenʃəl], *a.* (*gram.*) de una frase, de la oración.
sententious [sen'tenʃəs], *a.* sentencioso.
sententiousness, *s.* estilo sentencioso.
sentience, *s.* estado consciente; percepción; sensibilidad.
sentient ['senʃənt], *a.* sensible; consciente. — *s.* ente, criatura sensible o cosa que siente.
sentiment ['sentimənt], *s.* sentimiento; opinión, *f.*, dictamen, juicio; afecto, simpatía; concepto, frase, *f.*, pensamiento.
sentimental [senti'mentəl], *a.* sentimental; tierno, muy sensible.
sentimentalist [senti'mentəlist], *s.* sentimentalista, *m.f.*; romántico.
sentimentalism, sentimentality [sentimen'tæliti], *s.* sentimentalismo; sensiblería.
sentimentalize, *v.t., v.i.* idealizar sentimentalmente, mostrar sensiblería, regodearse.
sentinel ['sentinəl], **sentry** ['sentri], *s.* centinela, *m.f.*, guardia, *m.f.*; *sentry box*, garita de centinela; *to stand sentry*, estar de centinela.
sepal ['sepəl], *s.* sépalo.
separability [sepərə'biliti], *s.* calidad de separable; naturaleza separable.
separable ['sepərəbəl], *a.* separable.
separate ['sepəreit], *v.t.* separar, desunir, dividir, desviar, despegar, disgregar, desprender; divorciar, alejar, apartar, considerar separadamente, estimar como cosas distintas. — *v.i.* separarse, desunirse, apartarse. — *a.* separado, distinto, aparte, diferente; segregado, desunido.
separateness, *s.* estado de separación.
separation [sepə'reiʃən], *s.* separación; división, desunión, *f.*, disgregación, disociación, apartamiento; análisis químico; divorcio.
separatist ['sepərə'tist], *s.* separatista, *m.f.*; (*igl.*) cismático.
separative, *a.* separativo, distintivo.
separator, *s.* separador, divisor, escogedor, partidor.
separatory [sepə'reitəri], *a.* separativo, separatorio; (*quím.*) embudo de separación.
sepia ['si:piə], *s.* (*pint.*) sepia; dibujo a la sepia; (*ict.*) sepia, jibia; jibión. — *a.* de sepia, hecho en sepia.
sepoy ['si:pɔi], *s.* cipayo.
sepsis ['sepsis], *s.* sepsia.
sept [sept], *s.* clan (irlandés); tribu, *f.*, familia.
septal ['septəl], *a.* de septo.
septan ['septən], *a.* que se repite cada séptimo día (fiebre, calentura intermitente, etc.).
septangle ['septæŋgəl], *s.* heptágono.
septangular [sep'tæŋgjuːləɪ], *a.* heptagonal, heptágono.
September [sep'tembəɪ], *s.* septiembre.
septemia, septæmia [sep'ti:miə], *s.* septicemia.
septenary ['septenəri], *a.* septenario. — *s.* septena; septenio.
septennial [sep'teniəl], *a.* sieteñal.
septentrional [sep'tentrionəl], *a.* septentrional.
septet [sep'tet], *s.* septena; (*mús.*) septeto.
septic ['septik], *a.* séptico.
septicæmia [septi'si:miə], *s.* septicemia.
septicæmic, *a.* séptico.
septillion [sep'tiljən], *s.* septillón.
septuagenary, *a.* septuagenario.
septuagesima [septjuːə'dʒezimə], *s.* septuagésima.

septuagesimal, *a.* septuagésimo.
septum ['septəm], *s.* septo.
septuple ['septjuːpəl], *a.* séptuplo. — *v.t., v.i.* septuplicar, septuplicarse.
sepulchral [se'pʌlkrəl], *a.* sepulcral, fúnebre; (*fig.*) funesto, sombrío.
sepulchre ['sepʌlkəɪ], *s.* sepulcro, sepultura. — *v.t.* sepultar, enterrar, poner en un sepulcro.
sepulture ['sepʌltʃəɪ], *s.* inhumación, sepultura, entierro.
sequacious [se'kweiʃəs], *a.* secuaz; servil; consecutivo.
sequaciousness [se'kweiʃəsnes], **sequacity** [se'kwæsiti], *s.* servilismo.
sequel ['si:kwəl], *s.* secuela; resultado, éxito, consecuencia; conclusión, capítulo o párrafo final; *in the sequel*, después.
sequela [se'kwi:lə], *s.* secuela.
sequence ['si:kwəns], *s.* serie, *f.*; sucesión; ilación; arreglo; (en los naipes) runfla de un palo; efecto, consecuencia; (*mús.*) modulación.
sequent, *a.* siguiente, subsiguiente, consiguiente.
sequester [se'kestəɪ], *v.t.* separar, retirar, apartar; (*for.*) secuestrar.
sequestered, *a.* aislado, remoto.
sequestrable, *a.* que se puede secuestrar.
sequestrate ['sekwestreit], *v.t.* (*for.*) secuestrar; confiscar.
sequestration, *s.* (*for.*) secuestro; separación, reclusión, retiro.
sequestrator, *s.* secuestrador.
sequestrum [se'kwestrəm], *s.* (*cir.*) secuestro.
sequin ['si:kwin], *s.* lentejuela; (moneda) cequí.
sequoia [se'kwɔiə], *s.* sequoia.
seraglio [se'rɑːljou], *s.* serrallo.
seraph ['serəf], *s.* (*pl.* **seraphim**) serafín.
seraphic [se'ræfik], **seraphical** [se'ræfikəl], *a.* seráfico.
seraphina, seraphine ['serəfiːn], *s.* serafina, organillo de salón, órgano portátil.
Serb [səːɪb], **Serbian**, *s. y a.* servio.
Serbo-Croatian [səːɪboukrou'eiʃən], *s. y a.* servocroata, *m.f.* (idioma y raza).
sere [siəɪ], *a.* marchito, seco.
serein [se'ræŋ], *s.* sereno.
serenade [sere'neid], *s.* serenata. — *v.t.* dar una serenata.
serene [se'riːn], *a.* sereno, claro, despejado; apacible, tranquilo, sosegado; *Most Serene*, serenísimo.
sereneness, *s.* serenidad.
serenity [se'reniti], *s.* serenidad; claridad; serenidad (título de ciertos príncipes).
serf [səːɪf], *s.* siervo; esclavo.
serfdom, *s.* servidumbre.
serge [səːɪdʒ], *s.* estameña; anascote; sarga.
sergeant ['sɑːɪdʒənt], *s.* (*mil.*) sargento; (*ant.*) alguacil; (*ant.*) abogado de primera clase; *sergeant-at-arms*, macero; *sergeant-major*, sargento instructor.
sergeantship, *s.* sargentía.
serial ['siəriəl], *a.* en serie, consecutivo; (novela) por entregas. — *s.* novela por entregas.
serially, *adv.* en serie; por serie; por entregas.
sericate ['serikeit], *a.* sedoso; velludo.
sericeous [se'riʃəs], *a.* sérico, sedoso, lustroso como seda, cubierto de pelusa muy suave.

sericultural, *a.* sericícola.
sericulture ['serikʌltʃəɹ], *a.* sericicultura.
series [siəriːz], *s.* serie, *f.,* sucesión; (*mat.*) serie, *f.,* progresión.
serin ['serin], *s.* verderón, pinzoncillo.
seringa [se'riŋɡə], *s.* (*bot.*) siringa; (*fam.*) jeringuilla.
serio-comic [siəriou'kɔmik], **serio-comical** [siəriou'kɔmikəl], *a.* jocoserio, seriocómico.
serious ['siəriəs], *a.* serio; severo; grave; sincero; importante; *to take seriously,* tomar una cosa en serio.
seriousness, *s.* seriedad; gravedad; formalidad.
serjeant ['sɑːɹdʒənt], *s.* [SERGEANT].
sermon ['səːɹmən], *s.* sermón; amonestación; discurso cristiano, oración evangélica; *collection of sermons,* sermonario; *funeral sermon,* oración funebre.
sermonize, *v.t.* predicar, sermonear; reprender, echar sermones.
sermonizer, *s.* sermoneador.
seron ['siəron], **seroon** [si'ruːn], *s.* sera, sera grande, serón, zurrón; *seroon of cinnamon,* churla de canela; *seroon of cocoa,* sobornal de cacao.
serosity [se'rɔsiti], *s.* serosidad.
serotherapy [siəro'θerəpi], *s.* seroterapia.
serotine ['serotin], *s.* especie de murciélago.
serotinous, *a.* serondo, serotino.
serous ['siərəs], *a.* seroso.
serpolet ['səːɹpolet], *s.* tomillo silvestre.
serpent ['səːɹpənt], *s.* serpiente, *f.,* sierpe, *f.;* (*mús.*) serpentón; (*piro.*) buscapiés; (*astr.*) Serpiente.
serpentine ['səːɹpentain], *a.* serpentino; caracoleando, que anda caracoleando; *serpentine marble,* serpentina (marmol). — *s.* (*min.*) serpentina. — *v.i.* serpentear; andar caracoleando.
serpiginous [səɹ'pidʒinəs], *a.* serpiginoso.
serpigo [səɹ'paigou], *s.* serpigo.
serrate ['sereit], **serrated** [se'reited], *a.* dentellado; (*bot.*) serrado, endentado.
serration, *s.* endentadura, recortadura.
serrature ['seratʃəɹ], *s.* (*biol.*) estructura serrada, endentadura.
serried ['serid], *a.* apretado, apiñado.
serum ['siərəm], *s.* suero.
servable ['səːɹvəbəl], *a.* servible.
servant ['səːɹvənt], *s.* criado, sirviente; siervo, esclavo; servidor; *woman servant, servant girl, servant maid,* criada; *servant man,* criado.
serve [səːɹv], *v.t.* servir, trabajar para, estar al servicio de, estar sujeto a, servir de o para; ayudar, ser útil a; servir o asistir a la mesa; escanciar vino, etc.; manejar, mantener en acción, hacer maniobrar o funcionar; abastecer, surtir; divertir; obsequiar, agasajar; (*for.*) entregar una citación o requerimiento; cumplir una condena; prestar culto o adoración a Dios; (*mar.*) aforrar; tratar, recompensar; cubrir (el macho a la hembra). — *v.i.* servir; ser criado; desempeñar o cumplir los deberes de un empleo, servir a su país; estar en sujeción; bastar; (*dep.*) servir (la pelota); (en ciertos juegos de naipes) servir con naipe del mismo palo; *to serve for,* servir para; *to serve time,* cumplir una condena en presidio; *to serve one's turn,* bastar, ser suficiente; *to serve (out)*

one's time, acabar el tiempo de servicio; terminar el aprendizaje; *to serve another's ends,* servir para que otro consiga lo que intenta; *to serve someone a trick,* pegar a uno un chasco, jugar a uno una mala partida; *to serve an office,* desempeñar algún cargo; *to serve a warrant,* ejecutar un auto de prisión; *to serve someone in kind,* pagarle a uno en la misma moneda; *when occasion serves,* cuando la ocasión sea favorable.
server, *s.* servidor; criado de mesa; (*igl.*) acólito; bandeja; (*dep.*) saque.
service ['səːɹvis], *s.* servicio; desempeño; servidumbre; utilidad, ventaja; oficio; uso, favor, asistencia, obsequio, ayuda; acomodo; vajilla, servicio de mesa; (*igl.*) culto divino, servicio, misa, oficio; (*for.*) condición, trabajo u obligación de un criado, empleado, dependiente o arrendatario; entrega legal de una citación; (*mar.*) forro de cable; *at your service,* a la disposición de Vd.; *out of service,* sin acomodo, desacomodado, sin conveniencia; *to be of service to,* ser útil a, servir; *to see service,* prestar servicio, servir; *it is of no service,* no vale nada, no sirve para nada; *service(-tree),* serbal; *coffee service,* juego de café; *diplomatic service,* cuerpo diplomático; *on active service,* en acto de servicio; en el campo de batalla.
serviceable ['səːɹvisəbəl], *a.* servible, útil; duradero; oficioso; aprovechable; servicial.
serviceableness, *s.* calidad de servicial o duradero.
servient ['səːɹviənt], *a.* (*for.*) subordinado.
servile ['səːɹvail], *a.* servil, bajo, abyecto; adulador, lisonjero; abatido, humilde; (*gram.*) que no pertenece a la raíz de la palabra. — *s.* esclavo; letra o sílaba que no pertenece a la radical.
servility [səɹ'viliti], *s.* servilismo.
serving, *s.* acción de servir. — *a.* sirviente; ministrante; *serving maid,* criada, sirvienta; *serving man,* sirviente, criado; *serving mallet,* (*mar.*) maceta de forrar.
servitor ['səːɹvitəɹ], *s.* (*ant.*) servidor; asistente; fámulo (de colegio, etc.).
servitorship, *s.* famulato.
servitude ['səːɹvitjuːd], *s.* servidumbre, esclavitud; (*for.*) servidumbre; servicio militar o naval (angloindio); *penal servitude,* cadena.
sesame ['sesəmi], *s.* ajonjolí, sésamo, alegría; *Open, sesame!* ¡ábrete, sésamo!; (*fig.*) llave maestra.
sesamoid ['sesəmɔid], *s. y a.* (*anat.*) sesamoideo, que tiene nódulos.
sesquioxide [seskwi'ɔksaid], *s.* sesquióxido.
sesquipedal [ses'kwipidəl], **sesquipedalian** [seskwipe'deiliən], *a.* sesquipedal.
sesquitertian, *a.* sesquitercio.
sessile ['sesail], *a.* sesil, sentado.
session ['seʃən], *s.* sesión, asentada, junta; tribunal; término judicial; curso académico; *petty sessions,* tribunal de primera instancia.
sessional, *a.* perteneciente a una sesión.
sesterce ['sestəːɹs], *s.* sestercio.
set [set], *v.t.* (*pret., p.p.* set) fijar, poner, disponer, poner fijo, poner en pie, poner derecho, colocar, asentar, sentar; poner a empollar (una gallina); plantar; establecer, instalar, situar, destinar, ordenar, señalar, determinar; arreglar, alistar, poner en orden, preparar, ajustar; reducir a reglar; afilar (una

navaja); (*impr.*) parar (tipo), componer; (*joy.*) montar, engastar; (*mús.*) poner en música, componer; (*mús.*) dar o fijar el tono; embarazar, detener, impedir; inquietar, perturbar; engastar, embutir (una cosa en otra); trabar, triscar (los dientes de la sierra); hacer andar, poner en movimiento; (*cir.*) reducir una dislocación; encasar (un hueso roto); (*mar.*) tender, desplegar; (velas) tender, poner lazos; regular (un reloj). — *v.i.* (*astr.*) ponerse (un astro); cuajarse (un líquido); (*mús.*) poner en música; (*danza*) situarse en frente del compañero de baile; correr, moverse o fluir (una corriente); (*fam.*) empollar (la gallina); (*fam.*) sentar, ajustar, caer bien (una prenda de vestir); tender, inclinarse; dedicarse, aplicarse, ponerse a; detenerse, pararse, quedarse parado; fijarse, quedarse fijo; apuntar, señalar, parar (la caza); empezar a desarrollarse; *to set about doing something*, ponerse a hacer una cosa, dedicarse a una cosa; *to set about each other*, venir a las manos; *to set one person against another*, irritar a uno en contra de otro, poner mal a uno con otro; *to set against*, oponer, indisponer; *to be set against*, detestar, concebir odio contra; *to set apart o aside*, poner a un lado, dejar para otra vez; *to set aside*, despreciar, no hacer caso de, abrogar, anular; *to set at*, estimar, considerar, valuar, reputar, fijar un precio; *to set at liberty*, poner en libertad; *to set at naught*, tener en nada, no hacer caso de; *to set at rest*, poner en reposo; *to set back*, hacer retroceder, llevar hacia atrás; *to set before*, poner a la vista, dar a escoger, presentar; *to set down*, acusar, atribuir, imputar, poner en tierra, poner por tierra, desembarcar, depositar, poner por escrito, hacer un apunte, censurar, humillar; *to set fire to*, pegar fuego a; *to set forth*, exponer, promulgar, manifestar, dar a conocer, enunciar, hacer valer (razones), avanzar, adelantarse, ponerse en camino, poner en orden; *to set forward*, promover; animar, ponerse en camino; *to set free*, poner en libertad, libertar; *to set in* (de la marea), fluir con constancia hacia tierra; comenzar, embutir, encajar; *to set off*, poner hermoso, adornar, poner en relieve, embellecer, hermosear; partir, salir; *to set nets*, tender lazos; *to set on*, determinar, acometer, atacar, arremeter, animar, incitar, azuzar; *to set (the teeth) on edge*, dar dentera; *to set on fire*, pegar fuego a; *to set one's hand to*, poner su firma a; *to set one's house in order*, arreglar sus negocios; prepararse para la muerte; *to set one's heart on*, empeñarse en; tener ilusión por; *to set out*, ponerse en camino, emprender un viaje; dar principio a; adornar, hermosear; hacer ver, mostrar; señalar; *to set a price*, fijar un precio; *to set right, to set to rights*, rectificar, corregir, poner en orden; *to set sail*, hacer vela, hacerse a la vela; *to set (great) store by*, dar (mucha) importancia a; *to set a task*, imponer una tarea; *to set thinking*, hacer pensar; *to set a time*, señalar un plazo determinado; *to set to*, ponerse a trabajar, reñirse; *to set to work*, poner(se) a la obra, ponerse a trabajar; *to set together*, poner junto, juntar; *to set up*, exaltar, ensalzar; elevar, erigir, armar; fundar, instituir; enderezar; adelantarse, establecer(se); (*impr.*) componer; *to set*

up house, poner casa; *to set up a tent*, levantar una tienda; *to set up for*, erigirse en, hacer profesión de, darse uno (por lo que es o por lo que no es); *to set up for oneself*, trabajar por su cuenta; *to set upon*, asaltar, atacar, echarse sobre; *to be set upon*, determinar resueltamente, ser aficionado a.

set [set], *s.* juego, serie, *f.*, clase, *f.*, colección, agregado, conjunto, servicio; compañía, banda, grupo, cuadrilla; equipo; juego de herramientas; aderezo; tiro (de caballos); disposición, orden; posición; movimiento, curso; encorvadura; tendencia; porte; puesta (del sol), ocaso; plantel; ajuste, caída; triscamiento (de una sierra); (*teat.*) decoración; fraguado (del cemento, etc.); aparato (de radio); juego (de herramientas, etc.); tallo (para plantar); planta de transplantar; *set of teeth*, dentadura; *dinner set*, vajilla de mesa.

set [set], *a.* obstinado, resuelto, determinado, terco, de opinión fija; establecido, señalado, prescrito; arreglado, ajustado, regular, formal; reflexionado, estudiado; colocado, puesto, inmóvil, fijo; construído, hecho; fabricado; engastado, montado; *p.p.* [SET]; *set form*, formulario.

setaceous [se'teiʃəs], *a.* cerdoso, cerdudo.

setback ['setbæk], *s.* revés, contrariedad.

setbolt, *s.* prisionero, botador, perno de trabante.

set-down, *s.* reprimenda; (*fam.*) peluca.

set-off ['setɔːf], *s.* contraste; contraposición; compensación, contrapeso; (*for.*) contra-rreclamación; (*impr.*) repinte.

seton ['siːtən], *s.* (*cir.*, *vet.*) sedal.

setose, setous, *a.* cerdoso.

settee [se'tiː], *s.* banco, canapé; *settee bed*, cama turca.

setter ['setəɹ], *s.* persona que monta, asienta, etc.; perdiguero, sétter; espía, espión; *diamond setter*, joyero; *typesetter*, (*impr.*) cajista, *m.f.*

setting, *s.* acción o efecto de fijar, colocar, montar, etc.; puesta (del sol), ocaso; (*fam.*) nidada; (*joy.*) engaste, montadura, engastadura; (*mar.*) dirección; fraguado (del cemento, etc.); (*teat.*) decorado; (*mús.*) arreglo; marco; aliño (de huesos).

settle ['setəl], *v.t.* colocar, asentar; establecer, estatuir (leyes, reglamentos, etc.); hacer más compacto; casar; dar una profesión, estado, dar colocación a; sosegar, serenar, calmar; poblar, colonizar; quitar la hez, clarificar; poner en orden; poner fin a, acabar con, acabar; determinar, decidir, resolver, aclarar; señalar, fijar, afirmar, asegurar; hacer firme y transitable (un camino); saldar, liquidar, finiquitar, satisfacer; redondear, componer, arreglar, ajustar (cuentas); regularizar. — *v.i.* posarse, asentarse, reposarse; arraigar, fijarse, fijar su residencia, establecerse; casarse; calmarse, sosegarse, serenarse; ir al fondo, hacer sedimento; instalarse, poner casa; contraerse; tomar estado; (*for.*) dar en dote, constituir, señalar o asignar una pensión, etc.; liquidar con acreedores; determinarse, decidirse; saldar (una cuenta); elegir, escoger; *to settle down*, asentarse; fijarse; cobrar juicio; ponerse a; *to settle accounts*, ajustar cuentas; *to settle disputes*, zanjar las dificultades; hacer las paces. — *s.* banco, escaño; escalón, grada.

settled, *a.* fijo; arraigado; establecido; asentado; saldado; determinado; arreglado; poblado. — *p.p.* [SETTLE].

settledness, *s.* estabilidad, permanencia, estado fijo.

settlement ['setəlmənt], *s.* establecimiento, instalación; colonia, caserío; poblado; colonización; domicilio; asiento; (*for.*) dote; asiento de un edificio; poso, sedimento; acomodo, destino, empleo; convenio, ajuste; (*com.*) saldo, finiquito, liquidación.

settler ['setləɹ], *s.* persona que arregla, coloca, fija, asegura, etc.; poblador, colono; fundador, establecedor; *settler of averages*, medidor de averías.

settling, *s.* establecimiento, arreglo, colonización; instalación; ajustamiento.

settlings, *s.*, heces, *f.pl.*, zurrapas; poso, sedimento.

set-to [set'tu:], *s.* combate, lucha, debate, disputa.

set-up, *s.* disposición; sistema, *m.*; organización.

setwall ['setwɔ:l], *s.* valeriana.

seven ['sevən], *s.*, *a.* siete.

sevenfold ['sevənfould], *a.* séptuplo. — *adv.* siete veces.

sevenscore ['sevənskɔ:ɹ], *a.* ciento cuarenta.

seventeen [sevən'ti:n], *s.*, *a.* diez y siete, diecisiete.

seventeenth, *a.* décimo séptimo, diez y siete.

seventh ['sevənθ], *a.* séptimo, septeno; siete. — *s.* séptimo, séptima parte; (*mús.*) séptima.

seventhly, *adv.* en séptimo lugar.

seventieth, *a.* septuagésimo.

seventy ['sevənti], *s.*, *a.* setenta.

sever ['sevəɹ], *v.t.* separar, apartar, cortar, dividir, desunir; deshacer, partir, romper, separar con violencia; arrancar, sacar, quitar. — *v.i.* separarse, entreabrirse, desunirse, dividirse, partirse, arrancarse, romperse, apartarse.

several ['sevərəl], *a.* diversos, varios, ciertos, unos, algunos; distinto, respectivo; solo, individuo, separado. — *s.* varios.

severally, *adv.* separadamente, individualmente, distintamente; a parte, cada uno de por sí; *jointly and severally*, solidariamente, in sólidum.

severalty ['sevərəlti], *s.* (*for.*) posesión privativa de un terreno.

severance ['sevərəns], *s.* partición, separación.

severe [se'viəɹ], *a.* severo; riguroso; áspero, duro; rígido, austero; recio, fuerte; grave.

severity [se'veriti], **severeness** [se'viəɹnis], *s.* severidad; rigor, crueldad; aspereza; gravedad, seriedad; inclemencia (del tiempo); austeridad.

sew [sou], (*p.p.* **sewn, sewed**) *v.t.*, *v.i.* coser; *to sew up*, coser en.

sewage ['sju:idʒ], *s.* aguas de albañal; alcantarillado.

sewer [souəɹ], *s.* persona que cose, cosedor.

sewer ['sju:əɹ], *s.* albañal, desaguadero, cloaca, sumidero, alcantarilla; *sewer gas*, emanaciones de las cloacas.

sewerage ['sju:əɹidʒ], *s.* alcantarillado; sistema de cloacas.

sewing ['souiŋ], *s.* costura; el cosido; *sewing-thread*, hilo de coser; *sewing-machine*, máquina de coser; *sewing-needle*, aguja de coser; *sewing-bee*, reunión de amigas para hacer costura; *sewing-press*, telar de encuadernar.

sex [seks], *s.* sexo; *the sex*, (*ant.*) las mujeres; *the fair sex*, el bello sexo.

sexagenarian [seksəgeˈneəriən], *s.* sesentón.

sexagenary [sek'sædʒenəri], *a.* sexagenario.

sexagesima [seksə'dʒesimə], *s.* sexagésima.

sexagesimal [seksə'dʒesiməl], *a.* sexagesimal.

sexangular [seks'æŋgju:ləɹ], *a.* sexángulo, hexágono, sexangular.

sexennial [sek'seniəl], *a.* que dura seis años, que acontece cada seis años.

sexless, *a.* neutro; sin sexo.

sextain [seks'tein], *s.* sextilla.

sextant ['sekstənt], *s.* sexta parte de un círculo; sextante.

sextet [seks'tet], *s.* sexteto.

sextile ['sekstail], *s.* sextil.

sextillion [seks'tiljən], *s.* sextillón.

sexton ['sekstən], *s.* (*igl.*) sacristán; enterrador; sepulturero.

sextuple ['sekstju:pəl], *a.* séxtuplo.

sexual ['seksju:əl], *a.* sexual.

sexuality [seksju:'æliti], *s.* sexualidad, condición sexual.

sgraffito [zgræf'i:tou], *s.* esgrafiado.

shabbiness ['ʃæbinəs], *s.* pobreza; estado desharrapado; mezquindad, ruindad.

shabby ['ʃæbi], *a.* usado, en mal estado, raído, gastado; andrajoso, zarrapastroso, desharrapado; ruin, tacaño; despreciable, bajo, vil.

shack [ʃæk], *s.* choza, cabaña; pasto de bellotas para cerdos; derecho de pastoreo; vagabundo; caballo sin valor alguno.

shackle ['ʃækəl], *v.t.* encadenar, atar, ligar con cadenas, poner esposas o grilletes; poner obstáculos, estorbar; (*elec.*) poner un aislador en un corte de alambre; (*f.c.*, *E.U.*) enganchar vagones. — *s.* grillete, grillo, esposa; traba, impedimento; sujeción; maneota, arropea, trabón; (*f.c.*) cadena, perno de enganche; *shackle bolt*, cáncamo de grillete; eslabón de candado, perno de horquilla.

shad [ʃæd], *s.* alosa, saboga, sábalo, trisa.

shaddock ['ʃædək], *s.* pamplemusa.

shade [ʃeid], *s.* sombra, obscuridad; umbría; sitio sombreado; matiz, tinte; visillo, cortina, transparente; cantidad pequeña, poco, diferencia muy ligera; pantalla de lámpara; visera de gorra; máscara, sombraje, toldo; umbráculo; espectro, sombra, fantasma, *m.*; ilusión, ficción, imagen, *f.*; exterior, ligera apariencia; *glass shade*, guardabrisa, *m.*, brisero; *sun shade*, quitasol, parasol; *window shade*, visillo. — *v.t.* obscurecer, privar de la luz; asombrar, cubrir con la sombra; entoldar, cubrir con toldos; casar bien los colores, matizar; (*b.a.*) sombrear; esfumar; rasguear (las letras); (*fig.*) esconder, amparar, poner el abrigo de, proteger.

shadeless, *a.* privado de sombra.

shader, *s.* persona o cosa que obscurece.

shadily ['ʃeidili], *adv.* con sombra, en la sombra; sospechosamente, de una manera sospechosa.

shadiness, *s.* calidad de estar bajo la sombra; carácter sospechoso.

shading, *s.* (*b.a.*) degradación, sombreado.

shadow ['ʃædou], *s.* sombra; sombrajo; espectro, fantasma, *m.*, aparecido; lugar sombreado, retiro, seclusión; (*pint.*) toque de obscuro; (*poét.*) obscuridad, tinieblas; poco, cantidad muy pequeña; traza, vestigio, pizca; (*fig.*) refugio, protección, amparo;

(*fig.*) compañero inseparable; *to be a shadow of one's former self*, no ser ni su sombra. — *v.t.* anublar, dar sombra, obscurecer, sombrear; (con *forth* o *out*) indicar, representar vagamente, bosquejar, simbolizar, representar por medio de un símbolo; espiar, cazar, acompañar de cerca, seguir a uno como su sombra; (*b.a.*) sombrear, matizar. — *v.i.* anublarse, obscurecerse; cambiar gradualmente de color.

shadowy, *a.* umbroso, umbrío; tenebroso, sombreado, obscuro; visionario; vago, sin realidad; indefinido.

shady ['ʃeidi], *a.* sombreado; obscuro; umbrío, umbroso; sombrío; (*fam.*) sospechoso.

shaft [ʃɑːft], *s.* flecha, dardo, saeta; mango de un arma o de una herramienta; (*mec.*) eje, astil, árbol; (*arq.*) caña o fuste de columna; (*carr.*) limón, limonera; vara (de una silla de manos); chapitel de torre; humero, cañón de chimenea; cañón o tubo de pluma; (*min.*) socavón, pozo de mina; túnel de un horno de fundición; pozo de ascensor; *cam-shaft*, árbol de levas; *driving shaft*, árbol motor. — *pl.* **shafts**, varas y juego (de un coche).

shafting, *s.* (*mec.*) juego de ejes y correaje; aparato para transmisiones de fuerza.

shag [ʃæg], *s.* pelo áspero y lanudo; (*tej.*) felpa; (*Am.*) tripe; jergón; (*orn.*) cuervo marino, cormorán; tabaco fuerte y cortado muy finamente. — *v.t.*, *v.i.* (pret., *p.p.* **shagged**) hacer velludo o peludo, hacer escabroso, desigual.

shagbark ['ʃægbɑːːk], *s.* caria; nogal americano.

shagged ['ʃægid], *a.* velludo, peludo; achaparrado.

shagginess ['ʃægines], *s.* calidad de peloso, peludo o afelpado.

shaggy ['ʃægi], *a.* velludo, peludo, hirsuto; afelpado, lanudo; escabroso, áspero, rudo, desigual; cubierto de pelo enredado.

shagreen [ʃæ'griːn], *s.* piel de zapa, lija; chagrén.

shah [ʃɑː], *s.* cha, *m.*

shake [ʃeik], *v.t.* (pret. **shook**; *p.p.* **shaken**) sacudir, agitar, menear, mover con violencia, excitar, blandir, hacer bambolear; arrojar, lanzar; hacer temblar; hacer vacilar o flaquear, amilanar, desalentar; debilitar; despertar, agitar, excitar, poner en riesgo; (*mús.*) trinar (una nota); estrechar (la mano); despedir, desembarazarse de, librarse de. — *v.i.* bambolear, temblar, estremecerse, retemblar, temblequear; trepidar, cimbrar, vibrar; vacilar, titubear; (*mús.*) trinar, hacer gorgoritos; (*fam.*) dar un apretón de manos; *to shake hands*, darse un apretón de manos, estrechar la mano; (*fig.*) ponerse de acuerdo; *to shake one's head*, mover la cabeza; *to shake off*, sacudir, hacer caer una cosa a fuerza de sacudirla; arrojar con una sacudida; hacer perder la pista, despistar; *to shake in*, introducir una cosa sacudiéndola; *to shake up*, sacudir, remover; *to shake out*, hacer salir una cosa sacudiéndola; *to shake to pieces*, hacer caer una cosa en pedazos sacudiéndola; *to shake with laughter*, morirse (o desternillarse) de risa. — *s.* meneo, sacudida; vibración, sacudimiento, impulso, traqueteo, concusión, sacudidura, agitación; temblor; duela; tabla de ripia; acción de darse las manos, apretón

de manos; (*fam.*) periquete; instante; (*mús.*) trino; hendedura, grieta, rajadura. — *pl.* **shakes**, escalofrío (de la fiebre intermitente); *in two shakes*, o *in a brace of shakes*, (*fam.*) en un periquete.

shakedown ['ʃeikdaun], *s.* cama improvisada.

shaken ['ʃeikən], sacudido, meneado, agitado; rajado, hendido (madero). — *p.p.* [SHAKE].

shaker, *s.* temblador, temblante, temblón; sacudidor.

Shakespearean, **Shakespearian** [ʃeiks-'piəriən], *a.* shakespeariano.

shaking ['ʃeikiŋ], *s.* sacudimiento, sacudidura, meneo, concusión, traqueteo, vibración; estremecimiento, temblor. — *a.* temblante, tembloroso, temblón.

shako, shacko ['ʃækou], *s.* chacó.

shaky ['ʃeiki], *a.* trémulo; poco firme, vacilante, movedizo, débil; agrietado, hendido; (*com.*) falto de crédito; dudoso.

shale [ʃeil], *s.* esquisto, arcilla esquistosa, pizarra; *shale oil*, aceite de esquistos.

shall [ʃæl], *v. aux. defect.* (sin infinitivo, participio o imperativo) *I shall do it*, lo haré; *shall we come tomorrow?* ¿vendremos mañana?; expresa deber u obligación en la 2a y 3a persona; *he shall do it*, tiene que hacerlo.

shalloon [ʃæ'luːn], *s.* chalón.

shallop ['ʃæləp], *s.* chalupa; bote abierto.

shallot [ʃələt], *s.* chalote, ascalonia (o escalona).

shallow ['ʃælou], *a.* somero, vadoso, poco profundo; (*fig.*) trivial, superficial, vano, insípido, necio. — *s.* (*mar.*) bajío.

shallow-bodied, *a.* (*mar.*) de poco calado.

shallow-brained, **shallow-pated**, *a.* ligero de cascos, aturdido, necio, bobo.

shallowness, *s.* poca profundidad; (*fig.*) frivolidad; superficialidad.

shaly ['ʃeili], *s.* pizarreño, esquistoso.

sham [ʃæm], *v.t.*, *v.i.* simular, fingir; *to sham Abraham*, (*mar.*) fingirse enfermo. — *s.* impostura, ficción, camama, bambolla, farsa. — *a.* fingido, disimulado; postizo, falso; *sham quarrel*, contienda simulada; *sham-fight*, (*mil.*) simulacro.

shamble ['ʃæmbəl], *v.i.* andar arrastrando los pies; moverse renqueando. — *s.* bamboleo, paso vacilante.

shambles ['ʃæmbəlz], *s.pl.* matadero, degolladero; carnicería, mercado de carne.

shambling, *a.* pesado, lento.

shame [ʃeim], *s.* vergüenza; ignominia, deshonra; oprobio, afrenta; *for shame! shame on you!* ¡qué vergüenza! — *v.t.* avergonzar, causar vergüenza, abochornar; deshonrar, afrentar; *to shame into* o *to shame out of*, impeler (o incitar) por un sentimiento de vergüenza.

shamefaced ['ʃeimfeisd], *a.* tímido, vergonzoso; avergonzado.

shamefacedness, *s.* timidez, vergüenza, pudor.

shameful, *a.* vergonzoso, ignominioso, escandaloso; deshonroso; indecente.

shameless, *a.* desvergonzado, sin vergüenza, indecente, descarado.

shamelessness, *s.* desvergüenza; impudicia; descaro, cinismo.

shammy ['ʃæmi], *s.* gamuza [CHAMOIS]; *shammy leather*, piel de gamuza.

shampoo [ʃæm'puː], *v.t.* dar champú; dar un masaje. — *s.* champú; masaje.

shamrock ['ʃæmrɔk], *s.* trébol blanco.

shandygaff [ʃændi'gæf], *s.* refresco de cerveza y gaseosa.

shanghai [ʃæŋ'hai], *v.t.* (*mar.*, *vulg.*) emborrachar o narcotizar a un marinero y embarcarlo contra su voluntad.

shank [ʃæŋk], *s.* zanca; (*impr.*) cuerpo del tipo; (*mec.*) asta, mango, espiga, pierna; (*zap.*) enfranque de la suela; cola de botón; (*bot.*) pedicelo, pedúnculo; *shank painter*, (*mar.*) boza de la uña del ancla; *shank of an anchor*, (*mar.*) asta de ancla; *spindle shank*, pierna de un huso; *Shanks's mare* o *pony*, las piernas.

shanked, *a.* que tiene asta, ástil o mango; *long-shanked* o *spindle-shanked*, zancudo, de zancas largas.

shan't [ʃaːnt], (*fam.*) abreviación de *shall not*.

shanty ['ʃænti], *s.* (*pl.* **shanties**) cabaña, choza; *sea-shanty*, canción marinera.

shapable ['ʃeipəbəl], *a.* capaz de recibir una forma.

shape [ʃeip], *v.t.*, *v.i.* (*p.p.* **shaped**, (*ant.*) **shapen**) formar, dar forma, dar figura, ahormar, modelar, tallar; disponer, ordenar; ajustar, proporcionar, modificar; concebir, figurarse, imaginar; *to shape a course*, (*mar.*) ponerse en rumbo. — *s.* forma; contorno; bulto; talle; (*coc.*) molde; fantasma, *m.*; (*fam.*) manera, modo de hacer; *to put an idea into shape*, dar forma a una idea.

shapeless, *a.* informe; disforme, imperfecto.

shapelessness, *s.* irregularidad, informidad, deformidad.

shapeliness, *s.* simetría, forma hermosa, proporción, belleza.

shapely ['ʃeipli], *a.* simétrico, bien formado, proporcionado.

shaper, *s.* conformador; máquina de tallar o estampar.

shard [ʃaːd], *s.* tiesto, casco; élitro (de un coleóptero).

share [ʃeə], *v.t.* dividir, partir; compartir; alcanzar, participar de, tomar parte en; distribuir, repartir. — *v.i.* participar de; tomar parte en; *to share alike* (o *to share and share alike*), repartir igualmente, recibir (o tener) una parte igual; *to share out*, repartir, distribuir. — *s.* parte, *f.*, porción, cuota, escote; (*agr.*) reja (del arado, etc.); (*com.*) acción; interés, participación; (*anat.*) pubis; *deferred shares*, (*com.*) acciones postergadas; *paid-up share*, acción liberada; *preferred shares*, acciones privilegiadas; *to hold a share*, tener un interés (o una acción); *share and share alike*, por partes iguales; *on shares*, con condición de tener una parte; *to go shares*, entrar (o ir) a la parte; *to fall to the share of*, tocar a, caer en parte de; *let each have his share*, a cada uno su parte.

sharebone, *s.* hueso del pubis.

shareholder ['ʃeəhouldə], *s.* (*com.*) accionista, *m.f.*; porcionista, *m.f.*

sharer ['ʃeərə], *s.* partícipe, copartícipe, repartidor.

shark [ʃaːk], *s.* (*ict.*) tiburón; (*fam.*) caimán. — *v.t.*, *v.i.* estafar, hurtar, petardear, gatear, ratear; *to shark up*, reunir furtivamente.

sharker, *s.* petardista, *m.*, tahur.

sharp [ʃaːp], *a.* agudo; fino, perspicaz, astuto; vivo; mañoso; aguzado, cortante, puntiagudo, afilado, incisivo; penetrante; lince, de vista aguda; áspero; acre, picante, mordaz, agrio; de buen oído, fino de oído; sarcástico; rígido, acerbo severo; ansioso, violento, ardiente, vehemente; listo, pronto, sagaz, avisado; fogoso, impetuoso; atento, vigilante; claramente delineado, bien definido, distinto; (*mús.*) sostenido; *sharp features*, facciones enjutas; *sharp nosed*, de nariz puntiaguda; de finísmo olfato. — *s.* (*mús.*) sostenido (♯); aguja de coser muy larga y delgada; estafador; fullero. — *adv.* (*fam.*) exactamente, puntualmente; (*mús.*) demasiado alto de tono; *at two o'clock sharp*, a las dos en punto; *look sharp!* ¡ojo alerta! ¡está alerta! — *v.t.* afilar, aguzar; (*mús.*) elevar medio tono, marcar con un sostenido. — *v.i.* (*mús.*) cantar o tocar más alto que el tono debido; engañar, trampear, petardear, ratear.

sharp-edged, *s.* agilado, agudo, aguzado.

sharpen ['ʃaːpən], *v.t.* afilar, aguzar, sacar punta a, adelgazar, amolar; (*fig.*) aguzar (el apetito), aguzar, sutilizar (el ingenio); hacer más severo, intenso, acre, fogoso, etc. — *v.i.* hacerse más agudo, aguzarse; afilarse; hacerse más picante, agriarse, acedarse.

sharpener, *s.* amolador, aguzador, afilador; *pencil sharpener*, cortalápiz; *knife sharpener*, chaira.

sharper ['ʃaːpə], *s.* fullero, caballero de industria, trampista, *m.f.*, estafador, timador.

sharp-eyed, sharp-sighted, *a.* de vista penetrante, que tiene vista de lince, perspicaz.

sharp-faced, sharp-featured, *a.* cariaguileño.

sharpness ['ʃaːpnes], *s.* agudeza; viveza de ingenio, perspicacia, sutileza; acrimonia, mordacidad; aspereza; agrura, acritud, acidez; rigor, violencia; inclemencia (del tiempo); brusquedad.

sharp-pointed, *a.* de punta aguda, puntiagudo.

sharp-set, *a.* ansioso.

sharpshooter [ʃaːp'ʃuːtə], *s.* franco tirador

sharp-witted, *a.* agudo de ingenio.

shatter ['ʃætə], *v.t.* destrozar, hacer pedazos, hacer astillas, hacer añicos; romper, estrellar; frustrar (esperanzas); quebrantar, arruinar (la salud); perturbar, distraer. — *v.i.* hacerse pedazos, quebrarse, romperse; dar un estallido.

shatter-brained, *a.* aturdido, necio, bobo.

shattery, *a.* desmenuzable, quebradizo.

shave [ʃeiv], *v.t.* afeitar, rasurar; (*ten.*) descarnar; (*carp.*) acepillar; rozar, pasar rozando; raer, raspar. — *v.i.* afeitarse, hacerse la barba. — *s.* afeitada; cuchilla desbastadora; roce; *to have a close shave*, escapar por un pelo.

shaveling ['ʃeivliŋ], *s.* (*despec.*) hombre rapado; monje, fraile.

shaver ['ʃeivə], *s.* persona que afeita, barbero; navaja o máquina de afeitar; (*fam.*) jovencito, rapaz, muchacho.

shaving, *s.* raedura, afeitada, rasura, acepilladura, raspadura; *shaving-blade*, navaja de afeitar; *shaving-brush*, brocha de afeitar; *shaving-dish*, bacía; *shaving-soap*, jabón para afeitarse; *cloth shaving*, paño de afeitar. — *pl.* **shavings**, acepilladuras, alisaduras, virutas, raeduras.

shaw [ʃɔ], *s.* soto, bosquecillo.

shawl [ʃɔ:l], s. chal, pañolón, rebocillo, mantón, (*Am.*) manta, rebozo.

shawm [ʃɔ:m], s. (*mús.*) chirimía, dulzaina.

she [ʃi:], *pron. fem.* ella; hembra (*en composición*): *she-devil*, diabla; *she-goat*, cabra; *she-ass*, burra, borrica; *she who, etc.*, la que.

sheaf [ʃi:f], s. (*pl.* **sheaves**) (*agr.*) gavilla, garba; haz, *m.*; fajo; paquete, atado, lío; roldana. — *v.t.* (*agr.*) agavillar, garbear.

shear [ʃiəɹ], *v.t.* (*pret.* **sheared, shore**; *p.p.* **sheared, shorn**) tonsurar, rapar, trasquilar, equilar; (*tej.*) tundir; cortar; cizallar; romper. — *v.i.* romperse; *shear stress*, esfuerzo cortante; *shearing-machine*, esquiladora mecánica; *shearing-time*, esquileo.

shearer, s. esquilador, trasquilador, marceador.

shearing, s. esquileo, tonsura; corte, *m.*

shearman, s. esquilador, tundidor.

shears [ʃiəɹz], *s.pl.* tijeras grandes; (*mec.*) cizallas; correderas de un torno.

shearwater [ˈʃiəɹwɔːtəɹ], s. (*orn.*) pico-tijera.

sheat-fish, s. siluro.

sheath [ʃi:θ], s. vaina, caja, manguito, funda, estuche, cubierta.

sheathe [ʃi:ð], *v.t.* envainar, meter en la vaina; poner vaina a; embotar; (*mar.*) aforrar.

sheathing [ˈʃiθiŋ], s. forro exterior, cubierta, aforro, embono; *sheathing nails*, clavos de entablar; *copper sheathing*, (*mar.*) forro de cobre.

sheathless [ˈʃi:θles], *a.* desenvainado; sin vaina, sin estuche.

sheave [ʃi:v], s. roldana; rueda de polea, garrucha, monopastos, *m.*; (*mec.*) rueda excéntrica. — *v.t.* (*agr.*) garbar, agavillar.

sheave-holes, s. (*mar.*) escoteras.

shed [ʃed], *v.t.* (*pret.*, *p.p.* **shed**) arrojar, quitarse, desprenderse de; mudar; esparcir; dejar caer; exhalar; derramar, verter; *to shed feathers*, pelechar. — *v.i.* caer; mudar (los cuernos, la piel, las plumas), separarse, desunirse. — *s.* vertiente, declive, bajada, cuesta; efusión, derramamiento (*en composición*).

shed, s. cabaña, barraca; cobertizo, sotechado.

shedder [ˈʃedəɹ], s. derramador, persona que derrama; animal que muda la piel, las plumas, etc.

shedding, s. derramamiento, vertimiento; muda (de plumas, piel, etc.).

sheen [ʃi:n], s. brillo, lustre.

sheeny [ˈʃi:ni], *a.* brillante, luciente, lustroso.

sheep [ʃi:p], s. (*pl.* **sheep**) oveja; carnero; (*fig.*) simplón, papanatas, *m.*; (*enc.*) badana. — *pl.* (*fig.*) fieles, feligreses; *sheep-dip*, baño o desinfectante para ganado; *sheep shearer*, esquilador; *sheep master*, ganadero; *sheepshank*, pierna de un carnero; (*mar.*) margarita en un cabo; *black sheep*, (*fam.*) garbanzo negro.

sheep-cote [ˈʃi:pkout], s. [SHEEPFOLD].

sheep-dog, s. perro de pastor.

sheep-dung, s. sirria.

sheepfold, s. redil, majada.

sheephook [ˈʃi:phuk], s. cayado.

sheepish [ˈʃi:piʃ], *a.* vergonzoso, tímido, pusilánime; tonto.

sheepishness, s. timidez, cortedad, empacho, pusilanimidad.

sheep's-eye, s. mirada amorosa; *to cast sheep's eyes at*, lanzar miradas de carnero degollado.

sheepshead [ˈʃi:pshed], s. (*ict.*) sargo.

sheep-shearing, s. esquileo.

sheepskin, s. badana, piel de carnero.

sheeptick, s. garrapata.

sheepwalk, s. carneril, dehesa.

sheer [ʃiəɹ], *a.* puro, claro, consumado, absoluto, completo, sin mezcla, cabal; (*tej.*) transparente; acantilado, enhiesto, escarpado. — *adv.* de un golpe, de una vez; a pico. — *s.* (*mar.*) arrufo, arrufadura; *with a great sheer*, (*mar.*) muy arrufado. — *v.i.* (*mar.*) alargarse, desviarse; torcer, doblar; *to sheer off*, (*fam.*) huirse, escaparse, marcharse.

sheer-hulk [ˈʃiəɹhʌlk], s. chata de arbolar.

sheer-legs, s. cabria de arbolar.

sheers [ʃiəɹz], s. cabria de arbolar; machina, grúa de tijeras.

sheet [ʃi:t], s. hoja, lámina, plancha (de cualquier materia); sábana; pedazo, pliego u hoja (de papel); diario; extensión de agua; (*mar.*) escota; (*poét.*) vela; *sheet hole*, escotera; *sheet lightning*, fucilazo(s); *sheet cable*, cable mayor; *sheet piling*, pilotaje; *sheet anchor*, ancla de la esperanza; (*fig.*) áncora de salvación, apoyo seguro, esperanza principal; *top-sail sheets*, (*mar.*) escotines; *to sail with flowing sheets*, navegar a escota larga; *to haul aft the sheets*, cazar las escotas; *winding sheet*, mortaja. — *v.t.* ensabanar, envolver en sábanas, poner sábanas en, proveer de sábanas; amortajar; extender en láminas u hojas.

sheeting, s. tela para sábanas, (*Méx.*) manta; (*metal.*) laminado; (*hidr.*, *min.*) encofrado.

sheikh [ʃi:k, ʃeik], s. jeque.

shekel [ˈʃekəl], s. siclo. — *pl.* (*fam.*) dinero.

sheldrake [ˈʃeldreik], s. (*orn.*) tadorna, cataraña; mergánsar.

shelf [ʃelf], s. (*pl.* **shelves**) anaquel, estante; (*mar.*) bajío, banco de arena; (*geol.*) escalón (de roca); *to be on the shelf*, quedarse para tía.

shell [ʃel], s. casco; cáscara (de nuez, de huevo, etc.); (*bot.*) silicua; vaina, vainilla (de legumbres); concha; coraza (de tortuga); caparazón (de cangrejo, etc.); corteza, cubierta; casco de caldera; armazón, *f.*, casco; (*fund.*) camisa o revestimiento de horno; (*poét.*) la lira; (*arti.*) granada; bote largo y angosto para regatas; (*mar.*) casco o caja de motón; (*poét.*) lira; *shell work*, obra de concha; *tortoise shell*, carey, concha de tortuga; *shell proof*, a prueba de bomba; *shell fish*, mariscos; *shell silver*, plata de concha; *shell gold*, oro de concha, oro molido. — *v.t.* deshollejar, desvainar, descortezar, quitar las cáscaras, descascarar, pelar; encerrar en cáscara, vaina o cápsula; (*arti.*) bombardear; (*E.U.*) desgranar. — *v.i.* descascararse, desconcharse.

shellac [ʃelæk], s. goma laca en hojuelas. — *v.t.* barnizar con laca.

shellbark [ˈʃelbɑːɹk], s. caria.

sheller, s. desgranador, descascarador.

shellfish, s. marisco.

shelling, s. descascaramiento, desgranamiento, desgrane; bombardeo.

shelly, *a.* conchado, conchudo, cubierto de conchas.

shelter [ˈʃeltəɹ], s. resguardo, amparo, abrigo; asilo; protector, amparador, defensor, protección; (*mil.*, *etc.*) refugio. — *v.t.* guarecer, abrigar, resguardar, poner al abrigo *o* a cubierto de; acoger; amparar, defender, proteger, ocultar, encubrir, tapar. — *v.i.* refugiarse, acogerse, guarecerse.

sheltered, *a.* abrigado.

sheltering, *a.* protector.

shelterless, *a.* desamparado, sin refugio, sin asilo; desabrigado.

shelve [ʃelv], *v.t.* poner sobre un estante o anaquel; proveer de estantes o anaqueles; (*fig.*) poner a un lado, aplazar (*o* diferir) indefinidamente; dar carpetazo. — *v.i.* inclinarse, estar en declive, en pendiente.

shelves, *s.pl.* [SHELF].

shelving, *a.* inclinado, en declive, en pendiente. — *s.* estantería, anaquelería; carpetazo; declive, lugar en declive, lugar declinado.

shelvy, *a.* inclinado, con declive gradual.

shemozzle [ʃeˈmɔzəl], *s.* (*fam.*) barahúnda; alboroto.

shepherd [ˈʃepəɪd], *s.* pastor; zagal; (*fig.*) párroco, cura, *m.*; *shepherd's purse, shepherd's pouch*, (*bot.*) bolsa de pastor; *shepherd dog*, perro de pastor; *shepherd's crook*, cayado; *shepherd's watch*, hierba pajarera.

shepherdess [ˈʃepəɪdes], *s.f.* pastora, zagala.

sherbet [ˈʃəːɪbət], *s.* sorbete, granizado.

sherd [ʃəːɪd], *s.* tiesto, casco, tejoleta.

sherif [ʃeˈriːf], *s.* jerife (descendiente de Mahoma).

sheriff [ˈʃerif], *s.* sheriff (magistrado).

sheriffdom, *s.* jurisdicción del *sheriff*.

sherry [ˈʃeri], *s.* vino de Jerez.

shew [ʃou], *v.t.* (*pret.* **shewed**; *p.p.* **shewn**) [SHOW].

shibboleth [ˈʃiboleθ], *s.* mote; contraseña.

shie, *v.t.* [SHY].

shield [ʃiːld], *s.* escudo; broquel, rodela; (*fig.*) amparo, patrocinio; resguardo, defensa, reparo; defensor, protector; (*blas.*) escudo de armas; (*ent.*) falena; *shield fern*, aspidia. — *v.t.* escudar, amparar, defender, resguardar, proteger.

shield-bearer, *s.* escudero.

shift [ʃift], *v.t.* trasladar; mover; transferir, remover, transportar; conducir, llevar; (*teat.*) cambiar de decoración; quitar. — *v.i.* moverse, cambiar(se); menearse, mudar(se); variar; tergiversar; ingeniarse, darse maña, arreglárselas; (*mar.*) correrse; *to shift for oneself*, arreglárselas; mirar por sí mismo; *to shift a tackle*, (*mar.*) enmendar un aparejo; *to shift the royal*, (*mar.*) despasar el ayuste; *to shift the cargo*, volver la estiva. — *s.* cambio; sustitución; expediente, recurso; artificio, artimaña, evasión, subterfugio, astucia, fraude; camisa; tanda (de obreros); revezo; *to make shift to*, arreglarse para; *to make shift without*, pasarse sin.

shiftable, *a.* mudable; revecero.

shifter, *s.* (*mec.*) desviador; (*teat.*) carpintero, tramoyista, *m.*; invencionero; zorrocloco.

shiftless, *a.* desamparado; inútil, incapaz; perezoso; descuidado.

shifty [ˈʃifti], *a.* astuto; falso; furtivo.

shikar [ʃiˈkɑːɪ], *s.* (*Ang.-Ind.*) caza.

shikaree, *s.* cazador, deportista, *m.*

shillalah, shillelah [ʃiˈleilə], *s.* palo, cachiporra.

shilling [ˈʃiliŋ], *s.* chelín.

shilly-shally [ˈʃiliˈʃæli], *v.i.* (*fam.*) estar irresoluto, vacilar, estar vacilando, no saber qué hacer. — *s.* vacilación, irresolución. — *a.* irresoluto. — *adv.* con que sí y con que no.

shim [ʃim], *s.* cuña, chaveta, plancha, etc. que sirve de relleno. — *v.t.* tapar, rellenar, cuñar.

shimmer [ˈʃiməɪ], *v.i.* rielar, despedir luz trémula. — *s.* luz trémula; débil resplandor.

shimmy [ˈʃimi], *s.* especie de 'foxtrot' acompañado de movimientos temblorosos; (*vulg.*) camisa de mujer; (*aut.*) zigzagueo.

shin [ʃin], *s.* espinilla, canilla. — *v.t.*, *v.i.* trepar; (*E.U.*, *vulg.*) pedir dinero prestado.

shindy [ˈʃindi], *s.* (*fam.*) alboroto, zacapela.

shine [ʃain], *v.i.* (*pret. y p.p.* **shone**) lucir, relucir, resplandecer, brillar, relumbrar; rielar; favorecer, ser propicio; exceder, resaltar, distinguirse, sobresalir. — *v.t.* pulir, bruñir; dar lustre a (los zapatos), (*Méj.*) dar bola. — *s.* resplandor, brillo, lustre; buen tiempo, claridad.

shiner, *s.* persona o cosa que brilla; (*fam.*) moneda de oro; pez plateado.

shingle [ˈʃiŋgəl], *v.t.* cubrir con tablas de ripia (*o* tejamaníes); cortar (el pelo) a la garçonne; (*metal.*) cinglar. — *s.* tabla de ripia; tejamaní; pelo a la garçonne; guijarros; cascajo; (*E.U.*) letrero.

shingles [ˈʃiŋgəlz], *s.* (*med.*) zoster, zona.

shingly, *a.* guijarroso, guijarreño.

shining [ˈʃainiŋ], *a.* brillante, radiante, luciente, resplandeciente, luminoso, lustroso. — *s.* lucimiento, lustre, esplendor; resplandor, brillo.

shiningness, *s.* resplandor, lustre.

shiny [ˈʃaini], *a.* lustroso, brillante, luciente, resplandeciente.

ship [ʃip], *s.* buque, nave, *f.*, barco, bajel, navío, embarcación; *merchant ship*, buque mercante; *store ship*, navío almacén; *ship of the line*, navío de alto bordo, navío de línea; *ship of war*, buque de guerra; *ship's biscuit*, galleta de munición, galleta muy dura; *ship stores*, matalotaje; *ship's carpenter*, carpintero de ribera; *ship chandlery*, cabuyería; tienda de artículos de marina; *ship's boy*, paje de escoba, grumete; *ship fever*, tifus. — *v.t.* embarcar, poner a bordo; (*com.*) transportar, remesar, expedir; (*mar.*) tripular, recibir a bordo la tripulación; embarcar; armar, montar (mástiles, timón, remos, etc.); *to ship a heavy sea*, embarcar agua, encapillar un golpe de mar. — *v.i.* ir a bordo, embarcar(se); engancharse como marinero.

shipboard [ˈʃipbɔːɪd], *s.* (*mar.*) bordo; *a-shipboard, on shipboard*, a bordo.

shipbuilder [ˈʃipbildəɪ], *s.* ingeniero naval, constructor de buques.

shipbuilding, *s.* construcción naval.

shipload, *s.* cargazón, *f.*, cargamento.

shipmaster, *s.* patrón, capitán de buque.

shipmate [ˈʃipmeit], *s.* camarada de a bordo.

shipment [ˈʃipmənt], *s.* embarque; expedición; cargamento; envío, remesa.

ship-owner, *s.* naviero.

shipper, *s.* remitente; importador; exportador.

shipping [ˈʃipiŋ], *s.* barcos, buques; marina; (*com.*) embarque, expedición. — *a.* naval, marítimo, de la marina mercante, de embarque; *shipping-charges*, gastos de embarque; *shipping-clerk*, dependiente de muelle; *shipping-bill*, factura de embarque; *shipping-agent*, consignatario de buques; *shipping-articles*, contrata de marinero; *shipping-master*, persona que contrata marineros.

shipshape ['ʃipʃeip], *a.* en buen orden; bien arreglado, bien orientado, bien instalado.

shipworm, *s.* broma; teredo; tiñuela.

shipwreck ['ʃiprek], *s.* naufragio; (*fig.*) desastre, ruina, pérdida total. — *v.t.* causar naufragio, hacer naufragar, hacer zozobrar, echar a pique; *shipwrecked*, naufragado; *to be shipwrecked*, naufragar, zozobrar.

shipwright ['ʃiprait], *s.* constructor de buques; carpintero de ribera.

shipyard ['ʃipjɑːɹd], *s.* astillero; varadero.

shire [ʃaiəɹ], *s.* condado; *shire horse*, percherón.

shirk [ʃəːɹk], *v.t.*, *v.i.* evadir, eludir, evitar, esquivar; faltar a, desentenderse de, desatender; *to shirk one's duty*, faltar al deber.

shirk, shirker, *s.* persona que falta a su deber; gandul, vago.

shirr [ʃəːɹ], *v.t.* (*cost.*) fruncir, gandujar, acordonar; (*coc.*) pasar (huevos) por crema, escalfar (huevos) en crema. — *s.* (*cost.*) frunce, fruncimiento, acordonamiento; hilo de goma tejido en una tela para hacerla elástica.

shirred, *p.p.*, *a.* (*cost.*) acordonado, fruncido; (*tej.*) elástico; (*coc.*) pasado por crema, escalfado en crema.

shirt [ʃəːɹt], *s.* camisa (de hombre); blusa (de mujer); (*fund.*) revestimiento de horno de fundición; *shirt-sleeve*, manga de camisa; *to be in one's shirt-sleeves*, estar en mangas de camisa; *shirt-front*, pechera de camisa; *shirt-waist*, corpiño (o cuerpo) de camisa.

shirting, *s.* tela para camisas.

shist [ʃist], *s.* esquisto.

shittah-tree ['ʃitɑːtriː], *s.* especie de acacia de la India.

shittim ['ʃitim] (**-wood**), *s.* palo de setim.

shiver ['ʃivəɹ], *s.* temblor, escalofrío, tiritón, estremecimiento; pedazo, cacho, trozo, cachivache, fragmento, casco. — *v.i.* tiritar, temblequear, temblar; estallar, estrellarse; cascarse, hacerse pedazos, quebrantarse; (*mar.*) flamear; sacudir. — *v.t.* estrellar, romper de un golpe, hacer pedazos, hacer astillas, hacer añicos.

shivering, *s.* escalofrío; temblor, estremecimiento; desmembramiento, quebranto.

shivery ['ʃivəɹi], *a.* trémulo, tembloroso; friolento, friolero; friable, quebradizo.

shoal [ʃoul], *s.* bajo, bajío, banco de arena, alfaque; banco (de peces), cardumen; muchedumbre. — *a.* poco profundo, bajo; *shoal water*, agua poco profunda. — *v.t.*, *v.i.* disminuir en profundidad; reunirse en gran número; juntarse en tropas, atroparse.

shoaliness, *s.* falta de profundidad.

shoaly, *a.* vadoso, lleno de bajíos.

shoat, shote [ʃout], *s.* cochinillo, gorrino; pelafustán, pelagatos.

shock [ʃok], *s.* choque, golpe, sacudida, colisión, sacudimiento, concusión; combate, reencuentro; susto, sobresalto; encuentro violento, encontrón; ofensa; desazón, *f.*; (*med.*) postración nerviosa, choque; (*elec.*) electrochoque, sacudida eléctrica; (*agr.*) hacina, fascal, tresnal; mechón, greña; *shock-absorber*, (*mec.*) amortiguador; (*aut.*) amortiguador de los muelles; *shock-troops*, tropas de asalto. — *a.* afelpado, lanudo, desgreñado. — *v.t.*, *v.i.* sacudir, dar una sacudida; chocar; escandalizar, horrorizar, disgustar; (*agr.*) hacinar, hacer hacinas de grano.

shocking, *a.* espantoso, horrible, chocante, ofensivo.

shod [ʃod], *pret. y p.p.* [SHOE].

shoddy ['ʃodi], *s.* lana regenerada; (*fig.*) pacotilla. — *a.* inferior; de pacotilla; espurio.

shoe [ʃuː], *s.* (*pl.* **shoes**) zapato; calzado; herradura; suela de trineo; (*mec.*, *mar.*) zapata; galga de carruaje; (*mar.*) calzo, soler, solera; tornapunta; regatón, contera; canal para conducir trigo, etc., a la tolva; *horse-shoe*, herradura; *wooden shoes*, zuecos, chanclos; *shoe blacking*, betún para zapatos; *shoe polish*, lustre; *to cast a shoe*, desherrarse (un animal); *to be in someone's shoes*, (*fam.*) hallarse en el pellejo de uno. — *v.t.* (*pret.* **shod**; *p.p.* **shod, shodden**) calzar; herrar (un caballo); *to shoe an anchor*, (*mar.*) calzar el ancla.

shoe-black, shoe-cleaner, *s.* limpiabotas, *m.*

shoe-horn ['ʃuːhoːɹn], *s.* calzador.

shoeing ['ʃuːiŋ], *s.* acto de herrar.

shoe-lace, (*E.U.*) **shoe-string**, *s.* lazo de zapato, cordón de zapato.

shoemaker, *s.* zapatero.

shoemaking, *s.* zapatería, fabricación de calzado.

shoer ['ʃuːəɹ], *s.* herrador (de caballerías).

shoe-shop, *s.* zapatería.

shole [ʃoul], *s.* (*mar.*) solero, tornapunta.

shone [ʃon], *pret.* [SHINE].

shoo [ʃuː], *v.t.*, *v.i.* ahuyentar (gallinas, etc.); *shoo!* ¡so! *interj.* ¡so! ¡fuera!

shook [ʃuk], *pret.* [SHAKE]. — *s.pl.* **shooks,** paquete de duelas, bocoyes o barriles abatidos.

shoon, *s.pl.* (*ant.*) [SHOE].

shoot [ʃuːt], *v.t.* (*pret.*, *p.p.* **shot**) disparar, arrojar, tirar, lanzar; vaciar; descargar; fusilar; pegar un tiro (a); empujar, hacer salir; traspasar; volar; atravesar rápidamente; hacer saltar, dar barreno. — *v.i.* tirar, disparar; salir, espigar, brotar, nacer, germinar; crecer; pasar o correr rápidamente, lanzarse; latir, punzar (un dolor); sobresalir, proyectar; caer (una estrella); *to shoot an arrow*, lanzar o disparar una flecha, flechar; *to shoot rapids*, pasar, salvar el recial de un río; *to shoot forth*, lanzarse o abalanzarse; *to shoot a bolt*, echar (o correr) un cerrojo (o pestillo); *to shoot off*, tirar, descargar (un arma); llevarse; *to shoot out*, salir escapado; *to shoot over*, pasar rápidamente por encima de; *to shoot under*, pasar rápidamente por debajo de; *to shoot through*, atravesar, pasar rápidamente de parte a parte; *to shoot out of* (*a sack*), vaciar (los costales) de; *to shoot up*, espigarse (plantas, niños, etc.). — *s.* vástago, retoño, pimpollo, renuevo, brotón, mugrón, grillo; recial de río; partida de caza; tiro al blanco; artesa inclinada; (*arq.*) refuerzo de arco o bóveda; gorrín, gorrino.

shooter, *s.* tirador; *sharp-shooter*, francotirador.

shooting, *s.* caza con escopeta; tiro; tiroteo; latido doloroso, punzada; coto de caza; derecho de cazar; *shooting-star*, estrella fugaz; *shooting-match*, concurso de tiro; *shooting-range*, campo de tiro; *shooting-stick*, (*dep.*) bastón asiento; (*impr.*) acuñador, desacuñador; atacador.

shop [ʃop], *s.* tienda, comercio, almacén; (*ind.*)

taller; *baker's shop*, panadería; *bookseller's shop*, librería; *jeweller's shop*, joyería; *silversmith's shop*, platería; *chemist's shop*, farmacia; *stationer's shop*, papelería; *watchmaker's shop*, relojería; *to shut up shop*, cerrar la tienda; *(fam.)* desistir de (o terminar) una empresa; *to smell of the shop*, oler a tienda; *to talk shop*, hablar de negocios. — *v.i.* ir de compras; comprar, feriar.

shop-boy, *s.* mancebo de tienda, dependiente.

shop-girl, *s.f.* muchacha de tienda.

shopkeeper, *s.* tendero.

shoplifter, *s.* ladrón (ladrona) de tiendas.

shoplifting, *s.* ratería en las tiendas.

shopman, *s.* tendero; mercader; dependiente, mancebo de tienda.

shopping, *s.* compra, compras.

shopwalker, *s.* vigilante de almacén.

shopwoman, *s.f.* tendera.

shorage ['ʃɔːridʒ], *s.* derecho de costa o ribera.

shore ['ʃɔːəɹ], *s.* costa, playa, ribera; grao; orilla (de un río o lago); puntal; costón; *(min.)* entibo, ademe; *(mar.)* escora, botante; *shore of a pair of shears*, *(mar.)* puntal diagonal de cabria; *along shore*, cerca de tierra; *close inshore*, arrimado a la tierra. — *v.t.* apuntalar, acodalar, poner puntales; *(mar.)* escorar; llevar a tierra, a la orilla; circundar.

shoreless, *a.* que no tiene playa.

shorn ['ʃɔːɹn], *a.* mocho. — *p.p.* [SHEAR].

short [ʃɔːɹt], *a.* corto; reducido; bajo; breve; escaso, falto, limitado; conciso, sucinto, compendiado; insuficiente, deficiente, inadecuado; seco, brusco; cercano, próximo; corto de alcances; menguado, quebradizo; breve (vocal, etc.); *(com.)* alcanzado; *in short*, en resumen, en suma, para abreviar; *in (o within) a short time*, dentro de poco tiempo, pronto; *a very short while*, un ratito; *to come (o fall) short (of)*, faltar; no alcanzar, no llegar; estar lejos de, ser inferior a; *short of this*, fuera de esto, además de esto, amén de esto; *to be short of*, estar lejos de; no responder a; andar escaso de; *to be short*, *to cut a long story short*, para abreviar; *to cut someone short*, cortar la palabra a, interrumpir bruscamente; *to grow short*, acortarse, hacerse corto, comenzar a ser corto; *to run short*, faltar; *to take short*, coger de improviso; *short-handed*, falto de mano de obra; *short allowance*, media ración; *short-bodied*, pequeño de cuerpo; *short circuit*, corto circuito; *short cut*, atajo; *short-nosed*, de nariz aplastada, chato, romo; *short-sighted*, miope, corto de vista; *(fig.)* falto de perspicacia; *short-sightedness*, miopía, cortedad de vista; *(fig.)* falta de perspicacia; *short-waisted*, corto de talle; *short ton*, tonelada de 2000 lb. — *s.* sumario, compendio, resumen, substancia; *(com.)* déficit; vocal breve. — *pl.* **shorts**, salvado mezclado con harina; calzón corto; *in short*, en suma, en cuentas resumidas, en resumen; *the long and the short of it*, en resumidas cuentas, en resumen. — *adv.* brevemente, en breve, breve.

shortage ['ʃɔːɹtidʒ], *s.* falta, escasez, deficiencia; carestía.

shortbread ['ʃɔːɹtbred], **shortcake** ['ʃɔːɹtkeik], *s.* mantecada.

shortcoming [ʃɔːɹt'kʌmiŋ], *s.* defecto, omisión;

negligencia, mengua, falta, escasez, deficiencia.

shorten ['ʃɔːɹtən], *v.t.* hacer más corto, acortar; reducir, cercenar, disminuir; resumir, compendiar, abreviar; limitar, impedir, restringir; hacer quebradiza (la pastelería). — *v.i.* hacerse más corto, acortarse, disminuirse, abreviarse, encogerse.

shortening, *s.* acortamiento; aminoración; abreviación; dismínución; *(coc.)* manteca o mantequilla con que se hacen quebradizos los hojaldres, etc.

shorthand ['ʃɔːɹthænd], *s.* taquigrafía, estenografía. — *a.* taquigráfico; *shorthand-writer*, taquígrafo, taquígrafa.

shortlived, *a.* corto de vida, pasajero.

shortly, *adv.* presto, luego, al instante, en seguida, pronto, en breve; brevemente, en pocas palabras.

shortnecked, *a.* cuellicorto.

shortness, *s.* cortedad; pequeñez; defecto, deficiencia, imperfección; brevedad; flaqueza (de memoria); *shortness of breath*, respiración dificultosa.

short-sighted, *a.* [SHORT].

short-winded [ʃɔːɹt'winded], *a.* corto de respiración, asmático.

shot [ʃɔt], *pret.*, *p.p.* [SHOOT]. — *a.* *(tej.)* batido, tornasolado. — *v.t.* cargar con perdigones; limpiar botellas con perdigones. — *s.* perdigón, perdigones; bala, proyectil; golpe, tiro; tirador; tirada, jugada; alcance; *(min.)* barreno; escote; *fowling shot*, *bird shot*, munición menuda; *grape shot*, metralla; *deer shot*, *buck shot*, munición de balines; *a good shot*, un buen tirador; *cannon shot*, cañonazo; *shot pouch*, perdigonera; *shot gauge*, vitola para calibrar proyectiles; *shot plug*, tapabalazo; *shot tower*, torre para hacer municiones; *shot free*, libre de escote; *(fig.)* que no recibe el castigo merecido; *shot between wind and water*, balazo a flor del agua; *not by a long shot*, *(fam.)* ni mucho menos, ni con mucho.

shotgun ['ʃɔtgʌn], *s.* escopeta.

shotten, *a.* *(ant.)* dislocado; desovado. — *p.p.* *(ant.)* [SHOOT].

should [ʃud], *pret.* [SHALL]; auxiliar de modo condicional; indica el modo subjuntivo; también indica deber: *I should like to go*, me gustaría ir; *you should go*, deberías ir.

shoulder ['ʃouldəɹ], *s.* hombro; espalda; cuarto delantero, brazuelo; contera de bastón; virola de cuchillo; *(carp.)* can, pie de amigo; espaldón de espiga; parte saliente, soporte, sostén; *(fig.)* lo que apoya o sostiene; *to give someone the cold shoulder*, recibir a uno fríamente, negarse a recibirle o hablar con él, etc.; *shoulder-of-mutton sail*, *(mar.)* guaira, vela triangular; *shoulder of pork*, pernil; *shoulder strap*, correón; charretera; *shoulderknot*, *(mil.)* charretera mocha, capona; *shoulder to shoulder*, hombro a hombro; *(fig.)* apoyándose mutuamente. — *v.t.* echarse a la espalda, cargar al hombro, llevar a hombros; *(fig.)* cargar con, tomar sobre sí, asumir; empujar con indiferencia o insolencia; codear, meter el hombro; *shoulder arms*, *(mil.)* armas al hombro; *broadshouldered*, ancho de espaldas.

shoulder-blade, **shoulder-bone**, *s.* espaldilla, paletilla, omóplato, escápula.

shout [ʃaut], *v.t.*, *v.i.* vocear, gritar, dar voces, dar gritos, baladrar; exclamar, dar vivas, vitorear, aclamar; *to shout down*, silbar. — *s.* grito, gritería, baladro; alarido; aclamación, exclamación; *shout of applause*, aclamación.

shouter, *s.* gritador, baladrero.

shouting, *s.* vocerío, gritería; aclamación. — *a.* que vocea, que da gritos.

shove [ʃʌv], *v.t.*, *v.i.* empujar; mover con fuerza, llevar adelante, impeler; *to shove away*, rechazar, alejar; *to shove off*, (*mar.*) echar afuera; alejarse; *to shove back*, hacer retroceder, empujar hacia atrás; *to shove along* (o *forward*), empujar; hacer avanzar; *to shove from*, empujar, rechazar a empujones; *to shove out*, empujar hacia afuera, hacer salir. — *s.* empellón, empuje, empujón, impulso.

shovel [ʃʌvəl], *s.* pala; *shovel hat*, sombrero de teja; *fire shovel*, badila. — *v.t.* traspalar.

shovel-board, *s.* tabla para jugar al tejo; el tejo mismo.

shovelful, *s.* palada.

shovelling [ʃʌvəliŋ], *s.* traspaleo.

shoveller, *s.* palero.

show, shew [ʃou], *v.t.* (*pret.* **showed;** *p.p.* **showed, shown**) indicar, mostrar; hacer ver, enseñar; demostrar, probar; manifestar, descubrir, exponer; explicar; conducir, guiar. — *v.i.* parecer, tener apariencia o señales de; aparecer, mostrarse, asomarse, dar señal; *to show off*, hacer ver, exhibir; lucir; pavonearse; hacer alarde de; *to show forth*, exponer, mostrar; manifestar, publicar; *to show up*, hacer subir; descubrir o exponer un fraude; comparecer; (*fam.*) dejarse ver, presentarse; *to show one's teeth*, (*fig.*) alargar los dientes. — *s.* exhibición, exposición, cosa expuesta; espectáculo público; (*teat.*) función; boato, ostentación, pompa, tren, aparato; seña, manifestación, indicación, promesa; apariencia, exterioridad; máscara, pretexto, velo; (*fam.*) suerte, *f.*; lance; negocio; *a show of*, apariencia de, pretexto de; *to make a good show*, hacer gran papel; *in open show*, públicamente; *to make a show of*, aparentar, hacer gala de; *show card*, tarjetón, letrero; *show bill*, cartel, cartelón; *show case*, vitrina, aparador, caja de muestras; *show window*, escaparate; (*to vote*) *by show of hands*, alzando las manos; *cattle show*, exposición de ganado.

showbread, shewbread [ʃoubred], *s.* panes de proposición.

shower [ʃouəɹ], *s.* mostrador, el que muestra.

shower [ʃauəɹ], *s.* chubasco, aguacero, nubada; nubarrada; (*fig.*) lluvia; abundancia; *heavy shower*, turbión, nubada; (*fig.*) lluvia; abundancia; *shower bath*, ducha. — *v.t.* regar, mojar; derramar con abundancia; distribuir con liberalidad. — *v.i.* llover, caer un chubasco, caer agua, chaparrear; (*fig.*) llover.

showeriness, *s.* tiempo lluvioso.

showerless, *a.* sin lluvia, sin nubadas.

showery [ʃauəri], *a.* lluvioso.

showiness [ʃouines], *s.* visualidad, esplendor, ostentación, magnificencia.

showman [ʃoumən], *s.* director de espectáculos; empresario de circo, teatro, etc.

shown, shewn, *p.p.* [SHOW].

showy [ʃoui], *a.* vistoso, lujoso, aparatoso, magnífico, ostentoso, suntuoso; llamativo,

chillón; *to be showy*, tener vista; llamar la atención.

shrank [ʃræŋk], *pret.* [SHRINK].

shrapnel [ʃræpnəl], *s.* granada de metralla; shrapnel.

shred [ʃred], *v.t.* desmenuzar; hacer tiras, hacer pedazos muy pequeños. — *s.* tira, triza, girón, retazo, arambel, harapo; fragmento, pizca, partícula, pedazo pequeño; punto, jota, átomo.

shredded, *a.* trojezado, desmenuzado, hecho trizas.

shrew [ʃru:], *s.* (*zool.*) musgaño, musaraña; fiera, arpía, víbora.

shrewd [ʃru:d], *a.* sagaz, prudente, perspicaz, vivo; fino; sutil; (*ant.*) solapado; (*ant.*) agudo, cortante.

shrewdness, *s.* sagacidad, perspicacia, sutileza.

shrewish [ʃru:iʃ], *a.* regañón, regañador, malhumorado.

shrewishly, *adv.* de muy mal humor, a regañadientes.

shrewishness, *s.* mal genio, maldad.

shrewmouse [ʃru:maus], *s.* (*zool.*) musgaño, musaraña.

shriek [ʃri:k], *v.i.* chillar, gritar, dar gritos o chillidos. — *s.* chillido, grito agudo; *to utter a shriek*, dar un grito; *shriek of laughter*, risotada.

shrievalty [ʃri:vəlti], *s.* cargo a funciones de *sheriff*. — [SHERIFF].

shrift [ʃrift], *s.* (*igl.*) confesión; penitencia; *to give short shrift to*, echar con cajas destempladas.

shrike [ʃraik], *s.* pega reborda.

shrill [ʃrill], *a.* agudo, penetrante, estridente. — *v.t.*, *v.i.* chillar, dar un grito agudo.

shrillness, *s.* agudeza, estridencia.

shrimp [ʃrimp], *s.* camarón, quisquilla; gamba; (*despec.*) hombrecillo. — *v.i.* pescar camarones.

shrine [ʃrain], *s.* relicario; sepulcro de santo; altar, capilla, templete.

shrink [ʃriŋk], *v.i.* (*pret.* **shrank, shrunk;** *p.p.* **shrunk, shrunken**) encogerse, contraerse, estrecharse, acortarse, angostarse; mermar, disminuir; (*fig.*) temblar, estremecerse; retirarse; retroceder; apocarse; *to shrink from*, huir de, evitar. — *v.t.* encoger, reducir, contraer; *to shrink away*, desaparecer por grados, sustraerse; *to shrink away from*, recular ante; huir de; *to shrink back*, retirarse, retroceder; *to shrink up*, estrechar(se), arrugarse, encogerse; (*fig.*) estremecerse, temblar; *to shrink on*, (*mec.*) montar en caliente, enmangar en caliente. — *s.* encogimiento; *shrink-fit*, ajuste en caliente.

shrinkage [ʃriŋkidʒ], *s.* encogimiento, contracción; diminución, reducción; (*com.*) merma, pérdida.

shrinking, *a.* apocado, tímido.

shrive [ʃraiv], *v.t.*, *v.i.* (*pret.* **shrove, shrived;** *p.p.* **shriven, shrived**) (*igl.*) confesar; confesarse.

shrivel [ʃrivəl], *v.t.* arrugar; encoger; marchitar; secar. — *v.i.* arrugarse, encogerse, encarrujarse, ensortijarse (el hilo, etc.); avellanarse, acorcharse (las frutas); *to shrivel up*, encogerse.

shriven [ʃrivən], *p.p.* [SHRIVE].

shroud [ʃraud], *s.* mortaja; anillo refuerzo de

una rueda dentada; (*fig.*) velo, disfraz. — *pl.* **shrouds,** (*mar.*) obenques; vientos o tirantes de la chimenea de un vapor; retenidas; *futtock shrouds,* arraigadas; *bumkin shrouds,* pie de servioleta; *bowsprit shrouds,* mostachos del bauprés; *main shrouds,* obenques mayores; *preventer shrouds,* obenques volantes. — *v.t.* amortajar; cubrir, ocultar, velar.

shrove, úsase solamente en composición, v.g. *Shrove Tuesday,* martes de carnestolendas, martes de carnaval.

shrovetide ['ʃrouvtaid], *s.* carnaval.

shrub [ʃrʌb], *s.* arbusto; mata, matojo; limonada con aguardiente y azúcar.

shrubbery ['ʃrʌbəri], *s.* arbustos; maleza, matorral.

shrubbiness, *s.* abundancia de arbustos.

shrubby ['ʃrʌbi], *a.* lleno de arbustos; parecido a un arbusto; aparrado, fruticoso.

shrug [ʃrʌg], *v.t.* encoger, contraer; *to shrug off,* esquivar; tratar con indiferencia. — *v.i.* encogerse de hombros. — *s.* encogimiento de hombros.

shrunk [ʃrʌŋk], **shrunken** ['ʃrʌnkən], *pret.* y *p.p.* [SHRINK].

shuck, *v.t.* descascarar, descortezar, pelar, deshollejar; (*E.U.*) quitar la concha a una ostra. — *s.* cáscara, vaina, hollejo; (*E.U.*) concha de marisco.

shudder [ʃʌdəɪ], *v.i.* estremecerse, temblar; vibrar. — *s.* temblor, estremecimiento; vibración.

shuffle ['ʃʌfəl], *v.t.* mezclar, revolver; barajar (naipes); restregar (los pies). — *v.i.* arrastrar los pies; barajar; tergiversar; *to shuffle off,* esquivar (una dificultad); largarse arrastrando los pies; desprenderse o zafarse de; *to shuffle along,* andar arrastrando los pies; ir tirando, ir pasando; *to shuffle up,* hacer una cosa de mala manera. — *s.* barajadura; confusión, desorden, *m.f.*; mezcla; excusa, salida; restregamiento de pies en el suelo; fraude, embuste.

shuffler, *s.* tergiversador; embustero.

shuffling ['ʃʌfliŋ], *s.* barajadura; tergiversación. — *a.* tergiversador; (paso) arrastrante.

shun [ʃʌn], *v.t., v.i.* huir, rehuir, evitar, esquivar; retraerse de, apartarse de, escaparse de, recatarse de; *to shun the world,* enterrarse en vida.

shunt [ʃʌnt], *v.t.* desviar; (*f.c.*) apartar; (*elec.*) derivar, shuntar; eludir, evadir; echar el muerto o el cascabel a. — *v.i.* desviarse; (*f.c.*) hacer maniobras. — *s.* desviación; (*elec.*) derivador de corriente, shunt.

shunter, *s.* (*f.c.*) guardagujas, *m.*

shunting, *s.* (*f.c.*) maniobras.

shut [ʃʌt], *v.t.* (pret., *p.p.* **shut**) cerrar. — *v.i.* cerrarse; apretarse, juntarse (dientes, tijeras, etc.); *to shut down,* cerrar; parar (fábrica, taller); *to shut in,* encerrar; rodear; *to shut off,* cortar (agua, etc.); *to shut out,* excluir; *to shut up,* cerrar; encerrar; (*fam.*) hacer callar (a); callarse, achantarse.

shutter ['ʃʌtəɪ], *s.* cierre; juntura. — *a.* cerrado, entornado; persona o cosa que cierra; cerradura, cerrador; postigo de ventana, contraventana; (*foto.*) obturador.

shuttle ['ʃʌtəl], *s.* (*tej.*) lanzadera.

shuttlecock ['ʃʌtəlkɔk], *s.* volante, rehilete.

shy [ʃai], *a.* tímido; asustadizo, miedoso;

reservado; esquivo, vergonzoso, evasivo, huraño. — *v.t. to shy, shy off* o *shy away,* hacer desviar, apartar; arrojar, lanzar. — *v.i.* respingar; asustarse; desviarse repentinamente; *to fight shy of,* rehuir; *have a shy at,* probar. — *s.* lanzamiento; sobresalto; respingo; prueba, ensayo.

shyness, *s.* timidez; vergüenza; esquivez, reserva.

shyster ['ʃaistəɪ], *s.* (*fam., E.U.*) picapleitos.

si [si:], *s.* (*mús.*) si.

Siamese [saiə'mi:z], *s., a.* siamés.

Siberian [sai'biəriən], *a.* siberiano.

sibilant ['sibilənt], *a.* sibilante.

sibilation [sibi'leiʃən], *s.* silbido.

sibyl ['sibil], *s.* sibila, profetisa.

sibylline ['sibilain], *a.* sibilino; profético, oracular.

sicamore, *s.* [SYCAMORE].

siccate ['sikeit], *v.t.* secar.

siccation, *s.* acto de secar, desecación.

siccative ['sikətiv], **siccant** ['sikənt], *s., a.* (*pint.*) secante, secativo, desecativo.

siccity ['siksiti], *s.* sequedad, aridez.

Sicilian [si'siliən], *s., a.* siciliano.

sick [sik], *a.* malo, doliente, enfermo; (*Ingl.*) nauseado; cansado, hastiado, harto de; *sick bed,* lecho de enfermo; *sick headache,* jaqueca con náuseas; *sick to death,* enfermo de muerte; (*fam.*) harto de; *sick flag,* (*mar.*) bandera amarilla; *to be sick at heart,* llevar la muerte en el alma. — *v.t.* animar, excitar, incitar.

sicken ['sikən], *v.t.* poner enfermo; marear; dar asco a; hartar, hastiar. — *v.i.* enfermar(se), caer enfermo; cansarse, fastidiarse, hartarse; marearse, tener náuseas; flaquear; extenuarse, debilitarse.

sickening ['sikəniŋ], *a.* nauseabundo, asqueroso, repugnante; fastidioso; empalagoso.

sickish, *a.* indispuesto; nauseabundo.

sickle ['sikəl], *s.* hoz, *f.*, falce, *f.*, segadera.

sickliness ['siklinis], *s.* falta de salud, achaque, indisposición; estado enfermizo; insalubridad.

sickly ['sikli], *a.* enfermizo, achacoso; lánguido, endeble; malsano; nauseabundo; empalagoso; *to grow sickly* (o *become sickly*), perder la salud.

sickness ['siknis], *s.* enfermedad, mal, indisposición; falta de salud; náusea, basca.

sick-nurse, *s.* enfermera.

side [said], *s.* lado, costado; margen, orilla; ladera, falda; bando, facción, partido; parte, *f.*; (*mar.*) bordo, banda, costado; cara, faz, *f.*, lazo de parentesco; (*dep.*) equipo; ijada (de animal); *lee-side,* (*mar.*) costado de sotavento; *starboard side,* banda de estribor; *right* (o *wrong*) *side* (of cloth, stuff or material), cara (o revés) de una tela; *on this side,* a (de o por) este lado; *on that side,* de (o por) aquel lado; *to be on the side of,* estar por, estar del partido de; *by the side of,* al lado de, por el lado de; *on the other side,* del (o al) otro lado; *on the far* (o *other*) *side,* más allá; *on the maternal side,* por parte de madre; *on all sides,* por todas partes; *side arms,* (*mil.*) armas blancas; *to split one's sides,* reventarse de risa. — *a.* lateral, de lado; oblicuo, indirecto; *side show,* función (o exhibición) secundaria; *side light,* luz lateral, secundaria;

side saddle, silla de montar de mujer; *side wheel*, rueda lateral; *side track*, apartadero, desviadero; *side table*, trinchero. — *v.t.*, *v.i. to side with*, tomar parte por, declararse por, unirse con, ser de la opinión de.

sideboard ['saidbɔːɹd], *s.* aparador; copero.

side-car, *s.* sidecar.

sideface, *s.* perfil, cabeza de perfil.

sidelong ['saidlɔŋ, *a.* lateral, de lado. — *adv.* lateralmente, de lado.

sideral [sai'diərəl], **sidereal** [sai'diəriəl], *a.* sidéreo, sideral.

siderography [sidə'rɔgræfi], *s.* siderografía.

siderurgy [sidə'rəːɹdʒi], *s.* siderurgia.

side-track ['saidtræk], *v.t.* (E.U., *f.c.*) desviar, apartar; (*fig.*) desviar.

sidewalk, *s.* acera.

sideward, **sidewards**, *adv.* de lado, de costado.

sideways [saidweiz], **sidewise**, *adv.* de lado, oblicuamente, al través.

side-whiskers, *s.* patillas, *f.pl.*

siding ['saidiŋ], *s.* (*f.c.*) apartadero, desviadero; (*carp.*) entablado de los costados, costaneras; adhesión a un partido.

sidle ['saidəl], *v.i.* ir de lado; *to sidle up to*, acercarse a.

siege [siːdʒ], *s.* sitio, asedio; cerco; *to lay siege*, poner sitio; *to raise a siege*, levantar un sitio.

Sienese [siːə'niːz], *a.*, *s.* sienés.

sienite ['saiənait], *s.* sienita.

sienna [si'enə], *s.* tierra de siena; *burnt sienna*, tierra de siena tostada.

sieve [siv], *s.* tamiz, cedazo, harnero, zaranda, criba, cribo, coladera; persona gárrula; canasto. — *v.t.* tamizar, cerner, cribar.

sievemaker, *s.* cedacero, fabricante de tamices o cedazos.

sift [sift], *v.t.* cerner, tamizar, zarandear, cribar; escudriñar, examinar; separar, dividir, entresacar. — *v.i.* caer (o pasar) al través de un tamiz (o cedazo); *to sift out*, investigar, inquirir.

sifter, *s.* cernedor, cribador; garbillador; escudriñador; criba, cedazo, harnero, tamiz, zaranda.

siftings, *s.pl.* granzas; cerniduras.

sigh [sai], *v.i.* suspirar, dar suspiros; llorar, lamentar; *to sigh for*, desear, anhelar. — *v.t.* (*poét.*) decir suspirando; lamentar; *to sigh away the time*, consumir el tiempo en suspiros. — *s.* suspiro.

sighingly, *adv.* con suspiros, suspirando.

sight [sait], *s.* vista; visión; perspectiva; aspecto, facha; espectáculo, cuadro, escena; parecer, opinión, *f.*; acto de apuntar, puntería; agujero, abertura para mirar; mira (de fusil, etc.); pínula (de los instrumentos topográficos); *to come in* (o *into*) *sight*, asomarse, empezar a aparecer; *to pay at sight*, pagar a la vista; *ten days after sight*, a diez días vista; *at sight*, a primera vista; *in sight*, a la vista; *out of sight*, perdido de vista; *to catch sight of*, vislumbrar. — *v.t.* avistar, alcanzar con la vista; ver (o descubrir) con un instrumento; apuntar (un fusil, etc.); poner miras a una arma.

sighted, *a.* (*mar.*) señalado (un buque); (*en composición*) de vista, que tiene vista (buena, mala, etc.).

sightless, *a.* ciego, falto de vista; invisible; fuera de vista.

sightliness, *s.* hermosura, belleza.

sightly ['saitli], *a.* hermoso; deleitable, agradable a la vista.

sightseeing ['saitsiːiŋ], *a.* acto (o costumbre) de visitar objetos o puntos de interés; *to go sightseeing*, visitar los monumentos.

sightseer ['saitsiːəɹ], *s.* turista, *m.f.*

sigil ['sidʒil], *s.* sello, firma.

sigmoid ['sigmɔid], *a.* sigmoideo.

sign [sain], *s.* signo, señal, *f.*; marca, síntoma, *m.*, indicio, prueba, indicación; seña, santo y seña; firma, rúbrica; huella, vestigio, traza, rastro; signo del zodíaco; muestra, tablilla, letrero; *sign manual*, (*Ingl.*) firma del soberano; cualquier firma o rúbrica de propio puño; *to make the sign of the cross*, santiguarse, hacer la señal de la cruz. — *v.t.* firmar; signar, rubricar; (*igl.*) persignar; señalar, poner marca, firma o señal; significar, representar, hacer señas; *to sign away* (o *off*), firmar la cesión de una cosa.

signal ['signəl], *a.* señalado, insigne, notable, memorable. — *s.* seña, señal, *f.*, aviso; (*f.c.*) señal, *f.*; indicio, signo; señalado; *signal code*, (*mar.*) código (o sistema) de señales; *sailing signals*, señales de hacerse a la vela; *signal light*, fanal. — *v.t.*, *v.i.* hacer señas, señalar, indicar.

signal-box, *s.* garita de señales.

signalize ['signəlaiz], *v.t.* señalar, distinguir; hacer notable, singularizar, particularizar.

signally ['signəli], *adv.* insignemente, grandemente; señaladamente.

signalman, *s.* guardavía, *m.*

signatory ['signətəɹi], *s.*, *a.* firmante, signatario.

signature ['signətʃəɹ], *s.* firma, rúbrica; (*impr.*, *mús.*) signatura; (*ant.*) marca, señal, *f.*

sign-board ['sainbɔːɹd], *s.* muestra, letrero.

signer ['sainəɹ], *s.* firmante, persona que firma.

signet ['signet], *s.* sello; signáculo; timbre.

significance [sig'nifikəns], **significancy** [sig'nifikənsi], *s.* significación, expresión; significado; peso, consecuencia, importancia, momento; fuerza, eficacia, energía.

significant [sig'nifikənt], *a.* significante, significativo; expresivo; sugestivo; importante.

signification [signifi'keiʃən], *s.* significación, significado, sentido.

significative, *a.* significativo; indicativo, sugestivo; expresivo.

signify ['signifai], *v.t.* significar; expresar; declarar, anunciar, manifestar; dar a entender; denotar, representar, simbolizar; importar; ser indicio o signo de. — *v.i.* importar, ser de importancia o consecuencia; *it doesn't signify*, no importa.

signiory ['siːnjɔːɹi], *s.* señorío, dominio.

signpost, *s.* indicador de dirección.

Sikh [siːk], *s.* sik.

silage ['sailidʒ], *s.* forraje conservado en silo.

silence ['sailəns], *s.* silencio; *to put to silence*, reducir al silencio, hacer callar; *silence gives consent*, quien calla otorga. — *interj.* ¡silencio! ¡punto en boca! ¡chis! — *v.t.* imponer silencio a; mandar (o hacer) callar, cerrar la boca a; parar, acorralar; sosegar, aquietar, tranquilizar; silenciar; amortiguar; (*mil.*) apagar el fuego (del enemigo).

silencer, *s.* (*aut.*) silenciador; silencioso (de pistola, etc.).

silent ['sailənt], *a.* silencioso; mudo; tácito; callado, taciturno, sigiloso, quieto, sosegado, calmoso, tranquilo; *to remain silent,* callar, guardar silencio; *to keep silent with an effort,* morderse la lengua; *silent partner,* (*com.*) socio comanditario; *be silent,* calle Vd.

silentiary [sai'lenʃəri], *s.* silenciario.

silentness, *s.* silencio.

silex]'saileks], *s.* sílice, *f.*; pedernal.

silfast ['silfɑ:st], *s.* matadura.

silhouette [silu:'et], *v.t.* hacer aparecer en silueta. — *s.* silueta.

silica ['silikə], *s.* sílice, *f.*

silicate ['silikit], *s.* silicato.

silicic [si'lisik], *a.* silícico.

silicious [si'liʃəs], *a.* silíceo, silícico.

silicle ['silikəl], *s.* silícula, silicua pequeña.

silicon ['silikən], *s.* silicio.

silicone, *s.* silicona. — *a.* silicónico.

siliconize, *v.t.* siliciar.

silicosis [sili'kousis], *s.* silicosis, *f.*

siliqua ['silikwə], *s.* silicua.

siliquous, siliquose ['silikwəs], *a.* silicuoso.

silk [silk], *a.* de seda, sedoso, sedeño; *silk hat,* sombrero de copa. — *s.* seda; tejido de seda; *figured silk,* seda labrada; *raw silk,* seda en rama; *floss silk,* seda floja, atanquía, escarzo, filadiz; *shot silk,* seda tornasolada; *twilled silk,* tela cruzada de seda; *watered silk,* seda ondeada, muaré; *silk cotton,* seda vegetal; *waste silk,* borra de seda; *silk growing,* sericultura; *silk throwing,* torcedura de la seda; *silk-thrower* o *silk-throwster,* devanador (o torcedor) de seda. — *pl.* **silks,** sedería.

silken, *a.* sedoso, sedeño, de seda; blando, suave; lustroso; lujoso; vestido de seda.

silkiness, *s.* blandura, suavidad.

silkman, *s.* sedero.

silk-mercer, *s.* mercader de seda.

silkweed, *s.* asclepias.

silkworm ['silkwə:m], *s.* gusano de seda.

silky ['silki], *a.* de seda, sedeño, sedoso; suave; lustroso.

sill [sil], *s.* umbral de puerta; (*carp.*) solera, viga de carrera; *ground sill,* viga de carrera; *window sill,* antepecho de ventana; *cap sill,* (*min.*) cumbrera, cabezal.

sillabub ['siləbʌb], *s.* bebida de leche, vino (o sidra) y especias.

silliness ['silinis], *s.* simpleza, bobería, necedad, tontería, mentecatada.

sillometer [si'lɔmetəɪ], *s.* instrumento para medir la velocidad de un buque.

silly ['sili], *a.* necio, tonto, bobo, imbécil, mentecato; disparatado; (*ant.*) inocente, simple.

silo ['sailou], *s.* silo, silero.

silt [silt], *s.* aluvión, sedimentación. — *v.t., v.i.* obstruir(se) con aluvión.

Silurian [sai'lju:riən], *s., a.* siluriano.

silvan ['silvən], **sylvan,** *a.* selvático, silvático, silvestre; rústico, rural.

silver ['silvəɪ], *s.* plata; (*com.*) monedas de plata; vajilla de plata o plateada. — *a.* de plata, hecho de plata, argentino; plateado; sonoro como la plata; *silver alloy,* aleación de plata; *silver birch,* abedul; *silver foil,* (o *leaf*) hoja de plata; *silver fir,* (*bot.*) abeto; *silver plate,* vajilla o mercadería de plata o plateada, artículos plateados; *silver beater,* batihoja, *m.,* batidor de plata; *silver thistle,* (*bot.*) acanto, branca ursina; *silver lace,* galón de

plata; *every cloud has a silver lining,* cada semana tiene su día santo; *silver wedding,* bodas de plata. — *v.t.* platear; azogar; blanquear, dar la blancura de plata a.

silverfish ['silvəɪfiʃ], *s.* (*ict.*) lepisma.

silvering ['silvəriŋ], *s.* capa (o baño) de plata; plateado, plateadura; azogamiento.

silver-plated, *a.* plateado.

silversmith, *s.* platero; fabricante de artículos de plata.

silverware, *s.* plata labrada; efectos de plata; vajilla de plata.

silverweed, *s.* agrimonia.

silvery ['silvəri], *a.* plateado; argentino; sonoro o lustroso como la plata.

simian ['simiən], *s.* simio, mono. — *a.* símico.

similar ['similəɪ], *a.* similar, semejante, parecido.

similarity [simi'læriti], *s.* semejanza, parecido.

simile ['simili], *s.* símil; similitud, comparación.

similitude [si'militju:d], *s.* similitud, semejanza; comparación, ejemplo; parecido.

simioid ['simiɔid], **simious** ['simiəs], *a.* símico.

simitar ['simitəɪ], *s.* cimitarra.

simlin ['simlin], *s.* (*E.U.*) calabaza.

simmer ['siməɪ], *v.i.* hervir a fuego lento.

Simon Pure [saimən'pju:əɪ], *a.* verdero, genuino, puro.

simoniac [si'mouniək], **simoniacal** [simo'naiəkəl], *a.* simoníaco.

simony ['simoni], *s.* simonía.

simoom [si'mu:m], **simoon** [si'mu:n], *s.* simún.

simper ['simpəɪ], *v.i.* sonreírse afectadamente. — *s.* sonrisa afectada.

simperingly, *adv.* sonriendo tontamente o afectadamente.

simple ['simpəl], *a.* sencillo; simple; puro; llano; fácil; ingenuo, cándido, inocente; mero; bobo, necio, mentecato. — *s.* (*med.*) simple; elemento; planta o hierba medicinal.

simple-hearted, *a.* sencillo, franco, sincero.

simple-minded, *a.* simple, mentecato.

simple-mindedness, *s.* simpleza, mentecatez.

simpler, *s.* (*med., ant.*) simplista, *m.f.*

simpleton ['simpəltən], *s.* simplón, simplenazo, papanatas, *m.,* gaznápiro, bobalicón.

simplicity [sim'plisiti], **simpleness,** *s.* sencillez, llaneza, ingenuidad, candor; simplicidad; simpleza, sandez, bobería, imbecilidad, necedad.

simplification [simplifi'keiʃən], *s.* simplificación.

simplify ['simplifai], *v.t.* simplificar, hacer menos complicado.

simulacrum [simju:'leikrəm], *s.* (*pl.* **-cra**), simulacro; apariencia; farsa.

simulant ['simju:lənt], *a.* que simula, imita o finge; de forma de.

simulate ['simju:leit], *v.t.* simular, fingir.

simulation, *s.* simulación, fingimiento, hipocresía, doblez de ánimo.

simultaneity [siməltei'ni:iti], **simultaneousness,** *s.* simultaneidad, sincronismo.

simultaneous [siməl'teiniəs], *a.* simultáneo. sincrónico.

sin [sin], *s.* pecado; culpa; transgresión, ofensa, falta; *sin offering,* sacrificio propiciatorio. — *v.i.* pecar.

sinapism ['sinəpizm], *s.* sinapismo.

since [sins], *adv.* desde; desde hace; desde entonces; tiempo ha, antes de ahora, atrás; *some months since*, algunos meses ha; *ever since*, desde entonces; *long since*, hace mucho tiempo; *not long since*, hace poco, de poco acá. — *conj.* ya que, puesto que, en vista de; pues, pues que; como; *since it is so*, siendo (esto) así. — *prep.* desde, después.

sincere [sin'siəɹ], *a.* sincero; verdadero; abierto, franco; *Yours sincerely*, s.s.s. (su seguro servidor).

sincerity [sin'seriti], *s.* sinceridad; franqueza.

sinciput ['sinsipʌt], *s.* sincipucio, coronilla.

sine [sain], *s.* (*mat.*) seno; *coversed sine*, cosenoverso; *versed sine*, senoverso.

sine, *prep.* (*Lat.*) sin; *sine die*, indefinidamente, hasta nueva orden.

sinecure ['sainikju:əɹ], *s.* sinecura; (*igl.*) beneficio simple.

sinew ['sinju:], *s.* tendón; nervio, fuerza. — *v.t.* fortalecer, dar fuerza, proveer de tendones.

sinewed, sinewy ['sinju:i], *a.* fibroso; nervoso, nervioso; robusto, fuerte.

sinful ['sinfəl], *a.* pecaminoso; *sinful man*, pecador; *sinful woman*, pecadora.

sinfulness, *s.* pecado; culpabilidad; maldad, perversidad.

sing [siŋ], *v.t.*, *v.i.* (*pret.* **sang, sung**; *p.p.* **sung**) cantar; murmurar (el agua); gorjear, cantar (los pájaros), cantar (los oídos); celebrar, elogiar; *to sing out*, (*fam.*) vocear, anunciar (*o* avisar) gritando; *to sing a child to sleep*, dormir a un niño cantando; *to sing out of tune*, cantar falso, desafinar, desacordarse.

singe [sindʒ], *v.t.* chamuscar; socarrar; sollamar; (*coc.*) aperdigar (un ave); (*fig.*) dañar, perjudicar.

singeing ['sindʒiŋ], *s.* socarra, chamusquina.

singer ['siŋəɹ], *s.* cantor, cantora, cantante.

Singhalese, *s.*, *a.* cingalés.

singing ['siŋiŋ], *s.* canto; zumbido (de los oídos). — *a.* cantante; *singing master*, maestro de canto; *singing bird*, pájaro cantor; *singing book*, cuaderno de canto, cuaderno de solfa.

single ['siŋgəl], *a.* único; simple; sencillo; solo, singular, solitario; sin compañía, individual, particular; franco, sincero, soltero, soltera; (*mar.*) single; *single life*, celibato; *single loader*, arma de fuego de retrocarga de un solo cartucho; *single acting*, (*mec.*) de simple efecto; *single-phase*, (*elec.*) monofásico; *single plate clutch*, (*aut.*) embrague de un solo disco; *not a single word*, ni una (sola) palabra; *single combat*, combate singular; *single entry*, (*com.*) partida simple; *single file*, fila india. — *v.t.* singularizar; particularizar; retirar, separar, escoger, elegir; *to single out*, escoger, elegir.

single-handed, *a.* solo, sin ayuda.

single-hearted, single-minded, *a.* sincero, sin doblez.

singleness, *s.* unidad; sencillez, sinceridad, franqueza.

single-stick, *s.* (*esgr.*) bastón.

singlet ['siŋglet], *s.* camiseta.

singly, *adv.* invididuamente; a solas; separadamente, de uno en uno, uno a uno.

singsong ['siŋsɔŋ], *s.* tonillo; concierto espontáneo; *to talk in a singsong voice*, hablar con acento cantarín.

singular ['siŋgju:ləɹ], *a.* singular; aislado, aparte, peculiar, simple, sencillo; extraño, extraordinario, raro, distinguido, excelente; único; (*gram.*) singular. — *s.* (*gram.*) número singular.

singularity [siŋgju:'læriti], *s.* particularidad, singularidad, rareza, distinción.

singularize ['siŋgju:ləraiz], *v.t.* singularizar, individualizar, particularizar.

Sinic ['sinik], *a.* chinesco, chino.

sinical ['sinikəl], *a.* (*geom.*) relativo al seno de un arco.

sinister ['sinistəɹ], *a.* siniestro; sospechoso; infeliz, funesto, aciago.

sinistrous ['sinistrəs], *a.* siniestro; depravado, malvado.

sink [siŋk], *v.t.* (*pret.* **sank, sunk**; *p.p.* **sunk**; *p.a.* **sunken**) hundir, sumergir, echar a pique, echar al fondo; clavar en tierra; sumir, ahondar, excavar, abatir un pozo; bajar, disminuir, rebajar; abatir, hacer bajar, hacer caer; deprimir, humillar, abatir; ocultar, suprimir, hacer desaparecer, disipar; grabar, penetrar, cavar; extinguir, exterminar, destruir, derribar; invertir (dinero). — *v.i.* hundirse, sumirse, sumergirse; (*arq.*) sentarse, apretarse, asentarse; grabarse (en la memoria); caer, penetrar, introducirse; bajar, disminuir, menguar; bajarse, descender; disiparse, ir desapareciendo, desaparecer; naufragar, zozobrar, irse a pique o al fondo; dejarse caer, rendirse; abatirse, acoquinarse, amilanarse; debilitarse, sucumbir, perecer; decaer, empeorar, declinar, arruinarse, ir a menos; *to sink under*, atribularse en (*o* con), anonadarse; *to sink down*, caer, penetrar profundamente; *sinking fund*, (*com.*) fondo de amortización; *to sink on one's knees*, caer de rodillas. — *s.* fregadero (de cocina), artesón; sumidero, sentina, vertedero; (*fig.*) sentina.

sinkable, *a.* hundible, sumergible.

sinker, *s.* hundidor; plomada; *die sinker, punch sinker*, tallador, abridor o grabador en hueco.

sinking, *s.* hundimiento; sumergimiento; cavadura; abatimiento (de ánimo); abertura (de un pozo, etc.).

sinless ['sinles], *a.* sin pecado.

sinlessness, *s.* impecabilidad.

sinner ['sinəɹ], *s.* pecador, pecadora.

sinologist [si'nɔlɔdʒist], *s.* sinólogo.

sinology [si'nɔlɔdʒi], *s.* sinología.

sinople ['sinopəl], *s.* (*blas.*) sinople.

sinter ['sintəɹ], *s.* toba, incrustación de manantiales.

sinuate ['sinju:eit], *v.t.* formar oblicuidades o sinuosidades. — *a.* tortuoso, sinuoso, ondulado.

sinuation, *s.* corvadura, tortuosidad.

sinuosity [sinju:'ɔsiti], *s.* sinuosidad, tortuosidad, enroscadura.

sinuous ['sinju:əs], *a.* sinuoso, serpentino, tortuoso.

sinus ['sainəs], *s.* (*med.*, *etc.*) seno; cavidad, concavidad.

sip [sip], *v.t.*, *v.i.* sorber; saborear; chupar, churrupear. — *s.* sorbo; *little sip*, sorbito.

siphon ['saifɔn], *s.* sifón. — *v.t.*, *v.i.* sacar con sifón.

sipper ['sipəɹ], *s.* sorbedor.

sippet ['sipit], *s.* sopita, sopilla, sopa, pan empapado en agua u otra bebida.

sir [səːɹ], *s.* señor; caballero; (título inglés) sir.

sire [´saiəɹ], *s.* padre; progenitor; anciano; caballo semental; Señor (tratamiento del soberano); *grandsire*, abuelo. — *v.t.* engendrar, producir (*hablando de caballos*).

siren [´saiərən], *s.* sirena.

Sirius [´siriəs], *s.* (*astr.*) Sirio, canícula.

sirloin [´səːɹlɔin], *s.* lomo, solomillo.

sirocco [si´rɔkou], *s.* siroco.

sirrah [si´rɑː], *s.* (*desp.*) malandrín, pícaro.

sirup [´sirəp], *s.* [SYRUP].

sirupy [´sirəpi], *a.* [SYRUPY].

sisal [´sisəl], **sisal-grass, sisal-hemp,** *s.* henequén.

siskin [´siskin], *s.* (*orn.*) verderón.

sissy [´sisi], *a.* (*E.U.*) afeminado, adamado.

sister [´sistəɹ], *s.f.* hermana; (*igl.*) Sor; *Sister of Mercy,* Hermana de la Caridad; *foster sister,* hermana de leche; *step sister,* media hermana, hermanastra; *sister-blocks,* (*mar.*) motones herrados.

sisterhood, *s.* hermandad; conjunto de hermanas.

sister-in-law, *s.f.* cuñada, hermana política.

sisterly, *a.* con hermandad; de hermana.

sistrum [´sistrəm], *s.* sistro.

sit [sit], *v.t.* (*pret.* **sat;** *p.p.* **sat**) sentar, asentar. — *v.i.* sentarse, asentarse; estar sentado; posarse; empollar (las aves); fijarse, estar situado, estar colocado; celebrar junta o sesión; reunirse en junta para deliberar; formar parte de un tribunal; sentar (un vestido); descansar, apoyarse; montar, mantenerse a caballo; servir de modelo a; *to sit close,* acercarse, juntarse; *to sit by,* sentarse, animado (o junto) a (o al lado de); *to sit down,* sentarse; estar sentado, parar, detenerse; descansar; morar, residir; comenzar un asedio; *to sit down under insults* (*ill-treatment, etc.*) dejarse atropellar impunemente; *to sit up,* sentarse (un enfermo), incorporarse; velar; *to sit upon,* juzgar, estar reunida (una comisión, etc.) para juzgar; (*fam.*) desairar, dejar aplastado a; *to sit for one's portrait,* hacerse retratar; *to sit out,* quedarse sentado hasta el fin (de un espectáculo); dejar pasar un baile; perseverar; *to sit still,* estar quieto, no levantarse; *to sit well,* venir bien (una cosa con otra).

sitar [si´tɑːɹ], *s.* guitarra oriental.

site [sait], *s.* sitio, local, situación; solar.

sited, *a.* colocado, puesto, situado; ubicado.

sitiology [siti´ɔlodʒi], **sitology** [sit´ɔlodʒi], *s.* dietética.

sitiophobia [sitiou´foubiə], *s.* repugnancia a la comida.

sitter [´sitəɹ], *s.* el que se sienta, el que está sentado; el que se hace retratar; ave que está empollando huevos.

sitting, *s.* el sentarse; sentada, asentada; empolladura; nidada o cría (de pajarillos); legislatura; junta, sesión, reunión, *f.* — *a.* sentado; que empolla; (*bot.*) sesil; *sitting-room,* sala de estar.

situate [´sitjuːeit], *a.* sitio, situado, colocado, puesto.

situation [sitjuː´eifən], *s.* situación, posición, localidad, vecindad; colocación, empleo, plaza; *out of a situation,* sin empleo; *in a situation,* colocado, empleado.

six [siks], *s., a.* seis; *at sixes and sevens,* en estado de desorden; *to be all at sixes and sevens,* andar por los cerros de Úbeda.

sixfold, *adv.* seis veces.

sixpence [´sikspəns], *s.* seis peniques.

sixpenny [´sikspəni], *a.* de seis peniques; mezquino, miserable, ruin.

sixscore [´sikskɔːɹ], *a.* ciento veinte.

sixteen [siks´tiːn], *s., a.* diez y seis, dieciséis.

sixteenth, *a.* décimosexto.

sixth [´siksθ], *a.* sexto; seis (del mes). — *s.* sexto, sexta parte; (*mús.*) sexta.

sixthly, *adv.* en sexto lugar.

sixtieth [´sikstiəθ], *a.* sexagésimo, sesenta. — *s.* una sexagésima parte, sesentavo.

sixty [´siksti], *s., a.* sesenta.

sizable, sizeable [´saizəbəl], *a.* de tamaño considerable; bastante grande.

sizar [´saizəɹ], *s.* estudiante pensionado, estudiante con beca.

size [saiz], *s.* tamaño; medida; talle; volumen; calibre; dimensión; diámetro (de un tubo, alambre, etc.); talla, cuerpo, corpulencia, estatura; número (de zapatos, etc.); *size stick,* (*zap.*) cartabón. — *v.t.* medir, computar el tamaño de; ajustar; fijar, igualar, arreglar; calibrar; fijar (pesos y medidas); distribuir (o clasificar) según tamaño; avalorar, evaluar, tasar, apreciar; *to size up,* tomar las medidas a.

size, *s.* cola; cola de retazo, sisa de doradores. — *v.t.* encolar.

sized [saizd], *a.* encolado; sisado; calibrado; de (tal) tamaño.

siziness [´saizines], *s.* viscosidad.

sizing, *s.* encoladura, encolado, calibradura.

sizy, *a.* viscoso, pegajoso.

sizz [siz], *v.i.* silbar, chirriar, chillar, chisporrotear.

sizzle, *v.t., v.i.* chisporrotear, chirriar. — *s.* chisporroteo, chirrido.

sjambok [´zæmbɔk], *s.* fusta o látigo pesado hecho de cuero de rinoceronte.

skate [skeit], *v.t., v.i.* patinar. — *s.* patín; (*ict.*) raya; *roller skate,* patín de ruedas.

skater, *s.* patinador.

skating [´skeitiŋ], *s.* patinaje; *skating-rink,* pista de patinar.

skedaddle [ske´dædəl], *v.i.* (*fam.*) tomar las de Villadiego, largarse, poner pies en polvorosa.

skeet [skiːt], *s.* (*mar.*) bañadera.

skein [skein], *s.* cadejo, madeja, capillejo, majo.

skeletal [´skeletəl], *a.* de (del) esqueleto; esquelético.

skeleton [´skeletən], *s.* esqueleto; armazón, *f.*; armadura; esquema, *m.*, esbozo, plan; *skeleton-key,* llave maestra; *to be reduced to a skeleton,* (*fig.*) estar en los huesos. — *a.* en esqueleto, en armazón; perteneciente al esqueleto (o armazón); extenuado.

skeptic, skeptical, skeptically, skepticism [SCEPTIC].

sketch [sketʃ], *s.* esbozo, diseño, bosquejo, boceto, esquicio, rasguño, croquis, borrón, apunte; descripción; (*teat.*) entremés. — *v.t.* esquiciar, delinear, trazar, rasguñar; bosquejar, dibujar, apuntar; describir.

sketchily, *adv.* de un modo abocetado, a manera de bosquejo; superficialmente.

sketchiness, *s.* modo abocetado; estado incompleto; hechura ligera; superficialidad.

sketchy [´sketʃi], *a.* bosquejado, abocetado, esquiciado; incompleto; ligero; superficial.

skew [skjuː], *a.* oblicuo, sesgado, atravesado, torcido, al sesgo, de través. — *s.* movimiento,

curso o posición oblicuos; mirada de soslayo.
— *v.t.* sesgar, poner (o echar) de través,
poner al sesgo, dar forma oblicua. — *v.i.*
andar (o moverse) oblicuamente (o de
través); mirar de soslayo.

skewer [ˈskjuːəɹ], *s.* (*coc.*) brocheta, broqueta,
espetón; aguja de lardear. — *v.t.* espetar,
afianzar con espetones.

ski [skiː], *s.* esquí. — *v.i.* esquiar.

skiagraph [ˈskaiəgræf], *s.* radiografía.

skiascope [ˈskaiəskoup], *s.* fluoroscopo.

skid [skid], *v.t.* (*mar.*) proveer de varaderas;
arrastrar sobre varaderas. — *v.i.* (*aut.*)
patinar. — *s.* (*mar.*) varadera, baradero, care-
note; rastra, calzo; rodillo; (*aut.*) patinazo.

skidding, *s.* patinaje.

skiff [skif], *s.* esquife, bote pequeño, botecillo,
caique.

ski-ing [ˈskiːiŋ], *s.* el esquiar.

skilful [ˈskilfəl], *a.* diestro, hábil, mañoso;
ducho.

skilfulness, *s.* habilidad, pericia, destreza.

skill [skil], *s.* habilidad, destreza, pericia,
maña.

skilled, *a.* diestro, hábil; experto.

skilless [ˈskilles], *a.* inhábil.

skillet [ˈskilit], *s.* cacerola, marmita o cazuela
pequeña.

skim [skim], *v.t.* quitar la nata a, desnatar;
espumar, quitar la espuma; tocar ligeramente, rasar; examinar superficialmente. —
v.i. deslizarse, pasar rasando; *skim-milk*,
leche desnatada; (*fig.*) cosa insulsa; *to skim
the ocean*, (*mar.*) peinar las olas; *to skim over*,
resbalar, rozar; leer superficialmente, recorrer, hojear (un libro); tocar ligeramente
(una cuestión); *to skim along*, rozar, resbalar.
— *n.* acción de desnatar; espuma, nata.

skimmer, *s.* espumadera.

skimming, *s.* despumación.

skimmington [ˈskimiŋtən], *s.* procesión de
mofa ridiculizando a un marido cornudo,
esposa infiel, etc.

skimp [skimp], *v.t.* escatimar; frangollar. —
v.t., v.i. ser tacaño.

skin [skin], *s.* piel, *f.*, cutis, dermis, epidermis;
pellejo, tegumento; (*ten.*) cuero; pellejo,
corteza (de algunas frutas); odre, pellejo o
cuero para líquidos; (*mar.*) forros de un
buque; (*elec.*) parte de un conductor usado
para los circuitos fantasma; *skin effect*, (*elec.*)
efecto kelvin. — *pl.* **skins**, pieles, *f.pl.*,
corambre; *scarf-skin*, epidermis, cutícula;
skin-deep, superficial; *sheepskin*, badana,
zalea; *calfskin*, piel de becerro; *skin-tight*,
ajustado como un guante; *skin-game*, (*fam.*)
fullería, astucia, maña; *to be soaked to the
skin*, estar calado hasta los huesos; *to save
one's skin*, salvar el pellejo. — *v.t.* quitar el
pellejo, quitar la piel, desollar, despellejar,
escorchar; cubrir con piel, cubrir superficialmente; deshollejar, mondar, pelar;
(*fam.*) desollar. — *v.i., v.t.* cubrirse de
pellejo, de tegumento; cicatrizarse; *to skin
over*, cicatrizarse; hacerse costras.

skinflint [ˈskinflint], *s.* avaro, tacaño.

skinless, *a.* desprovisto de pellejo; de piel muy
delgada.

skinner, *s.* desollador; pellejero; peletero;
petardista, *m.f.*, estafador.

skinniness [ˈskininis], *s.* flaqueza, falta de
carnes; extenuación.

skinny, *a.* flaco, descarnado.

skip [skip], *v.t.* pasar por alto, omitir; saltar
por encima de. — *v.i.* saltar, brincar; saltar
a la comba; pasar por alto; escaparse. — *s.*
cabriola, salto, brinco; omisión; descuido;
(*min.*) cubo para elevar mineral.

skipper [ˈskipəɹ], *s.* saltador, brincador,
bailarín, bailarina; (*ict.*) escombresocio;
gusanillo de queso; (*ent.*) especie de mariposa; (*mar.*) patrón, mareante; paje de
escoba; *skipper's daughter*, cabrilla de mar.

skipping, *s.* acción de saltar; comba (juego);
skipping-rope, comba.

skippingly, *adv.* a saltos, a brincos.

skirmish [ˈskəːɹmiʃ], *s.* escaramuza. — *v.i.*
escaramuzar.

skirmisher, *s.* escaramuzador.

skirret [ˈskiret], *s.* chirivía.

skirt [skəːɹt], *s.* falda; saya; sayuela, enagua;
(*sast.*) faldón; faldones de la silla de montar;
orilla, borde, margen; (*fam.*) muchacha,
mujer; *divided skirt*, saya en forma de
pantalones muy anchos; *skirts of a city*,
contornos, alrededores de una ciudad;
skirts of a country, confines de un país. —
v.t., v.i. ladear; (*cost.*) orillar, poner cenefa.

skirting, skirting-board, *s.* zócalo.

skit [skit], *s.* sátira; burla; parodia, caricatura.

skite [skait], *v.i.* pasar, volar, precipitarse.
— *s.* golpe severo especialmente en sentido
terciado.

skitter [ˈskitəɹ], *v.i.* planear, deslizarse, pasar
rasando.

skittish [ˈskitiʃ], *a.* reacio, retozón, repropio,
terco (caballo, etc.); caprichoso, liviano;
juguetón.

skittishness, *s.* capricho; liviandad.

skittle [ˈskitəl], *s.* bolo. — *v.i.* jugar a los bolos.

skittles, *s.pl.* juego de bolos.

skive [skaiv], *v.t.* (*ten.*) raspar, adelgazar.

skiver [ˈskaivəɹ], *s.* cuero hendido con cuchillo; cuero para pastas; cuchillo (o
máquina) de adelgazar.

skulk [skʌlk], *v.i.* remolonear; andar a
sombra de tejado; acechar, ocultarse;
rondar.

skulker, *s.* socaire; acechador; remolón.

skull [skʌl], *s.* cráneo; calavera.

skull-cap, *s.* casquete, gorra; sincipucio; (*bot.*)
escutelaria.

skunk [skʌŋk], *s.* mofeta; (*Arg., Guat.,
Hond.*) zorrillo, mapurite; (*fam.*) sinvergüenza, *m.f.*; *skunk-cabbage*, (*bot.*) hierba
fétida de la familia del yaro.

sky [skai], *s.* cielo; firmamento; atmósfera;
sky-high, tan alto como el cielo; (*fig.*) por las
nubes; *sky-pilot*, (*fam.*) clérigo.

sky-blue, sky-coloured, *a.* azul celeste,
cerúleo.

sky-born, *a.* (*poét.*) nacido en el cielo.

skyey [ˈskaii], *a.* etéreo.

skyish, *a.* azulado.

skylark [ˈskailɑːɹk], *s.* (*orn.*) alondra, calandria.
— *v.i.* (*fam.*) chacotear; jaranear, estar de
chacota.

skylarking, *s.* chacota, jarana.

skylight [ˈskailait], *s.* claraboya, tragaluz, *m.*,
lumbrera.

sky-rocket, *s.* cohete, volador.

skysail [ˈskaisəl], *s.* (*mar.*) periquito, sosobre,
montera.

sky-scraper ['skaiskreipəɹ], s. (mar.) periquito, montera, sosobre; rascacielos, m.sing.

skyward ['skaiwəd], **skywards** ['skaiwədz], adv. hacia el cielo.

slab [slæb], s. plancha; losa; tabla, loncha, laja, lastra; costero.

slabber, v.i. [SLOBBER].

slack [slæk], a. flojo, laxo, poco apretado; poco firme, débil; negligente, perezoso, descuidado; tardo, sosegado, lento; espacioso; (com.) encalmado; slack ropes, (mar.) cabos sueltos (o en banda); slack water, repunte de la marea. — s. seno de un cabo; cabo de cuerda colgante; flojedad; cisco, carbón menudo; pl. pantalones.

slack, slacken, v.t., v.i. poner flojo, aflojar, desapretar; laxar, relajar, soltar, largar, tiramollar; poner blando, ablandar; diferir, descuidar, tardar, remitir; retardar; apagar (la cal); flojear, amortiguar, amainar; despegar(se); ser perezoso; dejar de trabajar; debilitarse, flaquear, entibiarse, decaer, ceder, cejar, desfallecer; to slack up, retardar, aflojar, detener, amainar, detener la rapidez de.

slacker, s. perezoso, gandul.

slackness, s. debilidad; flojedad; descuido; pereza; desanimación.

slag [slæg], s. escoria.

slain, p.p. [SLAY].

slake [sleik], v.t. apagar (la cal); (fig.) apagar (la sed); satisfacer; moderar.

slam [slæm], v.t. arrojar o tirar con violencia; cerrar de golpe; (en los juegos de naipes) dar capote. — v.i. cerrarse de golpe, arrojarse con estrépito. — s. portazo; capote (en el juego de naipes).

slander ['slɑːndəɹ], v.t. calumniar; denigrar, infamar. — s. calumnia; infamación, denigración.

slanderer, s. calumniador; murmurador, maldiciente.

slandering, s. murmuración, maledicencia, denigración. — a. calumnioso; maldiciente.

slanderous ['slɑːndərəs], a. calumnioso; infamatorio.

slang [slæŋ], s. argot; jerga; germanía. — v.t. poner como un trapo, poner verde.

slangy ['slæŋi], a. de argot; que habla en argot.

slant [slɑːnt], v.t., v.i. inclinar, oblicuar, sesgar; sesgarse, inclinarse. — a. oblicuo, sesgado, inclinado. — s. declive, inclinación, oblicuidad.

slanting, a. sesgado, oblicuo; inclinado, en declive. — s. oblicuidad, sesgo; plano inclinado, inclinación, declive.

slantingly, slantwise, adv. sesgadamente, de través, al través.

slap [slæp], v.t. pegar, abofetear, golpear, dar una bofetada, manotada, sopapo a. — s. manotada, revés, palmada, bofetada, bofetón, sopapo, golpe de plano. — adv. de golpe y porrazo, de sopetón.

slapdash ['slæpdæʃ], a. (fam.) descuidado; chapucero.

slash [slæʃ], v.t. acuchillar, dar cuchilladas. — v.i. tirar tajos y reveses. — s. cuchillada, jabeque, chirlo; azote, latigazo; (sast.) corte, cuchillo, cortadura.

slat [slæt], v.t., v.i. arrojar, tirar, lanzar, sacudir(se); (mar.) azotar (las velas). — s. tablilla, loncha; blind-slat, tablilla de persiana.

slatch [slætʃ], s. (mar.) socaire; seno de un cabo; intervalo de buen tiempo.

slate [sleit], s. pizarra, esquisto; pizarra (para escribir); (E.U., pol.) lista de candidatos, programa de partido; slate-coloured, de color de pizarra, apizarrado, pizarreño; slate quarry, pizarral, cantera de pizarra; slate-pencil, pizarrete, pizarrín; to wipe clean off the slate, borrar completamente. — v.t. cubrir con pizarra, empizarrar; (fam.) criticar severamente, censurar; (fam.) hacer polvo a.

slater ['sleitəɹ], s. pizarrero.

slattern ['slætəɹn], s. mujer desaliñada, pazpuerca.

slatternliness, s. desatavío, desaliño.

slatternly, a. puerco, desaliñado. — adv. desaliñadamente.

slaty ['sleiti], a. pizarreño.

slaughter ['slɔːtəɹ], s. matanza; carnicería. — v.t. matar (animales); matar, hacer una carnicería de; hacer pedazos.

slaughterer, slaughterman, s. matarife, jifero; asesino.

slaughterhouse, s. matadero.

Slav [slɑːv, slæv], s., a. eslavo.

slave [sleiv], s. esclavo, esclava; siervo. — v.i. trabajar como esclavo.

slave-born, a. nacido en la esclavitud.

slave-driver, s. capataz de esclavos.

slave-holder, s. proprietario de esclavos.

slaver ['sleivəɹ], s. negrero.

slaver ['slævəɹ], s. baba; (fig.) adulación rastrera. — v.i. babosear.

slaverer ['slævərəɹ], s. baboso, persona que babosea.

slavery ['sleivəri], s. esclavitud; servidumbre.

slave-trade, slave-traffic, s. trata de esclavos; white slave traffic, trata de blancas.

Slavic ['slævik], s., a. eslavo; esclavón.

slavish ['sleiviʃ], a. servil; esclavizado; humilde, bajo.

slavishness, s. servilismo; servidumbre; esclavitud; vileza, bajeza.

Slavism ['slɑːvizm], s. eslavismo.

Slavonian ['sləˈvouniən], s., a. esclavón, esclavonio, eslavo.

Slavonic [sləˈvɔnik], s., a. eslavo; esclavón.

slaw [slɔː], s. ensalada de col.

slay [slei], v.t. (pret. slew; p.p. slain) matar, quitar la vida.

slay, sley, s. (tej.) peine, carda.

slayer, s. matador, asesino; man-slayer, homicida, m.

sleave [sliːv], s. (ant.) seda en rama, hilo destorcido. — v.t. desenredar, destorcer.

sleaziness, s. textura débil y ligera.

sleazy, sleezy ['sliːzi], a. flojo, delgado, ligero.

sled [sled], s. narria, rastra; trineo. — v.t., v.i. usar una narria, ir o llevar en una narria, rastra o trineo.

sledge [sledʒ], s. rastra, narria, trineo. — v.t., v.i. transportar o viajar) en una narria, rastra o trineo.

sledge-hammer, s. mandarria, acotillo.

sleek [sliːk], a. liso, lustroso; pulcro, elegante; obsequioso, meloso, zalamero. — v.t. alisar; pulir; suavizar.

sleekness, s. lisura, lustre.

sleeky ['sliːki], a. liso; taimado, zalamero, socarrón.

sleep [sli:p], *v.t.*, *v.i.* (*pret.*, *p.p.* **slept**) dormir; descansar, reposar; (*fig.*) yacer muerto; *to sleep soundly*, dormir a pierna suelta; dormir profundamente; *to sleep away*, (*v.t.*) malgastar el tiempo durmiendo; *to sleep away* (*v.i.*) o *to sleep on*, seguir durmiendo; *to sleep on it*, consultar con la almohada; *to sleep like a top*, dormir como un lirón; *to sleep off one's liquor*, desollar la zorra, dormir la mona; *to sleep in the open air*, dormir al sereno. — *s.* sueño; inacción; (*fig.*) muerte, *f.*; *to put to sleep*, adormecer; *to go to sleep*, dormirse; *my leg has gone to sleep*, se me ha dormido la pierna.

sleeper, *s.* durmiente; (*f.c.*) coche-cama, *m.*; (*f.c.*) traviesa, durmiente; (*constr.*) travesaño, carrera; (*mar.*) carlinga, curva de yugo.

sleepiness ['sli:pinis], *s.* somnolencia, sueño, adormecimiento; letargo.

sleeping, *s.* sueño. — *a.* durmiente; *sleeping-partner*, (*com.*) (socio) comanditario; *sleeping-car*, *sleeping-coach*, (*f.c.*) coche-cama, *m.*; *sleeping-draught*, *sleeping-potion*, bebida calmante, narcótico; *sleeping sickness*, enfermedad del sueño, tripanosomíasis, *f.*

sleepless, *a.* desvelado, insomne.

sleeplessness, *s.* insomnio.

sleep-walker ['sli:pwɔ:kər], *s.* somnámbulo.

sleep-walking, *s.* somnambulismo.

sleepy ['sli:pi], *a.* soñoliento, adormecido, amodorrado; soporoso, soporífero; letárgico; *sleepy sickness*, encefalitis letárgica; *sleepy-head*, lirón.

sleet [sli:t], *s.* aguanieve, *f.*, cellisca. — *v.i.* caer aguanieve, cellisquear.

sleety, *a.* de aguanieve (tiempo); como aguanieve.

sleeve [sli:v], *s.* (*sast.*) manga; (*mec.*) dedal largo, manguito de enchufe, junta de manguito; *to wear one's heart on one's sleeve*, llevar el corazón en la mano; *to laugh in one's sleeve*, reírse con disimulo; *to hang on someone's sleeve*, depender de (o estar sujeto a) la voluntad de otro; *to say in one's sleeve*, decir para su capote (o para su sayo); *sleeve-band*, (*cost.*) tira del puño; (*sast.*) vuelta de manga; *sleeve-buttons*, gemelos, mancuernas, botones de manga; *sleeve-links*, gemelos, yugos; *sleeve-coupling*, (*mec.*) junta de manguito; *sleeve-nut*, (*mec.*) manguito de tuerca; *hanging sleeves*, mangas perdidas.

sleeved, *a.* que tiene mangas.

sleeveless, *a.* sin mangas, que no tiene mangas; (*ant.*) fútil.

sleigh [slei], *s.* trineo; *sleigh-bell*, cascabel; *sleigh ride*, paseo en trineo. — *v.i.* ir en trineo.

sleighing ['sleiiŋ], *s.* paseo en trineo.

sleight [slait], *s.* (*ant.*) habilidad; maña; ardid, estratagema; *sleight of hand*, juego de manos, prestidigitación.

slender ['slendər], *a.* delgado, tenue, sutil, fino; adelgazado; flaco, sin fuerza; delicado; sin fundamento, escaso; pequeño, corto, limitado; *slender waist*, cintura o talle delgado; *slender wit*, entendimiento limitado; *slender estate*, hacienda corta, pocos haberes; *slender income*, renta corta; *slender pittance*, escasa pitanza; *slender hope*, esperanza remota.

slenderness, *s.* delgadez, delicadeza, sutileza; tenuidad; pequeñez; escasez.

slept, *p.p. pret.* [SLEEP].

sleuth ['slu:θ], *s.* pista, rastro; (*fig.*) detective.

sleuth-hound ['slu:θhaund], *s.* sabueso ventor.

slew [slu:], *pret.* [SLAY].

slice [slais], *v.t.*, *v.i.* rebanar, hacer rebanadas, cortar en lonjas, tiras o tajadas; cortar, tajar, partir, dividir. — *s.* rebanada, lonja, tajada; pala (para pescado, etc.); espátula.

slicer, *s.* rebanador; (*joy.*) aparato de hender, sierra circular.

slick [slik], *a.* liso, lustroso; terso; resbaladizo; meloso, rendido, adulador; (*fam.*) diestro; mañoso, hecho diestramente.

slide [slaid], *v.i.* (*pret.* **slid**; *p.p.* **slid**, (*ant.*) **slidden**) resbalar, deslizarse; escabullirse, escurrirse; correr, pasar aprisa; pecar, errar, cometer un desliz; *to slide over*, pasar por alto; *to let things slide*, dejar rodar la bola. — *v.t.* hacer colar, introducir con cuidado o artificio; *to slide into*, introducir con artificio y maña. — *s.* tapa corrediza; (*foto.*) diapositiva; (*foto.*) portaplacas, *m.sing.*; resbalón, resbaladura; portaobjetos (para el microscopio); declive; encaje (de un bastidor); muesca; resbaladero; (*geol.*) falla, dislocación de una veta; desprendimiento (de rocas); (*mús.*) ligado, portamento; (*mec.*) guía; pasador (para el pelo); *slide-rule*, regla de cálculo.

slide-bolt, *s.* pestillo corredizo, cerrojo de seguridad.

slide-box, *s.* caja de válvulas de distribución; portaobjetos.

slider ['slaidər], *s.* resbalador; cursor.

slide-rail, *s.* (*f.c.*) aguja, contracarril.

slide-rest, *s.* (*mec.*) soporte de corredera.

slide-rule, *s.* medida (o escala) de corredera.

sliding, *s.* deslizamiento. — *a.* corredizo; resbaladizo, escurridizo; *sliding place*, deslizadero, resbaladero; *sliding-door*, puerta corrediza; *sliding-scale*, escala graduada; *sliding-seat*, banca corrediza (de bote).

slight [slait], *a.* ligero, leve, de poca importancia; escaso, breve, pequeño, corto, limitado; flojo. — *s.* desaire, menosprecio, desatención, desprecio; *to make slight of*, hacer poco caso de, despreciar, menospreciar. — *v.t.* menospreciar, despreciar, desairar; no hacer caso de, desatender.

slighting, *s.* menosprecio. — *a.* despreciativo.

slightness ['slaitnes], *s.* pequeñez; ligereza; insignificancia; poca importancia.

slim [slim], *a.* delgado; tenue, sutil; insuficiente, escaso, insubstancial; astuto, agudo. — *v.i.* adelgazar.

slime [slaim], *s.* mucilago, lama, limo, légamo, fango, cieno; babaza; chapapote, asfalto. — *v.t.*, *v.i.* enfangar, enlodar, ensuciar con limo, légamo, babaza, etc.; deslamar.

sliminess ['slaiminis], *s.* viscosidad, limosidad, mucosidad; servilismo.

slimming, *s.* el adelgazar; adelgazamiento. — *a.* que adelgaza, adelgazador; (vestido) que hace delgado.

slimy ['slaimi], *a.* viscoso, limoso, mucilaginoso, pegajoso, legamoso, mucoso; (*fig.*) servil; vil, repulsivo.

sling [sliŋ], *s.* honda; (*cir.*) cabestrillo, vendaje, barbiquejo; (*mil.*) charpa, portafusil; (*mar.*) eslinga, balso; (*E.U.*) bebida de ginebra con azúcar y nuez moscada; *slings of the buoy*, (*mar.*) guarnición de la boya; *slings of the* *yard*, (*mar.*) cruz de la verga, estribos de las vergas. — *v.t.* tirar con honda; tirar, arrojar, lanzar; eslingar, embragar, embalsar, izar; poner en cabestrillo, suspender, colgar. — *v.i.* oscilar repentinamente; girar, ir girando, dar vueltas.

slinger ['slɪŋəɹ], *s.* hondero, pedrero.

slink [slɪŋk], *v.i.* (*pret., p.p.* **slunk**) escabullirse, escurrirse, escaparse, huirse furtivamente; (*vet.*) abortar, malparir.

slip [slip], *v.t.* (*pret., p.p.* **slipped**) dejar; deslizar; meter o introducir secretamente; tirar, arrojar; soltarse, zafarse, escaparse, desprenderse; (*agr.*) cortar esquejes; soltar; (*vet.*) malparir, abortar; dislocar (un hueso, etc.); (*mar.*) largar o soltar (un cable o cabo). — *v.i.* deslizarse, resbalar, irse los pies; salirse de su sitio, escurrirse, errar, equivocarse; huirse, escapar, largarse; caer en una falta, cometer un desliz, incurrir en un error; pasar sin ser visto; olvidarse; *to slip the cable*, (*mar.*) alargar el cable por el chicote, lascar el cable; *to slip into*, introducirse, insinuarse, entremeterse en; *to slip down*, bajar sin ser observado, dejarse caer, escaparse (una palabra); *to slip away*, marcharse secretamente, desaparecerse, escabullirse, huirse; *to slip off*, quitarse de encima, soltar; *to slip out*, salir sin ser observado; dislocarse un hueso; *to slip on one's clothes*, vestirse de prisa; *to let a chance slip*, perder la ocasión. — *s.* resbalón, resbaladura, desliz, deslizamiento, tropiezo, traspié; falta, equivocación, error, engaño, lapso; (*geol.*) falla, dislocación; (*E.U.*) embarcadero; (*aer.*) varadero de hidroaviones; (*agr.*) esqueje, vástago, estaca; tira, lista (de papel o tela); escapada, huida; lengua de tierra; callejón; (*impr.*) galerada; combinación (de mujer); funda de almohada; calzones de baño; slip; traílla de un perro; requesón de leche; légamo, limo; portaobjetos (del microscopio); *slip of the tongue*, lapsus linguæ; *there's many a slip 'twixt cup and lip*, (*prov.*) de la mano a la boca desaparece la sopa; *to give the slip*, escaparse de. — *pl.* **slips**, (*mar.*) anguilas.

slip-board ['slipbɔːɹd], *s.* (*mar.*) corredera.

slip-cover, *s.* funda de mueble.

slip-knot ['slipnɔt], *s.* nudo corredizo.

slipper ['slipəɹ], *s.* zapatilla, chancleta, chinela, pantufla; galga de una rueda.

slippered, *a.* con zapatillas.

slipperiness ['slipəɹinis], *s.* carácter resbaladizo; informalidad; astucia.

slippery ['slipəɹi], *a.* resbaladizo, resbaloso, escurridizo, movedizo, poco firme; sin escrúpulos, sospechoso; *slippery-elm*, variedad de olmo.

slipshod ['slipʃɔd], *a.* en chancletas; (*fig.*) descuidado, abandonado.

slipslop ['slipslɔp], *s.* aguachirle; despropósito, error craso; trabajo casual, dislate.

slipstream ['slipstriːm], *s.* (*aer.*) torbellino de la hélice.

slipway, *s.* surtida, anguilas, *f.pl.*

slit [slit], *v.t.* (*pret., p.p.* **slit**) rajar, hender, tajar; cortar; *to slit the throat*, degollar. — *s.* raja, resquicio, hendedura, cortadura, ranura.

slitting, *s.* acción de cortar largas tiras, de hacer largas incisiones; *slitting-mill*, taller de hacer clavos, sierra múltiple; (*joy.*) sierra de disco; (*mec.*) tajadera mecánica.

sliver [slivəɹ], *v.t., v.i.* cortar en tiras; romper(se) a lo largo, desgajarse, desgajar. — *s.* brizna, astilla; lonja de pescado; borde sin pulir de un tablón; torzal.

slobber ['slɔbəɹ], *s.* baba. — *v.t., v.i.* babosear.

sloe [slou], *s.* endrino; endrina.

slog [slɔg], *v.t., v.i.* dar, pegar; trabajar como un negro.

slogan ['slougən], *s.* grito de combate, de partido; mote.

sloop [sluːp], *s.* (*mar.*) balandra, chalupa; *sloop of war*, (*mar.*) corbeta.

slop [slɔp], *v.t., v.i.* verter, derramar; ensuciar, mojar, enlodar; derramarse. — *s.* charco, lugar mojado, mojadura. — *pl.* **slops**, agua sucia, lavazas, zupia, purrela, aguachirle; (*despec.*) atole, gachas; te o café flojo; (*mar. y fam.*) ropa barata y mal hecha; *slop-work*, chapucería; (*argot*) policía; *slop-shop*, tienda de ropa barata; *slop-basin*, *slop-bucket*, barreño; *slop-bowl*, *slop-pail*, cubo o tina para aguas sucias.

slope [sloup], *s.* (*geol., min.*) inclinación, sesgo, escotadura; (*f.c.*) talud; declive, descenso, loma, falda, bajada, repecho, recuesto, desnivel, escarpadura; ladera, vertiente; (*fort.*) rampa, escarpa; *at the slope*, (*mil.*) al hombro. — *a.* sesgo, inclinado, en declive. — *adv.* oblicuamente, al sesgo. — *v.t.* sesgar, partir o cortar en sesgo; formar en declive; (*cost.*) escotar; *slope arms!* ¡armas al hombro! — *v.i.* inclinarse, declinar, estar en declive; ir oblicuamente, moverse en plano inclinado.

sloping, *a.* sesgo, inclinado, en declive.

sloppiness ['slɔpinis], *s.* estado lodoso, desaliñado, etc.; carácter empalagoso.

sloppy ['slɔpi], *a.* aguoso; cenagoso, lodoso; chapucero; desaliñado; empalagoso.

slosh [slɔʃ], *v.t.* salpicar, rociar; chapotear, enlodar, humedecer, hacer saltar (el agua). — *v.i.* chapotear, chapalear, golpear el agua. — *s.* aguanieve, *f.*; fango, cieno, lodo blando; aguachirle.

slot [slɔt], *s.* (*mec.*) muesca, ranura, canal o hendedura, estrecha; rastro, pista, huella; *slot-machine*, expendedor. — *v.t.* ajustar en una ranura, cortar una ranura; acanalar.

sloth [slouθ], *s.* pereza, dejadez, indolencia, negligencia, acidia; (*zool.*) perezoso.

slothful ['slouθfəl], *a.* perezoso, indolente, holgazán.

slothfulness, *s.* pereza, indolencia.

slouch [slautʃ], *s.* inclinación del cuerpo; persona desmañada; chapucero. — *v.t., v.i.* ir cabizbajo; poner gacho; *slouch-hat*, sombrero gacho.

slough [slau], *s.* lodazal, fangal, cenagal, pantano, sitio pantanoso; (*fig.*) abismo; (*E.U.*) charca; camisa (de serpiente); (*med.*) escara, tejido muerto.

slough [slʌf], *v.t., v.i.* echar fuera una costra; mudar la piel (la serpiente, etc.).

sloughy, *a.* fangoso, pantanoso, lodoso; (*med.*) que tiene escara.

Slovak ['slouvæk], *s., a.* eslovaco.

sloven ['slʌvən], *s.* persona desaseada, desaliñada; chapucero.

Slovene ['slouviːn], *s., a.* esloveno.

slovenliness ['slʌvənlinis], *s.* desaliño, desaseo; descuido, dejadez, negligencia; chapucería.

slovenly ['slʌvənli], a. desaliñado, desaseado; sucio; descuidado, dejado.

slow [slou], a. lento; tardo; tardío; paulatino; flemático, calmoso, cachazudo; torpe, lerdo, pesado, estúpido; *slow-witted*, torpe, estúpido; *on a slow fire*, a lumbre mansa; *the clock is five minutes slow*, el reloj lleva cinco minutos de atraso. — *v.t.*, *v.i.* to slow up, to slow down, retardar, ir más despacio, aflojar el paso.

slowcoach ['sloukoutʃ], s. perezoso; parado.

slowly ['slouli], adv. despacio.

slowness, s. lentitud; tardanza; dilación; torpeza; cachaza.

slow-paced, a. pesado en el andar.

slow-worm ['slouwə:ɹm], s. lución, m.

slub [slʌb], v.t. ovillar, torcer la lana antes de encanillar. — s. mechón, lana muy poco retorcida.

slubber ['slʌbəɹ], s. canillero; ovillador de lana; mechón. — v.t. ensuciar, manchar; frangollar.

sludge [slʌdʒ], s. lodo, cieno, fango; (mar.) pequeños trozos de hielo flotando en el mar.

slue [slu:], v.t., v.i. revirar, girar, mover como sobre un eje, volver. — s. giro, vuelta.

slug [slʌg], s. babaza, babosa; (arti.) posta; (impr.) lingote.

sluggard ['slʌgəɹd], s. haragán, holgazán, zángano.

sluggish ['slʌgiʃ], a. perezoso, indolente; pesado; flojo (Bolsa, etc.).

sluggishness, s. lentitud, pesadez; haraganería, pereza, poltronería.

slug-horn, s. trompeta.

sluice [slu:s], s. esclusa; canal, acequia, acueducto; (fig.) abertura. — v.t. mojar, regar, inundar; (min.) lavar; soltar la presa (de un canal, etc.).

sluice-gate, s. compuerta, paradera, ladrón, templadera.

sluice-way, s. saetín, conducto; bocacaz de presa.

slum [slʌm], s. barrio pobre, barrio bajo. — v.i. visitar los barrios bajos por filantropía.

slumber ['slʌmbəɹ], v.i. dormitar, estar medio dormido; (poét.) dormir; (fig.) descuidarse. — s. sueño ligero y tranquilo.

slumberous, a. soñoliento, soporífero; dormido; tranquilo.

slummock ['slʌmək], v.i. tragar con avidez; moverse o hablar groseramente.

slump [slʌmp], v.i. caerse; dejarse caer; hundirse; bajar. — s. hundimiento; (com.) baja repentina; crisis económica.

slung [slʌŋ], pret., p.p. [SLING].

slung-shot, s. rompecabezas, m.

slunk, pret., p.p. [SLINK].

slur [slə:ɹ], v.t. menospreciar, desdorar, rebajar; farfullar; juntar (o comerse) palabras, sílabas o letras; pasar ligeramente, pasar por encima, ocultar, suprimir; (mús.) ligar las notas; ensuciar, manchar; (impr.) repintar. — s. estigma, m.; reparo; borrón o mancha ligera en la reputación; (impr.) trozo manchado, repintado; (mús.) ligado.

slush [slʌʃ], v.t. ensebar, engrasar, embarrar; (con up) (alb.) llenar de argamasa, rellenar; lavar echando agua. — s. aguanieve, f.; fango, cieno, lodo blando; grasa lubricante; pintura (para evitar el enmohecimiento); ñoñería.

slushy, a. fangoso, lodoso; cubierto de aguanieve; ñoño, empalagoso.

slut [slʌt], s. mujer sucia; perra.

sluttish, a. asqueroso, puerco, sucio, despreciable, desaliñado, desaseado.

sly [slai], a. astuto, taimado, socarrón; disimulado, falso; *on the sly*, a hurtadillas; *slyblade*, *slyboots*, camastrón, socarrón, mosquita muerta, marrajo, gran perillán.

slyly ['slaili], adv. astutamente; a hurtadillas, callandito; con segunda intención.

slyness, s. socarronería, astucia, bellaquería; disimulo.

smack [smæk], v.t., v.i. saborear(se), rechuparse; hacer sonar un beso, besarse mutuamente; dar manotadas. — v.i. saber a, tener dejo o sabor de, tener un sabor; oler a; tener gusto. — s. sabor, dejo, gusto, gustillo; olor; resabio, semejanza; tintura, conocimiento ligero o superficial; beso sonado y fuerte; manotada; rechupete; chasquido de látigo; (mar.) cúter, lancha de pescar.

smacker, s. beso sonado, golpe fuerte; manotada.

small [smɔ:l], a. pequeño, menudo, diminuto, chico; corto, estrecho, escaso, exiguo; bajo (de estatura); despreciable, mezquino; insignificante; poco; delgado, fino; de poca importancia, de poco momento; bajo, obscuro; *small-arms*, armas portátiles; *small coal*, cisco, carbón menudo; *small-clothes*, ropa interior; *small beer*, cerveza débil o floja; (fig.) persona o cosa de poca importancia; *small craft*, embarcaciones menores; cosas o personas de poca importancia; *small print*, carácter de letra menuda; *small rate*, precio bajo; *small talk*, conversación de ninguna importancia, vulgaridades; *small fry*, pececillos; gente menuda, de poca importancia, cosas pequeñas; *small hours*, altas horas de la noche; *small pica*, (impr.) lecturita, (tipo de 11 puntos); *small wares*, mercería; *small voice*, vocecita, voz delgada; *to cut something small*, hacer pedazos menudos una cosa; *to make small*, achicar. — s. parte estrecha de cualquier cosa; cosa pequeña, cantidad pequeña. — pl. **smalls**, (fam.) ropa interior. — adv. en tono bajo o suave.

smallage ['smɔ:lidʒ], s. apio, apio silvestre.

smaller ['smɔ:ləɹ], a. comp., **smallest**, a. superl. [SMALL]; menor.

smallish, a. pequeñito, algo pequeño, menudo.

smallness, s. pequeñez; cortedad; insignificancia; exigüidad.

smallpox ['smɔ:lpɔks], s. viruelas, f.pl.

smalt [smɔ:lt], s. esmalte; (pint.) esmaltín.

smarmy ['smɑ:ɹmi], a. (fam.) zalamero, meloso.

smart [smɑ:ɹt], a. vivo; listo, ingenioso, hábil, eficaz, activo; despierto, vivaracho, despabilado, despejado; sutil, agudo; picante, acerbo. mordicante, agrio, punzante, mordaz; elegante, a la moda; garrido, gallardo, galano; astuto, inteligente, ladino. — s. escozor, aflicción, dolor. — v.i. escocer, picar; mordicar; requemar; dolerse, arrepentirse, pagar caro, sentir.

smarten, v.t. hermosear, embellecer, hacer gallardo. — v.i. escocer, picar.

smartness, s. agudeza, viveza, despejo,

vivacidad, vigor, habilidad, sutileza; astucia, perspicacia; elegancia.

smarty ['smɑːɪti], s. (fam.) persona que se pasa de listo.

smash [smæʃ], v.t., v.i. romper(se), machacar, allanar, quebrar, aplastar, destrozar, despachurrar, hacer pedazos, hacer añicos, hacer astillas; (fam.) fracasar, hacer bancarrota, quebrar, arruinarse. — s. rotura, acto de romper, rompimiento, machacamiento, destrozo; fracaso; refresco de aguardiente, hierbabuena y azúcar; ruina, quiebra; to go to smash (o to smash up), arruinarse, quebrar.

smash-and-grab [smæʃənd'græb], s. robo violento.

smatch [smætʃ], s. gusto, resabio; tintura.

smatter ['smætəɹ], v.i. saber (o hablar) muy por encima, superficialmente, hablar sin conocimiento.

smatterer, s. conocedor superficial.

smattering, s. tintura, conocimiento superficial.

smear [smiəɹ], v.t. untar, embarrar, tiznar, manchar, emporcar, ensuciar. — s. embarradura, mancha viscosa; media tapa (de artículos de alfarería); (biol.) frotis.

smeary ['smiəɹi], a. graso, lardoso, pegajoso.

smegma ['smegmə], s. esmegma.

smegmatic [smeg'mætik], a. jabonoso.

smell [smel], v.t. (pret., p.p. **smelt**, (ant.) **smelled**) oler, olfatear, oliscar, husmear, ventear; (fig.) percibir, conocer, descubrir; to smell a rat, (fig.) oler el poste; to smell someone out, descubrir a uno. — v.i. oler; tener olor; oler mal; apestar; to smell of, oler a; to smell strong, despedir un olor fuerte. — s. olfato; aroma, perfume, olor (bueno o malo); traza, vestigio; fragancia, hediondez; to have an offensive smell, oler que apesta.

smeller, s. persona o cosa que huele, oledor, rastreador, husmeador; (fam.) la nariz.

smell-feast, s. (ant.) gorrista, m.f., mogollón, parásito.

smelling, s. acción de oler, husmeo; smelling-salts, sales aromáticas (o inglesas); smelling-bottle, frasco de sales; sweet smelling, oloroso, odorífero; foul smelling, hediondo, que huele mal.

smelt [smelt], pret., p.p. [SMELL]. — s. (ict.) esperlán. — v.t. (fund.) derretir, fundir (minerales).

smelter ['smeltəɹ], s. fundidor, apartador.

smeltery, s. fundición.

smelting, s. fundición; smelting-furnace, horno de fundición; smelting-house, smelting works, fundición, apartado; smelting-pot, cubilote.

smew [smjuː], s. harla, mergo.

smift [smift], s. (min.) mecha.

smilax ['smailæks], s. esmílax, esmiláceo.

smile [smail], v.i. sonreír(se); reír; ser propicio, favorecer. — v.t. expresar con una sonrisa; to smile at, on (o upon) ser propicio a, sonreír a, favorecer; to smile one's thanks, dar las gracias con una sonrisa; to smile assent, consentir con una sonrisa. — s. sonrisa.

smiling ['smailiŋ], a. risueño, sonriente.

smilingly, adv. con cara risueña, sonriendo, con sonrisa.

smirch [sməːɹtʃ], v.t. ensuciar, tiznar, deslucir,

mancillar; (fig.) desorar, denigrar, deshonrar, difamar. — s. tiznón, tiznadura, tiznajo.

smirk [sməːɹk], v.i. sonreírse afectadamente. — s. sonrisa boba o afectada; visaje.

smirking, a. sonriente; afectado.

smite [smait], v.t. (pret. **smote**, (ant.) **smit**; p.p. **smitten**, (ant.) **smit**) herir, golpear; destruir, afligir, castigar, asolar; encantar, ganar (o robar) el corazón; llegar al alma, conmover, enternecer; doler, apenar, pesar; aplanar, aplastar; to smite off, cortar, partir (o romper) de un golpe. — v.i. chocar; venir con fuerza repentina. — s. golpe, porrazo.

smiter ['smaitəɹ], s. golpeador; persona o animal que hiere, que castiga, destruye, etc.

smith [smiθ], s. herrero; (en composición) artífice; smith and farrier, herrador; smith's hammer, destajador.

smithereens [smiðə'riːnz], s.pl. añicos, pedazos.

smithery ['smiθəri], s. herrería, taller u oficio del herrero.

smithy ['smiði], s. fragua, forja, hornaza.

smitten ['smitən], p.p. [SMITE].

smock [smɔk], s. (ant.) camisa (de mujer); blusa (de labrador); smock-frock, blusa de labrador.

smock-faced, a. (ant.) de cara afeminada.

smoke [smouk], s. humo; smoke-black, negro humo; to end in smoke, (fig.) volverse agua de cerrajas, volverse humo, reducirse a nada; smoke-burner, smoke-consumer, aparato fumívoro; smoke-consuming, fumívoro; smoke-jack, torno de asador movido por el humo; smoke-screen, cortina de humo; humo de protección; smoke-signal, ahumada; there's no smoke without fire, cuando el río suena, agua lleva. — v.t. fumar; curar al humo, poner al humo, ahumar, sahumar; ennegrecer; to smoke out, ahumar, ahogar con humo; hacer salir por medio del humo; echar fuera. — v.i. humear, echar humo; fumar; arder, estar encendido; oler; descubrir.

smoke-dry ['smoukdrai], v.t. ahumar, curar, secar al humo.

smokeless, a. sin humo, desahumado.

smoker, s. fumador; sahumador; caja de ahumar abejas; (fam.) vagón de fumar, coche para fumadores; (fam.) tertulia en que se permite fumar.

smoke-sail, s. (mar.) guardahumo.

smoke-stack, s. chimenea.

smoke-tight ['smouktait], a. impenetrable al humo.

smoke-tree, **smoke-plant**, s. arbusto que da penachos parecidos a plumas.

smokiness ['smoukinis], s. fumosidad, carácter humoso.

smoking, s. el fumar; el ahumar. — a. humeante, fumante; (E.U.) smoking-car, (Ingl.) smoking-carriage, (f.c.) vagón para fumadores; smoking-jacket, batín; smoking-room, fumadero, cuarto de fumar; no smoking allowed, se prohibe fumar; please do not smoke, se ruega no fumar.

smoky ['smouki], a. humeante; humoso; ahumado.

smolt [smoult], s. (ict.) murgón, esguín.

smolder ['smouldəɹ], v.i. [SMOULDER].

smooch [smuːtʃ], v.i. ensuciar; besuquear.

smooth [smuːð], *a.* liso; pulido, bruñido, alisado; suave; delicado; calmo, plácido, manso (del agua); dulce, tierno, tranquilo, terso; uniforme, sin variación; llano, plano, igual; lisonjero, meloso, halagüeño, carantoñero, adulador; afable, cortés; que no rasca; no aspirado (gramática griega); *smooth-faced*, sin barba, barbilampiño; pulido, alisado; cariparejo; *smooth-grained*, de vetas lisas; *smooth-sliding*, que se desliza con suavidad; *smooth-shaven*, bien afeitado; *smooth-paced*, que anda con paso igual; *smooth-tongued*, *smooth-spoken*, lisonjero, adulador, obsequioso, zalamero, meloso. — *v.t.* allanar, alisar, poner liso, suavizar, igualar, pulir; (*carp.*) acepillar; lijar; facilitar; pacificar, aquietar; ablandar, calmar, zanjar, atenuar (dificultades); *smoothing-iron*, alisador, plancha, raspa, hierro para alisar; *smoothing-plane*, cepillo corto; *to smooth the way for*, allanar el camino para.

smoother [ˈsmuːðəɹ], *s.* alisador.

smoothly [ˈsmuːðli], *adv.* lisamente; con suavidad; lisonjeramente.

smoothness, *s.* lisura, igualdad, llanura, tersura; bruñido, suavidad, blandura; dulzura, dulzor.

smote, *pret.* [SMITE].

smother [ˈsmʌðəɹ], *v.t.* ahogar, asfixiar, sofocar; suprimir, disfrazar, ocultar; apagar; (*coc.*) estofar. — *v.i.* carecer de respiración, ahogarse, asfixiarse. — *s.* efecto de suprimir, supresión, ocultación; humareda, polvareda; ahoguío, sofocación.

smoulder [ˈsmouldəɹ], *v.i.* arder lentamente, arder sin llama; arder en rescoldo; (*fig.*) estar latente, oculto o escondido; arder (una pasión).

smouldering, *a.* que arde lentamente o humeando; latente; ardiente.

smudge [smʌdʒ], *v.t.* tiznar; ensuciar, manchar; embarrar, embadurnar; (*E.U.*) fumigar, ahumar. — *s.* mancha; tizne, tiznajo, tiznadura, tiznón, hollín; fumigación, ahumadura.

smudgy, *a.* tiznado, ensuciado, holliniento; humeante.

smug [smʌg], *a.* de gran opinión propia, satisfecho de sí mismo; farisaico.

smuggle [ˈsmʌgəl], *v.t.* pasar de contrabando, matutear, alijar, introducir a escondidas. — *v.i.* hacer contrabando, matutear.

smuggler [ˈsmʌgləɹ], *s.* contrabandista, *m.f.*, alijador, matutero.

smuggling, *s.* contrabando, matute, metedoría.

smugness [ˈsmʌgnis], *s.* satisfacción de sí mismo; presunción.

smut [smʌt], *s.* tiznón, tiznajo, tiznadura, mancha; (*fig.*) indecencia, obscenidad; (*bot.*) tizón, tizoncillo. — *v.t.* tiznar, manchar, ensuciar; (*fig.*) mancillar la reputación, echar un baldón; (*bot.*) atizonar, añublar. — *v.i.* (*bot.*) atizonarse, anublarse.

smutch [smʌtʃ], *v.t.* tiznar, manchar, ensuciar. — *s.* mancha, tiznajo.

smuttiness [ˈsmʌtinis], *s.* tizne, tiznón; (*fig.*) indecencia.

smutty [ˈsmʌti], *a.* tiznado, manchado con tizne, humoso; (*bot.*) anublado, atizonado; indecente, verde.

snack [snæk], *s.* parte, *f.*, porción; merienda;

piscolabis; bocado; *to go snacks*, ir a medias; *snack-basket*, fiambrera.

snaffle [ˈsnæfəl], *s.* bridón; filete. — *v.t.* refrenar; (*fam.*) hurtar.

snag [snæg], *s.* (*carp.*) nudo en la madera; protuberancia; (*E.U.*) tronco o tocón sumergido; obstáculo inesperado; (*dent.*) raigón de una muela; pitón del asta del ciervo; *to strike a snag*, chocar contra un obstáculo.

snagged [snægd], *a.* lleno de raigones; nudoso.

snaggy [ˈsnægi], *a.* lleno de troncos (o tocones); (*carp.*) nudoso, parecido a un tócon.

snail [sneil], *s.* caracol (de tierra); (*E.U.*) babosa; persona lenta; *snail-clover*, alfalfa, mielga; *snail's pace*, paso de tortuga, de caracol.

snake [sneik], *s.* culebra, sierpe, *f.*, serpiente, *f.* — *v.t.* (*fam.*, *E.U.*) arrastrar y tirar de una cosa; enrollar. — *v.i.* serpentear.

snake-root, *s.* serpentaria.

snake-weed, *s.* bistorta, dragontea.

snaky [ˈsneiki], *a.* de culebra; culebrino, serpentino, tortuoso; que serpentea; solapado; traidor; (*E.U.*) lleno de culebras.

snap [snæp], *v.t.* tirar un mordisco, morder o tratar de morder; chasquear, hacer estallar; romper; cerrar de golpe; (*foto.*) sacar una instantánea de; decir bruscamente. — *v.i.* chasquear, dar un chasquido; estallar, partirse, romperse o quebrarse; hablar bruscamente; *to snap at*, coger de golpe, querer coger o morder, tirar una mordiscada, pegar una dentellada; *to snap in two*, quebrar, romper en dos pedazos; *to snap one's fingers*, castañetear; burlarse (de); *to snap off*, romperse, partirse; *to snap up*, coger, agarrar; lanzarse sobre. — *s.* chasquido; castañeteo (con los dedos); estallido; dentellada, mordiscón, mordedura; cierre de resorte, corchete, garra, cerrajita; galletica; (*fam.*) fuerza, vivacidad, vigor, energía; período corto (de frío); (*teat.*) bolo, contrata, casual; *soft snap*, (*fam.*) ganga; *snap-shot*, disparo rápido, sin apuntar; *snapshot*, (*foto.*) instantánea. — *a.* hecho de repente, repentino; inesperado.

snapdragon [ˈsnæpdrægən], *s.* hierba becerra, antirrino.

snapper [ˈsnæpəɹ], *s.* ratero, ladrón; punta del látigo; triquitraque, buscapiés; (*ict.*) pez comestible. — *pl.* **snappers**, castañuelas, castañetas.

snapping, *s.* acción de estallar, chasquear, etc. [SNAP]. — *a.* saltadizo; *snapping turtle*, gran tortuga voraz.

snappish [ˈsnæpiʃ], *a.* respondón, mordaz, agrio, irritable.

snappishness, *s.* irritabilidad.

snappy, *a.* irritable; vivo, vigoroso.

snare [snɛəɹ], *s.* cepo, lazo, trampa; acechanza, celada, red; artimaña; tirante para templar un tambor. — *v.t.* enredar, tender trampas o lazos, enmarañar. — *v.i.* cazar con trampas.

snarl [snɑːɹl], *v.i.* gruñir, regañar, arrufar. — *v.t.*, *v.i.* enredar(se), enmaranar(se); estampar, embutir (metales); confundir. — *s.* regaño, regañamiento, gruñido; maraña, hilo enredado; (*fam.*) contienda, riña; cabellos desgreñados; complicación, enredo.

snarler, *s.* regañón; perrengue.

snarly, *a.* enredoso, insidioso.

snatch [snætʃ], *v.t.* arrebatar, quitar; agarrar, echar mano o garra, arrapar, agarrar, apercollar; disfrutar (un descanso, etc.). — *v.i.* procurar (o tratar de) agarrar o arrebatar; tirar a morder; *to snatch at,* procurar arrebatar. — *s.* asimiento, agarro; arrebatamiento; arrebatiña; ratito; pedacito, bocado; fragmento; *by snatches,* a ratos, poco a poco, de vez en cuando.

snatch-block ['snætʃblɔk], *s.* pasteca.

snatcher, *s.* arrebatador, ladrón.

snath [snæθ], **snathe** [sneiθ], **snead** [sniːd], *s.* mango de guadaña.

sneak [sniːk], *v.i.* colarse (en); escurrirse, escabullirse; acusar, delatar; sisar, ratear; *(escuela)* ir con chismes al maestro; *sneakthief,* garduño; *to sneak along,* andar cabizbajo, ir a la sordina. — *s.* correveidile; mandilón.

sneak-boat, *s.* bote cubierto con ramas para cazar patos.

sneaker, *s.* correveidile. — *pl.* (*E.U.*) zapatos de playa.

sneaking ['sniːkiŋ], *a.* servil, bajo, vil; furtivo, oculto, secreto; *sneaking fondness* (o *affection* o *love*) afición secreta.

sneck, *s.* pasador, aldaba de puerta, colanilla; *sneck-drawer,* ladrón.

sneer [snɪəɹ], *v.i.* mirar o hablar con desprecio; mofarse, burlarse. — *s.* mirada de desprecio; escarnio, mofa; fisga.

sneerer, *s.* mofador, escarnecedor, fisgón.

sneering, *a.* burlón, escarnecedor, mofante. — *s.* escarnio, burla.

sneeringly, *adv.* con desprecio; escarneciendo.

sneeze [sniːz], *v.i.* estornudar; *not to be sneezed at,* no ser de despreciar; ser digno de consideración. — *s.* estornudo.

sneezewort ['sniːzwəɹt], *s.* estornutatorio; cebadilla.

sneezing, *s.* estornudo; *sneezing powder,* cebadilla, estornutatorio.

snell [snel], *s.* sedal del anzuelo; sotileza.

snick [snik], *v.t.* cortar (con tijeras). — *s.* corte pequeño, tijeretada; *snick or snee,* riña a cuchilladas.

snicker ['snikəɹ], **snigger** ['snigəɹ], *v.i.* reírse tontamente, dar risotadas. — *s.* risita.

snickersnee [snikəɹ'sniː], *s.* cuchillo; cuchillo de monte.

sniff [snif], *v.t.* husmear, olfatear, ventear, oliscar. — *v.i.* resollar, oler; dar un respingo para expresar el desdén. — *s.* acción de oler, olfatear, etc., olfateo; cosa olfateada.

snigger, *s.* [SNICKER].

sniggle ['snigəl], *v.t.*, *v.i.* pescar anguilas en presa; entrampar, enmarañar.

snip [snip], *v.t.* tijeretear, dar tijeretadas, cortar con tijeras; *to snip off,* cortar de un golpe. — *s.* tijeretada; recorte, retazo, pedazo pequeño, pedacito; parte, *f.*; persona pequeña o insignificante (*fam.*) ocasión, ganga; cosa hecha, éxito asegurado; *a snip of a girl,* (*fam.*) una muchachita.

snipe [snaip], *s.* agachadiza, becardón. — *v.t.*, *v.i.* cazar agachadizas; (*mil.*) paquear; (*fig.*) atacar esporádicamente.

sniper ['snaipəɹ], *s.* paco.

snipper ['snipəɹ], *s.* persona que corta con tijeras.

snippet ['snipet], *s.* recorte, retacito; porción pequeña.

snip-snap ['snipsnæp], *s.* diálogo picante.

snivel ['snivəl], *s.* moquita. — *v.i.* moquear; llorar como una criatura; hacer pucheros, jeremiquear.

sniveller, *s.* persona quejumbrosa, lloraduelos, llorón; mocoso.

snivelling, *a.* llorón, que hace pucheros; mocoso.

snob [snɔb], *s.* esnob.

snobbish ['snɔbiʃ], *a.* esnob.

snobbishness, *s.* esnobismo.

snood [snuːd], *s.* redecilla; moco (de pavo); cendal (de pesca).

snook [snuːk], *s.* pez tropical parecido al lucio.

snook, *s.* palmo de nariz; *to cock a snook,* hacer un palmo de nariz.

snoop [snuːp], *v.i.* ir husmeando; espiar.

snooper, *s.* husmeador; espía, *m.*

snooze [snuːz], *v.i.* (*fam.*) dormitar, descabezar el sueño, estar amodorrado. — *s.* (*fam.*) siestecita, sueño ligero.

snore [snɔːɹ], *v.i.* roncar. — *s.* ronquido.

snorer, *s.* roncador.

snoring, *s.* ronquido.

snort [snɔːɹt], *v.t.*, *v.i.* resoplar, bufar. — *s.* bufido, resoplido.

snot [snɔt], *s.* (*vulg.*) moco; (*fam.*) persona ruin y despreciable.

snotty ['snɔti], *a.* (*vulg.*) mocoso; sucio; insolente. — *s.* (*mar.*, *fam.*) guardiamarina, *m.*

snout [snaut], *v.t.* proveer de hocico o boquerel. — *s.* jeta, morro, hocico; cañón de un fuelle, tobera; embocadura de un cañón; boquerel de manguera.

snout-beetle, *s.* gorgojo.

snouted, *s.* hocicudo.

snout-ring, *s.* narigón para puercos.

snow [snou], *s.* nieve, *f.*; nevasca, nevada; (*germ.*, *E.U.*) cocaína; *snow-blind,* cegado por la nieve; *snow-blindness,* ceguera causada por el reflejo de la nieve; *snow-bird,* pinzón de las nieves; *snow-bunting,* verderón de las nieves. — *v.i.* nevar, caer nieve, ventiscar. — *v.t. to snow in, to snow under, to snow up,* cubrir, obstruir, detener o aprisionar con nieve; *to snow under,* (*fig.*) abrumar.

snowball, *v.t.* lanzar bolas de nieve. — *v.i.* ir ganando fuerzas. — *s.* bola de nieve.

snow-bound, *a.* sitiado por la nieve.

snow-capped, *a.* coronado de nieve.

snowdrift ['snoudrift], *s.* acumulación de nieve, ventisquero.

snowdrop ['snoudrɔp], *s.* campanilla de invierno.

snowfall ['snoufɔːl], *s.* nevada, nevasca.

snowflake ['snoufleik], *s.* copo de nieve; (*orn.*) verderol de las nieves; (*bot.*) campanilla.

snow-plough, *s.* (*f.c.*) arado quitanieves.

snow-shed, *s.* guardaaludes.

snow-shoe, *s.* raqueta de nieve.

snow-slip, *s.* alud.

snowstorm ['snoustɔːɹm], *s.* nevasca, borrasca de nieve, nevada, ventisca.

snow-white ['snouwait], *a.* nevado; blanco como la nieve; (*poét.*) de nieve, níveo.

snowy ['snoui], *a.* nevoso, de nieves, cargado de nieve; (*poét.*) níveo; sin mancha, puro.

snub [snʌb], *v.t.* desairar; repulsar; tratar con desdén; *to snub up,* parar de repente. — *s.* repulsa; desaire; nariz chata. — *a.* chato; *snub-nosed,* chato.

snuff [snʌf], *s.* moco o pavesa de candela; rapé;

(*fam.*) indignación. — *v.t.* olfatear, oliscar, oler, ventear; despabilar, quitar el pábilo (a una vela); introducir en la nariz con el aliento. — *v.i.* aspirar, resoplar hacia adentro; tomar rapé; *to snuff up*, tomar por la nariz.

snuff-box, *s.* caja de rapé, tabaquera.

snuffer ['snʌfəɹ], *s.* despabilador. — *pl.* **snuffers**, despabiladeras.

snuffiness ['snʌfinis], *s.* suciedad causada por el rapé.

snuffle ['snʌfəl], *v.i.* ganguear, hablar por las narices. — *v.t.* hablar o cantar con gangueo. — *s.* gangueo. — *pl.* **snuffles**, (*fam.*) catarro nasal, romadizo.

snuffy ['snʌfi], *a.* cubierto de rapé; que huele a rapé.

snug [snʌg], *a.* cómodo, acomodado, abrigado; compacto; caliente; escondido; *as snug as a bug in a rug*, (*fam.*, *E.U.*) con toda comodidad. — *v.t.* acomodar, ajustar, aparejar, apañar.

snuggery ['snʌgəri], *s.* (*fam.*) aposento cómodo, cuarto conveniente y bien arreglado.

snuggle ['snʌgəl], *v.i.* acomodarse; arrimarse; *to snuggle up to one another*, arrimarse a, apretarse contra.

so [sou], *adv.* así, de este modo, de esta manera; tal, tan, tanto; de igual modo, también; por tanto, por lo cual, por cuya razón; conque, aproximadamente, cosa así; poco más o menos; lo, ello, eso, lo mismo (para evitar la repetición de una frase), sea, así sea; bien, bueno; *so?* (*fam.*) ¿de veras? ¿verdad? *so much as*, tanto como, a lo menos; *so . . . as*, tan (o tanto) . . . como; *not so much as*, ni siquiera; *so as to*, de manera que; *and so forth*, y así de lo demás, etcétera; *so that*, de suerte que, de modo que, de forma que, de (tal) manera que; *if it be so that*, (o *if so be that*) si fuese así, si fuese verdad que; *so be it*, amén, así sea, quiéralo Dios; *so much as*, por mucho que; *it is not so*, no es cierto, no es así; *so-so*, así así, tal cual, bueno bueno, regular, medianamente; *if so*, si así es, de ese modo; *why so?* ¿por que? ¿por qué así? *how so?* ¿cómo es eso? ¿cómo? *just so* o *exactly so*, ni más ni menos, precisamente; *so-called*, llamado (así), seudo, supuesto; *I hope so*, así lo espero; *I think so*, así lo creo; *I should think so* (*indeed*)! ¡ya lo creo! *so far*, hasta aquí, hasta ahí; (*Mr.*) *So-and-So*, (Señor, Don) fulano, fulano de tal; *so much for*, he aquí lo que es; he ahí; *so to say*, o *so to speak*, por decirlo así; *ever so much*, (*fam.*) muchísimo; *ever so little*, (*fam.*) muy poco; *if ever so little*, por poco que; *be he never so powerful*, por poderoso que sea. — *conj.* con que, con tal que, por tal que, supuesto que, siempre que, a condición de que. — *interj.* ¡so!

soak [souk], *v.t.* empapar, mojar, remojar, humedecer, regar, poner en remojo; (*fam.*) clavar, abusar; *to soak in*, *to soak up*, chupar, absorber, embeber; beber con exceso. — *v.i.* estar en remojo; *to soak*, *soak in* o *soak through*, remojarse, esponjarse, calarse; beborrotear, empinar el codo. — *s.* remojo, calada; líquido en que se empapa alguna cosa; (*fam.*) bebedor, borrachín; borrachera.

soakage ['soukidʒ], *s.* merma.

soaker, *s.* remojador, persona o cosa que

remoja o empapa; chubasco, chaparrón; (*fam.*) borrachín.

soaky ['souki], *a.* empapado, calado, mojado, húmedo.

soap [soup], *s.* jabón; (*fam.*) lisonja, adulación; *soap-ball*, bola de jabón, jabonete; *soap-boiler*, caldera para jabón; jabonero; *soap-ashes*, cenizas de jabón; *soap-bubble*, pompa de jabón; *soap factory* (o *manufactory*), jabonería; *soap plant*, (*bot.*) amole. — *v.t.* jabonar, enjabonar, lavar con jabón; (*fam.*) adular.

soapberry-tree, *s.* sapindo, jaboncillo.

soap-dish, *s.* jabonera.

soap-maker, *s.* jabonero.

soapstone ['soupstoun], *s.* esteatita, galaxía; jaboncillo, jabón de sastre.

soap-suds, *s.pl.* jabonaduras.

soapwort ['soupwəɹt], *s.* saponaria, jabonera.

soapy ['soupi], *a.* jabonoso, saponáceo.

soar [sɔːɹ], *v.i.* remontarse, elevarse; sublimarse, encumbrarse; anhelar, aspirar; (*aer.*) volar a vela. — *s.* remonte, vuelo hacia lo alto.

soaring, *a.* que remonta; (*fig.*) sublime, elevado. — *s.* vuelo a vela.

sob [sɔb], *s.* sollozo. — *v.i.* sollozar.

sober ['soubəɹ], *a.* sobrio; sensato; moderado; serio, modesto; sombrío, oscuro, de color apagado; *to get sober*, recobrar la sobriedad, volverse formal; *in sober earnest*, con toda seriedad, de veras. — *v.t.* desemborrachar, desembriagar; poner grave, o pensativo. — *v.i.* volverse sobrio, cuerdo, etc.; *to sober down*, serenar(se), hacer volver (o volverse) cuerdo; sosegar(se).

sober-minded, *a.* sereno, grave, formal.

soberness ['soubəɹnis], **sobriety** [so'braiiti], *s.* sobriedad; templanza; moderación; seriedad; calma.

sobriquet ['soubrikei], *s.* apodo.

soccer ['sɔkəɹ], *s.* fútbol.

sociability [souʃə'biliti], *s.* sociabilidad, simpatía, franqueza, afabilidad.

sociable ['souʃəbəl], *a.* sociable, amigable, conversable.

social ['souʃəl], *a.* social; afable, sociable, amistoso. — *s.* reunión, *f.*, velada.

Socialism ['souʃəlizm], *s.* socialismo.

socialist ['souʃəlist], *s.*, *a.* socialista, *m.f.*

socialistic [souʃə'listik], *a.* socialista.

socialize ['souʃəlaiz], *v.t.* socializar.

society [so'saiiti], *s.* sociedad; comunidad; mundo elegante, alta sociedad; compañía, conversación amena; *to go into society*, frecuentar la sociedad; *fashionable society*, la alta sociedad.

Socinian [so'siniən], *a.* sociniano.

Socinianism, *s.* socinianismo.

sociological [souʃo'lodʒikəl], **sociologist** [souʃi'olodʒist], *a.*, *s.* sociólogo.

sociology [souʃi'olodʒi], *s.* sociología.

sock [sɔk], *s.* calcetín; (*ant.*) escarpín, zueco; (*ant.*, *fig.*) comedia; (*fig.*) reja de arado; golpe, puñetazo. — *v.t.* (*fam.*) pegar, dar, golpear.

socket ['sɔkit], *s.* hueco; cubo, caja, contera, encaje, cajera, cepo, ojo; cuenca (del ojo); fosa (de un hueso); (*elec.*) enchufe; casquillo, tubo o cañón de candelero; *socket of the capstan*, (*mar.*) concha de cabrestante; *socket of a tooth*, alvéolo (de un diente); *socket-*

joint, (*mec.*) articulación o juntura de encastre; *socket-wrench*, (*mec.*) llave de tubo o de vaso.

socle ['soukəl], *s.* (*arq.*) zócalo, rodapié, plinto.

Socratic [so'krætik], *a.* socrático.

sod [sɔd], *v.t.* cubrir de césped. — *s.* césped; turba, tepe, terrón, témpano (de tierra vegetal).

soda ['soudə], *s.* sosa, soda; carbonato u óxido de sodio; sal soda; *soda-water*, agua de soda; agua de seltz; *soda-fountain*, fuente de agua de soda.

sodaic [so'deiik], *a.* sódico.

sodality [so'dæliti], *s.* cofradía, hermandad.

sodden ['sɔdən], *v.t.* mojar, saturar, empapar. — *v.i.* empaparse, mojarse, ponerse blando; podrirse. — *a.* mojado, empapado, saturado; (*ant.*) cocido; (*fig.*) tonto, necio. — *p.p.* [SEETHE].

sodium ['soudiəm], *s.* sodio.

sodomite ['sɔdomait], *s.* sodomita, *m.*

sodomy ['sɔdomi], *s.* sodomía.

soever [so'evɹ], *adv.* que sea, por mucho que sea, por más que sea; *which way soever*, por donde quiera.

sofa ['soufə], *s.* sofá; canapé.

soffit ['sɔfit], *s.* (*arq.*) sófito; intradós.

soft [sɔːft, soft], *a.* suave; blando; flojo; muelle; dúctil, maleable, flexible; plástico, jugoso, pastoso; dulce, melodioso; manso, dócil, fácil; apacible, plácido; tierno, delicado, esponjoso, fofo; tonto; afeminado, débil de carácter; perezoso, poncho; delgada, fina (agua); bituminoso (carbón); templado, de matices delicados o apagados; (*hilado*) flojo, con poca torsión; (*gram.*) sibilante; sonante; *soft answer*, buenas palabras; *soft bread*, mollete, pan tierno; *soft-headed*, *soft-witted*, necio, tonto; *soft shell*, de cáscara blanda; *soft drinks*, *s.pl.* bebidas no alcohólicas. — *interj.* ¡despacio! ¡quedo! ¡quedito! — *adv.* blandamente, flexiblemente, suavemente.

softa, *s.* estudiante de teología y ley santa mahometana.

soften ['sɔːfən], *v.t.* ablandar, reblandecer; enternecer; suavizar, amansar, templar; calmar, aplacar, atemperar, mitigar; afeminar, enervar. — *v.i.* ablandarse, reblandecerse; templarse; enternecerse; amansarse.

softener ['sɔːfənɹ], *s.* persona o cosa que ablanda, aplaca, etc.; ablandador, suavizador; (*pint.*) brocha ancha para amortiguar los colores.

softening, *a.* que ablanda, aplaca, etc.; suavizador, emoliente. — *s.* reblandecimiento; blandura; ablandamiento; enternecimiento; suavidad; *softening iron*, (*ten.*) hierro de ablandar.

softish [sɔːftiʃ], *a.* blandito, blanducho.

softly, *adv.* blandamente; suavemente; quedito, tranquilamente, callandito, sin ruido; lentamente, con lentitud, paso a paso; *to speak softly*, hablar bajo.

softness ['sɔftnes], *s.* blandura, dulzura, suavidad; pastosidad; (*med.*) morbidez; (*metal.*) ductilidad, maleabilidad; ternura, dulzura; efeminación, debilidad de carácter; delicadeza.

soggy ['sɔgi], *a.* empapado, saturado; pesado y húmedo.

soho [so'hou], *interj.* ¡hola! (caza).

soil [sɔil], *v.t.* ensuciar, manchar; (*vet.*) purgar con alcacel; dar alcacel (al ganado). — *s.* tierra; país, región; suciedad; mancha; estiércol; *to take soil*, (caza mayor) empantanarse, refugiarse; *native soil*, país natal.

soiling, *s.* alcacel, alcacer; ensuciamiento.

soirée ['swɑːrei], *s.* (*fr.*) tertulia, velada, sarao.

sojourn ['sʌdʒəɹn], *v.i.* residir, morar, permanecer. — *s.* morada, permanencia, residencia, estancia.

sojourner, *s.* morador, transeúnte, residente temporal.

sol [sɔl], *s.* sueldo (moneda); sol (moneda); (*mús.*) sol; *Old Sol*, (*fam.*) Febo, el sol.

solace ['sɔləs], *v.t.* solazar, divertir; recrear, alegrar; confortar, consolar; *to solace oneself*, consolarse, solazarse, recrearse, divertirse. — *s.* solaz, alivio, recreo, consuelo, complacencia.

solan ['soulən], *s.* bubia.

solanaceous [soulə'neiʃəs], *a.* solanáceo.

solar ['souləɹ], *a.* solar; *solar spot*, mancha del sol; *solar print*, (*foto.*) impresión heliográfica; *solar plexus*, plexo solar.

solarium [so'lɛəriəm], *s.* habitación o cuarto para tomar baños de sol.

solatium [so'leiʃəm], *s.* compensación o indemnidad por daños o sufrimiento.

sold, *pret.*, *p.p.* [SELL].

solder ['sɔldəɹ], *v.t.* soldar; estañar. — *s.* soldadura.

solderer, *s.* soldador.

soldering ['sɔldəriŋ], *s.* soldadura; *soldering-iron*, soldador.

soldier ['souldʒəɹ], *s.* soldado; militar.

soldier-like, soldierly, *a.* soldadesco, militar, marcial.

soldiership, *s.* soldadesca; profesión de soldado.

soldiery ['souldʒəri], *s.* soldadesca; tropa; servicio militar.

sole [soul], *v.t.* (*zap.*) solar, echar suelas; *to half-sole*, poner (o echar) medias suelas. — *s.* planta del pie; suela del zapato; (*ict.*) lenguado; dado, tejuelo, base, *f.*, fondo, suelo; *sole of the rudder*, zapata del timón; *sole of a gun-carriage*, solera de cureña. — *a.* uno, único, solo, exclusivo, absoluto; (*for.*) soltero, soltera.

solecism [sɔli'sizm], *s.* solecismo.

solecistic [sɔli'sistik], *a.* incorrecto.

solecize ['sɔlisaiz], *v.i.* (*ant.*) cometer solecismos.

solemn ['sɔləm], *a.* solemne, grave; majestuoso, augusto.

solemnness, *s.* solemnidad, gravedad, seriedad.

solemnity [so'lemniti], *s.* solemnidad, ceremonia.

solemnization [solemnai'zeiʃən], *s.* solemnización, celebración.

solemnize ['sɔlemnaiz], *v.t.* solemnizar, celebrar, celebrar solemnemente.

solen ['soulən], *s.* navaja (marisco).

solenoid ['soulenɔid], *s.* solenoide.

soleus [so'liːəs], *s.* sóleo.

sol-fa [sɔl'fɑː], *s.* solfa; solfeo. — *v.t.*, *v.i.* (*mús.*) solfear.

solfeggio [sɔl'fedʒiou], *s.* solfeo.

solferino [sɔlfe'riːnou], *s.* solferino.

solicit [so'lisit], *v.t.* solicitar; pretender, procurar, importunar, pedir, rogar, implorar;

incitar, inducir; tentar. — *v.i.* pedir, hacer una petición o solicitud.

solicitation [solisit′eiʃən], *s.* solicitación, cuestación; incitación.

solicitor [so′lisitəɹ], *s.* abogado; pretendiente.

solicitous [so′lisitəs], *a.* solícito; deseoso, ansioso; inquieto.

solicitress [so′lisitres], *s.f.* solicitadora.

solicitude [so′lisitjuːd], *s.* solicitud; cuidado; preocupación.

solid [′sɔlid], *a.* sólido; macizo; duro; firme, serio, formal; unánime; verdadero. — *s.* sólido.

solidarity [soli′dæriti], *s.* solidaridad.

solidification [sɔlidifi′keiʃən], *s.* solidificación; consolidación.

solidify [so′lidifai], *v.t.* solidificar. — *v.i.* solidificarse.

solidity [so′liditi], **solidness** [′sɔlidnis], *s.* solidez; firmeza; unanimidad.

solidungulate [sɔli′dʌŋgjuːleit], **solidungulous**, *a.* solípedo.

soliloquize [so′lilokwaiz], *v.i.* soliloquiar, hacer un soliloquio.

soliloquy [so′lilokwi], *s.* soliloquio.

soliped [′sɔliped], *s.* solípedo.

solitaire [′sɔlitɛəɹ], *s.* (*joy.*) solitario; solitario (naipes, etc.).

solitariness [′sɔlitərines], *s.* soledad, retiro.

solitary [′sɔlitəri], *a.* solitario; solo, único, aislado, poco frecuentado; desierto; (*zool.*, *bot.*) solitario; simple, no compuesto, sencillo; *in solitary confinement*, incomunicado. — *s.* solitario, ermitaño.

solitude [′sɔlitjuːd], *s.* soledad, vida solitaria; paraje solitario, desierto.

sollar [′sɔləɹ], *s.* (*min.*) descanso; (*igl.*, *ant.*) camarín.

solmization [sɔlmai′zeiʃən], *s.* (*mús.*) solfa.

solo [′soulou], *s.* solo; *solo flight*, (*aer.*) vuelo a solas.

soloist [′soulouist], *s.* solista, *m.f.*

Solomon's seal [′sɔlomənz′siːl], *s.* (*bot.*) sello de Salomón.

solstice [′sɔlstis], *s.* solsticio.

solstitial [sɔl′stiʃəl], *a.* solsticial.

solubility [sɔlju:′biliti], *s.* solubilidad.

soluble [′sɔljuːbəl], *a.* soluble.

solute [′sɔljuːt], *a.* (*bot.*) libre, separado completamente.

solution [so′ljuːʃən], *s.* solución.

solutive [′sɔljuːtiv], *a.* solutivo; soluble; laxante, laxativo.

solvability [sɔlvə′biliti], **solvableness** [′sɔlvəbəlnes], *s.* solubilidad.

solvable [′sɔlvəbəl], *a.* disoluble, soluble.

solve [sɔlv], *v.t.* resolver.

solvency, *s.* solvencia.

solvent [′sɔlvənt], *a.* disolvente, disolutivo; (*com.*) solvente; resolvente. — *s.* disolvente; (*med.*) disolvente.

somatic [sou′mætik], *a.* somático.

somatology [soumə′tɔlodʒi], *s.* somatología.

somatome [′soumətoum], *s.* segmento teórico del cuerpo de un articulado.

sombre [′sɔmbəɹ], *a.* sombrío; obscuro; tétrico; lúgubre, melancólico.

sombrous [′sɔmbrəs], *a.* (*poét.*) sombrío.

some [sʌm], *a.* algo de, un poco, cerca de, poco más o menos, alguno, alguna, algún; unos cuantos, unos pocos, ciertos, algunos, algunas, unos, unas; *someone*, alguien,

alguno; *some persons say*, algunos dicen. — *pron.* los, las, les; algunos, algunas; unos y otros; parte, una parte (de), una porción (de). — *adv.* (*fam.*) cerca de, aproximadamente, poco más o menos.

somebody [′sʌmbɔdi], *s.* alguien, alguna persona; *he is a somebody*, es un personaje; *somebody else*, algún otro.

somehow [′sʌmhau], *adv.* de algún modo, de alguna manera.

somersault [′sʌməɹsɔːlt], **somerset**, *s.* salto mortal. — *v.i.* dar un salto mortal.

something [′sʌmθiŋ], *s.* alguna cosa, algo; *something else*, otra cosa; *to have something to do*, tener que hacer. — *adv.* algo, algún tanto; *this is something like*, (*fam.*) esto sí que me gusta.

sometime [′sʌmtaim], *adv.* algún día; antiguamente; en algún tiempo; en otro tiempo; *sometime last week*, durante la semana pasada; *sometime very soon*, dentro de muy poco tiempo.

sometimes, *adv.* algunas veces, de vez en cuando, a veces.

somewhat [′sʌmwɔt], *s.* algo; un poco. — *adv.* algo, algún tanto, un poco; *somewhat busy*, algo ocupado.

somewhere [′sʌmwɛəɹ], *adv.* en alguna parte; *somewhere else*, en alguna otra parte.

somite [′soumait], *s.* segmento teórico del cuerpo de un articulado.

somnambulism, *s.* somnambulismo.

somnambulist [sɔm′næmbjuːlist], *s.* somnámbulo.

somniferous [sɔm′nifərəs], *a.* somnífero, soporífero.

somnific [sɔm′nifik], *a.* narcótico, soporífero.

somniloquism [sɔm′nilokwizm], **somniloquy** [sɔm′nilokwi], *s.* somnilocuencia.

somniloquist [sɔm′nilokwist], *s.* somnilocuo.

somnolence, somnolency, *s.* somnolencia.

somnolent [′sɔmnolent], *a.* soñoliento; soporífero, adormecedor.

son [sʌn], *s.* hijo; *son-in-law*, yerno, hijo político; *son of a gun*, (*fam.*) camastrón, tuno, pillastre; *sonny*, hijito.

sonant [′sounənt], *a.* (*gram.*) sonante; sonoro.

sonata [so′nɑːtə], *s.* sonata.

song [sɔŋ], *s.* canción; cantar; copla, cantinela, tonada; canto; poesía, verso; balada, poema lírico; bagatela, poca cosa, nimiedad; *the Song of Songs*, el Cantar de los Cantares; *drinking song*, canción báquica; *to sell for a (mere) song*, vender por un pedazo de pan; *an old song*, bagatela; *to sing the same song*, cantar la misma cantinela, repetir la misma cosa.

song-bird, *s.* ave cantora.

song-book, *s.* cancionero.

songful, *a.* melodioso.

songless, *a.* sin canto, que no canta.

songster [′sɔŋstəɹ], *s.* cantor; poeta, *m.*; pájaro cantor.

songstress [′sɔŋstres], *s.f.* cantora, cantadora, cantarina, cantante, cantatriz.

sonifer [′sɔnifəɹ], *s.* sonífero.

soniferous [so′nifərəs], **sonorific** [sono′rifik], *a.* sonante, sonoro.

sonnet [′sɔnet], *v.i.* celebrar con sonetos; sonetear. — *s.* soneto.

sonneteer [sɔne′tiəɹ], *s.* sonetista, *m.f.*

sonometer [so'nɔmetəɹ], s. instrumento para medir sonidos, examinar sordos, etc.

sonority [so'nɔːriti], s. sonoridad.

sonorous ['sɔnərəs], a. sonoro; armonioso.

sonship ['sʌnʃip], s. filiación.

sonsy ['sɔnsi], a. alegre, feliz; rollizo, regordete; manso, domesticado (animales).

soon [suːn], adv. pronto; dentro de poco; too soon, demasiado temprano, demasiado pronto; as soon as, luego que, tan pronto como; how soon? ¿cuándo? soon after, poco después.

sooner, adv. comp. [SOON]; más pronto; antes; I would sooner die, antes la muerte; the sooner the better, cuanto antes mejor; sooner or later, tarde o temprano; no sooner said than done, dicho y hecho; no sooner had he come, when . . ., apenas había venido, cuando . . .; I would sooner go, preferiría ir.

soonest, adv. superl. [SOON]; lo más pronto posible; at the soonest, cuanto antes.

soot [sut], s. hollín. — v.t. manchar, ensuciar o cubrir de hollín.

sooth [suːθ], a. (ant.) real, verdadero; suave. — s. verdad.

soothe [suːð], v.t. calmar; aliviar, mitigar; suavizar; apaciguar.

soother, s. consolador; amansador, apaciguador; adulador.

soothing ['suːðiŋ], a. calmante, tranquilizador; consolador.

soothingly, adv. con dulzura, con tono acariciador.

soothsayer ['suːθseiəɹ], s. adivino, pronosticador.

sootiness ['sutinis], s. fuliginosidad.

sooty ['suti], a. holliniento, lleno de hollín; fuliginoso, tiznado, obscurecido.

sop [sɔp], s. sopa (pan empapado); soborno. — v.t. empapar, ensopar; hacer empapar, embeber o absorber.

sophism ['sɔfizm], s. sofisma, m.; falacia.

sophist, s. sofista, m.f.; ergotista, m.f.

sophistic [so'fistik], sophistical [so'fistikəl], a. sofístico.

sophisticalness, s. sofistería.

sophisticate [so'fistikeit], v.t. sofisticar, hacer sofismas; alterar, adulterar, falsificar. — a. adulterado, falsificado, viciado.

sophisticated, a. mundano; no sencillo; elaborado; culto.

sophistication [sofisti'keiʃən], s. adulteración; mundanería; cultura.

sophisticator, s. falsificador, adulterador.

sophistry ['sofistri], s. sofistería.

Sophoclean [sofo'kliːən], a. sofocleo.

sophomore ['sɔfomɔːɹ], s. (E.U.) estudiante de segundo año.

soporiferous [sɔpoː'rifərəs], a. soporífero, somnífero.

soporiferousness, s. virtud o calidad soperífera.

soporific [sɔpoː'rifik], a. soporífero, dormidero, soporoso, adormecedor. — s. soporífero.

sopping ['sɔpiŋ], a. calado, empapado.

soppy ['sɔpi], a. mojado, empapado, húmedo y blando; (fam.) débil, pusilánime, afeminado.

soprano [so'prɑːnou], s. tiple, soprano.

sora ['sɔːrə], s. ave zancuda (Porzona carolina).

sorb [sɔːb], s. sorba, serba, serbo, serbal.

sorb-apple, s. sorba o serba.

sorbefacient [sɔːbi'feiʃənt], a. absorbente.

sorbet ['sɔːbet], s. sorbete.

sorcerer ['sɔːɹsərəɹ], s. hechicero, mago, brujo, encantador.

sorceress, s.f. hechicera.

sorcery ['sɔːɹsəri], s. hechizo, encantamiento, encantación, hechicería, sortilegio.

sordid ['sɔːɹdid], a. sórdido; mercenario, interesado; vil, bajo.

sordidness, s. sordidez; bajeza, vileza.

sordine ['sɔːɹdiːn], s. sordina.

sore ['sɔːɹ], s. herida; llaga; úlcera; matadura (del ganado); lastimadura; memoria dolorosa; halcón de dos años. — a. dolorido; doloroso; vehemente, violento; extremo; enojado; sore (o sorry) sight, (ant.) espectáculo doloroso; sore eyes, mal de ojos; sore ears, mal de oídos; sore throat, mal de garganta. — adv. (poét.) penosamente, con gran pena.

soreness ['sɔːɹnis], s. dolencia, dolor, mal, lastimadura; amargura (o intensidad) de una pena; sensibilidad de una llaga, herida, etc.

sorghum ['sɔːɹgəm], s. sorgo, zahina; (E.U.) melaza de sorgo.

sorites [so'raitiːz], s. sorites.

sorority [so'rɔriti], s. (E.U.) club o hermandad de mujeres.

sorrel ['sɔrəl], a. alazán rojo. — s. color alazán o roano; alazán (de un animal); (bot.) acedera, acetosa, romaza; field-sorrel o meadow-sorrel, acedera pequeña; wood-sorrel, acederilla.

sorrow ['sɔrou], s. pesar, dolor, pesadumbre, sentimiento, pena, aflicción, tristeza; amargura; desgracia, infortunio; duelo, luto; to my great sorrow, con gran sentimiento mío. — v.i. entristecerse, apesararse, sentir pena, afligirse, ponerse triste.

sorrowful ['sɔrouful], a. pesaroso, afligido, doliente, angustiado, desconsolado; doloroso, lastimoso, melancólico, triste.

sorrowfulness, s. angustia, tristeza, aflicción, pesar.

sorrowing ['sɔrouiŋ], s. aflicción, pesar, lamentación, tristeza.

sorry ['sɔri], a. arrepentido; pesaroso, afligido, triste, desconsolado; despreciable, vil, ruin; I am sorry (for it), lo siento; I am so sorry, lo siento mucho; looking very sorry for himself, en un estado lastimoso.

sort [sɔːɹt], s. clase, f., especie, f., género; condición, calidad; forma, modo, manera, suerte, f.; all sorts of people, toda clase de gentes; after a (o in a) sort, de cierto modo, hasta cierto punto; in like sort, de la misma suerte; nothing of the sort, ni por semejas; out of sorts, indispuesto; malhumorado; (impr.) falto de una fundición especial de letra o guarismos. — v.t. separar, distribuir en grupos, dividir en clases; clasificar; escoger, colocar, arreglar, ordenar; to sort out, escoger y arreglar (u ordenar); to sort over, clasificar. — v.i. acomodarse, ajustarse, convenir; unirse, hermanarse; salir bien o mal.

sortable, a. (ant.) acomodado; apto, conveniente, oportuno.

sortie ['sɔːɹti], s. salida, surtida.

sortilege ['sɔːɹtilidʒ], s. sortilegio.

so-so ['sousou], a. mediano, regular, pasadero, mediocre. — adv. así así, medianamente, regularmente.

sot [sɔt], s. zaque, tumbacuartillos, borrachín, borracho.

sotadean [soutə'diːən], a. sotadeo, de Sotades.

soteriology, s. doctrina de la salvación.

sottish ['sɔtiʃ], a. borracho; entorpecido.

sottishness, s. entorpecimiento.

sou [suː], s. sueldo (moneda francesa).

soubrette [suː'bret], s. (teat.) graciosa.

soubriquet ['soubrikei], s. apodo.

souffle ['suːfəl], s. (cir.) murmullo, susurro.

sough [sʌf], v.i. suspirar, susurrar, murmurar. — s. susurro, murmullo, suspiro.

sought [sɔːt], pret., p.p. [SEEK].

soul [soul], s. alma; espíritu; ánima; ser; persona; corazón; upon my soul, en mi conciencia; (interj.) ¡Dios mío! with all my soul, con toda mi alma, con el mayor gusto; he cannot call his soul his own, no se atreve a decir, esta boca es mía; All Souls' Day, Día de los Difuntos.

souled, s. animado, con alma, que tiene alma.

soulful, a. conmovedor, espiritual.

soulfulness, s. sensibilidad, espiritualidad.

soulless ['soulles], a. desalmado; sin conciencia; sin conocimiento; despreciable, ruin, bajo, vil.

sound [saund], a. sano, bueno; puro; ileso, incólume; completo, perfecto, entero, cabal; (com.) solvente; justo, recto, firme; indudable, seguro, cierto; profundo; sólido; safe and sound, sano y salvo. — adv. sanamente, vigorosamente. — s. mar de sonda, mar poco profundo, estrecho; sonido, son, tañido; ruido; tienta, sonda; vejiga natatoria (del pez); importancia, significación; sound-post, alma del violín; sound wave, onda sonora; of sound and disposing mind and memory, (for.) de mente y memoria sanas (es decir, capaz de hacer testamento); sound-proof, aislado de todo sonido; sound-track, guía sonora. — v.t. tocar, sonar, pulsar, tañer; anunciar, proclamar, cantar, celebrar, aclamar, publicar; hacer emitir un sonido, probar por el sonido; inquirir, sondear, rastrear, tantear; (med.) auscultar; (cir.) sondar, tentar; (mar.) sondar, sondear, echar la sonda; to sound the alarm, tocar al arma. — v.i. sonar, hacer ruido, causar ruido; resonar, divulgarse, esparcirse; dar toque de aviso (o llamada), dar señal por medio de un toque; calarse (la ballena).

sounder ['saundəɹ], s. (elec.) resonador; (mar.) sondeador; (cir.) tienta; hato de puercos monteses.

sounding, a. sonante, sonable, sonoro; retumbante; high-sounding, sonoro, campanudo, retumbante. — s. (mar.) sonda, sondeo, sondadura, escandallada, braceaje; sounding-lead, (mar.) escandallo; sounding-line, sondaleza, bolina. — pl. **soundings**, sondas, cantidad de brazas; muestras (sacadas del agua por el sondeador); off (o out) of soundings, fuera de sondas.

sounding-board, s. tabla de armonía, caja armónica (de un piano); secreto, cajón de los órganos; tornavoz, sombrero de púlpito.

soundless, a. insondable; mudo, sin sonido.

soundly, adv. sanamente, con salud; firmemente, seguramente, verdaderamente, rectamente; to sleep soundly, dormir profundamente.

soundness, s. sanidad, salud, f.; firmeza, vigor, fuerza, validez, solidez; verdad, pureza; justicia, rectitud; ortodoxia.

soup [suːp], s. (coc.) sopa, caldo; clear soup, consommé; thick soup, puré; soup-tureen, sopera; soup-ladle, cucharón; soup-plate, plato sopero; milk soup, sopa de leche; pea soup, sopa de guisantes; mock-turtle soup, imitación de la sopa de tortuga; in the soup, (fam.) en apuros, en un dilema.

sour [sauəɹ], a. agrio, acedo, ácido, avinagrado; huraño, desabrido, áspero, acre; sour apple, manzana agria, manzana verde; sour-dock, acedera; sour-sop, guanabana, guanabano; sour-gourd, pan de mico; sour-grass, acedera pequeña; to turn sour, volverse agrio; to taste sour, tener gusto agrio; sour grapes, ¡están verdes! — v.t. poner acedo o agrio, agriar, acedar, avinagrar; descontentar, desagradar; irritar, exasperar, desabrir, indisponer los ánimos; hacer fermentar (la cal). — v.i. ponerse agrio, agriarse, cortarse, avinagrarse; fermentar, revenirse; corromperse, podrirse; irritarse, enojarse; (agr.) malearse, volverse áspera (la tierra) para las mieses.

source [sɔːɹs], s. fuente, f.; nacimiento; origen; cuna; foco; to have from a good source, saber de buena tinta.

sourish ['sauəɹiʃ], a. algo agrio, agrillo, asperillo, agrete, vinagroso.

sourness, s. acedía, acidez, agrura, agrio; desabrimiento, aspereza, acrimonia.

souse [saus], s. escabeche, adobo, salmuera; zambullida, chapuz; cabeza, patas u orejas de cerdo adobadas; ataque repentino (del halcón). — adv. zas, de golpe, con violencia. — v.t. zambullir, chapuzar; arrojar, derramar, verter un líquido; (coc.) poner en escabeche, escabechar, adobar; mojar; dar un golpe (o arrojarse) con violencia. — v.i. arrojarse, lanzarse de cabeza con violencia.

soutache [suː'tɑːʃ], s. sutás.

soutane, s. sotana.

souteneur, s. chulo.

south [sauθ], s. mediodía, m., sur. — a. meridional, del mediodía, del sur; to be south, dar a mediodía; South-American, sudamericano; South-African, sudafricano; south wind, viento del sur; South Pole, Polo Sur. — adv. hacia el sur; del sur (viento).

south-east, s. sudeste. — a. sudeste, del sudeste.

south-easter, s. temporal (o viento) de sudeste.

south-easterly, a., adv. al sudeste, hacia el sudeste; del sudeste.

south-eastern, a. del sudeste.

souther ['sauðəɹ], s. viento (o borrasca) del sur.

southerly ['sʌðəɹli], a. meridional, hacia el sur.

southern ['sʌðəɹn], a. meridional; del sur; situado al sur; Southern Cross, Cruz del Sur.

southernmost, a. superl. [SOUTHERN]; lo más al sur.

southern-wood, s. abrótano, lombriguera.

southing ['sauθiŋ], a. que camina hacia el sur. — s. diferencia de latitud medida hacia el sur.

southmost ['sauθmost], a. el más cercano al mediodía.

southron ['sʌðɹən], s. habitante del sur, meridional.

southward ['sauθwəd], a. situado hacia el sur. — adv. hacia el mediodía; southward of the line, al sur del ecuador.

south-west [sauθ'west], *s.* sudoeste. — *a.* sudoeste, del sudoeste.

south-wester, *s.* vendaval del sudoeste; (*mar.*) sueste.

south-westerly, *a., adv.* del sudoeste; hacia el sudoeste.

south-western, *a.* del sudoeste.

south-westward, *a.* hacia el sudoeste.

souvenir ['su:vəniəɹ], *s.* recuerdo.

sovereign ['sɔvrin], *s.* soberano; monarca, *m.f.*; (*Ingl.*) libra esterlina (moneda de oro). — *a.* soberano; preeminente; muy eficaz.

sovereignty ['sɔvrənti], *s.* soberanía.

soviet ['sɔvjet], *s.* soviet. — *a.* soviético.

sow [sau], *s.* puerca, marrana, cochina, guarra, cerda; (*fund.*) goa, galápago; *wild sow,* jabalina o puerca montés.

sow [sou], *v.t., v.i.* (*pret.* **sowed**; *p.p.* **sown, sowed**) (*agr.*) sembrar; desparramar, diseminar, esparcir; *to sow one's wild oats,* (*fig., fam.*) correr sus mocedades, hacer travesuras juveniles; *as a man sows, so must he reap,* tal siembras, tal recogerás. — *v.i.* sembrar.

sow-bread ['saubred], *s.* pan porcino, pamporcino.

sow-bug ['saubʌg], *s.* cochinilla de tierra.

sower ['souəɹ], *s.* sembrador; diseminador; desparramador; máquina para sembrar; sembradera.

sow-gelder ['saugeldəɹ], *s.* capador de marranas.

sowing ['souiŋ], *s.* sementera, siembra; sembradura; diseminación; *sowing machine,* sembradera; *sowing time,* sementera.

sown [soun], *p.p.* [SOW].

sow-pig ['saupig], *s.* lechona.

sow-thistle ['sauθisəl], *s.* cerraja, cardo ajonjero.

soy [sɔi], *s.* soja; salsa de soja.

soya-bean ['sɔiəbi:n], *s.* soja.

sozzled ['sɔzəld], *a.* borracho perdido.

spa [spɑ:], *s.* balneario; manantial de aguas minerales; caldas.

space [speis], *s.* espacio; lugar; trecho; área; cabida; intervalo; período, rato; (*impr.*) espacio; *space-ship,* astronave, *f.* — *v.t.* poner espacios entre (palabras, líneas, etc.); espaciar, ensanchar; regletear, interlinear.

spacious ['speiʃəs], *a.* espacioso, vasto, extenso, amplio, capaz, ancho.

spaciousness, *s.* espaciosidad, extensión, capacidad, amplitud.

spadassin [spə'dæsin], *s.* espadachín.

spade [speid], *s.* (*agr.*) pala; (*Cuba*) guataca; (*mil.*) zapa; espadas (de la baraja francesa); eunuco, animal castrado; *to call a spade a spade,* llamar al pan pan, y al vino vino; hablar en plata. — *v.t.* cavar con pala; (*Cuba*) guataquear.

spadeful, *s.* palada.

spadille [spə'dil], *s.* espadilla (juego de tresillo).

spadix ['speidiks], *s.* espádice.

spado ['speidou], *s.* eunuco.

spake [speik], *pret. ant.* [SPEAK].

spall [spɔ:l], *s.* astilla. — *v.t.* descascarar, alisar toscamente. — *v.i.* deshacerse en astillas.

spalt [spɔ:lt], *s.* (*fund.*) espalto; leño del largo de una ripia.

span [spæn], *s.* palmo; lapso, espacio, mo-

mento, rato, instante, trecho; vano (de puente, etc.); bóveda; envergadura (de ala); (*mar.*) amante, eslinga, traba; (*E.U.*) pareja (de caballos); braga, guía; *span-rope,* (*mar.*) nervio; *span-shackle,* (*mar.*) suncho, carlinga. — *v.t.* medir con la mano, medir a palmos; cruzar; abrazar, alcanzar; echar sobre, extenderse sobre; ligar, atar, amarrar. — *v.i.* emparejarse (caballos); proceder por etapas, por jornadas regulares; etc.

span, *pret. ant.* [SPIN].

spandrel ['spændrəl], *s.* (*arq.*) tímpano; enjuta, embecadura.

spangle ['spæŋgəl], *s.* lentejuela, bricho. — *v.t.* adornar con lentejuelas.

spangled, *a.* estrellado (del cielo).

Spaniard ['spænjəd], *s.* español.

spaniel ['spænjəl], *s.* perro de aguas.

Spanish ['spæniʃ], *s., a.* español; hispano; castellano (idioma); *Spanish-bayonet,* (*bot.*) yuca; *Spanish-American,* hispanoamericano; *Spanish broom,* retama de olor; *Spanish-black,* negro de España; corcho quemado; *Spanish chalk,* esteatita, jaboncillo; *Spanish-fly,* cantárida; *Spanish mackerel,* escombro; *Spanish leather,* cordobán; *Spanish main,* parte oriental del mar Caribe, camino entre España y América; *Spanish soap,* jabón de Castilla; *Spanish-moss,* musgo negro, musgo de Florida.

spank [spæŋk], *v.t.* zurrar, dar una zurra. — *v.i.* correr, ir de prisa. — *s.* nalgada.

spanker ['spæŋkəɹ], *s.* persona o cosa que da nalgadas; (*mar.*) maricangalla; (*fam.*) algo grande y hermoso; corredor.

spanking, *a.* pronto, veloz; (*fam.*) muy grande, muy hermoso, de mucho éxito. — *s.* zurra, azotaina.

spanless ['spænles], *a.* que no se puede abarcar (o medir).

spanner ['spænəɹ], *s.* (*mec.*) llave de tuercas, *f.*; llave inglesa; (*ent.*) oruga.

spar [spɑ:ɹ], *s.* (*min.*) espato; (*mar.*) berlinga, percha, borón, palo, mástil, verga; asna, cabrial, cabrio (de grúa o cabria); boxeo; tranca, cerreta, barra; riña, altercado; pelea de gallos con espolones cubiertos. — *v.t.* proveer de vergas, berlingas, o mástiles; mover o alzar por medio de mástiles, y poleas. — *v.i.* boxear. — *pl.* **spars,** arboladura.

sparable ['spærəbəl], *s.* (*zap.*) puntilla, tachuela.

spar-buoy, *s.* baliza.

spar-deck, *s.* cubierta de guindaste.

spare [spɛəɹ], *v.t.* ahorrar; escatimar; economizar; pasar, pasarse sin; guardar, reservar; evitar, dispensar de; perdonar; hacer gracia de. — *v.i.* abstenerse, refrenarse, detenerse, desistir; ser ahorrativo, ser frugal, vivir con economía; usar de clemencia, hacer gracia; *to have* (*enough and*) *to spare,* tener de sobra; *he does not spare himself,* no economiza sus esfuerzos; *spare the rod and spoil the child,* la letra con sangre entra. — *a.* sobrante, disponible, de sobra, adicional, suplementario, de repuesto, de respeto; mezquino, escaso, sobrio; flaco, enjuto, descarnado; débil, delicado; *spare hours,* horas de recreo, horas de ocio; *spare moments* (o *time*), tiempo desocupado, ratos perdidos; *spare cash* (o *money*), ahorros, dinero de repuesto (o de reserva); *spare-built*, flaco, delgado; *spare deck*, (*mar.*) crujías; *spare bed* (o *room*), cama (o cuarto) de repuesto (o de sobra); *spare part*, pieza de recambio, pieza de repuesto; *spare wheel*, rueda de recambio; *to spare at the spigot and let out at the bung-hole*, (*prov.*) economizar una gota y desperdiciar una bota.

spareness, *s.* magrura; escasez; frugalidad, ahorro.

sparer [ˈspɛərəɹ], *s.* ahorrador, persona que ahorra.

spare-rib [spɛəɹˈrib], *s.* costilla de puerco casi descarnada.

sparger [ˈspɑːɹdʒəɹ], *s.* regadera (fábricas de cerveza).

sparing [ˈspɛəriŋ], *a.* escaso, limitado, corto, poco; ahorrativo, frugal, parco, económico, sobrio; *sparing of speech* (o *words*), lacónico.

sparingness, *s.* ahorramiento, ahorro; escasez; parsimonia, frugalidad.

spark [spɑːk], *s.* chispa; vislumbre; (*poét.*) centella; (*joy.*) diamante pequeño; (*elec.*) chispa eléctrica, chispazo; (*fam.*) pisaverde, petimetre, galancete; galán; *spark of life*, átomo de vida; *spark-arrester* o *spark-catcher*, (*f.c.*) chispero, sombrerete; *spark-plug*, (*E.U.*) bujía de encendido. — *v.t.* centellear; (*fam.*) galantear. — *v.i.* chispear, centellear, echar chispas; formar chispas en el conmutador (de los dínamos, etc.).

sparking-plug, *s.* bujía de encendido.

sparkle [ˈspɑːkəl], *s.* centelleo, destello; brillo; vislumbre. — *v.i.* chispear, rutilar, destellar, centellear, brillar, relucir; ser espumoso (de ciertos vinos).

sparkler, *s.* (*vulg.*) diamante.

sparkling, *a.* brillante, centelleante, rutilante, chispeante; espumoso; *sparkling wine*, vino espumante.

sparrow [ˈspærou], *s.* gorrión, pardal.

sparrow-grass, *s.* (*fam.*) espárrago.

sparrow-hawk, *s.* gavilán, esparaván.

sparry [ˈspɑːri], *a.* espático, que contiene espato.

sparse [spɑːs], *a.* poco denso, esparcido, desparramado, ralo, claro.

sparsely, *adv.* aquí y allá, a grandes trechos, con poca densidad.

sparsity [ˈspɑːsiti], *s.* rareza; parquedad.

Spartan [ˈspɑːtən], *s.*, *a.* espartano, (habitante) de Esparta.

spasm [spæzm], *s.* espasmo, calambre.

spasmodic [spæzˈmɔdik], *a.* espasmódico.

spastic [ˈspæstik], *a.* espasmódico.

spat [spæt], *pret.*, *p.p.* [SPIT]. — *v.t.*, *v.i.* desovar (los mariscos); (*E.U.*) dar palmaditas; reñir ligeramente; batir, azotar (la lluvia). — *s.* huevas de los mariscos; manotada. — *pl.* **spats**, polainas.

spatangus [spəˈtæŋgəs], *s.* (*zool.*) género de erizo de mar de forma de corazon.

spate [speit], *s.* crecida, avenida; (*fig.*) torrente; *in spate*, crecido.

spathe [speiθ], *s.* espata, espádice.

spathic [ˈspæθik], *a.* espático, parecido el espado.

spatial, spacial [ˈspeiʃəl], *a.* del espacio, relativo al espacio.

spatter [ˈspætəɹ], *v.t.*, *v.i.* salpicar; regar, rociar, esparcir; manchar con agua sucia; (*fig.*) manchar, difamar, quitar la fama. — *s.* salpicadura; rociada, rociamiento.

spatterdashes [ˈspætəɹdæʃiz], *s.pl.* polainas.

spatula [ˈspætjuːlə], *s.* espátula.

spatulate, *a.* espatulado, en forma de espátula.

spavin [ˈspævin], *s.* (*vet.*) esparaván.

spawn [spɔːn], *s.* (*ict.*) freza, huevas; pececillos; (*despec.*) producto, fruto, resultado; (*vulg.*) hijo, hijos. — *v.t.*, *v.i.* (*ict.*) poner huevos (de los peces, etc.), desovar, frezar; (*despec.*) producir en abundancia, engendrar, procrear.

spawner, *s.f.* pez hembra.

spawning, *s.* freza, desove; *spawning time*, desove.

spay [spei], *v.t.* castrar (las hembras de los animales).

speak [spiːk], *v.t.*, *v.i.* (*pret.* **spoke**, (*ant.*) **spake**; *p.p.* **spoken**) hablar, decir; pronunciar; conversar; sonar; dirigirse (a uno); llamar (un buque a otro) con bocina; *to speak to*, (*fam.*) echar un sermón a, poner de oro y azul, reprender; *to speak one's mind*, decir lo que se piensa, hablar en plata; *to speak out*, hablar en romance, hablar claro; *to speak for*, hablar a favor de, hablar en nombre de; ser prueba de; *to speak for oneself*, hablar por sí mismo; *to speak for itself*, (*fig.*) ser manifiesto; *to speak thick*, hablar con media lengua; *to speak up*, elevar la voz, hablar en voz alta; decir claridades; *to speak through the nose*, ganguear, hablar gangoso; *so to speak*, por decirlo así; *to speak fair*, hablar bien de.

speakable [ˈspiːkəbəl], *a.* decible, capaz de decirse.

speak-easy, *s.* (*E.U.*) tienda de licor ilícito.

speaker [ˈspiːkəɹ], *s.* el que habla; orador; (*E.U.*) libro de declamación; presidente de un cuerpo cualquiera; *Speaker of the House of Commons*, Presidente de la Cámara de los Comunes.

speakership, *s.* presidencia de una asamblea legislativa.

speaking, *a.* parlante, hablante, que habla, para hablar; *speaking likeness*, retrato viviente; *speaking-trumpet*, bocina, portavoz; *speaking-tube*, tubo acústico; *they are not on speaking terms*, no se conocen sino de vista; no se hablan. — *s.* habla, discurso; declamación.

spear [spiəɹ], *s.* lanza; venablo, azagaya; (*poét.*) lancero; árpon de pesca; (*bot.*) brizna. — *v.t.* alancear, atravesar con arpón. — *v.i.* brotar.

spear-grass, *s.* hierba de los prados.

spear-head, *s.* punta de lanza.

spearmint [ˈspiəɹmint], *s.* hierbabuena punit-aguda, menta verde.

spearwood, *s.* eucalipto; acacia.

spearwort, *s.* especie de ranúnculo.

special [ˈspeʃəl], *a.* especial; extraordinario, singular; particular; específico.

specialist [ˈspeʃəlist], *s.* especialista, *m.f.*

speciality [speʃiˈæliti], *s.* especialidad; rasgo característico, peculiaridad.

specialize [ˈspeʃəlaiz], *v.t.* especializar. — *v.i.* especializarse.

specialness, *s.* especialidad.

specialty [ˈspeʃəlti], *s.* especialidad; (*for.*) obligacion firmada formalmente.

specie [ˈspiːʃiː], *s.* dinero contante, efectivo, moneda, metálico, numerario.

species [ˈspiːʃiːz], *s.* (*pl.* **species**) (*biol.*, *lóg.*)

especie, *f.*; clase, *f.*, variedad, género; naturaleza, forma.

specific [spe'sifik], *a.* específico; expreso, explícito; especificado, determinado; distinto; peculiar; (*med.*) específico; *specific gravity*, peso específico; *specific heat*, calor específico. — *s.* (*med.*) específico.

specification [spesifi'keiʃən], *s.* especificación; mención.

specificness [spe'sifiknis], *s.* carácter específico.

specify ['spesifai], *v.t.* especificar, detallar, mencionar específicamente, particularizar; determinar.

specimen ['spesimən], *s.* espécimen; ejemplo; muestra; *specimen-book*, muestrario.

speciology [spi:ʃi'olodʒi], *s.* especiología.

specious ['spi:ʃəs], *a.* especioso.

speciousness, *s.* carácter especioso; apariencia engañosa.

speck [spek], **speckle** ['spekəl], *s.* manchita, motita, mácula, señal, *f.*, lunar; nube (*f.*) en un ojo, punto, pizca, átomo, partícula; grasa de ballena, etc. — *v.t.* abigarrar, jaspear, manchar, motear, espolvorear.

spectacle ['spektəkəl], *s.* espectáculo; exhibición, exposición; escena. — *pl.* **spectacles**, anteojos, gafas.

spectacled, *a.* que lleva (o usa) gafas o anteojos.

spectacular [spek'tækju:lər], *a.* espectacular, aparatoso.

spectator [spek'teitər], *s.* espectador.

spectatress, *s.* espectadora.

spectral ['spektrəl], *a.* espectral; (*ópt.*) espectral.

spectre ['spektər], *s.* espectro, fantasma, *m.*; duende.

spectrology [spek'trolodʒi], *s.* espectrología.

spectroscope ['spektroskoup], *s.* espectroscopio.

spectroscopic, *a.* espectroscópico.

spectrum ['spektrəm], *s.* (*ópt.*) espectro; imagen o espectro ocular.

specular ['spekju:lər], *a.* especular, limpio, terso; *specular stone*, mica.

speculate ['spekju:leit], *v.t.*, *v.i.* especular, contemplar, meditar, considerar, reflexionar; (*com.*) especular.

speculation, *s.* especulación; teoría; (*com.*) especulación.

speculative ['spekju:lətiv], *a.* especulativo; pensativo, contemplativo; teórico; (*com.*) especulador.

speculativeness, *s.* carácter especulativo.

speculator ['spekju:leitər], *s.* especulador; teórico; (*teat.*) revendedor de billetes.

speculum ['spekju:ləm], *s.* (*cir.*) espéculum; (*ópt.*) espejo.

sped [sped], *pret., p.p.* [SPEED].

speech [spi:tʃ], *s.* palabra; lenguaje; habla; oración, discurso; conversación (*teat.*) parlamento; idioma, *m.*, dialecto, lengua; (*pol.*) *King's speech* (*from the throne*), discurso de la Corona; *after-dinner speech*, brindis.

speechify ['spi:tʃifai], *v.i.* (*fam.*) arengar.

speechless, *a.* mudo; cortado, callado, sobrecogido, turbado, sin habla; desconcertado.

speechlessness ['spi:tʃlesnes], *s.* mudez; turbación.

speech-maker, *s.* orador, persona que hace arengas.

speed [spi:d], *v.t.* (*pret., p.p.* **sped, speeded**) ayudar, dar ayuda, favorecer; despedir, acompañar; expedir, despachar, acelerar, resolver, apresurar, avivar, dar prisa; hacer salir bien, hacer que tenga buen éxito una cosa. — *v.i.* (*pret., p.p.* **sped**) correr, moverse con presteza, andar rápidamente, darse prisa, apresurarse; adelantar, progresar, prosperar, acertar, medrar, salir bien, tener buen éxito; marchar con velocidad excesiva. — *s.* rapidez; presteza, prontitud; velocidad; prisa; diligencia, apresuramiento; *speedometer*, cuentakilómetros; *speed-way*, pista de ceniza; *speed limit*, velocidad máxima; límite de velocidad; *with all speed*, a toda prisa, con toda celeridad; *full speed*, galope, carrera tendida; *at full speed*, a toda velocidad; a carrera tendida, a rienda suelta, a todo correr; *to make speed*, acelerarse, apresurarse, hacer diligencia.

speed-boat, *s.* lancha de carrera.

speediness ['spi:dinis], *s.* celeridad, rapidez, velocidad; diligencia, prontitud, prisa.

speedwell ['spi:dwel], *s.* verónica.

speedy ['spi:di], *a.* ligero, rápido, veloz; presuroso; diligente, pronto.

speleology, *s.* espeleología.

spell [spel], *s.* hechizo, ensalmo, encanto; orden, turno, tanda, revezo; arrobamiento, fascinación; (*fam.*) poco tiempo, período, rato, temporada; astilla; travesaño de silla; *by spells*, por turnos, a ratos. — *v.t.* (*pret., p.p.* **spelt**) deletrear; descifrar; significar; encantar, hechizar; revezar, reemplazar, relevar; *to spell out*, deletrear poco a poco; *how do you spell . . .?* ¿cómo se escribe . . .? — *v.i.* saber deletrear, escribir con buena ortografía.

spellbind ['spelbaind], *v.t.* encantar, conjurar.

spellbound, *a.* fascinado, encantado.

speller, *s.* deletreador, persona que deletrea.

spelling, *s.* acción de deletrear, deletreo, ortografía, manera de deletrear.

spelling-book, *s.* cartilla, abecedario.

spelt [spelt], *pret., p.p.* [SPELL].

spelter, *s.* (*com.*) cinc; peltre.

spelt-wheat, *s.* escanda, espelta.

Spencerian [spen'siəriən], *a.* referente a Herbert Spencer.

Spencerism ['spensərizm], *s.* sistema filosófico de Herbert Spencer.

spend [spend], *v.t.* (*pret., p.p.* **spent**) gastar; emplear el dinero en; expender; consumir; agotar, fatigar, cansar; disipar, malgastar, echar a perder; ocupar, pasar, emplear; *to spend a mast*, (*mar.*) perder un palo; *spend time*, pasar tiempo; haraganear. — *v.i.* gastar dinero, hacer gastos; gastarse, consumirse.

spender, *s.* persona que gasta, gastador.

spendthrift ['spendθrift], *s.* pródigo, maniroto, malgastador, derrochador.

spent, *pret., p.p.* [SPEND].

sperm [spə:m], *s.* esperma, semen; esperma de ballena.

spermaceti [spə.rmə'seti], *s.* esperma de ballena.

spermaceti-oil, *s.* aceite de esperma.

spermatic [spə.r'mætik], *a.* espermático.

spermatize, *v.i.* arrojar esperma.

spermatology [spəɹmə'tɔlodʒi], s. espermatología.

spermatorrhœa [spəɹməto'riːə], s. espermatorrea.

spermatozoon [spəɹməto'zouон], s. espermatozoide.

sperm-oil, s. aceite de esperma.

spermology [spəɹ'mɔlodʒi], s. espermatología.

sperm-whale, s. cachalote.

spew [spjuː], v.t., v.i. vomitar, arrojar. — s. vómito.

spewer, s. persona que vomita.

spewing, s. vómito.

sphacelate ['sfæseleit], v.t., v.i. gangrenar(se), esfacelar(se).

sphacelus ['sfæseləs], s. esfacelo.

sphagnous ['sfægnəs], a. esfagnoso, esfeñoso.

sphenoid ['sfenɔid], a. esfenoidal. — s. (anat.) esfenoides.

spheral ['sfiərəl], a. esférico; perteneciente a las esferas celestes.

sphere [sfiəɹ], s. esfera; globo, orbe; (geom.) esfera; sphere of influence, zona de influencia. — v.t. colocar en una esfera; rodear, abarcar; redondear, poner redondo.

spherical ['sferikəl], a. esférico; celestial.

sphericity [sfe'risiti], s. forma esférica, esfericidad, redondez, rotundidad.

spheroid ['sferɔid], s. esferoide.

spheroidal [sfe'rɔidəl], a. esferoidal.

spherule ['sferjuːl], s. esférula, glóbulo.

sphincter ['sfiŋktəɹ], s. esfínter.

sphinx, s. esfinge, f.; sphinx-like, (ent.) esfíngido.

sphygmic ['sfigmik], a. esfígmico; pulsátil.

sphygmograph ['sfigmogræf], s. esfigmógrafo.

sphygmomanometer [sfigmomə'nɔmetəɹ], s. esfigmómetro.

spical ['spaikəl], **spicate** ['spaikeit], **spicated** [spai'keitid], a. (bot.) espigado, espiciforme, dispuesto en espigas; (orn.) espolonado.

spice [spais], s. especia; (fig.) saborete, picante; dejo; (poét.) olor, fragancia, aroma, perfume; (fig.) flor y nata. — pl. spices, especiería; spice-bag, churla; spice-bush, benjuí. — v.t. (coc.) especiar, echar especias, sazonar, o condimentar con especias; (fig.) dar gusto (o picante) a.

spicery ['spaisəri], s. especiería, droguería; dispensa; carácter aromático; picante.

spick-and-span [spikənd'spæn], a. más limpio que una patena; pulcro; flamante (nuevo).

spicknel ['spiknel], s. tuero, pinillo oloroso.

spicular ['spaikjuːləɹ], a. agudo, puntiagudo; picante, mordaz.

spicule ['spaikjuːl], s. espiguilla, espina; (zool.) púa; (bot.) espiguita. — pl. spicules, agujas de la escarcha (o del hielo).

spicy ['spaisi], a. que contiene (o sabe a) especias; que abunda en (o lleno de) especias; especiado, aromático; (fig.) sabroso, picante.

spider ['spaidəɹ], s. araña; cazo con pies; spider's web, telaraña; spider-line, hilo de tela de araña para micrómetros.

spider-crab, s. cangrejo marino, araña de mar.

spider-wort, s. pasajera.

spidery, a. parecido a una araña.

spigot ['spigət], s. canilla, espiche, espita; tapón de espita; llave (f.) de fuente.

spike [spaik], s. (bot.) espiga de grano; espliego, alhucema; alcayata, clavo largo, espigón, perno. — v.i. clavar (o sujetar) con

alcayatas, espigones, etc.; empernar, aguzar, enclavijar; clavetear; (mil.) clavar (un cañón).

spikelet ['spaiklet], s. espiguita, espiguilla; espiga secundaria.

spikenard ['spaiknɑːɹd], s. espicanardo; nardo.

spiky ['spaiki], a. erizado, puntiagudo; armado de púas; claveteado.

spile [spail], v.t. horadar un barril y ponerle espita o tapón; clavar estacas o pilotes. — s. pilote (estaca); tarugo; espiche, clavija; (E.U.) llave de sangrar el arce azucarero.

spill [spil], s. astilla, calvija; pajuela, clavillo, mecha; (fam.) vuelco; derramamiento; spillway, aliviadero, bocacaz, vertedero (aljibe, presa, etc.); spilling-lines, (mar.) trapas de las velas. — v.t. (pret., p.p. **spilled, spilt**) derramar, desparramar, verter, dejar caer, esparcir; arrojar, volcar; desperdiciar, destruir, disipar, malbaratar; (mar.) apagar, descargar (el viento del seno de una vela para aferrarla). — v.i. derramarse, volcarse, verterse; rebosar; to spill the beans, (fam.) soltar el gato.

spiller, s. sedal (de caña de pescar).

spin [spin], v.t. (pret. **spun, span**; p.p. **spun**) hilar; retorcer, hacer girar; to spin out, alargar, prolongar; (fig.) parlotear, contar; (aer.) entrar (o caer) en barrena; to spin a yarn, contar un cuento; to spin out a speech, hacer un discurso muy largo. — v.i. hilar, correr hilo a hilo, girar. — s. giro, vuelta; (fam.) paseo, vuelta (en automóvil o bicicleta); (aer.) barrena.

spinach ['spinidʒ], s. espinaca.

spinal ['spainəl], a. espinal. — s. spinal column, columna vertebral, espinazo; spinal cord or marrow, médula espinal.

spindle ['spindəl], s. huso, broca; (mec.) gorrón, eje, carretel, torno, astil, aguja, peón, árbol; (mar.) pínola, fierro, maza; (fig.) persona larga y delgada. — v.i. (bot.) crecer (un tallo) muy alto y delgado.

spindle-legged, spindle-shanked, a. zanquivano.

spindle-shaped, a. ahusado, fusiforme.

spindle-tree, s. bonetero.

spindrift ['spindrift], s. rocío del mar.

spine [spain], s. espinazo, espina dorsal; (bot.) espina, púa delgada; (impr.) lomo de un libro.

spinel, s. espinela.

spinet [spi'net], s. espineta.

spiniferous [spai'nifərəs], a. espinoso, espinigero, espinoso.

spinnaker ['spinəkəɹ], s. ala (o arrastradera) grande para yates de regata.

spinner ['spinəɹ], s. hilador, hilandero, hilandera; máquina de hilar; araña de jardín.

spinneret ['spinəret], s. (ent.) fileras, órgano hilandero (de las arañas y gusanos de seda).

spinney ['spini], s. bosquecito, arboleda.

spinning ['spiniŋ], s. hila, hilado, hilatura, arte de hilar; spinning-wheel, torno de hilar; spinning-jenny, máquina de hilar; spinning tackle, curricán; spinning top, peonza, trompo; spinning-mule, máquina de hilar.

spinose ['spainous], a. espinoso.

spinosity [spai'nɔsiti], s. dificultad, enredo, perplejidad, cosa espinosa.

Spinozism [spi'nouzizm], s. espinosismo.
spinster ['spinstəɪ], s. soltera, solterona; (ant.) hilandera.
spiny ['spaini], a. espinoso, espíneo, de espinas; penoso, difícil.
spiracle ['spairəkəl], s. respiradero de un insecto o cetáceo; ventosa.
Spiræa [spai'riə], s. espíreas.
spiral ['spaiərəl], a. espiral, helicoidal. — s. (geom.) espira; espiral, f.; hélice, f.; (aer.) vuelo en espiral.
spiral-shaped, a. acaracolado.
spirant ['spaiərənt], s. consonante, continua.
spiration [spai'reiʃən], s. espiramiento.
spire ['spaiəɪ], s. (arq.) aguja, chapitel; cúspide, f., ápice, cima; brizna de hierba; espira, espiral, f., caracol. — v.t. edificar con chapitel. — v.i. rematar en punta; germinar.
spirit ['spirit], s. espíritu; ánima, alma; ánimo, energía, aliento, brío, esfuerzo, denuedo; agudeza; espectro, aparecido, sombra, fantasma, m.; fortaleza, grandeza de alma; humor, carácter, temple, temperamento; genio, talento, ingenio; motivo, móvil; verdadero sentido; espíritu de vino, alcohol; extracto, quinta esencia. — pl. **spirits**, espíritus; licor, aguardiente; alegría, viveza, vivacidad; humor, buen humor; spirits of wine, alcohol; wood spirit, éter piroleñoso, alcohol metílico; low spirits, abatimiento; high spirits, alegría, vivacidad; animal spirits, energía, fogosidad; to show spirit, mostrarse resuelto, mostrar buen ánimo; to have a high spirit, tener el alma grande; ser altivo; to lose one's spirits, amilanarse; to keep (up) one's spirits, mantener el valor; spirit-lamp, lámpara de alcohol; spirit-level, nivel de aire; the Holy Spirit, el Espíritu Santo. — v.t. to spirit, spirit off, spirit away, arrebatar, llevarse; (ant.) alentar, animar, incitar, dar espíritu.
spirited, a. vivo, fogoso, brioso; valiente, espiritoso, varonil, animoso, arrebatado; high-spirited, de alma grande, magnánimo; low-spirited, abatido, amilanado; mean-spirited, de ánimo estrecho, mezquino, miserable.
spiritedness, s. arrebato, calor, ardor, energía; valor, corazón; vigor, fuerza, brío, vivacidad, ánimo.
spiritism ['spiritizm], s. espiritismo.
spiritist, s. espiritista, m.f.
spiritless ['spiritles], a. abatido, amilanado; insípido, sin vigor, sin espíritu, sin carácter, sin imaginación; exánime, muerto.
spiritlessness, s. amilanamiento, abatimiento, falta de vigor o energía.
spiritous ['spiritəs], a. espiritoso, espirituoso, refinado, destilado.
spiritual ['spiritju:əl], a. espiritual; inmaterial, incorpóreo; santo, puro; mental, intelectual; místico; piadoso, religioso; eclesiástico; espiritista.
spiritualism ['spiritju:əlizm], s. espiritismo; espiritualismo; espiritualidad.
spiritualist ['spiritju:əlist], s. espiritista, m.f.; espiritualista, m.f.
spiritualistic [spiritju:ə'listik], a. espiritista.
spirituality [spiritju:'æliti], s. espiritualidad, inmaterialidad; bienes espirituales o eclesiásticos.
spiritualization, s. acto de espiritualizar.

spiritualize, v.t. espiritualizar; vivificar, animar.
spirituous ['spiritju:əs], a. espiritoso, espirituoso, destilado, refinado, embriagante, ardiente.
spirituousness, s. calidad de espirituoso.
spirt [spə:ɪt], [SPURT].
spissated ['spisətid], a. espesado.
spit [spit], v.t. (pret., p.p. **spat**, (ant.) **spit**) escupir; esputar; arrojar. — v.i. escupir; chisporrotear; caer en gotas. — v.t. (pret., p.p. **spitted**) (coc.) espetar; ensartar. — s. asador, espetón; saliva; salivazo, escupidura, escupitajo; lengua de tierra, banco de arena; espuma o huevos de ciertos insectos.
spitch-cock ['spitʃkɔk], s. anguila tajada y asada. — v.t. tajar y asar (anguilas, etc.).
spite [spait], s. rencor, despecho, ojeriza, odio, mala voluntad; (in) spite of, a pesar de, a despecho de, no obstante, contra la voluntad de. — v.t. causar (o mostrar) indignación o resentimiento, vejar, dar pique, dar pesar.
spiteful ['spaitful], a. rencoroso, malévolo, enconoso, maligno, malicioso.
spitefulness, s. despecho, rencor, malevolencia, malignidad, malicia, encono.
spitfire ['spitfaiəɪ], s. fierabrás; cascarrabias, m.f.; fiera.
spitter, s. el que espeta; escupidor; gamezno.
spittle ['spitəl], s. saliva, salivazo, esputo, escupido, gargajo.
spittoon [spi'tu:n], s. escupidera.
spitz [spits], s. perro de Pomerania.
splanchnic ['splæŋknik], a. esplácnico, relativo a las vísceras. — s. nervio esplánico.
splanchnology [splæŋk'nɔlodʒi], s. esplanalogía.
splash [splæʃ], v.t. salpicar, hacer saltar (el agua), rociar, enlodar; humedecer, chapotear. — v.i. chapotear, chapalear. — s. salpicadura, rociada; chapateo, chapaleo; to make a splash, (fam.) causar una sensación.
splash-board, s. alero, guardabarros.
splashy, a. cenagoso, sucio, lodoso, húmedo.
splatter ['splætəɪ], v.t., v.i. chapotear, guachapear, chapalear, chapurrear; hablar entre dientes.
splay [splei], v.t. hacer en chaflán, achaflanar, descantear; (vet.) despaldar, despaldillar (a un caballo). — a. extendido, ancho, desplegado, pesado. — s. (arq.) alféizar, derrame; chaflán, bisel.
splay-foot, splay-footed, a. zancajoso.
splay-mouth, a. boquiancho.
spleen [spli:n], s. (anat.) bazo; rencor, mal humor, resentimiento; tristeza; esplín, melancolía, hipocondría; to vent one's spleen, descargar la bilis.
spleened, a. privado del bazo.
spleenful, a. bilioso, colérico, regañón, adusto, enfadoso; melancólico, triste.
spleenwort ['spli:nwə:ɪt], s. escolopendra, doradillo, culantrillo.
spleeny, a. triste, bilioso, melancólico; irritable, enfadadizo.
splendent ['splendənt], a. esplendente; resplandeciente.
splendid ['splendid], a. resplandeciente, brillante; espléndido, magnífico, grandioso; glorioso, heroico, ilustre; splendid! ¡estupendo!

splendour ['splendəɹ], *s.* brillantez, resplandor, refulgencia; esplendor; pompa, magnificencia, esplendidez, gloria.

splenetic [sple'netik], *a.* bilioso, atrabilioso, atrabiliario, melancólico; regañón. — *s.* persona enferma del esplín; medicina para enfermos del bazo.

splenic ['splenik], *a.* esplénico.

splenius ['spli:niəs], *s.* esplenio.

splenotomy [splen'ɔtomi], *s.* esplenotomía.

splice [splais], *v.t.* ayustar, empalmar; empotrar, juntar, unir; (*fam.*) casar, unir en matrimonio; *to splice the main-brace,* (*mar.*) servir una ración de ron; beber. — *s.* (*mar.*) ayuste, gaza, empalme, costura; (*cine*) juntura de una cinta rota; *long-splice,* costura larga, ayuste largo; *short-splice,* empalmadura, costura corta; *eye-splice,* (*mar.*) costura de ojo.

splicing, *s.* ayuste, empalme; *splicing-fid,* (*mar.*) pasador.

splint [splint], *v.t.* (*cir.*) entablillar. — *s.* tira plana y delgada; astilla; (*cir.*) tablilla; (*vet.*) sobrehueso; *splint-bone,* (*vet.*) hueso metacarpiano (caballos).

splinter ['splintəɹ], *v.t.* astillar, hacer astillas, hender en pedazos; (*cir.*) entablillar, entabletar. — *v.i.* romperse en astillas, hacerse pedazos. — *s.* astilla, cacho, esquirla, brizna; rancajo o astilla de madera clavada en la carne; astillazo; *splinter-bar,* (*carr.*) balancín.

split [split], *v.t.* (*pret.,* *p.p.* **split**) hender, dividir, partir, cuartear, estrellar, rajar, resquebrar, separar a lo largo; (*fig.*) desunir, introducir discordia; *to split the difference,* partir la diferencia. — *v.i.* romperse, henderse, rajarse, partirse, dividirse a lo largo, grietarse, cuartearse, resquebrajarse; estallar; separarse en dos o más partidos; *to split* (o *to split one's sides*) *with laughing,* reventar de risa, despedazarse de risa; *to split on,* denunciar, delatar. — *s.* hendidura, hendedura, raja, grieta, quebraja, resquebradura, cuarteadura; cisma, división, rompimiento; *split nut,* tuerca hendida; *split pin,* chaveta hendida. — *a.* hendido, rajado, partido, cuarteado; curado (pescado).

splitter, *s.* persona que raja o hiende, hendedor.

splodge [splɔdʒ], **splotch,** *s.* mancha, manchita, borrón.

splurge [splə:ɹdʒ], *v.i.* fachendear, hacer gran papel, hacer alarde. — *s.* fachenda, ostentación vana.

splutter ['splʌtəɹ], *v.t.,* *v.i.* balbucear; farfullar; chisporrotear. — *s.* balbuceo; chisporroteo; baraúnda, barullo, confusión.

spoil [spɔil], *v.t.* (*pret.,* *p.p.* **spoilt, spoiled**) estropear, echar a perder, debaratar; corromper, pervertir, arruinar, podrir; ajar, destruir la utilidad de, deteriorar, inutilizar; mimar, malcriar, consentir; saquear, despojar, robar. — *v.i.* inutilizarse, estropearse, corromperse, dañarse, echarse a perder; hacer pillaje, ir al saqueo, robar; *spoiled* (o *spoilt*) *child,* niño mimado, gachón, mal criado. — *s.* saqueo, robo, pillaje; despojo, botín; tierra excavada; (*min.*) estériles, *m.pl.* — *pl.* (*E.U.,* *fam.*) enchufes.

spoiler, *s.* desposeedor, despojador, robador, ladrón; corruptor, consentidor, pervertidor.

spoke [spouk], *s.* (*carr.*) rayo; galga, retranca; escalón, travesaño, peldaño; (*mar.*) cabilla del timón; *to put a spoke in one's wheel,* (*fig.*) impedir que uno haga una cosa. — *v.t.* (*carr.*) enrayar, poner rayos a; *spoke-shave,* rebajador de rayos.

spoke, spoken, *pret.,* *p.p.* [SPEAK].

spokesman ['spoukzmən], *s.* portavoz.

spoliation [spouli'eiʃən], *s.* despojo, rapiña; (*for.*) expoliación.

spoliator, *s.* expoliador.

spondaic [spɔn'deiik], *a.* espondaico.

spondee [spɔn'di:], *s.* espondeo.

spondyl ['spɔndil], *s.* espóndil, espóndilo; vértebra.

spondylitis [spɔndi'laitis], *s.* espondilosis, *f.*

sponge [spʌndʒ], *s.* esponja; (*arti.*) lanada, escobillón; (*fig.*) gorrista, *m.f.,* mogollón; *sponge-cake,* bizcocho; *sponge-tree,* cuje; *to throw up the sponge,* darse por vencido. — *v.t.* mojar, limpiar o borrar con esponja, esponjar; (*fig.*) chasquear, comer de gorra, chupar, meterse de mogollón; escobillonar. — *v.i.* embeberse; pescar (o recoger) esponjas; vivir (o comer) de gorra.

spongelet ['spʌndʒlet], *s.* esponja pequeña, esponjita; (*bot.*) espongiola.

sponger ['spʌndʒəɹ], *s.* sablista, *m.f.;* gorrista, *m.f.,* gorrón, mogollón.

sponginess, *s.* esponjosidad.

sponging, *s.* gorronería, socaliña, estafa, pillería; limpiamiento, limpiadura.

spongiole ['spʌndʒioul], *s.* espongiola.

spongy ['spʌndʒi], **spongeous, spongious,** *a.* esponjoso, esponjado; lleno de poros, fofo; embebido, empapado.

sponsion ['spɔnʃən], *s.* fianza, acto de salir fiador por otro.

sponson ['spɔnsən], *s.* barbeta lateral saliente de los buques de guerra; (*aer.*) flotadores de las alas de un hidroavión.

sponsor ['spɔnsəɹ], *s.* fiador; padrino o madrina.

spontaneity [spɔntə'ni:iti], *s.* espontaneidad.

spontaneous [spɔn'teiniəs], *a.* espontáneo; voluntario; natural; esporádico.

spontaneousness, *s.* espontaneidad.

spontoon [spɔn'tu:n], *s.* espontón.

spook [spu:k], *s.* (*fam.*) fantasma, *m.,* aparición, aparecido.

spool [spu:l], *s.* canilla, carrete, carretel. — *v.t.* ovillar, encanillar, devanar, encañar.

spoom [spu:m], *v.i.* navegar a toda vela; ir o correr de prisa.

spoon [spu:n], *s.* cuchara; *tea-spoon,* cucharilla; *dessert-spoon,* cucharilla de postre; *table-spoon,* cuchara grande; *spoon-bait, spoon-hook,* anzuelo de cuchara. — *v.t.* sacar (o alzar) con cuchara. — *v.i.* usar una cuchara, pescar con anzuelo de cuchara; estar amartelado, requebrar, hacer cocos, estar enamorado.

spoonbill, *s.* espátula, ave de cuchara.

spoonful, *s.* cucharada.

spoonwort, *s.* coclearia.

spoony, *a.* (*fam.*) amartelado, acaramelado. — *s.* galán meloso.

spoor [spuəɹ], *s.* rastro, pista, huella de animal salvaje. — *v.i.* seguir el rastro o la pista.

sporadic [spɔ'rædik], *a.* (*med.*) esporádico, aislado, solo.

spore [spɔ:ɹ], *s.* (*bot.,* *biol.*) espora; organismo diminuto, germen.

sport [spɔ:ɹt], *s.* deporte; recreación, pasatiempo, placer, diversión; certamen de fuerza o destreza; cacería; broma, burla, chanza, chacota, chirigota; juguete, hazmerreír; objeto de broma; (*fam.*) aficionado a algún deporte; (*biol.*) animal o planta que exhibe variación espontánea del tipo normal; buen muchacho; *to make sport of*, burlarse de; *field-sports*, diversiones del campo, caza. — *v.i.* divertirse, alegrar(se), jugar, holgar, regocijarse, chancear(se), estar de chunga (o burla), bromear; (*biol.*) variar espontáneamente del tipo normal. — *v.t.* lucir, ostentar, estrenar, hacer alarde de.

sportful, *a.* (*ant.*) alegre, festivo, agradable, placentero, chistoso, retozón.

sportfulness, *s.* (*ant.*) diversión; buen humor, humor alegre, temperamento divertido.

sporting, *a.* de caza; de juego; perteneciente (o relativo) a cualquier deporte; *sporting man*, aficionado a algún deporte; (*fig.*) buen muchacho; *sporting chance*, posibilidad de éxito.

sportingness, sportiveness, *s.* retozo, alegría, festividad, holganza, temperamento de buen muchacho.

sportive [ˈspɔːtiv], *a.* juguetón, retozón, festivo, alegre, placentero, aficionado a bromear, chistoso.

sportless, *a.* sin diversión, sin gana de jugar.

sportsman [ˈspɔːtsmən], *s.* aficionado a algún deporte, deportista, *m.f.*; cazador; (*fam.*) caballero cumplido.

sportsmanlike, *a.* aficionado al deporte; conforme a las reglas del juego.

sportsmanship [ˈspɔːtsmənʃip], *s.* arte y pericia en el deporte, etiqueta de los deportes.

sportswoman [ˈspɔːtswumən], *s.* mujer aficionada a los deportes.

sporty, *a.* divertido; retozón; picante.

sporule [ˈspɔːrjuːl], *s.* espora, espora pequeña.

spot [spɔt], *s.* sitio, lugar, paraje, puesto, parte, *f.*, punto; mancilla, mácula, desgracia, baldón, deshonra, ignominia; mancha, borrón, maca, lunar, pinta, palo (de baraja); tacha; *on the spot*, en el sitio mismo, (*fam.*) en el acto, inmediatamente, puntual, alerta; *to put on the spot*, pegar un tiro a; *spot cash*, contante y sonante, al contado; *spot-light*, (*teat.*) foco de luz individual; *in spots*, (*fam.*) aquí y allí. — *v.t.* abigarrar, motear, manchar, tachonar, macular; mancillar, desdorar, deslustrar, corromper, mudar, alterar; (*fam.*) marcar, señalar, observar, distinguir, notar; poner en posición (una bola de billar). — *v.i.* salir (manchas).

spotless, *a.* limpio, sin mancha, inmaculado.

spotlessness, *s.* pulcritud; inocencia.

spotlight, *s.* proyector; luz del proyector.

spotted, *a.*, *p.p.* manchado, ensuciado con manchas, moteado, pintojo, mosqueado; apulgarado; esquizado (mármol); *spotted fever*, meningitis cerebroespinal, *f.*; tabardillo pintado (tifus exantemático).

spotter, *s.* persona que mancha, motea, etc.; vigilante.

spottiness, *s.* estado de tener manchas.

spotty, *a.* lleno de manchas; manchado.

spousal [ˈspauzəl], *a.* (*poét.*) nupcial, conyugal. — *s.pl.* nupcias, bodas, desposorio, casamiento.

spouse [spauz], *s.* esposo, esposa.

spouseless, *a.* soltero, viudo; sin esposo, sin esposa.

spout [spaut], *s.* caño, tubo, pitón, conducto, cañería, surtidor; canilla de tonel, espita; canalón, gárgola; cuello (de vasija); pico (de cafetera, de tetera); chorro; *rain-spout*, chaparrón, turbión; *water-spout*, surtidor; tromba o manga marina, remolino; *to put up the spout*, (*fam.*) dar en prenda, empeñar. — *v.t.*, *v.i.* arrojar, echar (un líquido); salir, saltar, hacer salir; surgir, borbotar, brotar, chorrear, correr a chorro; (*fam.*) soltar el rollo; hacer un discurso; *to spout up*, resaltar.

sprain [sprein], *v.t.* torcer(se) violentamente. — *s.* (*med.*) torcedura, torcimiento, relajación.

sprang [spræŋ], *pret.* [SPRING].

sprat [spræt], *s.* sardineta; arenque pequeño.

sprawl [sprɔːl], *v.t.* tender(se) a la larga; recostarse (en); (*agr.*) desparramarse. — *s.* acto de caer (o tenderse) sin gracia; posición poco graciosa; desparramamiento.

spray [sprei], *v.t.*, *v.i.* rociar, esparcir en menudas gotas, pulverizar (un líquido). — *s.* rociada, rocío; espuma del mar; rociador, pulverizador; ramita, ramaje menudo.

sprayer, *s.* rociador, pulverizador.

spread [spred], *v.t.* (*pret.*, *p.p.* **spread**) tender, extender, desplegar, alargar, desarrollar, desenvolver; difundir, desparramar, derramar, esparcir; publicar, divulgar; diseminar, propagar, propalar; exhibir; poner a la vista; dar una capa de, untar con; alejar; poner (la mesa), preparar; separar, apartar; (*impr.*) espaciar. — *v.i.* extenderse, alargarse, desplegarse; desparramarse, esparcirse; cundir, exhalarse, propagarse, desarrollarse, difundirse; apartarse, separarse; *to spread over*, cubrir (o untar) con; *to spread abroad*, esparcir, divulgar, propalar; *to spread oneself*, (*fam.*) echar el resto; *to spread the table*, poner la mesa. — *a.* extendido; (*joy.*) de poco brillo. — *s.* extensión, dilatación, amplitud; propagación, diseminación; ámbito; desarrollo; colcha (o cobertor) de cama; tapete de mesa, mantel; (*fam.*) festín, banquete; (*com.*) operación de bolsa con opción de compra o venta.

spreadeagle, *v.t.* espanzurrar; (*fig.*) desparramar.

spreader, *s.* esparcidor; divulgador; propagador; separador.

spreading, *a.* ancho, extenso; (*bot.*) divergente, frondoso (de un árbol).

spree [spriː], *v.i.* ir de parranda; beber mucho, emborracharse. — *s.* borrachera; franca chela, jarana.

sprig [sprig], *s.* ramita, mugrón, pimpollo, renuevo; puntilla, hita, espiga; vástago. — *v.t.* adornar con ramitas; formar ramajes.

spriggy, *a.* ramoso, lleno de ramitas.

sprightliness [ˈspraitlinis], *s.* viveza, despejo, vivacidad, desenvoltura, alegría.

sprightly [ˈspraitli], *a.* alegre, despejado, despierto, vivaracho, vivo.

spring [spriŋ], *v.t.* (*pret.* **sprang**; *p.p.* **sprung**) soltar (un resorte o muelle); sacar o presentar de golpe; hacer volar, saltar (una mina); rendir (un palo o verga); encorvar, combar, torcer, doblar; (*arq.*) arrancar, vaciar (un arco); pasar saltando; insertar (o meter) una cosa doblándola (o forzándola); pasar por arriba, saltar por encima; ojear, alzar (la caza). — *v.i.* brincar, saltar; brotar, nacer, arrojar, salir, manar (un líquido); presentarse súbitamente; emanar, originarse, tomar su origen, dimanar, venir, provenir; moverse como por resorte; alabearse, combarse, torcerse; elevarse, levantarse; (*arq.*) arrancar (un arco, etc.); *to spring again*, renacer, volver a brotar; *to spring back*, saltar hacia atrás; *to spring at*, lanzarse sobre; saltar a; *to spring away*, saltar a un lado; *to spring forth*, brotar, salir; precipitarse, arrojarse, lanzarse; *to spring up*, brotar, nacer; desarrollarse; *to spring forward*, dispararse, abalanzarse, arrojarse, tirarse, dispararse; *to spring upon*, abalanzarse a; *to spring a leak*, (*mar.*) hacer agua (un buque); *to spring an accusation*, hacer una acusación inesperadamente. — *a.* vernal, primaveral, de primavera. — *s.* primavera; muelle, resorte; brinco, salto, corcovo, bote, respingo; elasticidad, fuerza elástica; reculada, rechazo; entrada de agua, manantial, fuente, *f.*, fontana, surtidor; barloa, tangidera; principio o causa de acción, origen; combadura, alabeo; *spring-back*, lomo plegado (de un libro); *spring-mattress*, colchón de muelles; *spring-board*, trampolín; *spring halt*, cojera de caballo; *spring-latch*, picaporte; *spring water*, agua de manantial, agua de pie; *spring-lock*, cerradura de golpe; *spring-tide*, marea viva, marea del equinoccio vernal; primavera.

springbok ['spriŋbɔk], *s.* gacela del sur de África.

springe [sprindʒ], *s.* lazo, trampa (caza).

springer ['spriŋəɹ], *s.* saltador, brincador; (*arq.*) imposta, cojinete, sotabanco; sillar de arranque; perro ojeador.

springiness ['spriŋinis], *s.* elasticidad, resorte, fuerza elástica.

springtime, *s.* primavera.

springy ['spriŋi], *a.* elástico; lleno de manantiales.

sprinkle ['spriŋkəl], *v.t.* asperjar, rociar, esparcir; empolvar, salpicar, polvorear, despolvorear; regar, desparramar; bautizar rociando. — *v.i.* (*impers.*) caer en gotas, lloviznar, empezar a llover. — *s.* rocío, rociada; poco, pizca.

sprinkler, *s.* rociador, irrigador, regadera; (*igl.*) aspersorio, hisopo; (*arm.*) mangual; rociadura automática.

sprinkling, *s.* rociada, rociadura, aspersión; poco, pizca, migaja; *sprinkling of rain*, llovizna.

sprint [sprint], *v.t.*, *v.i.* (*dep.*) sprintar; correr. — *s.* sprint; carrera.

sprinter, *s.* corredor.

sprit [sprit], *s.* (*mar.*) botavara.

sprite [sprait], *s.* duende, trasgo, hada; espíritu del aire.

spritsail ['spritsəl], *s.* (*mar.*) cebadera.

sprocket ['sprɔket], *s.* diente de rueda; rueda dentada; *sprocket-wheel*, rueda de cabillas; *sprocket-gear*, engranaje de rueda y cadena.

sprout [spraut], *v.t.* hacer germinar (o brotar); quitar los botones (o vástagos). — *v.i.* germinar, retoñar, brotar, entallecer, echar botones (o renuevos), grillarse; crecer; ramificarse, extenderse en ramificaciones. — *s.* vástago, renuevo, grillo, retoño, serpollo, botón. — *pl.* **Brussels sprouts**, bretones.

spruce [spruːs], *a.* apuesto, majo, pulido, peripuesto, lindo. — *s.* (*bot.*) picea, abeto,

pinabete, pruche; *red spruce*, picea roja; *black spruce*, abeto falso (o negro); *Norway spruce*, pinabete, picea de Noruega; *hemlock spruce*, abeto del Canadá. — *v.t.* arreglar, poner elegante; *to spruce oneself up*, vestirse con esmero. — *v.i.* vestirse con esmero, ponerse majo, ponerse elegante.

spruceness, *s.* majeza, garbo, lindeza, gentileza, hermosura.

sprue [spruː], *s.* mazarota; bebedero de molde.

sprung [sprʌŋ], *p.p.* [SPRING]; *sprung mast*, palo rendido.

spry [sprai], *a.* vivo, listo, ágil, activo.

spryness, *s.* agilidad; presteza.

spud [spʌd], *s.* (*agr.*) escarda; especie de pala; horca; (*cir.*) limpiaojos; (*fam.*) patata, papa.

spue [spjuː], *v.t.*, *v.i.* [SPEW].

spume [spjuːm], *s.* espuma; espumarajo. — *v.i.* espumar, echar o hacer espuma.

spumescent [spju:'mesənt], *a.* espumante.

spumous ['spjuːməs], **spumy** ['spjuːmi], *a.* espumoso, espumajoso, espumante.

spun [spʌn], *pret.*, *p.p.* [SPIN]; *spun glass*, *s.* hilacha de vidrio; *spun gold, silver*, *s.* hilo de oro o plata; *spun silk*, *s.* borra de seda hilada.

spunk [spʌŋk], *s.* yesca; (*fam.*) corazón, valor, coraje; enojo.

spunky, *a.* (*fam.*) vivo, valiente, valeroso; enfadadizo, enojadizo.

spun-yarn, *s.* meollar.

spur [spəːɹ], *s.* espuela, acicate; aguijada, aguijón, estímulo; uña puntiaguda; corvejón, espolón del gallo; pincho; (*mar.*) curva, pernada; espolón; (*geog.*) espolón, estribo; (*arq.*) riostra, botarel, contrafuerte, machón, puntal, pilar; (*bot.*) espuela; *spur-gear*, *spur-wheel*, rueda dentada; *spur-gearing*, engranaje de ruedas dentadas; *on the spur of the moment*, de sopetón, de repente; *to win one's spurs*, ganar la dignidad de caballero, llevarse la palma. — *v.t.*, *v.i.* picar con la espuela; poner(se) (o calzar) espuelas; espolear; avivar, incitar, estimular; apretar el paso; viajar con toda prisa; *to spur on*, espolear, aguijar, avivar, estimular.

spurge [spəːɹdʒ], *s.* lechetrezna, titímalo, euforbio, tártago; *spurge-laurel*, lauréola, mecereón.

spurious [spju:'riəs], *a.* espurio; falso; contrahecho; bastardo, ilegítimo; (*biol.*) falso; (*bot.*) aparente.

spuriousness, *s.* falsificación, falsedad; adulteración; bastardía.

spurn [spəːɹn], *v.t.*, *v.i.* desdeñar, despreciar, mirar con desprecio, menospreciar; desechar con desdén, cocear, acocear, rechazar a puntapiés; oponerse con desprecio. — *s.* coz, *f.*; ajamiento.

spurning, *s.* menosprecio, desdén.

spurn-water, *s.* guardaaguas, *m.*

spurred [spəːɹd], *a.* con espuelas; con espolones; (*biol.*) atizonado.

spurrier ['spʌriəɹ], *s.* el que hace espuelas.

spurry ['spʌri], *s.* espérgula.

spurt [spəːɹt], *v.i.* chorrear, salir en chorro; borbotar; brotar, surgir; hacer un esfuerzo supremo. — *v.t.* hacer chorrear, hacer salir en chorro; espurriar; lanzar. — *s.* chorro, chorretada; explosión de ira; esfuerzo repentino, esfuerzo supremo; rato, momento.

sputter ['spʌtəɹ], *v.i.* escupir; chisporrotear;

farfullar; balbucir. — *v.t.* escupir; balbucir.
— *s.* chisporroteo; farfulla.
sputterer, *s.* escupidor, farfullador, persona que escupe mucho, que chisporrotea saliva.
sputtering, *s.* chisporroteo; balbuceo.
sputum ['spju:təm], *s.* esputo.
spy [spai], *s.* espía, *m.f.* — *v.t.* divisar; observar; atisbar, columbrar; *to spy out a country,* explorar, reconocer un país. — *v.i.* espiar, ser espía.
spy-boat, *s.* barca exploradora.
spy-glass, *s.* catalejo.
spy-hole, *s.* atisbadero.
squab [skwɔb], *a.* implume, acabado de salir de la cáscara; regordete, rechoncho, gordiflón. — *s.* (*orn.*) pichón, pichoncillo; persona regordeta o rechoncha; cojín, canapé, otomana. — *adv.* zas, de golpe y porrazo.
squabble ['skwɔbəl], *v.t.* (*impr.*) empastelar. — *v.i.* reñir, disputar; andar en pendencias, armar disputas. — *s.* pendencia, querella, riña, disputa.
squabbler, *s.* pendenciero, amigo de armar pendencias.
squad [skwɔd], *s.* escuadra; pelotón.
squadron ['skwɔdrən], *s.* (*mar.*) escuadra; (*mil.*) escuadrón, cuadro; (*aer.*) escuadrilla; *squadron-leader,* comandante.
squadroned, *a.* escuadronado.
squalid ['skwɔlid], *a.* escuálido; desaliñado; mezquino.
squalidness, *s.* escualor, escualidez; mezquindad; suciedad, inmundicia.
squall [skwɔ:l], *v.t.*, *v.i.* chillar; dar voces; berrear. — *s.* chillido, berrido; (*mar.*) ráfaga, racha, turbonada, chubasco, solana; tempestad.
squaller, *s.* chillador, chillón.
squally, *a.* chubascoso; borrascoso.
squalor ['skwɔləɹ], *s.* escualor, escualidez; suciedad, inmundicia, mugre, *f.*
squama ['skweimə], *s.* escama.
squamoid ['skweimɔid], *a.* escamoso.
squamose, squamous ['skweiməs], *a.* escamoso, lamelar.
squander ['skwɔndəɹ], *v.t.*, *v.i.* gastar, malgastar, disipar, despilfarrar, desperdiciar, arrojar por la ventana, prodigar, malbaratar, derrochar.
squanderer, *s.* malbaratador, derrochador, gastador, pródigo, disipador.
square [skwɛəɹ], *a.* cuadrado; en cuadro; a escuadra; exacto, perfecto, justo, cabal; honrado, formal; categórico, redondo; (*fam.*) opíparo, abundante; (*com.*) saldado, en paz; (*mar.*) en cruz; (*mat.*) cuadrado; *square measure,* medida de superficie; *square dealing,* buena fe, honradez en los tratos; *to be square,* estar justa la cuenta, estar pagados; *square root,* (*mat.*) raíz cuadrada; *square-sail,* (*mar.*) vela redonda; *square yard,* yarda cuadrada; *square timbers,* maderos escuadrados. — *s.* (*geom.*) cuadro, cuadrado; cuadratura; (*mat.*) cuadrado; cristal de ventana; escaque, casilla (de tablero de damas); plaza; (*E.U.*) manzana de casas; escuadra, cartabón; proporción debida, nivel, orden; integridad, exactitud, honradez, equidad; (*mil.*) cuadro; *on the square,* (*fam.*) honradamente, de buena fe; *out of the square,* que no está en ángulo recto o a escuadra. — *v.t.*

cuadrar, formar en cuadro; escuadrar; (*mat.*) elevar (o reducir) al cuadrado; (*carp.*) cuadrar, escuadrar; (*b.a.*) cuadricular; (*com.*) saldar; pasar balance; acomodar, conformar, arreglar, ajustar, justificar; sobornar; medir (una superficie) en metros (o pies, etc.) cuadrados; (*mar.*) bracear en cuadro. — *v.i.* cuadrar, estar en ángulos rectos; encajar, conformarse, convenir, estar en conformidad, ajustarse, concordarse (una cosa con otra); *to square up to,* tomar una actitud pugilística; *to square the yards,* (*mar.*) poner las vergas en cruz; *to square the circle,* cuadrar el círculo.
squareness, *s.* cuadratura; honradez.
square-rig, *s.* aparejo de cruzamen.
square-rigged, *a.* de aparejo de cruzamen.
squaring ['skwɛəriŋ], *s.* cuadratura; escuadreo; cuadriculación; escuadrición; *squaring shears,* cizallas de escuadrar.
squarrose ['skwɔ:rous], **squarrous** ['skwɔ:rəs], *a.* (*biol.*) áspero, escamoso.
squash [skwɔʃ], *s.* aplastamiento; (*bot.*) calabaza; cosa blanda o inmatura; agolpamiento, apiñamiento (de personas); limonada; pulpa; maceración; despachurramiento; (*dep.*) badminton; *summer squash,* cidracayote de verano. — *v.t.*, *v.i.* aplastar, macerar, magullar, despachurrar.
squash-beetle, *s.* coleóptero crisomélido.
squash-vine, *s.* cidracayote, cucúrbita.
squashy, *a.* blando, tierno; zumoso.
squat [skwɔt], *v.i.* agacharse, agazaparse, acurrucarse, ponerse (o sentarse) en cuclillas; ocupar (o establecerse en) sin derecho. — *a.* agachado, puesto en cuclillas; rechoncho, cachigordete, rehecho. — *s.* posición del que está en cuclillas.
squatter, *s.* advenedizo, intruso, colono usurpador.
squaw [skwɔ:], *s.* (*E.U.*) mujer o esposa india.
squawk [skwɔ:k], *v.i.* graznar; (*fam.*) chillar. — *s.* graznido.
squeak [skwi:k], *v.i.* chillar, dar un chillido; recrujir; chirriar, rechinar; (*fam.*) cantar. — *s.* chillido, chirrido, grito; *to have a narrow squeak,* escapar por milagro.
squeaker, *s.* el que rechina, etc.; (*fam.*) delator, traidor.
squeal [skwi:l], *v.i.* chillar, dar voces, dar chillidos, lanzar gritos agudos; (*fam.*) cantar. — *s.* chillido, grito agudo.
squeamish ['skwi:miʃ], *a.* delicado, escrupuloso, remilgado; asqueado.
squeamishness, *s.* remilgo, escrúpulo; asco, náusea, basca.
squeegee [skwi:'dʒi:], *s.* rodillo o escobilla de goma para restregar superficies mojadas. — *v.t.* restregar con rodillo de goma.
squeeze [skwi:z], *v.t.* apretar, comprimir; estrechar; exprimir, estrujar, prensar, apachurrar; atortujar, apretujar; tupir; oprimir, acosar, agobiar; rebajar (jornales); (*b.a.*) recalcar; imponer, tributos excesivos; *to squeeze through,* pasar (o hacer pasar) a través (por fuerza); *to squeeze in,* entrar (o hacer entrar) apretando; *to squeeze out,* salir con dificultad; hacer salir, exprimir; *to squeeze to death,* (*fam.*) matar a apretones. — *v.i.* escaparse, pasar, entrar o salir apretando. — *s.* estrujón, apretadura, compresión, presión, apretón; facsímile, recal-

cado de una moneda, etc.; *tight squeeze*, (*fam.*) aprieto, apuro.

squeezer, *s.* exprimidera; *lemon-squeezer*, exprimidor de limones; *cork-squeezer*, prensacorchos; *rotary squeezer*, (*fund.*) forja giratoria.

squelch [skweltʃ], *v.t.* despachurrar; (*fig.*) derrotar. — *v.i.* chapalear, chapotear; despachurrarse. — *s.* chapaleo; despachurramiento.

squib [skwib], *s.* (*piro.*) buscapiés, carretilla; pasquinada (sátira). — *v.t.*, *v.i.* atacar con pasquinadas; soltar carretillas.

squid [skwid], *s.* calamar.

squill [skwil], *s.* (*bot.*) escila, albarrama; (*ict.*) esquila.

squint [skwint], *a.* bizco, bisojo, ojizaino. — *s.* estrabismo; mirada bizca; mirada furtiva; tendencia; (*fam.*) vistazo; *to have a squint*, mirar bisojo, bizquear; *to give* (o *have*) *a squint at*, (*fam.*) mirar de soslayo. — *v.t.*, *v.i.* bizquear, bizcar, mirar bizco; mirar de soslayo.

squint-eyed, *a.* bizco, bisojo, ojizaino; avieso, atravesado, torcido; ambiguo, obscuro.

squinting, *s.* estrabismo.

squire ['skwəiəɹ], *s.* escudero; (*Ingl.*) hacendado; cacique. — *v.t.* acompañar (una señora).

squirm [skwə:ɹm], *v.i.* torcerse, retorcerse; serpear, serpentear; *to squirm out*, salir con dificultad (o escaparse) de un aprieto. — *s.* torcimiento, retorcimiento.

squirrel ['skwirəl], *s.* ardilla.

squirt [skwə:ɹt], *v.t.* lanzar; hacer salir a chorros; jeringar. — *v.i.* chorrear, salir a chorros. — *s.* chorro; jeringazo; jeringa; (*fam.*) majadero.

squirter, *s.* el que jeringa.

squirt-gun, *s.* jeringa.

St., *s. abrev.* [SAINT]; San, Santo, Santa.

stab [stæb], *v.t.* apuñalar, acuchillar. — *s.* puñalada, estocada, cuchillada.

stabber, *s.* heridor; asesino.

stability [stə'biliti], *s.* estabilidad; permanencia, duración; consistencia, solidez, fijeza, firmeza, constancia.

stable ['steibəl], *a.* estable; durable, permanente; decidido, fijo, firme, constante; sólido. — *s.* establo; cuadra, caballeriza; caballos de carrera. — *v.t.*, *v.i.* poner (o vivir, o estar colocado) en la cuadra (o establo).

stable-boy, stable-man, *s.* establero; mozo de caballos.

stableness, *s.* estabilidad.

stabling ['steibliŋ], *s.* estabulación; cabida en un establo; lugar en un establo.

stack [stæk], *s.* niara, almiar (de heno); rima, rimero; pila, hacina, montón; (*mil.*) pabellón de fusiles; cañón de chimenea; (*fam.*) abundancia, copia. — *v.t.* (*agr.*) hacinar; apilar, amontonar; poner (las armas) en pabellón.

stadia ['steidiə], *s.* estación de agrimensores; estadia, instrumento topográfico; estadal de nivelación.

stadium ['steidiəm], *s.* estadio.

stadtholder ['stɑ:thouldəɹ], *s.* estatúder.

staff [stɑ:f], *s.* (*pl.* **staffs**, (*mús., etc.*) **staves**) báculo; palo; bordón (de peregrino); alivio, sostén, apoyo, arrimo; porra, palo, garrote; bastón de mando, vara; pértiga, percha; vara de medir; jalón de mira; asta (de lanza, bandera, etc.); personal (de oficina, etc.); (*mil.*) estado mayor, plana mayor; cuerpo; (*mús.*) pentagrama, *m.*; (*arq., b.a.*) cartón piedra; (*cir.*) guía o sonda acanalada; (*igl.*) báculo pastoral; *staff-officer*, (*mil.*) oficial de estado mayor; *ensign-staff*, (*mar.*) asta de bandera de popa; *flag-staff*, asta de bandera; *jack-staff*, asta de bandera de proa; *medical staff*, cuerpo de sanidad militar; *staff-tree*, alaterno.

staff-wood, *s.* madera para duelas.

stag [stæg], *s.* ciervo, venado; (*fam.*) varón; toro castrado; (*fam.*) delator, traidor; (*Bolsa*) alcista a corto plazo, *m.*

stag-beetle, *s.* ciervo volante.

stage [steidʒ], *s.* (*teat.*) tablado, escenario, tablas, escena; teatro; andamio; escena de acción; entarimado, estrado, plataforma; parada, descansadero; jornada, etapa; estado, grado; progreso, período de una enfermedad; disco, portaobjetos (de microscopio, etc.); (*E.U.*) diligencia; (*arq.*) escalón, paso de escalera; *stage-manager*, (*teat.*) director de escena; *stage-hand*, metesillas, *m.*, tramoyista, *m.*; *by short stages*, a cortas jornadas; a pequeñas etapas; *hanging stage*, plancha de viento; *to go on the stage*, abrazar la carrera del teatro; *to produce* o *put upon the stage*, poner en escena; *to go off* (o *quit*) *the stage*, abandonar la escena, retirarse del teatro. — *v.t.* (*teat.*) poner en escena; representar.

stage-coach, *s.* diligencia.

stage-driver, *s.* mayoral; cochero de diligencia.

stage-fright, *s.* miedo al público.

stager ['steidʒəɹ], *s.* caballo de diligencia; *old stager*, veterano.

stage-struck, *a.* loco por dedicarse al teatro.

stage-whisper, *s.* aparte.

stagger ['stægəɹ], *v.i.* hacer eses, tambalear; bambolear; titubear, vacilar. — *v.t.* atontar; asombrar; desconcertar; hacer vacilar, hacer dudar, hacer tambalear; (*mil., etc.*) escalonar; *staggered hours*, horas escalonadas. — *s.* tambaleo; vacilación; (*aer.*) descalaje.

staggering, *a.* tambaleante; asombroso.

staggers, *s.* (*vet.*) vértigo, vahido.

staghound ['stæghaund], *s.* sabueso, perro para cazar ciervos.

staging ['steidʒiŋ], *s.* andamiaje; tráfico en diligencias y ómnibus.

stagnancy, *s.* estagnación, estancamiento, paralización.

stagnant ['stægnənt], *a.* estancado, detenido, estantío, encharcado; paralizado.

stagnate [stæg'neit], *v.i.* estancarse, detenerse; estar estancado, volverse muerto; embotarse, estar embotado.

stagnation, *s.* estagnación, estancación, estancamiento, paralización de los negocios.

stag-party, *s.* reunión (*f.*) de hombres solos.

staid [steid], *pret.*, *p.p.* [STAY]. — *a.* serio, grave, juicioso, sentado, sosegado.

staidness, *s.* sosiego, juicio, seriedad, gravedad.

stain [stein], *v.t.*, *v.i.* manchar; teñir(se), colorar(se), chafarrinar; descolorar; ensuciar; mancillar, ajar, desdorar, empañar (la fama, etc.); *stained glass*, vidrio de color. — *s.* mancha, mancilla, mácula, borrón; descoloramiento, descoloración; color, tinte, tintura; deslustre, deshonra, desdoro.

stainer, *s.* persona que ensucia (mancha, etc.), pintor; tintorero; *glass-stainer,* fabricante de vidrios de color.

stainless, *a.* limpio, sin manchas, inmaculado; *stainless steel,* *s.* acero inoxidable.

stair [stɛəɹ], *s.* escalón, peldaño. — *pl.* escalera; *spiral* (o *winding*) *stairs,* escalera de caracol; *upstairs,* arriba, en el piso superior; *downstairs,* abajo, en el piso inferior; *flight of stairs,* tramo de escalera; *to go* (o *come*) *upstairs,* subir (la escalera); *to go* (o *come*) *downstairs,* bajar (la escalera).

stair-carpet, *s.* alfombra de escalera.

staircase, *s.* escalera.

stair-rod, *s.* varilla para alfombra de escalera.

stairway, *s.* escalera.

stake [steik], *s.* estaca, poste, pilote, piquete, jalón, estaquilla; (*agr.*) rodrigón; pira; (*carr.*) telero; tas, bigorneta; (*com.*) interés, ganancia o pérdida contingente; premio (de contienda); azar, riesgo, peligro, contingencia; posta, apuesta (en los juegos). — *v.t.* estacar (en los juegos) poner, apostar; arriesgar, aventurar, exponer; *to stake (one's) all,* echar (o envidar) el resto, aventurarlo todo.

stalactic [stə'læktik], **stalactitic** [stælək-'titik], *a.* estalactítico.

stalactite ['stæləktait], *s.* estalactita.

stalagmite ['stæləgmait], *s.* estalagmita.

stalagmitic [stæləg'mitik], *a.* estalagmítico.

stale [steil], *a.* rancio; viejo; pasado, gastado, desusado, anticuado; deteriorado, alterado; cansado; *stale wine,* vino picado; *stale bread,* pan viejo; *stale beer,* cerveza pasada; *stale news,* noticia añeja; *stale olive,* aceituna zapatera; *to grow stale,* enranciarse. — *v.t.* añejar. — *v.i.* añejarse; perder interés.

stalemate ['steilmeit], *s.* tablas (ajedrez); empate. — *v.t.* hacer tablas (ajedrez).

staleness, *s.* rancidez, vejez, antigüedad.

stalk [stɔːk], *v.t.* cazar al acecho, a la espera. — *v.i.* andar con paso majestuoso, taconear; avanzar a paso de lobo, andar a hurtadillas. — *s.* (*bot.*) tallo, caña, pedúnculo; pecíolo; troncho (de ciertas hortalizas); raspa (de uva); pie (de copa); paso majestuoso, taconeo.

stalking horse, *s.* boezuelo para la caza; disfraz, máscara.

stalky, *a.* tronchudo, duro como un tallo.

stall [stɔːl], *s.* pesebre, casilla de establo; puestecillo, puesto, parada; (*Méx.*) tenderete; tabanco; (*teat.*) (asiento de) butaca; (*igl.*) sitial de coro; (*aut.*) pérdida de velocidad; (*aer.*) pérdida de sustentación; (*min.*) galería; tajo de carnicero; *cobbler's stall,* zapatería de viejo. — *v.t.* encerrar (o meter) en cuadra o establo; poner puestos (o casillas); instalar, investir; atascar, atollar; poner obstáculos. — *v.i.* estar atascado, atollado; hundirse (en la nieve, etc.); (*aer.*) perder sustentación; (*aut.*) calarse, pararse; disimular.

stall-fed, *a.* cebado en establo.

stallion ['stæljən], *s.* caballo padre, garañón.

stalwart [stɔːlwət], *a.* fornido, forzudo, membrudo; fiel, constante, leal a su partido, acérrimo.

stamen ['steimen], *s.* (*pl.* **stamens**) estambre.

stamina ['stæminə], *s.* fuerza vital, fibra, vigor.

staminal, *a.* (*bot.*) estaminal; vital, esencial.

staminate, *a.* estaminífero.

stamineous [stə'miniəs], *a.* estamíneo, estaminoso.

stammer ['stæməɹ], *v.t.,* *v.i.* tartamudear, balbucear, balbucir. — *s.* tartamudeo; balbuceo, balbucencia.

stammerer, *s.* tartamudo, farfalloso.

stamp [stæmp], *v.t.* estampar, marcar, señalar, imprimir; sellar; estampillar, marcar con una estampilla, timbrar (papel, cartas, etc.); fijar el sello de correo; acuñar; patear, golpear con los pies; (*min.*) triturar, quebrantar, bocartear; machacar, majar, moler; apisonar; (*fig.*) dar una cualidad distintiva a; infamar, estigmatizar. — *v.i.* patear, patalear, piafar, dar patadas en el suelo. — *s.* sello; timbre, estampa, sigilación, impresión, marca, señal,*f.*; estampilla; imagen grabada; estampador; cuño; troquel; mano de mortero; (*fig.*) temple, clase, *f.,* suerte, *f.;* laya, calaña; *postage stamp,* sello de correo; *stamp-duty,* derecho de papel sellado (o de sello); *stamp act,* ley del timbre; *stamp-mill,* (*min.*) bocarte; *to bear the stamp of,* llevar el timbre de, (*fig.*) llevar la señal (o marca o sello) de.

stampede [stæm'piːd], *v.t.,* *v.i.* ahuyentar, escampar; salir de estampía; (hacer) huir con pavor; dispersarse en desorden; (*fig.*) obrar por común impulso, tomar de repente un acuerdo (una reunión). — *s.* estampida, escampado, huida con terror, pánico; determinación repentina y unánime.

stamper ['stæmpəɹ], *s.* estampador; impresor; bocarte, pilón, punzón de forja, martinete de fragua; triturador de pólvora; mano de almirez; pisón.

stamping, *s.* selladura; timbre, timbrado; estampado (de telas); pateo, pataleo; *stamping-mill,* bocarte.

stanch [stɑːntʃ], *v.t.* restañar; estancar, detener el curso de. — *v.i.* (*ant.*) estancarse, detenerse. — *a.* firme, adicto, fiel; constante; fuerte, sano, seguro, sólido; en buen estado, bien acondicionado; *stanch ship,* buque marinero, fuerte, sólido; *stanch hound,* sabueso que no pierde la pista.

stanchion ['stænʃən], *s.* puntal, asnilla, pie derecho, candelero, montante.

stanchness ['stɑːntʃnis], *s.* firmeza, seguridad constancia, celo, adhesión, resolución, determinación.

stand [stænd], *v.t.* (*pret.,* *p.p.* **stood**) poner (o colocar) derecho (o de pie); soportar, someterse a, aguantar, tolerar, sufrir, resistir, llevar con paciencia, sostener, defender, hacer frente a; importar, ser de provecho, ser útil; pasar por; (*fam.*) convidar; pagar el coste de; *to stand treat,* pagar una convidada. — *v.i.* estar, ser, tener, hallarse; estar en pie (o de pie), estar (o tenerse) derecho, tieso o firme, mantenerse derecho, etc.; sostenerse, resistir; pararse, quedarse, permanecer, detenerse, hacer alto; estancarse (el agua); presentarse como candidato; durar, perdurar, mantenerse firme; tener valor, valer, estar vigente, tener fuerza; levantarse, erguirse, enderezarse; estar colocado (o situado), hallarse; (*mar.*) correr, navegar, dirigirse; *to stand* *about*, cercar, rodear; *to stand against*, oponerse a, mantenerse firme contra; *to stand alone*, estar solo, ser el único; *to stand aloof*, mantenerse separado, aparte; *to stand aside*, alejarse, dejar pasar, mantenerse separado; *to stand back*, recular, retroceder; *to stand by*, ayudar, auxiliar, estar al lado de, sostener; estar cerca, ser espectador (de un juego, etc.); atenerse a; (*mar.*) estar listo, velar; *to stand by itself*, ser único en su clase, estar solo; *to stand far away* (o *off*), estar muy lejos; *to stand fire*, aguantar el fuego; *to stand for*, sustituir, estar en lugar de; representar, indicar; querer decir, significar; presentarse (como candidato) para; *to stand (sponsor) for*, sacar de pila a; *to stand forth*, avanzar, adelantarse; *to stand in*, montar, importar tanto; *to stand in for*, sustituir; *to stand in awe of*, sentir temor de; *to stand in someone's light*, quitar la luz a uno, (*fig.*) causar perjuicio a uno; *to stand in need of*, necesitar; *to stand in good stead*, ser útil, servir; *to stand in the way* (*of*), cerrar el paso (a), ser un obstáculo, impedir; *to stand off*, mantenerse separado, no convenir, no ser amigos, volverse atrás, no acercarse; *to stand off and on*, (*mar.*) barloventear; *to stand on end*, erizarse, mantenerse derecho; *to stand on tiptoe*, ponerse de puntillas; *to stand out*, avanzar, adelantarse, oponerse resolutamente, hacer frente, no convenir; destacarse, resaltar, estar en relieve; (*mar.*) gobernar más afuera; hacerse a la mar; *to stand out of the way*, quitarse de en medio; *to stand to reason*, ser razonable; *to stand sentry*, estar de centinela; *to stand still*, estarse quieto, no moverse; *to stand together*, mantenerse juntos; *to stand up*, levantarse, alzarse, ponerse en pie; *to stand up for*, defender; volver por; *to stand upon*, estar en, adherirse a, picarse de; *to stand upon ceremony*, gastar (o andarse en) cumplimientos; *to stand upon end*, erizarse (el pelo); *to stand upon trifles*, pararse en fruslerías.

stand [stænd], *s.* posición; tribuna, plataforma; consola, velador; mesita; soporte, sostén; mostrador; puesto (en un mercado); atril (de música); estante; parada, pausa; resistencia, oposición; armamento; estado fijo; vegetación sobre el campo; *flower-stand*, jardinera, tenducho de flores; *to take one's stand on*, basarse en; hacer hincapié en.

standard ['stændəɪd], *s.* marca, norma, tipo, medida, pauta, patrón, modelo, dechado, marco, regla fija; nivel; (*joy.*) ley (del oro o la plata), *f.*; (*mec.*) poste, pilar, puntal, madrina, árbol, pie; mueble fijo; estandarte, pabellón, bandera, pendón; (*mar.*) curva capuchina. — *a.* regulador; de marca, normal, de ley; clásico; *standard-bearer*, porta-estandarte, portaguión; *standard author*, autor clásico; *standard gauge*, medida (o marco) que sirve de norma; (*f.c.*) entrevía común; *standard work*, obra maestra, obra clásica; *standard time*, hora de Greenwich; *gold standard*, patrón de oro.

standardize, *v.t.* hacer uniforme; controlar.

stand-by ['stændbai], *s.* adherente fiel, persona digna de confianza.

stander ['stændəɪ], *s.* persona que está de pie; resalvo.

standing ['stændiŋ], *a.* derecho, levantado, en

pie, de pie; erecto; con pedestal, con pie; estable, duradero, constante; sin salida, sin vertiente; permanente, establecido, fijo; fijado, estancado, encharcado; (*for.*) vigente; *standing army*, ejército permanente; *standing water*, agua estancada (o remansada); *standing room*, sitio para estar de pie; *standing room only*, (*teat.*) espacio solo para estar en pie; *standing rigging*, (*mar.*) jarcia muerta; *standing orders*, reglamento permanente. — *s.* posición, reputación, crédito; puesto, sitio, paraje; duración, antigüedad; alto, parada; *of four years' standing*, de hace cuatro años, de cuatro años de fecha; *of old (long) standing*, de mucho tiempo, antiguo; *of the same standing*, contemporáneo; *of good (o high) standing*, de importancia, de posición, de consecuencia.

stand-offish, *a.* reservado; altanero.

standpoint ['stændpɔint], *s.* punto de vista.

standstill ['stændstil], *s.* parada, detención, alto; pausa completa, descanso.

stanhope ['stænəp], *s.* cabriolé ligero.

stank [stæŋk], *pret.* [STINK].

stannic ['stænik], *a.* estannífero.

stannite ['stænait], *s.* (*min.*) estannita; (*quím.*) estannito.

stanza ['stænzə], *s.* estancia, estrofa.

stapes ['steipiːz], *s.* (*anat.*) estribo.

staphyle ['stæfili], *s.* úvula.

staphylitis, *s.* inflamación de la úvula.

staphylococcus, *s.* estafilococo.

staple ['steipəl], *s.* producto principal (de un país); material o asunto principal); fibra, hebra o filamento (de algodón o de lana); materia prima, materia bruta; (*mec.*) hembra de cerrojo; grapa; picolete (de cerradura); argolla, aro; armella; (*mar.*) grampa, cibica. — *a.* (*com.*) corriente, de uso general; principal, importante. — *v.t.* asegurar con armellas; clasificar (hebras textiles) según su longitud; *short-stapled*, de hebra corta; *long-stapled*, de hebra larga.

stapler ['steiplər], *s.* clasificador de lanas.

star [staːr], *s.* estrella; astro; (*teat.*) estrella; (*impr.*) asterisco; *star of Bethlehem*, (*bot.*) leche de gallina; *stars and stripes*, las barras y las estrellas; *north star* o *pole star*, estrella polar; *shooting star*, estrella errante. — *v.t.* estrellar, sembrar de estrellas; (*teat.*) presentar como estrella; señalar con asterisco. — *v.i.* ser estrella.

starboard ['staːɪbəd], *s.* estribor.

starch [staːɪtʃ], *s.* almidón; fécula; (*fig.*) tiesura. — *v.t.* almidonar.

starched, *a.* almidonado; tieso.

starcher, *s.* almidonador.

starch-maker, *s.* almidonero.

starchness, starchiness, *s.* almidonamiento; tiesura.

starchy ['staːɪtʃi], *a.* almidonado; (*fig.*) tieso, entonado; de almidón; (*med.*) feculoso.

stare [stɛər], *v.t.* clavar o fijar la vista; mirar de fijo, de hito en hito, descaradamente. — *v.i.* abrir grandes ojos; saltar a la vista; mirar con asombro (o con insolencia); ser muy vivo o chillón (un color); erizarse, levantarse (el pelo); *to stare in the face*, dar en cara, saltar a los ojos, estar cerca, estar a la vista; ser claro, evidente. — *s.* mirada fija, mirada de hito en hito.

starer, *s.* persona que mira fijamente.

starfish, *s.* estrella de mar.

star-gazer, s. astrónomo; astrólogo; despistado.

staring ['stɛərɪŋ], a. que mira fijamente; que salta a la vista, llamativo, vivo, chillón.

stark [stɑːk], a. tieso, rígido; árido, desierto (paisaje); poderoso; completo, puro; *stark and stiff*, rígido, muerto; *stark madness*, locura completa; *stark nonsense*, pura tontería. — *adv.* completamente, enteramente; *stark mad*, rematadamente loco; *stark-naked*, en cueros, completamente desnudo.

starless, a. sin estrellas.

starlight ['stɑːlait], s. luz de las estrellas. — a. estrellado.

starlike ['stɑːlaik], a. estrellado; brillante, rutilante, radiante.

starling ['stɑːlɪŋ], s. (orn.) estornino; (arq.) espolón de un puente.

starred [stɑːd], a. estrellado; señalado con asterisco; *ill-starred*, desafortunado, malogrado.

starriness, s. abundancia de estrellas.

starry, a. estrellado; estelar; esteliforme; sembrado de estrellas.

star-shaped, a. estrelular.

star-shell, s. granada luminosa.

star-spangled, a. sembrado de estrellas.

start [stɑːt], v.t. empezar; poner en marcha (o en movimiento), hacer marchar (o funcionar); ojear, espantar (caza); (hacer) levantar (un animal), desemboscar; dar la señal de partida; dislocar, aflojar; provocar, suscitar; iniciar; abrir; trasegar; alabear, despegar (madera); desfondar. — v.i. sobrecogerse, asustarse, sobresaltarse, estremecerse; dar un salto (o respingo); partir, ponerse en marcha; salir (un tren); arrancar (un coche, una carrera); emprender un negocio; comenzar, estrenarse; proceder, provenir, derivar; aflojarse de su lugar; alabearse; combarse; descoyuntarse; apartarse; *to start after*, salir en busca de, empezar a perseguir; *to start aside*, echarse a un lado, ladearse; *to start for*, ponerse en camino hacia; *to start back*, saltar hacia atrás, dar un respingo; emprender el viaje de regreso; partir a la vuelta; *to start from*, salir, partir, dimanar de; *to start in one's sleep*, despertarse sobresaltado; *to start out*, salir; *to start off*, partir, ponerse en marcha (o en camino); *to start up*, levantarse precipitadamente; salir de repente; ponerse en movimiento, ponerse derecho, empezar a funcionar; *to start a train*, (f.c.) dar la señal para que salga un tren; *to start a subject*, iniciar una discusión. — s. salto, sobresalto, bote, repullo, estremecimiento, respingo; comienzo, iniciativa, primer paso; principio; marcha, salida, partida; arranque; estampida; delantera, ventaja; raja, grieta, aflojamiento; *by starts*, a saltos, por botes; *to get the start*, coger la delantera; *by fits and starts*, a saltos y corcovos; a ratos; *to give a start*, dar un susto, asustar; *at the start*, al primer paso, al principio.

starter, s. iniciador; levantador, ojeador; stárter, juez de salida; (mec.) palanca de marcha; (aut.) motor de arranque, arranque automático.

starting, a. que inicia o comienza; *starting-point*, punto de partida; *starting-place*, (deporte) puesto de salida. — s. estremecimiento,

sobresalto; comienzo, partida; movimiento repentino; (mec.) arrancada, salida.

startle ['stɑːtəl], v.t. espantar, asustar, dar un susto; sobrecoger, alarmar; hacer estremecer.

starvation [stɑːˈveiʃən], s. hambre, f.; inanición; inopia, indigencia, miseria; *starvation diet*, régimen de hambre; *starvation wage*, ración de hambre.

starve [stɑːv], v.i. morir(se) de hambre; pasar hambre; morir de frío. — v.t. matar de hambre; hacer morir de frío; helar; *to starve oneself*, privarse de lo necesario para vivir, dejarse morir de hambre.

starveling ['stɑːvlɪŋ], s. animal extenuado por el hambre. — a. hambriento, muerto de hambre, famélico.

starwort ['stɑːwəːt], s. argamula, estrellada.

state [steit], s. estado, condición, situación; (pol.) estado; grandeza, dignidad, majestad; aparato, fausto, pompa, ceremonia; gobierno civil; *state affairs*, negocios públicos, asuntos de estado; *wedded state* o *married state*, matrimonio; *single state*, celibato; *King's (Queen's o State's) evidence*, cómplice que declara para eludir su culpabilidad; *in a state of* (o *to*), en estado de; *in state*, con gran pompa, de gran ceremonia; *to lie in state*, estar expuesto en la capilla mortuoria. — a. de estado; de lujo; político, público; de gala. — v.t. exponer, manifestar, expresar; mencionar; enunciar; declarar, decir; relatar, contar; informar; (for.) aseverar; (dlg.) proponer, plantear (un problema).

statecraft ['steitkrɑːft], s. política, arte de gobernar.

stated, a. indicado; establecido, regular, fijo. — p.p. [STATE].

stateliness, s. grandeza, majestad, pompa, dignidad, aparato, altivez.

stately ['steitli], a. augusto, elevado, sublime, imponente, noble, soberbio, majestuoso, grande, excelso.

statement ['steitmənt], s. declaración; exposición; resumen; manifestación; relación, narración; cuenta; informe, relato, memoria; (com.) estado de cuenta.

stater ['steitəɹ], s. estáter.

state room ['steitrum], s. (mar.) camarote de lujo; camarote; (f.c.) compartimiento; gran salón, salón de recepción (de un palacio, etc.).

statesman ['steitsmən], s. estadista, m., hombre de Estado.

statesmanlike ['steitsmənlaik], a. propio de un estadista.

statesmanship ['steitsmənʃip], s. arte de gobernar.

static ['stætik], **statical** ['stætikəl], a. estático.

statics ['stætiks], s. estática; (rad.) ruidos parásitos o atmosféricos.

station ['steiʃən], s. puesto; sitio; condición (o posición) social; (f.c.) estación; (rad.) emisora; (mar.) apostadero; (mil.) puesto militar; punto de marca (en agrimensura); (igl.) estación; *station-master*, (f.c.) jefe de estación. — v.t. apostar, disponer, situar, arreglar, colocar, alojar.

stationary ['steiʃənəri], a. estacionario, inmóvil, parado; estantío; (astr.) estacional.

stationer ['steiʃənəɹ], s. papelero.

stationery ['steiʃənəri], s. papelería, efectos de escritorio.

statist ['stætist], s.; **statistic** [stəˈtistik],

statistical [stə'tistikəl], *a.;* **statistician** [stætis'tiʃən], *s.* estadístico.
statistics [stə'tistiks], *s.* estadística.
statuary ['stætjuːəri], *s.* estatuaria, imaginería; estatuario, escultor.
statue ['stætjuː], *s.* estatua; imagen, *f.*
statuesque [stætjuː'esk], *a.* escultural; majestuoso, noble.
statuette [stætjuː'et], *s.* figurilla, estatua pequeña.
stature ['stætjuːəɹ], *s.* estatura, altura, talla, tamaño.
status, *s.* estado, posición; reputación.
statutable, *a.* según estatuto o reglamento.
statute, *s.* estatuto, ley, *f.*, ordenanza, reglamento, decreto.
statutory ['stætjuːtəri], *a.* establecido; reglamentario, estatutario.
staunch [stɔːntʃ], *a.* firme, adicto, leal, fiel; sano, constante, fuerte, sólido, seguro; en buen estado, bien acondicionado [STANCH].
stave [steiv], *v.t.* (*pret., p.p.* **staved, stove**) cubrir de duelas; poner (o romper) las duelas; abrir boquete, desfondar, agujerear, destrozar, quebrar, quebrantar; (*Cuba*) desguazar; *to stave off*, diferir, retardar, aplazar; evitar. — *s.* duela de barril; ladera de un pozo; (*mús.*) pentagrama, *m.*; estancia, estrofa.
staves, *s.pl. reg.* [STAVE]. — *pl. irreg.* [STAFF].
stavesacre ['steivzeikəɹ], *s.* estafisagra, albarraz.
stay [stei], *v.t.* (*pret., p.p.* **stayed**, (*ant.*) **staid**) parar, impedir, detener; contener, poner freno, reprimir; apoyar, sostener; acodar, ahorquillar, acodalar, apuntalar, ademar; aplazar, diferir, posponer. — *v.i.* permanecer, quedarse; parar(se); detenerse, tardar; aguardarse, esperarse; (*fam.*) hospedarse; *to stay out*, quedarse fuera, no entrar; *to stay in*, quedarse en casa, no salir; *to stay away*, no volver; quedarse fuera (o alejado); *to stay up*, velar, no acostarse; *to stay on*, permanecer, seguir o continuar en el mismo estado; *stay-a-while*, mata espinosa; *stay-at-home*, persona casera; el que no sale a veranear; *to stay the stomach*, tomar un bocado, tomar las once. — *s.* estada, estancia, permanencia, quedada, residencia; suspensión, espera; mansión, parada, morada; detención; (*mec.*) codal, contrete; (*for.*) cesación temporal de un procedimiento judicial; impedimento, embarazo, freno, obstáculo; entibo, puntal, sostén, apoyo; fiador, atesador, sustentáculo; (*arq.*) arbotante, estribo, apeo; (*mar.*) estay, nervio; tentemozo; ballena de corsé; perseverancia; *to make a stay*, detenerse, quedarse, permanecer. — *pl.* **stays**, corsé, cotilla; *main-stay*, estay mayor; *foretop-stay*, estay del velacho; *fore-stay*, estay de trinquete; *to miss stays*, (*mar.*) fallar la virada; *in stays*, (*mar.*) de bordada en bordada.
stay-lace, *s.* cordón de corsé.
stay-sail, vela de estay.
stead [sted], *s.* lugar, sitio; auxilio, ayuda; *in (the) stead of*, en lugar de, en vez de; *in his stead*, en su lugar; *to stand in good stead*, ser útil.
steadfast ['stedfəst], *a.* constante, fiel, leal, adicto, inmutable, firme, estable, determinado, resuelto.

steadfastness, *s.* inmutabilidad, fijeza, estabilidad, firmeza, resolución, constancia.
steadiness ['stedines], *s.* estabilidad; fijeza; entereza; seriedad, formalidad; firmeza, constancia.
steady ['stedi], *a.* firme, fijo, seguro, asegurado; formal, juicioso, prudente; asentado; constante, estable, invariable, continuo, uniforme. — *v.t.* hacer firme, sostener, fijar; estabilizar; hacer formal; calmar.
steak [steik], *s.* filete (de carne); *beef-steak*, biftec.
steal [stiːl], *v.t.*, *v.i.* (*pret.* **stole**; *p.p.* **stolen**) robar, hurtar, pillar; plagiar; colarse; escabullirse; introducirse clandestinamente, pasar furtivamente (o a hurtadillas); *to steal a march on*, sorprender; ganar por la mano; *to steal away from*, quitar del medio, esconder, ocultar; *to steal away* o *to steal off*, marcharse a hurtadillas, escabullirse; *to steal along*, pasar en silencio, avanzar a paso de lobo, deslizarse sin ruido; *to steal down* (*forth, in* o *into*), descender, (salir, entrar, o penetrar) furtivamente; *to steal up*, subir a ocultas; *to steal over*, ganar insensiblemente; *to steal upon*, aproximarse sin ruido a, sorprender, apoderarse tranquilamente de.
stealer, *s.* ladrón.
stealing, *s.* hurto, robo.
stealth [stelθ], *s.* astucia; cautela; *by stealth*, a hurtadillas, a escondidas; en secreto; furtivamente.
stealthy ['stelθi], *a.* furtivo; clandestino, secreto; cauteloso.
steam [stiːm], *s.* vapor; vaho; niebla; *the steam is on*, hay presión; *with all steam on*, a todo vapor; *superheated* (o *supercharged*) *steam*, vapor recalentado; *high-pressure steam*, vapor a alta presión. — *v.t.* saturar con vapor; (*coc.*) cocer al vapor; poner en vapor; empañar (ventanas, etc.). — *v.i.* generar vapor; echar vapor; empañarse; evaporarse.
steamboat ['stiːmbout], *s.* vapor, buque de vapor; vapor de río.
steam-chest, *s.* cámara de vapor.
steam-dome, *s.* cámara de distribución.
steam-engine, *s.* máquina de vapor.
steamer, *s.* buque de vapor; (*coc.*) marmita al vacío.
steam-gauge, *s.* manómetro.
steam-hammer, *s.* maza de fragua.
steam-plough, *s.* arado de vapor.
steam-roller, *s.* apisonadora.
steamship ['stiːmʃip], *s.* (*mar.*) vapor, embarcación, buque de vapor (más grande que un *steamboat*).
steam-whistle, *s.* silbato, sirena, pito.
stearic ['stiːərik], *a.* esteárico.
stearin ['stiːərin], *s.* estearina.
steatite ['stiːətait], *s.* esteatita, jaboncillo.
steed [stiːd], *s.* corcel.
steel [stiːl], *s.* acero; arma blanca; espada; afilón; eslabón; *cast steel*, acero colado (o fundido); *alloy steel*, acero de aleación; *steel works*, fábrica de acero; *tool steel*, acero superior para herramientas cortantes; *steel-engraving*, grabado en acero; *cold steel*, arma blanca. — *a.* acerado; de acero; insensible; duro. — *v.t.* acerar; poner acero, cubrir (o armar) de acero; endurecer; fortalecer.
steel-clad, *a.* cubierto (o armado) de acero.

steeliness ['sti:linis], s. dureza de acero, dureza; insensibilidad.

steely, a. acerado, acerino, de acero; (*fig.*) inflexible, de bronce, fuerte, duro, firme.

steelyard ['sti:lja:ɹd], s. romana.

steep [sti:p], a. escarpado, empinado, precipitoso; acantilado; (*fam.*) excesivo, exorbitante. — s. precipicio, despeñadero, derrumbadero; remojo. — v.t. empapar, impregnar, macerar; remojar; saturar. — v.i. estar en remojo.

steeper, s. remojadero, pelambrera.

steeping, s. remojo; maceración, mojadura; *steeping-tub* (o *trough* o *vat*), cuba de remojar.

steeple ['sti:pəl], s. aguja campanario.

steeplechase ['sti:pəltʃeis], s. (*equit.*) carrera de obstáculos.

steeplejack, s. reparador de campanarios, etc.

steepness, s. carácter escarpado.

steepy ['sti:pi], a. (*poét.*) escarpado, enriscado.

steer [stiəɹ], s. novillo, novillejo; buey joven. — v.t. (*mar.*, *aer.*, *aut.*) gobernar; guiar; conducir. — v.i. navegar; timonear; dirigirse, conducirse; obedecer al timón; *to steer clear of*, (*fig.*) evitar, huir de.

steerage ['stiəridʒ], s. entrepuente; popa; tercera clase; gobierno, dirección; *steerage passenger*, pasajero de tercera clase; *steerage way*, (*mar.*) velocidad mínima; *to have steerage way*, tener salida para navegar.

steering, s. (*mar.*) gobierno; mecanismo de gobierno; (*aut.*) mecanismo de dirección, gobierno.

steering-wheel ['stiəriŋwi:l], s. (*mar.*) rueda del timón; (*aut.*) volante.

steersman ['stiəɹzmən], s. (*mar.*) timonel, timonero.

stegnosis [steg'nousis], s. estenosis, f.

stegnotic [steg'nɔtik], a. astringente.

stellar ['stelaɹ], a. astral, estelar, estrellar.

stellate, a. estrellado, de forma estrellada.

stelliferous [stel'ifərəs], a. estelífero, abundante en estrellas.

stelliform ['stelifɔ:m], a. estrellado.

stellular ['stelju:ləɹ], a. estrellado; estelulado.

stem [stem], s. (*bot.*) tallo, tronco, pedúnculo, vástago, pecíolo; (*mec.*, *carp.*) caña, espiga, cabillo; cañón de pluma; pie (de copa); rabo (o rabito) de una nota de música; (*gram.*) raíz, f.; (*mar.*) roda, roa, tajamar, branque; *from stem to stern*, de proa a popa; *stem-winder*, reloj de remontar. — v.t. ir contra, navegar contra, hacer frente a, oponerse a, resistir; represar, contener; embestir con la proa; tapar o enlodar una juntura; quitar los pedúnculos; desgranar (uvas, pasas, etc.); poner pedúnculos postizos (para hacer ramilletes); poner pies; *to stem the tide*, rendir la marea; *to stem the torrent*, detener el torrente.

stemless, a. sin pedúnculo, sin pie; (*bot.*) acaule.

stempel, stemple ['stempəl], s. estemple, montante, asnado; travesaño.

stemson ['stemsən], s. (*mar.*) contrabranque, contrarroda, sobrerroda.

stench [stentʃ], s. hedor, hediondez, fetidez; tufo.

stencil ['stensəl], v.t. estarcir. — s. patrón para estarcir; estarcido, marca.

stenciller, s. estarcidor.

stenograph ['stenogræf], s. escritura taquigráfica; maquinita de taquígrafo.

stenographer [ste'nogrəfəɹ], s. taquígrafo, estenógrafo.

stenographic, a. estenográfico.

stenography [ste'nogrəfi], s. taquigrafía, estenografía.

stentor ['stentəɹ], s. estentor.

stentorian [sten'tɔ:riən], a. estentóreo.

step [step], v.t. (*pret.*, *p.p.* **stepped, stept**) poner (el pie); plantar un mástil. — v.i. dar un paso; pisar; caminar, andar; *to step aside*, desviarse, apartarse, ponerse a un lado; *to step after*, ir detrás; *to step back*, volver atrás; retroceder; *to step forth*, avanzar; *to step down*, bajar, descender; (*elec.*) reducir (voltajes); *to step in*, entrar; *to step on*, andar sobre, poner el pie sobre, pisar; *to step on it*, (*E.U.*, *fam.*) apresurarse; (*aut.*, *fam.*) acelerar; *to step off*, (*v.t.*) medir (tantos pasos); (*v.i.*) bajar; marcharse; *to step out*, salir; apearse; bailar; dar pasos grandes; *to step over*, atravesar; *to step short*, (*mil.*) acortar el paso; *to step up*, subir. — s. paso; escalón, grada, peldaño de escalera; grado; umbral de puerta; huella; pisada; (*mús.*) intervalo; pedestal de máquina; quicio de eje vertical; diente de una llave; (*mar.*) carlinga. — *pl.* **steps**, pasos, diligencias, gestiones, medios; gradería; escalera de mano; *to retrace one's steps*, volver sobre sus pasos; *to make a step*, dar un paso; *to take steps*, tomar medidas; *in step*, a compás, llevando el paso; *to keep in step*, llevar el paso; *watch your step!* ¡tenga Vd. cuidado!; *step-down transformer*, (*elec.*) transformador para reducir voltajes.

step-box, s. (*mec.*) rangua.

stepbrother, s.m. medio hermano, hermanastro.

stepdaughter, s.f. hijastra.

stepfather, s.m. padrastro.

stephanite ['stefənait], s. (*min.*) negrillo.

step-ladder, s. escalera de tijera.

stepmother, s.f. madrastra.

stepney ['stepni], s. rueda de recambio.

steppe [step], s. estepa; llanura, erial.

stepping-stone ['stepiŋstoun], s. estriberón; pasadera; (*fig.*) escabel.

stepsister, s.f. media hermana, hermanastra.

stepson, s.m. hijastro.

stercoraceous [stəɹko'reiʃəs], a. estercolizo, estercoráceo.

stere [stiəɹ], s. estéreo, metro cúbico.

stereographic ['steriogræfik], a. estereográfico.

stereography, s. estereografía.

stereometer [steri'ɔmetəɹ], s. estereómetro.

stereometry, s. estereometría.

stereophonic, a. estereofónico.

stereophony, s. estereofonía.

stereoscope, s. estereoscopio.

stereoscopic, a. estereoscópico.

stereotomy, s. estereotomía.

stereotype ['steriotaip], v.t. estereotipar, clisar. — s. estereotipia, estereotipo, clisé; *stereotype-plate*, plancha estereotípica, clisé.

stereotyper, s. estereotipador.

stereotypic, a. estereotípico.

stereotyping, s. estereotipia, clisado.

stereotypography [steriotai'pɔgrəfi], s. estereotipia.

sterile ['sterail], a. estéril, infecundo; árido; inútil.

sterility [ste'riliti], s. esterilidad, infecundidad; aridez.

sterilization, s. esterilización.

sterilize ['sterilaiz], v.t. esterilizar.

sterilizer, s. esterilizador.

sterling ['stə:liŋ], a. esterlina; genuino, verdadero, puro; hecho a ley.

stern [stə:n], a. austero, duro, torvo; rígido, inflexible; áspero. — s. (mar.) popa; (fam.) rabo, cola; stern-frame, cuaderna (o peto) de popa; stern-sheets, popa (de bote); stern-post, guardatimón, codaste, estambor; stern-port, (mar.) porta de popa; stern-fast, codera; tangidera; stern-chase, caza en que una nave va siguiendo en la estela de otra; stern-chaser, guardatimón, pieza de retirada.

sternmost ['stə:nməst], a. popel.

sternness, s. severidad, rigor, dureza, austeridad, aspereza.

sternson ['stə:nsən], s. talón de quilla.

sternum ['stə:nəm], s. esternón.

sternutation [stə:nju:'teiʃən], s. estornudo.

sternway ['stə:nwei], s. marcha atrás (un buque).

stertorous ['stə:tərəs], a. estertoroso.

stethograph ['steθogræf], s. neumatógrafo.

stethoscope ['steθoskoup], s. estetoscopio.

stethoscopic, a. estetoscópico.

stethoscopy [ste'θoskopi], s. estetoscopía.

stetson ['stetsən], s. sombrero vaquero.

stevedore ['sti:vidɔ:], s. estibador.

stew [stju:], v.t., v.i. (coc.) estofar; hervir; cocer. — s. estofado, guisado; (fam.) agitación; preocupación. — pl. (ant.) stews, burdel, lupanar.

steward ['stju:əd], s. administrador; mayordomo, senescal; ranchero, despensero; camarero (en los vapores); (Cuba) mayoral; steward's room, despensa.

stewardess ['stju:ədes], s.f. mayordoma, despensera, administradora; camarera.

stewardship, s. mayordomía.

stew-pan, s. cazuela, cacerola.

step-pot, s. olla.

sthenia ['sθi:niə], s. excitación nerviosa.

sthenic ['sθenik], a. demasiado activo, excitado.

stibial ['stibiəl], a. antimonial.

stibium, s. estibio.

stich [stik], s. versículo, verso.

stick [stik], s. palo, palillo; estaca; porra, garrote; leña; vara; bastón; (mús.) batuta; varilla (de abanico); ristra; estique de escultor; barra (de lacre); arco (de violín, etc.); (mar.) palo, verga; tallo (de espárrago, etc.); adhesión, pegadura; (fam.) individuo; (teat.) mal actor. — pl. sticks, leña; (mar.) arboladura; shooting-stick, (impr.) atacador; composing-stick, (impr.) componedor; blow with a stick, bastonazo, garrotazo; in a cleft stick, entre la espada y la pared. — v.t. (pret., p.p. stuck) hundir; clavar; meter; hincar; introducir, hacer entrar; pinchar; hacer penetrar; fijar (con tachuelas, etc.); llenar de puntas; punzar, picar; matar; herir; atravesar (de una puñalada o cuchillada); juntar, pegar, encolar, unir, adherir; fijar en la pared; (fam.) engañar; dar un sablazo a; (agr.) plantar jalones; (impr.) componer tipo. — v.i. estar clavado; clavarse; pegarse, unirse; adherirse; quedar; detenerse; fijarse; estar confundido; atascarse, atollarse; encallarse;

perseverar, ser constante; to stick at nothing, (fam.) no pararse en pelillos; to stick at, persistir en; detenerse ante; tener escrúpulos sobre; he sticks at everything, (fam.) se ahoga en poca agua; to stick fast, pegarse, adherirse; to stick close, mantenerse juntos; to stick by, sostener, apoyar; pegarse a alguno; to stick in, clavar, punzar; to stick in the mud, hundirse (o atascarse) en el fango; (E.U., fam.) stick them up! ¡manos arriba! to stick to, pegarse a, adherirse a; to stick to one's word, mantener su palabra; to stick to one's task (o guns), perseverar, persistir, obstinarse; to stick out, (v.t.) asomar, sacar; (v.i.) salir, sobresalir; proyectar; to stick up for, defender, volver por.

sticker, s. (E.U.) [LABEL, TAG].

stickiness ['stikinis], s. tenacidad, viscosidad, glutinosidad.

sticking-plaster ['stikiŋplɑstə], s. esparadrapo, parche.

stickle ['stikəl], v.i. porfiar, altercar, disputar acerca de menudencias.

stickleback ['stikəlbæk], s. (ict.) espino.

stickler ['stiklə], s. rigorista, m.f.; partidario.

stick-up, s. (E.U., fam.) atraco a mano armada.

sticky ['stiki], a. pegajoso, viscoso, tenaz; difícil.

stiff [stif], a. tieso; duro, firme; yerto, aterido; torpe, envarado; inflexible, rígido; espeso; viscoso; almidonado; estirado; terco; serio; difícil, severo; (com.) alto, excesivo (precio); (mar.) de aguante, que aguanta bien el viento; stiff breeze, brisa fuerte, brisote; stiff gale, viento fuerte; stiff neck, torticolis; to grow stiff, endurecerse, atiesarse. — s. (fam.) cadáver.

stiffen ['stifən], v.t. poner tieso, atiesar; endurecer; reforzar, fortalecer; espesar; envarar, aterir o arrecir de frío. — v.i. atiesarse, ponerse tieso; endurecerse; fortalecerse, robustecerse; obstinarse; espesarse; enderezarse; envararse, aterirse o arrecirse; refrescar (el viento).

stiffener, s. contrafuerte; atiesador, abultador; cojinillo, colchoncillo.

stiff-necked, a. obstinado, testarudo, terco.

stiffness, s. tesura, tiesura; inflexibilidad; envaramiento, rigidez; severidad; inflexibilidad, obstinación, terquedad; dureza de estilo; espesura; (med.) rigor.

stifle ['staifəl], v.t. ahogar, sofocar; apagar; ocultar, callar, suprimir. — v.i. ahogarse. — s. (vet.) rodilla.

stigma ['stigmə], s. estigma, m.; (bot., zool.) estigma, m.

stigmatic [stig'mætik], a. (bot.) estigmático; de estigma.

stigmatize ['stigmataiz], v.t. estigmatizar.

stile [stail], s. portillo con escalones; estilo; (carp.) larguero.

stiletto [sti'letou], s. estilete; (cost.) ojeteador, punzón.

still [stil], v.t. acallar, hacer callar; aplacar, sosegar, aquietar, calmar, apaciguar; detener, parar; (ant.) alambicar, destilar. — adv. todavía, aún, sin cesar, hasta ahora, siempre; no obstante, sin embargo, a pesar de eso; más, además; still more, todavía más, aún más. — a. inmóvil, fijo, quedo, tranquilo, quieto; sosegado, apacible; suave, suavizado, sordo (ruido); no espumoso, sin efervescencia

(vino); muerto, inanimado; *still life*, (*pint.*)
naturaleza muerta, bodegón; *still water*, agua
encharcada (o tranquila); *still waters run deep*,
(*prov.*) guárdate del agua mansa; *to stand
still*, detenerse, no moverse, permanecer
quedo. — *s.* silencio, tranquilidad, quietud,
sosiego; alambique, destiladera; (*cine*) retrato
de propaganda.

stillage ['stilidʒ], *s.* caballete.

stillborn ['stilbɔːɪn], *a.* nacido muerto.

stilling, *s.* poíno, codal.

stillness ['stilnis], *s.* silencio, calma, sosiego,
quietud, tranquilidad.

stilly, *a.* (*poét.*) tranquilo, silencioso, quieto,
suave. — *adv.* quietamente, tranquilamente.

stilt [stilt], *s.* zanco; esteva del arado.

stilted, *a.* hinchado, pomposo, enfático.

stimulant ['stimjuːlənt], *s.*, *a.* (remedio o
bebida) estimulante, que estimula. — *pl.*
stimulants, licores embriagantes.

stimulate ['stimjuːleit], *v.t.* estimular, excitar,
incitar, aguijonear, punzar, avivar. — *v.i.*
servir como estímulo o aguijón; tomar esti-
mulantes.

stimulation, *s.* estímulo; aguijón; excitación,
estimulación.

stimulating, *a.* estimulante; inspirador.

stimulative ['stimjuːlətiv], *a.* estimulante. —
s. estímulo; excitación.

stimulator, *s.* irritador, acuciador.

stimulus ['stimjuːləs], *s.* estímulo, incentivo;
(*med.*) estimulante (*bot.*) dardo, aguijón.

sting [stiŋ], *v.t.*, *v.i.* (*pret.*, *p.p.* **stung**) picar,
pinchar, morder (una culebra); mordicar,
pungir; estimular, aguijonear; carcomer,
atormentar, causar tormento; remorder la
conciencia. — *s.* aguijón; punzada, picadura,
picada, picazón, *f.*, mordedura (de culebra);
estímulo; remordimiento de conciencia;
(*bot.*) púa, aguijón.

stinginess ['stindʒinis], *s.* avaricia, tacañería,
ruindad.

stinging ['stiŋiŋ], *s.* picadura, punzadura,
punzada.

stingless, *s.* sin aguijón; sin púa.

stingy ['stindʒi], *a.* avaro, tacaño, agarrado;
escaso.

stink [stiŋk], *v.i.* (*pret.* **stank, stunk**; *p.p.*
stunk) heder, apestar, oler mal. — *s.* hedor,
hediondez, peste, *f.*

stinker, *s.* cosa hedionda, de mal olor.

stinking ['stiŋkiŋ], *a.* hediondo, apestoso.

stinkingness, *s.* hediondez.

stink-pot, *s.* bomba asfixiante.

stint [stint], *v.t.* limitar, escatimar, restringir;
señalar (o asignar) una tarea. — *v.i.* ser
económico, ser parco, ceñirse. — *s.* cuota,
tarea, destajo; restricción, límite.

stipe [staip], *s.* estipo.

stipend ['staipend], *s.* estipendio, salario,
sueldo, honorarios.

stipendiary [sti'pendiəri], *s.*, *a.* estipendiario,
soldadero.

stipitate ['stipiteit], *a.* estiposo.

stipple ['stipəl], *v.t.* (*b.a.*) picar, puntear. — *s.*
picado, punteado.

stipple-graver ['stipəlgreivəɪ], *s.* graneador.

stippling, *s.* (*b.a.*) graneo, picado.

stipulate ['stipjuːleit], *v.t.* estipular, especificar, detallar, mencionar, particularizar. —
v.i. estipular, contratar, pactar.

stipulation [stipjuː'leiʃən], *s.* estipulación,

artículo, capitulación, cláusula, condición;
convenio, contrato, pacto.

stipule ['stipjuːl], *s.* estípula.

stir [stəːɪ], *v.t.* agitar, mover, revolver;
excitar; perturbar; agitar, inquietar; irritar;
suscitar, animar, incitar; inspirar; conmover; discutir, ventilar; atizar, avivar (la
lumbre); *to stir up*, despertar; conmover, excitar; aguijonear; poner en movimiento. —
v.i. ponerse en movimiento, moverse,
menearse; madrugar, levantarse (de la cama,
etc.). — *s.* movimiento; conmoción; actividad; excitación, estruendo, bullicio, alboroto; interés.

stirrer ['stəːrəɪ], *s.* promovedor; incitador;
batidor; molinillo; mecedero (de vinos);
meneador.

stirring, *s.* movimiento, meneo; el revolver.
— *a.* conmovedor, emocionante; agitado.

stirrup ['stirəp], *s.* estribo; (*zap.*) tirapié;
(*mar.*) estribo; *stirrup-leather*, ación.

stitch [stitʃ], *v.t.* coser; hilvanar; (*cir.*) suturar,
dar puntos. — *v.i.* coser; bordar, hacer
bordados; *to stitch down*, ribetear; *to stitch
up*, remendar, recoser lo roto; (*cir.*) dar
puntos. — *s.* (*cost.*) puntada; punto; (*cir.*)
punto; punzada, dolor punzante; (*agr.*)
caballón, surco; distancia, jornada; *back-
stitch*, punto atrás; *cross-stitch*, punto cruzado, punto de escarpín; *chain-stitch*, punto
de cadena; *lock-stitch*, punto de cadeneta.

stitcher, *s.* cosedor, cosedora; ribeteadora;
(*enc.*) cosedor.

stitching, *s.* puntos, puntadas; costura;
pespunte, punto atrás.

stiver ['staivəɪ], *s.* moneda holandesa; ochavo,
blanca, ardite.

stoat [stout], *s.* armiño.

stob [stɔb], *s.* alzaprima.

stock [stɔk], *s.* tronco, cepa; injerto; (*for.*)
línea directa (de una familia); estirpe, *f.*,
linaje; (*com.*) valores, acciones, *f.pl.*; capital;
mercancías almacenadas, existencias; surtido
de mercancías; enseres, muebles; caldo para
guisar; provisión; reserva; ganado; cepo;
leño, tajo, zoquete; (*bot.*) alhelí; berbiquí de
barrena; culata (de fusil); corbatín, alzacuello; (*mar.*) astillero, grada de construcción; baceta o monte de una baraja; (*fig.*)
hombre necio (o tonto); *stock-blocks*, (*mar.*)
polines de la grada; *stock of an anchor*,
(*mar.*) cepo de ancla; *live stock*, ganado; *to
lay in a stock*, surtir sus almacenes, proveerse, hacer provisión; *to take stock*, hacer
inventario; *stock in hand*, o *stock in trade*,
mercancías en almacén; *joint-stock company*,
sociedad anónima, sociedad por acciones;
stock-farmer, ganadero; *stock-yard*, corral de
ganado; *rolling-stock*, (*f.c.*) material rodante o
móvil. — *v.t.* abastecer, llenar; acumular,
surtir, proveer, juntar, acopiar; poner en un
cepo, encepar.

stockade [stɔ'keid], *v.t.* empalizar, rodear de
empalizadas. — *s.* empalizada, estacada, palanquera, fila de estacas, vallado; pilotaje.

stock-breeder, *s.* ganadero.

stock-broker ['stɔkbroukəɪ], *s.* corredor de
valores; bolsista, *m.*

stock-dove, *s.* paloma torcaz.

stockfish, *s.* bacalao seco, pejepalo.

stockholder ['stɔkhouldəɪ], *s.* accionista, *m.f.*

stockinette, *s.* elástica; paño, tela basta.

stocking ['stɔkiŋ], s. media, calceta; *stocking-weaver*, tejedor de medias; *stocking-frame*, telar de medias.

stockish ['stɔkiʃ], a. duro, estúpido, obstinado, insensible.

stock-jobber ['stɔkdʒɔbəɹ], s. agiotista, m.

stock-jobbing, s. agiotaje.

stocks [stɔks], s.pl. [STOCK]; cepo (castigo); acciones, f.pl., valores públicos; (mar.) astillero, gradas de construcción.

stock-still, a. inmóvil, inmoble.

stock-taking, s. inventario.

stocky ['stɔki], a. rechoncho.

Stoic ['stouik], s. estoico.

stoic [stouik], **stoical** ['stouikəl], a. estoico.

stoicism ['stouisizm], s. estoicismo.

stoke [stouk], v.t., v.i. alimentar, atender (un horno); echar carbón (a un fuego); atizar.

stokehold, s. (mar.) cámara de calderas; sala de calderas.

stoker, s. fogonero.

stole [stoul], s. estola.

stole, stolen, pret., p.p. [STEAL].

stolid ['stɔlid], a. estólido; impasible.

stolidity [stoˈliditi], s. estolidez; impasibilidad.

stolon ['stoulon], s. estolón.

stoma ['stoumə], s. (pl. **stomata**) estoma, m., poro, orificio.

stomach ['stʌmək], s. estómago; vientre, barriga; (fig.) apetito; valor. — v.t. tragar, apechugar, digerir; (fig.) tragar(se), aguantar, sufrir.

stomachal ['stʌməkəl], a. estomacal; cordial.

stomacher ['stʌməkəɹ], s. peto, estomaguero.

stomachic [stoˈmækik], a. estomocal, estomático. — s. medicamento estomacal.

stomatitis [stouməˈtaitis], s. (med.) estomatitis, f.

stone [stoun], s. piedra; roca; china; piedra sepulcral; (joy.) piedra preciosa; (med.) piedra, cálculo; hueso, pepita (de las frutas); (Ingl.) peso de 14 libras; (vulg.) testículo; *millstone*, piedra de molino; *flint stone*, pedernal; *imposing-stone*, (impr.) piedra de imponer; *stone (colour)*, gris azulado; *stone hammer*, dolobre, marra; *stone-coal*, antracita; *stone-cold*, frío como la piedra; *stone-dead*, muerto como una piedra; *stone-blind*, completamente ciego; *stone-deaf*, completamente sordo; *stone-dumb*, completamente mudo; *stone-fruit*, fruta de hueso; *stone-pit*, o *stone-quarry*, pedrera, cantera; *stone's cast*, o *stone's throw*, tiro de piedra. — a. de piedra, hecho de piedra. — v.t. apedrear, atacar (o matar) a pedradas; deshuesar (la fruta); (alb.) revestir de piedras; *to leave no stone unturned*, no dejar piedra por mover, hacer todo lo posible.

stonebreak, s. quebrantapiedras, f., saxífraga.

stone-breaker, stone-crusher, s. bocarte de piedra.

stone-chat, s. collalba.

stone-crop, s. chubarba, fabacrasa, ombligo de Venus.

stone-cutter, s. picapedrero, cantero, dolador.

stone-cutting, s. labra de las piedras.

stone-hawk, s. halcón apedreado.

stone-mason, s. albañil; picapedrero.

stone-parsley, s. perejil perenne, amomo.

stoner, s. apedreador; despepitador de frutas.

stoneware ['stounwɛəɹ], s. gres.

stonework ['stounwəːɹk], s. obra de sillería.

stoniness ['stouninis], s. carácter pedregoso (o pétreo); dureza, inflexibilidad, insensibilidad.

stony ['stouni], a. lleno de piedras, pedregoso; de piedra, pétreo; (fig.) empedernido, duro, insensible; *stony-broke*, (fam.) sin cinco, sin dinero.

stood [stud], pret., p.p. [STAND].

stool [stuːl], s. banquillo, taburete, escabel; sillico (para excrementos), inodoro; tarimilla, banqueta; excremento; planta madre; vástago acodado; señuelo o añagaza. — pl. **stools**, (mar.) mesetas de los jardines; *stoo of repentance*, banquillo de la penitencia; *stool-pigeon*, cimbel, cimillo; cómplice; *close-stool*, o *night-stool*, sillico; *foot-stool*, escabel, taburete, tarimilla. — v.i. evacuar el vientre; echar tallos (plantas).

stoop [stuːp], v.i. agacharse, doblar o inclinar el cuerpo; ser cargado de espaldas; inclinarse; combarse, rebajarse; bajarse; someterse, humillarse, abatirse; rendirse, ceder; condescender; lanzarse, arrojarse (sobre la presa). — v.t. someter, abatir, bajar, hacer bajar. — s. inclinación; cargazón (f.) de espaldas; caída, descenso; caimiento, abatimiento, declinación; caída sobre la presa; (E.U.) gradería, pórtico exterior, escalinata de entrada.

stoop, stoup [stuːp], s. copa o frasco para beber; pila de agua bendita.

stooping, a. inclinado, encorvado; doblado; cargado de espaldas). — s. inclinación.

stop [stɔp], v.t. detener, retener, parar; atajar, interceptar, cortar; poner coto, reprimir, contener, refrenar; paralizar; descontinuar, suspender; cesar (de); obstruir; tapar, cubrir, cerrar, cegar; estancar, represar; restañar; empastar (un diente); *to stop payments*, hacer suspensión de pagos; *to stop up*, tapar, cerrar, obstruir; *to stop (up) the way*, cerrar el paso, obstruir el camino; *to stop someone's mouth*, tapar la boca a uno, no dejarle hablar. — v.i. parar(se), detenerse, hacer alto; cesar (de), dejar (de); (fam.) quedarse, permanecerse; acabarse, llegar al fin, terminar; (mús.) cambiar el tono (por medio de un agujero o un traste); (foto.) diafragmar; *stop a moment*, deténgase Vd. (o espere Vd.) un instante; *to stop short*, quedarse cortado; *not to stop at*, (fig.) no mirar en, no contentarse con. — s. parada, alto; cesación; detención; parada (de autobús); espera, interrupción; retardación; retardo, dilación; suspensión, paro (de trabajo); represión; obstrucción, impedimento, embarazo, obstáculo, oposición; (mús.) tecla, palanca, llave, f.; registro (de órgano); (foto.) abertura; traste de guitarra; (mec.) retén, fiador, seguro, tope, leva, paleta, linguete; (gram.) punto; *full stop*, punto, punto final; *to make a stop*, hacer alto, detenerse; *to put a stop to*, poner coto (o término) a; *dead stop*, parada súbita. — interj. ¡basta! ¡cuidado! ¡alto!; *stop-press*, noticias de última hora.

stopcock, s. llave (f.) de agua, grifo.

stop-gap, s. (mar.) abarrote; (fig.) tapagujeros.

stoppage ['stɔpidʒ], s. cesación, interrupción; interceptación, detención; embarazo, impedimento, obstrucción; represa; retención (sobre un pago); (med.) estrangulación;

stoppage in transit, (*for.*) embargo de mercancías durante su transporte en caso de insolvencia del comprador.

stopper ['stɔpəɪ], *v.t.* entaponar, tapar con tapón; (*mar.*) bozar, amarrar con bozas. — *s.* tapón; taco, tarugo; obturador, tapador; detenedor; (*mar.*) boza, estopor; *anchor-stopper*, (*mar.*) capón; *stopper-bolts*, argollas de boza.

stopping, *s.* acción de detener(se), parar(se), etc.; empaste (de un diente); *stopping-place*, paradero, escala, estala.

stopple ['stɔpcl], *v.t.* entaponar, atarugar, cerrar con tapón. — *s.* tapón, tarugo, taco, bitoque.

stop-watch, *s.* cronógrafo.

storage ['stɔːridʒ], *s.* almacenaje.

storax ['stɔːræks], *s.* estoraque; *storax-tree*, estoraque.

store ['stɔːɹ], *s.* copia, abundancia, acopio; repuesto, provisión; almacén, depósito; tienda, comercio. — *pl.* **stores**, pertrechos, equipos; víveres, provisiones; bastimentos, municiones; *store-ship*, buque nodriza; *store of victuals*, provisiones de boca; *army stores*, pertrechos de guerra. — *v.t.* proveer, surtir, abastecer; municionar, pertrechar; guardar, atesorar, acumular, acopiar; tener en reserva; almacenar.

storehouse ['stɔːɹhaus], *s.* almacén; depósito.

storekeeper, *s.* almacenista, *m.f.*, almacenero, guardalmacén; jefe de depósito; tendero, comerciante; (*mar.*) pañolero.

storeroom ['stɔːɹrum], *s.* despensa, bodega, cillero; (*mar.*) pañol de víveres.

store-ship, *s.* buque nodriza; navío almacén.

storied ['stɔːrid], *a.* referido por la historia, historiado; que tiene pisos, de (tantos) pisos: *three-storied*, de tres pisos.

stork [stɔːɹk], *s.* cigüeña.

stork's-bill, *s.* (*bot.*) geranio.

storm [stɔːɹm], *s.* tempestad, temporal, tormenta, borrasca; vendaval; (*fig.*) lluvia (de proyectiles, etc.); arrebato, explosión, furia, frenesí; alboroto, tumulto; (*mil.*) ataque, asalto; *thunderstorm*, tronada; *snowstorm*, nevasca; *rain and wind storm*, turbonada; *to take by storm*, tomar por asalto; *to raise* (o *stir up*) *a storm*, levantar cisco, promover desórdenes; *storm-door*, guardapuertas, cancel; *storm-sail*, (*mar.*) tallavientos; *a storm in a teacup*, (*fam.*) tempestad en un vaso de agua, mucho ruido y pocas nueces. — *v.t.* asaltar, tomar por asalto, atacar a viva fuerza. — *v.i. impers.* haber tormenta o tempestad, tempestar; bramar (o reventar o estallar) de cólera, prorrumpir en injurias.

storm-bird, *s.* procelaria.

storminess ['stɔːɹminis], *s.* estado borrasco (o tempestuoso).

stormy ['stɔːɹmi], *a.* tempestuoso, borrascoso; turbulento, violento.

story ['stɔːri], *s.* historia; cuento, fábula, relación, conseja; anécdota; (*fam.*) hablilla, cuento de viejas, trama, enredo, argumento; (*fam.*) bola, embuste; (*arq.*) alto, piso; *fairy story*, cuento de hadas; *true story*, historia verdadera; *as the story goes*, según cuenta la historia; *a four-story house*, casa de cuatro pisos; *story-teller*, cuentista, *m.f.*; (*fam.*) chismoso, chismeador, embustero. — *v.t.* narrar, historiar; colocar en pisos.

stoup [stuːp], *s.* (*ant.*) frasco, copa; pila (de agua bendita).

stout [staut], *a.* fornido, forzudo, robusto; corpulento, gordo; recio, fuerte, vigoroso, firme, sólido; resuelto, animoso, intrépido. — *s.* cerveza fuerte.

stoutness, *s.* corpulencia, gordura; solidez; inflexibilidad, fuerza; arrojo, ánimo, valor.

stove [stouv], *pret.*, *p.p.* [STAVE]. — *s.* horno, estufa.

stow [stou], *v.t.* aprensar, atestar, hacinar; ordenar, colocar, alojar, meter; ocultar, esconder; (*mar.*) estibar, arrumar, abarrotar; arrizar; *to stow oneself*, (*fam.*) alojarse.

stowage ['stouidʒ], *s.* almacenaje; dinero que se paga por el almacenaje; (*mar.*) estiba; arrumaje; arreglo, colocación.

stowaway ['stouəwei], *s.* polizón, llovido. — *v.i.* embarcarse clandestinamente.

stower, *s.* estibador.

strabismus [strə'bizməs], *s.* estrabismo.

straddle ['strædəl], *v.i.* despatarrarse, esparrancarse; ponerse (o montar) a horcajadas. — *v.t.* montar a horcajadas; (*arti.*) horquillar el blanco. — *s.* posición del que se esparranca; acción o estado de ponerse a horcajadas; (*com.*) operación de bolsa con opción de compra o venta.

strafe [straːf], *v.t.* bombardear intensamente; ametrallar en vuelo bajo; castigar.

straggle ['strægəl], *v.i.* extraviarse; dispersarse; rezagarse; desparramarse; estar disperso (o esparcido); *straggling branches*, ramas dispersas; *straggling soldier*, soldado rezagado.

straggler, *s.* rezagado; vagamundo, tunante; rama extendida; objeto aislado.

straggling, straggly, *a.* rezagado; disperso; esparcido; desordenado.

straight [streit], *a.* derecho; recto, directo, en línea recta; erguido, estirado, tieso; lacio (pelo); ordenado; justo, equitativo; honrado, íntegro; exacto, correcto; franco, libre de estorbos; seguido; *to tell straight out*, (*fam.*) decir sin ambages; *straight face*, cara seria; *straight away*, en seguida. — *adv.* derecho; en línea recta; directamente. — *s.* (póquer) runfla de cinco naipes del mismo palo.

straighten, *v.t.* poner derecho, enderezar, desencorvar; poner en orden, sacar del desorden, arreglar.

straightener, *s.* el que endereza (o pone en orden).

straightforward [streit'fɔːrwəd], *a.* recto, derecho; que no desvía; íntegro, honrado, sincero.

straightforward(ly), *adv.* de frente, a derechas.

straightness ['streitnes], *s.* rectitud, derechura; honradez.

strain [strein], *v.t.*, *v.i.* extender (o estirar) con esfuerzo, forzar; ensanchar, estirar; esforzar(se); torcer (un músculo); forzar (la vista); aguzar (el oído); obligar demasiado; (*mec.*) forzar, torcer, retorcer; abrazar, estrechar; colar(se), filtrar(se), trascolar(se); incomodar, inquietar, molestar; *to strain a point*, forzar un argumento; hacer un esfuerzo (una excepción); *to strain the voice* (o *the eyes*), forzar la voz, (o la vista). — *s.* tensión; tirantez, estiramiento, estirón; esfuerzo violento; torcedura; estilo, tono, modo de hablar, modo de pensar; abuso exceso; (*mús.*) aire, melodía, acentos; parte distintiva (de un poema o canto); estirpe, *f.*, raza; (*biol.*) cepa; verso; clase, *f.*; vena, disposición heredada; *strain of madness*, vena de locura.

strainer, *s.* colador, coladera, coladero, pasador.

strait [streit], *a.* estrecho, angosto, apretado, ajustado; riguroso; *strait-jacket*, o *strait-waistcoat*, camisa de fuerza. — *s.* (*geog.*) estrecho; apuro, aprieto.

straiten ['streitən], *v.t.* estrechar, angostar; ceñir; limitar.

strait-laced ['streitleisd], *a.* ceñido, apretado; mojigato.

straitness, *s.* estrechez, estrechura, angostura; aprieto, apuro; escasez, penuria; austeridad, severidad, rigor.

strake [streik], *s.* traca, hilada.

stramineous [strə'miniəs], *a.* de color de paja, amarillo claro.

stramonium [strə'mouniəm], *s.* estramonio.

strand [strænd], *v.t.*, *v.i.* encallar, embarrancar; romper uno de los cabos de una cuerda; torcer, retorcer los cabos de un cordel; *stranded wire*, cable de alambre; *to be stranded*, quedarse desamparado; (*fig.*) quedarse colgado; *to leave stranded*, (*fig.*) dejar colgado. — *s.* costa, playa, ribera; filamento, fibra, hebra; cabo, ramal.

stranding, *s.* encalladura, zaborda.

strange [streindȝ], *a.* extraño, singular, raro, extraordinario, peregrino; ajeno; forastero, desconocido; reservado. — *interj.* ¡cáspita! ¡cosa rara!

strangeness, *s.* rareza, extrañeza; novedad; reserva.

stranger ['streindȝəɪ], *s.* desconocido; forastero; *to be a stranger to one*, ser desconocido a uno; *to be a stranger to something*, desconocer, no conocer.

strangle ['stræŋgəl], *v.t.* estrangular; dar garrote a, agarrotar; sofocar, ahogar; suprimir, reprimir.

strangler, *s.* estrangulador.

strangles ['stræŋgəlz], *s.* estrangol, hinchazón, *f.*

strangulated ['stræŋgjuːleitid], *p.p.*, *a.* (*med.*) estrangulado.

strangulation [stræŋgjuːleiʃən], *s.* estrangulación; ahogamiento.

strangury ['stræŋgjuːri], *s.* estangurria, estrangurria.

strap [stræp], *s.* correa; tira, faja, banda; gamarra; trabilla, precinta; (*zap.*) tirador, tirante, oreja (de zapato); (*carr.*) correones, sopandas; (*mar.*) gaza; *razor-strap*, asentador de navajas; *strap-hanger*, (*fam.*) persona que viaja de pie en un tren, etc., y que se agarra a las correas que cuelgan del techo; *shoulder-strap*, (*mil.*) capona. — *v.t.* liar, fajar o atar con correas; precintar; asentar las navajas.

strappado [strə'paːdou], *s.* estrapada.

strapper, *s.* (*fam.*) persona alta y talluda.

strapping, *a.* (*fam.*) rollizo; robusto; *strapping girl* (o *woman*), mocetona, mujerona.

strata ['straːtə, 'streitə], *s.pl.* [STRATUM].

stratagem ['strætədȝəm], *s.* estratagema, ardid, treta.

strategic [strə'tiːdȝik], *a.* estratégico.

strategist, *s.* estratega, *m.*

strategy ['strætidȝi], *s.* estrategia.

strath [stræθ], *s.* (*Esco.*) valle extenso.

stratification [strætifi'keiʃən], *s.* estratificación.

stratiform ['strætifɔːɪm], *a.* estratiforme.

stratify ['strætifai], *v.t.* estratificar.

stratigraphic, stratigraphical, *a.* estratigráfico.

stratigraphy [strə'tigrəfi], *s.* estratigrafía.

stratocracy [strə'tɔkrəsi], *s.* dictadura militar.

stratosphere ['strætosfiəɪ], *s.* estratosfera.

stratum ['straːtəm, 'streitəm], *s.* estrato, capa; (*geol.*) estrato, capa; (*anat.*) capa de tejido.

stratus ['streitəs], *s.* estrato.

straw [strɔː], *s.* paja; fruslería, bledo, nonada; *stack of straw*, pajar, almear; *I don't care a straw*, no me importa un bledo; *to break a straw*, reñir; *to be the last straw*, ser el colmo; *the last straw breaks the camel's back*, a la bestia cargada, el sobornal la mata. — *a.* hecho (o relleno) de paja; de ningún valor, falso, ficticio; *straw-bail*, caución (o fianza) simulada; *straw bed*, jergón de paja; *straw colour*, color de paja, amarillo claro; *straw hat*, sombrero de paja.

strawberry ['strɔːbəri], *s.* fresa; madroncillo; *strawberry-tree*, madroño.

straw-coloured, *a.* pajizo claro, de color de paja.

straw-worm, *s.* gorgojo.

strawy, *a.* pajizo, hecho de paja.

stray [strei], *v.i.* descarriarse, extraviarse, perder el camino, andar descarriado; errar, vagar. — *a.* extraviado, perdido, descarriado. — *s.* persona o animal descarriado o perdido; descarriamiento, descarrío.

streak [striːk], *s.* raya, lista, faja, línea; rayo de luz; reguero; vena, rasgo de ingenio; pizca, traza; capricho, antojo; (*min.*) raspadura; (*mar.*) costura de tablas, traca, hilada; *streak of lightning*, relámpago; *yellow streak*, cobardía. — *v.t.* rayar, listar; gayar, abigarrar, entreverar colores.

streaky, *a.* rayado, veteado, listado, alistado, abigarrado; bordado.

stream [striːm], *s.* corriente, *f.*; arroyo, río; raudal, torrente; flujo; curso; chorro (de líquido, luz, etc.); *downstream*, agua abajo; *upstream*, agua arriba; *against the stream*, contra la corriente; *stream anchor*, anclote; *stream tin*, estaño de aluvión. — *v.t.*, *v.i.* correr, manar, fluir, brotar; salir a torrentes; chorrear; derramar (o arrojar) con abundancia; (*min.*) lavar en agua corriente; flotar, (hacer) ondear, (hacer) tremolar, flamear; *to stream the buoy*, (*mar.*) echar la boya al agua.

streamer, *s.* flámula, gallardete, bandera, pendiente, banderola.

streamlet ['striːmlet], *s.* arroyuelo, hilo de agua.

streamline ['striːmlain], *s.* línea de flujo; forma aerodinámica. — *a.* aerodinámico. — *v.t.* fuselar.

streamlined, *a.* aerodinámico, fuselado, currentilineal.

streamy, *s.* abundante en agua corriente; surcado de arroyos; que mana a chorros; radiante, parecido a rayos de luz.

street [striːt], *s.* calle, *f.*; *street-walker*, prostituta; *street railway*, tranvía, ferrocarril urbano; *by-street* (o *side street*), callejuela; *main street*, calle mayor (o principal); *cross-street*, calle traviesa.

streetcar, s. (*E.U.*) [TRAMCAR].
strength [streŋθ], s. fuerza, vigor, robustez, consistencia, fortaleza, firmeza, solidez, tenacidad, resistencia, virilidad, energía; virtud, eficacia; potencia, pujanza, poder; nervio; validez, fuerza legal; fortaleza, espíritu; vehemencia; intensidad; grado de potencia, intensidad o concentración; cuerpo (del vino); confianza, seguridad; (*mil.*) fuerza(s) militar(es).
strengthen ['streŋθən], v.t. fortalecer, dar fuerza a, fortificar; corroborar, reforzar, confirmar; animar, infundir brío, alentar. — v.i. fortalecerse, cobrar fuerzas, reforzarse, hacerse (más) fuerte.
strengthener, s. confortador, corroborante.
strengthless, a. débil, sin vigor, sin fuerza.
strenuous ['strenju:əs], a. estrenuo; enérgico; acérrimo, arduo.
strenuousness ['strenju:əsnis], s. estrenuidad; energía; arduidad; vigor, ardor, ánimo.
streptococcus [strepto'kɔkəs], s. estreptococo.
streptomycine [strepto'maisin], s. estrepto-micina.
stress [stres], s. importancia, tensión; violencia; compulsión, coacción; acento tónico; énfasis; (*mec.*) esfuerzo; *to lay great stress upon*, insister sobre, dar mucha importancia a; hacer hincapié. — v.t. sujetar a peso o tensión; dar énfasis o importancia a; insistir en; subrayar; poner en aprieto, acongojar.
stretch [stretʃ], v.t. extender, tender; alargar, alongar, estirar, atesar, entesar; dilatar; ensanchar; forzar, violentar; exagerar; (*mar.*) hacer toda fuerza de vela; *to stretch forth* (o *out*), alargar(se), extender(se), estirar(se), prolongar(se), desplegar(se); (*fam.*) tumbar; *to stretch out to sea*, (*mar.*) tirar a la mar. — v.i. alargarse; extenderse; desplegarse; dar de sí; estirarse; dilatarse; desperezarse; (*fig.*) esforzarse, hacer un gran esfuerzo; exagerar; *to stretch as far as*, extenderse hasta; *to stretch out*, extenderse. — s. tensión, tirantez; estirón; esfuerzo; (*fig.*) violencia o interpretación forzada; extensión; trecho; intervalo; (*mar.*) bordada; *at one stretch*, de una tirada, de un tirón.
stretcher, s. tendedor, estirador, atesador, dilatador, ensanchador; camilla; (*alb.*) soga; (*carp.*) viga, madero largo, tirante; (*mar.*) peana o pedestal de bote; (*fam.*) exageración; cuento chino; *glove-stretcher*, abridor (o ensanchador) de guantes; *carpet-stretcher*, atiesador de alfombras; *wire-stretcher*, estirador de alambre; *stretcher-bearer*, camillero.
stretching, s. tendedura, estiramiento, entesamiento, alargamiento, dilatación; esperezo.
strew [stru:], v.t. (*p.p.* **strewed**, **strewn**) esparcir, derramar, desparramar; salpicar, sembrar; espolvorear, polvorear.
stria ['straiə], s. (*arq.*) estría.
striate ['straiət], v.t. estriar, marcar con estrías.
striate, **striated**, a. estriado.
striation [strai'eiʃən], **striature** ['straiətʃər], s. estriación, estriadura, estriatura.
stricken ['strikən], a. herido (por un proyectil); atacado, agobiado, afligido; entrado en años. — *p.p.* [STRIKE].
strickle ['strikəl], s. rasero.
strict [strikt], a. estricto; riguroso; exacto; escrupuloso; severo; tieso; *strictly speaking*, en rigor.

strictness, s. exactitud; severidad, rigor.
stricture ['striktʃər], s. crítica, severa, censura; (*med.*) estrechez, constricción.
stride [straid], s. paso largo, tranco, trancada, zancada. — v.t. (*pret.* **strode**; *p.p.* **stridden**, **strid**) pasar a zancadas, cruzar a grandes trancos; montar a horcajadas. — v.i. andar a pasos largos; cruzar a grandes trancos.
strident ['straidənt], a. estridente, chillón; (*fig.*) chillón, llamativo.
stridor ['straidɔr], s. estridor, sonido chirriante, chirrido.
stridulate ['stridju:lit], v.i. estridular, chirriar.
stridulation, s. estridor, chirrido.
stridulous ['stridju:ləs], a. estridente, rechinante.
strife [straif], s. contienda, disputa, lucha, refriega; rivalidad; porfía; antipatía.
strike [straik], v.t. (*pret.* **struck**; *p.p.* **struck**, **stricken**) golpear, dar golpes; pegar, apuñear; herir; cutir, percutir, tocar, hacer resonar, batir, chocar con, arrojar contra; hacer eco; encender (un fósforo); sellar, acuñar (moneda); contratar, cerrar (un trato); dar (la hora); parecer, hacer (o causar) una impresión; ocurrírsele o ocurrirle a uno (una idea); convenir, concertar; descubrir, divisar, encontrar, dar con; asumir (una postura); bajar (una vela); calar, arriar (una bandera); parar el trabajo; pasar o hacer (balance); allanar, nivelar; imprimir en la memoria; sorprender(se), amedrentar; tropezar con, encontrar, hallar. — v.i. golpear, dar golpes; dar contra, tropezar; batir, aporrear; (*mar.*) varar, encallar, embarrancar; sonar, dar sonido; suceder casualmente; avanzar, ir adelante; declararse en huelga; arriar el pabellón, rendirse; brotar, manifestar, estallar; arraigar, echar raíces; (*geol.*) inclinarse, yacer; saturarse de sal; entrar repentinamente; *to strike back*, dar golpe por golpe; *to strike against* (o *upon*), chocar con, estrellarse contra; *to strike a lead*, (*min.*) hallar una veta; *to strike at*, atacar, acometer; *to strike for*, (*fam.*) dirigirse hacia; acometer; *to strike down*, derribar, echar abajo a fuerza de golpes, arriar; acometer (una enfermedad, el cansancio, etc.); *to strike home*, dar en el vivo (o hito, o clavo); *to strike in*, meterse; juntarse, unirse; interrumpir; *to strike in with*, conformarse con; *to strike into*, comenzar repentinamente; penetrar en; *to strike on*, dar contra; encontrar, descubrir; *to strike off*, anular, cancelar, borrar, tachar, rayar; tirar, imprimir; quitar (a fuerza de golpes); *to strike on a rock*, (*mar.*) escollar; *to strike out*, tachar, rayar, borrar, cancelar, testar; asestar un puñetazo; tomar una resolución; arrojarse, lanzarse; *to strike soundings*, (*mar.*) sondear; *to strike up*, tocar, empezar a tocar, tañer; trabar (amistad); *to strike through*, atacar (una persona) por medio de (otra); traspasar, atravesar; calar; *to strike fire*, sacar fuego (del pedernal); *to strike with admiration*, llenar de admiración; *to strike work*, hallar trabajo; *to strike blind*, cegar (o poner) ciego de repente; *it strikes me*, me parece, me ocurre el pensamiento; *so it strikes me*, así me parece, en mi opinión. — s. golpe; huelga, cesación (o paro) del trabajo; (*min.*) descubrimiento de un filón; (*fam.*) buen éxito, ganga; rasero; medida.

strike-breaker, *s.* esquirol.

striker ['straikəɹ], *s.* persona o cosa que golpea, golpeador, percusor; huelgista, *m.f.*

striking, *a.* sorprendente, notable, impresionante; semejante, parecido; evidente, patente, obvio; violento, fuerte; que llama la atención; que está en huelga, que hace huelga; percuciente.

string [striŋ], *s.* bramante, cordel, cuerdezuela, cuerdecita; ristra, cuelga; cinta, presilla; cuerda (de un arco); fila, hilera; (*mús.*) cuerda; (*fig.*) retahila, sarta, serie, *f.*, sinfín, cadena, encadenamiento; nervio, fibra, tendón; (*mar.*) durmiente del alcázar y castillo; *string-beans,* (*bot.*) habichuelas; *string of lies,* sarta de mentiras; *to have more than one string to one's bow,* tener el pie en dos zapatos; *string beans,* judías verdes. — *pl.* (*mús.*) (instrumentos de) cuerda. — *v.t.* (*pret., p.p.* **strung**) (*mús.*) encordar; templar (un instrumento de cuerdas); ensartar, enhilar, enhebrar, encordelar, atar con bramante; estirar, poner tenso, entiesar, entesar; quitar las fibras; *to string up,* (*fam.*) ahorcar; (*mús.*) encordar, templar; *to string out,* extender en fila. — *v.i.* extenderse en línea; parecer hebras (o fibras o briznas).

stringed [striŋd], *a.* encordado, encordelado; ensartado; *stringed instrument,* instrumento de cuerda.

stringency ['strindʒənsi], *s.* aprieto, apuro; estrechez, severidad.

stringent ['strindʒənt], *a.* estricto, riguroso, severo; que comprime, que aprieta; impedido por obstáculos; (*com.*) tirante.

stringer ['striŋəɹ], *s.* (*carp.*) zanca; (*f.c.*) durmiente; ensartador; encordador.

stringless ['striŋles], *a.* sin cuerdas, que no tiene cuerdas.

stringy ['striŋi], *a.* fibroso, filamentoso; correoso, duro.

strip [strip], *v.t.* (*pret., p.p.* **stripped, stript**) desnudar, dejar en cueros; despojar, desvestir, desguarnecer; robar; descortezar; desgarrar (o cortar) en tiras (o jirones); ordeñar hasta agotar; *to strip a mast,* (*mar.*) desparejar un palo; *to strip off,* desnudar; *to strip completely* (o *bare*), no dejar ni un clavo en la pared. — *v.i.* desnudarse, desvestirse; despojarse; perder el hilo (tornillos, tuercas). — *s.* tira, faja, listón, lista, lonja, jirón; *strip-cartoon,* dibujos (en periódicos), cartón comico; *weather-strip,* gualdrín; *narrow strip,* tirita, tirilla; *strip-tease,* 'strip-tease', número de cabaret en que la artista se desnuda total o parcialmente.

stripe [straip], *v.t.* rayar, hacer rayas, gayar. — *s.* raya, lista, banda, tira, línea, franja, barra, galón; azote, azotazo; cardenal (en el cuerpo), señal (o marca) de un golpe, *f.*

stripling ['striplin], *s.* mozalbete, mozuelo.

strive [straiv], *v.i.* (*pret.* **strove**; *p.p.* **striven**) empeñarse, esforzarse, procurar, hacer lo posible (para conseguir); disputar, contender, debatir; estar en oposición, oponerse, contrarrestar, competir.

striver, *s.* competidor.

strobile ['stroubil], *s.* estróbilo.

strode [stroud], *pret.* [STRIDE].

stroke [strouk], *s.* golpe, choque; (*mec.*) golpe (o curso o carrera) del émbolo; golpe del remo, boga, remada, brazada, braceo; toque, trazo, raya, rasgo, plumada, pincelada; golpe de fortuna; rasgo de ingenio; ataque fulminante; golpe de mano; campanada; tacada (en el billar); jugada; proeza, hazaña; acción eficaz; éxito, suceso, feliz encuentro; caricia con la mano; modo de obrar (o trabajar); proel (que maneja el remo de proa); *stroke-oar,* bogavante, primer remero; *stroke of a pen,* plumada; *stroke of a brush* (o *pencil*), pincelada; *stroke of genius,* ocurrencia genial, inspiración, idea genial, rasgo ingenioso; *stroke of* (*good*) *luck,* golpe de fortuna, racha de buena suerte (en el juego); *stroke of wit,* chiste, rasgo gracioso, humorada. — *v.t.* pasar la mano por la espalda, acariciar, halagar; frotar suavemente; ranurar (la piedra) con cincel; remar, halar, batir; (*cost.*) alisar (un plegado con la aguja).

stroll [stroul], *v.i.* deambular, pasear(se), vagar; vaguear, tunar, callejear. — *s.* paseo; callejeo, vagancia.

stroller, *s.* paseante, paseador; vagamundo, vagabundo; cómico ambulante.

strolling, *a.* que vaga, vagamundo, ambulante; cómico ambulante.

stroma ['stroumə] (*pl.* **stromata**), *s.* (*anat.*) estroma.

strong [stroŋ], *a.* fuerte, fornido, forzudo, vigoroso, muscular, robusto, sano; potente, poderoso, pujante; concentrado, espirituoso, de cuerpo (vino); firme, sólido, consistente; capaz, hábil; impetuoso, caluroso, violento; enérgico, activo, determinado, resuelto, eficaz; brillante, vivo, picante; intenso; celoso; acérrimo; marcado, pronunciado; numéricamente fuerte; (*com.*) pujante, con tendencia al alza; *strong-box,* caja (de caudales); cofre fuerte, caja de hierro; *ten thousand strong,* de diez mil hombres.

strong-bodied, *a.* corpulento, de mucho cuerpo, membrudo, fornido.

strong-handed, *a.* fuerte de manos y puños.

stronghold ['stroŋhould], *s.* plaza fuerte, fortín, castillo; (*fig.*) refugio.

strongly ['stroŋli], *adv.* fuertemente, vigorosamente; rigorosamente, severamente, sólidamente, firmemente; acérrimamente; vehementemente.

strong-minded, *a.* determinado, resuelto, obstinado; de firmes creencias.

strontia ['stronʃə], *s.* estronciana.

strontium ['stronʃəm], *s.* estroncio.

strop [strop], *v.t.* suavizar, asentar (una navaja). — *s.* suavizador (o asentador) de navajas; (*mar.*) estrovo.

strophe ['stroufi], *s.* (*poét.*) estrofa, estancia.

strove [strouv], *pret.* [STRIVE].

struck [strʌk], *pret., p.p.* [STRIVE].

structural ['strʌktʃərəl], *a.* estructural; *structural resistance,* (*aer.*) resistencia pasiva.

structure ['strʌktʃəɹ], *s.* construcción, edificio, fábrica, bastimento, máquina; hechura, estructura, textura.

struggle [strʌgəl], *v.i.* luchar, pugnar, pelear, bregar, batallar, forcejar; esforzarse, hacer esfuerzos, agitarse; contender, resistirse. — *s.* disputa, contención, contienda, pugna, forcejo, pelea, lucha, conflicto; esfuerzo; resistencia.

strum [strʌm], *v.t., v.i.* rasguear, rasgar (la guitarra); guitarrear; tocar mal un instrumento de cuerda.

struma ['struːmə], s. lamparón, lamparones, tumores escrofulosos.

strumming, s. rasgueo (de guitarra); guitarreo.

strumous ['struːməs], a. escrofuloso.

strumpet ['strʌmpet], s.f. ramera, meretriz, mujer abandonada.

strung [strʌŋ], pret., p.p. [STRING].

strut [strʌt], v.i. contonearse, pavonearse; farolear, fachendear, ensoberbecerse, inflarse. — s. contoneo, pavonada, paso arrogante; (carp.) jabalcón, tornapunta de caballete; (aer.) montante; (min.) adema; (cost.) plegadera.

struthious ['struːθiəs], a. parecido (o perteneciente) a los avestruces.

strychnine, s. estricnina.

stub [stʌb], s. (agr.) tocón, cepa; zoquete; cabo, colilla (de cigarrillo), fragmento, resto; talón, matriz, f. — v.t. tropezar contra una cosa baja; (agr.) rozar, extirpar, desarraigar; reducir a un tocón, hacer cachigordete, quitar los tocones.

stubbed [stʌbd], a. a modo de tocón; lleno de tocones; áspero, grosero.

stubbiness ['stʌbinis], s. forma parecida a un tocón, estado de grueso y corto.

stubble ['stʌbəl], s. (agr.) rastrojo; barba.

stub-book, s. libro talonario.

stubborn ['stʌbərn], a. cabezudo, obstinado, testarudo, contumaz, terco, porfiado, tenaz, tozudo; inquebrantable, irreducible, inflexible.

stubbornness, s. obstinación, terquedad, testarudez, aferramiento, pertinacia, porfía, tesonería.

stubby ['stʌbi], a. cachigordete, gordo, corto y tieso.

stub-iron, s. hierro para cañones de fusil.

stub-nail, s. puntilla, hita.

stub-pen, s. pluma de escribir de punta mocha.

stucco ['stʌkou], v.t., v.i. (alb.) estucar, cubrir (o revestir) de estuco, formar adornos de estuco. — s. estuco; stucco plasterer (o worker), estucador, estuquista, m.f.; stucco-work, guarnecido, estuco, estucado.

stuck [stʌk], pret., p.p. [STICK].

stud [stʌd], s. (carp.) poste de tabique, paral, pie derecho; tachuela grande, tachón, clavo de adorno; botón pasador de camisa; refuerzo de eslabón; potrero; yeguada, caballada; caballeriza; stud-horse, caballo padre; stud-book, registro genealógico de caballos; stud-farm, acaballadero, potrero; stud-work, (carp.) entramado. — v.t. tachonar, adornar con tachones; (fig.) adornar, salpicar.

studding-sails, s.pl. (mar.) alas, rastreras, arrastraderas.

student ['stjuːdənt], s. estudiante, discípulo, alumno, escolar; investigador, estudioso.

studied ['stʌdid], a. estudiado, premeditado, hecho con cuidado; culto, docto, cerebral, correcto, pedante, de mucha lima. — p.p. [STUDY].

studio ['stjuːdiou], s. estudio, taller; (radio, cine, etc.) estudio.

studious ['stjuːdiəs], a. estudioso, aplicado; asiduo, solícito, diligente, estudiado, premeditado.

studiously, adv. estudiosamente, asiduamente, diligentemente; a sabiendas, con intención.

studiousness, s. estudiosidad, diligencia, aplicación al estudio.

study ['stʌdi], s. estudio, aplicación, diligencia, cuidado; investigación; asignatura, materia que se estudia; ensayo, bosquejo; escritorio, gabinete, (ant.) retrete; meditación profunda; perplejidad, embarazo; solicitud, cuidado; (mús.) estudio, ejercicio; to be in a brown study, pensar en las musarañas. — v.t. estudiar, investigar, examinar, observar; considerar, meditar; idear, proyectar. — v.i. estudiar, dedicarse al estudio; prepararse (para un examen); meditar, contemplar.

stufa [stuːfə], s. chorro de vapor que emana de una grieta en la tierra.

stuff [stʌf], s. material, materia prima; materia substancial, parte elemental, f., esencia, elemento fundamental; mueblaje, mobiliario; cachivaches, chismes, baratijas; desechos, desperdicios; ideas (o sentimientos) sin valor, disparates, patrañas, fruslería; (fam.) trastos, cosas, utensilios; paño, género, tela, tejido, estofa; mejunje, jarope, pócima; (mar.) betún; (carp.) tablas, tablillas; thick stuff, (mar.) tablones; poor stuff, de pacotilla. — interj. ¡bagatela! ¡niñería! ¡fruslería! — v.t. henchir, llenar, colmar, rehenchir; empaquetar; embutir, atiborrar; apretar, atestar; atascar, tapar; (coc.) rellenar, embutir; practicar la taxidermia. — v.i. atracarse, engullir, tragar, llenarse de comida.

stuffiness, s. mala ventilación, bochorno.

stuffing, s. atestadura, material con que se atesta o rellena una cosa, rehenchimiento; (mec.) empaquetado; (coc.) relleno, efecto o acto de rellenar; stuffing-box, (mec.) caja de empaquetado.

stuffy ['stʌfi], a. que tupe, que impide la respiración, mal ventilado; (vulg.) hinchado, empinado, puntilloso.

stultification [stʌltifi'keiʃən], s. embobecimiento.

stultify ['stʌltifai], v.t. embrutecer, atontar, embobecer; invalidar; (for.) alegar locura (o estupidez).

stum [stʌm], s. mosto, vino fermentado en parte. — v.t. echar antiséptico al vino para que no fermente; azufrar un tonel.

stumble ['stʌmbəl], v.i. tropezar, dar un traspié; (en la pronunciación) titubear, tropezar, tartamudear; to stumble on (across o upon), hallar casualmente, encontrar, dar con, tropezar con. — s. traspié, tropiezo, tropezón, resbalón, trompicón; desliz; desatino.

stumbler, s. tropezador.

stumbling-block, s. tropiezo, tropezadero; piedra de escándalo.

stump [stʌmp], s. tocón, cepa, cachopo, toza; troncho (de col); muñón de brazo (o pierna); raigón (de una muela); poste; (b.a.) esfumino; tope de cerradura; estrado, tribuna pública; uno de los tres postes del juego cricket; (pol.) arenga electoral; (fam.) desafío, reto; stump speaker, orador callejero; stump speech, discurso enfático, absurdo; to be up a stump, estar en un aprieto, estar perplejo; to stir one's stumps, (fam.) moverse, ponerse en movimiento. — a. parecido a un tocón; perteneciente a una arenga política. — v.t. recorrer haciendo discursos políticos; (fam.) dejar perplejo, vencer, cachifollar; (fam.) desafiar, retar, provocar; tropezar contra, encontrar (obstáculos); (b.a.) esfumar. — v.i. andar renqueando; andar sobre los muñones; (*fam.*) pronunciar discursos políticos.

stumpy, *a.* lleno de tocones; tozo, rechoncho, cachigordete.

stun [stʌn], *v.t.* aturdir con un golpe, atontar, dejar pasmado, pasmar, privarse o privar (el sentido); atolondrar, atronar, ensordecer, aturrullar. — *s.* sacudimiento (o choque, o golpe) que aturde; aturdimiento.

stung [stʌŋ], *pret., p.p.* [STING].

stunk [stʌŋk], *pret., p.p.* [STINK].

stunner [ˈstʌnəɹ], *s.* persona o cosa que aturde, atolondra o aturrulla; (*fam.*) cosa rara, pasmosa; (*fam.*) chica guapa.

stunt [stʌnt], *v.t.* impedir el crecimiento o desarrollo, no dejar medrar, hacer achaparrado; hacer acrobacias (especialmente en público); *to grow stunted*, achaparrarse. — *s.* falta de crecimiento o desarrollo; cosa achaparrada; reclamo, señuelo, propaganda extravagante y llamativa; (*fam.*) suerte o ejercicio de habilidad; (*aer.*) acrobacias.

stupe [stjuːp], *s.* (*med.*) fomentación, fomento, compresa. — *v.t.* fomentar.

stupefacient [stjuːpiˈfæʃənt], *s., a.* estupefaciente, estupefactivo.

stupefaction [stjuːpiˈfækʃən], *s.* atolondramiento, aturdimiento, estupefacción, estupor, pasmo.

stupefied [ˈstjuːpifaid], *a.* estupefacto, turulato.

stupefier, *s.* persona o cosa que produce estupor.

stupefy [ˈstjuːpifai], *v.t.* causar estupor, dejar turulato (o estupefacto), embobecer, atontar, atolondrar, embrutecer, entorpecer; pasmar, causar sorpresa.

stupendous [stjuːˈpendəs], *a.* estupendo, vasto, inmenso, de tamaño grande; estupendo, maravilloso.

stupendousness, *s.* calidad de estupendo (o maravilloso), lo estupendo (o maravilloso).

stupid [ˈstjuːpid], *a.* estúpido, torpe, mentecato, grosero, tosco, necio, zote, estólido; estupefacto, turulato.

stupidity [stjuːˈpiditi], *s.* estupidez, torpeza, insensatez; necedad, mentecatada, tontería, embrutecimiento.

stupor [ˈstjuːpəɹ], *s.* estupor; atontamiento, gran torpeza, estupidez.

sturdily [ˈstəːɹdili], *adv.* robustamente, vigorosamente; tenazmente, resueltamente, firmemente, porfiadamente.

sturdiness, *s.* robustez, fuerza, fortaleza, vigor; tenacidad, obstinación, terquedad.

sturdy [ˈstəːɹdi], *a.* robusto, vigoroso, capaz de trabajar, fuerte; endurecido, terco, firme, bronco, tenaz, porfiado, obstinado. — *s.* (*vet.*) modorra.

sturgeon [ˈstəːɹdʒən], *s.* esturión, marón; sollo.

stutter [ˈstʌtəɹ], *v.i.* tartamudear, balbucear, hablar con dificultad, gaguear, tartelear; tartajear; titubear, tropezar. — *s.* tartamudeo, acción de tartamudear, (*fam.*) farfulla.

stutterer [ˈstʌtərəɹ], *s.* tartamudo, tartajoso, (*fam.*) farfulla, *m.f.*, balbuciente.

sty [stai], *s.* (*pl.* **sties**) zahúrda, pocilga, cochiquera; zaquizamí, tabuco, cuchitril; burdel, lupanar; (*med.*) orzuelo del ojo.

Stygian [ˈstidʒiən], *a.* estigio.

style [stail], *s.* estilo, dicción, lenguaje, manera de hablar (o escribir); manera de obrar; moda, estilo, modelo; manera, uso, modo, tono; escuela, género; (*arq.*) estilo; tratamiento, título; (*ant.*) buril, estilo o punzón para escribir; estilo o gnomon del reloj de sol; (*cir.*) estilete; (*zool.*) pira; (*bot.*) estilo. — *v.t.* intitular, nombrar, poner un nombre o título.

stylet, *s.* estilete, punzón; (*zool.*) púa.

stylish [ˈstailiʃ], *a.* elegante, de buen estilo, a la moda.

stylist, *s.* estilista, *m.f.*

stylize [ˈstailaiz], *v.t.* estilizar.

stylobate [ˈstailobeit], *s.* estilóbato.

stylograph [ˈstailogræf], *s.* estilógrafo.

styloid [ˈstailoid], *a.* estiloideo.

stylus [ˈstailəs], *s.* estilo, punzón; (*gramófono*) estilete, aguja.

styptic [ˈstiptik], *s., a.* estíptico, astrictivo.

stypticity [stipˈtisiti], *s.* estipticidad.

styracaceous [stairəˈkeiʃəs], *a.* estiracáceo.

styrax [ˈstairæks], *s.* estoraque.

Styx [stiks], *s.* (*mit.*) Estige, *f.*, laguna del infierno.

suable [ˈsjuːəbəl], *a.* que puede ser perseguido en justicia.

suasion [ˈsweiʒən], *s.* persuasión.

suasive [ˈsweiziv], (*ant.*) **suasory**, *a.* persuasivo, suasorio.

suave [sweiv], *a.* urbano, reposado, suave, tratable.

suavity [ˈswæviti], *s.* suavidad, urbanidad; dulzura, blandura, delicia.

subacid [sʌbˈæsid], *a.* agrillo; (*quím.*) subácido.

subacrid, *a.* asperillo.

subaerial [sʌbˈeiiriəl], *a.* subaéreo.

sub-agent, *s.* subagente, subejecutor.

sub-almoner, *s.* teniente de limosnero.

subaltern [ˈsʌbəltəɹn], *a.* subalterno, subordinado; (*lóg.*) (proposición) particular. — *s.* oficial subalterno; alférez, teniente.

subalternate [sʌbˈæltəɹnit], *a.* sucesivo; subalterno, subordinado. — *s.* (*lóg.*) proposición particular.

subaqueous [sʌbˈeikwiəs], *a.* subacuático.

sub-base [ˈsʌb-beis], *s.* (*arq.*) miembro más bajo de una base.

sub-bass [ˈsʌb-beis], *s.* (*mús.*) registro grave (de un órgano).

subcarbonate, *s.* subcarbonato.

subchanter, *s.* sochantre.

subcommittee [ˈsʌbkəmiti], *s.* subcomisión, comisión parcial.

subconscious, *s.* subconsciencia. — *a.* subconsciente.

subcontract [sʌbˈkɔntrækt], *s.* subcontrato. — *v.* hacer subcontratos.

subcontractor, *s.* subcontratista, *m.f.*

subcontrary, *a.* (*lóg.*) (proposición) subcontraria.

subcordate, *a.* subcordiforme.

subcutaneous [sʌbkjuːˈteiniəs], *a.* subcutáneo, hipodérmico.

subdeacon, *s.* subdiácono.

subdeaconship, *s.* subdiaconato.

subdean, *s.* subdecano, vice-decano.

subdecuple, *a.* subdécuplo.

subdelegate, *s.* subdelegado. — *v.t.* subdelegar.

subdelegation, *s.* subdelegación.

subdivide [sʌbdiˈvaid], *v.t.* subdividir.

subdivision [sʌbdi'viʒən], *s.* subdivisión.
subdominant, *s., a.* (*mús.*) subdominante, *f.*
subduce, subduct, *v.t.* (*ant.*) substraer, quitar.
subduction, *s.* substracción.
subdue [sʌb'dju:], *v.t.* sojuzgar, subyugar, reprimir, someter, rendir, mortificar, sujetar, dominar; domeñar, domar, amansar; amortiguar, suavizar, enternecer; *subdued tone,* tono sumiso, voz baja; (*pint.*) color amortiguado.
subduement, subduing, *s.* sujeción, subyugación, rendición; doma, domadura, amansamiento; amortiguamiento.
subduer [sʌb'djuəɹ], *s.* sojuzgador; domador, amansador.
sub-editor, *s.* subdirector (de un periódico).
suberic [sju:'berik], *a.* subérico.
suberin ['sju:berin], *s.* suberina.
subfamily, *s.* (*biol.*) tribu, *f.* subfamilia.
subfusc [sʌb'fʌsk], *a.* algo moreno, algo obscuro.
subgenus, *s.* (*biol.*) subgénero.
subjacent [sʌb'dʒeisənt], *a.* subyacente.
subjacency, *s.* calidad de subyacer.
subject ['sʌbdʒekt], *v.t.* sujetar, someter, subyugar, exponer, presentar; subordinar, poner en estado de dependencia, supeditar. — *a.* sujeto, expuesto, propenso; avasallado, sometido, supeditado, dominado. — *s.* súbdito, vasallo; tema, *m.,* materia, tópico, asunto, sujeto; plan, proyecto; (*gram.*) sujeto; (*med.*) individuo, cadáver destinado a la disección; *subject-matter,* materia, asunto, contenido.
subjection [səb'dʒekʃən], *s.* sujeción, sometimiento, ligadura.
subjective [səb'dʒektiv], *a.* subjetivo.
subjectivism, *s.* subjetivismo.
subjectivity [sʌbdʒek'tiviti], *s.* subjetividad.
subjoin [sʌb'dʒɔin], *v.t.* añadir, juntar, adjuntar.
subjugate ['sʌbdʒju:geit], *v.t.* subyugar, sojuzgar, someter, sujetar.
subjugation, *s.* sujeción, subyugación.
subjunctive [sʌb'dʒʌŋktiv], *s., a.* (*gram.*) subjuntivo.
sub-kingdom, *s.* subreino.
sublease [sʌb'li:s], *s.* subarriendo. — *v.t.* subarrendar.
sub-lessee [sʌbles'i:], *s.* subarrendatario.
sub-lessor, *s.* subarrendador.
sublet [sʌb'let], *v.t.* subarrendar. — *s.* subarriendo.
subletting, *s.* subarrendamiento.
sublimate ['sʌblimeit], *s.* (*quím.*) sublimado; *corrosive sublimate,* solimán, sublimado corrosivo. — *v.t.* (*quím.*) sublimar; (*fig.*) separar de la escoria, depurar.
sublimation [sʌbli'meiʃən], *s.* sublimación.
sublimatory, *a.* sublimatorio.
sublime [sʌb'laim], *a.* sublime, excelso; supremo, extremo; imponente, solemne, majestuoso. — *s.* lo sublime, sublimidad. — *v.t., v.i.* sublimar, engrandecer, ensalzar; (*quím.*) sublimar(se).
sublimity [sʌb'limiti], *s.* sublimidad, alteza.
sublingual, *a.* sublingual.
sublunar [sʌb'lu:nəɹ], **sublunary** [sʌb-'lu:nəri], *a.* sublunar.
submarine ['sʌbməri:n], *a.* submarino. — *s.* submarino.

submaxillary, *a.* submaxilar.
submediant, *s.* (*mús.*) superdominante, *f.*
submerge [səb'mə:ɹdʒ], *v.t.* sumergir, zambullir, inundar, empantanar; ahogar, anegar. — *v.i.* zambullirse, sumergirse.
submergence, submersion, *s.* sumersión, sumergimiento, zambullida; hundimiento.
submission [səb'miʃən], *s.* sumisión, rendimiento, obsequio, resignación, conformidad; sometimiento, rendición; (*for.*) sometimiento a arbitraje.
submissive [səb'misiv], *a.* sumiso, rendido, obsequioso, humilde.
submissiveness, *s.* sumisión, rendimiento, obsequio, conformidad.
submit [səb'mit], *v.t.* someter, sujetar; presentar, referir, trasladar, dejar a la decisión de uno; presentar (o exponer) como opinión propia. — *v.i.* someterse, estar sometido, conformarse, resignarse, sujetarse, rendirse, ceder.
submultiple, *s.* submúltiplo.
subnormal [sʌb'nɔ:ɹməl], *a.* anormal; (*temperatura*) bajo la normal. — *s.* (*mat.*) subnormal.
suboctave, *a.* subóctuplo.
suborder, *s.* (*bot., zool.*) suborden; (*arq.*) orden subordinado.
subordinacy, *s.* subordinación, sujeción.
subordinate [sʌb'ɔ:ɹdineit], *s., a.* subalterno, subordinado, dependiente, secundario. — *v.t.* subordinar, considerar como de importancia secundaria; posponer; someter, sujetar.
subordination, *s.* subordinación; menoría.
suborn [sʌ'bɔ:ɹn], *v.t.* sobornar, cohechar.
subornation [sʌbɔ:ɹ'neiʃən], *s.* soborno, cohecho.
suborner, *s.* sobornador, cohechador.
subpoena [sub'pi:nə], *s.* (*for.*) citación, comparendo. — *v.t.* (*for.*) citar, emplazar.
subpolar, *a.* subpolar.
subrector, *s.* subrector, vice-rector, subregente.
subreption, *s.* subrepción.
subrogation, *s.* subrogación.
subscribe [səb'skraib], *v.t., v.i.* subscribir, rubricar; aprobar, consentir, dar el consentimiento; subscribirse, abonarse.
subscriber, *s.* infrascrito, firmante, persona que firma (o subscribe); subscriptor, abonado.
subscript [səb'skript], *s., a.* cosa escrita debajo de otra.
subscription [səb'skripʃən], *s.* subscripción; abono; firma; cantidad subscrita.
subsection, *s.* subdivisión.
subsecutive, *a.* subsiguiente, subsecuente.
subsequence, *s.* subsecuencia.
subsequent ['sʌbsekwənt], *a.* subsecuente, subsiguiente.
subsequently, *adv.* posteriormente, subsiguientemente, luego, más tarde.
subserve [səb'sə:ɹv], *v.t.* servir, ayudar, estar subordinado a. — *v.i.* servir como subordinado.
subservience, subserviency, *s.* utilidad, provecho, servicio, ayuda; servilismo, adulación; subordinación.
subservient [səb'sə:ɹviənt], *a.* útil, servicial; servil, adulador; subordinado, subalterno, inferior.

subside [səb'said], *v.i.* apaciguarse, calmarse, callarse, cesar (una tempestad); bajar (un flúido); desplomarse, hundirse, irse a fondo; dejarse caer.

subsidence ['sʌbsidəns], *s.* hundimiento, desmoronamiento, desplume, sumersión; bajada (de un flúido); asiento, poso (de sedimento); (*fig.*) apaciguamiento, amortiguamiento, desencono, desenojo.

subsidiary [səb'sidiəri], *a.* subsidiario.

subsidize ['sʌbsidaiz], *v.t.* subvencionar, dar un subsidio a, suministrar fondos a.

subsidy ['sʌbsidi], *s.* subvención, subsidio.

subsist [səb'sist], *v.i.* subsistir, perdurar; existir, consistir; mantenerse, sustentarse, tener con que vivir. — *v.t.* sustentar, mantener.

subsistence [səb'sistəns], *s.* subsistencia, existencia; subsistencias, sustento, manutención, mantenimiento, sostenimiento.

subsistent, *a.* (*ant.*) subsistente.

subsoil ['sʌbsɔil], *s.* subsuelo.

substance ['sʌbstəns], *s.* substancia; materia, material; (*biol.*) tejido; miga, jugo, enjundia, fuste; hacienda, caudal, bienes.

substantial [sʌb'stænʃəl], *a.* substancial, sólido, fuerte, vigoroso, resistente; substancial, valioso, cuantioso, considerable; real, verdadero, existente; material, corpóreo; rico, acomodado; substancioso, enjundioso. — *s.* cosa real, realidad; parte esencial.

substantiality, *s.* substancia, solidez; substantividad, realidad; corporeidad.

substantialize, *v.t., v.i.* hacer efectivo, hacer real.

substantially [sʌb'stænʃəli], *adv.* substancialmente, sólidamente; realmente; principalmente, en gran parte.

substantiate [sʌb'stænʃieit], *v.t.* verificar, comprobar, establecer, justificar; substanciar.

substantiation [sʌbstænʃi'eiʃən], *s.* verificación, comprobación, justificación; substanciación.

substantival [sʌbstən'taivəl], *a.* (*gram.*) substantivo.

substantive ['sʌbstəntiv], *a.* (*gram.*) substantivo; substantivo, real, esencial, duradero; explícito. — *s.* (*gram.*) substantivo; persona o cosa independiente.

substantively, *adv.* substancialmente, en substancia, substantivamente.

substitute ['sʌbstitjuːt], *v.t.* substituir, reemplazar. — *s.* substituto, suplente, reemplazo.

substitution [sʌbsti'tjuːʃən], *s.* substitución, reemplazo.

substratum [sʌb'streitəm] (*pl.* **substrata**), *s.* lecho o capa inferior.

substructure ['sʌbstrʌktʃəɹ], *s.* parte inferior de un edificio.

subtangent, *s.* (*geom.*) subtangente.

subtend [sʌb'tend], *v.t.* (*geom.*) subtender.

subtense, *s.* (*geom.*) subtensa.

subterfuge ['sʌbtəɹfjuːdʒ], *s.* subterfugio, salida, efugio, evasión.

subterranean [sʌbtə'reiniən], **subterraneous** [sʌbtə'reiniəs], *a.* subterráneo.

subtile ['sʌtəl], *a.* sutil, delicado, tenue, etéreo; refinado; artificioso; perspicaz, ingenioso, agudo, astuto, penetrante.

subtilely, *adv.* (*ant.*) sutilmente, astutamente, ingeniosamente.

subtility [sʌb'tiliti], *s.* sutileza, sutilidad; refinamiento; delgadez, tenuidad; astucia, ingeniosidad.

subtilization, *s.* sutilidad, refinamiento; pedantería, discreteo, conceptuosidad.

subtilize, *v.t., v.i.* sutilizar; discretear, cultiparlar, pedantear.

subtle ['sʌtəl], *a.* sutil, mañoso, artero; sutil, penetrante, agudo, ingenioso; hábil, apto, perito; artificioso, primoroso.

subtlety, *s.* sutileza, maña; ingeniosidad, agudeza, sutilidad, alambicamiento; argucia, astucia; primor, artificio.

subtly ['sʌtli], *adv.* sutilmente, mañosamente; sutilmente, ingeniosamente; artificiosamente.

subtract [sʌb'trækt], *v.t.* substraer, deducir, apartar; (*arit.*) restar.

subtraction, *s.* substracción; (*arit.*) resta.

subtrahend ['sʌbtrəhend], *s.* substraendo, sustraendo.

subtreasurer, *s.* subtesorero.

subtropic, subtropical, *a.* subtropical, casi tropical.

suburb ['sʌbəɹb], *s.* suburbio, arrabal. — *pl.* **suburbs,** afueras, alrededores, suburbios, inmediaciones.

suburban [sʌb'əːɹbən], *s., a.* suburbano, arrabalero.

subvention [səb'venʃən], *s.* subvención, subsidio.

subversion [səb'vəːɹʃən], *s.* subversión, estrago, trastorno.

subversive, a. subversivo.

subvert [səb'vəːɹt], *v.t.* subvertir, trastornar.

subverter, *s.* subversor, trastornador.

subvertible, *a.* subvertible, trastornable.

subway ['sʌbwei], *s.* camino artificial subterráneo; (*E.U.*) metro.

succedaneous [sʌkse'deiniəs], *a.* sucedáneo.

succedaneum [sʌkse'deiniəm], *s.* substituto; (*med.*) sucedáneo.

succeed [sək'siːd], *v.t.* suceder a, seguir a, reemplazar a; heredar a. — *v.i.* salir bien, tener éxito, conseguir, acertar, lograr; ser el heredero o sucesor.

succeeder, *s.* (*ant.*) sucesor.

succeeding, *a.* subsiguiente, sucediente, siguiente, futuro.

success [sək'ses], *s.* éxito, logro, ventaja, medro, acierto; notabilidad, victorioso, triunfo, acierto.

successful, *a.* próspero, que sale bien, venturoso, afortunado, feliz, dichoso, fausto, airoso; *to be successful,* tener éxito, escuchar aplausos, salir bien.

successfully, *adv.* felizmente, prósperamente, con buen éxito.

successfulness, *s.* feliz éxito, dicha, buen suceso.

succession [sək'seʃən], *s.* sucesión; seguida, continuación; linaje, descendencia; herencia, derecho de sucesión; (*mús.*) serie, *f.*, escala; serie, *f.*, sarta; *in succession,* sucesivamente, uno tras otro.

successive [sək'sesiv], *a.* sucesivo, siguiente.

successively, *adv.* sucesivamente, arreo; *and so on successively,* y así sucesivamente.

successor [sək'sesəɹ], *s.* sucesor; heredero.

succinate ['sʌksineit], *s.* (*quím.*) succinato.

succinct [sʌk'siŋkt], *a.* sucinto, conciso, compendioso.

succinctly [sʌk'siŋktli], *adv.* sucintamente, con precisión, compendiosamente, en pocas palabras.

succinctness, *s.* brevedad, concisión.

succinic [sʌk'sinik], *a.* succínico.

succinite ['sʌksinait], *s.* succino, ámbar.

succory ['sʌkori], *s.* achicoria.

succotash ['sʌkotæʃ], *s.* (*E.U.*) potaje de maíz tierno, fréjoles y habas.

succour ['sʌkəɹ], *v.t.* socorrer, auxiliar, dar socorro. — *s.* socorro, favor, auxilio, asistencia. — *pl.* (*mil., ant.*) refuerzos.

succourer, *s.* socorredor, auxiliador.

succuba ['sʌkju:bə], **succubus** ['sʌkju:bəs], *s.* (*pl.* **succubæ, succubi**) súcubo.

succulence, succulency, *s.* jugosidad.

succulent ['sʌkju:lənt], *a.* suculento, jugoso, sucoso.

succumb [sə'kʌm], *v.i.* sucumbir, rendirse; morir.

succumbent, *a.* (*ant.*) sucumbiente.

succussion [sə'kʌʃən], *s.* sacudimiento.

such [sʌtʃ], *a.* tal, igual, semejante, parecido; extremo; *in such and such words*, en tales y cuales palabras. — *pron.* tal, un tal; el que, la que, lo que, los que, las que; aquel, aquella, aquello, aquellos, aquellas; cualquiera que.

suchlike, *a.* semejante, tal, de esta clase, de esta índole.

suck [sʌk], *v.t., v.i.* chupar, mamar, libar; sorber; *to suck in*, embeber, chupar; *to suck out* (o *up*), extraer (o sacar) chupando (o con una bomba), dar a la bomba, vaciar, agotar; *to suck up to*, (*vulg.*) dar coba, dar jabón, hacer la zalá. — *s.* succión; chupada; mamada; (*fam.*) engaño; *to give suck*, mamantar, dar de mamar.

sucker, *s.* lechón, gorrinillo; chupadero, chupador; mamón, chupón; mamador; (*mec.*) émbolo, sopapo de bomba; (*bot.*) pimpollo, vástago, retoño, serpollo, barbado; (*zool., etc.*) ventosa; (*ict.*) remora; lompo, liebre de mar; (*fam.*) pelele, primo; borrachín.

sucking, *s.* chupadura, (*fam.*) mamada. — *a.* mamante, chupadero; lechal, recental.

sucking-fish, *s.* rémora.

sucking-pig, *s.* lechón, lechoncillo.

suckle [sʌkəl], *v.t.* amamantar, dar de mamar, dar la teta, criar. — *v.i.* lactar, mamar.

suckling ['sʌkliŋ], *s.* mamón, mamantón de teta (o de cría).

sucrose ['sju:krous], *s.* sucrosa.

suction ['sʌkʃən], *s.* succión; *suction-hose*, manguera de alimentación; *suction-pump*, bomba aspirante.

suctorial [sʌk'tɔ:riəl], *a.* chupadero, chupador, chupón.

Sudanese [su:də'ni:z], *s., a.* sudanés.

sudation [sju:'deiʃən], *s.* sudor.

sudatory ['sju:dətori], *a.* sudorífero. — *s.* sudorífico; sudadero, estufa.

sudd [sʌd], *s.* masa vegetable flotante en el Nilo blanco.

sudden ['sʌdən], *a.* repentino, pronto, imprevisto, no prevenido, impensado, súbito; apresurado, precipitado; *on a sudden* o *all of a sudden*, de repente, súbitamente.

suddenly, *adv.* de repente, de pronto, de sopetón, sin esperarse, repentinamente, súbitamente.

suddenness, *s.* precipitación, calidad de repentino, brusquedad, rapidez.

sudoriferous [sju:do'rifərəs], *a.* sudorífero.

sudorific [sju:do'rifik], *s., a.* sudorífico.

suds [sʌdz], *s.pl.* jabonaduras, espuma; *to be in the suds*, (*fam.*) estar en apuros, apurado.

sue [sju:], *v.t., v.i.* demandar, poner pleito, pedir en juicio, poner por justicia, entablar juicio; (*ant.*) galantear; *to sue for*, rogar, pedir, suplicar, tratar de persuadir; *to sue for damages*, (*for.*) demandar por daños y perjuicios.

suède [sweid], *s.* ante, gamuza.

suet ['sju:et], *s.* sebo en rama, grasa dura.

suety ['sju:eti], *a.* seboso.

suffer ['sʌfəɹ], *v.t., v.i.* sufrir, padecer, sentir; soportar, tolerar, aguantar, comportar, conllevar; consentir, admitir, permitir, pasar; sufrir una pena, un castigo; *to suffer for another*, llevar la pena de otro; *it is not to be suffered*, es insoportable.

sufferable ['sʌfrəbəl], *a.* sufrible, sufridero, pasadero, tolerable, soportable.

sufferably, *adv.* de un modo soportable.

sufferance ['sʌfrəns], *s.* tolerancia, consentimiento tácito, permisión; (*ant.*) pena, sufrimiento, aguante, conformidad; (*com.*) permiso especial de la aduana.

sufferer ['sʌfərəɹ], *s.* sufridor, doliente, paciente; víctima, *f.*; *fellow-sufferer*, compañero de infortunio.

suffering, *s.* sufrimiento, pena, dolor, tormento, padecimiento. — *a.* sufriente, doliente.

suffice [sə'fais], *v.t., v.i.* bastar, alcanzar, ser suficiente.

sufficiency, *s.* suficiencia, lo suficiente, lo bastante; eficacia, cualidad; (*ant.*) presunción.

sufficient [sə'fiʃənt], *a.* suficiente, bastante, amplio; apto, idóneo.

sufficiently, *adv.* suficientemente, bastante, asaz, bastante bien.

suffix ['sʌfiks], *v.t.* añadir como sufijo. — *s.* (*gram.*) sufijo, afijo, postfijo.

suffocate ['sʌfokeit], *v.t.* sofocar, asfixiar, ahogar; extinguir, apagar (un fuego). — *v.i.* sofocarse, asfixiarse, ahogarse, no poder respirar.

suffocating, *a.* sofocante, sofocador, asfixiante, que asfixia, que impide la respiración, que ahoga.

suffocation, *s.* sofocación, asfixia, ahogo, ahogamiento.

suffragan ['sʌfrəgən], *s., a.* (*igl.*) sufragáneo.

suffrage ['sʌfridʒ], *s.* sufragio, voto; consentimiento, aprobación; (*igl.*) sufragio.

suffragette [sʌfrə'dʒet], *s.f.* sufragista.

suffragist ['sʌfrədʒist], *s.* votante; partidario del voto femenino, sufragista, *m.*

suffruticose [sʌ'fru:tikous], *a.* (*bot.*) leñoso y herbáceo.

suffuse [sə'fju:z], *v.t.* difundir, bañar, cubrir, verter; extender.

suffusion [sə'fju:ʒən], *s.* difusión, baño; (*med.*) sufusión.

sufi ['su:fi], *s.* sufí, sofí.

sugar ['ʃugəɹ], *s.* azúcar; cosa muy dulce; (*fig.*) lisonja, miel, *f.*; *brown sugar*, azúcar moreno (o terciado); *white sugar*, azúcar refinado; *sugar-candy*, azúcar piedra (candi o cande); *sugar-bowl*, azucarero; *maple sugar*, azúcar de arce; *grape-sugar*, glucosa; *loaf-sugar*, azúcar de pilón; *sugar of lead*, azúcar de plomo, sal de saturno; *sugar-house* o *sugar-plantation*, ingenio (de azúcar); *sugar-syrup*, miel de caña, melado; *sugar-tongs*, tenacillas. — *v.t.* azucarar, endulzar, confitar; *to sugar the pill*, (*fig.*) dorar la píldora.

sugar-beet, *s.* remolacha.

sugar-cane, *s.* caña de azúcar; cañamiel, *f.*, caña melar, caña dulce.

sugar-coated, *a.* confitado, garapiñado.

sugar-daddy, *s.* (*E.U.*, *vulg.*) viejo rico que mantiene con lujo a una mujer joven.

sugared, *a.* azucarado, endulzado. — *p.p.* [SUGAR].

sugar-plum, *s.* dulce, confite; golosina.

sugary [ˈʃugəri], *a.* azucarado, sacarino, goloso; (*fig.*) meloso, almibarado.

suggest [sʌˈdʒest, səˈdʒest], *v.t.* sugerir, insinuar, indicar, advertir, intimar; aconsejar; evocar, recordar; sugestionar; echar una indirecta; ocurrirse (una idea).

suggestion [səˈdʒestʃən], *s.* sugestión, insinuación, indicación, instigación.

suggestive [səˈdʒestiv], *a.* picante, chocarrero, verde, erótico; sugestivo, sugerente, que sugiere, que inspira, que estimula.

suicidal [sjuːɪˈsaidəl], *a.* suicida; (*fig.*) suicida.

suicide [ˈsjuːisaid], *s.* suicidio; suicida, *m.f.*; (*fig.*) ruina, suicidio.

suint [ˈsjuːint], *s.* grasa natural de la lana.

suit [sjuːt], *s.* petición, súplica, solicitación; cortejo, galanteo; (*for.*) pleito, litigio; serie, *f.*, colección, juego, surtido; (*sast.*) vestido, traje completo; palo (en la baraja); *suit of armour*, armadura completa; *to bring a suit*, entablar un pleito; *to follow suit*, jugar el mismo palo; (*fig.*) seguir el ejemplo. — *v.t.*, *v.i.* cuadrar, convenir, acomodar, ir (o venir) bien, sentar, caer, encajar, proporcionar; agradar, adecuar, contentar; ajustarse, acomodarse, casar, conformarse, hermanarse, concordar; parecer, ser aparente; *to suit oneself*, (*fam.*) hacer uno lo que le dé la gana.

suitability [sjuːtəˈbiliti], *s.* conformidad, conveniencia, aptitud, acomodamiento, igualdad.

suitable [ˈsjuːtəbəl], *a.* conforme, adecuado, apropiado, propio, apto, a propósito, conveniente, satisfactorio.

suitably [ˈsjuːtəbli], *adv.* apropiadamente, adecuadamente, conforme, de una manera conveniente, satisfactoriamente.

suit-case, *s.* maleta.

suite [swiːt], *s.* serie, *f.*, juego; séquito, tren, comitiva, acompañamiento; *suite of apartments*, juego de habitaciones, juego de piezas; *bedroom suite*, juego de dormitorio (muebles).

suitor [ˈsjuːtər], *s.* (*for.*) demandante, pleitante; pretendiente, cortejo, amante, suplicante, aspirante; postulante.

sulcate [ˈsʌlkət], **sulcated** [sʌlˈkeitid] (*ant.*) *a.* surcado, acanalado.

sulfa drugs [ˈsʌlfədrʌgz], *s.* nombre colectivo dado a los sulfanamidos.

sulk [sʌlk], *v.i.* ponerse mohino, estar de mal humor, amorrar(se) (*fam.*), coger una murria (*fam.*). — *s.* murria, mohina, ceño.

sulkiness, *s.* murria, mohina, mal humor, ceño.

sulky [ˈsʌlki], *a.* murrio, mohino, malhumorado, ceñudo; (*bot.*) achaparrado. — *s.* (*carr.*) solitario, calasín de un solo asiento.

sulien [ˈsʌlən], *a.* hosco, adusto, remolón, cazurro, intratable, sombrío, tétrico, malévolo, taciturno.

sullenly, *adv.* con hosco, con ceño, tercamente, ásperamente.

sullenness [ˈsʌlənnes], *s.* hosquedad, malhumor, taciturnidad, ceño, berrín; terquedad, obstinación.

sully [ˈsʌli], *v.t.* manchar, ensuciar, empañar; desdorar, mancillar, tachar, ennegrecer. — *v.i.* mancharse, ensuciarse, empañarse, etc. — *s.* mancha; mancilla.

sulphate [ˈsʌlfeit], *s.* sulfato. — *v.t.* sulfatar.

sulphide [ˈsʌlfaid], *s.* sulfuro.

sulphite [ˈsʌlfait], *s.* sulfito.

sulphonal [ˈsʌlfonəl], *s.* sulfonal.

sulphur [ˈsʌlfər], *s.* azufre. — *v.t.* azufrar.

sulphurate [ˈsʌlfjuːrit], *v.t.* sulfurar, azufrar; blanquear. — *a.* sulfúreo.

sulphuration [sʌlfjuːˈreiʃən], *s.* sulfatación, sulfatado.

sulphureousness, *s.* calidad de sulfúreo.

sulphuret, *s.* (*ant.*) sulfuro.

sulphuretted [ˈsʌlfjuːretid], **sulphureous** [sʌlˈfjuːriəs], **sulphurous** [ˈsʌlfjuːrəs], *a.* sulfúreo, azufrado, azufroso.

sulphuric [sʌlˈfjuːrik], *a.* sulfúrico.

sulphurous [ˈsʌlfərəs], *a.* sulfuroso.

sulphurwort [ˈsʌlfəːwəːt], *s.* servato.

sulphury [ˈsʌlfəri], *a.* sulfúreo, azufroso.

sulphydric [sʌlˈfaidrik], *a.* sulfhídrico.

sultan [ˈsʌltən], *s.* sultán, soldán.

sultana [sʌlˈtɑːnə], *f.* sultana; (fruta) sultana.

sultriness [ˈsʌltrines], *s.* bochorno.

sultry [ˈsʌltri], *a.* bochornoso, sofocante.

sum [sʌm], *s.* (*arit.*) suma; problema aritmético; total, monto, monta; (*com.*) cantidad; recopilación, resumen, sumario, compendio; lo sumo, lo último; *in sum*, en suma, en breve, en resumen; *good round sum*, cantidad considerable (de dinero); *sum agreed upon*, cantidad alzada. — *v.t.* sumar; abreviar; recopilar, compendiar; *to sum up*, resumir, recapitular.

sumac [ˈsjuːmæk, ˈʃuːmæk], *s.* zumaque.

sumless, *a.* innumerable.

summarily [ˈsʌmərili], *adv.* sumariamente, resumidamente, en resumen; someramente, superficialmente.

summarize [ˈsʌməraiz], *v.t.* epitomar, resumir, compendiar.

summary [ˈsʌməri], *a.* sumario, compendioso; somero, superficial. — *s.* sumario, resumen, compendio.

summer [ˈsʌmər], *a.* estival, veraniego, de verano. — *s.* verano, estío; (*arq.*) viga solera (o maestra); dintel; sotabanco; manto de chimenea; *Indian summer*, veranillo de San Martín; *summer-time*, estío, verano, hora (oficial) de verano. — *v.t.* calentar. — *v.i.* veranear, pasar el verano.

summer-boarder, *s.* veraneante.

summer-fallow, *v.t.* arar en verano y dejar en barbecho.

summer-house, *s.* cenador, glorieta.

summit [ˈsʌmit], *s.* ápice, cima, cumbre, *f.*, punta, tope, cúspide, *f.*, pináculo.

summon ['sʌmən], *v.t.* citar, emplazar; ordenar, mandar; llamar, convocar, reunir; notificar, requerir; intimar; *to summon up*, espolear, aguijar, animar, excitar; *to summon away*, llamar aparte, mandar ir; *to summon back*, mandar volver.

summoner, *s.* emplazador, persona que notifica o cita.

summons ['sʌmənz], *s.* (*for.*) citación, comparendo, requerimiento, emplazamiento, notificación, intimación.

sump [sʌmp], *s.* (*min.*) sumidero, pozanco; (*aut.*) sumidero del cárter.

sumpter ['sʌmptəɪ], *s.* acémila; *sumpter-horse, sumpter-mule*, caballo o mula de carga.

sumption ['sʌmpʃən], *s.* premisa mayor de un silogismo.

sumptuary ['sʌmptjuːəɪɪ], *a.* suntuario; *sumptuary law* o *edict*, leyes o edicto suntuario.

sumptuous ['sʌmptjuːəs], *a.* suntuoso, magnífico, espléndido, opíparo, pomposo.

sumptuously, *adv.* suntuosamente, con pompa, con ostentación, con esplendor.

sumptuousness ['sʌmptjuːəsnis], **sumptuosity** [sʌmptjuːˈɔsiti], *s.* suntuosidad, pompa, magnificencia.

sun [sʌn], *s.* sol; luz de sol; solana. — *v.t.* poner al sol, secar al sol, asolear; *to sun oneself*, tomar el sol; *to take* (o *shoot*) *the sun*, (*mar.*, etc.) tomar la altura del sol para fijar la latitud.

sun-bath, *s.* baño de sol, solana.

sun-bathing, *s.* baño de sol.

sunbeam ['sʌnbiːm], *s.* rayo de sol.

sun-bird, *s.* suimanga.

sun-blind, *s.* persiana; toldo para el sol.

sunbonnet, *s.* papalina.

sunburn ['sʌnbəːɪn], *s.* quemadura del sol, solanera; bronceado, tosteado.

sunburnt, *a.* tostado por el sol, asoleado; requemado, atezado.

sun-clad, *a.* (*poét.*) brillante.

sundae ['sʌndei], *s.* mantecado con frutas, nueces, etc.

Sunday ['sʌndi], *s.* domingo. — *a.* dominical; *Sunday-school*, escuela dominical; *Sunday letter*, letra dominical; *Easter Sunday*, domingo de resurrección; *Palm Sunday*, domingo de ramos; *Sunday best*, (*fam.*) los trapitos de cristianar.

sunder ['sʌndəɪ], *s.* separación; *in sunder*, (*poét.*) en dos. — *v.t., v.i.* separar(se), hender, rajar(se), apartar, romper(se).

sundew ['sʌndjuː], *s.* (*bot.*) rocío del sol; cualquier planta género *Drosera*.

sun-dial ['sʌndail], *s.* reloj de sol, cuadrante solar.

sundown ['sʌndaun], *s.* puesta del sol.

sundries ['sʌndriz], *s.pl.* (*com.*) géneros diversos.

sundry ['sʌndri], *a.* varios, diversos, muchos.

sunfish ['sʌnfiʃ], *s.* (*ict.*) rueda, ojón.

sunflower ['sʌnflauəɪ], *s.* girasol, mirasol, helianto.

sung [sʌŋ], *pret., p.p.* [SING].

sun-hemp, *s.* cáñamo de sol.

sunk [sʌŋk], *pret., p.p.* [SINK].

sunken, *a.* sumido, hundido.

sunless ['sʌnles], *a.* sombrío, sin luz, sin sol, sin calor.

sunlight ['sʌnlait], *s.* luz del sol, rayos del sol.

sunlike, *a.* semejante (o parecido) al sol; resplandeciente.

Sunna ['sʌna], *s.* parte tradicional de la ley Musulmana.

sunny ['sʌni], *a.* expuesto al sol, asoleado, resolano; claro, brillante, resplandeciente; (*fig.*) alegre, risueño; *to be sunny*, hacer sol.

sun-proof, *a.* a prueba de sol.

sunrise ['sʌnraiz], *s.* salida del sol, amanecer; (*poét.*) Oriente; *from sunrise to sunset*, de sol a sol.

sunset, *s.* ocaso, puesta del sol, anochecer.

sunshade, *s.* quitasol, parasol, sombrilla; sombrero.

sunshine ['sʌnʃain], *s.* luz (o claridad) del sol, día; *in the sunshine*, al sol.

sunshiny, *a.* lleno de sol, resplandeciente, claro como el sol; (*fig.*) risueño.

sunspot, *s.* mácula, mancha del sol.

sunstroke, *s.* insolación.

sunward, *adv.* hacia el sol.

sunwise, *adv.* con el sol.

sup [sʌp], *v.t.* sorber, beber a sorbos. — *v.i.* cenar. — *s.* sorbo.

superable ['sjuːpərəbəl], *a.* superable.

superableness, *s.* cualidad (o estado) de superable.

superabound [sjuːpərəˈbaund], *v.i.* superabundar, abundar con exceso.

superabundance, *s.* superabundancia, sobreabundancia.

superabundant [sjuːpərəˈbʌndənt], *a.* superabundante, sobreabundante.

superadd [sjuːpərˈæd], *v.t.* sobreañadir, requintar.

superaddition, *s.* sobreañadidura, adición excesiva.

superannuate [sjuːpərˈænjuːeit], *v.t.* jubilar, dar retiro a.

superannuated, *a.* jubilado; anticuado, fuera de servicio. — *p.p.* [SUPERANNUATE].

superannuation, *s.* (*ant.*) inhabilitación; jubilación.

superb [sjuːˈpəːɪb], *a.* soberbio, grandioso, espléndido, magnífico, majestuoso.

supercargo ['sjuːpəɪkɑːɪɡou], *s.* encomendero, sobrecargo.

superciliary, *a.* situado en la sobreceja, perteneciente a la ceja.

supercilious [sjuːpəɪˈsiliəs], *a.* desdeñoso, altivo, altanero, imperioso.

superciliousness, *s.* altanería, altivez, desdén.

supereminence, (*ant.*) **supereminency**, *s.* supereminencia.

supereminent [sjuːpərˈeminənt], *a.* supereminente, eminentísimo.

supererogate [sjuːpərˈerogeit], *v.i.* (*ant.*) realizar una supererogación.

supererogation, *s.* supererogación.

supererogatory [sjuːpərəˈrɔɡətori], *a.* supererogatorio.

superessential, *a.* sobreesencial.

superexcellence, *a.* sobreexcelencia.

superficial [sjuːpəɪˈfiʃəl], *a.* superficial.

superficiality [sjuːpəɪfiʃiˈæliti], *s.* superficialidad, exterioridad, frivolidad.

superficially, *adv.* superficialmente, ligeramente, someramente, por encima.

superficiary [sjuːpəɪˈfiʃəri], *s.* (*for.*) superficiario.

superficies [sjuːpəɪˈfiʃiiːz], *s.* superficie, *f.*

superfine [sju:pəɹˈfain], *a*. superfino, sobre-fino, florete.

superfineness, *s*. calidad de superfino.

superfluous [sju:ˈpəːɹflu:əs], *a*. superfluo, sobrante.

superfluity [sju:pəɹˈflu:iti], **superflux** [ˈsju:pəɹflʌks], *s*. superfluidad, sobra, redundancia.

superfluously [sju:ˈpəːɹflu:əsli], *adv*. superfluamente.

superfœtation, *s*. superfetación.

super-heterodyne, *s*. (*radio*.) superheterodino. — *a*. superheterodínico.

superhuman [sju:pəɹˈhju:mən], *a*. sobrehumano.

superimpose [sju:pəɹim'pouz], *v.t*. sobreponer.

superimposition, *s*. superposición.

superincumbent [sju:pəɹin'kʌmbənt], *a*. sobrepuesto, superyacente.

superinduce [sju:pəɹin'dju:s], *v.t*. sobreañadir, promover.

superinduction, *s*. sobreañadidura, acto de sobreañadir.

superintend [sju:pəɹin'tend], *v.t*. dirigir, superentender, vigilar.

superintendence, **superintendency**, *s*. superintendencia, dirección, inspección, intervención.

superintendent [sju:pəɹin'tendənt], *s*. superintendente, inspector, capataz, interventor.

superior [sju:ˈpiəɹiəɹ], *s*., *a*. superior, mejor; (*ant*.) superior, más alto; (*fam*.) altanero, altivo; *lady superior*, superiora; *Superior Court*, Audiencia.

superiority [sju:piəɹi'ɔriti], *s*. superioridad, excelencia, preeminencia, autoridad, dominio.

superlative [sju:ˈpəːɹlətiv], *s*., *a*. superlativo, más grande, más excelente; (*gram*.) superlativo; superlativo, extremado, supremo.

superlatively [sju:ˈpəːɹlətivli], *adv*. superlativamente; en sumo grado, en grado superlativo, extremadamente.

superlativeness, *s*. excelencia.

superman [ˈsju:pəɹmæn], *s*. superhombre.

supernal [sju:ˈpəːɹnəl], *a*. superno, supremo; celeste.

supernatural [sju:pəɹˈnætʃju:ɹəl], *a*. sobrenatural. — *s*. lo sobrenatural.

supernaturalism, *s*. creencia en lo sobrenatural.

supernaturally, *adv*. sobrenaturalmente.

supernaturalness, *s*. calidad de sobrenatural.

supernumerary [sju:pəɹˈnju:məɹəri], *a*. supernumerario, de sobra, suplementario; (*teat*.) figurante, comparsa.

superpose [sju:pəɹ'pouz], *v.t*. sobreponer, superponer.

superposition, *s*. superposición.

superscribe [sju:pəɹ'skraib], *v.t*. sobreescribir, poner un sobreescrito.

superscription, *s*. sobreescrito; lema, *m*.; mote, leyenda.

supersede [sju:pəɹ'si:d], *v.t*. (*for*.) sobreseer; reemplazar, suplantar.

supersedeas [sju:pəɹ'si:diəs], *s*. (*for*.) auto jurídico de sobreseimiento.

supersedure [sju:pəɹ'si:dʒəɹ], *s*. (*for*.) sobreseimiento.

superserviceable, *a*. demasiado servicial u oficioso.

supersession [sju:pəɹ'seʃən], *s*. sobreseimiento, anulación.

superstition [sju:pəɹ'stiʃən], *s*. superstición.

superstitious [sju:pəɹ'stiʃəs], *a*. supersticioso.

superstructure [ˈsju:pəɹstɹʌktʃəɹ], *s*. construcción que se levanta sobre otra; (*fig*.) fábrica, elaboración; superestructura.

super-tax [ˈsju:pəɹtæks], *s*. impuesto adicional sobre rentas o beneficios que exceden cierto nivel. Llámase también *sur-tax*.

supervene [sju:pəɹ'vi:n], *v.i*. sobrevenir, supervenir; acaecer, suceder; seguir, ir sucediendo.

supervenient [sju:pəɹ'vi:niənt], *a*. superveniente, adicional.

supervention [sju:pəɹ'venʃən], *s*. supervención, superveniencia, sobrevenida.

supervise [sju:pəɹ'vaiz], *v.t*. superentender, vigilar, dirigir, intervenir.

supervision [sju:pəɹ'viʒən], *s*. superintendencia, intervención.

supervisor, *s*. superintendente, interventor, sobrestante, veedor.

supination [sju:pi'neiʃən], *s*. supinación, posición supina.

supine [ˈsju:pain], *a*. supino, boca arriba; pendiente, inclinado; descuidado, negligente, indolente. — *s*. (*gram*.) supino.

supinely, *adv*. boca arriba; descuidadamente, con negligencia.

supineness, *s*. posición supina; negligencia, descuido, dejadez.

supper [ˈsʌpəɹ], *s*. cena; banquete; *suppertime*, hora de cenar; *The Lord's Supper*, la santísima comunión; *The Last Supper*, la (última) cena; *to have supper*, cenar, tomar la cena.

supperless, *a*. sin cenar.

supplant [sə'plɑ:nt], *v.t*. suplantar, desbancar, dar una zancadilla.

supplanter, *s*. suplantador, persona que suplanta a otra.

supplanting, *s*. suplantación.

supple [ˈsʌpəl], *a*. flexible, manejable; cimbreño, ágil; blando, dócil; servil, lisonjero, adulatorio. — *v.t*., *v.i*. hacer (o volverse) flexible, obediente, dócil o manejable.

supplement [ˈsʌplimənt], *s*. suplemento; apéndice; (*geom*., *gram*.) suplemento.

supplemental [sʌpli'mentəl], **supplementary** [sʌpli'mentəri], *a*. suplementario, suplemental; supletorio.

suppleness [ˈsʌpəlnis], *s*. flexibilidad; agilidad; blandura, docilidad; adulación, servilismo.

suppletory [ˈsʌplitori], *a*. (*for*.) supletorio.

suppliance [ˈsʌpliəns], *s*. ruego, súplica.

suppliant [ˈsʌpliənt], *s*., *a*. (*poét*.) suplicante.

supplicant [ˈsʌplikənt], *s*. suplicante.

supplicate [ˈsʌplikeit], *v.t*. suplicar, rogar, impetrar.

supplication, *s*. súplica, ruego, suplicación; (*igl*.) preces, *f.pl*., plegaria.

supplicatory [sʌpli'keitəri], *a*. suplicatorio.

supplier [sə'plaiəɹ], *s*. suministrador, proveedor, abastecedor, surtidor.

supply [sə'plai], *v.t*. surtir, proveer, abastecer, suministrar, proporcionar, facilitar, suplir, hacer las veces de, reemplazar; acabalar, habilitar. — *s*. suministro, provisión, proveimiento, abastecimiento; cantidad suficiente; suplente, substituto; (*com*.) abasto, oferta; surtido, repuesto. — *pl.* **supplies,** pertrechos, materiales, víveres, provisiones, enseres; *supply and demand,* (*com.*) oferta y demanda.

support, *v.t.* sostener, apoyar, servir de apoyo a; sustentar, mantener, proveer; sufrir, resistir, aguantar, tolerar; amparar, asistir, abogar por; atestiguar, defender, probar, justificar, vindicar; acompañar en público; (*teat.*) hacer (o desempeñar) un papel, hacer (o desempeñar) un papel subordinado a otro; *to support oneself,* ganarse la vida. — *s.* sostén; afianzamiento; sostenimiento, sustentación; ayuda, protección, apoyo; prueba, justificación; sufragio; manutención, sustento; *in support of,* en favor de, en pro de, en apoyo de.

supportable [sə'pɔːɹtəbəl], *a.* soportable, llevadero, tolerable; sostenible.

supportably, *adv.* de una manera soportable (o tolerable).

supporter [sə'pɔːɹtəɹ], *s.* mantenedor, defensor, partidario, sostenedor, sosteniente; aficionado; soporte, sostén, sustentáculo, sostenimiento; (*arq.*) atlante, telamón, columna; amparo, apoyo; (*blas.*) tenante.

supposable [sə'pouzəbəl], *a.* que se puede suponer (o imaginar), imaginable.

supposableness, *s.* probabilidad.

suppose [sə'pouz], *v.t.* suponer, presumir, creer, imaginar, figurarse; admitir, dar de barato; *supposing that,* dado caso que, suponiendo que.

supposer, *s.* suponedor.

supposition [sʌpo'ziʃən], *s.* suposición, hipótesis, *f.*

suppositional, *a.* hipotético, supositivo.

supposititious [səpɔsi'tiʃəs], *a.* supositicio.

suppositive [sə'pɔzitiv], *a.* supositivo.

suppositively, *adv.* en suposición.

suppository [sə'pɔzitəri], *s.* supositorio, cala.

suppress [sə'pres], *v.t.* suprimir, sofocar, acabar con, destruir, extinguir; reprimir, contener; omitir, ocultar, eliminar; parar, detener, impedir (o estorbar) el curso de.

suppression, *s.* supresión, extinción, represión; (*med.*) suspensión, falta de secreción.

suppressive, *a.* supresivo, represivo.

suppressor, *s.* supresor, represor; (*elec.*) supresor.

suppurate ['sʌpjuːreit], *v.i.* supurar.

suppuration [sʌpjuː'reiʃən], *s.* supuración.

suppurative, *a.,* *s.* supurativo.

supramaxillary [sjuːprəmæk'ziləri], *s.,* *a.* supramaxilar.

supramundane [sjuːprə'mʌndein], *a.* sobrenatural.

supra-renal [sjuːprə'riːnəl], *a.* suprarrenal.

supremacy [sjuː'preməsi], *s.* supremacía; autoridad suprema.

supreme [sjuː'priːm], *a.* supremo, sumo, extremado, (lo) más elevado, (lo) más grande; *the Supreme,* Dios; *Supreme Court of Judicature,* el tribunal supremo.

supremely, *adv.* supremamente, soberanamente, en el más alto grado.

sural ['sjuːrəl], *a.* sural.

surbase ['səːɹbeis], *s.* cornisa de pedestal.

surcease [səɹ'siːs], *v.i.* cesar, acabarse, suspenderse. — *s.* cesación.

surcharge [səɹ'tʃɑːɹdʒ], *s.* sobrecarga, sobre-

peso, recargo; resello. — *v.t.* sobrecargar, cargar con exceso, recargar; resellar.

surcingle ['səːɹsiŋgəl], *s.* sobrecincha; cíngulo, ceñidor.

surcoat ['səːɹkout], *s.* sobretodo, gabán; sobrevesta.

surculose ['səːɹkjuːlous], *a.* lleno de vástagos.

surd [səːɹd], *s.* (*mat.*) cantidad irracional; (*gram.*) consonante sorda. — *a.* (*mat.*) irracional; (*gram.*) sordo, no sonoro.

surdity ['səːɹditi], *s.* falta de sonoridad.

sure ['ʃjuːɹ], *a.* seguro, cierto, certero, indudable, infalible, positivo, efectivo; acertado; sentado, firme; puntual; estable, constante; *sure-footed,* de pie firme; *to be sure,* sin duda, seguramente; estar seguro, asegurarse; ser cierto; *to make sure,* asegurar, cerciorar. — *interj.* (*E.U.*) ya lo creo, ya se ve; claro, claro está; ya; *to make sure of,* asegurarse de; contar con; *as sure as fate,* como hay viñas. — *adv.* (*fam.*) ciertamente, indudablemente, sin duda alguna; *sure enough,* a buen seguro.

surely, *adv.* seguramente, sin duda, ciertamente, por cierto, por supuesto; acertadamente.

sureness, *s.* seguridad, certeza, acierto.

surety ['ʃjuːɹəti], *s.* fiador, garante, obligado; garantía, fianza, caución, seguridad, certeza, fieldad; *to be surety for,* responder de, salir garante (por).

suretyship, *s.* seguridad, fianza.

surf [səːɹf], *s.* rompiente, resaca, marejada, olaje.

surface ['səːɹfis], *s.* superficie, *f.,* cara, sobrefaz, *f.* — *a.* superficial. — *v.t.* allanar, igualar, alisar; poner una superficie; salir a la superficie (un submarino).

surfacer, *s.* cepillo mecánico, máquina de alisar (o cepillar) madera.

surfeit ['səːɹfit], *v.t.* ahitar, saciar, hartar, atracar, encebadar. — *v.i.* ahitarse, hartarse, saciarse, atracarse. — *s.* ahito, indigestión, empacho, atracón, encebadamiento; (*fig.*) empalago, empacho.

surge [səːɹdʒ], *s.* olaje, oleada. — *v.i.* agitarse, bullir; embravecerse (el mar); romper (las olas). — *v.t.* hacer undular como olas; (*mar.*) largar, lascar.

surgeon ['səːɹdʒən], *s.* cirujano; (*mil.*, *mar.*) médico, físico; *veterinary surgeon,* albéitar, veterinario; *surgeon-general,* (*E.U.*) médico mayor, jefe de sanidad (militar o naval).

surgery ['səːɹdʒəri], *s.* cirugía; dispensario, consultorio.

surgical ['səːɹdʒikəl], *a.* quirúrgico.

surlily ['səːɹlili], *adv.* desabridamente, acedamente, con displicencia, ásperamente.

surliness, *s.* desabrimiento, displicencia, acedía, aspereza, encono, mal genio, mal humor.

surloin ['səːɹloin], *s.* solomillo.

surly ['səːɹli], *a.* desabrido, arisco, agrio, displicente, enconoso, áspero, rudo, tosco.

surmise [səɹ'maiz], *v.t.* conjeturar, presumir, barruntar. — *s.* conjetura, suposición, noción, barrunto.

surmount [səɹ'maunt], *v.t.* vencer, superar, sobrepujar; coronar.

surmountable, *a.* superable, vencible.

surmullet [səɹ'mʌlet], *s.* mullo, barbo marino, salmonete.

surname ['səːɪneim], s. apellido, sobrenombre; (ant.) epíteto, apodo, renombre. — v.t. apellidar, denominar, nominar, nombrar.

surpass [səɪ'pɑːs], v.t. sobrepujar, superar, aventajar(se), exceder.

surpassing, a. sobresaliente, superior, sobrepujante; incomparable, sin par.

surplice ['səːɪplis], s. (igl.) sobrepelliz, f.

surpliced, a. con sobrepelliz.

surplus ['səːɪpləs], **surplusage** ['səːɪpləsidʒ], s. sobras, sobrante, excedente, exceso, demasía, (com.) superávit.

surprise [səɪ'praiz], **surprisal** [səɪ'praizəl], s. sorpresa, extrañeza, asombro, admiración; novedad. — v.t. sorprender, dejar admirado, sobrecoger, coger de improviso, asaltar, tomar por sorpresa.

surprising, a. sorprendente, maravilloso, asombroso, admirable.

surrealism, s. surrealismo.

surrealist, a., s. surrealista, m.f.

surrebut [səɪə'bʌt], v.i. (for.) triplicar.

surrebutter, s. (for.) tríplica.

surrejoinder, s. (for.) contrarréplica.

surrender [sə'rendəɪ], v.t. rendir, entregar; traspasar, ceder; renunciar a, abandonar, entregar. — v.i. entregarse, rendirse, ceder. — s. rendición, entrega; dejación, renuncia, abandono, sumisión; (for.) cesión de bienes.

surreptitious [sʌrep'tiʃəs], a. subrepticio.

surreptitiously, adv. subrepticiamente a hurtadillas, de rebozo.

surrey, s. (E.U.) vehículo ligero, victoria.

surrogate ['sʌrogeit], v.t. subrogar. — s. substituto; (igl.) vicario; (for.) juez de testamentarias, m.

surround [sə'raund], v.t. circundar, rodear, cercar, ceñir, circunvalar; acorralar; sitiar, asediar. — s. acorralamiento, rodeo, circunvalación; borde, orilla.

surrounding, a. circunstante, circunvecino, ambiente, vecino, alrededor, en rededor.

surroundings [sə'raundiŋz], s.pl. alrededores, contornos, cercanías, afueras; ambiente.

sursolid [səɪ'sɔlid], a. del quinto grado. — s. (mat.) quinta potencia.

surtout ['səːɪtuː], s. (sast., ant.) levitón, sobretodo.

surveillance, s. vigilancia.

survey [səɪ'vei], v.t. apear, acotar, deslindar o medir tierras; inspeccionar, mirar, reconocer, recorrer, examinar, registrar; vigilar; levantar un plano, mapa, etc.; ejecutar operaciones topográficas.

survey ['səːɪvei], s. apeo, medición, deslindamiento; vista, perspectiva, aspecto; inspección, reconocimiento, vista, examen; (E.U.) zona fiscal; survey ship, buque planero.

surveying, s. agrimensura.

surveyor [səɪ'veiəɪ], s. agrimensor, apeador, deslindador, medidor, demarcador, topógrafo; superintendente, sobrestante, inspector, perito; surveyor of the custom-house, vista de aduana.

surveyorship, s. profesión (o empleo) de agrimensor, inspector o visitador.

survival [səɪ'vaivəl], s. supervivencia; sobreviviente, reliquia.

survive [səɪ'vaiv], v.t., v.i. sobrevivir; (fig.) perdurar, subsistir.

survivor, s. sobreviviente, el que sobrevive.

survivorship, s. supervivencia.

susceptibility [səsepti'biliti], s. susceptibilidad, delicadeza; propensión, tendencia.

susceptible [sə'septəbəl], a. susceptible; delicado, sensible; impresionable, capaz de recibir impresiones; enamoradizo.

susceptibly, adv. de una manera susceptible.

susceptive, a. susceptivo, susceptible, sensible.

suspect [səs'pekt], v.t. sospechar, figurarse, imaginar, conjeturar, remusgar, barruntar; desconfiar, recelar, dudar, tener por sospechoso, sospechar de. — v.i. tener sospechas. — s. persona sospechosa, vigilada, o sospechada de un delito. — a. sospechoso.

suspectedly, adv. de una manera sospechosa.

suspend [səs'pend], v.t. suspender, colgar; suspender, mantener suspenso; sospesar; suspender, diferir; hacer depender; suspender a uno, privarle (temporalmente) de su empleo o ministerio; suspended animation, muerte aparente. — v.i. suspend payment, (com.) suspender pagos.

suspender, s. suspendedor. — pl. suspenders, ligas, tirantes (de las medias o calcetines); (E.U.) tirantes del pantalón.

suspense [səs'pens], s. suspensión, duda, incertidumbre; (ant.) detención, parada; (for.) entredicho.

suspension [səs'penʃən], s. suspensión; suspension-bridge, puente colgante; suspension of hostilities, (mil.) suspensión de armas.

suspensive, a. suspensivo.

suspensory, s., a. suspensorio.

suspicion [səs'piʃən], s. sospecha, desconfianza, recelo, suspicacia; conjetura, noción, idea; (fam.) pizca, grano, sombra.

suspicious [səs'piʃəs], a. sospechoso, dudoso; suspicaz, desconfiado, receloso.

suspiciously, adv. sospechosamente, con sospecha; suspicazmente, con recelo.

suspiciousness, s. recelo, desconfianza, suspicacia.

suspiration [sʌspi'reiʃən], s. (ant.) acción de suspirar, suspiro.

suspire [səs'paiəɪ], v.i. (poét.) suspirar por; suspirar; respirar.

sustain [səs'tein], v.t. sostener, sustentar, mantener; (mús.) prolongar, sostener; patrocinar, apoyar; establecer, probar; to sustain a loss, sufrir una pérdida; to sustain injuries, sufrir o recibir heridas.

sustainable, a. sostenible, sustentable, defendible.

sustainer, s. sostenedor, defensor, sustentador, protector.

sustenance ['sʌstənəns], s. sostenimiento, mantenimiento; sustento, alimentos.

sustentation [sʌsten'teiʃən], s. sostenimiento, sustentamiento, sustentación; sustento.

susurration [sʌsju:'reiʃən], s. susurro.

sutler ['sʌtləɪ], s. vivandero.

sutor ['sjuːtəɪ], s. zapatero remendón; chapucero.

suttle ['sʌtəl], s., a. (ant.) neto; peso limpio.

sutural, a. sutural.

suture ['sjuːtjəɪ], s. (anat.) sutura, comisura; (bot.) rafe; (cir.) sutura, costura.

suzerain ['suːzərin], s. soberano.

suzerainty ['suːzrənti], s. autoridad suprema o regia, soberanía, dominio.

swab [swɔb], s. escobín, estropajo, fregajo, (cir.) torunda, esponja de hilas; (arti.; escobillón; (mar.) lampazo. — v.t. limpiar)

fregar; (*mar.*) lampacear, limpiar con lampazo.
swabber, *s.* lampacero, galopín, paje de escoba.
swaddle ['swɔdəl], *v.t.* empañar, fajar, envolver con fajas; *swaddling-band* o *swaddling-cloth*, faja, pañal, pañales.
swag [swæg], *v.i.* bambolearse, tambalearse; colgar, pender. — *s.* (*fam.*) botín, despojo; (*b.a.*) guirnalda.
swag-bellied, *a.* (*fam.*) ventrudo, panzudo, de vientre abultado.
swage [sweidʒ], *v.t.* (*metal.*) estampar (con una matriz, etc.). — *s.* macho o punzón de estampar.
swage-block, *s.* matriz de estampar.
swagger ['swægɔɹ], *v.i.* fanfarrear, baladronear; pavonearse, darse tono, garbear, gallardear. — *s.* fanfarria, baladronada, fachenda; pavoneo, chulería.
swaggerer, *s.* jaque, jaquetón, fanfarrón, matasiete, baladrón, valentón.
swaggering, *a.* fanfarrón, fachendoso, baladrón; marchoso; chulo, flamenco, garboso, majo.
swain [swein], *s.* zagal, pastorcillo; enamorado, amante.
swallow ['swɔlou], *v.t.* tragar, deglutir, engullir; (*fig.*) tragar(se), creer a ciegas; hacer desaparecer; retractar, retirar, desdecir; tragar(se) (un insulto); *to swallow up*, tragar, sumir, absorber completamente. — *s.* trago, bocado, tragadero, esófago; deglución; abismo, sima; sumidero; (*orn.*) golondrina; vencejo, avión.
swallow-fish, *s.* (*ict.*) golondrina.
swallow-tail, *s.* (*carp.*) cola de milano.
swallow-tailed coat, *s.* frac.
swallow-wort, *s.* asclepiada, celidonia.
swam [swæm], *pret.* [SWIM].
swamp [swɔmp], *s.* pantano, marisma, ciénaga, lapachar, fangal. — *v.t.* sumergir, echar a pique, hacer zozobrar; empantanar, encenagar, encharcar; mojar; (*fig.*) hundir, arruinar. — *v.i.* empantanarse; irse a pique, zozobrar; (*fig.*) inundarse, enfrascarse, estar inundado; caer en grandes dificultades.
swamp-oak, *s.* (*bot.*) carrasco.
swampy, *a.* pantanoso, cenagoso.
swan [swɔn], *s.* (*orn.*) cisne; *swan-song*, canto de cisne.
swank [swæŋk], *v.i.* (*fam.*) fanfarrear, echar baladronadas; darse tono, pisto o charol. — *s.* (*fam.*) farolero, fachendoso, farolería, pavoneo, fachenda.
swan-like, *a.* semejante al cisne.
swansdown, *s.* plumón de cisne; (*tej.*) moletón, paño de vicuña.
swanskin, *s.* piel de cisne, *f.*; lanilla.
swap [swɔp], *v.t.* (*fam.*) cambiar, trocar, cambalachear. — *v.i.* hacer cambalaches o trueques. — *s.* (*fam.*) cambalache, cambio, trueque.
sward [swɔːɹd], *s.* césped, pasto, herbaje.
swarm [swɔːɹm], *s.* enjambre; caterva, gentío, hormiguero, multitud. — *v.i., v.t.* enjambrar, jabardear, arrebozarse, hacer mucha cría, desahijar; hervir, pulular, bullir, hormiguear; haber abundancia, abundar; trepar.
swart [swɔːɹt], *a.* (*ant.*) prieto, atezado, moreno; triste.
swarthily ['swɔːɹðili], *adv.* de color moreno.
swarthiness ['swɔːɹðinis], *s.* atezamiento, tez morena, color moreno.

swarthy ['swɔːɹði], *a.* tezado, atezado, moreno, curtido, negruzco.
swash [swɔʃ], *s.* chapoteo, chapalateo, chorretada; (*mar.*) canalizo. — *v.t.* lanzar una chorretada; derramar (agua) en cantidad. — *v.i.* chapotear, chapalear, borbotar, borbollar; salpicar (el agua), baladronear; meter bulla; *swash-plate*, *s.* (*mec.*) placa motriz.
swashbuckler ['swɔʃbʌklɔɹ], **swasher,** *s.* matasiete, espadachín, fanfarrón.
swashbuckling, *a.* valentón, fanfarrón, baladrón. — *s.* fanfarria, valentonada, baladronada.
swashing, *a.* valentón, fanfarrón; flamenco, garboso; violento, abrumador; que borbota o borbolla, estrepitoso. — *s.* fanfarria, baladronada.
swashy, *a.* lodoso, mojado.
swat, *v.t.* matar (moscas).
swath [swɔːθ], *s.* ringla o ringlera de mies segada.
swathe [sweið], *v.t.* fajar, liar, envolver, vendar. — *s.* faja, pañal, atadura, venda.
sway [swei], *v.t.* inclinar, ladear; ejercer influencia sobre, influir en el ánimo de, inducir, inspirar; blandir, cimbrar; cimbrarse, guapear; mandar, dominar, gobernar, regir; (*mar.*) guindar, izar. — *v.i.* ladearse, torcerse, inclinarse; mecerse, oscilar; bambolearse, bambalearse, bambonearse, tambalear, flaquear; tener domino o influencia; *to sway up*, guindar. — *s.* ascendente, influencia; poder, imperio, predominio, preponderancia; vaivén, balanceo, oscilación, vibración, bamboleo; estremecimiento, sacudimiento; *to hold sway*, gobernar, regir.
sweal [swiːl], *v.i.* derretirse y correrse; quemarse o consumirse despacio.
swear [sweɔɹ], *v.t., v.i.* (*pret.* **swore,** (*ant.*) **sware;** *p.p.* **sworn**) jurar; declarar, (confirmar, ratificar, etc.) bajo juramento; renegar, blasfemar, perjurar, echar juramentos, echar votos; juramentar, tomar o prestar juramento; hacer votos, votar; prometer solemnemente; *to swear by*, (*fam.*) poner confianza implícita en; *to swear in*, hacer prestar juramento a, juramentar.
swearer, *s.* jurador, renegador, votador; (*for.*) jurante.
sweat [swet], *v.t., v.i.* (*pret., p.p.* **sweated,** (*ant.*) **sweat**) sudar, trasudar, resudar; hacer sudar; secar en horno; (*ten.*) apelambrar; soldar; recortar o cercenar monedas; (*fig.*) sudar, trabajar mucho; *to sweat out*, (*med.*) curar por medio del sudor. — *s.* sudor, humedad; (*fig.*) sudor, trabajo; *to be in a sweat*, estar nadando en sudor; *sweat-shop*, taller donde se impone un trabajo excesivo por jornal insuficiente.
sweater, *s.* sudante, persona o animal que suda; patrón explotador; sueta, jersey.
sweatiness, *s.* estado del que suda, (*fam.*) sudadera; calor y humedad.
sweating, *s.* transpiración, exudación; explotación (de obreros); *sweating-room*, sudadero, estufa.
sweaty, *a.* ['sweti], *s.* sudoroso, sudado, sudoso; laborioso, trabajoso.
Swede [swiːd], *s.* sueco; nabo sueco.
Swedish, *a.* sueco. — *s.* idioma sueco.
sweeny ['swiːni], *s.* (*E.U., vet.*) atrofia de un

músculo de la espalda (caballos); pescuezo, engreimiento.

sweep [swiːp], *v.t.*, *v.i.* (*pret.*, *p.p.* **swept**) barrer, limpiar, deshollinar (chimeneas); pasar rápidamente por; arrebatar, arrastrar, arrebañar; marchar orgullosamente, majestuosamente; *to sweep down*, decender precipitadamente; (*mil.*) batir, barrer, enfilar con la artillería; *to sweep away*, barrer, llevar sin dejar nada, quitar completamente; *to sweep the bottom*, (*mar.*) rastrear, dragar; *to sweep the board*, alzarse con el dinero; *to sweep along*, arrastrar rápidamente o con fuerza; marchar o pasar majestuosamente; *to sweep aside*, rechazar o apartar con un gesto desdeñoso o majestuoso; *to sweep through*, pasar majestuosamente; *to sweep up*, barrer en montón; *new brooms sweep clean*, (*prov.*) escoba nueva barre bien; *to be swept off one's feet*, ser arrebatado, rendir el albedrío. — *s.* barredura, escobada, barrido; extensión, recorrido, alcance, vuelo, carrera; encorvadura, curva descrita, giro, vuelta; envergadura; barrendero, deshollinador; pieza de una máquina (a lo largo de la cual se efectúa un rozamiento); remo largo y pesado; cigoñal de pozo; aspa de molino; guimbalete de bomba; *chimney-sweep*, deshollinador, limpiachimeneas, *m.sing.*

sweeper, *s.* barrendero; *chimney-sweeper*, deshollinador, limpiachimeneas, *m.sing.*; *carpet-sweeper*, escoba mecánica para barrer alfombras; *sweeper-bar*, (*arti.*) travesaño de la amoladera; *mine-sweeper*, (*mar.*) buque dragaminas.

sweeping, *a.* arrastrador, arrebatador; vasto, comprehensivo, demasiado amplio o abstracto. — *s.* barrido. — *pl.* **sweepings**, barreduras, basura.

sweep-net, *s.* jabeca, esparavel.

sweepstake(s) [ˈswiːpsteik], *s.* lotería (espec. de carreras de caballos).

sweet [swiːt], *a.* dulce; azucarado, sabroso, gustoso, rico; oloroso, fragante; fresco, no salado; melodioso, suave, blando; encantador, amable, bonito; benigno, gentil, apacible. — *s.* dulzura, deleite, placer; dulce, bombón; persona querida, amor, cariño. — *pl.* **sweets**, dulces, golosinas, bombones; *sweet-basil*, (*bot.*) albahaca; *sweet-apple*, *sweet-sop*, (*bot.*) anona, chirimoya; *sweet-cicely*, (*bot.*) perifollo; *sweet-fern*, (*bot.*) helecho miricáceo; *sweet-corn*, mazorca, panoja; *sweet-flag*, *sweet-rush*, (*bot.*) cálamo aromático; *sweet-oil*, aceite de oliva; *sweet-gum*, ocozol; *sweet-potato*, batata, patata dulce; (*Am.*) camote; *sweet-pea*, (*bot.*) arveja olorosa, guisante de olor; *sweet-tongued* o *sweet-spoken*, melifluo, pico de oro; *sweet-smelling*, odorífero, fragante; *sweet-tempered*, de carácter dulce, complaciente; *sweet-scented*, perfumado; *sweet-toothed*, goloso; *sweet-willow*, *sweet-gale*, (*bot.*) mirto holandés; *sweet-william*, (*bot.*) dianto, clavel barbado; *sweet-and-twenty*, joven y hechicera.

sweetbread [ˈswiːtbred], *s.* lechecillas o mollejas de ternera.

sweetbrier [swiːtˈbraiər], *s.* escaramujo oloroso, agavanzo.

sweeten [ˈswiːtən], *v.t.* endulzar, dulzurar, azucarar, dulcificar, (*farm.*) edulcorar; em-

balsamar; hacer salubre; purificar. — *v.i.* endulzarse.

sweetener, *s.* dulcificante.

sweetheart [ˈswiːthɑːt], *s.* enamorada, dulce amiga, novia, querida; dulcinea; novio, amador, cortejo, galanteador, galán.

sweeting, *s.* (*bot.*) camuesa.

sweetish, *a.* algo dulce.

sweetmeat [ˈswiːtmiːt], *s.* dulce, bombón, golosina, confitura.

sweetness, *s.* dulzura, dulcedumbre, suavidad, melosidad; dulzura, bondad, apacibilidad, blandura; fragancia.

swell [swel], *v.t.* (*p.p.* **swollen, swelled**) hinchar, inflar, engrosar, entumecer, distender, abultar, aumentar, agravar; envanecer, engreír. — *v.i.* hincharse, entumecerse, engrosarse, abotagarse; henchirse; elevarse, subir, crecer; esponjarse, engreírse, envanecerse, ensoberbecerse; (*mar.*) embravecerse, agitarse (el mar); *to swell out*, ampollarse, espetarse, bufar; *swollen with pride* (o *conceit*), hinchado de orgullo. — *a.* hinchado por una torcedura; (*fam.*) elegantísimo, precioso, gallardo; peripuesto, tieso. — *s.* entumecencia, bulto, hinchazón, *f.*; ondulación del terreno, protuberancia, prominencia; oleada, oleaje, marejada; (*mús.*) unión de crescendo y diminuendo; pedal de expresión; (*fam.*) petimetre, dandi; *swell-organ*, (*mús.*) órgano de expresión; *swell-pedal*, (*mús.*) pedal de expresión.

swelling, *s.* hinchazón, *f.*, inflación; (*med.*) tumefacción, entumescencia, turgencia, abotagamiento; chichón, bollo; bulto, protuberancia, salida. — *a.* que se hincha, (se) infla, etc.; turgente; *swelling sea*, mar embravecido.

swelter [ˈsweltər], *v.t.* sofocar, achicharrar, abrumar de calor. — *v.i.* abrasarse, achicharrarse, ahogarse, sudar la gota gorda.

swept [swept], *pret.*, *p.p.* [SWEEP].

swerve [swəːv], *v.t.* desviar, apartar, torcer. — *v.i.* torcerse, desviarse; extraviarse. — *s.* esguince, desviación.

swift [swift], *a.* veloz, rápido, ligero, acelerado, presto; pronto; volador, andador; diligente, vivo, activo; repentino; (*mar.*) velero. — *s.* (*orn.*) vencejo, arrejaque; lagartija; carrete, devanadera; *swift-footed* o *swift of foot*, de paso rápido, ligero, alípedo.

swifter, *s.* (*mar.*) tortor, andaribel; falso obenque.

swiftly, *adv.* velozmente, rápidamente, ligeramente, aprisa, de prisa.

swiftness, *s.* velocidad, rapidez, ligereza, celeridad; prontitud.

swig [swig], *v.t.*, *v.i.* beber a grandes tragos. — *s.* (*fam.*) trago.

swill [swil], *v.t.* enjuagar, lavar; emborrachar, embriagar, beber con exceso. — *v.i.* emborracharse. — *s.* bazofia; tragantada, trago grande.

swiller, *s.* bebedor insaciable; persona que bebe demasiado.

swim [swim], *v.i.* (*pret.* **swam**; *p.p.* **swum**) nadar; flotar, sobrenadar; ir con la corriente, dejarse ir o llevar; resbalar o deslizarse suavemente; inundarse, anegarse; padecer vahidos; abundar (en una cosa); *my head swims*, se me va la cabeza. — *v.t.* pasar a nado; hacer flotar; calar, mojar, empapar;

to swim with the tide, seguir o ir con la corriente. — *s.* natación, nado; nadadera de pez; *to be in the swim*, sstar al corriente; estar de manga.

swimmer ['swimǝɹ], *s.* nadador.

swimming, *a.* nadante, natatorio. — *s.* natación, nado; vahido, vértigo; *swimming-costume*, traje de baño; *swimming-place*, nadadero; *swimming-bladder*, vejiga natatoria (de los peces); *swimming-bath* o *-pool*, piscina.

swimmingly, *adv.* a pie llano, como una seda, con creciente éxito.

swim-suit, *s.* (*fam.*) traje de baño.

swindle ['swindǝl], *v.t.* petardear, estafar, soflamar, sonsacar, trampear. — *s.* estafa, timo, petardo.

swindler ['swindlǝɹ], *s.* estafador, timador, petardista, *m.f.*, trampeador, tramposo, trampista, *m.f.*

swine [swain], *s.* (*pl.* **swine**) marrano, puerco, cochino, cerdo; (*fig.*) cochino, canalla, *m.f.*; *sea-swine*, (*ict.*) marsopa, marsopla; *wild-swine*, jabalí; *swine-fever*, peste (*f.*) de los puercos; *swine-thistle*, (*bot.*) cerraja, cardo ajonjero; *swine-pox*, variedad de viruelas locas.

swine-bread, *s.* (*bot.*) trufa, criadilla de tierra; pan de puerco.

swine-herd ['swainhǝːɹd], *s.* porquero, porquerizo.

swing [swiŋ], *v.i.* (*pret.*, *p.p.* **swung**) oscilar, vibrar, columpiarse, balancearse; dar vueltas, (*mar.*) bornear; (*vulg.*) ser ejecutado o ahorcado. — *v.t.* columpiar, cunear, mecer, hacer oscilar (vibrar, balancear, o bambolear); hacer engoznar; blandir (un arma); hacer girar (volverse, voltear, o dar vueltas); *to swing about*, dar vueltas alrededor de una cosa; *to swing around the circle*, pasar por la serie completa; *to swing clear*, evitar un choque, torcerse; *swing-back*, respaldo de articulación de una máquina fotográfica; *swing-block*, (*mec.*) gorrón; *swing-bar*, (*carr.*) balancín; *swing-plough*, arado de reja reversible. — *s.* vibración, oscilación, balanceo, vaivén, bamboleo, balance; ritmo; música rítmica de baile; columpio, mecedor; libre carrera, libre curso; (*mec.*) carrera, recorrido; alcance; golpe duro; *in full swing*, en plena operación; *to go with a swing*, ir como por viña vendimiada; *to swing a swing*, columpiar.

swinge [swindʒ], *v.t.* (*pret.*, *p.p.* **swinged**) (*metal.*) soldar a martillo, forjar; quemar, chamuscar; (*ant.*) azotar, castigar.

swingeing ['swindʒiŋ], *a.* (*fam.*) grande, pesado, monstruoso, extravagante.

swinger ['swiŋǝɹ], *s.* columpiador.

swinging ['swiŋiŋ], *s.* oscilación, vibración, balanceo, vaivén; borneo. — *a.* oscilante, mecedor; rítmico.

swingle ['swiŋgǝl], *v.t.* espadar, espadillar. — *s.* espadilla; brazo corto del mayal; (*carr.*) bolea.

swingle-tree, *s.* (*carr.*) bolea.

swinish ['swainiʃ], *a.* porcuno; (*fig.*) cochino, sucio.

swinishness, *s.* marranada, cochinada, cochinería; grosería, maldad.

swipe [swaip], *v.t.* (*fam.*) dar un golpe fuerte a, soplar, apuñear; engullir (comida o bebida); (*vulg.*) murciar, sisar, calar. — *s.* (*fam.*) torta, mojicón.

swirl [swǝːɹl], *v.t.*, *v.i.* arremolinar(se), (hacer) girar. — *s.* remolino, torbellino; torcedura.

swish [swiʃ], *v.t.*, *v.i.* blandir, agitar(se), menear; silbar, crujir, susurrar; azotar, dar un latigazo. — *s.* silbo, crujido, susurro, movimiento o silbido del látigo al cortar el aire. — *a.* (*germ.*) de buen tono, elegante.

Swiss [swis], *s.*, *a.* suizo, suiza; *Swiss Guards*, *s.* guardia suiza del Vaticano.

switch [switʃ], *s.* vara pequeña, varilla, bastoncillo, latiguillo; cuje; cabellera postiza; (*f.c.*) apartadero, desviadero, aguja; (*elec.*) conmutador, interruptor; desviación de un tren o una corriente eléctrica por medio de un *switch*; *switch-lever*, (*f.c.*) palanca de aguja; *switch-tender*, guardaagujas, *m.*, (*Amér.*) cambiavía, *m.* — *v.t.* varear, azotar, dar golpes o latigazos, fustigar; (*elec.*) cambiar la dirección de la corriente, mudar de un circuito a otro; *to switch off*, (*elec.*) desconectar, apagar, cortar; *to switch on*, (*elec.*) conectar, dar, poner, encender, enchufar.

switchback, *s.* (*dep.*) montaña rusa.

switch-board, *s.* (*elec.*) cuadro de distribución.

switch-man, *s.* (*f.c.*) guardaagujas, *m.*, (*Amér.*) cambiavía, *m.*, cambiador.

swivel ['swivǝl], *v.t.*, *v.i.* girar (o hacer girar) sobre un eje. — *s.* alacrán, torniquete, eslabón giratorio, lanzadera de un telar de cintas; *swivel-gun*, (*arti.*) colisa, pedrero; *swivel-chair*, silla giratoria; *swivel-door*, puerta giratoria; *swivel-joint*, junta articulada, rótula.

swollen ['swoulǝn], *a.* turgente, hinchado, henchido, crecido. — *p.p.* [SWELL].

swoon [swuːn], *v.i.* desmayarse, desvanecerse, desfallecer, perder el sentido. — *s.* desmayo, desfallecimiento, deliquio, síncope, (*fam.*) soponcio, pasmo.

swoop [swuːp], *v.t.*, *v.i.* abatirse, calarse (aves); abalanzarse, embestir, arrebatar; agarrar. — *s.* calada; embestida; agarro.

swop [swɔp], *v.t.* (*fam.*) cambiar, trocar, cambalachear. — *s.* cambalache, cambio, trueque.

sword [sɔːɹd], *s.* espada, sable; *to put to the sword*, pasar a cuchillo o a filo de espada; *sword-arm*, brazo derecho; *with* (o *to*) *fire and sword*, a sangre y fuego; *sword-guard*, *sword-hilt*, *sword's hilt*, empuñadura, puño, guarda de la espada; *sword-law*, ley del más fuerte.

sword-belt, *s.* talabarte, cinturón.

sword-fish, *s.* (*ict.*) pez espada, *m.*

sword-knot, *s.* borla de espada.

sword-play, *s.* esgrima, manejo de la espada.

sword-shaped, *a.* ensiforme.

swordsman ['sɔːɹdzmǝn], *s.* (*pl.* **swordsmen**) tirador, espada, *m.*, espadachín, hombre de espada.

swore [swɔːɹ], **sworn**, *pret.*, *p.p.* [SWEAR].

swot, *v.i.* (*fam.*) empollar.

swum [swʌm], *pret.*, *p.p.* [SWIM].

swung [swʌŋ], *pret.*, *p.p.* [SWING].

sybaritic [saibǝˈritik], *a.* sibarítico.

Sybarite ['saibǝrait], *s.* sibarita, *m.f.*

sycamore ['sikǝmɔːɹ], *s.* (*bot.*) sicómoro; (*E.U.*) falso plátano.

sycophancy, *s.* servilismo, gorronería, adulación.

sycophant ['sikofænt], *s.* adulador, parásito, mogollón, gorrista, *m.f.*, gorrón.

sycophantic [sikoˈfæntik], *a.* servil, gorrón, lisonjero, adulatorio; chismoso, parlón.

syenite ['saiǝnait], s. sienita.
syenitic, a. sienítico.
syllabary ['silǝbǝri], s. silabario.
syllabic [si'læbik], syllabical [si'læbikǝl], a. silábico.
syllabically, adv. por sílabas.
syllabicate, v.t. silabear.
syllabication, s. silabeo.
syllable ['silǝbǝl], s. sílaba; (poét.) pie.
syllabus ['silǝbǝs], s. programa, m., resumen, compendio, sílabo.
syllepsis [si'lepsis], s. silepsis, f.
sylleptic, sylleptical, a. que envuelve silepsis.
syllogism ['silɔdʒizm], s. silogismo.
syllogistic [silo'dʒistik], a. silogístico.
syllogistically, adv. en forma silogística.
syllogize ['silɔdʒaiz], v.i. silogizar, hacer silogismos.
sylph [silf], s. silfo, sílfide, f.; (orn.) colibrí.
sylva ['silvǝ], s. selva, conjunto de árboles.
sylvan ['silvǝn], a. selvático, silvático, silvestre; rural, rústico.
symbol ['simbǝl], s. símbolo, emblema, m., signo, tipo; marca, carácter, abreviatura, esquema, m., fórmula; (teol.) credo.
symbolic [sim'bɔlik], symbolical [sim'bɔlikǝl], a. simbólico.
symbolism ['simbolizm], s. simbolismo.
symbolist, s. simbolista, m.f.
symbolization [simbolai'zeiʃǝn], s. simbolización.
symbolize ['simbolaiz], v.t., v.i. simbolizar.
symbology [sim'bɔlodʒi], s. arte de simbolizar, tratado de los símbolos.
symmetrical [si'metrikǝl], a. simétrico.
symmetrize ['simetraiz], v.t. dar simetría a.
symmetry ['simetri], s. simetría.
sympathetic [simpǝ'θetik], a. compasivo, que simpatiza, afín; simpático.
sympathetically, adv. compasivamente; simpáticamente, con simpatía.
sympathize ['simpǝθaiz], v.i. simpatizar, condolerse, compadecerse; doler (o padecer o sentir) por simpatía; convenir, armonizarse, ajustarse, congeniar.
sympathizer, partidario; aficionado.
sympathy ['simpǝθi], s. compasión, conmiseración, lástima; afinidad; simpatía; pésame; (med., fís.) simpatía.
symphonic [sim'fɔnik], a. sinfónico; homónimo.
symphonious, a. armonioso.
symphonist ['simfonist], s. sinfonista, m.f.
symphony ['simfoni], s. sinfonía.
symphysis ['simfisis], s. sínfisis, f.
symposium [sim'pouziǝm], s. festín, banquete; colección de artículos, comentarios, etc.
symptom ['simptǝm], s. síntoma, m.; indicio, señal, f.
symptomatic [simpto'mætik], a. sintomático.
symptomatology [simptomǝ'tɔlodʒi], s. sintomatología.
synæresis [si'niǝresis], s. sinéresis, f.
synagogue ['sinǝgɔg], s. sinagoga.
synalepha [sinǝ'liːfǝ], s. sinalefa.
synalgia [sin'ældʒiǝ], s. dolor por acción simpática.
synartrosis [sinɑːɹ'trousis], s. (anat.) sinartrosis, f.
synchromesh gear ['siŋkromeʃ'giǝɹ], s. (aut.) cambio sincronizado, sincronizador.

synchronous ['siŋkronǝs], a. sincrónico.
synchronism ['siŋkronizm], s. sincronismo.
synchronize ['siŋkronaiz], v.t., v.i. sincronizar.
synclinal [sin'klainǝl], a. (geol.) sinclinal.
syncopate ['siŋkopeit], v.t. (gram., mús.) hacer una síncopa, sincopar.
syncopation [siŋko'peiʃǝn], s. (gram., mús.) síncopa.
syncope ['siŋkopi], s. (med.) síncope; (gram., mús.) síncopa.
syncretism ['sinkretizm], s. sincretismo.
syndic ['sindik], s. síndico.
syndicalism, s. sindicalismo, organización obrera por medio del sindicato.
syndicate ['sindikeit], v.t., v.i. (com.) sindicar(se). — s. (for.) sindicatura, sindicado; (com.) asociación de capitalistas para emprender un negocio magno; sindicato, sindicado.
syne [sain], adv. (Esco.) tiempo atrás, hace tiempo.
synecdoche [si'nekdoki], s. (ret.) sinécdoque, f.
synergism, s. doctrina según la cual la energía humana coopera con la gracia divina.
synergy ['sinǝɹdʒi], s. (fisiol.) sinergia.
synod ['sinǝd], s. sínodo.
synodal, synodic, synodical, a. sinódico.
synonym ['sinonim], s. sinónimo.
synonymize, v.t. hacer uso de sinónimos.
synonymous [si'nɔnimǝs], a. sinónimo, homólogo.
synonymy [si'nɔnimi], s. sinonimia.
synopsis [si'nɔpsis], s. sinopsis, f., reseña.
synoptic [si'nɔptik], a. sinóptico.
synovia [si'nouviǝ], s. sinovia.
synovial [si'nouviǝl], a. sinovial.
syntactic [sin'tæktik], a. sintáctico.
syntax ['sintæks], s. sintaxis, f.
synthesis ['sinθesis], s. síntesis, f.
synthesize, v.t. sintetizar.
synthetic, synthetical, a. sintético.
synthetize, v.t. sintetizar.
syntonic [sin'tɔnik], a. sintónico, sintonizado.
syntonization, s. sintonización.
syntonize ['sintonaiz], v.t. sintonizar.
syphilis ['sifilis], s. (med.) sífilis, f., mal gálico.
syphilitic [sifi'litik], a. sifilítico.
syphon ['saifǝn], s. sifón.
syren ['saiǝrǝn], s. sirena [SIREN].
Syriac ['siriǝk], s., a. siriaco, siríaco.
Syrian ['siriǝn], s. sirio, habitante de Siria. — a. sirio.
syringa [si'riŋgǝ], s. (bot.) jeringuilla.
syringe ['sirindʒ], s. jeringa, clistel, clister. — v.t. jeringar.
syringotomy [siriŋ'gɔtǝmi], s. siringotomía.
syrtis ['sǝːɹtis], s. sirte, f.
syrup ['sirǝp], s. jarabe, almíbar.
system ['sistǝm], s. sistema, m., método, régimen; (fisiol., biol.) sistema; (geol.) formación; railway-system, red de ferrocarriles, f.
systematic [sistǝ'mætik], systematical [siste'mætikǝl], a. sistemático, metódico, clasificado con orden.
systematize ['sistǝmǝtaiz], v.t. sistematizar, reducir a sistema, metodizar.
systemic [sis'temik], a. sistemático.
systole ['sistoli], s. (fisiol.) sístole, f.
systolic, a. sistólico.
systyle, a., s. (arq.) sístilo.
syzygy ['sizidʒi], s. (astr.) sicigia.

T

T, t [tiː], vigésima letra del alfabeto inglés.
T, s. (mec.) forma de T; *T-iron*, hierro en T; *T-rail*, riel o carril de hongo, en forma de T; *T-square*, (dibujo) regla T.
tab [tæb], s. proyección, apéndice; oreja de zapato; herrete de un cordón; cuenta.
tabard ['tæbəɹd], s. tabardo.
tabarder, s. (ant.) persona que lleva tabardo.
tabaret, s. tejido de seda y muaré para tapicería.
tabbinet ['tæbinet], s. (tej.) tabinete.
tabby [tæbi], s. (tej.) tabí; gato romano, moteado; (fam.) gata. — a. ondeado, abigarrado, moteado, mosqueado.
tabefaction [tæbi'fækʃən], s. marasmo, consunción, enflaquecimiento.
tabefy ['tæbifai], v.t., v.i. extenuarse, debilitarse.
tabernacle ['tæbəɹnækəl], s. tabernáculo, templo, santuario.
tabes ['teibiːz], s.; **tabetic,** a. (med.) tábido.
tablature ['tæblətʃəɹ], s. música cifrada o en cifra; pintura mural.
table ['teibəl], s. mesa; (fig.) mesa, comida, manjares; tabla, cuadro sinóptico o comparativo, estado; tablero; meseta; (arq.) entablamento; palma de la mano; *side-table*, aparador, bufete; *to keep a good table*, tener buena mesa; *to turn the tables*, volverse la tortilla, hacer cambiar la suerte, devolver la pelota; *table-linen*, adamascado, mantelería; *table-set*, *table-service*, vajilla; *table-talk*, conversación familiar o de sobremesa; *table-boarder*, pupilo, pensionista, m.f.; *table d'hôte*, (fr.) mesa redonda (en una fonda); *table-beer*, cerveza floja, cerveza de pasto. — v.t., v.i. entablar (una petición); (E.U., pol.) arrinconar, dar carpetazo; poner sobre la mesa; hacer un índice o catálogo, catalogar, poner índice; (carp.) ensamblar, acoplar.
tableau ['tæblou], s. (pl. **tableaux**) cuadro al vivo.
table-cloth ['teibəlklɔːθ], s. mantel; tela para manteles.
table-cover, s. cubremesa, sobremesa, m.
table-land, s. meseta.
table-spoon, s. cuchara de mesa o de sopa.
tablespoonful, s. cucharada.
tablet ['tæblet], s. tableta, tabla, tablilla; bloque o taco de papel; losa, lápida; (farm.) pastilla, pan; *votive tablet*, tablilla exvoto, plancha grabada conmemorativa de un voto.
taboo [tə'buː], v.t. declarar tabú; (fig.) prohibir, excluir, vedar. — s. tabú; prohibición, exclusión.
tabor ['teibəɹ], s. (ant.) tamboril.
taborer, s. (ant.) tamborilero.
tabouret ['tæboret], s. tamboril, tamborilete; taburete; tambor de bordar.
tabular ['tæbjuːlləɹ], a. tabular.
tabulate ['tæbjuːleit], v.t. formar tabla, catalogar, poner índice a.
tabulated, a. liso, plano; catalogado, puesto en (forma de) tablas.
tabulation, s. distribución en tablas, cuadros o listas, catalogación.
tabulator, s. tabulador (máquina de escribir).
tacamahac ['tækəməhæk], s. tacamaca, tacamahaca.

tachometer [tə'kɔmetəɹ], s. hemotocómetro, tacómetro; (aut.) cuentakilómetros, m.
tachygraph, s. taquígrafo.
tachygraphic, a. taquigráfico.
tachygraphy [tə'kigrəfi], s. taquigrafía.
tachymeter [tə'kimetəɹ], s. taquímetro.
tachymetry, s. taquimetría.
tacit ['tæsit], a. tácito.
taciturn ['tæsitəɹn], a. taciturno.
taciturnity [tæsi'təːɹniti], s. taciturnidad.
tack [tæk], v.t. atar, afianzar o clavar con tachuelas; puntear, embastar, hilvanar; (fig.) añadir, agregar, anexar. — v.i. (mar.) virar, virar de bordo, dar bordos, cambiar de bordada. — s. tachuela, clavija, clavete, clavito, puntilla; hilván, embaste; (mar.) amura, bordo, virada, bordada; cambio de política, nuevo plan de acción, nuevo rumbo.
tack-claw, s. sacatachuelas, m., sacabrocas, m.
tackle ['tækəl], v.t. agarrar, asir, forcejear; (fig.) luchar con, abordar, aplicarse a; (fútbol) cargar. — s. (mar.) aparejo, maniobra, motonería, jarcia, cuadernal; equipo, avíos, enseres; (fútbol) carga; *stay-tackle*, candelón, candeletón, estrinque; *fore-tackle*, aparejo del trinquete; *main-tackle*, aparejo real; *tack-tackle*, aparejo de amurar; *tackle-hooks*, ganchos de aparejos; *tackle-fall*, tira de aparejo; *tackle-block*, motón de aparejo, polea.
tackling, s. aparejo, palanquín; herramientas.
tact [tækt], s. discreción, tacto, tino, tiento, diplomacia, discernimiento.
tactic ['tæktik], **tactical** ['tæktikəl], a.; **tactician** [tæk'tiʃən], s. táctico.
tactics ['tæktiks], s.pl. táctica.
tactile ['tæktil], a. tangible, palpable, tocable; táctil.
tactility [tæk'tiliti], s. calidad de tangible.
tactless, a. falto de tacto o tino, indiscreto.
tadpole ['tædpoul], s. renacuajo.
ta'en [tein], (Esco. y poét.) p.p. [TAKE].
tænia ['tiːniə], s. banda, cinta, faja; tenia, solitaria.
taffeta ['tæfetə], **taffety** ['tæfeti], s. (tej.) tafetán.
taffrail ['tæfrəl], s. (mar.) coronamiento.
taffy ['tæfi], s. caramelo, melcocha, arropía; (fam.) galés; (E.U., vulg.) coba, halago, zalamería.
tag [tæg], s. herrete; marbete, etiqueta, rótulo, tejuelo; extremo del rabo, apéndice; tirador de una bota; pingajo, arrapiezo; estribillo, refrán, frase hecha, mote; marro (juego); *to play tag*, jugar al marro. — v.t. clavetear, herretear, poner herretes; afianzar, atar, marcar con marbete o rótulo; pisar los talones, seguir de cerca; *to tag on*, (fam.) juntarse (a), acompañar; *tagged-lace*, agujeta.
tag-rag, s., *tag, rag and bobtail*, chusma, gentuza.
tail [teil], s. cola, rabo; cabo, extremidad, apéndice; (astr.) cola de cometa; (mús.) rabito de una nota; pie de página; reverso o cruz de una moneda; (sast.) faldón; (alb.) cola o entrega de un sillar; fila o hilera de gente; escolta, acompañamiento; (for.) limitación de propiedad; (aer.) planos de cola, estabilizadores traseros; *bobbed tail*, o *bob-tail*, cola cortada; *to turn tail*, huirse, volver la espalda, mostrar los talones; *tail-block*, (mar.) motón de rabiza; *tail-piece*,

apendice; (*impr.*) florón, culo de lámpara; *tail-coat*, chaqué o frac, (*col.*) sacolevita; *tail-spin*, (*aer.*) barrena de cola; *tail-end*, extremo, rabera, zaga. — *v.t.* añadir, agregar; tirar de la cola; cortar la cola, desrabotar; seguir, perseguir, pisar los talones; *to tail after*, seguir a cierta distancia; *to tail on*, juntarse (a), unir(se); *to tail off* o *away*, menguar, disminuir, enmudecer, morir, perderse de vista, etc.

tailed, *a.* rabudo, de rabo, que tiene rabo o cola.

tailing, *s.* (*alb.*) cola, entrega. — *pl.* **tailings,** restos, desechos, partes inferiores.

tailless, *a.* rabón, sin rabo.

tailor ['teilə], *s.* sastre; *tailor-bird*, pájaro oriental.

tailoress, *s.f.* sastra.

tailoring, *s.* sastrería.

taint [teint], *v.t.* manchar, inficionar, envenenar, viciar, ensuciar, corromper, echar a perder. — *v.i.* inficionarse, corromperse, podrirse. — *s.* mácula, mancha, infección, corrupción, lunar, tacha.

taintless, *a.* incorrupto, sin mancha, no contaminado.

take [teik], *v.t.* (*pret.* **took**; *p.p.* **taken**) tomar, llevar, asir, agarrar, coger; aceptar, recibir; sacar, quitar; apropiarse, posesionarse, apoderarse de; llevar, arrebatar; hurtar, robar, pillar; percibir, cobrar; restar, deducir, substraer; hacer prisionero, prender; apresar, capturar; emplear, usar, adoptar; entender, interpretar en un sentido determinado, tener por, considerar; concebir, aceptar, asumir, admitir; emplear o necesitar (tiempo); coger, contraer (una enfermedad); tomar, tragar (medicina); tomar, prender (el macho a la hembra); atrapar, sorprender; guiar, acompañar; cruzar; pasar por encima de, saltar; sacar (una fotografía, una copia); copiar; dar (un paseo); hacer (ejercicio); visitar, incluir en un curso o una ronda; (*fam.*) gustar, deleitar, encantar. — *v.i.* lograr, pegar bien, tener éxito, salir bien, dar golpe, cuajar; ser popular, gustar, causar gusto, agradar; prender (la vacuna, el fuego, las plantas, etc.); hacer su efecto, ser eficaz; efectuarse; picar (el pez); sacar (buen o mal) un retrato; adherirse, pegar; arraigar(se), agarrar(se) (las plantas); moverse; encaminarse, dirigirse; tener afición (a), aplicarse (a), inclinarse (a); *to take aback*, desconcertar, dejar perplejo; *to take after*, parecerse a, salir a; *to take away*, sacar, quitar, separar, apartar; *to take back*, (*fig.*) retractar; *to take down*, bajar (con), poner más bajo; escribir al dictado; humillar, abatir; *to take down (a peg)*, bajar los humos (a), desentonar; *to take for*, tomar por (creer equivocadamente); *to take for a walk*, pasear, llevar de paseo a; *to take for granted*, dar por sentado; *to take from*, privar de, substraer, despojar; *to take ill*, (*v.t.*) llevar a mal; (*v.i.*) caer enfermo; *to take in*, incluir, comprender; recibir, admitir, recoger, dar asilo; encoger, disminuir; engañar, estafar; *to take in hand*, tomar en mano, tomar por su cuenta; *to take off*, quitar(se) (vestidos); quitar de delante; invalidar; ridiculizar; imitar, remedar; despegar, cortar, amputar; arrancar (un vehículo), despegar (avión); *to take the edge off a knife*, embotar un cuchillo; *to take the gilt off the*

gingerbread, (*prov.*) quitar el encanto, desilusionar; *to take on*, encargarse de, emprender, aceptar; (*fam.*) lamentarse, quejarse; *to take on* o *upon*, tomar, hacerse; *to take on* (o *upon*) *oneself*, entremeterse en, encargarse de; *to take on trust* (o *on someone's word*), creer bajo el crédito de otro, tomar a crédito; *to take out*, salir con; sacar; llevar afuera; quitar, extraer, arrancar; *to take out a patent*, obtener un privilegio de invención; *to take over*, tomar posesión de, encargarse de; *to take to*, tomar afición a, aplicarse **a**; *to take to heart*, tomar a pecho(s); *to take to pieces*, desarmar; *to take up*, subir con; empezar, dar principio a; arrestar, prender; amonestar, reprender; llenar u ocupar (un sitio); adoptar, hacer suyo; pagar (una letra de cambio, etc.); acortar (vestido); *to take up with*, (*fam.*) vivir con, contraer amistad con; *to take it up with*, hablar (de un asunto) con; *to take with*, satisfacer, contentar; *to be taken with* o *to take a fancy* (o *a liking*) *to*, aficionarse a; *to take advice*, aconsejarse; *to take the bit between the teeth*, beber el freno; *to take breath*, tomar aliento, reposarse después de algún esfuerzo; *to take care*, tener cuidado, ser cuidadoso; *to take care of*, cuidar; *to take the chair*, presidir, ocupar el sillón presidencial; *to take fire*, encenderse; *to take fright*, cobrar miedo, atemorizarse; *to take (to) flight*, huir; *to take to one's heels*, irse o salvarse por (sus) pies; *to take out of the way*, arrimar; *to take heed*, atender; *to take hold (on)*, agarrar, coger; *to take leave*, despedirse; *to take no notice*, no hacer caso; *to take an oath*, hacer juramento; *to take offence*, agraviarse; *to take pains*, darse molestia, esmerarse; *to take no pains to attain one's end*, no dar pie ni patada; *to take pity on*, apiadarse de, compadecerse de; *to take place*, tener efecto, suceder, verificarse, efectuarse, celebrarse; *to take refuge*, acogerse, buscar asilo; *to take sanctuary*, tomar sagrado, acogerse a sagrado; *to take shelter*, guarecerse, refugiarse; *to take ship*, embarcarse; *to take up the cudgels*, bajar a la arena.

take, *s.* acción de tomar, tomadura, toma; (*impr., fotogr.*) tomada.

taken ['teikən], *p.p.* [TAKE].

take-off ['teikɔːf], *v.t.*, *v.i.* separar, quitar, rebajar; llevarse, arrebatar; remedar, ridiculizar, copiar; despegar. — *s.* (*aer.*) despegue; recorrido de despegue; (*fam.*) remedo, caricatura, sátira.

taker, *s.* tomador.

taking, *a.* seductor, encantador, halagüeño, atractivo; contagioso. — *s.* toma, secuestro, embargo; afición, inclinación, afecto; (*fam.*) arrebato; (*ant.*) brete, trance apurado. — *pl.* **takings,** (*com.*) ingresos, recibos, (*teat.*) taquilla.

talaria [təˈlɛəriə], *s.pl.* talares.

talc [tælk], *s.* talco, esteatita.

talcoid [ˈtælkɔid], **talcose** [ˈtælkəs], **talcous** [ˈtælkəs], *a.* talcoso.

talc-schist, *s.* talquita.

talcum powder, *s.* polvo de talco.

tale [teil], *s.* cuento, narración, relato, relación; rondalla, fábula, conseja; engaño, embuste; hablilla, chisme; (*ant.*) cuenta, número; *to tell tales out of school*, (*fam.*) revelar secretos.

tale-bearer, s. chismoso, cuentero, soplón.
tale-bearing, a. soplón, chismoso. — s. soplo, hablilla.
talent ['tælənt], s. talento, capacidad, ingenio, aptitud, habilidad; persona que tiene alguna habilidad, artista, m.f.; (ant.) talento (peso o moneda).
talented, a. talentoso.
tales ['teili:z], s. (for.) auto o mandato para la citación de jurados suplentes; lista de personas para ese caso.
talesman ['teilzmən], s. (pl. **talesmen**) jurado suplente.
tale-teller ['teiltelɹ], s. enredador, chismeador, chismoso, correveidile.
talion ['tæljon], s. talión.
talipes ['tælipi:z], s. (zool.) pie de piña.
talipot ['tælipot], s. palma grande de las Indias.
talisman ['tælizmən], s. talismán.
talk [to:k], v.t. hablar de, tratar de, conversar sobre; hablar en, hablar (un idioma); decir. — v.i. hablar, conversar, departir, platicar; charlar, parlar; razonar, conferenciar, parlamentar; to talk at random, hablar a destajo; to talk into, convencer hablando, persuadir, inducir; to talk away (o on) seguir hablando, hablar siempre; to talk out of, disuadir, sonsacar; to talk over, persuadir, convencer; to talk to the point o purpose, hablar al alma, ir al grano; to talk for talking's sake, hablar por hablar; to talk to, (fam.) reprender, dar un jabón; to talk up, hablar claro; discutir; alabar, engrandecer, ensalzar. — s. plática, conversación, coloquio; habla; discurso; charla, parloteo, cháchara; voz común, f., rumor, fama, hablilla; small talk, charla, palique; to be the talk of the town, andar de boca en boca.
talkative ['to:kətiv], a. hablador, charlante, amigo de charlar, parlero, lenguaz.
talkativeness, s. garrulidad, locuacidad, charlatanería.
talker, s. hablador, parlador, charlador; fanfarrón; good talker, decidor.
talking, a. parlante, hablante; talking machine, fonógrafo, gramófono; talking doll, muñeca parlante; talking-to, (fam.) represión, jabón; to give someone a good talking-to, dar una jabonadura, decirle cuántas son cinco.
tall [to:l], a. alto, espigado, talludo; elevado; altisonante, exagerado.
tallboy, s. cajonería, cómoda.
tallage ['tælidʒ], **talliage** ['tæliidʒ], s. pecho, tributo antiguo; impuestos, contribuciones, portazgo.
tallness, s. altura, talla, estatura.
tallow ['tælou], v.t. untar con sebo, ensebar. — s. sebo; tallow-chandler, velero; tallow-chandler's shop, velería.
tallow-candle, s. vela de sebo.
tallow-faced, a. pálido como la cera.
tallow-tree, s. (bot.) árbol del sebo.
tallowy, a. seboso, sebáceo, grasoso.
tally ['tæli], s. tarja, tara, taja, cuenta; tally-stick, tarja; to keep tally, llevar la cuenta. — v.t. tarjar, llevar la cuenta; acomodar, ajustar; to tally the sheets, (mar.) cazar y atracar las escotas. — v.i. cuadrar, concordar, estar conforme, conformarse, ajustarse.
tally-ho [tæli'hou], interj. grito del cazador, jaleo. — s. coche de cuatro caballos.

tallyman ['tælimæn], s. tendero que vende a tarja, tarjador, tarjero.
tallywoman, s. tendera que vende a tarja, tarjadora, tarjero.
Talmud ['tælməd], s. talmud.
Talmudical, a. talmúdico.
Talmudist, s. talmudista, m.
talon ['tælən], s. garra, uña; monte de la baraja; talón de hoja de espada.
talus ['teiləs], s. (anat.) astrágalo, tobillo; (geol.) talud, inclinación, pendiente, f.
tamable ['teiməbəl], a. domable, domesticable.
tamarack ['tæməræk], s. alerce.
tamarind ['tæmərind], s. tamarindo.
tamarisk ['tæmərisk], s. tamarisco, taraje, tamariz, taray.
tambour ['tæmbəɹ], s. (mús.) tambor; (arq.) tambor, tamboril; tambour-frame, tambor, bastidor para bordar. — v.t. bordar a tambor.
tambourine ['tæmbori:n], s. pandereta, pándero.
tame [teim], a. amansado, manso, domado, domesticado; dócil, tratable; sumiso, sometido; soso, insulso, aburrido, pesado. — v.t. domar, domesticar, domeñar, poner dócil, amansar; abatir, avasallar; (fig.) domar, amansar, reprimir, suavizar.
tameness, s. domestiquez, mansedumbre, f.; sumisión, timidez; sosería, insulsez.
tamer, a. domador, amansador.
taming, s. doma, domadura, amansamiento, domesticación.
tam-o'-shanter [tæmo'ʃæntəɹ], (fam.) **tammy(-shanter),** s. boina escocesa.
tamp [tæmp], v.t. atacar un barreno; tupir, apelmazar; apisonar, pisonear.
tamper, v.i. entremeterse, meterse (en); estropear, falsificar.
tampion ['tæmpiən], s. (arti.) tapabocas, m.
tampon ['tæmpən], s. (cir.) tapón. — v.t. taponar.
tan [tæn], v.t. (ten.) zurrar, curtir, adobar, aderezar; quemar, tostar, poner moreno; to tan (the hide), (vulg.) zurrar, tundir, castigar. — a. tostado, de color de canela. — s. (ten.) casca, corteza (del roble) molida; moreno, color de canela; tostadura del sol, tostado, bronceado.
tanager ['tænədʒəɹ], s. (orn.) tánagra.
tan-bark, s. (ten.) casca.
tandem ['tændəm], a. colocados uno tras otro. — s. tándem. — adv. uno delante de otro, en tándem.
tang [tæŋ], s. dejo, gustillo, resabio, sabor; (mec.) cola, espiga, rabera; retintín, tañido. — v.t. hacer retiñir — v.i. retiñir, retumbar.
tangency, s. tangencia.
tangent ['tændʒənt], s., a. (geom.) tangente; to go o fly off at a tangent, echar (o ir o irse) por los cerros de Úbeda.
tangential [tæn'dʒenʃəl], a. de tangente, en línea tangente, que se mueve en tangente.
tangerine ['tændʒəri:n], s., a. tangerino; naranja tangerina.
tangibility [tændʒi'biliti], s. calidad de tangible.
tangible ['tændʒibəl], a. tangible, palpable.
tangle ['tæŋɡəl], v.t. enredar, embarazar, enmarañar, embrollar; confundir. — v.i. enmarañarse, enredarse; confundirse. — s.

enredo, embrollo, maraña; confusión, laberinto; laminaria, alga marina.

tank [tæŋk], *s.* tanque, cisterna, alberca,
aljibe, estanque, depósito o arca de agua;
(*mil.*) tanque; *tank-car*, (*f.c.*) carro tanque;
tank-engine, locomotora con tanque pero sin
ténder.

tankage ['tæŋkidʒ], *s.* conservación de flúidos;
depósitos de agua, etc.; precio que se paga
por guardar algo en tanques; cabida o
capacidad de un tanque; residuo de las
grasas.

tankard ['tæŋkəɹd], *s.* bock, caña (para
cerveza), pichel; (*ant.*) cangilón, cántaro
grande.

tanker ['tæŋkəɹ], *s.* (*mar.*) petrolero; buque
aljibe o cisterna (de agua).

tannate ['tænit], *s.* tanato.

tanned [tænd], *a.* curtido; tostado del sol,
bronceado. — *p.p.* [TAN].

tanner, *s.* curtidor, zurrador; (*vulg.*) pieza de
seis peniques.

tannery, *s.* tenería, curtiduría.

tannic ['tænik], *a.* tánico; *tannic acid,* ácido
tánico, ácido tanino.

tannin ['tænin], *s.* tanino.

tanning ['tæniŋ], *s.* zurra, curtimiento, tunda;
(*vulg.*) zurra, tunda, castigo.

tansy ['tænzi], *s.* tanaceto, balsamita menor,
argentina.

tantalize ['tæntə'laiz], *v.t.* atormentar mostrando cosas inasequibles, mortificar, torear,
provocar, picar, exacerbar; ponerle a uno los
dientes largos.

tantalum ['tæntələm], *s.* (*quím.*) tantalio.

tantamount ['tæntəmaunt], *a.* equivalente; *to
be tantamount,* equivaler.

tantivy [tæn'tivi], *adv.* (*ant.*) velozmente, de
prisa, a rienda suelta.

tantrum ['tæntrəm], *s.* berrinche, pataleta,
rabieta.

tan-yard ['tænjɑːɹd], *s.* tenería.

tap [tæp], *v.t.* decentar (un barril); horadar
(para sacar líquido); hacer incisión a (un
árbol), sangrar o resinar el jugo de (un
árbol); (*cir.*) hacer una puntura en un
absceso; (*elec.*) derivar o tomar (una corriente); (*mec.*) aterrajar (un tornillo);
golpear ligeramente, dar una palmadita;
perforar, taladrar; descubrir (información),
escuchar secretamente una conversación
telefónica; poner tacón a (un zapato); *to tap
at the door,* llamar dando golpecitos a la
puerta. — *s.* palmadita, golpecito; llave, *f.,*
grifo; espita, canilla, tubo, caño; tarugo,
tapón; (*mec.*) macho de tarraja; (*fam.*)
mostrador de taberna; (*elec.*) derivación;
cualidad, clase (de vino); remiendo echado al
talón de un zapato. — *pl.* **taps,** (*mil.*) toque
de apagar las luces; *on tap,* en un barril, que
se saca de un barril; (*fig.*) a la mano, a pedir
de boca.

tap-dance, *s.* zapateado, claqué. — *v.i.* zapatear.

tape [teip], *s.* cinta, cintilla, galoncillo, bocadillo, trencilla, (*E.U.*) melindre; cinta (de
papel o de metal); *linen tape,* cinta de
hiladillo; *tape-line* o *tape-measure,* cinta para
medir; *red tape,* balduque; expedienteo,
burocracia, formalismo; *tape-machine,* máquina de cinta magnética, telégrafo.

taper, *s.* bujía, cerilla, candela, vela pequeña;

cirio (de iglesia); blandón, hacha; diminución (*o* afilamiento gradual). — *a.* cónico,
piramidal. — *v.t.* afilar, adelgazar, ahusar. —
v.i. rematar en punta.

tape-recorder, *s.* registrador de cinta magneto-
fónica.

tapestry ['tæpestri], *v.t.* entapizar; adornar
con colgaduras. — *s.* tapiz; tapicería, colgadura.

tapeworm ['teipwəːm], *s.* tenia, lombriz
solitaria.

tapioca [tæpi'oukə], *s.* tapioca, mandioca.

tapir ['teipəɹ], *s.* (*zool.*) tapir, danta.

tapis ['tæpiː], *s.* tapete; *on the tapis,* sobre el
tapete.

tappet ['tæpet], *s.* (*mec.*) empujaválvula, *m.,*
levantaválvula, *m.,* leva.

tapping ['tæpiŋ], *s.* golpecitos, golpeteo; (*cir.*)
paracentesis, *f.*

tapster ['tæpstəɹ], *s.* mozo de cervecería,
tabernero; (*ant.*) tabernera.

tar [tɑːɹ], *s.* alquitrán, brea, pez líquida; (*fam.*)
marinero; *tar-water,* agua de alquitrán;
mineral-tar, betún, alquitrán mineral; *coal-
tar,* alquitrán de hulla; *tar-brush,* (*mar.*)
escopero; *tar-pot,* desca; *Jack Tar,* (*fam.*)
marinero. — *v.t.* alquitranar, brear, embrear, dar brea a, betunar; *to tar and
feather,* embrear y emplumar; *tarred with the
same brush,* otra o otro que bien baila, otra o
otro que tal.

tarantella [tærən'telə], *s.* tarantela.

tarantula [tə'ræntjuːlə], *s.* tarántula.

tardigrade ['tɑːɹdigreid], *s., a.* tardígrado.

tardily ['tɑːɹdili], *adv.* morosamente, tardíamente, lentamente, fuera de tiempo.

tardiness, *s.* lentitud, tardanza, cachaza,
morosidad, flema.

tardy ['tɑːɹdi], *a.* tardío, moroso, rezagado,
negligente, cachudo, tardo, lento.

tare [tɛəɹ], *s.* (*bot.*) veza, yero, algarroba,
vicia, (en la biblia) cizaña; (*com.*) tara,
merma. — *v.t.* destarar, restar la tara al
pesar una cosa.

target ['tɑːɹget], *s.* blanco (a que se tira); tarja,
escudo, rodela; *target practice,* tiro al blanco.

Targum ['tɑːɹgʌm], *s.* targum.

tariff ['tærif], *s.* tarifa, arancel; lista de platos,
menú.

tarlatan ['tɑːɹlətən], *s.* tarlatana.

tarn [tɑːɹn], *s.* lago pequeño entre montañas.

tarnish ['tɑːɹniʃ], *v.t.* deslustrar, deslucir,
empañar, mancillar, desflorar. — *v.i.* des-
lucirse, deslustrarse, perder el lustre,
enmohecerse. — *s.* deslustre, falta de lustre,
empañadura.

taro ['tɑːrou], *s.* (*bot.*) taro.

tarpaulin [tɑːɹ'pɔːlin], *s.* lienzo empegado o
alquitranado, cáñamo embreado, encerado,
sombrero de cuero encerado; (*fam.*) marinero; *tarpaulin-nails,* (*mar.*) estoperoles.

tarragon ['tærəgɔn], *s.* (*bot.*) tarragón,
estragón.

tarred [tɑːɹd], *a.* embreado, alquitranado. —
p.p. [TAR].

tarriance ['tæriəns], *s.* (*ant.*) tardanza,
demora.

tarrier ['tæriəɹ], *s.* (*ant.*) tardador, persona que
tarda.

tarring, *s.* embreadura.

tarry ['tæri], *v.i.* tardar, obrar con lentitud o
cachaza; rezagarse; demorar, pararse, de-

tenerse. — *a.* embreado, alquitranado; piceo.
— *s.* (*ant.*) embreadura; (*ant.*) demora; estancia, visita.

tarsal ['tɑːɹsəl], *a.* del tarso, relacionado con el tarso.

tarsus ['tɑːɹsəs], *s.* tarso.

tart [tɑːɹt], *a.* acre, ácido, asperillo, acerbo, picante, agridulce, acedo. — *s.* tarta, pastelillo (de fruta, etc.); (*vulg.*) mujercilla, mujerzuela, damisela.

tartan ['tɑːɹtən], *s.* (*tej.*) tartán; (*mar.*) tartana.

tartar ['tɑːɹtəɹ], *s.* tártaro; (*dent.*) tártaro, sarro, toba; *cream of tartar,* cremor tártaro.

Tartar, *s.* tártaro; *to catch a Tartar,* hallar uno la horma de su zapato.

Tartarean [tɑːɹ'tɛəriən], *a.* tartáreo.

tartareous [tɑːɹ'tɛəriəs], *a.* compuesto de tártaro; tartáreo.

tartaric [tɑːɹ'tærik], *a.* tártrico, tartárico.

tartarize ['tɑːɹtəraiz], *v.t.* tartarizar, impregnar con tártaro.

tartarous, *a.* (*ant.*) de tártaro.

tartly ['tɑːɹtli], *adv.* agriamente, acerbamente, acedamente, con aspereza.

tartness, *s.* acidez, agrura, acedía, acrimonia, aspereza.

tartrate ['tɑːɹtreit], *s.* tartrato.

task [tɑːsk], *s.* tarea, faena, labor, *f.*; empresa, misión, encargo; *to take* (o *bring*) *to task,* reprender, (*fam.*) solfear, regañar; *task-work,* destajo; *task-force,* brigada o cuadrilla de trabajadores. — *v.t.* atarear, señalar, poner tarea.

tasker, taskmaster, *s.* mayoral, capataz, obrajero.

tassel ['tæsəl], *s.* borla, borlita, campanilla, especie de botón de seda; (*bot.*) inflorescencia de ciertas flores. — *v.t.* adornar con borlas.

tasselled ['tæsəld], *a.* adornado con borlas (o campanillas).

tastable ['teistəbəl], *a.* gustable, sabroso, que tiene sabor.

taste [teist], *v.t.* gustar, saborear, paladear; catar, probar, gustar de; probar, ensayar, experimentar. — *v.i.* saber (a), tener sabor o gusto (de); *to taste of,* saber a. — *s.* gusto, gustadura, sabor, paladeo, saboreo; cata, sorbo; (*fig.*) ligera cantidad, poco, muy poco, pizca; ejemplar, muestra; prueba, ensayo, experimento; buen gusto, discernimiento; afición, inclinación, aptitud; manera con que está ejecutada una cosa; *to have a taste for something,* tener afición a, gustarle a uno una cosa; *in bad* (*good*) *taste,* de mal (buen) gusto.

tasted, *a.* que tiene (cierto) sabor.

tasteful, *a.* elegante, de buen gusto, hecho con gusto; (*ant.*) sabroso.

tastefully ['teistfəli], *adv.* con gusto, según el buen gusto, elegantemente.

tastefulness, *s.* buen gusto, discernimiento, elegancia.

tasteless ['teistles], *a.* insípido, insulso, desabrido, soso; de mal gusto.

tastelessly, *adv.* insulsamente, sosamente; sin gusto, de mal gusto.

tastelessness, *s.* insipidez, insulsez; falta de gusto, mal gusto.

taster, *s.* catador, probador; catavinos; catavino, probeta.

tasty ['teisti], *a.* sabroso, apetitoso, apetitivo, gustoso; elegante, de buen gusto.

tat [tæt], *v.t., v.i.* hacer encaje de frivolité.

ta-ta [tæ'tɑː], *interj.* adiós (lenguaje de niños).

Tatar ['tɑːtəɹ], *s.* tártaro [TARTAR].

tatter ['tætəɹ], *s.* andrajo, pingajo, arrapiezo, colgajo, harapo, guiñapo, trapajo, jirón, arambel; *to be* (*all*) *in* (*rags and*) *tatters,* estar hecho un andrajo. — *v.t.* hacer harapos o andrajos.

tatterdemalion [tætəɹde'meiliən], *s.* zarrapastrón, andrajoso.

tattered ['tætəɹd], *a.* andrajoso, trapajoso, harapiento, guiñapiento. — *p.p.* [TATTER].

tatting, *s.* encaje de frivolité.

tattle ['tætəl], *v.t., v.i.* chacharear, parlar, chismear, comadrear. — *s.* cháchara, chismografía, parlería, charlatanería.

tattler ['tætləɹ], *s.* hablador, chacharero, chismoso; (*orn.*) agachadiza de pico recio agudo.

tattoo [tæ'tuː], *s.* tatuaje; (*mil.*) retreta; tamboreo; (*mil.*) parada militar. — *v.t.* tatuarse el cutis. — *v.i.* tamborear, tabalear.

tattooing [tæ'tuːiŋ], *s.* tatuaje; tamboreo, tabaleo.

taught [tɔːt], *pret., p.p.* [TEACH].

taunt [tɔːnt], *v.t.* mofar, hacer zumba de, vilipendiar, echar en cara, vituperar. — *s.* escarnio, mofa, vituperio, improperio; *taunt-masted,* (*mar.*) de mucha guinda.

taunter, *s.* vituperador, mofador, zumbón.

tauntingly, *adv.* con vituperio, con mofa; en tono insultante.

tauriform ['tɔːrifɔːm], *a.* de forma de toro; (*astr.*) referente a Tauro.

taurine ['tɔːrain], *a.* taurino, de toro; (*astr.*) relativo a Tauro.

tauromachy [tɔː'rɔməki], *s.* tauromaquia.

Taurus ['tɔːrəs], *s.* (*astr.*) Tauro.

taut [tɔːt], *a.* tieso, tirante, tenso, tendido; tieso, severo; pulido, aseado; en regla; *to haul* o *make taut,* (*mar.*) tesar, atiesar, poner tieso.

tauten, *v.t.* tesar, atiesar, entesar.

tautness, *s.* tensión.

tautog, tautaug [tɔː'tɔg], *s.* (*E.U.*) pescado negruzco.

tautological [tɔːto'lɔdʒikəl], *a.* tautológico.

tautologist, *s.* tautológico.

tautologize, *v.i.* usar de tautologías.

tautology [tɔː'tɔlodʒi], *s.* tautología.

tavern ['tævəɹn], *s.* taberna, mesón, posada, venta, figón.

tavern-keeper, *s.* posadero, tabernero.

taw [tɔː], *v.t.* curtir pieles en blanco. — *s.* canica de vidrio que usan los niños para tirar a las otras.

tawdrily ['tɔːdrili], *adv.* charramente, chillonamente, vistosamente, de modo cursi.

tawdriness ['tɔːdrinis], *s.* charrería, brillo falso, oropel, cursilería.

tawdry ['tɔːdri], *a.* charro, chillón, curro, cursi.

tawny ['tɔːni], *a.* leonado.

tax [tæks], *s.* contribución, impuesto, tributo, gabela, carga, exacción; *tax-payer,* contribuyente; *tax-collector* o *tax-gatherer,* exactor, recaudador de contribuciones; *tax-list,* cédula o lista de contribuyentes; *tax-rate,* cupo; (*Biblia*) censo de contribuyentes. — *v.t.* imponer tributos o contribuciones; (*for.*) tasar (costas); acensuar; exigir demasiado, cargar, abrumar; abusar; (*fam.*)

pedir como precio; acusar, imputar, tachar; *to tax with*, tachar de, acusar de.

taxable ['tæksəbəl], *a.* sujeto a tributación.

taxation, *s.* tributación o imposición (de contribuciones o impuestos), sistema tributario.

taxer, *s.* exactor, recaudador (de impuestos); acusador.

taxi ['tæksi], *s.* taxi; *taxi-driver*, taxista, *m.* — *v.i.* ir en taxi; (*aer.*), correr por tierra, rodar por el suelo; deslizarse sobre el agua.

taxidermist [tæk'sidəɹmist], *s.* taxidermista, *m.f.*

taxidermy [tæk'sidəɹmi], *s.* taxidermia.

taxonomy [tæk'sɔnomi], *s.* taxonomía.

tea [ti:], *s.* té; (*Filip.*) cha; cocimiento o infusión o decocción medicinal; colación de la tarde, merienda.

tea-board, tea-tray, *s.* batea o bandeja para servir el té.

tea-caddy, *s.* pequeña caja para guardar té.

teach [ti:tʃ], *v.t.* enseñar, dar lecciones, aleccionar, adiestrar, instruir. — *v.i.* ejercer el magisterio, ser profesor.

teachable ['ti:tʃəbəl], *a.* dócil; susceptible de enseñanza.

teachableness, *s.* capacidad para aprender, docilidad.

teacher ['ti:tʃəɹ], *s.* maestro (de escuela), profesor, preceptor, instructor, enseñador; *woman teacher*, maestra, profesora, preceptora; *assistant teacher*, sotamaestra, pasante, ayo.

teaching, *a.* docente. — *s.* enseñanza, instrucción, doctrina; magisterio, enseñanza.

tea-cosy, *s.* cubretetera, *m.*

tea-cup ['ti:kʌp], *s.* taza para té.

teacupful ['ti:kʌpfəl], *s.* taza llena, cabida de una taza.

teak [ti:k], **teakwood,** *s.* teca.

tea-kettle ['ti:ketəl], *s.* tetera [TEA-POT].

teal [ti:l], *s.* cerceta, trullo, zarceta.

team [ti:m], *s.* yunta, tronco, pareja, par; fila; atelaje; (*deportes*) partido, equipo; manada de patos. — *v.t.*, *v.i.* guiar (un tronco o una yunta), enganchar, asociar; *to team up with*, juntar(se) con, asociar(se) con; *team-spirit* o *team-work*, colaboración, cooperación.

teamster, *s.* conductor de un tiro (de caballos, etc.), tronquista, *m.f.*

tea-pot, *s.* tetera.

teapoy ['ti:pɔi], *s.* mesita de adorno para el servicio de té.

tear [tɛəɹ], *v.t.* (*pret.* **tore**, (*ant.*) **tare**; *p.p.* **torn**) romper, desgarrar, despedazar, hacer pedazos, rasgar; rasguñar, arañar, arpar; arrancar, separar con violencia; atormentar. — *v.i.* rasgarse, separarse, dividirse; correr precipitadamente; *to tear to tatters*, hacer jirones; *to tear one's hair*, arrancarse los cabellos; *to tear away* (o *off*), arrancar, desmembrar; (*fam.*) irse precipitadamente, irse corriendo; *to tear down*, derribar, demoler; *to tear oneself away*, (*fam.*) arrancarse, despedirse o marcharse contra su voluntad; *to tear up*, arrancar, desarraigar completamente; hacer pedazos o jirones; subir corriendo. — *s.* rasgón, rasgadura, desgarradura; raja; precipitación; *wear and tear*, estropeo, desmejoramiento.

tear [tiəɹ], *s.* lágrima; llanto, lloro; (*fig.*) llanto, lloro; *tear-gas*, gas lacrimógeno; *tear-shell*, (*arti.*) granada cargada con gas lacrimógeno.

tearful ['tiəɹful], *a.* lagrimoso, lloroso.

tearless ['tiəɹles], *a.* sin lágrimas.

tease [ti:z], *v.t.* fastidiar, atormentar, jorobar, importunar, torear; tomar el pelo, pitorrearse, guasearse; cardar, rastrillar; (*tej.*) despinzar, carduzar. — *s.* jorobadura, toreo, fastidio, importunidad; burla, pitorreo, (*fam.*) guasa; (*fam.*) cócora, *m.f.*, guasón.

teasel ['ti:zəl], *s.* (*bot.*) cardencha; carda. — *v.t.* cardar paño; *teasling machine*, máquina de cardar paño.

teaseller, *s.* pelaire; carda.

teaser, *s.* (*fam.*) guasón, cócora, *m.f.*; (*elec.*) excitador de una dínamo; (*fam.*) rompecabezas, *m.*, acertijo; *teasing-machine*, (*tej.*) máquina de cardar paño.

tea-spoon ['ti:spu:n], *s.* cucharita, cucharilla.

teaspoonful ['ti:spu:nful], *s.* cucharadita, cabida de una cucharada.

teat [ti:t], *s.* pezón; teta, tetilla; ubre, *f.*

technical ['teknikəl], *a.* técnico, tecnológico.

technicality [tekni'kæliti], *s.* cosa técnica; tecnicismo, mecanismo; detalle técnico, cosa baladí.

technician [tek'niʃən], *s.* técnico.

technics ['tekniks], *s.* técnica; tecnicismo.

technique [tek'ni:k], *s.* técnica, ejecución; mecanismo.

technological [teknoˈlɔdʒikəl], *a.* tecnológico.

technologist [tek'nɔlodʒist], *s.* tecnólogo.

technology [tek'nɔlodʒi], *s.* tecnología.

tectonic [tek'tɔnik], *a.* tectónico. — *s.pl.* tectónica.

ted [ted], *v.t.* (*agr.*) henear, rastrillar o esparcir el heno; (*fig.*) esparcir; derrochar.

tedder, *s.* heneador.

tedding, *s.* henaje.

teddy-bear [tedi'bɛəɹ], *s.* osito de trapo.

Te Deum [ti:'di:əm], *s.* tedéum.

tedious ['ti:diəs], *a.* tedioso, fastidioso, molesto, aburrido, enfadoso, pesado.

tediousness ['ti:diəsnis], **tedium** ['ti:diəm], *a.* tedio, aburrimiento, fastidio, pesadez, molestia.

tee [ti:], *s.* nombre de la letra T o cualquier objeto en forma de T; (*deport.*) meta; (juego de golf) montoncillo donde se coloca la pelota antes de lanzarla, 'tee'. — *v.t.* colocar (la pelota) en el *tee*.

teem [ti:m], *v.t.* vaciar (un tanque, metal fundido). — *v.i.* rebosar, estar rebosando, abundar; pulular, hormiguear, bullir, estar lleno de; hervir; diluviar (la lluvia); (*ant.*) parir, encintarse.

teeming, *a.* prolífico, fecundo; lleno; abundante, rebosante.

teenage, *s.* adolescencia.

teenager, *s.* adolescente.

teens [ti:nz], *s.pl.* los números cuyos nombres terminan en *-teen*; edad de trece a diez y nueve años; *to be in one's teens*, no haber cumplido los veinte; *to be out of one's teens*, haber llegado a los veinte.

teetee ['ti:ti:], *s.* (*zool.*) tití.

teeter ['ti:təɹ], *v.i.* balancearse, columpiarse, bambolearse, tambalearse. — *s.* balance, vaivén, movimiento oscilante.

teeth [ti:θ], *s.pl.* [TOOTH]; *wisdom teeth*, muelas del juicio.

teethe [ti:ð], *v.i.* echar los dientes, endentecer.

teething ['ti:ðiŋ], *s.* dentición; formación de los dientes; *teething-ring*, chupador, chupadero.

teetotal [ti:'toutəl], *a.* que se abstiene por completo de bebidas alcohólicas, abstemio; (*ant.*) total, completo.

teetotal(l)er, *s.* persona que se abstiene absolutamente de bebidas alcohólicas, abstemio.

teetotalism [ti:toutəlizm], *s.* abstinencia completa de bebidas alcohólicas.

teetotum [ti:'toutəm], *s.* totón, perinola.

tegmen ['tegmən], *s.* (*anat.*) placa de hueso; (*ent.*) élitro; (*bot.*) túnica interior.

tegument ['tegju:mənt], *s.* tegumento.

tegumentary [tegju:mentəri], *a.* tegumentario.

tehee [ti:'hi:], *v.i.* reír entre dientes. — *s.* risica, retozo de la risa, risa nerviosa. — *interj.* ¡ji, ji!

teil [ti:l], **teil-tree,** *s.* (*bot.*) tilo; alfónsigo, terebinto.

telamon ['teləmɔn], *s.* telamón.

telar ['ti:lə.ɪ], *a.* relativo a un tejido.

telautograph [tel'ɔ:togræf], *s.* telautógrafo

telegram ['telegræm], *s.* telegrama, *m.*

telegraph ['telegræf], *s.* telégrafo. — *v.t., v.i.* telegrafiar.

telegrapher [te'legrəfə.ɪ], **telegraphist** [te-'legrəfist], *s.* telegrafista, *m.f.*

telegraphic [tele'græfik], *a.* telegráfico.

telegraph-line, *s.* línea telegráfica.

telegraphy [te'legrəfi], *s.* telegrafía; *wireless telegraphy*, telegrafía sin hilos.

telemeter [te'lemetə.ɪ], *s.* telémetro.

telemetry [te'lemetri], *s.* telemetría.

teleologic, *a.* teleológico.

teleology [tele'ɔlodʒi], *s.* teleología.

telepathy [te'lepəθi], *s.* telepatía.

telephone ['telefoun], *v.t., v.i.* telefonear, llamar por teléfono. — *s.* teléfono; *telephone call*, comunicación telefónica; *conversación telefónica*; *telephone box* o *booth*, cabina telefónica; *telephone directory*, guía telefónica; *telephone exchange*, central telefónica; *telephone number*, número de teléfono; *telephone operator*, telefonista, *m.f.*; *to come to the telephone*, ponerse al teléfono.

telephonic [tele'fɔnik], *a.* telefónico, relativo al teléfono.

telephonist [te'lefonist], *s.* telefonista, *m.f.*

telephony [te'lefoni], *s.* telefonía.

teleprinter, *s.* teleimpresor.

telescope ['teleskoup], *s.* (*astr.*) telescopio; catalejo, anteojo de larga vista. — *v.t., v.i.* enchufar(se); condensar.

telescopic ['teles'kɔpik], *a.* telescópico, de larga vista; (*mec.*) con secciones enchufadas.

teleview ['televju:], *v.t., v.i.* mirar, ver con un aparato receptor de televisión.

televiewer, *s.* (*neol.*) espectador de televisión; televisoespectador.

televise ['televaiz], *v.t.* transmitir por televisión, (*fam.*) televisar.

television [tele'viʒən], *s.* televisión.

telic ['telik], *a.* (*gram.*) que denota intención.

tell [tel], *v.t., v.i.* (*pret., p.p.* told) relatar, narrar, contar; decir; expresar; explicar, manifestar, comunicar, informar, hacer saber; revelar, descubrir; decidir, determinar; adivinar, predecir; descifrar; marcar (la hora); producir efecto; arreglar, disponer, ordenar; mandar, dar un mandato a; numerar; *to tell on* o *upon*, producir efecto;

delatar; *to tell off*, enumerar; mandar, despachar; (*fam.*) dar un jabón, regañar.

teller, *s.* relator, narrador; escrutador (de votos, etc.); computista, *m.f.*; (*E.U.*) cajero; *paying teller*, pagador; *receiving teller*, cobrador; *entering teller*, contador.

telling, *a.* eficaz, que produce efecto, notable.

tell-tale ['telteil], *s.* soplón, chismeador, correveidile; chismoso; contador, indicador, reloj de vigilancia; (*mar.*) axiómetro.

telluric [te'lju:rik], *a.* telúrico.

tellurion [tel'ju:riən], *s.* aparato para demostrar los movimientos reales y aparentes de la tierra.

tellurium [tel'ju:riəm], *s.* telurio.

telpherage ['telfəridʒ], *s.* transporte automático aéreo por medio de la electricidad.

temerarious [temə'rɛəriəs], *a.* temerario.

temerariously, *adv.* temerariamente, de modo temerario.

temerity [te'meriti], *s.* temeridad.

temper ['tempə.ɪ], *v.t.* templar, moderar, acomodar, calmar; atemperar; entibiar; mezclar, ajustar, modificar; ablandar suavizar, temperar; (*metal.*) templar, dar dureza a. — *s.* mal genio, carácter irascible; ira, cólera, irritación; índole, *f.*, genio, temple, natural, humor, temperamento, disposición; calma, moderación, ecuanimidad, sangre fría; (*metal.*) temple; punto o grado de densidad (de una mezcla, v.g. en la argamasa); cal de defecación (para el azúcar).

tempera ['tempərə], *s.* (*pint.*) templa.

temperament ['temprəmənt], *s.* temperamento, genio, natural, índole, *f.*, condición, naturaleza; (*mús.*) temple.

temperamental, *a.* complexional, propio del temperamento, relacionado con el temperamento; caprichoso, mudadizo, veleidoso, voluntarioso.

temperance ['tempərens], *s.* templanza, temperancia, sobriedad, moderación; total abstinencia de bebidas alcohólicas; *temperance hospital* o *hotel*, sitio en el que no se venden bebidas alcohólicas.

temperate ['tempərit], *a.* morigerado, sobrio, abstemio, moderado, contenido, templado, benigno.

temperateness, *s.* templanza, moderación; serenidad.

temperature ['tempərətʃə.ɪ], *s.* temperatura; temperie, *f.*; (*med.*) fiebre, *f.*; (*ant.*) temperamento, temple; templanza.

tempered ['tempəɪd], *a.* templado, acondicionado, dispuesto, inclinado; *good-tempered*, de buen temple, de genio benigno, de buen humor; *ill-tempered*, áspero, agrio de genio, de mal humor; *even-tempered*, de humor igual; *hot-tempered*, irascible.

tempest ['tempest], *s.* tempestad, tormenta, temporal, borrasca; (*fig.*) tormenta, borrasca, tumulto, alboroto; conmoción de ánimo, violencia de genio.

tempest-tossed, *a.* sacudido por la tormenta.

tempestuous [tem'pestju:əs], *a.* tempestuoso, proceloso, borrascoso; (*fig.*) borrascoso, turbulento, impetuoso.

tempestuousness, *s.* tiempo proceloso, tempestad; (*fig.*) impetuosidad.

Templar ['templə.ɪ], *s.* Templario, miembro del orden de los Templarios; (*Ingl.*) estudiante de leyes, que habita en el Temple de Londres.

template, templet ['templit], s. patrón, escantillón; gálibo; cuña, solera.

temple ['tempəl], s. templo, iglesia; (*anat.*) sien, *f.*; (*tej.*) regla, encuentro, vara de telar.

tempo ['tempou], s. (*mús.*) tiempo, movimiento.

temporal ['temporəl], a. temporal, pasajero, transitorio; secular; (*anat.*) perteneciente a las sienes. — s. (*anat.*) hueso temporal.

temporality [tempo'ræliti], s. temporalidad.

temporally ['temporəli], adv. temporalmente, transitoriamente; que se refiere a la vida presente.

temporalty ['temporəlti], s. seglares, no eclesiásticos; bienes seculares.

temporarily, adv. provisionalmente, temporáneamente.

temporariness ['temporərinis], s. duración temporal, interinidad.

temporary ['temporəri], a. temporáneo, temporal, interino, provisorio.

temporize ['temporaiz], v.i. temporizar, contemporizar, ganar tiempo, diferir.

temporizer, s. temporizador, entretenedor.

tempt [tempt], v.t. tentar, solicitar al mal, poner a prueba; atraer, inducir; provocar, desafiar, excitar.

temptable, a. capaz de dejarse tentar o seducir.

temptation [temp'teiʃən], s. tentación; aliciente, *f.*

tempter, s. tentador.

tempting ['temptiŋ], a. tentador, atractivo, seductor.

temptingly, adv. con tentación.

temptress ['temptres], s.f. tentadora.

ten [ten], s., a. diez, m.

tenable ['tenəbəl], a. defensible, capaz de ser sostenido.

tenacious [te'neiʃəs], a. tenaz; pegajoso, adhesivo; fuerte; terco, firme, porfiado.

tenaciously, adv. tenazmente, con tenacidad; con tesón, con firmeza, con obstinación, a pie juntillo.

tenaciousness, s. tenacidad; pertinacia, tesón, obstinación.

tenacity [te'næsiti], s. tenacidad; calidad de adhesivo; tesón, terquedad, porfía.

tenaculum [te'nækju:ləm], s. tenáculo.

tenail, tenaille [te'neil], s. (*fort.*) tenaza, doble.

tenancy ['tenənsi], s. tenencia; posesión temporal, inquilinato.

tenant ['tenənt], s. arrendatario, inquilino, arrendador, residente, usufructuario, morador, rentero. — v.i. tener en arriendo.

tenantable ['tenəntəbəl], a. habitable.

tenantless, a. desarrendado, sin inquilinos; deshabitado.

tenantry ['tenəntri], s. inquilinato, inquilinos en general; arriendo, conjunto de los arrendatorios de un hacendado.

tench [tentʃ], s. (*ict.*) tenca.

tend [tend], v.t. guardar, cuidar, tener cuidado de, vigilar, velar, atender; acompañar, asistir, servir. — v.i. tener tendencia, propender, tender; contribuir; llevar, conducir; ir o moverse hacia, dirigirse o encaminarse (a); (*ant.*) estar atento; ocuparse, pensar;

to tend on (o *upon*), servir **a**, estar atento a.

tendency ['tendənsi], s. tendencia, propensión, proclividad; dirección, inclinación.

tendentious [ten'denʃəs], a. tendencioso.

tender ['tendər], a. tierno; flexible, blando, delicado; mollar, muelle; compasivo, sensible; afeminado; tierno, amoroso, afectuoso, cariñoso; benigno, indulgente, solícito, cuidadoso; arriesgado, arduo; escrupuloso. — s. ofrecimiento, oferta, propuesta, proposición; (*for.*) oferta formal de pago; (*com.*) lo que se ofrece en pago de una deuda; oferta por escrito; (*mar.*) buque nodriza; patache, falúa; (*f.c.*) ténder, alijo; guarda, servidor, persona que cuida a otra; *legal tender*, moneda corriente. — v.t. ofrecer, proponer, presentar; (*for.*) ofrecer en pago sin condiciones; ablandar, enternecer, poner tierno. — v.i. hacer una oferta o propuesta.

tenderfoot, s. (E.U. y Aust., *fam.*) apodo que dan los naturales del país al recién llegado; bisoño, pipiolo.

tender-hearted, a. tierno de corazón, compasivo.

tenderling, s. pitón de asta de venado.

tenderloin ['tendərloin], s. filete.

tenderly ['tendərli], adv. tiernamente, con cariño.

tenderness, s. ternura, terneza, suavidad, delicadeza; benignidad, benevolencia; afecto, amor, cariño; miramiento, escrupulosidad, nimiedad.

tendinous ['tendinəs], a. tendinoso.

tendon ['tendən], s. (*anat.*) tendón.

tendril ['tendril], s. (*bot.*) zarcillo, tijeretas de las vides.

tendrilled, a. provisto de zarcillos.

tenebrous ['tenebrəs], a. (*ant., poét.*) tenebroso, obscuro.

tenement ['tenemənt], s. parte de una casa donde se aloja una familia; (*fig.*) habitación, vivienda, alojamiento; (*for.*) heredamiento; edificio, casa; *tenement house*, casa de vecindad.

tenementary, a. (*for.*) arrendable.

tenesmus [te'nezməs], s. (*med.*) tenesmo, pujo.

tenet ['tenet, 'ti:net], s. dogma, m., principio, credo, aserción, aserto.

tenfold ['tenfould], a. décuplo. — adv. diez veces, de modo décuplo.

tennis ['tenis], s. tenis; trinquete; *tennis ball*, pelota de tenis; *tennis court*, campo o pista de tenis.

tenon ['tenən], v.t. (*carp.*) espigar, formar espiga, despatillar, desquijerar; juntar a espiga y mortaja. — s. (*carp.*) espiga, almilla; *tenon saw*, sierra de ingletes.

tenor ['tenər], s. tenor, curso, método; tendencia; tenor, contenido, substancia de un escrito; (*mús.*) tenor; alto; viola; *the even tenor of one's way*, el curso regular de su vida. — a. (*mús.*) de tenor.

tenotomy [te'nɔtomi], s. tenotomía.

tenpenny ['tenpəni], a. de diez peniques, que vale diez peniques; clavo de cierto tamaño.

tenpins ['tenpinz], s. (E.U.) juego con diez bolos de madera.

tense [tens], a. tieso, tenso, estirado, tirante; dramático, emocionante, tenso; nervioso. — s. (*gram.*) tiempo (de un verbo).

tenseness, *s.* tirantez, tensión, contracción; intensidad, emoción, tensión; nerviosismo.

tensibility [tensi'biliti], *s.* facilidad en ponerse tenso.

tensible ['tensibəl], **tensile** ['tensail], *a.* capaz de tensión.

tension ['tenʃən], *s.* tensión, tirantez; dilatación, extensión; intensidad, emoción; esfuerzo mental; fuerza expansiva; (*mec.*) regulador del hilo (en una máquina de coser); (*pol.*) tirantez de relaciones.

tensive ['tensiv], *a.* tirante, tenso, estirado, causado por la tensión.

tensor ['tensɔɹ], *s.* músculo extensor.

ten-strike, *s.* jugada en que se derriban los diez bolos con una sola bocha. — *v.t.* (*fig.*) poner una pica en Flandes.

tent [tent], *s.* tienda de campaña; pabellón; (*fig.*) habitación provisional; tintillo (vino); (*cir.*) lechino, tapón, tienta; *to pitch tents,* acamparse, armar las tiendas de campaña; *to strike tents,* desarmar o plegar tiendas, levantar el campo. — *v.i.* acampar bajo tiendas, alojarse en pabellones. — *v.t.* (*cir.*) tentar.

tentacle ['tentəkəl], *s.* tentáculo, tiento.

tentacular, *a.* de tentáculo.

tentative ['tentətiv], *a.* tentativo. — *s.* tentativa, ensayo, tanteo, prueba.

tent-cloth, *s.* terliz.

tented ['tentid], *a.* cubierto con tiendas o pabellones; entoldado.

tenter ['tentəɹ], *s.* (*tej.*) tendedor. — *v.t.* (*tej.*) estirar (el paño). — *v.i.* estirarse, dilatarse.

tenter-hooks, *s.pl.* (*tej.*) escarpias, alcayatas, clavijas de rama; *to be on tenter-hooks,* estar en ascuas.

tenth [tenθ], *a.* décimo, deceno, diez. — *s.* decena, décimo, décima parte; (*igl.*) diezmo.

tenthly, *adv.* en décimo lugar.

tent-pole ['tentpoul], *s.* mástil, montante de tienda.

tent-wine, *s.* vino de Alicante.

tentwort ['tentwəːɹt], *s.* (*bot.*) culantrillo.

tenuirostral [tenjuːiˈɹɔstrəl], *a.* tenuirrostro.

tenuity [te'njuːiti], *s.* tenuidad, raridad, delgadez, sutileza; rarefacción.

tenuous ['tenjuːəs], *a.* tenue, delicado, fino, delgado, sutil.

tenure ['tenjuːəɹ], *s.* tenencia, posesión, dependencia, pertenencia, enfiteusis, *f.*

teocalli [teiou'kæli], *s.* teocalí.

tepefaction [tepi'fækʃən], *s.* templadura; acto de entibiar.

tepefy ['tepefai], *v.t.*, *v.i.* entibiar, hacer o ponerse tibio.

tepid ['tepid], *a.* tibio, templado.

tepidity [te'piditi], *s.* tibieza.

teratology [terə'tɔlodʒi], *s.* teratología.

terce [təːɹs], *s.* tercerola; (*igl.*) tercia.

tercentenary [tersen'tiːnəɹi], *a.* de tres siglos. — *s.* aniversario tricentésimo.

tercet ['təːɹset], *s.* (*poét.*) terceto.

terebinth ['terebinθ], *s.* terebinto, alfóncigo.

terebinthinate, terebinthine, *a.* terebintáceo.

terebrate ['terebreit], *v.t.* taladrar.

teredo [te'riːdou], *s.* (*ent.*) broma.

terete [te'riːt], *a.* cilíndrico, redondo.

tergal ['təːɹɡəl], *a.* dorsal.

tergiversate ['təːɹdʒivəɹseit], *v.i.* tergiversar, buscar rodeos.

tergiversation [təːɹdʒivəɹ'seiʃən], *s.* tergiversación, evasión, efugio; instabilidad.

term [təːɹm], *s.* plazo; término, período; vocablo, dicción, voz técnica, tecnicismo; trimestre (de escuela, universidad); (*for.*) tiempo en que un tribunal está en sesión; confín, límite; fin; (*lóg.*, *mat.*) término. — *pl.* **terms,** condiciones, estipulaciones; precio, tarifa; obligaciones impuestas; relaciones mutuas; arreglo, acuerdo; *in set terms,* en términos escogidos; *upon what terms?* ¿en qué términos? *not on any terms,* por ningún concepto, a ningún precio, de ningún modo; *to be on good terms with,* estar sobre buen pie o en buenas relaciones con; *to bring to terms,* imponer condiciones, traer a un arreglo; *to come to terms,* decidirse a un arreglo; *to make terms,* efectuar un acuerdo (o arreglo), ponerse de acuerdo. — *v.t.* nombrar, llamar.

termagancy, *a.* carácter pendenciero.

termagant ['təːɹməɡənt], *a.* (*de mujeres*) fiera, cruel, pendenciera; (*ant.*) pendenciero, turbulento, ruidoso. — *s.f.* fierecilla, fiera, arpía.

terminable ['təːɹminəbəl], *a.* limitable.

terminal ['təːɹminəl], *a.* terminal, último, final, extremo; trimestre, trimestral. — *s.* término, final; (*arq.*) término, remate, figura terminal; (*elec.*) borne, terminal; estación o aeropuerto terminal; (*fam.*) exámenes trimestres (de colegio, universidad); (*gram.*) terminación, desinencia.

terminate ['təːɹmineit], *v.t.*, *v.i.* terminar, ser término, ser fin, poner fin, acabar, concluir, rematar.

termination, *s.* terminación, limitación, remate, conclusión, fin, límite, cabo, extremidad, lindero; (*gram.*) terminación, desinencia.

terminative, *a.* terminativo.

terminer, *s.* (*for.*) audición, vista, audiencia.

terminology [təːɹmi'nɔlodʒi], *s.* terminología, nomenclatura.

terminus ['təːɹminəs], *s.* final, término, fin; (*f.c.*) estación terminal o de cabeza de línea, paradero; límite, mojón; remate, término arquitectónico.

termite ['təːɹmait], *s.* termita, *m.*, hormiga blanca.

termless, *a.* ilimitado, sin límites, sin términos.

tern [təːɹn], *s.* terna, terno; (*orn.*) golondrina de mar. — *a.* ternario.

ternary ['təːɹnəɹi], *a.* ternario, trino, compuesto de tres. — *s.* terna, terno, ternario.

ternate ['təːɹnit], *a.* ternario.

terne-plate, *s.* hojalata (con baño de aleación estaño-plomo).

Terpsichorean [təːɹpsi'kɔːɹiən], *a.* de Terpsícore, del baile.

terra ['terə], *s.*; *terra firma,* tierra firme; *terra alba,* tierra de pipa; *terra incognita,* tierra desconocida.

terrace ['terəs], *s.* terraplén, (*ant.*) terrapleno, bancal, parata; terraza, terrado, terrero, azotea; balcón, galería abierta. — *v.t.* terraplenar.

terra-cotta [terə'kɔtə], *s.* terracota.

terrain [te'rein], *s.* (*geol.*, *mil.*) terreno, campo, región.

terrapin ['terəpin], *s.* (*Am.*) emídido, tortuga de la costa atlántica.

terraqueous [te´reikwiəs], *a.* terráqueo.

terrene [´teriːn], *a.* térreo, terrenal, terreno, terrestre, mundano.

terreplein [´tɛəɹplein], *s. (fort.)* terraplén, plataforma.

terrestrial [te´restriəl], *a.* terrestre, terreno, terrenal.

terret [´teret], *s.* anilla, portarriendas, *m.*

terrible [´teribəl], *a.* terrible, pavoroso, horroroso, espantoso; *(fam.)* tremendo; muy grande, desmesurado.

terribleness, *s.* terriblez, terribilidad.

terribly [´teribli], *adv.* terriblemente, horriblemente, espantosamente; *(fam.)* tremendamente, terriblemente, muy, mucho.

terrier [´teriəɹ], *s.* (perro) zorrero o raposero, terrier; *(fam., Ingl.)* soldado del ejército territorial; descripción, o catálogo de posesiones, heredades o bienes raíces.

terrific [tə´rifik], *a.* terrorífico, terrífico, espantoso, formidable; *(fam.)* tremendo, atroz, estupendo.

terrify [´terifai], *v.t.* aterrar, poner miedo, arredrar, espantar, aterrorizar, horrorizar.

terrigenous [te´ridʒənəs], *a.* terrígeno.

territorial [teri´tɔːriəl], *a.* territorial.

territoriality [teritɔːri´æliti], *s.* territorialidad.

territory [´teritəri], *s.* territorio, región, distrito, comarca.

terror [´terəɹ], *s.* espanto, terror, pavor; objeto de miedo; *(fam.)* persona incorregible, bestia, fiera.

terrorism [´terɔrizm], *s.* terrorismo.

terrorize [´terɔraiz], *v.t.* aterrorizar.

terse [təːɹs], *a.* conciso, limado, sucinto; brusco; *(ant.)* terso, liso, pulido.

terseness, *s.* concisión, limo; brusquedad; *(ant.)* tersura, pulidez.

tertian [´təːɹʃən], *a.* terciano, tercianario. — *s. (med.)* terciana.

tertiary [´təːɹʃəri], *a.* terciario, tercero; *(geol.)* terciario, de la época terciaria. — *s.* (terreno terciario); *(orn.)* pluma terciaria de una ave.

tertiate [´təːɹʃiit], *v.t. (arti.)* medir el espesor de las piezas.

terzet [´təːɹset], *s. (poét.)* terceto [TERCET].

tessellate [´tesəleit], *v.t.* taracear.

tessellate, tessellated, *a.* taraceado, teselado, mosaico.

tessellation, *s.* taracea, obra taraceada, mosaico.

tessera [´tesərə], *s.* tesela; pieza.

tessitura [tesi´tuːrə], *s. (mús.)* tesitura.

test [test], *s.* prueba, ensayo, toque, experimento, probatura, tentativa; examen; juicio; distinción, criterio, piedra de toque; juramento o profesión de fe; análisis, *m.f.;* copela; reactivo, reacción; *(zool.)* concha; *(bot.)* tegumento de una semilla; concha; *to stand the test,* soportar la prueba; *to put to the test,* probar, poner a prueba; *test-tube,* *(quím.)* tubo de ensayo, probeta; *test-paper,* cuestionario, *(quím.)* papel reactivo; *test-match,* partido internacional de cricket; *test-pilot, (aer.)* piloto de pruebas. — *v.t.* probar, tentar, ensayar, experimentar, hacer la prueba, poner a prueba, sujetar a condiciones; *(for.)* atestiguar.

testable, *a.* que puede probarse; que puede legarse; que puede servir de testigo.

testacean [tes´teiʃən], *s., a.* testáceo, que tiene concha.

testaceous, *a.* testáceo.

testament [´testəmənt], *s.* testamento; *Old Testament,* Antiguo o Viejo Testamento; *New Testament,* Nuevo Testamento.

testamentary [testə´mentəri], *a.* testamentario.

testate [´testit], *a.* testado, que ha hecho testamento.

testator [tes´teitəɹ], *s.* testador.

testatrix [tes´teitriks], *s.f.* testadora.

tested, *a.* ensayado, experimentado, probado, examinado. — *p.p.* [TEST].

tester [´testəɹ], *s.* ensayador, probador, persona que pruęba; *(quím.)* reactivo; pabellón, baldaquín; *(ant.)* casco, testera.

testicle [´testikəl], *s.* testículo, teste, glándula seminal.

testicular [tes´tikjuːləɹ], *a.* testicular.

testiculate, *a.* en forma de testículo; que tiene testículos u órganos parecidos a ellos.

testification, *s.* acción de testificar, testificación.

testifier [´testifaiəɹ], *s.* testigo, testificante.

testify [´testifai], *v.t. (for.)* testificar, atestiguar, testimoniar, atestar, afirmar. — *v.i.* dar testimonio, aseverar, servir de testigo (o indicación o evidencia).

testimonial [testi´mouniəl], *a.* testimonial, testificativo, que da testimonio o fe. — *s.* recomendación, certificación, certificado, atestado, testimoniales.

testimony [´testiməni], *s.* testimonio, atestación, testificación, declaración; pruebas; *(Bibl.)* las Tablas de la Ley, Decálogo, libro de la Ley, Antiguo Testamento; *in testimony whereof,* en fe (o en testimonio) de lo cual.

testiness [´testinis], *s.* enojo, enfado, aspereza, mal humor, mal genio.

testis [´testis], *s. (pl.* **testes**) testículo, teste.

testudo [tes´tjuːdou], *s.* testudo; *(zool.)* tortuga.

testy [´testi], *a.* enojadizo, cosquilloso, quisquilloso, descontentadizo.

tetanic [te´tænik], *a.* tetánico.

tetanoid [te´tænɔid], *a.* parecido al tétano.

tetanus [´tetənəs], *s.* tétano(s).

tetchily [´tetʃili], *adv.* quisquillosamente, de mal humor.

tetchy, *a.* quisquilloso, cosquilloso, enojadizo, de mal humor.

tête-à-tête [´teitɑː´teit], *s., adv. (fr.)* cara a cara, de silla a silla, a solas. — *s.* confidente (mueble). — *a.* en privado, confidencial.

tether [´teðəɹ], *s.* traba, maniota, lazo, correa, brida, atadura; *to have come to* o *be at the end of one's tether,* quedarse sin recursos, acabarse o consumirse la paciencia. — *v.t.* apersogar, restriñir, atar, trabar.

tetrachord [´tetrəkɔːɹd], *s.* tetracordio.

tetragon [´tetrəgɔn], *a.* tetrágono, cuadrilátero.

tetragonal, *a.* tetrágono, cuadrangular.

tetrahedral [tetrə´hiːdrəl], *a.* tetraédrico, tetraedral.

tetrahedron [tetrə´hiːdrɔn], *s.* tetraedro.

tetralogy [te´trælodʒi], *s.* tetralogía.

tetrameter [te´træmetəɹ], *s. (poét.)* tetrámetro.

tetrarch [´tetrɑːk], *s.* tetrarca, *m.*

tetrarchate, tetrarchy, *s.* tetrarquía.

tetter [´tetəɹ], *s.* herpes, *m.f.pl.*

Teuton [´tjuːtən], *s.* teutón, tudesco.

Teutonic [tju´tɔnik], *a.* teutónico, tudesco. — *s.* teutón, tudesco.

tew [tju:], *v.t.* (*dial.*) cascar, agramar, espadillar; amasar, sobar, machacar; cansar, fatigar. — *v.i.* (*E.U.*, *dial.*) trabajar mucho.

Texan ['teksən], *s.*, *a.* tejano, de Tejas.

text [tekst], *s.* texto; tema, *m.*; tesis, *f.*; ejemplar, libro; (*impr.*) tipo; *text hand*, carácter de letra muy grueso; letra, libreto (de canto u ópera).

text-book, *s.* libro de texto, libro escolar o de escuela.

textile ['tekstail], *s.* textil, materia textil; tela, tejido. — *a.* textil, hilable, capaz de hilarse.

textual ['tekstju:əl], *a.* textual; versado en el texto.

textualist, *s.* textualista, *m.f.*

textually, *adv.* textualmente; según el texto.

texture ['tekstjəɹ], *s.* tejido, tejedura, tela, obra tejida; textura, configuración, estructura.

thaler ['tɑːləɹ], *s.* tálero; (*biol.*) tejido.

thallic ['θælik], *a.* tálico.

thallium ['θæliəm], *s.* talio.

Thames [temz], *s.* Támesis; *Not to set the Thames on fire*, No haber inventado la pólvora.

than [ðæn], *conj.* que, partícula comparativa; *you have more money than I*, Vd. tiene más dinero que yo; de, en sentido afirmativo delante de números: *fewer than ten*, menos de diez; *more than a hundred*, más de un centenar; *more than once*, más de una vez; del, de la, de los, de las que; de lo que.

thane [θein], *s.* (*ant.*) caballero, gentilhombre; hacendado, dueño de cierta extensión de terreno.

thank [θæŋk], *v.t.* agradecer, estimar, dar gracias a; *thank God*, a Dios gracias; *thank you*, gracias; (*I*) *thank you for*, le agradezco, muchas gracias por. — *s.pl.* **thanks**, gracias. — *interj.* ¡gracias! ¡muchas gracias!

thankful ['θæŋkful], *a.* agradecido, grato, reconocido.

thankfully, *adv.* con reconocimiento, con gratitud.

thankfulness, *s.* agradecimiento, reconocimiento, gratitud.

thankless, *a.* desagradecido, ingrato.

thanklessness, *s.* desagradecimiento, ingratitud.

thanksgiving [θæŋks'givin], *s.* acción de gracias, reconocimiento; celebración pública en reconocimiento del favor de Dios; *Thanksgiving Day*, (*E.U.*) el último jueves de Noviembre.

thankworthy ['θæŋkwəːɹði], *a.* digno de reconocimiento, meritorio.

that [ðæt], *a.* (*pl.* **those**) ese, esa, aquel, aquella. — *pron.* ése, ésa, eso; aquél, aquélla, aquello; que, quien, el cual, la cual, lo cual; el, la, lo; *that which*, el que, la que, lo que; *what of that?* ¿y qué? ¿qué importa eso? ¿qué quiere Vd. decir con eso? *that way*, por aquel camino, por allá; *that is*, es decir, a saber; *that may be*, puede ser, es posible; *to put this and that together*, atar cabos, deducir conclusiones. — *conj.* que; (*so*) *that*, para que, a fin de que, de modo que, de forma que, de manera que, de suerte que, con el objeto de; cuando. — *adv.* (*vulg.*) tan.

thatch [θætʃ], *s.* barda, techado de paja, cañas, etc. — *v.t.* bardar, techar con paja, cañas, etc.

thatcher, *s.* bardador, trastejador de paja, cañas, etc.

thaumaturgical [θɔːməˈtəːɹdʒikəl], *a.* taumatúrgo.

thaumaturgy ['θɔːmətəːɹdʒi], *s.* taumaturgia.

thaw [θɔː], *v.t.*, *v.i.* deshelar(se), desnevar(se), derretir(se); (*fig.*) suavizar(se), ablandar(se). — *s.* deshielo, derretimiento, desnieve.

the [ði:, ðə], *art.* el, la, lo, los, las. — *adv.* (precede a un comparativo): *the . . . the . . .* cuanto . . . tanto (más).

theatre ['θiəɹtəɹ], *s.* teatro, coliseo, (*ant.*) corral; teatro, drama, *m.*; teatro o escena (de algún acontecimiento); *theatre attendant* o *usherette*, acomodor(a).

theatrical [θiˈætrikəl], *a.* teatral, (*ant.*) teátrico; (*fig.*) teatral, afectado.

theatrically, *adv.* teatralmente, de un modo teatral.

theatricals [θiˈætrikəlz], *s.pl.* funciones teatrales; *amateur theatricals*, función de aficionados.

thee [ði:], *pron.* (*poét.*) te, a ti, caso objetivo de [THOU].

theft [θeft], *s.* hurto, robo, ladrocinio.

their [ðeəɹ], *pron. pos.* su, sus; suyo, suya, suyos, suyas, de ellos, de ellas.

theism ['θi:izm], *s.* teísmo; deismo.

theist, *s.* teísta, *m.f.*; deísta, *m.f.*

theistic [θi:ˈistik], **theistical** [θi:ˈistikəl], *a.* teísta, del teísmo, de los teístas; deísta, etc.

them [ðem], *pron.* caso objetivo de [THEY], los, las, les; ellos, ellas; a aquéllos, a aquéllas.

thematic [θeˈmætik], *a.* temático.

theme [θi:m], *s.* tema, *m.*; tesis, *f.*, disertación; (*mús.*) tema, *m.*, motivo.

themselves [ðemˈselvz], *pron. pl.* ellos mismos, ellas mismas; sí mismos.

then [ðen], *adv.* entonces, en aquel tiempo, a la sazón; luego, en seguida, después; en otro tiempo. — *conj.* pues, en tal caso, por consiguiente, luego, por esta razón; *now and then*, de vez en cuando, de cuando en cuando; *now . . . then . . .*, ya . . . ya . . .; ora . . . ora . . .; *now then*, pues, ahora pues, ahora bien; *well then*, pues bien, bien (pues); *and then*, con esto, y en seguida, y entonces; *and what then?* y ¿qué más? y ¿qué resultó, o ¿qué resultará? ¿qué es lo que pasó (o pasará)? — *a.* de entonces, de aquel tiempo.

thence [ðens], *adv.* (de lugar) de allí, desde allí; (de tiempo) desde entonces, desde aquel momento, de allí en adelante; (de modo) de ahí, por eso, por esa razón, por ese motivo.

thenceforth [ðensˈfɔːɹθ], **thenceforward** [θensˈfɔːɹwəɹd], *adv.* desde entonces, en adelante, de allí en adelante.

theocracy [θiˈɔkrəsi], *s.* teocracia.

theocratic [θiouˈkrætik], **theocratical** [θiouˈkrætikəl], *a.* teocrático.

theodicy [θiˈɔdisi], *s.* teodicea.

theodolite [θiˈɔdəlait], *s.* teodolito.

Theodosian [θioˈdousiən], *s.* teodosiano.

theogony [θiˈɔgoni], *s.* teogonía.

theologian [θioˈloudʒən], *s.* teólogo.

theological [θioˈlɔdʒikəl], *a.* teológico, teologal.

theologically, *adv.* teológicamente.

theologize, *v.t.* teologizar; hacer o convertir en teológico. — *v.i.* teologizar.

theologue [ˈθioloug], s. (E.U.) seminarista, m., estudiante de teología; (ant.) teólogo.
theology [θiˈɔlodʒi], s. teología.
theorbo [θiˈɔːɹbou], s. (mús.) tiorba.
theorem [ˈθiorem], s. teorema, m.
theoretic [θioˈretik], theoretical [θioˈretikəl], a. teórico.
theoric [θiˈɔrik], a. de la teoría (espectáculos públicos entre los griegos).
theorist [ˈθiərist], s. teórico.
theorize [ˈθioraiz], v.i. teorizar; discurrir sobre teorías.
theory, s. teoría, teórica; in theory, en teoría.
theosophic [θioˈsɔfik], theosophical [θioˈsɔfikəl], a. teosófico.
theosophist [θiˈɔsofist], s. teósofo.
theosophy [θiˈɔsofi], s. teosofía.
therapeutic [θerəˈpjuːtik], therapeutical [θerəˈpjuːtikəl], a. terapéutico.
therapeutics [θerəˈpjuːtiks], s. terapéutica.
therapeutist [θerəˈpjuːtist], s. terapeuta, m.f.
there [ðɛɹ], adv. ahí, allí, allá; there they are, allí están, hélos ahí; there is o there are, (impers.) hay; here and there, acá y acullá; who goes there? ¿quién vive? who's there? ¿quién es? ¿quién llama?; there was once, había o hubo una vez; out o over there, por allí, por allá, allí; there and back, ida y vuelta. — interj. ¡toma! ¡vaya! ¡ya ves!; There! there! ¡cálmate! ¡vamos!
thereabout(s) [ˈðɛərəbaut(s)], adv. por ahí, por allá, por allí, cerca, en los contornos; cerca de, aproximadamente, por ahí; tocante a eso.
thereafter [ðɛɹˈɑːftəɹ], adv. después de eso, en seguida; conforme, en conformidad; según.
thereat [ðɛɹˈæt], adv. de eso, en eso, por eso; entonces, en aquel punto (o paraje o lugar); allá.
thereby [ðɛɹˈbai], adv. con eso, con aquello, de ese (o aquel) modo, por medio de eso; ahí, por allí cerca.
therefor [ðɛɹˈfɔːɹ], adv. (ant.) para eso (o esto), por eso (o esto).
therefore [ˈðɛɹfɔːɹ], (E.U.) therefor, adv. por esto, por eso, por aquello, por esta razón, por tanto, por lo tanto, de consiguiente, por ello.
therefrom [ðɛɹˈfrɔm], adv. de allí, de allá; de eso, de aquello.
therein [ðɛɹˈin], adv. allí dentro; en esto, en eso, en aquello.
thereinafter [ðɛɹinˈɑːftəɹ], adv. (for.) posteriormente, más adelante.
thereinbefore [ðɛɹinbiˈfɔːɹ], adv. (for.) anteriormente, más arriba.
thereinto [ðɛɹˈintuː], adv. dentro de eso o de aquello.
thereof [ðɛɹˈɔv], adv. de esto, de eso, de aquello, de ello.
thereon [ðɛɹˈɔn], adv. en eso, encima, sobre eso.
thereout [ðɛɹˈaut], adv. de allí, fuera de allí; fuera de eso (o de aquello).
thereto [ðɛɹˈtuː], (ant.) thereunto [ðɛɹˈʌntuː], adv. a eso, a aquello, a ello; además.
thereunder [ðɛɹˈʌndəɹ], adv. debajo de eso.
thereupon [ðɛɹəˈpɔn], adv. sobre, encima; por lo tanto, por consiguiente, en consecuencia de eso; luego, en eso, en esto; al instante, luego.

therewith [ðɛɹˈwið], adv. con eso, con aquello; luego, inmediatamente.
therewithal [ˈðɛɹwiðɔːl], adv. a más, además; con todo; al mismo tiempo.
theriac [ˈθiəriæk], a. teriacal, triacal.
therm [θəːɹm], s. (fís.) unidad térmica.
thermal [ˈθəːɹməl], a. (fís.) térmico; termal, de las caldas.
thermic, a. térmico.
thermite [ˈθəːɹmait], s. (quím.) termita.
thermodynamics [θəːɹmodaiˈnæmiks], s. termodinámica.
thermoelectric, a. termoeléctrico.
thermoelectricity [θəːɹmoelekˈtrisiti], s. termoelectricidad.
thermometer [θəɹˈmɔmetəɹ], s. termómetro.
thermometric [θəːɹmoˈmetrik], a. termométrico.
thermometry, s. termometría.
thermonuclear, a. termonuclear.
thermoscope [ˈθəːɹmoskoup], s. termoscopio.
thermostat [ˈθəːɹmostæt], s. termostato.
thesaurus [θiːˈsɔːrəs], s. tesauro, tesoro, diccionario idealógico.
these [ðiːz], dem. a.pl. [THIS], estos, estas. — dem. pron. pl. [THIS], éstos, éstas.
thesis [ˈθiːsis], s. tesis, f.; (ret.) tesis, f., parte no acentuada del verso o de la palabra.
Thespian [ˈθespiən], a. relativo a Tespis, trágico, dramático.
theurgy [ˈθiːəɹdji], s. teurgia.
thew [θjuː], s. tendón, músculo. — pl. thews, fuerza muscular, energía, vigor.
they [ðei], (pron. pl. he, she o it) ellos, ellas.
thick [θik], a. espeso, grueso, corpulento, macizo; repetido, continuado, continuo, frecuente; tupido, fuerte, denso, condensado, lleno, apretado, amazacotado; turbio, feculento, cenagoso; tosco, basto, grosero; cargado, nebuloso, cerrado, brumoso, sombrío; (fig.) obtuso, embotado, torpe; apagado, borroso; (fam.) íntimo, excesivamente familiar; thick of hearing, duro de oído; to speak thick, hablar con media lengua; thick stuff, (mar.) tablones, palmejares; scarf thick stuff, (mar.) palmejares de los escarpes. — s. espesor, grueso; lo más denso (recio, tupido o nutrido); the thick of the fight, lo más reñido del combate; to go through thick and thin, atropellar por todo; to be a friend through thick and thin, ser un amigo leal (a pesar de todo). — adv. frecuentemente, continuadamente, repetidamente; fuertemente; espesamente.
thicken, v.t., v.i. espesar, condensar, aumentar, engrosar; reforzar; enturbiar(se), cerrar(se); dar fuerza (a), dar más vigor (a).
thickener, s. espesador, coagulante.
thickening, s. espesura; aumento; hinchamiento; (coc., alb.) espesador, coagulante.
thicket [ˈθikit], s. maleza, soto, bosquecito espeso, espesura, matorral, broza, fosca.
thick-headed, thick-skulled, a. torpe, lerdo, estúpido; (fig.) insensible, obstinado, de cabeza dura.
thickish, a. algo turbio, algo espeso o denso.
thick-lipped, a. bezudo.
thickly, adv. espesamente; profundamente; con frecuencia; thickly settled, muy poblado; to speak thickly, hablar con media lengua.
thickness, s. espesor, densidad, espesura, grueso, cuerpo, grosor, consistencia; (fig.)

media lengua, medias palabras, pronunciación indistinta.

thickset ['θikset], *a.* doblado, rechoncho, grueso; plantado muy espeso.

thick-skinned, *a.* paquidermo; (*fig.*) insensible, torpe, de cara dura.

thief [θi:f], *s.* ladrón, estafador; moco de vela; *thief-tube*, pipeta, tubo muestreador.

thieve [θi:v], *v.i.* hurtar, robar, latrocinar. — *v.t.* hurtar, robar.

thievery ['θi:vəri], *s.* robo, hurto, latrocinio.

thievish, *a.* ladrón, rapaz.

thievishly, *adv.* ladronamente, como ladrón.

thievishness, *s.* latrocinio, rapacidad.

thigh [θai], *s.* muslo.

thigh-bone, *s.* fémur.

thill [θil], *s.* limonera, lanza, vara de carruaje.

thimble ['θimbəl], *s.* (*cost.*) dedal; (*mec.*) manguito, virola, boquilla; (*mar.*) guardacabo.

thimble-berry, *s.* frambuesa negra.

thin [θin], *a.* delgado, flaco, magro, descarnado, falto de carnes; delgado, tenue, sutil, fino, diáfano, delicado; ralo, raro, claro; ligero, transparente, insubstancial, sin fundamento, superficial; aguado, seroso; (*fam.*) bautizado (vino); poco, poco numeroso, corto, diseminado, escaso; pequeño; *thin blood*, sangre clara o aguada; *thin air*, aire enrarecido; *to make thin*, descarnar; hacer enflaquecer; *to make thinner*, adelgazar; *to grow thin*, enflaquecer. — *v.t.* atenuar, enrarecer, poner ralo; adelgazar; entresacar (bosque, arboleda, etc.), aclarar, clarificar, dejar claro; *to thin out*, entresacar, disminuir, diluir. — *v.i.* enflaquecer, adelgazarse; menguar, reducirse, disminuir.

thine [ðain], *pron.* (*poét.*) tuyo, tuya, tuyos, tuyas. — *a.* tu, tus; (se emplea en vez de [THY], delante de una vocal).

thing [θiŋ], *s.* cosa, objeto; hecho, circunstancia, acontecimiento; (*despec.*) sujeto, persona, quídam; *poor thing!* ¡pobre! ¡el (o la) pobre! *poor little thing!* ¡pobrecito! o ¡pobrecita!; *above all things*, sobre todo, muy especialmente; *no such thing*, nada de eso, no hay tal (cosa), nada; *the thing*, lo que está de moda, lo que se desea, lo necesario; *to make a good thing out of it*, (*fam.*) aprovechar o sacar provecho de una cosa; *as things stand* o *are*, tal como están las cosas. — *pl.* **things,** trebejos, trastos, efectos, artículos, (*Amér.*) tarecos, equipaje; (*fam.*) trapos, trapitos, vestidos; (*vulg.*) suerte, *f.*, circunstancias.

think [θiŋk], (*pret. y p.p.* **thought**) *v.t., v.i.* pensar, meditar, figurarse, imaginar, discurrir, idear, considerar, reflexionar; intentar, proyectar, formar designio o plan, proponerse, tener intención de; creer, entender, juzgar, conceptuar, formar concepto (de); *to think of* o *on* o *upon*, acordarse de, recordar, pensar en; reflexionar acerca de, meditar, considerar; *to think of*, pensar de, tener opinión de; *to think well* (o *ill*) *of one*, tener buen (o mal) concepto de; *as you think fit*, como Vd. guste, como Vd. quiera; *to think highly* (o *badly*) *of*, tener buen (o mal) concepto de; *to think proper* o *right*, creer conveniente, parecerle oportuno; *to think to oneself*, pensar para sí; *to think too much of oneself*, estar o ponerse muy ancho,

darse pisto; *What do you think* (*of this*)? ¿Qué le parece?; *to think out*, resolver (un problema); planear, idear, proyectar; *to think* (*it*) *over*, pensar(lo), meditar sobre, reflexionar sobre.

thinker, *s.* pensador.

thinking, *s.* pensamiento, meditación, reflexión; juicio, concepto; *way of thinking*, parecer, opinión, modo de pensar; *to my* (*way of*) *thinking*, en mi concepto, en mi opinión, a mi parecer.

thinness ['θinnis], *s.* delgadez, flaqueza, magrez, falta de carnes; delgadez, tenuidad, sutileza, finura, delicadez, ligereza; raleza, raridad; escasez, falta, pequeño número; poca consistencia.

third [θə:rd], *a.* tercer(o); *third boiler*, meladora de azúcar; *third-class, -rate*, de tercera clase, de tercer orden; inferior sin valor, sin importancia. — *s.* tercio, tercera parte; (*mús.*) tercera.

thirdly, *adv.* en tercer lugar.

thirst [θə:rst], *s.* sed, *f.*; (*fig.*) sed, ansia, anhelo, deseo ardiente. — *v.t., v.i.* tener o padecer sed; ansiar, anhelar, desear vivamente; *to slake* o *satisfy one's thirst*, apagar o matar la sed; *to thirst after*, (*fig.*) desear ardientemente.

thirstiness, *s.* sed, *f.*

thirsty ['θə:rsti], *a.* que tiene sed, sediento; (*fig.*) que desea ardientemente; *to be thirsty*, tener sed; *to make thirsty*, hacer sed.

thirteen [θə:r'ti:n], *s., a.* trece.

thirteenth [θə:r'ti:nθ], *a.* décimotercio, trezavo, trece. — *s.* décimotercio, trezavo.

thirtieth ['θə:rtiəθ], *a.* trigésimo, treinta. — *s.* trigésimo, treintavo.

thirty ['θə:rti], *s., a.* treinta.

this [ðis], *a.* (*pl.* **these**) este, esta. — *pron.* éste, ésta, esto.

thistle [θisəl], *s.* (*bot.*) cardo; (*mil.*) abrojo; *carline thistle*, carlina, ajonjera; *fuller's thistle*, cardón, cardencha, cardo de batanero; *Our Lady's thistle* (o *milk-thistle*), cardo lechoso; *prickly thistle*, acanto; *cursed thistle*, cardo silvestre; *Scotch thistle*, cardo, emblema nacional de Escocia; *Order of the Thistle*, la más alta orden de nobleza en Escocia.

thistledown, *s.* papo o vilano (de cardo); (*fig.*) soplilla, ligereza.

thistle-finch, *s.* jilguero.

thistly, *adv.* lleno de cardos.

thither [ðiðər], *adv.* allá, hacia allá; a ese fin, a ese punto; *hither and thither*, acá y allá.

tho' [ðou], *conj., contr.* [THOUGH].

thole [θoul], *s.* (*mar.*) tolete, escálamo, gavilán; asidero del mango de la guadaña.

thole-pin, *s.* tolete.

tholus ['θouləs], *s.* (*arq.*) cúpula.

Thomist ['toumist], *s.* tomista, *m.*

thong [θoŋ], *s.* correa, correhuela, tireta de cuero, guasca, zurriaga.

thoracic [θo:'ræsik], *a.* torácico.

thorax ['θo:ræks], *s.* (*pl.* **thoraces**) (*anat.*) tórax.

thorium ['θo:riəm], *s.* torio.

thorn [θo:rn], *s.* espina, púa, pincho; espino, abrojo; (*fig.*) espina. — *v.t.* pinchar, traspasar o asegurar con una espina; *to be upon thorns*, estar en ascuas.

thorn-apple, *s.* (*bot.*) estramonio.

thornback, thornbut, s. (ict.) raya espinosa, lija raya.

thornless, a. sin espinas, falto de espinas.

thorny ['θɔːɪni], a. espinoso, lleno de espinas; (fig.) espinoso, arduo.

thorough ['θɔrə], a. entero, cabal, completo, perfecto, cumplido, acabado, perfecto, consumado; escrupuloso, concienzudo, esmerado.

thorough-bass ['θɔrəbeis], s. (mús.) bajo continuo.

thoroughbred ['θɔrə'bred], a. de casta, de pura sangre; (fig.) valeroso, osado; elegante.

thoroughfare ['θɔrəfɛəɪ], s. vía pública; No thoroughfare, Prohibido el paso, Calle cerrada.

thoroughgoing [θɔrə'gouiŋ], a. completo, cumplido, entero, eficaz; escrupuloso, concienzudo, esmerado.

thoroughly ['θɔrəli], adv. completamente, por completo, enteramente, a fondo, cabalmente, esmeradamente, minuciosamente.

thoroughness, s. esmero, minuciosidad.

thoroughpaced ['θɔrəpeisd], a. entero, completo, cabal.

thoroughwort, s. eupatorio, hierba fuerte.

thorp [θɔːɪp], s. pueblo, aldea, lugar, caserío.

those [ðouz], a. pl. [THAT]; esos, esas; aquellos, aquellas; los, las. — pr. pl. [THAT]; ésos, ésas, aquéllos, aquéllas; those who, o those which, los que, las que, quienes; those of, los de, las de.

thou [ðau], pr. pers. tú. — v.t. tutear; to thee-and-thou, tutear, dar trato demasiado familiar.

though [ðou], conj. aunque, bien que, aun cuando, siquiera; sin embargo, no obstante, si bien; as though, así es, como que; con todo; what though? ¿qué importa si . . .?

thought [θɔːt], s. (pret. y p.p. **think**) pensamiento, consideración, reflexión, meditación, cogitación; concepto, idea, juicio; proyecto, designio, propósito, plan; recuerdo, recordación, memoria; atención, solicitud, cuidado; inquietud; dictamen, opinión, f.; (fig.) migaja, poquito; on second thoughts, después de pensarlo bien o repensarlo.

thoughtful, a. pensativo, meditativo, meditabundo, considerado; precavido, previsor; contemplativo; atento, solícito.

thoughtfully ['θɔːtfuli], adv. contemplativamente; cuidadosamente; con provisión, con reflexión; solícitamente, atentamente.

thoughtfulness, s. recogimiento, reflexión, meditación; previsión; obsequio, atención, solicitud.

thoughtless, a. descuidado, irreflexionado, irreflexivo, incauto, impróvido, inconsiderado; atolondrado, necio; descuidado, negligente.

thoughtlessly, adv. descuidadamente, sin reflexión, sin consideración; neciamente; negligentemente, descuidadamente.

thoughtlessness, s. irreflexión, inadvertencia, descuido, omisión; aturdimiento, atolondramiento, indiscreción, inconsideración, necedad; negligencia.

thousand ['θauzənd], a. mil. — s. mil, millar.

thousandth, s. milésimo, milésima (parte). — a. milésimo.

thraldom ['θrɔːldəm], s. servidumbre, f., esclavitud.

thrall [θrɔːl], s. siervo, esclavo; servidumbre, f., esclavitud. — v.t. esclavizar, avasallar.

thrap [θræp], v.t. (mar.) atar, amarrar, ligar.

thrash [θræʃ], v.t. zurrar, azotar, golpear; menear (trigo), desgranar, trillar; batir, batanear; sacudir; (fam.) castigar, zurrar; (fam.) derrotar, aplastar.

thrasher, s. apaleador; trillador, trilladora; (orn.) malviz; (ict.) zorra marina (especie de tiburón).

thrashing, s. trilla, trilladura, desgranamiento; tunda, paliza, zurra; thrashing-floor, era; thrashing-machine, trilladora, trillo.

thread [θred], s. hilo, hilito, hebra, fibra, filamento, torzal, filete; (de tornillo) rosca, paso; (fig.) hilo. — v.t. enhebrar, ensartar; colarse o pasar a través de; roscar, aterrajar (tornillos); enfilar (telas).

threadbare ['θredbɛəɪ], a. raído, muy gastado, muy usado (hasta verse los hilos); (fig.) trillado, usado.

thread-like, a. filiforme.

threadworm, s. ascáride, f., lombriz intestinal.

thready ['θredi], a. filamentoso.

threat [θret], s. amenaza.

threaten ['θretən], v.t. amenazar, amagar, aterrar.

threatener, s. amenazador.

threatening, a. amenazador, amenazante, terrible, horroroso. — s. amenaza.

threateningly, adv. con amenaza(s), de una manera amenazante.

three [θriː], s., a. tres; three deep, en tres filas.

three-cleft, a. (bot.) trífido.

three-cornered, a. triangular, de tres cuernos, de tres picos, tricornio.

three-decker, s. navío de tres puentes.

threefold, a. triple, tresdoble.

three-forked, a. de tres dientes.

threepence ['θrepəns], s. tres peniques.

threepenny ['θrepəni], a. de tres peniques, a tres peniques; (fig.) de poco valor, despreciable; threepenny bit, pieza de tres peniques.

three-ply ['θriːplai], a. triple, de tres capas. — s. madera contrachapada de tres capas.

threescore ['θriːskɔːɪ], s., a. sesenta.

three-stringed, a. de tres cuerdas.

three-tonner, s. (fam.) camión de tres toneladas de carga.

three-valve(d), a. trivalvado, trivalvo, trivalvular.

threnody ['θrenodi], s. treno.

thresh [θreʃ], v.t. [THRASH].

thresher, s. (ict.) zorra marina (especie de tiburón); trilladora.

threshing, s. [THRASHING].

threshold ['θreʃould], s. umbral, entrada, tranco; (fig.) umbral, principio, comienzo.

threw [θruː], pret. [THROW].

thrice [θrais], adv. tres veces.

thrift [θrift], s. economía, ahorro, frugalidad; ganancia, medra, provecho, prosperidad; desarrollo, crecimiento; (bot.) planta, variedad de la especie del género Armeria, llamada también sea-pink.

thriftily ['θriftili], adv. frugalmente, económicamente.

thriftiness, s. economía, ahorro, frugalidad; espíritu de provecho, medra.

thriftless ['θriftles], a. derrochador, pródigo, manirroto.

thriftlessness, *s.* prodigalidad.

thrifty ['θrifti], *a.* económico, frugal; floreciente, próspero.

thrill [θril], *v.t.* conmover, emocionar; perforar, penetrar, taladrar. — *v.i.* emocionarse, estremecerse, conmoverse, sentir emoción viva. — *s.* estremecimiento, emoción, temblor; taladro.

thrilling, *a.* emocionante, conmovedor, espeluznante; agudo, penetrante, que penetra.

thrive [θraiv], (*pret.* **throve, thrived;** *p.p.* **thriven, thrived**) *v.i.* adelantar, salir bien, tener éxito, prosperar; medrar, hacer fortuna; crecer con vigor, desarrollarse con ímpetu.

thriving, *a.* próspero, floreciente, que prospera, que tiene éxito, vigoroso.

thrivingness, *s.* prosperidad.

throat [θrout], *s.* garganta, gaznate, gola, cuello; boca de chimenea; (*mar.*) quijada, cuello (de cuerva), diamante (de una áncora); *sore throat,* dolor de garganta; *to clear the throat,* aclarar la voz; *to seize* (o *take*) *by the throat,* andar al pescuezo; agarrar por la garganta; *throat-halliard,* (*mar.*) driza de cangreja.

throat-band, *s.* ahogadero.

throating, *s.* goterón.

throatwort, *s.* (*bot.*) campanilla.

throaty, *a.* ronco.

throb [θrɔb], *v.i.* palpitar, latir, vibrar. — *s.* palpitación, latido, pulsación.

throbbing, *a.* palpitante. — *s.* latido.

throe [θrou], *s.* tormento, angustia, dolor, agonía; *throes of childbirth,* dolores de parto; *throes of death,* agonía (de la muerte).

thrombosis [θrɔm'bousis], *s.* (*med.*) trombosis, *f.*

throne [θroun], *s.* trono; (*fig.*) corona; poder soberano. — *v.t.* colocar en el trono; elevar; ensalzar, exaltar.

throng [θrɔŋ], *s.* muchedumbre, *f.*, multitud, tropel, gentío, caterva. — *v.t.* apretar, estrujar, llenar de bote en bote. — *v.i.* venir en tropel, amontonarse, apiñarse.

throstle ['θrɔsəl], *s.* (*orn.*) tordo, malvís; máquina continua de devanar.

throttle ['θrɔtəl], *s.* (*dial.*) gorja, gaznate, garguero; (*mec.*) regulador, toma de vapor; mariposa de válvula (de vapor). — *v.t.* sofocar, ahogar, estrangular. — *v.i.* ahogarse; *to throttle down* o *back,* cerrar el regulador, decelerar; *to open* (o *close*) *the throttle,* abrir (o cerrar) el regulador o estrangulador.

through [θru:], *prep.* a través de, por entre, por; por causa de; por medio de; de un extremo a otro de; gracias a, por mediación de; de parte a parte, de medio a medio; por medio, agencia, falta, o cuenta de. — *adv.* de parte a parte, a través; enteramente, completamente, desde el principio hasta el fin; de un extremo a otro, de un lado a otro; todo el camino; *to carry through,* llevar a cabo; *to be wet through,* mojarse hasta los tuétanos, estar calado. — *a.* continuo; *through train,* tren directo; *through traffic,* tráfico de tránsito, tráfico interurbano.

throughout [θru:'aut], *prep., adv.* todo, en todas partes, por todo, en todo; de un extremo a otro (de); a lo largo (de), durante todo.

throve [θrouv], *pret.* [THRIVE].

throw [θrou], *v.t., v.i.* (*pret.* **threw;** *p.p.*

thrown) echar, lanzar, arrojar, botar; volcar, rechazar, echar al suelo, derribar; apear, desmontar; tirar, disparar; torcer (seda); impeler, estrellar, empujar; despojarse de; tender; echarse, arrojarse; desarzonar; parir (la coneja y otros animales); *to throw about,* arrojar de un lado y de otro, esparcir; *to throw aside,* poner de lado, desechar; *to throw away,* tirar; disipar, despilfarrar, desperdiciar, malgastar; desechar, arrinconar; *to throw back,* devolver, devolver con desprecio, rechazar; *to throw by,* arrinconar; *to throw down,* echar al suelo, derribar; *to throw a glance,* dirigir la mirada; *to throw in,* echar dentro, insertar, incluir, dar de más; *to throw in one's lot with,* acompañar, tomar el partido de, ayudar; *to throw into jail,* echar a presidio; *to throw off,* abandonar, quitar, arrojar, despojar, expeler, echar fuera; *to throw open,* abrir de par en par; *to throw out,* echar fuera, emitir (una opinión); rechazar (un proyecto de ley), expeler, excluir; *to throw out a hint,* insinuar; *to throw overboard,* echar a la mar; *to throw silk,* torcer seda; *to throw one's skin,* mudar la piel (la sierpe); *to throw up,* echar al aire, levantar, elevar; abandonar, renunciar a; (*fam.*) vomitar; *to throw up the sponge,* (*fig.*) rendirse, darse por vencido. — *s.* tiro, tirada; golpe; echamiento, echada, alcance; rato, momento; embolada, carrera, recorrido; (en el juego de dados) lance; *at one throw,* de un golpe.

thrower, *s.* lanzador, tirador, arrojador; jugador (de dados); torcedor (de seda).

throwing, *s.* tiro.

throwster ['θroustəɹ], *s.* torcedor (de seda).

thrum [θrʌm], *s.* cabos de hilo, hilo basto, hilo grueso; borla; rasgueo (de una guitarra, etc.); (*bot.*) estambres. — *v.t., v.i.* tejer; aporrear; rasguear (una guitarra, etc.); adornar con borlas.

thrush [θrʌʃ], *s.* (*orn.*) tordo, malvís, zorzal; (*vet.*) higo; (*med.*) afta.

thrust [θrʌst], *v.t.* (*pret., p.p.* **thrust**) impeler, introducir (con violencia), meter, empujar, hacer entrar; cerrar, apretar; tirar (una estocada); *to thrust aside,* empujar de lado; *to thrust away,* rechazar, abandonar; *to thrust back,* rechazar; *to thrust upon,* imponer. — *v.i.* empujar, embestir, acometer, arrojarse, precipitarse; clavar, pinchar, punzar, hincar, aguijonear; entremeterse; meterse, introducirse, tirar una estocada. — *s.* golpe; ataque, asalto, arremetida; empuje, empujón; lanzada, estocada, bote, pase; (*mec.*) tracción, empuje; (*min.*) derrumbe.

thud [θʌd], *s.* ruido sordo, baque. — *v.i.* hacer un ruido sordo.

thug [θʌg], *s.* miembro de una secta de asesinos fanáticos de la India (suprimida 1828–35); matón, rufián, tahur.

thumb [θʌm], *s.* (dedo) pulgar; *thumb-screw,* empulgueras; (*mec.*) tornillo de mariposa, tornillo de orejetas; *thumb-tack,* (E.U.) chinche (metálico), chincheta. — *v.t.* manejar, manosear, emporcar con los dedos; hojear; *to thumb through,* hojear.

thumb-stall ['θʌmstɔ:l], *s.* dedil, dedal.

thump [θʌmp], *s.* puñetazo, golpazo, porrazo, baque. — *v.t., v.i.* cascar, apuñear, aporrear.

thumping, *s.* golpeteo, sucesión de golpes fuertes. — *a.* grueso, enorme, pesado.

thunder ['θʌndəɹ], *s.* trueno; estruendo, tronido; (*fig.*) rayo. — *v.t.*, *v.i.* tronar, atronar; resonar, retumbar; (*fig.*) fulminar, arrojar rayos.

thunderbolt ['θʌndəɹboult], *s.* rayo; censura, fulminación; gran sorpresa.

thunderclap ['θʌndəɹklæp], *s.* trueno, tronada.

thunderer, *s.* tronador, fulminador, tonante.

thundering, *s.* trueno. — *a.* de trueno, que truena; (*fam.*) terrible; *thundering great,* (*fam.*) muy grande, enorme, colosal.

thunderous, *a.* tonante, atronador.

thunderstorm ['θʌndəɹstɔːɹm], *s.* tronada.

thunderstrike, *v.t.* fulminar, herir con rayo.

thunderstroke, *s.* trueno.

thunderstruck ['θʌndəɹstrʌk], *a.* fulminado, aterrado, estupefacto, anonadado.

thurible ['θjuːribəl], *s.* (*igl.*) turíbulo, incensario.

thuriferous [θjuːˈrifərəs], *a.* turífero, turibulario.

thurification, *s.* turificación.

Thursday ['θəːɹsdi], *s.* jueves; *Maundy Thursday,* jueves santo.

thus [ðʌs], *adv.* así, de esta suerte, de esta manera, de este modo, en estos términos, en estas condiciones; hasta este punto, a ese grado; tanto; siendo así, en este caso; *thus far,* hasta aquí; *that much,* hasta aquí, basta, no más. — *s.* incienso, resina aromática.

thuya ['θuːjə], *s.* (*bot.*) tuya.

thwack [θwæk], *s.* golpe violento, porrazo, latigazo. — *v.t.* golpear, zurrar, aporrear, pegar.

thwart [θwɔːɹt], *v.t.* contrariar, frustrar, desbaratar, desconcertar; (*ant.*) atravesar. — *s.* (*mar.*) banco (de remeros). — *a.* (*ant.*, *poét.*) transverso, transversal, de través, oblicuo, atravesado.

thwarting, *s.* oposición, contrariedad. — *a.* contrario, opuesto.

thy [ðai], *a. pos.* (*poét.*) tu, tus.

thyme [taim], *s.* tomillo, serpoleto.

thymol ['θaimɔl], *s.* timol.

thymus ['θaiməs], *s.* (*anat.*) timo.

thymy, *a.* cubierto de tomillo, oliente a tomillo.

thyroid ['θairɔid], *a.* tiroideo, en forma de escudo; *thyroid gland,* tiroides, *m.sing.*

thyrsus [θəːɹsəs], *s.* (*bot.*) tirso.

thyself [ðaiˈself], *pron. refl.* (*poét.*) tú mismo, ti mismo.

tiara [tiˈɑːrə], *s.* tiara, diadema.

tibia ['tibiə], *s.* (*ant.*) flauta.

tibial ['tibiəl], *a.* tibial, de la tibia; (*ant.*) de flauta.

tic [tik], *s.* (*med.*) tic (nervioso).

tick [tik], *v.i.* hacer tictac, tictaquear; señalar, marcar. — *v.t.* contramarcar, señalar, marcar contra; puntear (cuentas). — *s.* (*entom.*) garrapata, rezno; tictac; golpecito; contraseña, contramarca; (*fam.*) crédito, fiado; funda de almohada y de colchón.

ticket ['tikit], *s.* billete; entrada, pase; marbete, marca; papeleta; placa, medalla, número; bono; boleta, (*Amér.*) boleto; cédula de transporte por ferrocarril; rótulo, etiqueta; (*E.U.*, *pol.*) candidatura, balota; programa político; *ticket of leave,* libertad provisional;

return ticket, billete de ida y vuelta; *single ticket,* billete de ida; *season ticket,* billete de abono; *that's the ticket!* (*fam.*) ¡está bien! ¡justo! ¡eso es! — *v.t.* rotular, marcar, numerar.

ticking ['tikiŋ], *s.* tic-tac; (*tej.*) terliz, cutí.

tickle ['tikəl], *v.t.* hacer cosquillas (a), cosquillear; (*fig.*) divertir; (*fig.*) halagar, lisonjear. — *v.i.* tener o sentir cosquillas, titilar; dar comezón. — *s.* cosquillas; comezón, *f.*, picor, picazón, *f.*

tickler ['tikləɹ], *s.* el que hace cosquillas; (*fam.*) rompecabezas, *m.*; problema difícil.

tickling, *s.* cosquillas, cosquilleo, cosquillejas; comezón, *f.*, picor, picazón, *f.*; (*fig.*) prurito, deseo ardiente; pesca de truchas.

ticklish ['tikliʃ], *a.* cosquilloso; incierto, inseguro; puntilloso, susceptible; espinoso, delicado, difícil, arduo.

ticklishness, *s.* naturaleza cosquillosa o quisquillosa; sensibilidad.

tick-tack ['tiktæk], *s.* tic-tac.

tidal ['taidəl], *a.* de marea; periódico; *tidal wave,* aguaje, marejada; oleada o torrente de opinión pública.

tid-bit ['tidbit], *s.* golosina [TITBIT].

tide [taid], *s.* marea; época, estación, tiempo, temporada; torrente, corriente, *f.*, flujo; marcha, curso; (*min.*) vuelta; *ebb tide,* bajamar, *f.*, reflujo del mar; *flood tide,* flujo, creciente, *f.*; *high tide,* pleamar, *f.*, montante, *f.*, plenamar, *f.*, marea alta; *low tide,* bajamar, *f.*, menguante, *f.*, marea baja; *neap tide,* agua muerta; *spring tide,* agua viva, marea mayor; *time and tide,* tiempo y sazón; *to go with the tide,* seguir la corriente. — *v.i.* ir, flotar o navegar con la marea; *to tide over,* superar. — *v.t.* conducir, llevar.

tide-gate, *s.* compuerta de marea.

tideless, *a.* sin marea.

tidesman ['taidzmən], *s.* empleado de aduanas.

tide-way, *s.* canal de marea.

tidily ['taidili], *adv.* aseadamente, pulcramente, en orden.

tidiness, *s.* aseo, pulcritud, limpieza, buen orden.

tidy ['taidi], *a.* aseado, decente, ordenado, limpio, pulcro; oportuno, a propósito; (*fam.*) considerable, de bastante importancia. — *v.t.*, *v.i.* poner en orden, asear, limpiar. — *s.* delantal, cubierta de respaldar; *a tidy lot,* (*fam.*) bastante, mucho.

tidings ['taidiŋz], *s.pl.* nuevas, noticias, relato, (*ant.*) albricias.

tie [tai], *v.t.* (*pret. y p.p.* tied; *p.pr.* tying) atar, ligar, amarrar, trincar, enlazar, encadenar, sujetar; limitar, confinar; anudar, unir; (*mús.*) ligar; *to tie down, tie up,* sujetar, asegurar, ligar (abajo o arriba), amarrar; recoger; impedir, obstruir; envolver. — *v.i.* atarse, enlazarse; (deportes) empatar. — *s.* lazo, atadura, nudo; ligamento; (*mús.*) ligadura, ligazón, *f.*; corbata, corbatín; parentesco, vínculo; adhesión, apego; (*dep.*) empate; (*f.c.*) traviesa; (*fig.*) deber, obligación, peso; *tie beam,* (*arq.*) tirante.

tier [tiəɹ], *s.* fila, ringlera, ringla, tongada, tonga; andana.

tierce [tiəɹs], *s.* (*mús.*) tercera; (*igl.*) tercia; tercerola, tonel que contiene un tercio de pipa (42 galones); tercera en el juego de los cientos; (*esgr.*) la tercera posición.

tiercet ['təːɹset], s. (*poét.*) terceto [TERCET].

tiff [tif], s. riña; disgusto, pique; (*ant.*) trago, traguito, sorba. — v.i. enfadarse, disputarse, picarse, reñir. — v.t. (*vulg.*) beber a sorbos o traguitos.

tiffany ['tifəni], s. gasa de seda.

tiffin ['tifin], s. almuerzo, merienda.

tige [tiːʒ], s. (*arq.*) tronco, fuste de columna.

tiger ['taigəɹ], s. tigre; *tiger lily*, (*bot.*) tigridia.

tigerish ['taigəɹiʃ], a. de tigre, atigrado; feroz, terrible.

tight [tait], a. apretado, tieso, premioso, vendado, estrecho, tirante; diestro; bien cerrado, ajustado, bien apretado; severo, duro, que se hace con dificultad; hermético, compacto; (*mar.*) estancado, estanco; (*com.*) escaso; (*fam.*) borracho, embriagado; (*fam.*) mezquino, avaro, avariento; *air-tight*, hermético, impermeable al aire; *water-tight*, impermeable o estanco al agua; *tight fit*, empalme muy ajustado, (*mec.*) ajuste forzado; *tight corner* o *squeeze*, (*fam.*) apuro, aprieto; *to be tight*, (*fam.*) estar alumbrado, estar hecho una cuba; (*fam.*) *to be tight(-fisted)*, ser como un puño, ser estrecho, ser tacaño. — adv. fuertemente, bien; *to hold tight*, tener bien; *to tie tight*, apretar, estrechar.

tighten ['taitən], v.t. apretar, estrechar, estirar, atiesar, vendar.

tightly ['taitli], adv. estrechamente, apretadamente, ajustadamente, aseadamente; bien, firme; pronto.

tightness, s. tirantez, tensión, estrechez; impermeabilidad; (*fam.*) tacañería; (*mar.*) estado estancado.

tight-rope, s. cuerda de volatinero; *tight-rope walker*, volatinero, equilibrista, m.f.

tights [taits], s.pl. calzas muy ajustadas; (*teat.*) mallas.

tigress ['taigres], s. hembra del tigre.

tigrine ['taigrin], a. atigrado, de tigre, como un tigre.

tike [taik], s. (*dial.*) aldeano; persona mal instruida, mal hombre; (*despec.*) perro.

tile [tail], s. teja, baldosa, azulejo, loseta, baldosín (para pisos); chistera, sombrero de copa; *to have a tile loose*, (*vulg.*) tener flojos los tornillos. — v.t. tejar, trastejar, enlosar, baldosar, azulejar.

tiler ['tailəɹ], s. tejero, trastijador, solador; portero de una sociedad de francmasones.

tiling, s. trastijadura, tejado, enlosado.

till [til], prep. hasta. — conj. hasta que, mientras que, antes (de) que, que. — v.t. cultivar, labrar. — s. cajón o gaveta de mostrador.

tillable, a. labrantío.

tillage ['tilidʒ], s. labranza, cultura, cultivo, agricultura.

tiller ['tiləɹ], s. cultivador, labrador, agricultor; caña del timón; palanca; vástago, renuevo, gamonito, botón; *tiller hole*, (*mar.*) limera. — v.i. echar retoños de la raíz.

tilt [tilt], s. inclinación, ladeo, declive, sesgo; pabellón, tienda de campaña; tendal, toldo, toldillo; lanzada; justa, torneo; *to give a tilt to*, ladear, inclinar. — v.t. inclinar, ladear; entoldar; cubrir con una tela; dar una lanzada a; voltear, volcar; martillar; arrojar; vaciar. — v.i. inclinarse, ladear(se), estar o ponerse al sesgo; justar, luchar en un torneo; echarse, caer, echarse encima.

tilter, s. justador.

tilth [tilθ], s. cultivo, labranza.

tilting ['tiltiŋ], s. inclinación, ladeo, sesgo; justa, torneo; acción de justar.

timbal ['timbəl], s. timbal.

timber ['timbəɹ], s. madera de construcción, maderamen, maderaje; madero, viga maestra; tronco de árbol, palo, fuste; monte, árboles de monte; (*mar.*) cuaderna; armazón, f. — pl. **timbers**, (*mar.*) gambotas; *timber-work*, maderaje, maderamen; *timber-yard*, almacén de maderas; *standing timber*, árboles en pie. — v.t. construir con madera; plantar árboles en.

timbered ['timbəɹd], a. enmaderado, de madera, hecho de madera; cubierto de árboles, arbolado.

timbre ['timbəɹ], s. tono, timbre, calidad del sonido.

timbrel ['timbrəl], s. pandero, pandereta.

time [taim], s. tiempo, época, edad, período, era; estación, temporada, período; rato, momento, hora, instante; vez, f.; intervalo, prórroga, plazo; turno; coyuntura, ocasión, oportunidad, sazón, f.; (*mús.*) compás, cadencia, ritmo; (*mil.*) paso, movimiento; (*fam.*) angustia, detención, prisión; *at a time*, a la vez; *at times*, a veces; *at any time*, a cualquier hora; *at the same time*, al mismo tiempo; (*fig.*) no obstante, sin embargo; *behind time*, atrasado; *behind the times*, pasado de moda; *in time*, a tiempo, con tiempo; *in the course of time*, andando el tiempo; *at no time*, nunca, jamás, en ninguna época; *in the day time*, de día; *in the night time*, de noche; *in good time*, con tiempo suficiente, a su tiempo, a su vez; *every time*, todas las veces, cada vez; *in our times*, en nuestros días; *in the time to come*, en el porvenir, en lo futuro; *from time to time*, de vez en vez, de vez en cuando, de cuando en cuando; *from this time forward* (o *on*), desde hoy en adelante, desde ahora; *out of time*, (*mús.*) fuera de compás; (*fig.*) atrasado, fuera de moda; *many and many a time*, muchísimas veces; *time out of mind*, tiempo inmemorial; *for the time being*, por ahora; *to arrange* (o *appoint*) *a time*, fijar un día; *to beat time*, (*mús.*) llevar o marcar el compás; *to keep time*, guardar compás; *to mark time*, (*mil.*, *fig.*) marcar el paso; *to gain time*, (*fig.*) ganar tiempo; *to have a bad time*, pasar un mal rato; *to have a good time*, divertirse; tener un buen rato; *to take time*, tardar; necesitar tiempo; *to be in* o *on time*, llegar en punto, ser puntual; *what time is it?* ¿qué hora es? *time and tide wait for no man*, tiempo ni hora no se ata con soga. — v.t. calcular; reglar; poner a la hora, adaptar al tiempo; hacer con oportunidad; calcular el tiempo de, cronometrar; sincronizar.

timed [taimd], a. calculado, cronometrado.

time-exposure, s. (*fot.*) exposición.

timeful, a. oportuno.

time-honoured, a. venerable, anciano.

time-keeper, **time-piece**, s. reloj, cronómetro, reloj marcador.

timeless, a. eterno; (*ant.*) inoportuno, mal a propósito, prematuro, intempestivo.

timeliness ['taimlinis], s. oportunidad, tempestividad.

timely ['taimli], a. oportuno, a propósito, a

tiempo. — *adv.* oportunamente, a propósito.

time-server, *s.* adulador, contemporizador.

time-serving, *a.* complaciente, servil, contemporizador.

time-table, *s.* horario, itinerario, guía, *f.*

timeworn ['taimwɔːɪn], *a.* usado; (*fig.*)
gastado, trillado, vulgar.

timid ['timid], *a.* tímido, temeroso, encogido,
corto, medroso.

timidity [ti'miditi], **timidness** ['timidnis], *s.*
timidez, cortedad.

timocracy [ti'mɔkrəsi], *s.* timocracia.

timorous ['timorəs], *a.* tímido, timorato,
temeroso, medroso, miedoso.

timorously, *adv.* tímidamente, con temor,
temorosamente.

timorousness, *s.* timidez, naturaleza tímida,
encogimiento, temor.

timothy ['timoθi], *s.* planta gramínea que se
emplea como forraje (*Phleum pratense*).

tin [tin], *s.* estaño, lata, hojalata; (*vulg.*)
parné, dinero; *tin can,* lata. — *v.t.* estañar,
envasar en lata, cubrir con hojalata; estaño-
soldar; *tin-plate,* hojalata.

tincal ['tiŋkəl], *s.* atíncar, bórax crudo.

tincture ['tiŋktʃəɪ], *s.* (*farm.*) tintura, tinte,
color; saborcillo, gustillo, baño. — *v.t.*
tinturar, teñir, colorear.

tinder ['tindəɪ], *s.* mecha, yesca.

tinder-box, *s.* lumbres, *f.pl.,* yescas.

tine [tain], *s.* diente de tenedor, púa de rastrillo.
— *v.t.* inflamar, encender.

tinea ['tiniə], *s.* tínea, polilla; (*med.*) tiña.

tinfoil [tin'fɔil], *s.* alinde, hoja de estaño.

ting [tiŋ], *v.t.* repicar, sonar. — *v.i.* repicarse,
retiñir. — *s.* retintín.

tinge [tindʒ], *v.t.* teñir, colorar, tintar, dar un
tinte a, matizar; impregnar. — *s.* color
ligero, matiz, tinte; (*fig.*) gusto, gustillo,
dejo.

tingle ['tiŋgəl], *v.i.* picar, sentir o producir
picazón u hormigueo, hormiguear; zumbar;
estremecerse.

tingling, *s.* picazón, *f.,* comezón, *f.,* hormigueo,
picor, escozor, quemazón, *f.;* zumbido,
retintín.

tinker ['tiŋkəɪ], *s.* calderero, remendón. —
v.t., v.i. componer (calderos, etc.); desabollar; *to tinker with a job,* (*fam.*) chafallar,
remendar mal.

tinkerly, *adv.* como un calderero.

tinkle ['tiŋkəl], *v.t., v.i.* tintinear, tintinar,
cencerrear, retiñir; zumbar (los oídos).

tinkle, tinkling, *s.* retintín, tilín, cencerreo.

tinman ['tinmən], *s.* hojalatero, estañero.

tinned, *a.* en conserva, en latas; estañado, de
hojalata.

tinner, *s.* estañador, estañero, minero de
estaño.

tinning ['tiniŋ], *s.* estañadura, estañado.

tinny, *a.* de estaño; (*fam.*) frágil.

tinsel ['tinsəl], *s.* oropel, relumbrón; (*ant.*)
brocadillo, restaño; (*fig.*) oropel, relumbrón,
falso brillo. — *a.* de oropel, de relumbrón.
— *v.t.* adornar con oropel.

tin-smith, *s.* hojalatero, escañador.

tint [tint], *s.* matiz, color, tinte. — *v.t.* teñir,
matizar, colorar.

tinware, *s.* efectos de hojalata o de estaño.

tiny ['taini], *a.* muy pequeño, chiquitico, muy
menudo.

tip [tip], *s.* punta, cabo, extremo, extremidad;
virola, agujeta, casquillo, regatón; escorial (de
mineral); (*fig.*) propina, gratificación; aviso
útil y confidencial; toque ligero, golpecito.—
v.t. guarnecer el cabo de calzar, herrar; golpear ligeramente, dar un golpecito a; lanzar;
(*fam.*) dar una propina a. — *v.t., v.i.*
inclinar, ladear, voltear; *to give a tip,* (*fam.*)
dar información secreta o una sugerencia;
to tip the wink, (*fam.*) avisar al momento
oportuno.

tip-car, tip-cart, *s.* volquete, carro de volteo,
vagoneta basculadora.

tippet ['tipit], *s.* palatina, esclavina.

tipple ['tipəl], *v.t., v.i.* emborracharse, beber
con exceso, empinar el codo. — *s.* bebida
espirituosa, licor.

tippler, *s.* bebedor.

tippling, *s.* borrachera.

tipsily ['tipsili], *adv.* como borracho.

tipsy ['tipsi], *a.* ebrio, achispado, alegre,
chispo; (*fig.*) vacilante.

tipstaff ['tipstɑːf], *s.* palo herrado; vara de
alguacil; alguacil, ministril.

tiptoe ['tiptou], *s.* punta del pie; *to walk on
tiptoe,* andar de puntillas.

tiptop [tip'tɔp], *a.* (*fam.*) de órdago, espléndido,
soberbio. — *s.* (*fam.*) cumbre, *f.,* punto más
alto.

tirade [ti'reid], *s.* diatriba, invectiva.

tire ['taiəɪ], *v.t.* cansar, fatigar, importunar,
fastidiar, aburrir, enfadar; *to tire out,*
agotar, abrumar; *to be tired out,* reventar de
consancio; *to be tired of,* estar cansado o
aburrido de. — *v.i.* cansarse, fatigarse,
fastidiarse, aburrirse. — *s.* fila, hilera; atavío,
adorno, diadema; calce, loriga; llanta;
neumático [TYRE].

tired ['taiəɪd], *a.* cansado, fatigado, fastidiado,
aburrido. — *p.p.* [TIRE]; provisto de neumáticos, de llantas; *tired out,* muy cansado,
estropeado, molido.

tiredness, *s.* fatiga, cansancio.

tireless, *a.* infatigable, incansable.

tiresome ['taiəɪsəm], *a.* molesto, fastidioso,
tedioso, pesado, aburrido.

tiresomeness, *s.* fastidio, tedio, aburrimiento.

'tis [tiz], *abrev.* [IT IS.]

tisane [ti'zɑːn], *s.* tisana.

tissue ['tiʃjuː], *s.* (*biol.*) tejido; tisú, gasa;
tejido, brocado; (*fig.*) sarta, encadenamiento;
tissue paper, papel de seda. — *v.t.* tejer,
entretejer; recamar.

tit [tit], *s.* caballito, jaca; (*orn.*) paro; golpecito;
tit for tat, tal para cual.

titanic [tai'tænik], *a.* titánico, gigantesco,
vasto; *a titanic task,* obra de romanos.

titanium [tai'teiniəm], *s.* titanio.

tit-bit [tit'bit], *s.* golosina; bocado regalado.

tithable ['taiðəbəl], *a.* diezmable, sujeto al
diezmo.

tithe [taið], *s.* diezmo; décimo, décima parte;
pizca. — *v.t.* diezmar. — *v.i.* pagar el diezmo.

tithe-collector, tither, *s.* diezmero.

tithing, *s.* diezmo.

titillate ['titileit], *v.t.* titilar.

titillation, *s.* titilación, picazón, *f.*

titivate ['titiveit], *v.t., v.i.* emperifollar(se),
elegantizar(se), componer(se).

titlark ['titlɑːɪk], *s.* pipí o pitpit de matorral.

title ['taitəl], *s.* título, nombre, epíteto, in-

scripción, epígrafe, rótulo; derecho; documento, acta. — *v.t.* intitular, nombrar.
titled ['taitəld], *a.* titulado.
titleless, *a.* sin título.
title-page, *s.* frontispicio, portada, (*Amér.*) carátula.
titling ['titliŋ], *s.* gorrión silvestre; pipí [TITLARK]; paro.
titmouse ['titmaus], *s.* (*pl.* **titmice**) paro.
titrate ['taitrit], *v.t.* (*quím.*) graduar, dosificar, valorar.
titter ['titəɹ], *v.i.* reír a medias, reír entre dientes, reír nerviosamente o sofocadamente; risa nerviosa o sofocada o verde.
titterer, *s.* persona que ríe entre dientes.
tittering, *s.* sonrisa nerviosa o sofocada o verde.
tittle, *s.* vírgula, tilde, virgulilla; ápice, adarme, pizca.
tittle-tattle ['titəltætəl], *s.* cháchara, chismes, chismorreo.
titubate ['titju:beit], *v.i.* titubear.
titubation, *s.* titubeo.
titular ['titju:ləɹ], *a.* titular, nominal. — *s.* titular.
titulary ['titju:ləri], *a.* titular, con sólo el título.
to [tu:], *prep., adv.* a, hacia, por, para, de, en, hasta, con, que; menos (marcando la hora); partícula que indica el modo infinitivo de un verbo; *to and fro*, de un lado a otro; de aquí para allí, de acá para acullá; *to come to*, volver en sí; *to his face*, (*fig.*) en cara; *from . . . to . . .* (v.gr. *from house to house*), de . . . en . .
toad [toud], *s.* sapo, escuerzo.
toad-eater ['toudi:təɹ], **toady** [toudi], *s.* adulador, zalamero, sicofante, parásito.
toadflax ['toudflæks], *s.* linaria, lino bastardo.
toadstone, *s.* estelón, estelión.
toadstool ['toudstu:l], *s.* hongo, hongo venenoso.
toady, *v.t.* adular, hacer la zalá. — *a.* adulador, zalamero.
toast [toust], *s.* pan tostado, rebanada de pan tostada; brindis. — *v.t.* tostar, hacer asar; brindar, beber a la salud de; calentar o secar a la lumbre.
toaster, *s.* parrillas, tostador, tostadera; brindador.
tobacco [to'bækou], *s.* tabaco. — *a.* tabacalero, de tabaco.
tobacconist [to'bækonist], *s.* tabaquero, estanquero; *tobacconist's* (*shop*), tabaquería, estanco.
tobacco-pouch, *s.* petaca o bolsa para el tabaco, (*Amér.*) tabaquera.
toboggan [tə'bɔgən], *s.* tobogán. — *v.i.* deslizarse sobre la nieve en un tobogán.
tocsin ['tɔksin], *s.* campanada de alarma, somatén, toque de somatén.
tod [tɔd], *s.* espesura, matorral, zorro; peso de lana de unos 12·700 kgs. apxm.
to-day [tə'dei], *adv.* hoy, hoy día, actualmente. — *s.* día de hoy, actualidad, época presente.
toddle ['tɔdəl], *v.i.* hacer pinitos, titubear. — *s.* pinitos, titubeo.
toddy ['tɔdi], *s.* ponche.
to-do [tə'du:], *s.* bullicio, baraúnda; lío, confusión.
toe [tou], *s.* dedo del pie, punta del pie de calzado, media, etc.; pezuña (del caballo, etc.); (*fig.*) base, *f.*, pie; *great* (o *big*) *toe*,

dedo gordo del pie; *from top to toe*, de pies a cabeza. — *v.t.* tocar con los dedos del pie; (*vulg.*) dar patadas; *to toe the line*, conformarse.
toff [tɔf], *s.* (*fam.*) petimetre; prócer, dignatario, señorito.
toft [tɔft], *s.* (*prov.*) bosquecillo.
tog, *v.t., v.i.; to tog up*, ataviar(se), componer(se).
toga ['tougə], *s.* toga.
together [tə'geðəɹ], *adv.* juntamente, juntos, uno con otro, al mismo tiempo, simultáneamente; de continuo, de seguida; *together with*, con, a una con, juntamente con, así como.
toggery ['tɔgəri], *s.* (*fam.*) trajes, vestido, ropa.
toggle ['tɔgəl], *s.* (*mar.*) cazonete de aparejo; (*mec.*) palanca acodada; *toggle-joint*, junta de codillo.
togs, *s.* (*fam.*) trapos; trastos.
tog-up, *v.i.* ataviar; componer.
toil [tɔil], *v.i.* trabajar mucho, cansarse con trabajo, atrafagar, afanarse; *to toil up a hill*, subir una cuesta con pena. — *s.* trabajo penoso, faena, trabajo que cansa, afán, fatiga, pena; tela de araña; lazo, red, *f.*
toilet ['tɔilet], *s.* tocado, atavío, vestido; tocador; retrete, wáter; *toilet set*, juego de tocador; *toilet table*, mesa de tocador.
toilful, **toilsome**, *a.* penoso, laborioso, trabajoso, fatigoso.
toilsomeness ['tɔilsəmnis], *s.* naturaleza penosa, fatiga, laboriosidad, afán.
token ['toukən], *s.* signo, síntoma, *m.*, indicio, rasgo característico; marca, muestra, testimonio, prenda, recuerdo; *as a token of*, en señal de. — *v.t.* indicar, significar, hacer conocer.
told [tould], *pret., p.p.* [TELL].
tolerable ['tɔlərəbəl], *a.* tolerable, soportable, sufrible, pasadero, llevadero; mediocre, mediano, regular.
tolerableness, *s.* estado de tolerable.
tolerably, *adv.* tolerablemente, medianamente.
tolerance, *s.* tolerancia, indulgencia, paciencia; (*mec.*) tolerancia.
tolerant ['tɔlərənt], *a.* tolerante, indulgente, paciente, liberal.
tolerate ['tɔləreit], *v.t.* tolerar, soportar, permitir, consentir.
toleration [tɔlə'reiʃən], *s.* tolerancia.
toll [toul], *s.* tasa, peaje, portazgo, pontazgo; tarifa; derecho de molienda; tañido de campanas. — *v.t., v.i.* pagar o cobrar peaje o portazgo; tocar, tañer, repicar una campana (en los funerales), tocar a muerto; (*for.*) suprimir, quitar.
toll-bar, **toll-gate**, *s.* barrera de peaje.
toll-call, *s.* conferencia o comunicación (telefónica) interurbana.
toll-gatherer, *s.* peajero.
toll-house, *s.* oficina de portazgo.
tolling ['touliŋ], *s.* tañido, retintín.
tolu [to'lu:], *s.* (*farm.*) tolú; (*bot.*) árbol de tolú.
tomahawk ['tɔməhɔ:k], *s.* 'tomahawk', hacha de guerra de los indios. — *v.t.* matar de un golpe de tomahawk.
tomato [to'ma:tou], *s.* tomate; *tomato plant*, tomatera.
tomb [tu:m], *s.* sepulcro, tumba, túmulo, mausoleo.

tombac ['tɔmbæk], s. tumbaga, aleación de cobre y zinc.

tombless, a. sin sepultura, sin sepulcro.

tomboy ['tɔmbɔi], s.f. chica ahombrada, marimacho, machota, chica muy vigorosa.

tombstone ['tu:mstoun], s. lápida o piedra sepulcral.

tom-cat, s. gato no castrado.

tom-cod, s. pez comestible del género *microgadus*, común en las costas de los E.U.

tome [toum], s. tomo, volumen; libro importante.

tomentous [to'mentəs], a. (*bot.*) tomentoso, velloso.

tomfool [tɔm'fu:l], s. necio, tonto.

tomfoolery, s. tontería, mentecatada.

tommy ['tɔmi], s. (*fam.*) soldado británico.

to-morrow [tə'mɔrou], adv. mañana. — s. día de mañana, día siguiente.

tompion ['tɔmpiən], s. (*arti.*) tapabocas, m., tapón; (*impr.*) tampón.

tomtit [tɔm'tit], s. paro.

tomtom ['tɔmtɔm], s. tam-tam, tambor; tantarantán, tamborileo.

ton [tʌn], s. tonelada; (*fam.*) tons of, la mar de, un montón de.

tonal ['tounəl], a. tonal.

tonality [to'næliti], s. tonalidad.

tone [toun], s. tono, timbre, sonido; tono, tonillo, sonsonete, acento (de la voz); (*mús.*) tono; (*med.*) tono; (*fig.*) tono, tendencia, aspecto; (*fig.*) matiz; (*gram.*) inflexión, acento; (*pint.*) matiz de colores. — v.t. dar el tono, modificar (o suavizar) el tono, entonar; afinar, templar; amortiguar el sonido; *to tone down*, amortiguar, suavizar; *to tone in with*, (*mús., colores*) entonar con, armonizar con; *to tone up*, (*med., etc.*) entonar, tonificar, robustecer. — v.i. corresponder en tono, armonizar.

tongs [tɔŋz], s.pl. tenazas, alicates, mordazas, pinzas.

tongue [tʌŋ], s. lengua; lengua, idioma, m., habla, lenguaje; palabra; clavillo; lengüeta; espiga de madera; clavo de hebilla; lengua de tierra; badajo de campana; *to hold one's tongue*, callar. — v.t. acusar, echar en cara a; tomar la embocadura, modificar con la lengua el sonido de la flauta, trompeta, etc.; machihembrar madera. — v.i. charlar, picotear.

tongued [tʌŋd], a. de lengua, que tiene lengua; *soft tongued* o *smooth tongued*, zalamero.

tongueless, a. mudo, deslenguado.

tongue-tied, a. mudo, con frenillo; (*fig.*) turbado.

tongue-twister, s. trabalenguas, m.

tongue-worm, s. (*zool.*) landrilla.

tonic ['tɔnik], a. tónico; rígido, tenso. — s. (*med.*) tónico; (*mús.*) tónica.

tonicity [to'nisiti], s. estado de tónico, tonicidad.

to-night [tə'nait], adv., s. esta noche.

tonite ['tounait], s. poderoso explosivo preparado de algodón pólvora.

tonnage ['tʌnidʒ], s. tonelaje, arqueo, porte; alcabala, derecho de tonelaje.

tonsil ['tɔnsil], s. tonsila, agallas, amígdala.

tonsillar ['tɔnsilər], a. tonsilar.

tonsillitis [tɔnsi'laitis], s. amigdalitis, f.

tonsorial [tɔn'sɔ:riəl], a. barberil.

tonsure ['tɔnʃər], s. tonsura.

tontine ['tɔnti:n], s. tontina.

too [tu:], adv. demasiado; además, igualmente, también; aun, así mismo.

took [tuk], pret. [TAKE].

tool [tu:l], s. herramienta, instrumento, utensilio; (*fig.*) agente; *edged tools*, instrumentos cortantes; (*fig.*) medios peligrosos.

toot [tu:t], v.t., v.i. tocar (cuerno, bocina, etc.). — s. sonido de cuerno, bocina, etc.

tooth [tu:θ], v.t. dentar, endentar; (*mec.*) engranar. — s. (*pl.* **teeth**) diente, muela; (*fig.*) paladar, gusto; leva, púa, melladura, mella; *tooth and nail*, pico y uñas, con empeño, con todas sus fuerzas, hasta con los dientes; *to gnash the teeth*, regañar, echar chispas (de ira); *to cut one's teeth*, echar los dientes, endentecer; *to have a sweet tooth*, ser goloso; *to pick one's teeth*, curarse los dientes; *in the teeth of*, contra, contra los esfuerzos de; *to show one's teeth*, (*fig.*) enseñar o mostrar (los dientes); *false teeth*, dentadura postiza; *set of teeth*, dentadura.

toothache ['tu:θeik], s. dolor de muelas.

tooth-brush, s. cepillo para dientes.

toothed [tu:θd], a. dentado, de dientes, con dientes; dentellado, serrado.

toothless, a. desdentado.

toothpick, s. palillo, mondadientes, m.

toothsome ['tu:θsəm], a. al gusto de uno, de buen comer agradable, goloso, sabroso.

toothwort, s. (*bot.*) dentaria.

toothy ['tu:θi], a. con dientes.

top [tɔp], s. cima, pico, copa (de árbol); cumbre, f., pináculo, cúspide, f., ápice, remate, coronilla (de cabeza); coronamiento; lo más alto; superficie, f.; jefe; cabeza (de página); peón, peonza, trompo; cielo; (*fig.*) auge, cima, cumbre, f.; (*de vehículo*) capota; copete, tupé; *from top to bottom*, de arriba abajo; *at the top*, en lo alto, a la cabeza; *top heavy*, muy pesado por arriba; *from top to toe*, de pies a cabeza; *to sleep like a top*, dormir como un tronco (o una piedra); *whipping-top*, peonza. — a. de encima, de arriba, superior, principal, primero. — v.t. cubrir; coronar, rematar; llegar a la cima de; exceder, ser más alto que, aventajar, sobrepujar; descabezar, desmochar; (*mar.*) amantillar. — v.i. sobresalir, dominar, prevalecer, reinar.

topaz ['toupæz], s. topacio.

top-coat, s. (*E.U.*) sobretodo, abrigo.

top-dog, s. (*fam.*) gallito, pájaro gordo, vencedor.

tope [toup], v.i. emborracharse, achisparse. — s. (*ict.*) milandro.

toper ['toupər], s. bebedor, borracho, borrachín.

toper, s. (*orn.*) paro.

topful ['tɔpful], a. completamente lleno, lleno hasta arriba.

top-gallant, (*mar.*) juanete.

top-hat, s. chistera, sombrero de copa.

tophus ['toufəs], s. (*med.*) tofo; (*min.*) toba.

topic ['tɔpik], s. tema, m., materia, tópico, asunto.

topical ['tɔpikəl], a. tópico, local; oportuno, actual, a propósito.

topknot, s. moño, penacho, copete; (*orn.*) penacho, moño, copete, cresta; (*vulg.*) testa, cabeza.

top-mast, s. mastelero, mástil de cofa.
topmost ['tɔpməst], a. (lo) más alto.
topographer [to'pɔgrəfəɹ], s. topógrafo.
topographical [tɔpo'græfikəl], a. topográfico.
topography [to'pɔgræfi], s. topografía.
topping, a. que sobrepuja; distinguido, célebre; (fam.) muy bueno, espléndido, hermoso; (E.U.) tiránico, mandón, dominante. — s. cubierta; extremidad, punta.
topple ['tɔpəl], v.i. caer adelante, venirse abajo; tambalearse, bambolearse; to topple down, hundirse, venirse abajo; caer; to topple over, tambalearse, caerse, perder el equilibrio. — v.t. hacer caer, hacer volcar, derríbar.
top-sail, s. gavia.
topsy-turvy [tɔpsi'təɹvi], a., adv. de arriba abajo, trastornado, patas arriba.
top-timber, s. (mar.) barraganete.
toque [touk], s. cofia, toca, especie de gorra de mujer; mono que tiene en la parte superior de la cabeza un moño parecido a una cofia.
tor [tɔɹ], s. tolmo, tormo, pico, mojón.
torch [tɔɹtʃ], s. hacha, hachón, antorcha, tea; lámpara eléctrica de bolsillo, lamparilla, linterna.
torch-bearer, s. portahachón, hachero.
torchlight, s. luz de antorcha.
tore [tɔɹ], pret. [TEAR]. — s. (arq.) toro, bocel, tondino; (dial.) hierba muerta que queda en los campos en invierno.
torment ['tɔɹment], s. tormento, suplicio, tortura, pena, angustia.
torment [tɔɹ'ment], v.t. atormentar, torturar, dar tormento; molestar, atormentar.
tormentil ['tɔɹməntil], s. (bot.) tormentila.
tormentor, s. atormentador.
tormina ['tɔɹminə], s. dolor agudo y severo en los intestinos.
torn [tɔɹn], p.p. [TEAR].
tornado [tɔɹ'neidou], s. tornado, torbellino.
torpedo [tɔɹ'piːdou], s. torpedo; (ict.) tremielga, tembladera, pez o raya eléctrica; torpedo boat, torpedero; torpedo-boat destroyer, contratorpedero.
torpescence, s. entorpecimiento naciente.
torpescent [tɔɹ'pesənt], a. entorpecido.
torpid ['tɔɹpid], a. torpe, embotado; entorpecido, eletargado; (med.) tórpido.
torpidity [tɔɹ'piditi], **torpidness** ['tɔɹpidnis], **torpitude** ['tɔɹpitjuːd], **torpor** ['tɔɹpəɹ], entorpecimiento, embotamiento.
torporific [tɔɹpə'rifik], a. lo que entorpece.
torrefaction [tɔri'fækʃən], s. torrefacción.
torrefy ['tɔrefai], v.t. torrar, torrefactar.
torrent ['tɔrənt], s. torrente, raudal.
torrential [tɔ'renʃəl], a. torrencial.
torrid ['tɔrid], a. tórrido.
torridity [tɔ'riditi], s. estado de tórrido, calor abrasador.
torsel ['tɔɹsəl], s. torzal.
torsion ['tɔɹʃən], s. torsión, torcedura.
torso ['tɔɹsou], s. torso.
tort [tɔɹt], s. (for.) tuerto, agravio.
tortile ['tɔɹtil], a. torcido, enredado, doblado.
tortoise ['tɔɹtəs], s. (zool.) tortuga.
tortuous ['tɔɹtjuːəs], a. tortuoso.
tortuosity [tɔɹtjuː'ɔsiti], s. tortuosidad, torcedura.
torture ['tɔɹtʃəɹ], s. tortura, tormento, suplicio, martirio. — v.t. atormentar, torturar, dar tormento a, torcer; (fig.) martirizar, atormentar.

torturer, s. atormentador; verdugo.
torus ['tɔːɹəs], s. (arq.) toro.
Tory ['tɔːɹi], s. (pol.) conservador.
toss [tɔs], v.t. (pret. y p.p. **tossed,** poét. **tost**) lanzar, arrojar, tirar, echar, lanzar en el aire; acornear, dar una cornada; menear, agitar, sacudir, mover; to toss aside, echar a un lado; to toss in a blanket, mantear, dar una manta; to toss up, echar al aire; jugar a cara o cruz, jugar a castillo o león; to decide by tossing up, echar a la buena barba. — v.i. arrojarse; agitarse; corcovear, no estarse quieto; balancearse, cabecear (un navío). — s. tiro; golpe; sacudimiento; cabeceo; cornada, cogida (de toro); toss up, cara o cruz.
tossing, s. tiro; agitación, sacudimiento, meneo, manteamiento; cornada.
tosspot ['tɔspɔt], s. (ant.) borracho.
tot [tɔt], s. (vulg.) chiquitín, nene, crío, chacho; copita, vaso muy pequeño; gotita, suma, total; to tot up, sumar.
total ['toutəl], s. total, suma, todo. — a. total, entero, completo, cabal. — v.t. totalizar, sumar. — v.i. ascender a.
totality [tou'tæliti], s. totalidad, conjunto.
totally ['toutəli], adv. totalmente, enteramente, por completo.
totem, s. totem.
totter ['tɔtəɹ], v.i. bambolearse (personas), tambalearse (cosas), titubear; (fig.) estar para caerse, amenazar ruina.
tottering, s. vacilación, bamboleo. — a. vacilante, tambaleante.
totteringly, adv. vacilando, de un modo tambaleante.
toucan ['tuːkən], s. tucán.
touch [tʌtʃ], v.t. tocar, palpar, tentar, manosear, rozar; irritar, aguijonear; tropezar; alcanzar, influir; enternecer, conmover; probar, ensayar; herir; tañer; trazar, delinear, retocar, esbozar; tocar, concernir, importar. — v.i. tocar; bosquejar, acabar de prisa; (mar.) hacer escala; to touch down, (aer.) aterrizar; to touch off, descargar (un cañón); to touch up, retocar, corregir; to touch upon (o on), tratar ligeramente de. — s. tacto; contacto, tiento, tocamiento, palpamiento, palpadura; toque, piedra de toque; conmoción; facción; ataque; celada; rasgo; última mano, ejecución; punzada, dolorcito; ensayo ligero; indirecta; (mús.) pulsación; armonía, simpatía; experiencia, prueba; corazonada; touch-me-not, (bot.) nolimetángere; touch hole, fogón (del cañón); touch and go, marro (juego); (fig.) arriesgado, precario; (fig.) ligero de cascos; it was touch and go with him, (fam.) estuvo al punto de morir.
touchable ['tʌtʃəbəl], a. tangible, palpable.
touchdown ['tʌtʃdaun], s. (aer.) aterrizaje, momento de tocar el suelo (el avión).
touchily ['tʌtʃili], adv. susceptiblemente.
touchiness, s. susceptibilidad, irritabilidad.
touching, a. conmovedor, enternecedor, tierno, patético, emocionante. — s. tacto, toque, contacto, palpamiento. — prep. tocante a, respeto a, en cuanto a, acerca de.
touchingly, adv. patéticamente, tiernamente, de una manera emocionante o conmovedora.
touchstone ['tʌtʃstoun], s. piedra de toque.
touchwood, s. yesca.
touchy ['tʌtʃi], a. susceptible, irritable, quisquilloso.

tough [tʌf], *a.* duro, correoso; flexible, manejable, tenaz, resistente; sólido, fuerte, duro, tieso; vulgar, grosero, rudo; (*fam.*) penoso, arduo. — *s.* (*fam.*) matón, rufián.

toughen ['tʌfən], *v.t.* endurecer, hacer duro. — *v.i.* endurecer(se), atiesar.

toughish, *a.* algo duro.

toughly ['tʌfli], *adv.* fuertemente, sólidamente, con dureza, tenazmente.

toughness, *s.* dureza, correa; solidez, dureza, tesura, endurecimiento, rigidez; tenacidad, fuerza; flexibilidad.

toupet ['tuːpei], *s.* tupé.

tour [tuːə], *s.* vuelta, turno, circuito, excursión, viaje, peregrinación; *circular tour*, viaje redondo; *on tour*, (*teat., etc.*) de gira (artística), de viaje.

tourist ['tuːərist], *s.* turista, *m.f.*, excursionista, *m.f.*

tourmaline ['tuːəməliːn], *s.* turmalina.

tournament ['tuːənəmənt], *s.* torneo, justa; concurso.

tourney ['tuːəni], *s.* torneo, justa. — *v.i.* justar.

tourniquet ['tuːəniket], *s.* (*cir.*) molinete, torniquete.

tousle, towsle ['tauzəl], *v.t.* desmelenar, despeinar; manosear, desarreglar, maltratar.

tout [taut], *v.i.* (*fam.*) alcahuetear, pescar; solicitar; (*E.U.*) solicitar votos. — *v.t.* espiar; alcahuetear, pescar. — *s.* descubridor, buho; alcahuete.

tow [tou], *v.t.* remolcar, llevar a remolque, halar, atoar. — *s.* estopa; remolque; *on o in tow*, a remolque.

towage ['touidʒ], *s.* remolque, atoaje.

towboat, *s.* remolcador.

tow-headed, *a.* pelirrojo.

tow-line, tow-rope, *s.* cabo o cable de remolque; (*mar.*) cable de sirga.

toward [tə'wɔːd], **towards** [tə'wɔːdz], *prep.* del lado de, con dirección a, hacia; cerca, cerca de, acerca de, alrededor de, por, para con; tocante a, con respecto a.

toward, *adv.* (*ant.*) cerca; en preparación, preparado.

towel ['tauəl], *s.* toalla, servilleta de tocador.

tower ['tauə], *s.* torre, *f.*, torreón, ciudadela, fortaleza; campanario; altura. — *v.i.* elevarse, dominar, descollar, destacarse; (*fig.*) destacarse, sobresalir.

towered, *a.* torreado, flanqueado o guarnecido de torres.

towering ['tauəriŋ], *a.* muy alto, elevado, dominante; soberbio, altanero, orgulloso; furioso, violento, terrible.

towing ['touiŋ], *s.* remolque, tirada.

town [taun], *s.* ciudad, población, villa, poblado, municipio, metrópoli, *f.*; *town clerk*, escribano municipal; *town council*, ayuntamiento, concejo municipal; *town councillor*, concejero municipal; *town crier*, pregonero; *town hall*, ayuntamiento, casa de ayuntamiento; *town-planning*, urbanismo, proyectos urbanísticos; *town wall*, muralla.

township ['taunʃip], *s.* municipalidad, municipio.

townsman ['taunzmən], *s.* ciudadano, conciudadano, vecino.

towsle, *v.t.* [TOUSLE].

toxic ['tɔksik], *a.* tóxico.

toxicology [tɔksi'kɔlodʒi], *s.* toxicología.

toxin ['tɔksin], *s.* toxina.

toy [tɔi], *s.* juguete; trebejo, bagatela, cosa de ningún valor, futilidad; retozo, retozadura. — *v.i.* jugar, divertirse, juguetear, chancear; *to toy with*, (*fig.*) jugar con.

toyish, *a.* chancero, fútil.

toyishness, *s.* puerilidad, muchachada, niñería.

toyman, *s.* juguetero.

toyshop, *s.* juguetería.

trace [treis], *v.t.* trazar; calcar; seguir la huella de, rastrear; delinear, escudriñar, investigar; descubrir; *to trace back*, hacer remontar. — *s.* huella, rastro, trazas, vestigio, señal, *f.*, pisada; tirantes, ronzal (de caballo); (*fig.*) pizca, saborcillo, traza.

traceable ['treisəbəl], *a.* que se puede trazar o rastrear.

tracer, *s.* trazador; tiralíneas, *m.*; persona que traza, que calca.

tracery ['treisəri], *s.* (*arq.*) tracería.

trachea [trə'kiːə], *s.* tráquea.

tracheal, *a.* traqueal.

tracheotomy [træki'ɔtomi], *s.* traqueotomía.

trachyte ['trækait], *s.* (*min.*) traquita.

tracing, *s.* calco; descubrimiento, rastreo; *tracing-paper*, papel para calcar.

track [træk], *s.* traza, huella, pista, estampa, rastro, vestigio; rodada, pisada, dirección (de ruedas); vereda, senda, sendero; ruta, rumbo; (*f.c.*) vía, carril; región; (*E.U.*) andén; (*deportes*) pista; (*mar., aer.*) rumbo, derrota; estela; (*mec.*) carrilera, oruga, banda de rodamiento (de tractor, etc.); *beaten track*, sendero trillado; *off the track*, (*f.c.*) descarrilado; (*fig.*) extraviado, desorientado; *sidetrack*, desvío, vía muerta; *to keep track of*, seguir la pista de, no perder de vista. — *v.t.* seguir la pista; rastrear; (*mar.*) sirgar.

trackage, *s.* remolque, sirgadura; (*E.U.*) sistema de vías.

tracker, *s.* (*mar.*) sirguero; seguidor.

tracking, *s.* seguimiento, caza; (*mec.*) alineación o dirección (de las ruedas).

trackless, *a.* sin trazas, sin huellas; sin camino; impracticable.

trackway, *s.* senda, vereda; vía de ferrocarril.

tract [trækt], *s.* tracto, trecho; extensión, región, comarca, espacio; tratado, folleto, librito, opúsculo; (*anat.*) vía.

tractability [træktə'biliti], *s.* docilidad, naturaleza tratable, afabilidad.

tractable ['træktəbəl], *a.* dócil, tratable, manejable, complaciente.

tractably, *adv.* dócilmente, afablemente, de una manera tratable.

tractate ['trækteit], *s.* tratado, folleto, opúsculo.

tractile ['træktil], *a.* dúctil.

tractility [træk'tiliti], *s.* ductilidad.

traction ['trækʃən], *s.* tracción; (*fig.*) atracción; *traction-engine*, máquina de tracción; *traction-wheel*, rueda de tracción.

tractive, *a.* (*mec.*) de tracción, tractor, tractivo.

tractor ['træktə], *s.* tractor; instrumento de tracción.

trade [treid], *s.* comercio, tráfico, negocio, contratación; profesión, ocupación, empleo, oficio; industria; negocio, trato; gremio, conjunto de obreros; *free trade*, libre cambio; *trade winds*, vientos alisios. — *v.t., v.i.* comerciar, traficar, negociar, contratar, tratar; cambiar, vender; *to trade in*, entregar como pago parcial, entregar a cuenta; *to trade on,* sacar provecho de, explotar.

trade-mark, *s.* marca de fábrica.

trader, *s.* negociante, comerciante, traficante, mercader; buque de carga, carguero; *free trader,* librecambista, *m.*

tradesman ['treidzmən] (*pl.* **tradesfolk** ['treidzfouk], **tradespeople** ['treidzpiːpəl]), *s.* comerciante, tendero, artesano; *tradesmen's entrance,* puerta de servicio.

trade(s)-union, *s.* sindicato.

trade(s)-unionism, *s.* sindicalismo.

trade(s)-unionist, *s.* sindicalista, *m.f.*

tradeswoman, *s.f.* mercadera.

trading, *a.* de comercio, comercial, mercantil negociante. — *s.* compraventa; negocios, comercio, trato.

tradition [trə'diʃən], *s.* tradición.

traditional [trə'diʃənəl], **traditionary** [trə-'diʃənəri], *a.* tradicional.

traditionalism, *s.* tradicionalismo.

traditionary, *a.* tradicional. — *s.* tradicionalista, *m.f.*

traduce [trə'djuːs], *v.t.* vituperar, vilipendiar, difamar, denigrar, detractar.

traducer, *s.* difamador, detractor, calumniador.

traducing, *a.* difamatorio, calumnioso.

traduction [trə'dʌkʃən], *s.* (*ant.*) propagación; (*ant.*) calumnia; (*lóg.*) transferencia.

traffic ['træfik], *s.* tráfico, comercio, intercambio, negocio; circulación, movimiento; transporte, tránsito; productos, géneros, mercancías. — *v.t., v.i.* traficar, comerciar, negociar; *traffic jam* o *block* o *congestion,* obstrucción o atasco de la circulación; *traffic indicator,* (*aut.*) indicador de virada [TRAFFICATOR]; *traffic lights,* luces automáticas (para la circulación); *traffic roundabout,* (*E.U.*) *traffic circle,* glorieta o redondel de circulación giratoria.

trafficator ['træfikeitəɹ], *s.* (*aut.*) indicador de virada, indicador lateral para cambio de dirección.

trafficker, *s.* traficante, comerciante, mercader, baratista, *m.f.*

tragacanth ['trægəkænθ], *s.* tragacanto, adraganto.

tragedian [trə'dʒiːdiən], *s.* trágico, escritor de tragedias o actor trágico.

tragedienne [trədʒiː'diˈen], *s.f.* trágica.

tragedy ['trædʒedi], *s.* tragedia.

tragic ['trædʒik], **tragical** ['trædikəl], *a.* trágico.

tragically, *adv.* trágicamente.

tragi-comedy [trædʒi'kɔmedi], *s.* tragicomedia.

tragi-comic, tragi-comical, *a.* tragicómico.

trail [treil], *s.* traza, pista, pisada, rastro, huella; camino, senda, sendero; estela, cola, cabellera; indicio. — *v.t.* arrastrar; seguir la pista, rastrear; bajar (las armas); pisar (la hierba), remolcar; *to trail the anchor,* (*mar.*) garrar. — *v.i.* arrastrar, ir arrastrando, dejar rastro; *to trail (behind),* rezagarse.

trailer, *s.* cazador a la pista; (*aut.*) (coche de) remolque; (*cine*) 'trailer,' anuncio de película; (*bot.*) tallo rastrero.

trailing, *a.* rastrero.

train [trein], *s.* tren; acompañamiento, séquito, procesión, comitiva, recua, convoy; reguero (de pólvora); cola (de traje de corte); estela,

curso; curso, orden, serie, *f.,* continuación; movimiento, juego; celada, lazo; artimaña; *down train,* tren descendente; *up train,* tren ascendente; *goods train,* tren de mercancías; *through train,* tren directo; *express train,* tren expreso, exprés; *fast train,* (tren) rápido; *slow train,* tren correo, tren ómnibus. — *v.t., v.i.* disciplinar, amaestrar, adiestrar; instruir, enseñar, educar; podar; (*deportes*) entrenar; (*agr.*) poner en espaldera; apuntar (un cañón).

train-bearer, *s.* caudatario.

trainer, *s.* amaestrador, domador; instructor; (*deportes*) entrenador; (*agr.*) espaldera.

training, *s.* instrucción, educación; (*deportes*) entrenamiento; *training college,* escuela normal.

train-oil, *s.* aceite de ballena.

trait [trei], *s.* rasgo, característica, facción.

traitor ['treitəɹ], *s.* traidor.

traitorous, *a.* traidor, pérfido, alevoso, aleve.

traitorously, *adv.* traidoramente.

traitorousness, *s.* traición, perfidia, alevosía.

traitress ['treitres], *s.f.* traidora.

traject [trə'dʒekt], *s.* travesía. — *v.t.* trasladar, transferir.

trajection, *s.* trayecto, travesía, transporte; emisión, tiro.

trajectory [trə'dʒektəri], *s.* trayectoria.

tram [træm], *s.* tranvía, *m.*; carril liso, riel plano.

tram-car, tramway, tramway-car, *s.* tranvía, *m.,* coche de tranvía.

tram-line, *s.* vía, carril de tranvía.

trammel ['træməl], *v.t.* embarazar, estorbar, impedir. — *s.* trasmallo; compás de varas, compás de elipse; traba, embarazo, estorbo.

tramontane [træ'montein], *s., a.* tramontano, ultramontano, extranjero.

tramp [træmp], *s.* vagabundo; marcha pesada; caminata, camino largo, paseo a pie; ruido de pisadas; (*E.U.*) mujerzuela. — *v.t., v.i.* ir o andar a pie; corretear, vagabundear, patear, patullar, pisar con fuerza o con paso pesado; *tramp steamer,* vapor volandero.

tramper, *s.* vagabundo; buen andador.

trample ['træmpəl], *v.t., v.i.* pisar, pisotear, hollar; *to trample on,* atropellar, maltratar, ajar. — *s.* atropello, pisoteo.

trampler, *s.* pisador.

trance [trɑːns], *s.* rapto, arrobamiento, enajenamiento; (*med.*) catalepsia.

tranquil ['træŋkwil], *a.* tranquilo, apacible, sosegado, pacífico, calmoso.

tranquillity [træŋ'kwiliti], *s.* tranquilidad, calma, sosiego, reposo, quietud, paz, *f.*

tranquillize ['træŋkwilaiz], *v.t.* tranquilizar, calmar, aquietar, sosegar.

tranquilly ['træŋkwili], *adv.* tranquilamente, reposadamente, con calma, con sosiego.

transact [træn'zækt], *v.t.* ejecutar, negociar, despachar, tramitar; desempeñar, llevar a cabo.

transaction, *s.* negocio, gestión, operación, transacción, negociación; desempeño. — *pl.* **transactions,** actas, memorias o trabajos de una sociedad.

transactor, *s.* negociador, gestor, agente.

transalpine [trænz'ælpain], *a.* transalpino.

transatlantic [trænzət'læntik], *s., a.* transatlántico.

transcend [træn'send], *v.t., v.i.* sobrepujar, sobresalir, superar, descollar, elevarse sobre.

transcendence, transcendency, *s.* transcendencia, superioridad; exageración.

transcendent [træn'sendənt], **transcendental** [trænsen'dentəl], *a.* transcendental, sobresaliente, eminente.

transcendentalism [trænsen'dentəlizm], *s.* transcendentalismo.

transcendently, *adv.* de un modo transcendente.

transcribe [træn'skraib], *v.t.* transcribir, copiar, trasladar; (*mús.*) transcribir, arreglar.

transcriber, *s.* copista, *m.f.*, copiador; adaptador, arreglador.

transcript ['trænskript], **transcription** [træn'skripʃən], *s.* transcripción, copia, traslado, trasunto; (*mús.*) transcripción, arreglo, realización.

transept ['trænsept], *s.* (*arq.*) crucero.

transfer [træns'fəːɪ], *v.t.* trasladar, transportar, transferir; dar, ceder; pasar, transbordar; (*for.*) enajenar.

transfer ['trænsfəɪ], *s.* cesión, transferencia, trasbordo, traslación, traslado, traspaso, transporte; calcomanía; (*for.*) enajenamiento, cesión.

transferable, *a.* transferible, transitivo, convertible.

transferee [trænsfəɪ'iː], *s.* cesionario.

transference ['trænsfərəns], *s.* transferencia.

transferor, transferrer, *s.* cedente, cesionista, *m.f.*

transfiguration [trænsfigju:'reiʃən], *s.* transfiguración, transformación.

transfigure [træns'figəɪ], *v.t.* transfigurar, transformar, transmutar.

transfix [træns'fiks], *v.t.* traspasar.

transfixion, *s.* transfixión.

transform [træns'fɔːɪm], *v.t.* transformar, transmutar, metamorfosear.

transformable, *a.* transformable.

transformation [trænsfɔːɪ'meiʃən], *s.* transformación, metamorfosis, *f.*, transmutación, conversión, cambio.

transformative [træns'fɔːɪmətiv], *a.* que puede transformar.

transformer, *s.* transformador.

transfuse [træns'fjuːz], *v.t.* transfundir.

transfusion [træns'fjuːʒən], *s.* transfusión.

transgress [træns'gres], *v.t.*, *v.i.* transgredir, traspasar, exceder(se), contravenir, infringir, violar; pecar.

transgression, *s.* transgresión, traspaso, pecado, contravención, delinquimiento, ofensa.

transgressor, *s.* transgresor, violador; quebrantador, infractor.

tranship [træn'ʃip], *v.t.* (*mar.*) transbordar.

transient ['trænziənt], *a.* transitorio, pasajero, efímero, temporáneo, transeunte.

transiently, *adv.* de paso, transitoriamente, temporalmente.

transientness, *s.* naturaleza pasajera, brevedad.

transistor, *s.* transistor.

transit ['trænsit], *s.* tránsito, pasaje, paso; trámite. — *v.t.* pasar sobre; *in transit,* de tránsito.

transition [træn'siʒən], *s.* tránsito, paso; transición, mudanza.

transitional, transitionary, *a.* de transición, transitorio.

transitive ['trænsitiv], *a.* (*gram.*) transitivo.

transitively, *adv.* de un modo transitivo.

transitorily ['trænsitərili], *adv.* transitoriamente, pasajeramente.

transitoriness, brevedad, fugacidad, interinidad.

transitory ['trænsitəri], *a.* transitorio, pasajero, fugaz.

translatable [træns'leitəbəl], *a.* traducible.

translate [træns'leit], *v.t.* traducir, verter; interpretar, explicar, descifrar; cambiar; transportar, transferir; arrebatar al cielo; (*igl.*) trasladar.

translation [træns'leiʃən], *s.* traducción, versión; transporte, translación; arrebatamiento al cielo; traslación de un obispo de una sede a otra.

translator, *s.* traductor, intérprete, *m.f.*

transliterate [træns'litəreit], *v.t.* traducir o trasladar fonéticamente.

translocation [trænslo'keiʃən], *s.* cambio de sitio.

translucence, translucency, *s.* translucidez.

translucent [træns'luːsənt], **translucid** [træns'luːsid], *a.* translúcido, transluciente; transparente.

transmarine [trænzmə'riːn], *a.* ultramarino, transmarino, de ultramar.

transmigrant [trænz'maigrənt], *s.* emigrante.

transmigrate ['trænzmaigreit], *v.i.* transmigrar, emigrar.

transmigration, *s.* transmigración, emigración.

transmigrator, *s.* emigrante.

transmigratory, *a.* que transmigra.

transmissibility, *s.* transmisibilidad.

transmissible [trænz'misibəl], *a.* transmisible.

transmission, transmittal, *s.* transmisión.

transmissive, *a.* transmitido, transmisible, transmisor.

transmit, *v.t.* transmitir, transfundir; enviar, remitir.

transmittal, *s.* transmisión.

transmitter, *s.* remitente, transmisor; (*elec.*) transmisor, radiotransmisor.

transmogrify, *v.t.* (*fam.*) metamorfosear, cambiar.

transmutability, *s.* transmutabilidad.

transmutable, *a.* transmutable.

transmutably, *adv.* de una manera transmutable.

transmutation [trænzmju:'teiʃən], *s.* transmutación.

transmute [trænz'mjuːt], *v.t.* transmutar, metamorfosear.

transom ['trænsəm], *s.* (*arq.*) travesaño, crucero, claraboya, montante; (*mar.*) yugo o peto de popa; (*arti.*) telera.

transparence, transparency, transparentness, *s.* transparencia, diafanidad.

transparent [træns'pɛərənt], *a.* transparente, diáfano; (*fig.*) transparente, obvio; (*fig.*) sincero, franco; evidente.

transpierce [træns'piəɪs], *v.t.* traspasar, penetrar.

transpirable, *a.* transpirable.

transpiration [trænspai'reiʃən], *s.* transpiración.

transpire [træns'paiəɪ], *v.i.* transpirar, exhalarse, rezumarse; empezar a divulgarse; (*fam.*) acontecer, suceder. — *v.t.* transpirar, exhalar, sudar.

transplant [træns'plɑːnt], *v.t.* trasplantar.

transplantable, *a*. trasplantable.

transplantation, *s*. trasplantación, trasplante.

transplanter, *s*. trasplantador.

transplanting, *s*. trasplante, trasplantación.

transport ['trænspɔːɹt], *v.t.* transportar, trasportar, trasladar; deportar, desterrar; transportarse, arrebatar, enajenar. — *s*. transporte, transportamiento, acarreo; arrebato, arrobamiento, transporte, rapto.

transportable, *a*. transportable, capaz de ser transportado.

transportation [trænspɔːɹ'teiʃən], *s*. transportación, transporte, transmisión, conducción, conducta, acarreo; deportación, extrañamiento, destierro.

transporter, *s*. transportador; vehículo de transporte.

transposal [træns'pouzəl], **transposing** [træns'pouziŋ], *s*. transposición, traspaso.

transpose [træns'pouz], *v.t.* transponer, trasponer; (*mús.*) transportar.

transposer, *s*. (*mús.*) transpositor.

transposition [trænspo'ziʃən], *s*. transposición, transpuesta; (*mús.*) transporte.

transshipment, *s*. transbordo.

transubstantiate, *v.t.* transubstanciar.

transubstantiation [trænsʌbstænʃi'eiʃən], *s*. transubstanciación.

transudation [trænsju'deiʃən], *s*. transudación, resudación.

transude [træn'sjuːd], *v.i.* transudar, trazumarse, resudar.

transversal [træns'vɜːɹsəl], *a*. transversal; (*anat.*) transverso.

transversally, *adv.* transversalmente.

transverse [træns'vɜːɹs], *a*. transversal; (*anat.*) transverso.

transversely, *adv.* transversalmente, oblicuamente.

trap [træp], *v.t.* entrampar, atrapar, coger con trampa, hacer caer en el garlito; adornar, enjaezar. — *v.i.* tender un lazo, armar lazos. — *s*. trampa; armadijo, cepo; garlito, lazo, red, *f*.; tartana, coche; escalera de mano; sifón; *mouse-trap*, ratonera; *to be caught* o *to fall in a trap*, caer en la trampa, caer en la ratonera. — *pl*. **traps**, (*fam.*) trastos, efectos, equipaje.

trapdoor, *s*. escotillón, trampa.

trapeze [trə'piːz], **trapezium** [trə'piːziəm], *s*. trapecio.

trapezoid [trə'piːzɔid], *s*. (*geom.*) trapezoide.

trapper ['træpəɹ], *s*. cazador (con trampas).

trappings ['træpiŋz], *s.pl.* adornos, jaeces, *m.pl.*, aderezos, arreos.

trash [træʃ], *s*. cachivaches, trasto; hojarasca, paja, ñoñería, ñoñez, porquería; escamonda, desperdicio, zupia, heces, *f.pl.*; bagazo, bagacillo (de azúcar); quídam, un cualquiera, gentuza. — *v.t.* escamondar, podar.

trashy ['træʃi], *a*. de desperdicio, ñoño, soso, sin valor, despreciable.

trauma ['trɔːmə], *s*. (*cir.*) trauma, *m*.; traumatismo; trauma psíquico.

traumatic [trɔː'mætik], *a*. traumático.

traumatism ['trɔːmə'tizm], *s*. traumatismo.

travail ['træveil], *s*. parto, dolores de parto; fatiga, afán. — *v.i.* estar de parto, tener dolores de parto; afanarse, trabajar. — *v.t.* (*ant.*) atormentar, fatigar, mortificar.

travel ['trævəl], *v.i.* viajar, estar de viaje; caminar, andar, recorrer, dirigirse; marchar.

— *v.t.* recorrer, hacer (una distancia viajando). — *s*. el viajar, turismo, viajes; (*mec.*) carrera, desplazamiento.

travelled, *a*. que ha viajado mucho, que ha visto tierras.

traveller, (*E.U.*) **traveler**, *s*. viajero, pasajero, viajador, persona que ha vista mundo o tierras, persona que viaja mucho; *commercial traveller*, viajante; *fellow traveller*, compañero de viaje; (*pol.*) persona de inclinación o simpatías comunistas; *traveller's cheque*, cheque de viajero; *traveller's joy*, (*bot.*) clemátide, *f*.

travelling, *a*. de viaje. — *s*. viajes.

travel-stained, *a*. manchado por el polvo del camino.

traversable [trə'vɜːɹsəbəl], *a*. que se puede atravesar.

traverse ['trævəɹs], *v.t.* atravesar, cruzar; recorrer; impedir, contrariar, estorbar; examinar, escudriñar; (*for.*) negar, hacer oposición. — *v.i.* girar, dar vueltas; (*equit.*) atravesarse; (*esgr.*) evitar, hacer vaivén. — *s*. travesaño, travesero; tabique; (*for.*) denegación; (*fort.*) través, trinchera; (*fig.*) subterfugio, artificio, obstáculo, revés; (*geom.*) línea transversal; (*mar.*) bordada en dirección oblicua; *traverse course*, rumbo compuesto. — *adv.* al través. — *a*. transversal, oblicuo.

traverser, *s*. (*for.*) demandado.

travestied ['trævəstid], *a*. parodiado.

travesty ['trævəsti], *s*. parodia. — *v.t.* parodiar; disfrazar.

trawl [trɔːl], *s*. red, *f*. — *v.t.*, *v.i.* pescar con red, pescar a la rastra, pescar al albareque; *trawl-line*, palangre; *trawl-net*, traína.

trawler, *s*. chalupa pescadora, buque pesquero de rastreo.

trawling, *s*. pesca con red, pesca a la rastra.

tray [trei], *s*. bandeja, salvilla, azafate, cubeta, platel; cajón.

treacherous ['tretʃərəs], *a*. traidor, pérfido, traicionero, aleve, alevoso; engañador, resbaladizo.

treachery ['tretʃəri], *s*. traición, perfidia, falsedad.

treacle ['triːkəl], *s*. melaza, meladura, melado; (*farm.*, *ant.*) teriaca, triaca.

tread [tred], *v.t.* (*pret.* **trod**; *p.p.* **trodden**) pisar, pisotear, hollar, gallear. — *v.i.* poner el pie, pisar; andar, caminar; *to tread in the steps of*, seguir las huellas de; *to tread on*, pisar; *to tread under foot*, pisotear, hollar; *to tread on one's heels*, pisarle los talones a uno, seguir de cerca a. — *s*. paso, huella, pisada, pisadura; andadura (del caballo); senda, camino; huella (de escalón); llanta (de neumático); fecundación (de animales), galladura.

treading, *s*. compresión; fecundación.

treadle ['tredəl], *s*. pedal, cárcola; galladura.

treadmill ['tredmil], *s*. molino de rueda de escalones, molino de disciplina; (*fig.*) tráfago.

treason ['triːzən], *s*. traición, deslealtad; *high treason*, alta traición.

treasonable, *a*. traidor, traicionero, de traición, desleal, pérfido.

treasonableness, *s*. traición.

treasonably, *adv.* traidoramente, como traidor.

treasure ['treʒəɹ], *s*. tesoro, riqueza, caudal; *treasure trove*, tesoro hallado. — *v.t.* atesorar, guardar (con mucho cuidado); amontonar, acumular riquezas.

treasurer, *s.* tesorero.

treasurership ['treʒərəɪʃip], *s.* tesorería.

treasury ['treʒəri], *s.* tesorería, tesoro; hacienda, ministerio de hacienda.

treat [tri:t], *v.t., v.i.* tratar (de), dar trato; (*med.*) tratar, dar tratamiento, curar; negociar un tratado; versar (sobre), tratar (de), discurrir (sobre); (*fam.*) invitar, convidar, agasajar, obsequiar. — *s.* regalo, convite, festín, banquete; placer, solaz, gusto, deleite; agasajo, obsequio; *to stand treat,* (*fam.*) convidar, pagar la convidada.

treater, *s.* el que trata; negociador; huésped, *m.f.,* anfitrión.

treatise ['tri:tiz], *s.* tratado, opúsculo, disertación.

treatment, *s.* tratamiento, trato; (*med.*) tratamiento, terapia; trato, porte, conducta; manejo, procedimiento.

treaty ['tri:ti], *s.* tratado, negociación, convenio, pacto, ajuste.

treble ['trebəl], *s.* triple; (*mús.*) tiple. — *a.* triple; (*mús.*) agudo, sobreagudo, atiplado. — *v.t.* triplicar. — *v.i.* triplicarse.

trebly ['trebli], *adv.* triplemente, triplicadamente.

tree [tri:], *s.* árbol; madero, palo, leño; horma (de zapatos); arzón; *fruit tree,* árbol frutal; *tree fern,* helecho de árbol; *up a tree,* (*fam.*) en un apuro, entre la espada y la pared; *to bark up the wrong tree,* (*fam.*) errar el tiro, ir descaminado.

treeless, *a.* sin árboles, pelado.

treenail ['tri:neil], *s.* (*mar.*) cabilla, clavija de palo.

trefoil ['tri:fɔil], *s.* trébol, trifolio.

trek [trek], *v.i.* (*fam.*) viajar, caminar, vagar; (*fam.*) marcharse, emigrar; viajar en carromatos. — *s.* viaje, emigración.

trellis ['trelis], *s.* enrejado, espalera, varaseto.

trellised, *a.* enrejado.

tremble ['trembəl], *v.i.* temblar, retemblar, tiritar; estremecerse, trepidar; oscilar; trinar. — *s.* estremecimiento, temblor.

trembler, *s.* miedoso.

trembling ['tremblɪŋ], *s.* temblor; estremecimiento; vibración, oscilación. — *a.* trémulo, tembloroso, temblante.

tremblingly, *adv.* trémulamente, temblando, con miedo, con vergüenza.

tremendous [tre'mendəs], *a.* espantoso, terrible; tremendo, enorme, muy grande; (*fam.*) formidable, tremendo.

tremendously, *adv.* terriblemente, horrorosamente, furiosamente; (*fam.*) muy, mucho, enormemente.

tremendousness, *s.* carácter espantoso.

tremolo ['tremolou], *s.* (*mús.*) trémolo.

tremor ['tremər], *s.* temblor, tremor, estremecimiento, vibración.

tremulous ['tremjuləs], *a.* tembloroso, tremulante, trémulo; vacilante, trémulo.

tremulously, *adv.* trémulamente.

tremulousness, *s.* temblor; vacilación, timidez.

trench [trentʃ], *v.t., v.i.* abrir, cavar o hacer fosos, zanjas o surcos, surcar; (*mil.*) hacer trincheras, atrincherar; *to trench upon,* usurpar. — *s.* trinchera, foso, zanja, tajo; cauce, presa; *trench-coat,* trinchera.

trenchant, *a.* penetrante, agudo.

trencher, *s.* tajadero, trinchero; mesa de comedor; comida; *trencher-man,* comilón.

trend [trend], *s.* rumbo, dirección, curso, giro; tendencia, inclinación. — *v.i.* tender, dirigirse, inclinarse.

trendle ['trendəl], *s.* rodillo.

trental ['trentəl], *s.* treintenario de misas.

trepan [tre'pæn], *v.t.* (*cir.*) trepanar; (*ant.*) coger en el garlito, engañar, entrampar. — *s.* trépano.

trepanation [trepə'neiʃən], **trepanning** [tre-'pæniŋ], *s.* (*cir.*) trepanación.

trephine [tre'fi:n], *s.* trefino. — *v.t.* trepanar.

trepidation [trepi'deiʃən], *s.* trepidación.

trespass ['trespəs], *v.i.* traspasar, trasgredir, faltar, pecar, infringir reglamentarias; entrar en propiedad ajena sin derecho; *to trespass against* o *upon,* infringir, contravenir; *to trespass upon someone's patience,* abusar de la paciencia de uno; *to trespass upon someone's time,* hacer perder a uno su tiempo. — *s.* pecado, delito; (*for.*) violación.

trespasser, *s.* violador, transgresor, pecador.

tress [tres], *s.* trenza, rizo, bucle.

tressed, *a.* trenzado, rizado.

trestle ['tresəl], *s.* bastidor (de mesa), armadura, caballete, tijera; *trestle-table,* mesa de tijera; *trestle-trees,* (*mar.*) baos de los palos.

trews [tru:z], *s.pl.* (*Esco.*) pantalones hechos de tela tartán.

trey [trei], *s.* el tres en los naipes o dados.

triad ['traiəd], *s.* (*mús.*) acorde ternario; terno, terna, trinca.

triadic, *a.* trino.

trial ['traiəl], *s.* prueba, ensayo, esfuerzo, probadura, tentativa, experimento, experiencia; aflicción, desgracia, prueba; (*for.*) pleito, proceso, juicio, vista de una causa; *on trial,* a prueba, (*for.*) en proceso, enjuiciado; *to bring to trial,* enjuiciar, procesar; *to stand trial,* estar a derecho, comparecer, estar a juicio; *trial run* o *trial trip,* marcha o viaje de prueba o de ensayo.

triangle ['traiæŋgəl], *s.* triángulo.

triangular [trai'æŋgju:lər], *a.* triangular, triangulado.

triangularly, *adv.* triangularmente.

tribal ['traibəl], *a.* de la tribu.

tribe [traib], *s.* tribu, *f.,* raza, casta; (*fig.*) partido, bando; (*bot.*) grupo.

tribesman, *s.* miembro de una tribu.

triblet ['triblet], *s.* mandril de platero para hacer anillos.

tribrach ['tribræk], *s.* tribraquio.

tribulation [tribju:'leiʃən], *s.* tribulación, congoja, aflicción.

tribunal [trai'bju:nəl], *s.* tribunal, tribuna; (*for.*) juzgado, sala.

tribunate ['tribju:nit], *s.* tribunado.

tribune ['tribju:n], *s.* tribuna; tribuno.

tributary ['tribju:təri], *a.* tributario. — *s.* tributario, súbdito, vasallo; afluente (de un río).

tribute ['tribju:t], *s.* tributo, contribución; homenaje.

trice [trais], *v.t.* (*mar.*) izar, amarrar, ligar. — *s.* momento, instante, tris; *in a trice,* en un abrir y cerrar de ojos, en un (decir) Jesús.

tricennial [trai'seniəl], *a.* tricenal.

triceps ['traiseps], *s.* tríceps.

trichina [tri'ki:nə], *s.* (*med.*) triquina.

trichinosis [triki'nousis], s. triquinosis, f.

trick [trik], s. burla, engaño, fraude, socaliña, superchería; trampa, truco, burla, chasco; petardo, treta; costumbre, f., vicio, hábito; destreza, habilidad; estratagema, ardid, artería; parchazo, travesura; baza (juego de naipes); *dirty trick*, (fam.) (mala) pasada, perrada, bribonada; *to play a trick upon*, burlar, engañar; *to play (one's) tricks*, hacer suertes. — v.t. defraudar, engañar, petardear, embaucar; *to trick out* o *up*, ataviar, adornar, componerse. — v.i. vivir de trampas, trampear.

trickery ['trikəri], s. engaño, falsedad, trampería, ardid, trampa; compostura, adorno.

trickiness ['trikinis], s. astucia, habilidad, maña; (fam.) carácter difícil.

trickish, a. artificioso, embustero, astuto, trapacero, mañoso; (fam.) difícil.

trickle ['trikəl], v.i. gotear, correr gota a gota, destilar, chorrear, escurrir.

trickling, s. acción de gotear.

trickster ['trikstəɹ], s. engañador, trampista, m.f., petardista, m.f.

tricksy ['triksi], a. juguetón, retozón, travieso; aleve, artificioso, embustero; ataviado, compuesto.

tricky ['triki], a. tramposo, trapacero; (fam.) difícil, espinoso; (fam.) vicioso (de un animal).

tricolour ['trikələɹ], a. tricolor. — s. bandera tricolor.

tricycle ['traisikəl], s. triciclo.

trident ['traidənt], s. tridente.

tridentate [trai'denteit], a. tridente; (bot.) tridentado.

tried [traid], a. probado, leal, fiel. — p.p. [TRY].

triennial [trai'eniəl], a. trienal.

triennially, adv. cada tres años.

trier ['traiəɹ], s. (fam.) persona que porfía o que trabaja con tesón; experimentador, ensayador; censor, examinador, juez, m., verificador, experto; prueba, ensayo, toque.

trifid ['traifid], a. trífido.

trifle ['traifəl], v.t.; *to trifle with*, despilfarrar, malgastar, perder, desperdiciar; jugar con, burlarse de. — v.i. juguetear, chancear, bromear, holgar. — s. bagatela, friolera, fruslería, baratija, poca cosa; (coc.) dulce de crema. — adv. un poquito, algo.

trifler, s. chancero, necio; burlador.

trifling ['traifliŋ], a. pequeño, de poca importancia, insignificante; ligero, frívolo, fútil. — s. frivolidad, ligereza, broma.

triflingly, adv. de una manera frívola.

triflingness, s. frivolidad, insignificancia, futilidad.

trifoliate [trai'fouliət], a. trifoliado, trifoliáceo.

triform ['traifɔːɹm], a. triforme.

trig [trig], v.t. trabar (las ruedas), impedir que una rueda dé vueltas. — s. cuña, calza de rueda, galga. — a. acicalado, bien puesto, compuesto.

trigger, s. gatillo, disparador; tirante, calzo o pararruedas (de rueda).

triglyph ['traiglif], s. (arq.) tríglifo.

trigonal ['trigonəl], a. triangular.

trigonometric [trigənə'metrik], **trigonometrical** [trigənə'metrikəl], a. trigonométrico.

trigonometry [trigo'nɔmetri], s. trigonometría.

trihedral [trai'hiːdrəl], a.; **trihedron** [trai-'hiːdrɔn], s. triedro.

trilateral [trai'lætərəl], a. trilátero, trilateral.

trilingual [trai'liŋgwəl], a. trilingüe.

triliteral [trai'litərəl], a. trilítero.

trill [tril], v.t., v.i. trinar, hacer trinos; correr gota a gota, gotear. — s. trino, gorjeo, trinado.

trillion ['triljən], s. (Fr. y E.U.) trillón; (Ingl.) la tercera potencia de un millón.

trilobate ['trailobeit], a. (bot.) trilobado.

trilogy ['trilodʒi], s. trilogía.

trim [trim], v.t. componer, poner en orden, disponer, arreglar, asear, pulir; adaptar, ajustar; vestir, adornar, decorar, guarnecer (un vestido); despabilar (una lámpara); cortar un poco (cabellos, barba, etc.); atusar, recortar; arreglarse (las uñas); (carp.) desbastar, acepillar, alisar; (mar.) orientar; arrumar la cala; (agr.) podar, mondar. — v.i. vacilar, fluctuar; nadar entre dos aguas; *to trim off*, (mar.) atusar, recortar; *to trim (oneself) up*, arreglar(se), componerse, ataviar(se), hermosear. — a. compuesto, ajustado, adornado, ataviado, acicalado, elegante, en buen estado. — s. adorno, compostura, atavío, aderezo; vestido, traje; aparato, tocador; (mar.) calado; (mar.) disposición, orientación (de las velas); *in good trim*, en buen orden.

trimeter ['trimitəɹ], s. trímetro.

trimly, adv. bien, en buen orden, en regla, elegantemente.

trimmer ['triməɹ], s. guarnecedor, persona que arregla; contemporizador, persona que vacila; veleta; (carp.) solera; recortadora, desbastadora; (cost.) ribeteador.

trimming, s. guarnición (de vestido), galón, orla, franja; arreglo, ajuste; reprimenda, corrección; poda; (mar.) estiva (de la cala); orientación (de las velas); (carp.) desbaste, ajuste. — pl. accesorios.

trimness ['trimnis], s. aseo, buen orden, buen estado; elegancia, esbeltez.

trinal ['trainəl], a. trino, triple.

trine [train], s. juego de tres; (teol.) la Trinidad; (astr.) el aspecto de los planetas cuando distan entre sí 120°.

tringle ['triŋgəl], s. (arq.) tirante.

trinitarian [trini'tɛəriən], s., a. trinitario.

trinity ['triniti], s. trinidad.

trinket ['triŋket], s. joya; dije, chuchería.

trinomial [trai'noumiəl], s. (alg.) trinomio. — a. (biol.) con tres nombres; (mat.) de tres términos.

trio ['triːou], s. trío.

triolet ['triːolet], s. trioleto.

triones [trai'ouniːz], s.pl. (astr.) triones.

trip [trip], v.t.; *to trip (up)*, dar una zancadilla, hacer caer, trompicar; armar un lazo; (fig.) sorprender, descubrir, coger en falta, suplantar; (mar.) zarpar, levantar (el ancla); (mec.) disparar, soltar. — v.i. dar un paso falso, tropezar, resbalar, trompicar, titubear; faltar, engañarse; ir con paso ligero, andar con gracia, ir corriendo; *to trip up*, tropezar, trompicar; (fig.) tropezar, equivocarse; *to trip away* o *off*, irse con paso ligero, irse dando pasitos, irse corriendo. — s. zancadilla, paso falso, traspié, tropiezo; excursión, vuelta, viaje corto; (mar.) trayecto; (mar.) bordada, barloventeando; *trip hammer*, martinete de fragua.

tripartite [trai'pɑːɹtait], a. tripartito.

tripe [traip], s. callos, tripa(s), mondongo; (*vulg.*) barriga.

tripedal ['tripedəl], a. tripede.

tripetalous [trai'petələs], a. tripétalo.

triphthong ['trifθɔŋ], s. triptongo.

triple ['tripəl], a. triple, tresdoble. — v.t. triplicar.

triplet ['triplet], s. terno; cada uno de tres hermanos nacidos de un parto, tripleto, triplete; (*mús.*) tresillo; (*poét.*) terceto.

triplex ['tripleks], a. tríplice.

triplicate ['triplikit], a. triple, triplo, triplicado. — s. triplicata, tercera copia.

triplication, s. triplicación.

triplicity [tri'plisiti], s. triplicidad.

triply ['tripli], adv. triplemente, por triplicado.

tripod ['traipɔd], s. trípode.

tripos ['traipɔs], s. (*Univ. de Cambridge*) los exámenes para reválida y graduación.

tripper ['tripəɹ], s. excursionista, m.f., turista, m.f.; saltarín, bailador; el que da una zancadilla.

tripping, a. ligero, ágil, suelto. — s. error, falta, tropiezo, traspié; (*mar.*) acción de levantar (el ancla).

trippingly, adv. ligeramente, ágilmente, velozmente.

triptych ['triptitʃ], s. tríptico.

trireme ['trairi:m], s. trireme.

trisagion [tri'sægiən], s. trisagio.

trisect [trai'sekt], v.t. trisecar, tripartir.

trisection, s. trisección.

trisyllabic [traisi'læbik], a. trisilábico.

trisyllable [trai'siləbəl], s. trisílabo.

trite [trait], a. trillado, gastado, vulgar, envejecido, usado.

triteness, s. banalidad, vulgaridad, trivialidad, cosa muy usada.

tritheism ['trai'θi:izm], s. triteísmo.

triton ['traitən], s. tritón, gasterópodo.

tritone ['traitoun], s. trítono.

triturable, a. triturable.

triturate ['tritju:reit], v.t. triturar.

trituration, s. trituración.

triumph ['traiəmf], v.i. triunfar, vencer, salir victorioso, prosperar; gloriarse. — s. triunfo, victoria; alegría.

triumphal [trai'ʌmfəl], a. triunfal.

triumphant [trai'ʌmfənt], a. triunfante, triunfal, victorioso.

triumphantly, adv. triunfalmente, triunfantemente, victoriosamente, en triunfo.

triumpher ['traiəmfəɹ], s. triunfador.

triumvir [trai'ʌmvəɹ], s. triunviro.

triumvirate [trai'ʌmvəreit], s. triunvirato.

triune [trai'ju:n], a. trino y uno.

trivet ['trivit], s. trípode, trébedes, f.pl.

trivial ['triviəl], a. trivial, fútil, sin importancia, insignificante; bajo, vulgar, frívolo.

triviality [trivi'æliti], s. trivialidad, futilidad, frivolidad, vulgaridad.

trivium ['triviəm], s. trivio.

tri-weekly [trai'wi:kli], a. que sucede o sale tres veces por semana.

troat [trout], v.i. bramar. — s. bramido del venado cuando está en celo.

trochaic [tro'keiik], a. trocaico.

troche [trouk, trouʃ], s. tablilla, trocisco, comprimido medicinal.

trochee [tro'ki:], s. troqueo.

trochlea ['trokliə], s. (*anat.*) trocla, polea.

trochoid ['trokɔid], s. (*geom.*) trocoide. — a. (*anat.*) que gira sobre su propio eje.

trod [trɔd], **trodden** ['trɔdən], pret., p.p. [TREAD].

troglodyte ['trɔglodait], s. troglodita, m.f.

trogon ['trougən], s. (*orn.*) quetzal, trogón.

Trojan ['troudʒən], s., a. troyano.

troll [troul], v.t., v.i. corretear, andorrear; dar vueltas, voltear, girar, rodar; chirriar, canturrear, canturriar; pescar con caña por la popa de un bote. — s. (*mús.*) canon; giro, vuelta, rodeo; pesca con caña; duende, enano, (*ant.*) gigante.

trolley ['trɔli], s. trole, cangrejo; vagoneta; carro; *trolley(-bus)*, trolebús.

trollop ['trɔləp], s. gorrona, zangarilleja.

trombone ['trɔmboun], s. trom.bón.

troop [tru:p], s. tropel, turba, caterva; banda, compañía, cuadrilla, escuadrón; compañía de actores. — pl. tropas; *troop-carrier*, buque o avión para transporte de tropas. — v.i. venir de tropel; marchar en orden militar; atroparse, agavillarse, apiñarse, juntarse, agolparse; *to troop away, troop off*, retirarse juntos o en tropel.

trooper, s. soldado de caballería; corcel de guerra.

troopial ['tru:piəl], s. (*orn.*) turpial, turicha.

trope [troup], s. tropo.

trophied ['troufid], a. cargado o adornado de trofeos.

trophy ['troufi], s. trofeo.

tropic ['trɔpik], s. trópico.

tropical ['trɔpikəl], a. tropical, de los trópicos; (*ret.*) trópico.

tropically, adv. figuradamente, metafóricamente.

tropological [trɔpo'lɔdʒikəl], a. tropológico.

tropology [tro'pɔlodʒi], s. tropología.

trot [trɔt], v.i. trotar, ir al trote. — v.t. pasar al trote, hacer trotar; *to trot out*, salir al trote; (*fig., fam.*) salir con (un dicho), sacar o salir a relucir. — s. trote; (*fam.*) niño, niña; *jog-trot*, pequeño trote.

troth [trouθ], s. fe, f., promesa, palabra de honor; verdad; lealtad, fidelidad; *to plight one's troth*, prometerse, desposarse, dar palabra y mano.

trotter, s. trotador, trotón; (*fam.*) mano o pie de carnero.

trotting, s. trote. — a. trotador, trotón.

troubadour ['tru:bədɔ:ɹ], s. trovador, juglar.

trouble ['trʌbəl], v.t. molestar, turbar, incomodar, agitar, conturbar, perturbar, disturbar, importunar, enturbiar, revolver, desazonar, hostigar, atribular, atormentar, inquietar, afligir. — v.i. darse molestia, incomodarse, apurarse; *to trouble oneself*, inquietarse, preocuparse, apurarse, molestarse; *to trouble someone for something*, pedir a uno una cosa; *to trouble someone to do a thing*, rogar a uno que haga una cosa. — s. pena, congoja, aflicción, cuita, tormento; inquietud, perplejidad; molestia, dificultad, fatiga, turbación, perturbación, disturbio, confusión; desazón, f., disgusto, pesadumbre, f.; incomodidad, impertinencia, enfado, engorro; *it is not worth the trouble*, no vale la pena; *to be in trouble*, hallarse en un apuro; (*fam.*) estar encinta; *to cause* o *stir up trouble*, armar un lío (*fam.*), dar guerra.

troubled ['trʌbled], a. turbado, agitado,

turbio; preocupado, atormentado, inquieto; *to fish in troubled waters*, pescar en río revuelto.

troubler ['trʌbləɹ], *s.* alborotador, inquietador, perturbador.

troublesome ['trʌbəlsəm], *a.* molesto, pesado, aburrido, fastidioso, penoso, oneroso, fatigoso, gravoso, embarazoso, incómodo, impertinente, importuno; tormentoso; travieso, difícil.

troublesomeness, *s.* fastidio, pena, molestia, embarazo; dificultad, importunidad.

troublous ['trʌbləs], *a.* tumultuoso, turbado, turbulento, inquieto; turbulento, travieso.

trough [troːf], *s.* artesa, dornajo, gamella, (*Amér.*) batea, cubeta, gamellón, artesón; vivero; tragadero (del mar); *drinking-trough*, abrevadero; *kneading-trough*, artesa.

trounce [trauns], *v.t.* (*fam.*) zurrar, batir, dar de palos, castigar duramente.

troupe [truːp], *s.* compañía (de teatro, etc.).

trousering ['trauzəriŋ], *s.* paño para pantalones.

trousers ['trauzəɹz], *s.* pantalones, calzones; *plus four trousers*, pantalones de golf.

trousseau ['truːsou], *s.* ajuar (de novia).

trout [traut], *s.* (*ict.*) trucha.

trover ['trouvəɹ], *s.* (*for.*) adquisición *o* apropiación; causa *o* pleito para recuperar lo que otro posee ilegalmente.

trow [trau, trou], *v.t., v.i.* (*ant.*) meter mientes, parar mientes, discurrir.

trowel ['trauəl], *s.* trulla, paleta, llana; desplantador.

troy, *s.* peso para el oro, plata y drogas medicinales, que es de 12 onzas avoirdupois cada libra (0·373 kgs.).

truancy, *s.* tuna, briba.

truant ['truːənt], *s., a., v.i.* holgazanear, vagabundear, ausentarse. — *s.* novillero (*fam.*); tunante, holgazán, vagabundo, pícaro; *to play truant*, hacer novillos, andar a la tuna. — *a.* holgazán, perezoso.

truantly, *adv.* como holgazán, haraganamente; haciendo novillos.

truce [truːs], *s.* tregua.

truck [trʌk], *s.* carretón, carro; (*E.U.*) camión; carruaje *o* carretilla de mano; furgón de plataforma; rueda de madera; rueda de cureña; trueque, cambio; pago en mercancías; (*mar.*) bolas, vertellos; (*fam.*) artículos sin valor, cachivaches; (*fam.*) trato, relaciones. — *v.t.* trocar, cambiar. — *v.i.* trocar, cambiar, traficar, hacer trueques.

truckage, *s.* trueque, cambio; camionaje, acarreo, carreteo.

trucker, *s.* carretonero; verdulero.

truckle ['trʌkəl], *v.i.* arrastrarse, hacer la zalá, gitanear; someterse, ceder. — *s.* rodaja, rueda pequeña; *truckle bed*, carriola, cama con rodajas.

truckman, *s.* carretonero, carretero.

truculence ['trʌkjuːləns], *s.* agresividad, turbulencia; truculencia.

truculent ['trʌkjuːlənt], *a.* agresivo, turbulento; truculento.

trudge [trʌdʒ], *v.i.* ir a pie; marchar con pena, andar despacio con fatiga y afán.

true [truː], *a.* verdadero, verídico, seguro, cierto, justo; fiel, leal; sincero, ingenuo; genuino, propio, puro, natural; *true blue*, (*fig.*) patriótico; conservador.

true-born, *s.* legítimo, de casta, de buena cepa.

true-bred, *a.* de pura sangre, de casta legítima.

true-hearted, *a.* de corazón, sincero, leal, fiel.

trueness, *s.* verdad, fidelidad, sinceridad, autenticidad, candidez, franqueza.

truffle ['trʌfəl], *s.* trufa, criadilla de tierra.

truffled, *a.* guarnecido con trufas.

truism ['truːizm], *s.* axioma, *m.*, verdad incontestable; perogrullada.

trull [trʌl], *s.f.* peliforra, puta.

truly ['truːli], *adv.* verdaderamente, en verdad, a fe; efectivamente, realmente, exactamente; sinceramente.

trump [trʌmp], *s.* triunfo (juego de naipes); (*mús., ant.*) trompeta; (*fig., fam.*) persona preciosa, joya, preciosidad. — *v.t.* cortar con el triunfo, fallar (naipes). — *v.i.* jugar triunfo; tocar la trompeta; *to trump up lies*, inventar mentiras; *trump-card*, comodín, malilla, naipe de triunfo.

trumpery ['trʌmpəri], *s.* oropel(es), hojarasca, relumbrón, adorno falso, baratija; engaño, falsedad, fraude; sandeces, *f.pl.* — *a.* malo, falso, sin valor, de pacotilla.

trumpet ['trʌmpet], *s.* trompeta, trompetilla, bocina, clarín; *ear-trumpet*, trompetilla acústica; *to blow one's own trumpet*, darse importancia, alzar el gallo. — *v.t., v.i.* pregonar a son de trompeta; trompetear, tocar la trompeta; (*fig.*) divulgar.

trumpet-creeper, *s.* (*bot.*) jazmín trompeta.

trumpeter ['trʌmpetəɹ], *s.* trompeta, *m.*, trompetero; pregonero; (*orn.*) agamí.

trumpet-fish, *s.* centrisco.

trumpeting, *s.* trompeteo; divulgación; berrido (del elefante); (*fig.*) berrido, grito desaforado.

trumpet-tongued, *a.* vocinglero.

truncate [trʌŋ'keit], *v.t.* truncar.

truncate, truncated, *a.* (*bot.*) cortado, truncado.

truncation [trʌŋ'keiʃən], *s.* truncamiento, mutilación, tronca.

truncheon ['trʌntʃən], *s.* tranca, porra, cachiporra, garrote, bastón de mando. — *v.t.* dar palos a, apalear, dar garrotazos a.

trundle ['trʌndəl], *v.t., v.i.* rodar, hacer rodar. — *s.* rodaja, carretón; barra de linterna.

trundle-bed, *s.* carriola.

trunk [trʌŋk], *s.* tronco; tallo; (*f.c.*) línea principal; tronco, busto; trompa (del elefante); fuste de columna; baúl, maleta, cofre; *trunk hose*, bragas, calzas trusas; *trunk line*, línea principal (de ferrocarril, etc.); *trunk-line*, (*teléfonos*) línea interurbana; *trunk-call*, (*teléfonos*) conferencia interurbana; *trunk-road*, carretera principal, ruta nacional.

trunk-maker, *s.* cofrero.

trunnion ['trʌnjən], *s.* muñón.

truss [trʌs], *v.t.* (*mar.*) izar; apretar, atirantar, apuntalar; empaquetar; afianzar una ave antes de guisarla; (*fig.*) ahorcar un criminal. — *s.* lío, atado, haz, fardo; armadura, armazón; braguero, vendaje herniario; (*Ingl.*) 56 lbs de paja o 60 de heno; (*mar.*) guardín, troza; (*bot.*) racino, mazorca; *truss beam*, riostra; *truss work*, entramado.

trust [trʌst], *v.t.* fiarse a, confiar en, confiarse a, tener confianza en, creer en; contar con; vender al fiado. — *v.i.* esperar, tener confianza, esperar con confianza; *to trust to o in* *a person*, contar con uno; *to trust oneself to someone*, entregarse en brazos de uno. — *s.* confianza, creencia, expectación, esperanza, fe, *f.*; cargo de confianza; confidencia; depósito, cargo; seguridad; crédito sin fianza; (*for.*) fideicomiso; (*com.*) 'trust', gremio; *to hold in trust*, guardar en depósito, *to sell on trust*, vender a crédito; *to give on trust*, dar fiado; *on trust*, al fiado; *trust deed of sale*, (*for.*) escritura de venta condicionada.

trustee [trʌs'ti:], *s.* depositario, guardián; comisario, fideicomisario, fiduciario, administrador, síndico; director de una compañía.

trusteeship [trʌs'ti:ʃip], *s.* administración, cargo de fideicomisario; curatela, albaceazgo.

truster, *s.* persona que confía, que hace crédito.

trustful, *a.* confiado; leal, fiel.

trustfully, *adv.* confiadamente.

trustfulness, *s.* confianza entera.

trustily, *adv.* lealmente, fielmente, honradamente.

trustiness, *s.* lealtad, fidelidad, honradez, probidad, integridad.

trustingly, *adv.* con confianza.

trustless, *a.* inconstante, infiel.

trustworthy ['trʌstwə:ɹði], *a.* confiable, fiable, seguro, fidedigno.

trusty ['trʌsti], *a.* fiel, leal, seguro, constante, íntegro; fuerte, firme.

truth [tru:θ], *s.* verdad, veracidad, realidad; fidelidad, constancia, honradez, lealtad, probidad; exactitud; *of a truth*, en verdad, en realidad; *the plain truth*, la pura verdad.

truthful, *a.* veraz; verídico, verdadero, exacto.

truthless, *a.* mentiroso, falso, inconstante, fementido.

try [trai], *v.t., v.i.* (*pret.*, *p.p.* **tried**) procurar, intentar, tratar de, tentar; ensayar, experimentar, probar, poner a prueba; emprender; hacer lo posible; sondear, verificar, tantear; cansar, exasperar, fatigar, molestar, preocupar; (*for.*) juzgar, procesar, ver (un litigio); purificar, refinar, afinar (los metales por fundición, etc.); *to try on clothes*, ensayar un vestido; *to try one's luck*, probar ventura; *to try the experiment*, (*fig.*) hacer la prueba; *to try out*, poner a prueba; *to try hard*, esforzarse (para), porfiarse. — *s.* prueba, experiencia; ensayo, tentativa, esfuerzo; *try-sail*, (*mar.*) la vela mayor de un paquete; *try-out*, (*fam.*) prueba, ensayo.

trying, *a.* difícil, molesto, penoso, fatigoso, contrariador, cansado.

tryst [traist], *s.* cita, lugar de cita. — *v.t., v.i.* citar, dar una cita a; acudir a una cita.

tsetse ['setsi], *s.* tsetsé, *f.*

tub [tʌb], *v.t.* encajonar, encubar, entinar; (*fam.*) bañar. — *s.* cuba, cubeta; artesa, artesón; tonel, barril, batea, tina; *to have a tub*, (*fam.*) bañarse, tomar un baño; *wash-tub*, cuba o tina de lejía o de lavar; *bath-tub*, baño, bañera; *mash-tub*, cuba de bracear la cerveza; *tub-thumper*, (*fam.*) gerundio.

tuba, *s.* (*mús.*) tuba.

tube [tju:b], *v.t.* proveer de tubos. — *s.* tubo, cañón; cámara de aire (neumáticos); metro, ferrocarril subterráneo; (*anat.*) trompa; canal, conducto.

tubeless, *a.* sin cámara interior (neumáticos).

tuber ['tju:bəɹ], *s.* (*bot.*) **tubercle**, *s.* tubérculo.

tubercular [tju:'bə:ɹkjuːləɹ], **tuberculous** [tju:'bə:ɹkjuːləs], *a.* tuberculoso.

tuberose ['tju:bərous], *s.* tuberosa.

tuberosity [tju:bə'rɔsiti], *s.* (*anat.*) tuberosidad.

tuberous ['tju:bərəs], *a.* tuberoso.

tubing ['tju:biŋ], *s.* tubería; entubación, entubado, entubamiento.

tubular ['tju:bjuːləɹ], *a.* tubular.

tubulate ['tju:bjuːlit], *v.t.* dar forma de tubo a; poner en tubos.

tubulated, *a.* provisto o que tiene forma de tubo.

tubule, *s.* túbulo, tubito.

tuck [tʌk], *v.t.* remangar, asobarcar, arremangar; recoger; arropar, alforzar, hacer alforzas. — *s.* (*fam.*) dulces, golosinas; filete, pliegue, doblez; recogido, alforza; (*mar.*) falda, arca de popa; (*ant.*) espada estrecha y larga, estoque; *to tuck in*, arropar; (*fam.*) comerse, tragar, embuchar.

tucker, *s.* escote, camisolín; (*cost.*) alforzador; *in (his) best bib and tucker*, (*fam.*) hecho un brazo de mar o más galán que Mingo.

tucket ['tʌkit], *s.* (*ant.*) toque de trompetas.

Tuesday ['tju:zdi], *s.* martes; *Shrove Tuesday*, martes de carnestolendas o de carnaval.

tufa ['tju:fə], **tuff**, *s.* toba, tufa.

tufaceous [tju:'feiʃəs], *a.* tobáceo, tubáceo.

tuft [tʌft], *v.t.* adornar, guarnecer de copetes, penachos, etc. — *s.* penacho, borla, copete; ramillete, manojo; moño; tupé; penacho, copete, cresta de ave; (*bot.*) corimbo; *tuft-hunter*, zalamero, quitapelillos, *m.*; (*mil.*) pompón.

tufted, tufty, *a.* copetudo, frondoso; penachudo, sembrado de penachos, encopetado; como ramillete.

tug [tʌg], *v.t., v.i.* arrancar, tirar (de), tirar o sacar con esfuerzo; esforzarse, luchar; remolcar, halar. — *s.* tirón, esfuerzo; (*mar.*) remolcador; coyunda; *tug of war*, lucha a la cuerda.

tugboat, *s.* remolcador.

tugger ['tʌgəɹ], *s.* persona que tira con fuerza, que da tirones.

tuition [tju:'iʃən], *s.* enseñanza, educación, instrucción; (*ant.*) guarda, tutela.

tulip ['tju:lip], *s.* tulipán; *tulip tree*, tulipero.

tulle [tu:l], *s.* tul.

tumble ['tʌmbəl], *v.i.* saltar, dar saltos; dar brincos, voltear, dar vueltas como los volteadores; rodar, menearse, agitarse, volverse, revolverse; desplomarse, hundirse; dar en tierra, caer, venirse abajo; *to tumble down*, caer, dar en tierra, desplomarse; *to tumble into bed*, echarse en la cama; *to tumble out of bed*, saltar fuera de la cama; *to tumble over*, chocar (con), volcar; caerse; *to tumble to the meaning of something*, (*fam.*) caer en la cuenta, caer en ello. — *v.t.* hacer caer, lanzar o echar con violencia; echar abajo, derribar; volcar, trastornar; cazar al vuelo; precipitar; arrugar o ajar (ropa blanca o vestidos); desordenar, desarreglar. — *s.* caída, vuelco, voltereta.

tumble-down ['tʌmbəldaun], *a.* destrozado, ruinoso, en ruinas, desvencijado.

tumbler, *s.* saltador, saltimbanquis, saltabanco, titiritero; vaso para agua; cortadillo; dominguillo; (*orn.*) pichón volteador o derrocante; (*mec.*) tambor; conmutador oscilante.

tumbling, *s.* caída, hundimiento.

tumbrel, tumbril ['tʌmbrəl], *s.* banquillo de zambullida; carreta, chirrión; (*art.*) furgón, carro de artillería.

tumefaction [tju:mi'fækʃən], *s.* tumefacción, hinchazón, *f.*

tumefy ['tju:mifai], *v.t.* entumecer, hinchar. — *v.i.* entumecerse, hincharse.

tumid ['tju:mid], *a.* (*med.*) hinchado, turgente, tumescente; (*fig.*) túmido, hinchado.

tumidity [tju:'miditi], *s.* hinchazón, *f.*, turgencia; (*fig.*) hinchazón, *f.*

tumour ['tju:mər], *s.* tumor.

tump [tʌmp], *s.* terrero, montecillo; (*agr.*) terrón. — *v.t.* (*prov.*) formar un montón de tierra alrededor de una planta; *tump-line,* correa en la frente o pecho para ayudar a sobrellevar la carga de la espalda.

tumular, *a.* en montecillo, abultado.

tumulose ['tju:mju:lous], **tumulous** ['tju:-mju:ləs], *a.* montuoso.

tumult ['tju:mʌlt], *s.* tumulto, alboroto, conmoción, motín, agitación; desorden; agitación de ánimo.

tumultuarily, *adv.* tumultuariamente, en desorden.

tumultuary [tju:'mʌltju:əri], *a.* tumultuario.

tumultuous [tju:'mʌltju:əs], *a.* tumultuoso.

tumultuously, *adv.* tumultuosamente, en desorden, de tropel.

tumultuousness, *s.* tumulto, turbación, turbulencia; estado tumultuoso.

tumulus ['tju:mju:ləs], *s.* (*pl.* **tumuli**) túmulo.

tun [tʌn], *s.* cuba; tunel, tonel, tonelada de vino de 252 galones (981·38 l.); agujero. — *v.t.* embarrilar, envasar, entonelar.

tuna, *s.* (*E.U.*) atún.

tunable ['tju:nəbəl], *a.* musical, armonioso, cantable; que se puede templar o afinar.

tunably, *adv.* armoniosamente; templadamente.

tune [tju:n], *s.* aire, tono, tonada; concordancia, consonancia, armonía; afinación; humor, acuerdo; *in tune,* afinado, templado; acordado, armonioso; (*fig.*) de acuerdo; *out of tune,* desafinado, destemplado, desentonado, falso; *to sing in tune,* cantar justo; *to the tune of,* (*fam.*) por o hasta la suma de. — *v.t.* (*up*) templar, afinar, entonar; afinar, sintonizar (radio, etc.); poner a punto, ajustar (motores). — *v.i.* (*up*) templar (instrumentos); (*in*) sintonizar, coger (radio); poner a punto, adaptar (automóviles); (*fam.*) tararear.

tuneful, *a.* canoro, armonioso, melodioso, dulce.

tuneless, *a.* sin armonía, discordante, desentonado, disonante.

tuner ['tju:nər], *s.* templador, afinador; (sistema) sintonizador, selector (de receptor).

tungstate ['tʌŋsteit], *s.* tungestato.

tungsten ['tʌŋstən], *s.* tungsteno.

tungstic ['tʌŋstik], *a.* túngstico.

tunic ['tju:nik], *s.* túnica.

tunicated ['tju:nikeitid], *a.* (*bot.*) membranoso.

tunicle ['tju:nikəl], *s.* tegumento, túnica; (*igl.*) tunicela.

tuning ['tju:niŋ], *s.* afinación, templadura; sintonización (de radio).

tuning-fork, *s.* diapasón normal.

tuning-hammer, tuning-key, *s.* templador, llave de afinador.

tunnage ['tʌnidʒ], *s.* derecho de tonelaje.

tunnel ['tʌnəl], *s.* túnel; socavón; cañón de chimenea; embudo; especie de red; *tunnel-net,* red abocinada. — *v.t., v.i.* horadar un túnel, construir un túnel; formar en embudo.

tunnelling, *s.* construcción de túneles, horadación.

tunny ['tʌni], *s.* atún.

tup [tʌp], *v.t.* cubrir el macho a la hembra (carneros). — *v.i.* copularse (carneros). — *s.* (*zool.*) morueco, borrego; cabeza del martinete.

tupelo ['tju:pelou], *s.* (*bot.*) nisa (*Nyssa aquatica*).

turban ['tə:rbən], *s.* turbante.

turbaned, *a.* cubierto con un turbante.

turbary ['tə:rbəri], *s.* turbera; *common of turbary,* (*for.*) derecho de cavar turba en terreno ajeno.

turbid ['tə:rbid], *a.* turbio, túrbido.

turbidity [tə:r'biditi], *s.* turbia, turbiedad.

turbinal ['tə:rbinəl], **turbinate** ['tə:rbineit], *a.* (*anat., bot.*) en forma de peonza.

turbine ['tə:rbain], *s.* turbina.

turboprop, *s., a.* (de) turbohélice.

turbot ['tə:rbət], *s.* (*ict.*) rodaballo, rombo.

turbulence, turbulency, *s.* turbulencia, alboroto, confusión, tumulto.

turbulent ['tə:rbju:lənt], *a.* turbulento, agitado, tempestuoso, tumultuoso, revoltoso, levantisco; violento, insubordinado.

turcism ['tə:rsizm], *s.* (*ant.*) religión o costumbres turcomanas.

turcoman ['tə:rkomæn], *s., a.* turcomano.

turd, *s.* (*vulg.*) cámara, excremento.

turdus ['tə:rdəs], *s.* (*orn.*) tordo.

tureen [tju:'ri:n], *s.* sopera, salsera; *soup-tureen,* sopera; *sauce-tureen,* salsera.

turf [tə:rf], *s.* césped, tepe; turba (combustible); *the turf* o *Turf,* campo de carreras, hipódromo. — *v.t.* cubrir de céspedes, encespedar; *turf-pit,* hornaguera.

turfiness, *s.* naturaleza del césped, abundancia de césped; estado turboso.

turfing, *s.* encespedamiento.

turfy ['tə:rfi], *a.* cubierto de césped, encespado; turboso.

turgent ['tə:rdʒənt], **turgid** ['tə:rdʒid]; *a.* turgente, (*poét.*) túrgido; (*fig.*) hinchado, ampuloso.

turgescence [tə:r'dʒesəns], *s.* turgencia; (*fig.*) hinchazón, *f.*, ampulosidad.

turgidity [tə:r'dʒiditi], *s.* turgencia; hinchazón, *f.*, ampulosidad.

Turk [tə:rk], *s.* turco.

Turkish, *a.* turco, turquesco.

turkey ['tə:rki], *s.* pavo, pava; (*Cuba*) guanajo; (*Méj.*) guajalote.

turkey-buzzard, *s.* aura.

turkey-cock, *s.* gallipavo.

turkey-hen, *s. f.* pava.

turk's cap, *s.* (*bot.*) martagón.

turmeric ['tə:rmərik], *s.* cúrcuma.

turmoil ['tə:rmoil], *s.* tumulto, baraúnda, estruendo, alboroto, turbación, disturbio, zaragata, agitación. — *v.t.* turbar, agitar; atormentar. — *v.i.* atormentarse, inquietarse, agitarse.

turn [tə:rn], *v.t.* (*pret.* y *p.p.* **turned**) hacer girar, torcer, dar vueltas a; invertir, poner en sentido inverso, trastocar, volver al revés; (*fig.*) mirar a los diferentes lados de, volver y revolver en la mente; efectuar (saltos mortales); aplicar o dedicar a diferente uso u objeto; desviar, dar nueva dirección a; adaptar, convertir o pervertir, transformar, transmutar, volver; traducir, parafrasear; voltear, rodear un flanco (de un ejército); dar la vuelta a, torcer, encorvar, doblar hacia atrás; embotar (el filo de un cuchillo, etc.); hacer fermentar, hacer agriar o acedar; marear, dar nauseas o asco; infatuar; inquietar, perturbar, hacer vertiginoso; hacer marchar, despedir, enviar, echar, arrojar (fuera, etc.); enroscar (un tornillo); tornear, dar buena forma, redondear (una frase, un concepto, etc.); *to turn about*, volver, volver de nuevo; *to turn adrift*, despedir, rechazar, soltar; *to turn against*, hacerse enemigo de, hacer frente a; *to turn aside*, alejar, desviar; *to turn away*, despedir, echar, alejar, separar, rechazar; *to turn back*, volver atrás, devolver; *to turn one's back on*, volver la espalda a; *to turn down*, plegar, doblar, poner boca abajo, hacer bajar, hacer un pliegue a; (*fam.*) rechazar, abandonar; *to turn from*, hacer desistir de, desviar de; *to turn the head*, trastornar la cabeza; *to turn in*, volver adentro; (*fam.*) ir a la cama; *to turn into*, transformar o convertir en, cambiar en; *to turn into ridicule*, hacer chacota de; *to turn one's mind to*, aplicarse a, dedicarse, dirigir su espíritu hacia; *to turn off*, cerrar (una llave, etc.); despachar, doblar, apartar; *to turn on*, abrir (una llave, etc.); encender, dar (la luz, etc.); *to turn out*, expeler, arrojar, despedir; sacar hacia afuera; apagar (luz, etc.); volver del revés; (*fam.*) levantarse de la cama; *to turn over*, volver, volver de nuevo; recorrer; invertir, reversar, transferir a; entregar; negociar, comerciar por el montante de; *to turn over the leaves of (a book)*, hojear (un libro); *to turn over a new leaf*, (*fig.*) empezar vida nueva, enmendarse; *to turn round*, volver, volver de nuevo; *to turn the stomach*, dar asco; *to turn to good account*, poner a provecho; *to turn to ridicule*, volver en ridículo; *to turn up*, volver arriba, levantar, arremangar; (*agr.*) revolver; *to turn up the eyes*, levantar los ojos; *to turn up one's nose at*, (*fig.*) desdeñar; *to turn upon*, volver sobre, revolver sobre; *to turn upside down*, trastornar, volcar, zozobrar. — *v.i.* volver, volverse, retornar, torcer(se), girar; desviarse; ponerse, volverse, hacerse, convertirse, venir a ser; ponerse a, comenzar; avinagrarse (el vino), volverse, agriarse (la leche), acedarse; infatuarse, inquietarse, perturbarse; marearse; resultar, terminar; tornearse; (*mar.*) bornear, virar; *to turn about (o around)*, voltearse, volverse; *to turn aside*, separarse, desviarse; *to turn away*, volverse, desviarse; *to turn back*, retroceder, volverse (atrás); *to turn home*, irse a casa; *to turn in*, volver, entrar, volverse adentro; doblar(se) hacia dentro; (*fam.*) ir a la cama; *to turn into*, entrar en; transformarse en, convertirse en; *to turn off*, desviarse, apartarse; torcer, girar; *to turn on*, volverse contra; *to turn out*, volver afuera; hacerse, venir a ser, acabar por ser, resultar; suceder, pasar; levantarse de la cama; salir; *to turn over*, volcar, voltear, volverse, revolverse, voltar, dar vueltas; *to*

turn round, volverse; *to turn short*, dar media vuelta; *to turn to*, ponerse a, empezar a, volver a, recurrir a, acudir a, dirigirse hacia; *to turn up*, volver arriba, arremangarse; (*fam.*) llegar, presentarse; acontecer, suceder, pasar; *to turn upon*, volver sobre, recaer sobre; depender de; *my head turns*, la cabeza me da vueltas; *the wind turns*, el viento vuelve.

turn [təːʍn], *s.* giro, revolución, vuelta; paseo; viraje, vuelta, rodeo, rocodo; vez, *f.*, turno; tanda, revezo; dirección, marcha, curso; inclinación, genio, carácter, propensión; oportunidad, ocasión; vicisitud, fase, *f.*, cambio, mudanza; procedimiento, proceder; servicio, favor, asistencia, obsequio; (mala) pasada o partida; utilidad, provecho; aspecto, faz, *f.*; *friendly turn*, favor; *ill turn*, pasada, partida serrana; *at every turn*, a todo momento, a cada instante; *by turns*, por turno, alternativamente; *in his turn*, a su turno; *to do a good turn to*, prestar un servicio a; *to have a turn for*, ser aficionado a, tener aptitud para; *to take a turn*, dar un paseo, dar una vuelta; *one good turn deserves another*, amor con bien se paga.

turnbuckle ['təːʍnbʌkəl], *s.* tarabilla, torniquete, tensor de tornillo.

turncoat ['təːʍnkout], *s.* chaquetero, desertor, tránsfuga, *m.f.*, renegado; *to become a turncoat*, volver (la) casaca.

turner, *s.* tornero; gimnasta, *m.f.*

turnery ['təːʍnəri], *s.* tornería, arte del tornero.

turning, *s.* vuelta, revuelta, recodo, ángulo; bocacalle, *m.*; *turning-point*, punto decisivo.

turnip ['təːʍnip], *s.* nabo.

turnkey ['təːʍnkiː], *s.* carcelero, llavero de una cárcel.

turnout ['təːʍnaut], *s.* (*fam.*) vestidos, uniforme, gala; salida de personas; huelga; séquito, tren; tripulación; (*com.*) producto neto.

turnover ['təːʍnouvər], *s.* especie de pastel; (*com.*) suma del movimiento, ingresos totales, ventas; vuelta, vuelco, voltereta.

turnpike, *s.* (*ant.*) molinete; camino de portazgo, barrera de portazgo; *turnpike road*, carretera principal, autopista de peaje; *turnpike keeper*, guardabarrera, *m.f.*

turn-screw, *s.* destornillador.

turnsole, *s.* (*bot.*) heliotropo, tornasol, girasol, mirasol.

turnspit ['təːʍnspit], *s.* rueda de asador; galopín que revuelve el asador.

turnstile ['təːʍnstail], *s.* molinete, torniquete.

turn-stone, *s.* (*orn.*) revuelvepiedras, *m.*

turntable, *s.* plataforma o placa giratoria; plato (de fonógrafo).

turpentine ['təːʍpentain], *s.* trementina, aguarrás; *turpentine-tree*, (*bot.*) terebinto.

turpeth ['təːʍpeθ], *s.* turbit.

turpitude ['təːʍpitjuːd], *s.* depravación, vileza, infamia, torpeza, (*ant.*) turpitud.

turquoise ['təːʍkwɑːz], *s.* turquesa.

turret ['tʌret], *s.* torrecilla; (*mar.*) torreblindada.

turreted, *a.* en forma de torre, que tiene torre.

turtle ['təːʍtəl], *s.* (*orn.*) tórtolo, tórtola; (*zool.*) tortuga; *to turn turtle*, volcar o voltear patas arriba.

turtle-dove, *s.* tórtola.

turtle-shell, *s.* carey.

Tuscan ['tʌskən], *s.*, *a.* toscano.
tush [tʌʃ], *interj.* ¡bah! ¡ca!
tusk [tʌsk], *s.* canino, diente canino; colmillo, presa.
tusked, tusky, *a.* colmilludo.
tussle ['tʌsəl], *s.* lucha, agarrada, pelea. — *v.t.*, *v.i.* tener una agarrada, luchar.
tussock ['tʌsək], *s.* copete, penacho, montecillo de hierbas crecientes.
tussore [tʌ'sɔːɪ], *s.* gusano de seda de la India; seda tusá o tussá.
tut [tʌt], *interj.* ¡bah! ¡vaya! ¡basta! ¡mal haya!
tutelage ['tjuːtəlidʒ], *s.* tutela, tutoría, protección.
tutelar ['tjuːtelər], **tutelary** [tjuːteləri], *a.* tutelar; *tutelar angel*, ángel de la guarda; *tutelar saint*, santo patrón.
tutor ['tjuːtəɪ], *s.* tutor, preceptor, ayo, repetidor. — *v.t.* enseñar, instruir; reprender; hacer la lección a; ser curador de. — *v.i.* dar clases, dar clases particulares, dar seminarios.
tutorage ['tjuːtoridʒ], *s.* tutela, tutoría, funciones de preceptor, (*for.*) curaduría.
tutoress, *s.f.* tutora, tutriz; maestra de escuela; aya.
tutorial [tjuː'tɔːriəl], *s.* seminario (de universidad), clase particular.
tutoring, *s.* instrucción, enseñanza.
tutorship, *s.* funciones de tutor, repetidor, etc.
tutsan ['tʌtsən], *s.* (*bot.*) todabuena.
tutty ['tʌti], *s.* atutía, tutía.
tuxedo, *s.* (*E.U.*) smoking [DINNER JACKET].
tuwhit [tuː'wit], **tuwhoo** [tuː'wuː], *s.* grito del buho. — *v.i.* gritar el buho.
twaddle ['twodəl], *s.* habladuría, patrañas, disparates, tonterías. — *v.t.*, *v.i.* disparatar, parlotear.
twaddler, *s.* disparatador.
twain [twein], *s.*, *a.* (*ant.*) dos, un par.
twang [twæŋ], *s.* sonido vibrante; tan, tintín; gangueo, tonillo nasal; punteado de una cuerda. — *v.i.* ganguear; vibrar. — *v.t.* hacer vibrar; hablar gangueando.
'twas [twoz], *contr.* [IT WAS].
twayblade ['tweibleid], *s.* orquídea de dos hojas radicales.
tweak [twiːk], *v.t.* pellizcar retorciendo. — *s.* pellizco retorcido.
tweed [twiːd], *s.* paño asargado, cheviot, 'tweed'.
tweedle ['twiːdəl], *v.t.* atraer o seducir con música. — *v.i.* chirriar, tocar mal o con descuido.
tweet, *s.* piada, gorjeo. — *v.t.*, *v.i.* piar, gorjear.
tweeter, *s.* (*elec.*) altavoz para superfrecuencias.
tweezers ['twiːzəɪz], *s.pl.* alicates, tenacillas, pinzas.
twelfth ['twelfθ], *a.* duodécimo, doceno, doce; *Twelfth Night*, (víspera del) día de los Reyes; *Twelfth Day*, día de los Reyes. — *s.* dozavo, duodécima parte; (*mús.*) duodécima.
twelve [twelv], *s.*, *a.* doce; *twelve o'clock*, las doce, mediodía, *m.*, medianoche, *f.*
twelvemonth ['twelvmənθ], *s.* año, doce meses.
twentieth ['twentiəθ], *a.* vigésimo, veinte. — *s.* veintavo, vigésima parte.
twenty ['twenti], *a.* veinte.
'twere [twɛəɪ], *contr.* [IT WERE].

twice [twais], *adv.* dos veces, doble.
twice-told, *a.* repetido.
twiddle ['twidəl], *v.t.* hacer girar, garrapatear, jugar con.
twig [twig], *s.* ramita, rama pequeña, vástago; varilla; (*anat.*) rama pequeña de una arteria u otro vaso. — *v.t.* (*fam.*) observar; echar de ver, darse cuenta de, fijarse en.
twilight ['twailait], *s.* crepúsculo, media luz, nochecita; *at* o *by twilight*, entre dos luces. — *a.* crepuscular, obscuro.
twill [twil], *v.t.* plegar, cruzar, asargar. — *s.* tela cruzada, tela asargada.
twin [twin], *s.* gemelo, mellizo; (*Méj.*) cuate, (*Cuba*) jimagua, (*Amér.*) morocho; (*astr.*) Géminis. — *v.i.* nacer gemelo, hermanearse, parearse. — *v.t.* aparejar, parear, juntar; casar, desposar. — *a.* gemelo; doble.
twin-born, *a.* gemelo, mellizo.
twine [twain], *v.t.* torcer, retorcer, tejer, envolver, enroscar, acordonar, ceñir, estrechar, ligar. — *v.i.* ensortijarse, enroscarse, entrelazarse, entretejerse; dar vueltas, caracolear. — *s.* torzal, cordel, guita, bramante; abrazo, enroscadura, (*Amér.*) hilo mestizo, guita, (*Méj.*) mecate.
twin-engined, *a.* bimotor.
twinge [twindʒ], *s.* punzada, dolor agudo; (*fig.*) remordimiento. — *v.t.* pellizcar, causar un dolor agudo. — *v.i.* sufrir, sentir un dolor agudo.
twinkle ['twiŋkəl], *v.t.*, *v.i.* centellear, rutilar, destellar, chispear; brillar; pestañear, guiñar, parpadear.
twinkle, twinkling, *s.* resplandor, brillo, centelleo, titilación; instante; pestañeo, guiñada; *in a twinkling*, en un credo o en un santiamén; *in the twinkling of an eye*, en un abrir y cerrar de ojos.
twin-screw, *a.* (*aer.*, *mar.*) bihélice.
twirl [twəːɪl], *s.* giro, vuelta, rotación, pirueta; rasgueo. — *v.t.* hacer o dar vueltas, hacer girar, volver rápidamente. — *v.i.* hacer piruetas, girar, dar vueltas, volver, hacer el molinillo.
twist [twist], *v.t.* torcer, retorcer, enroscar; entretejer, entrelazar, enlazar; enrollar, arrollar; retortijar, bornear, ceñir, rodear; trenzar, tejer; pervertir, falsificar, fraguar (una historia); doblar, virar; trenzar (cabellos). — *v.i.* envolverse, torcerse, retorcerse, retortijarse, caracolear, serpentear. — *s.* cuerda, cordón, cordoncillo; torzal, mecha; sacudida, tirón; rasgo característico, peculiaridad; recodo, recoveco (de camino); quiebro; torsión, torcedura, contorsión, torcimiento; enroscadura; trenza; rollo (de tabaco); pan retorcido; (*arq.*) nervosidad.
twisted, *a.* torcido; torcido, contrahecho; (*fam.*) torcido, deshonrado.
twister, *s.* torcedor, soguero, cordelero, cabestrero, guitero; (*mar.*) torbellino; (*fam.*) estafador.
twisting, *s.* torcimiento, retorcedura, torcedura; serpenteo; entrelazamiento, enlazamiento, entretejido. — *a.* sinuoso, serpenteado; retorcido.
twit [twit], *v.t.* vituperar, reprender, echar en cara.
twitch [twitʃ], *v.t.* tirar bruscamente; crispar, torcer bruscamente; agitar, menear, mover; arrancar, coger. — *v.i.* encogerse, crisparse,

contraerse espasmódicamente. — *s.* sacudimiento, crispamiento, tirón; punzada, dolor agudo; contracción nerviosa de los músculos; remordimiento; (*vet.*) acial.
twitch-grass, *s.* (*bot.*) cantinodia, sanguinaria.
twitter ['twitəɹ], *v.i.* gorjear, piar; (*fig.*) gorjear, cantar; (*fig.*) parlotear. — *v.i.* (*dial.*) temblar. — *s.* gorjeo, piada; temblor, agitación, inquietud; (*fam.*) estado de agitación del ánimo.
twitting, *a.* que reprende, burlón.
twittingly, *adv.* burlonamente, con desaire.
'twixt [twikst], (*contr.* **betwixt**).
two [tu:], *s.*, *a.* dos; (*by*) *two and two* o *two by two,* dos a dos; *in two,* en dos partes o porciones; *to put two and two together,* caer en la cuenta, ver el juego; atar cabos.
two-cleft, *a.* bífido.
two-faced, *a.* doble, de dos caras; falso, disimulado; *to be two-faced,* (*fig.*) ser de dos haces.
twofold ['tu:fould], *a.* duplicado, doble. — *adv.* doblemente.
two-handed, *a.* de dos manos, para dos manos; ambidextro.
two-headed, *a.* de dos cabezas, bicéfalo, bícipite.
two-legged, *a.* bípedo.
twopence ['tʌpəns], *s.* dos peniques.
twopenny ['tʌpəni], *a.* (del valor) de dos peniques; (*fig.*) de tres al cuarto.
two-ply ['tu:plai], *a.* de dos tramas, de dos hilos.
two-seater, *s.* coche o avión etc. de dos asientos.
two-sided, *a.* de dos lados, de dos caras, disimulado.
two-step, *s.* pasodoble.
two-stroke engine, *s.* motor de dos tiempos.
two-way switch, *s.* conmutador bidireccional.
tyke [taik], *s.* perro; puerco, zascandil, petate, granuja, *m.*
tymbal ['timbəl], *s.* timbal.
tympan ['timpən], *s.* tímpano.
tympanitis [timpə'naitis], *s.* timpanitis, *f.*
tympanize ['timpənaiz], *v.i.* tocar el tambor.
tympanum ['timpənəm], *s.* (*anat.*) tímpano; (*bot.*) timpanillo; (*arq.*) tímpano, faldón.
type [taip], *s.* tipo, género; (*impr.*) tipo, letra de imprenta; ejemplar, modelo; figura, impresión, signo, emblema, *m.*; *type-case,* caja de imprenta; *type-founder,* fundidor de letras de imprenta; *type-foundry,* fundición de tipos; *type-metal,* metal de imprenta; *type-setting,* tipografía; *type-setter,* cajista, *m.f.*
typewrite, *v.t.* escribir a máquina, mecanografiar.
typewriter ['taipraitəɹ], *s.* máquina de escribir.
typewriting, *s.* dactilografía, mecanografía. — *a.* mecanográfico, dactilográfico.
typhoid ['taifɔid], *a.* tifoideo. — *s.* fiebre tifoidea.
typhoon [tai'fu:n], *s.* tifón.
typhous ['taifəs], *a.* tífico.
typhus, *s.* tifo, tifus.
typic ['tipik], **typical** ['tipikəl], *a.* típico, característico.
typically, *adv.* de una manera típica o característica.

typify ['tipifai], *v.t.* simbolizar, representar, tipificar (*neol.*).
typist ['taipist], *s.* mecanógrafa (-fo), dactilógrafa (-fo).
typographer, *s.* tipógrafo.
typographic [taipo'græfik], **typographical** [taipo'græfikəl], *a.* tipográfico.
typography [tai'pɔgrəfi], *s.* tipografía.
tyrannic [tai'rænik], **tyrannical** [tai'rænikəl], *a.* tiránico, despótico.
tyrannicide [ti'rænisaid], *s.* tiranicidio; tiranicida, *m.f.*
tyrannise, tyrannize ['tirənaiz], *v.t.*, *v.i.* tiranizar, obrar con tiranía.
tyrannous ['tirənəs], *a.* tiránico, despótico.
tyranny ['tirəni], *s.* tiranía, tiranización, despotismo.
tyrant ['tairənt], *s.* tirano, déspota, *m.f.*
tyre [taiəɹ], (*E.U.*) **tire,** *s.* neumático, llanta (de rueda de carro, etc.), cubierta (de rueda de automóvil); *tyre-puncture,* pinchazo; *punctured tyre,* neumático desinflado; *spare tyre,* neumático de repuesto.
Tyrian ['tiriən], *s.*, *a.* tirio.
tyro ['tairou], *s.* novicio, principiante, tirón [TIRO].
Tyrolese [tirɔ'li:z], *a.* tirolés, del Tirol.
tzar [zɑ:ɹ], *s.* zar, czar.
tzarina [zə'ri:nə], *s.f.* zarina, czarina.

U

U, u [ju:], *s.* vigésima primera letra del alfabeto inglés. Esta letra tiene tres sonidos principales: como la *u* española en *rule,* etc.; sonido intermedio entre la *a* y la *o* española en *but, cut,* etc.; como el diptongo *iu* en español en *due, cure,* etc.; *U-shaped,* en forma de U.
ubiquitarian, *s.*, *a.* ubiquitario.
ubiquitary [ju:'bikwitəri], *a.* ubicuo, omnipresente. — *s.* ubiquitario.
ubiquitous [ju:'bikwitəs], *a.* ubicuo, omnipresente.
ubiquity [ju:'bikwiti], *s.* ubicuidad, omnipresencia.
udder ['ʌdəɹ], *s.* ubre, *f.*, teta, mama.
uddered, *a.* con ubres, con tetas.
udometer [ju:'dɔmetəɹ], *s.* udómetro.
ugh [ʌ], *interj.* ¡puf! ¡pu! ¡uf!
uglily ['ʌglili], *adv.* feamente, perversamente; (*fam.*) con mal genio.
ugliness ['ʌglinis], *s.* fealdad, afeamiento, deformidad; perversidad, fiereza; (*fam.*) mal genio.
ugly ['ʌgli], *a.* feo; repugnante, perverso, asqueroso, endiablado; (*fam.*) pícaro, regañón; *to be as ugly as sin,* (*fam.*) parecer un coco.
uhlan ['u:lən], *s.* (*mil.*) ulano.
ukase ['ju:kais], *s.* ucase.
ulcer ['ʌlsəɹ], *s.* úlcera.
ulcerate ['ʌlsəreit], *v.t.* ulcerar. — *v.i.* ulcerarse.
ulceration, *s.* ulceración.
ulcered, *a.* ulcerado.
ulcerous ['ʌlsərəs], *a.* ulceroso.
uliginous [ju:'lidʒinəs], *a.* uliginoso.
ulmaceous [ʌl'meiʃəs], *a.* ulmáceo.
ulmic ['ʌlmik], *a.* úlmico.
ulna ['ʌlnə], *s.* (*anat.*) cúbito.
ulnar ['ʌlnəɹ], *a.* cubital.

ulster ['Alstəɹ], s. abrigo largo y ancho para ambos sexos, generalmente con un cinturón.

ulterior [Al'tiəriəɹ], a. ulterior, posterior; *ulterior motive*, segunda intención.

ultimate ['Altimit], a. último, extremo, final; esencial, elemental, fundamental, primario.

ultimately, adv. últimamente, finalmente, al fin, por fin.

ultimatum [Alti'meitəm], s. (pl. **ultimata**) ultimátum.

ultimo ['Altimou], adv. (contr. **ult.**) del mes pasado.

ultra- ['Altrə], pref. ultra, más allá, además.

ultra, a. extremo, exagerado. — s. extremista, m.f.

ultraism ['Altrəizm], s. exageración en las opiniones políticas, radicalismo.

ultraist, s. (pol.) exagerado o exaltado.

ultramarine [Altrəmə'riːn], a. ultramarino.

ultramontane [Altrə'montən], a. ultramontano; ultracatólico.

ultramundane, a. ultramundano.

ultra-violet [Altrə'vaiolet], a. ultravioleta.

ululate ['juːjuːleit], v.i. ulular.

ululation, s. ululato, aullido.

umbel ['Ambel], s. (bot.) umbela.

umbellate ['Ambəleit], **umbelliferous** [Ambe-'lifərəs], a. umbelífero.

umber ['Ambəɹ], v.t. sombrear, poner sombra en una pintura. — s. (dial.) sombra, tierra de sombra (color). — a. oscuro, pardo.

umbilic [Am'bilik], s. ombligo.

umbilic, umbilical [Am'bilikəl], a. umbilical.

umbilicus [Ambi'laikəs], s. ombligo.

umbles ['Ambəlz], s.pl. entrañas de ciervo.

umbo ['Ambou], s. cazoleta de broquel.

umbra ['Ambrə], s. (astr.) sombra, arrojada.

umbrage ['Ambridʒ], s. (poét.) sombraje, umbría; sombrajo; resentimiento, pique; *to take umbrage*, darse por sentido, picarse. — v.t. sombrear; (fig.) eclipsar.

umbrageous [Am'breidʒəs], a. umbroso, sombrío, umbrático, obscuro.

umbrageousness, s. sombra, sombrajo, umbría, umbrosidad.

umbrella [Am'brelə], s. paraguas, m., quitasol, sombrilla; *umbrella-stand*, portaparaguas, m., paragüero.

umpire ['Ampaiəɹ], s. árbitro, arbitrador, tercero en discordia, corredor; (ant.) secuestro, compromisario; (deportes) árbitro. — v.t., v.i. arbitrar.

unabased [Anə'beisd], a. que no está envilecido.

unabashed [Anə'bæʃd], a. descocado, desvergonzado, descarado; reposado, sereno, sosegado.

unabated [Anə'beitid], a. no disminuido; completo, entero, continuo.

unabbreviated, a. no abreviado, sin abreviar; íntegro.

unable [An'eibəl], a. incapaz, inhábil, impotente; *to be unable to do something*, no poder hacer una cosa.

unabridged [Anə'bridʒd], a. no abreviado, sin abreviar; completo, íntegro.

unabsolved, a. no absuelto.

unaccented [Anək'sentid], a. sin acento, no acentuado.

unacceptable [Anək'septəbəl], a. inaceptable; desagradable.

unacceptableness, s. naturaleza desagradable.

unaccepted, a. inaceptado, no aceptado.

unaccommodating [Anə'komodeitiŋ], a. poco servicial, poco complaciente.

unaccompanied [Anə'kʌmpənid], a. no acompañado, solo.

unaccomplished [Anə'kʌmpliʃd], a. inacabado, imperfecto, incompleto, no acabado; falto de habilidad o de gracias, inexperto.

unaccountable [Anə'kauntəbəl], a. inexplicable; irresponsable, extraño.

unaccountableness, s. irresponsibilidad; inconcebilidad, rareza.

unaccountably, adv. de una manera rara o inexplicable extrañamente; irresponsablemente.

unaccustomed [Anə'kʌstəmd], a. desacostumbrado, insólito, inhabituado, no habitual.

unacknowledged [Anək'nɔledʒd], a. inconfeso; no reconocido; no declarado, no admitido; sin contestación (de una carta), por contestar.

unacquainted [Anə'kweintid], a. desconocido, ignorante; ignorado, extraño; *to be unacquainted with*, no conocer, ignorar; no estar acostumbrado a.

unacquired, a. no adquirido, no comprado, natural.

unacquitted [Anə'kwitid], a. no absuelto.

unadaptable [Anə'dæptəbəl], a. inadaptable.

unadapted, a. impropio; no ajustado, no ordenado.

unaddicted [Anə'diktid], a. que no está dedicado o entregado.

unaddressed [Anə'drest], a. sin dirección.

unadjusted [Anə'dʒʌstəd], a. no ajustado.

unadmired [Anəd'maird], a. no admirado.

unadopted [Anə'doptid], a. no adoptado.

unadorned [Anə'dɔːɹnd], a. sin compostura, sin adorno(s), simple, liso, llano.

unadulterated [Anə'dʌltəreitid], a. inalterado, sin mezcla, natural, puro, genuino, sincero.

unadventurous [Anəd'vəntʃərəs], a. nada aventurero; tímido, prudente, circunspecto.

unadvisable [Anəd'vaizəbəl], a. poco conveniente, poco cuerdo, imprudente.

unadvised [Anəd'vaizd], a. inconsiderado, imprudente, poco advertido, desatentado.

unadvisedly [Anəd'vaizedli], adv. imprudentemente, sin reflexionar, desacordadamente.

unadvisedness, s. irreflexión, imprudencia, falta de prudencia o consideración.

unaffected [Anə'fektid], a. inafectado, sin afectación, natural, franco, sencillo, llano; leal, fiel; no afectado, impasible.

unaffectedly, adv. sin afectación, de una manera natural.

unaffectedness, s. ausencia de afectación, sencillez, naturalidad, lisura.

unaffectionate [Anə'fekʃənət], a. poco cariñoso, desafecto.

unafflicted [Anə'fliktid], a. que no está afligido, que no padece.

unaided [An'eidid], a. sin auxilio, sin ayuda.

unaired [An'ɛəɹd], a. no ventilado.

unalarmed [Anə'laːɹmd], a. sin estar alarmado.

unalienated [An'eiliəneitid], a. no contrariado, no enajenado, inalienado.

unallayed [ʌnə'leid], *a.* que no está apaciguado.

unalleviated [ʌnə'liːvieitid], *a.* que no está aliviado, monótono.

unallied [ʌnə'laid], *a.* no aliado, sin alianza; sin parientes; sin afín.

unallowable, *a.* inadmisible.

unallowed [ʌnə'laud], *a.* no permitido.

unalloyed [ʌnə'lɔid], *a.* sin mezcla, sin liga, puro, genuino.

unalterable [ʌn'ɔltərəbəl], *a.* inalterable, invariable, inmutable.

unaltered, *a.* inalterado, no cambiado.

unambiguous [ʌn'æmbigjuːəs], *a.* no ambiguo, claro, evidente.

unambitious [ʌn'æmbiʃəs], *a.* que no aspira a nada, que no es ambicioso, sin ambición.

unambitiously, *adv.* sin ambición.

un-American [ʌnə'merikən], *a.* contrario a las costumbres de los (norte)americanos.

unamiable [ʌn'eimiəbəl], *a.* poco amable.

unamiableness, *s.* falta de amabilidad.

unanimity [juːnə'nimiti], *s.* unanimidad.

unanimous [juː'næniməs], *a.* unánime.

unanimously, *adv.* unánimemente, de acuerdo, de común acuerdo.

unanimousness, *s.* unanimidad.

unannealed [ʌnə'niːld], *a.* irrecocido, no templado.

unannounced, *a.* sin ser anunciado; (*fig.*) de rebato, de súbito.

unanswerable [ʌn'ɑːnsərəbəl], *a.* incontestable, indisputable, irrefutable, incontrovertible.

unanswerably, *adv.* indisputablemente, incontestablemente.

unanswered, *a.* no contestado, incontestado, por contestar, sin respuesta; no correspondido.

unappalled [ʌnə'pɔːld], *a.* no asombrado, sin extrañar; sin miedo, intrépido.

unapparent [ʌnə'pɛərənt], *a.* invisible, oculto, obscuro, escondido.

unappeasable [ʌnə'piːzəbəl], *a.* implacable.

unapplied [ʌnə'plaid], *a.* inaplicado.

unappreciated [ʌnə'priːʃieited], *a.* que no es apreciado, desestimado, mal comprendido, que se pasa por alto.

unapprehended, *a.* libre, no preso.

unapprehensive [ʌn'æprehensiv], *a.* incauto; torpe, lerdo, necio.

unapprised [ʌnə'praizd], *a.* sin ser avisado.

unapproachable [ʌnə'proutʃəbəl], *a.* inaccesible, inabordable.

unapproachableness, *a.* inaccesibilidad.

unapproachably, *adv.* de una manera inaccesible.

unappropriated [ʌnə'prouprieitid], *a.* en reserva, sin empleo determinado, disponible, libre.

unapproved [ʌnə'pruːvd], *a.* no aprobado, desaprobado.

unapt [ʌn'æpt], *a.* impropio, inhábil, inepto, incapaz, poco propenso, poco inclinado [INEPT].

unaptly, *adv.* ineptamente, mal a propósito.

unaptness, *s.* inaptitud, ineptitud, incapacidad, falta de conveniencia [INEPTITUDE].

unarmed [ʌn'ɑːrmd], *a.* desarmado, sin armas, indefenso.

unarranged [ʌnə'reindʒd], *a.* no arreglado, no clasificado; accidental, imprevisto.

unarrayed [ʌnə'reid], *a.* no adornado; no ordenado.

unarrested [ʌnə'restid], *a.* no arrestado.

unasked [ʌn'ɑːskd], *a.* no solicitado, no pedido, no convidado, no llamado.

unaspirated [ʌn'æspireitid], *a.* que no se aspira.

unassailable [ʌnə'seiləbəl], *a.* inatacable, inexpugnable.

unassessed [ʌnə'sesd], *a.* no calculado; no tasado.

unassignable [ʌnə'sainəbəl], *a.* intransferible.

unassimilated [ʌnə'simileitid], *a.* no asimilado.

unassisted [ʌnə'sistid], *a.* sin socorro, sin auxilio.

unassuming [ʌnə'sjuːmiŋ], *a.* sin pretensión, modesto.

unassured [ʌnə'ʃjuːrd], *a.* poco seguro, no asegurado.

unattached [ʌnə'tætʃd], *a.* no agregado, despegado, suelto; (*mil.*) de reemplazo; (*for.*) no embargado; no casado, no desposado, soltero.

unattackable, *a.* inatacable.

unattainable [ʌnə'teinəbəl], *a.* inasequible, inaccesible, fuera del alcance.

unattained, *a.* no alcanzado.

unattempted [ʌnə'temtid], *a.* que no ha sido intentado o ensayado o experimentado.

unattended [ʌnə'tendid], *a.* sin compañía, sin séquito, solo, no acompañado; no concurrido.

unattested [ʌnə'testid], *a.* inatestiguado.

unattractive [ʌnə'træktiv], *a.* poco atractivo, falto de atracción, antipático.

unauthenticated [ʌnɔː'θentikeitid], *a.* no legalizado, no declarado auténtico.

unauthorized [ʌn'ɔːɪθəraizd], *a.* no autorizado, desautorizado.

unavailable [ʌnə'veiləbəl], *a.* inaprovechable, inaccesible, que no está al alcance; agotado (de libros).

unavailing, *a.* infructuoso, ineficaz, sin provecho, vano.

unavailingly, *adv.* inútilmente, sin resultado, sin provecho.

unavenged [ʌnə'venʒd], *a.* no vengado; impune, (*poét.*) inulto.

unavoidable [ʌnə'vɔidəbəl], *a.* inevitable, ineludible, indeclinable, ineluctable.

unavoidableness, *s.* inevitabilidad.

unaware [ʌnə'wɛəɪ], *a.* sin conocimiento de una cosa, que ignora cierta cosa, ignorante.

unaware, unawares, *adv.* impensadamente, de improviso, de repente, descuidado, inopinadamente.

unawed [ʌn'ɔːd], *a.* sin pavor, sin temor; no humillado, poco impresionado.

unbacked [ʌn'bækt], *a.* sin apoyo, sin ayuda; sin respaldo.

unbaked [ʌn'beikt], *a.* no cocido.

unbalanced [ʌn'bælənsd], *a.* desequilibrado, no balanceado, sin contrapeso; (*fig.*) desequilibrado, trastornado, destornillado; (*com.*) no balanceado.

unbaptized [ʌnbæp'taizd], *a.* no bautizado, no cristiano.

unbar [ʌn'bɑːɪ], *v.t.* quitar la barra, desatrancar; abrir.

unbearable [ʌn'bɛərəbəl], *a.* insoportable, intolerable, insufrible, inaguantable.

unbeaten [ʌn'biːtən], *a.* no batido; no frecuentado, no trillado, no pisado; no vencido, invicto.

unbecoming [ʌnbe'kʌmiŋ], *a.* impropio, inconveniente, indecente, informal, indecoroso; que sienta o cae mal.

unbecomingly, *adv.* indecorosamente, impropiamente, de una manera inconveniente; de un modo desgarbado, sin gracia.

unbefitting [ʌnbe'fitiŋ], *a.* inconveniente, impropio, informal.

unbefriended [ʌnbe'frendid], *a.* sin amigos, sin el apoyo de amigos.

unbegotten [ʌnbe'gɔtən], *a.* no concebido; (*teol.*) increado.

unbelief [ʌnbe'liːf], *s.* incredulidad; descreimiento, irreligión, infidelidad.

unbeliever, unbelieving, *s.* incrédulo; irreligioso, descreído, infiel.

unbend [ʌn'bend], *v.t.* (*pret., p.p.* **unbended, unbent**) soltar, aflojar; dilatar; desencorvar, enderezar; (*mar.*) desenvergar, desentalingar; (*fig.*) descansar; (*fig.*) enervar, debilitar. — *v.i.* enderezarse; descansar; ser afable, condescender.

unbending, *a.* inflexible, resuelto, determinado; tieso, rígido, severo.

unbenefited [ʌn'benefitid], *a.* sin ventaja.

unbias(s)ed [ʌn'baiəsd], *a.* sin prejuicios, imparcial.

unbid [ʌn'bid], **unbidden** [ʌn'bidən], *a.* no convidado, no invitado, sin ser convidado; sin orden, sin encargo, espontáneo.

unbiddenly, *adv.* espontáneamente.

unbind [ʌn'baind], *v.t.* (*pret., p.p.* **unbound**) desvendar, desatar, desligar, desamarrar.

unblamable [ʌn'bleiməbəl], *a.* irreprochable.

unblamed, *a.* no censurado.

unbleached [ʌn'bliːtʃd], *a.* crudo, sin blanquear.

unblemishable, *a.* que no se puede manchar.

unblemished [ʌn'blemiʃd], *a.* sin mancha, sin tacha, puro, inmaculado, perfecto.

unblenched [ʌn'blentʃd], *a.* no obscurecido, puro.

unblenching, *a.* intrépido, valiente.

unblended, *a.* puro, sin mezcla; no mezclado.

unblest [ʌn'blest], *a.* no bendito, no bendecido; maldito, infeliz, desgraciado.

unblown [ʌn'bloun], *a.* no inflado de viento, no abierto; (de motores) sin soplante.

unblushing [ʌn'blʌʃiŋ], *a.* que no se avergüenza, desvergonzado.

unbolt [ʌn'boult], *v.t.* desbarretar, tirar el cerrojo de, abrir.

unbooted [ʌn'buːtid], *a.* sin botas, descalzo.

unborn [ʌn'bɔːɪn], *a.* innato, que no ha nacido todavía.

unbosom [ʌn'buzəm], *v.t.* descubrir, abrir, confiar, revelar; *to unbosom oneself,* descubrir su pecho, desahogarse.

unbought [ʌn'bɔːt], *a.* no comprado.

unbound [ʌn'baund], *a.* desanudado, desligado, desatado, suelto, libre; (de un libro) no encuadernado.

unbounded, *a.* sin límites, infinito, inmenso, ilimitado; desenfrenado.

unbowed [ʌn'bawd], *a.* que no está humillado, invicto.

unbrace [ʌn'breis], *v.t.* desliar, desatar, desasegurar, desabrochar, aflojar, soltar.

unbraid [ʌn'breid], *v.t.* destrenzar, destejer, desenredar.

unbreathed [ʌn'briːðd], *a.* (secreto) no comunicado a otro.

unbred [ʌn'bred], *a.* mal educado, mal criado, grosero; no educado para.

unbreeched [ʌn'briːtʃd], *a.* sin calzones; (*arti.*) desmontado.

unbridle [ʌn'braidəl], *v.t.* desembridar, desencadenar.

unbridled, *a.* licencioso, irrefrenable, desencadenado, desenfrenado.

unbroken [ʌn'broukən], *a.* inviolado; entero, intacto, completo; no interrumpido; indómito; no adiestrado, indomado, cerril; (*deportes*) no batido.

unbrotherly [ʌn'brʌðəli], *a.* poco fraternal, sin cariño fraternal.

unbuckle [ʌn'bʌkəl], *v.t.* deshebillar, desatar.

unburden [ʌn'bəːɪdən], *v.t.* descargar, aliviar; *to unburden oneself,* descubrir el pecho, desahogarse.

unburied [ʌn'berid], *a.* insepulto, sin sepultura.

unburned [ʌn'bəːɪnd], **unburnt,** *a.* no quemado, no consumido, incombusto.

unbusinesslike [ʌn'biznislaik], *a.* inexperto en los negocios; contrario a la práctica del comercio; nada ceremonioso, afable.

unbutton [ʌn'bʌtən], *v.t.* desabotonar, desabrochar.

uncage [ʌn'keidʒ], *v.t.* hacer salir de una jaula, libertar.

uncalled [ʌn'kɔːld], *a.* sin ser llamado, no llamado, no pedido.

uncalled-for, *a.* innecesario, gratuito, inmerecido.

uncancelled [ʌn'kænsəld], *a.* no borrado, no anulado, no rescindido, sin cancelar.

uncanny [ʌn'kæni], *a.* misterioso, pavoroso, extraño; (*dial.*) peligroso, incauto, inseguro.

uncap [ʌn'kæp], *v.t.* destapar, descubrir.

uncared [ʌn'kɛəɪd], **uncared-for,** *a.* descuidado, desamparado, abandonado.

uncase [ʌn'keis], *v.t.* sacar de una caja o de un estuche; desenvainar; despojar; revelar; (*mil.*) desplegar la bandera.

uncaught [ʌn'kɔːt], *a.* no cogido, no agarrado.

unceasing [ʌn'siːsiŋ], *a.* incesante, sin cesar, continuo.

unceasingly, *adv.* incesantemente, continuamente, sin cesar.

uncensured [ʌn'senʃəɪd], *a.* no censurado.

unceremonious [ʌnseri'mouniəs], *a.*; **unceremoniously,** *adv.* sin ceremonia, familiar, llano; descortés, poco servicial.

unceremoniousness, *s.* falta de ceremonia, afabilidad; incivilidad, brusquedad.

uncertain [ʌn'səːɪtin], *a.* incierto, dudoso; irresoluto, indeciso, perplejo; inseguro, precario; inconstante, variable.

uncertainly, *adv.* inciertamente, con incertidumbre, inseguramente, inconstantemente.

uncertainty, *s.* incertidumbre, irresolución, duda, incierto; vaguedad, inseguridad, instabilidad.

uncertificated, *a.* (de profesores, etc.) sin título, sin certificados, no patentado.

uncertified [ʌn'səːɪtifaid], *a.* no certificado.

unchain [ʌn'tʃein], *v.t.* desencadenar, libertar.

unchallenged [ʌn'tʃæləndʒd], *a.* incontrovertible; inexpugnable; no provocado.

unchangeable [ʌn'tʃeindʒəbəl], *a.* invariable,

inmutable, impermutable, uniforme, igual, (el) mismo.

unchangeableness, s. invariabilidad, inmutabilidad, estabilidad.

unchangeably, adv. invariablemente, inmutablemente.

unchanged, a. invariable, inalterado, que no ha cambiado.

unchanging, a. invariable, inalterable, inmutable, uniforme.

uncharged [ʌnˈtʃɑːɹdʒd], a. (elec.) neutro, que no está cargado.

uncharitable [ʌnˈtʃæritəbəl], a. que no es caritativo, intransigente.

uncharitableness, s. falta de caridad, intransigencia.

unchaste [ʌnˈtʃeist], a. impúdico, incontinente, incasto, deshonesto.

unchastised, a. impune, no castigado.

unchecked [ʌnˈtʃekd], a. desenfrenado, sin freno; no verificado.

unchristened [ʌnˈkrisənd], a. no bautizado.

unchristian [ʌnˈkristʃən], a. anticristiano, poco cristiano; (fig.) poco caritativo.

uncial [ˈʌnsiəl], a. uncial. — s. letra uncial.

unciform [ˈʌnsifɔːɹm], a. unciforme.

uncinate [ˈʌnsineit], a. uncinado.

uncircumcised [ʌnˈsəːɹkəmsaizd], a. incircunciso, no circuncidado.

uncircumscribed [ʌnˈsəːɹkəmskraibd], a. incircunscrito.

uncivil [ʌnˈsivəl], a. incivil, descortés, desvergonzado.

uncivilized [ʌnˈsivilaizd], a. no civilizado, bárbaro.

uncivilly [ʌnˈsivili], adv. incivilmente, desvergonzadamente, descortésmente.

unclad [ʌnˈklæd], a. desnudo.

unclaimed [ʌnˈkleimd], a. no reclamado.

unclasp [ʌnˈklɑːsp], v.t. desabrochar; desengarzar; desatar, abrir.

unclassifiable [ʌnklæsiˈfaiəbəl], a. inclasificable.

uncle [ˈʌŋkəl], s.m. tío; (fam.) tío, persona respetable y venerada; (fam.) prestamista, m.f.; Uncle Sam, (fam.) símbolo de los Estados Unidos.

unclean [ʌnˈkliːn], a. impuro, sucio, desaseado; lascivo, inmundo, obsceno.

uncleanliness, uncleanness, s. impureza, suciedad; obscenidad.

uncleansed [ʌnˈklenzd], a. desaseado, sucio; no limpiado.

unclench [ʌnˈklentʃ], v.t. desencrespar, abrir (las manos).

uncloak [ʌnˈklouk], v.t. quitar la capa de; (fig.) revelar, descubrir. — v.i. quitar su capa.

unclose [ʌnˈklouz], v.t. abrir, revelar.

unclothe [ʌnˈklouð], v.t. desnudar.

uncloud, v.t. aclarar, desvelar, desembarazar de nubes.

unclouded [ʌnˈklaudid], a. sin nubes, claro, despejado.

uncloudedness, s. claridad, pureza.

unco [ˈʌnko], a. (Esco.) singular, extraordinario, extravagante, poco familiar. — adv. extraordinariamente, en extremo, demasiado.

uncock [ʌnˈkɔk], v.t. desmontar; (mil.) poner el seguro.

uncocked, a. desmontado, no remangado.

uncoffined [ʌnˈkɔfind], a. sin ataúd.

uncoil [ʌnˈkɔil], v.t. desenredar, desenrollar, desarrollar.

uncollected [ʌnkoˈlektid], a. no recogido, no juntado; separado, disperso; no clasificado, desordenado.

uncoloured [ʌnˈkʌləɹd], a. incoloro, descolorado; imparcial.

uncombed [ʌnˈkoumd], a. mal peinado, despeinado, desgreñado.

uncomeliness, s. desgarbo, falta de gracia; (ant.) indecencia.

uncomely [ʌnˈkʌmli], a. desgarbado, sin gracia; (ant.) indecente.

uncomfortable [ʌnˈkʌmfətəbəl], a. incómodo; inconveniente, molesto, desagradable, penoso, enfadoso, pesado.

uncomfortableness, s. incomodidad; molestia, desconsuelo, penalidad, malestar, desagrado.

uncommercial [ʌnkoˈməːɹʃəl], a. no comerciante; fuera de las buenas reglas y usos del comercio.

uncommitted [ʌnkoˈmitid], a. no cometido; no comprometido; imparcial, objetivo.

uncommon [ʌnˈkɔmən], a. poco común, poco frecuente, infrecuente, insólito, extraordinario; raro, extraño.

uncommonly, adv. extraordinariamente, extremadamente; raramente, con poca frecuencia.

uncommonness, s. infrecuencia; rareza.

uncommunicated, a. incomunicado.

uncommunicative [ʌnkoˈmjuːnikətiv], a. poco expresivo, taciturno, poco comunicativo.

uncommunicativeness, s. taciturnidad, reserva.

uncompassionate [ʌnkəmˈpæʃənit], a. no compasivo.

uncompensated [ʌnˈkɔmpenseitid], a. sin compensación.

uncomplaining [ʌnkəmˈpleiniŋ], a. que no se queja, complaciente.

uncompleted [ʌnkəmˈpliːtid], a. no terminado, incompleto, inacabado.

uncomplimentary [ʌnkɔmpliˈmentəri], a. poco halagüeño, desfavorable.

uncomplying [ʌnkəmˈplaiiŋ], a. intratable, poco complaciente, indócil.

uncompounded [ʌnkəmˈpaunded], a. no compuesto, simple, sencillo.

uncompressed [ʌnkəmˈpresd], a. no comprimido, no apretado.

uncompromising [ʌnˈkɔmpromaiziŋ], a. inflexible, intratable, firme, incondicional.

unconcealed [ʌnkənˈsiːld], a. no escondido, patente.

unconcern, s. indiferencia, desapego, frialdad; despreocupación, imparcialidad.

unconcerned [ʌnkənˈsəːɹnd], a. indiferente, desinteresado, impasible, frío; despreocupado.

uncondemned [ʌnkənˈdemd], a. no condenado, no denunciado.

uncondensed [ʌnkənˈdensd], a. no condensado.

unconditional [ʌnkənˈdiʃənəl], a. incondicional, sin condición, ilimitado.

unconditioned, a. exento de condiciones, no limitado, libre; no acondicionado.

unconfessed [ʌnkɔnˈfesd], a. no confesado, sin confesarse, inconfeso.

unconfined [ʌnkən'faind], *a.* sin límites, sin trabas, sin estorbo.

uncongealable, *a.* incongelable.

uncongealed [ʌnkən'dʒiːld], *a.* incongelado, no cuajado.

uncongenial [ʌnkən'dʒiːniəl], *a.* antipático; poco simpático, incompatible, sin afinidad, desagradable.

uncongeniality, uncongenialness, *s.* incompatibilidad.

unconnected [ʌnkə'nektid], *a.* inconexo; incoherente; sin parentesco; (*elec.*) desconectado, no enchufado.

unconquerable [ʌn'kɔŋkərəbəl], *a.* inconquistable, invencible, insuperable.

unconscientious, *a.* no concienzudo, desaplicado.

unconscionable [ʌn'kɔnʃənəbəl], *a.* irracional, injusto, desrazonable; desmedido, enorme, extraordinario, excesivo.

unconscionably, *adv.* irracionalmente, sin razón, sin conciencia.

unconscious [ʌn'kɔnʃəs], *a.* inconsciente, sin conocimiento, desmayado, insensible, sin sentido; inocente, sin querer; desconocido, ignorante.

unconsciously, *adv.* inconscientemente, involuntariamente, sin saberlo.

unconsciousness, *s.* insensibilidad; inconsciencia, ignorancia, falta de percepción.

unconsecrated [ʌn'kɔnsekreitid], *a.* no consagrado.

unconsenting [ʌnkən'sentiŋ], *a.* que no consiente.

unconsidered [ʌnkən'sidəɹd], *a.* inconsiderado, descuidado.

unconstitutional [ʌnkɔnsti'tjuːʃənəl], *a.* anticonstitucional, inconstitucional.

unconstrained [ʌnkən'streind], *a.* espontáneo, libre, voluntario.

unconsumed [ʌnkən'sjuːmd], *a.* no consumido.

uncontaminated [ʌnkən'tæmineitid], *a.* incontaminado, sin mancha, puro.

uncontested [ʌnkən'testid], *a.* incontestado.

uncontracted, *a.* incontratado.

uncontradicted, *a.* no contradicho.

uncontrite [ʌn'kɔntrait], *a.* incontrito, no arrepentido.

uncontrollable [ʌnkən'trouləbəl], *a.* irresistible, irrefrenable, indomable, ingobernable, incontestable, incontrolable.

uncontrolled, *a.* sin freno, no controlado, libre.

unconventional [ʌnkən'venʃənəl], *a.* nada convencional, estrafalario; poco convencional, original, extraordinario.

unconventionality, *s.* originalidad, novedad; extravagancia.

unconversant, *a.* poco versado (en), ignorante (de).

unconverted [ʌnkən'vəːɹted], *a.* inconverso, no convertido, infiel.

unconvertible, *a.* inconvertible.

unconvicted [ʌnkən'viktid], *a.* no declarado culpable.

unconvinced, *a.* no convencido.

unconvincing [ʌnkən'vinsiŋ], *a.* no convincente, que no convence, insubstancial.

uncord [ʌn'kɔːɹd], *v.t.* desliar, deshacer una cuerda.

uncork [ʌn'kɔːɹk], *v.t.* destapar, descorchar.

uncorrected [ʌnkə'rekted], *a.* que no está corregido.

uncorrupted [ʌnkə'rʌpted], *a.* incorrupto; que no está corrupto; no sobornado.

uncouple [ʌn'kʌpəl], *v.t.* desconectar, desatar, desengranar, desenganchar; soltar, zafar, separar.

uncoupled, *a.* suelto; soltero.

uncouth [ʌn'kuːθ], *a.* tosco, rústico, grosero, rudo, chabacano, patán; (*ant.*) extraño; (*ant.*) desolado.

uncouthness, *s.* grosería, patanería, tosquedad; (*ant.*) extravagancia, rareza.

uncover [ʌn'kʌvəɹ], *v.t.* descubrir, revelar, poner al descubierto; desnudar, desarropar, desabrigar; destapar. — *v.i.* descubrirse; desarrebozarse.

uncreated [ʌnkri'eitid], *a.* increado.

uncropped [ʌn'krɔpd], *a.* no segado, no recogido; no cortado.

uncross [ʌn'krɔːs], *v.t.* descruzar.

uncrossed, *a.* (cheques) sin cruzar; que no está borrado; sin oposición, no contrariado.

uncrown [ʌn'kraun], *v.t.* destronar.

uncrowned, *a.* destronado; no coronado.

unction ['ʌŋkʃən], *s.* unción, ungüento, ungimiento, untadura, untamiento, untura; (*igl.*) extremaunción; hipocresía; fervor; (*teo.*) gracia.

unctuous ['ʌŋktjuːəs], *a.* untuoso; zalamero.

unctuousness, *s.* untuosidad; hipocresía.

uncultivable [ʌn'kʌltivəbəl], *a.* incultivable.

uncultivated, *a.* inculto; (*fig.*) inculto.

uncurbable, *a.* indomable.

uncurbed [ʌn'kəːɹbd], *a.* indómito; desenfrenado.

uncurl [ʌn'kəːɹl], *v.t.* desrizar, desenrizar; desencrespar; destorcer; desarrollar. — *v.i.* deshacerse, desenrizarse, destorcerse.

uncurtailed, *a.* no abreviado, no acortado.

uncustomary [ʌn'kʌstəməri], *a.* no habituado, insólito.

uncut [ʌn'kʌt], *a.* no cortado, sin cortar; no abreviado.

undamaged [ʌn'dæmədʒd], *a.* indemne, ileso, en buen estado; (*com.*) no averiado.

undated [ʌn'deitid], *a.* sin fecha.

undaunted [ʌn'dɔːnted], *a.* impávido, intrépido, impertérrito; decidido; denodado, arrojado.

undecagon [ʌn'dekəgən], *s.* undecágono. endecágono.

undecayed [ʌnde'keid], *a.* intacto, no estropeado.

undeceive [ʌnde'siːv], *v.t.* desengañar, desilusionar.

undecided, *a.* indeciso, irresoluto, incierto.

undecipherable [ʌnde'saifərəbəl], *a.* indescifrable.

undecisive [ʌnde'saiziv], *a.* no decisivo, indeciso.

undecked [ʌn'dekd], *a.* sin adornos; despojado.

undeclinable [ʌnde'klainəbəl], *a.* indeclinable.

undefended [ʌnde'fendid], *a.* sin defensa, indefenso.

undefiled [ʌnde'faild], *a.* impoluto, sin mancha, incontaminado.

undefinable, *a.* indefinible.

undefined [ʌnde'faind], *a.* no definido, indefinido.

undelayed [ʌnde'leid], *a.* sin retardo.

undelivered [ʌnde'livəɹd], *a.* no librado; no entregado.

undeniable [ʌnde'naiəbəl], *a.* incontestable, innegable, irrefragable.

under ['ʌndəɹ], *prep.* bajo, debajo de; inferior a; sometido a; so (sólo con los substantivos capa, color, pena, etc.); soto (en substantivos compuestos: sotoministro, sotocargo, etc.); menos de, menos que; por menos, en menos; en, por, mediante; con relación a; en la época de, en tiempo de; según, conforme a; *under age,* menor de edad; *under arms,* (*mil.*) bajo (o debajo de) las armas; *under articles,* escriturado; *under cover,* a cubierto, al abrigo; *under consideration,* en consideración; *under lock and key,* debajo de (o bajo) llave; *under one's own hand,* de su propia mano; *under steam,* (*mar.*) al vapor; *under restraint,* sujeto; *under sail,* (*mar.*) debajo de velas, o a la vela; *under pain of,* bajo pena de, so pena de. — *a.* bajo, de debajo; subalterno, subordinado, inferior. — *adv.* abajo, debajo, menos.

underbid, *v.t.* ofrecer menos que.

underbred, *a.* mal instruido; mal educado; de casta impura.

underbrush, *s.* maleza.

undercarriage, *s.* (*aer.*) tren de aterrizaje, aterrizador.

underclerk, *s.* subsecretario.

underclothes, underclothing, undergarments, *s.pl.,* **underwear,** *s.* ropa interior, paños menores.

undercurrent, *s.* corriente submarina, resaca; (*fig.*) tendencia oculta; dejo.

undercut, *v.t.* socavar; (*com.*) baratear, ofrecer precios menores. — *s.* solomillo, filete (de carne); socavadura, socavón; (*boxeo*) puñetazo de abajo arriba.

underdo, *v.t.* (*coc.*) freír o asar poco.

underdone, *a.* (carne) poco frita, poco asada.

under-dose, *s.* (*med.*) dosis débil.

underestimate [ʌndəɹ'estimeit], *v.t.* apreciar demasiado bajo.

underfoot [ʌndəɹ'fut], *adv.* debajo de los pies.

undergo [ʌndəɹ'gou], *v.t.* (*pret.* **underwent;** *p.p.* **undergone**) padecer, sufrir; sostener, aguantar; experimentar; sobrellevar, arrostrar; pasar por.

undergraduate [ʌndəɹ'grædju:it], *s.* estudiante universitario no licenciado.

underground ['ʌndəɹgraund], *a.* subterráneo. — *adv.* bajo tierra, subterráneamente. — *s.* ferrocarril subterráneo, metro.

undergrowth, *s.* matorrales, maleza, breña.

underhand ['ʌndəɹhænd], *adv.* bajo mano, solapadamente. — *a.* solapado, oculto.

underhanded, *a.* solapado, oculto. — *adv.* bajo mano.

underlay, *v.t.* sostener, apoyar, reforzar. — *s.* (*min.*) buzamiento; (*impr.*) calzo, realce.

underlease, *s.* subescritura, subarriendo.

underlet, *v.t.* subalquilar, subarrendar.

underlie, *v.t.* (*pret.* **underlay;** *p.p.* **underlain**) estar debajo de, ser la razón fundamental de.

underline, *v.t.* rayar, subrayar.

underling, *s.* agente inferior, subordinado; hombre vil, despreciable.

underlying, *a.* fundamental; (*geol.*) subyacente.

undermine [ʌndəɹ'main], *v.t.* (*min.*) zapar, socavar, descalzar; (*fig.*) minar.

underminer, *s.* zapador, minador; (*fig.*) enemigo oculto.

undermost ['ʌndəɹmost], *a.* el más bajo, ínfimo. — *adv.* debajo de todo.

underneath [ʌndəɹ'ni:θ], *adv.* debajo, por debajo, por lo bajo. — *prep.* bajo, debajo de.

underpaid, *a.* mal pagado, mal retribuido.

underpants, *s.* (*E.U.*) [PANTS].

underpay, *v.t.* pagar insuficientemente.

underpin, *v.t.* socalzar, apuntalar.

underplot, *s.* intriga accesoria, trama secreta; (*teat.*) acción secundaria.

underprivileged, *a.* menesteroso, necesitado.

underprop, *v.t.* sostener, apuntalar, poner puntales.

underrate [ʌndəɹ'reit], *v.t.* desapreciar, menospreciar, estimar a un valor inferior al valor real.

underrun, *v.t.* correr por debajo; (*mar.*) resacar.

underscore, *v.t.* subrayar.

under-secretary, *s.* subsecretario.

undersell, *v.t.* vender a precio inferior, malbaratar; baratear, vender a precios menores.

underset, *v.t.* sostener, apuntalar. — *s.* (*mar.*) contracorriente, *f.,* resaca.

undershirt ['ʌndəɹʃə:ɹt], *s.* (*E.U.*) camiseta.

underside ['ʌndəɹsaid], *s.* cara inferior, revés, envés.

undersign, *v.t.* subscribir, firmar debajo de otro.

undersigned, *s., a.* infrascrito, abajo firmado.

undersized, *a.* de corta estatura, de dimensiones inferiores a lo normal, falto de tamaño.

underskirt, *s.* enagua, refajo, zagalejo.

understand [ʌndəɹ'stænd], *v.t., v.i.* (*pret., p.p.* **understood**) entender, comprender; saber; penetrar; aprender, conocer, ser informado, estar informado, tener entendido; sobrentender; *to give one to understand,* hacer comprender a uno; *to understand one another,* (*fig.*) estar en buena inteligencia, conocerse bien el uno al otro.

understanding, *s.* entendimiento, intelecto, inteligencia; comprensión, conocimiento; acuerdo, armonía, correspondencia; *to come to an understanding,* convenirse, ponerse de acuerdo.

understandingly, *adv.* de un modo inteligente, con inteligencia; con conocimiento de causa; con simpatía.

understate, *v.t.* representar, declarar como menos de lo que en verdad es, declarar dando poco énfasis o fuerza.

understood [ʌndəɹ'stud], *a.* sobrentendido. — *p.p.* [UNDERSTAND]; *be it understood,* entiéndase; *that is understood,* bien entendido.

understrapper, *s.* subordinato.

understudy, *s.* (*teat.*) sobresaliente. — *v.t.* sustituir.

undertake [ʌndəɹ'teik], *v.t., v.i.* (*pret.* **undertook;** *p.p.* **undertaken**) encargarse de, emprender, tomar en mano, tomar sobre sí, tomar por su cuenta, tomar a su cargo, responder de.

undertaker, *s.* director de pompas fúnebres, (*Cuba*) zacateca; emprendedor, contratista, *m.f.*

undertaking, s. empresa funeraria; (*for.*) garantía; empresa, encargo, contratación.
under-tenant [ʌndəɹˈtenənt], s. subarrendador, subarrendatario, subinquilino.
undertone [ˈʌndəɹtoun], s. voz baja, media voz; tonillo, doble sentido; (*art.*) matiz o color suavizado.
undertow, s. (*mar.*) resaca, contracorriente, f.
undervaluation, s. estimación muy baja, menosprecio.
undervalue, v.t. desapreciar, menospreciar; estimar a un valor inferior al valor real.
underwear, s. [UNDERCLOTHES].
underwood, s. matorrales, monte bajo.
underworld [ˈʌndəɹwəːɹld], s. el mundo del hampa, heces de la sociedad, f.pl.; averno, infierno.
underwrite [ˈʌndəɹɹait], v.t. (*pret.* **underwrote**; *p.p.* **underwritten**) subscribir (finanzas), asegurar, reasegurar. — v.i. hacer seguros.
underwriter, s. asegurador; agente asesor; suscriptor de valores.
underwriting, s. seguro, reaseguro.
undescribable [ʌndeˈskraibəbəl], a. indescriptible.
undescribed, a. que no está descrito.
undeserved [ʌndeˈzəːɹvd], a. inmerecido, injusto.
undeserver, s. persona sin mérito.
undeserving, a. desmerecedor, inmeritorio, indigno, que no merece.
undesigned [ʌndeˈzaind], a. sin designio, no premeditado.
undesignedly, adv. involuntariamente, casualmente, sin premeditación.
undesigning, a. que obra sin designio premeditado; sencillo, sincero, leal.
undesirable [ʌndeˈzairəbəl], a. no deseable, poco deseable, indeseable.
undesired, a. que no se desea.
undetected [ʌndeˈtektid], a. no descubierto.
undetermined [ʌndeˈtəːɹmind], a. indeterminado, incierto, indeciso.
undeterred [ʌndeˈtəːɹd], a. no asustado, no impedido, sin vacilar.
undeveloped [ʌndeˈveləpd], a. no desarrollado, sin desarrollo.
undeviating [ʌnˈdiːvieitiŋ], a. directo, regular, igual, sin rodeo, sin desviar.
undid, *pret.* [UNDO].
undigested [ʌndiˈdʒestid], a. no digerido, indigesto; (*fig.*) mal ordenado.
undignified [ʌnˈdignifaid], a. sin dignidad.
undiluted [ʌndiˈljuːtid], a. sin diluir, puro.
undiminished [ʌndiˈminiʃd], a. no disminuido; continuo, constante, entero, completo, íntegro.
undimmed [ʌnˈdimd], a. puro, claro; no amortiguado.
undirected [ʌndiˈrektid], a. sin dirección, sin señas; sin guía.
undiscerned [ʌndiˈsəːɹnd], a. inapercibido.
undiscernible, a. imperceptible, invisible.
undiscerning, a. sin discernimiento, sin juicio.
undischarged [ʌndisˈtʃɑːɹdʒd], a. no pagado; no librado.
undisciplinable, a. indisciplinable.
undisciplined [ʌnˈdisiplind], a. indisciplinado.
undisclosed [ʌndisˈklouzd], a. no descubierto, no revelado.

undiscouraged [ʌndisˈkʌrədʒd], a. no desanimado.
undiscoverable [ʌndisˈkʌvərəbəl], a. inaveriguable.
undiscovered, a. no descubierto; desconocido, oculto, ignoto.
undisguised [ʌndisˈgaizd], a. sin disfraz; abierto, franco, sencillo.
undismayed [ʌndisˈmeid], a. no asustado, sin miedo, que no se ha amilanado.
undisputed [ʌndisˈpjuːtid], a. incontestado, incontestable, incontrovertible.
undissolvable, a. indisoluble.
undissolved [ʌndiˈzɔlvd], a. no disuelto, no derretido.
undissolving, a. que no se derrite.
undistinguishable [ʌndiˈstiŋgwiʃəbəl], a. indistinguible.
undistinguished, a. no distinguido, sin distinción, indistinto, confuso.
undistinguishing, a. que no distingue.
undistorted [ʌndisˈtɔːɹtid], sin distorsión, no deformado.
undisturbed [ʌndiˈstəːɹbd], a. sin alterarse, no inquietado, no turbado; apacible, quieto.
undivided [ʌndiˈvaidid], a. entero, indiviso, íntegro.
undivulged, a. no revelado; no divulgado.
undo [ʌnˈduː], v.t. (*pret.* **undid**; *p.p.* **undone**) deshacer, desliar, desatar, zafar, desmontar, desarmar; destruir, perder, arruinar, corromper; anular, desvirtuar; *to be undone*, (*fig.*) estar arruinado o perdido; *to come undone*, deshacerse, desliarse; *to leave undone*, no hacer, dejar de hacer; *to remain undone*, quedar por hacer.
undock [ʌnˈdɔk], v.t. sacar un buque de un dique o dársena.
undoer [ʌnˈduːəɹ], s. el que deshace; el que arruina.
undoing [ʌnˈduːiŋ], s. pérdida, ruina, desfacimiento; anulación.
undoubted [ʌnˈdautid], a. indudable, evidente, fuera de duda.
undoubtedly, adv. indudablemente, sin duda.
undoubtful, a. indudable, no dudoso.
undoubting, a. que no duda, no desconfiado.
undrawn [ʌnˈdrɔːn], a. no sacado, no extraído; (*com.*) no girado; no sacado (de una lotería).
undreamed-of [ʌnˈdrimdɔv], a. inopinado.
undress [ʌnˈdres], v.t. desnudar, desvestir; desvendar (una herida). — v.i. desnudarse. — s. paños menores; ropa de casa; *undress o undress uniform*, (*mil.*) uniforme diario; *to be in undress*, (*fam.*) estar de trapillo.
undressed, a. desnudo, desnudado, no vestido; no preparado; (*agr.*) no podado; (*com.*) en bruto, en rama; sin curtir; no cepillado (madera).
undried [ʌnˈdraid], a. no secado, mojado.
undrinkable [ʌnˈdriŋkəbəl], a. impotable.
undue [ʌnˈdjuː], a. indebido; injusto, ilícito; irregular, desmedido, excesivo, no apropiado, innecesario.
undulate [ˈʌndjuːleit], v.i. undular, ondear, fluctuar. — v.t. hacer undular, hacer ondear, modular.
undulated, a. undulado.
undulating, a. ondulante, undoso, ondeante, (*poét.*) undante; (*geog.*) accidentado.
undulation, s. ondulación, undulación, ondeo.

undulatory, *a.* undulatorio; (*fís.*) oscilatorio, pulsatorio.

unduly [ʌn'djuːli], *adv.* indebidamente, ilícitamente, irregularmente, con exceso.

undutiful [ʌn'djuːtifəl], *a.* desobediente, indócil, irrespetuoso, insumiso.

undutifully, *adv.* irrespetuosamente, contra su obligación.

undutifulness, *s.* desobediencia.

undyed [ʌn'daid], *a.* sin teñir, crudo.

undying [ʌn'daiiŋ], *a.* inmortal, imperecedero.

unearned [ʌn'əːɪnd], *a.* inmerecido; no ganado.

unearth, *v.t.* desenterrar; desarraigar, sacar de la tierra o de la madriguera; (*fig.*) descubrir, revelar, sacar a luz.

unearthing, *s.* desenterramiento; (*fig.*) revelación, descubrimiento.

unearthly [ʌn'əːɪθli], *a.* sobrenatural, no terrestre; espantoso.

uneasily [ʌn'iːzili], *adv.* inquietamente; incómodamente, difícilmente.

uneasiness, *s.* inquietud, intranquilidad, desasosiego, malestar; incomodidad.

uneasy [ʌn'iːzi], *a.* inquieto, intranquilo, desasosegado; incómodo, incomodado; difícil, dificultoso; *to become uneasy,* desasosegarse, inquietarse.

uneatable [ʌn'iːtəbəl], *a.* incomible, no comestible.

unedifying [ʌn'edifaiiŋ], *a.* poco edificante.

uneducated [ʌn'edjuːkeited], *a.* sin educación, ignorante.

unembarrassed [ʌnem'bærəsd], *a.* no desconcertado, no perplejo, sin avergonzarse; no apurado, sin deudas.

unemployable, *a.* inservible, inútil, que no sirve.

unemployed [ʌnem'plɔid], *a.* no empleado, sin trabajo, sin empleo, sin ocupación, desocupado, cesante.

unenclosed [ʌnen'klouzd], *a.* no cercado.

unencumbered [ʌnen'kʌmbəɪd], *a.* sin cargas, sin trabas, libre de gravamen.

unending [ʌn'endiŋ], *a.* sin fin, inacabable, perpetuo, eterno.

unendowed [ʌnen'daud], *a.* indotado, sin dote.

unendurable [ʌnen'djuːrəbəl], *a.* intolerable, insoportable, inaguantable, insufrible.

unenduring, *a.* no duradero, de poca duración.

unengaged [ʌnen'geidʒd], *a.* no comprometido, libre, desocupado.

unengaging, *a.* que no seduce o no atrae, antipático.

unenlightened [ʌnen'laitənd], *a.* no ilustrado, ignorante.

unenterprising [ʌn'entəɪpraiziŋ], *a.* poco emprendedor, sin iniciativa, sin ánimo; no innovador, ordinario.

unentertaining [ʌnentəɪ'teiniŋ], *a.* de poco interés, insípido, poco divertido.

unenviable [ʌn'enviəbəl], *a.* poco envidiable.

unenvied, *a.* poco envidiado.

unequable [ʌn'ekwəbəl], *a.* desigual, inconstante.

unequal [ʌn'iːkwəl], *a.* desigual, dispar, disimilar, desproporcionado, poco simétrico; insuficiente; ineficaz; inferior.

unequalled, *a.* sin igual, sin rival, sin par.

unequally, *adv.* desigualmente.

unequipped [ʌne'kwipd], *a.* desprovisto.

unequivocal [ʌne'kwivokəl], *a.* inequívoco.

unerring [ʌn'əːriŋ], *a.* infalible, cierto, inerrable.

unessential [ʌne'senʃəl], *a.* no esencial. — *s.* cosa no esencial.

uneven [ʌn'iːvən], *a.* desigual; impar; irregular, quebrado, escabroso, barrancoso.

unevenness, *s.* desigualdad; irregularidad, escabrosidad, desnivelación, desnivel.

uneventful [ʌne'ventfəl], *a.* sin acontecimientos, sosegado, tranquilo.

unexamined [ʌnek'zæmind], *a.* no examinado.

unexampled [ʌnek'zɑːmpəld], *a.* sin ejemplo, único, raro.

unexceptionable [ʌnek'sepʃənəbəl], *a.* irrecusable, intachable, irreprensible.

unexceptional, *a.* no extraordinario, usual.

unexecuted [ʌn'eksekjuːted], *a.* inejecutado.

unexhausted [ʌnek'zɔːsted], *a.* inexhausto, no agotado.

unexpected [ʌnek'spekted], *a.* imprevisto, impensado, inopinado, inesperado, repentino.

unexpectedly, *adv.* de improviso, de una manera impensada, de repente, de improviso.

unexpensive, *a.* poco costoso, económico.

unexperienced [ʌneks'piəriənsd], *a.* inexperto.

unexplainable [ʌnek'spleinəbəl], *a.* inexplicable.

unexplored [ʌn'eksplɔːɪd], *a.* inexplorado.

unexplosive [ʌneks'plouziv], *a.* no explosivo.

unexposed [ʌneks'pouzd], *a.* no expuesto, no revelado.

unexpressed, *a.* tácito, sobrentendido; no expresado.

unexpressive [ʌnek'spresiv], *a.* sin expresión.

unfaded [ʌn'feidid], *a.* no marchitado, sin ajar, sin disminuir su frescura o colores.

unfading, *a.* que no se marchita, inmarcesible; inmortal, imperecedero.

unfailing [ʌn'feiliŋ], *a.* inagotable, indefectible; infalible, seguro, cierto.

unfair [ʌn'fɛəɪ], *a.* injusto, sin equidad; desleal, falso, doble, de mala fe.

unfairly, *adv.* injustamente; deslealmente, con doblez, de mala fe.

unfairness, *s.* injusticia; deslealtad, mala fe.

unfaithful [ʌn'feiθful], *a.* infiel, desleal, sin fe, infidente, pérfido; inexacto, incorrecto.

unfaithfulness, *s.* infidelidad, deslealtad, perfidia; inexactitud.

unfaltering [ʌn'fɔltəriŋ], *a.* firme, que no vacila.

unfalteringly, *adv.* sin vacilar, sin titubear, resuelto.

unfamiliar [ʌnfə'miliəɪ], *a.* poco familiar, poco común, no conocido.

unfashionable [ʌn'fæʃənəbəl], *a.* que no es de moda, fuera de moda.

unfashionableness, *s.* impopularidad; inelegancia.

unfashioned, *a.* informe, no pulido, no trabajado.

unfasten [ʌn'fɑːsən], *v.t.* desatar, deshacer, desligar, desabrochar, soltar, zafar, aflojar.

unfatherly [ʌn'fɑːðəɪli], *a.* indigno o impropio de un padre.

unfathomable [ʌn'fæðəməbəl], *a.* insondable, impenetrable; sin fondo.

unfavourable [ʌn'feivərəbəl], *a.* desfavorable, desventajoso, adverso, no propicio.

unfavoured, *a.* no favorecido.
unfeasible [ʌn'fiːzəbəl], *a.* impracticable, no factible.
unfed [ʌn'fed], *a.* falto de alimento, sin alimento, sin nutrición, no nutrido.
unfeeling [ʌn'fiːliŋ], *a.* duro, seco, insensible, impasible, apático, sin piedad.
unfeigned [ʌn'feind], *a.* no fingido, verdadero, sincero, real, genuino, ingenuo.
unfenced [ʌn'fensd], *a.* descercado, sin murallas; sin defensa.
unfermented [ʌnfəɹ'mentid], *a.* no fermentado.
unfertile [ʌn'fəɹtail], *a.* infecundo, estéril.
unfetter [ʌn'fetəɹ], *v.t.* desmanear, desencadenar, quitar los grillos a, libertar.
unfilial [ʌn'filiəl], *a.* indigno o impropio de un hijo.
unfinished [ʌn'finiʃd], *a.* imperfecto, incompleto; no acabado, no terminado, no concluido.
unfit [ʌn'fit], *v.t.* hacer incapaz, inhabilitar. — *a.* inepto, inconveniente, inhábil, inoportuno, incapaz, poco propio, poco hecho.
unfitly, *adv.* mal a propósito, impropiamente, ineptamente.
unfitness, *s.* ineptitud, incapacidad, insuficiencia, falta de conveniencia, incompetencia, inhabilidad, impropiedad.
unfitting, *a.* inconveniente, impropio, indigno.
unfix [ʌn'fiks], *v.t.* desliar, desatar, deshacer.
unfixed, *a.* no atado, desprendido, suelto; incierto, irresuelto, irresoluto.
unflagging [ʌn'flægiŋ], *a.* infatigable, porfiado, persistente.
unfledged [ʌn'fledʒd], *a.* implume.
unflinching [ʌn'flintʃiŋ], *a.* determinado, resuelto, firme, inmóvil.
unfold [ʌn'fould], *v.t.* desplegar, desdoblar, desenvolver, extender; abrir; deshacer; descubrir, revelar, manifestar, explanar, explicar, descifrar, poner en claro; desarrollar, exponer. — *v.i.* descubrirse, desarrollarse, abrirse, desenvolverse.
unfolding, *s.* despliegue; divulgación; desarrollo, exposición; (*mil.*) despliegue.
unforced [ʌn'fɔːɹsd], *a.* voluntario, espontáneo; no fingido, natural; no obligado.
unfordable [ʌn'fɔːɹdəbəl], *a.* invadeable.
unforeknown [ʌnfɔːɹ'noun], *a.* inesperado, impensado.
unforeseen [ʌnfɔːɹ'siːn], *a.* imprevisto, inopinado.
unforgettable [ʌnfə'getəbəl], *a.* inolvidable.
unforgiving [ʌnfə'giviŋ], *a.* implacable, que no perdona.
unforgotten [ʌnfə'gɔtən], *a.* no olvidado, fijo en la memoria.
unformed [ʌn'fɔːɹmd], *a.* informe, en embrión; rudimentario, no pulido; sin experiencia.
unforsaken [ʌnfɔɹ'seikən], *a.* no abandonado.
unfortified [ʌn'fɔːɹtifaid], *a.* no fortificado.
unfortunate [ʌn'fɔːɹtʃuːnit], *a.* desgraciado, desdichado, desventurado, infortunado, desafortunado, cuitado, infeliz, aciago. — *s.* desgraciado, desventurado; mujer perdida, moza de fortuna.
unfortunately, *adv.* desgraciadamente, por desgracia, infelizmente, desafortunadamente.
unfortunateness, *s.* infortunio, desgracia.

unfounded [ʌn'faundid], *a.* infundado, sin fundamento, no establecido, injustificado.
unframed [ʌn'freimd], *a.* no encuadrado, sin cuadro.
unfrequented [ʌnfre'kwentid], *a.* poco frecuentado, solitario.
unfrequently, *adv.* rara vez, raramente, pocas veces, poco.
unfriended [ʌn'frendid], *a.* solo, sin amigos.
unfriendliness, *s.* falta de amistad, hostilidad; desapego; insociabilidad.
unfriendly [ʌn'frendli], *a.* hostil, enemigo; antipático, poco amistoso; desfavorable, perjudicial; insociable.
unfrock [ʌn'frɔk], *v.t.* exclaustrar.
unfruitful [ʌn'fruːtfəl], *a.* infecundo, infructífero, improductivo, infructuoso.
unfruitfulness, *s.* infertilidad, infecundidad, esterilidad.
unfulfilled [ʌnful'fild], *a.* no ejecutado, no cumplido.
unfurl [ʌn'fʌɹl], *v.t.* desplegar, desdoblar; (*mar.*) desaferrar las velas.
unfurnished [ʌn'fʌɹniʃd], *a.* no amueblado; no aprovisionado, desprovisto.
unfurrowed [ʌn'fʌɹoud], *a.* no surcado (por el arado, etc.).
ungainliness, *s.* desgarbo, torpeza, falta de gracia; desmaña.
ungainly [ʌn'geinli], *a.* torpe, desgarbado; desmañado.
ungallant [ʌn'gælənt], *a.* poco galante, no gallardo, no airoso.
ungarnished [ʌn'gɑːɹniʃd], *a.* no guarnecido; sin adorno.
ungarrisoned [ʌn'gærisənd], *a.* desguarnecido, sin guarnición.
ungartered [ʌn'gɑːɹtəɹd], *a.* sin ligas.
ungathered [ʌn'gæðəɹd], *a.* no recogido.
ungauged [ʌn'geidʒd], *a.* no aforado, no medido.
ungenerous [ʌn'dʒenərəs], *a.* poco generoso, poco caritativo; mezquino, tacaño; indigno, bajo.
ungenerously, *adv.* sin generosidad, sin caridad; mezquinamente; indignamente.
ungenial [ʌn'dʒiːniəl], *a.* poco favorable, poco propicio; brusco, antipático.
ungenteel [ʌndʒen'tiːl], *a.* poco urbano, poco distinguido, informal, poco serio, mal criado.
ungenteelly, *adv.* de una manera informal o poco seria, de mala educación, sin urbanidad.
ungentle [ʌn'dʒentəl], *a.* poco suave; rudo, seco, duro, severo, mal educado.
ungentlemanlike [ʌn'dʒentəlmənlaik], **ungentlemanly**, *a.* de mal tono, informal, inurbano, poco señoril, indigno de un caballero.
ungentlemanliness, *s.* informalidad, inurbanidad, mal tono.
ungentleness, *s.* aspereza, dureza.
ungently [ʌn'dʒentli], *adv.* ásperamente, duramente, severamente.
ungird [ʌn'gəːɹd], *v.t.* desceñir, desfajar, descinchar, quitar la cintura de.
unglazed [ʌn'gleizd], *a.* sin cristales, sin vidrios, sin vidriar; no barnizado, no lustrado, deslustrado, mate; sin satinar (papel).
ungloved [ʌn'glʌvd], *a.* sin guantes.
ungodlily, *adv.* impíamente, irreligiosamente.

ungodliness, *s.* impiedad, irreligión.
ungodly [ʌnˈgɔdli], *a.* impío, irreligioso, malvado, profano.
ungovernable [ʌnˈgʌvənəbəl], *a.* ingobernable, indisciplinable, indomable; desarreglado.
ungraceful [ʌnˈgreisful], *a.* sin gracia, desagraciado, desairado, desgarbado.
ungracefully, *adv.* sin gracia, con desgarbo.
ungracious [ʌnˈgreiʃəs], *a.* desgraciado, desagradable, ofensivo.
ungraciously, *adv.* desagradablemente, groseramente, de mala gracia.
ungraciousness, *s.* inurbanidad, descortesía, aspereza.
ungrammatical [ʌngrəˈmætikəl], *a.* antigramatical, incorrecto.
ungrammatically, *adv.* incorrectamente.
ungrateful [ʌnˈgreitful], *a.* ingrato, desagradable, desagradecido.
ungratefully, *adv.* con ingratitud, ingratamente, desagradablemente, desagradecidamente.
ungratefulness, *s.* ingratitud, desagradecimiento.
ungratified [ʌnˈgrætifaid], *a.* no contentado, no satisfecho.
ungrounded [ʌnˈgraundid], *a.* mal fundado, infundido, sin fundamento.
ungrudging [ʌnˈgrʌdʒiŋ], *a.* generoso, liberal.
ungrudgingly, *adv.* con liberalidad, de buena voluntad, de buena gana.
ungual [ˈʌŋgjuːəl], *a.* ungular, ungulado.
unguarded [ʌnˈgɑːded], *a.* indefenso, sin defensa; imprudente, descuidado; desprevenido.
unguardedly, *adv.* sin tomar precauciones, inconsideradamente.
unguent [ˈʌŋgwənt], *s.* unto, ungüento.
unguided [ʌnˈgaidid], *a.* sin guía, no guiado, no dirigido.
ungulate [ˈʌŋgjuːlit], *s., a.* ungulado.
ungum [ʌnˈgʌm], *v.t.* desengomar, despegar.
unhabituated [ʌnhəˈbitjuːeitid], *a.* poco habituado, poco acostumbrado.
unhallowed [ʌnˈhæloud], *a.* profanado, profano, impío.
unhand [ʌnˈhænd], *v.t.* quitar las manos de, soltar.
unhandled, *a.* no manoseado.
unhandsome [ʌnˈhændsəm], *a.* desagraciado, poco hermoso; desleal, descortés; grosero, indecente.
unhandsomely, *adv.* sin gracia, sin elegancia; descortésmente, sin generosidad.
unhandy [ʌnˈhændi], *a.* torpe, poco hábil, desmanotado, desmañado; embarazoso, incómodo.
unhappily [ʌnˈhæpili], *adv.* desgraciadamente, por desgracia, infelizmente, desdichadamente.
unhappiness, *s.* desgracia, infelicidad, desdicha, infortunio, mala ventura.
unhappy [ʌnˈhæpi], *a.* desgraciado, infeliz, desdichado, infortunado, desventurado, malhadado, infausto.
unharmed [ʌnˈhɑːmd], *a.* sano y salvo, ileso, incólume.
unharness [ʌnˈhɑːnes], *v.t.* desenjaezar, desenganchar, desaparejar.
unhasp [ʌnˈhɑːsp], *v.t.* soltar el pestillo.

unhatched [ʌnˈhætʃd], *a.* no abierto, no incubado, no criado.
unhealthfulness, *s.* insalubridad.
unhealthily, *adv.* de un modo malsano o insalubre.
unhealthiness, *s.* insalubridad, estado enfermizo.
unhealthy [ʌnˈhelθi], *a.* achacoso, enfermizo; malsano, insalubre.
unheard [ʌnˈhəːd], *a.* sin ser oído; ignorado, desconocido.
unheard-of, *a.* inaudito, extraño, sin ejemplo.
unheavenly [ʌnˈhevənli], *a.* no celestial.
unheeded [ʌnˈhiːdid], *a.* descuidado, desapercibido, despreciado, desatendido.
unheedful, *a.* descuidado, distraído, negligente.
unheeding, *a.* descuidado, destraído, desatento.
unheedly, *a.* repentino, súbito, precipitado.
unhelm [ʌnˈhelm], *v.t.* quitar el casco a.
unhelmed, *a.* sin casco.
unhelped, *a.* no asistido, no ayudado, sin ayuda o auxilio.
unhelpful [ʌnˈhelpful], *a.* poco servicial; vano, inútil, estéril.
unhesitating [ʌnˈhesiteitiŋ], *a.* que no vacila; firme, resuelto, fijo; pronto, listo.
unhesitatingly, *adv.* sin vacilar, prontamente, inmediatamente, a ojos cerrados.
unhewn [ʌnˈhjuːn], *a.* bruto, en bruto; sin labrar; en rollo.
unhinge [ʌnˈhindʒ], *v.t.* desgoznar, quitar los goznes de; descolgar, desmontar, desquiciar; *(fig.)* trastornar, desequilibrar.
unhitch [ʌnˈhitʃ], *v.t.* desatar, descolgar, desaparejar, desenganchar.
unholiness, *s.* impiedad, falta de santidad, impureza.
unholy [ʌnˈhouli], *a.* profano, impío, impuro; *(fam.)* tremendo, extraordinario.
unhonoured [ʌnˈɔnəd], *a.* sin honor, despreciado, desdeñado.
unhook [ʌnˈhuk], *v.t.* descolgar, desenganchar, desabrochar.
unhoop, *v.t.* quitar los cercos de (barriles, toneles, etc.).
unhoped (for) [ʌnˈhoupdfɔːɹ], inesperado.
unhorse [ʌnˈhɔːɹs], *v.t.* desmontar, desarzonar.
unhoused, *a.* desalojado, sin casa.
unhung [ʌnˈhʌŋ], *a.* descolgado; no colgado.
unhurt [ʌnˈhəːɹt], *a.* ileso, incólume, sin herida, sano y salvo; intacto, indemne, sin daño.
unhurtful, *a.* inocente, inofensivo.
unicorn [ˈjuːnikɔːɹn], *s.* unicornio.
unicornous, *a.* de un solo cuerno.
unification [juːnifiˈkeiʃən], *s.* unificación.
uniflorous [juːˈniflɔrəs], *a.* unifloro.
uniform [ˈjuːnifɔːɹm], *a.* uniforme, invariable, semejante, igual; armonioso, acorde; constante, consistente. — *s.* uniforme.
uniformity [juːniˈfɔːɹmiti], *s.* uniformidad, conformidad, igualdad.
uniformly, *adv.* uniformemente, sin variación.
unify [ˈjuːnifai], *v.t.* unificar, unir.
unilateral [juːniˈlætərəl], *a.* unilateral.
unillumined [ʌniˈljuːmind], *a.* no alumbrado, no iluminado.
unimaginable [ʌniˈmædʒinəbəl], *a.* inimaginable.

unimpaired [ʌnim'pɛəɹd], *a.* no perjudicado, intacto, ileso, no deteriorado, inalterado, indemne, incólume.

unimpassioned [ʌnim'pæʃənd], *a.* sin pasión.

unimpeachable [ʌnim'piːtʃəbəl], *a.* irreprensible, intachable, inatacable, irrecusable.

unimpeded [ʌnim'piːdid], *a.* sin obstáculo.

unimportance, *s.* poca importancia.

unimportant [ʌnim'pɔːɹtənt], *a.* poco importante, sin importancia.

unimposing [ʌnim'pouziŋ], *a.* poco imponente, poco impresionante.

unimpressed [ʌnim'presd], *a.* no conmovido, no impresionado.

unimpressive, *a.* poco impresionante, poco conmovedor, de poca importancia.

unimproved [ʌnim'pruːvd], *a.* no mejorado, no perfeccionado, no adelantado; inculto, yermo.

uninfectious [ʌnin'fekʃəs], *a.* no infecto.

uninflamed [ʌnin'fleimd], *a.* no inflamado.

uninflammable [ʌnin'flæməbəl], *a.* incombustible.

uninfluenced [ʌn'influːənsd], *a.* no influido, sin preocupaciones.

uninfluential, *a.* sin influencia.

uninformed [ʌnin'fɔːɹmd], *a.* no instruido, ignorante, no informado (de cualquier cosa), inculto.

uninhabitable, *a.* inhabitable.

uninhabited [ʌnin'hæbitid], *a.* inhabitado, sin habitantes, despoblado, desierto, escueto.

uninitiated [ʌni'niʃieitid], *a.* no iniciado.

uninjured [ʌn'indʒəɹd], *a.* incólume, ileso, no perjudicado, no herido, sano y salvo, intacto, indemne.

uninspired [ʌnin'spaird], *a.* no inspirado, sin inspiración, sin emoción.

uninstructed [ʌnin'strʌktəd], *a.* sin instrucción, ignorante.

uninstructive, *a.* poco instructivo.

uninsulated [ʌn'insjuːleitid], *a.* (*elec.*) descubierto, inaislado.

uninsured [ʌnin'ʃjuːəɹd], *a.* no asegurado, sin seguro.

unintelligent [ʌnin'telidʒənt], *a.* no inteligente.

unintelligibility, unintelligibleness, *s.* incomprensibilidad, obscuridad.

unintelligible [ʌnin'telidʒəbəl], *a.* ininteligible.

unintelligibly, *adv.* de una manera ininteligible.

unintended [ʌnin'tendid], **unintentional** [ʌnin'tenʃənəl], *a.* no intencional, no premeditado, hecho sin intención.

unintentionally, *adv.* involuntariamente, sin querer, sin intención.

uninterested [ʌn'intərestid], *a.* desinteresado.

uninteresting, *a.* poco interesante, falto de interés, insípido, soso.

unintermitting [ʌnin'təɹ'mitiŋ], *a.* continuo, incesante.

unintermittingly, *adv.* continuamente, sin cesar.

uninterrupted [ʌnintəɹ'rʌptid], *a.* incesante, continuo, no interrumpido, sin interrupción.

uninterruptedly, *adv.* sin interrupción, continuamente.

uninvested [ʌnin'vestid], *a.* no investido, no colocado.

uninvestigable, *a.* inescrutable.

uninvestigated [ʌnin'vestigeitid], *a.* no investigado.

uninvited, *a.* no invitado, no convidado, sin invitación; (*fig., fam.*) de imprevisto.

union ['juːniən], *s.* unión, *f.*, reunión, *f.*, junta, coalición, allegamiento, coligación, confederación; asociación, liga, gremio, mancomunidad; simetría, proporción, acuerdo, armonía, concordia; estado matrimonial; (*mec.*) unión, *f.*, conexión, trabazón, *f.*; *Union Jack*, bandera nacional de Gran Bretaña e Irlanda reunidas; *trade(s)-union*, sindicato, gremio obrero.

unionism, *s.* sindicalismo.

unionist ['juːniənist], *a.* unionista, *m.f.*, sindicalista, *m.f.*; (*pol.*) miembro de un partido político formado para aponerse a la concesión de autonomía a Irlanda.

uniparous [juː'nipərəs], *a.* unípara.

unipersonal [juːni'pəːɹsənəl], *a.* (*gram.*) unipersonal.

unique [juː'niːk], *a.* único, singular, raro, sin igual.

uniquely, *adv.* de una manera única.

uniqueness, *s.* unicidad, lo singular.

unisexual [juːni'sekʃuːəl], *a.* unisexual.

unison ['juːnizən], *s.* (*mús.*) unisonancia, unísono; (*fig.*) acuerdo; *in unison*, al unísono. — *a.* unísono, unisón.

unisonal [juːni'sounəl], **unisonous** [juːni'sonəs], *a.* unísono.

unit ['juːnit], *s.* unidad.

unitarian [juːni'tɛəriən], *s.* unitario.

unite [juː'nait], *v.t.* unir, allegar, adunar, reunir; trabar, enlazar, juntar, mezclar, incorporar, mancomunar. — *v.i.* unirse, juntarse, asociarse, aliarse, renunirse, concertarse, coligarse, convenirse.

united [juː'naitid], *a.* unido, reunido, juntado. — *p.p.* [UNITE]; *United Kingdom*, Reino Unido; *The United States*, Los Estados Unidos.

unitedly, *adv.* unidamente, de un modo unido, juntamente; de acuerdo.

uniter, *s.* unificador, enlazador.

unity ['juːniti], *s.* unidad; unión, *f.*, conformidad, acuerdo, conjunto, concordia, armonía; (*mat.*) el número uno.

univalve ['juːnivælv], *s.*, *a.* univalvo.

univalved, univalvular, *a.* univalvo.

universal [juːni'vəːɹsəl], *a.* universal, general, común.

universal coupling, universal joint, *s.* junta cardánica.

universality [juːnivəɹ'sæliti], *s.* universalidad, generalidad.

universally [juːni'vəɹsəli], *adv.* universalmente, generalmente.

universe ['juːnivəɹs], *s.* universo.

university, *s.* universidad.

univocal [juː'nivokəl], *a.* unívoco.

unjointed [ʌn'dʒɔintid], *a.* desunido, desarticulado, desencajado.

unjudged [ʌn'dʒʌdʒd], *a.* no juzgado, no decidido; pendiente de juicio, en litigio.

unjust [ʌn'dʒʌst], *a.* injusto, inicuo.

unjustifiable [ʌndʒʌsti'faiəbəl], *a.* injustificable, inexcusable.

unjustifiably, *adv.* injustificadamente, de una manera injustificable, inexcusablemente.

unjustified, *a.* injustificado, injusto.

unjustly [ʌn'dʒʌstli], *adv.* injustamente, inicuamente.

unkempt [ʌn'kempt], *a.* despeinado, desmelenado, desgreñado, sin pulimento, desaseado.

unkennel [ʌn'kenəl], *v.t.* hacer salir (a un perro de la perrera); descubrir (un raposo); desemboscar (un ciervo); (*fig.*) desalojar.

unkind [ʌn'kaind], *a.* poco benévolo, poco amable, duro, adusto, áspero, seco; desfavorable, poco propicio.

unkindliness, *s.* falta de complacencia, severidad, dureza, rigor.

unkindly, *a.* maligno, perjudicial, contrario. — *adv.* sin benevolencia, sin bondad, con rigor, duramente, ásperamente.

unkindness, *s.* falta de cariño, rigor, dureza, malevolencia, desamor, carácter poco amable.

unkingly [ʌn'kiŋli], *a.* indigno de un rey.

unkink, *v.t.* quitar las cocas de.

unknit [ʌn'nit], *v.t.* deshacer (las medias, etc.); desliar.

unknot [ʌn'nɔt], *v.t.* desliar, desatar.

unknowing [ʌn'nouiŋ], *a.* ignorante.

unknowingly, *a.* sin darse cuenta, sin saberlo; involuntariamente.

unknown [ʌn'noun], *a.* desconocido, ignoto, obscuro, incógnito, oculto, ignorado; superior a todo cómputo; unknown quantity, (*mat.*) incógnita; *unknown to him*(*self*), sin saberlo él, o sin que él (mismo) lo supiese.

unlaboured [ʌn'leibəɹd], *a.* natural, espontáneo.

unlace [ʌn'leis], *v.t.* desatar, desenlazar, desabrochar.

unlade [ʌn'leid], *v.t.* descargar.

unlading, *s.* descarga.

unladylike [ʌn'leidilaik], *a.* indigno o impropio de una señora, de mal tono, informal.

unlamented [ʌnlə'mentid], *a.* no llorado, no sentido.

unlatch [ʌn'lætʃ], *v.t.* levantar el picaporte o el pestillo de; abrir.

unlawful [ʌn'lɔːful], *a.* ilegítimo, ilícito, ilegal.

unlawfulness, *s.* ilegalidad, ilegitimidad.

unlay [ʌn'lei], *v.t.* (*mar.*) destorcer (cuerdas, etc.).

unlearn [ʌn'ləːɹn], *v.t.* desaprender, olvidar.

unlearned, *a.* iletrado, indocto, ignorante.

unleavened [ʌn'levənd], *a.* sin levadura, ázimo.

unless [ʌn'les], *conj.* a menos (de) que, a menos de, a no ser que, excepto, si no, si no es, no siendo.

unlettered [ʌn'letəɹd], *a.* iletrado, ignorante.

unlicensed [ʌn'laisənsd], *a.* no autorizado; sin licencia, sin patente, sin permiso.

unlighted [ʌn'laitid], *a.* no iluminado, no encendido.

unlike [ʌn'laik], *a.* desemejante, disímil, distinto, desigual, diferente, dispar; improbable. — *adv.* a distinción de, a diferencia de.

unlikelihood, unlikeliness, *s.* inverisimilitud, improbabilidad.

unlikely [ʌn'laikli], *a.* inverosímil, inverisímil, poco probable, improbable, difícil, remoto. — *adv.* improbablemente.

unlikeness, *s.* desemejanza, disimilitud.

unlimber, *v.t.* (*mil.*) quitar el armón o el aventrén (a un cañón).

unlimited [ʌn'limitid], *a.* ilimitado, sin restricción, indeterminado, inmenso, infinito.

unlined [ʌn'laind], *a.* no forrado, sin forro; sin rayas; no arrugado, suave, liso.

unlink [ʌn'liŋk], *v.t.* deseslabonar.

unliquidated [ʌn'likwideitid], *a.* no liquidado, ilíquido.

unload [ʌn'loud], *v.t.* aligerar, descargar, exonerar; (*bolsa*) vender grandes partidas de valores.

unloading, *s.* descargue, descarga.

unlock [ʌn'lɔk], *v.t.* abrir una cerradura, abrir con llave; abrir, dar libre acceso a, revelar.

unlooked-for [ʌn'lukdfɔːɹ], *a.* inopinado.

unloose [ʌn'luːs], *v.t.* soltar, desatar, aflojar. — *v.i.* deshacerse, aflojarse.

unlovable, *s.* poco amable, antipático.

unloved [ʌn'lʌvd], *a.* que no es amado.

unlovely [ʌn'lʌvli], *a.* poco amable, poco seductor, sin gracia.

unloving, *a.* nada cariñoso.

unluckily, *adv.* por desgracia, desgraciadamente, infaustamente.

unluckiness, *s.* mala suerte, desgracia, infortunio, desastre.

unlucky [ʌn'lʌki], *a.* desgraciado, infortunado, desafortunado, desdichado; infausto, nefasto, funesto, azaroso, siniestro.

unmade [ʌn'meid], *a.* deshecho; desarmado; no hecho, increado.

unmaidenly [ʌn'meidənli], *a.* impropio de una doncella.

unmake [ʌn'meik], *v.t.* deshacer, desarmar; destruir, aniquilar; destituir, deponer.

unman [ʌn'mæn], *v.t.* acobardar, desanimar, abatir, afeminar; embrutecer, degradar; castrar; (*mil.*) desguarnecer, desarmar (un buque).

unmanageable [ʌn'mænidʒəbəl], *a.* inmanejable, intratable, ingobernable, indomable, indócil.

unmanlike, unmanly, *a.* indigno de un hombre; vil, bajo, afeminado, enervado; *to be unmanly*, tener mala mano.

unmannered [ʌn'mænəɹd], *a.* mal educado, mal criado, mal enseñado, rudo, brusco.

unmannerliness, *s.* brusquedad, rudeza, mala crianza.

unmannerly [ʌn'mænəɹli], *a.* mal educado, mal criado, brusco, descortés; impolítico. — *adv.* descortésmente, bruscamente.

unmanured [ʌnmə'njuːəɹd], *a.* no abonado, sin estiércol.

unmarked [ʌn'mɑːɹkd], *a.* sin marca, no marcado; no señalado; intacto, no perjudicado.

unmarketable [ʌn'mɑːɹketəbəl], *a.* invendible, incomerciable, echado a perder.

unmarriageable [ʌn'mæridʒəbəl], *a.* incasable, que no se puede casar.

unmarried [ʌn'mærid], *a.* soltero, soltera, célibe.

unmask [ʌn'mɑːsk], *v.t.* desenmascarar, quitar la máscara a, quitar el velo a, descubrir. — *v.i.* desenmascararse.

unmast [ʌn'mɑːst], *v.t.* (*mar.*) desarbolar.

unmastered [ʌn'mɑːstəɹd], *a.* indomado, no vencido o subyugado; aun no aprendido.

unmatchable, *a.* incomparable; único; dispar.

unmatched [ʌn'mætʃd], *a.* incomparable, único, sin igual, sin par; dispar.

unmeaning [ʌn'miːniŋ], *a.* insignificante, sin

significación, sin sentido, vacío, que no dice nada.

unmeant, *a.* involuntario.

unmeasurable, *a.* inmensurable, inmenso, ilimitado.

unmeasured [ʌn'meʒəɹd], *a.* sin límites, sin medida; no medido.

unmeet [ʌn'miːt], *a.* impropio, poco conveniente.

unmeetness, *s.* inconveniencia.

unmellowed [ʌn'meloud], *a.* inmaduro.

unmelodious [ʌnme'loudiəs], *a.* no melodioso.

unmelodiously, *adv.* sin melodía.

unmentionable [ʌn'menʃənəbəl], *a.* que no se debe mencionar. — *s.pl.* (*fest.*) pantalones.

unmentioned, *a.* no mencionado; desconocido.

unmerciful [ʌn'məːɹsiful], *a.* inclemente, despiadado, sin piedad.

unmercifully, *adv.* sin misericordia, rigurosamente, despiadamente, desapiadadamente.

unmercifulness, *s.* inhumanidad, crueldad, inclemencia.

unmerited [ʌn'meritid], *a.* desmerecido, inmerecido, inmérito.

unmindful [ʌn'maindful], *a.* desatento, descuidado, poco cuidadoso, olvidadizo, dejado, negligente.

unmindfully, *adv.* sin atención, negligentemente.

unmindfulness, *s.* negligencia, descuido, desatención.

unmistakable [ʌnmis'teikəbəl], *a.* inequívoco, indudable, evidente.

unmitigated [ʌn'mitigeitid], *a.* no mitigado; completo, absoluto; redomado.

unmixed [ʌn'miksd], *a.* sin mezcla, puro, sencillo, simple.

unmodified [ʌn'mɔdifaid], *a.* sin modificación.

unmolested [ʌnmo'lestid], *a.* no molestado, tranquilo, quieto.

unmoor [ʌn'muːəɹ], *v.t.* (*mar.*) desamarrar, desaferrar, levantar el ancla.

unmortgaged [ʌn'mɔːɹgidʒd], *a.* no hipotecado.

unmotherly [ʌn'mʌðəɹli], *a.* indigno o impropio de una madre.

unmounted [ʌn'mauntid], *a.* no montado, desmontado.

unmourned [ʌn'mɔːɹnd], *a.* no llorado, no lamentado.

unmoved [ʌn'muːvd], *a.* inmoto, inmóvil; constante, firme, fijo, inalterable; impasible, sin conmoverse.

unmuffle [ʌn'mʌfəl], *v.t.* descubrir, desembozar, destapar (la cara, etc.).

unmusical [ʌn'mjuːzikəl], *a.* poco aficionado a la música; poco armonioso; *to be unmusical*, no tener oído.

unmutilated [ʌn'mjuːtileitid], *a.* no mutilado, intacto.

unmuzzle [ʌn'mʌzəl], *v.t.* quitar el bozal.

unnamed [ʌn'neimd], *a.* innominado, no mencionado; sin nombre, anónimo.

unnatural [ʌn'nætʃərəl], *a.* innatural, no natural, contranatural, desnaturalizado; violento, cruel; artificial, afectado, forzado; contrario a la naturaleza, inhumano, monstruoso.

unnaturally, *adv.* contra naturaleza.

unnavigable [ʌn'nævigəbəl], *a.* innavegable.

unnavigated, *a.* que no ha sido navegado.

unnecessarily, *adv.* sin necesidad, innecesariamente, inútilmente.

unnecessariness, *s.* inutilidad, superfluidad.

unnecessary [ʌn'nesesəri], *a.* inútil, innecesario, superfluo, excusado.

unneeded [ʌn'niːdid], *a.* innecesario.

unneighbourly [ʌn'neibəɹli], *a.* descortés, adusto, áspero, poco amable con sus vecinos.

unnerve [ʌn'nəːɹv], *v.t.* amilanar, acobardar.

unnoted [ʌn'noutid], **unnoticed** [ʌn'noutisd], *a.* desapercibido, pasado por alto, inadvertido.

unnumbered [ʌn'nʌmbəɹd], *a.* innumerable, sin número.

unobjectionable [ʌnəb'dʒekʃənəbəl], *a.* irrecusable, irreprensible; libre de objeciones.

unobservable, *a.* imperceptible, insensible.

unobservant, unobserving, *a.* que no observa, descuidado, inobservante.

unobserved [ʌnəb'zəːɹvd], *a.* desapercibido.

unobstructed ['ʌnəb'strʌktid], *a.* no obstruido, libre; raso; despejado.

unobtainable [ʌnəb'teinəbəl], *a.* que no puede ser obtenido, inasequible.

unobtrusive [ʌnəb'truːziv], *a.* discreto, modesto.

unoccupied [ʌn'ɔkjuːpaid], *a.* desocupado, no ocupado, disponible; vacío, vacante, libre.

unoffending [ʌnə'fendiŋ], *a.* inofensivo, inocente.

unofficial [ʌnə'fiʃəl], *a.* no oficial; poco ceremonioso.

unopened [ʌn'oupənd], *a.* no abierto.

unoppressive [ʌnə'presiv], *a.* que no es opresivo.

unordered [ʌn'ɔːɹdəɹd], *a.* no ordenado, no clasificado; no mandado.

unorganized [ʌn'ɔːɹgənaizd], *a.* no organizado, inorganizado; inorgánico.

unorthodox [ʌn'ɔːɹθodɔks], *a.* heterodoxo; no convencional.

unostentatious [ʌnɔsten'teiʃəs], *a.* sencillo, llano, simple, modesto.

unostentatiously, *adv.* sin ostentación.

unowned [ʌn'ound], *a.* sin dueño; mostrenco; no reconocido.

unoxidizable [ʌnɔksi'daizəbəl], *a.* inoxidable.

unpacified [ʌn'pæsifaid], *a.* no pacificado.

unpack [ʌn'pæk], *v.t.* desempaquetar, desenfardar, desembalar.

unpaid [ʌn'peid], *a.* no pagado, a pagar; (*com.*) pendiente.

unpainted [ʌn'peintid], *a.* no pintado.

unpaired [ʌn'pɛəɹd], *a.* desapareado.

unpalatable [ʌn'pælətəbəl], *a.* ingustable, de sabor desagradable; (*fig.*) desagradable.

unparalleled [ʌn'pærəleld], *a.* sin paralelo, sin igual, único, sin par, incomparable.

unpardonable [ʌn'pæːɹdənəbəl], *a.* imperdonable, irremisible.

unpardonably, *adv.* irremisiblemente, imperdonablemente.

unpardoned, *a.* no perdonado.

unparliamentary [ʌnpɑːɹlə'mentəri], *a.* indigno o impropio del parlamento, contrario a las reglas del parlamento.

unpatriotic [ʌnpætri'ɔtik], *a.* antipatriótico.

unpatronized [ʌn'pætronaizd], *a.* sin protección; que no tiene clientela.

unpaved, unpaven, *a.* desempedrado, sin empedrar.

unpeg [ʌn'peg], *v.t.* desclavar, desenclavijar; desclavijar; deshacer.

unpensioned [ʌn'penʃənd], *a.* no jubilado, no pensionado; sin pensión.

unpeople [ʌn'pi:pəl], *v.t.* despoblar.

unperceived [ʌnpəɪ'si:vd], *a.* desapercibido; inadvertido.

unperformed [ʌnpəɪ'fɔ:ɪmd], *a.* inacabado, inejecutado; por hacer o cumplir.

unpin [ʌn'pin], *v.t.* quitar los alfileres; desenclavijar, deshacer, desprender, separar.

unpitied [ʌn'pitid], *a.* de que no se tiene lástima o compasión.

unpitifully, unpityingly, *adv.* con inclemencia, con rigor, sin piedad.

unpitying, *a.* sin piedad, inclemente.

unplaced [ʌn'pleisd], *a.* sin empleo, sin colocación.

unplanted [ʌn'plɑ:ntid], *a.* que no ha sido plantado; espontáneo.

unpleasant [ʌn'plezənt], *a.* desagradable, desapacible, ingrato, molesto, enfadoso.

unpleasantly, *adv.* de una manera desagradable, desabrida o enfadosa.

unpleasantness, *s.* fastidio, disgusto, desazón, *f.,* enfado; desavencia, desacuerdo.

unpleasing [ʌn'pli:ziŋ], *a.* desagradable, displicente, enfadoso, molesto, ofensivo.

unpleasurable, *a.* desagradable, que no agrada.

unpledged [ʌn'pledʒd], *a.* no empeñado.

unpliable [ʌn'plaiəbəl], *a.* inflexible.

unpointed [ʌn'pɔinted], *a.* sin punta; (*gram.*) sin puntuación; (*fig.*) poco picante.

unpoised [ʌn'pɔizd], *a.* que no está en equilibrio.

unpolished [ʌn'pɔliʃd], *a.* no pulido, deslustrado, mate; (*fig.*) rudo, grosero, tosco, bronco, áspero; (*joy.*) en bruto.

unpolluted [ʌnpɔ'lju:tid], *a.* impoluto, no mancillado; no profanado; incontaminado, limpio.

unpopular [ʌn'pɔpju:lə], *a.* impopular.

unpopularity, *s.* impopularidad.

unpractical [ʌn'præktikəl], *a.* impracticable, irrealizable, no ejecutable.

unpractised [ʌn'præktisd], *a.* inexperto, inhábil, imperito, poco acostumbrado; no practicado.

unprecedented [ʌn'presedented], *a.* sin precedente, sin ejemplar, inaudito.

unpremeditated [ʌnpri'mediteitid], *a.* impremeditado, improvisado, indeliberado.

unprepared [ʌnpre'pɛəɪd], *a.* sin preparación, desprevenido, desapercibido.

unpreparedness, *s.* falta de preparación, desapercibimiento, desprevención.

unprepossessing [ʌnpri:pɔ'zesiŋ], *a.* poco atractivo, antipático.

unpresentable [ʌnpre'zentəbəl], *a.* no presentable.

unpressed [ʌn'presd], *a.* no apretado; no forzado, voluntario.

unpretending [ʌnpre'tendiŋ], *a.* sin pretención, modesto, sencillo.

unprevailing [ʌnpre'veiliŋ], *a.* impotente, que no hace impresión, que no consigue lo deseado.

unpriestly [ʌn'pri:stli], *a.* indigno de un sacerdote.

unprincely [ʌn'prinsli], *a.* indigno de un príncipe.

unprincipled [ʌn'prinsipəld], *a.* sin principios, sin conciencia, inmoral.

unprinted [ʌn'printid], *a.* no impreso; liso (de tejidos).

unprivileged [ʌn'privilidʒd], *a.* sin privilegio.

unprized [ʌn'praizd], *a.* poco apreciado.

unproclaimed [ʌnpro'kleimd], *a.* no proclamado, no reconocido.

unproductive [ʌnpro'dʌktiv], *a.* improductivo.

unprofessional [ʌnpro'feʃənəl], *a.* contrario a las reglas de una profesión.

unprofitable [ʌn'prɔfitəbəl], *a.* improductivo, infructífero, sin provecho; vano, inútil.

unprofitableness, *s.* inutilidad, infructuosidad.

unprofitably, *adv.* sin utilidad, inútilmente, sin provecho.

unpromising [ʌn'prɔmisiŋ], *a.* que no promete (mucho), que da poca esperanza.

unpronounceable [ʌnpro'naunsəbəl], *a.* que no se puede pronunciar.

unpropitious [ʌnpro'piʃəs], *a.* poco propicio, desfavorable, infausto.

unprosperous [ʌn'prɔspərəs], *a.* impróspero, no lucrativo; desafortunado, infeliz, desgraciado.

unprotected [ʌnpro'tekted], *a.* desvalido, sin protección, no protegido.

unproved [ʌn'pru:vd], **unproven** [ʌn'prouvən], *a.* no probado, no demostrado.

unprovided [ʌnpro'vaidid], *a.* desprovisto, desproveído, desabastecido, desapercibido; *unprovided for,* sin recurso (para), desvalido.

unprovoked [ʌnpro'voukd], *a.* no provocado, sin provocación, sin motivo.

unprovoking, *a.* que no provoca.

unpublished [ʌn'pʌbliʃd], *a.* inédito, no publicado; (*fig.*) desconocido, secreto, oculto.

unpunctual [ʌn'pʌŋktju:əl], *a.* no puntual, tardador, tardo. ·

unpunished [ʌn'pʌniʃd], *a.* impune, sin castigo.

unqualified [ʌn'kwɔlifaid], *a.* impropio, inepto, poco apto, inhábil, inhabilitado, incapaz; sin título o licencia (para una profesión), desautorizado, incompetente; ilimitado, sin restricción; entero, completo, absoluto.

unqueenly [ʌn'kwi:nli], *a.* indigno o impropio de una reina.

unquenchable [ʌn'kwentʃəbəl], *a.* inextinguible, inapagable, insaciable.

unquenched, *a.* no apagado, no sosegado.

unquestionable [ʌn'kwestʃənəbəl], *a.* incontestable, fuera de duda, indudable, indiscutible, indisputable, incuestionable.

unquestionably, *adv.* incontestablemente, indudablemente, sin duda, sin disputa, a buen seguro.

unquestioned, *a.* incontestado, incontestable, fuera de duda, indisputable; no preguntado, no examinado.

unquiet [ʌn'kwaiət], *a.* inquieto, turbado, desasosegado; no callado, nada silencioso.

unquietly, *adv.* nada silenciosamente; con desasosiego, con inquietud, inquietamente.

unquietness, *s.* falta de silencio; inquietud, agitación, desasosiego.

unracked [ʌn'rækd], *a.* no clarificado, no trasegado (vinos).

unransomed [ʌn'rænsəmd], *a.* sin rescate, no rescatado.

unravel [ʌn'rævəl], *v.t.* deshilar, desenlazar, desenredar, desembrollar, desenmarañar, descifrar, desatar; (*fig.*) desenredar, desembrollar, descifrar. — *v.i.* desenredarse, desembrollarse, desenlazarse.

unravelling, *s.* deshiladura; desenlace.

unreached [ʌn'ri:tʃd], *a.* no alcanzado.

unread [ʌn'red], *a.* no leído, sin leer; iletrado, indocto, ignorante, iliterato.

unreadable [ʌn'ri:dəbəl], *a.* ilegible.

unreadiness, *s.* falta de preparación, desapercibimiento, desprevención; falta de facilidad, lentitud, dificultad.

unready [ʌn'redi], *a.* desprevenido, desapercibido; no dispuesto, no inclinado; torpe, grosero, lerdo.

unreal [ʌn'ri:əl], *a.* irreal, no real, incorpóreo, incorporal, inmaterial; ilusorio, quimérico, sin realidad, ficticio; falso, insincero.

unreality [ʌnri'æliti], *s.* irrealidad, inmaterialidad; ilusión, lo ilusorio, lo ficticio; falsedad, insinceridad.

unreaped [ʌn'ri:pd], *a.* no segado, no cosechado.

unreasonable [ʌn'ri:zənəbəl], *a.* irracional, irrazonable, desrazonable; extravagante, excesivo, inmoderado, exorbitante.

unreasonableness, *s.* extravagancia, exorbitancia; absurdidad, sinrazón, *f.*, falta de razón, despropósito.

unreasonably, *adv.* sin razón, irracionalmente, desatinadamente; excesivamente, exorbitantemente.

unreclaimed [ʌnre'kleimd], *a.* no reclamado; incorregible.

unrecognizable [ʌnrekəg'naizəbəl], *a.* que no puede reconocerse.

unreconciled [ʌn'rekənsaild], *a.* no reconciliado, enemistado.

unrecorded [ʌnre'kɔ:ɹdid], *a.* no inscrito, no registrado, no mencionado en los anales, no archivado; no grabado (en disco gramofónico).

unrecoverable [ʌnre'kʌvərəbəl], *a.* irrecuperable; irreparable, incurable.

unrecovered, *a.* no recobrado, no restablecido.

unredeemed [ʌnre'di:md], *a.* no rescatado, no redimido.

unredressed [ʌnre'dresd], *a.* no reformado, no enderezado.

unreduced [ʌnre'dju:sd], *a.* no reducido; no rebajado.

unrefined [ʌnre'faind], *a.* bruto, en bruto, no purificado, no depurado, no refinado; grosero, inculto, rudo, mal criado.

unreflecting [ʌnre'flektiŋ], *a.;* **unreflectingly,** *adv.* sin reflexionar.

unreformable, *a.* irreformable, incorregible.

unreformed [ʌnre'fɔ:ɹmd], *a.* no reformado, sin corregir; obstinado en el mal, impenitente.

unrefreshing [ʌnre'freʃiŋ], *a.* que no refresca, no refrescante; poco estimulante.

unrefunded [ʌnre'fʌndid], *a.* no reembolsado.

unregarded [ʌnre'gɑ:ɹded], *a.* desdeñado, desatendido; desconocido.

unregenerate [ʌnre'dʒenərit], *a.* no regenerado; incorrigible, malvado.

unregistered [ʌn'redʒistəɹd], *a.* no certificado, no registrado, no inscrito.

unregretted [ʌnre'gretid], *a.* no sentido, poco lamentado, no llorado.

unregulated [ʌn'regju:leitid], *a.* no ordenado, no arreglado.

unreined [ʌn'reind], *a.* sin freno, desenfrenado; (*fig.*) desenfrenado.

unrelated [ʌnre'leitid] **(to),** *a.* sin parentesco (con), sin relación (con); no relacionado, no afín.

unrelenting [ʌnre'lentiŋ], *a.* inexorable, implacable, inflexible.

unreliable [ʌnre'laiəbəl], *a.* poco serio, informal, no digno de fe, indigno de confianza, no fiable; incierto, inestable, mudadizo, errátil; (*de máquinas*) poco seguro de funcionamento, que funciona mal.

unrelieved [ʌnre'li:vd], *a.* no aliviado, sin socorro; continuo, monótono; (*mil.*) no relevado.

unrelinquished [ʌnre'liŋkwiʃd], *a.* no abandonado.

unrelished [ʌn'reliʃd], *a.* sin gusto, soso, insípido; no gustado.

unreluctant [ʌnre'lʌktənt], *a.* que no vacila.

unremarkable [ʌnre'mɑ:ɹkəbəl], *a.* poco notable.

unremarked, *a.* no notado.

unremedied [ʌn'remedid], *a.* no curado; irremediado.

unremembered [ʌnre'membəɹd], *a.* no recordado; pasado por alto.

unremembering, *a.* olvidadizo.

unremitting [ʌnre'mitiŋ], *a.* incesante, constante; infatigable, sostenido, incansable.

unremittingly, *adv.* incesantemente, sin descanso.

unremunerated [ʌnre'mju:nəreitid], *a.* irremunerado.

unremunerative, *a.* no remunerador, poco lucrativo.

unrepaired [ʌnre'pɛəɹd], *a.* no reparado, no arreglado, sin reparación.

unrepealable [ʌnre'pi:ləbəl], *a.* irrevocable.

unrepealed [ʌnre'pi:ld], *a.* no revocado; en vigor.

unrepeated [ʌnre'pi:tid], *a.* no repetido.

unrepentant [ʌnre'pentənt], *a.* impenitente, obstinado, contumaz.

unrepented, *a.* de que uno no se arrepiente.

unrepresented, *a.* sin representante, no representado.

unreprieved [ʌnre'pri:vd], *a.* (reo de muerte) a quien no se ha concedido la conmutación de pena.

unreproached [ʌnre'proutʃd], *a.* no reprochado, sin censura.

unrequested [ʌnre'kwestid], *a.* no solicitado, no invitado.

unrequired [ʌnre'kwaiəɹd], *a.* innecesario, no pedido, no deseado.

unrequited [ʌnre'kwaitid], *a.* no recompensado.

unreserve, *s.* ausencia de reserva, abandono, ingenuidad; candor.

unreserved [ʌnre'zə:ɹvd], *a.* ilimitado; abierto, franco, expansivo.

unreservedly, *adv.* sin reserva; sin reticencia, francamente, abiertamente.

unresisted, *a.* sin resistencia.

unresisting [ʌnre'zistiŋ], *a.* que no resiste, que no ofrece resistencia.

unresistingly, *adv.* sin resistencia.

unresolved [ʌnre'zɔlvd], *a.* irresoluto; sin solución.

unresolving, *a.* irresoluto.

unrespited [ʌnre'spaitid], *a.* sin descanso, sin suspensión; sin remisión de sentencia.

unrest [ʌn'rest], *s.* inquietud, desasosiego, agitación.

unrestored [ʌnre'stɔːɹd], *a.* no restituido, no restablecido, no devuelto; no restaurado, no renovado.

unrestrained [ʌnre'streind], *a.* sin freno, desenfrenado, no contenido, desarreglado.

unrestricted [ʌnre'striktid], *a.* sin restricción, libre.

unreturned [ʌnre'təːɹnd], *a.* no devuelto.

unrevenged [ʌnre'vendʒd], *a.* no vengado, (*poét.*) inulto.

unrevengeful, *a.* que no es vengativo.

unreversed [ʌnre'vəːɹsd], *a.* no revocado, no cambiado.

unrevised [ʌnre'vaizd], *a.* no revisto, no cambiado.

unrewarded [ʌnre'wɔːɹdid], *a.* no recompensado, no premiado; no reconocido.

unriddle [ʌn'ridəl], *v.t.* resolver, desembrollar, descifrar.

unrifled [ʌn'raifəld], *a.* no robado, saqueado o pillado.

unrig [ʌn'rig], *v.t.* (*mar.*) desaparejar.

unrighteous [ʌn'raitʃəs], *a.* injusto, inicuo, malo, perverso.

unrighteousness, *s.* injusticia, inicuidad, maldad, perversidad.

unrightful, *a.* injusto; ilegítimo.

unripe [ʌn'raip], *a.* prematuro, verde, agraz, crudo, precoz.

unripened, *a.* inmaturo.

unripeness, *s.* falta de madurez.

unrivalled [ʌn'raivəld], *a.* sin rival, sin igual, sin paralelo, incomparable, sin par.

unrivet [ʌn'rivit], *v.t.* quitar los remaches, desclavar.

unrobe [ʌn'roub], *v.t.* quitar el vestido a, desnudar. — *v.i.* quitar su vestido, desnudarse.

unroll [ʌn'roul], *v.t.* desarrollar, desenrollar; desplegar, desenvolver; abrir. — *v.i.* desarrollarse, desenvolverse, abrirse.

unromantic [ʌnro'mæntik], *a.* poco romántico, poco romancesco.

unroof [ʌn'ruːf], *v.t.* levantar el tejado de, destechar, destejar.

unroused [ʌn'rauzd], *a.* no despertado.

unroyal [ʌn'rɔiəl], *a.* poco real.

unruffle, *v.i.* apaciguarse, calmarse.

unruffled [ʌn'rʌfəld], *a.* reposado, sereno, tranquilo; terso, liso, no arrugado.

unruled [ʌn'ruːld], *a.* independiente, absoluto; (papel) sin rayar.

unruliness, *s.* desenfreno, desenfrenamiento; indisciplina, rebeldía; indocilidad.

unruly [ʌn'ruːli], *a.* indomable, indócil, inmanejable, intratable; ingobernable, indisciplinable; irrefrenable, desenfrenado.

unsaddle [ʌn'sædəl], *v.t.* desarzonar, desbastar, desensillar.

unsafe [ʌn'seif], *a.* inseguro, peligroso, aventurado.

unsafely, *adv.* sin seguridad, inseguramente, peligrosamente.

unsaid [ʌn'sed], *a.* no dicho; *to leave unsaid,* no decir, callar.

unsalable, unsaleable [ʌn'seiləbəl], *a.* (*com.*) invendible.

unsalted [ʌn'sɔːltid], *a.* soso, sin sal; desalado.

unsanctioned [ʌn'sæŋkʃənd], *a.* no sancionado, no permitido.

unsated [ʌn'seitid], *a.* no harto.

unsatisfactorily, *adv.* de una manera poco satisfactoria.

unsatisfactory [ʌnsætis'fæktəri], *a.* poco satisfactorio, que no satisface.

unsatisfied [ʌn'sætisfaid], *a.* descontento, no satisfecho; no convencido; no harto; no saldado, no liquidado.

unsatisfying, *a.* poco satisfactorio, insuficiente.

unsavourily, *adv.* sin sabor, desabridamente.

unsavoury [ʌn'seivəri], *a.* sin sabor, insípido, soso; desagradable, desabrido; fétido, hediondo; (*fig.*) desabrido, sucio, deshonrado.

unsay [ʌn'sei], *v.t.* retractar, desdecir(se).

unscared [ʌn'skɛəd], *a.* no asustado.

unscarred [ʌn'skɑːd], *a.* sin cicatrices.

unscathed [ʌn'skeiðd], *a.* sano y salvo, no herido, intacto.

unscholastic [ʌnsko'læstik], *a.* no escolar; no escolástico; no pedante.

unschooled [ʌn'skuːld], *a.* iletrado, ignorante; sin experiencia.

unscientific [ʌnsiən'tifik], *a.* no científico; inexacto.

unscorched [ʌn'skɔːtʃd], *a.* no quemado, sin chamuscar.

unscratched [ʌn'skrætʃd], *a.* no raspado, no arañado; intacto, no perjudicado, como nuevo.

unscreened [ʌn'skriːnd], *a.* no abrigado; (*elec.*) descubierto, no protegido contra contactos accidentales.

unscrew [ʌn'skruː], *v.t.* destornillar, desatornillar; (*fig.*) desenganchar. — *v.i.* destornillarse.

unscriptural [ʌn'skriptʃərəl], *a.* no conforme a la Escritura Santa.

unscrupulous [ʌn'skruːpjuːləs], *a.* poco escrupuloso, sin conciencia.

unscrupulously, *adv.* sin escrúpulos, sin conciencia, sin moralidad.

unseal [ʌn'siːl], *v.t.* desellar, abrir.

unsearchable [ʌn'səːtʃəbəl], *a.* inescrutable, impenetrable.

unseasonable [ʌn'siːzənəbəl], *a.* fuera de sazón, intempestivo, fuera de propósito, inoportuno, prematuro, inconveniente, indebido.

unseasonably, *adv.* intempestivamente, fuera de sazón.

unseasoned [ʌn'siːzənd], *a.* sin sazonar, soso; verde, nuevo, no preparado (de madera, etc.); intempestivo, fuera de sazón; sin experiencia, no aclimatado, no acostumbrado; no aguerrido (tropas); no endurecido.

unseat [ʌn'siːt], *v.t.* quitar de un asiento, desarzonar, derribar; (*pol.*) anular la elección de un miembro de la Cámara de Comunes; echar abajo (a un ministerio).

unseaworthy [ʌn'siːwəːɹði], *a.* en mal estado para hacerse a la mar, inservible.

unseconded [ʌn'sekəndid], *a.* no apoyado, no favorecido.

unsecured [ʌnse'kjuːəd], *a.* inseguro, peligroso.

unseeing [ʌn'siːiŋ], *a.* falto de vista; inobservante.

unseemliness, s. indecencia, inconveniencia.
unseemly [ʌn'siːmli], a. mal visto, mal parecido, indecente, inconveniente, indecoroso.
unseen [ʌn'siːn], a. inapercibido; invisible, oculto; *the Unseen,* el mundo de los espíritus.
unselfish [ʌn'selfiʃ], a. desinteresado, desprendido, generoso.
unselfishness, s. desinterés, abnegación, generosidad.
unsensitized [ʌn'sensitaizd], a. (*foto.*) no sensibilizado.
unserviceable [ʌn'səːɹvisəbəl], a. fuera de servicio, inútil, malo, inservible.
unserviceableness, s. inutilidad.
unset [ʌn'set], a. no puesto, no colocado; no cuajado.
unsettle [ʌn'setəl], v.t. desarreglar, descomponer, poner en desorden; trastornar, agitar, turbar, alterar. — v.i. turbarse, desarreglarse.
unsettled, a. vacilante, instable, inconstante, variable, incierto; descompuesto, desarreglado; agitado, turbado, trastornado; sin residencia fija, errante; sin colonizar, sin habitantes; indeterminado, irresuelto; (*com.*) no liquidado, pendiente, de pago, por pagar.
unsettledness, unsettlement, s. desarreglo; instabilidad; indecisión, irresolución, incertidumbre.
unsevered [ʌn'sevəɹd], a. no separado, indiviso.
unsew [ʌn'sou], v.t. descoser, deshilar.
unsex [ʌn'seks], v.t. privar, quitar las cualidades propias del sexo.
unsexual, a. asexual; no sexual, sin sexualidad.
unshackle [ʌn'ʃækəl], v.t. desencadenar, destrabar, desaherrojar; libertar.
unshaded [ʌn'ʃeidid], a. sin sombra, no sombreado; (*pint.*) no sombreado, sin esfumación.
unshakable, a. firme, constante, imperturbable.
unshaken [ʌn'ʃeikən], a. constante, firme; inmovible.
unshape [ʌn'ʃeip], v.t. desfigurar; desarreglar, trastornar, poner en confusión.
unshapely, unshapen, a. disforme, informe, desproporcionado.
unshaven [ʌn'ʃeivən], a. no afeitado, sin afeitar.
unsheathe [ʌn'ʃiːð], v.t. desenvainar.
unshed [ʌn'ʃed], a. no derramado.
unshielded [ʌn'ʃiːldid], **unsheltered** [ʌn'ʃeltəɹd], a. desabrigado, no abrigado, desvalido.
unship [ʌn'ʃip], v.t. (*mar.*) desembarcar, descargar; desmontar, desarmar.
unshod [ʌn'ʃod], a. descalzo, con pie desnudo; desherrado (de un caballo).
unshorn [ʌn'ʃɔːɹn], a. intonso, no cortado; no esquilado, por esquilar (de las ovejas).
unshrinkable [ʌn'ʃriŋkəbəl], a. inencogible (*neol.*), que no se encoge (de vestidos).
unshrinking, a. intrépido, sin vacilar.
unshrinkingly, adv. intrépidamente, sin vacilar.
unshriven [ʌn'ʃrivən], a. no confesado.
unshrouded [ʌn'ʃraudid], a. sin sudario.
unshut [ʌn'ʃʌt], a. no cerrado.
unsifted [ʌn'siftid], a. no cribado, no cernido.
unsightliness, s. deformidad, fealdad.

unsightly [ʌn'saitli], a. disforme, feo.
unsisterly [ʌn'sistəɹli], a. indigno o impropio de una hermana.
unsized [ʌn'saizd], a. (papel) desencolado, no encolado, sin cola.
unskilful [ʌn'skilfəl], **unskilled** [ʌn'skild], a. inhábil, desmañado, inexperto, imperito.
unskilfully, adv. torpemente, con poca maña, sin arte.
unskilfulness, s. inhabilidad, torpeza, impericia, desmaña.
unslaked [ʌn'sleikd], a. no apagado (de la sed); no apaciguado, no satisfecho.
unsling [ʌn'sliŋ], v.t. (*mar.*) quitar las relingas de, deslingar.
unsmoked [ʌn'smoukd], a. no ahumado.
unsociable [ʌn'souʃəbəl], a. insociable, intratable, huraño.
unsociableness, unsociability, s. insociabilidad, huraña.
unsocial [ʌn'souʃəl], a. insocial, huraño.
unsoiled [ʌn'sɔild], a. sin mancha, limpio, impoluto.
unsold [ʌn'sould], a. no vendido; por vender.
unsoldierlike [ʌn'souldʒəɹlaik], **unsoldierly** [ʌn'souldʒəɹli], a. poco militar, poco marcial, indigno de un soldado.
unsolicited [ʌnso'lisitid], a. no solicitado, sin ser solicitado.
unsolicitous, a. poco servicial, poco complaciente.
unsolved [ʌn'sɔlvd], a. no resuelto, no solucionado.
unsophisticated [ʌnso'fistikeitid], a. inurbano; cándido, puro, sencillo; inexperto.
unsorted [ʌn'sɔːɹtid], a. no surtido, mixto.
unsought [ʌn'sɔːt], a. no buscado, no solicitado.
unsound [ʌn'saund], a. poco sólido, falto de solidez, falto de fuerza; corrompido, podrido, vicioso, malsano; ligero, defectuoso; falso, erróneo; enfermo, enfermizo, achacoso; quebrado, rajado, hendido; heterodoxo; *unsound in health,* de mala salud; *of unsound mind,* insano, desequilibrado.
unsounded, a. que no se ha sondeado.
unsoundly, adv. de un modo poco sano; falsamente; ligeramente; poco sólidamente.
unsoundness, s. falta de solidez; corrupción; debilidad, mala salud; falsedad, error; heterodoxia.
unsoured [ʌn'sauəɹd], a. no agriado.
unsown [ʌn'soun], a. no sembrado.
unsparing [ʌn'spɛəriŋ], a. liberal, generoso, pródigo; sin piedad, inhumano, cruel.
unsparingly, adv. liberalmente, generosamente, pródigamente; sin piedad, inhumanamente.
unspeakable [ʌn'spiːkəbəl], a. inexplicable, inefable, inenarrable, indecible; incomparable, inmejorable; execrable.
unspeakably, adv. de una manera inexplicable, indeciblemente, inefablemente; de una manera execrable.
unspecified [ʌn'spesifaid], a. no indicado, sin precisar, no especificado.
unspent [ʌn'spent], a. no gastado, no disipado, inexhausto.
unspoiled [ʌn'spɔild], a. ileso, intacto; no despojado.
unspoilt, a. no mimado; no estropeado, ileso, intacto.

unspotted [ʌn'spɔtid], *a.* sin mancha, puro, limpio, inmaculado.

unsprung, *a.* sin muelles; no suspendido.

unstable [ʌn'steibəl], *a.* inestable, instable, movedizo; variable, vacilante, inconstante; desequilibrado, insano; desmoronable.

unstableness, *s.* inestabilidad; vacilación; desequilibrio.

unstaid [ʌn'steid], *a.* nada ceremonioso.

unstaidness, *s.* falta de ceremoniosidad, afabilidad.

unstained [ʌn'steind], *a.* inmaculado, no manchado; no teñido.

unstamped [ʌn'stæmpd], *a.* no sellado, sin franquear, sin sello.

unstanched [ʌn'stɑ:ntʃd], *a.* no restañado.

unstatesmanlike [ʌn'steitsmənlaik], *a.* no político, indigno o impropio de un político.

unsteadily, *adv.* sin seguridad, sin firmeza, de una manera tambaleante; inconstantemente, ligeramente.

unsteadiness, *s.* inestabilidad, poca seguridad, irresolución, inconsecuencia, inconstancia, falta de firmeza; tambaleo; ligereza, debilidad.

unsteady [ʌn'stedi], *a.* voluble, inestable, vacilante, poco firme; tambaleante; poco asegurado.

unstinted [ʌn'stintid], *a.* liberal, no restringido, no limitado.

unstirred [ʌn'stə:rd], *a.* no conmovido, poco emocionado; sin remover, sin revolver.

unstop [ʌn'stɔp], *v.t.* destapar; dar paso, abrir.

unstrained [ʌn'streind], *a.* libre, suelto; no colado, no filtrado.

unstrengthened [ʌn'streŋθənd], *a.* no fortificado.

unstring [ʌn'striŋ], *v.t.* (*pret., p.p.* **unstrung**) soltar, aflojar; desliar, desatar, deshacer, quitar las cuerdas de, desencordar; desensartar (perlas).

unstudied, *a.* no estudiado; no premeditado, impensado, natural.

unstudious [ʌn'stju:diəs], *a.* poco estudioso.

unsubdued [ʌnsəb'dju:d], *a.* no disminuido; sin vacilar, intrépido; indómito.

unsubject [ʌn'sʌbdʒekt], *a.* no sujeto, no sujetado, no sumiso.

unsubmissive [ʌnsəb'misiv], *a.* no sometido, rebelde, insumiso.

unsubmitting, *a.* que no se somete, indomable.

unsubstantial [ʌnsəb'stænʃəl], *a.* insubstancial, inmaterial, poco sólido.

unsuccessful [ʌnsək'sesful], *a.* sin éxito, infructuoso, desgraciado, desairado, desafortunado, adverso; *to be unsuccessful,* fracasar, no tener éxito, fallar.

unsuccessfully, *adv.* sin éxito, en vano, vanamente.

unsuccessfulness, *s.* falta de éxito, fracaso, desdicha, desgracia.

unsufferable [ʌn'sʌfrəbəl], *a.* insoportable.

unsuitable [ʌn'sju:təbəl], *a.* no apto, no adecuado, inapropiado, poco conveniente, inconveniente, impropio; incongruo, incompatible, fuera de lugar; indigno.

unsuitability, unsuitableness, *s.* inconveniencia, incongruencia, impropiedad, incapacidad, incompatibilidad, desacuerdo.

unsuitably, *adv.* poco convenientemente, mal a propósito.

unsuited, *a.* incompatible, desproporcionado.

unsullied [ʌn'sʌlid], *a.* sin mancha, no ensuciado, inmaculado, puro.

unsung [ʌn'sʌŋ], *a.* no cantado; no elogiado, no celebrado.

unsupplied [ʌnsə'plaid], *a.* no provisto, no abastecido.

unsupported [ʌnsə'pɔ:tid], *a.* sin sostenimiento, sin sostén, sin apoyo.

unsuppressed [ʌnsə'presd], *a.* no suprimido, no reprimido.

unsure [ʌn'ʃu:ər], *a.* poco seguro, incierto.

unsurmountable [ʌnsə'mauntəbəl], *a.* insuperable.

unsurpassed [ʌnsər'pɑ:st], *a.* no sobrepujado, incomparable, insuperable.

unsusceptible [ʌnsə'septibəl], *a.* no susceptible, incapaz.

unsuspected, *a.* no sospechado, inopinado.

unsuspecting [ʌnsə'spektiŋ], *a.* no sospechoso, no suspicaz; sin sospechas, confiado.

unsuspicious [ʌnsə'spiʃəs], *a.* sin sospechas, franco, abierto, confiado.

unswathe [ʌn'sweið], *v.t.* desfajar.

unswerving [ʌn'swə:rviŋ], *a.* inconmovible, tenaz, firme, inquebrantable.

unsworn [ʌn'swɔ:rn], *a.* no juramentado.

unsymmetrical [ʌnsi'metrikəl], *a.* poco simétrico, asimétrico, desproporcionado.

unsympathetic [ʌnsimpə'θetik], *a.* incompasivo, insensible; antipático.

unsympathizing, *a.* que no simpatiza, incompasivo.

unsynchronised, unsynchronized [ʌn'siŋkrənaizd], *a.* (*mec.*) asincronizado.

unsystematic [ʌnsiste'mætik], *a.* sin sistema, falto de sistema.

untack [ʌn'tæk], *v.t.* descoser; quitar tachuelas.

untainted [ʌn'teinted], *a.* fresco, puro, no corrompido.

untamable [ʌn'teiməbəl], *a.* indomable, indomesticable.

untamed, *a.* no domado, no domesticado, salvaje, cerril, bravío; indomado, insumiso.

untarnished [ʌn'tɑ:niʃd], *a.* no empañado, sin mancha, sin mancilla.

untasted [ʌn'teistid], *a.* no gustado, no probado.

untaught [ʌn'tɔ:t], *a.* iletrado, no instruido, ignorante.

unteachable [ʌn'ti:tʃəbəl], *a.* indócil, incapaz de ser enseñado.

untenable [ʌn'tenəbəl], *a.* insostenible.

untenantable [ʌn'tenəntəbəl], *a.* no habitable.

untenanted, *a.* desocupado, inhabitado, desalquilado, vacío.

untended [ʌn'tendid], *a.* no cuidado, no guardado.

untested [ʌn'testid], *a.* no probado, no examinado.

unthanked [ʌn'θæŋkd], *a.* sin agradecimiento, desestimado.

unthankful, *a.* ingrato, desagradecido.

unthankfully, *adv.* con ingratitud, ingratamente, desagradecidamente.

unthankfulness, *s.* ingratitud, desagradecimiento.

unthinking [ʌn'θiŋkiŋ], *a.* irreflexivo, inconsiderado, indiscreto, descuidado, desatento.

unthinkingly, *adv.* inconsideradamente, indiscretamente, irreflexivamente.

unthought-of, *a.* impensado, inesperado, inaudito, imprevisto.

unthread [ʌnˈθred], *v.t.* deshebrar, desenhebrar, deshilachar; desensartar.

untidily, *adv.* sin orden, sin cuidado, sin arreglo; sin aseo.

untidiness, *s.* desorden, desarreglo, desaliño, descompostura; desaseo.

untidy [ʌnˈtaidi], *a.* descuidado, desaliñado, desarreglado; desaseado.

untie [ʌnˈtai], *v.t.* desatar, desliar, desligar, desprender, desenlazar; desamarrar; desembrollar; aflojar, zafar, soltar; resolver.

until [ʌnˈtil], *prep.* hasta, antes de; *until now,* hasta aquí. — *conj.* hasta que, antes que, mientras que.

untile [ʌnˈtail], *v.t.* quitar las tejas de, destejar.

untilled [ʌnˈtild], *a.* no cultivado, no labrado, inculto, baldío.

untimeliness, *s.* inoportunidad, lo intempestivo.

untimely [ʌnˈtaimli], *a.* inoportuno, intempestivo, prematuro, extemporal, fuera de propósito. — *adv.* prematuramente, intempestivamente, antes del tiempo, fuera de sazón.

untinged [ʌnˈtindʒd], *a.* no teñido, incoloro, sin mancha.

untirable [ʌnˈtaiərəbəl], *a.* infatigable, incansable.

untiring, *a.* infatigable, incesante.

untitled [ʌnˈtaitəld], *a.* sin título (nobiliario); sin título, sin epígrafe.

unto [ˈʌntu:], *prep.* a, hacia, en, dentro.

untold [ʌnˈtould], *a.* no referido, no contado, no narrado, no dicho, nunca dicho; desmedido, incalculable, un sinnúmero de; *to leave untold,* no decir, no referir, dejar en el tintero.

untomb [ʌnˈtu:m], *v.t.* exhumar.

untouchable [ʌnˈtʌtʃəbəl], *s., a.* intangible, que no debe tocarse.

untouched, *a.* no alcanzado; no afectado; no tocado; no conmovido, insensible, impasible; ileso, intacto.

untoward [ʌnˈtoːrd], *a.* adverso, desfavorable, desgraciado; indecente, impropio; indócil, refractario; incómodo, enfadoso.

untowardness, *s.* desgracia, adversidad; indecencia, impropiedad, inconveniencia; indocilidad; enfado.

untraceable [ʌnˈtreisəbəl], *a.* que no se puede trazar o rastrear o averiguar.

untraced, *a.* sin huella, rastro o pisada; no descubierto; (*art.*) no calcado.

untractable [ʌnˈtræktəbəl], *a.* intratable, indócil, insumiso, testarudo.

untractableness, *s.* indocilidad; huraña.

untrained [ʌnˈtreind], *a.* imperito, inexperto, indisciplinado; (*deportes*) no entrenado.

untrammelled [ʌnˈtræməld], *a.* sin trabas, libre, desembarazado.

untransferable [ʌntrænsˈfəːrəbəl], *a.* intransferible, no enajenable.

untranslatable [ʌntrænsˈleitəbəl], *a.* intraducible.

untravelled [ʌnˈtrævəld], *a.* que no ha viajado; intransitado, inexplorado; provinciano.

untried [ʌnˈtraid], *a.* no ensayado, no experimentado, no probado; no inspeccionado, no verificado, no juzgado.

untrimmed [ʌnˈtrimd], *a.* no adaptado, sin arreglar, no arreglado; no guarnecido, sin guarniciones, sin adornos; (*carp.*) sin alisar o desbastar; (*agr.*) sin podar, sin mondar, sin escamondar.

untrod [ʌnˈtrod], **untrodden** [ʌnˈtrodən], *a.* no frecuentado, no pisado, no hollado, virgen.

untroubled [ʌnˈtrʌbəld], *a.* quieto, tranquilo, apacible, sosegado; transparente, claro.

untrue [ʌnˈtru:], *a.* falso, no verdadero, mendaz; engañoso, infiel, pérfido.

untruly [ʌnˈtru:li], *adv.* falsamente; pérfidamente, infielmente.

untruss [ʌnˈtrʌs], *v.t.* desempaquetar, desatar.

untrustworthy [ʌnˈtrʌstwəːˌiði], *a.* indigno de confianza, poco fiable, indigno de fe; poco serio, informal.

untrusty [ʌnˈtrʌsti], *a.* pérfido, desleal, infiel.

untruth [ʌnˈtru:θ], *s.* mentira, falsedad.

untruthful, *a.* mentiroso, inexacto, falso.

untuck [ʌnˈtʌk], *v.t.* deshacer un pliegue a.

untunable [ʌnˈtju:nəbəl], *a.* discordante, que no se puede acordar.

untune, *v.t.* (*mús.*) desafinar, desacordar; (*elec.*) desintonizar.

unturned [ʌnˈtəːrnd], *a.* no torneado.

untutored [ʌnˈtju:tərd], *a.* sin instrucción, ignorante, inculto.

untwine [ʌnˈtwain], **untwist** [ʌnˈtwist], *v.t.* destorcer, desenredar, desenrollar, desarrollar, desatar, deshacer.

unused [ʌnˈju:zd], *a.* no empleado, nuevo, poco usado; inusitado, insólito.

unusual [ʌnˈju:ʒju:əl], *a.* poco usual, nada usual, poco común, infrecuente, poco frecuente, inusitado, insólito, desacostumbrado.

unusually, *adv.* inusitadamente, rara vez, raramente; en extremo, extraordinariamente.

unutterable [ʌnˈʌtərəbəl], *a.* indecible, inefable, inenarrable.

unvalued [ʌnˈvælju:d], *a.* desestimado, desdeñado, menospreciado, descuidado.

unvanquished [ʌnˈvæŋkwiʃd], *a.* invicto.

unvaried [ʌnˈvɛərid], *a.* uniforme, invariable, monótono.

unvarnished [ʌnˈvɑːniʃd], *a.* no barnizado, sin barnizar, sin barniz; sin adorno.

unvarying [ʌnˈvɛəriiŋ], *a.* invariable, uniforme, constante.

unveil [ʌnˈveil], *v.t., v.i.* descubrir(se), quitar(se) el velo.

unventilated [ʌnˈventileitid], *a.* no ventilado, no aireado, ahogado sin aire.

unversed [ʌnˈvəːsd], *a.* poco versado, inexperto.

unviolated [ʌnˈvaioleitid], *a.* inviolado, ileso, intacto.

unwakened [ʌnˈweikənd], *a.* dormido, no despierto.

unwalled, *a.* abierto, sin murallas, sin muros, sin paredes.

unwarily [ʌnˈwɛərili], *adv.* aturdidamente, sin previsión, incautamente, imprudentemente.

unwariness, *s.* imprevisión, imprudencia, aturdimiento.

unwarned [ʌnˈwɔːnd], *a.* desprevenido, no prevenido, no advertido.

unwarrantable [ʌnˈwɔrəntəbəl], *a.* injustificable, indisculpable, insostenible.

unwarrantably, *adv.* sin excusa, injustamente, injustificablemente.

unwarranted [ʌnˈwɔrəntid], *a.* no autorizado,

sin motivo, injustificable; (*com.*) no garantizado, sin garantía.

unwary [ʌn'wɛəri], *a.* incauto, irreflexivo, improvisor, imprudente, inconsiderado.

unwashed [ʌn'wɔʃd], *a.* no lavado, sucio, puerco; *the great unwashed*, (*iron.*) el populacho, la turba, la gentuza.

unwasted [ʌn'weistid], *a.* no perdido, no malgastado, entero.

unwatched [ʌn'wɔtʃd], *a.* no vigilado.

unwatered [ʌn'wɔːtəɹd], *a.* no regado.

unwavering [ʌn'weivəriŋ], *a.* que no vacila, resuelto, decidido, determinado, firme, constante.

unweaned [ʌn'wiːnd], *a.* no destetado.

unwearable [ʌn'wɛəɹəbəl], *a.* que no puede ponerse más, usado; impropio para ponerse, inservible.

unwearied [ʌn'wiəɹid], *a.* infatigable.

unweariedly, unwearyingly, *adv.* sin cansarse.

unwearying, *a.* que no se cansa, tenaz, constante.

unweave [ʌnwiːv], *v.t.* destejer, destramar, deshilachar; destrenzar.

unwed [ʌn'wed], **unwedded** [ʌn'wedid], *a.* no casado, soltero.

unwelcome [ʌn'welkəm], *a.* mal venido, mal acogido, mal recibido; inoportuno; molesto, incómodo.

unwell [ʌn'wel], *a.* indispuesto, enfermizo, malo.

unwept [ʌn'wept], *a.* no llorado, no lamentado.

unwholesome [ʌn'houlsəm], *a.* insalubre, malsano; nocivo, pernicioso, malo.

unwholesomeness, *s.* insalubridad.

unwieldily, *adv.* pesadamente, dificultosamente.

unwieldiness, *s.* pesadez, dificultad, calidad de abultado.

unwieldy [ʌn'wiːldi], *a.* abultado, pesado, ponderoso, demasiado grande, difícil de manejar.

unwilling [ʌn'wiliŋ], *a.* maldispuesto, desinclinado, que no quiere, de mala voluntad.

unwillingly, *adv.* de mala voluntad, de mala gana, a regañadientes, mal de su grado.

unwillingness, *s.* mala gana, mala voluntad; aversión, repugnancia.

unwind [ʌn'waind], *v.t.* (*pret., p.p.* **unwound**) desenredar, desembrollar, desenmarañar, devanar, desenvolver, desarrollar. — *v.i.* devanarse, desarrollarse, desenvolverse.

unwise [ʌn'waiz], *a.* poco prudente, imprudente, indiscreto, mal aconsejado, ignorante.

unwitnessed [ʌn'witnisəd], *a.* sin testigo, falto de evidencia.

unwitting [ʌn'witiŋ], *a.* inconsciente.

unwittingly, *adv.* sin saberlo, inconscientemente.

unwomanly [ʌn'wumənli], *a.* indigno o impropio de una mujer; poco femenina.

unwonted [ʌn'wountid], *a.* no acostumbrado, inusitado, insólito.

unwontedly, *adv.* de una manera inusitada.

unwontedness, *s.* rareza.

unwooded [ʌn'wudid], *a.* pelado, sin árboles, sin bosques.

unwooed [ʌn'wuːd], *a.* no cortejado; no solicitado.

unworkable [ʌn'wəːɹkəbəl], *a.* (*de minas, etc.*) inexplotable.

unworkmanlike [ʌn'wəːɹkmənlaik], *a.* desmañado, chapucero, charanguero.

unworldliness [ʌn'wəːɹldinis], *s.* desapego del mundo, espiritualidad; inocencia, impericia.

unworldly [ʌn'wəːɹldli], *a.* poco mundano, espiritual; inocente, imperito.

unworn [ʌn'wɔːɹn], *a.* nuevo, sin llevar, no estrenado.

unworthily, *adv.* indignamente.

unworthiness, *s.* indignidad, falta de mérito, desmerecimiento.

unworthy [ʌn'wəːɹði], *a.* indigno, desmerecedor, sin mérito.

unwounded [ʌn'wuːndid], *a.* no herido, ileso, indemne.

unwoven [ʌn'wouvən], *a.* no tejido. — *p.p.* [UNWEAVE].

unwrap [ʌn'ræp], *v.t.* desenvolver, deshacer, quitar la carpeta de.

unwrinkled [ʌn'riŋkəld], *a.* no arrugado, sin arrugas, liso, terso, suave.

unwritten [ʌn'ritən], *a.* no escrito, oral, tradicional, verbal; en blanco.

unwrought [ʌn'rɔːt], *a.* no trabajado, no elaborado, (en) bruto.

unwrung [ʌn'rʌŋ], *a.* no torcido, no violentado.

unyielding [ʌn'jiːldiŋ], *a.* firme, inflexible, terco, reacio.

unyoke [ʌn'jouk], *v.t.* quitar el yugo a, desuncir, separar.

up [ʌp], *adv.* arriba, hacia arriba, alto, en lo alto; derecho, levantado, sublevado, en insurrección, en pie, en el aire; (*fam.*) bien enterado, adelantado, competente; (*fam.*) terminado, llegado, acabado; totalmente, completamente; *up and down*, arriba y abajo, acá y allá, de un lado y de otro, por todas partes, por todos lados; *up there*, allá arriba; *to go* o *come up*, subir; *to bear up* [UPBEAR]; *to lift up*, [UPLIFT]; *to heave up* [UPHEAVE]; *to speak up*, hablar alto; *to be up*, (*com.*) haber sabido; (*fam.*) haberse levantado; *it's not up to much*, (*fam.*) es poca cosa, no vale mucho; *it's up to you*, a ti te toca; tú dirás; *to be well up in*, estar al corriente de, estar al tanto en, estar fuerte en; *the sun is up*, el sol ha salido; *it's all up!* (*fam.*) ¡se acabó! *time's up*, la hora ha llegado, o ya es la hora; *what's up?* (*fam.*) ¿qué pasa? ¿qué te pasa? ¿ qué hay? *hard up*, con muy poco dinero, a la cuarta pregunta, en apuros; *to be up in arms*, tomar las armas, sublevarse. — *prep.* sobre, encima de, en lo alto de; hacia arriba de; a lo largo de; subiendo; en el interior de; *up (the) stairs*, en lo alto de la escalera, arriba; *up (the) country*, tierra adentro, en el interior del país; *to catch up* o *up with*, alcanzar; sorprender; *up to*, hasta, en; *up to date*, al día, moderno; hasta la fecha; al corriente de; *he's up to anything*, (*fam.*) tiene el hilo. — *interj.* ¡sus! ¡arriba! ¡upa!; *up-a-daisy*, (*fam.*) ¡upa! — *s.* alto; lo elevado; tierra alta; *the ups and downs*, los altos y los bajos, las vicisitudes, los vaivenes o altibajos. — *a.* levantado, erecto; que va hacia arriba; *up-grade*, cuesta ascendente; (*fig.*) valorización, progreso; *up train*, tren ascendente.

upas ['juːpəs], *s.* (*bot.*) antiaro.

upbear [ʌp'bɛəɹ], *v.t.* (*pret.* **upbore**, *p.p.* **upborne**) levantar, elevar, solevantar.

upbraid [ʌp'breid], *v.t.* echar en cara, vituperar, afrentar, afear, reprender, reconvenir.

upbraiding, s. reprimenda, reproche.

upburst ['ʌpbəːɪst], s. erupción, borbollón, reventón (hacia arriba).

upcast ['ʌpkɑːst], a. arrojado el aire, tirado a lo alto. — s. tiro por alto; (min.) pozo ascendente de ventilación.

upgrowth ['ʌpgrouθ], s. crecimiento, aumento.

upheaval, s. cataclismo, trastorno, solevantamiento; (geol.) levantamiento de la corteza terrestre.

upheave [ʌp'hiːv], v.t. solevantar. — v.i. solevantarse.

uphill ['ʌphil], a. ascendente; trabajoso, penoso, difícil, fatigoso. — adv. cuesta arriba.

uphold [ʌp'hould], v.t. (pret., p.p. **upheld**) apoyar, sostener, mantener, defender; levantar, elevar.

upholder, s. sostenedor, sostén, apoyo.

upholster [ʌp'houlstəɪ], v.t. cubrir, tapizar, entapizar (muebles), poner colgaduras, guarnecer (sofás, etc.).

upholsterer [ʌp'houlstərəɪ], s. tapicero.

upholstery [ʌp'houlstəri], s. tapicería; vestidura (de autos).

upkeep ['ʌpkiːp], s. manutención, conservación, entretenimiento; manutención, alimentación.

upland ['ʌplənd], s. terreno elevado, tierra alta, altura. — a. montuoso, elevado.

uplander, s. montañés.

uplift [ʌp'lift], v.t. levantar, elevar, alzar, levantar en vilo. — s. elevación; (geol.) levantamiento; (vulg., amenudo es despec.) influencia edificante, fervor.

upmost ['ʌpməst], a. superl. [UP]; lo más alto, lo más elevado.

upon [ə'pɔn], prep. sobre, encima de, en; cerca de; con; por; a; de; to depend upon, depender de; upon my word o honour, le doy mi palabra, a fe mía; upon this, con esto, o dicho esto; upon reading this book, leyendo o al leer, o después de leer este libro; upon pain of death, bajo o so pena de muerte.

upper ['ʌpəɪ], a. compar. [UP]; más alto, superior, más elevado, de arriba, de encima; etéreo; aristocrático; upper hand, (fig.) ventaja, superioridad; upper deck, (mar.) cubierta alta; Upper House, (pol.) Cámara Alta, (Ing.) Cámara de los lores; upper ten (thousand), (fam.) la minoría selecta, la aristocracia. — s. pala de zapato; borceguíes.

upper-case, a. (impr.) caja alta.

upper-cut, s. puñetazo de abajo arriba.

uppermost ['ʌpəɪməst], a. (lo) más alto, (lo) más elevado; de encima de todo; to say whatever comes uppermost, decir todo lo que pasa por la cabeza.

uppish ['ʌpiʃ], a. (fam.) encandilado, engreído, entonado; brusco.

uppishness, s. (fam.) altivez, engreimiento, entono; brusquedad.

upraise [ʌp'reiz], v.t. elevar, levantar.

uprear [ʌp'riəɪ], v.t. elevar, levantar, enderezar.

upright ['ʌprait], a. vertical, derecho, perpendicular, a plomo, recto, enhiesto; recto, justo, íntegro, probo, equitativo; bolt upright, (fam.) derecho como un huso. — s. (arq.)

elevación, plan de frontispicio; soporte, montante, pieza vertical.

uprightly, adv. verticalmente, perpendicularmente, derechamente, derecho; de aplomo; rectamente, honestamente, con justicia.

uprightness, s. aplomo; rectitud, probidad, derechura, justicia.

uprise [ʌp'raiz], v.i. levantarse. — s. acto de levantarse.

uprising, s. insurrección, sublevación, tumulto; acción de levantarse, levantamiento, solevantamiento; cuesta, subida.

uproar ['ʌprɔːɪ], s. alboroto, batahola, barahúnda, tumulto, estrépito, algazara, gritería, grita, conmoción.

uproarious [ʌp'rɔːriəs], a. tumultuoso, estrepitoso.

uproariously, adv. tumultuosamente, ruidosamente; a carcajadas.

uproot [ʌp'ruːt], v.t. desarraigar, extirpar, arrancar, (agr.) descuajar.

upset [ʌp'set], v.t. trastornar, desordenar, desarreglar, contrariar, derribar; tumbar, volcar, hacer volcar; perturbar, alterar, enfadar; fracasar, frustrar, dar al traste con; (mar.) hacer zozobrar. — v.i. volcarse. — a. upset price, primera oferta.

upset ['ʌpset], **upsetting**, s. trastorno, derribo, vuelco; trastorno, aflicción; fracaso.

upshot ['ʌpʃɔt], s. resultado, fin, conclusión.

upside ['ʌpsaid], s. parte superior, parte de arriba; turn upside down, poner lo de arriba abajo, poner al revés o patas arriba.

upstairs [ʌp'steəɪz], adv. arriba, en el piso superior o de arriba.

upstanding [ʌp'stændiŋ], a. recto, honrado, formal; recto, erecto, membrudo.

upstart ['ʌpstaɪt], v.i. levantarse de pronto. — s. advenedizo, presuntuoso. — a. advenedizo, repentino, súbito; presuntuoso.

upstream [ʌp'striːm], adv. aguas arriba, contra (la) corriente.

uptear [ʌp'teəɪ], v.t. arrancar de abajo arriba.

upthrust ['ʌpθrʌst], s. (geol.) solevantamiento, levantamiento.

upturn [ʌp'təːn], v.t. volver hacia arriba, trastornar, revolver; desterronar, labrar; levantar de nuevo.

upward ['ʌpwəd], **upwards** ['ʌpwədz], adv. (hacia) arriba, por arriba, hacia el cielo; upwards and downwards, arriba y abajo; upwards of an hour, más de una hora; from his youth upwards, desde su juventud. — a. vuelto (hacia) arriba, levantado; que sube; ascensional, ascendente.

uranite ['juərənait], s. uranita.

uranium [juːˈreiniəm], s. uranio; uranium-reactor, reactor nuclear de uranio.

uranoelectricity, s. uranoelectricidad.

uranographic, a. uranográfico.

uranography [juərəˈnɔgræfi], s. uranografía.

uranometry [juərəˈnɔmetri], s. uranometría.

Uranus ['juərənəs], s. (astr.) Urano.

urate ['juərət], s. urato.

urban ['əːbən], a. urbano, ciudadano.

urbane [əːˈbein], a. urbano, fino, servicial, civilizado.

urbanity [əːˈbæniti], s. urbanidad, cortesía, cultura, finura.

urceolate ['əːɪsioleit], a. urceolado.

urchin [əˈɪtʃin], s. (zool.) erizo; equino; niño

travieso, nene, granuja, *m.*, rapacejo, pilluelo, bribonzuelo.

uredo [juːˈriːdou], *s.* (*bot.*) uredo; (*med.*) urticario.

ureter [juːˈriːtər], *s.* uréter.

urethra [juːˈriːθrə], *s.* uretra.

urethral [juːˈriːθrəl], *a.* uretral, urético.

urethritis [juːriˈθraitis], *s.* uretritis, *f.*

urge [əːdʒ], *v.t.* empujar, impeler, hacer avanzar; solicitar o recomendar o proponer con urgencia, instar, pedir con ahinco, insistir en; estimular, excitar, incitar, provocar; apretar, acosar; acelerar, apresurar; hurgar, aguijonear; alegar, sostener. — *v.i.* aportar argumentos; insistir; urgir.

urgency, *s.* urgencia, necesidad urgente, solicitación urgente.

urgent [ˈəːdʒənt], *a.* urgente, apremiante; insistente, importuno.

urgently, *adv.* urgentemente, con urgencia; con instancia, encarecidamente.

urger [ˈəːdʒər], *s.* solicitador, acuciador.

urging, *a.* urgente, importuno.

uric [ˈjuːrik], *a.* (*quím.*) úrico.

urinal [ˈjuːrinəl], *s.* orinal; urinario, meadero.

urinary [ˈjuːrinəri], *a.* urinario.

urination, *s.* micción.

urinate [ˈjuːrineit], *v.i.* orinar, mear.

urine [ˈjuːrin], *s.* orina, orines.

uriniferous, *a.* urinífero.

urinous [ˈjuːrinəs], *a.* urinario.

urn [əːn], *s.* urna, jarrón; cafetera, tetera.

uroscopy, *s.* uroscopia.

Ursa [ˈəːsə], *s.* (*astr.*) osa.

ursiform [ˈəːsifɔːm], *a.* de figura de oso.

ursine, *a.* de oso.

urticaceous, *a.* urticáceo.

urticaria [əːtiˈkɑːriə], *s.* urticaria.

us [ʌs], *pr. pers. pl.* nos, nosotros.

usable [ˈjusəbəl], *a.* servible, que sirve, utilizable.

usage [ˈjuːzidʒ], *s.* uso, costumbre, *f.*; tratamiento, trato.

usance [ˈjuːzəns], *s.* uso, empleo, aprovechamiento; (*com.*) usanza; (*ant.*) interés.

use [juːz], *v.t.* usar (de), servirse de, hacer uso de, emplear, utilizar; habituar, acostumbrar; consumir; ejercer, practicar; usar de, tratar, dar buen o mal trato a; portarse bien o mal con; (*for.*) usufructuar; *to use up*, agotar, consumir. — *v.i.* soler, acostumbrar, tener costumbre de, estar acostumbrado a, estar en el uso de.

use [juːs], *s.* uso, empleo, servicio, aprovechamiento, utilidad, costumbre, *f.*, hábito, ejercicio; necesidad, ocasión; práctica; provecho, interés, ventaja; (*for.*) usufructo, goce, manejo; *of no use*, inútil; *to be of no use*, no servir para nada; *to be in use*, servir, estar en uso, usarse; *to make use of*, aprovechar; utilizar, hacer uso de; *to have no more* o *further use for*, no necesitar; *to put to good use*, poner a ganancias, sacar partido de; *what is the use of it?* ¿para qué sirve? *to use ill*, tratar mal, manosear.

useful [ˈjuːsful], *a.* útil, ventajoso, conveniente, servible, beneficioso, provechoso.

usefully, *adv.* útilmente, con utilidad, ventajosamente, provechosamente.

usefulness, *s.* utilidad.

useless, *a.* inútil, inservible; excusado; inepto, vano; ocioso.

uselessly, *adv.* inútilmente, infructuosamente, vanamente.

uselessness, *s.* inutilidad, infructuosidad.

user [ˈjuːzər], *s.* el que usa o emplea o se vale (de), utilizador, dueño.

usher [ˈʌʃər], *v.t.* introducir, anunciar, acomodar, aposentar; *to usher in*, introducir; (*fig.*) preceder; *to usher out*, acompañar hasta la puerta, despedir con cortesía. — *s.* ujier, conserje, portero; sotamaestro, submaestro; (*teat.*) acomodador.

usherette, *s.* (*teat.*, *cine.*) acomodadora.

ustion [ˈʌstjən], *s.* cauterización.

usual [ˈjuːʒjuəl], *a.* usual, usado, habitual, común, acostumbrado, general, normal, ordinario; *as usual*, como siempre, como de ordinario, como de costumbre.

usually, *adv.* usualmente, generalmente, por lo general, por lo común, habitualmente, de ordinario, comúnmente, regularmente.

usucapt [ˈjuːʒjuːkæpt], *v.t.* (*for.*) usucapir.

usufruct [ˈjuːʒjuːfrʌkt], *s.* (*for.*) usufructo.

usufructuary [juːʒjuːˈfrʌktjuːəri], *s.* usufructario.

usurer [ˈjuːʒərər], *s.* usurero.

usurious [juːˈʒuːriəs], *a.* usurario.

usurp [juːˈzəːrp], *v.t.* usurpar, arrogarse.

usurpation, *s.* usurpación.

usurper, *s.* usurpador.

usurpingly, *adv.* por usurpación.

usury [ˈjuːʒjuri], *s.* usura; *to practise usury*, usurear, usurar.

ut [ʌt], *s.* (*mús.*) ut.

utensil [juːˈtensəl], *s.* utensilio, herramienta.

uterine [ˈjuːtərain], *a.* uterino.

uterus [ˈjuːtərəs], *s.* útero, matriz.

utilitarian [juːtiliˈtɛəriən], *s.*, *a.* utilitario.

utilitarianism, *s.* utilitarismo.

utility [juːˈtiliti], *s.* utilidad, conveniencia, aprovechamiento, ventaja. — *pl.* **utilities**, servicios de agua, gas, luz eléctrica, etc.

utilizable [juːtilaizəbəl], *a.* utilizable, aprovechable.

utilize [ˈjuːtilaiz], *v.t.* servirse de, utilizar, hacer uso de, aprovechar, explotar.

utmost [ˈʌtməst], **uttermost** [ˈʌtəməst], *a.* extremo, sumo, postrero, último, más lejano, más distante, mayor. — *s.* más alto grado, grado supremo, sumo, mayor, más; *at the utmost*, a lo más; *to do one's utmost*, hacer (todo) lo posible, hacer cuanto pueda.

Utopia [juːˈtoupiə], *s.* Utopía, Utopia.

Utopian [juːˈtoupiən], *s.* utópico.

utricle [ˈjuːtrikəl], *s.* (*bot.*) utrículo; (*biol.*) célula; (*anat.*) bolsita del laberinto del oído interno.

utricular [juːˈtrikjuːlər], *a.* uterino.

utter [ˈʌtər], *v.t.* decir, expresar, pronunciar, articular, proferir; dar (gritos, etc.); (*ant.*) descubrir, revelar, publicar; emitir (moneda), poner en circulación; (*com.*) vender, despachar. — *a.* extremo; entero, todo, total, absoluto, sumo, completo; perentorio, terminante.

utterable [ˈʌtərəbəl], *a.* decible; que se puede proferir o pronunciar.

utterance [ˈʌtərəns], *s.* emisión, articulación, prolación, pronunciación; palabra; expresión, lenguaje; *to give utterance to*, pronunciar.

utterer, *s.* persona que pronuncia, que dice, que emite, que pone en circulación.

utterly ['ʌtəɹli], *adv.* enteramente, absoluta- mente, completamente, totalmente, del todo.
uttermost, *a.* [UTMOST].
utterness, *s.* calidad de completo, extremidad.
uva ['juːvə], *s.* grano de uva.
uvea ['juːviə], *s.* úvea, túnica úvea.
uveous ['juːviəs], *a.* úvea, de la úvea.
uvula ['juːvjuːlə], *s.* úvula, galillo, campanilla.
uvular ['juːvjuːləɹ], *a.* uvular.
uxorious [ʌk'zɔːriəs], *a.* gurrumino.
uxoriously, *adv.* con gurrumina.
uxoriousness, *s.* gurrumina.

V

V, v [viː], *s.* vigésima segunda letra del alfabeto inglés. Se pronuncia siempre como la *b* española. *v.* abrev. [VERSUS]; [VOLT]; [VIDE]; *V-shaped,* en V.
vacancy, *s.* vacío, vacuidad, laguna, hueco; vacante, *f.,* vacancia; (*ant.*) vacación, tiempo libre.
vacant ['veikənt], *a.* vacío, hueco; vacante, vacuo; exento, libre; vago, distraído; torpe, lerdo, estólido; desocupado, distraído, des- embarazado, ocioso.
vacantly, *adv.* distraídamente, vagamente; torpemente.
vacate [və'keit], *v.t.* vaciar, dejar vacío, evacuar, dejar vacante; (*for.*) invalidar, rescindir, anular; revocar. — *v.i.* marcharse, irse, salir.
vacation, *s.* vacación, vacaciones, *f.pl.*; vacante, *f.*; (*for.*) anulación, revocación.
vaccinate ['væksineit], *v.t.* vacunar.
vaccination, *s.* vacunación, inoculación, vacuna.
vaccinator, vaccinist, *s.* vacunador.
vaccine ['væksin], *a.* vacuno, de vaca.
vaccine, *s.* vacuna.
vacillate ['væsileit], *v.i.* vacilar, titubear, fluctuar, estar incierto.
vacillating, *a.* vacilante.
vacillation, *s.* vacilación, titubeo, fluctuación, vaivén.
vacuity [və'kjuːiti], *s.* vacuidad, vacío, vacuo, laguna, hueco; estupidez; ociosidad, inani- dad.
vacuous ['vækjuːəs], *a.* vacío; desocupado; mentecato, fatuo.
vacuum ['vækjuːəm], *s.* (*fís.*) vacío, vacuo; *vacuum-brake,* freno de vacío, vacuofreno; *vacuum-cleaner,* (vacuo)aspirador de polvo; *vacuum-flask,* termos, *m.sing.*
vade-mecum [veidi'miːkəm], *s.* vademécum, venimécum.
vagabond ['vægəbɔnd], *s., a.* mendigo; vagamundo, vagabundo, errante, fluctuante; *to be a vagabond,* vagamundear, vagabun- dear.
vagabondage ['vægəbɔndidʒ], **vagabondism** ['vægəbɔndizm], *s.* vagabundeo, vagancia.
vagabondize, *v.i.* vagamundear, vagabundear.
vagary [və'gɛəri], *s.* capricho, fantasía, ex- travagancia, humorada, antojo.
vagina [və'dʒainə], *s.* (*anat.*) vagina; (*bot.*) vaina; (*arq.*) parte superior de un término del cual parece que sale la figura.
vaginal [və'dʒainəl], *a.* vaginal.
vaginate ['vædʒinit], *a.* envainado, invagi- nado.

vagrancy, *s.* holgazanería, vagancia, tuna.
vagrant ['veigrənt], *a.* errante, vagabundo, vagamundo, errático, errante. — *s.* vaga- bundo; mendigo.
vague [veig], *a.* vago, indistinto, indefinido, incierto, dudoso.
vaguely ['veigli], *adv.* vagamente; *to speak vaguely,* hablar al aire.
vagueness, *s.* vaguedad, vago.
vail [veil], *v.t.* (*ant.*) bajar, abatir, quitarse el sombrero, etc. — *v.i.* inclinarse, ceder. — *s.* (*ant.*) velo; propina, gratificación.
vain [vein], *a.* vano, sin efecto, inútil, infruc- tuoso; vano, vanidoso, soberbio, presun- tuoso, desvanecido; suntuoso, llamativo, ostentoso; insubstancial, fútil; *in vain,* inútilmente, en vano, en balde.
vainglorious [vein'glɔːriəs], *a.* vanaglorioso, jactancioso, ufano.
vaingloriously, *adv.* vanagloriosamente, con jactancia.
vaingloriousness, vainglory, *s.* vanagloria, jactancia.
vainly ['veinli], *adv.* inútilmente, en vano; vanamente, arrogantemente, con vanidad.
vainness, *s.* vanidad, inutilidad, futilidad; vanidad, envanecimiento.
vair [vɛəɹ], *s.* (*blas.*) vero.
valance ['væləns], *s.* franja, orladura, doselera de cama, gotera del dosel o de cortina, cenefa.
vale ['veiliː], *s.* (*poét.*) valle, cañada, canalizo. — *interj., s.* vale, adiós.
valediction [væli'dikʃən], *s.* despedida, adiós, vale.
valedictory [væli'diktəri], *a.* de despedida. — *s.* discurso de despedida.
valence ['veiləns], **valency** ['veilənsi], *s.* (*quím.*) valencia.
valentine ['væləntain], *s.* billete amoroso que es costumbre entre los jóvenes ingleses de escribirse el día de San Valentín, 14 de Febrero.
valerian [və'liəriən], *s.* (*bot.*) valeriana.
valerianate, valerate, *s.* (*quím.*) valerianato.
valet ['vælet], *s.* servidor, criado, camarero.
valetudinarian [vælitjuːdi'nɛəriən], **vale- tudinary** [væle'tjuːdinəri], *s., a.* valetudi- nario.
valiant ['væljənt], *a.* valiante, animoso, vigoroso.
valiantly, *adv.* valientemente, esforzadamente, valerosamente.
valid ['vælid], *a.* valedero, válido; vigente, en vigor.
validate ['vælideit], *v.t.* validar.
validity [və'liditi], *s.* validez.
validly ['vælidli], *adv.* válidamente.
valise [və'liːz], *s.* saco de viaje, maleta.
valkyrie ['vælkiri], *s.* valquiria.
valley ['væli], *s.* valle, vallecillo, arroyada; (*min.*) quebradura; (*arq.*) gotera, limahoya.
valorous ['vælərəs], *a.* valiente, valeroso, animoso, bizarro, intrépido.
valour ['væləɹ], *s.* valor, valentía, brío, ánimo, intrepidez, bravura, fortaleza, bizarría.
valuable ['væljuːəbəl], *a.* precioso, de precio, de valor, valioso, costoso; estimable, apre- ciable.
valuableness, *s.* valor, precio.
valuables, *s.pl.* objetos de valor.
valuably ['væljuːəbli], *adv.* apreciadamente.

valuation [vælju:'eiʃən], s. valuación, tasación, tasa, valía, avalúo.

valuator ['vælju:eitəɹ], s. tasador, avaluador.

value ['vælju:], v.t. valuar, valorar, tasar, preciar; apreciar, estimar, tener en mucho; considerar, hacer caso de. — s. valor, precio, valuación, monta, justiprecio; importancia, valía, valor intrínseco; mérito, estimación, aprecio; entidad; sentido, significación; (mús.) valor, duración; to set a value upon, poner un precio a.

valueless, a. sin valor, sin importancia, insignificante, despreciable.

valuer ['vælju:əɹ], s. estimador, tasador, valuador, apreciador.

valvate ['vælveit], a. valvulado, valvular.

valve [vælv], s. (mec.) válvula; (anat., bot.) valva, ventalla; lámpara (de radio); hoja de puerta; alma de fuelle; overhead valve, (aut.) válvulas en la culata; slide-valve, cajón.

valvet, valvlet, valvule, s. valvulita, valvulilla.

valvular ['vælvju:ləɹ], a. valvular, con válvulas.

vamose [və'mous], v.t., v.i. (E.U., vulg.) dejar de repente, salir al trote, poner pies en polvorosa, tomar las de Villadiego.

vamp [væmp], v.t. poner capellada o empeine a; (mús.) improvisar un acompañamiento; (vulg.) seducir, engatusar, hechizar. — s. capellada, empeine; empella, remonta, remiendo; (fam.) acompañamiento músico improvisado; (vulg.) sirena, ninfa.

vamper, s. (fam.) hechicera, coqueta, sirena.

vampire ['væmpaiəɹ], s. vampiro; (orn.) vampiro; (teat.) escotillón.

vampirism ['væmpairizm], s. vampirismo.

van [væn], s. vanguardia, frente, f.; aspa, brazo de molinillo; camioneta, furgoneta, furgón de equipajes, carromato; (agr.) harnero; (f.c.) furgón de equipajes.

vanadium [və'neidiəm], s. vanadio.

vandal ['vændəl], s. vándalo.

vandalic, a. vandálico, de vándalo, bárbaro.

vandalism, s. vandalismo.

vane [vein], s. veleta; aspa, brazo de molino; barba (de pluma); pínula; (mar.) grímpola; dog vane, cataviento.

vang [væŋ], s. (mar.) osta.

vanguard ['væŋgɑːd], s. vanguardia; to be in the vanguard, ir o estar a vanguardia.

vanilla [və'nilə], s. vainilla.

vanish ['væniʃ], v.i. desaparecer, evaporarse, disiparse, desvanecerse.

vanishing, s. desaparición; fuga; vanishing point, punto de fuga; vanishing cream, crema (para el cutis).

vanity ['væniti], s. vanidad, deseo vano, presunción, engreimiento, futilidad; ostentación, alarde, fausto.

vanquish ['væŋkwiʃ], v.t. conquistar, derrotar, rendir, batir.

vanquishable, a. vencible.

vanquisher, s. vencedor.

vantage ['vɑːntidʒ], s. provecho, ganancia, superioridad, ventaja; ventaja (en el tenis); vantage ground, posición ventajosa.

vapid ['væpid], a. insípido, soso, insulso, pesado, aburrido.

vapidity, vapidness, s. insipidez, insulsez, sosería.

vaporific [væpə'rifik], a. que vaporiza.

vaporizable, a. que puede ser vaporizado.

vaporization, s. vaporización.

vaporize ['veipəraiz], v.t. vaporizar, volatilizar, evaporizar, evaporar, nebulizar (neol.). — v.i. vaporizarse, evaporizarse.

vaporous ['veipərəs], a. vaporoso, nebuloso, aéreo, etéreo; (fig.) vaporoso, tenue, diáfano; (fig.) vago, nebuloso.

vapour ['veipəɹ], (E.U.) **vapor**, s. vapor, niebla, humo, vaho, exhalación; nube ligera; fluido, gas; hálito; sahumerio; ventolera, hinchazón, f., engreimiento. — pl. **vapours**, vapores, hipocondría. — v.t. evaporar, echar en vapor; exhalar. — v.i. evaporarse, vaporizarse, exhalar vapor, avahar, humear; (fig.) baladronear, alardear, vanagloriarse.

vapourer, s. jactancioso, fanfarrón, baladrón.

vapourish, vapoury, a. vaporoso, húmedo.

variability [vɛəri'biliti], s. variabilidad.

variable ['vɛəriəbəl], a. variable, inconstante, veleidoso, vario, mudable, alterable; regulable, modificable.

variableness, s. variabilidad, inconstancia, instabilidad.

variably, adv. variablemente.

variance ['vɛəriəns], s. variación, fluctuación; cambio, mudanza; disidencia, desacuerdo, desavenencia, disensión; to be at variance, estar en desacuerdo, estar de punta.

variant ['vɛəriənt], a. variante, diverso; vario, inconstante, variable, mudable, veleidoso. — s. variante, f.

variation [vɛəri'eiʃən], s. variación, cambio; (fís.) declinación (de la aguja); (mús.) variación, diferencia; (gram.) inflexión; (astr.) desviación de los cuerpos celestes.

varicella [væri'selə], s. varicela.

varicocele ['værikosi:l], s. varicocele.

varicoloured, a. abigarrado, de colorines.

varicose ['værikous], **varicous** ['værikəs], a. varicoso.

varied ['vɛərid], a. variado, diverso; mezclado.

variegate ['vɛərigeit], v.t. abigarrar, jaspear, matizar, combinar (los colores); pintarrajar, pintorrear, gayar.

variegation [vɛəri'geiʃən], s. abigarramiento, jaspeadura, jaspeado.

variety [və'raiiti], s. variedad, diversidad.

variola [və'raiolə], s. (med.) viruela(s).

varioloid [və'raiolɔid], a. varioloide.

variolous [və'raioləs], a. varioloso, virolento.

various ['vɛəriəs], a. vario, diferente, diverso, desemejante, variado; variable, mudable, inconstante; abigarrado, veteado.

variously, adv. variamente, diversamente, de diversos modos.

varix ['vɛəriks], s. (pl. **varices**) (cir.) variz, f., varice, f., várice, f.

varlet ['vɑːlet], s. (ant.) lacayo, paje, mozo de espuelas; pícaro, bribón.

varnish ['vɑːniʃ], v.t. barnizar, charolar, acicalar, vidriar; (fig.) paliar, disimular. — s. barniz, charol, mogate, esmalte.

varnisher, s. barnizador, charolista, m.f., esmaltador.

varnishing, s. barnizado, vidriado, esmalte.

varsity ['vɑːsiti], s. (fam.) universidad.

vary ['vɛəɹi], v.t., v.i. variar, cambiar, mudar(se), diversificar; separar(se), desviar(se), discrepar, discordar, estar en desacuerdo.

varying, a. vario, variante, variable.

vascular ['væskju:ləɹ], a. vascular.

vascularity, s. vascularidad.

vasculose ['væskjuːlous], *a.* vasculoso.

vase [vɑːz], *s.* jarrón, florero, jarro.

vasomotor [vəˈzɔmetəɹ], *a.* (*anat.*) vasomotor.

vassal ['væsəl], *s.* vasallo, súbdito, siervo. — *a.* tributario.

vassalage, *s.* vasallaje, esclavitud, servidumbre.

vast [vɑːst], *a.* vasto, extendido, inmenso, muy extenso, dilatado, muy grande; poderoso, enorme, atroz. — *s.* (*poét.*) inmensidad, vastedad, infinito.

vastly, *adv.* inmensamente, enormemente, en sumo grado.

vastness, *s.* vastedad, inmensidad, enormidad, grandeza.

vasty, *a.* (*poét.*) vasto, inmenso.

vat [væt], *s.* cuba, tanque, tina; noque, hoyo de curtidor; depósito.

Vatican ['vætikən], *s.* vaticano.

vaticide ['vætisaid], *s.* asesinato (o asesino) de un profeta.

vaticinal [vəˈtisinəl], *a.* profético.

vaticinate [væˈtisineit], *v.i.* vaticinar, pronosticar, augurar.

vaticination, *s.* vaticinio, adivinación, augurio.

vaudeville ['voudvil], *s.* teatro de variedades; (*ant.*) jácara.

vault [vɔːlt], *s.* bóveda, cripta; caverna, cueva; bodega, subterráneo; sepultura, tumba; salto, voltereta; (*poét.*) bóveda celeste; (*ant.*) albañal, cloaca. — *v.t.* (*arq.*) abovedar, voltear. — *v.i.* voltear, saltar (por encima de), saltar con pértiga.

vaulted, vaulty, *a.* abovedado, arqueado.

vaulter, *s.* volteador, saltador, volatín.

vaunt [vɔːnt], *v.t.* alardear, hacer ostentación o gala de. — *v.i.* vanagloriarse, jactarse. — *s.* vanagloria, jactancia, alarde, fachenda, gala.

vaunter, *s.* alabancioso, fanfarrón, fachendista, *m.f.*

vaunting, *s.* jactancia.

vauntingly, *adv.* con jactancia.

vavasour ['vævəsəɹ], *s.* vasallo de un vasallo.

veal ['viːəl], *s.* ternera, carne de ternera; *veal-chop*, chuleta de ternera; *veal-cutlet*, filete de ternera.

vectis ['vektis], *s.* (*cir.*) fórceps.

vector ['vektəɹ], *s.* (*geom.*) radio vector; rumbo.

vectorial, *a.* vector.

vedette [veˈdet], *s.* (*mil.*) centinela o escucha de caballería; (*mar.*) escampavía.

veer [viəɹ], *v.i.* virar, cambiar de dirección; virar, rolar (el viento). — *v.t.* (*mar.*) virar, aflojar, arriar, alargar; *to veer and haul*, (*mar.*) lascar y halar; largar y escasear; *to veer away*, (*mar.*) arriar cables o amarras.

veering, *s.* (*mar.*) virada.

veery, *s.* (*orn.*) tordo canoro.

vegetable ['vedʒitəbəl], *s.* legumbre, vegetal, vegetable. — *a.* vegetal.

vegetables, *s.pl.* hortalizas, legumbres, verduras.

vegetal ['vedʒitəl], *a.* vegetal.

vegetarian [vedʒiˈtɛəriən], *s.* vegetariano, fitófago. — *a.* vegetal.

vegetarianism, *s.* vegetarianismo.

vegetate ['vedʒiteit], *v.i.* vegetar.

vegetation, *s.* vegetación.

vegetative, *a.* vegetativo, vegetante.

vegetativeness, *s.* vegetabilidad, potencia vegetativa.

vehemence ['viːəməns], **vehemency** ['viːəmənsi], *s.* vehemencia, intensidad, viveza.

vehement ['viːəmənt], *a.* vehemente, ardiente.

vehicle ['viːikəl], *s.* vehículo, carruaje; medio, instrumento.

vehicular [viˈhikjuːləɹ], *a.* de (los) vehículos, para vehículos.

veil [veil], *v.t.* cubrir con velo, velar, tapar(se); (*fig.*) velar, tapar, ocultar. — *s.* velo, cortina; máscara, disfraz; pretexto.

veilless, *a.* sin velo.

vein [vein], *v.t.* (*pint.*) vetear, jaspear. — *s.* (*anat.*) vena, vaso; (*min.*) capa, veta, filón; (*bot.*) nervio, hacecillo de hebras; (*carp.*) trepa, hebra; (*fig.*) humor, temperamento, disposición, genio.

veined, *a.* veteado, venoso, avetado.

veining, *s.* acción de vetear, veteado.

veinless, *a.* (*bot.*) sin vasos, sin nervosidades.

veinstone, *s.* (*min.*) ganga.

veiny, *a.* veteado, venoso, avetado.

velleity [veˈliːiti], *s.* veleidad.

vellicate ['velikeit], *v.i.* (*med.*) velicar; (*ant.*) punzar, pellizcar, cosquillear.

vellication, *s.* (*med.*) velicación; (*ant.*) comezón, *f.*, punzada, cosquilleo.

vellum ['veləm], *s.* vitela, pergamino.

velocipede [veˈlɔsipiːd], *s.* velocípedo.

velocity [veˈlɔsiti], *s.* velocidad, celeridad, rapidez.

velours, velour, velure [vəˈluːəɹ], *s.* terciopelo, velludillo, veludillo.

velvet ['velvet], *s.* terciopelo; (*zool.*) vello; lucro, ganancia, rendimiento; *velvet-weaver*, terciopelero. — *a.* terciopelado, de terciopelo, afelpado, felpudo; (*fig.*) dulce, meloso.

velveteen ['velvətiːn], *s.* veludillo, pana lisa, terciopelo de algodón.

velveting, *s.* afelpado.

velvet-like, velvety, *a.* terciopelado, aterciopelado.

venal ['viːnəl], *a.* (*anat.*) venoso, venal; venal, sobornable.

venality [veˈnæliti], *s.* venalidad.

venation [veˈneiʃən], *s.* (*ant.*) venación.

vend [vend], *v.t.* vender.

vendee [venˈdiː], *s.* (*for.*) adquiridor, comprador.

vendetta [venˈdetə], *s.* venganza personal, feudo de sangre.

vendibility, vendibleness, *s.* cualidad de vendible.

vendible ['vendəbəl], *a.* vendible.

vendor ['vendəɹ], *s.* vendedor; vendedor ambulante, buhonero.

veneer [veˈniəɹ], *v.t.* plaquear, enchapar, chapear; revestir, ocultar, tapar, disfrazar. — *s.* hoja para plaquear o chapear, madera contrachapada; chapa, capa exterior; (*fig.*) apariencia.

veneering, *s.* enchapado, chapeado.

venenate ['venəneit], *a.* (*med.*) envenenado.

venenation, *s.* envenenamiento.

venerable ['venərəbəl], *a.* venerable.

venerableness, *s.* carácter venerable, respetabilidad.

venerate ['venəreit], *v.t.* venerar, reverenciar.

veneration, *s.* veneración, reverencia, acatamiento.

venerator, *s.* venerador.

venereal, *a.* venéreo. — *s.* (mal) venéreo; *venereal disease*, (mal) venéreo, venus, *f.*

venery ['venəri], *s.* acto venéreo, venus, *f.*; (*ant.*) caza, montería.

venesection ['venesekʃən], *s.* (*cir.*) sangría, flebotomía.

Venetian [ve'niːʃən], *a.* veneciano; *Venetian blinds*, celosías, persianas; *Venetian chalk*, talco gráfico, jaboncillo de sastre; *Venetian window*, ventana de tres aberturas separadas.

venge [vendʒ], *v.t.* (*ant.*) vengar.

vengeance ['vendʒəns], *s.* venganza, vindicta; *with a vengeance*, (*fam.*) con fuerza, con violencia; con creces.

vengeful, *a.* vengativo, vengador.

venial ['viːniəl], *a.* venial.

venison ['venzən], *s.* carne montesina, carne de venado.

venom ['venəm], *s.* veneno, ponzoña; (*fig.*) ponzoña, veneno, despecho, rencor.

venomous, *a.* venenoso, envenenado, ponzoñoso, dañoso.

venomously, *adv.* con veneno, venenosamente.

venomousness, *s.* venenosidad, malignidad, ponzoña.

venous ['viːnəs], *a.* venoso, veteado.

vent [vent], *v.t.* dar salida a, dar paso a, dar libre carrera a; ventilar, expresar; desahogar, desfogar, descargar, desventar, dejar escapar. — *s.* abertura, agujero, pasaje, paso, oído; desahogo, expresión, emisión, salida; ventosa, resolladero, respiradero, tronera, lumbrera; (*arti.*) fogón; (*fund.*) bravera; (*com.*) venta; (*fig.*) divulgación; *to give vent to*, dar salida o expresión o rienda suelta a; *to give vent to one's feelings*, desahogarse.

ventail ['venteil], *s.* ventalla.

vental ['ventəl], *a.* del viento.

venter, *s.* (*anat.*) abdomen, vientre; (*for.*) matriz, *f.*, madre, *f.*; cavidad.

venthole ['venthoul], *s.* respiradero, orificio de ventilación, orificio de escape.

ventiduct ['ventidʌkt], *s.* (*arq.*) ventosa; resolladero, bravera, respiradero, conducto de ventilación.

ventilate ['ventileit], *v.t.* ventilar, airear, orear; (*agr.*) ahechar, aventar (granos); (*fig.*) ventilar, discutir.

ventilation, *s.* ventilación, (*med.*) aeración; ventilación, discusión.

ventilator, *s.* ventilador; aventador.

ventose ['ventous], *a.* ventoso, flatulento.

ventosity [ven'tɔsiti] *s.* ventosidad, flatulencia.

vent-peg, *s.* espita.

ventral ['ventrəl], *a.* ventral, abdominal.

ventricle ['ventrikəl], *s.* ventrículo.

ventricular [ven'trikjuːlər], *a.* ventricular.

ventriloquism [ven'trilokwizm], **ventriloquy** [ven'trilokwi], *s.* ventriloquia.

ventriloquist, *s.* ventrílocuo.

venture ['ventʃər], *v.t.* aventurar, arriesgar. — *v.i.* aventurarse, arriesgarse, atreverse, osar, correr riesgo, exponerse; *to venture abroad* o *out*, arriesgarse fuera, atreverse a salir; *nothing venture, nothing win*, quien no se aventura, no ha ventura; *at a venture*, a la (buena) ventura.

venturer, *s.* aventurero.

venturesome ['ventʃərsəm], **venturous** [ventʃərəs], *a.* aventurero, osado, emprendedor; aventurado, peligroso.

venturesomely, venturously, *adv.* aventuradamente, atrevidamente, arrojadamente, osadamente.

venturesomeness, venturousness, *s.* arrojo, atrevimiento, temeridad.

venue ['venjuː], *s.* (*for.*) vecindad; escena; (*esgr.*) pase.

Venus ['viːnəs], *s.* Venus; *Venus's flytrap*, (*bot.*) atrapamoscas, *m.*; *Venus's comb*, (*bot.*) peine de pastor; *Venus's looking-glass*, (*bot.*) campanilla; *Venus's slipper*, (*bot.*) zueco.

veracious [ve'reiʃəs], *a.* verídico, veraz, verdadero.

veracity [ve'ræsiti], *s.* veracidad, verdad.

veranda, verandah [ve'rændə], *s.* mirador, 'veranda', galería, pórtico.

verb [vəːb], *s.* verbo.

verbal, *a.* verbal, oral, de palabra; verbal, literal; (*gram.*) verbal.

verbalism, *s.* expresión oral; palabrería, verbalismo.

verbalize ['vəːbəlaiz], *v.t.* convertir en verbo. — *v.i.* gastar palabras, ser verboso.

verbally ['vəːbəli], *adv.* de palabra, verbalmente.

verbatim [vər'beitim], *adv., a.* palabra por palabra, al pie de la letra.

verbena [vər'biːnə], *s.* verbena.

verberation [vəːbə'reiʃən], *s.* verberación.

verbiage ['vəːbiədʒ], *s.* verbosidad, palabrería, palabreo, vaniloquio.

verbose [vəː'bous], *a.* verboso, prolijo, palabrero, palabrista, palabrón.

verbosely, *adv.* con verbosidad.

verboseness, verbosity, *s.* verbosidad, palabrería, ampulosidad, palabreo.

verdancy, *s.* verdor, verdura.

verdant ['vəːdənt], *a.* verde, floreciente, florido; novel, imperito.

verdict ['vəːdikt], *s.* (*for.*) veredicto, fallo; decisión, sentencia, juicio, fallo, dictamen, opinión, *f.*

verdigris ['vəːdigris], *s.* (*quim.*) cardenillo, verdete, verdía.

verditer ['vəːditər], *s.* verde de tierra.

verdure ['vəːdʒər], *s.* verdor, verdura, verde; vegetación, frondas, lozanía.

verdured, verdurous, *a.* verdoso, lozano, fresco.

verge [vəːdʒ], *s.* vara, varilla, varita, báculo; borde, límite, margen, extremidad, canto, lindero; distrito, esfera, alcance, jurisdicción; anillo, círculo; (*mec.*) eje de áncora, eje del volante (de relojes); (*arq.*) fuste de columna; *on the verge of*, al borde de, a orillas de; (*fig.*) en vísperas de, a vista de, a punto de.

verger, *s.* alguacil de vara; aposentador, pertiguero; macero, bedel.

veridical [ve'ridikəl], *a.* verídico.

verification [verifi'keiʃən], *s.* verificación, demostración, comprobación.

verify ['verifai], *v.t.* verificar, probar, comprobar, justificar, demostrar; ejecutar, cumplir; (*for.*) afirmar bajo juramento; acreditar.

verily ['verili], *adv.* en verdad, verdaderamente.

verisimilar, *a.* verosímil, verisímil.

verisimilitude [verisi'militjuːd], *s.* verosimilitud, verisimilitud.

veritable ['veritəbəl], *a.* verdadero, cierto, real, genuino.

verity ['veriti], *s.* verdad, realidad. — *pl.* **verities,** verdades, dogmas, *m.pl.*

verjuice ['vəːɹdʒuːs], *s.* agraz, agrazada; mordacidad, aspereza.

vermeil ['vəːɹmil], *s.* plata dorada; barniz de agua; (*poét.*) bermellón.

vermicelli [vəɹmiˈseli], *s.* fideos.

vermicide ['vəːɹmisaid], *s.* vermicida, vermífugo.

vermicular [vəɹˈmikjuːləɹ], *s.* (*anat.*) vermicular, vermiculado, vermiforme.

vermiculate, *v.t.* (*arq.*) adornar de vermiculares. — *a.* vermiforme.

vermicule ['vəːɹmikjuːl], *s.* verme, gusanillo.

vermiculose, vermiculous, *a.* vermicular.

vermiform, *a.* (*anat.*) vermicular, vermiforme.

vermifuge ['vəːɹmifjuːdʒ], *s.* vermífugo.

vermilion, vermillion [vəɹˈmiljən], *s.* bermellón, bermejo, cinabrio. — *v.t.* pintar con bermellón, teñir de rojo, enrojar.

vermin ['vəːɹmin], *s.* bicho, sabandija, insectos asquerosos; canalla, *m.*, puerco; gentuza, chusma.

verminous ['vəːɹminəs], *a.* verminoso; (*fig.*) lleno de miseria.

vermiverous, *a.* vermívoro.

vermouth ['vəːɹmuːθ], *s.* vermut.

vernacular [vəɹˈnækjuːləɹ], *a.* vernáculo, indígena, materno, del país, endémico, vulgar. — *s.* lengua vulgar; lenguaje vulgar.

vernal ['vəːɹnəl], *a.* vernal, primaveral, de la primavera; (*fig.*) joven, de la juventud.

vernier ['vəːɹniəɹ], *s.* nonio.

Veronese [veroˈniːz], *s.*, *a.* veronés.

veronica, *s.* (*bot.*) verónica.

verruca, *s.* (*med.*) verruga.

verrucose ['verjuːkous], *a.* verrugoso.

versant ['vəːɹsənt], *a.* versado, familiar.

versatile ['vəːɹsətail], *a.* de muchos talentos, adaptable; adaptable para varios usos; versátil, inconstante.

versatility, *s.* adaptabilidad, muchos talentos, variedad de conocimientos, pluriadaptabilidad (*neol.*); variedad de aplicaciones.

verse [vəːɹs], *s.* verso; poesía, versos, estrofa, copla; versículo; *verse-maker*, versificador; *verse-monger*, poetastro.

versed, *a.* versado, ejercitado, práctico, familiar.

versicle ['vəːɹsikəl], *s.* versículo.

versicolour, versicoloured, *a.* multicolor.

versification [vəɹsifiˈkeiʃən], *s.* versificación.

versificator, versifier, *s.* versificador, versista, *m.f.*

versify ['vəːɹsifai], *v.t.*, *v.i.* versificar, trovar, poner en verso.

version ['vəːɹʃən], *s.* versión.

verso ['vəːɹsou], *s.* reverso (de página o moneda).

verst [vəːɹst], *s.* versta.

versus ['vəːɹsəs], *prep.* contra.

vert [vəːɹt], *s.* (*blas.*) sinople; broza; (*for.*) derecho de tala.

vertebra ['vəːɹtebrə], *s.* (*pl.* **vertebræ**) (*anat.*) vértebra.

vertebral, *a.* (*anat.*) vertebral; (*zool.*) vertebrado.

vertebrate, vertebrated, *a.* (*zool.*) vertebrado.

vertex ['vəːɹteks], *s.* (*pl.* **vertices**) (*geom.*) vértice, cúspide, *f.*; (*anat.*) coronilla, vértice; (*bot.*) ápice; (*fig.*) cumbre, *f.*, cenit, cima, ápice.

vertical ['vəːɹtikəl], *a.* vertical. — *s.* línea vertical; montante.

verticality [vəɹtiˈkæliti], *s.* verticalidad, posición vertical.

verticity [vəɹˈtisiti], *s.* (*ant.*) verticidad.

vertiginous [vəɹˈtidʒinəs], *a.* vertiginoso.

vertiginousness, *s.* vértigo, aturdimiento.

vertigo ['vəːɹtigou], *s.* (*pl.* **vertigines**) vértigo, vahído.

vervain ['vəːɹvein], *s.* (*bot.*) planta silvestre del género verbena.

verve [vəːɹv], *s.* fuerza, vigor; brío; (*ant.*) numen, estro, vis, *f.*

very ['veri], *a.* verdadero, real, mismo, idéntico; grande, cabal, perfecto; sincero, franco; completo, entero. — *adv.* muy; mucho; precisamente, cabalmente, perfectamente; completamente, enteramente, sumamente.

vesania [veˈseiniə], *s.* vesania.

vesicate ['vesikeit], *v.t.* avejigar.

vesicatory, *s.* vejigatorio.

vesicle ['vesikəl], *s.* vejiguilla, vesícula.

vesicular [veˈsikjuːləɹ], **vesiculate** [veˈsikjuːlit], *a.* vejigular, vejiguloso, vesicular, vesiculoso.

vesper ['vespəɹ], *s.* (*poét.*) estrella vespertina, véspero, héspero; (*igl.*) víspera; (*ant.*) anochecer. — *a.* vespertino, de la tarde.

vespers, *s.pl.* (*igl.*) vísperas.

vessel ['vesəl], *s.* vasija, recipiente; (*anat.*) canal, vaso, vena; (*mar.*) bajel, buque, embarcación.

vest [vest], *s.* camiseta; chaleco, chaqueta antigua, chaqueta de niño; (*poét.*) vestidura, vestido. — *v.t.* (*poét.*) vestir; revestir, investir; hacer entrega, dar posesión; dar a cargo, colocar (fondos). — *v.i.* (*poét.*) vestirse; tener validez; caer, ser devuelto, pertenecer.

vestal ['vestəl], *s.*, *a.*, *f.* vestal; virgen; monja; virginal, pura, casta.

vestiary ['vestiəɹi], *s.* vestuario.

vestibule ['vestibjuːl], *s.* vestíbulo, zaguán, portal, recibimiento, atrio, pórtico; (*anat.*) vestíbulo.

vestige ['vestidʒ], *s.* vestigio, huellas, trazas, indicios, rastro.

vestigial [vesˈtidʒiəl], *a.* rudimentario, residual.

vesting, *s.* tela para chalecos, corte de chaleco.

vestment ['vestmənt], *s.* hábito, prenda de vestir, vestidura, ropa; (*igl.*) vestimentas.

vestry ['vestri], *s.* sacristía; vestuario de convento; asamblea parroquial, sesión de la junta de la parroquia.

vesture ['vestʃəɹ], *s.* vestido, vestidura, vestuario, ropa.

Vesuvian [veˈsuːviən], *a.* del Vesuvio. — *s.* vesuviana.

vet, *v.t.* (*fam.*) examinar *o* tratar (animales o hombres); (*fig.*, *fam.*) escudriñar, examinar, dar un vistazo.

vetch [vetʃ], *s.* (*bot.*) algarroba, alverjana, veza, almorta.

vetchling, *s.* arveja, áfaca.

vetchy, *a.* abundante en algarrobas.

veteran ['vetərən], *s.* veterano. — *a.* aguerrido, experimentado.

veterinarian [vetərinˈɛəriən], *s.* veterinario.

veterinary ['vetərinəri], *a.* veterinario; *veterinary science*, veterinaria; *veterinary surgeon*, veterinario.

veto ['viːtou], s. veto, prohibición. — v.t. poner su veto a, prohibir, vedar.

vex [veks], v.t. enfadar, enojar, irritar; hostigar, atormentar, provocar, exasperar, acosar, vejar; molestar, desazonar, incomodar. — v.i. enfadarse, irritarse, picarse, incomodarse.

vexation [vek'seiʃən], s. disgusto, contrariedad, enojo, enfado; vejación, vejamen, molestia, maltrato.

vexatious [vek'seiʃəs], a. enojoso, contrariador, fastidioso, provocativo; molesto, vejatorio, importuno.

vexatiousness, s. disgusto, contrariedad, enojo; molestia, vejación, vejamen.

vexed, a. fastidiado, contrariado; vejado, molestado; discutido, debatido, espinoso.

vexing, a. fastidioso, contrariador; importuno, vejador.

vexingly, adv. de una manera contrariadora; importunamente.

VHF [vːeitʃ'ef], (abrev.) very high frequency, ondas ultracortas; VHF radio, receptor por hiperfrecuencias.

via ['vaiə], s. vía, senda. — adv. por, por la vía de, por medio de; por, a través de, pasando por.

viability, s. viabilidad.

viable ['vaiəbəl], a. viable.

viaduct ['vaiədʌkt], s. viaducto.

vial ['vaiəl], s. frasco pequeño, ampolleta, redoma. — v.t. poner en una redomita.

viand ['vaiənd], s. vianda. — pl. **viands**, manjares, provisiones, comida.

viaticum [vai'ætikəm], s. viático, provisiones de camino; (igl.) viático.

vibrant ['vaibrənt], a. vibrante.

vibrate [vai'breit], v.t. vibrar, hacer vibrar. — v.i. vibrar, oscilar, vacilar, fluctuar, retemblar, cimbrar, retumbar, trepidar, jinglar.

vibratile ['vaibrətil], a. vibrátil, vibratorio.

vibrating, a. vibrante, trepidante.

vibration [vai'breiʃən], s. vibración, oscilación, trepidación, vaivén.

vibrative, vibratory, a. vibratorio, vibrante, oscilatorio.

viburnum [vai'bəːɪnəm], s. viburno, mundillo.

vicar ['vikəɪ], s. vicario, cura, m.

vicarage ['vikərid3], s. vicariato, vicaría; curato de parroquia.

vicarial [vi'kɛəriəl], a. vicario, delegado.

vicarious [vi'kɛəriəs], a. delegado, vicario, substituto, substituido; simpático, experimentado o padecido por otro.

vicariously, adv. por delegación; por simpatía ajena.

vicarship, s. vicariato, vicaría.

vice [vais], s. vicio, inmoralidad, depravación; falta, imperfección, defecto; maldad; resabio (de caballos); (fam.) suplente, sustituto; tornillo de banco. — prep. (prefijo) vice, en lugar de, en vez de.

vice-admiral, s. vicealmirante.

vice-admiralty, s. vicealmirantazgo.

vice-chancellor, s. vicecanciller.

vice-consul, s. vicecónsul.

vice-consulate, s. viceconsulado.

vicegerency, s. subadministración; virreinato.

vicegerent [vais'd3erənt], s. vicegerente, subadministrador, substituto, diputado. — a. delegado, representante.

vice-presidency, s. vicepresidencia.

vice-president, s. vicepresidente.

viceregal [vais'riːgəl], a. de virrey.

vicereine ['vaisrein], s. virreina.

viceroy ['vaisrɔi], s. virrey.

viceroyalty, viceroyship, s. virreinato.

vice-versa [vaisi'vɔːɪsə], adv. viceversa.

vicinage ['visinid3], s. [VICINITY].

vicinal ['visinəl], a. vecinal, vecino; vicinal, inmediato, adyacente.

vicinity [vi'siniti], s. vecindad, cercanías, inmediaciones; proximidad, cercanía.

vicious ['viʃəs], a. vicioso, defectuoso, depravado, maligno, imperfecto, corrompido, podrido; resabioso, espantadizo (caballos).

viciousness, s. naturaleza viciosa, depravación; lacra, resabio.

vicissitude [vai'sisitjuːd], s. vicisitud, altibajo, vaivén.

victim ['viktim], s. víctima, f.

victimize ['viktimaiz], v.t. hacer víctima, inmolar; embaucar, estafar; hacer víctima de, vejar, hacer el vacío a.

victor ['viktəɪ], s. vencedor, triunfador.

victoria [vik'tɔːriə], s. victoria (coche); (bot.) ninfea de las Amazonas.

victorious [vik'tɔːriəs], a. victorioso, vencedor.

victoriousness, s. carácter victorioso; victoria, triunfo.

victory ['viktori], s. victoria, conquista, triunfo.

victress, s.f. vencedora.

victual ['vitəl], v.t. abastecer, avituallar, bastimentar, proveer de víveres. — s. vianda. — pl. vituallas, víveres.

victualler, s. proveedor, abastecedor; comisario, hostalero, fondista, m.f.

victualling, s. abastecimiento; víveres, victuallas.

victuals ['vitəlz], s.pl. víveres, alimentos, provisiones.

vide ['vaidiː], v.t. vea Vd., véase, véanse.

videlicet [vi'diːliset], adv. (abrev.) **viz.,** a saber, o sea, es decir.

viduage ['vidjuːid3], s. viudez.

vie [vai], v.i. rivalizar, disputar, luchar, competir, contender.

view [vjuː], v.t. mirar, ver, contemplar, presenciar, considerar, especular, apercibir, examinar, inspeccionar. — s. vista, vistazo, visión, ojeada, mirada; paisaje, perspectiva, escena, panorama, m.; contemplación; modo de ver, idea, noción, parecer, opinión, f.; exterioridad, apariencia; at a view, de una ojeada; at first view, a primera vista; point of view, punto de vista; to take a closer view of, examinar de más cerca; with a view to, en vista de, con motivo de; in view of, en vista de, visto, a causa de; in the view of, en la opinión de, al modo de ver de; bird's-eye view, (a) vista de pájaro.

viewer, s. inspector, mirador, veedor, visor; (for.) experto.

viewless, a. invisible; que no da a un panorama pintoresco.

vigesimal [vi'd3eziməl], a. vigésimo.

vigil ['vid3il], s. vigilia, desvelo, vela, velación, vigilancia.

vigilance, vigilancy, s. vigilancia, desvelo, cuidado.

vigilant ['vid3ilənt], a. vigilante, despierto, atento, alerta, cuidadoso.

vigilantly, *adv.* con vigilancia, vigilantemente, alertamente.

vignette [vin'jet], *s.* (*impr.*) viñeta; (*arq.*) ramaje. — *v.t.* aviñetar; (*foto.*) hacer un retrato en viñeta.

vigorous ['vigərəs], *a.* vigoroso, recio, robusto, potente, fuerte.

vigorously, *adv.* vigorosamente, con fuerza, con energía.

vigorousness, **vigour**, *s.* vigor, fuerza, robustez.

Viking ['vaikiŋ], *s.* vikingo, antiguo pirata escandinavo.

vile [vail], *a.* vil, bajo, despreciable, indigno, infame, ruin, vergonzoso, perverso.

vileness, *s.* vileza, bajeza, abyección, infamia.

vilification [vilifi'keiʃən], *s.* difamación, envilecimiento, vilipendio.

vilifier ['vilifaiəɹ], *s.* difamador.

vilify ['vilifai], *v.t.* envilecer, degradar, difamar, vilipendiar.

villa ['vilə], *s.* finca, hotelito, casa de campo, quinta.

village ['vilidʒ], *s.* lugar, pueblo, pueblecito, aldea.

villager, *s.* lugareño, aldeano.

villain ['vilən], *s.* patán, plebeyo, pechero, villano; bellaco, malvado, pícaro.

villainous, *a.* vil, despreciable, infame, bellaco, pícaro, malvado; (*fam.*) repugnante.

villainousness, **villainy**, *s.* maldad, infamia, perversidad.

villeinage ['vilənidʒ], *s.* vasallaje.

villose, **villous** ['viləs], *a.* velloso, velludo, felpudo.

villosity, *s.* vellosidad.

vim [vim], (*fam.*) fuerza, energía, vigor.

vimineous [vi'miniəs], *a.* de mimbre, mimbroso.

vinaceous [vai'neiʃəs], *a.* vinario, vinoso.

vinaigrette [vinei'gret], *s.* redomilla para esencia; vinagreta.

vincible ['vinsibəl], *a.* vencible.

vinculum ['viŋkju:ləm], *s.* vínculo.

vindemial [vin'demiəl], *a.* (*ant.*) de la vendimia.

vindicable ['vindikəbəl], *a.* sostenible, justificable.

vindicate ['vindikeit], *v.t.* vindicar, sostener, defender, justificar, afirmar; desagraviar.

vindication, *s.* vindicación, justificación; desagravio.

vindicative, *a.* vindicativo, vindicador, justificativo.

vindicator, *s.* defensor, vindicador, protector.

vindicatory, *a.* vindicatorio, justificativo, vengador.

vindictive [vin'diktiv], *a.* vengativo, despiadado, cruel, rencoroso.

vindictively, *adv.* vengativamente, con crueldad.

vindictiveness, *s.* carácter vengativo, deseo de venganza, rencor, crueldad.

vine [vain], *s.* (*bot.*) enredadera, parra, vid, *f.*; sarmiento; *vine beetle*, (*entom.*) escarabajuelo; *wild vine*, vid silvestre; *vine-disease*, *vine-pest*, filoxera; *vine-fretter*, pulgón de la vid.

vine-branch, *a.* rama de viña, sarmiento.

vine-clad, *a.* cubierto de viñas.

vine-dresser, *s.* viñador.

vinegar ['vinigəɹ], *s.* vinagre; *vinegar cruet*, vinagrera.

vinegarish, **vinegary**, *a.* avinagrado, vinagroso.

vine-knife, *s.* podadera.

vine-like, *a.* aparrado.

vinery ['vainəri], *s.* invernadero, emparrado.

vine-shoot, *s.* sarmiento.

vine-stock, *s.* cepa.

vineyard ['vinjɑ:ɹd], *s.* viña, viñedo.

vinose ['vainous], *a.* vinoso.

vinosity, *s.* vinosidad.

vinous ['vainəs], *a.* vinoso.

vintage ['vintidʒ], *s.* vendimia; (*fig.*) vendimia. — *v.t.* vendimiar.

vintager, *s.* vendimiador, vinícola, *m.f.*, vinariego.

vintner ['vintnəɹ], *s.* vinatero, tabernero.

viny ['vaini], *a.* perteneciente a las vides.

viol ['vaiol], *s.* (*mús.*, *ant.*) viola, violón; (*mar.*) virador; *double bass viol*, (*mús.*, *ant.*) contrabajo.

viola, *s.* (*mús.*, *bot.*) viola.

violable ['vaiоləbəl], *a.* violable.

violaceous [vaio'leiʃəs], *a.* violáceo.

violate ['vaioleit], *v.t.* violar, interrumpir, turbar; violentar, insultar; violar, profanar, ultrajar, violar, atropellar, infringir, contravenir, quebrantar; violar, estuprar, forzar.

violation, *s.* violación.

violator, *s.* violador.

violence, *s.* violencia; *to do violence to*, violentar.

violent ['vaiolənt], *a.* violento, arrebatado, impetuoso, vehemente, fulminante; fuerte, duro, severo, intenso.

violently, *adv.* con violencia, con fuerza, violentamente, impetuosamente.

violet ['vaiolet], *s.* violeta. — *a.* violado.

violin [vaio'lin], *s.* (*mús.*) violín; violinista, *m.f.*

violinist, *s.* violinista, *m.f.*

violoncellist, *s.* violoncelista, *m.f.*

violoncello [vi:olən'tʃelou], *s.* violoncelo, violonchelo; violoncelista, *m.f.*

viper ['vaipəɹ], *s.* víbora; *viper grass*, (*bot.*) escorzonera.

viperine, **viperish**, **viperous**, *a.* viperino, de víbora; nocivo, venenoso.

virago [vi'reigou], *s.f.* mujer de mal genio, fiera, sierpe, *f.*, áspid; (*ant.*) marimacho, amazona, virago, *f.*

vireo ['viriou], *s.* (*orn.*) víreo.

virescent [vi'resənt], *a.* (*bot.*) verdoso.

Virgilian [vəɹ'dʒilien], *a.* virgiliano, de Virgilio.

virgin ['vəɹ.ɹdʒin], *s.f.* virgen, doncella; religiosa con voto de castidad; (*astr.*) virgo; (*zool.*) insecto hembra que produce huevos sin ser fertilizada o impregnada. — *a.* virgen, casto, puro, virginal; (*fig.*) virgen.

virginal, *a.* virginal. — *s.* (*mús.*) espineta.

virginity [vəɹ'dʒiniti], *s.* virginidad.

virgin's-bower, *s.* (*bot.*) clemátide, *f.*

viridescent [viri'desənt], *a.* verdoso.

viridity [vi'riditi], *s.* verdor; verdura.

virile ['virail], *a.* viril, varonil.

virility [vi'riliti], *s.* virilidad.

virole [vi'roul], *s.* (*blas.*) virol.

virose, **virous** ['virəs], *a.* ponzoñoso; (*bot.*) que emite olor fétido.

virtual ['vəɹːtjuːəl], *a.* virtual.

virtuality, *s.* virtualidad.

virtually, *adv.* virtualmente.

virtue ['vəɹːtjuː], *s.* virtud, castidad; excelencia,

valor; *by virtue of*, en virtud de. — *pl.* el quinto coro de los espíritus celestiales.

virtueless, *a.* sin virtud.

virtuosity [vəɹtjuːˈɔsiti], *s.* maestría, musicalidad virtuosa.

virtuoso [vəɹtjuːˈouzou], *s.* (artista) virtuoso.

virtuous [ˈvəːɹtjuːəs], *a.* virtuoso.

virtuousness, *s.* virtud.

virulence, virulency, *s.* virulencia.

virulent [ˈvirjuːlənt], *a.* virulento.

virulently, *adv.* con virulencia.

virus [ˈvairəs], *s.* (*med.*) virus; (*fig.*) virulencia, malignidad.

visage [ˈvizidʒ], *s.* rostro, cara, semblante, faz, *f.*, aspecto.

visaged, *a.* de rostro, de cara.

viscera [ˈvisərə], *s.pl.* vísceras, entrañas.

visceral, *a.* visceral.

viscid [ˈvisid], **viscous** [ˈviskəs], *a.* viscoso, pegajoso, glutinoso, conglutinativo.

viscidity [viˈsiditi], **viscosity** [visˈkɔsiti], *s.* viscosidad, gomosidad.

viscount [ˈvaikaunt], *s.* vizconde.

viscountess [ˈvaikauntes], *s.* vizcondesa.

viscountship, viscounty, *s.* vizcondado.

viscous [ˈviskəs], *a.* [VISCID].

vise [vais], *s.* (*E.U.*) tornillo de banco [VICE].

visé, *v.t.* visar. — *s.* visado.

visibility [viziˈbiliti], *s.* visibilidad.

visible [ˈvizibəl], *a.* visible; manifiesto, claro, evidente; conspicuo, externo.

visibleness, *s.* visibilidad.

visibly, *adv.* visiblemente; manifiestamente, evidentemente, claramente; a vista de ojos, cada vez más.

Visigoth [ˈvizigɔθ], *s.* visigodo.

Visigothic, *a.* visigótico, visigodo.

vision [ˈviʒən], *s.* vista, visión; visión, aparición, fantasma, *m.*, sueño, revelación.

visional, *a.* de visión.

visionary [ˈviʒənəri], *a.* visionario, quimérico; místico. — *s.* visionario, soñador; místico.

visit [ˈvizit], *v.t.* visitar, hacer una visita a, ir a ver, inspeccionar; visitar, acudir con frecuencia; (*med.*) visitar; (*teol.*) visitar. — *v.i.* hacer visitas, ir de visita, visitarse; *to go visiting*, ir de visita. — *s.* visita; investigación, inspección, reconocimiento; *on a visit*, en visita.

visitable, *a.* visitable, sometido a la visita, sujeto a inspección.

visitant, *a.* visitador, visitante.

visitation [viziˈteiʃən], *s.* visitación, visita, registro, inspección, reconocimiento; visitación del cielo; *death by visitation of God*, muerte natural.

visiting [ˈvizitiŋ], *s.* inspección, visita. — *a.* de visita; *visiting card*, tarjeta de visita.

visitorial, *a.* de inspección, de visita.

visor [ˈvaizəɹ], *s.* visera de casco; máscara.

visored, *a.* con la visera baja; enmascarado.

vista [ˈvistə], *s.* vista, perspectiva, panorama, *m.*

visual [ˈviʒjuːəl], *a.* visual, óptico.

visuality, *s.* visualidad.

visually, *adv.* visualmente.

vital [ˈvaitəl], *a.* vital; indispensable, esencial, de suma importancia; *vital air*, aire respirable.

vitalism, *s.* vitalismo.

vitalist, *s.* vitalista, *m.f.*

vitality [vaiˈtæliti], *s.* vitalidad, vigor, brío, energía.

vitalize [ˈvaitəlaiz], *v.t.* vivificar, animar; reanimar, dar vida.

vitally [ˈvaitəli], *adv.* vitalmente; esencialmente, indispensablemente.

vitals [ˈvaitəlz], *s.pl.* partes vitales; órganos esenciales del cuerpo; (*fig.*) entrañas.

vitelline [viˈtelin], *s.* (*quím.*) vitelina.

vitiate [ˈviʃieit], *v.t.* viciar, corromper, dañar, inficionar, infectar; invalidar, perjudicar.

vitiation *s.* depravación, alteración, corrupción; invalidación, perjuicio.

viticulture [ˈvitikʌltʃəɹ], *s.* viticultura.

viticultural, *a.* vitícola.

viticulturist, *s.* vitícola, *m.f.*, viticultor.

vitreous [ˈvitriəs], *a.* vítreo, vidrioso; *vitreous enamel*, esmalte vítreo.

vitreousness, *s.* vitreosidad, vidriosidad.

vitrescence, *s.* vitrificación.

vitrescent [viˈtresənt], **vitrescible,** *a.* vitrificable.

vitrifaction [vitriˈfækʃən], *s.* vitrificación.

vitrifiable, *a.* vitrificable.

vitrification [vitrifiˈkeiʃən], *s.* vitrificación.

vitriform, *a.* vítreo, vitriforme.

vitrify [ˈvitrifai], *v.t.* vitrificar. — *v.i.* vitrificarse.

vitriol [ˈvitriəl], *s.* vitriolo, aceite de vitriolo, ácido sulfúrico, sulfato vitriolo; *blue, roman* o *copper vitriol*, sulfato de cobre; *green vitriol*, sulfato de hierro, caparrosa; *white vitriol*, sulfato de cinc.

vitriolate, vitriolize, *v.t.* convertir en sulfato o en vitriolo.

vitriolate, vitriolated, *a.* vitriolado.

vitriolic [vitriˈɔlik], *a.* vitriólico; (*fig.*) cáustico, mordaz.

vituline [ˈvitjuːlin], *a.* becerril, de ternero.

vituperable, *a.* vituperable.

vituperate [vaiˈtjuːpəreit], *v.t.*, *v.i.* vituperar, censurar.

vituperation, *s.* vituperación, vituperio, reproche.

vivacious [vaiˈveiʃəs], *a.* vivaz, animado, vivo, vivaracho, despejado; (*bot.*) perenne.

vivaciously, *adv.* de una manera viva.

vivaciousness, vivacity, *s.* vivacidad, viveza.

vivarium [vaiˈvɛəriəm], **vivary,** *s.* vivera, vivero, vivar.

viva voce [ˈvaivəˈvousi], *adv.* de viva voz, de palabra.

vivid [ˈvivid], *a.* brillante, intenso, resplandeciente; gráfico, vivaz; vigoroso, (*poét.*) vívido.

vividness, *s.* brillo, resplandor, brillantez; vivacidad, intensidad, ardor.

vivification [vivifiˈkeiʃən], *s.* vivificación.

vivify [ˈvivifai], *v.t.* vivificar, dar vida.

viviparous [vaiˈvipərəs], *a.* vivíparo.

vivisect, *v.t.*, *v.i.* practicar la vivisección.

vivisection [viviˈsekʃən], *s.* vivisección.

vixen [ˈviksən], *s.f.* zorra, raposa; (*fig.*) arpía, fiera.

viz. [viz], *adv. contr.* [VIDELICET]; es decir, a saber, o sea.

vizard [ˈvizəɹd], *s.* visera, máscara. — *v.t.* enmascarar.

vizier [viˈziəɹ], *s.* visir.

vizierate, viziership, *s.* dignidad de visir.

vizor [ˈvaizəɹ], *s.* visera [VISOR].

vizored, *a.* con visera.

vocable [ˈvoukəbəl], *s.* vocablo, voz, *f.*

vocabulary [vo'kæbju:ləri], *s.* vocabulario.
vocal ['voukəl], *a.* vocal, oral, de la voz. — *s.* vocal, *f.*
vocalist, *s.* cantor, cantora, cantatriz, *f.*, cantante, *m.f.*
vocality [vo'kæliti], *s.* calidad de vocal.
vocalization, *s.* vocalización.
vocalize ['voukəlaiz], *v.t.* vocalizar. — *v.i.* vocalizar, solfear.
vocally, *adv.* vocalmente, verbalmente, oralmente, con la voz.
vocation [vo'keiʃən], *s.* vocación, ocupación, empleo, oficio; carrera, profesión.
vocational, *a.* profesional, para la carrera, relativo a la vocación.
vocative ['vɔkətiv], *s.* (*gram.*) vocativo. — *a.* del vocativo.
vociferate [vo'sifəreit], *v.t.*, *v.i.* vociferar, vocear, clamorear, aullar, gritar.
vociferation, *s.* vocería, grita, vociferación, vinglería.
vociferous [vo'sifərəs], *a.* vocinglero, clamoroso.
vociferously, *adv.* vociferando, desaforadamente, a gritos.
vogue [voug], *a.* boga, moda; *in vogue*, de moda, en boga.
voice [vɔis], *s.* voz, *f.*; lenguaje, habla, palabra; sufragio, voto; juicio, opinión, *f.*; admonición, instrucción, enseñanza; (*gram.*) voz del verbo; *to raise one's voice*, levantar la voz; *without a dissentient voice*, con unanimidad de votos; *in a loud voice*, a gritos, en voz alta; *in a low voice*, en voz baja. — *v.t.* proclamar, publicar; expresar, intepretar; votar; decir su parecer; dar el tono; acordar o templar un instrumento.
voiced, *a.* dicho, hablado, expresado; que tiene voz; (*gram.*) sonoro.
voiceless, *a.* sin voz, sin voto; mudo; (*gram.*) sordo, consonante muda.
void [vɔid], *a.* vacante, vacío, hueco, desocupado; (*for.*) nulo, inválido, sin valor, sin fuerza legal; desprovisto, privado, falto; ilusorio, vano. — *s.* vacío, oquedad, espacio vacío, vacuo. — *v.t.* vaciar, desocupar, evacuar; invalidar, anular; expulsar. — *v.i.* (*ant.*) anularse.
voidable, *a.* anulable; que se puede vaciar o expeler.
voidance, *s.* vacancia, vaciamiento, evacuación; invalidación; (*ant.*) subterfugio; expulsión.
voider, *s.* (*for.*) anulador, persona que anula; vaciador.
voiding, *a.* que anula; que recibe los residuos. — *s.* vaciamiento; invalidación.
voidness, *s.* vacío, vacuidad, nulidad.
volant ['vɔlənt], *a.* volante, ligero; (*poét.*) rápido, ligero, ágil.
volatile ['vɔlətail], *a.* volátil, volante; voluble, ligero, errátil; sutil, fugaz; transitorio, pasajero.
volatility [vɔlə'tiliti], *s.* volatilidad; volatariedad, volubilidad, inconstancia, ligereza.
volatilization, *s.* volatilización.
volatilize [vo'lætilaiz], *v.t.* volatilizar, volatizar, vaporizar. — *v.i.* volatilizarse.
volcanic [vɔl'kænik], *a.* volcánico.
volcano [vɔl'keinou], *s.* volcán.
vole [voul], *s.* bola (juegos de naipes); ratón campestre. — *v.t.* (juego de naipes) hacer todas las bazas.

volition [vo'liʃən], *s.* volición, voluntad.
volitional, *a.* volitivo.
volley ['vɔli], *s.* descarga, salva, andanada; (*deportes*) voleo (de la pelota). — *v.t.* enviar o hacer una descarga de; (*deportes*) volear. — *v.i.* estallar.
volplane ['vɔlplein], *v.i.* (*aer.*) planear.
volt [voult], *s.* (*elec.*) voltio; (*esgr.*, *etc.*) vuelta.
voltage ['voultidʒ], *s.* (*elec.*) voltaje.
voltaic [vɔl'teiik], *a.* voltaico.
voltaism, *s.* voltaísmo, galvanismo.
voltameter [vɔl'tæmetəɹ], *s.* voltámetro.
volubility [vɔlju:'biliti], *s.* volubilidad, verbosidad, picotería.
voluble ['vɔlju:bəl], *a.* gárrulo, hablador; (*bot.*) voluble, que trepa en espiral.
volubly, *adv.* con garrulidad.
volume ['vɔlju:m], *s.* volumen; bulto, masa; tomo, libro; gran cantidad, suma, importe; caudal (de río); potencia sonora (de radio); cilindrada (de motores); potencia sonora (de música); sonoridad.
volumetric [vɔlju:'metrik], *a.* volumétrico.
voluminous [vɔl'ju:minəs], *a.* voluminoso, abultado; copioso, prolijo, extenso.
voluminously, *adv.* de una manera voluminosa; copiosamente; en muchos tomos.
voluminousness, *s.* bulto, lo voluminoso.
voluntarily ['vɔləntərili], *adv.* voluntariamente, espontáneamente.
voluntariness, *s.* naturaleza voluntaria.
voluntary ['vɔləntəri], *a.* voluntario, independiente, espontáneo, libre; hecho con intención, deliberado. — *s.* voluntario; solo de órgano que se toca en la celebración del oficio divino.
volunteer [vɔlən'tiəɹ], *s.*, *a.* voluntario. — *v.t.* ofrecer voluntariamente. — *v.i.* ofrecerse voluntariamente, contribuir voluntariamente; (*mil.*) servir como voluntario.
voluptuary [vo'lʌptju:əri], *s.* hombre voluptuoso, sibarita, *m.f.* — *a.* voluptuoso, lujurioso.
voluptuous [vo'lʌptju:əs], *a.* voluptuoso, lujurioso.
voluptuously, *adv.* voluptuosamente, lujuriosamente.
voluptuousness, *s.* voluptuosidad, sensualidad.
volute [vo'lju:t], *s.* (*arq.*) voluta; arrollado, voluto. — *a.* de espiral.
voluted, *a.* de volutas.
volution, *s.* espiral.
volvulus ['vɔlvju:ləs], *s.* (*med.*) miserere.
vomit ['vɔmit], *v.t.*, *v.i.* vomitar, arrojar. — *s.* vómito; (*med.*) vomitivo; (*med.*) vómica.
vomiting, *s.* vómito.
vomit nut, *s.* nuez vómica.
vomitory ['vɔmitəri], *s.* vomitivo. — *a.* vomitivo, emético.
voodoo ['vu:du:], *s.* (*Am.*) tabú, vudú.
voracious [vo'reiʃəs], *a.* voraz, rapaz, devorador, tragón.
voraciously, *adv.* vorazmente.
voracity [vo'ræsiti], *s.* voracidad.
vortex ['vɔ:ɹteks], *s.* (*pl.* **vortexes**, **vortices**) remolino, torbellino, vórtice, vorágine, *f.*
vortical ['vɔ:ɹtikəl], **vortiginous** [vɔ:ɹtidʒinəs], *a.* vortiginoso.
votaress, *s.f.* sacerdotisa, mujer que cumple un voto.
votary ['voutəri], *s.* devoto; partidario, sectario.

vote [vout], *s.* voto; votación, sufragio, resolución; parecer, dictamen; *casting vote,* voto decisivo; *to put to the vote,* poner a votación. — *v.t.* votar por, elegir. — *v.i.* votar, dar su voto, opinar.

voter, *s.* votante, elector.

voting, *s.* votación.

votive ['voutiv], *a.* votivo.

vouch [vautʃ], *v.t.* afirmar, garantizar, responder (de), atestiguar, certificar, testificar. — *v.i.* dar testimonio, salir fiador. — *s.* testimonio, atestación.

voucher, *s.* (*for.*) garante, fiador; testigo; documento comprobante, certificado justificante; abono, vale, cargareme; resguardo, recibo.

vouchsafe [vautʃ'seif], *v.t.* otorgar, permitir, conceder, condescender. — *v.i.* condescender, dignarse.

voussoir ['vu:swa:ɹ], *s.* (*arq.*) clave de arco, dovela.

vow [vau], *s.* voto, ofrenda, promesa solemne; *to take (the) vows,* pronunciar sus votos. — *v.t.* votar, jurar, hacer voto de. — *v.i.* hacer voto, hacer promesa, prometer, jurar.

vowel ['vauəl], *s.* vocal, *f.* — *a.* vocal, de vocal. — *v.t.* poner vocales.

vowelled, *a.* que abunda en vocales.

vox [voks], *s.* voz, *f.*, registro de órgano que imita la voz humana.

voyage ['voiədʒ], *s.* viaje, travesía; *voyage out and home,* viaje redondo. — *v.i.* viajar por mar, navegar. — *v.t.* navegar, transitar por.

voyager, *s.* navegador; viajero, pasajero, viajante.

vulcan ['vʌlkən], *s.* vulcano.

vulcanist, *s.* vulcanista, *m.f.*

vulcanite ['vʌlkənait], *s.* vucanita.

vulcanization, *s.* vulcanización.

vulcanize ['vʌlkənaiz], *v.t.* vulcanizar.

vulgar ['vʌlgəɹ], *a.* ordinario, mal criado, cursi, de mal tono; grosero; vulgar, común. — *s.* vulgo, plebe, *f.*, populacho.

vulgarism, *s.* vulgaridad, vulgarismo, barbarismo.

vulgarity [vʌl'gæriti], **vulgarness** ['vʌlgəɹnis], *s.* cursilería, grosería, mal tono, chocarrería.

vulgarization, *s.* vulgarización.

vulgarize, vulgarise, *v.t.* vulgarizar.

vulgarly, *adv.* de mal tono, groseramente; vulgarmente, comúnmente.

Vulgate ['vʌlgeit], *s.* (*igl.*) Vulgata.

vulnerability [vʌlnəɹə'biliti], *s.* vulnerabilidad, calidad de vulnerable.

vulnerable ['vʌlnəɹəbəl], *a.* vulnerable.

vulnerary ['vʌlnəɹəri], *a.* vulnerario. — *s.* medicamento vulnerario.

vulpine ['vʌlpain], *a.* vulpino, raposuno, zorruno, (*fig.*) vulpino, ladino.

vulture ['vʌltʃəɹ], *s.* buitre.

vulturine, vulturish, vulturous, *a.* buitrero, de buitre, rapaz.

vulva ['vʌlvə], *s.* vulva.

vulvar, vulval, *a.* vulvario.

vying ['vaiiŋ], *a.* rivalizando [VIE].

W

W, w ['dʌbəlju:], vigésima tercera letra del alfabeto inglés. Su sonido es muy parecido a la *u* española; es muda cuando precede a la *r* como en *wrap,* y delante de la *h* seguida de *o* como en *who, whole*; también es muda en algunas voces como en *sword, answer,* etc.

wabble [wobəl], *v.i.* bambalearse, tambalearse, oscilar, vacilar, balancear(se) [WOBBLE]. — *s.* bamboleo, bamboneo, tambaleo.

wabbling, *s.* oscilación, bamboleo, tambaleo. — *a.* tambaleante, inestable.

wabblingly, *adv.* vacilando, bamboleándose, con mal equilibrio.

wabbly, *a.* inestable, tambaleante, que bambolea.

wacke ['wæki], *s.* (*geol.*) roca parda arcillosa.

wad [wod], *s.* rollo (de papeles), fajo (de billetes), manojo de paja; pelote o borra para rehenchir cojines, muebles, etc.; lápiz negro; (*cost.*) guata; (*arti.*) taco; (*min.*) quijo de manganeso y cobalto. — *v.t.* rehenchir, emborrar, acolchar; atacar; enhuatar.

wadded, *a.* emborrado, acolchado.

wadding, *s.* pelotes, guata, borra, algodón en rama; taco; entretela, entreforro, relleno.

waddle ['wodəl], *v.i.* anadear.

waddling, *s.* anadeo.

wade [weid], *v.i.* vadear, andar en el agua, etc.; atravesar, pasar con dificultad y trabajo; *to wade in,* (*fig.*) abalanzarse a, meterse en; *to wade through,* (*fig.*) leer detenida y trabajosamente. — *v.t.* vadear, atravesar a vado.

wader, wading-bird, *s.* (*orn.*) zancuda, ave zancuda.

wafer ['weifəɹ], *s.* oblea, hostia; barquillo; (*arti.*) fulminante. — *v.t.* poner una oblea en, cerrar con oblea.

waffle ['wofəl], *s.* fruta de sartén.

waft ['wa:ft], *v.t.* transportar o llevar (por el aire); hacer flotar, mecer; sobrenadar; (*ant.*) hacer señal a. — *v.i.* flotar, vogar. — *s.* ráfaga de aire, brisa; mecedura, fluctuación; (*ant.*) señal hecha con bandera; banderín.

waftage, *s.* transporte o conducción por el aire.

wafter, *s.* (*ant.*) buque de transporte.

wafture ['wa:ftʃəɹ], *s.* fluctuación, mecedura, agitación; conducción por el aire.

wag [wæg], *v.t.* sacudir, mover ligeramente, menear ligeramente; *to wag the tail,* menear la cola, colear, rabear. — *v.i.* oscilar, balancearse, agitarse; (*vulg.*) moverse, deslizarse, irse, ir pasando. — *s.* coleadura, coleada, movimiento de cabeza; guasón, bromista, *m.f.*, burlón, bufón, chancero; *to play the wag,* estar de chunga; (*vulg.*) hacer novillos.

wage [weidʒ], *s.* (*pl.* **wages**) salario, sueldo, paga, jornal; (*fig.*) premio, galardón, recompensa. — *v.t.* apostar; hacer, emprender, sostener; aventurar, probar, tentar; *to wage war,* hacer guerra.

wage-earner ['weidʒə:ɹnəɹ], *s.* asalariado; jornalero, trabajador.

wager ['weidʒəɹ], *s.* apuesta; cantidad apostada; *to lay a wager,* apostar, hacer una apuesta. — *v.t.* apostar, poner.

wages ['weidʒiz], *s.pl.* salario, sueldo, soldada, paga, jornal, prenda.

waggery ['wægəri], *s.* bufonada, guasa, jocosidad, travesura.

waggish ['wægiʃ], *a.* zumbón, guasón, chacotero, travieso, jocoso, juguetón.

waggishly, *adv.* de una manera zumbona, con guasa, estando de chunga, jocosamente.

waggishness, *s.* guasa, jocosidad, travesura, chacota, chunga.

waggle ['wægəl], *v.t.* mover blandamente, o agitar, menear ligeramente. — *v.i.* moverse, menearse; anadear. — *s.* meneo, oscilación; anadeo, pavoneo.

wag(g)on ['wægən], *s.* carro grande, carretón, carreta, galera; (*f.c.*) vagón, wagón; (*mil.*) furgón; *wagon maker*, carretero; *wagon load*, carretada. — *v.t.* acarrear, transportar con carros.

wag(g)onage, *s.* carretaje; precio de acarreo, precio de transporte.

wag(g)oner, *s.* carretero, carretonero, carromatero; (*astr.*) carro, la constelación auriga.

wag(g)onette [wægo'net], *s.* carricoche, birlocho; autobús ligero.

wagtail ['wægteil], *s.* nevatilla, aguzanieves, motacila, cerrojillo.

waif [weif], *s.* niño andorrero o sin hogar; niño expósito, niño abandonado; objeto abandonado, objeto extraviado, bienes mostrencos.

wail [weil], *v.t.* lamentar, deplorar, llorar, sollozar, gemir. — *v.i.* lamentarse, gemir. — *s.* lamentación, gemido, sollozo, lamento.

wailful, *a.* lamentoso, triste.

wailing, *s.* lamento, lamentación, gemidos, sollozos.

wain [wein], *s.* carreta, carretón; *Charles's Wain*, (*fam.*) Osa mayor.

wainscot ['weinskət], *s.* alfarje, friso de madera; revestimiento. — *v.t.* alfarjar, enfrisar, poner friso; revestir.

wainscoting, *s.* alfarje, friso de madera; revestimiento.

waist [weist], *s.* cintura, talle; cinto, cinturón; (*cost.*) corpecico, corpiño, jubón; (*mar.*) combés (de un buque).

waistband, *s.* cintura (de pantalones, etc.), pretina.

waistboards, *s.pl.* (*mar.*) falcas.

waistcloths, *s.pl.* (*mar.*) empavesadas.

waistcoat [weistkət], *s.* chaleco; justillo, monillo; chupa.

wait [wait], *v.i.* esperar, aguardar; ser mozo (de fonda, etc.), servir; estar listo; atender, despachar (en una tienda, etc.); *to wait at table*, servir a la mesa; *to wait for*, esperar a; *wait on* o *upon*, servir como criado; ir a ver, presentar sus respetos a; *to keep waiting*, hacer esperar; *to wait for*, aguardar, esperar; *to wait upon*, ir a casa de, pasar por casa de; acompañar; cuidar; servir. — *v.t.* (*ant.*) aguardar, esperar [AWAIT]; acompañar, seguir. — *s.* espera, dilación, pausa, detención, demora, tardanza; descanso, intervalo; murga de nochebuena; acechanza, celada, emboscada; *to lay wait*, formar emboscada; *to lie in wait*, acechar.

waiter ['weitəɹ], *s.* camarero, mozo (de café, fonda, etc.); (*E.U.*) sirviente; azafate, bandeja; *dumb-waiter*, bufete o aparador giratorio; (*E.U.*) ascensor para subir la comida de la cocina al comedor.

waiting, *a.* que aguarda; que sirve. — *s.* espera; servicio; *waiting-maid*, o *waiting-woman*, camarera, doncella; *gentleman-in-waiting*, gentilhombre de servicio; *lady-in-waiting*, dama se servicio.

waiting-room, *s.* sala de espera, antesala; sala de descanso.

waitress ['weitres], *s.f.* camarera; criada, doncella, moza.

waits [weits], *s.pl.* músicos que dan murgas o serenatas por nochebuena.

waive [weiv], *v.t.* abandonar, renunciar, repudiar.

wake [weik], *v.t.* (*pret. y p.p.* woke, waked) despertar; resucitar, excitar; velar (un muerto); *to wake up*, despertar, llamar. — *v.i.* despertar(se); velar, estar de velorio; despabilarse. — *s.* vela, velación, velada, vigilia; velorio; (*mar.*) estela, aguaje. — *pl.* (*prov., Ingl.*) fiesta de la dedicación de una iglesia que antiguamente se celebraba con romería y velando toda la noche.

wakeful, *a.* vigilante, que vela, desvelado, en vela, despierto; atento, vigilante; *to be wakeful*, velar, no dormir; estar atento.

wakefully, *adv.* vigilantemente, desveladamente.

wakefulness, *s.* vigilia, desvelo, velo; falta de sueño, insomnio.

waken ['weikən], *v.t.* despertar, llamar. — *v.i.* despertar(se), recordar(se).

wakener, waker, *s.* persona que (se) despierta; velador.

wake-robin, *s.* (*bot.*) aro, yaro.

waking, *s.* vela, velada, pervigilio; el despertar. — *a.* despierto, que despierta; de vela, de vigilia.

wale [weil], *s.* roncha, señal (del látigo, etc.), cardenal; (*mar.*) cinta; relieve (de tejidos). — *v.t.* levantar ronchas, azotar.

walk [wɔ:k], *v.i.* andar, ir a pie, caminar, ir andando, marchar; pasear(se), dar un paseo; conducirse, portarse, obrar; aparecer (fantasmas, espectros, etc.); (*fam.*) ser despedido; *to walk by one's self*, pasearse solo; *to walk about*, pasearse; *to walk after*, seguir, ir tras; *to walk away* o *off*, marcharse, irse; *to walk back*, volver a pie; *to walk down*, andar bajando, bajar a pie; *to walk in*, entrar, pasar adelante; *to walk on*, seguir andando; pisar, hollar; *to walk out*, irse afuera, salir; salir en huelga; *to walk up*, andar subiendo, subir a pie; acercarse, llegar; *to walk up and down*, ir y venir, pasearse de arriba a abajo. — *v.t.* recorrer, atravesar; pasear, hacer pasear, sacar a pasear; hacer ir al paso, hacer andar; dirigir, conducir; *to walk the hospitals*, estudiar clínica en los hospitales; *to walk the streets*, andorrear, callejear; prostituirse. — *s.* paseo, vuelta, caminata; modo de andar; paseo, avenida, alameda; acera; paso del caballo; vocación, empleo, carrera; porte, conducta, método de vida; *to go for a walk*, ir a paseo; *to go out for a walk*, salir a paseo; *to take a walk*, dar un paseo.

walker, *s.* paseante, caminante, andador, peatón; paseador; guarda forestal, guardabosque.

walkie-talkie [wɔ:ki'tɔ:ki], *s.* radioteléfono emisor-receptor portátil.

walking, *s.* paseo; el andar, el pasear; *walking-beam*, balancín; *walking-stick*, bastón; *walking-dress*, traje de paseo; *walking encyclopedia*, enciclopedia ambulante; *walking-pace*, paso de andadura; *walking-tour*, excursión a pie, caminata.

walk-over ['wɔ:kouvəɹ], *s.* (*fam.*) pan comido, triunfo o victoria fácil.

wall [wɔːl], s. pared, f., muro, tapia, muralla, (fig.) muralla, defensa; (fig.) pared, f., bulto; masa; main wall, pared maestra; partition wall, tabique; wall-creeper, (orn.) pico murario; garden-wall, tapia; wall-fruit, fruta de espalera; wall-louse, chinche; to be drawn to the wall, estar entre la espada y la pared; to be with one's back to o against the wall, estar entre la espada y la pared, estar en apuros; to take the wall, tomarse la acera; walls have ears, las paredes oyen. — v.t. murar, cercar con murallas, emparedar, fortificar, tapiar; to wall in, up o off, emparedar, tapiar, muriar.

wallaby ['wɔləbi], s. especie de canguro.

Wallachian [wɔ'leitʃən], s., a. valaco.

wallet ['wɔlit], s. cartera, bolsa de cuero; zurrón, alforja, mochila.

wall-eye, s. (med.) glaucoma.

wall-eyed ['wɔːlaid], a. (vet.) zarco, ojizarco; ojituerto, bizco.

wallflower ['wɔːlflauəɹ], s. (bot.) alelí doble; (vulg.) mujer sin pareja en un baile.

walling, s. murallas, muros; mampostería; materiales para hacer muros.

walloon [wɔ'luːn], s. valón.

wallop ['wɔləp], v.t. (vulg.) cardar, zurrar. — v.i. bullir, hervir; bambolearse. — s. tunda, zurra, golpe.

wallow ['wɔlou], v.i. revolcarse, chapalear, rodar (en el lodo), encenagarse; (fig.) encenagarse; regodearse; (fig.) nadar; to wallow in riches, nadar en la opulencia. — s. encenagamiento, revuelco.

wallower, s. persona o animal que se revuelca; (mec.) rueda de linterna.

wallowing, a. que chapalea, que se revuelca. — s. revuelco, encenagamiento; (fig.) regodeo; wallowing place, revolcadero.

wall-paper ['wɔːlpeipəɹ], s. papel pintado, papel de colgadura.

wall-pepper, s. (bot.) siempreviva.

wall-plug, -socket, s. (elec.) enchufe de pared, enchufe mural.

wall-tree, s. espaldera, espalera.

wallwart ['wɔːlwɔːt], s. (bot.) cañarroya, oreja de monja, parietaria oficinal.

walnut ['wɔːlnʌt], s. (bot.) nuez de nogal; madera de nogal; walnut-tree, nogal, noguera.

walrus ['wɔːlrəs], s. (zool.) morsa, rosmaro.

waltz [wɔlts], s. vals. — v.i. valsar, bailar el vals.

waltzer, s. valsador.

wamble ['wɔmbəl], v.i. padecer bascas, náuseas, ganas de vomitar.

wan [wɔn], a. pocho, paliducho, de cara de gualda, desvaído; pálido, descolorido; to grow wan, ponerse pálido o paliducho.

wand [wɔnd], s. vara (insignia de autoridad); varita (de virtudes o mágicas); batuta.

wander ['wɔndəɹ], v.i. vagar, andar vagando, errar, andorrear, corretear, rodar; desviarse, extraviarse; delirar. — v.t. recorrer, errar; (fam.) aturdir.

wanderer, s. vagamundo, andorrero, errante; viajero.

wandering, a. errático, errabundo, errante; descarriado, descaminado; vago, vagueante; delirante. — s. acción de errar, el vagar, el errar, el viajar; divagación; paseo sin objeto; extravío, aberración, distracción, devaneo; turbación de espíritu, delirio.

wane [wein], v.i. disminuir, menguar, decaer. — s. diminución, mengua, decadencia, decaimiento, declinación; menguante (de la luna), f.; (carp.) bisel.

wanly ['wɔnli], adv. con palidez, débilmente.

wanness, s. palidez, languidez, descaecimiento.

want [wɔnt], s. privación, necesidad; carencia, carestía, escasez, falta, penuria, miseria; demanda, solicitud, deseo; for want of, por falta de. — v.t. hacer falta, necesitar, tener necesidad de; estar desprovisto de; desear, querer, anhelar; pedir, exigir, requerir; pasarse sin, dispensarse de; you are wanted, preguntan por Vd. — v.i. carecer, faltar, estar ausente; estar necesitado; he is wanted, le necesitan, o preguntan por él; wanted, a teacher, se solicita o solicito (un) profesor.

wantage ['wɔntidʒ], s. deficiencia, déficit, merma.

wanting, a. defectuoso, falto, deficiente; menguado; ausente; escaso; to be wanting, faltar.

wanton ['wɔntən], a. protervo, desenfrenado, salaz, lascivo; (poét.) jovial, alegre, juguetón, retozón; travieso, extravagante; suelto, licencioso, disoluto, atrevido; frívolo, fútil; (poét.) frondoso, lozano; imperdonable, inexcusable, injustificable. — s. libertino, prostituta, persona frívola. — v.i. holgarse, regodearse, refocilarse, retozar, juguetear; travesear, hacer picardías; to wanton away, disipar, malgastar.

wantonly, adv. protervamente, lascivamente, inmodestamente; locamente; alegremente; desenfrenadamente; injustificadamente, sin motivo.

wantonness ['wɔntənnes], s. lascivia, impudicia, licencia; protervia; travesura; futilidad.

war [wɔːɹ], s. guerra, lucha, conflicto; man of war, buque de guerra; war to the death, guerra a muerte; to be on the war path, buscar pendencia. — a. bélico, de guerra, guerrero. — v.i. hacer la guerra, estar en guerra, guerrear; pelear, luchar; to declare war, declarar, o publicar, la guerra; declaration of war, declaración de guerra.

warble ['wɔːɹbəl], v.t. trinar, gorjear, gorgoritear; murmurar (agua). — s. gorjeo, trino, gorgorito.

warbler ['wɔːɹbləɹ], s. cantante, cantor, gorjeador; (orn.) cerrojillo, silvia, curruca, pájaro cantor.

warbling, a. melodioso (de un río, arroyo, corriente, etc.), canoro (de pájaros), susurrante, murmurante, que murmulla suavemente. — s. gorgoritos, trino, gorjeo, garganteo, murmullo (de un arroyo); acentos, acordes.

war-club, s. maza.

war-cry, s. grito de guerra, alarido.

ward [wɔːɹd], v.t. guardar, defender, proteger, preservar; parar (un golpe); to ward off, parar, desviar, evitar. — s. guarda, m.f., guardián, conserje; (for.) pupilo, menor; tutela, pupilaje; barrio, cuartel, distrito electoral o administrativo de una ciudad; sala de hospital, asilo, cárcel, etc.; guardas de una cerradura.

warden ['wɔːɹdən], s. guardián, gobernador, guarda, m.f.; carcelero, alcaide, calabocero;

conserje; bedel; director (o rector) de un colegio; (*mar.*) capitán (de un puerto).

wardenship, *s.* oficio (o dignidad) de un guardián, gobernador, etc., guarda, *f.*, conserjería, bedelía, alcaidía.

warder, *s.* guarda, *m.*, guardia, *m.*

wardrobe ['wɔːɹdroub], *s.* guardarropa, ropero; vestuario, vestido; (*teat.*) vestuario, guardarropía.

wardship, *s.* pupilaje, tutoría, tutela.

ware [wɛəɹ], *s.* mercadería; *table-ware,* vajilla de mesa; *earthenware,* loza, vajilla de barro; *hardware,* ferretería; *smallwares,* mercería, pasamanería. — *pl.* **wares,** mercancías, mercaderías, géneros.

warehouse ['wɛəɹhaus], *s.* almacén, depósito; *warehouse keeper,* guardaalmacén; *warehouse rent,* almacenaje. — *v.t.* almacenar.

warehouseman, *s.* almacenero, almacenador.

warehousing ['wɛəɹhauziŋ], *s.* almacenaje, depósito.

warfare ['wɔːɹfɛəɹ], *s.* servicio militar, vida militar, arte militar, guerra. — *v.i.* guerrear.

warily, *adv.* prudentemente, cautamente, cautelosamente.

wariness ['wɛərinis], *s.* prudencia, cautela, precaución.

warlike ['wɔːɹlaik], *a.* guerrero, belicoso, bélico, marcial, militar.

warlikeness, *s.* naturaleza belicosa.

warlock ['wɔːɹlɔk], *s.* hechicero, brujo.

warm [wɔːɹm], *a.* caliente, cálido, caloroso, caluroso, acalorado, ardiente, fogoso; animado, vivo, activo, violento, furioso, celoso; (*fam.*) reciente, fresco; (*fam.*) fastidioso, molesto; (*vulg.*) en buenas circunstancias, con el riñón cubierto; conmovido, apasionado, arrebatado, encariñado, amoroso, afectuoso; indelicado, erótico, picante; (*arte*) predominando los colores rojo o amarillo; (*juego de niños*) quemarse, estar cerca a lo que se busca; *to be warm,* tener calor; (*impers.*) hacer calor; *to get warm,* acalorarse, calentar(se); *to keep warm,* conservar caliente; *to make warm,* calentar; *warm work,* (*fig.*) fuerte tarea. — *v.t.* calentar, acalorar, caldear; encender, enfervorizar, animar, abrigar; *to warm over* o *up,* volver a calentar; (*aut.*) calentar (el motor). — *v.i.* calentar(se), animarse.

warm-blooded, *a.* de sangre caliente; (*fam.*) ardiente, entusiasmado.

warmer, *s.* escalfador.

warm-hearted, *a.* afectuoso, generoso, simpático.

warming, *s.* calefacción; *warming-pan,* calentador.

warmly ['wɔːɹmli], *adv.* con calor, ardientemente, acaloradamente, calurosamente, afectuosamente.

warmness ['wɔːɹmnis], **warmth** ['wɔːɹmθ], *s.* calor moderado; ardimiento, ardor, vigor, viveza, vivacidad, fervor, celo, cordialidad, entusiasmo.

warn [wɔːɹn], *v.t.* advertir, precaver, (*for.*) caucionar, prevenir, amonestar; avisar, enterar, informar, notificar, aconsejar, exhortar.

warner, *s.* amonestador.

warning, *s.* advertencia, amonestación, admonición, (*for.*) caución; escarmiento, lección; aviso; (*fam.*) despedida.

War Office, *s.* Ministerio de la Guerra.

warp [wɔːɹp], *s.* urdimbre, *f.*, urdiembre, *f.*, torcimiento, torcedura, alabeo; (*mar.*) espía, estacha, calabrote; depósito aluvial de agua introducida artificialmente en tierras bajas. — *v.t.* torcer, retorcer, hacer torcer, ladear; urdir; encorvar, combar, empandar; falsear, pervertir, corromper; (*agr.*) inundar; (*mar.*) remolcar. — *v.i.* torcerse, combarse, alabearse, bornearse; desviarse; alejarse; urdir; (*mar.*) espiarse, ser remolcado, ir a remolque.

warp-beam, *s.* plegador de urdimbre, enjullo.

warped, *a.* combo, adunco, combado; (*vulg.*) destornillado, chalado, desequilibrado.

warper, *s.* urdidor.

warping, *s.* combadura, alabeo; distorsión, deformación; urdimbre, *f.*, urdidura; (*agr.*) irrigación; ladeamiento.

warp-thread, *s.* lizo.

warrant ['wɔrənt], *v.t.* garantir, garantizar, responder por; apoyar, sostener; autorizar; apostar; fiar, asegurar, certificar, aseverar; justificar. — *s.* auto, autorización, documento comprobante o justificante, poder; garantía, sanción, póliza, motivo, razón; decreto, mandamiento, despacho; cédula; mandato de arresto, orden de prisión; (*com.*) certificado de depósito; *warrant-officer,* suboficial.

warrantable ['wɔrəntəbəl], *a.* autorizado, legítimo, justificable.

warrantableness, *s.* seguridad, justificación, certeza.

warrantably, *adv.* justificadamente.

warranted, *a.* garantizado, con garantía.

warrantee [wɔrən'tiː], *s.* (*for.*) afianzado; garantizado.

warranter, warrantor, *s.* (*for.*) fiador, fianza; garante.

warranty ['wɔrənti], *s.* (*for.*) garantía; autorización, seguridad, autoridad.

warren ['wɔrən], *s.* conejera; conejar, vivar, vivero, madriguera; (*for.*) caza reservada.

warrener, *s.* conejero; guardabosque.

warrior ['wɔriəɹ], *s.* guerrero, soldado.

wart [wɔːɹt], *s.* verruga.

warted, *a.* averrugado, verrugoso.

wartwort ['wɔːɹtwəːɹt], *s.* (*bot.*) verrucaria; (*ant.*) girasol.

warty, *a.* averrugado, verrugoso.

war-worn, *a.* aguerrido; gastado, abrumado por la guerra.

wary ['wɛəri], *a.* cauto, cauteloso, discreto, prudente, avisado, circunspecto, reservado.

was [wɔz], pret. del verbo *to be.*

wash [wɔʃ], *v.t.* lavar, bañar; limpiar, purificar, blanquear; recubrir (metal); (*pint.*) lavar, dar una capa de color; *to wash away* o *off* o *out,* quitar lavando, borrar; (*fam.*) anular, rechazar; *to wash up,* fregar o lavar la vajilla; arrojar, desechar (el mar). — *v.i.* lavarse, bañarse; colar; blanquear, hacer la colada; (*alb.*) deslavar; (*mar.*) baldear; mecerse (agua); gastarse por la acción del agua. — *s.* lavado, colada, lavadura, lejía; ropa lavada; ropa para lavar; lavazas; loción, cosmético; ablución, lavación, lavatorio; (*pint.*) aguada; (*pint.*) capa delgada, baño; remolinos, estela de un buque; batiente del mar; depósito, aluvión; (*mar.*) pala de remo.

wash-basin, o **wash-hand-basin,** *s.* jofaina, lavamanos, *m.*, palangana, lavabo.

wash-board, s. tabla (o tablilla) para jabonar; (*carp.*) rodapié; (*mar.*) falca, batidero.

wash-bowl, s. jofaina, lavamanos, *m.*, palangana.

washer, s. lavandero, lavador; lavadora, máquina de lavar; (*mec.*) arandela, volandera.

washerwoman, s.f. lavandera.

wash-hand-stand o **washstand,** s. lavabo, palanganero, aguamanil.

wash-house, s. lavadero.

washing, s. lavado, lavadura, lavamiento, ablución; blanqueadura; ropa lavada, ropa para el lavado; (*igl.*) lavatorio; (*mar.*) baldeo; *washing-machine,* lavadora.

wash-leather, s. gamuza, badana.

wash-out, s. (*min.*) derrumbe de aluvión, derrumbe por socavación; (*fam.*) fracaso completo, pifia; fracaso, persona inútil.

wash-pot, s. bacía.

wash-tub, s. gamella, cuba de lavar.

washy, a. aguado, mojado; flojo, débil, soso.

wasp [wɔsp], s. avispa; (*fig.*) persona enconosa; *wasp's nest,* avispero.

waspish, a. enojadizo, enconoso, mordaz.

waspishly, adv. enojadamente, ásperamente, con encono.

waspishness, s. irritabilidad, irascibilidad, mal genio, encono.

wassail ['wɔsəl], s. brindis; fiesta, francachela, borrachera, orgía; cerveza aderezada con manzanas, azúcar y especies.

wassailer, s. borrachón.

wast [wɔst], 2 *pers. sing. pret.* [BE].

wastage ['weistidʒ], s. despilfarro, desperdicio, desgaste; merma.

waste [weist], v.t. agotar, usar, consumir, gastar, mermar, debilitar; malgastar, disipar, malbaratar, derrochar, despilfarrar; perder (tiempo); desolar, arruinar, devastar, destruir, destrozar, desbaratar, talar, echar a perder. — v.i. consumirse, gastarse, desgastarse, usarse, alterarse, disiparse, dañarse; *to waste away,* disminuirse, descaecer, menguar, ir a menos; demacrarse. — a. desierto, inculto, baldío, yermo; inútil, desechado; asolado, desolado, devastado; superfluo, sobrante, de desperdicio; *to lay waste,* devastar. — s. desperdicio, decadencia; despilfarro, gasto inútil, derroche, consunción; desierto, erial, baldío; restos, desperdicios, despojos; disminución, merma, desgaste, pérdida; derrame, desagüe; inmensidad, extensión; devastación, asolamiento, destrozo, destrucción, daño; *wastepipe,* desaguadero, tubo de desagüe; *wastepaper,* papel de desecho; *waste-paper basket,* (*E.U.*) *waste-basket,* cesto para papeles; *wastebook,* borrador.

wasteful, a. pródigo, malgastador, manirroto; ruinoso, destructor; inútil.

wastefully, adv. inútilmente, pródigamente, con prodigalidad, despilfarradamente.

wastefulness, s. despifarro, pérdida, prodigalidad, gasto inútil.

waster, s. disipador, gastador; devastador; haragán, golfo, zángano.

wasting, a. que se consume, que se agota. — s. atrofia, extenuación, consunción, derramamiento, devastación.

wastrel ['weistrəl], s. desierto, erial; haragán, golfo; disipador, derrochador.

wasty ['weisti], a. baldío, yermo.

watch [wɔtʃ], s. vigilancia, observación, atención, cuidado; velada, vigilia, velación; vela, guarda, acecho, ronda; centinela, vigía, atalaya, *m.f.*; sereno, vigilante; (*mar.*) cuarto, guardia, servicio; reloj de bolsillo; *to be on the watch,* estar a quien vive, estar de acecho, estar de guardia, estar sobre sí; *dog watch,* (*mar.*) segunda guardia; *larboard watch,* (*mar.*) guardia de babor; *starboard watch,* (*mar.*) guardia de estribor; *morning watch,* guardia de la madrugada; *night watch,* guardia de noche; *watch and ward,* patrulla, ronda; *watch-glass,* cristal de reloj, (*mar.*) ampolleta de media hora; *lever-watch,* reloj de escape; *pocket-watch,* reloj de bolsillo; *wrist-watch,* reloj de pulsera; *repeating watch,* reloj de repetición; *stop-watch,* reloj de segundos muertos; *to set the watch,* (*mar.*) rendir la guardia; *to spell the watch,* (*mar.*) llamar la guardia. — v.t. mirar, observar, acechar, espiar, vigilar, guardar; cuidar de, velar sobre, custodiar. — v.i. velar, estar de guardia, hacer centinela, hacer guardia; *to watch someone eat,* contar los bocados (a uno).

watchbox, s. garita.

watch-case, s. relojera.

watch-chain ['wɔtʃtʃein], s. cadena de reloj, leontina.

watch-charm, s. dije.

watchdog, s. perro de guardia.

watcher ['wɔtʃəɹ], s. observador; velador, vigilante, persona que vela a un enfermo.

watchful ['wɔtʃful], a. vigilante, desvelado, observador, despabilado, atento, despierto.

watchfully, adv. desveladamente, atentamente, con vigilancia.

watchfulness, s. vigilancia, desvelo, atención, cuidado.

watch-house ['wɔtʃhaus], s. cuarto de guardia; cuerpo de guardia.

watching, s. desvelo, insomnio, vigilancia, atención.

watchkey ['wɔtʃkiː], s. llave de reloj, f.

watchmaker, s. relojero; *watchmaker's (shop),* relojería.

watchmaking, s. relojería.

watchman ['wɔtʃmən], s. sereno, guardia, *m.*, guardián; salvaguardia, *m.*, vigilante; (*mar.*) vigía, *m.*

watch-tower, s. atalaya, albarrana, mirador.

watchword ['wɔtʃwəːɹd], s. (*mil.*) palabra de orden, santo y seña, consigna; (*fig.*) lema, *m.*

water ['wɔːtəɹ], s. agua; (*med.*) orines, orina; (*poét.*) linfa; (*mar.*) marea; (*tej.*) viso; agua (de piedras preciosas); (*com.*) acciones emitidas sin el correspondiente aumento de capital pagado para representarlas; *of the first water,* (*fam.*) de primer rango; *fresh water,* agua dulce; *salt water,* agua salada o agua de mar; *rain-water,* agua de lluvia; *spring-water,* agua de manantial, agua de fuente; *holy water,* agua bendita; *orange-flower water,* agua de azahar; *still water,* agua mansa; *high water,* marea alta; *low water,* marea baja; *running water,* agua viva; *water-ballast,* lastre de agua; *water-cooled,* (*mec.*) enfriado por agua, hidroenfriado; *water-cure,* hidroterapia; *watergauge,* sonda, indicador de nivel de agua; *water-power,* fuerza hidráulica; *watertax,* censo de agua; *water-rate,* cupo del censo de agua; *water-supply,* servicio (púlico) de agua, traída de aguas. — *v.t.* regar, mojar, humedecer; bañar; aguar, bautizar (el vino), dar de beber a (los animales); (*mar.*) hacer aguada; *to make water*, hacer aguas, orinar; *to pour out money like water*, verter dinero a manos llenas. — *v.i.* tomar agua, sacar agua, chorrear agua; llorar; (*mar.*) hacer agua; *his mouth waters*, se le hace agua la boca.

waterage, *s.* barcaje.

water-bearer, *s.* (*astr.*) acuario.

water-boatman, *s.* (*entom.*) chinche de agua.

water-borne, *a.* flotante.

water-bottle, *s.* garrafa, cantimplora.

water-brash, *s.* (*med.*) pirosis, *f.*

water-bubble, *s.* ampolla.

water-butt, *s.* tonel, bota de agua.

water-carrier, *s.* aguador.

water-closet ['wɔːtəklɔzit], *s.* (*abrev.*) **W.C.**, wáter, retrete, letrina, excusado.

water-colour, *s.* acuarela; *water-colour painting*, acuarela.

watercourse ['wɔːtəkɔːʂs], *s.* curso de agua, corriente de agua; río, arroyo; lecho de río; derecho de aguas.

watercress, *s.* berro de agua, mastuerzo.

watered ['wɔːtəd], *a.* regado, mojado. — *p.p.* [WATER].

waterer, *s.* aguador de noria, abrevador, regador.

waterfall ['wɔːtəfɔːl], *s.* cascada, caída de agua, catarata.

water-fowl ['wɔːtəfaul], *s.* ave acuática.

water-fox, *s.* carpa.

water-hemlock, *s.* cicuta.

water-hen, *s.* polla de agua.

wateriness, *s.* abundancia de agua; humedad, acuosidad, aguanosidad.

watering ['wɔːtəɹiŋ], *s.* irrigación, riego, regadura; distribución de las aguas; acción de dar a beber (a los animales); lagrimeo; (*mar.*) aguada; prensado; *watering-boat*, barco aguador; *watering-can* o *-pot*, regadera; *watering-cart*, carro de regar; *watering-place*, abrevadero, aguadero; balneario, spa.

waterish, *a.* acuoso, ácueo, aguanoso, húmedo.

waterishness, *s.* aguosidad, aguanosidad.

water-jug, *s.* cántaro; jarro.

waterless, *a.* sin agua, seco.

water-level, *s.* nivel de agua.

water-lily, *s.* nenúfar, ninfea.

waterlogged ['wɔːtəlɔgd], *a.* (*mar.*) anegado en agua.

waterman ['wɔːtəmæn], *s.* barquero, marinero.

watermark ['wɔːtəmɑːk], *s.* nivel de las aguas; filigrana, corondel, marca de agua.

water-melon, *s.* melón de agua, sandía; (*Amér.*) patilla.

water-meter, *s.* hidrómetro.

water-mill, *s.* molino de agua, aceña.

water-mint, *s.* hierbabuena acuática.

water-mite, cresa de agua.

water-nymph, *s.* náyade, *f.*

water-pail, *s.* balde, cubo.

water-pipe, cañería, tubería de agua.

water-plant, *s.* planta acuática.

water-plantain, *s.* alisma.

water-pot, *s.* aguamanil.

waterproof ['wɔːtəpruːf], *a.* impermeable al agua. — *s.* impermeable. — *v.t.* impermeabilizar, hacer impermeable.

water-rat, *s.* rata de agua.

watershed ['wɔːtəʃed], *s.* vertiente, *f.*, divisoria de aguas; cuenca hidrográfica.

waterside ['wɔːtəsaid], *s.* orilla del agua.

water-skater, *s.* (*entom.*) tejedera.

water-skipper, *s.* (*entom.*) tejedor.

water-softener, ablandador del agua.

water-spider, *s.* (*entom.*) esquila.

waterspout ['wɔːtəspaut], *s.* bomba marina, manga, torbellino de agua, remolino.

waterspring, *s.* fuente, *f.*, manantial, ojo de agua.

water-sprite, *s.* ondina.

water-tank, *s.* aljibe, cisterna.

water-tap, *s.* grifo, llave, *f.*

watertight ['wɔːtətait], *s.* estanco o impermeable al agua.

water-trough ['wɔːtətrɔf], *s.* abrevadero.

waterway ['wɔːtəwei], *s.* cañería, (*mar.*) canalón, trancanil.

water-wheel, *s.* rueda hidráulica; turbina.

water-wings, *s.* nadaderas.

water-works ['wɔːtəwəːks], *s.* obras hidráulicas; establecimiento de abastecimiento de agua.

watery ['wɔːtəri], *a.* ácueo, aguanoso, acuoso, líquido, húmedo; seroso; evaporado; insípido; lloroso.

watt [wɔt], *s.* (*elec.*) vatio.

wattle ['wɔtəl], *s.* barbas de gallo, barba de pez; zarzo; sebe, *f.* — *v.t.* enzarzar, entrelazar o entretejer con mimbres.

wave [weiv], *s.* ola; onda, ondulación; ademán, gesto, movimiento de la mano; (*fís.*) onda; aguas, visos (de joyería y de tejidos); (*fig.*) onda, torrente, arrebato; *sound wave*, onda sonora; *wave-band*, (*elec.*) banda de frecuencias, banda de ondas; *wave-length*, frecuencia, longitud de onda; *long wave*, onda larga; *medium wave*, onda media; *short wave*, onda corta; *very short wave*, hiperfrecuencia, onda alta; *shock of a wave*, golpe de mar. — *v.t.*, *v.i.* ondear, flotar, tremolar, flamear, blandir, agitar, batir; moverse, agitarse; ondular (el pelo); hacer ademanes en señal de despedida, de saludo, etc., hacer señales, hacer señas.

waved, *a.* ondulado; ondeado.

waveless, *a.* sin olas, tranquilo.

wavelet ['weivlet], *s.* olita, cabrilla.

waver ['weivəɹ], *v.i.* ondear, oscilar, tambalear, balancearse; fluctuar, vacilar, estar incierto.

waverer ['weivəɹəɹ], *s.* persona indecisa, que vacila; veleta.

wavering, *a.* indeciso, irresoluto, vacilante, inconstante. — *s.* indecisión, irresolución, incertidumbre, titubeo, vacilación.

wavering ['weivəɹiŋ], *s.* ondulación; vacilación, indecisión. — *a.* ondulante; vacilante, titubeante.

waveringly, *adv.* vacilando, con incertidumbre, con vacilación.

waveringness, *s.* indecisión, vacilación.

waving, *s.* ondulación, agitación; ademanes (de despedida, de bienvenida, etc.). — *a.* ondulante, oscilante, que se agita.

wavy, *a.* ondulado (pelo, etc.); ondulante, ondeado, ondeante; sinuoso.

wax [wæks], *s.* cera; *ear wax*, cera de los oídos, cerilla; *cobbler's wax*, cerote; *sealing-wax*, lacre; *wax taper*, blandón, hacha de cera;

wax end, (*zap.*) hilo encerado. — *v.t.* encerar; sellar, cerrar. — *v.i.* crecer, aumentarse; crecer (la luna); (*poét.*) hacerse, ponerse.

waxen ['wæksən], *a.* de cera, plástico.

wax-flower, *s.* (*bot.*) ceriflor, *f.*

waxlight, *s.* vela de cera, cerilla, etc.

wax-like, waxy, *a.* semejante a cera; viscoso, blando.

waxwing, *s.* (*orn.*) picotera.

waxwork ['wækswə:ɹk], *s.* figura u obra de cera. — *pl.* **waxworks**, colección de figuras de cera.

way [wei], *s.* camino, senda, sendero, vía, ruta, calle, *f.*; trayecto, conducto, pasaje, calzada; (*anat.*) canal, vía; dirección, rumbo, curso; espacio recorrido, distancia, viaje; progreso, adelantamiento; hábito, costumbre, uso; medio, método, modo; manera, sistema, *m.*, forma, expediente; comportamiento, conducta, línea de conducta; (*mar.*) rota, derrota; velocidad, marcha, andar; (*fam.*) estado (de salud); *way in*, entrada; *way out*, salida; *way through*, pasaje; *ways and means*, propios y arbitrios, medios y arbitrios; *by way of*, a manera de, como; *by-way*, sendero; *high-way*, carretera, camino real; *Milky Way*, (*astr.*) vía láctea; *in no way*, de ningún modo; *right way*, buen camino; *to go the right way for*, ir bien para; *wrong way*, mal camino; *across* o *over the way*, en frente, al otro lado; *that way*, por ahí, por ese lado; *which way?* ¿por dónde? *all the way*, lo largo del camino; *any way*, (*fam.*) de cualquier modo; *by way of*, pasando por, por la vía de, a modo de; *by the way*, por (el) camino; (*fig.*) sea dicho de paso, a propósito; *every way*, de todos lados, por todas partes; *right of way*, servidumbre de paso; *to be in the way*, estar en el camino; (*fig.*) molestar, servir de estorbo, estorbar, incomodar; *to fetch way*, tener juego; *on the way*, de paso, en camino; *on the way to*, en camino de, con rumbo a; *out of the way*, fuera del camino; (*fig.*) extraordinario, curioso, raro, original; *to get out of the way*, alejarse, quitarse de ahí, retirarse, dejar el camino; *to get under way*, (*mar.*) zarpar, hacerse a la vela; *to go the same way*, llevar el mismo camino; *to go out of one's way*, extraviarse; *to go out of one's way (in order) to*, darse la molestia de, hacer todo lo posible para; *to give way*, ceder; romper; *to have one's own way*, (*fam.*) salirse con la suya; *to lead the way*, conducir, ir delante; *to lose one's way*, extraviarse, perder el camino; *to make way, to make one's way*, abrir paso, abrirse un paso, tener éxito; *to show the way*, enseñar el camino, dar ejemplo; *to take one's own way*, seguir su curso; *a long way* (*off*), muy lejos, a gran distancia; *a short way* (*off*), no muy lejos, a poca distancia.

way-bill, *s.* hoja de ruta.

wayfarer ['weifɛərəɹ], *s.* viajero, viajador, viajante, caminante, pasajero.

wayfaring, *a.* viajador, que viaja, que va de viaje. — *s.* el viajar.

wayfaring-tree, *s.* viburno.

waylay ['wei:lei], *v.t.* poner asechanzas (o celadas) a, insidiar, asechar.

waylayer, *s.* acechador, asechador, insidiador, trasechador.

wayless ['weiles], *a.* sin camino.

waymark, waypost, *s.* mojón, hito, poste indicador.

wayside, *s.* orilla del camino. — *a.* junto al camino, en el camino.

way-train, *s.* tren de escalas.

wayward ['weiwəɹd], *a.* travieso, voluntarioso, revoltoso; áspero, caprichudo, terco.

waywardly, *adv.* caprichosamente; perversamente, voluntariosamente, aviesamente.

waywardness, *s.* terquedad, obstinación; indocilidad, desobediencia, voluntariedad; malignidad; mal humor.

wayworn ['weiwɔ:ɹn], *a.* cansado, fatigado.

we [wi:], *pr. pers. pl.* nosotros, nosotras; *we are told*, se nos dice.

weak [wi:k], *a.* débil, debilitado, flaco, flojo, delicado, impotente, enclenque, feble, inseguro, poco fuerte, poco resistente; ineficaz; bobo, corto, simple, imbécil; (*fig.*) flojo, pobre, poco convincente; *to grow weak*, debilitarse; *weak point, weak side*, flaco, punto débil.

weaken, *v.t.* debilitar, enflaquecer, enervar, relajar, atenuar, disminuir.

weakener, *s.* persona que debilita.

weakening, *a.* debilitante. — *s.* debilitación, enflaquecimiento.

weak-eyed, *a.* que tiene los ojos débiles, de vista débil.

weak-handed, *a.* de manos débiles.

weak-headed, *a.* simple, de poca inteligencia, bobo.

weak-kneed, *a.* débil de energía; (*fig.*) impotente.

weakling ['wi:kliŋ], *s.* persona delicada, alfeñique.

weakly ['wi:kli], *a.* débil, flaco, canijo; achacoso, enfermizo. — *adv.* débilmente; tímidamente; sin fuerza, sin vigor.

weak-minded, *a.* débil de espíritu, pobre de espíritu, mentecato, simple, tonto.

weakness, ·*s.* debilidad, flojedad, flaqueza, encanijamiento; languidez, decaimiento; desliz; fragilidad; flaco, afición.

weal [wi:l], *s.* utilidad, bien, bienestar, bienandanza, prosperidad, felicidad; verdugón, cardenal; *common weal* o *public weal*, bien público, res pública.

weald [wi:ld], *s.* bosque.

wealth [welθ], *s.* riqueza, opulencia, fortuna, caudal, prosperidad, felicidad, abundancia.

wealthily ['welθili], *adv.* ricamente, opulentamente.

wealthiness, *s.* opulencia, abundancia de riquezas.

wean [wi:n], *v.t.* destetar, desahijar; desbecerrar; descordarar; apartar (de un vicio, hábito, costumbre, deseo, etc.), separar de, desaferrar, desapegarse.

weaning, *s.* destete.

weanling ['wi:nliŋ], *s.* niño o animal destetado, desteto. — *a.* recién destetado.

weapon ['wepən], *s.* arma; proyectil.

weaponed, *a.* armado.

weaponless, *a.* desarmado, sin armas.

weapons, *s.pl.* armas, armamentos; garras, riguijones; (*biol.*) púas, espinas.

wear [wɛəɹ], *v.t.* (*pret.* **wore**; *p.p.* **worn**), llevar, llevar puesto, traer puesto; tener aspecto de, exhibir, mostrar; usar, consumir, gastar, desgastar, deteriorar, agotar, apurar;

cansar, enfadar, aburrir; (*mar.*) virar (por redondo); *to wear away*, usar, gastar, consumir, borrar, destruir; *to wear down*, usar, gastar, etc., por el roce; *to wear off*, borrar; *to wear out*, gastar, desgastar, agotar, usar; *to wear one's heart on one's sleeve*, llevar el corazón en la mano, andar con la cara descubierta. — *v.i.* usarse, gastarse, consumirse; perdurar, durar; correr, pasar (el tiempo); (*mar.*) virar (por redondo); *to wear away* o *out*, consumirse, usarse, pasar, envejecer, perecer; decaer, deteriorar; *to wear off*, borrarse, gastarse, usarse, disiparse; pasar, desaparecer; *to wear on*, pasarse lentamente; *to wear well*, ser duradero, durar. — *s.* uso; gasto; deterioro; boga, moda; presa, represa [WEIR]; *for (one's) own wear*, para (su) propio uso; *for summer* (o *winter*) *wear*, para verano (o invierno); *wear and tear*, deterioro, uso, desgaste, desmejoramiento, depreciación por uso; *the worse for wear*, que deteriora, decae con el uso; *hardly* (o *little*) *the worse for wear*, casi sin usar.

wearable ['wɛərəbəl], *a.* que se puede llevar (o gastar, usar, etc.).

wearer ['wɛərəɹ], *s.* persona que lleva (gasta, o usa alguna cosa).

wearied ['wiərid], *a.* fatigado, cansado; enfadado, aburrido, fastidiado.

weariless, *a.* infatigable.

wearily ['wiərili], *adv.* con cansancio.

weariness, *s.* fatiga, cansancio, lasitud; enfado, enojo, fastidio, aburrimiento.

wearing ['wɛəriŋ], *a.* que se lleva; *wearing apparel*, vestidos, ropa de uso. — *s.* uso; desgaste, deterioro, decaimiento, pérdida; acción de llevar (vestidos).

wearisome ['wiərisəm], *a.* fatigante, enojoso, tedioso, pesado, fastidioso, cansado, aburrido.

wearisomely, *adv.* fastidiosamente, enojosamente, fatigosamente, pesadamente.

wearisomeness, *s.* fastidio, tedio, hastío, cansancio, fatiga.

weary ['wiəri], *a.* fatigado, molido, rendido, abrumado, laso, hastiado, cansado; fastidiado, fastidioso, enfadoso, aburrido. — *v.t.* cansar, fatigar; aburrir, abrumar, hastiar, molestar, enfadar.

weasand ['wi:zənd], *s.* traquea; gaznate.

weasel ['wi:zəl], *s.* (*zool.*) comadreja.

weather ['wɛðəɹ], *s.* tiempo, estado atmosférico; intemperie, *f.*; temporal, tempestad; (*fig.*) vicisitudes de la suerte; *bad weather*, mal tiempo; *cloudy weather*, tiempo cubierto; *fine weather*, buen tiempo; *wet* o *rainy weather*, mal tiempo, tiempo lluvioso; *weather permitting*, si el tiempo lo permite; *the weather is bad*, hace mal tiempo. — *v.t.* orear, airear; (*mar.*) doblar, montar (un cabo), ganar barlovento; resistir a, sobrevivir a, aguantar, sufrir, vencer (obstáculos); curtir a la intemperie; *to weather the storm*, resistir a la tempestad; *to weather a point*, ganar una ventaja. — *v.i.* curtirse a la intemperie, disgregarse, descolorarse (a la intemperie). — *a.* al viento, del lado del viento, de barlovento; del tiempo, metereológico.

weather-beaten, *a.* curtido a la intemperie.

weather-chart, *s.* mapa meteorológico.

weathercock ['wɛðəɹkɔk], *s.* veleta, giraldilla,

cataviento; (*fig.*) persona mudable o inconstante.

weather-forecast, *s.* prognosis, *f.*, pronóstico meteorológico.

weather-gage, -gauge, *s.* (*mar.*) barlovento.

weather-glass, *s.* barómetro.

weathering ['wɛðəriŋ], *s.* (*geol.*) desgaste (por la acción atmosférica); exposición a la intemperie.

weatherly, *a.* (*mar.*) de barlovento, de bolina.

weathermost, *a.* lo más al viento.

weatherproof ['wɛðəɹpru:f], *a.* a prueba de mal tiempo, resistente a la intemperie.

weave [wi:v], *v.t.* (*pret.* **wove**; *p.p.* **woven, wove**) tejer, tramar, unir, reunir; trenzar (los cabellos); entrelazar, entretejer; (*fig.*) tejer, inventar, forjar, urdir, forjar (cuentos); (*fig.*) serpentear. — *v.i.* tejer, trabajar en telar. — *s.* textura, tejido, ligamento del hilo; dibujo (del tejido).

weaver, *s.* tejedor; tramador; (*ent.*) araña tejedora.

weaver-bird, *s.* (*orn.*) tejedor.

weaving, *s.* tejeduría; tejido, textura; rumbo sinuoso, rumbo en zigzag.

weazen ['wizən], *a.* delgado, enjuto. — *v.i.* encogerse, contraerse.

web [web], *s.* tejido, tela, obra tejida; trama, lazo; encadenamiento; hoja (de sierra, de espada); tela de araña; barba o pelo de pluma; (*zool.*) membrana interdigital; (*f.c.*) cuello del riel; mancha blanca en el ojo; (*fig.*) trama, trampa, artificio; *web-foot*, pie palmado; *web-footed*, palmado, palmípedo.

webbed [webd], *a.* palmado, palmípedo; unido por una membrana.

webbing, *s.* cinta para cinchas, cincha, pretal.

webby, *a.* membranoso.

wed [wed], *v.t.* (*pret.* y *p.p.* **wedded**) casarse con; casar, dar en casamiento, unir en matrimonio; (*fig.*) encadenar. — *v.i.* casarse, contraer matrimonio.

wedded ['wedid], *a.* casado; conyugal; *wedded to*, (*fig.*) aficionado a; *wedded to one's opinions*, testarudo.

wedding ['wediŋ], *s.* boda, casamiento, nupcias, bodas, enlace, unión, *f.*; *silver wedding*, bodas de plata; *golden wedding*, bodas de oro; *wedding-day*, día de bodas; *wedding-cake*, pan de boda; *wedding-dress*, traje nupcial; *wedding-march*, marcha nupcial; *wedding-ring*, anillo de la boda; *wedding-trip*, viaje de novios.

wedge [wedʒ], *s.* cuña, calce, calza, alzaprima; (*geom.*) prisma triangular. — *v.t.* acuñar, meter cuñas, apretar con cuñas, calzar, enchavetar, sujetar.

wedlock ['wedlɔk], *s.* nupcias, himeneo, matrimonio.

Wednesday ['wenzdi], *s.* miércoles; *Ash Wednesday*, miércoles de ceniza.

wee [wi:], *a.* (*fam.*, *Esco.*) chiquito, pequeñín; *a wee bit*, un poquito, un poquitín.

weed [wi:d], *s.* mala hierba, hierbajo, cizaña; *the weed*, (*fam.*) tabaco; *seaweed*, alga. — *pl.* **weeds**, ropa de luto, gasa de luto, luto; *widow's weeds*, luto de una viuda. — *v.t.* escardar, desyerbar, sachar, sallar; (*fig.*) extirpar, quitar lo inútil de.

weeder, *s.* escardador, extirpador, desyerbador; sacho.

weedhook, *s.* escarda.

weeding, s. escardadura, escarda.
weed-killer, s. herbicida, m.
weedless, a. sin malas hierbas, limpio.
weedy ['wi:di], a. lleno de malas hierbas; (fig.) raquítico, flaco, mezquino.
week [wi:k], s. semana; week-day, día de trabajo; week-end, fin de semana, 'weekend'; this day week o to-day week, de hoy en ocho días.
weekly ['wi:kli], a. hebdomadario, semanal. — adv. todas las semanas, cada semana. — s. periódico semanal, semanario.
ween [wi:n], v.i. (poét.) pensar, creer, imaginar.
weep [wi:p], v.t., v.i. (pret., p.p. wept) llorar; deplorar, lamentar(se), gemir, gemir por, llorar por, condolerse (de); (bot.) destilar, rezumar, sudar; (fig.) estar pendiente, inclinarse hacia el suelo.
weeper, s. llorador, llorón, lloraduelos, plañidero; gasa de luto, velo de viuda.
weeping, a. llorón, plañidero; en lágrimas, que llora; weeping ash, fresno llorón; weeping willow, sauce llorón. — s. llanto, lloro, lágrimas.
weever ['wi:vər], s. traquino, dragón marino.
weevil ['wi:vəl], s. (ent.) gorgojo.
weft, s. trama (de tejidos).
weigh [wei], v.t. pesar, averiguar el peso; (fig.) estimar, apreciar, considerar, examinar, ponderar; suspender; sobrecargar, oprimir, agobiar; comparar; (mar.) levar (el ancla); to be under weigh, (naut.) llevar salida; to weigh down, exceder en peso, hundirse por su propio peso, sobrecargar; (fig.) oprimir, agobiar, sobrecargar; to weigh in with, (fig.) abalanzarse a, salir con; to weigh out, pesar en cantidades pequeñas. — v.i. pesar, ser pesado; pesar sobre, gravar, ser opresivo, ser gravoso; tener valor, tener peso, ser de importancia, ser digno de mucho aprecio.
weighable ['weiəbəl], a. que se puede pesar, capaz de ser pesado.
weigh-bridge, s. (puente) báscula.
weigher, s. pesador.
weighing, s. peso, pesada, cantidad pesada; ponderación, examen; weighing-machine, balanza, balancín, romana báscula.
weight [weit], s. peso, pesadez, pesantez, pesa; lastre, cargo; masa, masa pesada; obstáculo, gravamen, carga; (fig.) peso, gravedad, momento; by weight, al peso; defect in weight, desmedro; gross weight, peso bruto; net weight, peso neto; over-weight, sobrepeso, sobre el peso; standard weight, peso legal (o normal); to be worth one's weight in gold, valer su peso en oro; to make weight, completar el peso; to lose weight, ponerse delgado, adelgazar; enflaquecer; to put on weight, echar, tomar o cobrar carnes, ponerse gordo; to throw one's weight about, (fam.) tener horca y cuchillo, darse importancia, hombrear; to try the weight of, sopesar. — v.t. gravar, cargar; aumentar el peso de.
weightily ['weitili], adv. pesadamente, con fuerza.
weightiness, s. peso; solidez, firmeza; (fig.) peso, importancia, momento; pesadez, ponderosidad, gravedad, pesantez.
weightless, a. sin peso, ligero, leve.
weighty ['weiti], a. de peso, pesado, ponderoso, sólido; (fig.) de peso, serio, grave, importante.

weir [wiər], s. esclusa, presa, represa, paradera, parada de río; encañizada, nasa, cañal.
weird [wiəd], a. preternatural, extraño, raro, mágico, fantástico; the Weird Sisters, las Parcas. — s. sino, destino; encantamiento; predicción.
welcome ['welkəm], a. bienvenido, bien llegado; grato, agradable, dichoso, feliz; you are welcome to it, está a la disposición de Vd. — interj. ¡bien venido! ¡sea Vd. (el) bienvenido! ¡servidor de Vd.! — s. bienvenida, feliz llegada, buena acogida, recibimiento cordial, parabién, enhorabuena. — v.t. dar la bienvenida, saludar; recibir con agasajo, acoger, recibir con alegría, saber con alegría.
welcomer, s. persona que acoge, que da la bienvenida.
welcoming ['welkəmiŋ], s. bienvenida, salutación. — a. acogedor, hospitalario.
weld [weld], v.t. soldar; unir en un todo con golpe, martillo o compresión; (fig.) unir, hermanar, juntar. — s. soldadura; (bot.) gualda.
welder, s. soldador.
welding, s. soldeo, soldadura. — a. de soldadura.
weld-joint, s. junta de soldadura.
welfare ['welfɛər], s. bienestar, felicidad, prosperidad, bienandanza, salud, f.; welfare-state, estado nodriza, estado de bienestar social; welfare-work, servicio social.
welkin ['welkin], s. (poét.) bóveda celeste, azul, firmamento; to make the welkin ring, atronar el espacio.
well [wel], s. pozo; fuente, f., manantial; venero, origen, fuente; (mil.) zanja, aljibe, cisterna; (mar.) vivar, vivero (de barco de pesca); copa de tintero; caja (o pozo) de escalera; (mar.) caja de bombas, arca de bomba, sentina. — v.i. manar, fluir, brotar.
well [wel], adv. bien; correctamente, convenientemente; felizmente, favorablemente, diestramente; suficientemente, completamente; satisfactoriamente; muy, mucho. — a. bueno; dichoso, afortunado; satisfactorio; agradable, grato; sano. — interj. ¡bien! ¡bueno! ¡pues! ¡sea! ¡vamos! ¡vaya!; well, then, pues bien; as well as, así como, tanto como, lo mismo que; well and good, enhorabuena; all's well! ¡sereno!, (mil.) ¡centinela alerta! well enough, bastante bien; to be well off o well to do, tener el riñón bien cubierto, estar acomodado.
well-a-day, well-away, interj. ¡ay de mí!
well-aimed, a. certero.
well-appointed, a. bien provisto.
well-behaved, a. urbano, cortés, bien criado; (bien) domesticado, manso.
well-being, s. felicidad, bienestar.
well-beloved, a. bien amado.
well-borer, s. pocero.
well-born, a. bien nacido, de buena familia.
well-bred, a. bien educado, bien criado; de casta, de pura raza.
well-curb, s. brocal de pozo.
well-disposed, a. bien dispuesto, bien intencionado, benigno, generoso, caritativo.
well-doing, s. buenas obras, beneficencia, bienandanza, prosperidad.
well done! interj. ¡bien! ¡ánimo! ¡bien va!
well-drain, s. pozo de desagüe.

well-favoured, *a.* bien parecido, agraciado.
well-founded, *a.* bien fundado.
well-hole, *s.* pozo de escalera; boca de pozo.
wellington (boot) ['weliŋtən], *s.* bota alta hasta la rodilla, de goma impermeable.
well-intentioned, *a.* bien intencionado.
well-known, *a.* conocido, muy conocido.
well-meaning, *a.* bien intencionado, honrado, sincero.
well-read, *a.* erudito, instruido, muy leído.
well-spent, *a.* bien empleado, bien gastado.
well-spoken, *a.* que habla bien, urbano; bien dicho.
well-spring, *s.* fuente, *f.*, manantial.
well-stocked, *a.* bien provisto, bien aprovisionado, de buen surtido.
well-timed, *a.* oportuno, hecho a propósito.
well-to-do, *a.* acomodado, acaudalado, con el riñón bien cubierto.
well-turned, *a.* simétrico, bien hecho.
well-water, *s.* agua de pozo.
well-wisher, *s.* bienqueriente.
well-worded, *a.* bien expresado, bien dicho.
well-worn, *a.* usado, gastado, deteriorado; trillado, perogrullesco.
Welsh [welʃ], *a.* galo, del país de Gales. — *s.* galo, idioma galés; *Welsh rarebit* (o *rabbit*), tostada con queso hervido. — *v.t.*, *v.i.* estafar en las carreras de caballos, escapando para no pagar las apuestas.
welt [welt], *s.* vivo, ribete; vira de zapato; (*carp.*) refuerzo; verdugo, roncha, costurón; (*fam.*) tunda, azotaina. — *v.t.* ribetear; (*zap.*) poner viras; levantar ronchas, azotar.
welter ['weltər], *v.i.* revolcarse, encenagarse; (*fig.*) encenagarse, bañarse; hincharse (las olas). — *s.* oleaje; tumulto, conmoción, agitación; revolcadero, cenagal.
wen [wen], *s.* (*med.*) lobanillo, lupia.
wench [wentʃ], *s.f.* (*dial.*) moza, mozuela, muchacha; joven rústica; (*E.U.*, *fam.*) negra; (*ant.*) cantonera, amiga. — *v.i.* (*ant.*) putañear.
wend [wend], *v.i.* ir, rodear. — *v.t.* encaminar, dirigir; *to wend one's way*, dirigirse, seguir camino.
wennish ['weniʃ], *a.* que tiene un lobanillo, que parece lobanillo.
wept [wept], *pret.*, *p.p.* [WEEP].
were [wəːɹ], *pl.* [WAS]; *pret.* [BE]; *as it were*, por decirlo así; *as* (*if*) *it were*, como si fuese.
wert [wəːɹt], *2ª pers. sing. del pret.* [BE].
werwolf ['wəːɹwulf], *s.* (*folklore*) hechicero que tenía el poder de convertirse en lobo.
Wesleyan ['wezliən], *s.*, *a.* wesleyano, metodista, *m.f.*, discípulo de John Wesley.
west [west], *s.* oeste, occidente, poniente, ocaso. — *a.* occidental, de oeste, de occidente. — *adv.* al oeste, a poniente, hacia el poniente; *West Indies*, las Indias (Occidentales), las Antillas; *West Indian*, indiano, antillano; *west-north-west*, oesnorueste, oesnoroeste; *west-south-west*, oessudueste, oessudoeste; *west wind*, oeste, poniente, céfiro.
westerly ['westəɹli], *a.* occidental, hacia (el) oeste, del oeste. — *adv.* hacia el oeste u occidente.
western, *a.* occidental, de occidente, ponentino. — *s.* novela o película del lejano oeste.
westernmost ['westəɹnməst], *a.* enteramente al oeste, lo mas al oeste.
westing, *s.* dirección hacia el oeste.

westward, *a.* occidental, al oeste.
westwardly ['westwəɹdli], **westwards** ['westwəɹdz], *adv.* hacia (el) oeste, al oeste, hacia occidente, hacia el ocaso.
wet [wet], *a.* húmedo; mojado, regado, humedecido; lluvioso; (*vulg.*) necio, soso; *wet-nurse*, ama de cría, ama de leche; *wet plate*, (*foto.*) placa de colodión; (*fam.*) borracho; *to be wet through*, estar colado, estar mojado hasta los huesos. — *s.* humedad, tiempo húmedo; agua, lluvia. — *v.t.* humedecer, mojar, humectar, empapar; regar (plantas); *to wet one's whistle*, (*vulg.*) mojar el gaznate.
wether ['weðəɹ], *s.* carnero castrado.
wetness ['wetnis], *s.* humedad.
wetting ['wetiŋ], *s.* acción de mojar, mojada, mojadura, remojadura, remojo; humectación.
wettish, *a.* ligeramente mojado.
wey [wei], *s.* unidad de peso y de medida: lana, 82·55 Kgs.; avena y cebada, 17·454 Hectol.; queso, 101·6 Kgs.; sal, 14·545 Hectol.
whack [wæk], *v.t.* golpear, pegar, vapulear; (*vulg.*) repartir el botín (robo, saqueo, etc.). — *v.i.* dar una tunda; ajustar cuentas. — *s.* golpe, trastazo; (*vulg.*) lote, porción, participación.
whacker, *s.* vapuleador; (*vulg.*) masa, bola, cosa muy grande.
whacking, *s.* (*vulg.*) vapuleo, azotaina. — *a.* (*vulg.*) enorme, muy grande, desmesurado; *whacking big* o *great*, enormísimo.
whale [weil], *s.* (*ict.*) ballena. — *v.t.* (*E.U.*, *fam.*) vapulear, dar una tundar a. — *v.i.* dedicarse a la pesca de la ballena.
whale-boat, whaler, whale-ship, *s.* ballenero, buque ballenero.
whalebone ['weilboun], *s.* barba de ballena.
whaling ['weiliŋ], *a.* de ballena. — *s.* pesca de ballenas; (*E.U.*, *fam.*) zurra, vapuleo, azotaina, tunda.
whang [wæŋ], *s.* cuero fuerte, tunda. — *v.t.*, *v.i.* dar tundas.
wharf [wɔːɹf], *s.* (*pl.* **wharfs, wharves**) muelle, embarcadero, desembarcadero, descargadero; malecón. — *v.t.* proveer de muelle, poner sobre el muelle.
wharfage ['wɔːɹfidʒ], *s.* muellaje.
wharfinger ['wɔːɹfindʒəɹ], *s.* proprietario de muelle; estibador.
what [wɔt], *pr. rel.*, *pr. interr.* qué, que, qué cosa, quien, quién, cual, cuál, el cual, la cual, lo cual, el que, la que, lo que; cuanto, cuánto; *I'll tell you what*, le diré a Vd. lo que es; *what else?* ¿y qué más? *what ho!* (*fam.*) ¡hola! *what if?* ¿qué si? aun si, aun cuando; *what of that?* ¿qué importa eso? *what then?* ¿pues? ¿pues bien? *what though*, qué importa que, aun cuando. — *a. rel.*, *a. interr.* qué, que. — *adv.* cuán, cuanto; *what with* . . . *what with* o *what with* . . . *and* . . ., parte por . . . parte por . . ., o entre una cosa y otra.
what-d'ye-call-'em, -her, -him, -it, *pr.* (*vulg.*) (don) fulano (de tal), qué sé yo.
whatever [wɔt'evəɹ], **whatsoever** [wɔtsou-'evəɹ], *pr. rel.* todo lo que, cualquier cosa que, por cualquiera que sea, sea lo que fuere; *whatever you say*, diga lo que diga. — *a. rel.* todo . . . que, cual; cualquiera, ninguno; *whatever be the way*, sea cual fuere el camino.

whatnot ['wɔtnɔt], *s.* estante, juguetero, rinconera; y qué sé yo, cualquier cosa, lo que Vd. quiera.

what's-his-name ['wɔtsizneim], *pr.* (*vulg.*) (don) fulano (de tal).

wheal [wiːl], *s.* postilla, grano; roncha, cardenal.

wheat [wiːt], *s.* trigo.

wheatear ['wiːtiəɹ], *s.* (*orn.*) triguero.

wheaten, *a.* de trigo.

wheatfield ['wiːtfiːld], *s.* trigal.

wheedle ['wiːdəl], *v.t.* acariciar, halagar, lisonjear, adular; engaitar, engatusar, sonsacar, lagotear.

wheedler, *s.* adulador, zalamero, lagotero, engaitador.

wheel [wiːl], *s.* rueda; rodete, disco, círculo, roldana, rodaja; vuelta, rotación, revolución; carrete; bicicleta; polea; noria; *to break on the wheel*, enrodar; *wheel-barometer*, barómetro de cuadrante; *wheel-horse*, caballo de varas; *wheel-rope*, guardín (timón de buques); *wheel and axle*, cabria; *cog-wheel*, rueda dentada; *driving wheel*, rueda motriz; *fly-wheel*, volante (de máquinas); *fifth wheel*, rodete; *front wheel*, rueda delantera; *rear wheel*, rueda trasera; *to take the wheel*, (*aut.*) llevar el volante, conducir. — *v.t., v.i.* rodar, hacer rodar; girar, volver, dar vuelta(s); poner ruedas; ir en bicicleta; labrar con rueda de alfarero; acarrear, transportar sobre ruedas.

wheelband, *s.* llanta (de rueda).

wheelbarrow ['wiːlbærou], *s.* carretilla.

wheeled, *a.* de ruedas.

wheeler ['wiːləɹ], *s.* carretero; caballo de vara(s); biciclista, *m.f.*; rodador, girador; aperador; vapor de ruedas; policía montado en moto, motociclista, *m.f.*

wheeling, *s.* rotación; transporte sobre ruedas, rodaje; paseo en bicicleta; (*mil.*) vuelta; (*de aves*) vueltas.

wheelman, *s.* timonero; ciclista, *m.f.*

wheelwork, *s.* rodaje.

wheelwright ['wiːlrait], *s.* carretero, aperador.

wheeze [wiːz], *v.i.* jadear, silbar, respirar asmáticamente *o* con dificultad.

wheezing, *s.* jadeo. — *a.* asmático.

whelk [welk], *s.* caracol de mar, buccino; grano, pústula; (*vulg.*) roncha, cardenal.

whelm [welm], *v.t.* sumergir, anegar; aplastar; oprimir, subyugar; sobrepujar.

whelp [welp], *s.* lobato, perrito, perrezno, cachorro; mozalbete; (*mec.*) diente de engranaje. — *v.i.* parir (la hembra de un lobo, perro, etc.).

when [wen], *adv.* cuando; desde que, mientras que, al tiempo que, que, en que; en cuanto, tan pronto como, así que; y entonces. — *interr.* ¿cuándo? *at the moment when*, el momento en que; *since when*, desde entonces; ¿desde cuándo?

whence [wens], *adv.* de donde, desde donde, de que, de quien, de aquí; de qué causa, de ahí, por eso es, por lo que; por consiguiente, así pues. — *interr.* ¿de dónde?

whenever [wen'evəɹ], **whensoever** [wensou-'evəɹ], *adv.* cuandoquiera que, siempre que, todas las veces que, en cualquier tiempo que sea.

where [wɛəɹ], *adv.* donde, adonde, en donde, por donde, en qué lugar; *anywhere*, en cualquier sitio (que sea); *everywhere*, en todas partes; *nowhere*, en ninguna parte. — *interr.* ¿dónde? ¿adónde? etc.

whereabout ['wɛəɹəbaut], **whereabouts,** *adv.* donde, de qué lado, hacia donde, hacia qué sitio; poco más o menos.

whereabouts, *s.* lugar cercano; situación aproximada, paradero.

whereas [wɛəɹ'æz], *conj.* mientras (que), cuando; visto que, en vista de que, siendo así que, pues que, ya que; (*for.*) por cuanto, considerando.

whereat [wɛəɹ'æt], *adv.* a lo cual; ¿de qué? ¿por qué?

whereby [wɛəɹ'bai], *adv.* por (o con) el que, por (o con) lo cual, por medio del que; ¿por qué? ¿cómo?

wherefore ['wɛəɹfɔːɹ], *adv.* por lo cual, por cuyo motivo, por consiguiente; ¿por qué? ¿para qué? — *s.* porqué, motivo, causa.

wherefrom [wɛəɹ'frɔm], *adv., conj.* de donde, desde donde.

wherein [wɛəɹ'in], *adv.* donde, en donde, en que, en el que, en lo que.

whereinto, *adv.* en donde, dentro de lo cual.

whereof [wɛəɹ'ɔv], *adv.* de lo cual, del cual, de que, cuyo.

whereon [wɛəɹ'ɔn], *adv.* en que, sobre que, sobre lo cual; ¿en qué?

wheresoever [wɛəɹsou'evəɹ], *adv.* dondequiera, en cualquier parte (que), en cualquier sitio que sea (que).

whereto [wɛəɹ'tuː], **whereunto** [wɛəɹ'ʌntuː], *adv.* a que, a lo que.

whereupon, *adv.* sobre que, en esto, con lo cual, entonces.

wherever [wɛəɹ'evəɹ], *adv.* donde quiera (que), por donde quiera que, en donde quiera; ¿dónde?

wherewith [wɛəɹ'wið], **wherewithal,** *adv.* con que, con lo cual; ¿con qué?

wherewithal ['wɛəɹwiðɔːl], *s.* dinero necesario, recursos, medios, lo necesario.

wherry ['weri], *s.* barca de poco calado, esquife, barquilla, chalana; (*prov.*) bebida hecha de la pulpa de manzanas silvestres después de extraer el agraz.

wherryman, *s.* barquero.

whet [wet], *v.t.* afilar, aguzar, amolar; (*fig.*) estimular, excitar, exasperar, agriar; *to whet the appetite*, abrir el apetito, aguzar los dientes. — *s.* aguzadura, amoladura, afiladura; estímulo; aperitivo.

whether ['weðəɹ], *conj.* si, sea, sea que, que.

whetstone ['wetstoun], *s.* (piedra) aguzadera, amoladera, piedra de afilar.

whetter, *s.* amolador, afilador; estimulante.

whew [huː], *interj.* ¡uf! ¡caramba! ¡ay! ¡ah! ¡cáspita!

whey [wei], *s.* suero de la leche.

wheyey, wheyish, *a.* seroso.

which [witʃ], *pr. rel.* que, cual, cuyo; el cual, la cual, los cuales, las cuales, quien; *all of which*, todo lo cual, todo esto; *both of which*, los dos, ambos; *which way?* ¿por dónde? — *pr. interr.* ¿cuál? ¿qué? — *a. rel.* el que, la que, los (las) que, los (las) cuales.

whichever [witʃ'evəɹ], *pr. indef.* cualquiera, cualesquiera, quienquiera, el que.

whiff [wif], *s.* vaharada; soplo de viento; bocanada (de humo), fumarada, fumada. —

v.t., *v.i.* echar vaharadas (o bocanadas); olfatear, oler.

whiffle ['wifəl], *v.i.* virar, variar, cambiar; echar bocanadas; soplar; agitarse; ser voluble; silbar suavemente.

whiffler, *s.* (*fig.*) veleta, *m.f.*, quídam; fumador que echa bocanadas.

whiffle-tree ['wifəltri:], *s.* (*carr.*) balancín, volea.

whiffling, *s.* vacilación, inconstancia. — *a.* vacilante, mudable, errátil; despreciable, fútil, mezquino.

Whig [wig], *s.* (*pol.*) liberal.

whiggery ['wigəri], **whiggism** ['wigizm], *s.* partido de los Whigs.

while [wail], *s.* rato, momento, instante; espacio corto de tiempo; *between whiles*, a intervalos, de cuando en cuando; *a long while*, mucho tiempo; *a little while*, poco tiempo, un rato (o ratito), momento, instante; *a little while ago* (o *since*), hace poco, no hace mucho; *for a while*, durante (o por) algún tiempo; *to be worth while*, valer la pena, merecer la pena. — *conj.* (se usa en general en sentido elíptico con un *p.a.*) mientras (que), durante (que), al mismo tiempo que; (aun) cuando, si bien. — *v.t.* (hacer) pasar o entretener (el tiempo). — *v.i.* (*prov.*) pasar lentamente; remolonear.

whilom ['wailəm], *adv.* (*ant.*) antiguamente, en otro tiempo. — *a.* que fué, antiguo, del tiempo pasado.

whilst [wailst], *conj.* mientras (que), al mismo tiempo que.

whim [wim], *s.* capricho, antojo, manía, fantasía, extravagancia, chifladura; (*min.*) malacate, torno de izar.

whimbrel ['wimbrəl], *s.* (*orn.*) curlán, chorlito.

whimper ['wimpər], *v.i.* sollozar, gemir, plañir, lloriquear, quejarse. — *s.* quejido, plañido, lloriqueo.

whimperer, *s.* (*fam.*) lloriqueador.

whimpering, *s.* lloriqueo; queja.

whimsey, whimsy ['wimzi], *s.* capricho, fantasía.

whimsical ['wimzikəl], *a.* caprichoso, antojadizo, fantástico.

whimsicality [wimzi'kæliti], *s.* fantasía, extravagancia, singularidad, rareza.

whimsically, *adv.* caprichosamente, de una manera fantástica.

whin [win], *s.* (*bot.*) hiniesta, aulaga, aliaga, tojo; (*geol.*) roca fuerte y duro (especialmente el basalto).

whine [wain], *v.i.* gimotear, gemir, plañir, lloriquear. — *s.* gemido, plañido, quejido, lloriqueo.

whining ['wainiŋ], *a.* quejumbroso, que lloriquea. — *s.* lloriqueo, gimoteo, perra (de niño).

whinny ['wini], *v.i.* relinchar (especialmente en tono suave o con placer). — *s.* relincho.

whip [wip], *s.* azote, látigo, fusta, zurriago; (*Amér.*) fuete; mayoral; (*pol.*) miembro del parlamento que tiene a su cargo la disciplina de su partido, y la convocación de su grupo para votaciones, etc.; *stroke of a whip*, latigazo; *whip and spur*, a uña de caballo; *whip-hand*, mano derecha; (*fig.*) ventaja; *to have the whip-hand*, tener el mando y el palo, tener la sartén por el mango. — *v.t.* azotar, dar azotes, flagelar, fustigar, zurrar,

tundir, vapular; corregir (a un niño); batir (huevos); asir, arrebatar; sacar, desenvainar; filetear, hilvanar; (*agr.*) trillar; (*cost.*) sobrecoser; vencer, aplastar; (*fig.*) criticar; *to whip back*, hacer volver a latigazos; (*fam.*) volver muy de prisa; (*vulg.*) beber(se) rápidamente; *to whip down*, hacer bajar a latigazos; bajar muy de prisa, bajar volando; *to whip off*, echar a latigazos, despachar prontamente, quitar vivamente; salir corriendo, sacar rápidamente, llevar (afuera) rápidamente; *to whip out*, hacer salir a latigazos; sacar vivamente; salir vivamente; *to whip up*, hacer subir a latigazos; excitar, conmover, entusiasmar; batir (huevos, etc.); alzar de repente; reunir con éxito; (*mar.*) izar con la candeliza. — *v.i.* ir rápidamente, correr, echar a correr, andar de prisa, obrar con ligereza; *to whip about*, moverse vivamente; *to whip away*, marcharse de prisa; *to whip back*, volver vivamente; *to whip down*, bajar corriendo (o volando); *to whip in*, entrar muy de prisa; *to whip off*, escaparse, irse; *to whip out*, escaparse, zafarse; *to whip up*, subir corriendo (o vivamente).

whipcord ['wipkɔːrd], *s.* tralla del látigo; tela con bordones diagonales.

whipper ['wipər], *s.* azotador, batidor.

whipper-snapper ['wipərsnæpər], *s.* (*fam.*) pilluelo, mozalbete, quídam; cara dura, *m.*

whippet ['wipit], *s.* perro lebrero; especie de carro de asalto ligero.

whipping, *s.* flagelación, vapuleo, azotaina, latigazos.

whipple-tree ['wipəltri:], *s.* (*carr.*) balancín, bolea de coche.

whipsaw ['wipsɔː], *s.* serrucho, sierra cabrilla.

whipstaff ['wipstɑːf], *s.* piño del látigo; (*mar.*) pinzote del timón.

whipster ['wipstər], *s.* mequetrefe; hombre ágil.

whip-top ['wiptɔp], **whipping-top** ['wipiŋtɔp], *s.* peonza, trompa.

whirl [wəːl], *v.t.* rodar, girar rápidamente, dar vueltas, hacer girar, remolinar, voltejear, voltear; *to whirl along*, correr velozmente, andar volando, dejar atrás los vientos. — *s.* vuelta, rotación, giro; torbellino, remolino, volteo.

whirligig ['wəːligig], *s.* perinola; tiovivo; (*ent.*) girín.

whirling ['wəːliŋ], *s.* torbellino; rotación. — *a.* que gira.

whirlpool ['wəːlpuːl], *s.* vórtice, vorágine, *f.*, remolino de agua.

whirlwind ['wəːlwind], *s.* torbellino, remolino, tifón.

whirr [wəːr], *v.i.* girar con estruendo, zumbar; remolinar, dar vueltas. — *v.t.* agitar, batir; apremiar, apresurar.

whirring, *s.* zumbido de alas.

whish [wiʃ], *interj.* ¡zas! ¡chitón! ¡silencio! — *v.i.* moverse a través del aire o agua con sonido silbante.

whisk [wisk], *v.t.* cepillar, acepillar, sacudir, quitar, barrer; batir (los huevos). — *v.i.* pasar rápidamente; *to whisk away* (u *off*) (*tr.*), arrebatar, (*intr.*) marcharse de prisa. — *s.* manojo (de paja, heno, etc.); cepillo, escobilla; (*coc.*) batidor; movimiento rápido.

whisker ['wiskər], *s.* patilla, barba, bigote de gato, león, etc. — *pl.* bigotes; barba.

whiskered, *a.* de patillas, patilludo, barbudo, bigotudo.

whiskey, whisky ['wiski], *s.* aguardiente de centeno, maíz, etc., 'whisky'.

whisper ['wispəɹ], *v.t., v.i.* susurrar, cuchuchear, cuchichear, orejar, decir en voz baja, decir al oído, secretear; murmurar; apuntar, sugerir; soplar. — *s.* cuchicheo, susurro; murmullo; *in a whisper*, en voz baja.

whisperer, *s.* cuchicheador, susurrador; murmurador, parlero; indiscreto.

whispering, *s.* cuchicheo, susurro, susurración; murmullo, murmuración. — *a.* que cuchichea, susurra o murmulla.

whist [wist], *interj.* ¡chitón! ¡calla! ¡cierra la boca! — *a.* silencioso, callado, mudo. — *v.t.* hacer callar. — *v.i.* callarse. — *s.* 'whist' (juego de naipes parecido a la malilla).

whistle ['wisəl], *v.t., v.i.* silbar; chiflar; llamar silbando. — *s.* silbato, silbido, silbo; chifla, chiflate, chiflato, rechifla, pito; (*vulg.*) gaznate, pico; *to wet one's whistle*, (*fam.*) humedecerse el gaznate; *to pay dear for one's whistle*, pagar caro una chuchería.

whistler, *s.* silbador.

whistling, *s.* silbido. — *a.* silbante.

whit [wit], *s.* punto, poco, pizca, ápice, jota; *not a whit*, nada, ni pizca, ni por pienso.

white [wait], *a.* blanco; rubio, blondo, pálido, descolorido; (pelo) cano; puro, sin mancha, inmaculado, albo; feliz, propicio; (*blas.*) argén, *white elephant*, (*fig.*) elefante blanco (*Amér.*), cosa costosa e infructuosa; *white feather*, (*fig.*) cobardía; *white hot*, calentado al rojo blanco; *white lead*, albayalde, cerusa; *white lie*, mentirilla; *to get white, grow white*, blanquear, palidecer; *to turn white*, palidecer. — *s.* blanco, blancura, color blanco; pintura blanca; persona blanca; clara (de un huevo); ampo (de la nieve). — *pl.* whites, leucorrea, flores blancas; ropa blanca; harina superior, hecha de trigo candeal, flor de harina; *to turn up the whites of one's eyes*, poner los ojos en blanco.

whitebait ['waitbeit], *s.* (*ict.*) boquerones.

whitebeam, *s.* (*bot.*) aliso.

whitebines, *s.* (*bot.*) lúpulo.

whitecaps, *s.pl.* (*mar.*) cabrillas.

white-ear, *s.* (*orn.*) motoso.

whitefish, *s.* (*ict.*) merlán, cadoce, albur; pez de los lagos septentrionales de los E.U. parecido al salmón.

white-livered, *a.* cobarde; envidioso.

whiten ['waitən], *v.t.* blanquear. — *v.i.* ponerse blanco, blanquearse, emblanquecerse.

whitener, *s.* blanqueador.

whiteness ['waitnis], *s.* blancura, palidez; albura; candor, inocencia, pureza.

whitening ['waitəniŋ], *s.* blanqueo, blanqueamiento; yeso mate; enjalbegadura, lechada.

whitesmith ['waitsmiθ], *s.* hojalatero.

whitethorn ['waitθɔːɹn], *s.* (*bot.*) espino blanco.

whitewash ['waitwɔʃ], *s.* (*alb.*) lechada de cal, jalbegue, blanqueo; blanquete; agua para blanquear; enlucimiento. — *v.t.* blanquear, dar lechada a, encalar, enjalbegar; (*fig.*) excusar, disculpar, cubrir los defectos de otro.

whitewasher, *s.* blanqueador, enjalbegador.

whitewashing, *s.* blanqueo, enjalbegadura, jalbegue, encaladura, lechada; enlucido.

white-wood, *s.* (*bot.*) tulípero.

whither ['wiðəɹ], *adv.* adonde, hasta donde; ¿adónde? ¿hasta dónde?

whithersoever [wiðəɹso'evəɹ], *adv.* adondequiera, no importa donde.

whiting ['waitiŋ], *s.* (*ict.*) merlán, romero, albur; yeso mate, tiza, blanco de España, carbonato de cal.

whitish ['waitiʃ], *a.* blanquecino, blanquizco.

whitishness, *s.* color blanquizco, color blanquecino.

whitleather ['witleðəɹ], *s.* cuero baldés, ligamento de la nuca del buey.

whitlow ['witlou], *s.* (*med.*) panadizo, panarizo.

whitlow-wort, *s.* (*bot.*) nevadilla.

Whitmonday [wit'mʌndi], *s.* lunes de Pentecostés.

Whitsun ['witsən], *a.* de Pentecostés.

Whitsunday, *s.* domingo de Pentecostés.

Whitsuntide ['witsəntaid], *s.* pascua de Pentecostés, fiesta del Espíritu Santo.

whitten-tree ['witəntriː], *s.* sauco róseo.

whittle ['witəl], *v.t.* tallar, mondar, cercenar, aguzar, cortar poco a poco; (*fig.*) cercenar, disminuir, reducir poco a poco. — *s.* especie de manta, chal, pañolón, capa gruesa usada por las mujeres del campo; faca, navaja, cuchillo de carnicero, de marino, etc.

whity ['waiti], *a.* blanquizco.

whiz, whizz [wiz], *v.i.* silbar, zumbar, rehilar (la flecha, etc.). — *s.* silbido.

whizzing, *s.* silbido, zumbido. — *a.* silbante.

who [huː], *pr. rel.* quien, quienes, el que, la persona que. — *interr.* ¿quién? ¿quiénes?

whoa ['wouə], *interj.* ¡so! ¡jo! ¡cho! (voz usada por los carreteros, cocheros, etc. para hacer que paren las bestias).

whoever [huː'evəɹ], **whosoever**, *pr. indef.* quienquiera que, cualquiera que.

whole [houl], *a.* entero, todo, total; completo, íntegro, intacto, enterizo; ileso, sano. — *s.* totalidad, todo, conjunto, total; cantidad, suma; *on o upon the whole*, en suma, en general, en conjunto.

wholeness, *s.* todo, totalidad, integridad.

wholesale ['houlseil], *a., adv.* por mayor, al por mayor, en grande. — *s.* masa, grueso; venta al por mayor.

wholesome ['houlsəm], *a.* saludable, sano, salutífero; útil, edificante.

wholesomeness, *s.* sanidad, salubridad; utilidad.

wholly ['houlli], *adv.* completamente, totalmente, cabalmente, enteramente; del todo.

whom [huːm], *pr. rel.* que, el que, la que, el cual, la cual, los cuales, las cuales, los que, las que, quien, quienes, a quien, a quienes. — *pr. interr.* ¿quién? ¿a quién? ¿quiénes? ¿a quiénes?

whomever [huːm'evəɹ], **whomsoever** [huːmsou'evəɹ], *pr. indef.* cualquiera, cualquier, (a) quienquiera, (a) quienesquiera.

whoop [huːp], *s.* alarido, algarada, grito (de guerra o de alegría), chillido; chillido del buho; (*med.*) estertor (de la tos ferina). — *v.t., v.i.* vocear, huchear, gritar, dar gritos; toser; insultar a gritos.

whooping ['huːpiŋ], *s.* grita, alarido; paroxismo(s) de la tos ferina; *whooping cough*, tos ferina.

whop, *v.t.* (*vulg.*) zurrar, azotar; (*E.U.*) caerse con estruendo.

whopping, *s., a.* [WHAPPING].

whore [hɔːəɪ], *s.* ramera, prostituta, puta. — *v.t.* putear, prostituir. — *v.i.* putañear, putear; (*Bibl.*) practicar la idolatría.

whoredom [ˈhɔːəɪdəm], *s.* libertinaje.

whoremonger [ˈhɔːəɪmʌngəɪ], *s.* putañero, libertino.

whoreson [ˈhɔːɪzən], *s.* (*ant.*) hideputa, *m.*

whorl [wəːɪl], *s.* (*bot.*) verticilo; (*zool.*) una vuelta del espiral de una concha univalva; nuez de huso.

whorled, *a.* verticilado.

whort [wəːɪt], **whortleberry** [wəːɪtəlberi], *s.* arándano.

whose [huːz], *pr. rel., interr. poss.* [WHO, WHICH]; cuyo, del que, de la que, del cual, de la cual, de los que, de los cuales, de las que, de las cuales, de quien, de quienes, a quien, a quienes; ¿ de quién? ¿ de quiénes?

whoso [ˈhuːsou], **whosoever** [huːsouˈevəɪ], [WHOEVER].

why [wai], *adv., conj.* porqué, por qué, por qué razón; por eso; pero. — *interj.* ¡cómo! ¡vaya! ¡toma! ¡qué! — *s.* causa, razón, porqué.

wick [wik], *s.* mecha, torcida, pábilo; (*ant.*) pueblo, lugar, aldea.

wicked [ˈwikid], *a.* malo, perverso, malvado, impío, inicuo; malicioso, mal intencionado; juguetón, travieso, picaresco.

wickedly, *adv.* malvadamente, inicuamente, perversamente; con intención, maliciosamente; traviesamente.

wickedness, *s.* maldad, iniquidad, malignidad, perversidad; travesura; inmoralidad, irreligión, pecado, vicio.

wicker [ˈwikəɪ], *s.* mimbre, tejido de mimbres; *wicker work*, cestería. — *a.* de mimbre, mimbroso; *wicker basket*, cesto de mimbre; *wicker work*, cestería.

wicket [ˈwikit], *s.* postigo, portillo, barrera, portezuela; (*cricket*) los tres palos que forman la meta; espacio de terreno donde están los palos; turno de cada jugador con la pala; estado del terreno; *sticky-wicket*, (*fig.*) lance apretado, apuro.

wide [waid], *a.* ancho, anchuroso, amplio, vasto, dilatado, extenso, espacioso, inmenso; de ancho; lejano, apartado, remoto; abierto, liberal, comprensivo; *ten feet wide*, diez pies de ancho. — *adv.* lejos, a lo lejos, a gran distancia; extensamente, anchamente, completamente, enteramente; *far and wide*, por todos lados, en todas partes; completamente; *wide awake*, bien despierto, sobre sí, vigilante; *wide open*, abierto de par en par.

wideawake [ˈwaidəweik], *s.* especie de sombrero muy ancho.

wide-eyed [ˈwaidaid], *a.* que se le salta los ojos; asombrado; inocente.

widely [ˈwaidli], *adv.* extensivamente, anchamente; a gran distancia, lejos, a lo lejos; muy, mucho.

wide-mouthed, *a.* boquiancho, abocardado.

widen [ˈwaidən], *v.t.* ensanchar, dilatar, extender. — *v.i.* ensancharse, extenderse, dilatarse.

wideness, *s.* extensión, anchura.

widespread [ˈwaidspred], *a.* difuso, esparcido, que se extiende a lo lejos.

widgeon [ˈwidʒən], *s.* (*orn.*) cerceta, mareca.

widow [ˈwidou], *s.f.* viuda. — *v.t.* enviudar, dejar viuda; privar, despojar.

widowed, *a.* viudo, viuda.

widower [ˈwidouəɪ], *s.* viudo.

widowhood [ˈwidouhud], *s.* viudez.

width [widθ], *s.* extensión, anchura, ancho; (*fig.*) amplitud.

wield [wiːəld], *v.t.* manejar, dirigir, empuñar; llevar, tener; gobernar, mandar.

wieldless, *a.* no manejable.

wieldy [ˈwiːəldi], *a.* manejable.

wife [waif], *s.f.* (*pl.* **wives**) mujer, esposa; señora, ama de casa; mujer anciana *o* de condición humilde.

wifehood, *s.* estado de una mujer casada.

wifeless, *a.* sin mujer, sin esposa.

wifelike [ˈwaiflaik], **wifely** [ˈwaifli], *a.* de mujer, de esposa, como mujer casada.

wig [wig], *s.* peluca, cabellera, peluquín, pelucón, perico.

wigan [ˈwigən], *s.* forro basto que se usa para refuerzo.

wigged [wigd], *a.* con peluca.

wigging [ˈwigiŋ], *s.* (*fam.*) peluca, reprensión, censura.

wiggle [ˈwigəl], *v.i.* cimbrearse, pavonearse, garbear; culebrear; anadear, tambalearse; agitarse, menear. — *v.t.* menear, agitar, garbear. — *s.* cimbreo, garbeo; culebreo; tambaleo; agitación, movimiento.

wight [wait], *s.* (*prov.*) individuo, persona, personaje, criatura, sujeto. — *a.* (*prov.*) ágil, listo, fuerte, bravo.

wig-maker [ˈwigmeikəɪ], *s.* peluquero.

wigwam [ˈwigwɔm], *s.* tienda de los indios, (*Méj.*) jacal.

wild [waild], *a.* salvaje; silvestre, selvático, rusticano; montaraz, agreste; feroz, fiero; despoblado, inhabitado, yermo, desierto, solitario, inculto; violento, impetuoso, indómito, bravo, cerril; insensato, loco, alocado, descabellado, atronado; inconstante, fogoso; borrascoso; estrafalario; desordenado, turbulento, alborotado, disparatado, aturdido, desenfrenado. — *s.* yermo, desierto; *to run wild*, desencadenarse, volver al estado primitivo; *to sow one's wild oats*, correr sus mocedades; *wild beast*, fiera; *wild boar*, jabalí; *wild carrot*, (*bot.*) dauco; *wild cat*, gato silvestre; *wild-cat scheme*, proyecto fantástico (o quimérico); *wild goose chase*, empresa inútil, sus de gaita.

wilder [ˈwaildəɪ], *v.t.* (*poét.*) despistar. — *v.i.* extraviarse.

wilderness [ˈwildəɪnis], *s.* desierto, yermo, erial; soledad, confusión.

wildfire [ˈwaildfaiəɪ], *s.* fuego fatuo *o* griego; *to spread like wildfire*, extenderse como el fuego.

wilding, *s.* manzana silvestre. — *a.* inculto, indómito.

wildly, *adv.* de una manera salvaje, en estado salvaje, salvajemente; sin cultivo; desatinadamente; con extravagancia, caprichosamente; con pavor, frenéticamente.

wildness [ˈwaildnis], *s.* estado salvaje, carácter salvaje; violencia, brutalidad, impetuosidad, ferocidad; rudeza, selvatiquez; tumulto; travesura, desvarío, extravío; irregularidad; extravagancia; frenesí.

wile [ˈwaiəl], *s.* astucia, artificio, fraude, ardid, engaño, maña. — *v.t.* engañar, embaucar, engatusar; *to wile away an hour*, pasar un rato.

wilful [ˈwilful], *a.* caprichudo, obstinado,

terco, testarudo, voluntarioso, repropio; premeditado, intencionado.

wilfully, *adv.* tercamente, con terquedad, obstinadamente, voluntariosamente; intencionadamente, premeditadamente.

wilfulness, *s.* terquedad, obstinación, perversidad; intención.

wilily ['wailili], *adv.* fraudulentamente, engañosamente, artificiosamente, arteramente.

wiliness ['wailinis], *s.* astucia, maña, artería, engaño, fraude.

will [wil], *s.* albedrío, voluntad; deseo, voto; discreción; volición, elección, escogimiento; entusiasmo práctico, voluntad, energía de carácter; resolución, designio; testamento; *where there's a will there's a way*, donde hay gana, hay maña; *at will*, a voluntad; *free will*, libre arbitrio, libre albedrío; *good will*, benignidad, benevolencia, simpatía; *ill will*, malquerer, malevolencia, odio; *to get one's will*, salirse con la suya. — *v.t.*, *v.i.* (*pret. e imperf. subj.* would; (*fam. negativo*) **won't**, **wouldn't**) querer, desear; resolver, determinar; mandar; legar, dejar en testamento; sugestionar. — *v. auxil. del futuro y condicional; v. defect.* significa deseo, anhelo, etc.

willed, *p.p.* [will]; *ill-willed*, malévolo; *self-willed*, voluntarioso, testarudo.

willer, *s.* el que quiere, la que quiere.

willing, *a.* dispuesto, inclinado; complaciente, servicial, de buena voluntad, bien dispuesto; deseoso, pronto; franco, voluntario; *God willing*, Dios mediante, si Dios quiere.

willingly, *adv.* de buena gana, con gusto.

willingness, *s.* buena voluntad, complacencia.

will-o'-the-wisp ['wiloðəwisp], *s.* fuego fatuo.

willow ['wilou], *s.* (*bot.*) sauce; mimbrera, bardaguera; *weeping willow*, sauce llorón, sauce de Babilonia; (*mec.*) diablo, máquina para limpiar lana.

willowed, willowy, *a.* cubierto (o lleno) de sauces, mimbreño, sarguero; (*fig.*) cimbreño, esbelto.

willy-nilly ['wili'nili], *adv.* de buen o mal grado, de grado o por fuerza.

wilt [wilt], *v.t.* marchitar, ajar. — *v.i.* marchitarse, secarse, agostarse, descaecer; (*fam.*) amansarse; 2ª *pers. sing. pres. indic.* will.

wily ['waili], *a.* mañoso, astuto, marrullero, taimado.

wimble ['wimbəl], *s.* berbiquí, barrena de gusano. — *v.t.* horadar.

wimple ['wimpəl], *s.* griñón, toca; ardid, *f.*, artificio. — *v.t.* velar, tapar. — *v.i.* caer desplegado (como la toca).

win [win], *v.t.* ganar, alcanzar, obtener, lograr, conseguir; vencer, conquistar; seducir, persuadir, atraer. — *v.i.* llevar la victoria, llevar la palma; triunfar; prevalecer.

wince [wins], *v.i.* recular, retroceder; quejarse; vacilar, estremecerse; respingar, tirar coces. — *s.* respingo.

winch [wintʃ], *s.* cabria, torno, tornillo; manubrio, manivela; montacarga, *m.*, malacate.

wind [wind], *s.* viento, aire; soplo; resuello, aliento, respiración; ventosidad, flatuosidad, flatulencia, flato; *land-winds*, terrales; *light winds*, (*mar.*) ventolinos; *trade-winds*, vientos alisios; *wind in the teeth*, viento en pie; *gale of wind*, ventarrón; *gust of wind*, ráfaga, racha; *steady wind*, viento hecho; *to be in*

the wind, (*fig.*) tramarse; *to get wind of*, husmear, descubrir (intrigas, etc.); *to keep the wind*, navegar de bolina; *in the teeth of the wind*, de cara al viento. — *v.t.* airear, ventilar, ventear; sofocar, quitar el resuello; olfatear, husmear; recobrar el aliento. — *v.i.* soplar, resoplar.

wind [waind], *v.t.* arrollar, enrollar; dar cuerda (a un reloj); torcer, retorcer; devanar, ovillar, tejer; *to wind off*, desenrollar, devanar; *to wind round*, ceñir, envolver; (*fig.*) ir serpenteando, enroscar, cercar, rodear; *to wind up*, dar cuerda (a un reloj); (*fig.*) perorar, atar cabos; (*com.*) liquidar, saldar. — *v.i.* arrollarse, enrollarse; enroscarse, serpentear.

windage ['windidʒ], *s.* (*arti.*) viento (de un cañón).

winded ['winded], *a.* anhélito, jadeante, acezoso; *short winded*, corto de aliento (o resuello); *long winded*, de largo aliento; (*fig.*) interminable, prolijo.

winder, *s.* devanador; (*máquina*) devanadera; llave para dar cuerda; (*bot.*) enredadera; (*mar.*) carretel.

windfall ['windfɔ:l], *s.* fruta caída del arbol; ganga, un golpe de fortuna, ganancia inesperada, buena suerte.

windflower ['windflauəɪ], *s.* (*bot.*) anemone, *f.*

wind-gall, *s.* (*vet.*) aventadura.

wind-gauge ['windgeidʒ], *s.* anemómetro.

wind-gun, *s.* escopeta de viento.

wind-hatch, *s.* pozo de extracción.

wind-hover ['windhʌvəɪ], *s.* (*orn.*) cernícalo.

windiness ['windinis], *s.* ventolera, ventosidad, flatulencia; hinchazón, *f.*, presunción, vanidad.

winding ['waindiŋ], *s.* vuelta, revuelta, rodeo; tortuosidad; recodo (de camino); arrollamiento; (*elec.*) devanado. — *a.* sinuoso, tortuoso, serpentino; enrollado; en espiral, de caracol (escalera); *winding-sheet*, sudario; *winding staircase*, escalera de caracol; *winding-up*, fin, peroración; (*com.*) liquidación.

windlass ['windləs], *s.* árgano, árgana; argüe, cabria, torno; (*mar.*) molinete; (*min.*) malacate.

windless ['windles], *a.* encalmado, sin viento, sin resuello.

windmill ['windmil], *s.* molino de viento.

window ['windou], *s.* ventana; ventanilla; vidrio, vidriera; cortina, velo; *shop-* o *show-window*, escaparate, muestra (de una tienda); *bay window*, ventana cimbrada; *rose window*, rosetón; *window blind*, celosía; *window frame*, bastidor, marco (o cerco) de ventana; *window pane*, cristal; *window post*, jamba; *window shade*, visillo; *window shutter*, postigo, contraventana; *window sash*, hoja de ventana; *window sill*, repisa o antepecho de ventana; *window-dresser*, decorador de escaparates.

windowed, *a.* fenestrado.

windpipe ['windpaip], *s.* tráquea; gaznate.

windsails, *s.pl.* (*mar.*) mangueras de viento.

windscreen ['windskri:n], (*E.U.*) **windshield** *s.* (*aut.*) parabrisas, *m.*; *windscreen-wiper*, limpiaparabrisas, *m.*

windward ['windwəɪd], *adv.* al viento, a barlovento. — *a.* al viento, del viento, de barlovento. — *s.* barlovento; *to lie to windward*, barloventear.

windy ['windi], *a.* ventoso, expuesto al viento, ventiscoso, borrascoso, tempestuoso; de viento; (*fig.*) vano, hinchado, pomposo;

(*vulg.*) cobarde; (*med.*) flatulento; *it is windy*, hace viento.

wine [wain], *s.* vino; ebriedad; *red wine*, vino tinto, (*claret*) vino clarete; *white wine*, vino blanco.

winebibber ['wainbibəɹ], *s.* borracho, borrachín.

wine-cellar, wine-vault, *s.* bodega.

wine-cooler, *s.* garapiñera.

wine-grower, *s.* viticultor, viñador.

winepress ['wainpres], *s.* trujal, lagar.

winery ['wainəri], *s.* candiotera.

wine-taster, *s.* catavinos, *m.*

wing [wiŋ], *s.* ala; vuelo, impulso; lado, costado; (*aut.*) aleta; apéndice; (*mil.*, *aer.*, etc.) ala, flanco; (*teat.*) bastidor; apéndice foliáceo, los opuestos pétalos de la corola papilionácea; (*fam.*) brazo; *on the wing*, al vuelo; *under one's wing*, (*fig.*) bajo su protección. — *v.t.* llevar sobre las alas; dar (o prestar) alas a; proveer de alas; impeler; atravesar (o hender) volando, pasar volando; (*mil.*) proteger, flanquear; herir en el ala o en el brazo; (*fig.*) dañar, incapacitar, inhabilitar. — *v.i.* irse, volar, aletear, alear.

winged [wiŋd], *a.* alígero, alado; que vuela; (*fig.*) rápido; elevado.

wingless, *a.* sin alas; (*ent.*) áptero.

winglet ['wiŋlet], *s.* alita.

wink [wiŋk], *v.i.* abrir y cerrar los ojos rápidamente, guiñar; parpadear, pestañear; hacer señas guiñando; (*fig.*) dar luz trémula, centellear; *to wink at*, (*fig.*) cerrar los ojos sobre; hacer la vista gorda, pasar por alto, disimular, tolerar. — *s.* guiño, guiñada; pestañeo; (un) abrir y cerrar de ojos; (*fig.*) siesta, canóniga; *not to sleep a wink*, no cerrar los ojos; *to take forty winks*, descabezar el sueño.

winker, *s.* persona que guiña el ojo, guiñador; anteojera; (*fam.*) párpado.

winking, *s.* guiño; pestañeo; (*fig.*) centelleo, tintilación. — *a.* guiñador.

winkle ['wiŋkəl], *s.* caracol marino.

winner ['winəɹ], *s.* ganador, vencedor.

winning, *a.* que gana, que vence; victorioso, triunfante; persuasivo, encantador, atractivo; ganancioso, afortunado. — *s.* ganancia, suma ganada, lucro; triunfo, conquista; *winning-post*, poste de llegada; *winning-back*, desquite.

winnow ['winou], *v.t.* aventar, cerner, ventilar, zarandar, aechar; examinar, escoger, analizar; (*poét.*) batir el aire (con las alas). — *v.i.* abalear, aechar el grano.

winnower, *s.* aventador.

winnowing, *s.* aecho, aechadura, abaleo, despajadura, aventamiento; escogimiento, examen. — *pl.* **winnowings**, tamo.

winnowing-fork, *s.* bieldo.

winsome ['winsəm], *a.* divertido, alegre; amable, atractivo, simpático; hermoso, lindo; retrechero, saleroso.

winter ['wintəɹ], *s.* invierno; (*fig.*) año; *winter quarters*, cuartel de invierno; *winter season*, invernada. — *a.* invernal, de invierno. — *v.i.* invernar, pasar el invierno. — *v.t.* hacer invernar; conservar (mantener o guardar) durante el invierno.

winter-beaten, *a.* maltratado, gastado, curtido por el invierno.

winter-berry, *s.* apalachina.

winter-cherry, *s.* alquequenje.

wintergreen ['wintəɹgri:n], *s.* (*bot.*) pirola.

wintering ['wintəriŋ], *s.* invernada.

winterly, *a.* de invierno, hibernal, hiemal.

wintriness ['wintrinis], *s.* invernada; frío.

wintry ['wintri], *a.* de invierno, hibernal, invernal, hiemal; (*fig.*) glacial, frígido, desabrido.

winy [waini], *a.* vinoso.

winze [winz], *s.* (*min.*) pozo de comunicación, pozo ciego.

wipe [waip], *v.t.* enjugar, secar; restregar, cepillar; aplicar soldadura; *to wipe off* o *out*, borrar, cancelar, enjugar; *to wipe out*, (*fig.*) extirpar, destruir; *to wipe away*, secar o limpiar frotando. — *s.* limpiadura, limpión; (*fam.*) manotada, revés.

wiper, *s.* persona que enjuga; paño, pañuelo, trapo; toalla; (*mec.*) frotador; excéntrica, álabe, leva.

wiping, *s.* limpieza, acción de limpiar, enjugar, etc.

wire [waiəɹ], *s.* alambre, hilo metálico; (*mús.*) cuerda, varilla; telégrafo; (*fam.*) telegrama, *m.*; *wire coil*, carrete; *wire-cutters*, tenazas de corte para alambres; *wire edge*, filbán; *wire-netting*, tela metálica, alambrera; *wire-puller*, (*fam.*, *pol.*) intrigante; *wire-pulling*, (*fam.*, *pol.*) maquinaciones, intriga, enchufes. — *v.t.* liar, atar con hilo metálico; enrejar; proveer de alambre; coger (caza) con lazo o trampa de alambre. — *v.i.* (*fig.*) telegrafiar.

wiredraw ['waiəɹdrɔ:], *v.t.* estirar, prolongar, alargar en hilos; dar cuerda; extender; alambicar; deducir con sutileza.

wiredrawer, *s.* estirador, tirador (de oro, de plata).

wiredrawing, *s.* estiramiento, tirado.

wireless ['waiəɹles], *s.* radio, *f.*; radiorreceptor, *m.f.*; radiotelegrafía, telegrafía sin hilos, radiotelefonía; radiograma, *m.*, despacho telegráfico; *portable wireless*, radio portátil; *short-wave wireless*, radio de ondas cortas. — *a.* sin hilos, inalámbrico; radiotelegráfico. — *v.t.* radiotelegrafiar.

wireless-engineer, *s.* radiotelegrafista, *m.*

wireless-operator, *s.* telegrafista, *m.*

wireless-receiver o **-receiver**, *s.* radiorreceptor, *m.f.*; receptor.

wireless (transmitting) station, *s.* estación radioemisora, emisora; transmisor.

wireless-telegraphy, *s.* radiotelegrafía.

wireless-telephony, *s.* radiotelefonía.

wireless-transmission, *s.* emisión.

wirework, *s.* enrejado. — *pl.* fábrica de tirado, trefilería.

wiring ['waiəriŋ], *s.* alambrado; instalación o colocación de alambres (eléctricos); cablería.

wiry ['waiəri], *a.* de alambre, de hilo metálico; delgado pero fuerte y nervioso, nervudo; (*med.*) débil (pulso).

wisdom ['wizdəm], *s.* sapiencia, sabiduría, erudición; prudencia, buen criterio, juicio, cordura, discreción.

wise [waiz], *a.* sabio; erudito, docto; sagaz, prudente, sensato, cuerdo, juicioso, moderado, serio, grave, discreto. — *s.* manera, modo, forma, suerte, *f.*, uso, especie, *f.*; *a word to the wise is enough*, al buen entendedor pocas palabras bastan; *in no wise*, de ningún modo; *in any wise*, de cualquier modo; *wise guy*, (*E.U.*, *vulg.*) sábelotodo, toro corrido.

wiseacre ['waizeikəɹ], *s.* sabihondo, sabidillo, sábelotodo.

wisecrack ['waizkræk], *s.* (*E.U.*, *vulg.*) pulla, salida.

wisely ['waizli], *adv.* sabiamente, juiciosamente, con prudencia.

wish [wiʃ], *v.t.*, *v.i.* desear, querer, ansiar, apetecer, anhelar. — *s.* deseo, voto, ansia, anhelo; demanda, ruego, súplica, petición; *to make the wish the father to the thought,* el pintar como el querer; *I wish I knew* . . . ¡ojalá que supiese . . .! ¡quién supiese . . .!

wishbone ['wiʃboun], *s.* hueso de la pechuga (de aves), furcula; (*mec.*) horquilla oscilante (de la suspensión).

wisher, *s.* deseador, persona que desea.

wishful ['wiʃful], *a.* deseoso, ávido, ganoso, ansioso, anheloso; *wishful thinking,* sueños dorados, castillos en el aire.

wishfully, *adv.* con deseo, con anhelo, con vivo deseo, ansiosamente, ardientemente.

wishfulness, *s.* deseo.

wishy-washy, *a.* (*fam.*) ñoño, insípido, soso, aguado, flojo.

wisp [wisp], *s.* gavilla (de hierba); mechón; manojito (de paja); jirón, trocito, tira; fuego fatuo. — *v.t.* hacer un manojo, cepillar.

wistful ['wistful], *a.* cabizbajo, triste, pensativo, meditabundo; serio, atento; ansioso, anhelante, ávido.

wistfully, *adv.* tristemente; ardientemente, ansiosamente; pensativamente, reflexivamente.

wistfulness, *s.* recogimiento, meditación, tristeza; ansia, deseo, envidia, ansiedad, anhelos.

wit [wit], *s.* sutileza, ingenio, sal, *f.*, agudeza; concepto, imaginación, fantasía; (hombre de) ingenio, hombre de chispa, guasón, conversador, (*ant.*) conceptista, *m.f.*; (*ant.*) entendimiento, juicio, genio. — *pl.* **wits,** juicio, razón, *f.*, industria; *to live by one's wits,* vivir de invenciones, vivir de gorra, vivir a sablazos.

witch [witʃ], *s.* bruja, hechicera; vejarrona, mujer fea; mujer encantadora. — *v.t.* (*poét.*) embrujar, hechizar, maleficiar, encantar.

witchcraft ['witʃkræft], *s.* brujería, hechicería, maleficio, sortilegio.

witch-elm, *s.* olmo escocés.

witchery ['witʃəri], *s.* magia, brujería, hechicería, sortilegio, encantamiento, fascinación, aojadura.

witch-hazel, *s.* hamamelis virginiana.

witching ['witʃiŋ], *a.* encantador, halagüeño; mágico, de brujo.

with [wið], *prep.* con, en compañía de, juntamente con; de, entre, en, a, contra, por; así que, después de, luego que; hacia; con respecto a, concerniente, para con; *with all (due) speed,* a toda prisa; *away with you!* ¡fuera de aquí! ¡anda!; *with that* . . ., con esto . . ., dicho esto . . ., y luego . . .

withal [wið'ɔ:l], *adv.* al mismo tiempo; con todo; también; además; a más de esto, por otra parte.

withdraw [wið'drɔ:], *v.t.* (*pret.* **withdrew,** *p.p.* **withdrawn**) retirar, hacer retirar; apartar, separar, privar; llamar; arrebatar, quitar, sacar, remover; distraer; retractar, desdecirse. — *v.i.* retirarse, alejarse, apartarse, separarse, irse, salir.

withdrawal, withdrawment, *s.* retirada, recogida, retiro.

withdrawing, *s.* retirada.

withdrawn, *a.* (*fig.*) huraño, ensimismado, meditabundo, absorto.

withe [waið], *s.* brizna de mimbre, mimbre, junco; vencejo; (*mec.*) mango flexible.

wither ['wiðəɹ], *v.i.* secarse, marchitarse; consumirse, ajarse, decaer. — *v.t.* disecar, marchitar, deslucir, ajar, poner mustio, debilitar, descarnar; sonrojar, avergonzar. — *s.* vencejo.

withered ['wiðəɹd], *a.* mustio, seco, marchito. — *p.p.* [WITHER].

witheredness, *s.* desecamiento, sequedad, marchitamiento, marchitez, deterioro, languidez.

withering, *a.* que se marchita; cáustico, mordaz, desdeñoso. — *s.* acción de marchitarse.

withers ['wiðəɹz], *s.pl.* crucero, cruz (del caballo), *f.*

wither-wrung ['wiðəɹrʌŋ], *a.* (*vet.*) herido en la cruz.

withhold [wið'hould], *v.t.* (*pret.*, *p.p.* **withheld**) retener, detener, impedir, apartar, alejar, contener; rehusar, negar.

withholder, *s.* detentador.

within [wið'in], *prep.* dentro de, en, a, cerca de, en los límites de, en el interior de; en el espacio de; a la distancia de; a este lado de; al alcance de; por poco; *within hearing,* al alcance de la voz; *within a short distance,* a poca distancia; *within a short time,* dentro de poco (tiempo); *within an ace of,* por poco; *within an inch of,* a dos dedos de. — *adv.* dentro, adentro, en (su) casa, en (su) habitación, interiormente, en el interior; en el corazón (o la mente, el espíritu, etc.).

without [wið'aut], *prep.* fuera de, sin, a menos de, falto de. — *conj.* a menos que, sin que, si no, si no es que, a no ser que. — *adv.* fuera, afuera, por fuera, hacia fuera, en lo exterior, exteriormente, de la parte de afuera.

withstand [wið'stænd], *v.t.* (*pret.*, *p.p.* **withstood**) oponerse a, resistir a, hacer resistencia a.

withstander, *s.* antagonista, *m.f.*, adversario.

withstanding, *s.* resistencia, oposición.

withy ['wiði], *s.* mimbre. — *a.* de mimbre, flexible; cimbreño.

witless ['witles], *a.* sin inteligencia, sin talento, tonto, necio.

witlessly, *adv.* sin inteligencia, sin talento.

witlessness, *s.* necedad, imbecilidad.

witling ['witliŋ], *s.* fatuo, pelele.

witness ['witnis], *s.* testigo, espectador, declarante; testimonio, prueba, evidencia, atestación; *in witness whereof,* en fe de lo cual; *to bear witness,* testimoniar, dar testimonio, atestiguar; *eye-witness,* testigo de vista, testigo ocular; *witness for the defence,* testigo de descargo; *witness for the prosecution,* testigo de cargo. — *v.t.* ser testigo de, presenciar, ver; atestiguar, atestar; asistir a, concurrir a; mostrar, dar fe. — *v.i.* dar testimonio, testimoniar, testificar, servir de testigo.

witted, *a.* ingenioso; *quick witted,* vivo de ingenio; *slow witted,* o *heavy witted,* lerdo, estúpido.

witticism ['witisizm], *s.* ingeniosidad, ocurrencia, salida, pulla, rasgo de ingenio, dicho agudo, gracia, gracejo, epigrama, *m.*, (*ant.*) conceptismo.

wittily ['witili], *adv.* con gracia, ingeniosamente, agudamente, con sal, con donaire.

wittiness, *s.* agudeza, sal, *f.*, ingenio, gracia, donaire, donosura.

wittingly ['witiŋli], *adv.* de intento, a sabiendas, ex profeso, de propósito, adrede.

witty ['witi], *a.* ingenioso, gracioso, salado, sutil, agudo; (*ant.*) inteligente, talentoso; chistoso, conversador.

wive [waiv], *v.t.*, *v.i.* tomar (por) mujer, tomar (por) esposa, casarse (con).

wives [waivz], *s.pl.* [WIFE]; *an old wives' tale*, un cuento de viejas; *the Merry Wives of Windsor*, (Shakespeare) las Alegres Comadres de Windsor.

wizard ['wizəɹd], *s.* mago, brujo, adivino, nigromante, encantador. — *a.* hechicero, mago.

wizen ['wizən], *v.t.*, *v.i.* marchitar(se), secar(se), encoger(se).

wizened ['wizənd], *a.* encartonado, enjuto; marchito, mustio. — *p.p.* [WIZEN].

woad [woud], *s.* (*bot.*) glasto, gualda, pastel; isátida, y el tinte azul extraído de esta planta.

wobble ['wɔbəl], *v.i.* [WABBLE].

woe [wou], *s.* pena, dolor, aflicción, pesar, pesadumbre; angustia; calamidad, desgracia, infortunio, miseria, desastre. — *interj.* ¡ay de mí!; *woe is me*, ¡desgraciado de mí! ¡ay de mí! ¡pobre de mí!

woebegone ['woubigɔn], *a.* desconsolado, abrumado, angustiado.

woeful ['wouful], *a.* desconsolado, desgraciado, calamitoso, lastimero, triste, funesto, desastroso, afligido, angustiado; perverso, deplorable, ruin.

woefulness, *s.* infortunio, desgracia, miseria, aflicción, tristeza.

wold [would], *s.* llanura; campiña undulada.

wolf [wulf], *s.* (*pl.* **wolves**) lobo; (*fig.*) persona rapaz; (*mús.*) sonido discordante, esp. en un órgano; (*ent.*) especie de larva destructiva de varias mariposas nocturnas; (*vulg.*) don juan, tenorio; *to cry wolf*, gritar 'al lobo'; *to keep the wolf from the door*, cerrar la puerta al hambre; *to have the wolf by the ears*, ver las orejas al lobo; *to have a wolf in the stomach*, tener apetito voraz.

wolf-dog, wolf-hound, *s.* mastín; perro-lobo.

wolf-fish ['wulfiʃ], *s.* lobo marino.

wolfish ['wulfiʃ], *a.* lupino, lobero de lobo; (*fig.*) rapaz.

wolfishly, *adv.* como un lobo, con rapacidad.

wolfram ['wulfrəm], *s.* (*min.*) volframio.

wolf's bane, *s.* acónito.

woman ['wumən], *s.* (*pl.* **women**) mujer; hembra; mujer, sirvienta, criada; *woman-hater*, misógino. — *v.t.* afeminar; tratar de 'mujer'. — *v.i.* afeminarse; adamarse; cominear.

womanhood ['wumənhud], *s.* femineidad; sexo femenino.

womanish ['wuməniʃ], *a.* mujeril, de mujer, femenino, femenil; afeminado.

womanishness, *s.* femineidad; molicie, *f.*

womanize, *v.t.* afeminar. — *v.i.* (*vulg.*) putañear.

womanizer, *s.* (*vulg.*) putañero.

womankind ['wumənkaind], *s.* sexo femenino, la mujer.

womanliness, *s.* femineidad, feminidad; gallardía, garbo.

womanly ['wumənli], *a.* femenino, mujeril, de mujer. — *adv.* como mujer.

womb [wu:m], *s.* (*anat.*) matriz, *f.*, útero; seno, entrañas; madre, *f.*; (*fig.*) caverna, abismo, profundidad.

women ['wimin], [WOMAN].

wonder ['wʌndəɹ], *v.i.* estar admirado, admirarse, pasmarse, maravillarse (de), extrañarse, asombrarse, sorprenderse; desear saber; preguntarse. — *s.* admiración, sorpresa; maravilla, milagro, prodigio; pasmo.

wonderer, *s.* admirador.

wonderful ['wʌndəɹful], *a.* asombroso, maravilloso, estupendo, admirable; portentoso, pasmoso, prodigioso.

wonderfulness, *s.* naturaleza maravillosa, lo maravilloso; lo pasmoso.

wondering, *a.* admirado, desconcertado.

wonderland ['wʌndəɹlænd], *s.* país de las maravillas.

wonderment ['wʌndəɹmənt], *s.* admiración, maravilla, sorpresa, extrañeza.

wonderstruck ['wʌndəɹstrʌk], *a.* pasmado, admirado, maravillado.

wonder-worker ['wʌndəɹwəːɹkəɹ], *s.* hechicero, fabricador de milagros.

wondrous ['wʌndrəs], *a.* maravilloso, admirable, extraño, raro, prodigioso, colosal, portentoso, pasmoso.

wont [wount], *a.* acostumbrado, habituado, sólito. — *v. aux.* soler, habituar, acostumbrar. — *s.* costumbre, hábito, uso; *to be wont to*, soler, tener costumbre de, acostumbrar, estar habituado a.

won't [wount], (*fam.*) abreviatura de *will not*.

wonted ['wountid], *a.* acostumbrado, ordinario, habituado, habitual.

wontedness, *s.* costumbre, hábito.

woo [wu:], *v.t.* cortejar, solicitar, galantear, obsequiar, enamorar, requebrar, requerir de amores; instar, invitar con solicitud. — *v.i.* cortejarse.

wood [wud], *s.* madera; selva, bosque, monte; madero, leña, leño; *fire-wood*, leña; *coppice-wood*, monte tallar; *dye-wood*, madera de tinte; *drift-wood*, madera de flotación, madera de deriva; *sap-wood*, albura; (*carp.*) sámago; *small wood*, leña menuda, brusca. — *v.t.* proveer de leña; cubrir con bosques.

wood-ant, *s.* hormiga leonada.

woodbine ['wudbain], *s.* madreselva de Europa.

wood-carving, *s.* grabado en madera.

woodchuck, *s.* (*orn.*) marmota grande de América.

woodcock, *s.* becada, chochaperdiz, *f.*, pitorra.

woodcraft, *s.* conocimientos relativos a los bosques.

woodcut, *s.* viñeta, grabado en madera.

woodcutter, *s.* leñador; grabador en madera.

wooded ['wudid], *a.* arbolado, cubierto de bosques, plantado de árboles.

wooden ['wudən], *a.* de madera, en madera, de palo; embotado, torpe, rudo, imbécil; mecánico, glacial, poco expresivo; inflexible, antipático.

woodland ['wudlənd], *s.* monte, arbolado, selva, país cubierto de bosques.

woodlark ['wudlɑːɪk], *s.* alondra, calandria silvestre.

woodless, *a.* sin bosques.

woodlouse, *s.* cucaracha, carcoma.

woodman ['wudmən], *s.* leñador; guardabosque.

woodnymph ['wudnimf], *s.f.* napea, orea, oréade, oréada, dríade.

woodpecker ['wudpekəɪ], *s.* picaposte, picamaderos, pico barreno (o carpintero), pájaro carpintero.

wood-pigeon, *s.* paloma torcaz.

wood-pulp, *s.* pasta de madera, pasta papelera.

wood-rasp, *s.* escofina.

wood-reeve, *s.* guardabosque.

woodruff ['wudrəf], *s.* (*bot.*) aspérula.

woodshed ['wudʃəd], *s.* leñera.

wood-sorrel, *s.* (*bot.*) aleluya.

wood-thrush, *s.* tordo pardo.

wood-tick, *s.* (*ent.*) carcoma.

wood-wind, *s.* (*mús.*)(instrumentos de) madera.

woodwork ['wudwəːɪk], *s.* maderaje; enmaderamiento, obra de carpintería; carpintería.

woodworm, *s.* carcoma.

woody ['wudi], *a.* arbolado; leñoso.

wooer ['wuːəɪ], *s.* galanteador, pretendiente, cortejador, amoroso.

woof [wuːf], *s.* tejido, textura, trama.

wooing ['wuːiŋ], *s.* solicitación; galanteo, enamoramiento, obsequio.

wooingly, *adv.* amorosamente.

wool [wul], *s.* lana; pasa; *all wool*, pura lana, todo de lana; *fleece wool*, lana de vellón; *to pull the wool over someone's eyes*, embaucar, entruchar.

wool-bearing, *a.* lanar.

wool-comber, *s.* cardador.

wool-combing, *s.* cardadura.

woold [wuːld], *v.t.* (*mar.*) rostar, trincar.

wooled [wuld], *a.* con lana, que tiene lana.

wool-gatherer, *s.* (*fig.*) distraído, visionario.

wool-gathering, *s.* (*fig.*) ensimismamiento.

woollen, (*E.U.*) **woolen**, *a.* de lana, en lana; lanoso, lanudo; entapizado. — *s.* tela de lana; *woollen draper*, comerciante en paños, pañero; *woollen dyer*, tintorero de lana.

woolliness, (*E.U.*) **wooliness** ['wulinis], *s.* naturaleza lanuda, calidad de lanudo, lanosidad, vellosidad.

woolly, (*E.U.*) **wooly** [wuli], *a.* lanudo, lanoso, coposo, de lana; crespo (de cabello); aborregado (el cielo); (*fig.*) bobo, olvidadizo.

woolpack, *s.* fardo de lana; cúmulo (nube).

woolsack ['wulsæk], *s.* fardo de lana; asiento del Presidente (Cámara de los lores, Ing.).

wool-winder, *s.* vellonero.

word [wəːɪd], *s.* palabra, vocablo, voz, *f.*; lenguaje, habla; oferta, promesa; dicho, apotegma, *m.*; sentencia; orden, mandato; discusión; recado, aviso, mensaje; (*mil.*) santo y seña; (*Biblia*) el Verbo. — *pl.* **words**, disputa, contienda (de palabras); *high words*, palabras mayores, injurias; *by word of mouth*, de viva voz, verbalmente; *to bring word*, traer la noticia; *to have words*, trabarse de palabras, tener palabras; *to keep one's word*, cumplir su palabra; tener palabra; *to send word*, enviar a decir, avisar, dar aviso; *take my word (for it)*, bajo mi palabra, o créame Vd. — *v.t.* explicar, expresar, redactar, enunciar; hacer frases; instar con palabras.

wordiness ['wəːɪdinis], *s.* verbosidad, prolijidad, palabrería.

wording ['wəːɪdiŋ], *s.* redacción, términos, fraseología, manera de explicar, expresión; dicción, estilo.

wordless, *a.* sin palabras.

wordy ['wəːɪdi], *a.* verboso, difuso, prolijo, ampuloso.

wore ['woːɪ], *pret., p.p.* [WEAR].

work [wəːɪk], *s.* trabajo, tarea, faena; ocupación, empleo, producción; labor, *f.*; obras (públicas); obra, acción, acto; obra (artística). — *pl.* **works**, obras; taller, establecimiento, fábrica; movimiento (de un reloj), mecanismo, maquinaria; *work days*, días laborables, días útiles; *at work*, a la obra, al trabajo; *needle-work*, labor de aguja; *piece of work*, trabajo; obra; *piece work*, obra a destajo; *press work*, (*impr.*) tirada; *to be at work*, estar trabajando, estar ocupado; *to be hard at work*, estar atareado; *to set to work*, dar empleo, hacer trabajar. — *v.i.* (*pret.* y *p.p.* **worked**) obrar, trabajar; labrar, operar, fabricar; andar; formar; manufacturar; atormentar; fester, investigar; fermentar; moverse nerviosamente, agitarse; abrirse camino; funcionar, marchar; tener éxito, ser eficaz, hacer efecto; *to work at*, ocuparse de (o en); *to work in* (o *into*), entrar en, penetrar en, insinuarse en; *to work off*, irse, separarse poco a poco; *to work out*, tener (buen o mal) éxito; *to work loose*, aflojarse, soltarse; salir poco a poco; *to work round*, volverse lentamente; *to work up*, subir con grandes esfuerzos. — *v.t.* trabajar; explotar, fabricar, manufacturar; preparar, producir, componer; tallar (piedras preciosas); manipular, manejar; bordar; hacer funcionar, mover o andar; hacer fermentar; abrirse (camino); (*impr.*) imprimir, tirar; (*mar.*) maniobrar; *to work into*, entrar (o penetrar) en; *to work in*, hacer penetrar; (*fig.*) intercalar, insinuar en; *to work off*, terminar, acabar; deshacerse de, librarse de, desahogar; *to work out*, efectuar, ejecutar, resolver (un problema); borrar, expiar (culpas); conseguir, lograr con trabajo; *to work up*, servirse de, emplear; (*farm.*) amasar; dar forma a, labrar; agotar, consumir; inflamar, excitar; hacer subir (o levantar) con grandes esfuerzos; desarrollar, ponerse a aprender; *to work upon*, influir (o obrar) sobre, mover a compasión.

workable ['wəːɪkəbəl], *a.* explorable, laborable, labradero; practicable.

workaday ['wəːɪkədei], *a.* laborioso, industrioso; ordinario, practicable, de por ahí.

work-bag, *s.* saco de labor.

work-box, *s.* caja de labor.

workday ['wəːɪkdei], *s.* día de trabajo, día laborable.

worker, *s.* trabajador, obrero, operario.

workfellow ['wəːɪkfelou], *s.* compañero de trabajo.

workhouse ['wəːɪkhaus], *s.* hospicio, asilo (de los pobres), casa de misericordia; casa de corrección; taller.

working, *a.* laborioso, industrioso, trabajador, que trabaja bien; que trabaja, que funciona; de trabajo; obrero, proletario, práctico. — *s.* labor, *f.*; trabajo, obra; fermentación; laboreo, explotación (de minas); (*impr.*)

impresión, tirada; función, operación, movimiento, juego; faena, maniobra.

workman ['wəːkmən], s. obrero, trabajador, operario; autor, artista, m.f.

workmanlike, workmanly, a. diestro, hábil, primoroso; de obrero; bien hecho, bien acabado.

workmanship, s. habilidad, ejecución primorosa; manufactura; obra, mano de obra.

workmaster, s. oficial, maestro, encargado.

workroom, workshop, s. taller, obrador.

workwoman, s. obrera; costurera.

work-yard, s. taller, almacén.

world [wəːld], s. mundo; gentío, gente, f., muchedumbre; cantidad; for all the world as if . . ., bien así como . . ., exactamente como si . . .; world without end, para siempre jamás, por los siglos de los siglos.

worldliness ['wəːldlines], s. mundanalidad, mundanería.

worldling ['wəːldliŋ], s. mundano, persona mundana.

worldly ['wəːldli], a. mundano, del mundo, mundanal, carnal, terreno, humano; to be wordly-wise, tener (mucho) mundo. — adv. profanamente, mundanamente, mundanalmente.

world-wide, a. mundial, universal.

worm [wəːm], s. gusano, oruga, ascáride, f., larva; lombriz, f.; polilla, carcoma, gorgojo, coco; (mec.) tornillo sinfín, rosca, filete; (quím.) serpentín; persona vil, despreciable; (min.) barrena; (vet.) landrilla, lita; (arti.) sacatrapos; (fig.) gusano de la conciencia, remordimiento; still-worm, serpentín de alambique; glow-worm, luciérnaga, gusano de luz; silk-worm, gusano de seda; worm-gear, engranaje de tornillo sinfín. — v.t. arrastrar, introducir, insinuar; minar; taladrar, sacar con sacatrapos; arrancar mañosamente. — v.i. quitar gusanos; arrastrar(se), introducirse, trabajar por bajo mano, insinuarse; to worm (one's way) in (o into), insinuarse en, introducirse por bajo mano; to worm out, sonsacar (un secreto, etc.).

worm-eaten, a. comido de los gusanos, carcomido, apolillado.

worm-hole, s. lombriguera, carcoma, picadura de gusano.

wormseed, s. (bot.) santónico, simiente de Alejandría.

wormwood ['wəːmwud], s. ajenjo.

wormy ['wəːmi], a. verminoso, gusarapiento, gusaniento.

worn [wɔːn], p.p. [WEAR]; worn out, usado, raído, gastado; fatigado, rendido, hecho polvo.

worrier ['wʌriə], s. pesimista, m.f., persona que se preocupa o que molesta; aprensivo.

worry ['wʌri], v.t. preocupar, inquietar, molestar, incomodar, acosar, vejar, atormentar, abrumar, fastidiar, angustiar, perseguir, jorobar; morder, lacerar, desgarrar. — v.i. preocuparse, estar preocupado, incomodarse, atormentarse, inquietarse, desazonarse. — s. preocupación, fastidio, molestia, tormento, zozobra, ansiedad, vejación, ansia, cuidado; mordedura, desgarro, laceración.

worse [wəːs], a. compar. [BAD, ILL]; peor, inferior, más perverso; más enfermo; en peor situación, en peor estado; so much the worse, tanto peor; worse than ever, peor que nunca; worse and worse, de mal en peor, peor que

nunca, peor que peor; to be worse, estar peor, valer menos; to be worse off, ser menos feliz, estar peor; to grow o get worse, empeorarse, ponerse peor; to make worse, empeorar. — adv. compar. [BADLY, ILL]; peor. — s. lo peor.

worship ['wəːʃip], v.t. adorar, venerar, honrar, respetar, reverenciar. — v.i. dar culto, tomar parte en él. — s. adoración, culto, veneración, tratamiento, respeto, deferencia, honor; Your Worship, Vuestra Excelencia.

worshipful, a. venerable, honorable, adorable, respetable (se emplea como tratamiento a magistrados, etc.).

worshipfully, adv. respetuosamente, venerablemente, con adoración.

worshipper ['wəːʃipə], s. adorador, fiel, venerador, el que practica un culto.

worshipping, s. adoración, culto. — a. venerante, adorante.

worst [wəːst], v.t. batir, derrotar, vencer, triunfar de. — a. superl. [BAD]; lo peor, lo más malo; pésimo, malísimo. — adv. superl. [BADLY, ILL]; peor, lo peor, pésimamente, del peor modo posible. — s. peor, más malo; at (the) worst, a lo peor, en el peor estado posible; do your worst, haga Vd. todo lo que quiera; if the worst comes to the worst, si sucede lo peor; to make the worst of, sacar el peor partido de; the worst (of it) is, lo malo es, lo peor es.

worsted ['wustəd], p.p. [WORST]. — a. vencido; de estambre, de lana pura. — s. lana peinada, estambre.

wort [wəːt], s. (ant.) hierba, planta; repollo; cerveza nueva.

worth [wəːθ], s. valor, valía, monta, mérito, precio; consideración, importancia; excelencia, nobleza, dignidad. — a. digno, benemérito, que vale, que merece, que posee; equivalente a, del precio de; to be worth, valer, poseer, ser digno de; to be worth while, valer la pena, merecer.

worthily ['wəːðili], adv. dignamente, honorablemente, merecidamente.

worthiness ['wəːðinis], s. valor, mérito, valía, dignidad.

worthless ['wəːθles], a. sin mérito, sin valor, indigno, inútil, despreciable.

worthlessness, s. indignidad, inutilidad, falta de mérito, falta de valor.

worthy ['wəːði], a. digno, honorable, apreciable, benemérito, acreedor. — s. hombre ilustre, héroe, notable; (fam., despec.) individuo, tipo, tío. — pl. the Nine Worthies: Héctor de Troya, Alejandro el Grande, Julio César, Josué, David, Judas Macabeo, Rey Arturo, Carlomagno, y Godofredo de Bouillon.

wot [wɔt], (ant.) 1ª y 2ª pers. sing. indic. pres. [TO WIT].

would [wud], pret. y subj. [WILL]; querer; would to God, ¡plegue a Dios! ¡Ojalá!

would-be ['wudbiː], a. pretendido, supuesto, seudo, titulado, pretendiente, aspirante.

wound [waːnd], v.t., v.i. herir; ofender, lastimar, dañar, agraviar; to wound to the quick, tocar en lo vivo. — s. herida, llaga, lesión; golpe, daño, ofensa.

wound [waund], pret., p.p. [WIND].

wounding ['wuːndiŋ], a. injurioso; lastimador, mordaz; ofensivo. — s. heridas.

woundless ['wuːndles], *a.* sin herida; invulnerable.

woundwort ['wuːndwəːɪt], *s.* (*bot.*) vulneraria.

wove [wouv], **woven** ['wouvən], *pret.*, *p.p.* [WEAVE].

wrack [ræk], *v.t.* hacer zozobrar (un buque); atormentar [WRECK]. — *s.* (*bot.*) fuco, ova; celajes; (*poét.*) ruina, naufragio; *to go to wrack,* arruinarse.

wraith [reiθ], *s.* fantasma, *m.*, espectro, sombra, aparecido.

wrangle ['ræŋgəl], *v.i.* disputarse, denostarse, reñir, contender, altercar; regatear. — *s.* querella, disputa, pelotera, riña, camorra, pendencia, contienda, altercado.

wrangler ['ræŋgləɪ], *s.* disputador, pendenciero, querellador, quimerista, *m.f.*; estudiante de la primera clase en matemáticas (en la Universidad de Cambridge).

wrangling ['ræŋgliŋ], *s.* disputa, quimera, reyerta, altercación.

wrap [ræp], *v.t.* envolver, enrollar, arrollar; arropar, apañar; embozar; tapar(se), ocultar, cubrir. — *s.* bata, manto, capa; envoltorio.

wrapper ['ræpəɪ], *s.* envoltura, embalaje; cubierta, carpeta, funda, sobrepaño, cobertora; envolvedero, envolvedor; faja de periódico; capa de tabaco; peinador, bata.

wrapping, *s.* envoltura, cubierta, carpeta, faja de periódico.

wrath [rɔːθ], *s.* furor, rabia, cólera, ira.

wrathful, *a.* enojado, furioso, en cólera, colérico, airado.

wrathfully ['rɔːθfəli], *adv.* con cólera, coléricamente, furiosamente, airadamente.

wrathless, *a.* sin cólera, tranquilo.

wreak [riːk], *v.t.* ejecutar, infligir, descargar (la cólera); vengarse (de); *to wreak vengeance,* tomar venganza.

wreath [riːθ], *s.* guirnalda, corona; trenza; espiral; festón.

wreathe [riːð], *v.t.* guirnaldar, tejer guirnaldas, tejer coronas, enguirnaldar; trenzar, entretejer, entrelazar; rodear, ceñir.

wreathed [riːðd], *a.* rodeado de guirnaldas; enroscado, entrelazado; *wreathed in smiles,* deshecho en sonrisas, carialegre, sonrisueño.

wreathing ['riːðiŋ], *s.* enlazamiento, tejedura, trenzado, trenza.

wreathless ['riːθlis], *a.* sin guirnaldas.

wreathy, *a.* coronado; en espiral; enroscado.

wreck [rek], *v.i.* naufragar, zozobrar, chocar (buques), perderse, irse a pique; fracasar. — *v.t.* hacer naufragar o zozobrar, echar a pique; (*fig.*) echar a perder, arruinar, perder, destruir. — *s.* naufragio; despojos (*m.pl.*) de un naufragio; barco naufragado; destrozo, destrucción, ruina, pérdida; (*fig.*) consumido, desmedrado, muerto, sombra; *to be wrecked,* o *suffer wreck,* naufragar; *to go to wreck,* arruinarse, perderse.

wreckage ['rekidʒ], *s.* naufragios, restos (o despojos) de naufragio.

wrecker, *s.* demoledor; (*mar.*) raquero, salvador; ladrón de naufragios; camión de auxilio (para automóviles).

wren [ren], *s.* troglodito, reyezuelo, abadejo.

wrench [rentʃ], *v.t.* arrebatar, arrancar; torcerse, retorcer; dislocar, sacar de quicio, desencajar; *to wrench one's foot,* torcerse (o dislocarse) el pie. — *s.* torcedura, dislocación;

esfuerzo violento, tirón, arranque, arrancamiento; llave inglesa para tuercas.

wrest [rest], *v.t.* arrancar, arrebatar, torcer; pervertir, tergiversar, desvirtuar. — *s.* torcedura, torcimiento, torsión; arranque, acción de arrancar; violencia, esfuerzo violento; dislocación.

wrester, *s.* violador, infractor.

wrestle ['resəl], *v.i.* luchar (a brazo partido); esforzarse, disputar.

wrestler, *s.* luchador (atleta).

wrestling, *s.* lucha.

wretch [retʃ], *s.* desgraciado, miserable, desventurado; persona despreciable; pobre diablo.

wretched ['retʃid], *a.* desgraciado, miserable, triste, infeliz, cuitado, vil, ruin, mezquino, desdichado, desventurado, lastimero, calamitoso; malísimo, despreciable.

wretchedly, *adv.* miserablemente, desastradamente, ruinmente; malísimamente.

wretchedness, *s.* miseria, desgracia, pobreza, desventura, desdicha, vileza, bajeza, ruindad, escualidez.

wriggle ['rigəl], *v.i.* culebrear, serpentear, serpear, agitarse, moverse, torcerse, retorcerse; colear, undular; *to wriggle into,* introducirse (o insinuarse) en; *to wriggle away* (*o out of it*), escabullirse, escaparse. — *v.t.* agitar, torcer, retorcer, hacer colear.

wriggling, wriggle, *s.* retorcimiento, culebreo, serpenteo, torcedura, sacudida.

wright [rait], *s.* obrero, artesano, artífice (se usa generalmente en combinación: *shipwright,* calafate; *wheelwright,* tornero, etc.).

wring [riŋ], *v.t.* (*pret.*, *p.p.* **wrung**) torcer, arrancar, retorcer; aquejar, atormentar; exprimir, escurrir, estrujar; *to wring one's hands,* torcerse las manos; *to wring off,* arrancar retorciendo; *to wring out,* exprimir, hacer salir (torciendo); *to wring someone's neck,* torcerle el pescuezo. — *v.i.* torcerse. — *s.* torcedura, torsión.

wringer ['riŋəɪ], *s.* torcedor; exprimidor; máquina de exprimir (ropa húmeda).

wringing, *s.* torcedura, torsión; tormento, tortura.

wrinkle ['riŋkəl], *v.t.* arrugar, plegar, fruncir. — *v.i.* arrugarse, hacer arrugas, encarrujarse. — *s.* arruga, pliegue, surco; (*fam.*) capricho.

wrinkly, *a.* arrugado.

wrist [rist], *s.* muñeca.

wristband ['ristbænd], *s.* puño de camisa, tirillo del puño.

wristlet, *s.* pulsera; *wristlet-watch,* reloj de pulsera.

wrist-watch, *s.* reloj de pulsera.

writ [rit], *s.* escritura, escrito, orden, *f.*; (*for.*) auto, mandamiento, citación; (*pol.*) carta de convocación; *Holy Writ,* la Sagrada Escritura.

write [rait], *v.t.* (*pret.* **wrote**; *p.p.* **written**) escribir, poner por escrito, componer, redactar, describir, imprimir, grabar, trazar; *to write back,* contestar a una carta; *to write down,* poner por escrito, redactar, apuntar, anotar; (*fig.*) *to write on something,* escribir sobre una cosa; *to write on,* continuar escribiendo; *to write out,* copiar, transcribir, redactar; *to write over again,* volver a escribir, poner en limpio; *to write up,* redactar; (*fam.*) ensalzar por escrito; (*com.*) poner al día (el

writer

yarrow

libro mayor). — *v.i.* escribir, tener correspondencia; componer (como autor); *to write for,* hacer venir (por carta), solicitar, escribir para (pedir); escribir por o de parte de.

writer, *s.* escritor, autor; escribiente; articulista, *m.f.*; literato.

writhe [raið], *v.i., v.t.* torcer, torcerse; atormentar; alterar, falsear.

writing, *s.* escritura, escrito, obra; manuscrito, mano, *f.*; letra; estilo, composición; artículo, documento, acto; *in writing,* por escrito; *in one's own writing,* de su puño y letra.

writing-case, *s.* papelera.

writing-desk, *s.* atril, escritorio, escribanía, bufete.

writing-pad, *s.* bloc.

written, *p.p.* [WRITE].

wrong [rɔŋ], *v.t.* hacer daño a, agraviar a, ofender, causar perjuicio. — *a.* malo, injusto; erróneo, falso, incorrecto, desacertado, inexacto, equivocado; irregular, inoportuno, inconveniente; *to come at the wrong moment,* venir como pedrada en ojo de boticario; *wrong side,* o *wrong side outwards,* al revés; *to be wrong,* equivocarse, engañarse, no tener razón. — *s.* mal, perjuicio, injusticia; falta, error; culpa; sinrazón, *f.*, tuerto, daño, injuria, agravio; extravío, falsedad; *to be in the wrong,* no tener razón, tener mucha culpa; *to do wrong,* obrar mal, causar perjuicio, hacer daño. — *adv.* mal, injustamente, perversamente, sin razón, sin causa, al revés.

wrong-doer, *s.* malhechor.

wrong-doing, *s.* maleficencia.

wronger [ˈrɔŋəɪ], *s.* agraviador, injuriador.

wrongful [ˈrɔŋful], *a.* dañoso; inicuo, injusto.

wrongfully, *adv.* inicuamente, injustamente, sin razón, sin motivo ni causa; falsamente.

wronghead, *s.* calavera.

wrongheaded [rɔŋˈheded], *a.* obstinado, terco, testarudo.

wrongheadedness, *s.* terquedad, sinrazón, *f.*, perversidad, obstinación.

wrongly [ˈrɔŋli], *adv.* injustamente, equivocadamente, mal, sin razón ni causa.

wrongness, *s.* injusticia, maldad, falsedad, error, inexactitud, iniquidad.

wrote [rout], *pret.* [WRITE].

wroth [rouθ], *a.* irritado, encolerizado, airado.

wrought [rɔːt], *a.* forjado, trabajado; impelido; excitado; *wrought iron,* hierro forjado. — *p.p. irreg.* [WORK].

wrung [rʌŋ], *pret., p.p.* [WRING]; *wrung mast,* (*mar.*) palo torcido.

wry [rai], *a.* torcido, doblado, de través; oblicuo; falso, pervertido, tergiversado; *wry face,* gesto, visajes, mueca.

wryly [ˈraili], *adv.* secamente, irónicamente.

wryneck [ˈrainek], *s.* (*orn.*) torcecuello; (*med.*) torticolis, *f.*

wryness [ˈrainis], *s.* torcedura, contorsión; oblicuidad; gesto; mueca; ironía, desdén.

wych-elm [ˈwitʃelm], *s.* olmo escocés.

wych-hazel, *s.* (*bot.*) hamamelis virginiana.

wye [wai], *s.* la letra Y; horquilla; cualquier objeto en forma de Y.

X

X, x [eks], vigésima cuarta letra del alfabeto inglés. Tiene dos sonidos, uno fuerte y

otro suave. El primero equivale a *cs* en castellano, v.g. *axis, excise, executioner;* y el segundo a *gz,* pronunciando la *z* como en francés; v.g. *exempt, examination, executor.* A causa de su forma en cruz, sirve como abreviación de Cristo, v.g. *Xmas* por *Christmas, Xpher* por *Christopher. X-rays,* rayos X; *XX* o doble X, *XXX* o triple X, marcas indicando la graduación de la cerveza, coñac, etc.

xanthic [ˈzænθik], *a.* xántico.

xanthine [ˈzænθain], *s.* xantina, jantina.

xebec [ˈziːbek], *s.* (*mar.*) jabeque.

xenium [ˈzeniəm], *s.* (*pl. xenia*) golosina.

xenophobia [zenoˈfoubiə], *s.* xenofobia.

xerode [ˈzeroud], *s.* (*med.*) tumor seco.

xerophagy [zeˈrɔfəgi], *s.* jerofagía.

xerophthalmy [zerɔfˈθælmi], *s.* jeroftalmía.

xerosis [zeˈrousis], *s.* xerodermia.

xiphoid [ˈzifɔid], *a.* xifoideo.

Xmas [ˈkrismæs], *s.* (*fam.*) Navidad.

xylogen [ˈzailodʒən], *s.* xilógeno.

xylographical [zailoˈgræfikəl], *a.* xilográfico.

xylography, *s.* xilografía.

xylol [ˈzailəl], *s.* xilole, hidrocarbono líquido.

xylonite [ˈzailənait], *s.* xilonita.

Y

Y, y [wai], vigésima quinta letra del alfabeto inglés. Al principio de una voz se pronuncia como en castellano y en este caso se la considera en inglés como letra consonante. Al fin de palabra se pronuncia como *i* castellana pero corta. Su pronunciación en los otros casos es como *ai.* Como letra sola, *uai* y es vocal. — *s.* (*f.c.*) cambio de marcha en Y; triángulo de inversión de marcha. — *a.* en forma de Y; *Y-box,* (*elec.*) caja bifurcada; *Y-connection,* (*elec.*) conexión de estrella; *Y-gun,* cañón doble antisubmarino.

yacht [jɔt], *s.* yate. — *v.i.* viajar en yate.

yachting, *s.* deporte de 'yachting'.

yachtsman, *s.* propietario, dueño o timonel de un yate.

yah [jaː], *interj.* ¡bah! ¡ya! (exclamación de duda o burla).

yak [jæk], *s.* (*zool.*) yak.

Yale lock [jeil lɔk], *s.* cerradura de Yale (marca de fábrica).

yam [jæm], *s.* (*bot.*) batata, ñame.

yank [jæŋk], *v.t.* (*fam.*) dar un tirón; sucar de un tirón. — *s.* tirón, estirón; (*vulg.*) yanqui.

Yankee [ˈjæŋki], *s., a.* yanqui, *m.f.*; *Yankee doodle,* canción popular en los E.U.; yanqui.

yap [jæp], *v.i.* ladrar como un perrito; parlotear. — *s.* ladrido; perro mostrenco.

yard [jaːd], *s.* yarda, medida inglesa equivalente a 0·914 m.; corral; patio; cercado; depósito; (*mar.*) verga; *dock-yard,* arsenal, astillero; *lumber-yard,* depósito de madera; *yard-arms,* penoles de las vergas; *main-yard,* verga mayor; *yard-stick,* yarda de medir. — *v.t.* acorralar, apriscar.

yard-arm, *s.* penol de la verga.

yare [jɛəɹ], *a.* (*prov.*) ligero, pronto, diestro.

yarn [jaːɹn], *s.* hilo, hilado, hilaza; (*fam.*) cuento, historia, andaluzada; *to spin a yarn,* (*fig.*) contar una historia larga (o increíble).

yarrow [ˈjærou], *s.* (*bot.*) milenrama, milhojas.

[1443]

yataghan ['jætəgæn], *s.* yatagán.
yaw [jɔː], *v.i.* (*mar.*) guiñar, dar guiñadas; (*aer.*) derrapar. — *s.* (*mar.*) guiñada; (*aer.*) derrape.
yawl [jɔːl], *s.* (*mar.*) bote, yola, balandra.
yawn [jɔːn], *v.i.* bostezar, *to yawn open*, (*fig.*) abrirse. — *s.* bostezo.
yawner, *s.* bostezador.
yawning, *s.* bostezo. — *a.* bostezante, que bosteza; adormecido; abierto.
yclad [i'klæd], *a.* (*ant.*) vestido, cubierto.
ycleped, yclept [i'klept], *s.* (*ant.*) llamado.
ye [jiː], *pr. pl.* (*ant.*) [THOU]; vosotros, vos.
yea [jei], *adv.* (*ant.*) sí; en verdad, verdaderamente, ciertamente; y aun, y además, no solamente . . . sino; *yea or nay*, si o no. — *s.* sí; voto afirmativo; *the yeas and nays*, los votos en pro y en contra.
yean [jiːn], *v.i.* parir (las ovejas o cabras).
yeanling, *s.* cordero o cabrito mamantón.
year [jəːɹ], *s.* año. — *pl.* years, edad, vejez; *by the year*, al año; *last year*, el año pasado; *leap year*, año bisiesto; *once a year*, una vez al año; *every other year*, cada dos años, de dos en dos años; *to grow in years*, envejecer; *taking one year with another*, un año con otro; *year of grace*, año de gracia, año de la Era Cristiana.
year-book, *s.* anuario.
yearling ['jəːɹliŋ], *s.* añojo, primal, animal de un año. — *a.* de un año.
yearly ['jəːɹli], *a.* anual, de un año. — *adv.* anualmente, todos los años, cada año, una vez al año.
yearn [jəːɹn], *v.i.* (con *over*) conmoverse, afligirse; (con *for*) suspirar, anhelar; desear vivamente.
yearning, *s.* deseo ardiente, aspiración, anhelo; compasión, ternura.
yeast [jiːst], *s.* levadura, fermento, espuma; (*fig.*) fermento mental o moral.
yeasty, *a.* espumoso, ligero; frívolo, trivial.
yelk [jelk], *s.* yema de huevo [YOLK].
yell [jel], *v.t., v.i.* dar alaridos, gritar, vociferar, aullar, decir a gritos. — *s.* grito de terror; alarido, aullido, grito salvaje.
yelling, *a.* chillón. — *s.* alarido.
yellow ['jelou], *a.* amarillo, dorado, rubio; (*vulg.*) cobarde; *to get* (o *grow*) *yellow*, ponerse amarillo, amarillear. — *s.* amarillo.
yellow-bird, pintacilgo, jilguero; cerrojillo.
yellow-fever, *s.* fiebre amarilla.
yellow-hammer, *s.* emberizo, verderol.
yellowish, *a.* amarillento.
yellowishness, *s.* color amarillento.
yellowness, *s.* amarillez, color amarillo.
yelp [jelp], *v.i.* chillar; ladrar, latir, gañir (el perro).
yelp, yelping, *s.* aullido, gañido.
yen [jen], *s.* dólar japonés.
yeoman ['joumən], *s.* (*pl.* yeomen) hacendado; aldeano; soldado; (*mar.*) pañolero; (*E.U.*) auxiliar de oficinas; *Yeoman of the Guard*, alabardero de la Casa Real.
yeomanly, *a.* de hacendado; de soldado.
yeomanry ['joumənri], *s.* burguesía, hacendados; cuerpo voluntario de caballería formado por hacendados, etc.; guarda nacional.
yerk [jəːɹk], *v.t.* lanzar, arrojar, traquetear, sacudir. — *v.i.* cocear. — *s.* coz, *f.*

yes [jes], *adv., s.* sí, de veras, seguramente; *Yes?* ¿Qué hay? ¿De verdad?
yester ['jestəɹ], *a.* último, pasado; (*poét.*) de ayer.
yesterday ['jestəɹdei], *adv., s.* ayer.
yestereen, yestreen ['jestriːn], *s., adv.* (*poét.*) anoche.
yestern ['jestəɹn], *a.* de ayer.
yesternight ['jestəɹnait], *s., adv.* anoche.
yet [jet], *conj., adv.* todavía; sin embargo, no obstante, con todo; mas, pero; empero; *as yet*, hasta ahora, hasta aquí, todavía; *not yet*, todavía no, aun no.
yew [juː], *s.* (*bot.*) tejo.
Yiddish ['jidiʃ], *s.* dialecto del idioma alemán usado por judíos y empleando caracteres hebreos.
yield [jiːld], *v.t.* ceder, conceder, otorgar; dejar, admitir; rendir, redituar, producir, rentar; emitir, exhalar; deferir, condescender; devolver, restituir. — *v.i.* ceder, someterse, rendirse, sujetarse, conformarse, caer, sucumbir; asentir, consentir; producir, dar utilidad; flaquear, blandear, mollearse; *to yield up*, entregar, ceder. — *s.* producto, (*for.*) rédito, rendimiento, producción, beneficio; (*agr.*) cosecha; rendición.
yielding, *a.* complaciente, tratable, dócil; dúctil, flojo, elástico, fácil; obsequioso. — *s.* abandono, sumisión, rendición, consentimiento.
yieldingness, *s.* carácter complaciente, condescendencia; facilidad en ceder.
yodel ['joudəl], *v.t., v.i.* cantar o gritar modulando la voz desde el tono natural al falseto. — *s.* modo de cantar de los tiroleses y suizos.
yoke [jouk], *s.* yugo; horcajo; yunta, pareja; (*fig.*) yugo, sujeción, opresión, esclavitud, servidumbre; (*mar.*) barra de timón; (*cost.*) hombrillo de la camisa; culata (de imán); balancín (para llevar pesos); (*aer.*) palanca de mando. — *v.t.* poner al yugo, uncir, acoplar, acollarar, acoyundar; sujetar, oprimir, sujuzgar.
yokel ['joukəl], *s.* paisano rústico, patán, gañán.
yolk [jouk], *s.* yema de huevo, vitelo.
yon [jɔn], **yonder** ['jɔndəɹ], *adv.* allí, allá, acullá, allá abajo, a lo lejos. — *a.* que está allá abajo.
yore [jɔːɹ], *s.* (*poét.*) otro tiempo, antaño; *of yore*, antiguamente, de antaño, en otro tiempo.
you [juː], *pr. pers.* tú, vosotros, os; usted, ustedes; le, la, les; a usted(es).
young [jʌŋ], *a.* joven, juvenil, mozo, novicio, nuevo; inexperto, tierno, verde, reciente, fresco; *young child*, niño; *young face*, cara remozada; *to grow young again*, rejuvenecer. — *s.pl.* jóvenes, juventud; hijuelos (de los animales); *with young*, preñada, en cinta.
younger ['jʌŋgəɹ], *a. compar.* [YOUNG]; más joven; menor.
youngest ['jʌŋgest], *a. superl.* [YOUNG]; el más joven, el menor.
youngish ['jʌŋiʃ], *a.* algo joven, jovencillo, mozuelo, tierno.
youngling ['jʌŋliŋ], *s.* animal joven, animalito, pequeñuelo.
youngster ['jʌŋstəɹ], *s.* muchacho joven, chico, jovencito, mocito, mozalbete; (*fam.*) niño, chiquillo.

younker ['jʌŋkəɹ], *s.* muchacho, mozalbete.
your [jɔːɹ], *a. pos.* tu, tus, su, sus, de usted, de ustedes, vuestro, vuestros, vuestra, vuestras.
yours [jɔːɹz], *pr. pos.* de usted, de ustedes; (*fam.*) el tuyo, el vuestro; *yours truly*, su seguro servidor (S.S.S.).
yourself [jɔːɹ'self], *pr. refl.* (*pl.* **yourselves**) tú mismo, usted, usted mismo.
youth [juːθ], *s.* juventud, adolescencia, mocedad.
youthful, *a.* joven, de la juventud; vivo, vigoroso, fresco, juguetón.
youthfully, *adv.* como joven, como muchacho.
youthfulness, *s.* juventud, mocedad.
yowl [jaul], *v.i.* aullar, ladrar. — *s.* aullido.
yttrium ['itriəm], *s.* itrio.
yucca ['jʌkə], *s.* (*bot.*) yuca.
Yugoslav ['juːgouslæv], *s., a.* yugoeslavo.
yule [juːl], *s.* Navidad; *yule-log*, nochebueno; *yule-tide*, pascua de Navidad, Navidades.

Z

Z, z [zed], *s.* vigésima sexta y última letra del alfabeto inglés.   Se pronuncia siempre como *s* sonora.
zany ['zeini], *s.* bufón, simplón, truhán.
zea ['ziːə], *s.* (*bot.*) zea, género de altas plantas gramíneas; *Zea mays*, maíz.
zeal [ziːl], *s.* celo, entusiasmo, ardor, fervor.
zealot ['zelət], *s.* fanático, partidario ciego, entusiasta, *m.f.*
zealous ['zeləs], *a.* celoso, entusiasta, lleno de entusiasmo.
zealously, *adv.* con celo, con ardor, apasionadamente.
zealousness, *s.* celo, ardor, pasión.
zebra ['ziːbrə], *s.* cebra; *Zebra Crossing*, (*Ing.*) paso de peatones.
zebu ['ziːbjuː], *s.* cebú.
zechin ['zekin], *s.* cequí, moneda antigua de oro de la república de Venecia.
zed [zed], *s.* la letra zeta.
zedoary ['zedoəri], *s.* cedoaria.
zee, *s.* (*E.U.*) [zed].
zenith ['zeniθ], *s.* cenit, apogeo.
zeolite ['ziːolait], *s.* ceolito, zeolita.
zephyr ['zefəɹ], *s.* céfiro, favonio.
zero ['ziərou], *s.* cero, nada; *zero hour*, hora de ataque.
zest [zest], *s.* sabor, gusto, deleite; celo, entusiasmo; luquete. — *v.t.* dar gusto (o sabor) a.
zeta ['ziːtə], *s.* zeta.
zeugma ['zjuːgmə], *s.* zeugma.

zigzag ['zigzæg], *s.* zigzag. — *a.* en zigzag, serpentino. — *v.i.* zigzaguear, ir en zigzag.
zinc [ziŋk], *s.* zinc, cinc. — *v.t.* plaquear con cinc, galvanizar, cincar.
zincographer, *s.* cincógrafo.
zincography [ziŋ'kɔgrəfi], *s.* cincografía.
zincous ['ziŋkəs], *a.* de cinc.
zircon ['zəːɹkən], *s.* circón.
zither ['zitəɹ], *s.* cítara.
zodiac ['zoudiæk], *s.* zodiaco, zodíaco.
zodiacal [zo'dəiəkəl], *a.* zodiacal; *zodiacal light*, luz zodiacal.
zone [zoun], *s.* zona; faja, banda circular.
zoned, *a.* que lleva cinturón; marcado con zonas o fajas.
zoneless, *a.* que no tiene cinto o zona.
zonule ['zɔnjuːl], *s.* zona pequeña, aro pequeño.
zoo [zuː], *s.* (*fam.*) jardín zoológico.
zoogeny [zou'ɔdʒəni], *s.* zoogenia.
zoographer, *s.* zoógrafo.
zoographic, zoographical, *a.* zoográfico.
zoography [zou'ɔgrəfi], *s.* zoografía.
zoolatry [zou'ɔlətri], *s.* zoolatría.
zoolite ['zououlait], *s.* zoolito.
zoological [zuːo'lɔdʒikəl], *a.* zoológico; *zoological gardens*, jardín zoológico, parque zoológico.
zoologically, *adv.* zoológicamente.
zoologist [zuː'ɔlodʒist], *s.* zoólogo.
zoology [zuː'ɔlodʒi], *s.* zoología.
zoom [zuːm], *v.i.* zumbar; (*fam., aer.*) encabritarse, subir empinadamente; (*fam.*) aumentar.
zoophyte ['zououfait], *s.* zoófito.
zoophytic [zouou'fitik], *a.* zoofítico.
zoophytology, *s.* zoofitología.
zoospore ['zououspɔːɹ], *s.* zoosporo.
zootic [zou'ɔtik], *a.* zoótico.
zootomist, *s.* zootomista, *m.f.*
zootomy [zou'ɔtomi], *s.* zootomía.
zouave ['zuːɑːv], *s.* (*mil.*) zuavo.
zounds [zaundz], *interj.* (*ant.*) ¡juro a bríos! ¡por vida de sanes!
zurlite ['zəːɹlait], *s.* (*min.*) roca volcánica blanca o verde del Vesubio.
zygoma [zi'goumə], *s.* (*anat.*) cigoma, apófisis cigomática del temporal.
zygomatic [zigo'mætik], *a.* cigomático.
zyme [zaim], *s.* (*biol.*) fermento; germen de enfermedad cimótica.
zymologic [zaimo'lɔdʒik], *a.* cimológico.
zymology [zai'molodʒi], *s.* cimología.
zymometer [zai'mɔmetəɹ], **zymoscope** ['zaimoskoup], *s.* zimosímetro, zimóscopio.
zymome ['zaimoum], *s.* cimomo.
zymosis [zai'mousis], *s.* cimosis, *f.*
zymotic [zai'mɔtik], *a.* cimótico.

Y
Z

SPANISH VERBS

Verbs ending in *AR* in the infinitive belong to the FIRST conjugation.

,,	,,	*ER*	,,	,,	,,	SECOND	,,

,,   ,,   *ER*   ,,   ,,   ,,   SECOND   ,,
,,   ,,   *IR*   ,,   ,,   ,,   THIRD   ,,

Key to the Conjugation of Regular Verbs

Infinitive	Present	Indic. Pret.	Indic. Imperf.	Future	Imperative	Present Subjunctive
FIRST						
Amar	am-o	am-é	am-aba	am-aré		am-e
(*to love*)	am-as	am-aste	am-abas	am-arás	am-a	am-es
	am-a	am-ó	am-aba	am-ará	am-e	am-e
	am-amos	am-amos	am-ábamos	am-aremos	am-emos	am-emos
	am-áis	am-asteis	am-abais	am-aréis	am-ad	am-éis
	am-an	am-aron	am-aban	am-arán	am-en	am-en
SECOND						
Temer	tem-o	tem-í	tem-ía	tem-eré		tem-a
(*to fear*)	tem-es	tem-iste	tem-ías	tem-erás	tem-e	tem-as
	tem-e	tem-ió	tem-ía	tem-erá	tem-a	tem-a
	tem-emos	tem-imos	tem-íamos	tem-eremos	tem-amos	tem-amos
	tem-éis	tem-isteis	tem-íais	tem-eréis	tem-ed	tem-áis
	tem-en	tem-ieron	tem-ían	tem-erán	tem-an	tem-an
THIRD						
Vivir	viv-o	viv-í	viv-ía	viv-iré		viv-a
(*to live*)	viv-es	viv-iste	viv-ías	viv-irás	viv-e	viv-as
	viv-e	viv-ió	viv-ía	viv-irá	viv-a	viv-a
	viv-imos	viv-imos	viv-íamos	viv-iremos	viv-amos	viv-amos
	viv-ís	viv-isteis	viv-íais	viv-iréis	viv-id	viv-áis
	viv-en	viv-ieron	viv-ían	viv-irán	viv-an	viv-an

Formation of the Gerund

The FIRST conjugation forms the Gerund by adding -*ANDO* to the stem.
,,   SECOND   ,,   ,,   ,,   ,,   -*IENDO*   ,,   ,,
,,   THIRD   ,,   ,,   ,,   ,,   -*IENDO*   ,,   ,,

The past or passive participle is formed by adding
ADO to the stem for the FIRST
IDO for the SECOND and THIRD

The conditional is formed by adding -ía, -ías, -ía; -íamos, -íais,-ían to the infinitive: amar-ía, etc., temer -ía, etc., vivir-ía, etc.

Imperfect Subjunctive

am- ara,-ase	tem-iera, -iese	viv-iera, -iese
am- aras,-ases	tem-ieras, -ieses	viv-ieras, -ieses
am- ara,-ase	tem-iera, -iese	viv-iera, -iese
am-áramos,-ásemos	tem-iéramos, -iésemos	viv-iéramos, -iésemos
am- arais,-aseis	tem-ierais, -ieseis	viv-ierais, -ieseis
am- aran,-asen	tem-ieran, -iesen	viv-ieran, -iesen

Future Subjunctive

am-are	tem-iere	viv-iere
am-ares	tem-ieres	viv-ieres
am-are	tem-iere	viv-iere
am-áremos	tem-iéremos	viv-iéremos
am-areis	tem-iereis	viv-iereis
am-aren	tem-ieren	viv-ieren

NOTES ON REGULAR VERBS

Verbs ending in *car* change the radical *c* into *qu* before *e*: **tocar** becomes *toqué, toque, toquemos,* etc.

Verbs ending in *ear* double the *e* when the termination added to the stem begins also with *e*: **golpear**, preterite and subjunctive *golpeé, golpees.*

Verbs ending in *gar* add *u* after the radical *g* when the termination begins with *e*: **cargar**, *cargué*; **comulgar**, *comulgué, comulgues,* etc.

Verbs ending in *guar* change the plain *u* into *ü* when the termination begins with *e*: **santiguar**, *santigüéis*; **averiguar**, *averigüé.*

Verbs ending in *zar* change the *z* into *c* when followed by *e*: **alcanzar**, *alcance, alcancen*.

Verbs ending in *cer* or *cir* immediately preceded by a consonant change the *c* into *z* when followed by *a* or *o*: **vencer**, *venzo, venzamos*; **esparcir**, *esparzo, esparzas*.

Verbs ending in *ger* or *gir* change the *g* into *j* when followed by *a* or *o*: **proteger**, *protejo, proteja*; **afligir**, *aflijo, aflija*.

Verbs ending in *aer, eer, oer* change the *i* into *y* when it is followed by another vowel: **raer**, *rayó*; **creer**, *creyó, creyeron*; **roer**, *royendo*.

Verbs ending in *guir* drop the *u* from the stem after the *g* when followed by *a* or *o*: **distinguir**, *distingo, distinga*.

The verb **delinquir** changes the *qu* to *c* when followed by *a* or *o*: *delinco, delincamos*.

When the past part. in *ido* is immediately preceded by *a, e,* or *o*, the *i* in *ido* bears the written accent: *caído, leído, oído*.

Verbs ending in **ñir, ñer, llir,** and **ller** lose the *i* in the Gerund , the third person singular and plural Pret. and throughout the Past Subj.: *bullendo, tañó, ciñó, riñeron*, etc.

All verbs ending in *uir*, change the *i* into *y* before *a, e,* and *o*: **argüir**: (Pres.) *arguyo, arguyes, arguye, arguyen*; (Imper.) *arguye*; (Subj.) *arguya, arguyas, arguya, arguyamos, arguyáis, arguyan*; (Pret.) *argüí, argüiste, arguyó, argüimos, argüisteis, arguyeron*; (pres. part.) *arguyendo*.

IRREGULAR VERBS

NOTE. The past and future subjunctive may be formed from the third person plural of the preterit: hubieron: hubiera, -iese; -iere; dijeron: dijera, -ese; -ere.

1st group

Some verbs with an *e* in the penultimate syllable, change stressed *e* into *ie*:

acertar (Pres. Indic.) *acierto, aciertas, acierta, aciertan*
(Imper.) *acierta, acierte Vd., acierten Vds.*
(Subj.) *acierte, aciertes, acierte, acierten.*

Some verbs having an *o* in the penultimate syllable, change stressed *o* into *ue*:

acostar (Pres. Indic.) *acuesto, acuestas, acuesta, acuestan*
(Imper.) *acuesta, acueste Vd., acuesten Vds.*
(Subj.) *acueste, acuestes, acueste, acuesten*

2nd group

Some verbs ending in *ir* and having an *e* in the penultimate syllable, change this into *ie* when stressed and into *i* when unstressed if the following syllable contains *ie, io,* or stressed *a*: **sentir**: (Pres. *Indic.*) *siento, sientes, siente, sienten*; (Imper.) *siente*; (Pres. Subj.) *sienta, sientas, sienta, sintamos, sintáis, sientan*;(pres. part.) *sintiendo*; (Pret.) *sintió, sintieron*.

Some verbs ending in *ir* and having an *o* in the penultimate syllable, follow the same pattern in changing the *o* of the stem into *ue*, or into *u*: *duermo, durmiendo,* etc.

3rd group

Some verbs ending in *ir* and having an *e* in the penultimate syllable have the same irregularity as the *2nd group* but this change is always *e* into *i*: (Pres.) *pido, pides, pide, piden*;(Imper.) *pide*; (Pres. Subj.) *pida, pidas, pida, pidamos, pidáis, pidan*;(pres. part.) *pidiendo*; (Pret.) *pidió, pidieron*.

4th group

Some verbs ending in *acer, ecer, ocer, ucir*, add a *z* before the *c* when followed by *a* or *o*: **conocer**: (Pres.) *conozco*, etc.; (Subj.) *conozca, conozcas, conozcamos, conozcáis, conozcan*.

The verbs **cocer, escocer, torcer** change the *o* of the stem into *ue*, as **acostar**, and also the *c* into *z* before *a* or *o*: (Pres.) *cuezo, cueces*, etc.; (Subj.) *cueza, cuezas, cueza*, etc.

The verbs ending in *ducir*, as **conducir, reducir, traducir**, etc., have the same irregularity as **conocer**. They also change the *c* into *j*: **conducir**: (Pret.) *conduje, condujiste, condujo, condujimos, condujisteis, condujeron*; (Pres. Subj.) *conduzca, conduzcas, conduzca*, etc.

[1448]

LIST OF COMMON IRREGULAR VERBS

Verb	Group	Verb	Group	Verb	Group
Abastecer	IV	Blanquecer	IV	Denodar	I
Aborrecer	IV	Caber (*V. Note*)		Denostar	I
Acaecer	IV	Caer (*V. Note*)		Dentar	I
Acertar	I	Calentar	I	Derrengar	I
Acollar	I	Canecer	IV	Derretir	III
Acontecer	IV	Carecer	IV	Derrocar	I
Acordar	I	Cegar	I	Desbastecer	IV
Acostar	II	Ceñir	III	Descender	I
Acrecentar	I	Cerner	I	Descollar	I
Adherir	II	Cernir	I	Descordar	I
Adolecer	IV	Cerrar	I	Desertar	I
Adormecer	IV	Cimentar	I	Desmembrar	I
Aducir	IV	Clarecer	IV	Desolar	I
Advertir	II	Cocer	IV and I	Desollar	I
Afollar	I	Colar	I	Despertar	I
Aforar	I	Colegir	III	Desterrar	I
Agradecer	IV	Comedir	III	Desvergonzarse	I
Alborecer	IV	Comenzar	I	Dezmar	I
Alentar	I	Competir	III	Diferir	II
Almorzar	I	Complacer	IV	Digerir	II
Amolar	I	Concebir	III	Discernir	I
Amorecer	IV	Concernir	I	Discordar	I
Amortecer	IV	Concertar	I	Disolver	II
Anochecer	IV	Concordar	I	Divertir	II
Apacentar	I	Condescender	I	Doler	II
Aparecer	IV	Condoler	III	Dormir	III
Apetecer	IV	Conferir	I	Elegir	III
Apostar	I	Confesar	I	Embellecer	IV
Apretar	I	Conocer	IV	Embermejecer	IV
Aprobar	I	Conseguir	III	Embestir	III
Arrendar	I	Consentir	II	Emblandecer	IV
Arrepentir	II	Consolar	I	Embobecer	IV
Ascender	I	Constreñir	III	Embosquecer	IV
Asentar	II	Contar	I	Embravecer	IV
Asentir	I	Controvertir	IV	Embrutecer	IV
Aserrar	I	Convalecer	II	Emparentar	I
Asir (*V. Note*)		Convertir	III	Empedrar	I
Asolar	I	Corregir	IV	Empequeñecer	IV
Asoldar	I	Costar	I	Empezar	I
Asonar	I	Crecer	IV	Emplastecer	IV
Asosegar	I	Decentar	I	Emplumecer	IV
Atender	I	Decir (*V. Note*)		Empobrecer	IV
Aterrar	I	Defender	II	Empodrecer	IV
Atestar	I	Deferir	I	Emporcar	I
Atontecer	IV	Degollar	I	Enaltecer	IV
Atravesar	I	Demolar	I	Encallecer	IV
Atronar	I	Demostrar	I	Encanecer	IV
Aventar	I	Denegar	I	Encarecer	IV
Avergonzar	I				

Verb	Group	Verb	Group	Verb	Group
Encender	I	Fortalecer	IV	Probar	I
Encerrar	I	Forzar	I	Proferir	II
Encomendar	I	Fregar	I	Quebrar	I
Encontrar	I	Gemir	III	Reblandecer	IV
Encorar	I	Gobernar	I	Recordar	I
Encordar	I	Guarecer	IV	Recostar	I
Encornar	I	Guarnecer	IV	Recrudecer	IV
Encovar	I	Haber (*V. Note*)		Referir	II
Encrudecer	IV	Hacendar	I	Regar	I
Endurecer	IV	Heder	I	Regimentar	I
Enflaquecer	IV	Helar	I	Regir	III
Enfranquecer	IV	Henchir	III	Regoldar	I
Enfurecer	IV	Hender	I	Reír (*V. Note*)	
Engrandecer	IV	Heñir	III	Rejuvenecer	IV
Engrosar	I	Herir	II	Relentecer	IV
Engrumecer	IV	Herrar	I	Remanecer	IV
Enhestar	I	Hervir	II	Remendar	I
Enlenzar	I	Holgar	I	Rendir	III
Enloquecer	IV	Hollar	I	Renovar	I
Enmendar	I	Humedecer	IV	Reñir	III
Enmollecer	IV	Inferir	II	Repetir	III
Enmudecer	IV	Ingerir	II	Requebrar	I
Ennoblecer	IV	Invernar	I	Requerir	II
Enorgullecer	IV	Invertir	II	Rescontrar	I
Enrarecer	IV	Investir	III	Resollar	I
Enriquecer	IV	Ir (*V. Note*)		Resplandecer	IV
Enrobustecer	IV	Jugar	I	Restablecer	IV
Enrodar	I	Languidecer	IV	Restregar	I
Enrojecer	IV	Llover	I	Revejecer	IV
Enronquecer	IV	Manifestar	I	Reventar	I
Enroñecer	IV	Medir	III	Reverdecer	IV
Ensandecer	IV	Melar	I	Revolcar	I
Ensangrentar	I	Mentar	I	Robustecer	IV
Ensoberbecer	IV	Mentir	II	Rodar	I
Ensordecer	IV	Merecer	IV	Rogar	I
Entallecer	IV	Merendar	I	Saber (*V. Note*)	
Entender	I	Moblar	I	Salpimentar	I
Entenebrecer	IV	Mohecer	IV	Sarmentar	I
Enternecer	IV	Moler	I	Satisfacer (*V. Note*)	
Enterrar	I	Morder	I	Segar	I
Entesar	I	Morir	II	Seguir	III
Entontecer	IV	Mostrar	I	Sembrar	I
Entorpecer	IV	Mover	I	Sementar	I
Entortar	I	Nacer	IV	Sentar	I
Entristecer	IV	Negar	I	Sentir	II
Entullecer	IV	Negrecer	IV	Ser (*V. Note*)	
Entumecer	IV	Nevar	I	Serrar	I
Envanecer	IV	Obedecer	IV	Servir	III
Envejecer	IV	Obscurecer	IV	Solar	I
Enverdecer	IV	Ofrecer	IV	Soldar	I
Envestir	III	Oler (*V. Note*)		Soler (Defective)	I
Envilecer	IV	Oscurecer	IV	Soltar	I
Erguir (*V. Note*)		Pacer	IV	Sonar	I
Errar (*V. Note*)		Padecer	IV	Soñar	I
Escarmentar	I	Palidecer	IV	Sosegar	I
Escarnecer	IV	Parecer	IV	Soterrar	I
Esclarecer	IV	Pedir	III	Sugerir	II
Escocer	IV and I	Pensar	I	Temblar	I
Esforzar	I	Perder	I	Tender	I
Establecer	IV	Permanecer	IV	Tener (*V. Note*)	
Estar (*V. Note*)		Perniquebrar	I	Tentar	I
Estregar	I	Pertenecer	IV	Teñir	III
Estremecer	IV	Pervertir	II	Torcer	I and IV
Estreñir	III	Plastecer	IV	Tostar	I
Expedir	III	Plegar	I	Traer (*V. Note*)	
Extender	I	Poblar	I	Transferir	II
Fallecer	IV	Poner (*V. Note*)		Trascender	I
Favorecer	IV	Preferir	II	Trascordarse	I
Fenecer	IV	Preterir	II	Trasegar	I
Florecer	IV	Prevalecer	IV	Trastrocar	I
Follar	I				

Verb	Group	Verb	Group	Verb	Group
Travesar	I	Ventar	I	Volar	I
Trocar	I	Ver (*V. Note*)		Volcar	I
Tronar	I	Verdecer	IV	Volver	I
Tropezar	I	Verter	I	Yacer (*V. Note*)	
Venir (*V. Note*)		Vestir	III	Zaherir	II

Verbs with two Passive Participles

Some verbs have two passive participles, regular, and irregular (rarely used except as adjectives or nouns). A list of those in common use follows: bendecir (to bless), bendecido, *bendito*; convertir (to convert), convertido, *converso*; despertar (to awake), despertado, *despierto*; elegir (to choose), elegido, *electo*; expresar (to express), expresado, *expreso*; fijar (to fix), fijado, *fijo*; incluir (to include), incluido, *incluso*; prender (to arrest), prendido, *preso*; soltar (to loosen), soltado, *suelto*; suspender (to suspend), suspendido, *suspenso*, etc. (Irregular participles shown in italics.)

NOTE. These verbs have irregularities which are confined to them and their compounds:

Asir	Indic. Pres.	asgo, ases, ase; asimos, asís, asen.
	Subj.	asga, asgas, asga; asgamos, asgáis, asgan.
	Imper.	ase tú, asga él; asgamos, asid, asgan.
Caber	Indic. Pres.	quepo, cabes, cabe; cabemos, cabéis, caben.
	Past Def.	cupe, cupiste, cupo; cupimos, cupisteis, cupieron.
	Subj.	quepa, quepas, quepa; quepamos, quepáis, quepan.
	Imper.	cabe tú, quepa él; quepamos, cabed, quepan.
Caer	Indic. Pres.	caigo, caes, cae; caemos, caéis, caen.
	Past. Def.	caí, caiste, cayó; caimos, caisteis, cayeron.
	Subj.	caiga, caigas, caiga; caigamos, caigáis, caigan.
	Imper.	cae tú, caiga él; caigamos, caed, caigan.
Decir	Indic. Pres.	digo, dices, dice; decimos, decís, dicen.
	Past Def.	dije, dijiste, dijo; dijimos, dijisteis, dijeron.
	Subj.	diga, etc.
	Imper.	di tú, diga él, etc.
Erguir	Indic. Pres.	yergo, yergues, yergue; erguimos, erguís, yerguen.
	Past Def.	erguí, erguiste, irguió; erguimos, erguisteis, irguieron.
	Subj.	yerga, yergas, yerga; irgamos, irgáis, yergan.
	Imper.	yergue tú, yerga él; irgamos, erguid, yergan.
Errar	Indic. Pres.	yerro, yerras, yerra; erramos, erráis, yerran.
	Subj.	yerre, yerres, yerre; erremos, erréis, yerren.
	Imper.	yerra tú, yerre él; erremos, errad, yerren.
Estar	Indic. Pres.	estoy, estás, está; estamos, estáis, están.
	Past Def.	estuve, estuviste, estuvo; estuvimos, estuvisteis, estuvieron.
	Subj.	esté, estés, esté; estemos, estéis, estén.
	Imper.	está tú, esté él, etc.
Haber	Indic. Pres.	he, has, ha; hemos, habéis, han.
	Past Def.	hube, hubiste, hubo; hubimos, hubisteis, hubieron.
	Subj.	haya, hayas, haya; hayamos, hayáis, hayan.
Ir	Indic. Pres.	voy, vas, va; vamos, vais, van.
	Past Def.	fuí, fuiste, fué; fuimos, fuisteis, fueron.
	Subj.	vaya, vayas, vaya; vayamos, vayáis, vayan.
	Imper.	ve tú, vaya él; vamos, id, vayan.
	Imperf.	iba, ibas, iba; íbamos, ibais, iban.
Oler	Indic. Pres.	huelo, hueles, huele; olemos, oléis, huelen.
	Subj.	huela, huelas, huela; olamos, oláis, huelan.
	Imper.	huele tú, huela él; olamos, oled, huelan.
Poner	Indic. Pres.	pongo, pones, pone; ponemos, ponéis, ponen.
	Past Def.	puse, pusiste, puso; pusimos, pusisteis, pusieron.
	Imper.	pon tú, ponga él; pongamos, poned, pongan.
Reír	Indic. Pres.	río, ríes, ríe; reímos, reís, ríen.
	Past Def.	reí, reíste, rió; reímos, reísteis, rieron.
	Subj.	ría, rías, ría; riamos, riáis, rían.
	Imper.	ríe tú, ría él; riamos, reíd, rían.
	Imperf.	reía, reías, reía; reíamos, reíais, reían.
Saber	Indic. Pres.	sé, sabes, etc.
	Past Def.	supe, supiste, supo; supimos, supisteis, supieron.
	Subj.	sepa, sepas, sepa; sepamos, sepáis, sepan.

Satisfacer	Indic. Pres.	satisfago, satisfaces, satisface; satisfacemos, satisfacéis, satisfacen.
	Past Def.	satisfice, satisficiste, satisfizo; satisficimos, satisficiste, satisficieron.
	Imper.	satisfaz *or* satisface tú, satisfaga él, etc.
Ser	Indic. Pres.	soy, eres, es; somos, sois, son.
	Past Def.	fuí, fuiste, fué; fuimos, fuisteis, fueron.
	Subj.	sea, seas, sea; seamos, seáis, sean.
	Imper.	sé tú, sea él, etc.
	Imperf.	era, eras, era; éramos, erais, eran.
Tener	Indic. Pres.	tengo, tienes, etc.
	Past Def.	tuve, tuviste, tuvo; tuvimos, tuvisteis, tuvieron.
	Subj.	tenga, tengas, tenga; tengamos, tengáis, tengan.
	Imper.	ten tú, tenga él, etc.
Traer	(Conjugated as **caer** *exc*. Past Def. traje, -jiste, -jo; -jimos, -jisteis, -jeron)
Venir	Indic. Pres.	vengo, vienes, etc.
	Past Def.	vine, viniste, vino; vinimos, vinisteis, vinieron.
	Subj.	venga, vengas, venga; vengamos, vengáis, vengan.
	Imper.	ven tú, venga él, etc.
Ver	Indic. Pres.	veo, ves, ve; vemos, veis, ven.
	Past Def.	vi, viste, etc.
	Subj.	vea, veas, vea; veamos, veáis, vean.
	Imperf.	veía, veías, veía; veíamos, veíais, veían.
Yacer	Indic. Pres.	yazco, yazgo or yago; yaces, yace; yacemos, yacéis, yacen.
	Subj.	yazca, yazga or yaga; yazcas, etc.
	Imper.	yace tú or yaz.

NOTE. These verbs have irregular stems throughout the future and conditional:

		Future	Conditional
Caber	cabr-	é	ía
		ás	ías
		á	ía
		emos	íamos
		éis	íais
		án	ían

Decir	dir-
Haber	habr-
Hacer	har-
Poder	podr-
Poner	pondr-
Querer	querr-
Saber	sabr-
Salir	saldr-
Tener	tendr-
Valer	valdr-
Venir	vendr-

STRONG AND ANOMALOUS ENGLISH VERBS

*=obsolete.　　*A=obsolete, but still used adjectivally.　　†=becoming obsolete.　　R=rare.　　S=slang.

Pres. Inf.	Imperf. Indic.	Past Part.	Pres. Inf.	Imperf. Indic.	Past Part.
abide	abode	abode	fall	fell	fallen
arise	arose	arisen	feed	fed	fed
awake	awoke *or* awaked	awoke *or* awaked	feel	felt	felt
be *Pres. Indic.* am	was	been	fight	fought	fought
			find	found	found
bear	bore *bare	borne *or* born	flee	fled	fled
beat	beat	beaten	fling	flung	flung
become	became	become	fly	flew	flown
beget	begot *begat	begotten	forbear	forbore	forborne
begin	began	begun	forbid	forbade *or* forbad *forbid	forbidden *forbid
bend	bent *bended	bent *A bended[1]	forget	forgot	forgotten *forgot
bereave	bereaved *or* bereft	bereaved *or* bereft	forgive	forgave	forgiven
			forsake	forsook	forsaken
beseech	besought R beseeched	besought R beseeched	freeze	froze	frozen
			geld	gelded *or* gelt	gelded *or* gelt
*bestead	*bestead	*bestead	get	got *gat	got *A gotten[5]
bestride	bestrode *bestrid	bestridden *bestrid	gird	girded *or* girt	girded *or* girt
			give	gave	given
bid	bade †bid	bidden *bid	go	went	gone
bide	bode *or* bided	bided	grind	ground	ground
bind	bound	bound *A bounden[2]	grow	grew	grown
bite	bit	bitten	hang (to suspend. In the meaning 'to execute by hanging', the verb is weak)	hung	hung
bleed	bled	bled			
blow	blew	blown S blowed			
break	broke *brake	broken			
breed	bred	bred			
bring	brought	brought			
build	built *builded	built *builded	have	had	had
burn	burnt *or* burned	burnt *or* burned	hear	heard	heard
burst	burst	burst	heave	heaved *hove	heaved *hove
buy	bought	bought	hew	hewed	hewn *or* hewed
Pres. Indic. can	could	——	hide	hid	hidden *hid
cast	cast	cast	hit	hit	hit
catch	caught	caught	hold	held	held
chide	chid	chidden *chid	hurt	hurt	hurt
choose	chose	chosen	keep	kept	kept
cleave (*v.t.* to split)	cleft *clove	cleft *A cloven[3]	kneel	knelt *kneeled	knelt *kneeled
			knit	knitted *or* knit	knitted *or* knit[6]
cleave (*v.i.* to cling)	cleaved *clave	cleaved	know	knew	known
			lade	laded	laded *or* laden[7]
			lay	laid	laid
cling	clung	clung	lead	led	led
clothe	clothed †clad	clothed †clad	lean	leant *or* leaned	leant *or* leaned
come	came	come	leap	leapt *or* leaped	leapt *or* leaped
cost	cost	cost	learn	learnt *or* learned	learnt *or* learned
creep	crept	crept	leave	left	left
crow	crowed *or* †crew	crowed	lend	lent	lent
cut	cut	cut	let	let	let
dare	dared *durst	dared	lie (to recline. In the meaning 'to prevaricate', the verb is weak)	lay	lain
deal	dealt *dealed	dealt *dealed			
dig	dug *digged	dug *digged			
do	did	done			
draw	drew	drawn			
dream	dreamt *or* dreamed	dreamt *or* dreamed	light	lit *or* lighted	lit *or* lighted
			lose	lost	lost
drink	drank *drunk	drunk *A drunken[4]	make	made	made
			Pres. Indic. may	might	——
drive	drove	driven	mean	meant	meant
dwell	dwelt	dwelt *dwelled	meet	met	met
eat	ate *or* eat	eaten	melt	melted	melted *A molten[8]

[1] On *bended* knees.　　　[2] It is his *bounden* duty.　　　[3] *Cloven* hoof.　　　[4] A *drunken* man.
[5] Ill-*gotten* gains.　　　[6] Well-*knit*.　　　[7] *Laden* with corn.　　　[8] *Molten* metal.

[1453]

Pres. Inf.	Imperf. Indic.	Past Part.	Pres. Inf.	Imperf. Indic.	Past Part.
mow	mowed	mowed or mown	spell	spelt or spelled	spelt or spelled
Pres. Indic. must[1]	——		spend	spent	spent
pay	paid	paid	spill	spilt or spilled	spilt or spilled
pen (to confine. In the meaning 'to write', the verb is weak)	penned or pent	penned or pent	spin	spun *span	spun
			spit (to expectorate. In the meaning 'to put on a spit', the verb is weak)	spat †spit	spit
put	put	put			
quit	quitted or quit	quitted or quit	split	split	split
——	*quoth		spread	spread	spread
read	read	read	spring	sprang	sprung
rend	rent	rent		R sprung	
rid	rid	rid	stand	stood	stood
ride	rode	ridden *rode	stave	staved or stove	staved or stove
ring	rang *rung	rung	steal	stole	stolen
rise	rose	risen	stick	stuck	stuck
rive	rived	riven or rived	sting	stung *stang	stung
run	ran	run	stink	stank or stunk	stunk
saw	sawed	sawn R sawed	strew	strewed	strewed
say	said	said			*A strewn
see	saw	seen	stride	strode *strid	stridden
seek	sought	sought	strike	struck	struck
sell	sold	sold			*A stricken[5]
send	sent	sent	string	strung	strung
set	set	set	strive	strove	striven
shake	shook	shaken *shook		*strived	*strove
Pres. Indic. shall[2]	should	——	strow[6]	strowed	strown or strowed
shape	shaped	shaped *shapen	swear	swore	sworn
shear	sheared *shore	sheared	sweep	swept	swept
		*A shorn[3]	swell	swelled	swollen or swelled
shed	shed	shed	swim	swam *swum	swum
shew R	shewed R	shewn or shewed R	swing	swung *swang	swung
shine	shone	shone	take	took	taken
shoe	shod	shod	teach	taught	taught
shoot	shot	shot	tear	tore	torn
show	showed	shown or showed	tell	told	told
shrink	shrank or shrunk	shrunk	think	thought	thought
		*A shrunken	thrive	thrive or	thrived or
shut	shut	shut		throve	thriven
sing	sang †sung	sung	throw	threw	thrown
sink	sank †sunk	sunk *A sunken[4]	thrust	thrust	thrust
sit	sat *sate	sat *sate	tread	trod	trodden
slay	slew	slain	wake	woke or waked	waked or woke
sleep	slept	slept	wax	waxed	waxed *waxen
slide	slid	slid	wear	wore	worn
sling	slung	slung	weave	wove R weaved	woven
slink	slunk *slank	slunk			*A wove[7]
slit	slit	slit	weep	wept	wept
smell	smelt or smelled	smelt or smelled	wet	wetted or wet	wetted or wet
smite	smote	smitten	will	would	——
sow	sowed	sown or sowed	win	won	won
speak	spoke *spake	spoken	wind	wound	wound
speed	sped or speeded	sped or speeded	work	worked or	worked or
				wrought	wrought
			wring	wrung	wrung
			write	wrote	written

[1] Used as an auxiliary verb only, and has no inflections.   [2] Used as auxiliaries only.   [3] A *shorn* sheep.
[4] *Sunken* cheeks.   [5] Well-*stricken* in years.   [6] Obsolete form of strew.   [7] Vellum-*wove* paper.

COMMON SPANISH ABBREVIATIONS

A.	Alteza; Aprobado (en examen)—*Pass*
(a)	alias
@	arroba
@@	arrobas
AA.	Altezas; autores
ab.	abad
ab.^{l}	abril
A.C. *or* A. de C.	Año de Cristo
a/f	(*com.*) a favor—*in favor*
af.^{mo}	afectísimo
ag.^{to}	agosto
alc.^{de}	alcalde
am.^{o}	amigo
ap.	aparte; apóstol
art. *or* art.^{o}	artículo
arz. *or* arzbpo.	arzobispo
at.^{to}	atentísimo
Av.	Avenida
B.	Beato; Bueno (en examen)—*Good, or Credit*
B.L.M. *or* b.l.m.	besa la mano
B.L.P. *or* b.l.p.	besa los pies
B.^{mo} Padre	Beatísimo Padre
Br. *or* br.	bachiller
c.a.	(*elec.*) corriente alterna—*A.C.*
C.A.E.	Cóbrese al entregar—*C.O.D.*
c.c.	(*elec.*) corriente continua—*D.C.*
c./de	casa de—*care of, c/o*
c.^{a}	compañía
c. *or* cap. *or* cap.^{o}	capítulo
cap.^{n}	capitán
capp.^{n}	capellán
Card.^{l}	Cardenal
C. de J.	Compañía de Jesús
cénts.	céntimos
cf.	confesor; confirma (in old documents)
cg.	centigramo(s)
c.^{ia} *or* cía	compañía
cl.	centilitro(s)
cm.	centímetro(s)
C.M.B. *or* c.m.b.	cuyas manos beso
comp.^{a}	compañía
comps.	compañeros
conv.^{te}	conveniente
corr.^{te}	corriente
C.P.B. *or* c.p.b.	cuyos pies beso
cps.	compañeros
cs.	cuartos; céntimos
c.^{ta}	cuenta
c.^{to}	cuarto
cts.	cuartos; céntimos
D.	Don
D.^{a}	Doña
DD.	doctores
Dg.	decagramo(s)
dg.	decigramo(s)
dha., dho., dhas., dhos.	dicha, dicho, dichas, dichos
dic.^{e}, 10.e, *or* 10.bre	diciembre
Dl.	decalitro(s)
dl.	decilitro(s)
Dm.	decámetro(s)
dm.	decímetro(s)
D.^{n}	Don
Doct.	Doctor

docum.to	documento
dom.o	domingo
Dr. *or* dr.	doctor
dra., dro., dras., dros.	derecha, derecho, derechas, derechos
E.	este
Em.a	Eminencia
Em.mo *or* Emmo.	Eminentísimo
ENE.	estenordeste
en.o	enero
E.P.D.	En paz descanse—*R.I.P.*
ESE.	estesudeste
E.U.A. *or* EE.UU. *or* E.U.	Estados Unidos de América—*U.S.A.*
Exc.a	Excelencia
Exc.ma *or* Excma., Exc.mo *or* Excmo.	Excelentísima, Excelentísimo
F.	Fulano
F. de T.	Fulano de Tal
feb.o	febrero
fha., fho.	fecha, fecho
Fr.	Fray, Frey
g. *or* gr.	gramo(s)
Gen.l	general
Gob.no	gobierno
Gob.r	gobernador
gral.	general
hect.	hectárea(s)
Hg.	hectogramo(s)
Hl.	hectolitro(s)
Hm.	hectómetro(s)
igl.a	iglesia
Il.e	Ilustre
Il.ma, Il.mo, *or* Ilma., Ilmo.	Ilustrísima, Ilustrísimo
iz., izq.a, izq.o *or* izq.da, izq.do	izquierda, izquierdo
J.C.	Jesucristo
Jhs.	Jesús
juev.	jueves
Kg.	kilogramo(s)
Kl.	kilolitro(s)
Km.	kilómetro(s)
L.	Licenciado
l.	ley; libro; litro(s)
lbs.	libras
L.do, *or* l.do	licenciado
lun.	lunes
M.	Madre; Majestad; Merced; Maestro; Mediano (en examen)—*Fair*
m.	minuto(s); metro(s); mañana; muerto—*died*
mart.	martes
M.e	Madre
mg.	miligramo(s)
miérc.	miércoles
min.o	ministro
mm.	milímetro(s)
monast.o	monasterio
Mons.	Monseñor
Mr.	Monsieur—*Mr.*
mrd.	merced
M.S.	manuscrito
M.SS.	manuscritos
N.	norte; Notablemente aprobado (en examen)—*Credit*
n.	noche; nacido—*born*
N.aS.a	Nuestra Señora
NE.	nordeste
NNE.	nornordeste
NNO.	nornoroeste
NO.	noroeste
N.o	número: 1o, primero; 2o, segundo, etc.
nov.e, 9.e *or* 9.bre	noviembre
nra., nro., nras., nros.	nuestra, nuestro, nuestras, nuestros
núm. *or* núm.o, núms. *or* núm.s	número, números
N.S.	Nuestro Señor
N.S.J.C.	Nuestro Señor Jesucristo
ntra., ntro., ntras., ntros.	nuestra, nuestro, nuestras, nuestros

O.	oeste
ob. *or* obpo.	obispo
oct.ᵉ, 8.ᵉ *or* 8.bre	octubre
ONO.	oesnoroeste
onz.	onza
OSO.	oessudoeste
P.	Papa; Padre; Pregunta
P.A.	Por ausencia; Por autorización
p.ᵃ	para
pág., págs	página, páginas
P.D.	posdata—*P.S.*
P.ᵉ	Padre
p.ej.	por ejemplo
P.M.	Padre Maestro
P.O.	Por orden
P.P.	Porte pagado; Por poder (*law*)
p. p.do	próximo pasado
p.ʳ	por
prov.ᵃ	provincia
ps.	pesos
ptas. *or* pts.	pesetas
Q.B.S.M. *or* q.b.s.m.	que besa su mano
Q.B.S.P. *or* q.b.s.p.	que besa sus pies
Q.D.G. *or* q.D.g.	que Dios guarde
q.ᵉ	que
q.e.g.e.	que en gloria esté
q.e.p.d.	que en paz descanse—R.I.P.
q.ⁿ	quien
q.s.g.h.	que santa gloria haya
R.	Reverendo; Reverencia; Respuesta; Reprobado (*obs.*, en examen —*Fail, Suspended*)
Rda. M.	Reverenda Madre
Rdo. P.	Reverendo Padre
R.ˡ	Real
rte.	remite *or* remitente—sender, from
R.M.	Reverenda Madre
R.P.	Reverendo Padre
R.ˢ	Reales
S.	San *or* Santo; sur; Sobresaliente (en examen—*Distinction*)
S.ᵃ	Señora
S.A.	Su Alteza; Sudamérica; (*com.*) Sociedad Anónima—*Co. Ltd.*
sáb.	sábado
S.A.R.	Su Alteza Real
S.A.S.	Su Alteza Serenísima
S.C. *or* s.c.	su casa
S.D.	Se despide
SE.	sudeste
S.E.	Su Excelencia
sept.ᵉ, 7.ᵉ *or* 7.bre	septiembre
serv.º	servicio
set.ᵉ	setiembre
sig.te	siguiente
S.M.	Su Majestad
S.M.B.	Su Majestad Británica
S.M.C.	Su Majestad Católica
S.ⁿ	San
S.N.	Servicio Nacional—*N.S.*
SO.	sudoeste
S.ʳ *or* Sr.	Señor
Sra., Sras.	Señora, Señoras
Sres. *or* S.res	Señores
Sr.ta *or* Srta.	Señorita
S.S.	Su Santidad
S.S.ᵃ	Su Señoría
SS.AA.	Sus Altezas
SSE.	sudsudeste
SS.MM.	Sus Majestades
SS.mo	Santísimo
SS.mo P.	Santísimo Padre
SS.no	escribano
SSO.	sudsudoeste
S.S.S.	su seguro servidor

Sta.	Santa; (*frequently*) Señorita
Sto.	Santo
t.	tarde
test.º	testigo
t.º *or* tom.	tomo
tpo.	tiempo
U. *or* Ud., Uds.	Usted, Ustedes
V. *or* Vd., Vds.	Usted, Ustedes
V.A.	Vuestra Alteza
V.E.	Vuestra Excelencia
vg.	verbigracia—*e.g.*; virgen
v.g. *or* v.gr.	verbigracia—*e.g.*
vier.	viernes
V.M.	Vuestra Majestad
V.º B.º	Visto Bueno—*O.K.*
V.R.	Vuestra Reverencia
vra., vro., vras., vros.	vuestra, vuestro, vuestras, vuestros
v.ta, v.to	vuelta, vuelto
VV.	ustedes
xpiano	cristiano—*Xtian.*
Xpo.	Cristo
xptiano.	cristiano—*Xtian.*
Xpto.	Cristo

COMMON ENGLISH ABBREVIATIONS

A

a.	acre(s).
A.	alto (*Mus.*), ampere.
A 1	first class (*of ships, and fig.*).
A.A.	Automobile Association, Anti-Aircraft.
A.A.A.	Amateur Athletic Association, Anti-Aircraft Artillery, Agricultural Adjustment Administration (*Amer.*).
A.A.F.	Auxiliary Air Force, American Air Force.
A.A. of A.	Automobile Association of America.
a.a.r.	against all risks.
A.B.	able-bodied seaman.
A.B.A.	Amateur Boxing Association.
abbr.	abbreviation.
A.B.C.	Aerated Bread Company, American *or* Australian Broadcasting Company.
A.B.C.A.	Army Bureau of Current Affairs.
abl.	ablative.
Abp	archbishop.
abr.	abridged.
abs.	absolute.
A.C.	alternating current (*Elec.*), Alpine Club, Appeal Court.
A/C	aircraftsman (*Av.*).
a/c	account (*C.L.*).
A.C.A.	Associate of the Institute of Chartered Accountants.
A.C.C.	Allied Control Council.
acc.	acceptance, accepted, account, accusative, accompanied, according.
acct	account (*C.L.*).
A.C.P.	Associate of the College of Preceptors.
A.C.T.	Australian Capital Territory.
ad.	advertisement.
a.d.	after date (*C.L.*).
A.D.	Anno Domini.
A.D.A.	Atom Development Administration.
A.D.C.	aide-de-camp, Army Dental Corps.
adj.	adjective.
Adm.	Admiralty, admiral.
A.D.M.S.	Assistant Director of Medical Services (*Mil.*).
adv.	adverb, advocate.
ad val.	to the value of (*C.L.*).
advt	advertisement.
A.E.C.	Army Education Corps, Atomic Energy Commission.
A.E.F.	American Expeditionary Force.
A.E.U.	Amalgamated Engineering Union.
A.F.	audio frequency (*Rad.*).
A.F.A.	Amateur Football Association.
A.F.C.	Air Force Cross.
A.F.L.	American Federation of Labor.
A.F.M.	Air Force Medal.
A.F.N.	American Forces Network (*Rad.*).

A.F.S.	Auxiliary Fire Service.
A.F.V.	armoured fighting vehicle.
A.G.	Attorney-General (*Law*), Adjutant-General (*Mil.*), air gunner (*Av.*).
agr.	agriculture.
agt	agent (*C.L.*).
A.I.C.	Associate of the Institute of Chemistry.
A.I.C.E.	Associate of the Institute of Civil Engineers.
A.I.D.	Army Intelligence Department.
a.l.	autograph letter.
Ala.	Alabama.
A.L.A.	American Library Association.
Alas.	Alaska.
Ald.	alderman.
alg.	algebra.
alt	altitude.
a.m.	in the morning.
A.M.	Air Ministry, Albert Medal, Master of Arts (*Amer.*).
Am.	America, American.
A.M.C.	Army Medical Corps.
A.M.D.G.	to the greater glory of God.
Amer.	America, American.
A.M.G.(O.T.)	Allied Military Government (of Occupied Territory).
A.M.I.C.E.	Associate Member of the Institute of Civil Engineers.
A.M.I.E.E.	Associate Member of the Institute of Electrical Engineers.
A.M.I.Mech.E.	Associate Member of the Institute of Mechanical Engineers.
ammo	(*coll.*) ammunition.
amt	amount.
anal.	analogy, analogous.
anat.	anatomy, anatomical.
anc.	ancient.
angl.	in English.
ann.	annual.
anon.	anonymous.
ans.	answer.
Anzac	Australia and New Zealand Army Corps.
A.O.	Army Order.
a/o	to the account of (*C.L.*).
A.O.D.	Army Ordnance Department.
A. of F.	Admiral of the Fleet.
Ap.	apostle.
A.P.	Associated Press.
A/P	account purchase (*C.L.*)
A.P.D.	Army Pay Department.
A.P.O.	Army Post Office.
app.	appendix, apparently, appointed, apprentice.
appro.	approbation, approval.
approx.	approximate(ly).
A.P.T.C.	Army Physical Training Corps.
A.R.	annual return, in the year of the reign.
A.R.A.	Associate of the Royal Academy.
arch.	archaic, archipelago.

archit.	architecture.
A.R.C.	American Red Cross.
A.R.C.M.	Associate of the Royal College of Music.
A.R.I.B.A.	Associate of the Royal Institute of British Architects.
arith.	arithmetic.
Ariz.	Arizona.
Ark.	Arkansas.
A.R.P.	Air Raid Precautions.
arr.	arranged, arrival.
A.R.S.A.	Associate of the Royal Scottish Academy, Associate of the Royal Society of Arts.
art.	article, artificial, artillery.
A/S	account sales (*C.L.*).
A.-S.	Anglo-Saxon.
A.S.A.	Amateur Swimming Association.
asdic	Anti-Submarine Detection Investigation Committee (*used as name of a type of hydrophone equipment*).
A.S.E.	Amalgamated Society of Engineers.
A.S.L.E. & F.	Amalgamated Society of Locomotive Engineers and Firemen.
A.S.R.	air-sea rescue (*Mil.*).
A.S.R.S.	Amalgamated Society of Railway Servants.
Ass.	assistant.
assoc.	association.
asst	assistant.
astr(on).	astronomy.
A.T.	anti-tank, air temperature.
A.T.C.	Air Training Corps.
atm.	atmospheres.
A.T.S.	Auxiliary Territorial Service (*Mil.*).
A.T.T.	American Telephone and Telegraph Company.
Att.-Gen.	Attorney-General.
at. wt	atomic weight.
Å.U.	Ångström Unit (*Phys.*).
aux(il).	auxiliary.
A.V.	Authorized Version (*B.*).
a/v	ad valorem (*C.L.*).
av.	average.
avdp.	avoirdupois.
Ave.	avenue.
A.W.O.L.	absent without leave (*Mil.*).
A.W.V.S.	American Women's Voluntary Service (*Mil.*).

B

B	black (*on pencils*), bishop (*chess*).
b.	bowled (*Crick.*), born.
B.A.	Bachelor of Arts, British Association, British Academy.
bact.	bacteriology.
bal.	balance.
Bap(t).	Baptist.
bar.	barometer, barrister.
Bart	Baronet.
Bart's	Saint Bartholomew's Hospital.
batt.	battalion, battery (*Mil.*).
BB	double black (*on pencils*).
B.B.C.	British Broadcasting Corporation.
B.C.	before Christ, British Columbia.
B.Ch.	Bachelor of Surgery.
B.Com.	Bachelor of Commerce.
bd	bound.
B.D.	Bachelor of Divinity.
Bde	Brigade (*Mil.*).

bds	boards.
b.e.	bill of exchange (*C.L.*).
B.E.	Board of Education (*obs.*).
B/E	bill of exchange (*C.L.*).
B.E.A.	British European Airways.
Beds.	Bedfordshire.
B.E.F.	British Expeditionary Force.
Benelux	Belgium, Netherlands, and Luxemburg.
Beng.	Bengal.
Berks.	Berkshire.
B.E.S.A.	British Engineering Standards Association.
b.f. or B.F.	bloody fool (*vulg.*).
b/f	brought forward (*C.L.*).
B.F.B.S.	British and Foreign Bible Society.
B.F.N.	British Forces Network (*Rad.*).
B'ham	Birmingham.
b.h.p.	brake horse power.
B.I.	British India (*obs.*).
Bib.	Bible.
bibliog.	bibliography.
B.I.F.	British Industries Fair.
biog.	biography.
biol.	biology.
B.I.S.	Bank for International Settlements.
B.I.S.N.C.	British India Steam Navigation Company.
bk	book, bank.
bkg	banking.
bkt	basket.
bl	bale, barrel.
B.L.	Bachelor of Law.
B/L	bill of lading (*C.L.*).
bldg	building.
B.Litt.	Bachelor of Letters.
B.LL.	Bachelor of Laws.
B.M.	Bachelor of Medicine, British Museum, Brigade Major.
B.M.A.	British Medical Association.
B.Mus.	Bachelor of Music.
Bn	battalion (*Mil.*).
B.N.C.	Brasenose College (Oxford).
b.o.	buyer's option (*C.L.*), (*coll.*) body odour.
B/O	branch office (*C.L.*).
B.O.A.	British Optical Association, British Olympic Association.
B.O.A.C.	British Overseas Airways Corporation.
B. of E.	Board of Education (*obs.*).
B.O.P.	Boys' Own Paper.
bor.	borough.
bos'n	boatswain.
bot.	botany.
B.O.T.	Board of Trade.
b.p.	bills payable (*C.L.*), boiling point, below par.
B.P.	British Pharmacopœia.
Bp	bishop.
b.pl.	birthplace.
b.r.	bills receivable (*C.L.*).
B.R.	British Railways.
B.R.C.S.	British Red Cross Society.
b.rec.	see *b.r.*
'brev.	brevet (*Mil.*).
Brig.	Brigadier (*Mil.*).
Brig.-Gen.	Brigadier-General (*Mil.*).
Brit.	Britain, British.
bro.	brother, *bros.*, brothers.
b.s.	balance-sheet, bill of sale (*C.L.*).

B/S	bill of sale (*C.L.*).
B.S.	Bachelor of Surgery, (*Amer.*) Bachelor of Science.
B.S.A.	British South Africa, Birmingham Small Arms Company.
B.S.A.A.	British South American Airways.
B.Sc.	Bachelor of Science.
B.Sc. (Econ.)	Bachelor of Science (in Economics).
B.S.G.	British Standard Gauge.
bsh.	bushel.
bt	bought (*C.L.*).
bt fwd	brought forward (*C.L.*).
Bt	Baronet.
B.Th.U.	British Thermal Unit.
B.T.U.	Board of Trade Unit.
Bucks.	Buckinghamshire.
B.U.P.	British United Press.
Bur. St.	Bureau of Standards (*Amer.*).
B.V.M.	Blessed Virgin Mary (*R.C.*).
B.W.	Black Watch (42nd Highland Regiment).
B.W.G.	Birmingham Wire Gauge.
B.W.I.	British West Indies.
B.W.T.A.	British Women's Temperance Association.

C

c.	cent, centime, cubic, caught (*Crick.*), circa.
C.	Centigrade, Cape, Catholic, Conservative.
C. 3	unfit for military service.
C.A.	Chartered Accountant, Chief Accountant, Confederate Army (*Amer.*), Central America.
C/A	current account (*C.L.*).
Cal.	California.
Cambs.	Cambridgeshire.
Can.	Canada, canon, canto.
c. & b.	caught and bowled (*Crick.*).
Cant.	Canticles, Canterbury.
Cantab.	of Cambridge University.
Cantuar.	of Canterbury (*signature of the Archbishop*).
cap.	capital letter, chapter.
Capt.	Captain.
Card.	Cardinal.
Cards.	Cardiganshire.
Carmarths	Carmarthenshire.
carr. pd	carriage paid (*C.L.*).
cat.	catalogue, catechism.
Cath.	Cathedral, Catholic.
cav.	cavalry.
C.B.	Companion of the Order of the Bath, confined to barracks (*Mil.*), County Borough.
C.B.C.	Canadian Broadcasting Corporation.
C.B.E.	Commander *or* Companion of the Order of the British Empire.
C.B.S.	Columbia Broadcasting System (*Amer.*).
c.c.	cubic centimetre(s).
C.C.	County Council, County Court, Cricket Club, Cycling Club, Caius College (Cambridge), continuous current (*Elec.*).
C.C.C.	Central Criminal Court, Corpus Christi College (Oxford *or* Cambridge).

C.C.G.	Control Commission for Germany.
C.C.I.	International Chamber of Commerce.
C.C.P.	Court of Common Pleas.
c.d.	with dividend (*C.L.*).
C.D.	Chancery Division, Civil Defence.
C.E.	Church of England, Chief Engineer, Civil Engineer.
C.E.B.	Central Electricity Board.
Cels.	Celsius.
Celt.	Celtic.
cent.	hundred, century, central.
Cent.	Centigrade.
cert.	certificate, certified, (*coll.*) certainty.
Cestr.	of Chester (*signature of the Bishop*).
C.F.	Chaplain to the Forces.
cf.	compare.
c.f.i.	cost, freight, and insurance (*C.L.*).
C.G.	coastguard, Consul-General, Commissary-General, Coldstream Guards.
C.G.H.	Cape of Good Hope.
C.G.M.	Conspicuous Gallantry Medal.
C.G.S.	Chief of the General Staff, centimetre-gramme-second.
C.H.	Companion of Honour, clearing house, custom house.
ch.	chapter, chief, chain (*measure*).
Ch.	Church, Chancery.
Chamb.	Chamberlain.
chap.	chapter.
Chap.	Chaplain.
Ch.B.	Bachelor of Surgery.
Ch.Ch.	Christ Church (Oxford).
chem.	chemistry, chemical.
Ches.	Cheshire.
Ch.M.	Master of Surgery.
Chron.	Chronicles (*B.*).
C.I.	Channel Islands, Imperial Order of the Crown of India, certificate of insurance (*C.L.*).
C.I.C.	Counter-Intelligence Corps (*Amer.*).
Cicestr.	of Chichester (*signature of the Bishop*).
C.I.D.	Criminal Investigation Department.
C.I.E.	Companion of the Order of the Indian Empire.
c.i.f.c.	cost, insurance, freight, and commission (*C.L.*).
C.I.G.S.	Chief of the Imperial General Staff.
C.I.Mech.E.	Companion of the Institute of Mechanical Engineers.
C.-in-C.	Commander-in-Chief.
C.I.O.	Congress of Industrial Organizations (*Amer.*).
cit.	citation, cited.
C.I.V.	City Imperial Volunteers (*Mil.*).
civ.	civil, civilian.
C.J.	Chief Justice.
cl.	clause, class.
Clar.	Clarendon (*Typ.*).
C.L.B.	Church Lads' Brigade.
c.m.	by reason of death.
C.M.	Corresponding Member, Certified Master (*Naut.*), Master of Surgery.
Cmd.	Command Paper.
Cmdr.	Commodore (*Nav.*).
C.M.G.	Companion of the Order of Saint Michael and Saint George.

C.M.S.	Church Missionary Society.	C.U.	Cambridge University.
C.O.	Colonial Office, commanding officer, conscientious objector.	cub.	cubic.
		cum.	cumulative.
c/o	care of.	Cumb.	Cumberland.
Co.	company, County (Ireland, U.S.A.).	cum div.	with dividend (C.L.).
C.O.D.	cash on delivery.	Cum. Pref.	Cumulative Preference (Shares) (C.L.).
C. of E.	Church of England.		
cogn.	cognate.	C.U.P.	Cambridge University Press.
Col.	Colonel, Colossians (B.), colony, colonial, column, Colorado.	cur.	current, currency.
		C.V.	Common Version (B.).
coll.	colloquial, collection, collective(ly).	C.V.O.	Commander of the Royal Victorian Order.
Coll.	College.		
collat.	collateral.	c.w.o.	cash with order (C.L.).
colloq.	colloquial(ly).	C.W.S.	Co-operative Wholesale Society.
Colo.	Colorado.	cwt	hundredweight.
Col.-Sergt	Colour-Sergeant.	cyl.	cylinder.
com.	common, commerce, commission, comedy.	Cym.	Cymric.
Com.	Commander, Commissioner, Committee, Commodore (Nav.), Communist.		

D

Comdr	Commander.	d.	dead, died, penny, pence, departs, delete, daughter.
comm.	commentary.	D.	Doctor, Duke, diameter.
comp.	compare, comparative, compound.	D/A	deposit account (C.L.).
compl.	complement.	D.A.B.	Dictionary of American Biography.
con.	against, contra, conics.	D.A.G.	Deputy Adjutant General (Mil.).
Con.	Consul.	Dak.	Dakota.
conch.	conchology.	Dan.	Danish, Daniel (B.).
Cong.	Congress, congregation.	dat.	dative.
conj.	conjugation, conjunction, conjunctive.	dau.	daughter.
		d.b.	day-book (C.L.).
Conn.	Connecticut.	D.B.E.	Dame Commander of the Order of the British Empire.
conn.	connected.		
cons.	consonant.	D.C.	direct current (Elec.), from the beginning (Mus.), District of Columbia.
Consols	Consolidated Stock (C.L.).		
Co-op.	(coll.) Co-operative (Stores).		
Cor.	Corinthians (B.), Coroner.	D.C.L.	Doctor of Civil Law.
Corn.	Cornwall, Cornish.	D.C.L.I.	Duke of Cornwall's Light Infantry.
Corp.	Corporal (Mil.), Corporation.	D.C.M.	Distinguished Conduct Medal.
C.O.S.	Charity Organization Society.	D.D.	Doctor of Divinity.
cos	cosine.	d.d.	days after date (C.L.).
cosec	cosecant.	d...d or d—d	damned.
cosmog.	cosmogony, cosmography.	deb.	debenture (C.L.), (coll.) débutante.
cot	cotangent.		
cox	coxswain.	Dec.	December.
C.P.	(Court of) Common Pleas, Court of Probate, Clerk of the Peace, carriage paid (C.L.).	def.	definite, definition.
		Def.	defendant (Law).
		deg.	degree.
c.-p.	candle-power.	Del.	Delaware.
cp.	compare.	dele.	delete.
C.P.C.	Clerk of the Privy Council.	dent.	dental, dentist, dentistry.
Cpl	Corporal (Mil.).	dep.	deputy, departs, departure.
C.P.R.	Canadian Pacific Railway.	dept	department.
C.P.R.E.	Council for the Preservation of Rural England.	deriv.	derivation.
		Deut.	Deuteronomy (B.).
C.P.S.	Keeper of the Privy Seal.	D.F.	Dean of the Faculty, direction finding (Rad.).
Cr	credit, creditor (C.L.), Crown.		
cresc.	rising (Mus.).	D.F.C.	Distinguished Flying Cross.
crim. con.	criminal conversation (Law).	D.F.M.	Distinguished Flying Medal.
C.S.	Civil Service, Christian Science, Court of Session, Common Serjeant (Law), Chemical Society.	dft.	draft.
		D.G.	by the grace of God.
		dial.	dialect, dialogue.
C.S.A.	Confederate States of America (Hist.).	diam.	diameter.
		dict.	dictionary.
C.S.C.	Conspicuous Service Cross.	diff.	different, difference.
C.S.I.	Companion of the Star of India.	dim.	diminishing (Mus.).
C.S.M.	Company Sergeant Major.	dimin.	diminutive.
ct	caught (Crick.), cent.	Dioc.	diocese.
Ct	Count, Court.	Dir.	director.
C.T.	commercial traveller, certified teacher.	dis(c).	discount (C.L.).
		dist.	distance, district, distinguished.
C.T.C.	Cyclists' Touring Club.	div.	divide, dividend.

Div.	Division (*Mil.*).
D.L.	Deputy Lieutenant.
D.L.I.	Durham Light Infantry.
D.Lit.	Doctor of Letters.
D.L.O.	dead-letter office.
D.M.O.	Director of Military Operations.
d...n or *d—n*	damn.
D.N.B.	Dictionary of National Biography.
do.	ditto.
doc.	document, (*coll.*) doctor.
dom.	domestic.
Dom.	Dominus, Dominion.
Dor.	Doric.
D.O.R.A.	Defence of the Realm Act.
dow.	dowager.
doz.	dozen.
D.P.	displaced person.
D.P.H.	Department of *or* Diploma in Public Health.
Dpt	department.
dr.	dram, drawer (*C.L.*).
Dr.	Doctor.
Dr	debtor.
d.S. or *d/s.*	days after sight (*C.L.*).
D.Sc.	Doctor of Science.
D.S.O.	Distinguished Service Order.
d.s.p.	died without issue.
D.S.T.	Daylight Saving Time.
d.t. or *D.T.*	delirium tremens.
Du.	Dutch.
Dubl.	Dublin.
Dunelm.	of Durham (*signature of the Bishop*).
d.v.	God willing.
D.V.S.	Doctor of Veterinary Science.
dwt	pennyweight.
dyn.	dynamics.

E

E.	East.
E. & O.E.	errors and omissions excepted (*C.L.*).
Ebor.	of York (*signature of the Archbishop*).
E.C.	Eastern Central (*London postal district*).
E.C.A.	Economic Cooperation Administration.
Eccl(es).	ecclesiastical, Ecclesiastes (*B.*).
Ecclus.	Ecclesiasticus (*B.*).
econ.	economics.
E.C.U.	English Church Union.
ed.	edition, editor, edited.
E.D.C.	European Defence Community.
E.D.D.	English Dialect Dictionary.
Edin.	Edinburgh.
E.E.	errors excepted (*C.L.*).
E.E.T.S.	Early English Text Society.
e.g.	for example.
E.H.P.	effective horse-power.
E.I.	East Indies.
E.I.C.	East India Company.
elec(tr).	electric(al).
ellipt.	elliptical.
E.M.F.	electromotive force.
E.M.U.	electromagnetic unit(s).
E.N.E.	east-north-east.
Eng.	engineer.
Eng(l).	England, English.
ent(om).	entomology.
E.P.	electroplate.
Ep.	Epistle.

E.P.D.	Excess Profits Duty.
Eph.	Ephesians (*B.*).
Epiph.	Epiphany.
episc.	episcopal.
E.P.U.	European Payment Union.
E.R.P.	European Recovery Programme.
eq.	equal.
equiv.	equivalent.
E.R.	King Edward, Queen Elizabeth.
eschat.	eschatology.
E.S.E.	east-south-east.
esp.	especially.
Esq.	Esquire.
est.	established.
Esth.	Esther (*B.*).
E.S.U.	electrostatic unit(s).
et al.	among others.
etc.	and so on *or* so forth.
ethnol.	ethnology.
etym.	etymology, etymological.
Eucl.	Euclid.
euphem.	euphemism, euphemistic(ally)
ex.	example.
Ex.	Exodus (*B.*).
exam.	examination.
exc.	except(ing).
Exc.	Excellency.
Exch.	Exchange, Exchequer.
excl.	exclusive, excluding.
ex. div.	without dividend (*C.L.*).
ex. int.	without interest (*C.L.*).
Exod.	Exodus (*B.*).
exp.	export.
ext.	external.
Ezek.	Ezekiel (*B.*).

F

f.	farthing, fathom, foot, feminine following, loud (*Mus.*).
F.	Fellow (*Univ.*, *etc.*), Fahrenheit, focal length.
F.A.	Football Association.
f.a.a.	free of all average (*C.L.*).
fac.	facsimile.
facet.	facetious.
Fahr.	Fahrenheit.
fam.	familiar.
F.A.O.	Food and Agriculture Organization.
f.a.s.	free alongside ship (*C.L.*).
F.B.	Fenian Brotherhood, Fire Brigade, Free Baptist.
F.B.A.	Fellow of the British Academy.
F.B.I.	Federal Bureau of Investigation (*Amer.*), Federation of British Industries.
F.C.	Free Church (of Scotland), Football Club.
F.C.A.	Fellow of the Institute of Chartered Accountants.
fcap	foolscap.
F.C.G.I.	Fellow of the City and Guilds of London Institute.
F.C.P.	Fellow of the College of Preceptors.
F.C.S.	Fellow of the Chemical Society.
F.D.	Defender of the Faith.
fem.	feminine.
F.G.	Foot Guards (*Mil.*).
F.G.S.	Fellow of the Geological Society.
F.I.A.	Fellow of the Institute of Actuaries

F.I.A.A.	Fellow of the Incorporated Association of Architects and Surveyors.
F.I.C.	Fellow of the Institute of Chemists.
F.I.D.	Field Intelligence Division (*Mil.*).
fig.	figure, figurative(ly).
fl.	florin, guilder.
Fla	Florida.
flor.	flourished.
F.M.	Field-Marshal.
fm	fathom.
F.M.D.	foot-and-mouth disease.
F.O.	Foreign Office, field-officer (*Mil.*).
fo.	folio.
f.o.b.	free on board (*C.L.*).
f.o.r.	free on rail (*C.L.*).
F.P.	freezing point, fire point, field punishment (*Mil.*), former pupil (*Scots*).
f.p.	foot-pound.
F.Phys.S.	Fellow of the Physical Society.
F.P.S.	Fellow of the Philosophical Society.
Fr.	France, French.
fr.	franc(s).
F.R.A.M.	Fellow of the Royal Academy of Music.
F.R.C.M.	Fellow of the Royal College of Music.
F.R.C.P.	Fellow of the Royal College of Physicians.
F.R.C.S.	Fellow of the Royal College of Surgeons.
F.R.C.V.S.	Fellow of the Royal College of Veterinary Surgeons.
freq.	frequent.
F.R.G.S.	Fellow of the Royal Geographical Society.
Fri.	Friday.
F.R.Hist.S.	Fellow of the Royal Historical Society.
F.R.H.S.	Fellow of the Royal Horticultural Society.
F.R.I.B.A.	Fellow of the Royal Institute of British Architects.
Frisco	(*coll.*) San Francisco.
F.R.S.	Fellow of the Royal Society.
F.R.S.A.	Fellow of the Royal Society of Arts.
F.S.	foot-second.
F.S.A.	Fellow of the Society of Arts.
F.S.A.A.	Fellow of the Society of Incorporated Accountants and Actuaries.
F.S.I.	Fellow of the Surveyors' Institute.
F.S.R.	Field Service Regulations (*Mil.*).
ft	foot, feet.
Ft	fort.
fur.	furlong.
fut.	future.
F.W.B.	four-wheel brakes.
F.W.D.	four-wheel drive.
fwd	forward (*C.L.*).
F.Z.S.	Fellow of the Zoological Society.

G

g.	gramme(s), guinea, gauge.
Ga	Georgia.
G.A.	General Assembly.
Gael.	Gaelic.
gal.	gallon(s).
Gal.	Galatians (*B.*)

gaz.	gazette, gazetteer.
G.B.	Great Britain.
G.B.E.	Knight Grand Cross of the British Empire.
G.B.S.	George Bernard Shaw.
G.C.	George Cross.
G.C.B.	Knight Grand Cross of the Bath.
G.C.F.	greatest common factor (*Math.*).
G.C.I.E.	Knight Grand Commander of the Indian Empire.
G.C.M.	greatest common measure (*Math.*).
G.C.M.G.	Knight Grand Cross of Saint Michael and Saint George.
G.C.S.I.	Knight Grand Commander of the Star of India.
G.C.V.O.	Knight Grand Cross of the Royal Victorian Order.
Gdns	Gardens.
Gds	Guards (*Mil.*).
gen.	gender, genitive.
Gen.	General (*Mil.*), Genesis (*B.*).
gent.	(*coll.*) gentleman.
geog.	geography, geographical.
geol.	geology.
geom.	geometry.
Ger.	Germany, German.
G.F.S.	Girls' Friendly Society.
G.H.Q.	General Headquarters (*Mil.*).
G.I.	Government Issue (*Amer.*), (*coll.*) American soldier.
Gib	Gibraltar.
Gk	Greek.
G.L.	Grand Lodge.
Glam.	Glamorganshire.
Glos.	Gloucestershire.
gloss.	glossary.
G.M.	Grand Master.
G.M.T	Greenwich Mean Time.
gns	guineas.
G.O.	general order (*Mil.*).
G.O.C.	General Officer Commanding (*Mil.*).
G.O.C. in C.	General Officer Commanding in Chief (*Mil.*).
G.O.M.	Grand Old Man (i.e. Gladstone).
G.O.P.	Grand Old Party (i.e. Republican) (*Amer.*).
Goth.	Gothic.
Gov.	Government, Governor.
Gov.-Gen.	Governor-General.
Govt	Government.
G.P.	general practitioner (*Med.*).
G.P.I.	general paralysis of the insane (*Med.*).
G.P.O.	General Post Office.
G.R.	King George.
gr.	grain, gross.
Gr.	Greece, Greek.
gram.	grammar.
grm	gramme(s).
G.R.T.	gross registered tonnage (*Naut.*).
gr. wt	gross weight (*C.L.*).
gs.	guineas.
G.S.	gold standard, General Secretary, General Staff (*Mil.*).
G.S.N.C.	General Steam Navigation Company.
G.S.O.	General Staff Officer (*Mil.*).
Gt. Br.	Great Britain.
guar.	guaranteed.
G.W.R.	Great Western Railway (*obs.*).
gym.	gymnastics, gymnasium.

H

H	hard (*on pencils*).
H.	hydrant.
h.	hour(s).
H.A.	Horse Artillery.
hab.	habitat.
Hab.	Habakkuk (*B.*).
H.A.C.	Honourable Artillery Company.
Hag.	Haggai (*B.*).
h. & c.	hot and cold (water).
Hants.	Hampshire.
Harl.	Harleian.
HB	hard black (*on pencils*).
H.B.C.	Hudson's Bay Company.
H.B.M.	His *or* Her Britannic Majesty.
H.C.	House of Commons.
h.c.	honorary.
hcap	handicap.
H.C.F.	highest common factor.
H.C.J.	High Court of Justice.
hdbk	handbook.
hdqrs	headquarters.
H.E.	high explosive, horizontal equivalent, His Excellency (*not an English title*).
Heb	Hebrew, Hebrews (*B.*).
her.	heraldry.
Herts.	Hertfordshire.
H.F.	high frequency (*Rad.*).
hf	half. *hf-bd*, half-bound. *hf-cf*, half-calf. *hf-cl.*, half-cloth.
H.G.	His *or* Her Grace, Horse Guards.
HH	double hard (*on pencils*).
H.H.	His Holiness.
hhd	hogshead.
HICOG	High Commission(er) for Germany.
H.I.H.	His *or* Her Imperial Highness.
hist.	history, historical.
H.L.	House of Lords.
H.L.I.	Highland Light Infantry.
H.M.	His *or* Her Majesty.
H.M.A.	Headmasters' Association.
H.M.G.	His *or* Her Majesty's Government.
H.M.I.	His *or* Her Majesty's Inspector (*of schools*).
H.M.S.	His *or* Her Majesty's Ship.
H.M.S.O.	His *or* Her Majesty's Stationery Office.
H.O.	Home Office.
ho.	house.
Hon.	Honourable (*in titles*), Honorary.
Hon. Sec.	Honorary Secretary.
hor.	horizon.
horol.	horology.
hort.	horticulture.
Hos.	Hosea (*B.*).
h.p.	horse-power.
H.P.	hire-purchase, high pressure, horse-power, House Physician.
H.Q.	Headquarters.
H.R.	House of Representatives (*Amer.*), Home Rule.
H.R.H.	His *or* Her Royal Highness.
hr(s)	hour(s).
H.S.	House Surgeon.
H.S.H.	His *or* Her Serene Highness.
H.T.	high tension (*Elec.*).
Hunts.	Huntingdonshire.
h.w.	hit wicket (*Crick.*).
hydr.	hydraulics.

I

I(s).	Island(s).
I.A.	Indian Army, Incorporated Accountant.
ib.	in the same place.
i.b.	in bond (*C.L.*).
I.B.A.	Institute of British Architects.
ibid.	in the same place.
i/c	in charge of (*Mil.*).
icht(h).	ichthyology.
icon.	iconography.
I.C.S.	Indian Civil Service.
I.D.	Intelligence Department (*Mil.*).
id.	the same.
i.e.	that is (to say).
I.E.E.	Institute of Electrical Engineers.
I.F.S.	Irish Free State (*1921–37, now* Irish Republic).
I.H.P. *or* i.h.p.	indicated horse-power.
Ill.	Illinois.
ill.	illustrated, illustration.
I.L.O.	International Labour Organization.
I.L.P.	Independent Labour Party.
I.Mech.E.	Institute of Mechanical Engineers.
I.M.F.	International Monetary Fund.
Imp.	Imperial, Emperor *or* Empress.
imper.	imperative.
imperf.	imperfect.
impers.	impersonal.
I.M.S.	Indian Medical Service.
in.	inch(es).
Inc.	Incorporated.
incl.	including, inclusive.
incog.	incognito.
Ind.	India, Indiana.
ind.	independent.
indecl.	indeclinable.
indef.	indefinite.
indic.	indicative.
inf.	below, infantry, infinitive.
infra dig.	(*coll.*) beneath one's dignity.
in loc.	in the place of.
I.N.S.	ship of the Indian Navy.
ins.	insurance.
insc.	inscribed (*C.L.*).
Insp.	Inspector.
inst.	of the present month.
Inst.	Institute.
instr.	instrumental.
int.	interior, internal, international, interest (*C.L.*), interjection.
inter.	intermediate, interrogative.
interrog.	interrogative.
in trans.	on the way.
intran(s).	intransitive.
intro(d).	introduction.
inv.	invoice (*C.L.*), inventor.
I. of M.	Isle of Man.
I. of W.	Isle of Wight, Inspector of Works.
IOU	I owe you.
I.R.	Inland Revenue.
Ir.	Ireland, Irish.
I.R.A.	Irish Republican Army.
I.R.O.	International Refugee Organization.
iron.	ironical(ly).
irreg.	irregular.
Is.	Isaiah (*B.*).
I.S.S.	International Student Service.
isth.	isthmus.

I.T.	Inner Temple, Indian Territory (*Amer.*).
It.	Italy, Italian.
I.T.A.	Independent Television Authority.
ital.	italics.
itin.	itinerary.
I.W.	Isle of Wight.

J

J.	justice, judge, joule (*Elec.*).
J.A.	Judge-Advocate.
J/A	joint account (*C.L.*).
J.A.G.	Judge Advocate General.
Jam.	James (*B.*), Jamaica.
Jer.	Jeremiah (*B.*).
Jn	junction.
jnr	junior.
Jo.	Joel (*B.*).
joc.	jocular, jocose.
Jos.	Josiah (*B.*).
J.P.	Justice of the Peace.
jr.	junior.
Jud.	Judith (*B.*).
Judg.	Judges (*B.*).
jun. or *junr*	junior.
junc.	junction.

K

(N.B. With the change of sovereign, titles with 'King' change to 'Queen', except in the name of regiments and colleges.)

Kan.	Kansas.
K.B.	King's Bench, Knight Bachelor, Knight of the Bath.
K.B.E.	Knight Commander of the British Empire.
K.C.	King's Counsel, Knight Commander, King's College.
kc.	kilocycle(s) (*Rad.*).
K.C.B.	Knight Commander of the Bath.
K.C.I.E.	Knight Commander of the Indian Empire.
K.C.M.G.	Knight Commander of Saint Michael and Saint George.
K.C.S.I.	Knight Commander of the Star of India.
K.C.V.O.	Knight Commander of the Royal Victorian Order.
K.E.	kinetic energy.
K.G.	Knight of the (Order of the) Garter.
K.G.C.	Knight of the Grand Cross.
K.G.C.B.	Knight of the Grand Cross of the Bath.
K.H.B.	(*coll.*) King's hard bargain (*i.e. a no-good sailor*).
K.H.C.	Honorary Chaplain to the King.
K.H.P.	Honorary Physician to the King.
K.H.S.	Honorary Surgeon to the King.
K.K.K.	Ku-Klux-Klan (*Amer.*).
K.L.I.	King's Light Infantry.
K.M.	Knight of Malta.
Knt	Knight.
k.o.	knock-out.
K.O.S.B.	King's Own Scottish Borderers.
K.O.Y.L.I.	King's Own Yorkshire Light Infantry.
K.R.	King's Regulations (*Mil.*).

K.R.R.	King's Royal Rifles.
K.S.I.	Knight of the Star of India.
K.T.	Knight of the Order of the Thistle.
Kt	Knight.
kWh.	Kilowat-hour (*Elec.*).
Ky	Kentucky.

L

l.	line, left, litre, lire.
L.	Lake, Latin, Lance (*Mil.*), Linnaeus (*Bot.*), Liberal (Party).
£	pound sterling, *£A*, Australian pound, *£E*, Egyptian pound. *I£*, Israeli pound, *£NZ*, New Zealand pound, *£T*, Turkish pound.
La	Louisiana.
L.A.	Legislative Assembly, Law Agent.
Lab.	Labour (Party), Labrador.
Lam.	Lamentations (*B.*).
Lancs.	Lancashire.
lang.	language.
lat.	latitude.
Lat.	Latin.
lb.	pound (*weight*).
l.b.w.	leg before wicket (*Crick.*).
l.c.	lower case (*Typ.*), letter of credit (*C.L.*).
L.C.	Lower Canada, Lord Chancellor, Lord Chamberlain, left centre (*of stage*) (*Theat.*).
L.C.C.	London County Council.
L.C.J.	Lord Chief Justice.
L.C.M.	lowest common multiple.
L.C.P.	Licentiate of the College of Preceptors.
L.-Cpl	Lance-Corporal.
Ldp	Lordship.
L.D.S.	Licentiate in Dental Surgery.
Leics.	Leicestershire.
Lev.	Leviticus (*B.*).
L.F.	low frequency (*Rad.*).
l.h.	left hand.
lib.	book.
Lib.	Liberal (Party), library.
Lieut.	lieutenant.
Lieut.-Col.	Lieutenant-Colonel.
Lieut.-Gen.	Lieutenant-General.
Lieut.-Gov.	Lieutenant-Governor.
Lincs.	Lincolnshire.
liq.	liquid.
lit.	literally.
liter.	literature, literary.
Litt.D.	Doctor of Letters.
L.L.	Lord Lieutenant.
ll.	lines.
LL.B.	Bachelor of Laws.
LL.D.	Doctor of Laws.
L.M.S.(R.)	London Midland and Scottish (Railway) (*obs.*).
L.N.E.R.	London and North Eastern Railway (*obs.*).
L.N.U.	League of Nations Union (*obs.*).
loc. cit.	in the place cited.
log.	logarithm.
long.	longitude.
L.P.	Lord Provost (*Scots*), low pressure (*Meteor.*), long primer (*Typ.*).
L'pool	Liverpool.
L.P.T.B.	London Passenger Transport Board.

L.R.A.M.	Licentiate of the Royal Academy of Music.
l.s.	left side.
L.S.	Linnaean Society.
L.S.D.	Lightermen, Stevedores, and Dockers.
£. s. d.	pounds, shillings, and pence.
L.T.	low tension (*Elec.*).
Lt	Lieutenant.
L.T.A.	Lawn Tennis Association.
Lt-Col.	Lieutenant-Colonel.
Lt-Comm.	Lieutenant-Commander (*Nav.*).
Ltd	limited.
Lt-Gen.	Lieutenant-General.
L.W.L.	load-water-line.

M

m.	married, masculine, mile, minute(s).
M.A.	Master of Arts.
Macc.	Maccabees (*B.*).
mach.	machinery.
mag.	magazine.
magn.	magnetism.
Maj.	Major.
Maj.-Gen.	Major-General.
Mal.	Malachi (*B.*).
Mancun.	of Manchester (*signature of the Bishop*).
Man(it).	Manitoba.
mar.	married.
Mar.	March.
March.	Marchioness.
marg.	margin, (*coll.*) margarine.
Marq.	Marquess (*Engl.*), Marquis (*foreign*).
masc.	masculine.
Mass.	Massachusetts.
math.	mathematics.
matric.	matriculation.
Matt.	Matthew (*B.*).
M.B.	Bachelor of Medicine.
M.B.E.	Member of the (Order of the) British Empire.
M.C.	Member of Congress (*Amer.*), master of ceremonies, Member of Council, Military Cross.
M.C.C.	Marylebone Cricket Club.
M.D.	Doctor of Medicine.
Md	Maryland.
Md(d)x	Middlesex.
ME	Middle English.
Me	Maine.
meas.	measure.
M.E.C.	Member of the Executive Council.
mech.	mechanical, mechanics.
med.	medical, medicine, medieval.
mem(o).	memorandum.
Met.	Metropolitan.
metal(l).	metallurgy.
meteor.	meteorology.
Meth.	Methodist.
mfd	manufactured.
mfg	manufacturing.
M.F.H	Master of Foxhounds.
M.F.N.	most favoured nation.
mfr(s).	manufacturer(s).
M.G.	Military Government, machine-gun.
MHG	Middle High German.
M.H.R.	Member of the House of Representatives (*Amer.*).

Mic.	Micah (*B.*).
M.I.C.E.	Member of the Institute of Civil Engineers.
Mich.	Michigan.
M.I.E.E.	Member of the Institute of Electrical Engineers.
mil.	military.
Mil. Att.	Military Attaché.
Mil. Gov.	Military Government.
M.I.Mech.E.	Member of the Institute of Mechanical Engineers.
Min.	Ministry, minister.
min.	mineralogy.
Minn.	Minnesota.
misc.	miscellaneous.
Miss.	Mississippi.
mkt	market.
M.M.	Military Medal.
M.O.	money-order, Medical Officer (*Mil.*).
Mo.	Missouri.
mo.	month(s).
mod.	modern, moderate.
Mods.	Moderations (*Oxford University*).
M.O.H.	Medical Officer of Health.
mol. wt	molecular weight.
Mon.	Monday, Monmouthshire.
Mont.	Montana.
M.P.	Member of Parliament, Military Police.
m.p.	melting point.
m.p.h.	miles per hour.
M.P.S.	Member of the Pharmaceutical Society.
M.R.	Master of the Rolls.
Mr	Mister.
M.R.C.P.	Member of the Royal College of Physicians.
M.R.C.S.	Member of the Royal College of Surgeons.
M.R.I.	Member of the Royal Institute.
Mrs	Mistress.
M.S.	Military Secretary.
m.s.	months after sight (*C.L.*).
M.S.L.	mean sea level.
MS(S).	manuscript(s).
M.Sc.	Master of Science.
m.s.l.	mean sea-level.
M.T.	mechanical transport (*Mil.*).
Mt	Mount. *Mts*, Mountains.
M.T.B.	motor torpedo-boat.
mth	month.
mus.	music, museum.
Mus.B.	Bachelor of Music.
Mus.D.	Doctor of Music.
M.V.O.	Member of the Royal Victorian Order.
M.W.B	Metropolitan Water Board.
Mx	Middlesex.

N

n.	neuter, nominative, noon, noun.
N.	North, northern.
N.A.	North America, Nautical Almanack.
n/a	no account (*C.L.*).
N.A.A.F.I.	Navy, Army, and Air Force Institutes.
Nah.	Nahum (*B.*).
Nat.	national, nationalist, Natal, Nathaniel (*B.*).

nat. hist.	natural history.
N.A.T.O.	North Atlantic Treaty Organization.
nat. ord.	natural order.
naut.	nautical.
nav.	naval, navigation.
N.B.	note particularly, New Brunswick, North Britain, North Borneo.
n.b.	no ball (*Crick.*).
N.B.C.	National Broadcasting Corporation (*Amer.*).
N.C.	North Carolina.
N.C.B.	National Coal Board.
N.C.O.	non-commissioned officer.
N.C.U.	National Cyclists' Union.
n.d.	no date.
N. Dak.	North Dakota.
N.E.	north-east, New England.
Neb(r).	Nebraska.
N.E.D.	New English Dictionary.
neg.	negative.
Neh.	Nehemiah (*B.*).
nem. con.	no one contradicting.
nem. dis.	with no dissentient voice.
Neth.	Netherlands.
neut.	neuter.
Nev.	Nevada.
N.F.	Newfoundland.
N/F	no funds (*C.L.*).
N.F.C.	National Fitness Council.
Nfd(l).	Newfoundland.
N.F.U.	National Farmers' Union.
N.G.	no good.
N.H.	New Hampshire.
N.I.	Northern Ireland.
N.J.	New Jersey.
N.L.	Navy League.
N. lat.	north latitude.
N.L.I.	National Lifeboat Institution.
N. Mex.	New Mexico.
N.N.E.	north-north-east.
N.N.W.	north-north-west.
No. or N	number.
nom.	nominative.
non-com.	non-commissioned officer.
Noncon.	Nonconformist.
non obst.	notwithstanding.
non seq.	false conclusion.
Norm.	Norman.
Northants.	Northamptonshire.
Northumb.	Northumberland.
Norvic.	of Norwich (*signature of the Bishop*).
Norw.	Norway, Norwegian.
Nos. or Nº	numbers.
Notts.	Nottinghamshire.
n.p.	new paragraph.
N.P.	Notary Public.
N.P.F.A.	National Playing Fields Association.
n.p. or d.	no place or date.
N.R.	North Riding (*of Yorkshire*).
nr	near.
n.s.	not sufficient.
N.S.	New Style (*in dates*), Nova Scotia.
N.S.C.	National Sporting Club.
N.S.P.C.A.	National Society for the Prevention of Cruelty to Animals.
N.S.P.C.C.	National Society for the Prevention of Cruelty to Children.
N.S.W.	New South Wales.
N.T.	New Testament.

n.u.	name unknown.
Num.	Numbers (*B.*).
N.U.R.	National Union of Railwaymen.
N.U.T.	National Union of Teachers.
N.V.	New Version.
N.V.M.	Nativity of the Virgin Mary.
N.W.	north-west.
N.W.F.P.	North-West Frontier Province (*of Pakistan*).
N.W.T.	Northwest Territories (*of Canada*).
N.Y.	New York (*state*).
N.Z.	New Zealand.

O

o/a	on account of.
O.A.S.	Organization of American States.
ob.	died.
Obad.	Obadiah (*B.*).
obdt	obedient.
O.B.E.	Order of the British Empire.
obj.	object, objective.
obl.	oblong, oblique.
obs.	obsolete, observation.
ob. s.p.	died without issue.
obstet.	obstetrics.
O.C.	Officer Commanding.
Oct.	October.
o/d	on demand (*C.L.*).
OE	Old English.
O.E.D.	Oxford English Dictionary.
O.E.E.C.	Organization of European Economic Co-operation.
O.F.	Odd Fellow.
off.	official, officinal, offered.
offic.	official.
OF(r)	Old French.
OFris.	Old Frisian.
O.F.S.	Orange Free State.
OHG	Old High German.
O.H.M.S.	On His *or* Her Majesty's Service.
O.K.	(*coll.*) all correct.
Okla.	Oklahoma.
O.M.	Order of Merit.
ON	Old Norse.
Ont.	Ontario.
O.P.	out of print.
o.p.	over proof (*of spirits*), opposite the prompt side (*Theat.*).
op. cit.	in the work cited.
opp.	opposite, opposed.
opt.	optics, optional.
o.r.	owner's risk (*C.L.*).
ord.	ordained, order, ordinary, ordinance.
Ore(g).	Oregon.
orn(ith).	ornithology.
O.S.	Old Style (*of dates*), Ordnance Survey, ordinary seaman.
OS	Old Saxon.
O.S.A.	Order of Saint Augustine.
O.S.B.	Order of Saint Benedict.
O.S.D.	Order of Saint Dominic.
O.S.F.	Order of Saint Francis.
OSlav.	Old Slavonic.
O.T.	Old Testament.
O.T.C.	Officers' Training Corps.
O.U.P.	Oxford University Press.
Oxon.	Oxfordshire, of Oxford University, of Oxford (*signature of the Bishop*).
oz	ounce(s).

P

P.	pawn (*chess*).
p.	page, participle, person (*Gram.*), soft (*Mus.*).
P.A.	Press Association.
p.a.	each year.
Pa	Pennsylvania.
P.A.A.	Pan American Airways.
paint.	painting.
palaeog.	palaeography.
palaeont.	palaeontology.
pam.	pamphlet.
P. & O.	Peninsular and Oriental (Steamship Line).
par.	paragraph, parallel, parish.
parl.	parliament(ary).
pars.	paragraphs.
part.	participle.
pass.	passive (*Gram.*).
path.	pathology.
Pat. Off.	Patent Office.
P.A.U.	Pan American Union.
payt	payment.
P.B.	British Pharmacopœia.
P.B.I.	(*vulg.*) poor bloody infantry.
p.c.	postcard, per cent.
p/c	price current (*C.L.*).
P.C.	police constable, Privy Council(lor).
P.D.	potential difference (*Elec.*), printer's devil (*Typ.*).
pd	paid.
P.D.A.D.	Probate, Divorce, and Admiralty Division (*Law*).
pdr	pounder (*Artil.*).
P.E.I.	Prince Edward Island.
pen.	peninsula.
Penn.	Pennsylvania.
Pent.	Pentecost, Pentateuch.
P.E.P.	Political and Economic Planning.
PEPSU	Patiala and East Punjab States Union.
perf.	perfect (*Gram.*), perforated (*postage stamps*).
per pro.	by proxy.
pers.	person (*Gram.*), personal.
Pet.	Peter (*B.*).
P.G.	paying guest.
pharm.	pharmacy, pharmacology, pharmaceutical.
Ph.D.	Doctor of Philosophy.
phil.	philosophy.
Phil.	Philadelphia, Philippians (*B.*).
Philem.	Philemon (*B.*).
philol.	philology.
Phil. Trans	Philosophical Transactions of the Royal Society.
phon(et).	phonetics.
phot.	photography.
phren.	phrenology.
phys.	physics, physical.
physiol.	physiology, physiological.
pinx.	painted by.
pk	peck.
Pk	Park.
pkg.	package.
P/L	profit and loss (*C.L.*).
pl.	place, plural.
P.L.A.	Port of London Authority.
plen.	plenipotentiary.
plup.	pluperfect.
plur.	plural.
p.m.	afternoon.
P.M.	Prime Minister, Past Master, postmortem (examination).
pm	premium (*C.L.*).
P.M.G.	Postmaster-General.
P.M.L.A.	Publications of the Modern Language Association (of America).
p.n.	promissory note (*C.L.*).
pnxt	painted by.
P.O.	post-office, postal order, Petty Officer (*Nav.*), Pilot Officer (*Av.*).
p.o.a.	pay on delivery (*C.L.*).
pol.	politics, political.
P.O.O.	post-office order.
P.O.P.	printing-out paper (*Phot.*).
pop.	population, popular.
pos.	positive, position.
P.O.S.B.	post-office savings bank.
poss.	possession.
P.O.W.	prisoner of war.
p.p.	by proxy, past participle
pp.	pages.
ppa.	by proxy.
P.P.S.	additional postscript.
P.R.	proportional representation.
pr.	present, pronoun, price.
pr	pair.
P.R.A.	President of the Royal Academy.
Preb.	Prebendary.
prec.	preceding.
pred.	predicate, predicative.
Pref.	Preference (*C.L.*).
pref.	preface, prefix.
prelim.	preliminary.
prelims	preliminary matter (*Typ.*).
prem.	premium.
prep.	preparatory, preposition.
Pres.	President.
pres.	present (*Gram.*).
Presb.	Presbyter(ian).
pret.	preterite.
prev.	previous.
P.R.I.B.A.	President of the Royal Institute of British Architects.
P.R.O.	Public Record Office, Public Relations Officer.
pro.	professional.
prob	probably.
Proc.	Proceedings.
Prom.	(*coll.*) Promenade Concert.
pron.	pronoun, pronounced, pronunciation.
prop.	proposition, property.
propr.	proprietor, proprietary.
props	(*coll.*) properties (*Theat.*).
pros.	prosody.
pro tem.	for the time being.
prov.	provincial, proverbial.
Prov.	Proverbs (*B.*), Provençal.
prox.	next month.
prox. acc.	next in order.
P.S.	postscript, Permanent Secretary.
p.s.	prompt side (*Theat.*).
Ps.	Psalms (*B.*).
pseud.	pseudonym(ous).
P.S.N.C.	Pacific Steam Navigation Company.
psych.	psychic(al).
psychol.	psychology, psychological.
P.T.	physical training.

pt	pint(s), point, part, payment.
Pte	Private (*Mil.*).
P.T.O.	please turn over.
pub.	public, publication, published, (*coll.*) public house.
punct.	punctuation.
P.W.D.	Public Works Department.
P.X.	Post Exchange (*Amer. Mil.*).

Q

N.B. See also under K for titles in which 'Queen' was formerly 'King'.

q.	query, quasi.
Q.	Queen, question, coulomb (*Elec.*).
Q.A.B.	Queen Anne's Bounty.
Q.B.D.	Queen's Bench Division (*Law*).
Q.C.	Queen's Counsel (*Law*).
Q.E.D.	which was to be proved.
Q.F.	quick-firing.
Q.M.	Quartermaster.
Q.M.A.A.C.	Queen Mary's Army Auxiliary Corps.
Q.M.G.	Quartermaster-General.
Q.M.S.	Quartermaster-Sergeant.
qr	quarter.
Q.S.	Quarter Sessions.
q.s.	as much as is sufficient.
qt.	quantity.
q.t.	(*sl.*) on the quiet.
qu.	question, query, quasi.
quad.	quadrant, quadruple, quadrangle.
quart.	quarterly.
Q.U.B.	Queen's University, Belfast.
Que.	Quebec.
Queensl.	Queensland.
quot.	quotation (*C.L.*).
quote	(*coll.*) quotation (*literary*).
quotes	(*coll.*) quotation marks.
q.v.	which see, as much as you wish.
qy	query.

R

R.	King, Queen, river, resistance (*Elec.*), railway, Réaumur.
r.	right, radius, rood, runs (*Crick.*), rupee(s).
R.A.	Royal Academy, Royal Artillery.
R.A.C.	Royal Automobile Club.
R.A.F.	Royal Air Force.
R.A.M.	Royal Academy of Music.
R.A.M.C.	Royal Army Medical Corps.
R.A.N.	Royal Australian Navy.
R.A.O.C.	Royal Army Ordnance Corps.
R.A.P.C.	Royal Army Pay Corps.
R.A.S.C.	Royal Army Service Corps.
R.A.V.C.	Royal Army Veterinary Corps.
R.B.	Rifle Brigade.
R.B.A.	Royal Society of British Artists.
R.C.	Roman Catholic, Red Cross.
R.C.A.	Royal College of Art, Radio Corporation of America.
R.C.M.P.	Royal Canadian Mounted Police.
R.D.	Rural Dean, refer to drawer (*C.L.*).
Rd.	road.
R.D.C.	Rural District Council.
R.E.	Royal Engineers.
rec.	recipe.
recd	received.
recogns.	recognizances (*Law*).
recpt	receipt.

rect.	rectified.
redupl.	reduplicated.
ref.	reference, reformed, (*coll.*) referee.
refd	referred.
refl.	reflexive.
reg.	regular.
regd	registered.
Reg.-Gen.	Registrar-General.
Reg. Prof.	Regius Professor.
regt	regiment.
rel.	religion, relative (*Gram.*).
R.E.M.E.	Royal Electrical and Mechanical Engineers.
Rep.	representative, republic, report.
repr.	reprinted.
res.	resigned, reserve, residence.
ret.	retired.
retd	returned, retired.
retnr	retainer (*Law*).
rev.	revised, revision, reverse, revenue, revolution (*Mach.*).
Rev.	Revelations (*B.*), Reverend, review.
Rev. Ver.	Revised Version (*B.*).
R.F.A.	Royal Field Artillery.
R.G.S.	Royal Geographical Society.
r.h.	right hand.
R.H.	Royal Highness.
R.H.A.	Royal Horse Artillery.
rhet.	rhetoric.
R.H.S.	Royal Horticultural *or* Humane Society.
R.Hist.S.	Royal Historical Society.
R.I.	Rhode Island.
R.I.B.A.	Royal Institute of British Architects.
R.I.P.	(may he *or* she) rest in peace.
rit.	gradually slower (*Mus.*).
R.L.O.	returned letter office.
R.L.S.	Robert Louis Stevenson.
Rly	railway.
R.M.	Royal Mail, Royal Marines, Resident Magistrate.
R.M.A.	Royal Military Academy (*Woolwich*).
R.M.C.	Royal Military College (*Sandhurst*).
R.M.S.P.	Royal Mail Steam Packet Company.
R.N.	Royal Navy.
R.N.L.I.	Royal National Lifeboat Institution.
R.N.R.	Royal Naval Reserve.
R.N.V.R.	Royal Naval Volunteer Reserve.
R.N.V.S.R.	Royal Naval Volunteer Supplementary Reserve.
Roffen.	of Rochester (*signature of the Bishop*).
Rom.	Romans (*B.*), Roman, Romance.
rom.	roman type.
Rom. Cath.	Roman Catholic.
R.P. or *r.p.*	reply paid.
r.p.m.	revolutions per minute.
r.p.s.	revolutions per second.
R.P.S.	Royal Photographic Society.
rpt	report.
R.S.	Royal Society.
R.S.A.	Royal Society of Arts, Royal Scottish Academy.
R.S.M.	Regimental Sergeant-Major, Royal School of Mines.
R.S.P.C.A.	Royal Society for the Prevention of Cruelty to Animals.

R.S.P.C.C.	Royal Society for the Prevention of Cruelty to Children.	*sing.*	singular.
R.S.V.P.	please reply.	*S.J.C.*	Supreme Judicial Court (*Amer.*).
R.T. or *R/T*	radio-telegraphy *or* telephony.	*Skr.* or *Skrt*	Sanskrit.
R.T.C.	Royal Tank Corps.	*S.L.*	Solicitor at Law.
Rt Hon.	Right Honourable.	*S. lat.*	south latitude.
R.T.O.	Railway Transport Officer (*Mil.*).	*Slav.*	Slav(on)ic.
Rt Rev.	Right Reverend.	*s.l.p.*	without lawful issue.
R.T.S.	Religious Tract Society.	*S.M.M.*	Holy Mother Mary (*R.C.*).
R.U.	Rugby Union.	*Smith. Inst.*	Smithsonian Institution (*Amer.*).
R.V.	Rifle Volunteers, Revised Version (*B.*).	*s.m.p.*	without male issue.
		S.N.	shipping note.
R.V.O.	Royal Victorian Order.	*s.o.*	seller's option.
R.W.	Right Worthy *or* Worshipful.	*S.O.*	sub-office, Stationery Office.
Ry	railway.	*Soc.*	society, Socialist.
R.Y.S.	Royal Yacht Squadron.	*sociol.*	sociology.
		sol.	solution, solicitor.

S

		Som.	Somersetshire.
		Song of Sol.	Song of Solomon (*B.*).
		sop.	soprano.
S.	south, Saint, Society, Socialist, solo (*Mus.*), soprano (*Mus.*).	*S.O.S.* or *SOS*	distress signal.
s.	shilling, second(s), son, singular, see.	*sov.*	sovereign.
		s.p.	without issue.
S.A.	Salvation Army, South Africa, South America.	*Sp.*	Spain, Spanish.
		S.P.	small pica (*Typ.*), starting price.
s.a.	without date	*S.P.C.K.*	Society for the Promotion of Christian Knowledge.
Salop.	Shropshire.		
Sarum.	of Salisbury (*signature of the Bishop*).	*spec.*	special(ly), specification.
		specif.	specifical(ly).
Sask.	Saskatchewan.	*S.P.G.*	Society for the Propagation of the Gospel.
Sat.	Saturday.		
S.B.	simultaneous broadcast (*Rad.*).	*sp. gr.*	specific gravity.
Sc.	Scotland, Scottish, Scots, Scotch.	*spirit.*	spiritualism.
S.C.	South Carolina, Security Council.	*S.P.Q.R.*	(*coll.*) small profits and quick returns.
sc.	namely, scene (*Theat.*).		
s.caps.	small capitals (*Typ.*).	*S.P.R.*	Society for Psychical Research.
Scand.	Scandinavian.	*s.p.s.*	without surviving issue.
Sc.D.	Doctor of Science.	*S.P.V.D.*	Society for the Prevention of Venereal Disease.
sch.	school, scholar, schooner.		
sched.	schedule.	*sq.*	square.
sci.	science, scientific.	*Sqd. Ldr*	Squadron Leader (*Av.*).
S.C.M.	Student Christian Movement.	*S.R.*	Southern Railway (*obs.*).
Scot.	Scotland, Scottish.	*S.S.*	steamship, Straits Settlements, Secretary of State.
Script.	Scripture.		
sculp(t).	sculpture, sculptor.	*S.S.A.F.A.*	Soldiers', Sailors' and Airmen's Families Association.
s.d.	indefinitely, standard displacement (*Navy*).		
		S.S.E.	south-south-east.
S.D.	State Department (*Amer.*), Senior Dean.	*S.S.U.*	Sunday-School Union.
		S.S.W.	south-south-west.
S. Dak.	South Dakota.	*St*	saint, street, strait.
S.E.	south-east.	*st.*	stone(s), stanza, stumped (*Crick.*).
Sec.	secretary.	*Staffs.*	Staffordshire.
sec.	second, section.	*stat.*	statics, statistics, statute, stationary.
sect.	section.	*stereo.*	stereotype.
secy	secretary.	*St. Ex.*	Stock Exchange.
sel.	selected, select.	*stg*	sterling.
Sem.	Semitic, Seminary.	*Stip.*	Stipendiary.
Sen.	Senate, Senator.	*Stn*	Station.
sen. or *senr*	senior.	*str.*	stroke (oar).
Sept.	September, Septuagint (*B.*).	*sub.*	subaltern, subscription, substitute, suburb, submarine.
seq.	the following (*sing.*); *seqq.*, the following (*pl.*).		
		subj.	subject, subjunctive.
ser.	series.	*subst.*	substantive.
Sergt	sergeant (*Mil.*).	*suff.*	suffix, sufficient.
Serjt	Serjeant (*Law*).	*Suffr.*	Suffragan.
S.G.	screened grid (*Rad.*), Solicitor-General, specific gravity.	*sugg.*	suggestion, suggested.
		Sun.	Sunday.
Sgt	Sergeant.	*sup.*	superior, supine.
sh.	shilling.	*super.*	superfine, supernumerary, superintendent.
shd	should.		
sim.	similar(ly).	*superl.*	superlative.
sin	sine (*Math.*).	*suppl.*	supplement.
		supr.	supreme.

Supt	superintendent.
surg.	surgery, surgeon.
surv.	surveying, surviving.
s.v.	under the title, surrender-value (*C.L.*).
S.W.	south-west, South Wales.
Sw.	Sweden, Swedish.
S.W.G.	Standard Wire Gauge.
syll.	syllable.
syn.	synonym(ous).
syst.	system.

T

t.	ton, transitive.
T.A.	telegraphic address, Territorial Army.
tan	tangent.
Tasm.	Tasmania.
T.B.	tuberculosis.
Tce	Terrace.
T.D.	Territorial Decoration (*Mil.*).
tech.	technical(ly).
technol.	technology.
tel.	telephone, telegraph(y).
temp.	temperature, temporary, in the time of.
Tenn.	Tennessee.
term.	terminology, termination.
Terr.	Territory, Terrace.
Teut.	Teutonic.
Tex.	Texas.
T.G.W.U.	Transport and General Workers' Union.
theat.	theatre, theatrical.
theol.	theology, theological.
theor.	theorem.
theos.	theosophy.
therap.	therapeutics.
therm.	thermometer.
Thess.	Thessalonians (*B.*).
Thurs.	Thursday.
T.H.W.M.	Trinity High-Water Mark.
Tim.	Timothy (*B.*).
tinct.	tincture.
tit.	title.
Tit.	Titus (*B.*).
T.L.C.	tank-landing craft.
T.M.O.	telegraph money-order.
tn	ton(s).
TNT	trinitrotoluene.
T.O.	telegraph office, turn over.
Tob.	Tobit (*B.*).
tonn.	tonnage.
topog.	topography, topographical.
tp	troop.
Tpr	trooper (*Mil.*).
tr.	transpose (*Typ.*), transport, translate.
Tr.	trustee (*C.L.*).
trans.	transitive, transactions, translation.
transf.	transferred.
transl.	translated, translator, translation.
Treas.	Treasurer.
trig.	trigonometry.
Trin.	Trinity.
trop.	tropical, tropic(s).
Trs.	trustees.
trs.	transpose.
T.T.	teetotal(er).
T.U.	trade union.

T.U.C.	Trade Union Congress.
Tues.	Tuesday.
TV	television.
T.V.A.	Tennessee Valley Authority.
typ.	typography, typographical.

U

U.	Unionist.
u.c.	upper case (*Typ.*).
U.D.C.	Urban District Council.
U.F.C.	United Free Church (of Scotland).
U.G.C.	University Grants Committee.
U.K.	United Kingdom.
ult.	of last month.
U.N.	United Nations.
UNESCO	United Nations Education, Scientific, and Cultural Organization.
UNICEF	United Nations International Children's Emergency Fund.
Unit.	Unitarian.
Univ.	university.
unm.	unmarried.
U.N.S.C.	United Nations Security Council.
U.P.	United Press, United Provinces (*now* Uttar Pradesh).
u/s	unserviceable.
U.S.	United Services.
U.S.(A.)	United States (of America).
U.S.N.	United States Navy.
U.S.S.	United States Ship.
U.S.S.R.	Union of Soviet Socialist Republics.
usu.	usual(ly).
ut inf.	as below.
ut sup.	as above.
ux.	wife.

V

v.	against, see, verb, verse.
Va	Virginia.
V.A.	Royal Order of Victoria and Albert, Vicar Apostolic, Vice-Admiral.
V.A.D.	Volunteer Aid Detachment (*Mil.*).
val.	value.
var.	variety, variant.
vb	verb.
V.C.	Victoria Cross (*Mil.*), Vice-Chancellor (*Univ.*), Vice-Consul.
V.D.	venereal disease.
v.d.	various dates.
V.D.H.	valvular disease of the heart.
Ven.	Venerable.
verb. sap.	a word suffices to the wise.
Vert.	vertebrates.
vet.	(*coll.*) veterinary surgeon.
veter.	veterinary.
V.G.	Vicar-General.
v.g. or *V.G.*	very good.
V.H.F.	Very High Frequency.
v.i.	intransitive verb.
Vic.	Victoria (*Australia*).
vid.	see.
vil.	village.
v.imp.	impersonal verb.
V.I.P.	very important person.
v.ir.	irregular verb.
Vis.	Viscount.
viz	namely.
Vo. or *vᵒ*	on the left-hand page.
voc.	vocative.
vocab.	vocabulary.

Vol.	volunteer.
vol.	volume; *vols*, volumes.
V.O.A.	Voice of America (*Rad.*).
V.P.	Vice-President.
v.r.	reflexive verb.
V.R. (*et I.*)	Victoria Queen (and Empress).
v.s.	see above.
vs.	against.
V.S.	veterinary surgeon.
v.t.	transitive verb.
Vt	Vermont.
vulg.	vulgar.
Vulg.	Vulgate.
v.v.	conversely.
vv.	verses.

W

w.	with, wicket (*Crick.*).
W.	west, Welsh.
W.A.	Western Australia.
W.A.A.F.	Women's Auxiliary Air Force.
Warw.	Warwickshire.
Wash.	Washington (*state*).
W.B.	way-bill (*C.L.*), Water Board.
W.C.	West-Central (*London postal district*), water-closet.
w.c.	with costs.
W.D.	War Department, Works Department.
wd	would.
W.E.A.	Workers' Education Association.
Wed.	Wednesday.
w.f.	wrong fount (*Typ.*).
W.F.T.U.	World Federation of Trade Unions.
wh.	which.
whf	wharf.
W.H.O.	World Health Organization.
W.I.	West Indies.
Wilts.	Wiltshire.
Winton.	of Winchester (*signature of the Bishop*).

Wis(*c*).	Wisconsin.
Wisd.	Wisdom of Solomon (*B.*).
wk	week, weak.
W/*L*	wave-length (*Rad.*).
W.N.W.	west-north-west.
W.O.	War Office, Warrant Officer.
Worcs.	Worcestershire.
W.P.B. or *w.p.b.*	waste-paper basket.
W.R.	West Riding (*of Yorkshire*).
W.R.A.C.	Women's Royal Army Corps.
W.R.N.S.	Women's Royal Naval Service.
W.S.W.	west-south-west.
W.T. or *W*/*T*	wireless telegraphy.
wt	weight.
Wyo.	Wyoming.

X

x-d.	without dividend.
x-i.	without interest.
Xmas	Christmas.
Xt	Christ.
Xtian	Christian.

Y

y.	year.
yd(*s*)	yard(s).
Y.M.C.A.	Young Men's Christian Association.
Yorks.	Yorkshire.
yr	your, year, younger.
Y.W.C.A.	Young Women's Christian Association.

Z

Zech.	Zechariah (*B.*).
Zeph.	Zephaniah (*B.*).
Z.S.	Zoological Society.

ENGLISH GEOGRAPHICAL NAMES

A

Aachen or *Aix-la-Chapelle*, Aquisgrán.
Abyssinia, Abisinia.
Achæa, Acaya.
Addis Ababa, Addis Abeba.
Admiralty Islands, Islas del Almirantazgo.
Adrianople or *Edirne*, Adrianópolis.
Adriatic Sea, Mar Adriático.
Ægean Sea, Mar Egeo.
Aix-la-Chapelle [AACHEN].
Aleutian Islands, Islas Aleutianas.
Alexandria, Alejandría.
Algeria, Argelia.
Algiers, Argel.
Alps, Alpes.
Alsace-Lorraine, Alsacia-Lorena.
Amazon River, Río Amazonas.
Andalusia, Andalucía.
Antarctic Ocean, Océano Antártico.
Antilles, Greater, las Antillas Mayores.
Antilles, Lesser, las Antillas Menores.
Antioch, Antioquía.
Antwerp, Amberes.
Apennines, Apeninos.
Appalachian Mountains, Montes Apalaches.
Arabian Sea, Mar Arábigo.
Archipelago, El Archipiélago Griego o del Mar Egeo.
Arctic Ocean, Océano Ártico.
Ardennes, Sierra Ardenas.
Assisi, Asís.
Assyria, Asiria.
Athens, Atenas.
Atlantic Ocean, Océano Atlántico.
Attica, Ática.
Avignon, Aviñón.

B

Babylon, Babilonia.
Balearic Islands, Islas Baleares.
Balkans, Balcanes.
Baltic Sea, Mar Báltico.
Barbary Coast, Berbería.
Basle or *Basel*, Basilea.
Bavaria, Baviera.
Bayonne, Bayona.
Belgian Congo, Congo Belga.
Belgium, Bélgica.
Belgrade or *Beograd*, Belgrado.
Bengal, Bengala.
Berne or *Bern*, Berna.
Bethlehem, Belén.
Biscay, Vizcaya.
Black Forest, Selva Negra.
Black Sea, Mar Negro.
Blue Mountains, Montañas Azules.
Bologna, Bolonia.
Bordeaux, Burdeos.
Bosporus, Bósforo, el Estrecho del.
Brazil, el Brasil.
Britain, Great, la Gran Bretaña.
British Columbia, Colombia Británica.

British Guiana, Guayana Británica.
British Honduras, Honduras Británicas o Bélice.
British Isles, las Islas Británicas.
British Somaliland, Somalia Británica.
Bruges, Brujas.
Brussels, Bruselas.
Bucharest, Bucarest.
Burgundy, Borgoña.
Burma, Birmania.
Byzantium, Bizancio.

C

Calcutta, Calcuta.
Cambodia, Camboja.
Canal Zone [PANAMA CANAL ZONE].
Canary Islands, las Islas Canarias.
Cantabrian Mountains, Cordillera Cantábrica.
Cape Breton Island, Isla Cabo Bretón.
Cape Horn, Cabo de Hornos.
Cape of Good Hope, Cabo de Buena Esperanza.
Capetown, Ciudad del Cabo.
Cap Haitien, Cabo Haitiano.
Caribbean Sea, Mar Caribe o de las Antillas.
Carpathian Mountains, Montes Cárpatos.
Carthage, Cartago.
Cashmere or *Kashmir*, Cachemira.
Caspian Sea, Mar Caspio.
Castile, New, Castilla la Nueva.
Castile, Old, Castilla la Vieja.
Catalonia, Cataluña.
Caucasus, Cáucaso.
Cayenne, Cayena.
Central America, Centro América o América Central.
Ceylon, Ceilán.
Champagne, Champaña.
Cologne, Colonia.
Constantinople, Constantinopla.
Copenhagen, Copenhague.
Corinth, Corinto.
Corsica, Córcega.
Cracow or *Kraków*, Cracovia.
Crete or *Krete*, Creta.
Cyprus, Chipre.
Czechoslovakia, Checoslovaquia.

D

Dalmatia, Dalmacia.
Damascus, Damasco.
Danube, Danubio.
Dardanelles, Dardanelos.
Dead Sea, Mar Muerto.
Denmark, Dinamarca.
Dordogne, Dordoña.
Dresden, Dresde.
Dunkirk, Dunquerque.
Dutch Guiana or *Surinam*, Guayana Holandesa o Surinam.

E

East Indies, las Indias Orientales.
Edinburgh, Edimburgo.

Edirne [ADRIANOPLE].
Egypt, Egipto.
Elbe River, Río Elba.
England, Inglaterra.
English Channel, Canal de la Mancha.
Ephesus, Éfeso.
Epirus, Epiro.
Ethiopia, Etiopía.
Euphrates, Eufrates.

F

Falkland Islands, las Islas Malvinas *o* Falkland.
Finland, Finlandia.
Flanders, Flandes.
Florence, Florencia.
France, Francia.
French Equatorial Africa, África Ecuatorial
  Francesa.
French Guiana, Guayana Francesa.
French Somaliland, Somalia Francesa.
Friendly Islands, las Islas de los Amigos *o* de la
  Amistad.
Frisian Islands, las Islas Frisias.

G

Galilee, Galilea.
Garonne, Garona.
Gascony, Gascuña.
Gaul, Galia.
Geneva, Ginebra.
Genoa, Génova.
Germany, Alemania.
Ghent, Gante.
Gold Coast, Costa de Oro.
Great Britain, la Gran Bretaña.
Great Lakes, Grandes Lagos.
Greece, Grecia.
Greenland, Groenlandia.
Groningen, Groninga.

H

Hague, The, La Haya.
Haiti Island or *Hispaniola,* Haití *o* Santo Dom-
  ingo *o* Isla Española.
Haiti, Republic of, República de Haití.
Havana, La Habana.
Havre, Le, El Havre.
Hawaiian Islands, las Islas Hawai.
Hebrides, las Islas Hébridas.
Hellespont, Helesponto.
Hendaye, Hendaya.
Hispaniola, Isla Española *o* Haití *o* Santo
  Domingo.
Holland, Holanda.
Holy Land, Tierra Santa.
Hungary, Hungría.

I

Iberian Peninsula, Península Ibérica.
Iceland, Islandia.
Indian Ocean, Océano Índico.
Indus, Indo.
Ionian Sea, Mar Iónico.
Iraq, Irak.
Ireland, Irlanda.
Istanbul, Istambul.
Italian Somaliland, Somalia Italiana.
Italy, Italia.
Ivory Coast, Costa de Marfil.

J

Japan, el Japón.

Jerusalem, Jerusalén.
Jordan, Jordania.
Jutland, Jutlandia.

K

Kashmir, Cachemira.
Key West, Cayo Hueso.
Korea, Corea.

L

Lapland, Laponia.
Latin America, la América Latina.
Lausanne, Lausana.
Lebanon, Líbano.
Leeward Islands, las Islas de Sotavento.
Leghorn, Liorna.
Leningrad, Leningrado.
Libya, Libia.
Liège, Lieja.
Lille, Lila.
Lisbon, Lisboa.
Lithuania, Lituania.
London, Londres.
Lorraine, Lorena.
Louisiana, Luisiana.
Louvain, Lovaina.
Lower California, la Baja California.
Low Countries, los Países Bajos.
Lucerne or *Luzern,* Lucerna.

M

Magellan, Strait of, Estrecho de Magallanes.
Mainz, Maguncia.
Majorca or *Mallorca,* Mallorca.
Malaya, Malaya, Malasia, Archipiélago Malayo.
Malay Peninsula, Península de Malaca.
Maldive Islands, las Islas Maldivas.
Marmora or *Marmara, Sea of,* Mar de Már-
  mara.
Marseille or *Marseilles,* Marsella.
Martinique, Martinica.
Mauritius or *Ile de France,* Mauricio.
Mediterranean Sea, Mar Mediterráneo.
Memphis, Menfis.
Meuse, Mosa.
Mexico, Méjico *o* México.
Minorca or *Menorca,* Menorca.
Mississippi River, Río Misisipi.
Missouri, Misuri.
Moluccas or *Spice Islands,* las Islas Molucas *o*
  de las Especias.
Morocco, Marruecos.
Moscow, Moscú.
Moselle, Mosela.

N

Naples, Nápoles.
Near East, Cercano Oriente.
Netherlands, los Países Bajos *o* Holanda.
Newfoundland, Terranova.
New Orleans, Nueva Orleáns.
New South Wales, Nueva Gales del Sur.
New York, Nueva York.
New Zealand, Nueva Zelanda.
Niagara Falls, Cataratas del Niágara.
Nice, Niza.
Nile, Nilo.
Nineveh, Nínive.
Nippon, Nipón [JAPAN].
Normandy, Normandía.
North America, Norte América *o* América del
  Norte.

North Pole, Polo Norte.
Norway, Noruega.
Nova Scotia, Nueva Escocia.

O

Odessa, Odesa.
Olympus, Mount, Monte Olimpo.
Ostend, Ostende.

P

Pacific Ocean, Océano Pacífico.
Palestine, Palestina.
Panama Canal Zone, Zona del Canal de Panamá.
Papal States or *States of the Church*, Estados Pontificios.
Paris, París.
Parnassus, Mount, Parnaso.
Peking, Pekín.
Peloponnesus, Peloponeso.
Pennsylvania, Pensilvania.
Perugia, Perusa.
Philadelphia, Filadelfia.
Philippines, las Filipinas.
Phœnicia, Fenicia.
Piedmont, Piamonte.
Piræus, Pireo.
Poland, Polonia.
Pompeii, Pompeya.
Port-au-Prince, Puerto Príncipe.
Port of Spain, Puerto España.
Port Said, Puerto Said.
Prague, Praga.
Pyrenees, Pirineos.

R

Rangoon, Rangún.
Red Sea, Mar Rojo.
Rhine, Rhin *o* Rin.
Rhodes, Rodas.
Rhone, Ródano.
Rocky Mountains, Montañas Rocosas.
Rouen, Ruán.
Russia, Rusia.

S

Salonika or *Thessalonike*, Salónica.
Sardinia, Cerdeña.
Saudi Arabia, Arabia Saudita.
Saxony, Sajonia.
Scandinavia, Escandinavia.
Scheldt, Escalda.
Scotland, Escocia.
Seine, Sena.
Siam [THAILAND].
Sicily, Sicilia.
Smyrna, Esmirna.
Society Islands, Islas de la Sociedad.
South America, Sud América *o* América del Sur.
South Pole, Polo Sur.
Spain, España.
Sparta, Esparta.

Stockholm, Estocolmo.
St. Petersburg, San Petersburgo.
Surinam [DUTCH GUIANA].
Sweden, Suecia.
Switzerland, Suiza.
Syracuse, Siracusa.
Syria, Siria.

T

Tagus, Tajo or *Tejo*, Tajo.
Tangier, Tánger.
Taurus Mountains, Montañas Tauro.
Tehran or *Teheran*, Teherán.
Texas, Tejas.
Thailand or *Siam*, Thailandia *o* Siam.
Thames, Támesis.
Thebes, Tebas.
Thermopylæ, Termópilas.
Thessalonike [SALONIKA].
Thessaly, Tesalia.
Thrace, Tracia.
Tonga or *Friendly Islands*, Tonga *o* las Islas de los Amigos *o* de la Amistad.
Toulon, Tolón.
Toulouse, Tolosa.
Trent or *Trento*, Trento.
Troy, Troya.
Tunis, Túnez.
Turkey, Turquía.
Tuscany, Toscana.
Tyre, Tiro.
Tyrrhenian Sea, Mar Tirreno.

U

Ukraine, Ucrania.
Union of South Africa, la Unión Sudafricana.
Union of Soviet Socialist Republics (*U.S.S.R.*), la Unión de Repúblicas Socialistas Soviéticas (U.R.S.S.).
United Kingdom, el Reino Unido.
United States of America (*U.S.A.*), los Estados Unidos de América (E.U.).
Ural Mountains, Montes Urales.

V

Vatican City, la Ciudad del Vaticano.
Venice, Venecia.
Versailles, Versalles.
Vesuvius, Vesubio.
Vienna or *Wien*, Viena.
Virgin Islands, las Islas Vírgenes.

W

Wales, (País de) Gales.
Warsaw, Varsovia.
West Indies, las Indias, las Antillas.
Windward Islands, las Islas de Barlovento.

Y

Yellow River or *Hwang Ho*, Río Amarillo *o* Hoang Ho.
Yellow Sea or *Hwang Hai*, Mar Amarillo.

TABLE OF WEIGHTS AND MEASURES

ENGLISH TO SPANISH

Linear Measure—Medida de longitud
1 inch = 25,4 *milímetros*
1 foot (= 12 inches) = 0,3048 *metros*
1 yard (= 3 feet) = 0,9144 *metros*
1 furlong = 201,1684 *metros*
1 mile (= 8 furlongs) = 1,609347 *kilómetros* (statutory mile)
                  = 1,85324 *kilómetros* (geographical mile)
                  = 1,85318 *kilómetros* (nautical mile, *Ingl.*)
                  = 1,85324 *kilómetros* (nautical mile, *E.U.*)

Square Measure—Medida de superficie
1 square inch = 645 *milímetros cuadrados*
1 square foot = 0,0929 *metros cuadrados*
1 square yard = 0,8361 *metros cuadrados*
1 square mile = 2,59 *kilómetros cuadrados*

Liquid Measure—Medida de capacidad para líquidos
1 pint (*Ingl.*) = 0,56824 *litros*; (dry, *E.U.*) = 0,55059 *litros*; (liquid, *E.U.*) = 0,47316 *litros*
1 gallon (*Ingl.*) (= 8 pints) = 4,5459 *litros*; (dry, *E.U.*) = 4,4047 *litros*; (liquid, *E.U.*) = 3,7853 *litros*

Avoirdupois Weights—Pesos avoirdupois (o del comercio)
1 ounce (oz.) = 28,3495 *gramos*
1 pound (lb.) (= 16 ounces) = 0,453592 *kilogramos*
1 hundredweight (cwt.) (= 112 pounds) = 50,8023 *kilogramos*
1 ton (= 20 hundredweight) = 1016 *kilogramos*

Apothecaries Weights—Pesos usados en farmacia
1 grain   = 64,7989 *miligramos*
1 drachm = 3,8879 *gramos*
1 ounce   = 31,1034 *gramos*
1 pound   = 0,373241 *kilogramos*

SPANISH TO ENGLISH

Peso—Weights
1 *gramo*   = 15·4325 grains
1 *kilogramo* = 2·2046223 pounds (avoirdupois)
            = 2·679228 pounds (apothecary o troy)

Medida de longitud—Linear Measure
1 *milímetro* = 0·03937014 inch (*Ingl.*)
            = 0·03937 inch (*E.U.*)
1 *centímetro* = 0·3937014 inch (*Ingl.*)
            = 0·3937 inch (*E.U.*)
1 *metro*   = 3·280845 feet (*Ingl.*)
            = 3·280833 feet (*E.U.*)
1 *kilómetro* = 0·6213722 miles (statutory, *Ingl.*)
            = 0·6213699 miles (statutory, *E.U.*)

Medida de capacidad para líquidos—Liquid Measure
1 *litro* = 35·19609 ounces (fluid, *Ingl.*) = 1·759809 pints (*Ingl.*)
      = 33·81475 ounces (fluid, *E.U.*) = 2·113423 pints (*E.U.*)